Directory of Business Information Resources

2015

Twenty-Second Edition

Directory of Business Information Resources

- Associations
- Newsletters
- Magazines & Journals
- Trade Shows
- Directories & Databases
- Web Sites

Grey House Publishing

AMENIA, NY 12501

PUBLISHER: Leslie Mackenzie
EDITOR: Richard Gottlieb
EDITORIAL DIRECTOR: Laura Mars

PRODUCTION MANAGER & COMPOSITION: Kristen Thatcher
PRODUCTION ASSISTANTS: Brittany Goddard, Melissa Rose

MARKETING DIRECTOR: Jessica Moody

Grey House Publishing, Inc.
4919 Route 22
Amenia, NY 12501
518.789.8700
FAX 518.789.0545
www.greyhouse.com
e-mail: books@greyhouse.com

First edition published 1992
Twenty-Second edition published 2015
Printed in Canada
The directory of business information resources. – 1992-2015

v. ; 27.5 cm.
Annual
Other title: Business information resources

1. Business information services – United States – Directories. 2. Reference books – Business – Bibliography – Periodicals. 3. Association, institutions, etc. – United States – Directories. 4. Business – Databases – Directories. 5. Trade shows – Directories. I. Title: Business information resources.

HF54.52.U5 D56
016.65
ISBN: 978-1-61925-547-0 softcover
ISSN: 1549-7224

Table of Contents

Introduction

The Directory of Business Information Resources has been the premier reference book for business researchers since 1992. With comprehensive coverage of 101 industries – including two additions this year, it helps find new customers, increase customer loyalty, and improve the bottom line.

This twenty-second edition of *The Directory of Business Information Resources* offers an unequaled collection of valuable, industry-specific resources. Reach out to new customers through industry **Associations, Directories, Databases,** and **Trade Shows**. Find new ways to cut costs and improve efficiency through **Magazines, Journals** and **Newsletters**. Learn what your competitors are up to by visiting the latest, most important **Web Sites**. All industry chapters include an exhaustive number of these resource types. The 101 industries represented comprise a diverse list, including Alternative Energy (including Shale), Credit/Lending Services, **Cyber Security (NEW)**, E-Commerce, Healthcare, Machinery, Photography, Safety/Security, **Social Media (NEW)**, and Telecommunications. With 23,976 listings – 1,100 more than last edition – this twenty-second edition is the most comprehensive guide to business information on the market today.

Content

To keep pace with the changing face and challenges of industry in the twenty-first century, we have added two brand new chapters to this edition – Cyber Security and Social Media. As these areas continue to have an increasingly significant impact on how we do business, resources surrounding them have developed. This new edition captures Cyber Security and Social Media Associations, Trade Shows, Print and Online Media, and more. All listings include name, address, phone, fax, web site, email, key contacts and a brief description, making your research focused and productive. Also, when available, we have noted an association's presence on Facebook, Twitter and LinkedIn.

Online-only information is often confusing, unreliable, and outdated. The value of the focused, comprehensive data in *The Directory of Business Information Resources*, compiled with the business researcher in mind, cannot be overstated. This edition provides immediate assistance with your business: attend industry Trade Shows to **promote your product and find new customers;** subscribe to Publications to **stay competitive and ahead of the curve;** join Associations for **business support and educational opportunities.**

Numbers for 2015: 6,222 Associations, 2,938 Newsletters, 4,983 Magazines and Journals, 3,710 Trade Shows, 2,462 Directories and Databases, and 248 International Resources. Plus users will find 55,654 contact names, 18,473 fax numbers, 18,8774 web sites, and 14,978 e-mail addresses.

Features in 2015 Edition

User Guide: Defines fields for entry type. In addition to name, address, phone, fax, web site, e-mail, and description, *Associations* include number of members, dues, founding year. *Publications* include cost, frequency. *Trade shows* include location, number of exhibitors, attendees.

Content Summary of Chapter Listings: Lists more than 1,400 specific businesses under each of the 101 chapter names. For example, *Accounting* lists auditors, bookkeepers, payroll, and taxes; *Engineering* includes cost engineers, geologists, and robotics; *Restaurants* covers bakers, cookware, and caterers.

NAICS and SIC Reference Tables: Enable users to approach their topic based on the North American Industry Classification System (NAICS), or the Department of Labor's Standard Industrial Classification System (SIC).

Two Indexes:
Entry Index – Alphabetical list of all entries.

Publisher Index – Publishers of industry literature, sponsors of trade shows, etc. Number listed identifies the title of the material/trade show listed in this directory.

This premier reference offers organized, accessible business information for market researchers, advertising agencies, job placement and career planning offices, public relations personnel, and business schools and colleges.

The Directory of Business Information Resources is available for subscription online at http://gold.greyhouse.com for even faster, easier access to this vast array of information. Subscribers can search by keyword, geographic area, organization type, key contact name and so much more. Visit the site or call 800-562-2139 to set up a free trial of the Online Database.

Praise for previous editions:
"The 20th edition of this directory . . . continues to be an essential reference source . . . "

Choice

"A comprehensive directory . . . this volume is a worthy addition to academic and large public libraries serving business researchers."

Booklist

"This comprehensive resource [is] . . . very useful . . . {For} broad-based industry information, acquiring . . . regularly is recommended."

American Reference Books Annual

"…this substantial reference [is] easy to navigate . . . Recommended for marketing and industry research collections."

Library Journal

User Guide

Descriptive listings in *The Directory of Business Information Resources* are organized into 98 industry chapters. You will find the following types of listings throughout the book: Associations; Newsletters; Magazines & Journals; Trade Shows; Directories & Databases; and Web Sites.

Below is a sample listing illustrating the kind of information that is or might be included in an Association entry, with additional fields that apply to publication and trade show listings. Each numbered item of information is described in the paragraphs on the following page.

---

(1) **12345**

(2) **National Association of Big Band Musicians**

(3) 2061 Ryders Avenue
Westerville, OH 43081

(4) 002-208-0843

(5) 800-208-0845

(6) 002-208-0844

(7) info@bigb.com

(8) www.bigb.com

(9) Linda Whare, Executive Director
Keith Fallon, Secretary
Bill Jenkins, Editor

(10) A national organization that supports those musicians and instructors whose main interest is big band music. Committed to furthering the art of big bands through teaching, performance, compositions and scholarly research. Also promotes the growth and establishment of big band literature and libraries, and offers musicians and teachers guidance in instrument maintenance and performing venues.

(11) 1M *Members*

(12) *Founded*: 1984

(13) Bi Monthly

(14) $59.00

(15) 110,000

(16) **Special Issues:**
Top 100 Music Dealers
January

(17) 3,000 Attendees

(18) April

Resources User Key

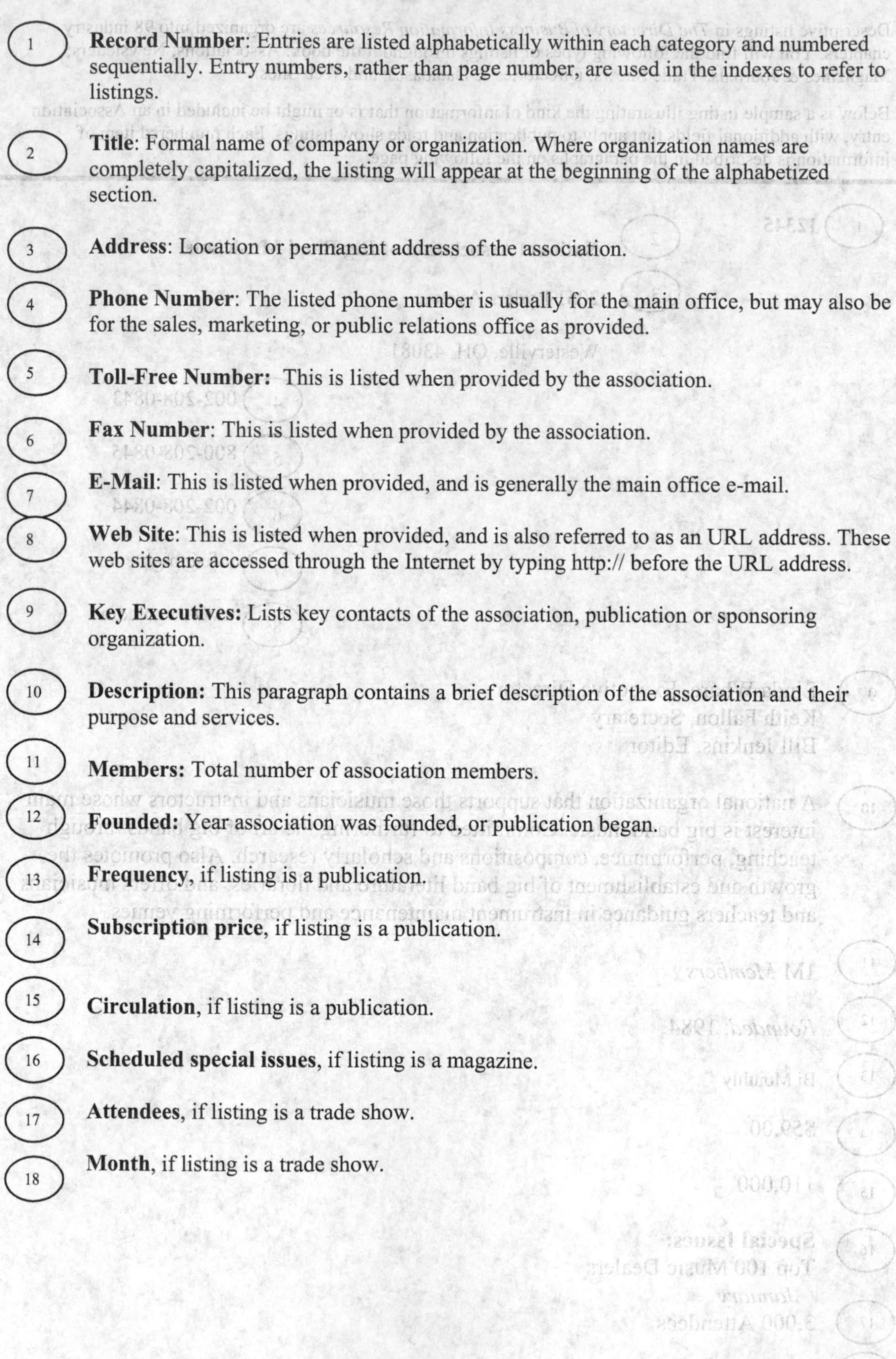

1 **Record Number**: Entries are listed alphabetically within each category and numbered sequentially. Entry numbers, rather than page number, are used in the indexes to refer to listings.

2 **Title**: Formal name of company or organization. Where organization names are completely capitalized, the listing will appear at the beginning of the alphabetized section.

3 **Address**: Location or permanent address of the association.

4 **Phone Number**: The listed phone number is usually for the main office, but may also be for the sales, marketing, or public relations office as provided.

5 **Toll-Free Number:** This is listed when provided by the association.

6 **Fax Number**: This is listed when provided by the association.

7 **E-Mail**: This is listed when provided, and is generally the main office e-mail.

8 **Web Site**: This is listed when provided, and is also referred to as an URL address. These web sites are accessed through the Internet by typing http:// before the URL address.

9 **Key Executives:** Lists key contacts of the association, publication or sponsoring organization.

10 **Description:** This paragraph contains a brief description of the association and their purpose and services.

11 **Members:** Total number of association members.

12 **Founded:** Year association was founded, or publication began.

13 **Frequency**, if listing is a publication.

14 **Subscription price**, if listing is a publication.

15 **Circulation**, if listing is a publication.

16 **Scheduled special issues**, if listing is a magazine.

17 **Attendees**, if listing is a trade show.

18 **Month**, if listing is a trade show.

Content Summary of Chapter Listings

Chapters in this directory often include a wide range of topics. The following list of keywords from the Association listings shows the subjects covered in each chapter.

Accounting
Accounting Historians
Accounting Standards
Accreditation
Auditors
Black Accountants
Bookkeepers
Broadcast Cable Financial Management
Budget & Program Analysis
Computerized Accounting
Construction Financial Management
Cost Estimating
Government Accountability
Government Financial Officers
Healthcare Financial Management
Hospitality Financial Management
Insolvency
Insurance
Latino Accountants
Military Comptrollers
Newspapers Financial Management
Payroll
Public Accountants
Taxes
Trucking Financial Management
Valuation
Women Accountants

Advertising
Advertising Agencies
Advertising Research
Cable TV Advertising
Children's Advertising
Commercials
Communications
E Marketing
Educational Advertising
Exhibition Management
Newspaper Advertising
Outdoor Advertising
Photographers
Point of Purchase
Public Opinion
Railroad Advertising
Signs
Transportation Advertising
Women in Advertising

Agriculture
4-H
Agricultural Aviation
Agricultural Communications
Agricultural Consultants
Agricultural County Agents
Agricultural Economics
Agricultural Education
Agricultural Engineers
Agricultural Fairs
Agricultural History
Agricultural Law
Agricultural Management
Agricultural Manufacturers
Agricultural Marketing
Agricultural Research
Agricultural Retail
Agricultural Teachers
Agronomy
Alfalfa
Angus
Animal Health
Animal Hides
Animal Science
Aquatics
Arid Lands
Bedding Plants
Bee Keeping
Beef
Bio-Dynamic Farming
Biomolecular Study
Blacksmiths
Blueberries
Brahman Beef
Canola
Cereal
Christmas Trees
Conservation
Corn
Cotton
Cottonseed
Cranberries
Crops
Dairy
Ecological Farming
Eggs
Enology
Entomology
Family Farming
Feed
Fertilizer
Fisheries
Florals
Foresters
Gardening
Grain
Grapes
Grasslands
Guernsey
Hay
Herbs
Hereford
Holstein
Horticulture
Irrigation
Jersey Cattle
Livestock
Maple Syrup
Millers
Oil Seed
Onions
Organic
Pesticides
Phytopathology
Pork
Potato
Poultry
Produce
Santa Gertrudis
Seeds
Sheep
Soil
Soybean
Sugar
Sunflowers
Veal
Walnuts
Weeds
Wheat

Alternative Energy
Biodiesel
Biogas
Biomass
Clean Energy
Energy Recovery
Ethanol
Geothermal Energy
Hydrogen
Lignite Energy
Low Impact Hydropower
Ocean Renewable Energy
Renewable Energy
Solar Energy
Sustainable Energy
Thermal Energy
Wind Energy

Amusement & Entertainment
Amusement Equipment Manufacturers
Amusement Equipment Rentals
Amusement Industry Marketing
Amusement Parks
Amusement Safety
Aquariums
Caves
Circus
Coin Operated
Concessions
Game Developers
Go-Karts
Haunted Attractions
Jugglers
Kiddie Rides
Laser Attractions
Motor Sports
Roller Coasters
Theaters
Themed Amusements
Ticketing
Water Parks
Zoos

Apparel & Accessories
Cashmere & Camel Hair Manufacturers
Clothing Contractors
Clothing Manufacturers
Costume Designers
Cotton
Cotton Shippers
Fashion Designers
Footwear
Fur Manufacturers
Fur Merchants
Headwear
Home Sewing/Crafts
Hosiery
Infant & Children Wear
Intimate Apparel
Knitting
Leather
Millners, Dressmakers & Tailors
Neckwear
Needlework
Sportswear
Sunglasses
Uniform Manufacturers
Union Manufacturers & Distributors
Western & English Tack Apparel

Appliances
Manufacturers
Parts Suppliers
Repair
Retail Dealers
Service

Architecture
Accessibility for the Disabled
Architectural Historians
Building Officials
Cast Stone
Code Administrators
Concrete
Conservation
Design Drafting
Education
Environmental Design
Impact Assessment
Insulated Cable Engineers
Intelligent Buildings
Landscape Architects
Livable Communities
Marine Engineers
Naval Architects
Precasts
Preservation
Schools of Architecture
Sustainable Buildings
Urban Design

Art & Antiques
Aesthetics
American History
Animal Artists
Antique Dealers
Appraisal
Art Dealers
Art Education
Art Libraries
Art Materials
Art Museums
Art Placement
Art Research
Art Therapy
Auctioneers
Blacksmiths
College Art
Collectors
Conservation
Fine Arts
Fine Print Dealers
Illustrators
Library Art
Limited Edition Dealers
Photography
Picture Framers
Preservation Technology
School Programs
State Art Agencies

Automotive
Aftermarkets
Air Conditioning
Antique Trucks
Auto Auctions
Autobody Work

Content Summary of Chapter Listings

Retail Lumber
Roof Coatings
Roof Tile
Rubber Pavements
Safety Glazing
Scaffolds
Screen Manufacturers
Senior Housing
Slag
Slurry Surfacing
Steel Joists
Steel Windows
Stone, Sand & Gravel
Structural Insulated Panel
Stucco Manufacturers
Subcontractors
Tech Home
Terrazzo & Mosaic
Tile Contractors
Tilt-Up Concrete
Timber Framers
Tools & Fasteners
Truck Mixer
Underground Construction
Unions
Utility Contractors
Wall & Ceiling Industries
Western Building Material
Women In Construction
Woodwork

Chemicals
Acrylonitrile
Adhesion
Aerosol
Agricultural Chemicals
Alkyl Amines
Analytical & Life Science Systems
Analytical Chemists
Analytical Communities
Bioanalysts
Biochemistry & Molecular Biology
Brewing Chemists
Cadmium
Catalysis
Chemical Engineers
Chemical Heritage
Chemical Manufacturers
Chemical Marketing Research
Chemical Recyclers
Chemical Strategies
Chlorine
Chlorine Chemistry
Chlorine Free
Chlorobenzene Producers
Clinical Chemistry
Coatings Technology
Coke & Coal Chemicals
Colorists
Consumer Specialty Chemicals
Cosmetic Chemists
Crystal Growth
Drug, Chemical & Allied Trades
Electrochemical
Embalming Chemical Manufacturers
Fiber Manufacturers
Hydrogen
Leather Chemists
Liquid Terminals
Lubricant Manufacturers
Mass Spectrometry
Materials Technology
Methanol
Oil Chemists
Oxygenated Fuels
Ozone
Pest Management
Pesticide Applicators
Phosphate Chemicals
Pine Chemicals
Polyisocyanurate Insulation
Polyurethane Foam
Powder Coating
Process Equipment Manufacturers
Spectroscopy
Synthetic Organic Chemicals
Textile Chemists
Toxicology

Cleaners & Laundries
Building Service Contractors
Diaper Services
Drycleaners
Environmental Management
Fabricare
Halogenated Solvents
Kitchen Exhaust
Linens
Power Washers
Uniform & Textile Service

Communications & Media
Abstracting & Information Services
Freedom Information Center
Information & Image Management
Information Systems
Information Technology
Medical Illustrators
Newspapers
Personal Achievement
Postal Commerce
Regional Magazines
Speakers
Technology in Education
Telecommunications Industry
Toastmasters
Translators
Writers

Computers & Data Processing
Alpha Micro Users
Artificial Intelligence
Audiovisual Catalogers
Automated Reasoning
Data Interchange Standards
Digital Dealers
Educational Communications & Technology
Electronic Engineers
Event Marketing
Identification Manufacturers
Imaging Science
Image Management
Information Display
Information Networking
Information Processing
Information Science
Information Systems Management
Intelligence
Interactive Multimedia
Knowledge Engineers
Language Instruction
Managing Human Resource Information
Medical Imaging
Medical Information
Open Applications
Optical Engineering
Precision Engineering
Recognition Technologies
Regional Sciences
Reprographic
Science Association
Security
Serial Storage Architecture
Software Users
Systems Management Technology
Technology in Education

Cosmetics, Perfumes & Personal Care
Aesthetics Manufacturers & Distributors
Aloe Science
Aromatics
Color
Consumer Healthcare Manufacturers
Cosmetology
Drug, Chemical & Allied Trades
Fragrance Research
Fragrances
Nail & Beauty
Nail Manufacturers
Tanning Manufacturers

Credit & Lending Services
Bankruptcy
Business Producers Credit
Commercial Collectors
Commercial Finance
Consumer Data
Consumer Debt Counseling
Credit Union Research & Consulting
Electronic Transactions
Financial Services
Fraud & Theft
Mortgage Brokers
Recovery Association
Risk Management

Cyber Security
Cyber Crime
Cyber Forensics
Automated Teller Machines
Intelligence Communities
Homeland Security
Defense Security
Microcomputers
Professional Certifications
Information Technology
Security Research
Firewalls
Intrusion Prevention
Advanced Technology Crimes
Information Security
Assurance
Risk Management
Governance
Federal Bureau of Investigation
National Security
Corporate Security
Cyber Crime Threats
Forensics
Cyber Watch

Direct Marketing
Art Directors
Digital Concepts
E-Marketing
Hispanic Marketing
Mail Marketing
Mobile Telecommunications
Publication Designers
Teleservices
Third Party Mailing
Writers

Drugs & Pharmaceuticals
Clinical
Clinical Laboratory
Distribution
Education
Efficient Operation
Ethical Pharmacies
Excipients
Generic
Health System
History of Pharmacy
Hospitals
Managed Care
Oil Chemists
Outsourcing Research
Parenteral & Enteral Nutrition
Pharmacy Law
Pharmaceutical Alliance
Pharmacy Cooperative
Senior Care
Standardization
Wholesale Druggists

E-Commerce & Internet
Advertising
Computing in Education
eMarketing
Hispanic Chamber
Public Technology
Security
Software Alliance
Uniform Council
Women in ECommerce

Electrical
Apparatus Service
Bioelectrmagnetics
Contractors
Electrical Instruments
Electrochemical
Electronic Assembly
Electronic Measuring Instruments
Engineers
Generating Systems
Insulated Cable
Intercommunications Applications
Laser and Electro-Optic
Magnetic
Microelectronics
Microwave
Overstress/Electrostatic
Public Owned Utilities
Relay Electronics
Research
Rural Electric Cooperative
Safety
Sound Systems
Technical Certifications
Testing
Variable Resistive Products

Electronics
Agricultural
Aircraft
Armed Forces
Assembly
Certified Technicians
Commercialization Research
Consumer Electronics
Environmental
Instrumentation & Measurement
Interactive Services
Marine Electronics
Metals
Microchip Industry
Microelectronics
Minerals

Content Summary of Chapter Listings

Optics and Photonics
Power Electronics
Progressive Rental Merchandise
Relay Manufacturers
Rural Electric
Service Dealers

Engineering
Abrasive Engineering
Acoustical
Adhesive & Sealant
Aerospace
Applied Technology
Automated Procedures
Biomedical
Black Engineers
Boiler and Pressure Inspectors
Cable
Chemical
Civil
Code Administrators
Cold Regions Research
Corrosion
Cost Engineers
Crystallographic
Design
Die Casting
Education
Energy
Environmental Engineering
Ergosyst
Evaluation
Examiners
Foundation
Gas
Gas Turbine
Geologists
Geoprofessional
Heating, Refrigeration & Air-Conditioning
Illuminating Engineering
Industrial Designers
Industrial Fabrics
Industrial Research
Information Networking
Instrumentation & Measurement
Maintenance Professionals
Management
Materials
Mechanical
Minority Engineers
Naval
Noise Control
Nondestructive Testing
Oil Chemists
Petroleum Operations
Physics
Plumbing
Potash and Phosphate
Precision Engineering
Railway Engineering
Refrigerating
Reliability Engineering
Reprographic
Robotics
Safety
Sanitary
Structural Connections
Tribologists
Vacuum
Voluntary Consensus Standards

Environment & Conservation
Adirondack Region
Aerosol Research
Agriculture
Agronomy
Air & Waste Management
Appropriate Technology
Aquatic Plant Management
Assessment of the Environment
Audobon Society
Balancing Bureau
Biological Sciences
Bison Control
Compliance
Education
Energy Economics
Family Planning
Fire Chiefs
Fisheries
Floodplan Managers
Food Protection
Forest History
Gas
Geologists
Great Lakes
Greenpeace
Hazardous Materials Control
Historic Preservation
Imaging and Geospacial Information
Indoor Air
Lake Ecology
Law
Marine Technology
Methanol Institute
Noise Control
Nuclear Society
Packaging
Pesticide Toxicity
Phytopathological
Renewable Energy & Fuels
River Ecosystems
Safe Buildings
Scrap Recycling
Seeding
Senior Involvement
Shore and Beach Preservation
Silicone Health
Soil and Foundation Engineers
Soil and Plant Analysis
Solid Waste Management
Steel Recycling
Treaty Support
Used Oil Services
Wildlife Federation
Woodland Owners
Zoo & Aquarium

Exhibits & Meeting Planners
Assembly Management
Business Media
Business-To-Business Information
Collegiate Conferences
Contractors
Cost Management Professionals
Healthcare Meetings
Hospitality
Information Technology
Museums
Religious Conferences
Science-Technology Centers

Financial Services
Aircraft Finance
Appraisers
Bankruptcy Institute
Broadcast Cable
Certified Divorce Planners
Collectors
Community Capital
Construction Financial Management
Consumer Data
Cost Engineering
Credit Union
Entrepreneurial Growth
Foreign Sales
Fraud & Theft Information
Individual Investors
Industrial Engineering
Internal Auditors
International Sales
Investor Responsibility Research
Life Insurance
Local Housing
Mutual Fund Investors
Neighborhood Reinvestment
Pension Plans
Tax Education
Urban Homesteading
Vehicle Leasing

Fishing
Atlantic States
Benthological Society
Great Lakes
Gulf and Caribbean
Middle Atlantic Fisheries
Inland
Pacific Coast
Pacific Seafood Processors
Southeastern
Women's Fisheries

Food & Beverage
African-American Natural Foods
Agricultural Research
Agronomy
Alfalfa Processors
Allergy & Anaphylaxis
Allied Purchasing
Aluminum Foil Container Manufacturers
Arborists
Association for Color
Association of Conservation
Automatic Merchandising
Bar and Restaurant Association
Beekeeping
Beverage Lincesees
Biodynamics Farming
Bio-Integrity
Biomolecular Screening
Biotechnology
Brewing Chemists
Cancer Research
Cereal Chemists
Chewing Gum
Club Management
Composite Cans and Tubes
Convenience Store Advisory
Cooperative Business
Correctional Food Service
Council on Science & Health
Crop Insurers
Deer Farmers
Distilled Spirits
Emu Associations
Enology and Viticulture
Enternal Nutrition
Entomological Society
Exporters and Importers
Extension 4-H Agents
Farm Managers
Feed Control
Fertilizer Institute
Food Information Council
Forage and Grassland
Fresh Produce and Floral
Ginseng Research
Glass Packaging
Grange Association
Healthy Water
Herbal Products
Horticulture Science
Hotel and Restaurant Industries
Hydroponic Society
Industrial Caterers
Inflight Food Service
Institute of Ammonia
Italian Trade Commission
Label Printin
Livestock Breeds
Mexican Restaurants & Cantinas
Nutritional Consultants
Ohytopathological Society
Organic Alliance
Ostrich Association
Packaging Education Forum
Pecan Shellers
Pomological Society
Poultry Association
Refrigeration
Roundtable of Food Professionals
Seed Trade
Sheep Industry
Special Supplement Nutrition
Spice Trade
Vegetarian Awareness
Women in Flavor & Fragrance

Foundations & Fund Raising
Black Foundation Executives
Campus Fund Raising
Catholic Development Conference
Center for Effective Philanthropy
Christopher Reeve Paralysis Center
Healthcare Philanthropy
Learning Institute
Music Performance Trust Funds
Nonprofit Organization
State and Provincial Lotteries

Freight & Packaging
Customs Brokers and Forwarders
Foodservice & Packaging
Glass Packaging
Healthcare Compliance Packaging
International Container Leasing
Petroleum Packaging
Transportation Intermediaries

Furnishings & Fixtures
Cotton Batting
Floorcovering
Futon Association
Glass & Ceramic Decorators
Housewares Manufacturers
Illuminating Engineering Society
Innerspring Manufacturers
Rental Dealers
Store Fixtures
Waterbed Retailers
Woodworking & Furnishings

Garden & Lawn
Consulting Arborists
Farm Equipment
Garden Writers
Grounds Management
Horticultural Therapy
Irrigation Consultants
Landscape Architects
Mailorder
Pest Management
Plants for Clean Air

Content Summary of Chapter Listings

Society of Indexers
Special Libraries Association
Substance Abuse Librarians

Literary Services
Before Columbus Foundation
Dramatists Guild of America
Self-Employed Writers &Artists Network
Translators Association

Liquor
Enology & Vinticulture
Home Wine and Beer Trade Association
Society of Brewing Chemists
Wine and Spirits Shippers Association

Lumber & Wood
Arborist
Forest Landowners
Helicopter Loggers
Kiln Drying
National Wood Tank
Railway Ties
Truss Plate
Wood and Synthetic Flooring

Machinery
Abrasive Grain
Fluid Power Society
Mechanical Engineers
Polycrystalline Products
Powder Actuated Tool Manufacturers
Robotic Industries

Management
Best Employers Association
Center for Creative Leadership
Decision Sciences Institute
Floodplain Management Association
Executive Secretaries /Admin Assistants
Third World Resources
Work in America Institute
Young Presidents Organization

Manufacturing, Miscellaneous
Agile Manufacturing Benchmarking
Bearings
Brushes
Cotton Batting
Fireworks
Ice
Punches, Dies and Retainers
Pressure Vessels
Quality
Refractory
Technology
Textile Machinery
Ultrasonic Materials

Marketing
Athletic Collegiate Directors
Chambers of Commerce
Communications
Construction
Consumer Science
Floral
Food
Gasoline
Graphic Arts
Healthcare
Innovative Marketing
Legal
Materials
Multi Cultural
Photography
Specialty Equipment

Metals & Metalworking
American Farriers Association
American Foundrymens' Society
Electrical Manufacturing & Coil Winding Association
Gold Prospectors
Magnet Distributors and Fabricators
National Blacksmiths and Welders
Silver Institute
Society of American Silversmiths
Systems Builders Association
Welding Research Council

Mining
American Coal Ash Association
American Geological Institute
Bureau of Land Management
Crystal Growth
Desert Research Institute
Mineral Information Institute
Ocean Industries
Stone, Sand & Gravel Association

Motion Pictures
Assistant Directors Training Program
Casting Society of America
Film Society of Lincoln Center
International Documentary Association
International Stunt Association
Studio Teachers Association
Sundance Institute
University Film and Video Association

Motorcycles
Harley Owners
HIstoric Racing
Legal Assistance
Riders Foundation
Safety Foundation
Women in the Wind

Music
Academy of Songwriters
American Kodaly Educators
American Music Scholarships
American Music Therapy Association
International Polka
Music Performance Trust Funds
Musical Box Society
Pitch Pipes

Office Supplies & Services
Business Forms
Copier Dealers
Express Carriers
Florists
Label Printing
Office Planners
Printing

Paper & Allied Products
Corrugated Container
Gummed Industries
International Union

Performing Arts
American Luthiers
Box Office Management
Composers, Authors
Conductors Guild
Costumers
Dance Critics
Disc Jockey
Drama Therapy
Jazz Education
Music Copyists
Music Publishers
Piano Manufacturers
Pipe Organ Builders
Square Dance
Theatre Equipment
Theatrical Mutual Association
Thespians
Ventriloquists

Petroleum & Allied Products
Drilling
Geologists
Nuclear Energy
Ocean Industries
Oil Scouts
Propane Gas
Royalty Owners
Spill Control
Stripper Well
Well Log Analysis

Pets & Pet Supplies
American Farriers
Animal Legal Defense
Delta Society
Pet Food Institute
Pet Sitters

Photography
Photogrammetry & Remote Sensing
Picture Archives
Picture Framers
Travelogue Sponsors
White House Press Photographers

Plastics
Composites Fabricators
Electrical Overstress/Electrostatic
Polyolefins Fire Performance
Rotational Molders
Thermoforming

Plumbing
Distributors
Drainage
Kitchen and Bath
Mechanical Contractors
Plastic Pipe and Fittings
Plumbing Engineers
Plumbing, Heating, Cooling
Sanitary Engineering
Suppliers
Valve and Fittings
Wholesalers

Printing
Binding Industries
Die Stampers
Engravers Union
Flexographic Technical
Foil Stamping and Embossing
Lithographics
Metal Decorators
Plate Printers
Screen Printing & Graphic Imaging
Web Offset

Public Relations
Career Skills Press
Consumer Affairs
Public Affairs

Publishing
Antiquarian Booksellers
Audit Bureau of Circulation
Book Dealers Exchange
Business Publications
Copyright Society
Desktop Publishing
Digital Imaging
Flexographic Technical
Free Community Papers
Free Papers
Independent Publishers
Rare Books
Study Groups

Real Estate
Affordable Housing
American Rental
Appraisers
Building Owners and Managers
Council of Shopping
Farm Managers
Homeowners Foundation
Housing Cooperatives
International Exchangers Association
Land Title Association
Lobbies for the Industry
Low Income Housing
Mortgage Bankers
Neighborhood Reinvestment
Resort Development
Surveying & Mapping

Restaurants
American Bakers
Chef & Child Foundation
Cookware Manufacturers
Culinary Professionals
Educational Training
Mobile Industrial Caterers

Retailing
Business Practices
Franchises
Map Trades
Pawnbrokers
Store Planners
Surplus Dealers
Rubber
Engineering with Rubber
Polyurethane Foam
Recycled Rubber
Retread and Repair
Rubber Pavements
Rubber Statistics
Single Ply
Synthetic Rubber
Tires
Tread Rubber

Safety & Security
Aerosol Research
Biological Safety
Biometrics
Bomb Technicians
Conveyor Equipment
Cotton Ginners
Counterterroism
Dive Rescue Specialists
Fire Protection
Floodplain Managers

The North American Industry Classification System (NAICS, pronounced Nakes) was developed as the standard for use by Federal statistical agencies in classifying business establishments for the collection, analysis, and publication of statistical data related to the business economy of the U.S. NAICS was developed under the auspices of the Office of Management and Budget (OMB), and adopted in 1997 to replace the old Standard Industrial Classification (SIC) system (see page xxiii). Below are all relevant NAICS codes and descriptions. For a more detailed explanation of the NAICS, visit www.naics.com.

11	**Agriculture, Forestry, Fishing and Hunting**
11141	Food Crops Grown Under Cover
11191	Tobacco Farming
114	Fishing, Hunting and Trapping
115	Support Activities for Agriculture and Forestry
21	**Mining**
211111	Crude Petroleum and Natural Gas Extraction
212	Mining (except Oil and Gas)
22	**Utilities**
22131	Water Supply and Irrigation Systems
23	**Construction**
236	Construction of Buildings
237	Heavy and Civil Engineering Construction
23815	Glass and Glazing Contractors
23821	Electrical Contractors
23822	Plumbing, Heating, and Air-Conditioning Contractors
2383	Building Finishing Contractors
31-33	**Manufacturing**
311	Food Manufacturing
3111	Animal Food Manufacturing
31121	Flour Milling and Malt Manufacturing
3113	Sugar and Confectionery Product Manufacturing
3114	Fruit and Vegetable Preserving and Specialty Food Manufacturing
3115	Dairy Product Manufacturing
3117	Seafood Product Preparation and Packaging
3118	Bakeries and Tortilla Manufacturing
31191	Snack Food Manufacturing
31192	Coffee and Tea Manufacturing
31193	Flavoring Syrup and Concentrate Manufacturing
31194	Seasoning and Dressing Manufacturing
312	Beverage and Tobacco Product Manufacturing
3141	Textile Furnishings Mills
315	Apparel Manufacturing
315211	Men's and Boys' Cut and Sew Apparel Contractors
315212	Women's, Girls', and Infants' Cut and Sew Apparel Contractors
315292	Fur and Leather Apparel Manufacturing
3159	Apparel Accessories and Other Apparel Manufacturing
316	Leather and Allied Product Manufacturing
3162	Footwear Manufacturing
321	Wood Product Manufacturing
322	Paper Manufacturing
323	Printing and Related Support Activities
324	Petroleum and Coal Products Manufacturing
325	Chemical Manufacturing
3252	Resin, Synthetic Rubber, and Artificial Synthetic Fibers and Filaments Manufacturing
3253	Pesticide, Fertilizer, and Other Agricultural Chemical Manufacturing
3254	Pharmaceutical and Medicine Manufacturing
3255	Paint, Coating, and Adhesive Manufacturing
3256	Soap, Cleaning Compound, and Toilet Preparation Manufacturing
32591	Printing Ink Manufacturing
32592	Explosives Manufacturing
325992	Photographic Film, Paper, Plate, and Chemical Manufacturing
326	Plastics and Rubber Products Manufacturing
3262	Rubber Product Manufacturing
32621	Tire Manufacturing
32622	Rubber and Plastics Hoses and Belting Manufacturing
32629	Other Rubber Product Manufacturing
327	Nonmetallic Mineral Product Manufacturing
32711	Pottery, Ceramics, and Plumbing Fixture Manufacturing
32712	Clay Building Material and Refractories Manufacturing
3272	Glass and Glass Product Manufacturing
3273	Cement and Concrete Product Manufacturing
3274	Lime and Gypsum Product Manufacturing
32791	Abrasive Product Manufacturing
331	Primary Metal Manufacturing
332	Fabricated Metal Product Manufacturing
3325	Hardware Manufacturing
333	Machinery Manufacturing
3331	Agriculture, Construction, and Mining Machinery Manufacturing
3333	Commercial and Service Industry Machinery Manufacturing
3334	Ventilation, Heating, Air-Conditioning, and Commercial Refrigeration Equipment Manufacturing
3335	Metalworking Machinery Manufacturing
3336	Engine, Turbine, and Power Transmission Equipment Manufacturing
334	Computer and Electronic Product Manufacturing
3342	Communications Equipment Manufacturing
33422	Radio and Television Broadcasting and Wireless Communications Equipment Manufacturing
3343	Audio and Video Equipment Manufacturing
3344	Semiconductor and Other Electronic Component Manufacturing
3345	Navigational, Measuring, Electromedical, and Control Instruments Manufacturing
334518	Watch, Clock, and Part Manufacturing
3346	Manufacturing and Reproducing Magnetic and Optical Media
335	Electrical Equipment, Appliance, and Component Manufacturing
3353	Electrical Equipment Manufacturing
336	Transportation Equipment Manufacturing
3361	Motor Vehicle Manufacturing
3363	Motor Vehicle Parts Manufacturing
3364	Aerospace Product and Parts Manufacturing
3365	Railroad Rolling Stock Manufacturing
3366	Ship and Boat Building
336991	Motorcycle, Bicycle, and Parts Manufacturing
336992	Military Armored Vehicle, Tank, and Tank Component Manufacturing
337	Furniture and Related Product Manufacturing
3372	Office Furniture (including Fixtures) Manufacturing
3391	Medical Equipment and Supplies Manufacturing
33991	Jewelry and Silverware Manufacturing
33992	Sporting and Athletic Goods Manufacturing
33993	Doll, Toy, and Game Manufacturing
33994	Office Supplies (except Paper) Manufacturing
33995	Sign Manufacturing
42	**Wholesale Trade**
423	Merchant Wholesalers, Durable Goods
424	Merchant Wholesalers, Nondurable Goods
425	Wholesale Electronic Markets and Agents and Brokers
44-45	**Retail Trade**
441	Motor Vehicle and Parts Dealers
442	Furniture and Home Furnishings Stores
443	Electronics and Appliance Stores
444	Building Material and Garden Equipment and Supplies Dealers
445	Food and Beverage Stores
446	Health and Personal Care Stores
451	Sporting Goods, Hobby, Book, and Music Stores
453	Miscellaneous Store Retailers
454	Nonstore Retailers
48-49	**Transportation and Warehousing**
481	Air Transportation
482	Rail Transportation
483	Water Transportation
484	Truck Transportation

485 Transit and Ground Passenger Transportation
486 Pipeline Transportation
487 Scenic and Sightseeing Transportation
4885 Freight Transportation Arrangement
493 Warehousing and Storage

51 Information
511 Publishing Industries (except Internet)
5111 Newspaper, Periodical, Book, and Directory Publishers
5121 Motion Picture and Video Industries
51223 Music Publishers
515 Broadcasting (except Internet)
516 Internet Publishing and Broadcasting
517 Telecommunications
518 Data Processing, Hosting and Related Services
51912 Libraries and Archives
51913 Internet Publishing and Broadcasting and Web Search Portals

52 Finance and Insurance
522 Credit Intermediation and Related Activities
52211 Commercial Banking
522292 Real Estate Credit
522293 International Trade Financing
52311 Investment Banking and Securities Dealing
52392 Portfolio Management
52399 All Other Financial Investment Activities
524 Insurance Carriers and Related Activities
525 Funds, Trusts, and Other Financial Vehicles
5251 Insurance and Employee Benefit Funds
52593 Real Estate Investment Trusts

53 Real Estate and Rental and Leasing
531 Real Estate
5321 Automotive Equipment Rental and Leasing
53212 Truck, Utility Trailer, and RV (Recreational Vehicle) Rental and Leasing
53221 Consumer Electronics and Appliances Rental
53223 Video Tape and Disc Rental
5324 Commercial and Industrial Machinery and Equipment Rental and Leasing
533 Lessors of Nonfinancial Intangible Assets (except Copyrighted Works)

54 Professional, Scientific, and Technical Services
5411 Legal Services
5412 Accounting, Tax Preparation, Bookkeeping, and Payroll Services
5413 Architectural, Engineering, and Related Services
54135 Building Inspection Services
54141 Interior Design Services
54143 Graphic Design Services
541613 Marketing Consulting Services
54162 Environmental Consulting Services
5418 Advertising and Related Services
54182 Public Relations Agencies
54183 Media Buying Agencies
541921 Photography Studios, Portrait

56 Administrative and Support and Waste Management and Remediation Services
561422 Telemarketing Bureaus
56145 Credit Bureaus
5615 Travel Arrangement and Reservation Services
5616 Investigation and Security Services
5617 Services to Buildings and Dwellings
56191 Packaging and Labeling Services
562 Waste Management and Remediation Services

61 Educational Services
6114 Business Schools and Computer and Management Training

71 Arts, Entertainment, and Recreation
711 Performing Arts, Spectator Sports, and Related Industries
713 Amusement, Gambling, and Recreation Industries
71321 Casinos (except Casino Hotels)
71394 Fitness and Recreational Sports Centers

72 Accommodation and Food Services
7211 Traveler Accommodation
72111 Hotels (except Casino Hotels) and Motels
72112 Casino Hotels
7212 RV (Recreational Vehicle) Parks and Recreational Camps
722 Food Services and Drinking Places
7221 Full-Service Restaurants

81 Other Services (except Public Administration)
8111 Automotive Repair and Maintenance
811211 Consumer Electronics Repair and Maintenance
8113 Commercial and Industrial Machinery and Equipment (except Automotive and Electronic) Repair and Maintenance
81141 Home and Garden Equipment and Appliance Repair and Maintenance
8121 Personal Care Services
81231 Coin-Operated Laundries and Drycleaners
813211 Grantmaking Foundations
813312 Environment, Conservation and Wildlife Organizations

92 Public Administration
921 Executive, Legislative, and Other General Government Support
922 Justice, Public Order, and Safety Activities
924 Administration of Environmental Quality Programs
92612 Regulation and Administration of Transportation Programs
92613 Regulation and Administration of Communications, Electric, Gas, and Other Utilities
92614 Regulation of Agricultural Marketing and Commodities
928 National Security and International Affairs

The Standard Industrial Classification (SIC) is a United States government system for classifying industries by a four-digit code. Established in 1937, it has been supplanted by the six-digit North American Industry Classification System (NAICS) (see page ixx), which was released in 1997; however certain government departments and agencies, such as the U.S. Securities and Exchange Commission (SEC), still use SIC codes. Below are all major SIC codes and descriptions. For a more detailed explanation of the SIC system, visit http://www.census.gov/epcd/www/sic.html.

01 Agricultural Production - Crops

07 Agricultural Services

09 Fishing, Hunting and Trapping

10 Metal Mining

12 Coal Mining

13 Oil and Gas Extraction

14 Mining and Quarrying of Nonmetallic Minerals, Except Fuels

15 Building Construction - General Contractors & Operative Builders

16 Heavy Construction, Except Building Construction - Contractors

17 Construction - Special Trade Contractors

20 Food and Kindred Products

21 Tobacco Products

22 Textile Mill Products

23 Apparel and Other Finished Products Made From Fabrics and Similar Materials

24 Lumber and Wood Products, Except Furniture

25 Furniture and Fixtures

26 Paper and Allied Products

27 Printing, Publishing, and Allied Industries

28 Chemicals and Allied Products

29 Petroleum Refining and Related Industries

30 Rubber and Miscellaneous Plastics Products

31 Leather and Leather Products

32 Stone, Clay, Glass, and Concrete Products

33 Primary Metal Industries

34 Fabricated Metal Products, Except Machinery and Transportation Equipment

35 Industrial and Commercial Machinery and Computer Equipment

36 Electronic and Other Electrical Equipment and Components, Except Computer Equipment

37 Transportation Equipment

38 Measuring, Analyzing, and Controlling Instruments; Photographic, Medical and Optical Goods; Watches

39 Miscellaneous Manufacturing Industries

41 Local and Suburban Transit and Interurban Highway Passenger Transportation

42 Motor Freight Transportation and Warehousing

44 Water Transportation

45 Transportation By Air

47 Pipelines, Except Natural Gas

47 Transportation Services

48 Communications

49 Electric, Gas and Sanitary Services

50 Wholesale Trade-Durable Goods

51 Wholesale Trade-Non-Durable Goods

60 Depository Institutions

61 Non-Depository Credit Institutions

63 Insurance Carriers

65 Real Estate

73 Business Services

75 Automotive Repair, Services, and Parking

76 Miscellaneous Repair Services

78 Motion Pictures

79 Amusement and Recreation Services

80 Health Services

81 Legal Services

82 Educational Services

84 Museums, Art Galleries, and Botanical and Zoological Gardens

87 Engineering, Accounting, Research, Management, and Related Services

92 Justice, Public Order, and Safety

94 Administration of Human Resource Programs

95 Administration of Environmental Quality and Housing Programs

96 Administration of Economic Programs

97 National Security and International Affairs

Associations

1 **AGN International - North America**
2851 S Parker Rd
Suite 850
Aurora, CO 80014-2744

303-743-7880
800-782-2272
Fax: 303-743-7660
E-Mail: rhood@agn.org
Home Page: www.agn-na.org
Social Media: LinkedIn

Rita J. Hood, Executive Director
Patsy Bowen, Director/Member Services
Mark Pigg, Director/Information Systems
Nathalie Champagne, Director/Member Programs
Irene Hayden, Staff Training Coordinator

Worldwide association of separate and independent accounting and consulting firms. Composed of CPA consulting firms who share information and resources via the association programs. AGN-NA operates under the premise that by sharing information and resources, members' growth and quality goals can be achieved more quickly.
53 Members
Founded in 1978

2 **ARMA International**
11880 College Blvd
Suite 450
Overland Park, KS 66210

913-341-3808
800-422-2762
Fax: 913-341-3742
E-Mail: headquarters@armaintl.org
Home Page: www.arma.org

Julie J. Colgan, President
Marilyn Bier, Chief Executive Officer
Brenda Prowse, Treasurer
Diane Carlisle, Deputy Executive Director
Candace Daniels, Product Marketing Manager

ARMA International is a not-for-profit association and a source for authoritative education, the latest legislative updates, standards & best practices. The association was established in 1955. Its approximately 10,000 members include records managers, archivists, corporate librarians, imaging specialists, legal professionals, IT managers, consultants, and educators, all of whom work in a wide variety of industries.
11000 Members
Founded in 1955

3 **Academy of Accounting Historians**
Case Western Reserve University
10900 Euclid Avenue
Cleveland, OH 44106

216-368-2058
Fax: 205-368-6244
E-Mail: acchistory@case.edu
Home Page: www.aahhq.org
Social Media: Facebook, Twitter, LinkedIn, YouTube

Joann Cross, President
Massimo Sargiacomo, President Elect
Robert Colson, VP, Partnerships
Yvette Lazdowski, VP,Communications
Stephanie Moussalli, Secretary

Subjects include modern prespectives of accounting history.
600 Members
Founded in 1973

4 **Accounting & Financial Women's Alliance**
2365 Harrodsburg Road
Lexington, KY 40504

859-219-3532
800-326-2163
Fax: 859-219-3533
E-Mail: afwa@afwa.org
Home Page: afwa.org
Social Media: Facebook, Twitter, LinkedIn

Berranthia Brown, President
Dianna Patton, President Elect
Mary E. Duff, Treasurer
Karyn Hartke, Secretary
Ericka Harney, Executive Director

To enable women in all accounting and related fields to achieve their full personal, professional and economic potential and to contribute to the future development of their profession.
Founded in 1938

5 **Accreditation Council for Accountancy and Taxation**
1010 N. Fairfax Street
Alexandria, VA 22314

888-289-7763
Fax: 703-549-2984
Home Page: www.acatcredentials.org

Roy Frick, President
Micahel P. Salazar, Vice President
Christine Giovetti, Secretary/Treasurer
Micahel D. Kinkade, Education Director
Peter M. Berkery, Public Director

To identify professionals in independent practice who specialize in providing financial, accounting and taxation services to individuals and small to mid-size businesses.
Founded in 1973

6 **Advancing Government Accountability**
2208 Mount Vernon Avenue
Alexandria, VA 22301-1314

703-684-6931
800-AGA-7211
Fax: 703-548-9367
E-Mail: agacgfm@agacgfm.org
Home Page: www.agacgfm.org
Social Media: Facebook, Twitter, LinkedIn, Twitter, GovLoop

Mary E. Peterman, 2013-2014 National President
Relmond P. Van Daniker, Executive Director
Maryann Malesardi, Director of Communications/Journal
Jennifer I. Curtin, MPA, Director/Public Affairs
Kevin Johnson, Director of Education & Research

AGA supports the careers and professional development of government finance professionals working in federal, state and local governments as well as the private sector and academia. Through education, research, publications, certification and conferences, AGA reaches thousands of professionals and offers more than 100,000 continuing professional education (CPE) hours annually.
15000 Members
Founded in 1950
Mailing list available for rent: 18,000 names

7 **Affordable Housing Association of Certified Public Accountants**
459 N 300 W
Suite 11
Kaysville, UT 84037

801-547-0809
800-532-0809
Fax: 801-547-5070
E-Mail: info@ahacpa.org
Home Page: www.ahacpa.org

Les Sparks, President
Kathy Christensen, Contact
Mike Olsen, Contact
Susan Harris, Contact

AHACPA is a national association of CPAs and financial professionals providing financial services, support and education for the affordable housing and HUD-approved lender communities, informing members of financial requirements and provide specific guidance on how to efficiently implement those requirements.
Founded in 1998
Mailing list available for rent

8 **American Accounting Association**
5717 Bessie Drive
Sarasota, FL 34233-2399

941-921-7747
Fax: 941-923-4093
E-Mail: info@aaahq.org
Home Page: www.aaahq.org
Social Media: Facebook, Twitter

Tracey Sutherland, Executive Director
Julie Smith David, Chief Innovation Officer
Dave Frazier, Finance Director
Diane Hazard, Publications Director
Lindsay Peters, Publications Assistant

The American Accounting Association promotes worldwide excellence in accounting education, research and practice. The Association is a voluntary organization of persons interested in accounting education and research.
9000 Members
Founded in 1916

9 **American Association for Budget and Program Analysis**
PO Box 1157
Falls Church, VA 22041

703-941-4300
Fax: 703-941-1535
E-Mail: aabpa@aabpa.org
Home Page: www.aabpa.org
Social Media: Facebook, Twitter, LinkedIn, GovLoop

Melissa Neuman, President
Anthony Rainey, Vice President for Symposia
Sandra Beattie, Vice President for Programs
Sarah McGrath, Vice President for Communications
Karen Kunz, Membership Director

Helps federal, state, and local government managers and analysts, corporate executives and academic specialists meet the unique challenges of their careers. By helping members keep up with the latest developments in their fields, establish and maintain contacts with colleagues, represent their interests and share opportunities, AABPA serves the key difference between simply having a job and being part of a highly respected and well trained profession.
400 Members
Founded in 1976

10 **American Association of Attorney-Certified Public Accountants**
8647 Richmond Hwy.
Suite 639
Alexandria, VA 22309

703-352-8064
888-288-9272
Fax: 703-352-8073
E-Mail: info@attorney-cpa.com
Home Page: www.attorney-cpa.com

Domenick R. Lioce, President
Joseph E. Cordell, President Elect/ Vice President
Nicole E. Ratner, Executive Director

Katie Cammer, Program Development
Kimmy Livingston, Director, Membership

The AAA-CPA is the only association in the nation whose members are comprised of professionals dually qualified as both attorneys and certified public accountants. Today, the AAA-CPA offers an array of products and services to help members succeed in their practice such as; networking and referral

1370 Members
Founded in 1964

11 **American Association of Finance & Accounting**

1702 E. Highland Ave
Suite 200
Phoenix, AZ 85016

602-277-3700
Fax: 602-926-2629
E-Mail: mnolan@afpersonnel.com
Home Page: www.aafa.com

An alliance of executive search firms specializing in the recruiting of finance and accounting professionals.

Founded in 1978

12 **American Association of Managing General Agents**

610 Freedom Business Center
Suite 110
King of Prussia, PA 19406

610-992-0022
Fax: 610-992-0021
E-Mail: mark@aamga.org
Home Page: www.aamga.org
Social Media: Facebook, Twitter, LinkedIn

Bernd G. Heinze, Esq, Executive Director
Matthew Letson, President
Roger Ware, Jr, President Elect
David Thomas, Senior Vice President
Ed Dickerson, Vice President

Trade association to international wholesale insurance professionals and leader in representing the interests of its members before federal, state,and local governments and regulatory agencies

Founded in 1926

13 **American College of Trust and Estate Counsel**

901 15th Street, NW
Suite 525
Washington, DC 20005

202-684-8460
Fax: 202-684-8459
Home Page: www.actec.org
Social Media: Twitter

Kathleen R. Sherby, President
Bruce Stone, President Elect
Cynda C. Ottaway, Vice President
Susan T. House, Treasurer
Charles D. Fox, Secretary

Nonprofit association of lawyers that advises clients on planning for tax efficient transfer of wealth during life and after death, preparing real estate planning documents, administering trusts, guardianships, planning for employee benefits, etc.

Founded in 1949

14 **American Council of Life Insurers**

101 Constitution Avenue
Suite 700
Washington, DC 20001-2133

202-624-2000
877-674-4659
E-Mail: contact@acli.com
Home Page: www.acli.com
Social Media: Facebook, Twitter, LinkedIn, YouTube

Roger W. Crandall, Chairman
Deanna Mulligan, Chairman-Elect
Dirk Kempthorne, President & Chief Executive Officer
Brian Waidmann, Chief of Staff
Kimberly Olson Dorgan, Senior Vice President

Trade association advocating federal, state, and international forums for public policy that supports the industry marketplace. ACLI members offer life insurance, annuities, retirement plans, long-term care, disability income insurance, and reinsurance.

15 **American Institute of Certified Public Accountants**

1211 Avenue of the Americas
New York, NY 10036

212-596-6200
888-777-7077
Fax: 212-596-6213
E-Mail: service@aicpa.org
Home Page: www.aicpa.org
Social Media: Facebook, Twitter, LinkedIn, RSS

William E. Balhoff, Chairman
Barry C Melancon, President & Chief Executive Officer
Susan Coffey, Senior Vice President
Mark Peterson, Senior Vice President
Anthony Pugliese, Senior Vice President

The American Institute of Certified Public Accountants is the national, professional organization for all Certified Public Accountants. Its mission is to provide members with the resources, information, and leadership that enable them to provide valuable services in the highest professional manner to benefit the public as well as employers and clients.

Founded in 1887

16 **American Institute of Professional Bookkeepers**

6001 Montrose Road
Suite 500
Rockville, MD 20852

800-622-0121
Fax: 800-541-0066
E-Mail: info@aipb.org
Home Page: www.aipb.org

Stanley Hartman, Executive Director
Stephen Sahlein, Director of Publishing
Carol Watson, Director
Robin Merrill, Assistant Manager
Kenia Salgado, Manager

Achieve recognition of bookkeepers as accounting professionals, keep bookkeepers up to date on changes in bookkeeping, accounting and tax, answer questions on bookkeeping and accounting, and certify bookkeepers.

30000 Members
Founded in 1987

17 **American Payroll Association**

660 North Main Avenue
Suite 100
San Antonio, TX 78205-1217

210-226-4600
Fax: 210-226-4027
E-Mail: apa@americanpayroll.org
Home Page: www.americanpayroll.org
Social Media: Facebook, Twitter, LinkedIn

Deborah Viers Traylor, President
Christine Avery, Managing Editor/Membership
Caren Jean Bennett, Editorial Assistant
Patricia Bowton, Director/Certification
Debbie Cervini, Production Coordinator

The American Payroll Association is the leading advocate for the advancement of payroll professionals and a catalyst for connecting the payroll industry with employers and government. Our vision is to create opportunities and forge a community by providing the education, skills, and resources necessary for payroll professionals to become successful leaders and strategic partners within their organizations.

21000 Members
Founded in 1982

18 **American Property Tax Counsel**

1970 East Grand Ave.
Suite 330
El Segundo, CA 90245

310-364-0193
Home Page: www.aptcnet.com
Social Media: LinkedIn

Provides property tax services locally and nationally.

19 **American Society of Military Comptrollers**

415 N Alfred St
Alexandria, VA 22314-2269

703-549-0360
800-462-5637
Fax: 703-549-3181
Home Page: www.asmconline.org
Social Media: Facebook, Twitter, LinkedIn

Marilyn M Thomas, President
Gretchen Anderson, Vice President
Al Runnels, Executive Director
Riitta Silverman, Associate Director for Finance
Phara G. Rodrigue, Associate Director

ASMC is the non-profit educational and professional organization for persons, military and civilian, involved in the overall field of military comptrollership. ASMC promotes the education and training of its members, and supports the development and advancement of the profession of military comptrollership. The society sponsors research, provides professional programs to keep members abreast of current issues and encourages the exchange of techniques and approaches.

18000 Members
Founded in 1948

20 **American Society of Women Accountants**

1760 Old Meadow Road
Suite 500
McLean, VA 22102

703-506-3265
800-326-2163
Fax: 703-506-3266
E-Mail: aswa@aswa.org
Home Page: www.aswa.org
Social Media: Facebook, Twitter, LinkedIn, ASWA Presidents Blog

Lee Lowery, Executive Director
Elizabeth Johnson, Manager/Association Services
Michelle Delarosa, Executive Adminstrator
Kate O'Donnell, Creative Services Manager
Elisa Perodin, Events Director

The American Society of Women Accountants (ASWA) was formed to increase the opportunities for women in all fields of accounting and finance. Members and their companies benefit from practical resources and benefit programs that strengthen their professional growth. ASWA members tap into an extensive knowledge base of accounting and finance professionals with technical expertise.

4000 Members
Founded in 1938

21 **American Woman's Society of Certified Public Accountants**
136 South Keowee Street
Dayton, OH 45402

937-222-1872
800-297-2721
Fax: 937-222-5794
E-Mail: info@awscpa.org
Home Page: www.awscpa.org
Social Media: Facebook, Twitter, LinkedIn

Kelly Welter, President
Kimberly Fantaci, Executive Director
Janet A. Young, VP/Membership
Cynthia Cox, VP/Affiliates
Bonnie L. Mackey, VP/Marketing

The American Woman's Society of Certified Public Accountants (AWSCPA) began in 1933 as a group of nine women CPAs united in facing the challenges affecting women in the profession at that time. Over the years, the organization has grown. Membership increased dramatically in 1982 when the membership amended the Society's bylaws to allow affiliated local groups. Today, AWSCPA has 25 affiliates located throughout the country with a membership of approximately 2,000.
1500 Members
Founded in 1933

22 **Appraisers Association of America**
212 West 35th Street
11th Floor South
New York, NY 10001

212-889-5404
Fax: 212-889-5503
E-Mail: referrals@appraisersassociation.org
Home Page: www.appraisersassociation.org
Social Media: Facebook, Twitter, LinkedIn

Betty Krulik, President
Deborah G. Spanierman, First Vice President
Elizabeth von Habsburg, Second Vice President
Linda Selvin, Executive Director
Daile Kaplan, Secretary

Develop and promote skills in the profession of appraising through education and professional practice.
Founded in 1949

23 **Association for Accounting Administration**
136 S Keowee Street
Dayton, OH 45402

937-222-0030
Fax: 937-222-5794
E-Mail: aaainfo@cpaadmin.org
Home Page: www.cpaadmin.org
Social Media: Facebook, Twitter, LinkedIn

Norman Saale, President
Janine Zirrith, Vice President
Kimberly A. Fantaci, Executive Director
Ann White, Director of Education
Sharon Trabbic, Director of Membership & Growth

The Association of Accounting Administrators enables accounting firm administrators to communicate with one another and provide each other with the benefits of everyone's experiences in what was a new and emerging profession.
900 Members
Founded in 1984

24 **Association for Accounting Marketing**
15000 Commerce Parkway
Suite C
Mount Laurel, NJ 08054

856-380-6850
Fax: 856-439-0525
E-Mail: info@accountingmarketing.org
Home Page: www.accountingmarketing.org
Social Media: Facebook, Twitter

Katie Tolin, President
Jack Kolmansberger, Vice President
Pete Pomilio, Executive Director
Bill Penczak, Chief Market Development Officer
Nancy Wine, Director of Marketing

The Association for Accounting Marketing (AAM) is a national organization and is the only trade association of its kind that provides resources, education, seminars, workshops, support and a global network to the accounting marketing industry. Our membership includes accounting firm marketers from Big Four and other national, regional, local and sole proprietor firms. Others include sales and business development professionals, accounting partners, firm administrators, and students.
843 Members
Founded in 1989

25 **Association for Management Information in Financial Services**
14247 Saffron Circle
Carmel, IN 46032

317-815-5857
E-Mail: ami2@amifs.org
Home Page: www.amifs.org
Social Media: Facebook, Twitter, LinkedIn

A nonprofit professional association dedicated to developing and advancing the profession of management information for the financial services industry.
Founded in 1980

26 **Association of Accounting Administrators**
136 South Keowee Street
Dayton, OH 45402

937-222-0030
E-Mail: aaainfo@cpaadmin.org
Home Page: www.cpaadmin.org
Social Media: Facebook, Twitter, LinkedIn

Janine Zirrith, President
Jim Fahey, Vice President
Jane Johnson, Secretary
Robert E. Biddle, Treasurer
Ann White, Director of Education
Founded in 1984

27 **Association of Certified Fraud Examiners**
716 West Ave
Austin, TX 78701-2727

512-478-9000
800-245-3321
Fax: 512-478-9297
E-Mail: memberservices@acfe.com
Home Page: www.acfe.com
Social Media: Facebook, Twitter, LinkedIn

Joseph T Wells, Chairman
James D Ratley, President/CEO
John D Gill, VP/Education
John Warren, VP/General Counsel
Jeanette LeVie, VP/Adminstration

The ACFE is reducing business fraud world-wide and inspiring public confidence in the integrity and objectivity within the profession.
65000 Members
Founded in 1988

28 **Association of Chartered Accountants in the United States**
3887 Punahele Road
Princeville, HI 96722

508-395-0224
E-Mail: admin@acaus.org
Home Page: www.acaus.org
Social Media: Facebook

Lindi Jarvis, President
Michael Dexter Smith, Executive Director
Natasha Holbeck, Secretary
Timothy Clackett, Treasurer
David Freeman, Board Member

ACAUS is a nonprofit professional and educational organization representing interests of U.S. based chartered accountants from the institutes of Chartered Accountants across the globe.
6000 Members
Founded in 1980

29 **Association of College and University Auditors**
PO Box 14306
Lenexa, KS 66285

913-895-4620
Fax: 913-895-4652
E-Mail: ACUA-info@goAMP.com
Home Page: www.acua.org
Social Media: Facebook, Twitter, LinkedIn

Douglas D. Horr, President
Sandy Jansen, Vice President
Francis Bossle, Executive Director
Robert Berry, Chief Audit Executive
Michael Bordoni, Chief Audit Officer

The Association of College and University Auditors (ACUA) is a professional organization comprised of audit professionals from all over the globe. We strive to continually improve the internal operations and processes of the individual institutions we serve, through continued professional development and the dissemination of individual internal audit experiences in an open forum with friends and colleagues.
Founded in 1958

30 **Association of Credit Union Internal Auditors**
PO Box 150908
Alexandria, VA 22315

703-688-2284
Fax: 703-348-7602
E-Mail: acuia@acuia.org
Home Page: www.acuia.org
Social Media: Facebook, Twitter, LinkedIn

Dana McCranie, Chairman
Amy Schaefer, Vice Chair
Nathan Cunningham, Secretary
Linda Goff, Treasurer
Jill Chase, Director

ACUIA is committed to being a quality provider of credit union internal audit resources. ACUIA is an international professional organization dedicated to the practice of internal auditing in credit unions. ACUIA's objectives are: to unify and encourage cooperative relationships among credit union internal auditors to facilitate the exchange of information and ideas; to provide educational opportunities for developing and enhancing audit and leadership skills; promote the IA profession.
600 Members
Founded in 1991

31 **Association of Government Accountants**
2208 Mount Vernon Ave
Alexandria, VA 22301-1314

703-684-6931
800-AGA-7211
Fax: 703-548-9367
E-Mail: agacgfm@agacgfm.org
Home Page: www.agacgfm.org
Social Media: LinkedIn

Mary E. Peterman, National President
Relmond P. Van Daniker, Executive Director
Cristina Barbudo, Director of

Finance/Administration
Maryann Malesardi, Director of Communications/Journal
Jennifer I Curtin, Director of Public Affairs

AGA supports the careers and professional development of government finance professionals working in federal, state and local governments as well as the private sector and academia. Through education, research, publications, certification and conferences, AGA reaches thousands of professionals and offers more than 100,000 continuing professional education (CPE) hours annually.
Founded in 1950

32 **Association of Healthcare Internal Auditors**
10200 W 44th Avenue
Suite 304
Wheat Ridge, CO 80003

303-327-7546
888-ASK-AHIA
Fax: 303-422-8894
E-Mail: ahia@ahia.org
Home Page: www.ahia.org

Robert Michalski, Chairman
Heidi Crosby, Vice Chair
David Stumph, Executive Director
Kelly Nueske, Managing Director
Dagmar Herrmann Estes, Director

The Association of Internal Auditors (AHIA) is a network of experienced healthcare internal auditing professionals who come together to share tools, knowledge and insight on how to assess and evaluate risk within a complex and dynamic healthcare environment. AHIA is an advocate for the profession, continuing to elevate and champion the strategic importance of healthcare internal auditors with executive management and the Board.
885 Members
Founded in 1981

33 **Association of Independent Accounting Professionals**
E-Mail: staff@aiaponline.com
Home Page: www.aiaponline.com

An online resource designed for today's independent accountant—provides practice expansion opportunities, information, and resources.

34 **Association of Insolvency Advisors and Restructuring Advisors**
221 Stewart Avenue
Suite 207
Medford, OR 97501-3647

541-858-1665
Fax: 541-858-9187
E-Mail: aira@aira.org
Home Page: www.aira.org
Social Media: Twitter, LinkedIn

Stephen Darr, Chairman
Anthony Sasso, President
Thomas Morrow, Vice President
Gina Gutzeit, Vice President - Member Services
Joel Waite, Vice President - Development

AIRA is a nonprofit professional association serving the bankruptcy, restructuring and turnaround practice area. AIRA's membership consists of accountants, financial advisors, investment bankers, attorneys, workout consultants, trustees, and others in the field of business turnaround, restructuring and bankruptcy. AIRA members are among the most trusted and sought-after professionals in matters dealing with limited capital resources and deteriorating operating performance.
2000+ Members
Founded in 1984

35 **Association of Insolvency and Reconstruction**
221 W. Stewart Avenue
Suite 207
Medford, OR 97501

541-858-1665
Fax: 541-858-9187
E-Mail: aira@aira.org
Home Page: www.aira.org

Anthony Sasso, Chairman
Matthew Schwartz, President
Thomas Morrow, President Elect
Angela Shortall, Vice President
Grant Newton, Executive Director
Founded in 1979

36 **Association of Latino Professionals in Finance and Accounting**
801 South Grand Avenue
Suite 650
Los Angeles, CA 90014

213-243-0004
Fax: 213-243-0006
E-Mail: info@national.alpfa.org
Home Page: www.alpfa.org
Social Media: Facebook, Twitter, LinkedIn, YouTube, Flickr

Manuel Espinoza, Chuief Executive Officer
Pamela Ravare Browne, Chief Operating Officer
Steve Calderon, Chief Financial Officer
Zenaida Medoza, Chief Creative Officer
Suri Surinder, Chief Operating Officer

ALPFA is the leading professsional association dedicated to enhancing opportunities for Latinos in the accounting, finance and related professions. ALPFA is a nonprofit entity registered with the IRS.
Founded in 1972

37 **Association of Local Government Auditors**
859-276-0686
E-Mail: tadams@ci.charlotte.nc.us
Home Page: algaonline.org
Social Media: Twitter, LinkedIn

Corrie Stokes, President
Kymber Waltmunson, President Elect
Bill Greene, Past President
David Givans, Treasurer
Tina Adams, Secretary

A professional organization committed to supporting and improving local government auditing through advocacy, collaboration, education, and training.

38 **Association of Public Pension Fund Auditors**
PO Box 16064
Columbus, OH 43216-6064

Home Page: www.appfa.org

Ryan Babin, President
Greg Beck, Vice President
Amy L. Barett, Secretary
Mary Kay Howard, Treasurer
Dave McKnight, Board Member

A professional association consisting of internal auditors dedicated to providing comprehensive professional development and networking opportunities for its members.
100 Members
Founded in 1991

39 **BCCA**
550 Frontage Road
Northfield, IL 60093

847-881-8757
Fax: 847-784-8059
E-Mail: info@bccacredit.com
Home Page: www.bccacredit.com
Social Media: Facebook, Twitter

Mary Collin, CEO
Jamie Smith, Director of Operations
Cindy Laser, Sales/Membership

BCCA is the media industry's credit association that functions as a central clearing house for credit information on advertisers, agencies and buying services, both locally and nationally. Also provides an Electronic Media Credit Application (EMCAPP.com) to members that helps streamline the application process. One app in one location!
545 Members
Founded in 1972

40 **Beta Alpha Psi**
220 Leigh Farm Road
Durham, NC 27707

919-402-4044
E-Mail: bap@bap.org
Home Page: www.bap.org
Social Media: Facebook, Twitter, LinkedIn

Jan Taylor Morris, President
Margaret Fiorentino, Executive Director
Cortney Sanders, Marketing & Communications
Amber Johnson, Manager/Events/Meetings
Lisa Wicker, Manager - Chapter Services

BETA ALPHA PSI is an honorary organization for Financial Information students and professionals. The primary objective of Beta Alpha Psi is to encourage and give recognition to scholastic and professional excellence in the business information field. This includes promoting the study and practice of accounting, finance and information systems; providing opportunities for self-development, service and association among members and practicing professionals.
300K Members
Founded in 1919

41 **Broadcast Cable Credit Association**
550 W Frontage Rd
Suite 3600
Northfield, IL 60093-1243

847-881-8757
Fax: 847-784-8059
E-Mail: info@bccacredit.com
Home Page: www.bccacredit.com
Social Media: Facebook, Twitter

Mary Collins, President/CEO
Jamie Smith, Director/Operations
Cindy Laser, BCCA Sales/Membership
Marylou Harris, Credit Investigator
Susan Graves, Credit Investigator

BCCA, a subsidiary of Media Financial Management Association, represents credit and collection professionals from TV, radio, cable, system operators, newspaper, and magazine organizations in the U.S. and Canada. BCCA functions as a central clearinghouse for credit information on advertisers, agencies and buying services, both locally and nationally.
600 Members
Founded in 1972

42 **CPA Associates International**
Meadows Office Complex
301 Route 17 North
Rutherford, NJ 07070-2599
201-804-8686
Fax: 201-804-9222
E-Mail: homeoffice@cpaai.com
Home Page: www.cpaai.com

Glenda A. Nixon, Chairman
Hans van den Besselaar, Chairman-Elect
James F. Flynn, President
Miguel Angel Vallejo, Treasurer
Ted A. Carnevale, Secretary

CPA Associates International was established as a global group of high-quality independent CPA and chartered accounting firms; it is market exclusive, with members in major cities throughout the world. The organized association provides members with the capabilities of the largest firm, yet allows each to maintain its local practice while avoiding costly overhead and unnecessary controls.
158 Members
Founded in 1960

43 **CPAsNET.com**
PO Box 7648
Princeton, NJ 8543

609-890-0800
Fax: 609-689-9720
E-Mail: solutions@cpasnet.com
Home Page: www.cpasnet.com

An association of accounting and business consulting firms who havepooled their resources to provide their clients with the local, national, and international perspective needed to prosper.
500 Members

44 **Construction Financial Management Association**
100 Village Blvd
Suite 200
Princeton, NJ 08540-5783

609-452-8000
888-421-9996
Fax: 609-452-0474
E-Mail: info@cfma.org
Home Page: www.cfma.org
Social Media: Facebook, Twitter, LinkedIn

Stuart Binstock, President/CEO
Brian Summers, Vice President, Content Management
Robert Rubin, Controller
Michael Verbanic, Director/Member Experience
Stacy Williams, Membership Assistant

CFMA is the only organization dedicated to bringing together construction financial professionals and those partners serving their unique needs. CFMA has 89 chapters located throughout the US and Canada.
7000 Members
Founded in 1981

45 **Construction Industry CPA/Consultants Association**
15011 East Twilight View Drive
Fountain Hills, AZ 85268

480-836-0300
800-864-0491
Fax: 480-836-0400
E-Mail: jcorcoran@cicpac.com
Home Page: www.cicpac.com

Bob Biehl, President
Chris Iannuzzi, Vice President
Ken Gardiner, Secretary/ Treasurer
Brad Gross, At Large Director
David Heier, At Large Director

The Construction Industry CPAs/Consultants Association (CICPAC) is a national association of CPA firms recognized in their respective markets for providing high quality financial and consulting services. Each firm is the exclusive member in its area and must demonstrate proficiency in construction industry services and a reputation for high-quality work and integrity.
7500 Members
Founded in 1989

46 **Construction Industry CPAs/Consultants Association**
15011 East Twilight View Drive
Fountain Hills, AZ 85268

480-836-0300
Fax: 480-836-0400
E-Mail: jcorcoran@cicpac.com
Home Page: www.cicpac.com

Dan Donofrio, President
Chris Iannuzzi, President Elect
Ken Gardiner, Vice President
Jacquelyn Daenen, Secretary/Treasurer
John Corcoran, Executive Director
Founded in 1989

47 **Federation of Schools of Accountancy**
220 Leigh Farm Road
Durham, NC 27707-8110

919-402-4825
E-Mail: mtarasi@aicpa.org
Home Page: www.thefsa.org

Robert Ricketts, President
Michael Roberts, Vice President
Rebecca Shortridge, Secretary
Timothy A. Pearson, Treasurer
Yvonne Hinson, Past President

Promotes and supports high-quality graduate accounting programs andachieves public trust in the accounting profession through leadership in supporting and shaping high quality accounting education.
Founded in 1978

48 **Federation of Tax Administrators**
444 N. Capitol Street NW
Suite 348
Washington, DC 20001

202-624-5890
Fax: 202-624-7888
Home Page: www.taxadmin.org

David Sullivan, President
Doug MacGinnitie, First Vice President
Michael Reissig, Second Vice President
Gale Garriott, Executive Director
Dawn Cash, Secretary

A nonprofit corporation designed to improve the quality of state tax administration by providing services to state tax authorities and administrators. These services include research and information exchange, training, and intergovernmental and interstate coordination.
Founded in 1937

49 **Financial Accounting Standards Board**
401 Merritt Boulevard
PO Box 5116
Norwalk, CT 06856-5116

203-847-0700
Fax: 203-849-9714
E-Mail: director@fasb.org
Home Page: www.fasb.org
Social Media: Twitter, RSS

Russell G. Golden, Chairman
Ronald W. Lott, Research Director
Susan M Cosper, Technical Director
Suzanne Q. Bielstein, Director-Planning and Support
Matthew Esposito, Assistant Director

The mission of the FASB is to establish and improve standards of financial accounting and reporting that foster financial reporting by nongovernmental entities that provides decision-useful information to investors and other users of financial reports. That mission is accomplished through a comprehensive and independent process that encourages broad participation, objectively considers all stakeholder views, and is subject to oversight by the Financial Accounting Foundation's Board of Trustees.
Founded in 1973

50 **Financial Executives International**
1250 Headquarters Plaza
West Tower, 7th Floor
Morristown, NJ 07960

973-765-1000
Fax: 973-765-1018
Home Page: www.financialexecutives.org
Social Media: Facebook, Twitter, LinkedIn, YouTube

Taylor Hawes, Sr., Chairman
Marie N Hollein, President/CEO
Tracy McBride, VP, Research and Accounting
Paul Chase, VP and CFO
Mark Steele, Vice President, IT and Web Services

FEI strives to be recognized globally as the leading organization for senior-level financial executives. Connects members through: interaction: providing local and international forums for connecting with peers, information: providing insight to assist with informed business decisions, influence: providing authoritative representation for members' interests, and integrity: providing the tools to advance the profession through ethical leadership.
15M Members
Founded in 1931

51 **Financial Management Association International**
University of South Florida
4202 E Fowler Ave
BSN 3331
Tampa, FL 33620-5500

813-974-2084
Fax: 813-974-3318
E-Mail: fma@coba.usf.edu
Home Page: www.fma.org

Jack S Rader, Executive Director
Douglas R Emery, President Elect
Franklin Allen, VP Program
Alexander J Triantis, VP Global Services
Ajay Patel, Secretary/Treasurer

Serving the global finance community by: Promoting the development of high-quality research that extends the frontier of financial knowledge; Promoting the understanding of basic and applied research and of sound financial practices; Enhancing the quality and relevance of education in finance; Providing opportunities for professional interaction between and among academics, practitioners, and students
Founded in 1970

52 **Financial Managers Society**
1 North LaSalle Street
Suite 3100
Chicago, IL 60602-4003

312-578-1300
800-275-4367
Fax: 312-578-1308
E-Mail: info@fmsinc.org
Home Page: www.fmsinc.org
Social Media: Facebook, Twitter, LinkedIn

Alan Renfroe, Chairman
Sydney K. Garmong, Vice Chairman
Dick Yingst, President
Darrell E. Blocker, Senior Vice President
Darrell Rains, CFO

Provides service to financial personnel such as savings and loan financial officers, and to community commercial banks and credit unions.
Founded in 1948

53 **Government Finance Officers Association**
203 N. LaSalle Street
Suite 2700
Chicago, IL 60601-1210

312-977-9700
Fax: 312-977-4806
Home Page: www.gfoa.org
Social Media: Facebook, Twitter, LinkedIn, YouTube

Robert W. Eichem, President
Heather A. Johnston, President Elect
Ade A. Ariwoola, Finance Director
Lori A. Economy Scholler, Chief Financial Officer
David C. Olsen, Treasurer

Represents public finance officials throughout the United States and Canada and promotes the professional management of governmental financial resources by indentifying, developing, and advancing fiscal strategies, policies, and practices for the public benefit.

54 **Government Officers Finance Association**
203 North Lasalle Street
Suite 2700
Chicago, IL 60601-1210

312-977-9700
Fax: 312-977-4806
Home Page: www.gfoa.org

Timothy L. Firestine, President
Robert W. Eichem, President-Elect
Jeffrey L. Esser, Executive Director CEO
Julia Harper Cooper, Board Member
Linda Cramer, Board Member

The purpose of the Government Finance Officers Association is to enhance and promote the professional management of governments for the public benefit by identifying and developing financial policies and best practices and promoting their use through education, training, facilitation of member networking, and leadership.
16000 Members
Founded in 1906

55 **Healthcare Financial Management Association**
3 Westbrook Corporate Center
Suite 7600
Westchester, IL 60154-5723

708-531-9600
800-252-4362
Fax: 708-531-0032
Home Page: www.hfma.org
Social Media: Facebook, Twitter, LinkedIn, YouTube

Joseph J. Fifer, FHFMA, CPA, President & Chief Executive Officer
Edwin P. Czopek, Senior Vice President
Susan Brenkus, VP, Human Resources
Richard L. Gundling, VP, Healthcare Financial
Lee Guthrie, VP, Marketing & Business

HFMA is the nation's leading membership organization for healthcare financial management executives and leaders. HFMA's vision is to be the indispensable resource for healthcare finance.
35000 Members
Founded in 1950

56 **Hospitality Financial and Technology Professionals**
11709 Boulder Lane
Suite 110
Austin, TX 78726

512-249-5333
800-646-4387
Fax: 512-249-1533
E-Mail: Membership@hftp.org
Home Page: www.hftp.org
Social Media: Facebook, Twitter, LinkedIn

Jerry Trieber, President
Daniel N. Conti, Jr., Vice President
Frank I Wolfe, Executive VP/CEO
Lucinda Hart, COO
Thomas Atzenhofer, CFO

HFTP is an international, professional association providing a global network, continuing education and resources to the hospitality, finance and technology communities.
4600 Members
Founded in 1952

57 **INPACT Americas**
PO Box 495
Frederick, MD 21705-0495

301-694-8580
Fax: 301-694-5804
E-Mail: inpactam@inpactam.org
Home Page: www.inpactam.org

Reynold P. Cicalese, President
Mara Ambrose, Executive Director
Kevin R. Hessler, Treasurer
Ralph J. Cetrulo, Director
Bruce C. Levine, Director

A nonprofit association focused on contributing to the profitability and success of North America's accounting and consulting firms through management and marketing programs and resources.

58 **Information Resources Management Association**
701 E Chocolate Ave
Suite 200
Hershey, PA 17033-1240

717-533-8845
Fax: 717-533-8661
E-Mail: member@irma-international.org
Home Page: www.irma-international.org

Jan Travers, Executive Director
Sherif Kamel, Communications Director
Lech Janczewski PhD, IRMA World Representative Director
Gerald Grant, IRMA Doctoral Symposium Director
Paul Chalekian, IRMA United States Representative

An international professional organization dedicated to advancing the concepts and practices of information resources management in modern organizations. The primary objective of IRMA is to assist organizations and professionals in enhancing the overall knowledge and understanding of effective information resource management in the early 21st century and beyond.

59 **Information Systems Audit & Control Association (ISACA)**
3701 Algonquin Rd
Suite 1010
Rolling Meadows, IL 60008-3124

847-253-1545
Fax: 847-253-1443
E-Mail: news@isaca.org
Home Page: www.isaca.org
Social Media: Facebook, Twitter, LinkedIn, Google+

Tony Hayes, International President
Allan Boardman, International Vice President
Juan Luis Carselle, International Vice President
Rams,s Gallego, International Vice President
Theresa Grafenstine, International Vice President

With members in more than 160 countries, ISACA is a recognized worldwide leader in IT governance, control, security and assurance. Sponsors international conferences, publishes the thw ISACA Journal and develops international information systems auditing and control standards.
75000 Members
Founded in 1969

60 **Institute for Professionals in Taxation**
600 Northpark Town Center
1200 Abernathy Rd., Suite L-2
Atlanta, GA 30328-1040

404-240-2300
Fax: 404-240-2315
E-Mail: website@ipt.org
Home Page: www.ipt.org

Arthur E. Bennett, President
Margaret C. Wilson, First Vice President
Chris G. Muntifering, Second Vice President
Margaret Dickson, Chief Financial Officer
Cass D. Vickers, Executive Director

A nonprofit educational association that provides educational programs, certifies, and establishes strict codes of conduct for state and local income, property, and sales.
4400 Members
Founded in 1976

61 **Institute of Internal Auditors**
247 Maitland Ave
Altamonte Springs, FL 32701-4201

407-937-1111
Fax: 407-937-1101
E-Mail: CustomerRelations@theiia.org
Home Page: na.theiia.org
Social Media: Facebook, Twitter, LinkedIn, Auditchannel.tv

Paul J. Sobel, CIA, CRMA, Chairman
Carolyn D. Saint, CIA, CRMA, CPA, Chairman
Richard F. Chambers, President and CEO

Independent, objective assurance and consulting activity designed to add value to an organization's operations. It helps an organization accomplish its objectives by bringing a systematic, disciplined approach to evaluate and improve the effectiveness of risk management, control and governance processes. Representation from more than 100 countries.
160M Members
Founded in 1941

62 **Institute of Management Accountants**
10 Paragon Dr
Suite 1
Montvale, NJ 07645-1760

201-573-9000
800-638-4427
Fax: 201-474-1600
E-Mail: ima@imanet.org
Home Page: www.imanet.org
Social Media: Facebook, Twitter, LinkedIn

William F. Knese, Chair
Jeffrey C. Thomson, President and CEO
Joseph A. Vincent, Chair-Elect
John C. Macaulay, Chair-Emeritus

Professional organization devoted exclusively to management accounting and financial management. Goals are to help members develop both personally and professionally, by means of education, certification and association with other business professionals.
67000 Members
Founded in 1919

63 **Institute of Management and Administration**
3 Bethesda Metro Center
Suite 250
Bethesda, MD 20814-5377

800-372-1033
703-341-3500
Fax: 800-253-0332

E-Mail: customercare@bna.com
Home Page: www.ioma.com

An independent source of exclusive business management information for experienced senior and middle management proessionals.

64 **Insurance Accounting & Systems Association, Inc.**
3511 Shannon Road
Suite 160
Durham, NC 27707

919-489-0991
Fax: 919-489-1994
E-Mail: info@iasa.org
Home Page: www.iasa.org
Social Media: Facebook, Twitter, LinkedIn, YouTube

Beth Mercier, Chairman
Forrest Mills, President
Joe Pomilia, Executive Director
Tom Ewbank, CFO
Mary Ellen Freyermuth, CIO

A nonprofit, education association that strives to enhance the knowledge of insurance professionals and participants from similar organizations closely allied with the insurance industry by facilitating the exchange of ideas and information.

65 **International Cost Estimating and Analysis Association**
8221 Old Courthouse Rd
Suite 106
Vienna, VA 22182

703-938-5090
Fax: 703-938-5091
E-Mail: iceaa@iceaaonline.org
Home Page: www.iceaaonline.org
Social Media: Facebook, Twitter

Brian Glauser, President
Paul Marston, Executive Vice President
Peter Braxton, VP, Professional Development
Patricia Zedaker, Secretary
Michael Thompson, Treasurer

A non-profit organization dedicated to improving cost estimating and analysis in government and industry by enhancing the competence and achievements of its professional members
2015 Members
Founded in 2012

66 **International Federation of Accountants**
529 Fifth Avenue
6th Floor
New York, NY 10017

212-286-9344
Fax: 212-286-9570
E-Mail: communications@ifac.org
Home Page: www.ifac.org
Social Media: Facebook, Twitter, LinkedIn, YouTube

Warren Allen, President
Olivia Kirley, Deputy President
Fayezul Choudhury, CEO
Russell Guthrie, Executive Director
Alta Prinsloo, Executive Director

IFAC is the global organization for the accountancy profession. It works with members and associates in 123 countries and jurisdictions to protect the public interest by encouraging high quality practices by the world's accountants.
173 Members
Founded in 1977

67 **National Academy of Public Administration**
1600 K Street NW
Suite 400
Washington, DC 20006

202-347-3190
Fax: 202-223-0823
E-Mail: feedback@napawash.org
Home Page: www.napawash.org
Social Media: Facebook, Twitter, LinkedIn, Vimeo

Robert J. Shea, Chair
Nancy R. Kingsbury, Vice Chair
Dan G Blair, President and CEO
B.J Reed, Secretary
Sallyanne Harper, Treasurer

An independent, nonprofit, and non-partisan organization that helpsthe Federal government address its critical management challenges through in-depth studies and analyses, advisory services and technical assistance, Congressional testimony, forums and conferences, and online stakeholder engagement.
800 Members
Founded in 1967

68 **National Association of Black Accountants**
7474 Greenway Center Drive
Suite 1120
Greenbelt, MD 20770

301-474-6222
Fax: 301-474-3114
E-Mail: customerservice@nabainc.org
Home Page: www.nabainc.org
Social Media: Facebook, Twitter, LinkedIn, YouTube

Calvin Harris Jr., President/CEO
Guillermo Hysaw, Executive Director and COO
Veda Stanley, Executive Vice President
Sheila Taylor-Clark, CPA
Ronald Walker, Chairman, Division of Firms

Nationwide professional association with the primary purpose of developing, encouraging and serving as a resource for greater participation by African-Americans and other minorities in the accounting and finance professions.
Founded in 1969

69 **National Association of Certified Valuators and Analysts (NACVA)**
5217 South State Street
Suite 400
Salt Lake City, UT 84107

801-486-0600
800-677-2009
Fax: 801-486-7500
E-Mail: nacva1@nacva.com
Home Page: www.nacva.com
Social Media: Y, Y

Terry Isom, Chairman
Scott Saltzman, President
Mark Kucik, Vice President
Parnell Black, CEO
Pam Bailey, Executive Director

Global, professional association that supports the business valuation and litigation consulting disciplines within the CPA and professional communities. Along with its training and certification progams, NACVA offers a range of support services, reference materials, software, and customized databases to enahnce the professional capabilities and capacities of its members.
6500 Members
Founded in 1990

70 **National Association of Computerized Tax Processors**
H&R Block
4400 Main Street
Kansas City, MO 64111

816-328-8485
Fax: 800-996-3526
Home Page: www.nactp.org

Todd Goldberg, President
Zeke Gikas, Vice President
Rebecca McCaulley, Treasurer
Vicki Massey, Secretary

Nonprofit association that represents tax processing software and hardware developers, electronic filing processors, tax form publishers and tax processing service bureaus. The association promotes standards in tax processing and works closely with the Internal Revenue Service and state governments to promote efficient and effective tax filing.
14100 Members
Founded in 1969

71 **National Association of Construction Auditors**
7305 Hancock Village Drive
Suite 519
Chesterfield, VA 23832

804-608-8703
Fax: 888-702-1059
E-Mail: info@thenaca.org
Home Page: www.thenaca.org
Social Media: Facebook, Twitter, LinkedIn

Brian D. Felix, Chairman
Carl E. Hansen, Vice Chairman
Larry G. Baker, Secretary/Treasurer

Provides resources, information, and leadership for NACA members, their clients, and the public to ensure the highest standard of construction control environments possible.

72 **National Association of Enrolled Agents**
1120 Connecticut Avenue NW
Suite 460
Washington, DC 20036-3953

202-822-6232
855-880-6232
Fax: 202-822-6270
E-Mail: info@naeahq.org
Home Page: www.naea.org
Social Media: Facebook, Twitter, LinkedIn

Betsey Buckingham, President
Michael S. Nelson, Executive Vice President
Marie Stravlo, Manager, Governance
Sam Matlick, Deputy Director
Bill Grutzkuhn, Director of Finance and Operations

Members are individuals who are enrolled to represent taxpayers before the Internal Revenue Service. We advise, represent and prepare tax returns for individuals, partnerships, corporations, estates, trusts and any entities with tax reporting requirements.
12000 Members
Founded in 1972

73 **National Association of Insurance and Financial Advisors**
2901 Telestar Court
Falls Church, VA 22042-1205

877-866-2432
Home Page: www.naifa.org
Social Media: Facebook, Twitter, LinkedIn, YouTube

Juli McNeely, President
Jules Gaudreau, President Elect
Paul R. Dougherty, Secretary
Matthew S. Tassey, Treasurer
Michael Gerber, Acting Chief Executive Officer

Serves and represents insurance and financial advisors, advocates for a positive legislative

and regulatory environment, enhances business and professional skills, and promotes the ethical conduct of its members.
Founded in 1890

74 **National Association of Mutual Insurance Companies**
3601 Vincennes Road
Indianapolis, IN 46268

317-875-5250
Fax: 317-879-8408
Home Page: www.namic.org
Social Media: Facebook, Twitter, LinkedIn, YouTube

Stuart Henderson, Chairman
Paul G. Stueven, Chairman Elect
Steve Linkous, Vice Chairman
Charles Chamness, President/CEO
Christopher P. Taft, Secretary/Treasurer

The largest property/casualty insurance trade association that has educational and advocacy programs to promote public policy solutions that benefit policyholders and the NAMIC member companies that exist to serve them.
Founded in 1920

75 **National Association of Personal Financial Advisors**
3250 North Arlington Heights Road
Suite 109
Arlington Heights, IL 60004

847-483-5400
888-333-6659
Fax: 847-483-5415
E-Mail: info@napfa.org
Home Page: www.napfa.org
Social Media: Facebook, Twitter, LinkedIn, YouTube

Robert Gerstemeier, Chair
Tim Kober, Vice Chair
Frank Moore, Treasurer
Geoffrey Brown, CEO
Chris Hale, Managing Editor

Professional association of Fee-Only financial advisors who advocate for client-focused financial planning with a Fee-Only compensation.

76 **National Association of State Auditors, Comptrollers and Treasurers**
449 Lewis Hargett Circle
Suite 290
Lexington, KY 40503

859-276-1147
Fax: 859-278-0507
Home Page: www.nasact.org

William G. Holland, President
Calvin McKelvogue, First Vice President
Richard K. Ellis, Second Vice President
R. Kinney Poynter, Executive Director
Debra K. Davenport, Secretary

Serves as the premier organization working to bring together state auditors, state comptrollers and state treasurers to cooperatively address government financial management issues.

77 **National Association of State Boards of Accountancy**
150 Fourth Ave. North
Ste. 700
Nashville, TN 37219-2417

615-880-4200
Fax: 615-880-4290
E-Mail: cpe@nasba.org
Home Page: nasba.org
Social Media: Facebook, Twitter, LinkedIn, YouTube

Walter C. Davenport, Chairman
Donald H. Burkett, Vice Chairman
Ken L. Bishop, President
Laurie J. Tish, Secretary
E. Kent Smoll, Treasurer

Enhances the effectiveness and advances the common interests of theBoards of Accountancy by creating a forum for accounting regulators and practitioners to address issues relevant to the viability of the accounting profession.
Founded in 1908

78 **National Association of State Budget Officers**
444 North Capitol Street NW
Suite 642
Washington, DC 20001

202-624-5382
Fax: 202-624-7745
E-Mail: nasbo-direct@nasbo.org
Home Page: www.nasbo.org
Social Media: Facebook, Twitter, LinkedIn, Google+

Mike Morrissey, President
Tom Mullaney, President Elect
Scott D. Pattison, Executive Director
Stacey Mazer, Senior Staff Associate
Brian Sigritz, Director of State Fiscal Studies

Provides a range of publications, services, and knowledge-sharing opportunities for its members and others interested in state finance issues.

79 **National Association of Tax Professionals**
PO Box 8002
Appleton, WI 54912-8002

800-558-3402
Fax: 800-747-0001
E-Mail: natp@natptax.com
Home Page: www.natptax.com
Social Media: Facebook, Twitter, LinkedIn, MySpace, YouTube

Jo Ann Schoen, EA, President
Jean Millerchip, EA, CFP, Vice President
Kathy Stanek, Chief Executive Officer
Matt Bone, CPA, Director of Finance/Administration
Susan Lucius, Director, Marketing & Communication

NATP members have access to a wide range of the most reliable industry resources, which ultimately save time and money. Members enjoy the support and knowledge that comes from joining the only professional organization that is 100% devoted to tax expertise.

80 **National CPA Health Care Advisors Association**
624 Grassmere Park Drive
Suite 15
Nashville, TN 37211

615-373-9880
800-231-2524
Fax: 615-377-7092
E-Mail: info@hcaa.com
Home Page: www.hcaa.com

Lee Ferber, President
Greg Papineau, Vice President
Hal Coons, III, Secretary

HCAA is an association of CPA firms that provide services to health care providers beyond traditional compliance work. Members are admitted on a territorial exclusive basis, one member in each territory.

81 **National Conference of CPA Practitioners**
22 Jericho Turnpike
Suite 110
Mineola, NY 11501

516-333-8282
888-488-5400
Fax: 516-333-4099
Home Page: go.nccpap.org/

NCCAP is a group of CPA professionals that allows small CPA firms and the sole practitioner to have a greater community impact and presence. This organization also gives back through its local chapters and at the national level.

82 **National Society of Accountants**
1010 N Fairfax St
Alexandria, VA 22314-1574

703-549-6400
800-966-6679
Fax: 703-549-2984
E-Mail: members@nsacct.org
Home Page: www.nsacct.org
Social Media: Facebook, Twitter, LinkedIn

Steven J. Hanson, President
Marilyn M. Niwao, First Vice President
Kathy Hettick, Second Vice President
John G. Ams, Executive Vice President
Jodi Goldberg, Vice President, Marketing

Professional society of practicing accountants and tax practitioners that sponsors the Accreditation Council for Accountancy and Taxation and supports the National Society of Public Accountants Political Action Committee and NSPA Scholarship Foundation.
30000 Members
Founded in 1945

83 **National Society of Accountants for Cooperatives**
136 South Keowee Street
Dayton, OH 45402

937-222-6707
Fax: 937-222-5794
E-Mail: info@nsacoop.org
Home Page: www.nsacoop.org
Social Media: Facebook

Kim Fantaci, Executive Director
Chris Headley, President
Carrie Parrish, Vice President
Stanley Mitchell, Chief Financial Officer
Jeff Brandenburg, Director

A professional society involved with the financial management and planning of cooperative business. It also provides educational programming, networking opportunities, and a directory of other professionals.
2000 Members
Founded in 1936

84 **National Tax Association**
725 15th St. NW
Ste. 600
Washington, DC 20005-2109

202-737-3325
Fax: 202-737-7308
E-Mail: natltax@aol.com
Home Page: www.ntanet.org

Alan Auerbach, President
Peter Brady, Vice President
Victoria Perry, Vice President
Charmaine J. Wright, Secretary
Eric Toder, Treasurer

A nonpartisan, nonpolitical educational association of tax professionals dedicatd to advancing understanding of the theory and practice of public finance.

85 **PKF North America**
1745 N. Brown Road
Suite 350
Lawrenceville, GA 30043

770-279-4560
Fax: 770-279-4566
E-Mail: tsnyder@pkfna.org

Home Page: www.pkfna.org
Social Media: Facebook, Twitter, LinkedIn

Terry Snyder, President
Debbie Kuhl, Vice President

An association of legally independently-owned accounting and consulting firms with offices in North America and throughout the world through its affiliation with PKF International.
402 Members

86 **PrimeGlobal**
3235 Satellite Bvld Bldg. 400
Suite 300
Duluth, GA 30096

678-417-7730
Fax: 678-999-3959
E-Mail: info@accountants.org
Home Page: www.accountants.org
Social Media: Facebook, Twitter, LinkedIn, YouTube

Jeffrey M. Mutnik, Chairman
Kevin Mead, President/CEO
Anne Hampson, CFO
Stacey Sanchez, Director of Events
Kathy Sautters, Communications Director

PrimeGlobal is an international affiliation of independent accounting and consulting firms.
200 Members
Founded in 1978

87 **Society of Actuaries**
475 N Martingale Rd
Suite 600
Schaumburg, IL 60173-2252

847-706-3500
Fax: 847-706-3599
E-Mail: webmaster@soa.org
Home Page: www.soa.org
Social Media: Twitter, LinkedIn

Greg Heidrich, Executive Director
Stacy Lin, Deputy Executive Director/CFO
Tiffany Berger, Director of Finance
Richard Veys, General Counsel
Michael Boot, Managing Director of Sections

An educational, research and professional organization dedicated to serving the public and society members. The vision is for actuaries to be recognized as the leading professional in the modeling and management of risk.
17000 Members
Founded in 1889
Mailing list available for rent: 17000 names at $300 per M

88 **Society of Financial Examiners**
12100 Sunset Hills Rd
Suite 130
Reston, VA 20190-3221

703-234-4140
800-787-7633
Fax: 888-436-8686
E-Mail: sofe@sofe.org
Home Page: www.sofe.org
Social Media: Facebook, LinkedIn

Richard Foster, President
Joanne Campanelli, Vice President, Examinations
Joseph Evans, Vice President, Publications
Mark Murphy, Vice President, Membership
Colette Sawyer, Vice President, Publications

The Society of Financial Examiners is a professional society for examiners of insurance companies, banks, savings and loans, and credit unions.
1600 Members
Founded in 1973

89 **Society of Financial Service Professionals**
19 Campus Boulevard
Suite 100
Newtown Square, PA 19073-3239

610-526-2500
Fax: 610-527-1499
Home Page: www.financialpro.org
Social Media: Facebook, Twitter, LinkedIn, YouTube, Flickr

Jim Christian, President
James B. Lammers, Immediate Past President
Michael P. Dow, President Elect
Anthony R. Bartlett, Secretary
Joseph E. Frack, Chief Executive Officer

Provides financial products and planning services in order to help individuals, families, and businesses achieve financial security.
11000 Members
Founded in 1928

90 **The American Society of IRS Problem Solvers**

Home Page: www.irsproblemsolvers.com

A select group of licensed tax professionals located in communities across the United States to help taxpayers end individual and business IRS problems.

91 **The Professional Accounting Society of America**

Home Page: www.thepasa.org

A professional organization designed specifically for entry-level and mid-level associates working at accounting firms across America.
Founded in 2005

Newsletters

92 **AAA Report**
Association for Accounting Administration
136 S Keowee Street
Dayton, OH 45402

937-222-0030
Fax: 937-222-5794
E-Mail: aaainfo@cpaadmin.org
Home Page: www.cpaadmin.org

Dennis Lemieux, President
Norman Saale, Vice President
Janine Zirrith, Secretary
Jim Fahey, Treasurer
Jane Johnson, Director of Education

Qarterly newsletter for the professional manager.
12 Pages
Frequency: Four/Year
Founded in 1984
Printed in 4 colors

93 **AGA Today**
Association of Government Accountants
2208 Mount Vernon Ave
Alexandria, VA 22301-1314

703-562-0900
800-242-7211
Fax: 703-548-9367
E-Mail: agacgfm@agacgfm.org
Home Page: www.agacgfm.org

Relmond Van Daniker, Executive Director
Evelyn Brown, National President

This publication acts as a clearinghouse for current government financial management information.
Frequency: Bi-Weekly
Circulation: 12,000

94 **ARCH**
Society of Actuaries
475 N Martingale Rd
Suite 600
Schaumburg, IL 60173-2252

847-706-3500
Fax: 847-706-3599
E-Mail: webmaster@soa.org
Home Page: www.soa.org

Greg Heidrich, Executive Director
Stacy Lin, Deputy Executive Director/CFO
Tiffany Berger, Director of Finance
Richard Veys, General Counsel

ARCH is an informal communication providing current actuarial research to friends and members of the actuarial community. Its primary goal is the speedy dissemination of current thinking and aids to research.

95 **ASMC Connections**
415 N Alfred St
Alexandria, VA 22314-2269

703-549-0360
800-462-5637
Fax: 703-549-3181
Home Page: www.asmconline.org
Social Media: Facebook, Twitter, LinkedIn

Marilyn Thomas, President
Art Hagler, VP
Kathy Watern, VP
Nancy Phillips, Treasurer

Provides insight into defense financial news, chapter spot lights, and other society news.
19m+ Members
Founded in 1948

96 **AWSCPA News**
American Woman's Society of CPAs
136 South Keowee Street
Dayton, OH 45402

937-222-1872
800-297-2721
Fax: 937-222-5794
E-Mail: info@awscpa.org
Home Page: www.awscpa.org

Amy Knowles-Jones, President
Kelly Welter, President Elect
Alexandra Miller, Secretary/Treasurer
Cynthia Cox, VP - Member Services

Available electronically.
Frequency: Quarterly
Circulation: 1500
Founded in 1933
Printed in 4 colors

97 **AcSEC Update**
American Institute of Certified Public Accountants
1211 Avenue of the Americas
Suite 6
New York, NY 10036-8701

212-596-6200
Fax: 212-596-6213
E-Mail: service@aicpa.org
Home Page: www.aicpa.org
Social Media: Facebook, Twitter, LinkedIn

Barry C Melancon, CEO
Susan Coffey, Senior Vice President
Lawson Carmichael, SVP - Strategy, People, Innovation
Arleen Thomas, SVP - Mgmt Accounting

Provides information about recently issued AcSEC pronouncments and current AcSEC projects.
Frequency: 4 Times/Year
Founded in 1887

98 **Accounting Alerts**
Grant Thornton

175 W Jackson Blvd
20th Floor
Chicago, IL 60604-2687

312-856-0001
Fax: 312-602-8099
Home Page: www.grantthornton.com
Social Media: Twitter

Stephen Chipman, CEO
Lou Grabowsky, COO
Russ Wieman, Chief Financial Officer

Periodic newsletter that highlights important accounting developments.
Founded in 1924

99 **Accounting Education News**
American Accounting Association
5717 Bessie Dr
Sarasota, FL 34233-2399

941-921-7747
Fax: 941-923-4093
E-Mail: info@aaahq.org
Home Page: aaahq.org

Tracey Sutherland, Executive Director
Deirdre Harris, Publication Contact
Diane Hazard, Publications Director

Information on industry development and associations, the newsletter is only available to members.
8600 Members
Frequency: Quarterly
Circulation: 8500
Founded in 1916
Printed in 3 colors on matte stock

100 **Accounting Historians Notebook**
Academy of Accounting Historians
10900 Euclid Avenue
Cleveland, OH 44106-7235

216-368-2058
Fax: 216-368-6244
E-Mail: acchistory@case.edu
Home Page: www.aahhq.org

Joanne Cross, President
Robert Colson, President Elect
Yvette Lazdowski, VP, Communications
Robert Colson, VP Communications
Stephanie Moussalli, Secretary

Published by the Academy of Accounting Historians, the Notebook provides information about the Academy, its members, conference, and publications. Subscription to the semi-annual publication is included in membership to the Academy.
600 Members
8 Pages
Frequency: Semi-Annual
Founded in 1973
Printed in one color

101 **Accounting Office Management & Administration Report**
Institute of Management and Administration
3 Bethesda Metro Center
Suite 250
Bethesda, MD 20814-5377

800-372-1033
703-341-3500
Fax: 800-253-0332
E-Mail: customercare@bna.com
Home Page: www.ioma.com

Designed for use by anyone responsible for the day-to-day management of a CPA firm. Provides actionable information that readers can use to manage their firms efficiently and profitably.
Cost: $469.00
Frequency: Monthly
Founded in 1984

102 **Accounting and Auditing Update Service**
Thomson Reuters
2395 Midway Rd
Carrollton, TX 75006

817-332-3709
800-431-9025
Fax: 888-216-1929
E-Mail: trta.lei-support@thomsonreuters.com
Home Page: www.ria.thomsonreuters.com

Elaine Yadlon, Plant Manager
Thomas H Glocer, CEO & Director
Robert D Daleo, Chief Financial Officer
Kelli Crane, Senior Vice President & CIO

Analyzes FASB and AICPA pronouncements.
Cost: $465.00
Frequency: Bi-Weekly
Founded in 1935

103 **Attorney/CPA Newsletter**
American Association of Attorney-CPAs
8647 Richmond Highway
Suite 639
Alexandria, VA 22309

703-352-8064
888-288-9272
Fax: 703-352-8073
E-Mail: info@attorney-cpa.com
Home Page: www.attorney-cpa.com

Robert Driegert, President
Domenick Lioce, President Elect
Joseph Cordell, Treasurer
John Pramberg, Secretary

To promote the study and understanding of law and accounting and those related professions.
Frequency: Quarterly
Founded in 1964

104 **Behavioral Research in Accounting**
American Accounting Association
5717 Bessie Dr
Sarasota, FL 34233

941-921-7747
Fax: 941-923-4093
E-Mail: info@aaahq.org
Home Page: www.aaahq.org

Tracey Sutherland, Executive Director
Julie Smith David, CIO
Diane Ledger, Director of Finance

To promote the wide dissemination of the results of systematic scholarly inquiries into the broad field of accounting.
Cost: $20.00
Frequency: Twice per Year
Circulation: 1400

105 **BusIndNews**
American Institute of Certified Public Accountants
1211 Avenue of the Americas
Suite 6
New York, NY 10036-8701

212-596-6200
Fax: 212-596-6213
E-Mail: service@aicpa.org
Home Page: www.aicpa.org
Social Media: Facebook, Twitter, LinkedIn

Barry C Melancon, CEO
Susan Coffey, Senior Vice President
Lawson Carmichael, SVP - Strategy
Arleen Thomas, SVP - Mgmt Accounting

The AICPA e-newsletter for members in business and industry, contains timely information on current issues and developments in areas related to business and industry.
Frequency: Monthly
Founded in 1887

106 **Business Valuation Monitor**
Grant Thornton
175 W Jackson Blvd
20th Floor
Chicago, IL 60604-2687

312-856-0001
Fax: 312-602-8099
Home Page: www.grantthornton.com
Social Media: Twitter, LinkedIn

Stephen Chipman, CEO
Lou Grabowsky, COO
Russ Wieman, CFO

Newsletter covering value creation perspectives for corporate executives and the investment community in the areas of financial reporting, transaction support, damage calculations in disputes, intellectual property, bankruptcy proceedings and corporate tax planning.
Founded in 1924

107 **CAE Bulletin**
Institute of Internal Auditors
247 Maitland Ave
Altamonte Spgs, FL 32701-4201

407-830-7600
Fax: 407-937-1101
E-Mail: custserv@theiia.org
Home Page: www.theiia.org

J. Michael Pepper, Chairman
Carolyn Saint, Senior Vice President
John Wxzelaki, Vice Chairman - Finance/Security

Newsletter that alerts members to news, guidance and information that helps professionals become as effective as possible in their jobs.
Frequency: Twice Monthly

108 **CPA Insider**
American Institute of Certified Public Accountants
1211 Avenue of the Americas
Suite 6
New York, NY 10036-8701

212-596-6200
Fax: 212-596-6213
E-Mail: service@aicpa.org
Home Page: www.aicpa.org
Social Media: Facebook, Twitter, LinkedIn

Barry C Melancon, CEO
Susan Coffey, Senior Vice President
Lawson Carmichael, SVP - Strategy
Arleen Thomas, SVP - Mgmt Accounting

Delivers need-to-know news of the profession, hard-hitting commentary, recommended products and professional development resources.
Frequency: Weekly
Founded in 1887

109 **Chapter Weekly**
National Association of Tax Professionals
PO Box 8002
Appleton, WI 54912-8002

800-558-3402
Fax: 800-747-0001
E-Mail: natp@natptax.com
Home Page: www.natptax.com
Social Media: Facebook, Twitter, MySpace

Jo Ann Schoen, President
Jean Millerchip, Vice President
Gerard Cannito, Treasurer
Patricia M. McNeer, Secretary

E-Newsletter features Chapter events and updates.
Frequency: Weekly

110 **Client Information Bulletin**
WPI Communications
55 Morris Ave
Springfield, NJ 07081-1422

973-467-8700
800-323-4995
Fax: 973-467-0368

E-Mail: info@wpicommunications.com
Home Page: www.wpicomm.com

Steve Klinghoffer, Owner
Lori Klinghoffer, Executive Vice President
Marilyn Lang, Circulation Manager
Sandy McMurray, Sales Manager
Anna Cooley, Managing Editor
This monthly newsletter covers important new tax developments, general business principles, financial planning, estate planning and other related topics.
4 Pages
Frequency: Monthly
Founded in 1952
Printed in 2 colors

111 **Controller's Report**
Institute of Management and Administration
3 Bethesda Metro Center
Suite 250
Bethesda, MD 20814-5377
800-372-1033
7033413500
Fax: 800-253-0332
E-Mail: customercare@bna.com
Home Page: www.ioma.com
Aimed at corporate controllers in companies of all sizes.
Cost: $437.00
20 Pages
Frequency: Monthly
Founded in 1984
Printed in 2 colors

112 **Controller's Tax Letter**
Institute of Management and Administration
3 Bethesda Metro Center
Suite 250
Bethesda, MD 20814-5377

800-372-1033
7033413500
Fax: 800-253-0332
E-Mail: customercare@bna.com
Home Page: www.ioma.com

Focuses on the tax implications of business decisions and provides readers in corporate finance/accounting details on recently settled cases from US Tax Court, with full citations for those who want to know more. CTL also shows controllers, accounting managers and tax managers the effects of business decisions as they relate to a company's strategic planning for new sales efforts, expanding their overseas or foreign presence, and exemptions and deductions available where laws have changed.
Cost: $259.00
Frequency: Monthly
Founded in 1984

113 **Controllers Update**
Institute of Certified Management Accountants
10 Paragon Drive
Suite 1
Montvale, NJ 07645-1718

800-638-4427
Fax: 201-474-1600
E-Mail: ima@imanet.org
Home Page: www.imanet.org
Social Media: Facebook, Twitter, LinkedIn

Jeffrey C. Thomson, President and CEO
Brian L. McGuire, Chair
John C. Macaulay, Chair-Elect
Sandra B. Richtermeyer, Chair-Emeritus
Monthly newsletter with useful information for chief financial officers, plant controllers and financial management personnel.
Frequency: Monthly
Circulation: 2,200

114 **Corporate Finance Insider**
American Institute of Certified Public Accountants
1211 Avenue of the Americas
Suite 6
New York, NY 10036-8701

212-596-6200
Fax: 212-596-6213
E-Mail: service@aicpa.org
Home Page: www.aicpa.org
Social Media: Facebook, Twitter, LinkedIn

Barry C Melancon, CEO
Susan Coffey, Senior Vice President
Lawson Carmichael, SVP - Strategy
Arleen Thomas, SVP - Mgmt Accounting
Covers financial management and corporate compliance issues, nationwide job opportunities, plus career advancement strategies from the experts, self assessment tools, compensation research and hiring trends for those who recruit, train and manage CPAs and other financial professionals.
Frequency: Monthly
Founded in 1887

115 **Corporate Taxation Insider**
American Institute of Certified Public Accountants
1211 Avenue of the Americas
Suite 6
New York, NY 10036-8701

212-596-6200
Fax: 212-596-6213
E-Mail: service@aicpa.org
Home Page: www.aicpa.org
Social Media: Facebook, Twitter, LinkedIn

Barry C Melancon, CEO
Susan Coffey, Senior Vice President
Lawson Carmichael, SVP - Strategy
Arleen Thomas, SVP - Mgmt Accounting
Delivers need-to-know news of the profession, hard-hitting commentary, recommended products and professional development resources to its subscribers.
Frequency: Monthly
Founded in 1887

116 **Currency**
Grant Thornton
175 W Jackson Blvd
20th Floor
Chicago, IL 60604-2687

312-856-0001
Fax: 312-602-8099
Home Page: www.grantthornton.com
Social Media: Twitter, LinkedIn

Stephen Chipman, CEO
Lou Grabowsky, COO
Russ Wieman, Chief Financial Officer
Electronic newsletter for bank executives that covers issues and trends in the financial institutions industry.
Founded in 1924

117 **E@lert**
National Association of Enrolled Agents
1120 Connecticut Avenue NW
Suite 460
Washington, DC 20036-3922

202-822-6232
Fax: 202-822-6270
E-Mail: info@naea.org
Home Page: www.naea.org
Social Media: Facebook, Twitter, LinkedIn

Frank I Degen, President
Betsey Buckingham, president-elect
Robert Reedy, Treasurer/Secretary
Newsletter that provides brief updates on the latest tax news affecting clients and practices.
11000 Members

118 **FSA Times**
Institute of Internal Auditors
247 Maitland Ave
Altamonte Spgs, FL 32701-4201

407-937-1100
Fax: 407-937-1101
E-Mail: custserv@theiia.org
Home Page: www.theiia.org

J. Michael Pepper, Chairman
Carolyn Saint, Senior Vice President
John Wxzelaki, Vice Chairman - Finance/Security
Quarterly publication provided to members of the Institute of Internal Auditors' Financial Services Auditor Group to support knowledge development for financial services auditors.
Frequency: Quarterly

119 **Financial Bulletin**
Grant Thornton
175 W Jackson Blvd
20th Floor
Chicago, IL 60604-2687

312-856-0001
Fax: 312-602-8099
Home Page: www.grantthornton.com
Social Media: Twitter, LinkedIn

Stephen Chipman, CEO
Lou Grabowsky, COO
Russ Wieman, Chief Financial Officer
Electronic publication that covers regulations and developments affecting financial services industry.
Founded in 1924

120 **Focus on Forensics**
Grant Thornton
175 W Jackson Blvd
20th Floor
Chicago, IL 60604-2687

312-856-0001
Fax: 312-602-8099
Home Page: www.grantthornton.com
Social Media: Twitter, LinkedIn

Stephen Chipman, CEO
Lou Grabowsky, COO
Russ Wieman, Chief Financial Officer
Periodic newsletter providing valuable forensic accounting insights into some of the most complex and critical challenges that businesses and legal counsel face today.
Founded in 1924

121 **General Ledger**
American Institute of Professional Bookkeepers
6001 Montrose Rd
Suite 500
Rockville, MD 20852-4873

800-622-0121
Fax: 800-541-0066
E-Mail: info@aipb.org
Home Page: www.aipb.org

Stan Hartman, Owner
The latest bookkeeping, accounting and tax news, keep current on bookkeeping and reporting techniques, time and money-saving charts, practical tips, sharpen skills with a Bookkeeper's Quiz in every issue, and monthly and annual rates and numbers are included.
Frequency: Monthly
Circulation: 30000
Founded in 1987
Mailing list available for rent

122 **Government Accounting and Auditing Update**
Thomson Reuters

2395 Midway Rd
Carrollton, TX 75006

817-332-3709
800-431-9025
Fax: 888-216-1929
E-Mail: trta.lei-support@thomsonreuters.com
Home Page: www.ria.thomsonreuters.com

Elaine Yadlon, Plant Manager
Thomas H Glocer, CEO & Director
Robert D Daleo, Chief Financial Officer
Kelli Crane, Senior Vice President & CIO

Includes changes taking place in government accounting and financial reporting, analysis of the latest developments, explanations of how they affect work and practical guidance on adapting to these changes.
Cost: $370.00
8 Pages
Frequency: Monthly
Founded in 1935
Mailing list available for rent: 5000 names
Printed in 2 colors on glossy stock

123 Government Financial Management TOPICS
2208 Mount Vernon Avenue
Alexandria, VA 22301

703-684-6931
800-AGA-7211
Fax: 703-548-9367
E-Mail: agacgfm@agacgfm.org
Home Page: www.agacgfm.org
Social Media: Facebook, Twitter, LinkedIn, GovLoop

Evelyn A. Brown, President
Relmond P Van Daniker, Executive Director

An AGA member service, designed to give national exposure to chapter events, community service projects and member accomplishments while offering the most up-to-date Association news.
15000 Members
Frequency: Bi-Weekly
Founded in 1950
Mailing list available for rent: 18,000 names

124 Governmental Accounting Standards Board Action Report
401 Merritt 7
PO Box 5116
Norwalk, CT 06856-5116

203-847-0700
Fax: 203-849-9714
E-Mail: webmaster@gasb.org
Home Page: www.gasb.org

Robert Attmore, Chairman
David Bean, Director Research/Technical Active

Action Report newsletter that includes developments in the standards-setting process and the status of technical projects.
Cost: $155.00
Frequency: Monthly

125 IIA Insight
Institute of Internal Auditors
247 Maitland Ave
Altamonte Spgs, FL 32701-4201

407-937-1100
Fax: 407-937-1101
E-Mail: custserv@theiia.org
Home Page: www.theiia.org
Social Media: Facebook, Twitter, LinkedIn

J. Michael Pepper, Chairman
Carolyn Saint, Senior Vice President
John Wxzelaki, Vice Chairman - Finance/Security

Member newsletter designed to instruct members on using IIA services, products, and training opportunities.
Frequency: Monthly

126 IIA Today
Institute of Internal Auditors
247 Maitland Ave
Altamonte Spgs, FL 32701-4201

407-830-7600
Fax: 407-937-1101
E-Mail: custserv@theiia.org
Home Page: www.theiia.org

J. Michael Pepper, Chairman
Carolyn Saint, Senior Vice President
John Wxzelaki, Vice Chairman - Finance/Security

Provides relevent and timely information on internal audit news. In print and electronic formats available.
Frequency: Twice Monthly

127 IMA Educational Case Journal
Institute of Management Accountants
10 Paragon Dr
Suite 1
Montvale, NJ 07645-1760

800-638-4427
Fax: 201-474-1600
E-Mail: ima@imanet.org
Home Page: www.imanet.org
Social Media: Facebook, Twitter, LinkedIn

Jeffrey C. Thomson, President and CEO
Brian L. McGuire, Chair
John C. Macaulay, Chair-Elect
Sandra B. Richtermeyer, Chair-Emeritus

The journal publishes teaching cases and research related to case writing or teaching with cases in management accounting and related fields.
Cost: $250.00
60000 Members
Frequency: Quarterly

128 IOMA's Report on Salary Surveys
Institute of Management and Administration
3 Bethesda Metro Center
Suite 250
Bethesda, MD 20814-5377

800-372-1033
7033413500
Fax: 800-253-0332
E-Mail: customercare@bna.com
Home Page: www.ioma.com

Analyzes data from major salary surveys released during the year by the biggest compensation survey companies, WorldatWork, SHRM, state HR societies, and the Big Four accounting firms, to give readers an overview of those expensive, hard-to-manage services.
Cost: $445.00
Founded in 1984

129 Infoline
Hospitality Financial & Technology Professionals
11709 Boulder Lane
Suite 110
Austin, TX 78726-1832

512-249-5333
800-646-4387
Fax: 512-249-1533
E-Mail: membership@hftp.org
Home Page: www.hftp.org

Frank I Wolfe, Executive VP/CEO
Lucinda Hart, COO
Thomas Atzenhofer, CFO
Eliza Selig, Director of Communications

Provides information regarding chapter and officer activities.
Frequency: Monthly
Founded in 1952

130 Information Management Newsletter
Information Resources Management Association
701 E Chocolate Ave
Suite 200
Hershey, PA 17033-1240

717-533-8845
Fax: 717-533-8861
E-Mail: member@irma-international.org
Home Page: www.irma-international.org

Jan Travers, Executive Director
Sherif Kamel, Communications Director
Lech Janczewski PhD, IRMA World Representative Director
Gerald Grant, IRMA Doctoral Symposium Director
Paul Chalekian, IRMA United States Representative

This practical, informative newsletter is a leading publication of information technology resources management. Short, concise articles give objective, professional views of newly emerging technologies and trends.
Cost: $60.00
Frequency: Semi-Annually
ISSN: 1080-286X

131 Internal Auditing Report
Thomson Reuters
2395 Midway Rd
Carrollton, TX 75006

817-332-3709
800-431-9025
Fax: 888-216-1929
E-Mail: trta.lei-support@thomsonreuters.com
Home Page: www.ria.thomsonreuters.com

Elaine Yadlon, Plant Manager
Thomas H Glocer, CEO & Director
Robert D Daleo, Chief Financial Officer
Kelli Crane, Senior Vice President & CIO

Perfect for keeping up to date on new auditing standards and developments. Offers guidance on managing internal auditing departments, covers new audit technology, offers new audit techniques used by successful audit management practices, and provides practitioner level feedback on current Institute of Internal Auditors standards.
Cost: $320.00
12 Pages
Frequency: Six Times/Year
Circulation: 5000
Founded in 1935
Mailing list available for rent: 5000 names
Printed in 2 colors on glossy stock

132 Jacobs Report
Offshore Press
PO Box 8137
Prairie Village, KS 66208-2824

913-362-9667
888-516-3177
Fax: 913-432-7174
E-Mail: jacobs@offshorepress.com
Home Page: www.offshorepress.com

Vernon K Jacobs, President

Contains International tax news.
Frequency: Daily
Founded in 1981

133 Letter Ruling Review
Tax Analysts

400 S Maple Ave
Suite 400
Falls Church, VA 22046-4245

703-533-4400
800-955-2444
Fax: 703-533-4444
E-Mail: cservice@tax.org
Home Page: www.taxanalysts.com

Chris Bergin, CEO
Martin Lobel, Chairman of the Board

Publication analyzes significant private letter rulings issued by the Internal Revenue Service during the month.
4 Pages
Frequency: Monthly
Founded in 1970
Printed in one color on matte stock

134 **Management & Administration Report (ADMAR)**
Institute of Management and Administration
3 Bethesda Metro Center
Suite 250
Bethesda, MD 20814-5377

800-372-1033
7033413500
Fax: 800-253-0332
E-Mail: customercare@bna.com
Home Page: www.ioma.com

How to manage corporate accounting departments more effectively, boost staff productivity, reduce operation costs and adopt new systems and technology, and take charge of your dealings with auditors and lenders.
Founded in 1984

135 **Managing Accounts Payable**
Institute of Management and Administration
3 Bethesda Metro Center
Suite 250
Bethesda, MD 20814-5377

800-372-1033
7033413500
Fax: 800-253-0332
E-Mail: customercare@bna.com
Home Page: www.ioma.com

The source of information for accounts payable and those responsible for the function. Each issue contains 5-7 articles, 6-10 short news clips, a manager's forum on the back page and calendar of upcoming seminars and conferences.
Cost: $419.00
Frequency: Monthly
Founded in 1984

136 **Managing the General Ledger**
Institute of Management and Administration
3 Bethesda Metro Center
Suite 250
Bethesda, MD 20814-5377

800-372-1033
7033413500
Fax: 800-253-0332
E-Mail: customercare@bna.com
Home Page: www.ioma.com

Aimed at controllers and corporate accounting managers and shows the most current techniques for efficient monthly closings and AICPA approved methods for general ledger entries.
Cost: $308.14
Frequency: Monthly
Founded in 1984

137 **NSPA Washington Reporter**
National Society of Public Accountants
1010 N Fairfax St
Alexandria, VA 22314-1574

703-549-6400
800-966-6679
Fax: 703-549-2984
E-Mail: members@nsacct.org
Home Page: www.nsacct.org
Social Media: Facebook, Twitter, LinkedIn

Harlan Rose, President
Steven Hanson, First Vice President
Marilyn Niwao, Second Vice President
Brian Thompson, Secretary-Treasurer

Coverage of NSPA activity with the government, and news on members in various states.
Frequency: Monthly
Founded in 1955

138 **National Estimator**
Society of Cost Estimating and Analysis
8221 Old Courthouse Rd
Suite 106
Vienna, VA 22182

703-938-5090
Fax: 703-938-5091
E-Mail: scea@sceaonline.org
Home Page: www.sceaonline.org

Erin Whittaker, Executive Director
Sharon Burger, Certification Program Admin
Brittany Walker, Membership Coordinator
Debra Lehman, Treasurer

Information on cost estimating and analysis, earned value management, budget and financial analysis, and program control.
Cost: $55.00
2015 Members
Frequency: Biannual
Founded in 1990

139 **National Newsletter**
415 N Alfred St
Alexandria, VA 22314-2269

703-549-0360
800-462-5637
Fax: 703-549-3181
Home Page: www.asmconline.org
Social Media: Facebook, Twitter, LinkedIn

Marilyn Thomas, President
Art Hagler, VP
Kathy Watern, VP
Nancy Phillips, Treasurer

Focuses on society information such as training, events, and other issues related to supporting the membership of ASMC.
19m+ Members
Frequency: Monthly
Founded in 1948

140 **New Developments Summary**
Grant Thornton
175 W Jackson Blvd
20th Floor
Chicago, IL 60604-2687

312-856-0001
Fax: 312-602-8099
Home Page: www.grantthornton.com
Social Media: Twitter, LinkedIn

Stephen Chipman, CEO
Lou Grabowsky, COO
Russ Wieman, Chief Financial Officer

Periodic bulletin providing a detailed summary of a recent technical development or accounting pronouncement.
Founded in 1924

141 **News Plus**
National Association of Black Accountants
7474 Greenway Center Dr
Suite 1120
Greenbelt, MD 20770-3504

301-474-6222
888-571-2939
Fax: 301-474-3114
E-Mail: newsplus@nabainc.org
Home Page: www.nabainc.org
Social Media: Facebook, Twitter, LinkedIn, YouTube

Calvin Harris Jr., President/CEO
Guillermo Hysaw, Executive Director and COO
Veda Stanley, Executive Vice President
Sheila Taylor-Clark, CPA
Ronald Walker, Chairman, Division of Firms

Updates on accounting proposals and regulations.
Cost: $20.00
Frequency: Quarterly
Founded in 1969

142 **Nonprofit Report: Accounting, Taxation Management**
Thomson Reuters
2395 Midway Rd
Carrollton, TX 75006

817-332-3709
800-431-9025
Fax: 888-216-1929
E-Mail: trta.lei-support@thomsonreuters.com
Home Page: www.ria.thomsonreuters.com

Elaine Yadlon, Plant Manager
Thomas H Glocer, CEO & Director
Robert D Daleo, Chief Financial Officer
Kelli Crane, Senior Vice President & CIO

Offers CPAs with nonprofit clients, and professionals working in the nonprofit sector. A practical, timely look at today's key nonprofit issues, including IRS rulings and pronouncements, AICPA changes and legislation governing the financial management of most nonprofit organizations.
Cost: $250.00
Frequency: Monthly
Founded in 1935
Mailing list available for rent
Printed in 2 colors on glossy stock

143 **On the Horizon**
Grant Thornton
175 W Jackson Blvd
20th Floor
Chicago, IL 60604 2687

312-856-0001
Fax: 312-602-8099
Home Page: www.grantthornton.com
Social Media: Twitter, LinkedIn

Stephen Chipman, CEO
Lou Grabowsky, COO
Russ Wieman, Chief Financial Officer

Updates on announcements, meetings and proposals from the accounting standards-setting bodies and industry regulators.
Frequency: Weekly
Founded in 1924

144 **Partner's Report for Law Firm Owners**
Institute of Management and Administration
3 Bethesda Metro Center
Suite 250
Bethesda, MD 20814-5377

800-372-1033
703-341-3500
Fax: 800-253-0332
E-Mail: customercare@bna.com
Home Page: www.ioma.com

Keeps partners up to date on salary guidelines and benefits, as well as provides the reader with tips on increasing profit margins and exercising leadership skills.
Cost: $464.00
Frequency: Monthly
Founded in 1984

145 **Payroll Currently**
American Payroll Association

660 N Main Ave
Suite 100
San Antonio, TX 78205-1217

210-226-4600
Fax: 210-226-4027
E-Mail: apamail@mindspring.com
Home Page: www.payroll.org
Social Media: Facebook, Twitter, LinkedIn

Daniel Maddux, President

Member newsletter containing breaking payroll compliance news and updates.
Frequency: Bi-Weekly

146 **Payroll Manager's Report**
Institute of Management and Administration
3 Bethesda Metro Center
Suite 250
Bethesda, MD 20814-5377

800-372-1033
703-341-3500
Fax: 800-253-0332
E-Mail: customercare.bna.com
Home Page: www.ioma.com

Written for payroll practitioners working with small and large employers. Provides how-to information on managing a payroll department cost effectively and service-efficiently.
Cost: $399.00
Frequency: Monthly
Founded in 1984

147 **Payroll Practitioner's Monthly**
Institute of Management and Administration
3 Bethesda Metro Center
Suite 250
Bethesda, MD 20814-5377

800-372-1033
703-341-3500
Fax: 800-253-0332
E-Mail: customercare@bna.com
Home Page: www.ioma.com

Shows payroll professionals what they need to do and how to do it when it comes to the many rules, regulations and laws they must follow to prepare and distribute a corporate payroll.
Cost: $399.00
16 Pages
Frequency: Monthly
Founded in 1984

148 **Payroll Tax Alert**
Institute of Management and Administration
3 Bethesda Metro Center
Suite 250
Bethesda, MD 20814-5377

800-372-1033
703-341-3500
Fax: 800-253-0332
E-Mail: customercare@bna.com
Home Page: www.ioma.com

Used by payroll managers and professionals in accounting or human resources. Provides quick, hard hitting updates on changes to federal and state payroll policy (wage-hour rules, industrial orders, new posting requirements and tax issues) from every agency that has a hand in corporate payroll & benefits administration.
Cost: $240.00
Frequency: Monthly
Circulation: 2000
Founded in 1984

149 **Pocket MBA**
Practising Law Institute
810 Seventh Avenue
21st Floor
New York, NY 10019-5818

212-824-5700
800-260-4754
Fax: 212-581-4670
E-Mail: info@pli.edu
Home Page: www.pli.edu
Social Media: Facebook, Twitter

Victor J Rubino, President
Nickola Francis, Subscription Manager

Provides information every lawyer needs to know about business and finance.
Cost: $1295.00
Frequency: Weekly
Founded in 1933

150 **Polaris International Newsletter**
Polaris International
9200 South Dadeland Boulevard
Suite 510
Miami, FL 33156

305-670-0580
Fax: 305-670-3818
E-Mail: info@accountants.org
Home Page: www.accountants.org
Social Media: Facebook, Twitter, LinkedIn, Youtube

Kevin Mead, President
Lydie Jubin, Chief Regional Officer
Anne Hampson, CFO
Pedro Figueroa, Administrative Manager

Newsletter containing information regarding events, activities and recent news for accounting and consulting firms.
Frequency: Quarterly
Founded in 1978

151 **Practicing CPA**
American Institute of Certified Public Accountants
1211 Avenue of the Americas
Suite 6
New York, NY 10036-8701

212-596-6200
Fax: 212-596-6213
E-Mail: service@aicpa.org
Home Page: www.aicpa.org
Social Media: Facebook, Twitter, LinkedIn

Barry C Melancon, CEO
Susan Coffey, Senior Vice President
Lawson Carmichael, SVP - Strategy
Arleen Thomas, SVP - Mgmt Accounting

Articles on development and management of firms.
Frequency: Monthly
Founded in 1887

152 **Public Accounting Desk Book**
Strafford Publications
590 Dutch Valley Road
PO Box 13729
Atlanta, GA 30324-0729

404-881-1141
800-926-7926
Fax: 404-881-0074
E-Mail: customerservice@straffordpub.com
Home Page: www.straffordpub.com
Social Media: Twitter

Richard Ossoff, President
Jon McKenna, Executive Editor

Provides public accounting firms with authoritative news and analysis of developments in the accounting profession today and emerging trends for the future. Also reports SEC auditor changes, mergers, acquisitions, personnel changes and related events.
Cost: $39.00
Frequency: Annual
ISSN: 0161-309X
Founded in 1984

153 **Public Accounting Report**
CCH
2700 Lake Cook Rd
Riverwoods, IL 60015-3867

847-940-4600
800-835-5224
Fax: 773-866-3095
Home Page: www.cch.com

Mike Sabbatis, President
Douglas M Winterrose, Vice President & CFO
Jim Bryant, EVP Software Products

Written for public accounting firm partners and professionals, it is renowned for its straight reporting and analysis of the news, developments, and trends that have influenced the profession for more than 20 years.
Cost: $449.00
8 Pages
Frequency: Bi-Weekly

154 **SEC Accounting Report**
Thomson Reuters
2395 Midway Rd
Carrollton, TX 75006

817-332-3709
800-431-9025
Fax: 888-216-1929
E-Mail: trta.lei-support@thomsonreuters.com
Home Page: www.ria.thomsonreuters.com

Elaine Yadlon, Plant Manager
Thomas H Glocer, CEO & Director
Robert D Daleo, Chief Financial Officer
Kelli Crane, Senior Vice President & CIO

For senior executives needing monthly news and insights on emerging SEC issues. The SEC Accounting Report can help you to understand SEC changes and their subsequent compliance requirements.
Cost: $365.00
8 Pages
Frequency: Monthly
Circulation: 5000
Founded in 1935
Mailing list available for rent: 5000 names
Printed in 2 colors on glossy stock

155 **Strategic TechNotes**
Institute of Management Accountants
10 Paragon Dr
Suite 1
Montvale, NJ 07645-1774

201-573-9000
800-638-4427
Fax: 201-474-1600
E-Mail: ima@imanet.org
Home Page: www.imanet.org
Social Media: Facebook, Twitter, LinkedIn

Jeffrey C. Thomson, President and CEO
Brian L. McGuire, Chair
John C. Macaulay, Chair-Elect
Sandra B. Richtermeyer, Chair-Emeritus

Award-winning technology e-newsletter designed for IMA members and others who want a look into the world of today's and tomorrow's technological trends and tools.
60000 Members
Frequency: 2 Times/Month

156 **TAXPRO Monthly**
National Association of Tax Professionals
PO Box 8002
Appleton, WI 54912-8002

800-558-3402
Fax: 800-747-0001
E-Mail: natp@natptax.com
Home Page: www.natptax.com
Social Media: Facebook, Twitter, MySpace

Jo Ann Schoen, President
Jean Millerchip, Vice President
Gerard Cannito, Treasurer
Patricia M. McNeer, Secretary
Kathy Stanek, CEO

Covers the latest news in detail and explores critical new developments in federal tax laws while providing practical applications of tax laws and procedures.
Frequency: Monthly

157 **TAXPRO Weekly**
National Association of Tax Professionals
PO Box 8002
Appleton, WI 54912-8002

800-558-3402
Fax: 800-747-0001
E-Mail: natp@natptax.com
Home Page: www.natptax.com
Social Media: Facebook, Twitter, MySpace

Jo Ann Schoen, President
Jean Millerchip, Vice President
Gerard Cannito, Treasurer
Patricia M. McNeer, Secretary
Kathy Stanek, CEO

Members receive e-Newsletter featuring tax alerts and news briefs hot off the press.
Frequency: Weekly

158 **TOPICS Newsletter**
Association of Government Accountants
2208 Mount Vernon Ave
Alexandria, VA 22301-1314

703-684-6931
800-AGA-7211
Fax: 703-548-9367
E Mail: agacgfm@agacgfm.org
Home Page: www.agacgfm.org

Relmond Van Daniker, Executive Director
Evelyn Brown, National President

Designed to give national exposure to chapter events, community service projects and member accomplishments while offering the most up-to-date Association news, released every other Monday morning by e-mail to members.
Frequency: 2x/Month

159 **Tax Hot Topics**
Grant Thornton
175 W Jackson Blvd
20th Floor
Chicago, IL 60604-2687

312-856-0001
Fax: 312 602-8099
Home Page: www.grantthornton.com
Social Media: Twitter, LinkedIn

Stephen Chipman, CEO
Lou Grabowsky, COO
Russ Wieman, Chief Financial Officer

Electronic newsletter addressing a wide range of tax issues, including Internal Revenue Service rulings, tax-related litigation, and state, local and international tax developments
Frequency: Biweekly
Founded in 1924

160 **Tax Incentives Alert**
Strafford Publications
590 Dutch Valley Road NE
PO Box 13729
Atlanta, GA 30324-0729

404-881-1141
800-926-7926
Fax: 404-881-0074
E-Mail: customerservice@straffordpub.com
Home Page: www.straffordpub.com

Richard Ossoff, President
Jon McKenna, Executive Editor

Reports on the new and ever-evolving array of federal and state tax credits, exemptions, deductions, abatements and other incentives.
Cost: $467.00
Frequency: Monthly
ISSN: 0161-309X
Founded in 1984

161 **Tax Insider**
American Institute of Certified Public Accountants
1211 Avenue of the Americas
Suite 6
New York, NY 10036-8701

212-596-6200
Fax: 212-596-6213
E-Mail: service@aicpa.org
Home Page: www.aicpa.org
Social Media: Facebook, Twitter, LinkedIn

Barry C Melancon, CEO
Susan Coffey, Senior Vice President
Lawson Carmichael, SVP - Strategy
Arleen Thomas, SVP - Mgmt Accounting

Delivers need-to-know news of the profession, hard-hitting commentary, recommended products and professional development resources to tax and financial planning professionals.
Frequency: 2x/Month
Founded in 1887

162 **Tax Letter and Social Security Report**
Scott Peyron & Associates
209 Main Street
Suite 200
Boise, ID 83702-7356

208-388-3800
Fax: 208-388-8898
E-Mail: info@peyron.com
Home Page: www.peyron.com

Scott Peyron, Owner

Covers taxes, social security tax, benefit tips and information for middle income individuals and professionals.
Cost: $56.00
4 Pages
Frequency: Monthly
Circulation: 2000
Printed in one color on matte stock

163 **The CPA Letter**
American Institute of Certified Public Accountants
1211 Avenue of the Americas
Suite 6
New York, NY 10036-8701

212-596-6200
Fax: 212-596-6213
E-Mail: service@aicpa.org
Home Page: www.aicpa.org
Social Media: Facebook, Twitter, LinkedIn

Barry C Melancon, CEO
Susan Coffey, Senior Vice President
Lawson Carmichael, SVP - Strategy
Arleen Thomas, SVP - Mgmt Accounting

A news source for certified public accountants.
Frequency: Monthly
Founded in 1887

164 **The Gaming Auditorium**
Institute of Internal Auditors
247 Maitland Ave
Altamonte Spgs, FL 32701-4201

707-937-1100
Fax: 407-937-1101
E-Mail: custserv@theiia.org
Home Page: www.theiia.org

J. Michael Pepper, Chairman
Carolyn Saint, Senior Vice President
John Wxzelaki, Vice Chairman - Finance/security

Quarterly publication provided to members of the Institute of Internal Auditors' Gaming Audit Group to support knowledge development for gaming audit professionals.
Frequency: Quarterly

165 **Tone at the Top**
Institute of Internal Auditors
247 Maitland Ave
Altamonte Spgs, FL 32701-4201

407-937-1100
Fax: 407-937-1101
E-Mail: custserv@theiia.org
Home Page: www.theiia.org

J. Michael Pepper, Chairman
Carolyn Saint, Senior Vice President
John Wxzelaki, Vice Chairman - Finance/security

Newsletter that provides executive management, boards of directors, and audit committees with concise, leading-edge information in issues such as risk, internal control, governance, ethics, and the changing role of internal auditing.
Frequency: Quarterly

166 **Wealth Management Insider**
American Institute of Certified Public Accountants
1211 Avenue of the Americas
Suite 6
New York, NY 10036-8701

212-596-6200
Fax: 212-596-6213
E Mail: service@aicpa.org
Home Page: www.aicpa.org
Social Media: Facebook, Twitter, LinkedIn

Barry C Melancon, CEO
Susan Coffey, Senior Vice President
Lawson Carmichael, SVP - Strategy
Arleen Thomas, SVP - Mgmt Accounting

Delivers need-to-know news of the profession, hard-hitting commentary, recommended products and professional development resources to CPAs who currently provide financial planning services or are looking to expand their practice.
Frequency: 2x/Month
Founded in 1887

Magazines & Journals

167 **AIRA Journal**
Association of Insolvency & Restructuring Advisors
221 W Stewart Ave
Suite 207
Medford, OR 97501-3647

541-858-1665
Fax: 541-858-9187
E-Mail: aira@aira.org
Home Page: www.airacira.org

Anthony Sasso, President
Thomas Morrow, Vice President
Mathew Schwartz, Treasurer
Joel Waite, VP

Publication provides accurate and authoritative information in regard to current issues and developments relevant to the insolvency and restructuring practice, as well as to inform members of upcoming Association events.
Frequency: Bi-Monthly

168 **Accountants SEC Practice Manual**
CCH
2700 Lake Cook Rd
Riverwoods, IL 60015-3867

847-940-4600
800-835-5224
Fax: 773-866-3095
Home Page: www.cch.com

Mike Sabbatis, President
Douglas M Winterrose, Vice President & CFO
Jim Bryant, EVP Software Products

Offers guidance for preparing and filing financial statements with the SEC, including regulations, forms and helpful summaries and

checklists.
Cost: $819.00
Frequency: Annual
Founded in 1913

169 **Accounting Historians Journal**
Academy of Accounting Historians
10900 Euclid Avenue
Cleveland, OH 44106-7235

216-368-2058
Fax: 216-368-6244
E-Mail: acchistory@case.edu
Home Page: www.aahhq.org

Joanne Cross, President
Robert Colson, President Elect
Yvette Lazdowski, VP, Communications
Robert Colson, VP Communications
Stephanie Moussalli, Secretary

Published by the Academy of Accounting Historians, the Journal provides research on the evolution of accounting thought and accounting practice. Subscription to the semi-annual publication is included in membership to the Academy.
600 Members
200 Pages
Frequency: Semi-Annual
Founded in 1973
Printed in one color

170 **Accounting Horizons**
American Accounting Association
5717 Bessie Dr
Sarasota, FL 34233-2399

941-921-7747
Fax: 941-923-4093
E-Mail: info@aaahq.org
Home Page: aaahq.org
Social Media: Facebook

Tracey Sutherland, Executive Director
Deirdre Harris, Publications Contact

Accounting and business information.
Cost: $100.00
8600 Members
Frequency: Quarterly
Circulation: 6000
Founded in 1916
Printed in 3 colors on matte stock

171 **Accounting Today**
Accountants Media Group & SourceMedia, Inc.
1 State Street Plaza
25th Floor
New York, NY 10004

212-258-8445
800-221-1809
Fax: 212-292-5216
E-Mail: william.carlino@sourcemedia.com
Home Page: www.accountingtoday.com
Social Media: Facebook, Twitter, LinkedIn

Michael Cohn, Editor-in-Chief
Tamika Cody, Managing Editor
Daniel Hood, Editor in Chief
Seth Fineberg, Technology Editor

Covers accounting and auditing standards, taxation and practice management.
Cost: $99.00
48 Pages
Circulation: 34991
ISSN: 1044-5714
Founded in 1987
Printed in 4 colors on glossy stock

172 **Accounting and Tax Highlights**
Thomson Reuters
2395 Midway Rd
Carrollton, TX 75006

817-332-3709
800-431-9025
Fax: 888-216-1929
E-Mail: trta.lei-support@thomsonreuters.com
Home Page: www.ria.thomsonreuters.com

Elaine Yadlon, Plant Manager
Thomas H Glocer, CEO & Director
Robert D Daleo, Chief Financial Officer
Kelli Crane, Senior Vice President & CIO

Covers current news and developments in the field. Audiocassette program for CPAs for continuing professional education. Accepts advertising.
Cost: $112.00
28 Pages
Frequency: Monthly
Founded in 1935

173 **Accounting and the Public Interest**
American Accounting Association
5717 Bessie Dr
Sarasota, FL 34233-2399
941-921-7747
Fax: 941-923-4093
E-Mail: deirdre@aaahq.org
Home Page: aaahq.org

Tracey Sutherland, Executive Director
Deirdre Harris, Publications Contact

An academic journal taking the view that accounting is a social activity with far-ranging consequences for every citizen, welcoming innovation and eclecticism, alternative theories and methodologies, as well as the more traditional ones. The common element in this diversity is the requirement that the study and its findings be linked to the public interest by situating them within a historical, social, and political context, and ultimately providing guidance.
8600 Members
Frequency: Periodically
Circulation: 400
Founded in 1916

174 **Achieve**
National Association of Black Accountants
7474 Greenway Center Dr
Suite 1120
Greenbelt, MD 20770-3504

301-474-6222
888-571-2939
Fax: 301-474-3114
E-Mail: customerservice@nabainc.org
Home Page: www.nabainc.org
Social Media: Facebook, Twitter, LinkedIn, YouTube

Calvin Harris Jr., President/CEO
Guillermo Hysaw, Executive Director and COO
Veda Stanley, Executive Vice President
Sheila Taylor-Clark, CPA
Ronald Walker, Chairman, Division of Firms

Magazine for NABA student members. Discussed are issues relevant to student academic, career, and personal aspirations.
Frequency: 2 Times/Year
Founded in 1969

175 **Actuary Magazine**
Society of Actuaries
475 N Martingale Rd
Suite 600
Schaumburg, IL 60173-2252

847-706-3500
Fax: 847-706-3599
E-Mail: webmaster@soa.org
Home Page: www.soa.org

Greg Heidrich, Executive Director
Stacy Lin, Deputy Executive Director/CFO

Provides informative feature articles that focus on a variety of actuarial topics, plus career information, SOA education initiatives and trends in international business.
Frequency: Bimonthly
Printed in 4 colors on glossy stock

176 **Armed Forces Comptroller**
415 N Alfred St
Alexandria, VA 22314-2269

703-549-0360
800-462-5637
Fax: 703-549-3181
Home Page: www.asmconline.org
Social Media: Facebook, Twitter, LinkedIn

Robert Hale, Executive Director
John Bunnell, Associate Director of Certification
Jennifer Sizemore, Chapter Management
Don W Fox, General Counsel

Leading industry journal, is one of the Society's means of sharing professional information. Articles are received from a variety of sources, such as academia, the government, and our members.
18000 Members
Founded in 1948

177 **Audit Report**
Association of Credit Union Internal Auditors
PO Box 150908
Alexandria, VA 22315

703-688-2284
866-254-8128
Fax: 703-683-0295
E-Mail: acuia@acuia.org
Home Page: www.acuia.org
Social Media: Facebook, Twitter, LinkedIn

Samuel Capuano, Chairman of the Board
Jill Chase, Vice Chair

Articles of interest to those in the auditing profession.
800 Members
Frequency: Quarterly
Founded in 1989
Printed in 4 colors

178 **Auditing: A Journal of Practice & Theory**
American Accounting Association
5717 Bessie Dr
Sarasota, FL 34233-2399

941-921-7747
Fax: 941-923-4093
E-Mail: deirdre@aaahq.org
Home Page: aaahq.org

Tracey Sutherland, Executive Director
Deirdre Harris, Publications Contact

The journal is distributed to members of the Auditing section of the Association, as well as libraries.
8600 Members
Frequency: Twice/Year
Circulation: 2000
Founded in 1916

179 **CFMA Building Profits**
Construction Financial Management Association
100 Village Blvd
Suite 200
Princeton, NJ 08540-5783

609-452-8000
888-421-9996
Fax: 609-452-0474
E-Mail: info@cfma.org
Home Page: www.cfma.org
Social Media: Facebook, Twitter, LinkedIn, YouTube

Stuart Binstock, President and CEO
Brian Summers, COO
Robert Rubin, CPA

Information for financial managers and CPAs concerned with financial management.
7000 Members
Frequency: Bi-Monthly

Circulation: 7,000
Founded in 1981

180 **CPA Practice Management Forum**
CCH
2700 Lake Cook Rd
Riverwoods, IL 60015-3867

847-940-4600
800-835-5224
Fax: 773-866-3095
Home Page: www.cch.com

Mike Sabbatis, President
Douglas M Winterrose, Vice President & CFO
Jim Bryant, EVP Software Products

Mini-journal that includes articles featuring best practices, tips and advice from the nation's leading practice management experts.
Cost: $529.00
24 Pages
Frequency: Monthly

181 **CPA Technology Advisor**
Cygnus Publishing
1233 Janesville Avenue
Fort Atkinson, W1 53538-0803

800-547-7377
E-Mail: shari.dodgen@cygnuspub.com
Home Page: www.cygnusb2b.com

John French, CEO
Paul Bonaiuto, CFO
Ed Wood, VP
Kris Flitcroft, EVP

The magazine is a resource for accountants and managers that features a Buyer's Guide that lists hundreds of businesses, manufacturers and professionals that can assist public accounting firms in delivering a variety of services to their clients in various industries.
Cost: $48.00
Circulation: 50,000+
Founded in 1991
Printed in 4 colors on glossy stock

182 **CPA Wealth Provider**
Accountants Media Group & SourceMedia, Inc.
One State Street Plaza
25th Floor
New York, NY 10004

212-258-8445
800-221-1809
Fax: 212-292-5216
E-Mail: howard.wolosky@sourcemedia.com
Home Page: www.accountingtoday.com
Social Media: Facebook

Michael Cohn, President and CEO
Joseph Wells, Chairman
John Gill, VP of Education
John Warren, VP and General Counsel

Offers financial planning strategies, product information and practivve-building advice in an environment that recognizes the special needs of accountants.
Frequency: Quarterly
Circulation: 37000
Founded in 1968
Printed in 4 colors on glossy stock

183 **Computers in Accounting**
Thomson Reuters
2395 Midway Rd
Carrollton, TX 75006

817-332-3709
800-431-9025
Fax: 888-216-1929
E-Mail: trta.lei-support@thomsonreuters.com
Home Page: www.ria.thomsonreuters.com

Elaine Yadlon, Plant Manager
Thomas H Glocer, CEO & Director
Robert D Daleo, Chief Financial Officer
Kelli Crane, Senior Vice President & CIO

Contains the latest information on accounting, tax and business software, electronic spreadsheets, and available hardware.
Cost: $58.00
40 Pages
Founded in 1935

184 **Controller's Cost & Profit Report**
Thomson Reuters
2395 Midway Rd
Carrollton, TX 75006

817-332-3709
800-431-9025
Fax: 888-216-1929
E-Mail: trta.lei-support@thomsonreuters.com
Home Page: www.ria.thomsonreuters.com

Elaine Yadlon, Plant Manager
Thomas H Glocer, CEO & Director
Robert D Daleo, Chief Financial Officer
Kelli Crane, Senior Vice President & CIO

Targets cash flow issues, risk/reward decisions, personnel trends, ways to increase productivity while reducing overhead costs, and technology updates for the new millennium.
Cost: $195.50
Frequency: SemiMonthly
Founded in 1935

185 **Current Issues in Auditing**
American Accounting Association
5717 Bessie Dr
Sarasota, FL 34233-2399

941-921-7747
Fax: 941-923-4093
E-Mail: info@aaahq.org
Home Page: www.aaahq.org

Tracey Sutherland, Executive Director
Julie Smith David, CIO
Diane Ledger, Director of Finance

This open-access journal offers free access to AAA members, non-members, and libraries.
Frequency: Periodically

186 **EA Journal**
National Association of Enrolled Agents
1120 Connecticut Avenue NW
Suite 460
Washington, DC 20036-3922

202-822-6232
Fax: 202-822-6270
E-Mail: info@naea.org
Home Page: www.naea.org
Social Media: Facebook, Twitter, LinkedIn

Frank I Degen, President
Betsey Buckingham, President elect
Robert Reedy, Treasurer/Secretary
Gigi Jarvis, Sr. Dir. Marketing/Communication
William Grutzkuhn, Director Finance/Administration

EA Journal brings information that helps set professionals apart from other tax practitioners.
12000 Members
Frequency: Every Other Month
Founded in 1972

187 **Financial Executive**
Financial Executives International
1250 Headquarters Plaza
West Tower, 7th Floor
Morristown, NJ 07960

973-765-1000
Fax: 973-765-1018
E-Mail: membership@financialexecutives.org
Home Page: www.financialexecutives.org
Social Media: Facebook, Twitter, LinkedIn, YouTube

Marie N Hollein, President & CEO
Marsha Hunt, VP
Mitch Danaher

Addresses accounting and treasury subjects, as well as overall strategies in corporate financial management.
Cost: $69.00
72 Pages
Frequency: 10x/yr
Circulation: 17000
ISSN: 0895-4186
Founded in 1931
Printed in 4 colors on glossy stock

188 **Financial Executive Magazine**
200 Campus Drive
PO Box 674
Florham Park, NJ 07932

973-360-0177
Fax: 973-898-4649
Home Page: www.financialexecutives.org

Marie N Hollein, President & CEO
Marsha Hunt, VP
Mitch Danaher
Paul Chase, VP/Chief Financial Officer
Christopher Allen, VP/Chief Marketing Officer

Award-winning flagship publication of FEI, providing senior-level financial executives with financial, business and management news, trends and strategies to help them work better, faster and smarter. Covers professional, strategic and technological practices and developments that affect financial executives' day-to-day and longer-term issues, reflecting the financial executive's increasing involvement in the general management of their companies.
15M Members
Frequency: 10x/ Year
Founded in 1931

189 **Financial Management**
Financial Management Association International
College of Business Administration
4202 East Fowler Avenue BSN 3331
Tampa, FL 33620-5500

813-974-2084
Fax: 813-974-3318
E Mail: fma@coba.usf.edu
Home Page: www.fma.org

William G Christie, Executive Editor

Financial Management serves the profession by publishing significant new scholarly research in finance that is of the highest quality. The principal criteria for publishability are originality, rigor, timeliness, practical relevance and clarity.
Frequency: Quarterly

190 **ISACA Journal**
Information Systems Audit & Control Association
3701 Algonquin Rd
Suite 1010
Rolling Meadows, IL 60008-3124

847-253-1545
Fax: 847-253-1443
E-Mail: news@isaca.org
Home Page: www.isaca.org
Social Media: Facebook, Twitter, LinkedIn

Susan Caldwell, CEO
Kristen Kessinger, Manager Of Media Relations

Provides professional development information to those spearheading IT governance and those involved with information systems audit, control and security.
Cost: $75.00
10000 Members
Frequency: Bimonthly
Circulation: 86000
Founded in 1969

191 **Information Management**
ARMA International

11880 College Blvd
Suite 450
Overland Park, KS 66215

913-341-3808
800-422-2762
Fax: 913-341-3742
E-Mail: hq@arma.org
Home Page: www.arma.org
Social Media: Facebook, Twitter, LinkedIn

Komal Gulich, President
Julie Colgan, President-elect
Brenda Prowse, Treasurer

ARMA International is a not-for-profit association and a source for authoritative education, the latest legislative updates, standards & best practices.
11000 Members
Founded in 1955

192 **Information Management Magazine**
ARMA International
11880 College Blvd
Suite 450
Overland Park, KS 66215

913-341-3808
800-422-2762
Fax: 913-341-3742
E-Mail: hq@arma.org
Home Page: www.arma.org
Social Media: Facebook, Twitter, LinkedIn

Komal Gulich, President
Julie Colgan, President-elect
Brenda Prowse, Treasurer

The leading source of information on topics and issues central to the management of records and information worldwide. Each issue features insightful articles written by experts in the management of records and information.
Cost: $115.00
Frequency: Bi-monthly
Circulation: 11000
ISSN: 1535-2897
Mailing list available for rent: 9000 names
Printed in 4 colors on glossy stock

193 **Insight**
Illinois CPA Society
550 W Jackson Blvd
Suite 900
Chicago, IL 60661-5742

312-993-0407
800-993-0407
Fax: 312-993-9954
E-Mail: jwinn@stametine.com
Home Page: www.icpas.org
Social Media: Facebook, Twitter, LinkedIn, YouTube

Elaine Weiss, President & CEO
Todd Shapiro, CFO & VP Finance & Administration
Judy Giannetto, INSIGHT Director

Editorial content focuses on practical issues affecting professional development.
Frequency: Monthly
Circulation: 23000
Founded in 1980

194 **Internal Auditing**
Thomson Reuters
2395 Midway Rd
Carrollton, TX 75006

817-332-3709
800-431-9025
Fax: 888-216-1929
E-Mail: trta.lei-support@thomsonreuters.com
Home Page: www.ria.thomsonreuters.com

Elaine Yadlon, Plant Manager
Thomas H Glocer, CEO & Director
Robert D Daleo, Chief Financial Officer
Kelli Crane, Senior Vice President & CIO

Provides solutions to internal auditing problems. Only professional resource written exclusively by leading practitioners.
Cost: $275.00
Frequency: Annual+
Founded in 1935

195 **Internal Auditor Magazine**
Institute of Internal Auditors
247 Maitland Ave
Altamonte Spgs, FL 32701-4201

407-937-1100
Fax: 407-937-1101
E-Mail: iia@theiia.org
Home Page: www.theiia.org
Social Media: Facebook, Twitter, LinkedIn

J. Michael Pepper, Chairman
Carolyn Saint, Senior Vice President
John Wxzelaki, Vice Chairman - Finance/security

World's leading publication covering the internal audit profession. Shares timely, helpful- indispensable -information for professionals who want to keep pace with the diverse, dynamic field of internal auditing.
160M Members
Founded in 1941

196 **International Journal of Business Data Communications and Networking**
Information Resources Management Association
701 E Chocolate Ave
Suite 200
Hershey, PA 17033-1240

717-533-8845
Fax: 717-533-8661
E-Mail: member@irma-international.org
Home Page: www.irma-international.org

Jan Travers, Executive Director
Sherif Kamel, Communications Director
Lech Janczewski PhD, IRMA World Representative Director
Gerald Grant, IRMA Doctoral Symposium Director
Paul Chalekian, IRMA United States Representative

This journal examines the impact of data communications and networking technologies, policies, and management on business organizatios, capturing their effect on IT-enabled management practices.
Cost: $545.00
Frequency: Quarterly
ISSN: 1548-0631

197 **Interpreter Magazine**
Insurance Accounting Systems Association
PO Box 51340
Durham, NC 27717-1340

919-489-0991
Fax: 919-489-1994
E-Mail: info@iasa.org
Home Page: www.iasa.org
Social Media: Facebook, Twitter

Ruth Estrich, President
Elizabeth Mercier, CIO
Ernie Pearson, Board Chair
Joseph Pomilia, Executive Director

This magazine includes reports on actions by the NAIC, interviews with business leaders, reports on industry trends and news about IASA activities.
Cost: $45.00
12 Pages
Frequency: Quarterly
Founded in 1940

198 **Issues in Accounting Education**
American Accounting Association
5717 Bessie Dr
Sarasota, FL 34233-2399

941-921-7747
Fax: 941-923-4093
E-Mail: deirdre@aaahq.org
Home Page: aaahq.org

Tracey Sutherland, Executive Director
Deirdre Harris, Publications Contact

Provides a forum for exchange of education-related ideas and techniques among accounting professors. A widley cited resource for academic members of the Association.
8600 Members
Frequency: Quarterly
Circulation: 5500
Founded in 1983

199 **Journal of Accountancy**
American Institute of Certified Public Accountants
1211 Avenue of the Americas
New York, NY 10036-8701

212-596-6200
Fax: 212-596-6213
E-Mail: service@aicpa.org
Home Page: www.aicpa.org
Social Media: Facebook, Twitter, LinkedIn, RSS

Barry C Melancon, CEO
Susan Coffey, Senior Vice President
Lawson Carmichael, SVP - Strategy
Arleen Thomas, SVP - Mgmt Accounting and Global

AICPA publication that focuses on the latest news and developments related to the field of accounting
Frequency: Monthly
Founded in 1887

200 **Journal of Accounting Research**
University of Chicago Booth School of Business
5807 S Woodlawn Ave
Chicago, IL 60637-1656

773-702-7743
Fax: 773-702-2225
E-Mail: jar@chicagobooth.edu
Home Page: www.chicagobooth.edu
Social Media: Facebook, Twitter, LinkedIn, YouTube

Ted Snyder, Manager
Nicholas Dopuch, Consulting Editor

Publishes original research using analytical, empirical, experimental, and field study methods in accounting research.
Cost: $49.00
Frequency: 5 Times/Year
Circulation: 2800
Founded in 1963

201 **Journal of Accounting and Public Policy**
Elsevier
3251 Riverport Lane
Maryland Heights, MO 63043

314-447-8878
877-839-7126
Fax: 314-447-8077
E-Mail: journalcustomerservice-usa@elsevier.com
Home Page: www.elsevier.com

Ron Mobed, CEO
David Lomas, CFO
Gavin Howe, EVP, Human Resources

Publishes research papers that focus on the intersection between accounting and public policy. It offers articles on accounting including public administration, political science and the

law.
Cost: $126.00
Frequency: 6x Yearly
ISSN: 0278-4254
Founded in 1997

202 **Journal of Applied Finance**
Financial Management Association International
College of Business Administration
4202 East Fowler Avenue BSN 3331
Tampa, FL 33620-5500

813-974-2084
Fax: 813-974-3318
E-Mail: fma@coba.usf.edu
Home Page: www.fma.org

Betty J Simkins, Editor
Ramesh P Rao, Editor
Charles W Smithson, Editor

The Journal of Applied Finance's goal is to be the leading bridging journal between practitioners and academics. The mission is to publish well-crafted papers of interest to practitioners and of use to academics in stimulating research and in their teaching function.
Frequency: 2 Times/Year

203 **Journal of Construction Accounting & Taxation**
Thomson Reuters
2395 Midway Rd
Carrollton, TX 75006
817-332-3709
800-431-9025
Fax: 888-216-1929
E-Mail: trta.lei-support@thomsonreuters.com
Home Page: www.ria.thomsonreuters.com

Elaine Yadlon, Plant Manager
Thomas H Glocer, CEO & Director
Robert D Daleo, Chief Financial Officer
Kelli Crane, Senior Vice President & CIO

Authoritative, targeted articles and experience-based columns cover several areas, including job-costing, risk assessment, dispute resolution, financial reporting, and benchmarking contractor performance.
Cost: $270.00
Frequency: 6 Times/Year
Circulation: 3400
Founded in 1935

204 **Journal of Cost Analysis and Parametrics**
Society of Cost Estimating and Analysis
8221 Old Courthouse Rd
Suite 106
Vienna, VA 22182

703-938-5090
Fax: 703-938-5091
E-Mail: scea@sceaonline.org
Home Page: www.sceaonline.org

Erin Whittaker, Executive Director
Sharon Burger, Certification Program Admin
Brittany Walker, Membership Coordinator

The Journal of Cost Analysis and Parametrics is a joint publication with the International Society of Parametric Analysts. It is dedicated to promoting excellence in cost estimating, cost analysis, and cost management.
Cost: $ 55.00
2015 Members
Frequency: Twice/Year
Founded in 1990

205 **Journal of Cost Management**
Thomson Reuters
2395 Midway Rd
Carrollton, TX 75006

817-332-3709
800-431-9025
Fax: 888-216-1929
E-Mail: trta.lei-support@thomsonreuters.com
Home Page: www.ria.thomsonreuters.com

Elaine Yadlon, Plant Manager
Thomas H Glocer, CEO & Director
Robert D Daleo, Chief Financial Officer
Kelli Crane, Senior Vice President & CIO

Journal of modern cost management (including cost and managerial accounting topics), especially activity-based costing, activity-based management, performance measurement, target costing and investment justification. Accepts advertising.
Cost: $275.00
64 Pages
Founded in 1935

206 **Journal of Emerging Technologies in Accounting**
American Accounting Association
5717 Bessie Dr
Sarasota, FL 34233-2399

941-921-7747
Fax: 941-923-4093
E-Mail: info@aaahq.org
Home Page: aaahq.org
Social Media: Facebook, Twitter

Tracey Sutherland, Executive Director
Deirdre Harris, Publications Contact

This journal is distributed to members of the AI/Emerging Technologies section of the Association, as well as libraries.
8600 Members
Frequency: Annually
Circulation: 300
Founded in 1916

207 **Journal of Government Financial Management**
Association of Government Accountants
2208 Mount Vernon Ave
Alexandria, VA 22301-1314

703-684-6931
800-242-7211
Fax: 703-548-9367
E-Mail: agacgfm@agacgfm.org
Home Page: www.agacgfm.org

Relmond Van Daniker, Executive Director
Evelyn Brown, National President

Provides valuable information for governmental decision makers. Examines budgeting, accounting, auditing and data process developments.
Cost: $60.00
Frequency: Quarterly
Circulation: 14,769
Mailing list available for rent: 18,000 names

208 **Journal of Information Systems**
American Accounting Association
5717 Bessie Dr
Sarasota, FL 34233-2399

941-921-7747
Fax: 941-923-4093
E-Mail: deirdre@aaahq.org
Home Page: aaahq.org

Tracey Sutherland, Executive Director
Deirdre Harris, Publications Contact

Covers developments relating to information systems in use in the accounting industry.
Cost: $35.00
8600 Members
Frequency: Twice/Year
Founded in 1916

209 **Journal of International Accounting Research**
American Accounting Association
5717 Bessie Dr
Sarasota, FL 34233-2399

941-921-7747
Fax: 941-923-4093
E-Mail: deirdre@aaahq.org
Home Page: aaahq.org

Tracey Sutherland, Executive Director
Deirdre Harris, Publications Contact

Has a diverse readership and is interested in articles in auditing, financial accounting, managerial accounting, systems, tax, and other specialties within the field of accounting.
8600 Members
Frequency: Twice/Year
Circulation: 1300
Founded in 1916

210 **Journal of Legal Tax Research**
American Accounting Association
5717 Bessie Dr
Sarasota, FL 34233-2399

941-921-7747
Fax: 941-923-4093
E-Mail: deirdre@aaahq.org
Home Page: aaahq.org

Tracey Sutherland, Executive Director
Deirdre Harris, Publications Contact

Publishes creative and innovative studies employing legal research methodologies that logically and clearly identify, decribe and illuminate important current tax issues, propose improvements in tax systems and unique solutions to problems, and critically analyze proposed or recent tax rule changes from both technical and policy perspectives.
8600 Members
Frequency: Twice/Year
Circulation: 900
Founded in 1916

211 **Journal of Management Accounting Research**
American Accounting Association
5717 Bessie Dr
Sarasota, FL 34233-2399

941-921-7747
Fax: 941-923-4093
E-Mail: deirdre@aaahq.org
Home Page: aaahq.org

Tracey Sutherland, Executive Director
Deirdre Harris, Publications Contact

Devoted exclusively to management accounting research. Contributingto the expansion of knowledge related to the theory and practice of management accounting. Covers all areas of management accounting including, budgeting, internal reporting, incentives, performance evaluation, and the interface between internal and external reporting.
8600 Members
Frequency: Annually, December
Circulation: 2000
Founded in 1916

212 **Journal of Organizational and End User Computing**
Information Resources Management Association
701 E Chocolate Ave
Suite 200
Hershey, PA 17033-1240

717-533-8845
Fax: 717-533-8661
E-Mail: member@irma-internationa.org
Home Page: www.irma-international.org

Jan Travers, Executive Director
Sherif Kamel, Communications Director
Lech Janczewski PhD, IRMA World Representative Director
Gerald Grant, IRMA Doctoral Symposium Director

Paul Chalekian, IRMA United States Representative

The Journal of Organizational and End User Computing (JOEUC) provides a forum to information technology educators, researchers, and practitioners to advance the practice and understanding of organizational and end user computing. The journal features a major emphasis on how to increase organizational and end user productivity and performance, and how to achieve organizational, strategic and competitive advantage.

Cost: $125.00
Frequency: Quarterly
ISSN: 1546-2234

213 **Journal of the American Taxation Association**
American Accounting Association
5717 Bessie Dr
Sarasota, FL 34233-2399

941-921-7747
Fax: 941-923-4093
E-Mail: info@aaahq.org
Home Page: aaahq.org

Tracey Sutherland, Executive Director
Deirdre Harris, Publications Contact

Dedicated to disseminating a wide variety of tax knowledge and publishes research that employs quantitative, analytical, experimental, and descriptive methods to address tax topics of interest to its readership.

8600 Members
Frequency: Twice/Year
Circulation: 1100
Founded in 1916

214 **National Public Accountant**
National Society of Accountants
1010 N Fairfax St
Alexandria, VA 22314-1574

703-549-6400
800-966-6679
Fax: 703-549-2984
E-Mail: members@nsacct.org
Home Page: www.nsacct.org
Social Media: Facebook, Twitter, LinkedIn

Harlan Rose, President
Steven Hanson, First Vice President
Marilyn Niwao, Second Vice President
Brian Thompson, Secretary-Treasurer

News for practicing accountants and tax practitioners.

48 Pages
Circulation: 20000
ISSN: 0027-9978
Founded in 1945

215 **New Accountant**
REN Publishing
3550 W Peterson Avenue
Suite 403
Chicago, IL 60659

773-866-9900
Fax: 773-866-9881
E-Mail: inquiries@RenPublishing.com
Home Page: www.renpublishing.com/

Steven N Polydoris, President/Publisher/Editor

A professional publication for accounting students and the accounting profession. Each issue includes articles to introduce students to the many and diverse career opportunities available to accounting majors and to prepare college accounting students and recent graduates to sit for the CPA exam. Also available in an online format.

Cost: $85.00
17 Pages
Frequency: Monthly
Circulation: 68000
Founded in 1883

216 **Newspaper Financial Executive Journal**
Interactive & Newsmedia Financial Executives
550 W. Frontage Road
Suite 3500
Northfield, IL 50093

847-715-7000
Fax: 847-715-7004
Home Page: www.infe.org
Social Media: Facebook, Twitter, LinkedIn

Trade publication for financial management of newspapers. More than 800 members.

Frequency: Weekly
Circulation: 1000
Founded in 1947

217 **North American Actuarial Journal**
Society of Actuaries
475 N Martingale Rd
Suite 600
Schaumburg, IL 60173-2252

847-706-3500
Fax: 847-706-3599
E-Mail: webmaster@soa.org
Home Page: www.soa.org

Greg Heidrich, Executive Director
Stacy Lin, Deputy Executive Director/CFO
Harry H Panjer, Editor

Scientically addresses domestic and international problems, interests and concerns of actuaries, their customers, and public policy decision makers.

Frequency: Quarterly
Circulation: 22800
ISSN: 1092-0277
Founded in 1997
Mailing list available for rent: 17000 names at $105 per M

218 **PayState Update**
American Payroll Association
660 N Main Ave
Suite 100
San Antonio, TX 78205-1217

210-226-4600
Fax: 210-226-4027
E-Mail: apamail@mindspring.com
Home Page: www.payroll.org
Social Media: Facebook, Twitter, LinkedIn

Daniel Maddux, President

Newsletter dedicated exclusively to state and local payroll compliance news and issues.

Cost: $289.00
Frequency: Bi-Weekly

219 **Payroll Administration Guide**
Bureau of National Affairs
3 Bethesda Metro Center
Suite 250
Bethesda, MD 20814

800-372-1033
Fax: 800-253-0332
E-Mail: customercare@bna.com
Home Page: www.bna.com

Gregory McCaffery, President and CEO
John Camp, VP and CTO
Lisa Fitzpatrick, VP and CMO

A notification and reference service for payroll professionals. Covers federal and state employment tax, wage-hour and wage-payment laws.

Cost: $896.00
Frequency: Bi-Weekly
Founded in 1929

220 **Paytech**
American Payroll Association
660 N Main Ave
Suite 100
San Antonio, TX 78205-1217

210-226-4600
Fax: 210-226-4027
E-Mail: apa@americanpayroll.org
Home Page: www.payroll.org
Social Media: Facebook, Twitter, LinkedIn

Daniel Maddux, President

Member magazine that includes case studies, topical articles, themed issues and comprehensive Buyer's Guides.

Cost: $200.00
Frequency: Monthly
Circulation: 40000
Founded in 1982

221 **Practical Tax Strategies**
Thomson Reuters
2395 Midway Rd
Carrollton, TX 75006

817-332-3709
800-431-9025
Fax: 888-216-1929
E-Mail: trta.lei-support@thomsonreuters.com
Home Page: www.ria.thomsonreuters.com

Elaine Yadlon, Plant Manager
Thomas H Glocer, CEO & Director
Robert D Daleo, Chief Financial Officer
Kelli Crane, Senior Vice President & CIO

Features offer in-depth articles and technical notes on taxation.

Cost: $185.00
64 Pages
Frequency: Monthly
Circulation: 12000
Founded in 1935

222 **Public Budgeting and Finance**
American Association for Budget and Program
PO Box 1157
Falls Church, VA 22041

703-941-4300
Fax: 703-941-1535
E-Mail: aabpa@aol.com
Home Page: www.aabpa.org
Social Media: Facebook, Twitter, LinkedIn, GovLoop

Judy Thomas, President
Melissa Neuman, President Elect
Anthony Rainey, VP
Patrick Vallely, Treasurer

Budget and program analysis professionals.

Frequency: Quarterly

223 **Real Estate Taxation**
Thomson Reuters
2395 Midway Rd
Carrollton, TX 75006

817-332-3709
800-431-9025
Fax: 888-216-1929
E-Mail: trta.lei-support@thomsonreuters.com
Home Page: www.ria.thomsonreuters.com

Elaine Yadlon, Plant Manager
Thomas H Glocer, CEO & Director
Robert D Daleo, Chief Financial Officer
Kelli Crane, Senior Vice President & CIO

Timely source of new ideas, trends and legal developments in real estate taxation. This journal gives you complete, ongoing coverage of all aspects of real estate tax planning.

Cost: $350.00
Frequency: Quarterly
Founded in 1935

224 **Review of Taxation of Individuals**
Thomson Reuters

2395 Midway Rd
Carrollton, TX 75006

817-332-3709
800-431-9025
Fax: 888-216-1929
E-Mail: trta.lei-support@thomsonreuters.com
Home Page: www.ria.thomsonreuters.com

Elaine Yadlon, Plant Manager
Thomas H Glocer, CEO & Director
Robert D Daleo, Chief Financial Officer
Kelli Crane, Senior Vice President & CIO

Offers information on the taxation of individuals, legislation, etc.
Cost: $58.00
Frequency: Monthly
Founded in 1935

225 **Sales & Use Tax Monitor**
Strafford Publications
590 Dutch Valley Road NE
PO Box 13729
Atlanta, GA 30324-0729

404-881-1141
800-926-7926
Fax: 404-881-0074
E-Mail: customerservice@straffordpub.com
Home Page: www.straffordpub.com
Social Media: Twitter

Richard Ossoff, President
Jon McKenna, Executive Editor

Provides updates on compliance requirements and tax avoidance opportunities in every state.
Cost: $487.00
Frequency: 2 Times/Month
ISSN: 0161-309X
Founded in 1984

226 **Spectrum Magazine**
National Association Of Black Accountants
7474 Greenway Center Dr
Suite 1120
Greenbelt, MD 20770-3504

301-474-6222
888-571-2939
Fax: 301-474-3114
Home Page: www.nabainc.org
Social Media: Facebook, Twitter, LinkedIn, YouTube

Calvin Harris Jr., President/CEO
Guillermo Hysaw, Executive Director and COO
Veda Stanley, Executive Vice President
Sheila Taylor-Clark, CPA
Ronald Walker, Chairman, Division of Firms

Provides a communication mechanism whereby readers are kept abreast of key topics of interest within the accounting, finance, and business professions.
Frequency: Annual

227 **State Income Tax Monitor**
Strafford Publications
590 Dutch Valley Road NE
PO Box 13729
Atlanta, GA 30324-0729

404-881-1141
800-926-7926
Fax: 404-881-0074
E-Mail: customerservice@straffordpub.com
Home Page: www.straffordpub.com

Richard Ossoff, President
Jon McKenna, Executive Editor

This journal is a comprehensive briefing on the latest revenue rulings, tax codes, regulations, court decisions and more in every state.
Cost: $467.00
Frequency: 2 Times/Month
ISSN: 0161-309X
Founded in 1984

228 **Strategic Finance**
Institute of Management Accountants
10 Paragon Dr
Suite 1
Montvale, NJ 07645-1774

201-573-9000
800-638-4427
Fax: 201-474-1600
E-Mail: ima@imanet.org
Home Page: www.imanet.org
Social Media: Facebook, Twitter, LinkedIn

Jeffrey C. Thomson, President and CEO
Brian L. McGuire, Chair
John C. Macaulay, Chair-Elect
Sandra B. Richtermeyer, Chair-Emeritus

IMA's award winning magazine that provides the latest information about practices and trends in finance, accounting, and information management that will impact members and their jobs.
Cost: $195.00
Frequency: Monthly
Printed in 4 colors on glossy stock

229 **TAXPRO Journal**
National Association of Tax Professionals
PO Box 8002
Appleton, WI 54912-8002

800-558-3402
Fax: 800-747-0001
E-Mail: natp@natptax.com
Home Page: www.natptax.com
Social Media: Facebook, Twitter, MySpace

Jo Ann Schoen, President
Jean Millerchip, Vice President
Gerard Cannito, Treasurer
Patricia M. McNeer, Secretary
Kathy Stanek, CEO

In-depth tax information and timely feature articles on such issues as new tax acts, practical tax applications, and solutions to the day-to-day challenges of running a tax practice.
Frequency: Quarterly

230 **Tax Management Estates, Gifts and Trusts Journal**
Bureau of National Affairs
3 Bethesda Metro Center
Suite 250
Bethesda, MD 20814

800-372-1033
Fax: 301-294-6760
E-Mail: www.customercare@bna.com
Home Page: www.bna.com

Gregory McCaffery, President and CEO
John Camp, VP and CTO
Lisa Fitzpatrick, VP and CMO

Provides articles by leading tax practitioners and proven techniques for estate planning and planning opportunities. It also features reviews of legislative, administrative and judicial developments.
Frequency: Bimonthly

231 **Tax and Business Advisor**
Grant Thornton
175 W Jackson Blvd
Suite 20
Chicago, IL 60604-2687

312-856-0001
Fax: 312-602-8099
Home Page: www.grantthornton.com
Social Media: Twitter, LinkedIn

Stephen Chipman, CEO
Lou Grabowsky, COO
Russ Wieman, Chief Financial Officer

Current tax and general business issues.
Founded in 1924

232 **The Accounting Review**
American Accounting Association
5717 Bessie Dr
Sarasota, FL 34233-2399

941-921-7747
Fax: 941-923-4093
E-Mail: info@aaahq.org
Home Page: aaahq.org
Social Media: Facebook, Twitter

Tracey Sutherland, Executive Director
Deirdre Harris, Publications Contact

A respected journal covering accounting theory and research, business problems and the teaching of business and accounting subjects. Read by businessmen, teachers, and students of accounting, as well as practicing accountants throughout the world.
Cost: $275.00
8600 Members
Frequency: 6/Year
Circulation: 8000
Founded in 1916

233 **The Bottom Line**
PO Box 1157
Falls Church, VA 22041

703-941-4300
Fax: 703-941-1535
E-Mail: aabpa@aabpa.org
Home Page: www.aabpa.org
Social Media: Facebook, Twitter, LinkedIn, GovLoop

Judy Thomas, President
Melissa Neuman, President Elect
Anthony Rainey, VP
Patrick Vallely, Treasurer

Helps federal, state, and local government managers and analysts, corporate executives and academic specialists meet the unique challenges of their careers. By helping members keep up with the latest developments in their fields, establish and maintain contacts with colleagues, represent their interests and share opportunities, AABPA serves the key difference between simply having a job and being part of a highly respected and well trained profession.
400 Members
Frequency: Monthly
Founded in 1976

234 **The Bottomline**
Hospitality Financial & Technology Professionals
11709 Boulder Lane
Suite 110
Austin, TX 78726-1832

512-249-5333
800-646-4387
Fax: 512-249-1533
E-Mail: membership@hftp.org
Home Page: www.hftp.org

Frank I Wolfe, Executive VP/CEO
Lucinda Hart, COO
Thomas Atzenhofer, CFO
Eliza Selig, Director of Communications

The Bottomline chronicles the most important industry news with focuses on both finance, technology and general management in hospitality.
4800 Members
Frequency: 10x/Year
Founded in 1952

235 **The Compass**
American Society of Women Accountants
1760 Old Meadow Road
Suite 500
McLean, VA 22102

703-506-3265
800-326-2163
Fax: 703-506-3266
E-Mail: aswa@aswa.org

Home Page: www.aswa.org
Social Media: Facebook, Twitter, LinkedIn

Cheryl E Heitz, President
Catherine Mulder, President-elect
Berranthia Brown, VP

Each e-magazine includes content in the areas of accounting & auditing, controllership, leadership, and tax and quick and easy links to the popular sections of the American Society of Women Accountants web site.
Frequency: Monthly
Founded in 1938

236 **The Tax Adviser**
American Institute of Certified Public Accountants
1211 Avenue of the Americas
New York, NY 10036-8701

212-596-6200
Fax: 212-596-6213
E-Mail: service@aicpa.org
Home Page: www.aicpa.org
Social Media: Facebook, Twitter, LinkedIn

Barry C Melancon, CEO
Susan Coffey, Senior Vice President
Lawson Carmichael, SVP - Strategy
Arleen Thomas, SVP - Mgmt Accounting

Monthly tax journal for CPAs and other tax professionals. It includes tax-planning techniques and tax-saving methods which make it a premier source of cutting-edge tax strategies.
Frequency: Monthly
Founded in 1887

237 **Today's CPA**
Texas Society of CPAs
14651 Dallas Pkwy
Suite 700
Dallas, TX 75254-7408

972-687-8500
800-428-0272
Fax: 972-687-8646
Home Page: www.tscpa.org
Social Media: Facebook, Twitter, LinkedIn

Fred Timmons, Chairman
William Hornberger, Chairman/Elect
Stephen W Parker, Treasurer
Roxie Samaniego, Secretary

Includes articles, news and professional tips.
Cost: $28.00
27000 Members
Frequency: Bimonthly

Trade Shows

238 **AAA Annual Meeting**
American Accounting Association
5717 Bessie Dr
Sarasota, FL 34233-2399
941-921-7747
Fax: 941-923-4093
E-Mail: info@aaahq.org
Home Page: aaahq.org

Tracey Sutherland, Executive Director
Karen Pincus, President
Deirdre Harris, Publications Contact

Highlighting the difference made when members are actively engaged in the profession. Striving for thought leadership through research, teaching, involvement in practice, and standard setting. 70 booths of accounting equipment, supplie and services. Accounting and business education, research and practice textbooks, publishers, software, etc.
8600 Members
Frequency: Annual/Summer
Founded in 1916

239 **AAH Research Conference**
Academy of Accounting Historians
10900 Euclid Avenue
Cleveland, OH 44106-7235

216-368-2058
Fax: 216-368-6244
E-Mail: acchistory@case.edu
Home Page: www.aahhq.org

Joanne Cross, President
Robert Colson, President Elect
Yvette Lazdowski, VP, Communications
Robert Colson, VP Communications
Stephanie Moussalli, Secretary

Subjects include modern perspectives of accounting history.
600 Members
Founded in 1973

240 **ACUA Annual Conference**
Association of College and University Auditors
PO Box 14306
Lenexa, KS 66285-4306
913-895-4620
Fax: 913-895-4652
E-Mail: acua-info@goamp.com
Home Page: www.acua.org

M Kevin Robinson, President
J Richard Dawson, Vice President
Karen R Hinen, Executive Director

Annual conference for professionals in the auditing profession.
Frequency: Annual

241 **ACUA Midyear Conference**
Association of College and University Auditors
PO Box 14306
Lenexa, KS 66285-4306

913-895-4620
Fax: 913-895-4652
E-Mail: acua-info@goamp.com
Home Page: www.acua.org
Social Media: Facebook, Twitter, LinkedIn

M Kevin Robinson, President
J Richard Dawson, Vice President
Karen R Hinen, Executive Director

The Midyear Conference was designed to offer a more intense type of training with two-and-a-half days spent on a particular subject matter.
273 Attendees
Frequency: Annual

242 **ACUIA Annual Conference & One-Day Seminar**
Association of Credit Union Internal Auditors
PO Box 150908
Alexandria, VA 22315

703-688-2284
866-254-8128
Fax: 703-683-0295
E-Mail: acuia@acuia.org
Home Page: www.acuia.org
Social Media: Facebook, Twitter, LinkedIn

Brad Feldman, Executive Director
Barry Lucas, Director

This four-day event covers the latest developments and features some of the industry's most popular speakers.

243 **AGA's Professional Development Conference & Exposition**
Association of Government Accountants
2208 Mount Vernon Avenue
Alexandria, VA 22301

703-684-6931
800-242-7211
Fax: 703-548-9367
E-Mail: agacgfm@agacgfm.org
Home Page: www.agacgfm.org

Relmond Van Daniker, Executive Director
Evelyn Brown, National President

Worth 24 CPE hours, the conferenc covers the latest research and information about the American Recovery Act, the constantly changing rules and standards, new management techniques, technological advances and practical tips for bringing greater efficiency to government operations. $800 for members, $1000 for nonmembers
Frequency: Annual

244 **AHIA Annual Conference**
The Association of Healthcare Internal Auditors
10200 W 44th Avenue
Suite 304
Wheat Ridge, CO 80033

888-275-2442
Fax: 303-422-8894
E-Mail: ahia@ahia.org
Home Page: www.ahia.org

Mark Eddy, Director
Pat Bogusz, Executive Director

Exhibits concerning cost containment and increased productivity in health care institutions through internal auditing.
1000 Attendees
Founded in 1981

245 **AM&AA Summer Conference**
Alliance of Merger and Acquisition Advisors
200 E. Randolph Street
24th Floor
Chicago, IL 60601

312-856-9590
877-844-2535
Fax: 312-729-9800
E-Mail: info@amaaonline.org
Home Page: www.amaaonline.com

Matthew C Hawkins, Conference Chairman

Hosts many of the world's leading mid-market M&A executives, top tier speakers, as well as an invaluable networking opportunity.
Frequency: Semi-Annual

246 **AM&AA Winter Conference**
Alliance of Merger and Acquisition Advisors
200 E. Randolph Street
24th Floor
Chicago, IL 60601
312-856-9590
877-844-2535
Fax: 312-729-9800
E-Mail: info@amaaonline.com
Home Page: www.amaaonline.com

Matthew C Hawkins, Conference Chairman

The conference covers a wide range of current topics of interest to members, such as new accounting and tax regulations, value-added intermediary services, financing, licensure, marketing and business development services and networking opportunities.
Frequency: Semi-Annual

247 **ARMA International Annual Conference & Expo**
ARMA International
11880 College Blvd
Suite 450
Overland Park, KS 66215

913-341-3808
800-422-2762
Fax: 913-341-3742
E-Mail: hq@arma.org
Home Page: www.arma.org

Social Media: Facebook, Twitter, LinkedIn, iConference

Marilyn Bier, Executive Director
Doug Allen, President
Elizabeth Zlitni, Exposition Manager

ARMA International is a not-for-profit association and a source for authoritative education, the latest legislative updates, standards & best practices.
11000 Members
Founded in 1955

248 **ARMA International Conference & Expo**
ARMA International
11880 College Blvd
Suite 450
Overland Park, KS 66215

913-341-3808
800-422-2762
Fax: 913-341-3742
E-Mail: hq@arma.org
Home Page: www.arma.org/conference
Social Media: Facebook, Twitter, LinkedIn

Carol Jorgenson, Meetings/Education Coordinator
Wanda Wilson, Senior Manager, Conferences
Elizabeth Zlitni, Exposition Manager

Conference, seminar, workshop, banquet, award ceremony and 175 exhibits of micrographics, optical disk, automated document storage and retrieval systems and more technology of interest to information professionals.
3500 Attendees
Frequency: Annual
Founded in 1956

249 **ASWA/AWSCPA Joint Annual Conference**
American Woman's Society of CPAs
136 S Keowee Street
Dayton, OH 45402

937-222-1872
800-297-2721
Fax: 937-222-5794
E-Mail: info@awscpa.org
Home Page: www.awscpa.org
Social Media: Facebook, Twitter, LinkedIn

Amy Knowles-Jones, President
Kelly Welter, President Elect
Alexandra Miller, Secretary/Treasurer
Cynthia Cox, VP - Member Services

The conference presents an opportunity to learn from leading experts on ways to develop a variety of your skills, leadership development, networking, education and fun.
Frequency: Annual/September
Founded in 2001

250 **ASWA/AWSCPA Joint National Conference**
American Society of Women Accountants
1760 Old Meadow Road
Suite 500
McLean, VA 22102

703-506-3265
800-326-2163
Fax: 703 506 3266
E-Mail: aswa@aswa.org
Home Page: www.aswa.org
Social Media: Facebook, Twitter, LinkedIn

Julia Merrill, Annual Conference Contact

Banquet, luncheon, tours and exhibits of accounting, business and employment opportunities. In conjunction with American Women's Society of CPAs
400 Attendees
Frequency: Annual

251 **Academy of Accounting Historians Annual Research Conference**
Academy of Accounting Historians
10900 Euclid Avenue
Cleveland, OH 44106-7235

216-368-2058
Fax: 216-368-6244
E-Mail: acchistory@case.edu
Home Page: www.aahhq.org

Joanne Cross, President
Robert Colson, President Elect
Yvette Lazdowski, VP, Communications
Robert Colson, VP Communications
Stephanie Moussalli, Secretary

Encourages research, publication, teaching and personal interchanges in all phases of accounting history and its inter-relation with business and economic history. Members are individuals and institutional affiliates with business and economic history.
600 Members
Frequency: Annual
Founded in 1973

252 **Accounting Technology New York Show & Conference**
Flagg Management
353 Lexington Avenue
New York, NY 10016

212-286-0333
Fax: 212-286-0086
E-Mail: flaggmgmnt@msn.com
Home Page: www.flaggmgmt.com

Russell Flagg, President

The free Show focuses on new computer-savvy systems for accounting practices and client operations. See new products offered for the first time. The Conference offers CPE sessions with more than 100 exhibitors and nationally recognized speakers.
Frequency: Annual

253 **All Star Conference**
Institute of Internal Auditors
247 Maitland Avenue
Altamonte Springs, FL 32701-4201

407-371-1100
Fax: 407-937-1101
E-Mail: iia@theiia.org
Home Page: www.theiia.org

J. Michael Pepper, Chairman
Carolyn Saint, Senior Vice President
John Wxzelaki, Vice Chairman - Finance/security

Event features concurrent sessions in tracks focusing on strategies for excellence, risk management, emerging issues, organization best practices, and preventing fraud.
400 Members
Frequency: October/Annual

254 **Alliance of Merger & Acquisition Advisors Semi-Annual Conference**
200 E Randolph St
24th Floor
Chicago, IL 60601-6435

312-856-9590
877-844-2535
Fax: 312-729-9800
E-Mail: info@amaaonline.org
Home Page: www.amaaonline.com

Michael Nall, Owner

AM&AA is the premier International Organization serving the educational and resource needs of the middle market M&A profession. Conferences cover a wide range of current topics of interest to our members, such as new accounting and tax regulations, value-added intermediary services, financing, licensure, marketing and business development services and networking.
Frequency: Semi-Annual
Founded in 1998

255 **American Association of Attorney-Certified Public Accountants Convention**
American Association of Attorney-CPAs
8647 Richmond Highway
Suite 639
Alexandria, VA 22309

703-352-8064
888-288-9272
Fax: 703-352-8073
E-Mail: info@attorney-cpa.com
Home Page: www.attorney-cpa.com

Robert Driegert, President
Domenick Lioce, President Elect
Joseph Cordell, Treasurer
John Pramberg, Secretary

Exhibits for persons licensed both as attorneys and CPAs.
Frequency: July/Annual
Founded in 1964

256 **American Payroll Association Annual Congress**
American Payroll Association
660 North Main Avenue
Suite 100
San Antonio, TX 78205

210-226-4600
Fax: 210-224-6038
E-Mail: apamail@mindspring.org
Home Page: www.americanpayroll.org
Social Media: Facebook, Twitter, LinkedIn, YouTube

Dave Maddux, Executive Director

The Annual Congress is the premier payroll event of the year. With over 190 workshops and special programs and entertainment, Congress is an excellent opportunity for payroll and other financial professionals to learn and network.
1500 Attendees
Frequency: Annual
Founded in 1982

257 **American Payroll Association Fall Forum**
American Payroll Association
660 North Main Avenue
Suite 100
San Antonio, TX 78205

210-226-4600
Fax: 210-224-6038
E-Mail: apamail@mindspring.org
Home Page: www.americanpayroll.org
Social Media: Facebook, Twitter, LinkedIn, YouTube

Dave Maddux, Executive Director

APA's Fall Forum is conducted under the auspices of APA's Strategic Payroll Leadership Task Force. This conference includes APA's Payroll Best Practices Survey and the presentation of APA's Prism Award winners.
1500 Attendees
Frequency: Annual
Founded in 1982

258 **Annual ACFE Fraud Conference and Exhibition**
716 West Ave
Austin, TX 78701-2727

512-478-9070
800-245-3321
Fax: 512-478-9297
E-Mail: accounting@acfe.com

Home Page: www.acfe.com
Social Media: Facebook, Twitter, LinkedIn

James D Ratley, President and CEO
Scott Grossfeld, Chief Executive Officer

The ACFE is the world's largest anti-fraud organization and premier provider of anti-fraud training and education.
50000 Members

259 Annual Conference for Women in Accounting
1760 Old Meadow Road
Suite 500
McLean, VA 22102

703-506-3265
800-326-2163
Fax: 703-506-3266
E-Mail: aswa@aswa.org
Home Page: www.aswa.org
Social Media: Facebook, Twitter, LinkedIn, ASWA Presidents Blog

Barbara W Cornington, President
Monika P Miles CPA, VP of Membership
Tracy L Johnson CPA, VP of Chapter Partnering
Vivian L Moller CPA, VP of Communications

Provides a program that offers a myriad of opportunities to help you meet your continuing education goals, whether technical or soft-skills focused, as well as an opportunity to network with other women of similar backgrounds.
4000 Members
Founded in 1938

260 BCCA Media Credit Seminar
550 W Frontage Rd
Suite 3600
Northfield, IL 60093-1243

847-881-8757
Fax: 847-784-8059
E-Mail: info@bccacredit.com
Home Page: www.bccacredit.com
Social Media: Facebook, Twitter

Cherryl Ingram, Chairman
Chad Richardson, Vice Chairman
Dalton Lee, Secretary
Ralph Bender, Treasurer

Subsidiary of the Media Financial Management Association. BCCA provides credit information, education, and networking opportunities which enables members to efficiently manage credit risk and increase profitability.
600 Members
Founded in 1972

261 CPAAI Regional Meetings
301 State Rt 17
Rutherford, NJ 07070-2599

201-804-8686
Fax: 201-804-9222
E-Mail: homeoffice@cpaai.com
Home Page: www.cpaai.com

James F Flynn, President
Glenda Nixon, Chairman
Ted Carnevale, Secretary

CPA Associates International was established as a global group of high-quality independent CPA and chartered accounting firms; it is market exclusive, with members in major cities throughout the world. The organized association provides members with the capabilities of the largest firm, yet allows each to maintain its local practice while avoiding costly overhead and unnecessary controls.
2050 Members
Founded in 1960

262 Capital Summit
American Payroll Association
660 North Main Avenue
Suite 100
San Antonio, TX 78205

210-226-4600
Fax: 210-226-4027
E-Mail: apamail@mindspring.org
Home Page: www.americanpayroll.org
Social Media: Facebook, Twitter, LinkedIn, YouTube

Dave Maddux, Executive Director

APA hosts the Capital Summit in Washington, D.C. This conference offers attendees the opportunity to meet with government officials and learn about the latest compliance initiatives.
Frequency: Annual
Founded in 1982

263 Club and Hotel Controllers Conference
11709 Boulder Lane
Suite 110
Austin, TX 78726

512-249-5333
800-646-4387
Fax: 512-249-1533
Home Page: www.hftp.org
Social Media: Facebook, Twitter, LinkedIn

Frank I Wolfe, Executive VP/CEO
Lucinda Hart, COO
Thomas Atzenhofer, CFO
Eliza Selig, Director of Communications

The program offers a range of sessions that reflect diverse responsibilities, from technology to taxes, human resource management to personal inspiration.
4600 Members
Founded in 1952

264 Current Financial Reporting Issues Conference
200 Campus Drive
PO Box 674
Florham Park, NJ 07932

973-360-0177
Fax: 973-898-4649
Home Page: www.financialexecutives.org

Marie N Hollein, President & CEO
Marsha Hunt, VP
Mitch Danaher
Paul Chase, VP/Chief Financial Officer
Christopher Allen, VP/Chief Marketing Officer

Get updated in all the areas of financial reporting critical to the sustainability of your company. FASB/IASB technical accounting, revenue recognition, accounting for leases by lessors and lessees, financial instruments-recognition, measurement, hedging and expected loss model, Washington tax update, and the latest SEC happenings.
15M Members
Founded in 1931

265 Detecting & Deterring Financial Reporting Fraud
200 Campus Drive
PO Box 674
Florham Park, NJ 07932

973-360-0177
Fax: 973-898-4649
Home Page: www.financialexecutives.org

Marie N Hollein, President & CEO
Marsha Hunt, VP
Mitch Danaher
Paul Chase, VP/Chief Financial Officer
Christopher Allen, VP/Chief Marketing Officer

Executive workshop for exploring strategies for building an ethical philosophy that deters fraud, employs skepticism-an enemy of fraud-in management's attitude and developing a culture of collaboration and knowledge sharing to deter and detect fraud.
15M Members
Frequency: 10x/Year
Founded in 1931

266 Distance Learning Seminar
550 W Frontage Rd
Suite 3600
Northfield, IL 60093-1243

847-881-8757
Fax: 847-784-8059
E-Mail: info@bccacredit.com
Home Page: www.bccacredit.com
Social Media: Facebook, Twitter

Cherryl Ingram, Chairman
Chad Richardson, Vice Chairman
Dalton Lee, Secretary
Ralph Bender, Treasurer

Credit & Collections 101 for the New Credit Professional
600 Members
Founded in 1972

267 Educational Institutions Payroll Conference
American Payroll Association
660 North Main Avenue
Suite 100
San Antonio, TX 78205

210-226-4600
Fax: 210-226-4027
E-Mail: apamail@mindspring.org
Home Page: www.americanpayroll.org
Social Media: Facebook, Twitter, LinkedIn, YouTube

Dave Maddux, Executive Director

This conference focuses on compliance issues impacting payroll professionals working in the higher education community.
Frequency: Annual
Founded in 1982

268 FMA Annual Meeting
University of South Florida
4202 E Fowler Ave
BSN 3331
Tampa, FL 33620-9951

813-974-2084
Fax: 813-974-3318
E-Mail: fma@coba.usf.edu
Home Page: www.fma.org

Jack S Rader, Executive Director
Douglas R Emery, President Elect
Franklin Allen, VP Program
Alexander J Triantis, VP Global Services
Ajay Patel, Secretary/Treasurer

The Financial Management Association International (FMA) is the global leader in developing and disseminating knowledge about financial decision making. FMA's members include adademicians and practitioners worldwide.
Founded in 1970

269 Financial Leadership Forum
200 Campus Drive
PO Box 674
Florham Park, NJ 07932

973-360-0177
Fax: 973-898-4649
Home Page: www.financialexecutives.org

Marie N Hollein, President & CEO
Marsha Hunt, VP
Mitch Danaher
Paul Chase, VP/Chief Financial Officer
Christopher Allen, VP/Chief Marketing Officer

Forum to help advance the success of senior-level financial executives.
15M Members
Frequency: 10x/Year
Founded in 1931

270 Gaming Conference
Institute of Internal Auditors
247 Maitland Avenue
Altamonte Springs, FL 32701-4201

407-371-1100
Fax: 407-937-1101
E-Mail: iia@theiia.org
Home Page: www.theiia.org

J. Michael Pepper, Chairman
Carolyn Saint, Senior Vice President
John Wxzelaki, Vice Chairman - Finance/security

A must attend event for knowledge-seeking auditors, compliance officers, regulators, and professionals from gaming sectors.
300 Members
Frequency: April/Annual

271 General Audit Management Conference
Institute of Internal Auditors
247 Maitland Avenue
Altamonte Springs, FL 32701-4201

407-371-1100
Fax: 407-937-1101
E-Mail: iia@theiia.org
Home Page: www.theiia.org

J. Michael Pepper, Chairman
Carolyn Saint, Senior Vice President
John Wxzelaki, Vice Chairman - Finance/security

The premiere opportunity for chief audit executives (CAEs), audit directors, and audit leaders to network with peers, benchmark against best practices, and tap into the knowledge of the profession's highest-level practitioners.
800 Members
Frequency: March/Annual

272 Governance, Risk and Control Conference
Institute of Internal Auditors
247 Maitland Avenue
Altamonte Springs, FL 32701-4201

407-371-1100
Fax: 407-937-1101
E-Mail: iia@theiia.org
Home Page: www.theiia.org

J. Michael Pepper, Chairman
Carolyn Saint, Senior Vice President
John Wxzelaki, Vice Chairman - Finance/security

Develop and enhance your auditing skills.
400 Members
Frequency: August/Annual

273 HITEC
11709 Boulder Lane
Suite 110
Austin, TX 78726

512-249-5333
800-646-4387
Fax: 512-249-1533
Home Page: www.hftp.org
Social Media: Facebook, Twitter, LinkedIn

Frank I Wolfe, Executive VP/CEO
Lucinda Hart, COO
Thomas Atzenhofer, CFO
Eliza Selig, Director of Communications

Attend HITEC and network with the industry's innovators, gain knowledge from an expert-led education program and find technology products and services to take your organization to the next level.
4600 Members
Founded in 1952

274 Hall of Fame Gala
200 Campus Drive
PO Box 674
Florham Park, NJ 07932

973-360-0177
Fax: 973-898-4649
Home Page: www.financialexecutives.org

Marie N Hollein, President & CEO
Marsha Hunt, VP
Mitch Danaher
Paul Chase, VP/Chief Financial Officer
Christopher Allen, VP/Chief Marketing Officer

Providing recognition to senior-level financial executives who have epitomized the performance, leadership and integrity of the most exemplary financial professionals throughout their careers and in doing so, have made significant contributions to the betterment of their respective organizations and to the profession as a whole.
15M Members
Founded in 1931

275 IASA Annual Conference
Insurance, Accounting & Systems Association
PO Box 51340
Durham, NC 27717-1340

919-489-0991
Fax: 919-489-1994
E-Mail: info@iasa.org
Home Page: www.iasa.org
Social Media: Facebook, Twitter

Ruth Estrich, President
Joseph Pomilia, Executive Director
Ernie Pearson, Board Chair
H. Louise Ziemann, president-elect
Tom Ewbank, CFO

Provides comprehensive education programs targeted for financial and technology professionals in the industry.
1800 Attendees
Frequency: Annual

276 IFRS Boot Camp
200 Campus Drive
PO Box 674
Florham Park, NJ 07932

973-360-0177
Fax: 973-898-4649
Home Page: www.financialexecutives.org

Marie N Hollein, President & CEO
Marsha Hunt, VP
Mitch Danaher
Paul Chase, VP/Chief Financial Officer
Christopher Allen, VP/Chief Marketing Officer

Provides an update on various recent convergence and regulatory/ statutory matters impacting U.S. GAAP and IFRS reporting companies. Provides financial executives with practical information for addressing global accounting convergence in their organizations, including potential operational considerations rellated to topics such as leases and revenue recognition.
15M Members
Frequency: 10x/Year
Founded in 1931

277 IMA's Annual Conference & Exposition
10 Paragon Dr
Suite 1
Montvale, NJ 07645-1774

201-573-9000
800-638-4427
Fax: 201-474-1600
E-Mail: ima@imanet.org
Home Page: www.imanet.org
Social Media: Facebook, Twitter, LinkedIn

Jeffrey C. Thomson, President and CEO
Brian L. McGuire, Chair
John C. Macaulay, Chair-Elect
Sandra B. Richtermeyer, Chair-Emeritus

Offers three days of knowledge building, education, networking, optional pre-conference workshops, and opportunities to earn NASBA-approved credits.
67000 Members
Founded in 1919

278 IMA's Student Leadership Conference
10 Paragon Dr
Suite 1
Montvale, NJ 07645-1774

201-573-9000
800-638-4427
Fax: 201-474-1600
E-Mail: ima@imanet.org
Home Page: www.imanet.org
Social Media: Facebook, Twitter, LinkedIn

Jeffrey C. Thomson, President and CEO
Brian L. McGuire, Chair
John C. Macaulay, Chair-Elect
Sandra B. Richtermeyer, Chair-Emeritus

Offers three days of learning and career networking opportunities for college students and educators. Accounting, finance, and business students will learn from veteran practitioners about the critical role of accountants and financial professionals within business.
67000 Members
Founded in 1919

279 Information Resources Management Association Conferences
Information Resources Management Association
701 E Chocolate Avenue
Suite 200
Hershey, PA 17033

717-533-8845
Fax: 717-533-8861
E-Mail: member@irma-international.org
Home Page: www.irma-international.org

Jan Travers, Executive Director
Sherif Kamel, Communications Director
Lech Janczewski PhD, IRMA World Representative Director
Gerald Grant, IRMA Doctoral Symposium Director
Paul Chalekian, IRMA United States Representative

Provides forums for researchers and practitioners to share leading-edge knowledge in the global information resource management area. Various seminars, conventions, conferences and other training programs are offered by IRMA throughout the year.

280 Joint ISPA/SCEA Conference & Workshop
Society of Cost Estimating & Analysis
8221 Old Courthouse Rd
Suite 106
Vienna, VA 22182

703-938-5090
Fax: 703-938-5091
E-Mail: scea@sceaonline.org
Home Page: www.sceaonline.net

Erin Whittaker, Executive Director
Sharon Burger, Certification Program Admin
Brittany Walker, Membership Coordinator
Debra Lehman, Treasurer

Speakers and panel sessions, integrated training tracks, informative workshops and vendor exhibits. Three of every four years, the annual conference is a joint conference with the Inter-

national Society of Parametric Analysts (ISPA). Certification exams are offered at the conference for a separate fee.
2015 Members
400 Attendees
Frequency: Annual/June
Founded in 1990

281 **NATP National Conference and Expo**
National Association of Tax Professionals
PO Box 8002
Appleton, WI 54912-8002

800-558-3402
Fax: 800-747-0001
E-Mail: natp@natptax.com
Home Page: www.natptax.com
Social Media: Facebook, Twitter, MySpace

Jo Ann Schoen, President
Jean Millerchip, Vice President
Gerard Cannito, Treasurer
Patricia M. McNeer, Secretary
Kathy Stanek, CEO

Four days filled with top-notch tax education, fun social events, networking, and much more.
Frequency: Annual

282 **National Leadership Conference**
Association of Government Accountants
2208 Mount Vernon Avenue
Alexandria, VA 22301

703-684-6931
800-242-7211
Fax: 703-548-9367
E-Mail: agacgfm@agacgfm.org
Home Page: www.agacgfm.org

Relmond Van Daniker, Executive Director
Evelyn Brown, National President

Presents new tools, and innovations, insights from financial management and accountability leaders, their strategies, mistakes, new management techniques, and the most current standards and regulations updates.
Frequency: Annual/February

283 **Performance Management Conference (PMC)**
Association of Government Accountants
2208 Mount Vernon Avenue
Alexandria, VA 22301

703-684-6931
800-242-7211
Fax: 703-548-9367
E-Mail: agacgfm@agacgfm.org
Home Page: www.agacgfm.org

Relmond Van Daniker, Executive Director
Evelyn Brown, National President

Leaders in performance reporting from all levels of goverment, the private sector and academia share how-tos, lessons learned and cooperative initiatives among governments. Registration begins at $395 for Members, $450 for nonmembers.
Frequency: Annual/November

284 **Practice Management Conference**
Association for Accounting Administration
136 S Keowee Street
Dayton, OH 45402

937-222-0030
Fax: 937-222-5794
E-Mail: aaainfo@cpaadmin.org
Home Page: www.cpaadmin.org
Social Media: Twitter, LinkedIn

Dennis Lemieux, President
Norman Saale, Vice President
Janine Zirrith, Secretary
Jim Fahey, Treasurer
Jane Johnson, Director of Education

Information and displays of accounting administration equipment and products.
200 Attendees
Frequency: Annual/June

285 **SCEA/ISPA Joint Annual Conference & Training Workshop**
Society of Cost Estimating and Analysis
8221 Old Courthouse Rd
Suite 106
Vienna, VA 22182

703-938-5090
Fax: 703-938-5091
E-Mail: scea@sceaonline.org
Home Page: www.sceaonline.org

Erin Whittaker, Executive Director
Sharon Burger, Certification Program Admin
Brittany Walker, Membership Coordinator

Features training sessions to help attendees enhance their skill set or prepare for the CCEA or CPP exams, study sessions, Professional Papers give attendees the chance to hear about best practices, lessons learned and the latest developments in the field.
2015 Members
500+ Attendees
Frequency: Annual
Founded in 1990

286 **Society of Actuaries Annual Meeting & Exhibit**
Society of Actuaries
475 N Martingale Road
Suite 600
Schaumburg, IL 60173

847-697-3900
E-Mail: customerservice@soa.org
Home Page: www.soa.org

Greg Heidrich, Executive Director
Stacy Lin, Deputy Executive Director/CFO

Sessions and keynote presentations about cutting edge research, and discussions, networking opportunities, the latest and greatest technologies, sponsorship opportunities; sometimes held in conjunction with the Academy Luncheon. Registration fees begin at $55 for the luncheon and go to $995 for full meeting attendance.
1,700 Attendees
Frequency: Annual/November

287 **SourceMedia Conferences & Events**
SourceMedia
One State Street Plaza
27th floor
New York, NY 10004

212-803-6093
800-803-3424
Fax: 212-803-8515
E-Mail: abconferences@sourcemedia.com
Home Page: www.sourcemedia.com/

James M Malkin, Chairman & CEO
William Johnson, CFO
Steve Andreazza, VP, Sales & Customer Service
Celie Baussan, SVP, Operations
Anne O'Brien, EVP Marketing & Strategic Planning

SourceMedia Conferences & Events attract over 20,000 attendees worldwide. The content embraces a variety of formats, including: conferences, executive roundtables, expositions, Web seminars, custom events and pod casts. With over 70 events annually, participants are provided with premier content as well as access to the industry's top solution providers. Markets served include: accounting; banking; capital markets; financial services; information technology; insurance; and real estate.

288 **Technology and Office Productivity (TOP) Conference**
National Association of Tax Professionals
PO Box 8002
Appleton, WI 54912-8002

800-558-3402
Fax: 800-747-0001
E-Mail: natp@natptax.com
Home Page: www.natptax.com
Social Media: Facebook, Twitter, MySpace

Jo Ann Schoen, President
Jean Millerchip, Vice President
Gerard Cannito, Treasurer
Patricia M. McNeer, Secretary
Kathy Stanek, CEO

Two days filled with valuable education on what it takes to run a small business, fun social events, networking, and more.
Frequency: Annual

289 **The IIA's International Conference**
The Institute of Internal Auditors
247 Maitland Avenue
Altamonte Springs, FL 32701-4201

407-937-1100
Fax: 407-937-1101
E-Mail: iia@theiia.org
Home Page: www.theiia.org

William J Mulcahy, Conference Chairman
Richard Chambers, President & CEO

Annual conference that features and unprecedented number of concurrent sessions on today's top issues, industry best practices, and unique challenges to help you add value to your organization.
84000 Attendees
Frequency: Annual
Founded in 1941

290 **The World Congress Annual Leadership Summit on Mergers & Acquisitions**
200 E Randolph St
24th Floor
Chicago, IL 60601-6435

312-856-9590
877-844-2535
Fax: 312-729-9800
E-Mail: info@amaaonline.org
Home Page: www.amaaonline.com

Michael Nall, Owner

AM&AA is the premier International Organization serving the educational and resource needs of the middle market M&A profession.
Founded in 1998

291 **Valcon**
Association of Insolvency & Restructuring Advisors
221 Stewart Avenue
Suite 207
Medford, OR 97501

541-858-1665
Fax: 541-858-9187
E-Mail: aira@aira.org
Home Page: www.airacira.org

Anthony Sasso, President
Thomas Morrow, Vice President
Mathew Schwartz, Treasurer
Joel Waite, VP
Matthew Schwartz, Treasurer

Join leading restructuring and valuation experts - attorneys, private equity investors, bankers, financial advisors and workout specialists - to discuss cutting-edge valuation issues and market developments.
Frequency: Annual/February
Founded in 1984

Directories & Databases

292 ARMA International's Buyers Guide
ARMA International
11880 College Blvd
Suite 450
Overland Park, KS 66215

913-341-3808
800-422-2762
Fax: 913-341-3742
E-Mail: hq@arma.org
Home Page: www.arma.org/conference
Social Media: Facebook, Twitter, LinkedIn

75-100 companies listed. Free.

293 Accountancy: A Professional Reference Guide
Georgia State University
35 Broad Street
5th Floor
Atlanta, GA 30302-3991

404-413-7200
Fax: 404-413-7203
E-Mail: admissions@gsu.edu
Home Page: robinson.gsu.edu/accountancy/index.html

Carla Hines, Administrative Coordinator
Allison Jacobs, Director of Student Services

Listings of accounting firms, associations, regulatory agencies and schools offering accredited accounting programs.
Cost: $99.95
450 Pages
Frequency: Hardcover

294 Accounting Research Directory
Markus Wiener Publishing
231 Nassau St
Princeton, NJ 08542-4601

609-921-1141
Fax: 609-921-1140
E-Mail: info@markusweiner.com
Home Page: www.markuswiener.com
Social Media: Facebook

Markus Wiener, Owner
Lawrence D Brown, Editor
Markus Wiener, President

Quick guide arranged by author's names for key articles. It can enable those interested in quantitative literature analysis to test and verify much of the work in this area by the authors in this book.
Cost: $79.95
Frequency: Hardcover
ISBN: 1-558760-68-7

295 Accounting and Tax Database
ProQuest Information and Learning
789 E Eisenhower Parkway
PO Box 1346
Ann Arbor, MI 48106-1346

734-761-4700
800-889-3358
Fax: 800-864-0019
E-Mail: support@il.proquest.com
Home Page: www.il.proquest.com
Social Media: Facebook, Twitter, LinkedIn

Offers comprehensive indexing and informative abstracts of articles in prominent accounting, taxation and financial management publications from the US and other countries. Over 260,000 citations.

296 American Association of Attorney-Certified Public Accountants Directory
American Association of Attorney-CPAs
8647 Richmond Highway
Suite 639
Alexandria, VA 22309
703-352-8064
888-288-9272
Fax: 703-352-8073
E-Mail: info@attorney-cpa.com
Home Page: www.attorney-cpa.com

Robert Driegert, President
Domenick Lioce, President Elect
Joseph Cordell, Treasurer
John Pramberg, Secretary
Driegert, Secretary

Offers names, addresses and biographical data on 1,400 individuals licensed as both attorneys and CPAs.
100 Pages
Frequency: Annual
Founded in 1964
Printed in one color

297 Directory of Actuarial Memberships
Society of Actuaries
475 N Martingale Rd
Suite 600
Schaumburg, IL 60173-2252

847-706-3500
Fax: 847-706-3599
E-Mail: webmaster@soa.org
Home Page: www.soa.org
Social Media: Twitter, LinkedIn

Greg Heidrich, Executive Director
Stacy Lin, Deputy Executive Director/CFO
Tiffany Berger, Director of Finance
Richard Veys, General Counsel
Francis P. Sabatini, Vice President

Lists member names, affiliations and contact information for major US and international actuarial professional associations.
Cost: $150.00
Mailing list available for rent: 17000 names at $300 per M

298 Federal Tax Coordinator 2D
Thomson Reuters
2395 Midway Rd
Carrollton, TX 75006
817-332-3709
800-431-9025
Fax: 888-216-1929
E-Mail: trta.lei-support@thomsonreuters.com
Home Page: www.ria.thomsonreuters.com

Elaine Yadlon, Plant Manager
Thomas H Glocer, CEO & Director
Robert D Daleo, Chief Financial Officer
Kelli Crane, Senior Vice President & CIO

Provides verbatim text of the Internal Revenue Code and IRS Regulations. Information is arranged by subject rather than in Code order. Professional tax preparers are heavy users of this service because of the thorough authoritative analysis it provides.
Cost: $2460.00
Founded in 1935

299 Future Actuary
Society of Actuaries
475 N Martingale Rd
Suite 600
Schaumburg, IL 60173-2252

847-706-3500
Fax: 847-706-3599
E-Mail: webmaster@soa.org
Home Page: www.soa.org

Greg Heidrich, Executive Director
Stacy Lin, Deputy Executive Director/CFO

Full coverage on topics like career development, non-traditional careers, grading systems, study tips, professional conduct and ethics and the structure of actuarial organizations.
Mailing list available for rent: 17000 names at $300 per M

300 International Guide to Accounting Journals
Markus Weiner Publishers
231 Nassau St
Princeton, NJ 08542-4601

609-921-1141
Fax: 609-921-1140
E-Mail: info@markuswiener.com
Home Page: www.markuswiener.com

Markus Wiener, Owner
Surendra Agrawal, Editor

Approximately 300 journals in accounting and related areas, including about 150 published in the US and 150 from 33 other countries that are published in English.
Cost: $49.95
ISBN: 1-558760-67-9

301 National Society of Public Accountants Yearbook
National Society of Public Accountants
1010 N Fairfax St
Alexandria, VA 22314-1574

703-549-6400
800-966-6679
Fax: 703-549-2984
E-Mail: members@nsacct.org
Home Page: www.nsacct.org
Social Media: Facebook, Twitter, LinkedIn

Harlan Rose, President
Steven Hanson, First Vice President
Marilyn Niwao, Second Vice President
Brian Thompson, Secretary-Treasurer

Association members and committees, lists of affiliated state organizations and members of governing board.
Frequency: Annual

Industry Web Sites

302 www.aabpa.org
American Assoc for Budget and Program Analysis
Social Media: LinkedIn

The American Association for Budget and Program Analysis helps federal, state and local government managers and analysts, corporate executives and academic specialists meet the unique challenges of their careers related to the fields of public budgeting and program analysis.

303 www.acatcredentials.org
Accreditation Council for Accountancy and Taxation
Identifies and accredits specialists in accountancy and federal taxation who serve the financial needs of individuals and small to mid-sized business entities. Offers 3 credentials: Accreditation in Accountancy/Accredited Business Accountant, Accredited Tax Preparer and Accredited Tax Advisor.

304 www.acaus.org
Association of Chartered Accountants in the U.S.
ACAUS is a nonprofit professional and educational organization representing interests of over 6,000 U.S. based chartered accountants from the institutes of Chartered Accountants across the globe.

305 **www.accountants.org**
IGAF Polaris
Association of over 136 independent accounting firms located throughout the world. We developed this comprehensive search site as a means of helping people locate an accounting or consulting firm anywhere in the world.

306 **www.acfe.com**
Association of Certified Fraud Examiners
The ACFE is the world's largest anti-fraud organization and premier provider of anti-fraud training and education.

307 **www.agacgfm.org**
Advancing Government Accountability
Educational organization dedicated to the enhancement of public financial management.

308 **www.agn.org**
Accountants Global Network International
Composed of CPA consulting firms who share information and resources via the associated programs.

309 **www.ahia.org**
Association of Healthcare Internal Auditors
Promotes cost containment and increased productivity in health care institutions through internal auditing. Serves as a forum for the exchange of experience, ideas, and information among members; provides continuing professional education courses and informs members of developments in health care internal auditing. Offers employment clearinghouse services.

310 **www.aicpa.org**
American Institute of Certified Public Accountants
The American Institute of Certified Public Accountants is the national, professional organization for all Certified Public Accountants. Its mission is to provide members with the resources, information, and leadership that enable them to provide valuable services in the highest professional manner to benefit the public as well as employers and clients.

311 **www.aipb.org**
American Institute of Professional Bookkeepers
Achieve recognition of bookkeepers as accounting professionals, to keep bookkeepers up-to-date on changes in bookkeeping, accounting and tax, to answer bookkeepers everyday bookkeeping and accounting questions, and to certify bookkeepers who meet high national standards.

312 **www.amaaonline.com**
Alliance of Merger & Acquisition Advisors
AM&AA is the premier International Organization serving the educational and resource needs of the middle market M&A profession.

313 **www.americanpayroll.org**
American Payroll Association
American Payroll Association provides numerous opportunities for payroll education and information.

314 **www.aswa.org**
American Society of Women Accountants
Organization for networking and information exchange in pursuit of professional development.

315 **www.attorney-cpa.com**
American Association of Attorney-CPAs
Seeks to safeguard the professional and legal rights of CPA attorneys.

316 **www.awscpa.org**
American Woman's Society of CPAs
Provides supportive environment that promotes equity and provides opportunities for the achievement of career goals in a competitive and rapidly changing profession.

317 **www.bap.org**
Beta Alpha Psi
Beta Alpha Psi is an honorary organization for Financial Information students and professionals. The primary objective is to encourage and give recognition to scholastic and professional excellence in the business information field.

318 **www.bccacredit.com**
Broadcast Cable Credit Association
Information on Credit Inquiry Service, credit and collection seminars yearly, credit personnel directories, surveys and on-line services.

319 **www.bna.com**
Bureau of National Affairs
A national organization that has a broad range of employment topics, designed for the small to medium-sized organization.

320 **www.computercpa.com**
Accountant's Home Page
Provides information on general accounting for manufacturing, contstruction, service, not-for-profit, e-commerce and more.

321 **www.cpa.net**
Mark Dietrich, CPA, PC
Includes information on social security and alternatives, bill presentation and payment.

322 **www.cpaadmin.org**
Association for Accounting Administration
Enables accounting firm administrators to communicate with one another and share experiences in the profession.

323 **www.cpaai.com**
CPA Associates International
CPA Associates International was established as a global group of high-quality independent CPA and chartered accounting firms; it is market exclusive, with members in major cities throughout the world. The organized association provides members with the capabilities of the largest firm, yet allows each to maintain its local practice while avoiding costly overhead and unnecessary controls.

324 **www.cpatechadvisor.com**
The CPA Technology Advisor
Online resource for accountants and managers. The Web site features a Buyer's Guide that lists hundreds of businesses, manufacturers, and professionals that can assist public accounting firms in delivering a variety of services to their clients in various industries.

325 **www.expresscarriers.com**
Express Carriers Association
A member organization of chief financial officers within the American Trucking Association.

326 **www.gasb.org**
Governmental Accounting Standards Board
Establishes and improves standards of state and local governmental accounting and financial reporting that will result in useful information for users of financial reports and guide and educate the public, including issuers, auditors and users of those financial institutions.

327 **www.grantthornton.com**
Grant Thornton LLP
Grant Thornton LLP is the U.S. member firm of Grant Thornton International Ltd., one of the six global audit, tax and advisory organizations.

328 **www.greyhouse.com**
Grey House Publishing
Authoritative reference directories for business information and general reference, including accounting, banking and financial markets. Users can search the online databases with varied search criteria allowing for custom searches by product category, geographic area, sales volume, keyword, subject and more. Full Grey House catalog and online ordering also available.

329 **www.hftp.org**
Hospitality Financial & Technology Professionals
HFTP is the global professional association for financial and technology personnel working in hotels, clubs, and other hospitality-related businesses.

330 **www.iasa.org**
Insurance, Accounting & Systems Association
The Insurance Accounting & Systems Association Web site offers information about membership in the organization, accounting seminars, events, publications and textbooks.

331 **www.ifac.org**
International Federation of Accountants
IFAC is the global organization for the accountancy profession. It works with its 157 members and associates in 123 countries and jurisdictions to protect the public interest by encouraging high quality practices by the world's accountants.

332 **www.igafworldwide.org**
International Group of Accounting Firms
IGAF Worldwide is one of the oldest, largest, and most well-respected accounting associations in the world. It was founded for the purpose of providing member firms with the tools and resources they need to furnish a broad spectrum of efficient, cost-effective accounting, auditing and management services to clients around the globe.

333 **www.imanet.org**
Institute of Management Accountants
Professional organization devoted exclusively to management accounting and financial management. Goals are to help members develop both personally and professionally, by means of education, certification, and association with other business professionals.

334 **www.infe.org**
Interactive & Newsmedia Financial Executives
Controllers, chief accountants, auditors, business managers, treasurers, secretaries and related newspaper executives, educators and public accountants.

335 **www.nabainc.org**
National Association of Black Accountants
Nationwide professional association with the primary purpose of developing, encouraging and serving as a resource for greater participation by African-Americans and other minorities in the accounting and finance professions.

336 **www.nactp.org**
Nat'l Association of Computerized Tax Processors
A nonprofit association that represents tax processing software and hardware developers,

electronic filing processors, tax form publishers and tax processing service bureaus. The association promotes standards in tax processing and works closely with the Internal Revenue Service and state governments to promote efficient and effective tax filing.

337 www.nacva.com
National Assoc of Certified Valuation Analysts
Global, professional association that supports the business valuation and litigation consulting disciplines within the CPA and professional communities. Along with its training and certification programs, NACVA offers a range of support services, marketing tools, software programs, reference materials and customized databases to enhance the professional capabilities of its members.

338 www.naea.org
National Association of Enrolled Agents
Members are enrolled to represent taxpayers before the Internal Revenue Service. We advise, represent and prepare tax returns for individuals, partnerships, corporations, estates, trusts and any entities with tax reporting requirements.

339 www.nsacct.org
National Society of Accountants
Professional society of practicing accountants and tax practitioners that sponsors the Acceditation Council for Accountancy and Taxation and supports the National Society of Public Accountants Political Action Committee and NSPA Scholarship Foundation.

340 www.sceaonline.org
Society of Cost Estimating and Analysis
Dedicated to improving cost estimating and analysis in government and industry. Offers a unique collection of educational and training materials on cost estimating, cost analysis, earned value management and related disciplines through its professional development program.

341 www.taxsites.com
Tax and Accounting Sites Directory
A comprehensive index of internet resources, designed to be a starting point for people who are searching for tax and accounting information and services.

342 www.theiia.org
Institute of Internal Auditors
International organization of internal auditors, corporate executives and board members. Contact and current development information.

Associations

343 **Ad Council**
815 Second Avenue
9th Floor
New York, NY 10017-4503

212-922-1500
Fax: 212-962-1676
E-Mail: info@adcouncil.org
Home Page: www.adcouncil.org
Social Media: Facebook, Twitter, LinkedIn, YouTube, Tumblr, Pinterest

Debra Lee, Chairman
Peggy Conlon, President and CEO
Jon Fish, Executive Vice President
Priscilla Natkins, Executive Vice President, Director
Paula Veale, Executive Vice President, Corporate

Our mission is to identify a select number of significant public issues and stimulate action on those issues through communications programs that make a measurable difference in our society. To that end, the Ad Council marshals volunteer talent from the advertising and communications industries, the facilities of the media, and the resources of the business and non-profit communities to create awareness, foster understanding and motivate action.
100 Members
Founded in 1942

344 **Ad Council Educational Resources**
815 Second Avenue
9th Floor
New York, NY 10017

212-922-1500
E-Mail: banners@adcouncil.org
Home Page: www.adcouncil.org
Social Media: Facebook, Twitter, LinkedIn, YouTube, Google+

Laura Desmond, Chair
David Christopher, Vice Chair
David Kenny, Vice Chair
Lisa Sherman, President & CEO
Nancy Hill, Secretary
Founded in 1942

345 **Advertising Council Inc**
1707 L Street NW
Suite 600
Washington, DC 20036

202-331-9153
Fax: 202-331-9186
E-Mail: info@adcouncil.org
Home Page: www.adcouncil.org
Social Media: Facebook, Twitter, LinkedIn, YouTube, Tumblr, Pinterest

Debra Lee, Chairman
Peggy Conlon, President and CEO
Jon Fish, Executive Vice President
Priscilla Natkins, Executive Vice President, Director
Paula Veale, Executive Vice President, Corporate

The Ad Council marshals volunteer talent from the advertising and communications industries, the facilities of the media, and the resources of the business and non-profit communities to create awareness, foster understanding and motivate action.

346 **Advertising Educational Foundation**
220 E 42nd St
Suite 3300
New York, NY 10017-5806

212-986-8060
Fax: 212-986-8061
E-Mail: pa@aef.com
Home Page: www.aef.com
Social Media: Facebook

John Partilla, Chairman
Sharon Hudson, VP/Manager
Paula Alex, Chief Executive Officer
Janice Spector, Deputy Director
Marcia Solling, Content Manager

The AEF is supported by ad agencies, advertisers and media companies. The AEF acknowledges that advertising is a vital and highly visible force in American society. Thus, a realistic understanding of how advertising is created, how it works and what it contributes to our social and economic life is important for all who play active roles in our complex society.
48 Members
Founded in 1983

347 **Advertising Media Credit Executives Association**
PO Box 740031
Louisville, KY 40201-7431

502-582-4327
Fax: 502-582-4330
E-Mail: myounger@gannett.com
Home Page: www.amcea.org

Mary Younger, President
Josie Salazar, Vice President
Vickie Bolinger, Secretary/Treasurer
J Dee Stevenson, Past President
Grace Carter, Director

The objectives of the AMCEA: To improve the professionalism, principles, understanding and techniques of media credit management by encouraging the exchange of ideas, methods and procedures within the membership; To provide additional education and training in the business fundamentals of media credit and credit policies; and in the related areas of finance, accounting, law and economics for the purpose of enhancing the career development of the members.
Founded in 1953

348 **Advertising Photographers of America**
2221-D Peachtree Rd, NE
Suite 553
Atlanta, GA 30309

800-272-6264
Fax: 888-889-7190
E-Mail: director@apaatlanta.com
Home Page: www.apaatlanta.com

Harold Daniels, Chairman
Judith Pishnery, National Chapter Rep
Bob Mahoney, Treasurer
David Fine, Board Member
Nate Dorn, Board Member

APA's mission is Successful Professional Photographers. Our goal is to establish, endorse, and promote professional practices, standards, and ethics in the photographic and advertising community. We seek to mentor, motivate, educate, and inspire in the pursuit of excellence. Our aim is to champion and speak as one common voice for advertising photographers and image makers to the advertising industry in the United States and the World.
Founded in 1981

349 **Advertising Research Foundation**
432 Park Ave South
6th Floor
New York, NY 10016-8013

212-751-5656
Fax: 212-319-5265
E-Mail: info@thearf.org
Home Page: www.thearf.org

Colleen Fahey Rush, Chairman
Gayle Fuguitt, CEO & President
Dr William Cook, EVP/Research/Standards
Felix Yang, Chief Revenue Officer
Navarrow Wright, Chief Technology Officer

The Advertising Research Foundation (ARF) is an open forum where the best and brightest from every avenue of advertising gather to exchange ideas and research strategies. Together, we challenge conventional maxims, take on the latest issues, and discover new insights that benefit us all. This collaboration yields something invaluable: knowledge. Knowledge that is meaningful, actionable, and indispensable. Knowledge that empowers our members to have a true impact on their marketing programs.
Founded in 1936

350 **Advertising Self-Regulatory Council**
112 Madison Avenue
3rd Floor
New York, NY 10016

212-705-0104
E-Mail: lbean@asrc.bbb.org
Home Page: www.asrcreviews.org
Social Media: Facebook, Twitter

C. Lee Peeler, President & CEO
Linda Bean, Director of Communication
Reshma Persaud, Marketing Manager
Sarah Agler, Administrative
Camille Sasena, Administration

Establishes the policies and procedures for advertising industry self-regulation. The self-regulatory system is administered by the Council of Better Business Bureaus.

351 **Advertising Specialty Institute**
4800 Street Rd
Langhorne, PA 19053-6698

215-953-4000
800-546-1350
Fax: 215-953-3045
E-Mail: info@asicentral.com
Home Page: www.asicentral.com

Norman Unger Cohn, Chairman
Timothy Andrews, President/CEO
Steve Bright, EVP/General Counsel
Richard Fairfield, EVP of Marketing
Vince Bucolo, Chief Operating Officer

The Advertising Specialty Institute, or ASI, has been providing award-winning products and services to the advertising specialty and promotional products industry for over 50 years. ASI publishes print and online business magazines, product catalogs, Web sites and informational directories. ASI's mission, then, is to bring together these participants by providing catalogs, information directories, newsletters, magazines, Web sites and databases, and offering interactive e-commerce, and marketing
26000 Members
Founded in 1950

352 **Advertising Women of New York**
28 West 44th Street
Suite 912
New York, NY 10036-4910

212-221-7969
Fax: 212-221-8296
E-Mail: assistant@awny.org
Home Page: www.awny.org
Social Media: Facebook, Twitter, LinkedIn, YouTube, Bloggr

Carol Watson, President
Amy Wilkins, First Vice President
Melissa Goidel, Second Vice President
Lynn Branigan, Executive Director
Suzanne Hogan, Associate Director, Events

AWNY was founded as the first women's association in the communications industry. It's active affiliate of the American Advertising Federation. Provides a forum for personal and professional growth; to serve as a catalyst for

the advancement of women in the communications field.
1500 Members
Founded in 1912

353 Alliance for Audited Media
48 W. Seegers Road
Arlington Heights, IL 60005-3913

224-366-6939
Fax: 224-366-6949
Home Page: auditedmedia.com
Social Media: Facebook, Twitter, LinkedIn, YouTube, Instagram

Christina Meringolo, Chairwoman
Scott Kruse, Vice Chair
David W. Leckey, Vice Chair
Chris Daly, Secretary
Liberta Abbondante, Treasurer

A nonprofit, member-based organization that works with media companies, advertising technology providers, ad agencies, and advertisers to provide them with independently verified data and information critical to evaluating and purchasing media.
Founded in 1914

354 American Academy of Advertising
24710 Shaker Blvd.
Beachwood, OH 44122

786-393-3333
E-Mail: patrose@aaasite.org
Home Page: www.aaoa.wildapricot.org
Social Media: Facebook, Twitter

Kim Sheehan, President
Karen Lancendorfer, Vice President
Patricia B. Rose, Executive Director
Gayle Kerr, Secretary
Nancy Mitchell, Treasurer

The American Academy of Advertising (AAA) is an organization of advertising scholars and professionals with an interest in advertising and advertising education. The Academy fosters research that is relevant to the field and provides a forum for the exchange of ideas among its academic and professional members.
600 Members
Founded in 1957

355 American Advertising Federation
1101 Vermont Ave NW
Suite 500
Washington, DC 20005-6306

202-898-0089
800-999-2231
Fax: 202-898-0159
E-Mail: aaf@aaf.org
Home Page: www.aaf.org
Social Media: Facebook, Twitter, YouTube

Wendy Clark, Chairman
James Edmund Datri, President & CEO
Joanne Schecter, EVP/Club Services
Karen Cohn, SVP/Marketing
Lisa Rubin, Executive Vice President

The AAF is the oldest national advertising trade association, and protects and promotes the well-being of advertising. The AAF accomplishes this through a unique, nationally coordinated grassroots network of advertisers, agencies, media companies, local advertising clubs and college chapters.
40000 Members
Founded in 1967

356 American Association for Public Opinion Research
111 Deer Lake Road
Suite 100
Deerfield, IL 60015

847-205-2651
Fax: 847-480-9282
E-Mail: custserv@jobtarget.com
Home Page: www.aapor.org
Social Media: Facebook, Twitter, LinkedIn, YouTube

Rob Santos, President
Michael Link, Vice President/President-Elect
Susan L. Tibbitts, Executive Director
Heidi Diederich, Administrative Director
Abra Alscher, Administrator

The AAPOR community includes producers and users of survey data from a variety of disciplines. Our members span a range of interests including election polling, market research, statistics, research methodology, health related data collection and education.
1700 Members
Founded in 1947
Mailing list available for rent: 1000 names at $400 per M

357 American Association of Advertising Agencies
1065 Avenue of the Americas
16th Floor
New York, NY 10018

212-682-2500
Fax: 212-682-8391
E-Mail: nhill@aaaa.org
Home Page: www.aaaa.org
Social Media: Facebook, Twitter, LinkedIn, YouTube, Google+

Nancy Hill, President/CEO
Michael D Donahue, Executive VP
Laura J. Bartlett, CFO & COO
Tom Finneran,

EVP, Agency Management Services
Mike Donahue, EVP, Strategic Partnerships

The national trade association reprsenting the advertising volume placed by agencies nationwide.
600 Members
Founded in 1917

358 American Marketing Association
311 S Wacker Dr
Suite 5800
Chicago, IL 60606-6629

312-542-9000
800-262-1150
Fax: 312-542-9001
Home Page: www.marketingpower.com
Social Media: Facebook, Twitter, LinkedIn, Youtube

Rick Dow, Chairman
Ric Sweeney, Chairman-Elect
Rob Malcolm, VP/Finance/Secretary
Mary Jo Bitner, Board Member
Jerome Williams, Board Member

The AMA is a professional association for individuals and organizations leading the practice, teaching and development of marketing knowledge worldwide. Our principle role is to serve as a forum to connect like-minded individuals and foster knowledge sharing, provide resources, tools and training and support marketing practice and thought leadership around the globe.
40000 Members
Founded in 1973

359 Asian American Advertising Federation
s230 Wilshire Blvd
Suite 1216
Los Angeles, CA 90048
E-Mail: ghomfranzen@3af.org
Home Page: www.3af.org
Social Media: Facebook, Twitter

Edward Chang, President
Jay Kim, Vice President
Iris Yim, Secretary
Sandra Lee, Treasurer
Genny Hom-Franzen, Executive Director

Consists of Asian American advertising agency principals, media, advertisers and strategic partners that seek to grow the Asian American advertising and marketing industry, raise public awareness of the Asian community, and increase professionalism within the industry.

360 Association of Canadian Advertisers
95 St Clair Avenue West
Suite 1103
Toronto, ON M4V 1N6

416-964-3805
800-565-0109
Fax: 416-964-0771
E-Mail: rlund@acaweb.ca
Home Page: www.acaweb.ca
Social Media: Twitter, LinkedIn

Dominique De Celles, Chair
Ron Lund, President, CEO
Paul Hetu, Vice President, Montreal
Bob Reaume, Vice President, Policy and Research
Randy Scotland, Vice President, Communications

The Association of Canadian Advertisers (ACA) is a national, not-for-profit association exclusively dedicated to serving the interests of companies that market and advertise their products and services in Canada. Membership in the ACA is restricted to client marketers only, making it the premier Canadian marketing association. It cuts across all products and service sectors, and speaks on behalf of over 200 companies.
Founded in 1914

361 Association of Hispanic Advertising Agencies
8400 Westpark Drive
Second Floor
McLean, VA 22102

703-610-9014
Fax: 703-610-0227
E-Mail: info@ahaa.org
Home Page: www.ahaa.org
Social Media: Facebook, Twitter, LinkedIn, YouTube, Storify

Aldo Quevedo, Chairman
Horacio Gavilan, Executive Director
Kristy Cartier, Director/Marketing
Carlos Santiago, Secretary
Gabriela Alc ntara-D¡az, Treasurer

Our mission is to grow, strengthen and protect the Hispanic marketing and advertising industry by providing leadership in raising awareness of the value of the Hispanic market opportunities and enhancing the professionalism of the industry.
100 Members
Founded in 1996

362 Association of Marketing Service Providers
1800 Diagonal Road
Suite 320
Alexandria, VA 22314-2862
703-836-9200
Fax: 703-548-8204

E-Mail: mfsa-mail@mfsanet.org
Home Page: www.amsp.org
Social Media: Facebook, Twitter, LinkedIn, RSS Feed, Youtube, Vimeo

Ken Garner, President/CEO
Leo Raymond, VP-Postal & Member Relations
Tyler Keeney, Director/Membership
Kimberly Kight, Special Publications Manager
Jennifer Root, Director of Conferences

MFSA is the national trade association for the mailing and fulfillment services industry and works to improve the business environment for mailing and fulfillment companies and to provide opportunities for the learning and professional development of the managers of these companies. MFSA provides: instant postal info; periodicals, surveys, and manuals unique to the industry; networking opportunities; and management education and information.
Founded in 1920

363 **Association of National Advertisers**
Association of National Advertisers
708 Third Avenue
33 Floor
New York, NY 10017

212-697-5950
Fax: 212-687-7310
E-Mail: info@ana.net
Home Page: www.ana.net
Social Media: Facebook, Twitter, LinkedIn, YouTube

Stephen F. Quinn, Chairman
Robert D Liodice, President and CEO
Brian Davidson, Senior Vice President
Nick Primola, Senior Vice President
Kristen McDonough, Vice President

The Association of National Advertisers (ANA) is the advertising industry's oldest trade association. Currently, the ANA leads the marketing community by providing its members insights, collaboration, and advocacy. ANA's membership includes 10,000 brands that collectively spend over $250 billion in marketing communications and advertising.
450 Members
Founded in 1910

364 **Better Business Bureau**
4200 Wilson Blvd
Suite 800
Arllington, VA 22203-1838

703-276-0100
Fax: 703-525-8277
Home Page: www.bbb.org
Social Media: Facebook, Twitter, LinkedIn, YouTube, Google+, Pinterest, F

Stephen Cox, President
Charles Underhill, EVP/ COO

The BBB is a leader in public services related to ethical business practices and dispute resolution. It is our passion to promote honesty and integrity in the marketplace. We are committed to and guided by trust, respect and fairness.
Founded in 1912

365 **Brand Activation Association**
650 First Avenue
Suite 2-SW
New York, NY 10016

212-420-1100
Fax: 212-533-7622
Home Page: www.baalink.org
Social Media: Facebook, Twitter, LinkedIn, Flickr

Bonnie J. Carlson, President
Edward M. Kabak, Chief Legal Officer
Lana Mavreshko, Chief Financial Officer
Christine Goonan, Director of Membership
Mike Kaufman, VP of Marketing

Organization that advocates networking, recognition, and provides educational resources to help brand marketers overcome the significant challengesthey face in a rapidly changing marketplace.

366 **Cabletelevision Advertising Bureau**
830 3rd Avenue
2nd Floor
New York, NY 10022

212-508-1200
Fax: 212-832-3268
Home Page: www.thecab.tv
Social Media: Facebook, Twitter, LinkedIn

Sean Cunningham, President & CEO
Charles (Chuck) Thompson, Executive Vice President
Danielle DeLauro, Senior Vice President
Gary Tietjen, Vice President
Evelyn Skurkovich, Sr. Director

367 **Eight-Sheet Outdoor Advertising Association**
1244 Lake Park Avenue
Galt, CA 95632

209-251-7622
800-874-3387
Fax: 209-251-7658
E-Mail: ddjesoaa@comcast.net
Home Page: www.esoaa.com
Social Media: Facebook

Carla Osmus, Chairman
Peter Maloney, President
David Jacobs, Executive Director
Mike Cossota, Vice President
Billboard Guru, Secretary/Treasurer

The Association has helped establish size, structure and location standards, has adopted a code of ethics and standards of business practices. These self-policing efforts have helped stabilize the industry and added the standardization needed for planning
140 Members
Founded in 1953

368 **Insurance and Financial Communications Association**
515 East Grant Rd Ste 141
Box 250
Tucson, AZ 85705

602-350-0717
Fax: 866-402-7336
E-Mail: info@ifcaonline.com
Home Page: www.ifcaonline.com
Social Media: Facebook, Twitter, LinkedIn, YouTube

Ralph Chaump, President
Kim Marchillo, Vice President Communications
Laurie Swinton, Second VP & Director, Membership
Brian Noonan, Director Strategic Planning
Becky Marrington, Director Awards & Recognition

IFCA's primary objective is to encourage and promote the exchange of experience and ideas among its members through an extensive program of formal schools, workshops, seminars, Newsletters, research studies, networking, international awards competition and IFCA's showcase event: the three-day annual meeting. The IFCA name reflects the diversity of our members and helps us recruit new members from more companies.
700 Members
Founded in 1933

369 **Interactive Advertising Bureau**
116 E 27th Street
7th Floor
New York, NY 10016

212-380-4700
Home Page: www.iab.net
Social Media: Facebook, Twitter, LinkedIn

David Moore, Chairman
Randall Rothenberg, President & Chief Executive Officer
Patrick Dolan, Executive Vice President
Sherrill Mane, Senior Vice President, Research
Mike Zaneis, Senior Vice President

The Interactive Advertising Bureau (IAB) is comprised of leading media and technology companies that are responsible for selling 86% of online advertising in the United States. On behalf of its members, the IAB is dedicated to the growth of the interactive advertising marketplace, of interactive's share of total marketing spend, and of its members' share of total marketing spend. The IAB educates marketers, agencies, and media companies about the value of interactive advertising.
500 Members
Founded in 1996

370 **Intermarket Advertising Network**
5307 S 92nd Street
Hales Corners, WI 53130

414-425-8800
Fax: 414-425-0021
E-Mail: camg@greenrubino.com
Home Page: www.intermarketnetwork.com
Social Media: LinkedIn

Deborah Pfluger, President
Joe Erwin, Vice President
Tom Wilson, Co-Chairman
Dan Borgmeyer, Co-Chairman

IAN (Intermarket Agency Network) is a forum for leaders of noncompetitive marketing agencies to openly exchange knowledge in a collaborative setting. A nationwide association of carefully selected agencies, its members meet twice annually to freely discuss important issues like new business, financials, HR, creativity, growth and much more. No topic is off limits.
19 Members
Founded in 1967

371 **International Communications Agency Network**
1649 Lump Gulch Road
PO Box 490
Rollinsville, CO 80474-0490

303-258-9511
Fax: 303-484-4087
E-Mail: info@icomagencies.com
Home Page: www.icomagencies.com
Social Media: Facebook, Twitter, Pinterest

Gary Burandt, Executive Director
Bob Morrison, Regional Director
Patrick Gaulon, Director Finance
Galina Epishkina, Director at Large
Miguel dos Santos, Vice Chairman

One of the world's largest networks of independent advertising and marketing communications agencies. Our mission is: To provide effective integrated communications resources to clients internationally; To provide a free exchange of ideas, information & support for members.
73 Members
Founded in 1950

372 **International Sign Association**
1001 N Fairfax Street
Suite 301
Alexandria, VA 22314

703-836-4012
866-WHY-SIGN
Fax: 703-836-8353
E-Mail: info@signs.org
Home Page: www.signs.org
Social Media: Facebook, Twitter, LinkedIn, YouTube

Lori Anderson, President
Rick Gottwald, VP Education/Technical Initiatives
David Hickey, Vice President, Government Relation
Bill Winslow, Vice President, Finance
Alison Kent, Executive Administrator

The International Sign Association (ISA) is devoted to supporting, promoting and improving the sign industry through government advocacy, education and training programs, technical resources, stakeholder outreach and industry networking events. Our members are manufacturers, users and suppliers of on-premise signs and other visual communications systems.
2600 Members
Founded in 1944

373 **Internet Marketing Association**
10 Mar Del Rey San
Clemente, CA 92673

949-443-9300
Fax: 949-443-2215
E-Mail: info@imanetwork.org
Home Page: imanetwork.org
Social Media: Facebook, Twitter, LinkedIn, YouTube, Google+

Sinan Kanatsiz, Chairman & Founder
Matthew Langie, Vice Chairman
David Steinberg, Vice President
Rachel Reenders, Account Executive
Vince Walden, Finance Director

374 **League of Advertising Agencies**
915 Clifton Avenue
Clifton, NJ 07013

973-473-6643
Fax: 973-473-0685
E-Mail: info@weinrichadv.com
Home Page: www.theweinrichgroup.com

Andy Weinrich, Executive Vice President
Robert Weinrich, Marketing Director

Provides marketing solutions that maximize success.

375 **MAGNET: Marketing & Advertising Global Network**
1017 Perry Hwy
Suite 5
Pittsburgh, PA 15237-2173

412-366-6850
Fax: 412-366-6840
E-Mail: cheri@magnetglobal.org
Home Page: www.magnetglobal.org
Social Media: Facebook, Twitter, RSS Feed

Dan Nelson, President
Joanne Kim, Vice President
Scott Morgan, Vice President - Membership
Mark Lethbridge, Vice President - Planning
Kevin Flynn, Vice President - Programs

Today, MAGNET is a group of non-competing, independently owned advertising agencies in major markets throughout the world. The network is comprised of leading agencies, with billings ranging from 8 million to 200 million US dollars, sharing a desire to pursue and achieve excellence in this profession we call marketing.
40 Members
Founded in 1999

376 **Newspaper Association of America**
4401 Wilson Blvd
Suite 900
Arlington, VA 22203

571-366-1000
Fax: 571-366-1009
Home Page: www.naa.org
Social Media: Facebook, Twitter, LinkedIn, YouTube, Google+

Robert J. Dickey, Chairman
Donna Barrette, Vice Chairman
Robert M. Nutting, Past Chairman
Stephen P. Hills, Secretary
Tony W. Hunter, Treasurer

377 **Outdoor Advertising Association of America**
1850 M St NW
Suite 1040
Washington, DC 20036-5821

202-833-5566
Fax: 202-833-1522
E-Mail: nfletcher@oaaa.org
Home Page: www.oaaa.org
Social Media: Facebook, Twitter, LinkedIn, YouTube

Wally Kelly, Chairman
Nancy J Fletcher, President/CEO
Ken Klein, Executive Vice President, Gov
Marci Werlinich, Vice President of Membership
Kerry Yoakum, Vice President, Government Affairs

The OAAA is the lead trade association representing the outdoor advertising industry and dedicated to promoting, protecting and advancing outdoor advertising interests in the US. With nearly 800 member companies, the OAAA represents more than 90 percent of industry revenues. OAAA Mission: To provide leadership, services, and standards to promote, protect and advance the outdoor advertising industry.
1000 Members
Founded in 1891

378 **Point of Purchase Advertising International**
440 N. Wells Street
Suite 740
Chicago, IL 60654
312-863-2900
Fax: 312-229-1152
E-Mail: info@popai.com
Home Page: www.popai.com
Social Media: Facebook, Twitter, LinkedIn

John Anderson, Chairman
Richard Carrigan, Treasurer
Elise Grosso, Office Manager
Tom Harris, Global Development Chair
Tammy Mulcahy, Director of Events

Education, globalization, technology, advocacy and elevating marketing at retail as a measured medium on a par with print, broadcast, and other advertising mediums are the driving strategies behind POPAI's direction. Throughout the years we have focused on strengthening global partnerships, enriching our research and educational programs, and utilizing technology to better serve our members.
1700 Members
Founded in 1936

379 **Promotional Products Association International**
3125 Skyway Circle North
Irving, TX 75038-3526

972-252-0404
888-426-7724
Fax: 972-258-3004
E-Mail: steves@ppa.org
Home Page: www.ppai.org
Social Media: Facebook, Twitter, YouTube, RSS

Paul Bellantone, President and CEO
Bob McLean, EVP
Lisa Beck, Executive Offices Manager
Sara Besly, Foundation Manager
Blake Bozeman, Business Development Sales Manager

Offers credibility, viability, visibility, community and opportunity to individuals and companies in the promotional products industry. PPAI's Mission: The Promotional Products Association International advocates the power and value of promotional products in the marketing and advertising professions to ensure the success of its members and the global industry.
7500 Members
Founded in 1904

380 **Retail Advertising and Marketing Association**
325 7th St NW
Suite 1100
Washington, DC 20004-2818
202-661-3052
Fax: 202-737-2849
E-Mail: gattim@nrf.com
Home Page: www.rama-nrf.org
Social Media: Facebook, Twitter, LinkedIn, Youtube, Pinterest, Google+, T

Kevin Brown, Chairman
Kelly Gilmore, Senior Vice President
Mike Gatti, Executive Director
Libby Landen, VP, Strategic Marketing
Lisa Marzotti, Sr. Director, Industry Relations

Provides visionary leadership that promotes creativity, innovation and excellence within all marketing disciplines that strategically elevates our members and our industry.
1600 Members
Founded in 1952

381 **Traffic Audit Bureau for Media Measurement**
271 Madison Ave
Suite 1504
New York, NY 10016-1012
212-972-8075
Fax: 212-972-8928
E-Mail: inquiry@tabonline.com
Home Page: www.tabonline.com

Joseph Philport, President/CEO
Larry Hennessey, Senior Vice President-Member Serv
Jeff Casper, Senior Vice President
Sean McCarthy, Senior Vice President - Information
Shawn Ballard, Vice President - Finance

The Traffic Audit Bureau for Media Measurement Inc. is a non-profit organization whose historical mission has been to audit the circulation of out of home media in the United States. Recently TAB's role has been expanded to lead and/or support other major out of home industry research initiatives.
450 Members
Founded in 1933

382 **Transworld Advertising Agency Network: TAAN**
814 Watertown Street
Newton, MA 02465

617-795-1706
Fax: 419-730-1706
E-Mail: info@taan.org
Home Page: www.taan.org

Bob Goranson, Chairman
Peter Gerritsen, President
Bill Ling, Board of Governors

TAAN exists to enhance the intelligence, expertise, reach and personal effectiveness of the owners of its member agencies: Intelligence, through the sharing of best practices, management information, processes and technologies; Expertise, through cooperative utilization of the talents, skills and experience of each member; Reach, through hands-on affiliations with local independent agencies around the world; Personal Effectiveness, through education and close, confidential, trusted relations.
47+ Members
Founded in 1936

383 **eMarketing Association**
40 Blue Ridge Dr.
Charlestown, RI 2813

Home Page: www.emarketingassociation.com
Social Media: Facebook, Twitter, LinkedIn

International association of emarketing professionals committed to enriching the marketing community and its members through recognition, research, advocacy, education, and service.

Newsletters

384 **A Formula for Fueling Ad Agency New Business Through Social Media**
American Association of Advertising Agencies
1065 Avenue of the Americas
16th Floor
New York, NY 10018

212-682-2500
Fax: 212-682-8391
Home Page: www.aaaa.org
Social Media: Facebook, Twitter, LinkedIn

Nancy Hill, President
Michael D. Donahue, Executive Vice President
Laura J. Bartlett, CFO & COO
Michele Adams, Board Secretary

Designed to focus and kick-start your agency's understanding, participation, credibility and leadership in social media with less expense, time and frustration. Created for C level and senior executives charged with the responsibility of new business development.

385 **AAA Newsletter**
American Academy of Advertising
24710 Shaker Blvd.
Beachwood, OH 44122

786-393-3333
E-Mail: director@aaasite.org
Home Page: www.aaasite.org
Social Media: Facebook, Twitter

Debbie Treise, President
Kim Sheehan, President Elect
Margie Morrison, Vice President
Nancy Mitchell, Treasurer
Glen Griffin, Secretary

The newsletter is designed to keep members up-to-date on activities of the Academy and to share information between members regarding their activities.
600 Members
Frequency: Quarterly
Founded in 1957

386 **ACT Newsletter**
Advertising Communications Times
29 Bala Ave
Suite 114
Bala Cynwyd, PA 19004

484-562-0063
Fax: 484-562-0068
E-Mail: adcomtimes@aol.com
Home Page: www.phillybizmedia.com

Joseph H. Ball, Publisher/Executive Editor
Elena Cruz, Executive Assistant

Business to business newsletter for company owners and executives in Philadelphia, Eastern Pennsylvania, Southern New Jersey & Delaware.
Frequency: Monthly
Circulation: 40000

387 **Associated Spring Newsletter**
Associated Spring
18 Main St
Bristol, CT 06010-6581

860-582-9581
800-528-3795
Fax: 860-589-3122
E-Mail: springs@asbg.com
Home Page: www.asbg.com

Paulo Coit, Manager

Offers news, conferences and seminars.
Frequency: Quarterly

388 **Business Owner**
Mailing & Fulfillment Service Association
1421 Prince Street
Suite 410
Alexandria, VA 22314-2806

703-836-9200
Fax: 703-548-8204
Home Page: www.mfsanet.org
Social Media: Facebook, Twitter, LinkedIn

Ken Garner, President/CEO
Leo Raymond, Vice President
Karen Loveridge, Executive Assistant

Distributed to the owner or CEO of all member companies as a dues-supported benefit of membership. Developed specifically to communicate with owners and CEOs on issues unique to them.
Frequency: Bi-Monthly

389 **Conexion Newsletter**
Association of Hispanic Advertising Agencies
8400 Westpark Drive
2nd Floor
McLean, VA 22102

703-610-9014
Fax: 703-610-0227
E-Mail: info@ahaa.org
Home Page: www.ahaa.org
Social Media: Facebook, Twitter, LinkedIn, YouTube

Ingrid Otero-Smart, President/CEO
Leo Olper, CEO
Roberto Orci, Chair

AHAA represents the best minds and resources dedicated to Hispanic-specialized marketing.
Frequency: Monthly

390 **Counselor**
Advertising Specialty Institute
4800 E Street Rd
Langhorne, PA 19053-6698

215-953-4000
800-546-1350
Fax: 215-953-3045
E-Mail: info@asicentral.com
Home Page: www.asicentral.com
Social Media: Facebook

Timothy M Andrews, CEO
Norman Cohn, Chairman
Matthew Cohn, Vice Chairman
Carol Albright, SVP-Human Resources

The voice of the promotional products industry, Counselor keeps you up to date with industry news and trends.
Frequency: 13x/Year
Circulation: 40000

391 **DMA Daily Digest**
Direct Marketing Association
1120 Avenue of the Americas
New York, NY 10036-6700

212-768-7277
Fax: 212-302-6714
E-Mail: customerservice@the-dma.org
Home Page: www.the-dma.org
Social Media: Facebook, Twitter, LinkedIn

Lawrence M Kimmel, CEO

A summary of today's industry news from trade publications and national media. Also available as an e-mail newsletter.

392 **Direct Hit**
Midwest Direct Marketing Association
PO Box 75
Andover, MN 55304

763-607-2943
Fax: 763-753-2240
E-Mail: mdma@mdma.org
Home Page: www.mdma.org

Beth Gervais, President
Vicki Erickson, Secretary/Treasurer

Brings members news of meetings, activities, local and regional events, pertinent articles and changes in legislation and postal requirements that affect the direct marketing industry.
Frequency: Bi-Monthly
Circulation: 600

393 **Display Newsletter**
Eight-Sheet Outdoor Advertising Association
1244 Lake Park Ave
Galt, CA 95632

209-251-7622
800-847-3387
Fax: 209-251-7658
E-Mail: ddjesoaa@comcast.net
Home Page: www.esoaa.com
Social Media: Facebook

David Jacobs, Executive Director
Nick Sr. Keyes, Chairman
Carla Osmus, President
Deb Justus, Vice President
Stuart Rayburn, Secretary/ Treasurer

Includes updates and supplements to the Rates and Allotments book.
Frequency: Monthly
Circulation: 350

394 **Dos and Dont's in Advertising**
Council of Better Business Bureaus
4200 Wilson Blvd
Suite 800
Arlington, VA 22203-1838

703-276-0100
Fax: 703-525-8277
E-Mail: webmaster@bbb.org
Home Page: www.bbb.org

Stephen A Cox, CEO

Provides in-depth coverage of the laws and regulations governing the advertising industry. Helps you to write, place and manage ads that foster consumer trust and confidence, follow federal and state ad rules, regulations and laws. It has helped legal and advertising professionals produce advertising that is ethical and correct for 50 years.
4000 Pages
Frequency: Monthly
Founded in 1970

395 **Education Adviser**
Advertising Specialty Institute
4800 E Street Rd
Langhorne, PA 19053-6698

215-953-4000
800-546-1350
Fax: 215-953-3045
E-Mail: info@asicentral.com
Home Page: www.asicentral.com

Timothy M Andrews, CEO
Norman Cohn, Chairman
Matthew Cohn, Vice Chairman
Carol Albright, SVP-Human Resources

Professional development and insight each month.
Frequency: Monthly

396 **Employment Points**
Mailing & Fulfillment Service Association
1421 Prince Street
Suite 410
Alexandria, VA 22314-2806

703-836-9200
Fax: 703-548-8204
E-Mail: mfsa-mail@mfsanet.org
Home Page: www.mfsanet.org

The content is written for business owners and operators who want to stay informed about current employment issues. The editorial is targeted on human resource issues and employment practices in the mailing and fulfillment services industry.
Frequency: 4x/Year
Circulation: 2000

397 **Globe Newsletter**
International Communications Agency Network
1649 Lump Gulch Road
PO Box 490
Rollinsville, CO 80474-0490

303-258-9511
Fax: 303-484-4087
E-Mail: info@icomagencies.com
Home Page: www.icomagencies.com
Social Media: Facebook, Twitter

Bob Morrison, Director
Joe Phelps, North American Member at Large

A review of industry trends, member agency news and network happenings.
Frequency: Monthly
Circulation: 150

398 **IAB Informer**
Interactive Advertising Bureau
116 E 27th Street
7th Floor
New York, NY 10016
212-380-4700
Home Page: www.iab.net
Social Media: Facebook, Twitter, LinkedIn

Randall Rothenberg, President/CEO

Features the latest need-to-know information from the IAB as well as research and other highlights from the world of Internet advertising and marketing
Frequency: Monthly

399 **IAB SmartBrief**
Interactive Advertising Bureau
116 E 27th Street
7th Floor
New York, NY 10016

212-380-4700
Home Page: www.iab.net
Social Media: Facebook, Twitter, LinkedIn

Randall Rothenberg, President/CEO

Designed specifically for advertising, marketing and media executives, providing the latest need-to-know news and industry information that maximizes your time, giving you and edge over your competition.
Frequency: Monthly

400 **ISA SmartBrief**
International Sign Association
1001 N Fairfax Street
Suite 301
Alexandria, VA 22314

703-836-4012
866-WHY-SIGN
Fax: 703-836-8353
E-Mail: info@signs.org
Home Page: www.signs.org

Duane Laska, Chairman
Harry Niese, Vice Chairman
Chad Jones, Secretary/Treasurer

ISA SmartBrief is a weekly e-newsletter, providing industry developments, new technology, and special offers from ISA.
2600 Members
Frequency: Weekly/Online

401 **InsideAPA Newsletter**
Advertising Photographers of America
27 W 20th Street
Suite 601
New York, NY 10011

212-807-0399
Fax: 212-727-8120
E-Mail: jocelyn@apany.com
Home Page: www.apanational.com

Theresa Raffetto, National President
Michael Grecco, VP
George Simian, Treasurer

InsideAPA is a blog style newsletter focused on photographers and the membership of the Advertising Photographers of America, APA.

402 **PPB Newslink**
Promotional Products Association International
3125 Skyway Cir N
Irving, TX 75038-3539

972-252-0404
Fax: 972-258-3004
E-Mail: ppb@ppai.org
Home Page: www.ppai.org
Social Media: Facebook, Twitter, LinkedIn, YouTube

Paul Bellantone, President
Steven Meyer, Chairman of the Board
Marc Simon, Chair-Elect

Electronic newsletter providing news and information about PPAI and the industry with links to articles in the online version of PPB Magazine.
Frequency: Weekly

403 **PostScripts**
Mailing & Fulfillment Service Association
1421 Prince Street
Suite 410
Alexandria, VA 22314-2806

703-836-9200
Fax: 703-548-8204
E-Mail: mfsa-mail@mfsanet.org
Home Page: www.mfsanet.org
Social Media: Facebook, Twitter, LinkedIn

Leo Raymond, Editor

Each issue of PostScripts highlights a theme relevant to mailing or fulfillment operations, such as production management or information technology.
Frequency: 18x/Year
Circulation: 2800

404 **Postal Points**
Mailing & Fulfillment Service Association
1421 Prince Street
Suite 410
Alexandria, VA 22314-2806

703-836-9200
Fax: 703-548-8204
E-Mail: mfsa-mail@mfsanet.org
Home Page: www.mfsanet.org
Social Media: Facebook, Twitter, LinkedIn

Leo Raymond, Editor

Deals exclusively with current and pending postal and delivery issues. Here you will find the facts and analysis of developing postal issues.
Frequency: 18x/Year

405 **STORES First Edition**
Retail Advertising & Marketing International
325 7th St Nw
Suite 1100
Washington, DC 20004-2818

202-661-3052
Fax: 202-737-2849
Home Page: www.rama-nrf.org
Social Media: Facebook, Twitter

Kevin Brown, RAMA Chairman
Rob Gruen, Vice Chairman
Gwen Morrison, CEO
Julie Gardner, CMO

E-newsletter alerting readers to new stories including web only content as well as STORES and NRF events taking place in the upcoming month.
Frequency: Monthly

406 **STORES Retail Deals**
Retail Advertising & Marketing International
325 7th St Nw
Suite 1100
Washington, DC 20004-2818

202-661-3052
Fax: 202-737-2849
Home Page: www.rama-nrf.org

Kevin Brown, RAMA Chairman
Rob Gruen, Vice Chairman
Gwen Morrison, CEO
Julie Gardner, CMO

Provides coverage of retail industry product and service provider news.
Frequency: Semi-Monthly

407 **Shopping Center Ad Trends**
National Research Bureau
320 Valley St
Burlington, IA 52601-5513

319-752-5415
Fax: 319-752-3421
E-Mail: contactus@supervisionmagazine.com
Home Page: www.national-research-bureau.com

Diane M Darnall, President
Nancy Heinzel, Editor

Advertising and marketing information for the clothing and furniture industry.
Frequency: Monthly
Founded in 1993

408 **Signals**
International Sign Association
1001 N Fairfax Street
Suite 301
Alexandria, VA 22314
703-836-4012
866-WHY-SIGN
Fax: 703-836-8353
E-Mail: info@signs.org
Home Page: www.signs.org

Duane Laska, Chairman
Harry Niese, Vice Chairman
Chad Jones, Secretary/Treasurer

ISA's legislative newsletter.
2600 Members
Frequency: Weekly/Online

409 **Signline**
International Sign Association
1001 N Fairfax Street
Suite 301
Alexandria, VA 22314
703-836-4012
866-WHY-SIGN
Fax: 703-836-8353
E-Mail: info@signs.org
Home Page: www.signs.org

Duane Laska, Chairman
Harry Niese, Vice Chairman
Chad Jones, Secretary/Treasurer

ISA's newsletter developed especially for sign users, sign companies, planners, building and zoning officials, and other government groups connected with the sign industry. Find important legal and planning information on signage, as well as information on traffic safety, amortization, the economic value of on-premise signs, and other related topics.
2600 Members
Frequency: Weekly/Online

410 **Weekly Information Newsletter**
MAGNET: Marketing & Advertising Global Network
1017 Perry Hwy
Suite 5
Pittsburgh, PA 15237-2173
412-366-6850
Fax: 412-366-6840
E-Mail: cheri@magnetglobal.org
Home Page: www.magnetglobal.org
Social Media: Facebook, Twitter

Jim Nash, President

Keeps members alert to such items as new business activities, personnel information, purchases of new equipment and software, industry trends and projections.
Frequency: Weekly

Magazines & Journals

411 **Advantages**
Advertising Specialty Institute
4800 E Street Rd
Langhorne, PA 19053-6698
215-953-4000
800-546-1350
Fax: 215-953-3045
E-Mail: info@asicentral.com
Home Page: www.asicentral.com
Social Media: Facebook

Timothy M Andrews, CEO
Norman Cohn, Chairman
Matthew Cohn, Vice Chairman
Carol Albright, SVP-Human Resources

Written especially for the promotional products sales professional, Advantages can help you sell more.
Frequency: 13x/Year
Circulation: 40000

412 **Advertiser**
The Pohly Company
253 Summer Street
Floor 3
Boston, MA 02210
617-451-1700
800-383-0888
Fax: 617-338-7767
E-Mail: info@pohlyco.com
Home Page: www.pohlyco.com
Social Media: Facebook, Twitter, LinkedIn

Diana Pohly, President & CEO
Bill Pryor, Media Sales General Manager
Kevin Miller, Chief Creative Officer
Bill Dugan, VP/General Manager, FuelNet
Matt Thorsen, Director of Operations & Production

Reports on today's most critical marketing issues such as measuring brand equity, using emerging technologies and global marketing. It also contains articles on key benchmarks and industry trends.
Frequency: 6x/Year

413 **Advertising & Society Review**
Advertising Educational Foundation
220 E 42nd St
Suite 3300
New York, NY 10017-5813
212-986-8060
Fax: 212-986-8061
Home Page: www.aef.com
Social Media: Facebook

John Partilla, Chairman
Paula Alex, CEO

Directed to professors and students in liberal arts colleges, universities and professional schools, Advertising & Society Review is an academic publication that publishes articles, essays and other scholarships about advertising in society, culture, history and the economy.

414 **Advertising Age**
Ad Age Group/Division of Crain Communications
711 3rd Ave
New York, NY 10017-4014
212-210-0785
Fax: 212-210-0465
E-Mail: kwheaton@adage.com
Home Page: www.adage.com
Social Media: Facebook, Twitter, LinkedIn

Norm Feldman, President

Editorial insights, exclusive analysis and proprietary data take readers beyond the day's news, helping our audience understand ongoing and emerging trends.
Frequency: Weekly
Circulation: 56650

415 **Adweek**
Prometheus Global Media
770 Broadway
7th Floor
New York, NY 10003-9595
212-493-4100
Fax: 646-654-5368
Home Page: www.prometheusgm.com
Social Media: Facebook, Twitter

Richard D. Beckan, CEO
James A. Finkelstein, Chairman
Madeline Krakowsky, Vice President Circulation
Tracy Brater, Executive Director Creative Service

Adweek is the source for advertising and agency news, information and opinion. Covering the industry from an agency perspective, Adweek focuses on the image makers and those who create the strategy and the ads as well as those who buy the media and handle client relations.
Cost: $149.00
Frequency: Weekly
Circulation: 36000
Founded in 1978

416 **Billboard Magazine**
Prometheus Global Media
770 Broadway
7th Floor
New York, NY 10003-9595
212-493-4100
Fax: 646-654-5368
Home Page: www.prometheusgm.com
Social Media: Facebook, Twitter, RSS

Richard D. Beckman, CEO
James Finkelstein, Chairman
Madeline Krakowsky, Vice President Circulation
Tracy Brater, Executive Director Creative Service

Packed with in-depth music and entertainment features including the latest in new media and digital music, global coverage, music and money, touring, new artists, radio news and retail reports.
Cost: $149.00
Frequency: Weekly
Founded in 1894

417 **Brandweek**
Prometheus Global Media
770 Broadway
7th Floor
New York, NY 10003-9595
212-493-4100
Fax: 646-654-5368
Home Page: www.prometheusgm.com

Richard D. Beckman, CEO
James A. Finkelstein, Chairman
Madeline Krakowsky, Vice President Circulation
Tracy Brater, Executive Director Creative Service

Focuses on marketing strategy and services, brand identity, sponsorships, licensing, media usage and distribution and promotions.
Frequency: Weekly
Circulation: 26000
Founded in 1991

418 **BtoB Magazine**
Crain Communications, Inc.
1155 Gratiot Ave
Detroit, MI 48207-2732
313-446-6000
E-Mail: info@crain.com
Home Page: www.crain.com

Keith Crain, Chairman
Rance Crain, President
Mary Kay Crain, Treasurer/Assistant Secretary
Merrilee P. Crain, Secretary/Assistant Treasurer
Robert Felsenthal, Vice President/Publisher

Dedicated to integrated business to business marketing. Every page is packed with substance news, reports, technologies, benchmarks, and best practices served up by the most knowledgeable journalists.
Frequency: Monthly
Circulation: 45000

419 **Corporate Logo Magazine**
Virgo Publishing LLC

3300 N Central Ave
Suite 300
Phoenix, AZ 85012-2532

480-675-9925
Fax: 480-990-0819
E-Mail: kkennedy@vpico.com
Home Page: www.vpico.com

Jenny Bolton, President

Provides promotional products distributors with tools to grow their businesses in a competitive marketplace.
Circulation: 20000
Founded in 1986
Printed in on glossy stock

420 **Counselor**
Advertising Specialty Institute
4800 E Street Rd
Langhorne, PA 19053-6698

215-953-4000
Fax: 215-953-3045
E-Mail: info@asicentral.com
Home Page: www.asicentral.com
Social Media: Facebook

Timothy M Andrews, CEO
Norman Cohn, Chairman
Matthew Cohn, Vice Chairman
Carol Albright, SVP-Human Resources

Counselor's coverage of marketing trends and new products is a must read for distributor principals.
Frequency: Monthly
Circulation: 11000

421 **Creativity**
Ad Age Group/Division of Crain Communications
1155 Gratiot Ave
Detroit, MI 48207-2732

313-446-6000
E-Mail: info@crain.com
Home Page: www.crain.com

Norm Feldman, Manager

Information, insight and inspiration in the brand creativity world. Each month we showcase the best work and take readers inside the making of ground breaking brand communications and experiences, while exploring the issues facing those in the idea business.
Frequency: Monthly
Circulation: 33000

422 **Government Relations: How To Guide for Clubs & Federations**
American Advertising Federation
1101 Vermont Ave NW
Suite 500
Washington, DC 20005-6306

202-898-0089
800-999-2231
Fax: 202-898-0159
E-Mail: aaf@aaf.org
Home Page: www.aaf.org
Social Media: Facebook, Twitter, YouTube

James Edmund Datri, President
Constance Cannon Frazier, COO
Joanne Schecter, Executive Vice President

The purpose of this manual is to help reduce the anxiety level that many feel when dealing with lawmakers.

423 **Hispanic Business Magazine**
Hispanic Business Inc
425 Pine Ave
Santa Barbara, CA 93117-3709

805-964-4554
Fax: 805-964-5539
E-Mail: info@hispanstar.com
Home Page: www.hirediversity.com

Jesus Chavarria, President

Our feature stories highlight significant trends in the US Hispanic market and include profiles of successful entrepreneurs, analysis of economic trends and news and data on such topics as government procurement, workplace diversity, politics, advertising, entertainment and events.
Frequency: Monthly
Circulation: 225000
Founded in 1979

424 **Hospitality Style**
ST Media Group International
11262 Cornell Park Dr
Cincinnati, OH 45242-1812

513-421-2050
800-421-1321
Fax: 513-421-5144
E-Mail: customer@stmediagroup.com
Home Page: www.stmediagroup.com

Tedd Swormstedt, CEO
Brian Foos, CFO

Publication for design and architecture of hotels, restaurants, spas, resorts, casinos, complexes or convention centers. Covers hospitality design with the eye of a fashion magazine, identifying trends and showcasing them seasonally in a photo-rich format.
Frequency: Monthly
Circulation: 17000
Founded in 1906

425 **IQ News Adweek**
Prometheus Global Media
770 Broadway
7th Floor
New York, NY 10003-9595

212-493-4100
Fax: 646-654-5368
Home Page: www.prometheusgm.com
Social Media: Facebook, Twitter, RSS

Richard D. Beckman, CEO
James A. Finkelstein, Chairman
Madeline Krakowsky, Vice President Circulation
Tracy Brater, Executive Director Creative Service

Adweek IQ Daily goes out every weekday morning with a briefing of the most important news on interactive advertising, the latest moves by major brands and agencies in terms of content creation, media partnerships and distribution strategies in the digital realm.
Frequency: Daily

426 **In-Store Marketer**
In-Store Marketing Institute
7400 Skokie Blvd
Skokie, IL 60077-3339

847-675-7400
Fax: 847-675-7494
E-Mail:
pdproducts_editor@instoremarketer.org
Home Page: www.instoremarketer.org
Social Media: Facebook, Twitter, LinkedIn

Peter Hoyt, President

Members-only e-newsletter highlights new content added to the Institute's website, including research, audio-enabled presentations, image galleries and trends articles.
Frequency: Bi-Monthly
Circulation: 15000
Printed in 4 colors on glossy stock

427 **Industrial + Specialty Printing**
ST Media Group International
11262 Cornell Park Dr
Cincinnati, OH 45242-1812

513-421-2050
800-421-1321
Fax: 513-421-5144
E-Mail: customer@stmediagroup.com
Home Page: www.stmediagroup.com

Tedd Swormstedt, CEO
Brian Foos, CFO

Covers functional and decorative printing done as part of the manufacturing process, examining the challenges printers face when setting up and maintaining efficient workflows and provides the solutions to keep production on track in industrial printing operations.
Frequency: Monthly
Circulation: 17000
Founded in 1906

428 **Insight Briefs**
Association of National Advertisers
708 Third Avenue
33 Floor
New York, NY 10017

212-697-5950
Fax: 212-661-8057
E-Mail: info@ana.net
Home Page: www.ana.net
Social Media: Facebook, Twitter, LinkedIn, YouTube

Bob Liodice, President & CEO
Christine Manna, COO
William Zengel, EVP

Association of National Advertisors collections of their best materials on a given subject. These resources incorporate information gathered from ANA's vast archive of proprietary information, including: best practices, case studies, charts, data, and quotes from client-side marketers. The purpose of the Briefs is to give high-level insights on a range of timely and important marketing topics.
Frequency: Monthly

429 **International Archive Magazine**
Luerzer's Archive Inc
106 West 29th St
New York, NY 10001

212-643-4297
Fax: 646-619-4264
E-Mail: office@luezersarchive.net
Home Page: www.luerzersarchive.net

Sandra Lehnst, CEO
Michael Weinzettl, Publisher
Christina Hrdlicka, Managing Editor
Michael Weinzettl, Editor in Chief

Presents new and innovative TV, magazine, poster and newspaper ads from 20 countries. Devoted to presentation of ads. Translations are provided.
Frequency: Bi-Monthly

430 **Journal of Advertising (JA)**
American Academy of Advertising
24710 Shaker Blvd.
Beachwood, OH 44122

512-471-8149
Fax: 512-471-7018
E-Mail: jaeditor@austin.utexas.edu
Home Page: www.journalofadvertising.org
Social Media: Facebook, Twitter

Herbert J Rotfeld, President
Debbie Treise, President Elect
Steve Edwards, Vice President
Margie Morrison, Treasurer
Wei-Na Lee, Ph.D, Editor

The premier academic publication covering significant intellectual development pertaining to advertising theories and their relationship with practice. The goal is to provide a public forum that reflects the current understanding of advertising as a process of communication, its role in the changing environment, and the relation-

ships between these and other components of the advertising business and practice.
600 Members
Frequency: Quarterly
Founded in 1957

431 **Journal of Advertising Research**
World Advertising Research Center Ltd
2233 Wisconsin Ave NW
Suite 535
Washington, DC 20007-4144

202-778-4544
Fax: 202-778-4546
E-Mail: americas@warc.com
Home Page: www.noralgroup.com
Social Media: Facebook, Twitter

Eva Kasten, President

The mission of the Journal of Advertising Research is to act as the research and development vehicle for professionals in all areas of marketing including media, research, advertising and communications
Frequency: Quarterly
Circulation: 1850

432 **Journal of Current Issues and Research in Advertising**
CTC Press
PO Box 290159
Columbia, SC 29229-0159

803-754-3112
800-382-8856
Fax: 803-754-3013
E-Mail: j-leigh@tamu.edu
Home Page: www.ctcpress.com

James H Leigh, Co-Editor

Educates advertising students, professionals and all others interested in advertising.

433 **Journal of Euromarketing**
Taylor & Francis Inc
325 Chestnut St
Suite 800
Philadelphia, PA 19106-2614

215-625-8900
800-354-1420
Fax: 215-625-2940
Home Page: www.taylorandfrancis.com

Kevin Bradley, President

Aims to meet the needs of academicians, practitioners, and public policymakers in the discussion of marketing issues pertaining to Europe. It helps to increase our understanding of the strategic planning aspects of marketing in Europe and the marketing aspects of the trading relationship between European and foreign firms.
Frequency: Quarterly
ISSN: 1049-6483

434 **Journal of Interactive Advertising**
American Academy of Advertising
24710 Shaker Blvd.
Beachwood, OH 44122

786-393-3333
E-Mail: patrose@aaasite.org
Home Page: www.aaasite.org
Social Media: Facebook, Twitter

Debbie Treise, President
Kim Sheehan, President Elect
Margie Morrison, Vice President
nancy Mitchell, Treasurer
Glen Griffin, Secretary

A refereed online publication designed to promote our understanding of interactive advertising, marketing and communication in a networked world.
600 Members
Frequency: 2x/Year
Founded in 1957

435 **Media**
Media Index Publishing
PO Box 24365
Seattle, WA 98124-0365

206-382-9220
800-332-1736
Fax: 206-382-9437
E-Mail: media@media-inc.com
Home Page: www.media-inc.com

Katie Sauro, Editor
James Baker, President

Contains the most up-to-date information and issues that are important to you as a member of the marketing, advertising, broadcast, film and video production, multimedia and creative services industries, along with special focus segments and lists each issue, helpful advice from industry leaders and insightful reporting.
Frequency: Bi-Monthly
Circulation: 10,000
Mailing list available for rent: 35M names

436 **Mediaweek**
Prometheus Global Media
770 Broadway
7th Floor
New York, NY 10003-9595

212-493-4100
Fax: 646-654-5368
Home Page: www.prometheusgm.com
Social Media: Facebook, Twitter, RSS

Richard D. Beckman, CEO
James A. Finkelstein, Chairman
Madeline Krakowsky, Vice President Circulation
Tracy Brater, Executive Director Creative Service

Highly targeted circulation covers media decision makers at the top 350 ad agencies in America, all top buying services and client media departments.
Frequency: Weekly
Circulation: 21000
Founded in 1991

437 **News & Views**
Advertising Media Credit Executives Association
8840 Columbia 100 Parkway
Columbia, MD 21045-2158

410-992-7609
Fax: 410-740-5574
E-Mail: amcea@amcea.org
Home Page: www.amcea.org

Sheila Wroten, President
Mary Younger, Vice President
Josie Salazar, Secretary/ Treasurer
Vickie Bolinger, Director
Grace Carter, Director

Our magazine reports on current trends and legal issues while offering tips on customer service, time management and collections.
Frequency: Quarterly

438 **Outdoor Advertising Magazine**
Outdoor Advertising Magazine
Rapid City, SD 57702

877-926-5406
E-Mail: publisher@oam.net
Home Page: www.oam.net
Social Media: Facebook, Twitter, LinkedIn

Randall Williamson, Publisher

A major source for the outdoor and out-of-home advertising industry. Contains the latest information on products, services, supplies, technology, creative ideas, financial and industry news.
Cost: $24.95
Founded in 1920

439 **PC Today**
Promotional Products Association International
3125 Skyway Cir N
Irving, TX 75038-3539

972-252-0404
Fax: 972-258-3004
E-Mail: ppb@ppai.org
Home Page: www.ppai.org
Social Media: Facebook, Twitter, LinkedIn, YouTube

Paul Bellantone, President
Steven Meyer, Chairman of the Board
Marc Simon, Chair-Elect

Quick-read, daily, electronic newsletter serves the unique educational needs of distributor salespeople.
Frequency: Weekly

440 **POP Design**
In-Store Marketing Institute
7400 Skokie Blvd
Skokie, IL 60077-3339

847-675-7400
Fax: 847-675-7494
E-Mail: pdproducts_editor@instoremarketer.org
Home Page: www.instoremarketer.org
Social Media: Facebook, Twitter, LinkedIn

Peter Hoyt, President

Serves the news and product information needs of producers and designers of in-store displays, signs and fixtures. Each issue features the latest trends and technologies vital to building and designing successful in-store merchandising.
Frequency: Bi-Monthly
Circulation: 15000
Printed in 4 colors on glossy stock

441 **PPB Magazine**
Promotional Products Association International
3125 Skyway Cir N
Irving, TX 75038-3539

972-252-0404
888-426-7724
Fax: 972-258-3004
E-Mail: ppb@ppai.org
Home Page: www.ppai.org
Social Media: Facebook, Twitter, YouTube

Paul Bellantone, President
Steven Meyer, Chairman of the Board
Marc Simon, Chair-Elect

Coverage concentrates on news activities and events of the promotional products industry.
Cost: $62.00
Frequency: Monthly

442 **Package Design Magazine**
ST Media Group International
11262 Cornell Park Dr
Cincinnati, OH 45242-1812

513-421-2050
800-421-1321
Fax: 513-421-5144
E-Mail: customer@stmediagroup.com
Home Page: www.stmediagroup.com

Tedd Swormstedt, CEO
Brian Foos, CFO

Full of the news and information professional package designers need to stay abreast of the latest innovations, materials, and technology driving the packaging industry. Presents readers with the useful insights they need to succeed in competitive retail markets.
Frequency: Monthly
Circulation: 17000
Founded in 1906

443 **Politically Direct**
Direct Marketing Association

1120 Avenue of the Americas
New York, NY 10036-6713

212-768-7277
Fax: 212-302-6714
E-Mail: customerservice@the-dma.org
Home Page: www.the-dma.org
Social Media: Facebook, Twitter, LinkedIn

Matt Blumberg, Chairman
Glenn Eisen, Vice Chairman
Rick Erwin, Treasurer

Published in both print and digital versions, this newsletter on DMA advocacy efforts keeps DMA members informed and involved in the politics and policies that impact them today and ahead of the curve on developments that will affect them tomorrow.
Frequency: Quarterly

444 **Promotional Consultant Magazine**
Promotional Products Association International
3125 Skyway Cir N
Irving, TX 75038-3539

972-252-0404
Fax: 972-258-3004
E-Mail: ppb@ppai.org
Home Page: www.ppai.org
Social Media: Facebook, Twitter, YouTube

Paul Bellantone, President
Steven Meyer, Chairman of the Board
Marc Simon, Chair-Elect

Featuring short, sales-specific articles, relevant trends, targeted strategies, expert voices and compelling case studies.
Frequency: Bi-Monthly
Circulation: 20000

445 **Public Opinion Journal**
American Association for Public Opinion Research
111 Deer Land Road
Suite 100
Deerfield, IL 60015-4943

913-895-4601
Fax: 913-895-4652
E-Mail: aapor-info@goamp.com
Home Page: www.aapor.org
Social Media: Facebook, Twitter, LinkedIn

Paul Lavrakas, President
Rob Santos, VP/President-Elect
Scott Keeter, Secretary-Treasurer

Offers articles about the science and practice of survey and opinion research to give people a voice in the decisions that affect their daily lives.
Frequency: Quarterly
Founded in 1948
Mailing list available for rent: 1000 names at $400 per M

446 **Public Relations Unplugged: PR Strategies For AAF Ad Clubs and Members**
American Advertisting Federation
1101 Vermont Ave NW
Suite 500
Washington, DC 20005-6306

202-898-0089
800-999-2231
Fax: 202-898-0159
E-Mail: aaf@aaf.org
Home Page: www.aaf.org

James Edmund Datri, President
Constance Cannon Frazier, COO
Joanne Schecter, Executive Vice President

In this text you will find guidance, instructions and examples to help your ad club deflect legislative threats and become a more prominent voice within your community.

447 **Response**
201 Sandpointe Ave
Suite 500
Santa Ana, CA 92707-8700

714-338-6700
800-854-3112
Fax: 714-513-8482
E-Mail: thaire@questex.com
Home Page: www.responsemagazine.com
Social Media: Facebook, Twitter, LinkedIn, YouTube

Thomas Haire, Editor
Don Rosenberg, VP
Kristina Kronenberg, Marketing Director

Magazine of direct response television reporting. Educates marketers and advertising executives on how to sell products, generate leads and drive store sales through infomercials, short-form commercials, televised shopping and multi-media retailing.
Frequency: Monthly
Circulation: 12000
Founded in 1987

448 **STORES Magazine**
Retail Advertising & Marketing International
325 7th St NW
Suite 1100
Washington, DC 20004-2818

202-661-3052
Fax: 202-737-2849
Home Page: www.rama-nrf.org

Kevin Brown, RAMA Chairman
Rob Gruen, Vice Chairman
Gwen Morrison, CEO
Julie Gardner, CMO

A publication devoted to retail news and trends as well as notification of conferences and meetings.
Frequency: Monthly

449 **Screen Printing Magazine**
ST Media Group International
11262 Cornell Park Dr
Cincinnati, OH 45242-1812

513-421-2050
800-421-1321
Fax: 513-421-5144
E-Mail: customer@stmediagroup.com
Home Page: www.stmediagroup.com

Tedd Swormstedt, CEO
Brian Foos, CFO

Leading publication and trusted source of information for the screen-printing industry. Landmark coverage of the latest techniques and technologies that save time, energy and money.
Frequency: Monthly
Circulation: 17000
Founded in 1906

450 **Shopper Marketing**
In-Store Marketing Institute
7400 Skokie Blvd
Skokie, IL 60077-3339

847-675-7400
Fax: 847-675-7494
E-Mail:
pdproducts_editor@instoremarketer.org
Home Page: www.instoremarketer.org
Social Media: Facebook, Twitter, LinkedIn

Peter Hoyt, President

The leading information source for news and information surrounding the shopper marketing industry. Each month, more than 18000 marketers, manufacturers, agencies and retailers of consumer products or services who buy and specify in-store marketing solutions turn to Shopper Marketing to learn about the latest insights, data and trends surrounding the industry.
Frequency: Bi-Monthly
Circulation: 15000
Printed in 4 colors on glossy stock

451 **Shopper Marketing Newswire**
In-Store Marketing Institute
7400 Skokie Blvd
Skokie, IL 60077-3339

847-675-7400
Fax: 847-675-7494
E-Mail:
pdproducts_editor@instoremarketer.org
Home Page: www.instoremarketer.org
Social Media: Facebook, Twitter, LinkedIn

Peter Hoyt, President

Delivered to a powerful audience of brands, retailers, agencies and solution providers. Offering personnel updates, company news, research/ data reports, path-to-purchase innovations, co-marketing initiatives across FDM and specialty chains and more.
Frequency: Bi-Monthly
Circulation: 15000
Printed in 4 colors on glossy stock

452 **Sign & Digital Graphics**
National Business Media Inc
2800 W Midway Boulevard
PO Box 1416
Broomfield, CO 80020

303-469-0424
800-669-0424
Fax: 303-469-5730
E-Mail: mdixon@nbm.com
Home Page: www.nbm.com/sb
Social Media: Facebook, Twitter

James Kochevar, Publisher
Ken Mergentime, Executive Editor
Matt Dixon, Managing Editor

A comprehensive monthly trade publication covering the business of visual communications offering a broad range of in-depth reporting for professionals. Topics covered include commercial signage, wide-format commercial printing, electric signs and letters, architectural signage, electronic displays, vehicle wraps and graphics and much more.
Cost: $38.00
120 Pages
Frequency: Monthly
Circulation: 18300
Founded in 1986
Mailing list available for rent: 1000 names at $225 per M
Printed in 4 colors

453 **Sign Builder Illustrated**
Simmons-Boardman Publishing Corporation
345 Hudson St
12th Floor
New York, NY 10014-7123

212-620-7200
Fax: 212-633-1165
E-Mail: jwoten@sbpub.com
Home Page: www.simmonsboardman.com

Arthur J McGinnis Jr, President

How-to magazine featuring the latest products, technology and techniques to enhance the sign maker's craft.
Frequency: Monthly
Circulation: 19055

454 **Sign Business**
National Business Media Inc
2800 W Midway Boulevard
PO Box 1416
Broomfield, CO 80020

303-469-0424
800-669-0424

Fax: 303-469-5730
E-Mail: mdixon@nbm.com
Home Page: www.nbm.com/sb

James Kochevar, Publisher
Ken Mergentime, Executive Editor
Matt Dixon, Managing Editor

Contains information on electrical illuminated signage, outdoor advertising and commercial sign shops.
Cost: $38.00
120 Pages
Frequency: Monthly
Circulation: 18348
Founded in 1986
Mailing list available for rent: 1000 names at $225 per M
Printed in 4 colors

455 SignCraft Magazine
SignCraft Publishing Company
PO Box 60031
Fort Myers, FL 33906

239-939-4644
800-204-0204
Fax: 239-939-0607
E-Mail: signcraft@signcraft.com
Home Page: www.signcraft.com

Tom McIltrot, Editor

Each issue includes an inside look at several sign shops, plus articles on techniques, materials, pricing, sales and computer aided sign making and puts hundreds of layout ideas at your fingertips.
Frequency: Monthly
Circulation: 14000
Mailing list available for rent: 25M names

456 Signs of the Times Magazine
ST Media Group International
11262 Cornell Park Dr
Cincinnati, OH 45242-1812

513-421-2050
800-421-1321
Fax: 513-421-5144
E-Mail: customer@stmediagroup.com
Home Page: www.stmediagroup.com

Tedd Swormstedt, CEO
Brian Foos, CFO

It is our mission to educate and inspire signage and graphics professionals worldwide through award winning editorial perspectives, technology updates, CAS reports, new product reviews, one of a kind Electric, CAS and Commercial State of the Industry reports, graphics techniques and much more.
Frequency: Monthly
Circulation: 17000
Founded in 1906

457 Supplier Global Resource
Advertising Specialty Institute
4800 E Street Rd
Langhorne, PA 19053-6698

215-953-4000
800-546-1350
Fax: 215-953-3045
E-Mail: info@asicentral.com
Home Page: www.asicentral.com
Social Media: Facebook

Timothy M Andrews, CEO
Norman Cohn, Chairman
Matthew Cohn, Vice Chairman
Carol Albright, SVP-Human Resources

The buying power of Supplier Global Resource readers is large-scale and powerful.
Frequency: 13x/Year
Circulation: 40000

458 Survey Practice
American Association for Public Opinion Research
111 Deer Land Road
Suite 100
Deerfield, IL 60015-4943

913-895-4601
Fax: 913-895-4652
E-Mail: aapor-info@goamp.com
Home Page: www.aapor.org
Social Media: Facebook, Twitter, LinkedIn

Paul Lavrakas, President
Rob Santos, VP/President-Elect
Scott Keeter, Secretary-Treasurer

AAPOR's e-journal with public opinion and survey research articles and commentary.
Frequency: Quarterly
Founded in 1948
Mailing list available for rent: 1000 names at $400 per M

459 TelevisionWeek
Crain Communications
1155 Gratiot Ave
Detroit, MI 48207-2732

313-446-6000
E-Mail: info@crain.com
Home Page: www.crain.com

Norm Feldman, Manager
Chuck Ross, Managing Director

Covers all aspects of the business programming and production, distribution and talent, broadcast, cable and satellite, advertising and media, government and regulation, finance and emerging technologies.
Founded in 1982

460 The Advertiser Magazine
Pohly Company
99 Bedford Street
Floor 5
Boston, MA 02111

617-457-3938
E-Mail: bliodice@ana.net
Home Page: www.ana.net

Kristina Sweet, Assoc Publisher, Director Sales

Reports on today's most critical marketing issues such as measuring brand equity, using emerging technologies and global marketing. It also contains articles on key benchmarks and industry trends. Offers news and events in the advertising industry. Produced by Association of National Adverstisers.
Frequency: 6x/Year
Circulation: 25000

461 The Big Picture
ST Media Group International
11262 Cornell Park Dr
Cincinnati, OH 45242-1812

513-421-2050
800-421-1321
Fax: 513-421-5144
E-Mail: customer@stmediagroup.com
Home Page: www.stmediagroup.com

Tedd Swormstedt, CEO
Brian Foos, CFO

Provides real-world solutions to today's design and production challenges. This publication reports on digital printing of visual communications with coverage of digital printing from image capture and processing to finishing and display.
Frequency: Monthly
Circulation: 17000
Founded in 1906

462 VMSD
ST Media Group International
11262 Cornell Park Dr
Cincinnati, OH 45242-1812

513-421-2050
800-421-1321
Fax: 513-421-5144
E-Mail: customer@stmediagroup.com
Home Page: www.stmediagroup.com

Tedd Swormstedt, CEO
Brian Foos, CFO

Leading magazine for retail designers and store display professionals, showcasing the latest store designs and visual presentations, presents merchandising strategies and new products, and reports on industry news and events.
Frequency: Monthly
Circulation: 17000
Founded in 1906

463 Wearables
Advertising Specialty Institute
4800 E Street Rd
Langhorne, PA 19053-6698

215-953-4000
800-546-1350
Fax: 215-953-3045
E-Mail: info@asicentral.com
Home Page: www.asicentral.com
Social Media: Facebook

Timothy M Andrews, CEO
Norman Cohn, Chairman
Matthew Cohn, Vice Chairman
Carol Albright, SVP-Human Resources

Serves the apparel and accessories segment of the advertising specialty industry.
Frequency: 13x/Year
Circulation: 40000

464 Winning at Retail
In-Store Marketing Institute
7400 Skokie Blvd
Skokie, IL 60077-3339

847-675-7400
Fax: 847-675-7494
E-Mail:
pdproducts_editor@instoremarketer.org
Home Page: www.instoremarketer.org
Social Media: Facebook, Twitter, LinkedIn

Peter Hoyt, President

Shares insights, case studies and lessons learned from thousands of studies conducted by Perception Research Services, the leading company in packaging and shopper marketing research.
Frequency: Bi-Monthly
Circulation: 15000
Printed in 4 colors on glossy stock

Trade Shows

465 AAPOR Annual Conference
American Association for Public Opinion Research
111 Deer Lake Road
Suite 100
Deerfield, IL 60015

847-205-2651
Fax: 847-480-9282
E-Mail: aapor-info@goamp.com
Home Page: www.aapor.org
Social Media: Facebook, Twitter, LinkedIn

Paul Lavrakas, President
Rob Santos, VP/President-Elect
Scott Keeter, Secretary-Treasurer

Features cutting edge research and informal access to leaders in the fields.
850 Attendees
Frequency: Annual
Mailing list available for rent: 1000 names at $400 per M

466 ADMERICA!
American Advertising Federation

1101 Vermont Ave NW
Suite 500
Washington, DC 20005-6306

202-898-0089
800-999-2231
Fax: 202-898-0159
E-Mail: aaf@aaf.org
Home Page: www.aaf.org
Social Media: Facebook, Twitter, YouTube

James Edmund Datri, President
Constance Cannon Frazier, COO
Joanne Schecter, Executive Vice President

Connects all aspects of the advertising industry. Influential agencies, clients, media companies, suppliers, and colleges from across the country will address how to thrive in a recovering economy and how the changing culture of business and consumers is impacting our industry.

467 **AMCEA Conference**
Advertising Media Credit Executives Association
8840 Columbia 100 Parkway
Columbia, MD 21045-2158

410-992-7609
Fax: 410-740-5574
E-Mail: amcea@amcea.org
Home Page: www.amcea.org

J Dee Stevenson, President
Kimberly Riley, VP
Vickie Bolinger, Director

The conference encompasses four days and is a networking extravaganza. Top attorneys discuss bankruptcy and legal issues. We invite advertising agencies to discuss network buying and liability problems.
Frequency: Annual

468 **ANA Advertising Financial Management Conference**
Association of National Advertisers
708 Third Avenue
33 Floor
New York, NY 10017

212-697-5950
Fax: 212-661-8057
E-Mail: info@ana.net
Home Page: www.ana.net
Social Media: Facebook, Twitter, LinkedIn, YouTube

Bob Liodice, President & CEO
Christine Manna, COO
William Zengel, EVP

Brings together top marketing finance and procurement professionals from the client side with agency CFOs and other key industry stakeholders interested in efficiencies, cost savings, return on investment, and delivering greater value to organizations.

469 **ANA Advertising Law & Public Policy Conference**
Association of National Advertisers
708 Third Avenue
33 Floor
New York, NY 10017

212-697-5950
Fax: 212-661-8057
E-Mail: info@ana.net
Home Page: www.ana.net
Social Media: Facebook, Twitter, LinkedIn, YouTube

Bob Liodice, President & CEO
Christine Manna, COO
William Zengel, EVP

Keeping up with the digital revolution is becoming a nearly impossible task. This conference enters the battlefield by putting together a stellar faculty, including leading regulators, top practitioners, and serious critics, capped off by a session that puts it all together led by a leading law professor.

470 **ANA Annual Conference - The Masters of Marketing**
Association of National Advertisers
708 Third Avenue
33 Floor
New York, NY 10017

212-697-5950
Fax: 212-661-8057
E-Mail: info@ana.net
Home Page: www.ana.net
Social Media: Facebook, Twitter, LinkedIn, YouTube

Bob Liodice, President & CEO
Christine Manna, COO
William Zengel, EVP

The conference offers an opportunity to learn from and engage with the leaders of the industry as they build brands, leverage the expanding array of media, make marketing more accountable and improve the quality of their marketing organizations.

471 **ANA Digital & Social Media Conference**
Association of National Advertisers
708 Third Avenue
33 Floor
New York, NY 10017

212-697-5950
Fax: 212-661-8057
E-Mail: info@ana.net
Home Page: www.ana.net
Social Media: Facebook, Twitter, LinkedIn, YouTube

Bob Liodice, President & CEO
Christine Manna, COO
William Zengel, EVP

Discussing how to use social media to impact the consumer decision journey and how to effectively partner with other companies to maximize social media reach and more.

472 **ANA TV & Everything Video Forum Presented by Google**
Association of National Advertisers
708 Third Avenue
33 Floor
New York, NY 10017

212-697-5950
Fax: 212-661-8057
E-Mail: info@ana.net
Home Page: www.ana.net
Social Media: Facebook, Twitter, LinkedIn, YouTube

Bob Liodice, President & CEO
Christine Manna, COO
William Zengel, EVP

The forum recognizes that the role of television in the media mix is being redefined and broadened. In addition to traditional television, the TV & Everything Video Forum will explore the use of video on any type of screen or device: the computer, Internet, mobile, point-of-purchase, gaming, and more. Registration starts at $595.
Frequency: Annual

473 **ANA/WFA Global Marketing Conference**
Association of National Advertisers
708 Third Avenue
33 Floor
New York, NY 10017

212-697-5950
Fax: 212-661-8057
E-Mail: info@ana.net
Home Page: www.ana.net
Social Media: Facebook, Twitter, LinkedIn, YouTube

Bob Liodice, President & CEO
Christine Manna, COO
William Zengel, EVP

Offers tips on marketing on a worldwide scale.

474 **Ad:tech Adweek**
Prometheus Global Media
770 Broadway
7th Floor
New York, NY 10003-9595

212-493-4100
Fax: 646-654-5368
Home Page: www.prometheusgm.com
Social Media: Facebook, Twitter, RSS

Richard D. Beckman, CEO
James A. Finkelstein, Chairman
Madeline Krakowsky, Vice President Circulation
Tracy Brater, Executive Director Creative Service

An interactive advertising and technology conference and exhibition. Worldwide shows blend keynote speakers, topic driven panels and workshops to provide attendees with the tools and techniques they need to compete in a changing world.

475 **Advertising Financial Management Conference**
Association of National Advertisers
708 Third Avenue
33 Floor
New York, NY 10017

212-697-5950
Fax: 212-661-8057
E-Mail: info@ana.net
Home Page: www.ana.net
Social Media: Facebook, Twitter, LinkedIn, YouTube

Bob Liodice, President & CEO
Christine Manna, COO
William Zengel, EVP

The agenda is developed with input from members of the Advertising Financial Management Committee and topics focus on efficiency, return on investment, cost savings and new ideas to bring greater value to organizations. Registration begins at $1,095.
Frequency: Annual

476 **Advertising Law & Public Policy Conference**
Association of National Advertisers
708 Third Avenue
33 Floor
New York, NY 10017

212-697-5950
Fax: 212-661-8057
E-Mail: info@ana.net
Home Page: www.ana.net
Social Media: Facebook, Twitter, LinkedIn, YouTube

Bob Liodice, President & CEO
Christine Manna, COO
William Zengel, EVP

Discuss new policy initiatives and how they will transform advertising; recent court decisions, regulatory changes reshaping the legal environment for advertising. Hear from FCC, FTC, and FDA experts and representatives. Registration begins at $795.
Frequency: Annual

477 **Advertising Media Credit Executives Association Annual Conference**
Advertising Media Credit Executives Association

PO Box 433
Louisville, KY 40201

502-582-4327
Fax: 502-582-4330
E-Mail: amcea@amcea.org
Home Page: www.amcea.org

Cheryl E Szluzer, President
Sheila Wroten, Vice President

Media credit managers, editors, business mangers and other professionals gather for exhibits of advertising media such as newspapers, magazines, radio and television.
400 Attendees
Frequency: Annual
Founded in 1896

478 **Annual Action Taker Series**
Retail Advertising & Marketing International
325 7th Street NW
Suite 1100
Washington, DC 20004

202-661-3052
Fax: 202-737-2849
Home Page: www.rama-nrf.org

Kevin Brown, RAMA Chairman
Rob Gruen, Vice Chairman
Gwen Morrison, CEO
Julie Gardner, CMO

Come hear real case studies and inspiring concepts from today's retail creative leaders.
400 Attendees
Frequency: Annual

479 **Annual Advertising Conference**
Advertising Women of New York
25 W 45th Street
Suite 403
New York, NY 10036

212-221-7969
Fax: 212-221-8296
E-Mail: awny@awny.org
Home Page: www.awny.org
Social Media: Facebook, Twitter, LinkedIn, You tube

Carol Watson, President
Melissa Goidel, VP

To meet some of the top people in the field of advertising; to discover techniques of career planning that can help you get the job of your choice with greater ease; to network with some of the most influential advertising executives of the time from a variety of disciplines.
600 Attendees

480 **Annual Conference and Mailing & Fulfillment Expo**
Mailing & Fulfillment Service Association
1421 Prince Street
Suite 410
Alexandria, VA 22314-2806

703-836-9200
Fax: 703-548-8204
E-Mail: mfsa-mail@mfsanet.org
Home Page: www.mfsanet.org

Ken Garner, President
Jennifer Root, Director
Bill Stevenson, Director Marketing

Quality educational sessions, industry specific exhibit hall, networking and more.
Frequency: Annual

481 **Annual Global Marketing Summit**
International Advertising Association - NY Chapter
World Serivce Center
275 Madison Avenue Suite 2102
New York, NY 10016

212-338-0222
Fax: 212-983-0455
E-Mail: coordinator@iaany.org
Home Page: www.iaany.org
Social Media: Facebook, Twitter, LinkedIn

Tom Brookbanks, President
Larry Levy, Treasurer
Sean Lough, Secretary

Designed to provide participants with the knowledge, tools and inspiration needed to market global brands. Various registration options. Visit website for details.
1000 Attendees
Frequency: Annual

482 **Annual MAPOR Conference- Public Opinion Frontiers**
American Association for Public Opinion Research
111 Deer Lake Road
Suite 100
Deerfield, IL 60015

847-205-2651
Fax: 847-480-9282
E-Mail: aapor-info@goamp.com
Home Page: www.aapor.org
Social Media: Facebook, Twitter, LinkedIn

Paul Lavrakas, President
Rob Santos, VP/President-Elect
Scott Keeter, Secretary-Treasurer

Focusing on emerging methods in data collection and analysis and research into attitude formation.
850 Attendees
Frequency: Annual
Mailing list available for rent: 1000 names at $400 per M

483 **Annual Proceedings Conference**
American Academy of Advertising
24710 Shaker Blvd.
Beachwood, OH 44122

786-393-3333
E-Mail: patrose@aaasite.org
Home Page: www.aaasite.org
Social Media: Facebook, Twitter

Debbie Treise, President
Kim Sheehan, President Elect
Margie Morrison, Vice President
nancy Mitchell, Treasurer
Glen Griffin, Secretary

Every year the American Academy of Advertising holds a conference at which advertising research findings and theories are presented, as well as papers concerning methods of teaching advertising.
600 Members
Founded in 1957

484 **Asian-Pacific Conference**
American Academy of Advertising
24710 Shaker Blvd.
Beachwood, OH 44122

786-393-3333
E-Mail: patrose@aaasite.org
Home Page: www.aaasite.org
Social Media: Facebook, Twitter

Debbie Treise, President
Kim Sheehan, President Elect
Margie Morrison, Vice President
nancy Mitchell, Treasurer
Glen Griffin, Secretary

Focusing on issues in the Asian-Pacific region, this conference welcomes research on any aspect of advertising as broadly defined in one or more Asian-Pacific countries or in multiple countries involving at least one Asian-Pacific country. This conference is co-sponsored by China Advertising Association of Commerce and Communication University of China.
600 Members
Founded in 1957

485 **Audience Measurement 7.0**
Advertising Research Foundation
432 Park Avenue S
6th Floor
New York, NY 10016-8013

212-751-5656
Fax: 212-319-5265
E-Mail: info@thearf.org
Home Page: www.thearf.org
Social Media: Facebook, Twitter, LinkedIn, youtube

Colleen Fahey Rush, Chief Research Officer
David Poltrack, Secretary
Bernard Bradpiece, Treasurer

Knowing the latest developments in audience composition and measurement across platforms is critical to ensuring your company's money is spent most effectively. Get up-to-the-minute on the latest evaluation approaches and technology.
400 Members
Founded in 1936

486 **Cable Advertising Conference**
Cabletelevision Advertising Bureau
830 3rd Avenue
2nd Floor
New York, NY 10022

212-508-1200
Fax: 212-832-3268
Home Page: www.thecab.tv

Sean Cunningham, President

Annual conference and exhibits of advertising-supported cable television networks and services to support local advertising sales.
2000 Attendees
Frequency: Annual/April

487 **Cannes Lion Advertising Festival Screening**
American Association of Advertising Agencies
1065 Avenue of the Americas
16th Floor
New York, NY 10018

212-682-2500
Fax: 212-682-8391
E-Mail: kipp@aaaa.org
Home Page: www.aaaa.org
Social Media: Facebook, Twitter, LinkedIn

Nancy Hill, President
Chris Weil, Chair
Andrew Bennett, Director at Large
Sharon Napier, Secretary/Treasurer

The screening will bring together hundreds of industry professionals to view the winning work of Cannes and celebrate the Philadelphia advertising community.

488 **Channel Partners Conference & Expo**
Virgo Publishing LLC
3300 N Central Ave
Suite 300
Phoenix, AZ 85012-2532

480-675-9925
Fax: 480-990-0819
E-Mail: kkennedy@vpico.com
Home Page: www.vpico.com

John Siefert, CEO
Kelly Ridley, CFO
Jon Benninger, VP
John LyBarger, Director of IT

The communications industry's only event designed exclusively for indirect sales organizations - agents, VARs, systems integrators, interconnects and consultants - focused on

transforming their businesses to become converged solutions providers.
Circulation: 20000
Founded in 1986
Printed in on glossy stock

489 **Co-Creation and the Future of Agencies**
American Association of Advertising Agencies
1065 Avenue of the Americas
16th Floor
New York, NY 10018

212-682-2500
Fax: 212-682-8391
E-Mail: kipp@aaaa.org
Home Page: www.aaaa.org
Social Media: Facebook, Twitter, LinkedIn

Nancy Hill, President
Chris Weil, Chair
Andrew Bennett, Director at Large
Sharon Napier, Secretary/Treasurer

Learn how to be part of the trend toward the disintermediation of agents, marketers are increasing going around agencies to work directly with the media, production companies, and even directly to creative talent via crowdsourcing.

490 **Comprehensive CRM & Database Marketing**
Direct Marketing Association
1120 Avenue of the Americas
New York, NY 10036-6700

212-768-7277
Fax: 212-302-6714
E-Mail: customerservice@the-dma.org
Home Page: www.the-dma.org
Social Media: Facebook, Twitter, LinkedIn

Lawrence M Kimmel, CEO

In an increasingly digital marketing landscape, metrics and ROI are being scrutinized and recalibrated like never before. Whether interested in classic database statistics or emerging trends in web analytics, the insights gained in our classes will add up to success.

491 **DMA Annual Conference & Exhibition**
Direct Marketing Association
1120 Avenue of Americas
New York, NY 10036-6700

212-768-7277
Fax: 212-302-6714
E-Mail: dmaconferences@the-dma.org
Home Page: www.the-dma.org
Social Media: Facebook, Twitter, LinkedIn

Lawrence M Kimmel, CEO
Julie A Hogan, SVP Conferences/Education Services

Offers a progressive marketers to help better engage customers and improve bottom line results in all channels, including social, search, monile, video and more.
12000 Attendees
Frequency: Annual/October

492 **Direct Marketing Institute**
Direct Marketing Association
1120 Avenue of the Americas
New York, NY 10036-6700

212-768-7277
Fax: 212-302-6714
E-Mail: customerservice@the-dma.org
Home Page: www.the-dma.org
Social Media: Facebook, Twitter, LinkedIn

Lawrence M Kimmel, CEO

A three-day intensive direct marketing seminar, the DMI iwll give step-by-step tactics to maximize the ROI of your campaigns.

493 **Effective Email Marketing**
Direct Marketing Association
1120 Avenue of the Americas
New York, NY 10036-6700

212-768-7277
Fax: 212-302-6714
E-Mail: customerservice@the-dma.org
Home Page: www.the-dma.org
Social Media: Facebook, Twitter, LinkedIn

Lawrence M Kimmel, CEO

The online world presents a myriad of options for establishing and developing customer and community relationships. If you want to segment and target your email database or launch a mobile campaign, we can teach you the best practices and strategies you need to meet and exceed your goals.

494 **Email Evolution Conference**
Direct Marketing Association
1120 Avenue of Americas
New York, NY 10036-6700

212-768-7277
Fax: 212-302-6714
E-Mail: www.dmaconference@the-dma.org
Home Page: www.the-dma.org
Social Media: Facebook, Twitter, LinkedIn

Lawrence M Kimmel, CEO
Julie A Hogan, SVP Conferences/Education Services

Focuses on the ever-changing and evolving world of email marketing, providing attendees with the best ways to capitalize on the high ROI this low-cost communication tool can provide both on its own, and integrated with social, search, mobile, video and other email enhancers.
10M Attendees
Frequency: Annual/February

495 **Giving and Receiving Feedback with Grace & Style**
American Association of Advertising Agencies
1065 Avenue of the Americas
16th Floor
New York, NY 10018

212-682-2500
Fax: 212-682-8391
E-Mail: kipp@aaaa.org
Home Page: www.aaaa.org
Social Media: Facebook, Twitter, LinkedIn

Nancy Hill, President
Chris Weil, Chair
Andrew Bennett, Director at Large
Sharon Napier, Secretary/Treasurer

The majority of professionals cringe when it comes time for performance evaluations, self assessments, and even everyday feedback. Participants learn how to speak assertively and deliver constructive criticism while also understanding how to receive feedback openly and grow professionally from the experience.

496 **Global Shop Conference**
Nielsen Business Media
1145 Sanctuary Parkway
Suite 355
Alpharetta, GA 30074

770-569-1540
Fax: 770-569-5105
E-Mail: kara.kobrzycki@nielsen.com
Home Page: www.globalshop.org
Social Media: Facebook, Twitter, LinkedIn

David Loechner, President
Michael Alicea, SVP/Human Resources
Denise Bashem, VP/Finance

Retail designers and brand marketers find the most innovative concepts, newest products and services to create unique store design and in-store marketing solutions.
50000 Attendees
Frequency: Annual/March

497 **Government Affairs Conference**
American Advertising Federation
1101 Vermont Avenue NW
Suite 500
Washington, DC 20005

800-999-2231
Fax: 202-898-0159
E-Mail: aaf@aaf.org
Home Page: www.aaf.org

James Edmund Datri, President
Constance Cannon Frazier, COO
Joanne Schecter, Executive Vice President

The conference is held annually in conjunction with the Association of National Advertisers and the American Association of Advertising Agencies.
807 Attendees
Frequency: Annual

498 **Hospitality Match**
ST Media Group International
11262 Cornell Park Dr
Cincinnati, OH 45242-1812

513-421-2050
800-421-1321
Fax: 513-421-5144
E-Mail: customer@stmediagroup.com
Home Page: www.stmediagroup.com

Tedd Swormstedt, CEO
Brian Foos, CFO

A series of targeted and exclusive invitation-only events that bring key decision makers from top design firms, purchasing companies and hotel groups together with relevan suppliers, face-to-face for a weekend of serious business and exceptional networking events. Suppliers will meet with pre-qualified hospitality buyers through pre-arranged one-on-one meetings.
Frequency: Monthly
Circulation: 17000
Founded in 1906

499 **IAB Annual Leadership Meeting**
Interactive Advertising Bureau
116 E 27th Street
7th Floor
New York, NY 10016

212-380-4700
Home Page: www.iab.net
Social Media: Facebook, Twitter, LinkedIn

Randall Rothenberg, President/CEO

Addresses head-on issues taking place right now in the digital industry.
Frequency: Monthly

500 **ICOM International World Management Conference**
International Communications Agency Network
1649 Lump Gulch Road
PO Box 490
Rollinsville, CO 80474-0490

303-258-9511
Fax: 303-484-4087
E-Mail: info@icomagencies.com
Home Page: www.icomagencies.com
Social Media: Facebook, Twitter, LinkedIn, YouTube

Bob Morrison, Director
Joe Phelps, North American Member at Large

Members will network and share ideas and success stories. Members will share learned information from the worst global economic crisis since 1929, what they learned about their busi-

nesses, their clients and their staffs and what they will do differently going forward.
80 Attendees
Frequency: Annual

501 IFCA Annual Conference
Insurance and Financial Communications Association
1037 N 3rd Ave
Tucson, AZ 85705

602-350-0717
E-Mail: info@ifcaonline.com
Home Page: www.ifcaonline.com
Social Media: Facebook, Twitter, LinkedIn, YouTube

Susan o'Neill, President
Ralph Chaump, VP
Kim Schultz, Secretary

Offers networking among peers, education through platform speeches and practical workshops, display of the best industry communications work being done and volunteer opportunities.

502 ISA International Sign Expo
International Sign Association
1001 N Fairfax Street
Suite 301
Alexandria, VA 22314

703-836-4012
866-WHY-SIGN
Fax: 703-836-8353
E-Mail: info@signs.org
Home Page: www.signs.org

Duane Laska, Chairman
Harry Niese, Vice Chairman
Chad Jones, Secretary/Treasurer

ISA's annual internation sign Expo is a premier platform for the sign industry to conduct business. 500 exhibitors. Admission from $15 to $40.
12800 Attendees

503 ISA Supplier & Distributor Conference
International Sign Association
1001 N Fairfax Street
Suite 301
Alexandria, VA 22314

703-836-4012
866-WHY-SIGN
Fax: 703-836-8353
E-Mail: info@signs.org
Home Page: www.signs.org

Duane Laska, Chairman
Harry Niese, Vice Chairman
Chad Jones, Secretary/Treasurer

The conference featured a slate of experts speaking on a wide range of topics specifically of interest to companies that sell to sign manufacturers.
Frequency: Annual

504 Integrated Marketing Members Only Conference by Microsoft Advertising
Pohly Company
99 Bedford Street
Floor 5
Boston, MA 02111

617-457-3938
E-Mail: ksweet@pohlyco.com
Home Page: www.ana.net

Kristina Sweet, Assoc Publisher, Director Sales

The development of new communications and the evolution of traditional communications have shifted power from the marketer to the consumer, which created enormous opportunities, providing marketers with the ability to better target their customers. Discover how top marketers develop, execute, and evaluate their overall marketing communications strategy based on consumer insight.
Frequency: 6x/Year
Circulation: 25000

505 International Career Developmemt Conference
DECA Inc
1908 Association Drive
Reston, VA 20191

703-860-5000
Fax: 703-860-4013
Home Page: www.deca.org

Jacklyn Schiller, President
Jim Brock, President-elect
Lynore Levenhagen

Gathering of members, advisors, businesspersons and alumni who attend. Most of the participants are competitors in one of DECA's competency based competitive events.
15000 Attendees

506 MFSA Midwinter Executive Conference
Mailing & Fulfillment Service Association
1421 Prince Street
Suite 410
Alexandria, VA 22314-2806
703-836-9200
Fax: 703-548-8204
E-Mail: mfsa-mail@mfsanet.org
Home Page: www.mfsanet.org

Ken Garner, President
Jennifer Root, Director
Bill Stevenson, Director Marketing

Addresses financial operations and business valuation, marketing your own company, the changing world of postal regulations, technology in fulfillment, building a sales team, being strong in digital printing and the landscape of employment law.

507 MIXX Conference & Expo
Interactive Advertising Bureau
116 E 27th Street
7th Floor
New York, NY 10016

212-380-4700
E-Mail: lisa@iab.net
Home Page: www.iab.net

Lisa Milgram, Events Director
Margaret Southwell, Events Coordinator

The preeminet event for marketing and agency professionals-and the publishers and technology firms who help drive their efforts. Brings together the industry's most prominent and influential figures to share insights on the most pressing topics in advertising.
Frequency: Annual

508 Mailer Strategies Conference
Mailing & Fulfillment Service Association
1421 Prince Street
Suite 410
Alexandria, VA 22314-2806

703-836-9200
Fax: 703-548-8204
E-Mail: mfsa-mail@mfsanet.org
Home Page: www.mfsanet.org

Ken Garner, President
Jennifer Root, Director
Bill Stevenson, Director Marketing

This conference will focus solely on postal issues that are important to your operations.

509 Media Conference & Tradeshow
American Association of Advertising Agencies
1065 Avenue of the Americas
16th Floor
New York, NY 10018

212-682-2500
Fax: 212-682-8391
E-Mail: kipp@aaaa.org
Home Page: www.aaaa.org
Social Media: Facebook, Twitter, LinkedIn

Nancy Hill, President
Chris Weil, Chair
Andrew Bennett, Director at Large
Sharon Napier, Secretary/Treasurer

Empowered consumers will be featured center stage in live focus groups during the conference.

510 Media and Account Management Conference
Association of Hispanic Advertising Agencies
8400 Westpark Drive
2nd Floor
McLean, VA 22102

703-610-9014
Fax: 703-610-0227
E-Mail: info@ahaa.org
Home Page: www.ahaa.org
Social Media: Facebook, Twitter

Horacio Gavilan, Executive Director
Melissa Chen, Membership/Directory
Ayanna Wiggins, Marketing

Examines the myriad of changes facing Hispanic agencies in and beyond including shifts in approaches to communications planning, demographics and client needs.

511 Multicultural Council Meeting
Interactive Advertising Bureau
116 E 27th Street
7th Floor
New York, NY 10016

212-380-4700
Home Page: www.iab.net
Social Media: Facebook, Twitter, LinkedIn

Randall Rothenberg, President/CEO

IAB members contributing information on the interactive advertising marketplace.
Frequency: Monthly

512 NCDM Conference
Direct Marketing Association
1120 Avenue of Americas
New York, NY 10036-6700

212-768-7277
Fax: 212-302-6714
E-Mail: dmaconferences@the-dma.org
Home Page: www.the-dma.org
Social Media: Facebook, Twitter, LinkedIn

Julie A Hogan, SVP Conferences/Events

Presents industry experts and hard-hitting case studies from a variety of verticles, such as financial services, retail, automotive, publishing, non-profit and many more, who will share the latest strategies and methodologies in gathering, analyzing, leveraging and protecting the most valuable business asset, customer data.
10M Attendees
Frequency: Annual/December

513 NRF Annual Convention & EXPO
Retail Advertising & Marketing International
325 7th Street NW
Suite 1100
Washington, DC 20004
202-661-3052
Fax: 202-737-2849
Home Page: www.rama-nrf.org

Kevin Brown, RAMA Chairman
Rob Gruen, Vice Chairman

Gwen Morrison, CEO
Julie Gardner, CMO

RAMA is undertaking in important transformation to become an organization that's representative of the changes that are affecting the retail marketing community with a strategic view that includes the integration of mobile, digital and traditional media.
400 Attendees
Frequency: Annual

514 **National Conference on Operations & Fulfillment (NCOF)**
Direct Marketing Association
1120 Avenue of Americas
New York, NY 10036-6700

212-768-7277
Fax: 211-302-6714
E-Mail: dmaconferences@the-dma.org
Home Page: www.the-dma.org
Social Media: Facebook, Twitter, LinkedIn

Julie A Hogan, SVP Conference/Events
Lawrence M Kimmel, CEO

Focuses on innovative solutions for the warehouse, distribution, operations, and ecommerce needs in the ever-changing world of operations and fulfillment.
10M Attendees

515 **New York Nonprofit Conference**
Direct Marketing Association
1120 Avenue of Americas
New York, NY 10036-6700

212-768-7277
Fax: 212-302-6714
E-Mail: dmaconferences@the-dma.org
Home Page: www.the-dma.org
Social Media: Facebook, Twitter, LinkedIn

Lawrence M Kimmel, CEO
Julie A Hogan, SVP Conferences/Education Services

Discover which acknowledgement problems work best and why, increase revenue with membership options-as well as traditional fund-raising appeals, learn how the internet and e-mail campaigns can improve fundraising, lowering costs and increase advocacy.
10M Attendees

516 **OAAA National Convention**
Outdoor Advertising Association of America
1850 M Street NW
Suite 1040
Washington, DC 20036

202-833-5566
Fax: 202-833-1522
E-Mail: nfletcheter@oaaa.org
Home Page: www.oaaa.org

Nancy Fletcher, President
Willliam reagan, Secretary
Kevin Reily, Treasurer

The national convention program will offer depth of content and a diverse schedule of activities with something important for everyone engaged in the out of home business.
Frequency: Biennial

517 **PPAI Brand**
Promotional Products Association International
3125 Skyway Cir N
Irving, TX 75038-3539

972-252-0404
Fax: 972-258-3004
E-Mail: ppb@ppai.org
Home Page: www.ppai.org
Social Media: Facebook, Twitter, LinkedIn, YouTube

Steve Slagel, President

The industry's most highly regarded incentive products showcase, gives an all-access pass to the $46 billion incentives market.

518 **PPAI Decorate**
Promotional Products Association International
3125 Skyway Cir N
Irving, TX 75038-3539

972-252-0404
Fax: 972-258-3004
E-Mail: ppb@ppai.org
Home Page: www.ppai.org
Social Media: Facebook, Twitter, LinkedIn, YouTube

Paul Bellantone, President
Steven Meyer, Chairman of the Board
Marc Simon, Chair-Elect

The best in screen printing, embroidery and digital technology. Experience demonstrations of the newest products and equipment.

519 **PPAI Expo**
Promotional Products Association International
3125 Skyway Circle N
Irving, TX 75038-3526

972-258-3104
Fax: 972-258-3012
E-Mail: ppb@ppai.org
Home Page. www.ppa.org

Paul Bellantone, President
Steven Meyer, Chairman of the Board
Marc Simon, Chair-Elect

Offering you the tools, opportunities and innovative ideas you need to excel, to grow your business beyond expectation and become the example to be followed.

520 **PPAI MASCAS**
Promotional Products Association International
3125 Skyway Cir N
Irving, TX 75038-3539

972-252-0404
Fax: 972-258-3004
E-Mail: ppb@ppai.org
Home Page: www.ppai.org
Social Media: Facebook, Twitter, LinkedIn, YouTube

Paul Bellantone, President
Steven Meyer, Chairman of the Board
Marc Simon, Chair-Elect

Master Advertising Specialist (MAS) and Certified Advertising Specialist (CAS) are the promotional products industry's professional designations.

521 **Powering Creativity Outside the Creative Department**
American Association of Advertising Agencies
1065 Avenue of the Americas
16th Floor
New York, NY 10018

212-682-2500
Fax: 212-682-8391
E-Mail: kipp@aaaa.org
Home Page: www.aaaa.org
Social Media: Facebook, Twitter, LinkedIn

Nancy Hill, President
Chris Weil, Chair
Andrew Bennett, Director at Large
Sharon Napier, Secretary/Treasurer

The success of any communication, any campaign, any brand, any company or community depends on smarter, more creative, more impactful thinking from everyone involved. Young professionals who work in account management, media, research and production disciplines should look to attend.

522 **RAMA CMO Summit**
Retail Advertising & Marketing International
325 7th Street NW
Suite 1100
Washington, DC 20004

202-661-3052
Fax: 202-737-2849
Home Page: www.rama-nrf.org

Kevin Brown, RAMA Chairman
Rob Gruen, Vice Chairman
Gwen Morrison, CEO
Julie Gardner, CMO

To provide a networking and discussion forum for senior retail marketing executives.
50 Attendees

523 **RAMACON: Thoughtful Topics, Fearless Ideas Remarkable People**
Retail Advertising & Marketing International
325 7th Street NW
Suite 1100
Washington, DC 20004

202-661-3052
Fax: 202-737-2849
Home Page: www.rama-nrf.org

Kevin Brown, RAMA Chairman
Rob Gruen, Vice Chairman
Gwen Morrison, CEO
Julie Gardner, CMO

RAMA is undertaking in important transformation to become an organization that's representative of the changes that are affecting the retail marketing community with a strategic view that includes the integration of mobile, digital and traditional media.
400 Attendees
Frequency: Annual

524 **Re:Think The ARF Annual Convention & Expo**
Advertising Research Foundation
432 Park Avenue S
6th Floor
New York, NY 10016-8013

212-751-5656
Fax: 212-319-5265
E-Mail: info@thearf.org
Home Page: www.thearf.org
Social Media. Facebook, Twitter, LinkedIn, YouTube

Colleen Fahey Rush, Chief Research Officer
David Poltrack, Secretary
Bernard Bradpiece, Treasurer

Re:Think is a research forum where the ad industry gathers to dispense, explore and challenge the latest knowledge driving the advertising and marketing industry. Showcases innovative market research services and products, high-level networking, free education, and leading-edge industry resources. Various registration options are available. Visit the ARF website for details.
400 Members
Founded in 1936

525 **Reinventing Account Management**
American Association of Advertising Agencies
1065 Avenue of the Americas
16th Floor
New York, NY 10018

212-682-2500
Fax: 212-682-8391
E-Mail: kipp@aaaa.org
Home Page: www.aaaa.org
Social Media: Facebook, Twitter, LinkedIn

Nancy Hill, President
Chris Weil, Chair

Andrew Bennett, Director at Large
Sharon Napier, Secretary/Treasurer

Next Practices for Senior Agency Professionals. The traditional account management function at advertising agencies and other marketing communications firms is changing dramatically to meet the needs of a 24/7 digitally connected multichannel marketplace.

526 **Response Expo**
201 Sandpointe Ave
Suite 500
Santa Ana, CA 92707-8700

714-338-6700
800-854-3112
Fax: 714-513-8482
E-Mail: thaire@questex.com
Home Page: www.responsemagazine.com
Social Media: Facebook, Twitter, LinkedIn, YouTube

Thomas Haire, Editor
Don Rosenberg, VP
Kristina Kronenberg, Marketing Director

Focuses on the evolution of consumers from passive watchers to active and empowered brand evangelists. Technology and social media have enabled and encouraged consumers to engage and interact with content. Learn how to take DR marketing from traditional campaign management to the future of customer engagement.
Frequency: Monthly
Circulation: 12000
Founded in 1987

527 **Shopper Marketing Expo**
In-Store Marketing Institute
7400 Skokie Blvd
Skokie, IL 60077-3339

847-675-7400
Fax: 847-675-7494
E-Mail:
pdproducts_editor@instoremarketer.org
Home Page: www.instoremarketer.org
Social Media: Facebook, Twitter, LinkedIn

Peter Hoyt, President

The premier annual event in the in-store industry filled with symposia, seminars, exhibits and awards dedicated to integrating the wide variety of solutions, tools and expertise needed to influence decision-making along the path to purchase.
Circulation: 15000
Printed in 4 colors on glossy stock

528 **Shopper Marketing Summit**
In-Store Marketing Institute
7400 Skokie Blvd
Skokie, IL 60077-3339

847-675-7400
Fax: 847-675-7494
E-Mail:
pdproducts_editor@instoremarketer.org
Home Page: www.instoremarketer.org
Social Media: Facebook, Twitter, LinkedIn

Peter Hoyt, President

A world-class senior level conference offering ideas and solutions to retailers, manufacturers and marketers of consumer products and services, agencies and other solution providers who are looking to achieve new heights at retail.
Printed in 4 colors on glossy stock

529 **Signage and Graphics Summit**
ST Media Group International
11262 Cornell Park Dr
Cincinnati, OH 45242-1812

513-421-2050
800-421-1321
Fax: 513-421-5144
E-Mail: customer@stmediagroup.com
Home Page: www.stmediagroup.com

Tedd Swormstedt, CEO
Brian Foos, CFO

Three days of education and networking for high-volume sign companies, screen printers and digital print shops.
Founded in 1906

530 **Speak to Be Heard! Influencing Others to Take Action**
American Association of Advertising Agencies
1065 Avenue of the Americas
16th Floor
New York, NY 10018

212-682-2500
Fax: 212-682-8391
E-Mail: kipp@aaaa.org
Home Page: www.aaaa.org
Social Media: Facebook, Twitter, LinkedIn

Nancy Hill, President
Chris Weil, Chair
Andrew Bennett, Director at Large
Sharon Napier, Secretary/Treasurer

Eliminate the static that plagues communicative delivery- to persuade, sell your ideas, motivate, influence or simply effectively communicate face-to-face with a clear message. Account executives, media directors, senior managers should attend.

531 **Stratconn**
In-Store Marketing Institute
7400 Skokie Blvd
Skokie, IL 60077-3339

847-675-7400
Fax: 847-675-7494
E-Mail:
pdproducts_editor@instoremarketer.org
Home Page: www.instoremarketer.org
Social Media: Facebook, Twitter, LinkedIn

Peter Hoyt, President

Gathering the leading designers/producers of displays, signs and fixtures together with teams of merchandising experts from leading CPG manufacturers and retailers.
Printed in 4 colors on glossy stock

532 **Strategy for Account Managers**
American Association of Advertising Agencies
1065 Avenue of the Americas
16th Floor
New York, NY 10018

212-682-2500
Fax: 212-682-8391
E-Mail: kipp@aaaa.org
Home Page: www.aaaa.org
Social Media: Facebook, Twitter, LinkedIn

Nancy Hill, President
Chris Weil, Chair
Andrew Bennett, Director at Large
Sharon Napier, Secretary/Treasurer

Workshop is designed for mid-an-higher-level account managers at marketing communication firms of all types who have clients that want them to think more strategically.

533 **SupplySide International Tradeshow and Conference**
Virgo Publishing LLC
3300 N Central Ave
Suite 300
Phoenix, AZ 85012-2532

480-675-9925
Fax: 480-990-0819
E-Mail: kkennedy@vpico.com
Home Page: www.vpico.com

John Siefert, CEO
Kelly Ridley, CFO
Jon Benninger, VP
John LyBarger, Director of IT

The world's largest event for healthy and innovative ingredients. Food, beverage, dietary supplement and cosmeceutical manufacturers, marketers and formulators attend to source cutting edge ingredients and learn from outstanding educational presentations at the largest event of its kind.
Founded in 1986

534 **Transformation LA**
American Association of Advertising Agencies
1065 Avenue of the Americas
16th Floor
New York, NY 10018

212-682-2500
Fax: 212-682-8391
E-Mail: kipp@aaaa.org
Home Page: www.aaaa.org
Social Media: Facebook, Twitter, LinkedIn

Nancy Hill, President
Chris Weil, Chair
Andrew Bennett, Director at Large
Sharon Napier, Secretary/Treasurer

Talent recruitment and retention; regulatory updates; mobility; social media; and growing your business are a few of the sessions scheduled. Tour some of the entertainment capital's most creative facilities, including innovative 4A's member agencies.

535 **VMSD International Retail Design Conference**
ST Media Group International
11262 Cornell Park Dr
Cincinnati, OH 45242-1812

513-421-2050
800-421-1321
Fax: 513-421-5144
E-Mail: customer@stmediagroup.com
Home Page: www.stmediagroup.com

Tedd Swormstedt, CEO
Brian Foos, CFO

The premier educational event created especially for members of the retail design community.
Circulation: 17000
Founded in 1906

Directories & Databases

536 **AMCEA Member Handbook & Roster**
Advertising Media Credit Executives Association
8840 Columbia 100 Parkway
Columbia, MD 21045-2158

410-992-7609
Fax: 410-740-5574
E-Mail: amcea@amcea.org
Home Page: www.amcea.org

J Dee Stevenson, President
Kimberly Riley, VP
Vickie Bolinger, Director

Inside you will find direct telephone numbers to every credit manager in our association along with numbers for credit references and fax inquiries. We also include their e-mail addresses and computer hardware and software information.

537 **Advertisers and Agency Red Book Plus**
Canon Communications Pharmaceutical Medial Group
300 American metro Bvld
Newtown, PA 18940
215-944-9800
Fax: 215-867-0053
E-Mail: sandra.baker@cancom.com
Home Page: www.pharmalive.com
Karl Engel, President
Styli Engel, Executive VP/Editor-in-Chief
James Hannan, CEO/Group Publisher
Lisa Aberman, CFO/COO
Advertising information.
Cost: $1788.00
Frequency: Quarterly
Founded in 1982

538 **Advertising Age: Leading National Advertisers Issue**
Ad Age Group/Crain Communications
711 3rd Ave
New York, NY 10017-4014
212-210-0785
Fax: 212-210-0200
E-Mail: subs@crain.com
Home Page: www.adage.com
Social Media: Facebook, Twitter, LinkedIn
Keith E Crain, Chairman/Publisher
Rance E Crain, President/Editor-In-Chief
David S Klein, VP Publishing/Editorial Director
Featuring comprehensive ad spending estimates on 100 elite, company profiles and sales and earnings reports for our annual 100 Leading National Advertisers Report.
Cost: $5.00
Frequency: Annual
Circulation: 59,000
Founded in 1930

539 **Advertising Growth Trends**
Schonfeld & Associates Inc
1931 Lynn Circle
Libertyville, IL 60048-1323
847-816-4870
800-205-0030
Fax: 847-816-4872
E-Mail: saiinfo@saibooks.com
Home Page: www.saibooks.com
Carol Greenhut, Publisher
Information on publicly owned corporations that spend on advertising. Measures of profitability and effectiveness of the company's advertising expenditures are shown.
Cost: $395.00
230 Pages
Frequency: Annual
ISBN: 1-932024-84-0

540 **Advertising Ratios & Budgets**
Schonfeld & Associates Inc
1931 Lynn Circle
Libertyville, IL 60048-1323
847-816-4870
800-205-0030
Fax: 847-816-4872
E-Mail: saiinfo@saibooks.com
Home Page: www.saibooks.com
Carol Greenhut, Publisher
The detailed annual report covers over 5,000 companies and 300 industries with information on current advertising budgets, ad-to-sales ratios and ad-to-gross margin ratios, as well as budgets and growth rate forecasts. Use it to track competition, win new ad agency clients, set and justify ad budgets, sell space and time or plan new media ventures and new products. Includes industry and advertiser ad spending rankings.
Cost: $395.00
190 Pages
Frequency: Annual
ISBN: 1-932024-80-8

541 **Advertising Red Books**
PO Box 1514
Summit, NJ 07902
800-908-5395
E-Mail: info@redbooks.com
Home Page: www.redbooks.com
Advertising Red Books has been providing competitive intelligence and prospecting data to media companies, advertising agencies, manufacturers, libraries, advertising service and suppliers.
Founded in 1922

542 **Advertising and Marketing Intelligence**
New York Times
1719 State Route 10
#A
Parsippany, NJ 07054-4507
E-Mail: hartman-center@duke.edu
Home Page: www.library.duke.edu
Contains abstracts of articles from over 75 publications on advertising, marketing and the media.

543 **Adweek Directory**
Prometheus Global Media
770 Broadway
7th Floor
New York, NY 10003-9595
212-493-4100
Fax: 646-654-5368
Home Page: www.prometheusgm.com
Social Media: Facebook, Twitter
Richard D. Beckman, CEO
James A. Finkelstein, Chairman
Madeline Krakowsky, Vice President Circulation
Tracy Brater, Executive Director Creative Service
Adweek Directories Online is where you will find searchable databases with comprehensive information on ad agencies, brand marketers and multicultural media.
Frequency: Annual
Circulation: 800
Founded in 1981

544 **Brands and Their Companies**
Gale/Cengage Learning
PO Box 09187
Detroit, MI 48209-0187
248-699-4253
800-877-4253
Fax: 248-699-8049
E-Mail: galee.galeord@cengage.com
Home Page: www.gale.com
Social Media: Facebook, Twitter, LinkedIn, YouTube
Patrick C Sommers, President
This source lists manufacturers and distributors from small businesses to large corporations, from both the public and private sectors offering complete coverage of more than 426,000 US consumer brands.
Frequency: Annual
ISBN: 1-414434-26-X

545 **Buyers Guide to Outdoor Advertising**
DoMedia LLC
247 Marconi Boulevard
Suite 400
Columbus, OH 43215
866-939-3663
E-Mail: contact@domedial.com
Home Page: www.domedia.com
FC Miller, Publisher
Robert Gainey, Circulation Manager
Offers valuable information on outdoor advertising companies and their markets.

546 **Circulation**
Standard Rate & Data Services
1700 E Higgins Rd
Des Plaines, IL 60018-5610
847-375-5000
800-851-7737
Fax: 847-375-5001
E-Mail: contact@srds.com
Home Page: www.srds.com
George Carens, Executive Vice President
Trish Delaurier, Publisher
This print service provides complete circulation, penetration and consumer demographic information on your newspaper options so you can make objective comparisons in multi newspaper markets and across markets. You'll be able to analyze circulation, number of households, retail sales, average household income and market rankings to determine what papers deliver your target audience.
Frequency: Annual
Circulation: 1000+

547 **Co-op Advertising Programs Sourcebook**
National Register Publishing
300 Connell Dr
Suite 20000
Berkeley Heights, NJ 07922
800-473-7020
Fax: 908-673-1189
E-Mail: nrpeditorial@marquiswhoswho.com
Home Page: www.co-opsourcebook.com
The best source for media companies, wholesalers, retailers and others for finding available advertising dollars to fund co-op programs. Includes 52 product classifications.
Frequency: Semi-Annual

548 **Consumer Magazine Advertising Source**
Standard Rate & Data Services
1700 E Higgins Rd
Des Plaines, IL 60018-5610
847-375-5000
800-851-7737
Fax: 847-375-5001
E-Mail: contact@srds.com
Home Page: www.srds.com
George Carens, Executive Vice President
Joseph Hayes, Publisher
This service provides complete planning information on US consumer magazines, including standardized ad rates, dates, contact information and links to online media kits, Web sites and audit statements that provide additional facts on readership information and positioning.
Frequency: Semi-Annual
Circulation: 2000+

549 **Creative Industry Director**
Black Book Inc
740 Broadway
Suite 202
New York, NY 10003-9518
212-979-6700
800-841-1246
Fax: 212-673-4321

E-Mail: eryder@blackbook.com
Home Page: www.blackbook.com

Joe Resudek, Janet

Designed to meet the needs of professionals who seek creative services in every aspect of media, advertising, production and the fashion industry.
Frequency: Annual

550 **Fashion and Print Directory: Madison Avenue Handbook**
Peter Glenn Publications
777 E Atlantic Ave
Suite C2337
Delray Beach, FL 33438

561-404-4209
888-332-6700
Fax: 561-892-5786
E-Mail: gjames@pgdirect.com
Home Page: www.pgdirect.com

Gregory James, Publisher
Todd Heustess, Editor

The most reliable and comprehensive entertainment resource includes over 400 pages of national information including everyone you need to know within the advertising, fashion and print industries.
Frequency: Annual
Founded in 1956

551 **IQ Directory Adweek**
Prometheus Global Media
770 Broadway
7th Floor
New York, NY 10003-9595

212-493-4100
Fax: 646-654-5368
Home Page: www.prometheusgm.com

Richard D. Beckman, CEO
James A. Finkelstein, Chairman
Madeline Krakowsky, Vice President Circulation
Tracy Brater, Executive Director Creative Service

Profile of companies at the leading edge of digital marketing, has the specifics you'll need to investigate, launch and/or expand your digital presence. Profiles over 2,200 interactive agencies, web developers, brand marketers, online media, CD-ROM developers, POP/Kiosk designers and multimedia creative companies
Founded in 1981

552 **IRS Corporate Financial Ratios**
Schonfeld & Associates Inc
1931 Lynn Circle
Libertyville, IL 60048-1323

847-816-4870
800-205-0030
Fax: 847-816-4872
E-Mail: saiinfo@saibooks.com
Home Page: www.saibooks.com

Carol Greenhut, Publisher

An ideal reference for CPAs, controllers, bankers, CFOs, tax lawyers, financial analysts, investment advisors and corporate planners, this reference book features 70-plus key financial ratios calculated from the latest income statement and balance sheet data available from the IRS.
Cost: $225.00
300 Pages
Frequency: Annual
ISBN: 1-932024-79-4

553 **ISA Membership & Buyer's Guide**
International Sign Association
1001 N Fairfax Street
Suite 301
Alexandria, VA 22314

703-836-4012
866-WHY-SIGN
Fax: 703-836-8353
E-Mail: info@signs.org
Home Page: www.signs.org

Duane Laska, Chairman
Harry Niese, Vice Chairman
Chad Jones, Secretary/Treasurer

Discover a new supplier or distributor. Use our database to search members by company, location, products, services or equipment.
2600 Members

554 **Illustrated Guide to P.O.P. Exhibits and Promotion**
Creative Magazine
31 Merrick Avenue
Merrick, NY 11566

516-378-0800
Fax: 516-378-0884
E-Mail: info@creativemag.com
Home Page: www.creativemag.com

Larry Flasterstein, Publisher

The Illustrated Guide serves over 15,000 P.O.P buyers, sales promotion and event managers in the leading corporations in North America with quick, up to the minute information about the resources in this industry.
Frequency: Annual

555 **Infomercial Marketing Sourcebook**
Prometheus Global Media
770 Broadway
7th Floor
New York, NY 10003-9595

212-493-4100
Fax: 646-654-5368
Home Page: www.prometheusgm.com

Richard D. Beckman, CEO
James A. Finkelstein, Chairman
Madeline Krakowsky, Vice President Circulation
Tracy Brater, Executive Director Creative Service

A complete resource guide for everyone involved in the infomercial industry.

556 **Internship Directory**
American Advertising Federation
1101 Vermont Ave NW
Suite 500
Washington, DC 20005-6306

202-898-0089
800-999-2231
Fax: 202-898-0159
E-Mail: aaf@aaf.org
Home Page: www.aaf.org

James Edmund Datri, President
Constance Cannon Frazier, COO
Joanne Schecter, Executive Vice President

More than 1,500 advertising and marketing internships are listed in this valuable resource.
Circulation: 50000

557 **Mediaweek Multimedia Directory**
Prometheus Global Media
770 Broadway
7th Floor
New York, NY 10003-9595

212-493-4100
Fax: 646-654-5368
Home Page: www.prometheusgm.com

Richard D. Beckman, CEO
James A. Finkelstein, Chairman
Madeline Krakowsky, Vice President Circulation
Tracy Brater, Executive Director Creative Service

Focuses on the most powerful segments covering 9,000 media companies from the top 100 media markets for radio, broadcast TV, cable TV and daily newspapers. Also includes the top 300 consumer magazines, the top 150 trade magazines, networks, syndicators, sales representatives, multi-media holding companies, trade associations and rating organizations.
Frequency: Annual
Circulation: 800

558 **Medical Marketing and Media**
Haymarket Media Inc
114 W 26th St
4th Floor
New York, NY 10001-6812

212-206-0606
Fax: 212-638-6117
E-Mail: custserv@haymarketmedia.com
Home Page: www.haymarket.com

William Bekover, Chief Executive Officer

Offers a comprehensive editorial resource to leaders, thinkers and executives dedicated to the promotion and commercialization of prescription drugs and other medical products and services in the US.
Frequency: Monthly
Circulation: 15000
Founded in 1996

559 **Navigator**
Promotional Products Association International
3125 Skyway Circle N
Irving, TX 75038-3539

972-252-0404
Fax: 972-258-3004
E-Mail: ppb@ppai.org
Home Page: www.ppai.org

Paul Bellantone, President
Steven Meyer, Chairman of the Board
Marc Simon, Chair-Elect

An invaluable resource designed to educate distributors about PPAI supplier and business services members and the products they offer.
Frequency: Annual

560 **Online Advertising Playbook**
John Wiley & Sons
111 River St
Hoboken, NJ 07030-5790

201-748-6000
Fax: 201-748-6088
E-Mail: info@wiley.com
Home Page: www.wiley.com

Stephen Smith, President & Chief Executive Officer
Vincent Marzano, Vice President

The book focuses on the enduring strategies necessary for marketers to have the knowledge base necessary to execute winning campaigns.

561 **Planning for Out of Home Media**
Traffic Audit Bureau for Media Measurement
271 Madison Ave
Suite 1504
New York, NY 10016-1012

212-972-8075
Fax: 212-972-8928
E-Mail: inquiry@tabonline.com
Home Page: www.tabonline.com

Joseph Philport, President
Larry Hennessy, Vice President

Reference book contains up-to-date descriptions of O-O-H media and their production specifications, O-O-H local and national case history success stories and creative guidelines, travel trend data, new technologies and a glossary of O-O-H terminology.

562 **Print Media Production Source**
Standard Rate & Data Services
1700 E Higgins Rd
Des Plaines, IL 60018-5610

847-375-5000
800-851-7737
Fax: 847-375-5001
E-Mail: contact@srds.com
Home Page: www.srds.com

Trish Delaurier, Publisher
George Carens, Executive Vice President

This service provides complete data on all critical ad production specifications for business and consumer magazines and newspapers. Production, traffic and graphic design personnel use this current, accurate resource to confirm essential production information so they can control production deadlines and budgets.
Frequency: Quarterly
Circulation: 800+

563 **R&D Ratios & Budgets**
Schonfeld & Associates Inc
1931 Lynn Circle
Libertyville, IL 60048-1323

847-816-4870
800-205-0030
Fax: 847-816-4872
E-Mail: saiinfo@saibooks.com
Home Page: www.saibooks.com

Carol Greenhut, Publisher

The comprehensive annual report covers over 4,700 companies and 280 industries with information on current R&D budgets, R&D-to-sales ratios and R&D-to-gross margin ratios. Use it to track competition, set and justify R&D budgets, screen potential acquisitions, sell the laboratory and technology markets or plan new ventures and develop new products. Includes industry and R&D spender rankings.
Cost: $395.00
186 Pages
Frequency: Annual
ISBN: 1-932024-81-6

564 **Radio Creative Resources Directory**
Radio Advertising Bureau
1320 Greenway Dr
Suite 500
Irving, TX 75038-2547

972-753-6700
800 232 3131
Fax: 972-753-6727
E-Mail: jhaley@rab.com
Home Page: www.rab.com

Erica Farber, President
Van Allen, EVP and CFO
Beverly Fraser, SVP

A list of radio production companies and studios in response to advertisers and agencies who want to find companies that specialize in writing, casting and producing great radio spots. Our current edition contains over 60 companies including many Radio-Mercury Award winners.
Frequency: Annual

565 **Research & Development Growth Trends**
Schonfeld & Associates Inc
1931 Lynn Circle
Libertyville, IL 60048-1323

847-816-4870
800-205-0030
Fax: 847-816-4872
E-Mail: saiinfo@saibooks.com
Home Page: www.saibooks.com

Carol Greenhut, Publisher

Information on publicly owned corporations that spend on R&D.
Cost: $395.00
277 Pages
Frequency: Annual
ISBN: 1-932024-85-9

566 **Standard Industry Directory**
Association of Hispanic Advertising Agencies
8400 Westpark Drive
2nd Floor
McLean, VA 22102

703-610-9014
Fax: 703-610-0227
E-Mail: info@ahaa.org
Home Page: www.ahaa.org
Social Media: Facebook, Twitter

Horacio Gavilan, President
Melissa Chen, Membership/Directory
Ayanna Wiggins, Marketing

AHAA represents the best minds and resources that are dedicated to Hispanic-specialized marketing.

567 **Suppliers Directory**
Eight-Sheet Outdoor Advertising Association
1244 Lake Park Ave
Galt, CA 95632

209-251-7622
800-847-3387
Fax: 209-251-7658
E-Mail: ddjesoaa@comcast.net
Home Page: www.esoaa.com

Rebecca Lambert, Editor

Lists suppliers to the Eight-Sheet outdoor billboard industry; arranged by specialty. Includes definitions of basic industry terms.
Frequency: Annual
Circulation: 800

568 **The Art & Science of Managing a Content Marketing Strategy**
Direct Marketing Association
1120 Avenue of the Americas
New York, NY 10036-6700

212-768-7277
Fax: 212-302-6714
E-Mail: customerservice@the-dma.org
Home Page: www.the-dma.org
Social Media: Facebook, Twitter, LinkedIn

Lawrence M Kimmel, CEO

Effective Search Engine Optimization and Search Engine Marketing can have a dramatic effect on a website's performance and ROI. From optimization techniques to keyword bidding, our Search course offerings will give the insights and strategies to improve search results and efficiency.

569 **Tie-In Promotion Service**
Association of National Advertisers
708 Third Avenue
33 Floor
New York, NY 10017

212-697-5950
Fax: 212-661-8057
E-Mail: info@ana.net
Home Page: www.ana.net
Social Media: Facebook, Twitter, LinkedIn, YouTube

Bob Liodice, President & CEO
Christine Manna, COO
William Zengel, EVP

Brand names listed by their companies as available for possible tie-in promotions with other companies.
Frequency: Annual/December

570 **U.S. Sourcebook of R&D Spenders**
Schonfeld & Associates Inc
1931 Lynn Circle
Libertyville, IL 60048-1323

847-816-4870
800-205-0030
Fax: 847-816-4872
E-Mail: saiinfo@saibooks.com
Home Page: www.saibooks.com

Carol Greenhut, Publisher

A directory of publicly owned corporations that spend on R&D, published annually. Corporate name, address, telephone number, and website are provided along with the names and titles of three senior executives, R&D budgets, sales, fiscal year closing, and more. Organized by state and ZIP code. The ideal reference for sales people who call on R&D centers and for economic development agencies.
Cost: $395.00
180 Pages
Frequency: Annual
ISBN: 1-932024-83-2

571 **US Source Book of Advertisers**
Schonfeld & Associates Inc
1931 Lynn Circle
Libertyville, IL 60048-1323

847-816-4870
800-205-0030
Fax: 847-816-4872
E-Mail: saiinfo@saibooks.com
Home Page: www.saibooks.com

Carol Greenhut, Publisher

A directory of publicly owned corporations that advertise. Corporate name, address, telephone number and website are provided along with the names and titles of three senior executives, ad budgets, sales, fiscal year closing and more. The ideal reference for media sales, ad agency new business development and selling corporate services.
Frequency: Annual
ISBN: 1-932024-55-7

572 **Who's Who: MASA Buyer's Guide to Blue Ribbon Mailing Services**
Mailing & Fulfillment Service Association
1421 Prince Street
Suite 410
Alexandria, VA 22314-2806

703-836-9200
Fax: 703-548-8204
E-Mail: mfsa-mail@mfsanet.org
Home Page: www.mfsanet.org

Ken Garner, President
Bill Stevenson, Director Marketing

Offers a detailed listing of suppliers of equipment, products and services to the direct mail industry, most containing a description of the specific products they provide.
Frequency: Annual

573 **Workbook**
Scott & Daughters Publishing
6762 Lexington Avenue
Los Angeles, CA 90038-2482

323-856-0008
800-547-2688
Fax: 323-856-4368
E-Mail: contributors@workbookstock.com
Home Page: www.workbook.com
Social Media: Facebook, Twitter

Alexis Scott, Owner
Susan Haller, Managing Editor
Bill Daniels, Publisher

This directory, offered in four volumes, lists over 25,000 advertising agencies, art directors and freelance illustrators in the United States.
Frequency: Annual
Circulation: 35,000

574 **Workforce Growth Trends**
Schonfeld & Associates Inc
1931 Lynn Circle
Libertyville, IL 60048-1323
847-816-4870
800-205-0030
Fax: 847-816-4872
E-Mail: saiinfo@saibooks.com
Home Page: www.saibooks.com
Carol Greenhut, Publisher
Information on all publicly owned corporations. Study is ordered by U.S. Department of Commerce SIC(Standard Industrial Classification) and alphabetically by company name within each SIC. Each companys historical information, average annual percent change, sales and shares are displayed.
Cost: $395.00
580 Pages
Frequency: Annual
ISBN: 1-932024-87-5

575 **Workforce Ratios & Forecasts**
Schonfeld & Associates Inc
1931 Lynn Circle
Libertyville, IL 60048-1323
847-816-4870
800-205-0030
Fax: 847-816-4872
E-Mail: saiinfo@saibooks.com
Home Page: www.saibooks.com
Carol Greenhut, Publisher
This comprehensive annual study by Schonfeld & Associates covers over 6,600 companies and 420 industries. The information reported includes current number of employees, a forecast of projected employee headcount and growth rates, as well as sales per employee and gross margin per employee. Use it to track competition, set and justify manpower budgets, screen potential acquisitions, plan new ventures and develop new businesses. Includes rankings by size and growth rate.
Cost: $395.00
250 Pages
Frequency: Annual
ISBN: 1-932024-86-7

Industry Web Sites

576 **www.aaaa.org**
American Association of Advertising Agencies
To improve and strengthen the advertising agency business in the United States by counseling members on operations and management.

577 **www.aaasite.org**
American Academy of Advertising
An organization of advertising scholars and professionals with an interest in advertising and advertising education.

578 **www.aaf.org**
American Advertising Federation
The American Advertising Federation protects and promotes the wellbeing of advertising.

579 **www.aapor.org**
American Association for Public Opinion Research
The American Advertising Federation protects and promotes the wellbeing of advertising.

580 **www.adcouncil.org**
Advertising Council
The Ad Council is a private, non-profit organization that marshals volunteer talent from the advertising and communications industries, the facilities of the media, and the resources of the business and non-profit communities to deliver critical messages to the American public.

581 **www.aef.com**
Advertising Educational Foundation
The advertising industry's provider and distributor of educational content to enrich the understanding of advertising and it's role in culture, society and the economy.

582 **www.ahaa.org**
Association of Hispanic Advertising Agencies
Mission to grow, strengthen and protect the Hispanic marketing and advertising industry by providing leadership in raising awareness of the value of the Hispanic market opportunities and enhancing the professionalism of the industry.

583 **www.ana.net**
Association of National Advertisers
Provides indispensable leadership that drives marketing excellence and champions, promotes and defends the interests of the marketing community.

584 **www.apanational.com**
Advertising Photographers of America
Our goal is to establish, endorse and promote professional practices, standards and ethics in the photographic and advertising community.

585 **www.awny.org**
Advertising Women of New York
The organization now consists of influential women and men representing the advertising, marketing, media, promotion and public relations fields.

586 **www.bbb.org**
Better Business Bureau
To be the leader in advancing marketplace trust.

587 **www.biznetis.net**
Biznet Internet Solutions
Biznet Internet Solutions is a full-service Web solutions company that focuses on business and mobile Web sites, provides advertising agency support, and Internet marketing.

588 **www.esoaa.com**
Eight-Sheet Outdoor Advertising Association
To provide leadership, services and standards to promote, protect and advance the eight sheet industry.

589 **www.greyhouse.com**
Grey House Publishing
Authoritative reference directories for business information and general reference including advertising, communications, marketing and media markets. Users can search the online databases with varied search criteria allowing for custom searches by product category, geographic area, sales volume, keyword, subject and more. Full Grey House catalog and online ordering also available.

590 **www.iaany.org**
International Advertising Association
Promoting the value of advertising globally, advocacy of freedom of commercial speech and consumer choice and encouraging industry self regulation.

591 **www.iab.net**
Interactive Advertising Bureau
Dedicated to the growth of the interactive advertising marketplace, of interactive's share of total marketing spend, and of its members' share of total marketing spend

592 **www.icomagencies.com**
International Communications Agency Network
The international organization of museums and museum professionals which is committed to the conservation, continuation and communication to society of the world's natural and cultural heritage, present and future, tangible and intangible.

593 **www.ifcaonline.com**
Insurance and Financial Communicators Association
An international association for insurance and financial communicators offering professional development and networking.

594 **www.magnetglobal.org**
MAGNET: Marketing & Advertising Global Network
Provides a way for member agencies to share their experience, knowledge and ideas with other agencies in other parts of the world.

595 **www.marketingpower.com**
American Marketing Association
It is a professional association for individuals and organizations involved in the practice, teaching and study of marketing and advertising worldwide.

596 **www.mfsanet.org**
Mailing & Fulfillment Service Association
The national trade association for the mailing and fulfillment services industry.

597 **www.oaaa.org**
Outdoor Advertising Association of America
To provide leadership, services and standards to promote, protect and advance the outdoor advertising industry.

598 **www.popai.com**
Point of Purchase Advertising International
Dedicated to promoting Marketing at Retail as a powerful advertising medium being rapidly integrated into the strategic marketing mix as retail programs deliver a critical combination of brand messaging and information at the critical moment of the consumer purchase decision.

599 **www.ppa.org**
Promotional Products Association International
To lead the industry by expanding the market, providing indispensable products and services, and enhancing our members' professionalism and success.

600 **www.rama-nrf.com**
Retail Advertising & Marketing International
Provides visionary leadership that promotes creativity, innovation and excellence within all marketing disciplines that strategically elevates our members and our industry.

601 **www.signs.org**
International Sign Association

Supports, promotes and improves the sign industry, which sustains the nation's retail industry.

602 **www.taan.org**
Transworld Advertising Agency Network
A network of independently owned advertising agencies that work closely together in the exchange of management information, reciprocal services and personal local contact.

603 **www.tabonline.com**
Traffic Audit Bureau for Media Measurement
An independent third party provider of standardized and valid circulation measures for out of home media.

604 **www.thearf.org**
Advertising Research Foundation
An open forum where the best and brightest from every avenue of advertising can gather to exchange ideas and research strategies

605 **www.thecab.tv**
Cabletelevision Advertising Bureau
Dedicated to providing advertisers and agencies with the most current, complete and actionable cable television media insights at the national, DMA and local levels.

606 **www.tradepromo.org**
Trade Promotion Management Association
Provides members with information, education and research on the dynamic world of trade promotion, including co op advertising, market development funds, slotting fees, off invoice deductions, channel promotions and more.

Associations

607 **AACC International**
3340 Pilot Knob Road
St. Paul, MN 55121-2055

651-454-7250
800-328-7560
Fax: 651-454-0766
E-Mail: aacc@scisoc.org
Home Page: www.aaccnet.org
Social Media: Facebook, Twitter, LinkedIn, Pinterest

David H. Hahn, Chair of the Board
Jan A. Delcour, President
Dave L. Braun, Treasurer
Marta S. Izydorczyk, Director
Matthew K. Morell, Director

Formerly the American Association of Cereal Chemists, a non-profit organization of members who are specialists in the use of cereal grains in foods.
154 Members
Founded in 1915

608 **Agribusiness Council(ABC)**
PO Box 5565
Washington, DC 20016

202-296-4563
Fax: 202-887-9178
E-Mail: info@agribusinesscouncil.org
Home Page: www.agribusinesscouncil.org

Nicholas E Hollis, President/CEO

The Agribusiness Council (ABC) is a private, nonprofit/tax-exempt, membership organization dedicated to strengthening U.S. agro-industrial competitiveness through programs which highlight international trade and development potentials as well as broad issues which encompass several individual agribusiness sectors and require a food systems approach. Examples of such issues are commercialization of new tech/crops, environmental impacts, human resource development, trade and investment policy.
Founded in 1967

609 **Agricultural & Applied Economics Association**
555 E Wells Street
Suite 1100
Milwaukee, WI 53202-6600

414-918-3190
Fax: 414-276-3349
E-Mail: info@aaea.org
Home Page: www.aaea.org
Social Media: Facebook, Twitter, LinkedIn, Blogger, Google+

Julie Caswell, President
Barry Goodwin, President-Elect
Richard Sexton, Past President
Michael Boland, Director
Keith H. Coble, Director

The Agricultural & Applied Economics Association (AAEA) is a not-for-profit association serving the professional interests of members working in agricultural and broadly related fields of applied economics. Members of the AAEA are employed by academic or government institutions, as well as in industry and not-for-profit organizations, and engage in a variety of teaching, research, and extension/outreach activities.
3000 Members
Founded in 1910

610 **Agricultural Communicators of Tomorrow**
PO Box 110180
Gainesville, FL 32611-0180

352-392-1971
Fax: 352-392-9589
Home Page: www.ifas.ufl.edu
Social Media: Facebook, Twitter

Dr Jack Payne, Senior Vice President

A national organization of college students professionally interested in communications related to agriculture, food, natural resources and allied fields. The Mission of UF/IFAS is to develop knowledge in agricultural, human and natural resources and to make that knowledge accessible to sustain and enhance the quality of human life.
Founded in 1853

611 **Agricultural Retailers Association**
1156 15th St NW
Suite 302
Washington, DC 20005-1745

202-457-0825
Fax: 202-457-0864
E-Mail: info@aradc.org
Home Page: www.aradc.org
Social Media: Facebook, Twitter

Johnny Council, Chairman
Daren Coppock, President & CEO
Richard Gupton, Senior Vice President
Donnie Taylor, Vice President of Membership & Corp
Michelle Hummel, Director of Marketing

The Agricultural Retailers Association (ARA) is a nonprofit trade association that serves as the political voice of agricultural retailers and distributors. We're advocates, educators, and champions for the American ag retailer. The Agricultural Retailers Association (ARA) is a nonprofit trade association that serves as the political voice of agricultural retailers and distributors. We're advocates, educators, and champions for the American ag retailer.
Frequency: Annual
Founded in 1993

612 **Agriculture Council of America**
11020 King St
Suite 205
Overland Park, KS 66210-1201

913-491-1895
Fax: 913-491-6502
E-Mail: info@agday.org
Home Page: www.agday.org
Social Media: Facebook, Twitter, Flickr, YouTube

Tres Bailey, Chair
Colin Woodall, Vice Chair
Curt Blades, Secretary/Treasurer
Lynn Henderson, Board Member
Nancy Barcus, Bard Member

The Agriculture Council of America (ACA) is an organization uniquely composed of leaders in the agriculture, food and fiber communities dedicated to increasing the public awareness of agriculture's vital role in our society.
75 Members
Founded in 1973

613 **Agriculture Federal Credit Union**
1400 Independence Ave SW
Room SM2
Washington, DC 20250

202-479-2270
800-368-3552
Fax: 202-479-3877
E-Mail: members@agriculturefcu.org
Home Page: www.agfed.org
Social Media: Facebook, Twitter

Margie Click, President/CEO
Theodora Ezekwerre, Senior Vice President
Tom Bowles, SVP/CFO
Clifton Jeter, Chair
Stephen J Hawkins, Vice Chair

Agriculture Federal Credit Union meets the highest standards for long term financial soundness. AgFed's workplace environment motivates and empowers employees to provide quality service to our members. AgFed offers a wide range of financial services and products to satisfy the diverse needs of our members throughout their lifetimes. AgFed has state-of-the-art technology designed to meet our members' needs.
23000 Members
Founded in 1934

614 **American Agricultural Law Association**
127 Young Road
Kelso, WA 98626

360-200-5699
Fax: 360-423-2287
E-Mail: roberta@aglaw-assn.org
Home Page: www.aglaw-assn.org

Peggy Kirk Hall, President
Robert Achenbach, Executive Director
Pat Jensen, President-Elect
David K Waggoner, Director
Ruth A Moore, Director

The AALA is a membership organization that focuses on the legal needs of the agricultural community.
600 Members
Founded in 1980

615 **American Agriculture Movement**
AAM National Secretary/Treasurer
11232 Road K
Liberal, KS 67901

620-482-6306
E-Mail: jrice@swko.net
Home Page: www.aaminc.org

Larry Matlack, President
Arthur Chaney, Executive Vice President
John Willis, Vice President
Lynn Kirkpatrick, Vice President of Marketing
Marc Wetzel, Vice President of Membership

The creation of the AAM has provided a farmer-created, farmer-built organization within which farmers themselves have been the leaders, speakers and organizers; empowering farmers as they had not been in the past, to speak for and advocate for themselves.
Founded in 1977

616 **American Angus Association**
3201 Frederick Ave
St Joseph, MO 64506-2997

816-383-5100
Fax: 816-233-9703
E-Mail: angus@angus.org
Home Page: www.angus.org
Social Media: Facebook, Twitter, Pinterest, Youtube, Vimeo

Bryce Schumann, CEO
Gordon Stucky, Vice President
Cathy Watkins, Treasurer
Bill Bowman, COO
Richard Wilson, CFO

The American Angus Association is the nation's largest beef registry association. Our goal is to serve the beef cattle industry, and increase the production of consistent, high quality beef that will better satisfy consumers throughout the world.
36000 Members
Founded in 1873

617 **American Association of Crop Insurers**
1 Massachusetts Ave NW
Suite 800
Washington, DC 20001-1401

202-789-4100
Fax: 202-408-7763
E-Mail: aaci@mwmlaw.com
Home Page: www.cropinsurers.com

Mike McLeod, Executive Director & Gen Counsel
David Graves, Manager, Secretary

The American Association of Crop Insurers is a nonprofit industry service organization representing the interests of insurance companies, agents, and adjusters involved in the Federal crop insurance program. AACI's reinsured company members write more than 80 percent of the crop insurance sold by private companies nationwide. AACI's primary purpose is governmental relations with Congress, the U.S. Department of Agriculture, and other executive agencies whose decisions influence the program.
25 Members
Founded in 1980

618 **American Beekeeping Federation**
3525 Piedmont Rd NE
Bldg 5 Suite 300
Atlanta, GA 30305-1509

404-760-2875
Fax: 404-240-0998
E-Mail: info@abfnet.org
Home Page: www.abfnet.org

Regina Robuck, Executive Director
Grayson Daniels, Membership Coordinator
Tara Zeravsky, Sr Conference Planner
Troy Fore, Director/Government Affairs
John Talbert, Director

The ABF is a national organization that continually works in the interest of all beekeepers, large or small, and those associated with the industry to ensure the future of the honey bee. Our members share a common interest to work toward better education and information for all segments of the industry in the hope of increasing our chances for survival in today's competitive world.
1000 Members
Founded in 1943

619 **American Brahman Breeders Association**
PO Box 14100
Kansas City, MO 64101-4100

816-595-2442
Fax: 816-842-6931
E-Mail: abba@abraonline.org
Home Page: www.brahman.org

Ricky Hughes, President
J. D. Sartwelle, Jr., Vice President
George Kempfer, Secretary/Treasurer
Neil Potter, Director
J Hnery oNovak, Director

American Brahman Breeders is a beef crossbreeding organization that plays a big role in the United States and beyond.
Founded in 1924

620 **American Dairy Science Association**
1800 South Oak Street
Suite 100
Champaign, IL 61820-6974

217-356-5146
Fax: 217-398-4119
E-Mail: adsa@assochq.org
Home Page: www.adsa.org
Social Media: RSS

Scott Rankin, President
Al Kertz, Vice President
Peter Studney, Executive Director
Roger Shanks, Editor-in-Chief
Vicki Paden, Administrative Assistant

The American Dairy Science Association (ADSA) is an international organization of educators, scientists, and industry representatives who are committed to advancing the dairy industry and keenly aware of the vital role the dairy sciences play in fulfilling the economic, nutritive, and health requirements of the world's population. Together, ADSA members have discovered new methods and technologies that have revolutionized the dairy industry.
3000 Members
Founded in 1998
Mailing list available for rent

621 **American Farm Bureau Federation**
600 Maryland Ave SW
Suite 1000W
Washington, DC 20024-2555

202-484-3600
Fax: 202-484-3604
E-Mail: bstallman@fb.org
Home Page: www.fb.org
Social Media: Facebook, Twitter, RSS, You Tube, Google+

Bob Stallman, President
Don Lipton, Executive Director
Julie Anna Potts, Executive Vice President/Treasurer
Ellen Steen, General Counsel & Secretary
Mace Thornton, Acting Director

Farm Bureau is an independent, non-governmental, voluntary organization governed by and representing farm and ranch families united for the purpose of analyzing their problems and formulating action to achieve educational improvement, economic opportunity and social advancement and, thereby, to promote the national well-being. Farm Bureau is local, county, state, national and international in its scope and influence and is non-partisan, non-sectarian and non-secret in character.
3M Members
Founded in 1919

622 **American Feed Industry Association**
American Feed Industry Association
2101 Wilson Blvd
Suite 916
Arlington, VA 22201-3047

703-524-0810
Fax: 703-524-1921
E-Mail: afia@afia.org
Home Page: www.afia.org
Social Media: Facebook, Twitter, LinkedIn

Jeff Cannon, Chairman
Joel G. Newman, President & Treasurer
Keith Epperson, VP/Manufacturing
Sarah Novak, VP/Membership
Steve Kopperud, SVP

AFIA is the world's largest organization devoted exclusively to representing the business, legislative and regulatory interests of the U.S. animal feed industry and its suppliers. AFIA also is the recognized leader on international industry developments. Members include more than 500 domestic and international companies and state, regional and national associations.
690 Members
Founded in 1909

623 **American Forage and Grassland Council**
PO Box 867
Berea, KY 40403

800-944-2342
E-Mail: tina.bowling@afgc.org
Home Page: www.afgc.org

Tina Bowling, Executive Director
Howard Straub, President
Ray Smith, Senior Vice President
Roger L Staff, Treasurer
Coy Fitch, Director

The American Forage and Grassland Council (AFGC) is an international organization made up of 20 affiliate councils in the United States and Canada. Our primary objective is to promote the profitable production and sustainable utilization of quality forage and grasslands. Mission is to be recognized as the leader and voice of economically and environmentally sound forage agriculture.
2700 Members

624 **American Guernsey Association**
1224 Alton Darby Creeek Road
Suite G
Columbus, OH 43228

614-864-2409
Fax: 614-864-5614
E-Mail: info@usguernsey.com
Home Page: www.usguernsey.com

David Trotter, President
Emily Hartmann, 1st Vice President
Duane Schuler, 2nd Vice President
David Trotter, Interim Executive Secretary
Brian Schnebly, Programs Coordinator

The AGA's mission is to provide and promote programs and services to enhance the value and profitability of the Guernsey breed for the members, owners and dairy industry worldwide.
900 Members
Founded in 1877

625 **American Hereford Association**
PO Box 014059
Kansas City, MO 64101

816-842-3757
Fax: 816-842-6931
E-Mail: aha@hereford.org
Home Page: www.hereford.org
Social Media: Facebook

Craig Huffhines, Executive Vice President
Jack Ward, COO
Angie Stump Denton, Communications Director
Amy Cowen, Youth Activities Director
Joe Rickabaugh, Field Mgmt Director

Association for people in the Hereford cattle industry.
Founded in 1910

626 **American Jersey Cattle Association**
6486 E Main Street
Reynoldsburg, OH 43068-2362

614-861-3636
Fax: 614-861-8040
Home Page: www.usjersey.com
Social Media: Facebook, Twitter

Neal Smith, CEO/Executive Secretary
Vickie White, Treasurer
Cherie L Bayer, Director
Cari Wolfe, Director/Research
Sarah Gilbert, Customer Service Coordinator

They improve and promote the Jersey cattle breed.
540 Members
Founded in 1868

627 **American Livestock Breeds Convervancy (ALBC)**
PO Box 477
Pittsboro, NC 27312

919-542-5704
Fax: 919-545-0022
Home Page: www.livestockconservancy.org
Social Media: Facebook, Blogger

Charles Bassett, Executive Director
Terry Wollen, President
Angelique Thompson, Operations Manager
James McConnell, Treasurer
Anneke Jakes, Manager of Breed Registry

The American Livestock Breeds Conservancy is a nonprofit membership organization working to protect over 180 breeds of livestock and poultry from extinction. Included are asses, cattle, goats, horses, sheep, pigs, rabbits, chickens, ducks, geese, and turkeys.
Founded in 1977

628 **American Meat Science Association**
201 W Springfield Ave
Ste 1202
Champaign, IL 61822-7676

217-356-5368
800-517-AMSA
Fax: 888-205-5834
Fax: 217-356-5370
E-Mail: information@meatscience.org
Home Page: www.meatscience.org

Robert J. Delmore, President
Thomas Powell, Executive Director
Deidrea Mabry, Director, Scientific Communications
Nancy Hayes, Event Manager
Meagan Igo, Youth Programs Coordinator

The American Meat Science Association is a broad-reaching organization of individuals that discovers, develops, and disseminates its collective meat science knowledge to provide leadership, education, and professional development. Our passion is to help meat science professionals achieve previously unimaginable levels of performance and reach even higher goals.
Founded in 1964

629 **American Phytopathological Society**
3340 Pilot Knob Road
Saint Paul, MN 55121-2097

651-454-7250
800-328-7560
Fax: 651-454-0766
E-Mail: aps@scisoc.org
Home Page: www.apsnet.org
Social Media: Facebook, Twitter, LinkedIn, YouTube

Steve Nelson, Exeutive Vice President
Amy Hope, Exeutive Vice President
Barbara Mock, VP of Finance
Michelle Bjerkness, Operations/Membership
Betty Ford, Event Manager

APS is a diverse global community of scientists that: provides credible and beneficial information related to plant health; advocates and participates in the exchange of knowledge with the public, policy makers, and the larger scientific community; and promotes and provides opportunities for scientific communication, career preparation, and professional development for its members.
4500 Members
Founded in 1908

630 **American Seed Trade Association**
1701 Duke Street
Suite 275
Alexandria, VA 22314-3415

703-837-8140
Fax: 703-837-9365
E-Mail: info@amseed.com
Home Page: www.amseed.com
Social Media: Facebook, Twitter, YouTube, Google+

Craig Newman, Chairman
Andrew LaVigne, President/CEO
Bernice Slutsky, Senior Vice President
Jane DeMarchi, Vice President, Government
Ric Dunkle, Ph.D., Senior Director of Seed Health

ASTA's mission is to be an effective voice of action in all matters concerning the development, marketing and movement of seed, associated products and services throughout the world. ASTA promotes the development of better seed to produce better crops for a better quality of life.
850 Members
Founded in 1883

631 **American Sheep Industry Association**
9785 Maroon Circle
Suite 360
Englewood, CO 80112

303-771-3500
Fax: 303-771-8200
E-Mail: eatlamb@wildblue.net
Home Page: www.sheepusa.org
Social Media: Facebook, Twitter

Clint Krebs, President
Burton Pfliger, Vice President
Peter Orwick, Executive Director
Larry Kincaid, Chief Financial Officer
Judy Malone, Industry Director

ASI is the national organization representing the interests of sheep producers located throughout the United States. From East to West, farm flocks to range operations, ASI works to represent the interests of all producers. ASI is a federation of 45 state sheep associations as well as individual members.
82000 Members
Founded in 1865

632 **American Society for Enology and Viticulture**
PO Box 1855
Davis, CA 95617-1855

530-753-3142
Fax: 530-753-3318
E-Mail: society@asev.org
Home Page: www.asev.org
Social Media: Twitter, LinkedIn, Picasa

James Kennedy, President
Lise Asimont, 1st Vice President
Mark Greenspan, 2nd Vice President
James Harbertson, Secretary/Treasurer
M Andrew Walker, Tech Program Director

The American Society for Enology and Viticulture (the sciences of winemaking and grape growing) is a 501 (c)(6), tax exempt professional society dedicated to the interests of enologists, viticulturists, and others in the fields of wine and grape research and production throughout the world. Our membership includes professionals from wineries, vineyards, academic institutions and organizations.
2400+ Members
Founded in 1950

633 **American Society for Horticultural Science**
1018 Duke Street
Alexandria, VA 22314

703-836-4606
Fax: 703-836-2024
E-Mail: webmaster@ashs.org
Home Page: www.ashs.org
Social Media: Facebook, Twitter, LinkedIn, Pinterest

Paul Bosland, Chairman
Mary Hockenberry Meyer, President
Sandra B. Wilson, Education Division Vice President
Jeffrey P. Norrie, Industry Division Vice President
Gary Bachman, VP/Extension Division

A cornerstone of research and education in horticulture and an agent for active promotion of horticultural science.
1200 Members
ISSN: 0018-5345
Founded in 1903

634 **American Society of Agricultural Consultants**
N78W14573 Appleton Ave
Suite 287
Menomonee Falls, WI 53051

262-253-6902
Fax: 262-253-6903
E-Mail: cmerry@country-marketing.com
Home Page: www.agconsultants.org
Social Media: Facebook, LinkedIn

Paige Gilligan, President
Peggy Raisanen, President-Elect
Gary Wagner, VP/Secretary

An association representing the full range of agricultural consultants which serves as an information, resource, and networking base for its members. The specific purpose of ASAC is to foster the science of agricultural consulting in all its varied fields; to promote the profession and maintain high standards under which the members conduct their service to the public; hold meetings for the exchange of ideas and the study of the profession of agricultural consulting;
181 Members
Founded in 1963

635 **American Society of Agricultural and Biological Engineers**
2950 Niles Rd
St Joseph, MI 49085-8607

269-429-0300
800-371-2723
Fax: 269-429-3852
E-Mail: hq@asabe.org
Home Page: www.asabe.org
Social Media: Facebook, Twitter, YouTube

Darrin Drollinger, Executive Director
Donna Hull, Publication Director
Dolores Jandeck, Director/Public Affairs
Scott Cedarquist, Director/Standards
Mark Crossley, Director/Membership

The American Society of Agricultural and Biological Engineers is an educational and scientific organization dedicated to the advancement of engineering applicable to agricultural, food, and biological systems. With members in more than 100 countries. The Society's Agricultural, Food and Biological Engineers develop efficient and environmentally sensitive methods of producing food, fiber, timber, and renewable energy sources.
8000 Members
Founded in 1907
Mailing list available for rent: 10000 names at $120 per M

636 **American Society of Agronomy**
5585 Guilford Road
Madison, WI 53711-5801

608-273-8080
Fax: 608-273-2021
E-Mail: headquarters@agronomy.org
Home Page: www.agronomy.org

Social Media: Facebook, Twitter, LinkedIn, RSS

Newell Kitchen, President
Wes Meixelsperger, Chief Financial Officer
Sara Uttech, Senior Manager - Governance
Alexander Barton, Director of Business Development
Ian Popkewitz, Director of IT and Operations

Promote human welfare through advancing the acquisition and dissemination of scientific knowledge concerning the nature, use improvement and interrelationships of plants, soils, water and environment. The society shall promote effective research, disseminate scientific information, facilitate technology transfer, foster high standards of education, strive to maintain high standards of ethics, promote advancements in this profession and cooperate with other organizations of similar objectives.
11000 Members
Founded in 1907

637 **American Society of Animal Science**
PO Box 7410
Champaign, IL 61826-7410

217-356-9050
Fax: 217-689-2436
E-Mail: asas@asas.org
Home Page: www.asas.org
Social Media: Facebook, Twitter, LinkedIn, YouTube

Gregory P. Lardy, President
Jacelyn Hemmelgarn, Chief Operations Officer
Meghan Wulster-Radcliffe, Chief Executive Officer
Melissa Burnett, Membership Manager
Liz Higgins, Events Manager

The American Society of Animal Science is a membership society that supports the careers of scientists and animal producers in the United States and internationally. The American Society of Animal Science fosters the discovery, sharing and application of scientific knowledge concerning the responsible use of animals to enhance human life and well-being.
ISSN: 0021-8812
Founded in 1908

638 **American Society of Consulting Arborists**
9707 Key West Ave
Suite 100
Rockville, MD 20850-3992

301-947-0483
Fax: 301-990-9771
E-Mail: asca@mgmtsol.com
Home Page: www.asca-consultants.org
Social Media: Facebook, Twitter, LinkedIn, Pinterest

Gordon Mann, President
Grace L. Jan, Vice President, Meetings
Beth W. Palys, Executive Director
Shannon Sperati, Member Services Manager
Julie Hill, Communications Manager

The industry's premier professional association focusing solely on arboricultural consulting. Consulting Arborists are authoritative experts on trees, consulting property owners, municipalities, attorneys, insurance professionals and others on tree disease, placement, preservation and dispute resolution in addition to providing consulting and expert testimony in the legal, insurance and environmental arenas.

639 **American Society of Farm Managers and Rural Appraisers (ASFMRA)**
950 S Cherry St
Suite 508
Denver, CO 80246-2664

303-758-3513
Fax: 303-758-0190
E-Mail: info@asfmra.org
Home Page: www.asfmra.org
Social Media: Facebook, Twitter, LinkedIn, Plaxo

Jim Rickert, President
Merrill E. Swanson, First Vice President
LeeAnn E. Moss, Academic Vice President
Debe Alvarez, Manager/Education
Cheryl Cooley, Manager/Info Technology

The ASFMRA provides members with the resources, information, and leadership that enable them to provide valuable services to the agricultural community. The focus of the ASFMRA is providing education and networking opportunities for a professional group of members providing farm and ranch management, rural and real property appraising, review appraisal, and agricultural consulting services to the private and public sectors and to the governmental and lending communities.
1900 Members
Founded in 1929
Mailing list available for rent

640 **American Soybean Association**
12125 Woodcrest Executive
Suite 100
Creve Coeur, MO 63141-5009

314-576-1770
800-688-7692
Fax: 314-576-2786
E-Mail: membership@soy.org
Home Page: www.soygrowers.com
Social Media: Facebook, Twitter, LinkedIn

Steve Wellman, Chairman
Danny Murphy, President
Ray Gaesser, 1st Vice President
Steve Censky, CEO
Julie Hawkins, Meeting Planner

The American Soybean Association (ASA) is recognized by the majority of U.S. soybean growers and industry for its vital role as their domestic and international policy advocate. ASA is clearly leading an expanding soybean value-chain, with farmers capturing a growing percentage. ASA's development of influential and effective grower leaders is recognized throughout the agriculture industry.
22000 Members
Founded in 1920

641 **Animal Agriculture Alliance**
2101 Wilson Blvd
Suite 916-13
Arlington, VA 22201

703-562-5160
Fax: 703-524-1921
E-Mail: info@animalagalliance.org
Home Page: www.animalagalliance.org
Social Media: Facebook

Christopher Ashworth, Chairman
Kay Johnson Smith, President and CEO
Emily Metz Meredith, Communications Director
Shakera Daley, Administrative Assistant
Morgan Hawley, Executive Assistant

The Animal Agriculture Alliance, is a broad based coalition of individual farmers, ranchers, producer organizations, suppliers, packer-processors, scientists, veterinarians and retailers. The Alliance with its members are interested in helping consumers better understand the role animal agriculture plays in providing a safe, abundant food supply to a hungry world.
3000 Members
Founded in 1987

642 **Aquatic Plant Management Society**
PO Box 821265
Vicksburg, MS 39182-1265

FAX 601-634-5502
E-Mail: dpetty@ndrsite.com
Home Page: www.apms.org
Social Media: Facebook, LinkedIn, Bloggr

Mike Netherland, President
Rob Richardson, Vice-President
Jeff Schardt, Secretary
Jason Ferrell, Editor
Sherry Whitaker, Treasurer

The Aquatic Plant Management Society, Inc. is an international organization of scientists, educators, students, commercial pesticide applicators, administrators, and concerned individuals interested in the management and study of aquatic plants. The Aquatic Plant Management Society (APMS) strives to promote environmental stewardship through scientific innovation and development of technology related to integrated plant management in aquatic and riparian systems.
Founded in 1961

643 **Association for Arid Lands Studies**
601 Indiana Avenue
PO Box 45004
Lubbock, TX 79409-5004

806-742-3667
Fax: 806-742-1286
E-Mail: gay.riggan@ttu.edu
Home Page: www.iaff.ttu.edu
Social Media: Facebook

Tibor Nagy, VP
Dr. A C Correa, International Director/ICASALS
Bob Crosier, Director
Dawn Cepica, International Faculty Counselor
Stephanie Cloninger, Special Projects Coordinator

To promote the university's special mission of the interdisciplinary study of arid and semi-arid environments and the human relationship to these environments from an international perspective.
200 Members
Founded in 1977

644 **Association of American Feed Control Officials**
1800 South Oak Street
Suite 100
Champaign, IL 61820-6974

217-356-4221
Fax: 217-398-4119
E-Mail: aafco@aafco.org
Home Page: www.aafco.org
Social Media: Facebook

Tim Darden, President
Doug Lueders, President Elect
Ali Kashani, Secretary/Treasurer
Mark LeBlanc, Senior Director
Ken Bowers, Junior Director

The Association of American Feed Control Officials (AAFCO) is a voluntary membership association of local, state and federal agencies charged by law to regulate the sale and distribution of animal feeds and animal drug remedies.Although AAFCO has no regulatory authority, the Association provides a forum for the membership and industry representation to achieve two main goals: Ensure consumer protection and safeguarding the health of animals and humans.
Founded in 1909

645 **Association of American Seed Control Officials**
Utah Department of Agriculture
350 N Redwood Road
PO Box 146500
Salt Lake City, UT 84114-6500

801-848-8543
Fax: 801-538-7189

E-Mail: stburningham@utah.gov
Home Page: www.seedcontrol.org

John Heaton, President
Steve Malone, First Vice President
Jim Drews, Second Vice President
Greg Helmbrecht, Treasurer
Larry Nees, Secretary

The Association of American Seed Control Officials is an organization of seed regulatory officials from the United States and Canada. The members meet to discuss mutual concerns of seed law enforcement, to be updated on new developments in the seed industry, and to update the Recommended Uniform State Seed Law which the organization developed and maintains as model law.
Founded in 1949

646 **Association of Equipment Manufacturers**
6737 W Washington Street
Suite 2400
Milwaukee, WI 53214-5647

414-272-0943
Fax: 414-272-1170
E-Mail: aem@aem.org
Home Page: www.aem.org
Social Media: Twitter

Stuart L. Levenick, Chairman
Nick Yaksich, Vice President, Government
Megan Tanel, Vice President, Exhibitions
Anne Forristall Luke, Vice President, Political & Public
Al Cervero, Vice President, Marketing

AEM is a trade association that provides services on a global basis for companies that manufacture equipment, products and services used worldwide in the following industries: Agriculture, Construction, Forestry, Mining and Utility. AEM's membership represents 200+ product lines.
850 Members
Founded in 1946

647 **Association of Equipment Manufacturers**
6737 W Washington St
Suite 2400
Milwaukee, WI 53214-5647

414-272-0943
866-236-0442
Fax: 414-272-1170
E-Mail: aem@aem.org
Home Page: www.aem.org
Social Media: Facebook, Twitter, LinkedIn, StumbleUpon, Google+

Richard A. Patek, Chairman
Dennis Slater, President
Anne Forristall Luke, Vice President
John Nowak, Chief Financial Officer
Judy Gaus, Senior Director, Human Resources

A trade association that provides services on a global basis for companies that manufacture equipment, products and services used worldwide in the following industries: Agriculture, Construction, Forestry, Mining and Utility. AEM's membership and represents 200+ product lines.
850 Members
Founded in 1894

648 **Bio-Dynamic Farming and Gardening Association**
1661 North Water Street
Sute 307
Milwaukee, WI 53202

262-649-9212
Fax: 262-659-9213
Fax: new
E-Mail: info@biodynamics.com
Home Page: www.biodynamics.com

Jean-Paul Courtens, President
Janet Gamble, Secretary
Steffen Schneider, Treasurer

The Bio-Dynamic Farming and Gardeing Association (BDA) is an association of individuals and organizations in North America who are committed to the transformation of the whole food system.

649 **Biodynamic Farming and Gardening Association**
1661 N Water Street
Suite 307
Milwaukee, WI 53202

262-649-9212
Fax: 262-649-9213
E-Mail: info@biodynamics.com
Home Page: www.biodynamics.com
Social Media: Facebook

Jean-Paul Courtens, President
Thea Maria Carlson, Director of Programs
Robert Karp, Executive Director
Jessica St. John, Director of Operations
Sarah Weber, Research Program Coordinator

The Biodynamic Farming and Gardening Association (BDA) is an association of individuals and organizations in North America who are committed to the transformation of the whole food system, from farm to table, and who draw inspiration from the spiritual-scientific insights of Rudolf Steiner. Biodynamics is a worldwide movement for the renewal of agriculture based on an understanding of the spiritual forces at work in nature and in human social life.
Founded in 1938

650 **Cape Cod Cranberry Growers' Association**
1 Carver Square Boulevard
PO Box 97
Carver, MA 02330

508-866-7878
Fax: 508-866-4220
E-Mail: info@cranberries.org
Home Page: www.cranberries.org
Social Media: Facebook

Brad Morse, President
Gary Garretson, 1st Vice President
Keith Mann, 2nd Vice President
Paul Kindinger, Executive Director
Henry Gillet, Jr,, Government Affairs Director

Promotes the success of US and Canadian cranberry growers through health, agricultural and environmental stewardship research and education.
Founded in 1888

651 **Committee on Organic and Sustainable Agriculture**
5585 Guilford Road
Madison, WI 53711-5801
608-273-8080
Fax: 608-273-2021
Home Page: www.cosagroup.org
Social Media: Facebook, Twitter, LinkedIn

Ann-Marie Fortuna, Chair

Develops programming for members and divisions interested in sustainable and organic agriculture for the Societies' annual meeting; obtain input and develop recommendations on ways to better serve members interested in sustainable and organic agriculture beyond the activities ata the annual meeting
Founded in 2003

652 **Communicating for AMERICA**
112 E Lincoln Avenue
PO Box 677
Fergus Falls, MN 56537

218-739-3241
800-432-3276
Fax: 218-739-3832
E-Mail: memberbenefits@cainc.org
Home Page: www.communicatingforamerica.org

Milt Smedsrud, Chairman
Patty Strickland, President/ Chief Operations Officer
Stephen Rufer, Vice President/General Counsel
Ben Shierer, Vice President of Government Rel
David Ramey, Owner

Strives to promote health, well-being and advancement of people in agriculture and agribusiness.
40M Members
Founded in 1972

653 **Community Alliance with Family Farmers**
36355 Russell Boulevard
PO Box 363
Davis, CA 95616

530-756-8518
800-892-3832
Fax: 530-756-7857
E-Mail: info@caff.org
Home Page: www.caff.org
Social Media: Facebook, Twitter, YouTube, Flickr

Carol Presley, Board Chair
Pete Price, Vice President
Diane Del Signore, Executive Director
Diana Aberella, Regional Food System Director
Bob Corshen, Farm to Market Director

Mission is to build a movement of rural and urban people to foster family-scale agriculture that cares for the land, sustains local economies and promotes social justice.
Cost: $47.95
Founded in 1978

654 **Corn Refiners Association**
1701 Pennsylvania Ave NW
Suite 950
Washington, DC 20006-5806

202-331-1634
Fax: 202-331-2054
E-Mail: aerickson@corn.org
Home Page: www.corn.org
Social Media: Facebook, Twitter, LinkedIn, StumbleUpon, Google+, Pinterest

Audrae Erickson, President
Thomas D Malkoski, Vice Chairman of the Board
J Patrick Mohan, Treasurer

Supports carbohydrate research programs through grants to colleges, government laboratories and private research centers.
8 Members
Founded in 1913

655 **Council for Agricultural Science and Technology**
4420 Lincoln Way
Ames, IA 50014-3447

515-292-2125
Fax: 515-292-4512
E-Mail: cast@cast-science.org
Home Page: www.cast-science.org
Social Media: Facebook, Twitter, LinkedIn, YouTube, Blogspot, Schooltube

Phillip Stahlman, President
Linda M. Chimenti, Executive Vice President
Dan Gogerty, Managing Communications

Editor
Carol Gostele, Managing Scientific Editor
Melissa Sly, Director of Council Operations

Assembles, interprets and communicates science based information regionally, nationally and internationally on food, fiber, agriculture, natural resources, and related societal and environmental issues.
2000+ Members
Founded in 1972

656 **Crop Insurance and Reinsurance Bureau Inc.**
201 Massachusetts Avenue, NE
Suite C5
Washington, DC 20002

202-544-0067
Fax: 202-330-5255
E-Mail: mtorrey@cropinsurance.org
Home Page: www.cropinsurance.org

Greg Mills, Chairman
Mike Torrey, Executive Vice President
Tara Smith, Federal Affairs Vice President
Sarah Hubbart, Director of Communications
Stephanie Butler, Director of Operations

The Crop Insurance Research Bureau is a national trade association made up of insurance providers and related organizations that provide a variety of insurance products to farmers. CIRB companies are big and small and offer private hail/fire coverage on growing crops, as well as participate in the federal crop insurance program which offers a greater variety of subsidized insurance products from yield based coverages to revenue products.
Founded in 1964

657 **Crop Science Society of America**
5585 Guilford Road
Madison, WI 53711-1086

608-273-8086
Fax: 608-273-2021
E-Mail: headquarters@crops.org
Home Page: www.agronomy.org
Social Media: Facebook, Twitter, LinkedIn

Ellen Bergsfeld, Chief Executive Officer
Wes Meixelsperger, Chief Financial Officer
Sara Uttech, Senior Manager - Governance
Alexander Barton, Director of Business Development
Luther Smith, Director of Certification Programs

Seeks to advance research, extension, and teaching of all basic and applied phases of the crop sciences.
4700 Members
Founded in 1955

658 **CropLife America**
1156 15th St NW
Suite 400
Washington, DC 20005-1752

202-296-1585
Fax: 202-463-0474
E-Mail: webmaster@croplifeamerica.org
Home Page: www.croplifeamerica.org
Social Media: Facebook, Twitter, LinkedIn, YouTube, RSS Feeds

Jay Vroom, President and CEO
Beau Greenwood, Executive Vice President of Gov
Barbara Glenn, Vice President, Science
Rachel G. Lattimore, Senior Vice President
Douglas T. Nelson, Senior Advisor for Trade

A trade association of the manufacturers, formulators, and distributors of agricultural crop protection, pest control, and biotechnology products. Membership is composed of companies that produce, sell and distribute virtually all the active ingredients used in crop protection chemicals.
86 Members
Founded in 1933

659 **Equipment Marketing & Distribution Association (EMDA)**
PO Box 1347
Iowa City, IA 52244

319-354-5156
Fax: 319-354-5157
Home Page: www.emda.net

Patricia A Collins, Executive VP

EMDA members are devoted to the marketing of specialized eqipment: agricultural, outdoor power, light industrial, forestry, irrigation, turf and grounds maintenance, lawn and garden and parts/components for those segments of industry.
250 Members
Founded in 1945

660 **Farm Equipment Manufacturers Association**
1000 Executive Parkway Dr
Suite 100
St Louis, MO 63141-6369

314-878-2304
Fax: 314-732-1480
E-Mail: info@farmequip.org
Home Page: www.farmequip.org

Andrew Cummings, President
Marc McConnell, 1st Vice President
Mike Kloster, 2nd Vice President
Vernon Schmidt, Executive Vice President
Hannah Hamontree, Communications Director

An information gathering and distributing organization for farm equipment manufacturers and suppliers. The Farm Equipment Manufacturers Association shall provide industry leadership to enhance business opportunities and profitability to the Membership by providing a forum for marketing shortline equipment through networking, communications, and technology, and a forum for purchasing materials and services required by the Members.
730+ Members
Founded in 1950

661 **Farm Foundation**
1301 W 22nd St
Suite 615
Oak Brook, IL 60523-2197

630 571 9393
Fax: 630-571-9580
Home Page: www.farmfoundation.org
Social Media: Facebook, Twitter, YouTube, RSS Feeds, Blogger

Jay Armstrong, Chairman
Neilson C. Conklin, President
Sheldon R. Jones, Vice President
Mary Thompson, Vice President, Communications
Tim Brennan, Director of Development

A publicly supported nonprofit organization working to improve the economic health and social well-being of US agriculture, the food system and rural people by helping private and public sector decision makers identify and understand forces that will shape the future.
Founded in 1993

662 **Fertilizer Institute**
425 Third Street, SW
Suite 950
Washington, DC 20024

202-962-0490
Fax: 202-962-0577
E-Mail: information@tfi.org
Home Page: www.tfi.org
Social Media: Facebook, Twitter, LinkedIn, Google+

Chris Jahn, President

Pamela Guffain, Vice President, Member Services
Carol Dorrough, Director, Administration & Finance
Melinda Giesler, Manager/Economic Services
Pamela D Guffain, Vice President, Member Services

TFI is the leading voice in the fertilizer industry, representing the public policy, communication and statistical needs of producers, manufacturers, retailers and transporters of fertilizer. Issues of interest to TFI members include security, international trade, energy, transportation, the environment, worker health and safety, farm bill and conservation programs to promote the use of enhanced efficiency fertilizer.
325 Members
Founded in 1970

663 **Foundation for Agronomic Research**
107 S State St
Suite 300
Monticello, IL 61856-1968

605-692-6280
E-Mail: pfixen@ipni.net
Home Page: www.farmresearch.com

Harold Reetz, President
Dr Paul Fixen, Senior Vice President

The Foundation for Agronomic Research (FAR) is a non-profit (501(c)(3) research and education foundation, created in 1980 by the Board of Directors of the Potash & Phosphate Institute (PPI), now the International Plant Nutrition Institute (IPNI), to expand its research efforts beyond that possible with PPI's resources and mandate. The mission of FAR is to improve the economic vigor and sustainability of agriculture in N.A. and around the world, while protecting and enhancing the environment.
Founded in 1980

664 **Fresh Produce Association of the Americas**
590 East Frontage Road
PO Box 848
Nogales, AZ 85628

520-287-2707
Fax: 520-287-2948
E-Mail: info@freshfrommexico.com
Home Page: www.freshfrommexico.com

Alejandro Canelos, Chairman
Lance Jungmeyer, President
Amy Adams, Public Affairs Director
Marlene Lopez, Events Director
Allison Moore, Director of Legislative Regulation

The Fresh Produce Association of the Americas and its members help to ensure North America's uninterrupted access to fresh, high-quality, healthy and delicious Mexican-grown fruits and vegetables. The FPAA is the leading agent of produce trade at the U.S.-Mexico border and across the country.
125+ Members
Founded in 1944

665 Fresh Produce and Floral Council
16700 Valley View Ave
Suite 130
La Mirada, CA 90638-5844

714-739-0177
Fax: 714-739-0226
E-Mail: info@fpfc.org
Home Page: www.fpfc.org

Mike Casazza, Chairman
Carissa Mace, President
Amy Wun, Manager Member Programs
Angela Steier, Events and Maketing Consultant
Brad Martin, Secretary/Treasurer

Promotes through communication and education, fresh fruit, vegetable and floral products. Acts as a trade organization providing an environment for better communication within the industry.
600+ Members
Founded in 1965

666 Herb Growing and Marketing Network
PO Box 245
Silver Springs, PA 17575-0245

717-393-3295
Fax: 717-393-9261
E-Mail: herbworld@aol.com
Home Page: www.herbworld.com

Maureen Rogers, Director

The Herb Growing & Marketing Network is the largest trade association for the herb industry. We are an information service. We have a library of over 3000 books, subscribe to over 200 periodicals, monitor blogs of all types and search the Web looking for resources and research on the herb industry that we can pass on to our members.
Cost: $48.00
1000 Members
Founded in 1990

667 Holstein Association USA
1 Holstein Place
PO Box 808
Brattleboro, VT 05302-0808
802-254-4551
800-952-5200
Fax: 802-254-8251
E-Mail: info@holstein.com
Home Page: www.holsteinusa.com
Social Media: Facebook, Twitter, You Tube

John Meyer, CEO
Lisa Perrin, Marketing

Holstein Association USA maintains records on over 22 million Registered Holsteinsr, collecting and analyzing production, type and genetic data to provide useable information that enables dairy producers to improve their businesses by breeding better cows. The Holstein Association works to help dairy producers recognize the full potential of their herds.
30000 Members
Founded in 1631

668 International Association of Fairs and Expositions
3043 E Cairo Street
PO Box 985
Springfield, MO 65802

417-862-5771
800-516-0313
Fax: 417-862-0156
E-Mail: iafe@fairsandexpos.com
Home Page: www.fairsandexpos.com
Social Media: Facebook, Twitter

Jim Tucker, President/CEO
Steve Siever, Director of Trade Shows, Membership
Max Willis, Max Willis, CFO/COO
Missy McCormack, Design and Production Manager
Rebekah Lee, Managing Editor - Fairs & Expos

The International Association of Fairs and Expositions (IAFE) is a voluntary, non-profit corporation whose members provide services and products that promote the overall development and improvement of fairs, shows, expositions, and allied fields. Mission is to lead in representing and facilitating the evolving interests of agricultural fairs, exhibitions and show associations.
1300 Members
Founded in 1885

669 International Association of Operative Millers
10100 West 87th Street
Suite 306
Overland Park, KS 66212

913-338-3377
Fax: 913-338-3553
E-Mail: info@iaom.info
Home Page: www.iaom.info
Social Media: Facebook, Twitter, LinkedIn

Joel Hoffa, President
Damon Sidles, Vice President
Melinda Farris, Executive Vice President
Shannon Henson, Director of Meetings and Exhibits
Carol Shankel, Director of Professional Dev

The International Association of Operative Millers (IAOM) is comprised of grain millers and allied trades representatives devoted to the advancement of education and training opportunities in the grain milling industries. Among its members, IAOM promotes a spirit of fellowship and cooperation, enhances their proficiency, and advances their interests in industry activities.
1500 Members
Founded in 1896

670 International Maple Syrup Institute
5072 Rock St.
RR#4
Spencerville, ON KOE 1XO

860-974-1235
Fax: 802-868-5445
E-Mail: agrofor@ripnet.com
Home Page: www.internationalmaplesyrupinstitute.com

Dave Chapeskie, Executive Director
Alfred Bolduc, Board Member
Roger Palmer, Board Member
Tim Perkins, Advisor
Steve Childs, Advisor

The International Maple Syrup Institute (IMSI) was founded to promote and protect pure maple syrup and other pure maple products. The organization provides an important international framework for communication, information exchange and cooperation on a variety of issues related to the production, sale and marketing of pure maple syrup. In addition, the Institute has been a strong monitor for adulteration around the world, protecting the integrity of maple products.
15M Members
Founded in 1975

671 International Weed Science Society
University of Arkansas
1366 W. Altheimer Drive
Fayetteville, AR 72704

479-575-3984
Fax: 479-575-3975
E-Mail: secretary@iwss.info
Home Page: www.iwss.info

Dr Albert Fischer, President
Dr Nilda Burgos, Vice President
Dr Frank Dayan, Secretary/Treasurer
Dr Baruch Rubin, Past President
Dr Bernal Valverde, Regional Coordinator

The International Weed Science Society (IWSS) was formed in 1975, by individuals from Europe, North America, South America, and the Asian-Pacific area, to deal with global weed science issues. The IWSS is a worldwide scientific organization, open to all who are interested in weeds and their control. The formation of IWSS was promoted actively by the six existing regional weed science societies. The purpose of IWSS is to supplement and complement their vital role.

672 Irrigation Association
6540 Arlington Blvd
Falls Church, VA 22042-6638

703-536-7080
Fax: 703-536-7019
E-Mail: info@irrigation.org
Home Page: www.irrigation.org

Robert D. Dobson, President
Aric J. Olson, Vice President
Deborah M. Hamlin, Executive Director
Chad Forcey, State Affairs Director
Rebecca J. Bayless, Finance Director

The Irrigation Association is the leading membership organization for irrigation equipment and system manufacturers, dealers distributors, designers, consultants, contractors and end users.
1600 Members
Founded in 1949

673 Livestock Marketing Association
10510 NW Ambassador Drive
Kansas City, MO 64153-1278

816-891-0502
800-821-2048
Fax: 816-891-0552
E-Mail: lmainfo@lmaweb.com
Home Page: www.lmaweb.com
Social Media: Facebook, Twitter

David Macedo, Chairman of the Board
Tim Starks, President
Dan Harris, VP
Mark Mackey, CEO
Vincent Nowak, CFO

We are committed to the support and protection of the local livestock auction markets. Auctions are a vital part of the livestock industry, serving producers and assuring a fair, competitive price through the auction method of selling.
800 Members
Founded in 1947

674 Maryland and Virginia Milk Producers Cooperative
1985 Isaac Newton Square West
Reston, VA 20190-5094

703-742-6800
Fax: 703-742-7459
Home Page: www.mdvamilk.com

Richard Mosemann, Second VP
Dwayne Meyers, NC President

Known for being a leader in the dairy industry, the Eastern Milk Producers Cooperative has a reputation for integrity, service and high quality products.
Founded in 1920

675 Midwest Equipment Dealers Association
5330 Wall St
Suite 100
Madison, WI 53718-7929

608-240-4700
Fax: 608-240-2069

E-Mail: gmanke@medaassn.com
Home Page: www.medaassn.com

Gary W. Manke, Executive Vice President, CEO
Antoniewicz Gaugert, Wisconsin & Illinois Legal Counsel
Julie Roisum, Executive Assistant
Jerry Deblaey, Vice President

Our mission is to promote the farm, industrial, outdoor power equipment, dairy and farmstead mechanization industry and to provide services that will assist Association members in becoming more profitable and better equipped to operate in today's business environment.
Founded in 1991

676 NCBA CLUSA

1401 New York Ave NW
Suite 1100
Washington, DC 20005-2160

202-638-6222
Fax: 202-638-1374
E-Mail: ncba@ncba.coop
Home Page: www.ncba.coop
Social Media: Facebook, Twitter, YouTube, Instagram

Wilson Beebe, Chair
Michael Beall, President & Chief Executive Officer
Patricia Brownell Sterner, Chief Operating Officer, NCBA
Amy Coughenour Betancourt, Chief Operating Officer
Anthony La Creta, Chief Financial and Administrative

Leading US organization strengthening the cooperative form of business to empower people and improve quality of life worldwide. To make cooperatives a strong, distinct and unified sector, recognized by the American public. Our member co-ops operate in the areas including, agricultural supply and marketing, children, energy, food distribution, healthcare and housing.
1800 Members
Founded in 1916

677 National 4-H Council

7100 Connecticut Ave
Chevy Chase, MD 20815-4934

301-961-2800
Fax: 301-961-2894
E-Mail: info@fourhcouncil.edu
Home Page: www.4-h.org
Social Media: Facebook, Twitter, google+, Pinterest

Donald Floyd, President/CEO
Jennifer Sirangelo, EVP/COO
Andy Ferrin, Senior Vice President
Paul Koehler, Senior Vice President
Jill Bramble, Senior Vice President

Works to advance the 4-H youth development movement, building a world in which youth and adults learn, grow, and work together as catalysts for positive change. National 4-H Council partners with the Cooperative Extension System and other organizations to provide technical support and training, develop curricula, create model programs and promote positive youth development to fulfill its mission. National 4-H Council also manages the National 4-H Conference.
7M Members
Founded in 1902

678 National Agri-Marketing Association

11020 King St
Suite 205
Overland Park, KS 66210-1201

913-491-6500
Fax: 913-491-6502
E-Mail: agrimktg@nama.org
Home Page: www.nama.org
Social Media: Facebook, Twitter, LinkedIn, Flicker, You Tube

Jennifer Pickett, CEO/EVP
Debbie Brummel, Manager/Chapter Services/Membership
Janae Prewitt, Information Services Coordinator
Jan Cichello, Manager, Programs & Information
Sherry Pfaff, Manager of Accounting Services

Marketing and communication suppliers, including trade publications, radio and television broadcast sales organizations, premium/incentive manufacturers, printers, marketing research firms, photographers and related professionals.
3500 Members
Founded in 1957

679 National Agricultural Aviation Association

1440 Duke Street
Alexandria, VA 22314

202-546-5722
Fax: 202-546-5726
E-Mail: information@agaviation.org
Home Page: www.agaviation.org
Social Media: Facebook

Dana Ness, President
Rick Boardman, Vice President
Andrew D. Moore, Executive Director
Jay Calleja, Manager of Communications
Lindsay Barber, Manager of Meetings, Marketing

NAAA supports the interests of small business owners and pilots licensed as professional commercial aerial applicators who use aircraft to enhance food, fiber and bio-fuel production, protect forestry and control health-threatening pests. NAAA provides networking, educational, government relations, public relations, recruiting and informational services to its members.
1800 Members
Founded in 1966

680 National Alliance of Independent Crop Consultants

349 E Nolley Dr
Collierville, TN 38017-3538

901-861-0511
Fax: 901-861-0512
E-Mail: AllisonJones@NAICC.org
Home Page: www.naicc.org

James E. Todd, President
Gary Coukell, President Elect
Marla Siruta, Secretary
Debra Keenan, Treasurer
Dennis Hettermann, Past President

The national society of agricultural professionals who provide research and advisory services. Memebers comprise 40 states and several foreign countries, and have expertise in the production of most crops grown around the world.
500+ Members
Founded in 1978

681 National Association of Agricultural Educators (NAAE)

300 Garrigus Building
University of Kentucky
Lexington, KY 40546-0215

859-257-2224
800-509-0204
Fax: 859-323-3919
E-Mail: jay_jackman@ffa.org
Home Page: www.naae.org

Farrah Johnson, President
Wm. Jay Jackman, Executive Director
Alissa Smith, Associate Executive Director
Savannah Robin, Meeting Planner & Advocacy
Julie Fritsch, Communications and Marketing

Professionals providing agricultural education for the global community through visionary leadership, advocacy and service. NAAE seeks to advance agricultural education and promote the professional interests and growth of agriculture teachers as well as recruit and prepare students who have a desire to teach agriculture.
7600 Members
Founded in 1948

682 National Association of Agricultural Fairs

Tennessee Department of Agriculture
440 Hogan Road
PO Box 40627
Nashville, TN 37220

615-837-5160
800-342-8206
Fax: 615-837-5194
E-Mail: pick.tn@tn.gov
Home Page: www.picktnproducts.org
Social Media: Facebook, Twitter

Ed Harlan, Agribusiness Coordinator
Dan Strasser, Director of Market Development
Nelson Owen, Livestock Grading/Market News

US and Canadian representatives of state/provincial agencies that are responsible for the support of educational and agricultural fairs.
35 Members
Founded in 1966

683 National Association of Animal Breeders

PO Box 1033
Columbia, MO 65205-1033

573-445-4406
Fax: 573-446-2279
E-Mail: naab-css@naab-css.org
Home Page: www.naab-css.org

Dr Charles Brown II, Chairman
Dr Gordon Doak, Secretary - Treasurer - President
Dr Roger Weigle, Vice Chairman
Jere R Mitchell, Service Director
Dr Roger Weigle, Vice Chairman

The purpose of the National Association of Animal Breeders (NAAB) as defined by its By-Laws is to unite those individuals and organizations engaged in the artificial insemination of cattle and other livestock into an affiliated federation operating under self-imposed standards of performance and to conduct and promote the mutual interest and ideals of its members.
20 Members
Founded in 1946

684 National Association of County Agricultural Agents

6584 W Duroc Road
Maroa, IL 61756

217-794-3700
Fax: 217-794-5901
E-Mail: exec-dir@nacaa.com
Home Page: www.nacaa.com
Social Media: Facebook, Twitter

Paul Craig, President
Henry Dorough, President-Elect
Mike Hogan, Vice President
Richard Fechter, Secretary
Parman Green, Treasurer

The NACAA strives to: Advance the professional status of Extension agents and specialists with agriculture-related Extension appointments. Encourage, promote, and provide professional improvement for all members. Provide for the exchange of ideas, methods, and techniques. Represent professional interests of members in matters of public

policy and affairs. Promote public confidence, esteem, and respect for Cooperative Extension. Recognize excellence in Cooperative Extension nationwide.
3850 Members
Founded in 1917
Mailing list available for rent: 3500 names at $500 per M

685 **National Association of Extension 4-H Agents**
University of Georgia
20423 State Road 7
Suite F6-491
Boca Raton, FL 33498

561-477-8100
Fax: 561-910-0896
E-Mail: jody@nae4ha.com
Home Page: www.nae4ha.org
Social Media: Facebook

Pam Van Horn, President
Shawn Tiede, Vice President for Finance
Thomas Manske, Vice President for Professional Dev
Melissa Henry, Vice President for Marketing
Vernon Parent, Policy & Resolutions Committee

Designed to meet the needs of youth development professionals by maximizing the use of technology, provide progressive levels of professional development, elevate the quality of youth development work through scholarship, research and practice, advocate for the 4-H youth development profession.
3600 Members
Founded in 1946

686 **National Association of State Departments of Agriculture**
4350 North Fairfax Drive
#910
Arlington, VA 22203

202-296-9680
Fax: 703-880-0509
E-Mail: nasda@nasda.org
Home Page: www.nasda.org
Social Media: Facebook, Twitter

Chuck Ross, President
Russell Kokubun, Vice President
Greg Ibach, Second Vice President
DeWitt Ashby, Director, Trade Shows & Grants
Carol Black, Project Manager, Pesticide Workers

Represents the state departments of agriculture in the development, implementation and communication of sound public policy and programs which support and promote the American agricultural industry, while protecting consumers and the environment.
Founded in 1915

687 **National Association of Wheat Growers**
415 2nd Street NE
Suite 300
Washington, DC 20002-4993

202-547-7800
Fax: 202-546-2638
E-Mail: wheatworld@wheatworld.org
Home Page: www.wheatworld.org
Social Media: Facebook, Twitter, RSS Feed, Youtube

Bling Von Bergen, President
Paul Penner, First Vice President
Brett Blankenship, Second Vice President
Jim Palmer, Chief Executive Officer
Hugh Whaley, Director of Corporate Relations

Nonprofit partnership of US wheat growers, by combining their strengths, voices and ideas are working to ensure a better future for themselves, their industry and the general public. NAWG's mission statement is: NAWG unites U.S. wheat growers to create beneficial policies for wheat growers; effective relationships with industry; and profitable opportunities through research and technology.
Founded in 1950

688 **National Bison Association**
8690 Wolff Court
Suite 200
Westminster, CO 80031

303-292-2833
Fax: 303-845-9081
E-Mail: david@bisoncentral.com
Home Page: www.bisoncentral.com

Peter Cook, President
Bruce Anderson, Vice President
Dave Carter, Executive Director
Jim Matheson, Assistant Director
Marilyn Wentz, Bison World Editor

Formed to promote the production, marketing and preservation of bison. The mission of the National Bison Association is to bring together stakeholders to celebrate the heritage of American bison/buffalo, to educate, and to create a sustainable future for our industry.
2400 Members
Founded in 1995

689 **National Christmas Tree Association**
16020 Swingley Ridge Rd
Suite 300
Chesterfield, MO 63017-6030

636-449-5070
Fax: 636-449-5051
E-Mail: info@realchristmastrees.org
Home Page: www.realchristmastrees.org
Social Media: Facebook, Twitter, YouTube, Blogger

Cline Church, President
Tom Dull, Vice President
Bob Schaefer, Vice President
Blake Rafeld, President-Elect and Vice President
Dustin McKissen, Executive Director

The National Christmas Tree Association (NCTA) is the national trade association representing the Christmas tree industry. NCTA represents more than 700 active member farms, 29 state and regional associations, and more than 4,000 affiliated businesses that grow and sell Christmas trees or provide related supplies and services.
700 Members
Founded in 1955
Mailing list available for rent: 5100 names

690 **National Cotton Council of America**
National Cotton Council of America
PO Box 2995
7193 Goodlett Farms Pkwy
Cordova, TN 38088-2995

901-274-9030
Fax: 901-725-0510
Home Page: www.cotton.org

James F. Dodson, Chairman
Mark D. Lange, President & Chief Executive Officer
Dr. Gary Adams, VP, Economy and Policy Analysis
Dr Bill Norman, VP, Technical Services
Craig Brown, VP Producer Affairs

The National Cotton Council is a unifying force of the U.S. cotton industry, bringing together representatives from the seven industry segments in the 17 cotton-producing states of the Cotton Belt to work out common problems and develop programs of mutual benefit.
35 Members

691 **National Cottonseed Products Association**
866 Willow Tree Circle
Cordova, TN 38018-6376

901-682-0800
Fax: 901-682-2856
E-Mail: info@cottonseed.com
Home Page: www.cottonseed.com

Ben Morgan, Executive Vice President
Bobby Crum, Vice President
Sandi Stine, Treasurer

National association of cottonseed products. NCPA is an organization of firms and individuals engaged in the processing of cottonseed and the marketing of cottonseed products, as well as cottonseed. These include oil mills, refiners, product dealers and product brokers.
200 Members
Founded in 1929

692 **National Council of Agricultural Employers**
8233 Old Courthouse Road
Suite 200
Vienna, VA 22182

703-790-9039
Fax: 202-728-0303
E-Mail: info@ncaeonline.org
Home Page: www.ncaeonline.org

Luawanna Hallstrom, President
Fred Leitz, Eastern Vice President
Ray Prescott, Western Vice President
Joe Young, Treasurer
Bryan Little, Secretary

NCAE represents Agricultural Employer interests before Congress and Regulatory/Administrative bodies such as the Departments of Labor, Homeland Security, Agriculture, the Occupational Safety and Health Administration, and the Environmental Protection Agency.
250 Members
Founded in 1964

693 **National Crop Insurance Services**
8900 Indian Creek Pkwy
Suite 600
Overland Park, KS 66210-1567

913-685-2767
Fax: 913-685-3080
E-Mail: webmaster@ag-risk.org
Home Page: www.ag-risk.org
Social Media: Facebook

Dr. Mark D. Lange, President and CEO
A. John Maguire, Senior Vice President
Dr. Gary Adams, Vice President, Economics

NCIS is an association of insurance companies writing insurance for damage by hail, fire and other weather perils to growing crops.
60+ Members
Founded in 1989

694 **National Dairy Herd Information Association**
421 S Nine Mound Round
PO Box 930399
Verona, WI 53593-0399

608-848-6455
Fax: 608-848-7675
E-Mail: dhia@dhia.org
Home Page: www.dhia.org

Dan Sheldon, President
Kent Butters, Vice President
Jay Mattison, CEO/Administrator
Leslie Thoman, Accounting/Bookkeeping
Steven Sievert, Quality Certification Services

The objective is to promote accuracy, credibility and uniformity of DHI records. To represent the DHI system on issues involving other National and International organizations
65M Members

695 **National Farmers Organization**
528 Billy Sunday Road
Suite 100, PO Box 2508
Ames, IA 50010-2508

515-292-2000
800-247-2110
Fax: 866-629-3976
E-Mail: nfo@nfo.org
Home Page: www.nfo.org

Paul Olson, President, Chairman of the Board
Paul Riniker, Vice President
Perry Gainer, Communications Director

National Farmers defines itself by its sophisticated commodity marketing and ag risk management programs and services. Through National Farmers MaximumMarketing, producers market their commodities in pooled groups, and their bank accounts benefit.
30M Members
Founded in 1955

696 **National Farmers Union**
20 F Street NW
Suite 300
Washington, DC 20001

202-554-1600
800-347-1961
Fax: 202-554-1654
Home Page: www.nfu.org
Social Media: Facebook, Twitter, Flickr, Youtube

Roger Johnson, President
Claudia Svarstad, Vice President
Jeff Knudson, Vice President of Operations
Leigh Slayden, VP of Membership
Robert Carlson, VP of International Relations

Farmers Union helped shape national policy, organized cooperative businesses that thrive today, delivered educational programs designed to build rural leaders, and provided farmers and ranchers with opportunities to be at the table.
25000 Members
Founded in 1902

697 **National Fisheries Institute**
7918 Jones Branch Dr
Suite 700
Mc Lean, VA 22102-3319

703-752-8880
Fax: 703-752-7583
E-Mail: contact@nfi.org
Home Page: www.aboutseafood.com
Social Media: Facebook, Twitter, LinkedIn, Pinterest, google+

John Connely, President
Gavin Gibbons, Director, Media Relations

The National Fisheries Institute is a non-profit organization dedicated to education about seafood safety, sustainability, and nutrition. From vessels at sea to your favorite seafood restaurant, our diverse member companies bring delicious fish and shellfish to American families. NFI promotes the US Dietary Guidelines that suggest Americans include fish and shellfish in their diets twice per week for longer, healthier lives.
241 Members
Founded in 1945

698 **National Future Farmers of America Organization**
6060 FFA Drive
P.O. Box 68960
Indianapolis, IN 46278-1370

317-802-4298
800-772-0939
Fax: 317-802-6051
E-Mail: membership@ffa.org
Home Page: www.ffa.org

Steve A. Brown, Board Chair
Brian Walsh, President
Dwight Armstrong, Chief Executive Officer
Joshua Bledsoe, Chief Operating Officer
Vicki Settle, Financial Services Director

Headquarters of the National FFA Organization, the organization's mission is to prepare students for successful careers and a lifetime of informed choices in the global agriculture, food, fiber and natural resources systems.
507M Members
Founded in 1928

699 **National Grain and Feed Association**
1250 I St NW
Suite 1003
Washington, DC 20005-3939

202-289-0873
Fax: 202-289-5388
E-Mail: ngfa@ngfa.org
Home Page: www.ngfa.org
Social Media: Facebook, Twitter, LinkedIn, Flickr

Randall C Gordon, President
Todd E. Kemp, Vice President of Marketing
Charles M. Delacruz, Vice President, General Counsel
David A. Fairfield, Vice President of Feed Services
Heather McElrath, Director of Communications

NGFA is the national trade association of grain elevators, feed and feed ingredient manufacturers, grain and oilseed processors, exporters, livestock and poultry integrators, and firms providing products and services to the industry.

700 **National Grange**
1616 H St NW
Suite 10
Washington, DC 20006-4999

202-628-3507
888-447-2643
Fax: 503-622-0343
Home Page: www.nationalgrange.org
Social Media: Facebook, Twitter, YouTube, RSS Feeds

Ed Luttrell, President/Master
Amanda Brozana, Communications Director
Nicole Palya Wood, Legislative Director
Charlene Shupp Espenshade, Youth and Young Adult Director
Beverley Mitchell, Marketing Coordinator

Promotes general welfare and agriculture through local organizations. Presides over the advancement and promotion of the farming and agriculture industry.
300K Members
Founded in 1867

701 **National Hay Association**
151 Treasure Island Cswy.
Suite 2
St. Petersburg, FL 33706-4734

727-367-9702
800-707-0014
Fax: 727-367-9608
E-Mail: haynha@aol.com
Home Page: www.nationalhay.org
Social Media: Facebook

Ron Bradtmueller, President
Stan Steffen, First Vice President
Larry Jones, Second Vice President
Rollie Bernth, Director
Carl Blackmer, Director

The National Hay Association is made up of people that are involved in the production, sale and transportation of forage products across the United States and the world. As an organization we work for the good of the hay industry through knowledge among members, to follow government legislation. We operate as an independent organization with no commitments or ties to any government groups.
750 Members
Founded in 1895

702 **National Institute for Animal Agriculture**
13570 Meadowgrass Dr
Suite 201
Colorado Springs, CO 80921-3058

719-538-8843
Fax: 719-538-8847
E-Mail: niaa@animalagriculture.org
Home Page: www.animalagriculture.org
Social Media: Facebook, LinkedIn

Annette Whiteford, Chairman of the Board
Katie Ambrose, Chief Operating Officer
Teres Lambert, Director of Communications
Mona Wolverton, Event Coordinator
Saralee Bonham, Administrative Assistant

NIAA is an organization that satisfies your needs, concerns and interests about the animal agriculture industry. NIAA's purpose is quite simple - to provide a source for individuals, organizations, and the entire animal agriculture industry to obtain information, education and solutions for challenges facing animal agriculture.
250 Members

703 **National Oilseed Processors Association**
1300 L St NW
Suite 1020
Washington, DC 20005-4168

202-842-0463
Fax: 202-842-9126
E-Mail: nopa@nopa.org
Home Page: www.nopa.org

Thomas Hammer, President
David J. Hovermale, Executive Vice President
David C. Ailor, Executive Vice President
Kathleen A. Pennington, Office Administrator

NOPA now represents oilseed crushers of soy beans, canola, flaxseed, safflower seed and sunflower seed. NOPA represents twelve (12) regular member firms engaged in the actual processing of oilseeds, and eight (8) associate member firms who are consumers of vegetable oil or oilseed meal, including some refiners.
Founded in 1989

704 **National Onion Association**
822 7th St
Suite 510
Greeley, CO 80631-3941

970-353-5895
Fax: 970-353-5897
E-Mail: kreddin@onions-usa.org
Home Page: www.onions-usa.org
Social Media: Twitter, LinkedIn

Gary Mayfield, President
Shawn Hartley, Vice President
John Rietveld, 2nd Vice President
Wayne Mininger, Executive VP
Kim Reddin, Director of Public & Industry Rel

The National Onion Association (NOA) is the official organization representing growers, shippers, brokers, and commercial representatives of the U.S. onion industry.
500 Members
Founded in 1913
Mailing list available for rent: 600 names

705 **National Pork Producers Council**
122 C Street NW
Suite 875
Washington, DC 20001

202-347-3600
800-937-7675
Fax: 202-347-5265

E-Mail: warnerd@nppc.org
Home Page: www.nppc.org
Social Media: Facebook, Twitter, LinkedIn, Pinterest, Flickr, Swinecast,

Randy Spronk, President
Ron Prestage, Vice President
Neil Dierks, Chief Executive Officer
Pat McGonegle, Vice President, State Relations
Pete Houska, Regional Director of Producer Ser

The National Pork Producers Council conducts public-policy outreach on behalf of its affiliated state associations, enhancing opportunities for the success of U.S. pork producers and other industry stakeholders by establishing the U.S. pork industry as a consistent and responsible supplier of high-quality pork to the domestic and world markets.
44 Members

706 **National Potato Council**
1300 L St NW
Suite 910
Washington, DC 20005-4107

202-682-9456
Fax: 202-682-0333
E-Mail: spudinfo@nationalpotatocouncil.org
Home Page: www.nationalpotatocouncil.org
Social Media: Facebook, Twitter, YouTube

Randy Mullen, President
Randy Hardy, First Vice President
Nels Iverson, Vice President, Finance
Jim Tiede, Vice President, Legislative
Dwayne Weyers, Vice President, Growers

The National Potato Council is the advocate for the economic well-being of U.S. potato growers on federal legislative, regulatory, environmental, and trade issues.
45000 Members
Founded in 1948

707 **National Potato Promotion Board**
4949 S. Syracuse St.
#400
Denver, CO 80237
303-369-7783
Fax: 303-369-7718
E-Mail: info@uspotatoes.com
Home Page: www.uspotatoes.com

Rob Davis, Chairman
Blair Richardson, President & CEO
Diana LeDoux, Vice President, Finance
David Fraser, Vice President, Industry
John Toaspern, Vice President, International

Also known as the US Potato Board. Organized to operate a national marketing program to position potatoes as low calorie, nutritious vegetables and to facilitate market expansion into domestic and export sales.
109 Members
Founded in 1971

708 **National Sunflower Association**
2401 46th Avenue SE
Suite 206
Mandan, ND 58554-4829

701-328-5100
888-718-7033
Fax: 701-328-5101
E-Mail: larryk@sunflowernsa.com
Home Page: www.sunflowernsa.com
Social Media: Facebook, YouTube

John Sandbakken, Executive Director
Tina Mittelsteadt, Business & Office Manager
Lerrene Kroh, Meeting Planner & Advertising Sales

Trade association for the sunflower industry.
20000 Members
Founded in 1981
Printed in 4 colors on glossy stock

709 **National Turkey Federation**
1225 New York Avenue
Suite 400
Washington, DC 20005
202-898-0100
Fax: 202-898-0203
E-Mail: info@turkeyfed.org
Home Page: www.eatturkey.com
Social Media: Facebook, Twitter, YouTube, Pinterest

John Burkel, Chairman
Joel Brandenberger, President
Damon Wells, Vice President, Gov Relations
Lisa Wallenda Picard, Vice President, Sceintific Reg

(NTF) is the national Advocate for all segments of the $8 billion turkey industry, providing services and conducting activities that increase demand for its members' products. The federation also protects and enhances its members' ability to effectively and profitably provide wholesome, high quality, nutritious turkey products.
264 Members
Founded in 1939

710 **National Young Farmer Educational Association**
PO Box 20326
Montgomery, AL 36120

334-546-9951
888-332-2668
Fax: 334-213-0421
E-Mail: nyfea-main@nyfea.org
Home Page: www.nyfea.org
Social Media: Facebook, Twitter, Flickr

Allen Tyler, President
Tim Kelley, President-Elect
Denise Sanner, Secretary

To promote the personal and professional growth of all people involved in agriculture.

711 **Nebraska Alfalfa Dehydrators Association**
8810 Craig Dr
Overland Park, KS 66212-2916

913-648-6800
Fax: 913-648-2648
E-Mail: wcobbkc@sbcglobal.net
Home Page: www.nebada.org

John Montgomery, President

Information for the processors and suppliers in the alfalfa industry.
Founded in 1941

712 **North American Farm Show Council**
590 Woody Hayes Drive
Columbus, OH 43210

614-292-4278
Fax: 614-292-9448
E-Mail: gamble.19@osu.edu
Home Page: fsc.cfaes.ohio-state.edu/

Doug Wagner, President
Dennis Alford, First Vice President
Chip Blalock, Second Vice President
Chuck Gamble, Secretary-Treasurer

Members are agriculture trade show sponsors and suppliers of services to these shows. Provides members with education, communication and evaluation. Provides the best possible marketing showcase for exhibitors and related products to the farmer/rancher/producer customer.
37 Members
Founded in 1972

713 **North American Millers' Association**
600 Maryland Ave SW
Suite 825 W
Washington, DC 20024

202-484-2200
Fax: 202-488-7416
E-Mail: generalinfo@namamillers.org
Home Page: www.namamillers.org

ÿJames M Meyer, Chairman
James A McCarthy, President and CEO
James A Blair, Vice President
Sherriÿ Lehman, Director of Government Relations

Trade association representing the wheat, corn, oat and rye milling industry. NAMA members operate one hundred and seventy mills in thirty-eight states and Canada. Their aggregate production of more than one hundred and sixty million pounds per day is approximately ninety-five percent of the industry capacity in the U.S.
45 Members
Founded in 1902

714 **Northeastern Weed Science Society**
PO box 307
Fredericksburg, PA 17206

81 -57 -406
E-Mail: northeasternweedscience@hotmail.com
Home Page: www.newss.org

William S Curran, President
Renee J Keese, Vice President
Brian S Manley, Secretary/Treasurer
Brent A Lockey, Public Relations Representative

Serves the Northeastern US by bringing together those who are concerned with the knowledge of weeds and their control, cooperates with other scientific societies to promote research, education and outreach activities and publishes scientific and practical information of value concerning weed sciences and other fields.
Founded in 1946

715 **Oregon Tilth**
260 SW Madison Ave.
Suite 106
Corvallis, OR 97333

503-378-0690
877-378-0690
Fax: 541-753-4924
E-Mail: andrew@tilth.org
Home Page: www.tilth.org

Susan Schechter, President
Chris Schreiner, Executive Director
JJ Haapala, Secretary
David Granatstein, Treasurer
Erin O'Donnell, Accounts Manager

Oregon Tilth is a nonprofit research and education membership organization dedicated to biologicaly sound and socially equitable agriculture. Oregon Tilth offers educational events throughout the state of Oregon, and provides organic certification services to organic growers, processors and handlers internationally.

716 **Organic Crop Improvement Association**
1340 North Cotner Boulevard
Lincoln, NE 68505-1838

402-477-2323
Fax: 402-477-4325
E-Mail: info@ocia.org
Home Page: www.ocia.org
Social Media: Facebook, Twitter

Kevin Koester, President
Jack Geiger, First Vice-President
Lyle Hamann, Second Vice-President

Demetria Stephens, Secretary
Terrence Sheehan, Treasurer

OCIA International is a farmer owned international program of certification, which adheres to strict organic standards. It currently certifies thousands of farmers and processors in North, Central and South America and Asia. OCIA International is IFOAM accredited and adheres to the USDA ISO Guide 65, Japan Agriculture Standards and the Quebec Accreditation Council. OCIA has also been accredited from the USDA National Organic Program and Costa Rica Ministry of Agriculture.
3500 Members
Founded in 1985
Mailing list available for rent: 3500 names at $50 per M

717 Organic Seed Alliance
PO Box 772
Port Townsend, WA 98368

360-385-7192
Fax: 360-385-7455
E-Mail: info@seedalliance.org
Home Page: www.seedalliance.org
Social Media: Facebook, Twitter

Sebastian Aguilar, President
Micaela Colley, Executive Director
Atina Diffley, Vice President
Tony Kleese, Secretary
Zea Sonnabend, Treasurer

Supports the ethical development and stewardship of the genetic resources of agricultural seed.
Founded in 2003

718 Produce Marketing Association
Po Box 6036
Newark, DE 19714-6036

302-738-7100
Fax: 302-731-2409
E-Mail: solutionctr@pma.com
Home Page: www.pma.com
Social Media: Facebook, Twitter

Bryan Silbermann, President and CEO
Tony Parassio, Chief Operating Officer
Yvonne Bull, Chief Financial Officer
Robert J Whitaker, Chief Science/Technology Officer
Margi Prueitt, Senior Vice President

The Produce Marketing Association is a not-for-profit trade association serving members who market fresh fruits, vegetables, and floral products worldwide. Its members are involved in the production, distribution, retail, and foodservice sectors of the industry.
2500 Members
Founded in 1949

719 Professional Farmers of America
1818 Market Street 31st Floor
Philadelphia, PA 19103

800-772-0023
E-Mail: editors@profarmer.com
Home Page: www.agweb.com/profarmer

Chip Flory, Editor/Publisher
Julianne Johnston, Sr. Markets Editor
Meghan Pederson, Pro Farmer Reporter
Brian Grete, Senior Market Analyst
Jim Wiesemeyer, Washington Consultant

Provides farmers with marketing strategies and market-trend data, as well as seminars and home study courses.
25M Members
Founded in 1973

720 Santa Gertrudis Breeders International
PO Box 1257
Kingsville, TX 78364-1257

361-592-9357
Fax: 361-592-8572
E-Mail: jford@santagertrudis.com
Home Page: santagertrudis.com/
Social Media: Facebook

John E Ford, Executive Director

America's First Beef Breed developed in 1918 at the famous King Ranch in Texas. Recognized in 1940 by the USDA. Famous for raid and efficient growth, solid red color, hardiness and good disposition. They are adaptable to many environments and are present throughout the US and in other countries.

721 Society of American Foresters
5400 Grosvenor Ln
Bethesda, MD 20814-2198

301-897-8720
Fax: 301-897-3690
E-Mail: membership@safnet.org
Home Page: www.safnet.org
Social Media: Facebook, Twitter, LinkedIn

Michael T Goergen Jr, Executive VP/CFO
Louise Murgia, Interim Executive Vice-President
Jorge Esguerra, Chief Financial Officer
Christopher Whited, Senior Director, Marketing
Elaine Cook, Office Manager, Marketing & Members

Provides access to information and networking opportunities to prepare members for the challenges and the changes that face natural resource professionals.
Founded in 1900

722 Society of Commercial Seed Technologists
1601 52nd Avenue
Suite 1
Moline, IL 61265
309-736-0119
Fax: 607-273-1638
E-Mail: scst@seedtechnology.net
Home Page: www.seedtechnology.net

Neal Foster, President
Barbara Cleave, Vice President
Brad Johnson, Director-at-Large
Sharon Davidson, Director-at-Large
Carol Betzel, Director-at-Large

Professionals involved in the testing and analysis of seeds, including research, production and handling based on botanical and agricultural sciences.
250 Members
Founded in 1922

723 Soil and Plant Analysis Council
347 North Shores Circle
Windsor, CO 80550

970-686-5702
Fax: 402-476-0302
E-Mail: rmiller@lamar.colostate.ed
Home Page: www.spcouncil.com

Rao Mylavarapu, President
Robert Mikkelsen, Vice President International Plant
Robert Miller, Secretary/Treasurer

Promotes uniform soil test and plant analysis methods, use, interpretation and terminology.
250 Members
Founded in 1969

724 Southern Cotton Ginners Association
874 Cotton Gin Pl
Memphis, TN 38106-2588

901-947-3104
Fax: 901-947-3103
E-Mail:
andrea.steadman@southerncottonginners.or
Home Page: www.southerncottonginners.org
Social Media: Facebook

George LaCour, Chairman of Board
Robert Royal, President
Riley James, Vice President
Tim Price, Executive Vice President
Andrea Steadman, Marketing Communications Specialist

Operates in a five state area as an information center covering safety and governmental regulations. Serves its members by providing safety, training and regulatory representation. Sponsors certification programs and hosts the industry's leading trade show, The Mid-South Farm & Gin Show.
700 Members
Founded in 1950

725 Texas Agribusiness Market Research Center
600 John Kimbrough Blvd.
Suite 371 - 2124 TAMU
College Station, TX 77843

979-845-5911
Fax: 979-845-6378
E-Mail: AFCER@tamu.edu
Home Page: afcerc.tamu.edu

Loren Schroeder, Program Manager
Senarath Dharmasena, Assistant Professor
Robin Hanselman, Graphic Design/Data Specialist

Provide a single point to all agricultural resources on the internet. Objective is to promote agribusiness and to enhance agricultural product marketing and research.

726 The William H. Miner Agricultural Research Institute
1034 Miner Farm Road
PO Box 90
Chazy, NY 12921
518-846-7121
Fax: 518-846-8445
Home Page: www.whminer.com

Dr Joseph C Burke, Chairman
Richard J. Grant, Ph.D., President
Kirk Beattie, VP/Administration
Catherine S. Ballard, Director of Research
Steve J. Fessette, Director of Physical Plant

Miner Institute conducts integrated, cutting-edge education, research, and demonstration programs that optimize the biological and economic relationships among forage-crop production, dairy and equine management, and environmental stewardship.We envision a vital agricultural community in northern New York and surrounding regions built on effective use of forage crops and management technologies that optimize animal production and well-being while sustaining the natural environment.
Founded in 1903

727 USA Dry Pea & Lentil Council
2780 W. Pullman Road
Moscow, ID 83843

208-882-3023
Fax: 208-882-6406
E-Mail: pulse@pea-lentil.com
Home Page: www.pea-lentil.com

Tim D. McGreevy, CEO
Pete Klaiber, Director of Marketing
Ali McDaniel, Food Marketing Manager
Todd Scholz, Director of Information &

Research
Dr. Janice Rueda, Director of Health & Nutrition

The USA Dry Pea & Lentil Council(USADPLC) is a non-profit organization to promote and protect the interests of growers, processors, warehousemen and sellers of dry peas, lentils and chickpeas in the United States.

728 **USA Rice Federation**
USA Rice Federation
2101 Wilson Bvld
Suite 610
Arlington, VA 22201
703-226-2300
Fax: 703-236-2301
E-Mail: riceinfo@usarice.com
Home Page: www.usarice.com
Social Media: Facebook, Twitter, LinkedIn, Pinterest, You Tube

Johnny Broussard, Director, Legislative Affairs
Lauren Echols, Manager, Government Affairs/PAC
Reece Langley, Vice President, Government Affairs
Steve Hensley, Senior Director, Regulatory Affairs

The global advocate for all segments of the U.S. rice industry with a mission to promote and protect the interests of producers, millers, merchants and allied businesses. USA Rice is made up of the USA Rice Grower's Assoc, USA Rice Millers' Assoc, USA Rice Council, and the USA Rice Merchants' Association.

729 **United Fresh Produce Association**
1901 Pennsylvania Ave NW
Suite 1100
Washington, DC 20006-3412
202-303-3400
Fax: 202-303-3433
E-Mail: united@unitedfresh.org
Home Page: www.unitedfresh.org
Social Media: Facebook, Twitter, YouTube

Thomas E Stenzel, CEO
Jeff Oberman, Vice President, Trade Relations
Victoria Backer, Senior Vice President
Jeff Oberman, Vice President, Trade Relations
Lorelei DiSogra, Ed.D., R.D., Vice President Nutrition & Health

Equipment, supplies, cartons, packaging machinery, computers, sorting and sizing equipment, harvesting equipment, film wrap manufacturing and commodity organizations.
1000+ Members
Founded in 1904

730 **United Producers**
8351 N High St
Sute 250
Columbus, OH 43235-1440
614-890-6666
800-456-3276
Fax: 614-890-4776
Home Page: www.uproducers.com
Social Media: Facebook, LinkedIn

Dennis Bolling, President/CEO
Joe Werstak, CFO

A cooperative marketing organization owned by farmers and ranchers in the United States' corn belt, midwest and southeast.
36000 Members
Frequency: Annual Meetings
Founded in 1962

731 **United States Animal Health Association**
PO Box 8805
St Joseph, MO 64508
816-671-1144
Fax: 816-671-1201
E-Mail: usaha@usaha.org
Home Page: www.usaha.org
Social Media: Facebook, Twitter

Dr. David Meeker, President
Dr. Bruce King, First Vice President
Dr. David Schmitt, Second Vice President
Dr. Boyd Parr, Third Vice President
Dr. Annette Whiteford, Treasurer

Seeks to prevent, control and eliminate livestock diseases.
1400 Members
Founded in 1897

732 **United States Canola Association**
600 Pennsylvania Ave SE
Suite 320
Washington, DC 20003-6300
202-969-8113
Fax: 202-969-7036
E-Mail: info@uscanola.com
Home Page: www.uscanola.com
Social Media: Facebook

John Gordley, Executive Director
Dale Thorenson, Assistant Director
Angela Dansby, Communications Director
Mary O'Donohue, Advertising Sales Representative

USCA members are producers and processors of canola and grapeseed.
Founded in 1989

733 **United States Egg Marketers**
4500 Hugh Howell Road
Suite 270
Tucker, GA 30084
770-360-9220
Fax: 770-360-7058
E-Mail: info@unitedegg.org
Home Page: www.unitedegg.org
Social Media: Facebook, Twitter, RSS Feed

Chad Gregory, President & CEO
David Inall, Senior Vice President
Sherry Shedd, Vice President of Finance
Derreck Nassa,

Director of Operations
Oscar Garrison, Director of Food Safety

A producer cooperative established specifically for the purpose of exporting large quantities of U.S. Shell Eggs.

734 **United States Grains Council**
20 F Street NW
Suite 600
Washington, DC 20001
202-789-0789
Fax: 202-898-0522
E-Mail: grains@grains.org
Home Page: www.grains.org
Social Media: Facebook, Twitter, LinkedIn, YouTube, Flickr, Pinterest

Julius Schaaf, Chairman
Thomas Sleight, President and CEO
Alan Tiemann, Secretary/Treasurer
Ron Gray, Vice Chairman
Kim Falcon, State Checkoff Sector Director

Motivated by the grain sorghum, barley and corn producer associations and representatives of the agricultural community. Provides commodity export market development.
175 Members
Founded in 1960

735 **United States Hide, Skin & Leather Association**
1150 Connecticut Ave, NW
12th Floor
Washington, DC 20036
202-587-4250
E-Mail: jreddington@meatami.com
Home Page: www.ushsla.org

Mike Larson, Chairman
John Reddington, President
Kelly Meine, Vice Chairman
Stephen Sothmann, Director/International Affairs

Exclusive representative of the hides and skin industry in the United States. Members range in size from small family-owned businesses to large corporations. Participates in two annual trade shows in Asia as a cooperator through the US Department of Agriculture's Foreign Agriculture Service.
35 Members

736 **Veal Quality Assurance Program & Veal Issues Management Program**
7501 NW Tiffany Springs Parkway
Suite 200
Kansas City, MO 64153
717-823-6995
E-Mail: info@vealfarm.com
Home Page: www.vealfarm.com

Members include veal producers and processors.
1300 Members
Founded in 1984

737 **Walnut Council**
1007 N 725 W
West Lafayette, IN 47906-9431
765-583-3501
Fax: 765-583-3512
E-Mail: walnutcouncil@walnutcouncil.org
Home Page: www.walnutcouncil.org

Donald Greene, President
Jerry Van Sambeek, VP
Liz Jackson, Executive Director
Bill Hoover, Treasurer
John Katzke, Quartermaster

A science based organization that encourages research, discussion, and application of knowledge about growing hardwood trees.
1000 Members
Founded in 1970

738 **Weed Science Society of America**
810 East 10th St.
Lawrence, KS 66044-7065
785-865-9250
800-627-0326
Fax: 785-843-1274
E-Mail: wssa@allenpress.com
Home Page: www.wssa.net
Social Media: RSS Feed

Joyce Lancaster, Executive Secretary
Tracy Candelaria, Managing Editor
John Madsen, Secretary
Ian Burkel, Treasurer

Promotes research, education and extension outreach activities related to weeds, provides science-based information to the public and policy makers; and fosters awareness of weeds and their impacts on managed and natural ecosystems.
2000 Members
Founded in 1956

739 **Western Fairs Association**
1776 Tribute Rd
Suite 210
Sacramento, CA 95815-4495

916-927-3100
Fax: 916-927-6397
E-Mail: stephenc@fairsnet.org
Home Page: www.fairsnet.org
Social Media: Facebook, Twitter, YouTube

Kent Hojem, President
Pat Kress, VP
Stephen Chambers, Executive Director
Tami Davis Triggs, Accounting Manager
Lori Hanley, Communications Manager

A non-profit association with members throughout the Western United States and Canada that strives to promote industry standards. Membership includes access to conventions and trade shows, educational training programs as well as legislative advocacy support.
2000 Members
Founded in 1922

740 **Western United States Agricultural Trade Association**
4601 NE 77th Avenue
Suite 240
Vancouver, WA 98662-2697

360-693-3373
Fax: 360-693-3464
E-Mail: export@wusata.org
Home Page: www.wusata.org

Andy Anderson, Executive Director
Janet Kenefsky, Deputy Director
Tricia Walker, Branded Program Manager
Amanda Hughart, Outreach Coordinator
Danielle Utter, Communications Coordinator

The Western United States Agricultural Trade Association (WUSATAr) is a non-profit trade association whose members are the thirteen western state departments of agriculture. WUSATA is administered by the USDA 's Foreign Agricultural Service (FAS) and funded through the Market Access Program (MAP) with a mission to support and assist members and agribusinesses in the thirteen Western States in developing and enhancing international markets for U.S. food and agricultural products.

Newsletters

741 **AAM Newsletter**
American Agriculture Movement
24800 Sage Creek Road
Scenic, SD 57780

605-993-6201
Fax: 605-993-6185
E-Mail: jjobgen@hotmail.com
Home Page: www.aaminc.org

Larry Matlack, President
Arthur Chaney, Executive Vice President
John Willis, Vice President
Jim Rice, Secretary/Treasurer
John Willis, Vice President

The creation of the AAM has provided a farmer-created, farmer-built organization within which farmers themselves have been the leaders, speakers and organizers; empowering farmers as they had not been in the past, to speak for and advocate for themselves. Updates about events, news, articles and letters to the editor.
Founded in 1977
Mailing list available for rent

742 **ALBC News**
American Livestock Breeds Conservancy
PO Box 477
Pittsboro, NC 27312

919-542-5704
Fax: 919-545-0022
Home Page: www.albc-usa.org
Social Media: Facebook, Blogger

Charles Bassett, Executive Director

Provides in-depth information about current ALBC activities, breed information, member updates, and more.
Frequency: Bi-Monthly

743 **ARA Retailer Facts**
Agricultural Retailers Association
1156 15th St Nw
Suite 500
Washington, DC 20005-1745

202-457-0825
Fax: 202-457-0864
E-Mail: ara@aradc.org
Home Page: www.aradc.org
Social Media: Facebook, Twitter, RSS Feed

Daren Coppock, President and CEO
Richard Gupton, SVP
Donnie Taylor, VP of Membership
Gary Baise, General Counsel

The Agricultural Retailers Association advocates before Congress and the Executive Branch to ensure a profitable business environment for members.
Frequency: Daily

744 **ARClight**
National Agri-Marketing Association
11020 King St
Suite 205
Overland Park, KS 66210-1201

913-491-6500
Fax: 913-491-6502
E-Mail: agrimktg@nama.org
Home Page: www.nama.org
Social Media: Facebook, Twitter, LinkedIn, Flicker, You Tube

Jennifer Pickett, CEO
Vicki Henrickson, President
Paul Redhage, Secretary/Treasurer
Matt Coniglio, Vice President

Agricultural Relations Council - a national association with members involved in agricultural public relations. Electronic newsletter of interest to association members.

745 **ASA Today**
American Soybean Association
12125 Woodcrest Executive
Suite 100
Saint Louis, MO 63141-5009

314-576-1770
800-688-7692
Fax: 314-576-2786
E-Mail: bcallanan@soy.org
Home Page: www.soygrowers.com
Social Media: Facebook, Twitter, RSS Feed

Steve Censky, CEO
Cassandra Schlef, Communications Coordinator

For members only
Frequency: Weekly

746 **ASAC News**
American Society of Agricultural Consultants
N78W14573 Appleton Ave
#287
Menomonee Falls, WI 53051

262-253-6902
Fax: 262-253-6903
E-Mail: cmerry@countryside-marketing.com
Home Page: www.agconsultants.org
Social Media: Facebook, LinkedIn

˜the American Society of Agricultural Consultants (ASAC) is a non-profit organization oriented around raising the standards and image of professional agricultural consultants. ASAC is the only association representing the full range of agricultural consultants.
Frequency: Quarterly
Founded in 1963

747 **Agri Times Northwest**
PO Box 1626
Pendleton, OR 97801

541-276-6202
Fax: 541-278-4778
E-Mail: editor@agritimesnw.com
Home Page: www.agritimesnw.com

Sterling Allen, Publisher
Jim Eardley, Editor
Brianna Walker, Graphics

Contains news stories and columns pertaining to rural life and agri-business, designed to keep farmers and ranchers up to date with agriculture in their backyard.
Cost: $20.00
Frequency: Bi Monthly
Founded in 1981

748 **AgriMarketing Weekly**
Henderson Communications LLC
1422 Elbridge Payne Rd
Suite 250
Chesterfield, MO 63017-8544

636-728-1428
Fax: 636-777-4178
E-Mail: info@agrimarketing.com
Home Page: www.agrimarketing.com

Lynn Henderson, Publisher/Editorial Director
Stephanie Wobbe, Editorial Assistant
Audrey Evans, Customer Service Manager

It includes a recap of the most important news within the industry during the prior week.
Frequency: Weekly
Circulation: 4500

749 **Agricultural Law Update**
American Agricultural Law Association
127 Young Rd
Kelso, WA 98626

360-200-5699
Fax: 360-432-2287
E-Mail: RobertA@aglaw-assn.org
Home Page: www.aglaw-assn.org

Amy Swanson, President
Robert Achenbach, Jr., Executive Director
David K Waggoner, Director
Ruth A Moore, Director
Beth Crocker, Director

Articles written about environmental and agricultural issues.

750 **Agweek**
Grand Forks Herald
375 2nd Avenue N
Grand Forks, ND 58206-6008

701-780-1100
Fax: 701-780-1211
E-Mail: kdeats@gfherald.com
Home Page: www.gfherald.com
Social Media: RSS Feed

Matthew C Cory, Managing Editor
Tom Dennis, Editorial/Opinion Page Editor
Mary Jo Hotler, Editor

Features classifieds, weather information, farming, ranch news and opinion for the Upper Midwest
Cost: $32.00
Frequency: Weekly

751 **Alliance Link Newsletter**
Animal Agriculture Alliance
2101 Wilson Blvd
Suite 916-B
Arlington, VA 22201

703-562-5160
Fax: 703-524-1921
E-Mail: info@animalagalliance.org
Home Page: www.animalagalliance.org
Social Media: Facebook, Twitter

Kay Johnson, Executive VP
Sarah Hubbart, Communications Coordinator

Helps members and industry stakeholders stay informed about the key issues impacting animal agriculture
Frequency: Monthly

752 **American Beekeeping Federation Newsletter**
American Beekeeping Federation
3525 Piedmont Rd NE
Bldg 5 Suite 300
Atlanta, GA 30305-1509

404-760-2875
Fax: 404-240-0998
E-Mail: info@abfnet.org
Home Page: www.abfnet.org

Robin D Lane, Executive Director
Grayson Daniels, Membership Coordinator
Troy Fore, Director of Government Relations

Newsletter for members of the American Beekeeping Federation.
Cost: $35.00
24 Pages
Frequency: Bi-Monthly
Circulation: 1750
Founded in 1943

753 **American Feed Industry Newlsetter**
American Feed Industry Association
2101 Wilson Boulevard
Suite 916
Arlington, VA 22201

703-524-0810
Fax: 703-524-1921
E-Mail: afia@afia.org
Home Page: www.afia.org
Social Media: Facebook, Twitter, LinkedIn

Al Gunderson, Chairman of the Board
Jeff Cannon, Chair/Elect
Joel Newman, President and Treasurer
Richard Sellers, VP and Corporate Security

Newsletter published every two weeks by the American Feed Industry for members only.
Frequency: Bi-Monthly
Circulation: 700
Founded in 1909

754 **Aquatic Plant News**
Aquatic Plant Management Society
PO Box 821265
Vicksburg, MS 39182-1265

FAX 601-634-5502
E-Mail: dpetty@ndrsite.com
Home Page: www.apms.org
Social Media: Facebook, LinkedIn

Terry Goldsby, President
Mike Netherland, President-elect
Sherry Whitaker, Treasurer

Aquatic Plant News is produced 3 times each year, and is distributed primarily by email.
Frequency: 3x Yearly
Founded in 1961

755 **Association of American Seed Control Officials Bulletin**
Utah Department of Agriculture
350 N Redwood Road
PO Box 146500
Salt Lake City, UT 84114-6500

801-538-7100
Fax: 801-538-7126
E-Mail: agriculture@utah.gov
Home Page: www.ag.utah.gov
Social Media: Facebook, Twitter, YouTube

Stephen T Burningham, Control Officer
Leonard Blachham, Commissioner
Jed Christenson, Marketing

Seed laws in the United States and Canada.
Frequency: Annual+
Circulation: 5000

756 **CSA News**
5585 Guilford Road
Madison, WI 53711-1086

608-273-8080
Fax: 608-273-2021
E-Mail: headquarters@agronomy.org
Home Page: www.agronomy.org
Social Media: Facebook, Twitter, LinkedIn

Ellen E Bergfeld, Executive VP
Luther Smith, Executive Director
Michela Cobb, Director Financial Services
Audrey Jankowski, Analyst/Programmer
Ian Popkewitz, Director IT/Operations

The official magazine for members of the American Society of Agronomy, Crop Science Society of America, and Soil Science Society of America.
11000 Members
Founded in 1907

757 **Chaff Newsletter**
American Association of Grain Inspection
PO Box 26426
Kansas City, MO 64196

816-569-4020
Fax: 816-221-8189
E-Mail: info@aagiwa.org
Home Page: www.aagiwa.org

Larry Kitchen, President
Mark Fulmer, VP

Welcomes member information about new products, business changes, personnel changes and other items that may be of interest to AAGIWA members.
Frequency: Monthly

758 **Council for Agricultural Science and Technology Newsletter**
Council For Agricultural Science and Technology
4420 Lincoln Way
Ames, IA 50014-3447

515-292-2125
Fax: 515-292-4512
E-Mail: info@cast-science.org
Home Page: www.cast-science.org
Social Media: Facebook, Twitter, LinkedIn, YouTube

Phillip Stahlman, President
Lowell Midla, President-elect
Turner Sutton, Treasurer

Identifies food, fiber, environmental and other agricultural issues for all stake holders, including legislators, policy makers and the public.
Founded in 1972

759 **Country Folks**
Lee Publications
6113 State Highway 5
PO Box 121
Palatine Bridge, NY 13428

518-673-3237
800-836-2888
Fax: 518-673-3245
E-Mail: info@leepub.com
Home Page: www.leepub.com
Social Media: Facebook, Twitter

Frederick Lee, Publisher
Scott Duffy, Sales Manager

Agricultural news from national, state and local levels. Some features on farm and agricultural industry, rural interest, etc.
75 Pages
Frequency: Weekly
Circulation: 27000
Founded in 1973

760 **Country World Newspaper**
Echo Publishing Company
401 Church St
Sulphur Springs, TX 75482-2681

903-885-0861
800-245-2149
Fax: 903-885-8768
E-Mail: scott@ssecho.com
Home Page: www.countryworldnews.com

Scott Key, President
Kari Arnold, Editor

A newspaper offering agricultural information to farmers, ranchers, dairyfarmers, and agribusinesses.
Frequency: Weekly
Founded in 1981

761 **Dair-e-news**
American Dairy Science Association
1800 S. Oak Street
Suite 100
Champaign, IL 61820-6974

217-356-5146
Fax: 217-398-4119
E-Mail: adsa@assochq.org
Home Page: www.adsa.org
Social Media: Facebook

Peter Studney, Executive Director
Cara Tharp, Executive Assistant

Timely topics and important announcements, industry calendar of events, and news of the Association.

762 **DairyProfit Weekly**
6437 Collamer Road
East Syracuse, NY 13057-1031

315-703-7979
800-334-1904
Fax: 315-703-7988
E-Mail: dgarno@dairybusiness.com
Home Page: www.dairybusiness.com
Social Media: Facebook, Twitter, YouTube

Keeps readers up to date with a quick, timely summary of news, markets and trends that impact your business.
Frequency: Weekly
Founded in 1904

763 **Decision Support Systems for Agrotechnology Transfer**
ICASA
2440 Campus Road
PO Box 527
Honolulu, HI 96822

808-956-2713
Fax: 808-956-2711
E-Mail: icasa@icasa.net
Home Page: www.icasa.net

Jeffrey White, Co-Chair
Martin Ittersum, Co-Chair
Gordon Tsuji, Secretariat

Systems analysis and crop simulation models for agrotechnology transfers and risk assessment. Reference guides and models for maize, wheat, rice, sorghum, millet, barley, soybean, peanut and potato are included. Linked to GIS software.

764 **Doane's Agricultural Report**
Doane Agricultural Services
77 Westport Plz
Suite 250
St Louis, MO 63146-3121

314-569-2700
866-647-0918
Fax: 314-569-1083
Home Page: www.doane.com

Rich Pottorff, Chief Economist
Marty Foreman, Senior Economist
Sam Funk, Senior Economist

Provides information to US farmers and agricultural professionals. Doane keeps you up to date on factors affecting your farm program benefits and production costs too.
Frequency: Weekly

765 **Farm Managers & Rural Appraisers News**
Amer. Society of Farm Managers & Rural Appraisers
950 S Cherry St
Suite 508
Denver, CO 80246-2664

303-758-3513
Fax: 303-758-0190
E-Mail: asfmra@asfmra.org
Home Page: www.asfmra.org
Social Media: Facebook, Twitter, LinkedIn, Plaxo

Paul Joerger, President
Jim Rickert, President-elect
Fred Hepler, First Vice President

Provides members and other agricultural professionals with current information relative to the industry and educational offerings.
Frequency: Bi-Monthly
Founded in 1929

766 **Farm and Ranch Guide**
2401 46th Avenue SE
Mandan, ND 58554

701-255-4905
Fax: 701-255-2312
E-Mail: office@farmandranchguide.com
Home Page: www.farmandranchguide.com
Social Media: Facebook, Twitter, RSS Feed

Brian Kroshus, Group Publisher
Mark Conlon, Editor
Patrick Sitter, General Manager
Andrea Johnson, Assistant Editor

Inform and entertain while serving as a conduit between our valued advertising customers and our loyal readers
Cost: $32.95
Frequency: Bi-Monthly
Circulation: 38,000

767 **Farmer's Friend**
116 Main Street
Towanda, PA 18846

570-265-2151
800-253-3662
Fax: 570-265-6130
E-Mail: kandrus@thedailyreview.com
Home Page: www.farmers-friend.com

Ronald W Hosie, Editor
Kelly Andrus, Managing Editor
Debbie Bump, Circulation

Farming news.
Frequency: Weekly
Founded in 1977

768 **Feedstuffs**
The Miller Publishing Company
5810 W. 78th St
Suite 200
Bloomington, MN 55339

952-931-0211
Fax: 952-938-1832
E-Mail: smuirhead@feedstuffs.com
Home Page: www.feedstuffs.com

Sarah Muirhead, Publisher/Editor
Rod Smith, Staff Editor/Livestock & Poultry
Tim Lundeen, Staff Editor/Nutrition & Health
Jacqui Fatka, Staff Editor/Policy
Kristin Bakker, Editorial Production Manager

A newspaper for agribusiness, each week of the month focuses on a different animal species. Topics include nutrition, health, marketing issues and the popular Bottom Line of Nutrition section.
Cost: $144.00
24 Pages
Frequency: Weekly
Circulation: 16600
Founded in 1895

769 **Fencepost**
The Fencepost
423 Main Street
Windsor, CO 80550-5129

970-686-5691
Fax: 970-686-5694
E-Mail: gloftus@thefencepost.com
Home Page: www.thefencepost.com

Gary Loftus, Publisher
Amiella Diaz, Editor
Robyn Scherer, Staff Reporter

Farming news and reports.
Cost: $39.00
Frequency: Weekly
Founded in 1980

770 **Forestry Source**
Society of American Foresters
5400 Grosvenor Ln
Bethesda, MD 20814-2198

301-897-8720
866-897-8720
Fax: 301-897-3690
E-Mail: safweb@podi.com
Home Page: www.safnet.org
Social Media: Facebook, Twitter, LinkedIn

Joe Smith, Editor
Michael T Goergen, Jr., Executive Vice President
Patricia Adadevoh, Leadership Services Manager

Offers the latest information on national forestry trends, the latest developments in forestry policy at the federal, state, and local levels, the newest advances in forestry-related research and technology, and up-to-date information about SAF programs and activities
Cost: $35.00
Frequency: Monthly
Founded in 1990

771 **Friday Notes**
Council For Agricultural Science and Technology
4420 West Lincoln Way
Ames, IA 50014-3447

515-292-2125
Fax: 515-292-4512
E-Mail: cast@cast-science.org
Home Page: www.cast-science.org

John Bonner, Executive VP/CEO
Phillip Stahlman, President
Turner Sutton, Treasurer

E-Newsletter featuring lead articles on current topics being discussed in agriculture, congressional updates, announcements of upcoming CAST publications and activities, and information about CAST's scientific society, company, and nonprofit members.
Frequency: Quarterly
Circulation: 4000
Founded in 1972

772 **Global Dairy Update**
DairyBusiness Communications
6437 Collamer Road
East Syracuse, NY 13057-1031

315-703-7979
800-334-1904
Fax: 315-703-7988
E-Mail: dgarno@dairybusiness.com
Home Page: www.dairybusiness.com
Social Media: Facebook, Twitter, YouTube

Dave Natzke, Editor
Scott Smith, Chairman/Co-CEO
John Montandon, President/Co-CEO
Joel Hastings, President, Dairy Business

Focuses on dairy developments throughout the world.
Founded in 1904

773 **Goats on the Move**
Meat & Livestock Australia
1401 K Street NW
Suite 602
Washington, DC 20005

202-521-2551
Fax: 202-521-2699
E-Mail: info@mla.com.au
Home Page: www.mla.com.au
Social Media: Facebook, Twitter, YouTube

Don Heatley, Chairman
David Palmer, Managing Director
Bernie Bindon, Director
Chris Hudson, Director

eNewsletter providing information on the latest developments in MLA's goat program and the broader Australian goatmeat industry.
Frequency: Quarterly
Founded in 1998

774 **Greenhouse Product News**
Scranton Gillette Communications
3030 W Salt Creek Lance
Suite 201
Arlington Heights, IL 60005-5025

847-391-1000
Fax: 847-390-0408
E-Mail: bbellew@sgcmail.com
Home Page: www.gpnmag.com

Bob Bellew, VP/Group Publisher
Tim Hodson, Editorial Director
Jasmina Radjevic, Managing Editor

Features the industry's leading Buyer's Guide directory, the PGR table and the bookstore are just a few reasons the industry's buyers keep coming back to GPN.
Frequency: Monthly
Mailing list available for rent: 19,000 names

775 **Hay Market News**
US Department of Agriculture
1400 Independence Ave., S.W.
Washington, DC 20250-0506

202-690-7650
Fax: 509-457-7132
E-Mail: shessman2@kda.state.ks.us
Home Page: www.usda.gov

Tom Vilsack, Secretary
Chris Smith, Chief Information Officer
Matt Paul, Director of Communications
Ramona Romero, General Counsel

Federal newsletter offering information and updates on crops and farming.
Cost: $40.00
8 Pages
Circulation: 180
Founded in 1862

776 **Holstein Association News**
Holstein Association
1 Holstein Place
PO Box 808
Brattleboro, VT 05302-0808

802-254-4551
800-952-5200
Fax: 802-254-8251
E-Mail: info@holstein.com
Home Page: www.holsteinusa.com

John Meyer, CEO/Executive Secretary
Chuck Worden, President
Glenn E Brown, Vice President
Barbara Casna, CFO/Treasurer

Bimonthly newsletter provides active customers with information on the association programs and services and how to integrate them into their dairy operations.
Founded in 1885

777 **Holstein Pulse**
Holstein Association USA Inc
1 Holstein Place
PO Box 808
Brattleboro, VT 05302-0808

802-254-4551
800-052-5200
Fax: 802-254-8251
E-Mail: info@holstein.com
Home Page: www.holsteinusa.com

Chuck Worden, President
Glenn E Brown, Vice President
Barbara Casna, Treasurer

Includes information relevant to our members, new developments in the industry, as well as updates from the CEO and President.
Cost: $2.00
Frequency: Quarterly
Founded in 1885

778 **Irrigation Association E-Newsletter**
Irrigation Association
6540 Arlington Blvd
Falls Church, VA 22042-6638

703-536-7080
Fax: 703-536-7019
E-Mail: info@irrigation.org
Home Page: www.irrigation.org

Deborah Hamlin, Executive Director
Noreen Rich, Foundation Manager
Kathleen Markey, Marketing Director

Published on a quarterly basis, this e-newsletter provides updates on Foundation activities and accomplishments.
Frequency: Monthly
Founded in 1949

779 **Irrigation Association IA Times**
Irrigation Association
6540 Arlington Blvd
Falls Church, VA 22042-6638

703-536-7080
Fax: 703-536-7019
E-Mail: info@irrigation.org
Home Page: www.irrigation.org

Deborah Hamlin, Executive Director
Kathleen Markey, Marketing Director

Reports on federal and state policies and legislation that affect the irrigation industry. Status updates on industry initiatives, and information on the latest association events, programs, services and awards.
1600 Members
Frequency: Monthly
Founded in 1949

780 **Kiplinger Agricultural Letter**
Kiplinger Washington Editors
1100 13th St. NW
Washington, DC 20005

202-887-6400
800-544-0155
Fax: 202-778-8976
E-Mail: sub.services@kiplinger.com
Home Page: www.kiplinger.com
Social Media: Facebook, Twitter, RSS

Knight A Kiplinger, President, Editor-in-Chief
Ed Maixner, Editor

Forecasts and judgments on wages, income, food packaging, processing and marketing techniques.
Cost: $137.00
Frequency: Biweekly
Founded in 1929

781 **NAMA Newsletter**
North American Millers' Association
600 Maryland Ave SW
Suite 825 W
Washington, DC 20024

202-484-2200
Fax: 202-488-7416
E-Mail: generalinfo@namamillers.org
Home Page: www.namamillers.org

Mary Waters, President
James Bair, Vice President
Paul B Green, Export Consultant
Sherri Lehman, Director of Government Relations
Mary Waters, President

Trade association representing the wheat, corn, oat and rye milling industry. NAMA members operate one hundred and seventy mills in thirty-eight states and Canada. Their aggregate production of more than one hundred and sixty million pounds per day is approximately ninety-five percent of the industry capacity in the U.S.
Frequency: Monthly
Circulation: 250

782 **NASDA News**
1156 15th St NW
Suite 1020
Washington, DC 20005-1711

202-296-9680
Fax: 202-296-9686
E-Mail: nasda@nasda.org
Home Page: www.nasda.org
Social Media: Facebook, Twitter

Stephen Haterius, CEO
Steve Troxler, President
Chuck Ross, Vice President

Represents the state departments of agriculture in the development, implementation and communication of sound public policy and programs which support and promote the American agricultural industry, while protecting consumers and the environment.
Founded in 1915

783 **NBA Weekly Update**
National Bison Association
8690 Wolff Ct
200
Westminster, CO 80031

303-292-2833
Fax: 303-845-9081
E-Mail: marilyn@bisoncentral.com
Home Page: www.bisoncentral.com

Dave Carter, Executive Director
Jim Matheson, Assistant Director
Marilyn Wentz, Bison World Editor

Mailed exclusively to all Life, Active and Allied Industry members. Contains the most up to date information available on the bison industry.
Frequency: Weekly

784 **NCPA Newsletter**
National Cottonseed Products Association
866 Willow Tree Cir
Cordova, TN 38018-6376

901-682-0800
Fax: 901-682-2856
E-Mail: info@cottonseed.com
Home Page: www.cottonseed.com

Ben Morgan, Executive VP & Secretary
Sandi Stine, Treasurer

Providing members with information on legislation, administrative rulings, federal regulations and court decisions affecting their business.
Founded in 1897

785 **National Honey Report**
Federal Market News Service
1400 Independence Avenue SW
STOP 0238
Washington, DC 20250

202-720-2175
Fax: 202-720-0547
Home Page:
www.ams.usda.gov/mnreports/fvmhoney.pdf

Billy Cox, Director
Becky Unkenholz, Deputy Director
Joan Shaffer, Senior Public Affairs Specialist

Current honey market information and colony conditions in the United States and other countries.
16 Pages
Frequency: Monthly
Founded in 1915

786 **National Onion Association Newsletter**
National Onion Association
822 7th St
Suite 510
Greeley, CO 80631-3941

970-353-5895
Fax: 970-353-5897
E-Mail: wmininger@onions-usa.org
Home Page: www.onions-usa.org
Social Media: Twitter

Mike Meyer, President
Gary Mayfield, Vice President
Kim Reddin, Director of Public & Industry

Newsletter published by and only for the National Onion Association.
Frequency: Monthly
Circulation: 600
Founded in 1913
Mailing list available for rent: 600 names

787 **Nebraska Alfalfa Dehydrators Bulletin**
Nebraska Alfalfa Dehydrators Association
8810 Craig Dr
Overland Park, KS 66212-2916

913-648-6800
Fax: 913-648-2648
E-Mail: wcobbkc@sbcglobal.net
Home Page: www.nebada.org

Jon Montgomery, President
David Rhea, Vice President
Dallas Buck, Director
Wanda Cobb, Executive Director/Secretary

Information for the processors and suppliers in the alfalfa industry.
Frequency: Weekly
Founded in 1941

788 **New England Farm Bulletin and Garden**
Jacob's Meadow Inc.

PO Box 67
Townton, MA 02780

E Mail: kimberlee@jacobsmeadow.org
Home Page: www.jacobsmeadow.org

Articles explore relevant topics; extensive farm clasifieds, doings around New England, book reviews and discount prices.

789 **News of the Association of Official Seed Analysts**
Association of Official Seed Analysts (AOSA)
101 East State Street
#214
Ithaca, NY 14850

607-256-3313
Fax: 607-273-1638
E-Mail: aosa.office@twcny.rr.com
Home Page: www.aosaseed.com

Dan Curry, President
Michael Stahr, Vice President
Janine Maruschak, Secretary/Treasurer

News items, technical reports, rules changes for testing seeds, surveys, identification and tax news, legislative updates and updates on the Association and publications in progress.

790 **No-Till Farmer**
Lessiter Publications
225 Regency Court
Suite 200
Brookfield, WI 53045

262-782-4480
800-645-8455
Fax: 262-782-1252
E-Mail: info@lesspub.com
Home Page: www.no-tillfarmer.com
Social Media: Facebook, Twitter, LinkedIn, YouTube

Frank Lessiter, Editor
Mike Lessiter, President
Darrell Bruggink, Executive Editor/Publisher
Amy Johnson, Production Manager

Management information for farmers interested in conservation tillage.
Frequency: Monthly
Circulation: 8000
Founded in 1972

791 **North American Millers' Association Newsletter**
600 Maryland Ave SW
Suite 825 W
Washington, DC 20024

202-484-2200
Fax: 202-488-7416
E-Mail: generalinfo@namamillers.org
Home Page: www.namamillers.org

Mary Waters, President
James Bair, VP

Trade association representing the wheat, corn, oat and rye milling industry. NAMA members operate one hundred and seventy mills in thrirty-eight states and Canada. Their aggregate production of more than one hundred and sixty million pounds per day is approximately ninety-five percent of the industry capacity in the U.S.
45 Members
Founded in 1902

792 **Northeastern Weed Science Society Newsletter**
PO Box 307
Fredericksburg, PA 17026

814-574-4067
E-Mail: northeasternweedscience@hotmail.com
Home Page: www.newss.org

Antonio DiTommaso, President
Greg Armel, Vice President
Melissa Bravo, Secretary/Treasurer
Darren Lycan, Editor
Javier Vargas, Public Relations

Serves the Northeastern US by bringing together those who are concerned with the knowledge of weeds and their control, cooperates with other scientific societies to promote research, education and outreach activities and publishes scientific and practical information of value concerning weed sciences and other fields.
Founded in 1946

793 **OCIA Communicator Newletter**
1340 North Cotner Boulevard
Lincoln, NE 68505-1838

402-477-2323
Fax: 402-477-4325
E-Mail: info@ocia.org
Home Page: www.ocia.org

Kevin Koester, President/ First Vice President
Jack Geiger, Second Vice President
Demetria Stephens, Secretary
Terrence Sheehan, Treasurer
Amy Krasne, Secretary

A quarterly newsletter published by the Organic Crop Improvement Association International (OCIA).
Cost: $50.00
Frequency: Quarterly
Circulation: 300
Mailing list available for rent: 3500 names at $50 per M

794 **Organic Report**
Organic Trade Association
28 Vernon Street
Suite 413
Brattleboro, VT 05301

802-275-3800
Fax: 802-275-3801
E-Mail: info@ota.com
Home Page: www.ota.com
Social Media: Facebook, Twitter, LinkedIn

Matthew McLean, President
Sarah Bird, Vice President
Tony Bedard, Treasurer
Kelly Shea, Secretary

Targets an audience of manufacturers, growers, retailers, importers, distributors, and consultants in the organic food and fiber industry.
Frequency: Monthly
Circulation: 2500
Founded in 1985

795 **Peterson Patriot**
Peterson Patriot Printers-Publishers
202 Main Street
PO Box 126
Peterson, IA 51047-0126

712-295-7711
E-Mail: patriot@iowatelecom.net

Roger Stoner, Publisher
Jane Stoner, Editor/Circulation Manager

Agricultural news.
Cost: $18.00
12 Pages
Frequency: Weekly
Circulation: 549

796 **Pro Farmer**
Farm Journal Media
1550 N Northwest HW
Suite 403
Park Ridge, IL 60068

215-578-8900
800-320-7992
Fax: 215-568-6782
E-Mail: rmurray@farmjournal.com
Home Page: www.farmjournalmedia.com

Andy Weber, Chief Executive Officer
Steve Custer, Executive Vice President/Publishing
Jeff Pence, Division President
Chuck Roth, Senior Vice President
Mitch Rouda, President, eMedia

Farm market news, analysis and management advice.
8 Pages
Frequency: Weekly
Founded in 1973

797 **SHORTLINER**
Farm Equipment Manufacturers Association
1000 Executive Parkway Dr
Suite 100
St Louis, MO 63141-6369

314-878-2304
Fax: 314-732-1480
E-Mail: info@farmequip.org
Home Page: www.farmequip.org
Social Media: Twitter

Andrew Cummings, President
Bob Atkinson, Treasurer
Marc McConnell, 1st Vice President
Mike Kloster, 2nd Vice President
Richard Kirby, Secretary

A review of news stories, press reports, and government actions affecting the industry.
Frequency: Bi-Monthly

798 **Salt & Trace Mineral Newsletter**
Salt Institute
700 N Fairfax Street
Suite 600
Alexandria, VA 22314-2040

703-549-4648
Fax: 703-548-2194
E-Mail: info@saltinstitute.org
Home Page: www.saltinstitute.org

Lori Roman, President
Morton Satin, VP/Science & Research

Information on animal nutrition.
Frequency: Quarterly
Founded in 1914

799 **Seed News**
PO Box 772
Port Townsend, WA 98368

360-385-7192
Fax: 360-385-7455
E-Mail: info@seedalliance.org
Home Page: www.seedalliance.org
Social Media: Facebook, Twitter

Sebastian Aguilar, President
Atina Diffley, Vice President
Zea Sonnabend, Treasurer

Information covering events, seminars and meetings.
Cost: $8.00
8 Pages

800 **Seed Technologist Newsletter**
Association of Official Seed Analysts (AOSA)
101 East State Street
#214
Ithaca, NY 14850

607-256-3313
Fax: 607-273-1638
E-Mail: aosa.office@twcny.rr.com
Home Page: www.aosaseed.com

Dan Curry, President
Michael Stahr, Vice President
Janine Maruschak, Secretary/Treasurer

News items, technical reports, rules changes for testing seeds, surveys, identification and tax

news, legislative updates and updates on the Association and publications in progress.
Cost: $20.00
Frequency: TriAnnual
Circulation: 500

801 Signals Newsletter
Association for Communication Excellence
ACE Headquarters
59 College Road, Taylor Hall
Durham, NH 03824

603-862-1564
Fax: 603-862-1585
E-Mail: ace.info@unh.edu
Home Page: www.aceweb.org

Faith Peppers, President
Joanne Littlefield, Vice President
Elaine Edwards, Treasurer
Emily Eubanks, Professional Development Director
Jason Ellis, Research Director

The newsletter includes articles with a professional development focus; updates from special interest groups, states and regions; announcements about upcoming workshops and conferences; and write-ups about members' awards and accomplishments, job changes and more.
Cost: $75.00
Frequency: Bimonthly

802 Smart Choices Newsletter
Communicating for America
112 E Lincoln Avenue
Fergus Falls, MN 56537

218-739-3241
80- 43- 327
Fax: 218-739-3832
E-Mail: info@cabenefits.org
Home Page: www.cabenefits.org

Milt Smedsrud, CEO
Wayne Nelson, President

Filled with updates on legislative accomplishments and advocacy, articles about healthy living and first-hand accounts from those participating in CA Education Programs.
40M Members
Founded in 1972

803 Society for Laboratory Automation and Screening
100 Illinois Street
Suite 242
St. Charles, IL 60174

630-256-7527
877-990-7557
Fax: 630-741-7527
E-Mail: slas@slas.org
Home Page: www.slas.org
Social Media: Facebook, Twitter, LinkedIn, YouTube

Greg Dummer, CEO
Mary Geismann, Manager
Carol Brady, Coordinator

Provides forums for education and information exchange to encourage the study of and advance science and technology for the drug discovery, agrochemical, biotechnology, chemical, clinical diagnostic, consumer product, energy, forensic, pharmaceutical, security and other industries.
Frequency: Bi-Monthly

804 Southern Cotton Ginners Association Newsletter
874 Cotton Gin Pl
Memphis, TN 38106-2588

901-947-3104
Fax: 901-947-3103
E-Mail: carmen.griffin@southerncottonginners.org
Home Page: www.southerncottonginners.org
Social Media: Facebook

George LaCour, President
Robert Royal, Vice President
Sledge Taylor, Treasurer
Timothy Price, Secretary

Operates in a five state area as an information center covering safety and governmental regulations. Serves its members by providing safety, training and regulatory representation. Sponsors certification programs and hosts the industry's leading trade show, The Mid-South Farm & Gin Show.
Founded in 1950

805 TecAGRInews
Clark Consulting International
435 Root Street
PO Box 68
Park Ridge, IL 60068-0068

847-836-5100
Fax: 847-589-8889
E-Mail: warren.clark@ccimarketing.com
Home Page: www.ccimarketing.com

Warren E Clark, President & Chief Executive Officer

News on new technology in agriculture reaching large computerized family farmers.
Frequency: Weekly
Circulation: 100000+
Founded in 1988

806 The Agrarian Advocate
36355 Russell Boulevard
P.O. Box 363
Davis, CA 95617

530-756-8518
800-892-3832
Fax: 530-756-7857
E-Mail: judith@fullbellyfarm.com
Home Page: www.caff.org
Social Media: Facebook, Twitter, YouTube

Carol Presley, Board Chair
Pete Price, Vice President
Judith Redmond, Secretary
Vicki Williams, Treasurer

Provides timely reporting on the food and farming issues
Cost: $47.95
Frequency: 3x/Year
Founded in 1978

807 The Alliance Link
Animal Agriculture Alliance
2101 Wilson Blvd
Suite 916-B
Arlington, VA 22201

703-562-5160
E-Mail: info@animalagalliance.org
Home Page: www.animalagalliance.org
Social Media: Facebook, Twitter

Kay Johnson, President and CEO
Emily Meredith, Communications Director

Provides information about specific animal rights organizations and their campaigns, referenced quotes by the activists themselves, as well as information to help with security at your facilities.
Frequency: Monthly

808 The Exchange
American Agricultural Economics Association
555 E Wells Street
Suite 1100
Milwaukee, WI 53202-6600

414-918-3190
Fax: 414-276-3349
E-Mail: info@aaea.org
Home Page: www.aaea.org
Social Media: Facebook

Richard Sexton, President
Julie Caswell, President-elect

Electronic newsletter for members of AAEA. Includes association announcements, membership news, and updates from the profession.
Frequency: Bi-Monthly
Founded in 1910

809 USA Rice Daily
USA Rice Federation
2101 Wilson Blvd
Suite 610
Arlington, VA 22201

703-226-2300
Fax: 703-236-2301
E-Mail: riceinfo@usarice.com
Home Page: www.usarice.com
Social Media: Facebook, Twitter, RSS, You Tube

Betsy Ward, President/CEO
Ann Banville, Vice President Domestic Promotion
Patricia Alderson, Vice President Member Services
Jim Guinn, Vice President International
Bob Cummings, Chief Operating Officer

The latest news on issues and activities for the U.S. rice industry.

810 Update
6060 FFA Drive
PO Box 68960
Indianapolis, IN 46268-0960

317-802-6060
888-332-2668
Home Page: www.ffa.org

Important news, information and program updates.
12 Pages
Frequency: Monthly
Circulation: 45,000
Founded in 1928

811 Vegetarian Journal
Vegetarian Resource Group
PO Box 1463
Baltimore, MD 21203
410-366-8343
Fax: 410-366-8804
E-Mail: vrg@vrg.org
Home Page: www.vrg.org
Social Media: Facebook, Twitter, RSS

Charles Stahler, President
Jeannie McStay, Catalog Manager
Debra Wasserman, Treasurer
Keryl Cryer, Senior Editor
Sonja Helman, Coordinator

Informative articles, recipes, book reviews, notices about vegetarian events, product evaluations, where to find vegetarian products and services. All nutrition information based on scientific studies.
Frequency: Quarterly
Circulation: 15000

812 WSSA Newsletter
P.O.Box 7065
Lawrence, KS 66044-7065

785-429-9622
800-627-0629
Fax: 785-843-1274
E-Mail: wssa@allenpress.com
Home Page: www.wssa.net

Rod Lym, President
Joe DiTomaso, Vice President
John Madsen, Secretary
Ian Burke, Treasurer
James Anderson, Director Publications

Promotes research, education and extension outreach activities related to weeds, provides science-based information to the public and policy makers; and fosters awarenes of weeds and their impacts on managed and natural ecosystems.
Founded in 1956

813 **Webster Agricultural Letter**
Webster Communications Corporation
3835 9th St N
Suite 401W
Arlington, VA 22203-5812

703-525-4512
Fax: 703-852-3534
E-Mail: editor@agletter.com
Home Page: www.agletter.com

James C Webster, President
Marilyn Webster, Vice President

Agricultural politics and policy issues.
Cost: $397.00
6 Pages
Frequency: 2x Monthly
ISSN: 1073-4813
Founded in 1980
Printed in one color on matte stock

814 **Weekly Livestock Reporter**
PO Box 7655
Fort Worth, TX 76111-0655

817-831-3147
Fax: 817-831-3117
E-Mail: service@weeklylivestock.com
Home Page: www.weeklylivestock.com

Ted Gouldy, Publisher
Phil Stoll, CEO/President
Mickey Schwarz, Circulation Manager

Offers comprehensive weekly information for cattle farmers and livestock agricultural professionals.
Cost: $18.00
Frequency: Weekly
Circulation: 10000
Founded in 1897

815 **Weekly Weather and Crop Bulletin**
NOAA/USDA Joint Agricultural Weather Facility
1400 Independence Ave SW
Washington, DC 20250

202-720-2791
E-Mail: jawfweb@oce.gov
Home Page: www.usda.gov

Douglas LeComte, Publisher
Annette Holmes, Secretary

Provides a vital source of information on weather, climate and agricultural developments worldwide, along with detailed charts and tables of agrometeorological information that are appropriate for the season.
Cost: $60.00
Frequency: Weekly
Circulation: 1,500
Founded in 1862

Magazines & Journals

816 **AFIA Journal**
American Feed Industry Association
2101 Wilson Boulevard
Suite 916
Arlington, VA 22201

703-524-0810
Fax: 703-524-1921
E-Mail: afia@afia.org
Home Page: www.afia.org
Social Media: Facebook, Twitter, LinkedIn

Joel Newman, President
Richard Sellers, VP and Corporate Secretary
Keith Epperson, Vice President
Sarah Novak, Vice President

Variety of topics about the animal feed industry and its suppliers.
Frequency: Quarterly
Founded in 1909

817 **Acreage Magazine**
Heartland Communications Group
1003 Central Avenue
Fort Dodge, IA 50501

515-955-1600
800-247-2000
Home Page: www.acreagelife.com
Social Media: Facebook

Francis McLean, Publisher

Cultural news and features edited for rural farm producers magazine.
Cost: $5.00
40 Pages
Frequency: Monthly
Founded in 1985

818 **Acres USA**
5321 Industrial Oaks Boulevard
Suite 128
Austin, TX 78735

800-355-5315
Fax: 512-892-4448
E-Mail: info@acresusa.com
Home Page: www.acresusa.com
Social Media: Facebook, Twitter, LinkedIn

Fred C Walters, CEO/President

Commercial-scale organic/ sustainable farming news.
Cost: $27.00
Frequency: Monthly
Circulation: 19000
ISSN: 1076-4968
Founded in 1970

819 **Agri Marketing Magazine**
Henderson Communications LLC
1422 Elbridge Payne Rd
Suite 250
Chesterfield, MO 63017-8544

636-728-1428
Fax: 636-777-4178
E-Mail: info@agrimarketing.com
Home Page: www.agrimarketing.com

Lynn Henderson, Editorial Director
Audrey Evans, Customer Service Manager
Stephanie Wobbe, Editorial Assistant
Judy Henderson, Artist

Covers the unique interests of corporate agribusiness executives, their marketing communications agencies, the agricultural media, ag trade associations and other ag-related professionals.
Circulation: 8000
Founded in 1962

820 **AgriSelling Principles and Practices**
Henderson Communications LLC
1422 Elbridge Payne Rd
Suite 250
Chesterfield, MO 63017-8544

636-728-1428
Fax: 636-777-4178
E-Mail: info@agrimarketing.com
Home Page: www.agrimarketing.com

Lynn Henderson, Editorial Director
Audrey Evans, Customer Service Manager
Stephanie Wobbe, Editorial Assistant
Judy Henderson, Artist

This 448-page book is utilized by many major agribusiness corporations and academic institutions for training its sales and marketing staff and or students.
Founded in 1962

821 **Agribusiness Fieldman**
Western Agricultural Publishing Company
4969 E Clinton Way
Suite 104
Fresno, CA 93727-1549

559-252-7000
E-Mail: westag@psnw.com
Home Page: www.westagpubco.com

For the professional agricultural consultant, featuring the latest information on chemical regulation, pest control techniques and feature stories on PCA and PCO community.

822 **Agrichemical Age**
Farm Progress Publishers
191 S Gary Ave
Carol Stream, IL 60188-2024
630-690-5600
800-441-1410
Fax: 630-462-2869
E-Mail: transf.tovm
Home Page: www.farmprogress.com

Jeffry M Lapin, President
John Vogel, Editor
Willie Vogt, Corporate Editorial Director
John Otte, Economics Editor
Dan Crummett, Executive Editor

Information for fertilizer/pesticide dealers, distributors, commercial applicators and crop consultants.

823 **Agricultural Aviation**
National Agricultural Aviation Association
1440 Duke Street
Alexandria, VA 22314

202-546-5722
Fax: 202-546-5726
E-Mail: information@agaviation.org
Home Page: www.agaviation.org

Dana Ness, President
Rick Boardman, Vice President
Doug Davidson, Secretary
Brenda Watts, Treasurer

Official publication for legislative updates, industry trends, new products and more.
Frequency: 6x Yearly
Founded in 1978

824 **Agricultural History**
The Sheridan Press
MSU History Department
PO Box H
Mississippi State, MS 39762

662-268-2247
E-Mail: aimarcus@history.msstate.edu
Home Page: www.aghistorysociety.org

Claire Strom, Editor
James C Giesen, Executive Secretary
Alan I Marcus, Treasurer

Traces historical lineage of agriculture in the US.
Cost: $47.00
Frequency: Quarterly
Circulation: 900
Founded in 1924

825 **Agriculture Research Magazine**
Agricultural Research Service
George Washington Carver Center
5601 Sunnyside Avenue
Beltsville, MD 20705-5130

301-504-1651
Fax: 301-504-1641

E-Mail: info@ars.usda.gov
Home Page: www.ars.usda.gov/ar

Robert Sowers, Editor/Circulation Manager
William Johnson, Art Director
Edward Knipling, CEO
Carol Durflinger, Secretary
Cost: $50.00
27 Pages
Frequency: Monthly
Circulation: 45000
Founded in 1954

826 **Agronomy Journal**
5585 Guilford Road
Madison, WI 53711-1086

608-273-8080
Fax: 608-273-2021
E-Mail: headquarters@agronomy.org
Home Page: www.agronomy.org
Social Media: Facebook, Twitter, LinkedIn

Ellen E Bergfeld, Executive VP
Luther Smith, Executive Director
Michela Cobb, Director Financial Services
Audrey Jankowski, Analyst/Programmer
Ian Popkewitz, Director IT/Operations

Journal of agriculture and natural resource sciences. Articles convey original research in soil science, crop science, agroclimatology, agronomic modeling, production agriculture, instrumentation, and more.
Founded in 1907

827 **Agweek**
Grand Forks Herald
375 2nd Avenue N
Grand Forks, ND 58203

701-780-1100
800-477-6572
Fax: 701-780-1123
E-Mail: onlineteam@gfherald.com
Home Page: www.agweek.com
Social Media: RSS

Michael Jacobs, Publisher/Editor
Tom Dennis, Editorial/Opinion Page Editor
Dawn Zimmey, Circulation Director
Cory Matt, Managing Editor

Agweek features classified, weather information, farming, ranch news and opinions for the Upper Midwest.
Cost: $32.00
80 Pages
Frequency: Weekly
Circulation: 25,000
Founded in 1879
Printed in 4 colors

828 **Alimentos Balanceados Para Animales**
WATT Publishing Company
303 N Main Street
Rockford, IL 61101

815-966-5400
Fax: 815-966-6416
E-Mail: gill@wattmm.com
Home Page: www.wattnet.com

Jim Watt, Chairman/CEO
Clayton Gill, Editorial Director
Christina Karmer, Human Resources Consultant

For feed industry professionals in Latin America.
Founded in 1994

829 **American Agriculturist**
Farm Progress Companies
5227 B Baltimore Park
Littlestown, PA 17340

717-359-0150
800-441-1410
Fax: 717-359-0250
E-Mail: jvogel@farmprogress.com
Home Page: www.farmprogress.com

John Vogel, Editor
Willie Vogt, Corporate Editorial Director
Dan Crummett, Executive Editor

Serves Northeast producers with information to help them maximize their productivity and profitability. Each issue is packed with information, ideas, news and analysis.
Cost: $26.95
Frequency: Monthly
Founded in 1842

830 **American Bee Journal**
Dadant and Sons
51 S 2nd St
Hamilton, IL 62341-1397

217-847-3324
888-922-1293
Fax: 217-847-3660
E-Mail: editor@americanbeejournal.com
Home Page: www.americanbeejournal.com
Social Media: Facebook, Twitter

Tim C Dadant, President
Marta Menn, Advertising
Dianne Behnke, Publisher
Joe Graham, Editor

Read by commercial and hobby beekeepers and entomologists.
Cost: $22.95
80 Pages
Frequency: Monthly
Circulation: 11000
ISSN: 0002-7626
Founded in 1861
Printed in 4 colors on glossy stock

831 **American Christmas Tree Journal**
National Christmas Tree Association
16020 Swingley Ridge Rd
Suite 300
Chesterfield, MO 63017-6030

636-449-5070
Fax: 636-449-5051
E-Mail: info@realchristmastrees.org
Home Page: www.realchristmastrees.org

Cline Church Ciocci, President
DeLaine Bender, Executive Director
Becky Rasmussen, Assistant Director
Rick Dungey, PR/Marketing Director
Lauren Mangnall, Project Coordinator

Covers production and research topics, marketing advice, feature stories, legislative updates, tax and business management info, NCTA news and more
Cost: $57.00
Frequency: Quarterly
Circulation: 1500
ISSN: 0569-3845

832 **American Feed Industry Association Journal**
2101 Wilson Blvd
Suite 916
Arlington, VA 22201-3047

703-524-0810
Fax: 703-524-1921
E-Mail: afia@afia.org
Home Page: www.afia.org
Social Media: Facebook, Twitter, LinkedIn

Joel Newman, President
Richard Sellers, VP/Feed Regulation & Nutrition
Keith Epperson, VP/Manufacturing & Training
Sarah Novak, VP/Membership & Public Relations
Leanna Nail, Director of Administration

Includes a variety of topics about the animal feed industry and its suppliers.
Founded in 1909

833 **American Fruit Grower**
Meister Media Worldwide
37733 Euclid Ave
Willoughby, OH 44094-5992
440-942-2000
800-572-7740
Fax: 440-975-3447
E-Mail: info@meistermedia.com
Home Page: www.meistermedia.com

Gary Fitzgerald, Chairman and CEO
Michael Deluca, President
Donald Hohmeier, VP and CFO

Specialized production and marketing information and industry-wide support for fruit growers.
Cost: $19.95
66 Pages
Frequency: Monthly
Circulation: 14000
Founded in 1880

834 **American Journal of Agricultural Economics (AJAE)**
American Agricultural Economics Association
555 E Wells Street
Suite 1100
Milwaukee, WI 53202-6600

414-918-3190
Fax: 414-276-3349
E-Mail: info@aaea.org
Home Page: www.aaea.org
Social Media: Facebook

Richard Sexton, President
Julie Caswell, President-elect

The leading journal for agricultural economics.
3000 Members
Frequency: 5x Yearly
Founded in 1910

835 **American Journal of Enology and Viticulture**
1784 Picasso Avenue, Suite D
PO Box 1855
Davis, CA 95617-1855
530-753-3142
Fax: 530-753-3318
E-Mail: society@asev.org
Home Page: www.asev.org
Social Media: Twitter, LinkedIn

Lyndie Boulton, Executive Director
Dan Howard, Assistant Executive Director
Leticia Chacon-Rodriguez, President
James Kennedy, First Vice President

The official journal of the American Society for Enology and Viticulture and is the premier journal dedicated to scientific research on winemaking and grapegrowing.
Frequency: Quarterly
Founded in 1950

836 **American Small Farm Magazine**
Back 40 Group
P.O. Box 8
Hartshorn, MO 65479

573-858-3244
866-284-9844
Fax: 573-858-3245
E-Mail: Publisher@SmallFarm.com
Home Page: www.smallfarm.com

Paul Berg, Editor
Herman Beck-Chenoweth, Publisher

Published for the owner/operator of farms from 5 to 300 acres. Focuses on production agriculture including alternative and sustainable farming ideas and technology, case studies, small farm lifestyle and tradition.
Cost: $18.00
Frequency: Monthly
Circulation: 62,444

ISSN: 1064-7473
Founded in 1992

837 **American Vegetable Grower**
Meister Media Worldwide
37733 Euclid Ave
Willoughby, OH 44094-5992

440-942-2000
800-572-7740
Fax: 440-975-3447
Home Page: www.growingproduce.com/americanvegetablegrower/

Gary Fitzgerald, President
Rosemary Gordon, Editor
Jo Monahan, Publisher
Brian Sparks, Group Editor
Paul Rusnak, Managing Editor

American Vegetable Grower magazine provides insight on field, greenhouse and organic production, marketing, and new varieties and products.
Cost: $19.95
Frequency: Monthly
Circulation: 26000
Founded in 1908

838 **Animal & Dairy News**
American Dairy Science Association
2441 Village Green Pl
Champaign, IL 61822-7676

217-356-5146
Fax: 217-398-4119
E-Mail: adsa@assochq.org
Home Page: www.adsa.org

Donald C Beitz, President
Philld C Tongz, VP
Peter Studney, Executive Director
William R Aimutis, Treasurer

A Publication of ADSA
Founded in 1898
Mailing list available for rent

839 **Applied Economic Perspectives and Policy (AEPP)**
American Agricultural Economics Association
555 E Wells Street
Suite 1100
Milwaukee, WI 53202-6600

414-918-3190
Fax: 414-276-3349
E-Mail: info@aaea.org
Home Page: www.aaea.org
Social Media: Facebook

Richard Sexton, President
Julie Caswell, President-elect

Formerly the Review of Agricultural Economics, each issue includes both featured and submitted articles.
3000 Members
Frequency: Quarterly
Founded in 1910

840 **Beef Today**
Farm Journal Media
1818 Market Street
31st Floor
Philadelphia, PA 19103-3654

215-578-8900
800-331-9310
Fax: 215-568-6782
E-Mail: jstruyk@farmjournal.com
Home Page: www.agweb.com/livestock/beef
Social Media: Facebook, Twitter, YouTube

Andy Weber, Chief Executive Officer
Steve Custer, Executive Vice President
Jeff Pence, President, Electronic Media
Chuck Roth, Senior Vice President
Boyce Thompson, Editorial Director

This is the only nationwide publication that currently serves beef producers of all sizes-large and small. It delivers the tools cattlemen need to make sustainable and profitable choices to transition their herd to the next generation. Topics include genetics, animal health, business planning, pasture management, wildlife management and market analysis.
Frequency: Weekly
Founded in 1973

841 **Belt Pulley**
Belt Pulley Pub Company
PO Box 58
Jefferson, WI 53549-1341

920-674-9732
Home Page: www.beltpulley.com

Katie Elmore, Publisher
Jane Aumann, Managing Editor

Covers antique tractors and farm machinery of all makes and models.
Cost: $20.00
Frequency: Monthly
Circulation: 3500
Founded in 1987

842 **Better Crops International Magazine**
Potash and Phosphate Institute
3500 Parkway Lane
Suite 550
Norcross, GA 30092-2844

770-447-0335
Fax: 770-448-0439
E-Mail: info@ipni.net
Home Page: http://www.ipni.net/wave

Terry Roberts, President
Steve Couch, VP Administration
Gavin Sulewski, Editor

Researchers report on nutrient-related topics for corn, wheat, groundnut, oil palm, sugarcane, rice, crop rotations, and fish ponds. The issue concludes with a back cover commentary explaining why support of agricultural development is the right thing to do.

843 **Biodynamics Journal**
PO Box 944
East Troy, WI 53120-0944

26- 6-9 92
888-516-7797
Fax: 26- 6-9 92
E-Mail: info@biodynamics.com
Home Page: www.biodynamics.com
Social Media: Facebook

Jean-Paul Courtens, President
Janet Gamble, Secretary
Steffen Schneider, Treasurer
Robert Karp, Executive Director

Provides a thoughtful collection of original articles centered on a theme of interest to the biodynamic community. Recent themes have included urban agriculture, biodynamic community, earth healing, raw milk, and the biodynamic preparations.

844 **Capital Press**
Press Publishing Company
1400 Broadway NE
PO Box 2048
Salem, OR 97308-2048

503-364-4431
800-882-6789
Fax: 503-370-4383
E-Mail: bnipp@capitalpress.com
Home Page: www.capitalpress.com
Social Media: Facebook, Twitter, LinkedIn, MySpace, Stumble Upon

Mike Forrester, President
John Perry, COO
Michael O'Brien, Publisher
Joe Beach, Editor

For the agricultural and forest community of the Pacific Northwest.
Cost: $44.00
60 Pages
Frequency: Weekly
Circulation: 37000
Founded in 1928
Printed in 4 colors

845 **Carrot Country**
Columbia Publishing
8405 Ahtanum Rd
Yakima, WA 98903-9432

509-248-2452
800-900-2452
Fax: 509-248-4056
E-Mail: dbrent@columbiapublications.com
Home Page: www.carrotcountry.com

Brent Clement, Editor/Publisher
Mike Stoker, Publisher

Includes information on carrot production, grower and shipper feature stories, carrot research, new varieties, market reports, spot reports on overseas production and marketing and other key issues and trends of interest to US and Canadian carrot growers.
Cost: $10.00
Frequency: Quarterly
Circulation: 2500
ISSN: 1071 6653
Founded in 1993
Printed in 4 colors on glossy stock

846 **Cattle Guard**
Colorado Cattlemen's Agricultrual Land Trust
8833 Ralston Road
Arvada, CO 80002-2239

303-431-6422
Fax: 303-431-6446
E-Mail: ccaglt@aol.com
Home Page: www.coloradocattle.org

T Wright Dickinson, President
Frank Daley, First VP
Tim Canterbury, Treasurer
Terry Frankhauser, Executive VP
Heidi Brown, Membership and Operations Manager

A full overview of information is given through this magazine for cattle farmers and breeders.
Founded in 1867

847 **Cattleman**
Texas & Southwestern Cattle Raisers Association
1301 W 7th St
Suite 201
Fort Worth, TX 76102-2665

817-332-7064
800-242-7820
Fax: 817-332-8523
E-Mail: tscra@tscra.org
Home Page: www.texascattleraisers.org
Social Media: Facebook, Twitter

Joe Parker, President
Eldon White, Executive VP and CEO
Clay Birdwell, First VP
Pete Bonds, Second VP
Matt Brockman, Manager

Full overview of information for the cattle producer in Texas and Oklahoma.
Cost: $25.00
130 Pages
Frequency: Monthly
Circulation: 16000
Founded in 1877
Printed in 4 colors on glossy stock

848 **Cereal Foods World**
AACC International

3340 Pilot Knob Rd
St. Paul, MN 55121-2055

651-454-7250
Fax: 651-454-0766
E-Mail: akohn@scisoc.org
Home Page: www.accnet.org

David H Hahn, President
Debi E Rogers, Chair of Board
Laura Hansen, Treasurer

Articles on scientific studies that focus on advances in grain based food science.
Founded in 1915

849 **Choices**
Agricultural & Applied Economics Association
1709 Darien Club Drive
Darien, IL 60561

630-271-1679
Fax: 630-908-3384
E-Mail: Walt@farmfoundation.org
Home Page: www.choicesmagazine.org

Walter J Armbruster, Editor
James Novak, Associate Editor

Provides current coverage regarding economic implications of food, farm, resource, or rural community issues directed toward a broad audience. Publishes thematic groupings of papers and individual papers.
Frequency: Quarterly
ISSN: 0886-5558
Founded in 1910
Printed in 4 colors on glossy stock

850 **Choices Magazine**
American Agricultural Economics Association
555 E Wells Street
Suite 1100
Milwaukee, WI 53202-6600

414-918-3190
Fax: 414-276-3349
E-Mail: info@aaea.org
Home Page: www.aaea.org
Social Media: Facebook

Richard Sexton, President
Julie Caswell, President-elect

Designed to provide current coverage regarding economic implications of food, farm, resource, or rural community issues directed toward a broad audience. Online only.
3000 Members
Frequency: Quarterly
Founded in 1910

851 **Christmas Tree Lookout**
Pacific Northwest Christmas Tree Association
4093 12th Street SE
PO Box 3366
Salem, OR 97302

503-364-2942
Fax: 503-581-6819
E-Mail: info@christmas-tree.com
Home Page: www.nwtrees.com

Bruce Wiseman, President
John Tillman, VP- Washington
Jan Hupp, Secretary/Treasurer
Mike Ramsby, V.P. Oregon
Bryan Ostlund, Executive Director

Marketing research and industry information for Christmas tree growers. Mailing list available.
Cost: $25.00
80 Pages
Frequency: Quarterly
Circulation: 1500
Founded in 1955
Printed in 4 colors on glossy stock

852 **Christmas Trees**
Tree Publishers
PO Box 107
Lecompton, KS 66050-0107

785-887-6324
E-Mail: ctreesmag@gmail.com
Home Page: www.christmastreesmagazine.com
Social Media: Facebook, Twitter

Catherine Howard, Publisher/Editor/Advertising

Magazine of plantation management for Christmas tree growers, shearing, shaping and marketing. Accepts advertising.
Cost: $16.00
44 Pages
Frequency: Quarterly
Circulation: 3200
ISSN: 0149-0217
Founded in 1973
Printed in 4 colors on glossy stock

853 **Citrus & Vegetable Magazine**
Vance Publishing
400 Knightsbridge Pkwy
Lincolnshire, IL 60069

847-634-2600
Fax: 847-634-4379
E-Mail: info@vancepublishing.com
Home Page: www.vancepublishing.com

Shawn Etheridge, VP and Publishing Director
Matthew Morgan, Director
Greg Johnson, Editorial Director
Vicky Boyd, Editor

Devlivers profitable production and management strategies to commercial citrus and vegetable growers in Florida.
Cost: $45.00
Frequency: Monthly
Circulation: 12000
Founded in 1937
Printed in 4 colors on glossy stock

854 **Citrus Industry**
Southeast AgNet Publications
5053 NW Hwy 225-A
Ocala, FL 34482

352-671-1909
Fax: 888-943-2224
E-Mail: office@southeastagent.com
Home Page: www.citrusindustry.net

William Cooper, President
Robin Loftin, Vice President
Ernie Neff, Editor

News, facts and data of interest to citrus growers, processors and shippers.
Cost: $24.00
64 Pages
Frequency: 6 issues per year
Circulation: 9900
Founded in 1920
Printed in 4 colors on glossy stock

855 **Cotton Farming**
One Grower Publishing, LLC
Collierville, TN 38117-5710

901-853-5067
Fax: 901-853-2197
E-Mail: lguthrie@onegrower.com
Home Page: www.cottonfarming.com
Social Media: Twitter, RSS, Flickr

Mike Rolfs, President
Lia Guthrie, Publisher
Tommy Horton, Editor
Carroll Smith, Senior Writer
Debbie Gibbs, Sales Manager

For commercial cotton growers across the United States Cotton Belt.
52 Pages
Frequency: Monthly
Circulation: 36300
Founded in 1993
Printed in 4 colors on glossy stock

856 **Country Living**
Arens Publications
395 S High Street
Covington, OH 45318-0069

937-473-2028
Fax: 937-473-2500
E-Mail: garyg@arnespub.com
Home Page: www.arenspub.com

Gary Godfrey, Owner
Connie Didier, Manager
Don Selanders, Sales Manager

Current news and features devoted to the agricultural industry.
Cost: $13.95
Frequency: Monthly
Circulation: 17000
Founded in 1954

857 **Country Woman**
Reiman Publications
5400 S 60th St
Greendale, WI 53129-1404

414-423-0100
888-861-1264
Fax: 414-423-1143
E-Mail: editors@countrywomenmagazine.com
Home Page: www.reimanpub.com
Social Media: Facebook, Twitter

Barbara Newton, President
Marylin Kruse, Editor
Lisa Karpinski, Director/Marketing
Reese Ludewig, Marketing Manager

Offers recipes, stories, profiles and articles pertaining to the country woman.
Cost: $14.98
68 Pages
Frequency: 6 issues in a year
Circulation: 50,000 +
Founded in 1970

858 **Countryside and Small Stock Journal**
Countryside Publications
145 Industrial Dr
Medford, WI 54451-1711

715-785-7979
800-551-5691
Fax: 715-785-7414
E-Mail: customerservice@countrysidemag.com
Home Page: www.countrysidemag.com

Mike Campbell, Publisher
Anne-Marie Belanger, Managing Editor
Elen Grunseth, Circulation & Fulfillment

Offers information for homesteaders seeking a self-reliant lifestyle.
Cost: $18.00
132 Pages
Circulation: 115000
ISSN: 8750-7595
Founded in 1917
Printed in on newsprint stock

859 **County Agents**
National Association of County Agricultural Agents
6584 W Duroc Road
Maroa, IL 61756

217-794-3700
Fax: 217-794-5901
E-Mail: exec-dir@nacaa.com
Home Page: www.nacaa.com
Social Media: Facebook, Twitter

Paul Craig, President
Henry Dorough, President-elect
Mike Hogan, Vice President
Richard Fetcher, Secretary
Parman Green, Treasurer

Members receive professional improvement, news of association activities, shared education

efforts from other states and reports from NACAA leadership and member states.
Cost: $10.00
Frequency: Quarterly
Circulation: 5000
Founded in 1916
Mailing list available for rent: 3850 names at $125 per M
Printed in 4 colors on matte stock

860 Cranberries Magazine
Cranberries Magazine
PO Box 190
Rochester, MA 02770

508-763-8080
Fax: 508-763-4141
E-Mail: cranberries@comcast.net

Carolyn Gilmore, Editor/Publisher

Containing up-to-date news, technical articles, new product information, grower profiles, economic data and other related features regarding the cranberry industry. Accepts advertising.
Cost: $25.00
28 Pages
Frequency: Monthly
Circulation: 850
Founded in 1936

861 Crop Insurance Today
National Crop Insurance Services
8900 Indian Creek Pkwy
Suite 600
Overland Park, KS 66210-1567

913-685-2767
Fax: 913-685-3080
E-Mail: webmaster@ag-risk.org
Home Page: www.ag-risk.org

Thomas Zacharias, President

A quarterly magazine published by the National Crop Insurance Services. Includes current rate information, tips and advice, industry news, forecasts, and resources.
Cost: $13.00
Frequency: Quarterly
Circulation: 18000
Founded in 1915
Printed in 4 colors on glossy stock

862 Crop Science
Crop Science Society of America
5585 Guilford Road,
Madison, WI 53711-5801

608-273-8080
Fax: 608-273-2021
E-Mail: headquarters@crops.org
Home Page: www.crops.org
Social Media: Facebook, Twitter, LinkedIn

Ellen Bergfeld, CEO
Wes Meixelsperger, CFO

Publishes original research in crop breeding and genetics, crop physiology and metabolism, crop ecology, production and management, and much more.
Founded in 1955

863 DVM Magazine
Advanstar Communications
8033 Flint St
Lenexa, KS 66214-3335

913-492-4300
800-225-6864
Fax: 913-871-3808
E-Mail: dverdon@advanstar.com
Home Page: www.dvm360.com
Social Media: Facebook, Twitter

Margaret Rampey, Editor
Marnette Falley, Principal
Sabrina Wilcox, COO
Dot Theisen, Sales Manager
Mindy Valcarcel, Senior Editor

The leading news in veterinary medicine covering news, features, practice management and new products and services.
Cost: $48.00
Frequency: Monthly
Circulation: 20000+
ISSN: 0012-7337
Founded in 1992

864 Dairy Herd Management
Vance Publishing
400 Knightsbridge Parkway
Lincolnshire, IL 60069

847-634-2600
Fax: 847-634-4379
E-Mail: info@vancepublishing.com
Home Page: www.vancepublishing.com

Tom Quaife, Editor/Associate Publisher
Matthew Morgan, Director

Helps top dairy producers prepare for and adapt to the different management skills needed in this increasingly evolving industry
Cost: $60.00
Frequency: Monthly
Circulation: 61638

865 Dairy Today
Farm Journal
30 S 15th Street
Suite 900
Philadelphia, PA 19102-4803

215-578-8900
800-320-7992
E-Mail: dcrisafulli@farmjournal.com
Home Page: www.farmjournal.com
Social Media: Facebook, Twitter, RSS, You Tube

Charlene Finck, Editor
Katie Humphreys, Managing Editor
Beth Snyder, Art Director
Sara Schafer, Business & Crops Online Editor

Award-winning editorial covers the broad spectrum of production, nutrition and marketing information. It serves dairy producers who milk 40+ cows or are members of the Dairy Herd Improvement Association.
Frequency: Monthly
Circulation: 125000
Founded in 1989

866 Dealer & Applicator
Vance Publishing
400 Knightsbridge Pkwy
Lincolnshire, IL 60069-3628

847-634-2600
Fax: 847-634-4379
Home Page: www.vancepublishing.com

Peggy Walker, President
Dean Horowitz, VP eMedia & Marketing
Steve Reiss, VP Salon & Woodworking
William C. Vance, CEO
Shawn Etheridge, VP Produce & Raw Crop

Serves as the reader's business partner to provide full-service dealers and custom applicators with management and business strategies to increase profitability.
Founded in 1937

867 Drovers
Vance Publishing
400 Knightsbridge Parkway
Lincolnshire, IL 60069

847-634-2600
Fax: 847-634-4379
E-Mail: info@vancepublishing.com
Home Page: www.vancepublishing.com

William C Vance, Chairman
Peggy Walker, President

Recognized as the beef industry leader for more than 130 years, valued for its management, production and marketing information.
Cost: $60.00
Frequency: Monthly
Circulation: 92000
Founded in 1873

868 Eastern DairyBusiness
DairyBusiness Communications
6437 Collamer Road
East Syracuse, NY 13057-1031

315-703-7979
800-334-1904
Fax: 315-703-7988
E-Mail: kjentz@dairybusiness.com
Home Page: www.dairybusiness.com
Social Media: Facebook, Twitter, YouTube

Joel P Hastings, President
John Montandon, President & Co-CEO
Scott A Smith, Chairman / Co-CEO

Reports on milk production and prices, quotes on hay and feed markets, animal health and nutrition, and the newest innovations in dairying technology, specifically tailored to the Eastern parts of the United States
Cost: $49.95
67 Pages
Frequency: Monthly
Circulation: 14000
ISSN: 1528-4360
Founded in 1904
Printed in 4 colors on glossy stock

869 Egg Industry
WATT Publishing Company
303 N Main Street
Suite 500
Rockford, IL 61101

815-966-5400
Fax: 815-966-6416
E-Mail: tokeefe@wattnet.net
Home Page: www.wattnet.com

James Watt, Chairman/CEO
Greg Watt, President/COO
Terrance O'Keefe, Editor

Regarded as the standard for information on current issues, trends, production practices, processing, personalities and emerging technology. A pivotal source of news, data and information for decision-makers in the buying centers of companies producing eggs and further-processed products.
Cost: $36.00
Frequency: Monthly
Circulation: 2500

870 Executive Guide to World Poultry Trends
WATT Publishing Company
303 N Main Street
Suite 500
Rockford, IL 61101

815-966-5400
Fax: 815-966-6416
Home Page: www.wattnet.com

James Watt, Chairman/CEO
Greg Watt, President/COO
Jeff Swanson, Publishing Director

Offers detailed analysis on a country-by-country and market-by-market basis.

871 FFA New Horizons
National FFA Organization
6060 FFA Drive
P.O. Box 68960
Indianapolis, IN 46268

317-802-6060
800-772-0939
Fax: 317-802-6051
E-Mail: newhorizons@ffa.org

Home Page: www.ffanewhorizons.org
Social Media: Facebook, Twitter

Jessy Yancey, Association Editor
Christina Carden, Associate Production Director
Julie Woodard, FFA Publications Manager

The official member magazine of the FFA contains information about agricultural education, career possibilities, chapter and individual accomplishments and news on FFA. Now available online.
100 Pages
Frequency: Bi-Monthly
Circulation: 525000
ISSN: 1069-806x
Founded in 1928
Printed in 4 colors

872 **FRONTIER**
Meat & Livestock Australia
1401 K Street NW
Suite 602
Washington, DC 20005

202-521-2551
Fax: 202-521-2699
E-Mail: info@mla.com.au
Home Page: www.mla.com.au
Social Media: Facebook, Twitter, YouTube

Don Heatley, Chairman
David Palmer, Managing Director
Bernie Bindon, Director
Chris Hudson, Director

Offers northern beef producers practical information on how to best manage their cattle enterprise and improve on-property profits and sustainability.
30000 Members
Frequency: Quarterly
Founded in 1998

873 **Farm Chemicals International**
Meister Media Worldwide
65 Germantown Ct.
Suite 202
Cordova, TN 38018

901-756-8822
800-572-7740
E-Mail: fci.circ@meistermedia.com
Home Page:
www.farmchemicalsinternational.com
Social Media: Facebook, Twitter, RSS

William Miller II, President
Rosemary Gordon, Editor
Robert White, COO
Roger Hercl, CFO
Richard Meister, Director

Information on production, marketing and application of crop protection chemicals and fertilizers.
Circulation: 8000
Founded in 1986

874 **Farm Equipment**
Cygnus Publishing
1233 Janesville Avenue
PO Box 803
Fort Atkinson, WI 53538-0803

920-000-1111
800-547-7377
Fax: 920-563-1699
E-Mail: editor@cpasn.com
Home Page: www.cygnus.com

John French, Chief Executive Officer
Paul Bonaiuto, Chief Financial Officer
Kathy Scott, Director of Public Relations
Ed Wood, Vice President, Human Resources
Kris Flitcroft, Executive Vice President

An industry-wide information and product news curriculum for farm equipment dealers that enhances their knowledge of business management principles.
Cost: $48.00
Frequency: Monthly
Circulation: 10000
Founded in 1937
Printed in 4 colors on glossy stock

875 **Farm Equipment Guide**
Heartland Communications
1003 Central Avenue
PO Box 1115
Fort Dodge, IA 50501-1115

515-955-1600
800-247-2000
Fax: 515-574-2182
E-Mail: dustin@agdeal.com
Home Page: www.farmershotline.com
Social Media: Facebook, Twitter

Sandra J Simonson, Group Publisher
Tracy Roper, Production Manager
Tammy Sweeney, Operational Manager
Dustin Hector, Sales Manager
Chet Frahm, Advertising Sales Associate

A subscription that includes an annual blue book of specifications, serial numbers and average pricing on farm machinery with monthly updates that list thousands of pieces for sale and thousands of actual auction values.
120 Pages
Frequency: Monthly
Circulation: 20,000
ISSN: 1047-725X
Founded in 1981
Printed in 4 colors on glossy stock

876 **Farm Impact**
314 E Church Street
Mascoutah, IL 62258-2100

618-566-8282
Fax: 618-566-8283

Greg Hoskins, Publisher
Michael King, Advertising Manager

Offers information to farmers.
Frequency: Monthly

877 **Farm Journal**
30 S 15th Street
Suite 900
Philadelphia, PA 19102-4803

215-557-8900
800-523-1538
Fax: 215-568-4436
E-Mail: scuster@farmjournal.com
Home Page: www.farmjournalmedia.com

Andrew J Weber Jr, CEO/President
Crain Freiberg, Editor
Steve Custer, President/Publishing
Chuck Roth, Senior Vice President/Project Dev

Published for operators and owners of commercial farms and ranches. Provides timely, useful marketing and management information to help them produce more efficiently, buy more wisely, sell their products at the highest possible prices, and retain as much of their income as possible.
Cost: $24.75
182 Pages
Frequency: Monthly
Circulation: 440,000
Founded in 1878

878 **Farm Reporter**
Meridian Star
814 22nd Avenue
PO Box 1591
Meridian, MS 39302

601-693-1551
Fax: 601-485-1210
Home Page: www.meridianstar.com
Social Media: Facebook, Twitter

Michael Stewart, Executive Editor
Steve Gillespie, Assistant Editor
Ida Brown, Staff Writer
Briand Livingston, Staff Writer
Otha Barham, Outdoors Page

Reports on every phase of farming including timber, cattle, poultry and all growing crops.
Cost: $2.00
Frequency: Monthly

879 **Farm Review**
Lewis Publishing Company
PO Box 153
Lynden, WA 98264-0153

360-354-4444
Fax: 360-354-4445
E-Mail: tribune@lyndentribune.com
Home Page: www.lyndentribune.com

Michael D Lewis, Publisher
Calvin Bratt, Editor
Diane Partlow, Circulation Manager

Offers a review of farming techniques and trends nationwide.
Cost: $30.00
Frequency: Quarterly
Circulation: 7000
Founded in 1888

880 **Farm Show Magazine**
Farm Show Publishing
Johnson Building
PO Box 1029
Lakeville, MN 55044-1029

952-469-5572
800-834-9665
Fax: 952-469-5579
Home Page: www.farmshow.com/
Social Media: Facebook

Mark Newhall, Editor/Publisher
Bill Gergen, Associate Editor

Focuses on latest agricultural products, and product evaluation. Contains no advertising.
Cost: $17.95
Founded in 1977

881 **Farm Talk**
Farm Talk
1801 S Highway 59
PO Box 601
Parsons, KS 67357-4900

620-421-9450
800-356-8255
Fax: 620-421-9473
E-Mail: farmtalk@terraworld.net
Home Page: www.farmtalknewspaper.com

Mark Parker, Publisher
Ted Gum, Manager

Agriculture for Eastern Kansas, Western Missouri, Northeast Oklahoma and Northwest Arkansas.
Cost: $30.00
60 Pages
Frequency: Weekly
Circulation: 10000
Founded in 1974

882 **Farm World (Farm Week)**
Mayhill Publications
27 N Jefferson Street
PO Box 90
Knightstown, IN 46148-1242

317-326-2235
800-876-5133
Fax: 765-345-3398

E-Mail: webmaster@mayhill-publications.com
Home Page: www.mayhill-publications.com/

Dave Blower Jr, Editor
Richard Lewis, Publisher
Diana Scott, Marketing Manager

Agriculture, farming, and related areas in Indiana, Ohio and Kentucky. Accepts advertising.
Cost: $28.50
84 Pages
Frequency: Monthly

883 **Farm and Dairy**
Lyle Printing and Publishing Company
185 E State Street
PO Box 38
Salem, OH 44460

330-337-3419
800-837-3419
Fax: 330-337-9550
E-Mail: farmanddairy@aol.com
Home Page: www.farmanddairy.com

Scot Darling, Chief Executive Officer, Publisher
Susan Crowell, Editor
Billy Sekely, Advertising Manager
Howard Marsh, Circulation Manager

Briefs of research reports from experiment stations in agriculture, success stories concerning farmers of Ohio, Pennsylvania and West Virginia, sale and livestock market reports, auctions and more. Accepts advertising.
Cost: $ 28.00
132 Pages
Circulation: 33500
ISSN: 0014-7826
Founded in 1914
Printed in 4 colors on n stock

884 **Farm and Ranch Living**
Reiman Publications
5400 S 60th St
Greendale, WI 53129-1404

414-423-0100
888-858-5417
Fax: 414-423-1143
E-Mail: editors@farmandranchliving.com
Home Page: www.reimanpub.com

Barbara Newton, President
Catherine Cassidy, SVP/Editor-in-Chief
Ann Kaiser, Editor
Lisa Karpinski, Marketing & Circulation Manager
Gretchen Trautman, Membership Director

Includes stories written by working farm families, antique tractor events and rural photo contests.
Cost: $3.99
68 Pages
Frequency: Bimonthly
Founded in 1978

885 **FarmWorld**
DMG World Media
27 N Jefferson Street
PO Box 90
Knightstown, IN 46148-1242

765-345-5133
800-876-5133
Fax: 765-345-5133
E-Mail: webmaster@farmworldonline.com
Home Page: www.farmworldonline.com

Tony Gregory, Publisher
David Blower Jr, Editor
Meggie Foster, Assistant Editor
Toni Hodson, Advertising Manager

Agriculture, farming, and related areas in Indiana, Ohio and Kentucky. Accepts advertising.
Cost: $38.95
84 Pages
Frequency: Weekly
Founded in 1955
Printed in 4 colors on newsprint stock

886 **Farmers Digest**
Heartland Communications
1003 Central Avenue
PO Box 1115
Fort Dodge, IA 50501-1115

515-955-1600
800-247-2000
Fax: 515-574-2182
E-Mail: fd@farmersdigest.com
Home Page: www.agdeal.com

Sandra J Simonsoa, Group Publisher
Melanie Filloon, Subscription Coordinator

Straightforwarded, commonsense articles on every aspect of farming and ranching edited with one goal in mind - to make you a better farmer or rancher.
Founded in 1941

887 **Farmers Hot Line**
Heartland Communications
1003 Central Avenue
Fort Dodge, IA 50501-1052

515-955-1600
800-247-2000
Fax: 515-955-1668
E-Mail: dustin@agdeal.com
Home Page: www.agdeal.com
Social Media: Facebook, Twitter

Gale W McKinney II, President/CFO
Mary Gonnerman, Vice President
Sandy Simonson, Publisher
Dustin Hector, Sales Manager
Chet Frahm, Advertising Sales Associate

Distributed to manufacturers, farmers, auctioneers and service companies nationwide. Designed to help buyers and sellers of new and used farm machinery, auctions, farm real estate, services and supplies.
Cost: $9.95
Circulation: 50000
Founded in 1988

888 **Farmers' Advance**
Camden Publications
331 E Bell Street
PO Box 130
Camden, MI 49232

517-368-0365
800-222-6336
Fax: 517-368-5131
E-Mail: transfer@ca.homecomm.net
Home Page: www.farmersadvance.com/
Social Media: Facebook

Don Lee, Circulation Manager
Richard Aginian, President
Ken Ungar, Senior Vice President
Kyle Hupfer, Director

Farming technology magazine.
Cost: $25.00
Frequency: Weekly
Circulation: 20000
Founded in 1898

889 **Farmers' Exchange**
Exchange
PO Box 490
Fayetteville, TN 37334

931-433-9737
Fax: 931-433-0053
E-Mail: exchange@vallnet.com
Home Page: www.fexonline.com

William Thomas, Publisher/Editor/CEO
Jim Bowers, Sales/Marketing Manager

Magazine offers a forum for the exchange of farming ideas and information country-wide.
56 Pages
Frequency: Monthly
Circulation: 30000
Founded in 1987

890 **Farmshine**
Dieter Krieg
State and Main Streets
PO Box 219
Brownstown, PA 17508

717-656-8050
866-724-6455
Fax: 717-656-8188
E-Mail: advertise@farmshine.com
Home Page: www.farmshine.com

Dieter Krieg, Publisher/Editor
Tammy Krieg, Ad Sales

Information pertaining to the farming community.
Cost: $12.00
Frequency: Weekly
ISSN: 0745-7553
Founded in 1979
Printed in on newsprint stock

891 **Fastline Productions**
Fastline Publications
4900 Fox Run Road
PO Box 248
Buckner, KY 40010

502-222-0146
800-626-6409
Fax: 502-222-0615
Home Page: www.fastline.com
Social Media: Facebook, Twitter, YouTube, Flickr

William G Howard, President/Editor
Gail Olzewski, Owner
Clifford Wolfe, CIO
Melanie Combs, Vice President
Crysten Minzenberger, Marketing Manager

Nationwide and regional picture buying guides for the farming industry.
Cost: $12.00
Frequency: Monthly
Founded in 1978

892 **Feed & Grain**
Cygnus Business Media
1233 Janesville Ave
Fort Atkinson, WI 53538

631-845-2700
800-547-7377
E-Mail: info@cygnus.com
Home Page: www.cygnusb2b.com

John French, CEO
Paul Bonaiuto, CFO
Edward Wood, Vice President, HR & Communications

Provides techniques and solutions on ways yo increase productivity and profitability for the commercial feed, grain and allied processing industry.
Frequency: Bi-Monthly
Circulation: 16,500

893 **Feed Additive Compendium**
The Miller Publishing Company
5810 W 78th St
Suite 200
Bloomington, MN 55439

952-931-0211
Fax: 952-938-1832
E-Mail: smuirhead@feedstuffs.com
Home Page: www.feedstuffs.com

Sarah Muirhead, Publisher
Rod Smith, Staff Editor/Livestock & Poultry
Sally Schuff, Staff Editor/Washington Bureau
Jacqui Fatka, Staff Editor/Grains & Ingredients
Kristin Baker, Editorial Production Manager

This magazine takes a closer look at the food additives and agriculture industries.
Cost: $260.00
Frequency: Weekly
Founded in 1935

894 Feed International
WATT Publishing Company
303 N Main Street
Suite 500
Rockford, IL 61101

815-966-5400
Fax: 815-966-6416
E-Mail: kjennison@wattnet.net
Home Page: www.wattnet.com

James Watt, Chairman/CEO
Greg Watt, President/COO
Ken Jennison, Editor

Provides feed formulators and manufacturers outside North America with the latest feed and grain market developments, management strategies, and information on nutrition and regulations to efficiently and safely formulate, process and market animal feeds and become more competitive in the world market.
Cost: $48.00
Frequency: Monthly
Circulation: 19191
ISSN: 9274-5771
Founded in 1980
Mailing list available for rent: 19,191 names at $225 per M
Printed in 4 colors

895 Feed Management
WATT Publishing Company
303 N Main Street
Suite 500
Rockford, IL 61101

815-966-5400
Fax: 815-966-6416
E-Mail: kjennison@wattnet.net
Home Page: www.wattnet.com

Jim Watt, Chairman/CEO
Greg Watt, President/COO
Ken Jennison, Editor

Covers the latest news in feed production, nutritional developments and trends, food safety and regulatory developments, grain markets, management strategies and new products.
Cost: $48.00
Circulation: 20,250
ISSN: 0014-956X
Founded in 1950
Mailing list available for rent: 20,249 names at $155 per M
Printed in 4 colors on glossy stock

896 Flue Cured Tobacco Farmer
Tabacco Farmer.Com
3101 Poplarwood Court
Suite 115
Raleigh, NC 27604

91- 8-2 47
Fax: 919-876-6531
E-Mail: publisher@tobaccofarmer.com
Home Page: www.tobaccofarmer.com

Dayton Matlick, Chairman
Taco Tuinstra, Editor in Chief
Noel Morris, Publisher

Business of farming publication for commercial tobacco producers. Feature articles deal with the research-backed production, harvesting and marketing aspects of the flue cured tobacco.
Cost: $25.00
Circulation: 14000
ISSN: 0015-4512
Founded in 1964
Printed in 4 colors on glossy stock

897 Food Aid Needs Assessment
US Department of Agriculture
1400 Independence Avenue SW
Washington, DC 20250

202-690-7650
800-999-6779
Fax: 202-720-2030
Home Page: www.usda.gov
Social Media: Facebook, Twitter, LinkedIn, YouTube, Flickr

Gene Mathia, Branch Chief

This annual report assesses the food situation in 60 developing countries. Most of the data are presented by region; crisis countries are covered individually.
Cost: $30.00
Founded in 1862

898 Forest Science
5400 Grosvenor Ln
Bethesda, MD 20814-2198

301-897-8720
866-897-8720
Fax: 301-897-3690
E-Mail: safweb@podi.com
Home Page: www.safnet.org
Social Media: Facebook, Twitter, LinkedIn

Michael T Goergen Jr, Executive VP/CFO
Brittany Brumby, Assistant to the CEO/Council
Amy Ziadi, Information Technology Manager
Larry D Burner CPA, Sr. Director Finance

Provides access to information and networking opportunities to prepare members for the challenges and the changes that face natural resource professionals.
Founded in 1900

899 Fresh Cut Magazine
Great American Publishing
75 Applewood Drive, Suite A
PO Box 128
Sparta, MI 49345

616-887-9008
Fax: 616-887-2666
E-Mail: fcedit@freshcut.com
Home Page: www.freshcut.com

Matt McCallum, Publisher
Kimberly Baker, Director of Media Services
Beecky Bosserd, Circulation Manager
Lee Dean, Editorial Director

Covers all sectors of the international value-added produce industry. Features industry profiles, research reports, governmental legislation coverage, industry columnists, news reports, new equipment showcases and much more.
Cost: $15.00
40 Pages
Frequency: Monthly
ISSN: 1072-2831
Founded in 1993
Printed in 4 colors on glossy stock

900 Fresh Digest
Fresh Produce & Floral Council
16700 Valley View Ave
Suite 130
La Mirada, CA 90638-5844

714-739-0177
Fax: 714-739-0226
E-Mail: info@fpfc.org
Home Page: www.fpfc.org

Carissa Mace, President
Pauleen Yoshikane, Director of Operations

Addresses issues concerning the Western US, with heavy emphasis on the important California market, read by thousands of professionals in the produce and floral industries.
600+ Members
Founded in 1965

901 Fruit Country
Clintron Publishing
PO Box 547
Yakima, WA 98907-0547

509-248-2452
800-869-7923
Fax: 509-248-4056

Clintke Withers, Publisher
John M Dahlin, Editor

Written for and about growers, their operations and their needs. Stories on growers and shippers, developments and trends in the fruit industry, human interest stories and politics, new products, chemicals and supplies, avant garde management techniques, cultural practices and tips on profitability. Advertising equipment and services to the fruit industry and distribution system.
Cost: $12.00
Frequency: Monthly
Circulation: 11,500

902 Futures Magazine
Futures Magazine
111 W Jackson Blvd
7th Floor
Chicago, IL 60604-4139

312-977-0999
Fax: 312-846-4638
Home Page: www.aip.com

Steve Lown, Manager
James T Holter, Editor

Agriculture commodities charted by various technical studies, plus analysis.
Cost: $39.00
24 Pages
Frequency: Monthly
Founded in 1972

903 Game Bird Breeders, Agiculturists, Zoologists and Conservationists
Game Bird Breeders
1155 W 4700 S
Salt Lake City, UT 84123
George Allen, Editor

Articles on how to keep and breed all types of game birds.
Cost: $18.00
45 Pages
Frequency: Monthly
Founded in 1974

904 Glimpsing Kentucky's Forgotten Heroes: Profiles & Lessons from an American
Agribusiness Council
PO Box 5565
Washington, DC 20016

202-296-4563
Fax: 202-887-9178
E-Mail: info@agribusinesscouncil.org
Home Page: www.agribusinesscouncil.org
Cost: $10.00

905 Grape Grower
Western Agricultural Publishing Company
4969 E Clinton Way
Suite 104
Fresno, CA 93727

559-252-7000
Fax: 559-252-7387
E-Mail: westag@psnw.com
Home Page: www.westagpubco.com

Paul Baltimore, Co Publisher
Jim Baltimore, Co Publisher
Randy Bailey, Editor
Robert Fujimoto, Assistant Editor

The West's most widely read authority on the cultivation of table grapes, raising grapes and wine grapes. All aspects of production are covered with the most current university, government and private research.

906 **Greenhouse Grower**
Meister Media Worldwide
37733 Euclid Ave
Willoughby, OH 44094-5992

440-942-2000
800-572-7740
Fax: 440-975-3447
E-Mail: gg.circ@meistermedia.com
Home Page: www.meistermedia.com

Gary Fitzgerald, President
Rick T Melnick, Corporate Editorial Director

Industry-leading voice for the commercial floriculture industry in the United States. Compiles buyers' directories and annual reports on the largest growers in the nation, produces vibrant emedia products and manages industry-leading events and awards programs.
Frequency: Monthly
Circulation: 20000
Founded in 1932

907 **Grower**
Vance Publishing
400 Knightsbridge Parkway
Lincolnshire, IL 60069

847-634-2600
Fax: 847-634-4379
E-Mail: info@vancepublishing.com
Home Page: www.vancepublishing.com

William C Vance, Chairman
Peggy Walker, President

Positioned as the key source of profitable production and management strategies to commercial producers who control 90% of the U.S. fruit and vegetable market.
Cost: $45.00
Frequency: Monthly
Circulation: 22,000
Founded in 1937

908 **Growertalks Magazine**
Ball Publishing
622 Town Road
PO Box 1660
West Chicago, IL 60186

630-231-3675
888-888-0013
Fax: 630-231-5254
E-Mail: info@ballpublishing.com
Home Page: www.growertalks.com

Chris Beytes, Editor/Publisher
Jennifer Zurko, Managing Editor

Specializes in the publishing of horticulture information, primarily related to floriculture production and marketing.
Frequency: Monthly
Circulation: 12000
Founded in 1937

909 **Guernsey Breeders' Journal**
Purebred Publishing Inc
1224 Alton Darby Creeek Road
Suite G
Columbus, OH 43228

614-864-2409
Fax: 614-864-5614
E Mail: info@usguernsey.com
Home Page: www.usguernsey.com

Seth Johnson, Executive Secretary-Treasurer
Brian Schnebly, Programs Coordinator
Katie Hensen, Editor
Ashley Shaffer, Assistant Editor

The journal discusses breeder stories, management trends and events in the Guernsey industry.
Frequency: 10x Yearly

910 **Gulf Coast Cattleman**
EC Larkin
11201 Morning Ct
San Antonio, TX 78213-1300

21- 3-4 77
Fax: 210-344-4258
E-Mail: info@gulfcoastcattleman.com
Home Page: www.gulfcoastpub.com

E C Larkin Jr, President
Joan Dover, Circulation
M'Lys Lloyd, Managing Editor

Services commercial cattlemen along the Gulf Coast states with industry news, management and herd health related articles.
Cost: $15.00
64 Pages
Frequency: Monthly
Circulation: 16000
ISSN: 0017-5552
Founded in 1935
Printed in 4 colors on glossy stock

911 **Hereford World**
American Hereford Association
PO Box 014059
Kansas City, MO 64101

81- 8-2 37
Fax: 816-842-6931
E-Mail: aha@hereford.org
Home Page: www.hereford.org

Craig Huffhines, Executive VP
Mary Ellen Hummel, Executive Assistant

Trade magazine for breeders of registered Polled Hereford cattle.
Frequency: Monthly
Circulation: 9500
Founded in 1742

912 **High Country News**
High Country Foundation
119 Grand Avenue
PO Box 1090
Paonia, CO 81428

970-527-4898
800-905-1155
Fax: 970-527-4897
E-Mail: circulation@hcn.org
Home Page: www.hcn.org

Paul Larmer, Executive Director
Greg Hanscom, Editor
Mike Maxwell, Director of Operations
Cindy Wehling, Art Director

Covers environmental and public lands issues.
Cost: $32.00
Circulation: 23000
Founded in 1970

913 **High Plains Journal/Midwest Ag Journal**
High Plains Publishing Company
1500 E Wyatt Earp Boulevard
PO Box 760
Dodge City, KS 67801

620-227-1834
800-452-7171
Fax: 620-227-7173
E-Mail: journal@hpj.com
Home Page: www.hpj.com

Tom Tayor, Publisher/CEO
Holly Martin, Editor
John Seatvet, Sales Manager
Sarah Farlee, Marketing Director

Farming news for the central states.
Cost: $46.00
Frequency: Weekly
Circulation: 50000
Printed in 4 colors on glossy stock

914 **Hoard's Dairyman The National Dairy Farm Magazine**
PO Box 801
Fort Atkinson, WI 53538-0801

920-563-5551
Fax: 920-563-7298
E-Mail: hoards@hoards.com
Home Page: www.hoards.com
Social Media: Facebook, Twitter

Steve A. Larson, Managing Editor
Corey A. Geiger, Senior Associate Editor
Demmos J. Hallady, Western Editor
Lucas S. Sjostrom, Associate Editor
Amanda C. Smith, Associate Editor

News aimed at the dairy farmer.
Cost: $18.00
5000 Members
Frequency: 20x/Year
Circulation: 63,000
Founded in 1885
Printed in 4 colors on glossy stock

915 **Hog Producer**
Farm Progress
6200 Aurora Avenue
Suite 609 E
Urbandale, IA 50322-2838

515-278-6693
Fax: 515-278-7797
E-Mail: jotte@farmprogress.com
Home Page: www.farmprogress.com

Sara Wyant, Publisher
John Otte, Editor

Management publication to help pork producers in the production, housing, genetics, health care and marketing of hogs.

916 **Holstein Pulse**
Holstein Association USA
PO Box 808
Brattleboro, VT 05302-0808

802-254-4551
800-965-5200
Fax: 802-254-8251
E-Mail: info@holstein.com
Home Page: www.holsteinusa.com

John Meyer, CEO
Lisa Perrin, Marketing
Frequency: Quarterly
Circulation: 19000

917 **Holstein World**
Dairy Business Communications
6437 Collamer Road
East Syracuse, NY 13057

315-703-7979
800-334-1904
Fax: 315-703-7988
Home Page: www.holsteinworld.com

Joel P Hastings, Publisher/Editor
Janice Barrett, Associate Editor

Showcases breeders who own America's genetically superior cattle. Elite group of progressive dairymen who have income, herd size, and milk production considerably above the national averages.
Cost: $38.95
123 Pages
Frequency: Monthly
Circulation: 12000
ISSN: 0199-4239
Founded in 1904
Printed in 4 colors on glossy stock

918 **HortScience**
American Society for Horticultural Science
1018 Duke Street
Alexandria, VA 22314-2851
703-836-4606
Fax: 703-836-2024

E-Mail: webmaster@ashs.org
Home Page: www.ashs.org

Michael Neff, Executive Director
Ruth Guamond, Managing Editor

HortScience is a bimonthly journal concentrating on significant research, education, extension findings, and methods.
Cost: $55.00
160 Pages
Frequency: Monthly
Circulation: 2500
ISSN: 0018-5345
Founded in 1903
Mailing list available for rent: 2500 names at $100 per M

919 **IMPACT Magazine**
Agricultural Communicators of Tomorrow
P.O. Box 110180
Gainesville, FL 32611-0180

352-392-1971
Fax: 352-392-9589
Home Page: www.ifas.ufl.edu
Social Media: Facebook, Twitter

Jack Payne, Senior Vice President

Features news about the statewide teaching, research and extension programs of the University of Florida's Institute of Food and Agricultural Sciences.
Founded in 1970

920 **Implement & Tractor**
Farm Journal Media
1818 Market Street
31st Floor
Philadelphia, PA 19103-3654

215-578-8900
800-331-9310
Fax: 215-568-6782
E-Mail: jstruyk@farmjournal.com
Home Page: www.agweb.com/machinery/implement_tractor.aspx

Andy Weber, Chief Executive Officer
Steve Custer, Executive Vice President
Jeff Pence, President, Electronic Media
Chuck Roth, Senior Vice President

Implement & Tractor is a bimonthly publication providing news and insights for dealers, distributors, OEMs, engineers and the associations that make up the more than $40 billion dealer and wholesaler equipment industry.
Frequency: Bimonthly
Founded in 1885

921 **International Journal of Vegetable Science**
Taylor & Francis Group LLC
325 Chestnut St
Suite 800
Philadelphia, PA 19106-2614

215-625-8900
800-354-1420
Fax: 215-625-2940
E-Mail: haworthorders@taylorandfrancis.com
Home Page: www.taylorandfrancis.com

Vincent M. Russo, Editor

Features innovative articles on all aspects of vegetable production, including growth regulation, pest management, sustainable production, harvesting, handling, storage, shipping and final consumption.
Frequency: Quarterly

922 **International Poultry Exposition Guide**
WATT Publishing Company
122 S Wesley Ave
Mt Morris, IL 61054-1451

815-734-7937
Fax: 815-734-4201
E-Mail: olentine@wattmm.com
Home Page: www.wattnet.com

Jim Watt, Chairman/CEO
Lisa Thornton, Managing Editor
Clay Schreiber, Publisher

923 **Invasive Plant Science and Management Journal**
P.O.Box 7065
Lawrence, KS 66044-7065

785-429-9622
800-627-0326
Fax: 785-843-1274
E-Mail: wssa@allenpress.com
Home Page: www.wssa.net

Dale Shaner, President
Jeff Derr, VP
Tom Mueller, Secretary
Dave Gealy, Treasurer
Michael Foley, Director Publications

Promotes research, education and extension outreach activities related to weeds, provides science-based information to the public and policy makers; and fosters awarenes of weeds and their impacts on managed and natural ecosystems.
2000 Members
Founded in 1956

924 **Jojoba Happenings**
John S Turner Public Relations
805 N 4th Avenue
Unit 404
Phoenix, AZ 85003-1304

FAX 602-252-5722

John Turner, Publisher
Ken Lucas, Editor

Jojoba farming. Accepts advertising.
8 Pages
Frequency: Bi-Monthly

925 **Journal of Agricultural & Food Chemistry**
American Chemical Society
1155 16th St NW
Washington, DC 20036-4892

202-872-4600
800-227-9919
Fax: 202-872-4615
E-Mail: jafc@ucdavis.edu
Home Page: www.pubs.acs.org

Madeleine Jacobs, CEO
John W Finley, Associate Editor
Elizabeth Waters, Associate Editor

Research results in pesticides, fertilizers, agricultural and food processing chemistry.
Cost: $146.00
Frequency: Monthly
Circulation: 159000
Founded in 1856

926 **Journal of Animal Science (JAS)**
PO Box 7410
Champaign, IL 61826

217-356-9050
Fax: 217-398-4119
E-Mail: asas@assochq.org
Home Page: www.asas.org
Social Media: Facebook, Twitter, RSS

Meghan Wulster-Radcli, CEO
Jacelyn Hemmelgarn, COO

Premier journal for animal science and serves as the leading source of new knowledge and perspective in this area. JAS consistently ranks as on of the top journals in the category of Agriculture, Dairy, and Animal Sciences.
Frequency: Monthly
ISSN: 0021-8812
Founded in 1908

927 **Journal of Applied Communications**
Association for Communications Excellence
University of Florida
407 Rolfs Hall
Gainesville, FL 32611-0540

352-273-2094
Fax: 352-392-8583
E-Mail: rwtelg@ufl.edu
Home Page: www.aceweb.org

Holly Young, Interim Executive Director
Faith Peppers, President
Joanne Littlefield, Vice President

A referred journal offering professional development for educational communicators who emphasize agriculture, natural resources, and life and human sciences.
Frequency: Quarterly
ISSN: 1051-0834

928 **Journal of Applied Communications (JAC)**
ACE
448 Agricultural Hall
Stillwater, OK 74078

40- 7-4 04
866-941-3048
E-Mail: editor@journalofappliedcommunications.or
Home Page: www.journalofappliedcommunications.org

Dwayne Cartmell, Executive Editor
Ricky Telg, Editorial Board Chair

The Journal of Applied Communications is a refereed journal offering professional development for educational communicators who emphasize agriculture, natural resources, and life and human sciences.
Frequency: Quarterly
Founded in 1970

929 **Journal of Aquatic Plant Management**
PO Box 821265
Vicksburg, MS 39182-1265

FAX 601-634-5502
E-Mail: webmaster@apms.org
Home Page: www.apms.org
Social Media: Facebook, LinkedIn

Terry Goldsby, President
Cody Gray, VP
Sherry Whitaker, Treasurer
Jeff Schardt, Secretary
Robert J. Richardson, Editor

A publication of the Aquatic Plant Management Society, Inc.
Founded in 1961

930 **Journal of Biomolecular Screening**
36 Tamarack Ave
Suite 348
Danbury, CT 06811

203-778-8828
Fax: 203-748-7557
E-Mail: email@aol.com
Home Page: www.sbsonline.org

Jeff Paslay, President
Michelle Palmer, Executive Director
Christine Giordano, Executive Director

The leading peer-reviewed journal focusing on drug-discovery sciences. Delivers the latest advancements in quantitative biomolecular sciences.
Cost: $175.00
Frequency: 10x/Year

931 **Journal of Dairy Science**
American Dairy Science Association
2441 Village Green Pl
Champaign, IL 61822-7676

217-356-5146
Fax: 217-398-4119
E-Mail: adsa@assochq.org
Home Page: www.adsa.org

Donald C Beitz, President
Philld C Tongz, VP
Peter Studney, Executive Director
William R Aimutis, Treasurer

Official Journal of the American Dairy Science Association
3000 Members
Founded in 1898
Mailing list available for rent

932 **Journal of Environmental Quality**
5585 Guilford Road
Madison, WI 53711-1086

608-273-8080
Fax: 608-273-2021
E-Mail: headquarters@agronomy.org
Home Page: www.agronomy.org
Social Media: Facebook, Twitter, LinkedIn

Ken Barbarick, President
Sharon Clay, President Elect
Ellen Bergfeld, CEO

Published by ASA, CSSA, and SSSA. Papers are grouped by subject matter and cover water, soil, and atmospheric research as it relates to agriculture and the environment.
11000 Members
Founded in 1907

933 **Journal of Forestry**
Society of American Foresters
5400 Grosvenor Ln
Bethesda, MD 20814-2198

301-897-8720
866-897-8720
Fax: 301-897-3690
E-Mail: safweb@podi.com
Home Page: www.safnet.org
Social Media: Facebook, Twitter, LinkedIn

Michael T Goergen Jr, Executive VP/CEO
Matthew Walls, Publications Dir./Managing Editor

To advance the profession of forestry by keeping professionals informed about significant developments and ideas in the many facets of forestry: economics, education and communication, entomology and pathology, fire, forest ecology, geospatial technologies, history, international forestry, measurements, policy, recreation, silviculture, social sciences, soils and hydrology, urband and community forestry, utilization and engineering, and wildlife management.
Cost: $85.00
Frequency: 8x Yearly
ISSN: 0022-1201
Founded in 1902

934 **Journal of Natural Resources & Life Sciences Education**
5585 Guilford Road
Madison, WI 53711-1086

608-273-8080
Fax: 608-273-2021
E-Mail: headquarters@agronomy.org
Home Page: www.agronomy.org
Social Media: Facebook, Twitter, LinkedIn

Ellen E Bergfeld, CEO
Wes Meixelsperger, CFO
Alexander Barton, Director of Business Development
Lisa Al-Moodi, Managing Editor

Today's educators look here for the latest teaching ideas in the life sciences, natural resources, and agriculture.
11000 Members
Founded in 1907

935 **Journal of Plant Registrations**
Crop Science Society of America
5585 Guilford Road
Madison, WI 53711-5801

608-273-8080
Fax: 608-273-2021
E-Mail: headquarters@crops.org
Home Page: www.crops.org
Social Media: Facebook, Twitter, LinkedIn

Maria Gallo, President
Jeffrey Volenec, President-elect

Publishes cultivar, germplasm, parental line, genetic stock, and mapping population registration manuscripts.
4700 Members
Founded in 1955

936 **Journal of Soil and Water Conservation**
Soil and Water Conservation Society
945 SW Ankeny Rd
Ankeny, IA 50021

515-289-2331
800-843-7645
Fax: 515-289-1227
E-Mail: pubs@swcs.org
Home Page: www.swcs.org

Oksana Gieseman, Editor
Jorge Delgado, Research Editor

The JSWC is a multidisciplinary journal of natural resource conservation research, practice, policy, and perspectives. The journal has two sections: the A Section containing various departments and features and the Research Section containing peer-reviewed research papers.
Cost: $99.00
Frequency: 6x Yearly
Circulation: 2000
ISSN: 0022-4561
Founded in 1945

937 **Journal of Sustainable Agriculture**
Taylor & Francis Group LLC
325 Chestnut St
Suite 800
Philadelphia, PA 19106-2614

215-625-8900
800-354-1420
Fax: 215-625-2940
Home Page: www.taylorandfrancis.com

Stephen R. Gliessman, Editor

Focuses on new and unique systems in which resource usage and environmental protection are kept in balance with the needs of productivity, profits, and incentives that are necessary for the agricultural marketplace. It increases professional and public awareness and gains support for these necessary changes in our agricultural industry.
Frequency: 8x Yearly

938 **Journal of Vegetable Science**
Taylor & Francis Group LLC
825 Chestnut Street
Suite 800
Philadelphia, PA 19106

215-625-8900
800-354-1420
Fax: 215-625-2940
Home Page: www.haworthpress.com

Vincent M Russo PhD, Editor

Features innovative articles on all aspects of vegetable production, including growth regulation, pest management, sustainable production, harvesting, handling, storage, shipping and final consumption.
Frequency: Quarterly
ISSN: 1931-5260

939 **Journal of the American Society of Farm Managers and Rural Appraisers**
950 S Cherry St
Suite 508
Denver, CO 80246-2664

303-758-3513
Fax: 303-758-0190
E-Mail: nhardiman@agri-associations.org
Home Page: www.asfmra.org
Social Media: Facebook, Twitter, LinkedIn

Nancy Hardiman, Director Education
Brian Stockman, Executive VP
Debe L Alvarez, Manager Education/Faculty

Provides the most up-to-date studies, research, practices, and methodologies proposed by the leading academic, management, appraisal and consulting members of our professions.
2300 Members
Founded in 1929
Mailing list available for rent

940 **Land**
Free Press Company
418 S 2nd Street
PO Box 3169
Mankato, MN 56001

507-344-6395
800-657-4665
Home Page: www.the-land.com

Kevin Schulz, Editor
Lynnae Schrader, Assistant Editor
Kim Henrickson, Advertising Manager
Ken Lingen, Manager

Agricultural news
Cost: $20.00
48 Pages
Frequency: Weekly
Circulation: 40000
ISSN: 0279-1633
Founded in 1976
Printed in 4 colors on newsprint stock

941 **Landscape Management**
Advanstar Landscape Group
7500 Old Oak Blvd
Cleveland, OH 44130-3343

440-243-8100
800-225-4569
Fax: 440-891-2740
Home Page: www.act-europe.org

Ron Hall, Editor-in-Chief
Jason Stahl, Managing Editor

Covers news, market trends, business and operations management, technical information on horticulture and agronomy for professional landscape contractors, lawncare operators and in-house grounds managers.
Cost: $3.83
Circulation: 60014
Founded in 1962
Printed in 4 colors on glossy stock

942 **Meat Science Journal**
American Meat Science Association
2441 Village Green Pl
Champaign, IL 61822-7676

217-356-5368
800-517-AMSA
Fax: 888-205-5834
Fax: 217-356-5370
E-Mail: information@meatscience.org
Home Page: www.meatscience.org

Thomas Powell, Executive Director

The official journal of AMSA. Peer-reviewed resource is the best way to stay current on the latest research in meat science across all meat products and in all aspects of meat production and processing.

943 MidAmerican Farmer Grower
MidAmerica Farm Publications
19 N Main Street
PO Box 323
Perryville, MO 63775

573-547-2244
877-486-6997
Fax: 573-547-5663
E-Mail: publisher@mafg.net
Home Page: www.mafg.net

John M LaRose, CEO/Publisher
Barbara Galeski, Editor
Jack Thompson II, Marketing

Offers farming news for the middle states.
Cost: $19.00
Frequency: Weekly

944 Midwest DairyBusiness
DairyBusiness Communications
6437 Collamer Road
East Syracuse, NY 13057-1031

315-703-7979
Fax: 315-703-7988
Home Page: www.dairybusiness.com/midwest

Dave Natzke, Editorial Director
Joel P Hastings, Publisher
JoDee Sattler, Associate Editor
Tom Vilsack, Secretary

Business resource for successful milk producers. Only business-oriented dairy publication exclusively for the large herd, Midwest milk producer.
Cost: $45.00
43 Pages
Frequency: Monthly
Circulation: 27500
ISSN: 1087-7096
Founded in 1904
Printed in 4 colors on glossy stock

945 Milling Journal
3065 Pershing Court
Decatur, IL 62526

217-877-9660
800-728-7511
Fax: 217-877-6647
E-Mail: webmaster@grainnet.com
Home Page: www.grainnet.com

Mark Avery, Publisher
Arvin Donley, Editor
Jody Sexton, Production Manager

Mailed to all active AOM members in the US, Canada, and internationally, including wheat flour/corn mills and corn/oilseed processors in US and Canada.
Frequency: Quarterly
Circulation: 1224

946 Mushroom News
American Mushroom Institute
1284 Gap Newport Pike
Suite 2
Avondale, PA 19311-9503

610-268-7483
Fax: 610-268-8015
E-Mail: ami@mwmlaw.com
Home Page: www.americanmushroom.org

For growers and scientists in the mushroom production.
Cost: $275.00
Frequency: Monthly
Founded in 1955

947 NWAC News: National Warmwater Aquaculture Center
127 Experiment Station Road
PO Box 197
Stoneville, MS 38776

662-686-3302
Fax: 662-686-3568
E-Mail: sharris@drec.msstate.edu
Home Page: www.msstate.edu/dept/tcnwac

Jammy Avery, Publisher
J Charles Lee, President
Frequency: Bi-annually
Circulation: 1000
Founded in 1993
Printed in 3 colors on matte stock

948 National Farmers Union News
National Farmers Union
11900 E Cornell Ave
Aurora, CO 80014-6201

303-368-7300
800-347-1961
Fax: 303-368-1390
Home Page: www.nfu.org

Dave Frederickson, President
Rae Price, Editor

Grass roots structure in which policy positions are initiated locally. The goal is to sustain and strengthen family farm and ranch agriculture.
Cost: $10.00
Frequency: Monthly
Circulation: 250000
Founded in 1902

949 National Hog Farmer
7900 International Dr
Suite 300
Minneapolis, MN 55425-2562
952-851-4710
Fax: 952-851-4601
Home Page: www.nationalhogfarmer.com

Dale Miller, Manager
Steve May, Publisher
John Frinch, President
Robert Moraczewski, Senior Vice President
Susan Rowland, Marketing Manager
Offers production information for hog farming business managers.
Cost: $35.00
Frequency: Monthly
Circulation: 31000
Founded in 1956
Mailing list available for rent: 84M names
Printed in 4 colors on glossy stock

950 National Wheat Growers Journal
National Association of Wheat Growers
415 2nd St NE
Suite 300
Washington, DC 20002-4993
202-547-7800
Fax: 202-546-2638
E-Mail: wheatworld@wheatworld.org
Home Page: www.wheatworld.org
Social Media: Facebook, Twitter

David Cleavinger, Publisher
Karl Scronce, Second Vice President
Dana Peterson, Second Vice President
Melissa George Kessler, Director of Communications

Information for wheat growers.
Founded in 1950

951 North Africa and Middle East Int'l Agricultural and Trade Report
US Department of Agriculture
200 Independence Ave SW
Washington, DC 20201-0007

202-690-7650
800-999-6779
Fax: 202-512-2250
Home Page: www.usda.gov

Michael Kurrzig, Editor
Chris Smith, Chief Information Officer
Matt Paul, Director of Communications
Ramona Romero, General Counsel

Information on current and projected agriculture production and trade in North Africa and the Middle East. Reports include trade and production data, highlights United States and European trade with the region.
Frequency: Annual
Founded in 1862

952 North American Deer Farmers Magazine
North American Deer Farmers Association
4501 Hills and Dales Rd NW
Suite C
Canton, OH 44708

330-454-3944
Fax: 330-454-3950
E-Mail: info@nadefa.org
Home Page: www.nadefa.org

Shawn Schafer, Executive Director
Tim Condict, First VP
Bill Pittenger, Second VP

National association of deer farming and ranching. Membership dues include this quarterly magazine.
Cost: $15.00
32 Pages
Frequency: Quarterly
Circulation: 1000
ISSN: 1084-0583
Founded in 1983
Printed in 4 colors on glossy stock

953 Northeast Dairy Business
DairyBusiness Communications
6437 Collamer Road
East Syracuse, NY 13057-1031

315-703-7979
800-334-1904
Fax: 315-703-7988
Home Page: www.dairybusiness.com/northeast

Eleanor Jacobs, Editor
Susan Harlow, Managing Editor
Joel Hasting, CEO/Publisher
Tom Vilsack, Secretary
Sue Miller, Circulation Manager

Business resource for successful milk producers. Devoted exclusively to the business and dairy management needs of milk producers in the 12 northeastern states.
Cost: $3.00
51 Pages
Frequency: Monthly
Circulation: 17500
ISSN: 1523-7095
Founded in 1904
Printed in 4 colors on glossy stock

954 Nut Grower
Western Agricultural Publishing Company
4969 E Clinton Way
Suite 119
Fresno, CA 93727-1549

559-252-7000
Fax: 559-252-7387
E-Mail: westag@psnw.com
Home Page: www.westagpubco.com

Paul Baltimore, Co Publisher
Jim Baltimore, Co Publisher
Randy Bailey, Editor
Robert Fujimoto, Assistant Editor

Covers production topics, the latest in research developments, and crop news on almonds, walnuts, pistachios, pecans and chestnuts.

955 **OEM Off-Highway**
1233 Janesville Avenue
Fort Atkinson, WI 53538-2738

920-563-6388
800-547-7377
Fax: 920-563-1701
E-Mail: Leslie.Shalabi@cygnuspub.com
Home Page: www.cygnusb2b.com

Richard Reiff, President
Leslie Shalabi, Publisher
Chad Elmore, Associate Editor
James S. Rank, VP
Kathy Scott, Director of Public Relations

Offers information on off-road machinery and farm equipment.
Founded in 1966

956 **Onion World**
Columbia Publishing
8405 Ahtanum Rd
Yakima, WA 98903-9432

509-248-2452
800-900-2452
Fax: 509-248-4056
Home Page: www.onionworld.net

Brent Clement, Editor
Mike Stoker, Publisher

Includes information on onion production and markcting, grower and shipper feature stories, onion research, from herbicide and pesticide studies to promising new varieties, martket reports, feedback from major onion meetings and conventions, spot reports on overseas production and marketing, and other key issues and trends of interest to US and Canadian onion growers.
Cost: $16.00
32 Pages
Circulation: 6500
Founded in 1984
Printed in 4 colors on glossy stock

957 **Organic World**
Loft Publishing
3939 Leary Way NW
Seattle, WA 98107-5043

206-632-2767
Fax: 206-632-7055

Covers the news of organic gardening.
Cost: $15.00
Frequency: Quarterly

958 **Pacific Farmer-Stockman**
999 W Riverside
PO Box 2160
Spokane, WA 99201

509-595-5385
800-624-6618
Fax: 509-459-5102
Home Page:
www.farmerstockmaninsurance.com

Michael R Craigen, General Manager
Tracy Sikes, Manager
Kathy Bergloff, Manager
Michelle Musgrave, Administrative Assistant

Offers farming news and information for farmers and herdsmen located in the Pacific states.

959 **Peanut Farmer**
Specialized Agricultural Publications
5808 Faringdon Place
Suite 200
Raleigh, NC 27609

919-872-5040
Fax: 919-876-6531
E-Mail: publisher@peanutfarmer.com
Home Page: www.peanutfarmer.com

Dayton H Matlick, Chairman
Mary Evans, Publisher/Sales Director
Mary Ann Rood, Editor

Offers peanut farmers profitable methods of raising, marketing and promoting peanuts, plus key related issues.
Cost: $15.00
24 Pages
Frequency: Monthly January-July
Circulation: 18,500
Founded in 1965
Printed in 4 colors on glossy stock

960 **Peanut Grower**
Vance Publishing
10901 W 84th Ter
Suite 200
Lenexa, KS 66214-1631

913-438-5721
Fax: 913-438-0697
E-Mail: mweeks@vancepublishing.com
Home Page: www.vancepublishing.com

Cliff Becker, VP
William C Vance, CEO

Written for the US peanut farmers. Covers disease, weed and insect control, legislation, farm equipment, marketing and new research.

961 **Pesticide Chemical News Guide**
FCN Publishing
2200 Clarendon Blvd
Suite 1401
Arlington, VA 22201

888-732-7070
Home Page: www.agra-net.com

Jason Huffman, Editor-in-Chief

Reference tool on pesticides and chemicals.
Frequency: Monthly

962 **Pig International**
WATT Publishing Company
303 N Main Street
Suite 500
Rockford, IL 61101

815-966-5400
Fax: 815-966-6416
E-Mail: rabbott@wattnet.net
Home Page: www.wattnet.com

James Watt, Chairman/CEO
Greg Watt, President/COO
Roger Abbott, Editor

Covers nutrition, animal health issues, feed procurement, and how producers can be profitable in the world pork market.
Frequency: Monthly
Circulation: 17600
ISSN: 0191-8834
Founded in 1971
Mailing list available for rent
Printed in 4 colors on glossy stock

963 **Plant Disease**
American Phytopathological Society
3340 Pilot Knob Road
St. Paul, MN 55121-2097

651-454-7250
800-328-7560
Fax: 651-454-0766
E-Mail: aps@scisoc.org
Home Page: www.apsnet.org
Social Media: Facebook, Twitter, LinkedIn, YouTube

R. Michael Davis, Editor-in-Chief

Published to stimulate plant disease research and to enable those throughout the world to benefit from the advances made in this environmentally important science.
Frequency: Monthly
Circulation: 1200
ISSN: 0191-2917

964 **Pork**
Vance Publishing
400 Knightsbridge Parkway
Lincolnshire, IL 60069

847-634-2600
Fax: 847-634-4379
E-Mail: info@vancepublishing.com
Home Page: www.vancepublishing.com

William C Vance, Chairman
Peggy Walker, President

Delivers practical, how-to information on production management, business techniques, industry trends and market analysis to the pork industry.
Cost: $50.00
Frequency: Monthly
Circulation: 16,000
Mailing list available for rent

965 **Pork Report**
PO Box 10383
Clive, IA 50325

515-223-6186
Fax: 515-223-2646

Charles Harness, Publisher

Hog farming news and information.

966 **Potato Country**
Columbia Publishing
8405 Ahtanum Rd
Yakima, WA 98903-9432

509-248-2452
800-900-2452
Fax: 509-248-4056
Home Page: www.potatocountry.com

Brent Clement, Editor/Publisher
Mike Stoker, Publisher

Edited for potato growers and allied industry people throughout the Western fall-production states. Editorial material covers production, seed, disease forecast, equipment, fertilizer, irrigation, pest/weed management, crop reports and annual buyers guide.
Cost: $18.00
32 Pages
Frequency: Daily
Circulation: 7500
ISSN: 0886-4780
Founded in 1993
Printed in 4 colors on glossy stock

967 **Potato Grower**
Harris Publishing Company
360 B Street
Idaho Falls, ID 83402

208-524-4217
Fax: 208-522-5241
Home Page: www.potatogrower.com

Jason Harris, Publisher
Gary Rawlings, Editor

Current news on growing potatoes, market trends, technology.
Cost: $20.95
48 Pages
Frequency: Monthly
Founded in 1971
Printed in on glossy stock

968 **Poultry Digest**
WATT Publishing Company
122 S Wesley Ave
Mt Morris, IL 61054-1451

815-734-7937
Fax: 815-734-4201
E-Mail: olentine@wattmm.com
Home Page: www.wattnet.com

Jim W Watt, Chairman/CEO
Charles G Olentine Jr PhD, VP/Publisher
Clay Schreiber, Publisher
Jim Wessel, Circulation Director

A magazine serving the production side of the entire poultry industry.

969 **Poultry International**
WATT Publishing Company
303 N Main Street
Suite 500
Rockford, IL 61101
815-966-5400
Fax: 815-966-6416
E-Mail: mclements@wattnet.net
Home Page: www.wattnet.com
James Watt, Chairman/CEO
Greg Watt, President/COO
Mark Clements, Editor
Viewed by commercial poultry integrators as the leading international source of news, data and information for their businesses.
68 Pages
Frequency: Monthly
Circulation: 20,000
ISSN: 0032-5767
Founded in 1962
Printed in 4 colors

970 **Poultry Times**
Poultry & Egg News
345 Green Street NW
PO Box 1338
Gainesville, GA 30503
770-536-2476
Fax: 770-532-4894
Home Page: www.poultrytimes.net
Social Media: Facebook
Christopher Hill, Publisher/Editor
David Strickland, Editor
Barbara Olejnik, Associate Editor
Dinah Winfree, National Sales Representative
Stacy Louis, National Sales Representative
The only newspaper in the poultry industry. We deliver the most up to date news in teh poultry industry.
Cost: $22.00
Frequency: Twice Monthly
Circulation: 13000
Founded in 1954

971 **Poultry USA**
WATT Publishing Company
303 N Main Street
Suite 500
Rockford, IL 61101
815-966-5400
Fax: 815-966-6416
Home Page: www.wattnet.com
James Watt, Chairman/CEO
Greg Watt, President/COO
Jeff Swanson, Publishing Director
The only resource focused on the entire integrated poultry market, delivering relevant and timely information to industry professionals across the entire poultry supply chain - from farm to table.
Frequency: Monthly

972 **Practical Winery & Vineyard**
58 Paul Dr
Suite D
San Rafael, CA 94903-2054
415-479-5819
Fax: 415-492-9325
E-Mail: Office@practicalwinery.com
Home Page: www.practicalwinery.com
A bi-monthly magazine of wine-growing and winemaking news and reviews.
Cost: $31.00
Circulation: 7500
Founded in 1985

973 **Prairie Farmer**
Prairie Farm Dairy
300 E Washington St
PO Box 348
Pana, IL 62557-1239
217-562-3956
Fax: 217-877-9695
E-Mail: info@prairiefarms.com
Home Page: www.prairiefarms.com
James R Smith, Manager
Mike Wilson, Editor
Agricultural news.

974 **Progressive Farmer**
2100 Lakeshore Drive
Birmingham, AL 35209-6721
205-445-6000
Fax: 205-445-6422
E-Mail: bruce_thomas@timeinc.com
Home Page: www.progressivefarmer.com
Bruce Thomas, Publisher
Jack Odle, Editor
Allen Vaughan, Business Manager
Farming news with regional focus on the midwest, midsouth and southwest.
Cost: $18.00
106 Pages
Frequency: 6 issues/Year
Circulation: 610000
ISSN: 0033-0760
Founded in 1886

975 **RF Design**
RFD News
131 E Main Street
Bellevue, OH 44811-1449
419-483-7410
Fax: 419-483-3737
Barry LeCerf, Publisher
Comprehensive source of rural agricultural news and information for farmers and the general public.
Frequency: Weekly

976 **Rice Farming**
Vance Publishing
400 Knightsbridge Pkwy
Lincolnshire, IL 60069-3628
847-634-2600
800-888-9784
Fax: 847-634-4379
E-Mail: vlboyd@worldnet.att.net
Home Page: www.vancepublishing.com
Peggy Walker, President
William Vance, Chairman
Judy Riggs, Director
Vicky Boyd, Editor
Profitable production strategies for commercial rice growers.
Founded in 1937

977 **Rice Journal**
Specialized Agricultural Publications
3000 Highwoods Boulevard
Suite 300
Raleigh, NC 27604-1029
919-878-0540
Fax: 919-876-6531
E-Mail: publisher@ricejournal.com
Home Page: www.ricejournal.com
Dayton H Matlick, President
Mary Evans, Publisher
Offers rice growers profitable methods of producing, marketing and promoting rice, plus key related issues.
Founded in 1897

978 **RuraLife**
William Johnston
1172 Orangeburg Mall Circle
Orangeburg, SC 29115-3439
803-534-1980
Jaun Maults, Executive Director
Gary Grimmond, Editor
Farm and agricultural news.

979 **Rural Heritage**
Allan Damerow
281 Dean Ridge Ln
Gainesboro, TN 38562-5039
931-268-0655
E-Mail: info@ruralheritage.com
Home Page: www.ruralheritage.com
Gail Damerow, Owner
Publication for people who farm and log with horses and other draft animals.
Cost: $26.00
100 Pages
Frequency: Bi-Monthly
Circulation: 8500
ISSN: 0889-2970
Founded in 1976
Printed in 4 colors on matte stock

980 **Rural Living**
Michigan Farm Bureau
7373 W Saginaw Highway
PO Box 30960
Lansing, MI 48909-8460
517-323-7000
Fax: 517-323-6793
E-Mail: mifarmnews@michfb.com
Home Page: www.michiganfarmbureau.com
Dennis Rudat, Editor
Paul W Jackson, President
Brigette Leach, Director
Earl Butz, Secretary
Editorial emphasis on consumer food news, travel information and issue analysis.
24 Pages
Frequency: Quarterly
Circulation: 200000

981 **Santa Gertrudis USA**
Caballo Rojo Publishing
PO Box 1257
Kingsville, TX 78364-1257
361-592-9357
Fax: 361-592-8572
Home Page: www.santagertrudis.com
Ervin Kaatz, Executive Director
Official Journal of the Breed developed in 1918 at the famous King Ranch in Texas. Famous solid red color, hardiness and good disposition. They are adaptable to many environments and are present throughout the US and in other countries.

982 **Seed Industry Journal**
Freiberg Publishing Company
2701 Minnetonka Dr
PO Box 7
Cedar Falls, IA 50613-1531
319-553-0642
Fax: 319-277-3783
Home Page: www.care4elders.com
Bill Freiberg, Owner
Carol Cutler, Editor
International seed industry news.

983 **Seed Technology Journal**
Society of Commerical Seed Technologists
101 E State Street
Suite 214
Ithaca, NY 14850
607-256-3313
Fax: 607-256-3313

E-Mail: scst@twcny.rr.com
Home Page: www.seedtechnology.net

Brent Reschly, President
Neal Foster, Vice President

Published jointly with the Association of Official Seed Analysts. an international journal containing scientific and technological papers in all areas of seed science and technology. The emphasis is on applied and basic research in seed physiology, pathology and biology that may relate to seed development, maturation, germination, dormancy and deterioration.
Cost: $125.00
Frequency: Members Cost: $75.00
Founded in 1922

984 **Seed Today**
Grain Journal Publishing Company
3065 Pershing Ct
Decatur, IL 62526-1564

217-877-9660
800-728-7511
Fax: 217-877-6647
E-Mail: webmaster@grainnet.com
Home Page: www.grainnet.com

Mark Avery, Publisher
Joe Funk, Editor
Kay Merryfield, Circulation Administrator
Ayanna Green, Manager

Information for individuals related to seeds.
Frequency: Quarterly
Circulation: 4000
Founded in 1978

985 **Seed World**
Scranton Gillette Communications
380 E Northwest Highway
Suite 200
Des Plaines, IL 60016-2282

847-298-6622
Fax: 847-390-0408
Home Page: www.seedworld.com

E S Gillette, Publisher
Angela Dansby, Editor

Seed marketers.
Cost: $30.00
48 Pages
Frequency: Monthly
Circulation: 5000
ISSN: 0037-0797
Founded in 1915

986 **Seed and Crops Industry**
Freiberg Publishing Company
2701 Minnetonka Dr
Cedar Falls, IA 50613-1531

319-553-0642
800-959-3276
Fax: 319-277-3783
E-Mail: informa@cfu.net
Home Page: www.care4elders.com

Bill Freiberg, Owner

Offers information for farmers related to crop protection.
Frequency: Monthly

987 **Self Employed Country**
Communicating for Agriculture & the Self Employed
112 E Lincoln Ave
Fergus Falls, MN 56537-2217

218-739-3241
800-432-3276
Fax: 218-739-3832
Home Page: www.selfemployedcountry.org

Milt Smedsrud, Owner
Jerry Barney, Production Manager

For members of Communicating for Agriculture, including legislation relating to CA activities, exchange program activities, rural seniors news, health and insurance material, feature stories and columns.
Cost: $6.00
Frequency: Quarterly
Founded in 1985

988 **Shorthorn Country**
Durham Management Company
5830 S 142nd St
Siote A
Omaha, NE 68137-2894

402-827-8003
Fax: 402-827-8006
Home Page:
www.durhamstaffingsolutions.com

Machael Durham, President
Tracy Duncan, Editor
Peggy Gilliland, Circulation Manager

Magazine published for cattle producers who breed and sell registered Shorthorn and Polled Shorthorn cattle.
Cost: $24.00
Circulation: 3000
ISSN: 0149-9319
Founded in 1956

989 **Soil Science**
Lippincott Williams & Wilkins
351 W Camden St
Baltimore, MD 21201-2436

410-949-8000
800-638-6423
Fax: 410-528-4414
Home Page: www.lww.com

J Arnold Anthony, Operations

Covers investigations in environmental soils.
Cost: $205.00
Frequency: Monthly
Circulation: 2800
ISSN: 0038-075X

990 **Soil Science of America Journal**
Soil Science Society of America
677 S Segoe Rd
Madison, WI 53711-1086

608-273-8095
Fax: 608-273-2021
E-Mail: headquarters@soils.org
Home Page: www.soils.org

Ellen Bergfeld, CEO

For those involved in research, teaching and extension activities in physics, chemistry, mineralogy, microbiology, soil fertility and plant nutrition
Cost: $600.00
Circulation: 4000
Founded in 1961

991 **Southeast Farm Press**
14920 US Highway 61
Clarksdale, MS 38614

662-624-8503
866-505-7173
Fax: 662-627-1977
Home Page: www.southeastfarmpress.com

Grey Frey, Publisher
Paul Hollis, Editor

Offers farming news for the southeastern states.
Founded in 1989

992 **Southeastern Peanut Farmer**
Southern Peanut Farmer's Federation
110 E 4th Street
Po Box 706
Tifton, GA 31794

229-386-3470
Fax: 229-386-3501
E-Mail: info@gapeanuts.com
Home Page: www.gapeanuts.com

Joy Carter, Editor

Offers information to peanut farmers.
Cost: $25.00
20 Pages
Frequency: Monthly
Circulation: 8400
ISSN: 0038-3694
Founded in 1961
Printed in 4 colors on glossy stock

993 **Southwest Farm Press**
Farm Press Publications
2104 Harvell Circle
Bellevue, NE 68005

402-505-7173
866-505-7173
Fax: 402-293-0741
E-Mail: sscs@pbsub.com
Home Page: southwestfarmpress.com

Greg Frey, Publisher
Ron Smith, Editor
Hembree Brandon, Editorial Director
Forrest Laws, Executive Editor
Darrah Parker, Marketing Manager

Farming news.
Cost: $40.00
Frequency: Fortnightly
Circulation: 33,100
Founded in 1974

994 **Soybean South**
6263 Poplar Avenue
Suite 540
Memphis, TN 38119-4736

901-385-0595
Fax: 901-767-4026

John Sowell, Publisher
Jeff Kehl, Circulation Director

Profitable prediction strategies for soybean farmers.
Frequency: 5 per year
Printed in 4 colors on glossy stock

995 **Speedy Bee**
American Beekeeping Federation
3525 Piedmont Road NE
Bldg 5 Suite 300
Atlanta, GA 30305-1509

404-760-2875
Fax: 404-240-0998
E-Mail: info@abfnet.org
Home Page: www.abfnet.org

Troy Fore, Publisher/Editor

The latest news affecting the beekeeping and honey industry.
Cost: $17.95
16 Pages
Frequency: Monthly
Circulation: 1500
ISSN: 0190-6798
Founded in 1972
Printed in on newsprint stock

996 **Spudman Magazine**
Great American Publishing
Po Box 128
Suite A
Sparta, MI 49345-0128

616-887-9008
Fax: 616-887-2666
Home Page: www.spudman.com

Matt McCallum, Owner
Kimberly Warren, Managing Editor
Erica Bernard, Circulation Manager
Marnie Draper, Advertising Manager
Jill Peck, Creative Director

Information for potato farming and marketing.
Circulation: 15500
Printed in on glossy stock

997 **Successful Farming**
Meredith Corporation

1716 Locust St
Des Moines, IA 50309-3023

515-284-3000
800-678-2659
Fax: 515-284-3563
E-Mail: shareholderhelp@meredith.com
Home Page: www.meredith.com

Stephen M Lacy, CEO
Sandy Williams, Production Manager
William Kerr, CEO
Tom Davis, Publisher

U.S. commerical farmers, ranchers and those employed in those operations or a directly related occupation.
Cost: $15.95
Frequency: Monthly
Circulation: 442000
Founded in 1902
Mailing list available for rent: 500M names at $75 per M
Printed in 4 colors on glossy stock

998 **Sugar: The Sugar Producer Magazine**
Harris Publishing Company
360 B Street
Idaho Falls, ID 83402

208-524-4217
800-638-0135
Fax: 208-522-5241
Home Page: www.sugarproducer.com

Jason Harris, Publisher
David FairBourn, Editor
Rob Erickson, Marketing
Eula Endecott, Circulation Manager

Sugar beet industry information.
Cost: $15.95
Frequency: Monthly
Circulation: 16000
Founded in 1975

999 **Sugarbeet Grower**
Sugar Publications
503 Broadway
Fargo, ND 58102-4416

701-476-2111
Fax: 701-476-2182
Home Page: www.sugarpub.com

Provides news and feature articles pertaining to sugarbeet production practices, research, legislation and marketing, along with profiles of industry leaders and outstanding producers. Primary audience is United States and Canadian sugarbeet growers.
Cost: $12.00
Circulation: 11,300
Founded in 1963

1000 **Sunflower Magazine**
National Sunflower Association
Ste 206
2401 46th Ave SE
Mandan, ND 58554-4829

701-328-5100
888-718-7033
Fax: 701-328-5101
Home Page: www.sunflowernsa.com

John Sandbakken, Executive Director
Sonia Mullally, Communications Director

Magazine geared to sunflower products.
Cost: $9.00
Circulation: 29300
Founded in 1981
Printed in 4 colors

1001 **Sunflower and Grain Marketing Magazine**
Sunflower World Publishers
3307 Northland Drive
Suite 130
Austin, TX 78731-4964

512-407-3434
Fax: 512-323-5118

Ed R Allen, Editor

Offers news and information on the sunflower and grain industries.
Circulation: 15,000

1002 **Super Hay Today Magazine**
Mt Adams Publishing and Design
14161 Fort Road
White Swan, DC 98552-9786

509-848-2706
800-554-0860
Fax: 509-848-3896
Home Page: www.hortexponw.com

Vee Graves, Editor
Julie LaForge, Advertising Manager

1003 **Swine Practitioner**
10901 W 84th Terrace
Suite 200
Lenexa, KS 66214-1649

913-438-8700
800-255-5113
Fax: 913-438-0695
E-Mail: info@vancepublishing.com
Home Page: www.vancepublishing.com

Kristal Arnold, Editor
Kevin Murphy, Sales/Marketing Manager
Bill Newham, Publishing Director
Cliff Becker, Group Publisher
Lori Eppel, Chief Financial Officer

Offers technical information, primarily on swine health and related production areas, to veterinarians and related industry professionals.
Frequency: Monthly
Circulation: 4800
Mailing list available for rent

1004 **The Forestry Source**
5400 Grosvenor Ln
Bethesda, MD 20814-2198

301-897-8720
Fax: 301-897-3690
E-Mail: safweb@safnet.org
Home Page: www.safnet.org
Social Media: Facebook, Twitter, LinkedIn

Michael T Goergen Jr, Executive VP/CFO
Brittany Brumby, Assistant to the CEO/Council
Amy Ziadi, Information Technology Manager
Larry D Burner CPA, Sr Director Finance

Provides access to information and networking opportunities to prepare members for the challenges and the changes that face natural resource professionals.
Founded in 1900

1005 **The Grower**
Vance Publishing
400 Knightsbridge Parkway
Lincolnshire, IL 60069

847-634-2600
Fax: 847-634-4379
E-Mail: info@vancepublishing.com
Home Page: www.vancepublishing.com
Social Media: Facebook, Twitter

William C Vance, Chairman
Peggy Walker, President

The key source of profitable production and management strategies to commercial producers who control 90% of the U.S. fruit and vegetable market.
Cost: $45.00
Frequency: Monthly
Circulation: 22,004
Founded in 1937
Printed in 4 colors on glossy stock

1006 **The Plant Genome**
Crop Science Society of America
5585 Guilford Road
Madison, WI 53711-5801

608-273-8080
Fax: 608-273-2021
E-Mail: headquarters@crops.org
Home Page: www.crops.org
Social Media: Facebook, Twitter, LinkedIn

Maria Gallo, President
Jeffrey Volenec, President-Elect

Electronic journal that provides readership with a short publication of the latest advances and breakthroughs in plant genomics research.
Founded in 1955

1007 **The Sunflower Magazine**
2401 46th Avenue SE
Suite 206
Mandan, ND 58554-4829

701-328-5100
888-718-7033
Fax: 701-663-8652
Home Page: www.sunflowernsa.com
Social Media: Facebook, YouTube

Larry Kleingartner, Executive Director
John Sandbakken, Marketing Director

Contains fresh, current and important articles on production strategies, ongoing research and market information.
Founded in 1981
Printed in 4 colors on glossy stock

1008 **Today's Farmer**
MFA
201 Ray Young Dr
Columbia, MO 65201-3599

573-874-5111
Fax: 573-876-5521
E-Mail: hr@mfa-inc.com
Home Page: www.mfa-inc.com

William Streeter, CEO
J Brian Griffith, Senior Vice President of Operations

Management and marketing news.
Cost: $12.00
Founded in 1914

1009 **Tomato Country**
Columbia Publishing
8405 Ahtanum Rd
Yakima, WA 98903-9432

509-248-2452
800-900-2452
Fax: 509-248-4056
Home Page: www.tomatomagazine.com

Brent Clement, Editor/Publisher
Mike Stoker, Publisher

Includes information on tomato production and marketing, grower and shipper feature stories, tomato research, from herbicide and pesticide studies to new varieties, market reports, feedback from major tomato meetings and conventions, along with other key issues and points of interest for USA and Canada tomato growers.

1010 **Top Producer**
Farm Journal Media
1818 Market Street
31st Floor
Philadelphia, PA 19103-3654

215-578-8900
800-320-7992
Fax: 215-568-6782

E-Mail: topproducer@farmjournal.com
Home Page: www.agweb.com/topproducer

Andy Weber, Chief Executive Officer
Steve Custer, Executive Vice President
Jeff Pence, President, Electronic Media
Chuck Roth, Senior Vice President

Top Producer is the premier magazine devoted to the business of farming. The focus on industry leaders, entrepreneurs and innovators in agriculture make this magazine the authoritative business resource for commercial farm operators.
Frequency: Weekly
Founded in 1973

1011 Tree Farmer Magazine, the Guide to Sustaining America's Family Forests
American Forest Foundation
1111 19th St NW
Suite 780
Washington, DC 20036

202-463-2700
Fax: 202-463-2785
E-Mail: info@forestfoundation.org
Home Page: www.forestfoundation.org

Tom Martin, President & CEO
Brigitte Johnson APR, Director
Communications, Editor

The official magazine of ATFS, this periodical provides practical, how-to and hands-on information and techniques, and services to help private fore landowners to become better stewards, save money and time, and add to the enjoyment of their land.

1012 Tree Fruit
Western Agricultural Publishing Company
4969 E Clinton Way
Suite 104
Fresno, CA 93727-1546

559-252-7000
Fax: 559-252-7387
E-Mail: westag@psnw.com
Home Page: www.westagpubco.com

Paul Baltimore, Co Publisher
Jim Baltimore, Co Publisher
Randy Bailey, Editor
Robert Fujimoto, Assistant Editor

For tree fruit growers in California.

1013 Valley Potato Grower
420 Business Highway 2
PO Box 301
East Grand Forks, MN 56721

218-773-7783
Fax: 218-773-6227
E-Mail: vpgsales@nppga.org
Home Page: www.nppga.org

Todd Phelph, CEO
Duane Maatz, Chairman

Information on potato farming.
Circulation: 10600
Founded in 1946

1014 Vegetable Growers News
Great American Publishing
75 Applewood Drive Suite A
PO Box 128
Sparta, MI 49345

616-887-9008
Fax: 616-887-2666
Home Page: www.vegetablegrowersnews.com

Matt McCallum, Executive Publisher
Brenda Bradford, Advertising
Kimberly Warren, Managing Editor
Erica Bernard, Circulation Department
Jill Peck, Creative Director

Market and marketing news.
Cost: $12.00
Frequency: Monthly

1015 Vegetables
Western Agricultural Publishing Company
4969 E Clinton Way
#104
Fresno, CA 93727-1549

559-252-7000
Fax: 559-252-7387
E-Mail: westag@psnw.com
Home Page: www.westagpubco.com

Paul Baltimore, Co Publisher
Jim Baltimore, Co Publisher
Randy Bailey, Editor
Robert Fujimoto, Assistant Editor

The definitive source for information on all aspects of western vegetable production.

1016 Vineyard and Winery Management
PO Box 2358
Winsdor, CA 95492

707-366-6820
800-535-5670
Fax: 607-535-2998
E-Mail: rmerletti@vwm-online.com
Home Page: www.vwm-online.com

Robert Merletti, Publisher
Tom Loid, General Manager
Dennis Black, General Manager
Suzanne Webb, Marketing Director

To be the bottom line resource for growers and vintners; to keep our readers tuned and primed for profit.
Cost: $37.00
100 Pages
Circulation: 6000
ISSN: 1047-4951
Founded in 1975
Printed in 4 colors on glossy stock

1017 Wallaces Farmer
Farm Progress Companies
255 38th Avenue
Suite P
St Charles, IL 60174-5410

630-462-2224
800-441-1410
E-Mail: rswoboda@farmprogress.com
Home Page: www.farmprogress.com

Rod Swoboda, Editor
Willie Vogt, Corporate Editorial Director
Frank Holdmeyer, Executive Editor

Serves Iowa farmers and ranchers with information to help them maximize their productivity and profitability. Each issue is packed with information, ideas, news and analysis.
Cost: $26.95
ISSN: 0043-0129
Founded in 1855

1018 Weed Science Journal
P.O.Box 7065
Lawrence, KS 66044-7065

785-429-9622
800-627-0629
Fax: 785-843-1274
E-Mail: wssa@allenpress.com
Home Page: www.wssa.net

Dale Shaner, President
Jeff Derr, VP
Tom Mueller, Secretary
Dave Gealy, Treasurer
Michael Foley, Director Publications

Promotes research, education and extension outreach activities related to weeds, provides science-based information to the public and policy makers; and fosters awarenes of weeds and their impacts on managed and natural ecosystems.
2000 Members
Founded in 1956

1019 Weed Technology Journal
P.O.Box 7065
Lawrence, KS 66044-7065

785-429-9622
800-627-0629
Fax: 785-843-1274
E-Mail: wssa@allenpress.com
Home Page: www.wssa.net

Dale Shaner, President
Jeff Derr, VP
Tom Mueller, Secretary
Dave Gealy, Treasurer
Michael Foley, Director Publications

Promotes research, education and extension outreach activities related to weeds, provides science-based information to the public and policy makers; and fosters awarenes of weeds and their impacts on managed and natural ecosystems.
Founded in 1956

1020 Western DairyBusiness
DairyBusiness Communications
6437 Collamer Road
East Syracuse, NY 13057 1031

315-703-7979
800-334-1904
Fax: 315-703-7988
E-Mail: bbaker@dairyline.com
Home Page: www.dairybusiness.com

Joel P Hastings, Editor
John Montandon, President & Co-CEO
Debbie Morneau, Marketing Coordinator

Business resource for successful milk producers. Covers 13 Western states. Provides information and news that is helpful in the daily operations of dairymen.
Cost: $49.95
67 Pages
Frequency: Monthly
Circulation: 14000
ISSN: 1528-4360
Founded in 1904
Printed in 4 colors on glossy stock

1021 Western Farm Press
Penton Media
249 W 17th Street
New York, NY 10011

212-204-4200
E-Mail: hbrandon@farmpress.com
Home Page: westernfarmpress.com

Greg Frey, VP
Hembree Brandon, Editorial Director
Harry Cline, Editor

Provides growers and agribusiness with in-depth coverage of the region's major crops plus the legislative, environmental and regulatory issues that affect their businesses.

1022 Western Fruit Grower
Meister Media Worldwide
37733 Euclid Ave
Willoughby, OH 44094-5992

440-942-2000
800-572-7740
Fax: 440-975-3447
E-Mail: rljones@meistermedia.com
Home Page: www.meisternet.com

Gary Fitzgerald, President
John Monahan, Publisher
Richard Jones, Editor

Edited for commercial growers of deciduous crops, citrus fruit and nut grape crops in the Western US.
Cost: $19.95
66 Pages
Frequency: Monthly
Circulation: 36000
Founded in 1933

1023 **Western Livestock Journal**
Crow Publications
7355 E Orchard Road
Suite 300
Greenwood Village, CO 80111

303-722-7600
800-850-2769
Fax: 303-722-0155
E-Mail: editorial@wlj.net
Home Page: www.wlj.net

Pete Crow, Publisher

Offers its readers the best coverage of timely, necessary news and information that affects the livestock industry, particularly cattle.
Cost: $45.00
Frequency: Weekly
Circulation: 30000+
Founded in 1922

Trade Shows

1024 **AACC International Annual Meeting**
3340 Pilot Knob Road
St. Paul, MN 55121-2055

651-454-7250
800-328-7560
Fax: 651-454-0766
E-Mail: aacc@scisoc.org
Home Page: www.aaccnet.org
Social Media: Facebook, Twitter, LinkedIn

Betty Ford, Director of Meetings
Rhonda Wilkie, Meetings Coordinator
Deborah Rogers, Chair
David Hahn, President
Steven C. Nelson, Executive Vice President

Formerly the American Association of Cereal Chemists, the AACC meeting offers a chance to come together, network with peers, discuss critical issues in the science and discover the methods of others.
Founded in 1915

1025 **AAEA Annual Meeting**
Agricultural & Applied Economics Association
415 S Duff Avenue
Suite C
Ames, IA 50010-6600

515-233-3202
Fax: 515-233-3101
E-Mail: nknight@iastate.edu
Home Page: www.aaea.org

Per Pinstrup-Anderson, President
Yvonne C Bennett, Executive Director
Nancy Knight, Manager Meetings
Joan Greiner, Events Coordinator

Annual meeting and trade show of 25 exhibitors.
1700 Attendees
Frequency: Annual/August
Founded in 1985

1026 **AAEA Symposia**
555 E Wells Street
Suite 1100
Milwaukee, WI 53202-6600

414-918-3190
Fax: 414-276-3349
E-Mail: info@aaea.org
Home Page: www.aaea.org

Otto C Doering III, President
Yvonne C Bennett, Executive Director

Providing a platform for research on the economics related to the role of consumers' food environments on their choices and health outcomes. The conference is aimed at providing insights into the influence of the food environment on the quality, price, and availability of food, associatec health or environmental impacts, and to uncover the impact of policies aimed at influencing the food production and choice.
3000 Members
Frequency: Annual
Founded in 1910
Mailing list available for rent

1027 **AAFCO Meeting**
Association of American Feed Control Officers
PO Box 478
Oxford, IN 47971

765-385-1029
Fax: 765-385-1032
E-Mail: sharon@aafco.org
Home Page: www.aafco.org

Sharon Krebs, Assistant Secretary/Treasurer
Frequency: Annual/July/August

1028 **AAW Annual Convention**
American Agri-Women
2103 Zeandale Road
Manhattan, KS 66502

785-537-6171
Fax: 785-537-9727
Home Page: www.americanagriwomen.org
Social Media: Facebook, Twitter

Karen Yost, President
Jody Elrod, Secretary
Peggy Clark, Treasurer

Tradeshow consisting of products of interest to women in agribusiness, farms and ranches.
350 Attendees
Frequency: Annual/November
Founded in 1974

1029 **AEM Annual Conference**
Association of Equipment Manufacturers
6737 W Washington St
Suite 2400
Milwaukee, WI 53214-5650

414-272-0943
866-236-0442
Fax: 414-272-1170
E-Mail: info@aem.org
Home Page: www.aem.org

Dennis Slater, President
Frequency: Annual/November

1030 **AFIA Pet Food Conference**
American Feed Industry Association
2101 Wilson Blvd
Suite 916
Arlington, VA 22201-3047

703-524-0810
Fax: 703-524-1921
E-Mail: afia@afia.org
Home Page: www.afia.org
Social Media: Facebook, Twitter, LinkedIn

Joel Newman, President
Richard Sellers, VP
Donald E Orr, Chairman
Anne Keller, Communications Director

Organization devoted to representing companies in the animal feed industry and its suppliers.
690 Members
Founded in 1909

1031 **ALBC Conference**
American Livestock Breeds Conservancy
PO Box 477
Pittsboro, NC 27312

919-542-5704
Fax: 919-545-0022
Home Page: www.albc-usa.org
Social Media: Facebook

Charles Bassett, Executive Director

An educational opportunity where members can share their knowledge with other members by sharing posters at the annual conference, subtting articles to the newsletter and more.
Frequency: Annual

1032 **AMSA Reciprocal Meat Conference**
American Meat Science Association
2441 Village Green Place
Champaign, IL 61822

217-356-5370
800-517-AMSA
Fax: 888-205-5834
Fax: 217-356-5370
E-Mail: information@meatscience.org
Home Page: www.meatscience.org\rmc

William Mikel, President
Scott J. Eilert, President-Elect
Casey B. Frye, Treasurer

RMC is the annual meeting for AMSA, featuring an interactive program tailored to bring attendees the very best and inspiring educational experience. Attendees are professionals in academia, government and industry, as well as students in the meat, food and animal science fields.

1033 **AOSA/SCST Annual Meeting-Association of Official Seed Analysts**
PMB #411
101 East State Street
Suite 214
Ithaca, NY 14850

607-256-3313
Fax: 607-273-1638
E-Mail: aosa.office@twcny.rr.com
Home Page: www.aosaseed.com

Ellen Chirco, President
Wayne Guerke, VP
Dan Curry, Secretary/Treasurer
Aaron Palmer, Certificate/Analysis
Larry Nees, Membership

Seed testing and laboratory equipment, supplies and services; workshops and discussions.
Frequency: Annual/J.ne

1034 **ARA Conference & Expo**
1156 15th St NW
Suite 500
Washington, DC 20005-1745

202-457-0825
Fax: 202-457-0864
E-Mail: info@aradc.org
Home Page: www.aradc.org

Jack Eberstacher, CEO
Jon Nienas, Secretary/Treasurer
Stacy Mayuga, Marketing Director

Advocates in the ag retail and distribution industry.
Frequency: Annual
Founded in 1993

1035 **ARBA National Convention**
American Rabbit Breeders Association
8 Westport Court
Bloomington, IL 61704

309-664-7500
Fax: 309-664-0941
Home Page: www.arba.net

Mike Avesing, President
Erik Bengtson, Vice-President
Eric Stewart, Executive Director
David Freeman, Treasurer

Seminar, banquet, luncheon and 1500 rabbit breeders exhibits.
3000 Attendees
Frequency: Annual/April
Founded in 1910

1036 **ASA-CSSA-SSSA International Annual Meeting**
American Society of Agronomy
5585 Guilford Road
Madison, WI 53711-5801
608-273-8080
Fax: 608-273-2021
E-Mail: pscullion@agronomy.org
Home Page: www.agronomy.org
Social Media: Facebook, Twitter, LinkedIn
Newell Kitchen, President
Kenneth Barbarick, President-Elect
Society members are dedicated to the conservation and wise use of natural resources to produce food, feed and fiber crops while maintaining and improving the environment. Annual meeting and exhibits of agricultural equipment, supplies and services.
Frequency: Annual/Fall

1037 **ASABE Annual International Meeting**
American Society of Agricultural & Bio-Engineers
2950 Niles Road
St. Joseph, MI 49085-9659
269-429-0300
800-371-2723
Fax: 269-429-3852
Home Page: www.asabe.org
Social Media: Facebook, Twitter, YouTube
Melissa Moore, Exec VP/Meetings & Conference Dir
Donna Hull, Publication Director
A forum to expand awareness of industry trends, promote and acknowledge innovations in design and technology, and provide opportunities for professional development. Networking, trade show, technical workshops and presentations, specialty sessions, and career fair.
Frequency: Annual/June
Founded in 1907

1038 **ASAS-ADSA Annual Meeting**
American Society of Animal Science
1800 S. Oak Street
Suite 100
Champaign, IL 61820-6974
217-356-9050
Fax: 217-398-4119
Home Page: www.asas.org
Social Media: Facebook, Twitter
Dr. Margaret E. Benson, President
Dr. James L. Sartin, President-Elect
Dr. Meghan Wulster-Radcliffe, CEO
Jacelyn Friedrich, COO
Professional organization for animal scientists designed to help members provide effective leadership through research, extension, teaching and service for the dynamic and rapidly changing livestock and meat industries. Containing 45 booths. Always a joint meeting with ADSA, and usually with one or more of these organizations: CSAS, AMPA, WSASAS, and PSA.
2000 Attendees
Frequency: Annual/July
Founded in 1908

1039 **ASCA Annual Conference**
American Society of Consulting Arborists
9707 Key West Ave
Suite 100
Rockville, MD 20850-3992
301-947-0483
Fax: 301-990-9771
E-Mail: asca@mgmtsol.com
Home Page: www.asca-consultants.org
Beth Palys, Executive Director
Recognized as a high quality, in depth conference with cutting edge speakers. Combining the best forum for discussion of current and relevant arboricultural issues, as well as consulting practice management issues and key consulting topics such as the role of the expert witness, risk assessment and tree appraisal
300 Attendees
Frequency: Annual/November/December

1040 **ASEV National Conference**
American Society for Enology and Vinticulture
PO Box 1855
Davis, CA 95617-1855
530-753-3142
Fax: 530-753-3318
E-Mail: society@asev.org
Home Page: www.asev.org
Social Media: LinkedIn
Dr. Sara Spayd, President
Leticia Chacon-Rodriguez, 1st Vice President
Dr. James Kennedy, 2nd Vice President
Dr. James Harbertson, Secretary/Treasurer
Provides a forum for the presentation of research in the fields of enology and viticulture or related sciences.
Frequency: Annual/June
Founded in 1950

1041 **ASFMRA Annual Meeting**
American Socitey of Farm Mgrs & Rural Appraisers
950 S Cherry Street
Suite 508
Denver, CO 80246-2664
303-758-3513
Fax: 303-758-0190
E-Mail: meetings@asfmra.org
Home Page: www.asfmra.org
Social Media: Facebook, Twitter, LinkedIn
Jeffrey Berg, President
Paul Joerger, President-Elect
Jim Rickert, 1st Vice President
Twenty-five exhibits of agricultural equipment, supplies and services; educational seminars and program sessions.
375 Attendees
Frequency: Annual/November

1042 **ASHS Annual Conference**
American Society for Horticultural Science
1018 Duke Street
Alexandria, VA 22314-2851
703-836-4606
Fax: 703-836-2024
E-Mail: webmaster@ashs.org
Home Page: www.ashs.org
Social Media: Facebook
Fred T Davies, Chair
Dewayne Ingram, President
Paul Bosland, President-Elect
Curt R. Rom, Treasurer
Facilitating the mutual exchange of ideas and information concerning horticultural research, extension, education, and industry.
Frequency: Annual/August

1043 **ATA Annual Conference**
Animal Transportation Association
12100 Sunset Hills Road
Suite 130
Reston, VA 20190
703-437-4377
Fax: 703-435-4390
E-Mail: info@animaltransportationassociation.org
Home Page: www.animaltransportationassociation.org
Robin Turner, Association Director
Lisa Schoppa, AATA President
Erik Liebegott, President-Elect
Chris Santarelli, Secretary/Treasurer
The latest information and technology relating to the transportation of animals. Subtopics include welfare, stress, meat quality, environmental control, biosecurity guidelines, training programs, and new transport designed crates and trailers.
150 Attendees
Frequency: Annual

1044 **AVMA Annual Convention**
American Veterinary Medical Association
1931 N Meacham Road
Suite 100
Schaumburg, IL 60173
800-248-2862
Fax: 847-925-1329
E-Mail: avmaininfo@avma.org
Home Page: www.avma.org
Social Media: Facebook, Twitter, Flickr, YouTube
Rene Carlson, President
Douglas Aspros, President-Elect
Jan Strother, Vice President
Barbara Schmidt, Treasurer
W. Ron DeHaven, Executive Vice President
Seminar and more than 300 exhibits of products, materials, equipment, data, and services for veterinary medicine. Education and hands-on labs, exhibit hall, charitable events and networking.
10000 Attendees
Frequency: Annual/July

1045 **Acres USA Conference**
5321 Industrial Oaks Boulevard
Suite 128
Austin, TX 78735
512-892-4446
800-355-5315
Fax: 512-892-4448
E-Mail: info@acresusa.com
Home Page: www.acresusa.com
Social Media: Facebook, Twitter, LinkedIn
Fred C Walters, Publisher/Editor
1300 Attendees
Founded in 1970
Printed in on newsprint stock

1046 **Ag Progress Days**
College of Agricultural Sciences
Penn State University
420 Agricultural Admin Building
University Park, PA 16802
814-865-2081
Fax: 814-865-1677
E-Mail: agprogressdays@psu.edu
Home Page: www.apd.psu.edu
Bob Oberheim, Manager
Agricultural trade show focusing on the innovations and progress made in the agricultural industry. More than 400 commercial exhibitors, interactive educational exhibits, guided tours and workshops, machinery and field demonstrations, live animals and equine seminars and demonstrations.
50M Attendees
Frequency: Annual/August
Founded in 1976

1047 Agri News Farm Show
Agri News
18 1st Avenue SE
Rochester, MN 55904-6118

507-857-7707
800-533-1727
Fax: 507-281-7436
Home Page: www.agrinew.com

John Losness, Publisher
Rosie Allen, Advertising Manager
Mychal Wilmes, Managing Editor

Annual show of 123 exhibitors of farming equipment, supplies and services.
7,500 Attendees
Frequency: Annual/March

1048 Agricultural Retailers Association Convention and Expo
Agricultural Retailers Association
1156 15th Street
Suite 302
Washington, DC 20005

202-570-0825
800-535-6272
Fax: 314-567-6808
E-Mail: kelly@aradc.org
Home Page: www.aradc.org
Social Media: Facebook, Twitter

Daren Coppock, President/CEO
Richard Gupton, Sr, VP, Public Policy
Michelle Hummel, VP
Marketing/Communications

Annual show of 120 manufacturers, suppliers and distributors of agricultural chemicals and fertilizers. Seminar, conference and banquet.
1200 Attendees
Frequency: Annual/December
Founded in 1993

1049 Allied Social Sciences Association Annual Meeting
555 E Wells Street
Suite 1100
Milwaukee, WI 53202-6600

414-918-3190
Fax: 414-276-3349
E-Mail: info@aaea.org
Home Page: www.aaea.org

Otto C Doering III, President
Yvonne C Bennett, Executive Director

The professional association for agricultural economists and related fields.
3000 Members
Frequency: Annual
Founded in 1910
Mailing list available for rent

1050 America Trades Produce Conference
590 East Frontage Road
PO Box 848
Nogales, AZ 85628

520-287-2707
Fax: 520-287-2948
E-Mail: info@freshfrommexico.com
Home Page: www.fpaota.org

Lee Frank, President
Alicia Bon Martin, Vice Chair
Allison Moore, Communications Director
Jose Luis Obregon, Deputy Director
Martha Rascon, Public Affairs Director

Represents companies involved in growing, harvesting, marketing and importing of Mexican produce entering the US.
125+ Members
Founded in 1944

1051 American Farriers Association Annual Convention Marketplace
American Farriers Association
4059 Iron Works Parkway
Suite 1
Lexington, KY 40511

859-233-7411
Fax: 859-231-7862
E-Mail: info@americanfarriers.org
Home Page: www.americanfarriers.org
Social Media: Facebook

Buck McClendon, President
Thomas Trosin, President Elect
John Blombach, Vice President
Alan Larson, Treasurer
Jason Knight, Secretary

One-hundred and seventy exhibits of equipment and supplies for farriers, seminar, banquet, luncheon and tours.
1500 Attendees
Frequency: Annual/February
Founded in 1971

1052 American Livestock Breeds Convervancy ALBC Conference
PO Box 477
Pittsboro, NC 27312

919-542-5704
Fax: 919-545-0022
Home Page: www.albc-usa.org
Social Media: Facebook, Blogger

Charles Bassett, Executive Director

Ensuring the future of agriculture through genetic conservation and the promotion of endangered breeds of livestock and poultry. A nonprofit membership organization working to protect over 180 breeds of livestock and poultry from extinction.

1053 American Seed Trade Association Annual Conference
1701 Duke Street
Suite 275
Alexandria, VA 22314-2878

703-837-8140
Fax: 703-837-9365
Home Page: www.amseed.com

Andy Lavigna, CEO

Producers of seeds for planting purposes. Consists of companies involved in seed production and distribution, plant breeding and related industries in North America.
850 Members
Founded in 1883

1054 Americas Food & Beverage Show
4601 NE 77th Avenue
Suite 200
Vancouver, WA 98662-2697

360-693-3373
Fax: 360-693-3464
Home Page: www.wusata.org

Andy Anderson, Executive Director
Eliza Lane, Outreach Coordinator

A nonprofit organization that promotes the export of food and agricultural products from the Western region of the US Comprised of 13 state funded agricultural promotion agencies.

1055 Annual Agricultural Law Symposium
127 Young Rd.
Kelso, WA 98626

360-200-5699
Fax: 360-423-2287
E-Mail: roberta@aglaw-assn.org
Home Page: www.aglaw-assn.org

Patricia A. Jensen, President
Amy Swanson, President-Elect
Robert P. Achenbach Jr., Executive Director

Bringing opportunities and ideas.
Frequency: Annual/October
Founded in 1980

1056 Annual Board of Delegates Meeting
1400 K St NW
Suite 1200
Washington, DC 20005-2449

202-789-0789
Fax: 202-898-0522
E-Mail: grains@grains.org
Home Page: www.grains.org

Kenneth Hobbie, President
Michael T Callahan, Director International Operations
Cheri Johnson, Manager Communications
Valerie Smiley, Manager Membership
Andrew Pepito, Director Finance/Administration

Motivated by the grain sorghum, barley and corn producer associations and representatives of the agricultural community. Provides commodity export market development.
Founded in 1960

1057 Annual Convention of the American Assoc. of Bovine Practitioners
American Association of Bovine Practicioners
PO Box 3610
Auburn, AL 36831-3610

334-821-0442
Fax: 334-821-9532
E-Mail: aabphq@aabp.org
Home Page: www.aabp.org

Brian J. Gerloff, President
Nigel B. Cook, President-Elect
Daniel L. Grooms, Vice President
Brian K. Reed, Treasurer
Charles W. Hatcher, Exhibits Chairman

130 exhibits of pharmaceutical and biological manufacturers, equipment and agricultural companies, computer programs and supplies.
1905 Attendees
Frequency: Annual/September
Founded in 1967

1058 Annual Meeting and Professional Improvement Conferences (AM/PIC)
6584 W Duroc Road
Maroa, IL 61756

217-794-3700
Fax: 217-794-5901
E-Mail: exec-dir@nacaa.com
Home Page: www.nacaa.com
Social Media: Facebook, Twitter

Rick Gibson, President

Hundreds of NACAA members from all over the country, every one relates to the same challenges faced every day on the job. Networking with other professional organizations.
Founded in 1917
Mailing list available for rent: 3500 names at $500 per M

1059 Aquatic Plant Management Society Annual Meeting
Aquatic Plant Management Socicty
PO Box 821265
Vicksburg, MS 39182-1265

FAX 601-634-5502
E-Mail: dpetty@ndrsite.com
Home Page: www.apms.org
Social Media: Facebook, LinkedIn

Tyler Koschnick, President
Mike Netherland, VP
Sherry Whitaker, Treasurer
Jeff Schardt, Secretary
Craig Aguillard, Director

An international organization of educators, scientists, commercial pesticide applicators, administrators and individuals interested in aquatic plant species and plant management.
Founded in 1961

1060 **Argi-Marketing Conference**
11020 King St
Suite 205
Overland Park, KS 66210-1201

913-491-6500
Fax: 913-491-6502
E-Mail: agrimktg@nama.org
Home Page: www.nama.org
Social Media: Facebook, Twitter, LinkedIn, YouTube, Flickr

Jennifer Pickett, CEO
Vicki Henrickson, Vice President

Marketing and communication suppliers, including trade publications, radio and television broadcast sales organizations, premium/incentive manufacturers, printers, marketing research firms, photographers and related professionals.
Founded in 1957

1061 **Asia Pacific Leather Fair**
1150 Connecticut Ave, NW
12th Floor
Washington, DC 20036

202-587-4250
E-Mail: jreddington@meatami.com
Home Page: www.ushsla.org

John Reddington, President
Susan Hogan, Manager
John Hochstein, Chairman

Exclusive representative of the hides and skin industry in the United States. Members range in size from small family-owned businesses to large corporations. Participates in two annual trade shows in Asia as a cooperator through the US Department of Agriculture's Foreign Agriculture Service.

1062 **Beltwide Cotton Conference**
National Cotton Council of America
7193 Goodlett Farms Parkway
Cordova, TN 38016

901-274-9030
Fax: 901-725-0510
Home Page: www.cotton.org

Dr. Mark D. Lange, President & CEO
A. John Maguire, Sr. Vice President
Charles H. Parker, Chairman
Chuck Coley, Vice Chairman
Meredith B. Allen, Vice President

Offers a forum for agricultural professionals.
Frequency: Annual/January

1063 **Big Iron Farm Show and Exhibition**
Red River Valley Fair Association
1201 West Main Avenue
PO Box 797
West Fargo, ND 58078-0797

701-282-2200
800-456-6408
Fax: 701-282-6909
E-Mail: info@redrivervalleyfair.com
Home Page: www.bigironfarmshow.com
Social Media: Facebook

Bryan Schulz, General Manager

Annual show of 750 manufacturers of agricultural machinery and related products with over 1,000 exhibit spaces.
70M Attendees
Frequency: Annual/September

1064 **Breeders of the Carolinas Field Day**
PO Box 1257
Kingsville, TX 78364-1257

361-592-9357
Fax: 361-592-8572
Home Page: www.santagertrudis.com

Ervin Kaatz, Executive Director

Devoted to the interests and the needs of the breed developed in 1918 at the famous King Ranch in Texas. Recognized in 1940 by the USDA, and famou for efficient growth, solid red color, hardiness and good disposition. They areadaptable to many environments and are present throughout the US and in other countries.

1065 **COSA Annual Meeting**
Committee on Organic and Sustainable Agriculture
5585 Guilford Road
Madison, WI 53711-5801

608-273-8080
Fax: 608-273-2021
Home Page: www.cosagroup.org

Ann-Marie Fortuna, Chair

COSA is a committee of the Tri-Societies for agronomy. The annual committee meeting is held in conjunction with the ASA-CSSA-SSSA Annual Meeting.
Frequency: Annual/Fall

1066 **CPMA Convention**
590 East Frontage Road
PO Box 848
Nogales, AZ 85628

520-287-2707
Fax: 520-287-2948
E-Mail: info@freshfrommexico.com
Home Page: www.fpaota.org

Lee Frank, President
Alicia Bon Martin, Vice Chair
Allison Moore, Communications Director
Jose Luis Obregon, Deputy Director
Martha Rascon, Public Affairs Director

Represents more than 125 member companies involved in growing, harvesting, marketing and importing of mexican produce entering the US at Nogales, Arizona.
125+ Members
Founded in 1944

1067 **Citrus Expo**
Southeast AgNet Publications/Citrus Industry Mag
5053 NW Hwy 225-A
Ocala, FL 34482

352-671-1909
Fax: 888-943-2224
E-Mail: CitrusExpo@southeastagnet.com
Home Page: www.citrusexpo.net

Maryann Holland, Show Manager

Citrus Trade Show with seminars, containing 150 exhibits. Complimentary attendance and lunch are provided to bona-fide grove owners & managers, citrus production managers, professional crop advisors, association execs & board members, government & legislative officials and the citrus research community.
1500 Attendees
Frequency: Annual/August
Founded in 1992

1068 **Commodity Classic**
Commodity Classic: ASA, NWGA, NCGA, NSP
632 Cepi Drive
Chesterfield, MO 63005 6397

636-733-9004
Fax: 636-733-9005
E-Mail: corninfo@ncga.com
Home Page: www.commodityclassic.com

Dave Burmeister, Registration Information
Kristi Burmeister, Exhibitor Information
Susan Powers, Media/Press Information
Beth Musgrove, General Information
Peggy Findley, Sponsorship Information

550 booths of equipment, seed and chemicals. Lecture series, classes, entertainment, awards, annual meetings of several agri-organziations/associations, and the trade show.
4000 Attendees
Frequency: February

1069 **Contractor Summit**
6540 Arlington Blvd
Falls Church, VA 22042-6638

703-536-7080
Fax: 703-536-7019
E-Mail: info@irrigation.org
Home Page: www.irrigation.org

Deborah Hamlin, Executive Director
Denise Stone, Meetings Director

Promotes education and use of irrigation in many areas of agriculture.
1600 Members
Founded in 1949

1070 **Country Elevator Conference & Trade Shows**
1250 I St NW
Suite 1003
Washington, DC 20005-3939

202-289-0873
Fax: 202-289-5388
E-Mail: ngfa@ngfa.org
Home Page: www.ngfa.org

Kendell Keith, President
Ronald D Olson, Chairman
Tom Coyle, Second Vice Chair
Randall Gordon, Vice President

NGFA is the national trade association of grain elevators, feed and feed ingredient manufacturers, grain and oilseed processors, exporters, livestock and poultry integrators, and firms providing products and services to the industry.
Founded in 1896

1071 **EMDA Industry Showcase**
Equipment Marketing & Distribution Association
PO Box 1347
Iowa City, IA 52244

319-354-5156
Fax: 319-354-5157
E-Mail: pat@edma.net
Home Page: www.edma.net

Patricia A Collins, Executive VP

Annual convention and 130 exhibits of equipment, supplies and services for wholesaler-distributors and independent manufacturer's representatives of shortline and specialty farm equipment, light industrial, lawn and garden, turf care equipment, estate and park maintenance equipment.
600 Attendees
Frequency: November

1072 **Eastern Milk Producers Cooperative Annual Meeting**
1985 Isaac Newton Square West
Reston, VA 20190-5094

703-742-6800
Fax: 703-742-7459
Home Page: www.mdvamilk.com

Known for being a leader in the dairy industry, the Eastern Milk Producers Cooperative has an 85-plus year reputation for integrity, service and high quality products.
ISSN: west-

1073 **El Foro**
WATT Publishing Company
122 S Wesley Avenue
Mount Morris, IL 61054

815-734-4171
Fax: 815-734-4201

E-Mail: olentine@wattmm.com
Home Page: www.wattnet.com

Jim Watt, Chairman/CEO

A trade show and technical symposium for the Latin American poultry, pig and feed industries. Containing 50 booths and 150 exhibits.
275 Attendees
Frequency: July

1074 Equipment Manufacturers Conference
American Feed Industry Association
2101 Wilson Blvd
Suite 916
Arlington, VA 22201-3047

703-524-0810
Fax: 703-524-1921
E-Mail: afia@afia.org
Home Page: www.afia.org
Social Media: Facebook, Twitter, LinkedIn

Joel Newman, President
Richard Sellers, VP
Donald E Orr, Chairman
Anne Keller, Communications Director

Organization devoted to representing companies in the animal feed industry and its suppliers.
690 Members
Founded in 1909

1075 European Seafood Exposition
4601 NE 77th Avenue
Suite 200
Vancouver, WA 98662-2697

360-693-3373
Fax: 360-693-3464
Home Page: www.wusata.org

Andy Anderson, Executive Director
Eliza Lane, Outreach Coordinator

A nonprofit organization that promotes the export of food and agricultural products from the Western region of the US Comprised of 13 state funded agricultural promotion agencies.

1076 FFA National Agricultural Career Show
National FFA Organization
PO Box 68960
6060 FFA Drive
Indianapolis, IN 46268-0960

888-332-2589
Fax: 800-366-6556
E-Mail: careershow@ffa.org
Home Page: www.ffa.org

850 booths encouraging high school youth to select careers in the agricultural industry. Held during the National FFA Convention.
45M Attendees
Frequency: Fall, Annually

1077 FPAA Convention & Golf Tournament
590 East Frontage Road
PO Box 848
Nogales, AZ 85628

520-287-2707
Fax: 520-287-2948
E-Mail: info@freshfrommexico.com
Home Page: www.fpaota.org

Lee Frank, President
Alicia Bon Martin, Vice Chair
Allison Moore, Communications Director
Jose Luis Obregon, Deputy Director
Martha Rascon, Public Affairs Director

Represents companies involved in growing, harvesting, marketing and importing of Mexican produce entering the US.
125+ Members
Founded in 1944

1078 Farm Bureau Showcase
American Farm Bureau Federation
1850 Howard Avenue
Suite C
Elk Grove, IL 60007

224-656-6600
Fax: 847-685-8696
E-Mail: webmaster@fb.org
Home Page: www.fb.org

Bob Stallman, President

Two-hundred plus booths featuring exhibits of agricultural equipment, supplies and services.
6-8M Attendees
Frequency: January

1079 Farm Equipment Manufacturers Association Spring Management Clinic
1000 Executive Parkway
Suite 100
St Louis, MO 63141-6369

314-878-2304
Fax: 314-732-1480
E-Mail: info@farmequip.org
Home Page: www.farmequip.org

Robert K Schnell, Executive VP
James Bearden, First VP
Richard W Heiniger, Second VP

An information gathering and distributing organization for farm equipment manufacturers and suppliers.
Founded in 1950

1080 Farm Progress Show
Farm Progress Companies
255 38th Avenue
Suite P
St Charles, IL 60174-5410
630-462-2224
800-441-1410
E-Mail: mjungmann@farmprogress.com
Home Page: www.farmprogressshow.com

Matt Jungman, National Shows Manager

Annual farm show of 400 exhibitors representing various types of agricultural products and services for farmers and agribusiness, including small operations to top producers.
Frequency: August/September

1081 Farm Science Review
Ohio State University
590 Woody Hayes Drive
232 Ag Engineering Building
Columbus, OH 43210-1057

614-926-6691
800-644-6377
Fax: 614-292-9448
E-Mail: gamble.18@osu.edu
Home Page: fsr.osu.edu

Chuck Gamble, Manager
Mattk Sullivan, Assistant Manager
Suzanne Steel, Media Coordinator

Annual show of 600 exhibitors of agricultural equipment, supplies and services.
140M Attendees
Frequency: Annual/September

1082 Farm/Ranch Expo
Bacon Hedland Management
475 S Frontage Road
Suite 101
Burr Ridge, IL 60527
630-323-6880
Fax: 630-898-3550

Gene Bacon, Show Manager
160 booths
7M Attendees
Frequency: January

1083 Farmfest
Farm Fairs
Highway 60 West
PO Box 731
Lake Crystal, MN 56055

507-726-6863
Fax: 507-726-6750

Annual show of 450 manufacturers, suppliers and distributors of farm equipment and machinery, computers and software products, chemicals, seeds and crops, and techniques of planting, tillage and harvesting.
50M Attendees

1084 Fertilizer Outlook and Technology Conference
425 Third Street SW
Suite 950
Washington, DC 20002-8037

202-962-0490
Fax: 202-962-0577
E-Mail: information@tfi.org
Home Page: www.tfi.org

Ford West, President
Ener Cunanan, Office Manager
Harry L Vroomen PhD, VP
Kathy Mathers, VP
Pamela D Guffain, Director/Government Relations

Gain perspective on the outlook for agriculture and major fertilizer materials and inputs from industry experts.
Founded in 1970

1085 Fresh Summit International Convention & Expo
1500 Casho Mill Road
PO Box 6036
Newark, DE 19714-6036

302-738-7100
Fax: 302-731-2409
E-Mail: pma@pma.com
Home Page: www.pma.com
Social Media: Facebook, Twitter, Flickr, YouTube, Xchange

Bryan Silbermann, President
Lorna Christie, VP/Industry Products & Services
Julie Stewart, Director Communications
Nancy Tucker, VP Global Business Development
Rayne Yori, VP Finance

PMA brings together leaders from around the world and from every segment of the supply chain. Participants throughout the global fresh produce and floral supply chains come together as a community to learn, network, build relationships, and do business.
Founded in 1949

1086 GEAPS Operations, Management, & Technology Seminar
Grain Elevator & Processing Society
4248 Park Glen Road
Minneapolis, MN 55416

952-928-4640
Fax: 952-929-1318
E-Mail: info@geaps.com
Home Page: www.geaps.com

David Krejci, Executive VP/Secretary
Darren Grahsl, Manager/Member & Chapter Services
Chuck House, Manager/Comm & Professional Dev
Amy McGarrigle, Manager/Member Ser & Information
Jason Stones, Manager/Member Ser & Publications

Offered in collaboration with the National Grain and Feed Association, boasted a faculty

of industry experts covering topics including contamination, purity and salvage; handling, storage and incident response; theft protection and inventory management beset practices; and natural disaster response and preparedness
2,000 Attendees
Frequency: March
Founded in 1937

1087 **GIE+EXPO - Green Industry & Equipment Expo**
Professional Lawncare Network, Inc
222 Pearl Street
Suite 300
New Albany, IN 47150

812-949-9200
800-558-8767
Fax: 812-949-9600
E-Mail: info@gie-expo.com
Home Page: www.gie-expo.com
Social Media: Facebook, Twitter

Annual show of 400 manufacturers, suppliers and distributors of lawn care equipment, supplies and services, including fertilizers, weed control materials, insurance information and power equipment, plus education sessions and presentations and demos.

1088 **Government Affairs Conference**
USA Rice Federation
4301 N Fairfax Drive
Suite 425
Arlington, VA 22203

703-226-2300
Fax: 703-236-2301
E-Mail: riceinfo@usarice.com
Home Page: www.usarice.com

Jamie Warshaw, Chairman

Discuss issues and activities for the U.S. rice industry, legislation, training, and seminars.
Frequency: Annual

1089 **Grain Feed Association Trade Show**
National Grain and Feed Association
1250 I Street NW
Suite 1003
Washington, DC 20005-3922

202-289-0873
Fax: 202-289-5388
E-Mail: ngfa@ngfa.org
Home Page: www.ngfa.org

Randall Gordon, President
Dave Hoogmoed, Chairman

One hundred and thirty booths exhibiting agribusiness products, supplies and services.
1.3M Attendees
Frequency: March

1090 **Grange Growth Summit**
1616 H St NW
Suite 10
Washington, DC 20006-4999

202-628-3507
888-447-2643
Fax: 202-347-1091
Home Page: www.nationalgrange.org

Ed Luttrell, President
Jennifer Dugent, Communications Manager
Leroy Watson, Legislative Director
Cindy Greer, Director Youth\Young Adult
DoriAnn Gedris, Marketing Director

Promotes general welfare and agriculture through local organizations. Presides over the advancement and promotion of the farming and agriculture industry.
300k Members
Founded in 1960

1091 **Grape Grower Magazine Farm Show**
Western Agricultural Publishing Company
4974 E Clinton Way
Suite 123
Fresno, CA 93727-1520

559-261-0396
Fax: 559-252-7387
Home Page: www.westagpubco.com

Phill Rhoads, Manager

Seminars, exhibits and prizes for grape growers. Contianing 80 booths and exhibits.

1092 **Green Industry Conference - GIC**
Professional Lawncare Network, Inc (PLANET)
950 Herndon Parkway
Suite 450
Herndon, VA 20170

703-736-9666
800-395-2522
Fax: 703-736-9668
E-Mail: info@gic-expo.com
Home Page: www.landcarenetwork.org/events/greenindustryconf/index.cfm

Held in conjunction with the GIE+EXPO, the conference offers leadership series, workshops, educational opportunities, events, and new member orientation.
Frequency: Annual

1093 **GrowerExpo**
Ball Publishing
335 N River Street
PO Box 9
Batavia, IL 60510-0009

630-208-9080
800-456-5380
Fax: 630-208-9350
E-Mail: info@ballpublishing.com

Diane Blazek, President

A trade show devoted to horticulture and floriculture production and marketing. 200 booths.
2M Attendees
Frequency: January

1094 **Hawkeye Farm Show**
Midwest Shows
PO Box 737
Austin, MN 55912

507-437-7969
Fax: 507-437-7752
E-Mail: salesfsu@farmshowsusa.com
Home Page: www.farmshowsusa.com

Penny Swank, Show Manager
18000 Attendees
Frequency: March

1095 **Holstein Association USA Regional Meeting**
1 Holstein Place
PO Box 808
Brattleboro, VT 05302-0808

802-254-4551
800-965-5200
Fax: 802-254-8251
E-Mail: info@holstein.com
Home Page: www.holsteinusa.com

John Meyer, CEO
Lisa Perrin, Marketing

Dairy cattle breed association with a membership base of people with strong interests in breeding, raising and milking Holstein cattle.
Founded in 1885

1096 **IAOM Conferences and Expos**
International Association of Operative Millers
10100 West 87th Street
Suite 306
Overland Park, KS 66212

913-338-3377
Fax: 913-338-3553
E-Mail: info@iaom.info
Home Page: www.aomillers.org
Social Media: Facebook, LinkedIn

Joe Woodard, President
Aaron Black, Vice President
Joel Hoffa, Treasurer
Melinda Farris, Executive Vice President

Premier educational events for grain milling and seed processing professionals. The annual events gather milling and allied trade professionals from around the world for several days of education, networking and fellowship.
Frequency: Annual/May
Founded in 1896

1097 **International Feed Expo**
American Feed Industry Association
2101 Wilson Blvd
Suite 916
Arlington, VA 22201-3047

703-524-0810
Fax: 703-524-1921
E-Mail: afia@afia.org
Home Page: www.afia.org
Social Media: Facebook, Twitter, LinkedIn

Joel Newman, President
Richard Sellers, VP
Donald E Orr, Chairman
Anne Keller, Communications Director

Organization devoted to representing companies in the animal feed industry and its suppliers.
Founded in 1909

1098 **International Hoof-Care Summit**
American Farriers Journal
223 Regency Court, PO Box 624
Suite 200
Brookfield, WI 53008-0624

262-782-4480
800-645-8455
Fax: 262-782-1252
E-Mail: info@lesspub.com
Home Page: www.americanfarriers.com

Alice Musser, Conference Manager

Conference held for America's leading most innovative hoof-care professionals.
800 Attendees
Frequency: January

1099 **International Marketing Conference & Annual Membership Meeting**
1400 K St NW
Suite 1200
Washington, DC 20005-2449

202-789-0789
Fax: 202-898-0522
E-Mail: grains@grains.org
Home Page: www.grains.org

Kenneth Hobbie, President
Michael T Callahan, Director International Operations
Cheri Johnson, Manager Communications
Valerie Smiley, Manager Membership
Andrew Pepito, Director Finance/Administration

Motivated by the grain sorghum, barley and corn producer associations and representatives of the agricultural community. Provides commodity export market development.
Founded in 1960

1100 **International Off-Highway and Power Plant Meeting and Exposition**
Society of Automotive Engineers

400 Commonwealth Drive
Warrendale, PA 15096-0001

724-776-4841
Fax: 724-776-4026
Home Page: www.sae.org

Diane Rogne, Show Manager
Sam Barill, Treasurer
Andrew Brown, Treasurer

Annual show of 270 suppliers of parts, components, materials and systems utilized in farm and industrial machinery and off-road and recreational vehicles.
5000 Attendees
Circulation: 84,000

1101 International Sweets & Biscuits Fair (ISM)
4601 NE 77th Avenue
Suite 200
Vancouver, WA 98662-2697
360-693-3373
Fax: 360-693-3464
Home Page: www.wusata.org

Andy Anderson, Executive Director
Eliza Lane, Outreach Coordinator

A nonprofit organization that promotes the export of food and agricultural products from the Western region of the US Comprised of 13 state funded agricultural promotion agencies.

1102 Irrigation Show
Irrigation Association
6540 Arlington Blvd
Falls Church, VA 22042-6638

703-536-7080
Fax: 703-536-7019
E-Mail: info@irrigation.org
Home Page: www.irrigation.org

Phil A. Burkart, President
Robert D. Dobson, President-Elect
Warren C. Thoma, Vice President
John E. Vikupitz, Treasurer

The Irrigation Show is the industry's one-stop event. Discover innovations on the show floor and in technical sessions, make connections with industry experts, business partners, and peers and build expertise with targeted education and certification.
3.5M Attendees
Frequency: Annual/November

1103 KFYR Radio Agri International Stock & Trade Show
KFYR Radio
3500 East Rosser Avenue
PO Box 1658
Bismarck, ND 58501

701-580-0550
800-472-2170
Fax: 701-255-8155
E-Mail: mwall@clearchannel.com
Home Page: www.kfyr.com

Syd Stewart, General Manager
Neil Cary, Manager
Jim Lowe, Manager

Annual show of 400 exhibitors of agricultural equipment, livestock and services.
15M Attendees
Frequency: February

1104 Kentucky Grazing Conference
151 Treasure Island Cswy. #2
St. Petersburg, FL 33706-4734

727-367-9702
800-707-0014
Fax: 727-367-9608
E-Mail: darthay@yahoo.com
Home Page: www.nationalhay.org

Ron Bradtmueller, President
Gary Smith, First VP
Richard Larsen, Second VP
Rollie Bernth, Director
Don Kieffer, Executive Director

NHA is the trade group that represents the interests of the hay industry throughout the United States and internationally.
Founded in 1895

1105 Kosherfest
4601 NE 77th Avenue
Suite 200
Vancouver, WA 98662-2697

360-693-3373
Fax: 360-693-3464
Home Page: www.wusata.org

Andy Anderson, Executive Director
Eliza Lane, Outreach Coordinator

A nonprofit organization that promotes the export of food and agricultural products from the Western region of the US Comprised of 13 state funded agricultural promotion agencies.

1106 Legislative Action Conference National Pork Producers Council
122 C Street NW
Suite 875
Washington, DC 20001

202-347-3600
800-937-7675
Fax: 202-347-5265
E-Mail: warnerd@nppc.org
Home Page: www.nppc.org
Social Media: Facebook, Twitter

Don Butler, President
Sam Carney, President-Elect
Doug Wolf, Vice President
Neil Dierks, CEO

National Pork Producers Council hosts a legislative action conference twice a year for pork producers from around the nation to learn about, discuss and lobby on agriculture legislation important to the U.S. pork industry.

1107 Legislative Conference
6540 Arlington Blvd
Falls Church, VA 22042-6638

703-536-7080
Fax: 703-536-7019
E-Mail: info@irrigation.org
Home Page: www.irrigation.org

Deborah Hamlin, Executive Director
Denise Stone, Meetings Director

Promotes education and use of irrigation in many areas of agriculture.
Founded in 1949

1108 Liquid Feed Symposium
American Feed Industry Association
2101 Wilson Blvd
Suite 916
Arlington, VA 22201-3047

703-524-0810
Fax: 703-524-1921
E-Mail: afia@afia.org
Home Page: www.afia.org
Social Media: Facebook, Twitter, LinkedIn

Joel Newman, President
Richard Sellers, VP
Donald E Orr, Chairman
Anne Keller, Communications Director

Organization devoted to representing companies in the animal feed industry and its suppliers.
Founded in 1909

1109 Mid South Farm Gin Supply Exhibit
Southern Cotton Ginners Association
874 Cotton Gin Place
Memphis, TN 38106
901-947-3104
Fax: 901-947-3103
Home Page: www.southerncottonginners.org

Chris Clegg, Chairman
Will Wade, President/Tennessee
Tim Price, Executive VP
Richard Kelly, VP/Tennessee
Allen Espey, Vice President/Tenessee

Exhibits new technology and practices for those in the cotton industry.
Frequency: Annual/February

1110 Mid-America Farm Show
Salina Area Chamber of Commerce
120 W Ash St.
PO Box 586
Salina, KS 67401

785-827-9301
Fax: 785-827-9758
Home Page: www.salinakansas.org

Don Weiser, Show Manager

Annual show of 325 exhibitors of agricultural equipment, supplies and services, including irrigation equipment, fertilizer, farm implements, hybrid seed, agricultural chemicals, tractors, feed, farrowing crates and equipment, silos and bins, storage equipment and farm buildings.
13M Attendees
Frequency: Annual/March
Founded in 1911

1111 Mid-America Horticulture Trade Show
Mid Am Trade Show
401 N. Michigan Ave.
Suite 2200
Chicago, IL 60611

312-321-5130
800-300-6103
Fax: 312-673-6882
E-Mail: mail@midam.org
Home Page: www.midam.org
Social Media: Facebook, Twitter, LinkedIn, YouTube

Barbara Rosborough, President
Bill Vogel, Vice President
Jim Melka, Secretary
Dave Story, Treasurer
Mid-Am is a green-industry event featuring more than 650 leading suppliers offering countless products, equipment, and services for the horticulture industry. Mid-Am also offers a variety of educational seminars featuring the best and the brightest in the horticultural and business communities to help keep you informed of the latest trends.
Frequency: Annual/January

1112 Midwest Ag Expo: OH
590 Woody Hayes Drive
Room 232
Columbus, OH 43210
614-292-4278
Fax: 614-292-9448
E-Mail: gamble.19@osu.edu
Home Page: www.farmshows.org

Doug Wagner, President
Dennis Alford, 1st Vice President
Chip Blalock, 2nd Vice President
Chuck Gamble, Secretary-Treasurer

Members are agriculture trade show sponsors and suppliers of services to these shows. Provides members with education, communication and evaluation. Provides the best possible marketing showcase for exhibitors and related

products to the farmer/rancher/producer customer.
Founded in 1972

1113 **Midwest Expo: IL**
Illinois Fertilizer & Chemical Association
130 W Dixie Highway
PO Box 186
Saint Anne, IL 60964-0186

815-939-1566
800-892-7122
Fax: 815-427-6573

Jean Trobec, President

Annual show of 130 manufacturers, suppliers and distributors of agricultural chemical and fertilizer application equipment, supplies and services.
2500 Attendees
Frequency: August, Danville

1114 **Midwest Farm Show**
North Country Enterprises
5330 Wall St
Suite 100
Madison, WI 53718

608-240-4700
Fax: 608-240-2069
Home Page: medaassn.com

Bill Henry, President
Massey Ferguson, Vice-President
Julie Roisum, Executive Assistant

250 booths. Top farm show exhibiting dairy and Wisconsin's tillage equipment, feed and seed.
175 Members
11M+ Attendees
Frequency: January

1115 **NCTA Convention & Trade Show**
National Christmas Tree Association
16020 Swingley Ridge Rd
Suite 300
Chesterfield, MO 63017-6030

636-449-5070
Fax: 636-449-5051
E-Mail: info@realchristmastrees.org
Home Page: www.realchristmastrees.org

Steve Drake, CEO
Pam Helmsing, Executive Director
Becky Rasmussen, Assistant Director
Rick Dungey, PR/Marketing Director

Draws christmas tree growers, retailers and suppliers from around the world for education, contests, networking and the trade show.
500 Attendees
Frequency: Annual/August

1116 **NDHIA Annual Meeting**
National Dairy Herd Improvement Association
421 S Nine Mound Round
PO Box 930399
Verona, WI 53593-0399

608-848-6455
Fax: 608-848-7675
E-Mail: info@dhia.org
Home Page: www.dhia.org

Jay Mattison, CEO
Dan Sheldon, President
Lee Maassen, VP
250 Attendees

1117 **NHA Annual Convention**
National Hay Association
151 Treasure Island Cswy
#2
St. Petersburg, FL 33706

727-367-9702
800-707-0014
Fax: 727-367-9608
E-Mail: darthay@yahoo.com
Home Page: www.nationalhay.org

Information and technology affecting the Hay industry.
Frequency: Annual/September

1118 **National Agri-Marketing Association Conference**
National Agri-Marketing Association
11020 King Street
Suite 205
Overland Park, KS 66210

913-491-6500
Fax: 913-491-6502
E-Mail: agrimktg@nama.org
Home Page: www.nama.org

Paul Redhage, President
Kenna Rathai, Ist Vice President

Annual show of 60 exhibitors of marketing and communication suppliers, including trade publications, radio and television broadcast sales organizations, premium/incentive manufacturers, printers, marketing research firms and photographers.
1400 Attendees
Frequency: April

1119 **National Agricultural Plastics Congress**
American Society for Plasticulture
526 Brittany Drive
State College, PA 16803

814-238-7045
Fax: 814-238-7051
E-Mail: contact@plasticulture.org
Home Page: www.plasticulture.org

William Tietjen, President
Jodi Fleck-Arnold, VP
Edward Cary, Secretary/Treasurer
Patricia Heuser, Executive Director

Congress of research presentations, with exhibit area of equipment, supplies and services relating to greenhouse production and mulch film production of agricultural and horticultural crops.
225 Attendees
Frequency: March

1120 **National Alliance of Independent Crop Consultants Annual Meeting**
349 E Nolley Dr
Collierville, TN 38017-3538

901-861-0511
Fax: 901-861-0512
E-Mail: jonesnaicc@aol.com
Home Page: www.naicc.org

Allison Jones, Executive VP
Shannon Gomes, Secretary

Represents individual crop consultants and contract researchers.
500+ Members
Founded in 1978

1121 **National Association Extension 4-H Agents Convention**
University of Georgia
Hoke Smith Annex
Athens, GA 30602

706-542-8804
E-Mail: freemand@vt.edu

Bo Ryles, State 4-H Leader
Heather Schultz, Live Stock Coordinator

50 booths for young people, youth staff and volunteers involved in 4-H.
1.2M Attendees
Frequency: November

1122 **National Association of Agricultural Educators (NAAE) Convention**
300 Garrigus Building
University of Kentucky
Lexington, KY 40545

859-257-2224
800-509-0204
Fax: 859-323-3919
E-Mail: jay_jackman@ffa.org
Home Page: www.naae.org

Greg Curlin, President
Ken Couture, President-elect
Jay Jackman PhD, CAE, Executive Director
Alissa Smith, Associate Executive Director
Julie Fritsch, Com. and Marketing Coordinator

A federation of 50 affiliated state vocational agricultural teacher associations.
7600 Members
Founded in 1948

1123 **National Association of County Agricultural Agents Conference**
National Association of County Agricultural Agents
6584 W Duroc Road
Maroa, IL 61756

217-794-3700
Fax: 217-794-5901
E-Mail: exec-dir@nacaa.com
Home Page: www.nacaa.com
Social Media: Facebook, Twitter

Paul Wigley, President
Paul Craig, President-Elect
Henry Dorough, Vice President
Richard Fechter, Secretary
Parman Green, Treasurer

Annual conference and exhibits for county agricultural agents and extension workers.
Frequency: Annual

1124 **National Association of Wheat Growers Convention**
National Association of Wheat Growers
415 2nd St NE
Suite 300
Washington, DC 20002-4993

202-547-7800
Fax: 202-546-2638
E-Mail: wheatworld@wheatworld.org
Home Page: www.wheatworld.org
Social Media: Facebook, Twitter

Wayne Hurst, President
Erik Younggren, 1st Vice President
Bing Von Bergen, 2nd Vice President
Paul Penner, Secretary/ Treasurer
Dana Peterson, CEO

Convention and trade show for the wheat, corn, soybean and sorghum industries.
Frequency: Annual/February
Founded in 1950

1125 **National Cotton Council Annual Meeting**
7193 Goodlett Farms Parkway
Cordova, TN 38016

901-274-9030
Fax: 901-725-0510
Home Page: www.cotton.org

Mark Lange, President/CEO
A. John Maguire, Senior Vice President

Membership consists of approximately 300 delegates named by cotton interests in the cotton-producing states.
35 Members

1126 **National Custom Applicator Exposition**
Agribusiness Association of Iowa

900 Des Moines Street
Suite 150
Des Moines, IA 50309-5549

515-262-8323
Fax: 515-262-8960
E-Mail: info@agribiz.org
Home Page: www.agribiz.org

Ed Beaman, President/CEO

Annual show of 70 manufacturers, suppliers and distributors of agrichemicals, fertilizers, spray equipment, tanks, agriplanes and agricomputer and flotation equipment.
2500 Attendees
Frequency: August

1127 National Farm Machinery Show & Tractor Pull
590 Woody Hayes Drive
Room 232
Columbus, OH 43210

614-292-4278
Fax: 614-292-9448
E-Mail: gamble.19@osu.edu
Home Page: www.farmshows.org

Doug Wagner, President
Dennis Alford, 1st Vice President
Chip Blalock, 2nd Vice President
Chuck Gamble, Secretary-Treasurer

Members are agriculture trade show sponsors and suppliers of services to these shows. Provides members with education, communication and evaluation. Provides the best possible marketing showcase for exhibitors and related products to the farmer/rancher/producer customer.
37 Members
Founded in 1972

1128 National Farm Machinery Show and Championship Tractor Pull
Kentucky Fair and Exposition Center
937 Phillips Lane
PO Box 37130
Louisville, KY 40233-7130

502-367-5000
Fax: 502-367-5299
Home Page: www.farmmachineryshow.org

Harold Workman, President/CEO

Annual show of 800 plus exhibitors of agricultural products, equipment, supplies and services.
293M Attendees
Frequency: February

1129 National Farmers Union Convention
20 F Street NW
Suite 300
Washington, DC 20001

202-554-1600
800-347-1961
Fax: 202-554-1654
Home Page: www.nfu.org
Social Media: Facebook, Twitter, YouTube

Roger Johnson, President
Claudia Svarstad, Vice President
Jeff Knudson, VP of Operations
Chandler Goule, VP of Government Relations

Promotes educational, cooperative and legislative activities of farm families in 26 states.
25000 Members
Founded in 1902

1130 National Grain Feed Association Annual Convention
National Grain Feed Association
1250 I Street NW
Suite 1003
Washington, DC 20005

202-289-0873
Fax: 202-289-5388
E-Mail: ngfa@ngfa.org
Home Page: www.ngfa.org

Kendall Keith, NGFA President
Todd Kemp, Director Marketing/Treasurer
Rachel Lyon, Meetings Manager
Marion Wimbush, Pressman

Committee meetings addressing issues essential to the business; Ag Village exhibitors and speakers.
1.3M Attendees
Frequency: March/April
Founded in 1896

1131 National Grange Convention
1616 H St NW
Suite 10
Washington, DC 20006-4999

202-628-3507
888-447-2643
Fax: 503-622-0343
Home Page: www.nationalgrange.org

Ed Luttrell, President
Jennifer Dugent, Communications Manager
Leroy Watson, Legislative Director
Cindy Greer, Director Youth\Young Adult
DoriAnn Gedris, Marketing Director

Promotes general welfare and agriculture through local organizations. Presides over the advancement and promotion of the farming and agriculture industry.
300k Members
Founded in 1960

1132 National No-Tillage Conference
No-Till Farmer
225 Regency Court, PO Box 624
Suite 200
Brookfield, WI 53008-0624

262-782-4480
800-645-8455
Fax: 262-782-1252
E-Mail: info@lesspub.com
Home Page: www.no-tillfarmer.com

Mike Lessitor, Executive VP
Alice Musser, Conference Manager

Conference held for America's leading most innovative no-till farmers.
Frequency: January

1133 National Orange Show Fair
National Orange Show
689 South E Street
San Bernardino, CA 92408

909-888-6788
Fax: 909-889-7666
Home Page: http://nationalorageshow.com
Social Media: Facebook

Five days of entertainment, art, exhibits, music, food and rides celebrating and educating the community on the California orange.
80000 Attendees
Frequency: Annual/May
Founded in 1889

1134 National Potato Council Annual Meeting
1300 L St NW
Suite 910
Washington, DC 20005-4107

202-682-9456
Fax: 202-682-0333
E-Mail: spudinfo@nationalpotatocouncil.org
Home Page: www.nationalpotatocouncil.org
Social Media: Twitter

John Keeling, Executive VP/CEO
Hollee Stubblebine, Director Industry Communications
Keith Masser, President
Jim Wysocki, VP Finance
Dan Elmore, VP Grower/Public Relations

Connect with other grower leaders from across the country on shaping national public policy impacting potato production and distribution. Such issues as keeping potatoes in schools, finalizing free trade agreements, and gearing up for the next Farm Bill will be reviewed and strategies will be developed.
45000 Members
Founded in 1948

1135 National Potato Council's Annual Meeting
National Potato Council
1300 L Street
Suite 910
Washington, DC 20005

202-682-9456
E-Mail: spudinfo@nationalpotatocouncil.org
Home Page: www.nationalpotatocouncil.org

John Keeling, CEO
Holly Stubblebine, Director of Public Relations
Mark Szymanski, Director of Public Relations

Annual meeting and exhibits of potato growing equipment, supplies and services.

1136 New England Grows
New England Grows
8-D Pleasant Street South
Natick, MA 01760

508-653-3009
Fax: 508-653-4112
E-Mail: info@newenglandgrows.org
Home Page: www.negrows.org

M. Virginia Wood, Executive Director
Jennifer A. Barich, Event Manager
Diane A. Zinck, Exhibit Sales & Marketing Manager
Owen J. Regan, Director of Operations
Elaine A. Kiesewetter, Conference Assistant

One of the largest and most visited horticulture and green industry events in North America, this event is known for its progressive educational conference and world-class trade show.
13000 Attendees
Frequency: Annual/February

1137 North American Beekeeping Conference
American Beekeeping Federation
3525 Piedmont Road
Bldg 5 Suite 300
Atlanta, GA 30305-1509

404-760-2875
Fax: 404-240-0998
E-Mail: info@abfnet.org
Home Page: www.abfnet.org

Robin D. Lane, Executive Director
Tara Zeravsky, Senior Conference Planner

Expert talks and discussions about beekeeping hot topics; exhibits and introduction of new products; and workshops.
1500 Attendees
Frequency: Annual/January
Founded in 1943

1138 North American Deer Farmers Association Annual Conference & Exhibit
North American Deer Farmers Association
104 S Lakeshore Drive
Lake City, MN 55041-1266

651-345-5600
Fax: 651-345-5603
E-Mail: info@nadefa.org
Home Page: www.nadefa.org

Carolyn Laughlin, President
Dave McQuaig, First VP
Glenn Dice Jr, Second VP

Annual show of 30+ exhibitors of deer farming equipment, supplies and services.
300 Attendees
Frequency: February
Founded in 1983

1139 **North American Farm and Power Show**
Tradexpos
811 W Oakland Avenue
PO Box 1067
Austin, MN 55912
507-437-4697
800-949-3976
Fax: 507-437-8917
E-Mail: steve@tradexpos.com
Home Page: www.tradexpos.com
Steve Guenthner, Show Director
Agri-business farm show for the 5-state region. Free admission and parking.
28M Attendees
Frequency: March

1140 **North American Fertilizer Transportation Conference**
425 Third Street SW
Suite 950
Washington, DC 20002-8037
202-962-0490
Fax: 202-962-0577
E-Mail: information@tfi.org
Home Page: www.tfi.org
Ford West, President
Ener Cunanan, Office Manager
Harry L Vroomen PhD, VP
Kathy Mathers, VP
Pamela D Guffain, Director/Government Relations
Co-hosted by The Fertilizer Institute and the Canadian Fertilizer Institute. Provides and opportunity for shippers and carriers to discuss issues of concern and work to reach mutually-beneficial solutions to logistical problems.
325 Members
Founded in 1970

1141 **North American International Livestock Exposition**
Kentucky Fair and Exposition Center
937 Phillips Lane
PO Box 37130
Louisville, KY 40209-7130
502-367-5000
Fax: 502-367-5139
Home Page: www.livestockexpo.org
Debbie Burda, Booking/Events
Ellen Anderson, Event Contact
Purebred livestock show with more than 20,000 entries in eight major divisions: dairy cattle, dairy goats, llamas, quarter horses, draft horses, market swine, beef cattle, sheep. Held at Kentucky Fair and Exposition Center in Louisville, Kentucky.
Frequency: November

1142 **Northwest Agricultural Congress**
4991 Drift Creek Rd SE
Sublimity, OR 97385-9764
503-769-8940
Fax: 503-769-8946
Home Page: www.nwagshow.com
Jim Heater, Show Manager
Second largest agricultural show on the west coast. Show is produced by the Northwest Horticultural Congress which is a partnership between Oregon Horticultural Society, the Oregon Association of Nurseries and Northwest Nut Growers Association. Show held in conjunction with annual meetings and seminars by all three of the horticultural groups.
21000 Members

1143 **Nut Grower Magazine Farm Show**
Western Agricultural Publishing Company
4974 E Clinton Way
Suite 123
Fresno, CA 93727-1520
559-252-7000
Fax: 559-252-7387
Phill Rhoads, Manager
Productions seminars, guest speakers, prizes and exhibits for nut growers. Containing 80 booths and exhibits.

1144 **Organic Seed Growers Conference**
PO Box 772
Port Townsend, WA 98368
360-385-7192
Fax: 360-385-7455
E-Mail: info@seedalliance.org
Home Page: www.seedalliance.org
Social Media: Facebook, Twitter
Dan Hobbs, Executive Director
Matthew Dillon, Executive Director
Supports the ethical development and stewardship of the genetic resources of agricultural seed.
Founded in 1975

1145 **Ozark Fall Farmfest**
Ozark Empire Fair
3001 North Grant Street
PO Box 630
Springfield, MO 65308
417-833-2660
Fax: 417-833-3769
Home Page: www.ozarkempirefair.com
Pat Lloyd, Manager
Annual show of 700 exhibitors with about 600 booths of agricultural products and services, including livestock.
40M Attendees
Frequency: October

1146 **PMA Convention & Exposition**
Produce Marketing Association
1500 Casho Mill Road
Newark, DE 19711-3547
302-738-7100
Fax: 302-731-2409
E-Mail: pma@pma.com
Home Page: www.pma.com
Social Media: Twitter, Flickr, YouTube
Bryan Silbermann, President & CEO
Lorna D. Christie, Vice President & COO
Yvonne Bull, CFO
A trade association of companies engaged in the marketing of fresh and safe produce and floral products. Show will inlcude 600 exhibitors with 1,600 booths.
16000 Attendees
Frequency: Annual/October
Founded in 1949

1147 **PMA Fresh Summit**
590 East Frontage Road
PO Box 848
Nogales, AZ 85628
520-287-2707
Fax: 520-287-2948
E-Mail: info@freshfrommexico.com
Home Page: www.fpaota.org
Lee Frank, President
Alicia Bon Martin, Vice Chair
Allison Moore, Communications Director
Jose Luis Obregon, Deputy Director
Martha Rascon, Public Affairs Director
Represents more than 125 member companies involved in growing, harvesting, marketing and importing of mexican produce entering the US at Nogales, Arizona.
125+ Members
Founded in 1944

1148 **Pest World**
National Pest Management Association
9300 Lee Highway
Suite 301
Fairfax, VA 22031
703-738-8330
Fax: 703-352-3031
Home Page: www.pestworld.org
Robert Lederer, Executive VP
Dominique Broyles, Director Conventions/Meetings
240 booths.
4000 Attendees
Frequency: October

1149 **Potato Expo**
1300 L St NW
Suite 910
Washington, DC 20005-4107
202-682-9456
Fax: 202-682-0333
E-Mail: spudinfo@nationalpotatocouncil.org
Home Page: www.nationalpotatocouncil.org
Social Media: Twitter
John Keeling, Executive VP/CEO
Hollee Stubblebine, Director Industry Communications
Keith Masser, President
Jim Wysocki, VP Finance
Dan Elmore, VP Grower/Public Relations
Largest conference and tradeshow for the potato industry held in North America. Offers educational programming covering the top issues facing the potato industry, provides networking opportunities with key decision makers and showcases the latest products and services for potato production and distribution.
45000 Members
Founded in 1948

1150 **Power Show**
590 Woody Hayes Drive
Room 232
Columbus, OH 43210
614-292-4278
Fax: 614-292-9448
E-Mail: gamble.19@osu.edu
Home Page: www.farmshows.org
Doug Wagner, President
Dennis Alford, 1st Vice President
Chip Blalock, 2nd Vice President
Chuck Gamble, Secretary-Treasurer
Members are agriculture trade show sponsors and suppliers of services to these shows. Provides members with education, communication and evaluation. Provides the best possible marketing showcase for exhibitors and related products to the farmer/rancher/producer customer.
37 Members
Founded in 1972

1151 **Prairie Farmer Farm Progress Show**
Farm Progress Publishers
1301 E Mound Road
Decatur, IL 62526-9394
217-877-9070
Fax: 217-877-9695
Sherry Stout, Editor
Jeffrey Smith, Advertising
One of the largest farm shows in the country.

1152 **Pro Farmer Midwest Crop Tour**
1818 Market Street 31st Floor
Philadelphia, PA 19103

800-772-0023
E-Mail: editors@profarmer.com
Home Page: www.profarmer.com
Social Media: Twitter

Sue King, Contact

Join the Pro Farmer editors at these seminars to discuss commodity markets, world economy, farm policy, land prices and more.
25M Members
Founded in 1973

1153 **Produce Executive Development Program**
1901 Pennsylvania Ave NW
Suite 1100
Washington, DC 20006-3412

202-303-3400
Fax: 202-303-3433
E-Mail: united@unitedfresh.org
Home Page: www.uffva.org
Social Media: Facebook, Twitter, YouTube

Thomas E Stenzel, CEO
Nicholas J Tompkins, Chair
Robert A Grimm, Executive Committee
Daniel G Vache, Secretary/Treasurer

Equipment, supplies, cartons, packaging machinery, computers, sorting and sizing equipment, harvesting equipment, film wrap manufacturing and commodity organizations.
1000+ Members
Founded in 1904

1154 **Produce Inspection Training Program**
1901 Pennsylvania Ave NW
Suite 1100
Washington, DC 20006-3412

202-303-3400
Fax: 202-303-3433
E-Mail: united@unitedfresh.org
Home Page: www.uffva.org
Social Media: Facebook, Twitter, YouTube

Thomas E Stenzel, CEO
Nicholas J Tompkins, Chair
Robert A Grimm, Executive Committee
Daniel G Vache, Secretary/Treasurer

Equipment, supplies, cartons, packaging machinery, computers, sorting and sizing equipment, harvesting equipment, film wrap manufacturing and commodity organizations.
1000+ Members
Founded in 1904

1155 **Produce for Better Health Annual Meeting**
590 East Frontage Road
PO Box 848
Nogales, AZ 85628

520-287-2707
Fax: 520-287-2948
E-Mail: info@freshfrommexico.com
Home Page: www.fpaota.org

Lee Frank, President
Alicia Bon Martin, Vice Chair
Allison Moore, Communications Director
Jose Luis Obregon, Deputy Director
Martha Rascon, Public Affairs Director

Represents companies involved in growing, harvesting, marketing and importing of Mexican produce entering the US.
125+ Members
Founded in 1944

1156 **Profit Briefing Professional Farmers of America**
1818 Market Street 31st Floor
Philadelphia, PA 19103

800-772-0023
E-Mail: editors@profarmer.com
Home Page: www.profarmer.com
Social Media: Twitter

Sue King, Contact

Join the Pro Farmer editors at these seminars to discuss commodity markets, world economy, farm policy, land prices and more.
25M Members
Founded in 1973

1157 **Purchasing & Ingredient Suppliers Conference**
American Feed Industry Association
2101 Wilson Blvd
Suite 916
Arlington, VA 22201-3047

703-524-0810
Fax: 703-524-1921
E-Mail: afia@afia.org
Home Page: www.afia.org
Social Media: Facebook, Twitter, LinkedIn

Joel Newman, President
Richard Sellers, VP
Donald E Orr, Chairman
Anne Keller, Communications Director

Organization devoted to representing companies in the animal feed industry and its suppliers.
690 Members
Founded in 1909

1158 **SAF National Convention**
5400 Grosvenor Ln
Bethesda, MD 20814-2198

301-897-8720
Fax: 301-897-3690
E-Mail: safweb@safnet.org
Home Page: www.safnet.org

Michael T Goergen Jr, Executive VP/CFO
Brittany Brumby, Assistant to the CEO/Council
Amy Ziadi, Information Technology Manager
Larry D Burner CPA, Sr Director Finance

Provides access to information and networking opportunities to prepare members for the challenges and the changes that face natural resource professionals.
Founded in 1900

1159 **SBS Conference & Exhibition**
Society for Biomolecular Sciences
100 Illinois Street
Suite 242
St. Charles, IL 60174

630-256-7527
877-990-7527
Fax: 630-741-7527
E-Mail: slas@slas.org
Home Page: www.slas.org
Social Media: Facebook, Twitter, LinkedIn

Michelle Palmer, Ph.D, President
David Dorsett, Vice President
Erick Rubin, Ph.D, Treasurer
Andy Zaayenga, Secretary

Scientists, innovators, researchers and industry analysts from around the world will converge to learn about the latest trends and basic and applied research that are transforming the way new pharmaceuticals are developed.
2000 Attendees
Frequency: Annual

1160 **Santa Gertrudis Breeders International Annual Meeting**
PO Box 1257
Kingsville, TX 78364-1257

361-592-9357
Fax: 361-592-8572
Home Page: www.santagertrudis.com

Ervin Kaatz, Executive Director

Information and issues regarding America's First Beef Breed developed in 1918 at the famous King Ranch in Texas. Recognized in 1940 by the USDA. Famous for rapid and efficient growth, solid red color, hardiness and good disposition. They are adaptable to many environments and are present throughout the US and in other countries.

1161 **Society for Biomolecular Screening**
Society for Biomolecular Screening
36 Tamarack Avenue
Suite 348
Danbury, CT 06810

203-788-8828
Fax: 203-748-7557
E-Mail: sbsemail@aol.com
Home Page: www.sbsonline.org

Al Kolbh, President
Christine Giordano, Executive Director
Larry Walker, Editor-in-Chief
Marietta Manono, Manager Meetings/Exhibitions

Technical sessions, exhibits, exhibitor tutorials, short courses, discussion groups related to discovery in the pharmaceutical and agrochemical industry and 181 exhibits.

1162 **Soil and Water Conservation Society Annual International Conference**
Soil and Water Conservation Society
945 SW Ankeny Road
Ankeny, IA 50021-9764

515-289-2331
800-843-7645
Fax: 515-289-1227
E-Mail: swcs@swcs.org
Home Page: www.swcs.org

Bill Boyer, President
Dan Towery, Vice-President
Clark Gantzer, Secretary
Jerry Pearce, Treasurer

Explores ways to improve the linkages among conservation science, policy and application at local, national, and international scales. The conference will provide participants an opportunity to teach skills, learn techniques, compare successes, and improve understanding.
1200 Attendees
Frequency: Annual

1163 **Southern Farm Show**
590 Woody Hayes Drive
Room 232
Columbus, OH 43210

614-292-4278
Fax: 614-292-9448
E-Mail: gamble.19@osu.edu
Home Page: www.farmshows.org

Doug Wagner, President
Dennis Alford, 1st Vice President
Chip Blalock, 2nd Vice President
Chuck Gamble, Secretary-Treasurer

Members are agriculture trade show sponsors and suppliers of services to these shows. Provides members with education, communication and evaluation. Provides the best possible marketing showcase for exhibitors and related products to the farmer/rancher/producer customer.
37 Members
Founded in 1972

1164 St. Louis All Equipment Expo
SouthWestern Association
P.O. Box 419264
Kansas City, MO 64141

816-762-5616
800-561-5323
Fax: 816-561-1249
E-Mail: oholcombe@swassn.com
Home Page: www.swassn.com

Jeffrey Flora, CEO
Cory Hayes, Director of Education

Manufacturers, suppliers and distributors of farm equipment, outdoor power equipment, supplies and agriculture products. Containing 350 booths.
15M Attendees
Frequency: December

1165 State Masters Conference
1616 H St NW
Suite 10
Washington, DC 20006-4999

202-628-3507
888-447-2643
Fax: 202-347-1091
Home Page: www.nationalgrange.org

Ed Luttrell, President
Jennifer Dugent, Communications Manager
Leroy Watson, Legislative Director
Cindy Greer, Director Youth\Young Adult
DoriAnn Gedris, Marketing Director

Promotes general welfare and agriculture through local organizations. Presides over the advancement and promotion of the farming and agriculture industry.
300k Members
Founded in 1960

1166 Sunbelt Agricultural Exposition
Sunbelt Ag Expo
290-G Harper Boulevard
Moultrie, GA 31788-2157

229-985-1968
Fax: 229-890-8518
E-Mail: info@sunbeltexpo.com
Home Page: www.sunbeltexpo.com
Social Media: Facebook

Over 1,200 exhibitors showing the latest agricultural technology in products and equipment plus harvesting and tillage demonstrations in the field. Largest farm show in North America's premier farm show.
200M Attendees
Frequency: Annual/October

1167 Sustainable Foods Summit
1340 North Cotner Blvd
Lincoln, NE 68505

402-477-2323
Fax: 402-477-4325
E-Mail: info@ocia.org
Home Page: www.ocia.org

Jeff See, Executive Director

OCIA International is a farmer owned international program of certification, which adheres to strict organic standards. It currently certifies thousands of farmers and processors in North, Central and South America and Asia. OCIA International is IFOAM accredited and adheres to the USDA ISO Guide 65, Japan Agriculture Standards and the Quebec Accreditation Council. OCIA has also been accredited from the USDA National Organic Program and Costa Rica Ministry of Agriculture.
3500 Members
Founded in 1985
Mailing list available for rent: 3500 names at $50 per M

1168 Sweetener Symposium
2111 Wilson Blvd
Suite 600
Arlington, VA 22201-3051

703-351-5055
Fax: 703-351-6698
E-Mail: info@sugaralliance.org
Home Page: www.sugaralliance.org

James Johnson, President
Jack Roney, Director Economics/Policy Analysis
Luther Markwart, Executive Vice President
Carolyn Cheney, Vice President

Covering a broad range of timely issues affecting the industry.
Founded in 1983

1169 TFI Fertilizer Marketing & Business Meeting
425 Third Street SW
Suite 950
Washington, DC 20002-8037

202-962-0490
Fax: 202-962-0577
E-Mail: information@tfi.org
Home Page: www.tfi.org

Ford West, President
Ener Cunanan, Office Manager
Harry L Vroomen PhD, VP
Kathy Mathers, VP
Pamela D Guffain, Director/Government Relations

Brings together members from each sector of the fertilizer industry for two days of networking and conducting business leading up to the spring planting season.
325 Members
Founded in 1970

1170 TFI World Fertilizer Conference
425 Third Street SW
Suite 950
Washington, DC 20002-8037

202-962-0490
Fax: 202-962-0577
E-Mail: information@tfi.org
Home Page: www.tfi.org

Ford West, President
Ener Cunanan, Office Manager
Harry L Vroomen PhD, VP
Kathy Mathers, VP
Pamela D Guffain, Director/Government Relations

Provides two days of networking and conducting business with industry leaders from as many as 60 different countries that represent all sectors of the fertilizer industry.
325 Members
Founded in 1970

1171 Tree Fruit Expo
Western Agricultural Publishing Company
4974 E Clinton Way
Suite 123
Fresno, CA 93727-1520

559-252-7000
Fax: 559-252-7387

Phill Rhoads, Manager

Productions seminars, dessert contest, guest speakers, prizes and exhibits for tree fruit growers. Containing 80 booths and exhibits.

1172 USA Rice Outlook Conference
USA Rice Federation
4301 N Fairfax Drive
Suite 425
Arlington, VA 22203

703-226-2300
Fax: 703-236-2301
E-Mail: riceinfo@usarice.com
Home Page: www.usarice.com

Jamie Warshaw, Chairman
Jeannette Davis, Conference Contact

Discuss issues and activities for the U.S. rice industry, legislation, training, and seminars.
Frequency: Annual

1173 USHSLA Annual Convention
United States Hide, Skin & Leather Association
1150 Connecticut Avenue, NW
12th Floor
Washington, DC 20036

202-587-4250
Home Page: www.ushsla.org

John Hochstein, Chairman
John Reddington, President

Represents the hide, skin and leather industries. Members range from small family-owned businesses to large corporations.
Frequency: Annual

1174 United Fresh Convention
590 East Frontage Road
PO Box 848
Nogales, AZ 85628

520-287-2707
Fax: 520-287-2948
E-Mail: info@freshfrommexico.com
Home Page: www.fpaota.org

Lee Frank, President
Alicia Bon Martin, Vice Chair
Allison Moore, Communications Director
Jose Luis Obregon, Deputy Director
Martha Rascon, Public Affairs Director

Represents companies involved in growing, harvesting, marketing and importing of Mexican produce entering the US.
125+ Members
Founded in 1944

1175 United Fresh Fruit and Vegetable Association Annual Convention
United Fresh Fruit & Vegetable Association
1901 Pennsylvania Avenue NW
Suite 1100
Washington, DC 20006

202-624-4989
Fax: 202-303-3433
E-Mail: united@uffva.org
Home Page: www.uffva.org

Thomas Stenzel, CEO
Mark Overbay, Manager Communications
30000 Attendees

1176 United States Animal Health Association Annual Meeting
4221 Mitchell Ave.
St Joseph, MO 64508

816-671-1144
Fax: 816-671-1201
E-Mail: usaha@usaha.org
Home Page: www.usaha.org

Benjamin Richey, Executive Director
Kelly Janicek, Executive Assistant

Seeks to prevent, control and eliminate livestock diseases.
1400 Members
Founded in 1897

1177 **United States Hide, Skin & Leather Assoc. - Asia Pacific Leather Fair**
1150 Connecticut Ave, NW
12th Floor
Washington, DC 20036

202-587-4250
E-Mail: jreddington@meatami.com
Home Page: www.ushsla.org

John Reddington, President
Susan Hogan, Manager
John Hochstein, Chairman
Stephen Sothmann, Director/International Affairs
Stephen Sothmann, Event Coordinator

Buyers will see the complete spectrum of the leather sector featuring the latest technology and products for leather making and footwear, as well as the widest range of leathers from around the globe displayed under one roof.
35 Members

1178 **Virginia Farm Show**
Lee Publications
6113 State Highway 5
PO Box 121
Palatine Bridge, NY 13428-0121

518-673-2269
800-218-5586
Fax: 518-673-3245
E-Mail: kmaring@leepub.com
Home Page: www.leepub.com

Ken Maring, Trade Show Manager

This show caters to the full-time farmer, with exhibits of all the major lines of equipment and services, and seminars presented by industry experts in dairy, beef and crop production.
Frequency: January
Founded in 1982

1179 **Walnut Council Annual Meeting**
1011 N 725 W
West Lafayette, IN 47906-9431

765-583-3501
Fax: 765-583-3512
E-Mail: walnutcouncil@walnutcouncil.org
Home Page: www.walnutcouncil.org

Liz Jackson, Executive Director
Larry R Frye, VP
William Hoover, Treasurer

Inviting scientists with the latest research on hardwood forestry, black walnut in particular, to present.
1000 Members
Founded in 1970

1180 **Washington Public Policy Conference**
United Fresh Produce Association
1901 Pennsylvania Ave NW
Suite 1100
Washington, DC 20006-3412

202-303-3400
Fax: 202-303-3433
E-Mail: united@unitedfresh.org
Home Page: www.uffva.org
Social Media: Facebook, Twitter, YouTube

Thomas E Stenzel, CEO
Nicholas J Tompkins, Chair
Robert A Grimm, Executive Committee
Daniel G Vache, Secretary/Treasurer

Equipment, supplies, cartons, packaging machinery, computers, sorting and sizing equipment, harvesting equipment, film wrap manufacturing and commodity organizations.
1000+ Members
Founded in 1904

1181 **Water Conference**
6540 Arlington Blvd
Falls Church, VA 22042-6638

703-536-7080
Fax: 703-536-7019
E-Mail: info@irrigation.org
Home Page: www.irrigation.org

Deborah Hamlin, Executive Director
Denise Stone, Meetings Director

Promotes education and use of irrigation in many areas of agriculture.
1600 Members
Founded in 1949

1182 **Western Fairs Association Convention & Trade Show**
1776 Tribute Rd
Suite 210
Sacramento, CA 95815-4495

916-927-3100
Fax: 916-927-6397
E-Mail: stephenc@fairsnet.org
Home Page: www.fairsnet.org

Stephen J Chambers, Executive Director
Jon Baker, VP

A non-profit association with members throughout the Western United States and Canada that strives to promote industry standards. Membership includes access to conventions and trade shows, educational training programs as well as legislative advocacy support.
2000 Members
Founded in 1922

1183 **Western Farm Show**
Investment Recovery Association
638 W 39th Street
Kansas City, MO 64111

816-561-5323
800-728-2272
Fax: 816-561-1991

Annual show of 700 manufacturers, suppliers and distributors of equipment, supplies and services relating to the agricultural industry.
35M Attendees
Frequency: February
Founded in 1962

1184 **Wheat Industry Conference**
415 2nd Street NE
Washington, DC 20002-4993

202-547-7800
Fax: 202-546-2638
E-Mail: wheatworld@wheatworld.org
Home Page: www.wheatworld.org
Social Media: Facebook, Twitter, YouTube

David Cleavinger, First Vice President
Karl Scronce, Second Vice President
Dana Peterson, CEO
Melissa George Kessler, Director of Communications

Nonprofit partnership of US wheat growers, by combining their strengths, voices and ideas are working to ensure a better future for themselves, their industry and the general public.
Founded in 1950

1185 **Winter Fancy Food Show**
4601 NE 77th Avenue
Suite 200
Vancouver, WA 98662-2697

360-693-3373
Fax: 360-693-3464
Home Page: www.wusata.org

Andy Anderson, Executive Director
Eliza Lane, Outreach Coordinator

A nonprofit organization that promotes the export of food and agricultural products from the Western region of the US Comprised of 13 state funded agricultural promotion agencies.

1186 **World Dairy Expo**
151 Treasure Island Cswy. #2
St. Petersburg, FL 33706-4734

727-367-9702
800-707-0014
Fax: 727-367-9608
E-Mail: darthay@yahoo.com
Home Page: www.nationalhay.org

Ron Bradtmueller, President
Gary Smith, First VP
Richard Larsen, Second VP
Rollie Bernth, Director
Don Kieffer, Executive Director

NHA is the trade group that represents the interests of the hay industry throughout the United States and internationally.
750 Members
Founded in 1895

1187 **World Pork Expo**
122 C Street NW
Suite 875
Washington, DC 20001

202-347-3600
800-937-7675
Fax: 202-347-5265
E-Mail: warnerd@nppc.org
Home Page: www.nppc.org
Social Media: Facebook, Twitter

Don Butler, President
Sam Carney, President-Elect
Doug Wolf, Vice President
Neil Dierks, CEO

The world's largest pork-specific trade show featuring business seminars, hundreds of exhibitors, breed shows and sales, and plenty of food and entertainment for everyone.
44 Members

Directories & Databases

1188 **AGRICOLA**
US National Agricultural Library
10301 Baltimore Ave
Beltsville, MD 20705-2351

301-504-5755
Fax: 301-504-5675
E-Mail: director@nalusda.gov
Home Page: www.agricola.nal.usda.gov/

Simon Y Liu, Director
Chris Cole, Acting Deputy Director

A database containing more than 3.3 million citations to journal literature, government reports, proceedings, books, periodicals, theses, patents, audiovisuals, electronic information, and other materials related to agriculture and its allied sciences.
Founded in 1962

1189 **ARI Network**
Ari Network Services
10850 W Park Pl
Suite 1200
Milwaukee, WI 53224-3636

414-973-4300
800-558-9044
Fax: 414-973-4619
Home Page: www.arinet.com
Social Media: Facebook, Twitter, LinkedIn, YouTube

Roy W. Olivier, President & CEO
Darin R. Janecek, CFO
Brian E. Dearing, Chairman

Offers current information on agricultural business, financial and weather information as well as statistical information for farmers.

1190 **Ag Ed Network**
ARI Network Services
10850 W Park Pl
Suite 900
Milwaukee, WI 53224-3636
414-973-4300
800-558-9044
Fax: 414-973-4619
E-Mail: info@arinet.com
Home Page: www.arinet.com
Roy W Olivier, Chief Executive Officer
John C Bray, New Market Development
Offers access to more than 1500 educational agriculture lessons covering farm business management and farm production.
Frequency: Full-text

1191 **AgriMarketing Services Guide**
Henderson Communications LLC
1422 Elbridge Payne Rd
Suite 250
Chesterfield, MO 63017-8544
636-728-1428
Fax: 636-777-4178
E-Mail: info@agrimarketing.com
Home Page: www.agrimarketing.com
Richard A Herrett, Executive Director
AgriMarketing Services Guide is published each December and is commonly referred to as the Who's Who in the North American ag industry sector.
Frequency: Annual/December

1192 **Agricultural Research Institute: Membership Directory**
Agricultural Research Institute
9650 Rockville Pike
Bethesda, MD 20814-3998
301-530-7122
Fax: 301-571-1816
Richard A Herrett, Executive Director
125 member institutions; also lists study panels and committees interested in environmental issues, pest control, agricultural meteorology, biotechnology, food irradiation, agricultural policy, research and development, food safety, technology transfer and remote sensing.
Cost: $50.00
Frequency: Annual

1193 **American Feed Industry Association: Software Directory**
American Feed Industry Association
2101 Wilson Blvd
Suite 916
Arlington, VA 22201-3047
703-524-0810
Fax: 703-524-1921
E-Mail: afia@afia.org
Home Page: www.afia.org
Joel Newman, President/CEO
Richard Sellers, Vice President
Anne Keller, Communications Director
Donald E Orr, Chairman
Companies that design software programs applicable to the feed industry.
Cost: $25.00

1194 **American Fruit Grower: Source Book Issue**
Meister Media Worldwide
37733 Euclid Ave
Willoughby, OH 44094-5992
440-942-2000
800-572-7740
Fax: 440-975-3447
E-Mail: joe_monahan@meistermedia.com
Home Page: www.meistermedia.com
Richard T Meister, Chairman
Gary T Fitzgerald, President
Joe Monahan, Group Publisher
Offers a list of manufacturers and distributors of equipment and supplies for the commercial fruit growing industry.
Cost: $19.95
66 Pages
Circulation: 35,143

1195 **American Meat Science Association Directory of Members**
American Meat Science Association
2441 Village Green Place
Champaign, IL 61822
217-356-5370
800-517-AMSA
Fax: 888-205-5834
Fax: 217-356-5370
E-Mail: information@meatscience.org
Home Page: www.meatscience.org
William Mikel, President
Scott J. Eilert, President Elect
Casey B. Frye, Treasurer
Directory for American Meat Science members only.
Cost: $20.00
230 Pages
Frequency: Biennial

1196 **American Society of Consulting Arborists: Membership Directory**
American Society of Consulting Arborists
9707 Key West Ave
Suite 100
Rockville, MD 20850-3992
301-947-0483
Fax: 301-990-9771
E-Mail: asca@mgmtsol.com
Home Page: www.asca-consultants.org
James R. Clark, Ph.D, President
Gordon Mann, President-Elect
Beth W. Palys, Executive Director
About 270 persons specializing in the growth and care of urban shade and ornamental trees; includes expert witnesses and monetary appraisals.
Frequency: Annual

1197 **Biological & Agricultural Index**
HW Wilson Company
950 Dr Martin Luther King Jr Blvd
Bronx, NY 10452-4297
718-588-8405
800-367-6770
Fax: 718-590-1617
Home Page: www.hwwilson.com
Harold Regan, President & CEO
Ann Case, Vice President, Editorial
Phillip Taylor, Customer Service Director
Amy Rosenbaum, Senior Manager
Kathleen McEvoy, Director of Public Relations
Provides fast access to core literature. In addition to citations to research and feature articles, users finding indexing of reports of symposia and conferences, and citations to current book reviews. Available on Web and disc.
359 Pages
Founded in 1898

1198 **Citrus & Vegetable Magazine: Farm Equipment Directory Issue**
Vance Publishing
10901 W 84th Ter
Suite 200
Lenexa, KS 66214-1631
913-438-5721
Fax: 913-438-0697
E-Mail: cvmscott@compuserve.com
Home Page: www.vancepublishing.com
Michael H Ross, President, Chief Operating Officer
William C Vance, Chairman, Chief Executive Officer
Judy Riggs, Director/Research Marketing
Offers information on a list of manufacturers of produce and citrus growing, handling, picking and packaging equipment.
Cost: $25.00
48 Pages
Frequency: Annual
Circulation: 12,000
ISSN: 0009-7586
Founded in 1938

1199 **Complete Guide to Gardening and Landscaping by Mail**
Mailorder Gardening Association
5836 Rockburn Woods Way
Elkridge, MD 21075-7302
410-540-9830
Fax: 410-540-9827
Home Page: www.mailordergardening.com
Bruce Frasier, President
Jim Bryant, First Vice President
Roberta Simpson, Second Vice President
Jean Vivlamore Norton, Treasurer
Camille Cimino, Executive Director
Member catalogers who sell gardening and nursery stock and supplies to consumers.
Cost: $2.00
Frequency: Annual
Founded in 1934

1200 **Contemporary World Issues: Agricultural Crisis in America**
ABC-CLIO
130 Cremona Drive
PO Box 1911
Santa Barbara, CA 93117-1911
805-681-1911
800 422 2546
Fax: 805-685-9685
E-Mail: CustomerService@abc-clio.com
Home Page: www.abc-clio.com
Ron Boehm, President/CEO
List of agencies and organizations in the US concerned with agricultural issues.
Cost: $50.00
Founded in 1953

1201 **Crop Protection Reference**
Vance Communications Corporation
315 W 106th St
Suite 504
New York, NY 10025-3473
212-932-1727
800-839-2420
Fax: 646-733-6010
E-Mail:
GreenbookCustomerService@Greenbook.net
Home Page: www.greenbook.net
Hilda Vazquez, Director Marketing, Sales
A single comprehensive source of up-to-date label information of crop protection products marketed in the United States by basic manufacturers and formulators. Extensive product indexing helps to locate products by: brand name, manufacturer crop site, mode of action, disease, insect, week, product category, common name, tank mix.
Cost: $50.00
Frequency: Annual

1202 **Directory for Small-Scale Agriculture**
US Department of Agriculture

Secretary oF Agriculture
Whitten Building/Room 200A
Washington, DC 20250-0001

202-012-2000

Offers information on persons involved with projects and activities relating to small-scale agriculture.
Cost: $5.50
119 Pages

1203 **Directory of American Agriculture**
Agricultural Resources & Communications
P.O.Box 283
Wamego, KS 66547-0283

785-456-9705
800-404-7940
Fax: 785-456-1654
E-Mail: chris@agresources.com
Home Page: www.agresources.com

Christina Wilson, President

This directory lists over 7,000 state and national associations involved in providing products and services related to food and fiber industries, in 27 categories. There are categorical indexes as well. Includes guide to Washington, D.C. offices, USDA listings, and guide to ag commodity commissions. Available on CD for $99.
Cost: $64.95
350 Pages
ISSN: 0897-1919
Founded in 1988
Printed in on matte stock

1204 **EMDA Membership Directory**
Equipment Marketing & Distribution Association
PO Box 1347
Iowa City, IA 52244-1347

319-354-5156
Fax: 319-354-5157
E-Mail: pat@edma.net
Home Page: www.emda.net

Patricia A Collins, Executive VP

Annual directory of FEWA-AIMRA members, includes address, phone, fax, web, e-mail, territory covered (with map) product descriptions, key personneland descriptive paragraph.
Cost: $50.00

1205 **Electronic Pesticide Reference: EPR II**
Vance Communications Corporation
315 W 106th St
Suite 504
New York, NY 10025-3473

212-932-1727
Fax: 646-733-6020
E-Mail:
GreenbookCustomerService@Greenbook.net
Home Page: www.greenbook.net

Hilda Vazquez, Director Marketing, Sales

Complete electronic reference to our 1,500 crop protection products; a full range of product information: full text labels and supplemental labels, full text MSDS's, product summaries, list of labeled tank mixes, worker protection information, DOT shipping information, SARA Title III reporting information. Search by brand name, manufacturer, common name crop, plant, site, weed, disease, insect plus much more. All versions of EPR II are provided on CD-ROM for windows.

1206 **Food & Beverage Marketplace**
Grey House Publishing
4919 Route 22
PO Box 56
Amenia, NY 12501

518-789-8700
800-562-2139
Fax: 845-373-6390
E-Mail: books@greyhouse.com
Home Page: www.greyhouse.com
Social Media: Facebook, Twitter

Richard Gottlieb, President
Leslie Mackenzie, Publisher

The most comprehensive resource in the food and beverage industry. Available in a three-volume printed directory, a subscription-based Online Database, as well as mailing list and database formats.
Cost: $595.00
2000 Pages
ISBN: 1-592373-61-5
Founded in 1981

1207 **Food & Beverage Marketplace: Online Database**
Grey House Publishing
4919 Route 22
PO Box 56
Amenia, NY 12501

518-789-8700
800-562-2139
Fax: 845-373-6390
E-Mail: gold@greyhouse.com
Home Page: www.gold.greyhouse.com
Social Media: Facebook, Twitter

Richard Gottlieb, President
Leslie Mackenzie, Publisher

This complete updated Food & Beverage Market Place: Online Database is the go-to source for the food and beverage industry. Anyone involved in the food and beverage industry needs this 'industry bible' and the important contacts to develop critical research data that can make for successful business growth.
Frequency: Annual
Founded in 1981

1208 **Food and Agricultural Export Directory**
National Technical Information Service
5285 Port Royal Rd
Springfield, VA 22161-0001

703-605-6000
800-553-6847
Fax: 703-605-6900
E-Mail: info@ntis.gov
Home Page: www.ntis.gov

Linda Davis, Vice President
Patrik Ekstr"m, Business Development Manager
Reuel Avila, Managing Director

Includes up to date listings of federal and state agencies, trade associations and a host of other organizations that can help you penetrate foreign markets. Includes phone and fax numbers.
100 Pages
Frequency: Annual

1209 **Food, Hunger, Agribusiness: A Directory of Resources**
Center For Third World Organizing
1218 E 21st St
Oakland, CA 94606-3132

510-533-7583
Fax: 510-533-0923
Home Page: www.ctwo.org

Lian Cheun, MAAP Director
Dan Ringer-Barwick, Operations Director

Offers information on organizations and publishers of books and other materials on food, hunger and agribusiness overseas.
Cost: $12.95
160 Pages

1210 **Grain & Milling Annual**
Sosland Publishing Company
4800 Main St
Suite 100
Kansas City, MO 64112-2513

816-756-1000
Fax: 816-756-0494
E-Mail: web@sosland.com
Home Page: www.sosland.com

Gordon Davidson, President

Offers a list of milling companies, mills, grain companies and cooperatives.
Cost: $115.00
Frequency: Annual
Circulation: 6,000
ISSN: 1098-4615

1211 **Guernsey Breeders' Journal: Convention Directory Issue**
Purebred Publishing Inc
7616 Slate Ridge Blvd
Reynoldsburg, OH 43068-3126

614-575-4620
Fax: 614-864-5614
E-Mail: sjohnson@usguernsey.com
Home Page: www.usguernsey.com

Seth Johnson, Manager
Dale Jensen, President
Tom Ripley, VP

A convention directory offering a list of officers and national members of the American Guernsey Cattle Association.
Cost: $20.00
Frequency: 10x Yearly

1212 **Hort Expo Northwest**
Mt Adams Publishing and Design
14161 Fort Road
White Swan, WA 98952-9786

509-848-2706
800-554-0860
Fax: 509-848-3896
Home Page: www.hortexponw.com

Vee Graves, Editor
Julie LaForge, Advertising Manager

The directory is mailed to subscribers and is also available complimentary at horticulture shows in the Northwest.
32 Pages
Frequency: Annually
Circulation: 8,700
Founded in 1989
Printed in 4 colors on glossy stock

1213 **Industrial Economic Information**
Global Insight
800 Baldwin Tower
Eddystone, PA 19022

610-490-4000
800-933-3374
Fax: 610-490-2557
E-Mail: info@globalinsight.com
Home Page: www.globalinsight.com

Joseph E Kasputys, Chair/President/CEO
Pricella Trumbull, Chief Operations Officer
Vicki Van Mater, VP
Kenneth J McGill, Product Management

Global Insight's unique perspective provides the most comprehensive economic and financial coverage of countries, regions and industries from any source.

1214 **International Green Front Report**
Friends of the Trees Society

PO Bo 253
Twisp, WA 98856

509-997-9200
Fax: 509-997-4812
Home Page: www.friendsofthetrees.net

Michael Pilarski, Director

Organizations and periodicals concerned with sustainable forestry and agriculture and related fields.
Cost: $7.00
192 Pages
Frequency: Irregular
Circulation: 8,000
Founded in 1978

1215 International Soil Tillage Research Organization
International Soil Tillage Research
1680 Madison Avenue
Wooster, OH 44691-4114

330-263-3700
Fax: 330-263-3658

A Franzluebbers, Editor-in-Chief

More than 750 individuals and institutions in 72 countries involved in the research or application of soil tilage and related subjects.
Cost: $100.00
Frequency: 10 per year

1216 Journal of the American Society of Farm Managers and Rural Appraisers
ASFMRA
950 S Cherry St
Suite 508
Denver, CO 80246-2664

303-758-3513
Fax: 303-758-0190
E-Mail: asfmra@agri-associations.org
Home Page: www.asfmra.org

Cheryl L Cooley, Manager Communications/PR
Frequency: Annually
Mailing list available for rent: 2500 names at $1M per M

1217 Landscape & Irrigation: Product Source Guide
Adams Business Media
11 Hanover Square
Suite 501
New York, NY 10005

212-566-7600
Fax: 212-566-7877
E-Mail: lenadams@acgresources.com
Home Page: www.acgresources.com

Len Adams, CEO

Offers information on suppliers, distributors and manufacturers serving the professional agriculture and landscaping community.
Circulation: 37,000

1218 Material Safety Data Sheet Reference
Vance Communications Corporation
315 W 106th St
Suite 504
New York, NY 10025-3473

212-932-1727
Fax: 646-733-6020
E-Mail: GreenbookCustomerService@Greenbook.net
Home Page: www.greenbook.net

Susan J Vannucci, Manager

Regulatory and product safety requirements. Contains full text MSDS's for products listed in the 1999 15th Edition Crop Protection Reference plus additional safety information such as DOT shipping information, SARA Title III regulations, Hazardous Chemical inventory reporting information plus much more.

1219 Meat and Poultry Inspection Directory
US Department of Agriculture
Administration Building
Room 344
Washington, DC 20250-0001

202-690-7650
Fax: 202-512-2250
Home Page: www.access.gpo.gov

Offers valuable information on all meat and poultry plants that ship meat interstate and therefore come under the US Department of Agriculture inspection.
Cost: $16.00
600 Pages
Frequency: SemiAnnual

1220 NASDA Directory
National Association of State Dept of Agriculture
1156 15th St NW
Suite 1020
Washington, DC 20005-1711

202-296-9680
Fax: 202-296-9686
E-Mail: nasda@nasda.org
Home Page: www.nasda.org

Stephen Haterius, Executive Director
Richard Kirchoff, Executive VP/CEO

Top agricultural officials in 50 states and four territories.
Cost: $100.00
Frequency: Annual

1221 National Agri-Marketing Association Directory
11020 King St
Suite 205
Overland Park, KS 66210-1201

913-491-6500
Fax: 913-491-6502
E-Mail: agrimktg@nama.org
Home Page: www.nama.org
Social Media: Facebook, Twitter, LinkedIn, Flickr, YouTube

Vicki Henrickson, President
Beth Burgy, 1st VP/ President-Elect
Paul Redhage, Secretary/Treasurer

Orginated as the Chicago Area Agricultural Advertising Association with 39 charter members. In 1963 the name was changed to the National Agricultural Advertising and Marketing Association and the present name was assumed in 1973.
Cost: $150.00
2500 Pages
Frequency: Annual
Founded in 1956

1222 National Organic Directory
Community Alliance with Family Farmers
36355 Russell Boulevard
PO Box 363
Davis, CA 95617-0363

530-756-8518
800-892-3832
Fax: 530-756-7857
E-Mail: info@caff.org
Home Page: www.caff.org

Judith Redmond, President
George Davis, VP
Pete Price, Secretary
Poppy Davis, Treasurer
Leland Swendon, Executive Director

Wriiten for all sectors of the booming organic food and fiber industry. Offers international listing with full contact information and extensive, cross-referenced index. Also provides regulatory updates, essays by industry leaders and other ressources.
Cost: $47.95
400 Pages
Frequency: Annual
Circulation: 2,500
ISBN: 1-891894-04-8
Founded in 1983

1223 Organic Pages Online North American Resource Directory
Organic Trade Association
28 Vernon St.
Suite 413
Brattleboro, VT 05301

802-275-3800
Fax: 802-275-3801
E-Mail: info@ota.com
Home Page: www.ota.com
Social Media: Facebook, Twitter, LinkedIn

Matt McLean, President
Sarah Bird, Vice President
Todd Linsky, Secretary
Kristen Holt, Treasurer

Provides over 1,300 listings by company name, brand name, business type, supply chain, product and service.

1224 Produce Marketing Association Membership Directory and Buyer's Guide
Produce Marketing Association
PO Box 6036
Newark, DE 19714-6036

302-738-7100
Fax: 302-731-2409
E-Mail: pma@pma.com
Home Page: www.pma.com

Bryan Silbermann, President
Julie Koch, Production Manager

A list of over 2,000 members that are involved in retail grocery and foodservice marketing businesses, including international companies.
Cost: $70.00
280 Pages
Frequency: Annual

1225 Professional Workers in State Agricultural Experiment Stations
US Department of Agriculture
200 Independence Ave SW
Whitten Bldg/Room 200A
Washington, DC 20201-0007

202-690-7650
Fax: 202-512-2250
Home Page: www.access.gpo.gov

Mike Johanns, Secretary of Agriculture

This directory offers information on academic and research personnel in all agricultural, forestry, aquaculture and home economics industries.
Cost: $15.00
289 Pages
Frequency: Annual
Founded in 1963

1226 Turf & Ornamental Reference
Vance Communications Corporation
315 W 106th St
Suite 504
New York, NY 10025-3473

212-932-1727
Fax: 646-733-6020
E-Mail: GreenbookCustomerService@Greenbook.net
Home Page: www.greenbook.net

Susan J Vannucci, Manager

Professional guide to plant protection problems. Provides the turf and ornamental industry with a single comprehensive source of up to

date label and MSDS information of plant protection products marketed in the United States by basic manufacturers and formulators. Extensive product indexing helps to locate products by: brand name; manufacturer; plant site; mode of action; disease, insect, weed; product category; common name; tank mix.
Cost: $159.00

1227 **USAHA Report of the Annual Meeting**
United States Animal Health Association
4221 Mitchelle Ave.
St Joseph, MO 64507

816-671-1144
Fax: 816-671-1201
E-Mail: usaha@usaha.org
Home Page: www.usaha.org

Benjamin Richey, Executive Director
Kelly Janicek, Executive Assistant

Held in conjunction with the American Association of Veterinary Laboratory Diagnosticians. (AAVLD)
Founded in 1897

1228 **Warehouses Licensed Under US Warehouse Act**
Farm Service Agency-US Dept. of Agriculture
1400 Independence Avenue SW
Stop Code 0506
Washington, DC 20013-2415

202-720-7809
Fax: 202-690-0014

Eric Parsons, Chief Public Affairs

Agricultural warehouses voluntarily licensed under the US Warehouse Act governing public storage facilities.
Frequency: Annual

1229 **Who's Who International**
WATT Publishing Company
303 N Main Street
Suite 500
Rockford, IL 61101

815-966-5400
Fax: 815-966-6416
Home Page: www.wattnet.com

James Watt, Chairman/CEO
Greg Watt, President/COO
Jeff Swanson, Publishing Director

Contains a detailed statistical section of key contacts in the industry. Includes industry phone book, genetic hatcheries and products, company directories, poultry marketers by city and state, refrigerated warehouses and federal agencies and associations.
310 Pages

1230 **Who's Who in the Egg & Poultry Industry in the US and Canada**
WATT Publishing Company
303 N Main Street
Suite 500
Rockford, IL 61101

815-966-5400
Fax: 815-966-6416
Home Page: www.wattnet.com

James Watt, Chairman/CEO
Greg Watt, President/CEO
Jeff Swanson, Publishing Director

Contains a detailed statistical section of key contacts in the industry. Includes industry phone book, genetic hatcheries and products, company directories, poultry marketers by city and state, refrigerated warehouses and federal agencies and associations.
Cost: $105.00
Frequency: Annual
ISSN: 0510-4130

1231 **World Databases in Agriculture**
National Register Publishing
300 Connell Drive
Suite 2000
Berkeley Heights, NJ 07922

800-473-7020
Fax: 908-673-1189
E-Mail: nrpeditorial@marquiswhoswho.com
Home Page: www.nationalregisterpub.com

Eileen Fanning, Managing Editor

Agricultural information on databases, including CD-ROM, magnetic tape, diskette, online, fax or databroadcast worldwide.

Industry Web Sites

1232 **http://gold.greyhouse.com**
G.O.L.D Grey House OnLine Databases

Grey House Publishing's online database platform, GOLD, includes Quick Search, Keyword Search and Expert Search for most business sectors including agriculture and food markets. The GOLD platform makes finding the information you need quick and easy. All of Grey House's directory products are available for subscription on the GOLD platform.

1233 **www.aaccnet.org**
AACC International

A non-profit organization of members who are specialists in the use of cereal grains in foods.

1234 **www.aaea.org**
Agricultural & Applied Economics Association

A not-for-profit association serving the professional interests of members working in agricultural and boradly related fields of applied economics.

1235 **www.aafco.org**
Association of American Feed Control Officials

Provides a mechanism for develping and implementing uniform and equitab;e laws, regulations, standrads and enforcement policies for regulating the manufacture, distribution and sale of animal feeds; resulting in safe, effective, and useful feeds.

1236 **www.aagiwa.org**
American Assoc of Grain Inspection & Weighing

The national association representing grain inspection and weighing agencies. These agencies provide official inspection services to measure the quantity of grain being bough and sold in the United States.

1237 **www.aaminc.org**
American Agriculture Movement

An umbrella organization composed of state organizations representing family farm producers.

1238 **www.aapausa.org**
AFIA Alfalfa Processors Council

Information for the processors and suppliers in the alfalfa industry.

1239 **www.abfnet.org**
American Beekeeping Federation

A national organiation with baout 1,000 members that continually works in the interest of all beekeepers, large or small, and those associated with the industry to ensure the future of the honeybee.

1240 **www.aceweb.org**
Agricultural Communicators in Education

An international association of communicators and information technologists. Develops professional skills of its members to extend knowledge about agriculture, natural resources and life and human sciences to people worldwide.

1241 **www.adsa.org**
American Dairy Science Association

Provides leadership in scientific and technical support to sustain and grow the global dairy through generation, dissemination, and exchange of information and services.

1242 **www.aem.org**
Association of Equipment Manufacturers

A trade association that provides services on a global basis for companies that manufacture equipment, products and services used worldwide in the following industries: Agriculture, Construction, Forestry, Mining and Utility. AEM's membership is made up of more than 750 companies and represents 200+ product lines.

1243 **www.afgc.org**
American Forage and Grassland Council

Dedicated to advancing the use of forage as a prime feed resource. Members present the academic community, producers, private industry, institutes and foundations.

1244 **www.afia.org**
American Feed Industry Association

Represents the total feed industry, as a key segment of the food chain, and member copmanies' interests, with one industry leadership voice on matters involving federal/state legislation and regulation

1245 **www.ag.ohio-state.edu/~farmshow**
North American Farm Show Council/Ohio State Univ

Strives to improve the value of its member shows through education, communication and evaluation. Provides the best possible marketing showcase for exhibitors of agricultural equipment and related products to the farmer/rancher/producer customer.

1246 **www.agconsultants.org**
American Society of Agricultural Consultants

A non-profit organization oriented around raising the standards and image of professional agricultural consultants.

1247 **www.agday.org**
Agriculture Council of America

A nonprofit organization composed of leaders in the agricultural, food and fiber community, dedicating its efforts to increasing the public's awareness of agriculture's role in modern society.

1248 **www.agnic.org**
Agriculture Network Information Center

A voluntary alliance of members based on the concept of centers of excellence. The member institutions are dedicated to enhancing collective information and services among the members and their partners for all those seeking agriculture information over the Internet.

1249 **www.agribusiness.com**
National Agri-Marketing Association

The nation's largest professional association for professionals in marketing and agribusiness

1250 **www.amseed.com**
American Seed Trade Association

Promotes the development of better seed to produce better crops for a better quality of life.

1251 **www.angus.org**
American Angus Association
The nation's largest beef registry association with over 30,000 adult and junior members. The goal is to serve the beef cattle industry, and increase the production of consistent, high quality beef that will better satisfy consumers throughout the world.

1252 **www.animalalliance.org**
Animal Agricultural Alliance
A non-profit organization that is dedicated to the protection of wildlife, the alleviation of animal suffering and the preservation of our environment.

1253 **www.aomillers.org**
International Association of Operative Millers
An international organization, comprised of flour millers, cereal grain and seed processors and allied trades representatives and companies devoted to the advancement of technology in the flour milling and cereal grain processing industries.

1254 **www.apms.org**
Aquatic Plant Management Society
An international organization of scientists, educators, students, commercial pedticide applicators, administrators, and concerned individuals interested in the management and study of aquatic plants.

1255 **www.asabe.org**
American Society of Agricultural & Biological Eng
An educational and scientific organization dedicated to the advancement of engineering applicable to agriculture, food, and biological systems.

1256 **www.asas.org**
American Society of Animal Science
Discover, disseminate and apply knowledge for sustainable use of animals for food and other human needs.

1257 **www.asca-consultants.org**
American Society of Consulting Arborists
The industry's premier professional association focusing solely on arboricultural consulting. Consulting Arborists are authoritative experts on trees, consulting property owners, municipalities, attorneys, insurance professionals and others on tree disease, placement, preservation and dispute resolution in addition to providing consulting and expert testimony in the legal, insurance and environmental arenas.

1258 **www.asev.org**
American Society for Enology and Viticulture
A tax exempt professional society dedicated to the interests of enologists, viticulturists, and others in the fields of wine and grape research and production throughout the world.

1259 **www.biodynamics.com**
Biodynamic Farming and Gardening Association
A non-profit, membership organization that fosters tknowledge of the practices and principles of the biodynamic method of agriculture, horticulture, and forestry in the North American continent

1260 **www.cast-science.org**
Council for Agricultural Science and Technology
A nonprofit organization composed of scientific societies an many individual, student, copmany, nonprofit, and associate society members.

1261 **www.christmastree.org**
National Christmas Tree Association
Strives to be one voice representing Christmas Tree Professionals and promoting the use of Real Christmas Trees

1262 **www.corn.org**
Corn Refiners Association
The national trade association representing the corn refining (wet milling) industry of the United States.

1263 **www.cottonseed.com**
National Cottonseed Products Association
An organization of firms and individuals engaged in the processing of cottonseed and the marketing of cottonseed products, as well as cottonseed. These include oil mills, refiners, product dealers and product brokers.

1264 **www.cropinsurance.org**
Crop Insurance Research Bureau
Working to improve crop insurance through unity and leadership

1265 **www.croplifeamerica.org**
CropLife America
Represents the developers manufacturers, formulators and distributors of plant science solutions for agriculture and pest management in the Unted States.

1266 **www.crops.org**
Crop Science Society of America
Seeks to advance research, extension, and teaching of all basic and applied phases of the crop sciences.

1267 **www.dhia.org**
National Dairy Herd Improvement Association
Promote accuracy, credibility, and uniformity of DHI records; represent the DHIA system on issues involving other National and International organizations; organize industry activities that benefit members of National DHIA

1268 **www.eap.mcgill.ca/cfbmc.htm**
Canadian Farm Business Management Council
To share and co-ordinate informatio non farm business management in order to help prevent duplication, encourage cost-sharing and build partnerships; to act as a forum for dialogue on farm business management issues of concern nationally or in more than on province of the country; to develop, adapt and distribute information products in farm business management to help increase the competitiveness of Canadian Agriculture.

1269 **www.fairsandexpos.com**
International Association of Fairs & Expositions
A voluntary, non-profit corporation, organizing state, provincial, regional, and county agricultural fairs, shows, exhibitions and expositions.

1270 **www.farmers-friend.com**
Farmers Friend
Farming news.

1271 **www.fb.org**
American Farm Bureau Federation
The unified national voice of agriculture, working through our grassroots organization to enhance and strengthen the lives of rural American and to build strong, prosperous agricultural communities

1272 **www.fewa-aimra.org**
FEWA-AIMRA Marketing & Distribution Association
Merged with AIMRA to form the leading association devoted to the marketing of specialized equipment.

1273 **www.fourhcouncil.edu**
National 4-H Council
Empowers youth to reach their full potential, working and learning in partnership with caring adults.

1274 **www.fpaota.org**
Fresh Produce Association of the Americas
A non-profit trade group of more than 100 members who are involved in the growth, harvest, import and distribution of the finest produce from Mexico.

1275 **www.fpfc.org**
Fresh Produce and Floral Council
Stimulates the promotion and sale of fresh fruit, vegetables and floral products; improves communications between all segments of the fresh produce and floral industries; and to exchange ideas on better and more economical handling of fresh fruit, vegetables and floral products from the farm to table.

1276 **www.freshcut.com**
Great American Publishing
Information on carrot production, growers and shippers.

1277 **www.grains.org**
US Grains Council
Develops export markets for U.S. barley corn, grain sorghum and related products. A private, non-profit corporation with nine international offices and programs in more than 50 countries.

1278 **www.greyhouse.com**
Grey House Publishing
Authoritative reference directories for business information and general reference, including agriculture and food markets. Users can search the online databases with varied search criteria allowing for custom searches by product category, geographic area, sales volume, keyword, subject and more. Full Grey House catalog and online ordering also available.

1279 **www.hereford.org**
American Hereford Association
For the raising and breeding of stock in the hereford cattle industry.

1280 **www.holsteinusa.com**
Holstein Association USA
The largest breed organization in the world, comprised of members who have a strong interest in breeding, raising and milking Holstein cattle.

1281 **www.iaff.ttu.edu/aals**
Association for Arid Land Studies

1282 **www.iaom.info**
International Association of Operative Millers
An international organization, comprised of flour millers, cereal grain and seed processors and allied trades representatives and companies devoted to the advancement of technology in the flour milling and cereal grain processing industries.

1283 **www.ifas.ufl.edu**
Institute of Food & Agriculture/Univ of Florida
For college students professionally interested in communications related to agriculture, food, natural resources and allied fields.

1284 **www.ipaa.net**
International Pesticide Applicators Association
Provides education and information for the professional horticultural applicator. Legislative work involves the states of Washington, Oregon, Idaho in the area of laws and regulations.

1285 **www.irrigation.org**
Irrigation Association
Membership organization for irrigation equipment and system manufacturers, dealers, distributors, designers, consultants, contractors and end users.

1286 **www.mailordergardening.com**
Mailorder Gardening Association
nonprofit organization serving the needs of companies involved in marketing gardening products to consumers

1287 **www.meatami.org**
American Meat Institute
Dedicated to increasing the efficiency, profitability and safety of meat and poultry worldwide.

1288 **www.naab-css.org**
National Association of Animal Breeders
To unite thos individuals and organizations engaged in the artificial insemination of cattle and other livestock into an affiliated federation operating under self-imposed standards of performance and to conduct and promote the mutual interest and ideals of its members.

1289 **www.nacaa.com**
National Association County Agricultural Agents
For agents focusing on educational programs for the youth of the community.

1290 **www.naicc.org**
National Alliance of Independent Crop Consultants
A professional society that represents the nation's crop porduction and research consultants.

1291 **www.nama.org**
National Agri-Marketing Association
Professional association for professionals in marketing and agribusiness.

1292 **www.nationalgrange.org**
Nat'l Grange of the Order of Patrons of Husbandry
Provides opportunities for individuals and families to develop to their highest potential in order to build stronger communities and states, as well as a stronger nation.

1293 **www.nationalplantboard.org**
National Plant Board
A non-profit organization of the plant pest regulatory agencies opf each of the staes and Commonwealth of Puerto Rico.

1294 **www.nationalpotatocouncil.Org**
National Potato Council
The advocate for the economic well-being of U.S. potato growers on federal legislative, regulatory, environmental and trade issues.

1295 **www.nfu.org**
National Farmers Union
Protects and enhances the economic well-being and quality of life for family farmers and ranchers and their rural communities

1296 **www.nppc.org**
National Pork Producers Council
Conducts public-policy outreach on behalf of its 43 affiliated state associations, enhancing opportunities for the success of U.S. pork producers and other industry stakeholders by establishing the U.S. pork industry as a consistent and responsible supplier of high-quality pork to the domestic and world markets.

1297 **www.ocia.org**
Organic Crop Improvement Association International
Dedicated to providing the highest quality organic certification serices and access to global organic markets

1298 **www.onions-usa.org**
National Onion Association
The official organization representing growers, shippers, brokers, and commerical representatives of the U.S. onion industry.

1299 **www.ota.com**
Organic Trade Association
A membership-based business association that focuses on the organic business community in North America. Promotes and protects the growth of organic trade to benefit the environment, farmers, the public and the economy.

1300 **www.pma.com**
Produce Marketing Association
Global trade association serving the entire produce and floral supply chains by enhancing the marketing of produce, floral, and related products and services worldwide.

1301 **www.profarmer.com**
Professional Farmers of America
Gives customers a competitive edge in marketing and financial management through timely delivery and accurate analysis of market-sensitive news and views.

1302 **www.sbsonline.org**
Society for Biomolecular Sciences
Non-profit scientific society dedicated to drug discovery and its related disciplines. Provides a forum for global educationand information exchange among professionals in the chemical, pharmaceutical, biotech and agrochemical industries.

1303 **www.seedtechnology.net**
Society Commercial Seed Technologists
An organization comprised of commercial, independent and government seed technologists.

1304 **www.sheepusa.org**
American Sheep Industry Association
The national organization representing the interests of sheep producers located throughout the United States.

1305 **www.southerncottonginners.org**
Southern Cotton Ginners Association
Serves its members by providing safety, training, and regulatory representation.

1306 **www.southwesternassn.com**
SouthWestern Association
Established by a progressive group of independent hardware and farm implement/mercantile dealers to help increase their profitability and solve common problems.

1307 **www.soygrowers.com**
American Soybean Association
Represents U.S. soybean farmers through policy advocacy and international market development.

1308 **www.sugaralliance.org**
American Sugar Alliance
A natinoal coalition of sugarcane and sugarbeet farmers, processoris, refiners, suppliers, workers and others dedicated to preserving a strong domestic sugar industry.

1309 **www.sunflowernsa.com**
National Sunflower Association
A non-profit commodity organization working on problems and opportunities for the improvement of all members.

1310 **www.tfi.org**
Fertilizer Institute
The leading voice in the fertilizer industry, representing the public policy, communication and statistical needs of producers, manufacturers, retailers and transporters of fertilizer.

1311 **www.turfweeds.net**
Turfgrass Weed Science/Virginia Polytech Institute
Provides weed management information and research reports to turfgrass managers.

1312 **www.unitedfresh.org**
United Fresh Produce Association
Commited to driving the growth and success of produce companies and their partners. Represents the interests of member companies throughout the global, fresh produce supply chain, including family-owned, private and publicly traded businesses as well as regional, national and international companies.

1313 **www.usguernsey.com**
American Guernsey Association
Register and deliver guernsey cattle throughout the United States.

1314 **www.uspotatoes.com**
United States Potato Board
The central organizing force in implementing programs that will increase demand for potatoes.

1315 **www.vealfarm.com**
Veal Quality Association Program
For veal producers and processors.

1316 **www.wawgg.org**
Washington Association of Wine Grape Growers
Advocates for the Washington wine growing industry by educating, promotin, representing, and unifying the industry and fostering a positive business environment for continued growth and production of world-class, Washington-grown wines.

1317 **www.wildblueberries.com**
Wild Blueberry Association of North America
For processors and growers of wild blueberries in Eastern Canada and Maine.

Associations

1325 **Advanced BioFuels USA**
507 North Bentz Street
Frederick, MD 21701
301-644-1395
E-Mail: info@AdvancedBiofuelsUSA.or
Home Page: advancedbiofuelsusa.info
Joanne Ivancic, Executive Director
Bob Kozak, Treasurer
A nonprofit organization that advocates for the adoption of advanced biofuels as an energy security, military flexibility, economic development andclimate change mitigation/pollution control solution though its promotion of public understanding, acceptance, and research.

1326 **Advanced Biofuels Association**
800 17th Street, NW
Suite 1100
Washington, DC 20006
Home Page:
www.advancedbiofuelsassociation.com
Social Media: Facebook, Twitter, LinkedIn, YouTube
Wayne Simmons, Chairman
Chris Ryan, Vice Chairman
Michael McAdams, President
Andrew Rojeski, Secretary
Christopher Higby, Treasurer
Organization that seeks to help America transform to a low carbon economy by supporting and advocating for public policies that are technology neutral, use sustainable feedstocks, and offering financial support to its member companies to bring products to market that are competitive and compatible with petroleum-based fuels and byproducts.
40 Members

1327 **Alliance for Affordable Energy**
P.O. Box 751133
New Orleans, LA 70175
504-208-9761
E-Mail: casey@all4energy.com
Home Page: all4energy.org
Social Media: Facebook, Twitter, LinkedIn, YouTube, Instagram
Casey DeMoss, Chief Executive Officer
Lynncal T. Bering, Program Director
Jessica Netto, Chief Operating Officer
Logan Atkinson, Office Development Manager
Annie Williams, Volunteer & Intern Manager
An environmental advocacy organization that promotes fair, affordable, environmentally responsible energy.
Founded in 1985

1328 **Alliance to Save Energy**
1850 M Street, NW
Suite 610
Washington, DC 20036
202-857-0666
Home Page: www.ase.org
Social Media: Facebook, Twitter, LinkedIn, YouTube, Google+
Sen Mark Warner, Chairman
Jorge Carrasco, Co-Chairman
Kateri Callahan, President
Ian Campbell, 1st Vice Chair
Willian Von Hoene, 2nd Vice Chair
Organization that leads worldwide energy efficiency initiatives in policy advocacy, research, education and technology deployment.

1329 **Alternative Energy Association**
1061 East Indiantown Road
Suite 400
Jupiter, FL 33477
561-776-8600
E-Mail: alternativeenergyassn@gmail.com
Home Page: www.alternativeenergyassn.com
Organization that uses marketing campaigns, seminars, and eduactional activities to promote awareness of clean, renewable sources of power generation as alternatives to the use of fossil fuels for energy production.

1330 **Alternative Energy Resources Organization**
432 N. Last Chance Gulch
Helena, MT 59601
406-443-7272
Fax: 406-442-9120
E-Mail: aero@aeromt.org
Home Page: www.aeromt.org
Social Media: Facebook, Twitter, Myspace, Pinterest, Google+
Bryan von Lossberg, Executive Director
Caroline Wallace, Membership and Communications
A grassroots nonprofit organization dedicated to solutions that promote resource conservation and local economic vitality. By bringing people together, AERO offers a vehicle for collective action and a sense of common purpose for citizens within their communities to shape a more sustainable future.
Founded in 1974

1331 **American Biogas Council**
1211 Connecticut Ave NW
Suite 600
Washington, DC 20036-2701
202-640-6595
E-Mail: info@americanbiogascouncil.org
Home Page: www.americanbiogascouncil.org
Wayne Davis, Chairman
Norma McDonald, Vice-Chair
Melissa VanOrnum, Treasurer
Amy McCrae Kessler, Vice-Chair
Mission is to create jobs, environmental sustainability and energy independence by growing the American biogas industry.
Mailing list available for rent

1332 **American Coalition for Ethanol**
5000 South Broadband Lane
Suite 224
Sioux Falls, SD 57108
605-334-3381
E-Mail: cbeck@ethanol.org
Home Page: ethanol.org
Social Media: Facebook, Twitter
Environmental advocacy organization that promotes the use of ethanol as the most successful renewable energy platform in the world.
Founded in 1987

1333 **American Council for an Energy-Efficient Economy**
529 14th Street N.W
Suite 600
Washington, DC 20045-1000
202-507-4000
Fax: 202-429-2248
Home Page: www.aceee.org
Alison Silverstein, President
Timothy M Stout, Treasurer
Peter A. Molinaro, Secretary
Roland J. Risser, Special Advisor
A nonprofit organization that seeks to advance energy efficiency policies, programs, technologies, investments, and behaviors.

1334 **American Council on Renewable Energy**
1600 K Street NW
Suite 650
Washington, DC 20006
202-393-0001
E-Mail: weirich@acore.org
Home Page: www.acore.org
Social Media: Facebook, Twitter, LinkedIn, YouTube
Michael R. Brower, Interim President and CEO
Todd Foley, Senior VP of Policy and Government
Dawn Butcher, Director of Event Planning
Cindi Ec, Director, Leadership Programs
Kevin Haley, Strategic Communications Manager
Works to bring all forms of renewable energy into the mainstream of America's economy and lifestyle. Members include every aspect and sector of the renewable energy industries and their trade associations, including wind, solar, geothermal, biomass and biofuels, hydropower tidal/current energy and waste energy.
Founded in 2001

1335 **American Hydrogen Association**
P.O. Box 4205
Mesa, AZ 85201

480-234-5070
E-Mail: 123GoH2@gmail.com
Home Page: www.americanhydrogenassociation.org

Providing information on the use of hydrogen as a fuel.

1336 **American Solar Energy Society**
2525 Arapahoe Ave
Ste E4-253
Boulder, CO 80302

303-443-3130
Fax: 303-443-3212
E-Mail: info@ases.org
Home Page: www.ases.org
Social Media: Facebook, Twitter, LinkedIn

David G. Hill, Chair
Susan Greene, President
Seth Masia, Executive Director
Jason Keyes, Secretary
Gina Johnson, Editor/Publisher

The nation's leading association of solar professionals & advocates. Mission is to inspire an era of energy innovation and speed the transition to a sustainable energy economy. Advancing education, research and policy.
13M Members
Founded in 1954

1337 **American Water Works Association**
6666 W. Quincy Ave.
Denver, CO 80235-3098

303-794-7711
Home Page: www.awwa.org
Social Media: Facebook, Twitter, LinkedIn, YouTube

John J. Donahue, President
Gene C. Koontz, President Elect
James A. Chaffee, Immediate Past President
Dave E. Rager, Treasurer

The largest nonprofit, scientific and educational association dedicated to managing and treating water.
Founded in 1881

1338 **American Wind Energy Association**
1501 M Street NW
Suite 1000
Washington, DC 20005

202-383-2500
Fax: 202-383-2505
E-Mail: windmail@awea.org
Home Page: www.awea.org
Social Media: Facebook, Twitter, LinkedIn, YouTube, Flickr

Gabriel Alonso, Chair
Pam Poisson, Chief Financial Officer
Rob Gramlich, Senior Vice President
Peter Kelley, Vice President, Public Affairs
Tom Kiernan, Chief Executive Officer

Promotes wind energy as a clean source of electricity for consumers around the world. Representing wind power project developers, equipment suppliers, services providers, parts manufacturers, utilities, researchers, and others involved in the wind industry - one of the world's fastest growing energy industries.
2500+ Members

1339 **Association of Energy Engineers**
3168 Mercer University Drive
Atlanta, GA 30341

770-447-5083
E-Mail: al@aeecenter.org
Home Page: www.aeecenter.org
Social Media: Facebook, Twitter, LinkedIn, YouTube

Randy Haines, President
Dr. Scott Dunning, President Elect
Bill Younger, Past President
Asit Patel, Secretary
Paul Goodman, Treasurer
17000 Members
Founded in 1977

1340 **Association of Energy Engineers (AEE)**
4025 Pleasantdale Rd.
Suite 420
Atlanta, GA 30340

770-447-5083
Fax: 770-446-3969
E-Mail: al@aeecenter.org
Home Page: www.aeecenter.org
Social Media: Facebook, Twitter, YouTube

Bill Younger, President
Albert Thumann, Executive Director
Stephenie Johnson, Information Services Director
Lauren Lake, Event and Marketing Coordinator
Patricia Ardavin, Membership Director

Information and networking in the dynamic fields of energy engineering and energy management, renewable and alternative energy, power generation, energy services, sustainability, and all related areas.
15M Members
Founded in 1977

1341 **Biomass Energy Research Association**
901 D Street, S.W
Suite 100
Washington, DC 20024

410-953-6202
Fax: 410-290-0377
E-Mail: bera@beraonline.org
Home Page: beraonline.org

Joan Pellegrino, President
Phillip C. Badger, Secretary
Mark A. Paisley, Director
Janis L. Tabor, Director
Dr. Evan Hughes, Director

An association of bioenergy researchers, companies, and advocates that promotes education and research on renewable biomass energy and waste-to-energy systems.

1342 **Biomass Power Association**
100 Middle St.
PO Box 9729
Portland, ME 04104-9729

703-889-8504
E-Mail: info@biomasspowerassociation.com
Home Page: www.usabiomass.org

Bob Cleaves, President & CEO
Gary Melow, State Projects Coordinator

The nation's leading organization working to expand and advance the use of clean, renewable biomass power. Educates policymakers at the state and federal level about the benefits of biomass and provides regular briefings and research to keep members fully informed about public policy impacting the biomass industry. Members include local owners and operators of existing biomass facilities, suppliers, plant developers and others.
80 Members

1343 **Biomass Thermal Energy Council**
1211 Connecticut Avenue NW
Suite 600
Washington, DC 20036-2701

202-596-3974
Fax: 202-223-5537
E-Mail: info@biomassthermal.org
Home Page: www.biomassthermal.org
Social Media: Facebook, Twitter

Dan Wilson, Chairman
Joseph Seymour, Executive Director
Jeffrey A. Serfass, Senior Advisor
Emanuel Wagner, Programs Director
Raymond Albrecht, Technical Advisor

An association of biomass fuel producers, appliance manufacturers and distributors, supply chain companies and non-profit organizations that view biomass thermal energy as a renewable, responsible, clean and energy-efficient pathway to meeting America's energy needs. BTEC engages in research, education, and public advocacy for the fast growing biomass thermal energy industry.
Founded in 2009

1344 **Business Council for Sustainable Energy**
505 9th Street NW
Suite 800
Washington, DC 20004

202-785-0507
Fax: 202-785-0514
E-Mail: bcse@bcse.org
Home Page: www.bcse.org
Social Media: Facebook, Twitter, LinkedIn

Mark Wagner, Chair
Rob Gramlich, Vice Chair
Scott Crider, Vice Chair
Lisa Jacobson, President
Ruth McCormick, Director

A coalition of companies and trade associations from the energy efficiency, natural gas and renewable energy sectors, and includes independent electric power producers, investor-owned utilities, public power, commercial end-users and project developers and service providers for environmental markets.

1345 **Canadian Renewable Fuels Association(CRFA)**
350 Sparks Street
Suite 605
Ottawa, ON K1R 7S8

613-594-5528
Fax: 613-594-3076
E-Mail: s.thurlow@greenfuels.org
Home Page: www.greenfuels.org
Social Media: Facebook, Twitter

W. Scott Thurlow, President
Deborah Elson, Vice President of Membership
Ellen Wightman, Director of Operations
Andrea Kent, Director of Communications
Lindsey Ehman, CRFA Coordinator

Promotes and advances the use of renewable fuels for transporation- to protect our environment by reducing harmful emissions and to grow our economy by creating the good, green-energy jobs of the future.
Founded in 1984

1346 **Center for Energy Efficiency and Renewable Technologies**
1100 11th Street
Suite 311
Sacramento, CA

916-442-7785
E-Mail: info@ceert.org
Home Page: ceert.org
Social Media: Twitter, LinkedIn

Jonathan M. Weisgall, Chairman
Ralph Cavanagh, Vice Chair
V. John White, Executive Director
John Shahabian, Director of Operations
Kevin Lynch, Secretary/Treasurer

A partnership of major environmental groups and private-sector clean energy companies that advocate for policies that promote global warming solutions and increased reliance on

clean, renewable energy sources for California andthe West.
Founded in 1990

1347 **Clean Energy Group**
50 State St.
Suite 1
Montpelier, VT 05602

802-223-2554
Fax: 802-223-4967
E-Mail: Lmilford@cleanegroup.org
Home Page: www.cleanegroup.org
Social Media: Facebook, Twitter

Lew Milford, President & Founder
Warren Leon, Executive Director, Clean Energy
Robert Sanders, Senior Finance Advisor
Valerie Stori, Project Director
Todd Olinksy-Paul, Project Director

A leading nonprofit advocacy organization working in the US and internationally on innovative clean energy technology, finance, and policy programs. Supported by major foundations, as well as state, federal and international energy agencies.
Founded in 1998

1348 **Distributed Wind Energy Association**
1065 Main Ave
Suite 209
Durango, CO 81301

928-380-6012
E-Mail: jjenkins@distributedwind.org
Home Page: distributedwind.org
Social Media: Facebook, Twitter, LinkedIn

Mike Bergey, President
Kevin Schulte, Vice President
Heather Rhoads, Secretary
Tal Mamo, Treasurer
Jim Duffy, Board Member

A collaborative group comprised of manufacturers, distributors, project developers, dealers, installers, and advocates, whose primary mission is to promote and foster all aspects of the American distributed wind energy industry.

1349 **Ducks Unlimited**
One Waterfowl Way
Memphis, TN 38120

901-758-3825
800-45D-UCKS
Home Page: www.ducks.org
Social Media: Facebook, Twitter, YouTube, Instagram

John W. Newman, Chairman
George Dunklin, President
Dale Hall, Chief Executive Officer
Paul R. Bonderson, First Vice President
Robert S. Hester, Treasurer

Conserves, restores, and manages wetlands and associated habitats for North America's waterfowl.
Founded in 1937

1350 **Efficient Windows Collaborative**
21629 Zodiac Street NE
Wyoming, MN 55092

E-Mail:
efficientwindowscollaborative@gmail.com
Home Page: www.efficientwindows.org
Social Media: Facebook, Twitter, LinkedIn

A nonprofit organization that partners with window, door, skylight,and component manufacturers, research organizations, federal, state and local government agencies, and others interested in expanding the market for high-efficiency fenestration products.

1351 **Energy Recovery Council**
1730 Rhode Island Avenue, NW
Suite 700
Washington, DC 20036

202-467-6240
E-Mail: tmichaels@energyrecoverycouncil.org
Home Page: www.energyrecoverycouncil.org

Ted Michaels, President

Represents the waste-to-energy industry and communities that own waste-to-energy facilities. Current ERC members own and operate modern waste-to-energy facilities that operate nationwide, safely disposing of municipal solid waste, while at the same time generating renewable electricity using modern combustion technology equipped with state-of-the-art emission control systems.

1352 **Environmental and Energy Study Institute**
1112 16th Street, NW
Suite 300
Washington, DC 20036-4819

202-628-1400
Fax: 202-204-5244
E-Mail: cwerner@eesi.org
Home Page: www.eesi.org
Social Media: Facebook, Twitter, LinkedIn, Vimeo

Jared Blum, Chairman
Carol Werner, Executive Director
David Robison, Director of Finance
Susan Williams, Director of Development
Alison Alford, Programs & Administrative Assistant

A nonprofit organization that advances innovative policy solutions that set us on a cleaner, more secure and sustainable energy path.
Founded in 1984

1353 **Export Council for Energy Efficiency**

E-Mail: laura@solarcities.org
Home Page: www.ecee.org

A nonprofit association that promotes the export of energy efficient products, services, and technologies worldwide.
Founded in 1994

1354 **Fuel Cell and Hydrogen Energy Association**
1211 Connecticut Avenue Northwest
Suite 650
Washington, DC 20036

202-261-1331
E-Mail: info@fchea.org
Home Page: www.fchea.org
Social Media: Facebook, Twitter, LinkedIn, Google+

Morry Markowitz, President & Executive Director
Bud DeFlaviis, Director of Government Affairs
Jennifer Gangi, Director of Comm. & Outreach
Sandra Curtin, Research & Comm. Manager
Connor Dolan, External Affairs Manager

A trade association for the fuel cell and hydrogen energy industry,and is dedicated to the commercialization of fuel cells and hydrogen energy technologies.
Founded in 2010

1355 **Geothermal Energy Association**
209 Pennsylvania Avenue SE
Washington, DC 20003

202-454-5261
Fax: 202-454-5265
E-Mail: jgreco@terra-genpower.com
Home Page: www.geo-energy.org
Social Media: Facebook, Twitter, LinkedIn, YouTube, Wordpress

Karl Gawell, Executive Director
Leslie Blodgett, Geothermal News Specialist
Kathy Kent, Sr. Director of Marketing
Mihaela-Daniela Lobontiu, Business Manager
Becky Little, Assistant to the Executive Director

Advocates for public policies that will promote the development and utilization of geothermal resources, provides a forum for the industry to discuss issues and problems, encourages research and development to improve geothermal technologies, presents industry views to governmental organizations, and conducts education and outreach projects.

1356 **Geothermal Exchange Organization**
312 S. Fourth St
Suite 100
Springfield, IL

888-255-4436
Home Page: www.geoexchange.org
Social Media: Facebook, Twitter, LinkedIn, Google+

Douglas Dougherty, President & CEO
Ted Clutter, Manager of Outreach

A nonprofit trade association that promotes the manufacture, designand installation of GeoExchange systems—an energy efficient and environmentallyfriendly heating and cooling technology.

1357 **Geothermal Resources Council**
20001 Second Street
Suite 5
Davis, CA 95618-5476

530-758-2360
Fax: 530-758-2839
E-Mail: grc@geothermal.org
Home Page: www.geothermal.org
Social Media: Facebook, Twitter, LinkedIn, YouTube, Flickr, Pinterest, Bl

Steve Ponder, Executive Director
Ian Crawford, Director of Communications, Editor
Estela M. Smith, GRC Office Manager
Anh Lay, Office Associate
Chi-Meng Moua, Library Associate & Web Master

Nonprofit, educational association actively seeking to expand its role as a primary professional educational association for the international geothermal community.
Founded in 1970

1358 **Intergovernmental Renewable Energy Organization**
884 2nd Avenue, UN Centre
No. 20050
New York, NY 10017

212-647-7000
Fax: 212-202-4100
Home Page: www.ireoigo.org
Social Media: Facebook, Twitter

Rand Neveloff, Chairman
Heidi Walters, Chief Protocol Officer
Ron Gardner, Executive Director
Tom Kelsey, Director of Communications
Gene Rurka, Director Humanitarian Services

Promotes the urgent transition to renewable energy sources and sustainable development through collaborative effort and the implementation of projects that improve the lives of people while preserving the environment and our resources for future generations of humans.
Founded in 2008

1359 **International Association for Energy Economics**
28790 Chagrin Blvd
Suite 350
Cleveland, OH 44122-4642
216-464-5365
Fax: 216-464-2737
E-Mail: iaee@iaee.org
Home Page: www.iaee.org
Social Media: Facebook, LinkedIn

David Newbery, President
Jacques Percebois, Vice President for Publications
Christophe Bonnery, Vice President for Business & Govt.
G□rkan Kumbaroglu, Vice President for Conferences
Ricardo B. Raineri, Vice President for Academic Affairs

Association for those involved in energy economics including publications, consultants, energy database software.
3400 Members
Founded in 1977
Mailing list available for rent

1360 **International Association for Hydrogen Energy**
Home Page: www.iahe.org

An association that stimulates the exchange of information in the Hydrogen Energy field through its publications and sponsorship of international workshops, short courses and conferences and endeavors to inform the general public of the important role of Hydrogen Energy in the planning of an inexhaustible and clean energy system.

1361 **International District Energy Association**
24 Lyman Street
Suite 230
Westborough, MA 1581
508-366-9339
Fax: 508-366-0019
E-Mail: idea@districtenergy.org
Home Page: www.districtenergy.org
Social Media: Facebook, Twitter, YouTube, Flickr

Ken Smith, Chair
Bruce Ander, Vice Chair
Tim Griffin, Second Vice Chair
James Adams, Secretary
Patrica Wilson, Past Chair

An organization that actively works to foster the success of its members as leaders in providing reliable, economical, efficient and environmentally sound district heating, district cooling and cogeneration (combined heat and power) services.

1362 **International Ground Source Heat Pump Association**
1201 S Innovation Way
Suite 400
Stillwater, OK 74074
405-744-5175
800-626-4747
Fax: 405-744-5283
E-Mail: igshpa@okstate.edu
Home Page: www.igshpa.okstate.edu
Social Media: Facebook, Twitter, Youtube, Google+

Jim Bose, Ph.D, Executive Director
Gail Ezepek, Conference & Membership Coordinator
Janet Reeder, Technical Writer
Ben Champlin, Graphic Designer
Roshan Revankar, Training Program Manager

Member-driven organization established to advance ground source heat pump technology on local, state, national and international levels. IGSHPA utilizes state-of-the-art facilities for conducting GSHP system installation training and geothermal research. Mission is to promote the use of ground source heat pump technology worldwide through education and communication.

1363 **Interstate Renewable Energy Council**
PO Box 1156
Latham, NY 12110-1156
518-458-6059
E-Mail: info@irecusa.org
Home Page: www.irecusa.org

David Warner, Chair
Jane Weissman, President and CEO
Larry Sherwood, Vice President, COO
Maryteresa Colello, Administrative Coordinator
Pat Fox, Director of Credentialing

Works with industry, government, educators and other stakeholders to ensure that the broader use of renewable energies is possible, safe, affordable and practical, particularly for the individual consumer.
Founded in 1994

1364 **Lignite Energy Council**
1016 E. Owens Avenue
PO Box 2277
Bismarck, ND 58502-2277
701-258-7117
800-932-7117
Fax: 701-258-2755
E-Mail: lec@lignite.com
Home Page: www.lignite.com
Social Media: Facebook, Twitter, YouTube, RSS Feeds

Jason Bohrer, President/CEO
Marie Hoerner, Director of Finance
Mike Jones, Ph. D., Mike Vice President of Research
Steve Van Dyke, Vice President of Communications
Renee Walz, Director of Member Services

Regional Trade Association - promotes policies and activities that maintain a viable lignite industry and enhance development of our regions' lignite resources.
355 Members
Founded in 1974

1365 **Low Impact Hydropower Institute**
34 Providence Street
Portland, ME 04103
207-773-8190
Fax: 206-984-3086
Home Page: www.lowimpacthydro.org

Richard Roos-Collins, President
Philip Raphals, Renewables Advisory Panel Chair
Michael J. Sale, PhD, Executive Director
Dana Hall, Deputy Director

Dedicated to reducing the impacts of hydropower generation through the certification of hydropower projects that have avoided or reduced their environmental impacts pursuant to the Low Impact Hydropower Institute's criteria. Mission is to reduce the impacts of hydropower dams through market incentives.

1366 **NABCEP**
56 Clifton Country Rd.
Suite 202
Clifton Park, NY 12065
800-654-0021
Fax: 518-899-1092
E-Mail: info@nabcep.org
Home Page: www.nabcep.org
Social Media: Facebook

Don Warfield, Chair
Richard Lawrence, Executive Director
Jeff Keller, Outreach and Operations Manager
Sue Pratt, Office Manager
Chad Wolf, Entry Level & Continuing Education

Mission is to support, and work with, the renewable energy and energy efficiency industries, professionals, and stakeholders. Goal is to develop voluntary national certification programs that will; promote renewable energy, provide value to practitioners, promote worker safety and skill, and promote consumer confidence.
Founded in 2000

1367 **National Association of Energy Service Companies**
1615 M Street, NW
Suite 800
Washington, DC 20036
202-822-0950
Fax: 202-822-095
E-Mail: info@naesco.org
Home Page: www.naesco.org
Social Media: Facebook, LinkedIn

David Weiss, Chairman
Mike Kearney, Vice Chair
Terry E. Singe, Executive Director
Donald Gilligan, President
Scott Ririe, Secretary

An organization that promotes energy efficiency at state, federal, and international facilities; ensures the key role of ESCOs in delivering energyefficiency resources; and builds new market opportunities while growing existingmarkets.

1368 **National Association of State Energy Officials**
2107 Wilson Boulevard
Suite 850
Arlington, VA 22201
703-299-8800
Fax: 703-299-6208
E-Mail: energy@naseo.org
Home Page: www.naseo.org
Social Media: Facebook, Twitter, LinkedIn, YouTube, Flickr

Janet Streff, Chair
Gene Therriault, Vice Chair
David Terry, Executive Director
John H. Davies, President
Mark Sylvia, Treasurer

A national nonprofit association that facilitates peer learning among state energy officials, serves as a resource for and about state energy offices, and advocates the interests of the state energy offices to Congress and federal agencies.

1369 **National Biodiesel Board**
605 Clark Ave
PO Box 104898
Jefferson City, MO 65101
573-635-3893
Fax: 573-635-7913
E-Mail: info@biodiesel.org
Home Page: www.biodiesel.org
Social Media: Facebook, Twitter, YouTube, RSS Feeds, Google+

Gary Haer, Chairman
Ed Ulch, Vice-Chair
Jim Conway, Treasurer
Ron Marr, Secretary

Mission is to advance the interests of its members by creating sustainable biodiesel industry growth. NBB serves as the industry's central coordinating entity and will be the single voice for its diverse membership base.

1370 National Fenestration Rating Council
6305 Ivy Lane
Suite 140
Greenbelt, MD

301-589-1776
E-Mail: info@nfrc.org
Home Page: www.nfrc.org
Social Media: Facebook, Twitter, LinkedIn, YouTube

James C. Benney, Chief Executing Officer
Deborah Callahan, Chief Operating Officer
Jessica Finn, Membership Coordinator
Cheryl Gendron, Meeting Manager
Scott Hanlon, Program Director

A nonprofit organization that administers an independent rating andlabeling system for the energy performance of windows, doors, skylights, and attachment products.
Founded in 1989

1371 National Hydropower Association
25 Massachusetts Ave, NW
Suite 450
Washington, DC 20001

202-682-1700
Fax: 202-682-9478
E-Mail: help@hydro.org
Home Page: www.hydro.org
Social Media: Facebook, Twitter

Marc Gerken, Executive Director
Jane Cirrincione, Vice President
Linda Church Ciocci, Executive Director
Jeffrey A. Leahey, Director of Government Affairs
Diane C. Lear, Membership Services

Dedicated to promoting the growth of clean, affordable US hydropower. Seeks to secure hydropower's place as a climate-friendly, renewable and reliable energy source that serves national environmental, energy, and economic policy objectives. Members are involved in projects throughout the US hydropower industry, including both federal and non-federal hydroelectric facilities.

1372 National Renewable Energy Association
629 North Main Street
Hattiesburg, MS 39401

601-582-3330
Fax: 601-582-3354
E-Mail: nrea@megagate.com
Home Page: www.nationalrenewableenergyassociation.org

A nonprofit organization dedicated to helping Americans use less energy and to use more renewable energy in the future.
Founded in 2007

1373 National Renewable Energy Laboratory
15013 Denver West Parkway
Golden, CO 80401

303-275-3000
Home Page: www.nrel.gov
Social Media: Facebook, Twitter, LinkedIn, YouTube

Dr. Dan Arvizu, President
Dr. Dana Christensen, Director, Science & Technology
Bobi Garrett, Director, Strategic Programs
Ken Powers, Director & Chief Operating Officer

Develops renewable energy and energy efficiency technologies and practices, advances related science and engineering, and transfers knowledge and innovations to address the nation's energy and environmental goals.

1374 National Wind Coordinating Collaborative
1110 Vermont Ave NW
Suite 950
Washington, DC 20005

202-656-3303
E-Mail: info@awwi.org
Home Page: nationalwind.org

Lauren Flinn, Facilitator
Abby Arnold, Senior Mediator

Provides a neutral forum for various stakeholders to pursue the shared objective of developing environmentally, economically, and politically sustainable commercial markets for wind power in the United States.
Founded in 1994

1375 Natural Resources Defense Council
40 West 20th Street
New York, NW 10011

212-727-2700
Fax: 212-727-1773
E-Mail: webmaster@nrdc.org
Home Page: www.nrdc.org
Social Media: Facebook, Twitter, YouTube

Daniel R. Tishman, Chairman
Frederick A.O. Schwarz, Chair Emeritus
Patricia Bauman, Vice Chair
Mary Moran, Treasurer
Alan F. Horn, Vice Chair

A nonprofit environmental action group that works to restore the natural elements, defend endangered species, and strives to safeguard the Earth: its people, its plants and animals and the natural systems on which all life depends.
14000 Members

1376 North American Board of Certified Energy Practitioners
56 Clifton Country Rd
Suite 202
Clifton Park, NY 12065

Home Page: www.nabcep.org
Social Media: Facebook

Don Warfield, Chair
Jane Weissman, Vice Chair
Jeff Irish, President
Jeff Spies, Secretary
Les Nelson, Treasurer

Offers entry level knowledge assessment, professional certification, and company accreditation programs to renewable energy professionals throughout North America.
Founded in 2002

1377 Northeast Sustainable Energy Association
50 Miles Street
Greenfield, MA 01301-3255

413-774-6051
Fax: 413-774-6053
E-Mail: nesea@nesea.org
Home Page: www.nesea.org
Social Media: Facebook, Twitter, LinkedIn, RSS

Jennifer Marrapese, Executive Director
Jeremy Koo, Program coordinator
Travis Niles, Manager of Communications
Gina Sieber, Business manager
Rayna Heldt, Membership coordinator

The nation's leading regional membership organization focused on promoting the understanding, development and adoption of energy conservation and non-polluting, renewable energy technologies.
1802 Members
Founded in 1974

1378 Ocean Renewable Energy Coalition
12909 Scarlet Oak Drive
Darnestown, MD 20878

301-869-3790
Fax: 301-869-5637
E-Mail: info@oceanrenewable.com
Home Page: www.oceanrenewable.com
Social Media: Facebook, Twitter, RSS

Sean O'Neill, President
Carolyn Elefant, General and Regulatory Counsel

Exclusively dedicated to promoting marine and hydrokinetic energy technologies from clean, renewable ocean resources. Organization embraces a wide range of renewable technologies; including wave, tidal, current, offshore wind, ocean thermal, marine biomass and all other technologies that utilize renewable resources from oceans, tidal areas and other unimpounded water bodies to produce electricity, desalinized water, hydrogen, mariculture and other by products.
40+ Members
Founded in 2005

1379 Office of Energy Efficiency & Renewable Energy
1000 Independence Avenue SW
Washington, DC 20585

Home Page: apps3.eere.energy.gov
Social Media: Facebook, Twitter, LinkedIn

David Danielson, Assistant Secretary
Mike Carr, Principal Deputy Secretary
Bindu Jacob, Director of Business Operations

Leads the U.S. Department of Energy's efforts to develop and deliver market-driven solutions for energy-saving homes, buildings, and manufacturing;sustainable transportation; and renewable electricity generation.

1380 One Sky
One Sky
3768 2nd Avenue
Box 3352
Smithers, BC V0J 2N0

250-877-6030
Home Page: www.onesky.ca

Michael S. Smithers, Executive Director
Lisa Gibson, Nigeria Integral Leadership Coord.
Gail Hochachka, Integral Program Coordinator

Explores and promotes practical solutions and appropriate technologies for our environmental. social and economic challenges in a global setting.
Founded in 2000

1381 Pellet Fuels Institute
1901 North Moore St
Suite 600
Arlington, VA 22209

703-522-6778
Fax: 703-522-0548
E-Mail: pfimail@pelletheat.org
Home Page: www.pelletheat.org
Social Media: Facebook, Twitter

Scott Jacobs, Chairman
Jennifer Hedrick, Executive Director
Jason Berthiaume, Membership & Government Affairs
John Crouch, Director of Public Affairs

Promotes energy independence throught the effiecient use of clean, renewable, densified biomass fuel.
Founded in 1985

1382 Portable Rechargeable Battery Association
1776 K Street
4th Floor
Washington, DC 20006
202-719-4978
Home Page: www.prba.org
Charlie Monahan, Chairman
Stephen P. Victor, President & COO
Chris Carlson, Vice President of Logistics
Andrew J. Sirjord, Vice President
Mark HickoK, Director
A nonprofit trade association that develops plans for workable battery recycling programs to be used industry wide and that serves as the voice of the Rechargeable Power Industry, representing its members on legislative, regulatory and standards issues at the state, federal and international level.

1383 Renewable Energy Markets Association (REMA)
1211 Connecticut Ave NW
Suite 600
Washington, DC 20036-2701
202-640-6597
Fax: 202-223-5537
E-Mail: info@renewablemarketers.org
Home Page: www.renewablemarketers.org
Social Media: Facebook, Twitter
Richard Anderson, President
Laura Pagliarulo, Vice President
Josh Lieberman, General Manager
Joseph Seymour, Program Coordinator
Kevin Maddaford, Treasurer
A nonprofit association dedicated to maintaining and growing strong markets for renewable energy in the United States. Representing organizations that sell, purchase, or promote renewable energy products.

1384 Renewable Energy and Efficiency Business Association, Inc.
185 Asylum Street
CityPlace I
Hartford, CT 06103-3469
E-Mail: pmichaud@murthalaw.com
Home Page: www.reeba.org
Jim Daylor, Chairman
John Michael Callahan, Vice Chairman
Christopher F. Haplin, President
Paul Michaud, Executive Director
Jackie Rowe, Director of Operations
An active business organization that promotes the sustainable deployment of renewable energy, DSM and energy efficiency advocacy, collaboration, networking, and information sharing.

1385 Renewable Fuels Association (RFA)
425 Third Street SW
Suite 1150
Washington, DC 20024
202-289-3835
Fax: 202-289-7519
Home Page: www.ethanolrfa.org
Neill McKinstray, RFA Chairman
Bob Dinneen, President & CEO
Christina Martin, Executive Vice President
Samantha Slater, Vice President, Government Affairs
Alex Obuchowski, Chief Financial Officer
The national trade association for the US ethanol industry promoting policies, regulations and research and development initiatives that will lead to the increased production and use of fuel ethanol. Membership includes a broad cross-section of businesses, individuals and organizations dedicated to the expansion of the US fuel ethanol industry.
Founded in 1981

1386 Rocky Mountain Institute
1820 Folsom Street
Boulder, CO 80302
303-245-1003
E-Mail: info@rmi.org
Home Page: www.rmi.org
Thomas Dinwoodie, Chair
Amory B. Lovins Cofounder, Chief Scientist
Jules Kortenhorst, Chief Executive Officer
Robert Hutchinson, Managing Director
Debbie Giallombardo, Executive Assistant
Emphasizes integrative design, advanced technologies working with the private sector as well as civil society and government to drive the transition from coal and oil to efficiency and renewables.

1387 Solar Electric Light Fund
1612 K Street NW
Suite 300
Washington, DC 20006
202-234-7265
E-Mail: info@self.org
Home Page: self.org
Social Media: Facebook, Twitter, YouTube
Robert A. Freling, Executive Director
Jeff Lahl, Project Director
John Alejandro, Communications Director
Darren Anderson, Project Manager
Lisa Esler, Finance Director
Designs and implements solar energy solutions to assist people living in energy poverty with their economic, educational, health care, and agricultural development.
Founded in 1990

1388 Solar Electric Power Association
1220 19th Street, NW,
Suite 800
Washington, DC 20036-2405
202-857-0898
Home Page: www.solarelectricpower.org
Social Media: Facebook, Twitter, LinkedIn, YouTube
Steve Malnight, Chair
Joseph Forline, Chair Elect
Julia Hamm, President & CEO
Jennifer Szaro, Secretary
Ervan Hancock, Treasurer
An educational nonprofit association dedicated to advancing utilityintegration of solar through collaborative solutions, objective information and shared benefits to the utility, its customers, and the public good.

1389 Solar Energy Industries Association
505 9th Street, N.W
Suite 800
Washington, DC 20004
202-682-0556
E-Mail: info@seia.org
Home Page: www.seia.org
Nat Kreamer, Chair
Tom Starrs, Vice Chair
Rhone Resch, President & CEO
Dave Sit, Chief Operating Officer
Scott Hennessey, Secretary
Works with its member companies to make solar a mainstream and significant energy source by expanding markets, removing market barriers, strenghtening the industry and educating the public on the benefits of solar energy.

1390 Solar Energy International
520 S. Third St.,
Room 16
Carbondale, CO 81623
970-963-8855
Home Page: www.solarenergy.org
Social Media: Facebook, Twitter, LinkedIn
Ed Marston, Chairperson
Sarah Bishop, President
A nonprofit educational organization that provides industry-leadingtechnical training and expertise in renewable energy to empower people, communities, and businesses worldwide.

1391 Solar Living Institute
PO Box 836
13771 S. Hwy 101
Hopland, CA 95449
707-472-2450
Fax: 707-472-2498
E-Mail: sli@solarliving.org
Home Page: solarliving.org
Social Media: Facebook, Twitter, LinkedIn, YouTube
Teresa Jodon-Manns, Executive Director
Karen Kallen, Managing Director
Hannah Bird, Programs Manager
Nop Panitchpakdi, Program Manager
Everardo Dominguez, Landscaper
A nonprofit solar training and sustainability organization. Mission is to promote sustainable living through inspirational environmental education.
Founded in 1998

1392 The Sustainable Biodiesel Alliance
P.O. Box 1677
Kahului, HI 96732
512-410-7841
Fax: 512-410-7841
E-Mail: infoadmin@fuelresponsibly.org
Home Page: test.sustainablebiodieselalliance.com/SBA/
Social Media: Facebook, Twitter
Kelly King, Chair
Annie Nelson, Vice-Chair
Mike Nasi, Treasurer
Ed Zwick, Secretary
An organization founded to support and encourage sustainable production and use of the renewable fuel biodiesel. Its primary mission is the completion of an independent sustainability certification system for U.S. Biodiesel Feedstock.
Founded in 2006

1393 UNEP SEF Alliance
Clean Energy Group
50 State St.
Suite 1
Montpelier, VT 05602
802-223-2554
Fax: 802-223-4967
E-Mail: RTyler@cleanegroup.org
Home Page: www.unepsefalliance.org
The only convening body in the international system for public finance agencies in the clean energy sector. Members are visionary organizations from various countries pushing the forefront of how to do public finance for clean energy.

1394 US Renewable Energy Association, LLC.
PO Box 0550
Lexington, MI 48450
810-359-2250
E-Mail: sales@usrea.org
Home Page: www.usrea.org

Social Media: Facebook, Twitter, LinkedIn, Google+

A volunteer renewable energy advocacy group working to educate and promote advanced technologies in the R.E. industry.

1395 United States Clean Heat & Power Association
1050 Thomas Jefferson Street, NW
Sixth Floor
Washington, DC 20007

202-298-3719
E-Mail: information@chpassociation.org
Home Page: www.chpassociation.org
Social Media: Facebook, Twitter, Rss Feeds

Joe Allen, Chair
Dale Louda, Executive Director
Wissam Balshe, Vice Chair
John Rathbun, Secretary
Paul Lemar, Treasurer

Providing superior advocacy, networking, education and market information to companies in the business of clean, local energy generation. Documents the benefits of clean heat and power to the public and to decision-makers. Also participates in federal agency programs to promote clean distributed energy.
Founded in 1999

1396 United States Energy Association
1300 Pennsylvania Avenue, NW
Suite 550
Washington, DC 20004-3022

202-312-1230
Fax: 202-682-1682
E-Mail: reply@usea.org
Home Page: www.usea.in
Social Media: Facebook, Twitter, LinkedIn

Vickey A. Bailey, Chairman
John E Futcher, Executive Vice President
Sheila Slocum Hollis, Treasurer
Barry K. Worthington, Executive Director
Brian Kerans, Chief Financial Officer

An association of public and private energy-related organizations, corporations, and government agencies that represent the broad interests of the U.S. energy sector by increasing the understanding of energy issues, both domestically and internationally.

1397 Wind Energy Foundation
1501 M Street, NW
Suite 900
Washington, DC 20005

202-580-6440
E-Mail: info@windenergyfoundation.org
Home Page: www.windenergyfoundation.org
Social Media: Facebook, Twitter, YouTube

A nonprofit organization dedicated to raising public awareness of wind as a clean, domestic energy source through communication, research, and education.
Founded in 1970

1398 Women's Council on Energy and the Environment
PO Box 33211
Washington, DC 20033-0211

202-997-4512
Fax: 202-478-2098
Home Page: www.wcee.org
Social Media: Facebook, Twitter

Ronke Luke, President
Robin Cantor, Vice President
Joyce Chandran, Executive Director
Alice Grabowski, Treasurer
Mary Brosnan-Sell, Secretary

Supports women involved in the environmental community with education, research, new trend information and several publications.

1399 World Resources Institute(WRI)
10 G Street NE
Suite 800
Washington, DC 20002

202-729-7600
Fax: 202-729-7610
E-Mail: cpotochny@gmail.com
Home Page: www.wri.org
Social Media: Facebook, Twitter, LinkedIn, YouTube, RSS

James A. Harmon, Chair
Andrew Steer, President & CEO
Steve Barker, CFO/VP Finance & Administration
Manish Bapna, Executive Vice President
Robin Murphy, Vice President For External Rel

WRI takes research and puts ideas into action, working globally with governments, business and civil society to build transformative solutions that protect the earth and improve people's lives.
Founded in 1982

Newsletters

1400 BTEC Newsletter
Biomass Thermal Energy Council
1211 Connecticut Avenue NW
Suite 600
Washington, DC 20036-2701

202-596-3974
Fax: 202-223-5537
E-Mail: info@biomassthermal.org
Home Page: www.biomassthermal.org
Social Media: Facebook, Twitter

Joseph Seymour, Executive Director
Charlie Niebling, Chairman
T.J. Morice, Vice-Chairman
Jon Strimling, Secretary
Bob Sourek, Treasurer

Provides member news, industry updates, upcoming events, and breaking BTEC news.
Frequency: Monthly
Founded in 2009

1401 Biogas News
American Biogas Council
1211 Connecticut Ave NW
Suite 600
Washington, DC 20036-2701

202-596-3974
Fax: 202-223-5537
E-Mail: info@americanbiogascouncil.org
Home Page: www.americanbiogascouncil.org

Paul Greene, Chairman
Norma McDonald, Vice-Chair
Melissa VanOrnum, Treasurer
Nora Goldstein, Secretary

Members only publication includes everything from legislative updates to industry news and funding opportunities.
Frequency: Bi-Weekly

1402 Clean Energy Direct
IHS, Inc.

855-417-4155
E-Mail: energy@omeda.com
Home Page: www.theenergydaily.com
Social Media: RSS

George Lobsenz, Executive Editor
Sabrina Ousmaal, Associate Publisher
Eric Lindeman, Contributing Editor

Get analysis of regulation, technology and industry news of renewables, top news in the clean energy industry as well as access to clean energy articles and archives.
Cost: $695.00
Frequency: Weekly

1403 Climate Change News
Environmental and Energy Study Institute
1112 16th Street, NW
Suite 300
Washington, DC 20036-4819

202-628-1400
Fax: 202-204-5244
E-Mail: cwerner@eesi.org
Home Page: www.eesi.org
Social Media: Facebook, Twitter, YouTube

Carol Werner, Executive Director
Jared Blum, Chair
Shelley Fidler, Treasurer
Richard L. Ottinger, Chair Emeritus

Recounts the top climate science, business, and politics stories of the week and includes a list of upcoming events and pending federal legislation.
Frequency: Weekly
Founded in 1984

1404 Coal Outlook
Pasha Publications
1600 Wilson Boulevard
Suite 600
Arlington, VA 22209-2509

703-528-1244
800-424-2908
Fax: 703-528-1253

Harry Baisden, Group Publisher
Michael Hopps, Editor
Kathy Thorne, Circulation Manager

Primary strategic information source that keeps coal marketing executives and utilities up-to-date on who's getting coal contracts and at what price.
Cost: $795.00
Frequency: Weekly

1405 Coal Week International
McGraw Hill
2 Penn Plz
Suite 25
New York, NY 10121-0101

212-904-2000
800-752-8878
Fax: 720-548-5701
E-Mail: support@platts.com
Home Page: www.mcgraw-hill.com

Peter C Davis, President
David Stellfox, Editor
Harry Sachinis, CEO
Larry Barth, Marketing Manager

A market management intelligence service for executives concerned with world trade metallurgical and steam coal.
Cost: $987.00
8 Pages
Frequency: Weekly
Founded in 1888

1406 Coal and Synfuels Technology
Pasha Publications
1600 Wilson Boulevard
Suite 600
Arlington, VA 22209-2510

703-528-1244
800-424-2908
Fax: 703-528-1253

Harry Baisden, Group Publisher
Michael Hopps, Editor

Reports on the US and international advances in clean coal technologies, synthetic fuels and clean air issues.
Cost: $790.00
Frequency: Weekly
Founded in 1985

1407 **Connecting to the Grid**
Interstate Renewable Energy Council
PO Box 1156
Latham, NY 12110-1156

518-458-6059
E-Mail: info@irecusa.org
Home Page: www.irecusa.org

Laurel Varnado, Editor
Ken Jurman, Chair
David Warner, Vice Chair
Jane Pulaski, Secretary
Jennifer Szaro, Treasurer

Focusing on the latest news on interconnection and net metering in the US.
Frequency: Monthly

1408 **Council on Women in Energy and Environmental Leadership Newsletter**
Association of Energy Engineers
4025 Pleasantdale Rd
Suite 420
Atlanta, GA 30340-4264

770-447-5083
Fax: 770-446-3969
E-Mail: info@aeecenter.org
Home Page: www.aeecenter.org
Social Media: Facebook, Twitter, LinkedIn, YouTube

Eric A. Woodroof, President
Gary Hogsett, President Elect
Bill Younger, Secretary
Paul Goodman, C.P.A., Treasurer

Addressing the high cost of energy, present and future sources of energy, and the impact of energy on the environment.
8.2M Members
Founded in 1977

1409 **EESI Update**
Environmental and Energy Study Institute
1112 16th Street, NW
Suite 300
Washington, DC 20036-4819

202-628-1400
Fax: 202-204-5244
E-Mail: cwerner@eesi.org
Home Page: www.eesi.org
Social Media: Facebook, Twitter, YouTube

Carol Werner, Executive Director
Jared Blum, Chair
Shelley Fidler, Treasurer
Richard L. Ottinger, Chair Emeritus

Updating supporters about the current work of EESI.
Frequency: 3x Yearly
Founded in 1984

1410 **Energy Insight**
Association of Energy Engineers (AEE)
4025 Pleasantdale Rd.
Suite 420
Atlanta, GA 30340

770-447-5083
Fax: 770-446-3969
E-Mail: al@aeecenter.org
Home Page: www.aeecenter.org
Social Media: Facebook, Twitter, YouTube

Albert Thumann, Executive Director

Written by, about and for the AEE member. Electronic publication includes information on AEE news, officers, award programs, nominations, certification, chapter news, operations report, presidents' message, study missions, upcoming events, and more.
15M Members
Frequency: Tri-Annually
Founded in 1977
Mailing list available for rent

1411 **GRC Bulletin**
Geothermal Resources Council
20001 Second Street
Suite 5
Davis, CA 95618-5476

530-758-2360
Fax: 530-758-2839
E-Mail: grc@geothermal.org
Home Page: www.geothermal.org
Social Media: Facebook, Twitter, LinkedIn, YouTube, Flickr

Curt Robinson, Ph.D, Executive Director

Features articles on technical topics and geothermal development issues, as well as commentaries and news briefs.
Frequency: 6x Yearly
Founded in 1970

1412 **Geothermal Energy Weekly**
Geothermal Energy Association
209 Pennsylvania Avenue SE
Washington, DC 20003

202-454-5241
E-Mail: jgreco@terra-genpower.com
Home Page: www.geo-energy.org

Karl Gawell, Executive Director
Leslie Blodgett, Editor-in-Chief
Paul Thomsen, President
Jonathan M. Weisgall, Chairman

Electronic newsletter providing updates on the national, state, and international levels, and includes news from GEA member companies. Upcoming events, job opportunities, and Requests for Proposals are also found here.
Frequency: Weekly

1413 **NABCEP News**
56 Clifton Country Rd.
Suite 202
Clifton Park, NY 12065

800-654-0021
Fax: 518-899-1092
E-Mail: info@nabcep.org
Home Page: www.nabcep.org

Ezra Auerbach, Executive Director
Don Warfield, Chair
Jane Weissman, Vice Chair
Les Nelson, Treasurer
Jeff Spies, Secretary

Newsletter from the North American Board of Certified Energy Practitioners featuring news, updates, technical issues and accomplishments of their certificants. Available electronically only.
Frequency: Bi-Monthly
Founded in 2000

1414 **NHA Today**
National Hydropower Association
25 Massachusetts Ave, NW
Suite 450
Washington, DC 20001

202-682-1700
Fax: 202-682-9478
E-Mail: help@hydro.org
Home Page: www.hydro.org
Social Media: Facebook, Twitter

Linda Church Ciocci, Executive Director
David Moller, President
James Crew, Treasurer
John Ragonese, Vice President
Tim Oakes, Secretary

Offers the latest information on regulatory and legislative policy, regional concerns, and issues on the horizon. Available electronically to members of NHA only.
Frequency: Bi-Weekly

1415 **OREC Newsletter**
Ocean Renewable Energy Coalition

301-869-3790
E-Mail: info@oceanrenewable.com
Home Page: www.oceanrenewable.com

Sean O'Neill, President
Carolyn Elefant, General Counsel

Striving to keep members, legislators, regulators, the media and the public at large up to date with OREC's activities as well as ongoing developments in this emerging industry.
40+ Members
Frequency: Weekly
Founded in 2005

1416 **Pellet Fuels Institute**
Pellet Fuels Institute.
1901 North Moore Street
Suite 600
Arlington, VA 22209

703-522-6778
Fax: 703-522-0548
E-Mail: pfimail@pelletheat.org
Home Page: www.pelletheat.org

Jennifer Hedrick, Executive Director
Jason Berthiaume, Membership/Gov't Affairs
John Crouch, Director of Public Affairs

Newsletter with industry news, updates published quarterly

1417 **Renewable Energy in the 50 States**
American Council on Renewable Energy(ACORE)
1660 K Street NW
Suite 650
Washington, DC 20006

202-393-0001
Home Page: www.acore.org

Dennis V. McGinn, President/CEO
Tom Weirich, VP of Corporate Relations
Dawn Butcher, Director of Event Planning/Mktg.

Executive summary on the status of renewable energy implementation at the state-level. A two-page overview on key developments including installed and planned projects.
Founded in 2001

1418 **Small Wind Energy**
Interstate Renewable Energy Council
PO Box 1156
Latham, NY 12110-1156

518-458-6059
E-Mail: info@irecusa.org
Home Page: www.irecusa.org

Larry Sherwood, Editor
Ken Jurman, Chair
David Warner, Vice Chair
Jane Pulaski, Secretary
Jennifer Szaro, Treasurer

Featuring updates and news about small wind energy issues.
Frequency: Quarterly

1419 **Solar@Work**
American Solar Energy Society
4760 Walnut Street
Suite 106
Boulder, CO 80301

303-443-3130
Fax: 303-443-3212
E-Mail: ases@ases.org
Home Page: www.ases.org
Social Media: Facebook, Twitter, LinkedIn

Susan Greene, President
David G. Hill, Chair
Bill Poulin, Treasurer
Jason Keyes, Secretary

Get the latest business and market analysis, technology breakthroughs and career advice from ASES professionals.
13M Members
Frequency: Bi-Monthly
Founded in 1954

1420 **Sun Times**
Alternative Energy Resources Organization
432 N. Last Chance Gulch
Helena, MT 59601
406-443-7272
Fax: 406-442-9120
E-Mail: aero@aeromt.org
Home Page: www.aeromt.org
Social Media: Facebook, Twitter, Myspace
Bryan von Lossberg, Executive Director
Stay up to date on AERO news and events.
Frequency: Monthly
Founded in 1974

1421 **Sustainable Bioenergy, Farms, and Forests**
Environmental and Energy Study Institute
1112 16th Street, NW
Suite 300
Washington, DC 20036-4819
202-628-1400
Fax: 202-204-5244
E-Mail: cwerner@eesi.org
Home Page: www.ccsi.org
Social Media: Facebook, Twitter, YouTube
Carol Werner, Executive Director
Jared Blum, Chair
Shelley Fidler, Treasurer
Richard L. Ottinger, Chair Emeritus
A look at sustainable bioenergy, farm, and forest policy issues.
Frequency: Weekly
Founded in 1984

1422 **The Biodiesel Bulletin**
National Biodiesel Board
605 Clark Ave
PO Box 104898
Jefferson City, MO 65110-4898
573-635-3893
Fax: 573-635-7913
E-Mail: info@biodiesel.org
Home Page: www.biodiesel.org
Social Media: Facebook, Twitter, YouTube
Gary Haer, Chairman
Ed Ulch, Vice-Chair
Jim Conway, Treasurer
Ron Marr, Secretary
Electronic publication keeping members up to date on the biodiesel industry and technology.
Frequency: Monthly
Mailing list available for rent

1423 **The Energy Daily**
IHS, Inc.
855-417-4155
E-Mail: energy@omeda.com
Home Page: www.theenergydaily.com
George Lobsenz, Executive Editor
Sabrinal Ousmaal, Associate Publisher
Erica Lengermann, Manager, Sales
Keeping readers at the forefront of all major developments in the energy industry. Through in-depth analysis of issues, cutting-edge reporting and unbiased journalism, The Energy Daily continues to deliver the news readers need for business success.
Cost: $2497.00
Frequency: Daily

1424 **The Energy Roundup**
IHS, Inc.
855-417-4155
E-Mail: energy@omeda.com
Home Page: www.theenergydaily.com
George Lobsenz, Executive Editor
Sabrinal Ousmaal, Associate Publisher
Erica Lengermann, Manager, Sales
The most important developing stories delivered weekly.
Frequency: Weekly

1425 **The IREC Report**
Interstate Renewable Energy Council
PO Box 1156
Latham, NY 12110-1156
518-458-6059
E-Mail: info@irecusa.org
Home Page: www.irecusa.org
Jane Pulaski, Editor
Ken Jurman, Chair
David Warner, Vice Chair
Jane Pulaski, Secretary
Jennifer Szaro, Treasurer
A monthly recap of the latest news about IREC's programs, policies and best practices in renewable energy.
Frequency: Monthly

1426 **The ISPQ Insider**
Interstate Renewable Energy Council
PO Box 1156
Latham, NY 12110-1156
518-458-6059
E-Mail: info@irecusa.org
Home Page: www.irecusa.org
Jane Pulaski, Editor
Ken Jurman, Chair
David Warner, Vice Chair
Jane Pulaski, Secretary
Jennifer Szaro, Treasurer
A monthly recap of the latest news, policies and best practices from the ISPQ credentialing program for renewable energy, weatherization and the energy retrofit sector.
Frequency: Monthly

1427 **The SITN Quarterly**
Interstate Renewable Energy Council
PO Box 1156
Latham, NY 12110-1156
518-458-6059
E-Mail: info@irecusa.org
Home Page: www.irecusa.org
Jane Pulaski, Editor
Ken Jurman, Chair
David Warner, Vice Chair
Jane Pulaski, Secretary
Jennifer Szaro, Treasurer
Summary of the latest news, policies and best practices from the Solar Instructor Training Network.
Frequency: Quarterly

1428 **Utility Reporter: Fuels, Energy and Power**
InfoTeam
PO Box 15640
Plantation, FL 33318-5640
954-473-9560
Fax: 954-473-0544
E-Mail: infoteamma@aol.com
Randy M Allen CPA, Editor
Focuses on activities involving: power generation, combustion, delivery and transmission; alternative energy devices and systems; heat transfer, storage and utilization; and myriad of related topics.
Cost: $289.00
20 Pages
Frequency: Monthly
ISBN: 0-890298-4 -
Printed in one color on matte stock

1429 **Wind Energy SmartBrief**
American Wind Energy Association
1501 M Street NW
Suite 1000
Washington, DC 20005
202-383-2500
Fax: 202-383-2505
E-Mail: windmail@awea.org
Home Page: www.awea.org
Social Media: Facebook, Twitter, YouTube, Flickr
Ned Hall, Chair
Thomas Carnahan, Chair-Elect
Gabriel Alonso, Secretary
Don Furman, Treasurer
Denise Bode, CEO
Delivers quickly digestible summaries of the day's wind energy-related stories from across the media, as well as links to those stories. SmartBrief not only keeps readers informed about the industry, it allows them to stay on top of what's being said about it.
2500+ Members
Frequency: Daily

1430 **Wind Energy Weekly**
American Wind Energy Association
1501 M Street NW
Suite 1000
Washington, DC 20005
202-383-2500
Fax: 202-383-2505
E-Mail: windmail@awea.org
Home Page: www.awea.org
Social Media: Facebook, Twitter, YouTube, Flickr
Ned Hall, Chair
Thomas Carnahan, Chair-Elect
Gabriel Alonso, Secretary
Don Furman, Treasurer
Denise Bode, CEO
Packed with detailed and up-to-date information on the world of wind energy that simply can't be obtained elsewhere. Readers have a professional interest in wind energy, need to keep up with wind energy development news or late-breaking legislative, economic, and environmental developments.
2500+ Members
Frequency: Weekly

Magazines & Journals

1431 **Biodiesel Magazine**
National Biodiesel Board
605 Clark Ave
PO Box 104898
Jefferson City, MO 65110-4898
573-635-3893
Fax: 573-635-7913
E-Mail: info@biodiesel.org
Home Page: www.biodieselmagazine.com
Social Media: Facebook, Twitter, YouTube
Gary Haer, Chairman
Ed Ulch, Vice-Chair
Jim Conway, Treasurer
Ron Marr, Secretary
Trade journal dedicated to objective, independent coverage of biodiesel news, events and information relevant to the global industry. With editorial focus on US and international methyl ester manufacturing, trade, distribution and

markets, Biodiesel Magazine also provides valuable insight into feedstock and market share competition from the non-ester renewable diesel sector.
Frequency: Monthly
Mailing list available for rent

1432 Biomass Power & Thermal
Biomass Thermal Energy Council
1211 Connecticut Avenue NW
Suite 600
Washington, DC 20036-2701

202-596-3974
Fax: 202-223-5537
E-Mail: info@biomassthermal.org
Home Page: www.biomassthermal.org
Social Media: Facebook, Twitter

Joseph Seymour, Executive Director
Charlie Niebling, Chairman
T.J. Morice, Vice-Chairman
Jon Strimling, Secretary
Bob Sourek, Treasurer

Tailored for industry professionals engaged in utilizing biomass for the generation of electricity, thermal energy, or both (CHP). Maintains a core editorial focus on biomass logistics; generating, cultivating, collecting, transporting, processing, marketing, procuring and utilizing sustainable biomass for power and heat.
Frequency: Monthly
Founded in 2009

1433 Distributed Generation & Alternative Energy Journal
Association of Energy Engineers (AEE)
4025 Pleasantdale Rd.
Suite 420
Atlanta, GA 30340

770-447-5083
Fax: 770-446-3969
E-Mail: al@aeecenter.org
Home Page: www.aeecenter.org
Social Media: Facebook, Twitter, YouTube

Albert Thumann, Executive Director
Jorge B. Wong, Ph.D, Editor-in-Chief

An authoritative publication which provides readers with detailed information on the latest innovations and developments in the distributed generation and related alternative energy fields.
15M Members
Frequency: Quarterly

1434 Energy Engineering
Association of Energy Engineers (AEE)
4025 Pleasantdale Rd.
Suite 420
Atlanta, GA 30340

770-447-5083
Fax: 770-446-3969
E-Mail: al@aeecenter.org
Home Page: www.aeecenter.org
Social Media: Facebook, Twitter, YouTube

Albert Thumann, Executive Director
Jorge B. Wong, Ph.D, Editor-in-Chief

The oldest journal exclusively written for engineers, energy managers, facility managers, utility professionals, VP's of operations, governmental energy managers and plant engineers involved in the design and application of energy management and facility improvement technologies.
15M Members
Frequency: Monthly
Founded in 1904

1435 Energy Law Journal
Federal Energy Bar Association
1990 M St Nw
Suite 350
Washington, DC 20036-3429

202-223-5625
Fax: 202-833-5596
E-Mail: admin@eba-net.org
Home Page: www.eba-net.org

Lorna Wilson, Administrator
Clinton A. Vince, Editor-in-Chief

Lawyers and consultants engaged in energy and public utility law.
Cost: $35.00
Frequency: Monthly
Circulation: 2600
ISSN: 0270-9163
Founded in 1946
Printed in 2 colors on matte stock

1436 Geo Outlook
International Ground Source Heat Pump Association
1201 S Innovation Way
Suite 400
Stillwater, OK 74074

405-744-5175
800-626-4747
Fax: 405-744-5283
E-Mail: igshpa@okstate.edu
Home Page: www.igshpa.okstate.edu

Jim Bose, Ph.D, Executive Director
Shelly Fitzpatrick, Conference & Membership Coordinator
John Turley, Chairman
Jack Henrich, Vice Chairman

The official publication of the geoexchange industry.
Frequency: Quarterly
Circulation: 50000

1437 Home Power Magazine
312 N. Main Street
Phoenix, OR 97535

541-512-0201
800-707-6585
Home Page: www.homepower.com
Social Media: Facebook, Twitter

Claire Anderson, Associate Editor

For renewable energy and sustainable living enthusiasts- homeowners and industry professionals alike. Specializing in hands-on, practical information about RE technologies, and presenting technical material in an easy-to-use format.
Frequency: Bi-Monthly

1438 IEEE Power and Energy Magazine
IEEE
PO Box 1331
Piscataway, NJ 08855

732-981-0061
Fax: 732-981-9667
E-Mail: custome-service@ieee.org
Home Page: www.ieee.org

Mel Olken, Editor
Susan Schneiderman, Business Development

Dedicated to disseminating information on all matters of interest to electric power engineers and other professionals involved in the electric power industry. Feature articles focus on advanced concepts, technologies, and practices associated with all aspects of electric power from a technical perspective in synergy with nontechnical areas such as business, environmental, and social concerns.
Cost: $260.00
82 Pages
Frequency: Monthly
Circulation: 23000
ISSN: 1540-7977
Founded in 2003
Mailing list available for rent
Printed in on glossy stock

1439 Renewables Global Status Report
REN21
REN21 Secretariat c/o UNEP
15, Rue de Milan 75441
Paris, France CEDEX 09

+33 1 44 3714 5090
E-Mail: secretariat@ren21.net
Home Page: www.new.ren21.net

Mohamed El-Ashry, Chair-UN Foundation
Michael Eckhart, VP- Citygroup
Kevin Nassiep, VP
Christine Lins, Executive Secretary

The Global Status Report(GSR) is the collaborative effort of over 400 authors, contributors and reviewers and is today the most frequently referenced report on renewable energy market, industry and policy trends. it provides testimony of the undeterred growth of electricity. heat and fuel production capacities from renewable energy sources including solar PV, wind power, solar hot water/heating, biofuels. hydropower and geothermal.

1440 SOLAR TODAY
American Solar Energy Society
4760 Walnut Street
Suite 106
Boulder, CO 80301

303-443-3130
Fax: 303-443-3212
E-Mail: ases@ases.org
Home Page: www.ases.org
Social Media: Facebook, Twitter, LinkedIn

Susan Greene, President
David G. Hill, Chair
Bill Poulin, Treasurer
Jason Keyes, Secretary

With the renewable energy industry changing at an unprecedented pace, SOLAR TODAY helps readers understand the changes, where the industry is headed, and how it's affecting the country.
13M Members
Frequency: 9x Yearly
Founded in 1954

1441 Solar Energy
Elsevier Science
655 Avenue of the Americas
PO Box 945
New York, NY 10010-5107

212-633-3800
Fax: 212-633-3850
Home Page: www.elsevier.com

Young Suk Chi, Manager

Devoted exclusively to the science and technology of solar energy applications. Presents information not previously published in journals on any aspect of solar energy research, development, application, measurement or policy.
Frequency: Monthly
Circulation: 6400

1442 Strategic Planning for Energy and the Environment
Association of Energy Engineers (AEE)
4025 Pleasantdale Rd.
Suite 420
Atlanta, GA 30340

770-447-5083
Fax: 770-446-3969
E-Mail: al@aeecenter.org
Home Page: www.aeecenter.org
Social Media: Facebook, Twitter, YouTube

Albert Thumann, Executive Director
Dr. Wayne C. Turner, Editor

Concentrates on the background, new developments and policy issues which impact corporate

planning for energy savings, operational efficiency, and environmental concerns.
15M Members
Frequency: Quarterly

1443 **The Ally**
BlueGreen Alliance
1020 19th Street NW
Suite 600
Washington, DC 20036

202-706-6910
E-Mail: ashley@bluegreenalliance.org
Home Page: www.bluegreenalliance.org
Social Media: Facebook, Twitter, flickr, YouTube

David Foster, Executive Director

A biweekly update providing reports, letters, press releases and other publications along with clean energy industry news.

1444 **The Energy Journal**
International Association for Energy Economics
28790 Chagrin Blvd
Suite 350
Cleveland, OH 44122-4642

216-464-5365
Fax: 216-464-2737
E-Mail: iaee@iaee.org
Home Page: www.iaee.org
Social Media: Facebook, LinkedIn

Mine Yucel, President
Lars Bergman, President-Elect
David L. Williams, Executive Director

Promotes the advancement and dissemination of new knowledge concerning energy and related topics. Publishing a blend of theoretical, empirical and policy related papers in energy economics.
3400 Members
Founded in 1977

Trade Shows

1445 **AERO Annual Meeting**
Alternative Energy Resources Organization
432 N. Last Chance Gulch
Helena, MT 59601

406-443-7272
Fax: 406-442-9120
E-Mail: aero@aeromt.org
Home Page: www.aeromt.org
Social Media: Facebook, Twitter, Myspace

Bryan von Lossberg, Executive Director

Sustainability Begins at Home.
Frequency: Annual/ October
Founded in 1974

1446 **AWEA Offshore Windpower Conference & Exhibition**
American Wind Energy Association
1501 M Street NW
Suite 1000
Washington, DC 20005

202-383-2500
Fax: 202-383-2505
E-Mail: windmail@awea.org
Home Page: www.awea.org
Social Media: Facebook, Twitter, YouTube, Flickr

Ned Hall, Chair
Thomas Carnahan, Chair-Elect
Gabriel Alonso, Secretary
Don Furman, Treasurer
Denise Bode, CEO

Brings together exhibitors and attendees from all over the world who are interested in becoming players in this new and highly promising market.
2500+ Members
1700 Attendees
Frequency: Annual/October

1447 **AWEA Windpower Conference & Exhibition**
American Wind Energy Association
1501 M Street NW
Suite 1000
Washington, DC 20005

202-383-2500
Fax: 202-383-2505
E-Mail: windmail@awea.org
Home Page: www.awea.org
Social Media: Facebook, Twitter, YouTube, Flickr

Ned Hall, Chair
Thomas Carnahan, Chair-Elect
Gabriel Alonso, Secretary
Don Furman, Treasurer
Denise Bode, CEO

Recognized as one of the world's premier wind energy trade shows, bringing together attendees and exhibitors from every aspect of the industry. Exhibitors display the latest industry products and services from manufacturing leaders, component suppliers, and other wind energy organizations. This conference combines education, exhibition, and networking creating a perfect venue for business development.
2500+ Members
16000 Attendees
Frequency: Annual/June

1448 **Annual Algae Biomass Summit**
Biomass Power Association
100 Middle St.
PO Box 9729
Portland, ME 04104-9729

703-889-8504
E-Mail: info@biomasspowerassociation.com
Home Page: www.usabiomass.org

Bob Cleaves, President & CEO
Gary Melow, State Projects Coordinator

This dynamic event unites industry professionals from all sectors of the world's algae utilization industries including, but not limited to; financing, algal ecology, genetic systems, carbon partitioning, engineering & analysis, biofuels, animal feeds, fertilizers, bioplastics, supplements and foods.
80 Members
Frequency: Annual/October

1449 **Annual National Ethanol Conference**
Renewable Fuels Association
425 Third Street SW
Suite 1150
Washington, DC 20024

202-289-3835
Fax: 202-289-7519
E-Mail: necregistration@bbiinternational.com
Home Page: www.ethanolrfa.org
Social Media: Facebook, Twitter, YouTube, Flickr

Bob Dinneen, President & CEO
Christina Martin, Executive Vice President
Alex Obuchowski, CFO

Recongnized as the preeminent conference for delivering accurate, timely information on marketing, legislative and regulatory issues facing the ethanol industry. Meet and interact with key stakeholders and take part in shaping the future of the ethanol industry.
1250+ Attendees
Frequency: Annual/February
Founded in 1981

1450 **Annual North American Waste-to-Energy Conference**
Solid Waste Association of North America - SWANA

800-GOS-WANA
Fax: 301-589-7068
Home Page: www.nawtec.org

Co-sponsored by ERC, ASME and SWANA, in partnership with WTERT, the conference and trade show focuses on municipal waste-to-energy operational issues and policy, technology and research initiatives.

1451 **Annual Renewable Energy Technology Conference & Exhibition (RETECH)**
American Council on Renewable Energy
1600 K Street NW
Suite 700
Washington, DC 20006

202-393-0001
E-Mail: vay@acore.org
Home Page: www.refindirectory.com
Social Media: Facebook, Twitter, LinkedIn, YouTube

Dennis V. McGinn, President

Conference sessions deliver unparalleled educational content including business development opportunities, topical professional development, current trends, the newest technologies and important up-to-date information on the changing legislative and regulatory landscapes. Exhibition offers the best opportunity to meet, network and connect with companies and organizations in the renewable energy industry.
3000+ Attendees
Frequency: Annual/October
Founded in 2001

1452 **Bioenergy Fuels & Products Conference & Expo**
Biomass Thermal Energy Council
1211 Connecticut Avenue NW
Suite 600
Washington, DC 20036-2701

202-596-3974
Fax: 202-223-5537
E-Mail: info@biomassthermal.org
Home Page: www.biomassthermal.org
Social Media: Facebook, Twitter

Joseph Seymour, Executive Director
Charlie Niebling, Chairman
T.J. Morice, Vice-Chairman
Jon Strimling, Secretary
Bob Sourek, Treasurer

Speakers and moderators who will address a range of topics including raw material, product and market developments and bio-process technologies.
Frequency: Annual/March
Founded in 2009

1453 **Biomass Thermal DC Summit**
Biomass Thermal Energy Council
1211 Connecticut Avenue NW
Suite 600
Washington, DC 20036-2701

202 596 3974
Fax: 202-223-5537
E-Mail: info@biomassthermal.org
Home Page: www.biomassthermal.org
Social Media: Facebook, Twitter

Joseph Seymour, Executive Director
Charlie Niebling, Chairman
T.J. Morice, Vice-Chairman
Jon Strimling, Secretary
Bob Sourek, Treasurer

Summit participants engage policy makers and renewable energy - related groups on the sub-

stantial benefits of biomass thermal energy use; increased rural economic activity, energy independence, healthier forests, and effective tax policy.
Frequency: Annual/November
Founded in 2009

1454 **Building Energy**
Northeast Sustainable Energy Association
50 Miles St
Greenfield, MA 01301-3255
413-774-6051
Fax: 413-774-6053
E-Mail: nesea@nesea.org
Home Page: www.nesea.org
Social Media: Facebook, Twitter, LinkedIn
David Barclay, Executive Director
Sonia Hamel, Vice Chair
Daniel Sagan, Secretary
Michael Skelly, Treasurer
Oldest and largest regional renewable energy event in the country, known for showcasing next-generation thinkers and game-changing ideas.
1802 Members
Founded in 1974
Mailing list available for rent

1455 **Energy Innovation Summit**
National Biodiesel Board
605 Clark Ave
PO Box 104898
Jefferson City, MO 65110-4898
573-635-3893
Fax: 573-635-7913
E-Mail: info@biodiesel.org
Home Page: www.biodiesel.org
Social Media: Facebook, Twitter, YouTube
Gary Haer, Chairman
Ed Ulch, Vice-Chair
Jim Conway, Treasurer
Ron Marr, Secretary
Designed to bring together key players from across the energy ecosystem - researchers, entrepreneurs, investors, corporate executives, and government officials - to share ideas for developing and deploying the next generation of clean energy technologies.
Frequency: Annual/February

1456 **Geothermal Energy Expo**
Geothermal Energy Association
209 Pennsylvania Avenue SE
Washington, DC 20003
202-454-5261
Fax: 202-454-5265
E-Mail: jgreco@terra-genpower.com
Home Page: www.geo-energy.org
Karl Gawell, Executive Director
Leslie Blodgett, Editor-in-Chief
Paul Thomsen, President
Jonathan M. Weisgall, Chairman
Kathy Kent, Director of Events
The world's largest gathering of vendors providing support for geothermal resource exploration, characterization, development, production and management. Provides a unique opportunity for exhibitors to showcase their projects, equipment, services and state of the art technology to the geothermal community.
Frequency: Annual/October

1457 **GlobalCon Conference & Expo**
Biomass Thermal Energy Council
1211 Connecticut Avenue NW
Suite 600
Washington, DC 20036-2701
202-596-3974
Fax: 202-223-5537
E-Mail: info@biomassthermal.org
Home Page: www.biomassthermal.org
Social Media: Facebook, Twitter
Joseph Seymour, Executive Director
Charlie Niebling, Chairman
Dan Arnett, Vice-Chairman
John Ackerly, Secretary
Mike Jostrom, Treasurer
Designed specifically to facilitate those seeking to expand their knowledge of fast-moving developments in the energy field, explore promising new technologies, compare energy supply options, and learn about innovative and cost-conscious project implementation strategies.
Frequency: Annual/March
Founded in 2009

1458 **IGSHPA Conference & Expo**
International Ground Source Heat Pump Association
1201 S Innovation Way
Suite 400
Stillwater, OK 74074
405-744-5175
800-626-4747
Fax: 405-744-5283
E-Mail: igshpa@okstate.edu
Home Page: www.igshpa.okstate.edu
Jim Bose, Ph.D, Executive Director
Shelly Fitzpatrick, Conference & Membership Coordinator
Jack Henrich, Chairman
Greg Wells, Vice Chairman
Jim Bose, Executive Director
The largest technical conference in the US dedicated solely to geothermal. Conference features technical classes, which attract many industry newcomers each year.
Frequency: Annual/October

1459 **International Bioenergy and Bioproducts Conference (IBBC)**
Technical Association of the Pulp & Paper Industry
15 Technology Parkway S
Norcross, GA 30092
770-446-1400
800-322-8686
Fax: 770-446-6947
E-Mail: webmaster@tappi.org
Home Page: www.tappi.org
Norman F. Marsolan, Chair
Thomas J. Garland, Vice Chair
Larry N. Montague, President & CEO
Focusing on technical advancements and commercialization of bioconversion technologies that leverage the forest products manufacturing infrastructure and will include technical presentations, expert panels, case studies, and reports from projects that address feedstock and harvesting improvements to increase yield and quality of biomass, and much more.
500 Attendees
Frequency: Annual/October

1460 **International Biomass Conference & Expo**
Biomass Thermal Energy Council
1211 Connecticut Avenue NW
Suite 600
Washington, DC 20036-2701
202-596-3974
Fax: 202-223-5537
E-Mail: info@biomassthermal.org
Home Page: www.biomassthermal.org
Social Media: Facebook, Twitter
Joseph Seymour, Executive Director
Charlie Niebling, Chairman
Dan Arnett, Vice-Chairman
John Ackerly, Secretary
Mike Jostrom, Treasurer
This dynamic event unites industry professionals from all sectors of the world's interconnected biomass utilization industries - biobased power, thermal energy, fuels and chemicals. Where future and existing producers of biobased power, fuels and thermal energy products go to network with waste generators and other industry suppliers and technology providers.
Frequency: Annual/April
Founded in 2009

1461 **International Topical Meeting on Advances in Reactor Physics**
555 N Kensington Ave
La Grange Park, IL 60526-5592
708-352-6611
800-323-3044
Fax: 708-352-0499
E-Mail: advertising@ans.org
Home Page: www.ans.org
Social Media: Facebook, Twitter, LinkedIn
Jack Tuohy, Executive Director
James S Tulenko, VP
William F Naughton, Treasurer
Advances in reactor physics being the main topic of discussion. Promoting the awareness and understanding of the application of nuclear science and technology.
10500 Members
Founded in 1954

1462 **NABCEP Continuing Education Conference**
NABCEP
56 Clifton Country Rd.
Suite 202
Clifton Park, NY 12065
800-654-0021
Fax: 518-899-1092
E-Mail: CEconference@nabcep.org
Home Page: www.nabcep.org
Ezra Auerbach, Executive Director
Don Warfield, Chair
Jane Weissman, Vice Chair
Les Nelson, Treasurer
Jeff Spies, Secretary
The objective of this conference is to offer NABCEP certified installers and technical sales professionals an opportunity that allows them to fulfill the majority of their CE requirements at a single event. In combination with manufacturer's training sessions, conference registrants will be able to attend workshops on the NEC, financial analysis, safety, and emerging fire codes.
Frequency: Annual/March
Founded in 2000

1463 **National Biodiesel Conference & Expo**
National Biodiesel Board
605 Clark Ave
PO Box 104898
Jefferson City, MO 65110-4898
573-635-3893
Fax: 573-635-7913
E-Mail: info@biodiesel.org
Home Page: www.biodiesel.org
Social Media: Facebook, Twitter, YouTube
Gary Haer, Chairman
Ed Ulch, Vice-Chair
Steven J. Levy, Treasurer
Ron Marr, Secretary
The only event that gathers biodiesel decision-makers from across the United States, and the world. Opportunities abound for attendees and exhibitors to network connect and learn. Event explores the topics of governmental pol-

icy, technical issues and marketing trends in the biodiesel industry.
Frequency: Annual/February

1464 **National Hydropower Association Annual Conference**
National Hydropower Association
25 Massachusetts Ave, NW
Suite 450
Washington, DC 20001

202-682-1700
Fax: 202-682-9478
E-Mail: help@hydro.org
Home Page: www.hydro.org
Social Media: Facebook, Twitter

Linda Church Ciocci, Executive Director
David Moller, President
Eric Van Deuren, Treasurer
Cherise Oram, Vice President
Suzanne Grassell, Secretary

Program will provide a unique opportunity to hear first-hand from the Administration, Congress, federal regulators and resource agencies on the issues and policies that directly affect individual businesses and projects.
Frequency: Annual/April

1465 **Pellet Fuels Institute Annual Conference**
1901 North Moore Street
Suite 600
Arlington, VA 22209

703-522-6778
Fax: 703-522-0548
E-Mail: pfimail@pelletheat.org
Home Page: www.pelletheat.org

Jennifer Hedrick, Executive Director
Jason Berthiaume, Membership/ Gov't Affairs Associate
John Crouch, Director of Public Affairs

Conference educates industry members on the latest information including new program development and what to expect in upcoming months. Speakers, roundtable panels, annual golf tournament and a beach bash.

1466 **Renewable Energy Finance Forum (REFF) -Wall Street**
American Council on Renewable Energy
1600 K Street NW
Suite 700
Washington, DC 20006

202-393-0001
E-Mail: vay@acore.org
Home Page: www.refindirectory.com
Social Media: Facebook, Twitter, LinkedIn, YouTube

Dennis V. McGinn, President
Estelle Lloyd, Managing Editor & Co-Founder
Tom, Naylor, Ronan
Murphy Managing Editor

Bringing together the top leaders of the USA's renewable energy industry, drawing attendees from the entire value chain, including financiers, manufacturers and developers.
700 Attendees
Frequency: Annual/June
Founded in 2001

1467 **Renewable Energy Markets Conference**
Renewable Energy Markets Association
1211 Connecticut Ave NW
Suite 600
Washington, DC 20036-2701

202-640-6597
Fax: 202-223-5537
E-Mail: info@renewablemarketers.org
Home Page: www.renewablemarketers.org
Social Media: Facebook, Twitter

Richard Anderson, President
Ian McGowan, Vice President
Kevin Maddaford, Treasurer
Sarah Smith, Secretary
Josh Lieberman, General Manager

Bridging the interests of renewable energy generators, sellers, and utilities with those of purchasers, policymakers, and the communities that benefit from clean energy, this is the nation's premier forum for the energy community to gather, learn from each other, and recognize best practices for promoting renewable energy.
400 Attendees
Frequency: Annual/November

1468 **Solar Thermal**
Interstate Renewable Energy Council
PO Box 1156
Latham, NY 12110-1156

518-458-6059
E-Mail: info@irecusa.org
Home Page: www.irecusa.org

Jane Weissman, Executive Director
Lary Sherwood, Vice Chaie
David Warner, Chair
Jane Pulaski, Secretary
Jennifer Szaro, Treasurer

A two-day conference and networking event for industry professionals including; installers, manufacturers, distributors, engineers, designers, policy makers, code officials, and trainers. A national solar heating and cooling conference.
Frequency: Annual/December

1469 **U.S. Clean Heat & Power Association's Annual Spring CHP Forum**
U.S. Clean Heat & Power Association
105 North Virginia Avenue
Suite 204
Falls Church, VA 22046
703-436-2257
E-Mail: info@uschpa.org
Home Page: www.uschpa.org
Social Media: Twitter

Jessica Bridges, Executive Director
Joe Allen, Chair
Warren Ferguson, Vice Chair
John Rathbun, Secretary
Paul Lemar, Treasurer

Showcasing a series of knowledgeable speakers sharing their expertise on policies and best practices that have facilitated CHP deployment in overseas markets and offering advice on how to break down barriers to CHP deployment and replicate those successes stateside. Listen to national and international trade and policy authorities, US government officials, and CHP business leaders discuss CHP challenges, success stories, and market expansion opportunities.
Frequency: Annual/May
Founded in 1999

1470 **UNEP SEF Alliance Annual Meeting**
Clean Energy Group/ UNEP SEF Alliance
50 State St.
Suite 1
Montpelier, VT 05602

802-223-2554
Fax: 802-223-4967
E-Mail: RTyler@cleanegroup.org
Home Page: www.unepsefalliance.org

Members engage in candid discussion with peer agencies about current challenges faced, latest programme developments, and plans for future programme design. Experts speak about specialized topics, and proposals for new areas of collaboration are presented and discussed.
Frequency: Annual/September

1471 **World Renewable Energy Forum**
American Solar Energy Society
4760 Walnut Street
Suite 106
Boulder, CO 80301
303-443-3130
Fax: 303-443-3212
E-Mail: ases@ases.org
Home Page: www.ases.org
Social Media: Facebook, Twitter, LinkedIn

Susan Greene, President
David G. Hill, Chair
Bill Poulin, Treasurer
Jason Keyes, Secretary

American Solar Energy Society annual conference and the bi-annual World Renewable Energy Congress have combined, providing a unique opportunity for renewable energy enthusiasts from around the world to share experiences.
13M Members
Frequency: Annual/May
Founded in 1954

1472 **World Shale Gas Conference & Exhibition**
Institute of Gas Technology
1700 S Mount Prospect Rd
Des Plaines, IL 60018-1804

847-768-0664
Fax: 847-768-0669
Home Page: www.gastechnology.org
Social Media: Facebook, Twitter, LinkedIn, YouTube

David Carroll, President & CEO
Ronald Snedic, Vice President/ Corporate Devel.
Paul Chromek, General Counsel & Secretary

Unique platform to uncover the real impact of shale on the global gas market. Provides a valuable opportunity to develop business, explore future prospects and unlock the potential of shale gas globally. Share knowledge and experience among industry professionals, government operators and solution providers.

Directories & Databases

1473 **American Solar Energy Society Membership Directory**
4760 Walnut Street
Suite 106
Boulder, CO 80301-2843

303-443-3130
Fax: 303-443-3212
E-Mail: ases@ases.org
Home Page: www.ases.org

Susan Greene, President
David G. Hill, Chair
Bill Poulin, Treasurer
Jason Keyes, Secretary

Offers information on over 2,000 manufacturers, professors, architects, engineers and others in the solar energy field.

1474 **Association of Energy Service Companies Directory**
Association of Energy Service Companies
6060 N Central Expy
Dallas, TX 75206-5209

214-692-0771
800-692-0771

Fax: 214-692-0162
Home Page: www.aesc.net

Patty Jordan, Publisher

About 750 energy service companies and industry suppliers.
Frequency: Bi-Monthly
Circulation: 10,000

1475 **Database of State Incentives for Renewables & Efficiency (DSIRE)**
North Carolina State University
Campus Box 7504
Raleigh, NC 27695-7504

919-515-3470
Fax: 919-515-2556
E-Mail: DSIREinfo@ncsu.edu
Home Page: www.dsireusa.org
Social Media: Facebook, Twitter

Amanda Vanega, Program Manager

Funded by the US Department of Energy's Office of Energy Efficiency and Renewable Energy. A comprehensive source of information on state, local, utility and federal incentives and policies that promote renewable energy and energy efficiency.
Founded in 1995

1476 **Energy**
WEFA Group
800 Baldwin Tower Boulevard
Eddystone, PA 19022-1368

610-490-4000
Fax: 610-490-2770
E-Mail: info@wefa.com
Home Page: www.wefa.com

Peter McNabb

This database covers energy supply and demand, including weekly rig count and gasoline prices by states; reserves, stocks, production, consumption and trade of petroleum products.

1477 **Energy Science and Technology**
US Department of Energy
PO Box 62
Oak Ridge, TN 37831-0062

865-574-1000
Fax: 865-576-2865
E-Mail: OSTIWebmaster@osti.gov
Home Page: www.osti.gov

This large database offers over 3 million citations, with abstracts, to literature pertaining to all fields of energy.

1478 **Handbook: Solar Energy System Design**
American Society of Plumbing Engineers
2980 S River Rd
Des Plaines, IL 60018-4203

847-296-0002
Fax: 847-296-2963
E-Mail: info@aspe.org
Home Page: www.aspe.org

Tom Govedarica, Executive Publisher
Richard Albrecht, Publication Coordinator
Gretchen Pienta, Managing Editor

This manual provides the know-how on solar hot-water systems, collectors, thermal storage and much more.
Cost: $20.00

1479 **Membership Roster and Registry of Geothermal Services & Equipment**
Geothermal Resources Council
20001 Second Street
Suite 5
Davis, CA 95618-5476

530-758-2360
Fax: 530-758-2839
E-Mail: grc@geothermal.org
Home Page: www.geothermal.org
Social Media: Facebook, Twitter, LinkedIn, YouTube, Flickr

Curt Robinson, Ph.D, Executive Director
Steve Ponder, Interim Executive Director
Estela M. Smith, Office Manager
Ian Crawford, Managing Editor
Chi-Meng Moua, Library Associate

A unique publication that provides business, consulting and research contacts throughout the international geothermal community.
Frequency: Annual
Founded in 1970

1480 **REFIN Directory**
American Council on Renewable Energy
1600 K Street NW
Suite 700
Washington, DC 20006

202-393-0001
E-Mail: vay@acore.org
Home Page: www.refindirectory.com
Social Media: Facebook, Twitter, LinkedIn, YouTube

Dennis V. McGinn, President
Douglas Llyod, CEO and Co-Founder
Estelle Llyod, Managing Editor

Connects suppliers of capital and expertise with industry participants engaged in the scale-up of renewable energy.
Frequency: Annually
Founded in 2001

1481 **The Source for Renewable Energy**
Momentum Technologies, LLC
PO Box 460813
Glendale, CO 80246
303-229-4841
Fax: 408-705-2031
E-Mail: energy@mtt.com
Home Page: energy.sourceguides.com

A comprehensive buyer's guide and business directory to more than 18,000 renewable energy businesses and organizations worldwide.

1482 **Wind Energy Conversion Systems**
South Dakota Renewable Energy Association
PO Box 491
Pierre, SD 57501-0491

605-224-8641

Offers valuable information for electrical-output wind machine manufacturers.
Cost: $2.00
45 Pages
Frequency: Annual

Industry Web Sites

1483 **energy.sourceguides.com**
Momentum Technologies, LLC

A comprehensive buyer's guide and business directory to more than 18,000 renewable energy businesses and organizations worldwide.

1484 **http://gold.greyhouse.com**
G.O.L.D Grey House OnLine Databases

Grey House Publishing's online database platform, GOLD, offers Quick Search, Keyword Search and Expert Search for most business sectors including mining, petroleum and alternative energy markets. The GOLD platform makes finding the information you need quick and easy. All of Grey House's directory products are available for subscription on the GOLD platform.

1485 **www.acore.org**
American Council on Renewable Energy

Works to bring all forms of renewable energy into the mainstream of America's economy and lifestyle. Members include every aspect and sector of the renewable energy industries and their trade associations, including wind, solar, geothermal, biomass and biofuels, hydropower tidal/current energy and waste energy.

1486 **www.aeecenter.org**
Association of Energy Engineers (AEE)

Information and networking in the dynamic fields of energy engineering and energy management, renewable and alternative energy, power generation, energy services, sustainability, and all related areas.

1487 **www.aeromt.org**
Alternative Energy Resources Organization

A grassroots nonprofit organization dedicated to solutions that promote resource conservation and local economic vitality. By bringing people together, AERO offers a vehicle for collective action and a sense of common purpose for citizens within their communities to shape a more sustainable future.

1488 **www.americanbiogascouncil.org**
American Biogas Council

Mission is to create jobs, environmental sustainability and energy independence by growing the American biogas industry.

1489 **www.americanhydrogenassociation.org**
American Hydrogen Association

Providing information on the use of hydrogen as a fuel.

1490 **www.ases.org**
American Solar Energy Society

The nation's leading association of solar professionals & advocates. Mission is to inspire an era of energy innovation and speed the transition to a sustainable energy economy. Advancing education, research and policy.

1491 **www.awea.org**
American Wind Energy Association

Promotes wind energy as a clean source of electricity for consumers around the world. Representing wind power project developers, equipment suppliers, services providers, parts manufacturers, utilities, researchers, and others involved in the wind industry - one of the world's fastest growing energy industries.

1492 **www.biodiesel.org**
National Biodiesel Board

Mission is to advance the interests of its members by creating sustainable biodiesel industry growth. NBB serves as the industry's central coordinating entity and will be the single voice for its diverse membership base.

1493 **www.biogaspower.org**
Bio-Gas Power Association

Dedicated to providing the industry with the knowledge needed to operate and maintain these facilities by providing a common ground to learn from each others' experiences. Developed as a way for owners, operators, technicians, and dealerships alike to come together and share ideas, experience, opinions, and tackle the tough issues that come with owning and operating Bio-Gas to Energy Facilities.

1494 **www.biomassthermal.org**
Biomass Thermal Energy Council

An association of biomass fuel producers, appliance manufacturers and distributors, supply chain companies and non-profit organizations that view biomass thermal energy as a renewable, responsible, clean and energy-efficient pathway to meeting America's energy needs. BTEC engages in research, education, and public advocacy for the fast growing biomass thermal energy industry.

1495 **www.cleanegroup.org**
Clean Energy Group
A leading nonprofit advocacy organization working in the US and internationally on innovative clean energy technology, finance, and policy programs. Supported by major foundations, as well as state, federal and international energy agencies.

1496 **www.dsireusa.org**
DSIRE Database
Funded by the US Department of Energy's Office of Energy Efficiency and Renewable Energy. A comprehensive source of information on state, local, utility and federal incentives and policies that promote renewable energy and energy efficiency.

1497 **www.eesi.org**
Environmental and Energy Study Institute
A nonprofit organization that advances innovative policy solutions that set us on a cleaner, more secure and sustainable energy path.

1498 **www.energyrecoverycouncil.org**
Energy Recovery Council
Represents the waste-to-energy industry and communities that own waste-to-energy facilities. Current ERC members own and operate modern waste-to-energy facilities that operate nationwide, safely disposing of municipal solid waste, while at the same time generating renewable electricity using modern combustion technology equipped with state-of-the-art emission control systems.

1499 **www.ethanolrfa.org**
Renewable Fuels Association
The national trade association for the US ethanol industry promoting policies, regulations and research and development initiatives that will lead to the increased production and use of fuel ethanol. Membership includes a broad cross-section of businesses, individuals and organizations dedicated to the expansion of the US fuel ethanol industry.

1500 **www.geo-energy.org**
Geothermal Energy Association
Advocates for public policies that will promote the development and utilization of geothermal resources, provides a forum for the industry to discuss issues and problems, encourages research and development to improve geothermal technologies, presents industry views to governmental organizations, and conducts education and outreach projects.

1501 **www.geothermal.org**
Geothermal Resources Council
Nonprofit, educational association actively seeking to expand its role as a primary professional educational association for the international geothermal community.

1502 **www.greyhouse.com**
Grey House Publishing
Authoritative reference directories for business information and general reference, including alternative energy, mining and petroleum markets. Users can search the online databases with varied search criteria allowing for custom searches by product category, geographic area, sales volume, keyword, subject and more. Full Grey House catalog and online ordering also available.

1503 **www.hydro.org**
National Hydropower Association
Dedicated to promoting the growth of clean, affordable US hydropower. Seeks to secure hydropower's place as a climate-friendly, renewable and reliable energy source that serves national environmental, energy, and economic policy objectives. Members are involved in projects throughout the US hydropower industry, including both federal and non-federal hydroelectric facilities.

1504 **www.iaee.org**
International Association for Energy Economics
Association for those involved in energy economics including publications, consultants, energy database software.

1505 **www.igshpa.okstate.edu**
International Ground Source Heat Pump Association
Member-driven organization established to advance ground source heat pump technology on local, state, national and international levels. IGSHPA utilizes state of the art facilities for conducting GSHP system installation training and geothermal research. Mission is to promote the use of ground source heat pump technology worldwide through education and communication.

1506 **www.irecusa.org**
Interstate Renewable Energy Council
Works with industry, government, educators and other stakeholders to ensure that the broader use of renewable energies is possible, safe, affordable and practical, particularly for the individual consumer.

1507 **www.ireoigo.org**
Intergovernmental Renewable Energy Organization
Promotes the urgent transition to renewable energy sources and sustainable development through collaborative effort and the implementation of projects that improve the lives of people while preserving the environment and our resources for future generations of humans.

1508 **www.lignite.com**
Lignite Energy Council
Regional Trade Association - promotes policies and activities that maintain a viable lignite industry and enhance development of our regions' lignite resources.

1509 **www.nabcep.org**
N. American Board of Cert. Energy Practitioners
Mission is to support, and work with, the renewable energy and energy efficiency industries, professionals, and stakeholders. Goal is to develop voluntary national certification programs that will; promote renewable energy, provide value to practitioners, promote worker safety and skill, and promote consumer confidence.

1510 **www.nationalrenewableenergyassociation.org**
National Renewable Energy Association
A nonprofit organization dedicated to helping Americans use less energy and to use more renewable energy in the future.

1511 **www.nesea.org**
Northeast Sustainable Energy Association
The nation's leading regional membership organization focused on promoting the understanding, development and adoption of energy conservation and non-polluting, renewable energy technologies.

1512 **www.oceanrenewable.com**
Ocean Renewable Energy Coalition
Striving to keep members, legislators, regulators, the media and the public at large up to date with OREC's activities as well as ongoing developments in this emerging industry.

1513 **www.renewablemarketers.org**
Renewable Energy Markets Association
A nonprofit association dedicated to maintaining and growing strong markets for renewable energy in the United States. Representing organizations that sell, purchase, or promote renewable energy products.

1514 **www.seia.org**
Solar Energy Industries Association
Works with its member companies to make solar a mainstream and significant energy source by expanding markets, removing market barriers, strenghtening the industry and educating the public on the benefits of solar energy.

1515 **www.solarliving.org**
Solar Living Institute
A nonprofit solar training and sustainability organization. Mission is to promote sustainable living through inspirational environmental education.

1516 **www.unepsefalliance.org**
UNEP SEF Alliance
The only convening body in the international system for public finance agencies in the clean energy sector. Members are visionary organizations from various countries pushing the forefront of how to do public finance for clean energy.

1517 **www.usabiomass.org**
Biomass Power Association
The nation's leading organization working to expand and advance the use of clean, renewable biomass power. Educates policymakers at the state and federal level about the benefits of biomass and provides regular briefings and research to keep members fully informed about public policy impacting the biomass industry. Members include local owners and operators of existing biomass facilities, suppliers, plant developers and others.

1518 **www.uschpa.org**
US Clean Heat & Power Association
Providing superior advocacy, networking, education and market information to companies in the business of clean, local energy generation. Documents the benefits of clean heat and power to the public and to decision-makers. Also participates in federal agency programs to promote clean distributed energy.

1519 **www.wcee.org**
Women's Council on Energy and the Environment
Supports women involved in the environmental community with education, research, new trend information and several publications.

Associations

1520 **Academy of Science Fiction Fantasy and Horror Films**
334 W 54th St
Los Angeles, CA 90037-3806

323-752-5811
Fax: 323-752-5811
E-Mail: scifiacademy@ca.rr.com
Home Page: www.saturnawards.org

Robert Holguin, CEO & President
David Bilbrey, Executive Administrator
Michael Laster, Director of Operations
Jeff Rector, Official Spokesperson
Kurt Reichenbach, Art Designer

Honors, recognizes and promotes genre films. Annually presents the prestigious Saturn Awards. In recent years, have added television and home entertainment categories to the media mix. Widened the scope of our awards by celebrating achievement in additional genres including action, adventure, and thrillers as well as international cinema.
Founded in 1972

1521 **American Alliance for Health, Physical Education, Recreation and Dance**
1900 Association Drive
Reston, VA 20191-1502

703-476-3400
800-213-7193
Fax: 703-476-9527
E-Mail: info@aahperd.org
Home Page: www.aahperd.org
Social Media: Facebook, Twitter, YouTube

Gale Wiedow, President
E. Paul Roetert, Chief Executive Officer
Dolly D. Lambdin, President-Elect
Frances Cleland, Member-at-Large
Neil Dougherty, Member-at-Large

Organization that provides educational programs, resources and support for professionals within the fields of health, physical education, recreation and dance. AAHPERD's mission is to promote and support leadership, research, education, and best practices in the professions that support creative, healthy, and active lifestyles.
25000 Members
Founded in 1885

1522 **American Amusement Machine Association**
450 E Higgins Rd
Suite 201
Elk Grove Vlg, IL 60007-1417

847-290-9088
866-372-5190
Fax: 847-290-9121
E-Mail: information@coin-op.org
Home Page: www.coin-op.org
Social Media: Facebook, Twitter, LinkedIn

John Schultz, President
Tina Schwartz, Business & Finance Manager
David Cohen, Chairman
Frank Consentino, Secretary
John Margold, Treasurer

Non profit trade association representing the manufacturers, distributors and part suppliers to the coin-operated and out of home amusement industry.
Founded in 1981

1523 **American Association of Cheerleading Coaches and Administration**
6745 Lenox Center Court
Suite 318
Memphis, TN 38115

800-533-6583
Fax: 901-251-5851
E-Mail: jimlord@aacca.org
Home Page: www.aacca.org
Social Media: Facebook, Twitter

Jim Lord, Executive Director
Mike Nordengran, Administration
Sheila Noone, Media Relations

AACCA,is a non-profit educational association for cheerleading coaches across the United States. Members of the association include: youth, junior high school, high school, all star, and college or university coaches/advisors, as well as leading national cheerleading instructional companies dedicated to the safe and responsible practice of student cheerleading.
70000 Members
Founded in 1987

1524 **American Coaster Enthusiasts**
1100-H Brandywine Boulevard
Zanesville, OH 43701-7303

740-450-1560
Fax: 740-452-2552
E-Mail: info@aceonline.org
Home Page: www.aceonline.org
Social Media: Facebook, Twitter, RSS

Dave Altman, President
Jerry Willard, Vice President
David Lipnicky, Public Relations Director
Lee Ann Draud, Publications Director
Brian Peters, Information Services Director

ACE is the world's largest ride enthusiast organization, and its members are the most educated, dedicated, and passionate amusement park guests. ACE's activities include publications, action-packed events, and preservation efforts. ACE is highly visible in the mainstream media. Local television stations and newspapers often consider ACE events in their area to be major news items.
7000 Members
Founded in 1978

1525 **American Disc Jockey Association**
20118 N 67th Avenue
Suite 300-605
Glendale, CA 85308

888-723-5776
Fax: 866-310-4676
E-Mail: office@adja.org
Home Page: www.adja.org
Social Media: Facebook, Twitter, YouTube

Rob Snyder, Director

An association of professional mobile entertainers. Encourages success for its members through continuous education, camaraderie, and networking. The primary goal is to educate Disc Jockeys so that each member acts ethically and responsibly.

1526 **Amusement Industry Manufacturers & Suppliers International**
3026 South Orange
Santa Ana, CA 92707

714-425-5747
Fax: 714-276-9666
E-Mail: info@aimsintl.org
Home Page: www.aimsintl.org
Social Media: Facebook

Brian D King, President

The Amusement Industry Manufacturers and Suppliers (AIMS) Trade Association evolved from the American Recreational Equipment Association. The Associations purpose is to establish communications and foster working relations using the highest degree of professionalism with other Amusement Industry Trade Associations, Local, State, and Federal Government entities in order to promote and preserve the prosperity of the Amusement Industry.
Founded in 1994

1527 **Amusement and Music Operators Association**
600 Spring Hill Ring Road
Suite 111
West Dundee, IL 60118

847-428-7699
800-937-2662
Fax: 847-428-7719
E-Mail: amoa@amoa.com
Home Page: www.amoa.com
Social Media: Facebook

John Pascaretti, President
Bobby Hogin, 1st Vice President
Jack Kelleher, Executive Vice President
Lori Schneider, Deputy Director
Jamie Griffiths, Office Coordinator

AMOA was created when 68 jukebox owners from around the country banded together to fight the repeal of the jukebox royalty exemption. The modest beginning, created by a common cause, revealed a fierce passion-shared by many-about their business. Harnessing the collective strength, energy, knowledge and entrepreneurial spirit of a growing number of volunteer members, AMOA quickly established itself as a major force.
Founded in 1948

1528 **Association of College Unions International**
120 W Seventh Street
One City Centre, Suite 200
Bloomington, IN 47404

812-245-2284
Fax: 812-245-6710
E-Mail: acui@acui.org
Home Page: www.acui.org
Social Media: Facebook, Twitter, YouTube

Mark C. Guthier, President
Marsha Herman-Betzen, Executive Director
Elizabeth Beltramini, Content Curation Director
Martha J. Blood, Corporate Partnerships Director
Jason Cline, Director of Membership and Sales

The association is a non-profit organization and has member institutions in a number of countries. ACUI members work at and attend urban and rural campuses at both the two and four year levels and are dedicated to building community on campus through programs, services and publications with the common goal of unifying the union and activities fields.
1000 Members
Founded in 1914

1529 **Association of Zoos and Aquariums**
8403 Colesville Rd
Suite 710
Silver Spring, MD 20910-3314

301-562-0777
Fax: 301-562-0888
E-Mail: membership@aza.org
Home Page: www.aza.org
Social Media: Facebook, Twitter

Jackie Ogden, PhD, Chairman
Jim Maddy, President & CEO
Jill Nicoll, Senior Vice President, Marketing
Phil Wagner, Vice President of Finance
Steven Feldman, Senior Vice President

A nonprofit organization dedicated to the advancement of accredited zoos and aquariums in

the areas of animal care, wildlife conservation, education and science.
200 Members
Founded in 1924

1530 **Circus Fans Association of America**
2704 Marshall Avenue
Lorain, OH 44052-4315

360-452-1919
E-Mail: circusvern@aol.com
Home Page: www.circusfans.org

Donald Covington, President
Cheryl Deptula, Executive Secretary-Treasurer
Peter Wagner, President Elect
Connie Thomas, Central Vice President
Mort Gamble, Public Relations Director

Established to enjoy and preserve the circus as an institution. CFA offers you an opportunity interact with fellow circus enthusiasts in many ways. Local geographic groups (called TENTS) provide a chance for folks who live in the same geographic area to attend shows together and to meet to discuss the circus scene. State organizations (called TOPS) organize larger gatherings and special events.
Founded in 1926

1531 **Circus Historical Society**
3100 Parkside Lane
Williamsburg, VA 23185

757-259-0412
E-Mail: CircusHistoricalSociety@gmail.com
Home Page: www.circushistory.org
Social Media: Facebook

Judith Griffin, President
Bruce Hawley, Vice President
Robert Cline, Secretary/Treasurer
Chris Berry, Trustee
Maureen Brunsdale, Trustee

The Circus Historical Society, Inc. (CHS) is a tax-exempt, not-for-profit educational organization dedicated to recording the history of the American circus from the first one in Philadelphia during 1793 to today. Membership includes historians, scholars, circus personnel, memorabilia collectors, Americana specialists who share both a love of the circus and a desire to preserve and disseminate its great heritage.
1000 Members
Founded in 1939

1532 **Clowns of America International**
PO Box 112
Eustis, FL 32727

352-357-1676
877-816-6941
E-Mail: coaioffice@aol.com
Home Page: www.coai.org

Glenn Kohlberger, President
Michael B. Cox, Vice-President
Catherine Hardebeck, Secretary
Paddee Embrey, Treasurer
Merilynn Barrett, Sergeant-at-Arms

The purpose of Clowns of America International Website is to share, educate, and act as a gathering place for serious minded amateurs, semiprofessionals, and professional clowns. COAI provides its membership with necessary resources that allow them to further define and improve their individual clown character. Visitors who are interested in the clown arts will find a variety of resources that will stimulate their interest, foster their curiosity and offer pathways to valuable information.

1533 **Council for Amusement & Recreational Equipment Safety**
PO Box 8236
Des Moines, IO 50301-8236

617-727-3200
217-558-7194
E-Mail: doug.rathbun@illinois.gov
Home Page: www.caresofficials.org

James Borwey, President
Chad Halsey, 1st Vice President
D. Scott Narreau, 2nd Vice President
Mike Triplett, Secretary/Treasurer

CARES is a voluntary organization of chief government officials who are responsible for the enforcement of amusement ride and recreational equipment regulations within their jurisdiction. Fosters cooperation among regulatory officials and amusement equipment industries to promote public safety. CARES membership has grown to more than two dozen regulatory agencies in the United States and Canada, and includes the informal participation of the U.S. Consumer Product Safety.

1534 **Game Manufacturers Association**
240 North Fifth Street
Suite 340
Columbus, OH 43215

614-255-4500
Fax: 614-255-4499
E-Mail: ed@gama.org
Home Page: www.gama.org
Social Media: Facebook

Joann Gain, Retail Chair
Mike Webb, Distributor Chair
Rick Loomis, President
Jamie Chambers, Vice President
John Ward, Executive Director

The Game Manufacturers Association (GAMA) is the non-profit trade organization dedicated to serving the tabletop game industry. Strengthens and supports industry professionals by advancing their interests, providing educational programs and opportunities, and promoting their form of quality social entertainment. Led by publishers and manufacturers, GAMA promotes the interests of all persons involved in the commerce of games and game-related products.
450 Members
Founded in 1977

1535 **International Amusement & Leisure Defense Association**
PO Box 4563
Louisville, KY 40204

502-473-0956
Fax: 502-473-7352
E-Mail: info@ialda.org
Home Page: www.ialda.org
Social Media: LinkedIn

Bryon T Pope, President
John W Grund, Vice-President
Gaylee Gillim, Secretary
David Bennett, Treasurer
Michael Amaro, Member-at-Large

The International Amusement & Leisure Defense Association, Inc. is a non-profit association of lawyers and other professionals who are actively engaged in representing the interests of the amusement and leisure industries. IALDA members work closely with those in the amusement and water park industries as well as those involved in the bowling, roller skating, and other leisure industries.

1536 **International Association of Amusement Parks and Attractions (IAAPA)**
1448 Duke St
Alexandria, VA 22314-3403

703-836-4800
Fax: 703-836-6742
E-Mail: iaapa@iaapa.org
Home Page: www.iaapa.org

Will Morey, Chairman
Paul Noland, President and CEO
Susan Mosedale, Executive Vice President
Andrew Lee, Vice President
David Mandt, Vice President, Communications

A non-profit organization with a membership consisting of fixed-site enterainment and attractions facilities and suppliers. The association is dedicated to the preservation and prosperity of the amusement industry worldwide.
4100 Members
Founded in 1918

1537 **International Association of Fairs Expositions**
3043 East Cairo St.
PO Box 985
Springfield, MO 65802

417-862-5771
800-516-0313
Fax: 417-862-0156
E-Mail: iafe@fairsandexpos.com
Home Page: www.fairsandexpos.com
Social Media: Facebook, Twitter

Jim Tucker, President/CEO
Max Willis, CFO, COO, and Director of Meetings
Steve Siever, Director of Trade Shows, Membership
Maria Calico, Education Director
Rachel Mundenhenke, Technology Director

The International Association of Fairs and Expositions (IAFE) is a voluntary, non-profit corporation, serving state, provincial, regional, and county agricultural fairs, shows, exhibitions, and expositions. Its associate members include state and provincial associations of fairs, non-agricultural expositions and festivals, associations, corporations, and individuals engaged in providing products and services to its members, all of whom are interested in the improvement of fairs, and expositions.
1300 Members
Founded in 1885

1538 **International Association of Haunted Attractions**
1001 Greenbay Road
Winnetka, IL 60093

888-320-8494
Fax: 609-799-7032
E-Mail: admin@iahaweb.com
Home Page: www.iahaweb.com
Social Media: Facebook

Patrick Konopelski, President
Gene Schopf, Vice President
John Eslich, Treasurer
Brett Bertolino, Secretary
Lore Callahan, Board Member

The Haunted Attraction Association assists and advances the thriving haunt industry through communication, education, and information. Our worldwide network of members exchange ideas, information, experiences and concerns via our conferences, exclusive networking events, message boards, newsletters, magazines and more. HAA members have been featured on national television shows such as Good Morning America, the Today Show, and our attractions have been featured in national publications.
400 Members
Founded in 1998

1539 **International Brotherhood of Magicians**
13 Point West Blvd
St Charles, MO 63301-4431

636-724-2400
Fax: 636-724-8566
E-Mail: info@magician.org

Home Page: www.magician.org
Social Media: Facebook, Twitter, YouTube

Bill Evans, International President
Joe M. Turner, International Vice President
Donald E. Wiberg, International Secretary
Roger Miller, International Treasurer
Shawn Farquhar, International President-Elect

The International Brotherhood of Magicians is the world's largest organization dedicated to the art of magic, with members in 88 countries. Our official publication, The Linking Ring, has linked magicians throughout the world. Local branches of the I.B.M., known as Rings, meet each month in hundreds of locations. Our Annual Convention features top professional magicians in our spectacular evening shows.
12000 Members
Founded in 1922

1540 **International Festivals and Events Association (IFEA)**
2603 W Eastover Ter
Boise, ID 83706-2800

208-433-0950
Fax: 208-433-9812
E-Mail: nia@ifea.com
Home Page: www.ifea.com
Social Media: Facebook, Twitter

Bruce Erley, Chair
Steven Wood Schmader, CFEE, President & CEO
Nia Hovde, CFEE, Vice President/Director Marketing
Beth Peterson, Director of Membership Services
Craig Sarton, Creative & Publications Director

The IFEA exists to serve the needs of our entire industry, who produce and support quality celebrations for the benefit of their respective 'communities' and all those who share our core values of excellence & quality; the sharing of experience, knowledge, creativity and best practices; and the importance of 'community' building both locally and globally. Our success lies in the success of those we serve through professional education, programming, products and resources, and networking.
2000 Members
Founded in 1956
Mailing list available for rent

1541 **International Game Developers Association**
19 Mantua Road
Mt Royal, NJ 08061

856-423-2990
Fax: 856-423-3420
E-Mail: contact@igda.org
Home Page: www.igda.org
Social Media: Facebook, Twitter, LinkedIn, YouTube, Flickr, Kickstarter,

Dustin Clingman, Chair
Kate Edwards, Executive Director
Tristin Hightower, Operations Manager
Tom Buscaglia, Vice Chair
Sheri Rubin, Secretary

The International Game Developers Association is the largest non-profit membership organization serving individuals who create video games. We bring together developers at conferences, in local chapters and in special interest groups to improve their lives and craft. The IGDA is dedicated to improving developers' careers and lives through: Community, Professional Development, and Advocacy.
Founded in 1994

1542 **International Jugglers' Association**
PO Box 7307
Austin, TX 78713-7307

702-798-0099
Fax: 702-248-2550
E-Mail: memberships@juggle.org
Home Page: www.juggle.org

Erin Stephens, Chair
Art Jennings, Chairman Emeritus
Martin Frost, Communications Director
Kyle Johnson, Marketing Director
Marilyn Sullivan, Membership Director

An organization of individuals dedicated to promoting juggling.
Founded in 1947

1543 **International Laser Display Association**
7062 Edgeworth Drive
Orlando, FL 32819-2700

407-797-7654
Fax: 503-344-3770
E-Mail: mail@laserist.org
Home Page: www.laserist.org

Christine Jenkin, President
Patrick Murphy, ILDA Executive Director
Olga Eser, Vice President
Dan Goldsmith, Secretary
Alex Henning, Treasurer

The International Laser Display Association (ILDA) is the world's leading organization dedicated to advancing the use of laser displays in the fields of art, entertainment and education. Promotes the use of laser displays in the international marketplace through awards programs, publications, technology standards and a code of ethics. ILDA also represents the industry on safety issues and provides forums for members to exchange ideas, forge partnerships and explore.
Founded in 1986

1544 **International Laser Tag Association: ILTA**
5351 E Thompson Road
Suite 236
Indianapolis, IN 46237

317-786-9755
Fax: 317-786-9757
E-Mail: info@lasertag.org
Home Page: www.lasertag.org

Ryan McQuillen, Executive Director
Eric Gaizat, Membership Director

The International Laser Tag Association (ILTA) is the non-profit developer and operator association for the laser tag industry. Help members become better informed through our research, services, and communications with all levels of the industry. Since the creation of the ILTA, no other source has been more reliable for information about our industry. Assist members by providing them with the most accurate infor available to date.
350 Members
Founded in 1996

1545 **International Magicians Society**
581 Ellison Avenue
Westbury, NY 11590

516-333-2377
Fax: 516-333-0018
E-Mail: info@imsmagic.com
Home Page: www.magicims.com

Tony Hassini, Chairman/CEO
Anthony Emin, World President
Remington Scott, Creative Director
William H. Mellhany, Magic Historian
John M. Caluwaert, Legal Counsel

Promotes and preserves the art of magic. IMS helps create new magicians in order to pass the torch to the next generation of magicians.
37000 Members
Founded in 1968

1546 **International Ticketing Association**
Two Meridian Plaza
10401 N. Meridian St, Suite 300
Indianapolis, IN 46290

212-629-4036
Fax: 212-628-8532
E-Mail: info@intix.org
Home Page: www.intix.org
Social Media: Facebook, Twitter, LinkedIn, YouTube

Jena L Hoffman, President/CEO
Tiffany Kelham, Membership Associate
Jane, Pelletier, Meeting Manager
Dorothea Heck, Sales & Service Manager
Mary Leaton, Accounting Associate

The International Ticketing Association is a nonprofit membership organization committed to leading the forum for the entertainment ticketing industry. INTIX represents ticketing, sales, technology, finance, and marketing professionals who work in arts, sports, and entertainment as well as a full range of public venues and institutions. Members represent organizations from across the United States, Canada and 20 countries from around the globe.
1000 Members
Founded in 1980

1547 **National Association of Amusement Ride Safety Officials**
PO Box 638
Brandon, FL 33509-0638

813-661-2779
800-669-9053
Fax: 813-685-5117
E-Mail: naarsoanswerman@aol.com
Home Page: www.naarso.com

Jack S. Silar, Chairman and Membership Chairman
Clyde D Wagner, President
Jonathan R. Brooks, Vice President
Leonard Cavalier, Executive Director
John Pierce, Treasurer

NAARSO is dedicated to the advancement of amusement ride and device safety through the doctrine of Safety Through Communication. NAARSO is a non-profit organization that provides resources for amusement industry professionals dedicated to the safety of the industry and its patrons.
800 Members
Founded in 1987

1548 **National Association of Teachers of Singing**
9957 Moorings Dr
Suite 401
Jacksonville, FL 32257-2416

904-992-9101
Fax: 904-262-2587
E-Mail: info@nats.org
Home Page: www.nats.org
Social Media: Facebook, Twitter, LinkedIn, YouTube, Flickr, Pinterest

Kathryn Proctor Duax, President
Carole Blankenship, Vice President (NATSAA)
Anne Christopherson, Vice President (Membership)
Kathleen H. Arecchi, Vice President (Workshops)
Mitra Sadeghpour, Vice President Discretionary Funds

Encourages the highest standards of the vocal art and of ethical principals in the teaching of singing; and promote vocal education and research at all levels, both for the enrichment of the general public and for the professional advancement of the talented.
7000 Members
Founded in 1944

1549 **National Caves Association**
PO Box 625
Cobleskill, NY 12043

270-492-2228
Fax: 931-688-3988
E-Mail: info@cavern.com
Home Page: www.cavern.com
Social Media: Facebook

Susan Berdeaux, Executive Director

Nonprofit organization of publicly and privately owned show caves and caverns - caves developed for public visitation.
Founded in 1965

1550 **National Independent Concessionaires Association, Inc.**
1043 E. Brandon Blvd.
Brandon, FL 33511

813-438-8926
Fax: 813-438-8928
E-Mail: nica@nicainc.org
Home Page: www.nicainc.org
Social Media: Facebook, RSS Feeds

Tom Sattler, CCE, President
Joseph Potillo, Jr., 2nd Vice President
Alta Mosley, Executive Director
Rey O'Day, NICA West Executive Manager
Paulette Keene, Treasurer

Striving towards better communication between fairs, festivals and independent concessionaires nationwide.
1200 Members

1551 **National Recreation and Park Association**
22377 Belmont Ridge Road
Ashburn, VA 20148-4501

703-858-0784
800-626-6772
Fax: 703-858-0794
E-Mail: customerservice@nrpa.org
Home Page: www.nrpa.org
Social Media: Facebook, Twitter, LinkedIn, YouTube

Robert F. Ashcraft, Chairman/Executive Director
Barbara Tulipane, President/CEO
Ted Mattingly, Director, Facilities
Kevin Conley, Director Information Technology
David Wenner, Administrator

NRPA is the leading advocacy organization dedicated to the advancement of public parks and recreation opportunities. Advances parks, recreation and environmental conservation efforts that enhance the quality of life.
Founded in 1965

1552 **New England Association of Amusement Parks and Attractions**
200 Allens Avenue
Suite 7D
Providence, RI 02903

877-999-8740
Fax: 401-288-7616
E-Mail: secretary@neaapa.com
Home Page: www.neaapa.com

David Daly, President
Jason Freeman, 1st VP

NEAAPA is the premier regional association representing amusement parks, attractions, and their suppliers. NEAAPA works with its members on education opportunities, legislative and policy issues, as well as promotion of the Association's members.
Founded in 1912

1553 **Outdoor Amusement Business Association**
1035 S Semoran Blvd
Suite 1045A
Winter Park, FL 32792-5512

407-681-9444
800-517-6222
Fax: 407-681-9445
E-Mail: oaba@oaba.org
Home Page: www.oaba.org
Social Media: Facebook, Twitter, YouTube

Mike Featherston, Chairman
Robert W Johnson, President
Dee Dee Alford, Vice President
Al DeRusha, Senior Vice President
Brenda Ruiz, Administration

The OABA manages and influences concerns for its members. OABA believes that all business owners and members of the trade association should continue to raise the level of safety and quality in the mobile amusement industry.
4000 Members
Founded in 1964

1554 **PLASA**
630 Ninth Avenue
Suite 609
New York, NY 10036

212-244-1505
Fax: 212-244-1502
E-Mail: info@plasa.org
Home Page: www.plasa.org
Social Media: Facebook, Twitter

Ed Pagett, Chairman
Matthew Griffiths, Chief Executive Officer
Shane McGreevy, Chief Operating Officer and Finance
Lori Rubenstein, Director of Membership
Jackie Tien, Director of Media, Sales

PLASA is the lead international membership body for those who supply technologies and services to the event, entertainment and installation industries. As the worldwide voice for those who supply and service the entertainment, event and installation markets, PLASA will develop, promote, support and grow our industry.
550 Members

1555 **Roller Skating Association International**
6905 Corporate Dr
Indianapolis, IN 46278-1927

317-347-2626
Fax: 317-347-2636
E-Mail: rsa@rollerskating.com
Home Page: www.rollerskating.org
Social Media: Facebook, Twitter, LinkedIn, YouTube

Tina Robertson, President
Robert Housholder, Vice President
Jim McMaho, Executive Director
Tina Robertson, Director of Conventions
Lynette Rowland, Director of Communications, Editor

The Roller Skating Association (RSA) is a trade association that serves commercial (for-profit) skating center owner/operators. It also serves those involved in various facets of the roller related industry such as teachers, coaches, manufacturers, distributors and other elements of the family entertainment industry. Promotes the success of members through education and advancing the roller skating business.
1000 Members
Founded in 1937

1556 **Showmen's League of America**
1023 W. Fulton Market
Chicago, IL 60607

312-733-9533
800-350-9906
Fax: 312-733-9534
E-Mail: joeb@showmensleague.org
Home Page: www.showmensleague.org
Social Media: Facebook, Twitter

Chris Atkins, President
Dale Merriam, 1st Vice President
Paul Kasin, 2nd Vice President
Ron Porter, 3rd Vice President
Joe Burum, Executive Secretary

It seeks to promote the success of our members through education and advancing the roller skating business.elp those in need through one of its many programs.
Founded in 1913

1557 **Society of Broadcast Engineers**
9102 N Meridian St
Suite 150
Indianapolis, IN 46260-1896

317-846-9000
Fax: 317-846-9120
Home Page: www.sbe.org
Social Media: Facebook, Twitter, LinkedIn

Josephn Snelson, President
Jerry Massey, Vice President
John L Poray CAE, Executive Director
Megan Clappe, Certification Director
Debbie Hennessey, Executive Assistant/Advertising

Committed to serving broadcast engineers. From the studio operator to the maintenance engineer and the chief engineer to the vice president of engineering, SBE members come from commercial and non-commercial radio and television stations and cable facilities. A growing segment of members are engaging the industry on their own as consultants and contractors, field and sales engineers.
5500 Members
Founded in 1964
Mailing list available for rent: 5700 names at $170 per M

1558 **Society of Camera Operators**
PO Box 2006
Toluca Lake, CA 91610

818-563-9110
818-382-7070
E-Mail: info@soc.org
Home Page: www.soc.org

Chris Tufty, President
Mark August, Vice President
David Frederick, Vice President
Michael Scott, Vice President
Douglas Knapp, Treasurer

Advances the art and creative contribution of the operating cameraman in the Motion Picture and Television Industries. The Society serves the purpose of bringing into the closest confederation Industry leaders in their fields.
Founded in 1978

1559 **Tennessee Department of Agriculture, Market Development Division**
Tennessee Department of Agriculture
440 Hogan Road
PO Box 40627
Nashville, TN 37204

615-837-5160
800-342-8206
Fax: 615-837-5194
E-Mail: pick.tn@tn.gov
Home Page: www.picktnproducts.org
Social Media: Facebook, Twitter

Ed Harlan, Assistant Commissioner
Debbie Ball, Director of Marketing

Nelson Owen, Livestock Grading/Market News
Erica Alexander, TAEP Producer
Diversification Coor
Art Colebank, Digital Media Specialist

US and Canadian representatives of state/provincial agencies that are responsible for the support of educational and agricultural fairs.
35 Members
Founded in 1966

1560 **Themed Entertainment Association**
150 East Olive Avenue
Suite 306
Burbank, CA 91502-1850

818-843-8497
Fax: 818-843-8477
E-Mail: info@teaconnect.org
Home Page: www.teaconnect.org
Social Media: Facebook, LinkedIn

Christine Kerr, President
Alexander Bresinsky, Vice President
Steve Birket, Treasurer
Louie Allen, Member
Scott Ault, Member

The Themed Entertainment Association (TEA) is an international non-profit association representing the world's leading creators, developers, designers and producers of compelling places and experiences.

1561 **Western Fairs Association**
1776 Tribute Rd
Suite 210
Sacramento, CA 95815-4495

916-927-3100
Fax: 916-927-6397
E-Mail: stephenc@fairsnet.org
Home Page: www.fairsnet.org
Social Media: Facebook, Twitter, YouTube

Kent Hojem, President
Pat Kress, Vice President
Stephen J Chambers, Executive Director
Louie A. Brown, Fairs Alliance Advocate
Lori Hanley, Communications Manager

Western Fairs Association (WFA) serves the fair industry throughout the Western United States and Canada. Assists in maintaining the highest professional standards within the fair industry through a voluntary network of individuals and organizations. Promotes the prosperity of fairs through education and training programs.
2000 Members
Founded in 1922

1562 **World Waterpark Association**
8826 Santa Fe Drive
Suite 310
Overland Park, KS 66212-3676

913-599-0300
Fax: 913-599-0520
E-Mail: wwamemberinfo@waterparks.org
Home Page: www.waterparks.org

Jim Basala, Chair
Rick Root, President
Kelly Harris, Director of Operations
Aleatha Ezra, Director of Park Member Development
Patty Miller, Director of Tradeshows

Provides forum for exchange of ideas related to the water amusement park industry.
1000 Members
Founded in 1981

Newsletters

1563 **ACE News**
American Coaster Enthusiasts
1100-H Brandywine Boulevard
Zanesville, OH 43701-7303

740-450-1560
Fax: 740-452-2552
E-Mail: info@aceonline.org
Home Page: www.aceonline.org

Lee Ann Draud, Publications Director
Mike Thompson, Editor
Dave Altman, President
Jerry Willard, Vice President
Susan Shick, Secretary

Up-to-date information about ACE, the events, roller coasters, and amusement parks.
20 Pages
Frequency: Bimonthly

1564 **Adams Gaming Report**
Casino City Press
95 Wells Ave
Newton, MA 02459-3299

617-332-2850
800-490-1715
Fax: 617-964-2280
E-Mail: customerservice@casinocitypress.com
Home Page: www.casinopromote.com

Michael A Corfman, CEO

Focuses on the gaming industry with nationwide coverage.
Cost: $149.00
Frequency: Monthly

1565 **Affaliate Connection**
International Festivals and Events Association
2603 W Eastover Ter
Boise, ID 83706-2800

208-433-0950
Fax: 208-433-9812
E-Mail: craig@ifea.com
Home Page: www.ifea.com

Steven Schmader, President
Nia Hovde, VP/Marketing
Craig Sarton, Creative &Publications Director
Bette Monteith, Director Of Finance

The IFEA newsletter provides information and news 24 hours a day, 7 days a week, keeping members, suppliers and affialiates up-to-date and current.
2000 Members
Circulation: 2,700
Founded in 1956
Mailing list available for rent: 20000 names at $235 per M

1566 **Celebrity Bulletin**
Celebrity Service
252 West 37th St
Suite 1204
New York, NY 10017-3632

212-757-7979
Fax: 212-582-7701
E-Mail: mark@celebrityservice.com
Home Page: www.celebrityservice.com

Mark Kerrigan, Manager
Nicole Bagley, COO
Nancy R. Bagley, President
Soroush Shehabi, CEO

A daily guide on the whereabouts and vital information of the famous. Includes celebrity contacts including agents, business managers, publicists, and record companies. Gives advanced notice of who's coming to town, what projects they're working on and how to get in touch with them. Features an International Page noting arrivals in cities worldwide.
Cost: $2245.00
4 Pages
Frequency: Daily
Founded in 1939

1567 **Connector**
Society of Broadcast Engineers
9102 N Meridian St
Suite 150
Indianapolis, IN 46260-1896

317-846-9000
Fax: 317-846-9120
Home Page: www.sbe.org

John L Poray CAE, Executive Director
Ralph Hogan, President
Joseph Snelson, Vice President
James Leifer, Secretary
Jerry Massey, Treasurer

To youth members and high schools across the country that have radio or television stations. Provides students with information on careers in broadcast engineering, post-secondary education, high school student stations, scholarships and technical information.
Frequency: 3x/Year
Circulation: 300

1568 **Entertainment Marketing Letter**
EPM Communications
19 W.21st St, # 303
New York, NY 10012-3208
212-941-0099
888-852-9467
Fax: 212-941-1622
E-Mail: info@epmcom.com
Home Page: www.epmcom.com

Ira Mayer, Owner
Michele Khan, Marketing
Terence Keegan, Editor

Covers marketing techniques used in the entertainment industry, and by others who link their goods and services marketing through entertainment properties.
Cost: $449.00
Frequency: 24x Year
ISSN: 1048-5112
Printed in on matte stock

1569 **INTIX e-Newsletter**
330 W 38th Street
Suite 605
New York, NY 10018

212-629-4036
Fax: 212-629-8532
E-Mail: info@intix.org
Home Page: www.intix.org

Jena L Hoffman, President/CEO
Kathleen O'Donnell, Deputy Director
Kevin McDonnell, Sales Manager
Mary Leaton, Accounting Associate
Tiffany Kelham, Membership Associate

E-mail bulletin which includes news from the association, promotions, replacements, clips from industry news sources; vendor updates, conferences and exhibitions, the latest job postings, and listings of members searching for a job.
Frequency: Monthly

1570 **SBE-News**
Society of Broadcast Engineers
9102 N Meridian St
Suite 150
Indianapolis, IN 46260-1896

317-846-9000
Fax: 317-846-9120
Home Page: www.sbe.org

John L Poray CAE, Executive Director
Ralph Hogan, President
Joseph Snelson, Vice President
James Leifer, Secretary
Jerry Massey, Treasurer

Email subscription of timely news and updates sent from the National Office.
Frequency: Semimonthly
Circulation: 4,000

1571 **Signal**
Society of Broadcast Engineers
9102 N Meridian St
Suite 150
Indianapolis, IN 46260-1896

317-846-9000
Fax: 317-846-9120
Home Page: www.sbe.org

John L Poray CAE, Executive Director
Ralph Hogan, President
Joseph Snelson, Vice President
James Leifer, Secretary
Jerry Massey, Treasurer

Provides members with timely articles on various broadcast-related topics, information on upcoming events, recognition of members' activities and achievements and details of SBE services.
Frequency: Bimonthly
Circulation: 5,500

Magazines & Journals

1572 **Amusement Business**
VNU Business Media
49 Music Sq W
Suite 300
Nashville, TN 37203-3213

615-321-4251
888-900-3782
Fax: 615-327-1575
E-Mail: mshear@amusementbusiness.com
Home Page: www.amusementbusiness.com

Michael Marchesano, President/CEO
Karen Oertley, Publisher
James Zoltak, Editor
Lisa Krugel, Classified Ad Manager

Serves the management of more than 10,000 mass entertainment and amusement facilities.
Cost: $129.00
Frequency: Monthly
Founded in 1894

1573 **Amusement Today**
Amusement Today
2012 E Randol Mill Rd
Suite 203
Arlington, TX 76011-8222

817-460-7220
Fax: 817-265-6397
E-Mail: gslade@amusementtoday.com
Home Page: www.amusementtoday.com

Gary Slade, Publisher
Bill Rea, Director
Sammy Piccola, Accounting/Circulation
Sue Nicholas, Advertising

Keeps decision makers in the amusement industry up-to-date with current events, business, international developments and new attractions at amusement parks and waterparks.
Cost: $50.00
Frequency: Monthly
Circulation: 36000
Mailing list available for rent: 3000 names

1574 **Balloons and Parties**
PartiLife Publications
65 Sussex Street
Hackensack, NJ 07601

201-441-4224
Fax: 201-342-8118
E-Mail: info@balloonsandparties.com
Home Page: www.balloonsandparties.com
Social Media: Facebook, Twitter

Andrea P Zettler, Editor
Janet Slowik, Director

A decorating resource offering tips and suggestions for parties, special occasions, holidays, banquets and events. Targeted, informative and practical ideas for the event decorating industry. Motivates readers to produce professional, innovative party services.
Cost: $9.95
2 Members
Frequency: 4x/Year
Circulation: 7000
Founded in 1986
Printed in 4 colors on glossy stock

1575 **Bandwagon**
Circus Historical Society
3100 Parkside Lane
Williamsburg, VA 23185

757-259-0412
E-Mail: rfsabia@widomaker.com
Home Page: www.circushistory.org

Judith L. Griffin, President
Neil C. Cockerline, Vice President
Robert Cline, Secretary/Treasurer

Publishes articles relating to circus history.
Cost: $5.00
Frequency: Bimonthly
Founded in 1939

1576 **Baseline**
Ziff Davis Media
28 E 28th St
Suite 1
New York, NY 10016-7914

212-503-3500
Fax: 212-503-5696
E-Mail: baseline@ziffdavisenterprise.com
Home Page: www.ziffdavis.com

Jason Young, CEO
Eileen Feretic, Editor
Stephanie McCarthy, Marketing

Publication that offers practical information and guidance on the management of information technology.
Cost: $205.00
Frequency: Monthly
Circulation: 125100

1577 **Billboard Magazine**
Prometheus Global Media
770 Broadwaye Blvd.
New York, NY 10003-9595

212-493-4100
Fax: 646-654-5368
Home Page: www.prometheusgm.com
Social Media: Facebook, Twitter

Richard D. Beckman, CEO
James A. Finkelstein, Chairman
Madeline Krakowsky, Vice President Circulation
Tracy Brater, Executive Director Creative Service

Packed with in-depth music and entertainment features including the latest in new media and digital music, global coverage, music and money, touring, new artists, radio news and retail reports.
Cost: $149.00
Frequency: Weekly
Founded in 1894

1578 **BoxOffice Magazine**
BoxOffice Media
9107 Wilshire Blvd.
Suite 450
Beverly Hills, CA 90210-4241

310-876-9090
Home Page: www.boxoffice.com

Peter Crane, Publisher
Kenneth James Bacon, Creative Director
Phil Contrino, Editor
Amy Nicholson, Editor

The premier trade magazine covering the latest developments in the movie industry, from films in production to digital cinema and everything in between.
Founded in 1948

1579 **Camera Operator**
Society of Camera Operators
PO Box 2006
Toluca Lake, CA 91610

818-382-7070
Fax: 323-856-9155
E-Mail: camopmag@soc.org
Home Page: www.soc.org

Chris Tufty, President
Steve Fracol, Vice President
Dan Turrett, Treasurer
Dan Gold, Recording Secretary

Features articles written by and about SOC members, presented from the camera operator's point of view. Encompassing the latest technological trends while reviewing historical productions, the Camera Operator seeks to enlighten and educate readers on the motion picture, television and commerical industries.
Cost: $20.00
Frequency: Semi-Annual
Printed in 4 colors

1580 **Carnival Magazine**
PO Box 4138
Salisbury, NC 28145-4138

704-638-0878
Fax: 704-636-1051
E-Mail: vicky@carnivalmag.com
Home Page: www.carnivalmag.com

Charles Dabbs, Publisher
Kevin Freese, Editor

Chronicles contemporary outdoor amusement history providing readers with information and news on carnivals, events, people, trade shows, manufacturers, suppliers and more.
Cost: $40.00
Frequency: Monthly

1581 **Carousel News and Trader**
11001 Peoria Street
Sun Valley, CA 91352

818-332-7944
Fax: 818-332-7944
E-Mail: roland@carouselnews.com
Home Page: www.carouselnews.com

Dan Horenberger, Publisher
Roland Hopkins, Editor
Ted McDonald, Webmaster

Articles devoted to the collecting, restoration and selling of carousel art.
Cost: $35.00
48 Pages
Frequency: Monthly
Founded in 1985

1582 **Casino Journal**
BNP Media
2401 W Big Beaver Rd
Suite 700
Troy, MI 48084-3333

248-362-3700
Fax: 248-332-0317

E-Mail: davidsonl@bnpmedia.com
Home Page: www.bnp.com

Taggert Henderson, CEO
Marian Green, Editor
Lynn Davidson, Marketing

A primary information source for the key decision makers in the worldwide casino, lottery, parimutuel, bingo and emerging internet wagering markets.
Frequency: Monthly
Circulation: 13034
Founded in 1995

1583 Connect Magazine
8403 Colesville Rd
Suite 710
Silver Spring, MD 20910-6331

301-562-0777
Fax: 301-562-0888
E-Mail: membership@aza.org
Home Page: www.aza.org
Social Media: Facebook, Twitter

Jim Maddy, President & CEO
Kris Vehrs JD, Executive Director
Jill Nicoll, SVP, Marketing & Corp Strategies
Laura Benson, SVP, Finance & Administration

Your window to the professional zoo and aquarium world. Each month, the magazine features fascinating stories that explore trends, educational initiatives, member achievements and conservation efforts.
200 Members
Founded in 1924

1584 Daily Variety
5900 Wilshire Blvd
Suite 3100
Los Angeles, CA 90036-7209

323-617-9100
Fax: 323-965-5375
E-Mail: dana.harris@variety.com
Home Page: www.variety.com

Jay Penske, President
Abe Burns, Marketing
Millie Chiavelli, Managing Director
Steve Gaydos, Executive Editor
Paula Taylor, Creative Director

Focuses on film, television, video, cable, music and theater. Includes coverage of financial, regulatory and legal matters pertaining to the entertainment industry.
Cost: $329.00
Frequency: Daily
Circulation: 38248

1585 Entertainment, Publishing and the Arts Handbook
Thomson West Publishing
610 Opperman Dr
St Paul, MN 55123-1340

651-687-7000
800-344-5008
Fax: 651-687-5581
Home Page: www.west.thomson.com

Charles B Cater, Executive VP
Laurie Zenner, VP

Provides information on the latest development in the expanding legal field of entertainment, publishing, and the arts. The articles focus on such issues as books, copyrights, right-of-publicity and more.
Cost: $538.00
Frequency: Annual

1586 Fair Dealer
Western Fairs Association
1776 Tribute Rd
Suite 210
Sacramento, CA 95815-4495

916-927-3100
Fax: 916-927-6397
E-Mail: stephenc@fairsnet.org
Home Page: www.fairsnet.org

Stephen J Chambers, Executive Director
Jon Baker, VP
Nichole Farley, Marketing

Offers information for fairground owners, managers and workers, fair related businesses.
Cost: $35.00
2000 Members
Frequency: Quarterly
Circulation: 1500
Founded in 1922
Printed in on glossy stock

1587 Fairs & Expos
International Association of Fairs & Expositions
3043 E Cairo
PO Box 985
Springfield, MO 65802

417-862-5771
800-516-0313
Fax: 417-862-0156
E-Mail: iafe@fairsandexpos.com
Home Page: www.fairsandexpos.com

Jim Tucker, President
Steve Siever, Director
Max Willis, CFO
Marla Calico, Director Of Education
Rachel Mundhenke, Director Of technology

The source for information on fair trends, innovative ideas, and association activities.
Circulation: 3250
Founded in 1885
Printed in 4 colors on glossy stock

1588 Hollywood Reporter
Prometheus Global Media
770 Broadway
New York, NY 10003-9595

212-493-4100
Fax: 646-654-5368
Home Page: www.prometheusgm.com
Social Media: Facebook, Twitter, YouTube

Richard D. Beckman, CEO
James A. Finkelstein, Chairman
Madeline Krakowsky, Vice President Circulation
Tracy Brater, Executive Director Creative Service

Gives fresh ideas for film and TV. Covers the full spectrum of craft and commerce in the entertainment industry.
Cost: $199.00
Frequency: Weekly
Circulation: 34770

1589 Inside Arts
Association of Performing Arts Presenters
1211 Connecticut Ave NW
Suite 200
Washington, DC 20036-2716

202-833-2787
888-820-2787
Fax: 202-833-1543
E-Mail: editor@artspresenters.org
Home Page: www.artspresenters.org

Mario Durham, President
Sean Handerhan, Marketing
Alicia Anstead, Editor
Margaret Stevens, Director
Laura Benson, Programme Manager

This publication explores issues critical to the performing arts, presenting and touring field.
Cost: $42.00
1900 Members
Frequency: Bi-Monthly
Founded in 1957
Printed in 4 colors

1590 International Gaming and Wagering Business
BNP Media
PO Box 1080
Skokie, IL 60076-9785

847-763-9534
Fax: 847-763-9538
E-Mail: igwb@halldata.com
Home Page: www.igwb.com

James Rutherford, Editor
Lynn Davidson, Marketing
Tammie Gizicki, Director

Focuses on business strategy, legislative information, food service and promotional concerns.
Frequency: Monthly
Circulation: 25000

1591 JUGGLE
International Jugglers' Association
3315 E Russell Road
Suite 203
Las Vegas, NV 89120

702-798-0099
Fax: 709-248-2550
E-Mail: editor@juggle.org
Home Page: www.juggle.org

Alan Howard, Editor
Scott Krause, Treasurer
Marilyn Sullivan, Membership Director
Martin Frost, Store Manager
Dave Pawson, Chair

Offers readers a variety of colorful articles and features on the art of juggling including interviews, a listing of jugggling clubs, upcoming events and more.
Cost: $30.00
Frequency: Quarterly
Founded in 1947

1592 Journal of Leisure Research
22377 Belmont Ridge Road
Ashburn, VA 20148

703-858-0784
800-626-6772
Fax: 703-858-0794
E-Mail: customerservice@nrpa.org
Home Page: www.nrpa.org
Social Media: Facebook, Twitter, LinkedIn, YouTube

Jodie H Adams, President
Jessica Lytle, Director
John Crosby, Marketing

Advancing parks, recreation and environmental conservation efforts that enhance the quality of life for all people.
Founded in 1965

1593 Journal of Physical Education, Recreation & Dance (JOPERD)
1900 Association Dr
Reston, VA 20191-1502

703-476-3400
800-213-7193
Fax: 703-476-9527
E-Mail: info@aahperd.org
Home Page: www.aahperd.org
Social Media: Facebook, Twitter, YouTube

Monica Mize, President
Judith C Young, VP
Paula Kun, Marketing

Provides a variety of information on health, physical education, recreation, and dance issues than any other publication in the field.
25000 Members
Founded in 1885

1594 Journal of Singing
National Association of Teachers of Singing

9957 Moorings Dr
Suite 401
Jacksonville, FL 32257-2416

904-992-9101
Fax: 904-262-2587
E-Mail: info@nats.org
Home Page: www.nats.org

Richard Dale Sjoerdsma, Editor-in-Chief

Provides current information regarding the teaching of singing as well as results of recent research in the field. A refereed journal, it serves as a historical record and is a venue for teachers of singing and other scholars to share the results of their work in areas such as history, diction, voice science, medicine, and especially voice pedagogy.
Frequency: 5x times/year

1595 **Laserist**
International Laser Display Association
7062 Edgeworth Drive
Orlando, FL 32819

407-797-7654
Fax: 503-344-3770
E-Mail: president@laserist.org
Home Page: www.laserist.org

Christine Jenkin, President
Patrick Murphy, Executive Director

Providing the latest news about the art and technology of laser displays.
Frequency: Quarterly
Founded in 1986
Printed in 4 colors

1596 **Linking Ring Magazine**
International Brotherhood of Magicians
11155 S Towne Square
Suite C
St Louis, MO 63123

314-845-9200
Fax: 314-845-9220
E-Mail: info@magician.org
Home Page: www.magician.org

Joan Pye, President
Shawn Farquhar, VP
Don Wiberg, Secretary
Roger Miller, Treasurer

Keeps IBM members informed about what's happening in the world of magic.
13000 Members
Frequency: Monthly
Founded in 1922

1597 **Magic-Unity-Might: MUM Magazine**
Society of American Magicians
7566 John Avenue
PO Box 510260
Saint Louis, MO 63129

314-846-5659
Fax: 314-846-5659
E-Mail: webmaster@magicsam.com
Home Page: www.magicsam.com

John Apperson, President
David Goodsell, National Secretary
Marlene Clark, National Secretary

You will find articles dealing with the business of magic, publicity, showmanship and the history of magic and the lives of famous magicians. Many of the creative minds in the business are regular contributors.
60 Pages
Frequency: Monthly
Circulation: 30,000
Founded in 1902

1598 **NRPA Express**
22377 Belmont Ridge Road
Ashburn, VA 20148

703-858-0784
800-626-6772
Fax: 703-858-0794
E-Mail: customerservice@nrpa.org
Home Page: www.nrpa.org
Social Media: Facebook, Twitter, LinkedIn, YouTube

Jodie H Adams, President
Jessica Lytle, Director
John Crosby, Marketing

Membership publication delivering the latest news and information about upcoming events, research projects, educational opportunities, grants, and initiatives about NRPA and the parks and recreation community.
Founded in 1965

1599 **New Calliope**
Clowns of America International
PO Box C
Richeyville, PA 15358-0532

724-938-8765
888-522-5696
Fax: 724-938-8765
Home Page: www.coai.org

Tom King, President
Pamela Bacher, VP

Contains informative articles regarding the art of clowning, such as make-up, costuming, props, skit development, etc. News of regional and local clown alley activities; resources for your clowning needs; information on the annual international conventions; information on the various regional conventions through the year.
Frequency: Bi-Monthly

1600 **Park & Rec Trades**
Trades Publishing Company
20 Our Way Dr
Crossville, TN 38555-5790

931-484-8819
Fax: 931-484-8825
E-Mail: subscribe@thetrades.com
Home Page: www.parktrades.com

Tim Wilson, Owner
Kristie Irvin, Marketing

Event calendar and buying guides for amusement and recreation park professionals.
Frequency: Monthly
Circulation: 32000
Printed in 4 colors on newsprint stock

1601 **Parks and Recreation Magazine**
National Recreation and Park Association
22377 Belmont Ridge Road
Ashburn, VA 20148

703-858-0784
Fax: 703-858-0794
E-Mail: info@nrpa.org
Home Page: www.nrpa.org

Douglas Vaira, Editor
Jessica Lytle, Director
John Crosby, Marketing
Barbara Tulipane, President
Michele White, Executive Assistant

NRPA's magazine keeps members informed about parks, recreation and envrionmental conservation efforts.
Circulation: Monthly
Founded in 1965

1602 **Play Meter**
Skybird Publishing Company
PO Box 337
Metairie, LA 70004-0337

504-488-7003
888-473-2376
Fax: 504-488-7083
E-Mail: news@playmeter.com
Home Page: www.playmeter.com

Bonnie Theard, Editor

Trade publication that provides members with information on the coin-operated entertainment industry, including upcoming trade shows, new products, ongoing trends and more.
Cost: $60.00
Frequency: Monthly
Circulation: 60000
Founded in 1974

1603 **Pollstar: Concert Hotwire**
4697 W Jacquelyn Ave
Fresno, CA 93722-6443

559-271-7900
Fax: 559-271-7979
E-Mail: info@pollstar.com
Home Page: www.pollstar.com

Gary Smith, COO
Shari Rice, VP
Gary Bongiovanni, CEO

Trade publication for the concert industry offering global coverage and information including concert tour schedules, ticket sales information and more.
Cost: $449.00
Frequency: Weekly
Circulation: 20000
Printed in 4 colors

1604 **Protocol**
Entertainment Services and Technology Association
875 Sixth Avenue
Suite 1005
New York, NY 10001

212-244-1505
Fax: 212-244-1502
E-Mail: info@esta.org
Home Page: www.esta.org

Beverly Inglesby, Editor
Lori Rubinstein, Executive Director
Bill Groener, President

Featuring columns and articles of interest to professionals in the entertainment technology industry on business and technical topics, current standards issues, certification developments, and trade shows.
550 Members
Frequency: Quarterly
Printed in 4 colors

1605 **RePlay Magazine**
PO Box 572829
Tarzana, CA 91357-7004

818-776-2880
Fax: 818-776-2888
E-Mail: editor@replaymag.com
Home Page: www.replaymag.com

Edward Adlum, Owner
Barry Zweben, Marketing

A trade publication for those within the coin-operated amusement machine industry, primarily distributors, manufacturers and operators of jukeboxes and games.
Cost: $65.00
Frequency: Monthly
Circulation: 36000
ISSN: 1534-2328
Founded in 1975
Printed in 4 colors on glossy stock

1606 **Research Quarterly for Exercise and Sport (RQES)**
1900 Association Dr
Reston, VA 20191-1502

703-476-3400
800-213-7193
Fax: 703-476-9527
E-Mail: info@aahperd.org

Home Page: www.aahperd.org
Social Media: Facebook, Twitter, YouTube

Monica Mize, President
Judith C Young, VP
Paula Kun, Marketing

Publishes research in the art and science of human movement that contributes to the knowledge and development of theory either as new information, reviews, substantiation or contradiction of previous findings, or as application of new or improved techniques.
25000 Members
Founded in 1885

1607 Rollercoaster!
American Coaster Enthusiasts
1100-H Brandywine Boulevard
Zanesville, OH 43701-7303

740-450-1560
Fax: 740-452-2552
E-Mail: info@aceonline.org
Home Page: www.aceonline.org

Dave Altman, President
Jerry Willard, VP
Paul Blick, Events Director

Magazine featuring in-depth articles of parks and coasters of the past along with profiles of today's coaster, parks, people, and places.
7000 Members
Founded in 1978

1608 Souvenirs, Gifts & Novelties Magazine
10 E Athens Avenue
Suite 208
Ardmore, PA 19003

610-645-6940
Fax: 610-645-6943
E-Mail: sgnmag@kanec.com
Home Page: www.sgnmag.com

Scott C Borowsky, President
Tony DeMasi, Editor

Trade magazine for the resort-gift, souvenir industry. Articles cover merchandising trends, profile successful operations, new products, trade show calendar, plus buyer's guide issue.
Cost: $40.00
Circulation: 42,362
Printed in 4 colors on glossy stock

1609 Strategies: A Journal for Physical and Sport Educators
1900 Association Dr
Reston, VA 20191-1502

703-476-3400
800-213-7193
Fax: 703-476-9527
E-Mail: info@aahperd.org
Home Page: www.aahperd.org
Social Media: Facebook, Twitter, YouTube

Monica Mize, President
Judith C Young, VP
Paula Kun, Marketing

Delivers practical ideas, how-to information, and tips for sport and physical educators.
25000 Members
Founded in 1885

1610 The Bulletin
120 W Seventh Street
One City Centre, Suite 200
Bloomington, IN 47404

812-245-2284
Fax: 812-245-6710
E-Mail: acui@acui.org
Home Page: www.acui.org
Social Media: Facebook, Twitter, YouTube

Rich Steele, President
Marsha Herman-Betzen, Executive Director
Andrea Langeveld, Marketing

Features everything from research analyses to best practices to practical reports about trends in the field.
1000 Members
Founded in 1914

1611 The New Calliope
PO Box 1171
Englewood, FL 34295-1171

941-474-4351
877-816-6941
Home Page: www.coai.org

Pamela Bacher, President
Michael B. Cox, Vice-President
Catherine Hardebeck, Secretary
Candyce Will, Treasurer

Contains informative articles regarding the art of clowning such as; makeup, costuming, props, skit development, etc. News of regional and local clown alley activities, resources for your clowning needs, information on the annual international convention, and information on various regional conventions through the year.

1612 Therapeutic Recreation Journal
22377 Belmont Ridge Road
Ashburn, VA 20148

703-858-0784
800-626-6772
Fax: 703-858-0794
E-Mail: customerservice@nrpa.org
Home Page: www.nrpa.org
Social Media: Facebook, Twitter, LinkedIn, YouTube

Jodie H Adams, President
Jessica Lytle, Director
John Crosby, Marketing

Advancing parks, recreation and environmental conservation efforts that enhance the quality of life for all people.
Founded in 1965

1613 Tourist Attractions & Parks
10 E Athens Avenue
Suite 208
Ardmore, PA 19003

610-645-6940
Fax: 610-645-6943
E-Mail: tapmag@kanec.com
Home Page: www.tapmag.com
Social Media: Facebook, Twitter

Scott C Borosky, President/Ex Editor
Caroline Burns, Managing Editor
Larry White, Publisher
Kittey White, Account Executive
Laurie O'Malley, Account Executive

Trade magazine for amusement, national & waterparks, zoos, and aquariums, bowling, skating + family entertainment centers, forest festivals.
Cost: $49.00
28124 Members
Circulation: 31,388
Founded in 1972

1614 Vending Times
Vending Times
55 Maple Avenue
Suite 102
Rockville Centre, NY 11570

212-302-4700
Fax: 212-221-3311
Home Page: www.vendingtimes.com

Alicia Lavay, President/Publisher
Nick Montano, VP/Executive Editor
Tim Sanford, Editor-in-Chief
Maria Ackies, Production Manager

Addresses the business, legal, legislative and regulatory concerns of companies providing industrial, institutional and public vending, refreshment, feeding and recreational services
Cost: $40.00
Frequency: Monthly
Circulation: 16,000
Founded in 1962

1615 White Tops
Circus Fans Association of America
1515 S Butler Street
Port Angeles, WA 98363

360-452-1919
E-Mail: feedback@circusfan.org
Home Page: www.circusfans.org

Vern Mendonca, President

Articles about the illustrious history of circus, including the greatest performers, famous acts and feats, logistical facts and figures, management and marketing, and the shows of yesteryear.
Circulation: 2000
Founded in 1926

Trade Shows

1616 ACE Coaster Con
American Coaster Enthusiasts
1100-H Brandywine Boulevard
Zanesville, OH 43701-7303

740-450-1560
Fax: 740-452-2552
E-Mail: info@aceonline.org
Home Page: www.aceonline.org

Dave Altman, President
Jerry Willard, VP
Susan Shick, Secretary
Cheri Armstrong, Treasurer
David Lipnicky, Public Relation Director

An annual convention, a great opportunity for fellow ACEers to gather together to ride coasters.
7000 Attendees
Frequency: Annual
Founded in 1978

1617 ACUI Conference
Association of College Unions International
120 W 7th Street
One City Centre, Suite 200
Bloomington, IN 47404-3925

812-245-ACUI
Fax: 812-245-6710
E-Mail: acui@acui.org
Home Page: www.acui.org

Michelle Smith, Director, Educational Prgms & Svcs
Marsha Herman, Executive Director
Tim Arth, Event and Corporate Sales Manager
Karen Keith, Financial Service Manager
Julie Sylvester, Office Administrator

Tours and outings, peer learning network, leadership meetings, orientation for new members, education sessions, seminars, networking fair, keynote speakers.
Frequency: Annual
Founded in 1914

1618 AIMS International Safety Seminar
Amusement Industry Manufacturers & Suppliers Intl
3026 S Orange
Santa Ana, CA 92707

714-425-5747
Fax: 714-276-9666
E-Mail: info@aimsintl.org
Home Page: www.aimsintl.org

Brian D King, President

This AIMS event is a comprehensive week of hands-on instruction taught by today's top in-

dustry professionals, for individuals responsible for the care and safety of the amusement industry's guests. Certification testing also available.
Frequency: January

1619 APAP Conference
Association of Performing Arts Presenters
1211 Connecticut Avenue NW
Suite 200
Washington, DC 20036
202-833-2787
888-717-APAP
Fax: 202-833-1543
E-Mail: info@apapconference.org
Home Page: www.apapconference.org
Sandra Gibson, President
Sean Handerhan, Marketing
Leah Yoon, Director
Judy Moore, Conference Manager
Providing valuable networking resources and opportunities for performing arts presenters, artists and artist managers throughout the world. Hundreds of exhibitors and performances: see who is doing what in the world of performing arts. Educational tracks are offered; special events; special interests; and clinics.
1900 Members
4000 Attendees
Frequency: January
Founded in 1957

1620 Amusement Expo
American Amusement Machine Association
450 E. Higgins Road
Suite 201
Elk Grove Village, IL 60007-1417
847-290-9088
866-372-5190
Fax: 847-290-9121
E-Mail: information@coin-op.org
Home Page: www.coin-op.org
Social Media: Facebook, Twitter, LinkedIn
John Schultz, President
Tina Schwartz, Business and Finance Manager
John Margold, Chairman
Frank Consentino, Secretary
Rich Babich, Treasurer
Featuring the latest in video games, digital-jukeboxes, dartboards, redemption games, plush toys, smart cards and more, as well as educational programs and seminars.

1621 Amusement Industry Expo
I-X Center
One I-X Center Drive
Cleveland, OH 44135
216-676-6000
800-897-3942
Fax: 216-265-2621
E-Mail: info@ixamusementpark.com
Home Page: www.ixcenter.com
John O'Brien, Director
Supplies and products for the amusement industry.
4100 Attendees
Frequency: March/April

1622 Amusement Showcase International: ASI
William T Glasgow Inc
10729 W 163rd Place
Orland Park, IL 60467
708-226-1300
Fax: 708-226-1310
E-Mail: info@asi-show.com
Home Page: www.asi-show.com
William T Glasgow, Executive Director
Features exhibits and seminars for the coin-operated amusement industry.
4000 Attendees
Frequency: Annual/March

1623 Amusement and Music Operators Association International Expo
William T Glasgow Inc
10729 W 163rd Place
Orland Park, IL 60467
708-226-1300
Fax: 708-226-1310
E-Mail: info@amoashow.com
Home Page: www.amoashow.com
William T Glasgow, Executive Director
The AMOA International Expo is designed for professionals from the amusement, music and vending industries.
8000 Attendees
Frequency: Annual/September
Founded in 1948

1624 BPAA Convention
PO Box 4563
Louisville, KY 40204
502-473-0956
Fax: 502-473-7352
E-Mail: info@ialda.org
Home Page: www.ialda.org
Lambert J. Hassinger, Jr., President
Bryan T. Pope, Vice-President
Nonprofit association of lawyers and other professionals who are actively engaged in representing the interests of the amusement and leisure industries.

1625 Broadcast Engineering Conference (BEC)
Society of Broadcast Engineers
9102 N Meridian Street
Suite 150
Indianapolis, IN 46260
317-846-9000
Fax: 317-846-9120
Home Page: www.sbe.org
John L Poray CAE, Executive Director
Vincent A Lopez CEV, CBNT, President
Held in conjunction with the National Association of Broadcasters, features SBE Ennes Workshop followed by sessions covering the latest in broadcast technology.
500 Attendees
Frequency: Annual/Spring
Mailing list available for rent: 4700 names

1626 COAI Annual Spring International Convention
Clowns of America International
PO Box C
Richeyville, PA 15358-0532
724-938-8765
888-522-5696
Fax: 724-938-8765
Home Page: www.coai.org
Glenn Kohlberger, President
Michael Cox, VP
Catherine Hardebeck, Secretary
Padee Embrey, Treasurer
The purpose of these conventions is to provide educational seminars, competitions for individuals and group skits, make up and costume competitions, as well as competitions in balloons and parade ability.
Frequency: Annual/Spring

1627 COAI Convention
PO Box 1171
Englewood, FL 34295-1171
941-474-4351
877-816-6941
Home Page: www.coai.org
Pamela Bacher, President
Michael B. Cox, Vice-President
Catherine Hardebeck, Secretary
Candyce Will, Treasurer
Offering classes, shows and competitions, theme party and banquet.

1628 CinemaCon
National Association of Theatre Owners
750 1st St NE
Suite 1130
Washington, DC 20002-4241
202-962-0054
Fax: 202-962-0370
Home Page: www.cinemacon.com
Social Media: Facebook
Mitch Neuhauser, Managing Director
A gathering of cinema owners and operators.
4000 Members
3500 Attendees
Frequency: Annual/March/ Las Vegas
Founded in 2010

1629 CoasterCon
American Coaster Enthusiasts
1100-H Brandywine Boulevard
Zanesville, OH 43701-7303
740-450-1560
Fax: 740-452-2552
E-Mail: info@aceonline.org
Home Page: www.aceonline.org
Dave Altman, President
Jerry Willard, VP
Susan Shick, Secretary
Cheri Armstrong, Treasurer
David Lipnicky, Public Relation Director
The flagship event of American Coaster.
Frequency: Annual/June

1630 Digital Out-of-Home Interactive Entertainment Conference (DNA)
450 E Higgins Rd
Suite 201
Elk Grove Vlg, IL 60007-1417
847-290-9088
866-372-5190
Fax: 847-290-9121
E-Mail: information@coin-op.org
Home Page: www.coin-op.org
Social Media: Facebook, Twitter, LinkedIn
John Schultz, President
Tina Schwartz, Business & Finance Manager
David Cohen, Chairman
Frank Consentino, Secretary
John Margold, Treasurer
Six dedicated sessions that speak directly to the industry and new opportunities, with a leading selection of speakers with direct experience in the sector and its future.
Founded in 1981

1631 Fun Expo
William T Glasgow
10729 W 163rd Place
Orland Park, IL 60467
708-226-1300
Fax: 708-226-1310
E-Mail: info@funexpo.com
Home Page: www.funexpo.com
William T Glasgow, Executive Director
Devoted to the family and location based entertainment industry and the trends that drive it. A focused and efficient event bringing buyers and

sellers together in an atmosphere that allows industry professionals to conduct business.
Frequency: Annual/March

1632 **GAMA Trade Show**
Game Manufacturers Association
240 N.Fifth St
Suite 340
Columbus, OH 43215

614-255-4500
Fax: 614-255-4499
E-Mail: ops@gama.org
Home Page: www.gama.org

John Ward, Executive Director
John Kaufeld, Marketing/Sales
Rick Loomis, President
Jamie Chambers, Vice President
Aaron Witten, Treasurer

For retailers, manufacturers, and industry professionals to network, see the newest products, and learn from others about ways to make their stores and businesses successful.
15000 Attendees

1633 **IAAPA Attractions Expo**
1035 S Semoran Blvd
Suite 1045A
Winter Park, FL 32792-5512

407-681-9444
800-517-6222
Fax: 407-681-9445
E-Mail: oaba@aol.com
Home Page: www.oaba.org
Social Media: Facebook, Twitter, YouTube

Robert W Johnson, President
Al DeRusha, VP
Anita Rockett, Director

The OABA manages and influences concerns for its members. OABA believes that all business owners and members of the trade association should continue to raise the level of safety and quality in the mobile amusement industry.
4000 Members
Founded in 1964

1634 **IAFE Annual Convention**
3043 East Cairo St.
PO Box 985
Springfield, MO 65802

417-862-5771
800-516-0313
Fax: 417-862-0156
E-Mail: iafe@fairsandexpos.com
Home Page: www.fairsandexpos.com
Social Media: Facebook, Twitter

Jim Tucker, President
Steve Siever, Director

The International Association of Fairs and Expositions (IAFE) is a voluntary, non-profit corporation whose members provide services and products that promote the overall development and improvement of fairs, shows, expositions, and allied fields.
1300 Members
Founded in 1885

1635 **IFEA Annual Convention & Expo**
International Festivals and Events Association
2603 W Eastover Terrace
Boise, ID 83706

208-433-0950
Fax: 208-433-9812
E-Mail: schmader@ifea.com
Home Page: www.ifea.com

Steven Wood Schmader, President
Nia Forster, VP/Marketing
Shauna Spencer, Director
Bette Monteith, Director Of Finance
Beth Petersen, Director Of Membership Services

Unites the world's leading festivals and events, suppliers, media, sponsors and related industry professionals to share information on every aspect of event production through in depth workshops, round table discussions and networking.
2000 Members
Frequency: Annual/Sept
Founded in 1956
Mailing list available for rent: 20000 names at $235 per M

1636 **IISF Trade Show**
1035 S Semoran Blvd
Suite 1045A
Winter Park, FL 32792-5512

407-681-9444
800-517-6222
Fax: 407-681-9445
E-Mail: oaba@aol.com
Home Page: www.oaba.org
Social Media: Facebook, Twitter, YouTube

Robert W Johnson, President
Al DeRusha, VP
Anita Rockett, Director

The OABA manages and influences concerns for its members. OABA believes that all business owners and members of the trade association should continue to raise the level of safety and quality in the mobile amusement industry.
4000 Members
Founded in 1964

1637 **ILDA Conference**
International Laser Display Association
7062 Edgeworth Drive
Orlando, FL 32819

407-797-7654
Fax: 503-344-3770
E-Mail: president@laserist.org
Home Page: www.laserist.org

Christine Jenkin, President
Patrick Murphy, Executive Director

One of the world's largest exhibitions of entertainment technology. Features international exhibitors from the fields of lighting, lasers, audio, video and staging.
70000 Attendees
Founded in 1986

1638 **INTIX Annual Conference & Exhibition**
INTIX
330 W 38th Street
Suite 605
New York, NY 10018

212-629-4036
Fax: 212-629-8532
E-Mail: info@intix.org
Home Page: www.intix.org

Jena L Hoffman, President
Kathleen O'Donnell, Deputy Director
Kevin McMacdonnell, Sales Manager

Combines educational workshops, committee and business meetings, networking and social events. Every major supplier serving he entertainment ticketing industry is represented at the exhibition. Launch new products and conduct user meetings for existing clients
Frequency: January

1639 **International Association of Amusement Parks and Attractions Expo**
Int'l Association of Amusement Parks & Attractions
1448 Duke Street
Alexandria, VA 22314

703-836-4800
Fax: 703-836-4801
Home Page: www.iaapa.org

Chip Cleary, President/CEO
Susan Mosedale, Executive VP
Jan MacCool, Executive Assistant

Features diverese entertainment exhibitions from high tech, to games, rides, food and beverage and much more. IAAPA showcases products and services for amusement parks, water parks, family entertainment centers, zoos, aquariums, museums — any company in the business of entertainment.
30M Attendees
Frequency: Annual/Nov
Founded in 1918

1640 **International Association of Fairs and Expositions Annual Convention**
International Association of Fairs & Expositions
3043 E Cairo
PO Box 985
Springfield, MO 65802

417-862-5771
800-516-0313
Fax: 417-862-0156
E-Mail: iafe@fairsandexpos.com
Home Page: www.fairsandexpos.com

Jim Tucker, President
Steve Siever, Director
Max Willis, CFO
Marla Calico, Director Of Education
Rachel Mundhenke, Director Of Technology

Largest event serving fairs and expositions. Convention attendees are able to network and learn from each other during the intensive four days of workshops, special seminars, and round table discussions. Companies showcase themselves while serving as a one-stop shop for all of a fair's booking, product, and service needs.
5000 Attendees
Frequency: Nov

1641 **International Brotherhood of Magicians Annual Convention**
International Brotherhood of Magicians
11155 S Towne Square
Suite C
St Louis, MO 63123

314-845-9200
Fax: 314-845-9220
E-Mail: info@magician.org
Home Page: www.magician.org

John Pye, President
Shawn Farquhar, VP
Jack White, Marketing
Don Wiberg, Secretary
Roger Miller, Treasurer

A place where members can meet and network with others sharing an interest in the art of magic.
13000 Members
Frequency: July
Founded in 1922

1642 **International Ticketing Association Annual Conference & Exhibition**
330 W 38th Street
Suite 605
New York, NY 10018

212-629-4036
Fax: 212-628-8532
E-Mail: info@intix.org
Home Page: www.intix.org

Social Media: Facebook, Twitter, LinkedIn, YouTube

Jena L Hoffman, President/CEO
Kathleen O'Donnell, Deputy Director

Non-profit association committed to the improvement, progress and advancement of ticket management. Provides educational programs, trade shows, conducts surveys, conference proceedings, and its valuable membership directory.
1000 Members
Founded in 1979

1643 Laser Tag Convention
International Laser Tag Association
5351 E Thompson Road
Suite 236
Indianapolis, IN 46237

317-786-9755
Fax: 317-786-9757
E-Mail: info@lasertag.org
Home Page: www.lasertag.org

Shane Zimmerman, Executive Director

The source for all things laser tag. Co-located with the Roller Skating Trade Show, this provides an opportunity to meet suppliers and manufacturers of laser tag equipment, video games, kitchen equipment and more.
Frequency: May

1644 Laughter Works
Laughter Works Seminars
PO Box 1220
Folsom, CA 95763-1220

916-985-6570
E-Mail: info@laughterworks.com
Home Page: www.laughterworks.com

Jim Pelley, President

Seminars and keynote speeches on humor, create positive team environment, unleash creativity and enhance productivity in the workplace.

1645 NATS National Conference
National Association of Teachers of Singing
9957 Moorings Dr
Suite 401
Jacksonville, FL 32257-2416

904-992-9101
Fax: 904-262-2587
E-Mail: info@nats.org
Home Page: www.nats.org

Allen Henderson, Executive Director
Deborah L Guess, Director of Operations
Tom Strother, Marketing & Communication
Elizabeth Zettler, Program Administrator
Frequency: June/July

1646 National Recreation and Park Association's Congress and Exposition
National Recreation and Park Association
22377 Belmont Ridge Road
Ashburn, VA 20148

703-858-0784
Fax: 703-858-0794
E-Mail: info@nrpa.org
Home Page: www.nrpa.org

Britt Esen, Director
Jodie H Adams, President
John Crosby, Marketing

Education and training opportunity plus a tradeshow for the park and recreation industry.
4000 Attendees
Frequency: October
Founded in 1965

1647 OABA Annual Meeting & Chairman's Reception
Outdoor Amusement Business Association
1035 S Semoran Blvd
Suite 1045A
Winter Park, FL 32792-5512

407-681-9444
800-517-6222
Fax: 407-681-9445
E-Mail: oaba@oaba.org
Home Page: www.oaba.org
Social Media: Facebook, Twitter, YouTube

Bill Johnson, Chairman
Jeanne McDonagh, 1st Vice Chair
Rober Johnson, President

The OABA manages and influences concerns for its members. OABA believes that all business owners and members of the trade association should continue to raise the level of safety and quality in the mobile amusement industry.
4000 Members
Founded in 1965

1648 Origins Game Fair
280 N High Street
Suite 230
Columbus, OH 43215

614-255-4500
Fax: 614-255-4499
E-Mail: ops@gama.org
Home Page: www.gama.org
Social Media: Facebook

John Ward, Executive Director
John Kaufeld, Marketing/Sales
Rick Loomis, President

A non-profit trade association dedicated to the advancement of the tabletop game industry
450 Members
Founded in 1977

1649 Pinball Expo
Pinball Expo
3869 Niles Road SE
Warren, OH 44484

330-369-1192
800-323-3547
Fax: 330-369-6279
E-Mail: brkpinball@aol.com
Home Page: www.pinballexpo.org

Robert Berk, Expo Chairman
Mike Pacak, Co-Expo Chairman

Annual show of manufacturers and related suppliers of pinball machines and supplies; tournaments and tours with over 50 exhibitors.
1,000 Attendees
Frequency: October

1650 RSA Convention and Trade Show
Roller Skating Association International
6905 Corporate Drive
Indianapolis, IN 46278

317-347-2626
Fax: 317-347-2636
E-Mail: rsa@rollerskating.com
Home Page: www.rollerskating.org

Bobby Braun, President
Ron Liette, VP
John Purcell, Executive Director

Helping roller skating industry professionals discover ways to build strong foundations for their businesses.
1000 Members
Frequency: Annual/August
Founded in 1937

1651 SLA Annual Meeting & Convention
Showmen's League of America
1023 W Fulton Market
Chicago, IL 60607

312-733-9533
800-350-9906
Fax: 312-733-9534
E-Mail: joeb@showmensleague.org
Home Page: www.showmensleague.org
Social Media: Twitter

Sam Johnston, President
Chris Atkins, 1st Vice President
Ron Porter, 2nd Vice President
Joe Burum, Executive Secretary
John Hanschen, Treasurer

Promotes friendship and fellowship between its members and the outdoor amusement industry, and pledges to help those in need through one of its many programs.
Founded in 1913

1652 World Waterpark Association Annual Tradeshow
World Waterpark Association
8826 Santa Fe Drive
Suite 310
Overland Park, KS 66212

913-599-0300
Fax: 913-599-0520
E-Mail: aezra@waterparks.org
Home Page: www.waterparks.org

Rick Root, President
Patty Miller, Director
Aleatha Ezra, Marketing

Exhibits include waterpark attractions, water quality equipment and apparel, with more than 300 booths.
1000 Members
2600 Attendees
Frequency: October
Founded in 1981

Directories & Databases

1653 American Casino Guide
Casino Vacations
PO Box 703
Dania, FL 33004-0703

954-989-2766
800-741-1596
Fax: 954-966-7048
Home Page: www.americancasinoguide.com

Steve Bourie, Author

A guide to every casino/resort, riverboat and Indian casino in the United States.
Cost: $16.95
448 Pages
Frequency: Annually
ISBN: 1-883768-11-X
Founded in 1992
Printed in one color

1654 Association of Performing Arts Presenters Membership Directory
1211 Connecticut Ave NW
Suite 200
Washington, DC 20036-2716

202-833-2787
888-820-2787
Fax: 202-833-1543
E-Mail: info@artspresenters.org
Home Page: www.artspresenters.org

Sandra Gibson, President
Sean Handerhan, Marketing

An invaluable resource for members to keep in touch with colleagues. Puts more than 1,450 presenters, service organizations, artists, management consultants, and vendors at your fingertips. An excellent networking tool for everyone on your staff.
1900 Members
Frequency: Annual
Founded in 1957

1655 Cavalcade of Acts and Attractions
Amusement Business

49 Music Square W
Nashville, TN 37203-3213

615-321-4250
Fax: 615-327-1575
E-Mail: info@amusementbusiness.com
Home Page: www.amusementbusiness.com

James Zoltak, Editor
Tom Powell, Senior Editor
Julie Wood, Managing Editor

Directory of personal appearance artist (musical and theatrical), touring shows, carnivals and other specialized entertainment such as fireworks firms, rodeos, etc. Also contains listings of booking agents, personal managers, promoters and producers.
Cost: $89.00
350 Pages
Frequency: Annual/December
Circulation: 7,000

1656 **Celebrity Access Directory**
Celebrity Access
2430 Broadway St
Suite 200
Boulder, CO 80304-4118

303-350-1700
Fax: 303-339-6877
E-Mail: sales@celebrityaccess.com
Home Page: www.celebrityaccess.com

Peter Denholtz, President
Marc Gentilella, Editor
Keri Mullin, Marketing

Database directory of more than 35,000 performers that includes contact information for agents as well as links to websites, record companies, touring schedules, box office info and more.
Cost: $899.00
Frequency: Annual
Founded in 1998

1657 **Data List & Membership Directory**
Western Fairs Association
1776 Tribute Rd
Suite 210
Sacramento, CA 95815-4495

916-927-3100
Fax: 916-927-6397
E-Mail: stephenc@fairsnet.org
Home Page: www.fairsnet.org

Stephen J Chambers, Executive Director
Jon Baker, Vice President
Nichole Farley, Marketing

A premier source of fair industry information for the Western United States and Canada. Referred to as the Bible of the fair industry, this directory contains a complete listing of every member fair, festival, special event, fair-related business, fair association, and agriculture-related organization.
2000 Members
Frequency: Annual
Founded in 1922
Printed in on glossy stock

1658 **Dinner Theatre: A Survey and Directory**
Greenwood Publishing Group
88 Post Road W
PO Box 5007
Westport, CT 06881-5007

203-226-3571
800-225-5800
Fax: 203-222-1502
E-Mail: customer-service@greenwood.com
Home Page: www.greenwood.com

Debra Adams, Editor
Listings of dinner theaters, including in-depth profiles are offered in this comprehensive directory.
Cost: $82.95
160 Pages
Frequency: Hardcover
ISBN: 0-313284-42-3

1659 **Directory of Fairs, Festivals & Expositions**
Amusement Business
49 Music Square W
Nashville, TN 37203-3213

615-321-4250
Fax: 615-327-1575
Home Page: www.amusementbusiness.com

James Zoltak, Editor
Tom Powell, Senior Editor
Mike Barnes, Executive Editor
Julie Wood, Managing Editor

Directory of over 5,000 state and county fairs, festivals and public expositions in the U.S. and Canada which run for three days or more. Contains dates, booking information, demographics, and other details.
Cost: $79.00
350 Pages
Frequency: Annual/January
Circulation: 7,000

1660 **Directory of Funparks & Attractions**
Amusement Business
49 Music Square W
Nashville, TN 37203-3213

615-321-4250
Fax: 615-327-1575
Home Page: www.amusementbusiness.com

James Zoltak, Editor
Tom Powell, Senior Editor
Mike Barnes, Executive Editor
Julie Wood, Managing Editor

Guide to over 2,800 amusement/theme parks, water parks, tourist attractions, zoos, kiddielands and family entertainment centers worldwide.
Cost: $69.00
130 Pages
Frequency: Annual/March
Circulation: 8,000

1661 **Directory of Historic American Theatres**
Greenwood Publishing Group
88 Post Road W
PO Box 5007
Westport, CT 06881-5007

203-226-3571
800-225-5800
Fax: 203-222-1502
E-Mail: customer-service@greenwood.com
Home Page: www.greenwood.com

Debra Adams, Editor

Directory of theaters built before 1915.
Cost: $86.95
367 Pages
Frequency: Hardcover
ISBN: 0-313248-68-0

1662 **EPM Entertainment Marketing Sourcebook**
EPM Communications
19 W.21st St,# 303
3rd Floor
New York, NY 10012-3208

212-941-0099
888-852-9467
Fax: 212-941-1622
E-Mail: info@epmcom.com
Home Page: www.epmcom.com

Ira Mayer, Owner
Michele Khan, Marketing

Over 4,000 media companies, sponsors and retailers that provide products and services to entertainment marketers.
Cost: $95.00
278 Pages
Frequency: Annual
Printed in on matte stock

1663 **Grey House Performing Arts Directory**
Grey House Publishing
4919 Route 22
PO Box 56
Amenia, NY 12501

518-789-8700
800-562-2139
Fax: 845-373-6390
E-Mail: books@greyhouse.com
Home Page: www.greyhouse.com
Social Media: Facebook, Twitter

Leslie Mackenzie, Publisher
Richard Gottlieb, Editor

The most comprehensive resource covering the Performing Arts. This directory provides current information on over 8,500 dance companies, instrumental music programs, opera companies, choral groups, theater companies, performing arts series and performing arts facilities.
Cost: $185.00
1200 Pages
Frequency: Annual
ISBN: 1-592373-76-3
Founded in 1981

1664 **Grey House Performing Arts Directory - Online Database**
Grey House Publishing
4919 Route 22
PO Box 56
Amenia, NY 12501

518-789-8700
800-562-2139
Fax: 845-373-6390
E-Mail: gold@greyhouse.com
Home Page: www.gold.greyhouse.com
Social Media: Facebook, Twitter

Leslie Mackenzie, Publisher
Richard Gottlieb, President

The Grey House Performing Arts Directory - Online Database provides immediate access to dance companies, orchestras, opera companies, choral groups, theater companies, series, festivals and perfoming arts facilities across the country, or in their region, state, or in your own backyard. It offers unequaled coverage of the Performing Arts - over 8,500 listings - of the major performance organization, facilities, and information resources.
Frequency: Annual
Founded in 1981

1665 **IAAPA Directory & Buyers Guide**
Int'l Association of Amusement Parks & Attractions
1448 Duke St
Alexandria, VA 22314-3403

703-836-3677
Fax: 703-836-2824
E-Mail: iaapa@iaapa.org
Home Page: www.iaapa.org

Will Morey, Chairman
Marion Mamon, Vice Chair

Directory of amusement parks, the attraction industry and related topics.
Founded in 1918

1666 **International Amusement Industry Buyers Guide**
Amusement Business

49 Music Square W
Nashville, TN 37203-3213

615-321-4250
Fax: 615-327-1575
Home Page: www.amusementbusiness.com

James Zoltak, Editor
Tom Powell, Senior Editor
Mike Barnes, Executive Editor
Julie Wood, Managing Editor

Complete source book containing comprehensive listings of manufacturers, importers and suppliers of all types of rides, games and merchandise, plus food and drink equipment and suppliers.
Cost: $69.00
130 Pages
Frequency: Annual/October
Circulation: 8,000

1667 **SBE Membership Directory & Buyer's Guide**
Society of Broadcast Engineers
9102 N Meridian St
Suite 150
Indianapolis, IN 46260-1896

317-846-9000
Fax: 317-846-9120
Home Page: www.sbe.org

Ralph Hogan, President
Joseph Snelson, VP

Provides a quick reference to all members and Sustaining Members' services. Offers a yellow-page guide section that contains categorical listings of all SBE Substaining Members and advertisements from leading equipment and service suppliers.
Frequency: Annually
Circulation: 5,500

1668 **Travel and Entertaiment Policies and Procedures Guide**
Institute of Management & Administration
1 Washington Park
Suite 1300
Newark, NJ 07102

973-718-4700
Fax: 973-622-0595
E-Mail: rcochran@ioma.com
Home Page: www.ioma.com

Joe Bremner, President
Perry Patterson, VP
Andy Dzamba, Editor
James Bell, Marketing

The report offers tips and suggestions to improve T&E operations, information on reim bursement policies and benchmark data, current trends, and more.
Cost: $329.00
Frequency: Annual
Circulation: 185,000

1669 **Who's Who in Festivals and Events Membership Directory & Buyers Guide**
International Festivals and Events Association
2603 W Eastover Terrace
Boise, ID 83706-2800

208-433-0950
Fax: 208-433-9812
E-Mail: craig@ifea.com
Home Page: www.ifea.com

Steven Schmader, President
Nia Forster, VP/Marketing
Craig Sarton, Director

Membership directory list hundreds of festivals and vendor members.
2000 Members
2000 Pages
Founded in 1956
Mailing list available for rent: 2000 names at $235 per M

Industry Web Sites

1670 **http://gold.greyhouse.com**
G.O.L.D Grey House OnLine Databases

Grey House Publishing's online database platform, GOLD, provides Quick Search, Keyword Search and Expert Search for most business sectors, including amusement, entertainment and recreation markets. The GOLD platform makes finding the information you need quick and easy. All of Grey House's directory products are available for subscription on the GOLD platform.

1671 **www.aceonline.org**
American Coaster Enthusiasts

ACE is a non-profit organization with members across the United States that promotes the roller coaster industry through a varicty of events and publications.
7000 Members

1672 **www.acui.org**
Association of College Unions International

Nonprofit educational organization. Dedicated to building community on campus through programs, services and publications with the common goal of unifying the union and activities fields.

1673 **www.amoa.com**
Amusement and Music Operators Association

Providing leadership for the amusement, music, entertainment and vending industry. AMOA works vigorously to protect and promote industry interests. Members include operators, manufacturers, suppliers, distributors, and consultants.

1674 **www.cavern.com**
National Caves Association

Nonprofit organization of publicly and privately owned show caves and caverns developed for public visitation. Provides access to a directory of caves for those seeking out adventure, fun and education.

1675 **www.circushistory.org**
Circus Historical Society

The Circus Historical Society is a not-for-profit educational organization whose mission is to record the history of the American circus. Members have the opportunity to meet and network at circus conventions where there are presentations, films and more.

1676 **www.coin-op.org**
American Amusement Machine Association

Non-profit trade association representing the manufacturers, distributors and part suppliers to the coin-operated and out of home amusement industry.

1677 **www.fairsnet.org**
Western Fairs Association

A non-profit association with members throughout the Western United States and Canada that strives to promote industry standards. Membership includes access to conventions and trade shows, educational training programs, as well as legislative advocacy support.

1678 **www.greyhouse.com**
Grey House Publishing

Reference directories for most business sectors, including amusement, entertainment and recreation markets. Users can search the online databases with varied search criteria allowing for custom searches by product category, geographic area, sales volume, keyword, subject and more. Full Grey House catalog and online ordering also available.

1679 **www.iaapa.org**
International Association of Amusement Parks &
Attractions

An international trade association that seeks to improve and support professional industry standards at permanently situated amustement facilities worldwide.
4,500 Members

1680 **www.ifea.com**
International Festivals and Events Association

A voluntary association of events, event producers, event suppliers and related professionals and organizations whose common purpose is the production and presentation of festivals, events, and civic and private celebrations.

1681 **www.intix.org**
International Ticket Association

Not-for-profit association representing 22 countries worldwide. Committed to the improvement, progress and advancement of ticket management through educational programs, trade shows, conducts surveys, conference proceedings, and produces a membership directory.
1,200 Members

1682 **www.laserist.org**
International Laser Display Association

Dedicated to advancing the use of laser displays, in art, entertainment and education. ILDA supports high industry standards, promotes safety and provides the opportunity for members to meet and network at trade shows and conventions.

1683 **www.lastertag.org**
International Laser Tag Association: ILTA

The ILTA helps individuals and companies start or add a lasertag facility.

1684 **www.magicsam.com**
Society of American Magicians

Promote and maintain harmonious fellowship among those interested in magic as an art, improve ethics of the magical profession, and foster, promote and improve the advancement of magical arts in the field of amusement and entertainment. Membership includes professional and amateur magicians, manufacturers of magical apparatus and collectors.

1685 **www.merchandisegroup.com**
Nielsen Business Media's Merchandise Group ASD/AMD

Leading producer of trade shows and publications in the variety and general merchandise industry.

1686 **www.music-rights.com**
Ad Producer.com

Provides music rights providers with the highest quality platform to leverage the Web to market your services around the world around the clock.

1687 **www.natoonline.org**
National Association of Theatre Owners

Exhibition trade organization, representing more than 30,000 movie screens in all 50 states, and additional cinemas in 50 countries worldwide.

1688 www.nats.org
National Association of Teachers of Singing
Encourage the highest standards of the vocal art and of ethical principals in the teaching of singing; and promote vocal education and research at all levels, both for the enrichment of the general public and for the professional advancement of the talented.

1689 www.oaba.org
Outdoor Amusement Business Association
Promotes interest of the outdoor amusement industry. Provides members with public relations and safety services as well as it's monthly Show Time magazine and annual publication The Midway Marquee.
4,000 Members

1690 www.rollerskating.org
Roller Skating Association International
A trade association representing skating center owners, operators; teachers, coaches and judges of roller skating; and manufacturers and suppliers of roller skating equipment.

1691 www.sbe.org
Society of Broadcast Engineers
Professional organization of television and radio engineers and those in the related fields. SBE has members in 114 chapters across the United States and Hong Kong.

1692 www.toyassociation.org
Toy Industry Association
National organization for U.S. producers and importers of toys, games and children's entertainment products. Represents more than 500 member companies including designers, safety consultants, testing laboratories, licensors, communication professionals and inventors.

1693 www.waterparks.com
World Waterpark Association
Official Web site for the waterpark and water-leisure industries provides a comprehensive listing of waterparks around the world. It was developed and is maintained by the World Waterpark Association, the international organization created to further safety and business effectiveness in the waterpark industry.

Associations

1694 **American Apparel & Footwear Association (AAFA)**
American Apparel & Footwear Association
1601 N Kent Street
12th Floor
Arlington, VA 22209
703-524-1864
800-520-2262
Fax: 847-522-6741
E-Mail: mrhowell@apparelandfootwear.org
Home Page: www.wewear.org
Social Media: Facebook, Twitter, LinkedIn, YouTube

Philip C. Williamson, Chairman
Kevin M Burke, President/CEO
Stephen E Lamar, Executive Vice President
Suzanne Shomers, Vice President, Finance
Susan Lapetine, VP/Industry Relations

The American Apparel & Footwear Association (AAFA) is the national trade association representing apparel, footwear and other sewn products companies, and their suppliers which compete in the global market. AAFA's mission is to promote and enhance its members' competitiveness, productivity and profitability in the global market by minimizing regulatory, legal, commercial, political, and trade restraints.
Founded in 2000

1695 **American Cotton Shippers Association**
88 Union Ave
Suite 1204
Memphis, TN 38103-5150
901-525-2272
Fax: 901-527-8303
E-Mail: bmay@acsa-cotton.org
Home Page: www.acsa-cotton.org
Social Media: RSS Feeds

Eduardo Esteve, Chairman
William E May, President
Vaniece C. Boone, Vice President/Memphis Operations
Linda Colston, Administrative Assistant/Accounting
Laura Skillern, Bookkeeper

ACSA members are engaged in a great enterprise, the purchasing, storing, tansporting and merchandising of America's most valuable cash crop and it's most abundant natural fiber.
Founded in 1924

1696 **American Flock Association**
469 Hospital Drive
Suite C
Gastonia, NC 28054
617-303-6288
Fax: 704-671-2366
E-Mail: info@flocking.org
Home Page: www.flocking.org

Steve Rosenthal, Managing Director

AFA members include manufacturers of roll-to-roll coated textiles, papers, and films as well as coaters of three dimensional objects and printers of apparel decoration and graphics art products. Industry suppliers are a key sector of the membership. The AFA is affiliated with the National Textile Association, a non-profit trade organization representing over 150 textile manufacturers and industry suppliers with operations in the U.S., and Canada.

1697 **American Sewing Guild**
9660 Hillcroft St
Suite 510
Houston, TX 77096-3866
713-729-3000
Fax: 713-721-9230
Home Page: www.asg.org
Social Media: Facebook, Twitter, YouTube

Janelle Archer, Chairman
Helen De Roo, Secretary
Jodell Larkin, Treasurer

ASG is a membership organization that welcomes sewing enthusiasts of all skill levels. Chapters are located in cities all across the country and members meet monthly to learn new sewing skills, network with others who share an interest in sewing and participate in community service sewing projects.
20000 Members
Founded in 1993

1698 **Cashmere and Camel Hair Manufacturers Institute**
3 Post Office Square
8th Floor
Boston, MA 02110
617-542-7481
Fax: 617-542-2199
E-Mail: jlomas@cashmere.org
Home Page: www.cashmere.org

Karl Spilhaus, President

The Cashmere & Camel Hair Manufacturers Institute (CCMI) is an international trade association representing the interests of producers and manufacturers of camel hair and cashmere fiber, yarn, fabric and garments throughout the world.
25 Members
Founded in 1984

1699 **Chemical Fabrics and Film Association**
1300 Sumner Avenue
Cleveland, OH 44115-2851
216-241-7333
Fax: 216-241-0105
E-Mail: cffa@chemicalfabricsandfilm.com
Home Page: www.chemicalfabricsandfilm.com

Charles M Stockinger, Executive Secretary

International trade association representing manufacturers of polymer-based fabric and film products, used in the building and construction, automotive, fashion and many other industries.
40 Members
Founded in 1927

1700 **Color Association of the United States**
33 Whitehall Street
Suite M3
New York, NY 10004
212-947-7774
Fax: 212-594-6987
E-Mail: info@colorassociation.com
Home Page: www.colorassociation.com
Social Media: Facebook, Twitter, LinkedIn, YouTube, Pinterest, Instagram

Sherrie Donghia, Chairman
Marcella Echavarria, Interior/Forecast
Linda De Franco, Fashion/Forecast
Kelly Kovak, Beauty/Forecast
Sal Cesarani, Men's Fashion/Forecast

The Color Association of The United States creates and delivers global color intelligence across industries. The Color Association serves as premier forecast agent, specialized educator, and trusted advisor to color professionals whose responsibility is to ensure marketplace success for their color decisions in the realm of brands, product and service, and spatial environments.
Founded in 1915

1701 **Costume Designers Guild**
11969 Ventura Boulevard
First Floor
Studio City, CA 91604-3570
818-752-2400
Fax: 818-752-2402
E-Mail: cdgia@cdgia.com
Home Page: www.costumedesignersguild.com
Social Media: Facebook, Twitter

Terry Gordon, Secretary
Marilyn Matthews, Treasurer

The Costume Designers Guild (CDG) is Local 892 of the International Alliance of Theatrical and Stage Employees (I.A.T.S.E.). The Guild represents Costume Designers, Assistant Costume Designers and Costume Illustrators working at the highest levels of skill and expertise in motion pictures, television and commercials. The CDG promotes and protects the economic status of its members while improving working conditions and raising standards for our craft.
810 Members
Founded in 1953

1702 **Cotton Incorporated**
6399 Weston Pkwy
Cary, NC 27513
919-678-2272
Fax: 919-678-2235
Home Page: www.cottoninc.com
Social Media: Facebook, Twitter, Youtube, RSS Feeds

J. Berrye AnkenyWorsham, President and CEO
Michael Watson, VP of Fiber Competition
Kater D. Hake, Ph.D., Vice President Agriculture
Edward M. Barnes, Senior Director of Agriculture
Linda De Franco, Director of Product Trend Analysis

To ensure that cotton remains the first choice among consumers in apparel and home products, Cotton Incorporated helps companies manufacture, market, and sell cotton products more efficiently and more profitably.
Founded in 1970

1703 **Council of Fashion Designers of America**
65 Bleecker St
11th Floor
New York, NY 10012
212-302-1821
Fax: 212-768-0515
E-Mail: info@cfda.com
Home Page: www.cfda.com
Social Media: Facebook, Twitter, Youtube, Google+, Pinterest, T

Diane von Furstenberg, President
Steven Kolb, Chief Executive Officer
Steven Kolb, Executive Director
Lisa Smilor, Deputy Director

The CFDA's goals are: to further the position of fashion design as a recognized branch of American art and culture, advance its artistic and professional standards, establish and maintain a code of ethics and practices of mutual benefit in professional, public, and trade relations, and promote and improve public understanding and appreciation of the fashion arts through leadership in quality and taste.
250 Members
Founded in 1962

1704 **Custom Tailors and Designers Association of America**
42732 Ridgeway Drive
Broadlands, VA 20148

888-248-2832
Fax: 866-661-1240
E-Mail: info@ctda.com
Home Page: www.ctda.com

Ron Brodeur, President
Mark Metzger, 1st Vice President
Peter Roberti, 2nd Vice President
Jeff Landis, Treasurer
Paco Fernandez, Vice Treasurer

Established as a venue through which ideas and techniques for design, pattern making, fitting, cutting and tailoring could be shared and exchanged.
300 Members
Founded in 1880

1705 **Fashion Footwear Association of New York**
274 Madison Avenue
Suite 1701
New York, NY 10016

212-751-6422
Fax: 212-751-6404
E-Mail: info@ffany.org
Home Page: www.ffany.org
Social Media: Facebook, Twitter, Instagram, Pinterest

Scott Silverstein, Chairman
Joseph Moore, President/CEO
Phyllis Rein, Executive Vice President
Marie Lou Campo, Chief Financial Officer
Shelley Berquist, Senior Vice President, Operations

FFANY's mission is to promote and assist the common business interests of its members. FFANY is committed to supporting New York City as the recognized national center of fashion trade and commerce and aims to ensure the city continues to be the best venue for both national and international footwear industry events.
300 Members
Founded in 1980

1706 **Fashion Scholarship Fund**
31 W 34Th Street
9th Floor
New York, NY 10001

646-308-5213
Fax: 212-279-6241
E-Mail: hharrison@fashionscholarshipfund.org
Home Page: www.the-yma.com

Kenneth Wyse, Chairman
Paul Rosengard, Chairman Emeritus
Debra Malbin, Scholarship Chair
Jim Rosenfeld, President
Harry Harrison, Executive Director

The YMA Fashion Scholarship Fund(FSF) is a national association dedicated to promoting education of the fashion arts and business by granting scholarships to talented students and facilitating internships, mentorships and career programs.
800+ Members
Founded in 1941

1707 **Hosiery Association**
7421 Carmel Executive Park Drive
Suite 200
Charlotte, NC 28226

704-365-0913
Fax: 704-362-2056
E-Mail: thainfo@hosieryassociation.com
Home Page: www.hosieryassociation.com
Social Media: Facebook, Twitter, LinkedIn, Pinterest

Sally Kay, President/CEO
Sheila Simpson, Director/Finance
Vicki Camp, Office Manager

The Hosiery Association(THA) is the only international nonprofit trade association exclusively representing the specific needs of legwear companies that produce and sell more than 90 percent of the products in the US. Supplier companies to the industry also play a major role in membership and sponsorship of THA.
Founded in 1905

1708 **International Glove Association**
PO Box 146
Brookville, PA 15825

814-328-5208
Fax: 814-328-2308
E-Mail: gloves@windstream.net
Home Page: www.iga-online.com

Kim O'Leary, President
Brent Fidler, Vice President
Carol Burdge, Executive Director
Matt Reid, Member
Larry Garner, Member

Our mission is to further build an association that improves manufacturing and distribution of hand protection. Studying, clarifying, and recommending government action to help promote proper glove selection and use, and the interests of glove manufacturers and distributors, will help association members achieve success with customers and maintain a financially sound organization.
Founded in 2003

1709 **Leather Apparel Association**
19 W 21st Street
Suite 403
New York, NY 10010

212-727-1210
Fax: 212-727-1218
Home Page: www.leatherassociation.com

Morris Goldfarb, President
Richard Harrow, Executive Director
Fran Harrow, Marketing

Represents the nation's leading leather retailers, manufacturers, cleaners and other businesses in promoting leather apparel in the US.
Founded in 1990

1710 **National Luggage Dealers Association**
1817 Elmdale Avenue
Glenview, IL 60026

847-998-6869
Fax: 847-998-6884
E-Mail: inquiry@nlda.com
Home Page: www.nlda.com

Alex Shapiro, President
George Morri, CEO
Felicia Libbin, Marketing Director

The National Luggage Dealers Association (NLDA) improves the buying power of the many stores it represents, giving the individual store owners the ability to compete with larger companies and department stores. Many of the founding members continue to be represented today by successive generations of family members.
Founded in 1925

1711 **National NeedleArts Association**
1100-H Brandywine Boulevard
Zanesville, OH 43701-7303

740-455-6773
800-889-8662
Fax: 740-452-2552
E-Mail: info@tnna.org
Home Page: www.tnna.org
Social Media: Facebook, Twitter, LinkedIn

Dona Zimmerman, Chair & Board Representative
Dale Lenci, Board President
Beth Casey, Board Vice President
Barbara Bergstan, Director
Sharon Crescent, Director

TNNA is an international trade organization representing retailers, manufacturers, distributors, designers, manufacturers' representatives, publishers, teachers and wholesalers of products and supplies for the specialty needlearts market. These businesses create and market hand painted needlepoint canvases, hand-dyed and specialty crochet and knitting yarns, embroidery, needlepoint and cross-stitch materials, kits, tools and more.
2650 Members
Founded in 1975

1712 **North American Association of Uniform Manufacturers & Distributors**
6800 Jericho Turnpike
Suite 120W
Syosset, NY 11791

516-393-5838
Fax: 516-393-5878
E-Mail: rjlerman@naumd.com
Home Page: www.naumd.com

Steve Robinson, Chairman
Richard J Lerman, President & CEO
Jackie Rosselli, Director of Communications
Jim Tewmey, Vice Chair
Brian Garry, Treasurer

The North-American Association of Uniform Manufacturers & Distributors (NAUMD) is a trade association representing the interests of all parties in the uniform & image apparel industry.
450+ Members
Founded in 1933

1713 **Private Label Manufacturers Association**
630 Third Avenue
New York, NY 10017-6506

212-972-3131
Fax: 212-983-1382
E-Mail: info@plma.com
Home Page: www.plma.com

John Shields, Former Chairman & CEO
Myra Rosen, VP

PLMA has steadily grown in size, reflecting the increasing importance of store brands to retailers and consumers. As you will see, PLMA member services have mirrored store brands new role in the marketplace, too.
3200+ Members
Founded in 1979

1714 **The Knitting Guild Association (TKGA)**
1100-H Brandywine Boulevard
Zanesville, OH 43701-7303

740-452-4541
Fax: 740-452-2552
E-Mail: tkga@tkga.com
Home Page: www.tkga.com
Social Media: Facebook, Twitter, Pinterest

Penny Sitler, Executive Director

Membership organization for knitters with focus on knitting education and enhancing knitters skills. TKGA seeks to advance creativity, knowledge and the quality of workmanship in knitting through education and communication.
11000 Members
Founded in 1984

1715 **The Vision Council of America**
Sunglass and Reader Division
225 Reinekers Lane
Suite 700
Alexandria, VA 22314-2846

703-548-4560
866-826-0290
Fax: 703-548-4580
E-Mail: info@thevisioncouncil.org
Home Page: www.thevisioncouncil.org
Social Media: Facebook, Twitter, YouTube

Ed Greene, Chief Executive Officer
Maureen Beddis, Vice President of Marketing
Deborah Malakoff-Castor, Vice President of Shows
Greg Chavez, Vice President of Member Services
Brian Carroll, Chief Operating Officer

Serving as the global voice for vision care products and services, The Vision Council represents the manufacturers and suppliers of the optical industry. We position our members to be successful in a competitive marketplace through education, advocacy, consumer outreach, strategic relationship building and industry forums.
263 Members
Founded in 1999

1716 **Tri-State Linen Supply Association**
1800 Diagonal Rd
Suite 200
Alexandria, VA 22314-2842

703-519-0029
877-770-9274
Fax: 703-519-0026
E-Mail: trsa@trsa.org
Home Page: www.trsa.org
Social Media: Facebook, Twitter, LinkedIn, YouTube, RSS Feeds

Roger Cocivera, President/CEO
George Ferencz, VP

Provides hygienic sustainable laundering services that offer cost-effective, energy-efficient solutions while protecting the environment and employing hundreds of thousands of individuals in highly safety-conscious workplaces nationwide.
1400 Members
Founded in 1913

1717 **Uniform Code Council**
Princeton Pike Corporate Center
1009 Lenox Drive Suite 202
Lawrenceville, NJ 08648

609-620-0200
Fax: 609-620-1200
Home Page: www.gs1us.org

W. Rodney McMullen, Chairman
Bob Carpenter, President and CEO
Laura DiSciullo, Senior Vice President, Solutions
Bernie Hogan, Senior Vice President
Yegneswaran Kumar, Senior Vice President

Barcodes, eCommerce and data synchronization, to EPC/RFID and business process automation standards.
Frequency: Members 280,000
Founded in 1974

1718 **Unite Here International Union**
275 Seventh Avenue
New York, NY 10001-6708

212-265-7000
Fax: 212-265-3415
E-Mail: ccarrera@unitehere.org
Home Page: www.unitehere.org
Social Media: Facebook, Twitter, Google+, RSS Feeds

D. Taylor, President
Tho Thi Do, General VP, Immigration
Sherri Chiesa, Secretary/Treasurer
Peter Ward, Recording Secretary

UNITE HERE represents workers throughout the U.S. and Canada who work in the hotel, gaming, food service, manufacturing, textile, distribution, laundry, and airport industries.
850k Members
Founded in 2004

1719 **Western and English Sales Association**
451 E 58th Avenue
Suite 4128
Denver, CO 80216

303-295-1040
800-295-1041
Fax: 303-295-0941
E-Mail: info@denver-wesa.com
Home Page: www.denver-wesa.com
Social Media: Facebook

Gene House, Chairman
Mark Broughton, President
Scott Piper, Vice President
Gerald Adame, Treasurer
Jay Phillips, Secretary

WESA began under the corporate name Men's Apparel Club of Colorado. The goal was to create a forum where retailers, manufacturers, and sales representatives could conduct business in an atmosphere of fair trade and fellowship.
1200 Members
Founded in 1921

Newsletters

1720 **AAFA Newsletter**
American Apparel & Footwear Association
1601 N Kent Street
Suite 1200
Arlington, VA 22209

703-524-1864
800-520-2262
Fax: 847-522-6741
Home Page: www.apparelandfootwear.org

Kevin M Burke, President
Stephen E Lamar, VP
Scott Elmore, Marketing

The nationwide trade association representing apparel, footwear and other sewn products companies and their suppliers which compete in the global market.
Founded in 2000

1721 **Barbara's View/Shopping Guides**
Barbara's View
PO Box 531006
Miami, FL 33153-1006

305-757-7638
Fax: 305-756-5353
E-Mail: barbara@barbarasview.com
Home Page: www.barbarasview.com

Barbara Wexner Levy, President

Shopping guides for fashion cities around the world.
Cost: $18.00
Frequency: Monthly
Founded in 1976

1722 **Clothing Manufacturers Association of the USA**
Clothing Manufacturers Association of the USA
770 Broadway
10th Floor
New York, NY 10003-9559

646-654-5000
Fax: 646-654-5001

David L Calhoun, CEO

Statistical report on profit sales, production and marketing trends for the men's and boy's tailored clothing industry.
Cost: $30.00
Frequency: Annual
Circulation: 300
Founded in 1933
Mailing list available for rent: 100 names at $200 per M

1723 **DNR-Daily News Record**
Fairchild Publications
7 W 34th St
New York, NY 10001-8100
212-630-3880
800-360-1700
Fax: 212-630-3868
E-Mail: info@dnrnews.com
Home Page: www.dnrnews.com

Samuel Farrel, President/CEO
John Birmingham, Editor-in-Chief
Jim Rossi, Marketing
Don Miller, Circulation Manager
Tom Beebe, Creative Director

Supplies retail fashion, product merchandising and marketing news for men's and boys' fashion.
Cost: $85.00
Frequency: Weekly
Circulation: 15755

1724 **International Association of Clothing Designers & Executives Newsletter**
475 Park Avenue South
Floor 9 No. 9
New York, NY 10016-6901

212-685-6602
E-Mail: newyorkiacde@cox.net
Home Page: www.iacde.com

Joachim Hensch, President
Mina Henry, Director

1725 **The Vision Voice**
The Vision Council Of America
225 Reinekers Lane
Suite 700
Alexandria, VA 22314

703-548-4560
866-826-0290
Fax: 703-548-4580
E-Mail: info@thevisioncouncil.org
Home Page: www.thevisioncouncil.org
Social Media: Facebook, Twitter

Ed Greene, CEO
Brian Carroll, CFO
Maureen Beddis, VP of Marketing & Communications
Greg Chavez, VP of Member Services

Newsletter for the membership of The Vision Council of America. A nonprofit association of manufacturers and distributors of sunglasses and sunglass parts.
12 Pages
Founded in 1940

1726 **Uniformer**
Professional Apparel Association
994 Old Eagle School Road
Suite 1019
Wayne, PA 19087-1802

610-971-4850
Fax: 610-971-4859

Sharon Tannahill, Executive Director

Seeks to enhance the growth of the professional apparel industry by educating uniform retailers.
1200+ Members
16 Pages
Frequency: Quarterly
Circulation: 500

1727 **UpFront Newsletter**
Embroidery Trade Association
P O Box 794534
Dallas, TX 75379-4534

888-628-2545
Fax: 972-755-2561
E-Mail: info@embroiderytrade.org
Home Page: www.embroiderytrade.org

John Swinburn, Executive Director
Dolores Cheek, Manager Of Member Services

A newsletter with advice and information on topics such as marketing, business operations and problem solving
1200 Members
Frequency: Weekly
Founded in 1990

Magazines & Journals

1728 **Accessories**
Business Journals
50 Day Street
Norwalk, CT 06854

203-853-6015
Fax: 203-852-8175
Home Page: www.busjour.com

Britton Jones, President/CEO
Stuart Nifoussi, VP
Mac Brighton, Chairman & COO
Christone Sullivan, Controller

This magazine profiles the national fashion trade for women's accessories.
Cost: $35.00
Frequency: Monthly
Circulation: 100000
Founded in 1931

1729 **Apparel Magazine**
Susan S. Nichols
801 Gervais St.
Suite 101
Columbia, SC 29201

803-771-7500
800-845-8820
Fax: 803-799-1461
E-Mail: cdeberry@apparelmag.com
Home Page: www.apparel.edgl.com

Susan S. Nichols, Publisher
Jordan Speer, Editor in Chief
Cindy DeBerry, Sales Manager

Trade publication for apparel/sewn products, manufacturing executives. Accepts advertising. Covers topics ranging from new products and technology to production management, sourcing, fabrics and financial news.
Cost: $48.00
180 Pages
Frequency: Monthly
Circulation: 18752
Printed in 4 colors on matte stock

1730 **California Apparel News**
MnM Publishing Corp
110 E 9th Street
Suite A-777
Los Angeles, CA 90079-1777

213-627-3737
E-Mail: info@apparelnews.net
Home Page: www.apparelnews.net

Alison A Nieder, Executive Editor
N Jayne Seward, Fashion Editor
Deborah Belgum, Senior Editor

News and analysis on the largest manufacturing center in the country, special supplements on denim, lingerie, trade shows, textiles and more. Contains the only comprehensive coverage of Los Angeles Fashion Week.
Cost: $89.00
450 Pages
Frequency: Weekly
Founded in 1945

1731 **Children's Business**
Fairchild Publications
Po Box 5121
New York, NY 10087-5121

212-630-3880
800-932-4724
Fax: 212-630-3868
E-Mail: debra.goldberg@fairchildpub.com
Home Page: www.fairchildmediakit.com

Debra Goldberg, Publisher
Tracy R Mitchell, Executive Editor
Ralph Erardy, Senior VP

Infants' and toddlers' wear, juvenile merchandise, footwear and toys.
Cost: $5.00
45 Pages
Frequency: Monthly
Circulation: 30458
ISSN: 0884-2280
Founded in 1985

1732 **Clothing & Textile Research Journal**
International Textile & Apparel Association
PO Box 70687
Knoxville, TN 37938-0687

865-992-1535
Fax: 916-722-8149
E-Mail: info@itaaonline.org
Home Page: www.itaaonline.org
Social Media: Facebook

Jana Hawley, President
Laurel E Wilsonn, VP
Nancy Rutherford,Ph.D, Executive Director

Offers the latest information on all areas of clothing and textiles.
Cost: $85.00
64 Pages
Frequency: Quarterly
Circulation: 1300
ISSN: 0887-3020
Founded in 1944
Printed in one color on matte stock

1733 **Costume! Business**
Gift Basket Review
815 Haines Street
Jacksonville, FL 32206-6025

904-634-1902
800-729-6338
Fax: 904-633-8764
Home Page: www.festivities-pub.com

Debra Paulk, Publisher
Kathy Horak, Editor

News and current issues in the costume retailing business.
Cost: $29.95
Frequency: Quarterly
Circulation: 8,000

1734 **Dress**
Costume Society of America
390 Amwell Road
Suite 402
Hillsborough, NJ 08844

908-359-1471
800-272-9447
Fax: 908-450-1118
Home Page: www.costumesocietyamerica.com/
Social Media: Facebook, Twitter

Sally Halverston, Associate Editor
Rosalyn M Lester, President
Linda Welters, Editor-in-Chief
Margaret Ordonez, Managing Editor

Journal of the Costume Society of America. The Costume Society of America advances the global understanding of all aspects of dress and appearance.
ISSN: 0361-2112
Founded in 1973
Printed in on matte stock

1735 **Fashion Accessories Magazine**
SCM Publications
10 DeGraaf Court
PO Box 859
Mahwah, NJ 07430

201-684-9222
Fax: 201-684-9228
Home Page: www.accessoriesmagazine.com

Lorrie Frost, Publisher
Lauren Parker, Editor

Offers information on the latest in fashion, jewelry and accessories.
Founded in 1951

1736 **Fashion Market Magazine**
Fashion Market Magazine Group
617 West 46th Street
New York, NY 10036

212-541-9350
Fax: 212-541-9340
Home Page: www.fmmg.com
Social Media: Facebook, Twitter

Victoria Monjo, Editor
Nicole Phillip, Fashion Editor

News for the apparel industry in New York, with original pictures and news in fashion, technology, finance and real estate.
Cost: $84.74
64 Pages
Frequency: Monthly
Circulation: 80000
Founded in 1985

1737 **Footwear Plus**
Symphony Publishing
36 Cooper Square
4th Floor
New York, NY 10003

646-278-1550
Fax: 646-278-1553
Home Page: www.footwearplusmagazine.com
Social Media: Facebook, Twitter

Greg Dutter, Editor-in-Chief
Pauline Lee, Associate Editor

Focuses on fashion, merchandising, trends and ideas in the retail footwear industry.
Cost: $50.58
Founded in 1989
Printed in on glossy stock

1738 **Hosiery News**
Home Sewing Association
105 Mall Boulevard
Po Box 369
Monroeville, PA 15146

412-372-5950
Fax: 412-372-5953
Home Page: www.sewing.org

Dotty Grexa, President
Dale Sutherland, Treasurer

Jenna Sheldon, Director Trade Show/Meetings
Jenny Prevatte, Director Information Services

It covers all THA activities, industry news, personnel changes, statistics, legislative and regulatory concerns, marketing, technology, financial reports and new product information.

1739 Impressions Magazine
1145 Sanctuary Parkway
Suite 355
Alpharetta, GA 30009-4772

800-241-9034
E-Mail: impressions@bill.com
Home Page: www.impressionsmag.com

Chris Casey, Publisher
Marcia Derryberry, Editor-in-Chief
Jamar Laster, Senior Editor

Offers news and information on the development or imprintable and imprinted sportswear and textiles.
Cost: $69.00
Circulation: 30000

1740 Industrial Fabric Products Review
U.S. Industrial Fabrics Association International
1801 County Road BW
Roseville, MN 55113-4061

651-222-2508
800-225-4324
Fax: 651-631-9334
E-Mail: generalinfo@ifai.com
Home Page: www.ifai.com

Stephen M Warner, President
JoAnne Ferris, Director Of Marketing

Keeps individuals up to date on the information needed to keep their business growing.
Cost: $69.00
Frequency: Monthly
Founded in 1915

1741 Juvenile Merchandising
EW Williams Publications Company
2125 Center Ave
Suite 305
Fort Lee, NJ 07024-5898

201-592-7007
Fax: 201-592-7171
E-Mail: philpl@ewwpi.com
Home Page: www.williamspublications.com

Andrew Williams, President
Phillip Russo, Publisher
Peter Berlinski, Editor-in-Chief

Offers news on the juvenile clothing, accessories and furniture industry.
Cost: $85.00
Circulation: 8000
Founded in 1938

1742 Knit Ovations Magazine
Woolknit Associates
267 5th Avenue
Suite 806-807
New York, NY 10016

212-683-7785
Fax: 212-683-2682

Eleanor Kairalla, Publisher

Fashions in knitwear for men and women trends in market; fashion color forecasts; guest features on knitwear by retail executives.

1743 Made to Measure
Halper Publishing Company
633 Skokie Blvd
Suite 490
Northbrook, IL 60062

224-406-8850
Fax: 224-406-8850
E-Mail: news@uniformmarket.com
Home Page: www.madetomeasuremag.com
Social Media: Facebook, Twitter

Rick Levine, President

Serves the uniform and career apparel industry.
Frequency: Bi-annually
Circulation: 25000
Founded in 1930
Printed in 4 colors on glossy stock

1744 Market Maker
Advanstar Communications
6200 Canoga Avenue
2nd Floor
Woodland Hills, CA 91367

818-593-5000
Fax: 818-593-5020
E-Mail: info@advanstar.com
Home Page: www.advanstar.com

Chirs DeMoulin, VP
Susannah George, Marketing Director
Joseph Loggia, President

Industry fashions
Cost: $2.00
Circulation: 14900
Founded in 1987

1745 Menswear Retailing Magazine
Business Journals Inc
1384 Broadway
Suite 11
New York, NY 10018-6111

212-686-4412
Fax: 212-686-6821
E-Mail: karena@mrketplace.com
Home Page: www.mrketplace.com

Bethany Raborn, Manager
Stuart Nifoussi, VP
Karen Alberg, Editor

Includes accurate information on the menswear retailing business, insightful analysis, bold ideas and real world fashion.
Circulation: monthly

1746 Needle's Eye
Union Special Corporation
1 Union Special Plz
Huntley, IL 60142-7007

847-669-5101
Fax: 847-669-4535
E-Mail: dkanies@unionspecial.com
Home Page: www.unionspecial.com

Terence A Hitpas, President

Industry events, developments in machine-sewed products, informs about improved manufacturing methods, and promotes interest in Union Special machinery.
Frequency: Monthly
Circulation: 28595
Founded in 1881

1747 Notions
American Sewing Guild
9660 Hillcroft St
Suite 510
Houston, TX 77096-3866

713-729-3000
Fax: 713-729-9230
Home Page: www.asg.org

Margo Martin, Executive Director

Contains articles written exclusively for us by the world's leading sewing experts, messages from the ASG Board of Directors and ASG National Headquarters, information about the latest sewing products and books.
Frequency: Quarterly

1748 Outerwear
Creative Marketing Plus
213-37 39th Avenue
Suite 228
Bayside, NY 11361

718-606-0767
Fax: 718-606-6345
E-Mail: rharrow@creativemarketingplus.com
Home Page: www.creativemarketingplus.com

Richard Harrow, Presidetn/CEO
Duke Wollsoncoft, Creative Director

Focuses on outerwear buyers' needs, fashion trends, as well as leading buying offices and promotional plans.
Cost: $62.00
30 Pages
Frequency: Monthly
Circulation: 16000
Founded in 1983
Printed in 4 colors on glossy stock

1749 Printwear Magazine
National Business Media Inc
PO Box 1416
Broomfield, CO 80038-1416

303-469-0424
800-669-0424
Fax: 303-465-3424
E-Mail: pweditor@nbm.com
Home Page: www.nbm.com

Bob Wieber, President
Mark Buchanan, Editor

Screen printing and embroidery equipment and technique, apparel styles and trends, heat-applied graphics, special effects printing and embroidery, business management and sales/marketing skills, digital transfers and sublimation, promotional products, embroidery digitizing, new products and the latest industry literature.
Frequency: Monthly
Circulation: 25000

1750 Promotional Sportswear
520 W Foothill Pkwy
Corona, CA 92882 6305

951-279-9327
Fax: 909-279-9327
E-Mail: customerservice@promowear.com
Home Page: www.promowear.com

Ted Taylor, Owner

Commercial direct screen printing, embroidery and complete art services on the highest quality sportswear available.

1751 Promowear
National Bussines Media Inc
P.O Box 1416
Broomfield, CO 80038

303-469-0424
800-669-0424
Fax: 303-469-5730
E-Mail: pweditor@nbm.com
Home Page: www.nbm.com/pr
Social Media: Facebook, Twitter

Bob Wieber, President
Mark Buchanan, Editor

The latest style trends, detailed product and sourcing information, sales and marketing tips, industry news.
Frequency: 6 Issues/Year
Founded in 1990

1752 Stitches
4800 Street Road
Trevose, PA 19053

800-546-1350
800-546-1350
Fax: 215-953-3107
E-Mail: mrollender@asicentral.com

Home Page: www.asipublications.com/stitches
Social Media: Facebook, Twitter

Nicole Rollender, Editor
Ed Koehler, Advertising Director

Information and the latest technology for embroidery professionals.
Circulation: 17233
Founded in 1987

1753 **Tack N' Togs Merchandising**
The Miller Publishing Company
12400 Whitewater Dr
Suite 160
Minnetonka, MN 55343-4590

952-931-0211
Fax: 952-938-1832
Home Page: www.tacntogs.com
Social Media: Facebook, Twitter

Sarah Muirhead, Publisher
Julie Golson-Richards, Associate Editor
Cindy Miller-Johnson, Adverting Sales Manager
Michelle Adaway, Advertising Account Excutive

Providing the latest news and information on equine retailing.
Frequency: Monthly
Circulation: 20424
Founded in 1970

1754 **Textile Rental Magazine**
Textile Rental Services Association
1800 Diagonal Rd
Suite 200
Alexandria, VA 22314-2842

703-519-0029
877-770-9274
Fax: 703-519-0026
E-Mail: trsa@trsa.org
Home Page: www.trsa.org

Roger Cocivera, President/CEO
Jack Morgan, Editor

Packed with valuable tips and ideas.
Frequency: Monthly

1755 **Uniformer**
Professional Apparel Association
994 Old Eagle School Road
Suite 1019
Wayne, PA 19087-1866

610-971-4850
Fax: 771-261-4859

Hope Silverman, Executive Director
Frequency: Quarterly

1756 **Vows Magazine**
Peter Grimes
24 Daisy St
Ladera Ranch, CA 92694-0709

949-388-4848
Fax: 949-388-8448
E-Mail: info@vowsmagazine.com
Home Page: www.vowsmagazine.com

Kori Grimes, Owner
Karlnon Nazarro, Director

Bridal retail, including how to survive as an independent retailer, how to merchandise and promote your business, how to effectively sell and train a sales staff, as well as identifying fashion and consumer shopping trends and preferences.
Founded in 1990

1757 **Wearables Business**
Advertising Specialty Institute
4800 E Street Rd
Langhorne, PA 19053-6698

215-953-4000
800-546-1350
Fax: 215-953-3045
E-Mail: nrollender@asicentral.com
Home Page: www.asicentral.com

Timothy M Andrews, President
Richard Fairfield, Publisher

Educational resource for promotional apparel distributors.
Cost: $1320.00
Frequency: Monthly
Circulation: 13533
Founded in 1987

1758 **Women's Wear Daily**
Fairchild Publications
750 3rd Ave
New York, NY 10017-2703

212-630-3500
800-289-0273
Fax: 212-630-3566
E-Mail: wwd@pubservice.com
Home Page: www.wwd.com
Social Media: Twitter

Mary G Berner, CEO
Christine Guilfoyle, Publisher
Edward Nardoza, Editor in Chief

Serves as the voice of authority, international newswire and agent of change for the fashion, beauty and retail industries
Cost: $195.00
Frequency: Daily
Circulation: 43618
Founded in 1892

Trade Shows

1759 **ASD/AMD Las Vegas Trade Show**
ASD/AMD Group
6255 W. Sunset Blvd
19th Floor
Los Angeles, CA 90028

323-817-2200
800-421-4511
Fax: 310-481-1900
Home Page: www.asdonline.com

Greg Farrar, President
Mark Hosbein, Marketing

Provides a portfolio of innovative face to face, print and online products for the wholesale industry.
10000 Attendees
Frequency: BiAnnual/August/March

1760 **ASG Conference**
American Sewing Guild
9660 Hillcroft
Suite 510
Houston, TX 77096

713-729-3000
Fax: 713-729-9230
Home Page: www.asg.org

Martha Ramey, President

Gives all Guild members the opportunity to meet sewing professionals, industry representatives, and other sewing enthusiasts from around the country, and to participate in sewing seminars and sewing related special events and tours.
20000 Attendees
Frequency: Annual/July

1761 **AccessoriesTheShow**
Accessories Magazine
50 Day Street
Norwalk, CT 06854

203-853-6015
800-358-6678
Fax: 203-852-8175
E-Mail: sharon@busjour.com
Home Page: www.accessoriestheshow.com

Britton Jonese, President
Sharon Enright, VP

All accessories trade event in the fashion capital of the US attracts thousands of fine specialty buyers
22k + Attendees

1762 **Action Sports Retailer Trade Exposition**
Miller Freeman Publications
PO Box 1899
Laguna Beach, CA 92652

847-296-6742
Fax: 847-391-9827
E-Mail: info@nsga.org
Home Page: www.nsga.org

Matt Carlson, President & Ceo

Manufacturers, suppliers, retailers, buyers, guides, outfitters, distributors, importers, exporters, press and industry influencers have converged at Fly-Fishing Retailer to chart the future of their business.

1763 **American Flock Association Annual Meeting**
American Flock Association
6 Beacon Street
Suite 1125
Boston, MA 02108

617-303-6288
Fax: 704-671-2366
E-Mail: info@flocking.org
Home Page: www.flocking.org

Karl Spilhaus, President
Steve Rosenthal, Managing Director

Provides positive leadership to foster a strong flock industry in North America.
60 Members
Founded in 1984

1764 **Apparel Show of the Americas**
Bobbin Publishing/Miller Freeman
PO Box 279
Euless, TX 76039

817-215-1600
800-693-1363
Fax: 817-215-1666
E-Mail: bobbin.expoinfo@mfi.com
Home Page: www.mfi.com

Betty Webb, Trade Show Director

Conference, seminar and 329 exhibits of equipment, fabrics, accessories and services for sewn products and apparel.
Founded in 1992

1765 **Arnold Sports Festival**
Arnold Sports Festival
1215 Worthington Woods Blvd.
Worthington, OH 43805

614-431-2600
Fax: 516-625-1023
E-Mail: lpinney@arnoldexpo.com
Home Page: www.arnoldsportsfestival.com
Social Media: Facebook, Twitter

Lucy Pinneyr, Event Chair
Brent LaLonda, Media Contact

Five days of fitness equipment, sports entertainment, supplements, apparel and athletic stars, with more than 17,000 competitive athletes in 40 sporting events. Over 500 exhibitors.
150M+ Attendees
Frequency: March
Founded in 1976

1766 **Bead and Button Show**
Kalmbach Publishing Company

21027 Crossroads Circle
PO Box 1612
Waukesha, WI 53187-1612

262-796-8776
800-533-6644
Fax: 262-796-1615
Home Page: www.beadandbuttonshow.com
Social Media: Facebook

Gerald Boettcher, President
The biggest bead show in the country.
3500 Attendees
Frequency: Annual/May
Founded in 1985

1767 **Big and Tall Men's Apparel Needs Show**
Specialty Trade Show
3939 Hardie Road
Coconut Grove, FL 33133-6137

305-663-6635
Fax: 305-661-8118
E-Mail: info@spectrade.com
Home Page: www.spectrade.com

A gathering of buyers and vendors of apparel and accessories for tall and plus sized men. 200 Exhibitors.
1,500 Attendees
Frequency: February/August

1768 **Chicago Men's Collective: Winter**
Merchandise Mart Properties Inc
222 Merchandise Mart Plaza
Suite 470
Chicago, IL 60654

312-527-7635
800-677-6278
E-Mail: bschedler@mmart.com
Home Page: www.mmart.com

Bruce Schedler, VP
Approximately 300 exhibitors and over 1,000 lines of product featuring men's fashion business attire.
5000 Attendees
Frequency: August

1769 **Convergence**
Handweavers Guild of America
1255 Buford Highway
Suite 211
Suwanee, GA 30024-1701

678-730-0010
Fax: 678-730-0836
E-Mail: hga@weavespindye.org
Home Page: www.weavespindye.org

Nancy Peck, President
Mary Ann Sanborn, VP
Elaine Bradley, Marketing
Sandra Bowles, Executive Director
Conference for everyone who loves and works in fiber.
3000 Attendees
Frequency: June, Biennial

1770 **E-Sports & Business Services Show at the Super Show**
Communications & Show Management
1450 NE 123rd Street
North Miami, FL 33161

305-893-8771
Fax: 305-893-8783
Home Page: www.bizbash.com
Social Media: Facebook, Twitter

Tom Cove, President
Retailers, distributors, wholesalers, importers/exporters and other buyers of sports related products come for 10,000 exhibits of sports apparel, footwear, accessories and e-commerce products and services.
100k Attendees
Frequency: Annual/January

1771 **EGA National Seminar**
Embroiderers' Guild of America
1355 Bardstown Road
Suite 157
Louisville, KY 40204

502-589-6956
Fax: 502-584-7900
E-Mail: sem2010@egausa.org
Home Page: www.egausa.org

Lorie Welker, President
Barbara Harrison, VP
Lectures, workshops and networking.
20000 Attendees

1772 **Eastern Men's Market/Collective**
AmericasMart Atlanta
240 Peachtree Street NW
Suite 2200
Atlanta, GA 30303-1327

404-220-3000
800-285-6278
Fax: 404-220-3030
E-Mail: webmaster@americasmart.com
Home Page: www.americasmart.com
Social Media: Facebook, Twitter

Jeff Portman, President/COO
Hank Almquist, VP
An outlet for the latest trends and designs in products and services.
500 Attendees

1773 **Embroidery Trade Association Convention**
Embroidery Trade Association
PO Box 794534
Dallas, TX 75379-4534

972-247-0415
888-628-2545
Fax: 972-755-2561
E-Mail: info@embroiderytrade.org
Home Page: www.embroiderytrade.org

John Swinburn, Executive Director
An organization with the objective to continually strengthen the commercial embroidery business.
1200 Members
Founded in 1990

1774 **FFANY Collections**
Fashion Footwear Association of New York
274 Madison Avenue
Suite 1701
New York, NY 10016

212-751-6422
Fax: 212-751-6404
E-Mail: info@ffany.org
Home Page: www.ffany.org
Social Media: Facebook, Twitter

Joseph C Moore, President/CEO
Phyllis Rein, Senior VP
The essential venue for fashion footwear. Held at FFANY participating show rooms.
300 Attendees
Frequency: August
Founded in 1980

1775 **Fabric Exhibition**
Advanstar Communications
2501 Colorado Avenue
Suite 280
Santa Monica, CA 90404

310-857-7500
Fax: 310-857-7500
E-Mail: info@advanstar.com
Home Page: www.advanstar.com

Joseph Loggia, President
Chris DeMoulin, VP
Susannah George, Marketing Director
Conference and exhibition of interest to those in the fabric and garment industry.
7000 Attendees

1776 **Fitness Show at the Super Show**
Communications & Show Management
1450 NE 123rd Street
North Miami, FL 33161

305-893-8771
Fax: 305-893-8783
Home Page: www.bizbash.com

Tom Cove, President
Retailers, distributors, wholesalers, importers/exporters and other buyers of sports related products come for 10,000 exhibits of sports apparel, footwear, accessories and e-commerce products and services.
100k Attendees
Frequency: Annual/January

1777 **Gatlinburg Apparel & Jewelry Market**
Norton Shows
PO Box 265
Gatlinburg, TN 37738

865-436-6151
Fax: 865-436-6152
Home Page: www.nortonshows.com

Tom Norton, Show Manager/Owner
Linda Norton, Owner
Trade show that has wholesale, cash-and-carry, ladies, men's, and children's apparel, fashion jewelry, accessories, fine jewelry and gifts from around the world. There are 500-700 booths.
20000 Attendees
Frequency: March/June/Sept/Nov
Founded in 1987
Mailing list available for rent: 70,000 names

1778 **Global Leather**
American Apparel & Footwear Association
1601 N Kent Street
Suite 1200
Arlington, VA 22205

703-524-1864
800-520-2262
Fax: 847-522-6741
E-Mail: info@globalleathers.com
Home Page: globalleathers.com

Kevin M Burke, President
Stephen E Lamar, VP
Dawn Van Dyke, Marketing
Showcases the best in new leather materials and components for footwear leather, needle and allied trades of North America. Brings together hundreds of exhibitors from the major sourcing cities around the world, showcasing thousands of products.
1500 Attendees
Frequency: February/August
Founded in 1981

1779 **Holiday Sample Sale**
San Francisco Design Center
635 8th Street
San Francisco, CA 94103
415-490-5800
Fax: 415-490-5885
Home Page: www.sfdesigncenter.com

Dianne Travalini, Show Director
Aruex Dalmacio, Show Manager

Open to the public and offers jewelry, accessories and leather items, gift items, home accessories, housewares, toys and apparel.
11000 Attendees
Frequency: November

1780 **Hospitality Design Expo**
American Flock Association
6 Beacon Street
Suite 1125
Boston, MA 02108

617-303-6288
Fax: 617-542-2199
E-Mail: info@flocking.org
Home Page: www.flocking.org

Steve Rosenthal, Director

Provides positive leadership to foster a strong flock industry in North America.
Frequency: May

1781 **IACDE Convention**
Internatl Assoc of Clothing Designers & Executives
835 NW 36th Terrace
Oklahoma City, OK 73118

405-602-8037
Fax: 405-602-8038
Home Page: www.iacde.com

Joachim Hensch, President
Mina Henry, Director

Focus is on the retail link in the apparel supply chain. The students and faculty of the Fashion Institute of Technology are involved in the planning and presentation of many of the convention programs.
Frequency: Annual
Founded in 1910

1782 **ISAM: International Swimwear and Activewear Market**
California Market Center
110 E 9th Street
Los Angeles, CA 90079

213-303-3688
800-225-6278
Fax: 213-630-3708
E-Mail: info@californiamarketcenter.com

Barbara Brady, Director

Serves the swimwear and resortwear industry.
Frequency: August/September
Founded in 1978

1783 **Imprinted Sportswear Shows (ISS)**
Imprinted Sportswear Shows (ISS)
Nielson Business Media
1145 Sanctuary Parkway, Ste 355
Alpharetta, GA 30004-4756

800-933-8735
Fax: 770-777-8700
E-Mail: issshows@xpressreg.net
Home Page: www.issshows.com

David Loechner, President
Michael Alicea, Senior VP

Shows in: Long Beach, Orlando, Atlantic City, Atlanta and Fort Worth. Showcases the newest products, apparel, and equipment featuring new technology, sublimation, and techniques with hands-on demos. There are new conferences at every show providing learning and networking opportunities. Discuss business opportunities, best practices, artistic trends, and techniques.
Founded in 1981

1784 **International Fashion Boutique Show**
Advanstar Communications
757 3rd Ave
New York, NY 10017-2013

212-951-6600
Fax: 212-951-6793
E-Mail: info@advanstar.com
Home Page: www.advanstar.com

Offers a variety of fashion trade shows throughout each year at the Javitz Convention Center in New York.
25000 Attendees

1785 **International Fashion Fabric Exhibition**
Advanstar Communications
641 Lexington Avenue
8th Floor
New York, NY 10022

212-951-6600
Fax: 212-951-6793
E-Mail: info@advanstar.com
Home Page: www.advanstar.com

Joseph Loggia, CEO
Tony Calanca, Executive Vice President
Steven Sturm, Executive Vice President

Conference and exhibits of interest to those in the fabric and garment industries.
15000 Attendees

1786 **International Hosiery Exposition**
Home Sewing Association
105 Mall Boulevard
PO Box 369
Monroeville, PA 15146

412-372-5950
Fax: 412-372-5953
Home Page: www.sewing.org

Dotty Grexa, President
Jenna Sheldon, Director Trade Show/Meetings
Jenny Prevatte, Director Information Services

Specialize in the latest hosiery and sewn products industries' supplies and services. 250 Exhibitors.
10000 Attendees

1787 **International Intimate Apparel Lingerie Show**
Specialty Trade Show
3939 Hardle Road
Coconut Grove, FL 33133-6437

305-663-6635
Fax: 305-661-8118
E-Mail: info@spectrade.com
Home Page: www.lingerieshow.cc

Jeff Yunis, President

Specializing in lingerie and adult products.
2,000 Attendees
Frequency: October

1788 **International Kids Fashion Show**
Advanstar Communications
641 Lexington Avenue
8th Floor
New York, NY 10022

212-951-6600
Fax: 212-951-6793
E-Mail: info@advanstar.com
Home Page: www.advanstar.com

Joseph Loggia, CEO
Thomas Ehardt, Executive Vice President

Children's fashions, accessories, gift items, and footwear.
3500 Attendees
Frequency: Jan/March/August/October

1789 **International Show at the Super Show**
Communications & Show Management
1450 NE 123rd Street
North Miami, FL 33161

305-808-3531
Fax: 305-893-8783
Home Page: www.bizbash.com

Richard Aaron, President
David Adler, CEO, Founder
Ann Keusch, COO

Retailers, distributors, wholesalers, importers/exporters and other buyers of sports related products come for 10,000 exhibits of sports apparel, footwear, accessories and e-commerce products and services.
100k Attendees
Frequency: January

1790 **International Vision Expo**
The Vision Council of America
225 Reinekers Lane
Suite 700
Alexandria, VA 22314

703-548-4560
866-826-0290
Fax: 703-548-4580
E-Mail: info@thevisioncouncil.org
Home Page: www.thevisioncouncil.org

Ed Greene, President
Brian Carroll, VP
Maureen Beddis, Marketing Director

Learn about new market information, statistics, training and industry trends.
Frequency: Biennial
Founded in 1999

1791 **International Western Apparel and Accessories Market**
Dallas Market Center
2100 Stemmons Freeway
Dallas, TX 75207

214-655-6100
800-325-6587
Fax: 800-637-6833
Home Page: www.dallasmarketcenter.com

Bill Winsor, President/CEO
Pat Zajac, Contact Home Expo

Offers array of services geared toward helping retailers expand business and increase profits.
200M Attendees
Frequency: March/August
Founded in 1957

1792 **Licensed Sports Show at the Super Show**
Communications & Show Management
1450 NE 123rd Street
North Miami, FL 33161

305-808-3531
Fax: 305-893-8783
Home Page: www.bizbash.com

Richard Aaron, President
David Adler, CEO, Founder
Ann Keusch, COO

Retailers, distributors, wholesalers, importers/exporters and other buyers of sports related products come for 10,000 exhibits of sports apparel, footwear, accessories and e-commerce products and services.
100k Attendees
Frequency: January

1793 **MAGIC International Show**
MAGIC International
2501 Colorado Avenue
Suite 280
Santa Monica, CA 90404

310-857-7500
Fax: 310-593-5020

E-Mail: cs@MAGIConline.com
Home Page: www.magiconline.com

Joe Loggia, President/CEO
Francine Rich, Womens Sales Contact
Christopher Giffin, Vice President Sales
Pam Thompson, Attendee Relations

Fashion trade show in Las Vegas. 3,000 exhibitors.
75000 Attendees
Frequency: February/August
Founded in 1933

1794 **Management Conference & Team Dealer Summit**
National Sporting Goods Association
1601 Feehanville Drive
Suite 300
Mount Prospect, IL 60056

847-296-6742
800-815-5422
Fax: 847-391-9827
E-Mail: info@nsga.org
Home Page: www.nsga.org

Bob Dickman, Chairman of the Board
Matt Carlson, President/CEO
Dustin Dobrin, Research and Information Director

The goal is to stimulate fresh, agile thinking. How you and your company can create a culture that encourages and stimulates action, focus on the solution and fresh thinking.

1795 **Manufacturers Wholesalers Outerwear Sportswear Show**
I. Spiewak & Sons
463 7th Avenue
10th Floor
New York, NY 10018-6505

212-695-1620
800-223-6850
Fax: 212-629-4803
E-Mail: jerry@spiewak.com
Home Page: www.spiewak.com

Gerald Spiewak, Executive Director
Roy Spiewak, President

180 booths for manufacturers and importers of outerwear and rainwear.
3M Attendees
Frequency: January

1796 **Material World**
Urban Expositions
1395 S Marietta Parkway
Building 400, Suite 210
Marietta, GA 30067

770-180-0972
800-318-2238
Fax: 678-285-7469
Home Page: www.material-world.com

Doug Miller, President
Tim von Gal, Executive VP
Suzanne Pruitt, Contact

From design to delivery, Material World is the international full package, sourcing and fashion information event for the fabric related industries.
10600 Attendees
Frequency: May

1797 **Men's and Boy's Apparel Show**
Miami International Merchandise Mart
777 NW 72nd Avenue
Miami, FL 33126

305-665-5630
Fax: 305-261-3659
Home Page: www.miamimart.net

Martiza Agudo, President
Glorys Coyo, Administrator

This is a three-day show where wholesale buyers will find an extensive display of apparel lines including Calvin Klein, Perruzo, Supreme, just to name a few.
1000 Attendees
Frequency: April/May

1798 **National Bridal Market: Fall**
Merchandise Mart Properties Inc
222 Merchandise Mart Plaza
Suite 470
Chicago, IL 60654

312-527-4141
800-677-6278
Fax: 312-527-7971
E-Mail: mmailand@mmart.com
Home Page: www.mmart.com

Christopher Kennedy, President
Stephanie Ambuehl, Marketing

Specializing in leading bridal and special occasion resources for department and specialty stores.
3000 Attendees
Frequency: October

1799 **National Halloween & Costume & Party Show**
Transworld Exhibits
1850 Oak Street
Northfield, IL 60093

847-784-6905
800-323-5462
Fax: 847-446-3523
Home Page: www.tweshows.com

Joe Thaler, CEO
Paul O'Connor, Executive Director

Attracts people from across the US and over 50 foreign countries to see what over 700 manufacturers and distributors are showcasing as new and exciting for parties, shops and haunted houses. Free educational seminars and workshops.
10000 Attendees
Frequency: February

1800 **National Needlework Market**
The National NeedleArts Association
1100-H Brandywine Blvd
Zanesville, OH 43701

740-455-6773
800-889-8662
Fax: 740-452-2552
E-Mail: info@tnna.org
Home Page: www.tnna.org

Enabling professionals to come together to share knowledge, products and experiences.
5M Attendees
Frequency: Annual

1801 **National Sewing Show**
Home Sewing Association
PO Box 369
Monroeville, PA 15146

412-372-5950
Fax: 412-372-5953
Home Page: www.sewing.org

Dotty Grexa, President

Offers free sewing projects, guidelines and also a chat room where you can share with other about your ideas and collaborate on others.
Frequency: September

1802 **New England Apparel Club**
New England Apparel Club
75 McNeil Way
Suite 207
Dedham, MA 02026

781-326-9223
Fax: 781- 32- 689
E-Mail: neacrlg@aol.com
Home Page: www.neacshow.com

Richard Usherwood, President
Donald Hurowitz, Vice President
Rhonda Goldberg, Executive Director

2500 regional sales reps exhibiting clothing and related equipment, supplies and services.
2000 Attendees
Frequency: October, Boston

1803 **Northstar Fashion Exhibitors**
Northstar Fashion Exhibitors
175 Kellogg Blvd West
St Paul, MN 55102

763-546-8717
800-272-6972
Fax: 763-546-9176
E-Mail: northstarfashion@aol.com
Home Page: northstarfashion.com

Rick Siegel, President
Stanley Kaye, Show Coordinator
Debi Higgins, Manager

Trade show collections for men's, women's, Childrens apparel, accessories and textiles. 250 Booths.
1,260 Attendees
Frequency: 5/Year

1804 **Northwest Shoe Traveler's Buying Shoe Market**
Northwest Shoe Traveler's
12630 12th Street N
Lake Elmo, MN 55042

651-436-2709
Fax: 651-436-2028

Teri Tompkins, Show Manager

Trade show collections for men's, women's and Childrens.
250 Attendees
Frequency: January

1805 **Off-Price Specialist Show**
Off Price Specialist Center
16985 W Bluemound Road
Suite 210
Brookfield, WI 53005

262-782-1600
Fax: 262-782-1601
E-Mail: info@offpriceshow.com
Home Page: www.offpriceshow.com
Social Media: Facebook, Twitter

Stephen Krogulski, President/CEO
David Lapidos, Executive Vice President
Faye Osvatic, Buyers Contact
Kevin Redlich, Product Manager

Premiere show for off-price apparel and accessories.
12000 Attendees
Frequency: May 8-10
Founded in 1995

1806 **Outdoor Retailer Summer Market**
Nielsen Sports Group
31910 Del Obispo
Suite 200
San Juan Capistrano, CA 92675

949-226-5722
Home Page: www.outdoorretailer.com

Kenji Haroutunian, Director
Margle Lelvis, Marketing
Krista Dill, Account Executive
Jennifer Holcomb, Marketing Manager
Kenji Haroutunian, Show Director

The leading growth vehicle for brands that are interested in progressing and advancing into multiple channels of the outdoor marketplace.
17000 Attendees
Frequency: August

1807 **Outdoor Retailer Winter Market**
VNU Expositions
PO Box 1899
Laguna Beach, CA 92652

949-226-5722
Fax: 949-226-5625
Home Page: www.outdoorretailer.com

Marisa Nicholson, National Sales Manager
Paul Dillman, Senior Account Executive
Peter Devin, Group Show Director
David Lockner, Manager

Features the most comprehensive collection of outdoor apparel, gear, equipment, climbing technology, footwear, ski mountaineering, hunting, rescue outerwear and accessory companies from which to buy products.

1808 **PGA Merchandise Show**
Reed Exhibition Companies
383 Main Avenue
Suite 3
Norwalk, CT 06851

203- 84- 562
800-840-5628
Fax: 203-840-9628
E-Mail: inquiry@pga.reedexpo.com
Home Page: www.pgaexpo.com

Andre Smith, Director Marketing/Special Events
Marc Simon, Group Sales Director
Sherry Major, Media Contact

World's largest golf industry trade event. Open to retail buyers and golf industry professionals. Not open to the public
38500 Attendees
Frequency: January
Founded in 1954

1809 **Performance & Lifestyle Footwear Show at the Super Show**
Communications & Show Management
1450 NE 123rd Street
North Miami, FL 33161

305-893-8771
Fax: 305-893-8783
Home Page: www.bizbash.com

Richard Aaron, President
David Adler, CEO/President
Chad Kaydo, Editor in Chief
Dana Price, COO

Retailers, distributors, wholesalers, importers/exporters and other buyers of sports related products come for 10,000 exhibits of sports apparel, footwear, accessories and e-commerce products and services.
100k Attendees
Frequency: January

1810 **Printwear Show**
National Business Media Inc
PO Box 1416
Broomfield, CO 80038

303-469-0424
800-669-0424
Fax: 303-465-3424
Home Page: www.nbmshows.com
Social Media: Twitter

Bob Wieber, President

The event for buyers involved in screen printing, embroidery, heat applied graphics, digital textile printing, sublimation and apparel.
Frequency: August

1811 **Professional Apparel Association Trade**
Professional Apparel Association
994 Old Eagle School Road
Suite 1019
Wayne, PA 19087-1866

610-971-4850
Fax: 610-971-4859

Dr. Sharon Tannahill, Executive Director

Exhibitors display health care and hospitality uniforms, shoes, and accessories, and career apparel. Workshops and seminars for uniform retailers are also available. Biennial.

1812 **Seattle Trend Show**
Pacific Northwest Apparel Association
P.O. Box 3050
Issaquah, WA 98027

206-767-9200
Fax: 206-767-0707
E-Mail: pnaa@nwtrendshow.com
Home Page: www.nwtrendshow.com

Jane Powell, Director
Gary Morgan, President

Show and exhibits of apparel and related accessories.
2000 Attendees
Frequency: Jan/Apr/Jun/Aug/Oct

1813 **Shoe Market of America**
Miami Merchandise Mart
2335 NW 107 Ave
Suite 2M31 Box 120
Miami, FL 33172

786-331-9000
Fax: 786-331-9955
E-Mail: info@smota.com
Home Page: www.smota.com

Dianne Travalini, Executive Director
Alex Meme, Manager

Features the entire spectrum of footwear companies.
2500 Attendees
Frequency: 3x per year

1814 **Southwestern Shoe Traveler's**
Southwestern Shoe Traveler's Association
1024 Oxfordshire Dr.
Cannollton, TX 75007

972-446-4089
Fax: 214-292-9691
E-Mail: southwestshoeexpo@verizon.net

Mona Bennight, Executive Director

Definitive footwear trade site for footwear retailers.
1800 Attendees
Frequency: June

1815 **Syracuse Super Show**
Oncenter Complex
800 So. State Street
Syracuse, NY

315-488-4201
E-Mail: abc43@juno.com
Home Page: www.syracusesupershow.com

Carol Sweet, Menswear Contact
Dick Pirozzolo, Footwear Contact
Rhonda Goldberg, Women's & Children's Contact

Largest assortment of fashions in Upstate New York. The show is open to the wholesale trade only - sales representatives, manufacturers and retailers.

1816 **THA Annual Convention**
The Hosiery Association
7421 Carmel Executive Park Drive
Suite 200
Charlotte, NC 28226

704-365-0913
Fax: 704-362-2056
E-Mail: THAinfo@hosieryassociation.com
Home Page: www.hosieryassociation.com
Social Media: Facebook, Twitter

Sally Kay, President/CEO

Promotes leg wear manufacturers & suppliers
Founded in 1905

1817 **TNNA Trade Shows**
National Needlework Association
1100-H Brandywine Boulevard
Zanesville, OH 43701

740-455-6773
800-889-8662
Fax: 740-452-2552
E-Mail: info@tnna.org
Home Page: www.tnna.org
Social Media: Facebook, Twitter

A market for serious needleart buyers and sellers learn about trends in fashion, color and design. With over 800 booths.
Frequency: 4x per year

1818 **Team Sports Show at the Super Show**
Communications & Show Management
1450 NE 123rd Street
North Miami, FL 33161

305-893-8771
Fax: 305-893-8783
Home Page: www.bizbash.com

Richard Aaron, President
David Adler, CEO/founder
Chad Kaydo, Editor in Chief
Dana Price, COO

Retailers, distributors, wholesalers, importers/exporters and other buyers of sports related products come for 10,000 exhibits of sports apparel, footwear, accessories and e-commerce products and services.
100k Attendees
Frequency: January

1819 **Tennis & Golf Show at the Super Show**
Communications & Show Management
1450 NE 123rd Street
North Miami, FL 33161

305-893-8771
Fax: 305-893-8783
Home Page: www.bizbash.com

Richard Aaron, President
David Adler, CEO/Founder
Chad Kaydo, Editor in Chief
Dana Price, COO

Retailers, distributors, wholesalers, importers/exporters and other buyers of sports related products come for 10,000 exhibits of sports apparel, footwear, accessories and e-commerce products and services.
100k Attendees
Frequency: January

1820 **Trimmings, Accessories, Fabrics Expo**
National Knitwear & Sportswear Association
386 Park Avenue S
Suite 5741
New York, NY 10016-8804

212-683-7520
Fax: 212-532-0766

Seth Bodner, Executive Director

The only all-inclusive trimmings show in the United States. 160 booths.
6M Attendees
Frequency: November

1821 **WAM: Western Apparel Manufacturers Show**
Dallas Market Center

2300 Stemmons Freeway
Dallas, TX 75207

214-556-6100
Fax: 214-638-7221
E-Mail: info@dmcmail.com
Home Page: www.dallasmarketcenter.com
Social Media: Facebook, Twitter

Apparel manufacturing equipment. Held to meet the needs of the TOLA retailers who take advantage of the early fall buying opportunities.
3.2M Attendees
Frequency: April

1822 WSA: Western Shoe Associates
Western Shoe Associates
20281 SW Birch Street
Newport Beach, CA 92660

949-851-8451
Fax: 949-851-8523

Mitch Fisherman, President
Steve Katz, VP
Marie Mussabini, Exhibitor Coordinator
Dave Darling, Treasurer

Trade show held twice a year and featuring footwear.

1823 WWD Magic
MAGIC International
2501 Colorado Avenue
Suite 280
Santa Monica, CA 90404

310-857-7500
Fax: 310-857-7510
E-Mail: cs@magiconline.com
Home Page: www.magiconline.com
Social Media: Facebook, Twitter

Joe Loggia, President/CEO
Laura McConnell, VP

WWD Magic, a joint venture with Women's Wear Daily, is the recognized leader in women's apparel and accessories expositions in the world. WWD Magic offers the opportunity to discover new resources, network with industry peers, attend trend seminars and fashion shows, and meet with major manufacturers in an exciting and efficient forum. Containing over 1,000 exhibitors and 2,000 booths.
85000 Attendees
Frequency: August
Founded in 1933

1824 Western Shoe Associates International
Western Shoe Associates
20281 SW Birch Street
Suite 100
Newport Beach, CA 92660

949-851-8451
Fax: 949-851-8523

Mitch Fisherman, President
Marie Mussabini, Exhibitor Coordinator

Footwear trade market.

1825 Western and English Sales Association Trade Show
Western and English Sales Association
451 E 58th Avenue
Suite 4128
Denver, CO 80216

303-295-1040
800-295-1041
Fax: 303-295-0941
E-Mail: info@denver-wesa.com
Home Page: www.denver-wesa.com

Toni High, Executive Director
Amy Thomas, Trade Show Director

Trade shows for Equestrian-related products; wholesalers to retailers
10000 Attendees
Frequency: 2x/Year

1826 Women and Children's Market
AMC Trade Shows/DMC Expositions
2140 Peachtree Street NW
Suite 2200
Atlanta, GA 30303

404-220-3000
800-285-6278
Fax: 404-220-3030

Sarah Adamson, Show Manager

Women and children's apparel.
9000 Attendees

1827 Women's and Children's Apparel Market
Dallas Market Center
2100 Stemmons Freeway
Dallas, TX 75207

214-556-6100
800-325-6587
E-Mail: ahood@dmcmail.com
Home Page: www.dallasmarketcenter.com
Social Media: Facebook, Twitter

Pat Zajac, Home Expo

Features the most comprehensive variety of apparel and accessories lines.
20000 Attendees
Frequency: October
Founded in 1957

1828 Women's and Children's Fall Market
Merchandise Mart Properties Inc
222 Merchandise Mart Plaza
Suite 470
Chicago, IL 60654

312-527-4141
800-677-6278
Fax: 312-527-7782
Home Page: www.merchandisemart.com

Christopher Kennedy, President

Hundreds of designers featuring women's and children's clothing and accessories
5000 Attendees
Founded in 1950

1829 Women's and Children's Summer/Fall Preview Market
Merchandise Mart Properties
222 Merchandise Mart Plaza
Suite 470
Chicago, IL 60654

312-527-4141
800-677-6278
Fax: 312-527-7782
Home Page: www.merchandisemart.com

H Brennen III, Executive VP

Women's and children's apparel.
5000 Attendees
Frequency: June

1830 Wonderful World of Weddings and Occasions
Expo Productions
510 Hartbrook Drive
Hartland, WI 53029

262-367-5500
800-367-5520
Fax: 262-367-9956
E-Mail: monica@epishows.com
Home Page: www.weddingshowepi.com

Monica Seeger, Sales Manager

Wedding and other special occasion products, services, ideas including live and recorded music, still and video photography, cakes and catering, formal wear, gifts and much more.
6000 Attendees
Frequency: January
Founded in 1967

1831 X-treme Sports Show at the Super Show
Communications & Show Management
1450 NE 123rd Street
North Miami, FL 33161

305-893-8771
Fax: 305-893-8783
Home Page: www.bizbash.com

Richard Aaron, President
David Adler, CEO/Founder
Chad Kaydo, Editor in Chief
Dana Price, COO

Retailers, distributors, wholesalers, importers/exporters and other buyers of sports related products come for 10,000 exhibits of sports apparel, footwear, accessories and e-commerce products and services.
100k Attendees
Frequency: January

Directories & Databases

1832 Action Sports Retailer Buyer's Guide Issue
Miller Freeman Publications
2655 Seely Avenue
San Jose, CA 95134

408-943-1234
Fax: 408-943-0513

Pat Cochran, Editor

Guide to 1,600 manufacturers and distributors of specialty watersports, beach, skateboarding, snowboarding, volleyball and bicycling equipment and clothing.
Cost: $25.00

1833 American Apparel Contractors Association Directory - American Made Apparel
4870 Nome Street
Denver, CO 80239-2728

303-373-2924
Fax: 703-522-6741

Sue C Strickland, Executive Director
Sunny Park, Owner

Over 300 listings are offered pertaining to contractors, manufacturers and suppliers to the apparel industry.
30 Members
100 Pages
Frequency: Annual
Founded in 1981

1834 Apparel Specialty Stores Directory
Chain Store Guide
10117 Princess Palm Dr
Tampa, FL 33610

813-627-6700
800-927-9292
Fax: 813-627-6888
E-Mail: webmaster@chainstoreguide.com
Home Page: www.csgis.com

Mike Jarvis, Publisher
Chris Leedy, Advertising Sales
Shami Choon, Manager

The facts on more than 4,800 companies operating more than 70,700 stores all involved in the sale of women's, men's, family and children's wear. Also included are sporting goods stores that offer apparel and active wear as well as related merchandise. Includes more than

15,000 key buyers and executives.
Cost: $335.00

1835 **Bobbin-Suppliers Sourcing Issue**
Bobbin Blenheim Media Corporation
1110 Shop Road
PO Box 1986
Columbia, SC 29201-4743
800-845-8820
Fax: 803-799-1461
Offers information on over 8,000 suppliers to the apparel/sewn products industry.

1836 **College Store Executive: Emblematics Directory Issue**
Executive Business Media
825 Old Country Road
Westbury, NY 11590
516-334-3030
Fax: 516-334-3059
E-Mail: ebm-mail@ebmpubs.com
Home Page: www.ebmpubs.com
Murry Greenwald, President
List of distributors of products with emblems or insignia; coverage includes Canada.
Cost: $5.00
Frequency: Annual, February

1837 **Complete Directory of Apparel**
Sutton Family Communications & Publishing Company
155 Sutton Lane
Fordsville, KY 42343
270-740-0870
E-Mail: jlsutton@apex.net
Home Page: www.fleamarketeer.net
Theresa Sutton, Editor
Lee Sutton, General Manager
Print-out from database of wholesalers, manufacturers, distributors, importers and close-out houses. Database is updated daily to guarantee the most current sources available.
Cost: $77.65
100+ Pages

1838 **Complete Directory of Apparel Close-Outs**
Sutton Family Communications & Publishing Company
155 Sutton Lane
Fordsville, KY 42343
270-740-0870
E-Mail: jlsutton@apex.net
Home Page: www.fleamarketeer.net
Theresa Sutton, Editor
Lee Sutton, General Manager
Print-out from database of wholesalers, manufacturers, distributors, importers and close-out houses. Database is updated daily to guarantee the most current sources available to the close-out apparel industry.
Cost: $55.20
100+ Pages

1839 **Complete Directory of Baby Goods and Gifts**
Sutton Family Communications & Publishing Company
155 Sutton Lane
Fordsville, KY 42343
270-740-0870
E-Mail: jlsutton@apex.net
Home Page: www.fleamarketeer.net
Theresa Sutton, Editor
Lee Sutton, General Manager
Print-out from database of wholesalers, manufacturers, distributors, importers and close-out houses for baby goods and gifts. Database is updated daily to guarantee the most current sources available.
Cost: $57.65
100+ Pages

1840 **Complete Directory of Belts, Buckles & Boots**
Sutton Family Communications & Publishing Company
155 Sutton Lane
Fordsville, KY 42343
270-740-0870
E-Mail: jlsutton@apex.net
Home Page: www.fleamarketeer.net
Theresa Sutton, Editor
Lee Sutton, General Manager
Print-out from database of wholesalers, manufacturers, distributors, importers and close-out houses. Database is updated daily to guarantee the most current sources available.
Cost: $55.20
100+ Pages

1841 **Complete Directory of Brand New Surplus Merchandise**
Sutton Family Communications & Publishing Company
155 Sutton Lane
Fordsville, KY 42343
270-740-0870
E-Mail: jlsutton@apex.net
Home Page: www.fleamarketeer.net
Theresa Sutton, Editor
Lee Sutton, General Manager
Print-out from database of wholesalers, manufacturers, distributors, importers and close-out houses. Database is updated daily to guarantee the most current sources available.
Cost: $92.70
100+ Pages

1842 **Complete Directory of Caps & Hats**
Sutton Family Communications & Publishing Company
155 Sutton Lane
Fordsville, KY 42343
270-740-0870
E-Mail: jlsutton@apex.net
Home Page: www.fleamarketeer.net
Theresa Sutton, Editor
Lee Sutton, General Manager
Print-out from database of wholesalers, manufacturers, distributors, importers and close-out houses. Database is updated daily to guarantee the most current sources available.
Cost: $55.20
100+ Pages

1843 **Complete Directory of Clothing & Uniforms**
Sutton Family Communications & Publishing Company
155 Sutton Lane
Fordsville, KY 42343
270-740-0870
E-Mail: jlsutton@apex.net
Home Page: www.fleamarketeer.net
Theresa Sutton, Editor
Lee Sutton, General Manager
Print-out from database of wholesalers, manufacturers, distributors, importers and close-out houses. Database is updated daily to guarantee the most current sources available.
Cost: $55.20
100+ Pages

1844 **Complete Directory of Hat Pins, Feathers and Fads**
Sutton Family Communications & Publishing Company
155 Sutton Lane
Fordsville, KY 42343
270-740-0870
E-Mail: jlsutton@apex.net
Home Page: www.fleamarketeer.net
Theresa Sutton, Editor
Lee Sutton, General Manager
Print-out from database of wholesalers, manufacturers, distributors, importers and close-out houses. Database is updated daily to guarantee the most current sources available.
Cost: $67.70
100+ Pages

1845 **Complete Directory of Purses & Handbags**
Sutton Family Communications & Publishing Company
155 Sutton Lane
Fordsville, KY 42343
270-740-0870
E-Mail: jlsutton@apex.net
Home Page: www.fleamarketeer.net
Theresa Sutton, Editor
Lee Sutton, General Manager
Print-out from database of wholesalers, manufacturers, distributors, importers and close-out houses. Database is updated daily to guarantee the most current sources available.
Cost: $55.20
100+ Pages

1846 **Complete Directory of Sunglasses & Eye Weather**
Sutton Family Communications & Publishing Company
155 Sutton Lane
Fordsville, KY 42343
270-740-0870
E-Mail: jlsutton@apex.net
Home Page: www.fleamarketeer.net
Theresa Sutton, Editor
Lee Sutton, General Manager
Print-out from database of wholesalers, manufacturers, distributors, importers and close-out houses. Database is updated daily to guarantee the most current sources available.
Cost: $55.20
100+ Pages

1847 **Complete Directory of T-Shirts, Heat Transfers & Supplies**
Sutton Family Communications & Publishing Company
155 Sutton Lane
Fordsville, KY 42343
270-740-0870
E-Mail: jlsutton@apex.net
Home Page: www.fleamarketeer.net
Theresa Sutton, Editor
Lee Sutton, General Manager
Print-out from database of wholesalers, manufacturers, distributors, importers and close-out houses. Database is updated daily to guarantee the most current sources available.
Cost: $55.20
100+ Pages

1848 **Complete Directory of Western Wear**
Sutton Family Communications & Publishing Company
155 Sutton Lane
Fordsville, KY 42343
270-740-0870
E-Mail: jlsutton@apex.net
Home Page: www.fleamarketeer.net
Theresa Sutton, Editor
Lee Sutton, General Manager

Print-out from database of wholesalers, manufacturers, distributors, importers and close-out houses. Database is updated daily to guarantee the most current sources available.
Cost: $55.20
100+ Pages

1849 Complete Directory of Women's Accessories
Sutton Family Communications & Publishing Company
155 Sutton Lane
Fordsville, KY 42343
270-740-0870
E-Mail: jlsutton@apex.net
Home Page: www.fleamarketeer.net
Theresa Sutton, Editor
Lee Sutton, General Manager
Print-out from database of wholesalers, manufacturers, distributors, importers and close-out houses. Database is updated daily to guarantee the most current sources available.
Cost: $55.20
100+ Pages

1850 Directory of Active Sportswear
Sutton Family Communications & Publishing Company
155 Sutton Lane
Fordsville, KY 42343
270-740-0870
E-Mail: jlsutton@apex.net
Home Page: www.fleamarketeer.net
Theresa Sutton, Editor
Lee Sutton, General Manager
Print-out from database of wholesalers, manufacturers, distributors, importers and close-out houses. Database is updated daily to guarantee the most current sources available. Approximately 740 wholesale sources in a 3-ring binder.
Cost: $67.20
100+ Pages

1851 Directory of Apparel Specialty Stores
AKTRIN Textile Information Center
164 S Main Street
PO Box 898
High Point, NC 27261
336-418-8583
Fax: 336-841-5435
E-Mail: aktrin@aktrin.com
Home Page: www.textile-info.com
Information resource for people seeking in-depth, up-to-date data on the apparel specialty stores marketplace. Fully searchable database, either in form of a CD-ROM or downloadable over the Internet.
Cost: $780.00
Frequency: Annual

1852 Directory of Hosiery Manufacturers
Hosiery Association
7421 Carmel Executive Park Drive
Suite 200
Charlotte, NC 28226
704-365-0913
Fax: 704-362-2056
E-Mail: thainfo@hosieryassociation.com
Home Page: www.hosieryassociation.com
Social Media: Facebook, Twitter
Sally Kay, President/CEO
Over 700 hosiery manufacturers and distributors.
Founded in 1905

1853 Directory of Mail Order Catalogs
Grey House Publishing
4919 Route 22
PO Box 56
Amenia, NY 12501
518-789-8700
800-562-2139
Fax: 518-789-0556
E-Mail: books@greyhouse.com
Home Page: www.greyhouse.com
Social Media: Facebook, Twitter
Leslie Mackenzie, Publisher
Richard Gottlieb, President
The premier source of information on the mail order catalog industry. Covers over 13,000 consumer and business catalog companies with 44 different product chapters including clothing and sportswear.
Cost: $395.00
1900 Pages
Frequency: Annual
ISBN: 1-592373-96-8
Founded in 1981

1854 Directory of Mail Order Catalogs - Online Database
Grey House Publishing
4919 Route 22
PO Box 56
Amenia, NY 12501
518-789-8700
800-562-2139
Fax: 518-789-0556
E-Mail: gold@greyhouse.com
Home Page: http://gold.greyhouse.com
Social Media: Facebook, Twitter
Leslie Mackenzie, Publisher
Richard Gottlieb, President
Reach over 10,000 consumer catalog companies in one easy-to-use source with The Directory of Mail Order Catalogs - Online Database. Filled with business-building detail, each company profile gives you the information you need to access that organization quickly and easily. Listings provide key contacts, sales volume, employee size, printing information, circulation, list data, product descriptions and much more.
Frequency: Annual
Founded in 1981

1855 Earnshaw's Buyer's Guide to the New York Market
Earnshaw Publications
36 Cooper Square
4th Floor
New York, NY 10003
646-278-1550
Fax: 646- 27- 155
Home Page: www.earnshaws.com
Noelle Heffernan, Publisher
A children's wear guide offering over 1,200 manufacturers and suppliers of clothing for infants, boys and girls apparel.
200 Pages
Frequency: Annual
Circulation: 10,000

1856 Earnshaw's Infants', Girls', Boys' Wear Review: Children's Wear Directory
Earnshaw Publications
36 Cooper Square
4th Floor
New York, NY 10003
646-278-1550
Fax: 646-278-1553
Home Page: www.earnshaws.com
Noelle Heffernan, Publisher
A directory of over 1,500 children's apparel and accessory firms with offices or showrooms in the United States.
Cost: $10.00
Frequency: Annual
Circulation: 10,000

1857 Financial Performance Profile of Public Apparel Companies
Kurt Salmon Associates
650 Fifth Avenue
New York, NY 10019
212-319-9450
Home Page: www.kurtsalmon.com
John Karonis, CEO
Information on over 60 publicly held apparel manufacturers are available.
Cost: $400.00
300 Pages
Frequency: Annual
Founded in 1935

1858 Garment Manufacturers Index
Klevens Publications
411 S Main Street
Suite 209
Los Angeles, CA 90013
213-625-9000
Fax: 213-625-5002
E-Mail: editor@klevenspub.com
Home Page: www.garmentindex.com
Herbert Schwartz, Editor
A list of over 5,000 manufacturers and suppliers of products and services such as fabrics, trimmings, factory equipment and sewing contractors used in the manufacture of apparel and other sewn products.
Cost: $105.00
264 Pages
Frequency: Annual
Circulation: 29,495
ISSN: 1065-1330
Founded in 1938
Printed in 4 colors on matte stock

1859 Hosiery and Bodywear: Buyer's Guide to Support and Control Top Pantyhose
Advanstar Communications
641 Lexington Ave
8th Floor
New York, NY 10022-4503
212-951-6600
Fax: 212-951-6793
E-Mail: info@advanstar.com
Home Page: www.advanstar.com
Joseph Loggia, CEO
List of about 50 hosiery manufacturers.
Cost: $3.00
Frequency: Annual September
Circulation: 10,500

1860 Impressions: Directory Issue
Miller Freeman Publications
501 W. President George Bush Hwy. #150
Richardson, TX 75080
813-366-2877
800-697-8859
E-Mail: nimp@omeda.com
Home Page: www.impressionsmag.com
Marcia Derrberry, Editor in Chief
A list of more than 1,500 suppliers of products, services and equipment used in the imprinted sportswear industry including textile screen print equipment, supplies, embroidery equipment and supplies, and all types of imprintables.
Cost: $18.00
Frequency: Annual
Circulation: 60,000

1861 **International Nonwovens Directory**
1100 Crescent Green Suite 115
PO Box 1288
Cary, NC 27518

919-233-1210
Fax: 919-233-1282
Home Page: www.inda.org

Rory Holmes, President
Annette Balint, Director Finance
Ian Butler, Director Market Research/Stats

A Who's Who directory of services and supplies to the nonwovens industry.
300 Members
750 Pages
Frequency: Biennial
Circulation: 2,000

1862 **Nationwide Directory of Men's & Boys' Wear Buyers**
Reed Reference Publishing RR Bowker
630 Central Ave
New Providence, NJ 07974-1544

908-286-1090
888-269-5372
Fax: 908-464-3553
E-Mail: info@bowker.com
Home Page: www.bowker.com

A who's who directory of services and supplies to the industry.
Cost: $147.00
700 Pages
Frequency: Annual
Circulation: 1,000

1863 **Outerwear Sourcebook: Directory Issue**
Creative Marketing Plus
213-37 39th Avenue
Suite 228
Bayside, NY 11361

718-606-0767
Fax: 718-606-6345
E-Mail: rharrow@creativemarketingplus.com
Home Page: www.creativemarketingplus.com

Richard Harrow, President

List of more than 3,500 outerwear manufacturers in the US and Canada; 1,000 companies providing products and services to the outerwear trade.
Cost: $40.00
Frequency: Annual

1864 **WWD Buyers Guide: Womens Apparel and Accessories Manufacturers**
Fairchild Publications
750 3rd Ave
New York, NY 10017-2703

212-630-4000
Fax: 212-630-3563

Mary G Berner, Chief Executive Officer
Christine Guilfoyle, Publisher

Over 5,500 apparel and accessory manufacturers.
Founded in 1892

1865 **WWD Suppliers Guide**
Fairchild Books and Visuals
750 3rd Ave
New York, NY 10017-2700
212-630-4320
Fax: 212-630-3566

Mary G Berner, Chief Executive Officer
Christine Guilfoyle, Publisher

Over 5,500 apparel and accessory manufacturers in the US. Supplement to WWD Magazine.
Founded in 1892

Industry Web Sites

1866 **http://gold.greyhouse.com**
G.O.L.D Grey House OnLine Databases

Grey House Publishing's online database platform, GOLD, offers Quick Search, Keyword Search and Expert Search in most business sectors, including apparel and accessories markets. The GOLD platform makes finding the information you need quick and easy - whether you're a novice searcher or an experienced database user. All of Grey House's directory products are available for subscription on the GOLD platform.

1867 **www.apparelandfootwear.org**
American Apparel & Footwear Association

The national trade association for the apparel and footwear industries. Conducts seminars, compiles statistics and produces industry reports.

1868 **www.cashmere.org**
Cashmere and Camel Hair Manufacturers Institute

For cashmere and camel hair product manufacturers.

1869 **www.chemicalfabricsandfilm.com**
Chemical Fabrics and Film Association

An international trade association representing manufacturers of polymer-based fabric and film products, used in the building and construction, automotive, fashion and many other industries.

1870 **www.colorassociation.com**
Color Association of the US

Information on color/design issues; issues color charts two years in advance of selling seasons in order to profile popular American colors. Forecasts are issued in women's fashions and men's and children's clothing.

1871 **www.costumedesignersguild.com**
Costume Designers Guild

Works to promote employment and to create improved working conditions for costume designers.

1872 **www.ctda.com**
Custom Tailors and Designers Assn of America

Seeks to promote awareness of designers and makers of men's custom tailored clothing.

1873 **www.embroiderytrade.org**
Embroidery Trade Association

An organization with the objective to continually strengthen the commercial embroidery business.

1874 **www.formalwear.org**
International Formalwear Association
For the formal wear industry.

1875 **www.greyhouse.com**
Grey House Publishing

Authoritative reference directories for most industries, including apparel and accessories. Users can search the online databases with varied search criteria allowing for custom searches by product category, geographic area, sales volume, keyword, subject and more. Full Grey House catalog and online ordering also available.

1876 **www.ifai.com**
Industrial Fabrics Association International

For geosynthetics, fabricators, installers, equipment manufacturers, suppliers, testing firms, consultants, and educators, who produce textiles, nets, mats, grids, and other products.

1877 **www.itaaonline.org**
Int'l Textile & Apparel Assn Membership Directory

For college professors of clothing and textile studies.

1878 **www.naumd.com**
North American Assoc. of Uniform Manufacturers

For manufacturers and distributors of uniforms and career wear.

1879 **www.sewing.org**
American Home Sewing and Craft Association

Handicraft and collectibles forum.

1880 **www.uc-council.org**
GS1 US

Members rely on the standards and services of GS1 US for the effective management and control of their supply chains. Everyday we strive to keep a leader's pace in developing, maintaining, supporting and expanding the services we offer to fulfill our mission.

1881 **www.uniteunion.org**
Union of Needletrade Industrial Textile Employees

A union fighting for working people.

1882 **www.vowsmag.com**
Grimes & Associates
Information on the business specifics necessary for today's wedding professional.

Associations

1883 **Air Conditioning Contractors of America**
2800 S Shirlington Rd
Suite 300
Arlington, VA 22206-3607

703-575-4477
E-Mail: info@acca.org
Home Page: www.acca.org
Social Media: Facebook, Twitter, LinkedIn, YouTube, RSS Feeds, Flickr

Paul T. Stalknecht, President & CEO
Kevin W. Holland, Senior Vice President
Chris Hoelzel, Vice President, Product Fulfillment
Kimya Bailey Cajchun, Vice President of Membership
Craig Gotthardt, Vice President of Information

ACCA is a non-profit association serving the HVACR community, working to promote professional contracting, energy efficiency, and healthy, comfortable indoor environments.
64000 Members
Founded in 1914

1884 **Air-Conditioning, Heating and Refrigeration Institute**
2111 Wilson Boulevard
Suite 500
Arlington, VA 22201

703-524-8800
Fax: 703-562-1942
E-Mail: ahri@ahrinet.org
Home Page: www.ahrinet.org
Social Media: Facebook, Twitter, RSS Feeds

Stephen Yurek, President and CEO
Stephanie Murphy, Chief Financial Officer
Francis Dietz, Vice President of Public Affairs
Bob Johnston, Director/Accounting
Doug Burkes, Manager/Office Operations

AHRI is one of the largest trade associations in the nation, representing heating, water heating, ventilation, air conditioning and commercial refrigeration manufacturers within the global HVACR industry.
300 Members
Founded in 1953

1885 **American Boiler Manufacturers Association**
8221 Old Courthouse Rd
Suite 207
Vienna, VA 22182-3839
703-356-7172
Fax: 703-356-4543
Home Page: www.abma.com
Social Media: Facebook, Twitter, LinkedIn

Kevin Hoey, Chairman
W. Randall Rawson, President & CEO
Geoffrey Hailey, Director of Technical Affairs
Hugh K. Webster, General Counsel
Cheryl Jamall, Director of Meetings

The American Boiler Manufacturers Association (ABMA) is the national, nonprofit trade association of commercial, institutional, industrial and electricity-generating boiler system manufacturing companies (400,000 Btuh heat input), dedicated to the advancement and growth of the boiler and combustion equipment industry.
Founded in 1888

1886 **American Society of Heating, Refrigeration & Air-Conditioning Engineers**
1791 Tullie Cir NE
Atlanta, GA 30329-2398

404-636-8400
800-527-4723
Fax: 404-321-5478
E-Mail: ashrae@ashrae.org
Home Page: www.ashrae.org
Social Media: Facebook, Twitter, LinkedIn

William P. Bahnfleth, President
Jeff H Littleton, Executive VP
Darryl K. Boyce, P.Eng., Vice President
Bjarne W. Olesen, Ph.D., Vice President
Daniel C. Pettway, Vice President

An international organization that fulfills its mission of advancing heating, ventilation, air conditioning and refrigeration to serve humanity and promote a sustainable world through research, standards writing, publishing and continuing education.
55000 Members
Founded in 1894

1887 **American Society of Mechanical Engineers**
Two Park Avenue
New York, NY 10016-5900

973-882-1170
800 843-2763
Fax: 202-429-9417
E-Mail: infocentral@asme.org
Home Page: www.asme.org
Social Media: Facebook, Twitter, LinkedIn

Madiha El Mehelmy Kotb, President
Thomas G. Loughlin, Executive Director
Chitra Sethi, Managing Editor
David Walsh, Editor
John Kosowatz, Senior Editor

ASME is a not-for-profit membership organization that enables collaboration, knowledge sharing, career enrichment, and skills development across all engineering disciplines, toward a goal of helping the global engineering community develop solutions to benefit lives and livelihoods.
12000 Members
Founded in 1880

1888 **American Vacuum Society (AVS)**
125 Maiden Lane
15th Floor
New York, NY 10038

212-248-0200
Fax: 212-248-0245
Home Page: www.avs.org
Social Media: Facebook, Twitter, LinkedIn, RSS Feeds

Susan B. Sinnott, President
Jeannette DeGennaro, Exhibition & Sales Manager
Yvonne Towse, Managing Director
Ricky Baldeo, Office Services Coordinator
Angela Klink, Member Services Administrator

As an interdisciplinary, professional Society, AVS supports networking among academic, industrial, government, and consulting professionals involved in a variety of disciplines - chemistry, physics, biology, mathematics, business, sales, etc through common interests related to the basic science, technology development and commercialization of materials, interfaces, and processing areas.
4500 Members
Founded in 1953

1889 **Association of Home Appliance Manufacturers**
1111 19th Street NW
Suite 402
Washington, DC 20036
202-872-5955
Fax: 202-872-9354
E-Mail: info@aham.org
Home Page: www.aham.org

Paul V. Sikir, Board Chair
Joseph M. McGuire, President
Peter Frank, Vice President, Finance
Nick Baker, Manager, Communications
Jennifer Cleary, Director/Regulatory Affairs

A not-for-profit trade association representing manufacturers of major and portable home appliance, floor care appliances and suppliers to the industry .
Founded in 1915

1890 **Industrial Heating Equipment Association**
5040 Old Taylor Mill Rd.
PMB 13
Taylor Mill, KY 41015
859-356-1575
Fax: 859-356-0908
E-Mail: ihea@ihea.org
Home Page: www.ihea.org
Social Media: Facebook

Tim Lee, President
Bill Pasley, 1st Vice President
Mike Shay, 2nd Vice President
Jay Cherry, Treasurer

The Industrial Heating Equipment Association (IHEA) is a voluntary national trade association representing the major segments of the industrial heat processing equipment industry.
Founded in 1929

1891 **International Housewares Association**
6400 Shafer Ct
Suite 650
Rosemont, IL 60018-4929

847-292-4200
Fax: 847-292-4211
E-Mail: pbrandl@housewares.org
Home Page: www.housewares.org
Social Media: Facebook, Twitter, LinkedIn, YouTube

Richard L. Boynton, Chairman
Phil J. Brandl, President
Dean Kurtis, Vice President, Finance
Mia Rampersad, Vice President, Trade Show
Perry Reynolds, Vice President, Marketing

A full-service trade association dedicated to promoting the sales and marketing of housewares.
Founded in 1938

1892 **International Institute of Ammonia Refrigeration**
1001 N. Fairfax Street
Suite 503
Alexandria, VA 22314

703-312-4200
Fax: 703-312-0065
E-Mail: info@iiar.org
Home Page: www.iiar.org
Social Media: Facebook, LinkedIn

Robert Port, Jr., Chairman
David L. Rule, President
Bruce Badger, Chief Operating Officer
Marcos Braz, Chair-Elect
Tom Leighty, Vice Chair

IAR is an organization providing advocacy, education, standards, and information for the benefit of the ammonia refrigeration industry worldwide. IIAR's vision is to be recognized as the world's leading advocate for the safe, reli-

able and efficient use of ammonia and other natural refrigerants for industrial applications.
1200 Members
Founded in 1971

1893 **International Kitchen Exhaust Cleaning Association**
100 North 20th Street
Suite 400
Philadelphia, PA 19103

215-320-3876
Fax: 215-564-2175
E-Mail: information@ikeca.org
Home Page: www.ikeca.org
Social Media: Facebook, Twitter, LinkedIn, YouTube

Jack SchulerGrace, CECS, CE, President
Sarah Hagy, Executive Director
Lisa Chester, Associate Director
Hanna Linn, Administrative Director
Gina Marinilli, Standard Development Director

Promotes fire safety in restaurants and professionalism in the kitchen exhaust cleaning industry. This not for profit trade association, has established stringent standards and practices for contractors engaged in kitchen exhaust cleaning, conducted a variety of educational programs, and worked with influential code setting bodies such as the National Fire Protection Association to improve existing codes and regulations.
Founded in 1989

1894 **International Microwave Power Institute**
PO Box 1140
PO Box 1140
Mechanicsville, VA 23111-5007

804-559-6667
Fax: 804-559-4087
E-Mail: info@impi.org
Home Page: www.impi.org
Social Media: Facebook, Twitter

Molly Poisant, Executive Director
Ben Wilson, Executive Committee
John Gerling, Executive Committee
Ric Gonzalez, Executive Committee
Bob Schiffman, Executive Committee

The International Microwave Power Institute (IMPI) was founded in 1966 in Canada to serve the information needs of specialists working with microwave and RF heating systems. In 1977, the Institute reorganized to expand its industrial and scientific base to meet the information needs evolving in consumer microwave ovens and related products.
Founded in 1966

1895 **National Air Duct Cleaners Association**
15000 Commerce Parkway
Suite C
Mt Laurel, NJ 08054

856-380-6810
Fax: 856-439-0525
E-Mail: info@nadca.com
Home Page: www.nadca.com

Bill Benito, President
Rick MacDonald, 1st Vice President
Michael Vinick, 2nd Vice President
Mike Dwyer, CAE, Chief Relationship Officer
Jodi Araujo, Executive Director

NADCA: The HVAC Inspection, Maintenance and Restoration Association, otherwise known as the National Air Duct Cleaners Association (NADCA), was formed in 1989 as a non-profit association of companies engaged in the cleaning of HVAC systems. Its mission was to promote source removal as the only acceptable method of cleaning and to establish industry standards for the association.
1000 Members
Founded in 1989

1896 **National Kitchen and Bath Association**
687 Willow Grove St
Hackettstown, NJ 07840-1731

908-850-1206
800-843-6522
Fax: 908-852-1695
E-Mail: feedback@nkba.org
Home Page: www.nkba.org
Social Media: Facebook, Twitter, LinkedIn, Pinterest

John K. Morgan, President
Carolyn F. Cheetham, CMKBD, Vice President
Bill Darcy, Chief Executive Officer
Stephen Graziano, Senior Director of Finance
Nancy Barnes, Director of Learning

The NKBA enhances the success of its members in the kitchen and bath industry through networking, education, certification, marketing and business tools, leadership opportunities, and the annual Kitchen/Bath Industry Show.
40000 Members
Founded in 1963

1897 **North American Retail Dealers Association**
222 South Riverside Plaza
Suite 2100
Chicago, IL 60606

312-648-0649
800-621-0298
Fax: 312-648-1212
E-Mail: nardasvc@narda.com
Home Page: www.narda.com
Social Media: Facebook, LinkedIn

Leon Barbachano, Chairman
Timothy W. Seavey, First Vice Chairman
Otto Papasadero, Executive Director
Pam Clark, Administrative Assistant
Bob Goldberg, Legal Counsel

To enhance the ability of independent appliance retailers to build progressive, profitable businesses. NARDA members sell and serve kitchen and laundry appliances, consumer home and mobile electronics, computers and other home and small office products, furniture, sewing machines, vacuum cleaners, room air conditioners, and other consumer home products.
3000 Members
Founded in 1943

1898 **Professional Service Association**
71 Columbia Street
Cohoes, NY 12047-2939

518-237-7777
888-777-8851
Fax: 518-237-0418
E-Mail: psaworld@aol.com
Home Page: www.psaworld.com

Don Holman, President
Carmine D'Alessandro, Vice President
Linda Knudsen, Administrative Vice President
Randy Carney, Executive Director
Tom Lundin, Director

PSA is an independent trade association dedicated to the highest standards of quality service. The purpose of PSA is to be the voice of the independent service provider and to assess and identify industry related problems and provide solutions. PSA is dedicated to providing educational training, certification, business management training, support and fairness to the independent service industry. PSA encourages professionalism and honesty identifies those techs who provide that kind of service.
Cost: $150.00
1105 Members
Frequency: Membership Fee
Founded in 1989

1899 **Refrigeration Service Engineers Society**
1911 Rohlwig Road
Suite A
Rolling Meadows, IL 60008-1397

847-297-6464
800-297-5660
Fax: 847-297-5038
E-Mail: general@rses.org
Home Page: www.rses.org
Social Media: Facebook, Twitter, LinkedIn, RSS Feeds, Pinterest, Tumblr,

Roger M. Hensley, CMS, E&E, Board Chairman
Joe Marchese, CMS, International President
Harlan Krepcik, International Vice President
Michael Thompson, International Secretary/Treasurer
Nick Reggi, CMS, RCT, International Sergeant at Arms

To provide opportunities for enhanced technical competence by offering comprehensive, cutting-edge education and certification to our members and the HVACR industry. To advance the professionalism and proficiency of our industry through alliances with other HVACR associations. To be the definitive industry leader in all segments of the HVACR industry by providing superior educational training.
15231 Members
Founded in 1933

1900 **Silicon Valley Compucycle**
1096 Pecten Ct
Milpitas, CA 95035

408-432-1239
866-989-2970
Fax: 408-432-1249
E-Mail: svcinfo@svc.com
Home Page: www.svc.com
Social Media: Facebook, Twitter

Vivienne Harwood Mattox, Executive Director
Yvonne Swartz, Executive Manager
Beth Strong, Marketing & Communications Manager

Association dedicated to promote technical excellence by providing a global forum to inform, educate, and engage the members, the technical community, and the public on all aspects of vacuum coating, surface engineering and related technologies.
Founded in 2001

Newsletters

1901 **ACCA Insider**
Air Conditioning Contractors of America
2800 Shirlington Rd
Suite 300
Arlington, VA 22206-3607

703-575-4477
E-Mail: info@acca.org
Home Page: www.acca.org
Social Media: Facebook, Twitter, LinkedIn, YouTube

Paul T Stalknecht, President & CEO

Each issue contains association and industry news, boiled down into a brief, easy to read format that will keep you up to date in just five minutes each Monday.
Frequency: Weekly

1902 **AVEM Newsletter**
Association of Vacuum Equipment Manufacturers
International
201 Park Washington Court
Falls Church, VA 22046-4527

703-538-3543
Fax: 703-241-5603
E-Mail: aveminfo@avem.org
Home Page: www.avem.org

Dennis S. Pellegrino, President

Association news, member company news and informational articles regarding government programs, standards, economics, international trade and other issues affecting business operations.
49 Members
Frequency: Quarterly
Founded in 1969
Mailing list available for rent

1903 **Insights**
1791 Tullie Cir NE
Atlanta, GA 30329-2398

404-636-8400
800-527-4723
Fax: 404-321-5478
E-Mail: ashrae@ashrae.org
Home Page: www.ashrae.org
Social Media: Facebook, Twitter

Lee Burgett, President
Jeff H Littleton, Executive VP

ASHRAE Insights is the Society's newsletter with articles of interest to members, including Chapter News, Obituaries, Membership Advancement and other news.
55000 Members
Frequency: 6x/Year
Founded in 1894

1904 **SVC Bulletin**
Society of Vacuum Coaters
71 Pinon Hill Place NE
Albuquerque, NM 87122

505-856-7188
Fax: 505-856-6716
E-Mail: svcinfo@svc.com
Home Page: www.svc.com
Social Media: Facebook, Twitter

Vivienne Harwood Mattox, Executive Director
Yvonne Swartz, Executive Manager
Beth Strong, Marketing & Communications Manager

The SVC bulletin is distributed to professionals working in the vacuum coating community and related sciences and technologies. Each issue contains contributed articles, previews, or reviews of the TechCon; SVC committee activities; technical articles from the Conference Proceedings; book reviews, Corporate Sponsor news and profiles; and Society news.
Frequency: 3x/Year
Circulation: 15000

1905 **The Buzz**
Air Conditioning Contractors of America
2800 Shirlington Rd
Suite 300
Arlington, VA 22206-3607

703-575-4477
E-Mail: info@acca.org
Home Page: www.acca.org
Social Media: Facebook, Twitter, LinkedIn, YouTube

Paul Stalknecht, President & CEO

Roundup of latest news and interesting links for HVACR professionals.
Frequency: Weekly
Founded in 1984

1906 **Your Business**
Air Conditioning Contractors of America
2800 Shirlington Rd
Suite 300
Arlington, VA 22206-3607

703-575-4477
E-Mail: info@acca.org
Home Page: www.acca.org
Social Media: Facebook, Twitter, LinkedIn, YouTube

Paul Stalknecht, President & CEO

Contains management advice for small business owners.
Frequency: Bi-Weekly
Founded in 1984

1907 **eSociety**
1791 Tullie Cir NE
Atlanta, GA 30329-2398

404-636-8400
800-527-4723
Fax: 404-321-5478
E-Mail: ashrae@ashrae.org
Home Page: www.ashrae.org
Social Media: Facebook, Twitter

Lee Burgett, President
Jeff H Littleton, Executive VP

The official electronic newsletter of ASHRAE. Contains monthly news form the society about its activities and chapters.
55000 Members
Frequency: Monthly
Founded in 1894

Magazines & Journals

1908 **ACCA Contractor Excellence**
Air Conditioning Contractors of America
2800 Shirlington Rd
Suite 300
Arlington, VA 22206-3607

703-575-4477
E-Mail: info@acca.org
Home Page: www.acca.org
Social Media: Facebook, Twitter, LinkedIn, YouTube

Paul T Stalknecht, President & CEO

Representing the HVACR contracting industry. We help our members acquire and satisfy customers while upholding the most stringent requirements for professional ethics, and advocating for improvements to the industry overall.
Founded in 1914

1909 **ACR Standard: Assessment, Cleaning & Restoration of HVAC Systems**
National Air Duct Cleaners Association
1518 K St NW
Suite 503
Washington, DC 20005-1203

202-737-2926
Fax: 202-347-8847
E-Mail: info@nadca.com
Home Page: www.nadca.com

Ken Sufka, Owner

1910 **AHRI Trends Magazine**
Air Conditioning & Refrigeration Institute
2111 Wilson Boulevard
Suite 500
Arlington, VA 22201

703-524-8800
Fax: 703-528-3816
E-Mail: ahri@ahri.net
Home Page: www.ari.org

A resource for HVAC contractors and technicians.

1911 **ASHRAE Journal**
American Society of Heating, Refrigeration & AC
1791 Tullie Cir NE
Atlanta, GA 30329-2398

404-636-8400
800-527-4723
Fax: 404-321-5478
E-Mail: ashrae@ashrae.org
Home Page: www.ashrae.org

Lee Burgett, President
Jeff H Littleton, Executive VP

Explores topical technical issues, such as: indoor air quality, energy management, thermal storage, alternative refrigerants, fire and life safety and more.
Cost: $59.00
Frequency: Monthly

1912 **ASME International Journal**
American Society of Mechanical Engineers
3 Park Ave
Floor 22
New York, NY 10016-5902

212-591-7000
800-843 2763
Fax: 212-591-8676
E-Mail: infocentral@asme.org
Home Page: www.asme.org

David Walsh, Editor
Chitra Sethi, Managing Editor

Provides advanced scientific and technological information for the mechanical engineering industry to facilitate the international exchange and transfer of technology.
Cost: $375.00
Frequency: Monthly

1913 **Appliance**
Dana Chase Publications
1110 Jorie Boulevard
PO Box 90919
Oak Brook, IL 60522-9019

630-990-3484
Fax: 630-990-0078
E-Mail: lisa@appliance.com
Home Page: www.appliancemagazine.com

George Shurtleff, Production Manager
Maria Nigro, Circulation Director
Dana Chase Jr, Chairman

Devoted to serving the appliance industry worldwide, producers of consumer, commercial, business and medical appliances. Editorial material serves product engineering and design, production management and supervision, purchasing, management, marketing, sales and service. Accepts advertising.
Cost: $75.00
90 Pages
Frequency: Monthly
Circulation: 34500
ISSN: 0003-6781
Founded in 1944

1914 **Appliance Design**
Business News Publishing
2401 W Big Beaver Rd
Suite 700
Troy, MI 48084-3333

248-362-3700
877-747-1625
Fax: 248-362-0317
E-Mail: info@asnews.com

Home Page: www.bnpmedia.com
Social Media: Facebook, Twitter

Mitchell Henderson, CEO
Richard Babyak, Editor-in-Chief
Amy Alef, Production Manager
Mary Lowe, Associate Editor

Devoted to providing solutions for design and engineering teams in the global, commercial, and medical appliance/durable goods industry.
Circulation: 25,000
ISSN: 0003-6803
Founded in 1955
Printed in 4 colors on glossy stock

1915 **Appliance Service News**
Gamit Enterprises
1917 S Street
PO Box 808
St Charles, IL 60174

630-845-9481
877-747-1625
Fax: 630-845-9483
E-Mail: info@asnews.com
Home Page: www.applianceservicenews.com

William Wingstedt, Editor/Publisher
Peggy Wingstedt, Sales Representative

Published for owners, managers and technicians of appliance repair dealers. Accepts advertising.
Cost: $59.95
36 Pages
Frequency: Monthly
Circulation: 33000
ISSN: 0003-6803
Founded in 1950
Printed in 4 colors on glossy stock

1916 **Boiler Systems Engineering Magazine**
American Boiler Manufacturers Association
8221 Old Courthouse Rd
Suite 202
Vienna, VA 22182-3839

703-356-7172
Fax: 703-522-2665
E-Mail: randy@abma.com
Home Page: www.abma.com
Social Media: Facebook, Twitter, LinkedIn

Randell Rawson, President
Diana McClung, Executive Assistant
Cheryl Jamall, Director Of Meetings
Frequency: Monthly
Founded in 1888

1917 **Contractor Excellence**
Air Conditioning Contractors of America
2800 S Shirlington Rd
Suite 300
Arlington, VA 22206-3607

703-575-4477
E-Mail: info@acca.org
Home Page: www.acca.org

Paul Stalknecht, President

A quality source of business information for the HVAC industry, available to members.
Frequency: Quarterly
Founded in 2002

1918 **HPE Magazine**
American Boiler Manufacturers Association
8221 Old Courthouse Rd
Suite 202
Vienna, VA 22182-3839

703-356-7172
Fax: 703-522-2665
E-Mail: randy@abma.com
Home Page: www.abma.com
Social Media: Facebook, Twitter, LinkedIn

Randell Rawson, President
Diana McClung, Executive Assistant
Cheryl Jamall, Director Of Meetings
Founded in 1888

1919 **HVAC&R Research Journal**
American Society of Heating, Refrigeration & AC
1791 Tullie Circle NE
Atlanta, GA 30329-2398

404-636-8400
800-527-4723
Fax: 404-321-5478
E-Mail: ashrae@ashrae.org
Home Page: www.ashrae.org

Tom Watson, President
Jeff H Littleton, Executive VP

Offers the most comprehensive reporting of archival research in the fields of environmental control for the built environment. Also covers cooling technolgies for a wide range of applications and related processes and concepts, including underlying thermodynamics, fluid dynamics, and heat transfer.
Frequency: Bi-Monthly
ISBN: 1-883413-98-2

1920 **Indoor Comfort News Magazine**
Institute of Heating and Air Conditioning
454 W Broadway
Glendale, CA 91204-1209

818-551-1555
Fax: 818-551-1115
E-Mail: ihaci@ihaci.org
Home Page: www.ihaci.org

Susan Evans, Senior VP

A tool for attaining the trade association's goal of educating and promoting the HVAC/R/SM industry. Readers are top buyers and decision makers. They service and install new construction and replacement/retrofit projects.
Frequency: Monthly
Founded in 1955

1921 **Journal of Microwave Power and Electromagnetic Energy**
International Microwave Power Institute
7076 Drinkard Way
P O Box 1140
Mechanicsville, VA 23111-5007

804-559-6667
Fax: 804-559-4087
E-Mail: info@impi.org
Home Page: www.impi.org

Molly Poisant, Executive Director

Designed for the information needs of professionals specializing in the research and design of industrial and bio-medical applications, the Journal exemplifies the highest standards of scientific and technical information on the theory and application of electromagnetic power.
Cost: $250.00
Frequency: Quarterly

1922 **RSES Journal**
Refrigeration Service Engineers Society
1911 Rohlwing Road
Suite A
Rolling Meadows, IL 60008-1397

847-297-6464
800-297-5660
Fax: 847-297-5038
E-Mail: general@rses.org
Home Page: www.rses.org
Social Media: Facebook, Twitter, LinkedIn

Mark Lowry, Executive Vice President
Lori A Kasallis, Editor

Providing quality technical content in digital and printed forms that can be applied on the job site.
Frequency: Monthly
Circulation: 15231

1923 **Today's Boiler**
American Boiler Manufacturers Association
8221 Old Courthouse Rd
Suite 202
Vienna, VA 22182-3839

703-356-7172
Fax: 703-522-2665
Home Page: www.abma.com

W Randy Rawson, President & CEO

Trends, Technologies & Innovations, The Official Magazine of the American Boiler Manufacturers Association.
Founded in 1888

Trade Shows

1924 **ABMA Annual Meeting**
American Boiler Manufacturers Association
8221 Old Courthouse Road
Suite 207
Vienna, VA 22182-3839

703-356-7172
Fax: 703-356-4543
Home Page: www.abma.com

Jack Rentz, Chairman
W Randall Rawson, President/CEO
Kevin Hoey, Vice Chairman
Tom Giaier, Secretary

The association's premier membership networking event where members have the opportunity to learn about developments and trends inside and outside the industry, and have the opportunity, through committee and product/market group meetings to focus on issues and concerns of specific relevance to their product and market segments.
Frequency: Bi-Annual

1925 **ABMA Manufacturers Conference**
American Boiler Manufacturers Association
8221 Old Courthouse Road
Suite 207
Vienna, VA 22182-3839

703-356-7172
Fax: 703-356-4543
Home Page: www.abma.com

Jack Rentz, Chairman
W Randall Rawson, President/CEO
Kevin Hoey, Vice Chairman
Tom Giaier, Secretary

Designed to bring together manufacturing plant, office and others concerned with the design, fabrication, sales and distribution of ABMA products and services to network, discuss trends and developments, and problem solve with others in the industry and with outside experts.
Frequency: Annual/October

1926 **ACCA Conference & Indoor Air Expo**
Air Conditioning Contractors of America
2800 Shirlington Rd
Suite 300
Arlington, VA 22206

703-575-4477
E-Mail: info@acca.org
Home Page: www.acca.org
Social Media: Facebook, Twitter, LinkedIn, YouTube

Paul Stalknecht, President & CEO
Rosemary Graeme, Executive Assistant
Kevin W. Holland, Senior Vice President

Workshops and learning opportunities for HVAC contractors.
Frequency: Annual/March

1927 **AHAM Annual Meeting**
Association of Home Appliance Manufacturers

1111 19th Street NW
Suite 402
Washington, DC 20036

202-872-5955
Fax: 202-872-9354
E-Mail: info@aham.org
Home Page: www.aham.org

Edward V McAssey III, Chairman
Nick Baker, Manager
Alan M Holaday, Treasurer
Joseph M McGuire, President
Kevin Messner, Vice President

Provides ideas for the solution of problems and concerns of the Cross Functional Design.
Frequency: Annual/April

1928 **AHRI Annual Meeting**
Air-Conditioning, Heating & Refrigeration Inst
2111 Wilson Boulevard
Suite 500
Arlington, VA 22201

703-524-8800
Fax: 703-528-3816
E-Mail: ahri@ahrinet.org
Home Page: www.ahrinet.org

Stephen R Yurek, President
Stephanie Murphy, CFO
AmandaE. Donahue, Executive Assistant

The premiere networking experience of the heating, ventillation, air conditioning and commercial refrigeration manufacturing industry addresses the topics and issues you want most. Offers opportunities to learn about the top issues facing the industry, network with industry leaders and colleagues, and participate in product section business
480+ Attendees
Frequency: November

1929 **ASME International Mechanical Engineering Congress and Exposition**
American Society of Mechanical Engineers
Three Park Avenue
New York, NY 10016-5990

973-882-1170
800-843-2763
E-Mail: infocentral@asme.org
Home Page: www.asme.org

Sam Y Zamrik PhD, President
David Walsh, Editor
Chitra Sethi, Managing Editor
John Kosowatz, Senior Editor

Hundreds of sessions, forums, exhibits, tours and social events keep you current on the latest trends in technology and industry, and provide the opportunity to trade tips and share ideas with engineers in different industries and companies around the world.
Frequency: Annual/Fall

1930 **Fall Tech Conference**
15000 Commerce Parkway
Suite C
Mt. Laurel, NJ 08054

856-380-6810
Fax: 856-439-0525
E-Mail: info@nadca.com
Home Page: www.nadca.com

Kenneth M Sufka, Executive Vice President
Jodi Araujo, Executive Director
Leanne Murray, Director Membership
Jess Madden, Director Publications
Claire MacNab, Director Meetings

One-stop shop for training and certification. Designed to help members stand out from the competition. NADCA's trainers are highly experienced and know what it takes to be ultra successful in the HVAC cleaning industry.
1000 Members
Founded in 1989

1931 **GAMA Annual Meeting**
Gas Appliance Manufacturers Association
2107 Wilson Boulevard
Suite 600
Arlington, VA 22201

703-525-7060
Fax: 703-525-6790
E-Mail: sheit@gamanet.org
Home Page: www.gamanet.org

Stacy Heit, Manager of Meetings/Events

National trade association whose members manufacture space and water heating appliances, components and related products.
405 Attendees
Frequency: Annual
Founded in 1935

1932 **HARDI Annual Fall Conference**
15000 Commerce Parkway
Suite C
Mt. Laurel, NJ 08054

856-380-6810
Fax: 856-439-0525
E Mail: info@nadca.com
Home Page: www.nadca.com

Kenneth M Sufka, Executive Vice President
Jodi Araujo, Executive Director
Leanne Murray, Director Membership
Jess Madden, Director Publications
Claire MacNab, Director Meetings

Conference offers information on profitability, confidence in navigating the economic waters, and finding the most effective and efficient means to achieve the market and profit objectives.
1000 Members
Founded in 1989

1933 **IIAR**
1001 N. Fairfax Street
Suite 503
Alexandria, VA 22314

703-312-4200
Fax: 703-312 0065
E-Mail: iiar_request@iiar.org
Home Page: www.iiar.org

David L. Rule, President

IIAR provides advocacy, education, and standards for the benefit of the global community in the safe and sustainable installation and operation of ammonia and other natural refrigerant systems.
2086 Members
Founded in 1971

1934 **IMPI Annual Symposium**
International Microwave Power Institute
7076 Drinkard Way
P O Box 1140
Mechanicsville, VA 23111

804-596-6667
Fax: 804-559-4087
E-Mail: info@impi.org
Home Page: www.impi.org

Molly Poisant, Executive Director
Neal Cooper, Treasurer

Brings together researchers from across the globe to share the latest findings related to non-communications uses of microwave energy.
Frequency: Annual/June

1935 **International Air Conditioning, Heating & Refrigerating Expo**
International Exposition Company
15 Franklin Street
Westport, CT 06880

203-221-9232
Fax: 203-221-9260
E-Mail: info@ahrexpo.com
Home Page: www.ahrexpo.com

Mark Stevens, VP
Jeff Stevens, Sales VP
Kelley Stevens, Sales Manager

Co-sponsored by American Society of Heating, Refrigeration and Air Conditioning Engineers and the Air Conditioning and Refrigeration Institute, this expo features exhibits that include equipment and services of industrial, commercial and residential heating, refrigeration, air conditioning and ventilation.
37292 Attendees
Frequency: Annual/January
Founded in 1930

1936 **International CES Show**
1111 19th Street NW
Suite 402
Washington, DC 20036

202-872-5955
Fax: 202-872-9354
E-Mail: info@aham.org
Home Page: www.aham.org

Paul Sikir, Chairman
Jennifer Mintman, First Vice Chairperson
Jennifer Mintman, Treasurer
Joseph M McGuire, President

World's largest consumer technology tradeshow.
Founded in 1915

1937 **International Home & Housewares Show**
International Housewares Associaton
6400 Shafer Court
Suite 650
Rosemont, IL 60018

847-292-4200
Fax: 847-292-4211
E-Mail: sjanota@houseares.org
Home Page: www.housewares.org

Mia Rampersad, VP, Trade Shows
Sharon Janota, Manager, Trade Show Operations
David Reeves, Manager, Information Technology
Dean Kurtis, Finance & Information Technology
Judy Colitz, Manager Special Events

International housewares marketplace, showcasing thousands of new products and designs.
18500 Attendees
Frequency: March

1938 **International Housewares Show**
1111 19th Street NW
Suite 402
Washington, DC 20036

202-872-5955
Fax: 202-872-9354
E-Mail: info@aham.org
Home Page: www.aham.org

Paul Sikir, Chairman
Jennifer Mintman, First Vice Chairperson
Jennifer Mintman, Treasurer
Joseph M McGuire, President

The center of the IHA's yearly activities. One of the top 20 largest trade shows in the U.S. and in the top 10 in Chicago.
Founded in 1915

1939 **Kitchen & Bath Industry Show**
1111 19th Street NW
Suite 402
Washington, DC 20036

202-872-5955
Fax: 202-872-9354

E-Mail: info@aham.org
Home Page: www.aham.org

Paul Sikir, Chairman
Jennifer Mintman, First Vice Chairperson
Jennifer Mintman, Treasurer
Joseph M McGuire, President

The ultimate Kitchen & Bath destination. The freshest designs, products and technology from 500 leading manufacturers and suppliers. The brightest and best in the industry assemble to spot trends, see and experience product introductions, acquire knowledge and find the practical solutions and valuable connections.
Founded in 1915

1940 **Kitchen/Bath Industry Show and Conference**
National Kitchen & Bath Association
687 Willow Grove Street
Hackettstown, NJ 07840

800-843-6522
Fax: 908-852-1695
E-Mail: feedback@nkba.org
Home Page: www.nkba.org

Alan Zielinski, CEO& President
Timothy Captain, PR Manager
John A Petrie, Vice President
Carolyn Cheetham, Treasurer
Bill Darcy, CEO

Showcases the latest products and cutting-edge design ideas of the kitchen and bath industry.
40000 Attendees
Frequency: May

1941 **NADCA's Annual Meeting & Exposition**
15000 Commerce Parkway
Suite C
Mt. Laurel, NJ 08054

856-380-6810
Fax: 856-439-0525
E-Mail: info@nadca.com
Home Page: www.nadca.com

Kenneth M Sufka, Executive Vice President
Jodi Araujo, Executive Director
Leanne Murray, Director Membership
Jess Madden, Director Publications
Claire MacNab, Director Meetings

Promises educational sessions, live equipment demonstrations, and opportunities to meet peers.
1000 Members
Founded in 1989

1942 **NASA Convention & Trade Show**
National Appliance Service Association
3407 Williams Drive
PO Box 2514
Kokomo, IN 46904

765-453-1820
Fax: 765-453-1895
E-Mail: nasahq2011@gmail.com
Home Page: www.nasa1.org

Scott Kopin, President
Gordon Daniels, VP/Treasurer
Carrie Giannakos, Executive Director
Mike Hanika, Director
Don Kehoe, Director

Classes on marketing, advertising, customer service, machine repair by experienced professionals in the industry. Attendees are informed about industry trends and products, and have the opportunity to take advantage of show specials offered by exhibitors.
Frequency: Annual

1943 **NCCA Annual Meeting**
National Coil Coaters Association
1300 Sumner Avenue
Cleveland, OH 44115

216-241-7333
Fax: 216-241-0105
E-Mail: ncca@coilcoating.org
Home Page: www.coilcoating.org

Jeff Alexander, President
Jeff Widenor, Vice President
John Favilla, Treasurer
Frequency: April

1944 **National Appliance Parts Suppliers**
National Appliance Parts Suppliers Association
4015 W MARSHALL AVE
Longview, TX 75604

903- 75- 398
E-Mail: board11@napsaweb.org
Home Page: www.napsaweb.org

Jim Bossman, President
Sherry Harrell, Secretary, Treasurer
Jason Cunningham, Secretary

For those in the appliance parts replacement business. Containing 62 booths and 60 exhibits.

1945 **RSES Annual Conference and HVAC Technology Expo**
Refrigeration Service Engineers Society
1911 Rohlwing Road
Suite A
Rolling Meadows, IL 60008-1397

847-297-6464
800-297-5660
E-Mail: general@rses.org
Home Page: www.rses.org
Social Media: Facebook, Twitter, LinkedIn

Mark Lowry, Executive Vice President
Lori Kasallis, Publisher Editor
Jean Birch, Conference & Seminar Manager

80 booths consisting primarily of products and services.

1946 **SMACNA Annual Convention**
15000 Commerce Parkway
Suite C
Mt. Laurel, NJ 08054

856-380-6810
Fax: 856-439-0525
E-Mail: info@nadca.com
Home Page: www.nadca.com

Kenneth M Sufka, Executive Vice President
Jodi Araujo, Executive Director
Leanne Murray, Director Membership
Jess Madden, Director Publications
Claire MacNab, Director Meetings

Business and skill tips for HVAC and Contractor professionals.
1000 Members
Founded in 1989

1947 **VDTA/SDTA International Trade Show**
1111 19th Street NW
Suite 402
Washington, DC 20036

202-872-5955
Fax: 202-872-9354
E-Mail: info@aham.org
Home Page: www.aham.org

Paul Sikir, Chairman
Jennifer Mintman, First Vice Chairperson
Jennifer Mintman, Treasurer
Joseph M McGuire, President

Featuring exhibits, and seminars for the vacuum and sewing business.
Founded in 1915

1948 **World Educational Congress for Laundering and Drycleaning (Clean Show)**
Riddle & Associates
3098 Piedmont Road NE
Suite 350
Atlanta, GA 30305

404-876-1988
Fax: 404-876-5121
E-Mail: info@cleanshow.com
Home Page: www.cleanshow.com
Social Media: Facebook, Twitter

John Riddle, Manager
Ann Howell, Communications

World's largest exposition for laundry, drycleaning and textile services industry featuring working equipment and educational program. Draws international attendance.
11000 Attendees
Frequency: Biennial, Odd Years
Founded in 1977

Directories & Databases

1949 **A Portrait of the US Appliance Industry**
UBM Canon
11444 W. Olympic Blvd.
Los Angeles, CA 90064

310-445-4200
Fax: 310-445-4299
E-Mail: www.ubm.com
Home Page: www.appliancemagazine.com

David J Chase, President
Susan Chase Korin, CEO

Appliance companies in the US.
Cost: $45.00
Frequency: Annual
Founded in 1944

1950 **Complete Directory of Small Appliances**
Sutton Family Communications & Publishing Company
920 State Route 54 East
Elmitch, KY 42343

270-276-9500
E-Mail: jlsutton@apex.net

Theresa Sutton, Publisher
Lee Sutton, Editor

Print-out from database of wholesalers, manufacturers, distributors, importers and close-out houses. Database is updated daily to guarantee the most current and up-to-date sources available.
Cost: $55.20
100 Pages

1951 **Directory of Certified Performance (Online)**
Air Conditioning & Refrigeration Institute
Ste 500
2111 Wilson Blvd
Arlington, VA 22201-3036

703-524-8800
Fax: 703-528-3816
E-Mail: ari@ari.org
Home Page: www.ari.org

Stephen R Yurek, President

The trusted source of performace certified heating, ventilation, air-conditioning, and commercial refrigeration equipment and components.

Industry Web Sites

1952 **http://gold.greyhouse.com**
G.O.L.D Grey House OnLine Databases
Grey House Publishing's online database platform, GOLD, offers Quick Search, Keyword Search and Expert Search for most business sectors including appliances and small electroincs. The GOLD platform makes finding the information you need quick and easy. All of Grey House's directory products are available for subscription on the GOLD platform.

1953 **www.abma.com**
American Boiler Manufacturers Association
Represents companies involved in utility, industrial and commercial steam generation.

1954 **www.acca.org**
Air Conditioning Contractors of America
Representing the HVACR contracting industry. We help our members acquire and satisfy customers while upholding the most stringent requirements for professional ethics, and advocating for improvements to the industry overall.

1955 **www.aga.org**
American Gas Association
Represents local energy utility companies that deliver natural gas to more than 56 million homes, businesses and industries throughout the United States.

1956 **www.aham.org**
Association of Home Appliance Manufacturers
Statistical information and summaries on appliances.

1957 **www.apda.com**
Appliance Parts Distributors Association
Promotes the sale of appliance parts through independent distributors.

1958 **www.appliancemagazine.com**
Dana Chase Publications
Appliance industry information content focused into 20 industry zones for targeted editorial coverage.

1959 **www.ari.org**
Air Conditioning & Refrigeration Institute
Representing manufacturers of central air-conditioning and commercial refrigeration equipment.

1960 **www.ashrae.org**
American Society of Heating, Refrigeration & A/C
Serving the heating, ventilation, air conditioning and refrigeration industries.

1961 **www.asme.org**
American Society of Mechanical Engineers
Focuses on technical, educational and research issues of the engineering and technology community.

1962 **www.bema.org**
Bakery Equipment Manufacturers Association
Serves the baking and snack food industries.

1963 **www.gamanet.org**
Gas Appliance Manufacturers Association
Serves the residential, commercial and industrial gas and oil fired appliance industries.

1964 **www.ge.com**
General Electric
Information on home appliances, lighting, home solutions, corporate trends and customer service.

1965 **www.greyhouse.com**
Grey House Publishing
Authoritative reference directories for most business sectors including appliances and small electronics markets. Users can search the online databases with varied search criteria allowing for custom searches by product category, geographic area, sales volume, keyword, subject and more. Full Grey House catalog and online ordering also available.

1966 **www.housewares.org**
International Housewares Association
Provides information on the international homc & housewares industry, with search tools, consumer purchase trend data, and access to global opportunities and discount business services.

1967 **www.ihea.org**
Industrial Heating Equipment Association
A voluntary national trade association representing the major segments of the industrial heat processing equipment industry.

1968 **www.impl.org**
International Microwave Power Institute
A forum for the exchange of information on all aspects of microwave and RF heating technologies.

1969 **www.napsaweb.org**
National Appliance Parts Suppliers Association
Provides distributors of replacement parts for major home appliances with information and services.

1970 **www.narda.com**
North American Retail Dealers Association
Serves the independent retailer industry.

1971 **www.nasa1.org**
National Appliance Service Association
Promotes interests of portable and commercial appliance service repair and sales to industry owners.

1972 **www.nkba.com**
National Kitchen & Bath Association
Protects the interests of members by fostering a better business climate, awarding certification, and conducting training and seminars.

1973 **www.psaworld.com**
Professional Service Association
Information for companies that service and repair electronics and appliances.

1974 **www.repairclinic.com**
RepairClinic
Installation tips and how-to information on all appliances.

1975 **www.reta.com**
Refrigerating Engineers & Technicians Association
Seeks to upgrade the skills and knowledge of experienced members. Offers home-study courses on refrigeration and air conditioning.

1976 **www.rses.org**
Refrigeration Service Engineers Society
The world's leading education, training and certification association for heating, ventilation, air conditioning and refrigeration professionals.

1977 **www.supco.com**
Sealed Unit Parts
Serves the precision electronic test and service instruments, and refrigeration & air conditioning components industries; dedicated to producing high quality, innovative products at affordable prices to a wide range of customers.

Associations

1978 **American Architectural Foundation**
2101 L Street NW
Suite 550
Washington, DC 20037

202-787-1001
Fax: 202-787-1002
E-Mail: info@archfoundation.org
Home Page: www.archfoundation.org

G. Sandy Diehl, III, Chair
Ron Bogle, Hon. AIA, President & CEO
John Syvertsen, Vice Chair & Secretary
James R. Tolbert, III, Treasurer

The American Architectural Foundation (AAF) is dedicated to the vibrant social, economic, and environmental future of cities. In the past decade alone, AAF has worked directly with local leaders through more than 500 city engagements. During this time, AAF has served every major metropolitan region and most second-tier cities in the United States.

1979 **American Architectural Manufacturers Association**
1827 Walden Office Square
Suite 550
Schaumburg, IL 60173-4268

847-303-5664
Fax: 847-303-5774
E-Mail: customerservice@aamanet.org
Home Page: www.aamanet.org

Rich Walker, President and CEO
Dean Lewis, Technical Information Manager
Maureen Knight, Government Affairs
Jannine Klemencic, Executive Assistant
Melissa McCord, Staff Accountant

Advocate for manufacturers and professionals in the fenestration industry with respect to product certification, standards development, education and training, legislative regulations, and building and energy codes.

1980 **American College of Healthcare Architects**
18000 W.105th St.
Olathe, KS 66061-7543

913-895-4604
Fax: 913-895-4652
E-Mail: acha-info@goamp.com
Home Page: www.healtharchitects.org

Connie S. McFarland, President

Provides certificate holders with networking, educational, and marketplace opportunities and distinguishes healthcare architects through certification, experience, and rigorous standards.

1981 **American Design Drafting Association & American Digital Design Association**
105 East Main Street
Newbern, TN 38059-1526

731-627-0802
Fax: 731-627-9321
Home Page: www.adda.org
Social Media: Facebook, Twitter, LinkedIn

Rick Frymyer, Chairman of the Board
Richard Button, Governor - CFO
Danny G. Lewis, Governor
Bruce Nielsen, Governor
H. Duane Moore, Governor

The American Design Drafting Association was conceived by a dedicated and enthusiastic group of oil and gas piping drafters who were involved in various phases of design drafting. This group consisted of highly specialized industry drafters, educational instructors, piping designers, and engineering personnel.
1000+ Members
Founded in 1948

1982 **American Institute of Architects (AIAA)**
1735 New York Ave Nw
Washington, DC 20006-5292

202-626-7300
800-242-3837
Fax: 202-626-7547
E-Mail: infocentral@aia.org
Home Page: www.aia.org
Social Media: Facebook, Twitter, LinkedIn, Youtube, RSS Feeds, Instagram,

Christine McEntee, Executive Vice President

Based in Washington, D.C., the AIA is the leading professional membership association for licensed architects, emerging professionals, and allied partners.
83000 Members
Founded in 1857

1983 **American Institute of Architecture Students**
1735 New York Ave, NW
Suite 300
Washington, DC 20006-5209

202-626-7472
Fax: 202-626-7414
E-Mail: mailbox@aias.org
Home Page: aias.org

Charlie Klecha, President
Obi Okolo, Vice President
Nick Serfass, AIA, CAE, Executive Director

An independent, non-profit, student-run organization dedicated to providing unmatched programs, information, and resources on issues critical to architectural education.
Founded in 1956

1984 **American Planning Association**
205 N. Michigan Ave.
Suite 1200
Chicago, IL 60601

312-431-9100
Fax: 312-786-6700
E-Mail: customerservice@planning.org
Home Page: www.planning.org
Social Media: Facebook, Twitter, LinkedIn, YouTube, Flickr

William Anderson, President
Carol Rhea, President Elect
Lee Brown, Director
James Drinan, Executive Director
Ann Simms, Chief Operating Officer

An independent, nonprofit educational organization that provides leadership in the development of vital communities.
Founded in 1978

1985 **American Society for Aesthetics**
11935 Abercorn Street
PO Box 915
Savannah, GA 31419

912-961-3189
Fax: 912-961-1395
E-Mail: asa@aesthetics-online.org
Home Page: www.aesthetics-online.org

Robert Stecker, Editor
Theodore Gracyk, Editor
James Harold, Book Review Editor
Jenefer Robinson, Past President
Sondra Bacharach, Member

The American Society for Aesthetics promotes study, research, discussion, and publication in aesthetics. Aesthetics, in this connection, is understood to include all studies of the arts and related types of experience from a philosophic, scientific, or other theoretical standpoint, including those of psychology, sociology, anthropology, cultural history, art criticism, and education. The arts include the visual arts, literature, music, and theater arts.
Founded in 1942

1986 **American Society for Healthcare Engineering**
155 N. Wacker Drive
Suite 400.
Chicago, IL 60606

312-422-3800
Fax: 312-422-4571
E-Mail: ashe@aha.org
Home Page: www.ashe.org

Philip C. Stephens, President
David A. Dagenais, President Elect
Dale Woodin, Senior Executive Director
Patrick J. Andrus, Deputy Executive Director
Susan B. McLaughli, Associate Member Director

One of the largest associations devoted to optimizing the health care built environment and is a personal membership organization of the American Hospital Association.

1987 **American Society of Architectural Illustrators**
294 Merrill Hill Road
Hebron, ME 4238

207-966-2062
E-Mail: HQ@asai.org
Home Page: www.asai.org

John Dollus, President
Jon Soules, Vice President
W. Daniel Church, Secretary
Columbus Cook, Treasurer
Tina Bryant, Executive Director

An international, nonprofit organization dedicated to the advancement and recognition of the art, science, and profession of architectural illustration. Through communication, education, and advocacy, this society strives to redefine and emphasize the role of illustration in the practice and appreciation of architecture.
Founded in 1986

1988 **American Society of Concrete Contractors**
2025 S. Brentwood Blvd.
Suite 105
St. Louis, MO 63144

314-962-0210
866-788-2722
Fax: 314-968-4367
E-Mail: questions@ascconline.org
Home Page: www.ascconline.org
Social Media: Facebook

Mike Poppoff, President
Scott M. Anderson, First Vice President
Rocky R. Geans, Vice President
Beverly Garnant, Executive Director
Bruce Suprenant, Technical Director

Provides knowledge on technical production and distribution of concrete construction, educates the industry on constructability, develops business savvy members, and helps them deliver a high quality product.
500 Members

1989 **American Society of Golf Course Architects**
125 N. Executive Drive
Suite 302
Brookfield, WI 53005
262-786-5960
Fax: 262-786-5919
Home Page: www.asgca.org
Lee Schmidt, President
Steve Smyers, Vice President
Greg Martin, Treasurer
John Sanford, Secretary
Chad Ritterbusch, Executive Director
The leader in advancing the interests of golf course architects andthe profession of golf course architecture for the benefit of ASGCA members and their clients, the golf industry, and the game of golf.
Founded in 1947

1990 **American Society of Landscape Architects**
636 Eye St NW
Washington, DC 20001-3736
202-898-2444
888-999-2752
Fax: 202-898-1185
E-Mail: info@asla.org
Home Page: www.asla.org
Social Media: Facebook, Twitter, LinkedIn, RSS Feeds, Pinterest, Instagra
Thomas Tavella, President
David L. Lycke, VP Finance
Annette P. Wilkus, VP Professional Practice
Shawn T. Kelly, VP Membership
Mark A. Hough, VP Communication
Residential and commercial real estate developers, federal and state agencies, city planning commissions and individual property owners are all among the thousands of people and organizations in America and Canada that will retain the services of a landscape architect this year.
15000 Members
Founded in 1899

1991 **Applied Technology Council**
201 Redwood Shores Parkway
Suite 240
Redwood City, CA 94065
650-595-1542
Fax: 650-593-2320
Home Page: www.atcouncil.org
Roberto Leon, President
James A. Amundson, Vice President
Victoria Arbitrio, Secretary/Treasurer
Nancy Gavlin, Past President
Chris Rojahn, Executive Director
A nonprofit, tax-exempt corporation that develops and promotes state-of-the-art, user-friendly engineering resources and applications for use in mitigating the effects of natural and other hazards on the built enviroment. ATC also identifies and encourages needed research and develops consensus opinions onstructural engineering issues in a nonproprietary format.

1992 **Architectural League**
594 Broadway
Suite 607
New York, NY 10012
212-753-1722
Fax: 212-486-9173
E-Mail: info@archleague.org
Home Page: www.archleague.org
Social Media: Facebook, Twitter, RSS Feeds, Vimeo
Annabelle Selldorf, President
Paul Lewis, Vice President
Leo Villareal, Vice President
Michael Bierut, Vice President
Kate Orff, Vice President
To advance the art of architecture.
Founded in 1881

1993 **Architectural Precast Association**
6710 Winkler Rd
Suite 8
Fort Myers, FL 33919-7274
239-454-6989
Fax: 239-454-6787
E-Mail: info@archprecast.org
Home Page: www.archprecast.org
Paul Rossi, President
Chris Cox, Vice President
Fred L. McGee, Executive Director
Cari Renfro, Project Manager & Event Planner
Chris Leonhardt, Associate Director
A national trade association organized to advance the interests of architectural precast in North America.
Founded in 1966

1994 **Architectural Research Centers Consortium, Inc.**
Home Page: www.arccweb.org
Keith Diaz-Moore, President
Michelle A. Rinehart, Vice President
Saif Haq, Treasurer
Leonard Bachman, Secretary
Michael D. Kroelinger, Past President
An international association of architectural research centers committed to the expansion of the research culture and a supporting infrastructure in architecture and related design disciplines.
Founded in 1976

1995 **Association for Computer Aided Design in Architecture**
E-Mail: membership@acadia.org
Home Page: acadia.org
Aron Temkin, President
Nancy Yen-wen Cheng, Vice President
Michael Fox, Secretary
Michael Christenson, Treasurer
Wei Yan, Membership
An international network of digital design researchers and professionals that facilitate critical investigations into the role of computation in architecture, planning, and building science, encouraging innovation in design creativity, sustainability, and education.

1996 **Association for Environment Conscious Building**
PO Box 32
Llandysul, SA
845-456-9773
Home Page: www.aecb.net
Keith & Sally Hall, Founder
Chris Baines, Honorary President
Andy Simmonds, Chief Executive Officer
Sally Hall, Finance and Administration Officer
Gill Rivers, Business Operations Manager
A network of individuals, students, educational establishments, andcompanies with a common aim of promoting sustainable building. It brings together builders, architects, designers, manufacturers, housing associations, and local authorities to develop, share, and promote best practice in environmentally sustainable building.
Founded in 1989

1997 **Association for Preservation Technology International**
3085 Stevenson Drive
Suite 200
Springfield, IL 62703
217-529-9039
Fax: 888-723-4242
E-Mail: info@apti.org
Home Page: www.apti.org
Social Media: Facebook, LinkedIn
Joan C. Berkowitz, President
Gretchen Pfaehler, Vice President, Co-chair Conference
Michael Schuller, Vice-President, Co-chair Training
Nathela Chatara, CAEAdministrative Director
Lesley Gilmore, Treasurer
The Association for Preservation Technology (APT) is a cross-disciplinary, membership organization dedicated to promoting the best technology for conserving historic structures and their settings.
Founded in 1968

1998 **Association of Architecture Organizations**
224 South Michigan Avenue
Suite 116
Chicago, IL 60604
312-561-2159
Fax: 312 922-2607
Home Page: www.aaonetwork.org
Lynn Osmond, Hon. AIA, Chair
Margie O'Driscoll, Hon. AIACC, Vice Chair
Nate Eudaly, Treasurer
Linda Sylvan, Secretary
Michael Wood, Executive Director
A member-based network that connects organizations around the worlddedicated to enhancing public dialogue about architecture and design.

1999 **Association of Collegiate Schools of Architecture**
1735 New York Ave NW
3rd Floor
Washington, DC 20006-5209
202-785-2324
Fax: 202-628-0448
E-Mail: info@acsa-arch.org
Home Page: www.acsa-arch.org
Social Media: Facebook, Twitter, LinkedIn, Vimeo
Norman R. Millar, President
Hsin-Ming Fung, Vice President/President-Elect
Michael J Monti, PhD, Executive Director
Eric Wayne Ellis, Director of Operations and Programs
Pascale J. Vonier, Director of Communications
Nonprofit membership association founded to advance the quality of architectural education.
500 Members
Founded in 1912

2000 **Association of Licensed Architects**
One East Northwest Hwy.
Suite 200
Palatine, IL 60067
847-382-0630
Fax: 847-382-8380
E-Mail: ala@alatoday.org
Home Page: alatoday.org
Jeffrey Budgell, President
James K. Zahn, Esq, Vice President
Patrick C. Harris, Treasurer
Mark V. Spann, Secretary
Joanne Sullivan, Executive Director
An organization open to all architects and professions related to architecture and it represents architects registered or licensed in any state,

territory, or possession of the United States or foreign country.

2001 **Association of Professional Landscape Designers**
2207 Forest Hills Drive
Harrisburg, PA 17112

717-238-9780
Fax: 717-238-9985
Home Page: www.apld.com

Denise Calabrese, Executive Director
Lisa M. (Frye) Ruggiers, Associate Executive Director
Angela Burkett, Membership Director
Michelle Keyser, Director of Communications
Jennifer Swartz, Bookkeeper

An international organization dedicated to advancing the professionof landscape design and promoting the recognition of landscape designers as qualified and dedicated professionals.

2002 **Association of University Architects**
17595 S Tamiami Trail
Fort Myers, FL 33908-4570

FAX 239-590-1010
E-Mail: information@auaweb.net
Home Page: www.auaweb.net

Evie Asken, Director Campus Planning
Steven Thweatt, President

Purpose is to achieve more effective planning in the field of higher education, improve the design and construction standards of university buildings and to develop common bonds and establish standards which will ensure clarity of communications and render effective the exchange of information.
Founded in 1955

2003 **Business Architecture Guild**
E-Mail: info@businessarchitectureguild.org
Home Page: www.businessarchitectureguild.org

Bob Carlston, Director of Business Management
John Machiski, Treasurer
Neal McWhorter, Founder
Jim Rhyne, Founder
Kathy Ulrich, Founder/ Executive Director

A professional association that offers exclusive content to its members. Additional benefits include a private online community, opportunities to provide feedback and collaborate with them on content, a knowledge repository, newsletters, webinars, and more.

2004 **Cast Stone Institute**
813 Chestnut Street
PO Box 68
Lebanon, PA 17042-7218

717-272-3744
Fax: 717-272-5147
E-Mail: staff@caststone.org
Home Page: www.caststone.org

Jesse Hawthorne, President
Scott Mathews, Vice President
Jan Boyer, Executive Director
Tim Michael, Director
David Owen, Director

An organization of cast stone manufacturers, associates, professional architects, engineers and concrete technologists formed for the purpose of improving the quality of cast stone and disseminating information regarding its use.
70 Members
Founded in 1927

2005 **Center for Environmental Design Research**
University of California at Berkeley
390 Wurster Hall
Suite 1839
Berkeley, CA 94720-1839

510-642-2896
Fax: 510-643-5571
E-Mail: earens@berkeley.edu
Home Page: www.cedr.berkeley.edu
Social Media: Facebook, Twitter, LinkedIn, Flickr, Youtube

Tom J. Buresh, M.Arch., Chair, Department of Architecture
Paul Waddell, M.S., Ph.D, Chair, Department of City
G. Mathias Kondolf, M.S., Ph.D., Chair, Department of Landscaping
Jennifer Wolch, Ph.D., Dean
Gary Brown, M.Arch, Associate Dean for Faculty Affairs

Mission is to foster research in environmental planning and design

2006 **Construction Sciences Research Foundation, Inc.**
E-Mail: info@csrf.org
Home Page: www.csrf.org

Raymond K. Best, President
Kurt T. Preston, VP Finance and Administration
Michael D. Dell'Isola, Vice President
Charles Chief Boyd, Secretary/Treasurer
Julie K Brown, Director

An independent, nonprofit construction industry research organization dedicated to unifying and integrating communication between programs and design/communications processes used in facilities design and construction.

2007 **Council on Tall Buildings and Urban Habitat**
SR Crown Hall, Illinois Institute of Technology
3360 S State Street
Chicago, IL 60616-3796

312-567-3487
Fax: 312-567-3820
E-Mail: info@ctbuh.org
Home Page: www.ctbuh.org
Social Media: Facebook, Twitter, YouTube

Timothy Johnson, Chairman
Antony Wood, Executive Director
Patti Thurmond, Operations
Carissa Devereux, Membership
Steven Henry, Design & Production

Supported by architecture, engineering, planning development and construction professionals, designed to facilitate exchanges among those involved in all aspects of the planning, design, construction and operation of tall buildings.
Founded in 1969

2008 **Environmental Design Research Association**
7918 Jones Branch Drive
Suite 300
McLean, VA 22102

703-506-2895
Fax: 703-506-3266
E-Mail: headquarters@edra.org
Home Page: www.edra.org
Social Media: Facebook, Twitter, LinkedIn

Shauna Mallory - Hill, Chair
Gowri Betrabet Gulwadi, Chair Elect
Paula Horrigan, Secretary
David Boeck, Treasurer
Kate O Donnell, Executive Director

An organization dedicated to advancing and distributing environmental design research, thereby improving understanding of the interrelationships between people, their built and natural surroundings. EDRA's goal is also to facilitate the creation of environments that are responsive to human needs.
Founded in 1968

2009 **Green Building Alliance**
33 Terminal Way
Suite 331
Pittsburgh, PA 15219

412-431-0709
E-Mail: info@gbapgh.org
Home Page: www.go-gba.org
Social Media: Facebook, Twitter, LinkedIn, YouTube

Michael Kuhn, President
Christine Mondor, Vice President
Mike Schiller, CEO
Kevin Clarke, Secretary
Mark Smith, Treasurer

An organization that promotes healthy, high performing places for everyone by inspiring and leading the market, demonstrating and proving value, and equipping the community with knowledge and resources.
1200 Members
Founded in 1993

2010 **Historic New England**
Soc for Preservation of New England Antiquities
141 Cambridge St
Boston, MA 02114-2702

617-227-3956
Fax: 617-227-9204
Home Page: www.historicnewengland.org
Social Media: Facebook, Twitter, YouTube, Tumblr, Zazzle

Carl R. Nold, President/CEO
Diane Viera, Executive Vice President/COO
Kimberlea Tracey, Vice President for Advancement
Wendy Gus, Director of Finance
Benjamin Haavik, Team Leader for Property Care

Focuses on buildings, landscapes and objects reflecting New England life from the 17th century to the present. Also publishes a magazine about the organizations objects, architectural holdings and activities.
6000 Members
Founded in 1910

2011 **Institute for Urban Design**
17 West 17th Street, 7th Floor
New York, NY 10014-3731
212-366-0780
Fax: 212-633-0125
E-Mail: info@ifud.org
Home Page: www.ifud.org
Social Media: Facebook, Twitter, LinkedIn, RSS Feeds, vimeo

Anne Guiney, Executive Director
Alexandra Sutherland-Brown, Program Coordinator

Responsible for city planning.
1M Members
Founded in 1979

2012 **Insulated Cable Engineers Association**
P.O. Box 2694
Alpharetta, GA 30023

Home Page: www.icea.net

R.O. Bristol, President
Rick Williamson, 1st VP
Kim Nuckles, 2nd VP

A professional organization dedicated to developing cable standardsfor the electric power, control, and telecommunications industries.
Founded in 1925

2013 **Interior Design Educators Council**
1833 Centre Point Circle
Suite 123
Naperville, IL 60563

630-544-5057
E-Mail: info@idec.org
Home Page: www.idec.org
Social Media: Facebook, Twitter, LinkedIn, YouTube, Flickr, Yahoo, Google

Katherine Ankerson, President
John Martin Rutherford, Past President
Cynthia Mohr, President Elect
Migette Kaup, Secretary/Treasurer
Jill Pable, Director

An organization dedicated to the advancement of interior design education, scholarship, and service.
Founded in 1972

2014 **International Association for Impact Assessment**
1330 23rd Street S
Suite C
Fargo, ND 58103-3705

701-297-7908
Fax: 701-297-7917
E-Mail: info@iaia.org
Home Page: www.iaia.org

Rita Hamm, CEO
Jennifer Howell, Publications/Meetings Specialist
Bridget John, Marketing/Financial Specialist
Shelli LaPlante, Member Liaison/Conference Registrar
Loreley Fortuny, Special Project Associate

A forum for advancing innovation, development, and communication of best practice in impact assessment. Exists to improve and better inform the decision-making of today that has environmental consequences for tomorrow.
2500 Members
Founded in 1980

2015 **International Association of Innovation Professionals**
4422 Castle Wood Street
Sugar Land, TX 77479

925-858-0905
E-Mail: hello@iaoip.org
Home Page: iaoip.org

Brett Trusko, President/ CEO
Lewis Archer, Webmaster
Charisma Aggarwal, Development Manager
Dana J. Landry, VP Certification Programs
Marco D. Mancin, Director

Creates events and provides resources to help professionals learn the latest innovation methodologies, and offer certification testing to help themadvance in their careers.

2016 **International Code Council**
4051 W Flossmoor Road
Country Club Hills, IL 60478

708-799-4981
888-422-7233
Fax: 708-799-4981
E-Mail: members@iccsafe.org
Home Page: www.iccsafe.org
Social Media: Facebook, Twitter, LinkedIn, Youtube

Stephen D. Jones, CBO, President
Guy Tomberlin, CBO, Vice President
Mark Johnson, Executive VP and Director, Business
Hamid Naderi, Sr. VP, Product Development
Laurence Genest, VP, Sales Marketing

A nonprofit membership association dedicated to preserving the public health, safety and welfare in the built environment through the promulgation of model codes suitable for adoption by governmental entities and assisting code enforcement officials, design professionals, builders, manufacturers and others involved in the design, construction and regulatory processes.
16000 Members
Founded in 1915

2017 **International Interior Design Association**
222 Mechandise Mart
Suite 567
Chicago, IL 60654

312-467-1950
888-799-4432
312-467-1950
E-Mail: iidahq@iida.org
Home Page: www.iida.org
Social Media: Facebook, Twitter, LinkedIn, YouTube, Instagram

Julio Braga, President
Scott Hierlinger, President Elect
Viveca Bissonnette, Vice President
Dennis Krause, Senior Vice President
Cheryl Dust, Executive Vice President

Association that provides its members with sources, knowledge, and contacts necessary in the interior design field.

2018 **Marine Engineers' Beneficial Association**
444 N. Capitol Street, NW
Suite 800
Washington, DC 20001

202-638-5355
Fax: 202-638-5369
Home Page: mebaunion.org
Social Media: Facebook, Twitter, YouTube

Marshall Ainley, President
Bill Van Loo, Secretary/ Treasurer
Mark Gallagher, Contracts Rep
Eric C. Pittman, Comptroller

The oldest maritime trade union that represents licensed mariners, deck and engine officers and has a training plan to provide further technical training. It has worked hard in Washington, DC to ensure proper examination and licensing of engineers and the abolition of controversial license fees.
Founded in 1875

2019 **Marine Technology Society**
1100 H St., NW
Suite LL-100
Washington, DC 20005

202-717-8705
Fax: 202-347-4302
E-Mail: membership@mtsociety.org
Home Page: www.mtsociety.org

Drew Michel, President
Jerry Boatman, Immediate Past President
Ray Toll, Vice President
Richard lawson, Executive Director
Chris Barett, Director

A growing organization with a membership that includes businesses, institutions, individual professionals, and students who are ocean engineers, technologists, policy makers, and educators. This group works to promote awareness, understanding, advancement, and the application of marine technology.
Founded in 1963

2020 **National Academy of Environmental Design**

E-Mail: info@naedonline.org
Home Page: www.naedonline.org

Daniel Friedman, President
Thomas R. Fisher, Vice President
Frederick Steiner, Immediate Past President
James F. Palmer, Secretary
Claudia Phillips, Treasurer

A nonprofit organization that provides the public with expertise and leadership in the creation of healthier, greener, safer, and more resilient American communitites through environmental design.

2021 **National Architectural Accrediting Board**
1101 Connecticut Avn., NW
Suite 410
Washington, DC 20036

202-783-2007
Fax: 202-783-2822
E-Mail: info@naab.org
Home Page: www.naab.org

Shannon B. Kraus, President
Scott Veazey, President Elect
Patricia Kucker, Treasurer
Brian R. Kelly, Secretary
Andrea S. Rutledge, Executive Director

Develops and maintains a system of accreditation in professional architecture education that is responsive to the needs of society and allows institutions with varying resources and circumstances to evolve according to their individual needs.

2022 **National Association of Home Builders**
1201 15th Street NW
Washington, DC 20005

202-266-8200
800-368-5242
Fax: 202-266-8400
Home Page: www.nahb.org

Kevin Kelly, Chairman
Tom Woods, Chairman-Elect
Ed Brady, Second Vice Chairman
Granger MacDonald, Third Vice Chairman
Gerald M. Howard, Chief Executive Officer

A trade association that helps promote the policies that make housing a national priority.

2023 **National Council of Architectural Registration Boards**
1801 K St NW
Suite 700k
Washington, DC 20006-1320

202-783-6500
Fax: 202-783-0290
Home Page: www.ncarb.org
Social Media: Facebook, Twitter, LinkedIn, YouTube

Blakely C. Dunn, Vice President
Michael Armstrong, CEO

Committed to protecting the health, safety, and welfare of the public through effective regualtion and exemplary service.
Founded in 1919

2024 **National Organization of Minority Architects**
2366 Sixth Street, N.W.
Room 100
Washington, DC 20059

202-686-2780
E-Mail: president@noma.net
Home Page: www.noma.net

Kathy Dixon, President
Kevin M. Holland, President Elect
Aminah Wright, Secretary
Walter Wilson, Treasurer
Gianna Pigford, Recording Secretary

A national organization that strives to minimize the effects of racism in the architecture profession and also battles against apathy, bigotry, and abuse of the natural environment.

2025 Organization of Women Architects and Designers
PO Box 10078
Berkeley, CA 94709
Home Page: owa-usa.org

Janet Crane, President
Mui Ho, Secretary
Bill Hocker, Webmaster
Anne Jakiemiec, Health Plan Consultant
Judy L. Rowe, FAIA, Treasurer

A nonprofit organization that is an active support network for women involved in architecture, engineering, planning, landscape architecture, interior and graphic design, and related environmental design fields.
Founded in 1970

2026 Partners for Livable Communities
1429 21st St Nw
Washington, DC 20036-5902

202-887-5990
Fax: 202-466-4845
E-Mail: fkoleszar@livable.org
Home Page: www.livable.com

Robert H. McNulty, President
Penny Cuff, Vice President of Programs
Irene Garnett, Vice President of Finance
Faith Koleszar, Executive Assistant
Arianna Koudounas, Program Officer

A non-profit leadership organization working to improve the livability of communities by promoting quality of life, economic development, and social equity.
Founded in 1977

2027 Society for Environmental Graphic Design
1000 Vermont Ave NW
Suite 400
Washington, DC 20005-4921

202-638-5555
Fax: 202-478-2286
E-Mail: segd@segd.org
Home Page: www.segd.org
Social Media: Facebook, Twitter, LinkedIn, RSS Feeds

Clive Roux, CEO
Ann Makowski, COO
Pat Matson Knapp, Director of Communications
Justin Molloy, Director of Education
Sara Naegelin, Director of Sponsorship

The global community of people who work at the intersection of communication design and the built environment.
Founded in 1974

2028 Society of American Registered Architects
14 E. 38th Street
New York, NY 10016

888-385-7272
Fax: 888-385-7272
E-Mail: cmoscato@sara-national.org
Home Page: www.sara-national.org

Ron Knabb, Jr., FARA, President
Gaetano Ragusa, FARA, President-Elect
John J. Di Benedetto, FARA, Vice-President
Francisco J. Urrutia, FARA, Treasurer
Cathie Moscato, Executive Director

A professional society that includes the participation of all architects, regardless of their roles in the architectural community, the opportunity to share information and ideas.
Founded in 1956

2029 Society of Architectural Historians
1365 N Astor St
Chicago, IL 60610-2144

312-573-1365
Fax: 312-573-1141
E-Mail: info@sah.org
Home Page: www.sah.org
Social Media: Facebook, Twitter, LinkedIn

Abigail Van Slyck, President
Prof. Ken Breisch, Vice President
Dr. Ken Tadashi Oshima, 2nd Vice President
Pauline Saliga, Executive Director
Mr. Jan M. Grayson, Treasurer

A not-for-profit membership organization and learned society that promotes the study and preservation of the built environment worldwide.
2500 Members
Founded in 1940

2030 Society of Naval Architects and Marine Engineers
601 Pavonia Ave
Suite 400
Jersey City, NJ 07306-2922

201-798-4800
800-798-2188
Fax: 201-798-4975
Home Page: www.sname.org

Edward N. Comstock, President
Erik Seither, Executive Director

Internationally recognized nonprofit technical, professional society of individual members serving the maritime and offshore industries and their suppliers. Dedicated to advancing the industry by recording information, sponsoring research, offering career guidance and supporting education.
10000 Members
Founded in 1893

2031 Sustainable Buildings Industry Council
1090 Vermont Avenue NW
Suite700
Washington, DC 20005

202-289-7800
Fax: 202- 28- 109
E-Mail: nibs@nibs.org
Home Page: www.sbicouncil.org
Social Media: Facebook, Twitter, LinkedIn, Pinterest

Bud DeFlaviis, Executive Director
Kimberly Lowry, Executive Assistant

Mission is to unite and inspire the building industry toward higher performance through education, outreach, advocacy and the mutual exchange of ideas.
Founded in 1980

2032 The National Institute of Building Sciences
1090 Vermont Avenue, NW
Suite 700
Washington, DC 20005-4950

202-289-7800
Fax: 202-289-1092
E-Mail: nibs@nibs.org
Home Page: www.nibs.org

James T. Ryan, Chairman
Stephen Ayers, Vice Chairman
Henry L. Green, President
John G Lloyrd, Vice President
John P. Kelly, Secretary

A nonprofit, non-governmental organization that brings together representatives of government, the professions, industry, labor and consumer interests, and regulatory agencies to focus on the identification and resolution of problems that hamper the contruction of safe, affordable structures for housing, commerce, and industry throughout the United States.

2033 U.S. Green Building Council
2101 L Street, NW
Suite 500
Washington, DC 20037

202-742-3792
800-795-1747
E-Mail: info@usgbc.org
Home Page: www.usgbc.org

Kunal Gulati, Product Marketing Specialist
Mark de Groh, Director, Philanthropy
Aline Peterson, Media & Communications Specialist
Lee Brown, Account Manager
Alex Hammack, Operations Associate

This organization is made up of tens of thousands of member organizations, chapters, and student and community volunteers that strive to transform the way buildings and communities are operated, enabling an environmentally and socially responsible, healthy, and prosperous environment that improves the quality of life.

2034 United States Access Board
Access Board
1331 F St Nw
Suite 1000
Washington, DC 20004-1111

202-272-0080
800-872-2253
Fax: 202-272-0081
E-Mail: info@access-board.gov
Home Page: www.access-board.gov

Karen L. Braitmayer, FAIA, Chair
David M. Capozzi, Executive Director
Neil Melick, Director
James J. Raggio, General Counsel
Lisa Fairhall, Deputy General Counsel

Independent federal agency devoted to accessibility for people with disabilities. Its key missions include developing and maintaining guidelines for the built environment, transit vehicles, telecommunications equipment and standards for electronic and information technology; providing technical assistance and training on these guidelines and standards and enforcing design standards for federally funded facilities.
Founded in 1968

2035 Urban Design Associates
707 Grant Street
Gulf Tower, 31st Floor
Pittsburgh, PA 15219

412-263-5200
Fax: 412-263-5202
Home Page: www.urbandesignassociates.com
Social Media: Facebook, Twitter, Vimeo

Designs resilient neighborhoods, towns, villages, districts, places, and buildings.
Founded in 1964

Newsletters

2036 A/E Business Review
6524 E Rockaway Hills Drive
PO Box 4808
Cave Creek, AZ 85331-7609

480-488-0311
Fax: 480-488-0311

Clare Ross, Publisher

The management and marketing newsletter of architects, engineers and planners.
7 Pages
Frequency: Monthly

2037 AIA Architect
American Institute of Architects
1735 New York Ave Nw
Washington, DC 20006-5292

202-626-7300
800-242-3837
Fax: 202-626-7547
E-Mail: infocentral@aia.org
Home Page: www.aia.org

Robert Ivy, CEO
Jeff Potter, President

News of America's community of architects
Frequency: Weekly

2038 Access Currents
Access Board
1331 F St Nw
Suite 1000
Washington, DC 20004-1135

202-272-0080
800-872-2253
Fax: 202-272-0081
E-Mail: info@access-board.gov
Home Page: www.access-board.gov

David Capozzi, Executive Director
Frequency: Bi-Monthly

2039 Certifier
Nat'l Council of Architectural Registration Boards
1801 K St Nw
Suite 700K
Washington, DC 20006-1320

202-879-0520
Fax: 202-783-0290
Home Page: www.ncarb.org

Michael Armstrong, CEO
Blakely Dunn, Vice President

State architectural registration boards.
Frequency: Annual
Founded in 1919

2040 Design Drafting News
American Design Drafting Association
105 E Main Street
Newbern, TN 38059-1526

731-627-0802
Fax: 731-627-9321
E-Mail: corporate@adda.org
Home Page: www.adda.org

Ron McDonald, President
Dennis Schwartz, Executive VP

Newsletter for the American Design Drafting Association and American Digital Design Association.
Frequency: Bi-Monthly
Circulation: 1800

2041 Design Firm Management & Administration Report
Institute of Management and Administration
3 Bethesda Metro Center
Suite 250
Bethesda, MD 20814-537

703-341-3500
800-372-1033
Fax: 800-253-0332
Home Page: www.ioma.com

Provides practical, hands-on, timely information to design firm managers and administrators about the marketing and management aspects of operating a firm.
Cost: $429.00
Frequency: Monthly

2042 Designline
American Institute of Building Design
529 14th St NW
Suite 750
Washington, DC 20045

202-249-1407
800-366-2423
Fax: 866-204-0293
E-Mail: info@aibd.org
Home Page: www.aibd.org

Dan Sater, President
Alan Kent, Vice President

Focuses on issues, education, and events as they happen in the building design industry.
Frequency: Quarterly

2043 Direct Connection
Nat'l Council of Architectural Registration Boards
1801 K St NW
Suite 700K
Washington, DC 20006-1301

202-870-0520
Fax: 202-782-0290
E-Mail: customerservice@ncarb.org
Home Page: www.ncarb.org

Ron McDonald, CEO
Blakely Dunn, Vice President

Offers information and news on licensing, board certification, architectural trends and more for the professional architect and intern architect.
16 Pages
Circulation: 50000
Printed in 2 colors on glossy stock

2044 Energy Design Update
Aspen Publishers
76 Ninth Avenue
7th Floor
New York, NY 10011

212-771-0600
800-638-8437
Home Page: www.aspenpublishers.com

Mark Dorman, CEO
Gustavo Dobles, VP Operations

For professionals concerned with residential load management and energy efficient design and construction in housing.
Cost: $297.00
16 Pages
Frequency: Monthly

2045 Guidelines Letter: New Directions and Techniques in the Design Profession
Guidelines
PO Box 2590
Alameda, CA 94501

510-235-5174
800-634-7779
Fax: 510-523-5175
E-Mail: info@sfia.net
Home Page: www.sfia.net

Fred Stitt, Director/Editor
Chandler Vienneau, Circulation Director

Business and technical information for design professionals including comprehensive survey information regarding fees and client costs. The Guidelines Letter is in its 28th year of publication.
Cost: $70.00
4 Pages
Frequency: Monthly
ISSN: 1089-2141
Founded in 1992

2046 Landscape Architectural News Digest
American Society of Landscape Architects
636 Eye St NW
Washington, DC 20001-3736

202-898-2444
800-787-2752
Fax: 202-898-1185
E-Mail: membership@asla.org
Home Page: www.asla.org

Jonathan Mueller, President
Seck Hardi, Editor

Provides a comprehensive view of the latest developments in regional, residential and corporate architecture.
Cost: $42.00
16 Pages
Frequency: Monthly

2047 Memo
American Institute of Architects
1735 New York Ave Nw
Washington, DC 20006-5292

202-626-7300
800-242-3837
Fax: 202-626-7547
E-Mail: infocentral@aia.org
Home Page: www.aia.org

Robert Ivy, CEO
Jeff Potter, President
Norman Koonce, Editor
Scott Frank, Director

Architectural news and information.
Frequency: Monthly
Circulation: 85000

2048 SARAscope
Society of American Registered Architects
P.O. Box 280
Newport, TN 37822

888-385-7272
E-Mail: cmoscato@sara-national.org
Home Page: www.sara-national.org

Suzette Stoler, President
Cathie Moscato, Executive Director

Listing society conventions, meetings and other activities. Discusses news about the Society of interest to members.
Frequency: BiWeekly
Founded in 1956

2049 SBIC Newsletter
Sustainable Buildings Industry Council
1090 Vermont Avenue NW
Suite 700
Washington, DC 20005

202-289-7800
Fax: 202-289-1092
E-Mail: nibs@nibs.org
Home Page: www.sbicouncil.org

Henry Green, President
John Lloyd, Vice President
Gretchen Hesbacher, Editor

Published to inform the members of the mission to advance the design, affordability, energy performance and environmental soundness of residential, institutional and commercial buildings. Newsletter is free to members.
6-8 Pages
Frequency: 2-3 per year
Circulation: 400
Founded in 1995
Printed in 2 colors on matte stock

2050 Society of Architectural Historians Newsletter
Society of Architectural Historians
1365 N Astor St
Chicago, IL 60610-2144

312-573-1365
Fax: 312-573-1141

E-Mail: info@sah.org
Home Page: www.sah.org

Dr. Abigail Van Slyck, President
Prof. Ken Breisch, Vice President

Keeps readers informed about upcoming SAH events, conferences, tours, awards, publications and exhibitors.
Frequency: Bi-Monthly

2051 Times
Council of Tall Buildings and Urban Habitat
Illinois Institute of Technology SR Crown
3360 S State Street
Chicago, IL 60616-3793

312-567-3487
Fax: 312-567-3820
E-Mail: info@ctbuh.org
Home Page: www.ctbuh.org

Patti Thurmond, Operations Manager
Antony Wood, Executive Director
Tansri Muliani, News Editor
Steven Henry, Publications

Newsletter for members of CTBUH.
Cost: $75.00
Frequency: Monthly
Circulation: 1200
ISSN: 1061-5121
Founded in 1969
Printed in 2 colors on matte stock

Magazines & Journals

2052 AI Communications
AIAA
1735 New York Ave NW
Washington, DC 20006-5209

202-626-7300
800-242-3837
Fax: 202-626-7547
E-Mail: infocentral@aia.org
Home Page: www.aia.org

Jeffery Potter, President
Mickey Jacob, Vice President

Student programs and issues dealing with architectural education.
Founded in 1857

2053 APT Bulletin: The Journal of Preservation Technology
Association for Preservation Technology Int'l
3085 Stevenson Drive
Suite 200
Springfield, IL 62705

217-529-9039
Fax: 888-723-4242
E-Mail: info@apti.org
Home Page: www.apti.org

Joan Berkowitz, President
Gretchen Pfaehler, Vice President

Articles showcase cutting-edge preservation techniques, as well as innovative applications of established restoration technologies.

2054 Adobe Magazine
Adobe Systems
345 Park Ave
San Jose, CA 95110-2704

408-536-6000
Fax: 408-537-6000
Home Page: www.adobe.com

Shantanu Narayen, CEO
Mark Garrett, SVP

Devoted to adobe and earthen architecture. Showing both old and new traditions of building the earth.
Cost: $4.00
Circulation: 4,500

2055 American School & University
PRIMEDIA Intertec Publication
9800 Metcalf Ave.
Overland Park, KS 66212

913-341-1300
Fax: 913-967-1898
E-Mail: jagron@primediabusiness.com
Home Page: www.penton.com

Nicola Alais, Senior VP
Gregg Herring, Publisher
David KIESELSTEIN, CEO

The industry's definitive educational facilities publication.
Cost: $50.00
508 Pages
Frequency: Monthly
Circulation: 63540
Founded in 1928
Printed in 4 colors on glossy stock

2056 Architectural Design
John Wiley & Sons
111 River St
Hoboken, NJ 07030-5790

201-748-6000
Fax: 201-748-6088
E-Mail: info@wiley.com
Home Page: www.wiley.com

Matthew Kissner, CEO/President
Jean-Lou Chameau, President

Continues to publish a vigorous and wide range treatment of architectural trends of topical importance.
Cost: $145.00
Founded in 1807

2057 Architectural Digest
4 Times Square
Suite 15
New York, NY 10036-6518
212-286-2860
Fax: 212-286-6790
Home Page: www.architecturaldigest.com

Giulio Capua, Publisher
Margaret Russell, Editor-in-Chief

For the connoisseur of interior design. The purpose is to cultivate an appreciation of excellence in the luxury world of design and furnishing.
Cost: $39.95
Frequency: Monthly
Circulation: 840,995
Founded in 1999

2058 Architectural Record
McGraw Hill
2 Penn Plaza
9th Floor
New York, NY 10121-2298

212-904-2594
Fax: 212-904-4256
E-Mail: william_hanley@mcgraw-hill.com
Home Page: archrecord.construction.com

William Hanley, Web Editor
Cathleen McGuigan, Editor in Chief
Ilan Kapla, Sr. Manager, Web Production
Rama Bandu, Web Producer
Elisabeth Broome, Managing Editor

Provides a compelling editorial mix of design ideas and trends, building science, business and professional strategies, exploration of key issues, news products and computer-aided practice.
Cost: $49.00
Frequency: Monthly

2059 Architecture Magazine
American Institute of Architects
One Thomas Circle, NW
Suite 600
Washington, DC 20005

202-452-0800
Fax: 202-785-1974
E-Mail: info@architecturemag.com
Home Page: www.architecturemag.com

Ned Cramer, Editor-in-Chief
Greig O'Brien, Managing Editor
Katie Gerfen, Senior Editor

Evaluation of new and existing buildings and related news that affects the profession.
Frequency: Monthly
Circulation: 63449

2060 Ballast Quarterly Review
Ballast
2022 X Avenue
Dysart, IA 52224-9767

E-Mail: ballast@netins.net

Roy Behrens, Editor

Examines an eclectic assortment of publications with an emphasis on graphic design and architecture.
16 Pages
Frequency: Quarterly

2061 Building Design & Construction
Reed Business Information
360 Park Ave S
New York, NY 10010-1737

1 -46 -46 6
Fax: 646-756-7583
E-Mail: subsmail@reedbusiness.com
Home Page: www.reedbusiness.com

Mark Kelsey, CEO
James Reed, President

Serves the needs of the design and construction professionals of commercial, industrial and institutional buildings that include new and retrofit projects. Geared towards the building team that includes professionals from building firms, owning firms and design firms.
Frequency: Monthly
Founded in 1946

2062 CRIT: Journal of the American Institute of Architecture Students
American Institute of Architecture Students
1735 New York Ave NW
Washington, DC 20006-5292

202-626-7472
Fax: 202-626-7414
E-Mail: mailbox@aias.org
Home Page: www.aias.org

Joshua Caulfield, CEO
Joshua Caulfield, Executive Director
Yurly Napelenok, Programs & Membership
Laura Meader, Editor in Chief

The premier source of and the only international journal of student design work.
Frequency: Bi-Annual
Circulation: 13,000
Founded in 1976

2063 CTBUH Review Journal
Council on Tall Buildings and Urban Habitat
S.R.Crown Hall,
3360 South State Street
Chicago, IL 60616

312-567-3487
Fax: 312-567-3820
E-Mail: info@ctbuh.org
Home Page:

www.ctbuh.org/Publications/Journal/tabid/72/language/en-GB/Defaul

Marshall Ali, Editor
Anthony Wood, Executive Director
Robert Lau, Associate Editor

CTBUH Review is the Professional Journal of the Council on Tall Buildings and Urban Habitat. It includes refereed papers submitted by researchers, scholars, suppliers, and practicing professionals engaged in the planning, design, construction, and operation of tall buildings and the urban environment throughout the world. Membership benefits include monthly e-updates, access to on-line buildings database, discounts on selected publications and registration at Council-sponsored activities.
Cost: $150.00
1400 Pages
Frequency: Quarterly

2064 Classicist
Transaction Publishing Rutgers
35 Berrue Circle
Piscataway, NJ 08854-8042

732-445-2280
888-999-6778
Fax: 732-445-3138
E-Mail: trans@transactionpub.com
Home Page: www.transactionpub.com

Mary Curtis, President
Prof. David Shulman, Editor

Dedicated to the theory and practice of architecture and artistic classicism.
Cost: $39.95
164 Pages

2065 Computer-Aided Engineering
Penton Media
1300 E 9th St
Suite 316
Cleveland, OH 44114-1503

216-696-7000
Fax: 216-696-1752
E-Mail: information@penton.com
Home Page: www.penton.com

David Kieselstein, CEO
Nicola Allais, EVP
Jasmine Alexander, Senior VP & CIO

Database applications in design and manufacturing.
Cost: $50.00
96 Pages
Founded in 1982

2066 Concrete Masonry Designs
13750 Sunrise Valley Drive
Herndon, VA 20171-4662

703-713-1900
Fax: 703-713-1910
E-Mail: ncma@ncma.org
Home Page: www.ncma.org

Mary Arntson-Terrell, Director of Sales
Robert Thomas, President

Highlights concrete masonry applications, best practice tips, specifications and details. Also showcases concrete masonry landscape products.
Cost: $2.50
Frequency: Monthly
Circulation: 25000
Founded in 1918
Printed in 4 colors on glossy stock

2067 Contemporary Stone & Tile Design
BNP Media
210 E State Rt 4
Suite 203
Paramus, NJ 07652-5103

201-291-9001
Fax: 201-291-9002
E-Mail: info@stoneworld.com
Home Page: www.stoneworld.com

Alex Bachrach, Publisher
Michael Reis, Editor
Jennifer Adams, Editor

Focuses on stone and ceramic tile use in interior design for architects, interior designers, specifiers and consumrs with the buying influence for stone or stone materials and a variety of architectural and construction products and services.

2068 Design Issues
MIT Press
55 Hayward Street
Cambridge, MA 02142-1315

617-253-5646
Fax: 617-258-6779
Home Page: www.mitpress.mit.edu

Michael Sims, Managing Editor
Ellen Faran, Director

Provokes inquiry into the cultural and intellecutual issues surrounding design. Regular features include theoretical and critical articles by professional and scholarly contributions, extensive book reviews, and illustrations.
110 Pages
Frequency: Quarterly
ISSN: 0747-9360
Founded in 1984

2069 Design Journal
Journal Communications Group
1720 20th St #201
Santa Monica, CA 90404

310-394-4394
Fax: 310-394-0966
E-Mail: customer.services@benjamins.nl
Home Page: designjournalmag.com

Kees Vaes, Editor
Karin Plijnaar, Marketing Manager

Focuses on the design and architecture marketplace. Includes newsbites and a calendar, as well as designer and lighting resources.
Frequency: Monthly
Circulation: 34000
Founded in 1982

2070 Design Solutions Magazine
Architectural Woodwork Institute
46179 Westlake Drive
Suite 120
Potomac Falls, VA 20165
571-323-3636
Fax: 571-323-3630
E-Mail: adsales@awinet.org
Home Page: www.awinet.org

Teresa McCain, Director of Operations
Philip Duvic, Executive VP

Featuring beautiful woodwork projects manufactured by members of the Architectural Woodwork Institute (AWI). Many other related publications, including woodworking quality standards used by woodwork manufacturers and design professionals.
Cost: $25.00
Frequency: Quarterly
Circulation: 25000
Founded in 1953

2071 Design/Build Business
Cygnus Publishing
12735 Morris Road
Bldg. 200
Alpharetta, GA 30152-0803

770-427-5290
800-547-7377
Fax: 404-935-9290
E-Mail: kathy.scott@cygnusb2b.com
Home Page: www.cygnusb2b.com

John French, CEO
Michael Martin, President

Serves builders, architects and designing and remodeling firms, nationwide. Edited to these professions serving the residential and light commercial marketplaces.
Cost: $24.00
72 Pages
Frequency: Monthly
Circulation: 60424
ISSN: 1068-9433
Founded in 1935

2072 Dodge Construction News
McGraw Hill
PO Box 182604
Columbus, OH 43272

614-866-5769
877-833-5524
Fax: 614-759-3749
E-Mail: customer.service@mcgraw-hill.com
Home Page: www.mcgraw-hill.com

Jennifer Hayes, Editor
Harold McGraw III, President/CEO

Consists of program edition and proceedings and recap edition for the National Conventions of the American Institute of Architects and Construction Specifications Institute.
Circulation: 86400
Founded in 1958

2073 Fabrics Architecture
U.S. Industrial Fabrics Association International
1801 County Road NW
Roseville, MN 55113-4061

651-222-2508
800-225-4324
Fax: 651-631-9334
E-Mail: fabarch@ifai.com
Home Page: www.usifi.com

Ruth Stephens, Executive Director

Strives to inform architects, designers, landscape architects, engineers and other specifiers about architectural fabric structures, the fibers and fabrics used to make them, their design possibilities, their construction, and issues regarding their applicability and acceptance.
Cost: $39.00
Frequency: Bi-Monthly

2074 Glass Magazine
National Glass Association
1945 Old Gallows Rd
Suite 750
Vienna, VA 22182

703-442-4890
866-342-5642
Fax: 703-442-0630
E-Mail: editorialinfo@glass.org
Home Page: www.glass.org

Phil James, CEO
Nicole Harris, Vice President

Offers readers experienced editorial direction and informative coverage including market segment surveys, resource guides, reader polls, industry profiles, industry states, and industry products.
Frequency: Monthly

2075 Harvard Design Magazine
Harvard University Graduate School of Design
48 Quincy St
Gund Hall
Cambridge, MA 02138-3000

617-495-5453
Fax: 617-495-8949
E-Mail: hdm@gsd.harvard.edu

Home Page: www.gsd.harvard.edu
Social Media: Facebook, Twitter, LinkedIn

Mohsen Mostafavi, Dean

Aims to provide a forum for thoughtful and articulate practitioners, journalists, and academics, primarily from architecture, landscape architecture and urban design and planning.
Frequency: Bi-Annual

2076 Impact Assessment and Project Appraisal (IAPA)
International Association for Impact Assessment
1330 23rd Street S
Suite C
Fargo, ND 58103-3705

701-297-7908
Fax: 701-297-7917
E-Mail: info@iaia.org
Home Page: www.iaia.org

Rita Hamm, CEO
Jennifer Howell, Publications

IAPA is an international refereed journal. It welcomes papers on the environmental, social, health, technology, integrated, sustainability, etc. assessment of projects, programs, plans and policies.
Frequency: Quarterly
Circulation: 1600
ISSN: 1461-5517

2077 Inland Architect
Real Estate News Corporation
3500 West Peterson Avenue
Suite 403
Chicago, IL 60659

773-866-9900
888-641-3169
Fax: 773-866-9881
E-Mail: rencorpil@aol.com
Home Page: www.inlandarchitectmag.com

Steven Polydoris, Publisher/Editor

Covers distinguished and historical buildings.
Cost: $27.00
120 Pages
Founded in 1883
Printed in 4 colors on glossy stock

2078 Journal of Architectural Education
Blackwell Publishing Inc
350 Main St
Suite 6
Malden, MA 02148-5089

781-388-8598
800-835-6770
Fax: 781-388-8210
E-Mail: cs-journals@wiley.com
Home Page: www.blackwellpublishing.com

Vincent Marzano, VP
Stephen Smith, CEO

Enhances architectural design education, theory and practice.
Frequency: Quarterly
ISBN: 0-262753-24-3
Founded in 1947

2079 Journal of Architectural and Planning Research
Locke Science Publishing
332 S. Michigan Avenue
Suite 1032 #L221
Chicago, IL 60604

E-Mail: japr@lockescience.com
Home Page: www.lockescience.com

Andrew Seidel, Editor-in-Chief
Ajay Garde, Editor

The major international disciplinary resource for professionals and scholars in architecture, design, and planning. Also provides a link between theory and practice for researchers and practicing professionals.

2080 Journal of Urban Technology
New York City Technical College
300 Jay St
Brooklyn, NY 11201-1909

718-260-5250
Fax: 718-260-5524
E-Mail: connect@citytech.cuny.edu
Home Page: www.cuny.edu

Russell Hotzler, President
Miguel Cairol, VP

Covers technological developments in the architecture and transporatation fields.
Circulation: 10000
Founded in 1946

2081 Journal of the Society of Architectural Historians
Society of Architectural Historians
1365 N Astor St
Chicago, IL 60610-2144

312-573-1365
Fax: 312-573-1141
E-Mail: info@sah.org
Home Page: www.sah.org

Prof. Ken Breisch, Vice President
Abigail Van Slyck, President

Offers three to four scholarly articles on American and International topics, reviews of recently-published books, reviews of architecture exhibitions, and a variety of editorials designed to place the discipline of architectural history within a larger intellectual context.
Frequency: Quarterly

2082 Metal Architecture
Modern Trade Communications
7450 Skokie Blvd
Suite 200
Skokie, IL 60077-3374

847-674-2200
Fax: 847-674-3676
E-Mail: circulation@moderntrade.com
Home Page: www.moderntrade.com
Social Media: Facebook, Twitter, LinkedIn

Paul Deffenbaugh, Editorial Director
Mark Robins, Senior Editor
John S. Lawrence, CEO
John Paul Lawrence, President

Low-rise construction involving architects, engineers and specifiers.
Frequency: Monthly
Circulation: 33000
Founded in 1980

2083 Metropolis Magazine
Bellerophon Publications
61 W 23rd St
4th Floor
New York, NY 10010-4246

212-627-9977
Fax: 212-627-9988
E-Mail: edit@metropolismag.com
Home Page: www.metropolismag.com
Social Media: Facebook, Twitter, LinkedIn

Horace Havemeyer, Publisher
Susan Szenasy, Editor-in-Chief

The only magazine that covers all facets of design: architecture, interiors, furniture, preservation, urban design, graphics and crafts.
Cost: $27.95
Circulation: 61000
Founded in 1980

2084 Old House Interiors
Gloucester Publishers Corporation
10 Harbor Rd
Gloucester, MA 01930-3222

978-283-3200
800-356-9313
Fax: 978-283-4629
E-Mail: info@oldhouseinteriors.com
Home Page: www.oldhouseinteriors.com

Regina Cole, Editor

Covers restoration techniques for the pre-1939 home.
Cost: $26.00
116 Pages
Circulation: 100000
Founded in 1995
Printed in 4 colors on glossy stock

2085 Places: A Forum of Environmental Design
Journal of Environmental Design
100 Higgans Hall
Brooklyn, NY 11205

FAX 718-399-4332

James F Fulton, Publisher

Covers architecture, landscape architecture, urban design, with a multidisciplinary view of all aspects of public and private places.
Cost: $35.00

2086 Preservation Magazine
National Trust for Historic Preservation
1785 Massachusetts Ave NW
Washington, DC 20036-2189

202-588-6000
800-944-6847
Fax: 202-588-6038
E-Mail: info@savingplaces.org
Home Page: www.preservationnation.org

Stephanie Meeks, CEO
David Brown, EVP

Offers lively writing by the nation's best journalists on controversies, trends, accomplishments, and events of importance to cities, towns, suburbs, and rural communities.

2087 Professional Builder
Reed Business Information
360 Park Ave S
New York, NY 10010-1737

646-746-6845
Fax: 646-756-7583
E-Mail: corporatecommunications@reedbusiness.com
Home Page: www.reedbusiness.com

Mark Kelsey, CEO
James Reed, President

New residential construction magazine with a tradition of providing builders the solutions they need to maximize profits.
Frequency: Monthly
Founded in 1936

2088 Reed Bulletin
Reed Business Informtion
30 Technology Parkway South
Suite 100
Norcross, GA 30092

800-424-3996
E-Mail: talisha.jackson@reedbusiness.com
Home Page: www.reedconstructiondata.com

Talisha Jackson, Media Contact

Provides contractors with project news and tools suppliers.

2089 Residential Architect
Hanley-Wood

1 Thomas Circle NW
Suite 600
Washington, DC 20005-5811

202-452-0800
888-269-8410
Fax: 202-785-1974
E-Mail: cconroy@hanleywood.com
Home Page: www.residentialarchitect.com

Claire Conroy, Editorial Director
Jennifer Lash, Managing Editor
Bruce Snider, Senior Editor

It delivers substantive editorial on marketing, presentation, products, technology and business management to architects and designers.
Cost: $39.95
Frequency: 9x Yearly
Circulation: 22000
Founded in 1976

2090 Society of Architectural Administrators News Journal
Society of Architectural Administrators
15 E 7th Street NW
Cincinatti, OH 45202

513-684-3451

Patsy Frost, Publisher

Society news for professionals in the architectural community.

2091 World Monuments Fund
350 Fifth Avenue
Suite 2412
New York, NY 10118

646-424-9594
Fax: 646-424-9593
E-Mail: wmf@wmf.org
Home Page: www.wmf.org

Bonnie Burnham, President
Jonathan Foyle, Chief Executive
Darlene McCloud, VP
Lisa Ackerman, Executive VP, COO

This magazine offers information on the latest architectural trends, specifically landmarks, monuments, antiquities.
Cost: $17.95
16 Pages
Frequency: Quarterly
Founded in 1965
Printed in 4 colors on glossy stock

Trade Shows

2092 AIA National Convention and Design Exposition
American Institute of Architects
1735 New York Avenue NW
Washington, DC 20006-5292

202-626-7300
800-242-3837
Fax: 202-626-7547
E-Mail: infocentral@aia.org
Home Page: www.aia.org

Christine McEntee, CEO

Offers the chance to meet with more than 800 exhibitors and discover new products and technologies that can be used in future projects.
Frequency: Annual/April

2093 ASLA Annual Meeting & EXPO
American Society of Landscape Architects
636 Eye Street NW
Washington, DC 20001-3736

202-988-2444
800-787-2752
Fax: 202-898-1185
E-Mail: info@asla.org
Home Page: www.asla.org

Thomas Tavella, President
Mark Hough, VP

Landscape architect educational session and workshop plus 500 exhibits of outdoor lighting, playground and park equipment, landscape maintenance equipment, computer hardware and software and much more.
6000 Attendees

2094 American Institute of Architects Minn. Convention & Products Exhibition
American Institute of Architects, Minnesota Chap.
275 Market Street
Suite 54
Minneapolis, MN 55405

612-339-6904
Fax: 612-338-7981
E-Mail: infocentral@aia.org
Home Page: www.aia-mn.org

Christine McEntee, CEO

175 exhibits of windows, concrete, roofing, millwork, tile and more, plus conference, seminar and dinner.
2500 Attendees
Frequency: Annual
Founded in 1934

2095 American Institute of Building Design Annual Convention
American Institute of Building Design
529 14th St NW
Suite750
Washington, DC 20045

800-366-2423
Fax: 866-204-0293
E-Mail: info@aibd.org
Home Page: www.aibd.org

Dan Sater, President
Alan Kent, VP

A four day convention and trade show for residential design professionals
Frequency: Annual/July

2096 American Society for Aesthetics Annual Conference
American Society for Aesthetics
PO Box 915
Pooler, GA 31322

912-921-3189
Fax: 912-961-1395
E-Mail: asa@aesthetics-online.org
Home Page: www.aesthetics-online.org

Paul Guyer, President
Dabney Townsend, Treasurer
Dominic McLver Lopes, VP

Seminar, conference, and exhibits related to the study of the arts, all disciplines.
500 Attendees
Frequency: Annual/October
Founded in 1942

2097 Annual Technical & Educational Conference
American Design Drafting Association
105 E Main St
Newbern, TN 38059-1526

731-627-0802
Fax: 731-627-9321
E-Mail: corprorate@adda.org
Home Page: www.adda.org

Ron McDonald, President
Dennis Schwartz, Executive VP

Annual professional educational conference dedicated to serve the professional growth and advancement of the individuals working in the extremely fast paced, professional graphic community.
100 Members
Frequency: Annual/April

2098 Computers for Contractors and A/E/C Systems Fall
AEC Systems International/Penton Media
1300 E 9th St
Suite 316
Cleveland, OH 44114

216-696-7000
Fax: 216-696-6662
E-Mail: information@penton.com
Home Page: www.aecsystems.com

Sharon Rowlands, CEO
Nicola Allais, EVP

Computers for construction is the only tradeshow and conference dedicated exclusively to computer use by contractors. A/E/C SYSTEMS Fall is the regional technology event for the entire design and construction industry.
7000 Attendees
Frequency: Annual/November

2099 Council on Tall Buildings & Urban Habitat Congress
Lehigh University
11 East Packer Avenue
Bethlehem, PA 18015

610-583-3000
Fax: 610-758-4522
E-Mail: inctbuh@lehigh.edu
Home Page: www.ctbuh.orh

Antony Wood, Executive Director

Brings the world's leading decision makers together. For additional information visit our website or email us.
600+ Attendees
Frequency: Annual/February
Founded in 1969
Mailing list available for rent: 4500 names

2100 EDM/PDM Expo
AEC Systems International/Penton Media
1300 E 9th St
Suite 316
Cleveland, OH 44114

216-696-7000
Fax: 216-696-7000
E-Mail: info@aecsystems.com
Home Page: www.aecsystems.com

Sharon Rowlands, CEO
Nicola Allais, EVP

Showcases ways to manage technical/engineering documents, product management, and drawing conversion. Over 500 exhibits are shown.
20M Attendees
Frequency: Annual/May

2101 International Manufacturing & Engineering Technology Congress
AEC Systems International/Penton Media
1300 E 9th St
Suite 316
Cleveland, OH 44114

216-696-7000
Fax: 216-696-6662
E-Mail: info@aecsystems.com
Home Page: www.aecsystems.com

Sharon Rowlands, CEO
Nicola Allais, EVP

Automotive, aeronautics, and aerospace, electrical and electronics, consumer products, industrial, heavy equipment, and process industries. 1000 exhibits.
15M Attendees
Frequency: Annual/November

2102 **LightFair**
AMC
120 Wall Street
17th Floor
New York, NY 10005
212-248-5000
Fax: 212-248-5017
E-Mail: ies@ies.org
Home Page: www.iesna.org
Chip Israel, President
Daniel Salinas, Vice President
A major lighting trade show in North America featuring architectural lighting products from all spectrons of the industry. Containing 600 booths and 400 exhibits.
17M Attendees
Frequency: Annual/June
Mailing list available for rent: 10M names at $100 per M

2103 **Lightfair International**
Atlanta Market Center
240 Peachtree Street NW
Suite 2200
Atlanta, GA 30303-1327
404-220-3000
800-ATL-MART
Fax: 404-220-3030
E-Mail: webmaster@americasmart.com
Home Page: www.americasmart.com
John Portman, CEO
Jeffery Portman, COO
The world's largest annual architectural/commercial lighting trade show and conference program. Lightfair International features the latest technology, products, education, information, awards and industry association events. 600 booths.
20M Attendees
Frequency: Annual/May

2104 **M/Tech**
AEC Systems International/Penton Media
1300 E 9th Street
Suite 316
Cleveland, OH 44114
216-696-7000
Fax: 216-696-6662
E-Mail: info@aecsystems.com
Home Page: www.aecsystems.com
Sharon Rowlands, CEO
Nicola Allais, EVP
Focuses on applications to improve every phase of the product development cycle including CAD/CAM/CAE, Internet/intra/extranct, rapid prototyping and tooling, project/financial management, simulation and analysis, EDM/PDM and much more. 300 exhibits.
15M Attendees
Frequency: Annual/November

2105 **M/Tech West**
AEC Systems International/Penton Media
1300 E 9th St
Suite 316
Cleveland, OH 44114
216-696-7000
Fax: 216-696-6662
E-Mail: info@aecsystems.com
Home Page: www.acesystems.com
Sharon Rowlands, CEO
Nicola Allais, EVP
Explores concurrent engineering practices, computer integrated manufacturing, and mechanical engineering applications. 50 exhibits.
20M Attendees
Frequency: Annual/May

2106 **National Council of Architectural Registration Boards Annual Meeting**
Natl. Council of Architectural Registration Boards
1801 K Street NW
Suite 700K
Washington, DC 20006
202-783-6500
Fax: 202-783-0290
E-Mail: customerservice@ncarb.org
Home Page: www.ncarb.org
Ronald Biltch, President
Blakely Dunn, VP
Annual meeting and exhibits of architecture equipment, supplies and services.

2107 **Retail Design & Construction Conference & Expo**
Primedia
3585 Engineering Drive
Suite 100
Norcross, GA 30092
678-421-3000
800-216-1423
Fax: 913-967-1898
Home Page: www.primedia.com
Charles Stubbs, President
Kim Payne, SVP
Annual show of 145 exhibitors of equipment, supplies and services for retail design, construction, development, operations and maintenance, including signage, building equipment and materials, fixtures, floor coverings, furnishings, lighting, landscaping, store fronts, roofing, HVAC, maintenance materials and contractor services.
1000 Attendees

2108 **SARA National Conference**
Society Of American Registered Architects
P.O. Box 280
Newport, TN 37822
888-385-7272
Fax: 888-385-7272
E-Mail: cmoscato@sara-national.org
Home Page: www.sara-national.org
Social Media: LinkedIn
Guy Ragusa, Membership Chair
Cathie Moscato, Executive Director
Suzette Stoler, President
Gaetano Ragusa, Vice President
Annual conference holding the National Board Meeting, Architecture & Design Banquet, President's Celebration Banquet & Installation of Officers, and the International & Distinguished Building Award Presentations
503 Members
Founded in 1956

2109 **TCAA Convention**
Tile Contractors Association of America
10434 Indiana Avenue
Kansas City, MO 64137
816- 86- 930
800-655-8453
Fax: 816-767-0194
E-Mail: info@tcaainc.org
Home Page: www.tcaainc.org
Chris Pattavina, Associate Director
Carole Damon, Executive Director
Architect/designer learning exchange, speakers, business meetings, new products and technology
Founded in 1903

2110 **Technology for Construction**
Hanley-Wood
6191 N State Hwy 161
Suite 500
Irving, TX 75038
972-366-6300
866-962-7469
Fax: 972-536-6301
E-Mail: rmcconnell@hanleywood.com
Home Page: www.technologyforconstruction.com
Rick McConnell, President
Tom Cindric, Group Director
Annual forum that showcases the technology, tools and solutions for the design, construction, maintenance and modification of commercial buildings, institutions and other structures. These tools and education are essential for the seamless collaboration and communication between all those involved throughout the asset lifecycle.
72M Attendees
Frequency: Annual
Founded in 1976

Directories & Databases

2111 **Akron School Design Institute**
American Architectural Foundation
1020 19th Street NW
Suite 525
Washington, DC 20036
202-787-1001
Fax: 202-78 -002
E-Mail: info@archfoundation.org
Home Page: www.archfoundation.org
Ron Bogie, President/CEO
Scott Lauer, VP of Programs
Frequency: Annual

2112 **Dodge Building Stock**
DRI/McGraw-Hill
148 Princeton Heights Town Road
Height Town, NJ 08520
609- 42- 500
800-393-6343
E-Mail: support@construction.com
Home Page: www.dodge.construction.com
Social Media: Facebook, Twitter, LinkedIn
Keith Fox, President
Linda Brennan, VP of Operations
This database contains more than 18,000 historical and forecast quarterly time series on US buildings, including total square footage, number of buildings, and roof area for groups of structures in the categories of commercial, institutionals, manufacturing and residential.

2113 **Pro File/Official Directory of the American Institute of Architects**
American Institute of Architects (AIAA)
1735 New York Avenue NW
Washington, DC 20006-5292
202-783-6500
800-242-3837
Fax: 202-626-7364
E-Mail: infocentral@aia.org
Home Page: www.aia.org
Christine McEntee, CEO
Over 18,000 architectural firms are listed. These listings have one or more principals who is a member of the American Institute of Architects.
Cost: $225.00
1800 Pages
Frequency: Annual

2114 **Progressive Architecture: Information Sources Issue**
Penton Media

1300 E 9th St
Suite 316
Cleveland, OH 44114-1503

216-696-7000
Fax: 216-696-1752
E-Mail: information@penton.com
Home Page: www.penton.com

David Rowlands, CEO
Nicola Allais, EVP

List of trade and professional architecture associations.
Cost: $48.00

2115 **Sweets Directory**
Grey House Publishing/McGraw Hill Construction
1221 Avenue of the Americas
New York, NY 10020-1095

212-512-2000
800 442-2258
Fax: 212-512-3840
E-Mail: webmaster@mcgraw-hill.com
Home Page: www.mcgraw-hill.com
Social Media: Facebook, Twitter

Harold W McGraw III, CEO
Jack Callahan, Vice President

The leading desktop reference and preliminary research guide, featuring more than 10,000 building product manufacturers and their products.
Cost: $145.00
950 Pages
Frequency: Annual
ISBN: 1-592378-50-1
Founded in 1906

2116 **ThomasNet**
Thomas Publishing Company, LLC
User Services Department
5 Penn Plaza
New York, NY 10001

212-695-0500
800-699-9822
Fax: 212-290-7362
E-Mail: contact@thomaspublishing.com
Home Page: www.thomasnet.com
Social Media: Facebook, Twitter, LinkedIn

Carl Holst-Knudsen, President
Robert Anderson, VP, Planning
Mitchell Peipert, VP, Finance
Ivy Molofsky, VP, Human Resources

A way to reach qualified businesses that list their company information on ThomasNet.com. Detailed profiles promote their products, services, capabilities and brands carried. The ThomasNet.com web site is the most up-to-date compilation of 650,000 North American manufacturers, distributors, and service companies in 67,000 industrial categories.
Founded in 1898

2117 **Visual Merchandising and Store Design**
ST Media Group International
P.O. Box 1060
Skokie, IL 60076

847-763-4938
800-421-1321
Fax: 847-763-9030
E-Mail: customer@stmediagroup.com
Home Page: www.stmediagroup.com

Steve Duccilli, Group Publisher
Wade Swormstedt, Editor/Publisher
Ted Swormstedt, President/CEO

Visual Merchandising and Store Design showcases the latest store designs and visual presentations, presents merchandising strategies and new products and reports on industry news and events.
Frequency: Monthly
Circulation: 27000
Founded in 1922

Industry Web Sites

2118 **http://gold.greyhouse.com**
G.O.L.D Grey House OnLine Databases

Grey House Publishing's online database platform, GOLD. offers Quick Search, Keyword Search and Expert Search for most business sectors including architecture, buidling and construction markets. The GOLD platform makes finding the information you need quick and easy. All of Grey House's directory products are available for subscription on the GOLD platform.

2119 **www.access-board.gov**
Architectural & Transportation Barriers Compliance

Devoted to accessibility for people with disabilities.

2120 **www.acsa-arch.org**
Association of Collegiate Schools of Architecture

A nonprofit, membership association founded to advance the quality of architectural education.

2121 **www.adda.org**
American Design Drafting Association

The premier professional organization for drafters, designers, engineers, architects, ilustrators, graphics artist, digital technicians, digitial imaging, visual communications and multimedia

2122 **www.aecsystems.com.au**
A/E/C Systems International/Penton Media

Focuses on Internet/Intranet for the design, engineering and construction industries.

2123 **www.aia.org**
American Institute of Architects

A professional membership association for licensed, emerging professionals, and allied partners.

2124 **www.apti.org**
Association for Preservation Technology Int'l

A cross-disciplinary, membership organization dedicated to promoting the best technology for conserving historic structures and their settings.

2125 **www.archprecast.org**
Architectural Precast Association

A national trade association organized to advance the interests of architectural precast concrete in North America.

2126 **www.asla.org**
American Society of Landscape Architects

The national professional association representing landscape architects.

2127 **www.builderspace.com**
BuilderSpace.com

An online directory for the building industry and resources created to help users find the services and information they need.

2128 **www.construction.com**
McGraw-Hill Construction

McGraw-Hill Construction (MHC), part of The McGraw-Hill Companies, connects people and projects across the design and construction industry, serving owners, architects, engineers, general contractors, subcontractors, building product manufacturers, suppliers, dealers, distributors and adjacent markets.

2129 **www.ctbuh.org**
Council on Tall Buildings and Urban Habitat

Studies and reports on all aspects of the planning, design, and construction of tall buildings.

2130 **www.greyhouse.com**
Grey House Publishing

Authoritative reference directories for most business sectors including architecture, building and construction markets. Users can search the online databases with varied search criteria allowing for custom searches by product category, geographic area, sales volume, keyword, subject and more. Full Grey House catalog and online ordering also available.

2131 **www.historicnewengland.org**
Soc. for Preservation of New England Antiquities

Focuses on buildings, landscapes and objects reflecting New England life from the 17th century to the present.

2132 **www.icea.net**
Insulated Cable Engineers Association

Professional organization dedicated to developing cable standards for the electric power, control and telecommunications industries. Ensures safe, economical and efficient cable systems utilizing proven state-of-the-art materials and concepts. ICEA documents are of interest to cable manufacturers, architects and engineers, utility and manufacturing plant personnel, telecommunication engineers, consultants and OEMs.

2133 **www.ihs.com**
International Code Council

Nonprofit membership association with more than 16,000 members who span the building community, from code enforcement officials to materials manufacturers. Dedicated to preserving the public health, safety and welfare in the built environment through the effective use and enforcement of model codes.

2134 **www.ncarb.org**
Nat'l Council of Architectural Registration Boards

For state registration boards in the United States regulating the practice of architecture.

2135 **www.reedconstructiondata.com**
Architects First Source Online

Comprehensive building products information.

2136 **www.sah.org**
Society of Architectural Historians

Provides an international forum for those who care about architecture and its related arts.

2137 **www.sara-national.org**
Society of American Registered Architects

Architects helping Architects by sharing ideas and information.

2138 **www.sarc.msstate.edu**
Small Town Center

To maintain and improve the quality of life in American small towns.

2139 **www.sbicouncil.org**
Sustainable Buildings Industry Council

Information on the design, affordability, energy performance, and enviromental soundness of residential, institutional and commercial buildings.

2140 **www.sname.org**
Society of Naval Architects and Marine Engineers
Internationally recognized nonprofit, technical, professional society of individual members serving the maritime and offshore industries and their suppliers. Dedicated to advancing the industry by recording information, sponsoring research, offering career guidance and supporting education.

2141 **www.sweets.construction.com**
McGraw Hill Construction
In depth product information that lets you find, compare, select, specify and make purchase decisions in the industrial product marketplace.

Associations

2142 American Academy of Equine Art
117 North Water Street
PO Box 1364
Georgetown, KY 40324

502-570-8567
Fax: 859-281-6043
E-Mail: fcconner@aaea.net
Home Page: www.aaea.net

Xochitl Barnes, AAEA Vice President
Frances Clay Conner, Executive Director

The AAEA serves to educate and encourage a broad awareness and appreciation of contemporary equine art as a specific and distinctively worthy segment of fine art in America.
90 Members
Founded in 1980

2143 American Art Therapy Association
4875 Eisenhower Avenue
Suite 240
Alexandria, VA 22304-3302

703-212-2238
888-290-0878
E-Mail: info@arttherapy.org
Home Page: www.arttherapy.org
Social Media: Facebook, Twitter, LinkedIn

Sarah Deaver, President
Susan Corrigan, Executive Director
Michele Basham, Director, Membership Information
Julia Connell, Communications Manager
Barbara Florence, Director, Communication, Education

An organization of professionals dedicated to the belief that the creative process involved in art making is healing and life enhancing. Its mission is to serve its members and the general public by providing standards of professional competence, and developing and promoting knowledge in, and of, the field of art therapy.
4500 Members
Founded in 1969

2144 American Association of Museums
1575 Eye Street
Suite 400
Washington, DC 20005-1113

202-289-1818
Fax: 202-289-6578
E-Mail: membership@aam-us.org
Home Page: www.aam-us.org
Social Media: Facebook, Twitter, LinkedIn

Meme Omogbai, Chairman
Ford W. Bell, President
Laura Lott, COO
Canan Abayhan, Senior Director, Information
Carol Constantine, Director, Finance & Administration

Dedicated to promoting excellence within the museum community. Through advocacy, professional education, information exchange, accreditation and guidance on current professional standards of performance, AAM assists museum staff, boards and volunteers across the country to better serve the public.
16000 Members
Founded in 1906

2145 American Society for Aesthetics
PO Box 915
Pooler, GA 31322

912-921-2124
E-Mail: asa@aesthetics-online.org
Home Page: www.aesthetics-online.org

Robert Stecker, Editor
Theodore Gracyk, Editor
James Harold, Book Review Editor
James Harold, Book Review Editor

Promotes study, research, discussion and publication in aesthetics, which includes all studies of the arts and related experience including philosophic, scientific and theoretical viewpoints.
Founded in 1942

2146 American Society of Bookplate Collectors & Designers
5802 Bullock Loop
Suite C1 #84404
Laredo, TX 78041-8807

414-228-7831
E-Mail: info@bookplate.org
Home Page: www.bookplate.org
Social Media: Facebook, Twitter, LinkedIn

For designers, owners and collectors of bookplates.
Founded in 1942

2147 Antique Appraisal Association of America
1403 Gloria Lane
Boulder City, NV 89005

702-629-4502
888-791-0033
E-Mail: aaaofamerica@att.net
Home Page: www.antiqueappraisalassn.com

Helen Nolan, Executive Director

Members are well known for their Code of Ethics in their dealing with their customers. Our qualified professional appraisers have expertise in all types of appraisals and appraisal-related services, including insurance damage claims, estate probate, estate liquidation, estate auctions, court testimony, consultants and much more.
Founded in 1972

2148 Antiques Council
PO Box 1508
Warren, MA 01083

413-436-7064
Fax: 413-436-0448
E-Mail: info@antiquescouncil.com
Home Page: www.antiquescouncil.com

Marty Shapiro, President
Alan Cunha, VP
John Copenhaver, Education Director
David Bernard, Facilities Director
Joel Fletcher, Communications Director

A nonprofit organization created by professional antique dealers to improve the confidence of the public in antiques and their dealers through education, service and example.
100 Members
Founded in 1990

2149 Art Dealers Association of America
205 Lexington Avenue
Suite 901
New York, NY 10016
212-488-5550
Fax: 646-688-6809
E-Mail: adaa@artdealers.org
Home Page: www.artdealers.org

Dorsey Waxter, President
Mary Sabbatino, Vice President
Adam Sheffer, Vice President
Laurence Shopmaker, Secretary
Mark Brady, Treasurer

Nonprofit organzation that works to improve the stature and standing of the art gallery business. Members deal primarily with paintings, sculpture, prints, drawings and photographs from the Renaissance to the present day. We have more than 160 member galleries in more than 25 US cities.
160 Members
Founded in 1962

2150 Art Libraries Society of North America
7044 S. 13th St.
Oak Creek, WI 53154

414-768-8000
800-817-0621
Fax: 414-768-8001
E-Mail: customercare@arlisna.org
Home Page: www.arlisna.org
Social Media: Facebook, Twitter, LinkedIn

Gregory P.J. Most, President
Carole Ann Fabian, Vice-President/President Elect
Eric Wolf, Secretary
Deborah Barlow Smedstad, Treasurer
Robert J. Kopchinski, Association & Conference Manager

Devoted to fostering excellence in art librarianship, visual resources and curatorship for the advancement of visual arts. See website for available publications.
1000 Members
Founded in 1972
Mailing list available for rentat $200 per M

2151 Art and Antique Dealers League of America
PO Box 2066
Lenox Hill Station
New York, NY 10021

212-879-7558
Fax: 212-772-7197
E-Mail: secretary@artantiquedealersleague.com
Home Page: www.artantiquedealersleague.com

Clinton Howell, President
Robert Simon, VP
David Mayer, Secretary-Executive Director
Susan Kaplan Jacobson, Treasurer

Nonprofit organization promotes interests of retailers and wholesalers of antiques and art objects.
109 Members
Frequency: November/50 Attendees
Founded in 1926

2152 Art and Creative Materials Institute/ACMI
99 Derby Street
Suite 200
Hingham, MA 02043

781-556-1044
Fax: 781-207-5550
E-Mail: debbieg@acminet.org
Home Page: www.acminet.org

Michael Storei, President
Joan Lilly, Vice President
Timothy Gomez, Treasurer
Debbie Gustafson, Associate Director
Debbie Munroe, Certification Director

A non-profit association of manufacturers of art, craft and other creative materials, ACMI sponsors a certification program for both children's and adult's art materials and products, certifying that these products are non-toxic and meet voluntary standards of quality and performance. ACMI seeks to create and maintain a positive environment for art, craft and other creative materials usage, promoting safety in the materials and providing information and service resources on such products.
210 Members
Founded in 1936
Mailing list available for rent: 199 names

2153 Association for Preservation Technology International
3085 Stevenson Drive
Suite 200
Springfield, IL 62703

217-529-9039
Fax: 888-723-4242
E-Mail: info@apti.org
Home Page: www.apti.org
Social Media: Facebook, LinkedIn

Gretchen Pfaehler, President
John Diodati, Vice President
Dean Koga, Vice President
Lesley Gilmore, Treasurer
Nathela Chatara, CAE, Administrative Director

The Association for Preservation Technology (APT) is a cross-disciplinary, membership organization dedicated to promoting the best technology for conserving historic structures and their settings.
Founded in 1968

2154 Association of Restorers
8 Medford Place
New Hartford, NY 13413

315-733-1952
800-260-1829
Fax: 315-724-7231
Home Page: www.assoc-restorers.com

Andrea Daley, Founder

It is the mission of the AOR, Association of Restorers Inc, to increase the awareness of choice to consere, refurbish or restore historical works of art, household furnishings and architectural constructions
Founded in 1997

2155 College Art Association
TERRA Foundation
50 Broadway
21st Floor
New York, NY 10004

212-691-1051
Fax: 212-627-2381
E-Mail: nyoffice@collegeart.org
Home Page: www.collegeart.org
Social Media: Facebook, Twitter, YouTube

Ann Collins Goodyear, President
Maria Ann Conelli, Vice President for External Affairs
DeWitt Godfrey, Vice President for Committees
Patricia McDonnell, Secretary
John Hyland Jr., Treasurer

Promotes excellence in scholarship and technology in the criticisim of the visual arts and in the creativity and technical skill in the teaching and practices of art.
13000 Members
Founded in 1911

2156 Indian Arts & Crafts Association
4010 Carlisle NE
Suite C
Albuquerque, NM 87107

505-265-9149
Fax: 505-265-8251
E-Mail: info@iaca.com
Home Page: www.iaca.com
Social Media: Facebook, Twitter

Joseph P. Zeller, President
Cliff Fragua, Vice President
Beth Hale, Secretary
Kathi Ouellet, Treasurer

Nonprofit trade association whose mission is to promote, protect and preserve Indian arts.
700 Members
Founded in 1974

2157 International Fine Print Dealers Association (IFPDA)
250 W 26th St
Suite 405
New York, NY 10001-6737
212-674-6095
Fax: 212-674-6783
E-Mail: info@ifpda.org
Home Page: www.ifpda.org
Social Media: Facebook, Twitter

Paula McCarthy Panczenko, President
David Cleaton-Roberts, Vice President
Barbara Krakow, Vice President
Joni Moisant Weyl, Treasurer
Armin Kunz, Secretary

A nonprofit organzation that aspires to create a greater awareness and appreciation of fine prints among collectors and the general public. Povides funding for a variety of print-related educational programs, including pubications, lectures and symposia.
160 Members
Founded in 1987

2158 International Foundation for Art Research
500 5th Avenue
Suite 935
New York, NY 10110
212-391-6234
Fax: 212-391-8794
E-Mail: kferg@ifar.org
Home Page: www.ifar.org

Jack A Josephson, Chairman
Sharon Flescher, Executive Director

Nonprofit educational and research organization working for the interests of art scholarship, law and the public interest.
Founded in 1969

2159 National Antique & Collectible Association
PO Box 4389
Davidson, NC 28036

704-895-9088
800-287-7127
Fax: 704-895-0230
E-Mail: info@acna.us
Home Page: www.acna.us
Social Media: Facebook, Twitter

Angie Becker, President
Mike Becker, Vice President

The largest trade association for antique dealers & private collectors in the country. Our association has members in all 50 states. We offer an array of benefits including our insurance programs, merchant services, quarterly newsletter, educational seminars, travel, supply discounts and many more.
4300 Members
Founded in 1991

2160 National Art Education Association
1806 Robert Fulton Drive
Suite 300
Reston, VA 20191

703-860-8000
Fax: 703-860-2960
E-Mail: info@arteducators.org
Home Page: www.naea-reston.org
Social Media: Facebook, Twitter, LinkedIn

Dennis Inhulson, President
Patricia Franklin, President Elect
Deborah B Reeve, Executive Director

Promote art education through professional development, service, advancment of knowledge and leadership.
22000 Members
Founded in 1947

Mailing list available for rent: 22,000 names at $95 per M

2161 National Art Materials Trade Association
20200 Zion Ave.
Cornelius, NC 28031

704-892-6244
E-Mail: info@namta.org
Home Page: www.namta.org
Social Media: Facebook, Twitter, LinkedIn

Hayley Prendergast, President
Kevin P Lavin, Executive VP & CFO
Howard Krinsky, Vice President
Reggie Hall, Executive Director
Rick Munisteri, Director of Meetings

International association of manufacturers, importers, wholesalers and retailers of art materials.
2.1M Members

2162 National Assembly of State Arts Agencies
1029 Vermont Ave NW
Suite 2
Washington, DC 20005-3517

202-347-6352
202-347-5948
Fax: 202-737-0526
E-Mail: nasaa@nasaa-arts.org
Home Page: www.nasaa-arts.org

Pam Breaux, President
Jonathan Katz, Chief Executive Officer
Laura S. Smith, CFRE, Chief Advancement Officer
Kelly J Barsdate, Chief Planning Officer
Sharon Gee, Director of Meetings and Events

NASAA's mission is to advance and promote a meaningful role for the arts in the lives of individuals, families and communities throughout the United States. We empower state art agencies through strategic assistance that fosters leadership, enhances planning and decision making, and increases resources. TDD 202-347-5948.
56 Members
Founded in 1968

2163 National Association of Fine Arts
1155 F Street NW
Suite 1050
Washington, DC 20004

414-332-9306
Fax: 888-884-6232
E-Mail: info@artmarketing.com
Home Page: www.nafa.com
Social Media: Facebook, Twitter, LinkedIn

Kim O'Brien, President & CEO
Chip Anderson, Vice Chair
S Christopher Johnson, Secretary
Nathan Zuidema, Treasurer

Seeks to provide services and networking opportunities to individuals in the arts community.
100 Members
Founded in 1986

2164 National Auctioneers Association
8880 Ballentine St
Overland Park, KS 66214

913-541-8084
Fax: 913-894-5281
E-Mail: support@auctioneers.org
Home Page: www.auctioneers.org
Social Media: Facebook, Twitter

Paul C Behr, President
Thomas W Saturley, VP
Chris Pracht, Treasurer
Hannes Combest, CEO

NAA promotes the auction method of marketing and enhances the professionalism of its practitioners
6,000 Members
Founded in 1948

2165 National Guild of Community Schools of the Arts
520 8th Avenue
3rd Floor, Suite 302
New York, NY 10018

212-268-3337
Fax: 212-268-3995
E-Mail: guildinfo@nationalguild.org
Home Page: www.nationalguild.org
Social Media: Facebook, Twitter, LinkedIn

Jonathan Herman, Executive Director
Ken Cole, Assosiate Director
Claire Wilmoth, Membership Associate
James Harton, Program Director
Traci Horgen, Business Manager

Arts Management in Community Institutions (AMICI) Summer Institute trains administrators to meet needs of growing and emerging arts schools. Other programs, services, guildnotes newsletter, job opportunities listings, and publications catalog available upon request on online. Mailing list $25 for non-members, free for members.
300 Members
Founded in 1937

2166 National Network for Art Placement
935 W Avenue 37
Los Angeles, CA 90065

323-222-4035
800-354-5348
E-Mail: NNAPnow@aol.com
Home Page: www.artistplacement.com

Warren Christensen, Consultant

An organization that helps any artist with start up capital and services for small businesses.

2167 National Trust for Historic Preservation
2600 Virginia Avenue
Suite 1000
Washington, DC 20037

202-588-6000
800-944-6847
Fax: 202-588-6038
E-Mail: info@savingplaces.org
Home Page: www.preservationnation.org
Social Media: Facebook, Twitter

Stephanie K. Meeks, President &CEO
David J. Brown, Vice President & CPO
Paul Edmondson, Chief Legal Officer
Terry Richey, Chief Marketing Officer
Rosemarie Rae, Chief Financial Officer

A private, nonprofit membership organization dedicated to saving historic places and revitlizing America's communities. Also provides leadership, education, advocacy, and resources to save America's diverse historic places and revitalize the communities.
270k Members
Founded in 1949

2168 Professional Picture Framers Association
2282 Springport Road
Suite F
Jackson, MI 49202
517-788-8100
800-762-9287
Fax: 517-788-8371
E-Mail: ppfa@ppfa.com
Home Page: www.ppfa.com

John Pruitt, President
Stuart M Altschuler, VP
Jim Esp, Secretary & Executive Director
Robin Gentry, Treasurer

A trade association of manufacturers, wholesalers, print publishers, importers and retailers selling art, framing and related supplies.
3000 Members
Founded in 1971

2169 Society of Animal Artists
5451 Sedona Hills Drive
Berthoud, CO 80513

970-532-3127
Fax: 970-532-2537
E-Mail: admin@societyofanimalartists.com
Home Page: www.societyofanimalartists.com
Social Media: Facebook

Diane Mason, President
Allen Bragden, VP
Marilyn Newmark, VP
Douglas Allen, VP
Renee Headings-Bemis, Treasurer

Devoted to promoting excellence in the portrayal of the creatures sharing our planet and to the education of the public through informative art seminars, lectures and teaching demonstrations.
360 Members
Founded in 1960

2170 Society of Illustrators
128 E 63rd St
New York, NY 10065

212-838-2560
Fax: 212-838-2561
E-Mail: info@societyillustrators.org
Home Page: www.societyillustrators.org
Social Media: Facebook, Twitter

Dennis Dittrich, President
Victor Juhasz, Vice President
Tim O'Brien, Executive VP
Karen Green, Secretary
David Ruess, Treasurer

A professional society of illustrators and art directors.
950 Members
Founded in 1901

2171 The American Institute for Conservation of Historic & Artistic Works
1156 15th Street
Suite 320
Washington, DC 20005-1714

202-452-9545
Fax: 202-452-9328
E-Mail: info@conservation-us.org
Home Page: www.conservation-us.org
Social Media: Facebook, Twitter, YouTube, Flickr

Eryl P. Wentworth, Executive Director
Ruth Seyler, Membership & Meetings Director
Eric Pourchot, Institutional Advancement Director
Sandy T. Nguyen, Finance Director
Abigail Choudhury, Development and Education

Conservators of artistic and cultural property.
3500 Members
Founded in 1961

2172 The Art Students League of New York
215 W 57th Street
New York, NY 10019

212-247-4510
Fax: 212-541-7024
E-Mail: info@artstudentsleague.org
Home Page: www.theartstudentsleague.org
Social Media: Facebook, Twitter, YouTube, Pinterest

Salvatore Barbieri, President
Susan Matz, Vice President
Howard A. Friedman, Vice President
Ira Golberg, Executive Director
Ken Park, Director of Communications

Educational organization that provides space, studios and offices to members.
Founded in 1875

2173 The Maven Co.
Maven Company
PO Box 937
Plandome, NY 11020-0937

51 -62 -880
Fax: 914-248-0800
E-Mail: fasttrack@erols.com
Home Page: www.mavencompany.com

N Chittenden, VP

An innovator of new and unique programs to help antique dealers sell their merchandise and to make their shows more successful.
5,000 Attendees
Frequency: January/Annual
Founded in 1970

2174 The National Antique & Art Dealers Association of America
220 E 57th St
New York, NY 10022

212-826-9707
Fax: 212-832-9493
Home Page: www.naadaa.org

James R McConnaughy, President
Mark Jacoby, VP
Arlie Sulka, Secretary
Steven J Chait, Treasurer

Works to promote the best interests of the antique art exhibitions and to promote just, honorable and ethical trade practices.
38 Members
Founded in 1954

2175 Volunteer Committees of Art Museums
5139 Thorncroft Court
Royal Oak, MI 48073

504-488-2631
Fax: 504-484-6662
E-Mail: co_presidents@vcam.org
Home Page: www.vcam.org
Social Media: Facebook, Twitter, LinkedIn

Peter Milne, President
Linda McGinty, Co President
Susan Colangelo, Secretary
Victoria Cather, Treasurer

An internationally recognized non-profit organization. VCAM is committed to provide a forum for information exchange, mutual education and enhancement of services to its art museum volunteer committee members through international conferences, regional meetings, published comprehensive conference reports, resource files and the VCAM NEWS publication.
19 Members
Founded in 1952

Newsletters

2176 ARTnewsletter
ARTnews Associates
48 W 38th Street
New York, NY 10018-6211

212-398-1690
800-284-4625

Fax: 212-819-0394
E-Mail: info@artnewsonline.com
Home Page: www.artnewsonline.com

Milton Esterow, Publisher/CEO
Robin Cembalest, Executive Editor
Debra Melson, Marketing
Elizabeth McNamara, Circulation Manager

Business report on the world art market. Targeted to private collectors, dealers, gallery owners, museum directors and curators, tax and estate buyers.
Cost: $279.00
Frequency: Bi-weekly
Circulation: 83375
Founded in 1902

2177 **ASA Newsletter**
P.O. Box 915
Pooler, GA 31322

912-921-2124
E-Mail: asa@aesthetics-online.org
Home Page: www.aesthetics-online.org

Paul Guyer, President
Dominic McIver Lopes, VP
Dabney Townsend, Secretary/Treasurer

Promotes study, research, discussion and publication in aesthetics, which includes all studies of the arts and related experience including philosophic, scientific and theoretical viewpoints.
Founded in 1942

2178 **Antique Appraisal Association of America Newsletter**
Antique Appraisal Association of America
1403 Gloria Lane
Boulder City, NV 89005

702-629-4502
888-791-0033
E-Mail: aaaofamerica@att.net
Home Page: www.antiqueappraisalassn.com

Marge Swenson, Publisher

Supplies members with additional knowledge of antiques from research.

2179 **Art Hazards Newsletter**
New York Foundation for the Arts
155 Avenue of the Americas
14th Floor
New York, NY 10013

212-366-6900
Fax: 212-366-1778
E-Mail: csa@tmn.com

Theodore Berger, Executive Director
Toni Lewis, Director Administration

Contains information on all hazardous materials; art materials and articles.
Cost: $24.00
Frequency: Quarterly
Founded in 1977

2180 **Art Research News**
500 5th Avenue
Suite 935
New York, NY 10110

212-391-6234
Fax: 212-391-8794
E-Mail: kferg@ifar.org
Home Page: www.ifar.org

Sharon Flescher, Executive Director

The latest news on authenticity, ownership, theft, and other artistic, legal and ethical issues concerning art objects.
Founded in 1969

2181 **Arts & Culture Funding Report**
Capitol City Publishers
4416 East West Hwy
Suite 400
Bethesda, MD 20814-4568

301-916-1800
800-637-9915
Fax: 301-528-2497
Home Page: www.capitolcitypublishers.com

A monthly newsletter on federal, state, private and nonprofit sector funding and financial assistance to arts and cultural organizations.
Cost: $198.00
Frequency: Monthly
ISSN: 1047-3297

2182 **Arts Management**
Radius Group
545 5th Ave
New York, NY 10017-3647

212-972-2929
Fax: 212-972-7581
E-Mail: postmaster@trflaw.com
Home Page: www.trflaw.com

Leonard A Rodes, Partner
David Trachtenberg, Partner
Barry Friedberg, Partner

The national news service for those who finance, manage and communicate the arts.
Cost: $18.00
Frequency: 5 per year

2183 **Artsfocus**
Colorado Springs Fine Arts Center
30 W Dale St
Colorado Spring, CO 80903-3249

719-634-5581
Fax: 719-634-0570
E-Mail: info@csfineartscenter.org
Home Page: www.csfineartscenter.org

Sam Gappmayer, CEO
Kari Torgerson, COO
Tom Jackson, Director of Development

Museum members publication.
Cost: $5.00
24 Pages
Frequency: Quarterly
Founded in 1936
Printed in 2 colors on matte stock

2184 **Aviso**
American Association of Museums
1575 Eye Street NW
Suite 400
Washington, DC 20005-1113

202-289-1818
Fax: 202-289-6578
E-Mail: membership@aam-us.org
Home Page: www.aam-us.org

Ford W Bell, President
Douglas Myers, CEO Executive Director

Reports on museums in the news, federal legislation affecting museums, upcoming seminars and workshops, federal grant deadlines and AAM activities and services.
Frequency: Monthly

2185 **Bookplates in the News**
Amer. Society of Bookplate Collectors & Designers
605 N Stoneman Avenue
Suite F
Alhambra, CA 91801-1406

626-579-9147
E-Mail: exlibris@att.net
Home Page: www.artisanale@hotmail.com

Audrey Spencer Arellanes, Publisher
Victor Amor, Owner

Collectors' news for designers, owners and collectors of bookplates.
Cost: $25.00
200 Pages
Frequency: Quarterly
Circulation: 250

2186 **Communique**
Association for Preservation Technology Int'l
3085 Stevenson Drive
Suite 200
Springfield, IL 62703

217-529-9039
Fax: 888-723-4242
E-Mail: info@apti.org
Home Page: www.apti.org

Joan Berkwitz, President
Gretchen Pfaehler, Vice President
Kyle Normandin, Treasurer
Nathela Chatara,CAE, Administrative Director

APT's electronic newsletter, enables APT members to exchange preservation information, publicize their news and awards, share project experience with colleagues, post calls for papers, and submit preservation queries to the readership.
Frequency: Quarterly

2187 **Cotton & Quail Antique Gazette**
F+W Media
38 E. 29th Street
New York, NY 10016

212-447-1400
Fax: 212-447-5231
E-Mail: contact_us@fwmedia.com
Home Page: www.fwpublications.com

Greg Smith, Publisher
Linda Kunkel, Editor
Dave Paul, Marketing

Contains articles about various collecting topics, announcements of upcoming shows, reviews of shows and auctions, a Q & A column on antiques, 'how-to' articles, regular features about collecting and selling, an extensive show and auction calendar.
Cost: $20.00
Frequency: Monthly
Circulation: 25000
Founded in 1965

2188 **Encouraging Rejection**
Noforehead Press
Box 55
Kearsarge, NH 03847-0130

Home Page: www.reuben.org

Mark Heath, Editor/Publisher

To inspire and encourage artists in the face of rejection.
Cost: $19.00
Frequency: Bi-Monthly
Founded in 1994

2189 **Folk Art Finder**
Gallery Press
117 N Main Street
Essex, CT 06426-1302

860-767-0313
Home Page: folkart.com

Florence Laffal, Editor/Publisher

Contains feature stories, a calendar of events, a readers exchange, news items, book reviews, and classified and display ads relating to 20th century American folk art. Other issues addressed are folk art preservation, laws affecting the arts and funding for the arts.
Cost: $14.00
24 Pages
Frequency: Quarterly
Mailing list available for rent
Printed in one color on matte stock

2190 **IFAR Journal**
International Foundation for Art Research
500 5th Avenue
Suite 935
New York, NY 10110

212-391-6234
Fax: 212-391-8794
E-Mail: kferg@ifar.org
Home Page: www.ifar.org
Social Media: Facebook

Sharon Flescher PhD, CEO
Jack A. Josephson, Chairman

Listings of stolen art and the legal developments of articles on art recovery, art law, cultural property and art authentication.
Cost: $65.00
32 Pages
Frequency: Quarterly
ISSN: 1098-1195
Founded in 1969

2191 **Indian Arts & Crafts Association Newsletter**
4010 Carlisle NE
Suite C
Albuquerque, NM 87107

505-265-9149
Fax: 505-265-8251
E-Mail: info@iaca.com
Home Page: www.iaca.com

Joseph Zeller, President
Don Standing Bear Forest, VP
Gail Chehak, Executive Director
Susan Pourian, Secretary
Kathi Ouellet, Treasurer

2192 **International Association of Auctioneers Newsletter**
Butterfield & Butterfield Auctioneers
220 San Bruno Ave
San Francisco, CA 94103-5018

415-861-7500
800-222-2854
Fax: 415-861-8951
E-Mail: appraisals.us@bonhams.com
Home Page: www.butterfields.com

Melcolm Barbar, CEO

A news bulletin with descriptions of upcoming auctions around the world.
8 Pages
Frequency: Quarterly
Circulation: 6500
Founded in 1865

2193 **Kovels on Antiques and Collectibles**
Antiques
2135 N Milwaukee Ave
Chicago, IL 44122

773-360-8162
Fax: 216-752-3115
Home Page: www.kovels.com
Social Media: Facebook, Twitter

Terry Kovel, Co-Publisher
Ralph Kovel, Co-Publisher

Newsletter for dealers, investors and collectors.
Cost: $27.00
12 Pages
Frequency: Monthly
Founded in 1995
Printed in 4 colors on matte stock

2194 **National Association of Antiques Bulletin**
National Association of Dealers in Antiques
PO Box 421
Barrington, IL 60011-0421

847-381-3101
Fax: 815-877-4282

Shirley Kowing, Publisher

Educational and association news.

2195 **Professional Picture Framers Association Newsletter**
4305 Sarellen Road
Richmond, VA 23231-4311

804-226-0430
Fax: 804-222-2175
E-Mail: framers@gnn.com

Rex P Boynton, Executive Director

Trade association news for manufacturers, wholesalers, print publishers, importers and retailers selling art, framing and related supplies.

2196 **Stolen Art Alert**
500 5th Avenue
Suite 935
New York, NY 10110

212-391-6234
Fax: 212-391-8794
E-Mail: kferg@ifar.org
Home Page: www.ifar.org

Sharon Flescher, Executive Director

Reports on art thefts and recoveries and also covered major art forgery cases.
Founded in 1969

2197 **VCAM NEWS**
Volunteer Communities of Art Museums
New Orleans Museum of Art
PO Box 19123
New Orleans, LA 70179

504-488-2631
Fax: 504-484-6662
E-Mail: president@vcam.org
Home Page: www.vcam.org

Peter Milne, President
Susan Colangelo, Secretary
Victoria Cather, Treasurer

Informs and invigorates the volunteers.
19 Members
Founded in 1952

2198 **World Fine Art**
Art Baron Management Corporation
1356 Cherry Bottom Road
Colombos, OH 43230-6771

614-476-9708

Jeffrey Coffin, Publisher
Steve Shipp, Editor
John Blackburn, Manager

Art history, values and projections regarding artists and movements.
Cost: $95.00
10 Pages
Frequency: 9 per year
Printed in one color

Magazines & Journals

2199 **A History of Art Therapy**
American Art History
4875 Eisenhower Avenew
Suite 240
Alexandria, VA 22304-3302

703-212-2238
888-290-0878
E-Mail: info@arttherapy.org
Home Page: www.arttherapy.org

Mercedes ter Maat, President
Charlotte Boston,MA,ATR, Secretary
Joseph Jaworek ATR-BC, Treasurer
Frequency: Yearly

2200 **AIC Guide to Digital Photography and Conservation Documentation**
American Institute for Conservation
1156 15th St NW
Suite 320
Washington, DC 20005-1714

202-452-9545
Fax: 202-452-9328
E-Mail: info@aic-faic.org
Home Page: www.aic-faic.org

Eryl Wentworth, Executive Director
Adam Allen, Meetings Associate
Steve Charles, Membership Assistant

2201 **Advocacy and Lobbying: Speaking up for the Arts**
National Assembly of State Arts Agencies
1029 Vermont Ave NW
2nd Floor
Washington, DC 20005-3517

202-347-6352
Fax: 202-737-0526
E-Mail: nasaa@nasaa-arts.org
Home Page: www.nasaa-arts.org

Dennis Dewey, Manager
Arlynn Fishbaugh, President
Pam Breaux, VP
Bobby Kadis, Treasurer
John Bracey, Secretary

2202 **Airbrush Action**
3209 Atlantic Avenue
PO Box 438
Allenwood, NJ 08720

732-223-7878
800-876-2472
Fax: 732-223-2855
E-Mail: customerservice@airbrushaction.com
Home Page: www.airbrushaction.com

Clifford S Stieglitz, President/Publisher

Offers information on the art and graphic design community. Airbrush Action's editorial includes features/coverage on: automotive customizing, hobby applications, illustration, signs, t-shirts, body art, home decorative and more.
Cost: $26.95
Circulation: 35000
Printed in 4 colors on glossy stock

2203 **Airbrush Art and Action**
Paisano Publishers
28210 Dorothy Drive
PO Box 3000
Agoura Hills, CA 91301

818-889-8740
800-247-6246
Fax: 818-889-1252
Home Page: www.paisanopub.com/

Joseph Teresi, Publisher

A look at new products, step by step instruction features, profiles of professionals in the airbrushing field, and examples of airbrushed artworks.
Frequency: Bi-annually
Circulation: 68500

2204 **American Artist**
Billboard
770 Broadway
New York, NY 10003-9589

646-654-4400
800-562-2706
Fax: 646-654-5514
E-Mail: billboard@espcomp.com
Home Page: www.billboard.com

Jessica Letkemann, Managing Editor
Lisa Ryan Howard, Publisher

A magazine devoted to the best of the best in the art industry.
Cost: $43.45
Frequency: Monthly
Circulation: 71,435
Founded in 1894

2205 **Antique Trader**
F+W Media
38 E. 29th Street
New York, NY 10016

212-447-1400
Fax: 212-447-5231
E-Mail: contact_us@fwmedia.com
Home Page: www.fwpublications.com

Jim Ogle, CFO
Sara Domville, President
Chad Phelps, Chief Digital Officer
David Nussbaum, CEO

For the antiques and collectibles hobby industry. Accepts advertising.
Cost: $38.00
100 Pages
Frequency: Weekly
Circulation: 27363
Founded in 1957

2206 **Antique Week**
Mayhill Publications
27 N Jefferson Street
PO Box 90
Knightstown, IN 46148

765-345-5133
800-876-5133
Fax: 800-695-8153
E-Mail: tony@antiqueweek.com
Home Page: www.antiqueweek.com

Gary Thoe, President
David Blower, Senior Editor

Antique dealers.
Cost: $38.95
Frequency: Weekly
Circulation: 65000
Founded in 1968

2207 **Aristos**
Aristos Foundation
PO Box 20845
Park West Station
New York, NY 10025

212-678-8550
E-Mail: aristos@aristos.org
Home Page: www.aristos.org

Louis Torres, Editor
Michelle Marder Kamhi, Editor

Independent online journal advocating objective standards in arts scholarship and criticism. Our aim is to present well-reasoned commentary on the arts and on the philosophy of art, for a broad audience of general readers and scholars.
Cost: $25.00
Frequency: Monthly
Founded in 1982

2208 **Art & Antiques**
Art & Antiques Worldwide Media LLC
1319-cc Military Cutoff Road #192
Wilmington, NC 28405

910-679-4402
888-350-0951
Fax: 919-869-1864
E-Mail: info@artandantiquesmag.com
Home Page: www.artandantiquesmag.com

Jon Dorfman, Senior Editor

Magazine for collectors of the fine and decorative arts.
Frequency: Monthly

2209 **Art & Auction**
Art & Auction
601 West 26th Street
Suite 410
New York, NY 10001

212-447-9555
800-777-8718
Fax: 212-447-5221
E-Mail: info@artandauction.com
Home Page: www.artinfo.com

Louise T Blouin, President/Owner
Benjamin Genocchio, Editor-in-Chief

Editorial covers the art market from antiquities to contemporary art, monthly calendar of gallery exhibitions and auction sales.
Cost: $80.00
Frequency: Monthly
Circulation: 38500
Founded in 1996

2210 **Art Business News**
Advanstar Communications
600 Unicorn Park Drive
Suite 400
Woburn, MA 01801

339-298-4200
800-552-4346
Fax: 781-939-2490
E-Mail: info@advanstar.com
Home Page: www.advanstar.com/

Julie MacDonald, Editor
Joseph Loggia, CEO

Publication addressing the business aspect of art and framing. Editorial covers everything from trends and sales to new colors and the latest tax changes.
Cost: $43.00
Frequency: Monthly
ISSN: 0273-5652
Founded in 1992

2211 **Art Materials Retailer**
Fahy-Williams Publishing
171 Reed Street
PO Box 1080
Geneva, NY 14456-2137

315-789-0458
800-344-0559
Fax: 315-789-4263
E-Mail: kfahy@fwpi.com
Home Page: www.fwpi.com

J Kevin Fahy, Publisher
Tina Manzer, Editorial Director
Bradley G. Gordner, Senior Editor
Frequency: Quarterly
Circulation: 12000
Printed in 4 colors on glossy stock

2212 **Art in America**
Brant Publications
575 Broadway
5th Floor
New York, NY 10012-3227

212-941-2900
Fax: 212-941-2885
E-Mail: interview_ad@brantpub.com
Home Page: www.interviewmagazine.com

Sandra Brant, Publisher
Elizabeth Baker, Editor

Includes show reviews, event schedules, profiles of artists and genres and updates on literature and materials.
Cost: $24.95
Frequency: Monthly
Circulation: 64,182
Founded in 1984

2213 **Arts and Activities**
Publishers' Development Corporation
12345 World Trade Dr
San Diego, CA 92128-3743

858-605-0200
Fax: 858-605-0247
E-Mail: promo@artsandactivities.com
Home Page: www.gunsmagazine.com

Tom Von Rosen, Owner
Maryellen Bridge, Editor

Offers information and news on the latest in the visual arts.
Cost: $24.95
Frequency: Monthly
Founded in 1932

2214 **Artweek**
PO Box 485
Hilo, HI 96721-0485

800-733-2916
800-733-2916
Fax: 262-495-8703
E-Mail: info@artweek.com
Home Page: www.artweek.com

Debra Koppman, Editor
Laura Richar Janku, Editor

Critical reviews of contemporary West Coast art as well as news, features, articles, interviews, special sections and opinion pieces.
Cost: $34.00
Frequency: Monthly
Founded in 1968

2215 **Breakthrough Magazine**
Breakthrough Magazine
2271 Old Baton Rouge Highway
PO Box 2945
Hammond, LA 70404-2945

985-345-7266
800-783-7266
Fax: 985-542-1831
E-Mail: info@breakthroughmagazine.com
Home Page: www.breakthroughmagazine.com

Larry Blomquist, Publisher

Artist profiles, tips, previews, and a calendar of events. Incorporates similar techniques related to wildlife carvings, sculpture and photography,
Cost: $32.00
Frequency: Quarterly
Circulation: 8932

2216 **CNA**
F+W Media
38 E. 29th Street
New York, NY 10016

212-447-1400
Fax: 212-447-5231
E-Mail: contact_us@fwmedia.com
Home Page: www.fwpublications.com

Jim Ogle, CFO
Sara Domville, President
Chad Phelps, Chief Digital Officer
David Nussbaum, CEO

A craft industry trade magazine reaching retailers and industry leaders. Readers turn to CNA each month in search of trends, innovative products, partnerships, corporate accomplishments, and retail strategies that positively impact their businesses. Regular editorial includes timely product showcases and special sections that target arts, crafts, scrapbooking, children's activities, sewing and needlework products. The editorial team has much experience in the industry.
Cost: $30.00
112 Pages
Circulation: 21777
Founded in 1945

2217 **Christie's International Magazine**
Christies Publications

20 Rockefeller Plaza
New York, NY 10020

212-636-2000
800-395-6300
Fax: 212-636-2399
E-Mail: info@christies.com
Home Page: www.christies.com

Mark Wrey, Publisher
Victoria Tremlett, Editor
John L Vogelstein, Chairman

Devoted to the promotion of Christie's fine art auctions worldwide.
Cost: $70.00
Circulation: 60000
Founded in 1766

2218 Craft and Needlework Age
F+W Media
38 E. 29th Street
New York, NY 10016

212-447-1400
Fax: 212-447-5231
E-Mail: contact_us@fwmedia.com
Home Page: www.fwpublications.com

Jim Ogle, CFO
Sara Domville, President
Chad Phelps, Chief Digital Officer
David Nussbaum, CEO

Trade magazine serving the crafts and needlework industry. Accepts advertising.
Cost: $20.00
Frequency: Monthly
Founded in 1952

2219 Decorative Artist's Workbook
F+W Media
38 E. 29th Street
New York, NY 10016

212-447-1400
Fax: 212-447-5231
E-Mail: contact_us@fwmedia.com
Home Page: www.fwpublications.com

Jim Ogle, CFO
Sara Domville, President
Chad Phelps, Chief Digital Officer
David Nussbaum, CEO

The leading how-to magazine for decorative painters, because it offers detailed step-by-step instruction and illustrations for fabulous projects, plus problem-solving tips, and articles on new techniques, products and books. Readers find a full range of decorative painting subjects and styles painted in a whole range of skill levels and mediums and on a variety of surfaces...and all designed by the most well known artists and instructors in decorative painting!
Cost: $27.00
72 Pages
Frequency: Quarterly
Circulation: 111573
Founded in 1987

2220 Folk Art
American Folk Art Museum
2 Lincoln Square
Columbus Avenue at 66th Street
New York, NY 10023

212-595-9533
Fax: 212-265-2350
E-Mail: info@folkartmuseum.org
Home Page: www.folkartmuseum.org

Irene Kreney, Manager
Linda Dune, Acting Director
Edward Blanchard, President, Treasurer

An award winning publication. The editorial content is geared toward collectors, scholars, and the museum community interested in traditional and contemporary American folk and decorative arts. A benefit of membership, and is delivered to a targeted national and international readership.

2221 HOW Magazine
F&W Publications
10151 Carver Road
Blue Ash, OH 45242

513-531-2690
Fax: 513-531-1843
E-Mail: contact_us@fwmedia.com
Home Page: www.fwpublications.com
Social Media: Facebook, Twitter, LinkedIn

David Nussbaum, CEO
Jim Ogle, COO/CFO
Sara Domville, President

The industry's leading creativity, business and technology magazine for graphic design professionals. Each issue provides a mix of essential business information, up-to-date technology tips, the creative whys and hows behind noteworthy projects, and profiles of professionals who are influencing design.
Cost: $27.73
140 Pages
Frequency: Monthly
Circulation: 44883
Founded in 1985

2222 Hammer's Blow
259 Muddy Fork Road
Jonesborough, TN 37659

423-913-1022
Fax: 423-913-1023
E-Mail: centraloffice@abana.org
Home Page: www.abana.org

David Hutchinson, President
Jack Parks, First VP
Peter Renzetti, Second VP
Bill Clemens, Secretary

Journal of the Artist-Blacksmiths' Association of North America
4500 Members
Frequency: Quarterly
Circulation: 2 Mag.
Founded in 1973

2223 I.D. Magazine
F+W Media
38 E. 29th Street
New York, NY 10016

212-447-1400
Fax: 212-447-5231
E-Mail: contact_us@fwmedia.com
Home Page: www.fwpublications.com

Jim Ogle, CFO
Sara Domville, President
Chad Phelps, Chief Digital Officer
David Nussbaum, CEO
Andr,a Pellegrino, Advertising Director

The international design magazine, showcases innovative products and technologies for sophisticated readers who are at the forefront of shaping the world through design. The multi-disciplinary coverage embraces design trends, theories, experiments and innovators.
Cost: $59.96
96 Pages
Frequency: 1 Year 8 Issues
Circulation: 31,424
Founded in 1954

2224 IFAR Journal
500 5th Avenue
Suite 935
New York, NY 10110

212-391-6234
Fax: 212-391-8794
E-Mail: kferg@ifar.org
Home Page: www.ifar.org

Sharon Flescher, Executive Director
Jack Josephson, Chairman

Emphasizes education and research regarding the ethical, legal and scholarly issues concerning art objects. In addition to news stories and book reviews, the Journal contains feature articles on art authenticity and attribution; forgery and fraud; art law and ethics; World War II-era art restitution issues; conserving, restoring and caring for art; and art theft.
Founded in 1969

2225 Journal of Aesthetics and Art Criticism
P.O. Box 915
Pooler, GA 31322

912-921-2124
E-Mail: asa@aesthetics-online.org
Home Page: www.aesthetics-online.org

Paul Guyer, President
Dominic McIver Lopes, VP
Dabney Townsend, Secretary/Treasurer

Promotes study, research, discussion and publication in aesthetics, which includes all studies of the arts and related experience including philosophic, scientific and theoretical viewpoints.
Founded in 1942

2226 Journal of the American Institute for Conservation (JAIC)
1156 15th Street
Suite 320
Washington, DC 20005-1714

202-452-9545
Fax: 202 452-9328
E-Mail: info@conservation-us.org
Home Page: www.conservation-us.org

Eryl Wentworth, Executive Director
Meg Loew Craft, President
Pamela Hatchfield, VP

Publication of peer-reviewed technical studies, research papers, treatment case studies and ethics and standards discussions relating to the broad field of conservation and preservation of historic and cultural works.
3500 Members
Founded in 1961

2227 Magazine Antiques
Brant Publications
575 Broadway
5th Floor
New York, NY 10012-3227

212-941-2900
Fax: 212-941-2885
E-Mail: interview_ad@brantpub.com
Home Page: www.interviewmagazine.com

Sandra Brant, Publisher
Allison Ledes, Editor
Donald Liebling, Circulation Manager
Jennifer Norton, Marketing Executive

Articles on American and European decorative and fine arts, architecture, historic preservation, and collecting.
Cost: $24.95
Frequency: Monthly
Circulation: 64402
Founded in 1969

2228 Memory Makers
F+W Media
38 E. 29th Street
New York, NY 10016

212-447-1400
Fax: 212-447-5231
E-Mail: contact_us@fwmedia.com
Home Page: www.fwpublications.com

Jim Ogle, CFO
Sara Domville, President
Chad Phelps, Chief Digital Officer
David Nussbaum, CEO
Buddy Redling, Editor in Chief

Entertains, informs, and inspires the burgeoning number of scrapbook enthusiasts. Features

the ideas and stories of its readers - people who believe in keeping scrapbooks and the tradition of the family photo historian alive. Two special newsstand-only issues are dedicated to specific areas of interest including holidays, heritage albums, and more.
Cost: $45.00
144 Pages
Frequency: Bi-annually
Circulation: 203287
Founded in 1996

2229 **Michaels Create!**
F+W Media
38 E. 29th Streett
New York, NY 10016
212-447-1400
Fax: 212-447-5231
E-Mail: contact_us@fwmedia.com
Home Page: www.fwpublications.com
Jim Ogle, CFO
Sara Domville, President
Chad Phelps, Chief Digital Officer
David Nussbaum, CEO
Features contemporary designs reflecting the latest trends with clear instructions. The home decorating, fashion, and gift ideas will inspire experienced crafters as well as seasonal crafters to explore new possibilities. Step-by-step instructions, tips, and techniques will engage crafters of all ages - including kids - with the creative skills of crafting to be enjoyed as a year-round activity.
Cost: $21.97
116 Pages
Frequency: Monthly
Circulation: 24991
Founded in 1975

2230 **Military Trader**
F+W Media
38 E. 29th Street
New York, NY 10016
212-447-1400
Fax: 212-447-5231
E-Mail: contact_us@fwmedia.com
Home Page: www.fwpublications.com
Social Media: Facebook, Twitter, LinkedIn
David Nussbaum, CEO
Jim Ogle, CFO/COO
Sara Domville, President
Monthly publication for collectors of military memorabilia.
Cost: $19.00
Frequency: Monthly
Founded in 1952

2231 **Museum**
American Association of Museums
1575 Eye Street NW
Suite 400
Washington, DC 20005-1113
202-289-1818
Fax: 202-289-6578
E-Mail: membership@aam-us.org
Home Page: www.aam-us.org
John Strand, Publisher
Susan Breitkopf, Editor In Chief
Ford Bell, President
Frequency: Bi-Monthly

2232 **Pastel Journal**
F+W Media
38 E. 29th Street
New York, NY 10016
212-447-1400
Fax: 212-447-5231
E-Mail: contact_us@fwmedia.com
Home Page: www.fwpublications.com
Jim Ogle, CFO
Sara Domville, President
Chad Phelps, Chief Digital Officer
David Nussbaum, CEO
Written by pastel artists for pastel artists. Content is geared toward artists, amateur & professional alike, who already work in pastels and who want to further develop their skills through in-depth information on pastel painting processes and thought-provoking ideas from successful pastel artists. Also included is information on workshops and exhibitions, as well as articles providing details on the business aspects of art - creating prints, creating Web sites, framing prints, and shipping.
Cost: $27.00
84 Pages
Circulation: 19167
Founded in 1999

2233 **Picture Framing Magazine**
Hobby Publications
83 South Street
Unit 307
Freehold, NJ 07728
732-536-5160
800-969-7176
Fax: 732-536-5761
E-Mail: www.pictureframingmagazine.com
Home Page:
www.pictureframingmagazine.com
David Gherman, President
Patrick Sarver, Editor
Bruce Gherman, Executive Publisher
News and trends in the picture framing trade, marketing strategies, and economic developments.
Cost: $20.00
Frequency: Monthly
Circulation: 25000
ISSN: 1052-9977
Founded in 1955

2234 **Postcard Collector**
F+W Media
38 E. 29th Street
New York, NY 10016
212-447-1400
Fax: 212-447-5231
E-Mail: contact_us@fwmedia.com
Home Page: www.fwpublications.com
Jim Ogle, CFO
Sara Domville, President
Chad Phelps, Chief Digital Officer
David Nussbaum, CEO
Monthly publication for postcard collectors.
Cost: $29.98
Frequency: Monthly
Founded in 1982

2235 **SchoolArts**
Davis Publications
50 Portland Street
Worcester, MA 01618
508-754-7201
800-533-2847
Fax: 508-753-3834
E-Mail: contactus@davis-art.com
Home Page: www.davisart.com
Social Media: Facebook, Twitter, LinkedIn
Wyatt Wade, Owner
John Carr, Marketing
For art educators.
Cost: $23.95
60 Pages
Frequency: Monthly
Circulation: 23717
Founded in 1901
Printed in 4 colors on matte stock

2236 **Sotheby's Preview Magazine**
Sotheby's
1334 York Ave
New York, NY 10021-4806
212-606-7000
541-312-5682
Fax: 212-606-7107
E-Mail: preview@sothebys.com
Home Page: www.sothebys.com
William F Ruprecht, CEO
Bruno Vinciguerra, Chief Operating Officer
Auction schedule listings, exhibition dates and catalogue pricing.
Cost: $75.00
48 Pages
Circulation: 80,000
Founded in 1976
Printed in 4 colors on newsprint stock

2237 **Style: 1900**
199 George Street
Lambertville, NJ 08530
609-397-4104
Fax: 609-397-4409
E-Mail: fred@style1900.com
Home Page: www.style1900.com
Social Media: Facebook, Twitter, LinkedIn
Fred Albert, Editor
Jennifer Strauss, Director Advertising
David Rago, Publisher
The only publication devoted solely to the works and thoughts of the arts and crafts movement.
Cost: $6.95
88 Pages
Frequency: Quarterly
Circulation: 20000
ISSN: 1080-451X
Founded in 1987
Mailing list available for rent: 7,000 names at $250 per M
Printed in 4 colors on glossy stock

2238 **The Anvil's Ring**
259 Muddy Fork Road
Jonesborough, TN 37659
423-913-1022
Fax: 423-913-1023
E-Mail: centraloffice@abana.org
Home Page: www.abana.org
David Hutchison, President
Jack Parks, First VP
Peter Renzetti, Second VP
The most comprehensive overview on what's happening in the artist- blacksmithing world or the inspiration to get you out to the forge.
4500 Members
Frequency: Quarterly
Circulation: 2 Mag.
Founded in 1973

2239 **The Chronicle of the Horse**
American Academy of Equine Art
117 North Water Street
PO Box 1364
Georgetown, KY 40324
859-281-6031
Fax: 859-281-6043
E-Mail: fcconner@aaea.net
Home Page: www.aaea.net
Frances Clay Conner, Executive Director
Xochitl Barnes, AAEA President
The official magazine of the American Academy of Equine Art.
90 Members
Founded in 1980

2240 **Visual Anthropology Review**
American Anthropoligical Association

2200 Wilson Blvd
Suite 600
Arlington, VA 22201-3357

703-528-1902
Fax: 703-528-3546
E-Mail: najwa@optonline.net
Home Page: www.aaanet.org

Bill Davis, Executive Director
Oona Schmid, Director of Publishing
Leith Mullings, President

Directed toward the study of visual aspects of human behavior including anthropology of art and museology and the use of media in anthropological research, representation, and teaching.
Cost: $25.00
Circulation: 1000
ISSN: 1053-7147
Founded in 1902
Mailing list available for rent
Printed in one color on glossy stock

2241 **Watercolor Magic**
F+W Media
38 E. 29th Street
New York, NY 10016

212-447-1400
Fax: 212-447-5231
E-Mail: contact_us@fwmedia.com
Home Page: www.fwpublications.com

Jim Ogle, CFO
Sara Domville, President
Chad Phelps, Chief Digital Officer
David Nussbaum, CEO

Offers valuable how-to instruction and creative inspiration for artists who work in water-based media. From page after page of inspirational ideas, to illustrations of the best techniques, to must-have painting tools and materials, watercolorists will find everything they need to know to help them create art from the inside out. Plus, each issue includes special reports and tons of tips from the foremost experts in the field. The definitive source of creative inspiration and technical info.
Cost: $27.00
72 Pages
Frequency: Monthly
Circulation: 94636
Founded in 1993

Trade Shows

2242 **AAM Meeting & MuseumExpo**
American Association of Museums
1575 Eye Street NW
Suite 400
Washington, DC 20005-1113

202-289-1818
Fax: 202-289-6578
E-Mail: membership@aam-us.org
Home Page: www.aam-us.org

Dean Phelus, Meetings/Education Director
Malena Malone, Senior Manager Meetings
45000 Attendees
Frequency: Annual/May

2243 **ABANA International Conferences**
Artist-Blacksmith's Association of North America
259 Muddy Fork Road
Jonesborough, TN 37659

423-913-1022
Fax: 423-913-1023
E-Mail: conference@abana.org
Home Page: www.abana.org

David Hutchison, President
Peter Renzetti, 2nd Vice President
Linda Tanner, Treasurer

Held biennially in the United States for members. Demonstrations, panel discussions and lectures by experts in the field from around the globe. Share knowledge of technical, aesthetic and business areas of the craft for beginners to established professionals.
1000 Attendees
Frequency: Biennial
Founded in 1975

2244 **American Art Therapy Association Conference**
American Art Therapy Association
4875 Eisenhower Avenue
Sute 240
Alexandria, VA 22304

703-548-5860
888-290-0878
Fax: 703-783-8468
E-Mail: info@arttherapy.org
Home Page: www.arttherapy.org

Mercedes ter Maat, President
Susan Corrigan, Executive Director

Over 20 exhibitors of art supplies, books, therapeutic materials and schools.
800 Attendees
Frequency: Annual
Founded in 1969

2245 **American Institute for Conservation Annual Meeting**
Amer Institute for Conservation of Historic Works
1156 15th Street NW
Suite 320
Washington, DC 20005

202-452-9545
Fax: 202-452-9328
E-Mail: info@conservation-us.org
Home Page: www.aic-faic.org

Eryl P Wentworth, Executive Director
Adam Allen, Meeting Manager
Meg Loew Craft, President

Annual meeting of conservators of artistic and cultural property, which includes seminars and workshops with over 1,000 members attending yearly. 50 booths.
1000 Attendees
Frequency: June
Founded in 1971

2246 **American Society for Aesthetics Annual Conference**
American Society for Aesthetics
11935 Abersorn Street
Savannah, GA 31419

912-921-2124
E-Mail: asastcar@vms.csd.mu
Home Page: www.aestheticsonline.org

Carolyn Korsmeyer, President
Stephen Davies, VP

Seminar, conference, and exhibits related to the study of the arts, all disciplines.
500 Attendees
Frequency: Annual
Founded in 1942

2247 **Antique Arms Show**
Beinfeld Productions
72 Sunrise Drive
Rancho Mirage, CA 92270

760-202-4489
Fax: 760-202-4793
Home Page: www.antiquearmsshow.com

Wallace Beinfeld, Show Manager

Public show with 1000 booths of antiques and collectibles.
5M/6M Attendees
Frequency: January

2248 **Art Expo New York**
Advanstar Communications
641 Lexington Avenue
8th Floor
New York, NY 10022

212-951-6600
Fax: 212-951-6793
E-Mail: info@advanstar.com
Home Page: www.advanstar.com

Joseph Loggia, CEO
Thomas Ehardt, Vice President
Tom Florio, CFO

Five hundred and eighty exhibitors of artwork including: paintings, sculpture, prints and graphics.
15000 Attendees
Frequency: Annual
Founded in 1985

2249 **Art Libraries Society of North America Annual Conference**
Art Libraries Society of North America
7044 S. 13th St.
Oak Creek, WI 53154

414-768-8000
800-817-0621
Fax: 414-768-8001
E-Mail: arlisna@mercury.interpath.com
Home Page: www.arlisna.org

Deborah Kempe, President
Gregory Most, VP

Annual conference and show of publishers, book dealers, library suppliers and visual resources suppliers.
500 Attendees
Frequency: April
Founded in 1977

2250 **Art Miami: International Art Fair**
Advanstar Communications
641 Lexinton Avenue
8th Floor
New York, NY 10022

212-951-6600
Fax: 212-951-6793
E-Mail: info@advanstar.com
Home Page: www.advanstar.com

Joseph Loggia, CEO
Thomas Ehardt, Vice President
Tom Florio, CFO

99 exhibits of fine arts, attended by professionals.
44500 Attendees

2251 **Art Supply Expo**
Marketing Association Services
1516 Pontius Avenue
Floor 2
Los Angeles, CA 90025-3306

310-478-0074

Randy Bauler, Executive Director

Exhibits consist of art and drafting equipment and computer graphics supplies.
10M Attendees
Frequency: October

2252 **Art and Creative Materials Institute/ACMI Annual Meeting**
99 Derby St.
Suite 200
Hingham, MA 02043

781- 55- 104
Fax: 781- 20- 555

E-Mail: debbief@acminet.org
Home Page: www.acminet.org

Van Foster, President
Deborah S Gustafson, Associate Director
Debbie Munroe, Certification Director
Carol Rourke, Program Director

A non-profit association of manufacturers of art, craft and other creative materials, ACMI sponsors a certification program for both children's and adult's art materials and products, certifying that these products are non-toxic and meet voluntary standards of quality and performance. ACMI seeks to create and maintain a positive environment for art, craft and other creative materials usage, promoting safety in the materials and providing information and service resources on such products.
210 Members
Founded in 1940
Mailing list available for rent: 199 names

2253 Conference of the Volunteer Committees of Art Museums of Canada and the US
Volunteer Committees of Art Museums
Philbrook Museum
2727 S Rockford
Tulsa, OK 74114

FAX 918-743-4230

Grace Robin, VCAM President

Triennial conference and exhibits of art museum equipment, supplies and services.
Founded in 1952

2254 Consumer Show
Maven Company
PO Box 937
Plandome, NY 11030-0937

51- 62- 880
E-Mail: fasttrack@erols.com
Home Page: www.mavencompany.com

N Chittenden, VP

Specialty show, doll, toy and teddy bear.
5,000 Attendees
Frequency: Semi-Annual
Founded in 1970

2255 Craftsmen's Christmas Classic Arts and Crafts Festival
Gilmore Enterprises
3514-A Drawbridge Pkwy
Greensboro, NC 27410-8584

336-282-5550
Fax: 336-274-1084
E-Mail: Contact@GilmoreShows.com
Home Page: www.gilmoreshows.com

Jennifer Palmer, Show Manager
Clyde Gilmore, Executive Director

Features work from over 305 talented artists and craftspeople. All juried exhibitors work has been hand made by the exhibitors and must be original design and creation. Visit Christmas Tree Village to view the uniquely decorated Christmas Trees by some of our exhibitors. Something from every taste and budget with items from the most contemporary to the most traditional.
Founded in 1982

2256 Craftsmen's Classic Arts and Crafts Festival
Gilmore Enterprises
3514-A Drawbridge Pkwy
Greensboro, NC 27410-8584

336-282-5550
Fax: 336-274-1084
E-Mail: Contact@GilmoreShows.com
Home Page: www.gilmoreshows.com

Jennifer Palmer, Show Manager
Clyde Gilmore, Executive Director

Features work from over 305 talented artists and craftspeople. All work has been hand made by the juried exhibitors and must be original design and creation. See the creative process in action with several exhibitors demonstrating their craft in their booths. Something from every style, taste and budget with items from the most contemporary to the most traditional.
15000 Attendees
Frequency: March/April/Aug/Sept/Oct.
Founded in 1982

2257 Decor Expo
Pfingsten Publishing
6000 Lombardo Center Drive
Suite 420
Seven Hills, OH 44131

216-328-8926
888-772-8926
Fax: 216-328-9452
E-Mail: iafg-info@pfpublish.com
Home Page: www.decor-expo.com

Hugh T Tobin, Group Show Director
Rob Spademan, Marketing Director

Five hundred booths exhibiting fine art, limited edition prints, graphics, oil paintings and reproductions. Three shows a year in Orlando (January), New York City (March), and Atlanta (September).
4M Attendees
Frequency: September

2258 Gilmore Shows
Craftsmen's Classic Art & Craft Festivals
3514-A Drawbridge Pkwy
Greensboro, NC 27410-8584

336-282-5550
Fax: 336-274-1084
E-Mail: contact@gilmoreshows.com
Home Page: www.gilmoreshows.com
Social Media: Facebook

Jennifer Palmer, Show Manager
Clyde Gilmore, Executive Director
Jan Donovon, Marketing Manager

10 shows annually in North Carolina, South Carolina and Virginia. Each show features work from 250-450 talented artists and craftspeople from across the nationa. All juried exhibitors work has been hand made by the exhibitors and must be original design and creation. There is something from every taste and budget with items from traditional to contemporary, functional to whimsical, decorative to fun & funky. Visit Christmas Tree Village to view the trees decorated by some or our exhibitors.
20000 Attendees
Frequency: October/November
Founded in 1973

2259 IACA Markets
Indian Arts & Crafts Association
4010 Carlisle NE
Suite C
Albuquerque, NM 87107

505-265-9149
Fax: 505-265-8251
E-Mail: info@iaca.com
Home Page: www.iaca.com

Joseph Zeller, President
Don Standing Bear Forest, VP
Susan Pourian, Secretary
Kathy Ouellet, Treasurer

Wholesale and retail markets of authentic, handmade Indian arts & crafts.
300 Attendees
Frequency: Semi-Annually

2260 IFPDA Print Fair
International Fine Print Dealers Association
250 W 26th St
Suite 405
New York, NY 10001-6737

212-674-6095
Fax: 212-674-6783
E-Mail: info@ifpda.org
Home Page: www.ifpda.org

Michele Senecal, Executive Director
Laura Beth Gencarella, PR/Marketing Manager
Tara Reddi, President
Elizabeth Fodde-Reguer, Executive Assistant

The largest and most celebrated art fair dedicated to fine prints.

2261 Morristown Antiques Show
Wendy Management
PO Box 222
Harrison, NY 10528

914-316-4700
Fax: 914-698-6273
Home Page: www.wendyantiquesshows.com

Meg Wendy, President
Perry Grosser, Marketing and Finance

Three day show of 85 important dealers from the Northeast. Covers the key periods of antiques for budget minded collectors.
Frequency: November/Annual
Founded in 1930

2262 NAMTA's World of Art Materials
National Art Materials Trade Association
20200 Zion Ave.
Cornelius, NC 28031

704-926-6244
Fax: 702-892-6247
E-Mail: info@namta.org
Home Page: www.namta.org

Reggie Hall, Executive Director
Richard Goodban, President

Seven hundred and fifty booths including educational programs to advance the welfare of the art materials and framing industry.
5M Attendees
Frequency: May

2263 National Art Education Association Convention
National Art Education Association
1806 Robert Fulton Drive
Suite 300
Reston, VA 20191-1590

703-860-8000
800-299-8321
Fax: 703-860-2960
E-Mail: info@arteducators.org
Home Page: www.naea-reston.org

Kathy Duse, Show Manager
Dr. Deborah Reeve, Executive Director
Dr. Robert Sabol, President

Annual show of 140-200 exhibitor booths displaying manufacturers, suppliers, distributors, publishing companies and universities latest art textbooks and high-tech software. Show draws approximately 4,000 or more attendees.
Frequency: April

2264 National Guild of Community Schools of the Arts Conference
National Guild of Community Schools of the Arts
520 Eighth Avenue, 3rd Floor
Suite 302
New York, NY 10018-8018

212-268-3337
Fax: 212-268-3995
E-Mail: guildinfo@nationalguild.org
Home Page: www.nationalguild.org

Jonathan Herman, Executive Director
Kenneth Cole, Director

Exhibits of equipment, supplies and services for the advancement of education in the performing and visual arts. Arts Management in Community Institutions (AMICI) Summer Institute trains administrators to meet needs of growing and emerging arts schools. Other programs, services, guildnotes newsletter, job opportunities listings, and publications catalog available upon request on online.
350 Attendees
Frequency: Annual

2265 **New York Antiques Show**
Wendy Management
PO Box 222
Harrison, NY 10528

914-316-4700
Fax: 914-698-6273
Home Page: www.wendyantiquesshows.com

Meg Wendy, President
Perry Grosser, Marketing and Finance

This unique, sophisticated show is an important convenient source for trend setting decorators. There are quality antiques for new, young, collectors as well as seasoned pros. This show is filled with 17th, 18th, and 19th Century American, English, French, Oriental and Continental furniture and decorative accessories, including rare books, clocks, silver, brass, paintings, prints, maps, porcelain, rugs, glass, lighting devices, sconces, candlesticks, garden urns, and so much more. 80/90 Dealers
Frequency: September
Founded in 1930

2266 **Professional Picture Framers Association Show**
Professional Picture Framers Association
4305 Sarellen Road
Richmond, VA 23231

517-788-8100
Fax: 517-788-8100
E-Mail: ppfa@ppfa.com
Home Page: www.ppfa.com

Mark Klostermeyer, President

Source for manufacturers, wholesalers, print publishers, importers and retailers selling art, framing and related supplies.
Frequency: Annual
Founded in 1971

2267 **Surtex**
George Little Management
1133 Westchester Avenue
White Plains, NY 10606-3547

914-421-3200
800-272-7469
Fax: 914-948-6180
Home Page: www.surtex.com

George(Jeff) Little II, President/COO
Penny Sikalis, VP, Show Manager
Rita Malek, Show Manager

In addition to providing the art and design component of this market we also include important home products.
5000 Attendees
Frequency: May/October

2268 **The AADLA Spring Show**
PO Box 2066
Lenox Hill Station
New York, NY 10021

212-879-7558
Fax: 212-772-7197
E-Mail: secretary@artantiquedealersleague.com
Home Page: www.artantiquedealersleague.com

Clinton Howell, President
Robert Simon, VP
Susan Caplan Jacobson, Treasurer
David Mayer, Secretary/Executive Director
Ira Spanierman, Vice Chairperson

The best choice of the very best in fine art. Unique chances to view and buy paintings as well as objects reflecting excellence in the applied arts.
109 Members
Frequency: November/50 Attendees
Founded in 1926

Directories & Databases

2269 **AADA Membership Directory**
Art Dealers Association of America
205 Lexington Avenue
Suite 901
New York, NY 10016

212-488-5550
Fax: 64- 68- 680
E-Mail: straussnatt.net
Home Page: www.artdealers.org

Lucy Mitchell-Innes, President
Michael Findlay, Vice President
Jeffery Fraenkel, Secretary

An annual directory listing the AADA members. Published by the Art Dealers Association of America.
77 Pages
Founded in 1962

2270 **ARTWEEK Gallery Calendar Section**
Spaulding Publishing
PO Box 52100
Palo Alto, CA 94303-0751
800-733-2916
Fax: 262-495-8703
E-Mail: info@artweek.com
Home Page: www.artweek.com

Richard J O'Brien, Chairman
John T Bourger, Vice Chairman

A screened list of galleries on the West coast and other Western states are profiled.
Cost: $34.00
Circulation: 14,500

2271 **Art Index**
HW Wilson Company
10 Estes Street
Ipswich, MA 01938

800-653-2726
Fax: 978-356-6565
E-Mail: information@ebscohost.com
Home Page: www.hwwilson.com

Tim Collins, President
Michael Gorrell, EVP of Technology, CIO

Offers more than 500,000 citations to articles and book reviews in over 300 periodicals, yearbooks and museum bulletins.
Founded in 1929

2272 **Art Museums of the World**
Greenwood Publishing Group
88 Post Road W
PO Box 5007
Westport, CT 06881-5007
203-226-3571
800-225-5800
Fax: 203-222-1502
E-Mail: customer-service@greenwood.com
Home Page: www.greenwood.com

Debra Adams, Editor

National and international art museum list.
Cost: $259.00
1696 Pages
ISBN: 0-313213-22-4

2273 **Art in America: Guide to Galleries, Museums, and Artists**
Brant Publications
575 Broadway
New York, NY 10012-3227

212-941-2900
Fax: 212-941-2885
E-Mail: interview_ad@brantpub.com
Home Page: www.interviewmagazine.com

David Nussman, CEO

A list of over 4,000 museums, galleries and other display areas.
Cost: $15.00
Frequency: Annual
Circulation: 70,000
Founded in 1969

2274 **Arts and Humanities Search**
Institute for Scientific Information
1500 Spring Garden St
Philadelphia, PA 19130-4067

215-386-0100
800-386-4474
Fax: 215-386-2911

Offers data from more than 1100 arts and humanities journals.

2275 **Directory of MA and PhD Programs in Art and Art History**
College Art Association
50 Broadway
21 Floor
New York, NY 10004

212-691-1051
Fax: 212-627-2381
E-Mail: nyoffice@collegeart.org
Home Page: www.collegeart.org
Social Media: Facebook, Twitter, LinkedIn

Linda Downs, Executive Director
Alan Gilbert, Editor
Anne Collins Goodyear, President

Institutions are profiled that offer M.A. and Ph.D. programs in art and art history.
Cost: $12.50
152 Pages
Founded in 1911

2276 **Films and Videos on Photography**
Program for Art on Film
200 Willoughby Avenue
Brooklyn, NY 11205

718-399-4506
Fax: 718-399-4507
E-Mail: info@artfilm.org
Home Page: www.artfilm.org

Nadine Covert, Executive Director

An annotated directory of over 500 films and videos on photography, photographers, and photographic techniques.
Cost: $15.00
132 Pages
ISBN: 0-870995-75-1
Founded in 1990

2277 **IACA Directory**
Indian Arts & Crafts Association
4010 Carlisle NE
Suite C
Albuquerque, NM 87107

505-265-9149
Fax: 505-265-8251
E-Mail: info@iaca.com
Home Page: www.iaca.com

Joseph Zeller, President
Don Standing Bear Forest, VP
Susan Pourian, Secretary
Kathy Ouellet, Treasurer

Directory of all IACA members (wholesalers, retailers, artists/craftspeople, collectors, muse-

ums and ancillary organizations)
Cost: $15.00

2278 **Illustrators Annual**
Society of Illustrators
128 E 63rd St
New York, NY 10065-7392

212-838-2560
Fax: 212-838-2561
E-Mail: info@societyillustrators.org
Home Page: www.societyillustrators.org

Denis Dittrich, President
Tim O'Brien, Executive Vice President
Victor Juhasz, Vice President
David Reuss, Treasurer

Published by the Society of Illustrators
Cost: $49.95
320 Pages
Circulation: 7000
Founded in 1959
Mailing list available for rent: 1000 names at $600 per M
Printed in 4 colors

2279 **Key Guide to Electronic Resources: Art and Art History**
Information Today
143 Old Marlton Pike
Medford, NJ 08055-8750

609-654-6266
800-300-9868
Fax: 609-654-4309
E-Mail: custserv@infotoday.com
Home Page: www.infotoday.com

Thomas H Hogan, President
Roger R Bilboul, Chairman of the Board

An evaluative directory of electronic reference in the fields of art and art history.
Cost: $39.50
120 Pages
ISBN: 1-573870-22-6

2280 **NAMTA International Convention & Trade Show Directory**
National Art Materials Trade Association
20200 Zion Ave.
Cornelius, NC 28031

704-892-6244
Fax: 704-892-6247
E-Mail: info@namta.org
Home Page: www.namta.org
Social Media: Facebook, Twitter, LinkedIn

Richard Fjordbotten, President
Reggie Hall, Executive Director

National Art Materials Trade Association directory.

2281 **Official Museum Directory**
National Register Publishing
300 Connell Drive
Suite 2000
Berkley Heights, NJ 07922

908-464-6800
800-473-7020
Fax: 908-673-1189
E-Mail: NRPeditorial@marquiswhoswho.com
Home Page: www.nationalregisterpub.com

Eileen Fanning, Editorial
Gene McGovern, Publisher

Comprehensive reference for those seeking information on the country's museums. Features profiles and statistics on more than 7,700 museums in the US.

2282 **The Artful Home: Furniture, Sculpture and Objects**
Kraus Sikes
931 E Main Street
Suite 106
Madison, WI 53703-2955

608-572-2590
877-223-4600
Fax: 608-257-2690
E-Mail: info@artfulhome.com
Home Page: www.guild.com

Lisa Bayne, CEO
Bill Lathrop, Vice President

A wealth of information on craft artists working in furniture, wall decor and accessories are listed.
Cost: $29.95
256 Pages
Frequency: Annual
Circulation: 15,000

2283 **What Museum Guides Need To Know:Access For Blind & Visually Impaired Visitors**
American Foundation for the Blind
2 Penn Plaza
Suite 1102
New York, NY 10121

212-502-7600
800-232-5463
Fax: 888- 54- 833
E-Mail: afbinfo@afb.net
Home Page: www.afb.org

Carl R Augusto, President/CEO
Paul Schroeder, Vice President, Programs

Provides practical, easy-to-use guidelines on how to greet blind and visually impaired museum goers. This handbook also covers aesthetics and visual impairment and a training outline for museum requirements for accessibility.
Cost: $16.95
64 Pages

2284 **Who's Who in Art Materials**
National Art Materials Trade Association
20200 Zion Ave.
Cornelius, NC 28031

704-892-6244
Fax: 704-892-6247
E-Mail: info@namta.org
Home Page: www.namta.org
Social Media: Facebook, Twitter, LinkedIn

Richard Fjordbotten, President
Reggie Hall, Executive Director

Membership directory of the National Art Materials Trade Association.

Industry Web Sites

2285 **http://gold.greyhouse.com**
G.O.L.D Grey House OnLine Databases

Grey House Publishing's online database platform, GOLD, offers Quick Search, Keyword Search and Expert Search for most business sectors including art, antique and renovation markets. The GOLD platform makes finding the information you need quick and easy - whether you're a novice searcher or an experienced database user. All of Grey House's directory products are available for subscription on the GOLD platform.

2286 **www.aam-us.org**
American Association of Museums

For the museum community, enhances the ability of museums to serve the public interest, works on behalf of museums in educating federal legislators, assists museums in improving technical standards.

2287 **www.acminet.org**
Art and Creative Materials Institute

For art and craft product makers who encourage safe use of materials and proper labeling through certification.

2288 **www.albemarle-nc.com/camden**
Watermark Association of Artisans

Provides marketing assistance to craft producers.

2289 **www.aristos.org/aristos2.htm**
Aristos Foundation

The Foundation's purpose is to deepen public understanding of the nature of art as well as to foster the understanding and appreciation of humanistic values in the arts. Publishes an online journal.

2290 **www.artantiquedealersleague.com**
Art and Antique Dealers League of America

Nonprofit organization promotes interests of retailers and wholesalers of antiques and art objects.

2291 **www.artdealers.org**
Art Dealers Association of America

Works to improve the stature and standing of the art gallery business. Members deal primarily in paintings, sculpture, prints, drawings and photographs from the Renaissance to the present day. We have over 160 member galleries in more than 25 US cities.

2292 **www.artnet.com**
Art Net United States

The place to buy, sell and research fine art online.

2293 **www.collegeart.org**
College Art Association

Association for institutions that offer MA and PhD programs in art and art history.

2294 **www.greyhouse.com**
Grey House Publishing

Authoritative reference directories for most business sectors, including art, antique and restoration markets. Users can search the online databases with varied search criteria allowing for custom searches by product category, geographic area, sales volume, keyword, subject and more. Full Grey House catalog and online ordering also available.

2295 **www.iaca.com**
Indian Arts & Crafts Association

Not for profit trade association. Our mission is to promote, protect and preserve Indian arts.

2296 **www.naadaaa.org**
National Association of Dealers in Antiques

Nonprofit trade association of America's leading dealers mutually pledged to safeguard the interests of those who buy, sell or collect antiques and works of art.

2297 **www.naao.net**
National Association of Artist's Organizations

For artists within nonprofit organizations. Dedicated to the presentation of alternative visual arts, media, literature, new music and performing arts.

2298 **www.naea-reston.org**
National Art Education Association

Manufacturers, suppliers, distributors, publishing companies and universities.

2299 **www.naled.com**
National Association of Limited Edition Dealers

For dealers, vendors and publishers involved with collectibles and gifts.

2300 **www.namta.org**
National Art Materials Trade Association
For manufacturers, importers, wholesalers and retailers of art materials.

2301 **www.nasaa-arts.org**
National Assembly of State Arts Agencies
For those in the arts agency field in the US.

2302 **www.societyillustrators.com**
Society of Illustrators
For professional illustrators and art directors.

2303 **www.sothebys.com**
Sotheby's
Auction schedule listings, exhibition dates and catalogue pricing.

Associations

2304 **AERA Engine Builders Association**
500 Coventry Lane
Suite 180
Crystal Lake, IL 60014

815-526-7600
815-526-7600
Fax: 815-526-7601
E-Mail: info@aera.org
Home Page: www.aera.org
Social Media: Facebook, Twitter

Steve Schoeben, Chairman
Rex B. Crumpton, First Vice Chairman
Steve Edmondson, Second Vice Chairman
Ron McMorris, Treasurer
Kevin Frische, Director

A specialized network of professional engine builders, rebuilders, production engine remanufacturers and installers.
Founded in 1922

2305 **AUTOMOTIVE WHO'S WHO, Inc.**
AUTOMOTIVE WHO'S WHO, Inc
2899 East Big Beaver Road
#400
Troy, MI 48083

248-368-0200
Fax: 248-368-0202
E-Mail: info@automotivewhoswho.com
Home Page: www.automotivewhoswho.com

David M Bennett, Managing Director

Publishes an automotive original equipment suppliers directory and database for users by a wide range of industry professionals including top executives, site managers, engineers, buyers, consultants and researchers. The comprehensive directory covers the automotive manufacturing supply chain comprised of Tier I, II and III suppliers of parts, components, assemblies and related services.
Founded in 1999

2306 **Advocates for Highway and Auto Safety**
750 1st St NE
Suite 901
Washington, DC 20002

202-408-1711
Fax: 202-408-1699
E-Mail: advocates@saferoads.org
Home Page: www.saferoads.org
Social Media: Facebook, Twitter

Judith Lee Stone, President
Jacqueline Gillan, VP
Judie Pasquini, Director

An organization whose members advocate the support and advancement of highway and auto safety through the implementation of state and federal laws, programs and policies.

2307 **Alliance of Automobile Manufacturers**
803 7th Street, N.W
Suite 300
Washington, DC 20001

202-326-5500
Home Page: www.autoalliance.org
Social Media: Facebook, Twitter

Mitch Bainwol, President/ CEO

An association of 12 of the largest car manufacturers, and is the leading advocacy group for the auto industry.

2308 **Alliance of State Automotive Aftermarket Associations**
5330 Wall Street
Suite 100
Madison, WI 53718

608-240-2066
Fax: 608-240-2069
E-Mail: info@asaaa.com
Home Page: www.asaaa.com

Skip Potter, President
Randy Lisk, VP
Gary Manke, Executive Director

ASAAA consists of more than 10,000 members from both regional and state associations that support and represent the automotive aftermarket industry including that of parts and accessories, supplies and services.
10000 Members
Founded in 1953

2309 **American Association of Motor Vehicle Administrators**
4301 Wilson Blvd
Suite 400
Arlington, VA 22203

703-522-4200
Fax: 703-522-1553
E-Mail: info@aamva.org
Home Page: www.aamva.org
Social Media: Facebook, Twitter

Neil D Schuster, President
Mark Saitta, VP
Claire O'Brian, Marketing

A nonprofit association that supports both state and provincial official members throughout North America who oversee the administration and enforcement of motor vehicle laws. Services include development and research in motor vehicle administration, law enforcement and highway safety as well as being an information clearinghouse.
Founded in 1933

2310 **American Autoimmune Related Diseases Association**
22100 Gratiot Ave.
Eastpointe, MI 48021

586-776-3900
800-598-4668
Fax: 586-776-3900
Home Page: www.aarda.org
Social Media: Twitter, LinkedIn, YouTube

Betty Diamond, Chairperson
Noel R. Rose, Chairman Emeritus
Stanley M. Finger, Vice Chairperson
Virginia T. Ladd, President
John Kaiser, Treasurer

Includes patient information about autoimmunity and autoimmune related diseases.
Founded in 1991

2311 **American Automobile Association**
1000 AAA Drive
Heathrow, FL 32746

407-444-4240
800-222-4357
Fax: 800-444-4247
Home Page: www.aaa.com

Robert Darbelnet, President
Jerry Cheske, Director Public Relations

Nation's largest motoring and leisure travel organization. AAA provides travel, insurance, financial and automotive related services. The not-for-profit, fully tax paying AAA has been a leader and advocate for the safety and security of all travelers.
45MM Members
Founded in 1902

2312 **American Automotive Leasing Association**
675 North Washington Street
Suite 410
Alexandria, VI 22314

703-548-0777
Fax: 703-548-1925
E-Mail: sederholm@aalafleet.com
Home Page: www.aalafleet.com

Pamela Sederholm, Executive Director
Traci Peters, Account Manager
Courtney Groff, Legislative Associate

A national industry association composed of commercial automotive fleet leasing and management companies.
Founded in 1955

2313 **American Bus Association**
111 K Street NE
9th Floor
Washington, DC 20002

202-842-1645
Fax: 202-842-0850
E-Mail: abainfo@buses.org
Home Page: www.buses.org
Social Media: Facebook, Twitter, LinkedIn

Thomas JeBran, Chair
John Meier, Vice Chair
Peter Pantuso, President & CEO
Frank Henry, Secretary/Treasurer

ABA supports 3,800 members consisting of motorcoach and tour companies in addition to organizations that represent the tourism and travel industry. ABA strives to educate consumers on the importance of highway and motorcoach safety.
Founded in 1926

2314 **American Coatings Association**
1500 Rhode Island Ave., NW
Washington, DC 20005

202-462-6272
Fax: 202-462-8549
E-Mail: members@paint.org
Home Page: www.paint.org
Social Media: Facebook, Twitter, LinkedIn, Hangout

J. Andrew Doyle, President/ CEO
Thomas J. Graves, Vice President
Allen Irish, Counsel/ Director
Jeff Wasikowski, Counsel
Nathan Perrine, CFO

2315 **American Highway Users Alliance**
1101 14th St NW
Suite 750
Washington, DC 20005-5608

202-857-1200
Fax: 202-857-1220
E-Mail: info@highways.org
Home Page: www.highways.org
Social Media: Facebook, Twitter

Greg Cohen, President & CEO

A nonprofit trade association that actively advocates and promotes safe and uncongested highways and America's freedom of mobility.
Founded in 1932

2316 **American International Automobile Dealers Association**
211 N Union St
Suite 300
Alexandria, VA 22314

703-519-7800
800-462-4232
Fax: 703-519-7810
E-Mail: goaiada@aiada.org

Home Page: www.aiada.org
Social Media: Facebook, Twitter

Jenell Rose, Chairwoman
Larry Kull, Chairman Elect
Bradley Hoffman, Vice Chair
Greg Kaminsky, Secretary/Treasurer

Lobbying and communications organization for American automobile dealerships that sell and service international nameplate brands.
11000 Members
Founded in 1970

2317 **American Public Transportation Association**
1666 K St NW
Suite 1100
Washington, DC 20006

202-496-4800
Fax: 202-496-4324
E-Mail: meetings2@apta.com
Home Page: www.apta.com
Social Media: Facebook, Twitter

Michael Melaniphy, President & CEO
Petra Mollet, Chief of Staff
Rosemary Sheridan, VP, Marketing
Jeff Popovich, Chief Information Officer
Mary L. Childress, Chief Financial Officer

APTA is an international organization that supports and represents the transportation industry. Membership benefits include an annual association meeting, an international expo, membership directory, access to online publications, newsletters and electronic news service.
Founded in 1882

2318 **American Society for Quality**
600 N Plankinton Avenue
PO Box 3005
Milwaukee, WI 53201-3005

414-272-8575
800-248-1946
Fax: 414-272-1734
E-Mail: help@asq.org
Home Page: www.asq.org
Social Media: Facebook, Twitter, LinkedIn

John C Timmerman, Chair
Paul E Borawski, CEO
Chava Scher, Treasurer
Fay Spano, Communications/Media Relations

An international organization with more than 90,000 members, the ASQ is an authoritative resource on quality that strives for improvement within the workplace and communities alike worldwide through the usage of advanced technology and training programs.
90M Members
Founded in 1946

2319 **American Society of Body Engineers**
2122 15 Mile Rd
Suite F
Sterling Height, MI 48310-4853

586-268-8360
Fax: 586-268-2187
E-Mail: asbe@asbe.com
Home Page: www.asbe.com

William Bonner, President
Jeff Grundy, Director

The American Society of Body Engineers is a non-profit corporation consisting of about 1,000 members within the industry including engineers, designers and suppliers. The organization strives to keep members current on the latest technological advancements within the field of automotive body engineering.
1000 Members
Founded in 1945

2320 **American Trucking Association**
950 North Glebe Road
Suite 210
Arlington, VA 22203-4181

E-Mail: media@trucking.org
Home Page: www.trucking.org
Social Media: Facebook, Twitter, YouTube, Flickr

Duane Long, Chairman
Pat Thomas, First Vice Chairman
Kevin W. Burch, Second Vice Chairman
Barry Pottle, Vice Chairman
Bill Graves, President
Founded in 1933

2321 **Antique Automobile Club of America**
E-Mail: lgawel@aaca.org
Home Page: www.aaca.org
Social Media: Facebook, YouTube

America's premiere resource for the collectible vehicle community—includes publications, calendars, membership information, merchandise, photos, and forum.
Founded in 1935

2322 **Antique Truck Club of America**
85 S Walnut St
PO Box 31
Boyertown, PA 19512

610-367-2567
Fax: 610-367-9712
E-Mail: office@antiquetruckclubofamerica.org
Home Page:
www.antiquetruckclubofamerica.org
Social Media: Facebook

Fred Chase, President
Dave Lewis, Vice President
Tom Oehme, Treasurer
Mike Fowler, Secretary

An organization of persons who own or have an interest in antique commercial vehicles, and who wish to promote the preservation, restoration, operation and history of antique commercial vehicles.
Cost: $36.00
Frequency: Membership Fee
Founded in 1971

2323 **Association for the Advancement of Automotive Medicine**
P.O. Box 4176
Barrington, IL 60011-4176

847-844-3880
Fax: 847-844-3884
E-Mail: info@aaam.org
Home Page: www.aaam.org
Social Media: LinkedIn

Frank A. Pintar, President
Brian N. Fildes, Immediate Past President
Gary A. Smith, President-Elect
Federico E. Vaca, Secretary
Kristy B. Arbogast, Treasurer

A professional multidisciplinary organization dedicated to limiting injuries from motor vehicle crashes.
Founded in 1957

2324 **Association for the Advancement of Automotive Medicine**
PO Box 4176
Barrington, IL 60011-4176

847-844-3880
Fax: 847-844-3884
E-Mail: info@aaam.org
Home Page: www.aaam.org

Frank A. Pintar, President
Gary A Smith, President Elect
Federico E Vaca, Secretary
Kristy B Arbogast, Treasurer

A professional multidisciplinary organization dedicated entirely to motor vehicle crash prevention and control.
Founded in 1957

2325 **Association of Diesel Specialists**
400 Admiral Boulevard
Kansas City, MO 64106

816-285-0810
888-401-1616
Fax: 847-770-4952
E-Mail: info@diesel.org
Home Page: www.diesel.org

Andy Girres, President
Charles Oliveros, VP
Carl Fergueson, Secretary
Laura Roundtree, Treasurer

The worldwide diesel industry's leading trade association, dedicated to the highest level of service on diesel fuel injection and related systems.
700+ Members
Founded in 1956

2326 **Association of International Automobile Manufacturers**
1050 K Street, NW
Suite 650
Washington, DC 20001

202-650-5555
Fax: 703-525-8817
E-Mail: info@globalautomakers.org
Home Page: www.globalautomakers.org
Social Media: Facebook, Twitter

Michael J Stanton, President
Ellen J Gleberman, Vice President/General Counsel

An international trade association that supports original equipment suppliers, automobile trade organizations and motor vehicle manufacturers. AIAM monitors government regulations and provides information and advocacy support relative to regulatory and legislative issues that directly affect the auto industry.

2327 **Auto Body Parts Association**
400 Putnam Pike
Suite J 503
Smithfield, RI 02917-2442

401-531-0809
800-323-5832
Fax: 401-262-0193
E-Mail: info@autobpa.com
Home Page: www.autobpa.com

Dan Morrissey, Chairman
Jim Smith, President
Eric Taylor, Vice President
Michael Koren, Secretary
Dolores Richardson, Treasurer

An association of manufacturers, distributors, insurance and repair professionals which provide the collision repair industry with quality replacement parts.
140 Members
Founded in 1980

2328 **Auto Care Association**
7101 Wisconsin Ave
Suite 1300
Bethesda, MD 20814-3415

301-654-6664
Fax: 301-654-3299
E-Mail: info@autocare.org
Home Page: www.autocare.org
Social Media: Facebook, Twitter, Google+

Richard Jago, Chairman
Michael Klein, Vice Chairman
Kathleen Schmatz, President & CEO
Mark Finestone, Vice President
Ira Davis, Secretary

Provides advocacy, educational, networking, technology, market intelligence and communications resources on auto care to its members.

2329 Auto International Association
7101 Wisconsin Avenue
Suite 1300
Bethesda, MD 20814

301-654-6664
Fax: 301-654-3299
E-Mail: aia@aftermarket.org
Home Page: www.aiaglobal.org
Social Media: Facebook, Twitter, LinkedIn

Steve Bearden, Chair
Peter Klotz, Vice Chair

The Auto International Association (AIA) segment of the Automotive Aftermarket Industry Association promotes global trade in automotive products by providing a bridge between the international automotive community and the North American aftermarket.
Founded in 1981

2330 Automatic Transmission Rebuilders Association
2400 Latigo Avenue
Oxnard, CA 93030

805-604-2000
866-464-2872
Fax: 805-604-2003
E-Mail: webmaster@atra.com
Home Page: www.atra.com
Social Media: Facebook, Twitter

Dennis Madden, CEO
Jim Lyons, VP
Lance Wiggins, Director

Not-for-profit professional organization dedicated to the improvement and welfare of the automatic transmission repair industry for the benefit of the motoring public.
2000 Members
Founded in 1954

2331 Automotive Aftermarket Industry Association
7101 Wisconsin Avenue
Suite 1300
Bethesda, MD 20814-3415

301-654-6664
Fax: 301-654-3299
E-Mail: aaia@aftermarket.org
Home Page: www.aftermarket.org
Social Media: Facebook, Twitter, LinkedIn

Kathleen Schmatz, President
Susan Medick, CEO & CFO
Rich White, Senior VP
Scott Luckett, Chief Information Officer

A trade association consisting of more than 23,000 member companies and affiliates representing over 100,000 repair shops, distribution outlets, and parts stores.
23000 Members
Founded in 1999

2332 Automotive Aftermarket Suppliers Association
PO Box 13966
Research Triangle Park, NC 27709-3966

919-549-4800
Fax: 919-549-4824
E-Mail: media@mema.org
Home Page: www.aftermarketsuppliers.org

Steve Handschuh, President
Bill Hanvey, Senior Vice President
Chris Gardner, Vice President
Ann Wilson, Senior Vice President
Margaret Beck, Senior Director

Automotive aftermarket supplier industry that provides a forum to address issues and resources that highlight the importance of purchasing quality parts backed by full-service suppliers.

2333 Automotive Body Parts Association
400 Putnam Pike
Suite J 503
Smithfield, RI 02917-2442

401-531-0809
800-323-5832
Fax: 401-262-0193
E-Mail: info@autobpa.com
Home Page: www.autobpa.com

Dan Morrissey, Chairman
Jim Smith, President
Eric Taylor, Vice President
Michael Koren, Secretary
Dolores Richardson, Treasurer

Members are companies that distribute, supply or manufacture automotive replacement body parts.
140 Members
Founded in 1980

2334 Automotive Consulting Group
Automotive Consulting Group
4370 Varsity Dr.
Suite D
Ann Arbor, MI 48108

734-973-1110
Fax: 734-973-1118
E-Mail: acg@autoconsulting.com
Home Page: www.autoconsulting.com

Dennis Virag, President

Management consulting firm providing top line and bottom line business performance improvement services to the worldwide automotive industry.
Founded in 1986

2335 Automotive Engine Rebuilders Association
500 Coventry Ln
Suite 180
Crystal Lake, IL 60014

815-526-7600
888-326-2372
Fax: 815-526-7601
E-Mail: info@aera.org
Home Page: www.aera.org
Social Media: Facebook, Twitter

Ron McMorris, Chairman
Steven Schoeben, First VC
Paul Hauglie, President
Dwayne J Dugas, Treasurer

Network of specialists including production engine remanufacturers, installers, and professional engine rebuilders, provide services and support for the engine rebuilding industry.
Founded in 1922

2336 Automotive Fleet & Leasing Association
N83 W13410 Leon Road
Menomonee Falls, WI 53051

414-386-0366
Fax: 414-359-1671
E-Mail: info@afla.org
Home Page: www.afla.org
Social Media: Facebook, LinkedIn

Brian Barber, President
Steve Gibson, Executive Vice President
Michael Bieger, Vice President
Bill Elliott, Executive Director
Theresa Belding, Secretary

Provides an advanced forum for corporate fleet professionals to work with industry leaders.
400 Members
Founded in 1969

2337 Automotive Fleet and Leasing Association
11950 W. Lake Park Drive
Milwaukee, WI 53224

414-386-0366
Fax: 414-359-1671
E-Mail: info@aflaonline.com
Home Page: www.aflaonline.com

John Dmochowsky, Executive VP
Tom Callahan, President
Bill Elliot, Executive Director

An organization consisting of more than 300 members that provides information, education and research on the fleet industry. Member benefits include annual conferences, educational seminars, the AFLA membership directory and more. The best source of information and contacts for automotive fleet and leasing professionals.
300 Members
Founded in 1969

2338 Automotive Industry Action Group
26200 Lahser Road
Suite 200
Southfield, MI 48033-7100

248-358-3003
Fax: 248-799-7995
E-Mail: order_inquiry@aiag.org
Home Page: www.aiag.org
Social Media: Facebook, Twitter

John Batchik, Chairman
David Kneisler, Vice Chairman
Scot Sharland, Executive Director

Composed of major North American vehicle manufacturers and their suppliers. Provides an open forum where members cooperate to develop and promote solutions that enhance prosperity in the automotive industry.
1000 Members
Founded in 1982

2339 Automotive Lift Institute
80 Wheeler Ave
PO Box 85
Cortland, NY 13045

607-756-7775
Fax: 607-756-0888
E-Mail: info@autolift.org
Home Page: www.autolift.org
Social Media: Facebook, Twitter

Bob O'Gorman, President
Jeff Kritzer, Board of Directors

An association of manufacturers and distributors of automotive lifts used to raise motor vehicles for undercarriage work. Promotes awareness of safety measures used in operating lifts.
20 Members
Founded in 1988

2340 Automotive Maintenance & Repair Association
725 E Dundee Road
Suite 206
Arlington Heights, IL 60004

847-947-2650
Fax: 202-318-0378
Home Page: amra.org

A nonprofit trade association formally organized to represent the interests, common policies, and purposes of companies engaged in providing automotive maintenance and repair services, their suppliers, and related companies in the automotive industry when dealing with consumers.
Founded in 1994

2341 **Automotive Oil Change Association**
330 N. Wabash Ave.
Suite 2000
Chicago, IL 60611

312-321-5132
800-230-0702
Fax: 312-673-6832
E-Mail: info@aoca.org
Home Page: www.aoca.org
Social Media: Facebook

Jim Grant, President
Scott Jameson, VP
Bob Falter, Treasurer
Len Minco, Secretary

AOCA is a non-profit trade association that supports and represents more than 3,500 member facilities within the convenient automotive service industry. AOCA strives to educate consumers on the benefits of preventative auto maintenance, and the reliability of fast lube service centers.
3500 Members
Founded in 1987

2342 **Automotive Parts Remanufacturers Association**
4460 Brookfield Corporate Drive
Suite H
Chantilly, VA 20151-1671

703-968-2772
Fax: 703-968-2878
E-Mail: mail@apra.org
Home Page: www.apra.org
Social Media: Facebook, Twitter, LinkedIn

William C Gager, President
Mark Kothe, CEO
Jeanie Magathan, Senior VP

Mission is to address the needs of the automotive and truck parts remanufacturing industry and to serve members by providing a wide range of quality products, services, workshops and education, through legislative advocacy, offering technical services, as well as arranging many networking opportunities for members of the remanufacturing community.
1000 Members
Founded in 1941

2343 **Automotive Public Relations Council**
Original Equipment Suppliers Association (OESA)
1301 W Long Lake Road
Suite 225
Troy, MI 48098

248-952-6401
Fax: 248-952-6404
E-Mail: info@oesa.org
Home Page: www.oesa.org

Neil De Koker, President & CEO
Greg Janicki, Executive Director, Marketing

APRC is a professional organization for those within public relations that work in the automotive industry. Member benefits include access to industry news, discounted vendor services, and APRC conferences where members have the opportunity to meet and network with colleagues and practitioners in the automotive industry.
Founded in 1974

2344 **Automotive Recyclers Association**
9113 Church St.
Manassas, VA 20110

571-208-0428
888-385-1005
Fax: 571-208-0430
Home Page: www.a-r-a.org
Social Media: Facebook, Twitter

Ricky Young, President
Mike Swift, First Vice President
RD Hooper, Second Vice President
Michael E. Wilson, Chief Executive
David Gold, Secretary

ARA is an international non-profit trade association with more than 3,000 members that supply equipment and services within the automotive recycling industry.
1000 Members
Founded in 1943

2345 **Automotive Service Association**
8190 Precinct Line Road
Suite 100
Colleyville, TX 76034-7675

817-514-2900
800-272-7467
Fax: 817-514-0770
E-Mail: asainfo@ASAshop.org
Home Page: www.asashop.org
Social Media: Facebook, Twitter, LinkedIn

Darrell Amberson, Chairman
Donny Seyfer, Chairman Elect
Roy Schnepper, Secretary/Treasurer

Leading organization for owners and managers of independent automotive service businesses that strive to deliver excellence in service and repairs to consumers.
8000 Members
Founded in 1951

2346 **Automotive Specialty Products Alliance**
1667 K Street
NW Suite 300
Washington, DC 20006

202-862-3902
Fax: 202-223-2636
E-Mail: qbradley@consumered.org
Home Page: www.inhalant.org
Social Media: Facebook, Twitter

Colleen Creighton, Executive Director

Provides a unified industry voice for its members engaged in the automotive chemical and vehicle appearance product markets before state, regional and federal legislators and regulators.
Founded in 1966

2347 **Automotive Warehouse Distributors Association**
7101 Wisconsin Avenue
Suite 1300
Bethesda, MD 20814-3415

301-654-6664
Fax: 301-654-3299
E-Mail: aaia@aftermarket.org
Home Page: www.aftermarket.org
Social Media: Facebook, Twitter, LinkedIn

Kathleen Schmatz, President

A trade association consisting of more than 600 members who are manufacturers and warehouse distributors, affiliates, marketing associations and others actively involved in the production, distribution and installation of motor vehicle parts, tools, services, accessories, equipment, materials and supplies. A segment of the Automotive Aftermarket Industry Association.
600 Members
Founded in 1947

2348 **Battery Council International**
330 N Wabash Ave
Suite 2000
Chicago, IL 60611

312-644-6610
Fax: 312-527-6640
E-Mail: info@batterycouncil.org
Home Page: www.batterycouncil.org

Mark O. Thornsby, CAE, Executive Vice President

A not-for-profit trade association formed to promote the interests of an international lead-acid battery industry.
265 Members
Founded in 1924

2349 **Bearing Specialists Association**
800 Roosevelt Rd
Bldg C, Suite 312
Glen Ellyn, IL 60137

630-858-3838
Fax: 630-790-3095
E-Mail: info@bsahome.org
Home Page: www.bsahome.org
Social Media: Twitter, LinkedIn

Jack Simpson, President
Brian Negri, VP
Tim Breen, Treasurer
Jerilyn J. Church, Executive Secretary

BSA is a not-for-profit association that consists of companies that distribute factory-warranted ball, roller, and anti-friction bearings through authorized dealers. BSA provides members with the opportunity to network with others in the industry through meetings, seminars and educational programs at their annual convention.
100 Members
Founded in 1966

2350 **Brake Manufacturers Council**
PO Box 13966
Research Triangle Park, NC 27709-3966

919-549-4800
Fax: 919-549-4824
E-Mail: media@mema.org
Home Page: www.brakecouncil.org

Steve Handschuh, President
Jack Cameron, VP

Obtaining and disseminating to members information on topics of interest to the brake parts industry.
Founded in 1973

2351 **California Autobody Association**
P.O. Box 660607
Sacramento, CA 95866-0607

916-557-8100
Fax: 916-405-3529
Home Page: www.calautobody.com

David Picton, 1st VP
Chuck Reyes, President

CAA is a non-profit trade association consisting of more than 1,000 members that support collision repair industry training and education with the goal of providing quality consumer repairs at reasonable prices.
1000+ Members
Founded in 1967

2352 **Car Care Council**
7101 Wisconsin Ave
Suite 1300
Bethesda, MD 20814

240-333-1088
Fax: 301-654-3299
E-Mail: webmaster@aftermarket.org
Home Page: www.carcare.org
Social Media: Facebook, Twitter

Rich White, Executive Director
Ruth Elhinger, President

A nonprofit 501 (c) (3) educational foundation whose purpose is to educate motorists about the importance of maintenance repairs and entertainment for safer, cleaner, better-performing vehicles. Provides editorial and public service material for media use.
2000 Members
Founded in 1968

2353 **Center for Auto Safety**
1825 Connecticut Ave NW
Suite 330
Washington, DC 20009-5708
202-328-7700
Fax: 202-387-0140
Home Page: www.autosafety.org
Clarence M Ditlow III, Executive Director
Provides consumers with advocacy support in Washington for auto quality and safety in addition to helping owners of unreliable vehicles by providing information relative to lemon laws, recalls, defect investigations, legislative issues in Congress and more.
15000 Members
Founded in 1970

2354 **Driving School Association of the Americas**
3125 Wilmington Pike
Kettering, OH 45429
800-270-3722
Fax: 937-290-0696
E-Mail: info@thedsaa.org
Home Page: www.thedsaa.org
Social Media: Facebook, Twitter
Charles Chauncy, President
Sheila Varnado, Executive VP
Robert Cole, Treasurer
Anthony Caracci, Secretary
A nonprofit organization for the purpose of raising the standards of educational methods in teaching drivers education, to promote traffic safety on the highways and streets, to publicize, inform and educate the general public to the need for more intensive driver training, safer roadways and all things relating there to.
58000 Members
Founded in 1973

2355 **Electric Auto Association**
323 Los Altos Drive
Aptos, CA 95003
831-688-8669
E-Mail: contact@eaaev.org
Home Page: www.electricauto.org
Social Media: Facebook
Ron Freund, Chairman
Marc Geller, Co-Chairman
Howard Clearfield, Treasurer
Guy Hall, Board Member
Terry Hershner, Board Member
A nonprofit educational organization that promotes the advancement and widespread adoption of battery electric vehicles.
Founded in 1967

2356 **Filter Manufacturers Council**
10 Laboratory Drive
PO Box 13966
Research Triangle Park, NC 27709-3966
919-549-4800
Fax: 919-549-4824
E-Mail: media@mema.org
Home Page: www.filtercouncil.org
Social Media: Facebook
Steve Handschuh, President
Jack Cameron, VP
For manufacturers of vehicular and industrial filtration products in North America. Active in efforts to educate people on proper disposal of used oil filters.
Founded in 1971

2357 **Ford Dealers Alliance**
401 Hackensack Avenue
Continental Plaza
Hackensack, NJ 07601
201-342-4542
Fax: 201-342-3997
E-Mail: fda@dealersalliance.org
Home Page: www.dealersalliance.org
A Michell Van Vorst, Executive Director
Edwin Mullane, President
Organization that strives to protect dealers against factory encroachment into retail.
15000 Members
Founded in 1969

2358 **Formula & Automobile Racing Association**
786-571-6965
E-Mail: info@farausa.com
Home Page: www.farausa.com
Social Media: Facebook, Twitter, YouTube, Instagram
Reinaldo "Tico Almeida, President
Carlos Mendez, Chief Operating Officer
Victor Leo, Driver Academy Director
Randy Almeida, Vice President
Bob Van Epps, Race Director
Provider of motorsports events for auto enthusiasts.

2359 **Global Auto Makers**
1050 K Street, NW
Suite 650
Washington, DC 20001
202-650-5555
E-Mail: info@globalautomakers.org
Home Page: www.globalautomakers.org
Social Media: Facebook, Twitter
Michael J Stanton, President & CEO
Ellen J Gleberman, Vice President/General Counsel
Tom Loveless, Treasurer
James Lentz, Secretary
Michael J. Stanton, President & CEO
Working with industry leaders, legislators, regulators, and other stakeholders to create the kind of public policy that improves vehicle safety, encourages technological innovation, and protects the planet. Goal is to foster an open and competitive automotive marketplace that encourages investment, job growth, and development of more vehicles that enhance Americans' quality of life.
Founded in 1961

2360 **Global Automakers**
1050 K Street, NW
Suite 650
Washington, DC 20001
202-650-5555
E-Mail: info@globalautomakers.org
Home Page: www.globalautomakers.org
Social Media: Facebook, Twitter
Jim Lentz, Chairman
John Mendel, Vice Chairman
John Bozella, Chief Executive Officer
David Zuchowski, Secretary
Scott Becker, Treasurer
A Washington, D.C.-based trade association and Lobby group whose members include international automobile and light duty truck manufacturers that design, build, and sell products in the United States.

2361 **Golden Era Automobile Association**
18021-150th Avenue East
Orting
Washington 98360
360-893-4227
E-Mail: AGW1886@aol.com
Home Page: www.geaaonline.org
Henry Moebius, President
A car club that celebrates original cars, trucks, and motorcycles from 1915-1942 and World War II.

2362 **Heavy Duty Manufacturers Association**
10 Laboratory Drive
PO Box 13966
Research Triangle Park, NC 27709-3966
919-549-4800
Fax: 919-506-1465
E-Mail: info@hdma.org
Home Page: www.hdma.org
Timothy R. Kraus, President
Jennifer Hjalmquist, Senior Director
Beth Barkovich, Director
Richard Anderson, Senior Market Research Analyst
Katelyn Litalien, Manager
Represents companies participating in the classes 4-8 medium and heavy truck original equipment and aftermarket parts manufacturing industry.
Founded in 1983

2363 **Independent Automotive Damage Appraisers Association**
P.O. Box 12291
Columbus, GA 31917-2291
800-369-IADA
Fax: 888-IAD- NOW
E-Mail: admin@iada.org
Home Page: www.iada.org
Mark Nathan, President
Bill Ambrosino, First Vice President
Michael E. Sellman, Secretary/ Treasurer
John Williams, Executive Vice President
Leader in the insurance/automotive industry in providing its members and the entire industry a forum for exchange of ideas and solutions to common problems in automotive appraisal and repair.
Founded in 1947

2364 **International Association of Auto Theft Investigators**
PO Box 223
Clinton, NY 13323-0223
315-853-1913
Fax: 315-883-1310
E-Mail: webmaster@iaati.org
Home Page: www.iaati.org
John P O Byrne, President
John V Abounader, Executive Director
John V. Abounader, Executive Director
Formed to improve communication and coordination among the growing family of professional auto theft investigators.
4904 Members
Founded in 1952

2365 **International Automotive Technician's Network**
640 W Lambert Road
Brea, CA 92821
714-257-1335
E-Mail: dmca-copyright@iatn.net
Home Page: www.iatn.net
Social Media: Facebook, Twitter, LinkedIn
Monica Buchholz, Marketing
A group of professional automotive technicians from 153 countries who exchange technical knowledge and information with other members from around the world.
64601 Members

2366 **International Carwash Association**
230 East Ohio Street
uite 603
Chicago, IL 60611
888-422-8422
E-Mail: info@carwash.org

Home Page: www.carwash.org
Social Media: Facebook, Twitter, LinkedIn

Gary Dennis, President
Pam Piro, Vice President
Eric Wulf, Chief Executive Officer
Claire Moore, Chief Operating Officer
Charnann Cox, Treasurer

A nonprofit trade group representing the retail and supply segmentsof the professional car wash industry in North America and around the globe.

2367 International Motor Press Association
4 Park Street
Harrington Park, NJ 07640

201-750-3533
Fax: 201-750-2010
Home Page: www.impa.org
Social Media: Facebook, Twitter

David Kiley, President
Mike Allen, First VP
Karl Greenberg, Second VP
Lisa Barrow, Secretary
Mike Geylin, Treasurer

Professional group of writers and editors producing auto articles for the press, radio or TV.

2368 International Show Car Association
1092 Centre Rd
Auburn Hills, MI 48326-2657

248-373-1700
Home Page: www.theisca.com
Social Media: Facebook, Twitter

Bob Larivee, Owner
Bob Millard, General Manager

An organization of automotive enthusiasts who enjoy building, showing and viewing customs (cars, bikes and trucks), hot rods, competition cars, street machines and antique/restored vehicles.
Founded in 1963

2369 Manufacturers of Emission Controls Association
2200 Wilson Blvd
Suite 310
Arlington, VA 22201

202-296-4797
Fax: 202-331-1388
E-Mail: asantos@meca.org
Home Page: www.meca.org

Joseph Kubsh, Executive Director
Dr. Rasto Brezny, Deputy Director

Nonprofit association of the world is leading manufacturers of mobile source emission control manufacturers. Serves as a source of technical information on motor vehicle emission control technology.
Founded in 1976

2370 Metropolitan Parking Association
1112 16th St NW
Suite 840
Washington, DC 20036

202-296-4336
800-647-7275
Fax: 202-296-3102
E-Mail: info@npapark.org
Home Page: www.npapark.org
Social Media: Facebook, Twitter, LinkedIn

Jeff Wolfe, Chairman
Mark Muglich, Chair Elect
John Udelson, Vice Chair
Robert A Zuritsky, Treasurer
Nicolle Judge, Secretary

To promote and encourage ethical business practices among the operators of parking facilities, and to instill in public and non-public users of parking services confidence in the integrity and skills of parking operators.
400 Members

2371 Micro-Reality Motorsports
1500 SW 7th Street
Atlantic, IA 50022

712-243-9035
Fax: 712-243-8552
E-Mail: nsei@metc.net
Home Page: www.microreality.com

Kerry Namanny, President

Manufactures and promotes NASCAR micro-reality racing centers, plus several other sports and entertainment/promotions.
321 Members
Founded in 1986

2372 Mobile Air Conditioning Society Worldwide
225 S Broad Street
PO Box 88
Lansdale, PA 19446

215-631-7020
Fax: 215-631-7017
E-Mail: macsworldwide@macsw.org
Home Page: www.macsw.org
Social Media: Facebook, Twitter, LinkedIn

Andrew Fiffick, Chairman
Gus Swensen, Vice Chair
Elvis Hoffpauir, President/COO
David Jack, Secretary
Peter Coll, Treasurer

Provides technical training, information and communication for the professionals in the automotive air conditioning industry.
1700 Members
Founded in 1981

2373 Motor & Equipment Manufacturers Association
1030 15th Street N.W
Suite 500 East
Washington, DC 20005

202-393-6362
Fax: 919-549-4824
E-Mail: info@mema.org
Home Page: www.mema.org

Steve Handschuh, President
Wendy Earp, Senior Vice President
Paul McCarthy, Vice President
Jo Anne Farr, Vice President
Leigh Merino, Senior Director

Represents more than 1,000 companies that manufacture motor vehiclecomponents and systems for the original equipment and aftermarket segments of the light vehicle and heavy-duty industries.

2374 Motor & Equipment Remanufacturers Association
26200 Lahser Rd
Suite 200
Southfield, MI 48033

248-750-1280
Fax: 248-750-1281
E-Mail: info@mera.org
Home Page: www.mera.org
Social Media: Twitter, LinkedIn, YouTube, Instagram, Flickr

Shawn K. Zwicker, Chairman
Peter M. Butterfield, Vice Chairman
Michael Cardone Jr, Immediate Past Chairman
John R. Chalifoux, President & COO
Jack Vollbrecht, Senior Vice President

A trade group of many businesses, both large and small, in the remanufacturing industry.
Founded in 1904

2375 Motor and Equipment Manufacturers Association
10 Laboratory Drive
PO Box 13966
Research Triangle Park, NC 27709-3966

919-549-4800
Fax: 919-406-1465
E-Mail: info@mema.org
Home Page: www.mema.org
Social Media: Facebook, Twitter, LinkedIn

Steve Handschuh, President
Robert E McKenna, CEO
Wendy Earp, CFO, Treasurer & Senior VP
Jo Ann Farr, VP, Human Resource

Serves manufacturers of all types of automotive and truck products through market research, legislative and regulatory representation and reporting, information services, industry networking and commercial services.
2000 Members
Founded in 1904

2376 Motorcycle Industry Council
2 Jenner Street
Suite 150
Irvine, CA 92618-3806

949-727-4211
Fax: 949-727-3313
E-Mail: memberservices@mic.org
Home Page: www.mic.org

A nonprofit, national trade association representing manufacturers and distributors of motorcycles, scooters, motorcycle/ATV parts and accessories.
Founded in 1914

2377 NAFA Fleet Management Association
125 Village Boulevard Princeton Forrestal Villa
Suite 200
Princeton, NJ 08540

609-720-0882
Fax: 609-452-8004
E-Mail: info@nafa.org
Home Page: www.nafa.org
Social Media: Facebook, Twitter, LinkedIn

Cluade T Masters, President
Ruth A Wolfson, Senior VP
Joanne Marsh, Director Marketing & Communications

Serving the needs of those managing fleets of automobiles, light duty trucks and/or vans for US and Canadian organizations. Offers statistical research, publications, including NAFA's Fleet Executive monthly magazine, regional meetings, government representation, conferences, trade shows and seminars.
3000+ Members
Founded in 1957

2378 NARSA - The International Heat Transfer Association
3000 Village Run Road
Suite 103
Wexford, PA 15090-6315

724-799-8415
Fax: 724-799-8416
E-Mail: info@narsa.org
Home Page: narsa.org

Maarten Taal, Chairman
Pat O' Connor, President
Mark Hicks, Vice President
Darlene Barlow, Secretary
Angelo Miozza, Treasurer

An association that has provided focus for the business of thermal management for transportation by providing commercial and technical forums that lead business development and product innovation for more than 58 years.
Founded in 1954

2379 **National Association of Automobile Museums**
P.O. Box 271
Auburn, IN 46706
260-925-1444
Fax: 260-925-6266
Home Page: www.naam.museum
Terry Ernest, President
Mary Ann Porinchak, President Elect
Matthew G. Anderson, Secretary
Judy Endelman, Treasurer
Laura Brinkman, Executive Director
A professional center for automobile museums and affiliated organizations that supports, educates, and encourages members to operate according to professional standards of the museum industry.
Founded in 1994

2380 **National Auto Auction Association**
5320 Spectrum Dr
Suite D
Frederick, MD 21703
301-696-0400
Fax: 301-631-1359
E-Mail: naaa@naaa.com
Home Page: www.naaa.com
Social Media: Facebook, Twitter
Jack Neshe, President
Ellie Johnson, President-Elect
Mike Browning, Vice President
Frank Hackett, CEO
Steve McCannoughey, CFO
NAAA represents more then 317 auto auctions both domestic and international. With more than 8.9 million units sold each year. If there is one dominant theme that runs through the colorful history and phenomenal success of this entrepreneurial industry it is that auction business is all about people. NAAA is the net result of the people who pioneered and built it into one of the most respected trade associations in the world.
Founded in 1948

2381 **National Auto Body Council**
7044 S. 13th St.
Oak Creek, WI 53154
414-908-4957
Fax: 414-768-8001
Home Page: www.nationalautobodycouncil.org
Social Media: Facebook, Twitter, YouTube
Nick Notte, President
Elizabeth Stein, Vice President
Brandon Devis, Past President
Rick E. Tuuri, Treasurer
Elizabeth Clark, Vice President
A nonprofit organization dedicated to promoting the professionalismand integrity of the collision industry through community service initiatives.
Founded in 1990

2382 **National Auto Sport Association**
P.O. Box 2366
Napa Valley, CA 94558
510-232-6272
Fax: 510-277-0657
E-Mail: bizdev@drivenasa.com.prx2.unblocksit.es
Home Page: www.nasaproracing.com
An American motorsports organization promoting road racing and high-performance driver education.
Founded in 1991

2383 **National Automobile Dealers Association**
8400 Westpark Drive
McLean, VA 22102
703-821-7000
800-252-6232
E-Mail: help@nada.org
Home Page: www.nada.org
Social Media: Facebook, Twitter, YouTube, Flickr
Forest McConnell, Chairman
William C Fox, Vice Chairman
Peter K Welch, President
Jeffrey B. Carlson, Secretary
George E. Nahas, Treasurer
Represents more than 19,700 new car and truck dealers, both domestic and international, with more than 43,000 separate franchises.
Founded in 1917

2384 **National Automotive Finance Association**
7250 Parkway Drive
Suite 510
Hanover, MD 21076-1343
410-712-4036
800-463-8955
Fax: 410-712-4038
E-Mail: inquire@nafassociation.com
Home Page: nafassociation.com
Social Media: LinkedIn
Asbel Perez-Viciedo, Chairman
Steve Hall, President
Scot Seagrave, Vice President
Ian Anderson, Vice President
Laurie Kight, Secretary
Founded in 1996

2385 **National Automotive Radiator Service Association**
3000 Villiage Run Road
Suite 103, #221
Wexford, PA 15090-6315
724-799-8415
800-551-3232
Fax: 724-799-8416
E-Mail: info@narsa.org
Home Page: www.narsa.org
Wayne Juchno, Executive Director
Douglas Shymoniak, Manager, Sales & New Business
Laressa Davis, Member Services Coordinator
Trade association serving the cooling system service industry and the public.
1500 Members
Founded in 1953

2386 **National Glass Association**
1945 Old Gallows Rd
Suite 750
Vienna, VA 22182
703-442-4890
866-342-5642
Fax: 703-442-0630
E-Mail: administration@glass.org
Home Page: www.glass.org
Social Media: Facebook, Twitter, LinkedIn
Philip J. James, President & CEO
Nicole Harris, Vice President/Publisher
Bill Evans, Jr., Chairman-Elect
Robert Brown, Treasurer
Provides information and education, as well as promote quality workmanship, ethics, and safety in the architectural, automotive and window and door glass industries. Acts as a clearinghouse for industry information, a catalyst in education and training matters, and a powerful voice on behalf of the members.
4000 Members
Founded in 1948

2387 **National Independent Automobile Dealers Association**
2521 Brown Boulevard
Arlington, TX 76006-5203
817-492-2377
800-682-3837
Fax: 817-649-5866
E-Mail: mike@naida.com
Home Page: www.niada.com
Karen Barbee, President
Michael R Linn, President
Steve Jordan, COO
Representing quality independent automobile dealers for almost 60 years. NIADA is here to assist members in becoming more successful within the used motor vehicle industry.
19000 Members
Founded in 1946

2388 **National Locksmith Automobile Association**
630-837-2044
E-Mail: customerservice@thenationallocksmith.com
Home Page: www.thenationallocksmith.com
Social Media: Facebook
An organization of automotive specialists that service mechanical locks, produce duplicate keys of all types, and program transponders.

2389 **National Motorists Association**
402 W 2nd St
Waunakee, WI 53597
608-849-6000
Fax: 888-787-0381
E-Mail: nma@motorists.org
Home Page: www.motorists.org
Social Media: Facebook, Twitter
James Baxter, President
Gary Biller, Executive Director
Advocates, represents and protects the interests of North American motorists.
Cost: $35.00
Frequency: Annual Membership Dues
Founded in 1982

2390 **National Parking Association**
1112 16th St NW
Suite 840
Washington, DC 20036
202-296-4336
800-647-7275
Fax: 202-296-3102
E-Mail: info@npapark.org
Home Page: www.npapark.org
Social Media: Facebook, Twitter, LinkedIn
Jeff Wolfe, Chairman
Mark Muglich, Chair Elect
John Udelson, Vice Chair
Nicolle Jugde, Secretary
Robert A Zuritsky, Treasurer
Our members are comprised of parking professionals in both the public and private sectors from across the country and around the world. NPA members are private operators, parking consultants, colleges and universities, municipalities, parking authorities, hospitals and medical centers and industry vendors.
2400 Members
Founded in 1951

2391 **National Truck Equipment Association**
37400 Hills Tech Dr
Farmington Hill, MI 48331-3414
248-489-7090
800-441-6832
Fax: 248-489-8590

E-Mail: info@ntea.com
Home Page: www.ntea.com

James Carney, Executive Director
Frank Livas, First Vice President

Represents small to mid-sized companies that manufacture, distribute, install, buy, sell and repair commercial trucks, truck bodies, truck equipment, trailers and accessories.
1600 Members
Founded in 1964

2392 National Wheel and Rim Association
3943-2 Baymeadows Road
Jacksonville, FL 32217

904-737-2900
Fax: 904-636-9881
E-Mail: info@cvsn.org
Home Page: www.nationalwheelandrim.org

Dave Willis, President
Edward Neeley, Vice President
Andy Robblee, Treasurer
Angelo Volpe, Sectretary/Executive VP

Represents warehouse distributors of wheels, rims and related parts.
230 Members
Founded in 1924

2393 North American Automobile Trade Association
10 Four Seasons Place
10th Floor
Etobicoke, ON M9B 6H7

877-227-8878
E-Mail: naata@naata.org
Home Page: naata.org
Social Media: Facebook, Twitter, LinkedIn, Flickr

Tahverlee Dunlop, President/ CEO
George Sahakian, Vice President
Andrew Pilsworth, Director
Jan Zurek, Director
Wouter VanEssen, Treasurer

Promotes the export of motor vehicles.
Founded in 1996

2394 North American Council of Automotive Teachers (NACAT)
PO Box 80010
Charleston, SC 29416

843-556-7068
Fax: 843-556-7068
E-Mail: office@nacat.com
Home Page: www.nacat.com

Rob Thompson, President
Curt Ward, Vice President/President Elect

Supports all educators in the automotive industry, with training and education, publications and seminars.
750 Members
Founded in 1974

2395 Original Equipment Suppliers Association
1301 W Long Lake Rd
Suite 225
Troy, MI 48098

248-952-6401
Fax: 248-952-6404
E-Mail: info@oesa.org
Home Page: www.oesa.org
Social Media: Facebook, LinkedIn

Julie A Fream, President &CEO
Neil De Koker, President Elect
Margaret Baxter, Senior VP, Operations
Dave Andrea, Senior VP, Industry Analysis
Glenn Stevens, Senior VP, Membership & Sales

Dedicated to advancing the business interests of companies supplying components, systems, modules, equipment, materials and services used in and by the original equipment automotive industry and to engage in activities in support of the welfare of the association membership. OESA is an affiliate of the Motor and Equipment Manufacturers Association.
340 Members
Founded in 1998

2396 Overseas Automotive Council
10 Laboratory Drive
PO Box 13966
Research Triangle Park, NC 27709-3966

919-406-8810
Fax: 919-549-4824
E-Mail: oac@mema.org
Home Page: www.oac-intl.org
Social Media: Facebook, Twitter, LinkedIn

Caroline M Perrotta, Chairman
Mick Jordan, Vice Chair
Tim Vehlewald, Second Vice Chair
Dan Pike, Executive Director

One of the oldest and most unique organizations in the global automotive aftermarket. Mission is to promote the sale of automotive products and services exported from North America, to enhance the prestige and goodwill of the global automotive aftermarket industry, to promote friendly trade relationships, cultural understanding and mutually beneficial cooperation among those engaged in the automotive aftermarket industry.
500+ Members
Founded in 1923

2397 Performance Warehouse Association
41-701 Corporate Way
Suite 1
Palm Desert, CA 92260

760-346-5647
Fax: 760-346-5847
Home Page: www.pwa-par.org

Larry Pacey, Chairman
Ken Woomer, Chairman Elect
Trent Lowe, Treasurer

An organization of specialty automotive parts wholesalers joined together and dealing with management, financial and legislative matters.
10000 Members
Founded in 1971

2398 Production Engine Remanufacturers Association
PO Box 250
Colleyville, TX 76034-0250

817-243-2646
Fax: 417-998-5056
E-Mail: jeopolich@pera.org
Home Page: www.pera.org
Social Media: Facebook, LinkedIn

Nancie J. Boland, Executive VP
Robert P. McGraw, President

The Production Engine Remanufacturers Association is an association of individual and firm who remanufacture internal combustion enhgines or their major components or supply necessay components, supplies and eqipment required in the manufacturing process. The goal of PERA is to provide members with the opportinity to exchange ideas, methods and procedures necessary to efficiently produce remanufactured products which are equal or superior to origianl products in quality and performance.
Founded in 1946

2399 Recreation Vehicle Dealers Association
3930 University Dr
Suite 300
Fairfax, VA 22030-2515

703-591-7130
Fax: 703-359-0152
E-Mail: info@rvda.org
Home Page: www.rvda.org

Mike Molino, President
Ronnie Hepp, VP of Administration
Hank Fortune, Director of Finance
Susan Charter, Associate Services Manager

National association advances the best interests of RV retailers through education, services, leadership and programs of market expansion that promote increased use and sale of RVs while enhancing their image.

2400 Recreational Vehicle Aftermarket Association
54 Westerly Road
Camp Hill, PA 17011

717-730-0300
Fax: 630-544-5055
E-Mail: ellenkietzmann@blueox.us
Home Page: www.rvaftermarket.org

Ellen Kietzmann, President
Ron Dempster, VP
Jess Fowler, Secretary
Bill Fudale, Treasurer

An organization for the suppliers, distributors and agents that represent the aftermarket segment of the RV industry.
110 Members
Founded in 1969

2401 Retread and Repair Information Bureau
1013 Birch Street
Falls Church, VA 22046

703-533-7677
877-394-6811
Fax: 703-533-7678
E-Mail: info@retread.org
Home Page: www.retread.org
Social Media: Facebook, Twitter, LinkedIn

David Stevens, Managing Director
Bob Majewski, President

Serving as the public relations arm of the retread industry. Gathering and disseminating information on retread passenger and truck tires to members and the general public.
500 Members
Founded in 1973

2402 Rubber Manufacturers Association
1400 K St NW
Suite 900
Washington, DC 20005

202-682-4800
Fax: 202-682-4854
E-Mail: info@rma.org
Home Page: www.rma.org
Social Media: Facebook, Twitter

Charlie Cannon, President, CEO
Tracey Norberg, Senior VP
Dan Zielinski, Senior VP

National trade association for makers of tires and other rubber products.
100 Members

2403 Service Specialists Association
4015 Marks Road
Suite 2B
Medina, OH 44256-8316

330-725-7160
800-763-5717
Fax: 330-722-5638

E-Mail: trucksvc@aol.com
Home Page: www.truckservice.org
Social Media: Facebook

Larry Schmitz, President
Matt Thompson, Vice President
Toni Nastali, Treasurer
Marc Gold, Director

Members are persons, firms or corporations who have operated a full line heavy duty repair service shop for at least one year with sufficient inventory to service market area, having rebuilding department capable of making all necessary repairs.
140 Members
Founded in 1981

2404 Society of Automotive Engineers
SAE Automotive Headquarters
755 W Big Beaver
Suite 1600
Troy, MI 48084-4906

724-776-4841
877-606-7323
Fax: 248-273-2494
E-Mail: CustomerService@sae.org
Home Page: www.sae.org
Social Media: Facebook, Twitter, LinkedIn

Donald J Hillebrand, President
Mircea Gradu, VP, Automotive
Carol Story, Treasurer
David Schutt, CEO

Offers automotive engineers the technical information and expertise used in building, maintaining and operating self propelled vehicles for use on land, sea, air or space.
84000 Members
Founded in 1905

2405 Society of Automotive Historians
E-Mail: webmaster@autohistory.org
Home Page: autohistory.org

John Heitmann, President
Andrew Beckman, Vice President
Bob Ebert, Secretary
Bob Casey, Director
Vince Wright, Director

Encourages research, preservation, recording, compilation, and publication of historical facts concerning the development of the automobile and related items throughout the world.
Founded in 1969

2406 Society of Collision Repair Specialists
PO Box 909
Prosser, WA 99350

877-841-0660
Fax: 877-851-0660
E-Mail: info@scrs.com
Home Page: www.scrs.com
Social Media: Facebook, Twitter

Ron Reichen, Chairman
Andy Dingman, Vice Chair
Rodes Brown, Treasurer
Kye Yueng, Secretary

For owners and managers of auto collision repair shops, suppliers, insurance and educational associates and suppliers in the US, Canada, Australia and New Zealand. Distributes technical, management, marketing and sales information. Works to promote professionalism within the collision repair industry.
Founded in 1983

2407 Society of Independent Gasoline Marketers of America
3930 Pender Drive
Suite 340
Fairfax, VA 22030

703-709-7000
Fax: 703-709-7007
E-Mail: sigma@sigma.org
Home Page: www.sigma.org

Kenneth Doyle, Executive VP
Thomas Schmidt, First VP
Brian Beaver, Second VP

Supports independent fuel marketers and suppliers, providing training and education, publications and seminars.
250 Members
Founded in 1958

2408 Specialty Equipment Market Association
1575 South Valley Vista Drive
Diamond Bar, CA 91765-0289

909-610-2030
Fax: 909-860-0184
E-Mail: sema@sema.org
Home Page: www.sema.org
Social Media: Facebook, Twitter, LinkedIn

Nate Shelton, Chairman
Doug Evans, Chair Elect
Christopher J Kirsting, President & CEO

This trade association consists of a diverse group of manufacturers, distributors, retailers, publishing companies, auto restorers, street rod builders, restylers, car clubs, race teams and more.
5700+ Members
Founded in 1963

2409 The Recreation Vehicle Industry Association
1896 Preston White Drive
Reston, VA 20191

703-620-6003
Fax: 703-620-5071
Home Page: www.rvia.org

Derald Bontrager, Chairman
Robert L. Parish, First Vice Chairman
Garry Enyart, Second Vice Chairman
Kevin Phillips, Secretary
Matthew Miller, Treasurer
Founded in 1963

2410 Tire Industry Association
1532 Pointer Ridge Pl
Suite G
Bowie, MD 301-430-72

301-430-7280
800-876-8372
Fax: 301-430-7283
E-Mail: info@tireindustry.org
Home Page: www.tireindustry.org
Social Media: Facebook, Twitter, LinkedIn

Roy Littlefield, Executive VP
Reece Hester, Executive Director

Representing all segments of the tire industry, including those that manufacture, repair, recycle, sell, service or use new or retreaded tires, and also those suppliers or individuals who furnish equipment, material or services to the industry.
5000 Members
Founded in 2002

2411 Tire and Rim Association
175 Montrose West Ave
Suite 150
Copley, OH 44321-2793

330-666-8121
Fax: 330-666-8340
E-Mail: tra@us-tra.org
Home Page: www.us-tra.org

Joseph Pacuit, Executive VP

Technical standardizing organization for tire, rim and valve manufacturers.
110 Members
Founded in 1903

2412 Triangle Electric Auto Association
3702 Burwell Rollins CIR
Raleigh, NC 27612-5239

E-Mail: pppayments@rtpnet.org
Home Page: rtpnet.org

An association focused on the conversion of gas cars into electric cars.
Founded in 1990

2413 United States Auto Club
USAC National Office
4910 West 16th Street
Speedway, IN 46224-0001

317-247-5151
Fax: 317-248-5584
Home Page: www.usacracing.com
Social Media: Facebook, Twitter

Kevin Miller, President

Supports all driving professionals and consumers with education, publications, driving and vacation tips. Publishes monthly magazine.

2414 United States Council for Automotive Research
1000 Town Center Drive
Suite 300
Southfield, MI 48075

248-223-9000
Home Page: www.uscar.org

Steve Zimmer, Executive Director
Matt Liddane, Vice President
Paul Mascarenas, Chief Technical Officer
Jon Lauckner, Council Member

The collaborative automotive technology company for Chrysler Group LLC, Ford Motor Company, and General Motors.
Founded in 1992

2415 Womens Automotive Association International
PO Box 2535
Birmingham, MI 48012

248-646-5250
Fax: 248-387-3550
E-Mail: lhswaai@aol.com
Home Page: www.waai.com

Lorraine H Schultz, Founder
Marcela Fink, President

Dedicated to the development and advancement of women as automotive industry leaders. Today, the organization continues to thrive throughout the United States and Canada as the leading women's global organization dedicated to this purpose.
600 Members
Founded in 1995

Newsletters

2416 AIAG e-News Brief
Automotive Industry Action Group
26200 Lahser Road
Suite 200
Southfield, MI 48033-7100

248-358-3570
Fax: 248-358-3253
E-Mail: inquiry@aiag.org
Home Page: www.aiag.org

John Batchik, Chairman
David Kneisler, Vice Chairman
J. Scot Sharland, Executive Director

Global automotive industry news, member succes stories and need to know information on AIAG products and events.
1000 Members
Frequency: Monthly
Founded in 1982

2417 Automotive Market Report
Automotive Auction Publishing
607 Laurel Drive
Monroeville, PA 15146-4405

412-373-6383
Fax: 412-373-6388

Clyde K Hillwig, Publisher

News items pertinent to auto auctions and the auto industry.
Frequency: BiWeekly
Circulation: 10000

2418 Automotive Week: Greensheet
Molinaro Communications
PO Box 355
Munroe Falls, OH 44262-0355

330-688-4960
877-694-6076
Fax: 866-926-0452
E-Mail: gary@thegreensheetonline.com
Home Page: www.thegreensheetonline.com

Gary Molinaro, Publisher/Editor
Marc Vincent, Managing Editor

Intelligence concerning the $270 billion independent automotive aftermarked. Breaking news & analysis not available anywhere else in the industry. Key moves in the retail and wholesale distribution channels, mergers & acquisitions; financial analysis of publicly-traded entities. Classified, non-product advertising accepted.
Cost: $225.00
4 Pages
Frequency: 48 issues
ISSN: 0889-3918
Founded in 1975
Printed in on matte stock

2419 Car Dealer Insider
United Communications Group
9737 Washingtonian Blvd.
Suite 100
Gaithersburg, MD 20878-7364

301-287-2700
Fax: 301-287-2039
Home Page: www.ucg.com

Jill Gardner, Publisher
Donna Lawrence, Editor
Bruce Levenson, Co-Founder
Nancy Becker, Partner, President

Marketing intelligence for new car dealers includes dealer-tested tactics, best management practices and breaking news stories.
Frequency: Bi-Monthly
Founded in 1977

2420 Chek-Chart Service Bulletin
Motor Information Systems/Chek-Chart
1301 W Long Lake Rd
Suite 200
Troy, MI 48098-6349

248-828-0000
800-426-6867
Fax: 248-828-0215

Paul M Eckstein, Manager
Anthony Mattar, Owner

Up-to-date information on all the new automotive developments from the car manufacturers. Information bulletin for service station dealers, mechanics, and instructors. Chek/Chart is part of MotorInformation Systems.

2421 EngiNEWS
Production Engine Remanufacturers Association
28203 Woodhaven Road
Edwards, MO 65326

417-998-5057
Fax: 417-998-5056
E-Mail: nancieboland@pera.org
Home Page: www.pera.org
Social Media: Facebook, LinkedIn

Nancie J. Boland, Exutive VP
Robert P. McGraw, President

An semi-annual e-newsletter covering problems from airline fees to the amount of cars on the road and postives of new businesses involved in remanufacturing.
Frequency: Quarterly
Founded in 1946
Mailing list available for rent: 200 names

2422 Executive Directors Report
Society of Collision Repair Specialists
PO Box 909
Prosser, WA 99350

509-735-0607
877-841-0660
Fax: 877-851-0660
E-Mail: info@scrs.com
Home Page: www.scrs.com

Aaron Schulenburg, Executive Director
Luis Alonso, Treasurer
Linda Atkins, Administrative Assistant

Newsletter for owners and managers of auto collision repair shops, suppliers, insurance and educational associates and suppliers in the US, Canada, Australia and New Zealand. Technical, management, marketing and sales information. Free to members.
Frequency: Bi-Annually
Circulation: 6000
Founded in 1982

2423 FirstUp: Daily News
American Int'l Automobile Dealers Association
211 N Union St
Suite 300
Alexandria, VA 22314-2643

703-519-7800
800-462-4232
Fax: 703-519-7810
E-Mail: goaiada@aiada.org
Home Page: www.aiada.org
Social Media: Twitter

Jim Smail, Chairman
Ray Mungenast, Chairman-Elect
Jenell Ross, Vice Chair
Larry Kull, Secretary/ Treasurer
Cody Lusk, President

Conveys the day's auto-related news quickly, concisely, and accurately. Topics covered in FirstUp range from new vehicle releases, to the latest legislation concerning the auto industry.
11M+ Members
Frequency: Daily
Circulation: 30000
Founded in 1970

2424 Fleet Administration News
PO Box 159
Litchfield Park, AZ 85340

623-772-9096
Fax: 623-772-9098
Home Page: ncsfa.state.ut.us

Joe O'Neill, Executive Director

NCSFA members are state government administrators responsible for vehicle fleet management.
Cost: $50.00
Frequency: Quarterly
Printed in on matte stock

2425 Fleet Perspectives
National Association of Fleet Administrators
125 Village Boulevard
Suite 200
Princeton, NJ 08540

609-720-0882
Fax: 609-452-8004
E-Mail: info@nafa.org
Home Page: www.nafa.org
Social Media: Facebook, Twitter, LinkedIn

Phillip E. Russo, Executive Director
Patrick McCarron, Deputy Executive Director
Joanne Marsh, Director Marketing & Communications

Official e-newsletter for Public Service and Corporate fleet managers. Contains special profiles on NAFA Members, important fleet news, and informative articles that won't be found anywhere else.
3000+ Members
Frequency: Quarterly
Founded in 1957

2426 FleetFOCUS
National Association of Fleet Administrators
125 Village Boulevard
Suite 200
Princeton, NJ 08540

609-720-0882
Fax: 609-452-8004
E-Mail: info@nafa.org
Home Page: www.nafa.org
Social Media: Facebook, Twitter, LinkedIn

Phillip E. Russo, Executive Director

The focus for quick-reading highlights designed to give professional fleet managers the latest industry news.
2600+ Members
Frequency: Bi-Weekly

2427 Highway & Vehicle/Safety Report
Stamler Publishing Company
178 Thimble Island Road
PO Box 3367
Branford, CT 06405-1967

203-488-9808
800-422-4121
Fax: 203-488-3129
Home Page: www.trafficsafetynews.com

S Paul Stamler, Publisher
Suzanne Reutenauer, Circulation Manager

Business to business newsletter on the latest developments in transportation safety, regulations and new legislation, and new technology in the automotive industry.
Cost: $467.00
Frequency: Monthly
Founded in 1973

2428 Highway Users In Action
American Highway Users Alliance
1101 14th St NW
Suite 750
Washington, DC 20005

202-857-1200
Fax: 202-857-1220
E-Mail: info@highways.org
Home Page: www.highways.org
Social Media: Facebook, Twitter, YouTube

Bill Graves, Chairman
Richard A. Coon, Vice Chairman
Thomas F. Jensen, Secretary
Roy E. Littlefield, Treasurer

e-Newsletter with the latest, most recent Highway Users work on behalf of membership. Offers information affecting members.
Frequency: Bi-Annually
Founded in 1932

2429 **Hybrid & Electric Vehicle Progress**
Alexander Communications Group
1916 Park Ave
8th Floor
New York, NY 10037-3733

212-281-6099
800-232-4317
Fax: 212-283-7269
Home Page: www.evprogress.com

Romauld Alexander, Owner
Laurence Alexander, CEO

News of hybrid and electric vehicle commercialization. Worldwide coverage focuses on news and data on both the technical and business aspects of the hybrid or electric vehicle industry.
Cost: $477.00
8 Pages
Frequency: Fortnightly
Circulation: 800
ISSN: 0190-4175
Founded in 1954
Printed in 2 colors on matte stock

2430 **IMPACT**
International Motor Press Association
4 Park Street
Harrington Park, NJ 07640

201-750-3533
Fax: 201-750-2010
E-Mail: mike@jalopnik.com
Home Page: www.impa.org

Mike Spinelli, President
John Matras, First VP
Mike Allen, Second VP
Frequency: Monthly

2431 **Independent Gasoline Marketing (IGM)**
Soc. of Independent Gasoline Marketers of America
3930 Pender Drive
Suite 340
Fairfax, VA 22030

703-709-7000
Fax: 703-709-7007
E-Mail: sigma@sigma.org
Home Page: www.sigma.org

Kenneth Doyle, Executive VP
Marilyn Selvitelle, VP

Information for independent fuel marketers and suppliers on legislative issues, new market trends, equipment use and management techniques.
32 Pages
Circulation: 4000
Founded in 1958
Printed in 4 colors on glossy stock

2432 **Lemon Times**
Center for Auto Safety
1825 Connecticut Ave NW
Suite 330
Washington, DC 20009-5725

202-328-7700
Fax: 202-387-0140
Home Page: www.autosafety.org

Clarence M Ditlow III, Executive Director
Sanja Pesek, Editor

Reports on the auto safety world of CAS, as well as covering safety litigation, secret warranties, crash tests, lemon laws, recalls, federal and state investigations.
Cost: $20.00
15000 Members
Frequency: Quarterly
Founded in 1970

2433 **Market Watch**
AIADA
211 N Union St
Suite 300
Alexandria, VA 22314-2643

800-462-4232
Fax: 703-519-7810
E-Mail: goaiada@aiada.org
Home Page: www.aiada.org
Social Media: Twitter

Jim Smail, Chairman
Ray Mungenast, Chairman-Elect
Jenell Ross, Vice Chair
Larry Kull, Secretary/ Treasurer
Cody Lusk, President

Emailed report providing a succinct rundown of the latest industry sales numbers and data. A summary of monthly trends, accompanied by easy-to-read charts and graphs, allows readers to track trends, note milestones, and react quickly to a shifting auto market.
11M+ Members
Frequency: Monthly
Founded in 1970

2434 **Motor**
Hearst Business Communications
567 Robbins Dr
Suite 200
Troy, MI 48083-4515

248-585-1700
Fax: 248-828-7004
E-Mail: jlypen@motor.com
Home Page: www.motor.com

Duane Harrison, Owner
Kevin Carr, President
Paul Moszak, Vice President/General Manager
Lori Aemiseqqer, Marketing
Richard Laimbeer, Publisher

Articles to keep readers up to date on the latest diagnostic techniques and service procedures. Management articles to help shop owners increase profitability, latest tools available, new products and industry news.
Cost: $48.00
Frequency: Monthly
Circulation: 138941
Founded in 1903

2435 **NACAT News**
North American Council of Automotive Teachers
PO Box 80010
Charleston, SC 29416

843-556-7068
Fax: 843-556-7068
E-Mail: office@nacat.com
Home Page: www.nacat.com

Patrick Brown Harrison, President
Rob Thompson, Vice President

Cutting edge automotive information for automotive educators. Also news of the organization and the automotive industry.
Circulation: 750
Founded in 1974

2436 **NAFA Fleetfocus**
National Association of Fleet Administrators
125 Village Boulevard
Suite 200
Princeton, NJ 08540

609-720-0882
Fax: 732-494-6789
E-Mail: info@nafa.org
Home Page: www.nafa.org

Philip Russo, Executive Director
Patrick McCarren, Deputy Executive Director
Joanne Marsh, Director Marketing

The focus for quick rading highlights designed to give professional fleet managers the latest industry news.
3000+ Members
Frequency: Weekly
Circulation: 3600
Founded in 1946
Printed in one color on matte stock

2437 **News & Views**
Bearing Specialists Association
800 Roosevelt Road
Building C, Suite 312
Glen Ellyn, IL 60137

630-858-3838
Fax: 630-790-3095
E-Mail: info@bsahome.org
Home Page: www.bsahome.org
Social Media: LinkedIn

Linda Miller, President
Richard W Church, Executive Director
Jerilyn J Church, Executive Secretary

Monthly newlsetter of BSA, the forum to enhance networking and knowledge sharing to promote the sale of bearings through authorized distributors. Available to members only.
100 Members
Frequency: E-Newsletter for Members
Circulation: 400
Founded in 1966

2438 **Nozzle Chatter**
Association of Diesel Specialists
400 Admiral Boulevard
Kansas City, MO 64106

816-285-0810
Fax: 847-770-4952
E-Mail: info@diesel.org
Home Page: www.diesel.org
Social Media: Facebook, LinkedIn

Chuck Hess, President
Andy Girres, Vice President
Chuck Oliveros, Treasurer
Carl Fergueson, Secretary
David Fehling, Executive Director

Member benefit focusing on a variety of news, tips and information on the diesel industry. Contains information that will encourage the exchange of ideas among members; provides a forum for discussion and debate; allow for the fostering of new relationships and contacts; provide members with the knowledge and expertise of colleagues; and provide immediate access to information concerning training materials and publications through monthly reviews.
700+ Members
Frequency: Monthly
Founded in 1956

2439 **OAC Global Report**
Overseas Automotive Council
PO Box 13966
Research Triangle Park, NC 27709-3966

919-549-4800
Fax: 919-549-4824
E-Mail: media@mema.org
Home Page: www.tune-up.org

Margaret Beck, Senior Director
Steve Handschuh, President

Free to members.
Frequency: Monthly
Founded in 1923

2440 **Passenger Transport**
American Public Transit Association
1666 K St NW
Suite 1100
Washington, DC 20006-1215

202-496-4800
Fax: 202-496-4324
E-Mail: ptsubscriptions@apta.com
Home Page: www.apta.com

Michael Melaniphy, President/CEO
Petra Mollet, VP
Rosemary Sherid, Marketing

Information on federal legislative, administrative and regulatory developments, management and operations, new technology, and state and local developments in public transit.
Frequency: Bi-Weekly
Circulation: 5000
Founded in 1882

2441 **Power Report**
JD Power and Associates Publications Division
2625 Townsgate Rd
Suite 100
Westlake Villag, CA 91361-5737
805-418-8000
888-537-6937
Fax: 805-418-8900
E-Mail: information@jdpa.com
Home Page: www.jdpower.com

Finbarr O'Neill, CEO
Mary Ann Maskery, Editor
JD Power, Chairman
Focuses on what car buyers and owners feel about their current vehicles.
Cost: $299.00
Frequency: Monthly
Founded in 1968

2442 **Quality**
BNP Media Company
155 N. Pfingsten Rd.
Suite 205
Deerfield, IL 60015
847-405-4044
Fax: 248-358-1024
E-Mail: dalpozzod@bnpmedia.com
Home Page: www.qulitymag.com
Social Media: Twitter

Taggart Henderson, Co-CEO
Darrell O. Dal Pozzo, Group Publisher
Chistopher Sheehy, Senior Audience Development Manager
A monthly business publication serving the quality assurance and process improvement needs of more than 64,000 manufacturing professionals. the magazine reports on the use of sound metrology methods, statistical analysis and process improvement techniques to significantly improve quality on the shop floor and in manufacturing planning.
1000 Members
Frequency: Monthly
Founded in 1962

2443 **Safety & Environment/ Working Conditions**
Automotive Industry Action Group
26200 Lahser Road
Suite 200
Southfield, MI 48033-7100
248-358-3570
Fax: 248-358-3253
E-Mail: inquiry@aiag.org
Home Page: www.aiag.org

John Batchik, Chairman
David Kneisler, Vice Chairman
J. Scot Sharland, Executive Director
Addresses emerging and global issues in safety, health and the environment affecting member companies and employees worldwide.
1000 Members
Frequency: Monthly
Founded in 1982

2444 **Service Executive**
Automotive Week Publishing
PO Box 3495
Wayne, NJ 07474-3495
973-694-7792
Home Page: www.auto-week.com

Marketing information for the independent automotive aftermarket. Fast-breaking news of new market entries and strategies; key retail and wholesale developments; merger, acquisition, bankruptcy reports; regular charts of the Top 25 market leaders in various segments (parts, chains, tune-up specialists, brake specialists, tire, fast lube, etc.). The market's sole weekly. Classified non-product advertising accepted.
Cost: $130.00
4 Pages
Frequency: Monthly
Founded in 1975
Printed in on matte stock

2445 **Shop Talk**
IMACA Education Foundation
6410 Southwest Boulevard
Suite 212
Fort Worth, TX 76109-3920
817-732-4600
Fax: 817-732-9610
Home Page: www.imaca.org

Joan M Jones, Circulation Director
Technical and industry information for the mobile air conditioning industry.
Cost: $20.00
Founded in 1958

2446 **Show Stopper**
International Show Car Association
1092 Centre Rd
Auburn Hills, MI 48326-2657
248-373-1700
Home Page: www.theisca.com

Bob Larivee, Owner
Car association report about shows.

2447 **Supply Chain Solutions**
Automotive Industry Action Group
26200 Lahser Road
Suite 200
Southfield, MI 48033-7100
248-358-3570
Fax: 248-358-3253
E-Mail: inquiry@aiag.org
Home Page: www.aiag.org

John Batchik, Chairman
David Kneisler, Vice Chairman
J. Scot Sharland, Executive Director
Important information on customs and supply chain security regulation; materials management and logistics best practices; and automatic identifications/ RFID standards.
1000 Members
Frequency: Monthly
Founded in 1982

2448 **The Insider**
American Bus Association
111 K Street NE
9th Floor
Washington, DC 20002
202-842-1645
Fax: 202-842-0850
E-Mail: abainfo@buses.org
Home Page: www.buses.org
Social Media: Facebook, Twitter, LinkedIn

James Jalbert, Chairman
Thomas JeBran, Vice Chairman
Frank Henry, Secretary/ Treasurer
Peter Pantuso, President & CEO
Brandon Buchanan, Director of Operations
First source of information for bus and tour operators, travel partners, manufacturers, suppliers, and policy-makers seeking original coverage on the motorcoach, tous, and travel industry, from legislation and regulation to news to grow readers' business.
Frequency: Bi-Monthly
Circulation: 10000
Founded in 1926

2449 **Tire Business**
Crain Communications Inc
1725 Merriman Rd
Suite 300
Akron, OH 44313-5283
330-836-9180
Fax: 330-836-2831
E-Mail: info@crain.com
Home Page: www.crain.com

William Morrow, Executive VP, Operations
Peter Brown, VP
Besides reporting on breaking news, Tire Business also compiles numerous rankings and industry statistics relating to the North American tire and automotive service markets, independent tire dealers, tire manufacturers, tire retreaders and the global tire market.
Frequency: Bi-Weekly
Circulation: 30000
Founded in 1983

2450 **Today's Tire Industry**
Tire Industry Association
1532 Pointer Ridge Pl
Suite G
Bowie, MD 20716-1874
301-430-7280
800-876-8372
Fax: 301-430-7283
E-Mail: info@tireindustry.org
Home Page: www.tireindustry.org

Kevin Rohlwing, Senior Vice President Of Training
Sandra Martinez, Director Operations
Dr.Roy Littlefield, Executive Vice President
Chris Marnett, Director Of Training
Features retail, management, personnel and industry related information.
Cost: $13.00

2451 **UPdate: Society of Automotive Engineers**
Society of Automotive Engineers
400 Commonwealth Dr
Warrendale, PA 15086-7511
724-776-4841
877-606-7323
Fax: 724-776-5760
E-Mail: update@sae.org
Home Page: www.saesections.org

Richard O Schaum, President
Martha Schanno, Circulation Manager
Published to enhance communications with and among SAE members on such non-technical issues as society activities, meetings and members. Recruitment advertising is accepted.
Frequency: Monthly
Circulation: 65000
Founded in 1905
Printed in 2 colors on newsprint stock

2452 **USAC News**
United States Auto Club
PO Box 24001
Indianapolis, IN 46224-0001
317-247-5151
Fax: 317-247-0123
Home Page: www.usacracing.com

Kevin Miller, President

Contains schedules and news from USAC divisions.
8 Pages
Frequency: Monthly
Founded in 1982

2453 **Ward's Automotive Reports**
Ward's Communications
3000 Town Center
Suite 2750
Southfield, MI 48075-1245
248-799-2622
877-825-1815
Fax: 248-357-9747
E-Mail: wards@wardsauto.com
Home Page: www.wardsauto.com
Tom Duncan, Publisher
Steve Finlay, Senior Editor
Jim Bush, Business Manager
Chris Lamphear, Marketing Manager
Automotive sales, production and inventory statistics, news and analysis.
Cost: $1195.00
8 Pages
Frequency: Weekly
Founded in 1924
Printed in 2 colors on matte stock

2454 **Ward's Dealer Business**
PRIMEDIA Intertec-Technology & Transportation
3000 Town Center
Suite 2750
Southfield, MI 48075-1245
248-799-2622
877-778-2512
Fax: 248-357-9747
E-Mail: wards@wardsauto.com
Home Page: www.wardsauto.com
Thomas Duncan, Group Publisher
Steve Finlay, Senior Editor
Steve Sindly, Editor
James Bush, Managing Director
Information for the management of US new car dealerships by covering profit building techniques and business expansions. Includes analysis of current automotive trends.
Cost: $36.00
Frequency: Monthly
Circulation: 32635

2455 **Ward's Engine and Vehicle Technology Update**
Ward's Communications
3000 Town Center
Suite 2750
Southfield, MI 48075-1245
248-799-2622
Fax: 248-357-9747
E-Mail: wards@wardsauto.com
Home Page: www.wardsauto.com
Thomas Duncan, Group Publisher
Steve Finlay, Senior Editor
Barbara McClellan, Senior International Edit
James Bush, Managing Director
John Sousanis, Publication Manager
Review of the latest advances in engine and vehicle technology.
Cost: $935.00
8 Pages
Printed in 2 colors on ³ stock

Magazines & Journals

2456 **ACTION Magazine**
Mobile Air Conditioning Society Worldwide
225 S Broad Street
Lansdale, PA 19446
215-631-7020
Fax: 215-631-7017
E-Mail: info@macsw.org
Home Page: www.macsw.org
Social Media: Facebook, Twitter, LinkedIn
The journal of record for the professional in the growing global mobile AC industry and changing heat transfer and engine cooling system marketplace. has access to the global design and service and repair experts in automotive, heavy-duty, off-road, and bus mobile A/C, heat transfer and engine cooling system industry.
1700 Members
Frequency: 8x Yearly
Circulation: 13000
Founded in 1981

2457 **AGRR**
Key Communications
PO Box 569
Garrisonville, VA 22463
540-720-5584
Fax: 540-720-5687
E-Mail: news@glassbytes.com
Home Page: www.agrrmag.com
Debra Levy, Publisher
Charles Cumpston, Editor
Source of unbiased, accurate information about the auto glass repair and replacement industry.
Frequency: Monthly
Circulation: 10,000
Founded in 2001

2458 **Accident Analysis & Prevention**
AAAM
PO Box 4176
Barrington, IL 60011-4176
847-844-3880
Fax: 847-844-3884
E-Mail: info@aaam.org
Home Page: www.aaam.org
Brian N. Fildes, Ph.D, President
Mary Pat McKay, MD, President-Elect
Kristy B. Arbogast, Ph.D, Secretary
Frances D. Bents, Treasurer
Provides wide coverage of the general areas relating to accidental injury and damage, including the pre-injury and immediate post-injury phases. Published papers deal with medical, legal, economic, educational, behavioral, theoretical or empirical aspects of transportation accidents, as well as with accidents at other sites.
Frequency: 6x Yearly
Founded in 1957

2459 **Aftermarket Business Magazine**
Advanstar Communications
6200 Canoga Avenue
2nd Floor
Woodland Hills, CA 91367
81 -22 -403
Fax: 818-593-5020
E-Mail: jsavas@advanstar.com
Home Page: aftermarketbusiness.com
Larry Silvey, Editor
Jim Savas, VP
Specializing in providing news, trends, research and analysis on aftermarket auto parts
Cost: $5.00
Frequency: Monthly
Circulation: 41,077
Founded in 1936
Printed in on glossy stock

2460 **Alt Fuels Advisor**
Alexander Communications Group
1916 Park Ave
8th Floor, Suite 501
New York, NY 10037-3733
212-281-6099
800-232-4317
Fax: 212-283-7269
Home Page: www.altfuels.com
Romauld Alexander, Owner
Laurence Alexander, CEO
News and developments in alternative fuel vehicles, including natural gas, propane, CNG, ethanol, electric, hybrid and fuel cells. Alt Fuels brings together news of technical and business developments, usage, infrastructure and regulations for all types of alternative and clean fuel vehicles.
Cost: $367.00
Frequency: Monthly
ISSN: 1528-6746

2461 **American Rodder**
Buckaroo Communications
701 Arcturus Avenue
Oxnard, CA 93033
805-986-0400
866-515-5600
Fax: 810-735-6765
Home Page: www.superrod.com
Gerry Burgel, Editor
Debby Wheeler, Customer Service
Covers the street-rod and custom-car industries. Accepts advertising.
Cost: $39.99
100 Pages

2462 **Auto Laundry News**
EW Williams Publications
2125 Center Ave
Suite 305
Fort Lee, NJ 07024-5898
201-592-7007
Fax: 201-592-7171
E-Mail: philpl@ewwpi.com
Home Page: www.williamspublications.com
Andrew Williams, President
Stefan Budricks, Editor
Janys Kuznier, Circulation Director
Provides technical, operational, marketing, advertising, and managerial information for owners, operators, and investors in self services and automatic carwashes, as well as auto detailing information.
Cost: $56.00
Frequency: Monthly
Circulation: 17292
Founded in 1953

2463 **Auto Remarketing**
Cherokee Publishing Company
301 Cascade Pointe Ln
Cary, NC 27513-5778
919-674-6020
800-608-7500
Fax: 919-674-6027
Home Page: www.autoremarketing.com
Ron Smith, CEO
Reports on changes in the automotive industry and their effects on the buying and selling of cars.
Cost: $24.95
Frequency: Monthly
Circulation: 22000
Founded in 1990

2464 **Auto Rental News**
Bobit Business Media

3520 Challenger St
Torrance, CA 90503-1640

310-533-2400
Fax: 310-533-2500
Home Page: www.bobit.com

Edward J Bobit, CEO
Cathy Stephens, Executive Editor

For those involved in the renting of cars and trucks.
Cost: $30.00
Frequency: Monthly
Circulation: 16000

2465 Auto Trim and Restyling News
Bobit Publishing
3520 Challenger St
Torrance, CA 90503-1640

310-533-2400
800-241-9034
Fax: 310-533-2500
Home Page: www.bobit.com

Edward J Bobit, CEO
Travis Weeks, Group Publisher

Latest information on enhancing the appearance of cars with new upholstery, convertible tops and more.
Cost: $19.95
Frequency: Monthly
Founded in 1955

2466 AutoDealer
AIADA
211 N Union St
Suite 300
Alexandria, VA 22314-2643

800-462-4232
Fax: 703-519-7810
E-Mail: goaiada@aiada.org
Home Page: www.aiada.org
Social Media: Twitter

Jim Smail, Chairman
Ray Mungenast, Chairman-Elect
Jenell Ross, Vice Chair
Larry Kull, Secretary/ Treasurer
Cody Lusk, President

Offers members an in-depth look at America's international auto industry and provides thoughtful analysis of everything from cutting edge vehicle technology to legislation making its way through the halls of Congress. Features include exclusive interviews with auto executives, detailed political coverage, vehicle reviews, and member spotlights.
11M+ Members
Frequency: Quarterly
Founded in 1970

2467 AutoInc
Automotive Service Association
8191 Precinct Line Road
Suite 100
Colleyville, TX 76034-7675

817-514-2900
800-272-7467
Fax: 817-514-0770
E-Mail: asainfo@ASAshop.org
Home Page: www.asashop.org

Ron Nagy, Chairman
Darrell Amberson, Chairman-Elect
Frequency: Monthly
Founded in 1951

2468 AutoSmart
Aegis Group-Publishers
30400 Van Dyke Avenue
Warren, MI 48093-2368

586-574-3400
Fax: 248-447-7566
E-Mail: campbell-ewald@c-e.com
Home Page: www.campbell-ewald.com

Jim Palmer, President
Bill Ludwig, Chairman, CEO
Jeremy Morris, Publisher

Published for Delco Electronics for car company decision makers who deal with such systems.
Frequency: Monthly

2469 Autoglass
National Glass Association
1945 Old Gallows Rd
Suite 750
Vienna, VA 22182

703-442-4890
866-342-5642
Fax: 703-442-0630
E-Mail: nicole@glass.org
Home Page: www.glass.org

Phil James, CEO
Nancy Davis, Editor-in-Chief

Forum for owners, managers and distributors in glass replacement, repair, tinting, and also auto security fields. News and reports on insurance and legislative regulations. New product updates, news and technology information.
Cost: $24.95
Circulation: 7000
ISSN: 1047-2061
Founded in 1948

2470 Automotive Cooling Journal
National Automotive Radiator Service Association
3000 Villiage Run Road
Suite 103, #221
Wexford, PA 15090-6315

724-799-8415
800-551-3232
Fax: 724-799-8416
E-Mail: info@narsa.org
Home Page: www.narsa.org

Wayne Juchno, Executive Director
Douglas Shymoniak, Manager
Maarten Taal, President
Pat O'Connor, Vice President
Darlene Barlow, Secretary

Auto cooling system service data. Free to members.
Cost: $30.00
60 Pages
Frequency: Monthly
Circulation: 10000
Founded in 1956

2471 Automotive Design & Production
Gardner Publications
705 S Main St
Suite 200
Plymouth, MI 48170-2089

734-416-9705
Fax: 734-416-9707
E-Mail: daver@autofieldguide.com
Home Page: www.adp.com

Mike Vohland, Publisher
Lawrence S Gould, Contributing Editor
Rick Kline Jr, Publisher

Coverage of the automotive industry: suppliers, manufacturers from design through delivery.
Cost: $65.00
Frequency: Monthly
Circulation: 60,404
Founded in 1928

2472 Automotive Engineering International Magazine
Society of Automotive Engineers
400 Commonwealth Dr
Warrendale, PA 15096-0001

724-772-8509
877-606-7323
Fax: 724-776-9765
E-Mail: customerservice@sae.org
Home Page: www.sae.org

David Schutt, CEO
Kevin Jost, Editor
Brian Kaleida, Chief Information Officer

Cars, aircraft, trucks, off highway equipment, engines, materials, manufacturing and fuels have the Society of Engineers in common. The SAE is your one stop resource for technical information and expertise used in building, maintaining and operating self propelled vehicles for use on land, sea, air or space.
Cost: $120.00
125 Pages
Frequency: Monthly
Circulation: 124451
Founded in 1905

2473 Automotive Executive Magazine
National Auto Dealers Association
8400 Westpark Dr
Mc Lean, VA 22102-3591

703-821-7150
800-252-6232
Fax: 703-821-7234
E-Mail: msaldana@nada.org
Home Page: www.aemag.com

Tom Choy, Owner
Mark Stertz, President

Devoted exclusively to the automotive executive. Features that take on the new topics in the industry, and columns filled with practical, solid business advice for each dealership department.
Cost: $24.00
40 Pages
Frequency: Monthly
Circulation: 23000
Founded in 1917

2474 Automotive Fleet
Bobit Publishing Company
3520 Challenger St
Torrance, CA 90503-1640

310-533-2400
847-647-9780
Fax: 310-533-2500
E-Mail: Bobitpubs@halldata.com
Home Page: www.bobit.com

Edward J Bobit, CEO
Ty Bobit, President

Improvements in operational, purchasing and management responsibilities.
Cost: $35.00
Frequency: Monthly
Circulation: 21037
Founded in 1961

2475 Automotive Industries
Worldwide Purchasing Ltd
Versailles, KY 40383

313-262-5702
E-Mail: jal@autoindustry.us
Home Page: www.ai-online.com

John Larkin, Publisher
Ed Richardson, Editor
Ben Adler, Finance
Nick Palmen, Associate Publisher

Offers information for vehicle producers and suppliers worldwide.
Cost: $70.00
Frequency: Monthly
Circulation: 85000
Founded in 1895
Printed in on glossy stock

2476 **Automotive Manufacturing & Production**
Gardner Publications
6915 Valley Ln
Cincinnati, OH 45244-3153

513-527-8800
800-950-8020
Fax: 513-527-8801
E-Mail: rkline2@autofieldguide.com
Home Page: www.gardnerweb.com

Rick Kline Sr, CEO/Publisher
Richard Kline, VP

For engineers and managers who are concerned with improving manufacturing.
Cost: $89.00
110 Pages
Frequency: Monthly
Founded in 1934

2477 **Automotive News**
Crain Communications
1155 Gratiot Ave
Detroit, MI 48207-2732

313-446-0450
877-812-1584
Fax: 313-446-1680
E-Mail: customerservice@autonews.com
Home Page: www.autonews.com

Richard Johnson, Managing Editor
Jason Stein, Editor
Tony Merpi, Director Of Marketing
Victor Galvan, Web Editor

Covers the manufacturing side of the automotive industry, including engineering, design, production and suppliers, with equal emphasis on the retail side of the industry, including the marketing, sales, service and resale of vehicles.
Frequency: Weekly
Circulation: 79000

2478 **Automotive Recycling**
Automotive Recyclers Association
9113 Church Street
Suite 1
Manassas, VA 20110-5457

571-208-0428
888-385-1005
Fax: 571-208-0430
E-Mail: michael@a-r-a.org
Home Page: www.a-r-a.org

Michael E Wilson, CEO
Linda Pitman, President
Randy Reitman, Secretary

Offers information on the recycling of automobiles and automotive parts.
Cost: $40.00
Frequency: Bi-Monthly
Circulation: 1100
ISSN: 1058-9376
Founded in 1943
Printed in on glossy stock

2479 **Body Language**
Automotive Body Parts Association
1510 Eldridge Parkway
Suite 110-168
Houston, TX 77077

281-531-0809
800-323-5832
Fax: 281-531-9411
E-Mail: info@autobpa.com
Home Page: www.autobpa.com

Stanley Rodman, Executive Director
Nicholas Scheid, President

Published six times per year by the Automotive Body Parts Association, this newsletter keeps body shop operators and insurance industry executives up-to-date on the latest information concerning the manufacturing, distribution and importing of aftermarket body parts.
Cost: $80.00
146 Members
167 Pages
Circulation: 400
Founded in 1980

2480 **BodyShop Business**
Babcox Publications
3550 Embassy Pkwy
Akron, OH 44333-8318

330-670-1234
Fax: 330-670-0874
Home Page: www.babcox.com

Bill Babcox, Owner
Georgina Carson, Editor
Bob Bissler, Senior Editor

Devoted to helping collision-repair shop owners and managers run more profitable businesses. Editorially, BodyShop business covers all aspects of collision repair, with a focus on how-to topics include management, dimensioning, straightening, welding, refinishing, law and technology.
Cost: $64.00
Frequency: Monthly
Circulation: 60145
Founded in 1920

2481 **Brake & Front End**
Babcox Publications
3550 Embassy Pkwy
Akron, OH 44333-8318

330-670-1234
Fax: 330-670-0874
E-Mail: amarkel@babcox.com
Home Page: www.babcox.com

Bill Babcox, Owner
Andrew Markel, Editor
Brad Mitchell, Circulation/IT Director

Has monthly service articles that feature the latest information on brake, chassis, exhaust, front end, front-wheel drive and wheel alignment. Each issue also profiles the newest product and service offerings from aftermarket suppliers.
Cost: $64.00
Frequency: Monthly
Circulation: 40,310
Founded in 1920

2482 **Cars & Parts**
Amos Press
PO Box 4129
Sidney, OH 45365-4129

937-498-2111
800-448-3611
Fax: 937-498-0807
E-Mail: editorial@carsandparts.com
Home Page: www.amospress.com

Bruce D Boyd, CEO
Margie Bruns, Advertising Manager
Mark Kaufman, Associate Publisher

Focused to the serious collector car lobbyist. Each issue has an array of how-to articles, detailed coverage of feature cars and intriguing historical views of the auto companies and their most influential players. Additionally there are reports on major collector car shows and auctions including analysis of price trends on major categories of cars. Also included is a calendar of upcoming events: shows, auctions and swap meets. Finally, each issue has an extensive classified section.
Cost: $31.95
124 Pages
Frequency: Monthly
Founded in 1957
Printed in 4 colors on glossy stock

2483 **Counterman**
Babcox Publications
3550 Embassy Pkwy
Akron, OH 44333-8318

330-670-1234
Fax: 330-670-0874
Home Page: www.babcox.com

Bill Babcox, Owner
Jon Owens, Publisher

Targeted at the needs of the jobber sales team — those who buy and sell parts, services, equipment, build brand awareness, preference and loyalty by recommending parts to the DIY customer and professional technician.
Cost: $ 110.00
Frequency: Monthly
Circulation: 50,000
Founded in 1920

2484 **Dealer**
Horizon Communications
5201 Great America Pkwy
Floor 20, Suite 320
Santa Clara, CA 95054-1122

408-969-4888
Fax: 408-969-4895
E-Mail: jh@horizonpr.com
Home Page: www.horizonpr.com

Mike Roscoe, Publisher

Information for automobile dealers on service, parts, used car merchandising, financing, body shop, planning and risk management.
Cost: $35.00
Frequency: Monthly
Circulation: 21178
Founded in 1995

2485 **Destinations**
American Bus Association
111 K Street NE
9th Floor
Washington, DC 20002

202-842-1645
Fax: 202-842-0850
E-Mail: abainfo@buses.org
Home Page: www.buses.org

Peter J Pantuso, CEO
Brandon Buchanan, Director of Operations
Clyde J. Hart Jr, Senior Vice President
Eric Braendel, CFO

Motorcoach travel across North America and Association news.
80 Pages
Frequency: Monthly
Circulation: 6000
Founded in 1926
Printed in 4 colors on glossy stock

2486 **Diesel Progress: North American Edition**
Diesel & Gas Turbine Publications
20855 Watertown Rd
Suite 220
Waukesha, WI 53186-1873

262-754-4100
Fax: 262-754-4175
E-Mail: mosenga@dieselpub.com
Home Page: www.dieselspec.com

Michael Osenga, President
S Bollwahn, Circulation Manager

Geared towards readers interested in state-of-the-art systems technology. Features include new product listings, systems design, research and product testing as well as systems maintenance and rebuilding.
Frequency: Monthly
Circulation: 26,011
Founded in 1837

2487 **Double Clutch**
Antique Truck Club of America

PO Box 91
Imgomar, PA 15127
412-366-0392
Fax: 724-727-9768
Home Page: www.atca-inc.net/

Bill Powell, Publisher
Greg Matecko, Publisher

Magazine for antique truck enthusiasts.
Cost: $50.00
Founded in 1971

2488 Dual News Magazine
Driving School Association of the Americas
3125 Wilmington Pike
Kettering, OH 45429
800-270-3722
Fax: 937-290-0696
E-Mail: info@thedsaa.org
Home Page: www.thedsaa.org
Social Media: Facebook, Twitter

Sharon Postigo Fife, President
Robert Cole, Treasurer
Sheila Varnado, Executive VP
Debbie Prudhomme, Secretary

Keeping all driving school professionals informed of upcoming educational seminars, sharing ideas & opinions and introducing products and the like to driving educators. Represents a continuing commitment to the driving school industry.
58000 Members
Founded in 1973

2489 Engine Builder
Babcox Publications
3550 Embassy Pkwy
Akron, OH 44333-8318
330-670-1234
Fax: 330-670-0874
Home Page: www.babcox.com

Bill Babcox, Owner
Doug Kaufman, Editor

Business magazine serving the machine shop, custom engine, production engine and small parts rebuilding markets. It delivers editorial excellence that reflects the growing sophistication of the rebuilding industry and aids its readers in the profitable operation of their businesses.
Cost: $64.00
72 Pages
Frequency: Monthly
Circulation: 19500
Founded in 1920
Printed in 4 colors on glossy stock

2490 Engine Professional
Automotive Engine Rebuilders Association
500 Coventry Ln
Suite 180
Crystal Lake, IL 60014-7592
815-526-7600
866-326-2372
Fax: 815-526-7601
E-Mail: info@aera.org
Home Page: www.aera.org
Social Media: Facebook, Twitter

David Bianchi, Chairman
John Goodman, President
Dean Yatchyshyn, Treasurer
Dwayne J. Dugas, 1st Vice Chairman
Ron McMorris, 2nd Vice Chairman

Packed with highly technical, application-driven articles that will help you and your business thrive.
Frequency: Quarterly
Founded in 1922

2491 FLEETSolutions
National Association of Fleet Administrators
125 Village Boulevard
Suite 200
Princeton, NJ 08540
609-720-0882
Fax: 609-452-8004
E-Mail: info@nafa.org
Home Page: www.nafa.org
Social Media: Facebook, Twitter, LinkedIn

Phillip E. Russo, Executive Director

Contains educational articles based on the eight disciplines of the fleet management profession.
2600+ Members
Frequency: Bi-Monthly

2492 Family Motor Coaching Magazine
8291 Clough Pike
Cincinnati, OH 45244-2796
513-474-3622
800-543-3622
Fax: 513-474-2332
E-Mail: membership@fmca.com
Home Page: www.fmca.com

Don Eversman, Executive Director

Official publication of the Family Motor Coach Association, an organization for owners of self-contained motor homes. Publishes articles regarding motor home maintenance and repair, new products, travel destinations of interest to RV travelers and association news.
Cost: $24.00
Frequency: Monthly
Circulation: 98000

2493 Fleet Financials
Bobit Publishing Company
23210 Crenshaw Blvd
Suite 101
Torrance, CA 90505-3181
310-539-1969
Fax: 310-539-4329
E-Mail: mike.antich@bobit.com
Home Page: www.fleet-central.com

John Bebout, Owner

Features profiles of successfully managed fleets and analysis of lease verses company ownership.
Cost: $28.00
Frequency: Monthly
Circulation: 15500

2494 Global Connection
Automotive Parts Remanufacturers Association
4215 Lafayette Center Dr
Suite 3
Chantilly, VA 20151-1243
703-968-2772
Fax: 703-968-2878
E-Mail: mail@apra.org
Home Page: www.apra.org

William Gager, President
Jeanie Magathan, Sr. VP
Morris Spector, Director, Advertising & Marketing
Marlene Koskinas, Executive Assistant

Association newsletter provides members with information on the remanufacturing industry including product updates, news features and more.
Cost: $35.00
1000 Members
Frequency: Monthly
Circulation: 10000+
Founded in 1941

2495 Global Insight
Motor and Equipment Manufacturers Association
10 Laboratory Drive
PO Box 13966
Research Triangle Park, NC 27709-3906
919-549-4800
Fax: 919-406-1465
E-Mail: info@mema.org
Home Page: www.mema.org

Bob McKenna, President
Wendy Earp, VP
Frank Hampshire, Marketing

Member publication examines critical issues and challenges facing today's original equipment, aftermarket and heavy duty suppliers. Subscriptions and advertising available.
Frequency: Quarterly
Circulation: 2400
Founded in 1904

2496 Hemmings Classic Car
Hemmings Motor News
PO Box 4317
Bennington, VT 05201
802-442-3101
800-227-4373
Fax: 802-447-9631
E-Mail: hmnmail@hemmings.com
Home Page: www.hemmings.com

Formerly the Special Interest Auto magazine, features contemporary road tests and in-depth automobile profiles, automotive design, engineering, styling and historical exposes, how-to restoration and technical articles, and profiles on specialists and shops specializing in the collector-car industry.
Frequency: Monthly
Founded in 1954

2497 Hemmings Motor News
PO Box 100
Bennington, VT 05201
802-442-3101
800-227-4373
Fax: 802-447-9631
E-Mail: hmnmail@hemmings.com
Home Page: www.hemmings.com

Terry Ehrich, Publisher
Eileen Desmarais, Marketing

The bible of the car collector, this monthly magazine serves to enhance the experience of the car collector-enthusiast. Regular departments include vehicle and parts search, price checkers, dealers tips, hobby directory and more.
Cost: $31.95
Frequency: Monthly
Circulation: 210000
Founded in 1954

2498 ImportCar
Babcox Publications
3550 Embassy Pkwy
Akron, OH 44333-8318
330-670-1234
Fax: 330-670-0874
E-Mail: mdellavalle@babcox.com
Home Page: www.babcox.com

Bill Babcox, Owner
David Wooldridge, Publisher

Complete import service magazine. It is geared exclusively to the vehicle repair needs of import specialist technicians. The in-depth, technical nature of the magazine's editorial content helps technicians of all abilities do their jobs more efficiently and effectively.
Cost: $64.00
Frequency: Monthly
Circulation: 29190
Founded in 1979

2499 Independent Battery Manufacturers
401 North Michigan Avenue
24th Floor
Chicago, IL 60611

312-644-6610
Fax: 312-527-6640
E-Mail: info@thebatteryman.com
Home Page: www.thebatteryman.com

Founded in 1921

2500 International Collision Parts Industry Suppliers Guide
Automotive Body Parts Association
1510 Eldridge Parkway
Suite 110-168
Houston, TX 77077

281-531-0809
800-323-5832
Fax: 281-531-9411
E-Mail: info@autobpa.com
Home Page: www.autobpa.com

Stanley Rodman, Executive Director
Nicholas Scheid, President

Covers the collision replacement parts industry.
146 Members
64 Pages
Frequency: Quarterly
Circulation: 2300
Founded in 1980
Printed in 4 colors on glossy stock

2501 Journal of Quality Technology
American Society for Quality
600 N Plankinton Avenue
PO Box 3005
Milwaukee, WI 53201-3005

414-272-8575
800-248-1946
Fax: 414-272-1734
E-Mail: help@asq.org
Home Page: www.asq.org

Roberto M Saco, President
Paul E Borawski, Executive Director
Erica Gumieny, Sales
Fay Spano, Communications/Media Relations

Published by the American Society for Quality, the JQT is a quarterly, peer-reviewed journal that focuses on the subject of quality control and the related areas of reliability and similar disciplines.
Cost: $30.00
100M Members
Frequency: Quarterly
Founded in 1946

2502 LCT Magazine
Bobit Publishing Company
3520 Challenger St
Torrance, CA 90503-1640

310-533-2400
800-380-8335
Fax: 310-533-2500
E-Mail: webmaster@bobit.com
Home Page: www.bobit.com

Edward J Bobit, CEO

Serves the limousine agency owner.
Cost: $28.00
Frequency: Monthly
Circulation: 10000
Founded in 1961

2503 Limousine Digest
Digest Publications
29 Fostertown Road
Medford, NJ 08055

609-953-4900
Fax: 609-953-4905
E-Mail: info@limodigest.com
Home Page: www.limodigest.com

Chris Weiss, Publisher
Susan Rose, Assistant Publisher
Iric Cohen, President

Information for owners and operators of limousine, livery and transportation fleets, including day to day operational information, industry trends, product reviews, technical advances, as well as success stories.
Cost: $24.95
100 Pages
Frequency: Monthly
Circulation: 12500
ISSN: 1095-8436
Founded in 1990
Printed in 4 colors on glossy stock

2504 Locator
John Holmes Publishing Company
521 Main Street
PO Box 286
Whiting, IA 51063

712-458-2213
800-831-0820
Fax: 712-458-2687
E-Mail: sales@partslocator.com
Home Page: www.partslocator.com

John Holmes, President
Charis Lloyd, VP
Wendy Lloyd, Marketing Director
Stacy Phillips, Editor

Nation's leading auto and truck parts magazine.
Cost: $29.00
250 Pages
Frequency: Monthly
Circulation: 18500
Founded in 1957
Printed in 4 colors on newsprint stock

2505 Lubes-N-Greases
LNG Publishing Company
6105 Arlington Blvd
Suite G
Falls Church, VA 22044-2708

703-536-0800
Fax: 703-536-0803
E-Mail: info@Lngpublishing.com
Home Page: www.lngpublishing.com

Gloria Stienberg Briskin, Advertising Director
Nancy DeMarco, Publisher
Lisa Tocci, Managing Editor

The magazine of industry in motion.
Frequency: Monthly
Circulation: 17300
ISSN: 1080-9449
Founded in 1995
Printed in 4 colors on glossy stock

2506 Lubricants World
4545 Post Oak Place
Suite 230
Houston, TX 77027

713-840-0378
Fax: 713-840-8585

Kathryn B Carnes, Editor

Professional journal for those in the oil and grease industry.

2507 MOVE
AAMVA
4301 Wilson Blvd
Suite 400
Arlington, VA 22203-1867

703-522-4200
Fax: 703-522-1553
E-Mail: info@aamva.org
Home Page: www.aamva.org

Neil D. Schuster, President & CEO
Marc Saitta, Vice President & CFO

Provides members with practical and in-depth how-to information on a wide range of topics. Provides feature articles and departments that tackle issues facing today's administrators.
Frequency: Quarterly
Founded in 1933
Printed in 4 colors

2508 MOVE Magazine
American Assn. of Motor Vehicle Administrators
Executive Plaza, 11350 McCormick Rd
Suite 900
Hunt Valley, MD 21031

410-584-1955
Fax: 410-584-1998
Home Page: www.aamva.org

Linda Lewis-Pickett, President/CEO
Bonnie L Rutledge, Editor

Journal of the voluntary, nonprofit, educational organization. AAMVA represents the state and provincial officials in the US, Canada and Mexico, who are responsible for the administration and enforcement of laws pertaining to the motor vehicle and its use.
Cost: $26.00
Frequency: Quarterly
Circulation: 32000
Founded in 1996
Printed in 4 colors on glossy stock

2509 Market Analysis
Motor and Equipment Manufacturers Association
10 Laboratory Drive
PO Box 13966
Research Triangle Park, NC 27709-3966

919-549-4800
Fax: 919-406-1465
E-Mail: info@mema.org
Home Page: www.mema.org

Bob McKenna, President
Wendy Earp, VP
Frank Hampshire, Marketing

Provides an analysis of how the vehicles parts industry is affected by the economy including informative news topics such as producer price indexes for parts and accessories, market data and more.
Frequency: Monthly
Founded in 1904

2510 Modern Car Care
Virgo Publishing LLC
3300 N Central Ave
Suite 300
Phoenix, AZ 85012-2532

480-990-1101
Fax: 480-990-0819
E-Mail: jsiefert@vpico.com
Home Page: www.vpico.com

John Seifert, CEO
Kelly Ridley, Executive VP, CFO
Heather Wood, VP,Human Resources

Magazine for automotive professionals.
Frequency: Monthly
Circulation: 20000
Founded in 1986

2511 Motor Age
Chilton Company
300 Park Ave
Suite 19
New York, NY 10022-7409
212-751-3596
888-527-7008
Fax: 212-371-4058
E-Mail: info@advanstar.com
Home Page: www.chiltonfunds.com

Richard L Chilton Jr, Chairman, CEO
Michael Clark, President, COO

Features developments in the auto industry.
Cost: $14.00
Frequency: Monthly
Circulation: 143,000
Founded in 1992

2512 Motor Magazine
Hearst Business Communications
1301 Long Lake Road
Suite 300
Troy, MI 48098

248-585-1700
800-288-6828
Fax: 248-879-8603
E-Mail: motorbookscallcenter@motor.com
Home Page: www.motor.com

Duane Harrison, Owner
John Lypen, Editor
Richard Laimbeer, Publisher

Emphasis on repair and service end of automobile business for owners and managers.
Cost: $63.00
Frequency: Monthly
Circulation: 140000
Founded in 1903

2513 Motor Trend
Primedia
6420 Wilshire Boulevard
Los Angeles, CA 90048-5502

323-822-2201
Fax: 323-782-2467
Home Page: www.motortrend.com

Tom Rogers, CEO
Eric Schwab, Advertising Manager
Peter Clancey, Marketing Executive

Comprehensive magazine offers the latest information and news on the automotive industry.
Cost: $47.88
Frequency: Monthly
Circulation: 999999
Founded in 1988
Printed in 4 colors on glossy stock

2514 NADA'S Automotive Executive
National Automobile Dealers Association
8400 Westpark Dr
9th Floor, Suite 1
Mc Lean, VA 22102-3591

703-821-7000
800-252-6232
Fax: 703-821-7075
E-Mail: nadainfo@nada.org
Home Page: www.nada.org

Phillip D Brady, President
Rick Wagoner, CEO

Provides up to the minute legislative, regulatory and state association news, also includes product development and implementation, labor relations and the economic climate.
Cost: $24.00
Frequency: Monthly
Circulation: 21850
Founded in 1975

2515 NAPA Outlook
National Auto Parts Association
2999 Circle 75 Pkwy SE
Atlanta, GA 30339-3050

770-956-2200
877-794-9511
Fax: 770-956 2211
E-Mail: customersupport@napaonline.com
Home Page: www.napaautocare.com

Thomas C Gallagher, CEO

Ideas for business procedures for jobber store owners.
28 Pages
Frequency: Monthly
Founded in 1925

2516 NASCAR Performance
Babcox Publications
3550 Embassy Pkwy
Akron, OH 44333-8318

330-670-1234
Fax: 330-670-0874
E-Mail: dkaufman@babcox.com
Home Page: www.babcox.com

Bill Babcox, Owner
Doug Kaufman, Editor

Focuses on what goes on behind the scenes in NASCAR racing, and how that advanced technology transfers to automotive aftermarket applications. Professional NASCAR Garage is a quarterly supplement to all Babcox publications.
Founded in 1920

2517 National Oil & Lube News
National Oil & Lube News
4418 74th St
Suite 66
Lubbock, TX 79424-2336

806-762-4464
800-796-2577
Fax: 806-762-4023
E-Mail: info@noln.net
Home Page: www.noln.net

Garrett McKinnon, Editor
Steve Hurt, Co Publisher

Geared towards fast oil change and lubrication shop owners and managers. Information on the latest technology and environment concerns, also provides a link between shops and suppliers.
Cost: $29.00
76 Pages
Frequency: Monthly
Circulation: 17000
ISSN: 1071-1260
Founded in 1986
Printed in 4 colors on glossy stock

2518 New England Automotive Report
Thomas Greco Publications
PO Box 734
Neptune, NJ 07753

732-922-8909
Fax: 732-922-9821
E-Mail: setlit4u@msn.com
Home Page: www.aaspnj.org

Thomas Greco, Owner
Alicia D'Aquila, Editor
Charles Bryant, Executive Director

Provides reports on ideas, products and services to enhance collision repair productivity, also identifies insurance issues.
Cost: $48.00
85 Pages
Frequency: Monthly
Circulation: 4500
Founded in 1996
Printed in 4 colors on glossy stock

2519 Old Cars Weekly
F+W Media
38 E. 29th Street
New York, NY 10016

212-447-1400
Fax: 212-447-5231
E-Mail: contact_us@fwmedia.com
Home Page: www.fwpublications.com

Jim Ogle, CFO
Sara Domville, President
Chad Phelps, Chief Digital Officer
David Nussbaum, CEO

Covers the entire field of collectible automobiles - from classic touring cars and roadsters of the early 1900s to the popular muscle cars of the 1960s and 1970s. Includes historical perspectives and facts on cars and their manufacturers, and reports on attractions at upcoming shows. Regular columns include 'New Products,' 'Questions & Answers,' 'Show Biz,' 'Bookmobile,' 'Restoration Basics,' and an extensive classified word ad section. Hundreds of car show listings are included.
Cost: $41.98
64 Pages
Frequency: Weekly
Circulation: 63104
Founded in 1971

2520 PWA Conference
Performance Warehouse Association
41-701 Corporate Way
Suite 1
Palm Desert, CA 92260

760-346-5647
Fax: 760-346-5847
E-Mail: donnie@pedistributors.com
Home Page: www.pwa-par.org

Donnie Eatherly, President
John Towle, Executive Director
Larry Pacey, Chairman
Trent Lowe, Treasurer
Frequency: September

2521 Parking Magazine
National Parking Association
1112 16th St NW
Suite 840
Washington, DC 20036-4880

202-296-4336
800-647-7275
Fax: 202-296-3102
E-Mail: info@npapark.org
Home Page: www.npapark.org

Jeff Wolfe, Chairman
Mark Muglich, Chair Elect
Christine Banning, President

Published by the National Parking Association.
Cost: $99.00
2500 Members
Frequency: Monthly
Circulation: 4000
ISSN: 0031-2193
Founded in 1952
Mailing list available for rent: 2600 names at $250 per M
Printed in 4 colors

2522 Parts & People
Automotive Counseling & Publishing
899 Logan Street
Denver, CO 80203

303-765-4664
Fax: 303-765-4650
Home Page: www.partsandpeople.com

Lance Buchner, Owner
Rob Merwin, Editor

Collision and mechanical local and national news.
Cost: $36.00
Frequency: Monthly
Circulation: 59000
Founded in 1986

2523 Parts Plus Magazine
3085 Fountainside Drive
#210
Germantown, TN 38138

901-727-8112
800-727-8112
Fax: 901-682-9098
E-Mail: info@networkhq.org
Home Page: www.partsplus.com

Alan Bostwick, Executive VP

Published by the Association of Automotive Aftermarkets Distributors.
Cost: $29.95
Frequency: Monthly
Circulation: 5000
Founded in 1965

2524 Professional Carwashing and Detailing
National Trade Publications
19 British American Blvd. West
Latham, NY 12110-2197

518-783-1281
Fax: 518-783-1386
Home Page: www.carwash.com

Tracy Aston-Martin, Vice President
Sandy Murphy, Publisher

Provides technical and marketing information to professional vehicle washing owners, managers and investors. Accepts advertising.
Cost: $42.00
76 Pages
Frequency: Monthly
Circulation: 19000
Founded in 1976
Mailing list available for rent: 18M names at $125 per M
Printed in 4 colors on matte stock

2525 Professional Tool & Equipment News
1233 Janesville Avenue
Fort Atkinson, WI 53538

920-563-6388
888-966-3976
Fax: 920-563-1699
E-Mail: sales@pten.com
Home Page: www.vehicleservicepros.com

Larry Greenberger, Publisher
Jacques Gordon, Editor
Sara Shelstrom, Publisher

Information for personnel and owners of general and specialty repair shops, including buying tools and equipment, technological innovations, new systems, time saving ideas and product releases.
Cost: $32.00
Frequency: Monthly
Circulation: 105044
Founded in 1996

2526 Quality Engineering
American Society for Quality
600 N Plankinton Avenue
PO Box 3005
Milwaukee, WI 53201-3005

414-272-8575
800-248-1946
Fax: 414-272-1734
E-Mail: help@asq.org
Home Page: www.asq.org

James Rooney, Chair
Paul E Borawski, CEO
Erica Gumieny, Sales
Brian LeHouillier, Managing Director

Co-published with Taylor and Francis, this journal is for professional practitioners and researchers whose goal is quality engineering improvements and solutions.
Cost: $34.75
100M Members
Frequency: Quarterly/Members Price
Founded in 1946

2527 Quality Management Journal
American Society for Quality
600 N Plankinton Avenue
PO Box 3005
Milwaukee, WI 53201-3005

414-272-8575
800-248-1946
Fax: 414-272-1734
E-Mail: help@asq.org
Home Page: www.asq.org

James Rooney, Chair
Paul E Borawski, CEO
Erica Gumieny, Sales
Brian LeHouillier, Managing Director

Published by the American Society for Quality, the QMT is a quarterly, peer-reviewed journal that focuses on the subject of quality management practice and provides a discussion forum for both practitioners and academics in the area of research.
Cost: $50.00
100M Members
Frequency: Quarterly
Founded in 1946

2528 Quality Progress
American Society for Quality
600 N Plankinton Avenue
PO Box 3005
Milwaukee, WI 53201-3005

414-272-8575
800-248-1946
Fax: 414-272-1734
E-Mail: help@asq.org
Home Page: www.asq.org

James Rooney, Chair
Paul E Borawski, CEO
Erica Gumieny, Sales
Brian LeHouillier, Managing Director

Published by the American Society for Quality, the QP is a peer-reviewed journal that focuses on the subject of quality control, discussing the usage and implementation of quality principles including the subject areas of organizational behavior, knowledge management and process improvement.
Cost: $55.00
100M Members
Founded in 1946

2529 RV Trade Digest
Cygnus Publishing
1233 Janesville Avenue
Fort Atkinson, WI 53538

920-000-1111
800-547-7377
Fax: 920-563-1699
E-Mail: editor@rvtradedigest.com
Home Page: www.cygnusb2b.com

John French, CEO
Tom Kohn, Executive Vice President
Paul Caplan, Senior Vice President
Paul Bonaiuto, CFO

Offers in-depth information to a trade audience of business professionals actively engaged in the manufacture, distribution and sales of RVs, supplies and accessories.
Cost: $40.00
Frequency: 9 issues (1year
Circulation: 16055
Founded in 1966
Printed in 4 colors on glossy stock

2530 Recyclers Power Source
PO Box 556
Spirit Lake, IA 51360

712-336-5614
800-336-5614
Fax: 712-336-5617
E-Mail: jstahly@qwestoffice.net
Home Page: www.rpowersource.com

Laura Kabele
Julie Stahly

Purchasing guide for automotive recycling.
Frequency: Monthly

2531 SAE Off-Highway Engineering
Society of Automotive Engineers
400 Commonwealth Dr
Warrendale, PA 15096-0001

724-776-4841
877-606-7323
Fax: 724-776-0790
E-Mail: sohe@sae.org
Home Page: www.sae.org

David Schutt, CEO
Brian Kaleida, Chief Information Officer

Member services and news, as well as activities including meetings, professional development seminars, publication introductions and education programs.
Cost: $70.00
Frequency: Monthly
Circulation: 58263
Founded in 1905

2532 SEMA News
Performance Aftermarket Publishers
1575 South Valley Vista Drive
Diamond Bar, CA 91765

909-860-2030
Fax: 909-860-0184
E-Mail: editors@semanews.com
Home Page: www.sema.org

Christopher Kersting, President
Peter MacGillivray, VP Communications

Covers specialty and performance segment of autos with the Auto Aftermarket, Specialty Equipment and Marketing Association.
Cost: $39.95
96 Pages
Frequency: Monthly
Circulation: 35000
Founded in 1988
Printed in 4 colors on matte stock

2533 School Bus Fleet
Bobit Publishing Company
3520 Challenger St
Torrance, CA 90503-1640

310-533-2400
Fax: 310-533-2500
E-Mail: sbf@bobit.com
Home Page: www.bobitbusinessmedia.com; www.schoolbusfleet.com
Social Media: Facebook, Twitter, LinkedIn

Edward J Bobit, CEO
Mark Hollenbeck, Associate Publisher
Frank DiGiacomo, Publisher

Published for persons involved with the transportation of school children grades K-12, includes articles on lowering costs, improving fleet operations, scheduling techniques, vehicle maintenance and federal regulatory issues.
Cost: $25.00
Frequency: Monthly
Circulation: 22000
Founded in 1961

2534 Software Quality Professional
American Society for Quality
600 N Plankinton Avenue
PO Box 3005
Milwaukee, WI 53201-3005
414-272-8575
800-248-1946
Fax: 414-272-1734
E-Mail: help@asq.org
Home Page: www.asq.org

James Rooney, Chair
Paul E Borawski, ASQ CEO
Erica Gumieny, Sales
William Mc Bee III, Treasurer
Brian Houillier, Managing

Published by the American Society for Quality, the SQP is a quarterly, peer-reviewed journal for software development professionals that focuses on the subject of quality practice principles in the implementation of software and the

development of software systems.
Cost: $45.00
100M Members
Frequency: Quarterly
Founded in 1946

2535 **Specialty Automotive Magazine**
Meyers Publishing
799 Camarillo Springs Rd
Camarillo, CA 93012-9468

805-445-8881
Fax: 805-445-8882
E-Mail: len@meyerspublishing.com
Home Page: www.meyerspublishing.com

Len Meyers, Owner
Len Meyers, Publisher
Andrew Meyers, Associate Publisher
Harriet Kaplan, Assistant Editor

For accessories and performance specialists, dedicated for car and truck product suppliers and installers. Various fatermaker segments are covered: street, track, van, truck, and off-road. Features cover: technology and trends, performance retailing, new product showcases, upgrade news, trade shows, legislation, advertising, OEM's industry news, and people on the move.
Cost: $10.00
Frequency: Monthly
Circulation: 25000
ISSN: 0894-7414
Founded in 1983
Printed in 4 colors on glossy stock

2536 **Sport Truck & SUV Accessory Business**
Cygnus Publishing
1233 Janesville Avenue
Fort Atkinson, WI 53538

920-000-1111
800-547-7377
Fax: 920-563-1699
Home Page: www.cygnusb2b.com

John French, CEO
Pat Walker, Editor
Tom Kohn, Executive Vice President
Founded in 1966

2537 **Supercharger**
Detroit Section Society of Automotive Engineers
28535 Orchard Lake Road
Suite 200
Farmington Hills, MI 48334

248-324-4445
Fax: 248 324 4449
E-Mail: jjablonski@sae-detroit.org
Home Page: www.sae-detroit.org

Charon Morgan, Chair
Terry Rhoades, Treasurer

The official publication of SAE Detroit Section that brings members together with news of upcoming tours, technical meetings, events and more.
Circulation: 16000
Printed in on glossy stock

2538 **Tire Retread Information Packet & Buyers Guide**
Tire Retread and Repair Information Bureau
1013 Birch Street
Falls Church, VA 22046

703-533-7677
877-394-6811
Fax: 703-533-7678
E-Mail: info@retread.org
Home Page: www.retread.org

David Stevens, Managing Director
Bob Majewski, President
Eddie Burleson, Vice President
Phil Boarts, Secretary/Treasurer
Norm Ball, Director

Published by the Tire Retread Information Bureau.
380 Pages
Frequency: Weekly
Founded in 1972

2539 **Tire Review**
Babcox Publications
3550 Embassy Pkwy
Akron, OH 44333-8318

330-670-1234
Fax: 330-670-0874
E-Mail: bbabcox@babcox.com
Home Page: www.babcox.com

Bill Babcox, Owner
David Modiz, Group Publisher
Dave Wooldridge, Publisher

Designed to assist the independent retail tire dealer in his number one concern — profitability. It focuses on pricing strategies, marketing and effective advertising to meet the challenges of today's industry.
Cost: $64.00
84 Pages
Frequency: Monthly
Founded in 1902

2540 **Tow Times**
TT Publications
203 West SR 434
Winter Springs, FL 32708

407-327-4817
800-308-3745
Fax: 407-327-2603
E-Mail: news@towtimes.com
Home Page: www.towtimes.com

Clarissa Powell, Publisher
Tim Jackson, Editor
Dave Jones, President

Edited to review various aspects of the towing and road services. Accepts advertising.
Cost: $34.00
56 Pages
Frequency: Monthly
Founded in 1983

2541 **Toy Cars & Models**
F+W Media
38 E. 29th Street
New York, NY 10016

212-447-1400
Fax: 212-447-5231
E-Mail: contact_us@fwmedia.com
Home Page: www.fwmedia.com

Jim Ogle, CFO
Sara Domville, President
Chad Phelps, Chief Digital Officer
David Nussbaum, CEO

Provides comprehensive coverage of the model car hobby without bias toward scale, subject, manufacturer or material. Offers columns and news stories featuring models made of die-cast, white metal, plastic, resin and more while getting readers in touch with the manufacturers, distributors and retailers who sell these model cars. Monthly giveaways, reader polls and an active letters column give readers a chance to participate in their hobby.
Cost: $29.98
88 Pages
Frequency: Monthly
Circulation: 17916
Founded in 1998

2542 **Traffic Injury Prevention**
AAAM
PO Box 4176
Barrington, IL 60011-4176

847-844-3880
Fax: 847-844-3884
E-Mail: info@aaam.org
Home Page: www.aaam.org

Brian N. Fildes, Ph.D, President
Mary Pat McKay, MD, President-Elect
Kristy B. Arbogast, Ph.D, Secretary
Frances D. Bents, Treasurer

Bridging the disciplines of medicine, engineering, public health and traffic safety in order to foster the science of traffic injury prevention. The journal focuses on research, interventions and evaluations within the areas of traffic safety, crash causation, injury prevention and treatment.
Frequency: 6x Yearly
ISSN: 1538-9588
Founded in 1957

2543 **Truck & SUV Performance**
Bobit Publishing Company
3520 Challenger St
Torrance, CA 90503-1640

310-533-2400
Fax: 310-533-2500
E-Mail: travis.weeks@bobit.com
Home Page: www.bobit.com

Edward J Bobit, CEO
John Jeffries, Editor
Circulation: 32,000
Founded in 1961

2544 **Underhood Service**
Babcox Publications
3550 Embassy Pkwy
Akron, OH 44333-8318

330-670-1234
Fax: 330-670-0874
E-Mail: bbabcox@babcox.com
Home Page: www.babcox.com

Bill Babcox, CEO
Jeff Stankard, VP/ Group Publisher
Jennifer McMullen, Managing Editor

Meets the special needs of those technicians where most of their jobs involve the service and repair of under-the-hood systems. Answers the challenge of a continuing expansion of automotive technology.
Cost: $64.00
Frequency: Monthly
Circulation: 40500
Founded in 1920

2545 **Used Car Dealer Magazine**
Nat'l Independent Automobile Dealers Association
2521 Brown Boulevard
Arlington, TX 76006-5203

817-492-2377
800-682-3837
Fax: 817-649-5866
Home Page: www.niada.com/

Michael R Linn, CEO/Publisher
Michael Harbour, Editor
Angela Ledbetter, Executive Assistant
Adrianne Argumaniz, Publication Manager

Information on auctions, profit center opportunities, trends in used car market, and updates on legislation. Coverage on association membership and the entire used vehicle industry.
Cost: $36.00
Circulation: 15000
Founded in 1946
Printed in 4 colors on glossy stock

2546 **Ward's Autoworld**
Ward's Communications

3000 Town Center
Suite 2750
Southfield, MI 48075-1245

248-799-2622
Fax: 248-357-9747
E-Mail: wards@wardsauto.com
Home Page: www.wardsauto.com

Thomas Duncan, Publisher
Drew Winter, Editor

News and analysis for automotive OEM professionals.
Cost: $55.00
130 Pages
Frequency: Monthly
Circulation: 102000
ISSN: 0043-0315
Founded in 1924
Mailing list available for rent: 99,000 names
Printed in 4 colors on glossy stock

2547 **Ward's Dealer Business**
Ward's Communications
3000 Town Center
Suite 2750
Southfield, MI 48075-1245

248-799-2622
Fax: 248-357-9747
E-Mail: wards@wardsauto.com
Home Page: www.wardsdealer.com

Thomas Duncan, Group Publisher
Drew Winter, Editor
Tony Noland, CEO
James Bush, Managing Director

News and analysis for auto dealership professionals.
80 Pages
Frequency: Monthly
Circulation: 27000
ISSN: 1086-1629
Founded in 1924
Mailing list available for rent: 98,861 names
Printed in 4 colors

Trade Shows

2548 **AAIW: Automotive Aftermarket Industry Week Expo**
Overseas Automotive Council
10 Laboratory Drive
Po Box 13966
Reserach Triangle, NC 27709-3966

919-549-4800
Fax: 919-549-4824
E-Mail: media@mema.org
Home Page: www.oac-intl.org

Jeremy Denton, Show Management

Containing 2,500 exhibits.
100M+ Attendees
Frequency: November

2549 **AAMVA Annual International Conference**
American Assoc. of Motor Vehicle Administrators
4301 Wilson Boulevard
Suite 400
Arlington, VA 22203
703-522-4200
Fax: 703-522-1553
E-Mail: info@aamva.org
Home Page: www.aamva.org

Neil D Schuster, President
Marc Saitta, VP &CFO
Kathy King, Director Business Services

The annual conference of the American Association of Motor Vehicle Administrators during August that provides numerous exhibits, programs and presentations and the opportunity for members to meet and network with colleagues.
800 Attendees
Frequency: August
Founded in 1933

2550 **ABPA Trade Show Fair**
Automotive Body Parts Association
1510 Eldridge Parkway
Suite 110-168
Houston, TX 77077

281-531-0809
800-323-5832
Fax: 281-531-9411
E-Mail: info@autobpa.com
Home Page: www.autobpa.com

Stanley Rodman, Executive Director
Dolores Richardson, President

Trade show with 35 exhibitors and over 43 booths.
146 Members
Frequency: September
Founded in 1980

2551 **AFLA Annual Meeting and Conference**
Automotive Fleet and Leasing Association
1000 Westgate Drive
St Paul, MN 55114

651-203-7247
Fax: 651-290-2266
E-Mail: info@aflaonline.com
Home Page: www.aflaonline.com

Theresa Belding, President
John Dmochowsky, VP
Edward Bobit, Executive Director

Providing the opportunity and a forum for the exchange of information and ideas between related segments of the fleet industry.
300 Members
300 Attendees
Frequency: September
Founded in 1969

2552 **AIAG AutoTech Conference**
Automotive Industry Action Group
26200 Lahser Road
Suite 200
Southfield, MI 48033

248-358-3003
Fax: 248-799-7995
E-Mail: inquiry@aiag.org
Home Page: www.aiag.org

Jhon Batchik, Chairman
David Kneisler, Vice Chairman

It's a venue where the collaboration between OEMs and suppliers is showcased through educational sessions, product and service exhibits and demonstrations, and networking opportunities.
3000 Attendees
Founded in 1982

2553 **AOCA Annual Convention & Fast Lube Expo**
Automotive Oil Change Association
1701 North Greenville Avenue
Suite 404
Richardson, TX 75081

972-458-9468
800-331-0329
Fax: 972-458-9539
E-Mail: info@aoca.org
Home Page: www.aoca.org

Pat Wirth, President
Randy Groover, VP
Bob Falter, Director
LeeAnn Stump, Executive Director

Brings hundreds of vendors offering thousands of products and services to the fast lube industry and ancillary profit centers.
3000 Members
Frequency: Annual/April-May
Founded in 1987

2554 **ARA Annual Convention & Exposition**
Automotive Recyclers Association
9113 Church Street
Manassas, VA 20110

571-208-0428
888-385-1005
Fax: 571-208-0430
E-Mail: michael@a-r-a.org
Home Page: www.a-r-a.org

Michael Wilson, CEO
Kim Glasscock, Meetings & Expositions

Automotive recycling trade show. Containing over 150 booths and more than 100 exhibits. The 2006 trade show is scheduled for September 27th to September 30th in Indianapolis, Indiana and the 2007 trade show is scheduled for September 26th to September 29th in Orlando, Florida.
800 Attendees
Frequency: Annual/September

2555 **ARTA Powertrain Expo**
Automatic Transmission Rebuilders Association
2400 Latigo Avenue
Oxnard, CA 93030

805-604-2000
866-464-2872
Fax: 805-604-2003
E-Mail: dmadden@atra.com
Home Page: www.atra.com

Dennis Madden, CEO
Jim Lyons, VP
Lance Wiggins, Director

Speakers on many subjects, providing information and tips for those within the transmission repair industry. Event provides the opportunity for members to meet and network.
2000 Members
Frequency: September
Founded in 1954

2556 **ASA Annual Convention**
Automotive Service Association
8190 Precinct Line Road
Suite 100
Colleyville, TX 76034-7675

817-514-2900
800-272-7467
Fax: 817-514-0770
E-Mail: asainfo@ASAshop.org
Home Page: www.asashop.org

Ron Pyle, President/Chief Staff Executive
Toni Slanton, Executive Director
Jhon Scully, Senior Vice President
Linda Ferguson, Program Administrator
Frequency: April/May

2557 **American Engine Rebuilders Association Expo**
American Engine Rebuilders Association
500 Coventry Lane
Suite 180
Crystal Lake, IL 60014

815-526-7600
888-326-2372
Fax: 815-526-7601
E-Mail: info@aera.org
Home Page: www.aera.org

John Goodman, President
Dwayne J. Dugas, Chairman
Ron McMorris, First Vice Chairman
David Bianchi, Treasurer

550 exhibits with automotive services equipment, parts, tools, supplies and services. Seminar and dinner also offered.
6000 Attendees
Frequency: Annual
Founded in 1974

2558 American Public Transportation Association Expo
American Public Transit Association
1666 K Street NW
Suite 1100
Washington, DC 20006
202-496-4800
Fax: 202-496-4324
E-Mail: meetings2@apta.com
Home Page: www.apta.com
Michael Melaniphy, President
Gary Thomas, Chair
Rosemary Sheridan, Marketing
Karen W. Harvey, Director Human Resources
Industry leaders from around the globe attend to meet suppliers of the latest public transportation products, services, and technologies designed to enhance the passenger experience and make your transit system more efficient and profitable.
15000 Attendees
Frequency: October 2008/2011
Founded in 1882

2559 Annual Lean Six Sigma Conference
American Society for Quality
600 N Plankinton Avenue
PO Box 3005
Milwaukee, WI 53201-3005
414-272-8575
800-248-1946
Fax: 414-272-1734
E-Mail: help@asq.org
Home Page: www.asq.org
James Rooney, Chair
Paul E Borawski, Executive Director
Erica Gumieny, Sales
Fay Spano, Communications/Media Relations
An exclusive two-day briefing and networking event designed by and for the top practitioners in the Six Sigma community.
100M Members
Frequency: Annual/February
Founded in 1946

2560 Annual Quality Audit Conference
American Society for Quality
600 N Plankinton Avenue
PO Box 3005
Milwaukee, WI 53201-3005
414-272-8575
800-248-1946
Fax: 414-272-1734
E-Mail: help@asq.org
Home Page: www.asq.org
James Rooney, Chair
Paul E Borawski, Executive Director
Erica Gumieny, Sales
Fay Spano, Communications/Media Relations
Topics of interest include: new innovating audit/process approaches, value added involvement, corporate expectations, corporate/social responsibility, auditing in the overall corporate scheme.
100M Members
Frequency: Annual/October
Founded in 1946

2561 Annual Service Quality Conference
American Society for Quality
600 N Plankinton Avenue
PO Box 3005
Milwaukee, WI 53201-3005
414-272-8575
800-248-1946
Fax: 414-272-1734
E-Mail: help@asq.org
Home Page: www.asq.org
James Rooney, Chair
Paul E Borawski, Executive Director
Erica Gumieny, Sales
Fay Spano, Communications/Media Relations
The sessions we plan will help you to navigate through unpredictable consumer behavior and increasing competition to build a strong foundation for reaching superior levels of quality service.
100M Members
Frequency: Annual/September
Founded in 1946

2562 Annual World Conference on Quality and Improvement
American Society for Quality
600 N Plankinton Avenue
PO Box 3005
Milwaukee, WI 53201-3005
414-272-8575
800-248-1946
Fax: 414-272-1734
E-Mail: help@asq.org
Home Page: www.asq.org
James Rooney, Chair
Paul E Borawski, Executive Director
Erica Gumieny, Sales
Fay Spano, Communications/Media Relations
Conference focuses on quality and improvement with more than 2,000 exhibits and attendees. Keynote speakers and sessions discuss quality tools, techniques and methodologies. Provides the opportunity for members to meet and network with colleagues in the industry.
100M Members
Frequency: Annual/May
Founded in 1946

2563 Atlantic City Classic Car Show & Auction
Atlantic City Convention Center
One Convention Center Boulevard
Atlantic City, NJ 04801
609-449-2000
Fax: 609-449-2090
Home Page: www.acclassiccars.com
Social Media: Facebook, Twitter
Held annually, the AC Classic Car Show and Auction is the east coast's largest classic car show and auction.
60000 Attendees

2564 Auto Remarketing Convention
Auto Remarketing
Westview At Weston
301 Cascade Pointe Lane # 101
Cary, NC 27513
800-608-7500
Fax: 919-674-6027
Home Page: www.autoremarketing.com
Ron Smith, President
Executive conference focused on remarketing strategies for manufacturer, bank, finance, commercial and rental fleet/lease vehicles.
Frequency: February
Founded in 1996

2565 Automotive Aftermarket Products Expo
Automotive Aftermarket Industry Association
7101 Wisconsin Avenue
Suite 1300
Bethesda, MD 20814-3415
301-654-6664
Fax: 301-654-3299
E-Mail: aaia@aftermarket.org
Home Page: www.aftermarket.org
Kathleen Schmatz, President
Largest aftermarket trade show in North America, featuring over 1700 exhibitors of auto parts, accessories and services.
100M Attendees
Frequency: November

2566 Automotive Engine Rebuilders Association Expo
Automotive Engine Rebuilders Association
500 Coventry Lane
Suite 180
Crystal Lake, IL 60014-7592
815-526-7600
888-326-2372
Fax: 815-526-7601
E-Mail: info@aera.org
Home Page: www.aera.org
John Goodman, President
Dwayne J. Dugas, Chairman
Ron McMorris, First Vice Chairman
David Bianchi, Treasurer
Demonstrations of the industry's latest technology in equipment, tools, supplies, parts, and services for automotive, heavy-duty, industrial, high-performance, marine, and specialty engines. Featuring the leading national and international companies showcasing the latest new products and services in the world of engine building, remanufacturing, and installation.

2567 BCI Annual Convention
Battery Council International
401 N Michigan Avenue
24th Floor
Chicago, IL 60611-4267
312-644-6610
Fax: 312-527-6640
E-Mail: info@batterycouncil.org
Home Page: www.batterycouncil.org
Maurice A Desmarais, Executive VP
Ann Noll, Account Manager
Offers members the opportunity to exchange ideas and views with industry members from around the world in a working meeting atmosphere.
Frequency: Annual/Spring

2568 BSA Convention
Bearing Specialists Association
800 Roosevelt Road
Building C, Suite 312
Glen Ellyn, IL 60137
630-858-3838
Fax: 630-790-3095
E-Mail: info@bsahome.org
Home Page: www.bsahome.org
Social Media: LinkedIn
Linda Miller, President
Richard W Church, Executive Director
Jerilyn J Church, Executive Secretary
Kathy Fatz, Association Manager
Janet Arden, Publications Editor
The world's premier bearing industry event for authorized distributors of bearing products and services and the manufacturers of those products.
100 Members
Frequency: Annual
Founded in 1966

2569 BSA Winter Meeting
Bearing Specialists Association

800 Roosevelt Road
Building C, Suite 312
Glen Ellyn, IL 60137

630-858-3838
Fax: 630-790-3095
E-Mail: info@bsahome.org
Home Page: www.bsahome.org

Linda Miller, President
Jack Simpson, Vice President
Brian Negri, Treasurer
Kathy Fatz, Association Manager
Janet Arden, Publications Editor

BSA committees will be addressing many important issues and association projects at the Winter Meeting. Attending this meeting will help to influence the direction the industry takes over the coming years.
Frequency: Annual

2570 **Chicago Auto Show**
Chicago Automobile Trade Association
McCormick Place
2301 S Lake Shore Drive
Chicago, IL 60616

630-495-2282
Fax: 630-495-2260
Home Page: www.chicagoautoshow.com
Social Media: Facebook, Twitter, YouTube

Paul Brian, Director of Communications, CATA
Mark Bilek, Internet Director, CATA
Michelle Ferm, Communications Specialist, CATA
Dave Sloan, Auto Show General Manager
Sandi Potempa, Dir., Special Events & Exhibits

The Chicago Auto Show is the largest auto show in North America and has been held more times than any other auto exposition on the continent.
Frequency: Annual
Founded in 1901

2571 **Convergence Conference and Exhibition**
Society of Automotive Engineers
755 W Big Beaver
Suite 1600
Troy, MI 48084

248-273-2455
Fax: 24- 27- 249
E-Mail: pkreh@sae.org
Home Page: www.sae.org/convergence

Patti Kreh, Meetings, Exhibits Contact
Nori Fought, Meetings, Exhibits Contact
David Schutt, Chief Executive Officer

Serving the automotive and transportation electronics community by delivering relevant technology solutions and an electrifying line-up invited speakers and presenters.
8900+ Attendees
Frequency: October

2572 **Dayton Auto Show**
Hart Productions
60 N Second Street
Batavia, OH 45103

513-797-7900
877-704-8190
Fax: 513-797-1013
E-Mail: vicki@hartproductions.com
Home Page: www.hartproductions.com

Chip Hart, Show Management
Vicki Hart, Show Management
Vicki Diebold, Show Management
Trisha Marshall, Production Assistant
Victoria Hart, CFO

Annual auto show presented by the Dayton area Auto Dealers Association.
Frequency: March

2573 **Heavy Duty Aftermarket Week**
Association of Diesel Specialists
400 Admiral Boulevard
Kansas City, MO 64106

816-285-0810
Fax: 847-770-4952
E-Mail: info@diesel.org
Home Page: www.diesel.org
Social Media: Facebook, LinkedIn

Chuck Hess, President
Andy Girres, Vice President
Chuck Oliveros, Treasurer
Carl Ferguseon, Secretary
David Fehling, Executive Director

A distributor-focused business conference created by the industry's leading trade associations and marketing groups with a long-term goal of consolidating the many annual events on the industry calendar and to create the most valuable annual event for the heavy duty aftermarket. Heavy Duty Aftermarket Week is the largest North American gathering of the independent heavy-duty industry.
700+ Members
1800+ Attendees
Frequency: Annual/January
Founded in 1956

2574 **IAATI Annual Training Seminar**
International Association of Auto Theft Investigators
PO Box 223
Clinton, NY

315-853-1913
Fax: 315-883-1310
E-Mail: jvabounader@iaati.org
Home Page: www.iaati.org
Social Media: LinkedIn

Joe Broslus, President
John O'Byrne, VP
John V. Abounader, Executive Director
Marianne Finney, Marketing

Provides members who are auto theft investigators with resources to develop and maintain professional standards within the industry. Some of the topics covered range from arson and marine investigations to staged accident investigations. The 2012 seminar is in Kansas City, MO.
4904 Members
350 Attendees
Founded in 1952

2575 **International Autobody Congress and Exposition**
Hanley-Wood
8600 Freeport Parkway
Suite 200
Irving, TX 75063

972-366-6324
888-529-1641
Fax: 972-536-6445
E-Mail: krobinson@hanleywood.com
Home Page: www.naceexpo.com

Linsay Roberts, Director
Ellen Pipkin, Show Manager

Specifically created for professionals involved in all aspects of the collision repair industry.
15M Attendees
Frequency: November

2576 **International Big R Show**
Automotive Parts Remanufacturers Association
4215 Lafayette Center Drive
Suite 3
Chantilly, VA 20151-1243

703-968-2772
Fax: 703-968-2878
E-Mail: mail@apra.org
Home Page: www.bigrshow.com

William Gager, President
Jeanie Magathan, Sr. VP
Morris Spector, Director, Advertising & Marketing
Marlene Koskinas, Executive Assistant

Designed to attract rebuilders of a wide range of automotive and truck parts, exposing them to the key suppliers in this industry. Rebuilders specializing in electrical, c.v. joints, brake, clutch, transmissions, mechanical hydraulic, fuel systems, rack and pinion and air conditioning products will visit the show.
1000 Members
3000 Attendees
Frequency: November / Las Vegas, NV
Founded in 1941

2577 **LA Auto Show**
Los Angeles Convention Center
1201 S Figueroa Street
Los Angeles, CA 90015

213-741-1151
Home Page: www.laautoshow.com

The Los Angeles Auto Show is one of the top automotive events worldwide, bringing together the latest new vehicles from auto manufacturers around the world.

2578 **MACS Convention and Trade Show**
Mobile Air Conditioning Society Worldwide
225 S Broad Street
PO Box 88
Lansdale, PA 19446

215-631-7020
Fax: 215-631-7017
E-Mail: macsworldwide@macsw.org
Home Page: www.macsw.org

David Jack, Secretary
Elvis Hoffpauir, President, CEO
Mary Koban, Director
Andrew Fiffick, Chairman
Peter Coll, Treasurer
2000 Attendees
Frequency: Annual

2579 **NAAA Annual Conference**
National Auto Auction Association
5320 Spectrum Drive
Suite D
Frederick, MD 21703

301-696-0400
Fax: 301-631-1359
E-Mail: naaa@naaa.com
Home Page: www.naaa.com

Frank Hackett, Executive Director
Tom Dozier, Meetings Manager

Annual convention and exhibits of automobile and truck auction equipment, supplies and services.
Frequency: Fall

2580 **NADA Convention & Expo**
National Automobile Dealers Association
8400 Westpark Drive
Mc Lean, VA 22102-3522

703-217-7000
800-252-6232
Fax: 703-821-7075
E-Mail: nadainfo@nada.org
Home Page: www.nada.org

Gary Heimes, Convention Director
Stephen R Pitt, Executive Director, Convention
Phillip Brady, President

Providing automobile dealers with the latest in cutting edge technology, products and services they need to impact the future success of their businesses.
25000 Attendees
Frequency: January/February

2581 **NAFA Fleet Management Seminar**
National Association of Fleet Administrators
125 Villiage Boulevard
Suite 200
Princeton, NJ 08540

609-720-0882
Fax: 609-452-8004
E-Mail: info@nafa.org
Home Page: www.nafa.org

Phillip E Russo, Executive Director
Patrick McCarren, Deputy Executive Director
Joanne Marsdh, Director Marketing & Membership

Designed to provide comprehensive education to fleet managers like you who seek the fundamental principles and practices of successful fleet management.
3000+ Members
Founded in 1957
Printed in on glossy stock

2582 **NAFA Institute & Expo**
National Association of Fleet Administrators
125 Villiage Boulevard
Suite 200
Princeton, NJ 08540

609-720-0882
Fax: 609-452-8004
E-Mail: info@nafa.org
Home Page: www.nafa.org

Phillip E Russo, Executive Director
Patrick McCarren, Deputy Executive Director
Joanne Marsh, Director Marketing & Communications

To provide attendees and exhibitors alike with a more dynamic interaction on the exhibit hall floor and within concurrent sessions. An excellent opportunity to attend valuable education courses designed to benefit the veteran fleet professional as well as challenge first-time attendees!
3000+ Members
Frequency: April
Founded in 1957
Printed in on glossy stock

2583 **NARSA Annual Convention & Trade Show**
National Automotive Radiator Service Association
3000 Villiage Run Road
Suite103, #221
Wexford, PA 15090-6315

724-799-8415
800-551-3232
Fax: 724-799-8416
E-Mail: info@narsa.org
Home Page: www.narsa.org

Wayne Juchno, Executive Director
Douglas Shymoniak, Manager, Sales & New Business
Maarten Taal, President
Pat O'Connor, Vice President
Angelo Miozza, Treasurer

180 booths featuring seminars and workshops of parts, equipment and supplies.
1.8M Attendees
Frequency: Annual/November

2584 **NPA Annual Parking, Transportation and Services Convention & Expo**
National Parking Association
1112 16th Street NW
Suite 300
Washington, DC 20036

202-296-4336
800-647-7275
Fax: 202-296-3102
E-Mail: info@npapark.org
Home Page: www.npapark.org

Lawrence McFadden, Director Mktg/Business Development
Christine Banning, President
Heather Seiber, VP Marketing and Communications

Bringing together parking professionals from around the world with leading experts from business and industry to explore the latest trends and developments. The Convention also affords members an opportunity to share ideas and experiences and to explore the latest equipment and technologies at the Exposition.
Frequency: Annual
Founded in 1955
Mailing list available for rent: 1700 names at $250 per M

2585 **National Auto Glass Conference & Expo**
National Glass Association
1945 Old Gallows Rd
Suite 750
Vienna, VA 22182

703-442-4890
Fax: 703-442-0630
E-Mail: attend@glass.org
Home Page: www.glass.org

Phil James, President/CEO

Visit with over 50 companies and get informed about the latest technology and see products demonstrated live. Get answers to your technical questions and find out which solutions are right for your business.
800 Attendees
Frequency: Annual/May

2586 **National Independent Automobile Dealers Association Convention & Expo**
National Independent Automobile Dealers Assoc.
2521 Brown Boulevard
Arlington, TX 76006-5203

817-492-2377
800-682-3837
Fax: 817-649-5866
E-Mail: kimberly@niada.com
Home Page: www.niada.com

Ginger Barrientez, Director of Events
Michael R Linn, President/CEO
Steven Jordan, COO

75 booths including automobile aftermarkets and finance companies.
Frequency: June

2587 **National Quality Education Conference**
American Society for Quality
600 N Plankinton Avenue
PO Box 3005
Milwaukee, WI 53201-3005

414-272-8575
800-248-1946
Fax: 414-272-1734
E-Mail: help@asq.org
Home Page: www.asq.org

James Rooney, Chair
Paul E Borawski, CEO
Erica Gumieny, Sales
Fay Spano, Communications/Media Relations

Provides teachers, administrators, and support personnel opportunities to examine continuous improvement principles used in education. It provides resources and best practices to help you address requirements of No Child Left Behind, while helping you increase student achievement and improve overall performance.
100M Members
Frequency: Annual/November
Founded in 1946

2588 **New York International Auto Show**
Jacob Javits Center
655 West 34th Street
New York, NY 10001

718-746-5300
800-282-3336
Fax: 718-746-9333
Home Page: www.autoshowny.com
Social Media: Facebook, Twitter, YouTube

The show offers virtually every make and model vehicle sold in the US under one roof giving consumers the unique opportunity to see everything the auto industry has to offer. From fuel-sipping economy cars to million dollar supercars, NYIAS has something for everyone.
Frequency: Annual

2589 **North American Council of Automotive Teachers International Conference**
North American Council of Automotive Teachers
PO Box 80010
Charleston, SC 29416

843-556-7068
Fax: 843-556-7068
E-Mail: office@nacat.com
Home Page: www.nacat.com

Patrick Brown Harrison, President
Rob Thompson, Vice President
Curt Ward, Secretary
Chuck Ginther, Treasurer

Annual show of 70 exhibits and 50 seminars, suppliers, distributors, publishing companies and other trade organizations.
Frequency: July
Mailing list available for rent: 750 names at $165 per M

2590 **North American International Auto Show**
Detroit Auto Dealers Association
1900 W Big Beaver
Troy, MI 48084

248-643-0250
Fax: 248-637-0784
E-Mail: naiasmail@dada.org
Home Page: www.naias.com

Rod Alberts, Executive Director
William Perkins, Chair

Annual show and exhibits of new automobiles and trucks, concept cars and van conversions.
808M Attendees
Frequency: January
Founded in 1907

2591 **PERA Annual Conference**
Production Engine Remanufacturers Association
28203 Woodhave Road
Edwards, MO 65326

417-998-5057
Fax: 417-998-5056
E-Mail: nancieboland@pera.org
Home Page: www.pera.org
Social Media: Facebook, LinkedIn

Nancie J. Boland, Executive VP
Robert P. McGraw, President

An opportunity to exchange ideas, methods and procedures necessary to efficiently produce remanufactured products which are equal or superior to original products in quality and performance. PERA adheres to and supports the premise that its members are dedicated to the highest business ethics, customer satisfaction,

employee consideration and to the continual up-grading of the engine remanufacturing industry.
150 Attendees
Frequency: September / Seatle, WA
Founded in 1946

2592 **PWA Annual Conference**
Performance Warehouse Association
41-701 Corporate Way
Suite 1
Palm Desert, CA 92260

760-346-5647
Fax: 760-346-5847
E-Mail: christina@pwa-par.org
Home Page: www.pwa-par.org

John Towle, President
Larry Pacey, Chairman
Trent Lowe, Treasurer

This is an exclusive opportunity for manufacturers and distributors to meet in a private, businesslike environment to discuss sales and marketing policies and programs.
165 Attendees
Frequency: Annual/September
Founded in 1974

2593 **Performance Racing Industry Trade Show**
Performace Racing Industry
31706 South Coast Highway
Laguna Beach, CA 92651

949-499-5413
Fax: 949-499-0410
E-Mail: mail@performanceracing.com
Home Page: www.performanceracing.com

John Kilroy, Publisher/General Manager
Dan Schechner, Editor
Merredith Kaplan Burns, Managing Editor

Annual show. Features the latest in motorsports technology from 1400 companies with 4000 booths.
42000 Attendees
Frequency: Annual

2594 **Philadelphia Auto Show**
Philadelphia Convention Center
1101 Arch Street
Philadelphia, PA 19107

215-418-4700
Home Page: www.phillyautoshow.com
Social Media: Facebook, Twitter

Recognized by the industry as one of the top shows in the country, the Philly Auto Show displays more than 700 vehicles from a variety of manufacturers.
Frequency: Annual

2595 **RV Dealers International Convention & Expo**
Recreation Vehicle Dealers Association
3930 University Drive
Fairfax, VA 22030-2515

703-591-7130
Fax: 703-359-0152
E-Mail: info@rvda.org
Home Page: www.rvda.org

Mike Molino, CAE, President
Mary Anne Shreve, Editor

For RV retailers from across the U.S. and Canada.
Frequency: September
Mailing list available for rent: 1500 names

2596 **RVAA Executive Conference**
Recreational Vehicle Aftermarket Association
1833 Centre Point Circle
Suite 123
Naperville, IL 60563-9306

630-596-9004
E-Mail: info@rvaahq.org
Home Page: www.rvaahq.org
Social Media: Facebook, Twitter

Patrick Farrey, Executive Director
Laura Hallen, Account Executive
Michael Greskiewicz, Expo Sales Manager
Meg Pawelski, Events & Awards Manager
Danielle Griffin, Communications Manager

An event which allows members to meet with each other to develop strategies for the coming year. It's the perfect opportunity for you to make the contacts and have the important face to face meeting time, with the potential partners that will enhance your success.
Frequency: October
Founded in 1969

2597 **SAE International Truck & Bus Meeting and Exhibition**
Society of Automotive Engineers
755 W Big Beaver
Suite 1600
Troy, MI 48084

248-273-2455
877-606-7323
Fax: 248-273-2494
E-Mail: automotive_hq@sae.org
Home Page: www.sae.org
Social Media: Facebook, Twitter, LinkedIn, YouTube, Google +

Dr. Rodica Baranescu, President
David Schutt, CEO
Nori Fought, Conference Service Representative
John Miller, Program Developer
Jack Pokrzywa, Operations Director

100 booths featuring suppliers of parts and components.
2.5M Attendees
Frequency: November

2598 **SEMA International Auto Salon Trade Show**
Specialty Equipment Market Association
1575 South Valley Vista Drive
Diamond Bar, CA 91765

909-610-2030
E-Mail: showinfo@sema.org
Home Page: www.sema.org
Social Media: Facebook, Twitter, Google+

Christopher Kersting, President and CEO
Gary Vigil, Trade Show Director
Marel Del Rio, Trade Show Coordinator

When the sport-compact scene was just beginning, the show was launched to educate members about the growing market and to bring new buyers and opportunities to manufacturers.
Frequency: May
Founded in 1998

2599 **SEMA Offroad Convention**
Specialty Equipment Market Association
1575 South Valley Vista Drive
Diamond Bar, CA 91765-0910

909-610-2030
E-Mail: sema@sema.org
Home Page: www.phillyautoshow.com

Chris Kersting, President/CEO
Geoege Afremow, Vice President & CFO
Scooter Brothers, Chairman

Designed as a companion event to the well established SEMA Spring Expo, and as an extension of the SEMA Show, will target companies serving the recreational and performance off-road segments and aims to create new opportunities for this growing market.
Frequency: February

2600 **SEMA Show**
Specialty Equipment Market Association
1575 South Valley Vista Drive
Diamond Bar, CA 91765-0910

909-610-2030
Fax: 909-860-0184
E-Mail: sema@sema.org
Home Page: www.sema.org

Chris Kersting, President/CEO
Geoege Afremow, Vice President & CFO
Scooter Scooter, Chairman

The premier automotive specialty performance products trade event in the world featuring performance, accessories, restoration and motorsports products.
100M Attendees
Frequency: November

2601 **SEMA Spring Expo**
Specialty Equipment Market Association
1575 South Valley Vista Drive
Diamond Bar, CA 91765-0910

909-610-2030
E-Mail: sema@sema.org
Home Page: www.sema.org

Chris Kersting, President/CEO
Geoege Afremow, Vice President & CFO
Scooter Scooter, Chairman

The only trade show delivering the SEMA Show experience to the doorsteps of regional auto and truck parts and accessory businesses. We feature the leading companies that produce truck caps and accessories, automotive trim and restyling products, wheels and tires, gauges and instruments, performance parts and more.
Frequency: February

2602 **SIGM Annual Meeting**
Society of Independent Gasoline Marketers
3930 Pender Drive
Suite 340
Fairfax, VA 22030

703-709-7000
Fax: 703-709-7007
E-Mail: sigma@sigma.org
Home Page: www.sigma.org

Kenneth Doyle, Executive Vice President
Susan Crosby, Director, Communication & Education
Mary Alice Kutyn, Director of Meetings
Nancy Muskett, Director, Advertising & Sponsorship
Marilyn Selvitelle, Director, Business Development

SIGMA meetings are valuable and varied, addressing topics of interest for branded or unbranded motor fuel marketers, those interested in alternative fuels, fuel suppliers, and of course administrative and financial discussions for all types of organizations.
Frequency: October

2603 **SOUTHCON**
Wescon
1230 Rosecrans Avenue
Suite 100
Manhattan Beach, CA 90266

310-524-4100
800-877-2668
Fax: 310-643-7328
E-Mail: j.cruz@ecishow.com
Home Page: www.southcon.org

Joey Quesada Cruz, Show Management
Rod Mann, Conference Management

Issues that concern design, manufacturing and test departments. Instructors are leading experts in the topics they present.
10M Attendees
Frequency: February

2604 **Supernationals Custom Auto Show**
TNT Promotions Inc
PO Box 50386
Albuquerque, NM 87181-0386
505-480-0056
800-300-9381
Home Page: www.thesupernationals.com
The premier annual automotive event in New Mexico. Attracts prominent street rods and customs from throughout the country, as well as local and regional vehicles for both show and competition display.
25000 Attendees
Frequency: Annual/February
Founded in 1992

2605 **TIA World Tire Expo**
Tire Industry Association
1532 Pointer Ridge Place
Suite G
Bowie, MD 20716-1883
301-430-7280
800-876-8372
Fax: 301-430-7283
E-Mail: info@tireindustry.org
Home Page: www.tireindustry.org
Gary Albright, President & CEO
Lary Brandt, CEO
Mike Berra Jr, Vice President
Eddie Burleson, General Manager
Providing an ideal forum for diverse individuals to meet, network and advance new business and marketing opportunities. This world-class exhibition is the number one showcase dedicated to those who have an interest in tire, rubber and transportation services.
Frequency: April

2606 **WMDA Mega Show Annual Convention**
WMDA Service Station & Automotive Repair Assoc.
1532 Pointer Ridge Place
Suite G
Bowie, MD 20716
301-390-0900
800-492-0329
Fax: 301-390-3161
E-Mail: mgates@wmda.net
Home Page: www.wmda.net
Social Media: Facebook
Rick Agoris, President
Marta Gates, Director of Operations
Kirk McCauley, Director of Member Relations
Tirika Williams, Director of Finance
Featuring Over 225 Exhibits for the service station, automotive repair, car wash, convenience store & tire industries.
1500 Attendees

Directories & Databases

2607 **American Bus Association's Motorcoach Marketer**
American Bus Association
111 K Street NE, 9th Floor
Washington, DC 20002
202-842-1645
Fax: 202-842-0850
E-Mail: abainfo@buses.org
Home Page: www.buses.org
Thomas JeBran, President
John Meier, Vice Chairman
Frank Henry, Secretary/Treasurer
This directory is a comprehensive guide of the bus and travel industry offering information on hotels and sightseeing services, attractions, museums, restaurants and more.
500 Pages
Frequency: Annual
Founded in 1926

2608 **American Public Transit Association Membership Directory**
American Public Transit Association
1666 K St NW
Suite 1100
Washington, DC 20006-1215
202-496-4800
Fax: 202-496-4324
E-Mail: hbrett@apta.com
Home Page: www.apta.com
Michael Melaniphy, President/CEO
Petra Mollet, VP
Rosemary Sheridan, VP Communications and Marketing
A who's who directory of services and supplies within the public transportation industry.
Founded in 1882

2609 **Automotive Aftermarket Suppliers**
Automotive Aftermarket Suppliers Association
10 Laboratory Drive
PO Box 13966
Research Triangle Park, NC 27709-3966
919-549-4800
Fax: 919-549-4824
E-Mail: media@mema.org
Home Page: www.aftermarketsuppliers.org
Steve Handschuh, President
Chris Gardner, VP
Margaret Beck, Marketing and Communications
Directory of automotive supply chains and jobbers/retailers in North America. Also, warehouse distributors and major programmed distribution groups.
Founded in 1974

2610 **Automotive Parts Rebuilders Association Membership Directory**
Automotive Parts Remanufacturers Association
4460 Brookfield Corporate Drive
Suite H
Chantilly, VA 20151-1671
703-968-2772
Fax: 703-968-2878
E-Mail: magathan@buyreman.com
Home Page: www.bigrshow.com
William Gager, President
Morris Spector, Marketing
Lists member companies and their products, addresses, phone and fax numbers, key personnel and sometimes even internet information. Keep this directory, your network resource for the automotive parts rebuilding industry, on your desk throughout the year.
Cost: $35.00
Frequency: Annual
Founded in 1941

2611 **ELM Guide to Automakers in North America**
ELM International
PO Box 1740
East Lansing, MI 48826-1740
517-332-4900
Fax: 517-351-3032
E-Mail: contact_us@automotivesuppliers.com
The third edition of this guide contains more than 400 profiles that highlight the North American manufacturing operations of Chrysler, Ford, GM and all of the foreign owned automakers.
Cost: $350.00
Frequency: Semiannual

2612 **ELM Guide to Japanese Affiliated Suppliers in North America**
ELM International
PO Box 1740
East Lansing, MI 48826-1740
517-332-4900
Fax: 517-351-3032
E-Mail: contact_us@automotivesuppliers.com
Home Page: www.automotivesuppliers.com
Mark Santucci
Offers information on approximately 290 Japanese owned automotive original equipment components manufacturers that operate in North America.
Cost: $350.00

2613 **ELM Guide to US Automotive Sourcing**
ELM International
PO Box 1740
East Lansing, MI 48826-1740
517-332-4900
Fax: 517-351-3032
E-Mail: contact_us@automotivesuppliers.com
Mark Santucci, Executive Director
Two volumes offering information on automotive original equipment manufacturer parts and components suppliers and profiles of plants belonging to 576 companies.
Cost: $775.00
1200 Pages

2614 **NAFA's Professional Directory**
National Association of Fleet Administrators
125 Village Boulevard
Suite 200
Princeton, NJ 08540
609-720-0882
Fax: 609-452-8004
E-Mail: info@nafa.org
Home Page: www.nafa.org
Social Media: Facebook, Twitter, LinkedIn
Phillip E. Russo, Executive Director
Patrick McCarren, Executive Director
Mary Sticha, Vice President
Joanne Marsh, Director of Marketing
Gladys Reyes, Meeting & Event Planners
NAFA Member and Affiliate contact information.
2600+ Members
Frequency: Quarterly

2615 **Old Cars Price Guide**
F+W Media
38 E. 29th Street
New York, NY 10016
212-447-1400
Fax: 212-447-5231
E-Mail: contact_us@fwmedia.com
Home Page: www.fwpublications.com
Rick Groth, Publisher
Ron Kowalke, Editor
David Nussbaum, CEO
Sara Domville, President
The nation's most respected authority for pricing antique and collectible automobiles. The

extensive price-guide section covers makes and models of domestic cars, from AMC to Willys, from model years 1901 to 1994. Also included are light-duty trucks and selected makes of imported cars. Cars are valued in six conditions - from 'Excellent' down to 'Parts Car.' Also includes columns and features on collectible cars.
Cost: $19.98
148 Pages
Frequency: Monthly
Circulation: 61000
Founded in 1978

2616 PXN Parts Exchange New
15030 Avenue of Science, Suite 100
San Diego, CA 92128
858-946-1900; 800-669-4237
Fax: 858-946-1073
E-Mail: ICSCUser@audatex.com
Home Page: www.adpclaims.com
Social Media: Facebook, Twitter, LinkedIn, YouTube
Tony Aquila, Chairman, President & CEO
Jack Sanders, COO
Kamal Hamid, Director Investor Relations
Lisa Collins, Marketing Coordinator
Provides an electronic link from your ADP estimating system to comprehensive database of new replacement parts. Data on over three and a half million parts facilitates the writing of complete, cost-effective damage reports.

2617 RV Trade Digest
Cygnus Publishing
1233 Janesville Avenue
Fort Atkinson, WI 53538
920-000-1111; 800-547-7377
Fax: 920-563-1699
E-Mail: info@cygnus.com
Home Page: www.cygnus.com
John French, CEO
Paul Bonaiuto, CFO
Ed Wood, VP, HR and Communications
Kris Flitcroft, EVP-Residential, Construction, Mfg.
Blair Johnson, SVP, Business Development
Propriety BASE technology connecting businesses with multi-media content.
Cost: $40.00
40 Pages
Frequency: Bi-Monthly
Circulation: 15,000; Founded in 1983
Printed in 4 colors on glossy stock

2618 Transmission Digest Buyer's Guide Issue
MD Publications
PO Box 2210, 3057 E Cairo Street
Springfield, MO 65801-2210
417-866-3917; 800-274-7890
Fax: 417-866-2781
E-Mail: bmace@mdpublications.com
Home Page: www.mdpublications.com
Carol Langsford, President
Michelle Dickeman, Vice President
Bob Mace, Publisher
Gary Sifford, Editor
Mike Anderson, Advertising Sales
List of over 500 manufacturers and distributors of products and services for the motor vehicle transmission repair industry.
Cost: $15.00; Printed in 4 colors on glossy stock

2619 Ward's Automotive Yearbook
Ward's Communications
3000 Town Center
Suite 2750
Southfield, MI 48075-1245
248-799-2622
Fax: 248-357-9747
E-Mail: tduncan@wardsauto.com
Home Page: www.wardsauto.com
Social Media: Facebook, Twitter
Thomas Duncan, Group Publisher
James Bush, Managing Editor
David Zoia, Editorial Director
Drew Winter, Senior Editor
Chris Lamphear, Marketing Director
Directory of suppliers to the vehicle manufacturing industry. New vehicle sales, production and inventory data and new vehicle product information and statistics.
Cost: $475.00
500 Pages
Frequency: Annual
Circulation: 26,000
ISBN: 0-910589-15-1
Founded in 1938

2620 Who Makes It and Where Directory
Tire Guides
1101 S Rogers Circle, Suite 6
Boca Raton, FL 33487-2748
561-997-9229; *Fax:* 561-997-9233
E-Mail: tireinfo@tireguides.com
Home Page: www.tireguides.com
Nancy Garfield, Owner
James Garfield, Editor-in-Chief
Al Snyder, Contributing Editor
Jeff Chychrun, Associate Editor
Brand listings with manufacturer & distributor information; worldwide listing of web site addresses, fax numbers & U.S. toll free numbers.
Cost: $7.00
62 Pages
Frequency: Annual
Founded in 1950

2621 Worldwide Automotive Supplier Directory
Society of Automotive Engineers
400 Commonwealth Drive
Warrendale, PA 15086-7511
724-776-4841; 877-606-7323
Fax: 724-776-0790
E-Mail: customerservice@sae.org
Home Page: www.sae.org
Social Media: Facebook, Twitter, LinkedIn, YouTube, Google+
David Schutt, President
Michael Thompson, Publisher
Melissa Bachman, Marketing
Peggy Bartlett, Corporate Sales
Directory features 10,000+ supplier listings from every major vehicle-producing region. And, it is the ONLY directory to provide information on a company's technical capabilities.
Cost: $329.00
Frequency: Annual
Circulation: 60,550; ISBN: 0-768015-36-7

Industry Web Sites

2622 http://gold.greyhouse.com
G.O.L.D Grey House OnLine Databases
Grey House Publishing's online database platform, GOLD, offers Quick Search, Keyword Search and Expert Search for most business sectors including automotive and transportation markets. The GOLD platform makes finding the information you need quick and easy - whether you're a novice searcher or an experienced database user. All of Grey House's directory products are available for subscription on the GOLD platform.

2623 www.aaam.org
Assn for the Advancement of Automotive Medicine
A professional multidisciplinary organization dedicated entirely to motor vehicle crash prevention and control.

2624 www.aamva.org
American Assn. of Motor Vehicle Administrators
Nonprofit organization represents state and provincial officials in the US and Canada who administer and enforce motor vehicle laws. Strives to develop model programs in motor vehicle administration, police traffic services and highway safety.

2625 www.aflaonline.com
Automotive Fleet & Leasing Association
Designed to improve communications among buyers, sellers, fleet administrators, lending institutions, lessors, used vehicle marketers and allied automotive service companies.

2626 www.aftermarket.org
Automotive Aftermarket Industry Association
For those involved in the motor vehicle replacement parts industry.

2627 www.aiada.org
American Int'l Automobile Dealers Assocation
Lobbying and communications organization for American automobile dealerships that sell and service international nameplate brands.

2628 www.aiag.org
Automotive Industry Action Group
Composed of major North American vehicle manufacturers and their suppliers. Provides an open forum where members cooperate to develop and promote solutions that enhance prosperity in the automotive industry.

2629 www.aoca.org
Automotive Oil Change Association
Representing the convenient automotive service industry. Dedicated to enhancing the competency of fast lube owners, educating the public about services our members offer and maintaining a favorable business environment for the industry as a whole.

2630 www.apra.org
Automotive Parts Rebuilders Association
Association of more than 1,500 member companies engaged in the rebuilding of automotive related hard parts, including starters, alternators, clutches, transmissions, brakes, drive shafts and other parts for passenger cars, trucks, off road, equipment and industrial uses.

2631 www.asq.org
American Society for Quality
The world's leading authority on quality that creates better workplaces and communitites worldwide by advancing learning, quality improvement, and knowledge exchange to improve business results.

2632 www.atra-gears.com
Automatic Transmission Rebuilders Association
Not for profit professional organization dedicated to the improvement and welfare of the automatic transmission repair industry for the benefit of the motoring public.

2633 www.autobpa.com
Automotive Body Parts Association
Members are companies that distribute, supply or manufacture automotive replacement body parts.

2634 **www.autoconsulting.com**
Automotive Consulting Group
Management consulting firm providing top line and bottom line business performance improvement services to the worldwide automotive industry.

2635 **www.automotivefleetmgt.com**
Automotive Fleet Management Corporation
Formed in order that financial institutions such as banks, credit unions and finance companies could repossess and dispose of their automotive collateral in a manner that is quick, efficient and cost effective.

2636 **www.awda.org**
Automotive Warehouse Distributors Association
Oldest organized group of warehouse distributors and their respective suppliers of parts, accessories tools and other supplies for the automotive aftermarket. In January 2004, AWDA joined forces with the Automotive Aftermarket Industry Association.

2637 **www.buses.org**
American Bus Association
Trade association for the North American bus industry.

2638 **www.busesintl.com**
Buses International Association
An organization of persons throughout the world who are professionally involved in the management of companies or organizations which operate or manufacture buses.

2639 **www.carcare.org**
Car Care Council
A nonprofit 501 (c) (3) educational foundation whose purpose is to educate motorists about the importance of maintenance repairs and entertainment for safer, cleaner better performing vehicles. Provides editorial and public service material for media use.

2640 **www.classiccar.com**
ClassicCar.Com
Offers classic car enthusiasts around the world an online community with chats, forums and discussion groups.

2641 **www.diesel.org**
Association of Diesel Specialists
The worldwide diesel industry's leading trade association, dedicated to the highest level of service on diesel fuel injection and related systems.

2642 **www.edmunds.com**
Edmunds.Com
Founded in 1966 for the purpose of publishing new and used automotive pricing guides for automobile buyers.

2643 **www.filtercouncil.org**
Filter Manufacturers Council
For manufacturers of vehicular and industrial filtration products in North America. Active in efforts to educate people on proper disposal of used oil filters.

2644 **www.forecast1.com**
Forecast International
An electronic information/data service sourced from thousands of worldwide publications, in 15 languages. Provides concise passenger vehicles e-mail news and analysis summaries, news, trends and contract information with hyper-links to the source or a related website. Delivered 100 times a year.

2645 **www.greyhouse.com**
Grey House Publishing
Authoritative reference directories for most business sectors including automotive and transportation markets. Users can search the online databases with varied search criteria allowing for custom searches by product category, geographic area, sales volume, keyword, subject and more. Full Grey House catalog and online ordering also available.

2646 **www.hemmings.com**
Hemmings Motor News
Hemmings Motor News for the car collector and enthusiast.

2647 **www.iaati.org**
Int'l Association of Auto Theft Investigators
To improve communication and coordination among the growing family of professional auto theft investigators.

2648 **www.impa.org**
International Motor Press Association
Professional group of writers and editors producing auto articles for the press, radio or TV.

2649 **www.macsw.org**
Mobile Air Conditioning Society Worldwide
Provides technical training, information and communication for the professionals in the automotive air conditioning industry.

2650 **www.mema.org**
Motor and Equipment Manufacturers Association
Serves manufacturers of all types of automotive and truck products through market research, legislative and regulatory representation and reporting, information services, EDI network and credit reporting.

2651 **www.naaa.com**
National Auto Auction Association
Represents dealer wholesale auto auctions. Promotes exchange of ideas and public relations in the used car merchandising industry.

2652 **www.nada.com**
National Automobile Dealers Association
Provides representation for franchised new car and truck dealers in government, industry and public affairs. Provides counsel on legal and regulatory and political representation on Capital Hill.

2653 **www.nafa.org**
National Association of Fleet Administrators
Serving the needs of those managing fleets of automobiles, light duty trucks and/or vans for US and Canadian organizations. Offers statistical research, publications, regional meetings, government representation, conferences, trade shows and seminars.

2654 **www.narsa.org**
National Automotive Radiator Service Association
Trade association serving the cooling system service industry and the public.

2655 **www.nascar.com**
Turner Sports Interactive
Providing up-to-the-minute coverage on a 24-hour basis, NASCAR.COM delivers news, statistics and information on races, drivers, teams and industry events.

2656 **www.nationalwheelandrim.org**
National Wheel and Rim Association
Represents warehouse distributors of wheels, rims and related parts in the US and Canada.

2657 **www.ncsfa.state.ut.us**
National Conference of State Fleet Administrators
For state government administrators responsible for vehicle fleet management.

2658 **www.ntea.com**
National Truck Equipment Association
Represents small to mid-sized companies that manufacture, distribute, install, buy, sell and repair commercial trucks, truck bodies, truck equipment, trailers and accessories.

2659 **www.partsplus.com**
Association of Automotive Aftermarkets
Purchases and markets automotive replacement parts. Headquarters office for Parts Plus program distributors.

2660 **www.pera.org**
Production Engine Remanufacturers Association
The goal of the Production Engine Remanufacturers Association is to provide it's members with the opportunity to exchange the ideas, methods and procedures necessary to efficiently produce remanufactured products which are equal or superior to original products in quality and performance.

2661 **www.pwa-par.com**
Performance Warehouse Association
An organization of specialty automotive parts wholesalers joined together and dealing with management, financial and legislative matters.

2662 **www.retread.org**
Tire Retread Information Bureau
Serving as the public relations arm of the retread industry. Gathering and disseminating information on retread passenger and truck tires to members and the general public.

2663 **www.rma.org**
Rubber Manufacturers Association
National trade association for makers of tires and other rubber products.

2664 **www.rvda.org**
National RV Dealers Association
National association advances the best interests of RV retailers through education, services, leadership and programs of market expansion that promote increased use and sale of RVs as well as enhancement of the RV's image.

2665 **www.scrs.com**
Society of Collision Repair Specialists
For owners and managers of auto collision repair shops, suppliers, insurance and educational associates and suppliers in the US, Canada, Australia and New Zealand. Distributes technical, management, marketing and sales information. Works to promote professionalism within the collision repair industry.

2666 **www.theautochannel.com**
Auto Channel
Auto news, commentary and other useful information.

2667 **www.tireindusty.org**
Tire Industry Association
Representing all segments of the tire industry, including those that manufacture, repair, recycle, sell, service or use new or retreaded tires and also those suppliers or individuals who furnish equipment, material or services to the industry.

Associations

2668 Aero Safety & Maintenance Association
P.O. Box 182604
Columbus, OH 43272
202-383-2378
877-833-5524
Fax: 614-759-3749
E-Mail: customer.service@mcgraw-hill.com
Home Page: www.mcgrawhill.com
Herald McGraw, President
Jim Mathews, Publisher
A nonprofit research organization that depends primarily upon tax-deductible contributions.

2669 Aeronautical Radio & Research Incorporated
2551 Riva Road
Annapolis, MD 21401-7435
410-266-4000
800-633-6882
Fax: 410-266-2020
E-Mail: corpcomm@arinc.com
Home Page: www.arinc.com
Social Media: Facebook, Twitter, LinkedIn
John M Belcher, Chairman & CEO
Stephen L Waechter, VP & CFO
Provider of communications, engineering and integration solutions, we help our customers in the defense, commercial and government industries mitigate risk, improve operational and systems performance and meet program requirements.
Founded in 1929

2670 Aeronautical Repair Station Association
121 N Henry St
Alexandria, VA 22314-2903
703-739-9543
Fax: 703-739-9488
E-Mail: arsa@arsa.org
Home Page: www.arsa.org
Social Media: Facebook, Twitter, LinkedIn, RSS
Gary Jordan, President
Jim Perdue, Vice President
Christian A Klein, Executive VP
Marshall S Filler, General Counsel/Managing Director
Sarah MacLeod, Executive Director
Helps develop guidance, policy and interpretations that are clear, concise and consistent, and applied uniformly to all similarly situated companies and individuals.
700 Members
Founded in 1984

2671 Aerospace Industries Association
23 E El Segundo Blvd
El Segundo, CA 90245-4609
310-336-5000
Fax: 310-336-7055
E-Mail: membership@aia-aerospace.org
Home Page: www.aero.org
Social Media: Facebook, Twitter, Youtube, Google+
W M Austin, President & CEO
R Clinton, Senior VP/General Counsel/Secretary
H J Mitchell, Vice President
M H Goodman, Principal Director
The Aerospace Industries Association shapes public policy that ensures the US aerospace, defense and homeland security industry remains preeminent and that its members are successful and profitable in a changing global market.
283 Members
Founded in 1919

2672 Aerospace Medical Association
320 S Henry St
Alexandria, VA 22314-3579
703-739-2240
Fax: 703-739-9652
E-Mail: jsventek@asma.org
Home Page: www.asma.org
Jeffery C. Sventek,MS,CASp, Executive Director
Gisselle Vargas, Operations manager
Gloria Carter, Director
Our mission is to apply and advance scientific knowledge to promote and enhance the health, safety and performance of those involved in aerospace and related activities.
3200 Members
Founded in 1929
Mailing list available for rent

2673 Air Force Association
1501 Lee Hwy
Suite 400
Arlington, VA 22209-1198
703-247-5800
800-727-3337
Fax: 703-247-5853
E-Mail: membership@afa.org
Home Page: www.afa.org
Social Media: Facebook, Twitter, LinkedIn, Youtube, Blogger
George Muellner, Chairman
Jerry E White, Vice Chairman
Craig R McKinley, President
Len Vernamonti, Treasurer
Marvin L Tooman, Secretary
Independent nonprofit, civilian organization promoting public understanding of aerospace power and the pivotal role it plays in the security of the nation.
1400 Members
Founded in 1946

2674 Air Taxi Association
300 Galleria Parkway
Atlanta, GA 30339
770-563-7400
Home Page: www.atxa.com
Social Media: Twitter, LinkedIn, Youtube
Gordon Wilson, President & CEO
Eric Bock, Executive VP/CLO/CAO
Philip Emery, Executive VP/CFO
Mark Ryan, Executive VP/CIO
Bryan Conway, Chief Marketing Officer
Backed by leading air taxi companies, ATXA's mission is to speed the adoption of the air taxi model so that more business, individuals, and communities can enjoy the benefits of direct, personal flights.
Founded in 2006

2675 Air Traffic Control Association
1101 King St
Suite 300
Alexandria, VA 22314
703-299-2430
Fax: 703-299-2437
E-Mail: info@atca.org
Home Page: www.atca.org
Social Media: Facebook, Twitter, LinkedIn, RSS
James Washington, Chairman
Neil Planzer, Chair Elect
Peter F Dumont, President & CEO
Jeff Griffith, Treasurer
Rachel Jackson, Secretary
Works to establish and maintain a safe and efficient air traffic control system.
2400+ Members
Founded in 1956

2676 Air Transport Association of America
1301 Pennsylvania Ave NW
Suite 1100
Washington, DC 20004-1738
202-626-4000
800-497-3326
Fax: 202-626-4166
E-Mail: a4a@airlines.org
Home Page: www.airlines.org
Nicholas Calio, President
Paul R Archambeault, Senior VP/CFO/Treasurer
David A Berg, VP/General Counsel/Secretary
John M Meenan, Executive VP/CIO
David A Castelveter, VP Of Communications
Supports and assists its members by promoting the air transport industry and the safety, cost effectiveness, and technical advancement of its operators; advocating common industry positions before state and local governments; conducting designated industry-wide programs; and assuring governmental and public understanding of all aspects of air transport.
25 Members
Founded in 1936

2677 Aircraft Electronics Association
3570 NE Ralph Powell Rd
Lees Summit, MO 64064
816-347-8400
Fax: 816-347-8405
E-Mail: info@aea.net
Home Page: www.aea.net
Social Media: Facebook, Twitter, LinkedIn, Youtube, Flickr
Gary Harpster, Chairman
David Loso, Vice Chair
Paula Derks, President
Debra McFarland, Executive Vice President
Kim Stephenson, Secretary
Persons interested in aviation and avionics.
1200 Members

2678 Aircraft Owners & Pilots Association
421 Aviation Way
Frederick, MD 21701-4756
301-695-2000
800-872-2672
Fax: 301-695-2375
E-Mail: phil.boyer@aopa.org
Home Page: www.aopa.org
Social Media: Facebook, Twitter, LinkedIn
Mark Baker, President & CEO
Robert Moran, Chief Operating Officer
Karen Gebhart, Executive VP, Communications
AOPA has achieved its prominent position through effective advocacy, enlightened leadership, technical competence, and hard work. Providing member services that range from representation at the federal, state, and local levels to legal services, advice, and other assistance, we have built a service organization that far exceeds any other in the aviation community. AOPA ePilot and AOPA ePilot Flight Training Edition unique e-mail newsletters issued every Friday morning only to AOPA members.
405k Members
Founded in 1939

2679 Airline Pilots Association International
1625 Massachusetts Ave NW
Suite 800
Washington, DC 20036
703-689-2270
Fax: 202-797-4052
Home Page: www.alpa.org
Social Media: Facebook, Twitter, LinkedIn
Lee Moak, President
Sean Cassidy, First VP
Bill Couette, VP Administration
Randolph Helling, VP Finance
Promotes airplane use and co-operates with government agencies and private and public flying organizations to increase general safety.
64000 Members
Founded in 1931

2680 Airport Consultants Council
908 King St
Suite 100
Alexandria, VA 22314
703-683-5900
Fax: 703 683-2564
E-Mail: info@acconline.org
Home Page: www.acconline.org
Paula P Hochstetler, President
T.J. Schulz, Executive VP
John B Reynolds, Manager of Communicatons
Colleen Flood, Manager, Marketing & Membership
Chris Spaulding, Assistant
Represents the majority of airport consulting firms in the United States.
200+ Members
Founded in 1978

2681 Airports Association Council International
1615 L Street NW
Suite 300
Washington, DC 20036
202-293-8500
888-424-7767
Fax: 202-331-1362
Home Page: www.aci-na.com
Social Media: Facebook, Twitter, LinkedIn, Youtube
Deborah McElroy, Interim President
Nancy Zimini, Senior VP
Kent George, Chairman
Ian A Redhead, VP Airport Services
Patricia Hahn, EVP Operations/General Counsel
Members are boards, commissions, local governmental entities operating public airport facilities and more.
240 Members
Founded in 1947

2682 Allied Pilots Association
14600 Trinity Blvd
Suite 500
Fort Worth, TX 76155-2512
817-302-2272
Fax: 817-302-2119
E-Mail: public-comment@alliedpilots.org
Home Page: www.alliedpilots.org
Social Media: Facebook, Twitter, Youtube
Dave Ahles, Executive Director
Captian Dave Bates, President
Officer Anthony Chapman, Vice President
Provides all the traditional union representation services for its members. This includes the lobbying of airline pilots views to Congress and government agencies. In addition, it devotes more than 20 percent of its dues income to support aviation safety.
11500 Members
Founded in 1963

2683 American Astronautical Society
6352 Rolling Mill Place
Suite 102
Springfield, VA 22152-2370
703-866-0020
Fax: 703-866-3526
E-Mail: aas@astronautical.org
Home Page: www.astronautical.org
Social Media: Facebook, Twitter, Youtube
Lyn D Wigbels, President
J. Walter Faulconer, EVP
Richard Burns, VP Publications
Harley A Thronson, VP Programs
Independent scientific and technical group in the United States exclusively dedicated to the advancement of space science and exploration.
1400 Members
Founded in 1954

2684 American Bonanza Society
Mid-Continent Airport
PO Box 12888
Wichita, KS 67277
316-945-1700
Fax: 316-945-1710
E-Mail: bonanza2@bonanza.org
Home Page: www.bonanza.org
Social Media: Facebook, Twitter, LinkedIn
Nancy Johnson, Executive Director
Tom Turner, Technical Manager
We are nearly 10,000 owners and pilots of Bonanza, Baron and Travel Air type aircraft who have banded together to share information and experiences involving the operation and maintenance of the Beech produced aircraft. Together, we offer an underwriter recognized flight proficiency program, and service clinics scheduled throughout the year at various locations. These clinics provide members the opportunity to have their aircraft evaluated by highly experienced ABS technical personnel.
10K Members
Founded in 1967

2685 American Helicopter Society
217 N Washington St
Alexandria, VA 22314
703-684-6777
855-247-4685
Fax: 703-739-9279
E-Mail: staff@vtol.org
Home Page: www.vtol.org
Social Media: Facebook, Twitter, LinkedIn
Mike Hirschberg, Executive Director
Kay Yosua Brackins, Deputy Director
Randy Johnson, Director Of Information Resource
David Renzi, Director Of Meetings & Advertising
Holly Cafferelli, Director Of Administration
Promotes the interests of designers, engineers and manufacturers of the vertical flight industry. Serving as a clearinghouse for technical information, the society publishes several periodicals, organizes the largest vertical flight technology display in the world, and maintains a comprehensive library.
6000 Members
Founded in 1944

2686 American Institute of Aeronautics and Astronautics
1801 Alexander Bell Dr
Suite 500
Reston, VA 20191-4344
703-264-7500
800-639-2422
Fax: 703-264-7551
E-Mail: custserv@aiaa.org
Home Page: www.aiaa.org
Social Media: Facebook, Twitter, LinkedIn, Youtube
David W. Thompson, President
Mark J Lewis, President-Elect
A. Tom Smith, VP Finance
Merri J. Sanchez, VP Education
Mary L. Snitch, VP Member Services
Advancing the arts, sciences and technology of aeronautics and astronautics and promotes the professionalism of those engaged in these pursuits.
31,00 Members
Founded in 1963

2687 Army Aviation Association of America
593 Main Street
Monroe, CT 06468-2830
203-268-2450
Fax: 203-268-5870
E-Mail: aaaa@quad-a.org
Home Page: www.quad-a.org
Social Media: Facebook, Twitter, LinkedIn, Youtube
Howard W Yellen, President
E J Sinclair, Senior VP
Jeffrey J Schloesser, Treasurer
Stephen D Mundt, Secretary
A professional force that holds the aviation community, both military and industry together.

2688 Association of Air Medical Services
909 N Washington Street
Suite 410
Alexandria, VA 22314
703-836-8732
Fax: 703-836-8920
E-Mail: jfiegel@aams.org
Home Page: www.aams.org
John Fiegel, Executive Director/CEO
Rick Sherlock, President &CEO
Kristin Discher, Office Manager
Voluntary nonprofit organization, encourages and supports its members in maintaining a standard of performance reflecting safe operations and efficient, high quality patient care. Built on the idea that representation from a variety of medical transport services and businesses can be brought together to share information, collectively resolve problems and provide leadership in the medical transport community. We provide a e-mail newsletter called Capitol Watch for AAMS Members.
581 Members
Founded in 1980

2689 Association of Flight Attendants-CWA
501 3rd St NW
Suite 1
Washington, DC 20001
202-434-1300
800-424-2401
Fax: 202-434-1411
E-Mail: info@afacwa.org
Home Page: www.afacwa.org
Social Media: Facebook, Twitter, Youtube
Veda Shook, International President
Sara Nelson, International VP
Kevin Creighan, International Secretary/Treasurer

Represents over 50,000 flight attendants at 26 airlines, serving as a voice for flight attendants at their workplace, in the industry, the media and on Capitol Hill.
55M Members
Founded in 1930

2690 Association of Naval Aviation
6551 Loisdale Road
Suite 221
Springfield, VA 22150
703-960-6806
Fax: 703-960-6807
E-Mail: anahqtr@aol.com
Home Page: www.anahq.org
Social Media: Facebook, Twitter, LinkedIn
James L Holloway, Chairman
David L Philman, President
Michael E Field, Secretary/Treasurer
Linda Bubien, Advertising Director
R M Rausa, Editor
Professional, nonprofit, educational and fraternal society of Naval Aviation, whose main purpose is to educate the public and our national leaders on the vital roles of the Navy, Marine Corp and Coast Guard Aviation as key elements of our national defense posture. ANA continuously seeks to elucidate the key current issues impacting Naval Aviation through published writing, symposia, speeches and discussions with various interest groups.

2691 Aviation Development Council
141-07 20th Ave
Suite 404
Whitestone, NY 11357
718-746-0212
Fax: 718-746-1006
E-Mail: shellyade@aol.com
Home Page: www.adcnynj.org
William Huisman, Executive Director
Addresses noise problems from air carriers in the New York - New Jersey region.
Founded in 1962

2692 Aviation Distributors and Manufacturers
Fernley & Fernley Inc
100 North 20th Street
Suite 400
Philadelphia, PA 19103-1404
215-320-3872
Fax: 215-564-2175
E-Mail: mtaft@fernley.com
Home Page: www.adma.org
Social Media: Facebook
Michael Shaw, President
Lise Pearson, VP
Steve Langston, VP
Q Bruner Rowello, Management Liaison
Meg Taft, Meetings Manager
Promotes interests of wholesalers and manufacturers of general aviation aircraft parts and supplies.
Founded in 1943

2693 Aviation Insurance Association
7200 W 75th Street
Overland Park, KS 66204
913-627-9632
Fax: 913-381-2515
E-Mail: mandie@aiaweb.org
Home Page: www.aiaweb.org
Social Media: Facebook
Daul Leonard, President
Todd McCredie, Vice President
Patrick Bailey, Secretary
Mary D'Alauro, Treasurer
Mandie Bannwarth, Executive Director
A not-for-profit association dedicated to expanding the knowledge of and promoting the general welfare of the aviation insurance industry through numerous educational programs and events.
900 Members
Founded in 1976

2694 Aviation Technician Education Council
2090 Wexford Ct
Harrisburg, PA 17112-1579
717-540-7121
E-Mail: info@atec-amt.org
Home Page: www.atec-amt.org
Raymond E Thompson, President
David Jones, Vice President
Doug Dunn, Treasurer
Organization of Federal Aviation Administration approved Aviation Maintenance Technician schools and supporting industries.
Founded in 1961

2695 Cessna Owner Organization
N7450 Aanstad Road
PO Box 5000
Iola, WI 54945
715-445-5000
888-692-3776
Fax: 715-445-4053
E-Mail: help@cessnaowner.org
Home Page: www.cessnaowner.org
Social Media: Facebook
Daniel Weiler, Executive Director
Joe Jones, Publisher
Ryan Jones, Executive Publisher
Dennis Piotrowski, Editor
Kara Grundman, Graphic Designer
Membership support organization for Cessna aircraft owners.
5000 Members
Founded in 1973

2696 Civil Aviation Medical Association
PO Box 2382
Peachtree City, GA 30269-2382
770-487-0100
Fax: 770-487-0080
E-Mail: civilavmed@yahoo.com
Home Page: www.civilavmed.com
Mark Eidson, President
Clawton T Cowl, President-Elect
Gordon L Ritter, Secretary/Treasurer
David P Millet, Executive VP
James Carpenter, VP Communications & Representation
Aviation medical equipment, supplies and services. Working on behalf of physicians engaged in the practice of aviation medicine and dedicated to civil aviation safety.
Cost: $5.00
800+ Members
Founded in 1948

2697 Experimental Aircraft Association
3000 Poberezny Road
PO Box 3086
Oshkosh, WI 54903-3086
920-426-4800
800-564-6322
Fax: 920-426-6761
E-Mail: webmaster@eaa.org
Home Page: www.eaa.org
Social Media: Facebook, Twitter
Tom Poberezny, President
David Berkley, Communications Director
Adam Smith, VP Member Services
Works to keep aviation history alive. Members are active restorers and enthusiasts working to keep vintage aircraft in the air and flying for the pleasure and education of themselves and the public at large. EAA's weekly electronic newsletter e-Hot Line.
170M Members
Founded in 1953

2698 Flight Safety Foundation
801 N Fairfax Street
Suite 400
Alexandria, VA 22314-1774
703-739-6700
Fax: 703-739-6708
E-Mail: wahdan@flightsafety.org
Home Page: www.flightsafety.org
Social Media: Facebook, Twitter, LinkedIn
David McMillan, Chairman
Kevin L Hiatt, President & CEO
Kenneth P Quinn, Secretary/General Counsel
David Barger, Treasurer
Supported by airlines, aerospace manufacturers, aviation professionals, corporate flight departments and others interested in flight safety.
900 Members
Founded in 1947

2699 Forecast International
Forecast International
22 Commerce Rd
Newtown, CT 06470
203-426-0800
800-451-4975
Fax: 203-426-1964
E-Mail: info@forecast1.com
Home Page: www.forecastinternational.com
Social Media: Facebook, Twitter
Ray Peterson, VP, Research & Editorial Svcs.
Raymond Jaworowski, Senior Aerospace Analyst
Richard Pettibone, Senior Government Analyst
Rebecca Barnett Edwards, Latin America & Caribbean Analyst
Nicole Loeser, Middle East & Africa Analyst
Premier provider of market intelligence, forecasting, proprietary research and consulting services.
Cost: $495.00
24 Pages
Frequency: Weekly
Founded in 1973
Printed in 4 colors on matte stock

2700 Future Aviation Professionals of America (FAPA)
4959 Massachusetts Boulevard
Atlanta, GA 30337
404-997-8097
Fax: 770-997-8111
Home Page: www.fapa.info/
Linda Nelson, Chairman
Provides career information for those seeking careers in aviation, publications, newsletter, interview briefings and Aviation Job Bank. Also provides personal financial planning for airline pilots.
15M Members
Founded in 1974

2701 General Aviation Manufacturers Association
1400 K St NW
Suite 801
Washington, DC 20005-2485
202-393-1500
Fax: 202-842-4063
E-Mail: bforan@gama.aero
Home Page: www.gama.aero
Pete Bunce, President & CEO
Mary Lynn J Rynkiewicz, Director of Communications
Jens Hennig, VP Operations
Paul H Feldman, VP Government Affairs
bree J Foran, Meeting/Office Coordinator

Manufacturers of general aviation aircraft and related equipment. Members also operate fleets of aircraft, fixed based operations and pilot training facilities.
50 Members
Founded in 1970

2702 Helicopter Association International
1920 Ballanger Ave
Alexandria, VA 22314-2898

703-683-4646
800-435-4976
Fax: 703-683-4745
E-Mail: rotor@rotor.org
Home Page: www.rotor.com

Anthony W Burson, Chairman
Gale Wilson, Vice Chairman
Matthew S Zuccaro, President
Max Lyons, Treasurer
Edward F DiCampli, Executive VP/Secretary

Nonprofit organization provides members with services that directly benefit their operations and advances the civil helicopter industry by providing programs to enhance safety, encourage professionalism and promote the unique societal contributions made by the rotary flight industry.
2500 Members
Founded in 1948

2703 Helicopter Safety Advisory Conference
Marathon Oil Company
PO Box 60136
Houston, TX 77205

281-892-4088
E-Mail: mark.fontenot@bp.com
Home Page: www.hsac.org

Mark Fontenot, Chairman
Joseph Gross, Treasurer
Ron Domonique, Secretary
Robert Hall, Vice Chair

Promotes safety and seeks to improve operations through establishment of standards of practice.
115 Members
Founded in 1978

2704 International Association of Machinists and Aerospace Workers
9000 Machinists Place
Upper Marlboro, MD 20772-2687

301-967-4500
E-Mail: websteward@iamaw.org
Home Page: www.goiam.org
Social Media: Facebook, Twitter

R Thomas Buffenbarger, International President
Richard Michalski, VP
Dave Ritchie, General VP
Bill Trbovitch, Director Communications
Warren L Mart, General Secretary/Treasurer

Has an annual budget of approximately $101.3 million.
700K Members

2705 International Council of Aircraft Owner and Pilot Associations
421 Aviation Way
Frederick, MD 21701

301-695-2220
Fax: 301-695-2375
E-Mail: iaopa@aopa.org
Home Page: www.iaopa.org

Craig Fuller, President
Craig Spence, Secretary General
Ruth Moser, Administrator

Nonprofit federation of 53 autonomous, nongovernmental, national general aviation organizations. Facilitates the movement of general aviation aircraft.
40000 Members
Founded in 1962

2706 International Flight Services Association
1100 Johnson Ferry Road
Suite 300
Atlanta, GA 30342

404-252-3663
Fax: 404-252-0774
E-Mail: ifsanet@gmail.com
Home Page: www.ifsanet.org
Social Media: Facebook, Twitter, Youtube

Vicky Stennes, President
Kenneth Samara, Chairman
Pam Chumley, Executive Administrator
Ellen Hoy, Membership Manager
Michelle Moore, Meetings Manager

The International Flight Services Association is a global professional association created to serve the needs and interests of airline and railway personnel, in-flight and rail caterers and suppliers responsible for providing passenger foodservice on regularly scheduled travel routes.
Founded in 1966

2707 International Society of Women Airline Pilots
ISA + 21
723 S. Casino Center Blvd.
2nd Floor
Las Vegas, NV 89101-6716

E-Mail: TianaD777@aol.com
Home Page: www.iswap.org

Nancy Novaes, Chair
Mary Ana Gilbert, Vice Chair
Liana B Hart, Treasurer
Tiana Daugherty, Secretary
Eva Marie Brock, Communications Director

Fosters cooperation and exchange among women airline pilots employed as flight crew members (Captain, First Officer or Second Officer) and holding seniority numbers with an air carrier which operates at least one aircraft with a gross weight of 90,000 pounds or more.
4000 Members
Founded in 1978

2708 Light Aircraft Manufacturers Association
2001 Steamboat Ridge Ct
Daytona Beach, FL 32128-6918

651-592-7565
301-693-2223
Fax: 651-226-1825
E-Mail: info@lama.bz
Home Page: www.lama.bz

Dan Johnson, Chairman/President

Promotes interests of kit-built light aircraft. Membership dues are $125 for voting members and $25 for non-voting members.
50 Members
Founded in 1984

2709 Lighter Than Air Society
Lighter Than Air Society
Martin Center, University Of Akron Campus
105 Fir Hill
Akron, OH 44311-3311

330-535-5827
E-Mail: suggest@blimpinfo.com
Home Page: www.blimpinfo.com

Joseph Huber, President
Ron Browning, Director Business Development

Nonprofit organization whose members are devoted to the study of the history, science and techniques of all forms of buoyant flight.
1000 Members
Founded in 1952

2710 Mount Diablo Pilots Association
PO Box 6632
Concord, CA 94524

925-370-0828
E-Mail: president@mdpa.org
Home Page: www.mdpa.org
Social Media: Facebook, Twitter

Stewart Bowers, President
Natasha Lantsor, VP, Activities
Madeleine Ferguson, VP Communications
Steve Mink, VP Programs
David Thacker, Treasurer

To promote good public relations between general aviation enthusiasts and the local community; to encourage participation in fly-ins and other aviation activities; to promote safety and educational activities for pilots; to provide mutual resources of information on flying for members; to furnish information and support to the Contra Costa Airport Advisory Committee and other governmental agencies concerned with aviation; to be a proxy on aviation matters of community concern for its membership

2711 National Aeronautic Association
1 Reagan National Airport
Hangar 7, Suite 202
Washington, DC 20001-6015

703-416-4888
800-644-9777
Fax: 703-416-4877
E-Mail: naa@naa.aero
Home Page: www.naa.aero

Jonathan Gaffney, President
Michelle Garwin, Director, Administration
Art Greenfield, Contest & Records Director

A non-profit association that is dedicated to the advancement of the art, sport and science of aviation in the United States.
3000 Members
Founded in 1905

2712 National Agricultural Aviation Association
1440 Duke Street
Alexandria, VA 22314

202-546-5722
Fax: 202-546-5726
E-Mail: information@agaviation.org
Home Page: www.agaviation.org
Social Media: Facebook, Youtube

Dana Ness, President
Rick Boardman, Vice President
Doug Davidson, Secretary
Brenda Watts, Treasurer

Voice of the aerial application industry, we work to preserve aerial application's place in the protection and production of America's food and fiber supply. Aerial application is one of the safest, fastest, most efficient and economical ways to apply pesticides. It is also the most environmentally friendly tool of modern agriculture.
1,300 Members
Founded in 1966

2713 National Air Traffic Controllers Association
1325 Massachusetts Ave Nw
Washington, DC 20005-4171

202-628-5451
800-266-0895
Fax: 202-628-5767
E-Mail: web_staff@list.natca.net
Home Page: www.natca.org

Social Media: Facebook, Twitter, Youtube, RSS

Paul Rinaldi, President
Trish Gilbert, Executive VP

Founded to ensure safety and longevity of air traffic controller positions around the nation. Represents over 15,000 air traffic controllers throughout the US, Puerto Rico and Guam, along with 2,508 other bargaining unit members that span all areas from engineers and architects to nurses and health care professionals to members of the accounting community.
15000 Members
Founded in 1987

2714 National Air Transportation Association
4226 King St
Alexandria, VA 22302

703-845-9000
800-808-6282
Fax: 703-845-8176
E-Mail: dgleason@NATA.aero
Home Page: www.nata.aero
Social Media: Facebook, Twitter, LinkedIn, RSS

Michael Scheeringa, Chairman
Gary Dempsey, Vice Chair
Thomas L Hendricks, President & CEO
Diane Gleason, Director, Meetings and Conferences

Aggressively promotes safety and the success of aviation service businesses through its advocacy efforts before government, the media and the public as well as by providing valuable programs and forums to further its members' prosperity.
Founded in 1940

2715 National Association of Flight Instructors
EAA Aviation Center
3101 E Milham Ave
Portage, MI 49002

866-806-6156
Fax: 920-426-6865
E-Mail: nafi@nafinet.org
Home Page: www.nafinet.org
Social Media: Facebook

Robert Meder, Chairman
John Niehas, Program Coordinator
David Hipschman, Mentor Editor
Phil Poynor, VP, Government & Industry Relations
John Gibson, Director Of Sponsorship

Dedicated exclusively to raising and maintaining the professional standing of the flight instructor in the aviation community. Maintains a benefits package available for everyone from the independent instructor to those teaching at flight schools. Every other week we'll send NAFI members with access to e-mail and electronic eMentor.
Founded in 1967

2716 National Business Aviation Association
1200 G St NW
Suite 1500
Washington, DC 20005

202-783-9000
Fax: 202-331-8364
E-Mail: info@nbaa.org
Home Page: www.nbaa.org
Social Media: Facebook, Twitter, LinkedIn

Ronald Duncan, Chairman
Paul Anderson, ViceChair
Edward M Bolen, President & CEO
Dan Hubbard, Senior VP
Todd Wormington, Director

An organization for companies that rely on general aviation aircraft to help make their businesses more efficient, productive and successful.
8000 Members
Founded in 1947

2717 National EMS Pilots Association
PO Box 2128
Layton, UT 84041-9128

877-668-0430
Fax: 866-906-6023
E-Mail: contactus@nemspa.org
Home Page: www.nemspa.org
Social Media: Facebook, Twitter

Ron Fergie, President
Stuart Buckingham, Treasurer

A professional organization dedicated to serving pilots involved in the air-medical transport industry, and to improving the quality and safety of those services
Founded in 1984

2718 Ninety-Nines
4300 Amelia Earhart Dr
Suite A
Oklahoma City, OK 73159

405-685-7969
800-994-1929
Fax: 405-685-7985
E-Mail: 99s@ninety-nines.org
Home Page: www.ninety-nines.org
Social Media: Facebook, Twitter, Youtube

Martha Phillips, President
Jan McKenzie, Vice President
Cynthia Madsen, Secretary
Leslie Ingham, Treasurer
Lin Caywood, Director

International organization of licensed women pilots from 35 countries. We are a nonprofit, charitable membership corporation holding 501(c)(3) US tax status. Members are professional pilots for airlines, industry and government; we are pilots who teach and pilots who fly for pleasure; we are pilots who are technicians and mechanics. First and foremost, we are women who love to fly.
5500 Members
Founded in 1929

2719 Piper Owners Society
N7450 Aanstad Rd
Iola, WI 54945

715-445-5000
866-697-4737
Fax: 715-445-4053
E-Mail: help@piperowner.org
Home Page: www.piperowner.org
Social Media: Facebook

Dan Weiler, Executive Director
Joe Jones, Publisher
Ryan Jones, Executive Publisher
Dennis Piotrowski, Editor
Kara Grundman, Graphic Designer

To support private owners of all models of Piper light aircraft. Members receive a full color monthly magazine which includes flying experiences, aircraft parts explained and historical features.
Founded in 1987

2720 Popular Rotorcraft Association
PO Box 68
Mentone, IN 46539

574-353-7227
Fax: 574-353-7021
E-Mail: praofficemgr@gmail.com
Home Page: www.pra.org
Social Media: Facebook, Youtube

Scott Lewis, President
Douglas Barker, Vice President
Stan Foster, Secretary
Robert Rymer, Treasurer

A nonprofit organization dedicated to the advancement of knowledge, public education and safety among Rotorcraft enthusiasts worldwide.
2000 Members
Founded in 1962

2721 Professional Aeromedical Transport
PO Box 7519
Alexandria, VA 22307

800-541-7517

Purpose is to standardize and upgrade services of aeromedical transport operations. Membership is open to companies and individuals active in the industry.
170 Members
Founded in 1986

2722 Professional Aviation Maintenance Association
972 E Tuttle Road
Building 204
Ionia, MI 48846

724-772-8536
800-356-1671
Fax: 616-527-1327
E-Mail: hq@pama.org
Home Page: www.pama.org
Social Media: Facebook, Twitter, LinkedIn

Roger Sickler, Chairman
Jeff Gruber, Vice Chairman
John Wicht, Secretary

Enhances professionalism and recognition of the Aviation Maintenance Technician through communication, education, representation and support for continuous improvement in aviation safety.
3300 Members
Founded in 1972

2723 Regional Airline Association
2025 M St NW
Suite 800
Washington, DC 20036-3309

202-367-1170
Fax: 202-367-2170
E-Mail: raa@raa.org
Home Page: www.raa.org
Social Media: Facebook, Twitter

Roger Cohen, President
Scott Foose, Vice President
Faye Malarkey Black, Senior VP, Legislative Affairs
Liam Connolly, Senior Director
Kelly Murphy, Media Relations

Membership consists of more than 70 airlines, plus 350 Associate members provide goods and services.
510 Members
Founded in 1975

2724 Reliability Engineering & Management Institute
University Of Arizona
1130 N Mountian Avenue
Building 119 Room N 517
Tucson, AZ 85721

520-621-6120
Fax: 520-621-8191
E-Mail: dimitri@u.arizona.edu
Home Page: www.u.arizona.edu/~dimitri/

Dr Dimitri Kececioglu PE, Prof Aerospace/Mech Engineering

An institute to help provide a working knowledge in reliability engineering.
Frequency: November

2725 Seaplane Pilots Association
3859 Laird Blvd
Lakeland, FL 33811

863-701-7979
888-772-8923
Fax: 863-701-7588
E-Mail: spa@seaplanes.org
Home Page: www.seaplanes.org

Walter Windus, Chairman
Phil Lockwood, President
Randy Juen, VP
Gordon Richardson, Treasurer
Lyle Panepinto, Secretary

Represents members in dozens of seaplane access issues annually and provides numerous exclusive benefits. Members who have provided SPA with a valid email address receive Water Flying Update, a bimonthly e-newsletter that provides recent news, advocacy updates, technical tips, upcoming events, and a tip for using SPA's web site.
375 Members
Founded in 1971

2726 Soaring Society of America
Jack Gomez Blvd & Ave A
Hobbs, NM 88240

505-392-1177
Fax: 505-392-8154
E-Mail: feedback@ssa.org
Home Page: www.ssa.org
Social Media: Facebook, Twitter, LinkedIn

Dennis Layton, Chief Administrative Officer
Chuck Coyne, Editor
Kathey Pope, Accounting Manager
Rhonda Copeland, Member Services Manager

Fosters and promote all phases of gliding and soaring, nationally and internationally.
16K Members
Founded in 1932

2727 Society of Experimental Test Pilots
44814 N Elm Avenue
Lancaster, CA 93534

661-942-9574
Fax: 661-940-0398
E-Mail: setp@setp.org
Home Page: www.setp.org

Kevin Prosser, President
Mark Stucky, President Elect
Timothy Morey, Vice President
Mike Wallace, Secretary
Todd Ericson, Treasurer

International organization that seek to promote air safety and contributes to aeronautical advancement by promoting sound aeronautical design and development; interchanging ideas, thoughts and suggestions of the members, assisting in the professional development of experimental pilots, and providing scholarships and aid to members and the families of deceased members.
2000 Members
Founded in 1955

2728 Society of Flight Test Engineers
44814 N Elm Avenue
Lancaster, CA 93534

661-949-2095
Fax: 661-949-2096
E Mail: sftc@sftc.org
Home Page: www.sfte.org
Social Media: Facebook, Twitter, LinkedIn

Peter Donath, President
Michael Bartlett, Vice President

Members are engineers whose principal professional interest is the flight testing of aircraft. Purpose is to improve communications in the fields of flight test operations, analysis, instrumentation and data systems. We offer an online newsletter called SFTE Flight Test News.
900 Members
Founded in 1968

2729 Space Foundation
4425 Arrowswest Drive
Colorado Spring, CO 80907

719-576-8000
800-691-4000
Fax: 719-576-8801
E-Mail: web@spacefoundation.org
Home Page: www.spacefoundation.org
Social Media: Facebook, Twitter, LinkedIn

Elliot Holokauahi Pulham, CEO
Holly Roberts, CFO
Kevin C Cook, VP, Marketing & Communications
Steve Eisenhart, Senior VP, Strategy
Art Rakewitcz, VP, Operations

To advance space-related endeavors to inspire, enable, and propel humanity.
- Members
Founded in 1983

2730 Tailhook Association
9696 Businesspark Ave
San Diego, CA 921313-164

858-689-9223
800-322-4665
E-Mail: jrdavis@tailhook.net
Home Page: www.tailhook.org
Social Media: Facebook, LinkedIn, Google+

Gregory McWherter, President
Capt. J R Davis, Executive Director
Capt. Dennis Irelan, Editor
CDR Mike Dechemedy, Managing Editor

An independent, fraternal, nonprofit organization internationally recognized as the premier supporter of the aircraft carrier and other sea-based aviation.

2731 Transportation-Communications International Union
3 Research Place
Rockville, MD 20850

301-948-4910
E-Mail: websteward@tcunion.org
Home Page: www.tcunion.org
Social Media: Facebook, Twitter

Robert A Scardelletti, President
Russell C Oathout, National General Counsel

Members come from diverse transportation industries. In addition to bargaining and representation of its members, provides mortgage and bankcard programs and other services to its members.
Founded in 1899

2732 Tripoli Rocketry Association
PO Box 87
Bellevue, NE 68005

402-884-9530
Fax: 402-884-9531
E-Mail: deb@tripoli.org
Home Page: www.tripoli.org

Stu Barrett, President
Bob Brown, VP
Bruce Lee, Treasurer
David Wilkins, Secretary

This is a non-profit organization dedicated to the advancement and operation of non-professional high power rocketry.

2733 United States Parachute Association
5401 Southpoint Centre Boulevard
Fredricksburg, VA 22407

540-604-9740
Fax: 540-604-9741
E-Mail: uspa@uspa.org
Home Page: www.uspa.org
Social Media: Facebook, Twitter, LinkedIn, YouTube, RSS

Sherry Butcher, President
Randy Allison, Vice President
Ray Lallo, Secretary
Albert Berchtold, Treasurer

The USPA is a voluntary membership organization of individuals who enjoy and support the sport of skydiving. The purpose of USPA is three-fold: to promote safe skydiving through training, licensing, and instructor qualification programs; to ensure skydiving's rightful place on airports and in the airspace system; and to promote competition and record-setting programs.
33000 Members
Founded in 1946

2734 United States Pilots Association
1652 Indian Point Road
Branson, MO 65616

417-338-2225
E-Mail: jan@uspilots.org
Home Page: www.uspilots.org

Arnold Zimmerman, Owner
Jan Hoynacki, Executive Director

Works to promote aviation safety and pilot education and also acts as a forum for exchange of ideas.
5000 Members

2735 United States Ultralight Association
16192 Coastal Highway
Lewes, DE 19958

717-339-0200
Fax: 717-339-0063
E-Mail: usua@usua.org
Home Page: www.usua.org

Dale Hooper, Executive VP
Reginald E DeLoach, President

Annual meeting and exhibits of ultralight and microlight aviation equipment, supplies and services. There will be 20 booths.
3000 Members
Founded in 1985

2736 University Aviation Association
2415 Moore's Mill Road
Suite 265-216
Auburn, AL 36830

334-528-0300
Fax: 334-844-2432
E-Mail: uaamail@uaa.aero
Home Page: www.uaa.aero
Social Media: Facebook, Twitter, Youtube

Carolyn Williamson, Executive Director
David McAlister, Member Services Coordinator
Mary Chandler, Coordinator Office Administration

The voice of collegiate aviation education to its members, the industry, government and the general public. Through the collective expertise of its members, this nonprofit organization plays a pivotal role in the advancement of degree-granting aviation programs that represent all segments of the aviation industry.
625+ Members
Founded in 1947

2737 Vintage Aircraft Association
3000 Poberezny Road
Oshkosh, WI 54902

920-426-4825
Fax: 920-426-6579
E-Mail: vintageaircraft@eaa.org

Home Page: www.vintageaircraft.org
Social Media: Facebook, Twitter

Geoff L Robison, President
George Daubner, Vice President
Steve Nesse, Secretary
Dan Knutson, Treasurer

Brings together people from around the world who share an interest in the aircraft of yesterday.
8000 Members
Founded in 1971

2738 World Airline Historical Society
P.O. Box 489
Ocoee, FL 34761

904-221-1446
Fax: 407-522-9352
E-Mail: Information@WAHSOnline.com
Home Page: www.wahsonline.com
Social Media: Facebook, Twitter, LinkedIn, Youtube, RSS

Duane Young, President
Craig Morris, VP

Open to all persons and groups interested in collecting airline memorabilia and the study of the airline industry, past and current.
500 Members
Founded in 1977

Newsletters

2739 AIA Update
Aerospace Industries Association
15049 Conference Center Drive
Suite 600
Chantilly, VA 20151-3824

571-307-0000
Fax: 571-307-1001
E-Mail: membership@aia-aerospace.org
Home Page: www.aero.org

Wanda Austin, President
Peter B. Teets, Chairman
Thomas S. Moorman, Vice chairman
Barbara M. Barrett, Ambasador
Frequency: 9x/Year

2740 ATCA Bulletin
Air Traffic Control Association
1101 King St
Suite 300
Alexandria, VA 22314-2963

703-299-2430
Fax: 703-299-2437
E-Mail: info@atca.org
Home Page: www.atca.org
Social Media: Facebook, Twitter, LinkedIn

Peter F Dumont, President
Monte Belger, Chairman
William Cotton, Director South Central
Jeff Greffith, Secretary

Provides information on activities of the association, important developments in the air traffic control industry.
Frequency: Monthly
ISSN: 0400-1915
Founded in 1956
Printed in on matte stock

2741 ATXA Newsletter
Air Taxi Association
400 Galleria Parkway
Suite 1500
Atlanta, GA 30339

678-390-0001
Home Page: www.atxa.com

Offers information and association news for professionals in the aviation industry.
Frequency: Bimonthly, E-Newsletter

2742 Accident Prevention
Flight Safety Foundation
801 N Fairfax Street
Suite 400
Alexandria, VA 22314-1774

703-739-6700
Fax: 703-739-6708
E-Mail: apparao@flightsafety.org
Home Page: www.flightsafety.org

J.A. Donoghue, Director Publications
Mark Lacagnina, Senior Editor
Wayne Rosenkrans, Senior Editor
Linda Werfelman, Senior Editor
Rick Darby, Associate Editor

Focuses on the flight deck, including in-depth reviews of accident reports. Authors offer tips and descriptions on pilot incapacitation, outlines techniques to prevent runway overrun and addresses a wide variety of other subjects aimed at the experienced cockpit crew. Subscription included with FSF membership. Others will be $280.00/year.
4-16 Pages
Frequency: Monthly
Circulation: 3,000
Founded in 1948
Printed in 2 colors

2743 Aerospace Daily
AviationNow
1200 G St Nw
Suite 900
Washington, DC 20005-3821

202-383-2378
800-525-5003
Fax: 202-383-2438
E-Mail: aviationdaily@aviationnow.com
Home Page: www.aviationnow.com

Lee Ewing, Editor-in-Chief
Brett Davis, Managing Editor
Mark Lipowicz, Publisher
George Hamilton, President

Daily intelligence on the defense and space industries. If you're a prime or subcontractor, an aviation, defense or space official, a consultant or analyst, or an engineering or research and development manager, you'll benefit from our news on policy and programs.
8 Pages
Frequency: Daily
Founded in 1963

2744 Air Safety Week
Phillips Publishing
7811 Montrose Road
Potomac, MD 20854

703-522-8502
Home Page: www.phillips.com

Dan Cook, Publisher

Weekly newsletter dealing with aviation safety, security, recreation, certification and accident investigation.
Cost: $695.00
10 Pages
Frequency: Monthly

2745 Airport Consultants Council News
Airport Consultants Council
908 King St
Suite 100
Alexandria, VA 22314-3067

703-683-5900
Fax: 703-683-2564
E-Mail: info@acconline.org
Home Page: www.acconline.org

Paula Hochstetler, President
Anthony Mavrogiannis, Editor
Sharon Brown, Operations Manager
Cassandra Lamar, Marketing Manager

Council newsletter offering information on important and relevant issues for the aviation consulting community.
Frequency: Quarterly
Circulation: 300
Founded in 1978

2746 Airport Operations
Flight Safety Foundation
801 N Fairfax Street
Suite 400
Alexandria, VA 22314-1774

703-396-6700
Fax: 703-739-6708
E-Mail: apparao@flightsafety.org
Home Page: www.flightsafety.org

J.A. Donaghue, Director Publications
Mark Lacagnina, Senior Editor
Wayne Rosenkrans, Senior Editor
Linda Werfelman, Senior Editor
Rick Darby, Associate Editor

Directs attention to ground operations that involve aircraft and other equipment, airport personnel and services, air traffic control and passengers. Subscription included with FSF membership. Others will be $280.00/year.
4-8 Pages
Frequency: Bi-Monthly
Founded in 1974
Printed in 2 colors on glossy stock

2747 Annual Conference Proceedings
Air Traffic Control Association
1101 King St
Suite 300
Alexandria, VA 22314-2963

703-299-2430
Fax: 703-299-2437
E-Mail: info@atca.org
Home Page: www.atca.org
Social Media: Facebook, Twitter, LinkedIn

Peter F Dumont, President
Monte Belger, Chairman
William Cotton, Director South Central
Jeff Greffith, Secretary

A compendium of fifty or more air traffic control technical papers, covering the entire range of ATC subjects, authored by ATC experts from the full spectrum of public and private organizations engaged in advancement of the science of air traffic control.

2748 Antique Airplane Association Newsletter
Antique Airplance Association
22001 Bluegrass Rd
Ottumwa, IA 52501-8569

641-938-2773
Fax: 641-938-2093
E-Mail: antiqueairfield@sirisonline.com
Home Page: www.antiqueairfield.com

Robert L Taylor, CEO
Lucinda Reis, Editor

Air museums, US and abroad historical aviation societies, for AAA chapters, flying aircraft company histories, etc. - For AAA Digest: antique and classic aircraft restorations, mystery aircraft, etc.
Founded in 1953
Printed in 4 colors on glossy stock

2749 **Aviation Accident Law & Practice**
LexisNexis Matthew Bender & Company
PO Box 933
Dayton, OH 45401-0933

212-448-2000
800-253-5624
Fax: 518-487-3584

R Kaye Esq., Publisher

Domestic and international laws.

2750 **Aviation Consumer**
Belvoir Publishers
PO Box 2626
Greenwich, CT 06836-2626

203-422-7300
Fax: 203-661-4802

Robert Englander, Publisher
Richard Weeghman, Editor

Offers valuable information to the consumer regarding airports, airlines, safety and values.

2751 **Aviation Daily**
Aviation Week
1200 G Street NW
Suite 922
Washington, DC 20005

202-383-2374
800-525-5003
Fax: 888-385 1428
E-Mail: aviationdaily@aviationnow.com
Home Page: www.aviationnow.com

Anthony Velocci, Editor-in-Chief
James Asker, Executive Editor
Gregory Hamilton, President
Guy Norris, Senior Editor

Daily intelligence information on the commercial aviation and air transportation industry worldwide.
Cost: $1985.00
10 Pages
Frequency: Daily
Founded in 1939
Printed in on n stock

2752 **Aviation Education News Bulletin**
Aviation Distributors & Manufacturers Association
100 North 20th Street
4th-Floor
Philadelphia, PA 19103-1443

215-320-3872
Fax: 215-564-2175
E-Mail: adma@fernley.com
Home Page: www.adma.org

F. Charles Elkins, President
Michael Shaw, VP
Kristen Olszewski, Executive Director
Meg Taft, Meeting Manager

Association news pertaining to suppliers, distributors and manufacturers of aviation materials.
Frequency: Monthly
Founded in 1943

2753 **Aviation Law Reports**
CCH
2700 Lake Cook Rd
Riverwoods, IL 60015-3867

847-940-4600
800-835-5224
Fax: 773-866-3095
Home Page: www.cch.com

Mike Sabbatis, President
Douglas M Winterrose, Vice President & CFO
Jim Bryant, EVP Software Products

News covering aviation law and regulations.
Cost: $2495.00
Frequency: Weekly
Founded in 1913

2754 **Aviation Maintenance**
Professional Aviation Maintenance Association
972 E Tuttle Road
Building 204
Ionia, MI 48846

724-772-4092
800-356-1671
Fax: 616-527-1327
E-Mail: hq@pama.org
Home Page: www.pama.org

Dale Forton, President
Roger Sickler, Chairman
Jeff Gruber, Vice Chairman
John Wicht, Secretary
Richard Wellman, Treasurer

The source for information on the worldwide aviation aftermarket. Covers the latest new business trends, regulatory developments, technical advancements, and new products and services

2755 **Aviation Mechanics Bulletin**
Flight Safety Foundation
801 N Fairfax Street
Suite 400
Alexandria, VA 22314-1774

703-739-6700
Fax: 703-739-6708
E-Mail: apparao@flightsafety.org
Home Page: www.flightsafety.org

William Voss, President/CEO
Roger Rozelle, Publisher
Jerry Lederer, Founder

Directed to the aviation maintenance technician, with an emphasis on airline and corporate operations. Other regular sections include maintenance safety alerts, mechanical-incident reports and reviews of new products of interest to maintenance technicians.
Cost: $24.00
16 Pages
Frequency: Bi-Monthly
Founded in 1953

2756 **Aviation Medical Bulletin**
Aviation Insurance Agency
475 N Central Avenue
PO Box 20787
Atlanta, GA 30320

404-767-7501
800-241-6103
Fax: 404-761-8326
E-Mail: Pilot@harveywatt.com
Home Page: www.harveywatt.com

Pat Hiebel, President
Sean Daigre, Claims Director

Health education for the professional airline pilot.
Cost: $13.95
Frequency: Monthly
Founded in 1951

2757 **Aviators Hot Line**
Heartland Communications
PO Box 1052
Fort Dodge, IA 50501-1052

515-955-1600
800-247-2000
Fax: 515-955-1668
Home Page: www.hlipublishing.com

Gale W McKinney Ii, CEO
Joseph W Peed, Chairman
Mary Gonnerman, VP

Airline Trade Magazine.
Cost: $24.95
Frequency: Monthly
Founded in 1968

2758 **Buoyant Flight**
Lighter Than Air Society
526 S Main Street
Suite 232
Akron, OH 44311

E-Mail: suggest@blimpinfo.com
Home Page: www.blimpinfo.com

Articles on the history, science and techniques of buoyant flight.
Founded in 1954

2759 **Cabin Crew Safety**
Flight Safety Foundation
801 N Fairfax Street
Suite 400
Alexandria, VA 22314-1774

703-739-6700
Fax: 703-739-6708
E-Mail: ostrcga@flightsafety.org
Home Page: www.flightsafety.org

William Voss, President
Roger Rozelle, Publisher
Rick Derby, Editor
Patzy Sepezy, Circulation Manager

Focuses attention on the cabin crew, especially in airline operations, but the special requirements of corporate operations are also presented. Explanations on how to deal with hijackers, advocates of child restraints, emergency action plans and tips to reduce stress. Subscription included with FSF membership. Others will be $280.00/year.
Cost: $240.00
4 Pages
Printed in 2 colors

2760 **Captain's LOG**
World Airline Historical Society
P.O. Box 489
Ocoee, FL 34761

904-221-1446
Fax: 407-522-9352
E-Mail: president@wahsonline.com
Home Page: www.wahsonline.com

Duane Young, President
Craig Morris, Vice President
Jay Prall, Treasurer
Bill Demarest, Secretary/Editor
Frequency: Quarterly

2761 **Command, Control, Communications and Intelligence**
American Defense Preparedness Association
22 Commerce Road
Newtown, CT 22201-3062

203-426-0800
800-451-4975
Fax: 203-426-1964
E-Mail: info@forecast1.com
Home Page: www.forecast1.com

Ray Peterson, Vice President
Andrew Briney, Editor

Programs and funding information.
Cost: $1640.00
Founded in 1973

2762 **Federal Air Surgeons Medical Bulletin**
US Federal Aviation Administration
800 Independence Avenue SW
Washington, DC 20591

866-835-5322
Home Page: www.faa.gov

Michael Huerta, Acting Administrator
David Grizzle, Chief Operating Officer
David Weingart, Chief of Staff
Victoria B. Wessmer, Assistant Administrator Of Finance

Published for aviation medical examiners and others interested in aviation safety and aviation medicine.
Frequency: Quarterly
Circulation: 8000
Founded in 1967

2763 **Flight Safety Foundation NEWS**
Flight Safety Foundation
801 N Fairfax Street
Suite 400
Alexandria, VA 22314-1774

703-396-6700
Fax: 703-739-6708
E-Mail: apparao@flightsafety.org
Home Page: www.flightsafety.org

William Voss, President/CEO
Roger Rozelle, Publisher
Allen Smith, Marketing Manager

A primary tool for communicating the Foundation's activities through seminars, workshops, special projects, committee actions, awards to its members.
Cost: $480.00
Frequency: Monthly

2764 **Flight Test News**
Society of Flight Test Engineers
44814 N Elm Avenue
PO Box 4037
Lancaster, CA 93539-4037

661-949-2095
Fax: 661-949-2096
E-Mail: sfte@sfte.org
Home Page: www.sfte.org

Peter Donath, President
Michael Barrlett, Vice President
Mark Mondt, Secretary
Steve Martin, Treasurer
Barbara A. Wood, Director

Offers specific information for flight test engineers.

2765 **Flightlog**
Association of Flight Attendants
501 3rd St NW
Washington, DC 20001

202-434-1300
Fax: 202-712-9792
E-Mail: info@afacwa.org
Home Page: www.afanet.org
Social Media: Facebook, Twitter, YouTube

Elliott Kindred, Manager
Veda Shook, International President
Sara Nelson, International President

Offers updated information and news for flight attendants.
Frequency: Monthly

2766 **General Aviation Accident Report**
Andrews Communications
175 Stafford Street Building 4
Suite 140
Wayne, PA 19087

610-225-0510
800-345-1101
Fax: 610-225-0501
Home Page: www.andrewspub.com

Robert Maroldo, Publisher
Nicholas Sullivan, Editor

General aviation laws.
20 Pages
Founded in 1972

2767 **Helicopter News**
Phillips Business Information
1201 Seven Locks Road
Potomac, MD 20854

301-354-1400
Fax: 301-309-3847

Thomas Phillips, Publisher
Holly Yeager, Editor

Information on the rapidly changing helicopter industry.
Cost: $797.00
Frequency: 25 Issues

2768 **Helicopter Safety**
Flight Safety Foundation
801 N Fairfax Street
Suite 400
Alexandria, VA 22314-1774

703-396-6700
Fax: 703-739-6708
E-Mail: apparao@flightsafety.org
Home Page: www.flightsafety.org

J.A. Donaghue, Director Publications
Mark Lacagnina, Senior Editor
Wayne Rosenkrans, Senior Editor
Linda Werfelman, Senior Editor
Rick Darby, Associate Editor

Highlights the broad spectrum of real-world helicopter operations. Subscription included with FSF membership. Others will be $280.00/year.
4-8 Pages
Frequency: Bi-Monthly
Founded in 1974
Printed in 2 colors

2769 **Hotline**
Aeronautical Repair Station Association
121 N Henry St
Alexandria, VA 22314-2903

703-739-9543
Fax: 703-739-9488
E-Mail: arsa@arsa.org
Home Page: www.arsa.org
Social Media: Facebook, Twitter, LinkedIn, YouTube

Gary M. Fortner, President
Gary Jordan, VP
Jim Perdue, Treasurer

Devoted to regulatory compliance in aircraft design, production and maintenance.
Frequency: Monthly

2770 **Human Factors & Aviation Medicine**
Flight Safety Foundation
801 N Fairfax Street
Suite 400
Alexandria, VA 22314-1774

703-396-6700
Fax: 703-739-6708
E-Mail: apparao@flightsafety.org
Home Page: www.flightsafety.org

J.A. Donaghue, Director Publications
Mark Lacagnina, Senior Editor
Wayne Rosenkrans, Senior Editor
Linda Werfelman, Senior Editor
Rick Darby, Associate Editor

Presents information important to the training and performance of all aviation professionals. Subscription included with FSF membership. Others will be $280.00/year.
4-8 Pages
Frequency: Bi-Monthly
Founded in 1953
Printed in 2 colors

2771 **IE News: Aerospace and Defense**
Institute of Industrial Engineers
3577 Parkway Lane
Suite 200
Norcross, GA 30092

770-449-0460
800-494-0460
Fax: 770-441-3295
E-Mail: boyeyemi@iienet.org
Home Page: www.iienet.org

Jane Gaboury, Editorial Director
Don Greene, Vice President
Michael Hughes, Editor

Offers information and updates for industrial engineers.

2772 **Inside the Air Force**
Inside Washington Publishers
PO Box 7167
Washington, DC 20044-7167

703-685-5009
800-424-9068
Fax: 703-416-8543

Donna Haseley, Editor

An executive weekly report on Air Force programs, procurement and policymaking.
Cost: $980.00
Frequency: Weekly
Printed in one color on matte stock

2773 **International Operations Bulletin**
National Business Aviation Association
1200 18th St Nw
Suite 400
Washington, DC 20036-2527

202-783-9000
Fax: 202-331-8364
E-Mail: info@nbaa.org
Home Page: www.ebace.com

Ed Bolen, President/CEO

Flight information for international business flight crews.
Frequency: Quarterly
Circulation: 4000
Founded in 1947

2774 **Jet Fuel Intelligence**
Energy Intelligence Group
5 E 37th St
Suite 5
New York, NY 10016-2807

212-532-1112
Fax: 212-532-4479
E-Mail: info@energyintel.com
Home Page: www.energyintel.com

Ivan Sandrea, President
Thomas Wallin, Executive Vice President and Editor
Raja W Sidawi, Chairman
Peter Kemp, Editor
Sarah Miller, Editor-at-Large

Offers the latest information on jets, fuel, cargo, safety and legislation.
Cost: $2595.00
Frequency: Weekly
Founded in 1951

2775 **Light Aircraft Manufacturers Association Newsletter**
Light Aircraft Manufacturers Association
2001 Steamboat Ridge Ct
Dayton Beach, FL 32128-6918

651-592-7565
Fax: 65- 22- 182
E-Mail: info@lama.bz
Home Page: www.lama.bz

Larry Burke, President
Dave Martin, Editor

Manufacturers, distributors and suppliers receive the latest information and news pertain-

ing to light aircraft, including updated news from Washington, DC.
Frequency: Quarterly
Circulation: 66
Founded in 1984
Printed in 2 colors on glossy stock

2776 Light Plane Maintenance
Belvoir Publishers
PO Box 5656
Norwalk, CT 06856-5656
203-422-7300
800-829-9085
Fax: 203-661-4802
Home Page: www.lightplane-maintenance.com
John Likakis, Publisher
Articles of interest for light aircraft owners.
Cost: $19.97
24 Pages

2777 Mx Newsletter
Professional Aviation Maintenance Association
972 E Tuttle Road
Building 204
Ionia, MI 48846
724-772-4095
800-356-1671
Fax: 724-772-4064
E-Mail: hq@pama.org
Home Page: www.pama.org
Social Media: Facebook, Twitter, LinkedIn
Roger Sickler, Chairman
Jeff Gruber, Vice Chairman
John Wicht, Secretary
Features news for and about members, relevant articles and hot legislative information.
Frequency: Six/Year
Printed in one color

2778 NAA Record
National Aeronautic Association
1 Reagan National Airport
Hangar 7
Washington, DC 20001-6015
703-416-4888
Fax: 703-416-4877
E-Mail: naa@naa.aero
Home Page: www.naa.aero
Jonathan Gaffney, President
Nancy Sack, Administration Director
Arthur W Greenfield, Contest & Records Director
Frequency: Monthly
Circulation: 3000

2779 NBAA Management Guide
National Business Aviation Association
1200 18th St Nw
Suite 400
Washington, DC 20036-2527
202-783-9000
Fax: 202-331-8364
E-Mail: info@nbaa.org
Home Page: www.nbaa.org
Ed Bolen, President
Steven Brown, Sr VP Operations/Administration
Designed to assist existing flight departments with their operational and administrative requirements and to provide overall guidance for operating a flight department. Available to members only.

2780 National Aeronautics
National Aeronautic Association
1737 King Street
Suite 220
Alexandria, VA 22314
703-527-0226
800-644-9777
Fax: 703-416-4877
Home Page: www.naa-usa.org
Shannon Chambers, Editor
David L Ivey, Publisher
Nancy Sack, Office Manager
Information on industry events for the aviation community, also opinion articles, records and awards, technology developments, education, and future events.
8 Pages
Circulation: 3500
Founded in 1905
Printed in 2 colors on glossy stock

2781 National Transportation Safety Board Digest Service
Hawkins Publishing Company
103 River Rd
Edgewater, MD 21037-3824
410-798-1098
Fax: 410-798-1098
Home Page: www.ntsb.gov
Mark V Rosenker, Chairman
Loose-leafed indexed-digested-analysis of the decisions of the National Transportation Safety Board and its predecessor (the CAB), dealing with Aviation Safety Enforcement matters.
Cost: $390.00
Frequency: Monthly

2782 News & Views
Association of Air Medical Services
909 N Washington Street
Suite 410
Alexandria, VA 22314
703-836-8732
Fax: 703-836-8920
E-Mail: information@aams.org
Home Page: www.aams.org
John Fiegel, Executive Director
David J Dries, Editor
Gloria Dow, Editor
This faxed/e-mailed newsletter contains information on association activity updates, community and member news, crew fitness and survival, member survey data, member profiles, editorials, and classifieds.
Frequency: Monthly

2783 Ninety-Nines News
Ninety-Nines
4300 Amelia Earhart Dr
Suite A
Oklahoma City, OK 73159-1106
405-685-7969
800-994-1929
Fax: 405-685-7985
E-Mail: 99s@ninety-nines.org
Home Page: www.ninety-nines.org
Laura Ohrenberg, Manager
Susan Larson, President
Pat Prentiss, VP
Donna Moore, Secretary
Liz Lundin, Headquarters Manager
News and events for licensed women pilots.
Founded in 1929

2784 Operations Update
Helicopter Association International
1635 Prince St
Alexandria, VA 22314-2898
703-683-4646
Fax: 703-683-4745
Home Page: www.rotor.com
Matthew Zuccaro, President
Provides useful information to helicopter owners and operators regarding issues, events and new technologies that may effect or enhance the operator's ability to conduct business with helicopters.
Frequency: Monthly

2785 Parachutist
United States Parachute Association
5401 Southpoint Centre Boulevard
Fredricksburg, VA 22407
540-604-9740
Fax: 540-604-9740
E-Mail: uspa@uspa.org
Home Page: www.uspa.org
Social Media: Facebook, Twitter, LinkedIn, YouTube, RSS
Elijah Florio, Editor in Chief
Laura Sharp, Managing Editor
Guilherme Cunha, Advertising Manager, Web Developer
David Cherry, Graphic Designer
The official newsletter of the USPA.
33000 Members
Founded in 1946

2786 Preliminary Accident Reports
Helicopter Association International
1635 Prince St
Alexandria, VA 22314-2898
703-683-4646
Fax: 703-683-4745
Home Page: www.rotor.com
Matthew Zuccaro, President
PARs summarize civil helicopter accident reports as received from the National Transportation Safety Board and the Transportation Safety Board of Canada. One subscription included upon request in Regular and Associate member dues.
Frequency: Quarterly

2787 Rotor Breeze
Bell Helicopter Textron
600 E Hurst Boulevard
PO Box 482
Hurst, TX 76053
817-280-2011
Fax: 817-280-2321
Home Page: www.bellhelicopter.com
Mike Redenbaugh, Chairman/CEO
Brandon Battles, Editor
Newsletter on Bell Helicopter products and customer support.
Frequency: Quarterly
Founded in 1935

2788 Space Calendar
Space Age Publishing Company
65-1230 Mamalahoa Hwy
Suite D-20
Kamuela, HI 96743-7301
808-885-3473
Fax: 808-885-3475
E-Mail: news@spaceagepub.com
Home Page: www.spaceagepub.com
Steve Durst, Owner
Publication for the space industry.
Cost: $59.00
Frequency: Weekly

2789 Space Fax Daily
Space Age Publishing Company
65-1230 Mamalahoa Hwy
Suite D-20
Kamuela, HI 96743-7301
808-885-3473
Fax: 808-885-3475

E-Mail: news@spaceagepub.com
Home Page: www.spaceagepub.com

Steve Durst, Owner
Charles Bohannan, Associate Editor
Michelle Gonella, Marketing Manager

Information covering the space industry.
Cost: $59.00
Frequency: Weekly
Founded in 1988

2790 Space Letter
Callahan Publications
6220 Nelway Drive
PO Box 1173
Mclean, VA 22101

703-356-1925

Vincent F Callahan Jr, Editor

Information from Washington on the US multi-billion dollar National Space Program. Legislation, budgets, marketing trends and contracting.
Cost: $190.00
8 Pages
Frequency: 24/Yr
Printed in one color

2791 Space Station News
Phillips Publishing
7811 Montrose Road
Potomac, MD 20854-3363

301-208-6787
Fax: 301-340-0877

Tom Phillips, President/CEO/Publisher

Information pertaining to the space station program.
Founded in 1974

2792 Speednews
Speednews
17383 W. Sunset Boulevard
Suite A 220
Pacific Palisades, CA 90272

310-203-9603
Fax: 310-203-9352
E-Mail: admin@speednews.com
Home Page: www.speednews.com

William Freeman III, Publisher
Stephen Costley, Editor
Joanna Speed, VP, Circulation
Stephen A. Costley, VP, Managing Editor
Pamela Leven, Subscription Sales

Market intelligence newsletter for the aviation industry.
Cost: $687.00
Frequency: Weekly
Circulation: 50000
ISSN: 0271-2598
Founded in 1979

2793 The NAA Record
1 Reagan National Airport
Hangar 7
Washington, DC 20001-6015

703-416-4888
800-644-9777
Fax: 703-416-4877
E-Mail: naa@naa.aero
Home Page: www.naa.aero

Jonathan Gaffney, President
Nancy Sack, Administration Director
Arthur W Greenfield, Contest & Records Director

A non-profit association that is dedicated to the advancement of the art, sport and science of aviation in the United States.
3000 Members
Frequency: Monthly
Circulation: 3000
Founded in 1905

2794 World Airline News
Phillips Publishing
7811 Montrose Road
Potomac, MD 20854

301-354-1400
Fax: 301-340-0877
Home Page: www.phillips.com

Tom Phillips, President/CEO/Publisher

Provides airline executives with news and analysis on route developments, codesharing agreements, and traffic statistics as well as aviation entertainment.
Cost: $697.00
Frequency: Weekly/Newsletter
Circulation: 1,850
Founded in 1974

2795 World Airport Week
Phillips Publishing
7811 Montrose Road
Potomac, MD 20854

301-354-1400
Fax: 301-340-0877
Home Page: www.phillips.com

Tom Phillips, CEO

Focuses on commercialization and privatization of airports around the world.
Cost: $597.00
Frequency: Weekly
Circulation: 1800

Magazines & Journals

2796 ABS Magazine
American Bonanza Society
PO Box 12888
Wichita, KS 67277

316-945-1700
Fax: 316-945-1710
E-Mail: ABSMail@bonanza.org
Home Page: www.bonanza.org

Nancy Johnson, Executive Director
Peggy L Fuksa, Events Coordinator

Offers a treasury of practical information on such topics as maintenance, piloting techniques, aircraft restoration, aircraft insurance and ot her important subjects especially chosen for those with a specific interest in Bonanza, Baron, and Travel Air models of aircraft. This colorful magazine also features aircraft owned by an ABS members on its cover every month, as well as schedules of the numerous member activities which are conducted all around the nation.
Frequency: Monthly

2797 AIAA Technical Reports
American Institute of Aeronautics and Astronautics
1801 Alexander Bell Dr
Suite 500
Reston, VA 20191-4344

703-264-7500
800-639-2422
Fax: 703-264-7551
E-Mail: tammym@aiaa.org
Home Page: www.aiaa.org

Cort Durocher, President
Kathy Watkins, Maketing Manager
Dr David S Dolling, VP Publications

Each year AIAA sponsors approximately 25 national meetings where professionals present technical papers on such subjects as guidance and control Computers in Aerospace, etc.
Cost: $3.00
Circulation: 1925
Founded in 1963

2798 AOPA Flight Training Magazine
Aircraft Owners & Pilots Association
421 Aviation Way
Frederick, MD 21701-4756

301-695-2000
800-872-2672
Fax: 301-695-2375
Home Page: www.aopa.org

Craig Fuller, President

Provides up-to-date aviation news and safety tips for student pilots and CFIs.

2799 AOPA Pilot Magazine
Aircraft Owners & Pilots Association
421 Aviation Way
Frederick, MD 21701-4756

301-695-2000
800-872-2672
Fax: 301-695-2375
Home Page: www.aopa.org

Craig Fuller, President
Phil Boyer, President

Will keep you up to date on all the hottest issues in general aviation from the newest technologies in avionics to the latest safety and techniques to enhance your flying. Available only to AOPA members. Membership costs only $39.00/annually.
Frequency: Monthly
Circulation: 34,000

2800 AUSA News
Association of the United States Army
2425 Wilson Boulevard
Arlington, VA 22201-3326

703-841-4300
800-336-4570
Fax: 703-525-9039
E-Mail: ausa-info@ausa.org
Home Page: www.ausa.org

Peter Murphy, Editor
Gordon R Sullivan, President

AUSA represents every American soldier by: being the voice for all components of America's army; fostering public support of the Army's role in national security; providing professional education and information programs.
Frequency: Monthly
Circulation: 10000
Founded in 1950

2801 Aerospace Engineering
400 Commonwealth Drive
Warrendale, PA 15096-1

724-776-4841
877-606-7323
Fax: 724-776-0790
E-Mail: magazines@sae.org
Home Page: www.sae.org

Richard Klien, President
Mircea Gradu, Executive VP

Serves the international aerospace design and manufacturing field which consists of producers of airliners, helicopters, spacecraft, missiles; their powerplants, propulsion systems, avionics, electronic/electrical systems, parts and components.
Cost: $75.00
Frequency: 10 issues
Circulation: 28440
Founded in 1905

2802 Agricultural Aviation
National Agricultural Aviation Association
1005 E St SE
Washington, DC 20003-2847

202-546-5722
Fax: 202-546-5726

E-Mail: information@agaviation.org
Home Page: www.agaviation.org

Andrew Moore, Executive Director
Peggy Knizer, Assistant Executive Director

Official publication of the National Agricultural Aviation Association. Typical subject matter includes information on agricultural aviation business, agricultural aircraft, legislative issues, pesticides, new products and services, safety, maintenance, people profiles.
Cost: $30.00
Circulation: 5200
Founded in 1921

2803 Air Classics
Challenge Publications
9509 Vassar Ave
Unit A
Chatsworth, CA 91311-0883

818-700-6868
800-562-9182
Fax: 818-700-6282
E-Mail: customerservice@challengeweb.com
Home Page: www.challengeweb.com

Edwin Schnepf, Owner

Magazine of military aviations.
Cost: $36.95
76 Pages
Frequency: Monthly
Founded in 1963

2804 Air Force Magazine
Air Force Association
1501 Lee Hwy
Suite 400
Arlington, VA 22209-1198

703-247-5800
800-727-3337
Fax: 703-247-5853
E-Mail: letters@afa.org
Home Page: www.afa.org

Michael Dunn, President
Robert S. Dudney, Editor in Chief
Stephen P. Condon, National President
Suzann Chapman, Editor
John A. Tirpak, Executive Editor

Analysis of all aspects of aerospace power, from military and scientific advances to political ramifications. Includes reports on new technology and studies missile management.
Cost: $36.00
Frequency: Monthly
Circulation: 202718
Founded in 1946

2805 Air Line Pilot
Air Lines Pilot Association International
1625 Massachusetts Ave NW
Suite 800
Washington, DC 20036-2204

703-689-2270
Fax: 202-797-4052
Home Page: www.alpa.org

Captain Lee Moak, President
Mary Jo McPherson, Associate Editor
Captain Sean Cassidy, Vice President

Emphasizes advances in air safety, flight technology, industry developments and aviation history.
Cost: $32.00
56 Pages
Frequency: Monthly
Circulation: 86,656
Founded in 1931

2806 Air Line Pilot Magazine
Airline Pilots Association International
1625 Massachusetts Ave NW
Suite 800
Washington, DC 20036-2204

703-689-2270
Fax: 202-797-4052
Home Page: www.alpa.org

Captain Lee Moak, President
Captain Sean Cassidy, Vice President
Frequency: Monthly

2807 Air Medical Journal
Elsevier, Health Sciences Division
3251 Riverport Lane
Maryland Heights, MO 63043

314-447-8000
800-401-9962
Fax: 314-447-8033
E-Mail: elspcs@elsevier.com
Home Page: www.elsevier.com

Ron Mobed, CEO
David J Dries, Editor
Adriaan Roosen, Executive Vice President

Is the industry's combined trade and research journal. Each issue contains research articles, abstracts and book reviews designed to keep you up-to-date on the latest discoveries. Membership benefits includes a complimentary subscription.
Cost: $82.00
Founded in 1986

2808 Air Progress
Challenge Publications
9509 Vassar Ave
Unit A
Chatsworth, CA 91311-0883

818-700-6868
Fax: 818-700-6282
E-Mail: customerservice@challengeweb.com
Home Page: www.challengeweb.com

Edwin Schnepf, Owner
Taccy Kruger, Editor

Covers all phases of aviation.
Cost: $36.95
84 Pages
Frequency: Monthly
Founded in 1963

2809 Air Progress - Warbirds International
Challenge Publications
9509 Vassar Ave
Unit A
Chatsworth, CA 91311-0883

818-700-6868
800-562-9182
Fax: 818-700-6282
E-Mail: customerservice@challengeweb.com
Home Page: www.challengeweb.com

Edwin Schnepf, Owner
Michael O'Leary, Editor
Tim Baudler, Associate Publisher

The magazine of veteran and vintage military aircraft.
Cost: $22.00
80 Pages
Frequency: Quarterly
Circulation: 3836
Founded in 1963

2810 Air Transport World
Penton Media
8380 Colesville Rd
Suite 700
Silver Spring, MD 20910

301-755-0200
Fax: 913-514-3909
Home Page: www.atwonline.com

JA Donoghue, Editorial Director
William A Freeman III, Publisher

Lists nationwide and international information on airports, airlines and the latest technology in the aviation industry.
Cost: $65.00
85 Pages
Frequency: Monthly
Circulation: 40000
Founded in 1964
Printed in 4 colors on glossy stock

2811 Air and Space/Smithsonian
National Air and Space Museum
Smithsonian Institution
PO Box 37012 ,Victor Bldg 7100 MRC
Washington, DC 20013-7012

202-633-6070
800-513-3081
Fax: 202-275-1886
Home Page: www.airspacemag.com/

Joseph Bonsignore, Publisher
George C Larson, Editor

Smithsonian magazine offering information on the latest developments, technology, and historical news of the aviation industry.
Cost: $24.00
124 Pages
Founded in 1986

2812 Aircraft Maintenance Technology
Cygnus Business Media
1233 Janesville Avenue
Fort Atkinson, WI 53538

800-547-7377
Fax: 920-563-1699
E-Mail: jjezo@amtonline.com
Home Page: www.cygnusb2b.com

Jon Jezo, Publisher
Ronald Donner, Editor

Provides in depth coverage of the critical technical and professional issues facing today's technicians.
Cost: $90.00
98 Pages
Frequency: Monthly
Circulation: 39000
ISSN: 1072-3145
Founded in 1989
Mailing list available for rent: 41M names
Printed in 4 colors on glossy stock

2813 Airline Pilot Careers
Aviation Information Resources
1029 Peachtree Parkway N
Suite 352
Peachtree City, GA 30269

404-592-6500
87- 33- 293
Fax: 770-487-6617
E-Mail: KitDarby@gmail.com
Home Page: www.jet-jobs.com

Kit Darby, President/Publisher

Information to assist pilots in their career development as a airline pilot. Includes feature airline news, personnel announcements, aviation medical information, classifieds and calendar events.
Cost: $29.95
40 Pages
Frequency: Monthly
ISSN: 1095-4317
Founded in 1989

2814 Airliners
World Transport Press
2854 Sterling Road
Hollywood, FL 33020

954-923-4474
800-875-6711
Fax: 954-923-4541

E-Mail: airlinesonline@earthlink.net
Home Page: www.airlinersonline.com

Jon Proctor, Editor

Dedicated solely to the exciting world of airlines and airliners, past, present, and future. Airline histories, travel adventures, color photos of the latest airlines, humorous articles and much more. Accepts advertising.
Cost: $26.95
80 Pages
Circulation: 80000

2815 Airport Business
Cygnus Business Media
1233 Janesville Avenue
Fort Atkinson, WI 53538

800-547-7377
E-Mail: john.infanger@cygnuspub.com
Home Page: www.cygnusb2b.com

John Infanger, Editorial Director

Targets professionals who manage aitports, airport-based businesses, and corporate flight facilities in North America. Helps managers more effectively operate their operations by sharing case studies of what others are doing successfully, combined with expert analysis, industry news, and product information.
Cost: $60.00
44 Pages
Frequency: Monthly
Circulation: 14100
ISSN: 1072-1797
Founded in 1986

2816 Airport Equipment & Technology
8380 Colesville Rd
Suite 700
Silver Spring, MD 20910-6257

301-755-0200
Fax: 913-514-3909
Home Page: www.atwonline.com

William A Freeman III, Publisher
Geoffrey Thomas, Editor-in-Chief

Related to airport and airport operations.
Cost: $65.00
Frequency: Quarterly
Circulation: 40000
Founded in 1965

2817 Airport Journal
Airport Journal
551 Revere Avenue
PO Box 66001
Westmont, IL 60559

630-986-8132
Fax: 630-986-5010
Home Page: www.airportjournal.com

John Andrews, Editor

This journal offers news, information, statistics and reviews pertaining to airports across the globe.
Cost: $13.00
Frequency: Monthly

2818 Airports
Aviation Week
1200 G St NW
Suite 900
Washington, DC 20005-3821

202-383-2378
800-525-5003
Fax: 202-383-2438
E-Mail: aw_intelligence@aviationnow.com
Home Page: www.aviationnow.com

Christopher Fotos, Editor
Kimberley Johnson, Associate Editor
Mark Lipowicz, Publisher

Airports, the weekly for airport managers, users and suppliers, gives you exclusive insider intelligence to meet business challenges with your eyes open.
Cost: $98.00
Frequency: Weekly
Founded in 1920

2819 Airpower
Sentry Books
Republic Press
PO Box 881526
San Diego, CA 92168

818-368-2012
E-Mail: support@airwingmedia.com
Home Page: www.wingsairpower.com

Joseph Mizrahi, Publisher
Mike Machat, Editor/Publisher

Military and commercial aviation history, contains photos, drawings and interviews.
Cost: $44.00
56 Pages
Frequency: Monthly
Circulation: 45000
ISSN: 1067-1048
Founded in 1971

2820 Airways
Airways International
120 McGhee Road
PO Box 1109
Sandpoint, ID 83864

360-457-6485
800-440-5166
Fax: 208-263-5906
E-Mail: airways@airwaysmag.com
Home Page: www.airwaysmag.com

John Wegg, Editor-in-Chief
Seija Wegg, VP Marketing

Written for airline and air travel professionals, and the consumer. Focuses on the current air transport industry: the airliner, manufacturers, the people, technologies, the airports and the airways. Plus takes a nostalgic look at the past.
Cost: $39.95
80 Pages
Frequency: Monthly
Circulation: 43000
ISSN: 1074-4320
Founded in 1994

2821 America's Flyways
United States Pilots Association
1652 Indian Point Road
Brandson, MO 65616

417-338-2225
Fax: 309-215-6323
E-Mail: jan@hoynacki.com
Home Page: www.uspilots.org

Arnold Zimmerman, Owner
Jan Hoynacki, Executive VP
Frequency: Monthly

2822 Army Aviation
Army Aviation Publications
755 Main St
Suite 4D
Monroe, CT 06468-2830

203-268-2450
Fax: 203-268-5870
E-Mail: aaaa@quad-a.org
Home Page: www.quad-a.org

William R Harris, Publisher
Maryann Stirling, Circulation Manager
Daniel Petrosky, President

Is a professional military publication reporting on news and developments pertinent to the field of U.S. Army Aviation and is the official publication of the Army Aviation Association of America. Each issue offers in-depth coverage of a specific development or program within U.S. Army Aviation along with dynamic, easy-to-read feature articles from key offices, agencies, and operational units worldwide.
Cost: $30.00
Frequency: Monthly
Founded in 1957
Printed in 4 colors on glossy stock

2823 Aviation Business Journal
National Air Transportation Association
4226 King St
Alexandria, VA 22302-1507

703-845-9000
800-808-6282
Fax: 703-845-8176
E-Mail: rmulholland@NATA.aero
Home Page: www.nata.aero
Social Media: Facebook, Twitter, LinkedIn

James K Coyne, President
Tim Heck, VP/CFO
Eric R Byer, Gov't & Industry Affairs

Authored by experienced aviation journalists and industry experts
Frequency: Quarterly

2824 Aviation Digest Associates
P.O. Box 2231
Danbury, CT 06810

203-264-3727

Robert Dorr, Publisher
Sharon Simmons, Associate Publisher

Newsmagazine/shopper distributed to owners of general aviation (private and corporate) aircraft.
Cost: $20.00
Frequency: Monthly
Circulation: 12,000

2825 Aviation Equipment Maintenance
Phillips Business Information
7811 Montrose Road
Potomac, MD 20854

301-354-1400
Fax: 301-309-3847
Home Page: www.phillips.com

Richard Koulbanis, Publisher
Clif Stroud, Editor
John J. Coyle, President

Produced monthly and is the leading publication for airline and general aviation maintenance managers. AEM provides information on maintenance techniques, management procedures, new products and ground support equipment.
Frequency: Monthly
Founded in 1974

2826 Aviation International News
Convention News Company
81 Kenosia Avenue
Danbury, CT 06810

203-798-2400
Fax: 203-798-2104
E-Mail: jhartford@ainonline.com
Home Page: www.ainonline.com

Anthony Ramodo, Publisher
Charles Alcock, Editor
Jeff Hartford, Circulation Manager
Wilson Leach, Executive Director

Update on business aviation, equipment and services, and business aviation news and events.
Cost: $74.98
116 Pages
Frequency: Monthly
Circulation: 39,000
ISSN: 0887-9877
Founded in 1972
Printed in 4 colors on glossy stock

2827 Aviation Safety
Belvoir Publishers

800 Connecticut Avenue
PO Box 5656
Norwalk, CT 06856

203-857-3100
Fax: 203-857-3103
E-Mail: customer_service@belvoir.com
Home Page: www.belvoir.com

Ken Ibold, Editor-in-Chief
Robert Englander, CEO
Tom Canfield, VP

Journal on risk management and accident prevention, includes interviews with officials of the FFA.
Cost: $65.00
Frequency: Monthly
Founded in 1972

2828 **Aviation Week & Space Technology**
Aviation Week
1200 G St NW
Suite 900
Washington, DC 20005-3821

202-383-2378
800-525-5003
Fax: 202-383-2438
Home Page: www.aviationnow.com

Anthony L Velocci Jr, Editor-in-Chief
James R Asker, Manager Editor
Jim Mathews, Publisher

Articles and features on the aviation/aerospace industry, including aircraft rockets, missiles, space vehicles, powerplants, avionics and related components and equipment.
Cost: $5.00
Frequency: Weekly
Circulation: 140000
Founded in 1884

2829 **Aviation, Space and Environmental Medicine**
Aerospace Medical Association
320 S Henry St
Alexandria, VA 22314-3579

703-739-2240
Fax: 703-739-9652
E-Mail: inquiries@asma.org
Home Page: www.asma.org

Gisselle Vargas, Manager

Provides contact with physicians, life scientists, bioengineers and medical specialists working in both basic medical research and in its clinical applications.
Frequency: Monthly

2830 **Avionics News**
Aircraft Electronics Association
3570 Ne Ralph Powell Rd
Lees Summit, MO 64064-2360

816-347-8400
Fax: 816-347-8405
E-Mail: info@aea.net
Home Page: www.aea.net
Social Media: Facebook, Twitter, LinkedIn

Gregory Vall, President/Publisher
Gary Harp, Chairman
Jenneie Flattery, Treasurer

A magazine devoted exclusively to persons interested in aviation and avionics. Complimentary within North America.
Cost: $132.00
Frequency: Monthly
Circulation: 8500
Founded in 1975

2831 **Avionics: The Journal of Global Airspace**
PBI Media
1201 Seven Locks Road
Potomac, MD 20854

301-354-1400
847-559-7314
Fax: 301-340-0542
Home Page: www.avionicsmagazine.com

Daniel E Comiskey, Publisher
Stuart Bonner, Circulation Manager
Don Pazour, CEO
David Jensen, Editor-In-Chief

Covers electronics carried aboard aircraft, ground navigational and systems for air traffic control.
Cost: $89.00
Frequency: Monthly
Founded in 1999
Printed in 4 colors on glossy stock

2832 **Balloon Life**
Balloon Life Magazine
9 Madelaine Avenue
Westport, CT 06880

203-629-1241
Fax: 206-935-3326
E-Mail: bill_armstrong@balloonlife.com
Home Page: www.balloonlife.com

Bill Armstrong, Publisher/Editor

Dedicated to the sport of hot air ballooning. Four-color magazine contains articles on major events, safety, education, news, calendar and special reports to bring alive the life of bal looning.
Cost: $21.00
40 Pages
Frequency: Bi-Monthly
Circulation: 4000
ISSN: 0887-6061
Founded in 1986
Printed in 4 colors on glossy stock

2833 **Business & Commercial Aviation**
McGraw Hill
4 International Drive
Suite 260
Rye Brook, NY 10573

914-939-0300
800-257-9402
Fax: 914-939-1184
E-Mail: p02cs@mcgraw-hill.com
Home Page: www.aviationnow.com

William Garvey, Editor-in-Chief
Mark Lipowicz, Publisher
Richard Aarons, Safety Editor

Information for the management and executive levels of aircraft companies on improvements in operations and news of today's general aviation industry.
Cost: $60.00
Frequency: Monthly
Circulation: 52329

2834 **Captain's Log**
World Airline Historical Society
PO Box 489
Ocoee, FL 34761

904-221-1446
Fax: 407-522-9352
E-Mail: president@WAHSOnline.com
Home Page: www.wahsonline.com
Social Media: Facebook, Twitter

Duane Young, President
Craig Morris, VP

The premiere magazine for collectors of airline memorabilia.
Frequency: Quarterly
Circulation: 500

2835 **Cessna Owner Magazine**
Cessna Owner Organization
N7450 Aanstad Rd
Iola, WI 54945-5000

715-445-5000
888-692-3776
Fax: 715-445-4053
E-Mail: help@cessnaowner.org
Home Page: www.cessnaowner.org

Dan Weller, Executive Director
Joe Jones, Publisher

The official publication of the Cessna Owner Organization, it includes pilot tips, owner/aircraft articles, alerts, maintenance tips, new product information, SDR summaries, AD's, insurance updates, and much more.
Cost: $9.95
Frequency: Monthly
Circulation: 5000

2836 **Controller**
Sandhills Publishing
PO Box 82545
Lincoln, NE 68501-5310

402-479-2181
800-331-1978
Fax: 402-479-2195
E-Mail: human-resources@sandhills.com
Home Page: www.sandhills.com

Tom Peed, Publisher

A magazine designed and edited to provide a means of communication between buyer and seller in today's general aviation marketplace.
Cost: $52.00
60 Pages
Frequency: Weekly
Circulation: 20,000 +
Founded in 1978

2837 **EAA Sport Aviation**
Experimental Aircraft Association
3000 Poberezny Road
PO Box 3086
Oshkosh, WI 54902

920-426-4800
800-564-6322
Fax: 920-426-6761
E-Mail: webmaster@eaa.org
Home Page: www.eaa.org

Tom Poberezny, President
David Berkley, Communications Director
Adam Smith, VP Member Services

For pilots, designers, and enthusiasts of sport and homebuilt aircraft.
Cost: $40.00
100 Pages
Frequency: Monthly
Circulation: 165000
ISSN: 0038-7835
Founded in 1953
Printed in 4 colors on glossy stock

2838 **EAA Sport Pilot Magazine**
Experimental Aircraft Association
3000 Poberezny Road
PO Box 3086
Oshkosh, WI 54902

920-426-4800
800-564-6322
Fax: 920-426-6761
E-Mail: webmaster@eaa.org
Home Page. www.eaa.org

Tom Poberezny, President
David Berkley, Communications Director
Adam Smith, VP Member Services

Dedicated to those to fly, buy, build/assemble, maintain, and have fun with light-sport aircraft, sport pilot eligible aircraft, and ultralights, as well as the full spectrum of member activities that give people the opportunity to participate in recreational aviation.

2839 **EAA Vintage Aircraft Association**
Experimental Aircraft Association
PO Box 3086
Oshkosh, WI 54903-3086

920-426-4825
800-564-6322
Fax: 920-426-6579
E-Mail: vintageaircraft@eaa.org
Home Page: www.vintageaircraft.org

Geoff Robison, President

Devoted to all aspects of antique, classic and contemporary aircraft. (All aircraft cinstructed by the original manufacturer, or its licensee on or before 12/31/1970).
Cost: $36.00
6000+ Members
32 Pages
Frequency: Monthly
Circulation: 10,000
Founded in 1971

2840 **FAA Aviation News**
Government Printing Office
AFS-805 Room 832
800 Independence Avenue, S.W.
Washington, DC 20591

202-512-0000
866-835-5322
E-Mail: webmasteravnews@faa.gov
Home Page: www.faa.gov/

Phyllis Duncan, Editor
Michael Huerta, Administrator
David Weingart, Chief of Staff
Daniel J. Mehan, Chief Information Officer

Contains regulations and approved operational techniques, also in depth accident and incident reports.
Cost: $21.00
Frequency: Bi-monthly
Circulation: 50,000
Founded in 1966

2841 **Flight Physician**
Civil Aviation Medical Association
P.O. Box 2382
Peachtree City, GA 30269-2382

770-487-0100
Fax: 770-487-0080
E-Mail: david.millett@yahoo.com
Home Page: www.civilavmed.com

David Millett MD, Executive VP
James Heins MD, President
Gordon L Ritter, Secretary/Treasurer
Cost: $5.00
Frequency: Bi-Monthly

2842 **Flight Safety Digest**
Flight Safety Foundation
801 N Fairfax Street
Suite 400
Alexandria, VA 22314-1774

703-247-0700
Fax: 703-739-6708
E-Mail: Marshall@flightsafety.org
Home Page: www.flightsafety.org

William Voss, President/CEO
Roger Rozelle, Publisher
Mark Lacagnina, Senior Editor

Analyzes controversial industry issues; and authors have shared observations of important, but sometimes subtle influences that affect the airline industry. Authors have described the latest innovations in training, technology and management. Monthly sections present analyses of aviation statistics, brief accident reports and abstracts of information received at FSF Jerry Lederer Aviation Safety Library. Subscription included with FSF membership. Others will be $520.00.
Cost: $520.00
Frequency: Monthly
Circulation: 1000
Founded in 1982
Printed in one color

2843 **Flight Training**
Aircraft Owners & Pilots Association
421 Aviation Way
Frederick, MD 21701-4756

301-695-2000
800-872-2672
Fax: 301-695-2375
E-Mail: flighttraining@aopa.org
Home Page: www.aopa.org

Craig Fuller, President
Thomas B Haines, Editor-in-Chief

Offers information to new pilots and their instructors as well as flight school managers and owners.
Cost: $21.00
Frequency: Monthly
Circulation: 40000+
Founded in 1939

2844 **Flightline Magazine**
Allied Pilots Association
14600 Trinity Blvd
Suite 500
Fort Worth, TX 76155-2559

817-302-2272
Fax: 817-302-2119
E-Mail: public-comment@alliedpilots.org
Home Page: www.alliedpilots.org

Dave Ahles, Executive Director
Captain Dave Bates, President
James Eaton, Secretary/Treasurer

2845 **Flyer**
Flyer Media
5611 76th Street W
PO Box 39099
Lakewood, WA 98439

253-471-9888
800-426-8538
Fax: 253-471-9911
E-Mail: comments@generalaviationnews.com
Home Page: www.generalaviationnews.com

Janice Wood, Editor
Ben Sclair, Publisher
Roy McGhee, Production Manager
Ron Boydston, Circulation Manager

For general and business aviation.
Cost: $35.00
72 Pages
Frequency: Monthly
Circulation: 50000
ISSN: 1052-9136
Founded in 1949
Printed in 4 colors on newsprint stock

2846 **Flying**
460 N Orlando Avenue
Suite 20
Winter Park, FL 32789

407-628-4802
Fax: 407-628-7061
E-Mail: flying@neodata.com
Home Page: www.flyingmag.com

J Mac McClellan, Editor-in-Chief
Wayne Lincourt, Associate Publisher
Rachel Goldstein, Sales Development Manager

Dedicated to general aviation and includes industry news, products, reports on every aircraft category, the latest new products, technology and photography.
Cost: $54.00
116 Pages
Frequency: Monthly
Circulation: 310321
Founded in 1918
Printed in 4 colors

2847 **Flying Magazine**
National Association of Flight Instructors
EAA Aviation Center
730 Grand Street
Allegan, MI 49010

920-426-6801
866-806-6156
Fax: 920-426-6865
E-Mail: nafi@eaa.org
Home Page: www.nafinet.org

Sean Elliot, President
Jason Blair, Executive Director

Provided to all NAFI members, this highly respected general aviation magazine is a great source of information. NAFI and Flying have entered into a partnership that directly benefits you - the NAFI member! Flying is the perfect compliment to the technical flight instruction how-to's contained in NAFI Mentor.

2848 **GPS World**
Advanstar Communications
201 Sandpointe Ave
Suite 500
Santa Ana, CA 92707-8700

714-513-8400
Fax: 714-513-8680
E-Mail: info@gpsworld.com
Home Page: www.gpsworld.com

Mike Weldon, Plant Manager
Alan Cameron, Editor in Chief
Tracy Cozzen, Managing Editor

Covers current news and developments in the area of GPS (global positioning system) technology.
Cost: $54.00
Frequency: Monthly
Circulation: 35010
Founded in 1987

2849 **Helicopter Association International Magazine**
1635 Prince St
Alexandria, VA 22314-2898

703-683-4646
800-435-4976
Fax: 703-683-4745
E-Mail: marty.lenehan@rotor.com
Home Page: www.rotor.com

Matthew Zuccaro, President
Edward DiCampli, Executive Vice President

Dedicated exclusively to the civil helicopter industry. It covers pertinent helicopter operational safety and regulatory issues, including FAA question and answer column, legislative and lobbying issues, and HAI committee and member activities. Accepts advertising.
Cost: $15.00
48 Pages
Frequency: Quarterly
ISSN: 0897-831X
Founded in 1988
Printed in 4 colors on matte stock

2850 **Hook Magazine**
Tailhook Association
9696 Businesspark Ave
San Diego, CA 92131

858-689-9223
800-322-4665
E-Mail: thookassn@aol.com
Home Page: www.tailhook.org

Dennis Trelan, Editor
Jan Jacobs, Managing Editor

Dedicated to telling the story of US Navy carrier aviation, both past and person. Contains a selection of carrier and squadron histories balanced with departments containing the latest

news of current units and aerospace industry developments affecting carrier aviation.
Frequency: Quarterly

2851 IAM Journal
International Association of Machinists and
9000 Machinists Pl
Upper Marlboro, MD 20772-2675

301-967-4500
Fax: 301-967-4588
E-Mail: websteward@goiam.org
Home Page: www.goiam.org
Social Media: Facebook, Twitter

R Thomas Buffenbarger, CEO

This advocacy magazine addresses the trends and forces that affect us all. It covers stories provide an indepth analysis of today's hot issues and are meant to spark discussion among IAM members. Its feature stories provide a glimpse of the men and women who belong to the IAM. IAM represents works primarily in the air transport, aerospace, metalworking, machinery, manufacturing and automotive industries.

2852 Journal of Aerospace Engineering
American Society of Civil Engineers
9000 Machinists Pl
Upper Marlboro, MD 20772-2675

301-967-4500
800-548-2723
Fax: 703-295-6222
E-Mail: marketing@asce.org
Home Page: www.goiam.org

R Thomas Buffenbarger, President
Bill Henry, Publisher
Richard Michalski, General Vice President

Covers lunar soil mechanics, aerospace structures, and materials, extraterrestrial construction, robotics, remote sensing, applications, and real time data collection systems. Defines the role of civil engineering in space and emphasizes the practical applications of civil engineering in space and on earth.
Cost: $140.00
Frequency: Quarterly
Founded in 1852

2853 Journal of Air Traffic Control
Air Traffic Control Association
1101 King St
Suite 300
Alexandria, VA 22314-2963

703-299-2430
Fax: 703-299-2437
E-Mail: info@atca.org
Home Page: www.atca.org

Peter F Dumont, President
Brian Courter, Meetings and Program Coordinator
Michele Townes, Communications Director

Devoted to developments in air traffic control. It contains articles on current issues involving ATC operations, innovative concepts and applications of technology to ATC, public policy debates impacting ATC, commentary by noted aviation experts and policy makers, ATC historical material, and reviews of books and videos of interest to the aviation community.
Frequency: Quarterly
Founded in 1956

2854 Journal of Astronautical Sciences
American Astronautical Society
6352 Rolling Mill Place
Suite 102
Springfield, VA 22152-2370

703-866-0020
Fax: 703-866-3526
E-Mail: aas@astronautical.org
Home Page: www.astronautical.org

Frank Slazer, President
James Kirkpatrick, Executive Director

An archival publication devoted to the sciences and technology of astronautics.
Cost: $170.00
Frequency: Quarterly
ISSN: 0021-9142

2855 Journal of Guidance, Control & Dynamics
American Institute of Aeronautics and Astronautics
1801 Alexander Bell Dr
Suite 500
Reston, VA 20191-4344

703-264-7500
800-639-2422
Fax: 703-264-7551
E-Mail: custserv@aiaa.org
Home Page: www.aiaa.org

Dr. Brian Dailey, President
George T Schmidt, Editor-in-Chief

Offers information on guidance control, navigation, electronics and more related to astronautical and aeronautical systems.
Cost: $675.00
Frequency: Fortnightly
Circulation: 3000
Founded in 1930

2856 Journal of Propulsion & Power
American Institute of Aeronautics and Astronautics
1801 Alexander Bell Dr
Suite 500
Reston, VA 20191-4344

703-264-7500
800-639-2422
Fax: 703-264-7551
E-Mail: custserv@aiaa.org
Home Page: www.aiaa.org

Dr. Brian Dailey, President
Vigor Yang MD, Editor

Offers information on new advances and technology in airbreathing, propulsion systems, fuels, power generation and more.
Cost: $730.00
Frequency: Fortnightly
Circulation: 1900
Founded in 1930

2857 Journal of Rocket Motor and Propellant Developers
California Rocketry Publishing
PO Box 1242
Claremont, CA 91711-1242

626-974-9417
Fax: 626-974-9407
E-Mail: 01rocket@gte.net
Home Page: www.v-serv.com/dpt

Jerry Irvine, Publisher

Technical journal covering propellant formulations, motor design, performance results and methods. Back issues available.
Cost: $499.00
16 Pages
Frequency: Annual
Circulation: 500
Founded in 1994
Printed in on matte stock

2858 Journal of the American Helicopter Society
American Helicopter Society International
217 N Washington St
Alexandria, VA 22314-2538

703-684-6777
855-247-4685
Fax: 703-739-9279
E-Mail: webmaster@vtol.org
Home Page: www.vtol.org

Mike Hirschberg, Executive Director
Ashis Bagai, Associate Editor

The scope of the Journal covers the full range of research, analysis, design, manufacturing, test, operations, and support. A constantly growing list of specialty areas is included within that scope. Is distributed to the AHS membership for $20.00 and is also available for subscription.
Cost: $95.00
Frequency: Quarterly

2859 KITPLANES
Light Aircraft Manufacturers Association
2001 Steamboat Ridge Ct
Daytona Beach, FL 94588-8233

65- 59- 756
Fax: 925-426-0771
E-Mail: info@lama.bz
Home Page: www.lama.bz

Dan Johnson, President

Experimental-category homebuilt aircraft.
Frequency: Monthly

2860 Maintenance Update
Helicopter Association International
1635 Prince St
Alexandria, VA 22314-2898

703-683-4646
Fax: 703-683-4745
Home Page: www.rotor.com

Matthew Zuccaro, President
Edward DiCampli, Executive Vice President

Provides a forum for mechanics and technicians to exchange information. It includes regulatory issues, airworthiness directives, aircraft alerts and items of special interest.
Cost: $50.00
Frequency: Quarterly

2861 Midwest Flyer Magazine
Flyer Publications
PO Box 199
Oregon, WI 53575-199

608-835-7063
Fax: 608-835-7063
E-Mail: info@midwestflyer.com
Home Page: www.midwestflyer.com

Dave Weinman, Publisher/Editor

Reaches all aircraft owners in the Upper Midwest. Articles include flying travel destinations, fly-in restaurants and the issues affecting general aviation in the Midwest and nationwide.
Cost: $15.00
32 Pages
Founded in 1978

2862 NAFI Magazine
National Association of Flight Instructors
730 Grand Street
Allegan, MI 49010

920-426-6801
866-806-6156
Fax: 920-426-6865
E-Mail: nafi@nafinet.org
Home Page: www.nafinet.org

Jason Blair, Executive Director

A monthly magazine published by the National Association of Flight Instructors.
Cost: $39.00
18 Pages
Frequency: Monthly
Circulation: 5400
Founded in 1967

2863 **NAFI Mentor**
National Association of Flight Instructors
730 Grand Street
Allegan, MI 49010

920-426-6801
866-806-6156
Fax: 920-426-6865
E-Mail: nafi@nafinet.org
Home Page: www.nafinet.org

Jason Blair, Executive Director
Rusty Sachs, Executive Director

Membership includes this magazine created exclusively for flight instructors.
20 Pages
Frequency: Monthly

2864 **NASA Tech Briefs**
Associated Business Publications International
261 5th Avenue
Suite 1901
New York, NY 10016

212-490-3999
Fax: 212-986-7864
E-Mail: linda@techbriefs.com
Home Page: www.techbriefs.com

Dominic Mucchetti, CEO
Linda Bell, Editor
Marie Claussell, Circulation Manager
Domenic Mucchetti, CEO
Zoe Wai, Manager

Features exclusive reports of innovations developed by NASA and its partners that can be applied to develop new and improved products and solve engineering or manufacturing problems.
Cost: $49.00
Frequency: Monthly
Circulation: 30000
Founded in 1985

2865 **Naval Aviation News**
Naval Historical Center
805 Kidder Breese Street SE
Washington Navy Yard
Washington, DC 20374-5060

202-433-4882
Fax: 202-433-8200
E-Mail: navymuseum@navy.mil
Home Page: www.history.navy.mil

Wendy Lelend, Managing Editor
Admiral Jay A. DeLoach, Director

Professional magazine of naval aviation.
Cost: $21.00
42 Pages
Frequency: Monthly
Circulation: 25,000
ISSN: 0028-1417
Founded in 1917
Printed in 4 colors on glossy stock

2866 **Ninety-Nines News**
Ninety-Nines
4300 Amelia Earhart Dr
Suite A
Oklahoma City, OK 73159-1106

405-685-7969
800-994-1929
Fax: 405-685-7985
Home Page: www.ninety-nines.org

Laura Ohrenberg, Manager
Susan Larson, President
Boby Row, Editor
Pat Theberge, Vice President

A bi-monthly magazine published by Ninety-Nines.
Cost: $20.00
Circulation: 6500
Founded in 1929

2867 **Northwest Airlifter**
PO Box 98801
Tacoma, WA 98498

253-584-1212
800-293-1216
Fax: 253-581-5962

Tom Swarner, CEO

Features news, mission stories and entertainment for military personnel and families of McChord AFB.
Frequency: Weekly

2868 **Overhaul & Maintenance**
McGraw Hill
1221 Avenue of the Americas
New York, NY 10020-1095

212-512-2000
800-525-5003
Fax: 212-512-3840
E-Mail: p18cs@mcgraw-hill.com
Home Page: www.mcgraw-hill.com

Harold W McGraw III, CEO

Information for people in airlines, flight departments, maintenance operations, maintenance bases, military logistics, issues on safety, quality, and compliance in the aviation aftermarket.
Cost: $54.00
Frequency: Monthly
Circulation: 35000
ISSN: 0031-1588

2869 **PRA Rotorcraft E-Zine**
Popular Rotorcraft Association
PO Box 68
Mentone, IN 46539

574-353-7227
Fax: 574-353-7021
E-Mail: prahq@medt.com
Home Page: www.pra.org

Igor Bensen, Founder
Douglas Barker, President
Tim O'Connor, VP
Cost: $42.00
Frequency: Monthly
Circulation: 1500

2870 **Parachutist Magazine**
United States Parachute Association
5401 Southpoint Centre Blvd
Fredericksburg, VA 22407-2612

540-604-9740
Fax: 540-604-9741
E-Mail: uspa@uspa.org
Home Page: www.uspa.org
Social Media: Facebook, Twitter

Jay Stokes, President
Ed Scott, Executive Director

Supporting safe skydiving and those who enjoy it.
Cost: $4.50
112 Pages
Frequency: Monthly
Circulation: 35000
Founded in 1946

2871 **Pipers**
Pipers Owner Society
N7450 Aanstad Rd
Iola, WI 54945

715-445-5000
866-697-4737
Fax: 715-445-4053
E-Mail: help@piperowner.org
Home Page: www.piperowner.org

Keith Mathiowetz, Editor
Daniel Weiler, Executive Director
Joe Jones, Publisher

The official magazine of the Piper Owners Society.
Cost: $9.95
55 Pages
Frequency: Monthly
Circulation: 8400
Mailing list available for rent: 2750 names
Printed in 4 colors

2872 **Plane and Pilot**
Werner Publishing
12121 Wilshire Blvd
12th Floor
Los Angeles, CA 90025-1168

310-820-1500
Fax: 310-826-5008
E-Mail: editors@planeandpilotmag.com
Home Page: www.wernerpublishing.com

Steve Werner, Owner

Articles on general aviation from light single-engine planes to medium weight twins and related products.
Cost: $11.97
Frequency: Monthly
Founded in 1965

2873 **Powered Sport Flying Mangazine**
Popular Rotorcraft Association
PO Box 68
Mentone, IN 46539

574-353-7227
Fax: 574-353-7021
E-Mail: prahq@medt.com
Home Page: www.pra.org

Igor Bensen, Founder
B Scott Lewis, President
Tim O'Connor, VP

Devoted exclusively to homebuilt rotorcraft. Also has information, technical articles, photos of autogyros and helicopters, safety tips and news of new products for rotorcraft builders and pilots.
2000 Attendees
Frequency: August

2874 **Professional Pilot**
Queensmith Communications
30 S Quaker Ln
Suite 300
Alexandria, VA 22314-4596

703-370-0606
Fax: 703-370-7082
E-Mail: editorial@propilotmag.com
Home Page: www.propilotmag.com

Murray Smith, Owner
Anthony Herrera, General Manager
Phil Rose, Managing Editor
Ivor Tafro, Communications Manager

Offers information for career pilots.
Cost: $50.00
Frequency: Monthly
Circulation: 35000
ISSN: 0191-6238
Founded in 1966
Printed in 4 colors on glossy stock

2875 **ROTOR Magazine**
Helicopter Association International
1635 Prince St
Alexandria, VA 22314-2898

703-683-4646
Fax: 703-683-4745
Home Page: www.rotor.com

Matthew Zuccaro, President

Dedicated to exclusively to the civil helicopter industry. It covers pertinent helicopter operations, safety and regulatory issues including an FAA question and answer column, legislative and lobbying issues, and HAI committee and member activities. Advertising space is available is this publication. Subscription included

with membership.
Cost: $15.00
Frequency: Quarterly

2876 Rotor & Wing
Access Intelligence
4 Choke Cherry Rd
2nd Fl
Rockville, MD 20850-4024

301-354-2000
Fax: 301-340-0542
E-Mail: asteinebach@pbimedia.com
Home Page: www.aviationtoday.com
Social Media: Facebook, Twitter, LinkedIn

Don Pazour, CEO
Julian Clover, Managing Editor
Jim McKenna, Manager

Semitechnical information for helicopter industry, both civil and military. Includes pilot reports, features, news and product section.
Cost: $90.99
88 Pages
Frequency: Monthly
Circulation: 33,400
Founded in 1977

2877 Rotorcraft Magazine
Popular Rotorcraft Association
PO Box 68
Mentone, IN 46539

574-353-7227
Fax: 574-353-7021
E-Mail: prahq@medt.com
Home Page: www.pra.org

B Scott Lewis, President
Tim O'Connor, VP

Devoted exclusively to homebuilt rotorcraft. Free to members.
Cost: $26.00
60 Pages
Founded in 1963

2878 Russian Aeronautics
Allerton Press
250 W 57th St
New York, NY 10107-2099

212-459-0535
Fax: 646-424-9695
E-Mail: journals@allertonpress.com
Home Page: www.allertonpress.com

W Shalof, Publisher
Vyacheslav A Firsov, Editor-in-Chief

The sole scientific-technical journal in Russia publishing articles on fundamental research, application, and developments in the field of aeronautical, space, rocket science and engineering that are carried out at institutes of higher education, research institutes, design bureaus, and branch enterprises.Published in English and Russian.
Cost: $1945.00
Frequency: Quarterly
ISSN: 1068-7998
Founded in 1971

2879 Soaring Magazine
Soaring Society of America
5425 W Jack Gomez Boulevard
PO Box 2100
Hobbs, NM 88241-2100

505-392-1177
Fax: 505-392-8154
E-Mail: dlayton@ssa.org
Home Page: www.ssa.org

Susan Dew, Staff Writer
Amaris Bradford, Editorial Assistant
Denise Layton, Managing Editor
Dennis Wright, Executive Director

Each issue brings you the latest developments on safety issues, delightful accounts of individual soaring accomplishments, a sharing of ideas and experiences, tips from the great soaring pilots of our times, and much more.
Cost: $26.00
60 Pages
Frequency: Monthly
Founded in 1932

2880 Space News
Army Times Publishing Company
6883 Commercial Dr
Springfield, VA 22151-4202

703-750-7400
800-368-5718
Fax: 703-750-8622
E-Mail: cust-svc@gannettgov.com
Home Page: www.armytimes.com

Elaine Howard, CEO
Tobias Naegele, Editor-in-Chief
Alex Neill, Managing Editor
Judy McCoy, Publisher

For top level executives in government and industry worldwide. Devoted exclusively to issues for military government and commercial space.
Cost: $55.00
Frequency: Weekly
Circulation: 360000
Founded in 1990

2881 Space Times
American Astronautical Society
6352 Rolling Mill Place
Suite 102
Springfield, VA 22152-2370
703-866-0020
Fax: 703-866-3526
E-mail: aas@astronautical.org
Home Page: www.astronautical.org

Frank Slazer, President
James Kirkpatrick, Executive Director
Lin D. Wigbels, Executive Vice President

The voice of the AAS, presenting thought provoking ideas and opinions, features articles on salient issues in space policy and future exploration, and reviews and notes of interest to both the professional and popular community of space flight advocates.
Cost: $85.00
Frequency: Bi-Monthly
Circulation: 1300
ISSN: 1933-2793

2882 The Airline Handbook
Air Transport Association of America
1301 Pennsylvania Ave NW
Suite 1100
Washington, DC 20004-1738

202-626-4000
800-497-3326
Fax: 202-626-4166
E-mail: a4a@airlines.org
Home Page: www.airlines.org
Social Media: Twitter, LinkedIn

Nicholas Calio, President
Steve Lott, VP Communications

2883 Trade-A-Plane
TAP Publishing Company
174 4th St
Crossville, TN 38555-4303

931-484-5137
800-337-5263
Fax: 931-484-2532
E-Mail: info@trade-a-plane.com
Home Page: www.trade-a-plane.com

Cosby A Stone, CEO
L Stone, Circulation Manager

World's largest advertising periodical for general aviation.
Cost: $14.95
Frequency: Monthly
Circulation: 118000
Founded in 1937

2884 Ultralight Flying
Glider Rider
1085 Bailey Avenue
Chattanooga, TN 37404

423-629-5375
Fax: 423-629-5379
Home Page: www.ultralightflying.com

Tracy Knauss, Publisher
Sharon Hill, Editor

Conventional and motorized ultralight flying.
Cost: $36.95
48 Pages
Frequency: Monthly
Circulation: 50000+
Founded in 1973
Printed in on newsprint stock

2885 Vertiflite
American Helicopter Society International
217 N Washington St
Alexandria, VA 22314-2538

703-684-6777
855-247-4685
Fax: 703-739-9279
E-Mail: staff@vtol.org
Home Page: www.vtol.org

Michael Hirschberg, Executive Director
Kim Smith, Editor
Mike Hirschberg, Managing Editor

Magazine published for the vertical flight industry, pursuing excellence within the business, stimulating research, debate and expert opinion.
Cost: $80.00
72 Pages
Frequency: Monthly
Circulation: 12000
ISSN: 0042-4455
Founded in 1943
Printed in 4 colors on glossy stock

2886 Water Flying
Seaplane Pilots Association
3859 Laird Blvd
Lakeland, FL 33811

863-701-7979
888-772-8923
Fax: 863-701-7588
E-Mail: spa@seaplanes.org
Home Page: www.seaplanes.org

Steve McCaughey, Executive Director
Randy Juen, Vice President
J.J. Frey, President

Features articles covering everything from pilot technique and safety to destinations and personalities. Each issue includes industry news and an update on regulatory issues across the country. The March/April issue is our Directory Special, with flight school and float directories.
Cost: $45.00
32 Pages
Circulation: 7500
ISSN: 0733-1754
Founded in 1972
Mailing list available for rent
Printed in on glossy stock

2887 Western Flyer
Northwest Flyer

PO Box 98786
Tacoma, WA 98498-0786

253-968-3422
Fax: 253-588-4005

Dave Sinclair, Publisher
Kirk Gormley, Editor

Covering general aviation, including all aspects of business and sport aviation.
Cost: $24.00
84 Pages
Frequency: BiWeekly
Circulation: 38,000

2888 Wings
Sentry Books
P.O. Box 881526
San Diego, CA 92168

818-368-2012
E-Mail: support@airwingmedia.com
Home Page: www.wingsairpower.com

Mike Machat, Publisher/Editor

Historic aviation, heavy on photos, artwork, drawings, interviews with aviation designers, pilots, engineers.
Cost: $44.00
56 Pages
Frequency: Monthly
Circulation: 30000
ISSN: 1067-0637
Founded in 1971

2889 Wings West
Wiesner Publishing
6160 South Syracuse
Suite 300
Greenwood Village, CO 80111

303-662-5200
Fax: 303-397-7619
Home Page: www.wiesnerpublishing.com

Babette Andre, Editor
Becky Stairs, Advertising Executive
Dan Wiesner, CEO

Information for the mountain aviation community on various facets of western flying, including travel and safety for active pilots.
Cost: $17.97
72 Pages
Frequency: Bi-Monthly

2890 Wings of Gold Magazine
Association of Naval Aviation
2550 Huntington Avenue
Suite 201
Alexandria, VA 22303-1400

703-960-6806
Fax: 703-960-6807
E-Mail: anahqtr@aol.com
Home Page: www.anahq.org

R M Rausa, Editor
Linda Bubien, Advertising Director
Walter Massenburg, President
Jacqueline M Hayes, Editorial Assistant

Articles and commentary designed to inform the public of the value of a strong maritime air posture to US national policy. Also, articles on subjects related to Navy, Marine Corps and Coast Guard aviation, such as personnel technology, history, readiness, aircraft and weapon systems and budgetary issues within DOD and before the Congress.
Cost: $25.00

2891 World Airshow News
Flyer Publications
PO Box 975
East Troy, WI 53120-0975

262-642-2450
Fax: 262-642-4374
E-Mail: jeffparnau@gmail.com
Home Page: www.airshowmag.com
Social Media: Facebook, Twitter, LinkedIn

Jim Froneberger, Editor
Sandra Ruka, Advertising Sales
Jim Froneberger, Editor
Cost: $24.95
Frequency: Nine Times a Year
Circulation: 6000

Trade Shows

2892 AAC Annual Conference & Exposition
Airport Consultants Council
908 King Street
Suite 100
Alexandria, VA 22314-3121

703-683-5900
Fax: 703-583-2564
E-Mail: info@acconline.org
Home Page: www.acconline.org
Social Media: Facebook, Twitter, LinkedIn

Paula P Hochstetler, President
Emily VanderBush, Marketing & Membership Coordinator
John B Reynolds, Coordinator of Communications
Sharon Brown, Director, Programs & Finance

Enhanced networking programs; workshops; keynote speakers; exhibitors.
Frequency: July

2893 AAC/AAAE Airport Planning, Design & Construction Symposium
Airport Consultants Council
908 King Street
Suite 100
Alexandria, VA 22314-3121

703-683-5900
Fax: 703-683-2564
E-Mail: info@acconline.org
Home Page: www.acconline.org
Social Media: Facebook, Twitter, LinkedIn

Paula P Hochstetler, President
Emily VanderBush, Marketing & Membership Coordinator
John B Reynolds, Coordinator of Communications
Sharon Brown, Director, Programs & Finance

Planning and development, land side/terminal facilities development, airside/airfield facility development, program and construction management, and information technology are the focus of the symposium.
600 Attendees
Frequency: Spring

2894 AAS National Conference
American Astronautical Society
6352 Rolling Mill Place
Suite 102
Springfield, VA 22152-2370

703-866-0020
Fax: 703-866-3526
E-Mail: aas@astronautical.org
Home Page: www.astronautical.org

Frank Slazer, President
James Kirkpatrick, Executive Director
350 Attendees
Frequency: Annual, November

2895 ADMA International Fall Conference
Aviation Distributors & Manufacturers Association
100 North 20th Street
Suite 400
Philadelphia, PA 19103-1442

215-320-3872
Fax: 215-564-2175
E-Mail: adma@fernley.com
Home Page: www.adma.org

Michael Shaw, President
F Charles Elkins, Past President
Kristen Olszewski, Executive Director
Meg Taft, Meeting Manager

Educational and informational presentations, group activities, and planned networking functions, including Private Conference Sessions.
Frequency: May, November

2896 AEA International Convention & Trade Show
Aircraft Electronic Association
3570 NE Ralph Powell Road
Lee's Summit, MO 64064

816-347-8400
Fax: 816-347-8405
E-Mail: info@aea.net
Home Page: www.aea.net
Social Media: Facebook, Twitter, LinkedIn, Youtube

Paula Derks, President
Debra McFarland, Executive Vice President
Aaron Ward, Information Services Director
Mike Adamson, VP, Member Training & Education

Workshops, training sessions, keynote speakers, and hundreds of exhibitors in the field of aviation electronics.
Frequency: April

2897 AHS International Annual Forum & Tech Display
American Helicopter Society
217 N Washington Street
Alexandria, VA 22314

703-684-6777
Fax: 703-739-9279
E-Mail: staff@vtol.org
Home Page: www.vtol.org
Social Media: Facebook, Twitter, LinkedIn, RSS, YouTube

Michael Hirschberg, Executive Director
Kay Brackins, Deputy Director/Production Mgr
David Renzi, Director of Meetings & Marketing

Exhibits for technical professionals in aircraft design, engineering, government, operators and industry executives. Over 200 presentations on aerodynamics, acoustics, dynamics, operations, product support, propulsion, testing and evaluation, and other areas. Technology display is concurrent with the Forum and is presented by leading manufacturers, service providers, defense contractors, universities and r&d organizations.
Founded in 1943

2898 AIAA New Horizons Forum & Expo at the Aerospace Science Meeting
American Institute of Aeronautics & Astronautics
1801 Alexander Bell Drive
Suite 500
Reston, VA 20191-4344

703-264-7500
800-639-2422
Fax: 703-264-7551
E-Mail: tammym@aiaa.org
Home Page: www.aiaa.org

Social Media: Facebook, Twitter, LinkedIn, Youtube

Cort Durocher, President
Tammy Marko, Director
Lawrence Garrett, Editor

A forum for scientists and engineers from industry, government and academia to share and disseminate knowledge and research. New Horizons will feature speakers discussing about new technology, challenges, opportunities, and trends, as well as panel discussions. The Aerospace Expo will showcase exhibits from industry, government and small businesses with hardware and software demos, discussions, and opportunities for side meetings.
Frequency: Annual
Founded in 1930

2899 Aerofast SAE Aerospace Automated Fastening Conference & Exposition
Society of Automotive Engineers
400 Commonwealth Drive
Warrendale, PA 15096-0001

72- 77- 484
877-606-7323
Fax: 724-776-0790
Home Page: www.sae.org

Diane Applegate, Meetings/Exhibits
David Shutt, CEO

Annual show of 45 manufacturers or suppliers of fasteners, assembly systems, CNC's, tooling and fixtures, fully automated systems.
400 Attendees
Frequency: September
Founded in 1990

2900 Aerospace Atlantic
Society of Automotive Engineers
400 Commonwealth Drive
Warrendale, PA 15096-0001

724-776-4841
877-606-7323
Fax: 724-776-0790
Home Page: www.sae.org

David Shutt, President

Annual show of 30 exhibitors of aircraft systems and components, engineering services, electronics, power systems and computer services.
700 Attendees
Frequency: 84,000 Members

2901 Aerospace Medical Association Meeting
Aerospace Medical Association
320 S Henry Street
Alexandria, VA 22314-3579

703-739-2240
Fax: 703-739-9652
E-Mail: inquiries@asma.org
Home Page: www.asma.org

Jeffrey Sventek, Executive Director
Gisselle Vargas, Operations Manager

Provides a multi-faceted forum for all aerospace medical disciplines and concurrently provides continuing education credits for those attending the meeting. Lectures, seminars, panels, poster presentations, workshops, film reports, and technical and scientific exhibits present data on the latest results of clinical and research studies.
Frequency: Annual

2902 Aerospace Testing Expo
Society of Flight Test Engineers
44814 N Elm Avenue
Lancaster, CA 93534
661-949-2095
Fax: 661-949-2096
E-Mail: sfte@sfte.org
Home Page: www.sfte.org
Social Media: Facebook, Twitter, LinkedIn, Youtube

Peter Donath, President
Michael Barrlett, Vice President
Frequency: April

2903 Aerotech: Society of Automotive Engineers Aerospace Technology Congress
Society of Automotive Engineers
400 Commonwealth Drive
Warrendale, PA 15096-0001

724-776-4841
877-606-7323
Fax: 724-776-0790
E-Mail: advertising@sae.org
Home Page: www.sae.org

David Shutt, President

Annual show of 80 suppliers to aerospace engineers and designers.
2500 Attendees
Frequency: October

2904 Agricultural Aviation Convention
National Agricultural Aviation Association
1440 Duke Street
Alexandria, VA 22314

202-546-5722
Fax: 202-546-5726
E-Mail: information@agaviation.org
Home Page: www.agaviation.org

Andrew Moore, Executive Director
Jay Calleja, Manager,Programs, & Events

Information on agricultural aviation business, agricultural aircraft, legislative issues, pesticides, new products and services, safety, maintenance, people, state and regional association news. 135 booths.
1300 Attendees

2905 Air Cargo Forum and Exposition
The International Air Cargo Association
PO Box 661510
Miami, FL 33266-1510

786-265-7011
Fax: 786-265-7012
E-Mail: secgen@tiacca.org
Home Page: www.tiaca.org

Tom Davis, Deputy Director, Exhibits
Michael Steen, Chairman
Oliver Evans, Vice Chairman

This is the premier show for the Air Cargo Industry.
3000 Attendees
Frequency: September

2906 Air Medical Transport Conference
Association of Air Medical Services
909 N Washington Street
Suite 410
Alexandria, VA 22314

703-836-8732
Fax: 703-836-8920
E-Mail: information@aams.org
Home Page: www.aams.org

John Fiegel, Executive Director/CEO
Blair Marie Beggan, Communications/Marketing Director
Natasha Ross, Education/Meetings Manager
Elena Sierra, Membership Manager

Attendees are emergency medical and critical care professionals from both hospital and independent providers of air and ground medical transport services. CEO's, program directors, medical directors, physicians, nurses, respiratory therapists, paramedics, pilots, communication specialists and mechanics.
1800 Attendees
Frequency: Annual/Fall
Founded in 1980
Mailing list available for rent: 1600 names

2907 Air Medical Transport Conference (AMTC)
Association of Air Medical Services
909 N Washington Street
Suite 410
Alexandria, VA 22314

703-836-8732
Fax: 703-836-8920
E-Mail: information@aams.org
Home Page: www.aams.org

Rick Sherlock, President
Natasha Ross, Education & Meetings Manager
Elena Sierra, Membership Manager
Blair Marie Beggan, Communication & Marketing Manager

Provides up-to-date information on the latest techniques and innovative approaches to air medical practice from community experts, and continuing education credits opportunities; keynote speakers and educational offerings, plus technology demos and networking opportunities; and the largest trade show of the industry with exhibits from hundreds of providers.
Frequency: March

2908 Air Show Trade Expo International
Dayton International Airport
3800 Wright Drive
Suite A
Vandalia, OH 45377

937-898-5901
877-359-3291
Fax: 937-898-5121
E-Mail: info@daytonairshow.com
Home Page: www.daytonairshow.com

Terry Greivous, Executive Director
Brenda Kerfoot, General Manager

One hundred and thirty three booths that encompass all aspects of the global aerospace industry. Commercial and military aircraft and equipment, plus major suppliers' products and services display.
12M Attendees
Frequency: July

2909 Air Traffic Control Association Convention
Air Traffic Control Association
1101 King St
Suite 300
Alexandria, VA 22314

703-299-2430
Fax: 703-299-2437
E-Mail: info@atca.org
Home Page: www.atca.org

Peter Dumont, President
Kenneth Carlisle, Director of Meetings & Expositions

Containing over 325 booths and exhibits of air traffic control products and services.
4,500 Attendees
Frequency: 3 times per year

2910 Aircraft Electronics Association Annual Convention & Trade Show
Aircraft Electronics Association
3570 NE Ralph Powell Road
Lee's Summit, MO 64064

816-347-8400
Fax: 816-347-8405
E-Mail: info@aea.net
Home Page: www.aea.net

Paula Derks, President
Debra McFarland, VP

Annual show of 131 exhibitors of industry related equipment and supplies.
1500 Attendees
Frequency: March/April Annual
Founded in 1980

2911 **Aircraft Owners & Pilots Association Expo**
Aircraft Owners & Pilots Association
421 Aviation Way
Frederick, MD 21701
301-695-2000
800-872-2672
Fax: 301-695-2375
E-Mail: aopahq@aopa.org
Home Page: www.aopa.org
Craig Fuller, President
Robert Moran, COO
From the latest technology, to tools and flight gear, you'll find today's best products. 500 Exhibit Booths.
Frequency: June

2912 **Aircraft Owners Pilots Association Expo**
Aircraft Owners & Pilots Association
421 Aviation Way
Frederick, MD 21701
301-695-2000
888-462-3976
Fax: 301-695-2375
Home Page: www.aopa.org
Craig Fuller, President
Robert Moran, COO
Annual exhibits of single-engine and multi-engine aircraft, avionics, financing information and related equipment, supplies and services. Expo offers 75 seminar hours covering the latest safety, medical, proficiency, ownership, and technology issues. Over 500 booths.
Frequency: November

2913 **Airliners International**
World Airline Historical Society
PO Box 489
Ocoee, FL 34761
904-221-1446
Fax: 407-522-9352
E-Mail: president@WAHSOnline.com
Home Page: www.wahsonline.com
Social Media: Facebook, Twitter
Duane Young, President
Craig Morris, VP
1000 Attendees
Frequency: Annual/August
Founded in 1977

2914 **Airlines Electronic Engineering Committee Conference**
Airlines Electronic Engineering Committee
2551 Riva Road
Annapolis, MD 21401-7435
410-266-4000
Fax: 410-266-2047
Home Page: www.arinc.com
Daniel A Martinec, Chairman
Roger S Goldberg, Show Contact
Annual show and exhibit of air transport avionics equipment and systems.
Frequency: October

2915 **Airport Systems Action Planning Meeting**
ARINC
2551 Riva Road
Annapolis, MD 21401
410-664-4000
80 -63 -688
Fax: 410-266-2329
E-Mail: flightops@arinc.com
Home Page: www.arinc.com
Social Media: Facebook, Twitter, LinkedIn
Lee Suarez, Staff VP
John M Belcher, Chairman/CEO
Stephen Waechter, VP Business Operations/CFO
Linda Hartwig, Sr Dir Corporate Communications
The meeting format will include organizational, technical, and project updates from the ARINC management team.
Frequency: September
Founded in 1920

2916 **Airports Council International - North America Annual Conference & Expo**
Airports Council International
1775 K Street NW
Suite 500
Washington, DC 20006
202-293-8500
Fax: 202-331-1362
E-Mail: apeters@aci-na,org
Home Page: www.aci-na.org
Social Media: Facebook, Twitter, LinkedIn, Youtube
Gregory Principato, President
Deborah McElroy, VP
Nancy Zimini, SVP Administration and Operations
Representatives from more than 100 airports around the world attend this exhibition and conference; seminars, discussions and speakers about air travel and the industry, developing legal affairs, challenges and best practices; hundreds of exhibitors.
Frequency: September
Founded in 1948

2917 **Airports Council International: North America Convention**
Airports Council International-North America
1775 K Street NW
Suite 500
Washington, DC 20006
202-293-8500
Fax: 202-331-1362
Home Page: www.aci-na.org
Deborah McElroy, Vice President
Nancy Zimini, SVP Administration & Operations
Juliet Wright, Senior Director Public Relations
Gregory Principato, President
Annual show and exhibit of air transportation equipment, supplies and services.
Frequency: Annual

2918 **American Bonanza Society Convention**
Midcontinent Airport
PO Box 12888
Wichita, KS 67277
316-945-1700
Fax: 316-945-1710
E-Mail: ABSMail@bonanza.org
Home Page: www.bonanza.org
Nancy Johnson, Executive Director
Peggy L Fuksa, Events Coordinator
Annual convention featuring educational seminars and 75-100 exhibits of equipment, supplies and services for the aviation industry, including aftermarket products, safety items and computer weather services.
1200 Attendees
Frequency: September
Founded in 1967

2919 **Annual Repair Symposium**
Aeronautical Repair Station Association
121 N Henry Street
Alexandria, VA 22314-2903
703-739-9543
Fax: 703-739-9488
E-Mail: arsa@arsa.org
Home Page: www.arsa.org
Social Media: Facebook, Twitter, LinkedIn, Youtube
Craig Fabian, VP
Daniel Fisher, VP
The Symposium will include a variety of sessions on topical subjects. Legislative Day will inform you about the issues that affect your business, and includes the opportunity for you to arrange Capitol Hill meetings with your representatives, senators and congressional staff.
Frequency: Annual/March

2920 **Annual Scientific Meeting**
Aerospace Medical Association
320 S Henry Street
Alexandria, VA 22314-3579
703-739-2240
Fax: 703-739-9652
E-Mail: rrayman@asma.org
Home Page: www.asma.org
Jeffrey Sventek, Executive Director
Gisselle Vargas, Operations Manager
Russell Rayman MD, Executive Director
Provides a multi-faceted forum for all aerospace medical disciplines and concurrently provides continuing education credits for those attending the meeting.
3000 Attendees
Frequency: Annual/May
Founded in 1929
Mailing list available for rent

2921 **Army Aviation Association of America Convention**
Army Aviation Association of America
755 Main Street
Suite 4D
Monroe, CT 06468-2830
203-268-2450
Fax: 203-268-5870
E-Mail: aaaa@quad-a.org
Home Page: www.quad-a.org
Social Media: Facebook, Twitter, Youtube
Daniel J Petrosky, President
Howard Yellen, Senior Vice President
E.J, Sinclair, Secretary
A show of 275 or more exhibitors both military and industry displaying technology and material pertinent to the army aviation community.
6000 Attendees
Frequency: Annual/May
Founded in 1978

2922 **Arnic Aviation Customer Meeting**
British Telecommunications
2551 Riva Road
Annapolis, MD 21401
410-266-4000
800-633-6882
Fax: 410-266-2329
E-Mail: flightops@arinc.com
Home Page: www.arinc.com
Social Media: Facebook, Twitter, LinkedIn, Youtube
Lee Suarez, Staff VP
John M Belcher, Chairman/CEO
Stephen Waechter, VP Business Operations/CFO
Linda Hartwig, Sr Dir Corporate Communications
Up to date information on the current and future products and services of Arnic and its strategic partners in Asia.
Frequency: May
Founded in 1920

2923 **Arnic Global Communications Workshop**
British Telecommunications
2551 Riva Road
Annapolis, MD 21401

410-266-4000
800-633-6882
Fax: 410-266-2329
E-Mail: flightops@arinc.com
Home Page: www.arinc.com
Social Media: Facebook, Twitter, LinkedIn, Youtube

Lee Suarez, Staff VP
John M Belcher, Chairman/CEO
Stephen Waechter, VP Business Operations/CFO
Linda Hartwig, Sr Dir Corporate Communications

Concentrates on the communications needs of the airlines serving the Latin America/Caribbean region, and provides information on the benefits of implementing a data link program and associated applications.
Frequency: May
Founded in 1920

2924 **Aviation Insurance Association Conference**
Aviation Insurance Association
400 Admiral Blvd
Kansas City, MO 64106

816-221-8488
Fax: 816-472-7765
E-Mail: mandie@aiaweb.org
Home Page: www.aiaweb.org
Social Media: Facebook

Trevor Light, President
Paul Herbers, Vice President
Meredith Carr, Director, Marketing & Membership

Provides a forum for the biggest names and best minds in the aviation insurance industry. Offers top-notch speakers, continuing education classes, time with vendors and opportunities to network and develop relationships that last a lifetime.
Frequency: Annual
Founded in 1976

2925 **Aviation Services and Suppliers Supershow**
National Air Transportation Association
4226 King Street
Alexandria, VA 22302

703-845-9000
800-808-6282
Fax: 703-845-8176
Home Page: www.nata.aero

James K Coyne, President
Eric Byer, VP
Diane Gleason, Manager Meetings/Conventions
Eric R Byer, Dir Government/Industry Affairs

Workshop, conference, seminar and 700 exhibits of aviation products & services for fixed base and air charter operators.
5000 Attendees
Frequency: May/Annual

2926 **Aviation Show South America**
American Aerospace & Defense Industries
212 Carengie Center
Suite 203
Princeton, NJ 08540

609-987-9050
Fax: 609-987-0277
E-Mail: info@aadi.net
Home Page: www.aadi.net

Marianne Ferrandi, Show Contact

One hundred and seven exhibitors of areospace information.
90000 Attendees
Frequency: July

2927 **Aviation Technician Education Council Conference**
Aviation Technician Education Council
2090 Wexford Court
Harrisburg, PA 17112-1579

717-540-7121
Fax: 717-540-7121
E-Mail: info@atec-amt.org
Home Page: www.atec-amt.org

Vince Jones, President
Richard Dumaresq, Executive Director

Annual conference and exhibits of aviation maintenance equipment, supplies and services.
150 Attendees
Frequency: April

2928 **Business Information Technology Conference**
Airports Council International - North America
1775 K Street NW
Suite 500
Washington, DC 20036-2463

202-293-8500
Fax: 202-331-1362
E-Mail: meetings@aci-na.org
Home Page: www.aci-na.org

Gregory Principato, President
Diedre Clemmons, Director, Conferences
Cassandra Jackson, Manager, Conferences

Hear from industry experts and peers on the latest way to deal with IT challenges, maximize the value of your IT infrastructure and anticipate new technologies.
Frequency: Annual

2929 **Civil Air Patrol Annual Conference**
Civil Air Patrol
105 S Hansell Street
Building 714
Maxwell AFB, AL 36112-6332

334-834-2236
877-227-9142
Fax: 334-953-4262
Home Page: www.capmembers.com

Brig Gen Amy Courter, Interim National Commander
1.2M Attendees
Frequency: August
Founded in 1930

2930 **Civil Aviation Medical Association Conference**
Civil Aviation Medical Association
PO Box 2382
Peachtree City, GA 30269-2382

77- 48- 010
Fax: 77- 48- 008
E-Mail: david.millett@yahoo.com
Home Page: www.civilavmed.com

James Heins MD, President
David Millet MD, Executive VP
Gordon Ritter, Secretary/Treasurer

Annual conference and exhibits of aviation medical equipment, supplies and services. Containing 15 booths.
250 Attendees
Frequency: October
Founded in 1948

2931 **Defense & Security Symposium**
International Society for Optical Engineering
PO Box 10
Bellingham, WA 98227-0010

360-676-3290
888-504-8171
Fax: 360-647-1445
E-Mail: CustomerService@SPIE.org
Home Page: www.spie.org

Dr John C Carrano, Contact Person
Dr Larry B Stotts, Contact Person
Dr. Katarina Svanberg, President
William Arnold, Vice President

A large, unclassified international symposium related to sensors and sensor networks.
5700 Attendees
Frequency: March

2932 **Economic Specialty Conference**
Airports Association Council International
1775 K Street NW
Suite 500
Washington, DC 20006

202-293-8500
Fax: 202-331-1362
Home Page: www.aci-na.org

Gregory Principato, President
Nancy Zimini, VP
Christopher Oswald, SVP Technical Affairs
Ian A Redhead, VP Airport Services
Patricia Hahn, EVP Operations/General Counsel

Provided with information on the latest economic trends for airports and the airport industry. Attendees include executive directors and CFOs from airports throughout North America, plys representatives from insurance companies and airport concessionaires.
Frequency: May

2933 **Experimental Aircraft Association AirVenture**
Experimental Aircraft Association
3000 Poberezny Road
PO Box 3086
Oshkosh, WI 54902

920-426-4800
800-236-4800
Fax: 920-232-7772
E-Mail: webmaster@eaa.org
Home Page: www.airventure.org

Tom Poberezny, President
David Berkley, Communications Dirctor
Adam Smith, VP Member Services

Recreational aviation event, with more than 765,000 people and 10,000 airplanes attending. Containing 900 booths and 730 exhibits.
765M Attendees
Founded in 1953

2934 **Fall Education Conference**
University Aviation Association
3410 Skyway Drive
Auburn, AL 36830-6444

334-844-2434
Fax: 334-844-2432
E-Mail: uaamail@uaa.aero
Home Page: www.uaa.aero

Carolyn Williamson, Executive Director
Mary Chandler, Coordinator Office Administration
Founded in 1947

2935 **GTO Annual Convention & Fly In**
Pipers Owner Society & Cessna Owner Organization
PO Box 5000
Iola, WI 54945

715-445-5000
888-692-3776
Fax: 715-445-4053
E-Mail: help@piperowner.org

Home Page: www.gto.aircraftownersgroup.com

Dan Weiler, Executive Director
Joe Jones, Publisher

Annual fly in prior to the EAA AirVenture.
150 Attendees
Frequency: Annual

2936 **Gate Way to Oshkosh**
Cessna Owner Organization
N7450 Aanstad Rd
Iola, WI 54945

715-445-5000
888-692-3776
Fax: 715-445-4053
E-Mail: help@cessnaowner.org
Home Page: www.cessnaowner.org

Dan Weiler, Executive Director
Joe Jones, Publisher
150 Members
Frequency: Annual

2937 **Heli-Expo**
Helicopter Association International
1635 Prince Street
Alexandria, VA 22314-2818

703-683-4646
Fax: 703-683-4745
E-Mail: heliexpo@rotor.com
Home Page: www.rotor.com

Matthew Zuccaro, President
Edward DiCampli, Executive Vice President
Elaine Little, Administrative Services Manager

The world's largest tradeshow dedicated to the international helicopter community. Attend for new ideas, business solutions, products and services, and networking. Over 550 exhibiting companies offering engines, avionics, instruments, modifications, helicopters for every mission, finance, insurance, software, uniforms and safety gear, mechanic and pilot training, parts, and accessories.
16000 Attendees
Frequency: February

2938 **IFSA Annual Conference & Exhibition**
Inflight Food Service Association
304 W Liberty Street
Suite 201
Louisville, KY 40202-3011

502-583-3783
Fax: 502-589-3602
Home Page: www.ifsanet.com

Pam Chumley, Executive Administrator
Jim Fowler, Executive Director
Jacqueline Petty, Manager of Communications
Caitlin Ellery, Membership Manager

An opportunity to experience excellent educational speakers, panel discussions, culinary demos, and general sessions focused on important issues in the in-flight and onboard foodservice industry. An exhibition is held in conjunction with the conference to exhibit the latest innovations while providing network opportunities with key leaders and decision makers in in-flight and railway catering.
Frequency: Annual

2939 **International Air Cargo Forum & Exposition**
International Air Cargo Association
5600 NW 36th Street
Suite 620
Miami, FL 33266-1510

786-265-7011
Fax: 786-265-7012
E-Mail: secgen@tiaca.org
Home Page: www.tiaca.org

Michael Steen, Chairman
George F Johnson, Treasurer
Daniel F Fernandez, Secretary General

Biennial trade show of the air cargo industry featuring services and products from aircraft manufacturers, airlines, airports, freight forwarders trade publications logistics consultants.
4,000 Attendees
Frequency: September
Founded in 1960

2940 **Joint Airports Environmental/Technical Committee Meeting**
Airports Association Council International
1615 L Street
Suite 300
Washington, DC 20006

202-293-8500
888-424-7767
Fax: 202-331-1362
E-Mail: memberservices@aci-na.org
Home Page: www.aci-na.org
Social Media: Facebook, Twitter, LinkedIn

Gregory Principato, President
Nancy Zimini, VP
Christopher Oswald, SVP Technical Affairs
Frequency: May
Founded in 1948

2941 **NATA FBO Leadership Conference**
National Air Transportation Association
4226 King Street
Alexandria, VA 22302

703-845-9000
800-808-6282
Fax: 703-845-8176
E-Mail: info@nata-online.org
Home Page: www.nata.aero
Social Media: Facebook, Twitter, LinkedIn

James Sweeney, Chairperson
Thomas Hendricks, President

An opportunity for business leaders to meet with their customers and learn about the latest challenges and opportunities facing their industry. d seminars. The Conference will focus on the changing climate of the industry and the developing environment. Opportunities to learn service and marketing techniques, network and exchange best practices.
Frequency: Annual

2942 **NBAA Annual Meeting & Convention**
National Business Aviation Association
1200 18th Street NW
Suite 400
Washington, DC 20036

202-783-9000
Fax: 702-331-8364
E-Mail: info@nbaa.org
Home Page: www.nbaa.org

Ed Bolen, President/CEO

Learning sessions, networking opportunities, 1,000 exhibitors, demonstrations and displays.
32000 Attendees
Frequency: September

2943 **National Space Symposium**
Space Foundation
4425 Arrowswest Drive
Colorado Springs, CO 80907

719-768-8000
800-691-4000
Fax: 719-576-8801
E-Mail: web@spacefoundation.org
Home Page: www.spacefoundation.org
Social Media: Facebook, Twitter, LinkedIn

Martin Faga, Chairman
Elliot G Pulham, President/CEO

The National Space Symposium is the premier U.S. policy and program forum, providing an opportunity for information and interaction on all sectors of space - civil, commercial, and national security. The conference is attended by industry leaders, military and government officials and general space enthusiasts, and covered locally and nationally by broadcast, print and industry trade media.
Frequency: Annually/April

2944 **Ninety Nines International Conference**
International Organization of Women Pilots
4300 Amelia Earhart Road
Oklahoma City, OK 73159-1140

405-685-7969
800-994-1929
Fax: 405-685-7985
E-Mail: 99s@ninety-nines.org
Home Page: www.ninety-nines.org

Susan Larson, President
Pat Theberge, VP
Corbi Bulluck, Director
Laura Ohrenberg, Headquarters Manager
Frances Luckhart, Secretary
Frequency: August

2945 **PAMA Aviation Maintenance & Management Symposium**
Professional Aviation Maintenance Association
972 E Tuttle Road
Building 204
Ionia, MI 48846

724-772-4092
800-356-1671
Fax: 616-527-1327
E-Mail: hq@pama.org
Home Page: www.pama.org
Social Media: Facebook, Twitter, LinkedIn

Roger Sickler, Chairman
Jeff Gruber, Vice Chairman
John Wicht, Secretary
Frequency: March
Founded in 1972

2946 **PRA International Conference**
Popular Rotorcraft Association
PO Box 68
Mentone, IN 46539

574-353-7227
Fax: 574-353-7021
E-Mail: prahq@medt.com
Home Page: www.pra.org

B Scott Lewis, President
Tim O'Connor, VP

Exhibits, flight demonstrations, contests, commercial exhibits, great food, forums on rotorcraft topics, and unlimited fun! There are also many other events sanctioned by PRA and its local chapters.
2000 Attendees
Frequency: August

2947 **PRA International Convention Fly-In**
Popular Rotorcraft Association
PO Box 68
Mentone, IN 46539

574-353-7227
Fax: 574-353-7021
Home Page: www.pra.org

Igor Bensen, Founder
Scott Lewis, President
Tim O'Connor, VP

The largest gathering of homebuilt rotorcraft in the world. It has exhibits, flight demonstrations, contests, commercial exhibits, great food, forums on rotorcraft topics, and unlimited fun.
3500 Attendees
Frequency: Annual/Summer

2948 **Professional Aviation Maintenance Symposium and Trade Show**
Professional Aviation Maintenance Association
972 E Tuttle Road
Building 204
Ionia, MI 48846

202-300-0258
800-356-1671
Fax: 616-527-1327
E-Mail: hq@pama.org
Home Page: www.pama.org

Dale Forton, President

Annual show of 200 exhibitors of aviation and aerospace products for the aviation maintenance industry.
2000 Attendees
Frequency: March

2949 **Regional Airline Association Convention**
Regional Airline Association
2025 M Street NW
Suite 800
Washington, DC 20036

202-367-1170
Fax: 202-367-2170
E-Mail: raa@raa.org
Home Page: www.raa.org
Social Media: Facebook, Twitter

Roger Cohen, President
Scott Foose, Vice President

A forum for airport and airline professionals held twice a year in the spring and fall.
Frequency: May/October

2950 **Regional Airline Association Spring Meeting**
Regional Airline Association
2025 M Street NW
Suite 800
Washington, DC 20036

202-367-1170
Fax: 202-367-2170
E-Mail: raa@raa.org
Home Page: www.raa.org
Social Media: Facebook, Twitter

Roger Cohen, President
Scott Foose, Vice President

Forum for airport and airline professionals.
1.6M Attendees
Frequency: May

2951 **Reliability Engineering and Management Institute Conference**
Univ of Arizona, Aerospace & Mechanical Engin Dept
1130 N Mountain Avenue
Building 119 Room N 517
Tucson, AZ 85721

520-621-6120
Fax: 520-621-8191
E-Mail: dimitri@u.arizona.edu
Home Page: www.u.arizona.edu/~dimitri/

Dr Dimitri B Kececioglu, Manager

Provides all engineers, and particularly Reliability Managers and Engineers, and Products Assurance Managers and Engineers in government and Industry, with a working knowledge of Reliability Engineering Theory and Practice; Mechanical Reliability Prediction; Reliability Testing and Demonstration; Failure Analysis (FAMECA); Complete Industry Product Assurance strategies; Maintainability Engineering; Reliability and Quality Management; Manufacturing Techniques, and more.
Frequency: Nov Arizona

2952 **Reliability Testing Institute**
University Of Arizona
1130 N Mountain Avenue
Tucson, AZ 85721

520-621-6120
Fax: 520-621-8191
E-Mail: dimitri@u.arizona.edu
Home Page: www.u.arizona.edu/~dimitri/

Dr Dimitri Kececioglu PE, Prof Aerospace/Mech Engineering

An institute to help provide a working knowledge in reliability engineering.
Frequency: May

2953 **SAE AeroTech Congress & Exhibition**
Society of Automotive Engineers
400 Commonwealth Drive
Warrendale, PA 15086-7511

724-776-4841
877-606-7323
Fax: 724-776-0790
E-Mail: jhudson@sae.org
Home Page: www.sae.org
Social Media: Facebook, Twitter, LinkedIn, Youtube

David Shutt, President

Provides a forum for the aerospace community to meet and discuss current and future challenges, opportunities and requirements of next-generation R&D, products, and systems, and to develop professional relationships among the worldwide community. Technical sessions, panel discussions, keynote speakers, presentations and demonstrations.
3M Attendees
Frequency: Annual

2954 **SAE Government/Industry Event**
Society of Automotive Engineers
400 Commonwealth Drive
Warrendale, PA 15086-7511

724-776-4841
877-606-7323
Fax: 724-776-0790
E-Mail: mjena@sae.org
Home Page: www.sae.org
Social Media: Facebook, Twitter, LinkedIn, Youtube

David Shutt, President

Awards and presentations, technical sessions, network receptions, and exhibits.
Frequency: Annual

2955 **SAE World Congress**
Society of Automotive Engineers
400 Commonwealth Drive
Warrendale, PA 15096-0001

724-776-4841
877-606-7323
Fax: 724-776-0790
E-Mail: agrech@sae.org
Home Page: www.sae.org
Social Media: Facebook, Twitter, LinkedIn, Youtube

David Shutt, President

Reinvented in 2010, the World Conference provides a highly relevant and engaging technical program, expanded and improved opportunities for networking and information exchange, and innovative exhibits.
3.5M Attendees
Frequency: Annual

2956 **SAFE Symposium**
SAFE Association
PO Box 130
Creswell, OR 97426

541-895-3012
Fax: 541-895-3014
E-Mail: safe@peak.org
Home Page: www.safeassociation.com
Social Media: Facebook

Robert Billings, President
Marcia Baldwin, President-Elect

The Symposium provides an internationally attended marketplace for the exchange of technical information, product and service exhibitions, and the showcasing of industry capabilities for meeting challenges in vehicular occupant protection and personnel worn safety equipment.
Frequency: October

2957 **SAMPE Fall Technical Conference**
Society for the Advancement of Material & Process
1161 Park View Drive
Suite 200
Covina, CA 91724

626-331-0616
800-562-7360
Fax: 626-332-8929
E-Mail: sampeibo@sampe.org
Home Page: www.sampe.org
Social Media: Facebook, LinkedIn

Priscilla Heredia, Conference & General Information
Karen Chapman, Exhibit Information

The Society for the Advancement of Material and Process Engineering's Fall event showcases the latest technology, applications and materials for the advanced manufacturing marketplace; educational sessions, and exhibits.
Frequency: Annual/Fall

2958 **SAMPE Spring Conference & Exhibition**
Society for the Advancement of Material & Process
1161 Park View Drive
Suite 200
Covina, CA 91724

626-331-0616
800-562-7360
Fax: 626-332-8929
E-Mail: sampeibo@sampe.org
Home Page: www.sampe.org
Social Media: Facebook, LinkedIn

Priscilla Heredia, Conference & General Information
Karen Chapman, Exhibit Information

The Society for the Advancement of Material and Process Engineering's Spring event showcases the latest technology, applications and materials for the advanced manufacturing marketplace; educational sessions, and exhibits.
Frequency: Annual/Spring

2959 **Sea-Air-Space**
Navy League of the United States
11208 Waples Mill Road
Suite 112
Fairfax, VA 22030

703-631-6200
800-564-4220
Fax: 703-818-9177
E-Mail: sales@jspargo.com
Home Page: www.jspargo.com

Paul doCarmo, Assistant Director/Exhibit Sales
Connie Shaw, Exhibit Sales Account Manager

Annual event to help promote and develop a technologically advanced naval force.
6000 Attendees
Frequency: April

2960 Seaplane Pilots Association Conference
Seaplane Pilots Association
3859 Laird Blvd
Lakeland, FL 33811
863-701-7979
888-772-8923
Fax: 863-701-7588
E-Mail: spa@seaplanes.org
Home Page: www.seaplanes.org
Steve McCaughey, Executive Director
Randy Juen, Vice President
Thirty booths and conference.
1.5M Attendees
Frequency: September

2961 Soaring Society of America Annual Convention
Soaring Society of America
5425 W Jack Gomez Boulevard
PO Box 2100
Hobbs, NM 88241-2100
505-392-1177
Fax: 505-392-8154
E-Mail: merchandise@ssa.org
Home Page: www.ssa.org
Meetings, exhibits, and displays.
Frequency: Annual

2962 Society of Automotive Engineers: Aerotech Expo
Society of Automotive Engineers
400 Commonwealth Drive
Warrendale, PA 15096-0001
772- 77- 484
877-606-7323
Fax: 248-273-2494
E-Mail: advertising@sae.org
Home Page: www.sae.org
David Shutt, President
Exhibits of commercial, military, business and general aviation.

2963 Society of Experimental Test Pilots
Society of Experimental Test Pilots
44814 Elm Avenue
Lancaster, CA 93534
661-942-9574
Fax: 661-940-0398
E-Mail: setp@setp.org
Home Page: www.setp.org
Steve Rainey, President
Paula Smith, Executive Director
These conferences provide major forums for the discussion of aspects of tax, accounting, administration, statute and case law, which are of general concern to practitioners, as well as providing advance knowledge of developments affecting trusts, estates and subjects of allied subjects. Twenty Booths.
1.5M Attendees
Frequency: September

2964 Strategic Space and Defense
Space Foundation
4425 Arrowswest Drive
Colorado Springs, CO 80907
719-576-8000
Fax: 719-576-8801
E-Mail: web@spacefoundation.org
Home Page: www.spacefoundation.org
Elliot G Pullman, President/CEO
Chuck Zimkas, Chief Operating Officer
Holly Roberts, CFO
The definitive global security conference where the senior leadership of U.S. Strategic Command, component and supported commands, and the executive leadership of the national security industrial base gather to gain insight on the Command's mission, global activities and relationships.
Frequency: October

2965 United States Pilots Association Meeting
United States Pilots Association
1652 Indian Point Road
Branson, MO 65616
417-338-2225
E-Mail: jan@hoynacki.com
Home Page: www.uspilots.org
Paul Hough, Chairman
Jan Hoynacki, Executive Director
Holds two meetings a year — in the spring and fall.
Frequency: June/Septemter

2966 United States Ultralight Association
United States Ultralight Association
PO Box 3501
Gettysburg, PA 17325-1810
717-339-0200
Fax: 717-339-0063
E-Mail: usua@usua.com
Home Page: www.usua.org
Steve McCaughey, Executive Director
Dale Hooper, Executive VP
Annual meeting and exhibits of ultralight and microlight aviation equipment, supplies and services. There will be 20 booths.
3000 Attendees
Frequency: February
Founded in 1998

2967 World Airline Historical Society Convention
World Airline Historical Society
PO Box 489
Ocoee, FL 34761
904-221-1446
Fax: 407-522-9352
E-Mail: Information@WAHSOnline.com
Home Page: www.wahsonline.com
Duane Young, President
Craig Morris, Vice President
Convention and exhibits of airline memorabilia, including airplane models, airline schedules, postcards, posters, photos and publications from airlines.
500 Members
Frequency: Annual
Founded in 1977

Directories & Databases

2968 AAMS Resource Guide
Association of Air Medical Services
909 N Washington Street
Suite 410
Alexandria, VA 22314
703-836-8732
Fax: 703-836-8920
E-Mail: information@aams.org
Home Page: www.aams.org
John Fiegel, Executive Director
Blair Marie Beggan, Communications & Marketing
Gloria Dow, Editor
The directory contains information on the association and its products and services; pertinent details on members, including demographic and historical information; and special crew listings that help community members perform their jobs better through enhanced networking opportunities. It also provides decision makers with a buyer's guide of community vendors and suppliers and the services they supply.

2969 ABD: Aviation Buyer's Directory
Air Service Directory
116 Radio Circle
Suite #302
Mt Kisco, NY 10549
914-242-8700
Fax: 914-242-5422
E-Mail: abd@abdonline.com
Home Page: abdonline.com/
Manufacturers and dealers of aviation equipment and aircraft are the focus of this directory.
Cost: $25.00
400 Pages
Frequency: Quarterly
Circulation: 17,000

2970 AOPA's Airport Directory
Aircraft Owners & Pilots Association
421 Aviation Way
Frederick, MD 21701-4756
301-695-2000
800-872-2672
Fax: 301-695-2375
Home Page: www.aopa.org
Craig Fuller, President
Includes information on over 7,400 airports, seaplane bases and heliports. Also covers more than 2,200 private use airports. In addition to basic airport information such as runways, lighting, approaches, frequencies, identifiers and lat/long, you'll also find listings of nearby hotels, transportation, restaurants, etc. Paperback.
Cost: $29.95
680 Pages
Frequency: Annual
Circulation: 300,000
Founded in 1962
Printed in one color on glossy stock

2971 Address List for Regional Airports Divisions and Airport Districts
US Federal Aviation Administration
800 Independence Avenue SW
Washington, DC 20591-0001
202-366-4000
866-835-5322
Fax: 202-493-5032
Home Page: www.faa.gov
David Grizzle, COO
David Weingart, Chief of Staff
Offers district offices and airports.
20 Pages

2972 Aerospace Database
Cambridge Scientific Abstracts
Aerospace Access
59 John Street, 7th Floor
New York, NY 10038
212-349-1120
Fax: 212-349-1283
Tony Lenti, Managing Editor
Earl Spencer, Owner
Provides bibliographic coverage of basic and applied research in aeronautics, astronautics, and space sciences. The database also covers technology development and applications in complementary and supporting fields such as chemistry, geosciences, physics, communications, and electronics. In addition to periodic literature, the database also includes coverage of reports issued by NASA, other US government agencies, international institutions, universities, and private firms.

2973 Airline Handbook
Air Transport Association

1301 Pennsylvania Ave NW
Suite 1100
Washington, DC 20004

202-626-4000
800-497-3326
Fax: 301-206-9789
E-Mail: a4a@airlines.org
Home Page: www.airlines.org

Nicholas Calio, President/CEO

Overview of the history, structure, economics and operations of the airline industry. Includes a glossary of commonly used airline terminology.
Cost: $10.00
Frequency: Hardcover
Founded in 2001

2974 **Airport Operators Council International**
1775 K St NW
Suite 500
Washington, DC 20006-1529

202-293-8500
Fax: 202-331-1362
E-Mail: webmaster@aci-na.org
Home Page: www.aci-na.com

Gregory Principato, President
Deborah McElroy, Executive VP External Affairs
Nancy Zimini, Senior Vice President

Contains an annual time series of aviation and airport data for more than 580 airports from the Worldwide Airport Traffic Report.
Founded in 1948

2975 **Airports**
CTB/McGraw Hill
20 Ryan Ranch Rd
Monterey, CA 93940-5770

831-393-0700
Fax: 831-393-6528

Ellen Haley, President

Offers information on airport management issucs, including funding. Congressional and regulatory activities, legal matters, noise and capacity problems are offered as well.
Frequency: Full-text

2976 **Aviation Businesses and the Service they Provide**
National Air Transportation Association
4226 King St
Alexandria, VA 22302-1507

703-845-9000
800-808-6282
Fax: 703-845-8176
E-Mail: csipes@nata-online.org
Home Page: www.nata.aero
Social Media: Facebook, Twitter, LinkedIn

Thomas Hendricks, President
Timothy Heck, Financial Officer, VP
Shannon Chambers, Director Mktg/Communications

A detailed fact book, complete with statistical data, on the aviation services industry.

2977 **Aviation Telephone Directory**
Aviation Telephone Directory
6619 Tumbleweed Ridge Lane
Suite 102
Henderson, NV 89015

800-437-2962
Fax: 702-943-8982
Home Page: www.aviationfinder.com

Is the leading source for General Aviation information with more than 14,000 Companies and 10,000 airports. Yellow pages, White pages, and Blue pages(by airport). Thousands of phone numbers.
Cost: $19.95
790 Pages
Frequency: BiAnnually
Circulation: 20000
ISSN: 1075-1378
Founded in 1949
Printed in 4 colors on newsprint stock

2978 **Collegiate Aviation Guide**
University Aviation Association
3410 Skyway Dr
Auburn, AL 36830-6444

334-844-2434
Fax: 334-844-2432
Home Page: www.uaa.aero

Carolyn Williamson, Executive Director
Mary Chandler, Coordinator Office Administration

A comprehensive guide of regionally accredited colleges and universities with aviation offerings ranging from academic completion certificates and associate degrees to doctoral programs. Contains listings of institutions throughout the United States, with some located in Canada.
Cost: $29.95
Founded in 1947

2979 **Commuter Flight Statistics and Online Origin & Destination Data**
US Department of Transportation
Kendall Square
Cambridge, MA 02142-1093

617-494-5906

Robin A Caldwell, Director

Covers all areas of the commuter airline flight industry, including statistical information on flights by commuter airlines.
Frequency: Statistical

2980 **Flying Annual and Buyers Guide**
Hachette Filipacchi Magazines
1633 Broadway
42nd Floor
New York, NY 10019-6708

212-767-6000
Fax: 212-767-5600
Home Page: www.hfmnewsstand.com/index

Alain Lemarchand, CEO
Richard Collins, Editor at Large

This substantial guide lists manufacturers, dealers, suppliers and professionals in the aviation industry.
Cost: $18.00

2981 **General Aviation Statistical DataBook**
General Aviation Manufacturers Association
1400 K St NW
Suite 801
Washington, DC 20005-2402

202-393-1500
Fax: 202-842-4063
E-Mail: bforan@gama.aero
Home Page: www.gama.aero

Pete Bunce, President, Chief Executive Officer

Statistics on US general aviation shipments, aircraft fleet, international trade, safety and the most current data on airport statistics and pilot population.
Cost: $10.00
Frequency: Annual

2982 **Guide to Selecting Airport Consultants and Membership Directory**
Airport Consultants Council
908 King Street
Suite 100
Alexandria, VA 22314-3067

703-683-5900
Fax: 703-683-2564
E-Mail: info@acconline.org
Home Page: www.acconline.org

Paula Hochstetler, President
T.J. Shultz, Executive VP

A full nationwide listing of airport consultants and association news.
Frequency: Annual

2983 **Helicopter Annual**
Helicopter Association International
1635 Prince St
Alexandria, VA 22314-2898

703-683-4646
Fax: 703-683-4745
Home Page: www.rotor.com

Matthew Zuccaro, President

A comprehensive reference guide for th civil helicopter industry. Includes specifications, industry statistics, HAI membership directories by class and geographic matrix, listings of international civil aviation contacts, key FAA personnel, association committees, and more. First copy included free with membership.
Cost: $50.00
360 Pages
Frequency: Annual
Circulation: 25,000

2984 **International Aerospace Abstracts**
American Institute of Aeronautics and Astronautics
1801 Alexander Bell Dr
Suite 500
Reston, VA 20191-4344

703-264-7500
800-639-2422
Fax: 703-264-7551
E-Mail: tammym@aiaa.org
Home Page: www.aiaa.org

Dr. Brian Dailey, President

This database contains more than 2 million references and abstracts of journal and monograph literature relating to aerospace science and technology.
Frequency: Monthly

2985 **Light Aircraft Manufacturers Association Directory**
2001 Steamboat Ridge Ct
Daytona Beach, FL 94588

651-592-7565
Fax: 925-426-0771
E-Mail: info@lama.bz
Home Page: www.lama.bz

Don Johnson, President
Jan Fridrich, Secretary General

A list of over 400 member manufacturers of light and ultralight aircraft and suppliers of related products and services.

2986 **Living with Your Plane**
Flyer Media
5611 76th Street W
PO Box 39099
Lakewood, WA 98499-0099

253-471-9888
800-426-8538
Fax: 253-471-9911
Home Page: www.flyer-online.com/airparks

Dave Sclair, Editor
Janice Wood, Editorial Coordinator

Offers a large amount of information including 400 residential airports with phones, addresses

and contact names.
Cost: $20.00
Frequency: Annual
Circulation: 1,000

2987 NBAA Directory of Member Companies, Aircraft & Personnel
National Business Aviation Association
1200 18th St NW
Suite 400
Washington, DC 20036-2527
202-783-9000
Fax: 202-331-8364
E-Mail: info@nbaa.org
Home Page: www.nbaa.org
Ed Bolen, President
Furnished to members only and contains a comprehensive listing of NBAA Member companies with their aircraft and flight department personnel.

2988 Space Law
Oceana Publications
198 Madison Avenue
New York, NY 10016
800-334-4249
Fax: 212-726-6476
E-Mail: custserv.us@oup.com
Home Page: www.oceanalaw.com
Paul Stephen Dempsey, Editor
Provides in-depth expert coverage by today's preeminent export of the most pressing issues currently being faced by international regulators in this dynamic and growing area of the law.
Cost: $625.00
40 Pages
Frequency: 5 Volume Set
Circulation: 2,000
ISBN: 0-379012-92-8
Printed in 4 colors

2989 United States Civil Aircraft Registry
Insured Aircraft Title Service
PO Box 19527
Oklahoma City, OK 73144-0527
405-681-6663
800-654-4882
Fax: 405-681-9299
E-Mail: iats@earthlink.net
Home Page: www.insuredaircraft.com
Matthew Kelly, Owner
This directory covers owners of over 275,000 aircraft.
Cost: $600.00
190 Pages
Frequency: Monthly
Founded in 1963

2990 Water Landing Directory
Seaplane Pilots Association
3859 Laird Blvd
Lakeland, FL 33811
863-701-7979
888-772-8923
Fax: 863-701-7588
E-Mail: spa@seaplanes.org
Home Page: www.seaplanes.org
Steve McCaughey, Executive Director
Is the only publication that combines federal, state, provincial and special agency regulations affecting seaplane operators. The directory includes waterway closures and restrictions, seaplane bases listed by state and city, informative seaplane base diagrams, customs information, flight planning charts and other miscellaneous quick reference materials.

2991 World Aviation Directory and Aerospace Database
McGraw Hill
1200 G St NW
Suite 922
Washington, DC 20005-3821
202-343-2300
Fax: 202-383-2347
Home Page: www.mcgraw-hillhomelandsecurity.com
John McNicholas, Marketing Director
Aviation and the aerospace industry are covered in this global directory offering information on manufacturers, subcontractors, support services and associations.
2500 Pages

Industry Web Sites

2992 http://gold.greyhouse.com
G.O.L.D Grey House OnLine Databases
Grey House Publishing's online database platform, GOLD, offers Quick Search, Keyword Search and Expert Search for most business sectors including aviation and aerospace markets. The GOLD platform makes finding the information you need quick and easy - whether you're a novice searcher or an experienced database user. All of Grey House's directory products are available for subscription on the GOLD platform.

2993 www.aams.org
Association of Air Medical Services
Air medical transport equipment, supplies and services.

2994 www.aci-na.org
Airports Council International-North America
Represents local, regional and state governing bodies that own and operate commercial airports throughtout the United States and Canada.

2995 www.aeronet.com
Aeronet Worldwide
Specializes in urgent shipping solutions. From computer and technical supplies, to medical equipment, to odd size, one of a kind machine parts, we have always been there for our clients, one shipment at a time.

2996 www.afa.org
Air Force Association
Independent nonprofit, civilian organization promoting public understanding of aerospace power and the pivotal role it plays in the security of the nation.

2997 www.afanet.org
Association of Flight Attendants
Represents over 50,000 flight attendants at 26 airlines, serving as a voice for flight attendants at their workplace, in the industry, the media and on Capitol Hill.

2998 www.agaviation.org
National Agricultural Aviation Association
Voice of the aerial application industry, we work to preserve aerial application's place in the protection and production of America's food and fiber supply. Aerial application is one of the safest, fastest, most efficient and economical ways to apply pesticides. It is also the most environmentally friendly tool of modern agriculture.

2999 www.aia-aerospace.org
Aerospace Industries Association
The Aerospace Industries Association shapes public policy that ensures the US aerospace, defense and homeland security industry remains preeminent and that its members are successful and profitable in a changing global market.

3000 www.aiaa.org
American Institute of Aeronautics and Astronautics
Advances the arts, sciences, and technology of aeronautics and astronautics and promotes the professionalism of those engaged in these pursuits.

3001 www.airlines.org
Air Transport Association
Supports and assits its members by promoting the air transport industry and the safety, cost effectiveness, and technical advancement of its operators; advocating common industry positions before state and local governments; conducting designated industry-wide programs; and assuring governmental and public understanding of all aspects of air transport.

3002 www.airship-association.org
Airship Association
Circulates information on all matters affecting airships.

3003 www.anahq.org
Association of Naval Aviation
Professional, nonprofit, educational and fraternaL society of Naval Aviation, whose main purpose is to educte the public and our national leaders on the vital roles of the Navy, Marine Corp and Coast Guard Aviation as key elements of our national defense posture. ANA continuosly seeks to elucidate the key current issues impacting Naval Aviation through published writing, symposia, speeches and discussions with various interest groups.

3004 www.aopa.org
Aircraft Owners & Pilots Association
Works to make flying safer, more economical and enjoyable for private aircraft owners.

3005 www.arinc.com
Aeronautical Radio
Aeronautical Radio provides transportation communications and systems engineering solution for five major industries: aviation, airports, defense, government, and transportation

3006 www.arsa.org
Aeronautical Repair Station Association
Helps develop guidance, policy and interpretations that are clear, concise and consistent, and applied uniformly to all similarly situated companies and individuals.

3007 www.asma.org
Aerospace Medical Association
Our mission is to apply and advance scientific knowledge to promote and enhance the health, safety and performance of those involved in aerospace and related activities.

3008 www.astronautical.org
American Astronautical Society
Independent scientific and technical group in the United States exclusively dedicated to the advancement of space science and exploration.

3009 www.atec-amt.org
Aviation Technician Education Council
Organization of Federal Aviation Administration approved Aviation Maintenance Technician schools and supporting industries.

3010 **www.blimpinfo.com**
Lighter Than Air Society
Nonprofit organization whose members are devoted to the study of the history, science and techniques of all forms of buoyant flight.

3011 **www.bonanza.org**
American Bonanza Society
ABS is a group of members who own, fly or have a sincere interest in Bonanza, Baron, and Travel air type aircraft. Because of this common interest we share information and experiences involving the operation and maintenance of the Beech produced aircraft.

3012 **www.cessnaowner.org**
Cessna Owner Organization
Membership support organization for Cessna aircraft owners.

3013 **www.civilavmed.com**
Civil Aviation Medical Association
Aviation medical equipment, supplies and services. Working on behalf of physicians engaged in the practice of aviation medicine, dedicated to civil aviation safety.

3014 **www.eaa.org**
Experimental Aircraft Association
Equipment, supplies and services for sport and recreational flying.

3015 **www.generalaviation.org**
General Aviation Manufacturers Association
Manufacturers of general aviation aircraft, and related equipment.

3016 **www.greyhouse.com**
Grey House Publishing
Authoritative reference directories for most business sectors including aviation and aerospace markets. Users can search the online databases with varied search criteria allowing for custom searches by product category, geographic area, sales volume, keyword, subject and more. Full Grey House catalog and online ordering also available.

3017 **www.iaopa.org**
Int'l Council of Aircraft Owner & Pilot Assns.
Nonprofit federation of 53 autonomous, nongovernmental, national general aviation organizations. Facilitates the movement of general aviation aircraft.

3018 **www.ifsanet.com**
International Inflight Food Service Association
For airline and railway personnel, caterers and suppliers responsible for providing passenger food service.

3019 **www.iswap.org**
International Society of Women Airline Pilots
Organization for all women pilots who are employed as flight crew members (Captain, First Officer, or Second Officer) and hold senority numbers with an airline carrier that operates at least one aircraft with a gross wieght of 90,000 pounds or more.

3020 **www.naa.usa.org**
National Aeronautic Association
For aerospace corporations, aero clubs, affiliates and major national sporting aviation organizations.

3021 **www.nafinet.org**
National Association of Flight Instructors
Dedicated to raising and maintaining the professional standing of the flight instructor in the aviation community. Maintains a benefits package available for everyone from the independent instructor to those teaching at flight schools.

3022 **www.nata.aero**
National Air Transportation Association
National association of aviation business service providers.

3023 **www.natca.org**
National Air Traffic Controllers Association
Founded to ensure the safety and longetivity of air traffic controller positions around the nation. Represents over 15,000 air traffic controllers throughout the US, Puerto Rico and Guam, along with 2,508 other bargaining unit members that span the areas of engineers and architects to nurses and health care professionals to members of the accounting community.

3024 **www.nbaa.org**
National Business Aviation Association
Not-for-profit, nonpartisan corporation dedicated to the success of the business aviation community.

3025 **www.ninety-nines.org**
Ninety-Nines
International organization of licensed women pilots from 35 countries. We are a nonprofit, charitable membership corporation holding 501(c)(3) US tax status. Members are professional pilots for airlines, industry, government; we are pilots who teach and pilots who fly for pleasure; we are pilots who are technicians and mechanics. First and foremost, we are women who love to fly.

3026 **www.ofainc.com.**
Organization of Flying Adjusters
Dedicated to the highest standard of professional ethics in handling aviation insurance claims, investigating causes of aircraft accidents objectively and promoting every aspect of air safety.

3027 **www.piperowner.org**
Pipers Owner Society
Independent group of Piper owners, pilots, and enthusiasts, the POS is committed to the goal of safe, fun, and affordable flying. Membership benefits include: pre-buy referral service; free STC summaries, free parts locating and a referral service. Pipers magazine is exclusively for POS members.

3028 **www.pra.org**
Popular Rotorcraft Association
A nonprofit organization dedicated to the advancement of knowledge, public education and safety among Rotorcraft enthusiasts worldwide.

3029 **www.quad-a.org**
Army Aviation Association of America
Aerospace products, helicopters, rotor blades, engines, tires, helmets and related aviation equipment. Representing membership interests to the Army and the Legislative Branch.

3030 **www.rotor.com**
Helicopter Association International
Receives and disseminates information concerning the use, operation, hiring, contracting and leasing of helicopters.

3031 **www.safeassociation.com**
SAFE Association
Website of the nonprofit organization dedicated to the preservation of human life. It provides a common meeting ground for the sharing of problems, ideas and information.

3032 **www.seaplanes.org**
Seaplane Pilots Association
Represents our members in dozens of seaplane access issues annually and provides numerous exclusive benefits.

3033 **www.ssa.org**
Soaring Society of America
Fosters and promote all phases of gliding and soaring, nationally and internationally.

3034 **www.tcunion.org**
Transportation-Communications International Union
Members come from diverse transportation industries. In addition to bargaining and representation of its members, provides mortgage and bankcard programs and other services to its members.

3035 **www.tiaca.org**
International Air Cargo Association
For air cargo industry services and products from aircraft manufacturers, airlines, airports, freight forwarders trade publications logistics consultants, etc.

3036 **www.ussf.org**
Space Foundation
Nonprofit organization advancing the exploration, development and use of space and space education for the benefit of humankind.

3037 **www.vtol.org**
AHS International
For designers, engineers and manufacturers of the vertical flight industry.

3038 **www.wahsonline.com**
World Airline Historical Society
Open to all persons and groups interested in collecting airline memorabilia and the study of the airline industry, past and current.

Associations

3039 ARMA International
11880 College Blvd
Suite 450
Overland Park, KS 66210
913-341-3808
800-422-2762
Fax: 913-341-3742
E-Mail: hq@arma.org
Home Page: www.arma.org
Social Media: Facebook, Twitter, LinkedIn

Julie J Colgan, President
Fred Pulzello, President Elect
Brenda Prowse, Treasurer

A not-for-profit professional association and the authority on managing records and information.
11000 Members
Founded in 1955

3040 Advancing Financial Crime Professionals Worldwide
80 Southwest 8th Street
Suite 2350
Miami, FL 33130
305-373-0020
Fax: 305-373-5229
E-Mail: info@acams.org
Home Page: www.acams.org

Ted Weissberg, Chief Executive Officer
John Byrne, Executive Vice President
Ari House, Chief Financial Officer
Ms. Hue Dang, Head of Asia
Geoffrey Fone, Director of Sales

The largest international membership organization dedicated to enhancing the knowledge and expertise of financial crime detection and prevention professionals from a wide range of industries in both public and private sectors.

3041 American Association of Bank Directors
1250 24th Street, NW
Suite 700
Washington, DC 20037
202-463-4888
Fax: 202-349-8080
E-Mail: info@aabd.org
Home Page: aabd.org

David Baris, President
Richard M. Whiting, Executive Director
Charles J. Thayer, Chairman Emeritus
Andrew Baris, VP and Director of Marketing
Betty Pelton, Membership Director

Devoted to serving the information, education and advocacy needs of individual bank and savings institution directors. This nonprofit organization has members nationwide.

3042 American Association of Residential Mortgage Regulators
1025 Thomas Jefferson Street, NW
Suite 500 East
Washington, DC 20007
202-521-3999
Fax: 202-833-3636
E-Mail: efreundel@aarmr.org
Home Page: www.aarmr.org

Promotes the exchange of information and education concerning the licensing, supervision, and regulation of the residential mortgage industry.

3043 American Bankers Association
1120 Connecticut Avenue NW
Washington, DC 20036
202-663-5000
800-226-5377
Fax: 202-828-4540
E-Mail: custserv@aba.com
Home Page: www.aba.com
Social Media: Facebook, Twitter, LinkedIn

Jeff L Plagge, Chairman
John A Ikard, Chair Elect
R Daniel Blanton, Vice Chair
Frank Keating, President & CEO
Gary D Hemmer, Treasurer

Brings together all categories of banking institutions to best represent the interests of this rapidly changing industry. Its membership includes community, regional and money center banks and holding companies, as well as savings associations, trust companies and savings banks.
Founded in 1875

3044 American Bankers Insurance Association
American Bankers Association
1120 Connecticut Avenue NW
Washington, DC 20036
202-663-5163
800-226-5377
Fax: 202-828-4546
E-Mail: vbarton@aba.com
Home Page: www.theabia.com
Social Media: Facebook, Twitter, LinkedIn

Paul Petrylak, President/Chairman
Neal Aton, Vice President
David Cissell, Secretary
Val Teagarden, Treasurer

The American Bankers Insurance Association (ABIA) is the insurance subsidiary of the American Bankers Association (ABA). The ABIA's mission is to develop policy and provide advocacy for banks in insurance and to support bank insurance operations through research, education, compliance assistance, and peer group networking opportunities.
300 Members
Founded in 2001

3045 American Bankruptcy Institute
66 Canal Center Plaza
Suite 600
Alexandria, VA 22314
703-739-0800
Fax: 703-739-1060
E-Mail: support@abiworld.org
Home Page: www.abiworld.org
Social Media: Facebook, Twitter, LinkedIn

Geoffrey L Berman, Chairman
Patricia A Redmond, President
Brian L Shaw, President Elect
John Tittle Jr., Treasurer
Rudy J Cerone, Secretary

Multidisciplinary, non-partisan organization dedicated to research and education on matters related to insolvency. Engaged in numerous educational and research activities as well as the production of a number of publications both for the insolvency practitioner and the public.
11700 Members
Founded in 1982

3046 American Payroll Association
660 North Main Avenue
Suite 100
San Antonio, TX 78205-1217
210-226-4600
Fax: 210-226-4027
Home Page: www.americanpayroll.org

Conducts payroll training conferences and seminars across the country and publishes a complete library of resource texts and newsletters.

3047 Arab Bankers Association of North America
150 West 28th Street
Suite 801
New York, NY 10001
212-599-3030
Fax: 212-599-3131
E-Mail: info@arabbankers.org
Home Page: www.arabbankers.org

Dr. Amer Bisat, President
Susan Peters, Executive Director/COO
Dueaa Elzin, Membership Coordinator
Lameece Issaq, Event Manager
Ryah Aqel, Administrative Associate

Provides news, job listings, and resources for financial institutions in the U.S. and the Middle East.
Founded in 1983

3048 Association For Financial Professionals
4520 East West Highway
Suite 750
Bethesda, MD 20814
301-907-2862
Fax: 301-907-2864
E-Mail: afp@afponline.org
Home Page: www.afponline.org

Susan Glass, Chairman
Jeff Johnson, Vice Chairman
Anita Patterson, Vice Chairman
Ann Anthony, CTP
Robert Eiseman, CTP

The Association for Financial Professionals (AFP) serves a network of more than 16,000 treasury and finance professionals. Headquartered in Bethesda, MD, AFP provides members with breaking news, economic research and data on the evolving world of treasury and finance, as well as world-class treasury certification programs, networking events, financial analytical tools, training, and public policy representation to legislators and regulators.

3049 Association for Financial Technology
34 North High Street
New Albany, OH 43054-8507
614-895-1208
Fax: 614-895-3466
E-Mail: aft@aftweb.com
Home Page: www.aftweb.com
Social Media: Twitter, LinkedIn

David Culbertson, President
Russ Bernthal, Vice President
Andrew Grinstead, Treasurer
James R Bannister, Executive Director
Erin Thomas, Managing Director

Association founded to promote high standards of professionalism in the planning, development, implementation and application of technology to the financial services industry.
Founded in 1972

3050 Association for Management in Financial Services
14247 Saffron Circle
Carmel, IN 46032-7769
317-815-5857
Fax: 317-815-5877

E-Mail: ami2@amifs.org
Home Page: www.amifs.org

Andy Streiff, President
Jeff Nathasingh, Executive Vice President

The Association for Management Information in Financial Services is the preeminent organization for management information professionals in the financial services industry, and counts among its members individuals who set the policies and advance the concepts of management information at major financial institutions worldwide.
300 Members
Founded in 1980

3051 Association of Independent Trust Companies
2213 North Broadway
Ada, OK 74820

405-680-7869
Fax: 580-332-4714
E-Mail: ato@trustorgs.com
Home Page: www.trustorgs.com

Daniel Carter, President
Tony Guthrie, Treasurer
Thomas Blank, General Counsel/Secretary

To provide a forum of leaders, owners and operators of trust companies and wealth management providers.
150 Members
Founded in 1989

3052 Association of Military Banks of America (AMBA)
PO Box 3335
Warrenton, VA 20188

540-347-3305
Fax: 540-347-5995
E-Mail: info@ambahq.org
Home Page: www.ambahq.org

Vince E Barfield, Chairman
Terry Tuggle, Vice Chairman
Andrew M Egeland, Jr, President/Treasurer/Secretary
James A Cerrone, Vice Chair

AMBA is a not-for-profit association of banks operating on military installations, banks not located on military installations but serving military customers, and military banking facilities designated by the US Treasury.
130 Members
Founded in 1959

3053 Association of Residential Mortgage Compliance Professionals
167 West Hudson Street
Suite 200
Long Beach, NY 11561

516-442-3456
Home Page: armcp.org

The first and only national organization in the Unites States devoted exclusively to residential mortgage compliance professionals offering discussion groups, educational forums, panels, lectures, and other venues for residential mortgage compliance professionals.

3054 Bank Administration Institute
115 S LaSalle St
Suite 3300
Chicago, IL 60603-3801

312-683-2464
888-224-0037
Fax: 312-683-2373
E-Mail: info@bai.org
Home Page: www.bai.org
Social Media: Facebook, Twitter, LinkedIn

Lewis C Fischer, Chairman
Scott M Peters, Vice Chair
Deborah L Bianucci, President & CEO
Charles G Kim, Secretary
Rilla S Delorier, Treasurer

The financial services industry's partner for breakthrough information and intelligence needed to innovate and stay relevant in an evolving marketplace. Serves a wide segment of the financial services industry, from the largest multinational banks to community-based institutions.

3055 Bank Insurance and Securities Association
2025 M Street NW
Suite 800
Washington, DC 20036

202-367-1111
Fax: 202-367-2111
E-Mail: bisa@BISAnet.org
Home Page: www.bisanet.org
Social Media: Facebook, Twitter, StumbleUpon

Sam Guerrieri Jr., President
Dan Overbey, President Elect
Frank A Consalo, VP
Daniel J McCormack, VP
Thomas N Howe, Treasurer/Secretary

Dedicated to serving the needs of those responsible for marketing securities, insurance and other investment and risk management products through commercial banks, trust companies, savings institutions, and credit unions.
Founded in 2002

3056 Bankers' Association for Finance & Trade
1120 Connecticut Avenue NW
Washington, DC 20036

202-663-7575
Fax: 202-663-5538
E-Mail: info@baft-ifsa.com
Home Page: www.baft.org
Social Media: Facebook, Twitter

Rita Gonzalez, Chairman
James H Peterson, Vice Chairman
Tod R Burwell, CEO
Kimberley A Burdette, Treasurer/Secretary
Michael Quinn, Managing Director

A financial services trade association headquartered in Washington, DC, whose membership primarily represents a broad range of financial institutions and service members that provide services throughout the global financial community.
180 Members
Founded in 1921

3057 Community Development Bankers Association
1444 Eye Street NW
Suite 201
Washington, DC 20005

202-689-8935
E-Mail: info@cdbanks.org
Home Page: www.cdbanks.org

Jane Henderson, Chairman
Brian Argrett, Vice-Chair
Huey Townsend, Treasurer
Robert Patrick Cooper, Secretary
Robert McGill, Emeritus Director

The national trade association of the community development bank sector.

3058 Conference of State Bank Supervisors
1129 20th Street, N.W.
9th Floor
Washington, DC 20036

202-296-2840
Fax: 202-296-1928
Home Page: www.csbs.org

Ms. Candace A. Franks, Chairman
Mr. David J. Cotney, Chairman Elect
Mr. Charles G. Cooper, Vice Chairman
Mr. Charles J. Dolezal, Secretary
Mr. Lauren Kingry, Treasurer

The nationwide organization of banking regulators from all 50 states, the District of Columbia, Guam, Puerto Rico, and the U.S. Virgin Islands.
Founded in 1984

3059 Consumer Bankers Association
1225 Eye St., NW
Suite 550
Washington, DC 20005

202-552-6382
E-Mail: rhunt@cbanet.org
Home Page: www.cbanet.org

Richard Hunt, President/ Chief Executive Officer
Janet Pike, Executive Assistant
Steven I. Zeisel, General Counsel/ EVP
Reagan Anderson, SVP, Congressional Affairs
Kristen Fallon, VP, Congressional Affairs

The recognized voice on retail banking issues in the nation's capital.

3060 Council for Electronic Billing and Payment
13450 Sunrise Valley Drive
Suite 100
Herndon, VA 20171

703-561-1100
E-Mail: runger@nacha.org
Home Page: cebp.nacha.org

Robert Unger, Senior Director
Liz Millard, Assistant Director

Promotes electronic consumer and business-to-business billing and payment programs and services across any delivery channel. It also provides an open forum for education, resource development, solution innovation, research and the exchange of information about the electronic billing and the electronic payment industries.

3061 Credit Union National Association
5710 Mineral Point Rd
Madison, WI 53705-4454

800-356-9655
Fax: 608-231-4333
Home Page: www.cuna.org

Dennis E. Pierce, Chairman
Susan Streifel, Vice Chairman
Rodney Staatz, Secretary
Patrick S. Jury, Treasurer
Jim Nussle, President/CEO

A national trade association for both state and federally charteredcredit unions located in the United States.

3062 Electronic Funds Transfer Association
4000 Legato Road
Suite 1100
Fairfax, VA 22030

571-318-5556
Fax: 571-318-5557
Home Page: www.efta.org
Social Media: Twitter

Kurt Helwig, President & CEO
Dennis Ambach, Sr Director/Government Relations

Melanie Renner, Meeting Coordinator
Bob Bucceri, Media Relations

The Electronic Funds Transfer Association (EFTA) is the nation's leading inter-industry professional association promoting the adoption of electronic payment systems and commerce.

3063 Electronic Payments Association NACHA

13450 Sunrise Valley Drive
Suite 100
Herndon, VA 20171

703-561-1100
Fax: 703-787-0996
E-Mail: info@nacha.org
Home Page: www.nacha.org
Social Media: Facebook, Twitter, LinkedIn

Donna Schwartze, Media Contact
Joshua Maze, Sponsorship

NACHA manages the development, administration, and governance of the ACH Network, the backbone for the electronic movement of money and data. The ACH Network provides a safe, secure, and reliable network for direct account-to-account consumer, business, and government payments. Annually, it facilitates billions of Direct Deposit via ACH and Direct Payment via ACH transactions. Used by all types of financial institutions, the ACH Network is governed by the fair and equitable NACHA Operating Rules

3064 Electronic Transactions Association

1101 16th STREET NW #402
WASHINGTON, DC 20036

202-828-2635
800-695-5509
Home Page: www.electran.org

Debra Rossi, President
Greg Cohen, President-Elect
Jeff Rosenblatt, Treasurer
Jeff Sloan, Secretary
Kim Fitzsimmons, Immediate Past-President

A trade organization representing independent sales organizations, merchant service providers and those help them serve their merchant clients.

3065 Environmental Bankers Association

510 King St
Suite 410
Alexandria, VA 22314

703-549-0977
800-966-7475
Fax: 703-548-5945
E-Mail: eba@envirobank.org
Home Page: www.envirobank.org
Social Media: Facebook, Twitter, LinkedIn

Rick Ferguson, President
Sharon Valverde, Vice President
Stephen Richardson, Secretary & Communication
Scott Beckerman, Treasurer & Finance
Dan Richardson, General Counsel

EBA voting members are banks, trust companies, credit unions, savings and loan associations, and other financial services organizations with an interest in environmental risk management and related issues. Active participants are bankers from Trust or Credit offices with responsibility for environmental liability, and financial services officers with environmental interests. Affiliate members are from law firms, consulting and insurance organizations.
Founded in 1994

3066 Financial Managers Society

1 North LaSalle Street
Suite 3100
Chicago, IL 60602-4003

800-275-4367
Fax: 312-578-1308
E-Mail: info@fmsinc.org
Home Page: www.fmsinc.org

Dick Yingst, President/ CEO
Tom King, Director Professional Development
Autumn Wolfer, Director of Marketing/Membership
Mark Loehrke, Editor/Writer
Christine Smith, Marketing/Membership Coordinator

A nonprofit professional society serving the financial services industry.

3067 Financial Services Roundtable

600 13th Street, NW
Suite 400
Washington, DC 20005

202-289-4322
E-Mail: info@fsroundtable.org
Home Page: www.fsround.org

Larry D. Zimpleman, Chairman
Frederick H. Waddell, Chairman-Elect
John G. Stumpf, Immediate-Past Chairman
Thomas R. Watjen, Treasurer
Richard K. Davis, Director

The leading advocacy organization for America's financial services industry. Its members include banking, insurance, asset management, finance, andcredit card companies.

3068 Financial Women International

1027 W Roselawn Avenue
Roseville, MN 55113

651-487-7632
866-807-6081
Fax: 651-489-1322
E-Mail: info@fwi.org
Home Page: www.fwi.org

Melissa Curzon, President
Cindy Hass, VP
Carleen DeSisto, Secretary

FWI is dedicated to developing leaders, accelerating careers, and generating results for professionals in the banking and financial services industry.
1000 Members
Founded in 1921

3069 Financial Women's Association

215 Park Avenue South
Suite 1712
New York, NY 10003

Home Page: fwa.org

Maureen Adolf, President
Katrin Dambrot, President-Elect
Kimberly Weinrick, Pat President
Jennifer Openshaw, Executive Director
Kalinka Mondrova-Rothman, Secretary

A nonprofit organization established by a group of Wall Street Women to support the role and development of women in the financial services industry.

3070 Global Association of Risk Professionals

111 Town Square Pl
Suite 1215
Jersey City, NJ 07310

201-719-7210
Fax: 201-222-5022
E-Mail: info@garp.com
Home Page: www.garp.com
Social Media: Facebook, Twitter, LinkedIn

Richard Apostolik, President
Kenneth Abbott, Managing Director
Mark Wallace, Chief Operating Officer
Brenda Boultwood, Chief Risk Officer

To be the leading professional association for risk managers, managed by and for its members dedicated to the advancement of the risk profession through education, training and the promotion of best practices globally. Members come from over 100 countries.
52330 Members
Founded in 1996

3071 Impact Mortgage Management Advocacy & Advisory Group

2740 S. Newland Street
Lakewood, CO 80227

303-674-1200
Fax: 303-674-1664
E-Mail: bill@immaag.com
Home Page: www.immaag.com

Provides thousands of state licensed mortgage loan originators the information and advocacy support necessary for the industry to deal with absorbing the results of the financial crisis being dealt with by the nation.

3072 Independent Community Bankers of America

1615 L St NW
Suite 900
Washington, DC 20036

202-659-8111
866-843-4222
Fax: 202-659-9216
E-Mail: info@icba.org
Home Page: www.icba.org
Social Media: Facebook, Twitter, LinkedIn, Youtube

William A Loving Jr., Chairman
John H Buhrmaster, Chairman Elect
Jack Hartings, Vice Chair
Timothy Zimmerman, Secretary
Nancy Ruyle, Treasurer

Trade association for the nations community banks.
5000 Members

3073 Institute of Certified Bankers

American Bankers Association
1120 Connecticut Avenue NW
Washington, DC 20036

202-663-5092
800-226-5377
Fax: 202-828-4540
E-Mail: icb@aba.com
Home Page: www.aba.com/ICB/default.htm
Social Media: Facebook, Twitter, LinkedIn

Frank Keating, President/CEO

A national association of certified professionals in the financial services industry whose mission is to provide financial services professionals with confidence, credibility and recognition through its certifications.
Founded in 1990

3074 Institute of International Bankers

299 Park Ave
17th Floor
New York, NY 10171

212-421-1611
Fax: 212-421-1119
E-Mail: iib@iib.org
Home Page: www.iib.org
Social Media: Facebook, Twitter, LinkedIn

Roger Blissett, Chairman
Sarah Miller, CEO
Angelo R Aldana, Vice Chair

Betty A Whelchel, Secretary
Andy Lebron, Events Registration Coordinator

To help resolve the many special legislative, regulatory and tax issues confronting internationally headquartered financial institutions that engage in banking, securities and/or insurance activities in the United States.
Founded in 1966

3075 International Financial Services Association
9 Sylvan Way
Suite 130
Parsippany, NJ 07054-3817

973-656-1900
Fax: 973-656-1915
E-Mail: info@intlbanking.org
Home Page: www.ifsaonline.org

Tod Burwell, Vice President
Colleen Kennedy, Manager, Programs & Events

Represents the international operations areas of financial services providers, their customers, suppliers and partners. Dedicates itself to meeting the specific needs of those who provide, use, and support trade and payments with particular focus on documentary credits, funds transfer, treasury operations, compliance, and regulatory reporting.
Founded in 1924

3076 Investment Bankers Association

E-Mail:
info2@investmentbankersassociation.org
Home Page:
www.investmentbankersassociation.org

A national organization for businesses that want to go public and raise capital to meet small regional and independent brokerage firms, investment bankers, capital sources and other capital market service providers.

3077 MasterCard Worldwide
2000 Purchase St
Purchase, NY 10577-2405

914-249-2000
Fax: 914-249-4135
Home Page: www.mastercardinternational.com
Social Media: Facebook, Twitter, LinkedIn

Robert W Selander, CEO
Sharon Gamsin, VP
Chris Harral, Director
Chris A McWilton, Chief Financial Offcier
Lawrence Flanagan, Chief Marketing Officer

Administers the MasterCard credit and other MasterCard products fo member financial institutions around the world.
25000 Members
Founded in 1940

3078 Mortgage Bankers Association
1919 M Street NW
5th Floor
Washington, DC 20036

202-557-2700
Fax: 202-721-0248
E-Mail: membership@mortgagebankers.org
Home Page: www.mortgagebankers.org
Social Media: Facebook, Twitter, LinkedIn, Youtube

Edward J Burke, Chairman
Bill Cosgrove, Chair Elect
William C Emerson, Vice Chair
Richard A Aneshansel, President & CEO
Dan Thoms, VP Education/Business Development

Seeks to improve methods of originating, servicing and marketing loans.
2900 Members
Founded in 1914

3079 Mortgage Bankers Association of America
1919 M Street NW
5th Floor
Washington, DC 20036

202-557-2700
800-793-6222
Home Page: www.mbaa.org

Bill Cosgrove, CMB, Chairman
Bill Emerson, Chairman-Elect
Rodrigo Lopez, CMB, Vice Chairman
David H. Stevens, President/ CEO
Marcia Davies, Chief Operating Officer

A national association representing the entire real estate finance industry. This association develops innovative business tools and provides education and training for industry professionals.

3080 NACHA: Electronic Payments Association
13450 Sunrise Valley Drive
Suite 100
Herndon, VA 20171

703-561-1100
Fax: 703-787-0996
E-Mail: info@nacha.org
Home Page: www.nacha.org
Social Media: Facebook, Twitter, LinkedIn

Elliott McEntee, President/CEO
William B Nelson, Executive VP
Deb Evans-Doyle, Senior Director Conference Mktg
Julie Hedlund, Senior Director Electronic Commerce
Michael Herd, Director Public Relations

To promote the development of electronic solutions that improve the payments for the benefit of its members and their customers.
11000 Members
Founded in 1974

3081 National Association of Affordable Housing Lenders
1667 K Street NW
Suite 210
Washington, DC 20006

202-293-9850
Fax: 202-293-9852
E-Mail: info@naanl.org
Home Page: www.naahl.org

Judith Kennedy, President/CEO
Paul Haaland, COO
Sara Olson, Administrator

Represents America's leaders in moving private capital to those in need. Encompasses 200 organizations committed to increasing private lending and investing in low and moderate-income communities.
Founded in 1990

3082 National Association of Bankruptcy Trustees
One Windsor Cove
Suite 305
Columbia, SC 29223

803-252-5646
800-445-8629
Fax: 803-765-0860
E-Mail: info@nabt.com
Home Page: www.nabt.com

Christina Hicks, Executive Director
Nancy H Cooper, Executive Liaison

A non profit association formed to address the needs of bankruptcy trustees throughout the country and to promote the effectiveness of the bankruptcy system as a whole.
Founded in 1982

3083 National Association of Chapter 13 Trustees
1 Windsor Cove
Suite 305
Columbia, SC 29223

803-252-5646
800-445-8629
Fax: 803-765-0860
E-Mail: Info@NACTT.com
Home Page: www.nactt.com

Margaret A Burks, President
Robert B Wilson, President Elect
Mary Ida Townson, VP
D Sims Crawford, Secretary
Joyce Bradley Babin, Treasurer

Provides a forum within which Chapter 13 Trustees will act as an information and communication resource to advance education, leadership, and continuous improvement in the administration of bankruptcy. We will provide the means to establish and implement professional standards and participate in the national legislative and administrative processes while promoting the highest ethical principles.
1000 Members
Founded in 1965

3084 National Association of Credit Union Supervisory & Auditing Committees
PO Box 160
Del Mar, CA 92014

800-287-5949
Fax: 858-792-3884
E-Mail: nacusac@nacusac.org
Home Page: www.nacusac.org

Celeste Shelton, Executive Director
Lauren Clark, Associate Director
Bob Spinder, Associate Director

A unique organization of, by and for credit union supervisory committee members. Provides leadership, support and education to enhance the capability of credit union supervisory and auditing committee members to fulfill their responsibilities.
Founded in 1985

3085 National Association of Federal Credit Unions
3138 10th St N
Suite 3
Arlington, VA 22201-2149

703-522-4770
800-336-4644
Fax: 703-524-1082
Home Page: www.nafcu.org

Michael J Parsons, Chairman
Ed Templeton, Vice Chairman
Richard L Harris, Treasurer
Jeanne Kuckey, Secretary

A respected and influential trade association that exclusively represents the interests of federal credit unions before the federal government and the public.
Founded in 1967

3086 National Association of Government Guaranteed Lenders
215 East 9th Avenue
Stillwater, OK 74074

405-377-4022
Fax: 405-377-3931
E-Mail: bfortune@naggl.com
Home Page: www.naggl.org

Tony Wilkinson, President/CEO
Jane Butler, EVP/COO
Jennifer Brake, Assistant VP Marketing
Jennifer Sterret-O'Neill, Assistant VP Communications

Promotes professional and governmental affairs interests of financial institutions and small

businesses who participate in Small Business Administration guaranteed lending and secondary market programs.
600 Members
Founded in 1984

3087 National Association of Independent Housing Professionals
601 Pennsylvania Ave. NW
South Building, Suite 900
Washington, DC 20004
202-587-9300
Fax: 304-267-9046
Home Page: www.naihp.org
Marc Savitt, CRMS, President
Peter Gallo, Vice President
Kate Crawford, Secretary/Treasurer
Brian Benjamin, Legislative Chair
William Howe, Director
A legislative and regulatory organization comprised of all housing industry professionals.

3088 National Association of Mortgage Professionals
2701 W. 15th Street
Suite 536
Plano, TX 75075
972-758-1151
Fax: 530-484-2906
E-Mail: membership@namb.org
Home Page: www.namb.org
John Councilman, President
Rocke Andrews, President Elect
Fred Kreger, Vice President
Rick Bettencourt, Secretary
Andy W. Harris, Treasurer
The only national trade association representing the mortgage professional industry. It promotes the industry through programs and services such aseducation, professional certification and government affairs representation.

3089 National Association of Mortgage Brokers
2701 West 15th Street
Suite 536
Plano, TX 75075
972-758-1151
Fax: 530-484-2906
E-Mail: membership@namb.org
Home Page: www.namb.org
Social Media: Facebook, Twitter, LinkedIn, Youtube, RSS
Donald J Frommeyer, President
John Councilman, President Elect
Rocke Andrews, VP
Kay A Cleland, Secretary
Andy W Harris, Treasurer
Mortgage brokers who seek to increase professionalism and to foster business relationships among members.
27000 Members
Founded in 1973

3090 National Association of Professional Mortgage Women
PO Box 451718
Garland, TX 75045
800-827-3034
Fax: 469-524-5121
E-Mail: napmw1@aol.com
Home Page: www.napmw.org
Social Media: Facebook, LinkedIn, Google+, RSS
Jill Kinsman, President
Christine Pollard, President Elect
Cynthia Nutter, Secretary
Jeanne Evans, Treasurer
Serves all mortgage professionals and employers who want to excel. Provides business, personal, and leadership development opportunities advancing women in mortgage-related professions.
4500 Members
Founded in 1964

3091 National Association of State Credit Union Supervisors
1655 Fort Myer Dr
Suite 650
Arlington, VA 22209
703-528-8351
800-728-7927
Fax: 703-528-3248
E-Mail: offices@nascus.org
Home Page: www.nascus.org
Social Media: Facebook, Twitter, LinkedIn
John Kolhoff, Chairman
Michael Wettrich, Chair Elect
Mary Ellen O'Neill, Secretary/Treasurer
State chartered credit unions and state credit union supervisors.
900 Members
Founded in 1965

3092 National Bankers Association
1513 P St NW
Washington, DC 20005
202-588-5432
Fax: 202-588-5443
E-Mail: webmaster@nationalbankers.org
Home Page: www.nationalbankers.org
Michael Grant, President
Members are minority and women's banking institutions, minority individuals employed by majority banks and institutions.
16000 Members
Founded in 1927

3093 National Credit Union Administration
1775 Duke St
Suite 4206
Alexandria, VA 22314-6115
703-518-6300
800-755-1030
Fax: 703-518-6539
E-Mail: pacamsil@ncua.gov
Home Page: www.ncua.gov
Social Media: Facebook, Twitter, LinkedIn
Deborah Matz, Chairman
David Marquis, Executive Director
Governed by a three member board appointed by the President and confirmed by the US Senate, this independent federal agency charters and supervises federal credit unions. NCUA, with the backing of the full faith and credit of the US government, operates the National Credit Union Share Insurance Fund, insuring the savings of 80 million account holders in all federal credit unions and many state chartered credit unions.
700 Members
Founded in 1909

3094 National Investment Banking Association
PO Box 6625
Athens, GA 30604
706-208-9620
Fax: 706-993-3342
E-Mail: emily@nibanet.org
Home Page: www.nibanet.org
Social Media: Facebook, Twitter, LinkedIn, Youtube, RSS
James E Hock, Co-Chair/Secretary/Treasurer
Erick Paulson, Co-Chair
Vicky Barone, Director
Gerald A Adler, Director
Lynne Bolduc, Director
A national trade association of regional and independent brokerages, investment banking firms, and related capital market service providers.
Founded in 1932

3095 National Marine Bankers Association
231 South LaSalle Street
Suite 2050
Chicago, IL 60604
312-946-6260
E-Mail: info@marinebankers.org
Home Page: www.marinebankers.org
Micheal Bryant, President
Peggy Bodenreider, VP
Willaim B Otto, Treasurer
Jayme B Yates, Secretary
Jackie Forese, Director
Created to educate current and prospective lenders in marine financing procedures and to promote the extension of credit to consumer and trade borrowers.
70 Members
Founded in 1980

3096 National Mitigation Banking Association
1155 15th Street NW
Suite 500
Washington, DC 20005
202-457-8409
E-Mail: info@mitigationbanking.org
Home Page: www.mitigationbanking.org
Wayne White, President
Michael Sprague, Vice President
Donna Collier, Treasurer
Randy Vogel, Secretary
Doug Lashley, Immediate Past-President
Promotes federal legislation and regulatory policy that encourages mitigation banking and conservation banking as a means of compensating for adverse impacts to America's wetlands and other natural resources.

3097 National Reverse Mortgage Lenders Association
1400 16th St., NW
Suite 420
Washington, DC 20036
202-939-1760
Fax: 202-265-4435
Home Page: www.nrmlaonline.org
Joe DeMarkey, Co-Chairman
Reza Jahangiri, Co-Chairman
Sherry Apanay, Vice-Chairwoman
Mark Browning, Vice-Chairman
Steve McClellan, Secretary
Trade association that serves as an educational resource, policy advocate and public affairs center for reverse mortgage lenders and related professionals.

3098 Nonprofit Risk Management Center
204 South King Street
Leesburg, VA 20175
703-777-3504
Fax: 202-785-3891
Home Page: www.nonprofitrisk.org
Michael A. Schraer, President
Lisa Prinz, Treasurer
Carolyn Hayes-Gulston, Secretary
Peter Andrew, Director
Kitty Holt, Director
Provides risk management assistance and resources for community-serving nonprofit organizations.

3099 Public Risk Management Association
700 S. Washington St.
Suite 218
Alexandria, VA 22314

703-528-7701
Fax: 703-739-0200
E-Mail: info@primacentral.org
Home Page: www.primacentral.org

Regan Rychetsky, President
Betty Coulter, Past-President
Dean Coughenour, President-Elect
Ed Beecher, Director
Terri Evans, Director

Member based organization which is dedicated to providing practicaleducation, training, and information for public sector risk management practitioners.

3100 Risk Management Association
1801 Market Street
Suite 300
Philadelphia, PA 19103-1628

215-446-4000
Fax: 215-446-4101
E-Mail: customers@rmahq.org
Home Page: www.rmahq.org
Social Media: Facebook, Twitter, LinkedIn, WordPress

Michael J Loughlin, Chairman
Nancy J Foster, Vice Chair
William F Githens, CEO

A not-for-profit, member driven professional association whose sole purpose is to advance the use of sound risk principles in the financial services industry.
3000 Members
Founded in 1914

3101 Securities Industry and Financial Markets Association (SIFMA)
1101 New York Ave Nw
Suite 800
Washington, DC 20005-4279

202-962-7300
Fax: 202-962-7305
Home Page: www.fisma.org
Social Media: Facebook, Twitter, LinkedIn

T Timothy Ryan Jr, President/CEO
Randy Snook, Senior Managing Director/EVP
Donald D Kittell, CFO

SIFMA's mission is to champion policies and practices that benefit investors and issuers, expand and perfect global capital markets, and foster the development of new products and services. SIFMA provides an enhanced member network of access and forward-looking services, as well as premiere educational resources for the professionals within the industry and the investors whom they serve.

3102 Society of Financial Examiners
12100 Sunset Hills Rd
Suite 130
Reston, VA 20190-3221

703-234-4140
800-787-7633
Fax: 888-436-8686
E-Mail: sofe@sofe.org
Home Page: www.sofe.org

L. Brackett, Executive Director
Judy Estus, Administrator
William Latza, General Counsel

Professional society for examiners of insurance companies, banks, savings and loans, and credit unions.

3103 Society of Risk Management Consultants
330 S. Executive Drive
Suite 301
Brookfield, WI 53005-4275

Home Page: www.srmcsociety.org

An international organization of professionals engaged in risk management, insurance and employee benefits consulting.

3104 The Association of Executives in Finance, Credit, & International Business
8840 Columbia 100 Parkway
Columbia, MD 21045-2158

410-423-1840
888-256-3242
Fax: 410-740-5574
E-Mail: fcib_global@fcibglobal.com
Home Page: www.fcibglobal.com
Social Media: Twitter, LinkedIn, RSS

Marta Chacon, Director, The Americas
Ron Shepherd, Director, Business Dev.
Noelin Hawkins, Director, Europe, Middle East

The premier Association for Finance, Credit and International business professionals. The leading resource for global credit information, professional development and education.
1000+ Members
Founded in 1919

3105 The Bankers Association for Finance and Trade
1120 Connecticut Avenue, NW
Washington, DC 20036

202-663-7575
Fax: 202-663-5538
E-Mail: info@baft.org
Home Page: www.baft.org

Rita Gonzalez, Chair
Sara K. Joyce, Vice chair
Tod R. Burwell, CEO
Michael Quinn, Secretary-Treasurer
John Ahearn, Director

3106 The Fiduciary and Investment Risk Management
Post Office Box 507
Stockbridge, GE 30281

678-565-6211
Fax: 678-565-8788
E-Mail: info@thefirma.org
Home Page: www.thefirma.org

Bruce K. Goldberg, President
Jennifer De Vries, Vice President
Jeffrey S. Kropschot, Secretary
Bradley F. Beshea, Director
Angela M. Frozena, Director

Provider of current and relevant fiduciary and investment risk management education and networking opportunities to risk management professionals.

3107 The First
7054 Jefferson Highway
Baton Rouge, LA 70806

225-228-7275
Fax: 225-228-7276
Home Page: www.thefirstbank.com

Personal and commercial banking. Offers information about services,products, and locations.

3108 University Risk Management and Insurance Association
PO Box 1027
Bloomington, IN 47402-1027

812-855-6683
Fax: 812-856-3149
E-Mail: urmia@urmia.org
Home Page: www.urmia.org

Marjorie F.B. Lemmon, President
Donna McMahon, President-Elect
Kathy E. Hargis, Secretary
Tish Gade-Jones, Treasurer

Advances the discipline of risk management in higer education.

3109 Urban Financial Services Coalition
1200 G St NW
Suite 800
Washington, DC 20005

202-289-8335
800-996-8335
Fax: 202-434-8707
E-Mail: ufsc@ufscnet.org
Home Page: www.ufscnet.org
Social Media: Facebook, Twitter, LinkedIn, Youtube

Walter Brown Jr., President
Roderick Hayes, Vice President
Adrian Johnson, Treasurer
Renee Coffiel, Secretary

Formerly known as the National Association of Urban Bankers is an organization of minority professionals in the financial services industry and related fields.
Founded in 1974

3110 Western Independent Bankers
555 Montgomery Street
Suite 750
San Francisco, CA 94111

415-352-2323
Fax: 415-352-2314
E-Mail: info@wib.org
Home Page: www.wib.org

Richard T. Beard, Chair
Russell A. Colombo, Chair-elect
Bryan Luke, Secretary/Treasurer
Janet Garufis, Immediate Past Chair

A trade association that informs, educates, and connects community banks with the resources and services to achieve the highest standards of personal and organizational performance.

3111 Women's World Banking
122 East 42nd Street
42nd Floor
New York, NY 10168

212-768-8513
Fax: 212-768-8519
Home Page: www.womensworldbanking.org

Jennifer Riria, Chair
Mary Houghton, Vice Chair
Connie Collingsworth, Secretary
Mary Ellen Iskenderian, President and CEO
J. Thomas Jones, Chief Operating Officer

A global nonprofit organization devoted to giving more low-income women access to the financial tools and resources they require to build security and prosperity.

Newsletters

3112 ABA Bank Directors Briefing
American Bankers Association
1120 Connecticut Avenue NW
Washington, DC 20036

202-663-5000
800-226-5377
Fax: 202-828-4548
Home Page: www.aba.com
Social Media: Facebook, Twitter, LinkedIn

Frank Keating, President/CEO
Stephen Crowe, Treasurer

Published by the editors of ABA Banking Journal in cooperation with the American Bankers Association. Focuses on keeping bank directors informed about legislative and regulatory developments, summarizing important banking industry trends, updating all directors on the latest thinking in corporate governance, educating new directors in the basics of community bank directorship
Frequency: Monthly

3113 **ABA Bankers News**
American Bankers Association
1120 Connecticut Avenue NW
Washington, DC 20036-3902

202-635-5000
800-226-5377
Fax: 202-663-7543
E-Mail: custserv@aba.com
Home Page: www.aba.com
Social Media: Facebook, Twitter, LinkedIn

Frank Keating, President/CEO
Stephen Crowe, Treasurer

For everyone in the banking industry especially CEOs and compliance officers. Learn to use the internet effectively, retain your best customers, reduce risk, nurture a sales culture and more.
Cost: $450.00
Frequency: Bi-Weekly
Founded in 1875

3114 **ABIA Insurance News**
American Bankers Association
1120 Connecticut Avenue NW
Washington, DC 20036

202-663-5163
800-226-5377
Fax: 202-828-4546
E-Mail: vbarton@aba.com
Home Page: www.theabia.com

Paul Petrylak, President/Chairman
Neal Aton, Vice President
David Cissell, Secretary
Val Teagarden, Treasurer

The American Bankers Insurance Association (ABIA) is the insurance subsidiary of the American Bankers Association (ABA). The ABIA's mission is to develop policy and provide advocacy for banks in insurance and to support bank insurance operations through research, education, compliance assistance, and peer group networking opportunities.
300 Members
Frequency: Bi-Weekly
Founded in 2001

3115 **AITCO Advisor**
Association of Independent Trust Companies
8 S Michigan Ave
Suite 802
Chicago, IL 60603-3452

312-223-1611
Fax: 312-580-0165
E-Mail: atico@gss.net
Home Page: www.aitco.net

Marcia Williams, Treasurer
Doug Nunn, President
Tom Blank, General Counsel/Secretary

Features professionally written articles on marketing and legislative issues as well as association updates.
Frequency: Quarterly

3116 **AMI Bulletin**
Assn for Management Information in Financial Svcs
14247 Saffron Circle
Carmel, IN 46032

317-518-5857
Fax: 317-518-5877
E-Mail: ami2@amifs.org
Home Page: www.amifs.org

Andy Schrieff, President
Jeff Nathasingh, Executive VP
Lynn Courchaine, Treasurer

News, calendars, events, and industry articles.
Frequency: Quarterly

3117 **Access**
American Safe Deposit Association
5433 S 200 E
Franklin, IN 46131-8982

317-738-4432
Fax: 317-738-5267
E-Mail: jmclin@aol.com
Home Page: www.tasda.com

Bill Lee, Publisher
Thomas Cullinan, President
J Wayne Merrill, First VP
Winnifred Howard-Hommack, Second Vice President
Kevin Fanning, Treasurer

A newsletter full of timely articles on safe deposit procedures, policies, problems and solutions.
Cost: $10.00

3118 **Advocacy Bulletins**
CFA Institute
Po Box 3668
Charlottesville, VA 22903-0668

434-951-5499
800-247-8132
Fax: 434-951-5262
E-Mail: info@amir.org
Home Page: www.cfainstitute.org

Alan Meder, Chair
John Rogers, President

To communicate time-sensitive information to interested AIMR/CFA Member Societies and members.
Frequency: Periodically

3119 **Allied News**
Allied Finance Adjusters Conference
P.O.Box 41368
Raleigh, NC 27629

800-621-3016
800-843-1232
Fax: 888-949-8520
E-Mail: alliedfinanceadjusters@gmail.com
Home Page: www.alliedfinanceadjusters.com
Social Media: Facebook, Twitter, LinkedIn

George Badeen, President

Trade Association of recovery specialists.
Cost: $200.00
Founded in 1936

3120 **American Banker**
SourceMedia
1 State Street Plaza
27th floor
New York, NY 10004-1561

212-803-8200
800-803-3424
Fax: 212-843-9608
E-Mail: custserv@sourcemedia.com
Home Page: www.sourcemedia.com

Douglas Manoni, CEO
Richard Antoneck, CFO
Cost: $99.00
Frequency: Monthly
Founded in 2005

3121 **BNA's Banking Report**
Bureau of National Affairs
3 Bethesda Metro Center
Suite 250
Bethesda, MD 20814

800-372-1033
Fax: 800-253-0332
E-Mail: customercare@bna.com
Home Page: www.bna.com

Donna Ives, VP Operations
Gregory McCaffery, President

Legal and regulatory developments in the financial services industry.
Cost: $1780.00
Frequency: Weekly
ISSN: 1522-5984
Founded in 1929

3122 **Bank Alerts**
Consumer Bankers Association
1000 Wilson Blvd
Suite 2500
Arlington, VA 22209-3912

703-276-1750
Fax: 703-528-1290
E-Mail: research@cbanet.org
Home Page: www.cbanet.org
Social Media: Facebook, Twitter, LinkedIn

Richard Hunt, President
Janet Pike, Executive Assistant

Federal legislative developments.
Frequency: Monthly
Circulation: 10,000
Founded in 1919
Printed in on newsprint stock

3123 **Bank Directors Briefing**
American Bankers Association
1120 Connecticut Avenue NW
Washington, DC 20036-3902

202-635-5000
800-226-5377
Fax: 202-663-7597
Home Page: www.aba.com

Matthew Williams, Chair
John Ikard, Vice Chairman

Newsletter reporting on legislative developments and management issues affecting community banks and their boards of directors.
Frequency: Monthly
Circulation: 33130

3124 **Bank Rate Monitor**
Bank Rate
11760 US Highway 1
Suite 500
North Palm Beach, FL 33408-8888

561-630-2400
Fax: 561-625-4540
Home Page: www.bankrate.com

Don Munsell, Production Director

Independent national source for the financial industry.
Cost: $499.00
4 Pages
Frequency: Weekly
Mailing list available for rent: 750 names
Printed in 3 colors

3125 **Bank Technology News**
SourceMedia
1 State Street Plaza
27th floor
New York, NY 10004-1561

212-803-8200
800-803-3424
Fax: 212-843-9608

E-Mail: custserv@sourcemedia.com
Home Page: www.sourcemedia.com

Douglas Manoni, CEO
Richard Antoneck, CFO
Cost: $99.00
Frequency: Monthly
Founded in 2005

3126 **Bank Tellers Report**
Sheshunoff Information Services
4120 Freidrich Lane
Suite 100
Austin, TX 78744

512-305-6500
800-456-2340
Fax: 512-305-6575
E-Mail: customercare.sis@sheshunoff.com
Home Page: www.sheshunoff.com

Bob Mate, CEO
Marge Simmons, Author

General interest publication for bank tellers.
Cost: $449.00
Frequency: Monthly
Founded in 1975

3127 **Bank and S&L Quarterly Rating Service**
Sheshunoff Information Services
4120 Freidrich Lane
Suite 100
Austin, TX 78744

512-305-6500
800-456-2340
Fax: 512-305-6575
E-Mail: customercare.sis@sheshunoff.com
Home Page: www.sheshunoff.com

Bob Mate, CEO

Statistical reports and research on savings and loan institutions.
Cost: $580.00
Frequency: Quarterly
Circulation: 5000
Mailing list available for rent: 5000 names

3128 **Banks in Insurance Report**
John Wiley & Sons
111 River St
Hoboken, NJ 07030-5790

201-748-6000
800-225-5945
Fax: 201-748-6088
E-Mail: info@wiley.com
Home Page: www.wiley.com

Mari Baker, CEO
Jean-Lou Chameau, President
Linda Katehi, Chancellor

Highlights the steps necessary for expansion into insurance products and services through articles that report on legislative activities, regulatory concerns, business and strategies.
Cost: $745.00
16 Pages
Frequency: Monthly
ISSN: 8756-6079
Founded in 1807
Printed in one color on matte stock

3129 **Cheklist**
BKB Publications
98 Greenwich Avenue
1st Floor
New York, NY 10011-7743

212-807-7933
Fax: 212-807-1821
E-Mail: bkbpub1@ix.netcom.com

Brian Burkart, Publisher
Charlene Komar Storey, Editor

Features general news, feature articles, legislative updates, reports on trends, legal advice, marketing ideas, product information and news of state and national association activities.
Cost: $35.00
Frequency: Quarterly
Circulation: 16,000
ISSN: 1066-3029

3130 **Client Quarterly**
WPI Communications
55 Morris Ave
Suite 300
Springfield, NJ 07081-1422

973-467-8700
800-323-4995
Fax: 973-467-0368
E-Mail: info@wpicommunications.com
Home Page: www.wpicomm.com

Steve Klinghoffer, Owner/Publisher
Lori Klinghoffer, Executive Vice President

Information and advice on financial, business and tax matters.
Frequency: Quarterly
Founded in 1952

3131 **Community Bank President**
Siefer Consultants
525 Cayuga Street
PO Box 1384
Storm Lake, IA 50588-1384

712-660-1026
Fax: 866-680-5866
E-Mail: info@siefer.com
Home Page: www.siefer.com

Dan Siefer, Publisher

Profit making opportunities for financial institutions.
Cost: $297.00
8 Pages
Frequency: Monthly

3132 **Compliance & Management Bulletin**
American Bankers Association
1120 Connecticut Avenue NW
Washington, DC 20036-3902

202-663-5000
800-226-5377
Fax: 202-828-4540
E-Mail: custserv@aba.com
Home Page: www.aba.com

Frank Keating, President/CEO
Albert Kelly, Chair

Includes the information you need to keep up with and respond to the latest in new and revised laws and regulations affecting your institution's management and operations.
Cost: $375.00
Frequency: Published, As Needed
Circulation: 2000
Founded in 1992

3133 **Consumer Bankers Association**
Consumer Bankers Association
1000 Wilson Blvd
Suite 2500
Arlington, VA 22209-3912

703-276-1750
Fax: 703-528-1290
E-Mail: webmaster@cbanet.org
Home Page: www.cbanet.org

Richard Hunt, President
Janet Pike, Executive Assistant

Legislative newsletter on retail banking for association members.
Founded in 1919

3134 **Credit Card Management**
Thomson Financial Publishing
1 State St
27th Floor
New York, NY 10004-1481

212-825-8445
800-328-9378
Fax: 212-292-5216
E-Mail: general.info@thomson.com
Home Page: www.sourcemedia.com

Douglas Manoni, CEO
Richard Antoneck, CFO

Information on the major developments in the credit card industry.
Cost: $98.00
74 Pages
Frequency: Monthly
Circulation: 19000
Printed in 4 colors on glossy stock

3135 **Credit Union Journal**
SourceMedia
1 State St
27th Floor
New York, NY 10004-1561

212-803-8200
800-803-3424
Fax: 212-843-9608
E-Mail: custserv@sourcemedia.com
Home Page: www.sourcemedia.com

Douglas Manoni, CEO
Richard Antoneck, CFO
Cost: $99.00
Frequency: Monthly
Founded in 2005

3136 **Current Issues in Bank Auditing**
Bank Research Associates
5866 Kootenai Lane
PO Box 7812
Boise, ID 83707-1812

208-322-3508
Home Page: www.bankresearchassociates.com

Don L Raymond CPA, Editor

Offers information and updates on auditing of financial institutions.
Cost: $98.00
6 Pages
Frequency: Monthly
Founded in 1979

3137 **DTCC Newsletter**
Depository Trust Company
55 Water St
New York, NY 10041-0024

212-855-1000
Fax: 212-855-2350
E-Mail: info@dtcc.com
Home Page: www.dtcc.com

Robert Druskin, Chairman
Michael Bodson, President

Information for the banking and securities industry.
Frequency: Monthly
Circulation: 7000
Founded in 1999

3138 **Daily Treasury Statement**
Financial Management Service
3700 E West Highway
Room 502A
Hysttaville, MD 20782

202-874-9790
800-826-9434
Fax: 202-874-8447
E-Mail: dts.Questions@fms.treas.gov
Home Page: www.fms.treas.gov

Richard L Gregg, Commissioner
Melanie Rigney, Editor

This report offers the latest news of the Treasury Department.
Frequency: Daily
Founded in 1974

3139 **Digest for Corporate & Securities Lawyers**
Bowne & Company
55 Water Street
New York, NY 10041
212-924-500
212-229-3400
Home Page: www.bowne.com
Bruce Brumberg, Editor-in-Chief
Johanna McKenzie, Editor
Susan Koffman, Editor
Karen Axelrod, Managing Editor
David Shea, Chairman/CEO
Summaries of articles on corporate finance, mergers acquisitions, initial public offerings (ipos) and restructuring. Selects articles from hundreds of publications focusing on articles trends, strategies and advice on deal structuring.
2700 Members
Frequency: Monthly
Founded in 1775

3140 **Direct Deposit Authorization Forms**
NACHA: Electronic Payments Association
13450 Sunrise Valley Drive
Suite 100
Herndon, VA 20171
703-561-1100
Fax: 703-787-0996
E-Mail: info@nacha.org
Home Page: www.nacha.org
Janet O Estep, CEO
Maurice Haitema, Chairperson
These authorizations are for companies looking for generic authorization forms that market ACH benefits to consumers.
Cost: $30.00
Frequency: Monthly

3141 **Directors & Trustees Digest**
American Bankers Association
1120 Connecticut Avenue NW
Washington, DC 20036-3902
202-663-5000
Fax: 202-828-4540
E-Mail: custserv@aba.com
Home Page: www.aba.com
Frank Keating, President/CEO
Albert Kelly, Chairman
Steven Crowe, Treasurer
Monique Hanis, Marketing/Business Development
Provides corporate governance guidance, outlines board legal and fiduciary responsibilities and offers resourceful information on board management relations.
Frequency: Monthly

3142 **Examiner**
Conference of State Bank Supervisors
1129 20th Street, N.W.
9th Floor
Washington, DC 20036-4327
202-296-2840
Fax: 202-296-1928
Home Page: www.csbs.org
Neal Milner, CEO
Thomas Harlow, CFO
Cecelia Smith, Senior Manager, Administration
John Gorman, General Counsel
Provides news, analysis and commentary on the important events affecting the state banking system.
Frequency: Weekly

3143 **FSPA Newsletter**
Financial & Security Products Association
Plaza Ladera, 5300 Sequoia NW
Suite 205
Albuquerque, NM 87120
505-839-7958
800-843-6082
Fax: 505-839-0017
E-Mail: info@fspa1.com
Home Page: www.fspa1.com
Mark Thatcher, Chairman
Bill Mercer, President
John M Vrabec, Executive Director
Offers timely ideas and techniques to help you compete and run your business more effectively. Also provides low-cost opportunities for members to advertise their products and/or services within the body of the newsletter, or in an insert included with the newsletter mailing.
Frequency: Monthly

3144 **Federal Reserve Bulletin**
Board of Governors of the Federal Reserve System
20th St & Constitution Ave N
Washington, DC 20551-0001
202-452-3284
Fax: 202-452-3101
Home Page: www.federalreserve.gov
Social Media: Facebook, Twitter, LinkedIn
Ben S Bernanke, Chairman
Janet Yellen, Vice Chairman
Reports on analysis on economic developments, regulatory issues and new data. The quarterly version will no longer be published, however the Board will print an annual compendium.
Frequency: Annual
Founded in 1913

3145 **Federal Reserve Regulatory Service**
Federal Reserve Board Publishers
20th St & Constitution Ave N
Washington, DC 20551-0001
202-452-3000
Fax: 202-452-3819
E-Mail: publication-bog@frbog.frb.gov
Home Page: www.federalreserve.gov
Social Media: Facebook, Twitter, LinkedIn
Ben S Bernanke, Chairman
Janet Yellen, Vice Chairman
Consumer and community affairs.
Cost: $200.00
Frequency: Monthly

3146 **Financial Services Daily**
SNL Securities
One SNL Plaza
PO Box 2124
Charlottesvle, VA 22902
434-977-1600
Fax: 434-977-4466
E-Mail: CustomerService@snl.com
Home Page: www.snl.com
Mike Chinn, President/CEO
Nick Cafferillo, COO
Comprehensive daily coverage of the financial services and technology sectors.
Cost: $795.00
40 Pages
Frequency: Monthly
Founded in 1987

3147 **Funds Transfer Report**
Bankers Research
PO Box 431
Westport, CT 06881-0431
Ted Volckhausen Sr, Publisher/Co-Editor
Ted Volckhausen Jr, Editor
Offers banking and financial information to professionals and consumers.
Cost: $324.00
Frequency: Monthly

3148 **Global Investment Technology**
Global Investment Technology
909 Third Avenue
27th Floor
New York, NY 10022
212-370-3700
Fax: 212-370-4606
E-Mail: info@globalinv.com
Home Page: www.globalinv.com
Micheal Horton, Publisher
Paven Saeghel, Editor-in-Chief
Focuses exclusively on strategic business trends, operations, and automation issues facing US and non-US investment institutions and banks.
Cost: $695.00
Frequency: Bi-Weekly
Circulation: 1800
Founded in 1991

3149 **Global Survey of Regulatory & Market Developments in Banking**
Institute of International Bankers
299 Park Ave
17th Floor
New York, NY 10171-3896
212-421-1611
Fax: 212-421-1119
E-Mail: iib@iib.org
Home Page: www.iib.org
Social Media: Facebook, Twitter, LinkedIn
Sarah ""sally"" Miller, CEO
Richard Coffman, General Counsel
William Goodwin, Communications Director
The study documents the economic contributions that international banks make to the United States, and also addresses the benefits that other countries enjoy from the extensive activities of United States and other non-domestic banks in their markets.
Frequency: Annual

3150 **IBES Monthly Comments**
Lynch, Jones and Ryan
1633 Broadway
48th Floor
New York, NY 10019
212-310-9500
800-992-7526
Fax: 646-223-9081
E-Mail: ljrinfo@ljr.com
Home Page: www.ljr.com
Stanley Chamberlin, Publisher
Todd W Burns, President
Monitors changes in global earning estimates database.
Founded in 1966

3151 **ICBA Washington Report**
Independent Community Bankers of American
1615 L Street NW
Suite 900
Washington, DC 20036
202-659-8111
E-Mail: info@icba.org
Home Page: www.icba.org
Camden R Fine, President/CEO
Rachael Solomon, Advertising Contact
Provides detailed coverage of important federal legislative and regulatory developments specifically for community bankers.
Cost: $60.00
Frequency: Monthly

3152 IFSA Newsletter
International Financial Services Association
1120 Connecticut Avenue, NW
Washington, DC 20036

20 -66 -757
Fax: 202-663-5538
E-Mail: info@baft-ifsa.com
Home Page: www.ifsaonline.org
Social Media: Facebook, Twitter, LinkedIn

Tod Burwell, Vice President
250 Pages
Frequency: Quarterly
Founded in 1924

3153 In Focus
National Assn of Government Guaranteed Lenders
215 East 9th Avenue
Stillwater, OK 74074

405-377-4022
Fax: 405-377-3931
E-Mail: bfortune@naggl.com
Home Page: www.naggl.org

Tony Wilkinson, President/CEO
Jennifer Sterrett O'Neill, EVP/COO
Jenifer Brake, Assistant VP Marketing
Jennifer Sterrett-O'Neill, Assistant VP Communications

Practical tips that will help you build the little efficiencies that make a big difference.
Frequency: Monthly

3154 Inside Mortgage Compliance
Inside Mortgage Finance Publishers
7910 Woodmont Ave
Suite 1000
Bethesda, MD 20814-7019

301-951-1240
Fax: 301-656-1709
E-Mail: imce@imfpubs.com
Home Page: www.imfpubs.com

Guy Cecala, Owner/Publisher

Keeps executives on top of crucial and evolving legal and regulatory issues. Covers fair housing, predatory lending, consumer protection, RESPA, TILA, lawsuits. Features monthly CRA ratings.
Cost: $571.00
14 Pages
Frequency: Monthly
ISSN: 1093-605X
Founded in 1990
Mailing list available for rent: 750 names
Printed in 2 colors on matte stock

3155 Inside Strategy
Strategy Research Corporation
100 NW 37th Avenue
Miami, FL 33125

305-649-5400
Fax: 305-643-5584
E-Mail: strategy@canect.net
Home Page: www.strategyresearch.com

Johanna Strouss, Editor
Richard Tobin, President

Inside Strategy is a newsletter that covers trends and developments in Latin America and the US Hispanic market mostly obtained from SRC, studies, products services and reports.
38511 Pages
Frequency: Monthly
Founded in 1998

3156 Inside The GSEs
Inside Mortgage Finance Publishers
7910 Woodmont Ave
Suite 1000
Bethesda, MD 20814-7019

301-951-1240
Fax: 301-656-1709
E-Mail: service@imfpubs.com
Home Page: www.imfpubs.com

Guy Cecala, Owner
Greg Johnson, Editor
John Bancroft, Managing Editor
Mary L Probka, Director Marketing/Circulation

Subscribers know the latest on GSE finance, products, political contributions, their critics and supporters, and news on potential reform, controversies and regulatory activities.
Cost: $763.00
14 Pages
Frequency: Bi-Weekly
ISSN: 1093-605X
Founded in 1985
Mailing list available for rent: 400 names
Printed in 2 colors on matte stock

3157 MSRB Manual
Municipal Securities Rulemaking Board
1900 Duke St
Suite 600
Alexandria, VA 22314-3461

703-797-6600
Fax: 703-797-6700
E Mail: MSRBsupport@msrb.org
Home Page: www.msrb.org

Lynnette Hotkis, Executive Director
Marcelo Vieira, Director Research

Rules of the Municipal Rule-Making Board.
Cost: $7.00
Founded in 1975

3158 NACHA: Electronic Payments Association Newsletter
NACHA: The Electronic Payments Association
13450 Sunrise Valley Drive
Suite 100
Herndon, VA 20171

703-561-1100
Fax: 703-787-0996
E-Mail: info@nacha.org
Home Page: www.nacha.org

Marcie Haitema, Chairperson
Janet O Estep, CEO

Articles on industry self regulatory organizations for automated clearing house payment systems and other electronic payments.
Cost: $120.00
Printed in 2 colors on matte stock

3159 NAGGL News Flash
National Assn of Government Guaranteed Lenders
215 East 9th Avenue
Stillwater, OK 74074

405-377-4022
Fax: 404-377-3931
E-Mail: bfortune@naggl.com
Home Page: www.naggl.org

Tony Wilkinson, President/CEO
Jennifer Sterrett O'Neill, EVP/COO
Jenifer Brake, Assistant VP Marketing
Jennifer Sterrett-O'Neill, Assistant VP Communications

This email is an at-a-glance review of recent industry news.
Frequency: Bi-Monthly

3160 Nilson Report
HSN Consultants
1110 Eugenia Place
Suite 100
Carpinteria, CA 930113-992

805-684-8800
Fax: 805-684-8825
E-Mail: info@nilsonreport.com
Home Page: www.nilsonreport.com

H Spencer Nilson, Publisher

Credit card newsletter.
Cost: $945.00
12 Pages
Frequency: BiWeekly

3161 Opportunities for Banks in Life Insurance
American Association of Bank Directors
1250 24th Street, NW
Suite 700
Washington, DC 20037

20 -46 -488
Fax: 202-349-8080
E-Mail: info@aabd.org
Home Page: www.aabd.org

David Baris, Executive Director

The guide reviews best insurance sales practices, distribution strategies, selling through investment brokers, using licensed branch bankers, referrals from investment specialists, referrals from licensed branch bankers, stand alone life specialists, direct sales and more.
Cost: $12.50

3162 Origination News
Thomson Financial
One State Street Plaza
27th floor
New York, NY 10004

212-803-8760
Fax: 212-292-5216
Home Page: www.originationnews.com

Elaine Yadlon, Plant Manager
Richard J Harrington, President/CEO

Information for mortgage industry executives on mortgage brokers, mortgage bankers and mortgage executives in commercial banks, savings banks, savings and loan associations and credit unions.
Cost: $78.00
Frequency: Monthly

3163 Payments System Report
National Automated Clearing House Association
13450 Sunrise Valley Drive
Suite 100
Herndon, VA 20171-4607

703-561-1100
800-487-9180
Fax: 703-787-0996
E-Mail: info@nacha.org
Home Page: www.nacha.org
Social Media: Facebook, Twitter, LinkedIn

Janet O Estep, CEO

Official source for Automated Clearing House (ACH) news and information. Contains reports on rule changes, legislative and regulatory developments, policy issues, market research, product developments and marketing solutions.
Frequency: Monthly

3164 Peer News
American Bankers Association
1120 Connecticut Avenue NW
Washington, DC 20036

202-635-5000
800-226-5377
Fax: 202-828-4540
E-Mail: icb@aba.com
Home Page: www.aba.com/icbcertifications

Frank Keating, President/CEO
Albert Kelly, Chairman
Steven Crowe, Treasurer
Monique Hanis, Marketing/Business Development
Mark DeBaugh, Marketing/Communications Manager

ICB members receive a newsletter that shares program developments, member career notes,

insights from ICB leadership, the latest continuing education opportunities, and more.
Frequency: Quarterly

3165 Pratt's Bank Security Report
AS Pratt & Sons
805 15th St. NW
Third Floor
Washington, DC 20005-2207
800-572-2797
E-Mail: customercare.sis@sheshunoff.com
Home Page: www.aspratt.com
Peter Knopp, Editor
Security officers and consultants can keep up with the latest developments affecting bank security by subscribing to Pratt's Bank Security Report.
Cost: $455.00
Frequency: Monthly
Founded in 1867

3166 RTC Suits Against Savings Institution Directors and Officers
American Association of Bank Directors
1250 24th Street, NW
Suite 700
Washington, DC 20037
20 -46 -488
Fax: 202-349-8080
E-Mail: info@aabd.org
Home Page: www.aabd.org
David Baris, Executive Director
This study reviews all 90 of the cases in the RTC's public files that were filed by the RTC against directors and officers.
Cost: $85.00

3167 Regional Mortgage Market Report
Mortgage Bankers Association
1717 Rhode Island Avenue, NW
Suite 400
Washington, DC 20036
202-557-2700
E-Mail: membership@mortgagebankers.org
Home Page: www.mortgagebankers.org
Social Media: Facebook, Twitter, LinkedIn
The Regional Mortgage Market Report for MSAs and/or states has been designed to provide mortgage professionals with a primary source of information to help identify mortgage lending opportunities and manage the risks associated with mortgage servicing.
Cost: $395.00
Frequency: Quarterly
Founded in 1914

3168 Report of Task Force on Asset Freezes of Bank Directors and Officers
American Association of Bank Directors
1250 24th Street, NW
Suite 700
Washington, DC 20037
20 -46 -488
Fax: 202-349-8080
E-Mail: info@aabd.org
Home Page: www.aabd.org
David Baris, Executive Director
Cost: $25.00

3169 SCOR Report
Stewart Gordon Associates
PO Box 781992
Dallas, TX 75378-1992
972-620-2489
Fax: 972-406-0213
E-Mail: tsg@scor-report.com
Home Page: www.scor-report.com
Tom Stewart Gordon, Publisher
C Delton Simmons, Circulation Manager
Anne D Hall, Production Manager
Capital information alternatives for small business. Target audience: small business, their lawyers and accountants.
Cost: $280.00
Founded in 1994

3170 SNL Bank & Thrift Daily
SNL Securities
212 7th Street NE
Charlottesville, VA 22902-2124
434-977-1600
Fax: 434-977-4466
E-Mail: subscriptions@snl.com
Home Page: www.snl.com
Social Media: Twitter, Youtube
Michael Chinn, President/CEO
Nick Cafferillo, COO
Summary of previous week's acquisition announcements, branch sales, merger conversions, FDIC transactions and deal updates and perspectives.
Cost: $1700.00
Frequency: Weekly
Founded in 1987

3171 SNL REIT Weekly
SNL Securities
212 7th Street NE
Charlottesvle, VA 22902
434-977-1600
Fax: 434-977-4466
E-Mail: subscriptions@snl.com
Home Page: www.snl.com
Social Media: Twitter, Youtube
Michael Chinn, President/CEO
Nick Cafferillo, COO
Fax newsletter that summarizes the previous week's activity involving REITs. Includes comprehensive articles on current industry trends, condensed news stories, recent capital offerings and the latest market information.
Cost: $496.00
15 Pages
Frequency: Weekly
Founded in 1987

3172 Secondary Mortgage Markets
Federal Home Loan Mortgage Corporation
8200 Jones Branch Drive
McLean, VA 22102-3110
703-903-2000
800-424-5401
Fax: 703-903-4045
E-Mail: smm@frediemac.com
Home Page: www.freddiemac.com
Charles E. Haldeman, CEO
Ralph Boyd, Executive VP Community Relations
Covers buying and selling residential and commercial mortgage-backed and asset-backed loans, marketing, and risk management.
Frequency: Monthly
Circulation: 15000
Founded in 1970

3173 Securities & Investments M&A
SNL Securities
212 7th Street NE
Charlottesvle, VA 22902
434-977-1600
Fax: 434-977-4466
E-Mail: CustomerService@snl.com
Home Page: www.snl.com
Social Media: Twitter, Youtube
Michael Chinn, President/CEO
Nick Cafferillo, COO
Fully devoted to M&A in the securities and asset management sectors.
Cost: $795.00
40 Pages
Frequency: Monthly
Founded in 1987

3174 Specialty Finance M&A
SNL Securities
212 7th Street NE
Charlottesvle, VA 22902
434-977-1600
Fax: 434-977-4466
E-Mail: CustomerService@snl.com
Home Page: www.snl.com
Social Media: Twitter, Youtube
Michael Chinn, President/CEO
Nick Cafferillo, COO
A unique source dedicated exclusively to specialty finance M&A.
Cost: $795.00
40 Pages
Frequency: Monthly
Founded in 1987

3175 Study of Leading Banks in Insurance
American Bankers Insurance Association
1120 Connecticut Avenue NW
Washington, DC 20036
202-663-5163
800-226-5377
Fax: 202-828-4546
E-Mail: vbarton@aba.com
Home Page: www.aba.com
Frank Keating, President/Chairman
Albert Kelly, Chairman
David Cissell, Secretary
Neal Aton, Treasurer
Presents the findings from the eighth research of the current and planned insurance activities of U.S. banks. Designed as a management tool for executives who need to understand how the bank-insurance industry is developing.
300 Members
Frequency: Annual
Founded in 2001

3176 Thrift Insider
Inside Mortgage Finance Publishers
7910 Woodmont Ave
Suite 1000
Bethesda, MD 20814-7019
301-951-1240
Fax: 301-656-1709
E-Mail: service@imfpubs.com
Home Page: www.imfpubs.com
Guy Cecala, Owner
Complete coverage of regulatory, legislative, legal, accounting, and market issues in the thrift industry.
Cost: $485.00
Frequency: Bi-Weekly

3177 U.S. Banker
SourceMedia
1 State St
27th Floor
New York, NY 10004-1561
212-803-8200
800-803-3424
Fax: 212-843-9608
E-Mail: custserv@sourcemedia.com
Home Page: www.sourcemedia.com
Douglas Manoni, CEO
Richard Antoneck, CFO
Cost: $99.00
Frequency: Monthly
Founded in 2005

3178 World Bank News
World Bank

1818 H St Nw
Room U11-147
Washington, DC 20433-0002

202-473-1000
Fax: 202-477-6391
Home Page: www.mehr.org

Graeme Wheeler, CEO
Paul Wolfowitz, President
Cynthia Delgadillo, Production Manager

For journalists and the developing community
Frequency: Fortnightly
Circulation: 9000
Founded in 1980

Magazines & Journals

3179 **A Guide to Implementing Direct Payment**
NACHA: Electronic Payments Association
13450 Sunrise Valley Drive
Suite 100
Herndon, VA 20171

703-561-1100
Fax: 703-787-0996
E-Mail: info@nacha.org
Home Page: www.nacha.org
Social Media: Facebook, Twitter, LinkedIn

Janet O Estep, CEO

A complete overview of these popular ACH applications. Also discussed are benefits, costs, operational/implementation concerns and promotional efforts. Included are sample promotional materials and implementation checklists.

3180 **A Profile of State Chartered Banking**
1129 20th Street, N.W.
9th Floor
Washington, DC 20036-4327

202-296-2840
800-886-2727
Fax: 202-296-1928
E-Mail: rstromberg@csbs.org
Home Page: www.csbs.org

John Ryan, President/CEO
Cecelia Smith, Senior Manager, Administration
54 Pages
Frequency: Monthly
Founded in 1902

3181 **ABA Bank Compliance**
American Bankers Association
1120 Connecticut Avenue NW
Washington, DC 20036-3971

202-635-5000
800-226-5377
Fax: 202-663-7543
E-Mail: custserv@aba.com
Home Page: www.aba.com

Frank Keating, President
Albert Kelly, Chairman

The source for timely, authoritative analysis of the ever-changing regulatory environment. Covers all the current regulatory issues, such as Privacy and E-Commerce, and perennial Compliance focus areas, such as lending, the Community Reinvestment Act, risk management, training and technology.
Cost: $450.00
Frequency: Bi-Monthly
Founded in 1875

3182 **ABA Bank Marketing**
American Bankers Association
1120 Connecticut Avenue NW
Washington, DC 20036-3971

202-635-5000
800-226-5377
Fax: 202-828-4540
E-Mail: custserv@aba.com
Home Page: www.aba.com

Frank Keating, President
Albert Kelly, Chairman

A designed package of marketing intelligence, featuring essential industry news, in-depth articles, award-winning columnists and opinions, useful case studies and time-saving advice.
Cost: $120.00
Frequency: Monthly
Founded in 1875

3183 **ABA Bank Marketing Survey Report**
ABA Marketing Network
1120 Connecticut Avenue NW
Washington, DC 20036-3971

202-663-5000
800-226-5377
Fax: 202 828-4540
E-Mail: marketingnetwork@aba.com
Home Page: www.aba.com/marketingnetwork/

Frank Keating, President
Albert Kelly, Chairman

The ABA Bank Marketing Survey Report provides comprehensive detailed benchmarks of bank marketing in such areas as marketing expenditures, marketing functions, market segmentation strategies, cross-selling/sales incentives, direct marketing, Internet marketing and advertising agency use.

3184 **ABA Banking Journal**
Simmons-Boardman Publishing Corporation
345 Hudson St
12th Floor
New York, NY 10014-7123

212-620-7200
Fax: 212-633-1165
E-Mail: bstreeter@sbpub.com
Home Page: www.simmonsboardman.com

Arthur J McGinnis Jr, President

The official journal of the American Bank Association, reporting on the banking industry.
Frequency: Monthly
Circulation: 32867
Founded in 1908
Mailing list available for rent

3185 **ABA Consumer Banking Digest**
American Bankers Association
1120 Connecticut Avenue NW
Washington, DC 20036-3902

202-635-5000
800-226-5377
Fax: 202-828-4547
E-Mail: drhodes@aba.com
Home Page: www.aba.com

Frank Keating, President
Albert Kelly, Chairman

Provides perspectives on the latest developments, shifts and changes in the e-commerce sector. The goal is to provide a comprehensive, yet concise, description of current events shaping the rapidly emerging world of e-commerce and banking.
Cost: $450.00
Frequency: Bi-Monthly
Founded in 1875

3186 **ABA Reference Guide for Regulatory Compliance**
American Bankers Association
1120 Connecticut Avenue NW
Washington, DC 20036-3200

202-635-5000
800-226-5377
Fax: 202-663-7597
Home Page: www.aba.com

Frank Keating, President
Albert Kelly, Chairman

Ideal source for Compliance Managers, Department Managers and Staff, Product Managers, and Retail/Branch Managers and those preparing for the Certified Regulatory Compliance Manager Exam.
Cost: $350.00
Frequency: Annual

3187 **ABA Trust & Investments**
American Bankers Association
1120 Connecticut Avenue NW
Washington, DC 20036

202-635-5000
800-226-5377
Fax: 202-828-4540
E-Mail: custserv@aba.com
Home Page: www.aba.com

Frank Keating, President
Albert Kelly, Chairman

Brings current, authoritative, wide-ranging coverage and updates on all aspects of the trust and investments industry
Cost: $120.00
15 Pages
Frequency: Bi-Monthly

3188 **ACH Marketing Handbook: A Guide for Financial Institutions & Companies**
NACHA: The Electronic Payments Association
13450 Sunrise Valley Drive
Suite 100
Herndon, VA 20171

703-561-1100
Fax: 703-787-0996
E-Mail: info@nacha.org
Home Page: www.nacha.org

Marcie Haitema, Chairperson
Janet O Estep, CEO

Designed for financial institutions and companies to assist them in understanding ACH products and services-their benefits, risk management considerations, and consumer perspectives.
Cost: $70.00
Frequency: Annual+

3189 **ACH Operating Rules & Guidelines**
NACHA: Electronic Payments Association
13450 Sunrise Valley Drive
Suite 100
Herndon, VA 20171

703-561-1100
Fax: 703-787-0996
E-Mail: info@nacha.org
Home Page: www.nacha.org

Janet O Estep, CEO
Marcie Haitema, Chairperson

Reflects the results of the Rules Simplifications initiative.
Cost: $78.00

3190 **ACH Operating Rules, Corporate Edition**
NACHA: Electronic Payments Association
13450 Sunrise Valley Drive
Suite 100
Herndon, VA 20171

703-561-1100
Fax: 703-787-0996
E-Mail: info@nacha.org
Home Page: www.nacha.org

Janet O Estep, CEO
Marcie Haitema, Chairperson

Reflects the results of the Rules Simplification initiative. Previously organized around major topics, the simplified Rules framework is structured around the rights and responsibilities of participants in the ACH Network.
Cost: $46.00

3191 ACH Settlement Guide
NACHA: Electronic Payments Association
13450 Sunrise Valley Drive
Suite 100
Herndon, VA 20171

703-561-1100
Fax: 703-787-0996
E-Mail: info@nacha.org
Home Page: www.nacha.org
Social Media: Facebook, Twitter, LinkedIn

Janet O Estep, CEO

Designed to provide a thorough working knowledge of how money flows through the ACH Network and to equip financial institutions with the necessary tools to reconcile the daily ACH. Included in this publication are examples of statements, ACH advices and a sample balancing worksheet that financial institutions can use as a model for daily reconciling. This document was written as a direct result of financial institutions losing money due to the mismanagement of the ACH settlement function.

3192 AFP Exchange
Association for Financial Professionals
4520 East West Hwy
Suite 750
Bethesda, MD 20814-3319

301-907-2862
Fax: 301-907-2864
E-Mail: afp@afponline.org
Home Page: www.afponline.org

Michael Connolly, Chairman of the Board
Susan Glass, Vice Chairman
James Kaitz, President & CEO

AFP Exchange is published for financial professionals. Editorial highlights include case studies and practical business information. Regular departments include outlook, new products and services, calendar and book reviews.
Cost: $90.00
80 Pages
Frequency: Bi-Monthly
Circulation: 12000
Founded in 1979
Printed in 4 colors on glossy stock

3193 AITCO Membership Directory
Association of Independent Trust Companies
8 S Michigan Ave
Suite 1000
Chicago, IL 60603-3452

312-223-1611
Fax: 312-580-0165
E-Mail: aitco@gss.net
Home Page: www.aitco.net

Douglas Nunn, President
Marcia Williams, Treasurer
Tom Blank, General Counsel/Secretary

Provides members with contact information on peers as well as industry vendors. This reference tool also include a listing of key officers as well as detailed descriptions of the company's product line and specialty areas.
50+ Pages

3194 American Banker
American Banker/SourceMedia
1 State St
27th Floor
New York, NY 10004-1561

212-803-8450
800-221-1809
Fax: 212-843-9600
E-Mail: adam.silverstone@sourcemedia.com
Home Page: www.sourcemedia.com

Douglas Manoni, CEO
Richard Antoneck, CFO

Focuses on the continuing changes in banking, including lending, money market shifts, developments in operations and technology, marketing, mortgages and mergers.
Cost: $945.00
Circulation: 18754
Founded in 1835

3195 BAI Banking Strategies
Bank Administration Institute
115 S. LaSalle Street
Suite 3300
Chicago, IL 60603-3801

312-683-2464
888-284-4078
Fax: 312-683-2373
E-Mail: info@bai.org
Home Page: www.bai.org
Social Media: Facebook, Twitter, LinkedIn, Youtube

Lewis Fischer, Chairman of the Board
Scott Peters, Vice Chairman

Offers insightful editorial perspective in-depth unbiased coverage of important strategic issues and industry best practices.
Frequency: Monthly

3196 Bank Director News
American Association of Bank Directors
1250 24th Street, NW
Suite 700
Washington, DC 20037

202-463-4888
Fax: 202-349-8080
E-Mail: info@aabd.org
Home Page: www.aabd.org

David Baris, Executive Director
Frequency: quarterly

3197 Bank Insurance & Securities Marketing
Bank Insurance and Securities Association
2025 M Street NW
Suite 800
Washington, DC 20036

202-367-1111
Fax: 202-367-2111
E-Mail: bisa@BISAnet.org
Home Page: www.bisanet.org

Jim McNeil, Executive Director
Marc A Vosen, President

The official publication of the Bank Insurance & Securities Association, sets the standard for in-depth industry reporting. Offers readers expert advice, exemplary editorials, in-depth articles and timely news updates.
Founded in 2002

3198 Bank News
Bank News Publications
PO Box 29156
Shawnee Mission, KS 66205-9156

913-261-7000
800-336-1120
Fax: 913-261-7010
E-Mail: info@banknews.com
Home Page: www.banknews.com

Janet Holman, President & Publisher
Joel Holman, CEO & Publisher

News and features for banks and bankers.
Cost: $79.00
64 Pages
Frequency: Monthly
Circulation: 7000
Founded in 1901
Printed in 4 colors on glossy stock

3199 Bank Notes
510 King Street
Suite 410
Alexandria, VA 22314

703-549-0977
800-966-7475
Fax: 703-548-5945
E-Mail: eba@envirobank.org
Home Page: www.envirobank.org

Rick Ferguson, President
Scott Beckerman, Treasurer
76 Pages
Frequency: Bi-Monthly
Founded in 1994

3200 Bank Systems & Technology
CMP Media
240 West 35th Street
New York, NY 10001

212-928-8400
Fax: 212-600-3080
E-Mail: siannuz@cmp.com
Home Page: www.cmp.com

David Leven, CEO
Dame Helen Alexander, Chairman

In-depth look into the new age of banking where total integration of technology is the driving force of new product business growth. Features deliver critical information on the strategic use of technology for increased profitability and productivity, in turn providing bankers with the tools to gain the competitive advantage on today's changing financial services landscape.
Cost: $52.00
Frequency: Monthly
Circulation: 23753
Founded in 1918

3201 Bank Technology News
Thomson Media
1 State St
27th Floor
New York, NY 10004-1481

212-803-8200
Fax: 212-843-9600
E-Mail: custserv@sourcemedia.com
Home Page: www.banktechnews.com
Social Media: Facebook, Twitter

Penny Crosman, Editor in Chief
Douglas J. Manoni, CEO

The leading source for financial services technology coverage, written for those individuals who are responsible for the front, middle and back office technology needs of their financial institutes.
52 Pages
Frequency: Monthly
Founded in 1987
Mailing list available for rent

3202 Bankers Digest
P.O. Box 743006
Dallas, TX 75374-3006

214-221-4544
Fax: 214-221-4546
E-Mail: bankersdigest@bankersdigest.com
Home Page: www.bankersdigest.com

Bonnie J Blackman, Owner
R Blackman Jr, Managing Editor

A weekly news magazine devoted to the southwest banking news. Accepts advertising.
Cost: $29.00
16 Pages
Frequency: Weekly
Circulation: 3100
ISSN: 0140-1800
Founded in 1942
Printed in 2 colors on glossy stock

3203 Bankers' Magazine
Thomson Reuters
195 Broadway
Suite 4
New York, NY 10007-3124
646-822-2000
800-231-1860
Fax: 646-822-2800
E-Mail: trta.lei-support@thomsonreuters.com
Home Page: www.ria.thomsonreuters.com
Elaine Yadlon, Plant Manager
Thomas H Glocer, CEO & Director
Robert D Daleo, Chief Financial Officer
Kelli Crane, Senior Vice President & CIO
Written by bank professionals who offer urgent information about the banking industry to the banking community.
Cost: $115.00
Frequency: Bi-Monthly
Founded in 1935

3204 Banking Strategies
Bank Administration Institute
115 S. LaSalle Street
Suite 3300
Chicago, IL 60603
312-683-2464
800-224-9889
Fax: 312-683-2373
E-Mail: info@bai.org
Home Page: www.bai.org
Social Media: Facebook, Twitter, LinkedIn, Youtube
Lewis Fischer, Chairman of the Board
Scott Peters, Vice Chairman
Includes information on finance, economics, planning, operations, regulations, retail, technology and human resources management.
Cost: $66.50
66 Pages
Circulation: 42175
ISSN: 1091-6385

3205 Banking Strategies Magazine
Bank Administration Institute
115 S LaSalle St
Suite 3300
Chicago, IL 60603
312-683-2464
888-284-4078
Fax: 312-683-2373
E-Mail: info@bai.org
Home Page: www.bai.org
Social Media: Facebook, Twitter, LinkedIn, Youtube
Lewis Fischer, Chairman of the Board
Scott Peters, Vice Chairman
To present the latest in best practices and thought leadership through high-quality, in-depth, unbiased editorial coverage of strategic and managerial issues in today's complex and dynamic financial services business.
Frequency: Annual

3206 Broker Magazine
Thomson Media
1 State St
27th floor
New York, NY 10004-1481
212-825-8445
888-501-8850
Fax: 212-292-5216
E-Mail: Custserv@thomsonmedia.com
Home Page: www.brokermagazine.com
Mark Fogarty, Editorial Director
Brad Finkelstein, Editor
Timothy Murphy, Group Publisher
Features on training, motivation, technology, legislation and marketing
Cost: $60.00
Frequency: Bi-Monthly

3207 Business Credit
Assn of Executives in Finance, Credit & In'tl Bus
8840 Columbia 100 Parkway
Columbia, MD 21045-2158
410-423-1840
888-256-3242
Fax: 410-740-5574
E Mail: fcib_info@fcibglobal.com
Home Page: www.fcibglobal.com
Social Media: Twitter, LinkedIn
Kelly Bates, Chairperson
Robin Schauseil, President
Tom Demovic, Director
For professionals responsible for extending credit and collecting receivables. Topics include business law, lien law, technology, credit management, collections, deductions, fraud, credit risk, credit scoring, outsourcing, information services, trade finance and more.
Cost: $54.00
72 Pages
Frequency: 10x/Year
Circulation: 32000
Founded in 1896
Printed in 4 colors on matte stock

3208 Business Credit Magazine
8840 Columbia 100 Parkway
Columbia, MD 21045-2158
410-423-1840
888-256-3242
Fax: 410-740-5574
Home Page: www.fcibglobal.com
Social Media: LinkedIn
Marta Chacon, Director, The Americas
Ron Shepherd, Director, Business Dev.
Noelin Hawkins, Director, Europe, Middle East
Business Credit
1000+ Members
Frequency: Monthly
Circulation: 38000
Founded in 1919

3209 CFA Digest
CFA Institute
PO Box 3668
Charlottesville, VA 22903-0668
434-951-5499
800-247-8132
Fax: 434-951-5262
E-Mail: info@cfainstitute.org
Home Page: www.cfainstitute.org
Social Media: Facebook, Twitter, LinkedIn
John Rogers, CEO
Daniel J Larocco, Co-Editor
Distills selected current industry research into short, easy-to-read summaries.
Frequency: Quarterly
Founded in 1971

3210 CFA Magazine
CFA Insitute
Po Box 3668
Charlottesville, VA 22903-0668
434-951-5499
800-247-8132
Fax: 434-951-5262
E-Mail: info@cfainstitute.org
Home Page: www.cfainstitute.org
Social Media: Facebook, Twitter, LinkedIn
John Rogers, CEO
Roger Mitchell, Associate Editor
A practice-based, professional member magazine. Created on the feedback from a series of worldwide focus groups and a member survey.
Frequency: Bi-Monthly
Founded in 2003

3211 CMBS World
30 Broad Street
28th Floor
New York, NY 10004
212-509-1844
Fax: 212-509-1895
E-Mail: info@crefc.org
Home Page: www.cmbs.org
Social Media: Facebook, Twitter, LinkedIn
Stephen Renna, CEO
Ed DeAngelo, VP
To inform, educate and stimulate meaningful discussions and exchanges among CMBS members on the risks and benefits of commercial mortgage-backed securities.
309 Pages
Frequency: Quarterly
Founded in 1994

3212 Commercial Mortgage Insight
Zackin Publications
PO Box 2180
Waterbury, CT 06722-2180
800-325-6745
Fax: 203-262-4680
E-Mail: info@cmi-online.com
Home Page: www.cmi-online.com/cmi
Paul Zackin, Publisher
Jessica Lillian, Editor
For decision-making executives in commercial mortgage banking and brokerage firms, commercial banks and community/savings institutions. Provides professionals with timely and comprehensive market news, trends and know-how needed to make informed decisions and choices.
Cost: $48.00
32 Pages
Frequency: Monthly
Circulation: 16089
ISSN: 1095-0729
Founded in 1997
Printed in 4 colors on glossy stock

3213 Community Bank President
Siefer Consultants
PO Box 1384
Storm Lake, IA 50588-1384
712-732-7340
Fax: 712-732-7906
E-Mail: siefer@ncn.net
Dan Siefer, Publisher
Analysis of trends, new ideas and implementation strategies, regulatory compliance, and bank profitability. Provides a glimpse at the latest deposit and loan statistics, marketing and new technology updates and bank management issues.
Frequency: Monthly
Circulation: 1800

3214 Community Banker Magazine
America's Community Bankers
1120 Connecticut Avenue NW
Washington, DC 20036
202-857-3100
80- 22- 537
Fax: 202-296-8716
E-Mail: info@acbankers.org

Home Page: www.americascommunitybankers.org

Frank Keating, President
Monique Hanis, Senior VP Marketing
Leann Shepp, Circulation Manager
Diane Casey-Landry, President

Community Banker presents engaging, practical and timely reporting and analysis on industry issues. Enhanced coverage of major interest to community bank leaders includes mortgages, management, technology and wealth.
Cost: $66.00
Frequency: Monthly
Circulation: 10500+
ISSN: 1529-1332
Printed in 4 colors on glossy stock

3215 **Community Banking Advisor**
624 Grassmere Park Drive
Suite 15
Nasvhille, TN 37211

615-377-3392
800-231-2524
Fax: 615-377-7092
E-Mail: info@bankingcpas.com
Home Page: www.bankingcpas.com

Brian Blaha, President

A publication for banking professionals that features articles on management, tax, operational, and other issues confronting community banks.
24 Pages
Frequency: Quarterly
Founded in 1995

3216 **Compliance Manual**
NACHA: The Electronic Payments Association
13450 Sunrise Valley Drive
Suite 100
Herndon, VA 20171

703-561-1100
Fax: 703-787-0996
E-Mail: info@nacha.org
Home Page: www.nacha.org

Janet O Estep, CEO
Marcie Haitema, Chairperson

Covers authorizations, disclosures, processing, funds availability, settlement, error resolution, returns, reversals, retention, audit, all Standard Entry Class Codes and much, much more.
Cost: $90.00

3217 **Credit Union Journal**
Thomson Media
1 State St
27th Floor
New York, NY 10004-1481

212-803-8200
800-221-1809
Fax: 800-843-9600
E-Mail: Richard.Scalise@sourcemedia.com
Home Page: www.cujournal.com

Frank J Diekmann, Editor/Co-Publisher
Lisa Freeman, Managing Publisher

A surging economy, combined with competitive pricing policies and regulatory changes allowing credit unions to expand their field of membership.
Cost: $119.00
Frequency: Weekly

3218 **Credit Union Management Magazine**
Credit Union Executives Society
5510 Research Park Drive
PO Box 14167
Madison, WI 53708-167

608-271-2664
800-252-2664
Fax: 608-271-2303
E-Mail: cues@cues.org
Home Page: www.cues.org
Social Media: Facebook, Twitter, LinkedIn

Fred Johnson, President/CEO
Mary Arnold, VP Publications
George Hofheimer, VP Professional Development
Barbara Kachelski, CAE, SVP/CIP

Published for credit union CEOs and senior management, the magazine focuses each month on general management, operations, marketing and human resource functions. Includes in-depth coverage of technology, facilities, finance, lending, staffing and card services, among other topics.
Cost: $129.00
11067 Members
Frequency: Monthly
Circulation: 8000
Founded in 1962

3219 **Documentary Credit World**
International Financial Services Association
1120 Connecticut Avenue NW
Washington, DC 20036

20 -66 -757
Fax: 202-663-5538
E-Mail: info@baft-ifsa.com
Home Page: www.ifsaonline.org

Frank Keating, President
Albert Kelly, Chairman

Published jointly by the Institute of International Banking Law and Practice and the IFSA. DCW is your source for information on LCs.
Cost: $595.00
Frequency: 10x/Year

3220 **Electronic Payments Journal**
NACHA: Electronic Payments Association
13665 Dulles Technology Dr
Suite 300
Herndon, VA 20171-4607

703-561-1100
Fax: 703-787-0996
E-Mail: info@nacha.org
Home Page: www.nacha.org

Janet O Estep, CEO

Helps industry professionals to track the latest developments in electronic payments and provides in-depth coverage of a broad array of payment issues.
Founded in 1978

3221 **Electronic Payments Review and Buyer's Guide**
NACHA: Electronic Payments Association
13450 Sunrise Valley Drive
Suite 100
Herndon, VA 20171

703-561-1100
Fax: 703-787-0996
E-Mail: info@nacha.org
Home Page: www.nacha.org

Janet O Estep, CEO
Marcie Haitema, Chairperson

A directory of payment services with listings for ACH Services, Authentication & Security Solutions, B2B Invoicing & Presentment Services, Card Services, Check/Electronic Check Services, Consultants & Industry Associations, Consumer-Based Bill Payment & Presentment, Electronic Government Services, Electronic Consumer Services, International Payment Resources, Payment & Processing Software & Hardware, Thrid-Party Service Providers, and Wireless Payment & Commerce
Cost: $3.50
Frequency: Annual

3222 **Federal Credit Union Magazine**
National Association of Federal Credit Unions
3138 10th St N
Suite 3
Arlington, VA 22201-2160

703-522-4770
800-336-4644
Fax: 703-524-1082
E-Mail: tfcu@nafcunet.org
Home Page: www.nafcu.org

Fred Becker, President

Written for CEOs, senior staff and volunteers of Federal Credit Unions. Offers legislative and regulatory news, as well as technology and operational issues.
Cost: $99.00
80 Pages
Frequency: Bi-Monthly
Circulation: 11136
ISSN: 1043-7789
Founded in 1967
Printed in 4 colors on glossy stock

3223 **Finance and Development**
International Monetary Fund
700 19th St NW
Washington, DC 20431-0002

202-623-7000
Fax: 202-623-6220
E-Mail: publicaffairs@imf.org
Home Page: www.imf.org

David Lipton, First Deputy Managing Director
Christine Lagarde, Managing Director

Analysis of financial and economic developments and explanation of the policies and work of the International Monetary Fund and the World Bank.
Cost: $10.00
Frequency: Quarterly
Circulation: 130000
Founded in 1945
Mailing list available for rent: 120M names
Printed in 4 colors

3224 **Financial Analyst**
CFA Institute
PO Box 3668
Charlottesville, VA 22903-0668

434-951-5499
800-247-8132
Fax: 434-951-5262
E-Mail: info@cfainstitute.org
Home Page: www.cfainstitute.org

John Rogers, CEO
Rodney N Sullivan, Associate Editor

Is to advance the knowledge and understanding of the practice of investment management through the publication of high-quality, practitioner-relevant research.

3225 **Financial Review**
Blackwell Publishing
350 Main St
Commerce Place
Malden, MA 02148-5089

781-388-8200
Fax: 781-388-8210
Home Page: www.blackwellpublishing.com

Steven Smith, President/CEO
Vincent Marzano, Vice President, Treasurer

Publishes original empirical, theoretical and methodological research providing new insights into issues of importance in financial economics.
Frequency: Quarterly
ISSN: 0732-8516

3226 **Financial Women Today Magazine**
Financial Women International

1027 W Roselawn Avenue
Roseville, MN 55113

651-487-7632
866-807-6081
Fax: 651-489-1322
E-Mail: info@fwi.org
Home Page: www.fwi.org

Melissa Curzon, President
Cindy Hass, VP
Carleen DeSisto, Secretary

Serves nearly 10,000 female financial service professionals, helping them to attain their economic, professional and personal goals.
Cost: $24.00
Frequency: Quarterly
Circulation: 19000
ISSN: 1059-3950
Founded in 1921
Mailing list available for rent
Printed in 4 colors on matte stock

3227 **Global Custodian**
Asset International
1055 Washington Blvd
Stamford, CT 06901

203-295-5015
888-374-3722
Fax: 203-595-3201
E-Mail: education@globalcustodian.com
Home Page: www.globalcustodian.com

Dominic Hobson, Editor-in-Chief
Charles Ruffel, Founder/CEO
Maredith Hughes, VP

Written for international institutional investors. Stories cover engineering markets, cross border investing, securities lending and more.
Cost: $185.00
Frequency: 5x/Year
Circulation: 20000
Founded in 1989

3228 **Government Affairs Bulletin**
Financial Services Roundtable
1001 Pennsylvania Ave NW
Suite 500 S
Washington, DC 20004-2508

202-289-4322
Fax: 202-289-1903
E-Mail: info@fsround.org
Home Page: www.fsround.org
Social Media: Facebook, Twitter

Tim Pawlenty, CEO
Richard Whiting, Executive Director

This bulletin keeps the members of the Roundtable informed on issues in the financial services industry and how the Roundtable views them.
100 Pages
Frequency: Weekly
Founded in 1993

3229 **ICBA Independent Banker Magazine**
Independent Community Bankers of America
518 Lincoln Road
PO Box 267
Sauk Centre, MN 56378

320-526-6546
800-422-7285
Fax: 320-352-5766
E-Mail: info@icba.org
Home Page: www.icba.org

Camden R Fine, President/CEO
Rachael Solomon, Advertising Contact

ICBA members rely on for community banking news.
Cost: $60.00
Frequency: Monthly

3230 **Independent Banker**
Inside Mortgage Finance Publishers
7910 Woodmont Ave
Suite 1000
Bethesda, MD 20814-7019

301-951-1240
800-422-8439
Fax: 301-656-1709
E-Mail: service@imfpubs.com
Home Page: www.imfpubs.com
Social Media: Twitter, LinkedIn, Youtube

John Bancroft, VP
George Brooks, Editor

Features strategies for high-performance community banks. Also includes profiles of success stories in community banks and assesses developments in legislation and regulation.
Frequency: Monthly
Circulation: 9,800
Mailing list available for rent

3231 **Information Management Magazine**
ARMA International
11880 College Blvd
Suite 450
Overland Park, KS 66215

913-341-3808
800-422-2762
Fax: 913-341-3742
E-Mail: hq@arma.org
Home Page: www.arma.org

Komal Gulch, President
Brenda Prowse, Treasurer

The leading source of information on topics and issues central to the management of records and information worldwide. Each issue features insightful articles written by experts in the management of records and information.
Cost: $115.00
Frequency: Bi-monthly
Circulation: 11000
ISSN: 1535-2897
Mailing list available for rent: 9000 names
Printed in 4 colors on glossy stock

3232 **International Banking Focus**
Institue of International Bankers
299 Park Ave
17th Floor
New York, NY 10171-3896

212-421-1611
Fax: 212-421-1119
E-Mail: iib@iib.org
Home Page: www.iib.org

Sarah Miller, Chief Executive Officer
Richard Coffman, General Counsel
Robin Wilks, Chief Administrative Officer

The Focus describes the latest legislative, regulatory and tax developments in Washington and various states, along with the Institute's efforts to address particular problems that affect international banks.
Frequency: Bi-Monthly
Founded in 1966

3233 **Journal of Performance Management**
Assn for Management Information in Financial Svcs
14247 Saffron Circle
Carmel, IN 46032

317-815-5857
Fax: 317-815-5877
E-Mail: ami2@amifs.org
Home Page: www.amifs.org

Andy Streiff, President
Jeff Nathasingh, Executive VP
Cost: $200.00
Frequency: 3/year
Circulation: 350

3234 **Mortgage Banking**
Mortgage Bankers Association
1717 Rhode Island Avenue, NW
Suite400
Washington, DC 20036

202-557-2700
E-Mail: membership@mortgagebankers.org
Home Page: www.mortgagebankers.org

Janet Reilley Hewett, Editor-in-Chief
Michael Young, Chairman

Provides in-depth coverage of the real estate finance industry. Intelligent analysis of news and the most important issues and trends affecting the industry. Association discount available.
Cost: $60.00
120 Pages
Frequency: 14x/Year
Circulation: 6000
ISSN: 0730-0212
Founded in 1914
Mailing list available for rent: 2800 names at $100 per M
Printed in 4 colors on glossy stock

3235 **Mortgage Servicing News**
Thomson Media
1 State Street Plaza
27th Floor
New York, NY 10004-1481

212-825-8445
800-221-1809
Fax: 212-292-5216
E-Mail: custserv@thomsonmedia.com
Home Page:
www.mortgageservicingnews.com/

Mark Fogarty, Editor
Timothy Murphy, Group Publisher
Timothy Reifschneider, Marketing Manager
Virginia Wiese, Custom Publishing

Information on cross serving techniques, legislative decisions, management strategies, and professional profiles.
Cost: $98.00
Frequency: Monthly
Circulation: 20,000

3236 **NABTalk It**
National Association of Bankruptcy Trustees
One Windsor Cove
Suite 305
Columbia, SC 29223

803-252-5646
800-445-8629
Fax: 803-765-0860
E-Mail: info@nabt.com
Home Page: www.nabt.com

Nancy H Cooper, Staff Editor
Neil Gordon, President
Frequency: Quarterly

3237 **NACTT Quarterly**
National Association of Chapter 13 Trustees
1 Windsor Cove
Suite 305
Columbia, SC 29223
803-252-5646
800-445-8629
Fax: 803-765-0860
E-Mail: info@nactt.com
Home Page: www.nactt.com

Debra Miller, President
Margaret Burks, VP

The Quarterly emphasizes current local and national developments in Chapter 13. Each Quarterly provides a summary of the most recent Chapter 13 Bankruptcy court decisions.

3238 **NACUSAC News**
NACUSAC

PO Box 160
Del Mar, CA 92014

800-287-5949
Fax: 858-792-3884
E-Mail: nacusac@nacusac.org
Home Page: www.nacusac.org

Gerald Dunning, Chairman
Robert Butler, Director

Official magazing of the National Association of Credit Union Supervisory & Auditing Committees that keeps you up to date on the latest developments and events affecting supervisory/auditing committee members.
Frequency: Quarterly

3239 **NMB Magazine**
National Association of Mortgage Brokers
2701 West 15th Street
Suite536
Plano, TX 75075

972-758-1151
Fax: 530-484-2906
E-Mail: pr@nmpmediacorp.com
Home Page: www.namb.org
Social Media: Facebook, Twitter, LinkedIn, Youtube

Mike Anderson, VP
Donald Frommeyer, President
Debbie Maxwell, Production Manager
Cost: $59.95
Frequency: Monthly
Founded in 1973

3240 **National Mortgage Broker Magazine**
Banat Communications
23425 N 39th Drive
104-193
Glendale, AZ 85310

623-516-2723
Fax: 623-516-7738
E-Mail: jon@banatcommunications.com
Home Page:
www.nationalmortgagebroker.com

Mike Anderson, VP
Donald Frommeyer, President
Debbie Maxwell, Production Manager
Cost: $59.95
Frequency: Monthly
Founded in 1984

3241 **New England Economic Indicators**
Federal Reserve Bank of Boston
600 Atlantic Avenue
Suite 100
Boston, MA 02210-2204

617-973-3000
Fax: 617-973-5918
E-Mail: boston.library@bos.frb.org
Home Page: www.bos.frb.org

Eric S Rosengren, President/CEO
Kenneth Montgomery, VP COO

Contains current and historical economic data for the states of CT, ME, MA, NH, RI, and VT, as well as the US data include employment, unemployment, prices and construction activity.
80 Pages
Frequency: Monthly
Circulation: 7000
Founded in 1914

3242 **North Western Financial Review**
NFR Communications
7400 Metro Blvd
Suite 217
Minnieapolis, MN 55439

952-835-2275
Fax: 612-831-1464
E-Mail:
info@northwesternfinancialreview.com
Home Page:
www.northwesternfinancialreview.com

Tom Bengston, Publisher

Provides useful information and useful data regarding developments without trade association bias.
Frequency: Annual+
Circulation: 9,000
Founded in 1989

3243 **RMA Journal**
Risk Management Association
1801 Market Street
Suite 300
Philadelphia, PA 19103-1628

215-446-4000
800-677-7621
Fax: 215-446-4101
E-Mail: customers@rmahq.org
Home Page: www.rmahq.org
Social Media: Facebook, Twitter, LinkedIn

William Githens, President/CEO
Linda O'Loughlin, Director Marketing
Dwight Overturf, CFO

Expanded both format and content to address an array of risk management issues while respecting and preserving essentials of commercial lending
Cost: $95.00
Frequency: Monthly
Founded in 1914
Printed in 4 colors on glossy stock

3244 **Reg/Ops**
America's Community Bankers
1120 Connecticut Ave NW
Washington, DC 20036

202-857-3100
800-226-5377
Fax: 202-296-8716
E-Mail: custserv@aba.com
Home Page:
www.americascommunitybankers.com

Frank Keating, President
Albert Kelly, Chairman

Offers detailed reporting and analysis of the latest banking legislation, regulations, and agency compliance guidance.
Cost: $405.00
16 Pages
Frequency: Monthly
Founded in 1950

3245 **Regional Review**
Federal Reserve Bank of Boston
600 Atlantic Ave
Boston, MA 02210-2204
617-973-3000
800-409-1333
Fax: 617-973-4292
E-Mail: bostonlibrary@bos.frb.org
Home Page: www.bos.frb.org

Erin Rosengren, President/CEO

Magazine on economics, banking, business topics, designed for the busy professional.
Frequency: Quarterly
Circulation: 15000
ISSN: 1062-1865
Founded in 1913
Printed in 5 colors on glossy stock

3246 **Regulatory Report**
America's Community Bankers
1120 Connecticut Avenue NW
Washington, DC 20036

202-857-3100
80- 22- 537
Fax: 202-296-8716
E-Mail: info@acbankers.org
Home Page:
www.americascommunitybankers.com

Frank Keating, President
Harry P Doherty, Editor

Dedicated to thoroughly analyzing regulations and laws of key importance to banks.
Cost: $680.00
38702 Pages
Frequency: Monthly

3247 **SNL Quarterly Bank & Thrift Digest**
SNL Securities
212 7th Street NE
Charlottesvle, VA 22902

434-977-1600
Fax: 434-977-4466
E-Mail: customerservice@snl.com
Home Page: www.snl.com
Social Media: Facebook, Twitter, LinkedIn, Youtube

Mike Chinn, President & CEO

Contains all relevant information on every publicly traded bank and thrift providing insight into each individual institution and allowing quick and accurate comparisons with both peer institutions and industry benchmarks.
Cost: $799.00
600 Pages
Frequency: Quarterly
Founded in 1987
Mailing list available for rent

3248 **SNL Real Estate Securities Quarterly**
SNL Securities
212 7th Street NE
Charlottesville, VA 22902

434-977-1600
Fax: 434-977-4466
E-Mail: subscriptions@snl.com
Home Page: www.snl.com
Social Media: Facebook, Twitter, LinkedIn, Youtube

Mike Chinn, President & CEO

This data digest provides comprehensive corporate, market, and financial information and portfolio level property data on more than 240 publicly traded and privately held real estate companies. SNL Real Estate Securities Quarterly is the industry's most comprehensive publication for evaluating real estate company performance at both a property and financial level.
Cost: $696.00
Frequency: Quarterly
Founded in 1987
Mailing list available for rent

3249 **Secondary Marketing Executive**
Zackin Publications
70 Edwin Avenue
PO Box 2180
Waterbury, CT 6708

203-755-0158
800-325-6745
Fax: 203-262-4680
E-Mail: info@sme-online.com
Home Page: www.sme-online.com/sme

Vanessa Williams, Account Executive
John Clapp, Editor
June Han, Marketing

Offers how-to information for buyers and sellers of mortgage loans.
Cost: $48.00
48 Pages
Frequency: Monthly
Circulation: 95000
ISSN: 0891-2947
Founded in 1970

3250 **Servicing Management**
LDJ Corporation

70 Edwin Avenue
PO Box 2180
Waterbury, CT 06722-2330

203-755-0158
800-325-6745
Fax: 203-262-4680
E-Mail: info@sm-online.com
Home Page: www.sm-online.com

Paul Zackin, Publisher
John Clapp, Editor
June Han, Marketing

Includes updates on industry and regulatory trends, and advise on operating their departments more profitably and efficiently.
Cost: $48.00
Frequency: Monthly
Circulation: 22500
Founded in 1989

3251 US Banker
Thomson Media
1 State St
27th Floor
New York, NY 10004-1481

212-803-8200
800-221-1809
Fax: 212-843-9600
E-Mail: ustserv@sourcemedia.com
Home Page: www.americanbanker.com

Neil Weinberg, Editor-in-Chief
John Ceasar, Group Publisher
James Malkin, Chairman/CEO

Features on news and technological developments in the banking industry. Includes reports on companies, personalities and industry trends.
Cost: $109.00
Frequency: Monthly
Circulation: 80000
Founded in 1955

3252 Washington Perspective
America's Community Bankers
1120 Connecticut Avenue NW
Washington, DC 20036

202-857-3100
800-226-5377
Fax: 202-296-8716
E-Mail: info@acbankers.org
Home Page:
www.americascommunitybankers.com

Frank Keating, President
Albert Kelly, Chairman

Zeroes in on the issues developing on Capital Hill and at the regulatory agencies that affect community banking.
Cost: $595.00
4 Pages
Frequency: Weekly
Circulation: 2200
Founded in 1992

Trade Shows

3253 ABA National Conference for Community Bankers
American Bankers Association
1120 Connecticut Avenue NW
Washington, DC 20036

800-226-5377
800-226-5377
E-Mail: custserv@aba.com
Home Page: www.aba.com

Frank Keating, President
Albert Kelly, Chairman

Features educational sessions, exceptional speakers, networking opportunities and world class exhibit hall.
2 mil Members
1500 Attendees
Frequency: Annual, February
Founded in 1875

3254 ABA Sales Management Workshop
American Bankers Association
1120 Connecticut Avenue NW
Washington, DC 20036

202-635-5000
800-226-5377
E-Mail: custserv@aba.com
Home Page: www.apa.com

Frank Keating, President
Albert Kelly, Chairman

Workshop on creating and keeping customers, over 13 exhibitors, visited by community bank executives, managers, sales and marketing staff.
Frequency: Annual, September

3255 ABA Wealth Management & Trust Conference
American Bankers Association
1120 Connecticut Avenue NW
Washington, DC 20036

800-226-5377
E-Mail: custserv@aba.com
Home Page: www.aba.com

Frank Keating, President
Albert Kelly, Chairman

Delivers practical, inventive ideas for wealth management and trust professionals.
Frequency: Annual, May

3256 AMIFS Annual Profitability & Performance Measurement Conference
Assn for Management Information in Financial Svcs
14247 Saffron Circle
Carmel, IN 46032

317-815-5857
Fax: 317-815-5877
E-Mail: ami2@amifs.org
Home Page: www.amifs.org

Andy Streiff, President
Jeff Nathasingh, EVP
Kevin W Link, Executive Director

3-day conference consisting of one day of workshops, and two days of educational sessions. 10 exhibitors.
Frequency: April

3257 ARMA International Conference & Expo
ARMA International
11880 College Blvd
Suite 450
Overland Park, KS 66215

913-341-3808
800-422-2762
Fax: 913-341-3742
E-Mail: Conference@armaintl.org
Home Page: www.arma.org/conference

Carol Jorgenson, Meetings/Education Coordinator
Wanda Wilson, Senior Manager, Conferences
Elizabeth Zlitni, Exposition Manager

Conference, seminar, workshop, banquet, award ceremony and 175 exhibits of micrographics, optical disk, automated document storage and retrieval systems and more technology of interest to information professionals.
3500 Attendees
Frequency: Annual
Founded in 1956

3258 American Bankers Insurance Association Annual Conference
American Bankers Insurance Association
1120 Connecticut Avenue NW
Washington, DC 20036

202-663-5163
800-226-5377
Fax: 202-828-4546
E-Mail: vbarton@aba.com
Home Page: www.aba.com

Paul Petrylak, President/Chairman
Thomas Anderson, VP
David Cissell, Secretary
Neal Aton, Treasurer

The Conference highlights Best Practices Panel presentations as well as numerous break-out sessions with case studies by bankers and providers of insurance products and services.
300 Members
Frequency: September
Founded in 2001

3259 American League of Financial Institutions Annual Conference
America's Community Bankers
900 19th Street NW
Suite 400
Washington, DC 20006

202-857-3176
Fax: 202-296-8716
E-Mail: webmaster@alfi.org
Home Page: www.businessfinance.com

William W Zuppe, Chairman
Mark Macomber, First Vice Chairman
Edwin R Maus, Second Vice Chairman
Diane Casey-Landry, President/CEO
Monique Hanis, Marketing/Business Development

Exhibits for financial institutions, federal and state chartered minority savings and loan associations in 25 states and DC.
Frequency: Annual

3260 American Safe Deposit Association Conference
American Safe Deposit Association
PO Box 519
Franklin, IN 46131-0519

317-738-4432
Fax: 317-738-5267
Home Page: www.tasda.com

Thomas Cullinan, President
J Wayne Merrill, First VP
Winnifred Howard-Hammack, Second VP
Joyce A McLin, Executive Director
Kevin Fanning, Treasurer

Offers jam-packed sessions full of information and ideas that can be implemented immediately after conference.
200 Attendees
Frequency: June

3261 Association for Financial Professionals Annual Conference
Association for Financial Professionals
4520 East West Highway
Suite 750
Bethesda, MD 20814

301-907-2862
Fax: 301-907-2864
E-Mail: AFP@AFPonline.org
Home Page: www.AFPonline.org

Social Media: Facebook, Twitter, LinkedIn, Youtube

Susan Glass, Chairman
Anita Patterson, Vice Chairman

Workshop and 642 exhibits of lockboxes, check processing systems, computers, investments, pensions, foreign exchange, consulting, mergers, acquisitions and more information of interest to financial professionals.
6000 Attendees
Frequency: October
Founded in 1979

3262 Association of Independent Trust Companies Conference
Association of Independent Trust Companies
8 South Michigan Avenue
Suite802
Chicago, IL 60603

312-223-1611
Fax: 312-580-0615
E-Mail: aitco@gss.net
Home Page: www.aitco.net

Douglas Nunn, President
Marcia Williams, Treasurer
Tom Blank, General Counsel/Secretary

Typically attracts more than 50 financial executive to an information-packed program which addresses the practical issues and challenges of doing business within the trust and financial advisory industry.
Frequency: Annual

3263 Association of Military Banks of America Conference
Association of Military Banks of America(AMBA)
PO Box 3335
Warrenton, VA 20188

540-347-3305
Fax: 540-347-5995
E-Mail: christiane.jacobs@ambahq.org
Home Page: www.ambahq.org

Andrew Egeland, President
John Mitchell, Chairman
Terry Tuggle, Vice Chairman
Frequency: September

3264 Bank Insurance and Securities Association Annual Conference
Bank Insurance and Securities Association
2025 M Street, NW
Suite 800
Washington, DC 20036

202-367-1111
Fax: 20 -36 -211
E-Mail: bisa@BISAnet.org
Home Page: www.bisanet.org

Jim McNeil, Executive Director
Marc A Vosen, President

Focus on the internal administration of the supervisory and compliance functions of the bank broker-dealer and its related activities.
Frequency: June
Founded in 2002

3265 Bankers' Association for Finance & Trade Annual Conference
Bankers' Association for Finance & Trade
1120 Connecticut Avenue NW
6th Floor
Washington, DC 20036-3902

202-663-7575
Fax: 202-663-5538
E-Mail: info@baft-ifsa.com
Home Page: www.baft.org

Tom Burwell, Vice President
Colleen Kennedy, Manager,Programs, & Events
Donna K Alexander, President

Focused on the global environment and the impact of economic developments in specifications and markets including consecutive breakouts on compliance, risk mitigation and key issues.
Frequency: April

3266 Boot Camp for BSA Professionals
Conference of State Bank Supervisors
1129 20th Street, N.W.
9th Floor
Washington, DC 20036

202-296-2840
Fax: 202-296-1928
E-Mail: rstromberg@csbs.org
Home Page: www.csbs.org

Greg Gonzales, Chairman
Candace Franks, Vice Chairman
David Cotney, Secretary

Will provide BSA Compliance knowledge and value to your regulatory agency, financial institution or money service business.
Frequency: May

3267 CPSA Annual Meeting
Check Payment Systems Association
2025 M Street NW
Suite 800
Washington, DC 20036-2422

202-671-1144
Fax: 202-367-2144
E-Mail: info@cpsa-checks.org
Home Page: www.cpsa-checks.org

Steven Antolick, Executive Director
Renee Lurker, Senior Associate

In addition to the business meeting, there are presentations from top industry performers and innovators.
Frequency: May

3268 CSBS Annual Meeting & Conference
Conference of State Bank Supervisors
1129 20th Street NW
9th Floor
Washington, DC 20036

202-296-2840
Fax: 202-296-1928
E-Mail: mbquist@csbs.org
Home Page: www.csbs.org

Mary Beth Quist, Meetings/Conference Contact
Neil Milner, President

The largest gathering of State 7 Federal banking regulators, state bank CEOs, industry policy makers and representatives of companies who support the banking industry.
Frequency: May

3269 Combating Payments & Check Fraud Conference
Bank Administration Institute
115 S LaSalle St
Suite 3300
Chicago, IL 60603-3801

312-683-2464
888-224-0037
Fax: 312-683-2373
E-Mail: info@bai.org
Home Page: www.bai.org
Social Media: Facebook, Twitter, LinkedIn, Youtube

Lewis Fischer, Chairman of the Board
Scott Peters, Vice Chairman
Frequency: September

3270 Commercial Mortgage Securities Association Conference
Commercial Mortgage Securities Association
900 7th Street, NW
Suite 820
New York, NY 10004-2304

212-509-1844
Fax: 212-509-1895
E-Mail: info@crefc.org
Home Page: www.cmbs.org
Social Media: Facebook, Twitter, LinkedIn

Steven Renna, CEO

Intensive educational offerings and presentations on the CMBS industry's biggest challenges.
Frequency: June

3271 Commerical Real Estate Finance/Multifamily Housing Convention & Expo
Mortgage Bankers Association
1717 Rhode Island Avenue NW
Suite 400
Washington, DC 20036

202-557-2700
E-Mail: meetiings@mortgagebankers.org
Home Page: www.mortgagebankers.org

David H Stevens, President/CEO
Elaine Howard, VP Meetings/Conferences

Thousands of commerical real estate industry professionals gathered from across the country to do business with and learn the latest in industry trends, regulatory develoments and strategies to succeed in today's dynamic marketplace.
Frequency: Annual/February

3272 Community & Regional Bank Forum
Bank Insurance and Securities Association
2025 M Street, NW
Suite 800
Washington, DC 20036

202-367-1111
Fax: 202-367-2111
E-Mail: bisa@BISAnet.org
Home Page: www.bisanet.org

Jim McNeil, Executive Director
Marc A Vosen, President
Frequency: September
Founded in 2002

3273 Community Bank Director's Conference
American Association of Bank Directors
1250 24th Street, NW
Suite 700
Washington, DC 20037

202-463-4888
Fax: 20 -34 -808
E-Mail: info@aabd.org
Home Page: www.aabd.org

Keith Dalrymple, President/CEO
David Baris, Executive Director

Sponsored by the AABD and Bank CEO Network, designed to provide information community bank directors need
Frequency: Annual

3274 Community Banking Advisory Network Super Conference
HCAA
624 Grassmere Park Drive
Suite 15
Nasvhille, TN 37211

615-377-3392
800-231-2524
Fax: 615-377-7092
E-Mail: info@hcaa.com
Home Page: www.hcaa.com

Keith Kamperschroer, President

3275 **Credit Congress**
8840 Columbia 100 Parkway
Columbia, MD 21045-2158

410-423-1840
888-256-3242
Fax: 410-740-5574
Home Page: www.fcibglobal.com
Social Media: LinkedIn

Marta Chacon, Director, The Americas
Ron Shepherd, Director, Business Dev.
Noelin Hawkins, Director, Europe, Middle East

Business Credit
1000+ Members
1500 Attendees
Founded in 1919

3276 **Eastern Finance Association Meeting**
Eastern Finance Association
220 Holman Hall
PO Box 1848
University, MS 38677

404-498-8937
Fax: 404-498-8956
E-Mail: admin@easternfinance.org
Home Page: www.easternfinance.org

Mark Lion, President
Jacqueline Garner, VP Local Arrangements

Annual meeting and exhibits relating to any aspect of finance, including financial management, investments and banking.
Frequency: April

3277 **Environmental Bankers Association Membership Meeting**
Environmental Bankers Association
510 King Street
Suite 410
Alexandria, VA 22314

703-549-0977
800-966-7475
Fax: 703-548-5945
E-Mail: eba@envirobank.org
Home Page: www.envirobank.org

Rick Ferguson, President
Scott Beckerman, Treasurer
Frequency: January/June
Founded in 1994

3278 **Federal Reserve Board Conference**
Federal Reserve Board Publishers
20th Street & Constitution Avenue NW
Washington, DC 20551

202-452-3000
Fax: 202-728-5886
Home Page: www.federalreserve.gov

Lucrezia Reichlin, Conference Organizer
Dale Henderson, Conference Organizer
Deborah Lagomarsino, Media Contact

Organized by the International Research Forum on Monetary Policy. Its purpose is to encourage research on monetary policy issues that are relevant for monetary policy making in interdependent economies.
Frequency: December

3279 **Financial & Security Products Association Annual Conference**
Financial & Security Products Association
Plaza Ladera, 5300 Sequoia NW
Suite 205
Albuquerque, NM 87120

505-839-7958
800-843-6082
Fax: 919-648-0670
E-Mail: info@fspa1.com
Home Page: www.fspa1.com

Mark Thatcher, Chairman
Bill Mercer, President
John M Vrabec, Executive Director
Frequency: June
Founded in 1973

3280 **Financial Women International Annual Conference**
Financial Women International
1027 W Roselawn Avenue
Roseville, MN 55113

651-487-7632
866-807-6081
Fax: 651-489-1322
E-Mail: info@fwi.org
Home Page: www.fwi.org

Melissa Curzon, President
Cindy Hass, VP
Carleen DeSisto, Secretary
Frequency: September

3281 **GARP Annual Risk Management Convention & Exhibit**
Global Association of Risk Professionals
111 Town Square Place
Suite 1215
Jersey City, NJ 07310

201-719-7210
Fax. 201-222-5022
E-Mail: rich.apostolik@garp.com
Home Page: www.garp.com
Social Media: Facebook, Twitter, LinkedIn

Richard Apostolik, President/CEO
Kenneth Abbott, Managing Director
Mark Wallace, Chief Operating Officer
Thomas Daula, Chief Risk Officer
Frequency: February
Founded in 1996

3282 **Global Association of Risk Professionals Annual Exhibition**
111 Town Square Place
Suite 1215
Jersey City, NJ 07310

201-719-7210
Fax: 201-222-5022
E-Mail: rich.apostolik@garp.com
Home Page: www.garp.com
Social Media: Facebook, Twitter, LinkedIn

Richard Apostolik, President/CEO
Kenneth Abbott, Managing Director
Mark Wallace, Chief Operating Officer
Thomas Daula, Chief Risk Officer

GARP's flagship event for Asia, with Keynote presentations, multi-track forum and separate workshops.
Frequency: Annual
Founded in 1996

3283 **Independent Community Bankers of America National Convention and Techworld**
Independent Community Bankers of America
518 Lincoln Road
PO Box 267
Sauk Centre, MN 56378

320-526-6546
800-422-7285
Fax: 320-352-5766
E-Mail: mark_traeger@icba.org
Home Page: www.icba.org

Jan Meyer, Director Conferences
Mark Traeger, Associate Dir Conferences/Exhibits
Sandy Zehrer, Supervisor Conference/Exhibits
Greg Martinson, Executive Director

Only national trade show exclusively representing America's independent/community banks. Containing 200+ booths and 175+exhibitors.
3000 Attendees
Frequency: March

3284 **Institute of International Bankers Annual Washington Conference**
Institute of International Bankers
299 Park Avenue
17th Floor
New York, NY 10171

212-421-1611
Fax: 212-421-1119
E-Mail: iib@iib.org
Home Page: www.iib.org

Sarah Miller, CEO
Maura Christ, Executive Assistant
William Harris, Controller
Andy Lebron, Membership Associate

A two-day conference featuring senior U.S. and international government policy makers and financial industry leaders. As part of the conference, which is widely attended by general manager and other senior officers of Institute member banks, there is an evening reception for the Washington community, including Administration officials, Members of Congress, banking regulators and senior staff.
Frequency: March
Founded in 1966

3285 **International Financial Services Association Annual Conference**
International Financial Services Association
1120 Connecticut Avenue NW
Washington, DC 20036

202- 66- 757
Fax: 202-663-5538
E-Mail: info@baft-ifsa.com
Home Page: www.ifsaonline.org

Renee Wigfall, Manager, Meetings/Events
Todd Burwell, Vice President
Frequency: September

3286 **Legal Issues and Regulatory Compliance Conference**
Mortgage Bankers Association
1717 Rhode Island Avenue NW
Suite 400
Washington, DC 20036

202-557-2700
E-Mail: meetings@mortgagebankers.org
Home Page: www.mortgagebankers.org

David H Stevens, President/CEO
Elaine Howard, VP Meetings/Conferences

Learn about all the legal and regulatory developments facing the industry.
Frequency: Annual/May

3287 **Microbanker**
Microbanker
PO Box 708
Lake George, NY 12061

518-745-7071
Fax: 518-745-7071
E-Mail: webmaster@microbanker.com
Home Page: www.microbanker.com

Annual show and exhibits of microcomputer software, hardware and services for banking, savings and loans, and credit unions.
200 Attendees

3288 **Mid-Year Technical Conference**
National Assn of Government Guaranteed Lenders
424 South Squires Street
Stillwater, OK 74074

405-377-4022
Fax: 405-377-3931

E-Mail: bfortune@naggl.com
Home Page: www.naggl.com

Tony Wilkinson, President/CEO
Karen High, EVP/COO
Jenifer Brake, Assistant VP Marketing
Jennifer Sterrett-O'Neill, Assistant VP Communications
Cheryl Stone, VP Conferences
Frequency: May

3289 **NACUSAC Annual Conference & Exposition**
NACUSAC
PO Box 160
Del Mar, CA 92014

800-287-5949
Fax: 858-792-3884
E-Mail: nacusac@nacusac.org
Home Page: www.nacusac.org

Celeste Shelton, Executive Director
Laura Clark, Associate Director
Bob Spindler, Associate Director
These events sponsored by the National Association of Credit Union Supervisory & Auditing Committees offer second-to-none networking and educational opportunities for supervisory and auditing committees.
Frequency: June

3290 **National Association of Bankruptcy Trustees Annual Convention**
National Association of Bankruptcy Trustees
One Windsor Cove
Suite 305
Columbia, SC 29223

803-252-5646
800-445-8629
Fax: 803-765-0860
E-Mail: info@nabt.com
Home Page: www.nabt.com

Christina Hicks, President
Kelly Hagen, VP
Frequency: September

3291 **National Association of Chapter 13 Trustees Annual Seminar**
National Association of Chapter 13 Trustees
1 Windsor Cove
Suite 305
Columbia, SC 29223

803-252-5646
800-445-8629
Fax: 803-765-0860
E-Mail: info@nactt.com
Home Page: www.nactt.com

Debra Miller, President
Margaret Burks, VP
This seminar is NAACO's educational highlight. National experts discuss complex issues and recent developments in the Chapter 13 areas.

3292 **National Association of Federal Credit Unions Conference**
National Association of Federal Credit Unions
3138 10th Street N
Suite 300
Arlington, VA 22201-2149

703-522-4770
800-336-4644
Fax: 703-524-1082
E-Mail: fbecker@nafcu.org
Home Page: www.nafcu.org

Fred Becker, President/CEO
Patrick Morris, Executive Vice President/COO
Stands as a national forum for the federal credit union community where new ideas, issues, concerns and trends can be identified, discussed and resolved.
Frequency: July

3293 **National Association of Mortgage Brokers Annual Conference**
National Association of Mortgage Brokers
2701 West 15th Street
Suite 536
Plano, TX 75075

972-758-1151
Fax: 530-484-2906
E-Mail: membership@namb.org
Home Page: www.namb.org

Donald Frommyer, President
George Hanzimanolis CRMS, VP
Frequency: June

3294 **National Association of Professional Mortgage Women Annual Conference**
National Assn of Professional Mortgage Women
PO Box 451718
Garland, TX 75045

425-778-6162
800-827-3034
Fax: 425-771-9588
E-Mail: napmw1@napmw.org
Home Page: www.napmw.org

Laurie Abshier, President
Candice Smith, President-Elect
Liz Roberts, Senior Vice President
Patricia Hull, Executive Director
Frequency: May

3295 **National Fraud Issues Conference**
Mortgage Bankers Association
1717 Rhode Island Avenue NW
Suite 400
Washington, DC 20036

202-557-2700
E-Mail: meetings@mortgagebankers.org
Home Page: www.mortgagebankers.org

David H Stevens, President/CEO
Elaine Howard, VP Meetings/Conferences
Where industry professionals can learn about the issues related to the growing incidence and complexity of mortgage fraud.
Frequency: Annual/March

3296 **National Investment Banking Association Annual Conference**
National Investment Banking Association
PO Box 6625
Athens, GA 30604

706-208-9620
Fax: 706-993-3342
E-Mail: emily@nibanet.org
Home Page: www.nibanet.org

James Hock, Co Chair
Gerald Alder, Director
Emily Foshee, Executive Director
D Scott Foshee, Chief Technology Officer
Vicki Barone, Treasurer/Secretary
Provides member firms with regularly scheduled forums where they are able to exchange ideas and information, evaluate presentations made by companies being underwritten or sponsored by member firms, collectively voice their positions on issues impacting their livelihood, and enhance their knowledge and expertise through ongoing educational programs designed to enable them to remain competitive.
Frequency: May

3297 **National Marine Bankers Association Annual Conference**
National Marine Bankers Association
231 South LaSalle Street
Suite 2050
Chicago, IL 60604

312-946-6260
E-Mail: bmcardle@nmma.org
Home Page: www.marinebankers.org

Bernice McArdle, Associate Manager
A three-day member conference where the latest trends issues relating to the marine industry are discussed in detail.
Frequency: September

3298 **National Mortgage Servicing Conference & Expo**
Mortgage Bankers Association
1717 Rhode Island Avenue NW
Suite 400
Washington, DC 20036

202-557-2700
E-Mail: meetings@mortgagebankers.org
Home Page: www.mortgagebankers.org

David H Stevens, President/CEO
Elaine Howard, VP Meetings/Conferences
Gives companies the opportunity to reach key servicing executives from residential mortgage companies. Showcase the product offerings, network with key decision makers, and obtain qualified leads.
Frequency: Annual/February

3299 **National Policy Conference**
Mortgage Bankers Association
1717 Rhode Island Avenue NW
Suite 400
Washington, DC 20036

202-557-2700
E-Mail: meetings@mortgagebankers.org
Home Page: www.mortgagebankers.org

David H Stevens, President/CEO
Elaine Howard, VP Meetings/Conferences
Brings togethers key officials, cabinet members and special guest speakers to address issues of what is happening in the community as well as the practical effect proposed changes may have on the business and industry
Frequency: Annual/March

3300 **National Technology in Mortgage Banking Conference**
Mortgage Bankers Association
1717 Rhode Island Avenue NW
Suite 400
Washington, DC 20036

202-557-2700
E-Mail: meetings@mortgagebankers.org
Home Page: www.mortgagebankers.org

David H Stevens, President/CEO
Elaine Howard, VP Meetings/Conferences
Forum to learn about the newest industry solutions and how they can increase the company's competitive edge. Focuses on relevant topics, including legal/regulatory updates, eMortgages, investor reporting changes adn technology advances such as mobile computing.
Frequency: Annual/March

3301 **Payments**
NACHA: Electronic Payments Association
13450 Sunrise Valley Drive
Suite 100
Herndon, AV 20171

703-561-1100
Fax: 703-787-0996
E-Mail: info@nacha.org
Home Page: www.nacha.org

Marcie Haitema, Chairperson
Janet O Estep, CEO

The premier source for payments professionals from across industries and around the globe to get the most vital and actionable information needed to help address the myriad of issues and opportunities in today's rapidly changing environment.
Frequency: Annual/April-May

3302 RMA Annual Conference of Lending & Credit Risk Management
Risk Management Association
1801 Market Street
Suite 300
Philadelphia, PA 19103-1628
215-446-4000
800-677-7621
Fax: 215-446-4100
E-Mail: customers@rmahq.org
Home Page: www.rmahq.org
William Githens, President/CEO
Sonny B Lyles, Vice Chair
Containing 31 booths and 28 exhibits.
600 Attendees
Frequency: October

3303 Retail Delivery Conference & Expo
Bank Administration Institute
115 S. LaSalle Street
Suite 3300
Chicago, IL 60603-3801
312-683-2464
888-284-4078
Fax: 312-683-2373
E-Mail: info@bai.org
Home Page: www.bai.org
Social Media: Facebook, Twitter, LinkedIn, Youtube
Lewis Fischer, Chairman of the Board
Scott Peters, Vice Chairman
2M Attendees
Frequency: November

3304 Sales Management Workshop
Bank Insurance and Securities Association
2025 M Street NW
Suite 800
Washington, DC 20036
202-367-1111
Fax: 20 -36 -211
E-Mail: bisa@BISAnet.org
Home Page: www.bisanet.org
Jim McNeil, Executive Director
Marc A Vosen, President
Frequency: May/October/December
Founded in 2002

3305 Securities Industry and Financial Markets Association (SIFMA) Annual Meeting
SIFMA
1101 New York Avenue NW
8th Floor
Washington, DC 20005
202-962-7300
Fax: 202-962-7305
Home Page: www.sifma.org/
Timothy Ryan, President/CEO
Cheryl Crispen, Executive Vice President
The Securities Industry and Financial Markets Association/SIFMA Annual Meeting and Conference program addresses a variety of topics that may include competitiveness of the U.S. capital markets, global exchange consolidation, regulatory and legal initiatives, and trends in the fixed-income and capital markets.

3306 TransPay Conference & Expo
Bank Administration Institute
115 S LaSalle St
Suite 3300
Chicago, IL 60603
312-683-2464
800-375-5543
Fax: 312-683-2373
E-Mail: info@bai.org
Home Page: www.bai.org
Social Media: Facebook, Twitter, LinkedIn, Youtube
Lewis Fischer, Chairman of the Board
Scott Peters, Vice Chairman
Offers top solutions providers, innovators and your peers at BAY TransPay - focused on your financial institution profitability in payments.
Frequency: May

3307 Treasury & Risk Management Conference
Bank Administration Institute
115 S LaSalle St
Suite 3300
Chicago, IL 60603
312-683-2464
800-375-5443
Fax: 312-683-2373
E-Mail: info@bai.org
Home Page: www.bai.org
Social Media: Facebook, Twitter, LinkedIn, Youtube
Lewis Fischer, Chairman of the Board
Scott Peters, Vice Chairman
Frequency: May

3308 Urban Financial Services Coalition Annual Conference
Urban Financial Services Coalition
1200 G Street NW
Suite 800
Washington, DC 20005
202-289-8335
800-996-8335
Fax: 202-434-8707
E-Mail: ufsc@ufscnet.org
Home Page: www.ufscnet.org
Diane Evans, President
Brenda Joseph, Vice President
Linda Smith, Treasurer
Audrey Williams, Secretary
Frequency: June

Directories & Databases

3309 ABA Directory of Trust Banking
4709 Golf Road
Skokie, IL 60076
847-676-9600
800-321-3373
Fax: 847-933-8101
E-Mail: custserv@accuitysolutions.com
Home Page: www.accuitysolutions.com
Hugh Jones, President
Kerry Hewson, VP
An official publication of the American Bankers Association. Listings include information such as national and state rankings, collective investment funds and corporate trusts.
Cost: $403.00
Circulation: 2800
ISBN: 1-563103-53-2

3310 ABA Financial Institutions Directory
4709 Golf Road
Skokie, IL 60076
847-676-9600
800-321-3373
Fax: 847-933-8101
E-Mail: custserv@accuitysolutions.com
Home Page: www.accuitysolutions.com
Hugh Jones, President
Kerry Hewson, VP
This two-volume Executive Desktop Edition includes a special ABA Resource Guide with a Quick Reference Guide to Banking Regulations.
Cost: $500.00
Frequency: January/July
Circulation: 31850

3311 ABA Key to Routing Numbers
4709 Golf Road
Skokie, IL 60076
847-676-9600
800-321-3373
Fax: 847-933-8101
E-Mail: custserv@accuitysolutions.com
Home Page: www.accuitysolutions.com
Hugh Jones, President
Kerry Hewson, VP
Cost: $184.00
Frequency: January/July
Circulation: 83300
Founded in 1911

3312 ACH Participant Directory
4709 Golf Road
Skokie, IL 60076
847-676-9600
800-321-3373
Fax: 847-933-8101
E-Mail: custserv@accuitysolutions.com
Home Page: www.accuitysolutions.com
Hugh Jones, President
Kerry Hewson, VP
Cost: $207.00
Frequency: February/August
Circulation: 54600

3313 American Financial Directory
4709 Golf Road
Skokie, IL 60076
847-676-9600
800-321-3373
Fax: 847-933-8101
E-Mail: custserv@accuitysolutions.com
Home Page: www.accuitysolutions.com
Hugh Jones, President
Kerry Hewson, VP
Cost: $558.00
Frequency: January/July
Circulation: 41300
ISBN: 1-563103-47-8
Founded in 1836

3314 Annual Membership Directory & Buyers' Guide
Financial & Security Products Association
Plaza Ladera, 5300 Sequoia NW
Suite 205
Albuquerque, NM 87120
505-839-7958
800-843-6082
Fax: 505-839-0017
E-Mail: info@fspa1.com
Home Page: www.fspa1.com
Mark Thatcher, Chairman
Bill Mercer, President
Who's Who of independent firms serving financial institutions hleps readers locate new dealers, products/service suppliers and strategic business partners.

3315 Annual Report of the Board of Governors of the Federal Reserve System
Board of Governors

20th St & Constitution Ave N
Washington, DC 20551-0001

202-452-3284
Fax: 202-452-3101
Home Page: www.federalreserve.gov

Rick McKinney, Manager
Janet Yellen, Vice Chair

Listing of directors, advisory councils and officers of banks and branches involved in mergers and acquisitions.
Frequency: Annual

3316 **Annual Software Guide**
Financial & Security Products Association
Plaza Ladera, 5300 Sequoia NW
Suite 205
Albuquerque, NM 87120

505-839-7958
800-843-6082
Fax: 505-839-0017
E-Mail: info@fspa1.com
Home Page: www.fspa1.com

Mark Thatcher, Chairman
Bill Mercer, President
John Vrabec, Executive Director

This detailed evaluation of the latest software to enhance business performance is provided by Brown Smith Wallace (BSW) only to members of participating associations, including FSPA.

3317 **BankNews Montain States Bank Directory**
BankNews Publications
PO Box 29156
Shawnee Mission, KS 66201-9156

913-261-7000
800-336-1120
Fax: 913-261-7010
Home Page: www.banknews.com

Janet Holman, President & Publisher
Joel Holman, CEO & Publisher

Over 600 commercial banks, savings and loans, and holding companies are listed in this directory, state banking and regulatory agencies are also studied in the areas of Colorado, Wyoming, New Mexico, Montana and Utah.
Cost: $ 35.00
350 Pages
Frequency: Annual
Circulation: 3,500

3318 **BankRoll II**
US Federal Reserve System, Board of Governors
20th Street & Constitution Avenue NW
Washington, DC 20551-0001

Home Page: www.federalreserve.gov/
Social Media: Twitter, LinkedIn

This database contains descriptive information and financial information from the Financial Report Bank Holding Companies (Y9) submitted to the Federal Reserve Board.

3319 **Bankcard Barometer**
RAM Research Corporation
1230 Avenue of the Americas
7th Floor, Rockefeller Center
New York, MD 21702-0700

301-954-4660
Fax: 301-695-0160
Home Page: www.ramresearch.com

Robert B McKinley, Publisher/Editor

Database of nation's capital largest bank credit card issuers.
Cost: $1295.00
600 Pages
Frequency: Monthly
Founded in 1986
Printed in one color on matte stock

3320 **Branches of Your State: Banks, Savings & Loans, Credit Unions & Savings**
Sheshunoff Information Services
901 South Mopac
Suite 140
Austin, TX 78746-7970

512-472-4000
800-477-1772
Fax: 512-305-6575
E-Mail: sales@smslp.com
Home Page: www.smslp.com
Social Media: Facebook, Twitter, LinkedIn

Gabrielle Sheshunoff, CEO

State editions list banks, savings and loan branches and credit unions. Individual banks are listed for states without branch banking.
Cost: $345.00
Frequency: Annual

3321 **Data Book**
FDIC Public Information Center
550 17th St Nw
Washington, DC 20429-0001

202-898-3631
877-275-3342
Fax: 202-898-3984
E-Mail: publicinfo@fdic.gov
Home Page: www.fdic.gov
Social Media: Facebook, Twitter, LinkedIn

Martin Gruenberg, Chairman
Thomas Hoenig, Vice Chairman
Jeremiah Norton, Director

Offers information on bank names, locations, bank numbers and branches for each banking office, in seven volumes, divided geographically and aggregate bank deposits also known as Summary of Deposits.
Frequency: Quarterly

3322 **Directory of Minority and Women-Owned Investment Bankers**
San Francisco Redevelopment Agency
1 S Van Ness Avenue
Suite 5
San Francisco, CA 94103-5416

415-749-2400
Fax: 415-749-2565
Home Page: www.sanfranciscofcu.org

Marcia Rosen, Executive Director
Erwin Tanjuaquio, Director Public Affairs

Lists 18 minority-owned investment banking firms.
Frequency: Biennial

3323 **Directory of Venture Capital & Private Equity Firms - Online Database**
Grey House Publishing
4919 Route 22
PO Box 56
Amenia, NY 12501

518-789-8700
800-562-2139
Fax: 518-789-0556
E-Mail: gold@greyhouse.com
Home Page: www.gold.greyhouse.com
Social Media: Facebook, Twitter

Leslie Mackenzie, Publisher
Richard Gottlieb, Editor

Packed with need-to-know information, this database offers immediate access to 2,300 VC firms, over 10,000 managing partners, and over 11,500 VC investments.
Frequency: Annual

3324 **Directory of Venture Capital and Private Equity Firms**
Grey House Publishing
4919 Route 22
PO Box 56
Amenia, NY 12501

518-789-8700
800-562-2139
Fax: 845-373-6390
E-Mail: books@greyhouse.com
Home Page: www.greyhouse.com
Social Media: Facebook, Twitter

Leslie Mackenzie, Publisher
Richard Gottlieb, Editor

Offers access to over 2,300 domestic and international venture capital and private equity firms, including detailed contact information and extensive data on investments and funds.
Cost: $685.00
1,200 Pages
Frequency: Annual
ISBN: 1-592372-72-4

3325 **Financial Institutions Directory of New England**
4709 Golf Road
Skokie, IL 60076

847-676-9600
800-321-3373
Fax: 847-933-8101
E-Mail: custserv@accuitysolutions.com
Home Page: www.accuitysolutions.com

Hugh Jones, President
Kerry Hewson, VP
Cost: $114.00
Frequency: January/July

3326 **Financial Management**
University of South Florida COBA
3821 Holly Drive
Tampa, FL 33620-7360

813-974-4133
Fax: 813-974-5130
E-Mail: caminfo@arts.usf.edu
Home Page: www.ira.usf.edu

Margaret Miller, Director
Alexa Favata, Associate Director

Financial management of individual firm, governmental unit or nonprofit institution, as opposed to financial structure of whole economy for practitioners and professors of financial management.
Cost: $20.00
Circulation: 11,500
Founded in 1970

3327 **National Credit Union Administration Directory**
National Credit Union Administration
1775 Duke St
Alexandria, VA 22314-6115

703-518-6300
800-755-1030
Fax: 703-518-6539
E-Mail: consumerassistance@ncua.gov
Home Page: www.ncua.gov

J Leonard Skiles, Executive Director
Robert Fenner, Director/General Counsel
Jane Walters, Deputy Executive Director

Directory of credit unions governed by a three member board appointed by the President and confirmed by the US Senate, by the independent federal agency that charters and supervises federal credit unions. NCUA, with the backing of the full faith and credit of the US government, operates the National Credit Union Share Insurance Fund, insuring the savings of 80 million account holders in all federal credit unions and many state chartered credit unions.

3328 North American Financial Institutions Directory
4709 Golf Road
Skokie, IL 60076
847-676-9600
800-321-3373
Fax: 847-933-8101
E-Mail: custserv@accuitysolutions.com
Home Page: www.accuitysolutions.com
Hugh Jones, President/CEO
Cost: $495.00
Frequency: January/July
Circulation: 31850
Founded in 1895

3329 Ranking the Banks
American Banker
1 State St
27th Floor
New York, NY 10004-1561
212-803-8450
Fax: 212-843-9600
Home Page: www.sourcemedia.com
Douglas Manoni, President/CEO
David Longobardi, Editor-in-Chief
Richard Melville, Managing Editor
Timothy Reifschneider, Advertising Director
A comprehensive database of banking and financial services rankings, league tables, and vital statistics. Includes all tables published in the print edition of American Banker, and more. Organized by category with historical data.
Cost: $945.00
128 Pages

3330 State and Local MBA Directory
Mortgage Bankers Association of America
1717 Rhode Island Avenue, NW
Suite 400
Washington, DC 20036
202-557-2700
E-Mail: membership@mortgagebankers.org
Home Page: www.mortgagebankers.org
Michael Young, Chairman
All state and local MBA officers and a calendar of significant meeting dates.
Cost: $50.00
Frequency: SemiAnnual

3331 Thomson Bank Directory
4709 Golf Road
Skokie, IL 60076
847-676-9600
800-321-3373
Fax: 847-933-8101
E-Mail: custserv@accuitysolutions.com
Home Page: www.accuitysolutions.com
Hugh Jones, President
Kerry Hewson, VP
Cost: $684.00
Frequency: June/December
Circulation: 35000
ISBN: 1-563103-45-1

3332 Thomson Credit Union Directory
4709 Golf Road
Skokie, IL 60076-1231
847-676-9600
800-321-3373
Fax: 847-933-8101
E-Mail: custserv@accuitysolutions.com
Home Page: www.accuitysolutions.com
Hugh Jones, President
Kerry Hewson, VP
Semi-annual directory that includes valuable industry statistics, a quick telephone lookup index of all credit unions and a resource guide featuring vendors within the credit union marketplace. Includes over 12,500 major credit unions and 5,500 branches, with asset rankings, membership totals and more. Published in partnership with the Credit Union National Association.
Cost: $247.00
Frequency: January/July
ISBN: 1-563103-24-9

3333 Thomson Regulation CC Directory
4709 Golf Road
Skokie, IL 60076
847-676-9600
800-321-3373
Fax: 847-933-8101
E-Mail: custserv@accuitysolutions.com
Home Page: www.accuitysolutions.com
Hugh Jones, President
Kerry Hewson, VP
Cost: $144.00
Frequency: January/July
Circulation: 30100

3334 Thomson Savings Directory
4709 Golf Road
Skokie, IL 60076-1231
847-676-9600
800-321-3373
Fax: 847-933-8101
E-Mail: custserv@accuitysolutions.com
Home Page: www.accuitysolutions.com
Hugh Jones, President
Kerry Hewson, VP
Semi-annual directory dedicated to the thrift industry. Listings include primary correspondent information, national industry statistics and breakdowns of mortgage portfolios.
Cost: $316.00
Frequency: January/July

3335 World Bank Directory
4709 Golf Road
Skokie, IL 60076-1231
847-676-9600
800-321-3373
Fax: 847-933-8101
E-Mail: custserv@accuitysolutions.com
Home Page: www.accuitysolutions.com
Hugh Jones, President
Kerry Hewson, VP
Contains detailed listings for 10,000 international banks and their branches worldwide plus the top 1,000 US banks. The information in this annual directory includes world and country rankings, international and correspondent contact information, principal correspondent institutions an standard settlement instructions.
Cost: $495.00
Frequency: September
Founded in 1895

3336 Worldwide Correspondents & Resource Guide
4709 Golf Road
Skokie, IL 60076-1231
847-676-9600
800-321-3373
Fax: 847-933-8101
E-Mail: custserv@accuitysolutions.com
Home Page: www.accuitysolutions.com
Hugh Jones, President
Kerry Hewson, VP
A convenient one-volume directory listing the principal correspondent relationships for banks worldwide.
Cost: $184.00
Frequency: June/December

3337 Y-9 Report Analyzer
Sheshunoff Information Services
901 South Mopac
Suite 140
Austin, TX 78746-7970
512-472-4000
800-477-1772
Fax: 512-305-6575
E-Mail: sales@smslp.com
Home Page: www.smslp.com
Social Media: Facebook, Twitter, LinkedIn
Gabrielle Sheshunoff, CEO
Sheshunoff Information Services provides bank holding companies (BHC) a tool to prepare and electronically file the following government forms: Y-9C, Y9-LP, Y11Q, and Y11I. Built in edit checks ensure the BHC's file the most accurate report possible.
Cost: $495.00
Frequency: Annual w/Quarterly Update

Industry Web Sites

3338 http://gold.greyhouse.com
G.O.L.D Grey House OnLine Databases
Grey House Publishing's online database platform, GOLD, offers Quick Search, Keyword Search and Expert Search, for most business sectors including banking and financial markets. The GOLD platform makes finding the information you need quick and easy - whether you're a novice searcher or an experienced database user. All of Grey House's directory products are available for subscription on the GOLD platform.

3339 www.aabd.org
American Association of Bank Directors
Devoted to serving the information, education and advocacy needs of individual bank and savings institution directors. This non-profit organization has members nationwide.

3340 www.aba.com
American Bankers Association
Brings together all categories of banking institutions to best represent the interests of this rapidly changing industry. It's membership — which includes community, regional and money center banks and holding companies, as well as savings associations, trust companies and savings banks makes ABA one of the largest banking trade associations in the country.

3341 www.aba.com/ICB/default.htm
Institute Of Certified Bankers
A national association of certified professionals in the financial services industry whose mission is to provide financial services professionals with confidence, credibility and recognition through its certifications.

3342 www.abiworld.org
American Bankruptcy Institute
Dedicated to research and education on matters related to insolvency.

3343 www.aftweb.com
Association for Financial Technology
Association founded in 1972 to promote high standards of professionalism in the planning, development, inplemtation and application of technology to the financial services industry.

3344 www.aitco.net
Association of Independent Trust Companies
Dedicated to provide a forum of leaders, owners and operators of trust companies and wealth management providers.

3345 **www.ambahq.org**
Association of Military Banks of America (AMBA)
Non-profit association of banks operating on military installments serving military customers and military banking facilities designated by the U.S. Treasury.

3346 **www.baft.org**
Bankers' Association for Finance & Trade
Financial trade association whose membership represents a broad range of internationally active financial institutions and companies that provide important services to the global financial community. BAFT serves as a forum for analysis, discussion and action among international financial professionals on a wide range of topics affecting international trade and finace, including legislative/regulatory issues.

3347 **www.bai.org**
Bank Administration Institute
The financial services industry's partner for breakthrough information and intelligence needed to innovate and stay relevant in an evolving marketplace. Serves a wide segment of the financial services industry, from the largest multinational banks to community-based institutions.

3348 **www.bisanet.org**
Bank Insurance and Securities Association
Dedicated to serving the needs of those responsible for marketing securities, insurance and other investment and risk management products.

3349 **www.bmaatlanta.com**
Business Marketing Association: Atlanta
BMA offers an information-packed website, online skills-building, marketing, certification programs and industry surveys and papers.

3350 **www.cbanet.org**
Consumer Bankers Association
Recognized voice on retail banking issues in the nation's capital. Member institutions are the leaders in consumer financial services, including auto finance, home equity lending, card products, education loans, small business services, community development, investments, deposits, and delivery.

3351 **www.cfainstitute.org**
CFA Institute
The CFA Institute is the global, non-profit professional association that administers the Chartered Financial Analyst curriculum and examination program.

3352 **www.envirobank.org**
Environmental Bankers Association
Dedicated to providing services for individuals with an interest in environmental risk management and related issues.

3353 **www.freddiemac.com**
Freddie Mac
Freddie Mac is a stockholder-owned corporation chartered by Congress to create a continuous flow of funds to mortgage lenders in support of homeownership and rental housing.

3354 **www.fwi.org**
Financial Women International
Formerly the National Association of Bank Women, the Association was founded in 1921 - one year after women won the right to vote, by a group of New York City women bankers. FWI serves women in the financial services industry that seeks to expand their personal and professional capabilities through self-directed growth in a supportive environment.

3355 **www.garp.org**
Global Association of Risk Management
This association is dedicated to being the leading professional association for risk managers, managed by and for its members.

3356 **www.greyhouse.com**
Grey House Publishing
Authoritative reference directories for most business sectors including banking and financial markets. Users can search the online databases with varied search criteria allowing for custom searches by product category, geographic area, sales volume, keyword, subject and more. Full Grey House catalog and online ordering also available.

3357 **www.icba.org**
Independent Community Bankers of America
Dedicated exclusively to enhancing the franchise value of the nation's community banks for the benefit of their customers and the communities they serve.

3358 **www.ifsaonline.org**
International Financial Services Association
Represents the international operations areas of financial services provider, their customers, suppliers and partners.

3359 **www.iib.org**
Institute of International Bankers
Created to help resolve the many special legislative, regulatory and tax issues confronting internationally headquartered financial institutions.

3360 **www.jpmorganchase.com**
JPMorgan Chase
A leading global financial services firm with assets of $1.3 trillion and operations in more than 50 countries.

3361 **www.marinebankers.org**
National Marine Bankers Association
Formed in 1980 in response to a request by the National Marine Manufacturers Association - NMMA - for additional sources of financing for it's members products. The purpose of the NMBA is to educate prospective lenders in marine finacing procedures, create new lenders to help finance the sales of the manufacturers products, and to create an information exchange for its members.

3362 **www.mastercardinternational.com**
MasterCard Worldwide
Administers the MasterCard credit card and other products for 25,000 member institutions around the world.

3363 **www.mbaa.org**
Mortgage Bankers Association of America
Representing the real estate finance industry, MBA serves its membership by representing their legislative and regulatory interests before the US Congress and federal agencies; by meeting their educational needs through programs and a range of periodicals and publications; and by supporting their business interests with a variety of research initiatives and other products and services.

3364 **www.mortgagebankers.org**
Mortgage Bankers Association
Seeks to improve methods of originating, servicing and marketing loans.

3365 **www.naahl.org**
National Association of Affordable Housing Lenders
For financial institutions and others with an interest in affordable housing and development lending.

3366 **www.nabt.com**
National Association of Bankruptcy Trustees
Nonprofit association formed in 1982 to address the needs of the bankruptcy trustees thoughout the country and to promote the effectiveness of the bankruptcy system as a whole. While the majority of trustees who are members of the NABT are Chapter 7 trustees who primarily liquidate nonexempt assets for the benefit of creditors, many Chapter 7 trustees also serve as Chapter 11 trustees, who operate and reorganize companies. Some of our members are also Chapter 12 or Chapter 13 trustees.

3367 **www.nacha.org**
NACHA: Electronic Payments Association
Organization developing electronic solutions to improve the payments system. Representing more than 12,000 financial institutions through direct memberships and a network of regional payments associations, and 650 organizations through its industry councils, NACHA develops operating rules and business practices for the Automated Clearing House network and for electronic payments in the areas of internet commerce, electronic bill and invoice presentment and payment and other electronic payments.

3368 **www.nactt.com**
National Association of Chapter 13 Trustees
Provides a forum within which Chapteer 13 trustees will act as an information and communication resource to advance education, leadership, and continuous imporvement in the administration of bankruptcy.

3369 **www.nacusac.org**
Nat'l Assoc. of Credit Union Super. & Audit. Comm.
A unique organization of, by and for credit union supervisory committee members.

3370 **www.nafcu.org**
National Association Of Federal Credit Unions
A respected and influential trade association that exclusively represents the interests of federal credit unions before the federal government and the public.

3371 **www.naggl.com**
Nat'l Assoc. of Government Guaranteed Lenders
Promotes professional and governmental affairs interests of financial institutions and small businesses who participate in the Small Business Administration guaranteed lending and secondary market programs.

3372 **www.namb.org**
National Association of Mortgage Brokers
Mortgage brokers who seek to increase professionalism and to foster business relationships among members.

3373 **www.napmw.org**
Nat'l Association of Professional Mortgage Women
Serves all mortgage professionals and employers who want to excel.

3374 **www.nascus.org**
Nat'l Assoc. of State Credit Union Supervisors
State chartered credit unions and state credit union supervisors.

3375 **www.nationalbankers.org**
National Bankers Association

Members are minority and women's banking institutions, minority individuals employed by majority banks and institutions.

3376 **www.ncua.gov**
National Credit Union Administration

Charters and supervises federal credit unions.

3377 **www.nibanet.org**
National Investment Banking Association

A national trade association of regional and independent brokerages, investment banking firms, and related capital market service providers.

3378 **www.rmahq.org**
Risk Management Association

Topics relating to all aspects of commercial lending, financial statement analysis and credit information exchange and managerial aspects of consumer lending.

3379 **www.sifma.org/**
Securities Industry and Financial Markets Assoc.

SIFMA's mission is to champion policies and practices that benefit investors and issuers, expand and perfect global capital markets, and foster the development of new products and services.

3380 **www.snl.com**
SNL Securities

News articles on banks and thrifts, insurance and other financial services. Also features vital company information.

3381 **www.sourcemedia.com**
SourceMedia

Provides market information, including news, analysis, and insight to the financial services and related industries.

3382 **www.ufscnet.org**
Urban Financial Services Coalition

An organization of minority professionals in the financial services industry and related fields.

3383 **www.wiley.com**
John Wiley & Sons

Wiley is a global publisher of print and electronic products, specializing in science, technical, and material books and journals, professional and consumer books and subscription services, textbooks and other educational materials for undergraduate and graduate students as well as lifelong learners. Wiley has approximately 22,700 active titles and about 400 journals, and publishes about 2000 new titles in a variety of print and electronic formats each year.

Associations

3384 **Aesthetics' International Association**
310 E. Interstate 30
Suite B107
Garland, TX 75043
972-203-8530
877-968-7539
Fax: 972-226-2339
E-Mail: AIAthekey@aol.com
Home Page: www.aestheticsassociation.com/
Patricia Strunk, President
Michelle D'Allaird, Vice President
International professional organization for aestheticians that represents every facet of the aesthetics industry. We offer something for the student, aesthetician, make-up artist, reflexologist, aromatherapist, massage therapist, nutritionist, nurse, holistic practitioner and physician to the day spa and salon owner.
Founded in 1972

3385 **American Association of Cosmetology Schools**
9927 East Bell Road
Suite 110
Scottsdale, AZ 85260
480-281-0424
800-831-1086
Fax: 480-905-0708
E-Mail: jim@beautyschools.org
Home Page: www.beautyschools.org
Social Media: Facebook, Twitter
Scott Buchanan, Chairman
Rueben Carranza, Vice Chair
Chris Cox, Member Services
Jenn Lyles, Communications Coordinator
Susan Miller, Public Relations
National non-profit association open to all privately owned schools of Cosmetology Arts and Sciences. AACS specializes in updating our members with information about new teaching methods, current industry events, and Washington, DC updates.
1100 Members
Founded in 1924

3386 **American Beauty Association**
15825 N 71st St
Suite 100
Scottsdale, AZ 85254-1521
480-281-0431
E-Mail: info@probeautyassociation.org
Social Media: Facebook, Twitter, LinkedIn
James Cox, Executive Director
Bruce Selan, VP
George Schaeffer, Secretary/Treasurer
ABA members are manufacturers, manufacturer reps and consultants in the professional beauty industry. Associate members are made up of trade publications, distributors and salons. The ABA's mission is to expand, serve and protect the interests of the professional beauty industry.
250 Members
Founded in 1985

3387 **American Electrology Association**
1616 Cherry Street
Wenatchee, WA 98801
509-663-6874
Fax: 509-663-6874
E-Mail: infoaea@electrology.com
Home Page: www.electrology.com
Social Media: Facebook
Pearl Warner, CPE, President
Barbara Greathouse, CPE, 1st VP
Deborah Cassin, CPE, Treasurer
The American Electrology Association (AEA), is the largest international nonprofit membership organization for permanent hair removal professionals. Promotes the highest standards in Electrology education, practice and ethics and champions state licensing and regulation of the profession to protect the public interest.
1500 Members
250 Attendees
Frequency: 3 times a year
Circulation: 1500
Founded in 1958

3388 **American Hair Loss Council**
30 South Main
Shenandoah, PA 17976
412-765-3666
Fax: 412-765-3669
E-Mail: info@ahcl.org
Home Page: www.ahlc.org
Susan Kettering, President
A not-for-profit agency, dedicated to sorting through this information, discovering what works and what doesn't, and presenting findings to the consumer.

3389 **American Society of Hair Restoration Surgery**
737 North Michigan Avenue
Suite 2100
Chicago, IL 60611
312-981-6760
Fax: 312-981-6787
E-Mail: info@cosmeticsurgery.org
Home Page: www.cosmeticsurgery.org
Social Media: Facebook, Twitter, LinkedIn
Angelo Cuzalina, President
Gerald Edds, President-Elect
Neil Sadick, Treasurer
Susan Hughes, Secretary
1600 Members

3390 **Association of Cosmetologists and Hairdressers**
15825 N. 71st Street
Suite 100
Scottsdale, AZ 85254-1521
480-281-0424
800-468-2274
Fax: 480-905-0708
E-Mail: info@probeauty.org
Home Page: www.ncacares.org
Scott Buchanan, Chariman
Reuben Carranza, Vice Chair
Steve Sleeper, Executive Director
Association of Cosmetologists membership includes salon owners, hairdressers, nail technicians, estheticians, educators, and students, and is the world's largest association of salon professionals.
3910 Members
Founded in 1985

3391 **Cosmetologists Chicago**
330 N Wabash Ave
Chicago, IL 60611-4255
312-321-6809
800-883-7808
Fax: 312-245-1080
E-Mail: info@americasbeautyshow.com
Home Page:
www.chicagomidwestbeautyshow.com
Social Media: Facebook, Twitter, Youtube, Pinterest, WordPress
Joseph Cartagena, President
Denise Provenzano, First VP
Larry Silvestri, 2nd VP
Karen Gordon, Treasurer
Robert Passage, Secretary
Voice of the salon industry, a beauty authority and presenter of the Chicago Midwest Beauty Show, stylists, estheticians, color technicians, salon owners, educators and nail technicians.
35000 Members

3392 **Cosmoprof North America (CPNA)**
15825 N 71st Street
Suite 100
Scottsdale, AZ 85254
480-281-0424
800-468-2274
Fax: 480-905-0708
E-Mail: info@cosmoprofnorthamerica.com
Home Page: www.cosmoprofnorthamerica.com
Social Media: Facebook, Twitter, LinkedIn, Pinterest
Max Wexler, Chariman
Scott Buchanan, Vice Chair
Bruce Selan, Treasurer
Supports all those involved with industry related equipment, supplies and services.
Frequency: Annual
Founded in 1892

3393 **Intercoiffure of America**
5151 Reed Road
Columbus, OH 43220-2543
614-457-7712
Fax: 614-457-7794
Home Page: www.intercoiffure.com
Social Media: Facebook, Twitter, Google+
Lois Christie, President & CEO
Maryanne McCormick, VP
Andreas Zafiriadis, 2nd VP
Coral Pleas, Secretary
Darlene Gage, Treasurer
Sponsors semiannual hair fashion shows in New York City.
260 Members
Founded in 1933

3394 **International Guild of Hair Removal Specialists**
1918 Bethel Road
Columbus, OH 43220
800-830-3247
Home Page: www.ighrs.org
Formerly known as the International Guild of Professional Electrologists. A non-profit organization dedicated to providing the latest information about permanent and long-term hair removal to the consumer.
2000 Members
Founded in 1979

3395 **International Nail Technicians Association**
330 N Wabash Ave
Chicago, IL 60611
312-321-6809
800-883-7808
Fax: 312-245-1080
E-Mail: info@americasbeautyshow.com
Home Page: www.isnow.com
Social Media: Facebook, Twitter, Youtube, Pinterest, WordPress
Joseph Cartagena, President
Denise Provenzano, First VP
Larry Silvestri, 2nd VP
Karen Gordon, Treasurer
Robert Passage, Secretary
An international organization for nail professionals. In 2001 it was acquired by Cosmetologists Chicago with the purpose of providing an association 'home' to nail care professionals that is dedicated to the needs of technicians and the industry

3396 **International Salon Spa Business Network**
207 E Ohio Street
#361
Chicago, IL 60611
440-846-6022
866-444-4272
Fax: 866-444-5139
E-Mail: margie@salonspanetwork.org
Home Page: www.icsa.cc
Social Media: Facebook, Twitter
Jason Volk, President
Paul Brown, Vice President
Scott Colabuono, Vice President
Larry Walt, Treasurer
Philip Gould, Secretary
Dedicated to helping its members grow their business, effect positive change politically, provide a forum for members to share their views and ideas and interface with the professional beauty industry on behalf of the chain salons and spas.
70 Members
Founded in 1973

3397 **National Beauty Culturists' League**
25 Logan Circle NW
Washington, DC 20005-3725
202-332-2695
Fax: 202-332-0940
E-Mail: nbcl@bellsouth.net
Home Page: www.nbcl.org
Katie B Catalon, President
Established as the National Hair System Culture League, members are black beauticians and cosmetologists who embrace diversity.
3000 Members
Founded in 1919

3398 **National Cosmetology Association**
15825 N. 71st Street
Suite 100
Scottsdale, AZ 85254
480-281-0424
800-468-2274
Fax: 480-905-0708
E-Mail: info@probeauty.org
Home Page: www.ncacares.org
Max Wexler, Chariman
Scott Buchanan, Vice Chair
Bruce Selan, Treasurer
Membership includes salon owners, hairdressers, nail technicians, estheticians, educators, and students. Members live and work in all 50 states, and also have the option to participate in the state and local affiliate, along with national activities.
25000 Members
Founded in 1921

3399 **Professional Beauty Association**
15825 N 71st Street
Suite 100
Scottsdale, AZ 85254-1521
480-281-0424
800-468-2274
Fax: 480-905-0708
E-Mail: info@probeauty.org
Home Page: www.probeauty.org
Social Media: Facebook, Twitter
Scott Buchanan, Chariman
Reuben Carranza, Vice Chair
Steve Sleeper, Executive Director
The Professional Beauty Association (PBA) is a non-profit trade association that represents the interests of the professional beauty industry from manufacturers and distributors to salons and spas. PBA serves the industry through five core competencies: education, government advocacy, commerce opportunities, research/statistics and public relations/image building.
1400 Members
Founded in 1904

3400 **Society of Clinical and Medical Hair Removal**
2424 American Lane
Madison, WI 53704-3102
608-443-2470
Fax: 608-443-2474
E-Mail: homeoffice@scmhr.org
Home Page: www.scmhr.org
Nedra Lockhart, President
William Moore, Exectuive VP
Rosalind Finkelstein, Treasurer
Denise MacIsaac, Secretary
An international non profit organization with members in the United States, Canada, Australia, Japan and beyond. Supports all methods of hair removal and is dedicated to the research of new technology that will keep its members at the pinnacle of their profession, offering safe, effective hair removal to their clients.
600 Members
Founded in 1985

Newsletters

3401 **AEA Newsletter**
American Electrology Association
1616 Cherry Street
Wenatchee, WA 98801
509-663-6874
Fax: 509-663-6874
E-Mail: presaea@electrology.com
Home Page: www.electrology.com
Sharon Ortiz, CPE, President
Barbara Greathouse, CPE, 1st VP
Deborah Cassin, CPE, Treasurer
The largest international not for profit membership organization. Promotes the highest standards in Electrology education, practice and ethics and champions state licensing and regulation of the profession to protect public interest.
1500 Members
Frequency: Three/Year
Circulation: 1200
Founded in 1958

3402 **ISNOW Cosmetologists Chicago**
401 N Michigan Avenue
Chicago, IL 60611-4255
312-321-6809
800-883-7808
Fax: 312-245-1080
E-Mail: info@americasbeautyshow.com
Home Page: www.isnow.com
Frank Gironda, President
Joseph Cartagena, First VP
Denise Provenzano, Secretary
Larry Silvestri, Treasurer
Represents the industries various constituencies and salon owners.
Cost: $18.95
Frequency: Monthly
Circulation: 5000
Founded in 2004

3403 **National Beauty News**
10405 E 55th Place
Suite B
Tulsa, OK 74146-6502
918-627-8000
Fax: 918-627-8660
Douglas Von Allmen, Owner
Offers news of shows, seminars, product information and columns for the professional beauty industry.
Cost: $12.00
Frequency: Monthly
Circulation: 35,500

3404 **Pink Sheet**
685 Route 202/206
Bridgewater, NJ 08807
800-332-2181
908-547-2159
Fax: 908-547-2200
E-Mail: custcare@elsevier.com
Home Page: www.elsevierbi.com
Social Media: RSS
Mike Squires, President
Cathy Kelly, Executive Editor
Brooke McManus, Managing Editor
Jim Chicca, Executive Director
Melissa Carlson, Editorial Operations Manager
Chronicles regulatory and legal news, major scientific developments and testing methodologies, and their effect on these industries. Product marketing news, new product launches, and promotions and advertising at the retail level, are also included.
Cost: $1050.00
Frequency: Weekly
Founded in 1939

Magazines & Journals

3405 **AEA Journal of Electrology**
American Electrology Association
1616 Cherry Street
Wenatchee, WA 98801
509-663-6874
Fax: 509-663-6874
E-Mail: presaea@electrology.com
Home Page: www.electrology.com
Sharon Ortiz, CPE, President
Barbara Greathouse, CPE, 1st VP
Deborah Cassin, CPE, Treasurer
The Journal of Electrology is a membership news publication, published twice per year and is designed to inform and educate the professional electrologist by offering articles of interest and value by reputable authors who are well qualified in the topic area.
Cost: $40.00
1500 Members
Frequency: Semi-Annual
Circulation: 1200
Founded in 1958

3406 **Beauty Store Business**
Creative Age Publications
7628 Densmore Ave
Van Nuys, CA 91406-2042
818-782-7328
800-442-5667
Fax: 818-782-7450
E-Mail: webmaster@creativeage.com
Home Page: www.creativeage.com
Deborah Carver, President/CEO
Mindy Rosiejka, Vice President/COO
Karie Frost, Executive Director
Industry trends and valuable tips concerning real estate, banking, insurance, product liability, advertising, merchandising, and more.
Frequency: Monthly
Circulation: 15000
ISSN: 1098-0660
Founded in 1971

3407 **BeautyLink**
American Association of Cosmetology Schools

9927 E. Bell Road
Suite 110
Scottsdale, AZ 85260

480-281-0431
800-831-1086
Fax: 480-905-0993
E-Mail: jim@beautyschools.org
Home Page: www.beautyschools.org

Jim Cox, Executive Director
Lisa Zarda, General Manager

Quarterly magazine of the AACS, with cosmetology industry updates and features on new trends and best practices.
Frequency: Quarterly
Circulation: 7000

3408 **Cosmetic World**
Ledes Group
16 East 40th Street
Suite 700
New York, NY 10016

212-840-8800
Fax: 212-840-7246
Home Page: www.cosmeticworld.com

Debra Davis, Advertising Director
Brittany Burhop, Executive Editor
Debbie Ward, Managing Editor

Current industry events, legislation, management changes and corporate activities, as well as marketing developments and financial analysis.
Cost: $175.00
Circulation: 5397
Printed in on glossy stock

3409 **DaySpa Magazine**
Creative Age Publications
7628 Densmore Ave
Van Nuys, CA 91406-2042

818-782-7328
Fax: 818-782-7450
E-Mail: sverba@creativeage.com
Home Page: www.creativeage.com

Deborah Carver, President/CEO
Mindy Rosiejka, Vice President/COO
Karie Frost, Executive Director

DaySpa is dedicated to helping premium salon and spa owners better serve their client enhance their bottom line. Presents the most accurate, up-to-date information available on trends, products, equipment, services, and management and management tools in easy-to-read, entertaining articles.
Cost: $17.50
Frequency: Annual+
Circulation: 24,000+
Founded in 1972

3410 **Dermascope Magazine**
Aesthetics International Association
310 East I-30,
SuiteB107
Garland, TX 75043

469-429-9300
800-961-3777
Fax: 469-429-9301
E-Mail: press@dermascope.com
Home Page: www.dermascope.com

William Strunk, Publisher
Amy McKay, Editor
Wes Wynne, Marketing Director

Provides education for skin care professionals. One of the oldest magazines in the industry.
Cost: $45.00
148 Pages
Frequency: Monthly
Circulation: 16000
ISSN: 1075-055X
Founded in 1972

3411 **Looking Fit Magazine**
Virgo Publishing LLC
3300 N Central Ave
Suite 300
Phoenix, AZ 85012-2532

48 - 9 - 11
Fax: 480-990-0819
E-Mail: swhitley@vpico.com
Home Page: www.vpico.com

John Siefert, CEO
Kelly Ridley, Executive VP/ CFO

Educational resource for professionals in the indoor tanning industry.
Cost: $70.00
300 Pages
Frequency: Monthly
Founded in 1986

3412 **Modern Salon**
Vance Publishing
400 Knightsbridge Pkwy
Lincolnshire, IL 60069

847-634-2600
Fax: 847-634-4379
E-Mail: info@vancepublishing.com
Home Page: www.vancepublishing.com

William C Vance, Chairman
Peggy Walker, President

The constant leader and voice of the professional salon industry. Delivers step-by-step education for the stylist and paid circulation for the advertiser.
Frequency: Monthly
Circulation: 117000
Founded in 1924
Printed in 4 colors on glossy stock

3413 **NW Stylist and Salon**
Porter Publishing
1750 Sw Skyline Blvd
Suite 8
Portland, OR 97221-2543

503-296-4889
888-297-7010
Fax: 503-296-4893
Home Page: www.portlandpsinc.com

James Pettigrove, President
Lisa Kind, Managing Editor
Joel Holland, VP
Marcy Avenson, Advertising Director

Business trade journal mailed free to every salon school and practitioner in Oregon. Accepts advertising.
Cost: $20.00
36 Pages
Frequency: Monthly
Circulation: 22000
Founded in 1983

3414 **NailPro**
Creative Age Publications
7628 Densmore Ave
Van Nuys, CA 91406-2042

818-782-7328
800-442-5667
Fax: 818-782-7450
E-Mail: webmaster@creativeage.com
Home Page: www.creativeage.com

Deborah Carver, President/CEO
Mindy Rosiejka, Vice President/COO
Karie Frost, Executive Director

Nail care how-to's, business related articles, information on nail anatomy and pathology, as well as new products, trends, profiles and a calendar of events.
Cost: $21.95
Frequency: Monthly
Circulation: 50713
Founded in 1971

3415 **Nails Magazine**
Bobit Publishing Company
3520 Challenger St
Torrance, CA 90503-1640

310-533-2400
Fax: 310-533-2500
E-Mail: Hannah.Lee@bobit.com
Home Page: www.bobit.com

Edward J Bobit, CEO
Hannah Lee, Executive Editor
Uyonna Beckham, Sales Assistant
Sarah Paredes, Senior Production Manager
Ty Bobit, CEO

Offers business information on products and application techniques for professional manicurists and salon owners.
Cost: $20.00
Frequency: Monthly
Circulation: 62274
Founded in 1961

3416 **Salon News**
Fairchild Publications
750 3rd Ave
New York, NY 10017-2703
212-630-4000
Fax: 212-630-3563
Home Page: www.fairchildpub.com

Mary G Berner, CEO

Profitability and stability, salon services and resale, and on motivation and education.
Frequency: Monthly
Circulation: 77,603

3417 **Salon Today**
Vance Publishing
400 Knightsbridge Pkwy
Lincolnshire, IL 60069

847-634-2600
Fax: 847-634-4379
E-Mail: info@vancepublishing.com
Home Page: www.vancepublishing.com

William C Vance, Chairman
Peggy Walker, President

Content is modeled as a monthly exchange of ideas on how to grow salon business. Special issues include annual Salon Today 200, Salon of the Year, Technology and Spa Business.
Frequency: Monthly
Circulation: 25000

3418 **Skin Magazine**
Allured Publishing Corporation
PO Box 50
Congers, NY 10920
845-267-3008
866-616-3008
Fax: 845-267-3478
E-Mail: skininc@cambeywest.com
Home Page: www.skininc.com

Janet Ludwig, President
Lin Getner, Controller

The business magazine preferred by owners and managers of salons and spas and the official publication of the American Aestheticians Education Association. Recently awarded a Gold award for editorial from the American Business Publication editors association.
Cost: $49.00
120 Pages
Frequency: Monthly
Circulation: 16000
Founded in 1988

3419 **WWD Beauty Biz**
Fairchild Publications
7 W 34th St
New York, NY 10001-8100

212-630-3880
Fax: 212-630-3868

E-Mail: summits@fairchildpub.com
Home Page: www.fairchildpub.com

Mary Berner, President/CEO
Patrick McCarthy, Chairman/Editorial Director
Jenny B. Fine, Editor-in-Chief
Sarah Murphy, Publisher

The premier guide to the beauty industry. Provides in-depth coverage and analysis on all aspects of the industry, including trends, brands, retailers, and personalities driving both the general consumer and insider sides of the business.
Cost: $60.00
Frequency: Monthly
Circulation: 40,056
Founded in 1892

Trade Shows

3420 **AACS Annual Convention & Expo**
American Association of Cosmetology Schools
9927 E. Bell Road
Suite 110
Scottsdale, AZ 85260

480-281-0431
800-831-1086
Fax: 480-905-0993
E-Mail: jim@beautyschools.org
Home Page: www.beautyschools.org

Jim Cox, Executive Director
Lisa Zarda, General Manager

An opportunity to bring your professional team together to lead your school into the future. Education tracks, classes, social events, and the expo hall complete the experience.
800 Attendees
Frequency: November

3421 **AEA Annual Convention**
American Electrology Association
1616 Cherry Street
Wenatchee, WA 98801

509-663-6874
Fax: 509-663-6874
E-Mail: presaea@electrology.com
Home Page: www.electrology.com

Sharon Ortiz, CPE, President
Barbara Greathouse, CPE, 1st VP
Deborah Cassin, CPE, Treasurer

Annual convention usually in October. Includes 15 hours of CEUs as well as exhibitors.
1500 Members
300 Attendees
Frequency: Annual/Fall
Founded in 1958

3422 **Aesthetics' World Expositions**
Aesthetics' International Association
2611 N Belt Line Road
Suite 140
Sunnyvale, TX 75182-9357

972-203-8530
877-968-7539
Fax: 972-226-2339
Home Page: www.beautyworks.com/aia

150-250 exhibits of skin care, body therapy products make up and equipment. Salon owners, body massage therapists, and dermatologists attend.
3000 Attendees
Frequency: Biennial
Founded in 1979

3423 **American Electrology Association Convention**
American Electrology Association
1616 Cherry Street
Wenatchee, WA 98801

509-663-6874
Fax: 509-663-6874
E-Mail: presaea@electrology.com
Home Page: www.electrology.com

Sharon Ortiz, CPE, President
Barbara Greathouse, CPE, 1st VP
Deborah Cassin, CPE, Treasurer

AEA is the largest international nonprofit membership organization for permanent hair removal. The convention features the largest number of exhibitors with the latest state of the art equipment.
1500 Members
300 Attendees
Frequency: Annual
Founded in 1958

3424 **Big Show Expo**
Big Show Expo
1841 Broadway
Room 812
New York, NY 10023-7603

212-580-1407
Fax: 212-757-3611

Bernice Calvin, President
Maggie Smallwood, Conference Coordinator

Largest group of ethnic beauty shows. 200 booths updating the skills and expertise of hairdressers with ethnic clientele and spotlighting new trends in hair fashions, with all new styles for today's fashion looks.
15M Attendees
Frequency: August, September

3425 **COSMOPROF North America**
COSMOPROF North America
15825 North 71st Street
Suite 100
Scottsdale, AZ 85254

480-281-0424
800-468-2274
Fax: 480-905-0708
E-Mail: cpnainfo@probeauty.org
Home Page: www.cosmoprofnorthamerica.com

Eric Horn, Show Director
Ebony King, Show Manager
Wendy Forakis, Business Relations Manager

The most comprehensive and international professional beauty industry show on the continent. Attendees include manufacturers to distributors , salon owners to spa professionals, importers to retail buyers with hundreds of exhibitors.
25000 Attendees
Frequency: July
Mailing list available for rent

3426 **Hairworld**
National Cosmetology Association
15825 North 71st Street
Suite 100
Scottsdale, AZ 85254

480-281-0424
800-468-2274
Fax: 480-905-0708
E-Mail: info@probeauty.org
Home Page: www.ncacares.org

Max Wexler, Chairman
Scott Buchanan, Vice Chair
Bruce Selan, Treasurer

Annual show of 125 exhibitors of hair products, cosmetics and jewelry.
3000 Attendees
Frequency: July
Circulation: 30,000

3427 **International Congress of Esthetics**
Aesthetics' International Association
310 East I-30
Suite B107
Garland, TX 75043

469-429-9300
800-961-3777
Fax: 469-429-9301
E-Mail: press@dermascope.com
Home Page: www.dermascope.com

Will Strunk, Publisher
Amy McKay, Editor

Biennial show of skin care, makeup and body therapy products and equipment.
3000 Attendees
Frequency: February
Founded in 1977

Directories & Databases

3428 **AEA Online Directory**
American Electrology Association
1616 Cherry Street
Wenatchee, WA 98801

509-663-6874
Fax: 509-663-6874
E-Mail: presaea@electrology.com
Home Page: www.electrology.com

Sharon Ortiz, CPE, President
Barbara Greathouse, CPE, 1st VP
Deborah Cassin, CPE, Treasurer

Available on the AEA Web site.
1500 Members
Founded in 1958

3429 **Drug Store and HBC Chains Database**
Chain Store Guide
3922 Coconut Palm Dr
Tampa, FL 33619-1389

813-627-6700
800-927-9292
Fax: 813-627-6888
E-Mail: webmaster@chainstoreguide.com
Home Page: www.csgis.com

Mike Jarvis, Publisher
Arthur Sciarrotta, Senior VP

Tap into the lucrative drug industry with profiles on more than 1,700 US and Canadian companies operating two or more retail drug stores, deep discount stores, health and beauty care (HBC) stores, cosmetic stores or vitamin stores that have industry sales of at least $250,000. This powerful database empowers you to sell and market your products successfully by reaching more than 8,300 key decision-makers.
Cost: $335.00
Circulation: 8,300

3430 **Hayes Chain Drug Store Directory**
Hayes Directories
PO Box 3436
Mission Viejo, CA 92690

949-583-0537
Fax: 949-583-7419
E-Mail: enhayes@pacbell.net
Home Page: www.hayesdir.com

James Edward Hayes, Editor

Comes in two volumes and contains information for 34,773 chain pharmacies in the United States, 8 stores or more. First volume lists the chain headquarters, and includes the total count of stores with pharmacies. The second volume groups the individual chain stores alphabetically by chain name followed by the name and address information for the headquarters of the parent company.
Cost: $250.00
Frequency: Annual,November

3431 **Hayes Drug Store Directory**
Hayes Directories
PO Box 3436
Mission Viejo, CA 92690

949-583-0537
Fax: 949-583-7419
E-Mail: enhayes@pacbell.net
Home Page: www.hayesdir.com

James Edward Hayes, Editor

Contains information for the 53,821 retail drug stores in the United States.
Cost: $335.00
Frequency: Annual,November

3432 **Hayes Independent Drug Store Directory**
Hayes Directories
PO Box 3436
Mission Viejo, CA 92690

949-583-0537
Fax: 949-583-7419
E-Mail: enhayes@pacbell.net
Home Page: www.haynesdir.com

James Edward Hayes, Editor

Published annually and contains information for 19,048 independent retail pharmacies in the United States. Independent stores are 7 stores or less.
Cost: $300.00
Frequency: Annual,November

Industry Web Sites

3433 **http://gold.greyhouse.com**
G.O.L.D Grey House OnLine Databases

Grey House Publishing's online database platform, GOLD, offers Quick Search, Keyword Search and Expert Search for most business sectors including beauty and cosmetics markets. The GOLD platform makes finding the information you need quick and easy - whether you're a novice searcher or an experienced database user. All of Grey House's directory products are available for subscription on the GOLD platform.

3434 **www.bbsi.org**
Beauty and Barber Supply Institute

Our members are wholesaler-distributors, manufacturers and manufacturers' representatives from around the world. Our mission is to maximize the potential of the professional salon industry.

3435 **www.beautyschools.org**
American Association of Cosmetology Schools

Serves privately owned schools of Cosmetology Arts & Sciences.

3436 **www.dermascope.com**
Aesthetics' International Association

International professional organization for aestheticians representing every facet of the aesthetics industry. From the student, aesthetician, make-up artist, reflexologist, aromatherapist, massage therapist, nutritionist, nurse, holistic practitioner and physician to the day spa/salon owner.

3437 **www.electrology.com**
American Electrology Association

Organization of professional hair removal practitioners promoting the highest standards of electrology education through our annual and state conventions with seminars following a prescribed learning standard.

3438 **www.greyhouse.com**
Grey House Publishing

Authoritative reference directories for most business sectors including beauty and cosmetics markets. Users can search the online databases with varied search criteria allowing for custom searches by product category, geographic area, sales volume, keyword, subject and more. Full Grey House catalog and online ordering also available.

3439 **www.isnow.com**
Cosmetologists Chicago

Voice of the salon industry. Presenter of the Chicago Midwest Beauty Show, we are stylists, estheticians, color technicians, salon owners, educators and nail technicians.

3440 **www.oneroof.org**
American Beauty Association

Serves the interests of the professional beauty industry.

3441 **www.salons.org**
The Salon Association

Non-profit organization representing 7,000 employment-based salons and spas across the United States and Canada

Associations

3442 American Association for Medical Chronobiology & Chronotherapeutics
E-Mail: editorial@aamcc.org
Home Page: www.aamcc.net

Erhard Haus, President
Michael Smolensky, Vice President
Linda Sackett-Lundeen, Secretary-Treasurer
Molly Bray, Director
Martin Young, Director

Provides a forum for the exchange and discussion of new findings, methods, and applications in medical chronobiology and chronotherapeutics.

3443 American Association of Bioanalysts
906 Olive Street
Suite 1200
St Louis, MO 63101-1448

314-241-1445
Fax: 314-241-1449
E-Mail: aab@aab.org
Home Page: www.aab.org

Mark S Birenbaum PhD, Administrator

AAB is committed to the pursuit of excellence in clinical laboratory services by enhancing the professional skills of each of its members; promoting more efficient and productive operations; offering external quality control programs; collaborating with other professional associations and government agencies; promoting safe laboratory practices; and educating legislators, regulators, and the general public about clinical laboratory tests and procedures.
Founded in 1956

3444 American Association of Immunologists
9650 Rockville Pike
Bethesda, MD 20814

301-634-7178
Fax: 301-634-7887
E-Mail: infoaai@aai.org
Home Page: www.aai.org
Social Media: Facebook

Marc K Jenkins, President
M Michele Hogan, Executive Director

AAI is a professional organization founded to advance the knowledge of immunology and related disciplines, foster interchange of ideas and information among scientists, and promote understanding of the field of immunology.
Cost: $50.00
6500 Members
Founded in 1913

3445 American Geophysical Union
2000 Florida Ave Nw
Washington, DC 20009

202-462-6900
800-966-2481
Fax: 202-328-0566
E-Mail: service@agu.org
Home Page: www.agu.org
Social Media: Facebook, Twitter, LinkedIn, Youtube, RSS

Carol Finn, President
Margaret Leinen, President Elect
Susan Webb, International Secretary
Christine W McEntee, Executive Director/CEO
Lisa Tauxe, General Secretary
52000 Members
Founded in 1919
Mailing list available for rent

3446 American Institute of Biological Sciences
1900 Campus Commons Drive
Suite 200
Reston, VA 20191

703-674-2500
800-992-2427
Fax: 703-674-2509
E-Mail: rogrady@aibs.org
Home Page: www.aibs.org
Social Media: Facebook, Twitter, LinkedIn, Youtube, RSS

Joseph Travis, President
John Tobin, Treasurer
Judith Skog, Secretary

Supports professionals involved with the biological sciences, including research, products, education; sponsors annual conference.
Mailing list available for rent

3447 American Registry of Magnetic Resonance Imaging Technologists
8815 Commonwealth Blvd.
Bellerose, NY 11426

718-347-8690
Fax: 718-347-8691
E-Mail: ARMRIT@msn.com
Home Page: armrit.org

James F. Coffin, President & Executive Director
Thomas K. Schrack, Director
Charles G. Fiore, Senior Director & Legal Counsel
William J. Woodward, Director
Charles W. Kreines, Director

MRI schools, educational resources, certified tech resumes, practice tests, and verification of a tech's certification.

3448 American Society for Biochemistry and Molecular Biology
11200 Rockville Pike
Suite 302
Rockville, MD 20852-3110

240-283-6600
Fax: 301-881-2080
E-Mail: asbmb@asbmb.org
Home Page: www.asbmb.org
Social Media: Facebook, Twitter, LinkedIn

Susan Pfeffer, President
Mark Lemmon, Secretary
Merle Olson, Treasurer

A professional and educational association for biochemists and molecular biologists which seeks to extend and utilize the field of biochemistry and molecular biology.
Cost: $18.50
11900 Members
Founded in 1906
Mailing list available for rent: 11000 names

3449 American Society for Reproductive Medicine
1209 Montgomery Highway
Birmingham, AL 35216-2809

205-978-5000
Fax: 205-978-5005
E-Mail: asrm@asrm.org
Home Page: www.asrm.org

Rebecca Sokol, President
Owen K. Davis, President Elect
Richard Paulson, Vice President
Linda Giudice, Past President
Richard H. Reindollar, Executive Director

Organization devoted to advancing knowledge and expertise in the study of reproduction and reproductive disorders.

3450 American Society of Plant Biologists
15501 Monona Drive
Rockville, MD 20855-2768

301-251-0560
Fax: 301-279-2996
Home Page: my.aspb.org

Crispin Taylor, Executive and Governance
Jotee Pundu, Administrative Staff
Melanie Binder, Member Services
Susan Cato, Member Services
Annette Kessler, Publications

A professional society devoted to the advancement of the plant sciences. It publishes research and organizes conferences that are key to the advancement of plant biology.

3451 American Soybean Association
12125 Woodcrest Executive Drive
Suite 100
St. Louis, MO 63141-5009

314-576-1770
800-688-7692
Fax: 314-576-2786
E-Mail: membership@soy.org
Home Page: soygrowers.com

Sam Butler, Director
Ted Glaub, Director
Richard Wilkins, Director
Walter Godwin, Director
Ray Gaesser, Director

Domestic and international policy advocate of increasing market opportunities and value for U.S. soybean farmers.

3452 Association for Women Geoscientists
12000 N. Washington St.
Suite 285
Thornton, CO 80241

303-412-6219
Fax: 303-253-9220
Home Page: www.awg.org

A professional organization which promotes the professional development of its members, provides geoscience outreach to girls, and encourages womento become geoscientists.

3453 Association for Women in Science
1321 Duke Street,
Suite 210
Alexandria, VA 22314

703-894-4490
E-Mail: awis@awis.org
Home Page: www.awis.org
Social Media: Facebook, Twitter, LinkedIn

Susan Fitzpatrick, President
Ann Lee Karlon, President Elect
Gail Gasparich, Secretary
Donna Gerardi Riordan, Treasurer

Provides support for female scientists and bioengineers. Also dedicated to achieving equity and full participation for women in science, mathematics, engineering and technology.
5000 Members
Founded in 1971
Mailing list available for rent

3454 Association of Biomolecular Resource Facilities
9650 Rockville Pike
Bethesda, MD 20814

301-634-7306
Fax: 301-634-7455
E-Mail: abrf@abrf.org
Home Page: www.abrf.org

Bill Hendrickson, President
Paula Turpen, Secretary/Treasurer
George Grills, Director
Tim Hunter, Director
Anoja Perera, Director

Dedicated to advancing core and research biotechnology laboratoriesthrough research, communication, and education.
Founded in 1988

3455 **Association of Women Soil Scientists**
9611 S. Riverbend Ave.
Parlier, CA 93648

E-Mail: Suduan.Gao@ars.usda.gov
Home Page: www.womeninsoils.org

Wendy Greenberg, Chair
A nonprofit organization of women and men in soil science that promotes a better understanding of the role of soil scientists and that provides assistance and encouragement for women in non-traditional fields and for women seeking employment in the field of soil science.

3456 **BioSpace**
6465 South Greenwood Plaza
Suite 400
Centennial, CO 80111

877-277-7585
Fax: 800-595-2929
E-Mail: support@biospace.com
Home Page: www.biospace.com

The leading online community for industry news and careers for lifescience professionals.

3457 **Biotechnology Industry Organization**
1201 Maryland Ave SW
Suite 900
Washington, DC 20024

202-962-9200
E-Mail: info@bio.org
Home Page: www.bio.org
Social Media: Facebook, Twitter, LinkedIn, Youtube

James C Greenwood, President
Scott Whitaker, COO
Joanne Duncan, CFO/SVP, Finance & Adminstration
Tom DiLenge, General Counsel/SVP, Legal

Provides support for all those involved in biotechnology from a government, corporate, and trade viewpoint. Also represents biotechnology companies, academic institutions, biotechnology centers and related organizations in all 50 US states and 31 other nations. Researchers expand the boundaries of science to benefit mankind by providing better healthcare, enhanced agriculture, and a cleaner and safer environment.
1100+ Members
Founded in 1993
Mailing list available for rent

3458 **Biotechnology Institute**
1201 Maryland Avenue, SW
Suite 900
Washington, DC 20024

202-312-9269
Fax: 202-355-6706
E-Mail: info@biotechinstitute.org
Home Page: www.biotechinstitute.org

Thomas G. Wiggans, Chairman
Scott W. Morrison, Treasurer
Lawrence Mahan, Ph.D., President
Bianca Blanks, Director of Programs
Quinta Jackson, VP Finance & Administration

An independent nonprofit organization founded to teach the public about the benefits of biotechnology.

3459 **Council for Biotechnology Information**
1201 Maryland Ave SW
Suite 900
Washington, DC 20024-2149

202-962-9200
Fax: 202-589-2547
E-Mail: cbi@whybiotech.com
Home Page: www.whybiotech.com
Social Media: Facebook, Twitter

James C Greenwood, CEO
Scott Whitaker, COO
Joanne Duncan, CFO/SVP, Finance & Adminstration
Tom DiLenge, General Counsel/SVP, Legal

A coalition of six of the world's leading biotechnology companies and two trade associations. Its mission is to improve the understanding and acceptance of biotechnology by collecting balanced, science-based information and communicating it through a variety of channels.
Founded in 2000
Mailing list available for rent

3460 **Crop Science Society of America**
5585 Guilford Rd.
Madison, WI 53711-5801

608-273-8080
Fax: 608-273-2021
E-Mail: membership@crops.org
Home Page: www.crops.org

An educational and scientific organization comprised of more than 4,700 members dedicated to the advancement of crop science.

3461 **CropLife America**
1156 15th St. NW
Washington, DC 20005

202-296-1585
Fax: 202-463-0474
Home Page: www.croplifeamerica.org

Jay Vroom, President &CEO
Beau Greenwood, EVP Government Relations
William F. Kuckuck, EVP/ COO
Rachel G. Lattimore, SVP & General Counsel
Priscilla Hammett, CFO
U.S. trade association representing the major manufacturers, formulators, and distributors of crop protection and pest control products.
Founded in 1933

3462 **Electrophoresis Society**
1202 Ann Street
Madison, WI 53713

608-258-1565
Fax: 608-258-1569
E-Mail: matt-aes@tds.net
Home Page: www.aesociety.org
Social Media: Facebook, LinkedIn

Mark A Hayes, President
Christa Hestekin, VP
Shashi Murthy, Executive VP
Phil Beckett, Secretary
Lawrence I Grossman, Treasurer
Unique international organization founded to improve and promote technologies necessary for biomolecular separation and detection.
200 Members
Founded in 1972
Mailing list available for rent

3463 **Enzyme Technical Association**
1111 Pennsylvania Avenue, NW
Washington, DC 20004-2541

202-739-5612
Fax: 202-739-3001
E-Mail: apavel@morganlewis.com
Home Page: www.enzymeassociation.org

Anthony T. Pavel, Jr., General Counsel and Secretary
Lynne Marie Brown, Administrator
Promotes the development, preservation, maintenance and general welfare of the industry to the world of manufacturing and distributing enzyme preparations from any source for direct and indirect addition or application to foods, drugs, and other articles of use by humans or animals.
Founded in 1970

3464 **Federation of American Societies for Experimental Biology**
9650 Rockville Pike
Bethesda, MD 20814

301-634-7000
Fax: 301-634-7001
E-Mail: info@faseb.org
Home Page: www.faseb.org

Joseph R. Haywood, PhD, President
Parker B. Antin, PhD, President-Elect
Hudson H. Freeze, PhD, Vice President for Science Policy
Mark O. Lively, PhD, Treasurer
Guy Fogleman, PhD, CFA, Federation Secretary
A nonprofit organization that is the principal umbrella organization of U.S. societies in the field of biological and medical research.

3465 **International Society for Biomedical Polymeric Biomaterials**
2415 Westwood Ave.
Suite B.
Richmond, VA 23230

804-523-2913
Fax: 804-288-3551
E-Mail: info@isbppb.org
Home Page: isbppb.org

Mia Galijasevic, Executive Director
Munmaya Mishra, Founding Chairman
Gary L. Bowlin, President

An organization engaged in educating, networking, advocating, and advancing the field of biomedical polymers and polymeric biomaterials internationally.
Founded in 2011

3466 **International Society for Chronobiology**
University of Texas-Medical Branch
301 University Boulevard
Galveston, TX 77555

409-611-1011
E-Mail: prf@unife.it
Home Page: www.chronoint.org

Promotes studies on temporal parameters of biological variables and pursues related scientific and educational purposes. Encourages research centers and the establishment of chronobiology as an academic discipline in its own right.
300 Members
Founded in 1937
Mailing list available for rent

3467 **International Society for Magnetic Resonance in Medicine**
2030 Addison Street
7th Floor
Berkeley, CA 94704

510-841-1899
Fax: 510-841-2340
E-Mail: info@ismrm.org
Home Page: www.ismrm.org
Social Media: Facebook, Twitter, RSS

Roberta A Kravitz, Executive Director
Jennifer Olson, Associate Executive Director

Sandra Daudlin, Director of Meetings
Mariam Barzin, Finance Director
Jacob Coverstone, Education Director

Nonprofit professional association devoted to furthering the development and application of magnetic resonance techniques in medicine and biology. Also holds annual scientific meeting and sponsors other major educational and scientific workshops.
5000 Members
Founded in 1994
Mailing list available for rent

3468 International Union of Biochemistry and Molecular Biology

Home Page: www.iubmb.org

Michael P. Walsh, General Secretary

An international non-governmental organization concerned with biochemistry and molecular biology.
Founded in 1955

3469 Massachusetts Biotechnology Council

300 Technology Sq
8th Floor
Cambridge, MA 02139

617-674-5100
Fax: 617-674-5101
E-Mail: info@massbio.org
Home Page: www.massbio.org
Social Media: Facebook, Twitter, LinkedIn, Youtube

Geoff MacKay, Chairman
Glenn Batchelder, Vice Chair
Michael Ohara, Treasurer

Not for profit organization that provides services and support for the Massachusetts biotechnology industry. Committed to advancing the development of critical new science technology and medicines that benefit people worldwide.
400+ Members
Founded in 1985
Mailing list available for rent

3470 National Center for Biotechnology Information

US National Library of Medicine
8600 Rockville Pike
Building 38A
Bethesda, MD 20894

301-496-2475
Fax: 301-480-9241
E-Mail: info@ncbi.nlm.nih.gov
Home Page: www.ncbi.nlm.nih.gov
Social Media: Youtube

To develop new information technologies to aid in the understanding of fundamental molecular and genetic processes that control health and disease.
Founded in 1988

3471 National Corn Growers Association

632 Cepi Drive
Chesterfield, MO 63005

636-733-9004
Fax: 636-733-9005
E-Mail: corninfo@ncga.com
Home Page: www.ncga.com

Chris Novak, Chief Executive Officer
Kathy Baker, Executive Assistant
Susan Claiborne, Receptionist
Rodger Mansfield, Vice President of Administration
Darcy Wolf, Director, Accounting

News, facts, and information for growers, media, educators, and anyone else interested in corn.

3472 New York Biotechnology Association

25 Health Sciences Dr
Suite 202
Stony Brook, NY 11790

631-444-8895
Fax: 631-444-8896
E-Mail: info@newyorkbio.org
Home Page: www.newyorkbio.org
Social Media: Facebook, LinkedIn

Robert Easton, Chairman
Nathan Tinker, Executive Director
Joseph Tortorice, VP, Operations
Patricia Wadington, Director, Membership Services

NYBA has been an active & vocal champion for New York's life science industry. Through the Association's education & advocacy efforts in both Albany and Washington DC, NYBA has focused it's resources on building a powerful innovation force in New York state by working to create an economic atmosphere that rewards entrepreneurism, expands access to capital, invests in the industry's future, and protects patient access to life saving therapies.
250 Members
Founded in 1990

3473 North American Benthological Society

5400 Bosque Blvd.
Suite 680
Waco, TX 76710

254-399-9636
Fax: 785-843-1274
E-Mail: webmaster@benthos.org
Home Page: www.benthos.org

The Society for Freshwater Science (SFS) is an international scientific organization whose purpose is to promote further understanding of freshwater ecosystems (rivers, streams, lakes, reservoirs, and estuaries) and ecosystems at the interface between aquatic and terrestrial habitats. The society fosters exchange of scientific information among the membership, and with other professional societies, resource managers, policy makers, educators, and the public.
Founded in 1953

3474 North Carolina Biotechnology Center

15 TW Alexander Drive
PO Box 13547
Research Triangle Park, NC 27709-3547

919-541-9366
Fax: 919-990-9544
E-Mail: info@ncbiotech.org
Home Page: www.ncbiotech.org
Social Media: Facebook, Twitter, LinkedIn, Youtube

John L Atkins III, Chairman
E Norris Tolson, President & CEO
Doug Edgeton, SVP, Financial Planning
Kenneth R Tindall, SVP, Science & Business Dev
Lynne Runyan, VP, Human Resource

To provide long-term economic and societal benefits to North Carolina through support of biotechnology research, business and education.
65 Members
Founded in 1981

3475 Pennsylvania Biotechnology Association

650 East Swedesford Road
Suite 190
Wayne, PA 19087

610-578-9220
Fax: 610-947-6801
E-Mail: president@pennsylvaniabio.org
Home Page: www.pabio.org

Christopher P Molineaux, President & CEO
Jim Manser, VP, Policy & Public Affairs

A catalyst to ensure Pennsylvania is a global leader in the biosciences by developing a cohesive community that unites the region's biotechnology, pharmaceutical research, and financial strategies.

3476 Protein Society

1450 S Rolling Road
Suite 3.007
Baltimore, MD 21227

301-634-7277
Fax: 301-634-7271
E-Mail: staff@proteinsociety.org
Home Page: www.proteinsociety.org
Social Media: Facebook, Twitter, LinkedIn

James Bowie, President
Jacquelyn Fetrow, Secretary/Treasurer

The Protein Society is a not-for-profit scientific and educational membership organization. Our mission is to provide international forums to facilitate communication and collaboration with respect to all aspects of the study of protein molecules, the building blocks of life.
2100 Members
Founded in 1986
Mailing list available for rent: 3,000 names at $200 per M

3477 Section for Magnetic Resonance Technologists

2030 Addison Street
7th Floor
Berkeley, CA 94704

510-841-1899
Fax: 510-841-2340
Home Page: www.ismrm.org

Roberta A. Kravitz, Executive Director
Kerry Crockett, Associate Executive Director
Mariam Barzin, Director of Finance
Julia White, Accounting Coordinator
Mary Day, Office Manager

A professional organization in the medical imaging community providing education, professional advice and support for magnetic resonance (MR) technologists and radiographers throughout the world.

3478 Sino-American Pharmaceutical Professionals Association

P. O. Box 282
Nanuet, NY 10954

E-Mail: information@sapaweb.org
Home Page: www.sapaweb.org

Dr. Ning Yan, President
Dr. Jiwen Chen, Immediate-past President
Dr. Weiguo Dai, President-elect

An independent, nonprofit and professional organization with over 4,000 members in the U.S.A., China, Hong Kong, Taiwan, and Japan. It promotes pharmaceutical science and technology.
Founded in 1993

3479 Society for Biological Engineering

120 Wall Street
FL 23
New York, NY 10005-4020

Home Page: www.aiche.org/sbe

Georges Belfort, Director
Bill Bentley, Director
Brian Davison, Director
Paula T. Hammond, Director
Pankaj Mohan, Director

A global organization of leading engineers and scientists dedicatedto advancing the integration of biology with engineering.

3480 **Society for Biomaterials**
15000 Commerce Pkwy
Suite C
Mt Laurel, NJ 08054

856-439-0826
Fax: 856-439-0525
E-Mail: info@biomaterials.org
Home Page: www.biomaterials.org
Social Media: Facebook, LinkedIn

Antonios Mikos, President
Nicholas Ziats, President Elect
David Kohn, Secretary/Treasurer

Promotes advances in all phases of materials, research and development by encouragement of cooperative educational programs, clinical applications, and professional standards in the biomaterials field.
1550 Members
Founded in 1969

3481 **Society for Biomolecular Screening**
36 Tamarack Ave
Suite 348
Danbury, CT 06811-4822

203-778-8828
Fax: 203-748-7557
E-Mail: email@sbsonline.org
Home Page: www.slas.org
Social Media: Facebook, Twitter, LinkedIn, Youtube

Al Kolb, President
Christine Giordano, Executive Director

Provides a forum for education and information exchange among professionals within drug discovery and related disciplines.
2000+ Members
Founded in 1994

3482 **Society for Cardiovascular Magnetic Resonance**
19 Mantua Road
Mt. Royal, NJ 8061

856-423-8955
Fax: 856-423-3420
E-Mail: hq@scmr.org
Home Page: www.scmr.org

Orlando Simonetti, PhD, President
Victor A. Ferrari, MD, Vice-President
Jeanette Schulz-Menger, MD, Treasurer
Matthias G. Friedrich, MD, Vice Secretary-Treasurer
Albert de Roos, MD, PhD, Immediate Past President

The leading international society for physicians, scientists, and technologists working in cardiovascular magnetic resonance.

3483 **Society for Freshwater Science, Formerly NABS**
5400 Bosque Blvd
Suite 680
Waco, TX 76710-4446

254-399-9636
Fax: 254-776-3767
E-Mail: membership@benthos.org
Home Page: www.freshwater-science.org

Randy Fuller, President
Brian Shelley, President Assistant
Dave Strayer, President Elect
Sue Norton, Secretary
Mike Swift, Treasurer

International Scientific organization with the purpose to promote better understanding of the biotic communitites of lake and stream bottoms and their role in aquatic ecosystems, by providing media and disseminating new investigation results , new interpretations and other benthological informatoin to aquatic biologists and the scientific community. Also publishes a journal.
Founded in 1953

3484 **Society for Industrial Microbiology and Biotechnology**
3929 Old Lee Highway
Suite 92A
Fairfax, VA 22030

703-691-3357
Fax: 703-691-7991
Home Page: www.simbhq.org

Christine Lowe, Executive Director
Jennifer Johnson, Director of Member Services
Suzannah Citrenbaum, Web Manager
Espie Montesa, Accountant
Katherine Devins, Publications Coordinator

A nonprofit international association dedicated to the advancement of microbiology sciences, especially as they apply to industrial products, biotechnology, materials, and processes.
Founded in 1949

3485 **Society for Laboratory Automation and Screening**
100 Illinois Street
Ste. 242
St. Charles, IL 60174

630-256-7527
877-990-7527
E-Mail: slas@slas.org
Home Page: www.slas.org

Daniel G. Sipes, President
Dean Ho, Vice President
Robyn Rourick, Treasurer
Richard Eglen, Secretary
Alastair Binnie, Director

A global community of more than 18,000 life science research and development professionals.

3486 **Strategic Information for the Life Sciences**
BioAbility™
PO Box 14569
Research Triangle Park, NC 27709-4569

919-544-5111
Fax: 919-544-5401
E-Mail: info@bioability.com
Home Page: www.bioability.com

Mark D Dibner, President/Founder
Tracey V du Laney, Research Director

BioAbility has provided the knowledge and experience to evaluate any area of the life sciences or biotechnology markets. Partnered with expert life science affiliates to bring a world-class level of expertise to our service offerings.

3487 **The American Society for Cell Biology**
8120 Woodmont Avenue
Suite 750
Bethesda, MD 20814

301-347-9300
Fax: 301-347-9310
E-Mail: ascbinfo@ascb.org
Home Page: ascb.org

Jennifer Lippincott-Schwartz, President
Don Cleveland, Past President
Shirley Tilghman, President-Elect
Kathleen Green, Secretary
Thoru Pederson, Treasurer

A professional society that provides the exchange of scientific knowledge in the area of cell biology.

3488 **Virginia Biotechnology Association**
800 E Leigh St
Suite 14
Richmond, VA 23219-1534

804-643-6360
Fax: 804-643-6361
E-Mail: questions@vabio.org
Home Page: www.vabio.org

Jeffrey M Gallagher, CEO
Sherry Halloran, Director, Membership Services
Susan Moore, Senior Administrative Assistant

Promotes the biotechnology industry in Virginia, to expand the knowledge and expertise of Virginia's businesses concerning biotechnology through seminars, educational publications and other means.
200 Members
Founded in 1992

3489 **Women in Cognitive Science**
Home Page: womenincogsci.org

Laurie Feldman, Officer
Judith Kroll, Officer
Suparna Rajaram, Officer
Debra Titone, Officer
Natasha Tokowicz, Officer

Organization that works to create an environment that encourages young women to join the field of cognitive psychology/science, particularly in cognitive neuroscience and computational modeling areas.

Newsletters

3490 **AAI Newsletter**
American Association of Immunologists
9650 Rockville Pike
Bethesda, MD 20814-3999

301-634-7178
Fax: 301-634-7887
E-Mail: infoaai@aai.org
Home Page: www.aai.org

Leslie Berg, President
Gail Bishop, Vice President
Mitchell Kronenberg, Treasurer/Secretary
Frequency: Bi-Monthly

3491 **BioPeople Magazine**
PO Box 5778
Walnut Creek, CA 94596
925-932-6364
Home Page: www.biotechmedia.com

Lisa Wagner, Advertising Executive
Charlene Carpentier, Production Manager
Sukaini Virji-Jeganathan, Editor

Provides information and analysis of the international biotechnology industry, including corporate agreements, product status, financial transactions and new technologies.
Cost: $675.00
Frequency: Quarterly
Circulation: 10,000
Printed in on glossy stock

3492 **BioWorld Financial Watch**
BioWorld
3525 Piedmont Road
Building 6, Suite 400
Atlanta, GA 30305-4031

404-262-5476
800-688-2421
Fax: 404-814-0759

E-Mail: customerservice@bioworld.com
Home Page: www.bioworld.com

Donald R Johnston, Publisher
Brady Huggett, Managing Editor
Chris Walker, Marketing Manager

Tracks public financing and portfolio performance offering expert analysis. The weekly source for biotechnology financial news.
Cost: $1197.00
Frequency: Weekly

3493 **Biotechnology News**
CTB International Publishing
PO Box 218
Maplewood, NJ 07040-218

973-966-0997
Fax: 973-966-0242
Home Page: www.ctbintl.com

F G Racioppi, Marketing Director

A leading biotechnology publication for executives. Provides incisive intelligence on the ever-changing biotechnology industry and includes news on research, product development and corporate doings.
Cost: $634.00
Founded in 1985
Printed in one color on newsprint stock

3494 **Biotechnology Newswatch**
McGraw Hill
1221 Avenue of the Americas
Suite C3A
New York, NY 10020-1095

212-512-2000
Fax: 212-512-3840
E-Mail: customer.service@mcgraw-hill.com
Home Page: www.mcgraw-hill.com

Harold W McGraw III, CEO
Mara Bovsun, Editor
Kenneth M Vittor, VP

Covers the business and technical news affecting companies engaged in serving the biotechnology sciences.
Cost: $737.00
12 Pages
Frequency: Monthly
Founded in 1910

3495 **Genetic Technology News**
John Wiley & Sons
111 River St
Hoboken, NJ 07030-5790

201-748-6000
Fax: 201-748-6088
E-Mail: info@wiley.com
Home Page: www.wiley.com

William J Pesce, CEO

Covers technical and business developments in every area of genetic engineering and related techniques, analyzing their applications in the chemical, pharmaceutical and energy industries as well as in agriculture, animal breeding and medicine.
Cost: $585.00
18 Pages
Frequency: Monthly
Founded in 1807

3496 **Industrial Bioprocessing**
John Wiley & Sons
111 River St
Hoboken, NJ 07030-5790

201-748-6000
Fax: 201-748-6088
E-Mail: info@wiley.com
Home Page: www.wiley.com

William J Pesce, CEO

Focuses on industrial processes involving biological routes to produce chemicals/energy; the conversion of biomaterials via fermentation, process monitoring and more.
Cost: $545.00
10 Pages
Frequency: Monthly
Founded in 1807
Mailing list available for rentat $180 per M
Printed in one color on matte stock

3497 **J Biomolecular Screening**
Society for Biomolecular Screening
100 Illinois Street
Suite 242
St.Charles, IL 60174

630-256-7527
Fax: 630-741-7527
E-Mail: slas@slas.org
Home Page: www.sbsonline.org

Michelle Palmer, President
David Dorsett, Vice President
Erik Rubin, Treasurer
Andy Zaayenga, Secretary

Biomolecular industry news and information.
Cost: $478.00
Founded in 1992

3498 **Life Sciences & Biotechnology Update**
InfoTeam
PO Box 15640
Plantation, FL 33318-5640

954-473-9560
Fax: 954-473-0544

Merton Allen, Editor

Medical and biological technology; health and disease; genetics and genetic engineering; bodily fluids, bones, tissues and organs, cancer, medical diagnoisis and treatment; medical instrumentation and procedures; medical care systems; public health; mental health; child care; medical costs; research; and more.
Frequency: Monthly

3499 **Technotrends Newsletter**
Burrus Research Associates
PO Box 47
Hartland, WI 53029-2347

262-367-0949
800-827-6770
Fax: 262-367-7163
E-Mail: office@burrus.com
Home Page: www.burrus.com/

Dan Burrus, CEO
Patti A Thomsen, Editor
Jennifer Metcalf, Marketing

This newsletter researches the latest innovations in science and technology. Provides access to information that can give an edge on tomorrow, today and shows how you might benefit from each innovation.
Cost: $39.95
Frequency: Monthly
Circulation: 1000
Founded in 1984
Printed in 4 colors on matte stock

Magazines & Journals

3500 **AWIS Magazine**
Association for Women in Science
1200 New York Avenue
Suite 650
Washington, DC 20005

202-326-8940
Fax: 202-326-8960
E-Mail: awis@awis.org
Home Page: www.awis.org

Janet Bandows, Executive Director

Focuses on issues relevant to women scientists. Contains articles about current events, career advancement, financial planning, work-life balance, and creating a diverse work environment.
Frequency: Quarterly
Circulation: 3500

3501 **American Biotechnology Laboratory**
International Scientific Communications
PO Box 870
Shelton, CT 06484-0870

203-926-9300
Fax: 203-926-9310
E-Mail: webmaster@iscpubs.com
Home Page: www.iscpubs.com

Brian Howard, Publisher
Robert G Sweeny, Publisher

American Biotechnology Laboratory serves Industry, Universities, Government and others allied to the field with special interest in life science research.
Cost: $173.12
64 Pages
Frequency: Monthly
Circulation: 60058
Mailing list available for rent: 60M names at $170 per M
Printed in 4 colors on glossy stock

3502 **Antiretroviral Resistance in Clinical Practice**
National Center for Biotechnology Information
8600 Rockville Pike
Bethesda, MD 20894

301-496-2475
Fax: 301-480-9241
E-Mail: info@ncbi.nlm.nih.gov
Home Page: www.ncbi.nlm.nih.gov

Anna Maria Geretti, Editor

3503 **Applied Biochemistry and Biotechnology**
Humana Press
999 Riverview Drive
Suite 208
Totowa, NJ 07512-1165

973-256-1699
Fax: 973-256-8341
Home Page: www.humanapress.com

David Watt, Editor
Ashok Mulchandani, Editor-in-Chief
Paul Dolgert, Director
Fran Lipton, Production Manager

Reports on new techniques and original research in biotechnology and biochemistry with a focus on the application of new technologies.
Cost: $1505.00
Frequency: Monthly
Circulation: 373
Founded in 1977

3504 **BioTechniques**
52 Vanderbilt Avenue
7th Floor
New York, NY 10017

212-520-2777
Fax: 212-520-2705
E-Mail: webmaster@biotechniques.com
Home Page: www.biotechniques.com

Nathan Blow, Editor in Chief
Bill Moran, Director of Sales
John C. Yarosh, Production Manager

Serves the biotechnical and pharmaceutical industries.
Cost: $145.00
254 Pages
Frequency: Monthly
Circulation: 85,000
Founded in 1983
Printed in 4 colors on glossy stock

3505 **Biotechnology Progress**
American Chemical Society
1155 16th St NW
Suite 600
Washington, DC 20036-4892

202-872-4600
80 - 2 - 55
Fax: 202-872-4615
E-Mail: service@acs.org
Home Page: www.acs.org

Nancy Jackson, President

Information on new technology.
Cost: $924.00
Founded in 1876

3506 **Biotechnology and Bioengineering**
John Wiley & Sons
111 River St
Hoboken, NJ 07030-5790

201-748-6000
Fax: 201-748-6088
E-Mail: info@wiley.com
Home Page: www.wiley.com

William J Pesce, CEO
Richard M Hochhauser, CEO

A scientific journal publishing new papers in the field of biotechnology and bioengineering.
Cost: $750.00
Frequency: 1 Year 28 Issue
Founded in 1807

3507 **CleanRooms Magazine**
PennWell Publishing Company
98 Spit Brook Rd
Suite L11
Nashua, NH 03062-5737

603-891-0123
80 - 2 - 05
Fax: 603-891-9294
E-Mail: mikel@pennwell.com
Home Page: www.pennwell.com

Christine Shaw, VP
Mark A Desorbo, Associate Editor
James Enos, Publisher

Serves the contamination control and ultrapure materials and process industries. Written for readers in the microelectronics, pharmaceutical, biotech, health care, food processing and other user industries. Provides technology and business news and new product listings.
Frequency: Monthly
Circulation: 35031
Founded in 1987

3508 **Engineering in Medicine and Biology**
3 Park Avenue
17th Floor
New York, NY 10016

212-419-7900
800-272-6657
Fax: 212-752-4929
E-Mail: jenderle@bme.uconn.edu
Home Page: www.ieee.org

Dr. John D Enderle, Editor
Desir,e de Myer, Managing Editor
Susan Schneiderman, Advertising Sales Manager

Focuses on up-to-date biomedical engineering applications for engineers who are at the forefront of electrotechnology innovation.
Cost: $300.00
Circulation: 7983
ISSN: 0739-5175
Founded in 1963

3509 **Freshwater Science**
Society for Freshwater Science
5400 Bosque Blvd.
Suite 680
Waco, TX 76710-4446

254-399-9636
Fax: 254-776-3767
Home Page: www.freshwater-science.org

Pamela Silver, Editor
Rosemary J. Mackay, Managing Editor
Irwin Polls, Business Manager

Publishes timely, peer-reviewed scientific research that promotes a better understanding and environmental stewardship of biological communities living on the bottom of streams, rivers, lakes, and wetlands, with an emphasis on freshwater inland habitats. Theoretical discussions, speculative and philosophical articles, and critical appraisals of rapidly developing research fields.
Cost: $65.00
Frequency: Quarterly

3510 **Journal of Biological Chemistry**
American Society for Biochemistry
11200 Rockville Pike
Suite 302
Rockville, MD 20852-3110

240-283-6620
Fax: 301-881-2573
E-Mail: asbmb@asbmb.org
Home Page: www.asbmb.org

Martha Fedor, Editor-in-Chief
Herbet Tabor, Co-Editor

3511 **Journal of Biomolecular Screening**
Sage Publications
2455 Teller Rd
Newbury Park, CA 91320-2234

805-499-9774
800-818-7243
Fax: 805-499-0871
E-Mail: journals@sagepub.com
Home Page: www.sagepub.com

Blaise R Simqu, CEO
Mark Beggs, Associate Editor
Stein Roaldset, Advertising Editor
Christine Giordano, Society Updates Editor
Charles Hart, New Products Editor

An official publication of the Society for Biomolecular Sciences. Peer-reviewed publication on drug discovery sciences, with an emphasis on screening methods and technologies; Information on the latest biomolecular sciences, with regular topics including: target identification/validation assay development methods, and technologies, lead generation/optimization, virtual screening/chemo-informatics, data and image analysis, sample management, biomarkers and legal/licensing issues.
Cost: $610.00
Frequency: 10x year/Price Varies
ISSN: 1087-0571
Founded in 1994

3512 **Journal of the North American Benthological Society**
The North American Benthological Society
PO Box 7065
Lawrence, KS 66044-7065

254-399-9636
Fax: 785-843-1274
E-Mail: info@freshwater-science.org
Home Page: www.benthos.org

Pamela Silver, Managing Editor
Irwin Polls, Business Manager

Articles that will promote further understanding of benthic communities and their role in aquatic ecosystems

3513 **Lab Animal**
Nature Publishing Group
1270 Broadway
6th Floor, Suite 807
New York, NY 10001-3224

212-278-8600
Fax: 212-564-0217
E-Mail: info@labanimal.com
Home Page: www.labanimal.com

Angelo Notaro, Partner
Rachel Burley, Publisher
Richard Charkin, CEO

A peer-reviewed journal for professionals in animal research, emphasizing proper management and care. Offers the latest on animal models, breeds, breeding practices, in vitro and computer models, lab care, nutrition, and improved animal handling techniques. Offers timely and informative material, reaching both the academic research world and applied research industries, including genetic engineering, human therapeutics and pharmaceutical companies.
Cost: $159.00
Founded in 1869

3514 **Molecular Plant: Microbe Interactions**
American Phytopatholgical Society
3340 Pilot Knob Road
Saint Paul, MN 55121-2097

651-454-7250
800-328-7560
Fax: 651-454-0766
E-Mail: aps@scisoc.org
Home Page: www.apsnet.org

Steve Nelson, Executive VP
Amy Hope, VP of Operations
Barbara Mock, VP Finance

Molecular biology and molecular genetics of pathological, symbiotic and associative interactions of microbes with plants, including plant response.
Frequency: Monthly
ISSN: 0894-0282
Mailing list available for rent

3515 **Nature**
Nature Publishing Group
1270 Broadway
Suite 807
New York, NY 10001-3224

212-278-8600
800-221-2123
Fax: 212-564-0217
E-Mail: nature@natureny.com
Home Page: www.nature.com

Angelo Notaro, Partner
Josie Natori, CEO

A reliable source of up-to-date scientific information. Publishes papers from any area of science with great potential impact. Also publishes a broad range of informal material in the form of opinion articles, news stories, briefings and recruitment features, and contributed material.
Frequency: Monthly
Circulation: 60289

3516 **Nature Biotechnology**
Nature America
345 Park Avenue S
10th Floor
New York, NY 10010-1707

212-726-9200
800-221-2123
Fax: 212-696-9635
E-Mail: biotech@natureny.com
Home Page: www.biotech.nature.com

Andrew Marshall, Editor
Richard Charkin, CEO
Annette Thomas, Managing Director

Philip Campbell, Editor-in-Chief
Peter Collins, Publishing Director

A monthly magazine of biotechnology news and research.
Cost: $178.00
550 Pages
Frequency: Monthly
Circulation: 18798
ISSN: 1054-0156
Founded in 1983
Printed in 4 colors on glossy stock

3517 **Protein Science**
Protein Society
9650 Rockville Pike
Bethesda, MD 20814-3999

301-634-7240
800-992-6466
Fax: 301-634-7271
E-Mail: cyablonski@proteinsociety.org
Home Page: www.proteinsociety.org

Cynthia A Yablonski, Executive Officer
Arthur G Palmer III, President
Jean Baum, Secretary/Treasurer
2100 Members
Founded in 1986
Mailing list available for rent: 3,000 names at $200 per M

3518 **Science Illustrated**
Communications Solutions
8428 Holly Leaf Drive
McLean, VA 22102-2224

703-356-1688
Fax: 202-296-1857
Home Page: http://www.scienceillustrated.com/

Tod Herbers, Editor

Provides physicians with information on research and development in the fields of science related to medicine.
Cost: $18.00
Circulation: 103200
Printed in 4 colors on glossy stock

Trade Shows

3519 **AAB Annual Meeting and Education Conference**
American Association of Bioanalysts
906 Olive Street
Suite 1200
Saint Louis, MO 63101-1448

314-241-1445
Fax: 314-241-1449
E-Mail: aab@aab.org
Home Page: www.aab.org
Social Media: Facebook, Twitter, LinkedIn

Mark S Birenbaum PhD, Administrator

Educational programs, abstract presentations, poster presentations and exhibits
Founded in 1956

3520 **Biometrics Technology Expo and Consortium Conference**
J Spargo & Associates
11208 Waples Mill Road
Suite 112
Fairfax, VA 22030

703-631-6200
800-564-4220
Fax: 703-654-6931
E-Mail: info@biometrics.org
Home Page: www.biometrics.org

Jeffrey Dunn, Chair
Fernando Podio, Chair

Co-located with the Biometric Consortium Conference, this event offers unparalleled opportunities to reach top buyers, federal and state agencies and leading industry corporations.
2000 Attendees
Frequency: September

3521 **Biophysical Society Annual Meeting**
Biophysical Society
11400 Rockville Pike
Suite 800
Bethesda, MD 20852

240-290-5600
Fax: 240-290-5555
E-Mail: society@biophysics.org
Home Page: www.biophysics.org

Ro Kampman, Executive Officer
Harris Povich, Director of Finance and Operations
Vida Ess, Programs Coordinator

Includes 3,000 poster presentations, 200 exhibits, 20 symposias, workshops, platform sessions, and subgroup meetings. It is also the worlds largest meeting for biophysicists.
6M Attendees
Frequency: February/March
Mailing list available for rent

3522 **Biotechnology Investment Conference**
Massachusetts Biotechnology Council
One Cambridge Center
Cmabridge, MA 02142

617-674-5100
Fax: 617-674-5101
E-Mail: inforequest@massbio.org
Home Page: www.massbio.org
Social Media: Facebook, Twitter, LinkedIn, Youtube

Geoffrey Cox, Chairman
Geoff McKay, Vice Chair
Michael Ohara, Treasurer

New England's largest biotechnology investor forum. Allows more than 70 local public and private companies to showcase their technologies and products in front of portfolio managers, analysts, venture capitalists and other investment professionals.
700 Attendees
Frequency: November

3523 **Int'l Conference on Strategic Business Information in Biotechnology**
Institute for Biotechnology Information
3200 Chapel Hill/Nelson Boulevard Suite 201
PO Box 14569
Research Triangle Park, NC 27709-4569

919-544-5111
Fax: 919-544-5401
E-Mail: info@bioability.com
Home Page: www.biotechinfo.com

For strategists, company managers, information specialists, financial analysts or users of strategic business information in biotechnology.
150 Attendees
Frequency: October

Directories & Databases

3524 **BioWorld Online**
3525 Piedmont Road
Building 6, Suite 400
Atlanta, GA 30305

404-262-5476
800-688-2421
Fax: 404-814-0759
E-Mail: customerservice@bioworld.com
Home Page: www.bioworld.com

Randy Osborne

This database contains a variety of information on biotechnology companies, products, and services.
Frequency: Full-text

3525 **Biosis/Thomson Scientific**
BIOSIS
1500 Spring Garden St
Fourth Floor
Philadelphia, PA 19130-4067

215-386-0100
800-336-4474
Fax: 215-386-2911
Home Page: www.biosis.org/support; scientific.thomson.com
Social Media: Facebook, Twitter, LinkedIn

Vin Caraher, President/CEO
Keith MacGregor, Executive VP
Andrea Degutis, Senior VP/Communications

A bibliographic database covering worldwide research on all biological and biomedical topics. Records contain bibliographic data, indexing information, and abstracts for most references. Biosis joined with the Thomson Corporation in early 2006 to expand its global presence.
Frequency: Updated Weekly

Industry Web Sites

3526 **http://gold.greyhouse.com**
G.O.L.D Grey House OnLine Databases

Grey House Publishing's online database platform, GOLD, offers Quick Search, Keyword Search and Expert Search for most business sectors, including scientific, technical and biotechnical markets. The GOLD platform makes finding the information you need quick and easy - whether you're a novice searcher or an experienced database user. All of Grey House's directory products are available for subscription on the GOLD platform.

3527 **www.aesociety.org**
Electrophoresis Society

International organization founded to improve and promote technologies necessary for biomolecular separation and detection.

3528 **www.asbmb.org**
American Society for Biochemistry and Molecular

Serves members who teach and conduct research at colleges and universities and in various government laboratories, nonprofit research institutions and industry.

3529 **www.asrm.org**
American Society for Reproductive Medicine

Organization devoted to advancing knowledge and expertise in reproductive medicine and biology. Members of this voluntary nonprofit organization must demonstrate the high ethical principals of the medical profession, evince an interest in reproductive medicine and biology, and adhere to the objectives of the Society.

3530 **www.benthos.org**
North American Benthological Society

International scientific organization whose purpose is to promote better understanding of the biotic communities of lake and stream bottoms and their role in aquatic ecosystems, by providing media and disseminating new investigation results, new interpetations, and other benthological information to aquatic biologists and to the scientific community at large.

3531 **www.bio.org**
Biotechnology Industry Organization
For firms involved in the use of recombinant DNA, hybridoma and immulogical technologies in a wide range of applications including human health care, animal husbandry, agriculture and specialty chemical production.

3532 **www.greyhouse.com**
Grey House Publishing
Authoritative reference directories for most business markets including science, technical and biotechnical markets. Users can search the online databases with varied search criteria allowing for custom searches by product category, geographic area, sales volume, keyword, subject and more. Full Grey House catalog and online ordering also available.

3533 **www.ismrm.org**
Int'l Society for Magnetic Resonance in Medicine
For physicians and scientists promoting the applications of magnetic resonance techniques to medicine and biology. The Society holds annual scientific meetings and sponsors other major educational and scientific workshops.

3534 **www.massbio.org**
Massachusetts Biotechnology Council
Organization that provides services and support for the Massachusets biotechnology industry.

3535 **www.proteinsociety.org**
Protein Society
Formed in 1986 to promote international interactions among investigators in order to explore all aspects of the building blocks of life, protien molecules. Members come from universities, foundations, institutes and corporations to provide leadership in this broad field of research. The Society and its members are making a strong impact on the advancements of protien science.

3536 **www.whybiotech.com**
Council for Biotechnology Information
Serves to improve understanding and acceptance of biotechnology by collecting balanced, credible and science based information, then communicating this information through a variety of channels.

Associations

3537 **American Boat Builders and Repairers Association**
1075 SE 17th Street
Fort Lauderdale, FL 33316

954-654-7821
Fax: 954-239-2600
E-Mail: info@abbra.org
Home Page: www.abbra.org
Social Media: Facebook, Twitter, LinkedIn

John Fitzgerald, President
Graham Wright, VP
Peter Sabo, Treasurer
Ron Gift, Secretary

Trade association for marinas, boat builders and repairers. Also offers a monthly newsletter and training seminars.
300 Members
Founded in 1943

3538 **American Boat and Yacht Council Association**
613 Third Street
Suite 10
Annapolis, MD 21403

410-990-4460
Fax: 410-990-4466
E-Mail: info@abycinc.org
Home Page: www.abycinc.org
Social Media: Facebook, Twitter, LinkedIn, Youtube

John Adey, President

A not-for-profit membership organization that has been developing and updating the safety standards for boat building and repair.
4000+ Members
Founded in 1954

3539 **American Boating Association**
PO Box 690
New Market, MD 21774

614-497-4088
E-Mail: admin@americanboating.org
Home Page: www.americanboating.org
Social Media: Facebook, RSS

Bill Condon, Founder/President

Through their membership in the American Boating Association, boaters and boating enthusiasts from across the nation share a common mission - working together to improve the safety, affordability, environmental cleanliness, growth and fun of our sport.
Cost: $10.00
30000 Members

3540 **American Power Boat Association**
17640 E. Nine Mile Road
Po Box 377
Eastpointe, MI 48021-0377

586-773-9700
Fax: 586-773-6490
E-Mail: apbahq@apba-racing.com
Home Page: www.apba-racing.com
Social Media: Facebook, Twitter, LinkedIn, Youtube, RSS

Dan Wiener, Executive Director
John Flynn, Creative Director
Sabrina Haudek, Membership Coordinator

The nation's authority on power boat racing which sanctions over 200 races each year.
6000 Members
Founded in 1903

3541 **American Sail Training Association**
29 Touro Street
PO Box 1459
Newport, RI 02840

401-846-1775
Fax: 401-849-5400
E-Mail: asta@tallshipsamerica.org
Home Page: www.tallships.sailtraining.org
Social Media: Facebook, Twitter, LinkedIn

Mike Rauworth, Chairman
Caleb Pifer, Vice Chair
Eric Shaw, Vice Chair
Dexter Donham, Treasurer
Capt. Christoph Rowsom, Secretary

Supports all those involved with sail training ships and programs, as well as ships under construction or renovation.
300 Members
Founded in 1973

3542 **American Society of Marine Artists**
P.O.Box 247
Smithfield, VA 23430

757-357-3785
E-Mail: asma1978@verizon.net
Home Page: www.americansocietyofmarineartists.com
Social Media: Facebook, Twitter, LinkedIn

Russ Kramer, President
Kim Shaklee, Vice President
Mike Killelea, Secretary
Peter Maytham, Treasurer/Managing Director

A non-profit, tax exempt organization, whose objective is to recognize and promote marine art and history, and to encourage cooperation among artists, historians, marine enthusiasts and others in activities related to marine art and maritime history.
500+ Members
Founded in 1978

3543 **Antique & Classic Boat Society**
422 James St
Clayton, NY 13624

315-686-2628
Fax: 315-686-2680
E-Mail: hqs@acbs.org
Home Page: www.acbs.org
Social Media: Facebook, Twitter, LinkedIn

Teresa Hoffman, President
Brian Gagnon, Senior VP
Jeff Funk, Second VP
Kathy Parker, Secretary
Dick Winn, Treasurer

Society devoted to disseminating information on building and restoring wooden and antique boats.
12000 Members
Founded in 1975

3544 **Association of Marina Industries**
50 Water Street
Warren, RI 02885

866-367-6622
Fax: 401-247-0074
E-Mail: info@marinaassociation.org
Home Page: www.marinaassociation.org
Social Media: Facebook, Twitter, LinkedIn

Jim Frye, CMM, Chairman/President
Gary Groenewold, Vice Chairman
Jeff Rose, Treasurer

The Association of Marina Industries is the international trade marine association for the marina industry.
800+ Members
Founded in 1986

3545 **Boat Owners Association of the US**
880 South Pickett Street
Alexandria, VA 22304

703-412-2770
800-395-2628
Fax: 703-461-2847
E-Mail: mail@baotus.com
Home Page: www.boatus.com
Social Media: Facebook, Twitter, Youtube

Richard Schwartz, Chairman/Founder
Bill Oakerson, CEO
Margaret Podlich, President

Supports all who are involved with legislation, regulations and consumer aspects of the industry.
62500 Members
Founded in 1966

3546 **Boating Writers International**
108 Ninth Street
Wilmette, IL 60091

847-736-4142
E-Mail: info@bwi.org
Home Page: www.bwi.org
Social Media: LinkedIn

John Woolridge, President
Alan Wendt, 1st VP
Lindsey Johnson, 2nd VP

A non-profit professional organization consisting of writers, broadcasters, editors, photgraphers, public relations specialists and others in the communications profession associated with the boating industry.
Founded in 1970

3547 **Coastal Yachting Academy**
PO Box 10441
St. Petersburg, FL 33733

727-867-9466
E-Mail: info@yachtdeliveries.com
Home Page: www.charternet.com/charters/donharper/index.html

Don Harper, Captain/Owner

To provide the recreational boater reasonably priced training equal to the training of professional mariners.
Founded in 1970

3548 **Marine Retailers Association of America**
8401 73rd Ave N
Suite 71
Minneapolis, MN 55428

763-315-8043
E-Mail: matt@mraa.com
Home Page: www.mraa.com

Steve Baum, Chairman
Randy Wattenbarger, Vice Chair
Joe Lewis, Secretary/Treasurer

Manufacturers and dealers of boats, equipment, supplies and services.
3000 Members
Founded in 1971

3549 **Marine Safety Foundation**
5050 Industrial Rd
Suite 2
Wall Township, NJ 07727-4044

732-751-0295
Fax: 732-751-0508
E-Mail: msf@marinesafety.org
Home Page: www.marinesafety.org

Burt Thompson, Executive Director

Advances the safety of life at sea through research, education and coordination.
131 Members
Founded in 1993

3550 **National Association of Charterboat Operators**
PO Box 7208
Diberville, MS 39540

866-981-5136
Fax: 877-263-8548
E-Mail: info@nacocharters.org
Home Page: www.nacocharters.org

Capt. Tom Baker, President
Ed O'Brien, Vice President
Robert Rush, Second Vice President
Gary Krein, Secretary
Ron Maglio, Treasurer

A national association of charterboat owners and operators that represent thousands of individuals across the United States.
3600+ Members
Founded in 1991

3551 **National Association of Sailing**
15 Maritime Drive
PO Box 1260
Portsmouth, RI 02871-0907

401-683-0800
800-877-2451
Fax: 401-683-0840
E-Mail: info@ussailing.org
Home Page: www.ussailing.org
Social Media: Facebook, Twitter, LinkedIn

Tom Hubbell, President
Bruce Burton, Vice President
Patty Lawrence, Secretary
Taran Teague, Treasurer
Jack Gierhart, Executive Director

Accredits sailing schools, certifies instructors and provides teaching and management information. Publishes a newsletter and directory of American sailing schools and charter operators. Provides free consulting services for start-ups of new schools.
100 Members
Frequency: Quarterly
Founded in 1980
Mailing list available for rent

3552 **National Association of State Boating Law Administrators**
1648 McGrathiana Parkway
Suite 360
Lexington, KY 40511

859-225-9487
Fax: 859-231-6403
E-Mail: info@nasbla.org
Home Page: www.nasbla.org
Social Media: Facebook, Twitter, LinkedIn, Flickr, Foursquare

John Johnson, Executive Director
Tom Hayward, Finance & Administration
Ron Sarver, Deputy Director

Representing the recreational boating authorities of all 50 States and U.S. territories. To strengthen the ability of the State and territorial boating authorities to reduce death, injury and property damage associated with recreational boating.
56 Members
Founded in 1960

3553 **National Marine Bankers Association**
231 South LaSalle St
Suite 2050
Chicago, IL 60604

312-946-6260
E-Mail: info@marinebankers.org
Home Page: www.marinebankers.org
Social Media: LinkedIn

Michael Bryant, President
Peggy Bodenreider, VP
William B Otto, Treasurer
Jayme B Yates, Secretary
Jackie Forese, Executive Director

Created for the purpose of educating current and prospective lenders in marine financing procedures, promoting the extension of credit to consumer and trade borrowers.
81 Members
Founded in 1979

3554 **National Marine Distributors Association**
37 Pratt St
Suite 3
Essex, CT 06426-1159

860-767-7898
Fax: 860-767-7932
E-Mail: executivedirector@nmdaonline.com
Home Page: www.nmdaonline.com

Nancy Cueroni, Executive Director
John Rothermel, President
Rick Chang, Vice President
Ryan Barber, Secretary/Treasurer

Wholesale distributors of marine accessories and hardware.
200 Members
Mailing list available for rent

3555 **National Marine Electronics Association**
7 Riggs Ave
Severna Park, MD 21146

410-975-9425
800-808-6632
Fax: 410-975-9450
E-Mail: info@nmea.org
Home Page: www.nmea.org
Social Media: Facebook

David Gratton, Chairman
Johnny Lindstrom, Vice Chairman
Christopher Harley, Secretary
Marilyn S Quarders, Treasurer
Ken Harrison, International Executive Director

Is the unifying force behind the entire marine electronics industry, bringing together all aspects of the industry for the betterment of all in our business.
400 Members
Founded in 1957

3556 **National Marine Manufacturers Association**
231 South LaSalle St
Suite 2050
Chicago, IL 60604

312-946-6200
Home Page: www.nmma.org
Social Media: Twitter

Thomas Dammrich, President
Ben Wold, EVP
Craig Boskey, VP Finance, CFO

Dedicated to creating, promoting and protecting an environment where members can achieve financial success through excellence in manufacturing, selling and service for their customers.
1400+ Members
Founded in 1979

3557 **National Marine Representative Association**
1333 Delany Road #500
PO Box 360
Gurnee, IL 60031

847-662-3167
Fax: 847-336-7126
E-Mail: info@nmraonline.org
Home Page: www.nmraonline.org

Ken Smaga, President
Brandon Flack, VP
Rob Gueterman, Treasurer
Dave Borgaard, Secretary

A national organization serving marine industry independent sales reps and the marine manufacturers who sell through reps.
300 Members
Founded in 1960

3558 **National Safe Boating Council**
PO Box 509
Bristow, VA 20136

703-361-4294
Fax: 703-361-5294
Home Page: www.safeboatingcouncil.org
Social Media: Facebook, Twitter, LinkedIn, Youtube

Chris Edmondston, Chairman
Richard Moore, Vice Chairman
Chris Stec, Treasurer
Betsy Woods, Secretary

NSBC has an interest in boating safety and education to reduce accidents and enhance the boating experience.
350 Members
Founded in 1958
Mailing list available for rent

3559 **Northwest Marine Trade Association**
1900 N Northlake Way
Suite 233
Seattle, WA 98103-9087

206-634-0911
Fax: 206-632-0078
E-Mail: info@nmta.net
Home Page: www.nmta.net
Social Media: Facebook, Twitter, LinkedIn, Youtube, Pinterest, RSS

Bruce Hedrick, Chairman
Mark Helgen, Vice Chair
Patricia Segulja Lau, Secretary/Treasurer
700+ Members
Founded in 1947

3560 **Offshoreonly**
PO Box 10868
St Petersburg, FL 33733

954-463-1101
Fax: 727-394-2451
E-Mail: offshoreonly@offshoreonly.com
Home Page: www.offshoreonly.com

Kathe Walker, President
Scott Ryerson, VP

OSO is a nonprofit organization catering to fun loving boaters in the Tampa/Clearwater/St. Petersburg areas of Florida.
Mailing list available for rent

3561 **Personal Watercraft Industry Association**
National Marine Manufacturers Association
231 South Lasalle Street
Suite 2050
Chicago, IL 60604

202-737-9761
Fax: 202-280-6951
E-Mail: ddickerson@nmma.org
Home Page: www.pwia.org

David Dickerson, Executive Director
Nicole Vasilaros, State Gov't Relations Manager
Trade association representing manufacturers of personal watercraft.
Founded in 1987

3562 **Propeller Club of the United States**
3927 Old Lee Hwy
Suite 101A
Fairfax, VA 22030-2422

703-691-2777
Fax: 703-691-4173

E-Mail: shannon@propellerclubhq.com
Home Page: www.propellerclubhq.com

Thomas Allegretti, President/CEO
Niels Aalund, Sr. Vice President
Shannon Hendrickson-Pluta, Admin Asst

Dedicated to the enhancement and well-being of all interests of the maritime community on a national and international basis.
10000 Members
Founded in 1927
Mailing list available for rent

3563 **Recreational Boaters of California**
925 L Street
Suite 220
Sacramento, CA 95814

E-Mail: rboc@rboc.org
Home Page: www.rboc.org
Social Media: Twitter

Jack Michael, President
Otis Brock, Secretary/Treasurer
Jerry Desmond Jr., Director Govt. Relations
Jerry Desmond, EVP

Monitors the proceedings in the State Capitol, reviewing each of the bills that are introduced and/or amended as to whether they would have an impact on boating.
Founded in 1968

3564 **Shipbuilders Council of America**
655 Fifteenth St NW
Suite 225
Washington, DC 20005

202-347-5462
Fax: 202-347-5464
E-Mail: preever@balljanik.com
Home Page: www.shipbuilders.org
Social Media: Facebook

Matt Paxton, President

Represents the U.S. shipyard industry. SCA members build, repair and service America's fleet of commercial vessels.
73 Members
Founded in 1920

3565 **Society of Accredited Marine Surveyors**
7855 Argyle Forest Blvd
Suite 203
Jacksonville, FL 32244

904-384-1494
800-344-9077
Fax: 904-388-3958
E-Mail: samshq@marinesurvey.org
Home Page: www.marinesurvey.org

Joseph B Lobley, President
Stuart J. McLea, Executive Vice President
Llyod E. Kittredge, Secretary/Treasurer

Dedicated to the advancement of the profession of marine surveying
1000 Members
Founded in 1986

3566 **Texas Dragon Boat Association**
PO Box 980972
Houston, TX 77098

832-687-7208
E-Mail: info@texasdragonboat.com
Home Page: www.houstondragonboat.com
Social Media: Facebook, Twitter

Michael Jhin, Chairman
Eve Marie Ruhlman, President/Executive Director

Promotes the tradition and sport of dragon boating; increases the awareness of Asian and Asian-American culture; and enhances cross-cultural understanding.

3567 **Traditional Small Craft Association**
PO Box 350
Mystic, CT 06355

Home Page: www.tsca.net
Social Media: Facebook

Andy Wolfe, President
Tom Shephard, Vice President
Pete Mathews, Secretary
Chuck Meyer, Treasurer

Nonprofit, tax-exempt educational organization which works to preserve and continue the living traditions, skills, lore and legends surrounding working and pleasure watercraft whose origins predate the marine gasoline engine.

3568 **U.S. Industrial Fabrics Association International**
1801 County Road B W
Roseville, MN 55113-4061

651-222-2508
800-225-4324
Fax: 651-631-9334
E-Mail: generalinfo@ifai.com
Home Page: www.ifai.com
Social Media: Facebook, LinkedIn

Mary J Hennessy, President & CEO
Todd V Lindemann, VP, Conference Management
Dan McCarthy, VP, Finance/CFO
Pam Egan-Blahna, Director, Human Resource
Andrew M Aho, Director, Memberships & Divisions

The mission of the United States Industrial Fabrics Institute (USIFI) is to build a strong coalition of US fiber, fabric, and end product manufacturers and to serve member company interests both domestically and internationally. USIFI is part of the not-for-profit Industrial Fabrics Association International (www.ifai.com), the global association for the specialty fabrics industry.
2000 Members
Founded in 1912

3569 **United States Power Squadrons**
1504 Blue Ridge Rd
Raleigh, NC 27607-3906

919-821-0281
888-367-8777
Fax: 888-304-0813
Home Page: www.usps.org
Social Media: Facebook, Twitter, LinkedIn, Youtube

Frank A. Dvorak, Executive Officer

A non-profit, educational organization dedicated to making boating safer and more enjoyable by teaching classes in seamanship, navigation and related subjects.
45000 Members
Founded in 1914

3570 **United States Rowing Association**
2 Wall Street
Princeton, NJ 08540

609-751-0700
800-314-4769
Fax: 609-924-1578
E-Mail: members@usrowing.org
Home Page: www.usrowing.org
Social Media: Facebook, Twitter, Flickr, Youtube

Peter Cipollone, President
Christine Collins, VP

Non-profit membership organization, recognized by the U.S. Olympic Committee as the national governing body for the sport of rowing in the United States.
16000 Members
Founded in 1982

3571 **United States Sailing Association**
15 Maritime Drive
PO Box 1260
Portsmouth, RI 02871-0907

401-683-0800
800-877-2451
Fax: 401-683-0840
E-Mail: info@ussailing.org
Home Page: www.ussailing.org
Social Media: Facebook, Twitter, LinkedIn, Youtube, RSS

Tom Hubbell, Us Sailing President
Jack Gierhart, Executive Director

National governing body for the sport of sailing.
100 Members
Founded in 1980

3572 **Yacht Brokers Association of America**
105 Eastern Avenue
Suite 104
Annapolis, MD 21403

410-940-6345
Fax: 410-263-1659
E-Mail: info@ybaa.com
Home Page: www.ybaa.com
Social Media: Facebook, Twitter, LinkedIn

Linda Warren, President
Gerry Laster, VP
Hal Slater, Treasurer
Vincent J Petrella, Executive Director
Joseph Thompson, General Manager

Sets the standards for professional yacht brokers throughout North America
250 Members
Founded in 1920

3573 **Yachting Club of America**
PO Box 1040
Marco Island, FL 34146

239-642-4448
Fax: 239-642-5284
E-Mail: ycaol@hotmail.com
Home Page: www.ycaol.com

David Martin, Owner

A membership organization dedicated to the advancement of yachting.
30000 Members
Founded in 1963

Newsletters

3574 **ASMA News**
American Society of Marine Artists
P.O.Box 247
Smithfield, VA 23430

757-357-3785
E-Mail: asma1978@verizon.net
Home Page:
www.americansocietyofmarineartists.com

Keeps you up to date with all of the Society's activities, along with providing space where artists like yourself can share ideas, inspirations, tips and even frustrations. Provides you access to the Society's network of members, local and national marine art news and information about art exhibitions and exhibition opportunities.
Frequency: Quarterly

3575 **American Boat & Yacht Council News**
American Boat and Yacht Council
613 Third Street
Suite 10
Annapolis, MD 21403

410-990-4460
Fax: 410-990-4466

E-Mail: info@abycinc.org
Home Page: www.abycinc.org

George Bellwoar, Chairman
Jack Horner, Vice Chair
F. Steven Herb, Treasurer

News and technical information of interest to ABYC members.
4000+ Members
8 Pages
Frequency: Quarterly
Founded in 1954
Mailing list available for rent

3576 **American Boat Builders and Repairers Association Newsletter**
American Boat Builders and Repairers Association
50 Water Street
Warren, RI 02885

401-247-0318
866-367-6622
Fax: 401-247-0074
Home Page: www.abbra.org

Jonathan Jones Haven, President
Peter Sabo, VP
Mark Amaral, Managing Director
Charles Teran, Treasurer/Secretary

Accepts advertising.
300 Members
4 Pages
Frequency: Monthly
Founded in 1943

3577 **Anchor Line Newsletter**
National Safe Boating Council
PO Box 509
Bristow, VA 20136

703-361-4294
Fax: 703-361-5294
Home Page: www.safeboatingcouncil.org
Social Media: Facebook, Twitter

Joyce Shaw, Chairman
Lynda Nutt, Vice Chairman
Virgil Chambers, Executive Officer
Sandy Smith, Chief Financial Officer
350 Members
Founded in 1958

3578 **Business of Pleasure Boats**
National Marine Bankers Association
231 South LaSalle St
Suite 2050
Chicago, IL 60604

312-946-6260
E-Mail: bmcardle@nmma.org
Home Page: www.marinebankers.org
Social Media: LinkedIn

Karen Trostle, President
Jackie Forese, Director
Mike Ryan, Vice President
Bernice McArdlen, Manager
81 Members
Frequency: Quarterly
Founded in 1979

3579 **MRAA Bearings**
Marine Retailers Association of America
P.O.Box 725
Boca Grande, FL 33921-0725

941-964-2534
Fax: 941-531-6777
E-Mail: mraa@mraa.com
Home Page: www.mraa.com

Phil Keeter, President
Marge Eckenroad, Executive Administrator
Larry Innis, Director Government Affairs
Marge Eckenroad, Executive Administrator

A publication encompassing issues that you need to know about, issues such as legislation, environment and compliance, legal, association and industry news, and much more.
3000 Members
Frequency: Monthly
Circulation: 2000
Founded in 1971

3580 **Mainsheet**
Rhodes 19 Class Association
174 Walnut Street
Reading, MA 01867

781-944-2697
E-Mail: info@rhodes19.org
Home Page: www.rhodes19.org
Social Media: Facebook

Steve Uhl, President
Mary Kovats, Secretary
Tom Carville, Treasurer

Newsletter concerning the Rhodes 19 design sailboat. Our mission is to promote Rhodes 19 racing by encouraging and supporting local fleet development nationally, and by working to maintain the one-design integrity of the boat.
Founded in 1965

3581 **Marine Safety and Security Report**
Stamler Publishing Company
178 Thimble Islands Rd
PO Box 3367
Branford, CT 06405-1967

203-488-9808
800-422-4121
Fax: 203-488-3129
E-Mail: sstamler@ix.netcom.net

S Paul Stamler, President/CEO

Business-to-business newsletter providing information on boating and shipping safety and enforcement issues, including federal regulations and Coast Guard Actions, state safety programs, IMO activity, classification studies, vessel recalls, and safety equipment. Accepts no advertising and is solely supported by subscribers worldwide.
Cost: $77.00
4 Pages
Founded in 1973
Printed in 2 colors on matte stock

3582 **Maritime Reporter and Engineering News**
118 East 25th Street
New York, NY 10010

212-477-6700
Fax: 212-254-6271
E-Mail: jomalley@marinelink.com
Home Page: www.marinelink.com

John O'Malley, Publisher
Greg Trauthwein, Associate Publisher
Michael Martino, Owner
Lucia M Annunziata, VP
Jennifer Rabulan, Technical Editor

Provides unparalleled coverage of the maritime industry covering the inland, Coastal and Great Lakes region.
95000 Members
Frequency: Monthly
Circulation: 50000
Founded in 1999

3583 **NACO Newsletter**
National Association of Charterboat Operators
PO Box 2990
Orange Beach, AL 36561

251-981-5136
Fax: 251-981-8191
E-Mail: info@nacocharters.org
Home Page: www.nacocharters.org

Bob Zales II, President
Ed O'Brien, Vice President
Tom Becker, Second Vice President
Gary Krein, Secretary
3600+ Members
Frequency: Quarterly
Circulation: 3500
Founded in 1991

3584 **Propeller Club Newsletter**
Propeller Club of the United States
3927 Old Lee Hwy
Suite 101A
Fairfax, VA 22030-2422

703-691-2777
Fax: 703-691-4173
E-Mail: shannon@propellerclubhq.com
Home Page: www.propellerclubhq.com

Thomas Allegretti, President/CEO
Niels Aalund, Sr. Vice President
Shannon Hendrickson-Pluta, Admin Asst
Virgil R Allen, VP Development

Features expanded coverage of Propeller Club activities, including legislative and regulatory reports, feature-length member profiles, regional news and expanded coverage of national maritime issues.
10000 Members
Frequency: Quarterly
Founded in 1927

3585 **Rudder**
Antique & Classic Boat Society
422 James St
Clayton, NY 13624-1136

315-686-2628
Fax: 315-686-2680
E-Mail: hqs@acbs.org
Home Page: www.acbs.org
Social Media: Facebook, Twitter

Jim Mersman, President
Dunc Hawkins, First VP
Teresa Hoffman, Second VP
Dick Winn, Treasurer
Brian Gagnon, Secretary

Historical news and how-to-restore wooden and antique boats.
12000 Members
Frequency: Quarterly
Founded in 1975
Printed in 4 colors

3586 **SAMS Newsletter**
Society of Accredited Marine Surveyors
7855 Argyle Forest Blvd
Suite 203
Jacksonville, FL 32244

904-384-1494
800-344-9077
Fax: 904-388-3958
E-Mail: samshq@marinesurvey.org
Home Page: www.marinesurvey.org

Joseph B Lobley, President
Stuart J. McLea, Executive Vice President
Llyod E. Kittredge, Secretary/Treasurer

For members.
1000 Members
Frequency: 4/Year
Circulation: 1000
Founded in 1986

3587 **Seamanship Training**
American Boating Association
PO Box 456
Centerville, MA 02632

508-534-9893
E-Mail: admin@americanboating.org
Home Page: www.americanboating.org
Social Media: Facebook

Bill Condon, Founder/President

Free to all ABA (American Boating Association) members as well as all boaters. Informative content on boating skills and safety issues.
30000 Members
Frequency: Bi-Monthly

3588 Shipyard Chronicle Newsletter
Shipbuilders Council of America
655 Fifteenth St NW
Suite 225
Washington, DC 20005
202-347-5462
Fax: 202-347-5464
E-Mail: preever@balljanik.com
Home Page: www.shipbuilders.org
Social Media: Facebook
Matt Paxton, President, Vice Chairman
Allen Walker, President
Irene Ringwood, Manager
The publication is devoted to keeping members up to date on the latest legislative and regulatory developments. It also includes a schedule of upcoming association and industry related government meetings, as well as news regarding SCA member companies.
73 Members
Founded in 1920

3589 Soundings Trade Only
Soundings Publications
10 Bokum Rd
Essex, CT 06426-1536
860-767-3200
Fax: 860-767-1048
E-Mail: info@soundingspub.com
Home Page: www.soundingsonline.com
Social Media: Facebook
Ian Bowen, Manager
Peter Mitchel, Publisher
Nation's boating business newspaper. Coverage of the recreational boating business; for marine dealers, marine operators, distributors and manufacturers. BPA audited.
Cost: $13.97
15500 Members
33 Pages
Frequency: Monthly
Circulation: 34,000
Founded in 1965

3590 Tidings
National Marine Representatives Association
1333 Delany Road #500
PO Box 360
Gurnee, IL 60031
847-662-3167
Fax: 847-336-7126
E-Mail: info@nmraonline.org
Home Page: www.nmraonline.org
Chris Kelly, President
Kathy Munzinger, VP
Ken Smaga, Treasurer
Brandon Flack, Secretary
Chris Kelly, Secretary
Contains informative articles to help manufacturers develop sound and profitable relationships with independent sales representatives and keep informed about the marine market in general.
300 Members
500+ Pages
Frequency: Quarterly
Founded in 1960

3591 Water Life
Northwest Marine Trade Association
1900 N Northlake Way
Suite 233
Seattle, WA 98103-9087
206-634-0911
Fax: 206-632-0078
E-Mail: info@nmta.net
Home Page: www.nmta.net
Social Media: Facebook, Twitter, LinkedIn
George Harris, President
Laura Snodgrass, Finance Director
John Thorburn, Vice President
Liz Manning, Membership Director
Provides industry information, member benefits, committee activity and new member announcements and anniversaries. Water Life continues to evolve into a valuable tool for Pacific Northwest marine leaders.
700+ Members
Founded in 1947

3592 Yacht Broker News
Yacht Brokers Association of America
105 Eastern Avenue
Suite 104
Annapolis, MD 21403
410-940-6345
Fax: 410-263-1659
E-Mail: info@ybaa.com
Home Page: www.ybaa.com
Vincent J. Petrella, Executive Director
Rod Rowan, President
Amy Luckado, Membership Director
Reports on latest business issues, industry concerns, legislation, regulatory activities and includes a member-to-member section(WayPoints), where members can report on their own company news, personnel updates and business expansion.
250 Members
Frequency: Quarterly
Founded in 1920

Magazines & Journals

3593 American Sailor
US Sailing Association
15 Maritime Drive
PO Box 1260
Portsmouth, RI 02871-0907
401-683-0800
800-877-2451
Fax: 401-683-0840
E-Mail: info@ussailing.org
Home Page: www.ussailing.org
Social Media: Facebook, Twitter, LinkedIn
Tom Hubbell, Us Sailing President
Jack Gierhart, Executive Director
Fred Hagedorn, Secretary
Jack Gierhart, Executive Director
Boating news.
100 Members
Frequency: Monthly
Founded in 1980

3594 Ash Breeze
Traditional Small Craft Association
PO Box 350
Mystic, CT 06355
E-Mail: drathmarine@rockisland.com
Home Page: www.tsca.net
Mike Wick, Co-Editor
Ned Asplundh, Co-Editor
Devoted to topics ranging from reports from the chapters to technical details and specific designs with lines and offsets. You may find anecdotal accounts of experiences in traditional boats, and tips on how to spile a plank.
Frequency: Quarterly

3595 Boat & Motor Dealer
Preston Publications
6600 W Touhy Ave
PO Box 48312
Niles, IL 60714-4516
847-647-2900
Fax: 847-647-1155
E-Mail: circulation@boatmotordealer.com
Home Page: www.prestonpub.com
Tinsley Preston, Owner
Jerome Koncel, Editorial Director
Dedicated to providing businesses in the recreational marine industry with the information, commentary and analysis needed to expand their businesses and improve profitability.
Founded in 1959
Mailing list available for rent: 30000 names at $100 per M

3596 BoatUS Magazine
Boat Owners Association of the US
880 South Pickett Street
Alexandria, VA 22304-4606
703-461-2864
Fax: 703-461-2845
E-Mail: emagazine@boatus.com
Home Page: www.boatus.com
Social Media: Facebook, Twitter
Michael Vatalaro, Executive Editor
Richard Schwartz, Chairman/Founder
Chris Landers, Associate Editor
Boating magazine includes legislative, travel, safety, DIY, and consumer news of interest to recreational boat owners.
Cost: $19.00
62500 Members
Frequency: Annual/6
Circulation: 500K+
Founded in 1966

3597 Boatbuilder
Belvoir Publishers
PO Box 5656
Norwalk, CT 06856-5656
203-857-4880
Fax: 203-661-4802
E-Mail: customer_service@belvoir.com
Home Page: www.belvoir.com
Robert Englander, Owner/CEO
The magazine is for those who build, modify and repair boats.
Founded in 1972

3598 Boating Industry
Ehlert Publishing Group
6420 Sycamore Ln N
Suite 100
Maple Grove, MN 55369-6014
763-383-4400
800-848-6247
Fax: 763-383-4499
E-Mail: acollins@ehlertpublishing.com
Home Page: www.boatingindustry.com
Social Media: Facebook, Twitter, LinkedIn
Jonathan Sweet, Editor in Chief
Tom Kaiser, Senior Editor
Links together all sectors of the boating market from boat and motor dealers to marinas, boatyards, builders and suppliers. It also provides strategic analysis, in-depth coverage and proprietary research of the most critical issues.
Frequency: 8 Issues/2 Special Issues

3599 Boating Magazine
Bonnier Corporation
460 N. Orlando Ave
Suite 200
Winter Park, FL 32789
407-628-4802
Fax: 407-628-7061

E-Mail: editor@boatingmag.com
Home Page: www.boatingmag.com
Social Media: Facebook, Twitter

John McEver, Publisher
Glenn Hughes, VP
Jonas Bonnier, Chairman

Offers up-to-date information on boats, manufacturers, suppliers, distributors related to the boating industry.
Cost: $17.95
Frequency: Monthly

3600 Canoe & Kayak Magazine
Canoe & Kayak
12025 115th Ave. NE
Suite D200
Kirkland, WA 98034

425-827-6363
800-692-2663
Fax: 425-827-1893
E-Mail: letters@canoekayak.com
Home Page: www.canoekayak.com
Social Media: Facebook, Twitter

Jeff Moag, Editor
Dave Shively, Managing Editor

Published by the Canoe American Associates.
Cost: $17.95
Frequency: 7 Issues
Circulation: 62000
Founded in 1973
Mailing list available for rent

3601 Dry Stack Marina Handbook
Association of Marina Industries
50 Water Street
Warren, RI 02885

866-367-6622
Fax: 401-247-0074
E-Mail: info@marinaassociation.org
Home Page: www.marinaassociation.org
Social Media: Twitter, LinkedIn

Jim Frye, CMM, Chairman/President
Gary Groenewold, Vice Chairman
Jeff Rose, Treasurer
Keith Boulais, Secretary

This book covers: Dry stack buildings and racks, Boat handling equipment, Statistics, Site planning, Typical costs, Fire protection problems & solutions, Comparision of dry stack vs. wet slip demand, Marketing, Facility operations, Lease or purchase decision, Loss control considerations.
Cost: $90.00
800+ Members
Frequency: 61 Illustrations
Founded in 1986

3602 Ensign
United States Power Squadrons
1504 Blue Ridge Rd
Raleigh, NC 27607-3906

919-821-0281
888-367-8777
Fax: 888-304-0813
Home Page: www.usps.org
Social Media: Facebook, Twitter

Frank A. Dvorak, Executive Officer

Ensign magazine is the official magazine of United States Power Squadrons. The mission is to promote recreational boating safety through education and civic activities while providing fellowship for our members.
Cost: $10.00
45000 Members
48 Pages
Frequency: Monthly
Circulation: 35,000
Founded in 1914
Printed in 4 colors on glossy stock

3603 Fabric Architecture
U.S. Industrial Fabrics Association International
1801 County Road B W
Roseville, MN 55113-4061

651-222-2508
800-225-4324
Fax: 651-631-9334
E-Mail: generalinfo@ifai.com
Home Page: www.usifi.com

Stephen Warner, CEO
JoAnne Ferris, Marketing Director

Targets architects, designers, specifiers, contractors and developers promoting the architectural advantages of fabric. Educates the industry about designing with fabric and promoting it as an environmentally-responsible choice.
Frequency: Bimonthly
Circulation: 8,000

3604 Fabric Graphics
Industrial Fabrics Association International
1801 County Road B W
Roseville, MN 55113-4061

651-222-2508
800-225-4324
Fax: 651-631-9334
E-Mail: generalinfo@ifai.com
Home Page: www.ifai.com
Social Media: Facebook, Twitter, LinkedIn

Mary J. Hennessy, Executive VP
JoAnne Farris, Marketing Director
Steven C. Rider, CFO, VP

Created to educate and inspire professionals to use fabric to expand their business. Promotes the use of textiles as a printing medium, showcasing the numerous applications for fabric and the technology needed to achieve good results.
Frequency: Bimonthly
Circulation: 8,000
Founded in 1912

3605 Geosynthetics
Industrial Fabrics Association International
1801 County Road B W
Roseville, MN 55113-4061

651-222-2508
800-225-4324
Fax: 651-631-9334
E-Mail: generalinfo@ifai.com
Home Page: www.ifai.com
Social Media: Facebook, Twitter, LinkedIn

Mary J. Hennessy, Executive VP
JoAnne Farris, Marketing Director
Steven C. Rider, CFO, VP

Targeting those who rely on the publication for the most professional presentation of Geosynthetic products, design, and applications.
Frequency: Bimonthly
Circulation: 14,000
Founded in 1912

3606 InTents
Industrial Fabrics Association International
1801 County Road B W
Roseville, MN 55113-4061

651-222-2508
800-225-4324
Fax: 651-631-9334
E-Mail: generalinfo@ifai.com
Home Page: www.ifai.com
Social Media: Facebook, Twitter, LinkedIn

Mary J. Hennessy, Executive VP
JoAnne Farris, Marketing Director
Steven C. Rider, CFO, VP

Focuses on tents, fabric structures, and accessories that tent renters need to operate a profitable business. The magazine and its website work together to deliver the total tent experience to readers and visitors.
Frequency: Bimonthly
Circulation: 11,000
Founded in 1912

3607 Marina/Dock Age
Preston Publications
6600 W Touhy Ave
Niles, IL 60714-4516

847-647-2900
Fax: 847-647-1155
E-Mail: atownshend@marinadockage.com
Home Page: www.marinadockage.com/
Social Media: Twitter, LinkedIn

Tinsley Preston, Owner
Anna Townshend, Editor

Provide marina/boatyard owners and managers with the information they need to meet ever-changing government regulations, operate more efficiently, expand their business, and improve their profitability.
Cost: $50.00
16500 Members
Frequency: Monthly
Circulation: 24000
Founded in 1989

3608 Marinas and Small Craft Harbors
Association of Marina Industries
50 Water Street
Warren, RI 02885

866-367-6622
Fax: 401-247-0074
E-Mail: info@marinaassociation.org
Home Page: www.marinaassociation.org
Social Media: Twitter, LinkedIn

Jim Frye, CMM, Chairman/President
Gary Groenewold, Vice Chairman
Jeff Rose, Treasurer
Keith Boulais, Secretary

The new edition includes updated and redrawn tables, charts, figures and text editing and additions, as well as newly created information on marina design characteristics of megyachts and test data, design loads, and recommendations on design and performance of dock cleats.
Cost: $89.95
800+ Members
Founded in 1986

3609 Marine Fabricator
Industrial Fabrics Association International
1801 County Road B W
Roseville, MN 55113-4061

651-222-2508
800-225-4324
Fax: 651-631-9334
E-Mail: generalinfo@ifai.com
Home Page: www.ifai.com
Social Media: Facebook, Twitter, LinkedIn

Mary J. Hennessy, Executive VP
JoAnne Farris, Marketing Director
Steven C. Rider, CFO, VP

Educates professionals in the techniques of quality marine craftsmanship and upholstery. Marine shop professionals rely on the magazine to stay informed on the latest techniques, technologies, business management and news. .
Cost: $34.00
Frequency: Bi-Monthly
Circulation: 5,000
Founded in 1912

3610 Marine Log
Simmons-Boardman Publishing Corporation
345 Hudson St
12th Floor, Suite 1201
New York, NY 10014-7123

212-620-7200
Fax: 212-633-1165

E-Mail: marinelog@sbpub.com
Home Page: www.marinelog.com
Social Media: Facebook, Twitter, LinkedIn

Arthur J McGinnis Jr, President
John Snyder, Publisher/Editor in Chief

For more than 130 years, maritime executives worldwide have turned to Marine Log as the source for news and analysis on issues impacting vessel design, construction and operations.
Frequency: Monthly
Circulation: 29934
Founded in 1878

3611 **Marine News**
Maritime Activity Reports
118 East 25th Street
New York, NY 10010

212-477-6700
Fax: 212-254-6271
E-Mail: jomalley@marinelink.com
Home Page: www.marinelink.com

John O'Malley, Publisher
Greg Trauthwein, Associate Publisher
Michael Martino, Owner
Lucia M Annunziata, VP
Jennifer Rabulan, Technical Editor

Features marine industry news and issues effecting maritime activity. Includes updates on vessel building and acquisitions as well as regular columns on research and devleopment, equipment reports and an events calendar.
95000 Members
Frequency: Monthly
Circulation: 23000
Founded in 1999

3612 **Motor Boating**
Time4 Media Marine Group
460 N. Orlando Ave
Suite 200
Winter Park, FL 32789

407-628-4802
Fax: 407-628-7061
E-Mail: editor@motorboating.com
Home Page: www.motorboating.com
Social Media: Facebook, Twitter

Ed Baker, Associate Publisher
John McEver, Publisher
Glenn Hughes, VP

Helps its readers buy, maintain and get the most out of their powerboats. It focuses on powerboats, people, products, destinations, trends and technological developments in the boating market, as well as cruising, water sports and safety.
Frequency: Monthly
Founded in 1907
Printed in on glossy stock

3613 **National Numbering & Titling**
National Association of State Boating Law
1500 Leestown Rd
Suite 330
Lexington, KY 40511-2047

859-225-9487
Fax: 859-231-6403
E-Mail: info@nasbla.org
Home Page: www.nasbla.org
Social Media: Facebook, Twitter, LinkedIn, Flickr, Foursquare

John Johnson, Executive Director
Tom Hayward, Finance & Administration
Ron Sarver, Deputy Director

Facilitate ongoing efforts to evaluate and improve the programs' internal procedures and external interactions in the face of resource constraints and in preparation for implementing the Coast Guard's Vessel Identification System.
Cost: $14.95
56 Members
Founded in 1960
Mailing list available for rent: 56 names

3614 **Paddle Magazine**
Paddle Sport Publishing
12025 115th Ave. NE
Suite D200
Kirkland, WA 98034

970-879-1450
Fax: 970-870-1404
E-Mail: Eugene@paddlermagazine.com
Home Page: www.paddlermagazine.com
Social Media: Facebook, Twitter

Eugene Buchanan, Publisher/Editor
Jeff Moag, Editor
Kevin Thompson, Account Manager

Information to keep the paddle sport equipment dealer up-to-date on issues that will effect their business, industry trends in boats, apparel and accessories, how to articles to assist the reader in selling boats.
Cost: $18.00
Circulation: 5527
Printed in 4 colors on glossy stock

3615 **Paddlesports Business**
Canoe & Kayak
12025 115th Ave. NE
Suite D200
Kirkland, WA 98034

425-827-6363
800-692-2663
Fax: 425-827-1893
E-Mail: letters@canoekayak.com
Home Page: www.canoekayak.com
Social Media: Facebook, Twitter

Jeff Moag, Editor
Dave Shively, Managing Editor

Trade publication for the paddlesports industry.
Founded in 1973
Mailing list available for rent

3616 **Professional BoatBuilder**
WoodenBoat Publications
41 Wooden Boat La
PO Box 78
Brooklin, ME 04616-0078

207-359-4651
800-877-5284
Fax: 207-359-8920
E-Mail: proboat@proboat.com
Home Page: www.proboat.com
Social Media: Facebook

Paul Lazarus, Sr. Editor
Aaron Porter, Editor
Carl Cramer, Co-Director

Focuses on materials, design, and construction techniques and repair solutions chosen by marine professionals. Regular technical articles provide detailed, real-world examples to improve the efficiency and quality of their work.
Cost: $35.95
76 Pages
Circulation: 27500
ISSN: 1043-2035
Founded in 1974
Printed in 4 colors on glossy stock

3617 **Propeller**
American Power Boat Association
17640 E. Nine Mile Road
PO Box 377
Eastpointe, MI 48021-0377

586-773-9700
Fax: 586-773-6490
E-Mail: propeller@apba-racing.com
Home Page: www.apba-racing.com

Mark Weber, President
Gloria Urbin, Executive Director
Tana Moore, News, Propellor

Propeller magazine is the mouthpiece of the American Power Boat Association, the nation's leading authority on power boat racing which sanctions over 200 races each year.
Cost: $2.50
22 Pages
Frequency: Monthly
ISSN: 0194-6218
Printed in 4 colors on glossy stock

3618 **Small Craft Advisory**
National Association of State Boating Law Admnstrs
1500 Leestown Rd
Suite 330
Lexington, KY 40511-2047

859-225-9487
Fax: 859-231-6403
E-Mail: info@nasbla.org
Home Page: www.nasbla.org
Social Media: Facebook, Twitter, LinkedIn, Flickr, Foursquare

John Johnson, Executive Director
Tom Hayward, Finance & Administration
Ron Sarver, Deputy Director

Small Craft Advisory, published bimonthly, is for and about the nation's boating law administration professionals. Authoritative articles featuring practices, procedures, and research in recreational boating safety, marine law enforcement, and boating safety education are presented to enhance the efficiency and effectiveness of recreational boating safety. Each issue highlights successful recreational boating safety programs, NASBLA activities, professional news, and legislative updates
Cost: $14.00
56 Members
Frequency: Bi-Monthly
Circulation: 11000
Founded in 1960
Mailing list available for rent: 56 names

3619 **Southern Boating Magazine**
330 N Andrews Ave
Suite 200
Fort Lauderdale, FL 33301-1025

954-522-5515
888-882-6284
Fax: 954-522-2260
E-Mail: sboating@southernboating.com
Home Page: www.southernboating.com
Social Media: Facebook, Twitter

Skip Allen, Owner/Chairman/Publisher/Editor
L.J. Wallace, Executive Editor
Cathryn Allen-Zubi, VP
Rain Hernandez Rouveroy, VP of Finance
Kellie Mackenroth, Circulation Manager

Focus is on boating in the southern US, Bahamas, and Caribbean.
Cost: $22.95
Frequency: Monthly
Circulation: 42000
Founded in 1972
Printed in 4 colors on matte stock

3620 **Specialty Fabrics Review**
Industrial Fabrics Association International
1801 County Road B W
Roseville, MN 55113-4061

651-222-2508
800-225-4324
Fax: 651-631-9334
E-Mail: generalinfo@ifai.com

Home Page: www.ifai.com
Social Media: Facebook, Twitter, LinkedIn

Mary J. Hennessy, Executive VP
JoAnne Farris, Marketing Director
Steven C. Rider, CFO, VP

In print since 1915, this international publication targets specialty fabric professionals. Each issue brings timely reporting on industry topics, helpful business articles and a review of global news and market updates.
Frequency: Monthly
Circulation: 13000
Founded in 1912

3621 The Reference Point
American Boat and Yacht Council Association
613 Third Street
Suite 10
Annapolis, MD 21403

410-990-4460
Fax: 410-990-4466
E-Mail: info@abycinc.org
Home Page: www.abycinc.org
Social Media: Facebook

George Bellwoar, Chairman
Jack Horner, Vice Chair
F. Steven Herb, Treasurer

ABYC's technical professional quarterly journal.
4000+ Members
Frequency: Quarterly
Founded in 1954

3622 US Yacht Racing Union
US Sailing
15 Maritime Drive
PO Box 1260
Portsmouth, RI 02871-0907

401-683-0800
800-877-2451
Fax: 401-683-0840
E-Mail: info@ussailing.org
Home Page: www.ussailing.org
Social Media: Facebook, Twitter, LinkedIn

Gary Jobson, Us Sailing President
Tom Hubbell, Vice President
Fred Hagedorn, Secretary
Jack Gierhart, Executive Director

National news of the Union, the latest in yacht racing, and dealers of yachts are covered.
100 Members
Founded in 1986

3623 UnderWater Magazine
Naylor, LLC
5950 NW 1st Place
Gainesville, FL 32607

800-369-6220
E-Mail: sgarrity@naylor.com
Home Page: www.underwater.com

Jamie Williams, Publication Director
Sean Garrity, Editorial
Rebecca Roberts, Marketing Manager

It covers the entire spectrum of underwater contracting, vehicles and technology.
Cost: $50.00
500 Members
Founded in 1968

3624 WoodenBoat
WoodenBoat Publications
41 Wooden Boat La
PO Box 78
Brooklin, ME 04616-0078

207-359-4651
800-877-5284
Fax: 207-359-8920
E-Mail: info@woodenboat.com
Home Page: www.woodenboat.com
Social Media: Facebook

Tom Jackson, Sr. Editor
Carl Cramer, Publisher
Matt Murphy, Editor

Provides readers with a dynamic editorial environment that combines technologies with traditional methods of boat design, construction and repair. The magazine is about craftmanship in wood, and its active boating audience works at all levels of expertise to build, restore, and maintain their boats.
Cost: $29.95
160 Pages
Frequency: Bi-Monthly
Circulation: 98000
Founded in 1974

3625 WorkBoat
Diversified Business Communications
121 Free Street
Portland, ME 04101

207-842-5600
Fax: 207-842-5611
E-Mail: info@divcom.com
Home Page: www.workboat.com
Social Media: Facebook, Twitter

Mike Lodato, VP
Ken Hocke, Senior Editor
David Krapf, Editor In Chief
Jerry Fraser, Publisher

Commercial marine publication serving the North American inland and coastal waterways — the most active sector in the commercial marine market today. Consisting of captains, owners, managers, operators, chief engineers and other industry professionals, the Workboat audience represents important and influential purchasing power in the commercial marine industry.
Cost: $39.00
Frequency: Monthly
Circulation: 25000
ISSN: 0043-8014
Founded in 1949

3626 Yachting Magazine
Time4 Media Marine Group
PO Box 420235
Palm Coast, FL 32142-0235

386-597-4382
800-999-0869
E-Mail: letters@yachtingmagazine.com
Home Page: www.yachtingmagazine.com
Social Media: Facebook, Twitter

Ed Baker, Associate Publisher
Rich Rasor, East Coast Sales Director

Covers the finest boats, electronics and equipment, including large yachts and yacht charters. It also covers the passions, adventures and lifestyles of active, affluent boat owners.
Frequency: Monthly
Founded in 1907

3627 Young Mariners Guide
Yachting Club of America
PO Box 1040
Marco Island, FL 34146

239-642-4448
Fax: 239-642-5284
E-Mail: ycaol@hotmail.com
Home Page: www.ycaol.com

David Martin, Owner

Designed to inform and teach young people about boating in simple and handy pocket book to help them on their way to becoming the future of the yachting fraternity in America.
Cost: $5.00
30000 Members
32 Pages
Frequency: Softbound
Founded in 1963
Mailing list available for rent

Trade Shows

3628 Annual American and Canadian Sport, Travel and Outdoor Show
Expositions, Inc.
Edgewater Branch
PO Box 550
Cleveland, OH 44107-0550

216-529-1300
Fax: 216-529-0311
E-Mail: showinfo@expoinc.com
Home Page: www.expoinc.com

Chris Fassnacht, President
Robert Attewell, Vice President
David Rosar, CFO, VP

975 exhibits of hunting and fishing equipment, travel services, boats, recreational vehicles and related equipment, supplies and services.
300k Attendees
Frequency: March
Founded in 1937

3629 Annual Boat & Fishing Show at the Lansing Center
Show Span, Inc
2121 Celebration Drive NE
Grand Rapids, MI 49525

616-447-2860
800-328-6550
Fax: 616-447-2861
E-Mail: events@showspan.com
Home Page: www.showspan.com

John Loeks, President
Henri Boucher, Vice President
Mike Wilbraham, VP, Show Producer

Held in Lansing, Michigan.
Frequency: March
Founded in 1945

3630 Annual Boat Show
General Sports Shows/NMMA
231 S. LaSalle St
Suite 2050
Chicago, IL 60604

312-946-6200
800-777-4766
E-Mail: bmcardle@nmma.org
Home Page: www.generalsportshows.com

Jennifer Thompson, Show Manager
Bonnie Schuenemann, Special Events Coordinator
Patty Gibbs, Media Contact

Enjoy 5 days of boating fun, education and one-stop shopping with hundreds of boats and exhibits and special attractions all under one roof.
Frequency: January

3631 Annual Boat Show & Fishing Exposition
Greenband Enterprises
3450 South Highland Drive
Suite 105
Salt Lake City, UT 84106

801-485-7399
800-657-3050
Fax: 801-485-0687
E-Mail: showinfo@greenband.com
Home Page: www.greenband.com
Social Media: Facebook

Jonathan D Greenband, Show Manager
Debra Greenband, Sales Manager

See the latest in Ski Boats, Cruisers, Fishing Boats, everything for boating fun.
45000 Attendees
Frequency: Annual, February
Founded in 1965

3632 Annual Boat, Vacation and Outdoor Show
Showtime Productions, Inc.
PO Box 4372
Rockford, IL 61110
815-877-8043
Fax: 815-877-9037
E-Mail: brenda@showtimeproduction.net
Home Page: showtimeproduction.net
Tom Pellant, President
Brenda Rotoco, Event Coordinator
Boat, travel, outdoor equipment, supplies, and services plus demonstrations.
28000 Attendees
Frequency: February
Founded in 1970

3633 Annual Conference & Educational Symposia
Society of Accredited Marine Surveyors
7855 Argyle Forest Blvd
Suite 203
Jacksonville, FL 32244
904-384-1494
800-344-9077
Fax: 904-388-3958
E-Mail: samshq@marinesurvey.org
Home Page: www.marinesurvey.org
Joseph B Lobley, President
Stuart J. McLea, Executive Vice President
Llyod E. Kittredge, Secretary/Treasurer
1000 Members
350 Attendees
Frequency: Annual/Fall
Founded in 1986

3634 Annual Conference on Sail Training and Tall Ships
American Sail Training Association
29 Touro Street
PO Box 1459
Newport, RI 02840
401-846-1775
Fax: 401-849-5400
E-Mail: asta@sailtraining.org
Home Page: www.tallships.sailtraining.org
Social Media: Facebook, Twitter, LinkedIn, Youtube
Mike Rauworth, Chairman
Robert Rogers, Executive Director
Caleb Pifer, Vice Chair
300 Members
Frequency: November
Founded in 1973

3635 Annual Iowa Boat and Vacation Show
Iowa Show Productions
PO Box 2460
Waterloo, IA 50704-2460
319-232-0218
Fax: 319-235-8932
E-Mail: info@iowashows.com
Home Page: www.iowashows.com
John Bunge, Show Manager
Over 25 dealers, 40 brands, 100's of models. Family runabouts, fishing boats, cabin cruisers, cuddies, power boats, waterski boats, personal watercraft, jet boats, bass boats, walleye boats, deck boats, pontoons, fish/ski boats, and marine accessories.
Frequency: January
Founded in 1975
Mailing list available for rent

3636 Annual Lido Yacht Expo
Duncan McIntosh Company
17782 Cowan, Ste A
Irvine, CA 92614
949-757-5959
Fax: 949-660-6172
E-Mail: boatshow@goboating.com
Home Page: www.lidoyachtexpo.com
Social Media: Facebook
Duncan McIntosh, President
Jeff Fleming, Associate Publisher
An upscale in-the-water show of yachts and big boats. More than 2,000 feet of floating dock.
Frequency: May
Founded in 1973

3637 Annual National Capital Boat Show
Royal Productions
PO Box 4197
Chester, VA 23831
804-256-6556
Fax: 804-288-7132
E-Mail: info@royalshows.com
Home Page: www.royalshows.com
David Posner, President
Nearly 40 dealers form throughout Maryland and Virginia bring a wide range of boats to the National Capital Boat Show including saltware fishing boats, ski boats, runabouts, motor yachts, jet boats, jon boats, PWC, bass boats, inflatables, deck boats and pontoons.
20000 Attendees
Frequency: March

3638 Annual Spring Boat Show
Southern California Marine Association
1006 East Chapman Ave
Orange, CA 92866
714-633-7581
Fax: 714-633-9498
E-Mail: scma@scma.com
Home Page: www.scma.com
Social Media: Facebook, Twitter
Richard Tressler, President
Renee Acencio, Vice President
You'll find a assortment of marine accessory booths featuring the latest and newest products filled with everything that floats, affordable family runabounts, ski boats, fishing boats, cruisers, pontoons, performance sportboats and personal watercraft.
Frequency: June
Founded in 1956

3639 Annual Spring New Products Show
Pacific Expositions c/o Tihati Productions
3615 Harding Ave
Suite 506
Honolulu, HI 96816
808-732-6037
Fax: 808-732-6039
E-Mail: info@pacificexpos.com
Home Page: www.pacificexpos.com
Tara Chanel-Thompson, Director/General Manager
The newest and most exciting products on land and sea with 320 exhibits for trade professionals, buyers, and the general public.
17000 Attendees
Frequency: Annual, April
Founded in 1974

3640 Association of Marina Industries Annual Conference
Association of Marina Industries
50 Water Street
Warren, RI 02885
866-367-6622
Fax: 401-247-0074
E-Mail: info@marinaassociation.org
Home Page: www.marinaassociation.org
Social Media: Twitter, LinkedIn
Jim Frye, CMM, Chairman/President
Gary Groenewold, Chairman
Brad Gross, Treasurer
Keith Boulais, Secretary
800+ Members
Frequency: May
Founded in 1986

3641 Atlanta Boat Show
National Marine Manufacturers Association
200 E Randolph Drive
Suite 1500
Chicago, IL 60601
954-441-3228
E-Mail: lberryman@nmma.org
Home Page: www.atlantaboatshow.com
Social Media: Facebook, Twitter
Larry Berryman, Show Manager
Scott Cohens, Relationship Manager
Sarah Ryser, PR Manager
Venus Berryman, Show Administrator
Debbie Harewood, Director, Shows Administration
Showcases the latest in boating products and marine technology. 225 exhibitors.
Frequency: January
Founded in 1961

3642 Atlantic City In-Water Power Boat Show
In-Water Power Boat Show
1650 Market St
36th Floor
Philadelphia, PA 19103
215-732-8001
Fax: 215-732-8266
E-Mail: info@acinwaterboatshow.com
Home Page: www.acinwaterboatshow.com
Social Media: Facebook, Twitter
Jerry Flaxman, Executive VP
This show provides space for over 700 boats on land and in-water and over 200 booths in the marine marketplace, including 2 tents and walkways along the piers. Showcases the new models for each coming year.
Frequency: September
Founded in 1983

3643 Atlantic City International Power Boat Show
National Marine Manufacturers Association
37-18 Northern Blvd
Suite 311
Long Islang City, NY 11101
718-707-0719
Fax: 888-649-7786
E-Mail: jpritko@nmma.org
Home Page: www.acboatshow.com
Social Media: Facebook, Twitter
Jon Pritko, Show Manager
Josh Rosales, Operations Manager
Showcases more than 700 all-new models of motor and express yachts, sports fisherman, cruisers and sport boats. Attracts boaters from all of the East Coast.
50000 Attendees
Frequency: February

3644 Boat Show of Grand Rapids
Show Span
2121 Celebration Drive NE
Grand Rapids, MI 49525
616-472-2860
800-328-6550
Fax: 616-447-2861

E-Mail: events@showspan.com
Home Page: www.showspan.com

John Loeks, President
Henri Boucher, Vice President
Mike Wilbraham, VP, Show Producer

Over 400 exhibits of power and sail boats, accessories, clocks, dockominiums and vacation destinations. Held at the Grand Center in Grand Rapids, Michigan.
Frequency: February
Founded in 1945

3645 **Boat Show of New England**
North America Expositions Company
33 Rutherford Avenue
Boston, MA 02129-3795

617-472-1442
800-225-1577
Fax: 617-242-1817
E-Mail: joneal@nmma.org
Home Page: www.naexpo.com
Social Media: Facebook, Twitter

Joseph B O'Neal, Managing Partner
Bob McAlpine, Operations Manager

Over 600 boats on display, both power and sailboats ranging from dinghies to 45 foot yachts, along with every conceivable accessory for your new or present boat.
215M Attendees
Frequency: February

3646 **Brokerage Yacht Show**
Yachting Promotions
1115 NE 9th Avenue
Fort Lauderdale, FL 33304-2110

954-764-7642
800-940-7642
Fax: 954-462-4140
E-Mail: info@showmanagement.com
Home Page: www.showmanagement.com
Social Media: Facebook, Twitter

Steve Sheer, Director Advertising
Kaye Pearson, President

The totally in-water presentation features over 500 new and pre-owned vessels.
Frequency: February
Founded in 1976
Mailing list available for rent

3647 **Education Under Sail Forum**
American Sail Training Association
29 Touro Street
PO Box 1459
Newport, RI 02840

401-846-1775
Fax: 401-849-5400
E-Mail: asta@sailtraining.org
Home Page: www.tallships.sailtraining.org
Social Media: Facebook, Twitter, Youtube

Mike Rauworth, Chairman
Robert Rogers, Executive Director
300 Members
Frequency: Biennial
Founded in 1973

3648 **IBEX Annual Conference**
National Marine Manufacturers Association
231 S. LaSalle St
Suite 2050
Chicago, IL 60604

312-946-6200
Fax: 312-946-0401
Home Page: www.nmma.org

Thomas Dammrich, President
Ben Wold, Executive Vice President
Craig Boskey, VP Finance/CFO

Exhibition features the products and processes now available that will streamline your boatbuilding business. See the advanced technologies ready for the upcoming model-year. Featuring 800 OEMs and suppliers, the exhibit halls offer you an opportunity to source and compare every tool available to boatbuilders.
Frequency: November
Founded in 1979

3649 **IFAI Expo Americas**
Internationl Fabrics Association International
1801 County Road B W
Roseville, MN 55113-4061

651-222-2508
800-225-4324
Fax: 651-631-9334
E-Mail: generalinfo@ifai.com
Home Page: www.ifaiexpo.com
Social Media: Facebook, Twitter, LinkedIn

Mary J. Hennessy, Executive VP
JoAnne Farris, Marketing Director
Steven C. Rider, CFO, VP

A trade event in the Americas for the technical textiles and specialty fabrics industry.
Frequency: Annual/October
Founded in 1912

3650 **International Boating and Water Safety Summit**
National Safe Boating Council
PO Box 509
Bristow, VA 20136

703-361-4294
Fax: 703-361-5294
E-Mail: office@safeboatingcouncil.org
Home Page: www.safeboatingcouncil.org
Social Media: Facebook, Twitter, Youtube

Joyce Shaw, Chair
Chris Edmonston, Vice Chair
Veronica Floyd, Past Chair
Frequency: April

3651 **International Conference of Professional Yacht Brokers**
Yacht Brokers Association of America
105 Eastern Avenue
Suite 104
Annapolis, MD 21403

410-940-6345
Fax: 410-263-1659
E-Mail: info@ybaa.com
Home Page: www.ybaa.com
Social Media: Facebook, Twitter, LinkedIn

Vincent J. Petrella, Executive Director
Rod Rowan, President
250 Members
Frequency: Annual
Founded in 1920

3652 **International Marina & Boatyard Conference**
American Boat Builders and Repairers Association
50 Water Street
Warren, RI 02885

401-247-0318
866-367-6622
Fax: 401-247-0074
E-Mail: info@marinaassociation.org
Home Page: www.abbra.org
Social Media: Twitter, LinkedIn

Jim Frye, CMM, Chairman/President
Gary Groenewold, Chairman
Brad Gross, Treasurer
Keith Boulais, Secretary

The conference is designed to meet the growing demand among those delivering the boating experience for an international forum for education and exposition.
800+ Members
Frequency: Annual
Founded in 1986

3653 **International WorkBoat Show**
The International WorkBoat Show
121 Fine Street
PO Box 7437
Portland, ME 04101-7437

207-842-5500
Fax: 207-842-5503
E-Mail: customerservice@divcom.com
Home Page: www.workboatshow.com
Social Media: Facebook, Twitter

Chris Dimmerling, Sales Director
Bob Callahan, Show Director
Denielle Christensen, Marketing Manager

The largest commercial marine tradeshow in North America, serving people in coastal, inland and offshore waters. It features 1000 exhibiting companies and is produced in partnership with WorkBoat magazine.
Frequency: Annual
Founded in 1978

3654 **MEGATEX**
Industrial Fabrics Association International
1801 County Road B W
Roseville, MN 55113-4061

651-222-2508
800-225-4324
Fax: 651-631-9334
E-Mail: generalinfo@ifai.com
Home Page: www.ifai.com
Social Media: Facebook, Twitter, LinkedIn

Mary J. Hennessy, Executive VP
JoAnne Farris, Marketing Director
Steven C. Rider, CFO, VP
Jeffrey W Kirk, President

Will be held at the Georgia World Congress Center in Atlanta, Georgia, and is anchored by the IFAI Expo and the ATMW-I shows. Together, the shows are expected to have more than 1,000 exhibitors.
20000 Attendees
Founded in 1912

3655 **Marine Retailers Association of America Annual Convention**
Marine Regtailers Association of America
PO Box 1127
Oak Park, IL 60304

708-763-9210
Fax: 708-763-9236
E-Mail: mraa@mraa.com
Home Page: www.mraa.com

Matt Gruhn, President
Liz Walz, Director
Larry Innis, Legislative Affairs
Frequency: November

3656 **Mid-America Sail & Power Boat Show**
Lake Erie Marine Trade Association
1269 Bassett Road
Cleveland, OH 44145-1116

440-899-5009
Fax: 440-899-5013
E-Mail: lemta@aol.com
Home Page: www.clevelandboatshow.com
Social Media: Facebook

Norm Schultz, President Emeritus

Annual show of 325 manufacturers and suppliers of pleasure boats and related marine equipment, supplies and services.
140M Attendees
Frequency: January

3657 **Midwest Boat Show**
Lake Erie Marine Trade Association

1269 Bassett Road
Cleveland, OH 44145-1116

440-899-5009
Fax: 440-899-5013

Norm Schultz, President

Annual show and exhibits of boats, equipment, supplies and services.
23M Attendees
Frequency: August
Founded in 1980

3658 **NMBA Annual Conference**
National Marine Bankers Association
231 South LaSalle Street
Suite 2050
Chicago, IL 60604

312-812-2777
E-Mail: bmcardle@nmma.org
Home Page: www.marinebankers.org
Social Media: LinkedIn

Michael Bryant, President
Jayme Yates, Secretary
Jackie Forese, Director

NMBA hosts a three day member conference where the latest trends relating to marine industry are discussed in detail.
180 Attendees
Frequency: September

3659 **National Association of State Boating Law Administrators Annual Conference**
National Association of State Boating Law
1500 Leestown Road
Suite 330
Lexington, KY 40511

859-225-9487
Fax: 859-231-6403
E-Mail: info@nasbla.org
Home Page: www.nasbla.org/

Toby Velasquez, President
Herb Angell, VP
Kevin Bergerson, Treasurer

Conference provides information that focuses on boating education, industry trends, workshops, and programs that discuss the history of recreational boating safety programs including an overview of state-by-state regulatory laws.
Frequency: September

3660 **National Capital Boat Show**
Royal Productions
PO Box 4197
Chester, VA 23831-8475

804-425-6556
Fax: 804-425-6563
Home Page: www.royalshows.com

Serving the Washington DC and suburban Virginia/Maryland markets. 40 dealers.
Frequency: March

3661 **National Dry Stack Conference**
Association of Marina Industries
444 North Capitol Street NW
Suite 645
Washington, DC 20001

202-379-9768
Fax: 202-628-8679
E-Mail: info@imimarina.org
Home Page: www.imimarina.org

Gregg Kenney, Chairman
Alex Laidlaw, Vice Chairman
Maureen Healey, Executive Director
Cris McSparen, Treasurer
Brooke Fishel, Manager Communications

The Dry Stack is a three-day hybrid school which combines an educational program along with networking among leading operations, developers and vendors.
Frequency: October

3662 **National Marine Bankers Association Annual Conference**
National Marine Bankers Association
231 South LaSalle Street
Suite 2050
Chicago, IL 60604

312-812-2777
E-Mail: bmcardle@nmma.org
Home Page: www.marinebankers.org
Social Media: LinkedIn

Michael Bryant, President
Jayme Yates, Secretary
Jackie Forese, Director

A three-day member conference where the latest trends issues relating to the marine industry are discussed in detail.
Frequency: September

3663 **North American Sail & Power Show**
Lake Erie Marine Trade Association
1269 Bassett Road
Cleveland, OH 44145-1116

440-899-5009
Fax: 440-899-5013
E-Mail: lemta@aol.com

Norm Schultz, President

Annual show and exhibits of marine equipment, supplies and services.
31M Attendees
Frequency: September

3664 **Portland Boat Show**
O'Loughlin Trade Shows
3600 SW Multnomah Boulevard
PO Box 80750
Portland, OR 97219-1750

503-246-8291
Fax: 503-246-1066
E-Mail: otssport@earthlink.net
Home Page: www.oloughlintradeshows.com

Peter O'Loughlin, Show Manager
Robert O'Loughlin Sr, President

Offers hundreds of makes and models, accessories and plenty of expert advice through seminars and hands on demonstrations.
Frequency: January

3665 **Professional Boatbuilder: International Boatbuilders Expo and Conference**
WoodenBoat Publications
86 Great Cove Drive
PO Box 78
Brooklin, ME 04616

207-359-4651
Fax: 207-359-8920
E-Mail: info@bibexshow.com
Home Page: www.ibexshow.com

Carl Cramer, Publisher
Anne Dunbar, Show Director
Joanne Miller, Registration Manager

Over 450 booths offering products for boat builders, designers, repairers, surveyors, and boatyard/marina operators.
2.5M Attendees
Frequency: November
Founded in 1989

3666 **SCA Spring Safety Seminar**
Shipbuilders Council of America
655 Fifteenth St NW
Suite 225
Washington, DC 20005

202-347-5462
Fax: 202-347-5464
E-Mail: preever@balljanik.com
Home Page: www.shipbuilders.org
Social Media: Facebook

Matt Paxton, President

Represents the U.S. shipyard industry. SCA members build, repair and service America's fleet of commercial vessels.
73 Members
Frequency: March
Founded in 1920

3667 **Seattle Boat Show**
Northwest Marine Trade Association
1900 North Northlake Way
Suite 233
Seattle, WA 98103

206-634-0911
Fax: 206-632-0078
E-Mail: info@seattleboatshow.com
Home Page: www.nmta.net
Social Media: Facebook, Twitter, LinkedIn

George Harris, President
John Thorburn, VP

The ten-day event features more than 1,000 recreational watercraft, seminars and the latest innovations in accessories at Qwest Field Event Center, plus 200 world-class boats in their natural habitat on South Lake Union.
Frequency: January-February
Founded in 1947

3668 **St. Petersburg Boat Show**
Show Management
1115 NE 9th Avenue
Fort Lauderdale, FL 33304

954-764-7642
800-940-7642
Fax: 954-462-4140
E-Mail: info@showmanagement.com
Home Page: www.showmanagement.com
Social Media: Facebook, Twitter

Kaye Pearson, Owner/Promoter
Elise Lipoff, Director Public Relations
Steve Sheer, Director Advertising

More than 600 boats of all types and sizes, electronics, engines and a vast selection of marine accessories will be displayed on land and in water.
10000 Attendees
Frequency: December
Founded in 1977
Mailing list available for rent

3669 **Suncoast Boat Show**
Show Management
1115 NE 9th Avenue
Fort Lauderdale, FL 33304
954-764-7642
800-940-7642
Fax: 954-462-4140
E-Mail: info@showmanagement.com
Home Page: www.showmanagement.com
Social Media: Facebook, Twitter

Kaye Pearson, Owner/Promoter
Elise Lipoff, Director Public Relations
Steve Sheer, Director Advertising
Chuck Bolt, Director Sales

Annual show and exhibits of boats and marine equipment, supplies and services.
30000 Attendees
Frequency: April
Founded in 1982
Mailing list available for rent

3670 **U.S. Rowing Association Annual Convention**
United States Rowing Association
2 Wall Street
Princeton, NJ 08540

609-751-0700
800-314-4769
Fax: 609-924-1578

E-Mail: members@usrowing.org
Home Page: www.usrowing.org
Social Media: Facebook, Twitter, Youtube

Elizabeth Webb, Events Manager

Coaching programs and information, referee clinics, speakers, and competitions.
Frequency: December

3671 US Sailboat Show
Annapolis Boatshows
100 Severn Drive
PO Box 4997
Annapolis, MD 21401-4997

410-268-8828
Fax: 410-280-3903

Dee Newman, Show Manager
Jim Barthold, General Manager

In-water sailboat show offering over 350 booths.
150M Attendees
Frequency: October

Directories & Databases

3672 American Boat and Yacht Council
613 Third Street
Suite 10
Annapolis, MD 21403

410-990-4466
Fax: 410-956-2737
E-Mail: info@abycinc.org
Home Page: www.abycinc.org

George Bellwoar, Chair
Jack Horner, Vice Chair
Steven Herb, Treasurer

Marine suppliers, engineers and underwriters, as well as architects and designers for the marine industry are listed.
105 Pages
Frequency: Biennial
Founded in 1954

3673 Boater's Source Directory
Boat US Foundation
880 S Pickett St
Alexandria, VA 22304-4606

703-461-8952
800-336-2628
Fax: 703-461-2855
Home Page: www.boatus.com/foundation
Social Media: Facebook, Twitter, LinkedIn, Youtube

Richard Schwartz, President

Pocket guide for boaters containing safety and regulatory information and resources.
Cost: $5.00
Frequency: Paperback, SemiAnnual
Founded in 1966

3674 Boating Industry: Marine Buyers' Guide Issue
Ehlert Publishing Group
6420 Sycamore Ln N
Suite 100
Maple Grove, MN 55369-6014

763-383-4400
800-848-6247
Fax: 763-383-4499
E-Mail: dvoll@ehlertpublishing.com
Home Page: www.bowhuntingworld.com
Social Media: Facebook, Twitter, Youtube

Steven Hedlund, President
Liz Walz, Senior Editor
Jon Mohrm, Associate Editor
Tammy Galvin, Group Publisher

A who's who directory of services and supplies for the industry.
Cost: $29.95
Frequency: Annual
Circulation: 30,000
Mailing list available for rent

3675 Confined Space Entry Video and Manual
Shipbuilders Council of America
655 Fifteenth St NW
Suite 225
Washington, DC 20004-1166

202-347-5462
Fax: 202-347-5464
E-Mail: preever@balljanik.com
Home Page: www.shipbuilders.org
Social Media: Facebook

Matt Paxton, President

This manual, in combination with the video program, covers some of the more common hazards associated with confined space entry. It also provides you with the information you will need to prevent accidents and injuries.
Cost: $ 50.00
73 Members
Founded in 1920

3676 Consumer Protection Database
Boat Owners Association of the US
800 South Pickett Street
Alexandria, VA 22304

703-412-2770
Fax: 703-461-2847
Home Page: www.boatus.com
Social Media: Facebook, Twitter, LinkedIn, Youtube

Richard Schwartz, Chairman/Founder
Jim Ellis, President/CEO

Contains consumer complaints and safety information reported by boat owners, the US Coast Guard, manufacturers, marine surveyors and marine technicians.
Founded in 1966

3677 ISSPA Sports and Vacation Show Directory and Calendar
International Sport Show Producers Association
PO Box 480084
Denver, CO 80248-0084

303-892-6800
800-457-2434
Fax: 303-892-6322
E-Mail: dseymour@iei-expos.com
Home Page: www.sportshow.org

Dianne Seymour, Executive Secretary

Products of outdoor recreation shows which include boating, travel, RV, hunting, and fishing.
Frequency: Annual

3678 Marine Products Directory
Underwriters Laboratories
12 Laboratory Drive
PO Box 13995
Research Triangle Park, NC 27709-3995

919-549-1400
Fax: 919-547-6363
E-Mail: paul.r.ouellette@us.ul.com
Home Page: www.ul.com/marine
Social Media: Facebook, Twitter, Youtube

Keith E. Williams, President
Sanjeev Jesudas, President

UL has been testing and certifying products for marine use since 1969. With a UL Marine Mark on your product, you can show consumers, retailers, surveyors, insurers, government agencies, regulatory and ABTC, NFPA and UL Safety Standards.
Cost: $10.00
176 Pages
Frequency: Annual

3679 Membership Directory: Boating Industry Administration
National Association of State Boating Laws
1500 Leestown Road
Suite 300
Lexington, KY 40511-2047

859-225-9487
Fax: 859-231-6403
E-Mail: info@nasbla.org
Home Page: www.nasbla.org

Toby Velasquez, President
Herb Angell, VP
Kevin Bergerson, Treasurer

Published by the National Association of State Boating Law Administration.

3680 NMRA Membership Directory
National Marine Representative Association
1333 Delany Road #500
PO Box 360
Gurnee, IL 60031

847-662-3167
Fax: 847-336-7126
E-Mail: info@nmraonline.org
Home Page: www.nmraonline.org

Norm McLeod, Past President
Tim Luehmann, President
Jeff Gueterman, VP
Rick Silverlake, Treasurer
Chris Kelly, Secretary

Provides a complete listing of all NMRA sales representatives. Includes contact information for their main and associate offices, the territories they cover, the markets they represent, and the list of companies they represent.
Cost: $10.00

3681 National Marine Manufacturers Association Membership List
231 S. LaSalle St
Suite 2050
Chicago, IL 60601-6539

312-946-6200
Fax: 312-946-0388
Home Page: www.nmma.org

Thomas Dammrich, President
Ben Wold, Executive Vice President
Craig Boskey, VP Finance/CFO

Directory of services and supplies to the industry.
160 Pages
Frequency: Quadrennial

3682 Pacific Boating Almanac
ProStar Publications
3416 Wesley Street
Suite B
Culver City, CA 90232-2901

310-280-1010
800-481-6277
Fax: 310-280-1025
E-Mail: editor@prostarpublications.com
Home Page: www.prostarpublications.com

Peter Griffes, Owner

Consists of three regional volumes. This information includes the latest Coast Pilot, Tide & Current Tables, First Aid, Electronics, Navigation and Safety, Weather, and Yacht Club Burgees.
Cost: $26.95
Frequency: Annual
Circulation: 20,000
ISBN: 1-577857-05-4
Mailing list available for rent: 19,000 names
Printed in on matte stock

3683 **Portbook of Marine Services**
Portbook Publications
PO Box 462
Belfast, ME 04915

207-338-1619
Fax: 207-338-6025
E-Mail: info@portbook.net
Home Page: www.portbook.net

Sandra Squire, Publisher

Marinas, yacht clubs, boatyards, dealers, marine supply stores, repair facilities, and other services for yachtsmen. For Annapolis, Maryland and Newport/Narragansett Bay, Rhode Island. Distributed free through advertisers, or four dollars by mail.
Cost: $40.00
100 Pages
Frequency: Annual
Circulation: 35M
Founded in 1982
Printed in on matte stock

3684 **Register of American Yacht Clubs**
Yachting Club of America
PO Box 1040
Marco Island, FL 34146-1040

239-642-4448
Fax: 239-642-5284
E-Mail: info@ycaol.com
Home Page: www.ycaol.com

A reciprocity guide for yacht and sailing clubs in the United States, Hawaii, Alaska, and the Virgin Islands registered with the Yachting Club of America. 800 yacht clubs registered with the Yachting Club of America.
Cost: $35.00
200 Pages
Frequency: Softbound
Founded in 1963
Printed in on glossy stock

3685 **Sail Tall Ships: Directory of Sail Training and Adventure at Sea**
American Sail Training Association
240 Thames Street
PO Box 1459
Newport, RI 02840

401-846-1775
Fax: 401-849-5400
E-Mail: asta@sailtraining.org
Home Page: www.ycaol.com

Lori Aguiar, Editor
Peter A Mello, Executive Director

Offers information on sail training ships, shoreside sail training programs and ships under construction or restoration.
Cost: $50.00
400 Pages
Frequency: Annual
Circulation: 15,000
ISBN: 0-963648-36-5
Founded in 1963

3686 **Seafarers**
Admiralty Insurance
6353 Argyle Forest Boulevard
Jacksonville, FL 32244

904-777-0042
800-456-8936
Fax: 904-777-0279
Home Page: www.seafarers.com

Searchable database of boating associations, yacht clubs, boating clubs and source of nautical information and links.

3687 **Ship Agents, Owners, Operators**
Maritime Association of the Port of New York
17 Battery Place
Suite 913
New York, NY 10004-1194

212-747-1284
Fax: 212-635-9498
E-Mail: themaritimeassoc@erols.com
Home Page: www.nymaritime.org

Edward Morgan, President
Brian McAllister, VP
Edward J Kelly, Executive Director

Directory of Atlantic, Gulf and West Coasts listing every steamship, owner, and operator in the major ports with lines that they represent and the countries that they serve.
Cost: $50.00
Frequency: Annual
Circulation: 2,000
Mailing list available for rent

3688 **Shipyard Ergonomics Video and Workbook CD**
Shipbuilders Council of America
655 Fifteenth St NW
Suite 225
Washington, DC 20004-1166

202-347-5462
Fax: 202-347-5464
E-Mail: awalker@vesselalliance.com
Home Page: www.shipbuilders.org
Social Media: Facebook

Matt Paxton, President

Designed to instruct shipyard employees, supervisors and trainers in identifying ergonomic risks and providing tools to allow the development of creative solutions to reduce the hazards.
Cost: $75.00
73 Members
Founded in 1920

Industry Web Sites

3689 **http://gold.greyhouse.com**
G.O.L.D Grey House OnLine Databases

Grey House Publishing's online database platform, GOLD, offers Quick Search, Keyword Search and Expert Search, for most business sectors including boating manufacture and service markets. GOLD is quick and easy - whether you're a novice searcher or an experienced database user. All of Grey House's directory products are available for subscription on the GOLD platform.

3690 **www.acbs.org**
Antique & Classic Boat Society

Dedicated to the preservation and enjoyment of historic, antique and classic boats. ACBS brings people with this common interest together to share fellowship, information, experiences and ideas.

3691 **www.americanboating.org**
American Boating Association

ABA's mission is to promote boating safety, affordability, growth, and a clean environment. It provides exclusive services and benefits for boaters and boating enthusiasts.

3692 **www.apba-racing.com**
American Power Boat Association

The sole authority for UIM approved powerboat racing ine United States.

3693 **www.by-the-sea.com**
By the Sea

Everything for the boat professional and enthusiast alike. News of sales and events, message boards and contact information.

3694 **www.greyhouse.com**
Grey House Publishing

Authoritative reference directories for most business segments incluidng boat manufacturing and service markets. Users can search the online databases with varied search criteria allowing for custom searches by product category, geographic area, sales volume, keyword, subject and more. Full Grey House catalog and online ordering also available.

3695 **www.ifai.com**
Industrial Fabrics Association International

The only trade association in the world representing the entire specialty fabrics/technical textiles industry. Member products range from fiber and fabric suppliers to manufacturers of end products, equipment and hardware.

3696 **www.imimarina.org**
International Marina Institute

International Marina Institute's educational resources include specialized training courses and seminars on fundamental and advanced levels, workshops, conferences the advanced marina management school and the Certified Marina Manager program along with a wide selection of publications.

3697 **www.lemta.com**
Lake Erie Marine Trade Association

Trade association of more than 100 recreational boat dealers, marina operators and pleasure boat service companies located across northern Ohio; also plays the key role in looking out for the consumer.

3698 **www.marinebankers.org**
National Marine Bankers Association

The purpose of the NMBA is to educate prospective lenders in marine financing procedures, create new lenders to help finance the sales of the manufacturers products, and to create an information exchange for its members.

3699 **www.mraa.com**
Marine Retailers Association of America

Manufacturers and dealers of boats, equipment, supplies and services.

3700 **www.nauticalworld.com**

Dedicated to bringing all related web sites within easy access to watersports enthusiasts, including advertiser's information. Offers sections on marine electronics and hardware, sailing, boats, dock supplies, fishing accessories, diving accessories, industry news, watersports, weather forecasting and more.

3701 **www.nauticexpo.com**
NauticExpo

This Virtual Boat Show is accessible in five languages and presents all the boats and nautical equipment available on the international market. It offers an accurate and up-to-date source of information to yachtsmen and professionals.

3702 **www.nmdaonline.com**
National Marine Distributors Association

Engages in exclusively nonprofit activities designed to promote the common business interests and improve the business conditions of wholesale distributors of marine accessories and of the marine industry in general.

3703 **www.nmraonline.org**
National Marine Representatives Association

Members are independent boat and marine accessory sales representatives national association.

3704 **www.nmta.net**
Northwest Marine Trade Association
Oldest and largest regional boating trade organization in the nation representing the interests of approximately 800 member companies. Each year it produces the Seattle Boat Show at the Stadium Exhibition Center and the Seattle Boat Show at Shilshole Bay Marina on behalf of its members.

3705 **www.propellerclubhq.com**
Propeller Club of the United States
Grassroots, nonprofit organization, whose membership resides throughout the United States and the world. It is dedicated to the enhancement and well-being of all interests of the maritime community on a national and international basis.

3706 **www.pwia.org**
Personal Watercraft Industry Association
Ensuring that personal watercraft and personal watercraft users are treated fairly when local, state, and federal government officials consider boating regulations. PWIA supports and actively advocates for reasonable regulations, strong enforcement of boating and navigation laws, and mandatory boating safety education for all personal watercraft operators.

3707 **www.rbbi.com**
Polson Enterprises
Offering research tools and papers on new product development and new product development services for boat builders, plus experience in the fields of marine drives, engine, marine vessels, propellar guards, boating safety. Industry and regulation updates are also available on this site.

3708 **www.tsca.com**
Traditional Small Craft Association
Nonprofit, tax-exempt educational organization which works to preserve and continue the living traditions, skills, lore and legends surrounding working and pleasure watercraft including construction and use of boats.

3709 **www.ussailing.org**
United States Sailing Association
Encourages participation and promotes excellence in sailing and racing in the US.

Associations

3710 **Academy of Canadian Cinema & Television**
49 Ontario Street
Suite 501
Toronto, ON M5A 2V1
416-366-2227
800-644-5194
Fax: 416-366-8454
E-Mail: info@academy.ca
Home Page: www.academy.ca
Martin Katz, Chair
Robin Mirsky, Vice Chair
Gabriel Nachman, Treasurer
A national non-profit, professional association dedicated to the promotion, recognition, and celebration of exceptional achievements in Candian film, television, and digital media.
Founded in 1979

3711 **Academy of Television Arts and Science**
5200 Lankershim Blvd
North Hollywood, CA 91601
818-754-2800
Fax: 818-761-2827
Home Page: www.emmys.com
Social Media: Facebook, Twitter, Youtube
Bruce Rosenblum, Chairman
Kevin Hamburger, Vice Chair
Frank Scherma, 2nd Vice Chair
Marcelino Ford, Secretary
Susan Nessanbaum-Goldberg, Treasurer
Nonprofit corporation devoted to the advancement of telecommunications arts and sciences and to fostering creative leadership in the telecommunications industry. In addition to recognizing outstanding programming and individual achivements for Primetime and Los Angeles area programming, ATAS sponsors meetings, conferences and activities for collaboration on a variety of topics involving traditional broadcast interests, new media and emerging digital technology.
12000 Members
Founded in 1957

3712 **Alaska Broadcasters Association**
700 W 41st Street
Suite 102
Anchorage, AK 99503
907-258-2424
Fax: 907-258-2414
E-Mail: akba@gci.net
Home Page: www.alaskabroadcaster.org
Social Media: Facebook
Matt Wilson, President
Charlie Ellis, VP
Ric Schimdt, Secretary/Treasurer
Dick Olson, VP, Sales Manager
Darlene Simono, Executive Director
To provide assistance, which enables members to serve their communities of license through education, representation and advocacy.
Founded in 1964

3713 **Alliance for Community Media**
4248 Park Glen Road
Minneapolis, MN 55416
952-928-4643
Fax: 202-393-2653
E-Mail: acm@alliancecm.org
Home Page: www.alliancecm.org
Social Media: Facebook, Twitter, LinkedIn, Youtube, Flickr
Keri Stokstad, Chair
Michael Heylin, Vice Chair
John Donovan, Treasurer
Todd Thayer, Treasurer Elect
Participants include cable access television and community programmers. Individual membership dues are $70.00, organization $350.00.
1000 Members
Founded in 1976
Mailing list available for rent: 1000 names at $200 per M

3714 **Alliance for Women in Media**
1760 Old Meadow Rd
Suite 500
Mc Lean, VA 22102
703-506-3290
Fax: 703-506-3266
E-Mail: info@allwomeninmedia.org
Home Page: www.allwomeninmedia.org
Social Media: Facebook, Twitter, LinkedIn, Youtube
Kay Olin, Chair
Kristen Welch, Chair Elect
Sarah Foss, Treasurer
Carol Grothem, Treasurer Elect
Sylvia Strobel, Interim CEO
Leverages the promise, passion, and power of women in all forms of media carrying forth with its mission by educating, advocating, and acting as a resource to its members and the industry at large via inspired thought leadership that illuminates areas of social need.
Founded in 1951

3715 **Alliance of Motion Picture and Television Producers**
15301 Ventura Blvd
Building E
Sherman Oaks, CA 91403
818-995-3600
Fax: 818-382-1793
Home Page: www.amptp.org
Nick Counter, President
Trade association with respect to labor issues in the motion picture and television industry. Negotiate industry wide collective bargaining agreements that cover actors, craftspersons, directors, musicians, technicians and writers.
350 Members
Founded in 1982

3716 **American Auto Racing Writers and Broadcasters Association**
922 North Pass Avenue
Burbank, CA 91505-2703
818-842-7005
Fax: 818-842-7020
E-Mail: aarwba@aarwba.org
Home Page: www.aarwba.org
Norma Brandel, President/Executive Director
Kathy Seymour, VP
Rhonda Williams, Treasurer
Patrick Reynolds, Secretary
The American Auto Racing Writers & Broadcasters Association is the oldest and largest organization devoted to auto racing coverage.
400 Members
Founded in 1955

3717 **American Center for Children and Media**
5400 North St Louis Avenue
Chicago, IL 60625
703-509-5510
Fax: 773-509-5303
E-Mail: info@centerforchildrenandmedia.org
Home Page: www.centerforhildrenandmedia.org
David Kleeman, President
James Fellows, President Emeritus
Mission is to support a vibrant children's media industry by convening key constituencies to develop, implement and promote policies and practices that respect young people's well being, and are sustainable.
Founded in 1985

3718 **American Disc Jockey Association**
20118 N 67th Avenue
Suite 300-605
Glendale, CA 85308
888-723-5776
Fax: 866-310-4676
E-Mail: office@adja.org
Home Page: www.adja.org
Social Media: Facebook, Twitter, Youtube
Rob Snyder, Director
An association of professional mobile entertainers. Encourages success for its members through continuous education, camaraderie, and networking. The primary goal is to educate Disc Jockeys so that each member acts ethically and responsibly.

3719 **American Federation of Television and Radio Artists**
5757 Wilshire Blvd
7th Floor
Los Angeles, CA 90036
212-532-7633
Fax: 212-532-2242
E-Mail: info@aftra.com
Home Page: www.aftra.com
Social Media: Facebook, Twitter, Youtube, RSS
David White, Executive Director
Mathis Dunn, Associate Executive Director
Duncan Crabtree-Ireland, CAO/General Counsel
Represents its members in four major areas: news and broadcasting; entertainment programing; the recording business; and commercials and non-broadcast, industrial, educational media.
80000 Members
Founded in 1952

3720 **American Private Radio Association (APRA)**
PO Box 4221
Scottsdale, AZ 85261-4221
480-661-5000
Association members are from private radio stations.

3721 **American Sportscasters Association**
225 Broadway
Suite 2030
New York, NY 10007
212-227-8080
Fax: 212-571-0556
E-Mail: lschwa8918@aol.com
Home Page: www.americansportscastersonline.com
Louis O Schwartz, President/Founder
Dick Enberg, Chairman
National Association of Sportscasters, radio, television and cable covering the US, Puerto Rico and Canada. Very active web site. Offers seminars, compiles statistics and operates a placement service, maintains a Hall of Fame and biographical archives and library.
500 Members
Founded in 1980

3722 American Sportscasters Association, Inc.
225 Broadway
Suite 2030
New York, NY 10007-3742

212-227-8080
Fax: 212-571-0556
E-Mail: lschwa8918@aol.com
Home Page:
www.americansportscastersonline.com

Louis O Schwartz, President/Founder
Dick Enberg, Chairman
Jim Nantz, Board of Directors
Jon Miller, Board of Directors
Bill Walton, Board of Directors

National Association of Sportscasters, radio, television and cable covering the US, Puerto Rico and Canada. Very active web site. Offers seminars, compiles statistics and operates a placement service, maintains a Hall of Fame and biographical archives and library.
500 Members
Founded in 1980

3723 Associated Press Broadcasters
1825 K Street NW
Suite 800
Washington, DC 20006-1202

212-621-1500
Fax: 202-736-1107
E-Mail: info@ap.org
Home Page: www.apbroadcast.com
Social Media: Facebook, Twitter, LinkedIn, Youtube

Mary E Junck, Chairman
Gary Pruitt, President & CEO
Kathleen Carroll, Senior VP/Executive Editor
Jessica Bruce, VP/Director, Human Resource
Ken Dale, CFO/Senior VP

Seeks to advance journalism through radio and television, and cooperates with the AP to promote accurate and impartial news.
5.9m Members
Founded in 1846

3724 Association for Maximum Service Television
4100 Wisconsin Avenue NW
PO Box 9897
Washington, DC 20036-2224

202-966-1956
Fax: 202-966-9617
E-Mail: mstv@mstv.org
Home Page: www.mstv.org

David Donovan, President

Assures the maintenance of an effective nationwide system of free television and seeks to meet present and future needs of the VHF and UHF system.
400+ Members
Founded in 1956

3725 Association of Independent Commercial Producers
3 W 18th St
5th Floor
New York, NY 10011
212-929-3000
Fax: 212-929-3359
E-Mail: info@aicp.com
Home Page: www.aicp.com
Social Media: Facebook, Twitter, LinkedIn, Youtube, Flickr, RSS

Matt Miller, President & CEO
Renee Paley, VP Communications

The national trade association of television commercial producers who account for in excess of 80% of the commercial production done in the United States annually.
500 Members
Founded in 1972

3726 Association of Local Television Stations
1320 19th Street NW
Washington, DC 20036

202-887-1970
Home Page: www.altv.com

3727 Association of Public Television Stations
2100 Crystal Drive
Suite 700
Arlington, VA 22202

202-654-4200
Fax: 202-654-4236
Home Page: www.apts.org
Social Media: Facebook, Twitter

Patrick Butler, President & CEO
Lonna Thompson, Executive VP/COO & General Counsel
Jennifer Kieley, VP, Government Relations
Stacey Karp, VP, Communications
Emil Mara, VP, Finance & Administration

Nonprofit membership organization that supports the continued growth and development of a strong and financially sound noncommercial television service for the American public. Provides advocacy for public television interests at the national level, as well as consistent leadership and information in marshaling grassroots and congressional support for its members: the nation's public television stations.
153 Members
Founded in 1980

3728 Audio Engineering Society
60 E 42nd St
Room 2520
New York, NY 10165-2520

212-661-8528
Fax: 212-682-0477
E-Mail: HQ@aes.org
Home Page: www.aes.org
Social Media: Facebook, Twitter, LinkedIn, Youtube, Google+, RSS

Roger Furness, Executive Director
Jim Anderson, President
Robert E Lee, Jr, Secretary
Louis Fielder, Treasurer

Professional society devoted to audio technology. Membership includes leading engineers, scientists and other authorities in the field. Serves its members, the industry and the public by stimulating and facilitating advances in the constantly changing field of audio.

3729 Broadcast Designers' Association International
145 W 45th Street
Room 1100
New York, NY 10036-4008

212-376-6222
Fax: 212-376-6202

Association for manufacturers or suppliers of broadcast design equipment, supplies and services.

3730 Broadcast Education Association
1771 N St NW
Washington, DC 20036-2891

202-429-5355
888-380-7222
Fax: 202-429-4199
E-Mail: beamemberservices@nab.org
Home Page: www.beaweb.org
Social Media: Facebook, Twitter, LinkedIn

Heather Birks, Executive Director
J D Boyle, Director, Sales & Marketing
Traci Bailey, Manager, Business Operations

Serves as a higher education association of professors and industry professionals who teach college students worldwide and prepares them to go into the broadcasting and related emerging technologies professions upon graduation from college.
1400 Members
Founded in 1955
Mailing list available for rent: 1300 names at $100 per M

3731 Broadcast Pioneers
7 World Trade Center
250 Greenwich Street
New York, NY 10007-0030

212-220-3000
Fax: 212-246-2163
Home Page: www.bmi.com
Social Media: Facebook, Twitter

Del Bryant, President & CEO

Honors radio or television stations for excellence in art and community service. Maintains library documents on television broadcasting history.
1.4M Members
Founded in 1942

3732 Broadcasters Foundation of America
125 West 55th Street
3rd Floor
New York, NY 10019-5366

212-373-8250
Fax: 212-373-8254
E-Mail: info@thebfoa.org
Home Page: www.broadcastersfoundation.org

Philip J. Lombardo, Chairman
Richard A Foreman, Vice Chair
James B Thompson, President
Peter Doyle, VP
Jeff Haley, VP

Provides financial assistance to radio and television broadcasters who are in financial need.

3733 Cable & Telecommunications Association for Marketing
120 Waterfront Street
Suite 200
National Harbor, MD 20745

301-485-8900
Fax: 301-560-4964
E-Mail: info@ctam.com
Home Page: www.ctam.com
Social Media: Facebook, Twitter, LinkedIn, Youtube

David Juliano, Chair
Jonathan Hargis, Vice Chair
David Preschlack, Secretary/Treasurer

Dedicated to the discipline and development of consumer marketing excellence in cable television, news media and telecommunications services. Members have the advantage of progressive research, insightful publications and forward thinking conferences all designed to help you and your company gain a competitive edge.
5500 Members
Founded in 1976

3734 Canadian Association of Broadcast Consultants
130 Cree Crescent
Winnepeg, MB R3J 3W1

204-889-9202
Fax: 204-831-6650

E-Mail: jsadoun@yrh.com
Home Page: www.cabc-accr.ca

Joseph Sadoun, Ing P Eng, President
Kerry Pelser, Secretary/Treasurer

Prepares technical briefs, coverage studies and frequencies.

3735 **Canadian Association of Broadcasters**
770-45 O'Connor St
Ottawa, ON K1P 1A4

613-233-4035
Fax: 613-233-6961
E-Mail: sbissonette@cab-acr.ca
Home Page: www.cab-acr.ca

Rick Arnish, Chairman
Kevin Goldstein, Vice Chair
Susan Wheeler, Secretary
Glenda Spenrath, Treasurer

Serves as the eyes and ears of the private broadcasting community to advocate and lobby on its behalf and to act as a cebtral point on matters of joint interest.

3736 **Canadian Association of Ethnic Broadcasters (Radio)**
622 College Street
Toronto, ON M6G 1B6

416-531-9991
Fax: 416-531-5274
E-Mail: info@chinradio.com
Home Page: www.chinradio.com
Social Media: Facebook, Twitter

Johnny Lombardi, Founder, President

Pioneer in multicultural radio broadcasting and has lead the way for similar briadcast operations to be established.

3737 **Caribbean Broadcasting Union**
Suite 1B, Building 6A
Harbor Industrial Estate
St Michael, BB 11145

246-430-1006
Fax: 242-228-9524
E-Mail: patrick.cozier@caribsurf.com
Home Page: www.caribunion.com

Patrick Cozier, President

Stimulates the flow of broadcast material among the radio and television systems in the Caribbean region.
Founded in 1970
Mailing list available for rent

3738 **Coalition Opposing Signal Theft**
25 Massachusetts Ave NW
Suite 100
Washington, DC 20001

202-222-2300
E-Mail: webmaster@ncta.com
Home Page: www.ncta.com

Michael Powell, President & CEO
James M Assey, Executive VP
K Dane Snowden, Chief of Staff
Bruce Carnes, Senior VP, Finance & Administration
William Check, Senior VP, Science & Technology

Acts as a clearinghouse of information regarding cable signal theft.

3739 **Community Antenna Television Association**
PO Box 1005
Fairfax, VA 22030-1005

202-775-3550

An association of over 3,000 cable television systems.
3M Members

3740 **Content Delivery & Security Association**
39 N Bayles Ave
Port Washington, NY 11050

519-767-6782
Fax: 516-883-5793
E-Mail: info@CDSAonline.org
Home Page: www.cdsaonline.org

James Dunkelberger, Chairman
Paul W Scott, VP
Tom Moran, Secretary/Treasurer

International trade association dealing with every facet of recording, media and related industries. Membership includes raw material providers, manufacturers, replicators, duplicators, packagers, and copyright holders.

3741 **Corporation for Public Broadcasting**
401 9th St NW
Washington, DC 20004-2129

202-879-9600
800-272-2190
Fax: 202-879-9700
E-Mail: oigemail@cpb.org
Home Page: www.cpb.org
Social Media: Facebook, Twitter

Patricia De Stacy Harrison, Chair
Vincent Curren, EVP & COO
William P Tayman Jr., CFO/Treasurer
Westwood Smithers Jr., Senior VP/General Counsel
Michael Levy, Executive VP

Facilitate the development of, and ensure universal access to, non-commercial high-quality programming and telecommunications services. It does this in conjunction with non-commercial educational telecommunications licensees across the country.
Founded in 1967

3742 **Country Radio Broadcasters**
1009 16th Ave South
Nashville, TN 37212

615-327-4487
Fax: 615-329-4492
E-Mail: info@crb.org
Home Page: www.crb.org
Social Media: Facebook, Twitter

Bill Mayne, Executive Director
Chasity Crouch, Business Manager

Broadcasting forum.

3743 **Educational Broadcasting Association**
825 Eighth Ave
New York, NY 10019

212-560-3063
Fax: 212-560-3199
E-Mail: programming@thirteen.org
Home Page: www.thirteen.org
Social Media: Facebook, Twitter, Pinterest

William F. Bakerns, President & CEO
Stella Giammasi, VP Communication
Daisy Pommer, Manager

Association members are producers and directors of public educational programming, channel 13, PBS.
500 Members
Mailing list available for rent

3744 **Enterprise Wireless Alliance**
8484 Westpark Drive
630
Mc Lean, VA 22102

703-528-5115
800-482-8282
Home Page:
www.enterprisewirelessalliance.org

Bart Fisher, Chariman
Catherine Leonard, Vice Chair
Mark E Crosby, President/CEO
William Jenkins, Treasurer

Provides a license renewal reminder service. Maintains liaison with major radio manufacturers and mediates problems between licensees.
15 Members
Founded in 1953

3745 **Geospatial Information and Technology Association**
1360 University Ave W
Suite 455
St. Paul, MN 55104-4086

303-337-0513
Fax: 303-337-1001
E-Mail: bsamborski@gita.org
Home Page: www.gita.org
Social Media: Facebook, Twitter, LinkedIn

Talbot Brooks, President

Provides unbiased educational programs, forums and publications for professionals involved with geospatial information and technology.
2200 Members
Founded in 1960

3746 **Hollywood Radio and Television Society**
13701 Riverside Dr
Suite 205
Sherman Oaks, CA 91423

818-789-1182
Fax: 818-789-1210
E-Mail: info@hrts.org
Home Page: www.hrts.org
Social Media: Facebook, Twitter, LinkedIn

Sean Perry, President
Jennie Nevin, Director of Operations
Ruzzo Martinelli, Events
Meshak Vallesillas, Marketing & Communications
Elvia Gonzalez, Member Services

Sponsors monthly luncheons featuring top industry and government speakers and seminars about broadcasting, maintains film and audio library.
100 Members
Founded in 1947
Mailing list available for rent

3747 **Intercollegiate Broadcasting Systems**
367 Windsor Highway
New Windsor, NY 12553-7900

845-565-0003
Fax: 845-565-7446
E-Mail: ibs@ibsradio.org
Home Page: www.ibsradio.org
Social Media: Facebook, Twitter

Len Mailloux, Chairman
Norman Prusslin, President/Chair Emeritus
Fritz Kass, CEO

Nonprofit association of student staffed radio stations based at schools and colleges across the country. Some 800 member stations operate all sizes and types of facilities including Internet-Webcasting, closed circuit, AM carrier-current, cable radio and FCC-licensed FM and AM stations.
800 Members
Founded in 1940

3748 **International Association of Broadcast Monitors**
PO Box 986
Irmo, SC 29063

803-749-9833
800-236-1741
Fax: 888-732-9004

E-Mail: iabm@iabm.com
Home Page: www.iabm.com

Mike Ross, Executive Director
Kevin Repka, President
Ron Coucil, VP International
John Croll, Secretary
Holly Wine, Treasurer

Worldwide trade association made up of news retrieval services which monitor television, radio, internet and print news mediums. It acts as a clearinghouse or forum for discussion on topics of collective concerns and acts as a united voice for the news monitoring industry.
Founded in 1981

3749 **International Council-National Academy**
25 W 52nd Street
New York, NY 10019

212-489-6969
Fax: 212-489-6557
E-Mail: iemmys@iemmys.tv
Home Page: www.iemmys.tv
Social Media: Facebook, Twitter, LinkedIn

Fred Cohen, Chairman
Bruce Paisner, President & CEO
MJ Sorenson, Director Marketing

Furthers the arts and sciences by bestowing International Emmy Awards, George Movshon Fellowship and the Joan Wilson memorial scholarship.
250+ Members
Founded in 1969

3750 **International Radio and Television Society Foundation**
420 Lexington Ave
Suite 1601
New York, NY 10170

212-867-6650
Fax: 212-867-6653
Home Page: www.irts.org

Joyce M. Tudrynff, President
Jim Cronin, Dir, Member Prgms & Development
Marilyn L. Ellis, Director, Program Administration
Lauren Kruk-Winokur, Dir, Academic Prgms & Communication
Tom Kane, Chairman

The lines between broadcast televison and radio, cable, telephony and the computer industry may be blurring, but one thing remains clear, we all have an affinity for a business that entertains, informs, educates and serves the American public in a meaningful way. The foundation provides a unique common forum for all segments of the communication industry. Members can enjoy sharing insight and ideas with colleagues during the season's numerous events.
750 Members
Founded in 1939

3751 **International Television Academy**
25 W 52nd Street
New York, NY 10019

212-489-6969
Fax: 212-489-6557
E-Mail: zoe.dyck@iemmys.tv
Home Page: www.iemmys.tv

Bruce Paisner, President
Fred Cohen, Chairman

Organization of global broadcasters, with representatives from over 50 countries based outside of the US, and represents the world's largest production, distribution and broadcast companies.
Founded in 1969

3752 **Jones/NCTI-National Cable Television Institute**
9697 E Mineral Ave
Centennial, CO 80112

303-792-3111
800-525-7002
Fax: 303-797-0829
E-Mail: info@jones.com
Home Page: www.jones.com

Glenn R Jones, CEO
Michael Guilfoyle, Director Market Strategy
Jerry Neese, Director Sales

Workforce performance products, services and education.
30 Members
Founded in 1969
Mailing list available for rent

3753 **Library of American Broadcasting**
University of Maryland
College Park, MD 20742-7011

301-405-9160
Fax: 301-314-2634
E-Mail: bp50@umail.umed.edu
Home Page: www.lib.umd.edu

Malachy Wienges, Chair
Barbara Williams Perry, 1st Vice Chair
Alison Gibson, 2nd Vice Chair
Jamie Jensen, Secretary
Terry D Peterson, Treasurer

Holds a wide ranging collection of audio and video recordings, books, pamphlets, periodicals, personal collections, oral histories, photographs, scripts and vertical files devoted exclusively to the history of broadcasting.
Founded in 1972

3754 **Manufacturers Radio Frequency Advisory Committee**
8900 Dicks Hill Parkway
Toccoa, GA 30577

316-832-9213
800-262-9206
E-Mail: jpakla@mrfac.com
Home Page: www.mrfac.com

Tom Fagan, President
Joe Cramer, VP
Don Tyree, Secretary
Rich Elersich, Treasurer

Representing the voice of the manufacturing industry and private land mobile radio users before the Federal Communications Commision, the responsibe federal regulatory agency for the nation's industrial communications. The leaders of the manufacturing industry, individually and collectively, have an obligation to influence the policies, plans, and procedures which govern the growth, structure and use of our national radio spectrum and telecommunications systems.
14000 Members

3755 **Media Communications Association International**
P.O.Box 5135
Madison, WI 53705-0135

608-836-0722
800-899-6224
Fax: 888-899-6224
E-Mail: loiswei@aol.com
Home Page: www.mca-i.org
Social Media: Facebook, Twitter, LinkedIn

Brian Alberth, President
Jennifer Salci, President Elect
Clayton Vandiver, Treasurer
Liz De Nesnera, Secretary

The Media Communications Association-International is a global community that provides professional development seminars and events, opportunities for networking, members-only benefits, forums for education, and information resources for media communications professionals.
Founded in 1968

3756 **Media Financial Management Association**
550 W Frontage Road
Suite 3600
Northfield, IL 60093

847-716-7000
Fax: 847-716-7004
E-Mail: info@mediafinance.org
Home Page: www.mediafinance.org
Social Media: Twitter, LinkedIn

Mary M Collins, President/CEO
Jamie L Smith, Director of Operations
Arcelia Pimentel, Membership Manager & Sales
Andy Holdgate, Public Relations Consultant

Professional society of media's top financial, MIS Credit and HR executives, plus associates in auditing, data processing, software development, law, tax and credit and collections
1300 Members
Founded in 1961
Mailing list available for rent

3757 **Museum of Broadcast Communications**
360 North State Street
Chicago, IL 60654

312-245-8200
Fax: 312-245-8207
E-Mail: info@museum.tv
Home Page: www.museum.tv
Social Media: Facebook, Twitter

Bruce DuMont, President, CEO
David Plier, VP, Secretary
Jack Weinberg, VP

Collects, preserves, and presents historic and contemporary radio and television content as well as educate, inform , and entertain the public through its archives, public programs, screenings, exhibits, publications, and online access to its resources.

3758 **National Academy of Television Arts and Sciences**
1697 Broadway
Suite 404
New York, NY 10019

212-586-8424
Fax: 212-246-8129
Home Page: www.emmyonline.tv
Social Media: Facebook, Twitter

Brent Stanton, Executive Director
David Winn, Director
Christine Chin, Manager

Dedicated to the advancement of the arts and sciences of television and the promotion of creative leadership for artistic, educational and technical achievements within the television industry. It recognizes excellence in television with the coveted Emmy Award.
12M Members
Founded in 1957
Printed in on glossy stock

3759 **National Association of Black Owned Broadcasters (NABOB)**
1201 Connecticut Avenue NW
Suite 200
Washington, DC 20036

202-463-8970
Fax: 202-429-0657
E-Mail: nabobinfo@nabob.org
Home Page: www.nabob.org

Micheal L Carter, VP
Karen E Slade, Treasurer

James L Winston, Executive Director/General Counsel

Largest trade organization representing the interests of African-American owners of radio and television stations across the country.

3760 National Association of Broadcasters
1771 N St Nw
Washington, DC 20036

202-429-5300
Fax: 202-429-4199
E-Mail: nab@nab.org
Home Page: www.nab.org
Social Media: Facebook, Twitter, LinkedIn

David K Rehr, CEO
Philip J Lombardo, Chairman
Dean Goodman, COO
Ann Young-Orr, Executive Director
Michelle Duke, Development Director

Full service trade association that represents the interests of free, over-the-air radio and television broadcasters. Offers seminars and workshops to members and holds local meetings that offer support on legal and industry issues. Sponsors the National Association of Broadcasters Educational Foundation, dedicated to serving the public interest via education and training programs, strategies to increase diverse initiatives, community support and philanthropy.
7000 Members
Founded in 1923

3761 National Association of College Radio/TV Stations
71 George Street
Providence, RI 02912-1824

401-863-2225
Fax: 401-863-2221
E-Mail: nacb@aol.com

Members are student radio/TV stations and interested individuals. Has an annual budget of approximately $300,000.
1600 Members
Founded in 1988

3762 National Association of Farm Broadcasters
1100 Platte Falls Road
PO Box 500
Platte City, MO 64079

816-431-4032
Fax: 816-431-4087
E-Mail: info@nafb.com
Home Page: www.nafb.com
Social Media: Facebook, Twitter

Janet Adkison, President
Susan Littlefield, President Elect
Brian Winnekins, VP

Works to improve quantity and quality of farm programming and serves as a clearinghouse for new ideas in farm broadcasting.
600 Members
Founded in 1944

3763 National Association of Television Program Executives
5757 Wilshire Blvd
Penthouse 10
Los Angeles, CA 90036-5810

323-937-4465
Fax: 310-453-5258
E-Mail: info@natpe.org
Home Page: www.natpe.org
Social Media: Facebook, Twitter, Youtube

Rod Perth, President/CEO
Olivia Thomas, Executive Assistant to President
Eric Low, Director, Registration
Jordan Ryder, VP, Event Programming
Dann Novak, Programming Producer

A global, non-profit organization dedicated to the creation, development and distribution of televised programming in all forms across all mature and emerging media platforms.
2800 Members
Founded in 1963
Mailing list available for rent

3764 National Cable Television Association
25 Massachusetts Ave NW
Suite 100
Washington, DC 20001

202-775-3550
Fax: 202-775-3604
E-Mail: webmaster@ncta.com
Home Page: www.ncta.com
Social Media: Facebook, Twitter, LinkedIn

Michael Powell, President & CEO
Brian Dietz, VP

Association for those interested in programs about cable television.
200+ Members
Founded in 1940

3765 National Council for Families & TV
3801 Barham Boulevard
Los Angeles, CA 90068-1000

323-953-7300
Fax: 310-208-5984
Home Page: www.salonprofessionals.org

Advances and promotes television awareness for family television shows.

3766 National Federation of Community Broadcasting
2751 Hennepin Avenue South #41
Minneapolis, MN 55408

612-998-9619
Fax: 510-451-8208
E-Mail: comments@nfcb.org
Home Page: www.nfcb.org

Maxie C Jackson III, President/CEO
Brian Terhorst, Board Chair
Kim Bosler, Secretary
Peggy Berryhill, Treasurer

A national alliance of stations, producers, and others committed to community radio. NFCB advocates for national public policy, funding, recognition, and resources on behalf of its membership while providing services to empower and strengthen community broadcasters through the core values of localism, diversity, and public service.

3767 National Public Radio Association
1111 North Capitol Street NW
Washington, DC 20002

202-686-0516
Fax: 202-513-3329
Home Page: www.npr.org
Social Media: Facebook, Twitter

Gary E Knell, President/CEO
Joyce MacDonald, Chief of Staff/Vice President
Jeff Perkins, Chief People Officer
Robert Kempf, General Manager
Deborah Cowan, VP/Chief Financial Officer

Works in partnership with member stations to create a more informed public, one challenged and invigorated by a deeper understanding and appreciation of events, ideas, and cultures.
750 Members
Founded in 1970

3768 National Religious Broadcasters
9510 Technology Dr
Manassas, VA 20110

703-330-7000
Fax: 703-330-7100
E-Mail: info@nrb.org
Home Page: www.nrb.org
Social Media: Facebook, Twitter, LinkedIn

Frank Wright, President/CEO
Linda Smith, President Assistant
Craig Parshall, Senior VP/General Counsel
Aaron Mercer, VP of Government Relations

Represents evangelical Christian radio and television stations, program producers, multimedia developers and related organizations around the worldMembers are responsible for much of the world's Christian radio and television.
1700 Members
Founded in 1944
Mailing list available for rent

3769 National Sportscasters and Sportswriters Association
PO Box 1545
Salisbury, NC 28145

704-633-4275
Fax: 704-633-2027
E-Mail: nssahalloffame@aol.com
Home Page: www.nssahalloffame.com
Social Media: Facebook, Twitter

Dave Goren, Executive Director
Katy Temple, Adminstrative Assistant

Meet annually.
1000 Members
Founded in 1959
Mailing list available for rent

3770 New England Cable & Telecommunications Associatoin Inc
Ten Forbes Road
Suite 440W
Braintree, MA 02184

781-843-3418
Fax: 781-849-6267
E-Mail: info@necta.info
Home Page: www.necta.info

Mark Reilly, President
Paul Cronin, Vice Chair
Tom Cohan, Treasurer
Melinda Poore, Secretary
William D Durand, Executive VP/Chief Counsel

NECTA is a six state regional trade association representing sbtstantially all private cable telecommunications companies in Connecticut, Maine, Massachusetts, New Hampshire, Rhode Island and Vermont.

3771 North American Broadcasters Association (N ABA)
205 Wellington Street West
Suite 6C300
Toronto, ON M5V 3G7

416-598-9877
Fax: 416-598-9774
E-Mail: contact@nabanet.com
Home Page: www.nabanet.com

Michael McEwan, Director General
Anh Ngo, Director, Administration
Jason Paris, Senior Coordinator

A non-profit association of broadcasting organizations in the United States, Mexico, and Canada committed to advancing the interests of broadcasters at home and internationally.

3772 **North American Network**
3700 Crestwood Pkwy NW
Suite 350
Duluth, GA 30096-7154

770-279-4560
Fax: 770-279-4566
E-Mail: rbeilfuss@pkfnan.org
Home Page: www.pkfnan.org

Terry Snyder, President

Radio broadcasting agency that provides news and programming services to radio stations and organizations. Programming is sponsored by the corporations, government angencies, associations and nonprofit organizations who are indentified in the program notes and scripts.

3773 **Public Radio in Mid-America (PRIMA)**
3651 Olive Street
St Louis, MO 63108

314-516-5968
Fax: 307-766-6184
E-Mail: info@kmwu.org
Home Page: www.kmwu.org

Tim Eby, General Manager
Terrence Dupuis, Chief Engineer
Shelley Kerley, Director, Development

Trusted source of informationa nd entertainment that opens minds and nourishes the spirit.

3774 **Radio Advertising Bureau**
1320 Greenway Dr
Suite 500
Irving, TX 75038-2547

972-753-6700
800-232-3131
Fax: 972-753-6727
E-Mail: jhaley@rab.com
Home Page: www.rab.com
Social Media: Facebook, Twitter

Bayard Walters, Chairman
Van Allen, CFO/EVP
Hartley Adkins II, Vice Chair
Kim Guthrie, Secretary

Our mission is to lead industry initiatives and provide organizational, educational, research and advocacy programs and services that benefit the RAB membership and the Radio industry as a whole.
7000 Members

3775 **Radio Television Digital News Assn.**
529 14th Street NW
Suite 425
Washington, DC 20045

800-807-8632
Fax: 202-223-4007
E-Mail: mikec@rtdna.org
Home Page: www.rtdna.org
Social Media: Facebook, Twitter, LinkedIn

Mike Cavender, Executive Director
Ryan Murphy, Communications
Katie Switchenko, Programs

An association dedicated to setting new standards for newsgathering and reporting.

3776 **Radio Television Digital News Association (Canada)**
529 14th Street NW
Suite 1240
Washington, DC 20045

800-807-8632
Fax: 202-223-4007
E-Mail: mikec@rtdna.org
Home Page: www.rtdna.org
Social Media: Facebook, Twitter, LinkedIn

Mike Cavender, Executive Director
Derrick Hinds, Communications, Marketing & Digital
Katie Switchenko, Programs

An association dedicated to setting new standards for newsgathering and reporting.

3777 **Radio Television News Directors Association**
529 14th Street NW
Suite 1240
Washington, DC 20045

800-807-8632
Fax: 202-223-4007
E-Mail: barbarac@rtnda.org
Home Page: www.rtnda.org
Social Media: Facebook, Twitter, LinkedIn

Mike Cavender, Executive Director
Derrick Hinds, Communications, Marketing & Digital
Katie Switchenko, Programs

Largest professional organization exclusively serving the electronic news profession. Dedicated to setting standards for newsgathering and reporting. Represents electronic journalists in radion, television and all digital media, as well as journalism educators and students.
3000+ Members
Founded in 1946

3778 **Radio Television News Directors Assn. - Canada**
2175 Shepherd Avenue E
Suite 310
Toronto, ON M2J 1W8

416-756-2126
877-257-8632
Fax: 416-364-8896
E-Mail: info@rtndacanada.com
Home Page: www.rtndacanada.com

Ian Koenigsfest, President

Progressive organization offering a forum for open discussion and action in the broadcast news industry. Speaks for the leaders of Canada's radio and television news operations on the issues that impact the newsroom.

3779 **Radio and Television Research Council**
234 5th Ave
#417
New York, NY 10001

212-028-8933
Fax: 212-481-3071

Robert M Purcell, Executive Director

Members are professionals actively engaged in radio/television research.
200 Members
Founded in 1941

3780 **Satellite Broadcasting and Communication Association (SBCA)**
1100 17th Street NW
Suite 1150
Washington, DC 20036

202-349-3620
800-541-5981
Fax: 202-349-3621
E-Mail: info@sbca.org
Home Page: www.sbca.com
Social Media: Facebook, Twitter, LinkedIn

Jeffrey Blum, Chairman
Andrew Reinsdorf, Vice Chair
Joseph Widoff, Executive Director

National trade organization representing all segments of the satellite consumer services industry. The association is committed to expanding the utilization of satellite technology for the delivery of video, data, voice, interactive and broadband services.
1000 Members
Founded in 1986

3781 **Society of Broadcast Engineers**
9102 N Meridian St
Suite 150
Indianapolis, IN 46260

317-846-9000
Fax: 317-846-9120
E-Mail: mclappe@sbe.org
Home Page: www.sbe.org

Joseph Snelson, President
Jerry Massey, VP
James E Leifer, Secretary
Andrea Cummins, Treasurer

SBE provides members with the opportunity to network and share ideas and information in keeping current with the ongoing changes within the industry. Members can attend annual conferences and expositions, have access to educational opportunities and obtain professional certification.
5500 Members
Founded in 1964
Mailing list available for rent: 5700 names at $170 per M

3782 **Society of Motion Picture & Television Engineers**
3 Barker Ave
5th Floor
White Plains, NY 10601

914-761-1100
Fax: 914-761-3115
Home Page: www.smpte.org
Social Media: Facebook, Twitter, LinkedIn

Wendy Aylsworth, President
Robert P. Seidel, Executive VP
Hans Hoffman, Standards VP
Peter Wharton, Secretary/Treasurer

The Society of Motion Picture and Television Engineers (SMPTE), is the leading technical society for the motion imaging industry. SMPTE members are spread throughout 64 countries worldwide. Sustaining (institutional) Members belong to SMPTE, allowing networking and contacts to occur on a larger scale. Touching on every discipline, our members include engineers, technical directors, cameramen, editors, technicians, manufacturers, designers, educators, consultants and field users.
6000 Members
Founded in 1916

3783 **Statenets National Association of State Radio Networks**
17911 Harwood Avenue
Homewood, IL 60430

708-799-6676
804-364-3075
Fax: 708-799-6698
E-Mail: idobrez@statenets.com
Home Page: www.statenets.com
Social Media: Facebook, Twitter, LinkedIn, RSS

Tom Dobrez, Executive Director
Sharon Kitchell, Deputy Director

Works with hundreds of regional and national marketers and political campaigns solve marketing challenges.

3784 **Syndicated Network Television Association**
One Penn Plaza
Suite 5310
New York, NY 10119

212-259-3740
Fax: 212-259-3770

E-Mail: mburg@snta.com
Home Page: www.snta.com

Mitch Burg, President
Jordan Harris, Director, Marketing
Hadassa Gerber, Director. Research

Communicates to advertisers, their agencies and media planners and buyers the benefits of syndication, from the wide range of programming choices to their high ratings and national reach, and the reliability and cost effectiveness of advertising in syndicated programming.

3785 Television Bureau of Advertising
120 Wall Street
15th Floor
New York, NY 10005-3908

212-486-1111
Fax: 212-935-5631
E-Mail: info@tvb.org
Home Page: www.tvb.org

Steve Lanzano, President
Abby Auerbach, Executive VP/CMO
Michael Bollo, VP, Business Development
Jack Poor, VP, Marketing Insights
Scott Roskowski, SVP, Business Development

Not-for-profit trade association of America's broadcast television industry. TVB provides a diverse variety of tools and resources to support its members and to help advertisers make the best use of local television.
600 Members
Founded in 1954

3786 Television Bureau of Canada
160 Bloor Street East
Suite 1005
Toronto, ON M4W 1B9

416-923-8813
800-231-0051
Fax: 416-413-3879
E-Mail: tvb@tvb.ca
Home Page: www.tvb.ca

Theresa Treutler, President, CEO
Duncan Robertson, Director, Media Insights
Rhonda Lynn Bagnall, Director, Telecaster Services

TVB markets the benefits and effectiveness of the TV medium in all its forms to advertisers and agencies. TVB collects, interprets, develops, identifies, and communicates information and data to be used.

3787 Television Critics Association
825 East Douglas Avenue
Witchita, KS 67202

316-268-6394
Fax: 316-288-6627
E-Mail: info@tvcritics.org
Home Page: www.tvcritics.org

Candy Havens, President
Scott Pierce, Vice President
Amber Dowling, Secretary
Brian Gianelli, Treasurer

Represents journalists writing about television for print and online outlets.
220 Members

3788 Television Operators Caucus
1176 K Street NW
9th Floor
Washington, DC 20006

202-719-7090
Fax: 202-719-7548
E-Mail: info@fundraise.com
Social Media: Facebook, Twitter, Google+

Nate Drouin, Founder/CEO
Kurt Schneider, COO
Kevin Bedell, CTO

Non-profit group of memebers that support television issues and its impacts on the world today.

3789 The Alliance for Community Media
4248 Park Glen Road
Minneapolis, MN 55416

952-928-4643
Fax: 703-506-3266
E-Mail: info@allcommunitymedia.org
Home Page: www.allcommunitymedia.org
Social Media: Facebook, Twitter

Keri Stokstad, Chair
Michael Heylin, Vice Chair
John Donovan, Treasurer
Todd Thayer, Treasurer Elect

Promotes civic engagement through community medias.
1000 Members
Founded in 1976

3790 The Association for Maximum Service Televi sion
4100 Wisconsin Avenue NW
PO Box 9897
Washington, DC 20016

202-966-1956
Fax: 202-966-9617
E-Mail: lmillory@mstv.org
Home Page: www.mstv.org

Craig Dubow, CEO

MSTV has endeavored to insure that American public receive the highest quality, interference free, over-the-air local television signals. Recognized as the industry leader in broadcasting technology and spectrum policy issues.

3791 The Broadcasters Hall of Fame
1240 Ashford Lane, 1A
PO Box 8247
Akron, OH 44320

330-867-3779
Fax: 330-867-4907
E-Mail: info@briadcastershalloffame.com
Home Page: www.broadcastershalloffame.com

C S (Doc) Williams, Founder, CEO
Henry Dunn, Chairman

A wealth of memorabilia from the early days of broadcasting, clippings from newspapers and magazines, taped recorded portions of early radio shows and other gems of broadcasting history.
Founded in 1982

3792 WGBH Educational Foundation
One Guest Street
Boston, MA 02135

617-300-5400
Home Page: www.wgbh.org

Jonathan C Abbott, President/CEO
Benjamin Godley, Executive VP & COO
Vinay Mehra, CFO/VP, Finance & Adminstration
Susan L Kantrowitz, VP & General Counsel
Stacey Decker, CTO

Make knowledge and the creative life of the arts, sciences, and humanities available to the widest possible public
Founded in 1836

Newsletters

3793 American Sportscasters Association Insiders Newsletter
American Sportscasters Association
225 Broadway
Suite 2030
New York, NY 10007-3742

212-227-8080
Fax: 212-571-0556
E-Mail: lschwa8918@aol.com
Home Page: www.americansportscastersonline.com
Social Media: Facebook, Twitter

Louis O Schwartz, CEO
Dick Enberg, Chairman Of The Board

Newsletter keeps sportscasters up to date on important issues for the profession.
24 Pages
Frequency: Quarterly
Circulation: 2500
Founded in 1980

3794 Bandwidth Investor
Kagan World Media
126 Clock Tower Place
Carmel, CA 93923-8746

831-624-1536
Fax: 831-625-3225
E-Mail: sgoldberg@kagan.com
Home Page: www.kagan.com

George Niesen, Editor
Harvy Carft, Marketing Manager
Tim Baskerville, CEO/President
Harvy Carft, Circulation Manager
Cost: $945.00
Frequency: Monthly
Founded in 1969

3795 Broadband Fixed Wireless
Kagan World Media
126 Clock Tower Place
Carmel, CA 93923-8746

831-624-1536
Fax: 831-625-3225
E-Mail: info@kagan.com
Home Page: www.kagan.com

George Niesen, Editor
Tom Johnson, Marketing Manager
Cost: $845.00
Frequency: Monthly

3796 Broadband Systems & Design
Gordon Publications
301 Gibraltar Drive
#650
Morris Plains, NJ 07950-3400

973-292-5100
Fax: 973-539-3476

Terry McCoy Jr, Publisher
Andrea Frucci, Editor

The only product tabloid serving buying influencers, engineers, corporate managers and purchasing professionals in the cable television marketplace.
Circulation: 26,400

3797 Broadband Technology
Kagan World Media
126 Clock Tower Place
Carmel, CA 93923-8746

831-624-1536
Fax: 831-625-3225
E-Mail: info@kagan.com
Home Page: www.kagan.com

George Niesen, Editor
Tom Johnson, Marketing Manager
Cost: $1450.00
Frequency: Monthly
Founded in 1969

3798 Broadcast Banker/Broker
Kagan World Media

126 Clock Tower Place
Carmel, CA 93923-8746

831-624-1536
800-307-2529
Fax: 831-625-3225
E-Mail: info@kagan.com
Home Page: www.kagan.com

George Niesen, Editor
Tom Johnson, Marketing Manager

A readers guide to equity deals and debt financing for radio and TV Station buying and selling analyzed. Key details on station trades with critical yardsticks of value. Three month trial is available.
Cost: $925.00
Frequency: Monthly
Founded in 1969

3799 **Broadcast Investor**
Kagan World Media
1 Lower Ragsdale Drive
Building One, Suite 130
Monterey, CA 93940-5749

831-624-1536
800-307-2529
Fax: 831-625-3225
E-Mail: info@kagan.com
Home Page: www.kagan.com/

Tim Baskerville, President
Tom Johnson, Marketing Manager

The newsletter on investments in radio and TV stations and publicly held companies. Comprehensive analysis of cash flow multiples and trends that impact value. Three month trial available.
Cost: $1295.00
Frequency: Monthly
Founded in 1969

3800 **Broadcast Stats**
Kagan World Media
126 Clock Tower Place
Carmel, CA 93923-8746

831-624-1536
800-307-2529
Fax: 831-624-5882
E-Mail: info@kagan.com
Home Page: www.kagan.com

George Niesen, Editor
Tom Johnson, Marketing Manager

The numbers behind the broadcast companies. Exclusive data, analysis and projections of radio and TV market billings, revenues, and cash flows, plus complete data on the buy-sell market. The industry's key reference source. Three month trial available.
Cost: $795.00
Frequency: Monthly
Founded in 1969

3801 **Business Radio**
Nt'l Association of Business & Educational Radio
500 Montgomery Street
Alexandria, VA 22314

703-548-1500
Fax: 703-836-1608

AE Goetz, Publisher

Association news for professionals, owners and consumers regarding radio stations.
Cost: $65.00
Circulation: 3,000

3802 **Cable Program Investor**
Kagan World Media
1 Lower Ragsdale Dr
Building One, Suite 130
Monterey, CA 93940-5749

831-624-1536
800-307-2529
Fax: 831-625-3225
E-Mail: info@kagan.com
Home Page: www.kagan.com/

Tim Baskerville, President
Tom Johnson, Marketing Manager
Robin Flynn, Senior VP
Sharon Armbrust, Senior Consultant
Derek Baine, Senior Vice President

Covers the economics of basic cable programming networks. Numbers, perspective unavailable from any other source. Programmers applaud its accuracy. Three month trial available.
Cost: $1045.00
Frequency: Monthly
Founded in 1969

3803 **Cable TV Advertising**
Kagan World Media
126 Clock Tower Place
Carmel, CA 93923-8746

831-624-1536
Fax: 831-624-5882
E-Mail: info@kagan.com
Home Page: www.kagan.com

George Niesen, Editor
Tom Johnson, Marketing Manager

Analysis of sales of commercial time by cable TV networks, interconnects and local systems. Detailed reports on national and local spot sales. Case studies and projections, all about the industry's upside. Three month trial available.
Cost: $795.00
Frequency: Monthly

3804 **Cable TV Finance**
Kagan World Media
126 Clock Tower Place
Carmel, CA 93923-8746

831-624-1536
800-307-2529
Fax: 831-624-5882
E-Mail: info@kagan.com
Home Page: www.kagan.com

George Niesen, Editor
Tom Johnson, Marketing Manager
Larry Gerbrandt, CEO/President
Judy Pinney, Circulation Manager
Tim Baskerville, Publisher

Cable's financial bible. Analyzes sources of funding for cable TV. Selling and buying of cable systems. Financing strategies and trends. Exclusive surveys of capital sources. Three month trial available.
Cost: $795.00
Frequency: Monthly
Founded in 1969

3805 **Cable TV Investor**
Kagan World Media
1 Lower Ragsdale Dr
Building One, Suite 130
Monterey, CA 93940-5749

831-624-1536
800-307-2529
Fax: 831-625-3225
E-Mail: info@kagan.com
Home Page: www.kagan.com

Tim Baskerville, President
Tom Johnson, Marketing Manager

Readers road map to cable stock trends. Chart service tracking stock price movements of 37 publicly held cable TV companies. Each graph shows two years of stock price activity. Three month trial available.
Cost: $1295.00
Frequency: Monthly
Founded in 1969

3806 **Cable TV Law Reporter**
Kagan World Media
1 Lower Ragsdale Dr
Building One, Suite 130
Monterey, CA 93940-5749

831-624-1536
800-307-2529
Fax: 831-625-3225
E-Mail: info@kagan.com
Home Page: www.kagan.com

Tim Baskerville, President
Tom Johnson, Marketing Manager

The quintessential library of cable court cases, arbitrations, legal precedents. Labeled and catalogued for easy reference. Required reading for attorneys, government regulators and top executives. Three month trial available.
Cost: $995.00
Frequency: Monthly
Founded in 1969

3807 **Cable TV Technology**
Kagan World Media
1 Lower Ragsdale Dr
Building One, Suite 130
Monterey, CA 93940-5749

831-624-1536
800-307-2529
Fax: 831-625-3225
E-Mail: info@kagan.com
Home Page: www.kagan.com

Tim Baskerville, President
Tom Johnson, Marketing Manager

Incisive, thorough reports on technical advances in cable TV, in terms operating executives can grasp and use to implement strategies. Analyzes growth in addressable converters, high definition TV, fiber optics and other advancements. Three month trial available.
Cost: $925.00
Frequency: Monthly
Founded in 1969

3808 **Community Radio News**
National Federation of Community Broadcasting
1970 Broadway
Suite 1000
Oakland, CA 94612

510-451-8200
Fax: 510-451-8208
E-Mail: comments@nfcb.org
Home Page: www.nfcb.org
Social Media: Facebook, Twitter

Ryan Bruce, Publications Manager

Contains calendar of events and information on public broadcasting, job listings, and legislative and regulatory updates. Annual Community Radio Conference and Community Radio Program Awards Competition.
Cost: $75.00
12-16 Pages
Frequency: Monthly
Circulation: 400
Founded in 1975
Mailing list available for rent: 300 names at $25 per M
Printed in one color on matte stock

3809 **Community Television Review**
National Federation of Local Cable Programmers
666 11th Street NW
Suite 806
Washington, DC 20001

202-393-2650
Fax: 202-393-2653

Andrew Lewis, Publisher

Issues of importance to community programming on cable and other areas of telecommuni-

cations.
Cost: $15.00
36 Pages

3810 **DBS Report**
Kagan World Media
1 Lower Ragsdale Dr
Building One, Suite 130
Monterey, CA 93940-5749

831-624-1536
800-307-2529
Fax: 831-625-3225
E-Mail: info@kagan.com
Home Page: www.kagan.com

Tim Baskerville, President
Tom Johnson, Marketing Manager
Cost: $1045.00
Frequency: Monthly
Founded in 1969

3811 **Dance on Camera Journal**
Dance Films Association
48 W 21st St
Suite 907
New York, NY 10010-6989

212-727-0764
Fax: 212-727-0764
E-Mail: christy@dancefilms.org
Home Page: www.dancefilms.org

Deidra Towers, Executive Director
Louise Spain, President

The only service organization in the world dedicated to both the dance and the film community.
ISSN: 1098-8084
Founded in 1956
Printed in on matte stock

3812 **Digital Television**
Kagan World Media
126 Clock Tower Place
Carmel, CA 93923-8746

831-624-1536
800-307-2529
Fax: 831-624-5882
E-Mail: info@kagan.com
Home Page: www.kagan.com

George Niesen, Editor
Tom Johnson, Marketing Manager

News of the Digital Television. Three month trial available.
Cost: $945.00
Frequency: Monthly
Founded in 1969

3813 **Hearsay**
Association of Radio Reading Services
600 Forbes Ave
Pittsburgh, PA 15219-3002

412-488-3944
Fax: 412-488-3953
E-Mail: info@readingservice.org
Home Page: www.readingservice.org
Social Media: Facebook, Twitter

Andy Ai, President
Erica Hacker, Vice President

Newsletter for the Radio Reading industry.

3814 **Inside Sports Letter**
American Sportscasters Association
225 Broadway
Suite 2030
New York, NY 10007-3742

212-227-8080
Fax: 212-571-0556
E-Mail: lschwa8918@aol.com
Home Page: www.americansportscastersonline.com
Social Media: Facebook

Louis O Schwartz, President/Editor
Dick Enberg, Chairman
Elaine Graifer, Associate Editor
Patrick Turturro, Assistant Editor

A quarterly newsletter published by the American Sportscasters Association.
38513 Pages
Frequency: Quarterly
Circulation: 2000
Founded in 1980

3815 **Interactive Mobile Investor**
Kagan World Media
1 Lower Ragsdale Dr
Building One, Suite 130
Monterey, CA 93940-5749

831-624-1536
800-307-2529
Fax: 831-625-3225
E-Mail: info@kagan.com
Home Page: www.kagan.com

Tim Baskerville, President
Tom Johnson, Marketing Manager
Cost: $945.00
Frequency: Monthly
Founded in 1969

3816 **Interactive TV Investor**
Kagan World Media
1 Lower Ragsdale Dr
Building One, Suite 130
Monterey, CA 93940-5749

831-624-1536
Fax: 831-625-3225
E-Mail: info@kagan.com
Home Page: www.kagan.com

Tim Baskerville, President
Tom Johnson, Marketing Manager
Cost: $895.00
Frequency: Monthly
Founded in 1970

3817 **Interactive Television**
Kagan World Media
1 Lower Ragsdale Dr
Building One Suite 130
Monterey, CA 93940-5749

831-624-1536
800-307-2529
Fax: 831-625-3225
E-Mail: info@kagan.com
Home Page: www.kagan.com

Tim Baskerville, President
Tom Johnson, Marketing Manager

News of the Interactive Television. Three month trial available.
Cost: $795.00
Frequency: Monthly
Founded in 1969

3818 **Internet Media Investor**
Kagan World Media
126 Clock Tower Place
Carmel, CA 93923-8746

831-624-1536
Fax: 831-625-3225
E-Mail: info@kagan.com
Home Page: www.kagan.com

George Niesen, Editor
Tom Johnson, Marketing Manager
Cost: $945.00
Frequency: Monthly
Founded in 1969

3819 **Interval**
Society of Cable Telecommunications Engineers
140 Philips Road
Exton, PA 19341-1318

610-363-6888
800-542-5040
Fax: 610-363-5898
E-Mail: scte@scte.org
Home Page: www.scte.org

Howard Whitman, Senior Editor
Marci Dodd, President

A monthly member newsletter. Subscription price of $25.00 is for non-members.
Cost: $25.00
Frequency: Monthly
Circulation: 16000
Founded in 1969

3820 **Kagan Broadband**
Kagan World Media
1 Lower Ragsdale Dr
Building One, Suite 130
Monterey, CA 93940-5749

831-624-1536
800-307-2529
Fax: 831-625-3225
E-Mail: info@kagan.com
Home Page: www.kagan.com

Tim Baskerville, President/CEO
Harvy Craft, Marketing Manager
Robert Nayoor, Circulation Manager
Sandie Borthwick, Executive Director

Daily e-mail or fax.
Cost: $1295.00
Frequency: Monthly
Founded in 1970

3821 **Kagan Media Money**
Kagan World Media
1 Lower Ragsdale Dr
Building One, Suite 130
Monterey, CA 93940-5749

831-624-1536
800- 30- 252
Fax: 831-625-3225
E-Mail: info@kagan.com
Home Page: www.kagan.com

Tim Baskerville, President
Tom Johnson, Marketing Manager
Sandie Borthwick, Executive Director

Analysts dissect deals, anticipate trends, project revenues, track financings, and value the debt and equity of hundreds of priovately held and publicly traded advertising, broadcasting, cable TV digital TV, home video, Internet media, motion picture, newspaper, pay TV, professional sports and wireless telecommunications companies in the US and abroad.
Cost: $1245.00
Founded in 1970

3822 **Kagan Music Investor**
Kagan World Media
1 Lower Ragsdale Dr
Building One,Suite 130
Monterey, CA 93940-5749

831-624-1536
800-307-2529
Fax: 831-625-3225
E-Mail: info@kagan.com
Home Page: www.kagan.com

Tim Baskerville, President
Tom Johnson, Marketing Manager
Sandie Borthwick, Executive Director

News and analysis of the music industry for investors.
Cost: $945.00
Frequency: Monthly
Founded in 1969

3823 **Marketing New Media**
Kagan World Media

1 Lower Ragsdale Dr
Building One, Suite 130
Monterey, CA 93940-5749

831-624-1536
800-307-2529
Fax: 831-625-3225
E-Mail: info@kagan.com
Home Page: www.kagan.com

Tim Baskerville, President
Tom Johnson, Marketing Manager

News of the Marketing New Media. Three month trial available.
Cost: $795.00
Frequency: Monthly
Founded in 1969

3824 Media Communications Association News
Media Communications Association International
P.O.Box 5135
Madison, WI 53705-0135

608-836-0722
Fax: 888-899-6224
E-Mail: loiswei@aol.com
Home Page: www.mca-i.org
Social Media: Facebook, Twitter, LinkedIn

Gary Shifflet, President
Lois Weiland, Executive Director
Mike Brown, Treasurer
Jim Powell, Secretary
John Coleman, Board Member

Coverage of the multimedia industry and association activities.
Frequency: Quarterly
Circulation: 3,000
Founded in 1968
Printed in on glossy stock

3825 Media Mergers & Acquisitions
Kagan World Media
126 Clock Tower Place
Carmel, CA 93923-8746

831-624-1536
Fax: 831-624-5882
E-Mail: info@kagan.com
Home Page: www.kagan.com

George Niesen, Editor
Tom Johnson, Marketing Manager

Where it all comes together. Exclusive scorecard of deals done by media companies. Dollar amounts, multiples paid, trends captured in succinct summaries of complex transactions. Three month trial available.
Cost: $795.00
Frequency: Monthly

3826 Media Sports Business
Kagan World Media
1 Lower Ragsdale Dr
Building One, Suite 130
Monterey, CA 93940-5749

831-624-1536
800-307-2529
Fax: 831-625-3225
E-Mail: info@kagan.com
Home Page: www.kagan.com

Tim Baskerville, President
Tom Johnson, Marketing Manager
Cost: $945.00
Frequency: Monthly
Founded in 1969

3827 Monitoring Times
Grove Enterprises
7540 Highway 64 W
Brasstown, NC 28902-8079

828-837-9200
800-438-8155
Fax: 828-837-2216
E-Mail: order@grove-ent.com
Home Page: www.grove-ent.com

Bob Grove, President
Judy Grove, Office Manager
Belinda McDonald, Office Manager

News on radio communication, scanner monitoring, international radio broadcasts and technical advice.
Cost: $28.95
92 Pages
Frequency: Monthly
Circulation: 50000
ISSN: 0889-5341
Founded in 1970
Printed in 4 colors on glossy stock

3828 Motion Picture Investor
Kagan World Media
1 Lower Ragsdale Dr
Building One Suite 130
Monterey, CA 93940-5749

831-624-1536
Fax: 831-625-3225
E-Mail: info@kagan.com
Home Page: www.kagan.com

Tim Baskerville, President
Tom Johnson, Marketing Manager
Cost: $845.00
Frequency: Monthly
Founded in 1969

3829 Multichannel News
360 Park Ave S
New York, NY 10010-1710

212-887-8387
Fax: 212-463-6703
E-Mail: crucker@nbmedia.com
Home Page: www.multichannel.com

Lawrence Oliver, Publisher
Marianne Paskowski, Editorial Director
Kent Gibbons, Editor
Heather Tatrow, Production Manager
Michael Demenchuk, Managing Editor

News of the electronic media industries.
Frequency: Weekly
Circulation: 18,875
Founded in 1980

3830 NRB Today
National Religious Broadcasters
9510 Technology Dr
Manassas, VA 20110-4149

703-330-7100
Fax: 703-330-7100
E-Mail: info@nrb.org
Home Page: www.nrb.org
Social Media: Facebook

Frank Wright, President/CEO
Linda Smith, EVP/COO
Kenneth Chan, Director of Communications

This weekly newsletter by National Religious Broadcasters covers the latest news from the association and NRB's member organizations. The newsletter also serves as a source for tips, trends, and insights relevant to Christian communicators across the spectrum. Topics include audience building, branding, business strategy, innovation, job hunting, leadership, management, marketing, social media, and web strategy. NRB Today also features occasional columns, movie reviews, and product reviews.
Founded in 1944

3831 National Cable Television Association
National Cable Television Association
25 Massachusetts Ave Nw
Suite 100
Washington, DC 20001-1434

202-775-3550
Fax: 202-775-3604
E-Mail: webmaster@ncta.com
Home Page: www.ncta.com

Robert Sachs, CEO
Brian Dietz, VP of Communications

Convention newsletter with programs about cable television.
8-200 Pages
Frequency: 7 per year

3832 Networks
Geospatial Information & Technology Association
14456 E Evans Ave
Aurora, CO 80014-1409

303-337-0513
Fax: 303-337-1001
E-Mail: bsamborski@gita.org
Home Page: www.gita.org

Bob Samborski, Executive Director
Lisa Connor, Membership Services Manager
Elizabeth Roberts, Marketing

A bi-monthly newsletter published by the Geospatial Information & Technology Association.
Cost: $125.00
28 Pages
Frequency: Monthly
Circulation: 2200
Founded in 1978

3833 Pay TV Newsletter
Kagan World Media
126 Clock Tower Place
Carmel, CA 93923-8746

831-624-1536
Fax: 831-624-5882
E-Mail: info@kagan.com
Home Page: www.kagan.com

George Niesen, Editor
Tom Johnson, Marketing Manager

The pay TV industry's publication of record since 1973. Exclusive estimates of network subscribers and economics. The pay-per-view business, event-by-event, film-by-film. Three month trial available.
Cost: $795.00
Frequency: Monthly

3834 Public Broadcasting Report
Warren Communications News
2115 Ward Ct Nw
Washington, DC 20037-1209

202-872-9200
800-771-9202
Fax: 202-318-8350
E-Mail: info@warren-news.com
Home Page: www.warren-news.com

Brig Easley, Manager
Daniel Warren, President/Editor

Industry news, personnel announcements and calendar listings for public broadcasting, digital TV, congress, FCC, and allied friends.
Cost: $575.00
Founded in 1945
Mailing list available for rent

3835 Radio & Records
Radio & Records
10100 Santa Monica Boulevard
3rd Floor
Los Angeles, CA 90067-4003

310-553-4330
Fax: 310-203-8450
E-Mail: radioandrecords@billboard.biz
Home Page: www.radioandrecords.com

Erica Farber, Publisher/CEO
Henry Mowry, Director Sales

A music newspaper that covers all aspects of the radio and recording industry.
Cost: $325.00
100 Pages
Frequency: Weekly
Circulation: 8006
Printed in 4 colors on n stock

3836 **Radio Business Report**
2050 Old Bridge Rd
Suite B-01
Woodbridge, VA 22192-2481
703-492-8191
Fax: 703-997-8601
Home Page: www.rbr.com

Jim Carnegie, Publisher
Jack Messmer, Executive Editor
Cathy Carnegie, VP Administration
Carl Marcucci, MD/Senior Editor
June Barnes, Sales

Focuses on radio business issues, inside news on people and controversial topics.
Cost: $220.00
Frequency: Daily
Circulation: 5100
Founded in 1983
Printed in 4 colors on matte stock

3837 **Radio Ink**
Streamline Publishing
224 Datura St
Suite 1015
West Palm Beach, FL 33401-5638
561-655-8778
800-610-5771
Fax: 561-655-6164
Home Page: www.radioink.com

Eric Rhoads, Owner
Reed Bunzel, Editor
Marty Sacks, Marketing
Tom Elmo, Circulation

Geared toward radio broadcast management professionals contains information on marketing trends, special reports, sales and programming issues.
Cost: $199.00
Circulation: 5000
Founded in 1992

3838 **Radio World**
Industrial Marketing Advisory Services
5827 Columbia Pike
Suite 310
Falls Church, VA 22041-2027
703-998-7600
800-336-3045
Fax: 703-998-2966
Home Page: www.totse.com

Steve Dana, President/Publisher
Lucia Cobo, Editor

A technical trade newspaper for the broadcast radio industry. Accepts advertising.
48 Pages
Circulation: 18000
Founded in 1978
Printed in 4 colors on newsprint stock

3839 **Streaming Media Investor**
Kagan World Media
126 Clock Tower Place
Carmel, CA 93923-8746
831-624-1536
Fax: 831-624-5882
E-Mail: info@kagan.com
Home Page: www.kagan.com

George Niesen, Editor
Harvy Craft, Marketing Manager
Tim Baskerville, CEO/President

News of the Streaming Media Investor. Three month trial available.
Cost: $895.00
Frequency: Monthly
Founded in 1969

3840 **TV Program Investor**
Kagan World Media
1 Lower Ragsdale Dr
Building One, Suite 130
Monterey, CA 93940-5749
831-624-1536
800-307-2529
Fax: 831-625-3225
E-Mail: info@kagan.com
Home Page: www.kagan.com

Tim Baskerville, President
Tom Johnson, Marketing Manager

More than just a newsletter, practically a seminar on how much programs cost and what they are worth. Exclusive spreadsheets with estimates of what goes between the commercials. Three month trial available.
Cost: $895.00
Frequency: Monthly
Founded in 1969

3841 **Television Digest with Consumer Electronics**
Warren Communications News
2115 Ward Ct Nw
Washington, DC 20037-1209
202-872-9200
800-771-9202
Fax: 202-318-8350
E-Mail: info@warren-news.com
Home Page: www.warren-news.com

Brig Easley, Manager
Daniel Warren, President/Editor

A weekly newsletter providing continuous coverage of broadcasting, cable, consumer electronics and related industries.
Cost: $943.00
12 Pages
Frequency: Weekly
Mailing list available for rent

3842 **The Signal**
Society of Broadcast Engineers
9102 N Meridian St
Suite 150
Indianapolis, IN 46260-1896
317-846-9000
Fax: 317-846-9120
E-Mail: mclappe@sbe.org
Home Page: www.sbe.org
Social Media: Facebook, Twitter, LinkedIn

John Poray, Executive Director
Vincent A Lopez, President

Provides members with timely articles on various broadcast-related topics, information on upcoming events, recognition of members' activities and achievements and details of SBE services.
Frequency: Bi-Monthly
Circulation: 5500
Mailing list available for rent: 4700 names at $100 per M
Printed in 4 colors on glossy stock

3843 **Video Investor**
Kagan World Media
126 Clock Tower Place
Carmel, CA 93923-8746
831-624-1536
Fax: 831-624-5882
E-Mail: info@kagan.com
Home Page: www.kagan.com

George Niesen, Editor
Harvy Craft, Marketing Manager
Tim Baskerville, CEO/President

Authoritative look inside the business of renting and selling video cassettes. Exclusive estimates of retail and wholesale transactions and inventories. Tracking movies into the home. Three month trial is available.
Cost: $ 795.00
Frequency: Monthly
Founded in 1969

3844 **Warren Communications News**
Warren
2115 Ward Ct Nw
Washington, DC 20037-1209
202-872-9200
800-771-9202
Fax: 202-318-8350
E-Mail: info@warren-news.com
Home Page: www.warren-news.com
Social Media: Facebook, Twitter, LinkedIn

Brig Easley, Manager
Daniel Warren, President/Editor

Commercial and noncommercial television stations and networks, including educational, low-power and instructional TV stations, and translators. Lists over 11,000 operating cable systems including subscribers, channel capacities, programming, fees and personnel.
Cost: $6.45
Mailing list available for rent

3845 **Wireless Market Stats**
Kagan World Media
1 Lower Ragsdale Dr
Building One, Suite 130
Monterey, CA 93940-5749
831-624-1536
800-307-2529
Fax: 831-625-3225
E-Mail: info@kagan.com
Home Page: www.kagan.com

Tim Baskerville, President
Tom Johnson, Marketing Manager

News of the Wireless Market Stats. Three month trial available.
Cost: $995.00
Frequency: Monthly
Founded in 1969

3846 **Wireless Telecom Investor**
Kagan World Media
1 Lower Ragsdale Dr
Building One, Suite 130
Monterey, CA 93940-5749
831-624-1536
800-307-2529
Fax: 831-625-3225
E-Mail: info@kagan.com
Home Page: www.kagan.com

Tim Baskerville, President
Tom Johnson, Marketing Manager

Exclusive analysis of private and public values of wireless telecommunications companies, including cellular telephone, ESMR and PCS. Exclusive databases of subscribers, market penetrations, market potential, industry growth. Catching super-fast growth in a capsule. Three month trial available.
Cost: $895.00
Frequency: Monthly
Founded in 1969

3847 **Wireless/Private Cable Investor**
Kagan World Media
1 Lower Ragsdale Dr
Building One, Suite 130
Monterey, CA 93940-5749
831-624-1536
800-307-2529
Fax: 831-625-3225

E-Mail: info@kagan.com
Home Page: www.kagan.com/

Tim Baskerville, President
Tom Johnson, Marketing Manager

The original bible of the wireless cable, multipoint distribution pay TV industry. Published continuously since 1972, this newsletter is the window on cable competition. Three month trial available.
Cost: $1095.00
Frequency: Monthly
Founded in 1969

Magazines & Journals

3848 ARRL The National Association for Amateur Radio
American Radio Relay League
225 Main St
Newington, CT 06111-1494

860-594-0200
800-326-3942
Fax: 860-594-0259
E-Mail: hq@arrl.org
Home Page: www.arrl.org

David Sumner, CEO
Kay Craigie, President
Bob Inderbitzen, Marketing Manager

Devoted to amateur radio information.
156M Members
Frequency: Monthly
Circulation: 146000
Founded in 1914

3849 Album Network
110 Spazier
Burbank, CA 91502-1852

818-842-2600
Fax: 818-972-2899
Home Page: www.musicbiz.com

Steve Smith, Publisher

Editorial emphasis on chart ratings, sales performances, music reviews, and industry news.
Cost: $400.00
Frequency: Weekly
Circulation: 2,500

3850 Alliance for Community Media
1100 G St NW
Suite 740
Washington, DC 20005-7415

202-393-2650
Fax: 202-393-2653
E-Mail: info@allcommunitymedia.org
Home Page: www.alliancecm.org

Hellen Soule, Executive Director
Denise M Woodson, Treasurer
Todd Thayer, Treasurer

Participants include cable access television and community programmers. Individual membership dues are $60.00, organization $305.00.
Cost: $35.00
36 Pages
Frequency: Quarterly
Circulation: 1500
ISSN: 1074-9004
Founded in 1985

3851 Almanac
International Council of NATAS
888 7th Avenue
5th floor
New York, NY 10019-3300

212-489-6969
Fax: 212-489-6557
E-Mail: info@iemmys.tv
Home Page: www.iemmys.tv/

Camille Bide Roizen, Executive Director
Eva Obadia, Marketing Manager
Georges Leclere, Senior VP

An annual publication with highlights of the International Emmy Program, global preference guides, articles on various facets in and around television today.
Founded in 1969

3852 BE Radio
Primedia
98 Metcalf Avenue
PO Box 12901
Shawnee Mission, KS 66282-2901

913-341-1300
800-441-0294
Fax: 913-514-6895
E-Mail:
CorporateCustomerService@penton.com
Home Page: www.penton.com

Eric Jacobson, Senior VP
Chriss Scherer, Editor
Kirby Asplund, Marketing Director

Provides radio station managers and engineers the information they need to make critical equipment purchase decisions. Presents need-to-know technical information to help readers solve the challenges of technology and the equipment problems they face. BE Radio serves the needs of radio engineers, managers and owners who need to make informed equipment and services buying decisions.
Cost: $30.00
Frequency: Monthly
Circulation: 12000
Founded in 1959

3853 Broadband Advertising
Kagan World Media
1 Lower Ragsdale Dr
Building One, Suite 130
Monterey, CA 93940-5749

831-624-1536
800-307-2529
Fax: 831-625-3225
E-Mail: sgoldberg@snl.com
Home Page: www.kagan.com

Tim Baskerville, President

Reports and analysis of the sale of commercial time by cable TV networks, interconnects and local spot sales.
Cost: $1095.00
Frequency: Monthly
Founded in 1969
Printed in 2 colors on n stock

3854 Broadcast Engineering
Primedia
PO Box 12914
Overland Park, KS 66282-2914

913-341-1300
800-441-0294
Fax: 913-967-1903
E-Mail: emily.kalmus@penton.com
Home Page: www.broadcastengineering.com
Social Media: Facebook, Twitter, LinkedIn

Brad Dick, Editor

Aimed at the market that includes corporate management, engineers/technicians and other management personnel at commercial and public TV stations, post-production and recording studios, broadcast networks, cable, telephone and satellite production centers and networks.
Circulation: 35000
Founded in 1960

3855 Broadcasting
Reed Business Information
2000 Clearwater Dr
Oak Brook, IL 60523-8809

630-574-0825
800-446-6551
Fax: 630-288-8781
E-Mail: webmaster@reedbusiness.com
Home Page: www.reedbusiness.com

Jeff Greisch, President
Larry Dunn, Publishing Director
Jim Casella, CEO

Offers comprehensive coverage of television, radio, cable, satellite and the attendant equipment and emerging technologies. Accepts advertising.
Cost: $189.00
Founded in 1894

3856 CQ Amateur Radio
CQ Communications
25 Newbridge Rd
Suite 405
Hicksville, NY 11801-2887

516-681-2922
Fax: 516-681-2926
E-Mail: cq@cq-amateur-radio.com
Home Page: http://www.cq-amateur-radio.com

Richard Ross, CEO
Rich Moseson, Managing Editor
Gail Sheehan, Managing Editor
Mellisa Gillgan, Circulation

Information for people interested in the developments of in the field radio communications and electronics. Coverage includes reviews of new operating programs, new products and seasonal promotional ideas.
Cost: $32.00
Frequency: Monthly
Circulation: 87000
Founded in 1950

3857 CTAM Quarterly Marketing Journal
Cable Television Administration & Marketing
201 N Union Street
Suite 440
Alexandria, VA 22314-2642

703-549-4200
Fax: 703-684-1167
E-Mail: info@ctam.com
Home Page: www.ctam.com/

Char Beales, President
Patrick Dougherty, Marketing Manager

A journal offering financial information to persons in the cable television management and executives.
Cost: $295.00
Frequency: Quarterly

3858 Cable Plus/Cable TV Publications
Cable TV Publications/TV Host
PO Box 1665
Harrisburg, PA 17105-1665

800-922-4678
Fax: 610-687-2965

Frank Dillahey, Sales Manager
Bob Newell, Marketing Director

Custom cable TV listing guides incorporating exclusive cable programming, editorial, movie reviews and TV listings that are sold to cable subscribers nationally. Circulation of this guide is over 1.75 million.
Cost: $24.00
Frequency: Monthly

3859 Communicator
Radio Television News Directors Association

1025 Thomas Jefferson St
7th Floor, Suite 700E
Washington, DC 20007-5214

202-625-3500
800-807-8632
Fax: 202-223-4007
E-Mail: barbarac@rtnda.org
Home Page: www.rtnda.org
Social Media: Facebook

The latest information on technological breakthroughs, cutting edge newsroom practices, and contemporary management techniques.
Cost: $75.00
Frequency: 11x/yr
Circulation: 4,000

3860 **DV Digital Video Magazine**
Miller Freeman Publications
PO Box 1212
Skokie, IL 60076

888-776-7002
888-776-7002
Fax: 847-763-9614
E-Mail: dv@halldata.com
Home Page: www.dv.com

Dominic Milano, Editorial Director
Armand DerHacobian, Associate Publisher
Jarett Cory, Sales Manager

Video production, animation and audio film, broadcast and new media. Includes discussions on training and communications.
Frequency: Monthly
Circulation: 64382
Founded in 1993

3861 **Digital TV/Television Broadcast**
United Entertainment Media
810 7th Avenue
27th Fl
New York, NY 10019

212-378-0400
Fax: 212-378-2160
E-Mail: sedorusa@optonline.net
Home Page: www.governmentvideo.com
Social Media: Facebook

Gary Rhodes, International Sales Manager

Digital TV/Television Broadcast is an in depth analysis and insider views of the business of television. It discusses the individuals, market trends, technology, products and policies that drive the television industry in the digital age.
Frequency: Monthly
Circulation: 22000
Founded in 1978
Mailing list available for rent

3862 **EQ Magazine**
Miller Freeman Publications
810 7th Ave
27th Fl, Suite 4
New York, NY 10019-5818

212-636-2700
Fax: 212-636-2750
E-Mail: sedorusa@optonline.net
Home Page: www.governmentvideo.com
Social Media: Facebook

Gary Rhodes, International Sales Manager

Articles on recording techniques and tips for musicians, producers, and engineers in the broadcast industry.
Frequency: Monthly
Circulation: 40000
Mailing list available for rent

3863 **Emmy Magazine**
Academy of Television Arts & Sciences
5200 Lankershim Blvd
North Hollywood, CA 91601-3155

818-754-2800
818-754-2860
Fax: 818-761-2827
E-Mail: emmymag@emmys.org
Home Page: www.emmys.com/

John Shaffner, CEO
Laurel Whitcomb, VP Marketing
Barbara Chase, Director Membership
Juan Morales, Editor
Gail Polevoi, Manager

This magazine tells of association news, EMMY information and awards for the broadcasting and media industries.
Cost: $28.00
Founded in 1995

3864 **FTTX**
Information Gatekeepers
1340 Soldiers Field Rd
Suite 302
Brighton, MA 02135-1000

617-782-5033
800-323-1088
Fax: 617-782-5735
E-Mail: info@igigroup.com
Home Page: www.igigroup.com

Paul Polishuk, CEO
Beverly Wilson, Controller
Yesim Taskor, Controller
Brian Mark, Editor

Covers developments, products, competition, technology, and standards for the use of fiber optics and related techniques in the cable TV industry.
Cost: $695.00
Frequency: Monthly
Circulation: 2000
Founded in 1977

3865 **Financial Manager**
Broadcast Cable Financial Management Association
550 W Frontage Rd
Suite 3600
Northfield, IL 60093-1243

847-716-7000
Fax: 847-784-8059
E-Mail: info@bccacredit.com
Home Page: www.bcfm.com

Mary Collins, President
Jamie Smith, Director of Operations
Rachelle Brooks, BCCA Sales

A bi-monthly magazine published by the Broadcast Cable Financial Management Association.
Cost: $69.00
36 Pages
Frequency: 6 issues per ye
Circulation: 2000
Mailing list available for rent: 1100 names at $495 per M

3866 **Folio**
Pacifica Foundation
1925 Martin Luther King Jr Way
Berkeley, CA 94704-1037

510-849-2590
Fax: 510-849-2617
E-Mail: contact@pacifica.org
Home Page: www.pacificafoundation.org

Lonnie Hicks, Manager
Dan Coughlin, Executive Director

Listing of programs heard on Pacific Radio Stations.
Cost: $40.00
28 Pages
Frequency: Monthly
Founded in 1949

3867 **GBH: Member's Magazine**
WGBH Educational Foundation
PO Box 55875
Boston, MA 02205-5875

617-300-5400
Fax: 617-300-1026
E-Mail: feedback@wgbh.org
Home Page: www.wgbh.org

Diane Dion, Editor
Jon Abbott, Owner
Mary Cotton, Owner

Offers information on station programming, personalities and more for members of WGBH, Boston's PBS and NPR station.
Cost: $50.00
Frequency: Monthly
Circulation: 175000
Founded in 1951

3868 **Hits Magazine**
Color West
3405 Pacific Avenue
Burbank, CA 91505

818-840-8881
Fax: 818-840-2753
E-Mail: info@colorwestprinting.com
Home Page: www.colorwestprinting.com

Dennis Lavinthal, Publisher
Lynn Jensen, President
Karen Jensen, Controller

Chartmakers and hits in contemporary pop music, industry news and happenings, also includes radio news and playlists.
Cost: $300.00
Frequency: Weekly
Circulation: 10000
Founded in 1971

3869 **Inside Radio**
Inside Radio
365 Union St
Littleton, NH 03561-5619

603-444-5720
800-248-4242
Fax: 603-444-2872
E-Mail: info@insideradio.com
Home Page: www.insideradio.com

Cathy Devine, Research Director
Kelli Grisez, Operations Manager

Features issues that effect the radio industry and individuals involved in it.
Cost: $455.00
Frequency: Daily
Circulation: 7000

3870 **International Cable**
Phillips Business Information
1201 Seven Locks Road
Potomac, MD 20854-2931

301-354-1400
Fax: 301-340-0542
E-Mail: edmerson@internationalcable.tv
Home Page: www.phillips.com

Nancy Umberger-Maynard, Publisher

Articles on technological advances internationally and the businesses that are making it possible.
Cost: $73.75
Frequency: Monthly
Circulation: 11,000

3871 **Journal of Broadcasting and Electronic Media**
Broadcast Education Association
1771 N St NW
Washington, DC 20036-2800

202-429-5355
888-380-7222
Fax: 301-869-8608

E-Mail: Don.Godfrey@asu.edu
Home Page: www.beaweb.org

Heather Birks, Executive Director
Steven D Anderson, President
Donald G Godfrey, Editor
Cost: $50.00
Frequency: Quarterly
ISSN: 0883-8151
Founded in 1955
Printed in one color on matte stock

3872 **Journal of College Radio**
Intercollegiate Broadcasting System
367 Windsor Highway
New Windsor, NY 12553-7900

845-534-0003
Fax: 845-565-7446
E-Mail: IBSHQ@aol.com
Home Page: www.collegeradio.tv/

Norman Prusslin, President
Jeff Tellis, VP

Magazine of the nonprofit association of student staffed radio stations based at schools and colleges across the country. Accepts advertising.
Cost: $20.00
24 Pages
Frequency: Quarterly
Founded in 1940

3873 **Journal of Radio & Audio Media**
Broadcast Education Association
1771 N St NW
Washington, DC 20036-2800

202-429-5355
Fax: 202-775-2981
E-Mail: beamemberservices@nab.org
Home Page: www.beaweb.org

Heather Birks, Executive Director
Traci Bailey, Manager, Business Operations
Phylis Johnson, Editor
Mary Schaffer, President
Cost: $30.00
Frequency: Bi-annually
Founded in 1955

3874 **Journal of the Audio Engineering Society**
Audio Engineering Society
60 E 42nd Street
Room 2520
New York, NY 10165-2520

212-661-8528
Fax: 212-682-0477
E-Mail: hq@aes.org
Home Page: www.aes.org
Social Media: Facebook, Twitter

Roger Furness, Executive Director
William T McQuaide, Managing Editor

The Journal contains state-of-the-art technical papers and engineering reports; feature articles covering timely topics; ore and post reports of AES conventions and society activities; news from AES sections; Standards and Education Committee work; membership news, patents, new products, and noteworthy developments. Subscriptions available in print, electronic and combination options.
Cost: $280.00
Frequency: 10/Year
Circulation: 12000
ISSN: 0004-7554
Printed in 4 colors on glossy stock

3875 **Ku-Band World Magazine**
Opportunities Publishing
305 Jackson Avenue W
Oxford, MS 38655-2154

FAX 662-236-5541

Ed Meek, Editor

Business application of developing Ku-band satellite communications systems.
Cost: $25.00
52 Pages
Frequency: Monthly
Founded in 1985

3876 **Millimeter Magazine**
2104 Harvell Circle
Bellevue, NE 68005

402-505-7100
866-505-7173
Fax: 402-293-0741
E-Mail: llcs@pbsub.com
Home Page: www.millimeter.com

Cynthia Wisehart, Editorial Director
Gayle Grooms, Audience Marketing
Christina Heil, Marketing
Jeff Victor, Associate Editor

Authoritative resource for more than 33,000 qualified professionals in production, postproduction, animation, streaming and visual effects for motion pictures, television and commercials.
Cost: $25.00
150 Pages
Frequency: Monthly

3877 **NRB Magazine**
National Religious Broadcasters
9510 Technology Dr
Manassas, VA 20110-4149

703-330-7100
Fax: 703-330-7100
E-Mail: info@nrb.org
Home Page: www.nrb.org
Social Media: Facebook, Twitter

Frank Wright, President
Linda Smith, President Assistant

Trade publication for Christian communicators, including radio, TV, Internet and international media.
Cost: $24.00
56 Pages
Frequency: Monthly
Circulation: 9000
ISSN: 1521-1754
Founded in 1969
Printed in 4 colors on glossy stock

3878 **RPM Weekly**
Novasound Productions
PO Box 630071
Irving, TX 75063-71

972-432-8100
Fax: 972-432-8102
E-Mail: jv@rapmag.com
Home Page: www.rapmag.com

Jerry Vigil, Publisher
Shardan Azat, Manager

Information on radio stations and independent production houses, engineering and production directors that manage these studios, industry news and latest technology information.
Cost: $115.00
Frequency: Monthly
Circulation: 7500
Founded in 1988

3879 **Radio**
1930 Century Park W
Los Angeles, CA 90067-6803

323-263-6991
Fax: 310-203-8450

Dwight Case, Editor

A magazine covering all aspects of the radio communications industry.
Cost: $215.00
Frequency: Monthly
Founded in 1973

3880 **Radio Science**
American Geophysical Union
2000 Florida Ave NW
Washington, DC 20009-1231

202-462-6900
800-966-2481
Fax: 202-328-0566
E-Mail: service@agu.org
Home Page: www.agu.org
Social Media: Facebook, Twitter

Fred Spilhaus, Executive Director

Coverage of radio propagation, communication, and upper atmospheric physics.
Cost: $10.00
Circulation: 1200
Founded in 1919

3881 **Radio-TV Interview Report**
Bradley Communications
135 E Plumstead Avenue
PO Box 1206
Lansdowne, PA 19050-8206

610-591-1070
Fax: 610-284-3704
E-Mail: Circ@rtir.com
Home Page: www.rtir.com

Bill Harrison, President

A source for finding authors and experts to interview about a wide variety of subjects.
88 Pages
Frequency: Monthly
Circulation: 4000
Founded in 1986

3882 **SMPTE Motion Imaging Journal**
Society of Motion Picture & Television Engineers
3 Barker Ave
Floor 5
White Plains, NY 10601-1509

914-761-1100
Fax: 914-761-3115
Home Page: www.smpte.org

Barbara Lange, Executive Director

The gateway to the world of motion imaging featuring industry-leading papers and standards, the Journal keeps its members on the cutting edge of this ever-changing industry.
Cost: $140.00
Frequency: Monthly

3883 **Satellite Retailer**
Triple D Publishing
1300 S Dekalb St
Shelby, NC 28152-7210

704-482-9673
Fax: 704-484-6976

Douglas G Brown Sr, President

Edited for the satellite industry.
Cost: $12.00
72 Pages
Frequency: Monthly
Founded in 1985

3884 **Satvision Magazine**
Satellite Broadcasting/Communications Association
1730 M St NW
Suite 600
Washington, DC 20036-4557
202-349-3620
Fax: 202-349-3621
E-Mail: info@sbca.org
Home Page: www.sbca.org

Joseph Widoff, Executive Director

Offers information for television satellite dealers.
Cost: $35.00
Frequency: Monthly
Circulation: 10000

3885 **Secure Signals**
National Cable Television Association
25 Massachusetts Ave NW
Suite 100
Washington, DC 20001-1434
202-775-3550
Fax: 202-775-3604
E-Mail: webmaster@ncta.com
Home Page: www.ncta.com
Robert Sachs, CEO
Brian Dietz, VP Communications
Covers legal aspects of theft of cable television services and how to prevent it from happening.
Frequency: Quarterly
Circulation: 4,000

3886 **Teleguia USA: Novedades USA - Buscando Amor**
Echo Media
900 Circle 75 Pkwy SE
Suite 1600
Atlanta, GA 30339-6014
770-955-3346
E-Mail: salesinfo@echo-media.com
Home Page: www.echo-media.com
Michael Puffer, CEO
Kelly Elarbee, Media Director
Frequency: Weekly
Circulation: 100,000
Founded in 1986
Mailing list available for rent
Printed in 4 colors on newsprint stock

3887 **Via Satellite**
Phillips Business Information
1201 Seven Locks Rd
Suite 300
Potomac, MD 20854
301-541-1400
Fax: 301-309-3847
Home Page: www.kftv.com/company-30086.html
Scott Chase, Publisher
Richard Summers, Managing Editor
Covers voice, video and data in global commercial communications, including company profiles, market analysis and new products.
Cost: $49.00
Frequency: Monthly
Circulation: 17446

3888 **WNYC Wavelength**
1 Centre St
Suite 2453
New York, NY 10007-1699
212-669-7800
Fax: 212-669-3312
Home Page: www.wnyc.org
Lori Krushefski, Marketing
Laura Walker, President
Relays broadcasting news. Accepts advertising.
16 Pages
Frequency: Monthly

3889 **Women on the Job: Careers in the Electronic Media**
American Women in Radio and Television
1760 Old Meadow Rd
Suite 800
Mc Lean, VA 22102-4306
703-506-3290
Fax: 703-506-3266
E-Mail: info@awrt.org
Home Page: www.awrt.org
Maria Brennan, President
Association news focusing on women in the workplace, particularly media and communications industries.

3890 **World Screen News**
1123 Broadway
Suite 1201
New York, NY 10010-2007
212-924-7620
Fax: 212-924-6940
E-Mail: mdaswani@worldscreen.com
Home Page: www.worldscreen.com
Ricardo Duise, Manager
Anna Carugati, Managing Editor
Kristin Brzoznowski, Managing Editor
Rafael Dlanco, Executive Editor
Cesar Suero, Advertising Sales Director
Serves the international television cable and satellite industries including advertising agencies within the industry and others allied to the field. Also publishes the following supplements; TV Kids, TV Europe, TV Docs, TV Latina.
Cost: $50.00
Frequency: Monthly
Circulation: 4038
Founded in 1985

Trade Shows

3891 **AES Convention**
Audio Engineering Society
60 E 42nd Street
Room 2520
New York, NY 10165-2520
212-661-8528
Fax: 212-682-0477
E-Mail: HQ@aes.org
Home Page: www.aes.org
Bob Moses, Executive Director
Roger Furness, Deputy Director
Jan Pederson, President
Frank Wells, President-Elect
Robert Breen, Vice President
An international organization that unites audio engineers, creative artists, scienists and students worldwide by promoting advances in audio and desseminating new knowledge and research.
Frequency: October

3892 **Alaska Broadcasters Association Conference**
Alaska Broadcasters Association
700 W 41st Street
Suite 102
Anchorage, AK 99503
907-258-2424
Fax: 907-258-2414
E-Mail: akba@gci.net
Home Page: www.alaskabroadcaster.org
Social Media: Facebook
Gary Donovan, President
Matt Wilson, Vice President
Provides assistance which enables members to serve their communities of license through educations, representation and advocacy.
225 Attendees
Frequency: Annual

3893 **Annual Community Radio Conference**
National Federation of Community Broadcasters
1970 Broadway
Suite 1000
Oakland, CA 94612
510-451-8200
Fax: 510-451-8208
E-Mail: comments@nfcb.org
Home Page: www.nfcb.org
Carol Pierson, President/CEO
Virginia Z Berson, VP Federation Services
National conference for public community radio stations offering opportunities for staff development, skill building, networking, affinity group, inspiration, new ideas, discussion and exchanges; exhibit area; programming awards. Business meetings for National Federation of Community Broadcasters.
300 Attendees
Frequency: April

3894 **Annual IBS Broadcasting & Webcasting Conference**
Intercollegiate Broadcasting System
367 Windsor Highway
New Windsor, NY 12553-7900
845-565-0003
Fax: 845-565-7446
E-Mail: ibshq@aol.com
Home Page: www.ibsradio.org
Norman Prusslin, President
Fritz Kass, Chief Operating Officer
Over 110 seminars, live music, over 250 top broadcasting professionals, and 1,200 student radio & webcasters from around the world. Live webstream during conference.
1.2M Attendees
Frequency: March

3895 **Audio Engineering Society Meeting**
Audio Engineering Society
60 E 42nd Street
Room 2520
New York, NY 10165-2520
212-661-8528
Fax: 212-682-0477
Home Page: www.aes.org
Roger K Furness, Executive Director
250 booths, held in the fall and spring of each year.
5M Attendees
Frequency: October

3896 **Broadcast Designers' Association International Conference & Expo**
Broadcast Designers' Association International
145 W 45th Street
Room 1100
New York, NY 10036-4008
212-376-6222
Fax: 212-376-6202
Annual show and exhibits of broadcast design equipment, supplies and services.

3897 **Broadcast Engineering Conference (BEC)**
Society of Broadcast Engineers
9102 N Meridian Street
Suite 150
Indianapolis, IN 46260
317-846-9000
Fax: 317-846-9120
E-Mail: mclappe@sbe.org
Home Page: www.sbe.org
John Poray, Executive Director
Vincent A Lopez, President

Offers broadcast engineers the opportunity to attend educational sessions, see the latest equipment and supplies, and meet with peers.
500 Attendees
Frequency: Annual/Spring

3898 **CRS - Country Radio Show**
Country Radion Broadcasters
819 18th Avenue South
Nashville, TN 37203
615-327-4487
Fax: 615-329-4492
E-Mail: info@crb.org
Home Page: www.crb.org
Ed Salamon, Executive Director
Chasity Crouch, Business Manager
Jams, discussions, introduction of new comers, Hall of Fame presentations.
2,000 Attendees
Frequency: March

3899 **Cable Television Trade Show and Convention: East**
Convention Show Management Company
6175 Barfield Road NE
Suite 220
Atlanta, GA 30328-4327
404-252-2454
Fax: 404-252-0215
Nancy Horne, Show Manager
Nine hundred booths.
6M Attendees
Frequency: August

3900 **Cable and Satellite: European Broadcasting/Communications Show**
Reed Exhibition Companies
255 Washington Street
Newton, MA 02458-1637
617-584-4900
Fax: 617-630-2222
Elizabeth Hitchcock, International Sales
Communications forum for professionals in the broadcasting industry.
7.9M Attendees
Frequency: April

3901 **MFMA/BCCA Annual Conference**
Media Financial Management Association
550 W Frontage Road
Suite 3600
Northfield, IL 60093
847-716-7000
Fax: 847-716-7004
E-Mail: info@mediafinance.org
Home Page: www.bcfm.com
Mary Collins, President/CEO
Jamie Smith, Director of Operations
Offers professional education targeting media financial and business executives; CPE opportunities; exhibitors; roundtables; and networking opportunities.
800 Attendees
Frequency: Annual
Mailing list available for rent: 1,200 names at $495 per M

3902 **MIP-TV: International Television Program Market**
Reed Exhibition Companies
255 Washington Street
Newton, MA 02458-1637
617-584-4900
Fax: 617-630-2222
Elizabeth Hitchcock, International Sales
Spring market for the television industry to buy, sell and distribute television programming.
9M Attendees
Frequency: April

3903 **NAB Radio Show**
National Association of Broadcasters
1771 N Street NW
Washington, DC 20036
202-429-5300
888-140-4622
301-682-7962
Fax: 202-429-4199
E-Mail: NABSHOW@expressreg.net
Home Page: www.nabshow.com
David Wharton, EVP Media Relations
Jennifer Landry-Jackson, Exhibit Sales
Kelly Bryant, Event Operations
A unique networking opportunity for station professionals representing all format and market sizes, with exhibits showcasing technologies, tools and solutions for the industry.
Frequency: Annual

3904 **NAB Show**
National Association of Broadcasters
1771 N Street NW
Washington, DC 20036
202-429-5300
800-342-2460
202-429-3189
Fax: 202-429-4199
E-Mail: NABSHOW@expressreg.net
Home Page: www.nabshow.com
David Wharton, EVP Media Relations
Jennifer Landry-Jackson, Exhibit Sales
Kelly Bryant, Event Operations
A global event for boradcasting news, legislation, networking, education and technology. Over 150 countries represented by 85,000+ attendees and exhibitors; conferences, and training sessions, and over 1,500 exhibitors.
85M Attendees
Frequency: April

3905 **NATPE Market & Conference**
National Association of TV Program Executives
5757 Wilshire Boulevard
Penthouse 10
Los Angeles, CA 90036-3681
310-453-4440
Fax: 310-453-5258
E-Mail: info@natpe.org
Home Page: www.natpe.org
Nick Orfanopoulos, Senior VP Exhibitions
Beth Braen, Senior VP Marketing
The National Association of Television Program Executives (NATPE) is a global alliance of business professionals engaged in the creation, development and distribution of content as well as advertising and financial activities. NATPE is the world's largest non-profit association dedicated to facilitating the continued growth and convergence of all content across all distribution platforms.
8000 Attendees
Frequency: Annual
Founded in 1963

3906 **NATPE: The Alliance of Media Content**
National Association of TV Program Executives
6868 Wilshire Boulevard
Penthouse 10
Los Angeles, CA 90036-3681
310-453-4440
800-NAT-PEGO
Fax: 310-453-5258
E-Mail: info@natpe.org
Home Page: www.natpe.org
Pam Silverman, Exhibition & Advertising
Linda Nichols, Exhibitor Services
Eric Low, Registration & Membership
The National Association of Television Program Executives (NATPE) is a global alliance of business professionals engaged in the creation, development and distribution of content as well as advertising and financial activities. NATPE is the world's largest non-profit association dedicated to facilitating the continued growth and convergence of all content across all distribution platforms.
1000 Attendees
Frequency: January
Founded in 1963

3907 **NECTA Convention & Exhibition**
New England Cable And Telecommunications Assn
10 Forbes Road
Suite 440W
Braintree, MA 02184-2648
781-843-3418
Fax: 781-849-6267
E-Mail: info@necta.info
Home Page: www.necta.info
Paul Cianelli, President
William Durand, Executive Vice President
Donna Nolan, Office Manager
A six state regional trade association representing substantially all private cable telecommunications companies in Connecticut, Maine, Massachusetts, New Hampshire, Rhode Island, and Vermont.
1.1M Attendees
Frequency: July

3908 **National Cable Television Association**
National Cable Television Association
25 Massachusetts Avenue NW
Suite 100
Washington, DC 20001
202-222-2300
E-Mail: webmaster@ncta.com
Home Page: www.ncta.com
Robert Sachs, CEO
Convention newsletter and programs concerning cable television. 2,000 booths.
14M Attendees
Frequency: Spring

3909 **National Public Radio Association**
National Public Radio Association
635 Massachusetts Avenue NW
Washington, DC 20001-3753
202-513-2000
Fax: 202-513-3329
Home Page: www.npr.org
Vivian Schiller, President & CEO
Howard Stevenson, Chair of the Board of Directors
Mitch Praver, COO
Seventy five booths for public radio professionals and providers of resource materials for public radio.
1.2M Attendees
Frequency: April/May

3910 **National Religious Broadcasters Annual Convention and Exposition**
National Religious Broadcasters
9510 Technology Drive
Manassas, VA 20110
703-330-7000
Fax: 703-330-7100

E-Mail: info@nrb.org
Home Page: www.nrb.org

Dr Frank Wright, President/CEO
Linda Smith, President Assistant
David Keith, VP Operations

Containing 280 exhibits. Broadcast and communications emphasis.
5,700 Attendees
Frequency: February

3911 OAB Broadcast Engineering Conference
Society of Broadcast Engineers
9102 N Meridian Street
Suite 150
Indianapolis, IN 46260

317-846-9000
Fax: 317-846-9120
E-Mail: mclappe@sbe.org
Home Page: www.sbe.org

Vincent A Lopez, President
John Poray, Executive Director

Offers broadcast engineers the opportunity to attend educational sessions, see the latest equipment and supplies, and meet with peers.
5500 Members
Frequency: Annual/November
Founded in 1964
Mailing list available for rent: 5700 names at $170 per M

3912 RAB2009 Conference
Radio Advertising Bureau
1320 Greenway Drive
Suite 500
Irving, TX 75038

972-536-6700
800-232-3131
Fax: 972-753-6727
E-Mail: jhaley@rab.com
Home Page: www.rab.com

Erica Ferber, President
Van Allen, CFO

Learn about new media opportunities from new digital platforms and monetizing streams to HD strategies that will empower you to compete at a new level and be an innovator at your station.
1600 Attendees
Frequency: Annual/March

3913 Recruiting Conference and Expo
Kennedy Information
1 Phoenix Mill Lane
Floor 3
Peterborough, NH 03458

603-924-1006
800-531-0007
E-Mail: conferences@kennedyinfo.com
Home Page: www.recruiting2006.com

Matt Lyons, Director, Recruiting Group

Learn about the winning strategies, best practices, and tools ou will need to succeed in a challenging talent market.
Frequency: Nov New York

3914 SCTE Cable-Tec EXPO
Society of Cable Telecommunication Engineers
140 Philips Road
Exton, PA 19341-1318

610-363-6888
800-542-5040
Fax: 610-363-5898
E-Mail: scte@scte.org
Home Page: www.scte.org

Lori Bower, Director
John Clark, CEO

Five hundred booths and, exhibits featuring telecommunications and programming equipment; dozens of workshops, with new technologies showcased.
12M Attendees
Frequency: Annual
Mailing list available for rent

3915 SMPTE Annual Tech Conference & EXPO
Society of Motion Picture & Television Engineers
3 Barker Avenue
5th Floor
White Plains, NY 10601

914-761-1100
Fax: 914-761-3115
E-Mail: smpte@smpte.org
Home Page: www.smpte.org
Social Media: Facebook, Twitter, LinkedIn

Barbara Lange, Executive Director
Sally Ann D'Amato, Director, Operations
Roberta Gorman, Manager, Member Relations
Aimee Ricca, Product Marketing Manager

The Technical Conference and Exhibition which is held in the fall. This alternates between the east and west coasts, usually in Pasadena and New York.
Frequency: Annual

3916 Satellite Broadcasting and Communication Association (SBCA)
Show Management & Services
900 Jorie Boulevard
Suite 200
Oak Brook, IL 60523-3835

800-654-9276
Fax: 630-990-2077

Diana Bubalo, Show Manager

Four hundred fifty booths.
2.5M Attendees

3917 Television Bureau of Advertising Annual Meeting
Television Bureau of Advertising
3 E 54th Street
New York, NY 10022

212-486-1111
Fax: 212-935-5631
E-Mail: info@tvb.org
Home Page: www.tvb.org

Steve Lanzano, President
Abby Auerbach, EVP
Gary Bellis, VP/Communications

Annual show of 20-25 exhibitors of services for television stations, including research, sales and management training programs, incentives, collection agencies, advertiser contests and computer software.

3918 Western Cable Television Conference and Expo
Trade Associates
11820 Parklawn Drive
Suite 250
Rockville, MD 20852-2505

301-519-1610

Susan Rosenstock, Expo Director

One thousand three hundred booths featuring exhibits of programming, mobile aerial devices, video equipment and products and services for the communications and related industry fields.
10M Attendees
Frequency: November/December

3919 Western Show
Trade Associates
11820 Parklawn Drive
Suite 250
Rockville, MD 20852-2505

301-519-1610
Fax: 301-468-3662

Susan Rosenstock, Director

One thousand booths featuring exhibits from cable operators and suppliers to the cable industry. The California Cable Television Association and the Arizona Cable Television Association sponsor this annual event.
10M Attendees
Frequency: December

Directories & Databases

3920 AES E-Library
Audio Engineering Society
60 E 42nd St
Room 2520
New York, NY 10165

212-661-8528
Fax: 212-682-0477
E-Mail: HQ@aes.org
Home Page: www.aes.org
Social Media: Facebook

Bob Moses, Executive Director
Roger K Furness, Deputy Director

The library contains over 12,000 fully searchable PDF files documenting the progression of audio research from 1953 to the present, and includes every AES paper published at a convention, conference or in the Journal. Available as a subscription or pay per paper download: $135 for members, $245 for non, or $5 per paper for members or $20 for non.
Cost: $5.00
Frequency: Annual or Per-Paper

3921 Arbitron Radio County Coverage
Arbitron Company
142 5th Ave
New York, NY 10011-4312

212-887-1300
Fax: 212-887-1558
Home Page: www.arbitron.com

Stephen Morris, CEO
Marilou Legge, Executive Vice President

This database offers access to audience listening estimates by county.
Frequency: Statistical

3922 Audio Engineering Society: Directory of Educational Programs
Audio Engineering Society
60 E 42nd St
Room 2520
New York, NY 10165
212-661-8528
Fax: 212-682-0477
E-Mail: HQ@aes.org
Home Page: www.aes.org
Social Media: Facebook

Bob Moses, Executive Director
Roger K Furness, Deputy Director

Institutions offering postsecondary programs and seminars in audio technology and engineering are searchable by program type or geographic area. Available free online. Educators are asked to confirm the information for their institutions.
Frequency: Free Online

3923 Bacon's Newspaper & Magazine Directories
Cision U.S., Inc.

322 South Michigan Avenue
Suite 900
Chicago, IL 60604

312-263-0070
866-639-5087
E-Mail: info.us@cision.com
Home Page: us.cision.com

Joe Bernardo, President & CEO
Heidi Sullivan, VP & Publisher
Valerie Lopez, Research Director
Jessica White, Research Director
Rachel Farrell, Research Manager

Two volume set listing all daily and community newspapers, magazines and newsletters, news service and syndicates, syndicated columnists, complete editorial staff listings of each publication provided, covers U.S., Canada, Mexico, and Carribean.
Cost: $350.00
4,700 Pages
Frequency: Annual
ISSN: 1088-9639
Founded in 1951
Printed in one color on matte stock

3924 Bacon's Radio/TV/Cable Directory
Cision U.S., Inc.
332 South Michigan Avenue
Suite 900
Chicago, IL 60604

312-263-0070
866-639-5087
E-Mail: info.us@cision.com
Home Page: www.us.cision.com

Joe Bernardo, President & CEO
Heidi Sullivan, VP & Publisher
Valerie Lopez, Research Director
Jessica White, Research Director
Rachel Farrell, Research Manager

Includes comprehensive coverage for contact and programming information for more than 3,500 televsion networks, cable networks, television syndicators, television stations, and cable systems in the United States and Canada.
Cost: $350.00
Frequency: Annual
ISSN: 1088-9639
Printed in one color on matte stock

3925 Broadcast Engineering Equipment Reference Manual
Penton
249 W 17th Street
New York, NY 10011

212-204-4200
E-Mail:
corporatecustomerservice@penton.com
Home Page: www.penton.com

Sharon Rowlands, Chief Executive Officer

Offers a list of more than 1,400 manufacturers and distributors of communications equipment for radio, television and recording applications.
Cost: $20.00
Frequency: Annual
Circulation: 35,500
ISSN: 0007-1994

3926 Burrelle's Media Directory
BurrellesLuce
75 E Northfield Rd
Livingston, NJ 07039-4532

973-992-6600
800-631-1160
Fax: 973-992-7675
Home Page: www.burrellesluce.com
Social Media: Facebook, Twitter, LinkedIn

Robert C Waggoner, CEO

Offers media outreach, media monitoring and media reporting products.
Cost: $795.00

3927 CPB Public Broadcasting Directory
Corporation for Public Broadcasting
401 9th St NW
Suite 200
Washington, DC 20004-2129

202-879-9600
Fax: 202-879-9700
E-Mail: oigemail@cpb.org
Home Page: www.cpb.org
Social Media: Twitter

Robert T Coonrod, CEO

Offers information on public television stations, national and regional public broadcasting association and networks.
Cost: $15.00
152 Pages
Frequency: Annual
Circulation: 14,000

3928 Cable Online Data Exchange
Prometheus Global Media
770 Broadway
New York, NY 10003-9595

212-493-4100
Fax: 646-654-5368
Home Page: www.prometheusgm.com

Richard D. Beckman, CEO
James A. Finkelstein, Chairman
Madeline Krakowsky, Vice President Circulation
Tracy Brater, Executive Director Creative Service

This database contains information on more than 10,000 US cable television system franchises.

3929 Complete Television, Radio and Cable Industry Directory
Grey House Publishing
4919 Route 22
PO Box 56
Amenia, NY 12501

518-789-8700
800-562-2139
Fax: 845-373-6390
Fax: new
E-Mail: books@greyhouse.com
Home Page: www.greyhouse.com

Richard Gottlieb, President
Leslie Mackenzie, Publisher

The most comprehensive industry data on the US and Canadian Televison, Radio and Cable Industries. Can also subscibe to the database found online.
Cost: $350.00
2000 Pages
ISBN: 9-781619-25-1
Founded in 1981

3930 Directory of Field Contacts for the Coordination of the Use of Radio
Federal Communications Commission
445 12th Street SW
Washington, DC 20554

202-180-0450
Fax: 866-418-0232
E-Mail: fccinfo@fcc.gov
Home Page: www.fcc.com

Radio frequency coordinating agencies are listed.
170 Pages
Frequency: Annual

3931 Directory of Religious Media
National Religious Broadcasters
9510 Technology Dr
Manassas, VA 20110-4149

703-330-7100
Fax: 703-330-7100
E-Mail: info@nrb.org
Home Page: www.nrb.org

Frank Wright, President
Linda Smith, President Assistant
David Keith, VP Operations

Comprehensive guide to radio, television, music and book publishers.
Frequency: 10 per year

3932 Editors Guild Directory
Motion Picture Editors Guild
7715 Sunset Boulevard
Suite 200
Hollywood, CA 90046

323-876-4770
Fax: 323-876-0861
E-Mail: info@editorsguild.com
Home Page: www.editorsguild.com

Lisa Churgin, Guild President
Dede Allen, VP
Diane Adler, Secretary
Rachel Igel, Treasurer
Tris Carpenter, Manager

An invaluable resource for producers, directors and post production professionals alike. It lists contact, credit, award and classification information for all of the Guild's active members at the time of publication, as well as a list of Oscar and Emmy winners for every year since the awards began. It also include a retirees section.
Cost: $25.00

3933 GMRS National Repeater Guide
Personal Radio Steering Group
PO Box 2851
Ann Arbor, MI 48106-2851

734-662-4533
Home Page: gmrs.org

Corwin Moore, Administrative Director

Lists the 3,500 GMRS repeaters nationally, along with names and addresses of station licensees.
Frequency: Monthly

3934 Gale Directory of Publications and Broadcast Media
Gale/Cengage Learning
PO Box 09187
Detroit, MI 48209-0187

248-699-4253
800-877-4253
Fax: 248-699-8049
E-Mail: gale.galeord@cengage.com
Home Page: www.gale.com

Patrick C Sommers, President

This media directory contains thousands of listings for radio and television stations and cable companies.
Frequency: Annual
ISBN: 1-414434-71-5
Founded in 2008

3935 International Motion Picture Almanac Intern Television & Video Almanac
Quigley Publishing Company, Incorporated
64 Wintergreen Lane
Groton, MA 01450

978-448-0272
Fax: 978-448-9325
E-Mail: quigleypub@aol.com
Home Page: www.quigleypublishing.com

William J Quigley, President/Publisher
Jayme Kulesz, Editor
Michael Quigley, Associate Editor/Ops Manager
Dee Quigley, Associate Editor

Invaluable completely updated information to the most sucscessful people in the business. Are you one of them? With thousands of corpo-

rations, 5,000 plus career profiles and the most comprehensive information available on the second largest industry in the US.
Cost: $250.00
780 Pages
Frequency: Annual
ISBN: 0-900610-74-3
ISSN: 0074-7084
Founded in 1915

3936 Kagan Media Index
Kagan World Media
126 Clock Tower Place
Carmel, CA 93923-8746
831-624-1536
Fax: 831-625-3225
E-Mail: info@kagan.com
Home Page: www.kagan.com
George Niesen, Editor
Tom Johnson, Marketing Manager
The most comprehensive collection of media industry databases found anywhere. Current estimates of industry growth for a dozen different media businesses, shown on a 145 line spreadsheet, projected forward and updated monthly. Three month trial available.
Cost: $795.00
Frequency: Monthly

3937 National Radio Publicity Outlets
Volt Directory Marketing
1800 Byberry Road
Suite 800
Huntingdon Valley, PA 19006-3520
800-677-3839
Fax: 610-832-0878
Offers valuable information on over 7,000 radio stations in all major United States and Canadian markets.
Cost: $188.00
640 Pages
Frequency: SemiAnnual

3938 Radio & Records
Radio & Records
10100 Santa Monica Boulevard
5th Floor
Los Angeles, CA 90067-4003
310-553-4330
Fax: 310-203-8450
Home Page: www.rronline.com
Erica Farber, Publisher/CEO
Sky Daniels, Vice President
Ron Rodriguez, Editor-in-Chief
Page Beaver, Operations Manager
Henry Mowry, Sales Executive
A music newspaper that covers all aspects of the radio and recording industry.
Cost: $299.00
Frequency: BiAnnual
Circulation: 10,000

3939 Radio Marketing Guide
Radio Advertising Bureau
1320 Greenway Dr
Suite 500
Irving, TX 75038-2547
972-753-6700
800-232-3131
Fax: 972 753 6727
E-Mail: jhaley@rab.com
Home Page: www.rab.com
Mike Mahone, VP
Leah Kamon, SVP Marketing
A multi dimensional tool for Radio sales management and advertising professionals.
1600 Attendees

3940 Radio Talk Shows Need Guests
Pacesetter Publications
PO Box 101330
Denver, CO 80250-1330
303-722-7200
Fax: 303-733-2626
Home Page: www.joesabah.com
Over 950 radio talk shows that interview guests over the telephone are profiled.
Cost: $198.00
Frequency: SemiAnnual
Founded in 1992

3941 SBE Members Directory
Society of Broadcast Engineers
9102 N Meridian St
Suite 150
Indianapolis, IN 46260-1896
317-846-9000
Fax: 317-846-9120
E-Mail: mclappe@sbe.org
Home Page: www.sbe.org
John Poray, Executive Director
Vincent A Lopez, President
List of all members of SBE, Includes a history, awards earned, leadership, suppliers and other information. Free to members.
108 Pages
Mailing list available for rent: 4700 names at $170 per M

3942 TV Cable Publicity Guide
Volt Directory Marketing
1 Sentry Pkwy E
Blue Bell, PA 19422-2310
610-825-7720
Fax: 610-941-6874
Home Page: www.volt.com
Jerry Di Pippo, CEO
Ronald Kochman, Vice President
Bruce Goodman, General Counsel
Over 5,000 cable and broadcast television stations and systems are profiled.
Cost: $188.00
545 Pages
Frequency: SemiAnnual

3943 TV Facts
Cabletelevision Advertising Bureau
830 3rd Ave
2nd Floor
New York, NY 10022-7523
212-508-1200
Fax: 212-832-3268
Home Page: www.onetvworld.org
Sean Cunningham, President
An essential pocketsized media planning tool that contains 120 pages of essential data, graphs and charts highlighting the extraordinary growth and value of Cable in the changing TV landscape.
Frequency: Annual
Circulation: 20000

3944 Talk Show Selects
Broadcast Interview Source
2233 Wisconsin Ave NW
Suite 301
Washington, DC 20007-4132
202-333-5000
800-932-7266
Fax: 202-342-5411
Home Page: www.expertclick.com
Mitchell Davis, Owner
More than 700 contacts at radio and television talk shows.
Cost: $185.00
240 Pages
Frequency: Annual
ISBN: 0-934333-35-1
Founded in 1984
Printed in on matte stock

3945 Television Yearbook
BIA Research
15120 Enterprise Ct
Suite 100
Chantilly, VA 20151-1275
703-818-8115
800-331-5086
Fax: 703-803-3299
E-Mail: pob@bia.com
Home Page: www.bia.com
Tom Bruno, Owner
US television markets and their inclusive stations, television equipment manufacturers and related service providers and trade associations.
Cost: $64.00
Frequency: Annual

3946 Television and Cable Factbook
Warren Communications News
2115 Ward Ct NW
Washington, DC 20037-1209
202-872-9200
800-771-9202
Fax: 202-318-8350
E-Mail: info@warren-news.com
Home Page: www.warren-news.com
Brig Easley, Manager
Daniel Warren, President/Editor
Commercial and noncommercial television stations and networks are profiled in this comprehensive directory. Educational and instructional stations are also included as one of the many categories of information.
Cost: $595.00
10M Pages
Frequency: 5 Volumes
Founded in 1932

3947 Top 200 National TV, News, Talk and Magazine Shows
Todd Publications
PO Box 635
Nyack, NY 10960-0635
845-358-6213
800-747-1056
Fax: 845-358-6213
B Klein, Publisher
The 200 most popular information shows on US television.
Cost: $40.00
Frequency: Annual

3948 World Broadcast News: International 500 Issue
Penton
PO Box 12901
Shawnee Mission, KS 66282-2901
913-341-1300
Fax: 913-514-6895
Home Page: www.penton.com
Eric Jacobson, Senior VP
Directory of services and supplies to the industry.
Cost: $10.00
Frequency: Annual

Industry Web Sites

3949 http://gold.greyhouse.com
G.O.L.D Grey House OnLine Databases
Grey House Publishing's online database platform, GOLD, offers Quick Search, Keyword Search and Expert Search for most business sectors including broadcasting, communications and media markets. The GOLD platform makes finding the information you need quick and easy - whether you're a novice searcher or

an experienced database user. All of Grey House's directory products are available for subscription on the GOLD platform.

3950 **www.aicp.com**
Association of Independent Commercial Producers
Represents exclusively, the interests of US companies that specialize in producing commercials on various media - film, video, computer- for advertisers and their agencies. AICP members account for 85 percent of all domestic commercials aired nationally, whether produced for traditional braodcast channels or nontraditional use.

3951 **www.alliancecm.org**
Alliance for Community Media
Committed to assuring everyone's access to electronic media, through public education, a progressive legislative and regulatory agenda, coalition building and grassroots organizing. A nonprofit, national membership organization founded in 1976, the Alliance represents over 1,000 Public, Educational and Governmental access organizations and community media centers.

3952 **www.americansportscasters.com**
American Sportscasters Association
Covers the U.S., Puerto Rico, and Canada. Offers seminars, compiles statistics and operates a placement service, maintains a Hall of Fame and biographical archives and library.

3953 **www.amptp.org**
Alliance of Motion Picture & Television Producers
Trade association with respect to labor issues in the motion picture and television industry. We negotiate 80 industry wide collective bargaining agreements and represents over 350 production companies and studios.

3954 **www.apts.org**
Association of Public Televsion Stations
Nonprofit membership organization established in 1980 to support the continued growth and development of a strong and financially sound noncommercial television service for the American public. We provide advocacy for public television interests at the national level, as well as consistent leadership and information in marshalling grassroots and congressional support.

3955 **www.bcfm.com**
Broadcast Cable Financial Management Association
A professional society of over 1,200 of television, radio and cable TV's top financial, MIS and HR executives, plus associates in auditing, data processing, software development, credit and collections.

3956 **www.bdaonline.org**
Broad Designers Association
For broadcast designers. Conferences annually in Asia, Australia, Europe, South and North America.

3957 **www.ctam.com**
Cable Telecommunications Association for Marketing
Dedicated to the discipline and development of consumer marketing excellence in cable television, new media and telecommunication services. Members have the advantage of progressive research, insightful publications and forward thinking conferences.

3958 **www.emmyonline.org**
National Academy of Television Arts & Sciences
Dedicated to the advancement of the arts and sciences of television and the promotion of creative leadership for artistic, educational and technical achievements within the television industry. Bestows the Emmy Award.

3959 **www.genehrts.com**
Hollywood Radio and Television Society
Featuring top industry and government speakers and seminars about broadcasting, maintains film and audio library.

3960 **www.gita.org**
Geospatial Information & Technology Association
A variety of information and useful references for your professional and technical needs, with descriptions of new programs and services, and a stable source of important member contacts, industry news and association related ongoing programs.

3961 **www.greyhouse.com**
Grey House Publishing
Authoritative reference directories for most business sectors including broadcasting, communications and media markets. Users can search the online databases with varied search criteria allowing for custom searches by product category, geographic area, sales volume, keyword, subject and more. Full Grey House catalog and online ordering also available.

3962 **www.halloffame.com**
National Sportscasters & Sportswriters Association

3963 **www.i-newsrelease.com**
Tellmedia Communications
Media research, Internet news, satelite media tours and video news releases.

3964 **www.iabm.com**
International Association of Broadcast Monitors
Website of world wide trade association made up of news retrieval services which monitor television, radio, Internet and print news mediums.

3965 **www.ibsradio.org**
Intercollegiate Broadcasting System
For college and university broadcasting stations.

3966 **www.iemmys.tv**
International Television Academy
Organization of global broadcasters, with representatives from over 50 countries. Sixty percent of the 100-member board of directors come from countries outside the US, and represent the world's largest production, distribution and broadcast companies.

3967 **www.irts.org**
Int'l Radio & Television Society Foundation
For professionals in radio, broadcast and cable televison, corporate video production, collaborative communication, DVD and new media production, marketing and advertising plus related areas, as well as interested laypeople.

3968 **www.kagan.com**
Kagan World Media
For those interested in investments in radio and TV stations and publicly held companies.

3969 **www.lib.umd.edu/LAB**
Library of American Broadcasting
Devoted to television and radio broadcasting materials and archives.

3970 **www.lostremote.com**
Lost Remote
Television industry news, job listings and resources.

3971 **www.mca-i.org**
Media Communications Association International
Website of the global community of professional devoted to the business and art of visual communication.

3972 **www.mediabistro.com**
Media Bistro
News and articles especially for those in broadcasting and publishing.

3973 **www.millimeter.com**
Millimeter Magazine
Authoritative resource for more than 33,000 qualified professionals in production, postproduction, animation, streaming and visual effects for motion pictures, television and commercials.

3974 **www.mrfac.com**
Manufacturer's Radio Frequency Advisory Committee
Representing the voice of the manufacturing industry and private land mobile radio users before the FCC.

3975 **www.nab.org**
National Association of Broadcasters
Full service trade association that represents the interests of free, over-the-air radio and television broadcasters.

3976 **www.naed.org**
National Association of Electrical Distributors
Nonprofit organization dedicated to serving and protecting the electrical distribution channel; provides networking opportunities through approximately 50 meetings and conferences a year, training, industry information and research through TED Magazine, and a marketing campaign for the industry through the NAED Advocacy Initiative.

3977 **www.nafb.org**
National Association of Farm Broadcasters
Works to improve quantity and quality of farm programming and serves as a clearinghouse for new ideas in farm broadcasting.

3978 **www.natpe.org**
Nat'l Association of Television Program Executives
Our mission is a commitment to furthering the quality and quantity of content, offering the wealth of our resources and experience to every content creator, no matter what the medium. Because the industry encompasses so much more today than ever before, NATPE too is expanding to accommodate this change and encourage progress while continuing to keep our members constantly appraised of changes.

3979 **www.ncta.com**
National Cable & Telecommunications Asssociation
National Cable and Telecommunications Association, formerly the National Cable Television Association, is the principal trade association of the cable television industry in the United States. Provides a strong national presence by providing a single, unified voice on issues affecting the cable and telecommunications industry.

3980 **www.ncti.com**
National Cable Television Institute

Independent provider of broadband communications training. Broadband cable system operators, contractors and industry vendors have turned to NCTI to train their employees who construct, operate and maintain broadband systems.

3981 www.necta.info
New England Cable & Telecommunications Association

NECTA is a six state regional trade association representing sbtstantially all private cable telecommunications companies in Connecticut, Maine, Massachusetts, New Hampshire, Rhode Island and Vermont.

3982 www.nrb.org
National Religious Broadcasters

For religious broadcasters and religious media. Hosts national convention featuring trade show and educational workshops.

3983 www.pcia.com
Personal Communications Industry Association

Represents companies that develop, own, manage and operate towers, commercial rooftops and other facilities for the provision of all types of wireless, broadcasting and telecommunications services. PCIA is dedicated to advancing an understanding of the benefits of wireless services and required infrastructure.

3984 www.productionhub.com
Production Hub

Television producers' news, listings, classifieds, casting notices and events.

3985 www.rab.cpm
Radio Advertising Bureau

For marketing personnel and raises awareness of radio among advertising and business communities.

3986 www.radiospace.com
North American Network

All information contained is provided to radio stations and networks for their free and unrestricted use.

3987 www.rtndf.org
Radio Television News Directors Association

Provides training programs, seminars, scholarship support and research in areas of critical concern to electronic news professionals and their audience. Offers professional development opportunities for working and aspiring journalists and journalism educators.

3988 www.sacredheartprofram.org
Sacred Heart Hour

Producers and syndicators of Public Service Radio Programs, Contact Radio available in, thirty minute, fifteen minute, five minute versions, Pathways, one minute radio spots.

3989 www.sbca.com
Satellite Broadcasting/Communications Association

National trade association representing all segments of the satellite consumer services industry. The association is committed to expanding the utilization of satellite technology for the delivery of video, data, voice, interactive and broadband services.

3990 www.sbe.org
Society of Broadcast Engineers

Offers a cooperative educational program intended to assist in the ongoing rollout of digital television.

3991 www.smpte.org
Society of Motion Picture & Television Engineers

Serves the needs of film and TV engineers.

3992 www.thirteen.org
Educational Broadcasting Association

For producers and directors of public educational programming, channel 13, PBS.

3993 www.tvspy.com
TVSpy

Television industry news, articles and links to other sites of interest.

Associations

3994 **ADSC: The International Association of Foundation Drilling**
8445 Freeport Parkway
Suite 325
Irving, TX 75063
469-359-6000
Fax: 469-359-6007
E-Mail: adsc@adsc-iafd.com
Home Page: www.adsc-iafd.com
Social Media: Facebook, Twitter, LinkedIn
Tom Tuozzolo, President
Al Rasband, VP
Martin McDermott, Treasurer
ADSC seeks to advance technology in the foundation of drilling and anchored earth retention industries. Represents drilled shaft, andchored earth retention, micropile contractors, civil engineers and manufacturing firms world wide.
Founded in 1972

3995 **Adhesive & Sealant Council**
7101 Wisconsin Ave
Suite 990
Bethesda, MD 20814
301-986-9700
Fax: 301-986-9795
E-Mail: info@ascouncil.org
Home Page: www.ascouncil.org
C Russell Thompson Jr., President & CEO
Amdrew Johnston, Treasurer
Christine A Bryant, Director
John P Carroll, Director
A North American trade association dedicated to representing the adhesive and sealant industry. ASC is bound by the collective efforts of its members, and strives to improve the industry operating environment and strengthen its member companies.
124 Members
Founded in 1958

3996 **American Architectural Manufacturers Association**
1827 Walden Office Square
Suite 550
Schaumburg, Il 60173-4268
847-303-5664
Fax: 847-303-5774
E-Mail: customerservice@aamanet.org
Home Page: www.aamanet.org
Social Media: Facebook, Twitter, LinkedIn, YouTube, Flickr, SlideShare
Rich Walker, President, CEO
Dean Lewis, Educational Information Mgr.
Maureen Knight, Govt. Affairs Manager
Jannine Klemencic, Executive Assistant
Karen Allen, Accounting/HR Mgr.
Trade association that advocates for manufacturers and professionals in the fenestration industry and is dedicated to the promotion of quality window, door, curtain wall, storefront and skylight products.
Founded in 1936

3997 **American Concrete Pipe Association**
8445 Freeport Parkway
Suite 350
Irving, TX 75063-2595
972-506-7216
Fax: 972-506-7682
E-Mail: info@concrete-pipe.org
Home Page: www.concrete-pipe.org
Social Media: Facebook, LinkedIn, Youtube
Matt Childs, President
Josh Beakley, PE, Technical Services Director
Kim Spahn, PE, Engineering Services Director
The American Concrete Pipe Association (ACPA) is a nonprofit organization, composed primarily of manufacturers of concrete pipe and related conveyance products located throughout the United States, Canada and in over 40 foreign countries. ACPA provides members with research, technical and marketing support to promote and advance the use of concrete pipe for drainage and pollution control applications.
145 Members
Founded in 1907

3998 **American Concrete Pressure Pipe Association**
3900 University Drive
Suite 110
Fairfax, VA 22030-2513
703-273-7227
Fax: 703-273-7230
E-Mail: support@acppa.org
Home Page: www.acppa.org
Jim Tully, Chairman
Alexander Narcise, Vice Chaiman
Mark Carpenter, Secretary
David Tantalean, Treasurer
The American Concrete Pressure Pipe Association (ACPPA) is a nonprofit trade association representing manufacturers of concrete pressure pipe around the world. ACPPA sponsors research projects and conducts educational programs to promote and advance the use of concrete pressure pipe in water and wastewater applications. We also manage an independent audit program to certify compliance with all applicable American Water Works Association (AWWA) standards for the manufacturers.
5 Members
Founded in 1949

3999 **American Concrete Pumping Association**
606 Enterprise Drive
Lewis Center, OH 43035
614-431-5618
Fax: 614-431-6944
E-Mail: christi@concretepumpers.com
Home Page: www.concretepumpers.com
Social Media: Facebook, Twitter, LinkedIn, Youtube, Flickr, RSS
Carl Walker, President
Beth Langhauser, Vice President
Scott Savage, Treasurer
Matt Kaminsky, Secretary
Dennis Andrews, Past President
The American Concrete Pumping Association promotes concrete pumping as the choice method of placing concrete, and to encourage and educate the concrete pumping industry on safe concrete pumping procedures. The ACPA Operator Certification Program is the only industry-recognized certification program for testing concrete pumping practices.
270 Members
Founded in 1974

4000 **American Congress on Surveying and Mapping**
5119 Pagasus Court
Suite Q
Frederick, MD 21704
240-439-4615
Fax: 240-439-4952
E-Mail: curtis.summer@acsm.net
Home Page: www.acsm.net
Social Media: Facebook, Twitter, Blogger
Curtis W Sumner, Executive Director
Bob Jupin, Accounting Manager
Sara Maggi, CST Program
Trish Milburn, Office Manager/Membership Services
A professional organization representing those who communicate the earth's spatial information using precisely prepared plats, charts, maps, and digital cartographic and related data systems.
7000 Members
Founded in 1941

4001 **American Council for Construction Education**
1717 N Loop 1604 East
Suite 320
San Antonio, TX 78232-1570
210-495-6161
Fax: 210-495-6168
E-Mail: acce@acce-hq.org
Home Page: www.acce-hq.org
John Gaver, President
Allan J Hauck, VP
Michael M Holland, Executive VP
Robert T Meyer, Treasurer
The accrediting agency for postsecondary construction education programs. The mission of ACCE is to be a global advocate for programs of post-secondary construction higher education. To accomplish this mission, ACCE will develop, periodically update, and promulgate comprehensive standards for programs of construction higher education and aAccredit programs meeting these standards through a rigorous, formal process of peer review.
Cost: $150.00
115 Members
Founded in 1974

4002 **American Fence Association**
800 Roosevelt Rd
Building C-312
Glen Ellyn, IL 60137
630-942-6598
800-822-4342
Fax: 630-790-3095
E-Mail: afa@mindspring.com
Home Page: www.americanfenceassociation.com
Social Media: Facebook, Twitter
Santo Pernicano, President
Mike Robinson, President Elect
Nate Prewitt, VP
David Gregg, Secretary
Susan Colson, Treasurer
The American Fence Association benefits the fence, deck and railing industry - as well as the consumer - by promoting the highest levels of professionalism, ethics and product standards by disseminating information and educating its members. With 31 member chapters serving the association, AFA offers several educational, certification options and networking opportunities to keep its members above and beyond their competition.
Cost: $365.00
2400 Members
Founded in 1962

4003 **American Institute of Building Design**
529 14th Street NW
Suite 750
Washington, DC 20045
202-249-1407
800-366-2423
Fax: 866-204-0293
E-Mail: info@aibd.org
Home Page: www.aibd.org
Social Media: Facebook, Twitter, LinkedIn, RSS
Steven Mickley, Executive Director
Whit Peterson, General Manager
Dan Sater, President
Alan Kent, Internal Vice President
Viki Wooster, External Vice President

AIBD provides building designers with educational resources, and has developed nationwide design standards and a code of ethics for the building design profession. Today, AIBD is a nationally recognized association with professional and associate members in 48 states, throughout Canada and in Europe, Asia, Australia and the Bahamas. Its chartered state societies are active in their respective legislative arenas and work to promote public awareness of the bldg design profession.
Founded in 1950

4004 American Institute of Constructors
700 North Fairfax Street
Suite 510
Alexandria, VA 22314

703-683-4999
Fax: 703-683-5480
E-Mail: info@professionalconstructor.org
Home Page: www.professionalconstructor.org
Social Media: Facebook, Twitter, LinkedIn

David F Fleming, President
Joseph Sapp, Executive Director
Charles L Sapp, Director, Association Management

AIC is the organization that seeks to give Constructors the professional status they deserve. The Institute is the constructor's counterpart of professional organizations found in architecture, engineering, law and other fields. As such, the Institute serves as the national qualifying body of professional constructor. AIC membership identifies the individual as a true professional.
Founded in 1971

4005 American Institute of Steel Construction
One East Wacker Drive
Suite 700
Chicago, IL 60601-1802

312-670-2400
Fax: 312-670-5403
E-Mail: ferch@aisc.org
Home Page: www.aisc.org

Roger Ferch, President
Jacques Cattan, VP, Certification
John Cross, VP, Market Development & Finance
Scott Melnick, VP, Communications, Member Services

The American Institute of Steel Construction (AISC), headquartered in Chicago, is a not-for-profit technical institute and trade association serving the structural steel design community and construction industry in the United States. AISC's mission is to make structural steel the material of choice by being the leader in structural-steel-related technical and market-building activities, including: specification and code development, research, education, and tech assistance.
2.7M Members
Founded in 1921

4006 American Iron and Steel Institute
25 Massachusetts Ave., NW
Suite 800
Washington, D. 20001

202-452-7100
Home Page: www.steel.org
Social Media: Facebook, Twitter

Michael Rippey, Chairman
Michael T. Rehwinkel, Vice Chairman
Thomas J. Gibson, President, CEO
Lisa Harrison, SVP, Communications
David E. Bell, VP, Finance & Admin.

An association of North American steel producers that features steel information for consumers, engineers, and other professionals.
145 Members

4007 American Public Works Association
2345 Grand Blvd
Suite 700
Kansas City, MO 64108-2625

816-472-6100
800-848-2792
Fax: 816-472-1610
E-Mail: ddancy@apwa.net
Home Page: www.apwa.net
Social Media: Facebook, Twitter, Youtube

Edward A Gottko, President
Ann Daniels, Director/Credentialing
Brad Patterson, Chapter Membership Manager
Mark Leinwetter, Lead Development Manager
David Dancy, Director/Marketing

APWA exists to develop and support the people, agencies, and organizations that plan, build, maintain, and improve our communities. Just as communities count on their public works professionals, APWA strives to be the organization those professionals know they can count on. APWA offers the most comprehensive resources available in the areas of professional development tools, advocacy efforts, networking opportunities, and outreach activities.
26000 Members
Founded in 1937

4008 American Society for Nondestructive Testing
1711 Arlingate Lane
PO Box 28518
Columbus, OH 43228-0518

614-274-6003
800-222-2768
Fax: 614-274-6899
E-Mail: wholliday@asnt.org
Home Page: www.asnt.org
Social Media: Twitter, LinkedIn, Youtube

Wayne Holliday, President
Mike Boggs, Quality Manager
Michael O'Toole, Manger/Conferences
Betsy Blazar, Manager/Marketing
Tim Jones, Manager/Publications

Technical society which is involved in nondestructive testing. ASNT publishes journals, including materials evaluation. The fall conference and quality testing show of this association is the society's largest annual show.
12000 Members
Founded in 1941

4009 American Society of Heating, Refrigerating and Air-Conditioning Engineers
1791 Tullie Circle NE
Atlanta, GA 30329

404-636-8400
800-527-4723
Fax: 404-321-5478
E-Mail: ashrae@ashrae.org
Home Page: www.ashrae.org

William B Bahnfleth, President
Thomas H Phoenix, President Elect
T David Underwood, Treasurer
Darryl K Boyce, Vice President
Jeff Littleton, Secretary

ASHRAE is a building technology society. The Society and its members focus on building systems, energy efficiency, indoor air quality and sustainability within the industry. Through research, standards writing, publishing and continuing education, ASHRAE shapes tomorrow's built environment today.
55000 Members
Founded in 1894

4010 American Society of Professional Estimators
2525 Perimeter Place Dr
Suite 103
Nashville, TN 37214

615-316-9200
888-378-6283
Fax: 615-316-9800
E-Mail: SBO@aspenational.org
Home Page: www.aspenational.org
Social Media: Facebook, Twitter

Patsy Smith, Executive Director
Tina Cooke, Membership Database, Bookkeeper
Tanya Graham, Certification Program

The American Society of Professional Estimators was created with dedication and commitment to the idea of providing its members with tangible benefits.
2500 Members
Founded in 1956

4011 American Subcontractors Association, Inc.
1004 Duke St.
Alexandria, VA 22314ÿ

703-684-3450
Fax: 703-836-3482
E-Mail: ASAoffice@asa-hq.com
Home Page: www.asaonline.com
Social Media: Facebook, Twitter, LinkedIn, YouTube, Google+, RSS

Richard Bright, Chief Operating Officer
Colette Nelson, Chief Advocacy Officer
Marc Ramsey, Director, Communications
Linda Wilson, Director, Chapter Services
Robert Abney, Board of Directors

A nonprofit, national, membership trade association of constructionspecialty trade contractors, suppliers, and service providers in the United States and Canada.

4012 Asbestos Information and Training Centers
Georgia Institute of Real Estate
5784 Lake Forrest Drive
Atlanta, GA 30328

404-252-6768
800-633-3583
Fax: 404-257-0354
E-Mail: gire@learningrealestate.com
Home Page: www.learningrealestate.com
Social Media: Facebook, Twitter, RSS

Rebecca Fletcher, School Director
Mendalyn Harper, Information Central Manager

Sponsors the Regional Asbestos Information and Training Centers. The Centers provide information and training in identification and abatement of asbestos hazards with the ultimate goal of training contractors for eventual certification. Each center offers a variety of specialized courses including identification of asbestos hazards and possible remedies of problems and solutions for those involved in the asbestos hazard abatement process.
Founded in 1959

4013 Asphalt Emulsion Manufacturers Association
Three Church Circle
PO Box 250
Annapolis, MD 21401

410-267-0023
Fax: 410-267-7546
E-Mail: krissoff@aema.org
Home Page: www.aema.org
Social Media: Facebook

Bucky Brooks, President
Mark McCollough, Vice President

Archie Reynolds, Secretary/Treasurer
Barry Baughman, Past President
Diane Franson, Director

The Asphalt Emulsion Manufacturers Association is the International Organization representing the asphalt emulsion industry. AEMA's mission is to expand the use and applications of asphalt emulsions. Asphalt emulsions are the most environmentally sound, energy efficient and cost effective products used in pavement maintenance and construction.
150 Members
Founded in 1973

4014 **Asphalt Institute**
2696 Research Park Dr
Lexington, KY 40511-8480

859-288-4960
Fax: 859-288-4999
E-Mail: info@asphaltinstitute.org
Home Page: www.asphaltinstitute.org
Social Media: Facebook, Twitter, LinkedIn

Peter T Grass, President
Alexander Brown, Regional Director
Bob Horan, Regional Director
Mark Blow, Senior Regional Director
Bob Humer, Senior Regional Director

The Asphalt Institute is the international trade association of petroleum asphalt producers, manufacturers and affiliated businesses. Our mission is to promote the use, benefits and quality performance of petroleum asphalt, through engineering, research, marketing and educational activities, and through the resolution of issues affecting the industry.
113 Members
Founded in 1919

4015 **Associated Builders & Contractors, Inc.**
440 1st St., N.W.
Ste., 200
Washington, D. 20001

202-595-1505
E-Mail: gotquestions@abc.org
Home Page: www.abc.org
Social Media: Facebook, Twitter, LinkedIn, YouTube

Dan Brodbeck, Chairman
Phil Hoppman, Chairman-Elect
Greg Hoberock, Immediate Past Chairman
Anthony Stagliano, Treasurer
Michael Bellaman, President, CEO

A national construction industry trade association representing nearly 21,000 chapter members and whose activities include government representation, legal advocacy, education, workforce development, communications, technology,etc.
21000 Members
Founded in 1950

4016 **Associated Builders and Contractors**
4250 Fairfax Drive
9th Floor
Arlington, VA 22203-1607

703-812-2000
Fax: 703-812-8201
E-Mail: gotquestions@abc.org
Home Page: www.abc.org
Social Media: Facebook, Twitter, LinkedIn, Youtube

Mike Bellaman, President/CEO
Jason Daisy, Chief Financial Officer
Tea Gennaro, Controller
Kim Greene, Executive Assistant
Kurt Becker, HR Business Partner

A national association representing merit shop construction and construction-related firms. ABC's membership represents all specialties within the U.S. construction industry and is comprised primarily of firms that perform work in the industrial and commercial sectors of the industry.
23000 Members
Founded in 1950

4017 **Associated Construction Distributors**
1605 SE Deleware Avenue, Suite B
PO Box 14552
Ankeny, IA 50021

515-964-1335
Fax: 515-964-7668
E-Mail: acdi@acdi.net
Home Page: www.acdi.net

Tom Goetz, Executive VP
Dave Hill, Director/Sales/Marketing
Jane Zieser, Controller
Linda Phipps, Meeting Manager

Associated Construction Distributors International, Inc. (ACDI) was founded when a group of independent, entrepreneurial businessmen came together and realized they had much to offer and much to learn. Sharing business information continues today at the core of the organization. It has allowed the members to succeed individually and as group. ACDI distributors account for nearly one billion dollars in the sale of materials and equipment to the construction industry.
34 Members
Founded in 1974

4018 **Associated Construction Publications**
1200 Madison Ave
LL20
Indianapolis, IN 46225

317-423-7080
800-486-0014
Fax: 317-423-7094
Home Page: www.acppubs.com

Wayne Curtis, Publisher
Royce Morse, Production Director

Strives to assist the heavy construction industry with local and regional news on a nationwide basis.
14 Members
Founded in 1938

4019 **Associated Equipment Distributors**
600 22nd Street
Suite 220
Oak Brook, IL 60523

630-574-0650
800-388-0650
Fax: 630-574-0132
E-Mail: info@aednet.org
Home Page: www.aednet.org
Social Media: Facebook, Twitter

Bob Henderson, EVP/COO
Dave Gordon, VP, Sales/Publisher
Janet L Dixon, Director, Meetings & Conferences
Kim Phelan, Programs Director
Jenny Choe, Communications Director

Associated Equipment Distributors (AED) is an international trade association representing companies involved in the distribution, rental and support of equipment used in construction, mining, forestry, power generation, agriculture and industrial applications.
1200 Members
Founded in 1919

4020 **Associated General Contractors of America**
2300 Wilson Blvd
Suite 400
Arlington, VA 22201

703-548-3118
Fax: 703-548-3119
E-Mail: info@agc.org
Home Page: www.agc.org
Social Media: RSS

Paul W Diederich, President
Alan L Landes, Senior Vice President
Charles L Greco, Vice President
Brian Burgett, Treasurer
Stephen E Sandherr, Chief Executive Officer

The Associated General Contractors of America (AGC) is the leading association for the construction industry. Operating in partnership with its nationwide network of 95 chartered Chapters, AGC provides a full range of services satisfying the needs and concerns of its members, thereby improving the quality of construction and protecting the public interest.
33000 Members
Founded in 1918

4021 **Association of Equipment Manufacturers**
6737 W Washington St
Suite 2400
Milwaukee, WI 53214-5647

414-272-0943
Fax: 414-272-1170
E-Mail: aem@aem.org
Home Page: www.aem.org
Social Media: Twitter

Richard A Patek, Chair
Robert A Kolb, Vice Chair
Dennis J Slater, Secretary
Michael A Haberman, Treasurer

Formed from the consolidation of the Construction Industry Manufacturers Association and Equipment Manufacturers Institute. The international trade and business development resource for companies that manufacture equipment, products and services used worldwide in the construction, agricultural, mining, forestry, and utility fields.
Founded in 2002

4022 **Association of Union Constructors (TAUC)**
1501 Lee Highway
Suite 202
Arlington, VA 22209-1109

703-524-3336
Fax: 703-524-3364
Home Page: www.tauc.org

Steven Lindauer, Chief Executive Officer
David Acord, Communications Manager
Ben Cahoon, Data Systems Manager
Wayne Creasap, Health Director
Michael Dorsey, Industrial Relations Director

TAUC's mission is to act as an advocate for union contractors and enhance cooperation between the three entities involved in the successful completion of construction projects: the union, the contractor and the owner-client, the company for which the work is being completed. By encouraging this tripartite dialogue, many potential issues and delays are eliminated before work even begins.
5000+ Members
Founded in 1969

4023 **Association of the Wall and Ceiling Industry**
513 West Broad Street
Suite 210
Falls Church, VA 22046

703-538-1600
Fax: 703-534-8307
E-Mail: info@awci.org
Home Page: www.awci.org
Social Media: Facebook, Twitter, LinkedIn, Youtube

Steven Etkin, EVP/CEO
Brenton C Stone, Associate Publisher
Karen Bilak, Convention Director

Laura Porinchak, Communications Director
Annemarie Selvitelli, Education Director

Represents acoustics systems, ceiling systems, drywall systems, exterior insulation and finishing systems, fireproofing, flooring systems, insulation, and stucco contractors, suppliers and manufacturers and those in allied trades. The mission of the Association of the Wall and Ceiling Industry is to provide services and undertake activities that enhance the members' ability to operate a successful business.
2400 Members
Founded in 1918

4024 Barre Granite Association

PO Box 481
Barre, VT 05641

802-476-4131
Fax: 802-476-4765
E-Mail: BGA@barregranite.org
Home Page: www.barregranite.org

Robert Couture, President
John Castaldo, VP/Executive Directors

Manufacturers of cemetery monuments, mausoleums, statuary, landscape and architectural granite products. It has been estimated that one-third of the public and private monuments and mausoleums in America — and they are millions in number — are products of the Barre quarries and Barre's international community of sculptors, artisans, mechanics and laborers. All this has been largely accomplished since the closing decades of the last century.
35 Members
Founded in 1889

4025 Brick Industry Association

1850 Centennial Park Drive
Suite 301
Reston, VA 20191

703-620-0010
Fax: 703-620-3928
E-Mail: brickinfo@bia.org
Home Page: www.gobrick.com
Social Media: Facebook, Twitter, LinkedIn, Youtube, Pinterest

Richard Jennison, President

National trade association representing distributors and manufacturers of clay brick and suppliers of related products and services. The Association is involved in a broad range of technical, research, marketing, government relations and communications activities. It is the recognized national authority on brick construction.
175 Members
Founded in 1934

4026 Bridge Grid Flooring Manufacturers Association

201 Castle Drive
West Mifflin, PA 15122

412-469-3985
Fax: 419-257-0332
Home Page: www.abcdpittsburgh.org

Stephen Shanley, President
Todd Carroll, Secretary
Monica O'Neil, Treasurer
Bill Ferko, Awards
Roxanne Podlipsky, Scholarships

Comprised of companies who manufacture steel grid flooring systems for bridges, and other companies with an interest in the steel grid market. The role of the Association is to promote the use of Grid Reinforced Concrete Bridge Decks through data collection, research/development, and education.

4027 Building Industry Association of Southern California

17444 Sky Park Circle
Suite 170
Irvine, CA 92614

949-553-9500
Fax: 949-769-8943
Home Page: www.biasc.org
Social Media: Facebook, Twitter, LinkedIn

Leonard Miller, President
Paul Johnson, Secretary/Treasurer
W Wes Keusder, Immediate Past President

The Building Industry Association of Southern California is a nonprofit trade association representing companies involved in planning and building Southern California's communities. Our members are involved in all aspects of construction and green building - from architecture to roofing to landscape design.
1850 Members
Founded in 1923

4028 Building Material Dealers Association

1006 SE Grand Street
Suite 301
Portland, OR 97214

503-208-3763
888-960-6329
Fax: 971-255-0790
E-Mail: bmda@bmda.com
Home Page: www.bmda.com

Gwyn Matras, Executive Director

BMDA provides Notice of Right to a Lien service for all states and Construction Lien service for Oregon and Washington. We offer current lien law manuals for Oregon and Washington, which assists our members with all areas of the construction lien laws. At BMDA, we believe attorneys who specialize in construction lien law are your best choice for answering legal questions. Therefore, we offer attorney referrals for Oregon and Washington. BMDA will not provide legal advice at any time.
3500 Members
Founded in 1915

4029 Building Stone Institute

5 Riverside Drive, Bldg 2
PO Box 419
Chestertown, NY 12817

518-803-4336
866-786-6313
Fax: 518-803-4338
Home Page: www.buildingstoneinstitute.org
Social Media: Facebook

Jane Bennett, Executive Vice President
Kayla Carlozza, Association Services Coordinator
Gina De Nardo, Communications
Rob Teel, President
Bernard Buster, Vice President

The Building Stone Institute works on behalf of the quarries, fabricators, retailers, importers, exporters, carvers, sculptors, restorers, designers, and installers that comprise our diverse membership. BSI provides programs and services that empower our member companies to offer the highest level of quality products and services. BSI is a not-for-profit trade association dedicated to serving its member firms, and providing educational materials and continuing education.
350 Members
Founded in 1919

4030 Building Trades Association

6353 W. Rogers Circle
Unit 3
Boca Raton, FL 33487

800-326-7800
E-Mail: info@buildingtrades.com
Home Page: www.buildingtrades.com
Social Media: Facebook

An association made up of thousands of companies involved in all phases of the building and construction industries.

4031 California Redwood Associates

818 Grayson Road
Suite 201
Pleasant Hill, CA 94523

925-935-1499
Fax: 925-935-1496
E-Mail: info@calredwood.org
Home Page: www.calredwood.org
Social Media: Youtube

Christopher Grover, President

A trade association for redwood lumber producers.

4032 Cedar Shake and Shingle Bureau

PO Box 1178
Sumas, WA 98295-1178

604-820-7700
Fax: 604-820-0266
E-Mail: info@cedarbureau.org
Home Page: www.cedarbureau.org

Lynne Christensen, Director of Operations
Barbara Enns, Accountant
Kelly Vaille, Marketing Coordinator
Suzie Quigley, Customer Service
Sharron Beauregard, Accounting Assistant

The Cedar Shake and Shingle Bureau is a non-profit organization that promotes the use of Certi-label cedar roofing and sidewall products. On June 9, 1915, at a meeting of the Trustees of the West Coast Lumber Manufacturers Association, it was agreed to establish a branch of the association to serve those members who manufactured shingles. Our influence grew, and as we survived both the Great Depression and World War II, manufacturers continued their quality commitment.
350 Members
Founded in 1915

4033 Construction Financial Management Association

100 Village Blvd
Suite 200
Princeton, NJ 08540

609-452-8000
Fax: 609-452-0474
E-Mail: info@cfma.org
Home Page: www.cfma.org
Social Media: Facebook, Twitter, LinkedIn, Youtube

Stuart Binstock, President & CEO
Erica O'Grady, VP, Operations
Robert Rubin, VP, Finance & Administration
Brian Summers, VP, Content Management & Education
Brigitte Meinders, Director, Marketing

CFMA is the only organization dedicated to bringing together construction financial professionals and those partners serving their unique needs. CFMA serves members located throughout the US and Canada.
7000 Members
Founded in 1981

4034 Construction Industry Service Corporation

2000 Spring Road
Suite 110
Oak Brook, IL 60523

630-472-9411
877-562-9411
Fax: 630-472-9413

Home Page: www.cisco.org
Social Media: Facebook, Twitter, LinkedIn

David Henderson, President
Mark Maher, VP
Frank Furco, Treasurer
Dan Divane, Interim Secretary

The Construction Industry Service Corporation (CISCO) is a non-profit labor management association bringing union construction labor and management representatives together to work cooperatively in order to better the construction industry as a whole. CISCO currently represents union contractors and workers in Cook, DuPage, Lake, Kane, Kendall and McHenry Counties.
14800 Members
Founded in 1988

4035 Construction Owners Association of America
5000 Austell Powder Springs Rd
Suite 217
Austell, GA 30106

770-433-0820
800-994-2622
Fax: 404-577-3551
E-Mail: coaa@coaa.org
Home Page: www.coaa.org
Social Media: Facebook, Twitter, LinkedIn

Ted Argyle, President
Kevin Lewis, Vice President
Gwen Glattes, Secretary/Treasurer
Boyd Black, Past President
A Miles Albertson, Director

National association dedicated to supporting project Owners' success in the design and construction of buildings and facilities through education, information and developing relationships within the industry. Comprised of public and private owners who manage facilities development and capital improvement projects.
530 Members
Founded in 1994

4036 Construction Specifications Institute
110 South Union Street
Suite 100
Alexandria, VA 22314

703-684-0300
800-689-2900
Fax: 703-684-8436
E-Mail: csi@csinet.org
Home Page: www.csinet.org
Social Media: Facebook, Twitter, LinkedIn, Youtube, Flickr

Casey F Robb, President
Robert W Simmons, President Elect
Ronald L Geren, Vice President
Stephen E Nash, Vice President
Kevin D Corkern, Secretary

A national association dedicated to creating standards and formats to improve construction documents and project delivery. The organization is unique in the industry in that its members are a cross section of specifiers, architects, engineers, contractors and building materials suppliers.
15000 Members
Founded in 1948

4037 Continental Automated Buildings Association (CABA)
1173 Cyrville Road
Suite 210
Ottawa, Canada, ON K1J 7S6

613-686-1814
888-798-2222
Fax: 613-744-7833
E-Mail: caba@caba.org
Home Page: www.caba.org
Social Media: Facebook, Twitter, LinkedIn, Youtube, Flickr

Ronald J Zimmer, President & CEO
Rawlson O'Neil King, Communications Director
Erin Mills, Research Director
George Grimes, Business Development Director
Sonia D'Ambrosio, Database Administrator

An association for the furtherance of automated buildings.
Founded in 1988

4038 Deep Foundations Institute
326 Lafayette Avenue
Hawthorne, NJ 07506

973-423-4030
Fax: 973-423-4031
E-Mail: staff@dfi.org
Home Page: www.dfi.org
Social Media: Facebook, LinkedIn

Robert B Bittner, President
Patrick Bernmingham, Vice President
Matthew Janes, Secretary
John Wolosick, Treasurer
James Morrison, Immediate Past President

DFI gathers professionals in the deep foundations sector of the construction industry, to create a place for discussion, inquiry and debate. In so doing, DFI brings the disciplines together where they have learned from each other, creating a better informed, more communicative foundations industry.
3000 Members
Founded in 1976

4039 Design-Build Institute of America
1331 Pennsylvania Ave., NW
4th Floor
Washington, D. 20004

202-682-0110
Fax: 202-682-5877
E-Mail: dbia@dbia.org
Home Page: www.dbia.org/Pages/default.aspx
Social Media: Facebook, Twitter, LinkedIn

Timothy J. Heck, Chief Financial Officer
Louis J. Jenny, VP, Advocacy & Outreach
Lisa Washington, CAE, Executive Director/CEO
Allison Leisner, Executive Assistant
Richard Thomas, Dir., State Legislative Affairs

An organization that defines, teaches, and promotes best practices in design-build and represents the entire design and construction industry.

4040 Door & Access Systems Manufacturers Association International
1300 Sumner Avenue
Cleveland, OH 44115-2851

216-241-7333
Fax: 216-241-0105
E-Mail: dasma@dasma.com
Home Page: www.dasma.com

John H. Addingtonÿ, Executive Director
R. Christopher Johnson, Assistant Executive Director
Joseph R. Hetzelÿ, Technical Director
Louise M.ÿ Shellhammer, Administrative Assistant
Eva Brunk, Technical Assistant

Trade association of manufacturers of garage doors, rolling doors, high performance doors, garage door operators, vehicular gate operators, and access control products.
Founded in 1996

4041 Elberton Granite Association
1 Granite Plaza
PO Box 640
Elberton, GA 30635

706-283-2551
Fax: 706-283-6380
E-Mail: granite@egaonline.com
Home Page: www.egaonline.com

Manuel Fernadez, President

The Elberton Granite Association, Inc. is the largest trade association of granite quarriers and manufacturers in the United States. More than 250,000 granite memorials are manufactured annually by E.G.A. firms and shipped throughout the United States.
150 Members
Founded in 1951

4042 Expanded Metal Manufacturers Association
800 Roosevelt Rd. Bldg. C
Suite 312
Glen Ellyn, IL 60137

630-942-6591
Fax: 630-790-3095
E-Mail: wlewis7@cox.net
Home Page: www.emma-assoc.org

Chris Steward, President
Jeff Church, Executive Vice President
Debra Lenahan, Immediate Past President
Wes Lewis, Technical Consultant
Randall Schievelbein, Secretary/Treasurer

Educational resources that promote the use of Expanded Metal which reduces scrap materials.

4043 Hollow Metal Door and Buck Association
National Assn of Architectural Metal Manufacturer
800 Roosevelt Rd
Bldg C Suite 312
Glen Ellyn, IL 60137

630-942-6591
Fax: 630-790-3095
E-Mail: wlewis7@cox.net
Home Page: www.naamm.org

Chris Steward, President
Randall Schievelbein, Secretary/Treasurer
Tony Leto, Division Chair
Joseph Karpen, Division Vice Chair

The largest of four operating divisions of the National Association of Architectural Metal Manufacturers. HMMA is a group composed of companies that manufacture, distribute and promote the use of hollow metal door and frame products.
60 Members
Founded in 1938

4044 Hollow Metal Manufacturers Association
800 Roosevelt Rd. Bldg. C
Suite 312
Glen Ellyn, IL 60137

630-942-6591
Fax: 630-790-3095
E-Mail: wlewis7@cox.net
Home Page: www.hollowmetal.org

Chris Steward, President
Jeff Church, Executive Vice President
Debra Lenahan, Immediate Past President
Wes Lewis, Technical Consultant
Randall Schievelbein, Secretary/Treasurer

Develops standards, conducts product performance testing and delivers education to promote the use of hollow metal doors and frames.

4045 ICC: International Code Council
500 New Jersey Avenue, NW
6th Floor
Washington, DC 20001
888-422-7233
Fax: 202-783-2348
E-Mail: webmaster@iccsafe.org
Home Page: www.iccsafe.org
Social Media: Facebook, Twitter, LinkedIn, RSS

Stephen D Jones, President
Guy Tomberlin, VP
Alex Olszowy III, Secretary/Treasurer
David Decourcey, EVP/General Counsel
Hamid Naden, SVP/Product Development

The International Code Council is a member-focused association dedicated to helping the building safety community and construction industry provide safe, sustainable and affordable construction through the development of codes and standards used in the design, build and compliance process. Mission: To provide the highest quality codes, standards, products and services for all concerned with the safety and performance.
Founded in 1994

4046 Interlocking Concrete Pavement Institute
13921 Park Center Rd
Suite 270
Herndon, VA 20171
703-657-6900
800-241-3652
Fax: 703-657-6901
E-Mail: icpi@icpi.org
Home Page: www.icpi.org
Social Media: Facebook, Twitter, LinkedIn, Youtube, Pinterest

Dave Carter, Chairman
David Pitre, Vice Chairman
Mike Mueller, Secretary/Treasurer
Roberto Nicolia, Immediate Past Chair
Elliot Bender, Member

Self governed, self funded autonomous association representing the interlocking concrete pavement industry in North America. Membership is open to producers, contractors, suppliers, consultants and others who have an interest in the industry.
600+ Members
Founded in 1993

4047 International Door Association
PO Box 246
West Milton, OH 45383
937-988-8042
800-355-4432
Fax: 937-698-6153
E-Mail: info@longmgt.com
Home Page: www.doors.org
Social Media: Facebook, Twitter, LinkedIn, Youtube

Chris Long, Managing Director
Dawn Jennings, Accounting Manager
Shawn Hicks, Marketing Manager
Art Komorowski, Publications Manager
Jane Treiber, Membership Manager

The International Door Association plays an important role in the process of quality creation and control by providing helpful programs and services to those who sell, install, and service the superb products produced by the industry's list of manufacturers. Door and access systems dealers are the front line businesses that serve the customer face-to-face.
750 Members
Founded in 1996

4048 International Slurry Surfacing Association
Three Church Circle
PO Box 250
Annapolis, MD 21401-1933
410-267-0023
Fax: 410-267-7546
E-Mail: krissoff@slurry.org
Home Page: www.slurry.org

Christine Deneuvillers, President
Rusty Price, Vice President
Carter Dabney, Secretary
Eric Reimschiisel, Treasurer
W Pierre Peltier, Immediate Past President

The International Slurry Surfacing Association (ISSA) is an international non-profit trade association comprised of contractors, equipment manufacturers, research personnel, consulting engineers and other industry professionals, working together to promote the concept of pavement preservation. ISSA promotes the highest standards of ethics and quality while providing its members with information, tech assistance and ongoing opportunities for networking and professional development.
Cost: $500.00
220+ Members
Founded in 1963

4049 International Zinc Association
1822 East NC Highway 54
Suite 120
Durham, NC 27713
919-361-4647
Fax: 919-361-1957
E-Mail: contact@zinc.org
Home Page: www.zinc.org
Social Media: Facebook, Twitter

A nonprofit global organization dedicated to the interests of zinc and its users.
Founded in 1990

4050 Interstates Construction Services
1520 North Main
PO Box 260
Sioux Center, IA 51250
712-722-1662
Fax: 712-722-1667
E-Mail: bdev@interstates.com
Home Page: www.interstates.com

Larry Den Herder, Chairman & CEO
Dave Crumrine, President
Scott Peterson, Chief Financial Officer
Doug Post, President/Interstate Engineering
Jack Woelber, President/Control Systems

Combine the strengths of teams with processing industry expertise to develop the best solutions for clients' project needs. From the planning table to the plant floor, Interstates is with clients every step of the way. Assists with preliminary budgeting and help develop cost effective designs, setting the stage for a quick and efficient startup.
Founded in 1953

4051 Manufactured Housing Institute
1655 North Fort Myer Road
Suite 104
Arlington, VA 22209
703-558-0400
Fax: 703-558-0401
E-Mail: info@mfghome.org
Home Page: www.manufacturedhousing.org
Social Media: Facebook, Twitter

Nathan Smith, President/CEO
Phyllis Knight, Vice Chair
Kevin Clayton, Secretary
Howard Walker, Treasurer
Lois Starkey, VP/Regulatory Affairs

MHI is the national trade organization representing all segments of the factory-built housing industry. MHI serves its membership by providing industry research, promotion, education and government relations programs, and by building and facilitating consensus within the industry.

4052 Mason Contractors Association of America: Advancing the Masonry Industry
1481 Merchant Drive
Algonquin, IL 60102
224-678-9709
800-536-2225
Fax: 224-678-9714
Home Page: www.masoncontractors.org
Social Media: Facebook, Twitter, LinkedIn

John Smith, Chairman
Mark Kemp, Vice Chair
Michael Sutter, Treasurer
Paul Odom, Secretary
Angie Parisi, Administration

The Mason Contractors Association of America (MCAA) is the national trade association representing mason contractors. The MCAA is committed to preserving and promoting the masonry industry by providing continuing education, advocating fair codes and standards, fostering a safe work environment, recruiting future manpower, and marketing the benefits of masonry materials.
1000 Members
Founded in 1950

4053 Masonry Society
105 South Sunset Street
Suite Q
Longmont, CO 80501-6172
303-939-9700
Fax: 303-541-9215
E-Mail: info@masonrysociety.org
Home Page: www.masonrysociety.org
Social Media: LinkedIn

Scott Walkowicz, President
Jerry M Painter, VP
Darrell McMillian, Secretary/Treasurer
Philip Samblanet, Executive Director
Susan Scheurer, TMS Meeting Planner

Dedicated to the advancement of scientific engineering, architechtural and construction knowledge of masonry. Promotes research and education and disseminates information on masonry materials, design, construction. Publishes newsletters, codes & specifications and material on masonry design.
700 Members
Founded in 1977

4054 Mechanical Contractors Association of America
1385 Piccard Drive
Rockville, MD 20850
301-869-5800
Fax: 301-990-9690
Home Page: www.mcaa.org

Provides high-quality educational materials and programs for 2,500 firms involved in heating, air conditioning, refrigeration, plumbing, piping, and mechanical service.

4055 Metal Building Manufacturers Association
1300 Sumner Avenue
Cleveland, OH 44115-2851
216-241-7333
Fax: 216-241-0105
Home Page: www.mbma.com
Social Media: LinkedIn

John H. Addington, General Manager
W. Lee Shoemaker, Ph.D., P.E., Dir., Research & Engineering
Jay D. Johnson, LEED AP, Dir., Architectural

Services
Daniel J. Walker, P.E., Assistant General Manager
Andres A. Carvallo, Staff Engineer

Promotes the design and construction of metal building systems in the low-rise, non-residential building marketplace.

4056 **Metal Construction Association**
8735 W. Higgins Rd.
Suite 300
Chicago, IL 60631

847-375-4718
Fax: 847-375-6488
E-Mail: mca@metalconstruction.org
Home Page: www.metalconstruction.org
Social Media: Facebook, Twitter, LinkedIn

Karl Hielscher, Chair
Norbert Schneider, Vice Chair
Todd E. Miller, Past Chair
Dale Nelson, Treasurer
Ed Karper, Secretary

An organization of manufacturers and suppliers whose metal products are used in structures.
Founded in 1983

4057 **Metal Framing Manufacturers Association**
330 N Wabash Ave
Chicago, IL 60611

312-644-6610
Fax: 312-321-4098
E-Mail: MFMAstats@smithbucklin.com
Home Page: www.metalframingmfg.org

Mark Thorsby, Executive Director
Amanda Frjelich, Member Services

The Members of the Metal Framing Manufacturers Association (MFMA) focus on the manufacture of ferrous and nonferrous metal framing (continuous slot metal channel systems) which consist of channels with in-turned lips and associated hardware for fastening to the channels (Strut) at random points.
Founded in 1981

4058 **Mississippi Valley Equipment Association**
11140 E Woodmen Rd
Falcon, CO 80831-8127

719-495-2283
800-388-9881
Fax: 719-495-3014
E-Mail: oholcombe@swassn.com
Home Page: www.mvea.com
Social Media: Facebook

Jim C Herron, CEO
Olivia Holcombe, Director of Marketing

A regional affiliate of the North American Equipment Dealers Association provides members with a multitude of services designed to assist them in maintaining a profitable business operation.
165 Members
Founded in 1941

4059 **Modular Building Institute**
944 Glenwood Station Ln
Suite 204
Charlottesville, VA 22901-1480

434-296-3288
888-811-3288
Fax: 434-296-3361
E-Mail: info@modular.org
Home Page: www.mbinet.org
Social Media: Facebook, Twitter, LinkedIn, Youtube, Google+

Michael Bollero Sr., President
Harry Klukas, VP
Kathy Wilmot, VP Elect
Kelly Williams, Secretary
Christopher Peterson, Treasurer

The Modular Building Institute (MBI) is the international non-profit trade association serving modular construction. Members are manufacturers, contractors, and dealers in two distinct segments of the industry - permanent modular construction (PMC) and relocatable buildings (RB). Associate members are companies supplying building components, services, and financing.
211 Members
Founded in 1983

4060 **National Asphalt Pavement Association**
5100 Forbes Blvd
Suite 200
Lanham, MD 20706

301-731-4748
888-468-6499
Fax: 301-731-4621
E-Mail: mcervarich@hotmix.org
Home Page: www.asphaltpavement.org
Social Media: Facebook, Twitter

Mike Acott, President
Margaret Cervarich, VP Marketing/Public Affairs
Audrey Copeland, VP/Engineering
Jay Hansen, Executive Vice President
Kent Hansen, Director/Engineering

The only trade association that represents the interests of the asphalt pavement producer and paving contractor on the national level with Congress, government agencies, and other national trade and business organizations. NAPA supports an active research program designed to answer questions about environmental issues and to improve the quality of asphalt pavements and paving techniques used in the construction of roads, streets, highways, parking lots, and environmental facilities.
1100+ Members
Founded in 1955

4061 **National Association of Architectural Metal Manufacturers**
800 Roosevelt Rd. Bldg. C
Suite 312
Glen Ellyn, IL 60137

630-942-6591
Fax: 630-790-3095
E-Mail: wlewis7@cox.net
Home Page: www.naamm.org

Chris Steward, President
Jeff Church, Executive Vice President
Debra Lenahan, Immediate Past President
Wes Lewis, Technical Consultant
Randall Schievelbein, Secretary/Treasurer

An association that represents a wide variety of architectural metal products for building construction.

4062 **National Association of Church Design Builders**
1000 Ballpark Way
Suite 306
Arlington, TX 76011

817-200-2622
866-416-2232
Fax: 817-275-4519
Home Page: www.nacdb.com

Dale Reiser, President
Steve Shehorn, Vice President
Amanda McFerren, Executive Director

An established, board-certified, nationwide association of firms committed to focusing on the ministry needs and styles of the churches they serve.

4063 **National Association of Elevator Contractors**
1298 Wellbrook Cir Ne
Suite A
Conyers, GA 30012-8031

770-760-9660
800-900-6232
Fax: 770-760-9714
E-Mail: info@naec.org
Home Page: www.naec.org

Mark Boelhouwer, President
John Sweeney, Vice President
Craig Jones, Secretary
Alison Whittaker, Treasurer
Hugh Bertshin, Director

NAEC is an association of elevator contractors and suppliers serving primarily the interests of independent elevator contractors and independent suppliers of products and services; promoting safe and reliable elevator, escalator and short-range transportation and promoting excellence in the management of member companies.
631 Members
Founded in 1950

4064 **National Association of Home Builders**
1201 15th Street NW
Washington, DC 20005

202-822-0200
800-368-5242
Fax: 202-266-8400
E-Mail: info@nahb.com
Home Page: www.nahb.org
Social Media: Facebook, Twitter, LinkedIn, Google+, Pinterest

Rick Judson, Chairman
Kevin Kelly, First Vice Chair
Tom Woods, Second Vice Chair
Ed Brady, Third Vice Chair
Gerald M Howard, CEO

Represents the building industry by serving its members and affiliated state and local builders associations.
220M Members
Founded in 1942

4065 **National Association of Women in Construction**
327 S Adams Street
Fort Worth, TX 76104

817-877-5551
800-552-3506
Fax: 817-877-0324
E-Mail: nawic@nawic.org
Home Page: www.nawic.org

Debra Gregoire, President
Cindy Johnsen, VP

Founded by women working in the construction industry. The founders organized NAWIC to create a support network for women in construction.
5800 Members
Founded in 1953

4066 **National Association of the Remodeling Industry**
PO Box 4250
Des Plaines, IL 60016

847-298-9200
800-611-6274
Fax: 847-298-9225
E-Mail: info@nari.org
Home Page: www.nari.org
Social Media: Facebook, Twitter

Art Donnelly, CEO
Dean Herriges, Chairman
Kevin Anundson, President Elect

Judy Mozen, Treasurer
H Dale Contant, Secretary

NARI has an inclusive, encompassing purpose to; establish and maintain a firm commitment to developing and sustaining programs that expand and unite the remodeling industry; to ensure the industry's growth and security; to encourage ethical conduct, sound business practices and professionalism in the remodeling industry; and to present NARI as the recognized authority in the remodeling industry.
Founded in 1935

4067 National Concrete Masonry Association
13750 Sunrise Valley Dr
Herndon, VA 20171-4662

703-713-1900
Fax: 703-713-1910
E-Mail: ncma@ncma.org
Home Page: www.ncma.org

Robert Thomas, President

Consists of manufacturers of concrete masonry products and suppliers of products to the industry. Offers a variety of technical of technical services and design aids through publications, computer programs, slide presentations and technical training.
Founded in 1918

4068 National Conference of States on Building Codes & Standards
505 Huntmar Park Dr
Suite 210
Herndon, VA 20170-5103

703-437-0100
Fax: 703-481-3596
E-Mail: dbecker@ncsbcs.org
Home Page: www.ncsbcs.org

Kevin Egilmez, Project Manager
Debbie Becker, Administrative Assistant

Serves as a forum for the interchange of information and provides technical services, education and training to our members to enhance the public's social, economic well-being through safe, durable, accessible and efficient buildings.
Founded in 1967

4069 National Council of Acoustical Consultants
9100 Purdue Rd
Suite 200
Indianapolis, IN 46268

317-328-0642
Fax: 317-328-4629
E-Mail: info@ncac.com
Home Page: www.ncac.com

Bennett Brooks, President
Michael Yantis, VP Membership

Strives to safeguard the interests of professional acoustical consulting firms. Managing physics and psychoacoustics to provide optimum lisning environments.
130 Members
Founded in 1962

4070 National Demolition Association
16 N Franklin Street
Suite 203
Doylestown, PA 18901-3536

215-348-4949
800-541-2412
Fax: 215-348-8422
E-Mail: info@demolitionassociation.com
Home Page: www.demolitionassociation.com

Jeff Kroeker, President
Peter Banks, VP
Scott Knightly, Secretary
Christopher Godek, Treasurer

Represents the demolition industry including demolition contractorsto foster goodwill and the exchange of ideas with the public, governmental agencies and contractors engaged in the demolition industry, and for manufacturers or suppliers of demolition equipment, supplies and services.
900 Members
Founded in 1972

4071 National Electrical Contractors Association
3 Bethesda Metro Ctr
Suite 1100
Bethesda, MD 20814

301-657-3110
Fax: 301-215-4500
E-Mail: beth.margulies@necanet.org
Home Page: www.necanet.org
Social Media: Facebook, Twitter, LinkedIn, Youtube, Flickr

John Grau, CEO
Dan Walter, VP & COO
Traci Pickus, Secretary/Treasurer
Geary Higgins, VP, Labor Relations

Represents a segment of the construction market comprised of electrical contracting firms.
70000 Members
Founded in 1897

4072 National Environmental Balancing Bureau
8575 Grovemont Cir
Gaithersburg, MD 20877

301-977-3698
Fax: 301-977-9589
E-Mail: stevej@nebb.org
Home Page: www.nebb.org

Robert Linder, President
James Huber, President Elect
Jean Paul Le Blance, VP
Stephen Archer, Treasurer

NEBB is an international certification assocaition for firms that deliver high performance building systems. Members perform testing, adjusting and balancing (TAB) of heating, ventilating and air-conditioning systems, commission and retro-commission building systems commissioning, execute sound and vibration testing, and test and certify lab fume hoods and electronic and bio clean rooms. NEBB holds the highest standards in certification.
Founded in 1971

4073 National Housing Endowment
1201 15th St Nw
Washington, DC 20005

202-293-9072
800-368-5242
Fax: 202-266-8177
E-Mail: nhe@nahb.org
Home Page: www.nationalhousingendowment.org

Robert L Mitchell, Chairman
Mark Ellis Tipton, Vice Chair
Kent Colton, Treasurer
F Gary Garczynski, Secretary

Provides a permanaent source of funds to address long-term industry concerns at the national level including: supporting scholarship progams that encourage students to select home building and related fields as their life's work, assisting colleges and universities in the development of housing related curricula and activities, revitalizing the industry's labor pool and enhancing its professionalism through apprenticeship programs, seminars and continuing education.
Founded in 1987

4074 National Lumber & Building Material Dealers Association
2025 M St NW
Suite 800
Washington, DC 20036-3309

202-367-1169
800-634-8645
Fax: 202-367-2169
E-Mail: info@dealer.org
Home Page: www.dealer.org
Social Media: Facebook, Twitter, LinkedIn

Chuck Bankston, Chair
Chris Yenrick, Chair Elect
JD Saunders, First Vice Chair
Scott Yates, Second Vice Chair
Linda Nussbaum, Treasurer

To advance the national agenda for America's building material suppliers.
6000 Members
Founded in 1916

4075 National Organization of Minority Architects
2366 Sixth Street, N.W.
Room 100
Washington, D. 20059

202-686-2780
Home Page: www.noma.net
Social Media: Facebook, Twitter, LinkedIn

Kathy Dixon, President
Kevin M. Holland, President Elect
Anzilla Gilmore, Vice President - South
Andrew Thompson, Vice President - Northÿ
Rod Henmi, Vice President - West

A national organization that strives to minimize the effects of racism in the architecture profession and also battles against apathy, bigotry, and abuse of the natural environment.

4076 National Paint and Coatings Association
1500 Rhode Island Ave Nw
Washington, DC 20005

202-462-6272
Fax: 202-462-8549
E-Mail: npca@paint.org
Home Page: www.paint.org

J Andrew Doyle, President
Thomas J Graves, VP, General Counsel
Allen Irish, Counsel/Director, Industry Affairs

Manufacturers of paints and industrial coatings and suppliers to the industry.
400+ Members
Founded in 1886

4077 National Railroad Construction & Maintenance Association
500 New Jersey Ave NW
Suite 400
Washington, DC 20001

202-715-2919
Fax: 202-318-0867
E-Mail: info@nrcma.org
Home Page: www.nrcma.org
Social Media: Facebook, Twitter, LinkedIn

Terry Benton, Chairman
Bill Dorris, Vice Chair
Chris Daloisio, Secretary/Treasurer

Members are railroad construction and maintenance contractors, engineering firms, manufacturing suppliers and professional associate firms.
100+ Members
Founded in 1978

4078 National Ready Mixed Concrete Association
900 Spring St
Silver Spring, MD 20910-4015

301-587-1400
888-846-7622
Fax: 301-585-4219
E-Mail: info@nrmca.org
Home Page: www.nrmca.org
Social Media: Facebook, Twitter, LinkedIn

Terry Benton, Chairman
Bill Dorris, Vice Chair
Chris Daloisio, Secretary/Treasurer

Our mission is to provide exceptional value for our members by responsibly representing and serving the entire ready mixed concrete industry through leadership, promotion, education and partnering; to ensure ready mixed concrete is the building material of choice.

1200 Members
Founded in 1930

4079 National Roofing Contractors Association
10255 W. Higgins Road
Suite 600
Rosemont, IL 60018-5607

847-299-9070
Fax: 847-299-1183
Home Page: www.nrca.net
Social Media: Facebook, Twitter, LinkedIn, YouTube

Richard M. Nugent, President
Lindy Ryan, Senior Vice President
Scott Baxter, Vice President
Dennis Conway, Vice President
Bob Kulp, Vice President

An association of roofing, roof deck, and waterproofing contractors; industry-related associate members; and international members worldwide.

Founded in 1886

4080 National Slag Association
P.O Box 1197
Pleasant Grove, UT 84062

801-785-4535
Fax: 801-785-4539
E-Mail: info@nationalslag.org
Home Page: www.nationalslag.org

Members are processors of iron and steel slags for use as a aggregate in construction and manufacturing applications.

77 Members
Founded in 1918

4081 National Stone, Sand & Gravel Association
1605 King St
Alexandria, VA 22314

703-525-8788
800-342-1415
Fax: 703-525-7782
E-Mail: jwilson@nssga.org
Home Page: www.nssga.org

Mike Johnson, President & CEO
Gus Edwards, President Emeritus

Represents the crushed stone, sand and gravel — or aggregate — industries. Our members account for 90 percent of the crushed stone and 70 percent of the sand and gravel produced annually in the US.

570 Members
Founded in 1985

4082 National Systems Contractors Association
3950 River Ridge DR NE
Cedar Rapids, IA 52402

319-366-6722
800-446-6722
Fax: 319-366-4164
E-Mail: nsca@nsca.org
Home Page: www.nsca.org
Social Media: Facebook, Twitter, LinkedIn

Ingolf De Jong, President
Kelly McCarthy, VP
Michael Hester, Treasurer
Ray Bailey, Secretary
Chuck Wilson, Executive Director

A not for profit association representing the commercial electronic systems industry. Also a powerful advocate of all who work within the low voltage industry, including systems contractors/integrators, product manufacturers, consultants, sales representatives, a growing number of architects, specifying engineers and others.

2800 Members
Founded in 1980

4083 National Terrazzo and Mosaic Association
P.O. Box 2605
Fredericksburg, TX 78624

800-323-9736
Fax: 888-362-2770
E-Mail: info@ntma.com
Home Page: www.ntma.com

George Hardy, Executive Director

The association establishes national standards for all terrazzo floor and wall systems and provides complete specifications, color plates and general information to architects and designers at no cost.

4084 National Tile Contractors Association
626 Lakeland E Drive
PO Box 13629
Jackson, MS 39232

601-939-2071
Fax: 601-932-6117
E-Mail: webmaster@tile-assn.com
Home Page: www.tile-assn.com

Dan Welch, President
James Woelfel, First VP
Martin Howard, Second VP
Bart Bettiga, Executive Director
James Olson, Ass. Executive Director

Serving every segment of the industry, and is recognized as the largest and most respected tile contractors association in the world.

675 Members
Founded in 1947
Mailing list available for rent

4085 National Utility Contractors Association
3925 Chain Bridge Road
Suite 300
Fairfax, VA 22230

703-358-9300
Fax: 703-358-9307
E-Mail: bill@nuca.com
Home Page: www.nuca.com
Social Media: Facebook, Twitter, LinkedIn

Bonnie Williams, VP, Marketing & Communications
Eben Wyman, VP, Government Relations
Bill Hillman, CEO

A national association that provides a forum for continuing education and promotes effective public policy, through its grassroots network, to protect and enhance your industry.

1400 Members
Founded in 1964

4086 North American Insulation Manufacturers Association
44 Canal Center Plaza
Suite 310
Alexandria, VA 22314-1548

703-684-0084
Fax: 703-684-0427
Home Page: www.naima.org

Kate Offringa, President/CEO
Angus Crane, EVP

Manufacturers of fiber glass, rock wool, and slag wool insulation products. NAIMA members manufacture the vast majority of fiber glass, rock and slag wool insulations produced and used in North America.

Founded in 1933

4087 Northeastern Retail Lumber Association
585 N Greenbush Rd
Rensselaer, NY 12144

518-286-1010
800-292-6752
Fax: 518-286-1755
E-Mail: rferris@nrla.org
Home Page: www.nrla.org

Jonas Kelly, Chair
Rita Ferris, President
Joe Miles, Chair Elect
Charles Handley, Vice Chair
Richard Tarr, Treasurer

A resource for industry members, consumers, and public officials independent lumber and building material suppliers and associated businesses in New York and the six New England states.

1150 Members
Founded in 1894

4088 Operative Plasterers' and Cement Masons' International Association
11720 Beltsville Dr
Suite 700
Beltsville, MD 20705

301-623-1000
Fax: 301-623-1032
E-Mail: opcmiaintl@opcmia.org
Home Page: www.opcmia.org

Patrick Finley, President
Earl F Hurd, General Secretary/Treasurer
Daniel Stepano, EVP

Represents and trains plasterers and cement masonsn for the purpose of protecting and promoting the quality of the industry and the livelihood of the members.

Founded in 1864

4089 Outdoor Power Equipment Institute
341 S Patrick St
Alexandria, VA 22314

703-549-7600
Fax: 703-549-7604
E-Mail: info@opei.org
Home Page: www.opei.org
Social Media: Facebook, Twitter, LinkedIn

Todd Teske, President & CEO
Paul Mullet, Chairman
Lee Sowell, Secretary/Treasurer

International trade association whose members are manufacturers of powered lawn and garden maintenance products, components and attachment supplies, as well as industry related services.

85 Members
Founded in 1952

4090 **Painting and Decorating Contractors of America**
2316 Millpark Drive
Maryland Heights, MO 63043

314-514-7322
800-332-7322
Fax: 314-890-2068
Home Page: www.pdca.org
Social Media: Facebook, Twitter, LinkedIn, Youtube

David Ayala, Chair
David Ryker, Vice Chair
Micheal Walker, Treasurer
James Anderson, Corporate Counsel

PDCA exists to lead the industry by providing quality products, programs, services, and opportunities essential to the success of our members.
5M Members
Founded in 1884

4091 **Perlite Institute**
4305 North 6th Street
Suite A
Harrisburg, PA 17110

717-238-9723
Fax: 717-238-9985
E-Mail: info@perlite.org
Home Page: www.perlite.org
Social Media: Facebook, LinkedIn

Kathryn Louis, President
Linda Chirico, VP

An international trade association which establishes product standards and specifications, and which encourages the development of new product uses through research.
183 Members
Founded in 1949

4092 **Pile Driving Contractors Association**
1857 Wells Rd.
Suite 6
Orange Park, FL 32073

904-215-4771
888-311-7322
Fax: 904-215-2977
E-Mail: execdir@piledrivers.org
Home Page: www.piledrivers.org
Social Media: Facebook, Twitter, LinkedIn

Rusty Signor, President
Mike Justason, VP
Bill Marczewski, Treasurer
Eric Albergini, Secretary

An organization of pile driving contractors that advocates the incresed use of driven piles for deep foundations and earth retention systems. Promotes the use of driven pile solutions in all cases where they are effective, support educational programs for engineers on the design and efficiency of driven piles and for contractors on improving installation procedures and give contractors a larger voice in establishing procedures and standards for pile installation and design.
450 Members
Founded in 1996

4093 **Pipe Fabrication Institute**
511 Ave Of Americas
#601
New York, NY 10011

514-634-3434
866-913-3434
Fax: 514-634-9736
E-Mail: pfi@pfi-institute.org
Home Page: www.pfi-institute.org

Michael R Cables, Chairman
Jeff Huggard, Vice Chair
Tim Monday, Treasurer
Guy Fortin, Executive Director
Scott Zimmerman, Legal Counsel

Members are companies producing sophisticated high temperature, high pressure piping systems that employ specialists from the United Association of Journeymen and Apprentices of the Plumbing and Pipe Fitting Industry. We exist solely for the purpose of ensuring a level of quality in the pipe fabrication industry that is without compromise.
65-70 Members
Founded in 1913

4094 **Portable Sanitation Association International**
7760 France Avenue South
11th Floor
Minneapolis, MN 55435

952-854-8300
800-822-3020
Fax: 952-854-7560
E Mail: info@psai.org
Home Page: www.psai.org
Social Media: Facebook, Twitter

Ron Crosier, President
Tim Petersen, VP
John Pausma, Secretary
Karen Holm, Treasurer

International trade association that represents firms engaged in the leasing, renting, selling and manufacturing of portable sanitation equipment, services and supplies for construction, recreation, emergency and other uses. Devoted to the proper handling of human waste by the most modern, sanitary means, giving the greatest concern to the preservation of an unspoiled environment.
550+ Members
Founded in 1971

4095 **Portland Cement Association**
5420 Old Orchard Road
Skokie, IL 60077

847-966-6200
Fax: 847-966-8389
E-Mail: info@cement.org
Home Page: www.cement.org
Social Media: Facebook, Twitter, LinkedIn

Brian McCarthy, President/CEO

The Portland Cement Association represents cement companies in the United States and Canada. It conducts market development, engineering, research, education, and public affairs programs.
Founded in 1916

4096 **Precast Prestressed Concrete Institute**
200 W Adams St
Suite 2100
Chicago, IL 60606

312-786-0300
Fax: 312-621-1114
E-Mail: info@pci.org
Home Page: www.pci.org
Social Media: Facebook, Twitter, RSS

James G Toscas, President
Michelle Burgess, Managing Editor
Roger Becker, Managing Director, R&D
Jeff Appel, Controller

Dedicated to fostering understanding and use of precast and prestressed concrete, maintains a full staff of techniocal and marketing specialists.
1400 Members
Founded in 1954

4097 **Professional Construction Estimators Association of America**
PO Box 680336
Charlotte, NC 28216

704-484-1494
877-521-7232
Fax: 704-489-1495
E-Mail: pcea@pcea.org
Home Page: www.pcea.org

Matt Solomon, President
Patty Delgado, President Elect
Glenn Hessee, VP
Amanda Sauls, Secretary
Wesley Ferree, Treasurer

Promotes construction estimating as a profession by upholding the code of ethics, and expanding public awareness.
1000 Members
Founded in 1956

4098 **Resilient Floor Covering Institute**
115 Broad Street
Sutie 201
La Grange, GA 30240

301-340-8580
E-Mail: info@rfci.org
Home Page: www.rfci.com

Douglas Wiegand, Executive Director

Industry trade association of North American manufacturers who produce resilient flooring products. Associate members of RFCI supply raw materials to the industry and manufacture installation and maintenance products.
7 Members
Founded in 1975

4099 **Retail Contractors Association**
400 North Washington Street
Suite 300
Alexandria, VA 22314ÿ

800-847-5085
703-683-5637ÿ
Fax: 703-683-0018
Home Page: www.retailcontractors.org

Mike Wolffÿ, President
Bob Moore, Vice President
Brad Bogart, Secretary/Treasurer
Steve Bachman, Director
Jack Grothe, Director

A national organization of retail contractors united to provide a solid foundation of ethics, quality, and professionalism within the retail construction industry.

4100 **Roof Coatings Manufacturers Association**
750 National Press Building
529 14th Street NW
Washington, DC 20045

202-207-0919
Fax: 202-223-9741
E-Mail: questions@roofcoatings.org
Home Page: www.roofcoatings.org

John Ferraro, Executive Director
Mike Fischer, Codes & Standard Director
Shawn Richardson, Communications Coordinator
Kelly Franklin, Industry Affairs Coordinator

Represents the interests of manufacturers of cold applied roof coatings, cements and waterproofing agents, as well as the suppliers of products, equipment and services to and for the industry.
70+ Members
Founded in 1983

4101 **Rubber Pavements Association**
1801 S Jentilly Ln
Suite A-2
Tempe, AZ 85281-5738

480-517-9944
877-517-9944
Fax: 480-517-9959

E-Mail: mbelshe@rubberpavements.org
Home Page: www.rubberpavements.org

Cliff Ashcroft, VP
Mark Belshe, Executive Director
Guadalupe Dickerson, Office Manager

Dedicated to encouraging greater usage of high quality, cost effective asphalt pavements containing recycled tire rubber. Conducts national and international seminars.
20 Members
Founded in 1985

4102 SPRI: Single Ply Roofing Industry
411 Waverley Oaks Road
Suite 331b
Waltham, MA 02452

781-647-7026
Fax: 781-647-7222
E-Mail: info@spri.org
Home Page: www.spri.org

Al Janni, President
Linda King, Managing Director

Comprised of manufacturers and marketers of sheet applied membrane roofing systems and components to the commercial roofing industry.
58 Members
Founded in 1982

4103 Safety Glazing Certification Council
P.O. Box 730
Sackets Harbor, NY 13685

315-646-2234
Fax: 315-646-2297
E-Mail: staff@amscert.com
Home Page: www.igcc.org

John Kent, Administrative Staff
Erin Ackley, Administrative Staff

Nonprofit corporation that provides for the certifacation of safety glazing materials, comprised of safety glazing manufacturers and other parties concerned with public safety. SGCC is managed by a board of directors comprised of representatives from the safety glazing industry and the public interest sector.
105 Members
Founded in 1977

4104 Scaffold Industry Association
400 Admiral Blvd
Kansas City, MO 64106-1508

602-257-1144
866-687-7115
Fax: 602-257-1166
E-Mail: info@scaffold.org
Home Page: www.scaffold.org
Social Media: Facebook, Twitter, LinkedIn

Marty Coughlin, President
Daryl Hare, Treasurer

Promotes safety by developing educational and informational material, conducting educational seminars and training courses, providing audio-visual programs and codes for safe practices, and other training and safety aids; to work with state, federal and other agencies in developing more effective safety standards; to reduce accidents, thereby reducing insurance costs; and to assist members in becoming more efficient and profitable in their businesses.
1000 Members
Founded in 1972

4105 Screen Manufacturers Association
2850 S Ocean Boulevard
Suite 114
Palm Beach, FL 33480-6242

561-533-0991
Fax: 561-533-7466
Home Page: www.smainfo.org

Alan Gray, VP

Manufacturers of insect screens, screen frames, window screens, detention screens, sliding screen doors, swinging screen doors, fiberglass insect screening and aluminum insect screening.
Cost: $1000.00
20 Members
Founded in 1955

4106 Specialty Tools and Fasteners Distributors Association
500 Elm Grove Rd.
Suite 210
Elm Grove, WI 53122

262-784-4774
800-352-2981
Fax: 262-784-5059
E-Mail: info@stafda.org
Home Page: www.stafda.org
Social Media: Facebook, LinkedIn

Rick Lamb, President
Rod Gowett, VP
Georgia Foley, Executive Director

International trade association composed of distributors and manufacturers and rep agents of light construction, industrial and related products. Members also include publishers of industry press serving the construction and industrial trades.
Cost: $350.00
2603 Members
Founded in 1976

4107 Spray Polyurethane Foam Alliance
3827 Old Lee Hwy
Suite 101B
Fairfax, VA 22030

800-523-6154
Fax: 703-222-5816
E-Mail: info@sprayfoam.org
Home Page: www.sprayfoam.org

Bonnie Strickler, Chair
Robert Duke, President
Dennis Vandewater, VP
Peter Davis, Secretary/Treasurer

A trade association representing interests associated with rigid and semi-rigid polyurethane foam products that are typically applied with spray equipment as roofing and insulation.
Founded in 1987

4108 Steel Door Instituteÿ
30200 Detroit Road
Westlake, OH 44145

440-899-0010
Fax: 440-892-1404
E-Mail: info@steeldoor.org
Home Page: www.steeldoor.org

A voluntary, nonprofit business association that develops quality and performance standards for steel doors and frames.

4109 Steel Joist Institute
234 W Cheves Street
Florence, SC 29501

843-407-4091
Fax: 843-626-5565
E-Mail: sji@steeljoist.org
Home Page: www.steeljoist.org
Social Media: Twitter, LinkedIn

J Kenneth Charles III, Managing Director

Composed of active manufacturers, the SJI cooperates with government and business agencies to establish steel joint standards.
40 Members
Founded in 1928

4110 Steel Window Institute
1300 Sumner Ave
Cleveland, OH 44115-2851

216-241-7333
Fax: 216-241-0105
E-Mail: swi@steelwindows.com
Home Page: www.steelwindows.com

John Addington, Executive Director

An association of the leading manufacturers of windows made from either solid or formed sections of steel, and such related products as casings, trim, mechanical operators, screens, and moldings when manufactureed and sold by members of the industry for use in conjunction with windows.

4111 Structural Insulated Panel Association
PO Box 1699
Gig Harbor, WA 98335

253-858-7472
Fax: 253-858-0272
Home Page: www.sips.org
Social Media: Facebook, Twitter, RSS

Al Cobb, President
Ard Smits, First VP
Mike Tobin, Second VP
Charlie Ewalt, Secretary/Treasurer

A trade association representing manufacturers, suppliers, fabriators, distributors, design professionals and builders committed to providing quality structural insulated panels for all segments of the construction industry.
250 Members
Founded in 1990

4112 Stucco Manufacturers Association
2402 Vista Nobleza
Newport Beach, CA 92660-3545

949-640-9902
Fax: 949-701-4476
E-Mail: info@stuccomfgassoc.com
Home Page: www.stuccomfgassoc.com
Social Media: Facebook, Youtube

Kevin Wensel, President
Nick Brown, VP
Buck Buchanan, Secretary
Rui Bronze, Treasurer
Norma S Fox, Executive Director

Our main purpose is to promote the advantage of 3 coat colored cementitious stucco by educating the building industry and consumers.
50 Members
Founded in 1957

4113 Subcontractors Trade Association
1430 Broadway
Suite 1600
New York, NY 10018

212-398-6220
Fax: 212-398-6224
E-Mail: hkita@stanyc.com
Home Page: www.stanyc.com
Social Media: Facebook, Twitter, LinkedIn

Jerry Liss, President
Robert J Ansbro, VP
Robert Weiss, VP
Peter Cafiero, Treasurer
John A Finamore, Secretary

Members are specialty and supply companies in the construction industry. Our goal is to improve the economic well being of our members through representation, support and assistance through the process of legislation, legal action, public relations, education and other public information programs.
350+ Members
Founded in 1966

4114 **Textile Care Allied Trades Association**
271 Route 46 West
Suite C-106
Fairfield, NJ 07004-2432

973-244-1790
Fax: 973-244-4455
E-Mail: info@tcata.org
Home Page: www.tcata.org
Social Media: Facebook, Twitter, LinkedIn

Bryant Dunivan, President
Bryant Dunivan, President-Elect

Represents the interests of distributors and manufacturers of equipment and supplies for the cleaning industry.

4115 **The American Institute of Architects**
1735 New York Ave., NW
Washington, D. 20006-5292

800-AIA-3837
Fax: 202-626-7547
E-Mail: docstechsupport@aia.org
Home Page: www.aia.org
Social Media: Facebook, Twitter, LinkedIn, YouTube, RSS, Flickr

Based in Washington D.C., the AIA is the leading professional membership association for licensed architects, emerging professionals, and allied partners.
Founded in 1857

4116 **The Construction Specifications Institute**
110 South Union Street
Suite 100
Alexandria, VA 22314ÿ

800-689-2900
Fax: 703-236-4600
E-Mail: csi@csinet.org
Home Page: www.csinet.org

An organization that keeps and changes the standardization of construction language as it pertains to building specifications. It provides technical information and products, continuing education, professional conferences, and product shows.
Founded in 1948

4117 **Tile Contractors' Association of America**
10434 Indiana Avenue
Kansas City, MO 64137

816-508-9900
800-655-8453
Fax: 816-767-0194
E-Mail: info@tcaainc.org
Home Page: www.tcaainc.org

Carole Damon, Executive Director
Chris Pattavina, Associate Director

Union contractor association featuring; Architect/designer learning exchange, speakers, business meetings, new products and technology.
175 Members
Founded in 1903

4118 **Tile Roofing Institute**
23607 Highway 99
Suite 2C
Edmonds, WA 98026

425-778-6162
Fax: 425-771-9588
E-Mail: info@tileroofing.org
Home Page: www.tileroofing.org
Social Media: Facebook, Twitter, LinkedIn

Manufacturers of clay and concrete roof tiles. Emphasis is on technical issues and codes that involve tile.
Founded in 1971

4119 **Timber Frame Business Council**
46 Chambersburg
Gettysburg, PA 17325

717-334-5234
888-560-9251
Fax: 717-334-5571
E-Mail: info@timberframe.org
Home Page: www.timberframe.org
Social Media: Facebook

Pam Hinton, Executive Director
Bruce Bode, President

Advances the business, communications and research interests of companies engaged in the timber framing industry.
Founded in 1995

4120 **Timber Framers Guild**
12100 Sunset Hills Rd
Suite 130
Reston, VA 20190

703-234-4055
888-453-0879
Fax: 703-435-4390
E-Mail: info@tfguild.org
Home Page: www.tfguild.org

Joel McCarty, Executive Director

The Guild is dedicated to establishing training programs for dedicated timber framers, disseminating information about timber framing and timber frame building design, displaying the art of timber framing to the public, and generally serving as a center of timber framing information for the professional and general public alike.
Cost: $85.00
1700 Members
Founded in 1984

4121 **Truck Mixer Manufacturers Bureau**
900 Spring St
Silver Spring, MD 20910-4015

301-587-1400
888-846-7622
Fax: 301-585-4219
E-Mail: nmaher@cpmb.org
Home Page: www.cpmb.org

Robert Garbini, President
Deana Angelastro, Executive Administrator

An association of ready mixed concrete truck manufacturers who have joined together in support of the ready mixed industry. TMMB members are required to manufacture equipment in accordance to the TMMB Standards.
Founded in 1958

4122 **Western Building Material Association**
909 Lakeridge Drive SW
PO Box 1699
Olympia, WA 98507

360-943-3054
888-551-9262
Fax: 360-943-1219
E-Mail: wbma@wbma.org
Home Page: www.wbma.org

Regional trade association serving material dealers throughout the states of Alaska, Idaho, Montana, Oregon and Washington and a federated association of the National Lumber and Building Material Dealers Association.
600 Members
Founded in 1903

Newsletters

4123 **ACSM Bulletin**
American Congress on Surveying and Mapping
6 Montgomery Village Ave
Suite 403
Gaithersburg, MD 20879-3557

240-632-9716
Fax: 240-632-1321
E-Mail: ilse.genovese@acsm.net
Home Page: www.acsm.net

Ilse Genovese, Editor

A bi-monthly professional magazine published by ACSM to inform the public about current developments taking place within the geospatial community.
Frequency: Bi-Monthly

4124 **AHW Reporter**
Duane Publishing
51 Park St
Dorchester, MA 02122-2643

617-282-4885
Fax: 617-282-0320
Home Page: www.rubblemakers.com

Herb Duane, Owner
Toby Duane, Director

Asbestos and hazardous waste information.

4125 **Asbestos & Lead Abatement Report**
Business Publishers
2222 Sedwick Dr
Suite 101
Durham, NC 27713

800-223-8720
Fax: 800-508-2592
E-Mail: custserv@bpinews.com
Home Page: www.bpinews.com

Tracks the major legislative, regulatory and technological developments in asbestos and lead abatement industries. Includes highlights of major research studies on the effect of lead and asbestos on human health.
Cost: $371.54
Frequency: BiWeekly

4126 **Brick News**
Brick Industry Association
1850 Centennial Park Drive
Suite 301
Reston, VA 20191-1542

703-620-0010
Fax: 703-620-3928
E-Mail: brickinfo@bia.org
Home Page: www.gobrick.com

Richard Jennison, President/CEO

News, information and programs of interest to brick distributors.

4127 **Building Products News**
Palgrave Macmillan
175 5th Ave
Suite 4
New York, NY 10010-7728

212-982-3900
888-330-8477
Fax: 212-307-5035
Home Page: www.macmillan.com

Winston Jeune, Director

A unique publication researching the commercial renovation and retrofit market.

4128 **Building Stone**
Building Stone Institute

5 Riverside Dr
Building 2
Chestertown, NY 12817

518-803-4336
866-786-6313
Fax: 518-803-4336
Home Page: www.buildingstoneinstitute.org

Duffe Elkins, President
Rob Teel, VP

State of the industry publication for architects, designers and people in the natural stone industries: granite, marble, limestone, etc.
Cost: $65.00
Frequency: Quarterly
Circulation: 17,000
Founded in 1919

4129 Building and Construction Market Forecast
Reed Business Information
360 Park Ave S
New York, NY 10010-1737

646-746-6400
Fax: 646-756-7583
E-Mail: corporatecommunications@reedbusiness.com
Home Page: www.reedbusiness.com

Mark Kelsey, CEO
Stuart Whayman, CFO

Forecasts and analysis on the construction industry.
Cost: $187.00
6 Pages
Frequency: Monthly
Founded in 1946

4130 Catalyst Newsletter
Adhesive & Sealant Council
7101 Wisconsin Ave
Suite 990
Bethesda, MD 20814-4805

301-986-9700
Fax: 301-986-9795
E-Mail: info@ascouncil.org
Home Page: www.ascouncil.org

Matt Croson, President

4131 Concrete Pipe News
American Concrete Pipe Association
8445 Freeport Parkway
Suite 350
Irving, TX 75063

972-506-7216
Fax: 972-506-7682
E-Mail: info@concrete-pipe.org
Home Page: www.concrete-pipe.org

Matt Childs, President
Josh Beakley, Technical Services Director
Wanda Cochran, Events Manager

Concrete Pipe News is designed to provide information on the use and installation of precast concrete pipe products for a wide variety of applications, including drainage and pollution control systems. Industry technology, research and trends are also important subjects of the publication. Readers include engineers, specifiers, public works officials, contractors, suppliers, vendors and members of the American Concrete Pipe Association.
Cost: $3.50
16 Pages
Frequency: Quarterly
Founded in 1907

4132 Construction Company Strategist
Brownstone Publishers
149 5th Ave
10th Floor
New York, NY 10010

212-473-8200
Fax: 212-564-0465

Douglas Lowey, CEO
Andrew Shapiro, VP

Strategies, legal tips, and how-to advice for successfully managing a construction company in the 1990's. Features model contract language, forms, guidelines and more.
Cost: $269.00
Frequency: Monthly
Circulation: 180000
Founded in 1971
Printed in 2 colors on matte stock

4133 Construction Contractor
Federal Publications
1100 13th Street NW
Washington, DC 20005

202-772-8295
888-494-3696
Fax: 202-772-8298
Home Page: fedpubseminars.com

Michael Canavan, Director

Bi-weekly newsletter providing in-depth legal insight and analysis for all construction professionals.
Cost: $592.00
Frequency: BiWeekly

4134 Construction Equipment Monthly
Heartland Communications
1003 Central Avenue
PO Box 1052
Fort Dodge, IA 50501-1052

515-955-1600
800-247-2000
Fax: 515-574-2107
E-Mail: personnel@hlipublishing.com
Home Page: www.hlipublishing.com

Patrick Van Arnam, President
Gale McKinney, CFO

Listings by category, equipment and parts for sale.
Cost: $125.00
Frequency: Annual+
Founded in 1988

4135 Construction Labor Report
Bureau of National Affairs
3 Bethesda Metro Center
Suite 250
Bethesda, MD 20814

800-372-1033
Fax: 800-253-0332
E-Mail: customercare@bna.com
Home Page: www.bna.com

Donna Ives, VP Operations
Gregory McCaffery, President

A weekly information service that covers union-management relations in the construction industry, reporting on significant legislative, judicial, economic, management and union developments.
Cost: $1543.00
Frequency: Weekly
Circulation: 1600
ISSN: 0010-6836

4136 Constructor Newsletter
Associated General Contractors of America
2300 Wilson Blvd
Suite 400
Arlington, VA 22201

703-548-3118
Fax: 703-837-5400
E-Mail: info@agc.org
Home Page: www.agc.org

Kristine Young, President
Joe Jarboe, SVP

Reports on contractors and items of interest to the construction community.
Frequency: Monthly
Circulation: 33000
Founded in 1918

4137 Crow's Weekly Letter
CC Crow Publications
3635 N Farragut St
Portland, OR 97217-5954

503-241-7382
Fax: 503-646-9971
E-Mail: info@chadcrowe.com
Home Page: www.chadcrowe.com

Chad Crowe, President

Weekly report on trends and prices in the wood products industry.
Cost: $285.00
12 Pages
Frequency: Weekly
Founded in 1921
Printed in 4 colors on matte stock

4138 Demo-Memo
Duane Publishing
51 Park Street
PO Box 130
Dorchester, MA 02122

617-282-4885
Fax: 617-282-0320
Home Page: www.demolitionconsulting.com

Herbert Duane, President

Demolition news and information.

4139 Dodge Report & Bulletins
McGraw Hill
PO Box 182604
Columbus, OH 43272-1095

614-866-5769
877-833-5524
Fax: 614-759-3749
E-Mail: customer.service@mcgraw-hill.com
Home Page: www.mcgraw-hill.com

Jennifer Hayes, Editor
Harold McGraw III, President/CEO

Dodge Reports gives you the information you need to prepare a bid or enter negotiations. The detailed project information will also enable you to sell products or services.
Frequency: Daily
Founded in 1884

4140 Environmental Building News
BuildingGreen
122 Birge St
Suite 30
Brattleboro, VT 05301-6703

802-257-7300
Fax: 802-257-7304
E-Mail: info@buildinggreen.com
Home Page: www.buildinggreen.com

Alex Wilson, Owner
Nadav Malin, President
Tristan Roberts, Editorial Director
Jennifer Atlee, Research Director

Featuring comprehensive, practical information on a wide range of topics related to sustainable building—from energy efficiency and recycled-content materials to land-use planning and indoor air quality.
Cost: $99.00
Frequency: Monthly
Founded in 1992

4141 Hard Hat News
Lee Publications

6113 State Highway 5
PO Box 121
Palatine Bridge, NY 13428

518-673-3237
800-218-5586
Fax: 518-673-2699
E-Mail: info@leepub.com
Home Page: www.leepub.com

Fred Lee, Owner
Wendell Jennings, Sales Manager

Construction and heavy equipment.
72 Pages
Frequency: Monthly

4142 **Housing Marketing Report**
CD Publications
8204 Fenton St
Silver Spring, MD 20910-4571

301-588-6380
800-666-6380
Fax: 301-588-6385
E-Mail: info@cdpublications.com
Home Page: www.cdpublications.com

Michael Gerecht, President
Charles Wisniowski, Editor

Concise analysis of national and regional housing markets, materials and supplies.
Cost: $169.00
Founded in 1961
Mailing list available for rent: 2,000 names at $160 per M
Printed in on matte stock

4143 **Indoor Air Quality Update**
Aspen Publishers
76 Ninth Avenue
7th Floor
New York, NY 10011

212-771-0600
800-638-8437
Fax: 301-695-7931
Home Page: www.aspenpublishers.com

Mark Dorman, CEO
Gustavo Dobles, VP Operations

A guide to the practical control of building materials.
Cost: $440.00
Circulation: 20000
ISSN: 1040-5313

4144 **Industry News**
Modular Building Institute
944 Glenwood Station Ln
Suite 204
Charlottesville, VA 22901-1480

434-296-3288
888-811-3288
Fax: 434-296-3361
E-Mail: info@mbinet.org
Home Page: www.mbinet.org

Tom Hardiman, Executive Director
Steven Williams, Operations Director

For members only.
Circulation: 650

4145 **Machinery Outlook**
Manfredi & Associates
20934 W Lakeview Pkwy
Mundelein, IL 60060-9502

847-949-9080
Fax: 847-949-9910
E-Mail: frank@manfredi.com
Home Page: www.machineryoutlook.com

Frank Manfredi, President
James Manfredi, Editor

A newsletter about and for the construction and mining machinery industry.
Cost: $550.00
14 Pages
Frequency: Monthly
Founded in 1984
Printed in one color on matte stock

4146 **Manufactured Structures Newsletter**
Bobbitt Group
1710 S Gilbert Rd
Ste 1167
Mesa, AZ 85204

480-982-6173
E-Mail: wsbobbitt@hotmail.com
Home Page: www.thebobbittgroup.com

William Bobbitt, Editor/Publisher
Marci Bobbitt, Associate Editor/Business Manager

Covers all aspects of the automated building industry with a monthly collection of original feature stories profiling leading and emerging companies in the industry as well as other informative information on the industry, business tips, proven sales and marketing and featured editorials.
Frequency: Monthly
ISSN: 1068-4962
Founded in 1969

4147 **NAWIC Image**
National Association of Women in Construction
327 S Adams Street
Fort Worth, TX 76104

817-877-5551
800-552-3506
Fax: 817-877-0324
E-Mail: nawic@nawic.org
Home Page: www.nawic.org

Debra Gregoire, Presdient
Cindy Johnsen, VP

Management, trends and techniques in the construction business.
Cost: $50.00
Frequency: Bi-Monthly
Circulation: 6000

4148 **NRCMA Biweekly Email Bulletin**
National Railroad Construction & Maintenance Assoc
500 New Jersey Ave NW
Suite 400
Washington, DC 20001-2065

202-715-2919
Fax: 202-318-0867
E-Mail: info@nrcma.org
Home Page: www.nrcma.org

Chuck Baker, President
Matt Ginsberg, Director of Operations
Frequency: Biweekly

4149 **News Brief**
Granite State Designers & Installers Association
53 Regional Drive
Ste 1
Concord, NH 03301-3520

603-228-1231
Fax: 603-228-2118
E-Mail: info@gsdia.org
Home Page: www.gsdia.org

Carl Hagstrom, Director
Randy Orvis, Director

Newsletter for members of GSD1 relative to septic system design, installation and maintenance.
Cost: $150.00
Frequency: Monthly

4150 **RCMA Newsletter**
Roof Coatings Manufacturers Association
750 National Press Building
529 14th Street NW
Washington, DC 20045

202-207-0919
Fax: 202-223-9741
E-Mail: questions@roofcoatings.org
Home Page: www.roofcoatings.org

Steve Heinje, Director
Frequency: Quarterly

4151 **Redwood Reporter**
California Redwood Association
818 Grayson Road
Suite 201
Pleasant Hill, CA 94523

925-935-1499
Fax: 925-935-1496
E-Mail: info@calredwood.org
Home Page: www.calredwood.org

Pamela Allsebrook, Publisher
Christopher Grover, President

Information about the redwood business of interest to redwood dealers.
8 Pages
Circulation: 8000

4152 **Reed Construction Data**
700 Longwater Drive
Norwell, MA 02061

770-209-3730
800-334-3509
Fax: 800-632-6732
Home Page: www.rsmeans.com

Offers statistical information for building contractors.

4153 **SPEC-DATA Program**
Construction Specifications Institute
110 S Union St
Ste 100
Alexandria, VA 22314-3351

703-684-0300
800-689-2900
Fax: 703-684-8436
E-Mail: csi@csinet.org
Home Page: www.csinet.org

Walter Marlowe, CEO
Stacy Vail, Operations Director
Cost: $75.00
Frequency: Monthly

4154 **Scaffold Industry Association Newsletter**
Scaffold Industry Association
400 Admiral Blvd
Kansas City, MO 64106-1508

602-257-1144
866-687-7115
Fax: 602-257-1166
E-Mail: info@scaffold.org
Home Page: www.scaffold.org

Steve Smith, President
Daryl Hare, Treasurer

Information on scaffold safety in the construction industry. Offers safe training programs for competent person and hazard awareness.
Cost: $65.00
Frequency: Monthly
Circulation: 1600
Founded in 1972

4155 **Scantlings**
Timbers Framers Guild
PO Box 295
Alstead, NH 03602

559-834-8453
888-453-0879
Fax: 888-453-0879

E-Mail: info@tfguild.org
Home Page: www.tfguild.org

Joel McCarty, Executive Director

It is a member benefit that is not available by subscription. Reports on timber framing events, news, business, and people.
Circulation: 1700
Founded in 1984

4156 **Specialty Tools and Fasteners Distributors Association Newsletter**
Specialty Tools and Fasteners Distributors
PO Box 44
Elm Grove, WI 53122

262-784-4774
800-352-2981
Fax: 262-784-5059
E-Mail: info@stafda.org
Home Page: www.stafda.org

Georgia Foley, President
Catherine Usher, Member Service Director

Members distribute or manufacture power equipment, anchors, fastening systems, drilling equipment and other related industrial supplies.
Circulation: 4,500
Founded in 1976

4157 **TAUC About Construction**
The Association of Union Constructors
1501 Lee Highway
Suite 202
Arlington, VA 22209-1109

703-524-3336
Fax: 703-524-3364
E-Mail: dacord@tauc.org
Home Page: www.tauc.org

Stephen R Lindauer, CEO
Kevin J Hilton, Senior VP

E-Newsletter containing exclusive TAUC content, with the latest collective bargaining agreements, wage rates, OSHA directives, legislative activity on Capitol Hill, and much more.
Frequency: Annual/May
Founded in 1970

4158 **TIDINGS Newsletter**
Textile Care Allied Trades Association
271 Route 46 West
#D203
Fairfield, NJ 07004-2432

973-244-1790
Fax: 973-244-4455
E-Mail: info@tcata.org
Home Page: www.tcata.org
Social Media: LinkedIn

Lawton Jones, President
Bryant Dunivan, President-Elect

Keeps members informed about relevant news in and affecting the industry, such as legislative/ regulatory developments, benefits and services.

4159 **Tilt-Up eNews**
Tilt-Up Concrete Association
113 First Street W
PO Box 204
Mount Vernon, IA 52314-0204

319-895-6911
Fax: 320-213-5555
E-Mail: info@tilt-up.org
Home Page: www.tilt-up.org

Ed Sauter, Executive Director
James Baty, Technical Director

A monthly newsletter published by the Tilt-Up Concrete Association, Tilt-Up eNews is free for members, however non-members can also sign up to receive these publications. The mission of the Tilt-Up Concrete Association is to expand and improve the use of Tilt-Up as the preferred construction method by providing education and resources that enhance quality and performance.
Cost: $25.00
Frequency: Quarterly
Circulation: 5500
Founded in 1986
Printed in 4 colors on glossy stock

4160 **Trade News**
Specialty Tools and Fasteners Distributors Assn.
500 Elm Grove Rd.
Suite 210
Elm Grove, WI 53122

262-784-4774
800-352-2981
Fax: 262-784-5059
E-Mail: info@stafda.org
Home Page: www.stafda.org
Social Media: Facebook, LinkedIn

Mike Kangas, President
Kramer Darragh, Vice President

Provides insight into the construction and industrial world, member news, Convention details, Trend Reports, and more.
4000 Attendees
Frequency: Monthly

4161 **Western Building Material Association Newsletter**
Western Building Material Association
PO Box 1699
Olympia, WA 98507-1699

360-943-3054
888-551-9262
Fax: 360-943-1219
E-Mail: wbma@wbma.org
Home Page: www.wbma.org

38511 Pages
Frequency: Monthly
Circulation: 700
Printed in on matte stock

4162 **World Fence News**
World Fencing Data Center
6101 W Courtyard Dr
Building 3 Suite 115
Austin, TX 78730-5031

512-349-2536
800-231-0275
Fax: 512-349-2567
E-Mail: editor@worldfencenews.com
Home Page: www.worldfencenews.com

Roger Duke, Publisher
Rick Henderson, Editor

Includes the most up to date information on events, products, trends, and services that effect the industry.
Cost: $29.95
Frequency: Monthly
Circulation: 12500
Founded in 1983

Magazines & Journals

4163 **ABC Today**
Associated Builders and Contractors
4250 Fairfax Dr
9th Floor
Arlington, VA 22203-1665

703-812-2000
Fax: 703-812-8201
Home Page: www.abc.org

Mike Bellaman, CEO
Todd Mann, COO

The purpose of this magazine is to offer industry updates on the latest trends and developments that affect general construction, labor, management, legislation, education, products and techniques for the building industry.
Cost: $36.00
Frequency: Monthly
Circulation: 25000
Founded in 1950

4164 **American Painting Contractor**
Douglas Publications
2807 N Parham Road
Suite 200
Richmond, VA 23294

703-519-2341
800-223-1797
E-Mail: ehoward@douglaspublications.com
Home Page: www.douglaspublications.com

Emily Howard, Editor
Jaimy Ford, Executive Editor

Features include business management, market research, decorating trends, techniques and developments in preparation and specialty coatings. News includes association activities, personnel changes and government actions.
Frequency: Monthly
Circulation: 25000
Founded in 1985

4165 **American Public Works Magazine**
2345 Grand Blvd
Suite 700
Kansas City, MO 64108-2625

816-472-6100
800-848-2792
Fax: 816-472-1610
E-Mail: ddancy@apwa.net
Home Page: www.apwa.net

Brian Van Norman, Director
David Dancy, Director of Marketing
Kevin Clark, Editor

International educational and professional association of public agencies, private sector companies, and individuals dedicated to providing high quality public works goods and services. The magazine is a forum for public works professionals, agencies and companies. It includes public works-related topics to public attention in local, state and federal areas.
Cost: $100.00
40 Pages
Frequency: Monthly
ISSN: 0092-4873
Founded in 1937

4166 **Architectural Record**
McGraw-Hill Construction
2 Penn Plz
9th Floor
New York, NY 10121-2298

212-904-2594
Fax: 212-904-4256
E-Mail: william_hanley@mcgraw-hill.com
Home Page: www.mcgraw-hill.com

William Hanley, Editor
Lamar Clarkson, Editor

Provides original, reliable and useful information to the architectural marketplace worldwide, setting the standards for excellence in architectural design and presenting insights and practical solutions for current challenges in the design, building construction and business practices.
Cost: $49.00
Frequency: Monthly
Circulation: 102,000
ISSN: 0003-858X

4167 **Asphalt Magazine**
Asphalt Institute

2696 Research Park Dr
Lexington, KY 40511-8480

859-288-4960
Fax: 859-288-4999
E-Mail: info@asphaltinstitute.org
Home Page: www.asphaltinstitute.org
Social Media: Facebook, Twitter, LinkedIn

Peter Grass, President
Frequency: 3x/Year
Circulation: 18000

4168 **Automated Builder**
CMN Associates
2401 Grapevine Dr
Oxnard, CA 93036

805-351-5931
800-344-2537
Fax: 805-351-5755
Home Page: www.automatedbuilder.com/

Donald Carlson
Agnes Carlson, Circulation
Distributed free of charge in the US to executive and management personnel upon written request in companies that are production (big volume) site builders, panelized home manufacturers, modular home manufacturers, special unit manufacturers, component manufacturers and HUD-Code, modular, panelized and commercial building dealers.
Cost: $50.00
Frequency: Monthly
Circulation: 25000
ISSN: 0899-5540
Founded in 1964
Printed in 4 colors on glossy stock

4169 **BUILDER**
Hanley-Wood
1 Thomas Cir NW
Suite 600
Washington, DC 20005-5811
202-452-0800
Fax: 202-785-1974
E-Mail: bthompson@hanleywood.com
Home Page: www.builderonline.com

Frank Anton, CEO
Hanley Wood, Publisher
Boyce Thompson, Editoral Director
BUILDER is the leading brand in residential new construction and serves as the magazine of the National Association of Home Builders (NAHB). For more than three decades, BUILDER has provided essential news, information and resources about products, technologies, trends, regulatory requirements and best practices to help home building professionals navigate challenges for success. BUILDER is the trusted source for top builders, architects and other industry professionals across the country.
Cost: $29.95
Frequency: Monthly
Circulation: 104852
ISSN: 0744-N93
Founded in 1977
Mailing list available for rent: 100M names
Printed in 4 colors on glossy stock

4170 **Bonded Builders News**
Richard K Nicholson Enterprises
2201 Corporate Boulevard
Suite 100
Boca Raton, FL 33431-7337

561-278-6968
800-749-0381
Fax: 561-368-1781
Home Page: www.bondedbuilders.com

Whit Ward, President
Howard Head, Editor-in-Chief
Provides builders and developers with information involving new technologies and changing trends in the home building industry.
Cost: $18.00
Frequency: Quarterly
Circulation: 7000

4171 **Builder Insider**
PO Box 191125
Dallas, TX 75219-8105

214-988-9181
866-930-1950
Fax: 214-871-2931
Home Page: www.builderinsider.com

Michael Anderson, Editor
Independent trade publications covering the residential and light commercial building industry.
Cost: $12.00
28 Pages
Frequency: Monthly
Circulation: 5200
Founded in 1976

4172 **Builders Trade Journal**
Lee Publications
6113 State Highway 5
PO Box 121
Palatine Bridge, NY 13428
518-673-3237
800-836-2888
Fax: 518-673-3245
E-Mail: info@leepub.com
Home Page: www.leepub.com

Fred Lee, Editor
Wendell Jennings, Sales Manager
Edited for the building industry.
Frequency: Monthly
Founded in 1982

4173 **Building Design & Construction**
Reed Business Information
360 Park Ave S
New York, NY 10010-1737

646-746-6400
Fax: 646-756-7583
E-Mail: corporatecommunications@reedbusiness.com
Home Page: www.reedbusiness.com

Mark Kelsey, CEO
Stuart Whayman, CFO
James Reed, Owner
Serves the needs of the design and construction professionals of commercial, industrial and institutional buildings that include new and retrofit projects. Geared towards the building team that includes professionals from building firms, owning firms and design firms.
Frequency: Monthly
Circulation: 76,005
Founded in 1993

4174 **Building Environment Report**
IAQ Publications
7920 Norfolk Ave
Suite 900
Bethesda, MD 20814-2539

301-913-0115
Fax: 301-913-0119
Home Page: www.eschoolnews.com

Robert Morrow, Owner
Nancy David, Editor
Covers information to help manage building environmental hazards, meet environmental compliance requirements, protect building occupants, conference coverage and meetings of note.
Cost: $325.00
Frequency: Monthly
Circulation: 1,500

4175 **Building Material Dealer**
National Lumber & Building Material Dealers Assoc.
2025 M Street Nw
Ste 800
Washington, DC 20036

202-367-1169
Fax: 202-367-2169
E-Mail: info@dealer.org
Home Page: www.dealer.org

Michael O'Brien, President
Scott Lynch, EVP
Content focuses on a mixture of regional and national news relating to governmental regulations, dealer and supplier news, meetings and seminars affecting the independent building retailer.
Frequency: Monthly
Circulation: 24,647

4176 **Building Operating Management**
Trade Press Publishing Corporation
2100 W Florist Avenue
Milwaukee, WI 53209-3799

414-228-7701
Fax: 414-228-1134
Home Page: www.tradepress.com

Brad Ehlert, Group Publisher
Brian Terry, Publisher
Serves the field of facilities management, encompassing commercial building: office buildings, real estate/property management firms, developers, financial institutions, insurance companies, apartment complexes, civic/convention centers, including members of the Building Owners and Managers Association
Cost: $120.00
Frequency: Monthly
Circulation: 70000
Founded in 1954
Printed in 4 colors on glossy stock

4177 **Building Stone Magazine**
Building Stone Institute
5 Riverside Dr
Building 1
Chestertown, NY 12817

518-803-4336
866-786-6313
Fax: 518-803-4336
Home Page: www.buildingstoneinstitute.org
Social Media: Facebook

Duffe Elkins, President
Rob Teel, VP
State of the industry publication for architects, designers and people in the natural stone industries: granite, marble, limestone, etc.
Cost: $65.00
350 Members
Circulation: 18000
Founded in 1919
Printed in 4 colors on glossy stock

4178 **Building Supply Home Centers**
Reed Business Information
360 Park Ave S
New York, NY 10010-1737

646-746-6400
Fax: 646-756-7583
Home Page: www.reedbusiness.com

Mark Kelsey, CEO
James Reed, Owner
For owners, manufacturers and other executives of the retail building market.
Cost: $60.00
Frequency: Monthly
Founded in 1917

4179 **Buildings: Facilities Construction & Management Magazine**
Stamats Communications
PO Box 1888
Cedar Rapids, IA 52406-1888

319-364-6167
800-553-8878
Fax: 319-365-5421
E-Mail: info@stamats.com
Home Page: www.stamats.com

Guy Wendler, CEO
Peter Stamats, EVP/CFO

Information on construction costs, building design, space planning, fire safety, environment solutions, energy effiency, accessibilty, security, and strategic facilities planning.
Cost: $70.00
Frequency: Monthly
Circulation: 56500
Founded in 1906

4180 **CIM Construction Journal**
Construction Industries of Massachusetts
1500 Providence Highway Suite 14
PO Box 667
Norwood, MA 02062

781-551-0182
Fax: 781-551-0916
E-Mail: info@cimass.org
Home Page: www.cimass.org

Mark Drummey, Editor/Publisher
John Pourbaix, Executive Director

Digest of horizontal public works projects.
Frequency: Weekly
Circulation: 2000
Founded in 1921

4181 **Carpenter**
United Brotherhood of Carpenters & Joiners
6801 Placid St
Las Vegas, NV 89119-4205

702-938-1111
Fax: 702-938-1122
E-Mail: dshoemaker@carpenters.org
Home Page: www.ubcmillwrights.com

William Irwin, Executive Director

Contains news and information on the union and its members, the craft, and the construction industry as a whole.
Founded in 1881

4182 **Catholic Cemetery**
National Catholic Cemetery Conference
1400 S Wolf Rd
Building # 3
Hillside, IL 60162

708-202-1242
888-850-8131
Fax: 708-202-1255
Home Page: www.ntriplec.com

Christine Kohut, Editor
Dennis Fairbank, Executive Director

News on products and manufacturers and also gives information on cemetery maintenance and repairs.
Frequency: Monthly
Circulation: 2100
Founded in 1949

4183 **Commerical Modular Construction**
Emlen Publications/Modular Building Institute
1241 Andersen Dr
North Suite
San Rafael, CA 94901-5374

415-460-6185
800-965-8876
Fax: 415-460-6288
E-Mail: info@emlenmedia.com
Home Page: www.emlenmedia.com

Eli Gage, Publisher
Ahavah Revis, Managing Editor

Contains articles on modular for architects, engineering and spec writers who need building product, specification and address information.

4184 **Computer-Aided Engineering**
Penton Media
1300 E 9th St
Suite 316
Cleveland, OH 44114-1503

216-696-7000
Fax: 216-696-6662
E-Mail: information@penton.com
Home Page: www.penton.com

Sharon Rowlands, CEO

Database applications in design and manufacturing.
Cost: $50.00
96 Pages
Founded in 1982

4185 **Concrete InFocus**
National Ready Mixed Concrete Association
900 Spring St
Silver Spring, MD 20910-4015

240-485-1139
Fax: 301-585-4219
E-Mail: info@nrmca.org
Home Page: www.nrmca.org
Social Media: Facebook, LinkedIn, YouTube

Robert Garbini, President
Deana Angelastro, Executive Administrator

The top resource for industry news, trends, research, legislative articles and company profiles.
1200 Members
Frequency: Quarterly
Circulation: 5000+
Founded in 1930

4186 **Concrete Pressure Pipe Digest**
American Concrete Pressure Pipe Association
3900 University Drive
Suite 110
Fairfax, VA 22030-2513

703-273-7227
Fax: 703-273-7230
Home Page: www.acppa.org

Richard Mueller, Chair
Mike Leathers, Vice Chair

4187 **Concrete Pumping Magazine**
American Concrete Pumping Association
606 Enterprise Dr
Lewis Center, OH 43035-9432

614-431-5618
Fax: 614-431-6944
Home Page: www.concretepumpers.com

Carl Walker, President
Christi Collins, Executive Director

Packed with articles on industry leaders, new products, and on-site examples.
Frequency: Quarterly
Circulation: 2,100

4188 **Construction Bulletin**
1200 Madison Ave
Indianapolis, IN 46225

317-423-7080
Fax: 317-422-7034
Home Page: www.acppubs.com

Greg Sitek, Editor
Kenny Veach, Advertising Sales Manager

Serves heavy highway and building construction.
Cost: $199.00
Frequency: Weekly
Circulation: 4000
ISSN: 0010-6720
Founded in 1893

4189 **Construction Dimensions**
Association of the Wall and Ceiling Industry
513 W Broad St
Suite 210
Falls Church, VA 22046-3257

703-538-1600
Fax: 703-534-8307
E-Mail: info@awci.org
Home Page: www.awci.org

Tim Wies, President
Jeffrey Burley, VP

A monthly magazine for manufacturers and suppliers in the wall and ceiling, and related industries. Construction Dimensions is the official publication of the Association of the Wall and Ceiling Industries International.
Cost: $ 40.00
115 Pages
Frequency: Monthly
Circulation: 23000
Founded in 1918

4190 **Construction Distribution**
Cygnus Business Media
1233 Janesville Avenue
Fort Atkinson, WI 53538

800-547-7377
E-Mail: nancy.terrill@cygnusb2b.com
Home Page: www.cygnusb2b.com

Nancy Terrill, Publisher
Rebecca Wasieleski, Editor

Resource for product, marketing and management information for construction supply distributors and the manufacturers and reps who serve them.
Frequency: Quarterly
Circulation: 14,800
Founded in 1966

4191 **Construction Equipment Distribution**
Associated Equipment Distributors
615 W 22nd St
Oak Brook, IL 60523-8807

630-574-0650
800-388-0650
Fax: 630-574-0132
E-Mail: info@aednet.org
Home Page: www.aednet.org

Toby Mack, President
Mike Quirk, SVP

Offers valuable information for executives who sell and rent construction equipment.
Cost: $71.40
72 Pages
Frequency: Monthly
Circulation: 5500
Founded in 1918

4192 **Construction Equipment Operation and Maintenance**
Construction Publications
PO Box 1689
Cedar Rapids, IA 52406-1689

319-366-1597
Fax: 319-362-8808

Clark Parks, Editor

Use and maintenance of construction equipment.
Cost: $10.00
24 Pages
Frequency: Monthly
Founded in 1948

4193 **Construction Executive**
Associated Builders and Contractors
4250 Fairfax Drive
9th Floor
Arlington, VA 22203-1665

703-812-2000
Fax: 703-812-8201
Home Page: www.abc.org

Lisa A Nardone, Editor-in-Chief
Lauren Pinch, Assistant Editor
Mike Bellaman, CEO

Focus on commercial and industrial construction.
Cost: $24.00
Frequency: Monthly
Circulation: 49,000

4194 **Construction Industry International**
Quarto International
10 Whirling Dun
Collinsville, CT 06022-1239
Andrew Webster, Editor

Serves the administrative construction industry.
80 Pages
Frequency: Monthly
Founded in 1975

4195 **Construction News West**
McGraw Hill
PO Box 182604
Columbus, OH 43272-1095

614-866-5769
877-833-5524
Fax: 614-759-3749
E-Mail: customer.service@mcgraw-hill.com
Home Page: www.mcgrawhill.com/

Jennifer Hayes, Editor
Harold McGraw III, President/CEO

Provides F.W. Dodge information for general contractors, suppliers, architects and owners in Arizona, Nevada and New Mexico.
Cost: $368.00
Frequency: Weekly
Circulation: 3000
Founded in 1902

4196 **Construction Specifier**
266 Elmwood Ave
Suite 289
Buffalo, NY 14222

716-572-5633
866-572-5633
Fax: 866-572-5677
E-Mail: sales@constructionspecifier.com
Home Page: www.constructionspecifier.com

Jill Kaletha, Editor

The offical magazine of Construction Specifications Institute. Focused on the job functions of its core readership-professionals involved in the specification process. Offers insight and analysis on industry topics through news, product announcements, legal columns, case studies and other research as well as providing in-depth features on industry-related issues.
Frequency: Monthly
Founded in 1956
Printed in on glossy stock

4197 **Constructioneer**
Associated Construction Publication
30 Technology Pkwy S
Suite 100
Norcross, GA 30092-2925

770-209-3730
800-424-3996
Fax: 770-209-3712
E-Mail: rcdwebmaster@reedbusiness.com
Home Page: www.reedconstructiondata.com

Iain Melville, CEO
Steve Ritchie, VP Marketing
Marco Piovesan, VP Data

Information directed to construction industry of New York, Pennsylvania, New Jersey, and Delaware.
100 Pages
Frequency: Bi-Monthly
Circulation: 18889
Founded in 1975
Printed in 4 colors on matte stock

4198 **Constructor Magazine**
Associated General Contractors of America
2300 Wilson Blvd
Suite 400
Arlington, VA 22201-5426

703-548-3118
Fax: 703-837-5400
E-Mail: info@agc.org
Home Page: www.agc.org

Kristine Young, President
Joe Jarboe, SVP

Voice of the construction industry.
Frequency: Monthly
Circulation: 40,000
Founded in 1918

4199 **Contractors Guide**
Painting and Decorating Contractors of America
1801 Park 270 Drive
Suite 220
St Louis, MO 63146-4020

314-514-7322
800-332-7322
Fax: 314-514-9417
Home Page: www.pdca.org

Darylene Dennon, Chair

What every painting and decorating contractor needs to know, organized for easy use by painting and decorating contractors of all sizes.
Cost: $68.00

4200 **Custom Home**
Hanley-Wood
1 Thomas Cir NW
Suite 600
Washington, DC 20005-5811

202-452-0800
Fax: 202-785-1974
E-Mail: fanton@hanleywood.com
Home Page: www.residentialarchitect.com

Frank Anton, CEO
Matt Flynn, CFO

Features materials, products, trends and the latest in designs for custom home construction.
Cost: $24.00
Frequency: 7 issues yearly
Circulation: 40000
Founded in 1976

4201 **DBA Automated Builder Magazine**
CMN Associates
2401 Grapevine Dr
Oxnard, CA 93036

805-351-5931
800-344-2537
Fax: 805-351-5755
E-Mail: info@automatedbuilder.com
Home Page: www.automatedbuilder.com/

Don O Carlson, Editor/Publisher
Agnes Carlson, Circulation Manager

Magazine for manufacturers and suppliers who have a product line that is of interest to the factory-built housing industry. Covering all seven segments of US, Canadian and foreign housing industry, including: production builders; panelizers; component producers; modular; commercial modular; hud code; and all builder/dealers.
Frequency: Monthly
Circulation: 25000
ISSN: 0899-4450
Founded in 1964

4202 **DFI Journal**
Deep Foundations Institute
326 Lafayette Avenue
Hawthorne, NJ 07506

973-423-4030
Fax: 973-423-4031
E-Mail: staff@dfi.org
Home Page: www.dfi.org

Publishes practice-oriented, high quality papers related to broad area of Deep Foundations Engineering.
Frequency: Bi-Annual

4203 **Daily Construction Service**
Construction Market Data
142 Arena Street
El Segundo, CA 90245

310-322-9990
Fax: 858-573-0485

Jeanne Peterson, Editor

Offers valuable information for construction workers.
Cost: $365.00
Frequency: Monthly
Founded in 1933

4204 **Daily Journal of Commerce**
Dolan Media Company/New Orleans Publishing Grp
111 Veterans Memorial Blvd., Suite 1440
3445 North Causeway Blvd., Suite 90
Metairie, LA 70005-3028

504-834-9292
Fax: 504-832-3435
E-Mail: djc@nopg.com
Home Page: www.djcgulfcoast.com

Lisa Blossman, Publisher
Christian Moises, Editor
Anne Lovas, General Manager
Becky Naquin, Assistance Editor

Reports on building and engineering industries.
Cost: $456.00
Frequency: Monthly
Founded in 1922

4205 **Deep Foundations Magazine**
Deep Foundations Institute
326 Lafayette Avenue
Hawthorne, NJ 07506

973-423-4030
Fax: 973-423-4031
E-Mail: dfihq@dfi.org
Home Page: www.dfi.org

James Morrison, President
Virginia Fairweather, Executive Editor

Distributed to members.
Frequency: Quarterly
Circulation: 2753

4206 **Demolition**
National Demolition Association
16 N Franklin St
Suite 203
Doylestown, PA 18901-3536

215-348-4949
800-541-2412
Fax: 215-348-8422
E-Mail: info@demolitionassociation.com
Home Page: www.demolitionassociation.com

Don Rachel, President
Jeff Kroeker, VP

Trade publication for the demolition industry.
Cost: $40.00
Circulation: 5000
ISSN: 1522-5690
Founded in 1972
Printed in 4 colors on matte stock

4207 Design Build
144 Lexington Street
Woburn, MA 01801

781-937-9265
Fax: 781-937-9241
Home Page: www.designbuild.construction.com

Gary Merrill, Sales Director
William Angelo, Editor-in-Chief

Received by all subscribers of Engineering News Record plus 7,500 owners identified by FW Dodge as having an interest in the design-build project delivery system, and 1,000 members of the Design-Build Institute of America.
84 Pages
Frequency: Quarterly
Circulation: 20000
ISSN: 1096-7095
Founded in 1953

4208 Design Cost & Data
Rector Communications
2300 Chestnut St
Suite 340
Philadelphia, PA 19103-4398

215-963-9661
Fax: 215-963-9672
Home Page: www.rector.com

Marion Rector, Owner

Cost estimating magazine for architects, builders, developers, appraisers, specifiers, insurers and construction financiers.

4209 Design Lines
American Institute of Building Design
7059 Blair Rd NW
Suite 201
Washington, DC 20012

800-366-2423
Fax: 866-204-0293
E-Mail: info@aibd.org
Home Page: www.aibd.org
Social Media: Facebook, Twitter, LinkedIn

Dan Sater, President
Alan Kent, Internal Vice President
Viki Wooster, External Vice President
Kerry Dick, Secretary/ Treasurer

Publication that focuses on issues, education, and events as they happen in the building design industry.
1500 Attendees
Frequency: Monthly
Founded in 1950

4210 Design Solutions Magazine
Architectural Woodwork Institute
46179 Westlake Dr
Suite 120
Potomac Falls, VA 20165

571-323-3636
Fax: 571-323-3630
E-Mail: info@awinet.org
Home Page: www.awinet.org

Robert Stout, President
Mike Bell, Vice President

Each issue showcases beautiful examples of fine architectural woodwork manufactured by AWI Manufacturing Member companies. With beautiful four-color images, crisp detailed drawings and thought provoking articles, Design Solutions offers our readers a bountiful resource that's sure to inspire and delight all.
Cost: $25.00
Frequency: Quarterly
Circulation: 27,000

4211 Dodge Construction News
McGraw Hill
2 Penn Plaza
9th Floor
New York, NY 10121-1299

212-904-3507
Fax: 212-904-2820
E-Mail: customerservice@mcgraw-hill.com
Home Page: www.mcgraw-hill.com

Jennifer Hayes, Editor
Harold McGraw, III, CEO/President

Consists of program edition and proceedings and recap edition for the National Conventions of the American Institute of Architects and Construction Specifications Institute.
Circulation: 86400
Founded in 1884

4212 Door & Window Maker
Key Communications
PO Box 569
Garrisonville, VA 22463-0569

540-720-5584
Fax: 540-720-5687
E-Mail: key-com@glass.com
Home Page: www.glass.com

Debra Levy, Owner
Brigid O'Leary, Assistant Editor
Frequency: 9 issues yearly
Circulation: 23,947
Founded in 1993

4213 Engineering News Record
McGraw Hill
2 Penn Plaza
9th Floor
New York, NY 10121-2298

212-904-3507
Fax: 212-904-2820
E-Mail: scott_lewis@mcgraw-hill.com
Home Page: www.enr.com

Richard Korman, Managing Senior Editor
Ilan Kapla, Senior Manager
Keith Wallace, Production Editor

Provides the news, analysis, commentary and data that construction industry professionals need to do their jobs more effectively. ENR is the national news magazine for the construction industry.
Cost: $82.00
Frequency: Weekly
Circulation: 60000
Founded in 1874

4214 Environmental Design & Construction
Business News Publishing Company
2401 W Big Beaver Rd
Suite 700
Troy, MI 48084-3333

248-362-3700
Fax: 248-362-0317
E-Mail: brownd@bnpmedia.com
Home Page: www.edcmag.com

Derrick Teal, Editor
Diana Brown, Publisher
Laura Zielinski, Associate Editor

Magazine dedicated to integrated high-performance buildings, and efficient and sustainable design and construction.
Founded in 1926

4215 Equipment Today
Cygnus Business Media
1233 Janesville Avenue
Fort Atkinson, WI 53538

800-547-7377
E-Mail: becky.schultz@cygnuspub.com
Home Page: www.cygnusb2b.com

Becky Schultz, Editor

Contractors and other users of construction machinery. Editorial is focused on the selection, application and maintenance of equipment as well as new and improved product introductions. Accepts advertising.
Cost: $60.00
54 Pages
Frequency: Monthly
Circulation: 77,000
Founded in 1966

4216 FW Dodge Northwest Construction
McGraw Hill
800 S Michigan St
Seattle, WA 98108-2655

206-378-4715
800-393-6343
Fax: 206-378-4741
E-Mail: support@construction.com
Home Page: www.construction.com

Keith Fox, President
Linda Brennan, VP Operations

Project news, plans, specifications and analysis data for the construction professional.
Cost: $40.00
Frequency: Monthly
Founded in 1884

4217 Fabric Architecture
Industrial Fabrics Association International
1801 County Road B W
Roseville, MN 55113-4061

651-222-2508
800-225-4324
Fax: 651-631-9334
E-Mail: generalinfo@ifai.com
Home Page: www.ifai.com

Stephen Warner, President
Chris Tschida, Editorial Manager

Strives to inform architects, designers, landscape architects, engineers and other specifiers about architectural fabric structures, the fibers and fabrics used to make them, their design possibilities, their construction, and issues regarding their applicability and acceptance.
Cost: $39.00
Frequency: Bi-monthly

4218 Facility Management Journal
International Facility Management Association
1 Greenway Plz
Suite 1100
Houston, TX 77046-0194

713-623-4362
Fax: 713-623-6124
E-Mail: ifma@ifma.org
Home Page: www.ifma.org

Andrea Sanchez, Editor-in-Chief
Laurie Steiner, Senior Associate Editor

Covers industry economic, financial trends and the industries legislative, special emphasis on developments in technology.
Cost: $75.00
Circulation: 14000
Founded in 1990

4219 Facility News Magazines
National Lead Abatement Council

PO Box 535
Olney, MD 20830

301-924-5490
800-590-6522
Fax: 301-924-0265

Stephen Weil, Publisher
Wendy Faxon, Editor

Information on facility maintenance management.
Cost: $36.00
20 Pages
Frequency: Monthly
Circulation: 7500
Founded in 1981

4220 **Fenestration Magazine**
Ashlee Publishing
18 E 41st Street
20th Floor
New York, NY 10017-6009

212-376-7722
Fax: 212-376-7723
Home Page: www.fenestrationmagazine.com

Joel Bruinooge, Editor

Windows and door industry.
Cost: $40.00
80+ Pages
Frequency: 10x yearly
Circulation: 17,000
ISSN: 0895-450X

4221 **Fine Homebuilding**
Taunton Press
63 S Main St
Box 5506
Newtown, CT 06470-2344

203-426-8171
Fax: 203-426-3434
E-Mail: fh@tauton.com
Home Page: www.taunton.com

Harrison McCampbell, Editor
Rob Yagid, Assistant Editor

Reviews of new equipment and related building materials and guidelines to successful work techniques and general industry news.
Cost: $37.95
Circulation: 308,000
Founded in 1980

4222 **Floor Covering Installer**
Business News Publishing Company
22801 Ventura Blvd
#115
Woodland Hills, CA 91364

818-224-8035
818-224-8042
Home Page: www.fcimag.com

John Moore, Editor
Jennifer Allen, Production Manager

Provides the varied information needed by those who engage in floor covering installation with how-to and skill-building articles, how-to-do-it photographic presentations, new installation product information, news of the industry, as well as how and where to get further training in various aspects of floor covering installation.
Frequency: Bi-Monthly
Circulation: 40,000

4223 **Foundation Drilling**
ADSC
8445 Freeport Parkway
Suite 325
Irving, TX 75063

469-359-6000
Fax: 469-359-6007
E-Mail: adsc@adsc-iafd.com
Home Page: www.adsc-iafd.com

Tim Wies, President
Jeffrey Burley, VP

Written for foundation drilling and anchored earth retention contractors and their project managers, superintendents, foremen, civil and structural engineers, soils engineers, public engineering officials, architects, manufacturers and distributors of industry related equipments.
Frequency: 8x yearly
Circulation: 5000

4224 **Frame Building News**
F+W Media
38 E. 29th Street
New York, NY 10016

212-447-1400
Fax: 212-447-5231
E-Mail: contact_us@fwmedia.com
Home Page: www.fwpublications.com

David Nussbaum, CEO
Sara Domville, President

Edited for the diversified town & country builders of light-industrial, commercial, agricultural, and residential structures. The majority of the coverage is about post-frame structures. Readers look for the latest in post-frame research and techniques, building code information, equipment, and materials. Regular features include 'Builder Spotlight,' 'New Products,' 'Supplier News,' 'OSHA Updates,' 'Legal Issues,' 'Business Strategies,' and 'Calendar of Events.' Official magazine of NFBA.
56 Pages
Circulation: 19211
Founded in 1952

4225 **Glass Digest**
Ashlee Publishing
18 E 41st Street
New York, NY 10017-6009

212-376-7722
Fax: 212-376-7723
Home Page: www.glassdigestmagazine.com/ashlee/glassdigest/index.html

Jordan Wright, Publisher

Merchandising/technical publication for the flat glass industry.
Cost: $25.00
140 Pages
Frequency: Monthly
Founded in 1922

4226 **Hanley-Wood's Tools of the Trade**
Hanley Wood
1 Thomas Cir NW
Suite 600
Washington, DC 20005-5803

202-452-0800
Fax: 202-785-1974
Home Page: www.hanleywood.com

Frank Anton, CEO
Matt Flynn, CFO

The wide array of tools and equipment in the construction and renovation industries.
Cost: $36.00
Circulation: 65,000
Founded in 1976

4227 **Home Builders Magazine**
Work-4 Projects
4819 Saint Charles Boulevard
Pierrefonds, QC H9H-3C7

514-620-2200
Fax: 514-620-6300
E-Mail: editor@work4.ca
Home Page: www.homebuildercanada.com/

Nachmi Artzy, Publisher
Cheryl Carvery, Sales

Specializes in educating readers on the latest installation tips, building techniques and materials that can be put into on-site practice everyday.
Cost: $30.00
Frequency: Bi-Monthly
Circulation: 23265
Founded in 1988

4228 **Hot Mix Asphalt Technology**
National Asphalt Pavement Association
5100 Forbes Blvd
Suite 200
Lanham, MD 20706-4407

301-731-4748
888-468-6499
Fax: 301-731-4621
E-Mail: mcervarich@hotmix.org
Home Page: www.hotmix.org

Mike Acott, President
Margaret Cervarich, VP Marketing/Public Affairs

The leading journal for the asphalt pavement contractor
Frequency: Bi-Monthly
Circulation: 10000

4229 **IEEE Power and Energy Magazine**
IEEE
PO Box 1331
Piscataway, NJ 08855-1331

732-981-0060
Fax: 732-981-1721
E-Mail: customer-service@ieee.org
Home Page: www.ieee.org

Fran Zappulla, Staff Director, Publishing
Susan Hassler, Editor

Network analysis, system stability studies, fault protection and construction management.
Cost: $285.00
82 Pages
Frequency: Monthly
Circulation: 23000
ISSN: 1540-7977
Founded in 1885
Mailing list available for rent
Printed in on glossy stock

4230 **InTents**
Industrial Fabrics Association International
1801 County Road B W
Roseville, MN 55113-4061

651-222-2508
800-225-4324
Fax: 651-631-9334
E-Mail: generalinfo@ifai.org
Home Page: www.ifai.com

Stephen Warner, CEO
Chris Tschida, Editorial Manager

Promotes the use of tents and accessories to the special-event and general-rental industries.
Cost: $39.00
Frequency: Bi-Monthly
Circulation: 12,000

4231 **Insulation Outlook**
National Insulation Association
12100 Sunset Hills Road
Suite 330
Reston, VA 20190-3295

703-683-6422
Fax: 703-549-4838
E-Mail: editor@insulation.org
Home Page: www.insulation.org

Michele Jones, EVP/CEO
Julie McLaughlin, Director of Publications

Contains information on new products, industry trends, asbestos abatement and installation practices.
Cost: $45.00
Frequency: Monthly
Circulation: 7000
Founded in 1973
Printed in 4 colors on glossy stock

4232 **Interior Construction**
Ceilings & Interior Systems Construction Assn
1010 Jorie Boulevard
Suite 30
Oak Brook, IL 60223
630-584-1919
Fax: 866-560-8537
Home Page: www.cisca.org
Shirley Wodynski, Executive Director
Rick Reuland, Editor
Offers information designed to keep contractors abreast of the changes in interior construction.
Cost: $35.00
Frequency: Monthly
Circulation: 10000
Founded in 1950

4233 **Interlocking Concrete Pavement Magazine**
Interlocking Concrete Pavement Institute
13921 Park Center Road
Suite 270
Herndon, VA 20171-3269
202-080-0285
800-241-3652
Fax: 202-408-0285
E-Mail: icpi@icpi.org
Home Page: www.icpi.org
Ericka Giles, Editor
Charles McGrath, Executive Director
Cost: $5.00
32 Pages
Frequency: Quarterly
Circulation: 20,000
Founded in 1993
Printed in 4 colors

4234 **Intermountain Contractor**
McGraw Hill
1114 W 7th Avenue
Suite 100
Denver, CO 80204
303-756-9995
800-393-6343
Fax: 303-756-4465
E-Mail: mark_shaw@mcgraw-hill.com
Home Page: www.intermountain.construction.com
Seth Horositz, Publisher
Mark Shaw, Editor
For general contractors. Serves Colorado, Idaho, Montana, Utah and Wyoming.
Cost: $40.00
88 Pages
Frequency: Weekly
Circulation: 5,247

4235 **International Construction**
Primedia
3585 Engineering Drive
Suite 100
Norcross, GA 30092
678-421-3000
800-216-1423
Home Page: www.primedia.com
Charles Stubbs, President
Kim Payne, SVP
Provides valuable information to help readers succeed in every aspect of their jobs, from planning strategies to targeting growth, from solving engineering problems to selecting the right equipment and materials.

4236 **Job-Site Supervisor**
FMI Corporation
5171 Glenwood Ave
Suite 200
Raleigh, NC 27612-3266
919-787-8400
Fax: 919-785-9320
E-Mail: webmasters@fminet.com
Home Page: www.fminet.com
Hank Harris, President
Delivers articles on safety, regulations and management; with a special section that examines a challenging construction project. Editorial is presented from a field manager's point-of-view, including charts, graphs, illustrations and industry advice.
Cost: $179.00
Circulation: 4000
Founded in 1953

4237 **Journal of Light Construction**
Hanley-Wood
186 Allen Brook Lane
Williston, VT 05495
802-879-3335
800-552-1951
Fax: 802-879-9384
E-Mail: jlc-cs@hanley-wood.com
Home Page: www.jlconline.com
Don Jackson, Editor
Rick Strachan, Publisher
Written for builders, remodelers, contractors and architects involved in the design and construction of residential and light commercial buildings. Accepts advertising.
Cost: $39.95
150 Pages
Frequency: Monthly
Circulation: 73000
ISSN: 1040-5224
Founded in 1982
Mailing list available for rent: 70,000 names at $120 per M
Printed in 4 colors on glossy stock

4238 **Journal of Protective Coatings & Linings**
Technology Publishing Company
2100 Wharton St
Suite 310
Pittsburgh, PA 15203-1951
412-431-8300
800-837-8303
Fax: 412-431-5428
E-Mail: webmaster@paintsquare.com
Home Page: www.paintsquare.com
Marian Welsh, Publisher
Mary Chollet, Editor-in-Chief
The right tools to help you reach the protective and marine coatings industry.
Cost: $80.00
Frequency: Monthly
Circulation: 15,000
ISSN: 8755-1985

4239 **Kitchen & Bath Design News**
Cygnus Business Media
2 University Plaza
Suite 310
Hackensack, NJ 07601
201-487-7800
Fax: 201-487-1061
E-Mail: kathy.scott@cygnusb2b.com
Home Page: www.cygnusb2b.com
Eliot Sefrin, Editorial Director/Publisher
Scott, Director of Public Relations
Serving the kitchen and bath industry, a key niche within the residential construction and remodeling marketplace.
Frequency: Monthly
Circulation: 48667
Founded in 1966

4240 **Manufactured Home Merchandiser**
RLD Group
PO Box 269149
Suite 800
Chicago, IL 60626-9149
312-236-3529
Fax: 312-236-4024
Herb Tider, President
Wayne Beamer, Editor
Offers information for home builders and professionals in the manufactured home industry.
Cost: $36.00
Frequency: Monthly
Circulation: 18600
Founded in 1952

4241 **Masonry Magazine**
Mason Contractors Association of America
1481 Merchant Drive
Algonquin, IL 60102
224-678-9709
800-536-2225
Fax: 224-678-9714
Home Page: www.masoncontractors.org
Jeff Buczkiewicz, Executive Director
Tim O'Toole, Marketing Director
This periodical covers every aspect of the mason contractor profession, not only equipment and techniques but topics such as building codes and stanards.
Cost: $29.00
Frequency: Monthly
Circulation: 17,000

4242 **Metal Roofing**
F+W Media
38 E. 29th Street
New York, NY 10016
212-447-1400
Fax: 212-447-5231
E-Mail: contact_us@fwmedia.com
Home Page: www.fwpublications.com
David Nussbaum, CEO
Sara Domville, President
Circulation: 25000
ISSN: 1533-8711
Founded in 1900
Printed in 4 colors on glossy stock

4243 **Midwest Contractor**
Associated Construction Publication
1200 Madison Ave
LL20
Indianapolis, IN 46225
317-423-7080
800-486-0014
Fax: 317-423-7094
Home Page: www.acppubs.com
Tad Smith, CEO
Greg Sitek, Managing Editor
Annual equipment buyers' guide, a complete cross reference listing of manufacturers, area distributors and their construction equipment lines.
Cost: $96.00
Founded in 1905

4244 **Muir's Original Log Home Guide for Builders and Buyers**
Gary J Schroder

1101 SE 7th Ave
Grand Rapids, MN 55744-4087
218-326-4434
800-359-6614
Fax: 218-326-2529
Home Page: www.loghelp.com
Gary Schroeder, Owner
Allan Muir, Author
Log home industry.
Cost: $12.95
Frequency: Monthly
ISBN: 0-967786-90-8
Founded in 1978

4245 **National Association of Demolition Contactors**
National Demolition Association
16 N Franklin Street
Suite 203
Doylestown, PA 18901
215-348-4949
800-541-2412
Fax: 215-348-8422
E-Mail: info@demolitionassociation.com
Home Page: www.demolitionassociation.com
Don Rachel, President
Jeff Kroeker, VP
Bimonthly magazine.
Cost: $40.00
Circulation: 5000
ISSN: 1522-5690
Founded in 1969
Printed in 4 colors on matte stock

4246 **New England Construction**
Associated Construction Publication
1200 Madison Ave
LL20
Indianapolis, IN 46225
317-423-7080
800-486-0014
Fax: 317-423-7094
Home Page: www.acppubs.com
Tad Smith, CEO
Greg Sitek, Managing Editor
Complete reports on contracts awarded, low bids and proposed work; features on highway construction and earthmoving, land development projects, utility construction, industrial building construction in the six-state New England region.
Cost: $96.00
Frequency: Monthly
Circulation: 10490
Founded in 1975

4247 **Northwest Construction**
McGraw Hill
800 S Michigan St
Seattle, WA 98108-2655
206-378-4715
800-393-6343
Fax: 206-378-4741
E-Mail: support@construction.com
Home Page: www.construction.com
Jeff Greisch, President
Heather McCune, Editor-in-Chief
A regional, monthly magazine with features on Washington and design construction projects. Accepts advertising.
Cost: $60.00
64 Pages
Frequency: Monthly
Circulation: 6,200
Founded in 1997

4248 **Occupational Hazards**
Penton Media
1300 E 9th St
Suite 316
Cleveland, OH 44114-1503
216-696-7000
Fax: 216-696-6662
E-Mail: information@penton.com
Home Page: www.penton.com
Sharon Rowlands, CEO
Analysis of qualified recipients who have indicated that they recommend, select and/or buy the safety equipment, fire protection and other occupational health products.
65 Pages
Frequency: Monthly
Circulation: 65,777
ISSN: 0029-7909
Founded in 1892
Printed in 4 colors on glossy stock

4249 **Old House Journal**
Old House Journal Group
PO Box 420235
Palm Coast, FL 32142-235
800-826-3893
Fax: 978-283-4629
E-Mail: dapospors@homebuyerpubs.com
Home Page: www.oldhousejournal.com
Demetra Aposporos, Editor-in-Chief
Danielle Small, Advertising Manager
Covers restoration techniques for the pre-1939 home.
Cost: $27.00
Circulation: 140119
Founded in 1999

4250 **Pacific Builder & Engineer**
Associated Construction Publication
30 Technology Pkwy S
Suite 100
Norcross, GA 30092-2925
770-209-3730
800-424-3996
Fax: 770-209-3712
Home Page: www.acppubs.com
Tad Smith, CEO
Greg Sitek, Managing Editor
For management level personnel in the highway and heavy construction and non-residential building industries in Washington, Oregon, Idaho, Montana and Alaska. Includes notice of bid calls, low bidders, contract awards on area projects; cost cutting construction methods, unusual techniques and equipment applications, analysis of market conditions and industry trends, new products and literature, general industry news and views, personal news and legal advice. Accepts advertising.
Cost: $50.00
Circulation: 100000
Founded in 1902

4251 **Pavement**
Cygnus Business Media
1233 Janesville Avenue
Fort Atkinson, WI 53538
E-Mail: amy.schwandt@cygnusb2b.com
Home Page: www.cygnusb2b.com
Amy Schwandt, Publisher
Allan Heydorn, Editor/Associate Publisher
Reaches contractors in the pavement maintenance and commercial paving sector. Covers the four main segments of the market in each issue: sealcoating, striping, paving and sweeping.
Circulation: 18,500
Founded in 1985

4252 **Period Homes**
Restore Media
5185 MacArthur Blvd NW
Suite 725
Washington, DC 20016
202-339-0744
Fax: 202-339-0749
E-Mail: info@restoremedia.com
Home Page: www.restoremedia.com
Michael Tucker, Chairman/CEO
Paul Kitzke, EVP
Peter Miller, President/Publisher
Lists sources of products for restoration and new construction of residential architecture.
Cost: $18.00
120 Pages
Circulation: 24,600
ISSN: 0898-0284

4253 **Products Finishing**
Scott Walker/Gardner Publications
6915 Valley Ln
Cincinnati, OH 45244-3153
513-527-8800
800-950-8020
Fax: 513-527-8801
Home Page: www.gardnerweb.com
Rick Kline, CEO
Serves the finishing field, including educational services, public administration and other manufacturing industries.
Cost: $89.00
Frequency: Monthly
Circulation: 42000
Founded in 1928
Printed in 4 colors on glossy stock

4254 **Professional Builder**
Reed Business Information
2000 Clearwater Dr
Oak Brook, IL 60523-8809
630-288-8000
Fax: 630-288-8781
Home Page: www.reedbusiness.com
Iain Melville, CEO
Andrew Rak, SVP
New residential construction magazine with a more than 63 year tradition of providing builders the solutions they need to maximize profits.
Frequency: Monthly
Circulation: 127002
Founded in 1931

4255 **Professional Door Dealer Magazine**
Virgo Publishing LLC
3300 N Central Ave
Suite 300
Phoenix, AZ 85012-2532
480-675-9925
Fax: 480-990-0819
E-Mail: danielle@vpico.com
Home Page: www.vpico.com
Jenny Bolton, President
Educational resource for residential and commercial door and access-control professionals.
Circulation: 20000
Founded in 1986
Printed in on glossy stock

4256 **Professional Remodeler**
Reed Business Information
360 Park Ave S
New York, NY 10010-1737
646-746-6400
Fax: 646-756-7583
E-Mail: corporatecommunications@reedbusiness.com
Home Page: www.reedbusiness.com
Iain Melville, CEO
Andrew Rak, SVP
Designed to accomodate the needs of residential remodelers and light commercial renova-

tors and focuses on news, features, new products, tech-takes, and management and marketing approaches.
Frequency: Monthly
Circulation: 18131
Founded in 2002

4257 Professional Roofing
National Roofing Contractors Association
10255 W Higgins Rd
Suite 600
Rosemont, IL 60018-5613
847-299-9070
800-323-9545
Fax: 847-299-1183
E-Mail: nrca@nrca.net
Home Page: www.professionalroofing.net

William Good, EVP
Ambika-Punia Bailey, Editor
Chrystine Hanus, Associate Editor
Carl Good, Publisher

Articles on both technical and business aspects of professional roofing.
Cost: $35.00
3500 Members
Frequency: Monthly
Circulation: 16000
ISSN: 0896-5552
Founded in 1886

4258 Professional Spraying
88-11th Avenue NE
Minneapolis, MN 55413
612-623-6000
Fax: 612-623-6580
E-Mail: CustomerService@graco.com
Home Page: www.graco.com

Patrick McHale, President/CEO
James Graner, CFO

Targets new products, industry news, and trade literature.
Frequency: Monthly
Circulation: 40000
Founded in 1926

4259 Qualified Remodeler
Cygnus Publishing
1233 Janesville Avenue
Fort Atkinson, WI 53538
920-563-6388
Fax: 920-563-1704
E-Mail: john.huff@cygnusb2b.com
Home Page: www.cygnusb2b.com

John Huff, Publisher

Serving contractors who specialize in residential and light commercial remodeling.
72 Pages
Frequency: Monthly
Circulation: 82000
Founded in 1975
Mailing list available for rent: 84,000 names
Printed in 4 colors on glossy stock

4260 RSI
7300 N Linder Ave
Skokie, IL 60077
847-983-2000
E-Mail: roofingsidinginsulation@halldata.com
Home Page: www.rsimag.com

Delivers timely news, technical and business management information, including a monthly analysis of key industry trends and techniques to help roofing, siding and insulation contractors run progressive, profitable businesses
Cost: $36.00
64 Pages
Frequency: Monthly
Circulation: 23658
Founded in 1945

4261 Reed Bulletin
Reed Business Informtion
30 Technology Parkway South
Suite 100
Norcross, GA 30092
800-424-3996
E-Mail: talisha.jackson@reedbusiness.com
Home Page: www.reedconstructiondata.com

Talisha Jackson, Media Contact

Provides contractors with project news and tools suppliers.

4262 Reeves Journal
Business News Publishing Company
23421 South Pointe Dr.
Suite 280
Laguna Hills, CA 92653
949-830-0881
Fax: 949-859-7845
E-Mail: ellyn@reevesjournal.com
Home Page: www.reevesjournal.com

Souzan Azar, Production
Ellyn Fishman, Publisher/Sales
Kati Larson, Advertising Sales
Jack Sweet, Editor

Reeves Journal, has been an invaluable tool for contractors & plumbing industry professionals for the last 85 years. Their goal is to address the regional opportunities and challenges facing PHC contractors, wholesalers and engineers in the 14 western United States.
Cost: $55.00
Frequency: Monthly
Circulation: 15,535
Founded in 1922

4263 Remodeling
Hanley-Wood
1 Thomas Cir NW
Suite 600
Washington, DC 20005-5811
202-452-0800
Fax: 202-785-1974
E-Mail: rm@omeda.com
Home Page: www.residentialarchitect.com

Frank Anton, CEO
Claire Conroy, Editorial Director
Jennifer Lash, Managing Editor

News on state-of-the-art in remodeling management, products, construction and techniques. Appeals to the residential and light commercial remodeling contractor.
Cost: $44.95
Frequency: Monthly
Circulation: 93612
Founded in 1955

4264 Rental Equipment Register
17383 W Sunset Blvd
Suite A220
Pacific Plsds, CA 90272-4187
310-230-7160
Fax: 310-230-7169
E-Mail: michael.roth@penton.com
Home Page: rermag.com

Michael Roth, Editor
Brandey Smith, Managing Editor

Edited for owners and managers of equipment rental and sales centers.
Cost: $45.00
125 Pages
Frequency: Monthly
Circulation: 21000
Founded in 1886

4265 Residential Architect
Hanley-Wood
1 Thomas Cir NW
Suite 600
Washington, DC 20005-5811
202-452-0800
888-269-8410
Fax: 202-785-1974
E-Mail: jlash@hanleywood.com
Home Page: www.residentialarchitect.com

Frank Anton, CEO
Jennifer Lash, Managing Editor
Bruce Snider, Senior Editor

An award-winning national magazine focusing exclusively on the residential architecture profession.
Cost: $39.95
Frequency: 9x Yearly
Circulation: 22000
Founded in 1976

4266 Rock and Dirt
174 4th St
Crossville, TN 38555-4303
931-484-5137
800-251-6776
Fax: 931-484-2532
E-Mail: subs@rockanddirt.com
Home Page: www.rockanddirt.com

Mike Stone, Publisher

Comprehensive buy/sell publications for heavy construction. Primary target audiences worldwide are contractors and other heavy equipment buyers. A non-editorial tabloid, each issue contains display and classified ads that feature thousand of pieces of heavy machinery and related products and services. The magazine also has a large auction section.
Cost: $14.33
Circulation: 170,000
Founded in 1950
Printed in 4 colors on newsprint stock

4267 Roofing Contractor
BNP Media
PO Box 5125
Naperville, IL 60540
630-554-2200
Fax: 630-554-3817
E-Mail: mward@illinoisroofing.com
Home Page: www.illinoisroofing.com

Focuses on coverage of new technology and its implementation in the field. Regular issues include equipment comparisons, new product information, safety tips and legal advice.
Frequency: Monthly
Circulation: 27205
Founded in 1926

4268 Rural Builder
F+W Media
38 E. 29th Street
New York, NY 10016
212-447-1400
Fax: 212-447-5231
E-Mail: contact_us@fwmedia.com
Home Page: www.fwpublications.com

Scott Tappa, Editor

Focuses on the post frame and metal frame industry.
Cost: $18.94
64 Pages
Circulation: 32000
Founded in 1952
Printed in 4 colors on glossy stock

4269 Scaffold & Access
Scaffold Industry Association

2001 E Campbell Avenue
Suite 101
Phoenix, AZ 85016

602-257-1144
866-687-7115
Fax: 602-257-1166
Home Page: www.scaffold.org

Steve Smith, President
Marty Coughlin, President Elect
Daryl Hare, Treasurer
Mike Russell, Secretary

The official publication of the SAIA. Striving to elevate the standard of practice in the scaffold and access industry by educating professionals on safety issues, better business practices and innovative solutions to difficult problems.
Frequency: Monthly

4270 **Services Magazine**
Building Service Contractors Association Int'l
401 N Michigan Avenue
22nd Floor
Chicago, IL 60611

312-321-5167
800-368-3414
Fax: 312-673-6735
E-Mail: info@bscai.org
Home Page: www.bscai.org

Sally Schopmeyer, President
Kevin Rohan, VP

The Building Service Contractors Association International is the trade association serving the facility services industry through education, leadership, and representation.
Cost: $30.00
56 Pages
Frequency: Monthly
Circulation: 20,504
ISSN: 0279-0548
Founded in 1981
Printed in 4 colors on glossy stock

4271 **Shelter**
Association Publications
1168 Vickery Ln
Suite 3
Cordova, TN 38016-1664

901-843-8226

James Powell, Editor

For the national distribution and retail segments of the building products industry.
Cost: $6.00
Frequency: Monthly
Founded in 1962

4272 **Southern Building**
Southern Building Code Congress International
900 Montclair Rd
Birmingham, AL 35213-1206

205-591-1853
888-422-7233
Fax: 205-599-9871
E-Mail: webmaster@iccsafe.org
Home Page: www.iccsafe.org

Gary Nichols, VP Operations

Publishes and maintains a set of model building codes called the Standard Codes. Also provides educational and technical support to the codes enforcement industry.
Cost: $25.00
40 Pages
Circulation: 12000
Founded in 1943

4273 **Southwest Contractor**
McGraw Hill
4747 E Elliot Rd
Suite 29-339
Phoenix, AZ 85044

602-274-2155
800-393-6343
Fax: 602-631-3073
E-Mail: scott_blair@mcgraw-hill.com
Home Page: www.southwest.construction.com

Seth Horowitz, Publisher
Scott Blair, Editor

We cover all aspects of the commercial construction industry in Arizona, Nevada and New Mexico. Our mission is to provide news about the projects, the people and the events that affect the building and highway/heavy segments market.
Cost: $40.00
48 Pages
Frequency: Monthly
Circulation: 7000
Founded in 1938

4274 **State of Seniors Housing**
American Seniors Housing Association
5225 Wisconsin Ave NW
Suite 502
Washington, DC 20015

202-237-0900
Fax: 202-237-1616
Home Page: www.seniorshousing.org

David Schless, President
Doris Maultsby, VP
Frequency: Yearly

4275 **Structural Insulated Panel**
Structural Insulated Panel Association
PO Box 1699
Gig Harbor, WA 98335

253-858-7472
Fax: 253-858-0272
Home Page: www.sips.org

Terry Dieken, President
Al Cobb, VP

A comprehensive, full color book on building with energy efficient SIPs.
Frequency: Quarterly
Circulation: 5000
Founded in 1990

4276 **Structures**
Business Journal of Portland
851 Sw 6th Ave
Suite 500
Portland, OR 97204-1342

503-274-8733
866-246-0424
Fax: 503-219-3450
E-Mail: portland@bizjournals.com
Home Page: www.bizjournals.com/portland

Craig Wessel, Publisher

Special edition of The Business Journal that spotlights top construction projects and highlights the design, architecture and construction
Cost: $89.00
52 Pages
Frequency: Daily
Circulation: 400000
ISSN: 0742-6550
Printed in 4 colors on newsprint stock

4277 **Subcontractor**
Subcontractors Education Trust
1004 Duke St
Alexandria, VA 22314-3588

703-684-3450
800-221-0415
Fax: 703-836-3482
E-Mail: asaoffice@asa-hq.com
Home Page: www.asaonline.com

Colette Nelson, EVP
Franklin Davis, Director Government Relations

News from the construction industry, including up-to-date information on legislative and regulatory affairs, and business news concerning the subcontracting industry.
24 Pages
Frequency: Quarterly
Circulation: 9000
Founded in 1966
Printed in 2 colors

4278 **The Construction User**
The Association of Union Constructors
1501 Lee Highway
Suite 202
Arlington, VA 22209-1109

703-524-3336
Fax: 703-524-3364
E-Mail: dacord@tauc.org
Home Page: www.tauc.org

Stephen R Lindauer, CEO
Kevin J Hilton, Senior VP

TAUC's official magazine, giving readers a fresh and thought-provoking perspective on union construction and the issues contractors, labor and owner-clients face on a daily basis.
Frequency: Monthly
Founded in 1970

4279 **Tileletter**
National Tile Contractors Association
626 Lakeland E Drive
PO Box 13629
Jackson, MS 39232

601-939-2071
Fax: 601-932-6117
E-Mail: bart@tile-assn.com
Home Page: www.tile-assn.com

Bart Bettiga, Executive Director
Lesley Goddin, Editor

A trade publication to the tile industry: contractors, distributors and manufacturers.
Cost: $35.00
100 Pages
Frequency: Monthly
Circulation: 20000
Mailing list available for rent: 20,000 names at $150 per M
Printed in on matte stock

4280 **Tiling & Decorative Surfaces**
Ashlee Publishing
18 E 41st Street
New York, NY 10017

212-376-7722
Fax: 212-376-7723
Home Page: www.ashlee.com

Jordan M Wright, President

Provides information about industry trends and events throughout the world including interviews with manufacturers, distributors and contractors, offering tips on successful merchandising and sales techniques. Issues include product listings and project articles.
Cost: $50.00
Frequency: Monthly
Circulation: 27181
Founded in 1950

4281 **Tilt-Up TODAY**
Tilt-Up Concrete Association
113 First Street West
PO Box 204
Mount Vernon, IA 52314-0204

319-895-6911
Fax: 320-213-5555
E-Mail: info@tilt-up.org

Home Page: www.tilt-up.org
Social Media: Facebook

Ed McGuire, President
Glenn Doncaster, President-Elect
Kimberly Corwin, Vice-President
Shane Miller, Treasurer
David Tomasula, Secretary

With continuing advancements in Tilt-Up innovation and architectural achievement, Tilt-Up TODAY highlights the wide variety of outstanding Tilt-Up construction that is taking place all across the world.
Frequency: Monthly
Founded in 2005
Printed in 4 colors on glossy stock

4282 **Timber Framing**
Timbers Framers Guild
PO Box 295
Alstead, NH 03602

559-834-8453
888-453-0879
Fax: 888-453-0879
E-Mail: info@tfguild.org
Home Page: www.tfguild.org

Joel McCarty, Executive Director

Contains in-depth articles on timber framing history, technology, theory, practice, design, and engineering, as well as the work of the guild and its members
Cost: $25.00
Frequency: Quarterly
Founded in 1984

4283 **Timber Home Living**
Home Buyer Publications
4200 Lafayette Center Drive
Suite 100
Chantilly, VA 20151-1239

703-222-6951
800-850-7279
Fax: 703-222-3209
E-Mail: store@homebuyerpubs.com
Home Page: www.loghomeliving.com
Social Media: Facebook, LinkedIn

Lara Sloan, Publisher

For individuals wishing to plan, build, decorate, or design a log or timber frame home.
Cost: $3.99
Frequency: Bi-Monthly

4284 **Traditional Building**
Restore Media
45 Main Street
Suite 411
Brooklyn, NY 11201

718-636-0788
Fax: 718-636-0750
E-Mail: theditors@restoremedia.com
Home Page: www.traditional-building.com

Ray Shepherd, Production Manager
Clem Labine, Editor

Lists sources of products for restoration and new construction of traditional buildings.
Cost: $19.95
Frequency: Bi-Monthly
Circulation: 29,000
ISSN: 0898-0284
Founded in 1988
Printed in on glossy stock

4285 **Underground Construction**
Oildom Publishing Company of Texas
PO Box 941669
Houston, TX 77094-8669

281-558-6930
Fax: 281-558-7029
E-Mail: oklinger@oildompublishing.com
Home Page: www.oildompublishing.com

Oliver Klinger, President & Publisher
Robert Carpenter, Editor
Cost: $25.00
Frequency: Monthly
Printed in 4 colors on glossy stock

4286 **Underground Focus**
Canterbury Communications
411 South Evergreen
Manteno, IL 60950

815-468-7814
Fax: 815-468-7644
Home Page: www.underspace.com

Ron Rosencrans, Editor-in-Chief
Paula Miller, Advertising Manager

People read Underground Focus magazine because it documents the importance of their work and helps them get the budgets to do the job. It powerfully dramatizes the need for underground damage prevention and excavation safety.
Cost: $25.00
46 Pages
Circulation: 18,000
ISSN: 1090-400X
Founded in 1986
Printed in 2 colors

4287 **Utility Contractor**
3925 Chain Bridge Road
Suite 300
Fairfax, VA 22030

703-358-9300
Fax: 703-358-9307
E-Mail: bill@nuca.com
Home Page: www.nuca.com

Bill Hillman, CEO

Serves the underground utility construction industry, including contractors, manufacturers, suppliers, engineering firms, municipal/public/private utilities, and others allied to the field.
Frequency: Monthly
Circulation: 20983
ISSN: 1098-0342
Founded in 1967

4288 **Walls & Ceilings**
Business News Publishing Company
2401 West Big Beaver Road
Suite 700
Troy, MI 48084

248-362-3700
Fax: 248-362-5103
E-Mail: mark@wwcca.org
Home Page: www.wconline.com

Lynette Barwin, Production Manager
John Wyatt, Editor
Mark Fowler, Editorial Directort

Information regarding management, building methods, technology, government regulations, consumer trends, and product information for the contractor involved in exterior finishes, waterproofing, insulation, metal framing, drywall, fireproofing, partitions, stucco and plaster.
Cost: $49.00
140 Pages
Frequency: Monthly
Circulation: 30000
Founded in 1938
Printed in 4 colors

4289 **Welding Journal**
American Welding Society
550 NW 42nd Ave
Miami, FL 33126-5699

305-443-9353
800-443-9353
Fax: 305-443-7559
E-Mail: info@aws.org
Home Page: www.aws.org

Annette O'Brien, Senior Editor
Mary Ruth Johnsen, Editor

Serves the metal working field, individuals and organizations engaged in welding, cutting or related processes and equipment for the fabrication, maintenance, design or repair of metal products.
Cost: $80.00
Frequency: Monthly
Circulation: 50,000
ISSN: 0043-2296
Founded in 1919

4290 **Western Builder**
Western Builder Publishing Company
30 Technology Pkwy S
Suite 100
Norcross, GA 30092-2925

770-209-3730
Fax: 770-209-3712
Home Page: www.acppubs.com

Tad Smith, CEO
Greg Sitek, Editorial Director

Regional construction publication serving the heavy, highway and non-residential construction industry in Wisconsin and the Upper Peninsula of Michigan.
Cost: $53.00
Frequency: Monthly
Circulation: 100,000
Founded in 1905

4291 **Window & Door**
National Glass Association
1945 Old Gallows Rd
Suite 750
Vienna, VA 22182

703-442-4890
866-342-5642
Fax: 703-442-0630
Home Page: www.glass.org

Philip James, President/CEO
Nicole Harris, VP

The focus is on technical, new product information, business management and industry issues which focus on manufacturing both new and replacement windows and doors.
Cost: $29.95
Circulation: 20000
Founded in 1948

4292 **Window Film Magazine**
Key Communications
PO Box 569
Garrisonville, VA 22463

540-720-5584
Fax: 540-720-5687
E-Mail: boleary@glass.com
Home Page: www.windowfilmmag.com/

Debra Levy, Publisher
Penny Beverage, Assistant Editor
Katie Hodge, Editor

Provides industry news, supplier and film manufacturer profiles, technical and installation tips, as well as state-by-state legislative breakdowns and consumer marketing issues relevant to the film industry.
Cost: $35.00
Frequency: Monthly
Circulation: 7000

4293 **Window World Magazine**
Work-4 Projects
4819 St. Charles Boulevard
Pierrefonds, Quebec H9H-3C7

514-620-2200
Fax: 514-620-6300

E-Mail: editor@work4.ca
Home Page: www.homebuildercanada.com

Nachmi Artzy, Publisher

Provides new products, announcements, calendar events, and coverage of industry news, technical and maketing information to small and medium window and door manufacturers of North America.
Cost: $30.00
Frequency: Bi-Monthly
Circulation: 9,877

4294 **Wrecking and Salvage Journal**
Duane Publishing
51 Park St
Dorchester, MA 02122-2643

617-282-4885
Fax: 617-282-0320
Home Page: www.rubblemakers.com

Herb Duane, Owner
Toby Duane, Director

Business related information for those engaged in demolition and urban renewal.
Cost: $35.00
Frequency: Monthly
Circulation: 2500
Founded in 1967

Trade Shows

4295 **ACSM Annual Spring Conference**
American Congress on Surveying and Mapping
6 Montgomery Village Avenue
Suite 403
Gaithersburg, MD 20879

240-632-9716
Fax: 240-632-1321
E-Mail: info@acsm.net
Home Page: www.acsm.net

Curtis Sumner, Executive Director
Colleen Campbell, Conference Director

Four hundred booths of products and services offered by companies involved in the aerial mapping industry.
2000 Attendees
Frequency: Annual/April

4296 **ACSM/APLS Annual Conference & Technology Exhibition**
American Congress on Surveying & Mapping
6 Montgomery Village Avenue
Gaithersburg, MD 20879

240-632-9716
Fax: 240-632-1321
E-Mail: curtis.sumner@acsm.net
Home Page: www.acsm.net

Curtis Sumner, Executive Director
Colleen Campbell, Conference Director

The American Congress on Surveying & mapping and the Arizona Professional Land Surveyors organizations have come together to produce this exhibition with four hundred booths of products and services offered by companies involved in the aerial mapping industry.
1500 Attendees
Frequency: Annual

4297 **AEMA Annual Meeting**
Asphalt Emulsion Manufacturers Association
3 Church Circle
PO Box 250
Annapolis, MD 21401-1933

410-267-0023
Fax: 410-267-7546
E-Mail: krissoff@aema.org
Home Page: www.aema.org

Michael Krissoff, Executive Director

Representing close to 150 of the world's leading companies in the pavement preservation and rehabilitation industry. A combined annual meeting with the International Slurry Surfacing Association and the Asphalt Recycling & Reclaiming Association.
400 Attendees
Frequency: Annual/March

4298 **AGC Building Contractors Conference**
Associated General Contractors of America
2300 Wilson Blvd
Suite 400
Arlington, VA 22201

703-548-3119
Fax: 703-837-5405
E-Mail: meetings@agc.org
Home Page: www.agc.org

Carolyn Coker, Executive Director
Joe Jarboe, SVP

One hundred and seventy-five exhibiors of heavy and light construction equipment, trucks, building materials, management services, computer hardware and software. Contractors, subcontractors and trade professionals attend.
4500+ Attendees
Frequency: Annual

4299 **AIBD Annual Convention**
American Institute of Building Design
7059 Blair Rd NW
Suite 201
Washington, DC 20012

800-366-2423
Fax: 866-204-0293
E-Mail: info@aibd.org
Home Page: www.aibd.org
Social Media: Facebook, Twitter, LinkedIn

Dan Sater, President
Alan Kent, Internal Vice President
Viki Wooster, External Vice President
Kerry Dick, Secretary/ Treasurer

Exhibition of 25 manufacturers, suppliers, distributors and plan publishers of building products including: roofing, windows, doors, floor covering, fire places, spas/jacuzzis, lumber, intercom systems, alarm systems and appliances; computer-aid design technology, computer hardware/software and plan publishers. Containing 30 booths and 30 exhibits.
1500 Attendees
Frequency: Annual/July
Founded in 1950

4300 **AIC Annual Forum**
American Institute of Constructors
PO Box 26334
Alexandria, VA 22314

703-683-4999
Fax: 703-683-5480
E-Mail: dwright@professionalconstructor.org
Home Page: www.aicnet.org

David Wright, Executive Director
Andy Wasiniak, President
Paul Mattingly, Treasurer

Educational presentations from leading practitioners and educators in the world of construction, panel discussions with major voices in the industry, opportunities to network with other emerging leaders in the construction profession as they fine-tune their leadership skills.
Frequency: Annual/April

4301 **AISC Annual Meeting**
American Institute of Steel Construction
1 E Wacker Drive
Suite 700
Chicago, IL 60601-2000

312-670-2400
Fax: 312-670-5403
E-Mail: ferch@aisc.org
Home Page: www.aisc.org

Roger Ferch, President
Katey Lenihan, Meeting Planner

One hundred booths attended by structural engineers, steel fabricators, educators and construction managers. Those interested in the design fabrication and erection of structural steel for non-residential buildings and bridges.
100 Attendees
Frequency: Annual/September

4302 **APWA International Public Works Congress & Expo**
American Public Works Association
2345 Grand Boulevard
Suite 700
Kansas City, MO 64108 2625

816-472-6100
800-848-2792
Fax: 816-472-1610
E-Mail: ddancy@apwa.net
Home Page: www.apwa.net

Brian Van Norman, Director
David Dancy, Director of Marketing

Offers the benefit of a variety of educational sessions, depth of the exhibit program and endless opportunities for networking. The latest cutting-edge technologies, managerial techniques and regulatory trends designed to keep you focused on the right solutions at the right time.
6500 Attendees
Frequency: Annual/September

4303 **APWA North American Snow Conference**
American Public Works Association
2345 Grand Boulevard
Suite 700
Kansas City, MO 64108-2625

816-472-6100
800-848-2792
Fax: 816-472-1610
E-Mail: ddancy@apwa.net
Home Page: www.apwa.net

Brian Van Norman, Director
David Dancy, Director of Marketing

Education, technical and hands-on for snow and ice management.
1000 Attendees
Frequency: Annual/April
ISSN: 0092-4873

4304 **ASPE Estimating Academy & Annual Convention**
American Society of Professional Estimators
2525 Perimeter Place Drive
Suite 103
Nashville, TN 37214

615-316-9200
888-378-6283
Fax: 615-316-9800
E-Mail: sbo@aspenational.org
Home Page: www.aspenational.com

Karen Hinen, Executive Director
Patsy Smith, Convention Planning

Provides two days of presentations by nationally known speakers in the construction industry. ASPE's Technical Documents Committee prepares a book for each convention attendee

that contains papers submitted by the speakers at these educational sessions.
Frequency: Annual/July

4305 AWI Annual Meeting/Convention
Architectural Woodwork Institute
46179 Westlake Dr
Suite 120
Potomac Falls, VA 20165

571-323-3636
Fax: 571-323-2330
E-Mail: info@awinet.org
Home Page: www.awinet.org

Kimberly Kennedy, Meeting/Conventions Director
Robert Stout, President

Seminar, workshop and woodwork products such as casework, fixtures and panelings, equipment and supplies.
Frequency: Annual/October

4306 Adhesive and Sealant Council Fall Convention
Adhesive & Sealant Council
7101 Wisconsin Avenue
Suite 990
Bethesda, MD 20814

301-986-9700
Fax: 301-986-9795
E-Mail: bob.willis@ascouncil.org
Home Page: www.ascouncil.org

Bob Willis, Senior Manager Conventions/Meetings
Frequency: October

4307 AeroMat Conference and Exposition
ASM International
9639 Kinsman Road
Materials Park, OH 44073-0002

440-338-5151
800-336-5152
Fax: 440-338-4634
E-Mail: natalie.nemec@asminternational.org
Home Page: www.asminternational.org

Stanley Theobald, Managing Director
Kelly Thomas, Exposition Account Manager
Natalie Nemec, Event Programming Manager

Conference for Aerospace Meterials Engineers, Structural Engineers and Designers. The annual event focuses on affordable structures and low-cost manufacturing, titanium alloy technology, advanced intermetallics and refractory metal alloys, materials and processes for space applications, aging systems, high strength steel, NDT evaluation, light alloy technology, welding and joining, and engineering technology. 150 exhibitors.
1500 Attendees
Frequency: Annual/June
Founded in 1984

4308 American Institute of Building Design Annual Convention
American Institute of Building Design
7059 Blair Road NW
Suite 201
Washington, DC 20012

202-249-1407
800-366-2423
Fax: 202-249-2473
E-Mail: info@aibd.org
Home Page: www.aibd.org

Dan Sater, President

A four day convention and trade show for residential design professionals.
Frequency: Annual/July

4309 Annual Conference on Deep Foundations
Deep Foundations Institute
326 Lafayette Avenue
Hawthorne, NJ 07506

973-423-4030
Fax: 973-423-4031
E-Mail: dfihq@dfi.org
Home Page: www.dfi.org

James Morrison, President
Katie Criqui, Event Coordinator

The premier event for industry members from across the globe to gather and share experiences, exchange ideas and learn the current state-of-the-practice from various disciplines such as engineers, contractors, suppliers, manufacturers and academicians.
600 Attendees
Frequency: Annual/October
Founded in 1975

4310 Arrowhead Home and Builders Show
Shamrock Productions
14552 Judicial Rd
Suite 111
Burnsville, MN 55306

952-431-9630
Fax: 952-431-9633
E-Mail: info@shamrockprod.com
Home Page: www.shamrockprod.com/dh.htm

Randy Schauer, President/CEO

Home building, remodeling, landscaping and more.
41960 Attendees
Frequency: Annual/April

4311 Associated Builders and Contractors National Convention
Associated Builders and Contractors
4250 N Fairfax Dr
9th Floor
Arlington, VA 22203

703-812-2000
Fax: 703-812-8200
E-Mail: meetings@abc.org
Home Page: www.abc.org

Michael Bellaman, President/CEO
Tina Schneider, Meetings/Conventions Director

Exhibits for construction contractors, subcontractors, and associated trades.

4312 Brick Show
Brick Industry Association
1850 Centennial Park Drive
Suite 301
Reston, VA 20191-1525
703-620-0100
Fax: 703-620-3928
E-Mail: brickinfo@bia.org
Home Page: www.bia.org

Susan Ludwig, Show Manager

The only national tradeshow and conference for the clay brick industry.
950 Attendees
Frequency: Annual/March

4313 Builders Trade Show
Maryland National Capital Building Industry Assn.
1738 Elton Road
Suite 200
Silver Spring, MD 20903-5730

301-445-5400
Fax: 301-445-5499
E-Mail: building@mncbia.org
Home Page: www.mncbia.org

Jean Mathis, Events Director
Diane Swenson, EVP

Annual show and exhibits of construction equipment, supplies and services.

4314 Building Industry Show
Building Industry Assn. of Southern California
17444 Sky Park Circle
Irvine, CA 92614

949-553-9500
Fax: 949-769-8942
E-Mail: sfrias@biasc.org
Home Page: www.buildingindustryshow.com

Wes Keusder, President

Annual show of about 400 exhibitors of products and services for the building industry.
8000+ Attendees
Frequency: Annual/November

4315 Business Administration Conference
National Ready Mixed Concrete Association
900 Spring Street
Silver Spring, MD 20910

301-587-1400
888-846-7622
Fax: 301-585-4219
E-Mail: info@nrmca.org
Home Page: www.nrmca.org

Robert Garbini, President
Deana Angelastro, Executive Administrator

A 3-day educational program for financial, information technology, and human resources professionals in the construction and construction materials business.
Frequency: Annual/October

4316 CFMA Annual Conference & Exhibition
Construction Financial Management Association
100 Village Blvd
Suite 200
Princeton, NJ 08540

609-452-8000
Fax: 609-452-0474
E-Mail: info@cfma.org
Home Page: www.cfma.org

Joseph Burkett, Chairman
Pat Cebelak, Treasurer

The source and resource for construction financial professionals.
6000 Attendees
Frequency: Annual/May

4317 CONEXPO-CON/AGG
Association of Equipment Manufacturers
6737 W Washington St
Suite 2400
Milwaukee, WI 53214-5647

414-272-0943
800-867-6060
Fax: 414-272-1170
Home Page: www.conexpoconagg.com

Ken Snover, Expo Managing Director
Jim Eldredge, Exhibits Coordinator

The international gathering place for the worldwide construction, aggregates and ready mixed concrete industries.
124M Attendees
Frequency: March/Every 3 Years
Founded in 2002

4318 Composites & Polycon
American Composites Manufacturers Association
1010 North Glebe Road
Suite 450
Arlington, VA 22201

703-525-0511
Fax: 703-525-0743
E-Mail: info@acmanet.org
Home Page: www.acmashow.org

Lori Luchak, President

World's largest trade association serving the composites industry. Provides education and support for composites fabricators in the successful operation of businesses, and offers leading-edge services in regulatory compliance and formulation, education and training, management, and market expansion.
1.5M Attendees
Frequency: Annual/September

4319 **Coverings: The Ultimate Tile & Stone Experience**
NTP, Coverings Show Management
313 S Patrick Street
Alexandria, VA 22314
703-683-8500
800-687-7469
Fax: 703-836-4486
E-Mail: coverings@ntpshow.com
Home Page: www.coverings.com
Karin Fendrich, COO
Showcasing the newest in tile and natural stone, the event provides opportunities for: continuing education, live demonstrations, networking and new business. 1200 international exhibitors, attracting 33,000+ distributors, retailers, fabricators, contractors, and design professionals.
33M Attendees
Frequency: Annual
Mailing list available for rent

4320 **Delmarva Ag & Construction Show**
Lee Publications
6113 State Highway 5
Palatine Bridge, NY 13428
518-732-2269
800-218-5586
Fax: 518-673-3237
E-Mail: info@leepub.com
Home Page: www.leepub.com
Ken Maring, Trade Show Manager
Hundreds of agriculture and construction exhibitors with products and equipment. Skid steer rodeo for fun. Held at the Wicomico Youth and Civic Center in Maryland.
Frequency: Annual/December

4321 **Design & Construction Exposition**
Construction Association of Michigan
43636 Woodward
PO Box 3204
Bloomfield Hills, MI 48302
248-972-1000
Fax: 248-972-1001
E-Mail: marketing@cam-online.com
Home Page: www.cam-online.com
Ron Riegel, Exposition Manager
Jeanny Snowden, Marketing Coordinator
Annual show of 250 manufacturers, suppliers and distributors of construction industry equipment, supplies and services.
11M Attendees
Frequency: Annual/February
Founded in 1985

4322 **EdCon & Expo**
Associated Builders and Contractors
4250 Fairfax Drive
9th Floor
Arlington, VA 22203-1665
703-812-2000
Fax: 703-812-8201
E-Mail: meetings@abc.org
Home Page: www.abc.org
Michael Bellaman, CEO
Todd Mann, COO
Jason Daisey, CFO
1700 Attendees
Frequency: Annual/April

4323 **Elevator Escalator Safety Awareness Annual Meeting**
Elevator World
356 Morgan Avenue
Mobile, AL 36606
251-479-4514
800-730-5093
Fax: 251-479-7043
E-Mail: admin@elevator-world.com
Home Page: www.elevator-world.com
Linda Williams, Director of Administration
Patricia Cartee, Director of Operations
Meetings, discussions and exhibits on the safety of elevators.
Frequency: Annual/February

4324 **Environmental Management Conference and Exposition**
Environmental Information Association
6935 Wisconsin Avenue
Suite 306
Chevy Chase, MD 20815-6112
301-961-4999
888-343-4342
Fax: 301-961-3094
E-Mail: info@eia-usa.org
Home Page: www.eia-usa.org
Kelly Rutt, Developement Manager
Brent Kynoch, Managing Director
Annual conference of 85-100 exhibitors of equipment, supplies and services for quantifying, managing or remediating environmental hazards in buildings and facilities.
1200 Attendees

4325 **Equipment Distributors Association Annual Meeting**
Associated Equipment Distributors
600 Hunter Dr
Suite 220
Oak Brook, IL 60523-8807
630-574-0650
Fax: 630-574-0132
E-Mail: info@aednet.org
Home Page: www.aednet.org
Toby Mack, President/CEO
Janet Dixon, Convention & Meetings Director
A place where distributor, manufacturer and supplier executives meet, build relationships, do business, and learn new skills.
3.5M Attendees
Frequency: Annual/January

4326 **FENCETECH Convention & Expo**
American Fence Association
800 Roosevelt Rd
Building C-312
Glen Ellyn, IL 60137-5899
630-942-6598
Fax: 630-790-3095
E-Mail: afa@mindspring.com
Home Page: www.americanfenceassociation.com
Rod Wilson, President
Mike Robinson, Vice President
Four hundred and eighty booths for the fence industry. Educational opportunities that will inform you of the most up-to-date technology.
5883 Attendees
Frequency: Annual/January/February

4327 **GlassBuild America: Glass, Window & Door Expo**
National Glass Association
1945 Old Gallows Rd
Suite 750
Vienna, VA 22182
703-424-4890
866-342-5642
Fax: 703-442-0630
Home Page: www.glass.org
Philip James, President
Nicole Harris, VP
Provides one central showcase for the class processing equipment, window and door manufacturing equipment, and the latest technology for all types of glass and fenestration products used in residential and commercial construction and related applications.
Frequency: Annual/October

4328 **Great Lakes Building Products Exposition**
Michigan Lumber & Building Materials Association
5815 Executive Drive
Suite B
Lansing, MI 48911
517-394-5225
Fax: 517-394-5228
E-Mail: assn@mlbma.org
Home Page: www.mlbma.org
Jodi Barber, VP
Rick Seely, President
Offering new products and presentations on industry topics for the building material dealer and builders/contractors.
Frequency: Annual/January

4329 **Hard Hat Show**
Lee Publications
6113 State Highway 5
Palatine Bridge, NY 13428-0121
518-732-2269
800-218-5586
Fax: 518-673-3237
E-Mail: kmaring@leepub.com
Home Page: www.leepub.com
Ken Maring, Trade Show Manager
Larry Price, Sales Manager
Beth Snyder, Trade Show Manager
The premier showcase for heavy construction in the Northeast sharing information about the latest innovations in the construction industry!
3.5M Attendees
Frequency: Annual/March
Founded in 1989

4330 **Home Improvement & Remodeling Exposition**
Dmg World Media
325 Essjay Road
Suite 100
Williamsville, NY 14221
716-631-2266
800-274-6948
Fax: 716-631-2425
Home Page: www.dmgevents.com
Mark Carr, President
Featuring a spectacular garden, the latest in home technology, thousands of products, celebrity appearances and over 350 exhibits where consumers can find what they need to create their own unique spaces and put their special style to work.
60000 Attendees
Frequency: Annual/March

4331 **IDA International Garage Door Expo**
International Door Association
PO Box 246
West Milton, OH 45383-0246
937-988-8042
800-355-4432
Fax: 937-698-6153
E-Mail: info@longmgt.com
Home Page: www.doors.org
Chris Long, Managing Director
Steve Smith, Accounting Manager

Workshops and Exhibits featuring the latest product innovations as well as the traditional products and services for which the industry is known for.
Frequency: Annual/April

4332 INTEX Expo System Construction Association
Association of the Wall and Ceiling Industry
513 W Broad Street
Suite 210
Falls Church, VA 22046
703-538-1600
Fax: 703-534-8307
E-Mail: info@awci.org
Home Page: www.awci.org
Tim Wies, President
Jeffrey Burley, VP
The premier interior/exterior wall and ceiling commercial construction trade show. This annual show host exhibitors such as, wall and ceiling contractors, general contractors, architects, specifiers, suppliers, and distributors.
3000 Attendees
Frequency: Annual/April

4333 Independent Electrical Contractors National Convention
Independent Electrical Contractors
4401 Ford Avenue
Suite 1100
Alexandria, VA 22302
703-549-7351
Fax: 703-549-7448
E-Mail: info@ieci.org
Home Page: www.ieci.org
Tim Welsh, Executive VP
Trayvia Watson, Meetings Manager
One hundred booths of electrical equipment, products and services.
1000 Attendees
Frequency: Annual/October

4334 International Builders Show
National Association of Home Builders
1201 15th Street NW
Washington, DC 20005
202-266-8200
800-368-5242
Fax: 202-266-8400
E-Mail: info@nahb.com
Home Page: www.nahb.org
Gerald Howard, CEO
More than 1,600 suppliers, representing the most comprehensive showcase of home building products and services, are ready to demonstrate how their offerings can help you to corner the market.
90000 Attendees
Frequency: Annual/January

4335 International Conference Building Official
International Code Council
5360 Workman Mill Road
Whittier, CA 90601-2298
888-422-7233
Fax: 562-908-5524
Home Page: www.iccsafe.org
Jay Peters, Executive Director
Mark Johnson, SVP
1,2M Attendees
Frequency: Annual/September

4336 International Construction and Utility Equipment Exposition
Association of Equipment Manufacturers
6737 W Washington Street
Suite 2400
Milwaukee, WI 53214-5647
414-272-0943
Fax: 414-272-1170
E-Mail: aem@aem.org
Home Page: www.aem.org
Sara Mooney Truesdale, Show Director
Paul Flemming, Exhibits Sales Manager
The only exposition for outdoor demonstrations of utility and construction equipment. Experience the newest technologies for their electric, phone, cable, water, sewer, gas, general construction, landscape, and government jobs.
15000 Attendees
Frequency: Annual/September

4337 International Thermal Spray Conference & Exposition
ASM International
9639 Kinsman Road
Materials Park, OH 44073
440-338-5151
800-336-5152
Fax: 440-338-4634
E-Mail: natalie.nemec@asminternational.org
Home Page: www.asminternational.org
Charles Hayes, Executive Director
Pamela Kleinman, Senior Event Manager
Global annual event attracting professional interested in thermal spray technology focusing on advances in HVOF, plasma and detonation gun, flame spray and wire arc spray processes, performance of coatings, and future trends. 150 exhibitors.
1000 Attendees
Frequency: Annual/May

4338 Lumber and Building Material Expo
Northeastern Retail Lumber Association
585 N Greenbush Road
Rensselaer, NY 12144
518-286-1010
800-292-6752
Fax: 518-286-1755
E-Mail: rferris@nrla.org
Home Page: www.nrla.org
Donna Berger, Events Coordinator
Rita Ferris, President
Largest regional trade show in the lumber and building material industry. Retail lumber dealers in the Northeast are afforded the opportunity to interact with manufacturers, wholesalers, and distributors of lumber, building materials, and related technologies.
7000 Attendees
Frequency: Annual/February

4339 MBI World of Modular Conference
Modular Building Institute
944 Glenwood Station Ln
Suite 204
Charlottesville, VA 22901-1480
434-296-3288
888-811-3288
Fax: 434-296-3361
E-Mail: info@modular.org
Home Page: www.modular.org
Steven Williams, Operations Director
Tom Hardiman, Executive Director
High-profile speakers, educational sessions, exhibits, discussion on trends in commercial modular, entertainment and prizes
500 Attendees
Frequency: Annual

4340 MCAA Annual Convention & Masonry Showcase
Mason Contractors Association of America
1481 Merchant Drive
Algonquin, IL 60102
224-678-9709
800-536-2225
Fax: 224-678-9714
Home Page: www.masoncontractors.org
Tim O'Toole, Marketing Director
Jeff Buczkiewicz, Executive Director
Featuring in-depth education seminars, high-profile international skills competitions and exhibit display. Attendees includes masonry contracting firms representing all facets of masonry installation, including the largest commercial, residential, institutional, landscape, paving, retaining, glass block, and stone contractors.
Frequency: Annual/March

4341 MIACON Construction, Mining & Waste Management Show
Finocchiaro Enterprises
2921 Coral Way
Miami, FL 33145
305-441-2865
Fax: 305-529-9217
Home Page: www.miacon.com
Michael Finocchiaro, President
Jose Garcia, VP
Justine Finocchiaro, Chief Operations
Annual show of 650 manufacturers, suppliers, distributors and exporters of equipment, machinery, supplies and services for the construction, mining and waste managment industries. There will be 600 booths.
10M Attendees
Frequency: Annual/October
Founded in 1994

4342 Metalcon International
PSMJ Resources
10 Midland Avenue
Newton, MA 02458-1021
617-965-0055
Fax: 617-928-1670
E-Mail: metalcon@psmj.com
Home Page: www.metalcon.com
Claire Kilcoyne, Show Manager
Suzanne Maher, Conference Director
Paula Parker, Exhibit Sales
Architects, builders, craftspeople, designers, framers, contractors, and other industry leaders will share their expertise, hone their skills, and make connections that will help their businesses reach new heights.
8000 Attendees
Frequency: Annual/October

4343 NCSBCS/AMCBO Annual Conference
Int'l Conference of State Bldg Codes & Standards
505 Huntmar Park Drive
Suite 210
Herndon, VA 20170
703-437-0100
Fax: 703-481-3596
E-Mail: dbecker@ncsbcs.org
Home Page: www.ncsbcs.org
Kevin Egilmez, Project Manager
Carolyn Fitch, Membership Services
Providing a wide variety of technical and administrative information of immediate value to the nation's construction and code enforcement community, trade associations, information technology firms and professional societies, academicians, students, and elected officials regarding building codes administration and public safety.
Frequency: Annual/Sept-Oct

4344 NECA Convention
National Electrical Contractors Association
3 Bethesda Metro Center
Suite 1100
Bethesda, MD 20814

301-657-3110
Fax: 301-215-4500
Home Page: www.necanet.org

Russell Alessi, President
Katie Nolan, Convention Manager

The event brings the largest manufacturers, utilities, contractors, engineers, consultants, plant engineers, and distributors from all over North America and 31 foreign countries.
8000 Attendees
Frequency: Annual/September

4345 NRCMA Conference
National Railroad Construction & Maintenance Assoc
500 New Jersey Avenue NW
Suite 400
Washington, DC 20001

202-715-2919
Fax: 202-318-0867
E-Mail: info@nrcma.org
Home Page: www.nrcma.org

Chuck Baker, President
Matt Ginsberg, Director of Operations

For railroad personnel, managers and purchasers in design, construction and maintenance. Information on breakthrough innovations in rail construction, railroad safety, new rail projects of national significance and more. 60-80 exhibitors.
750 Attendees
Frequency: Annual/January

4346 NSSGA Dredging Seminar & Expo
National Stone, Sand & Gravel Association
1605 King Street
Alexandria, VA 22314

703-525-8788
800-342-1415
Fax: 703-525-7782
E-Mail: jwilson@nssga.org
Home Page: www.nssga.org

Jennifer Wilson, President/CEO
Cynthia McDowell, Conventions Director

Created to specifically meet the needs of aggregate producers who use dredges or have an interest in using dredges in the future. This seminar uses educational seminars, plant tours and manufacturer's exhibits to provide information useful to both novice and experienced dredgers.
Frequency: Annual/June

4347 National Congress & Expo for Manufactured and Modular Housing
Manufactured Housing Institute
2111 Wilson Boulevard
Suite 100
Arlington, VA 22201-3040

703-558-0400
Fax: 703-558-0401
E-Mail: info@mfghome.org
Home Page: www.manufacturedhousing.org

Thayer Long, President/CEO
Lisa Quinn Brechtel, VP/Executive Director

The opportunity to network with over 1500 industry captains who make a positive difference in the modular and manufactured housing industries.
Frequency: Annual/April

4348 National Demolition Association Conference and Trade Show
National Demolition Association
16 North Franklin Street
Suite 203
Doylestown, PA 18901

215-348-4949
800-541-2412
Fax: 215-348-8422
E-Mail: info@demolitionassociation.com
Home Page: www.demolitionassociation.com

Don Rachel, President
Jeff Kroeker, VP
1700 Attendees
Frequency: Annual

4349 National Hardware Show
Reed Exhibitions
383 Main Avenue
Norwalk, CT 06851

203-404-4800
888-425-9377
Fax: 203-840-9622
E-Mail: inquiry@hardware.reedexpo.com
Home Page: www.nationalhardwareshow.com

Richard Russo, Event Director
Juliana Van Der Beek, Sales Manager

The only housing after-market show, bringing together manufacturers and resellers of all products used to remodel, repair, maintain and decorate the home and its surroundings.
3M Attendees
Frequency: Annual/May

4350 New England Home Show
Dmg World Media
45 Braintree Hill Office Park
Suite 302
Braintree, MA 02184

781-849-0990
800-469-0990
Fax: 781-849-7544
E-Mail: lauriemyette@us.dmgworldmedia.com
Home Page: www.newenglandhomeshow.com

Laurie Myette, Show Manager
Amy Kimball, Administrative Assistant

Annual show of 379 exhibitors of homebuilding and improvement equipment, supplies and services, including bathroom and kitchen supplies, building materials, appliances, doors and windows, swimming pools, hot tubs and spas.
100M Attendees
Frequency: Annual/February

4351 North American Quarry Recycling Show
Lee Publications
6113 State Highway 5
PO Box 121
Palatine Bridge, NY 13428-0121

518-732-2269
800-218-5586
Fax: 518-673-3245
Home Page: www.leepub.com

Ken Maring, Trade Show Manager
Matt Stanley, Sales Manager

The North American Quarry Show is the largest trade show in North America for the aggregates industry.
Frequency: Annual/October

4352 North American Steel Construction Conference
American Institute of Steel Construction
One East Wacker Drive
Suite 700
Chicago, IL 60601

312-670-2400
Fax: 312-670-5403
Home Page: www.aisc.org

David Ratterman, General Counsel
Roger Ferch, President

A premier education event aimed at providing structural engineers, steel fabricators, erectors, and detailers with practical information and the latest design and construction techniques.
2300 Attendees
Frequency: Annual/April

4353 Northwestern Building Products Expo
Northwestern Lumber Association
5905 Golden Valley Road
Suite 110
Minneapolis, MN 55422-4528

763-544-6822
888-644-6822
Fax: 763-595-4060
Home Page: www.nlassn.org

Jodie Fleck, Director of Conventions
Paula Siewert, President

Building materials and their contractors attend this trade show and conference for continuing educataion and cammeraderie
1200 Attendees
Frequency: Annual

4354 PACE: Paint and Coatings Expo
Painting and Decorating Contractors of America
1801 Park 270 Drive
Suite 220
St Louis, MO 63146-4020

314-514-7322
800-332-7322
Fax: 314-514-9417
Home Page: www.pdca.org

Richard Greene, CEO
Libby Loomis, Event Coordinator

This mega show is the culmination of months of research and planning by members of the two professional associations (PDCA & SSPC), who joined forces in search of a 'one-stop shop' solution for convening the maximum number of industry professionals in the most cost-effective and productive way.
Frequency: Annual/January

4355 PowerGen
Scaffold Industry Association
2001 E Campbell Avenue
Suite 101
Phoenix, AZ 85016

602-257-1144
866-687-7115
Fax: 602-257-1166
Home Page: www.scaffold.org

Steve Smith, President
Marty Coughlin, President Elect
Daryl Hare, Treasurer
Mike Russell, Secretary

Companies from all sectors of the industry exhibit and attendees come together for a look at the industry with key emphasis on new solutions and innovations for the future.
Frequency: Annual/July

4356 RCMA Meeting
Roof Coatings Manufacturers Association
750 National Press Building
529 14th Street NW
Washington, DC 20045

202-207-0919
Fax: 202-223-9741
E-Mail: questions@roofcoatings.org
Home Page: www.roofcoatings.org

Steve Heinje, Director

An educational program focusing on Technical, Marketing, and regulatory updates regarding roof coatings.
100 Attendees
Frequency: Annual

4357 **SIA Annual Convention & Exposition**
Scaffold Industry Association
2001 E Campbell Avenue
Suite 101
Phoenix, AZ 85016
602-257-1144
866-687-7115
Fax: 602-257-1166
Home Page: www.scaffold.org
Steve Smith, President
Marty Coughlin, President Elect
Daryl Hare, Treasurer
Mike Russell, Secretary
Exhibits and classes on scaffold safety and education.
Frequency: Annual/July

4358 **SIPA Annual Meeting & Conference**
Structural Insulated Panel Association
PO Box 1699
Gig Harbor, WA 98335
253-858-7472
Fax: 253-858-0272
Home Page: www.sips.org
Social Media: Facebook, Twitter
Frank Baker, President
A valuable networking event for both longtime veterans and newcomers to the SIP industry. If you're a builder, architect, developer or entrepreneur interested in employing SIPs in your next commercial or residential project, you'll be interested in this conference
Frequency: Annual/April

4359 **STAFDA Annual Convention & Trade Show**
Specialty Tools and Fasteners Distributors Assn.
500 Elm Grove Rd.
Suite 210
Elm Grove, WI 53122
262-784-4774
800-352-2981
Fax: 262-784-5059
E-Mail: info@stafda.org
Home Page: www.stafda.org
Social Media: Facebook, LinkedIn
Mike Kangas, President
Kramer Darragh, Vice President
Members distribute or manufacture power equipment, anchors, fastening systems, drilling equipment and other related industrial supplies.
4000 Attendees
Frequency: Annual/November

4360 **Spray Foam Conference & EXPO**
Spray Polyurethane Foam Alliance
4400 Fair Lakes Court
Suite 105
Fairfax, VA 22033
800-523-6154
Fax: 703-222-5816
Home Page: www.sprayfoam.org
Sig Hall, President
Bob Duke, Vice President
Peter Davis, Secretary/ Treasurer
Training and accreditation programs, general and breakout sessions, awards, networking receptions, and the exhibit hall
Frequency: Yearly
Founded in 1987

4361 **TAUC Annual Meeting**
The Association of Union Constructors
1501 Lee Highway
Suite 202
Arlington, VA 22209-1109
703-524-3336
Fax: 703-524-3364
E-Mail: dacord@tauc.org
Home Page: www.tauc.org
Stephen R Lindauer, CEO
Kevin J Hilton, Senior VP
The prime meeting of the year, bringing together our membership from around the country in a relaxed and informal setting. The meeting will provide an opportunity to network and meet our union contractors.
Frequency: Annual/May
Founded in 1970

4362 **TCA Annual Convention**
Tilt-Up Concrete Association
113 First Street West
PO Box 204
Mount Vernon, IA 52314-0204
319-895-6911
Fax: 320-213-5555
E-Mail: info@tilt-up.org
Home Page: www.tilt-up.org
Social Media: Facebook
Ed McGuire, President
Glenn Doncaster, President-Elect
Kimberly Corwin, Vice-President
Shane Miller, Treasurer
David Tomasula, Secretary
Tilt-up Concrete Association/TCA's annual convention that features intensive training and education seminars for contractors and engineers, as well as a trade show, building tour and focused sessions on marketing and architecturald design.
Frequency: Annual/October
Founded in 2005

4363 **Technology for Construction**
Hanley-Wood
8600 Freeport Parkway
Suite 200
Irving, TX 75063
972-366-6300
866-962-7469
Fax: 972-536-6402
E-Mail: TCindric@hanleywood.com
Home Page: www.technologyforconstruction.com
Tom Cindric, Show Director
Jackie James, Show Manager
Todd Gilmore, Sales Manager
International conference and tradeshow focused on the technology needs and interests of architects and interior designers; civil engineers, contractors, builders, and construction managers, facility managers, building engineers, owners, GIS, surveyors and mapping professionals for private, commercial, institutional and government sectors.
33M Attendees
Frequency: Annual/January

4364 **Utility Construction Expo**
National Utility Contractors Association
3925 Chain Bridge Road
Suite 300
Fairfax, VA 22030
703-358-9300
Fax: 703-358-9307
E-Mail: bill@nuca.com
Home Page: www.nuca.com
Bill Hillman, CEO
Bonnie Williams, VP
The latest technologies, products, and services being offered by the leading manufacturers and suppliers in the underground utility construction industry. Next trade show is scheduled to take place in Las Vegas, Nevada.
Frequency: Annual/February

4365 **WBMA Annual Convention**
Western Building Material Association
909 Lakeridge Drive SW
PO Box 1699
Olympia, WA 98507
360-943-3054
888-551-9262
Fax: 360-943-1219
E-Mail: wbma@wbma.org
Home Page: www.wbma.org
One hundred and fourty booths of products stocked and sold by building material dealers.
1.6M Attendees
Frequency: Annual/November

4366 **World Adhesive Conference & Expo**
Adhesive & Sealant Council
7101 Wisconsin Avenue
Suite 990
Bethesda, MD 20814
301-986-9700
Fax: 301-986-9795
E-Mail: bob.willis@ascouncil.org
Home Page: www.ascouncil.org
Bob Willis, Senior Manager Conventions/Meetings
Frequency: April

4367 **World of Asphalt Show & Conference**
National Asphalt Pavement Association
5100 Forbes Boulevard
Suite 200
Lanham, MD 20706
301-731-4748
888-468-6499
Fax: 301-731-4621
E-Mail: mcervarich@hotmix.org
Home Page: www.hotmix.org
Mike Acott, President
Margaret Cervarich, VP Marketing/Public Affairs
The leading trade show for the asphalt pavement industry, bringing together the Asphalt Pavement Conference and the People, Plants and Paving training program.
6000 Attendees

Directories & Databases

4368 **ANSI/SPRI Standard Field Test Procedure**
Single Ply Roofing Institute
411 Waverley Oaks Road
Suite 331B
Waltham, MA 02542
781-647-7026
Fax: 781-647-7222
E-Mail: info@spri.org
Home Page: www.spri.org
Linda King, Managing Director
Standard Field Test Procedure for determining the withdrawal resistance of roofing fasteners.
Cost: $5.00
Frequency: Free to members

4369 **ANSI/SPRI Wind Design Standard**
Single Ply Roofing Institute
411 Waverley Oaks Road
Suite 331B
Waltham, MA 02452
781-647-7026
Fax: 781-647-7222
E-Mail: info@spri.org
Home Page: www.spri.org
Linda King, Managing Director
Written for those who design, specify and install smooth-surfaced, low-slope flexible mem-

brane roof systems.
Cost: $5.00
23 Pages

4370 **Affirmative Action Compliance Manual for Federal Contractors**
Bureau of National Affairs
1801 S Bell St
Arlington, VA 22202-4501
703-341-3000
800-372-1033
Fax: 800-253-0332
E-Mail: customercare@bna.com
Home Page: www.bnabooks.com
Paul N Wojcik, CEO
Gregory C McCaffery, President
Employers and attorneys can more easily monitor and measure affirmative action requirements, implement policies, and quickly access other compliance information with this complete resource guide.
Cost: $611.00
Frequency: Monthly

4371 **Automated Builder: Top Component Producers Survey Issue**
Automated Builder
2401 Grapevine Dr
Oxnard, CA 93036
805-351-5931
Fax: 805-351-5755
E-Mail: info@automatedbuilder.com
Home Page: www.automatedbuilder.com
Don Carlson, Publisher
Over 100 leading industrialized building producers are profiled on the basis of sales. Top HUD-Code home producers, TOP pakelizers, TOP commercial modular builders. Features articles on technology, methods and machinery, sales and marketing for in-plant building.
Cost: $6.00
48 Pages
Frequency: Monthly
Circulation: 25000
ISSN: 0899-5540
Founded in 1964

4372 **Blue Book of Building and Construction**
Contractors Register
PO Box 500
Jefferson Valley, NY 10535
914-450-0200
800-431-2584
Fax: 914-243-0287
E-Mail: info@thebluebook.com
Home Page: www.thebluebook.com
Social Media: YouTube
Jeff Fandl, Editor
Regional construction directories in most major markets throughout the US. Online, thebluebook.com provides easy access to continually updated information for each of our regional editions.
4500 Pages
Frequency: Annual
Circulation: 615,000
Founded in 1913

4373 **Building & Construction Trades Department**
815 16th St NW
Suite 209
Washington, DC 20006-4101
202-347-1461
Fax: 202-628-0724
Home Page: www.bctd.org
Social Media: Facebook
Mark Ayers, President
Joseph Maloney, Secretary/Treasurer
Coordinates activity and provides resources to 15 affiliated trades unions in the construction industry.
386 Pages
Founded in 1908

4374 **Building Materials Directory**
Underwriters Laboratories
333 Pfingsten Rd
Northbrook, IL 60062-2096
847-412-0136
877-854-3577
Fax: 847-272-8129
E-Mail: cec@us.ul.com
Home Page: www.ul.com
Keith E Williams, CEO
John Drengenberg, Manager Consumer Affairs
Offers information on companies that have qualified to use the UL listing mark or classification marking on products that have been found to be in compliance with UL requirements.
Cost: $30.00
512 Pages
Frequency: Annual/February

4375 **Cedar Shake and Shingle Bureau Membership Directory/Buyer's Guide**
Cedar Shake & Shingle Bureau
PO Box 1178
Sumas, WA 98295-1178
604-820-7700
Fax: 604-820-0266
Home Page: www.cedarbureau.org
Jim Tuffin, Chairman
Len Taylor Jr., Vice-Chairman
Rav Dhaliwal, Secretary/Treasurer
About 102 member manufacturing mills in the Pacific Northwest and British Columbia, Canada; approximately 163 affiliated roofing applicators, builders, architects, remodelers and suppliers of related products and services.
Cost: $17.00
Frequency: SemiAnnual
Circulation: 450

4376 **Cement Americas**
Penton Media Inc
249 W 17th St
New York, NY 10011-5390
212-204-4200
Fax: 212-206-3622
E-Mail: steven.prokopy@penton.com
Home Page: www.penton.com
Sharon Rowlands, CEO
Offers 100 cement manufacturing companies in the United States, Canada, Mexico, Central and South America.
Cost: $78.00
225 Pages
Frequency: Annual
Circulation: 300
Mailing list available for rent
Printed in on glossy stock

4377 **Construction Equipment: Construction Giants Issue**
Reed Business Information
2000 Clearwater Dr
Oak Brook, IL 60523-8809
630-574-0825
Fax: 630-288-8781
Home Page: www.reedbusiness.com
Mark Kelsey, CEO
Stuart Whayman, CFO
Dan Olley, CIO
Listing of approximately 250 of the largest equipment-owning heavy construction contractors, engaged in earthmoving, paving, building and materials production owning over $10 million in equipment.
Frequency: Monthly
Circulation: 77010
Founded in 1949

4378 **Construction Planning & Scheduling Manual**
National Insulation Association
Ste 330
12100 Sunset Hills Rd
Reston, VA 20190-3295
703-683-6422
Fax: 703-549-4838
E-Mail: niainfo@insulation.org
Home Page: www.insulation.org
Melissa Jackson, Director of Publications
Beth Michaels, Vice President
Kristin DiDomenico, Vice President
This manual from the Associated General Contractors (AGC) was written to provide guidance to the contractor in the effective use of modern project management techniques. Its primary objective is to provide an educational tool that can be used within the construction industry to teach the concepts of construction planning and scheduling. The content of the book is written for all project personnel, from the working foreman to the project executive.
Cost: $155.00

4379 **Construction Specifier: Member Directory Issue**
Construction Specifications Institute
990 Canal Center Plaza
Suite 300
Alexandria, VA 22314
703-684-0300
800-689-2900
Fax: 703-684-8436
E-Mail: csi@csinet.org
Home Page: www.csinet.org
Eugene A Valentine, President
W Richard Cooper, VP
Roster of construction specifiers certified by the institute and approximately 17,200 members.
Cost: $203.00
Frequency: Annual/January
Circulation: 19500

4380 **Constructor: AGC Directory of Membership and Services Issue**
Associated General Contractors of America
333 John Carlyle Street
Sutie 200
Alexandria, VA 22314
703-548-3118
Fax: 703-548-3119
E-Mail: constructinfo@riagc.org
Home Page: www.agc.org
Donald Scott, Production Manager
Michael Kennedy, General Counsel
Norman Walton, Treasurer
List of more than 8,500 member firms and 24,000 national associate member firms engaged in building, highway, heavy, industrial, municipal utilities and railroad construction.
Frequency: Annual/July
Circulation: 34,000
ISSN: 0162-6191

4381 **Directory of Architectural and Construction Information Resources**
Grey House Publishing
4919 Route 22
PO Box 56
Amenia, NY 12501
518-789-8700
800-562-2139
Fax: 845-373-6390

E-Mail: books@greyhouse.com
Home Page: www.greyhouse.com
Social Media: Facebook, Twitter

Richard Gottlieb, President
Leslie Mackenzie, Publisher

The leading desktop reference and preliminary research guide, featuring more than 10,000 building product manufacturers and their products.
194 Pages
Frequency: Annual
ISBN: 1-519250-00-0

4382 Directory of Building Codes & Regulations
National Conference of States on Building Codes
505 Huntmar Park Dr
Herndon, VA 20170-5103

703-437-0100
800-362-2633
Fax: 703-481-3596

Robert Wible, Executive Director
Carolyn Fitch, Membership Services

This directory is a comprehensive guide to the building codes and regulations adopted and enforced in each of the 50 states, Puerto Rico, the District of Columbia, and 53 major U. S. cities in 14 different code areas - building, mechanical, plumbing, electrical, energy conservation, gas, fire prevention, life safety, accessibility, one & two family, modular, ventilation/indoor air quality, manufactured home installation, and elevator.
Cost: $78.00
Frequency: Annual

4383 Dodge Construction Analysis System
McGraw-Hill
1221 Avenue of the Americas
New York, NY 10020-1095

212-512-2000
800-393-6343
Fax: 212-512-3840
E-Mail: webmaster@mcgraw-hill.com
Home Page: www.mcgraw-hill.com

Harold W McGraw III, CEO
Joseph A Scott, National Marketing Director

This database lists over 4 million time series for construction projects involving more than 200 structural types.

4384 Dodge DataLine
McGraw-Hill
1221 Avenue of the Americas
New York, NY 10020-1095

212-512-2000
800-393-6343
Fax: 212-512-3840
E-Mail: webmaster@mcgraw-hill.com
Home Page: www.mcgraw-hill.com

Harold W McGraw III, CEO
Joseph A Scott, National Marketing Director
Dodge DataLine offers the most advanced searching of project leads in the industry. You can search the largest U.S. database of 500,000+ active construction projects.
Frequency: Daily

4385 ENR Top 100 Construction Managers
Engineering News Record/McGraw Publishing
2 Penn Plaza
9th Floor
New York, NY 10121-2298

212-512-2000
888-877-8208
Fax: 212-512-4039
E-Mail: support@construction.com
Home Page: www.construction.com

Gary Graizzaro, Plant Manager
John J Kosowatz, Managing Editor
William G. Krizan, Assistant Managing Editor

List of the top 100 leading construction and program management firms with the largest dollar volume in new construction management contracts on a for-fee only basis and an at-risk basis in the previous year.
Cost: $250.00
Frequency: Annual/June
Circulation: 90000

4386 ENR Top 400 Contractors Sourcebook
Engineering News Record/McGraw Publishing
2 Penn Plaza
9th Floor
New York, NY 10121-2298

212-512-2000
888-877-8208
Fax: 212-512-4039
E-Mail: support@construction.com
Home Page: www.construction.com

Gary Graizzaro, Plant Manager
Joann Gonchar, Associate Editor
William G. Krizan, Assistant Managing Editor
Debra K. Rubin, Managing Senior Editor

Market analysis rankings of the largest U.S.-based general contractors in eight major industry sectors: general building, transportation, manufacturing, industrial process, petroleum, power, environmental and telecommunications.
Cost: $85.00
112 Pages

4387 ENR Top 600 Specialty Contractors Issue
Engineering News Record/McGraw Hill
2 Penn Plaza
9th Floor
New York, NY 10121-2298

212-512-2000
Fax: 212-512-4039
E-Mail: support@construction.com
Home Page: www.construction.com

Gary Graizzaro, Plant Manager
John J Kosowatz, Managing Editor

Lists of the 600 largest US specialty subcontractors with sub-lists of top firms in mechanical contracting, electrical, excavation-foundation, steel erection, rofing, sheet metal, demolition-wrecking, glazing curtain wall, masonry, concrete, utilities, painting, wall/ceiling and asbestos abatement.
Cost: $350.00
Frequency: Annual/September
Circulation: 90000

4388 ENR Top Owners Sourcebook
Engineering News Record/McGraw Hill
2 Penn Plaza
9th Floor
New York, NY 10121-2298

212-512-2000
Fax: 212-512-4039
E-Mail: constructioninfo@ecnext.com
Home Page: www.construction.com

Gary Graizzaro, Plant Manager
John J Kosowatz, Managing Editor

List of 700 companies that had the largest expenditures for building construction and building acquisition in the previous year.
Cost: $300.00
Frequency: Annual/December
Circulation: 90000

4389 Electrical Construction Materials Directory
Underwriters Laboratories
333 Pfingsten Rd
Northbrook, IL 60062-2096

847-412-0136
877-854-3577
Fax: 847-272-8129
E-Mail: cec@us.ul.com
Home Page: www.UL.com

Keith E Williams, CEO
John Drengenberg, Manager Consumer Affairs

Companies that have qualified to use the UL listing mark or classification marking on or in connection with products which have been found to be in compliance with UL's requirements.
Cost: $30.00
Frequency: Annual
Printed in on glossy stock

4390 Fastener Selection Guide
Single Ply Roofing Institute
411 Waverley Oaks Road
Suite 331B
Waltham, MA 02452

781-647-7026
Fax: 781-647-7222
E-Mail: info@spri.org
Home Page: www.spri.org

Linda King, Managing Director

Identifies the various fastener options for each desk type and typical pullout values.
Cost: $15.00

4391 Flexible Membrane Roofing: Guide to Specifications
Single Ply Roofing Institute
411 Waverley Oaks Road
Suite 331B
Waltham, MA 02452

781-647-7026
Fax: 781-647-7222
E-Mail: info@spri.org
Home Page: www.spri.org

Linda King, Managing Director

Now in it's 7th edition, this is the most complete reference guide on materials, systems and designs for commerical roofing.
Cost: $50.00

4392 GreenSpec Directory
BuildingGreen
122 Birge Street
Suite 30
Brattleboro, VT 05301-6703

802-257-7300
Fax: 802-257-7304
E-Mail: info@buildinggreen.com
Home Page: www.buildinggreen.com

Alex Wilson, Owner
Nadav Malin, Editor
Daniel Woodbury, Publisher
Charlotte Snyder, Circulation Manager

Information on more than 1,850 green building products carefully screened by the editors of Environmental Building News. Directory listings cover more than 250 categories, from access flooring to zero-VOC paints. Included are product descriptions, environmental characteristics and considerations, and manufacturer contact information with internet addresses.
Cost: $89.00
464 Pages
ISBN: 1-929884-15-X

4393 MasterFormat
Construction Specifications Institute

110 South Union Street
Suite 100
Alexandria, VA 22314-3351

800-689-2900
Fax: 703-236-4600
E-Mail: csi@csinet.org
Home Page: www.csinet.org
Social Media: Facebook, Twitter, LinkedIn, YouTube

Paul R. Bertram Jr., President
Gregory J. Markling, President-Elect
Mitch A. Miller, Vice President
Casey F. Robb, Vice President
Lane J. Beougher, Secretary

The reengineering of this industry standard sets the present and future pace for organizing construction communication. MasterFormat 2004 Edition simplifies the process of determining where specific subject matter is located.
Cost: $159.00
516 Pages
ISBN: 0-976239-90-6
Founded in 2004

4394 NRCMA Membership Directory
National Railroad Construction & Maintenance Assoc
500 New Jersey Ave NW
Suite 400
Washington, DC 20001-2065

202-715-2919
Fax: 202-318-0867
E-Mail: info@nrcma.org
Home Page: www.nrcma.org
Social Media: Facebook, Twitter, LinkedIn

Chuck Baker, President
Matt Ginsberg, Director of Operations
Jim Perkins, Chairman
Terry Benton, Vice Chairman

A book of the railroad contracting industry, lists all members of the NRC, including their technical specialities ang geographic regions of operation.
Cost: $35.00
Frequency: Free to Members

4395 Public Works Manual
Hanley-Wood
426 S Westgate Street
Addison, IL 60101

630-543-0870
800-524-2364
Fax: 630-543-3112
E-Mail: arozgus@hanleywood.com
Home Page: www.pwmag.com

William D Palmer Jr., Editor-in-Chief
Amara Rozgus, Managing Editor
Sharon Glorioso, Associate Editor
Colette Palait, Editorial Assistant

Over 4,000 manufacturers and distributors of equipment, materials, services, computers and software used in the design, construction and maintenance of streets and highways, water systems, wastewater and solid wastes processing and recreation areas.
Cost: $30.00
Frequency: Annual
Circulation: 55000

4396 Roofing/Siding/Insulation: Trade Directory Issue
PO Box 1269
Skokie, IL 60076-8269

847-763-9594
Fax: 847-763-9694
E-Mail: roofingsidinginsulation@halldata.com
Home Page: www.rsimag.com

Thomas Skernivitz, Editor
Jacke Lyttle, Publisher

Lists thousands of contractors, manufacturers and distributors of equipment and products.
Cost: $20.00
Frequency: Annual
Circulation: 22,000

4397 STAFDA Directory
Specialty Tools & Fasteners Distributors Assn
500 Elm Grove Rd.
Suite 210
Elm Grove, WI 53122

262-784-4774
800-352-2981
Fax: 262-784-5059
E-Mail: info@stafda.org
Home Page: www.stafda.org
Social Media: Facebook, LinkedIn

Mike Kangas, President
Kramer Darragh, Vice President

This is a Who's Who of the industry. Listings include who makes over 900 different products: nearly 2,570 member addresses and contacts; brand names; fax numbers: 800 numbers; e-mail; www; and a recap of association services and activities.
500 Pages
Frequency: Annual
Circulation: 4500

4398 Scaffold Industry Association Directory & Handbook
Scaffold Industry Association
400 Admiral Blvd.
Kansas City, MO 64106-1508

816-595-4860
E-Mail: info@saiaonline.org
Home Page: www.scaffold.org
Social Media: Facebook, Twitter, LinkedIn

Steve Smith, President
Marty Coughlin, President-Elect
Daryl Hare, Treasurer
Mike Russell, Secretary

The SIA Directory and Handbook contains complete membership information, company and individual listings. It also includes federal OSHA scaffold standards for general industry, construction and maritime, scaffold plank grading rules, map and listing of OSHA regional and area offices, scaffold standards for the state of California, glossary of scaffold terms, illustrations of various types of scaffolds, and codes of safe practices.
Cost: $125.00
355 Pages
Circulation: 5000

4399 Source: Buyer's Guide & Dealer Directory
Northeastern Retail Lumber Association
585 N Greenbush Rd
Rensselaer, NY 12144-9615

518-286-1010
800-292-6752
Fax: 518-286-1755
E-Mail: rferris@nrla.org
Home Page: www.nrla.org
Social Media: Facebook

Rita Ferris, President
Tony Shepley, Chair
Jon Hallgren, Chair Elect
Jonas Kelly, Vice Chair

The industry's guide to names, addresses, phone numbers, fax numbers, and product lines of companies that comprise the independent retail lumber dealers of the Northeast.
Cost: $89.95
Frequency: Annual

4400 Sourcebook
Ray Publishing
P.O.Box 992
Morrison, CO 80465-0992

303-467-1776
Fax: 303-467-1777
Home Page: www.compositesworld.com

Judith Hazen, Publisher
Mike Mussleman, Managing Editor

A comprehensive directory of composites industry suppliers, manufacturers and service companies for the entire composites industry.
60 Pages
Founded in 1993
Printed in 4 colors on glossy stock

4401 Store Fixture Buyers' Guide and Membership Directory
Nat'l Association of Store Fixture Manufacturers
3595 Sheridan
Suite 200
Hollywood, FL 33322

954-893-7300
Fax: 954-893-7500
E-Mail: nasfm@nasfm.org
Home Page: www.nasfm.org
Social Media: Facebook, Twitter, LinkedIn

Jo Rossman, Senior Editor
Klein Merriman, Executive Director

This buyers' guide features the products and services of some 400 store fixture manufacturers. Contact information, plant size, number of employees, and company descriptions of all member manufacturers, plant listings by location, and contact and company information on products and services of 200 supplier members is included.
Cost: $175.00
80 Pages
Frequency: Free to Members

4402 Sweets Directory
Grey House Publishing/McGraw Hill Construction
1221 Avenue of the Americas
New York, NY 10020-1095

212-512-2000
800-442-2258
Fax: 212-512-3840
E-Mail: webmaster@mcgraw-hill.com
Home Page: www.mcgraw-hill.com
Social Media: Facebook, Twitter

Harold W McGraw III, CEO

The leading desktop reference and preliminary research guide, featuring more than 10,000 building product manufacturers and their products.
Cost: $145.00
950 Pages
Frequency: Annual
ISBN: 1-592378-50-1
Founded in 1906

4403 ThomasNet
Thomas Publishing Company, LLC
User Services Department
5 Penn Plaza
New York, NY 10001

212-695-0500
800-699-9822
Fax: 212-290-7362
E-Mail: contact@thomaspublishing.com
Home Page: www.thomasnet.com
Social Media: Facebook, Twitter, LinkedIn

Carl Holst-Knudsen, President
Robert Anderson, VP, Planning
Mitchell Peipert, VP, Finance
Ivy Molofsky, VP, Human Resources

A way to reach qualified businesses that list their company information on ThomasNet.com. Detailed profiles promote their products, services, capabilities and brands carried. The

ThomasNet.com web site is the most up-to-date compilation of 650,000 North American manufacturers, distributors, and service companies in 67,000 industrial categories.
Founded in 1898

4404 **Wind Design Guide**
Single Ply Roofing Institute
411 Waverley Oaks Road, Suite 331B
Waltham, MA 02452
781-647-7026, *Fax:* 781-647-7222
E-Mail: info@spri.org
Home Page: www.spri.org

Linda King, Managing Director

Wind Design Guide for Edge Systems Used with Low Slope Roofing Systems outlines design and construction of edge details for wind resistance, including test methods, calculations of design pressures and commentary.
Cost: $20.00

Industry Web Sites

4405 **http://gold.greyhouse.com**
G.O.L.D Grey House OnLine Databases

Grey House Publishing's online database platform, GOLD, offers Quick Search, Keyword Search and Expert Search for most business sectors including architecture, building and construction markets. The GOLD platform makes finding the information you need quick and easy - whether you're a novice searcher or an experienced database user. All of Grey House's directory products are available for subscription on the GOLD platform.

4406 **www.abc.org**
Associated Builders and Contractors

National trade association representing about 23,000 contractors, subcontractors, material suppliers and related firms from across the country and from all specialties in the construction industry.

4407 **www.acdi.net**
Associated Construction Distributors International

Cooperative association of independently owned and locally opearated distributors of specialty construction products and equipment.

4408 **www.acesystems.com**
AEC Systems International/Penton Media

Focuses on Internet/Intranet for the design, engineering and construction industries.

4409 **www.aednet.org**
Associated Equipment Distributors

Membership association of 1,200 independent distributors, manufacturers, and other organizations involved in the distribution of construction equipment and related products and services in North America and throughout the world.

4410 **www.agc.org**
Associated General Contractors of America

The voice of the construction industry, an organization of qualified construction contractors and industry related companies dedicated to skill, integrity and responsibility.

4411 **www.aibd.org**
American Institute of Building Design

Our members consist of professional building designers and architects, who have for the most part chosen residential design as the focus of their practice.

4412 **www.aisc.org**
American Institute of Steel Construction

Serving the structural steel industry in the US. Our purpose is to promote the use of structural steel through research activities, market development, education, codes and specifications, technical assistance, quality certifacation and standardization.

4413 **www.akropolis.net**
Akropolis

To enable firms at all levels of the design and building industry to operate more efficiently with the help of cutting edge technology solutions.

4414 **www.anodizing.org**
Aluminum Anodizers Council

Represents the interests of aluminum anodizers worldwide and is the principal trade organization for the anodizing industry in North America. It promotes the interests of its members through technical exchange, ongoing education, statistical data, market promotion, and industry representation.

4415 **www.apwa.net**
American Public Works Association

An international educational and professionals association of public agencies, private sector companies, and individuals dedicated to providing high quality public works goods and services.

4416 **www.aspenational.com**
American Society of Professional Estimators

Serving the construction estimators by providing education, fellowship and opportunity for professional development. ASPE represents individual members involved in the construction industry.

4417 **www.asphaltinstitute.org**
Asphalt Institute

Conducts education, research and engineering services related to asphaltic products; conducts seminars and sells publications and videos on asphalt technology.

4418 **www.asphaltpavement.org**
National Asphalt Pavement Association

The only trade association that exclusively represents the interest s of the Hot Mix Asphalt producer and paving contractor on the national level with Congress, government agencies, and other national trade and business organizations.

4419 **www.automatedbuilder.com**
CMN Associates

Association of manufacturers and suppliers who have a product line that is of interest to the manufactured and pre-fabricated housing industry.

4420 **www.awci.org**
Association of the Wall and Ceiling Industries

Represents acoustics systems, ceiling systems, drywall systems, exterior insulation and finishing systems, fireproofing, flooring systems, insulation, and stucco contractors, suppliers and manufacturers and those in allied trades.

4421 **www.build.com**
Build.com

Providing consumers, contractors and industry professionals with a valuable resource of products, service and information related to the building and home improvement industry.

4422 **www.buildingstone.org**
Building Stone Institute

Quarries, fabricators, dealers, installers and restorers of all types of natural stone. Membership dues based on sales volume.

4423 **www.calredwood.org**
California Redwood Association

A trade association for redwood lumber producers.

4424 **www.cfma.org**
Construction Financial Management Association

Non-profit organization dedicated to serving the financial professional in the construction industry.

4425 **www.cisco.org**
Construction Industry Service Corporation

Labor management association that promotes union construction, union contractors and union apprenticeship programs throughout Northeastern Illinois.

4426 **www.coaa.org**
Construction Owners Association of America

To act as a focal point and voice for the interests of owners in construction. Comprised of a diverse group of men and women representing construction owners.

4427 **www.concretepumpers.com**
American Concrete Pumping Association

Provides education, insurance, marketing and much more to companies involved with the concrete pumping industry. Our dedication to the concrete pumping industry has led us to become a key part in the education of safety and business management to everyone involved, from the operators to the management.

4428 **www.construction.com**
McGraw-Hill Construction

McGraw-Hill Construction (MHC), part of The McGraw-Hill Companies, connects people and projects across the design and construction industry, serving owners, architects, engineers, general contractors, subcontractors, building product manufacturers, suppliers, dealers, distributors and adjacent markets.

4429 **www.csinet.org**
Construction Specifications Institute

Our mission is to continuously improve the process of creating and sustaining the built environment. We do this by facilitating communication among all those involved in that process.

4430 **www.demolitionassociation.com**
National Association of Demolition Contractors

Representing the demolition industry including demolition contractors, formed to foster goodwill and the exchange of ideas with the public, governmental agencies and constractors engaged in the demolition industry. Also for manufacturers or suppliers of demolition equipment, supplies and services.

4431 **www.dfi.org**
Deep Foundations Institute

We can best be described as being a technical association of firms and individuals in the deep foundations and related industry. DFI covers the gamut of deep foundation construction and earth retention systems.

4432 **www.ebmda.org**
Eastern Building Material Dealers Association

Established to foster, protect and promote the welfare and best interest of its members engaged in the retail lumber and building materials business.

4433 **www.floorbiz.com**
Floor Biz
Internet's leading creator and operator of a vertical business community for the flooring industry. FloorBiz leverages the interactive features and global reach of the Internet to create a multi-national, targeted business community vertically integrated from consumer to manufacturer.

4434 **www.gobrick.com**
Brick Industry Association
A national trade association representing distributors and manufacturers of clay brick and suppliers of related products and services.

4435 **www.greyhouse.com**
Grey House Publishing
Authoritative reference directories for most business sectors including architecture, building and construction markets. Users can search the online databases with varied search criteria allowing for custom searches by product category, geographic area, sales volume, keyword, subject and more. Full Grey House catalog and online ordering also available.

4436 **www.homeimprovement.com**
Hometime
Hometime is a home-improvement television show broadcast on public television, The Learning Channel and in syndication. A comprehensive online resource for your remodeling and home-improvement needs.

4437 **www.iccsafe.org**
International Code Council
Formerly known as the Building Officials and Code Administrators International, we publish codes that establish minimum performance requirements for all aspects of the construction industry.

4438 **www.icpi.org**
Interlocking Concrete Pavement Institute
Self governed, self funded, autonomous association representing the interlocking concrete pavement industry in North America. Membership is open to producers, contractors, suppliers, consultants and others who have an interest in the industry. As an industry voice, the membership represents a majority of concrete paver production in North America.

4439 **www.iilp.org**
International Institute for Lathe and Plaster
Federation of organizations representing contractors, unions and makers of lathing and manufacturing.

4440 **www.manufacturedhousing.org**
Manufactured Housing Institute
National trade organization representing all segments of the factory built housing industry. MHI serves its membership by providing industry research, promotion, education, and government relations programs, and by building and facilitating consensus within the industry.

4441 **www.masoncontractors.org**
Mason Contractors Association of America
Through strong programs, publications and services, the MCAA avtively promotes the interests of its members. By promoting the use of masonry, influencing resonable codes and standards, work force development and public affairs, the association advances the use of masonry.

4442 **www.masonrysociety.org**
Masonry Society
Dedicated to the advancement of scientific engineering, architechtural and construction knowledge of masonry. Promotes research and education and disseminates information on masonry materials, design, construction. Publishes a newsletter.

4443 **www.mbinet.org**
Modular Building Institute
Serving the commercial factory-built buildings industry on an international scale. Our regular members are manufacturers and dealers of commercial modular structures, while our associate members are companies supplying building components, services, and financing.

4444 **www.naamm.org**
Nat'l Assn of Architectural Metal Manufacturers
The largest of four operating divisions of the National Association of Architectural Metal Manufacturers. HMMA is a group composed of companies that manufacture, distribute and promote the use of hollow metal door and frame products.

4445 **www.nahb.org**
National Association of Home Builders
Represents the interests of concrete, log, modular, and panel manufacturers, builders, and suppliers.

4446 **www.nam.org**
National Association of Manufacturers
The nation's largest industrial trade association, representing small and large manufacturers in every industrial sector and in all 50 states.

4447 **www.nari.org**
National Association of the Remodeling Industry
A voice in the remodeling industry, NARI has an exclusive, encompasing purpose to; establish and maintain a firm commitment to developing and sustaining programs that expand and unite the remodeling industry; to ensure the industry's growth and security; to encourage ethical conduct, sound business practices and professionalism in the remodeling industry; and to present NARI as the recognized authority in the remodeling industry.

4448 **www.nationalslag.org**
National Slag Association
Members are processors of iron and steel slags for use as a aggregate in construction and manufacturing applications.

4449 **www.nawic.org**
National Association of Women in Construction
Founded by 16 women working in the construction industry. The founders organized NAWIC to create a support network for women in construction.

4450 **www.ncac.com**
National Council of Acoustical Consultants
Strives to safeguard the interests of professional acoustical consulting firms. Managing physics and psychoacoustics to provide optimum listning environments.

4451 **www.ncma.org**
National Concrete Masonry Association
Manufacturers of concrete masonry products and suppliers of products to the industry. Offers a variety of technical services and design aids through publications, computer programs, slide presentations and technical training.

4452 **www.ncsbcs.org**
National Conference of States on Building Codes
Serving as a forum for the interchange of information and provides technical services, education and training to our members to enhance the public's social, economic well-being through safe, durable, accessible and efficient buildings.

4453 **www.necanet.org**
National Electrical Contractors Association
Represents a segment of the construction market comprised of over 70,000 electrical firms.

4454 **www.newhomes.move.com**
HomeBuilder.com
The web's leading provider of information on newly built homes, with listings for over 125,000 new home and planned developments throughout the US. Supplier of media and technology solutions that promote and connect real estate professionals to consumers before, during and after a move.

4455 **www.nrcma.org**
National Railroad Construction & Maintenance Assn
Railroad construction and maintenance contractors, engineering firms, manufacturing suppliers and professional associate firms.

4456 **www.nrla.org**
Northeastern Retail Lumber Association
A resource for industry members, consumers, and public officials in dependent lumber and building material suppliers and associated businesses in New York and the six New England states.

4457 **www.nrmca.org**
National Ready Mixed Concrete Association
Our mission is to provide exceptional value for our members by responsibly representing and serving the entire ready mixed concrete industry through leadership, promotion, education and partnering; to ensure ready mixed concrete is the building material of choice.

4458 **www.nssga.org**
National Stone, Sand & Gravel Association
Represents the crushed stone, sand and gravel — or aggregate — industries. Our members account for 90 percent of the crushed stone and 70 percent of the sand and gravel produced annually in the US.

4459 **www.ntma.com**
National Terrazzo and Mosaic Association
Full service nonprofit trade association headquartered in Northern Virginia. The association establishes national standards for all terrazzo floor and wall systems and provides complete specifications, color plates and general information to architects and designers at no cost.

4460 **www.nuca.com**
National Utility Contractors Association
A national association that provides a forum for continuing education and promotes effective public policy, through its grassroots network, to protect and enhance your industry.

4461 **www.oikos.com**
Oikos
Devoted to serving professionals whose work promotes sustainable design and construction. Oikos is a Greek word meaning house. Oikos serves as the root for two English words: ecology and economy.

4462 **www.opcmia.org**
Operative Plasterers' & Cement Masons' Int'l Assn
Represents and trains plasterers and cement masons for the purpose of protecting and promoting the quality of our industry and the livelihood of our members.

4463 **www.opei.org**
Outdoor Power Equipment Institute
International trade association whose members are manufacturers of powered lawn and garden maintenance products, components and attachment supplies, as well as industry related services.

4464 **www.pbmdf.com**
Composite Panel Association
The association of North American wood and agrifiber based particle board and medium density fiberboard producers, to broaden the base of participation in industry outreach programs.

4465 **www.pci.org**
Precast Prestressed Concrete Institute
Dedicated to fostering greater understanding and use of precast and prestressed concrete, maintains a full staff of technical and marketing specialists.

4466 **www.perlite.org**
Perlite Institute
International trade association which establishes product standards and specifications, and which encourages the development of new product uses through research.

4467 **www.pfi-institute.org**
Pipe Fabrication Institute
Members are companies producing sophisticated high temperature, high pressure piping systems that employ specialists from the United Association of Journeymen & Apprentices of the Plumbing & Pipe Fitting Industry. We exist solely for the purpose of ensuring a level of quality in the pipe fabrication indusrty that is without compromise.

4468 **www.piledrivers.org**
Pile Driving Contractors Association
Organization of pile driving contractors that advocates the increased use of driven piles for deep foundations and earth retention systems.

4469 **www.pipefitters537.org**
American Pipe Fittings Association
Trade association for any domestic corporation, firm or individual engaged in manufacture in the US or Canada of piping components and accessories, including pipe hangers and supports.

4470 **www.psai.org**
Portable Sanitation Association International
International trade association that represents firms engaged in the leasing, renting selling and manufacturing of portable sanitation equipment, services and supplies for construction, recreation, emergency and other uses. devoted to the proper handling of human waste by the most modern, sanitary means, giving the greatest concern to the preservation of an unspoiled environment.

4471 **www.reedconstructiondata.com**
First Source Online
Provides A/E/C professionals free access to the industry's most comprehensive, up-to-date library of formatted commercial building product information, plus manufacturers' addresses, telephone numbers, trade names, and regional distributors.

4472 **www.rfci.com**
Resilient Floor Covering Institute
Industry trade association of North American manufacturers who produce resilient flooring products. Associate members of RFCI supply raw materials to the industry and manufacture installation and maintenance products.

4473 **www.roofcoatings.org**
Roof Coatings Manufacturers Association
Represents the interests for manufacturers of cold applied roof coatings, cements and waterproofing agents, as well as the suppliers of products, equipment, and services to and for the industry. Currently RCMA boasts more than 70 member companies.

4474 **www.rubberpavements.org**
Rubber Pavements Association
Dedicated to encouraging greater usage of high quality, cost effective asphalt pavements containing recycled tire rubber. Conducts national and international seminars.

4475 **www.saiaonline.org**
Scaffold Industry Association
Promotes scaffold safety and education through its publications, conventions, tradeshows and training programs. Marketing of your product is available through the monthly magazine, convention and trade show.

4476 **www.sgcc.org**
Safety Glazing Certification Council
Provides for the certification of safety glazing materials, comprised of safety glazing manufacturers and other parties concerned with public safety. SGCC is managed by a board of directors comprised of representatives from the safety glazing industry and the public interest sector.

4477 **www.sips.org**
Structural Insulated Panel Association
A trade association representing manufacturers, suppliers, fabricators, distributors, design professionals and builders committed to providing quality structural insulated panels for all segments of the construction industry.

4478 **www.spri.org**
Single Ply Roofing Institute
Comprised of manufacturers and marketers of sheet applied membrane roofing systems and components to the commerical roofing industry.

4479 **www.stafda.org**
Specialty Tools & Fasteners Distributors Assn
International trade association composed of distributors and manufacturers and rep agents of light construction, industrial and related products. Members also include publishers of industry press serving the construction and industrial trades.

4480 **www.stanyc.com**
Subcontractors Trade Association
Members are specialty and supply companies in the construction industry. Our goal is to improve the economic well being of our members through representation, support and assistance through the process of legislation, legal action, public relations, education and other public information programs.

4481 **www.steelwindows.com**
Steel Window Institute
For United States manufacturers of windows made from hot-rolled, solid steel sections and such related products as castings, trim, mechanical operators, screens and moldings.

4482 **www.sweets.construction.com**
McGraw Hill Construction
In depth product information that lets you find, compare, select, specify and make purchase decisions in the industrial product marketplace.

4483 **www.swensongranite.com**
Swenson Granite Works
Family owned business that has been quarrying and cutting granite in New England since 1883.

4484 **www.tcaainc.org**
Tile Contractors Association of America
TCAA is an organization representing the finest union tile contractors in the United States. Founded in 1903, it is the only association which serves the needs of the union tile contractor.

4485 **www.tfguild.org**
Timber Framers Guild of North America
Dedicated to establishing training programs for dedicated timber framers, disseminating information about timber framing and timber frame building design, displaying the art of timber framing to the public, and generally serving as a center of timber framing information for the professional and general public alike.

4486 **www.thebluebook.com**
Contactors Register
Regional construction directories in most major markets throughout the US. Provides easy online access to continually updated information for each of our regional editions.

4487 **www.tile-assn.com**
National Tile Contractors Association
Serving every segment of the industry, and is recognized as the largest and most respected tile contractors association in the world.

4488 **www.tilt-up.org**
Tilt-up Concrete Association
Represents builders, engineers and suppliers involved with tilt-up concrete construction. Makes a continuing and increasingly important contribution to the success of each member through the most imaginative and efficient application of every appropriate skill, tool and service of the association.

4489 **www.wbma.org**
Western Building Material Association
Regional trade association serving building material dealers throughout the states of Alaska, Idaho, Montana, Oregon and Washington and a federated association of the National Lumber and Building Material Dealers Association.

4490 **www.wfca.org**
World Floor Covering Association
Shapes and defines public policy through agressive, national legislative advocacy on behalf of our members. Provides continuing professional educational programming through educational forums and the Regional Installation and Training Education (RITE) program.

4491 **www.windowanddoor.com**
WindowDoor.net
Anyone who is interested in window and door products can find the latest information on products, components and how-to information here.

Associations

4492 **AACC International**
3340 Pilot Knob Road
St. Paul, MN 55121

651-454-7250
800-328-7560
Fax: 651-454-0766
E-Mail: aacc@scisoc.org
Home Page: www.aaccnet.org
Social Media: Facebook, Twitter, LinkedIn

Jan A Delcour, President
David H Hahn, Chair
Gerard Downey, President Elect
Dave L Braun, Treasurer
Marta S Izydorczyk, Director

Formerly the American Association of Cereal Chemists, a non-profit organization of members who are specialists in the use of cereal grains in foods.
Founded in 1915

4493 **AOAC International**
481 N Frederick Ave
Suite 500
Gaithersburg, MD 20877-2450

301-924-7077
800-379-2622
Fax: 301-924-7089
E-Mail: aoac@aoac.org
Home Page: www.aoac.org
Social Media: Facebook, Twitter, LinkedIn

E James Bradford, CEO & Executive Director
Joyce L Schumacher, CFO
Delia A Boyd, Program Manager

Serves the communities of analytical sciences by providing the tools and porcesses necessary for community stakeholders to collaborate and through, consensus building, develop fit for purpose methods and services for assuring quality measurments.
3700 Members
Founded in 1887

4494 **Acrylonitrile Group**
1250 Connecticut Ave NW
Suite 700
Washington, DC 20036-2657

202-419-1500
Fax: 202-659-8037
E-Mail: angroup@regnet.com
Home Page: www.angroup.org

Robert J Fensterheim, Group Executive Director, President

Affiliated with the Synthetic Organic Chemical Manufacturers, (TAG) was formed under the Chemical manufacturers Association to do research. TAG represents producers and users of the industrial chemical used to make plastics, fibers and synthetic rubber products.
Founded in 1960

4495 **Adhesion Society**
2 Virginia Tech
Blacksburg, VA 24061

540-231-7257
Fax: 540-231-3971
E-Mail: adhesoc@vt.edu
Home Page: www.adhesionsociety.org

Ken Shull, President
Anand Jagota, Vice President
Charles Shuster, Treasurer
Leonardo Lopez, Secretary

Supports all those who are involved in adhesion's role in coatings, compostie materials, biological tissues and bonded structures.
400 Members
Founded in 1978

4496 **Alkyl Amines Council**
1850 M St NW
Suite 700
Washington, DC 20036

202-721-4100
Fax: 202-296-8120
E-Mail: info@socma.com
Home Page: www.socma.com

Lawrence D Sloan, President/CEO
Todd Brown, Director
Dolores Alonso, Senior Director

Data relating to production, processing and application.
6 Members
Founded in 1985

4497 **Alkylphenols and Ethoxylates Research Council**
1250 Connecticut Ave NW
Suite 700
Washington, DC 20036

202-419-1506
866-273-7262
Fax: 202-659-8037
E-Mail: info@aperc.org
Home Page: www.alkylphenol.org

Robert J Fensterheim, Executive Director

Monitors regulatory developments affecting manufacturers in the chemical industry
5 Members
Founded in 1998

4498 **Alliance for Responsible Atmospheric Policy**
2111 Wilson Blvd
Suite 850
Arlington, VA 22201

703-243-0344
Fax: 703-243-2874
E-Mail: fay@alliancepolicy.org
Home Page: www.alliancepolicy.org

Phil Lapin, Chair
Robert Wilkins, Vice Chair
William McQuade, Treasurer
Kevin Fay, Executive Director
Tonya Hunt, Finance & Membership Director

Made up of companies who rely on alternatives to ozone depleting chlorofluorocarbons(CFCs). Theses alternatives are HCPCs and HFCs, used primarily as refrigerants, speciality solvents, agents for foamed plastics.
300 Members
Founded in 1980

4499 **American Association Textile Chemists and Colorists**
PO Box 12215
Research Triangle Park, NC 27709-2215

919-549-8141
800-360-5380
Fax: 919-549-8933
E-Mail: danielsj@aatcc.org
Home Page: www.aatcc.org
Social Media: Facebook, Twitter, LinkedIn, Youtube

John Y Daniels, Executive VP
Debra Hibbard, Executive Assistant
Amy Holland, Office Manager
Bonnie Green, Membership Services
Suzanne Holmes, Program Manager/Technical Product

Supports all those working with colorants and chemical finishes for textile and related industries.
3000 Members

4500 **American Association for Clinical Chemistry**
1850 K St NW
Suite 625
Washington, DC 20006

202-857-0717
800-892-1400
Fax: 202-887-5093
Home Page: www.aacc.org
Social Media: Facebook, Twitter, LinkedIn, YouTube

Robert H Christensen, President
Steven H Wong, President Elect
Elizabeth L Frank, Secretary
Michael Bennett, Treasurer
Dennis J Dietzen, Director

AACC is an international scientific/medical society of clinical laboratory professionals, physicians, research scientists and other individuals involved with clinical chemistry and other clinical laboratory science related disciplines.
Founded in 1948

4501 **American Association for Crystal Growth**
6986 St. Wadsworth Court
Littleton, CO 80128

303-539-6907
888-506-1271
Fax: 303-482-2775
E-Mail: AACG@comcast.net
Home Page: www.crystalgrowth.org/index.php

Peter Schunemann, President
Robert M Biefeld, VP
Dave Vandewater, Treasurer
Joan M Redwing, Secretary

Provides support for all professionals in the field of crystal and crystal growth.

4502 **American Association of Bioanalysts**
906 Olive Street
Suite 1200
Saint Louis, MO 63101-1448

314-241-1445
Fax: 314-241-1449
E-Mail: aab@aab.org
Home Page: www.aab.org

Mark S Birenbaum PhD, Administrator

Professional association whose members are clinical laboratory directors, owners, supervisors, managers, medical technologists, medical laboratory technicians, physician office laboratory technicians, and phlebotomists.
Founded in 1956

4503 **American Chemical Society**
1155 16th St NW
Washington, DC 20036

202-872-4600
800-227-5558
Fax: 202-872-4615
E-Mail: service@acs.org
Home Page: www.acs.org
Social Media: Facebook, Twitter, LinkedIn

Madeleine Jacobs, CEO

Self-governed individual membership organization that provides a range of opportunities for peer interaction and career development, regardless of professional or scientific interests.
15900 Members
Founded in 1876

4504 **American Chemistry Council**
700 Second St. NE
Washington, DC 20002

202-249-7000
Fax: 202-249-6100
Home Page: www.americanchemistry.com

Social Media: Facebook, Twitter, LinkedIn, Youtube

Calvin M Dooley, President & CEO
Raymond J O'Bryan, CFO & CAO
Dell Perelman, Chief of Staff & General Counsel
Anne Womack Kolton, VP, Communications
Roger D Bernstein, VP, State Affairs

Committed to improved environmental, health and safety performance through responsible care, common sense advocacy designed to address major public policy issues, health and environmental research and product testing.
190 Members

4505 American Coatings Association
1500 Rhode Island Ave Nw
Washington, DC 20005

202-462-6272
Fax: 202-462-8549
E-Mail: members@paint.org
Home Page: www.paint.org

J. Andrew Doyle, President & CEO
Thomas J. Graves, Vice President, General Counsel
Allen Irish, Counsel/Director, Industry Affairs
Alison Keane, Vice President, Government Affairs
Robin Eastman Caldwell, Senior Government Affairs

Supports all those involved in the manufacturer of chemicals.

4506 American Coke & Coal Chemicals Institute
25 Massachusetts Ave NW
Suite 800
Washington, DC 20001

202-452-7198
Fax: 202-463-6573
E-Mail: information@accci.org
Home Page: www.accci.org

Ronald Schoen, Chairman
David Smith, Vice Chairman
Richard Owens, Secretary/Treasurer

Formed by companies interested in establishing a forum to discuss and act upon issues of common concern to their industry. Today, ACCI represents 7 of the 8 independently owned and operated US merchant coke producers; several integrated steel companies which produce coke; and all 4 of the US and 1 Canadian coal chemical companies which refine coal tar. Nearly 50 companies contribute their knowledge and expertise to enhance the effectiveness of the Institute.
160 Members
Founded in 1944

4507 American College of Toxicology Annual Meeting
1821 Michael Faraday Drive
Suite 300
Reston, VA 20190

703-547-0875
Fax: 703-438-3113
E-Mail: acthx@actox.org
Home Page: www.actox.org
Social Media: Facebook, Twitter, LinkedIn

Robert Snyder PhD, President
Patricia Frank PhD, VP
Robert W Kapp Jr. PhD, Treasurer
Suzanne W McMaster PhD, Secretary
Carol C Lemire, Executive Director

Multidisciplinary society composed of professionals having a common interest in toxicology. Our mission is to educate and lead professionals in industry, government and related areas of toxicology and actively promote the exchange of information and perspectives on the current status of safety assessment and the application of new developments in toxicology. Annual meeting,education courses, symposia and exhibits.
500 Members
Founded in 1979

4508 American Fiber Manufacturers Association
1530 Wilson Blvd
Suite 690
Arlington, VA 22209-2418

703-875-0432
Fax: 703-875-0907
E-Mail: afma@afma.org
Home Page: www.afma.org

Paul O'Day, President
Robert Baker, VP
Frank Horn, President Economics Bureau Div

Trade association for US companies that manufacture synthetic and cellulosotic fibers.
33 Members
Founded in 1933

4509 American Hydrogen Association
PO Box 4205
Mesa, AZ 85201

480-234-5070
E-Mail: 123GoH2@gmail.com
Home Page: www.clean-air.org

Abe Fouhy, President
Erik Szewczyk, Vice President

Stimulates interest and helping to establish the renewable hydrogen energy economy.

4510 American Institute of Chemical Engineers
120 Wall Street
FL 23
New York, NY 10005-4020

212-591-7338
800-242-4363
Fax: 203-775-5177
E-Mail: xpress@aiche.org
Home Page: www.aiche.org
Social Media: Facebook, Twitter, LinkedIn

John Sofranko, Executive Director
William D Byers, President
Cathy Diana, Director Human Resources
Ken Gruber, Finance/IT Manager

A professional association of members that provide leadership in advancing the chemical engineering profession.
50000 Members
Founded in 1908

4511 American Institute of Chemists
315 Chestnut St
Philadelphia, PA 19106-2702

215-873-8224
Fax: 215-629-5224
E-Mail: aicoffice@theaic.org
Home Page: www.theaic.org

David Manuta, President
E Ray McAfee, President Elect
E Gerry Meyer, Secretary
J Stephen Duerr, Treasurer
Jerry P Jasinski, Chairman

Supports all individual chemists and chemical engineers involved in the chemical industry.
Founded in 1923

4512 American Leather Chemists Association
1314 50th Street
Suite 103
Lubbock, TX 79412

806-744-1798
Fax: 806-744-1785
E-Mail: alca@leatherchemists.org
Home Page: www.leatherchemists.org

Steve Lange, President
Sarah Drayna, VP
David Peters, VP Elect
Carol Adcock, Executive Secretary

Group of leather chemists interested in the development of methods that could be utilized to standardize both the supply and application of the tanning agents utilized by the industry
500 Members
Founded in 1903

4513 American Society Biochemistry and Molecular Biology
11200 Rockville Pike
Suite 302
Rockville, MD 20852-3110

240-283-6600
Fax: 301-881-2080
Home Page: www.asbmb.org

Barbara A Gordon, Executive Director
Jennifer Dean, Director, Marketing
Ben Corb, Director, Public Affairs
Mary Ann Gunselman, Executive Assistant
Steve Miller, CFO

A professional and educational association for biochemists and molecular biologists which seeks to extend and utilize the fields of biochemistry and molecular biology.
13000 Members
Founded in 1906
Mailing list available for rent

4514 American Society for Mass Spectrometry
2019 Galisteo Street, Building I-1
Santa Fe, NM 87505

505-989-4517
Fax: 505-989-1073
E-Mail: office@asms.org
Home Page: www.asms.org
Social Media: Facebook, Twitter, LinkedIn

Susan T Weintraub, President
Jennifer Brodbelt, VP, Programs
Gary Valaskovic, VP, Arrangements
Neil L Kelleher, Treasurer
Rebecca Jockusch, Secretary

Formed to promote and disseminate knowledge of mass spectrometry and allied topics. Members come from academic, industrial and govermental laboratories. Their interests include advancement of techniques and instrumentation in mass spectrometry, as well as fundamental research in chemistry, geology, biological sciences and physics.
3500 Members
Founded in 1969

4515 American Society for Neurochemistry
9037 Ron Den Lane
Windermere, FL 34786

407-909-9064
Fax: 407-876-0750
E-Mail: asnmanager@asneurochem.org
Home Page: www.asneurochem.org

Etty Benveniste, President
Babette Fuss, President Elect
Vlad Parpura, Secretary
Susan McGuire, Treasurer

Organized by US, Canadian and Mexican members of the International Society for Neurochemistry and incorporated in the District of Columbia. Membership dues are $75/year.
1000 Members
Founded in 1969

4516 American Society of Brewing Chemists
3340 Pilot Knob Rd
Eagan, MN 55121-2055
651-454-7250
800-328-7560
Fax: 651-454-0766
E-Mail: asbc@scisoc.org
Home Page: www.asbcnet.org
Social Media: Facebook, LinkedIn
Steven C Nelson, VP
Amy Hope, VP Operations
Jody Grider, Operations Director
700 Members
Founded in 1934

4517 Analytical, Life Science, and Diagnostics Association
500 Montgomery Street
Suite 400
Alexandria, VA 22314
703-647-6214
Fax: 703-647-6368
E-Mail: cstarke@alssa.org
Home Page: www.alssa.org
Joseph D. Keegan, Chair
Timÿ Harkness, Vice Chair & Chair-Elect
Greg Herrema, Past Chairman
Michael J. Duff, President
ALSSA is the primary trade association for companies that supply instruments, chemical reagents, consumables and software used for analysis and measurement in chemistry and the life sciences.

4518 Association of Consulting Chemists and Chemical Engineers Inc.
A C C & C E
P.O. Box 902
Murray Hill, NJ 07974-0902
908-464-3182
Fax: 908-464-3182
E-Mail: accce@chemconsult.org
Home Page: www.chemconsult.org
Linda Townsend, Executive Secretary
Dr John Bonacci, Executive Director
The only organization of its kind that attracts qualified technical consultants of all kinds who assist their clients in creating and using chemical knowledge and technology.
150 Members
Founded in 1928

4519 Association of Defensive Spray Manufacturers
906 Olive Street
Suite 1200
St Louis, MO 63101-1448
314-241-1445
Fax: 314-241-1449
E-Mail: ADSM@pepperspray.org
Home Page: www.pepperspray.org
Mark S Birenbaum, Executive Director
To permit manufacturers of non lethal chemical weapons to join together to promote the industry as well as to address safety, quality control, marketing and other issues relevant to the industry
6 Members
Founded in 1992

4520 Association of Official Racing Chemists
1021 Storrs Rd
Storrs, CT 06268
860-487-3755
Fax: 860-487-3756
Home Page: www.aorc-online.org
Dennis Hill, Executive Director
The international membership consits of individuals concerned with detection of drugs in racing samples.
200 Members
Founded in 1947

4521 Basic Acrylic Monomer Manufacturers
17260 Vannes Court
Hamilton, VA 20158
540-751-2093
Fax: 540-751-2094
E-Mail: ehunt@adelphia.net
Home Page: www.bamm.net
Elizabeth K Hunt, Executive Director
Addresses the issues facing the basic acrylates. Also represents manufacturers and importers of acrylic acid and its esters.
5 Members
Founded in 1986
Mailing list available for rent

4522 CIIT Centers for Health Research
Six Davis Drive
PO Box 12137
Research Triangle Park, NC 27709-2137
919-581-1200
Fax: 919-558-1400
E-Mail: wgreenlee@ciit.org
Home Page: www.thehamner.org
Social Media: Twitter
John G. Dent, Ph.D., Chair & Treasurer
Charles E. Hamner, Jr., D.V.M., P, Vice Chair
William F. Greenlee, Ph.D., President/CEO
Joseph S. Pagano, M.D., Secretary
Jamie H. Wilkerson, CPA, CGMA, Assistant Treasurer
Studies toxicological and human health risk issues associated with the manufacture, distribution and disposal of industrial chemicals.
130 Members
Founded in 1974

4523 Center for the Polyurethanes Industry
1300 Wilson Blvd
Arlington, VA 22209-2307
703-841-0012
Fax: 202-249-6100
Home Page: www.polyurethane.org
Calvin M. Dooley, President/CEO
Dell Perelman, Chief of Staff & General Council
Raymond J. O'Bryan, Chief Financial Officer
Roger D. Bernstein, Vice President, State Affairs
Nacole B. Hinton, Managing Director
CPI of the American Chemistry Council promotes the sustainable growth of the polyurethane industry, by identifying and managing issues that could impact the industry, in cooperation with user groups. Members are producers and distributors of chemicals and equipment used to make polyurethane and manufacture polyurethane products.

4524 Chemical Coaters Association International
PO Box 54316
Cincinnati, OH 45254
513-624-6767
800-926-2848
Fax: 513-624-0601
E-Mail: aygoyer@one.net
Home Page: www.ccaiweb.com
Anne Goyer, Executive Director
A technical and professional organization that provides information and training on surface coating technologies. Users and suppliers of industrial cleaners, paints, coatings, and equipment.
1000 Members
Founded in 1970
Mailing list available for rent

4525 Chemical Development and Marketing Association (CDMA)
401 North Michigan Ave
Suite 2200
Chicago, IL 60611
312-321-5145
800-232-5241
Fax: 312-673-6885
E-Mail: CDMA@pdma.org
Home Page: www.cdmaonline.org/home.html
Theodre D. Goldman, President/Treasurer
Tom Regino, Executive Vice President
Eileen Strauss, Vice President/Webmaster
Maricy Bourgis, Vice President
A forum for networking, learning and sharing best practices in business development and marketing for the chemical and allied industries. Keeps members informed on commercial/business development and marketing as well as industrial marketing research via its two meetings per year (spring and fall), seminars and business schools.
Founded in 1999

4526 Chemical Fabrics and Film Association
1300 Sumner Avenue
Cleveland, OH 44115-2851
216-241-7333
Fax: 216-241-0105
E-Mail: cffa@chemicalfabricsandfilm.com
Home Page: www.chemicalfabricsandfilm.com
Charles Stockinger, Executive Secretary
International trade association representing manufacturers of polymer-based fabric and film products, used in the building and construction, automotive, fashion and many other industries.
40 Members
Founded in 1927

4527 Chemical Heritage Foundation
315 Chestnut St
Philadelphia, PA 19106
215-925-2222
Fax: 215-925-1954
E-Mail: info@chemheritage.org
Home Page: www.chemheritage.org
Tom Tritton, President/CEO
Miriam Schaeter, Special Advisor to the President
Michael Meyer, Editor-in-Chief
An independent, nonprofit organization, CHF maintains major collections of instruments, fine art, photographs, papers, and books. We host conferences and lectures, support research, offer fellowships, and produce educational materials.
29 Members

4528 Chemical Industry Data Exchange
401 North Michigan Avenue
Chicago, IL 60611-4267
312-321-5145
Fax: 312-212-5971
E-Mail: memberservices@cidx.org
Home Page: www.cidx.org
JoAnne Norton, Executive Director
Laura Field, Communications
Promotes standards to improve the efficiency of transactions across the chemical industry supply chain. Members include chemical producers and companies active in the chemicals industry.

4529 Chemical Strategies Partnership
423 Washington St
4th Floor
San Francisco, CA 94111

415-421-3405
Fax: 415-421-3304
Home Page: www.chemicalstrategies.org

Jill Kauffman Johnson, Executive Director
Angeline Kung, Senior Associate
Aarthi Ananthanarayanan, Associate
Max Pike, Communications Associate
Mark Stoughton, Ph.D., Research Advisor

CSP seeks to reduce chemical use, waste, risks and cost through the transformation of the chemical supply chain by redefining the way chemicals are used and sold.
Mailing list available for rent

4530 Chemtrec
1300 Wilson Blvd
Arlington, VA 22209-2323
703-741-5500
800-262-8200
Fax: 703-741-6086
E-Mail: chemtrec@chemtrec.com
Home Page: www.chemtrec.com

A 24 hour emergency communication service center that helps fire fighters and emergency responders protect the public and helps shippers of hazardous materials comply with the US Department of Transportation regulations.
Founded in 1971

4531 Chlorinated Paraffins Industry Association
1250 Connecticut Ave NW
Suite 700
Washington, DC 20036

202-419-1500
Fax: 202-659-8037
E-Mail: info@regnet.com
Home Page: www.regnet.com/cpia

Robert J Fensterheim, Executive Director

Composed of manufacturers, distributors, and users of chlorinated paraffins, used in lubricants, plastics and flame retardants.
Founded in 1970

4532 Chlorine Chemistry Division of the American Chemistry Counsil
1300 Wilson Blvd
Arlington, VA 22209-2323

703-741-5000
Fax: 703-741-6086
Home Page: www.americanchemistry.com/s_chlorine/index.asp

Calvin M. Dooley, President/CEO
Raymond J. O'Bryan, CFO & CAO
Robert J. Simon, Vice President, Chemical Products
Roger D. Bernstein, Vice President, State Affairs
Nacole B. Hinton, Managing Director

This division represents major producers and users of chlorine in North America, working to promote and protect the sustainability of chlorine chemsitry processes, products and applications in accordance with the Responsible Care initiative.

4533 Chlorine Free Products Association
1304 S Main St
Algonquin, IL 60102-2757

847-658-6104
Fax: 847-658-3152
E-Mail: info@chlorinefreeproducts.org
Home Page: www.chlorinefreeproducts.org

Archie Beaton, Executive Director

A nonprofit association that's primary purpose is to promote total chlorine free policies, programs and technologies throughtout the world.

4534 Chlorine Institute
1300 Wilson Blvd
Suite 525
Arlington, VA 22209

703-894-4140
Fax: 703-894-4130
E-Mail: info@cl2.com
Home Page: www.chlorineinstitute.org

Frankÿ Reiner, President
Henry Ward, VP, Emergency Preparedness
Terry Cirone, VP Health, Environment
Robyn Kinsley, Director, Transportation
Anna Belousovitch, Project Coordinator

Supports the chlo-alkali industry and serves the public by promoting the safe handling of chlorine and caustic materials.
204 Members
Founded in 1924

4535 Chlorobenzene Producers Association
1850 M St Nw
Suite 700
Washington, DC 20036-5810

202-721-4154
Fax: 202-296-8120
E-Mail: helmest@socma.com
Home Page: www.socma.com

C. Tucker Helmes PhD, Executive Director, SOCMA VISIONS

Addresses health and environmental issues in response to Environmental Protection Agency.
40 Members
Founded in 1979

4536 Color Pigments Manufacturers Association
300 N Washington St
Suite 105
Alexandria, VA 22314

703-684-4044
Fax: 703-684-1795
E-Mail: cpma@cpma.com
Home Page: www.pigments.org

J Lawrence Robinson, President

An industry trade association representing color pigment companies in Canada, Mexico and the US. Represents small, medium, and large color pigments manufacturers accounting for 95% of the production of color pigments in North America
50 Members
Founded in 1925

4537 Combustion Institute
5001 Baum Blvd
Suite 635
Pittsburgh, PA 15213-1851

412-687-1366
Fax: 412-687-0340
E-Mail: office@combustioninstitute.org
Home Page: www.combustioninstitute.org

Prof. Katrina Kohse-Hoinghaus, President
Prof. James F. Driscoll, VP, President Elect
Prof. Marcus Alden, Vice President Section Affairs
Prof. Reginald Mitchell, Secretary
Prof. Derek Dunn-Rankin, Treasurer

International organizaton with sections in several foreign countries including Canada. A non profit, educational organization with the purpose of promoting and disseminating knowledge in the field of combustion science.
4000 Members
Founded in 1954

4538 Consumer Specialty Products Association
1667 k street,NW
Suite 300
Washington, DC 20006

202-872-8110
Fax: 202-223-2636
E-Mail: info@cspa.org
Home Page: www.cspa.org
Social Media: LinkedIn, Flickr

Christopher Cathcart, President and CEO
Keith Fulk, Senior Vice President, Controller
Holly Schroeder SPHR, Director, Administrative Services
Phil Klein, Executive Vice President
Laura Madden, Director, Government Affairs

Supports all professionals involved in the manufacturer of chemical specialties.
Mailing list available for rent

4539 Consumer Specialty Products Association
1667 K Street, NW
Suite 300
Washington, DC 20006-2501

202-872-8110
Fax: 202-223-2636
E-Mail: info@cspa.org
Home Page: www.cspa.org
Social Media: LinkedIn, Flickr

Christopher Cathcart, President
Phil Klein, Executive Vice President
Colleen Creighton, Executive Director
Susan Little, Executive Director
Keith Fulk, Senior VP & Controller
Nonprofit organization composed of many companies involved in the formulation, manufacture, testing and marketing of chemical specialty products. Its line includes disinfectants that kill germs in homes, hospitals and restaurants, candles and fragrances that eliminate odors, pest management products for home and garden, cleaning products and much more.
200 Members
Founded in 1914

4540 Council for Chemical Research
1550 M St NW
Ste 1200
Washington, DC 20005-1703

202-429-3971
Fax: 202-429-3976
E-Mail: info@ccrhq.org
Home Page: www.ccrhq.org
Social Media: Facebook, LinkedIn

Dr. Marc Donohue, Chair
Dr. Eriv Lin, 1st Vice Chair
Dr. Jeffrey Reimer, 2nd Vice Chair
Dr. Seth W. Snyder, President
Dr. Kelly O. Sullivan, Treasurer

Promotes cooperation in basic research and encourage high quality education in the chemical sciences and engineering. Membership represents industry, academia, and government.
200 Members
Founded in 1980

4541 Council of Producers & Distributors of Agrotechnology
1730 Rhode Island Avenue
Suite 812
Washington, DC 20036

202-386-7407
Fax: 202-386-7409
Home Page: www.cpda.com

Dr Susan Ferenc, President
Diane Schute, Communications/Program Director
John Boling, Legislative Affairs
Dr. Michael White, Director, Regulatory

Affairs
Melvin A. Moore-Adams, Administrative Coordinator
The voice of the generic pesticide, inert, adjuvant and surfactant manufacturer, as well as crop protection product formulators and distributors on federal legislative and regulatory issues affecting the crop protection industry.
56 Members
Founded in 1975

4542 CropLife America
1156 15th St NW
Suite 400
Washington, DC 20005-1752
202-296-1585
Fax: 202-463-0474
E-Mail: webmaster@croplifeamerica.org
Home Page: www.croplifeamerica.org
Social Media: Facebook, Twitter, LinkedIn, Youtube
Jay Vroom, President and CEO
Beau Greenwood, Executive VP
Bill Kuckuck, Executive Vice President
Dr. Barbara Glenn, Senior Vice President, Science
Rachel Lattimore, Senior Vice President
A trade association of the manufacturers, formulators, and distributors of agricultural crop protection, pest control, and bitechnology products. Membership is composed of companies that produce, sell and distribute virtually all the active ingredients use in crop protection chemicals.
86 Members
Founded in 1933
Mailing list available for rent

4543 Drug, Chemical & Associated Technologies Association
1 Washington Blvd
Suite 7
Robbinsville, NJ 08691-3162
609-448-1000
800-640-3228
Fax: 609-448-1944
E-Mail: info@dcat.org
Home Page: www.dcat.org
Social Media: Facebook, LinkedIn
Lyra Myers, President
George Svokos, Senior VP & Annual Dinner Chair
Folker Ruchatz, Finance Officer
Milton Boyer, Vice President
Margaret M. Timony, Executive Director
The not for profit, member supported business development association whose membership is comprimsed of companies that manufacture, distribute or provide services to the pharmaceutical, chemical, nutritional and related industries.
350 Members
Founded in 1890

4544 Embalming Chemical Manufacturers
1370 Honeyspot Road Ext
Stratford, CT 06615-7115
Works to develop scientific, technological, and economic data about safety issues of the product.
Founded in 1951

4545 Emulsion Poylmers Council
1250 Connecticut Ave NW
Suite 700
Washington, DC 20036-2657
202-419-1500
Fax: 202-659-8037
E-Mail: epc@regnet.com
Home Page: www.regnet.com/epc/
Robert J Fensterheim, Executive Director
Represents regulatory professionals at companies which produce emulsion polymers, chemical compounds used in a variety of coating and other industril applications.
7 Members
Founded in 1995

4546 Ethylene Oxide Sterlization Association, Inc.
PO Box 33361
Washington, DC 20033
866-235-5030
Fax: 202-557-3836
E-Mail: eosainfo@eosa.org
Home Page: www.eosa.org
Randy Viscomi, President
Fenil Sutaria, Vice President
Dale Stucker, Treasurer
Chris Klosen, Secretary
EOSA is a non-profit organization that works to educate industry, regulators, and the public on the uses and benefits of ethylene oxide. EOSA also works to improve safety standards, foster industry communication, and provide a forum for issues related to ethylene oxide sterilization.
23 Members
Founded in 1995

4547 Federation of Analytical Chemistry and Spectroscopy Societies
2019 Galisteo St
Building I-1
Santa Fe, NM 87505
505-820-1648
Fax: 505-989-1073
E-Mail: facssc@facssc.org
Home Page: www.facss.org
Social Media: Facebook, Twitter, LinkedIn
Ian R. Lewis, Governing Board Chair 2012 and 2013
Greg Klunder, Governing Board Chair 2014 and 2015
Cindy Lilly, Executive Assistant
Christopher Palmer, Secretary 2009-2013
Mark Druy, Treasurer 2013 - 2015
Exists to combine many small meetings previously organized bythe individual societies into one joint meeting that covers the whole field of Analytical Chemistry.
12 Members
Founded in 1972

4548 Federation of Societies for Coatings Technology
527 Plymouth Rd
Plymouth Meetin, PA 19462-1641
610-940-0777
Fax: 610-940-0292
E-Mail: fsct@coatingstech.org
Home Page: www.coatingstech.org
Social Media: Facebook, Twitter, LinkedIn
Frederick H Walker, President
Rose A Ryntz, Secretary/Treasurer
John F Bartlett, VP
Provides technical education and professional development to its members and to the global industry through its multi-national constituent societies and collectively as a federation.
6000 Members
Founded in 1922

4549 Independent Liquid Terminals Association
1005 North Glebe Road
Suite 600
Arlington, VA 22201
703-875-2011
Fax: 703-875-2018
E-Mail: info@ilta.org
Home Page: www.ilta.org
Burton S. Russell, Chairman
Earl J. Crochet, Vice Chairman
Eric W. Thomas, Treasurer
David A. Ellis, Secretary
James F. Dugan, Director
Provides members with essential informational tools to facilitate regulatory compliance and improve operations, safety and environmental performance.
80 Members
Founded in 1974

4550 Independent Lubricant Manufacturers Association
400 N Columbus St
Suite 201
Alexandria, VA 22314
703-684-5574
Fax: 703-836-8503
E-Mail: ilma@ilma.org
Home Page: www.ilma.org
Celeste Powers, Executive Director
Martha Jolkovski, Associate Director
James A Taglia, President
Jay Covert, Publications Manager
Brenda Gillinson, Sr. Communications Manager
Supports all those involved in the US and international independent lubricant industry.
Founded in 1948

4551 Institute for Polyacrylate Absorbents
1850 M St NW
Suite 700
Washington, DC 20036
202-721-4100
Fax: 202-296-8120
Home Page: www.superabsorbents.com
C. Tucker Helmes, Executive Director
Represents manufacturers and users of absorbent polymers made of cross-linked polyacrylates and manufacturers and users of acrylic acid or its salts. It addreses the scientific, regulatory and related issues which are likely to impact the manufacture, use and disposal of fluid-absorbing polyacrylates.
Founded in 1985

4552 International Cadmium Association
9222 Jeffrey Road
Great Falls, VA 22066
703-759-7400
Fax: 703-759-7003
E-Mail: icdamorrow@aol.com
Home Page: www.cadmium.org
Hugh Morrow, Consultant
Provides marketing research and promotion to the industry. Hosts seperate annual meetings in the United States and Europe.
30 Members
Mailing list available for rent

4553 International Ozone Association: Pan American Group Branch
PO Box 28873
Scottsdale, AZ 28873
480-529-3787
Fax: 480-522-3080
E-Mail: infO3zone@io3a.org
Home Page: www.ioa-pag.org
Robert Jarnis, Executive Director
Represents the interests of environmental and other scientific communities, application engineers, users, and manufacturers of ozone generation and contacting equipment.
810 Members
Founded in 1973

4554 **Materials Technology Institute, Inc.**
1215 Fern Ridge Pkwy
Suite 206
St Louis, MO 63141

314-576-7712
Fax: 314-576-6078
E-Mail: mtiadmin@mti-global.org
Home Page: www.mtiproducts.org

James Macki, Executive Director
Deborah Ehret, Operations Director
Albert Krisher, President

Provides leadership in materials technology for chemical processing to improve reliability, profitability and safety.
52 Members
Founded in 1977

4555 **Methanol Institute**
124 South West Street
Suite 203
Alexandria, VA 22314

703-248-3636
Fax: 703-248-3997
E-Mail: MI@methanol.org
Home Page: www.methanol.org
Social Media: Facebook, Twitter, LinkedIn

Gregory A. Dolan, Executive Director; Americas/Europe
Dom LaVigne, Director of Gov & Public Affairs
Cliff Jackson, Manager Gov. & Public Affairs
Dr. Michael Quah, CEO
Larry Navin, Sr. Manager of External Affairs

Our mission is to expand markets for the use of methanol as a chemical commodity and an energy fuel.
35 Members
Founded in 1989

4556 **National Aerosol Association**
PO Box 5510
Fullerton, CA 92838

714-525-1518
Fax: 714-526-1295
E-Mail: NAA@nationalaerosol.com
Home Page: www.nationalaerosol.com

Mary Metzner, Executive Director
Larry Midtbo, Vice President

Individuals, firms and agencies engaged in the development, manufacture, packaging, sale or distribution of aerosol products.
30 Members
Founded in 1986

4557 **National Association of Chemical Recyclers**
1900 M Street NW
Washington, DC 20036

202-296-1725
Fax: 202-296-2530
E-Mail: 103612.514@compuserve.com

Christopher Goebel, Executive Director

Members are companies whose primary business is the reclamation of solvents and other chemicals from industrial waste streams and recycling.
Founded in 1979

4558 **National Chemical Credit Association**
1100 Main Street
Buffalo, NY 14209-2356

716-887-9527
Fax: 716-878-0479
E-Mail: robert.gagliardi@abc-amega.com
Home Page: www.ncca1.org

Don Peters, Contact
Pam Kelly, Executive Board Co-Chair
Mark Walker, Executive Board Co-Chair
Gordon Miller, Treasurer
Glenn Lifrieri, Member at Large

Members are major producers of basic chemicals and allied products.
100 Members
Founded in 1938

4559 **National Pest Management Association**
10460 North Street
Fairfax, VA 22030

703-352-6762
800-678-6722
Fax: 703-352-3031
Home Page: www.npmapestworld.org
Social Media: Facebook, Twitter

Enrique Iglesia, President
Bob Rosenberg, Eecutive Vice President
Gary McKenzie, CFO
Susan Pettit, Accounting Manager
Jean Neun, Executive Asst.

Represents the interests of its members and the structural pest control industry.
7000 Members
Frequency: October
Founded in 1933

4560 **North American Catalysis Society**
PO Box 80262
Wilmington, DE 19880

302-695-2488
Fax: 302-695-8347
E-Mail: michael.b.damore@usa.dupont.com
Home Page: www.nacatsoc.org

John N Armor, President
Gary B McVicker, VP
Umit S Ozkan, Secretary
John W Byrne, Treasurer

Fosters an interest in heterogeneous and homogeneous catalysis. Organizes national meetings. Members are chemists and chemical engineers engaged in the study and use of reactions involving catalysts. Publishes a newsletter.
1400 Members
Founded in 1956
Mailing list available for rent: 3400 names

4561 **Pine Chemicals Association**
PO Box 17136
Fernandina Beach, FL 32035

404-994-6267
Fax: 404-994-6267
E-Mail: wjones@pinechemicals.org
Home Page: www.pinechemicals.org

Charles Morris, President/COO
Gary Reed, Chairman/Board of Directors
Amanda Young, Executive Director
Alan Philips, Vice-Chairman
Lee Godina, Chairman & CEO

An association of producers, processors and consumers of pine chemicals. Promotes innovative, safe and environmentally responsible practices to assure a reliable supply of high quality products.
50 Members
Founded in 1947

4562 **Polyisocyanurate Insulation Manufacturers Association**
7315 Wisconsin Ave
Bethesda, MD 20814-3202

301-654-0000
Fax: 301-951-8401
E-Mail: pima@pima.org
Home Page: www.pima.org
Social Media: Facebook, Twitter

Renee Lamura, Director of Member Services
Jared O Blum, President

Represents the interests of polyisocyanurate manufacturers and suppliers to the industry. Efforts include education, environmental responsibility, government partnerships and energy conservation.
32 Members
Founded in 1970
Mailing list available for rent

4563 **Polyurethane Foam Association**
334 Lakeside Plz
Loudon, TN 37774

865-657-9840
Fax: 865-381-1292
E-Mail: rluedeka@pfa.org
Home Page: www.pfa.org

Pat Martin, Chairman
Robert Luedeka, Executive Director

Suppliers of raw material and equipment. Associate members are manufacturers of flexible polyurethane foam. Our mission is to educate customers and other groups about flexible polyurethane foam and promote its use in manufactured and industrial products. This includes providing facts on environmental, health and safety issues related to polyurethane foam to the membership of PFA, polyurethane foam users, regulatory officials, business leaders and the media.
63 Members
Founded in 1980

4564 **Powder Coating Institute**
PO Box 2112
Montgomery, TX 77356

936-597-5060
800-988-COAT
Fax: 936-597-5059
E-Mail: pci-info@powdercoating.org
Home Page: www.powdercoating.org

Dave Lurie, Executive Director
Chris Reding, President
Bob Allsop, Vice President
Tonya Farmer, Operations & Events Director
John Cole, Secretary/ treasurer

A trade association representing suppliers of powder coating materials, equipment, and related products and services in North America.
325 Members
Founded in 1981
Mailing list available for rent

4565 **Process Equipment Manufacturers Association**
201 Park Washington Ct
Falls Church, VA 22046

703-538-1796
Fax: 703-241-5603
E-Mail: info@pemanet.org
Home Page: www.pemanet.org

Susan A. Denston, Executive Director & Secretary
Harry W. Buzzerd, Management Counsel
Charlie Ingram, Treasurer
Chuck Weilbrenner, President
Jay Brown, Vice-President

Manufacturers and suppliers of equipment for food, chemical, pulp and paper, water, wastewater processing.
50 Members
Founded in 1960

4566 **Society of Chemical Manufacturers and Affiliates**
1850 M St Nw
Suite 700
Washington, DC 20036-5810

202-721-4100
Fax: 202-296-8120

E-Mail: info@socma.com
Home Page: www.socma.com

David Hurder, Chairman
Larry Sloan, President/ CEO
Dolores Alonso, Managing Director
Rebecca Dobbins, Sr. Manager
Reisa Tomlinson, Asst. Manager

Conducts workshops and seminars. Maintains a library on cancer policies and related subjects. Its member companies have more than 2,000 manufacturing sistes and 100,000 employees.
300 Members
Founded in 1921

4567 **Society of Cosmetic Chemists**
120 Wall St
Suite 2400
New York, NY 10005-4088

212-668-1500
Fax: 212-668-1504
E-Mail: scc@scconline.org
Home Page: www.scconline.org

Guy Padulo, President
Dawn Burke-Colvin, Vice President
David Smith, Executive Director
Dawn Thiel Glaser, Secretary
Peter Tsolis, Treasurer

Supports all those involved in working with and developing cosmetic chemicals.
4000 Members
Founded in 1948

4568 **Society of Toxicology**
1821 Michael Faraday Drive
Suite 300
Reston, VA 20190

703-438-3115
Fax: 703-438-3113
E-Mail: sothq@toxicology.org
Home Page: www.toxicology.org

Lois D. Lehman McKeeman, President

Members are scientists concerned with the effects of chemicals on man and the environment. Promotes the acquisition and utilization of knowledge in toxicology, aids in the protection of public health and facilitates disciplines. The society has a strong commitment to education in toxicology and to the recruitment of students and new members into the profession.
5000 Members
Founded in 1961

4569 **Spray Polyurethane Foam Alliance**
3827 Old Lee Hwy.
#101B
Fairfax, VA 22030

800-523-6154
Fax: 703-222-5816
E-Mail: info@sprayfoam.org
Home Page: www.sprayfoam.org

Robert Duke, President
Dennis Vandewater, Vice President
Peter Davis, Secretary/Treasurer
Bill Baley, Board Member
Mac Sheldon, Board Member

A trade association representing interests associated with rigid and semi-rigid polyurethane foam products that are typically applied with spray equipment as roofing and insulation.
Founded in 1987
Mailing list available for rent

4570 **The Electrochemical Society**
65 South Main St
Building D
Pennington, NJ 08534-2839

609-737-1902
Fax: 609-737-2743
E-Mail: esc@electrochem.org
Home Page: www.electrochem.org
Social Media: Twitter

Roque J Calvo, Executive Director
Mary E. Yess, Deputy Executive Director
Dinia Agarwala, Interface Production manager
Karen Chmielewski, Finance Associate
Paul B. Cooper, Editorial Manager

An international nonprofit, educational organization concerned with a broad range of phenomena relating to electrochemical and solid-state science and technology. The Electrochemical Society has scientists and engineers in over 70 countries worldwide who hold individual membership, as well as roughly 100 corporations and laboratories that hold corporate membership.
8000 Members
Founded in 1902

Newsletters

4571 **AAB Bulletin**
American Association of Bioanalysts
906 Olive Street
Suite 1200
Saint Louis, MO 63101-1448

314-241-1445
Fax: 314-241-1449
E-Mail: aab@aab.org
Home Page: www.aab.org

Mark S Biernbaum PhD, Administrator

Newsletter that provides the latest information on meetings, conferences, legislative and regulatory issues and developments.
Frequency: Quarterly
Founded in 1956

4572 **AACG Newsletter**
American Association for Crystal Growth
25 4th Street
Somerville, NJ 08876-3205

908-575-0649
Fax: 908-575-0794
E-Mail: aacg@att.net
Home Page: www.crystalgrowth.org

Candace Lynch, Chief Editor
Lara Keefer, Editor
Peter Schunemann, President
Robert Biefeld, Vice President

Technical articles and includes calendar of upcoming meetings.
Circulation: 600
ISSN: 1527-2389
Founded in 1966
Printed in 4 colors on glossy stock

4573 **AATCC News**
PO Box 12215
Research Triangle Park, NC 27709-2215

919-549-8141
800-360-5380
Fax: 919-549-8933
E-Mail: danielsj@aatcc.org
Home Page: www.aatcc.org
Social Media: Facebook, Twitter, LinkedIn

John Daniels, Executive VP
Debra Hibbard, Executive Assistant
Chris Leonard, Technical Director

Free, emailed newsletter providing up-to-date news and feature articles.
3000 Members

4574 **APE Newsletter**
Alkylphenols & Ethoxylates Research Council
1250 Connecticut Ave Nw
Suite 700
Washington, DC 20036-2657

202-419-1506
866-273-7262
Fax: 202-659-8037
E-Mail: angroup@regnet.com
Home Page: www.angroup.org

Robert J Fensterheim, Editor

4575 **Adhesion Society Newsletter**
Adhesion Society
2 Davidson Hall
Blacksburg, VA 24061-0001

540-231-7257
Fax: 540-231-3971
E-Mail: adhesoc@vt.edu
Home Page: www.adhesionsociety.org

Esther Brann, Manager

4576 **Advanced Coatings and Surface Technology**
John Wiley & Sons
111 River St
Hoboken, NJ 07030-5790

201-748-6000
Fax: 201-748-6088
E-Mail: info@wiley.com
Home Page: www.wiley.com

William J Pesce, CEO

Provides intelligence service reports and puts into perspective significant developments in coatings and surface modification across a broad range of industry lines. ACT interprets developments ranging from traditional coating processes to chemical vapor deposition and iron beam methods, which offers interdisciplinary analyses of those that have true commercial potential.
Cost: $530.00
10 Pages
Frequency: Monthly
Founded in 1807

4577 **Amber-Hi-Lites**
Rohm And Haas Company
100 S Independence Mall W
Suite 1A
Philadelphia, PA 19106-2399

215-592-3000
Fax: 215-592-3377
Home Page: www.rohmhaas.com

Raj L Gupta, CEO

Offers discussions of ion exchange resin use in fields of water conditioning.

4578 **Analytical Chemistry**
American Chemical Society
1155 16th St Nw
Suite 600
Washington, DC 20036-4892

202-872-4600
800-227-5558
Fax: 202-872-4615
E-Mail: service@acs.org
Home Page: www.acs.org

Madeleine Jacobs, CEO
Elizabeth Zubritsky, Manager

Information and news on the chemical industry.
Founded in 1876

4579 **Biochemistry**
American Chemical Society
1155 16th St Nw
Suite 600
Washington, DC 20036-4892

202-872-4600
800-333-9511
Fax: 202-872-4615

E-Mail: service@acs.org
Home Page: www.acs.org

Madeleine Jacobs, CEO

News and information for the scientific community.
Cost: $137.00
Frequency: Weekly
Founded in 1876

4580 ChemEcology
Chemical Manufacturers Association
1300 Wilson Boulevard
Arlington, VA 22209-2307

703-741-5502
Fax: 703-741-6807

Rebecca Swinehart, Editor

Issues on health, safety and the environment.

4581 ChemWeek Association
ChemWeek
110 William St
Suite 11
New York, NY 10038-3910

212-621-4900
Fax: 212-621-4800
E-Mail: ltattum@chemweek.com
Home Page: www.chemweek.com

John Rockwell, VP
Joe Mennella, Global Sales Director

Comprehensive coverage of the latest developments, uses, production, distribution, and manufacturing of chemicals for all industries.
Cost: $159.00
Frequency: Monthly
Circulation: 20779
Founded in 1977

4582 Chemical Bond
American Chemical Society
1155 16th St Nw
Suite 600
Washington, DC 20036-4892

202-872-4600
800-227-5558
Fax: 202-872-4615
E-Mail: service@acs.org
Home Page: www.acs.org

Madeleine Jacobs, CEO

Covers organization activities.

4583 Chemical Bulletin
American Chemical Society
Ste 312
1400 Renaissance Dr
Park Ridge, IL 60068-1336

847-647-8405
Fax: 847-647-8364
E-Mail: chicagoacs@ameritech.net
Home Page: www.chicagoacs.org

Gail Wilkening, Office Manager

Highlights events and meetings of local chapters, profiles prominent society members, and reports on research and technological advancements in the field.
Cost: $20.00
Frequency: Monthly
Circulation: 5700

4584 Chemical Economics Handbook Program
SRI Consulting
4300 Bohannon Dr
Suite 200
Menlo Park, CA 94025-1042

650-384-4300
Fax: 650-330-1190
Home Page: www.sriconsulting.com

John Pearson, President/CEO

Ongoing multiclient program focusing on the chemical and allied products industries. History, status and projected trends for hundreds of chemicals, chemical raw materials, and end-use products. Service includes access to on-line data base and client inquiry privileges.
Cost: $12000.00
Frequency: Monthly
Founded in 1946

4585 Chemical Industries Newsletter
SRI International
333 Ravenswood Ave
Menlo Park, CA 94025-3493

650-859-3711
Fax: 650-326-8916
Home Page: www.srifcu.org

Steve Bowles, President

Articles discuss the activities of SRI International Chemical Industries Centers.

4586 Chemical Industry Monitoring
Cyrus J Lawrence
1290 Avenue of the Americas
New York, NY 10006
Don Pattison, Editor

Prices and technological developments in the industry.

4587 Chemical Product News
US Dept. of Commerce, Business & Defense Service
200 Constitution Ave Nw
Washington, DC 20210-0001

202-693-5000
Fax: 202-219-8822
Home Page: www.dol.gov

Hilda L Solis, CEO

Offers information about chemical products and related issues.

4588 Chemical Regulation Reporter
Bureau of National Affairs
1801 S Bell St
Arlington, VA 22202-4501

703-341-3000
800-372-1033
Fax: 202-452-4084
E-Mail: customercare@bna.com
Home Page: www.bnabooks.com

Paul N Wojcik, Chairman

A notification and reference service consisting of six binders that comprehensively covers federal chemical regulations.
Cost: $1103.00
Frequency: Weekly
Founded in 1929

4589 Chemical and Engineering News
American Chemical Society
1155 16th St Nw
Suite 600
Washington, DC 20036-4892

202-872-4600
800-227-5558
Fax: 202-872-4615
E-Mail: service@acs.org
Home Page: www.acs.org

Madeleine Jacobs, CEO

Covers news relating to chemical engineering and technology.
Frequency: Weekly
Circulation: 137,664
ISSN: 0009-2347
Founded in 1876

4590 Chemweek's Business Daily
Chemical Week/Access Intelligence
110 William St
Suite 11
New York, NY 10038-3910

212-621-4900
Fax: 212-621-4800
E-Mail: ltattum@chemweek.com
Home Page: www.chemweek.com

John Rockwell, VP
Joe Minnella, Global Sales Manager

Daily electronic newsletter covering the latest chemical industry business and financial news, including markets, pricing, regulatory and security issues, research, technologies and new services.
Cost: $1049.00
Frequency: Daily
Founded in 2002
Printed in 4 colors

4591 Chlor-Alkali Marketwire
Chemical Week/Access Intelligence
110 William St
Suite 11
New York, NY 10038-3910

212-621-4900
Fax: 212-621-4800
E-Mail: ltattum@chemweek.com
Home Page: www.chemweek.com

John Rockwell, VP
Joe Mennella, Global Sales Director

Weekly electronic newsletter covering chlor-alkali market sector, including market trends in supply and demand, pricing fluctuations, production rates in caristic soda and chlorine. Also covers vinyls, soda ash and related derivatives
Cost: $1699.00
Frequency: Weekly
Founded in 2002
Printed in 4 colors

4592 Chlorine Institute Newsletter
Chlorine Institute
1300 Wilson Blvd
Arlington, VA 22209-2323

703-741-5760
Fax: 703-894-4130
E-Mail: aonna@cl2.com
Home Page: www.chlorineinstitute.org

Arthur Dungan, President

Articles featuring safe handling of chlorine and caustic materials.
5 Pages
Printed in 2 colors on matte stock

4593 Clinical & Forensic Toxicology News
1850 K St NW
Suite 625
Washington, DC 20006-2215

202-857-0717
800-892-1400
Fax: 202-887-5093
Home Page: www.aacc.org
Social Media: Facebook, Twitter, LinkedIn, YouTube

Greg rd Miller, President
Nancy Sasavage, Ph.D., Editor
Robert Dofour, Treasury

Online only newsletter provides practical and timely information on the clinical, forensic, technical, and regulatory issues faced by toxicology laboratories.

4594 Clinical Laboratory Strategies
1850 K St NW
Suite 625
Washington, DC 20006-2215

202-857-0717
800-892-1400
Fax: 202-887-5093
Home Page: www.aacc.org

Social Media: Facebook, Twitter, LinkedIn, YouTube

Richard Flaherty, VP
Penelope Jones, Director

Online newsletter for laboratory directors and managers gives strategic information on how to better manage the changes faced in jobs every day.

4595 Composites and Adhesives Newsletter
T/C Press
223 S Detroit Street
PO Box 36006
Los Angeles, CA 90036

323-938-7023
Fax: 323-938-6923
E-Mail: tcpress@msn.com

Mark Albert, Editor-In-Chief
Sherry Baranek, Senior Editor
Tom Beard, Senior VP
Lori Beckman, Managing Editor

News about composites and adhesives industry. Accepts very limited and selective advertising.
Cost: $190.00
20 Pages
Frequency: Quarterly
Circulation: 300
ISSN: 0888-1227
Founded in 1984

4596 Electronic Chemicals News
Chemical Week Associates
2 Grand Central Tower
140 E. 45th St., 40th Floor
New York, NY 10017

212-884-9528
Fax: 212-884-9514
E-Mail: lyn.tattum@ihs.com
Home Page: www.chemweek.com

Lyn Tattum, Publisher & Director
Natasha Alperowicz, Executive Editor

Written for and about the chemicals industry and contains industry developments, environmental news, new products, and financial and corporate briefs.
Cost: $699.00

4597 Government Affairs Update
American Association for Clinical Chemistry
1850 K St NW
Suite 625
Washington, DC 20006-2215

202-857-0717
800-892-1400
Fax: 202-887-5093
Home Page: www.ashrae.org
Social Media: Facebook, Twitter, LinkedIn, YouTube

Richard Flaherty, VP
Penelope Jones, Director

Online government affairs newsletter presents a comprehensive summary of legislative and government news that affect clinical labs and manufacturers.

4598 ILTA Newsletter
Independent Liquid Terminals Association
1444 I St Nw
Suite 400
Washington, DC 20005-6538

202-842-9200
Fax: 202-326-8660
E-Mail: info@ilta.org
Home Page: www.ilta.org

E David Doane, President

International trade association representing bulk liquid terminal companies that store commercial liquids in aboveground storage tanks and transfer products to and from oceangoing tank ships, tank barges, pipelines, tank trucks, and tank rail cars.
Frequency: Monthly
Circulation: 1200
Founded in 1974
Printed in 2 colors on matte stock

4599 Inside R&D
John Wiley & Sons
111 River St
Hoboken, NJ 07030-5790

201-748-6000
Fax: 201-748-6088
E-Mail: info@wiley.com
Home Page: www.wiley.com

William J Pesce, CEO

Weekly service offering information about current research and development, concentrating on new and significant developments that create new products/markets in the near-term and this are valuable to a company's bottom line.
Cost: $790.00
6 Pages
Frequency: Weekly
Founded in 1807
Mailing list available for rent

4600 Langmuir: QTL Biosystems
American Chemical Society
1322 Pouseo de Peralta
Santa Fe, NM 87501

505-989-1907
Fax: 505-989-1979
E-Mail: service@acs.org
Home Page: www.pubs.acs.org

David Whitten PhD, Editor

Edited for an audience involved with high-vacuum surface chemistry and spectroscopy, heterogeneous catalysis, all aspects of interface chemistry involving fluid interfaces and disperse systems.
Frequency: BiWeekly
Circulation: 1,200

4601 North American Catalysis Society Newsletter
PO Box 80262
Wilmington, DE 19880-262

302-695-2488
Fax: 302-695-8347
E-Mail: michael.b.damore@usa.dupont.com
Home Page: www.nacatsoc.org

Michael B D Amore, Editor
John N Armor, President
Gary McVicker, VP

Fosters an interest in heterogeneous and homogeneous catalysis. Organizes national meetings. Members are chemists and chemical engineers engaged in the study and use of reactions involving catalysts.
Cost: $45.00
38448 Pages
Frequency: Monthly
Founded in 1956
Mailing list available for rent: 3,500 names at $160 per M

4602 Pine Chemicals Association Newsletter
3350 Riverwood Parkway SE
Suite 1900
Atlanta, GA 30339

770-984-5340
Fax: 404-994-6267
E-Mail: wjones@pinechemicals.org
Home Page: www.pinechemicals.org

Walter L Jones, President/COO
Gary Reed, Chairman/Board of Directors

An association of producers, processors and consumers of pine chemicals. Promotes innovative, safe and environmentally responsible practices to assure a reliable supply of high quality products.
Frequency: Quarterly

4603 SOCMA Newsletter
Synthetic Organic Chemical Manufacturers Assn
1850 M St Nw
Suite 700
Washington, DC 20036-5803

202-721-4100
Fax: 202-296-8120
E-Mail: info@socma.com
Home Page: www.socma.com

Joseph Acker, President
Vivian Diko, Executive Assistant & CEO
Liesa Brown, Editor/Marketing/Communications

Offers information on the organic chemical industry.
10 Pages
Frequency: Bi-monthly
Founded in 1921

Magazines & Journals

4604 AATCC Review Journal
PO Box 12215
Research Triangle Park, NC 27709-2215

919-549-8141
800-360-5380
Fax: 919-549-8933
E-Mail: danielsj@aatcc.org
Home Page: www.aatcc.org
Social Media: Facebook, Twitter, LinkedIn

John Daniels, Executive VP
Debra Hibbard, Executive Assistant
Charles E Gavin, Treasurer
Chris Shaw, Advertising Sales

Covers fibers to finished products, and chemical synthesis to retail practices.
3000 Members

4605 AICHE Journal
American Institute of Chemical Engineers
3 Park Ave
New York, NY 10016-5991

212-591-7338
800-242-4363
Fax: 212-591-8888
E-Mail: CustomerService@aiche.org
Home Page: www.aiche.org
Social Media: Facebook, Twitter, LinkedIn

June Wispelway, Executive Director
Steve Smith, Publications Director
Bette Lawler, Director of Operations
Neil Yeoman, Treasurer

Serves as a journal emcompassing data and results of the latest information in significant research and trends in the field.
Cost: $1250.00
Frequency: Monthly
ISSN: 0001-1541
Founded in 1908

4606 Accounts of Chemical Research
American Chemical Society
1155 16th St NW
Suite 600
Washington, DC 20036-4892

202-872-4600
800-227-5558
Fax: 202-872-4615
E-Mail: service@acs.org
Home Page: www.acs.org

Madeleine Jacobs, CEO

Chemical research and statistical information.
Cost: $526.00
Frequency: Monthly
Circulation: 159,000
Founded in 1968

4607 Advanced Coatings and Surface Technology
605 3rd Avenue
9th Floor
New York, NY 10158
212-850-6824
Fax: 212-850-8643

4608 American Laboratory
International Scientific Communications
395 Oyster Pint Blvd.
#321
South San Francisco, CA 94080
650-243-5600
E-Mail: info@americanlaboratory.com
Home Page: www.americanlaboratory.com
Brian Howard, Editor-In-Chief
Robert G Sweeny, Publisher
Donna Frankel, Directetor Of Editorial
Susan Messinger, Managing Editor
American Laboratory serves industry, university, government, independent and foundation research laboratories.
50 Pages
Frequency: Monthly
Circulation: 91611
ISSN: 0044-7749
Founded in 1969
Printed in 4 colors on glossy stock

4609 An Energy Efficient Solution
Alliance for Responsible Atmoshperic Policy
2111 Wilson Blvd
Suite 850
Arlington, VA 22201-3001
703-243-0344
Fax: 703-243-2874
E-Mail: info@arap.org
Home Page: www.arap.org
David Stirpe, Executive Director

4610 Asia Pacific Chemicals
Reed Chemical Publications
360 Park Avenue South
10th Floor
New York, NY 10010
713-525-2613
888-525-3255
E-Mail: jlucas@chemexpo.com
Home Page: www.reedchemicals.com
Stanley F Reed
Bernard Petersen, Sales Manager
Karen Yanard, Sales Executive
Alan Taylor, Editor

4611 Asian Chemical News
Reed Chemical Publications
360 Park Avenue South
10th Floor
New York, NY 10010
212-791-4208
888-525-3255
E-Mail: csc@icis.com
Home Page: www.reedchemicals.com
Stanley F Reed
Bernard Petersen, Sales Manager
Karen Yanard, Sales Executive
Alan Taylor, Editor

4612 CPI Purchasing
Reed Business Information
2000 Clearwater Dr
Oak Brook, IL 60523-8809
630-574-0825
Fax: 630-288-8781
E-Mail: k.doyle@reedbusiness.com
Home Page: www.reedbusiness.com
Jeff Greisch, President
Kathy Doyle, Publisher
Trade magazine for purchasing professionals in the chemical/process industry. Accepts advertising.
Cost: $74.95
100 Pages
Circulation: 95078
Founded in 1983

4613 Cereal Chemistry
American Association of Cereal Chemists
3340 Pilot Knob Rd
Eagan, MN 55121-2055
651-454-7250
Fax: 651-454-0766
E-Mail: akohn@scisoc.org
Home Page: www.mbaa.com
Mary Ellen Camire, President
Bernie Bruinsma, Chair of Board
Laura Hansen, Treasurer
Cereal chemistry explores raw materials, processes and products utulizing cereal.
Cost: $79.00
Frequency: Bi-Monthly
ISSN: 0009-0352

4614 Chemical Engineering
Chemical Week Associates
2 Grand Central Tower
140 East 45th Street,40th Floor
New York, NY 10017
212-884-9528
Fax: 212-884-9514
E-Mail: ltattum@chemweek.com
Home Page: www.chemweek.com
Lyn Tattum, Publisher/Director
Robert Westervelt, Editor-In-Chief
Highlights include a calendar of related trade shows, new products listings, operations and maintenance techniques and marketing services ideas.
Cost: $59.00
Frequency: Monthly
Circulation: 69000
ISSN: 0009-2460
Founded in 1902
Printed in 4 colors on glossy stock

4615 Chemical Engineering Progress
American Institute of Chemical Engineers
3 Park Ave
New York, NY 10016-5991
203-702-7660
800-242-4363
Fax: 203-775-5177
E-Mail: CustomerService@aiche.org
Home Page: www.aiche.org
June Wispelwey, Executive Director
Marty Clancy, Director Membership/Cust. Service
Offers updated information for chemical engineers.
Cost: $245.00
Frequency: Quarterly
Founded in 1908

4616 Chemical Equipment
Reed Business Information
301 Gibraltar Drive
PO Box 650
Morris Plains, NJ 07950-650
973-920-7000
Fax: 973-539-3476
E-Mail: privacymanager@reedbusiness.com
Home Page: www.reedbusiness.com
Bud Ramsey, Publisher
Geoffery Bridgman, Editor
Gerard Van de Aast, CEO/President
Chemical Equipment is for engineers, plant management personnel, maintenance engineering and others concerned with design, building, engineering, operating and maintaining chemical process plants.
Frequency: Monthly
Circulation: 106032
Founded in 1959

4617 Chemical Equipment Literature Review
Reed Business Information
St 600
Rockaway
New Jersey, NJ 07866
973-920-7000
800-222-0289
Fax: 973-920-7531
E-Mail: plundy@reedbusiness.com
Home Page: www.chemicalequipment.com
Geoff Bridgman, Editor
Gail Kirberger, Circulation Manager
Patrick Lundy, Publisher
Covers reviews of new catalogs and brochures on products for the chemical industry.
8 Pages
Frequency: Monthly
Circulation: 106038
Founded in 1985

4618 Chemical Heritage
Chemical Heritage Foundation
315 Chestnut St
Philadelphia, PA 19106-2793
215-925-2222
Fax: 215-925-1954
E-Mail: info@chemheritage.org
Home Page: www.chemheritage.org
Michal Meyer, Editor
Dedicated to sharing the story chemistry and related sciences, technologies, and industries.
48 Pages
Circulation: 25000
ISSN: 0736-4555

4619 Chemical Intelligencer
Springer Verlag
233 Spring St
Suite 6
New York, NY 10013-1578
212-460-1500
800-777-4643
Fax: 212-460-1575
E-Mail: serviceny@springer.com
Home Page: www.springer.com
William Curtis, President
Written for the scientist interested in the history and culture of chemistry. Includes articles and essays that develop and comment on the current directions and concerns in chemistry, new discoveries and experiments as well as present trends and opportunities in chemistry, philosophy and education.
Cost: $79.00
Frequency: Quarterly
Circulation: 1,000

4620 Chemical Management Review
Reed Chemical Publications
2 Wall St
26th Floor, Suite 13
New York, NY 10005-2044
212-732-3200
Fax: 212-791-4311
E-Mail:

helga.tilton@chemicalmarketreporter.com
Home Page: www.reedchemicals.com

Stanley F Reed
Helga Tilton, Editor
Keith Jones, CEO/President
Jane Burgess, Marketing

Provides information for senior managers in the chemical industry and other industrial markets.
Cost: $195.00
Frequency: Monthly
Founded in 1871
Printed in 4 colors on glossy stock

4621 Chemical Market Reporter
Schnell Publishing Company
2 Rector St
26th Floor
New York, NY 10006-1819

212-791-4267
Fax: 212-791-4321
E-Mail: editor@chemexpo.com
Home Page: www.chemexpo.com

James Hannan, Publisher
Helga Tilton, Editor in Chief

Regular issue highlights include news of the week, coverage of pertinent industry trade shows/meetings, a review of new materials, and periodic insight reports on segments of the industry.
Cost: $109.00
Frequency: Weekly
Circulation: 14714

4622 Chemical Processing
Putman Media
555 W Pierce Rd
Suite 301
Itasca, IL 60143-2626

630-467-1300
Fax: 630-467-0197
E-Mail: chemicalprocessing@putman.net
Home Page: www.putman.net

Mark Rosenzweig, Editor-in-Chief
Amanda Joshi, Managing Editor

Carries technical overview and case history articles presented in a problem-solving environment geared to operations, engineering and R&D management. Topics include instrumentation, pumping, corrosion, heat transfer, mixing and energy conservation. Accepts advertising.
60 Pages
Frequency: Monthly
Circulation: 55000
ISSN: 0009-2630
Founded in 1938
Printed in 4 colors

4623 Chemical Times & Trends
Allen Press
900 17th St NW
Washington, DC 20006-2106

202-872-8110
Fax: 202-872-8114
E-Mail: info@cspa.org
Home Page: www.cspa.org

Christopher Cathcart, President
Keith Fulk, Vice President & Controller

Editorial focus emphasizes trends in legislation, industry events, packaging topics, and marketing concepts.
Cost: $27.00
Frequency: Quarterly
Circulation: 7000
Founded in 1935

4624 Chemist
American Institute of Chemists
315 Chestnut St
Suite 420
Philadelphia, PA 19106-2702

215-873-8224
Fax: 215-925-1954
E-Mail: info@theaic.org
Home Page: www.theaic.org

Davidah Manuta, President
Ray Mcafel, President-Elect
Jerry d Jasinski, Chair

Topics of professional, economic, social and legislative interest to individual chemists or chemical engineers.
Cost: $35.00
32 Pages
Frequency: Quarterly
Circulation: 5000
Founded in 1923

4625 Chemistry Research in Technology
American Chemical Society
1155 16th St NW
Suite 600
Washington, DC 20036-4892

202-872-4600
800-227-5558
Fax: 202-872-4615
E-Mail: service@acs.org
Home Page: www.acs.org

Madeleine Jacobs, CEO/Executive Director
Elizabeth Zubritsky, Manager

Information and research summaries of the latest in the chemical industry.
Cost: $49.00
Frequency: 1 Year 3 Issues
Founded in 1876

4626 Clinical Chemistry
1850 K St NW
Suite 625
Washington, DC 20006-2215

202-857-0717
800-892-1400
Fax: 202-887-5093
Home Page: www.aacc.org
Social Media: Facebook, Twitter, LinkedIn, YouTube

Nadar Rifai, Editor-In-Chief
Tom Annesley, Deputy Editor
James Boyd, Deputy Editor

The leading forum for peer-reviewed, original research on innovative practices in today's clinical laboratory.

4627 Clinical Laboratory News
1850 K St NW
Suite 625
Washington, DC 20006-2215

202-857-0717
800-892-1400
Fax: 202-887-5093
Home Page: www.aacc.org
Social Media: Facebook, Twitter, LinkedIn, YouTube

Robert Christenson, President
Dennis Dietzen, Director
Elizabeth Frank, Secretary

News magazine that is the authoritative source for timely analysis of issues and trends affecting clinical laboratorians and clinical laboratories.
Founded in 1948

4628 Coatings World
Rodman Publishing
70 Hilltop Rd
3rd Floor, Suite 3000
Ramsey, NJ 07446-1150

201-825-2552
Fax: 201-825-0553
E-Mail: info@rodpub.com
Home Page: www.nutraceuticalsworld.com

Rodman Zilenziger Jr, President
Matt Montgomery, VP

Cutting edge technical information and the most advanced and pertinent management and distribution techniques.
Frequency: 10 issues per y
Circulation: 17000
Founded in 1964

4629 Combustion and Flame
Combustion Institute
5001 Baum Blvd.
Suite 635
Pittsburgh, PA 15213-1851

412-687-1366
Fax: 412-687-0340
E-Mail: office@combustioninstitute.org
Home Page: www.combustioninstitute.org

Barbara Waronek, Executive Administrator
Prof. Katherine Kohs-Hosinghaus, President
Derek Dunn-Rankin, Treasurer

A monthly publication that focuses on combustion phenomena and related topics.
6000 Members
Frequency: Monthly
Founded in 1954

4630 Compoundings Magazine
Independent Lubricant Manufacturers Association
651 S Washington Street
Alexandria, VA 22314

703-684-5574
Fax: 703-836-8503
E-Mail: ilma@ilma.org
Home Page: www.ilma.org

Tom Osborne, Editor
Martha Jolkovski, Director Publications & Advertising
Carla Mangone, Managing Editor

Association and marketing news, meetings and programs, as well as employment and business opportunities to the US and international independent lubricant industry.
Cost: $150.00
Frequency: Monthly
Circulation: 2050
ISSN: 1042-508X
Founded in 1948
Printed in 4 colors on glossy stock

4631 Energy Process
American Institute of Chemical Engineers
3 Park Ave
New York, NY 10016-5991

212-591-7338
800-242-4363
Fax: 212-591-8888
Home Page: www.aiche.org

John Sofranko, Executive Director

Offers updated information for chemical engineers.
Cost: $20.00
Frequency: Quarterly

4632 European Chemical News
Reed Chemical Publications
Wall St
26th Floor, Suite 13
New York, NY 10005-2044

212-732-3200
Fax: 212-791-4311
E-Mail: jonathan.sismey@icis.com
Home Page: www.europeanchemicalnews.com

Stanley F Reed
Simon Platt, Director

Christopher Flook, Managing Director
Cost: $711.00
Frequency: Weekly
Circulation: 14112

4633 **European Journal of Clinical Chemistry and Clinical Biochemistry**
Walter De Gruyter
200 Saw Mill Road
Hawthorne, NY 1052

Home Page: journalseek.net/

Water De Gruyler, Editor

Up-to-date information on the chemistry industry.
Frequency: Monthly

4634 **HAPPI Household and Personal Products Industry**
Rodman Publishing
70 Hilltop Rd
3rd Floor
Ramsey, NJ 07446-1150

201-825-2552
Fax: 201-825-0553
E-Mail: info@rodpub.com
Home Page: www.nutraceuticalsworld.com

Rodman Zilenziger Jr, President
Matt Montgomery, VP

Highlights current developments, marketing, production, formulations, technical innovations, packaging, and management problems. Includes in-depth news on developments abroad as well as in the United States.
Cost: $52.00
Frequency: Monthly
Circulation: 140000
Founded in 1964

4635 **I&EC Research**
American Chemical Society
1155 16th St NW
Suite 600
Washington, DC 20036-4892

202-872-4600
800-227-5558
Fax: 202-872-4615
E-Mail: service@acs.org
Home Page: www.acs.org

Madeleine Jacobs, CEO/Executive Director

Offers information and statistical updates for chemists.
Circulation: 4600
Founded in 1876

4636 **Industrial & Engineering Chemistry Research**
American Chemical Society
1155 16th St NW
Suite 600
Washington, DC 20036-4892

202-872-4600
800-227-5558
Fax: 202-872-4615
E-Mail: help@acs.org
Home Page: www.acs.org

Madeleine Jacobs, CEO/Executive Director
Judith Benham, Chair
Elizabeth Zubritsky, Manager

Features fundamental research, design methods, process design and development, product research and development for chemists and chemical engineers.
Circulation: 4600
Founded in 1876

4637 **Inform**
American Oil Chemists' Society
2710 S Boulder
Urbana, IL 61802-6996

217-359-2344
Fax: 217-351-8091
E-Mail: keine@aocs.org
Home Page: www.aocs.org

Lori Stewart, Publications Director
Kimmy Farris, Production Editor
Kethy Heine, Managing Editor
Patrick Donnelly, CEO

A member benefit that provides international news on fats, oils, surfactants, detergents, and related materials.
Cost: $175.00
100 Pages
Frequency: Monthly
Circulation: 4500
ISSN: 0897-8026
Founded in 1990
Printed in 4 colors on glossy stock

4638 **International Laboratory**
International Scientific Communications
PO Box 870
Shelton, CT 06484-0870

203-926-9300
Fax: 203-926-9310
E-Mail: webmaster@iscpubs.com
Home Page: www.iscpubs.com/

Brian Howard, Publisher
Robert G Sweeney, Publisher

International Laboratory serves the industry, universities, government, independent and foundation research laboratories.
50 Pages
Circulation: 50036
ISSN: 0010-2164
Founded in 1971
Printed in 4 colors on glossy stock

4639 **International Laboratory Pacific Rim Edition**
International Scientific Communications
PO Box 870
Shelton, CT 06484-0870

203-926-9300
Fax: 203-926-9310
E-Mail: webmaster@iscpubs.com
Home Page: www.iscpubs.com

Brian Howard, Publisher
Robert G Sweeney, Publisher

Edited for chemists and biologists throughout Far East Asia and Australia who have a professional interest in various aspects of modern laboratory practice and basic research.
40 Pages
Founded in 1986

4640 **Journal of AOAC International**
AOAC International
481 N Frederick Ave
Suite 500
Gaithersburg, MD 20877-2450

301-924-7078
800-379-2622
Fax: 301-924-7089
E-Mail: aoac@aoac.org
Home Page: www.aoac.org

James Bradford, Executive Director

Publishes fully refereed contributed papers in the fields of chemical and biological analysis: on original research on new techniques and applications, collaborative studies, authentic data of composition, studies leading to method development, meeting symposia, newly adopted AOAC approved methods and invited reviews.
Cost: $98.00

4641 **Journal of Analytical Toxicology**
Preston Publications
6600 W Touhy Ave
PO Box 48312
Niles, IL 60714-4516

847-647-2900
Fax: 847-647-1155
E-Mail: circulation@jatox.com
Home Page: www.prestonpub.com

Tinsley Preston, Owner
Dr. Bruce A. Goldberger, Editor
Maria Tamacho, Circulation Manager

An international publication for toxicologists, pathologists, analytical chemists, researchers, educators and others. Dedicated to the isolation, indentification, and quantification of potentially toxic substances. Emphasis is on the practical applications for use in clinical, forensic, industrial, and other toxicology laboratories, drug abuse testing, therapeutic drug monitoring, and environmental pollution. Includes new products and litrature, meetings and short courses.
Cost: $475.00
Frequency: 8 issues per ye
Circulation: 1148
Founded in 1977
Mailing list available for rent: 9939 names at $125 per M

4642 **Journal of Biological Chemistry**
9650 Rockville Pike
Suite 300
Bethesda, MD 20814-3999

301-530-7150
Fax: 301-634-7126
E-Mail: publicaffairs@asbmb.org
Home Page: www.asbmb.org

Herbert Taber, Editor
Barbara Gordon, Executive Director

Features research papers on biochemistry and molecular biology and other articles of interest to the professional.
Frequency: TriAnnual

4643 **Journal of Chemical Education**
Division of Chemical Education
Department of Chemistry
University of Georgia
Athens, GA 30602-2556

706-542-6559
Fax: 706-542-9454
E-Mail: norbert-pienta@jce.acs.org
Home Page: www.pubs.acs.orgorg
Social Media: Facebook, Twitter

Norbert J Oienta, Editor-in-Chief
Renee S. Cole, Associate Editor

Provides information about and examples of teaching techniques for classroom and laboratory, curricular innovations, chemistry content, and chemical education research.
Cost: $45.00
136 Pages
Frequency: Monthly
ISSN: 0021-9584
Founded in 1924
Printed in on glossy stock

4644 **Journal of Chemical Information & Computer Sciences**
American Chemical Society
1155 16th St NW
Suite 600
Washington, DC 20036-4892

202-872-4600
800-227-5558
Fax: 202-872-4615
E-Mail: service@acs.org
Home Page: www.acs.org

Madeleine Jacobs, CEO/Executive Director
George A. Milne, Editor

Offers the latest technological information and news directed at the chemical industry.
Cost: $27.00
Frequency: Bi-Monthly

4645 Journal of Chemical Physics
American Institute of Physics
2 Huntington Quadrangle
Suite 101
Melville, NY 11747-4502

516-576-2200
Fax: 516-349-7669
E-Mail: jcp@aip.org
Home Page: www.aip.org

H. Frederick Dylia, Executive Director/CEO
Darlene Walters, Senior VP
John Haynes, VP Publishing

Targets both chemists and physicists involved in research and applications of chemical physics technology.
Frequency: Weekly
Circulation: 5,000

4646 Journal of Chemical and Engineering Data
American Chemical Society
180 Fitzpatrick Hall
University of Notre Dame
Notre Dame, IN 46556

574-631-1149
Fax: 516-349-9704
E-Mail: squarles@aip.org
Home Page: www.aip.org

Joan F. Brennecke, Ph.D., Editor
Marc Brodsky, CEO

Offers the latest updates and new information in the chemical industry.
Cost: $458.00
Frequency: Weekly
Circulation: 5000
Founded in 1931

4647 Journal of Chromatographic Science
Preston Publications
6600 W Touhy Ave
Niles, IL 60714-4516

847-647-2900
Fax: 847-647-1155
E-Mail: tpreston@prestonpub.com
Home Page: www.prestonpub.com

Tinsley Preston, Owner
Kevin Bailey, Managing Editor
Janice Gordon, Director Marketing

An international publication for scientists, analytical chemists, researchers, educators, and other allied to the field. Provides in depth information about analytical techniques, applications, sample preparation methods, systems problem solving, etc. Articles cover more practical information on all types of separations—gas, liquid, thin layer, supercritical fluid, electrophoresis, spectrometry, hyphenated methods, etc. any other single source. Also problem solving/troubleshooting answers.
Cost: $405.00
Frequency: Monthly
Circulation: 1000
Founded in 1961

4648 Journal of Colloid & Interface Science
Academic Press
525 B St
Suite 1900
San Diego, CA 92101-4401

619-235-6336
800-321-5068
Fax: 619-699-6280
Home Page: www.aceparking.com

D.T. Wasan, Editor-in-Chief
Claudia Romas, Publisher

Presents chemical and physiochemical aspects of theory and practice of colloids.
Cost: $883.00
Frequency: Monthly
Circulation: 2000
Founded in 1885

4649 Journal of Medicinal Chemistry
American Chemical Society
1155 16th St NW
Suite 600
Washington, DC 20036-4892

202-872-4600
800-227-5558
Fax: 202-872-4615
E-Mail: service@acs.org
Home Page: www.acs.org

Madeleine Jacobs, CEO/Executive Director

Information on the chemistry industry, dealing with aspects directly pertaining to the medical profession.
Founded in 1876

4650 Journal of Organic Chemistry
American Chemical Society
1155 16th St NW
Washington, DC 20036-4892

202-872-4600
800-227-5558
Fax: 202-872-4615
E-Mail: service@acs.org
Home Page: www.acs.org

Madeleine Jacobs, CEO/Executive Director

Areas emphasized are the multiple facets of organic reactions, natural products, studies of mechanism, theoretical organic chemistry and the various aspects of spectroscopy related to organic chemistry.
Cost: $1260.00
Frequency: BiWeekly
Circulation: 8,500

4651 Journal of Physical Chemistry
American Chemical Society
GA Institute of Technology
Boggs Building
Atlanta, GA 30332

404-894-0293
800-227-5558
Fax: 404-894-0294
E-Mail: jphyschm@chemistry.gatech
Home Page: www.pubs.acs.org

Mostafa A El-Sayed, Editor

Reports on both experimental and theoretical research dealing with the fundamental aspects of physical chemistry and chemical physics.
Frequency: Weekly
Circulation: 3774

4652 Journal of Society of Cosmetic Chemists
Society of Cosmetic Chemists
120 Wall St
Suite 2400
New York, NY 10005-4088

212-668-1500
Fax: 212-668-1504
E-Mail: societycoschem@worldnet.att.net
Home Page: www.scconline.org

Theresa Cesario, Administrator
Mindy Goldstein, Journal Editor
Doreen Scelso, Publication Coordinator

Features highlight new products, processing techniques, safety issues, and pharmacological features.
Cost: $200.00
Circulation: 4200
Founded in 1945

4653 Journal of Surfactants and Detergents
AOCS Press
12024 Vista Parke Drive
PO Box 200135
Austin, TX 78720-0135

512-331-2441
Fax: 512-331-2387
E-Mail: mfcox@cvcnet.com

Michael F Cox, Editor-in-Chief

Reports on the development and performance of surfactants in all areas, from household detergents to industrial uses, as well as on the development and manufacture of other detergent ingredients and their formulation into finished products.
Cost: $85.00
Frequency: Quarterly
Circulation: 1,500

4654 Journal of the American Chemical Society
American Chemical Society
1155 16th St NW
Suite 600
Washington, DC 20036-4892

202-872-4600
800-227-5558
Fax: 202-872-4615
E-Mail: service@acs.org
Home Page: www.acs.org

Madeleine Jacobs, CEO/Executive Director

Association news, member information and chemical industry information.
Cost: $125.00
Frequency: Weekly

4655 Journal of the American Leather Chemists Association
American Leather Chemists Association
1314 50th Street
Suite 103
Lubbock, TX 79412

806-744-1798
Fax: 806-744-1785
E-Mail: alca@leatherchemists.org
Home Page: www.leatherchemists.org

Carol Adcock, Executive Secretary
Cost: $175.00
Frequency: Monthly
Circulation: 500

4656 Journal of the Electrochemical Society
Electrochemical Society
65 S Main St
Building D
Pennington, NJ 08534-2839

609-737-1902
Fax: 609-737-2743
E-Mail: ecs@electrochem.org
Home Page: www.electrochem.org

Roque J. Calvo, Executive Director
Annie Goedkoop, Publications Director
Paul B. Cooper, Editorial Manager

Leader in the field of solid-state and electrochemical science and technology. This peer-reviewed journal publishes an average of 450 pages of 70 articles each month. Articles are posted online, with a monthly paper edition following electronic publication. The ECS membership benefits package includes access to the electronic edition of this journal.
450 Pages
Frequency: Monthly
ISSN: 0013-4651

4657 LCGC North America
Advanstar Communications

Woodbridge Corporate Plaza
485 Route 1 S, Building F
Iselin, NJ 08830

732-225-9500
Fax: 732-225-0211
E-Mail: lcgcedit@lcgcmag.com
Home Page: www.lcgcmag.com/lcgc/
Social Media: Facebook

David Esola, VP/General Manager
Michael Tessalone, Group Publisher
Tria Deibert, Marketing Director

Includes product and literature reports along with meeting and seminar listings.
Cost: $67.00
100 Pages
Frequency: Monthly
Circulation: 56000
Founded in 1987
Mailing list available for rent: 47,543 names at $155 per M
Printed in 4 colors on glossy stock

4658 **Laboratorio y Analisis**
Keller International Publishing Corporation
150 Great Neck Rd
Suite 400
Great Neck, NY 11021-3309

516-829-9210
Fax: 516-829-9306
Home Page: www.supplychainbrain.com

Terry Beirne, Publisher
Bryan DeLuca, Editor
Jerry Keller, President
Mary Chavez, Director of Sales

4659 **Lipids**
American Oil Chemists' Society
2710 S Boulder
Urbana, IL 61802-6996

217-359-2344
Fax: 217-351-8091
E-Mail: general@aocs.org
Home Page: www.aocs.org

Jody Schonfeld, Publications Director
Pam Landman, Journals Coordinator
Kimmy Farris, Production Editor
Lori Stewart, Books and Publications
Jenna Tatar, Customer Service

Scientific journal features full-length original research articles, short communications, methods papers and review articles on timely topics. All papers are meticulously peer-reviewed and edited by some of the foremost experts in their respective fields.
Cost: $461.00
Frequency: Monthly
Circulation: 2400
Founded in 1966

4660 **Nucleus**
American Chemical Society — Northeast
12 Corcoran Ave.
Burlington, MA 01803

800-872-2054
800-872-2054
Fax: 508-653-6329
E-Mail: webmaster@nesacs.org
Home Page: www.nesacs.org

Vincent J Gale, Editor
Amy Tapper, Secretary
Anna Singer, Administrative Secretary
Liming Shao, Chair

Content includes local meeting announcements; news of members of the Northeastern Section, American Chemical Society; historical articles; book reviews; calender of events covering all chemistry disciplines in the area. No Company or product information is published. Advertising is accepted.
Frequency: Monthly
Circulation: 7500
Founded in 1888
Printed in 2 colors on matte stock

4661 **PaintSquare**
PaintSquare
2100 Wharton Street
Suite 310
Pittsburgh, PA 15203

412-431-8300
800-837-8303
Fax: 412-431-5428
E-Mail: webmaster@paintsquare.com
Home Page: www.paintsquare.com
Social Media: Facebook, Twitter

Harold Hower, Publisher

Mission is to make PaintSquare a viable and useful tool to make your job easier and more efficient.
Founded in 2002

4662 **Performance Chemicals Europe**
Reed Chemical Publications
Quadrant House, The Quadrant
Sutton, Surrey, UK SM2 5AS

212-732-3200
+44 20 8652 3335
Fax: 212-791-4311
Fax: +44 20 8652 3375
E-Mail: csc@icis.com
Home Page: www.performancechemicals.com

Stanley F Reed
Neil Sinclair, Director
Simon Platt, Director
Christopher Flook, Managing Director
Cost: $711.00

4663 **PetroChemical News**
William F Bland Co.
709 Turmeric Ln
Durham, NC 27713-3103

919-544-1717
Fax: 919-544-1999
E-Mail: pcn@petrochemical-news.com
Home Page: www.petrochemical-news.com

Susan Kensil, Editor
Michelle Zard, Circulation Director

Covers new plants and projects, awards of contracts, mergers and acquisitions, current technology, and related government actions.
Cost: $807.00
Frequency: Weekly
Founded in 1963

4664 **Pine Chemicals Review**
Kriedt Enterprises
3803 Cleveland Ave.
New Orleans, LA 70119

504-482-3914
Fax: 504-482-4205
E-Mail: info@pinechemicalsreview.com
Home Page: www.pinechemicalsreview.com

Romney Richard, Publisher
Charley Richard, Editor

Pine Chemicals Review is the only trade journal covering pine and pulp chemicals within the naval stores industry. It is directed to producers and processors of pine gum and wood naval stores; pulp chemicals and pine derivative chemicals for the adhesives, coatings, printing ink, paper chemicals, flavor and fragrance.
Cost: $110.00
24 Pages
Frequency: Monthly
Circulation: 300
ISSN: 0164-4580
Founded in 1890
Printed in 4 colors on glossy stock

4665 **Polyurethane Professional Development Program**
Center for the Polyurethanes Industry
1300 Wilson Blvd
Suite 990
Arlington, VA 22209-2307

703-841-0012
Fax: 703-841-0525
Home Page: www.polyurethane.org
Social Media: Facebook, Twitter

Calvin Dooley, President
Frequency: Yearly

4666 **Powder and Bulk Engineering**
CSC Publishing
1155 Northland Dr
St Paul, MN 55120-1288

651-287-5600
Fax: 651-287-5650
Home Page: www.cscpublishinginc.com

Richard R Cress, Publisher
Terry O'Neill, Editor
Katherine Davich, Senior Editor

Featured editorial includes technical articles, case histories, test centers, product news and literature, and industry news items.
Frequency: Monthly
Circulation: 35379
Founded in 1986

4667 **Powder/Bulk Solids**
Reed Business Information
301 Gibralter Drive
Box 650
Morris Plains, NJ 07950

973-920-7000
Fax: 973-539-3476
E-Mail: scrow@reedbusiness.com
Home Page: www.reedbusiness.com

Mark Kelsey, CEO

Equipment and technological news for dry particulates processors.
Cost: $74.95
Frequency: Monthly
Circulation: 45,070
ISSN: 8740-6653
Founded in 1993

4668 **Proceedings of The Combustion Institute**
Combustion Institute
5001 Baum Blvd.
Suite 635
Pittsburgh, PA 15213-1851

412-687-1366
Fax: 412-687-0340
E-Mail: office@combustioninstitute.org
Home Page: www.combustioninstitute.org

Barbara Waronek, Executive Administrator
Prof. Katharina Kohse-Hoinghaus, President
Marcus Alden, VP
Derek Dunn-Rankin, Treasurer

Contains forefront contributions in fundamentals and applications of combustion science.
6000 Members
Frequency: Biennially
Founded in 1954

4669 **Processing**
Putman Media Company
555 W Pierce Rd
Suite 301
Itasca, IL 60143-2626

630-467-1300
Fax: 630-467-0197

E-Mail: webmaster@putman.net
Home Page: www.putman.net

John Cappelletti, CEO
Mike Bacidore, Editor-in-Chief
Tonia Becker, Publisher

Product areas covered include mechanical and pneumatic conveying, material handling, packaging, and storage. Each issue includes a specific editorial spotlight, product showcase and new literature section.
Frequency: Monthly
Circulation: 95035
ISSN: 0896-8659
Founded in 1972
Printed in 4 colors

4670 **Quimica Latinoamericana**
Reed Chemical Publications
2 Wall St
26th Floor, Suite 13
New York, NY 10005-2044

212-732-3200
888-525-3255
Fax: 212-791-4311
E-Mail: cnihelp@cnionline.com
Home Page: www.quimicalatinoamericana.com/

Stanley F Reed
Christopher Flook, Publisher
Neil Sinclair, Managing Editor
Jeff Evans, CEO/President
Jing Huang, Project Manager

Publication of Latin American petrochemicals.

4671 **Soap/Cosmetics/Chemical Specialties**
Cygnus Publishing
445 Broad Hollow Road
Suite 21
Melville, NY 11747-3601

631-845-2700
800-308-6397
Fax: 631-845-2798
E-Mail: soap@erols.com
Home Page: www.cygnuspub.com

Anita Hipius Shaw, Editor-in-Chief
Paul Bonaiuto, CFO
Kathy Scott, Director of Public Relations
John French, CEO

Includes tips on general management, purchasing, as well as new products and market trends, personal care, industrial and institutional markets, especially as they affect chemical, packing and equipment suppliers and their R and D professionals.
Cost: $30.00
Frequency: Monthly
Circulation: 6,491

4672 **Spray Technology & Marketing**
Industry Publications
3621 Hill Rd
Parsippany, NJ 07054-1001

973-331-9545
Fax: 973-331-9547
E-Mail: info@spraytechnology.com
Home Page: www.spraytechnology.com

Cynthia Hundley, Publisher
Michael L. SanGiovanni, Executive Editor
Shirleen Dorman, Editor

Features include articles on marketers, chemical and fragrance manufacturers and components manufacturers.
Frequency: Monthly
Circulation: 6,491
ISSN: 1055-2340
Founded in 1954
Mailing list available for rent
Printed in 4 colors on glossy stock

4673 **Sulfuric Acid Today**
PO Box 3502
Covington, LA 70434

985-893-9692
Fax: 985-893-8693
E-Mail: h2s04today.com
Home Page: www.h2so4today.comm

Earl B Heard, Publisher

Editorial covers industry news, engineering, technology and upcoming events.
Cost: $39.00
Frequency: SemiAnnual
Circulation: 5,000

4674 **Today's Chemist at Work**
American Chemical Society
1155 16th St NW
Washington, DC 20036-4892

202-872-4600
800-227-5558
Fax: 202-872-4615
E-Mail: service@acs.org
Home Page: www.acs.org

Madeleine Jacobs, CEO/Executive Director
William F Carroll, VP

Covers reports on materials, new products, chemical education, analytical chemistry and instrumentation.
Cost: $18.00
Frequency: Monthly
Circulation: 120000
Founded in 1876

Trade Shows

4675 **AACC International Annual Meeting**
3340 Pilot Knob Road
St. Paul, MN 55121-2055

651-454-7250
800-328-7560
Fax: 651-454-0766
E-Mail: aacc@scisoc.org
Home Page: www.aaccnet.org
Social Media: Facebook, Twitter, LinkedIn

Betty Ford, Meetings Director
Rhonda Wilkie, Meetings Coordinator
Deborah Rogers, Chair
David Hahn, President
Steven C. Nelson, Executive Vice President

Formerly the American Association of Cereal Chemists, the AACC meeting offers the chance to come together, network with peers, discuss critical issues in the science and discover the methods of others.
1200 Attendees
Frequency: October

4676 **ACOS Annual Meeting & Expo**
American Oil Chemists' Society
2710 S Boulder
Urbana, IL 61802-6996

217-693-4813
Fax: 217-351-8091
E-Mail: meetings@aocs.org
Home Page: www.aocs.org

Greg Hatfield, General Chairperson
Doreen Berning, Registration
Jeff Newman, Meeting Management/Logistics

The premier global science and business forum on fats, oils, surfactants, lipids and related materials. Includes oral and poster presentations, short courses, and exhibit, and networking with more than 1,600 colleagues from 60 countries.
2000 Attendees
Frequency: Annual/April-May

4677 **ACS Mid-Atlantic Regional Meeting**
American Chemical Society
1155 Sixteenth Street, NW
Washington, DC 20036

202-872-4600
800-227-5558
Fax: 989-835-8356
E-Mail: service@acs.org
Home Page: www.acs.org

Madeleine Jacobs, CEO/Executive Director

Attend poster sessions, symposia and workshops to experience the most exciting and cutting-edge research in the field of chemistry.
1M Attendees
Frequency: Annual/Spring

4678 **ACS Spring & Fall National Meeting & Expos**
American Chemical Society
1155 Sixteenth Street NW
Washington, DC 20036

202-872-4600
800-227-5558
Fax: 202-776-8044
E-Mail: conf_vendorrel@acs.org
Home Page: www.acs.org

Madeleine Jacobs, CEO/Executive Director

Symposia, poster sessions, and workshops around cutting-edge chemistry research.
1.2M Attendees
Frequency: Biennial

4679 **ALCA Annual Meeting**
American Leather Chemists Association
1314 50th Street
Suite 103
Lubbock, TX 79412

806-744-1798
Fax: 806-744-1785
E-Mail: alca@leatherchemists.org
Home Page: www.leatherchemists.org

Carol Adcock, Executive Secretary
100 Attendees

4680 **AOAC International Annual Meeting & Expo**
AOAC International
481 North Frederick Avenue
Suite 500
Gaithersburg, MD 20877-2417

301-924-7077
800-379-2622
Fax: 301-924-7089
E-Mail: aoac@aoac.org
Home Page: www.aoac.org
Social Media: Facebook, LinkedIn

Lauren Chelf, Director, Meetings & Exposition

The meeting offers a diverse program of symposia, workshops, and poster and scientific sessions. Specific educational tracks are offered for analytical chemists, microbiologists, laboratory managers, and other laboratory personnel.
Frequency: August

4681 **ASBC Annual Meeting**
American Society of Brewing Chemists
3340 Pilot Knob Road
Saint Paul, MN 55121

651-454-7250
800-328-7560
Fax: 651-454-0766
Home Page: www.meeting.asbcnet.org
Social Media: Facebook, Twitter

Charles F. Strachan, President
Steven Nelson, Executive Officer

Karen Cummings, Director of Publications
A. Hope, VP Operations
300 Attendees
Frequency: June/Non-Members Fee
Founded in 1934

4682 Agricultural Retailers Association Convention and Expo
Agricultural Retailers Association
1156 15th Street
Suite 500
Washington, DC 20005
202-457-0825
800-844-4900
Fax: 314-567-6808
E-Mail: kelly@aradc.org
Home Page: www.aradc.org
Daren Coppock, President/CEO
Richard Gupton, Sr. VP, Public Policy
Michelle Hummel, VP Marketing/Communications
Annual show of 120 manufacturers, suppliers and distributors of agricultural chemicals and fertilizers. Seminar, conference and banquet.
1200 Attendees
Frequency: Annual
Founded in 1993

4683 American Assn of Textile Chemists & Colorists International Conference
American Assn of Textile Chemists & Colorists
PO Box 12215
Research Triangle Park, NC 27709-2215
919-549-8141
800-360-5380
Fax: 919-549-8933
E-Mail: danielsj@aatcc.org
Home Page: www.aatcc.org
John Daniels, Executive VP
Debra Hibbard, Executive Assistant
Charles E Gavin, Treasurer
Colorants and chemical finishes for the textile trade are on display.
Frequency: Annual

4684 American Chemical Society: Southeastern Regional Conference & Exhibition
American Chemical Society
1155 16th Street NW
Washington, DC 20036
202-872-4600
800-227-5558
Fax: 202-872-4615
E-Mail: service@acs.org
Home Page: www.acs.org
Madeleine Jacobs, CEO/Executive Director
Booths featuring exhibits of the chemicals industry.
Frequency: Annual

4685 American College of Toxicology Annual Meeting
9650 Rockville Pike
Bethesda, MD 20814
301-634-7840
Fax: 301-634-7852
E-Mail: clemire@actox.org
Home Page: www.actox.org
Carol Lemire, Executive Director
Eve Gamzu Kagan, Asst. Executive Director
Education courses and scientific symposia, exhibits of contract laboratories, toxicology supplies and equipment and science journal publishing companies.
500 Attendees
Frequency: November

4686 American Institute Chemical Engineers Petrochemical Refining Expo
3 Park Avenue
New York, NY 10016-4363
212-591-8100
800-242-4363
Fax: 212-591-8888
Home Page: www.aiche.org
Social Media: Facebook, Twitter, LinkedIn
Marie Stewart, Director
A marketplace for materials used in processing chemicals.
20M Attendees
Frequency: April

4687 American Society Biochemistry and Molecular Biology Expo
American Society of Biochem & Molecular Biology
9650 Rockville Pike
Bethesda, MD 20814-3996
301-634-7145
Fax: 301-881-2080
E-Mail: asbmb@asbmb.org
Home Page: www.asbmb.org
600 booths of products used in biomedical research.
8M Attendees

4688 Annual Green Chemistry & Engineering Conference
ACS Green Chemistry Institute
1155 16th Street NW
Washington, DC 20036
202-872-6102
800-227-5558
Fax: 202-872-4615
E-Mail: gci@acs.org
Home Page: www.GCandE.org
Speakers, sessions, education, exhibits.
Frequency: Annual

4689 CPMA Conference
Color Pigments Manufacturers Association
300 N Washington St
Suite 105
Alexandria, VA 22314-2530
703-684-4044
Fax: 703-684-1795
E-Mail: cpma@cpma.com
Home Page: www.pigments.org
J Lawrence Robinson, President
Brings together pigments manufacturers their suppliers and users, and others with an interest in color pigments including regulators, consultants, and exhibitors.
Frequency: Annual

4690 Chem Show: Chemical Process Industries Exposition
International Exposition Company
15 Franklin Street
Westport, CT 06880-5903
203-221-9232
Fax: 203-221-9260
E-Mail: info@chemshow.com
Home Page: www.chemshow.com
Mark Stevens, VP
Jeff Stevens, Sales VP
Kelley Stevens, Sales Manager
Bringing together in one place major manufacturers of equipment, systems and services for the CPI. Product categories include; process equipment, fluid handling equipment and systems, solids handling equipment and sytems, engineered materials, instruments and controls, environmental and safety equipment and systems and services.
7481 Attendees
Frequency: Biennial/Oct
Founded in 1915

4691 Chem-Distribution
PennWell Publishing Company
1421 S Sheridan Road
Tulsa, OK 74112-6619
918-835-3161
800-331-4463
Fax: 918-831-9834
E-Mail: headquarters@pennwell.com
Home Page: www.pennwell.com
Bill Pryor, CEO/President
Junior Isles, Publisher/Editor
Exhibits of technology for the distribution, transfer and storage of chemicals and petrochemicals.

4692 Chem-Safe
PennWell Conferences and Exhibitions
1421 S Sheridan Road
Tulsa, OK 74112-6619
918-835-3161
800-331-4463
Fax: 918-831-9834
E-Mail: headquarters@pennwell.com
Home Page: www.pennwell.com
Bill Pryor, CEO/President
Junior Isles, Publisher/Editor
Exhibits of environmental, safety and health technology for the chemical and process industries.

4693 Chlorine Institute Annual Meeting & Trade Show
Chlorine Institute
1300 Wilson Blvd
Arlington, VA 22209-2323
703-741-5760
Fax: 703-894-4130
E-Mail: aonna@cl2.com
Home Page: www.chlorineinstitute.org
Arthur Dungan, President
Frequency: Annual/Spring

4694 Conchem Exhibition and Conference
Reed Exhibition Companies
255 Washington Street
Newton, MA 02458-1637
617-584-4900
Fax: 617-630-2222
Elizabeth Hitchcock, International Sales
The international event featuring specialty additives and chemicals for the building industry.
Frequency: November

4695 Consumer Specialty Products Association
Chemical Specialties Products Association
900 17th Street NW
Suite 300
Washington, DC 20006
202-872-8110
Fax: 202-872-8114
E-Mail: info@cspa.org
Home Page: www.cspa.org
Christopher Cathcart, President
Nonprofit organization trade show for the many companies involved in the formulation, manufacture, testing and marketing of chemical specialty products. 100 booths.
2M Attendees

4696 Eastern Analytical Symposium & Exposition
Eastern Analytical Symposium, Inc

PO Box 633
Montchanin, DE 19710-0633

610-485-4633
Fax: 610-485-9467
E-Mail: easinfo@aol.com
Home Page: www.eas.org

Sheree Gold, Exposition Director

The world's leading community for analytcal chemists seeking education and career advancement. Technical programs, speakers, and the expo. 240 booths.
6M Attendees
Frequency: Annual

4697 **Electrochemical Society Meetings**
Electrochemical Society
65 S Main St
Building D
Pennington, NJ 08534-2827

609-737-1902
Fax: 609-737-2743
E-Mail: meetings@electrochem.org
Home Page: www.electrochem.org

Roque J Calvo, Executive Director
Colleen Keepser, Executive Administrator
Mary Yess, Deputy Executive Director
Corey Eberhart, Global Sales Director
Karen Baliff Ornstein, Marketing Manager

Providing a forum for exchanging information on the latest scientific and technical developments in the fields of electrochemical and solid-state science and technology. ECS meetings bring together scientists, engineers, and researchers from academia, industry, and government laboratories to share results and discuss issues on related topics through a variety of formats, such as oral presentations, poster sessions, panel discussions, and tutorial sessions.
8000 Members
Frequency: Biannual/Spring & Fall
Founded in 1902

4698 **Federation of Spectroscopy Societies**
13 N Cliffe Drive
Wilmington, DE 19809-1623

302-656-0771

Dr. Edward Brame Jr, Show Manager

120 booths of analytical chemistry.
2M Attendees
Frequency: October

4699 **GlobalChem Conference and Exhibition**
1850 M St NW
Suite 700
Washington, DC 20036-5810

202-721-4100
Fax: 202-296-8120
E-Mail: info@socma.com
Home Page: www.socma.com

Larry Sloan, President/CEO
Alicia Massey, Senior Manager

Provides information and interaction with experts on the U.S. Toxic Substances Control Act, emerging issues and trends in the product stewardship arena and equivalent international regulations.
6 Members
Founded in 1985

4700 **ILTA Storage Tank & Bulk Liquid Terminal Int'l Operating Conf. & Trade Show**
Independent Liquid Terminals Association
1005 North Glebe Road
Suite 600
Arlington, VA 22201

703-875-2011
Fax: 703-875-2018
E-Mail: info@ilta.org
Home Page: www.ilta.org

E David Doane, President
Melinda Whitney, Director/Government Affairs
Renita Gross, Director of Mtgs/Info. Services

Containing 202 booths and 161 exhibits.
2,700 Attendees
Frequency: June

4701 **IUPAC World Polymer Congress**
2 Davidson Hall
Blacksburg, VA 24061-0001

540-231-7257
Fax: 540-231-3971
E-Mail: adhesoc@vt.edu
Home Page: www.adhesionsociety.org

Lynn Penn, President
Paul J Clark, Treasurer
Esther Brann, Manager

Enabling technologies for a safe, sustainable, healthy world.
400 Members
Founded in 1978

4702 **InformexUSA**
1850 M St NW
Suite 700
Washington, DC 20036-5810

202-721-4100
Fax: 202-296-8120
E-Mail: info@socma.com
Home Page: www.socma.com

Jill Aker, President

Serving businesses across a broad range of end-use markets such as pharmaceuticals, biopharmaceuticals, agrochemicals, adhesives, electronics, paints, and plastics. Utilizing an advisory committee, made up of industry executives and decision makers from across markets to help us make decisions that come directly from the chemical industry.
6 Members
Founded in 1985

4703 **International Conference on the Methods and Applications**
American Nuclear Society
555 N Kensington Ave
La Grange Park, IL 60526-5592

708-352-6611
800-323-3044
Fax: 708-352-0499
E-Mail: advertising@ans.org
Home Page: www.ans.org
Social Media: Facebook, Twitter, LinkedIn

Stephen Kuczynski, General Chair
Sedatel Goluoglu, Program Chair
Mikey Brady Raap, Treasurer

Of Radioanalytical Chemistry
10500 Members
Founded in 1954

4704 **International Thermal Spray Conference & Exposition**
ASM International
9639 Kinsman Road
Materials Park, OH 44073

440-338-5151
800-336-5152
Fax: 440-338-4634
E-Mail: natalie.nemec@asminternational.org
Home Page: www.asminternational.org

Natalie Neme, Event Manager
Kelly Thomas, Exposition Account Manager

Global annual event attracting professional interested in thermal spray technology focusing on advances in HVOF, plasma and detonation gun, flame spray and wire arc spray processes, performance of coatings, and future trends. 150 exhibitors.
1000 Attendees
Frequency: Annual/May

4705 **Optimizing Your Lab Automation: Lessons from the Front Line**
1850 K St NW
Suite 625
Washington, DC 20006-2215

202-857-0717
800-892-1400
Fax: 202-887-5093
Home Page: www.aacc.org
Social Media: Facebook, Twitter, LinkedIn, YouTube

Robert Christenson, President
Steven Wong, President-Elect
Patricia Jones, Director

The premiere event for clinical laboratorians, industry representatives, and health care executives to network and get ahead.

4706 **PCA International Conference**
Pine Chemicals Associations, Inc
3350 Riverwood Parkway SE
Suite 1900
Atlanta, GA 30339

770 981-5340
Fax: 770-984-5341
E Mail: wjones@pinechemicals.org
Home Page: www.pinechemicals.org

Walter L Jones, President/COO
Gary Reed, Chairman/Board of Directors
200 Attendees
Frequency: September

4707 **Powder Bulk Solids Conference and Expo**
Reed Business Information
2000 Clearwater Drive
Oak Brook, IL 60523

630-740-0825
Home Page: www.reedbusiness.com

Angela Piermartini, Show Manager

1,300 booths.
11M Attendees
Frequency: May

4708 **Spray Foam Conference & EXPO**
Spray Polyurethane Foam Alliance
4400 Fair Lakes Court
Suite 105
Fairfax, VA 22033

800-523-6154
Fax: 703-222-5816
E-Mail: info@sprayfoam.org
Home Page: www.sprayfoam.org

Sig Hall, President
Robert Duke, Vice President
Peter Davis, Secretary/Treasurer

Training and accreditation programs, general and breakout sessions, awards, networking receptions, and the exhibit hall.
Frequency: Annual/February
Founded in 1987

4709 **TRADEWORX**
Chemical Specialties Products Association
900 17th Street NW
Suite 300
Washington, DC 20006

202-872-8110
Fax: 202-872-8114
E-Mail: info@cspa.org
Home Page: www.cspa.org

Christopher Cathcart, President

Not-for-profit organization composed of many companies involved in the formulation, manu-

facture, testing and marketing of chemical specialty products.
2M Attendees
Frequency: May

Directories & Databases

4710 **Adhesives Digest**
International Plastics Selector/DATA Business Pub.
15 Inverness Way E
#6510
Englewood, CO 80112-5710

303-904-0407

A who's who directory of services and supplies to the industry.
Cost: $180.00
Frequency: Biennial

4711 **Advanced Coatings and Surface Technology**
John Wiley & Sons
111 River St
Hoboken, NJ 07030-5790

201-748-6000
Fax: 201-748-6088
E-Mail: info@wiley.com
Home Page: www.wiley.com

William J Pesce, Chief Executive Officer

Offers information on coatings and surface technology, covering breakthroughs in traditional coating processes, chemical vapor deposition and ion beam methods.
Frequency: Full-text

4712 **American Coke & Coal Chemicals Institute Directory and By-Laws**
1140 Connecticut Ave NW
Suite 705
Washington, DC 20036-4011

202-452-7177
Fax: 202-496-9702
E-Mail: information@accci.org
Home Page: www.recycle-steel.org

Chip Foley, VP
Charles Stewart, Chairman

Represents merchant oven coke producers, integrated coke producers, tar distillers, sales agents, and industry suppliers.
75 Pages
Founded in 1944

4713 **American Laboratory Buyers Guide**
International Scientific Communications
PO Box 870
Shelton, CT 06484-0870

203-926-9300
Fax: 203-926-9310
E-Mail: webmaster@iscpubs.com
Home Page: www.iscpubs.com

Brian Howard, Editor
Robert G Sweeny, Publisher

Manufacturers of and dealers in scientifi instruments, equipment, apparatus, and chemicals worldwide.
Cost: $25.00
Frequency: Annual

4714 **Available Chemicals Directory**
MDL Information Systems
3100 Central Expressway
Santa Clara, CA 05051-6608

408-764-2000
800-635-0064
Fax: 408-748-0175
E-Mail: info@mdli.com
Home Page: www.mdli.com

Magnetic tape, covers approximately 240,000 commercially available chemicals, including organic, and inorganic chemicals.
Frequency: Semiannual

4715 **CEH On-Line**
SRI International
333 Ravenswood Ave
Menlo Park, CA 94025-3493

650-859-3711
Fax: 650-326-8916
Home Page: www.srifcu.org

Steve Bowles, President

Database containing economic data for more than 1300 major commodity and specialty chemical products.
Frequency: Full-text

4716 **CERCLIS Database of Hazardous Waste Sites**
Environmental Protection Agency
Ariel Rios Building
1200 Pennsylvania Avenue NW
Washington, DC 20460

202-272-0167
E-Mail: r9.info@epa.gov
Home Page: www.epa.gov

Bob Zachariasiewicz, Acting Director
Shushona Hyson, Contact
Curt Spalding, Regional

Stands for Comprehensive Environmental Response, Compensation, and Liability Information System. This database contains information on more than 36,000 releases of hazardous substances reported to the US Environmental Protection Agency.
Frequency: Directory

4717 **CHEMEST**
Technical Database Services
62 W 39th Street
Rm 704
New York, NY 10018

212-245-0384
Fax: 212-556-0036

Mildred Green, Principal

This database contains information for estimating the properties of pharmaceuticals and chemicals of environmental concern.
Frequency: Properties

4718 **CLAIMS/Comprehensive Data Base**
IFI/Plenum Data Corporation
PO Box 1148
Madison, CT 06443

203-779-5301
Fax: 203-583-4521
E-Mail: info@ificlaims.com

Harry M Allcock, VP

This database contains enhanced indexing of the US chemical and chemically related patents included in the CLAIMS/UNITERM database.

4719 **Chem Source USA**
Chemical Sources International
PO Box 1824
Clemson, SC 29633

864-646-7840
Fax: 864-642-6168
E-Mail: information@chemsources.com
Home Page: www.chemsources.com

Mike Desing, Editor

Book containing information on where to obtain chemicals in the US and Canada.
Cost: $495.00
1700 Pages
Frequency: Annual January
Circulation: 10000
Founded in 1958

4720 **Chem Sources International**
PO Box 1824
Clemson, SC 29633-1824

864-646-7840
800-222-4531
Fax: 864-646-6168
E-Mail: csinfo@chemsources.com
Home Page: www.chemsources.com

Mike Desing, Editor
Dale Krohn, Owner

The most comprehensive directory ever compiled on the world's chemical industry. Includes the products of more than 8,000 chemical firms spanning 128 countries.
Cost: $750.00
Frequency: Biennial
Founded in 1958

4721 **Chemcyclopedia**
American Chemical Society
676 East Swedesford Road
Suite 202
Wayne, PA 19087-1612

610-964-8061
Fax: 610-964-8061
E-Mail: carroll@acs.org
Home Page: www.acs.org
Social Media: 1

Madeleine Jacobs, Executive Director/CEO
Ken Carroll, Publisher

List of over 900 chemical manufacturers in the US.
Cost: $60.00
Frequency: Annual

4722 **Chemical Abstracts**
American Chemical Society
1155 16th St NW
Suite 600
Washington, DC 20036-4892

202-872-4600
800-227-5558
Fax: 202-872-4615
E-Mail: service@acs.org
Home Page: www.acs.org

Madeleine Jacobs, CEO

Newsletter covering this branch of the American Chemical Society.
Frequency: Monthly

4723 **Chemical Exposure and Human Health**
McFarland & Company Publishers
PO Box 611
Jefferson, NC 28640-0611

336-246-4460
800-253-2187
Fax: 336-246-5018
E-Mail: info@mcfarlandpub.com
Home Page: www.mcfarlandpub.com

Cynthia Wilson, Editor

A list of organizations concerned with the effects of chemical exposure. Government exposure standards on over 300 chemicals.
Cost: $55.00
ISBN: 0-899508-10-3

4724 **Chemical Regulations and Guidelines System**
Network Management CRC Systems
11242 Waples Mill Road
Fairfax, VA 22030-6079

703-219-3865

This database contains citations, with abstracts, to US government statutes and federal guidelines.

4725 **Chemical Week: Financial Survey of the 300 Largest Companies in the US**
Chemical Week Associates
110 William St
New York, NY 10038-3910
212-621-4900
Fax: 212-621-4800
Home Page: www.chemweek.com
John Rockwell, Vice President
Offers information on over 300 chemical process companies in the United States.
Cost: $8.00
7 Pages
Frequency: Annual
Circulation: 50,615

4726 **DRI Chemical**
DRI/McGraw-Hill
24 Hartwell Ave
Lexington, MA 02421-3103
781-860-6060
Fax: 781-860-6002
E-Mail: support@construction.com
Home Page: www.construction.com
Keith Fox, President
Linda Brennan, VP Operations
Bob Stuono, Senior VP And General Manager
The coverage of this database encompasses the chemical industry in the United States, including imports and exports, inventories, production, sales, shipments and uses.

4727 **DRI Chemical Forecast**
DRI/McGraw-Hill
24 Hartwell Ave
Lexington, MA 02421-3103
781-860-6060
Fax: 781-860-6002
E-Mail: support@construction.com
Home Page: www.construction.com
Keith Fox, President
This time series contains over 700 quarterly forecasts on US supply and demand for more than 120 chemical products.

4728 **Directory of Bulk Liquid Terminal and Storage Facilities**
Independent Liquid Terminals Association
1005 North Glebe Road
Arlington, VA 22201
703-875-2011
Fax: 703-875-2018
E-Mail: info@ilta.org
Home Page: www.ilta.org
E David Doane, President
Melinda Whitney, Director/Executive VP
Published annually in April.
Cost: $95.00

4729 **Directory of Chemical Producers: East Asia**
SRI Consulting/IHS Global
333 Ravenswood Ave
Menlo Park, CA 94025-3493
650-859-3711
Fax: 650-326-8916
Home Page: www.srifcu.org
Steve Bowles, President
Over 2,000 companies producing over 14,000 chemicals in 2,600 plant locations in Indonesia, Japan, Korea, Taiwan and the Philippines.
Cost: $1800.00
800 Pages
Frequency: Annual

4730 **Directory of Chemical Producers: U.S.**
SRI Consulting/IHS Global
333 Ravenswood Ave
Menlo Park, CA 94025-3493
650-859-3711
Fax: 650-326-8916
Home Page: www.srifcu.org
Steve Bowles, President
Over 1,500 United States basic chemical producers manufacturing almost 10,000 chemicals in commercial quantities at 4,500 plant locations. Providing comprehensive, accurate and timely coverage of the international chemical industry since 1961.
Cost: $1460.00
1100 Pages
Frequency: Annual

4731 **Directory of Chemical Producers: Western Europe**
SRI Consulting/IHS Global
333 Ravenswood Ave
Menlo Park, CA 94025-3493
650-859-3711
Fax: 650-326-8916
Home Page: www.srifcu.org
Steve Bowles, President
Covered are over 2,500 western European chemical producers, chemicals and plant locations.
Cost: $1930.00
Frequency: Annual
Circulation: 2,100

4732 **Directory of Custom Chemical Manufacturers**
Delphi Marketing Services
400 E 89th Street
Apartment 2J
New York, NY 10128-6728
Newman Giragosian, Editor
A list of over 280 custom chemical manufacturers.
Cost: $295.00
220 Pages

4733 **Directory of Suppliers of Services**
Independent Liquid Terminals Association
1005 North Glebe Road
Arlington, VA 22201
703-875-2011
Fax: 703-875-2018
E-Mail: info@ilta.org
Home Page: www.ilta.org
E David Doane, President
Melinda Whitney, Director/Executive VP
Cost: $25.00

4734 **Environmental Fate Data Bases**
Syracuse Research Corporation
6225 Running Ridge Rd
North Syracuse, NY 13212-2510
315-452-8000
800-724-0451
Fax: 315-452-8100
Cheryl Wolfe, President
This database, consisting of 4 interrelated files of information on the fate of organic chemicals. The files include information in physical/chemical properties, degradation and transport, and monitoring for 16,000 chemicals.

4735 **Environmental Industry Yearbook and The Gallery**
Environmental Economics
1026 Irving Street
Philadelphia, PA 19107-6707
215-877-2063
Fax: 215-440-0116
More than 80 publicly traded companies, plus Fortune 500 firms that have an impact on environmental concerns.
Cost: $75.00
250 Pages
Frequency: SemiAnnual

4736 **Fine Chemicals Database**
Chemron
PO Box 2299
Paso Robles, CA 93447
210-340-8121
800-423-1148
Fax: 210-340-8123
This large database provides supplier information for more than 27,000 chemical products available from over 50 manufacturers and distributors in North America.
Frequency: Directory

4737 **Index to Chemical Regulations**
Bureau of National Affairs
1801 S Bell St
Arlington, VA 22202-4501
703-341-3000
800-372-1033
Fax: 800-253-0332
E-Mail: customercare@bna.com
Home Page: www.bnabooks.com
Paul N Wojcik, Chairman
Gregory C McCaffery, President
A one-binder index containing more than 80,000 citations by chemical name to the Code of Federal Regulations and the Federal Register.
Cost: $988.00
Frequency: Monthly

4738 **Information Officers of Member Companies**
Chemical Manufacturers Association
1300 Wilson Boulevard
Arlington, VA 22209-2307
703-741-5502
Fax: 703-741-6807
Thomas J Gilroy, Associate Media Director
About 180 companies.
Frequency: Biennial

4739 **International Chemical Regulatory Monitoring System**
Ariel Research Corporation
4320 East West Highway
Suite 440
Bethesda, MD 20814-3319
301-951-2500
Fax: 301-986-1681
Home Page: www.3ecompany.com
John Wyatt, CEO
This database contains references to regulations and precautionary data on more than 100,000 chemical substances.
Frequency: Full-text

4740 **Kirk-Othmer Encyclopedia of Chemical Technology Online**
John Wiley & Sons
111 River St
Hoboken, NJ 07030-5790
201-748-6000
800-825-7550
Fax: 201-748-6088
E-Mail: info@wiley.com
Home Page: www.wiley.com
Warren J Baker, President
Richard M Hochhauser, CEO
This comprehensive database offers complete text, citations, tables and abstracts of all 1,200 chapters in the 25-volume Encyclopedia of the same name. With no concurrent usage restriction, you can call up information covering the

entire chemical industry and allied fields any time with a click of your mouse from the library, office or laboratory.

4741 McCutcheons Functional Materials
McCutcheons Division
P.O.Box 2249
New Preston Marble Dale, CT 06777-0249

201-652-2655
Fax: 201-652-3419
E-Mail: mcinfo@gomc.com
Home Page: www.gomc.com

Michael Allured, Publisher

List of materials commonly used in conjunction with surfactants such as enzymes, lubricants, waxes, corrosion inhibitors, and other chemicals produced worldwide.
Cost: $40.00
Frequency: Monthly
Founded in 1921

4742 Multilingual Thesaurus of Geosciences
Information Today
143 Old Marlton Pike
Medford, NJ 08055-8750

609-654-6266
800-300-9868
Fax: 609-654-4309
E-Mail: custserv@infotoday.com
Home Page: www.infotoday.com

Thomas H Hogan, President
Roger R Bilboul, Chairman Of The Board

Represents the state of the art use of geoscience terminology by information centers around the world.
Cost: $99.00
654 Pages
ISBN: 1-573870-09-9

4743 OPIS/STALSBY Electric Power Industry Directory
OPIS/STALSBY
1255 Highway 70
Suite 32-N
Lakewood, NJ 08701

732-901-8800
877-210-4287
Fax: 732-901-9632
Home Page: www.opisnet.com

Karen England, Senior Editor
Karen Reng, Marketing Manager
Christine Kaniuk, Production/Advertising Coordinator

Provides detailed listings of over 1,200 companies and more than 2,700 personnel of the electric power industry. Company categories include producer, marketer, trader, broker, transmission, investor-owned, municipal, rural/co-op/fed/local government and independent. Personnel listings include sales/marketing, supply/purchasing, operations/transmissions, finance/treasury. Company listings include address, direct telephone, fax numbers and e-mails. CD-ROM $495.
Cost: $141.00
Frequency: 2 per year
Circulation: 625
Printed in 4 colors

4744 OPIS/STALSBY Petrochemicals Directory
OPIS/STALSBY
3349 State Route 138
Unit D
Wall Township, NJ 07719-9671
732-730-2500
877-210-4287
Fax: 732-280-0542
Home Page: www.ucg.com

Ben Brockwell, Manager
Karen Reng, Marketing Manager
Christine Kaniuk, Production/Advertising Coordinator
Bruce Levenson, Co-Founder

Provides detailed listings of over 2,100 companies and more than 7,000 personnel covering all segments of the petrochemical gas industry, including manufacturing, trading and distributing of petrochemicals. Company listings include addresses, telephone, fax, TLX, personal phone/fax numbers, cell phones and home addresses, area of responsibility and job titles. Five separate indices are provided for complete cross-referencing. CD-ROM $995.
Cost: $175.00
Frequency: 2 per year
Circulation: 425
Printed in 4 colors

4745 OPIS/STALSBY Petroleum Supply Americas Directory
OPIS/STALSBY
1255 Highway 70
Suite 32-N
Lakewood, NJ 08701

732-901-8800
877-210-4287
Fax: 732-901-9632
Home Page: www.opisnet.com

Karen England, Senior Editor
Karen Reng, Marketing Manager
Christine Kaniuk, Production/Advertising Coordinator

Helps traders, marketers and suppliers of crude oil, refined products and gas liquids to access detailed information on over 2,500 companies and 10,000 personnel in North, Central and South America. Company listings include company address, telephone, fax, TLX, personal phone/fax numbers, car phones, home addresses, area of responsibility and job title. Four separate indices are provided for complete cross-referencing. CD-ROM $995.
Cost: $235.00
Frequency: 2 per year
Circulation: 2,045
Printed in 4 colors

4746 OPIS/STALSBY Petroleum Supply Europe Directory
OPIS/STALSBY
1255 Highway 70
Suite 32-N
Lakewood, NJ 08701

732-901-8800
877-210-4287
Fax: 732-901-9632
Home Page: www.opisnet.com

Karen England, Senior Editor
Karen Reng, Marketing Manager
Christine Kaniuk, Production/Advertising Coordinator

Helps traders, marketers and suppliers of crude oil, refined products and gas liquids to access detailed information on over 1,500 companies and 6,600 personnel in Europe, Eastern Europe, Africa and the Middle East. Listings include company address, telephone, fax, TLX, personal phone/fax numbers, car phones, home addresses, area of responsibility and job titles. Four separate indices are provided for complete cross-referencing. CD-OM $995.
Cost: $190.00
Frequency: 2 per year
Circulation: 425
Printed in 4 colors

4747 OPIS/STALSBY Petroleum Terminal Encyclopedia
OPIS/STALSBY
1255 Highway 70
Suite 32-N
Lakewood, NJ 08701

732-901-8800
877-210-4287
Fax: 732-901-9632
Home Page: www.opisnet.com

Karen England, Senior Editor
Karen Reng, Marketing Manager
Christine Kaniuk, Production/Advertising Coordinator

Provides detailed listings of over 2,800 petroleum terminals. Information includes pipeline and rail interconnections and truck facilities for each terminal; berth, waterway and docking information for marine terminals; details on both public and private terminals for market analysis and exchange planning. Three separate indices are provided for complete cross-referencing. CD-ROM $995.
Cost: $245.00
Frequency: 2 per year
Circulation: 825
Printed in 4 colors

4748 OPIS/STALSBY Who's Who in Natural Gas
OPIS/STALSBY
1255 Highway 70
Suite 32-N
Lakewood, NJ 08701

732-901-8800
877-210-4287
Fax: 732-901-9632
Home Page: www.opisnet.com

Karen England, Senior Editor
Karen Reng, Marketing Manager
Christine Kaniuk, Production/Advertising Coordinator

Provides detailed listings of over 2,600 companies and more than 11,000 personnel covering all segments of the natural gas industry, including producers, processors, marketers, traders, transporters, major buyers, LDCs, brokers, gas storage, regulatory, etc. Company listings include addresses, telephone, fax, TLX, personal phone/fax numbers, car phones and home addresses, area of responsibility and job titles. Four separate indices are provided for complete cross-referencing. CD-ROM $995.
Cost: $200.00
Frequency: 2 per year
Circulation: 950
Printed in 4 colors

4749 Purchasing/CPI Edition: Chemicals Yellow Pages
Reed Business Information
2000 Clearwater Dr
Oak Brook, IL 60523-8809

630-574-0825
Fax: 630-288-8781
Home Page: www.reedbusiness.com

Jeff Greisch, President

Manufacturers and distributors of 10,000 chemicals and raw materials; manufacturers and distributors of containers and packaging.
Cost: $85.00
Frequency: Annual

4750 Refining & Gas Processing
Midwest Publishing Company
PO Box 4468
Suite E
Tulsa, OK 74159-0468

918-583-9999
800-829-2002
Fax: 918-587-9349

E-Mail: info@midwestdirectories.com
Home Page: www.midwestpub.com

Will L Hammack, Owner

Over 5,200 refineries, gas processing plants, engineering contractors, equipment manufacturers and supply companies.
Cost: $145.00
Frequency: Annual, May
Founded in 1943

4751 **Regulated Chemical Directory**
Kluwer Academic Publishers
101 Philip Drive
Norwellk, MA 02061

617-871-6600
Fax: 617-871-6528
E-Mail: kluwer@wkap.com
Home Page: www.hcirn.com

List of major federal and selected state and international regulatory and advisory sources of information regarding chemicals in the US, Canada, Australia, Germany and Israel.
Cost: $375.00
Frequency: Annual, January

4752 **STN Easy**
Chemical Abstracts Service
PO Box 3012
Columbus, OH 43210 0012

614-473-3600
800-848-6538
Fax: 614-447-3713
E-Mail: help@cas.org
Home Page: www.cas.org

Easy web acccess to scientific research and patents. STN Easy provides access to more than 60 databases covering all types of sci/tech information including chemistry, life sciences, buisiness, MSDS, math/computer science, engineering, medicine, pharmaceuticals, general science, food and agriculture, and regulatory information.

4753 **Soap/Cosmetics/Chemical Specialties: Blue Book Issue**
Cygnus Publishing
445 Broad Hollow Road
Suite 21
Melville, NY 11747-3601

631-845-2700
Fax: 631-845-2723
Home Page: www.cygnuspub.com

Anita Shaw, Editor-in-Chief
Shelley Colwell, CFO
Paul Bonaiuto, CFO
Kathy Scott, Director of Public Relations

Sources of raw materials, equipment and services for the chemical, soap and cosmetics industries. Includes a list of trade associations.
Cost: $15.00
Frequency: Annual, April
Circulation: 19,000

Industry Web Sites

4754 **http://gold.greyhouse.com**
G.O.L.D Grey House OnLine Databases

Grey House Publishing's online database platform, GOLD, offers Quick Search, Keyword Search and Expert Search for most business sectors including chemical and agriculture markets. The GOLD platform makes finding the information you need quick and easy - whether you're a novice searcher or an experienced database user. All of Grey House's directory products are be available for subscription on the GOLD platform.

4755 **www.aaccnet.org**
American Association of Cereal Chemists

Nonprofit international organization of nearly 4,000 members who are specialists in the use of cereal grains in foods. AACC has been an innovative leader in gathering and disseminating scientific and technical information to professionals in the grain based foods industry worldwide for over 85 years.

4756 **www.accci.org**
American Coke & Coal Chemicals Institute Directory

For merchant oven coke producers, integrated coke producers, tar distillers, sales agents, and industry suppliers.

4757 **www.actox.org**
American College of Toxicology

Multidisciplinary society composed of professionals having a common interest in toxicology. Our mission is to educate and lead professionals in industry, government and related areas of toxicology by actively promoting the exchange of information and perspectives on the current status of safety assesment and the application of new developments in toxicology.

4758 **www.aiche.org**
American Institute of Chemical Engineers

Professional association of more than 50,000 members, providing leadership in advancing the chemical engineering profession. Members develop processes and design and operate manufacturing plants, as well as research the safe and environmentally sound manufacture, use and disposal of chemical products.

4759 **www.americanchemistry.com**
American Chemistry Council

Committed to improved environmental, health and safety performance through responsible care, common sense advocacy designed to address major public policy issues, health and environmental research and product testing.

4760 **www.aoac.org**
Association of Official Analytical Communities

Calender, publications and training courses. AOAC serves as the primary resource for timely knowledge exchange, networking and high quality laboratory information for its members.

4761 **www.aocs.org**
American Oil Chemists Society

Encourages advancement of technology and research in fats, oils and other associated substances.

4762 **www.asms.org**
American Society for Mass Spectrometry

Formed to disseminate knowledge of mass spectrometry and allied topics. Members come from academic, industrial and governmental laboratories. Their interests include advancement of techniques and instrumentation in mass specrometry, as well as fundamental research in chemistry, geology, biological sciences and physics.

4763 **www.chemheritage.org**
Chemical Heritage Foundation

An independent, nonprofit organization, CHF maintains major collections of instruments, fine art, photographs, papers, and books. We host conferences and lectures, support research, offer fellowships, and produce educational materials.

4764 **www.chemistry.org**
American Chemical Society

Encourages advancement in all branches of chemistry. There are 34 ACS divisions and 188 local sections.

4765 **www.chemtrec.org**
American Chemistry Council

Serves as a referral service for non-emergency health and safety information, maintains library and speakers bureaus. Offers 24 hour emergency communication service center for hazardous materials, material data sheets, lending library, audio-visual training programs.

4766 **www.coatingstech.org**
Federation of Societies for Coatings Technology

Provides technical education and professional development to its members and to the global industry through its multi-national constituent societies and collectively as a federation.

4767 **www.combustioninstitute.org**
Combustion Institute

A non-profit, educational, scientific society whose purpose is to promote and disseminate research combustion science.

4768 **www.csma.org**
Chemical Specialties Manufacturers Association

For companies involved in the formulation, manufacture, testing and marketing of chemical specialty products.

4769 **www.cspa.org**
Consumer Specialty Products Association

Nonprofit organization composed of many companies involved in the formulation, manufacture, testing and marketing of chemical specialty products. Our line includes disinfectants that kill germs in homes, hospitals and restaurants, candles that eliminate odors, pest management products for home and garden, cleaning products and much more.

4770 **www.dupont.com/nacs**
DuPont Experimental Station

For chemists and chemical engineers engaged in the study and use of reactions involving catalysts. Publishes a newsletter

4771 **www.electrochem.org**
Electrochemical Society

The society is an international nonprofit, educational organization concerned with phenomena relating to electrochemical and solid state science and technology. Members are individual scientists and engineers, as well as corporations and laboratories.

4772 **www.fibersource.com**
American Fiber Manufacturers Association

Trade association for US companies that manufacture synthetic and cellulostic fibers. The industry employs 30,000 people and produces over 9 billion pounds of fiber in the US. The association maintains close ties to other manufactured fiber trade associations worldwide.

4773 **www.greyhouse.com**
Grey House Publishing

Authoritative reference directories for most business sectors incluidng chemical and agricultural markets. Users can search the online databases with varied search criteria allowing for custom searches by product category, geographic area, sales volume, keyword, subject and more. Full Grey House catalog and online ordering also available.

4774 **www.ilta.org**
Independent Liquid Terminals Association

Representing bulk liquid terminal companies that store commercial liquids in aboveground storage tanks and transfer products to and from oceangoing tanks ships, tank barges, pipelines, tank trucks, and tank rail cars.

4775 www.ioza.org
International Ozone Assn-Pan American Group Branch
Not for profit educational association which performs its information sharing functions through sponsorship of international symposia, seminars, publications, and the development of personal relationships among ozone specialists throughout the world.

4776 www.leatherchemists.org
American Leather Chemists Association
Publishes the Journal of the American Leather Chemists Association where original research reports are published along with abstracts of foreign articles. A four-day technical meeting is held annually. Promotes the advancement of the knowledge of science and engineering in their application to the problems facing the leather and leather products industries.

4777 www.methanol.org
American Methanol Institute
Our mission is to expand markets for the use of methanol as a chemical commodity building block, a hydrogen carrier for fuel cell applications, and an alternative fuel. AMI was formed in 1989, during the height of the Clean Air Act debate, and worked to help create the highly successful reformulated gasoline program.

4778 www.mti-link.org
Materials Tech. Institute of the Chemical Process
MTI provides leadership in materials technology for chemical processing to improve reliability, profitability and safety.

4779 www.nacatsoc.org
North American Catalysis Society
Fosters an interest in heterogeneous and homogeneous catalysis. Organizes national meetings. Members are chemists and chemical engineers engaged in the study and use of reactions involving catalysts. Publishes a newsletter.

4780 www.pemanet.org
Process Equipment Manufacturers' Association
Organized in 1960, we represent more than 40 companies in the process equipment field. Member companies serve the liquid-solids separation, food processing, pulp and paper, waste water treatment industry and others.

4781 www.pestworld.org
National Pest Control Association
For over 65 years, the NPMA has represented the interests of its members and the structural pest control industry. Through the efforts of NPMA, the pest control industry is stronger, more professional, and more unified. Guiding its members and industry through legislative and regulatory initiatives on the federal and state levels, the creation of verifiable training, the changing technologies used by the industry, and public and media relations, NPMA has been a clear, positive voice.

4782 www.pfa.org
Polyurethane Foam Association
Educating customers and other groups about flexible polyurethane foam and to promote its use in manufactured and indutrial products. This includes providing facts on environmental, health and safety issues related to polyurethane foam to the memebership of PFA, polyurethane foam users, regulatory officials, business leaders and the media.

4783 www.pigments.org
Color Pigments Manufacturers Association
An industry trade association representing color pigment companies in Canada, Mexico and the US. Represents small, medium, and large color pigments manufacturers accounting for 95% of the production of color pigments in North America

4784 www.pima.org
Polyisocyanurate Insulation Manufacturers Assn
National association that advances the use of polyisocyanurate (polyiso) insulation. Polyiso is one of the nation's most widely used and cost-effective insulation products. PIMA's membership consiosts of manufacturers as well as suppliers to the industry.

4785 www.pinechemicals.org
Pine Chemicals Association
Association of producers, processors and consumers of pine chemicals. The PCA promotes innovative, safe and environmentally responsible practices to assure a reliable supply of high quality products.

4786 www.powdercoating.org
Powder Coating Institute
Founded in 1981 as a nonprofit organization, PCI works to advance the utilization of powder coating as an economical, non-polluting and high quality finish for industrial and consumer products.

4787 www.scisoc.org/asbc
American Society of Brewing Chemists
News, information, member directory and publications.

4788 www.simaflavor.org
Flavor & Extract Manufacturers Assn of the US
Locates suppliers and manufacturers of rare chemicals and oils used in the flavor and fragrance industry.

4789 www.socma.com
Synthetic Organic Chemical Manufacturers Assn
Trade association serving the specialty batch and custom chemical industry since 1921. Its more than 320 member companies have more than 2,000 manufacturing sites and 100,000 employees. SOCMA members encompass every segment of the industry - and manufacture 50,000 products annually that are valued at $60 billion dollars.

4790 www.toxicology.org
Society of Toxicology
Members are scientists concerned with the effects of chemicals on man and the environment. Promotes the aquisition and utilization of knowledge in toxicology, aids in the protection of public health and facilitates disiplines. The society has a strong commitment to education in toxicology and to the recruitment of students and new members into the profession.

Associations

4791 American Cleaning Institute
1331 L St NW
Suite 650
Washington, DC 20005

202-347-2900
Fax: 202-347-4110
E-Mail: Info@CleaningInstitute.org
Home Page: www.cleaninginstitute.org
Social Media: Facebook, Twitter, LinkedIn, RSS Feed, SchoolTube, YouTube

Ernie Rosenberg, President & CEO
Helen Benz, CFO
Sandra Andrade, Program Coordinator, Meetings
Leonardo Bellisario, Govt. Affairs Coordinator
Melissa Bernardo, Manager of Sustainibility Programs

Nonprofit trade association representing manufacturers of household, industrial and institutional cleaning products; their ingredients and finished packaging. Dedicated to advancing public understanding of the safety and benefits of cleaning products and protecting the ability of its members to formulate products that best meet consumer needs.
100+ Members
Founded in 1926
Mailing list available for rent

4792 Building Service Contractors Association International
330 N. Wabash Ave.
Suite 2000
Chicago, IL 60611

312-321-5167
800-368-3414
Fax: 312-673-6735
E-Mail: info@bscai.org
Home Page: www.bscai.org

Chris Mundschenk, EVP/ CEO
Kevin S. Rohan, President
Janelle Bruland, Treasurer
Paul Greenland, Vice President
Lance Ford, Director

Trade association for companies offering security, maintenance and cleaning services. The international membership now represents over 10% of the association's professional membership.
Cost: $30.00
2500 Members
Founded in 1965
Mailing list available for rentat $75 per M

4793 Chlorine Free Products Association
1304 S Main St
Algonquin, IL 60102-2757

847-658-6104
Fax: 847-658-3152
E-Mail: info@chlorinefreeproducts.org
Home Page: www.chlorinefreeproducts.org

Archie Beaton, Executive Director
Richard Albert, Technical Staff Manager
Dr. Kevin Lyons, Chief Procurement Officer
Frank Perkowski, President, Business Development
Jane Bloodworth, Business Manager

A nonprofit association that's primary purpose is to promote total chlorine free policies, programs and technologies throughtout the world.

4794 Cleaning Equipment Trade Association
PO Box 270908
Oklahoma City, OK 73137-0908

704-635-7362
800-441-0111
Fax: 651-982-0030
E-Mail: info@ceta.org
Home Page: www.ceta.org

Steve Bowie, Vice-President
Terry Murray, President
Rick Wendt, SVP
Frank Jonkman, Secretary
Linda Chappell, Treasurer

International nonprofit reade association made up of manufacturers, distributors, and suppliers who coordinate their efforts to promote public awareness, professionalism, industry wide safety standards, and education for the advancement of the powered cleaning equipment industry.
300 Members
Founded in 1996

4795 Cleaning Management Institute
19 British American Blvd. West
Latham, NY 12110

518-783-1281
Fax: 518-783-1386
E-Mail: cmi@ntpmedia.com
Home Page: www.cminstitute.net

Maicah Ogburn, Director
Pat Harrington, Administrative Manager
Brant Insero, Training Sales Specialist
Matt Moberg, Training Development

CMI provides education, training and career improvement opportunities for building cleaning and maintenance professionals.
1000 Members
Founded in 1964

4796 Coin Laundry Association
1 S. 660 Midwest Rd.
Suite 205
Oakbrook Terrace, IL 60181

630-953-7920
800-570-5629
Fax: 630-953-7925
E-Mail: info@coinlaundry.org
Home Page: www.coinlaundry.org

Brian Wallace, President & CEO
Keith Griffin, Chairman
Jeff Gardner, Treasurer
Michael Sokolowski, EVP
Craig Kirchner, Vice-Chairman

Association for self-service laundry and dry cleaning industry.
2700+ Members
Founded in 1960

4797 Environmental Management Association
Vickie Lewis, EMA President
38575 Mallast
Harrison Township, MI 48045

313-875-9450
866-999-4EMA
Fax: 586-463-8075
E-Mail: emadirector@gmail.com
Home Page: www.emaweb.org

Nancy Kapral, EMA Director
Vickie Lewis, President
Karen Terry-Johnson, VP & Membership Chair

Association for manufacturers, suppliers and distributors of sanitation maintenance supplies, products, services.
11 Members
Founded in 1994

4798 Halogenated Solvents Industry Alliance
1530 Wilson Boulevard
Suite 690
Arlington, VA 22209

703-875-0683
Fax: 703-875-0675
E-Mail: info@hsia.org
Home Page: www.hsia.org

Steve Risotto, Executive Director

Represents manufacturers of perchloroetheylene and related solvents.

4799 ISSA
7373 N Lincoln Ave
Lincolnwood, IL 60712-1799

847-982-0800
800-225-4772
Fax: 847-982-1012
E-Mail: info@issa.com
Home Page: www.issa.com

John Garfinkel, Executive Director
Lydia Work, President
Ted Stark III, Secretary
Ken Vuylsteke Hospeco, Treasurer

The worldwide cleaning industry association.
5700+ Members
Founded in 1923

4800 International Drycleaners Congress
9016 Oak Branch Dr.
Apex, NC 27502

919-363-5062
Fax: 919-387-8326
Home Page: www.idcnews.org

Manfred Wentz, Executive Director
Nobuyasu Igarashi, President

International organization for cleaners.

4801 International Kitchen Exhaust Cleaning Association
100 N. 20th St.
Suite 400
Philadelphia, PA 19103

215-320-3876
Fax: 215-564-2175
E-Mail: information@ikeca.org
Home Page: www.ikeca.org

Sarah Hagy, Executive director
Lisa Chester, Associate Dir.
Hanna Lin, Administrative Dir.
Gina Marinilli, Standard Development Dir.
Tina Phelan, Meeting Manager

Promotes fire safety in restaurants through stringent standards and practices for contractors engaged in kitchen exhaust cleaning. Conducts a variety of educational programs, and works with influential code setting bodies such as the National Fire Protection Association to improve existing codes and regulations.
Founded in 1989

4802 International Maintenance Institute
PO Box 751896
Houston, TX 77275

281-481-0869
Fax: 281-481-8337
E-Mail: iminst@swbell.net
Home Page: www.imionline.org
Social Media: Facebook, Twitter, LinkedIn

George Masterson, Chairman
Gerard Goudreau, President
Joyce Rhoden, Executive Secretary
Edward Stedman, Secretary
Kevin O'Rourke, Treasurer

Focuses on plant workers and vendors who have products tailored to the maintenance industry. The philosophy of the organization is to professionalize the maintenance function by helping maintenance managers to work smarter through the exchange of ideas and education.
2.5M Members
Founded in 1960

4803 **Laundry and Dry Cleaning International**
14700 Sweitzer Lane
Laurel, MD 20707

301-622-1900
800-638-2627
Fax: 240-295-0685
E-Mail: techline@ifi.org
Home Page: www.ifi.org

Patrick Jones, Manager

Sponsors and supports The League of Voter Education Political Action Committee.

4804 **Multi-Housing Laundry Association**
1500 Sunday Drive
Suite 102
Raleigh, NC 27607-5151

919-861-5579
800-380-3652
Fax: 919-787-4916
E-Mail: nshore@mla-online.com
Home Page: www.mla-online.com
Social Media: Facebook, Twitter, LinkedIn

David Feild, Executive Director
Penny DePas CAE, Asst Exec Director/Conference Mgr

Furnishes information on tax and business development and promotes high business standards. Annual meetings held in June.
15M Members
Founded in 1959

4805 **National Association of Diaper Services**
994 Old Eagle School Rd
Suite 1019
Wayne, PA 19087-1802

610-971-4850
Fax: 610-971-4859
E-Mail: nads@diapernet.org
Home Page: www.diapernet.org

John Shiffert, Executive Director

The international professional trade association for the diaper service industry.
Founded in 1938

4806 **National Association of Institutional Linen Management**
2130 Lexington Road
Richmond, KY 40475-7923

800-669-0863
Fax: 859-624-3580
Home Page: www.nailm.org

Jim Thacker, Executive Director

Seeks improvement of laundry technology. Conducts formal schools.
1.4M Members
Founded in 1959

4807 **National Cleaners Association**
252 W 29th St
New York, NY 10001

212-967-3002
800-888-1622
Fax: 212-967-2240
E-Mail: info@nca-i.com
Home Page: www.nca-i.com

Debra Kravet, President
Nora Nealis, Executive Director
Simon Bai, Member Services Staff
Clint Lee, Member Services Staff
Vivian Benn, Office Staff

Professional trade association dedicated to the welfare of well groomed consumers and the professional cleaners who serve them. Elected officials, government angencies, consumer groups, fashion designers and major media outlets have recognized and responded to NCA's activities, reports and tradition of excellence.
4000 Members
Founded in 1946

4808 **North East Fabricare Association**
P.O.Box 920
Pelham, NH 03076

781-942-7630
800-442-6848
Fax: 781-942-7393
E-Mail: peteblke@aol.com
Home Page: www.nefabricare.com

Robert Joel, Vice-President
Jim Desjardins, President
Robert Gervais, Treasurer
John Dallas, Secretary

Serves cleaners in the New England, New Jersey and New York with information and news about the fabricare industry.
Founded in 1992

4809 **Power Washers of North America**
PO Box 270634
Saint Paul, MN 55127

800-393-7962
800-393-7962
Fax: 651-213-0369
E-Mail: pwnahq@pwna.org
Home Page: www.pwna.org

Eric Clark, President
Tom Bickett, Treasurer
John Nearon, VP
Charlie Arnold, Secretary
Jackie Gavett, Executive Dir.

Developing and communicating high standards in ethical business practices, environmental awareness and safety through continuing education and active representation of the membership. PWNA educated and trained contractors raise the level of professionalism and value to their customers.
550 Members
Founded in 1992
Mailing list available for rent: 500 names

4810 **Restoration Industry Association**
12339 Carroll Ave.
Rockville, MD 20852

301-231-6505
800-272-7012
Fax: 301-231-6569
E-Mail: info@restorationindustry.org
Home Page: www.restorationindustry.org
Social Media: Facebook, Twitter, LinkedIn

Timothy Shaw, Executive Director
Patricia L Harman, Communications Director
Samuel J. Bergman, President
Michael E. Gallahan, Secretary
michael Goldberg, Treasurer

A trade association for cleaning and restoration professionals worldwide, and the foremost authority, trainer and educator in the industry.
1100 Members
Founded in 1946

4811 **Rocky Mountain Fabricare Association**
2110 65th Ave.
Greely, CO 80634

970-330-0124
866-964-RFMA
Fax: 303-458-0002
E-Mail: info@rmfa.org
Home Page: www.rmfa.org
Social Media: Facebook

Colleen Mulhern, Executive Director
Brad Ewing, Secretary/Treasurer
Jim Nixon, President

Enhancing the image and viability of the fabricare industry through education and development of the skills, talents and professionalism of its membership. Serves cleaners in Colorado, Utah and Wyoming.
900 Members

4812 **South Eastern Fabricare Association**
14700 Sweitzer Lane
Laurel, MD 20707

877-707-7332
877-707-7332
Fax: 912-355-3155
E-Mail: peter@sefa.org
Home Page: www.sefa.org

Tim Morrow, President
Mark Watkins, VP-Alabama
Julia Campbell, Secretary
Wash Respress, Chairman
Russ Ballard, VP- South Carolina
Trade association that represents its members who have an interest in the dry cleaning and laundry industry.
900+ Members
Founded in 1972
Mailing list available for rent

4813 **Southwest Drycleaners Association**
5750 Balcones Dr.
Suite 201
Austin, TX 78731

512-873-8195
Fax: 512-873-7423
E-Mail: de.sda@sbcglobal.net
Home Page: www.sda-dryclean.com

Andrew Stanley, Executive Director
Michael E. Nesbit, CED, President
Allan Cripe, CED, CPD, 1st Vice President
John Walter, 2nd Vice President
Jeff Schwarz, Sergeant at Arms

Serves cleaners in Louisiana, Mississippi, Missouri, Kansas, Arkansa, New Mexico, Oklahoma and Texas.

4814 **Sponge and Chamois Institute**
10024 Office Center Ave.
Suite 203
St. Louis, MO 63128

314-842-2230
Fax: 314-842-3999
E-Mail: scwaters@swbell.net
Home Page: www.chamoisinstitute.org

Jules Schwimmer, Executive Secretary

Members are dealers and suppliers of natural sponges and chamois leather.
Founded in 1933

4815 **Uniform and Textile Service Association**
12587 Fair Lakes Cir
Fairfax, VA 22033-3822

703-247-2600
800-486-6745
Fax: 703-841-4750
E-Mail: info@utsa.com
Home Page: www.utsa.com

David Hobson, President
Jennifer Kellar, Executive Coordinator
Larry Patton, Director Plant Operations
Deborah Hodges, Director Finance/Administration

Represents textile supply and service companies. Represents 95% of the annual sales generated by the uniform service industry and 65% of the annual sales generated by the linen supply industry. UTSA members provide, clean, and maintain reusable textile products, such as uniforms, sheets, table linen, shop and print towels, floor mats, mops and other items to thousands of businesses.
100 Members
Founded in 1933

Newsletters

4816 Bulletin
Neighborhood Cleaners Association
252 W 29th St
New York, NY 10001-5271
212-967-3002
Fax: 212-967-2240
E-Mail: ncaiclean@aol.com
Home Page: www.nca-i.com
Debra Kravet, President
Technical info for the dry cleaning industry. Government regulation compliance.
Frequency: Bi-Monthly

4817 Coin Laundry Association: Journal
Coin Laundry Association
1315 Butterfield Road
Suite 212
Downers Grove, IL 60515-5602
630-963-5547
Fax: 630-963-5864
E-Mail: info@coinlaundry.org
Home Page: www.coinlaundry.org
Clay Pederson, Chairman
Brian Wallace, President
Bob Nieman, Editor
Laurie Moore, Circulation Manager
Bill Gilbert, Marketing Manager
Committed to offering coin-op owners the information necessary to become and remain competitive in today's changing market.
4 Pages
Frequency: Monthly
Founded in 1960

4818 Fabricare News
Drycleaning & Laundrey Institute International
14700 Sweitzer lane
Laurel, MD 20707
301-622-1900
800-638-2627
Fax: 240-295-4200
E-Mail: techline@dlionline.org
Home Page: www.dlionline.org
Social Media: Facebook
David MacHesny, President
Charlie Smith, Chair
Mary Scalco, CEO
Information of interest to dry cleaners and launderers.
8 Pages
Frequency: Monthly
Circulation: 5000
Founded in 1883

4819 Maytag Commercial Newsletter
Whirlpool Corporation
553 Benson Road
Benton Harbor, MI 49022-2692
269-923-5000
800-344-1274
Home Page: www.maytag.com
Mike Klosterman, Publisher
Debbie White, Executive Director
Self-service laundry industry news.
8 Pages
Frequency: BiWeekly

4820 Reclaimer
South Eastern Fabricare Association
7373 Hodgson Memorial Dr
Building 3, Suite C
Savannah, GA 31406-1595
912-355-3364
877-707-7332
Fax: 912-355-3155
E-Mail: barry@sefa.org
Home Page: www.sefa.org
Billy Stewart, President
Ron McLamb, VP
A monthly newsletter dedicated to the service of the drycleaning industry.
Cost: $5.00
Frequency: Monthly
Circulation: 2200

Magazines & Journals

4821 American Coin-Op
Crain Communications Inc
360 N Michigan Ave
Suite 7
Chicago, IL 60601-3800
312-649-5200
Fax: 312-649-7937
E-Mail: info@crain.com
Home Page: www.crain.com
Keith Crain, CEO
Offers operators, manufacturers and suppliers in-depth coverage of the latest industry trends, new products, energy-saving methods and management strategies.
Frequency: Monthly
Circulation: 17622
Mailing list available for rent

4822 American Drycleaner
Crain Communications Inc
360 N Michigan Ave
Suite 7
Chicago, IL 60601-3800
312-649-5200
Fax: 312-649-7937
E-Mail: info@crain.com
Home Page: www.crain.com
Keith Crain, CEO
Brings news, expert advice and indepth features to drycleaning businesses and suppliers nationwide every month. Stories focus on management, equipment and operations to help owners build their skills and profits.
Frequency: Monthly
Circulation: 24217

4823 American Laundry News
Crain Communications Inc
360 N Michigan Ave
Suite 7
Chicago, IL 60601-3800
312-649-5200
Fax: 312-649-7937
E-Mail: info@crain.com
Home Page: www.crain.com
Keith Crain, CEO
Focuses on the widely varied issues facing the industry: productivity, technology, labor, workplace safety, the environment and more.
Frequency: Monthly
Circulation: 15350
Founded in 1974

4824 American Window Cleaner Magazine
12 Twelve Publishing Corporation
750-B NW Broad Street
Southern Pines, NC 28387
910-693-2644
Fax: 910-246-1681
E-Mail: info@awcmag.com
Home Page: www.awcmag.com
Norman J Finegold, President
Information on new products, add-on businesses, association and convention news and safety.
Frequency: 6x/Year
Circulation: 8000

4825 Broom Brush & Mop
Rankin Publishing Company
204 E Main St
PO Box 130
Arcola, IL 61910-1416
217-268-0130
Fax: 217-268-4815
E-Mail: DRankin125@aol.com
Home Page: www.ragsmag.com
Don Rankin, Owner
Harrell Kerkhoff, Editor
Ron White, Associate Editor
Reports on import and export totals as well as updates on new products and trade show coverage, also industry trends and market conditions.
Cost: $25.00
Frequency: Monthly
Circulation: 1,700
Founded in 1912

4826 Brushware
Brushware
750-B NW Broad St
Southern Pines, NC 28387
910-693-2644
Fax: 910-246-1681
E-Mail: editors@brushwaremag.com
Home Page: www.brushwaremag.com/
Karen Grinter, Publisher
Norman J Finegold, President
Information on products that apply materials, clean and polish surfaces, covers also industry news, products, methods and trends, market reports, profiles and interviews.
Cost: $45.00
Circulation: 2000
Founded in 1898

4827 Cleaner
COLE Publishing
1720 Maple Lake Dam Road
PO Box 220
Three Lakes, WI 54562
715-546-3346
800-257-7222
Fax: 715-546-3786
Home Page: www.cleaner.com
Ted Roulphe, Editor
Geoff Bruss, CEO
The latest tools and equipment promoting safety and efficiency, employment and environmental concerns, as well as industry profiles.
Cost: $15.00
Frequency: Monthly
Circulation: 24000
Founded in 1979

4828 Cleaner Times
Advantage Publishing Company
1000 Nix Rd
Little Rock, AR 72211-3235
866-828-9267
800-525-7038
Fax: 501-280-9233
E-Mail: advpub@adpub.com
Home Page: www.adpub.com
Charlene Yarbrough, Publisher
Gerry Plus, Circualtion Manager
Jim McMurry, Editor
Application, information, and productivity for persons engaged in the manufacturing, distribu-

tion, or the use of high pressure water systems and accessories. The emphasis is on safety, regulatory, which affect the industry as well as cleaning applications.
Cost: $36.00
72 Pages
Frequency: Monthly
Circulation: 25,000
ISSN: 1073-9602
Founded in 1989
Printed in 4 colors on glossy stock

4829 Cleanfax Magazine
National Trade Publications
19 British Amer. Blvd. West
Latham, NY 12110-2197

518-783-1281
Fax: 518-783-1386
E-Mail: webmaster@cleanfax.com
Home Page: www.cleanfax.com

Micah Ogburn, Publisher
Jeff Cross, Senio Editor
Barry Lovette, General Manager

Information on carpet cleaning, water and fire damage restoration, industry news and updates.
80 Pages
Frequency: Monthly
Circulation: 20,000
Founded in 1981
Printed in 4 colors on glossy stock

4830 Cleaning & Restoration Magazine
Restoration Industry Association
9810 Patuxent Woods Dr
Suite K
Columbia, MD 21046-1595

443-878-1000
800-272-7012
Fax: 443-878-1010
E-Mail: info@restorationindustry.org
Home Page: www.restorationindustry.org

Donald E Manger, Executive Director
Patricia L Harman, Communications Director

Trade journal covering fire and water damage restoration, rug and textile cleaning, indoor air quality and business issues.
Frequency: Monthly
Circulation: 6000

4831 Commercial Floor Care
Business News Publishing Company
22801 Ventura Blvd
Suite 115
Woodland Hills, CA 91364-1230

818-224-8035
800-835-4398
Fax: 818-224-8042
E-Mail: stoufferj@bnpmedia.com
Home Page: www.bnpmedia.com

Phil Johnson, Publisher
Jeffrey Stouffer, Editor
Amy Levin, Production Manager
Jim Michaelson, Associate Publisher

Dedicated to floor care in the commercial environment.
40 Pages
Frequency: Monthly
Circulation: 26700
Founded in 1926
Printed in 4 colors on glossy stock

4832 Fabricare
Drycleaning & Laundry Institute International
14700 Sweitzer Lane
Laurel, MD 20707

301-622-1900
800-638-2627
Fax: 240-295-0685
E-Mail: techline@dlif.org
Home Page: www.dlifi.org

Charlie Smith, Chairman
Jan Barlow, President
Dave MacHesny, President-Elect

The central publication of the International Fabricare Institute. This publication provides information, knowledge and education about drycleaning and laundry issues, the industry, as a whole, and the association.
8 Pages
Frequency: Monthly
Circulation: 8,000
Founded in 1883

4833 ICS Cleaning Specialist
Business News Publishing Company
2401 West Big Beaver Road
Troy, MI 48054

818-224-8035
800-835-4398
Fax: 818-224-8042
Home Page: www.bnpmedia.com

Phil Johnson, Publisher
Evan Kessler, Publisher
Eric Fish, Editor
Amy Levin, Production Manager
Jim Michaelson, Associate Publisher

For carpet cleaning, restoration and floor care service providers.
68 Pages
ISSN: 1522-4708
Founded in 1928
Printed in on glossy stock

4834 Industrial Launderer Magazine
Uniform & Textile Service Association
1501 Lee Hwy.kes Cir
Suite 304
Arlington, VA 22209

703-247-2600
800-486-6745
Fax: 703-841-4750

George Harrinton Jr, President

The authoritative source for information for the uniform and textile service industry. It provides practical guidance and assistance for businesses that rent, lease or sell uniforms and other textiles including linen supply.
Cost: $100.00
Frequency: Monthly
Circulation: 6000

4835 International Fabricare Institute
12251 Tech Rd
Silver Spring, MD 20904-1901

301-622-1900
800-638-2627
Fax: 301-236-9320
E-Mail: techline@ifi.org
Home Page: www.ifi.org

William E Fisher, Publisher

The association of Professional Dry Cleaners, wetcleaners, and launderers. With its education, research, testing and professional training, IFI offers solutions that help member businesses provide expert garment care.
Founded in 1883

4836 Journal of the Coin Laundering and Drycleaning Industry
Coin Laundry Association
1315 Butterfield Road
Suite 212
Downers Grove, IL 60515-5602

630-963-5547
800-570-5629
Fax: 630-963-5864
E-Mail: info@coinlaundry.org
Home Page: www.coinlaundry.org

Brian Wallace, President
Clay Pederson, Chairman

The official voice of the coin laundry and drycleaning industry. It's the most cost effective way to reach over 28,000 small business entrepreneurs. Besides industry specific items these owners operate over 38,000 company vehicles, utilize business management materials and more. Accepts advertising.
52 Pages
Frequency: Monthly

4837 Maintenance Sales News
Rankin Publishing Company
204 E Main St
PO Box 130
Arcola, IL 61910-0130

217-268-4959
800-598-8083
Fax: 217-268-4815
E-Mail: drankin125@aol.com
Home Page: www.ragsmag.com

Don Rankin, Owner
Linda Rankin, Co-Publisher
Harrell Kerkhoff, Editor
Rick Mullen, Editor

Information on selling techniques, business management, training, merchandise, and seminars.
Circulation: 18,000

4838 Maintenance Solutions
Trade Press Publishing Corporation
2100 W Florist Avenue
Milwaukee, WI 53209

414-228-7701
Fax: 414-228-1134
E-Mail: contact@facilitiesnet.com
Home Page: www.facilitiesnet.com

Dick Yake, Editoridal Director
Dan Hounsell, Editor
Brad Ehlert, VP Publisher
Robert Geissler, Publisher
Stephen Bolte, Publisher

How to articles and features designed to alleviate reader problems as well as new product information and applications.
Cost: $45.00
42 Pages
Frequency: Monthly
Circulation: 35000
ISSN: 1072-3560
Founded in 1993

4839 Maintenance Supplies
Cygnus Publishing
3 Huntington Quadrangle
Suite 301N
Melville, NY 11747-3601

631-845-2700
800-308-6397
Fax: 720-945-2798
E-Mail: Rich.DiPaolo@cygnuspub.com
Home Page: www.cygnusb2b.com

Tracy Rossi, Publisher
Paul Mackler, President
Rich Di Paolo, Editor
Kathy Scott, Director of Public Relations
Elise Schafer, Assistant Editor

Case histories and general industry news, also supply distributors, new methods and equipment in the field.
Cost: $66.00
Frequency: Monthly
Circulation: 16,500
Founded in 1966

4840 **National Association of Institutional Linen Management News Magazine**
2161 Lexington Rd
Suite 2
Richmond, KY 40475-7952

859-624-0177
800-669-0863
Fax: 859-624-3580
Home Page: www.nlmnet.org

Linda Fairbanks, Executive Director
Randy Wendland, Corporate Director

Offers information for cleaners of fine fabrics.
Frequency: Monthly

4841 **Sanitary Maintenance**
Trade Press Publishing Corporation
2100 W Florist Avenue
Milwaukee, WI 53201-3799

414-228-7701
Fax: 414-228-1134
E-Mail: info@tradepress.com
Home Page: www.tradepress.com

Dick Yake, Editorial Director
Brian Terry, Publisher
Pat Foran, Editor
Robert Wisniewski, CEO

Business management, inventory control and product trends, also includes industrial paper products, cleaning chemicals, safety supplies, janitorial supplies and packaging products.
58 Pages
Frequency: Monthly
Circulation: 16052
ISSN: 0036-4436
Founded in 1943

4842 **Services Magazine**
Building Service Contractors Association Int'l
401 N Michigan Avenue
22nd Floor
Chicago, IL 60611

312-321-5167
800-368-3414
Fax: 312-673-6735
E-Mail: info@bscai.org
Home Page: www.bscai.org

Oliver Yandle, Executive VP/CEO
Karen Lawver, Director Membership Services

The Building Service Contractors Association International is the trade association serving the facility services industry through education, leadership, and representation.
Cost: $30.00
56 Pages
Frequency: Monthly
Circulation: 20064
ISSN: 0279-0548
Founded in 1981
Mailing list available for rent: 20000 names

4843 **Textile Rental Magazine**
Textile Rental Services Association
1800 Diagonal Rd
Suite 200
Alexandria, VA 22314-2842

703-519-0029
877-770-9274
Fax: 703-519-0026
E-Mail: trsa@trsa.org
Home Page: www.trsa.org

Roger Cocivera, President/CEO
Jack Morgan, Editor
Steven Biller, Editorial Director

Packed with valuable tips and ideas.
Frequency: Monthly

4844 **Water Conditioning & Purification Magazine**
Publicom, Incorporated
2800 E. Ft. Lowell Road
Tucson, AZ 85716

520-323-6144
Fax: 520-323-7412
E-Mail: info@wcponline.com
Home Page: www.wcponline.com

Kurt C. Peterson, Publisher
Sharon Peterson, Business Manager
Denise Roberts, Executive Editor

Water Conditioning & Purification Magazine(WC&P) has been the premier source for news, technical artticles and water science features sine 1959. We are committed to the water treatment industry. Our pro bono participation includes event and activity sponsorship, committe members, task force cahiras and association leadership.

Trade Shows

4845 **Association of Specialists in Cleaning & Restoration Convention**
Restoration Industry Association
9810 Patuxent Woods Drive
Suite K
Columbia, MD 21046-1595

443-878-1000
800-272-7012
Fax: 443-878-1010
E-Mail: info@restorationindustry.org
Home Page: www.restorationindustry.org

Donald E Manger, Executive Director
Patricia L Harman, Communications Director

Annual convention and exhibits of carpet, upholstery and draperies cleaning and restoration equipment, duct cleaning supplies and services, 100+ booths.
600 Attendees
Frequency: Annual
Founded in 1945

4846 **Building Service Contractors Association International Trade Show**
401 N Michigan Avenue
22nd Floor
Chicago, IL 60611

312-321-5167
800-368-3414
Fax: 312-673-6735
E-Mail: info@bscai.org
Home Page: www.bscai.org

Oliver Yandle, Executive VP/CEO
Karen Lawver, Director Membership Services

Containing 400 booths and 185 exhibits.
2000 Attendees
Frequency: March/April
Founded in 1965

4847 **Clean Show**
Riddle & Associates
1874 Piedmont Road
Suite 360
Atlanta, GA 30305

404-876-1988
Fax: 404-876-5121
E-Mail: info@cleanshow.com
Home Page: www.cleanshow.com

John Riddle, Manager
Ann Howell, Communications

World's largest exposition for laundry, drycleaning and textile services industry featuring working equipment and educational program. Draws international attendance.
17000 Attendees
Frequency: Biennial, Odd Years
Founded in 1977

4848 **Educational Congress for Laundering & Drycleaning**
Coin Laundry Association
1315 Butterfield Road
Suite 212
Downers Grove, IL 60515-5602

630-963-5547
800-570-5629
Fax: 630-963-5864
E-Mail: info@coinlaundry.org
Home Page: www.coinlaundry.org

Brian Wallace, President
Clay Pederson, Chairman

Two thousand one hundred booths of equipment and products for the cleaning industry. Service schools and other events planned.
22M Attendees
Frequency: July

4849 **National Educational Exposition and Conference**
Environmental Management Association
Fishbones In Greektown
400 Monroe Street
Detroit, MI 48226-3333

Annual show of 15 manufacturers, suppliers and distributors of sanitation maintenance supplies, products, services.
150 Attendees

4850 **Power Clean**
Cleaning Equipment Trade Association
P0 Box 1710
Indian Trail, NC 28079

704-635-7362
800-441-0111
Fax: 704-635-7363
Home Page: www.ceta.org

Troy Tranquill, President
Karl Loeffelholz, Manager

Annual show of 100 manufacturers and suppliers of cleaning equipment, high pressure washers and related component accessories and products.
1200 Attendees
Frequency: October, Dallas

4851 **Southern Drycleaners Show**
South Eastern Fabricare Association
P0 Box 912
Cumming, GA 30028

877-707-7332
Fax: 770-998-1441
Home Page: www.sefa.org

Joel Deutsch, Manager

Trade show for the drycleaning industry with 120 exhibitors and 250 booths.
2500 Attendees
Frequency: August

4852 **Tex Care**
National Cleaners Association
252 W 29th Street
New York, NY 10001

212-967-3002
Fax: 212-967-2240
E-Mail: ncaiclean@aol.com
Home Page: www.nca-i.com

Joseph Hallak, President
Ted Aveni, First Vice President

Containing 350 exhibits of interest to member cleaners.
5000+ Attendees
Frequency: April

Directories & Databases

4853 Carpet Cleaners Institute of the Northwest Membership Roster
147 SE 102nd Avenue
Portland, OR 97216-2703
503-253-9091
805-261-8222
Fax: 503-253-9172
E-Mail: info@ccinw.org
Home Page: www.ccinw.org
Over 330 member companies involved in the carpet cleaning industry in Washington, Oregon, and Montana, USA and Alberta and British Columbia, Canada.
Frequency: Annual

4854 Cleaning and Maintenance Management: Buyer's Guide Directory Issue
National Trade Publications
13 Century Hill Drive
Latham, NY 12110-2197
518-783-1281
Fax: 518-783-1386
Home Page: cmmonline.com
Alice J Savino, Group Publisher
Chris Sanford, Executive Editor
Over 500 manufacturers are profiled that supply equipment used in building maintenance and housekeeping.
Cost: $42.00
84 Pages
Frequency: Annual
Circulation: 42000
ISSN: 1051-5720
Founded in 1966
Mailing list available for rent: 42M names at $125 per M
Printed in 4 colors on glossy stock

4855 Coin Laundry Association of Suppliers
Coin Laundry Association
1315 Butterfield Road
Downers Grove, IL 60515
630-963-5547
800-570-5629
Fax: 630-963-5864
E-Mail: info@coinlaundry.org
Home Page: www.coinlaundry.org
Brian Wallace, President
Clay Pederson, Chairman
Bob Nieman, Editor
Kathy Sherman, Director Administration
Sue Lally, Director Membership
Lists over 500 manufacturers and suppliers of products and services to the coin and dry cleaning laundry industries.
2700+ Pages
Founded in 1960

4856 Inside Textile Service - Directories
Uniform & Textile Service Association
12587 Fair Lakes Cir
Fairfax, VA 22033-3822
703-247-2600
800-486-6745
Fax: 703-841-4750
E-Mail: info@utsa.com
Home Page: www.utsa.com
David Hobson, President
Jennifer Kellar, Executive Coordinator
The uniform and textile service industry's most comprehensive guide to US textile service companies. Includes contact data for UTSA's membership, and for hundreds of other textile service companies as well. Contains listings of all UTSA affiliated suppliers with catalog-like data on their products and services. Free to members.
Circulation: 3,000

4857 Textile Rental Services Association Roster
Textile Rental Services Association
1800 Diagonal Rd
Suite 200
Alexandria, VA 22314-2842
703-519-0029
Fax: 703-519-0026
E-Mail: trsa@trsa.org
Home Page: www.trsa.org
Roger Cocivera, President
Scott Mallan, Finance Manager
Michael Wilson, Director Government Affairs
Jack Morgan, Editor
Offers a list of over 1,800 companies that supply linen, uniforms and other textile products to other industries.
1300 Pages
Founded in 1913

Industry Web Sites

4858 http://gold.greyhouse.com
G.O.L.D Grey House OnLine Databases
Grey House Publishing's online database platform, GOLD, offers Quick Search, Keyword Search and Expert Search for most business sectors inlcuding the cleaning and laundry markets. Finding the information you need quick and easy - whether you're a novice searcher or an experienced database user. All of Grey House's directory products are available for subscription on the GOLD platform.

4859 www.ascr.org
Assn of Specialists in Cleaning and Restoration
For professionals involved in the cleaning and restoration of interior textiles and structures, including air handling systems.

4860 www.bscai.org
Building Service Contractors Association Int'l
For companies offering security, maintenance and cleaning services.

4861 www.ceta.org
Cleaning Equipment Trade Association
For manufacturers and suppliers of cleaning equipment, high pressure washers and related component accessories and products.

4862 www.cminstitute.net
Cleaning Management Institute
CMI provides education, training and career improvement opportunities for building cleaning and maintenance professionals.

4863 www.coinlaundry.org
Coin Laundry Association
For self-service laundry and dry cleaning industry. CLA is a not for profit trade association representing the 30,000 coin laundry owners in the US and the world.

4864 www.greyhouse.com
Grey House Publishing
Authoritative reference directories for most business sectors including cleaning and laundry markets. Users can search the online databases with varied search criteria allowing for custom searches by product category, geographic area, sales volume, keyword, subject and more. Full Grey House catalog and online ordering also available.

4865 www.ifi.org
International Fabricare Institute
With its education, research, testing and professional training, IFI offers solutions that help member businesses provide expert garment care.

4866 www.ikeca.org
International Kitchen Exhaust Cleaning Association
Education for members about safety, cleaning techniques and many other areas. Since its inception, IKECA, a not for profit trade association, has established stringent standards and practices for contractors engaged in kitchen exhaust clening, conducted a variety of educational programs, and worked with influential code setting bodies such as the National Fire Protection Association to improve existing codes and regulations.

4867 www.imionline.org
International Maintenance Institute
Focuses on plant workers and vendors who have products tailored to the maintenance industry. The philosophy of the organization is to professionalize the maintenance functiuon by helping maintenace managers to work smarter through the exchange of ideas and function.

4868 www.jriddle.com
Riddle & Associates
For the laundering, drycleaning and textile care industry - from single-owner coin-operated laundry and drycleaning establishments to giant industrial and institutional laundries. Our management capabilities work for any type of trade show - large or small. Our experience with heavy utility shows, and shows with highly technical requirements, gives us an expertise in these areas that is difficult to find.

4869 www.nailm.org
National Assn of Insurance Litigation Management
National educational and research group concerned primarily with the advancement of the art of manageing litigated claims.

4870 www.natclo.com
National Clothesline
News of interest to drycleaners. Links to regional and state associations, calendar of events.

4871 www.nca-i.com
Neighborhood Cleaners Association
Professional trade association dedicated to the welfare of well-groomed consumers and the professional cleaners and suppliers who serve them. for over 50 years, NCA has been at the vanguard of education, research and information distribution concerning garment and household fabric care. Elected officials, goverment agencies, consumer groups, fashion designers and major media outlets have recognized and responded to NCA's activities, reports and tradition of excellence.

4872 www.pwna.org
Power Washers of North America
Developing and communicating the highest standards in ethical business practices, environmental awareness and safety through continuing education and active representation of the membership. PWNA educated and trained contractors raise the level of professionalism and value to their customers.

4873 **www.rmfa.org**
Rocky Mountain Fabricare Association
Enhancing the image and viability of the fabricare industry through education and development of the skills, talents, and professionalism of its membership.

4874 **www.sdahq.org**
Soap and Detergent Association
Nonprofit tade association representing over 100 North American manufacturers of household, industrial and institutional cleaning products; their ingredients and finished packaging. Established in 1926, SDA is dedicated to advancing public understanding of the safety and benefits of cleaning products and protecting the ability of its members to formulate products that best meet consumer needs.

4875 **www.sefa.org**
South Eastern Fabricare Association
Trade association that represents its members who have an interest in the dry cleaning and laundry industry. The not for profit asscoiation provides value through education, research, legislative representation, industry specific information programs, products and services.

4876 **www.uniforminfo.com**
Uniform & Textile Service Association
Uniform companies provide more than just corporate apparel programs. Companies on this site offer a wide variety of products and services that will not only ensure that your unique corporate identity is conveyed consistently, but will help your workplace run more smoothly.

4877 **www.utsa.com**
Uniform & Textile Service Association
One stop place for important industry and UTSA news. It has complete information on upcoming events and activities, including online meeting brochures and secure online registration. Each department at UTSA has its own page where you will find information about committees, projects, regulations, and links to dozens of other pertinent sites such as the Clean Show or government sites.

Associations

4878 **Accuracy in Media**
4350 East West Highway
Suite 555
Bethesda, MD 20814

202-364-4401
800-787-4567
Fax: 202-364-4098
E-Mail: info@aim.org
Home Page: www.aim.org
Social Media: Facebook, Twitter, LinkedIn, YouTube

Don Irvine, Chairman
Deborah Lambert, Director of Special Projects
Roger Aronoff, Editor
Cliff Kincaid, Dir. AIM Center

Accuracy in Media is a non-profit, grassroots citizens watchdog of the news media that critiques botched and bungled news stories and sets the record straight on important issues that have received slanted coverage.
3500 Members
Founded in 1969

4879 **Advanced Television Systems Committee**
1776 K Street NW
8th Floor
Washington, DC 20006-2304

202-872-9160
Fax: 202-872-9161
E-Mail: atsc@atsc.org
Home Page: www.atsc.org
Social Media: Facebook, Twitter

Mark Richer, President
Jerry Whitaker, Vice President
Lindsay Shelton Gross, Director, Communications
Daro Bruno, Office Manager

ATSC is an international, non-profit organzation developing voluntary standards for digital television.

4880 **Agricultural Communications in Education**
University of Florida
Mowry Road
Building 16
Gainesville, FL 32611

352-392-9588
Fax: 603-862-1585
E-Mail: ace@ifas.ufl.edu
Home Page: www.aceweb.org

Kristina Boone, President
Steve Dodrill, VP
Hugh Maynard, Associate Director

Members are writers, editors, broadcasters and communicators who are involved in the dissemination of agricultural, food sciences and natural resource information in land-grant colleges, federal and state agencies, international agencies and other private communications work.
700+ Members
Founded in 1970

4881 **Alliance for Telecommunication Industry Solutions**
1200 G St NW
Suite 500
Washington, DC 20005

202-628-6380
Fax: 202-393-5453
E-Mail: membership@atis.org
Home Page: www.atis.org

Susan Miller, President/CEO
Andrew White, VP of Technology & Standards
Lauren Layman, VP of Marketing & Public Relations
Kris Rinne, Chairman
Bill Klein, VP Finance/Operations

Membership organization that provides the tools necessary for the industry to identify standards, guidelines and operating procedures that make the inoperability of existing and emerging telecommunications products and services possible.
1400 Members
Founded in 1983

4882 **Alliance for Telecommunications Industry Solutions**
1200 G Street, NW
Suite 500
Washington, DC 20005

202-628-6380
Home Page: www.atis.org
Social Media: Twitter, LinkedIn

Susan Miller, President & CEO
Thomas Goode, General Counsel
Lauren Layman, VP, Marketing and Public Relations
Andrew White, VP, Technology and Standards

A standards organization that develops technical and operational standards and solutions for the ICT industry.

4883 **American Communication Association**
College of Business Administration
The University of Northern Iowa
1227 W 27th Street
Cedar Falls, IA 50614-0125

209-667-3374
E-Mail: pdecaro@csustan.edu
Home Page: www.americancomm.org

Dr. Phillip J. Auter, Executive Director
Prof. Jim Parker, President
Vernon Humphrey, CFO
Myrene Augustin Magabo, Secretary
Dr. John Malalala, CIO

Founded for the purposes of fostering research and scholarship in all areas of human communication behavior, promoting and improving excellence in the pedagogy of communication, providing a voice in communication law and policy, providing evaluation and certification services for academic programs in communication study.
Founded in 1993

4884 **American Public Communications Council**
625 Slaters Ln
Suite 104
Alexandria, VA 22314

703-739-1322
Fax: 703-739-1324
E-Mail: APCC@apcc.net
Home Page: www.apcc.net

Willard R. Nichols, President
Deborah Sterman, CFO
Helly Shareefy, Office Manager
Dan Collins, Corporate Counsel
Evelyn Bruggeman, Account Manager

Formed to promote and address, at the FCC and on Capitol Hill, the legal and regulatory issues facing payphone service providers.
1200 Members
Founded in 1988

4885 **Armed Forces Broadcasters Association**
Po Box 447
Sun City, CA 92586-0447

951-672-7299
Fax: 951-679-5484
E-Mail: webmaster@afbanational.org
Home Page: www.afbanational.org

Mary Carnes, President

Enhances comaraderie among former, present, and future members of the military broadcasting community; provides employment search assistance.
600 Members
Founded in 1982

4886 **Armed Forces Communications & Electronics Association**
4400 Fair Lakes Ct
Fairfax, VA 22033-3899

703-631-6100
800-336-4583
Fax: 703-631-6169
Home Page: www.afcea.org
Social Media: Facebook, Twitter, LinkedIn, YouTube, Flickr

Kent Schneider, President/CEO
Nancy Temple, International Secretary
James L. Griggs, Jr., VP, CIO & CTO
Al Grasso, Chairman
Pat Morin, CPA, EVP, CFO & International Treasurer

A non-profit membership association serving the military, government, industry, and academia as an ethical forum for advancing professional knowledge and relationships in the fields of communications, IT, intelligence, and global security.
31000 Members
Founded in 1946

4887 **AscdiNatd**
131 NW First Avenue
Delray Beach, FL 33444

561-266-9016
Fax: 561-431-6302
Home Page: www.ascdi.com

Rob Neumeyer, Board Member
Jerry Roberts, Board Member
Todd A. Bone, Board Member
Thomas Weltin, Board Member
Scott Fluty, Board Member

An international trade association made up of companies who providetechnology solutions, technical support, and value added services to the business community.

4888 **Association Media & Publishing**
12100 Sunset Hills Road
Suite 130
Reston, VA 20190

703-234-4063
Fax: 703-435-4390
E-Mail: info@associationmediaandpublishing.org
Home Page: associationmediaandpublishing.org
Social Media: Facebook, Twitter, LinkedIn

Erin Pressley, President, BOD
Angel Alvarez-Mapp, Vice President, BOD
Kim Howard, CAE, Immediate Past President
Leslie McGee, Treasurer
John Falcioni, Assistant Treasurer

Serves the needs of association publishers, communications professionals and the media they create.
Founded in 1963

4889 **Association for Business Communication**
181 Turner St, NW
Blacksburg, VA 24061

540-231-8460
Fax: 646-349-5297
E-Mail: abcoffice@businesscommunication.org

Home Page: businesscommunication.org
Social Media: Facebook, Twitter

Kathy Rentz, First VP
Peter W. Cardon, Second VP
Nancy Schullery, President
James Dubinsky, Executive Dir.
Marilyn Buerkens, Office Manager

International organization commited to fostering excellence in business communication scholarship, research, education, and practice.
72 Members
Founded in 1935

4890 Association for Conservation Information
Division of Fish Game and Wildlife
Po Box 400
Trenton, NJ 08625-0400

609-984-0837
Fax: 609-984-1414
Home Page: www.aci-net.org
Social Media: Facebook

Don King, President
Micah Holmes, Vice-President
Robin Cahoon, Secretary
Judy Stokes Weber, Treasurer
Rachel Bradley, Board Member

Works to upgrade the quality of all forms of communication in and among agencies devoted to the protection and management of natural resources and wildlife.
110 Members
Founded in 1984

4891 Association for Educational Communications and Technology
320 W. 8th St.
Suite 101
Bloomington, IN 47404-3745

812-335-7675
877-677-AECT
Fax: 812-335-7678
E-Mail: aect@aect.org
Home Page: www.aect.org
Social Media: Facebook, Twitter

Phillip Harris, Executive Director
Larry Vernon, Electronic Services
Mark Childress, President

For audiovisual and instructional materials specialists, educational technologists, audiovisual and television production personnel, school media specialists.
2200 Members
Founded in 1923
Mailing list available for rentat $159 per M

4892 Association for Information Systems
Po Box 2712
Atlanta, GA 30301-2712

404-651-0348
Fax: 404-651-4938
E-Mail: WebMaster@ALSNe.org
Home Page: www.aisnet.org
Social Media: Twitter, LinkedIn

Pete Tinsley, Executive Director
Jane Fedorowicz, President
Mary C. Jones, Secretary
Matthew Nelson, Treasurer
Richard Baskerville, VP of Communications

AIS members are academics with interest in information systems and related fields.
4300 Members
Founded in 1994

4893 Association for Information and Image Management
1100 Wayne Avenue
Suite 1100
Silver Spring, MD 20910

301-587-8202
800-477-2446
E-Mail: aiim@aiim.org
Home Page: www.aiim.org
Social Media: Facebook, Twitter, LinkedIn, YouTube, Google+, RSS

Paul Engel, Chair, Finance Committee
John F. Mancini, President, CEO
Atle Skjekkeland, Chief Evangelist
Felicia Dillard, Chief Financial Officer
Peggy Winton, Vice President and CMO

A nonprofit membership organization that provides education, marketresearch, certification, and standards for information professionals.

4894 Association for Interactive Marketing
1430 Broadway Avenue
8th Floor
New York, NY 10018

888-337-0008
Fax: 212-391-9233
E-Mail: info@interactivehq.org
Home Page: www.interactivehq.org

Kevin Noonan, Executive Director

AIM is a non-profit trade association for interactive marketers and service providers.

4895 Association for Multi-Media International
PO Box 1897
Lawrence, KS 66044

866-393-4264
Fax: 785-843-1274
E-Mail: hq@ami.org

Vanessa Reilly, Executive Director

The professional objectives of the AMI are to promote the safety and advancement of medical illustration and allied fields of visual communication, and to promote understanding and cooperation with the medical profession and related health science professions.
1M Members
Founded in 1974

4896 Association for Postal Commerce
1800 Diagonal Rd.
Suite 320
Alexandria, VA 22314-2862
703-524-0096
Fax: 703-997-2414
Home Page: www.postcom.org

Gene Del Polito, President

National organization representing those who use, or who support, the use of mail as a medium for communication and commerce. Publishes a weekly newsletter covering postal policy and operational issues.
231 Members
Founded in 1947

4897 Association for Service Managers International
11031 Via Frontera
Suite A
San Diego, CA 92127

239-275-7887
800-333-9786
Fax: 239-275-0794
E-Mail: info@afsmi.org
Home Page: www.afsmi.org

J.B. Wood, President
Thomas Lah, Executive Director

A global organization dedicated to furthering the knowledge, understanding, and career development of executives, managers and professionals in the high technology service industry.
3000+ Members
Founded in 1975

4898 Association for Women in Communications
3337 Duke Street
Alexandria, VA 22314

703-370-7436
Fax: 703-342-4311
Home Page: www.womcom.org
Social Media: Facebook, Twitter, LinkedIn, YouTube, Google+

Mitzie Zerr, Chair
Sheila Scarborough, Vice Chair
Jill Randolph, Treasurer
Judy Arent-Morency, Immediate Past Chair
Lisa Angle, Secretary

An American professional organization for women in the communications industry.
Founded in 1909

4899 Association of Alternative Newsmedia
116 Cass Street
Traverse City, MI 49684ÿ

703-470-2996
Fax: 866-619 9755
E-Mail: web@aan.org
Home Page: www.altweeklies.com
Social Media: Facebook, Twitter, RSS, Google+

Sally Freeman, President
Amy Austin, Vice President
Ellen Meany, Treasurer
Tiffany Shackelford, Executive Director
Jason Zaragoza, Editor / Advertising Director

A trade association of alternative weekly newspapers in North America.
Founded in 1978

4900 Association of Cable Communicators
PO Box 75007
Washington, DC 20013-5007

202-222-2370
800-210-3396
Fax: 202-222-2371
E-Mail: services@cablecommunicators.org
Home Page: www.cablecommunicators.org
Social Media: Facebook, Twitter, LinkedIn

Rosa Gatti, President
Catherine Frymark, Secretary
Steven R. Jones, Executive Dir.
Annie Howell, EVP, Communications
Catherine Frymark, Communications

ACC is the only national, professional organization specifically addressing the issues, needs and interests of the cable industry's communications and public affairs professionals.
Founded in 1985

4901 Association of Federal Communications Consulting Engineers
PO Box 19333
Washington, DC 20036

941-329-6000
Fax: 703-591-0115
Home Page: www.afcce.org
Social Media: Facebook

David Snavely, President
Ben Evans, VP
Eric Wandel, secretary
Ron Chase, treasurer
Rich Biby, Director

An organization of professional engineering consultants serving the telecommunications industry.
250 Members
Founded in 1948

4902 Association of Information Technology Professionals
1120 Route 73
Suite 200
Mount Laurel, NJ 08054-5113

856-380-6910
800-224-9371
Fax: 856-439-0525
E-Mail: aitp_hq@aitp.org
Home Page: www.aitp.org
Social Media: Twitter, LinkedIn

Michael Welch, Board of Director
Barbara Viola, Board of Director
Melissa Baldwin, Executive Director
Heather Blush, Membership Director
Vanessa Smith, Membership/Chapter Relations Coor

A professional association that focuses on information technology education for business professionals.
Founded in 1951

4903 Association of Medical Illustrators
201 E. Main St.
Suite 1405
Lexington, KY 40507

866-393-4264
Fax: 859-514-9166
E-Mail: hq@ami.org
Home Page: www.ami.org
Social Media: RSS Feed

John Dorn, MA, Treasurer
Emily Shaw, Secretary
Joanne Haderer Muller, Chairman
Melanie Bowzer, Account Executive
Tonya Hines, President

An international organization of media professionals who promote, produce and utilize a wide range of presentation media.
1M Members
Founded in 1944

4904 Association of Professional Communication Consultants
211 E 28th st
Tulsa, OK 74114-3329

918-743-4793
Fax: 918-745-0932
Home Page: www.consultingsuccess.org
Social Media: LinkedIn

Reva Daniel, Association Manager
Lee Johns, Treasurer

Professional community of communication consultants where members can increase their knowledge, grow their business and achieve high standards of professional practice. Services include professional development workshops, online newsletter and referral database and active listserve discussions.
200 Members
Founded in 1982

4905 Association of Schools of Journalism & Mass Communications
234 Outlet Pointe Boulevard
Columbia, SC 29210-5667

803-798-0271
Fax: 803-772-3509
E-Mail: aejmchq@aol.com
Home Page: www.asjmc.org

Jennifer McGill, Executive Director
Donald Heider, President
Brad Rawlins, Vice-President
Ann Bill, President Elect
Mary Arnold, Executive Committee Representative

Promotes excellence in journalism and mass communication education. Non-profit, educational association composed of some 190 JMC programs at the college level. Eight international journalism and communication schools have joined the association in recent years.
202 Members
Founded in 1917

4906 Association of Teachers of Technical Writing
Department Of Linguistics And Technical Comm.
1155 Union Circle #305298
Denton, TX 76203-5017

940-565-4458
E-Mail: sims@unt.edu
Home Page: www.attw.org
Social Media: Facebook, Twitter, LinkedIn

TyAnna Herrington, Information officer
Michele Simmons, President
Michelle Eble, Vice-President
Brenda Sims, Secretary
Ann Blakeslee, Treasurer

Provides communication among teachers of technical writing and develops technical communications as an academic discipline.
600 Members
Founded in 1973

4907 Association of Women in Communications
3337 Duke Street
Alexandria, VA 22314

703-370-7436
Fax: 703-342-4311
E-Mail: info@womcom.org, members@womcom.org
Home Page: www.womcom.org
Social Media: Facebook, Twitter, LinkedIn, Youtube

Maria Henneberry, Chair
Mitzie Zerr, Treasurer
Pamela Vanlenzuela, Executive Dir.
Beth Veney, Communications & programs Manager
Caitlin Sloan, Membership Coordinator

Professional organization that champions the advancement of women across all communications disciplines by recognizing excellence, promoting leadership and positioning its members at the forefront of the evolving communications era. Hosts an internal, bi-annual meeting.
3500 Members
Founded in 1909
Mailing list available for rent

4908 BioCommunications Association
220 Southwind Lane
Hillsborough, NC 27278

919-245-0906
E-Mail: office@bca.org
Home Page: www.bca.org
Social Media: Facebook, Twitter, LinkedIn

Joseph Kane, President
Connie Johansen, RBP, Vice President
James Koepfler, FBCA, Treasurer/Secretary
Susanne Loomis, FBCA, Immediate Past President
Keith Bullis, Director at Large

An international association of photographers and media professionals who create and use quality images in visual communications for teaching, documentation and presentations in the life sciences and medicine.
Founded in 1931

4909 Business Information Technology Network
414 Locust Street
Suite 203
Burlington, ON L7S 1T7

E-Mail: info@bitnet.ca
Home Page: www.bitnet.ca
Social Media: Facebook, Twitter, LinkedIn, YouTube

Ron Durkin, President
Steve Rieck, Vice President
Barrie Haywood, Treasurer
Kathryn Rogers, Secretary

An association of individuals, business and organizations with a common interest in the practical and innovative use and development of technology.
Founded in 1992

4910 Cable in the Classroom
25 Massachussetts Ave NW
Suite 100
Washington, DC 20001

202-222-2335
Fax: 202-222-2336
E-Mail: help@ciconline.org
Home Page: www.ciconline.org
Social Media: Facebook, Twitter

Frank Gallagher, Executive Director
Helen Chamberlin, Deputy Executive Director
Kat Stewart, Director, Strategic Initiatives
Beverly Hicks, Assistant Director

Promotes the visionary, sensible, responsible and effective use of cable's broaband technology, services, and content in teaching and learning. CIC also advocates digtial citizenship and supports the complimentary provision, by cable industry companies, of broadband and multichannel video services and educational content to the nation's schools.

4911 CanWest Media Sales
121 Bloor Street East
Suite 1500
Toronto, ON M4W 3M5

416-967-1174
Fax: 416-967-1285
E-Mail: info@shawmedia.ca
Home Page: www.shawmedia.ca

Andrew Akman, VP

Televison and newspaper advertising, marketing, and sales company.

4912 Center for Communication
110 East 23rd Street
Suite 900
New York, NY 10010

216-686-5005
Fax: 212-504-2632
E-Mail: info@cencom.org
Home Page: www.cencom.org
Social Media: Facebook, Twitter, Youtube

David Barrett, Chairman
Tim Armstrong, CEO & chairman
Catherine Williams, Executice Dir.
Alaina Bendi, VP Membership/Business Development
Kate Stanley, Program Dir.

Exposes young people to the issues, the ethics, the people, and the creative product that defines the media business. Offers students interested in media careers a unique opportunity to learn about the world of communications.

4913 **Center for International Media Assistance**
1025 F Street NW
Suite 800
Washington, DC 20004

202-378-9700
Fax: 202-378-9407
E-Mail: CIMA@ned.org
Home Page: cima.ned.org
Social Media: Facebook, Twitter

Mark Nelson, Senior Director
Don Podesta, Manager and Editor
Valerie Popper, Assist Program & Officer
Rosemary D'Amour, Associate Editor
Paul Rothman, Assistant Partnerships Officer

Provides information, builds networks, conducts research, and highlights the role media play in the creation and development of sustainable democracies.

4914 **Center for Media Literacy**
22837 Pacific Coast Highway
#472
Malibu, CA 90265

310-804-3985
E-Mail: cml@medialit.org
Home Page: www.medialit.org
Social Media: YouTube

Elizabeth Thoman CHM, Founder
Tessa Jolls, President, CEO
Beth Thornton, Communications

An educational organization that provides leadership, public education, professional development and educational resources nationally and internationally.

4915 **Communication Media Management Association**

Home Page: www.cmma.org
Social Media: Facebook, Twitter, LinkedIn, RSS

Chris Barry, President
Gregg Moss, President-Elect
Clifton Brewer, Vice President
Thomas M. Densmore, Treasurer
Susan Kehoe, Secretary

Provides professional development and networking opportunities for communications media managers.
Founded in 1946

4916 **CompTIA**
3500 Lacey Road
Suite 100
Downers Grove, IL 60515

630-678-8300
Fax: 630-678-8384
E-Mail: techvoice@comptia.org
Home Page: www.comptia.org
Social Media: Facebook, Twitter, LinkedIn, Google+, YouTube, Pinterest

Todd Thibodeaux, President/ Chief Executive Officer
Nancy Hammervik, Senior VP, Industry Relations
Kelly Ricker, SVP, Events and Education
David Sommer, Chief Financial Officer
Randy Gross, Chief Information Officer

A nonprofit trade association created by representatives of five microcomputer leaderships and is a provider of professional certifications for theinformation technology (IT) industry.

4917 **Computer and Communications Industry Association**
900 17th Street, NW
Suite 1100
Washington, DC 20006

202-783-0070
Fax: 202-783-0534
Home Page: www.ccianet.org
Social Media: Facebook, Twitter, RSS

Edward Black, President, CEO
Daniel Johnson, Vice President & General Counsel
Catherine Sloan, VP, Government Relations
Matthew Schruers, Vice President, Law & Policy
Dan O'Connor, Vice President, Public Policy

Association of computer product vendors and communications firms lobbying for free trade and open markets.

4918 **Consolidated Tape Association**
C/O New York Stock Exchange
11 Wall Street, 21st Floor
New York, NY 10005

212-656-2052
Fax: 212-656-5848
E-Mail: phussey@nyse.com

Patricia Hussey, Administrator

Members are stock exchanges and the National Association of Securities Dealers. CTA melds the reporting of transactions from the various stock exchanges.
9 Members
Founded in 1974

4919 **Consortium for School Networking**
1025 Vermont Ave NW
Suite 1010
Washington, DC 20005

202-861-2676
866-267-8747
Fax: 202-393-2011
E-Mail: info@cosn.org
Home Page: www.cosn.org
Social Media: Facebook, Twitter, LinkedIn

Randy Wilhelm, CEO & Co-Founder
Jean Tower, Chair
Michael Jamerson, Treasurer
Alice Owen, Ph.D., Secretary
Walter l. Fox, Executive Director

Promotes the development and use of internet and information technologies for K-12 learning. Members are school districts, states, nonprofits and commercial organizations, all of whom share the goal of promoting the state of the art in computer networking technologies in schools.
450 Members
Founded in 1992

4920 **Cooperative Communicators Association**
174 Crestview Dr
Bellefonte, PA 16823-8516

877-326-5994
Fax: 814-355-2452
E-Mail: CCA@communicators.coop
Home Page: www.communicators.coop
Social Media: Facebook, Twitter

Katrice Bryant Graham, President
Marian Douglas, Director
Alexa Stoner, Treasurer
Marian Douglas, Secretary
Chandra Allen, VP

A teaching and news tool for the Cooperative Communicators Association, CCA consists communicators, editors, photographers, graphics, designers, public relations specialists who work for cooperatives in 35 states, Canada and Poland.
350 Members
Founded in 1953

4921 **Council of Communication Management**
65 Enterprise
Aliso Viejo, CA 92656

866-463-6226
Fax: 949-715-6931
E-Mail: info@thecommunicationexchange.org
Home Page: www.ccmconnection.com
Social Media: Facebook, Twitter, LinkedIn

Barry Mike, President
Steve Forsyth, VP
John Jensen, Secretary
Sherry Scott, Past President
Leila Bryner, Director

Provides a network through which managers, consultants and educators, who work at the policy level in organizational communication can help one another advance the practice of communication in business.
270 Members
Founded in 1955

4922 **Council of Science Editors**
10200 W 44th Ave.
Suite 304
Wheat Ridge, CO 80033

720-881-6046
Fax: 703-435-4390
E-Mail: CSE@CouncilScienceEditors.org
Home Page: www.councilscienceeditors.org

Heather Goodell, President
Barbara Gomez, Executive Vice President
Tim Cross, President-Elect
Angela Cochran, VP
ken Heideman, Past President

Membership consists of individuals concerned with writing, editing and publishing in the life sciences and related fields.
1200 Members
Founded in 1957

4923 **Digital Media Association (DiMA)**
1050 17th St., NW
Suite 220
Washington, DC 20036

202-639-9509
E-Mail: info@digmedia.org
Home Page: www.digmedia.org

Lee Knife, Executive Director
Greg Barnes, General Counsel
Ann Brown, Communications Consultant
Aileen Atkins, SVP/General Counsel
Bill Way, VP/ General Counsel

National trade organization devoted primarily to the online audio and video industries, and more generally to commercially innovative digital media opportunities.

4924 **Drug Information Association**
800 Enterprise Road
Suite 200
Horsham, PA 19044-3595

215-442-6100
Fax: 215-442-6199
E-Mail: DIA@diahome.org
Home Page: www.diahome.org
Social Media: Facebook, Twitter, LinkedIn, YouTube, Weibo, Digg, Reddit

Ling Su, President
John Roberts, Treasurer
Barbara Lopez Kunz, Global Chief Executive
Bayard Gardineer, CPA, CFO
Elizabeth Lincoln, MA, Worldwide Dir., HR

Provides a neutral global forum for the exchange and dissemination of information on the discovery, development, evaluation and utilization of medicines and related health care technologies. Through these activities the DIA

provides development opportunities for its members.
20000 Members
Founded in 1964

4925 EDUCAUSE
1150 18th St NW
Suite 900
Washington, DC 20036

202-872-4200
Fax: 202-872-4318
E-Mail: info@educause.edu
Home Page: www.educause.edu
Social Media: Facebook, Twitter, LinkedIn, Flickr

Mark Luker, VP

EDUCAUSE is a nonprofit association whose mission is to advance higher education by promoting the intelligent use of information technology.
17M Members
Founded in 1962

4926 Eastern Communication Association
600 Forbes Ave
340 College Hall
Pittsburgh, PA 15282

E-Mail: info@ecasite.org
Home Page: www.ecasite.org
Social Media: Facebook, Twitter

Thomas R. Flynn, President
J. Kanan Sawyer, Vice President
Jason S. Wrench, First Vice President Elect
Danette Ifert Johnson, Immediate Past President
Ronald C. Arnett, Executive Director

A professional organization of scholars, teachers, and students of Communcation Studies.
Founded in 1910

4927 Electronic Retailing Association
607 14th St., NW
Suite 530
Washington, DC 20005

703-841-1751
800-987-6462
Fax: 425-977-1036
E-Mail: webadmin@retailing.org
Home Page: www.retailing.org
Social Media: Facebook, Twitter, LinkedIn, YouTube, Flickr

Julie Coons, President & CEO
Kevin S. Kelly, CFO & COO
Bill McClellan, VP, Govt Affairs
Dave Martin, VP, Marketing & Content
Cecilia Mason, Accounting Manager

To foster growth, development and acceptance of the rapidly growing direct response industry worldwide for the companies who use the power of electronic media to sell goods and services to the public.
Founded in 1991
Mailing list available for rent

4928 Enterprise Wireless Alliance (EWA)
8484 Westpark Drive
Suite 630
McLean, VA 22102

703-528-5115
800-482-8282
Fax: 703-524-1074
E-Mail:
customerservice@enterprisewireless.org
Home Page: www.enterprisewireless.org

Mark Crosby, President/CEO
Andre Cote, Senior VP
Ila Dudley, VP of Spectrum Solutions
Ron Franklin, Customer Service Manager
Karen Fouchie, Accounting Manager

Formerly ITA and AMTA, works to preserve spectrum rights and assets for enterprise wireless customers.
1200 Members
Founded in 1953

4929 Forest Industries Telecommunications
1565 Oak St
Eugene, OR 97401

541-485-8441
Fax: 541-485-7556
E-Mail: license@landmobile.com
Home Page: www.landmobile.com

Kevin Mc Carthy, President

Organized to assist the forest industry in radio matters before the FCC.
600 Members
Founded in 1947

4930 Forestry Conservation Commications Association
122 Baltimore St.
Gettysburg, PA 17325

717-398-0815
Fax: 717-778-4237
E-Mail:
ralph.haller@frequencycoordination.org
Home Page: www.fcca-usa.org

Lloyd M. Mitchell, President
Roy Mott, VP
John McIntosh, Secretary/Treasurer
Matt Hogan, Executive Dir.
Michelle Fink, National Frequency Coordinator

Certified by the FCC as the radio frequency coordinator for the Forestry Conservation Radio Service.
200 Members
Founded in 1944

4931 Foundation for American Communications
44 Avenue Road South
Suite 1200
Arlington, VA 22203
703-276-0100
Fax: 703-525-8277
E-Mail: info@facsnet.org
Home Page: www.facsnet.org

John E Cox, CEO, President
Peter C McCarthy, Senior VP, COO
Paul Davis, Senior VP, Programs
Randy Reddick, Director
Christina Gardner, VP, Operations

A national non-profit educational organization with the mission of improving the quality of information reaching the public through the news.
Mailing list available for rent

4932 Freedom Information Center
133 Neff Annex University of Missouri
Columbia, MO 65211

573-882-4856
Fax: 573-884-6204
E-Mail: edwardsm@missouri.edu
Home Page: web.missouri.edu/~foiwww/

Hyde Post, President
Peter Scheer, VP

Maintains files documenting actions by government, media and society affecting the flow and content of information. Call or write for assistance with researching media topics or instruction in using access laws.
Founded in 1958

4933 Fulfillment Services Association of America
3030 Malmo Drive
Arlington Heights, IL 60005-4728

847-364-1222
Fax: 847-364-1268

Frederick J Herzog, Executive VP

Formerly Association of Publishing and fulfillment services.
1450 Members
Founded in 1986

4934 Geospatial Information & Technology Association
1360 University Ave. West
Suite 455
St. Paul, MN 55104-4086

E-Mail: president@gita.org
Home Page: www.gita.org
Social Media: Facebook, Twitter, LinkedIn, YouTube

Talbot Brooks, President
Daniel Shannon, Immediate Past President
Mark Limbruner, President Elect
Eric Hoogenraad, Treasurer
Jerry King, Secretary

A nonprofit educational association dedicated to promoting the use and benefits of geospatial information technologies.

4935 Health Industry Business Communications Council
2525 E Arizona Biltmore Circle
Suite 127
Phoenix, AZ 85016

602-381-1091
Fax: 602-381-1093
E-Mail: info@hibcc.org
Home Page: www.hibcc.org

Robert A Hankin PhD, President & CEO
DuWayne Schlittenhard, Chair
Patrick DeGrace, Immediate Past Chair
Greg Stivers, At Large

An industry-sponsored nonprofit council organized by major health care associations to develop a standard for data transfer using uniform bar code labeling, and later as the focal point for many other electronic data interchange standards.
12000 Members
Founded in 1984

4936 IEEE Communications Society

Home Page: www.comsoc.org
Social Media: Facebook, Twitter, LinkedIn, Tumblr, Instagram, Pinterest

Sergio Benedetto, President
Vijay Bhargava, Past President
Stan Moyer, Treasurer
Hikmet Sari, Vice President - Conferences
Susan Brooks, Executive Director

A diverse group of industry professionals with a common interest inadvancing all communications technologies.
Founded in 1952

4937 InfoComm International
11242 Waples Mill Road
Suite 200
Fairfax, VA 22030

703-273-7200
Fax: 800-659-7469
Home Page: www.infocomm.org

Tony Warner, CTS-D, CDT, LSC Chair
Johanne Belanger, President
Matt Emerson, CTS, President-Elect
Craig Janssen, LEED, Treasurer, Secretary
David Labuskes, CTS, RCDD, Executive Director, CEO

Educating, training, and certifying the communications industry.

4938 Information Resources Group
Ste A
2721 Industrial Dr
Jefferson City, MO 65109
573-632-6IRG
877-600- IRG
Fax: 877-295-7989
E-Mail: webmaster@irginc.net
Home Page: www.irginc.net

Shyam Goel, President

A national organization that offers MIS and corporate professionals at over 150,000 companies throughout the United States.
1M Members

4939 Information Systems Consultants
4131 Idlevale Drive
Tucker, GA 30084
770-491-1500
800-832-7767

Nonprofit organization of small businesses and individuals providing consulting services to all industries and government.
350 Members
Founded in 1986

4940 Information Systems Management Benchmarking Consortium
Houston, TX
281-440-5044
Home Page: ismbc.org

An international resource for business process research and metrics.
Founded in 1992

4941 Information Technology Industry Council
1101 K St., NW
Suite 610
Washington, DC 20005
202-737-8888
Fax: 202-638-4922
E-Mail: info@itic.org
Home Page: www.itic.org
Social Media: Facebook, Twitter, Google+, RSS, YouTube, Blog

Dean C. Garfield, President, CEO
Andy Halataei, SVP, Government Affairs
John Neuffer, SVP, Global Policy
Rick Goss, SVP, Environment and Sustainability
A.R. Trey Hodgkins, SVP, Public Sector

A Washington, D.C.-based trade association that represents companies from the information and communications technology (ICT) industry.
Founded in 1916

4942 Instructional Telecommunications Council
426 C St., NE
Washington, DC 20002-5839
202-293-3110
Fax: 651-450-3679
E-Mail: cullins@itcnetwork.org, cmeredith@itcnet
Home Page: www.itcnetwork.org

Anne Johnson, Chair
Christine Mullins, Executive Director
Carol Spalding, Ed.D., Treasurer
Mickey Slimp, Executive Director
Loraine Schmitt, Chair-Elect

Members are educators and organizations involved in higher education instructional telecommunications and distance learning
500 Members
Founded in 1977

4943 Interactive Multimedia and Collaborative Communications Association
PO Box 756
Syosset, NY 11797-0756
516-818-8184
Fax: 516-922-2170
Home Page: www.imcca.org
Social Media: Facebook, LinkedIn, RSS Feed

Carol Zelkin, Executive Director
Rick Snyder, Chairperson
Anne Hardwick, Treasurer
Ken Scaturro, Vice chairperson
David J. Danto, Dir., Emerging Technology

Provides a clearinghouse for the exchange of information between users, researchers, and providers in the field of teleconferencing.
1000 Members
Founded in 1998

4944 International Academy of Television Arts a nd Sciences
25 West 52nd Street
New York, NY 10019
212-489-6969
Fax: 212-489-1946
E-Mail: iemmys@iemmys.tv
Home Page: www.iemmys.tv
Social Media: Facebook, Twitter, YouTube

Max Newman, Membership & Office Coordinator
Bruce Paisner, President & CEO
Simon Sutton, Treasurer
Blair Westlake, Secretary
Tracy Oliver, General Manager

Member based organization comprised of leading media and entertainment figures from over 50 countries and 500 companies from all sectors of television including internet, mobile and technology.
Founded in 1969

4945 International Association of Audio Informa tion Services
1090 Don Mills Road
Suite 303
Toronto, ON M3C 3R6
416-422-4222
800-280-5325
Fax: 416-422-1622
E-Mail: info@iaais.org
Home Page: www.iaais.org

Kim Walsh, President
Lori Kessinger, Chairperson
Stuart Holland, 1st Vice President
Mark Dewitt, Awards Committee Chair
Lori Kesinger, Co-Chair

Encourages and supports the establishment and maintenance of audio information services that provide access to printed information for individuals who cannot read conventional print because of blindness or any other visual, physical, or learning disability.

4946 International Association of Audio Visual Communicators
The Cindy Competitions
57 West Palo Verde Avenue
PO Box 250
Ocotillo, CA 92259-0250
760-358-7000
Fax: 760-358-7569
E-Mail: sheemonw@cindys.com
Home Page: www.cindys.com

Sheemon Wolfe, Contact

Members are audio-visual professionals using the media of film, video, slides, filmstrips, multi-image and interactive media to communicate information
5200 Members
Founded in 1957

4947 International Association of Business Communicators
601 Montgomery St.
Suite 1900
San Francisco, CA 94111
415-544-4700
800-776-4222
Fax: 415-544-4747
E-Mail: service_centre@iabc.com
Home Page: www.iabc.com

Robin R. McCasland, Chair
Robin McCasland, Vice Chair
Ann Lazarus, Executive Dir.
Mari Pavia, Dir., HR Administration
Aaron Heinrich, Dir. Of Communications

International knowledge network for professionals engaged in stategic business communication management.
13,00 Members
Founded in 1982

4948 International Association of Information Technology Asset Managers
4848 Munson St. NW
Canton, OH 44718ÿ
330-628-3012
877-942-4826
Fax: 330-628-3289
E-Mail: info@iaitam.org
Home Page: www.iaitam.org
Social Media: Facebook, Twitter, LinkedIn, YouTube

Barbara Rembiesa, President, Founder, CEO

The professional association for individuals and organizations involved in any aspect of IT Asset Management ("ITAM"), Software Asset Management ("SAM"), Hardware Asset Management, and the lifecycle processes supporting IT Asset Management in organizations of every size and industry across the globe.
Founded in 2002

4949 International Communication Association
1500 21st Street, NWÿ
PO Box 418950
Washington, DC 20036ÿ
202-955-1444
Fax: 202-955-1448
E-Mail: icahdq@icahdq.org
Home Page: www.icahdq.org
Social Media: Facebook, Twitter, LinkedIn

Peter Vorderer, President
Amy B. Jordan, President Elect
Cynthia Stohl, Past President
Michael L. Haley, Executive Director
Sam Luna, Member Services Director

An academic association for scholars interested in the study, teaching, and application of all aspects of human and mediated communication.
Founded in 1950

4950 International Communications Association
1500 21st St NW
Washington, DC 20036
202-955-1444
Fax: 202-955-1448
E-Mail: icahdq@icahdq.org
Home Page: www.icahdq.org
Social Media: Facebook, Twitter, LinkedIn, Tumblr, Pinterest

Francois Heinderyckx, President
Michael L. Haley, Executive Dir.

John Paul Gutierrez, Communication Dir.
Francois Cooren, Finance Chair
Peter Vorderer, President Elect

International association for scholars interested in the study, teaching and application of all aspects of human mediated communication. ICA began as a small association of US reseachers and has matured into a international association with members in 65 countries.
3400+ Members
Founded in 1950

4951 International Communications Industry Association
11242 Waples Mill Road
Suite 200
Fairfax, VA 22030

703-273-7200
800-659-7469
Fax: 703-278-8082
E-Mail: customerservice@infocomm.org
Home Page: www.infocomm.org
Social Media: Facebook, Twitter, LinkedIn, Flickr, YouTube, SlideShare

Jim Ford, Chairman
Greg Jeffreys, Chair
Tony Warner, President
Matt Emerson, Secretary-Treasurer
David J. Labuskes, Executive Director

Centers on the technologies, products and systems for visual display, audio reproduction, video and audio production, interfacing and signal distribution, lighting, control systems, interactive display and audio presentation systems, remote video and web conferencing.

4952 International Digital Enterprise Alliance
1600 Duke St.
Suite 420
Alexandria, VA 22314

703-837-1070
Fax: 703-837-1072
E-Mail: info@idealliance.org
Home Page: www.idealliance.org
Social Media: Facebook, Twitter, LinkedIn

Chip Harding, Chairman
Laura Reid, Vice Chair
David J. Steinhardt, President & CEO
Frank Balser, VP of operations & Managing Dir.
Steve Bonoff, EVP

IDEAlliance programs and activities enable its members to strengthen their staff skills, participate in the development of standards, influence the development of tools and technologies, develop strategies and partnerships to deploy technology solutions, and position themselves as industry leaders.
200 Members
Founded in 1966

4953 International Documentary Association
3470 Wilshire Blvd.
Los Angeles, CA 90010

213-232-1660
Fax: 213-232-1669
E-Mail: michael@documentary.org
Home Page: www.documentary.org
Social Media: Facebook

Michael Lumpkin, Executive Director
Jon Curry, Office Manager
Cindy Chyr, Development

A nonprofit membership organization dedicated to supporting the efforts of nonfiction film and video makers throughout the United States and the world; promoting the documentary form; and expanding opportunities for the production, distribution, and exhibition of documentary.
2800+ Members
Founded in 1982
Mailing list available for rent: 2800 names at $250 per M

4954 International Interactive Communications Society
10160 SW Nimbus Avenue
Portland, OR 97223-4338

503-968-9210
Fax: 503-620-7857
E-Mail: worldhq@iics.org
Home Page: www.iste.org

Briam Lewis, CEO

Association of communications industry professionals dedicated to the advancement of interactive technologies. Provides a forum to share ideas, applications and techniques for effective use of interactive media.
3000 Members
Founded in 1983
Mailing list available for rent: 8000 names

4955 International Regional Magazine Association
38 Burgess Ave.
Toronto, ON M4E 1W7

416-705-6884
Fax: 888-806-1533
E-Mail: us002848@mindspring.com
Home Page: www.regionalmagazines.org

Win Holden, President
Cathy Murphy CMP, VP
Letitia Pollard, Director
Joan Henderson, Director
Kelly Roberson, Treasurer

IRMA provides a forum for regional magazine publishers to exchange ideas with the view to improving their respective publications.
250-3 Members
Founded in 1960

4956 International Society for Technology in Education
180 W 8th Avenue
Suite 300
Eugene, OR 97401-2916

541-302-3777
800-336-5191
Fax: 541-302-3778
E-Mail: iste@iste.org
Home Page: www.iste.org

Brian Lewis, CEO
Leslie Conery, Deputy CEO
Anne Tully, COO
Jessica Medaille, Chief Membership Officer
Jodie Pozo-Olano, Chief Communications Officer

A large nonprofit organization serving the technology-using educator.
10000 Members
Founded in 1979

4957 International Society of Business
7159 Navajo Road
San Diego, CA 92119-1606

619-687-3450

Audio and videotape professionals.
Founded in 1983

4958 Internet Society
1775 Wiehle Ave
Suite 201
Reston, VA 20190-5158

703-439-2120
Fax: 703-326-9881
E-Mail: isoc@isoc.org
Home Page: www.isoc.org
Social Media: Facebook, Twitter, LinkedIn, YouTube

Terry Weigler, Manager
Gregory Kapfer, CFO
Nicole Armstrong, Sr. Events Manager
Jane Coffin, Dir.,Development Strategy

Members are technologists, developers, educators, researchers, government representatives, business people and other with an interest in internet technologies and applications.
20000 Members
Founded in 1992

4959 Land Mobile Communications Council
8484 Westpark Drive
Suite 630
McLean, VA 22102-5117

703-528-5115
Fax: 703-524-1074
E-Mail: mark.crosby@enterprisewireless.org
Home Page: www.lmcc.org

Donald Vasek, President
Ralph Haller, VP
Mark Crosby, Secretary

A nonprofit association of organizations representing land mobile radio carriers and manufacturers equipment; LMCC membership represents diverse telecommunications sectors such as public safety, industrial/land transportation, private radio, specialized mobile radion and critical infrastructure.
Founded in 1967

4960 Local Media Association
116 Cass Street
Traverse City, MI 49684

888-486-2466
Fax: 231-932-2985
E-Mail: hq@localmedia.org
Home Page: www.localmedia.org
Social Media: Facebook, Twitter, LinkedIn, Tumblr, Instagram, Google+

Clifford Richner, Board Chairman
Gordon Borrell, First Vice Chairman
Suzanne Schlicht, Second Vice Chairman
Nancy Lane, President
Al Cupo, Vice President, Operations

A nonprofit, professional trade association specifically serving the local media industry.

4961 Media Alliance
1904 Franklin St
Suite 818
Oakland, CA 94612

510-684-6853
Fax: 510-238-8557
E-Mail: information@media-alliance.org
Home Page: www.media-alliance.org
Social Media: Facebook, Twitter

Tracy Rosenberg, Executive Director
Eloise Rose Lee, Program Director

A nonprofit training and resource center for media workers, community organizations and political activists.

4962 Media Communications Association-Internati onal
PO Box 5135
Madison, WI 53705-0135

888-899-MCAI
Fax: 888-862-8150
E-Mail: loiswei@aol.com
Home Page: www.mca-i.org
Social Media: Facebook, Twitter, LinkedIn

Gary Shifflet, President
Lois Weiland, Executive Director
Mike Brown, Treasurer
Jim Powell, Secretary
John Coleman, Board Member

Global community that provides its members opportunities for networking, learning and career advancement. Members work in video, film, collaborative communication, distance learning, web design and creation, and all forms of interactive visual communication, along with associated crafts; serving businesses, nonprofit organizations, the government, educational institutions, the medical field, and electronic media. Chapters are throughout the US, with affiliates in Asia and Europe.
Founded in 1968

4963 Media Institute
2300 Clarendon Blvd
Suite 602
Arlington, VA 22201
703-243-5700
Fax: 703-243-8808
E-Mail: info@mediainstitute.org
Home Page: www.mediainstitute.org
Social Media: Twitter, RSS Feed, You Tube
Patrick Maines, President
Richard T. Kaplar, Vice President
Susanna Coto, Director, Public Events
Wendy Wood, Webmaster
Non-profit research foundation specializing in communications policy isssues.
Founded in 1979

4964 Media Research Center
1900 Campus Commons Drive
Suite 600
Reston, VA 20191
571-267-3500
800-672-1423
Fax: 571-375-0099
Home Page: www.mrc.org
Social Media: Facebook, Twitter
A politically conservative content analysis organization.
Founded in 1987

4965 Media Research Directors Association
Ogilvy and Mather
309 W 49th Street
New York, NY 10019-7316
212-375-5502
Home Page: www.mrda.org
Provides support for research and maintains library.

4966 Minority Media and Telecommunications Coun cil
3636 16th Street NW
Suite B 366
Washington, DC 20010
202-332-0500
Fax: 202-332-0503
E-Mail: info@mmtconline.org
Home Page: www.mmtconline.org
Hon Julia L Johnson, Chairperson
Hon Deborah Taylor Tate, Vice Chair
David Honig, President
Ari Fitzgerald, Secretary
Ronald Johnson, Treasurer
National non-profit organization dedicated to promoting and oreserving equal opportunity and civil rights in the mass media, telecommunications and broadband industries, and closing the digital divide.

4967 NTCA-The Rural Broadband Association
4121 Wilson Boulevard
Suite 1000
Arlington, VA 22203
703-351-2000
Fax: 703-351-2001
Home Page: www.ntca.org
Shirley A. Bloomfield, CEO
Michael L. Viands, CFO
Laura B. Withers, Director, Communications
Scott Lively, Director of Government Affairs
Tammie S Logan, Director of Government Affairs
A nonprofit association representing small and rural telephone cooperatives and commercial companies.

4968 National Association for Media Literacy Education
10 Laurel Hill Drive
Cherry Hill, NJ 8003
888-775-2652
Home Page: namle.net
Social Media: Facebook, Twitter, Google+, Flickr, RSS
Sherri Hope Culver, President
Erin Reilly, 1st Vice President
Ethan Delavan, Treasurer
Rhys Daunic, Secretary
Lynda Bergsma, PhD, Past President
A national membership organization dedicated to media literacy as abasic life skill for the 21st century.

4969 National Association for Multi-Ethnicity in Communications
320 West 37th Street
8th Floor
New York, NY 10018
212-594-5985
Fax: 212-594-8391
E-Mail: info@namic.com
Home Page: www.namic.com
Social Media: Facebook, Twitter, LinkedIn
Kathy A Johnson, President
James Jones, VP Programs
Michael D. Armstrong, Chair
Mark DePietro, Treasurer
Jamie J. Rodriguez, Secretary
Works for diversity in the telecommunications industry.
2000 Members
Founded in 1980

4970 National Association of Air Medical Communication Specialists
Po Box 19240
Topeka, KS 66619
877-396-2227
Fax: 866-827-2296
E-Mail: info@naacs.org
Home Page: www.naacs.org
Social Media: Facebook, Twitter, LinkedIn
David Ross, President
Lisa Martin, Treasurer
Steven R. Goff, President-Elect
Professional organization whose mission is to represent the air medical communications specialist on a national level through education, standardization and recognition.
200 Members

4971 National Association of Broadcasters
1771 N Street NW
Washington, DC 20036
202-429-5300
E-Mail: nab@nab.org
Home Page: www.nab.org
Social Media: Facebook, Twitter, LinkedIn, YouTube
Gordon H. Smith, President, CEO
A trade association, workers union, and lobby group representing the interests of for-profit, over-the-air radio and television broadcasters in theUnited States.

4972 National Association of Communication Centers
Home Page: commcenters.org
Social Media: Facebook
Marlina Davidson, Chair
Bonnie Wentzel, Vice Chair
Anand Rao, Vice Chair Elect
Russell Carpenter, Past Chair
Brandi Quesenberry, Secretary
An organization devoted to the support of communication centers on college and university campuses across the country.

4973 National Association of Hispanic Publications
529 14th St, NW.
Suite 1126
Washington, DC 20045
202-662-7250
Fax: 703-610-9005
E-Mail: info@nahp.org
Home Page: www.nahp.org
Clara Padilla-Andrews, President
Kerry Stackpole, Interim CEO
Nile Wendorf, Treasurer
Jose Luis B. Garza, Trustees
Eddie Escobedo Jr., Vice Chair
Founded in the belief that the most effective way to reach the more than 29 million Hispanic Americans in the country is through their own language.
234 Members
Founded in 1982

4974 National Association of Independent Writers and Editors
P.O. Box 549
Ashland, VA 23005
804-767-5961
Home Page: naiwe.com
Janice Campbell, Director
A professional association for writers and editors, providing individual member websites and other benefits.
Founded in 2007

4975 National Association of Media Women
601 Pennsylvania Avenue NW
South Building, Suite 900
Washington, DC 20004
800-556-2926
Fax: 202-403-3788
E-Mail: national@nawbo.org
Home Page: www.nawbo.org
Social Media: Facebook, Twitter, LinkedIn
Xerona Brady, Executive Director
Billie Dragoo, Chair
Crystal Arredondo, Secretary/ Treasurer
Laura Yamanaka, Immediate Past Chair
Darla Beggs, Chair Elect
Sponsors studies, research and seminars to find solutions to problems and create opportunities for women. Presents annual awards.
300 Members
Founded in 1965

4976 **National Association of State Technology Directors**
PO Box 11910
Lexington, KY 40578-1910
859-244-8186
Fax: 859-244-8001
Home Page: www.nastd.org
Jack Ries, President
Mark McCord, Executive Dir.
Pamela Johnson, Meetings & Member Services Manager
Paul Czarnecki, Technology Analyst
Concerned with providing a forum for the exchange of ideas and practices and the development of a unified position on matters of national telecommunications policy and regulatory issues.
1000 Members
Founded in 1978

4977 **National Association of Telecommunications Officers and Advisors**
3213 Duke St.
Suite 695
Alexandria, VA 22314
703-519-8035
Fax: 703-997-7080
E-Mail: info@natoa.org
Home Page: www.natoa.org
Steve Traylor, Executive Director
Jennnifer Harman, Manager of Operations
Tonya Rideout, Deputy Dir.
Tony Perez, President
Todd Barnes, Communications Manager
A national association that represents the communications and interests of local governments, and those who advise local governments.
800 Members
Founded in 1980

4978 **National Cable & Telecommunications Association**
25 Massachusetts Avenue, NW
Suite 100
Washington, DC 20001ÿ
202-222-2300
Fax: 202-222-2514
E-Mail: info@ncta.com
Home Page: www.ncta.com
Social Media: Facebook, Twitter, LinkedIn
Michael Powell, President, CEO
Bruce Carnes, SVP, Finance & Administration
William Check, SVP, Science & Technology
Barbara York, SVP, Industry Affairs
Rick Chessen, SVP, Law & Regulatory Policy

4979 **National Cable and Telecommunications Association**
25 Massachusetts Ave Nw
Suite 100
Washington, DC 20001-1434
202-222-2300
Fax: 202-222-2514
E-Mail: webmaster@ncta.com
Home Page: www.ncta.com
Social Media: Facebook, Twitter
Micheal Powell, President & CEO
Brian Dietz, Vice President, Communications
James M. Assey, Executive Vice President
K. Dane Snowden, Chief of Staff
Jill Luckett, Senior Vice President
Members are cable TV systems; associate members are manufacturers, distributors, suppliers of hardware, programmers and other services
3189 Members
Founded in 1948

4980 **National Captioning Institute**
3725 Concorde Parkway
Suite 100
Chantilly, VA 20151
703-917-7600
Fax: 703-917-9853
E-Mail: info@ncicap.org
Home Page: www.ncicap.org
Social Media: Facebook, Twitter, LinkedIn
Gene Chao, Chairman
Drake Smith, Chief Technology Officer
Jill Toschi, Vice President for Operations
Juan Mario Agudelo, Director, Sales & Marketing
Beth Nubbe, Director, Administration
Non-profit organization whose primary purposes are to deliver effective captioning services and encourage, develop and fund the continuing development of captioning, subtitling, and other media access services for the benefit of peopl who require additional access to the auditory and visual information.
Founded in 1979

4981 **National Communication Association**
1765 N Street NW
Washington, DC 20036
202-464-4622
Fax: 202-464-4600
E-Mail: inbox@natcom.org
Home Page: www.natcom.org
Social Media: Facebook, Twitter, YouTube, Blog
Kim Griffin, CPAÿ, CFO
Nancy Kidd, Ph.D.ÿ, Executive Director
Mark Fernandoÿ, Chief of Staff
Trevor Parry-Giles, Ph.D., Dir., Academic & Prof. Affairs
Michelle Randallÿ, Dir., Conventions and Meetings
A not-for-profit membership-based scholarly society.
Founded in 1914

4982 **National Communications Association**
1765 N Street NW
Washington, DC 20036
202-464-4622
Fax: 202-464-4600
E-Mail: inbox@natcom.org
Home Page: www.natcom.org
Social Media: Facebook, Twitter, YouTube, NCA Blog
Nancy Kidd, Ph.D., Executive Director
Mark Fernando, Chief Of Staff
Kim Griffin, CPA, CFO
Wendy Fernando, Dir. Of Publications
Andy G. Riskind, Dir. Of Public Affairs
The NCA is the most dynamic and responsive of the communication-related organizations. It has achieved this prominance by serving the needs of departmental administrators in the communication arts and sciences.
7700 Members
Founded in 1914
Mailing list available for rent

4983 **National Council of Writing Program Administrators**
Department of English
Miami University
Oxford, OH 45056
513-529-5221
Fax: 513-529-1392
Home Page: www.wpacouncil.org
Social Media: Facebook, Twitter, LinkedIn
John Tassoni, Chair
National organization that fosters professional development, communication and community among college and university writing progrma administrators and other interested faculty.
700 Members
Founded in 1975

4984 **National Federation Abstracting & Information Services**
1518 Walnut Street
Suite 1004
Philadelphia, PA 19102-3403
215-893-1561
Fax: 215-893-1564
E-Mail: nfais@nfais.org
Home Page: www.nfais.org
Social Media: Twitter, LinkedIn
Suzanne BeDell, President
Mary Sauer-Games, Treasurer
Bonnie Lawlor, Executive Director
Jill O'Neill, Director of Communication
Margaret Manson, Manager, Member and Customer
Serves those groups that aggregate, organize, and facilitate access to information. To improve member capabilities and contribute to their ongoing success. Provides opportunities for education, advocacy, and a forum to address common interests.
60 Members
Founded in 1958
Printed in on matte stock

4985 **National Newspaper Association**
P.O. Box 7540
Columbia, MO 65205-7540
573-777-4980
Fax: 573-777-4985
E-Mail: tonda@nna.org
Home Page: nnaweb.org
Social Media: Facebook, Twitter, RSS
John Edgecombe Jr., President
Chip Hutcheson, Vice President
Robert M. Williams Jr.ÿ, Immediate Past President
Tonda Rush, Chief Executive Officer
Carol Pierce, Managing Director
An association representing community newspapers, publishers, and editors. Lists resources, events, membership benefits, and jobs.

4986 **National Newspaper Publishers Association**
1816 12th Street, NW
Washington, DC 20009
202-588-8764
Fax: 202-588-8960
E-Mail: admin@nnpa.org
Home Page: nnpa.org
Social Media: Facebook, Twitter
Cloves C. Campbell, Chair
Mollie F. Belt, 1st Vice Chair
John B. Smith, Srÿ, 2nd Vice Chair
Lenora Alexander, Treasurer
Natalie Cole, Secretary
A trade association composed of more than 200 black newspapers in the United States and the Virgin Islands. It also created an electronic news service which enables newspapers to provide real time news and information to its national constituency.

4987 **National Speakers Association**
1500 S Priest Dr
Tempe, AZ 85281-6203
480-968-2552
Fax: 480-968-0911
E-Mail: memberservices@NSAspeaker.org
Home Page: www.nsaspeaker.org
Social Media: Facebook, Twitter, Google+, YouTube, Instagram
Stacy Tetschner, CAE, FASAE, CEO
William Peterson, MBA, Director Of Finance

Michelle Reynolds, Director of Member Experiences
Christie Turley, Director of Marketing, Consultant
Barbara Parus, Director of Publications

The leading organization for experts who speak professionally. NSA's members include experts in a variety of industries and disciplines, who reach audiences as trainers, educators, humorists, motivators, consultants, authors and more. NSA provides resources and education designed to advance the skills, integrity, and value of its members and speaking profession. NSA the voice of the speaking profession.
3500 Members
Founded in 1973
Mailing list available for rent: 3200 names

4988 National Telemedia Council
1922 University Avenue
Madison, WI 53726
608-218-1182
Fax: 608-218-1183
E-Mail: ntelemedia@aol.com
Home Page: www.nationaltelemediacouncil.org

Marieli Rowe, Director

Promotes media literacy through workshops and telemediun.
Founded in 1953

4989 National Translator Association
5611 Kendall Court
Suite 2
Arvada, CO 80002
303-378-8209
Fax: 303-465-4067
E-Mail: stcl@comcast.net
Home Page: www.tvfmtranslators.com

Byron St. Clair, President
Arnold Cruze, Vice President
Alan Greager, Secretary/Treasurer

Dedicated to the preservation of free over-the-air TV in all geographical areas. It works to improve the technology of rebroadcast translators and regulatory climate which governs them. It continously promotes the concept of universal free over-the-air TV and reprsents the ineterests of translator operators before the FCC and other government agencies such as the Forest Service and the Bureau of Land Management. Membership is open to all individuals and organizations that are interested.
Founded in 1967

4990 National Writers Association

Home Page: www.nationalwriters.com

A nonprofit organization that provides education and an ethical resource for writers at all levels of experience. It also awards scholarships and provides no or low cost workshops and seminars.

4991 Networking Institute
PO Box 650037
West Newton, MA 02465-1928
617-965-3340
Fax: 617-965-2341
E-Mail: info@netage.com
Home Page: www.netage.com

Jessica Lipnack, Owner
Jeffrey Stamps, Co-Founder
Carrie Kuempel, Director Training
Rich Carpenter, Strategy Advisor

Promotes networks to help people work together. Offers consulting services, educational workshops and seminars. To order: The Age of the Network and The TeamNet Factor call Oliver Wright productions at 800-343-0625.
Founded in 1982

4992 Newspaper Association Managers
32 Dunham Road
Beverly, MA
978-338-2555
Home Page: nammanagers.com

Greg Sherrill, President
Lisa Hills, Vice President
Michael MacLaren, Immediate Past President
George White, Director
Layne Bruce, Secretary

An organization of executives representing newspaper associations in the United States and Canada.

4993 Newspaper Association of America
4401 Wilson Blvd
Suite 900
Arlington, VA 22203-4195
571-366-1000
Fax: 571-366-1195
E-Mail: joan.mills@naa.org
Home Page: www.naa.org
Social Media: Facebook, Twitter, LinkedIn, Google+, YouTube

Robert M. Nutting, Chairman
Robert J. Dickey, Vice Chairman
Donna Barrett, Secretary
Stephen P. Hills, Treasurer
Caroline Little, President and CEO

Focuses on the major issues that affect today's newspaper industry public policy and legal matters, advertising revenue growth and audience development across the medium's broad portfolio of products and digital platforms.
2000 Members
Founded in 1992

4994 North American Serials Interest Group
1902 Ridge Rd
West Seneca, NY 14224-3312

E-Mail: info@nasig.org
Home Page: www.nasig.org

Joyce Tenney, President
Steve Kelley, Vice President/President-Elect
Shana McDanold, Secretary
Jennifer Arnold, Treasurer
Beverly Geckle, Treasurer-Elect

An independent organization taht promotes communication and sharing of ideas among all members of the serials information chain, anyone working with or concerned about serial publications.
1200 Members
Founded in 1985

4995 Organization for the Promotion and Advance of Small Telecommunications Co.
21 Dupont Cir NW
Suite 700
Washington, DC 20036-1109
202-833-2775
Fax: 202-659-4619
E-Mail: membership@ncta.org
Home Page: www.opastco.org

John Rose, President
Corey Watkins, Network Administrator

Protects the interests of small, rural, independent commercial telephone companies and cooperatives that have less than 50,000 access lines.
675 Members
Founded in 1963

4996 PCIA- The Wireless Industry Association
500 Montgomery Street
Suite 500
Alexandria, VA 22314
703-971-7100
800-759-0300
Fax: 703-836-1608
E-Mail: andrewd@pcia.com
Home Page: www.pcia.com
Social Media: Facebook, Twitter, LinkedIn

W. Benjamin Moreland, Chairman
Thomas A. Murray, Vice Chairman
Steven Marshall, Treasurer
Jonathan S. Adelstein, President & CEO
Tim House, Vice President, External Relations

Represents companies that develop, own, manage and operate towers, commercial rooftops and other facilities for the provision of all types of wireless, broadcasting and telecommunications services.
3000 Members
Founded in 1949

4997 Paley Center for Media
25 West 52nd Street
New York, NY 10019
212-621-6800
Fax: 212-621-6600
E-Mail: coman@paleycenter.org
Home Page: www.paleycenter.org
Social Media: Facebook, Twitter, YouTube, Google+, Hulu

Pat Mitchell, President, CEO
John Lanaway, Interim CFO
Maxim Thorne, Executive Vice President
Diane Lewis, Vice President, Public Affairs
Maureen J. Reidy, Chief Marketing Officer

Leads the discussion about the cultural, creative, and social significance of television, radio, and emerging platforms for the professional community and media-interested public.

4998 Personal Achievement Institute
1 Speaking Success Road
Box 6543
Kingman, AZ 86402-6543
928-753-5315
800-321-1225
Fax: 928-753-7554
Home Page: www.speakingsuccess.com

Burt Dubin, President

Education that provides advice and business strategies for both novices and experts in mastering the field of professional speaking. Free monthly newsletter is accessible through Website.
Founded in 1978
Printed in one color on matte stock

4999 Portable Computer and Communications Association
PO Box 680
Hood River, OR 97031
541-490-5140
Fax: 413-410-8447
E-Mail: pcca@pcca.org
Home Page: www.pcca.org

Gloria Kowalski, Director
Peter Rysavy, Executive Director

Represents firms, organizations, and individuals interested in moblie communications.
65 Members

5000 **Railway Systems Suppliers**
9306 New La Grange Rd
Suite 100
Louisville, KY 40242-3672

502-327-7774
Fax: 502-327-0541
E-Mail: rssi@rssi.org
Home Page: www.rssi.org

Patti jon Goff, President
John Paljug, Executive Vice President
N. Michael Choat, First Vice President
Walter Winzen, Second Vice President

A trade association serving the communication and signal segment of the rail transportation industry. Primary activity is to organize and manage a trade show for its members to exhibit their products and services.
260 Members
Founded in 1966

5001 **Real Estate Information Professionals Association**
2501 Aerial Center Parkway
Suite 103
Morrisville, NC 27560

919-459-2070
Fax: 919-459-2075
Home Page: www.reipa.org

Sarah Gillian, Executive Director

Supports professional information providers in the real estate industry.
110 Members
Founded in 1995

5002 **Religious Communication Association**
Department of Communication
University of Texas at Tyler
3900 University Blvd
Tyler, TX 75799

903-566-7093
Fax: 903-566-7287
E-Mail: eiden@mail.uttyl.edu
Home Page: www.americanrhetoric.com/rca

Michael E Eidenmuller, Coordinator of E-Communication
Janie Harden Fritz, Executive Secretary
J. Matthew Melton, President
Kathleen M. Edelmayer, Immediate Past President
Mark A. E. Williams, 1st Vice President

An academic society of individuals interested in the study of all aspects of public religious communication, members include teachers, students, clergy, broadcasters and other scholars and professionals.
210 Members
Founded in 1973

5003 **Republican Communications Association**
PO Box 550
Washington, DC 20515

E-Mail: RCA@mail.house.gov
Home Page: www.rcaweb.org

Lisa Boot, President
Neal Patel, Vice President
Shea Snider, Treasurer
Michael Tadeo, Social Director
Justin LaFranco, Social Director

Sponsors professional development and networking programs. Conducts seminars, briefings, and tours.
165 Members
Founded in 1970

5004 **Satellite Broadcasting and Communications Association**
1100 17th Street NW
Suite 1150
Washington, DC 20036-4557

202-349-3620
800-541-5981
Fax: 202-349-3621
E-Mail: info@sbca.org
Home Page: www.sbca.com

Jeffrey Blum, Chairman
Andrew Reinsdorf, Vice Chairman
Joseph Widoff, Executive Director
Benjamin Rowan, Education Manager
Lisa Volpe McCabe, Director Public Policy and Outreach

The national trade organization representing all segments of the satellite industry. It is committed to expanding the utilization of satellite technology for the broadcast delivery of video, audio, data, music, voice, interactive and broadband services.
100 Members
Founded in 1986

5005 **Society for Technical Communication**
9401 Lee Hwy
Suite 300
Fairfax, VA 22031-1803

703-522-4114
Fax: 703-522-2075
E-Mail: stc@stc.org
Home Page: www.stc.org

Nicky Bleiel, President
Jane Wilson, Treasurer
Katherine Brown-Hoekstra, Vice President
Alyssa Fox, Secretary
Chris Lyons, Executive Director

Seeks to advance the theory and practice of technical communication in all media. Presents awards and sponsors high school writing contests.
19000 Members
Founded in 1953
Mailing list available for rent: 9000 names at $120 per M

5006 **Society of Satellite Professionals International**
250 Park Avenue
7th Floor
New York, NY 10177

212-809-5199
Fax: 212-825-0075
E-Mail: rbell@sspi.org
Home Page: www.sspi.org

Robert Bell, Executive Director
Louis Zacharilla, Director Development
Tamara Bond, Membership Director
Matthew Owen, Communications Manager

Members are individuals in the fields of businesss, education, entertainment, media, science and industry who share common interests in satellite technology.
1700 Members
Founded in 1983

5007 **Society of Telecommunications Consultants**
13275 State Highway 89
PO Box 70
Old Station, CA 96071

530-335-7313
800-782-7670
Fax: 530-335-7360
E-Mail: stchdq@stcconsultants.org
Home Page: www.stcconsultants.org

Cathy Cimaglia, Administrative Manager

The STC is an international organization of independent telecommunications and information technology consultants who serve clients in business and government
180 Members
Founded in 1976

5008 **Telecommunications Benchmarking International Group**
4606 Fm 1960 Rd W
Suite 250
Houston, TX 77069-4617
281-440-5044
888-739-8244
Fax: 281-440-6677
E-Mail: tbig@benchmarkingnetwork.com
Home Page: www.benchmarkingnetwork.com

Mark Czarnecki, President

An association of contact center professionals within telecommunications companies dedicated to providing members with an opportunity to identify, document and establish best practices through benchmakring to increase value, effiencies, and profits.
3500+ Members
Founded in 1992

5009 **Telecommunications Industry Association (TIA)**
1320 N. Courthouse Rd
Suite 200
Arlington, VA 22201-3834
703-907-7700
Fax: 703-907-7727
E-Mail: gseiffert@tiaonline.org
Home Page: www.tiaonline.org

Thomas Stanton, Chair
Susan Schramm, Vice Chair
Fred McDuffee, Treasurer
Grant Seiffert, President
Danielle Coffey, Vice President Government Affairs

The Telecommunications Industry Association/TIA represents providers of communications and information technology products and services for the global marketplace through its core competencies in standards development, domestic and international advocacy, as well as market development and trade promotion programs.

5010 **The Association of Business Information and Media Companies**
675 Third Avenue
Suite 2200
New York, NY 10017-5704

212-661-6360
Fax: 212-370-0736
E-Mail: info@abmmail.com
Home Page: www.abmassociation.com
Social Media: Facebook, Twitter, LinkedIn, WordPress

Neal Vitaleÿ, Chair
Doug Manoni, Vice Chair
James Casella, Treasurer
William Pollak, Past Chair
Marion Minor, Secretary

An association that focuses on the integrated business-to-business media model—which includes print publications, events, digital media and business information.
Founded in 1906

5011 **The Center for Media and Public Affairs**
933 N. Kenmore St.
Suite 405
Arlington, VA 22201

571-319-0029
Fax: 571-319-0029
E-Mail: rieckd@cmpa.com

Home Page: www.cmpa.com
Social Media: Facebook, Twitter

Truman Anderson, Chairman of the Board
Dr. Robert Lichter, Founder, President
Nell Minow, Treasurer & Secretary of the Board
Donald Rieck, Executive Director
Dan Amundson, Research Director

A nonpartisan, nonprofit research organization in Washington, D.C.,conducting scientific studies of the news and entertainment media.
Founded in 1985

5012 **The Energy Telecommunications and Electrical Association**
5005 W Royal Lane
Suite 116
Irving, TX 75063

972-929-3169
888-503-8700
Fax: 972-915-6040
Home Page: www.entelec.org
Social Media: Twitter, LinkedIn

Blaine Siske, Executive Manager
Richard Nation, Secretary/Treasurer
Tiffany Chase, Operations Coordinator
James C. Coulter, President
Kenneth Clouse, 1st VP

A user association focusing on communications and control technologies used by petroleum, natural gas, pipeline and electric utility companies.
Founded in 1928

5013 **The International Foundation for Information Technology**
P. O. Box 907
Summit, NJ 07901-2508

Home Page: www.if4it.com
Social Media: Facebook, Twitter, LinkedIn

A global industry best practices association that promotes the interests and career development of practitioners, educators, and students who wish to extend their knowledge and understanding of IT operations, management, and leadership.

5014 **Toastmasters International**
23182 Arroyo Vista
Rancho Santa Margarita
Mission Viejo, CA 92688-2620

949-858-8255
949-835-1300
Fax: 949-858-1207
E-Mail: newsletters@toastmasters.org
Home Page: www.toastmasters.org

Publishes educational articles on the subjects of communication and leadership. Topics include language, listening, humor, self-improvement, goal setting, success and logical thinking.
19500 Members
Founded in 1924

5015 **United States Internet Service Providers**
700 12th St NW
Suite 700 E
Washington, DC 20005-4052

202-904-2351
E-Mail: kdean@usispa.org
Home Page: www.usispa.org

John Albertine, President

Will serve both as the ISP community's representative during policy debates and as a forum in which members can share information and develop best practices for handling specific legal matters.
7 Members
Founded in 1991

5016 **United States Telecom Association**
607 14th Street, NW
Suite 400
Washington, DC 20005

202-326-7300
Fax: 202-315-3603
Home Page: www.ustelecom.org
Social Media: Facebook, Twitter, LinkedIn, YouTube

Steve Davis, Chairman of the Board
Walter B. McCormick, Jr., President, CEO
Mark Kulish, SVP, Administration, CFO
Alan J. Roth, Senior Executive Vice President
Anne Veigle, SVP, Communications

A trade association that represents telecommunications-related businesses based in the United States.

5017 **United Telecom Council**
1129 20th Street
Suite 350
Washington, DC 20036

202-872-0030
Fax: 202-872-1331
E-Mail: bill.moroney@utc.org
Home Page: www.utc.org
Social Media: Facebook, Twitter, LinkedIn

Connie Darshak, President/CEO
Kathleen Fitzpatrick, VP and General Counsel
Brett Kilbourne, Vice President, Government
Mike Oldak, Vice President, Strategy
Karnel Thomas, Vice President - Member & Industry

Represents organizations using telecommunications in their operations before various federal and state legislative and regulatory agencies, particularly the FCC
1500 Members
Founded in 1948

5018 **Utility Communicaotrs International**
229 E Ridgewood Road
Georgetown, TX 78628

512-869-1313
Fax: 512-864-7203
E-Mail: eboardman@att.net
Home Page: www.uci-online.com

Elliot Boardman, Executive Director

International organization comprimsed of advertising, public relations and marketing professionals from electric, gas and water utlities, energy companies, telephone companies, advertising and public relations agencies, and suppliers who communicate for and about the utility and energy industries.
400 Members
Founded in 1922

5019 **Wikibon**
5 Mount Royal Ave.
Suite 280
Marlborough, MA 1752

774-463-3400
Fax: 774-463-3405
Home Page: wikibon.org
Social Media: Facebook, Twitter, LinkedIn, Blog

A professional community solving technology and business problems through an open source sharing of free advisory knowledge.
Founded in 2007

5020 **Wireless Communications Association International**
1333 H St NW
Suite 700 W
Washington, DC 20005-4754

202-452-7823
Fax: 202-452-0041
E-Mail: president@wcai.com
Home Page: www.wcai.com
Social Media: Facebook, Twitter, LinkedIn

Fred Campbell, President

The non-profit trade and professional association for the Wireless Broadband industry. Mission is to advance the interests of the wireless carriers that provide high-speed data, internet, voice and video services on broadband spectrum through land-based systems using reception/transmit devices in all broadband spectrum bands.
250 Members
Founded in 1987

5021 **Wireless Dealers Association**
9746 Tappenbeck Dr
Houston, TX 77055-4102

713-467-0077
800-624-6918
E-Mail: contact@wirelessindustry.com
Home Page: www.wirelessindustry.com

Robert Hutchinson, President

Business association made up of cellular and wireless communications agents, dealers, resellers, carriers, manufacturers, distributors and importers.
2500 Members
Founded in 1986

5022 **Women in Cable and Telecommunications**
2000 K Street, NW
Suite 350
Washington, DC 20006

202-827-4794
Fax: 202-450-5596
E-Mail: membership@wict.org
Home Page: www.wict.org
Social Media: Facebook, Twitter, YouTube

Maria E. Brennan, CAE, President & CEO
Mary Meduski, Chair
Kim Martin, Treasurer
Sean Bratches, Governance Committee Chair
Parthavi Das, Chief of Staff

Provides opportunitites for leadership, networking, and advocacy in the industry.
4600 Members
Founded in 1979

5023 **World Teleport Association**
250 Park Avenue
Suite 14B
New York, NY 10004-3712

212-825-0218
Fax: 212-825-0075
Home Page: www.intelligentcommunity.org

Robert Bell, Executive Director

Promotes the understanding, development, and use of eleports as a means to achieve economic, political and social progress locally, regionally and worldwide.
606 Members
Founded in 1985

Newsletters

5024 **411 Newsletter**
United Communications Group
11300 Rockville Pike
Suite 1100
Rockville, MD 20852-3030

301-287-2700
Fax: 301-816-8945
E-Mail: webmaster@ucg.com
Home Page: www.ucg.com

Benny Dicecca, President

Business newsletter for professionals in the communications industry.
Cost: $339.00
Founded in 1977

5025 **ATTW Bulletin**
Association of Teachers of Technical Writing
Department of Linguistics and Technical Comm
1155 Union Circle #305298
Denton, TX 76203-5017

940-565-4458
E-Mail: sims@unt.edu
Home Page: www.attw.org

Barbara Sims, Executive Secretary

Publishes news about members, the association, and the profession as well as bibliographic resources for teachers, teaching techniques, suggested assignments, implications of current research for the classroom, opinions on professional issues, notices and highlights of conferences, calls for papers and proposals, job announcements, and other information that will interest new and experienced teachers in undergraduate or graduate curricula.
Frequency: Semi-Annual

5026 **Advertising & Newspaper Media**
Newspaper Association of America
4401 Wilson Blvd
Suite 900
Arlington, VA 22203-4195

571-366-1000
Fax: 571-366-1195
E-Mail: joan.mills@naa.org
Home Page: www.naa.org

Reggie Hall, Senior VP

Electronic newsletters delivers retail, national and classified advertising ideas plus updates on your most important customers. If your job responsibilities include any type advertising revenue you need to be a subscriber.
Frequency: Monthly

5027 **Bandwidth Minutes and IP Transport Markets Will Capacity Traders Succeed?**
Probe Research
3 Wing Drive
Suite 240
Cedar Knolls, NJ 07927-1000

973-285-1500
Fax: 973-285-1519
Home Page: www.proberesearch.com

We look into capacity exchanges and determine how they add value, whter participants will find exchanges useful, what are the presequisites for a robust capacity market, what are the risk to telcos if they use exchanges, and what do the exchanges need to do in order to increase trading volume.

5028 **Bandwidth Pricing Trends**
Probe Research
3 Wing Drive
Suite 240
Cedar Knolls, NJ 07927-1000

973-285-1500
Fax: 973-285-1519
Home Page: www.proberesearch.com

Provides an analysis of the trends in capacity pricing and the expected effects on demand. It provides a view of the drivers that determine what the bandwidth cost will be on a particular route. Also looks at how these determinants have contributes to the level of price erosion each of the routes analyzed.

5029 **Big Ideas Newsletter**
Newspaper Association of America
4401 Wilson Blvd
Suite 900
Arlington, VA 22203-4195

571-366-1000
Fax: 571-366-1195
E-Mail: joan.mills@naa.org
Home Page: www.naa.org

Reggie Hall, Senior VP

Designed especially for smaller market newspapers, featuring ways to increase revenues, cut costs or otherwise improve your newspaper.
Frequency: Bi-Monthly

5030 **Brandwidth Supply and Demand Analysis WIT IP Traffic Demand Update**
Probe Research
3 Wing Drive
Suite 240
Cedar Knolls, NJ 07927-1000

973-285-1500
Fax: 973-285-1519
Home Page: www.proberesearch.com

Provides an analysis of the bandwidth supply and demand on number of interregional routes. Describes methodology of building up the bandwidth supply and demand picture on these routes. Analyzes what the supply and demand balance is on these routes. Concludes what the business ramifications are for ISPs and backbone providers, banks and vendors.

5031 **Broadband Wireless**
Probe Research
3 Wing Drive
Suite 240
Cedar Knolls, NJ 07927-1000

973-285-1500
Fax: 973-285-1519
Home Page: www.proberesearch.com

In this bulletin, we take a look into is going on with terrestrial fixed wireless last mile solutions in the MMDS, LMDS spectrums. LMDS is emerging as the next platform for CLECs. However, these CLECs will be entering the market at the end of a long line of competitors in many cities.

5032 **Business Publisher**
JK Publishing
3105 N Newhall Street
Milwaukee, WI 53211

414-332-1625
Fax: 414-332-0916

John Kenney, Editor
Jean O'Brien, Circulation Manager

Offers information and full coverage of the magazine and business/trade publishing industry.
Cost: $335.00
8 Pages
Frequency: BiWeekly

5033 **CMA Newsletter**
College Media Advisers
University
#300
Memphis, TN 38152

512-471-5084
Fax: 901-678-4798
Home Page: www.collegemedia.org

Ken Rosenauer, Publisher

Provides news and information to those who advise/supervise college media run by students (i.e. newspapers, magazines, yearbooks, radios, and TV stations).
Cost: $60.00
6 Pages
Circulation: 750
Founded in 1954

5034 **Cantu's Newsletter**
Cantu's Comedy Newsletter
PO Box 210495
San Francisco, CA 94121

415-668-2402
E-Mail: info1@HumorMall.com
Home Page: www.humormall.com

John Cantu, Publisher

Articles of interest to public speakers, writers, comedians, comedy writers.
Cost: $29.95
Circulation: 3000
Founded in 1999

5035 **Chamber Executive**
American Chambers of Congress Exec Communications
4875 Eisenhower Ave
Suite 250
Alexandria, VA 22304-4850

703-998-0072
Fax: 703-212-9512
E-Mail: webmaster@acce.org
Home Page: www.acce.org

Mick Flemming, Manager

Newsletter aimed at management level communications professionals.
Cost: $99.00
12 Pages
Founded in 1914
Mailing list available for rent
Printed in 4 colors on matte stock

5036 **Circulation Update E-Newsletter**
Newspaper Association of America
4401 Wilson Blvd
Suite 900
Arlington, VA 22203-4195

571-366-1000
Fax: 571-366-1195
E-Mail: joan.mills@naa.org
Home Page: www.naa.org
Social Media: Facebook, Twitter

Reggie Hall, Senior VP

Focused on newspaper executives with responsibility for marketing their newspapers to readers. You will find a balance of recent headline stories, consumer marketing research, information about your retailers, and regulatory information blended with success stories and resources to help you in your mission of building circulation and readership.
Frequency: Weekly

5037 **Classified Communications Newsletter**
PO Box 4242
Prescott, AZ 86302

520-778-6788
E-Mail: classa@northlink.com

Agnes Franz, Publisher

Information and ad-writing tips for small budget advertisers. Both display and word classifieds addressed. Will also review books on advertising and marketing.
Cost: $35.00
8 Pages
Frequency: Monthly
Circulation: 2000
Founded in 1989
Printed in 2 colors on glossy stock

5038 **Communication Briefings**
Briefings Publishing Group

1101 King St
Suite 110
Alexandria, VA 22314-2944

703-548-3800
Fax: 703-684-2136
Home Page: www.combriefings.com

William G Dugan, Group Publisher
Susan Marshall, Executive Editor
Lois Willingham, Marketing Manager
Charles Blakeney, Owner

This newsletter provides subscribers with communications ideas and techniques to use to persuade clients, and motivate employees.
Cost: $79.00
8 Pages
Frequency: Monthly
Circulation: 55000
Founded in 1981

5039 **Communications Business Daily**
Warren Communications News
2115 Ward Ct Nw
Washington, DC 20037-1209

202-872-9200
800-771-9202
Fax: 202-318-8350
E-Mail: info@warren-news.com
Home Page: www.warren-news.com

Brig Easley, Manager
Daniel Warren, President/Editor
Founded in 1945

5040 **Communications Concepts**
Communication Concepts
508 Mill Stone Dr
Beavercreek, OH 45434-5840

937-426-8600
Fax: 937-429-3811
E-Mail: cci.dayton@pobox.com
Home Page:
www.communication-concepts.com

Rodger L Southworth, President

Ideas and methods for professional communications.

5041 **DBS Report**
Kagan World Media
1 Lower Ragsdale Dr
Building One, Suite 130
Monterey, CA 93940-5749

831-624-1536
800-307-2529
Fax: 831-625-3225
E-Mail: info@kagan.com
Home Page: www.kagan.com

Tim Baskerville, President
Cost: $1045.00
Frequency: Monthly
Founded in 1969

5042 **Daily Deal**
Vicki King
105 Madison Avenue
New York, NY 10016

212-313-9200
888-667-3325
E-Mail: customerservice@thedeal.com
Home Page: www.thedeal.com

Mickey Hernandez, Advertising Sales
Elena Freed, Marketing

Reports and analyzes all the aspects of the booming, high stakes world of the deal economy. Areas of coverage include mergers and aquisitions, private equity, venture capital and bankruptcies.
Cost: $498.00
26 Pages
Frequency: Daily
Circulation: 40893
Founded in 1999

5043 **EHS News Briefs**
Newspaper Association of America
4401 Wilson Blvd
Suite 900
Arlington, VA 22203-4195

571-366-1000
Fax: 571-366-1195
E-Mail: joan.mills@naa.org
Home Page: www.naa.org

Reggie Hall, Senior VP

These news briefs spotlight what is happening in Congress, the Administration, Courts and around the industry.
Frequency: Weekly

5044 **Emerging Media Report**
Knight MediaCom International
2400 Kettner Boulevard
Suite 237
San Diego, CA 92101

619-338-9885
Fax: 619-338-9886
E-Mail: knightsmedia@hotmail.com
Home Page: www.knightmedia.com

Covers VR, TV, CD, PC, and entertainment marketing.
Founded in 1978

5045 **Fusion Magazine**
Newspaper Association of America
4401 Wilson Blvd
Suite 900
Arlington, VA 22203-4195

571-366-1000
Fax: 571-366-1195
E-Mail: joan.mills@naa.org
Home Page: www.naa.org

Reggie Hall, Senior VP

This newsletter focuses on the business of diversity within the newspaper industry. In it you will find new strategies for making diversity work in advertising, news and editorial, circulation, marketing, production, human resources and the business office.
Frequency: Quarterly

5046 **Growing Audience E-Newsletter**
Newspaper Association of America
4401 Wilson Blvd
Suite 900
Arlington, VA 22203-4195

571-366-1000
Fax: 571-366-1195
E-Mail: joan.mills@naa.org
Home Page: www.naa.org

Reggie Hall, Senior VP

This newsletter provides an unparalleled array of information to keep you informed on the most current newspaper readership issues, experiments, results, ideas, successes and failures.
Frequency: Weekly

5047 **Information Broker**
Burwell Enterprises
5619 Plumtree Drive
Dallas, TX 75252

972-331-1951
Fax: 972-733-1951
Home Page: www.burwellinc.com

Helen Burwell, Publisher
Jeanne Paulino, Marketing Director

Covers fee-based information services for practitioners and users of information services. Accepts advertising.
Cost: $40.00
12 Pages
Frequency: Bi-Monthly
Circulation: 500
Printed in one color on matte stock

5048 **Intercom**
Society for Technical Communication
9401 Lee Hwy
Suite 300
Fairfax, VA 22031-1803

703-522-4114
Fax: 703-522-2075
E-Mail: stc@stc.org
Home Page: www.stc.org

Susan Burton, Executive Director
Anita Dosik, Publications Director
Maurice P. Martin, Editor
Antoinette DeSalvo, Marketing Coordinator
Suzanna Laurent, President

A monthly magazine offering Society members with information and articles on communication industry trends and activities.
Cost: $95.00
Circulation: 20000
Founded in 1957
Mailing list available for rent: 1000 names at $120 per M

5049 **Labor & Employment Law Letter**
Newspaper Association of America
4401 Wilson Blvd
Suite 900
Arlington, VA 22203-4195

571-366 1000
Fax: 571-366-1195
E-Mail: joan.mills@naa.org
Home Page: www.naa.org

Reggie Hall, Senior VP

This newsletter offers readers information on critical employment issues facing the newspaper industry.
Frequency: Bi-Monthly

5050 **Lifestyle Media-Relations Reporter**
InfoCom Group
5900 Hollis Street
Suite L
Emeryville, CA 94608

510-596-9300
800-959-1059
Home Page: www.infocomgroup.com

This newsletter offers information on media placement in lifestyle and consumer media.
Cost: $369.00
Frequency: Monthly
Founded in 1980

5051 **MAPNetter**
Architecture Technology Corporation
9977 Valley View Rd
Suite 300
Eden Prairie, MN 55344-3586

952-829-5864
Fax: 952-829-5871
E-Mail: info@atcorp.com
Home Page: www.atcorp.com
Social Media: Facebook

Kenneth Thurber, President

Monthly newsletter covering important developments in the field of factory communication systems.
Cost: $432.00
12 Pages
Frequency: Monthly
Founded in 1981

5052 **MRC Cyberalert**
Media Research Center
325 S Patrick St
Alexandria, VA 22314-3501

703-683-9733
800-672-1423
Fax: 703-683-9736
E-Mail: mrc@mediaresearch.org

Home Page: www.mrc.org
Social Media: Facebook

Brent Bozell, CEO

A news-daily report which documents and exposes liberal media bias. MRC is the nation's leading media watchdog.
Cost: $29.00
Frequency: Monthly
Circulation: 13000
Founded in 1987

5053 Marketing Library Services
Information Today
143 Old Marlton Pike
Medford, NJ 08055-8750
609-654-6266
800-300-9868
Fax: 609-654-4309
E-Mail: custserv@infotoday.com
Home Page: www.infotoday.com

Thomas H Hogan, President
Roger R Bilboul, Chairman of the Board

Provides information professional in all types of libraries with specfic ideas for marketing their services.
Cost: $79.95
Frequency: Bi Monthly
ISSN: 0896-3908

5054 Marketing New Media
Kagan World Media
1 Lower Ragsdale Dr
Building One, Suite 130
Monterey, CA 93940-5749
831-624-1536
800-307-2529
Fax: 831-625-3225
E-Mail: info@kagan.com
Home Page: www.kagan.com

Tim Baskerville, President
Tom Johnson, Marketing Manager

News of the Marketing New Media. Three month trial available.
Cost: $795.00
Frequency: Monthly
Founded in 1878

5055 Media Access
WGBH Educational Foundation
PO Box 200
Boston, MA 02134-1008
617-300-2000
Fax: 617-300-1032
E-Mail: feedback@wgbh.org
Home Page: www.wgbh.org

Jonathan Abbott, President
Russell Peotter, Owner
Mary Cotton, Owner

Includes information on NCAM's research and development projects, which strive to make media and technology accessible to disabled populations.
2 Pages
Circulation: 15000
Founded in 1951
Printed in 2 colors on matte stock

5056 Media File
Media Alliance
1904 Franklin St
Suite 500
Oakland, CA 94612-2926
510-832-9000
Fax: 510-238-8557
Home Page: www.media-alliance.org

Tracy Rosenberg, Executive Director
Eloise Rose Lee, Program Director

Information about media and media workers.
8 Pages
Frequency: Quarterly

5057 Media Law Reporter
Bureau of National Affairs
1801 S Bell St
Arlington, VA 22202-4501
703-341-3000
800-372-1033
Fax: 800-253-0332
E-Mail: customercare@bna.com
Home Page: www.bnabooks.com

Paul N Wojcik, CEO

A weekly reference service containing the full-text of federal and state court decisions and selected agency rulings affecting newspapers, magazines, radio, television, film and other media.
Cost: $1856.00
Frequency: Weekly
ISSN: 0148-1045
Founded in 1929

5058 Media Mergers & Acquisitions
Kagan World Media
1 Lower Ragsdale Dr
Building One, Suite 130
Monterey, CA 93940-5749
831-624-1536
800-307-2529
Fax: 831-625-3225
E-Mail: info@kagan.com
Home Page: www.kagan.com

Tim Baskerville, President
Tom Johnson, Marketing Manager

Where it all comes together. Exclusive scorecard of deals done by media companies. Dollar amounts, multiples paid, trends captured in succinct summaries of complex transactions. Three month trial available.
Cost: $795.00
Frequency: Monthly
Founded in 1969

5059 Media Sports Business
Kagan World Media
1 Lower Ragsdale Dr
Building One, Suite 130
Monterey, CA 93940-5749
831-624-1536
Fax: 831-625-3225
E-Mail: info@kagan.com
Home Page: www.kagan.com

Tim Baskerville, President
Tom Johnson, Marketing Manager
Cost: $945.00
Frequency: Monthly
Founded in 1969

5060 Motion Picture Investor
Kagan World Media
1 Lower Ragsdale Dr
Building One, Suite 130
Monterey, CA 93940-5749
831-624-1536
800-307-2529
Fax: 831-625-3225
E-Mail: info@kagan.com
Home Page: www.kagan.com

Tim Baskerville, President
Tom Johnson, Marketing Manager
Cost: $845.00
Frequency: Monthly
Founded in 1969

5061 NAMIC E-Newsletter
Natl Assoc for Multi-Ethnicity in Communications
320 West 37th Street
8th Floor
New York, NY 10018
212-594-5985
Fax: 212-594-8391
E-Mail: info@namic.com
Home Page: www.namic.com
Social Media: Facebook, Twitter

Kathy A Johnson, President
James Jones, VP Programs

For members only, provides timely and useful national and local information about industry-related issues, trends and events
Frequency: Bi-Monthly

5062 NFAIS e-Notes
National Federation Abstracting & Info Services
1518 Walnut St
Suite 1004
Philadelphia, PA 19102
215-893-1561
Fax: 215-893-1564
E-Mail: nfais@nfais.org
Home Page: www.nfais.org
Social Media: Facebook, Twitter, LinkedIn

Bonnie Lawlor, Executive Director
Jill O'Neil, Director Communications

Membership organization for all organizations that create, aggregate or provide ease of access to credible information.
80 Members
Frequency: Monthly
Founded in 1958

5063 Newspaper Investor
Kagan World Media
1 Lower Ragsdale Dr
Building One, Suite 130
Monterey, CA 93940-5749
831-624-1536
800-307-2529
Fax: 831-625-3225
E-Mail: info@kagan.com
Home Page: www.kagan.com

Tim Baskerville, President
Tom Johnson, Marketing Manager
Cost: $845.00
Frequency: Monthly
Founded in 1969

5064 Online Publishing Update E-Newsletter
Newspaper Association of America
4401 Wilson Blvd
Suite 900
Arlington, VA 22203-4195
571-366-1000
Fax: 571-366-1195
E-Mail: joan.mills@naa.org
Home Page: www.naa.org

Reggie Hall, Senior VP

A round-up of news, research, industry trends, best practices and more, focusing on items of interest to newspaper and digital media executives. Online Publishing Update e-newsletter is published every Monday, Wednesday and Friday.
Frequency: 3x/Weekly

5065 Pacific Dialogue
Robert Miko
33 Ferry Ct
Stratford, CT 06615
203-378-2803
E-Mail: bmiko@pacificdialogue.com
Home Page: www.pacificdialogue.com

Robert Miko, Publisher

Corporate communications of the Pacific Region.
Cost: $196.00
4 Pages
Frequency: Weekly
Circulation: 1,000

5066 **Party Line**
Party Line Publishing Company
35 Sutton Place
New York, NY 10022-2464
212-755-3487
Fax: 212-755-4859
Home Page: www.partylinepublishing.com
Morton Yarmon, Publisher
Betty Yarmon, Editor
Betty Yarmon, Marketing
Weekly media placement newsletter with up-to-date news of the media for public relations executives in all aspects of business, hospitals, publishers and associations.
Cost: $200.00
Frequency: Weekly
Circulation: 2000
Founded in 1960
Mailing list available for rentat $100 per M
Printed in 2 colors on matte stock

5067 **Pay TV Newsletter**
Kagan World Media
126 Clock Tower Place
Carmel, CA 93923-8746
831-624-1536
Fax: 831-625-3225
E-Mail: info@kagan.com
Home Page: www.kagan.com
George Niesen, Editor
Tom Johnson, Marketing Manager
Cost: $845.00
Frequency: Monthly

5068 **SIGNAL Connections**
4400 Fairfax Lakes Court
Fairfax, VA 22033
703-631-6100
800-336-4583
Fax: 703-631-6169
E-Mail: promo@afcea.org
Home Page: www.afcea.org
Social Media: Facebook, Twitter, LinkedIn
Richard K Ackerman, Editor in Chief
Bridges the gap between issues of SIGNAL by providing additional news and feature articles about the industry and the Association.
Frequency: Monthly

5069 **Satellite Week**
Warren Communications News
2115 Ward Ct Nw
Washington, DC 20037-1209
202-872-9200
800-771-9202
Fax: 202-318-8350
E-Mail: info@warren-news.com
Home Page: www.warren-news.com
Brig Easley, Manager
Daniel Warren, President/Editor
Founded in 1945

5070 **Smaller Market E-Newsletter**
Newspaper Association of America
4401 Wilson Blvd
Suite 900
Arlington, VA 22203-4195
571-366-1000
Fax: 571-366-1195
E-Mail: joan.mills@naa.org
Home Page: www.naa.org
Social Media: Facebook, Twitter
Reggie Hall, Senior VP
Stay ahead of industry news and trends with the latest reports outlining how to improve your smaller market newspaper. Also receive a synopsis on new NAA products and services and how they can benefit smaller market newspapers.
Frequency: Monthly

5071 **Speech Technology Magazine**
2628 Wilhite Court
Suite 100
Lexington, KY 40503
859-278-2223
877-993-9767
Fax: 859-278-7364
Home Page: www.speechtechmag.com/
John Kelly, Publisher & Editor
Sheila Willison, Circulation Director
Stephanie Owens, Associate Editor
Devon Taylor, Magazine Sales
Kerrie Porath, Sales Coordinator
Divided into four sections: applications, technology, new products, and a special focus section. Authors from the field contribute their expertise to this trade magazine.
73 Pages
Frequency: Fortnightly
Circulation: 25000
Founded in 1996

5072 **Telecom A.M.**
Warren Communications News
2115 Ward Ct Nw
Washington, DC 20037-1209
202-872-9200
800-771-9202
Fax: 202-318-8350
E-Mail: info@warren-news.com
Home Page: www.warren-news.com
Brig Easley, Manager
Daniel Warren, President/Editor
Founded in 1945

5073 **Telemarketing Update: The Regulations and the Impact**
Newspaper Association of America
4401 Wilson Blvd
Suite 900
Arlington, VA 22203-4195
571-366-1000
Fax: 571-366-1195
E-Mail: joan.mills@naa.org
Home Page: www.naa.org
Social Media: Twitter
Reggie Hall, Senior VP
Perspective on the Federal Telemarketing Regulations and an explanation of how newspapers are being impacted by the changes. What's working and what's not and what the Federal Government has in store for newspapers.

5074 **Television A.M.**
Warren Communications News
2115 Ward Ct Nw
Washington, DC 20037-1209
202-872-9200
800-771-9202
Fax: 202-318-8350
E-Mail: info@warren-news.com
Home Page: www.warren-news.com
Brig Easley, Manager
Daniel Warren, President/Editor
Founded in 1945

5075 **The RCA News**
Grove City College
Attn: Daniel Brown
100 Campus Drive, Box 3014
Grove City, PA 16127
724-458-3793
E-Mail: dsbrown@gcc.edu
Home Page: www.americanrhetoric.com/rca
Daniel S Brown, Newsletter Editor
Ken Danielson, Executive Secretary
Janie Harden Fritz, President
A newsletter for the academic society of individuals interested in the study of all aspects of public religious communication, members include teachers, students, clergy, broadcasters and other scholars and professionals.
210 Members
Founded in 1973

5076 **Washington Internet Daily**
Warren Communications News
2115 Ward Ct Nw
Washington, DC 20037-1209
202-872-9200
800-771-9202
Fax: 202-318-8350
E-Mail: info@warren-news.com
Home Page: www.warren-news.com
Brig Easley, Manager
Daniel Warren, President/Editor
Founded in 1945

Magazines & Journals

5077 **15 Minutes Magazine.Com**
7334 173rd Street
Fresh Meadows, NY 11366-1428
718-969-0404
Fax: 718-591-3660
E-Mail: editor@15minutesmagazine.com
Home Page: www.15minutesmagazine.com
Tim Boxer, Editor/Publisher
Nina Boxer, Associate Editor
Bernie Ilson, PR Consultant
Stanley Donen, Founder
Michael Fredo, Owner
Monthly magazine online covering society benefits, with reviews of arts and entertainment, travel and new products. Targets 715,000 readers in affluent market
Cost: $50.00
Frequency: Monthly
Circulation: 4,45,000
Founded in 1999
Printed in 4 colors

5078 **AV Video and Multimedia Producer**
Knowledge Industry Publications
701 Westchester Ave
Suite 101W
West Harrison, NY 10604-3077
914-328-9157
Fax: 914-328-9093
Home Page: www.kipinet.com/av_mmp/
Ollie Bieniemy, Publisher
Covers product development, graphics and animation, software and equipment, and industry news for readers involved in professional production, multimedia production, and presentation technology.
Cost: $53.00
Frequency: Monthly
Circulation: 100,000

5079 **Archive Magazine**
Luerzer's Archive Inc
410 Park Avenue
Suite 1530
New York, NY 10022-9441
212-941-2496
Fax: 212-941-5490
E-Mail: office@showcase.com
Home Page: www.lurzersarchive.net
Social Media: Twitter, LinkedIn
Walter Lurzer, Editor
Read by advertising agency executives in 35 countries, archive presents tv commercials and print ads that are currently running around the world.
Frequency: 6x a year
Circulation: 40000

5080 Business Communications Review
BCR Enterprises
3025 Highland Pkwy
Suite 200
Downers Grove, IL 60515-5668
630-986-1432
800-227-1234
Fax: 630-323-5324
E-Mail: bcrsubscriptions@cmp.com
Home Page: www.bcr.com

Offers a complete package of the latest information for persons associated with the communications industry.
Cost: $46.00
80 Pages
Frequency: Monthly

5081 Communication World
Int'l Association of Business Communicators
601 Montgomery Street
Suite 1900
San Francisco, CA 94111
415-544-4700
Fax: 415-544-4747
E-Mail: cwmagazine@iabc.com
Home Page: www.iabc.com

Natasha Nicholson, Executive Editor
Sue Khodarahmi, Managing Editor
Sue Cavallaro, Production Editor

Covers the leatest in communication research, technology and trends through in-depth reports and insightful interviews.
Cost: $150.00
Frequency: Bi-Monthly
Circulation: 13,000
ISSN: 0744-7612
Founded in 1982
Printed in on matte stock

5082 Communications ASP
Technology Marketing Corporation
1 Technology Plz
Norwalk, CT 06854-1936
203-852-6800
800-243-6002
Fax: 203-853-2845
E-Mail: tmc@tmcnet.com
Home Page: www.tmcnet.com

Rich Tehrani, CEO

Communication solution magazine.
Cost: $2000.00
Frequency: Monthly
Founded in 1972

5083 Communications Arts
Coyne & Blanchard
110 Constitution Dr
Menlo Park, CA 94025-1107
650-326-6040
800-688-1971
Fax: 650-326-1648
E-Mail: ca@commarts.com
Home Page: www.commarts.com

Patrick Coyne, Publisher/Editor

The leading professional journal in the US on graphic arts, commercial photography, illustration and interactive design. Features profile individuals, studios, and agencies with examples of their work. Accepts advertising.
Cost: $53.00
140 Pages
Frequency: 1 Year 8 Issues
Circulation: 74,834
ISSN: 0010-3519
Founded in 1959
Printed in on glossy stock

5084 Communications Daily
Warren Publishing
2115 Ward Ct NW
Washington, DC 20037-1209
202-872-9200
800-771-9202
Fax: 202-318-8350
E-Mail: info@warren-news.com
Home Page: www.warren-news.com

Brig Easley, Manager
Daniel Warren, President/Editor

Covers the entire spectrum of the telephone, data communications, broadcasting, cable TV, electronic information distribution, cellulars, PCS and satellite.
Cost: $4295.00
Frequency: Daily
Founded in 1945

5085 Computers in Libraries
Information Today
143 Old Marlton Pike
Medford, NJ 08055-8750
609-654-6266
800-300-9868
Fax: 609-654-4309
E-Mail: custserv@infotoday.com
Home Page: www.infotoday.com

Thomas H Hogan, President
Roger R Bilboul, Chairman of the Board

Coverage of news and issues in the field of library information technology. Focuses on practical applications of technology in community, school, academic and special libraries. Includes discussions of the impact of emerging computer technologies on library systems and services and on the library community itself.
Cost: $99.95
Frequency: 10 issues/yr
Mailing list available for rent: 4M names
Printed in 4 colors on glossy stock

5086 Digital Magic
PennWell Publishing Company
10 Tara Boulevard
5th Floor
Nashua, NH 03062-2800
603-891-0123
Fax: 603-891-0539
Home Page: www.digitalmagicmag.com

Dennis Allen, Publisher

Insights on new technology trends and techniques, covers the latest in hardware and software products to keep digital effects professional competitive and up to date.
Cost: $19.95
Frequency: Bi-Monthly
Circulation: 30,000

5087 Documentary
International Documentary Association
1201 W 5th St
Suite M270
Los Angeles, CA 90017-1476
213-534-3600
Fax: 213-534-3610
E-Mail: michael@documentary.org
Home Page: www.documentary.org

Michael Lumpkin, Executive Director
Jon Curry, Office Manager
Cindy Chyr, Development

Offers essential information and keeps readers on track with the industry.
Cost: $45.00
Frequency: Quarterly

5088 Extra!
Fairness & Accuracy in Publishing
112 W 27th Street
New York, NY 10001
212-633-6700
Fax: 212-727-7668
E-Mail: fair@fair.org
Home Page: www.fair.org

Deborah Thomas, Publisher
Jeff Cohen, Founder

Progressive media criticism.
Cost: $21.00
Frequency: Bi-monthly
Circulation: 21800
Founded in 1987

5089 Folio: Magazine for Magazine Management
Red 7 Media, LLC
10 Norden Place
Norwalk, CT 06855
203-854-6730
Fax: 203-854-6735
E-Mail: tsilber@red7media.com
Home Page: www.foliomag.com

Stefanie Botelho, Associate Editor
Kerry Smith, President/CEO
Dan Trombetto, Group Creative Director
Tony Silber, General Manager
John Ellertson, Director Advertising Sales Manager

Written for the people who run the nation's magazines. Offers authoritative intelligence on the magazine market to enable industry professionals to navigate the widening range of strategic options. Every issue delivers features on the people and technologies that are transforming the magazine business, along with useful columns and departments, thought-provoking analysis and tactical advice for building successful magazines.
Cost: $96.00
Frequency: Monthly
Circulation: 11550
Founded in 1971

5090 Government Video
Miller Freeman Publications
810 7th Ave
27th Fl, Suite 4
New York, NY 10019-5818
212-636-2700
Fax: 212-636-2750
E-Mail: sedorusa@optonline.net
Home Page: www.governmentvideo.com

Gary Rhodes, International Sales Manager

Articles on audio, video production and technologies, training and presentation, multimedia, video conferencing, and medical and scientific applications.
Frequency: Monthly
Circulation: 18,000

5091 IEEE Wireless Communications
IEEE Communications Society
3 Park Ave
17th Floor
New York, NY 10016-5997
212-705-8920
Fax: 212-705-8999
E-Mail: publications@comsoc.org
Home Page: www.ieee.org

Laura Book, Manager
Jack Howell, Executive Director

An interdisciplinary bimonthly magazine, covers technical and policy issues relating to personal, location-independent communications in all media and at all protocol layers.
Frequency: Bi-Monthly

5092 Information Week
UBM LLC
600 Community Drive
Manhasset, NY 11030
516-562-5000
Fax: 516-562-5036

E-Mail: rpreston@techweb.com
Home Page: www.informationweek.com

Rob Preston, VP/Editor In Chief
Laurianne McLaughlin, Editor In Chief
Fritz Nelson, VP/Editorial Director

Delivers breaking news, blogs, high-impact image galleries, proprietary research as well as analysis on IT trends, a whitepaper library, video reports and interactive tools, al i a 24/7 environment.
Circulation: 440,000

5093 International Communications Association
1500 21st St NW
Washington, DC 20036-1000

202-955-1444
Fax: 202-955-1448
E-Mail: publications@icahdq.org
Home Page: www.icahdq.org

M Haley, Executive Director
Wolfgang Donfback, Administrative Assistant
Colleen Brady, Administrative Assistant
James Danowski, Secretary

Bi-monthly newsletter that supports all students and professionals in the international communications industry.
Cost: $30.00
Circulation: 3500
Founded in 1950
Printed in on matte stock

5094 Journal of Applied Communications
Agricultural Communicators in Education
University of Florida
PO Box 110810
Gainesville, FL 32611

352-392-9588
Fax: 352-392-8583
E-Mail: ace@ifas.ufl.edu
Home Page: www.aceweb.org/jac/jac.html

Amanda Aubuchon, Managing Editor
Mark Tucker, Executive Editor

A peer-reviewed professional journal which accepts original contributions about communications, research, innovations and other pertinent information. The Journal is provided to all members, libraries and other interested people.
Cost: $75.00
Frequency: Quarterly
Circulation: 700
ISSN: 1051-0834
Founded in 1990

5095 Journal of Open Computing
Association for Communication Administration
1765 N Street NW
Washington, DC 20036

202-464-4622
Fax: 202-464-4600
Home Page: www.natcom.org

5096 Journal of the Association of Information Systems
Case Western Reserve University
PO Box 2712
Atlanta, GA 30301-2712

404-413-7440
Fax: 404-413-7443
E-Mail: publications@aisnet.org
Home Page: www.aisnet.org

Doug Vogel, President

Publishes the highest quality scholarship in the field of information systems. Covers all aspects of Information Systems and Information Technology. Publishes rigorously developed and forward looking conceptual and empirical contributions.Encourages multidisciplinary and nontraditional approaches.
Frequency: Quarterly

5097 Journal of the Relgious Communication Association
Department of Communication & Rhetorical Studies
340 College Hall
600 Forbes Ave
Pittsburgh, PA 15282

E-Mail: owner@americanrhetoric.com
Home Page: www.americanrhetoric.com/rca

Kathleen Edelmayer, President
Matthew Melton, VP

The JCR addresses the concerns of the religious communicator and the communication scholar and includes reviews of current publications in the field of religious communication. The journal is semi-annual and is included with membership.
Circulation: 675

5098 MAIL: Journal of Communication Distribution
Gold Key Box 2425
Milford, PA 18337

607-746-7600
Fax: 607-746-2750
E-Mail: mailmagazine@msn.com
Home Page: www.mailomg.com

Offers updated information on electronic mail and mail messaging systems.
Cost: $6.00
105 Pages
Frequency: Monthly

5099 Managing Media Relations in a Crisis
NACHA: The Electronic Payments Association
13450 Sunrise Valley Drive
Suite 100
Herndon, VA 20171

703-561-1100
Fax: 703-787-0996
E-Mail: info@nacha.org
Home Page: www.nacha.org

Janet O Estep, CEO
Marcie Haitema, Chairperson

Designed to assist your organization to develop, test and execute a crisis communication plan. With this guide, you will understand how to address issues, whom to call and in what order to alert them, which vendors you can count on to help and how to develop a means to track the crisis as it grows or abates.
Cost: $30.00

5100 Media Studies Journal
Columbia University, Freedom Forum Media Center
2960 Broadway
New York, NY 10027-6902

212-854-1754
Fax: 212-678-4817
Home Page: www.columbia.edu

Lee C Bollinger, President

Aimed at scholars, practitioners and commentators. Offers information on mass communications issues involving the media and the public at large.
Cost: $20.00
Frequency: Quarterly
Circulation: 9000
Founded in 1754

5101 Novedades USA
Echo Media
900 Circle 75 Pkwy SE
Suite 1600
Atlanta, GA 30339-6014

770-955-3346
E-Mail: sales@echo-media.com
Home Page: www.echo-media.com

Michael Puffer, CEO
Stacey Reece, VP
Frequency: Weekly
Circulation: 100,000
Founded in 1986
Printed in 4 colors on newsprint stock

5102 Presstime Magazine
Newspaper Association of America
4401 Wilson Blvd
Suite 900
Arlington, VA 22203-4195

571 366-1000
Fax: 571-366-1195
E-Mail: joan.mills@naa.org
Home Page: www.naa.org
Social Media: Twitter

Reggie Hall, Senior VP

The flagship publication reaches top executives across all departments with information about the issues that affect newspaper operations today and in the future.
Frequency: Monthly
Mailing list available for rent

5103 Professional Journal: Sbusiness Publication
AFSM International
11031 Via Frontera
Suite A
San Diego, CA 92127-1709

858-673-3055
800-333-9786
Fax: 239-275-0794
E-Mail: info@afsmi.org
Home Page: www.afsmi.org

JB Wood, President
Thomas Lah, Executive Director

A global organization dedicated to furthering the knowledge, understanding, and career development of executives, managers, and professionals in the high-technology services and support industry as well as to provide leadership and direction that helps our individual and corporate members expand their capabilities to meet the growing complexities and challenges of the industry. Sbusiness publication is distributed bi-monthly serving international decision makers.
Cost: $ 95.00
114 Pages
Circulation: 10000
ISSN: 1049-2135
Founded in 1975
Printed in 4 colors on matte stock

5104 Publishers Weekly
PO Box 51593
Harlan, IA 51593

800-278-2991
Fax: 712-733-8019
E-Mail: pwycustserv@cdsfulfillment.com
Home Page: www.publishersweekly.com
Social Media: Facebook, Twitter

Jim Milliot, Co-Editorial Director
Michael Coffey, Co-Editorial Director
Diane Roback, Children's Book Editor
Louisa Ermelino, Reviews Director
Calvin Reid, News Editor

PW is the international journal of book publishing and bookselling including business news, reviews and bestseller lists targeted at

publishers, booksellers, librarians and literary agents.
Frequency: Weekly
Founded in 1872

5105 **Red Herring: The Business of Technology**
Red Herring
1900 Alameda De Las Pulgas
Suite 1
San Mateo, CA 94403-1222

650-428-2900
Fax: 650-428-2901
E-Mail: info@redherring.com
Home Page: www.redherring.com

Alex Vieux, Publisher
Christopher Alden, Editorial Director
Joel Dreyfuss, Editor-in-Chief

Offers information on new and rising companies, as well as current industrial technology issues and topics.
Frequency: Weekly
Circulation: 45000
Founded in 1993

5106 **Replication News**
Miller Freeman Publications
810 7th Ave
27th Fl, Suite 4
New York, NY 10019-5818

212-636-2700
Fax: 212-636-2750
E-Mail: sedorusa@optonline.net
Home Page: www.governmentvideo.com
Social Media: Facebook, Twitter

Gary Rhodes, International Sales Manager

Information on electronic and recording media through news coverage and analysis to provide executives with the market for strategic business planning.
Frequency: Monthly
Circulation: 16,490
Mailing list available for rent

5107 **SIGNAL Magazine**
4400 Fair Lakes Court
Fairfax, VA 22033-3899

703-631-6100
800-336-4583
Fax: 703-631-6133
E-Mail: promo@afcea.org
Home Page: www.afcea.org
Social Media: Facebook, Twitter, LinkedIn

Robert K Ackerman, Editor in Chief

International news magazine serving the critical information needs of government, military and industry professionals active in the fields of command, control, communications, computers, intelligence, surveillance and reconnaissance (C4ISR); information security, research and development; electronics; and homeland security.
Frequency: Monthly
Circulation: 90000

5108 **Signal Magazine**
Armed Forces Communications & Electronics Assoc
4400 Fair Lakes Court
Fairfax, VA 22033-3899

703-631-6100
800-336-4583
Fax: 703-631-6405
E-Mail: service@afcea.org
Home Page: www.afcea.org
Social Media: Facebook, Twitter, LinkedIn

Kent Schneider, President/CEO
Becky Nolan, Executive VP
John A Dubia, Executive VP

5109 **Speaker Magazine**
National Speakers Association
1500 S Priest Dr
Tempe, AZ 85281-6203

480-968-2552
Fax: 480-968-0911
E-Mail: andrea@nsaspeaker.org
Home Page: www.nsaspeaker.org

Ronald Culberson, President

Trends, issues and perspectives about and for the professional speaking industry.
Cost: $49.00
Frequency: 10x/Year

5110 **TV Guide**
United Video Satellite Group
1211 Avenue of the Americas
4th Floor
New York, NY 10036-8701

212-852-7500
Fax: 212-852-4914

Richard Porter, Publisher

Focuses on all aspects of network, cable and pay television programming and how it affects and reflects their audience.
Cost: $39.88
Frequency: Weekly
Circulation: 13mm

5111 **TV Technology**
IMAS Publishing
PO Box 1214
Falls Church, VA 22041

703-998-7600
Fax: 703-998-2966
E-Mail: webmaster@imaspub.com
Home Page: www.tvtechnology.com

Steven Dana, President
Tom Butts, Editor
Eric Trabb, Publisher
Kwentin Keenan, Circulation Manager
Bob Moses, Executive Director

News of a technical nature covering topics ranging from regulatory developments through maintenance and new products.
Cost: $39.95
Frequency: Fortnightly
Circulation: 37,000
Founded in 1978

5112 **Tech Trenda**
Association for Educational Comm and Technology
1800 N Stonelake Drive
Suite 2
Bloomington, IN 47404

812-335-7675
Fax: 812-335-7678
Home Page: www.aect.org

Mark Childress, President
Cost: $125.00
Frequency: Bi-Monthly
Circulation: 3500

5113 **Television International Magazine**
Television International Magazine
PO Box 2473
Universal City, CA 91610-8471

323-462-1099
Fax: 702-939-4725
E-Mail: tvi@smart90.com
Home Page: www.tvimagazine.com

Josie Cory, Publisher
Mark Soval, Advertising Director

News and information regarding the television industry, includes the who's who of the business; geared toward the executives and professionals of the industry.
Cost: $129.00
Frequency: Monthly
Circulation: 16000
Founded in 1956
Printed in 4 colors on glossy stock

5114 **xchange**
Virgo Publishing LLC
3300 N Central Ave
Suite 300
Phoenix, AZ 85012-2532

480-675-9925
Fax: 480-990-0819
E-Mail: mikes@vpico.com
Home Page: www.vpico.com
Social Media: Twitter, LinkedIn

Jenny Bolton, President

Provides in-depth, executive-level news and analysis regarding strategy, technology and regulation to help communications service providers create new revenue, lower costs and achieve sustainable business models.
Cost: $75.00
Frequency: Monthly
Circulation: 35,003
Founded in 1986

Trade Shows

5115 **AFCEA TechNet International**
Armed Forces Communications and Electronics Assn
4400 Fair Lakes Court
Fairfax, VA 22033-3899

703-631-6200
800-564-4220
Fax: 703-654-6931
E-Mail: technetinternational@jspargo.com
Home Page: www.afcea.org
Social Media: Facebook, Twitter, LinkedIn

Paul doCarmo, Sales Manager
Connie Shaw, Sales Manager

This event draws commanders and staff from every branch of the military, including warfighting integration organizations charged with the most critical responsibilities of synthesizing military power on land, at sea, and in the air.
7500 Attendees
Frequency: June

5116 **AM&AA Summer Conference**
Alliance of Merger and Acquisition Advisors
150 North Michigan Avenue
Suite 2700
Chicago, IL 60601

877-844-2535
Fax: 312-729-9800
E-Mail: aemerson@amaaonline.org
Home Page: www.amaaonline.org

Ainsley Emerson, Director

Premier international organization serving the educational and resource needs of the middle market and M&A profession.
Frequency: Annual

5117 **ATTW Conference**
Association of Teachers of Technical Writing

Department of Linguistics and Technical Comm
1155 Union Circle #305298
Denton, TX 76203-5017

940-565-4458
E-Mail: sims@unt.edu
Home Page: www.attw.org

Bill Davidson, President
Brenda Sims, Secretary
600 Members
Frequency: Annual/April
Founded in 1973
Mailing list available for rent

5118 **American Public Communications Council Conference & Expo**
American Public Communications Council
625 Slaters Lane
Suite 104
Alexandria, VA 22314

703-739-1322
Fax: 703-739-1324
Home Page: www.apcc.net

Willard Nichols, President
Michael Bright, Director
Conference, luncheon and 100 exhibits of public communications equipment and information including, pay phones, internet, atm, multimedia and more. Discussions include lobbying, the political climate, legal regulatory and legislative updates.
Founded in 1988

5119 **Association for Business Communication Annual Symposium**
Po Box 6143
Nacogdoches, TX 75962-0001

936-468-6280
Fax: 646-468-6281
E-Mail: abcjohnson@sfasu.edu
Home Page: www.businesscommunication.org

Nancy Schullery, President
Workshop and displays from textbook publishers, speech and business writing, technical publications and corporate communication.
400 Attendees
Founded in 1935

5120 **DISA Customer Partnership AFCEA Technology Showcase**
Armed Forces Communications and Electronics Assn
4400 Fair Lakes Court
Fairfax, VA 22033

703-631-6200
800-564-4220
Fax: 703-654-6931
E-Mail: disaexhibits@jspargo.com
Home Page: www.afcea.org
Social Media: Facebook, Twitter, LinkedIn

Paul doCarmo, Assistant Director/Exhibit Sales
Connie Shaw, Exhibit Sales Account Manager
This conference facilitates a continuing interface with customers and strategic partners by allowing attendees to benefit from the perspective of DoD (Department of Defense) and industry speakers. It offers information sessions that provide a forum for questions, concerns and problem resolution.
1200 Attendees
Frequency: April-May

5121 **Entelec Conference & Expo**
Energy Telecommunications and Electrical Assoc
5005 W Royal Lane
Suite 116
Irving, TX 75063

972-929-3169
888-503-8700
Fax: 972-915-6040
E-Mail: info@entelec.org
Home Page: www.entelec.org

Michael Burt, President
James Coulter, VP
To bring together communications and control technology professionals from the petroleum, natural gas, pipeline, and electric utility companies for three days of quality training, seminars, exhibits and networking.
Frequency: Annual/May

5122 **Graphic Communications Conference of the Int'l Brotherhood of Teamsters**
1900 L Street NW
Washington, DC 20036

202-462-1400
Fax: 202-721-0600
E-Mail: wcbmessenger@gciu.org
Home Page: www.gciu.org

James Hoff, President
Robert Lacey, Secretary/Treasurer
Combines three independent shows: Printing XPO, Type-X, and Art-X and gives you a complete overview of the most recently introduced technologies and the newest information in the field of graphic arts.
15000 Members
Founded in 1983

5123 **LandWarNet Conference**
Armed Forces Communications and Electronics Assn
4400 Fair Lakes Court
Fairfax, VA 22033

703-631-6200
800-564-4220
Fax: 703-654-6931
E-Mail: landwarnet@jspargo.com
Home Page: www.afcea.org
Social Media: Facebook, Twitter, LinkedIn

Nathan Wills, Account Manager
Thousands of key communications/information technology buyers and influencers attend the conference every year. This is an opportunity to network with the best and develop crucial relationships with some of the Army's most influential decision-makers.
3700 Attendees
Frequency: August

5124 **MILCOM**
Armed Forces Communications and Electronics Assn
4400 Fair Lakes Court
Fairfax, VA 22033

703-631-6200
800-564-4220
Fax: 703-654-6931
E-Mail: milcom@jspargo.com
Home Page: www.afcea.org
Social Media: Facebook, Twitter, LinkedIn

Paul doCarmo, Assistant Director/Exhibit Sales
Connie Shaw, Exhibit Sales Account Manager
For over 20 years, MILCOM has been the premeir international conference for military communications, with over 3,000 attendees every year. It attracts decision-makers from government, military, academia and industry, including heads of multi-national forces from around the globe, all who contribute key technologies decisions and investments for their agency.
3000 Attendees
Frequency: October

5125 **Mailcom**
The Art & Science of Mail Communications
Po Box 7045
Philadelphia, PA 19149

732-280-8865
Fax: 732-280-7854
E-Mail: ljhumphries@msn.com
Home Page: www.mailcom.org

Lance Humphries, Managing Director
Learn how business communications can become strategic corporate tools
9000 Attendees
Frequency: Oct Las Vegas
Mailing list available for rent

5126 **NAA Annual Convention**
Newspaper Association of America
4401 Wilson Boulevard
Suite 900
Vienna, VA 22203-1867

571-366-1000
Fax: 571-366-1195
E-Mail: joan.mills@naa.org
Home Page: www.naa.org

James Moroney, President
Donna Barret, Treasurer
This event will welcome industry executives from across the country and is the opportunity for senior level newspaper professionals to learn, share ideas and network. The agenda will showcase the strategies and tactics necessary to address the key issues of revenue, audience, digital and infrastructure.
Frequency: Annual
Mailing list available for rent

5127 **NAMIC Conference**
Natl Assoc for Multi-Ethnicity in Communications
320 West 37th Street
8th Floor
New York, NY 10018

212-594-5985
Fax: 212-594-8391
E-Mail: info@namic.com
Home Page: www.namic.com
Social Media: Facebook, Twitter, LinkedIn

Kathy A Johnson, President
James Jones, VP Programs
Educational forum focused on leadership development, corporate diversity and inclusion, digital media and multi-ethnic content and programming. Content emphasizes diversity as a strategic business imperative
700 Attendees
Frequency: Annual

5128 **NFAIS Annual Conference**
National Federation Abstracting & Info Services
1518 Walnut St
Suite 1004
Philadelphia, PA 19102

215-893-1561
Fax: 215-893-1564
E-Mail: nfais@nfais.org
Home Page: www.nfais.org

Bonnie Lawlor, Executive Director
Jill O'Neil, Director Communications
300 Attendees
Frequency: February/March

5129 **NSA Convention**
National Speakers Association
1500 S Priest Dr
Tempe, AZ 85281-6203

480-968-2552
Fax: 480-968-0911

E-Mail: andrea@nsaspeaker.org
Home Page: www.nsaspeaker.org

Ronald Culberson, President
1500 Attendees
Frequency: Annual

5130 National Hispanic Market Trade Show and Media Expo (Se Habla Espanol)
Hispanic Business
425 Pine Avenue
Santa Barbara, CA 93117-3709

805-964-4554
Fax: 805-964-5539
E-Mail: info@hispanstar.com
Home Page: www.hispanstar.com
Social Media: Facebook, Twitter, LinkedIn

John Pasini, Cfo/Coo

Annual show of 100 exhibitors of market/research, media, advertising, public relations, information services and recruitment.
1500 Attendees

5131 Toastmasters Trade Show
Toastmasters International
PO Box 9052
Mission Viejo, CA 92690-9052

949-858-8255
949-835-1300
Fax: 949-858-1207
E-Mail: newsletters@toastmasters.org
Home Page: www.toastmasters.org

Focuses on communication in general and public speaking in particular. Topics include language, listening, humor, self improvement, goal setting, success and logical thinking.
2M Attendees
Frequency: August

Directories & Databases

5132 ACCE Communications Council Directory
4875 Eisenhower Ave
Suite 250
Alexandria, VA 22304-4850

703-998-0072
Fax: 703-212-9512
E-Mail: webmaster@acce.org
Home Page: www.acce.org
Social Media: Facebook, Twitter, LinkedIn

Michael Flemming, President

Offers member information on the council activities.
Frequency: Annual+
Founded in 1914

5133 Adweek Directory
Prometheus Global Media
770 Broadway
New York, NY 10003-9595

212-493-4100
Fax: 646-654-5368
Home Page: www.prometheusgm.com

Richard D. Beckman, CEO
Jame A. Finkelstein, Chairman
Madeline Krakowsky, Vice President Circulation
Tracy Brater, Executive Director Creative Service

Adweek Directories Online is where you will find searchable databases with comprehensive information on ad agencies, brand marketers and multicultural media.
Frequency: Annual
Circulation: 800
Founded in 1981

5134 American Showcase Illustration
Luerzer's Archive Inc
Ste 1530
410 Park Ave
New York, NY 10022-9441

212-941-2496
Fax: 212-941-5490
E-Mail: office@showcase.com
Home Page: www.lurzersarchive.net

Walter Lurzer, Editor

Illustrators and graphic designers.
Mailing list available for rent

5135 Association for Educational Communications and Technology Membership Directory
Association for Educational Comm and Technology
1800 N Stonelake Drive
Suite 2
Bloomington, IN 47404

812-335-7675
Fax: 812-335-7678
Home Page: www.aect.org

Mark Childress, President
Mary Beth Jordan, Secretary/Treasurer

5,000 audiovisual and instructional materials specialists, educational technologists, audiovisual and television production personnel, school media specialists
Frequency: Annual

5136 Bacon's Newspaper & Magazine Directories
Cision U.S., Inc.
322 South Michigan Avenue
Suite 900
Chicago, IL 60604

312-263-0070
866-639-5087
E-Mail: info.us@cision.com
Home Page: us.cision.com

Joe Bernardo, President & CEO
Heidi Sullivan, VP & Publisher
Valerie Lopez, Research Director
Jessica White, Research Director
Rachel Farrell, Research Manager

Two volume set listing all daily and community newspapers, magazines and newsletters, news service and syndicates, syndicated columnists, complete editorial staff listings of each publication provided, covers U.S., Canada, Mexico, and Carribean.
Cost: $350.00
4,700 Pages
Frequency: Annual
ISSN: 1088-9639
Founded in 1951
Printed in one color on matte stock

5137 Bacon's Radio/TV/Cable Directory
Cision U.S., Inc.
332 South Michigan Avenue
Suite 900
Chicago, IL 60604

312-263-0070
866-639-5087
E-Mail: info.us@cision.com
Home Page: www.us.cision.com

Joe Bernardo, President & CEO
Heidi Sullivan, VP & Publisher
Valerie Lopez, Research Director
Jessica White, Research Director
Rachel Farrell, Research Manager

Includes comprehensive coverage for contact and programming information for more than 3,500 televsion networks, cable networks, television syndicators, television stations, and cable systems in the United States and Canada.
Cost: $350.00
Frequency: Annual
ISSN: 1088-9639
Printed in one color on matte stock

5138 Burrelle's Media Directory
BurrellesLuce
75 E Northfield Rd
Livingston, NJ 07039-4532

973-992-6600
800-631-1160
Fax: 973-992-7675
Home Page: www.burrellesluce.com
Social Media: Facebook, Twitter, LinkedIn

Robert C Waggoner, CEO

Approximately 60,000 media listings in North America. Listings cover newspapers, magazines (trades and consumer), broadcast, and internet outlets.
Cost: $795.00
Frequency: Annual

5139 Corporate Yellow Book
Leadership Directories
104 5th Ave
New York, NY 10011-6901

212-627-4140
Fax: 212-645-0931
E-Mail: corporate@leadershipdirectories.com
Home Page: www.leadershipdirectories.com

David Hurvitz, CEO

Contact information for over 48,000 executives at over 1,000 companies and 6,000 subsidiaries and divisions, and more than 9,000 board members and their outside affiliations.
Cost: $360.00
1,400 Pages
Frequency: Quarterly
ISSN: 1058-2908
Founded in 1986
Mailing list available for rent: 50,000 names at $105 per M

5140 Film & Video Finder
Information Today
143 Old Marlton Pike
Medford, NJ 08055-8750

609-654-6266
800-300-9868
Fax: 609-654-4309
E-Mail: custserv@infotoday.com
Home Page: www.infotoday.com

Thomas H Hogan, President
Roger R Bilboul, Chairman Of The Board

Contains information on 130,000 films and videos. The most comprehensive reference available to educational films and videos. A three volume hardbound set.
Cost: $295.00
6434 Pages
Frequency: Annual
ISBN: 0-937548-29-4

5141 Gale Database of Publications and Broadcast Media
Gale/Cengage Learning
PO Box 09187
Detroit, MI 48209-0187

248-699-4253
800-877-4253
Fax: 248-699-8049
E-Mail: gale.galeord@cengage.com
Home Page: www.gale.com
Social Media: Facebook, Twitter, LinkedIn

Patrick C Sommers, President

This media directory contains thousands of listings for radio and television stations and cable companies.
Founded in 2008

5142 **Gale's Ready Reference Shelf**
Gale/Cengage Learning
PO Box 09187
Detroit, MI 48209-0187
248-699-4253
800-877-4253
Fax: 248-699-8049
E-Mail: gale.galeord@cengage.com
Home Page: www.gale.com
Social Media: Facebook, Twitter, LinkedIn
Patrick C Sommers, President
Gale's Ready Reference Shelf allows you to search the entire database of integrated content at one time and the data updates are automatic allowing the user to access the latest information available.

5143 **Gebbie Press All-in-One Directory**
Gebbie Press
PO Box 1000
New Paltz, NY 12561-0017
845-255-7560
Fax: 845-256-1239
Home Page: www.gebbieinc.com
Mark Gebbie, Editor/Publisher
TV and radio stations, daily and weekly newspapers, consumer and trade magazines, black and Hispanic media, news syndicates, networks, AP/UPI bureaus. Compact spiral bound 6x9 inches.
Cost: $140.00
500 Pages
Frequency: Also on Disk
Founded in 1970

5144 **Hudson's Washington News Media Contacts Directory**
Grey House Publishing
4919 Route 22
PO Box 56
Amenia, NY 12501
518-789-8700
800-562-2139
Fax: 845-373-6390
E-Mail: books@greyhouse.com
Home Page: www.greyhouse.com
Social Media: Facebook, Twitter
Leslie Mackenzie, Publisher
Richard Gottlieb, President
A comprehensive guide to the entire Washington, D.C. press corps, broken down into categories.
Cost: $289.00
350 Pages
ISBN: 1-592378-53-6
Printed in one color on matte stock

5145 **Hudson's Washington News Media Contacts - Online Database**
Grey House Publishing
4919 Route 22
PO Box 56
Amenia, NY 12501
518-789-8700
800-562-2139
Fax: 845-373-6390
E-Mail: gold@greyhouse.com
Home Page: www.gold.greyhouse.com
Social Media: Facebook, Twitter
Leslie Mackenzie, Publisher
Richard Gottlieb, President
With 100% verification of data, Hudson's is the most accurate, most up-to-date source for media contacts in our nation's capital. With the largest concentration of news media in the world, having access to Washington's news media will get your message heard by these key media outlets.

5146 **Journalism and Mass Communication Directory**
AEJMC
234 Outlet Pointe Boulevard
Suite A
Columbia, SC 29210-5667
803-798-0271
Fax: 803-772-3509
E-Mail: aejmchq@aol.com
Home Page: www.aejmc.org
Social Media: Facebook, Twitter, LinkedIn
Kyo Hum, President
Over 3,000 professionals, academics and graduate students; more than 400 journalism and mass communications schools and departments in four-year colleges and universities, including 200 members of the Association of Schools of Journalism and Mass Communication.
Cost: $25.00
Frequency: Annual
Circulation: 5000
Founded in 1983
Mailing list available for rent

5147 **Kagan Media Index**
Kagan World Media
126 Clock Tower Place
Carmel, CA 93923-8746
831-624-1536
Fax: 831-625-3225
E-Mail: info@kagan.com
Home Page: www.kagan.com
George Niesen, Editor
Tom Johnson, Marketing Manager
The most comprehensive collection of media industry databases found anywhere. Current estimates of industry growth for a dozen different media businesses, shown on a 145-line spreadsheet, projected forward and updated monthly. Three month trial available.
Cost: $795.00
Frequency: Monthly

5148 **M Street Radio Directory**
M Street Corporation
81 Main Street, Suite 2
PO Box 442
Littleten, NH 03561
603-444-5720
800-248-4242
Fax: 603-444-2872
E-Mail: info@insideradio.com
Home Page: ww.mstreet.net
Cathy Devine, Research Director
Kelli Grisez, Operations Manager
Frank Saxe, Senior Editor
Approximately 14,000 AM and FM radio stations in the US and Canada.
Cost: $79.00
Frequency: Annual
Printed in on matte stock

5149 **News Media Directories**
PO Box 316
Mount Dora, FL 32757
352-589-9020
800-749-6399
Fax: 866-586-7020
Home Page: www.newsmediadirectories.com
Dean Highberger, Editor
Directory for lists, daily papers, new services, magazines, weekly papers, special publications and radio stations. We have directories covering eight states , Alabama, Florida, Georgia, Mississippi, North Carolina, Ohio, South Carolina and Tennessee. Also, we have a condensed southeast edition. Listings include address, phone, fax, e-mail, and key associates.
Frequency: Annual

5150 **News Media Yellow Book**
Leadership Directories
104 5th Ave
New York, NY 10011-6901
212-627-4140
Fax: 212-645-0931
E-Mail: newsmedia@leadershipdirectories.com
Home Page: www.leadershipdirectories.com
Social Media: Facebook, Twitter
David Hurvitz, CEO
James M Petrie, Associate Publisher
Contact information for over 39,000 journalists at over 2,500 new services, networks, newspapers, television, radio stations, as well as independent journalists and syndicated columnists.
Cost: $325.00
1,200 Pages
Frequency: Quarterly
ISSN: 1071-8931
Founded in 1989
Mailing list available for rent: 32,000 names at $125 per M

5151 **O'Dwyer's Directory of Public Relations Firms**
JR O'Dwyer Company
271 Madison Ave
Suite 600
New York, NY 10016-1013
212-679-2461
Fax: 212-683-2750
E-Mail: jack@odwyerpr.com
Home Page: www.odwyerpr.com
Jack O'Dwyer, Publisher
Kevin McCauley, Editor
Sharlene Spingler, Associate Publisher
Exclusive ranking of public relations firms and lists more than 1,700 firms in the US and 55 countries.
Cost: $125.00
400 Pages
Frequency: Annual
Founded in 1968

5152 **Pocket Media Guide**
Media Distribution Services
307 W 36th St
Department P
New York, NY 10018-6519
212-279-4800
800-637-3282
Fax: 212-643-0576
Home Page: www.mdsconnect.com
Dan Cantelmo, President
Designed to fit easily into a wallet, the palm size guide includes names and addresses, with phone numbers, of more than 700 major print and media in North America, plus a calendar, annual media statistics, and a publicity primer.
40 Pages
Frequency: Annual

5153 **Power Media Selects**
Broadcast Interview Source
2233 Wisconsin Ave NW
Suite 301
Washington, DC 20007-4132
202-333-5000
800-932-7266
Fax: 202-342-5411
Home Page: www.expertclick.com
Mitchell Davis, Owner
Alan Caruba, Production Manager
Approximately 3,000 media contacts throughout the US, including newswire services, syndicates, syndicated columnists, national newspapers, magazines, radio and television talk shows, etc.
Cost: $166.50
Frequency: Annual

5154 **Sound & Communications**
Testa Communications
25 Willowdale Avenue
Port Washington, NY 11050-3779

516-767-2500
Fax: 516-767-9335

David Silverman, Editor
Bob Beoder, Advertising Manager

The systems magazine for contractors and consultants who design, specify, sell, and install audio and display systems. Installation profiles, news, business and product updates, incisive theory and applications reporting.
Cost: $15.00
Frequency: Monthly
Circulation: 23,000
Founded in 1955

Industry Web Sites

5155 **http://gold.greyhouse.com**
G.O.L.D Grey House OnLine Databases
Grey House Publishing's online database platform, GOLD, offers Quick Search, Keyword Search and Expert Search for most business markets including boradcasting, communications and media markets. The GOLD platform makes finding the information you need quick and easy - whether you're a novice searcher or an experienced database user. All of Grey House's directory products are available for subscription on the GOLD platform.

5156 **www.acce.org**
American Chamber of Commerce Executives
National organization uniquely serving individuals involved in the management of chambers of all sizes. Chamber executives and their staffs can capitalize on a wealth of information, leadership, skill development, management techniques and innovative program offerings. Also works diligently to upgrade the economic status and professional standing of those active in the chamber field.

5157 **www.adweek.com**
Adweek
Leading decision makers in the advertising and marketing field go to Adweek.com every day for breaking news, insight, buzz, opinion, analysis, research and classifieds. The resources of all six regional editions of Adweek, as well as the national edition of Brandweek are combined with the knowledge of our editors and the multimedia-interactive capabilities of the Web to deliver vital information quickly and effectively to our target audience.

5158 **www.aim.org**
Accuracy in Media
Nonprofit, grassroots citizens watchdog of the news media that critiques botched and bungled news stories and sets the record straight on important issues that have recieved slanted coverage.

5159 **www.americomm.org**
American Communication Association
Founded for the purposes of fostering research and scholorship in all areas of human communication behavior, promoting and improving excellence in the pedagogy of communication, providing a voice in communication law and policy, and providing evaluation and certification services for academic programs in communication study.

5160 **www.amta.org**
Antenna Measurement Techniques Association
Nonprofit professional organization, open to individuals with an interest in antenna measurements. Areas of interest include: measurement facilities, unique or innovative measurement techniques, test instrumentation and systems, RCS measurements, compact range design and evaluation, near-field techniques and their applications, and the practical aspects of measurement problems problems and their solutions.

5161 **www.apcc.net**
American Public Communications Council
APCC proudly offers offers a wide array of services to the public communications industry, from Perspectives magazine to our annual trade show to our involvement in legal and regulatory issues. This site is a place for the public to find out about our industry and for our members to learn of legal and regulatory developments, to become aware of APCC programs events, and to have a forum for discussion.

5162 **www.apco911.org**
Association of Public-Safety Communications
The world's oldest and largest professional organization dedicated to the enhancement of public safety communications and to serving its more than 15,000 members, the people who use public safety communications systems and services.

5163 **www.attw.org**
Association of Teachers of Technical Writing
Provides communication among teachers of technical writing and develops technical communications as an academic discipline.

5164 **www.bowker.com**
Reed Reference Publishing RR Bowker
Offers, in four separate volumes, syndicates, newspapers, radio and television stations, feature writers, photographers, illustrators and internal house organs.

5165 **www.consultingsuccess.org**
Assn of Professional Communication Consultants
Professional community where communication consultants increase their knowledge, grow their business, achieve high standards of professional practice. APCC's mission is to support members as they help clients reach their goals through better communication.

5166 **www.digmedia.org**
Digital Media Association
National trade organization devoted primarily to the online audio and video industries, and more generally to commercially innovative digital media opportunities.

5167 **www.drudgereport.com**
Links to international news sources and columnists.

5168 **www.entelec.org**
Energy Telecommunications and Electrical Assoc
A user association focusing on communications and control technologies used by petroleum, natural gas, pipeline and electric utility companies.

5169 **www.greyhouse.com**
Grey House Publishing
Authoritative reference directories for most business sectors including broadcasting, communications and meida markets. Users can search the online databases with varied search criteria allowing for custom searches by product category, geographic area, sales volume, keyword, subject and more. Full Grey House catalog and online ordering also available.

5170 **www.iaais.org**
Int'l Association of Audio Information Services
Formerly the National Association of Radio Reading Services, we are an organization of services that provide audio access to information for people who are print disabled. People served are blind, visually impared, learning disabled or physically disabled.

5171 **www.iabc.com**
Int'l Association of Business Communications
International knowledge network for professionals engaged in strategic business communication management. IABC links communicators in a global network that inspires, establishes and supports the highest professional standards.

5172 **www.icahdq.org**
International Communications Association
International association for scholars interested in the study, teaching and application of all aspects of human mediated communication.

5173 **www.iics.org**
International Interactive Communication Society
For communications industry professionals dedicated to the advancement of interactive technologies. Provides a forum to share ideas, applications amd techniques for effective use of interactive media.

5174 **www.iste.org**
International Society for Technology in Education
Nonprofit professional organization with a worldwide membership of leaders and potential leaders in educational technology.

5175 **www.kagan.com**
Kagan World Media
For those interested in investments in radio and TV stations and publicly held companies.

5176 **www.kausfiles.com**
Kausfiles
Site for journalists and media specialists.

5177 **www.liberty.uc.wlu.edu**
Journalism Resources
Lists of newspapers, film resources, jobs and internships and political advocacy groups.

5178 **www.missouri.edu/~foiwww**
Affiliation of University of Missouri
Maintains files documenting actions by government, media and society affecting the flow and content of information. Call or write for assistance with researching media topics or instruction in using access laws.

5179 **www.netage.com**
Networking Institute
Promotes networks to help people work together. Offers consulting services, educational workshops and seminars.

5180 **www.nfais.org**
National Federation Absrtacting & Info Services
Serves those groups that aggregate, organize, and facilitate access to information. To improve member capabilities and contribute to their on-

going success. Provides opportunities for education, advocacy, and a forum to address common interests.

5181 **www.nsaspeaker.org**
National Speakers Association

The leading organization for experts who speak professionally. NSA's 4000 members include experts in a variety of industries and disciplines, who reach audiences as trainers, educators, humorists, motivators, consultants, authors and more. NSA provides resources and education designed to advance the skills, integrity, and value of its members and speaking profession. NSA the voice of the speaking profession.

5182 **www.postcom.org**
Association for Postal Commerce

National Organization representing those who use, or support the use, of mail as a medium for communication and commerce. Postcom publishes a weekly newsletter covering postal policy and operational issues.

5183 **www.poynter.org**
Poynter Online

Poynter Institute is dedicated to teaching and inspiring journalists and media leaders. Promotes excellence and integrity in the practice of craft and in the practical leadership of successful businesses.

5184 **www.regionalmagazines.org**
International Regional Magazine Association

Promotes the interests of international and regional magazine professionals.

5185 **www.retailing.org**
Electronics Retailing Association

For infomercial producers, marketers, product developers, broadcasters and other industries serving the infomercial market.

5186 **www.speakingsuccess.com**
Personal Achievement Institute

5187 **www.theabc.org**
Association for Business Communication

International organization commited to fostering excellence in business communication scholarship, research, education, and practice.

5188 **www.toastmasters.org**
Toastmasters International

Publishes educational articles on the subjects of communication and leadership. Topics include language, listening, humor, self-improvement, goal setting, success and logical thinking.

5189 **www.wgbh.org**
WGBH Educational Foundation

WGBH productions are seen and heard on stations around the country.

Associations

5190 **AIM Global**
One Landmark North, 20399 Route 19
Suite 203
Cranberry Township, PA 16066

724-934-4470
Fax: 724-742-4476
E-Mail: info@aimglobal.org
Home Page: www.aimglobal.org
Social Media: LinkedIn

Charles Evanhoe, Chairperson
Mary Lou Bosco, COO
Diana Bowser, Manager, Finance and Administration

International trade association representing automatic identification and mobility technology solution providers.
900+ Members
Founded in 1972

5191 **ARMA International**
11880 College Blvd
7th Floor
Overland Park, KS 66210

913-341-3808
800-422-2762
Fax: 913-341-3742
E-Mail: headquarters@armaintl.org
Home Page: www.arma.org

Julie J. Colgan, CRM, President
Brenda Prowse, CRM, Treasurer
Fred Pulzello, CRM, President-Elect
Komal Gulich, CRM, Chair / Immediate Past President

A not-for-profit professional association and the authority on managing records and information.
11000 Members
Founded in 1955

5192 **Alpha Micro Users Society**
210 N Iris Avenue
Rialto, CA 92376-5727

909-874-6214
Fax: 909-874-2143
E-Mail: info@amus.org
Home Page: www.amus.org

Jeff Kreider, President

An organization supported by members to promote the uses of computers manufactured by Alpha Micro Products of Irvine, California. This basic purpose has expanded, over the years, from merely a focal point for the exchange of technical information on its use and versatility, to promotion of products (Software and Hardware) from Alpha Micro and various third party organizations having an interest in users of Alpha Micro computers.
125 Members
Founded in 1978

5193 **American Association for Artificial Intelligence**
2275 East Bayshore Road
Suite 160
Palo Alto, CA 94303

650-328-3123
Fax: 650-321-4457
E-Mail: info@aaai.org
Home Page: www.aaai.org

Alan Mackworth, President
Ted Senator, Treasurer/Secretary

Nonprofit society devoted to advancing the scientific understanding of the mechanisims underlying thought and intellegent behavior and their embodiment in machines.
6000 Members
Founded in 1979
Mailing list available for rent

5194 **American Council for Technology**
3040 Williams Dr
Suite 610
Fairfax, VA 22031-4618

703-208-4800
Fax: 703-208-4805
E-Mail: act-iac@actgov.org
Home Page: www.actgov.org
Social Media: Facebook, Twitter, LinkedIn, YouTube

Ken Allen, Executive Director
Don Arnold, Director
April Davis, Director Of Member Service
Jim Beaupre, Director, ACT-IAC Academy
Don Becker, Associate Director, Communications

A non-profit educational organization established to assist government in acquiring and using information technology, resources effectively and efficiently. Working with all levels of the government, ACT provides education, programming, and networking opportunities that enhance and advance the government IT profession.
50000 Members
Founded in 1979

5195 **American Medical Informatics Association**
4720 Montgomery Lane
Suite 500
Bethesda, MD 20814-6052

301-657-1291
Fax: 301-657-1296
E-Mail: mail@mail.amia.org
Home Page: www.amia.org
Social Media: Facebook, Twitter, LinkedIn, YouTube, Flickr

Kevin M. Fickenscher, MD, CPE,, AMIA President and CEO
Sara Ward, Executive Assistant
Karen Greenwood, Executive Vice President & COO
Ross D. Martin, MD, MHA, Vice President Corporate Relations
Jeffrey Williamson, M.Ed, Vice President, Education

Support all those involved with commercial and scientific medical informatics software and hardware, supplies and services. Hosts annual trade show.
3200 Members
Founded in 1990
Mailing list available for rent: 2000 names

5196 **American Society for Information Science and Technology**
1320 Fenwick Lane
Suite 510
Silver Spring, MD 20910

301-495-0900
Fax: 301-495-0810
E-Mail: asis@asis.org
Home Page: www.asis.org
Social Media: Facebook, Twitter

Andrew Dillon, President
Vicki Gregory, Treasurer
Richard Hills, Executive Director
William Senn, Chapter Assembly Director
Naresh Agarwal, Deputy Chapter Assembly Director

ASIS&T has been the society for information professionals leading the search for new and better theories, techniques, and technologies to improve access to information.
4000 Members
Founded in 1937

5197 **American Society for Precision Engineering**
PO Box 10826
Raleigh, NC 27605-0826

919-839-8444
Fax: 919-839-8039
E-Mail: webmaster@aspe.net
Home Page: www.aspe.net

Alexander H. Slocum, President
John S. Taylor, Vice President
Thomas A. Dow, Executive Director
Ilka Lee, Publications and Office Manager
Wendy Shearon, Meetings & Membership Manager

Members are from academia, industry and government, and include professionals in engineering, materials science, physics, chemistry, mathematics and computer science. Multidisciplinary professional and technical society concerned with precision engineering research and development, design and manufacturing of high accuracy components and systems.
Founded in 1986

5198 **Armed Forces Communications & Electronics Association (AFCEA)**
4400 Fair Lakes Ct
Fairfax, VA 22033-3899

703-631-1397
800-336-4583
Fax: 703-631-4693
E-Mail: service@afcea.org
Home Page: www.afcea.org
Social Media: Facebook, Twitter, LinkedIn

Kent Schneider, President/CEO
Becky Nolan, Executive VP
John A Dubia, Executive VP

A non-profit membership association serving the military, government, industry, and academia as an ethical forum for advancing professional knowledge and relationships in the fields of communications, IT, intelligence, and global security.
31000 Members
Founded in 1946

5199 **Association for Computing Machinery**
2 Penn Plz
Suite 701
New York, NY 10121-0799

212-868-5716
800-342-6626
Fax: 212-944-1318
E-Mail: acmhelp@acm.org
Home Page: www.acm.org
Social Media: Facebook, Twitter, LinkedIn, YouTube

John R White, Executive Director/CEO
Patricia Ryan, Deputy Exec Director Operations/COO
Wayne Graves, Director of Information Systems
Russell Harris, Director of Financial Services

Association for advancing the skills of information technology professionals and for interpreting the impact of information technology on society.
80000 Members
Founded in 1947

5200 Association for Educational Communication and Technology
320 W. 8th St
Suite 101
Bloomington, IN 47404

812-335-7675
877-677-AECT
Fax: 812-335-7678
E-Mail: aect@aect.org
Home Page: www.aect.org
Social Media: Facebook, Twitter

Mark Childress, President
Stephen Harmon, President-Elect
Ellen Hoffman, Executive Secretary
Ana Donaldson, Past President

A professional association of thousands of educators and others whose activities are directed towards improving instruction through technology.
Founded in 1923

5201 Association for Information and Image Management International
1100 Wayne Avenue
Suite 1100
Silver Spring, MD 20910

301-587-8202
800-477-2446
Fax: 301-587-2711
E-Mail: aiim@aiim.org
Home Page: www.aiim.org
Social Media: Facebook, Twitter, LinkedIn, YouTube

John F. Mancini, President and CEO
Felicia Dillard, CFO
Atle Skjekkeland, Chief Operating Officer
Peggy Winton, Vice President and CMO
Georgina Clelland, Director, Events

Global authority on enterprise content management (ECM). ECM Technologies are used to create, capture, customize, deliver, and manage information to support business process.
Founded in 1943

5202 Association for Services Management International
11031 Via Frontera
Suite A
San Diego, CA 92127

239-275-7887
800-333-9786
Fax: 239-275-0794
E-Mail: info@afsmi.org
Home Page: www.afsmi.org

JB Wood, President
Thomas Lah, Executive Director

Provides the knowledge, fellowship and career connections that customer services and support managers for technology based products and solutions needed for professional and career development.
Cost: $375.00
Frequency: Membership Fee
Founded in 1975

5203 Association for the Advancement of Computing in Education
P.O. Box 308
Waynesville, NC 28786

828-246-9558
Fax: 703-997-8760
E-Mail: info@aace.org
Home Page: www.aace.org
Social Media: Facebook

Dr Gary H Marks, Executive Director

An international, educational and professional nonprofit organization dedicated to the advancement of the knowledge, theory and quality of learning and teaching at all levels with information technology.
Founded in 1981

5204 Association of Information Technology Professionals
330 N. Wabash Ave
Suite 2000
Chicago, IL 60611

312-245-1070
800-224-9371
Fax: 312-673-6659
E-Mail: aitp_hq@aitp.org
Home Page: www.aitp.org

William W. Fly, President
Michael Welch, Executive Vice-President
W. Paul Ziems, Association Treasurer
John Council, Association Secretary
Norbert J. Kubilus, Immediate Past President

Comprised of career minded individuals who seek to expand their potential employers, employees, managers, programmers, and many others. The organization seeks to provide avenues for all their members to be teachers as well as students and to make contacts with other members in the IS field, all in an effort to become more marketable in rapidly changing, technological careers.
Founded in 1951

5205 Business Software Alliance
20 F Street, NW
Suite 800
Washington, DC 20001

202-872-5500
Fax: 202-872-5501
E-Mail: info@bsa.org
Home Page: www.bsa.org
Social Media: Facebook, Twitter

Victoria A. Espinel, President and CEO
Jodie L. Kelley, General Counsel and SVP
Matthew Reid, Senior Vice President
Scott Van Hove, CFO and Vice President

An organization dedicated to promoting a safe and legal digital world. BSA educates consumers on software management and copyright protection, cyber security, trade, e-commerce and other internet related issues.
Founded in 1988

5206 Business Technology Association
12411 Wornall Rd
Suite 200
Kansas City, MO 64145-1212

816-941-3100
800-826-6159
Fax: 816-941-2829
E-Mail: info@bta.org
Home Page: www.bta.org
Social Media: Facebook, Twitter, LinkedIn

Terry Chapman, President
Brent Hoskins, Executive Director
Valerie Briseno, Marketing Manager
Elizabeth Marvel, Associate Editor
Brian Smith, Membership Sales Representative

Serving independent dealers, value-added resellers, systems integrators, manufacturers and distributors in the business equipment and systems industry. BTA helps its members profit through a wide variety of services, including free legal advice and guidance; business benchmarking studies and reports; information on the latest news, trends, and products in the industry.

5207 CEMA: Computer Event Marketing Association
1512 Weiskopf Loop
Round Rock, TX 78664-6128

512-310-8330
Fax: 512-682-0555
E-Mail: info@cemaonline.com
Home Page: www.cemaonline.com
Social Media: Facebook, Twitter, LinkedIn

Liz Lathan, President
Chris Meyer, Vice President
Heather Shatz, Treasurer
Ashley Muntan, Secretary
Kimberley Gishler, Executive Director

Serving marketing professionals in the high technology industry. CEMA has grown to represent the interest of marketing communications professionals in the information technology industry.
500 Members
Frequency: $275-$775 Membership Fee
Founded in 1990

5208 Carnegie Mellon University: Information Networking Institute
4616 Henry Street
Pittsburgh, PA 15213

412-268-7195
Fax: 412-268-7196
E-Mail: ini@cmu.edu
Home Page: www.ini.cmu.edu
Social Media: Facebook, Twitter, LinkedIn

Dena Haritos-Tsamitis, Director
Terri Weinberg, Administrative Assistant
Tracey Bragg, Business & Enrollment Manager
Sean O'Leary, Manager

Established as the nation's first research and education center devoted to Information Networking. INI focuses on professional degree programs that combine technologies, economics, and policies of global communication networks and information security.
300 Members
Founded in 1989

5209 CompTIA
3500 Lacey Road
Suite 100
Downers Grove, IL 60515

630-678-8300
Fax: 630-678-8384
E-Mail: info@comptia.org
Home Page: www.comptia.org
Social Media: Facebook, Twitter, LinkedIn, YouTube, Flickr

MJ Shoer, Chairman
Robert Stegner, Vice Chair
Todd Thibodeaux, President and CEO
Nancy Hammervik, Senior Vice President, Industry
David Sommer, Chief Financial Officer

CompTIA is a trade association representing the international technology community. Its goal is to provide a unified voice, global advocacy and leadership, and to advance industry growth through standards, professional competence, education and business solutions.
20000 Members
Founded in 1984

5210 Computer Assisted Language Instruction Consortium
Texas State University
214 Centennial Hall
San Marcos, TX 78666

512-245-1417
Fax: 512-245-9089
E-Mail: info@calico.org
Home Page: www.calico.org
Social Media: Twitter

Robert Fischer, Executive Director
Esther Horn, Manager

A professional organization involved in language teaching and technology.
780 Members
Founded in 1983

5211 Computer Security Institute
350 Hudson Street
Suite 300
New York, NY 10014

415-947-6320
Fax: 415-905-2218
E-Mail: csi@ubm.com
Home Page: www.gocsi.com
Social Media: Facebook, Twitter, LinkedIn

Robert Richardson, Director
Nancy Baer, Marketing Manager
Mary Griffin, Membership Director
Fran Timmerman, Operations Manager

The world's leading membership organization specifically dedicated to serving and training the information, computer and network security professional.
Cost: $224.00
Frequency: Membership Fee
Founded in 1974

5212 Computerized Medical Imaging
National Biomedical Research Foundation
3900 Reservoir Road NW
Washington, DC 20007

202-687-2121
Fax: 202-687-1662
E-Mail: ledley@nbrf.georgetown.edu
Home Page: www.georgetown.edu
Social Media: Facebook, Twitter, LinkedIn, YouTube, Flickr

Blaire V Mossman, Chief Administrator
Dr. John J. DeGioia, President
Paul Tagliabue, Chair
William R. Berkley, Vice Chair

Formerly the Computerized Radiology Society. A source for the exchange of information concerning the medical use of computerized tomography in radiological diagnosis.
Founded in 1977

5213 Computing Research Association
1828 L Street
Suite 800
Washington, DC 20036-4632

202-234-2111
Fax: 202-667-1066
E-Mail: info@cra.org
Home Page: www.cra.org

J Strother Moore, Chair, Board of Directors
Ronald Brachman, Treasurer
Laura M. Haas, Vice Chair, Board of Directors
Susan B. Davidson, Secretary, Board of Directors
Andrew Bernat, Executive Director

Our mission is to seek to strengthen research and advanced education in computing and allied fields.
200 Members
Founded in 1972

5214 Data Interchange Standards Association (DISA)
7600 Leesburg Pike
Suite 430
Falls Church, VA 22043-2004

703-970-4480
888-363-2334
Fax: 703-970-4488
E-Mail: info@disa.org
Home Page: www.disa.org

Jerry C. Connors, President
Jim Taylor, Chair
Ken Hutcheson, Vice Chair
Jim Leach, Treasurer
Jonathan Lyon, Secretary

Nonprofit home for the development of cross-country electronic business interchange standards.
350+ Members
Founded in 1986

5215 Data Management Association
220 Regency Court
Suite 210
Brookfield, WI 53045

262-784-0444
Fax: 262-782-9489
Home Page: www.dmreview.com
Social Media: Facebook, Twitter, LinkedIn

Tony Carrini, Associate Publisher

A vendor independent professional organization dedicated to the advancement of data asset management concepts.
Founded in 1986

5216 Electronics Industries Alliance
2500 Wilson Boulevard
Arlington, VA 22201

703-907-7500
Fax: 703-907-7602
Home Page: www.eia.org

Dave McCurdy, President/CEO
Charles L Robinson, COO
James Shiring, Secretary/Treasurer

A national trade organization that includes a full spectrum of U.S. manufacturers. The alliance is a partnership of electronic and high-tech associations and companies whose mission is promoting the market development and competitiveness of the U.S. high-tech industry through domestic and international policy efforts.
1300 Members
Founded in 1952

5217 Enterprise Computing Solutions
26024 Acero
Mission Viejo, CA 92691-2768
949-609-1980
Fax: 949-609-1981
E-Mail: cbulter@thinkecs.com
Home Page: www.thinkecs.com

David Buttler, President
Cheryl Butler, CFO
John Foley, CTO

A leading provider of IT infrastructure solutions for Fortune 500 and mid-tier companies throughout California. ECS builds sophisticated IT infrastructure solutions for mission-critical applications, provides enterprise storage solutions that ensure data protection and business continuity, and delivers state-of-the-art server solutions for optimal computing capacity.
500 Members
Founded in 1995

5218 Independent Computer Consultants Association (ICCA)
11131 S Towne Sq
Suite F
St Louis, MO 63123-7817

314-892-1675
Fax: 314-487-1345
E-Mail: execdirector@icca.org
Home Page: www.icca.org

Joyce Burkard, Executive Director

Provides professional development opportunities and business support programs for independent computer consultants. Chapters are in many major metropolitan areas representing consulting firms nationwide.
1000 Members
Founded in 1976

5219 Information Resources Management Association
701 E Chocolate Ave
Suite 200
Hershey, PA 17033-1240

717-533-8845
Fax: 717-533-8661
E-Mail: member@irma-international.org
Home Page: www.irma-international.org

Jan Travers, Executive Director
Sherif Kamel, Communications Director

An international professional organization dedicated to advancing the concepts and practices of information resources management in modern organizations. The primary objective of IRMA is to assist organizations and professionals in enhancing the overall knowledge and understanding of effective information resources management in the early 21st century and beyond.
Mailing list available for rent

5220 Information Systems Audit & Control Association (ISACA)
3701 Algonquin Rd
Suite 1010
Rolling Meadows, IL 60008-3124

847-253-1545
Fax: 847-253-1443
E-Mail: news@isaca.org
Home Page: www.isaca.org
Social Media: Facebook, Twitter, LinkedIn

Susan Caldwell, CEO

With members in more than 160 countries, ISACA is a recognized worldwide leader in IT governance, control, security and assurance. Sponsors international conferences, publishes the thw ISACA Journal and develops international information systems auditing and control standards.
75000 Members
Founded in 1969

5221 Information Technology Management Institute
PO Box 890
Merrifield, VA 22116

703-208-9610
Fax: 703-208-9604
E-Mail: info@itm-inst.com
Home Page: www.itm-inst.com

Dr. Diane Murphy, CEO/Founder

Association for information technology organizations primarily in the US.
90 Members
Founded in 1996

5222 Institute of Electrical & Electronics Engineers Computer Society
2001 L Street N.W.
Suite 700
Washington, DC 20036-4928

202-371-0101
Fax: 202-728-9614
E-Mail: help@computer.org
Home Page: www.computer.org
Social Media: Facebook, Twitter, LinkedIn, YouTube, Google+

Angela Burgess, Executive Director
Anne Marie Kelly, Director, Governance
Chris Jensen, Director of Marketing and Sales
Ray Kahn, Director of Information Technology
John G. Miller, Director of Finance and Accounting

Supports all those involved in use and design of multimedia hardware, software and systems in industry, business, academia and the arts.
10000 Members
Founded in 1946

5223 International Association for Computer Systems Security
6 Swarthmore Lane
Dix Hills, NY 11746-4829

631-499-1616
Fax: 631-462-9178
E-Mail: iacssjalex@aol.com
Home Page: www.iacss.com

Robert J Wilk, President/Founder

Offers a testing program and upholds professional ethics. Supports education through workshops and sponsors lectures.
Founded in 1981

5224 International Association of Knowledge Engineers
973 Russell Avenue
Gaithersburg, MD 20879-3292

301-948-5390
Fax: 301-926-4243
Home Page: www.iake.org

Milton White, Owner
Julie Walker-Lowe, Executive Director

An international association of computer professionals concerned with designing reasoning machines and computer systems to receive, organize and maintain human knowledge.
Founded in 1987

5225 International Society for Technology in Education
180 W 8th Avenue
Eugene, OR 97401-2916

541-302-3777
800-336-5191
Fax: 541-302-3778
E-Mail: iste@iste.org
Home Page: www.iste.org

Kekia Ray, President
Paige Johnson, Treasurer
Mike Lawrence, Secretary
Brian Lewis, M.A., CAE, Chief Executive Officer
Jessica Medaille, Chief Membership Officer

A large nonprofit organization serving the technology-using educator.

5226 International Technology Law Association/ ITechLaw
401 Edgewater Place
Suite 600
Wakefield, MA 01880-6200

781-876-8877
Fax: 781-224-1239
E-Mail: memberservices@itechlaw.org
Home Page: www.itechlaw.org

Kiran Sandford, President
Sajai Singh, Vice President
Jenna Karadbil, Treasurer
Susan Barty, Secretary
Robert Weiss, Assistant Secretary

Computer Law Association changed its identity to ITechLaw to better reflect its global activities and expanded focus. Providing benefit to the worldwide community of information technology law professionals.
2000 Members
Founded in 1971

5227 Internet Alliance
1615 L Street NW
Suite 1100
Washington, DC 20036-5624

202-861-2407
E-Mail: tammy@internetalliance.org
Home Page: www.internetalliance.org

Kris Larsen, Manager
Kaye Caldwell, California Policy Director

Formerly the Interactive Services Association, the Alliance has been the only consisted voice representint internet companies in the 50 states. We have a proven track record of blocking or mitigating privacy and anti-spam legislation, and a high level of expertise in the Internet state tax area.
Founded in 1999

5228 NaSPA: Association for Corporate Computing Technical Professionals
NaSPA
7044 S 13th Street
Oak Creek
Milwaukee, WI 53154

414-908-4945
Fax: 414-768-8001
E-Mail: j.tucker@naspa.com
Home Page: www.naspa.com
Social Media: LinkedIn

Scott Sherer, Chairman
Leo Wrobel, President / Director
Sharon Wrobel, Director / Secretary / Treasurer
Radi Shourbaji, VP of Marketing
Edward J. Krueger, Director of Membership Services

Our mission is to serve the means to enhance the status and promote the advancement of all network and systems professionals; nurture member's technical and managerial knowledge and skills and many more.
50000 Members
Founded in 1986

5229 National Association of Computer Consultant Businesses
1420 King St
Suite 610
Alexandria, VA 22314-2750

703-838-2050
Fax: 703-838-3610
E-Mail: staff@naccb.org
Home Page: www.naccb.org
Social Media: Facebook, Twitter, LinkedIn

Susan Thaden, Chair
Chris Walters, President
Jim Carteris, Vice-President
Tom Nunn, Treasurer
Mark Roberts, Chief Executive Officer

Members are companies providing technical support services to clients such as programming, systems analysis and software/hardware engineering.
300 Members
Founded in 1987

5230 Online Audiovisual Catalogers
Minnesota State University
Memorial Library 3097
PO Box 8419
Mankota, MN 56002-2645

507-892-2147
Fax: 904-620-2719
E-Mail: gerhart@u.washington.edu
Home Page: www.olacinc.org

Liz Miller, President
Marcia Barrett, Vice President/Presidnet Elect
Scott Dutkiewicz, Secretary
Heather J. Pretty, Treasurer/Membership Coordinator
Marcy A. Strong, Newsletter Editor

To establish and maintain a group that could speak for catalogers of audiovisual materials. Provides a means for exchange of information, continuing education, and communication among catalogers of audiovisual materials and with the Library of Congress. Maintaining a voice with the bibliographic utilities that speak for catalogers of audiovisual materials, works toward common understanding of AV cataloging practices and standards.
Founded in 1980

5231 Open Applications Group
PO Box 4897
Marietta, GA 30061

404-402-1962
Fax: 801-740-0100
E-Mail: inquiry@oagi.org
Home Page: www.openapplications.org

David M Connelly, CEO
Mike Rowell, Chief Architect
Ralph Hertlein, VP, Operations
Jim Wilson, Chemical Industry Architect
Michelle Rascoe, Business Manager

A not-for-profit open standards group building process-based XML standards for both B2B and A2A integration.
Founded in 1994

5232 Optical Society of America
2010 Massachusetts Ave Nw
Washington, DC 20036-1023

202-223-8130
Fax: 202-223-1096
E-Mail: info@osa.org
Home Page: www.osa.org
Social Media: Facebook, Twitter, LinkedIn, YouTube

Donna Strickland, President
Philip Russell, Vice President
Stephen D. Fantone, Treasurer
Elizabeth A. Rogan, Chief Executive Officer
Donna Strickland, President

The Optical Society of America (OSA) was organized to increase and diffuse the knowledge of optics, pure and applied; to promote the common interests of investigators of optical problems, of designers and of users of optical apparatus of all kinds; and to encourage cooperation among them. The purposes of the Society are scientific, technical and educational.
Cost: $95.00
15000 Members
Frequency: Membership Fee
Founded in 1916

5233 Personal Computer Memory Card International Association
2635 N 1st St
Suite 218
San Jose, CA 95134-2048

408-433-2273
Fax: 408-433-9558
E-Mail: office@pcmcia.org
Home Page: www.pcmcia.org

Patrick Maher, Executive Director
Ken Stufflebeam, President
Brian Ikeya, Secretary
Jim Koser, Treasurer

Created to establish standards for Integrated Circuit cards and to promote interchangeability among mobile computers where ruggedness, low power, and small size were critical.
200+ Members
Founded in 1989

5234 Polar Microsystems
Po Box 403
Huntingdon Valley, PA 19006

215-676-1590
Fax: 215-676-1596
E-Mail: polar@netaxs.com
Home Page: www.polarmicro.com

Doug C Baer, Senior Systems Engineer

Provides consulting services that enable our clients to advance their businesses through full utilization of the Apple Macintosh hardware and software platform.

5235 **Portable Computer and Communications Association**
PO Box 680
Hood River, OR 97031

541-490-5140
Fax: 413-410-8447
E-Mail: pcca@pcca.org
Home Page: www.pcca.org

Peter Rysavy, Executive Director

Represents firms, organizations and individuals interested in mobile communications. PCCA publishes information, standards, software and other materials.
Cost: $100.00
75 Members
Frequency: Individual Membership Fee
Founded in 1992

5236 **Society For Modeling Simulation International**
2598 Fortune Way
Suite I
Vista, CA 92081

858-277-3888
Fax: 858-277-3930
E-Mail: scs@scs.org
Home Page: www.scs.org
Social Media: Facebook

John Sokolowski, President
Bill Tucker, Treasurer
Oletha Darensburg, Executive Director
Vicki Pate, Publications Manager & Editor
Aleah Hockridge, Conferences Director

The only technical Society dedicated to advancing the use of modeling & simulation to solve real-world problems. SCS is the principal technical society devoted to the advancement of simulation and allied computer arts in all fields.
Cost: $55.00
Frequency: Regular Membership Dues
Founded in 1952

5237 **Society for Imaging Science and Technology**
7003 Kilworh Lane
Springfield, VA 22151-4088

703-642-9090
Fax: 703-642-9094
E-Mail: info@imaging.org
Home Page: www.imaging.org

Alan Hodgson, President
Geoff J. Woolfe, Executive VP
Scott Silence, Treasurer
Ingeborg Tastl, Secretary
Suzanne E. Grinnan, Executive Director

Our goal is to keep members aware of the latest scientific and technological developments in the field of imaging through conferences, journals and other publications. We focus on imaging in all its aspects, with particular emphasis on silver halide, digital printing, electronic imaging, photofinishing, image preservation, image assessment, pre-press technologies and hybrid imaging systems.
2000+ Members
Founded in 1947

5238 **Society for Information Display**
1475 S Bascom Ave
Campbell, CA 95008-0628

408-879-3901
Fax: 408-879-3833
E-Mail: office@sid.org
Home Page: www.sid.org
Social Media: Twitter, LinkedIn

Brian Berkeley, President
Yong-Seog Kim, Treasurer
Helge Seetzen, Secretary
Dave Eccles, VP-Americas
Bao Ping Wang, VP -Asia

Representing the international and local display communities. Offers opportunites to network, recieve information and publications and news about trade shows.
6000 Members
Founded in 1962

5239 **Society for Materials Engineers and Scientists**
3440 E University Drive
Phoenix, AZ 85034

602-470-5700
Fax: 602-437-8497
E-Mail: general.inquiries@asm.com
Home Page: www.asm.com
Social Media: Twitter

Chuck D del Prado, Chairman of the Management Board
Peter A.M Van Bommel, Member of the Management Board
Per Ove Hansson, General Manager Thermal Products
Tominori Yoshida, General Manager Plasma Products
Fokko LeutScher, Vice President of Front-end Global

A leading supplier of semiconductor process equipment in both front and back end markets. The Company possesses a strong technological base, state-of-the-art manufacturing facilities, a competent and qualified workforce and a highly trained, strategically distributed support network.
Founded in 1968

5240 **Society of Manufacturing Engineers International**
1 SME Drive
Po Box 930
Dearborn, MI 48121

313-425-3000
800-733-4763
Fax: 313-425-3401
E-Mail: service@sme.org
Home Page: www.sme.org
Social Media: Facebook, Twitter, LinkedIn, YouTube

Dennis S. Bray, PhD, FSME, President
Mark C. Tomlinson, CMfgE, EMCP, SME Executive Director/CEO
Wayne F. Frost, CMfgE, Vice President
Dean L. Bartles, PhD, FSME, Secretary/Treasurer
Nancy S. Berg, Executive Director/General Manager

An association that provides information on various automated and computerized systems.
33 Members
Founded in 1932

5241 **Software Engineering Institute**
Carnegie Mellon University
Pittsburgh, PA 15213-3890

412-687-7700
Fax: 412-268-5758
E-Mail: customer-relations@sei.cmu.edu
Home Page: www.sei.cmu.edu
Social Media: Facebook, Twitter, LinkedIn, YouTube

Paul D Nielsen, CEO
Clyde Chittister, Chief Operating Officer

A federally funded research and development center sponsored by the U.S. Department of Defense through the Office of the Under Secretary of Defense for Acquisition, Technology, and Logistics. Supports all those engineers involved in the software industry.

5242 **Software Management Network**
55 Madison Avenue
STE400
Morristown, CA 07960

973-285-3264
Fax: 973-538-0503
E-Mail: jmgolub@softwaremanagement.com
Home Page: www.softwaremanagement.com

Nicholas Zvegintzov, President/Chief Technical Officer
Judith Marx Golub, VP/CFO

A publishing, consulting, and training group that serves professional software teams responsible for working, installed software systems. Its unique mission is to make available the most effective resources for managing active software.
Founded in 1981

5243 **Uni Forum Association**
PO Box 3177
Annapolis, MD 21403

800-333-8649
E-Mail: afedder@uniforum.org
Home Page: www.uniforum.org

Alan Fedder, President
Deborah Murray, VP
John Lehmann, Board Member
Phil Hughes, Board Member
Jon Hall, Board Member

Professional association for end users, developers and vendors. Promotes and exchanges information about the practices and benefits of open technologies and related hardware, software, applications and standards.
Founded in 1981

5244 **Vmebus International Trade Association**
PO Box 19658
Fountain Hills, AZ 85269
480-837-7486
E-Mail: info@vita.com
Home Page: www.vita.com

Ray Alderman, Executive Director
Jerry Gipper, Marketing Director

Association for manufacturers of microcomputer boards, hardware, software, military products, controllers, bus interfaces and other accessories compatible with VMEbus architecture.
Cost: $2500.00
150 Members
Frequency: Regular Membership Fee
Founded in 1984

Newsletters

5245 **AAR Newsletter**
School of Information Technology & Engineering
University of Ottawa
800 King Edward Avenue
Ottawa, Canada

613-562-5738
Fax: 613-562-5664
E-Mail: pieper@mcs.anl.gov
Home Page: www-unix.mcs.anl.gov

Gail W Pieper, Editor
Mary Dzielski, Secretary
Janet Werner, Executive Secretary

Represents research notes and problem sets, discusses software advances and announces conferences and workshops.
Frequency: Quarterly

5246 **ADAIC News**
Ada Information Clearinghouse
201 ILR Extension Building
Cornell University
Ithaca, NY 14853-3901
607-255-2763
800-949-4232
E-Mail: northeastada@cornell.edu
Home Page: www.northeastada.org
Susan Carlson, Publisher
Lorrie Fessenden, Administrative Assistant
Information on Ada-an internationally standardized, general purpose computer language used in a variety of applications includes news of the Ada community.
Circulation: 20,000
Founded in 2001

5247 **AEC Automation Newsletter**
Technology Automation Services
PO Box 3593
Englewood, CO 80155-3593
303-770-1728
Fax: 303-770-3660
Home Page: www.aecnews.com
Jeff Rowe, Editor
David Weisberg, Circulation Director
Randall S Newton, Editor-In-Chief
W Bradley Holtz, Group Publisher
Joel N Orr, Senior Editor
Reports on computer hardware and software issues relevant to architectural design, civil engineering, structural design, process plant design and geographic information management. Includes articles on software developments, new computer hardware, business issues, operating systems, application software, networking and technology developments.
Cost: $235.00
16 Pages
Frequency: Monthly
Founded in 1977
Printed in one color on matte stock

5248 **AI Interactions**
Academy of International Business
Michigan State University
7 Eppley Center
East Lansing, MI 48824-1121
517-432-4336
Fax: 517-432-1009
E-Mail: ciber@msu.edu
Home Page: aib.msu.edu
G Tomas M Hult, Executive Secretary
Tunga Kiyak, Managing Director
Irem Kiyak, Treasurer
Calls for papers, meeting notices and membership news of interest to professors of international business around the world.
Circulation: 3000
Mailing list available for rent: 3000 names at $250 per M

5249 **AIM Connections**
AIM Global
125 Warrendale Bayne Rd
Suite 100
Warrendale, PA 15086-7570
724-934-4470
Fax: 724-934-4495
E-Mail: info@aimglobal.org
Home Page: www.aimglobal.org
Mary Lou Bosco, President
Linda Young, Business Development Director
E-newsletter focused on automatic identification and mobile computing for a broad audience. Each issue contains analysis and news about the industry with a focus on what's happeneing in the market today.
900+ Members
Founded in 1972
Mailing list available for rent

5250 **Acronyms**
Computer Laboratory Michigan State University
40F Computer Ctr
East Lansing, MI 48824-1042
517-355-3600
Fax: 517-355-5176
Linda Dunn, Publisher
A listing of procedures, policies, hardware and software for computer users.
Frequency: Quarterly

5251 **Advanced Office Technologies Report**
DataTrends Publications
Po Box 4460
Leesburg, VA 20177-8541
703-779-0574
800-766-8130
Fax: 703-779-2267
E-Mail: info@stemcellresearchnews.com
Home Page: www.stemcellresearchnews.com
Paul G Ochs, Owner
Offers information on products, technological breakthroughs and industry developments in office automation technology.
Frequency: Full-text

5252 **Alpha Forum**
Pinnacle Publishing
316 N Michigan Avenue
Suite 300
Chicago, IL 60601
312-272-2401
800-493-4867
Fax: 312-960-4106
E-Mail: pinpub@ragan.com
Home Page: www.pinpub.com
Brent Smith, Publisher
David Stevenson, Editor
Technical newsletter for application developers and users. Hands-on articles with specific usage and programming techniques, tips and product updates.
16 Pages
Frequency: Monthly
Circulation: 8000
Founded in 1990
Mailing list available for rent
Printed in 2 colors on matte stock

5253 **Applications Software**
Thomson Media
1 State St
27th Floor
New York, NY 10004-1481
212-825-8445
Fax: 212-843-9600
James Malkin, President/CEO
William Johnson, CFO
General business management and word processing, reference services, custom services and CD-ROM services.
Frequency: Monthly

5254 **Artificial Intelligence Letter**
Kluwer Academic Publishers
101 Philip Drive
Norwell, MA 02061-1677
781-871-6600
Fax: 781-871-6528
Masoud Yazdani, Publisher
Provides a forum for the work of researchers and application developers from artificial intelligence, cognitive science and related disciplines.
Circulation: 625

5255 **Bits and Bytes Review**
Bits and Bytes Computer Resources
623 Iowa Ave
Whitefish, MT 59937-2336
406-862-7280
800-361-7280
Fax: 406-862-1124
E-Mail: Info@bitsbytescomputer.com
Home Page: www.bitsbytescomputer.com
John J Hughes, Owner
Resources and products for the academic field.
Cost: $56.90
Frequency: Monthly

5256 **Branch Automation News**
Phillips Publishing
7811 Montrose Road
Potomac, MD 20854
301-340-2100
E-Mail: feedback@healthydirections.com
Home Page: www.healthydirctions.com
Strategies for planning, implementing and managing bank technology.
Cost: $495.00
Circulation: 1000
Founded in 1974
Mailing list available for rent: 30342 names at $125 per M
Printed in 2 colors on matte stock

5257 **Business Computer Report**
Guidera Publishing Corporation
3 Myrtle Bank Road
Hilton Head Island, SC 29926-1809
Lawrence C Oakley, Editor
Hands-on review of business related software, as well as hardware, primarily for the PC world (as opposed to the MAC World). Readers are primarily owners of small to medium-sized businesses.
Cost: $95.00
8 Pages
Frequency: Monthly
Circulation: 125,000
Printed in one color on matte stock

5258 **Business Software News**
110 N Bell Avenue
Suite 300
Shawnee, OK 74801-6967
405-275-3100
Fax: 405-275-3101
Home Page: www.cpatechadvisers.com
Shari Bodger, Publisher
Melody Wrinkle, Editor
Shari Bodger, Marketing Manager
Offers updated information on computer software, marketing and technology news. Columnists address networks, sales and management with every issue including independent, comparative software reviews.
Cost: $40.00
8 Pages
Circulation: 1000
Founded in 1991
Printed in 4 colors on matte stock

5259 **C/C & Users Journal**
Miller Freeman Publications
2800 Campus Drive
San Mateo, CA 94403
650-513-4300
800-365-1364
Fax: 650-513-4601

E-Mail: cuj@neodata.com
Home Page: www.cuj.com

Peter Westerman, Publisher
Jon Erickson, Editorial Director
Jessica Marty, Director of Marketing
Amy Stephens, Managing Editor

Information for intermediate and advanced C and C++ programmers. Includes programming techniques, tutorials and software reviews.
Cost: $29.95
Frequency: Monthly
Circulation: 39,048
Founded in 1988

5260 C/Net News.Com
CNET
100 Pine St
Suite 1775
San Francisco, CA 94111-5127

415-409-8900
Fax: 415-395-9254
Home Page: www.ccolaw.com

Therese Cannata, Partner
John Morris, Editor
Christina Koukkos, Managing Editor

Provides information for high end audiences in the market for tech news, including the IS community, the technology business itself and the financial community.
Frequency: Daily
Founded in 1992

5261 COM-AND: Computer Audit News & Developments
Management Advisory Services & Publications
PO Box 81151
Wellesley Hills, MA 02481-0001

781-235-2895
Fax: 781-235-5446
E-Mail: info@masp.com
Home Page: www.masp.com

New standards and practices. Tutorials on impact of EDP on audit and control matters. Practical coverage of technical EDP developments for auditors and internal controls specialists.
Cost: $70.00
8 Pages
Founded in 1972
Mailing list available for rent
Printed in 2 colors on matte stock

5262 COMDEX Show Daily
Key 3 Media Group
795 Folsom Street
6th Floor
San Francisco, CA 94107-1243

415-905-2300
Fax: 415-905-2329
Home Page: www.medialiveinternational.com

Sean Cassidy, Marketing Manager
Robert Priest-Heck, President/CEO

Tabloid newspaper of computer related exhibits.
Frequency: Daily
Circulation: 3445

5263 CPA Technology Advisor
Harcourt Brace Professional Publishing
9720 Carroll Centre Rd
Suite 1900
San Diego, CA 92126-4551

858-271-7390
800-831-7799
Home Page: www.hbpp.com

Bruce Ta, Owner
Frank Peterson, Editor

Concise unbiased recommendations on hardware and software for CPA's.
Cost: $19.00

5264 Client/Server Economics Letter
Computer Economics
2082 Business Center Drive
Suite 240
Irvine, CA 92612

949-831-8700
Fax: 949-442-7688
Home Page: www.computereconomics.com

Frank Scavo, President
Dan Husiak, VP

Economic look at the client/server revolution. Provides critical economic data on costs and risks of client/server computing, backed up with research and presentation-quality graphs and tables. Provides the information you need to make sound business decisions.
Cost: $395.00
Frequency: Daily
Founded in 1978

5265 Comp-U-Fax Computer Trends Newsletter
Microcomputers Software and Consulting
28 S 12th Avenue
Mount Vernon, NY 10550-2913
Bob James, Publisher
Corporate information resource newsletter.

5266 Computer Aided Design Report
CAD/CAM Publishing
7100 N Broadway
Suite 2-P
Denver, CO 80221

303-482-2813
Fax: 303-484-3610
E-Mail: info@cadcamnet.com
Home Page: www.cadcamnet.com

Randall Newton, Editor

Uses of computers by engineers in the manufacturing trades.
Cost: $195.00

5267 Computer Architecture
IEEE Computer Society
1730 Massachusetts Avenue NW
Washington, DC 20036-1992

202-371-1013
Fax: 202-728-9614

Henry Ayling, Publisher
Lee Blue, Production Manager

Current trends in computer networks, hardware description languages, performance.
Circulation: 2303

5268 Computer Business
Round Table Association SAB
5340 W 57th Street
Los Angeles, CA 90056-1339

310-649-2846

A Hassan, Publisher/Editor
J Hassan, Circulation Manager

Best computer/communications articles of previous month, briefly abstracted.
Cost: $20.00

5269 Computer Economics Report
Computer Economics
2082 Business Center Drive
Suite 240
Irvine, CA 92612

949-831-8700
Fax: 949-442-7688
Home Page: www.computereconomics.com

Frank Scavo, President
Dan Husiak, VP

Written from an end-user perspective, this monthly newsletter provides analyses of new IBM technologies, plus acquisition and financial management strategies. Regular features include cost comparisons, price/performance analysis, new product forecasts, and evaluations of acquisition techniques for medium and large computer systems.
Cost: $595.00
Frequency: Monthly
Founded in 1978

5270 Computer Industry Report
International Data Corporation
5 Speen Street
Framingham, MA 01701

508-872-8200
E-Mail: leads@idc.com
Home Page: www.idc.com/

Kirk Campbell, President/CEO

Research and analysis of the computer processing industry.
Founded in 1964

5271 Computer Integrated Manufacture and Engineering
Lionheart Publishing
2555 Cumberland Pkwy Se
Suite 299
Atlanta, GA 30339-3921

770-432-2551
Fax: 770-432-6969

Explores cutting edge developments in manufacturing systems operation management.
Circulation: 24,000

5272 Computer Modeling and Simulation in Engineering
Sage Science Press
2455 Teller Rd
Newbury Park, CA 91320-2234

805-499-9774
800-818-7243
Fax: 805-499-0871
E-Mail: info@sagepub.com
Home Page: www.sagepub.com

Blaise R Simqu, CEO/President

Publishes application-oriented papers that utilize computer modeling and simulation techniques to understand and resolve industrial problems or processes that are of immediate and contemporary interest.
Frequency: Monthly

5273 Computer Protocols
Worldwide Videotex
PO Box 3273
Boynton Beach, FL 33424-3273

561-738-2276
E-Mail: markedit@juno.com
Home Page: www.wvpubs.com

Mark Wright, Editor/President
Linda Dera, Marketing Manager
Linda Dera, Circulation Manager

Covers news and developments of bridges, gateway and LAN. Coverage also provided on the development of internal protocols.
Cost: $165.00
Frequency: Monthly
Circulation: 30000
Founded in 1981

5274 Computer Reseller News
CMP Publications
One Jericho Plaza
Jericho, NY 11753-1680

516-562-5000
Fax: 516-562-7243

E-Mail: shadowram@mcimail.com
Home Page: www.crn.com

John Russell, Publisher

Computer news for resellers and distributors.

5275 **Computer and Communications Buyer**
Technology News of America Company
PO Box 20008
New York, NY 10025-1510

212-222-1123
E-Mail: subs@eintelligence.com
Home Page: www.eintelligence.com

Annotated statistical reports on capital equipment. $450.00 outside of United States.
Cost: $395.00
8 Pages
Frequency: Monthly
ISSN: 1042-4296
Founded in 1984
Mailing list available for rent

5276 **Computer and Computer Management News and Developments**
Management Advisory Services & Publications
PO Box 81151
Wellesley Hills, MA 02481-0001

781-235-2895
Fax: 781-235-5446
E-Mail: info@masp.com
Home Page: www.masp.com

Newsletter aimed at the management level of the computer industry.

5277 **Computers & Security**
Elsevier Science
6277 Sea Harbor Drive
Orlando, FL 32887

407-345-4020
877-839-7126
Fax: 407-363-1354
E-Mail: usjcs@elsevier.com
Home Page: www.elsevier.com

Andrew Fletcher, Publisher
E Schultz, CEO/President
Ann Dudley, Circulation Manager
Carl Lampert, Editor

International newsletter for the management of computer and information security.
Circulation: 1500

5278 **Computers & Structures**
Elsevier Science
PO Box 945
New York, NY 10010-945

212-989-5800
888-437-4636
Fax: 212-633-3680
E-Mail: usinfo@sciencedirect.com
Home Page: www.sciencedirect.com

Keith Lambert, Publisher/Editor

Analyzes the many relationships between computer technology and the different fields of engineering.
Circulation: 1500
Founded in 1962

5279 **Computers, Foodservice and You**
Mike Pappas
Po Box 338
Raton, NM 87740-0338

575-445-9811
Fax: 575-445-3080

Mike Pappas, Owner

A newsletter focusing on computers for the hospitality industry.
Cost: $119.00
16 Pages
Frequency: Bi-Monthly
Circulation: 450
Printed in one color on matte stock

5280 **DM Direct**
220 Regency Court
Suite 210
Brookfield, WI 53045

262-784-0444
Fax: 262-782-9489
Home Page: www.dmreview.com

Tony Carrini, Associate Publisher

In this e-mail newsletter you will find articles, online columnists, news and industry events exclusive to you, the online reader. Our goal is to ensure that DM Direct provides the information you need to compete in the business intelligence, data warehousing and analytics marketplace.

5281 **DP Budget**
Computer Economics
2082 Business Center Drive
Suite 240
Irvine, CA 92612

949-831-8700
Fax: 949-442-7688
Home Page: www.computereconomics.com

Frank Scavo, President
Dan Husiak, VP

Report analyzing DP expenses, salary issues and acquisition costs. Focuses on increasing productivity and improving the return on your DP investment.
Cost: $495.00
Frequency: Monthly

5282 **DPFN**
Directory & Database Publishers Forum & Network
352 Seventh Avenue
New York, NY 10001-546

212-643-5458
845-358-8034
E-Mail: gstone@ptmcomm.com
Home Page: www.dpfn.com

Barry Lee, Membership Chair
Jeff Fandl, President

Contains events, seminar information, publishers story, industry snapshots, and news pertaining to the industry. Members are large and small directory publishers, vendors to the trade and consultants. Provides networking opportunities and exposure to industry experts through their meetings and workshops.
Founded in 1990
Printed in on matte stock

5283 **Data Channels**
Phillips Publishing
7811 Montrose Road
Potomac, MD 20854

301-340-2100
E-Mail: feedback@healthydirections.com
Home Page: www.healthydirections.com

Source of intelligence for executives making data communications decisions. Accepts advertising.
Cost: $397.00
9 Pages

5284 **Data Security Management**
Auerbach Publications
535 5th Avenue
Room 806
New York, NY 10017-3610

800-737-8034
Home Page: www.auerbach-publications.com

Rich O'Hanley, Editor

Technical and management information for security managers, networks and systems administrators and data center managers.
Cost: $495.00
Frequency: Bi-Monthly
Circulation: 1,500
ISSN: 1096-7907
Printed in on matte stock

5285 **Dental Computer Newsletter**
Andent
1000 N Avenue
Waukegan, IL 60085

847-223-5077
E-Mail: info@andent.net
Home Page: www.andent.net

For and by an international group of Dentists, Physicians and allied health professionals interested in computers. Emphasis is on the practical use of all brands of computers for the professional office.
Cost: $25.00
Frequency: Quarterly
Circulation: 3100

5286 **Digital Directions Report**
Computer Economics
2082 Business Center Drive
Suite 240
Irvine, CA 92612

949-831-8700
Fax: 949-442-7688
Home Page: www.computereconomics.com

Frank Scavo, President

Provides details on the financial ramifications of future DEC products. The information is critical for decision makers involved with cost-control, strategy planning and new product analysis.
Cost: $525.00
Frequency: Monthly

5287 **Directory of Top Computer Executives**
Applied Computer Research
Po Box 41730
Phoenix, AZ 85080

602-216-9100
800-234-2227
Fax: 602-548-4800
E-Mail: tara@topitexecs.com
Home Page: www.acrhq.com

Computer performance and management.
Cost: $370.00
Circulation: 1000
ISSN: 0193-9920
Founded in 1972
Printed in one color on matte stock

5288 **Document Imaging Report**
Corry Publishing
5539 Peach Street
Erie, PA 16509

814-380-0025
Fax: 814-864-2037
E-Mail: corrypub@corrypub.com
Home Page: www.corrypub.com

John Coiston, Publisher
Terry Peterson, CEO
Micole Hykes, Editor
Karrie Boocious, Marketing
Melinda Fadden, Circulation Manager

Timely and actionable information on electronic imaging applications, products and user implementation.
Frequency: Monthly
Circulation: 43000

5289 **Dvorak Developments**
Freelance Communications
PO Box 666
Ridgway, CO 81432

970-626-2255

Randy Cassingham, Publisher

Promotes the use of the Dvorak keyboard for typewriters and computers. Dvorak is more ergonomic than the common Qwerty keyboard. Accepts advertising.
8 Pages

5290 **E-News**
Patricia Seybold Group
Po Box 240565
Boston, MA 02129

617-742-5200
800-826-2424
Fax: 617-742-1028
E-Mail: feedback@psgroup.com
Home Page: www.psgroup.com

Patricia Seybold, Founder/CEO

E-mail newsletter includes perspectives on the e-commerce industry, research and upcoming events.

5291 **EDI News**
Phillips Publishing
7811 Montrose Road
Potomac, MD 20854

301-340-2100
E-Mail: feedback@healthydirections.com
Home Page: www.healthydirections.com

Electronic data interchange marketplace information.
Cost: $397.00
9 Pages

5292 **Education Technology News**
Business Publishers
2222 Sedwick Dr
Suite 101
Durham, NC 27713

800-223-8720
Fax: 800-508-2592
E-Mail: custserv@bpinews.com
Home Page: www.bpinews.com

Information on educational hardware and software, trends in computer-aided teaching and computer uses in the classroom.
Cost: $217.00
Circulation: 500
Founded in 1963

5293 **Electronic Education Report**
Simba Information
60 Long Ridge Rd
Suite 300
Stamford, CT 06902-1841

203-325-8193
888-297-4622
Fax: 203-325-8915
E-Mail: info@simbanet.com
Home Page: www.simbanet.com

Linda Kopp, Publisher

News and analysis from a business perspective on software, multimedia/CD-ROM, videodisc, distance learning, Internet/online services and educational videocassettes.
Cost: $625.00
Founded in 1989

5294 **Electronic Marketing News**
Software Assistance International
PO Box 750
Morris Plains, NJ 07950-0750

973-644-0022
Fax: 973-539-3253

George Papov, Editor

Supplier of electronic catalogs to business and industries.
Circulation: 6,000

5295 **End-User Computing Management**
Auerbach Publications
535 5th Avenue
Room 806
New York, NY 10017-3610

800-737-8034
Fax: 212-297-9176

Kim Hovan Kelly, Publisher

Technical and mangement information.
Cost: $495.00
Frequency: BiWeekly
Circulation: 1,000

5296 **Federal Computer Week**
101Communications
3141 Fairview Park Drive
#777
Falls Church, VA 22042-4507

703-876-5100
Fax: 703-876-5126
Home Page: www.fcw.com

Anne Armstrong, Publisher
Jeff Calore, General Manager

The Federal Computer Week provides practical news, analysis and insight on how to buy, build and manage technology in government.
Circulation: 93000

5297 **Forestry Computer Applications**
Michaelsen's Micro Magic Publishers
PO Box 7332
Fredericksburg, VA 22404-7332
Nancy Michaelsen, Publisher

Offers news and information on computers and electronics used in the forestry services industry, including manufacturing, building, construction and architecture.
Cost: $29.95

5298 **Frontline**
Computer Security Institute
600 Harrison Street
San Francisco, CA 94107
415-947-6320
Fax: 818-487-4550
Home Page: www.gocsi.com

Robert Richardson, Editorial Director
Chris Keating, Director

This quarterly newsletter is to improve the security practices of your entire organization to increase end-user awareness of critical security topics pertaining to them.
Cost: $1860.00
4 Pages
Frequency: Annual Subscription

5299 **GCN Tech Edition**
Post Newsweek Tech Media
10 G St Ne
Suite 500
Washington, DC 20002-4228

202-772-2500
866-447-6864
Fax: 202-772-2511
E-Mail: editorial@gcn.com
Home Page: www.gcn.com

David Greene, President
Tom Temin, Editor-in-Chief
Kirstin Crane, Marketing Manager
Bar Blaskowsky, Circulation Manager

Evaluates performance, cost and applications of hardware, software, peripheral and communication products available to government agencies and businesses.
Cost: $95.00
Circulation: 87500
Founded in 1998
Printed in on glossy stock

5300 **Government Computer News**
Reed Business Information
2000 Clearwater Dr
Oak Brook, IL 60523-8809

630-574-0825
Fax: 630-288-8781
Home Page: www.reedbusiness.com

Jeff Greisch, President

The national newspaper of government computing.
Cost: $53.00
55 Pages
Frequency: Monthly
Founded in 1982

5301 **Graphic Communications Today**
IDEA Alliance
1421 Prince Street
Suite 230
Alexandria, VA 22314-2805

703-837-1070
Fax: 703-837-1072
Home Page: www.idealliance.org

Alan Kotok, Editor
David Steinhardt, CEO

Electronic commerce, direct marketing, printing and paper aspects, and graphics updates.
Frequency: Daily
Circulation: 200
Founded in 1966

5302 **HIS Insider**
United Communications Group
11300 Rockville Pike
Street 1100
Rockville, MD 20852-3030

301-287-2700
Fax: 301-816-8945
E-Mail: webmaster@ucg.com
Home Page: www.ucg.com

Benny Dicecca, President

News and reports on new hospital and clinical information system technologies, upcoming vendor merger acquisitions, analyses of telecommunicaiton systems used in health care.
Cost: $427.00
Frequency: Weekly
Founded in 1977

5303 **IN SYNC Magazine**
Agate Publishing
21 West 26th Street
New York, NY 10010

847-475-4457
E-Mail: seibold@agatepublishing.com
Home Page: www.agatepublishing.com

Doug Seibold

News and how-to for distributed and cooperative applications. Particularly how to link multiple computer systems to gain best advantage from each.
Cost: $8.00
Circulation: 1000

5304 **IS Budget**
Computer Economics

2082 Business Center
Dr. Ste 240
Irvine, CA 92612

949-831-8700
Fax: 949-442-7688
Home Page: www.computereconomics.com

Frank Scavo, President
Dan Husiak, VP

Tackles today's toughest IS budgeting issues head-on with exhaustively researched line-item cost comparisons by type of industry, installation size, company revenue and type of expenditure. Regular features include MIS spending comparisons, analyses of budgeting issues and inside information on vendor discounts.
Cost: $495.00
Frequency: Monthly
Founded in 1978

5305 Independent Computer Consultants Newsletter
Independent Computer Consultants Association
11131 S Towne Sq
Suite F
St Louis, MO 63123-7817

314-892-1675
Fax: 314-487-1345
E-Mail: execdirector@icca.org
Home Page: www.icca.org

Joyce Burkard, Executive Director

Promotes professional standards in the industry. Conducts educational programs and maintains local chapters in many major cities. Available to members only.
Circulation: 1000
Founded in 1976
Mailing list available for rent: 1200 names at $500 per M
Printed in 2 colors

5306 Inside the Internet
Cobb Group
115 6th Ave
Dayton, KY 41074-1111

859-291-1146
800-733-2040
Fax: 859-655-2482
E-Mail: tomherman@cobbinc.com
Home Page: www.cobbinc.com

Tom Herman, President
Adam Browning, Production Manager

Practical advice and instructions for Internet users.

5307 Intelligence: The Future of Computing
Intelligence
PO Box 20008
New York, NY 10025-1510

212-222-1123
800-638-7257
Home Page: www.eintelligence.com

Edward Rosenfeld, Editor/Publisher

Provides coverage of advanced computing: neutral networks, AI, genetic algorithms, fuzzy systems, wavelets, et. al., and the Net, the Web, Nanotechnologies quanteum, molecular and DNA computing.
Cost: $395.00
8 Pages
Frequency: Monthly
ISSN: 1042-4296
Founded in 1984
Printed in one color on matte stock

5308 International Spectrum
International Spectrum Magazine & Conferences
8956 Fox Drive
Suite 102
Thornton, CO 80260

720-259-1356
Fax: 603-250-0664
E-Mail: nathan@intl-spectrum.com
Home Page: www.intl-spectrum.com

Nathan Rector, President
Monica Giobbi, Manager
Clif Oliver, Editor

Trade magazine for PICK/UNIX/DOS computer industry which covers hardware, software and peripherals. Company produces major trade show held annually in Southern California and regional exhibitions and conferences across the country.
88 Pages
Frequency: 6 issues/Yr
Circulation: 50,000
Founded in 1982
Mailing list available for rent: 80M names
Printed in 4 colors on glossy stock

5309 Managing Human Resource Information Systems
Institute of Management and Administration
1 Washington Park
Suite 1300
Newark, NJ 07102

212-244-0360
Fax: 973-622-0595
Home Page: www.ioma.com

Covers management issues critical to building and maintaining state-of-the-art HRIS software, hardware, and Internet/intranet activities. It is intended to help control costs of HRIS, make better use of new technologies, migrate HRIS from mainframe, mini, and client/server systems.
Cost: $259.00
Frequency: Monthly
Circulation: 180000
Founded in 1982

5310 Micro Publishing
Cygnus Publishing
445 Broad Hollow Road
Melville, NY 11747

631-845-2700
800-308-6397
Fax: 631-845-2798
Home Page: www.cygnuspub.com

James Cavuoto, Publisher
Nancy Whelan, Advertising/Sales
Kenneth Spears, Production
Mark Erikson, Circulation Manager
Paul Bonaiuto, CFO

A newsletter for hardware and software vendors that examines the micro-based publishing systems market, including workstation publishing, printers, scanners, networks, technology and data-based publishing, production methods and page layout software. The editorials consists of microcomputer publishing product reviews, notes, and trend analysis, and new product announcements.
Cost: $295.00
10 Pages
Frequency: Monthly
Printed in on matte stock

5311 Network Economics Letter
Computer Economics
5841 Edison Place
Carlsbad, CA 92008-6500

760-438-8100
800-326-8100
Fax: 760-431-1126
Home Page: www.computereconomics.com

Bruno Bassi, Publisher
Don Trevillian, Editor

Provides an executive overview for MIS and network professionals who are involved in network strategic planning and implementation. It covers such topics as comparative analysis of hardware and software systems, cost of ownership studies, analysis of emerging protocols and standards and cost-saving opportunities.
Cost: $395.00
Frequency: Monthly

5312 OSINetter Newsletter
Architecture Technology Corporation
9977 Valley View Rd
Suite 300
Eden Prairie, MN 55344-3586

952-829-5864
Fax: 952-829-5871
E-Mail: info@atcorp.com
Home Page: www.atcorp.com

Noel Schmidt, Executive VP

Covers products and company activity in the area of open systems interconnection.
Cost: $50.00
Founded in 1955

5313 Official Memory News
Phillips Publishing
7811 Montrose Road
Potomac, MD 20854

301-340-2100
E-Mail: feedback@healthydirections.com
Home Page: www.healthydirections.com

Provides the latest news and analysis on OSI standards developments. Accepts advertising.
Cost: $497.00
9 Pages
Founded in 1974

5314 Open Systems Economics Letter
Computer Economics
2082 Business Center Drive
Suite 240
Irvine, CA 92612

949-831-8700
Fax: 949-442-7688
Home Page: www.computereconomics.com/

Dan Husiak, Vo
Frank Scavo, President

Addresses the critical economic issues associated with the worldwide transformation to open systems. In a concise, monthly format, this report provides the information that you must have to successfully adopt an open systems strategy, manage your transition to open standards, and protect your corporate investment in new technology.
Cost: $395.00
Frequency: Monthly

5315 Optical Memory News
Phillips Publishing
7811 Montrose Road
Potomac, MD 20854

301-340-2100
E-Mail: feedback@healthydirections.com
Home Page: www.healthydirections.com

Provides the latest news and analysis on the optical storage marketplace from vendor perspective. Accepts advertising.
Cost: $397.00
9 Pages
Frequency: BiWeekly
Printed in one color on matte stock

5316 Product Data Management Report
CAD/CAM Publishing
7100 N Broadway
Suite 2-P
Denver, CO 80221

303-482-2813
Fax: 303-484-3610

E-Mail: info@cadcamnet.com
Home Page: www.cadcamnet.com

Randall Newton, Editor

Devoted to product data management software and systems that are used by major manufacturing firms to store, control, and distribute CAD and other engineering data.
Cost: $345.00

5317 **Public and Policy**
American Public Human Services Association
1133 19th St NW
Suite 400
Washington, DC 20036

202-682-0100
Fax: 202-204-0071
Home Page: www.aphsa.org

Tracy Wareing, Executive Director
Frequency: Bimonthly

5318 **Rapid Prototyping Report**
CAD/CAM Publishing
2880 Stone Trail Dr
Bethesda, MD 20817-4556

240-425-4004
Fax: 301-365-4586
E-Mail: info@cadcamnet.com
Home Page: www.cadcamnet.com

Geoff Smith-Moritz, Editor
L Wolf, Production Manager

Gives in-depth objective appraisals of strengths and weaknesses of rapid prototyping technology. Includes applications on how RP technology is used in the industry.
Cost: $295.00
Frequency: Monthly

5319 **Report on IBM**
DataTrends Publications
Po Box 4460
Leesburg, VA 20177-8541

703-779-0574
Fax: 703-779-2267
Home Page: www.stemcellresearchnews.com

Paul G Ochs, Owner

For information technology professionals.
Cost: $495.00
Founded in 1983

5320 **Retail Price Week**
Personal Technology Research
63 Fountain Street
#400
Framingham, MA 01702-6262

508-875-5858

Casey Dworkin, Publisher

Product-specific advertising and pricing data on microcomputer software, perhipherals and desktop retail commodities.
Frequency: Weekly
Circulation: 300

5321 **Semiconductor Economics Report**
Relayer Group
8232 E Buckskin Trail
Scottsdale, AZ 85255-2132
Howard Dicken, Publisher

Economics in the microelectronics industry.

5322 **Small Business Systems**
Charles Moore Associates
277 Alexander Street
Suite 410
Rochester, NY 14607

585-325-5242
Fax: 585-325-5242

Charles Moore, Editor
Nancy Hannigan, Circulation Manager

Case histories which apply computers to solve small business problems.

5323 **Softletter**
Mercury Group
990 Washington Street
Suite 308 S
Dedham, MA 02026

781-518-8600
860-663-0552
Fax: 301-816-8945
E-Mail: customer@softletter.com
Home Page: www.softletter.com

Merrill R Chapman, Publisher
Gail Wertheimer, Editor
Rick Chapman, Marketing Manager
Ruth Greenfield, Director

Trends in the microcomputer software industry.
Cost: $596.00
Frequency: Fortnightly
ISSN: 0882-3499
Founded in 1983
Printed in 2 colors

5324 **Softrader**
Amerasia Group
PO Box 53114
Indianapolis, IN 46253-0114
Ben Yanto, Publisher

Shareware public domain programs guide. Accepts advertising.
16 Pages
Frequency: BiWeekly

5325 **Software Economics Letter**
Computer Economics
5841 Edison Place
Carlsbad, CA 92008-6500

760-438-8100
800-326-8100
Fax: 760-431-1126
Home Page: www.computereconomics.com

Bruno Bassi, Publisher
Don Trevillian, Editor

Devoted to management and cost control of software investments. Provides the corporate user and information systems communities with a concise analysis of software issues. Profiles the latest trends in software and software licensing and includes analysis of vendor policies and practices.
Cost: $395.00
Frequency: Daily

5326 **Step-By-Step Electronic Design**
Dynamic Graphics
6000 N Forest Park Drive
Peoria, IL 61614-3592

309-688-8851
Fax: 309-688-6579
Home Page: www.dgusa.com

Tom Biederbeck, Editor
Kris Elwell, Publisher
Alan Meckler, CEO/President
Mike Demilt, Marketing
Marcy Slane, Manager

For electronic designers, illustrators and prepress professionals, how-to articles with step-by-step techniques.
Cost: $36.00
Circulation: 24000
Founded in 1995

5327 **System Development**
Applied Computer Research
PO Box 41730
Phoenix, AZ 85080

602-216-9100
800-234-2227
Fax: 602-548-4800
E-Mail: tara@topitexecs.com
Home Page: www.acrhq.com

Philip Howard, Publisher
Allen Howard, CEO
Tara Saenz, Circulation Manager

Improvement ideas and techniques for software development.
Cost: $630.00
12 Pages
Frequency: Bi-annually
Founded in 1971
Mailing list available for rent: 20M names at $105 per M
Printed in one color on matte stock

5328 **Systems Reengineering Economics Letter**
Computer Economics
2082 Business Center Drive
Suite 240
Irvine, CA 92612

949-831-8700
Fax: 949-442-7688
Home Page: www.computereconomics.com

Frank Scavo, President
Dan Husiak, VP

Economic look at the re-engineering explosion, delivering critical information on the methods, costs and risks of systems and business process re-engineering. Updates on the analyses, data, opinions, and case studies you need to make sound business decisions and capitalize on your re-engineering process.
Cost: $395.00
Frequency: Daily
Founded in 1978

5329 **TechTarget**
TechTarget
117 Kendrick St
Suite 800
Needham Heights, MA 02494-2728

781-657-1000
888-274-4111
Fax: 781-657-1100
E-Mail: info@techtarget.com
Home Page: www.techtarget.com

Greg Strakosch, CEO
Don Hawk, President
Lisa Johnson, VP Marketing
Catherine Engelke, Director Public Relations

IBM iSeries focused media. The IBM e-Server iSeries (formerly the AS/400) is considered to be the world's most often used multi-user business computer. The installed base worldwide is huge and will get bigger, fueled by incresed Web development. The iSeries come with an integrated Web application server and all the tools needed to build internet, intranet, extranet, and e-commerce sites quickly and will figure promenently into IT strategy and implementation for years to come.
Frequency: Monthly
Founded in 1999

5330 **Technology Advertising & Branding Report**
Simba Information
60 Long Ridge Rd
Suite 300
Stamford, CT 06902-1841

203-325-8193
888-297-4622
Fax: 203-325-8915
E-Mail: info@simbanet.com
Home Page: www.simbanet.com

Linda Kopp, Publisher

Offers news, statistics and analysis of advertising strategies in the technology industry. Provides competitive information on the advertising and marketing activities of com-

puter hardware and software companies. Helps computer publishers target advertising sales by reporting the plans of computer advertisers. Shows computer advertisers how to get best buys.
Cost: $549.00
8 Pages

5331 Techweek
Metro States Media
1156 Aster Avenue
#B
Sunnyvale, CA 94086-6810
408-249-8300
Fax: 408-249-0727
Home Page: www.techweek.com
John Leggett, Publisher
Provides articles for the local high technology industry programmers. Includes information about the internet, finances, job market, and new products for technology professionals.
Frequency: BiWeekly
Circulation: 100,000

5332 TidBITS
TidBITS
50 Hickory Road
Ithaca, NY 14850
E-Mail: ace@tidbits.com
Home Page: www.tidbits.com
Adam Engst, Publisher
Tonya Engst, Managing Editor
Jeff Carlson, Managing Editor
Online newsletter and web site, devoted to the person behind the most personal of personal computers, the Macintosh. TidBITS relates events and products to real life uses and concerns. New TidBITS issues go out every Monday night; breaking news and important updates appear on the web site more frequently.
Frequency: Weekly
Circulation: 150000
Founded in 1990

5333 Wireless LAN
Information Gatekeepers
1340 Soldiers Field Rd
Suite 3
Brighton, MA 02135-1000
617-782-5033
800-323-1088
Fax: 617-782-5735
E-Mail: info@igigroup.com
Home Page: www.igigroup.com
Paul Polishuk, CEO
Cathey Mallen, Production Manager
Brian Mark, Newsletter Managing Editor
Bev Wilson, Managing Editor
Yesim Taskor, Controller
LAN technological trends and market opportunities.
Cost: $695.00
Frequency: Monthly
Founded in 1977

5334 Work Process Improvement Today
Recognition Technologies Users Association
75 Federal Street
Suite 901
Boston, MA 02110-1413
617-426-1167
800-99 -2974
Fax: 617-521-8675
E-Mail: kguarino@tawpi.org
Home Page: www.tawpi.org
Dan Bllida, Editor
Debra Sanderson, Publisher
Frank Moran, Owner
Accepts advertising.
Cost: $60.00
Circulation: 10000

5335 iACTion Newsletter
American Council for Technology
3040 Williams Dr
Suite 610
Fairfax, VA 22031-4618
703-208-4800
Fax: 703-208-4805
E-Mail: act-iac@actgov.org
Home Page: www.actgov.org
Ken Allen, Executive Director
Frequency: Monthly

Magazines & Journals

5336 2600 Magazine
PO Box 752
Middle Island, NY 11953
631-751-2600
Fax: 631-474-2677
E-Mail: webmaster@2600.com
Home Page: www.2600.com/
Emanuel Golstein, Editor
Written for computer hackers.
Cost: $20.00
Frequency: Quarterly
Founded in 1984

5337 ACM QUEUE
1515 Broadway
17th Floor
New York, NY 10036-5701
212-869-7440
800-342-6626
Fax: 212-302-5826
E-Mail: acmhelp@acm.org
Home Page: www.acm.org
Mark Mandelbaum, Director Publication
John R White, Associate Director
Robert Okajima, Associate Director
Alain Chesnais, Founder
Liliana Cintron, Administrative Assistant
Published by the Association for Computing Machinery.
Circulation: 25000
Founded in 1947

5338 AFSM International Professional Journal and High-Technology Service Mgmt.
AFSM International
11031 Via Frontera
Suite A
San Diego, CA 92127-1709
858-673-3055
800-333-9786
Fax: 239-275-0794
E-Mail: info@afsmi.org
Home Page: www.afsmi.org
John Shoenewald, Executive Director
Jb Wood, President/Ceo
For trade association members.
Cost: $150.00
86 Pages
Frequency: Monthly
Circulation: 20000
Founded in 1975
Printed in 4 colors on glossy stock

5339 AI Expert
Miller Freeman Publications
2655 Seely Avenue
San Jose, CA 95134
408-943-1234
Fax: 408-943-0513
Regina Star Ridley, Editor
Practical applications of artificial intelligence in any field.
Cost: $37.00
42 Pages
Frequency: Monthly
Founded in 1986

5340 AI Magazine
American Association for Artificial Intelligence
445 Burgess Drive
Menlo Park, CA 94025-3442
650-328-3123
Fax: 650-321-4457
Home Page: www.aimagazine.org
David Leake, Editor
David M Hamilton, Managing Editor
Michael Wellman, Book Review Editor
Carol McKenna Hamilton, Executive Director, AAAI
Alanna Spencer, Director
Quarterly issued magazine, available through AAAI membership. AI Magazine features articles regarding research in the field of artificial intelligence.
128 Pages
Frequency: Quarterly
Circulation: 7000
ISSN: 0738-4602
Founded in 1980
Printed in on matte stock

5341 ASR News
Voice Information Associates
P.O.Box 2861
Acton, MA 01720-6861
978-266-1966
Fax: 978-263-3461
Home Page: www.asrnews.com
Walt Tetschner, Publisher and Editor
Developments in products, marketing, technology, and investments in the automatic speech recognition industry.
Cost: $345.00
Frequency: Monthly
Founded in 1990

5342 Advanced Imaging
Cygnus Publishing
3 Huntington Quadrangle
Suite 301N
Melville, NY 11747-3601
631-845-2700
800-308-6397
Fax: 631-845-2736
E-Mail: info@advancedimaging.com
Home Page: www.advancedimagingmag.com
Dave Brambert, Publisher
Larry Adams, Editor-in-Chief
Paul Mackler, CEO
The only international magazine specifically designed to meet the needs of professionals using all forms of electronic imaging technologies. Offering monthly coverage of imaging application solutions for medical/diagnostic, industrial machine vision, government/security, and scientific imaging markets.
Frequency: Monthly
Circulation: 44009
Founded in 1966

5343 Aixpert
IBM Corporation

1133 Westchester Avenue
White Plains
New York, NY 10604-3406

914-423-3000
Fax: 866-722-9226
Home Page: www.ibm.com

George Noren, Editor-in-Chief

Provides timely up-to-date technical material to help developers plot, develop, and enhance applications for IBM AIX products.
Frequency: Quarterly
Circulation: 10,000

5344 **Aldus Magazine**
Aldus Corporation
801 N 34th Street
Seattle, WA 98103-8882
Carla Noble, Publisher
Harry Edwards, Editor

Supports and educates graphics professionals using ALDUS software. Covers tips, tricks and how-to pointers for maximizing PageMaker, Freehand, PhotoStyler and Persuasion. Also covers trends in electronic publishing.
Cost: $ 24.00
68 Pages
Frequency: 8 per year
Circulation: 220,000
Founded in 1989

5345 **Algorithmica**
Springer Verlag
233 Spring St
New York, NY 10013-1578

212-460-1500
Fax: 212-460-1575
E-Mail: service@springer-ny.com
Home Page: www.springer-ny.com

William Curtis, President
D T Lee, Managing Editor
Rubin Wang, Managing Editor

Provides an in-depth look into distributed computing, parellel processing, automated design, and software tools.
Cost: $1008.00
Frequency: Quarterly
Circulation: 1000
Founded in 1855

5346 **Analysis Solutions**
ConnectPress
2530 Camino Entrada
Santa Fe, NM 87505-4807

505-474-5000
Fax: 505-474-5001
Home Page: www.analysismag.com

Carolyn Mascarenas, Publisher

Design analysis and optimization for ANSYS technology users. Covers engineering simulation, acousitc analysis, model meshing, new products and case studies.
Cost: $90.00
Frequency: Quarterly
Circulation: 27,575

5347 **Application Development Trends**
600 Worcester Road
Suite 301
Framingham, MA 01702

508-875-6644
Fax: 508-875-6622
Home Page: www.adtmag.com

Sheryl Katz, Publisher
Michael Alexander, Editorial-in-Chief
Tracy S. Cook, Marketing Director
Christina Schaller, Managing Editor

The number one information source on today's key application development options delivering a high powered, management-oriented editorial that covers the application development industry in greater depth and breadth than any other publication.
Frequency: Monthly
Circulation: 45000
Founded in 1998

5348 **Applied Computing Technologies**
9041 Executive Park Dr
Suite 222
Knoxville, TN 37923-4603

865-675-0508
Fax: 865-694-9096

Peyman Dehkordi, Owner

5349 **Applied Optics**
Optical Society of America
2010 Massachusetts Ave Nw
Washington, DC 20036-1023

202-223-8130
Fax: 202-223-1096
E-Mail: info@osa.org
Home Page: www.osa.org

Elizabeth Rogan, Executive Director

5350 **Automatic ID News**
Advanstar Communications
641 Lexington Ave
8th Floor
New York, NY 10022-4503

212-951-6600
Fax: 212-951-6793
E-Mail: info@advanstar.com
Home Page: www.advanstar.com

Joseph Loggia, CEO

Information for decision-makers in all industries seeking definitive information about automatic data collection technology. The technology includes optical, magnetic, radio frequency and voice recognition systems and peripherals.
Frequency: Monthly
ISSN: 0890-9768

5351 **BAM Publications**
BAM Publications
3470 Buskirk Avenue
Pleasant Hill, CA 94523-4340

925-932-5900

Dennis Erokan, Editor

Provides regionally focused product and channel news to computer products and services.
Cost: $120.00
60 Pages
Frequency: Monthly
Founded in 1988

5352 **Better Channel**
ABCD: The Microcomputer Industry Association
450 E 22nd Street
Suite 230
Lombard, IL 60148-6158

630-268-1818
Fax: 630-268-1384

John Venator, Executive VP

A professional magazine that is exclusively dedicated to representing and serving all segments of the microcomputer industry. Accepts advertising.
Cost: $150.00
32 Pages
Frequency: Monthly

5353 **CADALYST**
Advanstar Communications
641 Lexington Ave
8th Floor
New York, NY 10022-4503

212-951-6600
Fax: 212-951-6793
E-Mail: info@advanstar.com
Home Page: www.advanstar.com

Joseph Loggia, CEO

Expert coverage of the latest developments in auto CAD systems, their products and the various CAD applications.
Cost: $4.00
Frequency: Monthly
Circulation: 70000

5354 **CALICO Journal**
Texas State University
214 Centennial Hall
San Marcos, TX 78666

512-245-1417
Fax: 512-245-9089
E-Mail: info@calico.org
Home Page: www.calico.org

Robert Fischer, Editor

Devoted to the dissemination of information concerning the application of technology to language teaching and language learning. The CALICO Journal is fully refereed and publishes articles, research studies, reports, software reviews, and professional news and announcements.
Cost: $85.00
Frequency: 3x/Year
Circulation: 800
ISSN: 0742-7778

5355 **CASE Strategies**
Cutter Information Corporation
37 Broadway
Suite 1
Arlington, MA 02474-5500

781-648-1950
Fax: 781-648-1950
Home Page: www.cutter.com

Verna Allee, Senior Consultant

Implementation strategies, reviews and case studies in areas of computer-aided systems engineering.
Cost: $295.00

5356 **CBT Solutions**
SB Communications
183 Whiting Street
#15
Hingham, MA 02043-3845

781-749-2151
E-Mail: cbstol@ziplink.net
Home Page: www.cbtsolutions.com

Steve Blumberg, Publisher

Featured editorials include advanced technology in the past and future, interactive web programs, new methods to access and control information, and personal profiles.
Frequency: Bi-Monthly
Circulation: 15,000

5357 **CD-ROM Enduser**
Disc Company
6609 Rosecroft Pl
Falls Church, VA 22043-1828
Linda Helgerson, Editor

For people who use CD-ROM applications.
Cost: $3.00
Frequency: Monthly
Founded in 1989

5358 **CD-ROM Librarian**
Mecklermedia Corporation

20 Ketchum Street
Westport, CT 06880-5808

203-226-6967
Fax: 203-454-5840

Alan Meckler, Editor

A periodical intended for the library professional.
Cost: $80.00
Frequency: Monthly
Founded in 1986

5359 CHANCE: New Directions for Statistics and Computing
Springer Verlag
233 Spring St
New York, NY 10013-1578

212-460-1500
Fax: 212-460-1575
E-Mail: service@springer-ny.com
Home Page: www.springer-ny.com

William Curtis, President
John E Rolph, Editor
Derk Haank, CEO
Peter Hendriks, President of Marketing
Rubin Wang, Managing Editor

Covers both statistics and computing. Designed for everyone who has an interest in the analysis of data. The informal style highlights and encourages sound statistical practice.
Cost: $7.00
Frequency: Monthly
Circulation: 4500
Founded in 1842

5360 CRN
UBM LLC
550 Cochituate Road
First Floor-West Wing, Suite 5
Framingham, MA 01701

508-416-1100
E-Mail: kelley.damore@ec.ubm.com
Home Page: www.crn.com

Kelley Damore, VP/Editorial Director
Steven Burke, Editor
Jane O'Brien, Managing Editor

Delivers strategic information and useful business tools that Solution Providers and other Channel professionals
Cost: $89.00
Frequency: BiWeekly
Circulation: 95,072

5361 Cadence
Miller Freeman Publications
2655 Seely Avenue
San Jose, CA 95134

408-468-8603
Fax: 408-468-1902
E-Mail: info@gartner.com
Home Page: www.gartner.com

Johanna Kleppe, Publisher
Kathleen Maher, Managing Editor
Michael Fister, CEO
Tom McCall, Senior Director Public Relations
Michael Bingle, Director

For users of Autocad - a construction/architecture program.
Cost: $6.00
Circulation: 72664

5362 Catalyst
Western Center for Microcomputers
1259 El Camino Real
#275
Menlo Park, CA 94025

650-855-8064
Home Page: www.home.earthlink.net/~thecatalyst/index.html

Sue Swezey, Editor
Robert Scott, Chief Information Officer

Reporting on both the increasing sophistication of technology and the increasing complexity special education. We've covered the profound changes in the lives of children and adults with special needs as they have benefited from computer use, as well as on the obstacles confronting them and those who serve them.
Cost: $18.00
Frequency: Quarterly

5363 Christian Computing
PO Box 319
Belton, MO 64012-0319

800-456-1868
Fax: 800-456-1868
E-Mail: steve@ccmag.com
Home Page: www.ccmag.com

Steve Hewitt, Editor-in-Chief
Frequency: Monthly
Founded in 1989

5364 CircuiTree
Business News Publishing Company
1050 IL Route 83
Suite 200
Bensenville, IL 60106-1096

630-377-5909
Home Page: circuitree.com

Katie Rotella, Manager
Tom Esposito, Group Publisher
Darryl Seland, Associate Publisher/
Karl Dietz, Technical Editor
Cost: $64.00
Frequency: Monthly
Circulation: 12000
Founded in 1926

5365 Civic.com
FCW Government Technology Group
3141 Fairview Park Drive
Suite 777
Falls Church, VA 22042-4507

FAX 703-876-5126
Home Page: www.fcw.com

Edith Holmes, President
Steve Vito, Publisher
Agnes Vanek, Circulation Director
Margo Dunn, Production Manager
Anne Armstrong, Editor

A print magazine and electronic companion designed for volume IT buyers, chief information officers and IT planners in state and local government.

5366 CleanRooms Magazine
PennWell Publishing Company
98 Spit Brook Rd
Suite 100
Nashua, NH 03062-5737

603-891-0123
Fax: 603-891-9294
E-Mail: johnh@pennwell.com
Home Page: www.pennwell.com

Christine Shaw, VP
James Enos, Publisher
Angela Godwin, Managing Editor
Steve Smith, News Editor
Bob Johnson, National Sales Manager

Serves the contamination control and ultrapure materials and process industries. Written for readers in the microelectronics, pharmaceutical, biotech, health care, food processing and other user industries. Provides technology and business news and new product listings.
Cost: $97.00
Frequency: Monthly
Circulation: 35031
Founded in 1987

5367 Com-SAC, Computer Security, Auditing & Controls
Management Advisory Services & Publications
PO Box 81151
Wellesley Hills, MA 02481-0001

781-235-2895
Fax: 781-235-5446
E-Mail: info@masp.com
Home Page: www.masp.com

A quarterly journal of in-depth tutorials in computer security, auditing and the most comprehensive digest service of all publications in computer security and controls.
Cost: $98.00
Frequency: Quarterly
Founded in 1973

5368 Common Knowledge
230 W Monroe St
Suite 220
Chicago, IL 60606-4802

312-416-3656
800-777-6734
Fax: 312-201-9588
E-Mail: info@knowledgenetworks.com
Home Page: www.knowledgenetworks.com

Kris Neeley, Publisher

Features interviews with industry experts, case studies, tutorials, the latest industry news and overviews of management concerns.
Frequency: Quarterly
Circulation: 15,000

5369 Communications of the ACM
Association for Computing Machinery
2 Penn Plz
Suite 701
New York, NY 10121-0799

212-868-5716
800-342-6626
Fax: 212-944-1318
E-Mail: acmhelp@acm.org
Home Page: www.acm.org

Jerry Ashton, President
John R White, CEO
Edward Grossman, Publisher
Diane Crawford, Executive Editor
Brian Hebert, Marketing/Communications Manager

Technical magazine covering developments in computer science for professional scientific and business dp, systems programming, database techniques and more.
Cost: $17.00
Frequency: Monthly
Circulation: 82,867
Founded in 1947

5370 CompactPCI Systems
CompactPCI Systems
13253 La Montana
Dr 207
Fountain Hills, AZ 85268-5328

480-967-5581
Fax: 480-837-6466
Home Page: www.compactpci-systems.com

Mike Hopper, Publisher
Joe Pavlat, Editor

Features application success stories that demonstrate how and where CompactPCI technology has provided solutions.
Circulation: 20000

5371 **Component Development Strategies**
Cutter Information Corporation
37 Broadway
Suite 1
Arlington, MA 02474-5500

781-648-1950
800-964-5118
Fax: 781-648-1950
E-Mail: press@cutter.com
Home Page: www.cutter.com

Karen Coburn, President and CEO
Tom Welsh, Senior Consultant
Hillel Glazer, Senior Consultant
Ron Blitstein, Director

Editorial content covers the latest information and technology on object-oriented programming, databases, and analysis and design.
Cost: $2400.00
Frequency: Monthly
Founded in 1991

5372 **CompuServe Magazine**
5000 Arlington Centre Blvd
Columbus, OH 43220-5439

614-326-1002
800-848-8199
Home Page:
webcenters.netscape.compuserve.com/menu/

Offers updated and statistical information for computer professionals.

5373 **Computer**
IEEE Computer Society
10662 Los Vaqueros Circle
P. O. Box 3014
Los Alamitos, CA 90720-1314

714-821-8380
800-272-6657
Fax: 714-821-4010
E-Mail: volunteer.services@computer.org
Home Page: www.computer.org/

Matt Loeb, Publisher
Doris L. Carver, Editor in Chief
Bill Schilit, Associate Editor
Judi Prow, Managing Editor
Jim Sanders, Senior Editor

Information on late breaking news, business trends, and a variety of technology specific departments.
Cost: $63.00
Frequency: Monthly
Circulation: 84340
Founded in 1988

5374 **Computer Business Review**
ComputerWire
245 5th Avenue
4th Floor
New York, NY 10016

212-770-0409
Fax: 212-686-2626
E-Mail: info@computerwire.com
Home Page: www.computerwire.com/cbr

Jake Sharp, Publisher
Micheal Danzon, CEO
Jason Stamper, Editor

Company profiles, computer market coverage and technology trends and news for investors and professionals in the computer, communications and microelectronics industries.
Cost: $195.00
Frequency: Monthly
Circulation: 20450
Founded in 1984

5375 **Computer Buyer's Guide & Handbook**
Bedford Communications
1410 Broadway
21st Floor
New York, NY 10018-5008

212-807-8220
Fax: 212-807-1098
Home Page: www.techworthy.com

Ed Brown, Owner

A guide to buying peripherals and software, as well as general advice and news on the world of computing.
Cost: $36.00
128 Pages
Frequency: Monthly
Circulation: 50000
Founded in 1981

5376 **Computer Design**
PennWell Publishing Company
10 Tara Boulevard
5th Floor
Nashua, NH 03062-2800

603-891-0123
Fax: 603-891-0514
Home Page: www.computer-design.com

John Carroll, Group Publisher

Each issue contains in-depth articles and timely features written by experienced senior editors who concentrate on the critical technologies, components and tools needed to design microprocessor and computer based OEM products and systems.
Frequency: Monthly
Circulation: 105,028

5377 **Computer Graphics Review**
Primedia
Po Box 12901
Shawnee Mission, KS 66282-2901

913-341-1300
Fax: 913-514-6895
E-Mail: inquiries@primediabusiness.com uirie
Home Page: www.penton.com

Eric Jacobson, Senior VP

To identify and interpret significant technological and business developments.
Cost: $48.00
120 Pages
Frequency: Monthly
Founded in 1986

5378 **Computer Graphics World**
PennWell Publishing Company
98 Spit Brook Rd
Nashua, NH 03062-5737

603-891-0123
800-225-0556
Fax: 603-891-9294
E-Mail: phil@pennwell.com
Home Page: www.pennwell.com

Christine Shaw, VP
Jenny Donelan, Managing Editor

Covers specific applications of computer graphics, written by users and vendors of equipment and services to the industry. The magazine of 3D computer graphics for engineering and animation professionals.
Frequency: Monthly
Founded in 1978
Printed in 4 colors on glossy stock

5379 **Computer Industry Almanac**
304 W White Oak
Arlington Heights, IL 60005

847-758-3687
Fax: 847-758-3686
E-Mail: ej@c-i-a.com
Home Page: www.c-i-a.com

Egil Juliussen, President

Annual reference book for and about the computer industry. The Almanac has ranking and awards of products, people and companies. Includes salary information, market forecasts, technology trends and directories of companies, publications, market research firms, associations and trade shows.
Cost: $45.00
Frequency: Annual

5380 **Computer Journal**
Oxford University Press
2001 Evans Rd
Cary, NC 27513-2010

919-677-0977
800-852-7323
Fax: 919-677-2673
Home Page:
www3.oup.co.uk/computer_journal/

F Leroy, Editorial Assistant:
F Murtagh, Editor-in-Chief
Julie Gribben, Special Sales Manager

Provides information on web sites, personal computers, hardware, software and online uses.
Cost: $920.00
Circulation: 18000

5381 **Computer Language**
600 Harrison Street
6th Floor
San Francisco, CA 94107

415-947-6000
Fax: 415-941-6055

Computer news and information.

5382 **Computer Link Magazine**
Millennium Publishing
100 Mobile Dr
Suite 1
Rochester, NY 14616-2145

585-797-4399
E-Mail: info@computerlinkmag.com
Home Page: www.techny.com

Justin Ziemniak, Editor-in-Chief

Website reviews, employment opportunities, and women's involvement in the technology age. Includes reports on the Western New York computer market.
Cost: $20.00
Frequency: Monthly
Circulation: 20000

5383 **Computer Manager**
Story Communications
116 N Camp Street
Seguin, TX 78155-5600

830-303-3328
Fax: 830-372-3011
E-Mail: story@storycomm.com
Home Page: www.compumgr.com

James M Story, Publisher
K Wiemann, Circulation Manager

Information to help corporate end users purchase computers and communications equipment easily.
Frequency: Quarterly
Circulation: 50000

5384 **Computer Price Guide**
Computer Merchants
22 Saw Mill River Road
Hawthorne, NY 10532-1533

914-347-0290
Fax: 914-347-0292

Svend Hartmann, Publisher

Market trends and developments, prices on used IBM computer equipment.
Cost: $70.00
Frequency: Quarterly
Circulation: 3500

5385 **Computer Security Journal**
Computer Security Institute
600 Harrison Street
San Francisco, CA 94107

415-947-6320
866-271-8529
Fax: 415-947-6023
Home Page: www.gocsi.com

Russell Kay, Publisher
Chris Keating, Director
Robert Richardson, Editorial Director
Nancy Baer, Marketing Manager

Keeps you informed with comprehensive, practical articles, case studies, reviews and commentaries written by knowledgeable computer security professionals.
Cost: $25.00
Frequency: Quarterly
Circulation: 3000
Founded in 1974

5386 **Computer Security, Auditing and Controls (COM-SAC)**
Management Advisory Services & Publications
PO Box 81151
Wellesley Hills, MA 02481-0001

781-235-2895
Fax: 781-235-5446
E-Mail: info@masp.com
Home Page: www.masp.com

Indepth tutorials in computer security and auditing and the most comprehensive digest service of all publications in computer security, auditing and internal controls. Security hardware-software news.
Cost: $98.00
Frequency: Quarterly
ISSN: 0738-4262
Founded in 1973
Printed in on glossy stock

5387 **Computer Shopper**
Segal Company
1 Battery Park Plz
New York, NY 10004-1487

212-858-1000
Fax: 212-251-5490
E-Mail: info@segalco.com

Glenn E Siegel

A buyer's guide of sorts, listing the latest information and equipment for the world of computers.

5388 **Computer Survival Journal**
Enterprise Publishing
Po Box 328
Blair, NE 68008-0328

402-426-2121
Fax: 402-426-2227
E-Mail: mrhoades@enterprisepub.com
Home Page: www.enterprisepub.com

Mark Rhoades, President
Dave Smith, Production Manager
Tracy Prettyman, Business Manager

Reviews and features on all areas of computer, office and home products (hardware and software). Also includes information on cellular phones, TV's and appliances, home electronics and television.
Cost: $250.00
50 Pages

5389 **Computer Technology Review**
West World Productions
420 N Camden Dr
Beverly Hills, CA 90210-4507

310-276-9500
888-889-3130
Fax: 310-276-9874
E-Mail: sinan@kanatsiz.com
Home Page: www.wwpi.com

Yuri R Spiro, Publisher

Computer Technology Review is an all-inclusive tabloid that covers the full spectrum of new and emerging technologies vital to systems integrators, high-end VARS, and OEM.
Cost: $10.00
60 Pages
Frequency: Monthly
Circulation: 64044
ISSN: 0278-9647
Founded in 1981
Printed in 4 colors on matte stock

5390 **Computer User Magazine**
Key Professional Media
220 S 6th St
Suite 500
Minneapolis, MN 55402-4501

612-339-7571
800-788-0204
Fax: 612-333-5806
E-Mail: info@computeruser.com
Home Page: www.computeruser.com

Nat Opperman, President
Elizabeth Millard, Associate Publisher

For small to medium-size business professionals and computer owners, ComputerUser is published in 13 markets nationally.
Cost: $14.00
60 Pages
Frequency: Monthly
Circulation: 64000
Founded in 1981
Printed in 4 colors on newsprint stock

5391 **Computer World/Focus**
PO Box 9171
Framingham, MA 01701-9171
Joe Maglitta, Feature Editor

A comprehensive magazine offering information on the computer industry.

5392 **Computer-Aided Engineering**
Penton Media
1300 E 9th St
Cleveland, OH 44114-1503

216-696-7000
Fax: 216-696-6662
E-Mail: caenetmaster@penton.com
Home Page: www.penton.com

Jane Cooper, Marketing

Applications, news, trends and products for CAD/CAM technology as applied in manufacturing, electronics, architectural and construction industries.
Cost: $50.00
Frequency: Monthly
Circulation: 56,062

5393 **Computers User**
220 S 6th Street
Suite 500
Minneapolis, MN 55042

612-339-7571
E-Mail: info@computeruser.com
Home Page: www.computeruser.com

David Needle, Editor
Matt Kusilek, Publisher

End user computer magazine for business and professional users of PC and Macintosh computers, software and peripherals.
Cost: $24.99
Frequency: Monthly

5394 **Computers and Biomedical Research**
Academic Press
1901 E South Campus Drive
Suite 1195
Salt Lake City, UT 84112-9359

801-581-6461
Fax: 801-585-5414
Home Page: www.aoce.utah.edu

T Allan Pryor, Editor
Liz McCoy, Executive Assistant
Brynn Roundy, Executive Secretary

Information on application of computer technology in biomedical research for medical professionals. Evaluates and discusses various techniques. Accompanied by photographs, charts, graphs and figures.
Cost: $325.00
Frequency: 6 per year
Circulation: 1,425

5395 **Computers in the Schools**
Taylor & Francis Group LLC
325 Chestnut St
Suite 800
Philadelphia, PA 19106-2614

215-625-8900
800-354-1420
Fax: 215-625-2940
E-Mail: haworthorders@taylorandfrancis.com
Home Page: www.taylorandfrancis.com

Kevin Bradley, President

Articles emphasize the practical aspect of any application but also tie theory to practice, relate present accomplishments to past efforts and future trends, identify conclusions and their implications and discuss the theoretical and philosophical basis for the application.
Frequency: Quarterly

5396 **Computertalk**
Computertalk Associates
492 Norristown Road
Suite 160
Blue Bell, PA 19422

610-825-7686
Fax: 610-825-7641
E-Mail: wal@computertalk.com
Home Page: www.computertalk.com

William A Lockwood Jr, President
Maggie L Lockwood, Director of Publications

Profiles on various sytems available for pharmacists purchasing and using computers.
Cost: $50.00
Frequency: Monthly
Circulation: 32,000
Founded in 1980
Printed in 4 colors on glossy stock

5397 **Computerworld**
CW Publishing
One Speen Street
PO Box 9171
Framingham, MA 01701-4653

508-879-0700
800-343-6474
Fax: 508-626-2705
E-Mail: editor@computerworld.com
Home Page: www.computerworld.com

Mitch Betts, Executive Editor
Don Tennant, VP/Editor in Chief
Matt Sweeney, CEO

For computer professionals who evaluate and implement information systems.
Cost: $99.99
170 Pages
Circulation: 170000
Founded in 1967

5398 **Computing Surveys**
Association for Computing Machinery

One Astor Place
1515 Broadway
New York, NY 10036-5701

212-869-7440
800-342-6626
Fax: 212-302-5826
E-Mail: acmhelp@acm.org
Home Page: www.acm.org

Mark Mandelbaum, Director Publication
John R. White, CEO
Gul Agha, Editor in Chief
Robert Okajima, Associate Director
Alain Chesnais, Founder

Carefully planned and presented introductions to complex issues, supported by exhaustive and comprehensive notations on the relevant literature.
Cost: $170.00
Frequency: Quarterly
Founded in 1947

5399 **Computing in Science & Engineering**
American Institute of Physics
2 Huntington Quad
Melville, NY 11747-4502

516-576-2200
Fax: 516-349-7669
Home Page: www.aip.org

Darlene Walters, Senior VP
Angela Burgess, Publisher
Georgann Carter, Marketing Manager

Computer science's interdisciplinary juncture with physics, astronomy and engineering.
Cost: $55.00

5400 **Control Solutions**
PennWell Publishing Company
1421 S Sheridan Rd
Tulsa, OK 74112-6619

918-831-9421
800-331-4463
Fax: 918-831-9476
Home Page: www.pennwell.com

Robert Biolchini, President
Ron Kuhfeld, Editor-in-Chief

Represents control technology for engineers and engineering manage4ment.

5401 **Cryptosystems Journal**
Cryptosystems Journal
485 Middle Holland Road
Holland, PA 18966-2870
Tony Patti, Publisher/Editor

Unique international journal devoted to implementation of cryptographic systems on IBM-PC's and compatibles.

5402 **Cyber Defense Magazine**
PO Box 71748
Phoenix, AZ 85050

480-990-0407
866-487-6652
Fax: 480-990-7306
Home Page: www.cyberdefensemag.com

John Riccio, Publisher
Curt Blakeney, Editor

Computer/Network security magazine.
Cost: $31.00
64 Pages
Frequency: 12 issues
Circulation: 64,000
Founded in 2003
Printed in 4 colors on glossy stock

5403 **DBMS-Database Management Systems**
Miller Freeman Publications
2655 Seely Avenue
San Jose, CA 95134

408-943-1234
Fax: 408-943-0513

Phillip Chapnick, Publisher
David Kohman, Editor

Covers the database and database applications marketplace.
Circulation: 69,029

5404 **DG Review**
Data Base Publications
9390 Research Blvd
Suite 300
Austin, TX 78759-7374

512-418-9590
Fax: 512-418-8165
Home Page: www.bancvue.com

Gabe Krajicek, CEO
Gloria Trent, Editor

For Data General and compatible computer users.
Cost: $48.00
64 Pages
Frequency: Monthly
Founded in 1981

5405 **DM Review**
Powell Publishing Company
16655 W Bluemound Rd
Suite 201
Brookfield, WI 53005-5935

262-780-0202
Fax: 414-771-8058
Home Page: www.b-eye-network.com

Ron Powell, Owner
Val Latzke, Editor
Jean Schauer, Editor in Chief
Mary Jo Nott, Executive Editor

Provides a wealth of knowledge through columns by top industry experts, data warehouse success stories, timely and informative articles, third-party product reviews, and executive interviews.
Frequency: Monthly
Circulation: 75012
Founded in 1994

5406 **DSP Engineering**
13253 La Montana Dr
Suite 207
Fountains Hills, AZ 85268

480-967-5581
Fax: 480-837-6466
Home Page: wwwdspengineering.com

Rosemary Kristoff, VP
Phyllis Thompson, Circulation Manager
Patrick Hopper, VP Marketing
Mike Hopper, Publisher

5407 **Data Bus**
AM Publications
PO Box 20044
Saint Petersburg, FL 33742

727-577-5500
Fax: 727-576-0622
E-Mail: ampubs@aol.com

Al Martino, Publisher/Editor

Contains new product reviews, trade literature and personnel announcements.
Frequency: Monthly
Circulation: 24000

5408 **Data Communications**
McGraw Hill
PO Box 182604
Columbus, OH 43272

614-866-5769
Fax: 614-759-3759
E-Mail: customer.service@mcgraw-hill.com
Home Page: www.mcgraw-hill.com

Kevin Harold, Publisher
Steve Weiss, Production Manager

Networking magazine edited for the technical managers responsible for the implementation and integration of computer information networks.
Cost: $5.00
Circulation: 112,941

5409 **Data Sources**
Ziff Davis Publishing Company
28 E 28th St
New York, NY 10016-7940

212-503-5772
E-Mail: info@ziffdavis.com
Home Page: www.ziffdavis.com

Steve Weitzner, CEO
Leo Greisman, General Counsel
Stephen Hicks, General Counsel
Steve Horowitz, COO
Cost: $240.00
Frequency: Monthly
Circulation: 700000
Founded in 1981

5410 **Data Storage**
PennWell Publishing Company
PO 91372
Calabasas, CA 91372

818-348-1240
Fax: 818-348-1742
Home Page: www.datastorage.com

Becky Adams, Publisher
David Simpson, Editor
Kevin Komiega, Senior Editor

Features news and information on all types of systems such as magnetic disk drives, media and magnetic tape drives, CD-ROM, optical, magneto-optical, holographic and nonvolatile semiconductor storage devices.
Frequency: Monthly
Circulation: 15,140

5411 **Data to Knowledge**
Business Rule Solutions
2476 Bolsover Street
#488
Houston, TX 77005-2518

713-681-1651
Fax: 604-681-7223
E-Mail: datatoknow@brsolutions.com
Home Page: www.brcommunity.com

Gladys S W Lam, Publisher
Ronald G Ross, Executive Editor
Keri Anderson Healy, Editor
Marie Yang, Director, Marketing & Business Dev
John Hall, Technology Review Editor

Provides analysis, news and tutorials for data management professionals, data administrators, DBA's and other involved in the planning, design and construction of large-scale information systems.
Circulation: 4603
Founded in 1973

5412 **Database Searcher**
Mecklermedia Corporation
11 Ferry Lane W
Westport, CT 06880-5808
Alan Meckler, Editor

Covers online and micro-computer techniques.
Cost: $95.00
Frequency: Monthly
Founded in 1985

5413 **Datamation**
Reed Business Information

2000 Clearwater Dr
Oak Brook, IL 60523-8809

630-574-0825
Fax: 630-288-8781
Home Page: www.reedbusiness.com

Jeff Greisch, President
William Semich, Editor-in-Chief

The magazine that interprets products, events and technologies for computer professionals in large companies worldwide.
Cost: $4.00
Circulation: 189,101

5414 **Design Automation**
Miller Freeman Publications
2655 Seely Avenue
San Jose, CA 95134

408-943-1234
Fax: 408-943-0513

Lindsey Vereen, Editor

Targeted to computer design engineers.
Frequency: Monthly

5415 **Designfax**
NP Communications, LLC
2500 Tamiami Trail N
Nokomis, FL 34275

941-966-9521
Fax: 941-966-2590
E-Mail: mfoley@nelsonpub.com
Home Page: www.designfax.net

Mike Foley, Editor
John W Holmes, National Sales Manager

eMagazine whose primary content focuses on the latest exciting applications and products for Electrical/Electronic, Mechanical, Motion Control, Fluid Power, and Materials engineering, including articles on powerful software programs that serve as a primary engineering tool.
Cost: $54.00
Frequency: Weekly
Circulation: 128,000
Founded in 1979
Printed in 4 colors on glossy stock

5416 **Desktop Engineering**
Helmers Publishing
174 Concord Street
PO Box 874
Peterborough, NH 03458

603-924-9631
Fax: 603-924-4004
E-Mail: jgooch@deskeng.com
Home Page: www.deskeng.com

Brian Vaillancourt, Publisher
Anthony J Lockwood, Editorial Director
Bill Fahy, Circulation Director
Carol Laughner, Marketing Director

Magazine providing design solutions from concept throughout manufacture, focuses on hardware, software, and technologies for hands-on design engineers and engineering management in the manufacturing solutions throughout extensive product reviews, comparisions, technology updates, real-world application stories, news, product resource guides, and new product reports.
60 Pages
Frequency: Monthly
Circulation: 63000
ISSN: 1085-0422
Founded in 1995
Printed in 4 colors on glossy stock

5417 **Distributed Computing Monitor**
Patricia Seybold Group
Po Box 240565
Boston, MA 02129

617-742-5200
800-826-2424
Fax: 617-742-1028
E-Mail: feedback@psgroup.com
Home Page: www.psgroup.com

Patricia Seybold, Founder/CEO

The editors give advanced technologists and strategic technology architects the technical details and business perspective necessary to sell upper management on how, why and when to implement the leading edge.
Frequency: Monthly
Founded in 1978

5418 **Distributing Computing**
DC Corporation
236 W 26th Street
#7SW
New York, NY 10001-6736

212-446-9330
Home Page: www.distributedcomputing.com

Hal Avery, Publisher

Editorial includes case studies of applications, technical, management, organizational, and cultural techniques.
Frequency: Monthly
Circulation: 40000

5419 **E-doc**
Association for Information and Image Management
1100 Wayne Avenue
Suite 1100
Silver Spring, MD 20910-5603

301-587-8202
800-477-2446
Fax: 301-587-2711
E-Mail: aiim@aiim.org
Home Page: www.aiim.org

Jan Andersson, Chair
Robert Zagami, Vice Chair
Peggy Winton, Marketing Director

Association magazine on electronic document management.
Circulation: 40000
Founded in 1943

5420 **EServer Magazine**
IBM Corporation
220 S 6th Street
Suite 500
Minneapolis, MN 55402

612-339-7571
Fax: 612-336-9220
Home Page: www.eservercomputing.com

Doug Rock, Editor/Publisher
Mari Adamson-Bray, Marketing Manager
Kelly McManus, Production Manager

New products and services, technological information, and related topics that benefit the decision makers in the optimization and management of these systems are included.
80 Pages
Frequency: Monthly
Circulation: 45000
ISSN: 1074-7082
Founded in 1993
Printed in 4 colors on glossy stock

5421 **Educational Technology**
Educational Technology Publications
700 Palisade Avenue
PO Box 1564
Englewood Cliffs, NJ 07632-564

201-871-4007
800-952-2665
Fax: 201-871-4009
E-Mail: edtecpubs@aol.com
Home Page: www.bookstoread.com/etp

Lawrence Lipsitz, Publisher/Editor

Systematic design of software and applications, and their impact on the educational community worldwide. Emphasis on computer-based instruction, the Internet, multimedia, electronic performance support, television and videoconferencing.
Cost: $139.00
Frequency: Bi-annually
ISSN: 0013-1962
Founded in 1960
Printed in on glossy stock

5422 **Educational Technology Research and Development**
Association for Educational Comm and Technology
1800 N Stonelake Drive
Suite 2
Bloomington, IN 47404

812-335-7675
Fax: 812-335-7678
Home Page: www.acct.org

Mary Herring, President
Mary Beth Jordan, Secretary/Treasurer

Communcations, technology and instructional development news.
Cost: $75.00
Frequency: Quarterly
Founded in 1923

5423 **Educational Technology Review**
AACE International
PO Box 3728
Norfolk, VA 23514

757-623-7588
Fax: 703-977-8760
E-Mail: info@aace.org
Home Page: www.aace.org

Gary H Marks, Editor

Promotes the use of information technology in education. New products including software, hardware and related materials.
Cost: $38.00
Founded in 1981

5424 **Electronic Design**
Penton Media
1300 E 9th St
Suite 310
Cleveland, OH 44114-1503

216-696-7000
Fax: 216-696-6662
E-Mail: information@penton.com
Home Page: www.penton.com

Jane Cooper, Marketing
David B Nussbaum, CEO

Celebrating 50 years of innovation, this authoritative magazine provides leading-edge technical information to electronic and engineering managers around the world.
Cost: $105.00
Circulation: 145000
Founded in 1890

5425 **Embedded Systems Programming**
Miller Freeman Publications
600 Harrison Street
6th Floor
San Francisco, CA 94107

415-947-6000
Fax: 415-947-6055
Home Page: www.mfi.com

Frequency: Monthly
Circulation: 45,000
Founded in 1986

5426 **Enterprise Management Issues**
AFCOM
742 E Chapman Ave
Orange, CA 92866-1644

714-997-7966
Fax: 714-997-9743

E-Mail: afcom@afcom.com
Home Page: www.afcomchicago.com

Jill Eckhaus, President

Content includes an in-depth cover story and features on current developments and the impact of advancing technology. Regular departments are devoted to automation issues and data processing news.
Frequency: Bi-Monthly
Circulation: 4,000

5427 **European Sources and News**
SSC Group
3126 Woodley Road NW
Washington, DC 20008-3448

202-232-0822
Fax: 202-337-5354
Home Page: www.euroreseller.com

Robert Snyder, Publisher
Steve Solomon, Editor

Provides European resellers, VAR, systems integrators and OEM with information on product sources and reseller management strategies.
Circulation: 49000

5428 **Federal Computer Week**
FCW Government Technology Group
3141 Fairview Park Drive
Suite 777
Falls Church, VA 22042-4507

703-876-5100
866-293-3194
Fax: 703-876-5126
Home Page: www.fcw.com

Jeffrey Calore, General Manager, Sales & Marketing
Anne Armstrong, Publisher
John Zyskowski, Senior Editor

The markets leading newspaper for influential users and volume buyers of federal information technology.
Cost: $100.00
48 Pages
Frequency: Weekly
Circulation: 100000
Founded in 1987

5429 **Foghorn**
FOG Publications
PO Box 1030
Dixon, CA 95620-1030
Gale Rhoades, Editor

For users of 16 and 32 bit systems.
Cost: $30.00
64 Pages
Frequency: Monthly
Founded in 1985

5430 **GEOWorld**
Bel-Av Communications
359 Galahad Road
Bolingbrook, IL 60440-2108

E-Mail: tdanielson@geoplace.com
Home Page: www.geoplace.com

Jo Treadwell, VP/Group Publisher
Todd Danielson, Editor

Offers a wealth of knowledge through features, news and commentary covering the geospatial industry. Covers local and federal government, emergency management, infrastructure, natural resource management, industry trends and onnovations and much more.
Cost: $72.00
Frequency: Monthly
Circulation: 25,000

5431 **Game Developer Magazine**
Think Services
600 Harrison Street
6th Floor
San Francisco, CA 94107

Home Page: www.gdmag.com

Simon Carless, Publisher
Brandon Sheffield, Editor-In-Chief
Jeffrey Fleming, Production Editor

Written specifically for creators of entertainment software, provides technical and industry information to professional game developers. Features articles written by professional game developers on cutting-edge game development techniques in the areas of graphics and AI programming, audio design and engineering, art and animation.
Cost: $49.95
Frequency: Monthly
Circulation: 35,000
Founded in 1971

5432 **Genealogical Computing**
Ancestry
360 W 4800 N
Provo, UT 84604-5675

801-705-7000
800-262-3787
Fax: 801-705-7001
Home Page: www.myfamily.com

Timothy P Sullivan, CEO
Elizabeth Kelley Kerstens, Managing Editor
Jennifer Browning, Senior Editor

For readers who use computers and technology to organize and enhance their research into accounts of ancestries and descent.
Cost: $25.00
Frequency: Quarterly

5433 **Gilder Technology Report**
Gilder Publishing
291 Main St
Suite A
Great Barringto, MA 01230-1608

413-644-2100
Fax: 413-644-2123
E-Mail: info@gilder.com
Home Page: www.gildertech.com

George Gilder, Editor in Chief

Focuses on the ascendence of the telecoms and the centrality of the Internet.
Cost: $195.00
Frequency: Monthly
Founded in 1995

5434 **Global Technology Business**
Global Technology Business Publishing
1157 San Antonio Road
Mountain View, CA 94043
650-934-2300
Fax: 650-934-2306
Home Page: www.gtbusiness.com

Alex Vieux, Publisher
Laurence Scott, Editor
Bob Beauchamp, CEO

Emphasizes the business aspects of the global computer and communications industries through corporate strategies, financial performance, technological directions.
Frequency: Monthly
Circulation: 45000

5435 **Global Techventures Report**
Miller Freeman Publications
2655 Seely Avenue
San Jose, CA 95134

408-943-1234
Fax: 408-943-0513

Annie Feldman, Publisher

Editorial content profiles vital capital investments and start-up companies, and addresses a variety of legislation, security and communication issues as they relate to today's technology.
Frequency: SemiMonthly

5436 **Government Best Buys**
FCW Government Technology Group
3141 Fairview Park Drive
Suite 777
Falls Church, VA 22042-4507

703-876-5100
866-293-3194
Fax: 703-876-5126
Home Page: www.fcw.com

Edith Holmes, President
John Stein Monroe, Editor-in-Chief
Christopher J. Dorobek, Executive Editor

Covers the hardware and software products available to government buyers on agency contracts and the General Services Administration schedule.
Founded in 1987

5437 **Hard Copy Observer**
Lyra Research
320 Nevada Street 1st Floor
PO Box 9143
Newtonville, MA 02640-9143

617-454-2600
Fax: 617-454-2601
Home Page: www.lyra.com

Charles LeCompte, President
Ann Priede, Director of Marketing
Carolyn ODonnell, Director of Marketing

News on the latest products, market news, supplies, end-user reponse and product testing for the computer printer industry.
Cost: $617.00
80 Pages
Frequency: Monthly
Founded in 1991

5438 **Heller Report on Educational Technology Markets**
Nelson B Heller & Associates
810 S Alfred Street
#1
Alexandria, VA 22314

303-209-9410
Fax: 303-209-9444
E-Mail: info@hellerreports.com
Home Page: www.hellerreports.com

Anne Wujcik, Publisher/Managing Editor

Information on the marketing of technology and telecommunications equipment to educators at all levels.
Cost: $395.00
Frequency: Monthly
Circulation: 1,100

5439 **Home Networking News**
111 Spleen
Suite 200
Framingham, MA 01701-2000

508-663-1500
Fax: 508-663-1599
E-Mail: kmoyes@ehpub.com
Home Page: www.ehpub.com

Kenneth Moyes, CEO/Publisher
Cindy Tazis, Editor
Elizabeth Cruze, Marketing Manager
Christine Ayers, Circulation Manager
Cost: $14.95
Frequency: Monthly
Circulation: 100000
Founded in 1994

5440 **IEEE Computational Science & Engineering**
IEEE Computer Society

PO Box 3014
Los Alamitos, CA 90720-1314

714-821-8380
Fax: 714-821-4010
E-Mail: mloeb@computer.org
Home Page: computer.org

Matt Loeb, Publisher
Scott Andresen, Editor
Monette Velasco, Production Manager
Paul Croll, Treasurer
David Grier, VP Publications

Developments in computation and algorithms, high-performance evaulation, and visualization techniques in the computational science field.
Cost: $98.00
Frequency: Quarterly
Circulation: 5713
Founded in 1946

5441 **IEEE Computer**
IEEE Computer Society
10662 Los Vaqueros Circle
PO Box 3014
Los Alamitos, CA 90720-1314

714-218-8380
800-272-6657
Fax: 714-821-4010
E-Mail: aburgess@computer.org
Home Page: www.computer.org

Angela Burgess, Executive Director
Marilyn Potes, Managing Editor
Rakesh Gupta, Editor in Chief
Paul Croll, Treasurer
David Grier, VP Publications

Examines a wide range of computer-related technologies. Written and refereed by experts, it features articles on the latest developments in computer technology, applications and research in the computer field.
Cost: $37.00
Circulation: 85930
Founded in 1946

5442 **IEEE Computer Graphics and Applications**
IEEE Computer Society
10662 Los Vaqueros Circle
PO Box 3014
Los Alamitos, CA 90720-1314

714-821-8380
800-272-6657
Fax: 714-821-4010
E-Mail: help@computer.org
Home Page: www.computer.org/

Angela Burgess, Executive Director
Sandy Brown, Marketing Director
Robin Baldwin, Managing Editor
Christine Kelly, Staff Editor
Tammi Titsworth, Staff Editor

Focuses on the design and use of computer graphics and systems. Addresses topics such as solid modeling, animation, CAD/CAM, tools for rendering graphics and graphics in medicine, science and business.
Cost: $70.00
Circulation: 10028
Founded in 1946

5443 **IEEE Computer Society of Computing Software Magazine**
Po Box 3014
Los Alamitos, CA 90720-1314

714-821-8380
Fax: 714-821-4010
E-Mail: volunteer.services@computer.org
Home Page: www.computer.org

Angela Burgess, Executive Director
Warren Harrison, Treasurer
Paul Croll, Treasurer
David Grier, VP Publications

Offers information on the latest software programs for computer professionals.
Circulation: 10000
Founded in 1945

5444 **IEEE Expert**
IEEE Computer Society
10662 Los Vaqueros Circle
PO Box 3014
Los Alamitos, CA 90720

714-821-8380
800-272-6657
Fax: 714-821-4010
E-Mail: volunteer.services@computer.org
Home Page: www.computer.org

Crystal Shif, Managing Editor
Angela Burgess, Executive Director
Matthew Bertholf, Advertising Manager
Sandy Brown, Senior Business Development Manager
Paul Croll, Treasurer

Accepts advertising.
Cost: $58.00
Circulation: 3,463
Founded in 1986

5445 **IEEE Intelligent Systems**
IEEE Computer Society
10662 Los Vaqueros Circle
PO Box 3014
Los Alamitos, CA 90720-1314

714-821-8380
800-272-6657
Fax: 714-821-4010
E-Mail: volunteer.services@computer.org
Home Page: www.computer.org

Angela Burgess, Executive Director
Paul Croll, Treasurer
Doris L Carver, Editor-in-Chief
David Grier, VP Publications

Features emphasize advanced research that is ready to be used in the real world. Departments include interviews, books and product reviews, opinion pieces, and conference calendars.
Cost: $47.00
Circulation: 15355
Founded in 1946

5446 **IEEE Network**
Institute of Electrical & Electronics Engineers
3 Park Ave
17th Floor
New York, NY 10016-5997

212-419-7900
Fax: 212-752-4929
E-Mail: society-info@ieee.org
Home Page: www.ieee.org

Daniel J Senese, CEO
Dr. Warren Gifford, Editor

Technical magazine serving both users and designers of multimedia hardware, software and systems in industry, business, academia and the arts.
Circulation: 14388
Founded in 1871

5447 **IEEE Transactions on Computers**
IEEE Computer Society
10662 Los Vaqueros Circle
PO Box 3014
Los Alamitos, CA 90720

714-821-8380
Fax: 714-821-4010
E-Mail: help@computer.org
Home Page: www.computer.org

Jean-Luc Gaudidt, Editor-in-Chief
Angela Burgess, Treasurer
Paul Croll, Treasurer
David Grier, VP Publications

Includes technical research reports and papers on the theory, design and applications of computer systems.
Cost: $72.00
Frequency: Monthly
Circulation: 8000
Founded in 1979

5448 **ISACA Journal**
Information Systems Audit & Control Association
3701 Algonquin Rd
Suite 1010
Rolling Meadows, IL 60008-3124

847-253-1545
Fax: 847-253-1443
E-Mail: publication@isaca.org
Home Page: www.isaca.org

Susan Caldwell, CEO

Provides professional development information to those spearheading IT governance and those involved with information systems audit, control and security
Cost: $75.00
Circulation: 35000
Founded in 1969
Printed in 4 colors

5449 **ISR: Intelligent Systems Report**
Lionheart Publishing
2555 Cumberland Pkwy SE
Suite 299
Atlanta, GA 30339-3921

770-432-2551
Fax: 770-432-6969
E-Mail: llewellyn@lionhrtpub.com
Home Page: www.lionhrtpub.com

John Llewellyn, Publisher
Marvin Diamond, Advertising Sales Manager

Provides an in-depth look into the integration and application of advanced decision support technologies including artificial intelligence, speech recognition, neural networks, fuzzy logic, expert systems, multimedia and virtual reality, and artificial life.
Frequency: Monthly

5450 **Imaging World**
American Business Media
1300 Virginia Drive
Suite 400
Fort Washington, PA 19034-3297

215-643-8000
Fax: 215-643-8159
Home Page: www.boucher1.com

Robert Boucher Jr, President/CEO
Dan Marsh, Publisher, Eyecare Business
Stephanie De Long, Editor-in-Chief, Eyecare

Serves the needs of vendors wishing to reach the North American market for electronic imaging and document-based information management and workflow.
Frequency: Monthly
Circulation: 75000
Founded in 1997

5451 **InTech Computing Magazine**
ISA Services
67 Alexander Drive
PO Box 12277
Research Triangle Park, NC 27709

919-549-8411
Fax: 919-549-8288
E-Mail: info@isa.org
Home Page: www.isa.org

Gregory Hale, Editor
Richard T Simpson, Publisher

Key source of information on automating manufacturing processes.
Cost: $45.00
Frequency: Monthly
Founded in 1945
Printed in 4 colors on glossy stock

5452 **Info Log Magazine**
BBS Press Service
785-286-4272
Fax: 239-992-4862
Alan Bechtold, Editor
A comprehensive magazine offering the latest information on aspects of the computer industry.
Frequency: Monthly
Founded in 1982

5453 **Information Display**
Ste 114
1475 S Bascom Ave
Campbell, CA 95008-0628
408-977-1013
Fax: 408-977-1531
E-Mail: office@sid.org
Home Page: www.sid.org
Ken Werner, Editor
Jenny Needham, Circulation Manager
Shigeo Nikoshiba, CEO/President
A magazine published by the Society for Information Display.
Cost: $55.00
Frequency: Monthly
Circulation: 12000
Founded in 1964

5454 **Information Management Magazine**
ARMA International
11880 College Blvd
Suite 450
Overland Park, KS 66215
913-341-3808
800-422-2762
Fax: 913-341-3742
E-Mail: hq@arma.org
Home Page: www.arma.org
Marilyn Bier, Executive Director
Jody Becker, Associate Editor
The leading source of information on topics and issues central to the management of records and information worldwide. Each issue features insightful articles written by experts in the management of records and information.
Cost: $115.00
Frequency: Bi-monthly
Circulation: 11000
ISSN: 1535-2897
Mailing list available for rent: 9000 names
Printed in 4 colors on glossy stock

5455 **Information Systems Management**
Auerbach Publications
3701 Algonquin Road
Suite 1010
Rolling Meadows, IL 60008
847-253-1545
Fax: 847-253-1443
E-Mail: publication@isaca.org
Home Page: www.isaca.org
Debra Cutts, Marketing
Jen Blader, Editorial
Susan Caldwell, CEO
Coverage includes information technology developments and business applications, financial issues, IS staff development, and relationships with business management.
Cost: $75.00
Frequency: Bi-monthly
Circulation: 40,000
ISSN: 1058-0530
Founded in 1969

5456 **Information World Review**
143 Old Marlton Pike
Medford, NJ 08055-8750
609-654-7777
Fax: 609-654-4309
Offers a full overview of the computer industry overseas.

5457 **InformationWEEK**
CMP Publications
600 Community Dr
Manhasset, NY 11030-3810
516-562-5000
Fax: 516-562-5036
E-Mail: llally@cmp.com
Home Page: www.cmp.com
Stephanie Stahl, Editor-in-Chief
Mike Friedenberg, Publisher
For information systems management.
Frequency: Weekly
Circulation: 440,000
Founded in 1985

5458 **Infostor**
PennWell Publishing Company
98 Spit Brook Rd
Nashua, NH 03062-5737
603-891-0123
Fax: 603-891-9294
E-Mail: mark@pennwell.com
Home Page: www.pennwell.com
Christine Shaw, VP
Jill Davis, Marketing Communications
News and information for enterprise storage professionals.
Cost: $120.00
Frequency: Monthly
Circulation: 38000
Founded in 1997

5459 **Infoworld Magazine**
Infoworld
501 Second Street
San Francisco, CA 94107
847-291-5217
E-Mail: feedback@infoworld.com
Home Page: www.infoworld.com/
Bob Ostrow, President/Publisher
Paul Calento, VP Marketing
Kevin McKean, Chairman
Steve Fox, Editor-in-Chief
Kathy Badertscher, Executive Managing Editor
Offers information for computer professionals.
Frequency: Weekly

5460 **Inside DPMA**
Data Processing Management Association
505 Busse Highway
Park Ridge, IL 60068-3143
847-825-0880
Fax: 847-825-1693
Paul Zuziak, Editor
A monthly newspaper for the DPMA and the information management profession. Accepts advertising.
Cost: $16.00
Frequency: Monthly
Founded in 1988

5461 **Inside Technology Training**
Ziff Davis Publishing Company
500 Unicorn Park Drive
Woburn, MA 01801
781-938-2600
E-Mail: editor@itrain.com
Home Page: www.itrain.com/
Nancy J Weingarten, Publisher
Targets management level executives, technology trainers, information technology training managers, CIO's and independent training consultants. Includes reports on new software, new media and new career paths. Also features designed to help training managers create and successfully implement strategy training and reskilling programs that anyone on any level can use.
Frequency: 10 per year
Circulation: 40,000

5462 **Inside Visual Basic**
ZD Journals
500 Canal View Boulevard
Rochester, NY 14623-2800
585-407-7301
Fax: 585-240-7760
Home Page: www.zdjournals.com
Jon Pyles, Publisher
Authors discuss subjects covering the building and creating of external objects, as well as topics surrounding class development. The publication informs readers of Visual Basic online resources, and addresses real world questions reagrding controls written in the program, uses of the status bar and extending functions capabilities.
Frequency: Monthly

5463 **Integrated System Design**
Verecom Group
954 San Rafael Avenue
Mountain View, CA 94043-1926
650-988-9677
Home Page: www.isdmag.com
James Uhl, Publisher
Richard Wallace, VP
Articles are written by designers who explain unique methods for solving design challenges. Publication supplies information on design methodologies and the use of tools and semiconductor capabilities.
Frequency: Monthly
Circulation: 58082

5464 **Intelligent Enterprise**
Miller Freeman Publications
411 Boral Avenue
#100
San Mateo, CA 94402-3522
650-573-3210
Fax: 650-655-4350
Home Page: www.intelligententerprise.com
David Kalman, Publisher
Each issue provides detailed analyses of the products, trends and strategies that help accelerate the creation of the enterprise's information infrastructure. Topics include: business intelligence; enterprise resource planning; knowledge management; transaction processing and performance monitoring; applications and systems management.
Frequency: 18 per year
Circulation: 103,000

5465 **Interactions**
Association for Computing Machinery
2 Penn Plz
Suite 701
New York, NY 10121-0799
212-868-5716
800-342-6626
Fax: 212-944-1318
E-Mail: acmhelp@acm.org
Home Page: www.acm.org
Mark Mandelbaum, Director Publication
Jonathan Arnowitz, Editors in Chief
Editorial content covers business, design, methods and tools, book previews, conference

previews and current events pertaining to designers, developers and researchers.
Founded in 1947

5466 International Journal of IT Standards and Standardization Research
Information Resources Management Association
701 E Chocolate Ave
Suite 200
Hershey, PA 17033-1240
717-533-8879
Fax: 717-533-8661
E-Mail: members@irma-international.org
Home Page: www.irma-international.org
Jan Travers, Executive Director
Koichi Asatani, Associate Editors
Carl Cargill, Associate Editor
Tineke Egyedi, Associate Editor
Richard Hawkins, Associate Editor
An authoritative source and information outlet for the diverse community of IT standards researchers, publishing research findings with the goal of advancing knowledge and research in all aspects of IT standards and standardization in modern organizations.
Cost: $115.00
Frequency: Semi-Annual
ISSN: 1539 3062

5467 International Journal of Information and Communication Technology Education
Information Resources Management Association
701 E Chocolate Ave
Suite 200
Hershey, PA 17033-1240
717-533-8879
Fax: 717-533-8861
E-Mail: member@irma-international.org
Home Page: www.irma-international.org
Jan Travers, Executive Director
Tonya Barrier, Associate Editor
Dencho Batanov, Associate Editor
David Carbonara, Associate Editor
Martin Crossland, Associate Editor
Includes new applications of technology for teaching and learning, and document those practices that contribute irrefutable verification of information technology education as a discipline.
Cost: $115.00
Frequency: Quarterly
ISSN: 1550-1876
Printed in

5468 Interpersonal Computing and Technology Journal
Association for Educational Comm and Technology
1800 N Stonelake Drive
Suite 2
Bloomington, IN 47404
812-335-7675
Fax: 812-335-7678
Home Page: www.aect.org
Mary Herring, President
Mary Beth Jordan, Secretary/Treasurer
The focus is on computer-mediated communication, and the pedagogical issues surrounding the use of computers and technology in educational settings.
Frequency: 2-4 times a year

5469 Iris Universe: Magazine of Visual Computing
Silicon Graphics
1500 Crittenden Lane
Mountain View, CA 94043
650-960-1980
800-800-7441
Fax: 650-932-6102
Home Page: www.sgi.com
Warren C Pratt, CEO/President
Gaye Graves, Features Editor
Anne Marie Gambelin, Publisher
Dominic Martinelli, Chief Information Officer
Written to appeal to all users of computer visualization, from the most technically oriented to the novice. Devoted to cutting edge techniques and technology used and presents the best in new products available.
Frequency: Quarterly
Founded in 1981

5470 Journal of American Society for Information Science
John Wiley & Sons
111 River St
Hoboken, NJ 07030-5790
201-748-6000
Fax: 201-748-6088
E-Mail: info@wiley.com
Home Page: www.wiley.com
William J Pesce, CEO
Richard M Hochhauser, CEO
Communications, management, applications, economics, and other news of interest in the science field.
Cost: $95.00
72 Pages
Frequency: Bi-Monthly

5471 Journal of Imaging Science and Technology
Society for Imaging Science & Technology
7003 Kilworh Lane
Springfield, VA 22151-4088
703-642-9090
Fax: 703-642-9094
E-Mail: info@imaging.org
Home Page: www.imaging.org
George T.C. Chin, Editor
Donna Smith, Managing Editor
Provides the imaging community documentation of a broad range of research, development, and applications in imaging. The selection of papers reflects the role of IS&T as the window on imaging, promoting communication and understanding across the boundaries of the many disciplines involved in modern imaging.
Cost: $95.00
Circulation: 2000
ISSN: 1062-3701
Founded in 1947

5472 Journal of Interactive Learning Research
AACE International
1 Morton Drive
Suite 500
Charlottesville, VA 22903
434-977-5029
Fax: 434-977-5431
E-Mail: info@aace.org
Home Page: www.aace.org
John Self, Editor
Reports on the research, developments, applications, and integration of intelligent computer technologies in education.
Frequency: Quarterly
Circulation: 3M

5473 Journal of Object-Oriented Programming
SIGS Publications
9121 Oakdale Avenue
Chatsworth, CA 91311
818-734-1520
Fax: 818-734-1522
Home Page: www.101com.com
Richard S Weiner, Editor
Mike Valenti, Executive Vice President
Provides an international forum for research, developments, applications, and new products in the field.
Circulation: 3,50,000
Founded in 1998

5474 KM World
Information Today
143 Old Marlton Pike
Medford, NJ 08055-8750
609-654-6266
800-300-9868
Fax: 609-654-4309
E-Mail: custserv@infotoday.com
Home Page: www.infotoday.com
Thomas H Hogan, President
Roger R Bilboul, Chairman of the Board
Serves the knowledge management industry by offering components and processes, including success stories, designed to improve business.
Cost: $23.95
Mailing list available for rent: 4M names
Printed in 4 colors on glossy stock

5475 LAN Magazine
Miller Freeman Publications
600 Harrison Street
6th Fl
San Francisco, CA 94107
415-947-6000
Fax: 415-947-6055
Home Page: www.mfi.com
Covers Local Area Networks.
Cost: $20.00
180 Pages
Frequency: Monthly
Founded in 1986

5476 Law Office Computing
James Publishing
PO Box 25202
Santa Ana, CA 92799-5202
714-755-5450
Fax: 714-751-5508
E-Mail: jamessale@jamespublishig.com
Home Page: www.jamespublishing.com
Jamie Tyo, Managing Editor
Amanda Flatten, Editor & Publisher
Jim Pawell, Marketing and Circulation
Legal software reviews, productivity enhancing tips and resources to improve law office automation.
Cost: $39.00
Founded in 1981

5477 Learning and Leading with Technology
International Society for Technology in Education
180 W 8th Avenue
Eugene, OR 97401-2916
541-302-3777
800-336-5191
Fax: 541-302-3778
E-Mail: iste@iste.org
Home Page: www.iste.org
Don Knezek, CEO
Leslie Conery, Deputy CEO
Authors and teachers include school and state administrators, classroom and lab teachers, tech coordinators, and teachers educators. Most are involved in tech-purcahsing decisions for their school and district. Every issue of L&L in-

cludes: a feature subject of broad appeal, articles about using tech in specific subject areas, lesson plans, reproducible worksheets, professional development advice, and referral to supplementary information on the L&L web site at www.iste.org.
Cost: $89.00
Circulation: 17000
ISSN: 1082-5754
Founded in 1989

5478 **Library Software Review**
Sage Publications
Vanderbilt University
419 21st Avenue S
Nashville, TN 37240-0001

615-343-6094
Fax: 615-343-8834
E-Mail: info@sagepub.com
Home Page: www.sagepub.com

Marshall Breeding, Editor

Provides the library professional with information necessary to make intelligent software evaluation, procurement, integration and installation decisions. Issues review software and software books and periodicals.
Cost: $52.00
Frequency: Quarterly
Circulation: 1M

5479 **Link-Up Digital**
Information Today
143 Old Marlton Pike
Medford, NJ 08055-8750

609-654-6266
800-300-9868
Fax: 609-654-4309
E-Mail: custserv@infotoday.com
Home Page: www.infotoday.com

Thomas H Hogan, President
Roger R Bilboul, Chairman Of The Board

A web-only product featuring articles, reviews and more for users and producers of electronic information products and services.
Mailing list available for rent: 4M names
Printed in 4 colors on glossy stock

5480 **MD Computing**
Springer Verlag
175 5th Ave
New York, NY 10010-7703

212-477-8200
Fax: 212-473-6272
Home Page: www.mdcomputing.com

Nhora Cortes-Comerer, Executive Editor
Kelley Suttenfield, Assistant Editor

Provides comprehensive and up-to-date information about the various segments of medical and healthcare informatics, such as clinical computing, health care information and delivery systems, telemedicine, radiology, and many others.
Cost: $69.00
74 Pages
Frequency: Bi-Monthly
Circulation: 19,771
ISSN: 0724-6811
Printed in 4 colors on glossy stock

5481 **MacWeek**
MacWorld Communications
501 2nd St
San Francisco, CA 94107-1496

415-243-0505
Fax: 415-442-0766

Mike Kisseberth, CEO
David Ezequelle, Publisher
Rick Lepage, President

Covers Apple's Macintosh computers. Accepts advertising.
Cost: $99.00
72 Pages
Frequency: 44 per year
Founded in 1987

5482 **MacWorld Magazine**
Mac Publishing
501 2nd St
San Francisco, CA 94107-1496

415-243-0505
Fax: 415-442-0766
E-Mail: letters@macworld.com
Home Page: www.macworld.com

Mike Kisseberth, CEO
Dan Miller, Executive Editor
Scholle Sawyer McFarland, Senior Editor
Dan Frakes, Senior Writer

The ultimate resource for Mac professionals and savvy Mac users. Each issue is packed with practical how-tos, in-depth features, the latest troubleshooting tips and tricks, industry news, future trends and more.
Cost: $19.97
Frequency: Year Subscription

5483 **Marketing Computers**
V&U
770 Broadway
F18
New York, NY 10003-9595

646-654-5000
Fax: 646-654-5374
Home Page: www.marketingcomputers.com

Donna Tapellini, Editor
Tony DiCamillo, Publisher

Edited for advertising and marketing executives in the high-tech industries. The publication covers interpretive news, timely big picture features, departments and analysis by staff editors and industry experts.
Cost: $149.00
100 Pages
Frequency: Weekly
Circulation: 15484

5484 **Mobile Office**
4845 West 111th Street
Alsip, IL 60658

708-636-5400
Fax: 708-636-8637
E-Mail: sales@mobileofficeinc.com
Home Page: mobileofficeinc.com

Jeff Hecox, Editor

Office equipment, computer technology and information.

5485 **Motion System Distributor**
Penton Media
1300 E 9th St
Cleveland, OH 44114-1503

216-696-7000
Fax: 216-696-6662
E-Mail: information@penton.com
Home Page: www.penton.com

Jane Cooper, Marketing
David B. Nussbaum, CEO
Larry Berardinis, Editor

Provides selling and technical information to individuals and distributors, specializing in power transmission, motion control and fluid products.
Frequency: Monthly
Circulation: 54000
Founded in 1892

5486 **NCR Connection**
Publications & Communications
505 Cypress Creek Road
Suite B
Cedar Park, TX 78613

512-250-9023
Fax: 512-331-3900

Mary Wilson, Editor

For users of NCR computer systems.
Cost: $92.00
32 Pages
Frequency: Monthly
Founded in 1983

5487 **NEWS 3X/400**
Duke Communications International
221 E 29th Street
Loveland, CO 80538-2769

970-634-4700
Fax: 970-667-2321

Tim Fixmer, Publisher
Trish Faubion, Editor

Leading technical journal for IBM Systems.
Cost: $119.00
220 Pages
Frequency: 16 per year
Circulation: 31,000
Founded in 1982

5488 **Network Support Magazine**
Technical Enterprises
7044 S 13th Street
Oak Creek, WI 53154-1429

414-768-8000
Fax: 414-768-8001
E-Mail: customercare@naspa.com
Home Page: www.naspa.com

Denise Rockhill, Publisher/Advertising Sales
Rachael Zimmerman, Editor
Matthew Jossart, Art Director

The most comprehensive how to publication in the industry. Orientedtoward professionals involved with a myriad of computing technologies and discusses the topic of importance in mainframe, host based and network oriented environments.
Cost: $5.00
68 Pages
Frequency: Monthly
Circulation: 50,000
Founded in 1987

5489 **Network World**
Network World
118 Turnpike Road
Southborough, MA 01772-9108

508-756-6400
800-622-1108
Fax: 508-460-1192
Home Page: www.networkworld.com

Evilee T Ebb, CEO/Publisher
John Gallant, CFO
Dylan Smith, CFO

For network IS professionals with direct responsibility for planning and managing their companies network computing environment.
Cost: $129.00
100 Pages
Frequency: Weekly
Circulation: 170,000
Founded in 1986

5490 **Newmedia Age**
HyperMedia Communications
PO Box 299
Brooklin, ME 04616

207-359-6573
800-935-0040
Fax: 207-359-9809
E-Mail: support@hypernet.com

Ben Calica, Editor

Covers new products and technology trends in audio and video computing.
Cost: $24.00
Frequency: Quarterly
Circulation: 40,000

5491 **OfficeWorld News**
366 Ramtown Greenville Road
Howell, NJ 07731-2789

732-785-5976
Fax: 732-785-1347

William Urban, Publisher
Kim Chandlee McCabe, Editor-in-Chief

Provides a diverse population of business products resellers the news and information to best serve the needs of small, mid and large business customers. Provides insight into partnering with their peers in this diverse marketplace.
Frequency: Monthly
Circulation: 31,500
Printed in 4 colors on glossy stock

5492 **PC Arcade**
Softdisk Publishing
606 Common Street
Shreveport, LA 71101-3437

318-218-8718
Fax: 318-221-8870

Al Vekovius, President
Ronda Farries, Circulation Director

Publisher of software subscriptions for DOS, Windows and Macintosh computers.
Cost: $19.95
Frequency: Monthly
Founded in 1990

5493 **PC Sources**
Ziff Davis Publishing Company
500 Unicorn Park Drive
Woburn, MA 01801

781-938-2600
Fax: 781-938-2626
E-Mail: info@ziffdavis.com
Home Page: www.ziffdavis.com

Peter McKie, Editor
Robert F Callahan, CEO
Michael J Miller, Editor-in-chief
Stephen Hicks, General Counsel

Serves experienced PC users.
Cost: $149.75
Frequency: Monthly
Founded in 1985

5494 **PC Systems and Support**
Technical Enterprises
7044 S 13th Street
Oak Creek, WI 53154

414-325-3366
Fax: 414-768-8001

Scott Sherer, President
Amy Birschbach, Editor

Offers solutions with tutorials on hardware and software implementation/upgrade techniques, workstation customization, integration and optimization. The how-to material presented each month guides those professionals in evaluating, selecting, acquiring, implementing, and supporting PC distributed resources. Presents in-depth technical information that can be applied at work.

5495 **PC Techniques**
Coriolis Group
14455 N Hyden Road
Suite 220
Scottsdale, AZ 85260

480-483-0192

Keith Weiskamp, Publisher
Jeff Duntemann, Editor

Covers information on a wide variety of computer systems and language technology.
Cost: $22.00
104 Pages
Frequency: Bi-Monthly
Founded in 1990

5496 **Pen Computing Magazine**
Aeon Publishing Group
PO Box 408
Plainview, NY 11803-0408

Home Page: www.pencomputing.com

Conrad H Blickenstorfer, Editor-in-Chief
Howard Borgen, Publisher
Wayne Laslo, Advertising Manager

In-depth coverage of pen technology, wireless communications and mobile computing.
Cost: $18.00
Frequency: Monthly
Circulation: 79515
Founded in 1993

5497 **Physicians & Computers**
Moorhead Publications
600 S Waukegan Road
#200
Lake Forest, IL 60045-2672

847-615-8333
Home Page: www.physicians-computers.com

Tom Moorhead, Publisher

Provides physicians with information on computer advances helpful in the private practice of medicine. Practice management, current medical and nonmedical software, computer diagnostics, etc.
Cost: $50.00
Frequency: Monthly

5498 **Powerbuilding Developer's Journal**
SYS-CON Publications
135 Chestnut Ridge Rd
Montvale, NJ 07645-1152

201-782-9600
800-513-7111
Fax: 201-782-9601
Home Page: www.powerbuilderjournal.com

Fuat Kircaali, Publisher

Covers provide an advanced look at Powerbuilder techniques, new products, reader feedback and interaction, and training in the Powerbuilder language.
Frequency: Monthly
Circulation: 20000

5499 **Precision Engineering Journal**
Elsevier Science Publishing
6277 Sea Harbor Drive
Orlando, FL 32887-4800

407-345-4020
877-839-7126
Fax: 407-363-1354
E-Mail: usjcs@elsevier.com
Home Page: www.elsevier.com /www.aspe.net

W T Estler, Editor-in-Chief
D G Chetwynd, Editor
T. Moriwaki, Co-Editor
Bill Godfrey, Chief Information Officer

Provides an integrated approach to all subjects related to the development, design, manufacture, and application of high-precision machines, systems, and components. International news, reviews, conference reports, informed comment, and a calendar of forthcoming events complete the spectrum of coverage designed to keep readers abreast with a fast-moving technology.
Cost: $1014.00
ISSN: 0141-6359
Founded in 1979

5500 **Processor**
Peed Corporation
PO Box 85518
Lincoln, NE 68501-5518

402-479-2141
800-819-9014
Fax: 402-479-2120
E-Mail: feedback@processor.com
Home Page: www.processor.com

Susy Miller, Publisher
Rhonda Peed, CEO

Information on computer products and services.
Cost: $26.00
84 Pages
Frequency: Weekly
Founded in 1978

5501 **Products for Document Management**
Acron Publishing
1306 Gaskins Road
Richmond, VA 23233-4919

804-754-2101
Fax: 804-754-1534

Irwin Posner, Publisher

News and reviews of latest technology and applications for document management world, including hardware, software, supplies and services.
Frequency: Quarterly
Circulation: 10.963

5502 **Pure Java Developer's Journal**
ZD Journals
500 Canal View Boulevard
Rochester, NY 14623-2800

585-407-7301
Fax: 585-240-7760
E-Mail: purejavadj@zdjournals.com
Home Page: www.elementkjournal.com

Jon Pyles, Publisher

Offers tips for Java developers and answers questions regarding serving side and the aspects of BeanInfo, writing, and mathematical equations
Frequency: Monthly

5503 **RIS/Retail Info Systems News**
Edgell Communications
4 Middlebury Boulevard
Randolph, NJ 07869-4221

973-252-0100
Fax: 973-252-9020
Home Page: www.risnews.com

Andrew Gaffney, Publisher
Jeff Zabe, Circualtion Manager
Gabriele A. Edgell, CEO
Gerald C Ryerson, President

Updates on the latest development in retail management technologies with articles that focus on the application of managerial and hi-tech advancements.
Frequency: Monthly
Founded in 1984
Printed in 4 colors on glossy stock

5504 **RTC**
RTC Group
27312 Calle Arroyo
San Juan Capistrano, CA 92675-2768

949-443-4400
Fax: 949-489-8502
E-Mail: johnr@rtcgroup.com
Home Page: www.rtcgroup.com

John Reardo, Publisher

Provides information to answer real life questions about the open systems computer market.

Also news, product updates, tech updates and standard tracking.
Frequency: Monthly
Circulation: 29,500

5505 Real Time Graphics
Computer Graphic Systems Development Corporation
2483 Old Middlefield Way
#140
Mountain View, CA 94043-2330
650-903-4920
Fax: 650-967-5252
Home Page: www.cgsd.com
Roy Latham, Owner
In-depth information on the technology of real time graphics, VR, simulations and coverage of industry news.
Cost: $205.00
Frequency: Monthly
Circulation: 1M

5506 Real-Time Engineering
Micrology PBT
2618 S Shannon
Tempe, AZ 85282-2936
480-967-5581
Fax: 480-968-3446
E-Mail: micrology@aol.com
Home Page: www.realtime-engineering.com
John Black, Editor-in-Chief
Focuses on software and operating systems.
Frequency: Quarterly
Circulation: 10,000

5507 Red Herring: The Business of Technology
Red Herring Communications
1550 Bryant St
Suite 450
San Francisco, CA 94103-4832
415-486-2819
Fax: 415-865-2280
E-Mail: info@redherring.com
Home Page: www.redherring.com

5508 Report on Healthcare Information Management
Aspen Publishers
1101 King Street
#444
Alexandria, VA 22314
703-683-4100
Fax: 703-739-6517
Home Page: www.healthcarenet.com
Mike Brown, Publisher
H. Stephen Lieber, CEO/President
Timothy B Clark, Marketing & Business Dev
System development, clinical information systems, cost-effective clinical integration, data collection, network security and confidentiality for the health care industry.
Cost: $358.00
Frequency: Monthly

5509 Retail Systems Alert
Retail Systems Alert Group
377 Elliot Street
PO Box 332
Newton Upper Falls, MA 02464
617-527-4626
Fax: 617-527-8102
Home Page: www.retailsystems.com
Tom Friedman, President
Hideo Funamoto, Contributing Editor
Provides updated information on automation news and trends, including decision systems, information systems implementation, in-store merchandise management, and case studies of retailers.
Cost: $295.00
8 Pages
Frequency: Monthly
Founded in 1988

5510 Retail Systems Reseller
Edgell Communications
4 Middlebury Boulevard
Suite 1
Randolph, NJ 07869-1111
973-252-0100
Fax: 973-252-9020
Home Page: www.edgellcommunications.com
michael Kachmar, Publisher
Joe Skorupa, Editor-in-Chief
Gabriele Edgell, CEO
Gerald C. Ryerson, President
John Chiego, Vice President
Offers information to retailers, dealers, systems integraters, VARs, VADs, etc., on retail technology for small to mid-size retailers.
Cost: $190.00
Frequency: Monthly
Founded in 1984

5511 RetailTech
Progressive Grocer Associates
23 Old King's Highway South
Darien, CT 06820-4538
646-654-7561
Fax: 203-656-3800
E-Mail: info@progressivegrocer.com
Home Page: www.progressivegrocer.com
John Failla, Publisher
Jenny McTaggart, Senior Editor
Stephen Dowdell, Editor-in-Chief
Joseph Tarnowski, Tech Editor, Equipment & Design
Editoral content covers software, computer peripherals, communications, electronic retailing, point-of-sale systems, networking, data warehousing, logistics/distribution systems, and the Internet.
Cost: $99.00
Frequency: Monthly

5512 Robot Explorer
Appropriate Solutions
85 Grove Street
PO Box 458
Peterborough, NH 03458
603-924-6079
Fax: 603-924-8668
E-Mail: asi@appropriatesolutions.com
Home Page: www.appropriatesolutions.com
Raymond Cote, Editor
Targets the world of non-industrial robots. From eight-legged walking machines exploring Antarctic volcanoes, to microscopic nano-machines, Robot Explorer provides practical construction details and fascinating reviews of current technology.
Cost: $14.95
Circulation: 500

5513 SCO Magazine
600 Community Drive
Manhasset, NY 11030-3847
516-562-5836
Fax: 516-562-5466
H Newton Barrett, Publisher

5514 SIGNAL Magazine
4400 Fair Lakes Center
Fairfax, VA 22033-3899
703-631-6100
800-336-4583
Fax: 703-631-6169
E-Mail: bmowery@afcea.org
Home Page: www.afcea.org
Beverly Mowery, Associate Publisher
Robert K Ackerman, Editor-in-Chief
A news magazine targeted to serve the critical information needs of government, military and industry professionals active in the fields of command, control, communications, computers, intelligence, surveillance and reconnaissance, or C4ISR; information security; research and development; electronics; and homeland security.
Cost: $56.00
Frequency: Monthly/Year Subscription
Mailing list available for rent

5515 SQL Forum Online
Informant Communications Group
10519 E Stockton Boulevard
Suite 100
Elk Grove, CA 95624-9703
916-863-3700
Fax: 916-379-0610
Home Page: www.informant.com
Forrest Freeman, Owner
Tom Bondur, Publisher
Written for data-base professionals to share and exchange ideas. Has papers and articles that are filled with answers to common data-base questions.
Frequency: Monthly

5516 Sawtooth News
Sawtooth Technologies
1500 Skokie Boulevard
Suite 510
Northbrook, IL 60062
847-239-7300
Fax: 847-239-7301
E-Mail: info@sawtooth.com
Home Page: www.sawtooth.com
Nicole Garneau, Editor
Articles on computer aided telephone interviewing, computer interviewing, conjoint analysis, and other advanced research techniques.
Founded in 1995

5517 Scan Tech News
Reed Business Information
2000 Clearwater Dr
Oak Brook, IL 60523-8809
630-574-0825
Fax: 630-288-8781
Home Page: www.reedbusiness.com
Jeff Greisch, President
Updates in trends in ADC technology and standards, the latest news from leading industry events, and product developments that streamline the flow of essential information in industrial settings.
Frequency: Monthly
Circulation: 82M

5518 Scan: Data Capture Report
Corry Publishing
5905 Beacon Hill Lane
Erie, PA 16509
814-380-0025
Fax: 814-864-2037
E-Mail: rickm@scandcr.com
Home Page: www.rmgenterprises.com/
Larry Roberts, CEO and Publisher
(Jon) Rick Morgan, President and Editor
Developments in bar code scanning, biometric identification, electronic commerce and areas of automatic data capture.
Cost: $597.00
Frequency: Fortnightly
Founded in 1996

5519 **Scientific Computing & Automation**
Reed Business Information
2000 Clearwater Dr
Oak Brook, IL 60523-8809

630-574-0825
Fax: 630-288-8781
E-Mail: mlally@cahners.com
Home Page: www.reedbusiness.com

Jeff Greisch, President

Provides the scientists working in industrial/analytical labs, clinical labs, life science labs and electronics R&D labs with information on developments in computing and automation technology for the laboratory.
Cost: $60.00
Frequency: Monthly
Circulation: 50,059

5520 **Scientific Computing & Instrumentation**
Reed Business Information
45 E 85th St
4th Floor
New York, NY 10028-0957

212-772-8300
Fax: 630-288-8686
E-Mail: subsmail@reedbusiness.com
Home Page: www.scimag.com

Lawrence S Reed
Suzanne Tracy, Editor in Chief

5521 **Semiconductor Magazine**
Semiconductor Equipment & Materials International
3081 Zanker Road
San Jose, CA 95134

408-943-6900
Fax: 408-428-9600
E-Mail: semihq@semi.org
Home Page: www.semi.org

T Buehler, Editor-in-Chief
Chris Bucholtz, Editor
Marie Claussell, Circulation Manager
Barbara Wietzel, Marketing Manager

Covers the technical and business information needs of inportant worldwide semiconductor manufacturers, including captive manufacturers, merchant manufacturers, research and development laboratories, equipment suppliers, government/military installations and consortiums.
Cost: $125.00
Frequency: Monthly
Founded in 1980

5522 **Sensors Magazine**
Advanstar Communications
275 Grove Street
Suite 2-130
Newton, MA 02466

603-924-5400
Fax: 603-924-5401
Home Page: www.sensormag.com

Barbara Goode, Group Editorial Director
Stephanie Henkel, Executive Editor
Jill Thiry, Group Publishing Director

Source among design and production engineers of information on sensor technologies and products, and topic integral to sensor-based systems and applications. Provides practical and in-depth yet accessible information on sensor operation, design, application, and implementation within systems. Covers the effective use of state-of-the-art resources and tools that enable readers to get the maximum benefit from their use of sensors.
Frequency: Monthly
Circulation: 66676
Founded in 1999

5523 **Serverworld Magazine**
Publications & Communications
11675 Jollyville Rd
Suite 150
Austin, TX 78759

512-250-9023
800-678-9724
Fax: 512-331-3900
E-Mail: pci@pcinews.com
Home Page: www.pcinews.com

David Wohlbrueck, Editor
Gary Pittman, CEO/President
Bill Lifland, VP Operations

Dedicated to Hewlett-Packard computing.
Cost: $45.00
60 Pages
Frequency: Monthly
Founded in 1979

5524 **Simulation**
Simulation Councils
PO Box 17900
San Diego, CA 92177-7900

858-277-3888
Fax: 858-277-3930
E-Mail: info@scs.org
Home Page: www.scs.org

William Gallagher, Publisher
Richard Fujimoto, Editor-in-Chief
Steve Branch, Executive Director

Information on computer simulation including, applications, methodologies and techniques of computer simulation.
Cost: $195.00
Frequency: Monthly
Circulation: 3800
Founded in 1952

5525 **Small Business Advisor: Software News**
Software News Publishing Company
110 N Bell Avenue
Suite 300
Shawnee, OK 74801-6967

405-275-3100
800-456-0864
Fax: 405-275-3101
Home Page: www.cpatechadvisor.com

Sharie Dodgen, Publisher
Melody Wrinkle, Manager
Isaac OBannon, Manager
Thomson Reuters, Executive Editor

Published for advisers to small businesses and for software installers for small businesses.
Cost: $48.00
Circulation: 50000
Founded in 1991

5526 **Smart Reseller**
Ziff Davis Publishing Company
500 Unicorn Park Drive
Woburn, MA 01801-4874

781-938-2600
Fax: 781-938-2626
Home Page: www.smartreseller.com

Sloan Seymour, Publisher

Identifies the most lucrative new business opportunities and details how to profitably take advantage of them. In-depth business management strategies and trusted new technology solutions-based reviews.
Frequency: SemiMonthly
Circulation: 60M

5527 **Software Development**
Miller Freeman Publications
2655 Seely Avenue
San Jose, CA 95134

408-943-1234
800-227-4675
Fax: 408-943-0513

Veronica Costanza, Publisher
Nicole Freeman, Editor
Laura Merling, Executive Director

For corporate developers and technical managers involved in the development of software applications within the industries.
Circulation: 73297

5528 **Software Digest**
National Software Testing Laboratories
670 Sentry Pkwy
2nd Floor
Blue Bell, PA 19422-2325

610-832-8400
Fax: 610-941-9952
E-Mail: info@nstl.com
Home Page: www.nstl.com

Lowrenie Goldstein, Publisher
Andrew Froning, Editor

Independent and comparative ratings on IBM PC software. All categories tested free of bias. No advertising is accepted.
Frequency: Monthly
Founded in 1983

5529 **Solid Solutions**
ConnectPress
551 W Cordova Road
Suite 701
Santa Fe, NM 87505-4100

505-474-5000
Fax: 505-474-5001
E-Mail: info@solidprofessor.com
Home Page: www.solidmag.com

Dale Bennie, Publisher

Covers the latest market developments and tracks the growth of SolidWorks software in the CAD/CAM/CAE market. Reviews of workstations, 3D printers, and Windows NT graphic accelerators.
Cost: $99.00
Frequency: Monthly

5530 **Solutions Integrator**
International Data Group
3 Post Office Sq
4th Floor
Boston, MA 02109-3939

617-423-9030
Fax: 617-423-0240
Home Page: www.solutionsintegrator.com

Bob Carrigan, CEO
Joel Shore, Editor-In-Chief

Provides accessment of technology, IT buying practices and plans, business strategies and vendor technology roadmaps.
Circulation: 90000

5531 **Speech Recognition Update**
CI Publishing
PO Box 570730
Tarzana, CA 91357-730

818-708-0962
888-632-7419
Fax: 818-345-2980
E-Mail: info@tmaa.com
Home Page: www.tmaa.com

William S Meisel, President
Bill Meisel, Editor

News and analysis of speech recognition markets, companies and technologies.
Cost: $195.00
Frequency: Monthly
Founded in 1993

5532 **Storage Management Solutions**
West World Productions
420 N Camden Dr
Beverly Hills, CA 90210-4507

310-276-9500
Fax: 310-276-9874
Home Page: www.wwpi.com

Yuri R Spiro, Publisher/CEO
Steve Schone, Circulation Manager

Articles on tutorials, case studies, lab tests and new products that offer solutions to issues of data accessibility, availablity and protection and network storage.
Cost: $10.00
72 Pages
Frequency: Monthly
Circulation: 64044
ISSN: 1097-5152
Founded in 1995
Printed in 4 colors on glossy stock

5533 **Studio City**
Resource Central
4126 Pennsylvania Avenue
Suite 3
Kansas City, MO 64111-3018
Tom Weishaar, President

Information on using the multimedia package Hyper Studio, mailed on 3.5 inch disk, 6 times a year. Available in Macintosh and Apple II versions.
Frequency: Bi-Monthly

5534 **Sun Observer**
Publications & Communications
11675 Jollyville Rd
Suite 150
Austin, TX 78759

512-250-9023
800-678-9724
Fax: 512-331-3900
E-Mail: pci@pcinews.com
Home Page: www.pcinews.com

Gary Pittman, CEO/President
Robert Martin, Editor

Journal of news and information devoted to the users of Sun Microsystems.
Cost: $14.95
80 Pages
Founded in 1980

5535 **Supply Chain Systems Magazine**
Helmers Publishing
174 Concord Street
P O Box 874
Peterborough, NH 03458-1291

603-924-9631
Fax: 603-924-7408
Home Page: www.scs-mag.com

David Andrewso, Publisher/Editorial
Bill Fahy, Circulation Director
Paul Quinn, Editor/Senior Writer

Educates its readers about the benefits and bast practices of supply chain management in manufacturing and service industries. We educate our readers about how e-business, Enterprises Resource Planning, asset management, data capture, warehouse management and management can be integrated to create effective and efficient supply chain systems.
60 Pages
Frequency: Weekly
Circulation: 53000
Founded in 1979
Printed in 4 colors on glossy stock

5536 **Synapps**
Synergis Technologies
472 California Rd
Quakertown, PA 18951-2463

215-643-6620
Fax: 215-536-9249
E-Mail: marketingsupport@synergis.com
Home Page: www.synergis.com

Barbara White, VP

Information for professional management of AutoCAD systems and includes application articles.
Frequency: Quarterly
Circulation: 25000

5537 **Sys Admin**
CMP Media
4601 West 6th Street
Suite B
Lawrence, KS 66046

785-841-1631
Fax: 785-841-2047
E-Mail: samag@neodata.com
Home Page: www.sysadminmag.com

Edwin Rothrock, Publisher
Amber Ankerholz, Editor
Gary Marshall, President
Bob Cucciniello, Marketing
Deirdre Blake, Managing Editor

SYS ADMIN serves the Unix and Linux system administration market.
Cost: $43.00
100 Pages
Frequency: Monthly
Circulation: 29121
Founded in 1992
Printed in on glossy stock

5538 **Systematic Magazine**
American Payroll Association
711 Navarro Street
Suite 100
San Antonio, TX 78205-1710

210-226-4600
Fax: 210-226-4027
Home Page: www.americanpayroll.org

Daniel J Maddux, Publisher

Covers new systems and implementation, the latest technology and its relation to human resources, payroll and accounting for CFOs, MIS department heads and top management in companies that use information technology for communication.
Frequency: Quarterly
Circulation: 14M

5539 **Systems Development Management**
Auerbach Publications
535 5th Avenue
Room 806
New York, NY 10017-3610

800-737-8034
Fax: 212-297-9176
Home Page: www.auerbach-publications.com

Rich O'Hamley, Publisher
Janet Butler, Editor

Technical and managerial information on systems development.
Cost: $495.00
Frequency: Bi-Monthly
Circulation: 1,000
ISSN: 1096-7893
Printed in on matte stock

5540 **Systems Integration**
Reed Business Information
360 Park Ave S
New York, NY 10010-1737

646-746-6400
Fax: 646-756-7583
E-Mail: slebris@reedbusiness.com
Home Page: www.reedbusiness.com

John Poulin, CEO
Thomas Temin, Editor
James Reed, Owner
Jim Casella, CEO

Covers trade and developments for mini-micro based computer systems.
Cost: $75.00
Frequency: Monthly
Founded in 1968

5541 **TAAR: The Automated Agency Report**
Automation Management Group
4964 Sundance Square
Boulder, CO 80301-3739

303-581-0525
Home Page: www.taan.com

Rick Morgan, Editor

Covers trends, developments and news, reviews new and current technology, and offers ideas and profiles on the productivity benefits.
Cost: $175.00
Frequency: Monthly

5542 **Tech Week**
1156 Aster Avenue
Suite B
Sunnyvale, CA 94086

408-249-8300
Fax: 408-249-0727

5543 **Techlinks**
3350 Riverwood Parkway
Suite 1900
Atlanta, GA 30339

678-627-8157
Fax: 678-627-8159

5544 **Technical Services Quarterly**
Taylor & Francis Group LLC
325 Chestnut St
Suite 800
Philadelphia, PA 19106-2614

215-625-8900
800-354-1420
Fax: 215-625-2940
E-Mail: haworthorders@taylorandfrancis.com
Home Page: www.taylorandfrancis.com

Kevin Bradley, President

This journal publishes up to the minute information that technical services professionals and paraprofessionals need in order to successfully negotiate changes in the field and take full advantage of automated systems that ultimately make collections more accessible to users.
Frequency: Quarterly

5545 **Technical Support Magazine**
Technical Enterprises
7044 S 13th Street
Oak Creek, WI 53154

414-908-4945
Fax: 414-768-8001
E-Mail: customercare@naspa.com
Home Page: www.naspa.com

Rachael Zimmerman, Editor
Denise Rockhill, President

Provides tips and techniques for MVS, VM and VSE mainframe operating systems and NT environments. It also examines security and system performance, product installation experiences and a host of other related enterprise concerns.
68 Pages
Frequency: Monthly

Circulation: 50,000
Founded in 1986
Printed in 4 colors on glossy stock

5546 **Technical Training**
American Society for Training & Development
1640 King St
Box 1443
Alexandria, VA 22314-2743
703-683-8100
Fax: 703-683-8103
E-Mail: customercare@astd.org
Home Page: www.astd.org
Tony Bingham, President
Industry trends, technologies and techniques within computer, manufacturing, telecommunications and government industries.
Cost: $59.00
Frequency: Bi-Monthly
Circulation: 11M

5547 **Technology & Learning**
Tech & Learning
1111 Bayhill Drive
Suite 125
San Bruno, CA 94066
650-238-0260
Fax: 650-238-0263
E-Mail: techlearning@nbmedia.com
Home Page: www.techlearning.com
Allison Knapp, Publisher
Kevin Hogan, Editorial Director
Christine Weiser, Managing Editor
Serves the K-12 education community with practical resources and expert strategies for transforming education through integration of digital technologies. Often used as a professional development tool to help educators across the board get up to speed with the newest technologies and products in order to best prepare students for the global digital workforce.
Frequency: Monthly
Circulation: 81000
Founded in 1971
Printed in on glossy stock

5548 **Technology and Practice Guide**
ABA Publishing
321 N Clark St
Chicago, IL 60654-7598
312-988-5000
800-285-2221
Fax: 312-988-5280
E-Mail: askaba@abanet.org
Home Page: www.abanet.org
Tommy H Wells Jr, President
Helps law professionals of general practice in making decisions about legal information management and technology.
Cost: $18.00
Frequency: SemiAnnual
Circulation: 13,477

5549 **Techscan: The Managers Guide to Technology**
Richmond Research
266 W 37th St
PO Box 537
New York, NY 10018-6609
212-594-9795
E-Mail: techscan@pipeline.com
Larry Richmond, President
Information and insights on how various new technologies, products and design techniques are used to solve business problems.
Cost: $87.50
Frequency: Monthly
Circulation: 2,500

5550 **Text Technology: The Journal of Computer Text Processing**
McMaster University
1280 Main Street W
Hamilton, On 0
905-525-9140
Fax: 905-577-6930
E-Mail: buckleyj@mcmaster.ca
Home Page: texttechnology.mcmaster.ca
Joanne Buckley, Editor
Edie Rasmussen, Editor
Tips, techniques and programs for TEXT, Icon, Macintosh and other software and word-processing programs, desktop publishing and Internet as they apply to educational applications.
Cost: $45.00
Frequency: Quarterly
Circulation: 800

5551 **Trends in Computing**
Scientific American
415 Madison Ave
New York, NY 10017-7934
212-451-8200
800-333-1199
Fax: 212-832-2998
E-Mail: webmaster@sciam.com
Home Page: www.sciam.com
Gretchen G Teichgraeber, CEO
Elias Arnett, Owner
Targets computer managers and professionals.
Cost: $24.97
Frequency: Annual+
Founded in 1845

5552 **Unicenter TNG Advisor**
Advisor Media
P.O.Box 503350
San Diego, CA 92150-3350
858-278-5600
Fax: 858-278-0300
Home Page: www.advisor.com
John Hawkins, CEO
Advice on TNG programs and equipment, covers end to end management in support of multi-platform infrastructure, integration of management functions and open extensibility.
Cost: $39.00
Frequency: Monthly
Circulation: 35000

5553 **Unisys World/Network Computing News**
Publications & Communications
505 Cypress Creek Road
Suite B
Cedar Park, TX 78613-1868
512-250-9023
Fax: 512-331-3900
Larry Storer, Editor
Dedicated to the users and OEMs of convergent technologies products.
Cost: $48.00
24 Pages
Frequency: Monthly
Founded in 1983

5554 **Varindustry Products**
VIPublishing
30506 Palos Verdes Drive W
Rancho Palos Verdes, CA 90275-4471
Kenneth Allen, Editor
Focuses on new products and services.
Frequency: Monthly
Founded in 1990

5555 **Vision Systems Design**
PennWell Publishing Company
98 Spit Brook Rd
5th Floor
Nashua, NH 03062-5737
603-891-0123
Fax: 603-891-9294
E-Mail: cholton@pennwell.com
Home Page: www.pennwell.com
Christine Shaw, VP
Andrew Wilson, Editor
Bonnie Heines, Managing Editor
Each issue discusses the development of leading edge industrial, scientific, medical, military, and aerospace machine vision applications.
Cost: $85.00
Frequency: Monthly
Circulation: 32000
Founded in 1910
Mailing list available for rent
Printed in 4 colors

5556 **Visual Basic Programmer's Journal**
Fawcette Technical Publications
2600 S El Camino Real
Suite 300
San Mateo, CA 94403-2381
650-378-7100
800-848-5523
Fax: 650-853-0230
Home Page: www.fawcette.com/vsm/
James Fawcette, President
Tina Fontenot, Marketing
Karin Becker, Associate Publisher
Karen Koenen, Sr. Circulation Director
Provides technical news on how to increase productivity and process applications more efficiently.
Cost: $71.40
Frequency: Monthly
Circulation: 109874
Founded in 1990

5557 **WINDOWS Magazine**
CMP Publications
600 Community Dr
Manhasset, NY 11030-3810
516-562-5000
Fax: 516-562-5995
Scott Wolfe, Publisher
Offers the latest information and updates for the WINDOWS user.

5558 **Wall Street Computer Review**
Miller Freeman Publications
1199 S Belt Line Rd
Suite 100
Coppell, TX 75019-4666
972-906-6500
Fax: 972-419-7825
Elizabeth Katz, Publisher
Pavan Sahgal, Editor
For financial and investment professionals and individual investors.
Cost: $5.00
Circulation: 34,000

5559 **Waters**
Waters Information Services
270 Lafayette St
Suite 700
New York, NY 10012-3311
212-925-6990
Fax: 212-925-7585
E-Mail: jkotz@riskwaters.com
Home Page: www.watersinfo.com
Andrew Delaeny, Editor-in-Chief
Phil Albinus, Editor
John Waters, CEO
Farrell McManus, Advertising Manager

Articles on technology applications leading strategic business success, career enhancements and workplace changes.
Cost: $240.00
Frequency: Monthly
Circulation: 20000
Founded in 1993

5560 **Windows & Dot Net**
Duke Communications International
221 E 29th Street
Loveland, CO 80538

970-663-4700
800-621-1544
Fax: 970-667-2321
E-Mail: CorporateCustomerService@penton.com
Home Page: www.penton.com

Bart Taylor, Group Publisher
Kim Paulsen, Publisher
David B. Nussbaum, CEO
Cost: $49.95
Frequency: Monthly
Circulation: 100000
Founded in 1982

5561 **Windows Developer's Journal**
600 Harrison Street
San Francisco, CA 94107

415-947-6000
Fax: 415-947-6027
Home Page: www.wdj.com

John Dorsey, Editor in Chief
Kerry Gates, Publisher
Holly Vessichelli, Director of Marketing
Deirdre Blake, Managing Editor

Publication for professional Windows developers.
Founded in 1990

5562 **Windows NT Magazine**
Duke Communications International
221 E 29th Street
PO Box 447
Loveland, CO 80539-447

970-663-4700
800-621-1544
Fax: 970-203-2996
Home Page: www.winntmag.com

Mark Smith, Publisher
Karen Forster, Manager
John Savill, Manager

Serves technical decision makers using the Windows NT application, and related systems.
Cost: $49.95
Frequency: Monthly
Circulation: 75000

5563 **Windows/DOS Developer's Journal**
R&D Associates
6701 W 121st Street
Suite 310
Overland Park, KS 66209

913-491-0345
Fax: 785-841-2624
Home Page: www.rndassociates.com

Ron Burk, Editor

Information for professional Windows and DOS programmers.
Cost: $29.00
Frequency: Monthly
Circulation: 22000
Founded in 1996

5564 **Windowspro Magazine**
Ziff Davis Publishing Company
500 Unicorn Park Drive
Woburn, MA 01801

781-938-2600
Fax: 781-938-2626
Home Page: www.windowspro.com

Jason Young, Publisher
Jacquelyn Gavron, Editor-in-Chief

Serves technology-experts responsible for Windows NT based support. Includes technologies, products, solutions, and how-to instructions.
Frequency: Monthly
Circulation: 150,000

5565 **Wired**
Wired News
520 3rd St
1st Floor
San Francisco, CA 94107-6805

415-276-8400
800-769-4733
Fax: 415-276-8500
E-Mail: info@wired.com
Home Page: www.wired.com

Evan Hansen, Editor-in-Chief
Jeremy Barna, Production Manager
Alison Macondray, General Manager
Drew Schutte, Publisher

Focuses on people and ideas behind digital technology.
Frequency: Monthly
Circulation: 305097

5566 **Workstation News**
Data Base Publications
9390 Research Blvd
Suite 300
Austin, TX 78759-7374

512-418-9590
Fax: 512-418-8165
Home Page: www.bancvue.com

Gabe Krajicek, CEO

Aimed at workstation users and volume buyers.
Frequency: Monthly
Founded in 1990

Trade Shows

5567 **AAAI National Conference**
American Association for Artificial Intelligence
445 Burgess Drive
Menlo Park, CA 94025-3442

650-328-3123
800-968-1738
Fax: 650-321-4457
Home Page: www.aaai.org

Keri Vasser Harvey, Senior Conference Coordinator
Corina Anzaldo, Conference Coordinator

The conference provides a forum for a broad range of topics, including knowledge representation and automated reasoning, planning, machine learning and data mining, autonomous agents, robotics and machine perception, probabilistic inference, constraint satisfaction, search and game playing, natural language processing, neural networks, multi-agent systems, computational game theory and cognitive modeling.
1.2M Attendees
Frequency: July
Founded in 1980

5568 **ACT Management of Change Conference**
American Council for Technology
3040 Williams Drive
Suite 610
Fairfax, VA 22031

703-208-4800
Fax: 703-208-4805
E-Mail: act-iac@actgov.org
Home Page: www.actgov.org

Kelly Olsen, Conference Director

For government and industry executives who are interested in unleashing the tremendous innovation potential of their organizations. It will explore the processes and effects of creative ideas, experiments and ventures that hold the promise of a better and safer America.
Frequency: June

5569 **AIA Business Conference**
Automated Imaging Association
900 Victors Way
Suite 140
Ann Arbor, MI 48108

734-994-6088
800-994-6099
Fax: 734-994-3338
E-Mail: jburnstein@robotics.org
Home Page: www.machinevisiononline.org

Jeff Burnstein, Executive Director

The annual AIA Business Conference has become the machine vision industry's most important networking event. The Conference gathers top industry executives to do business with their peers and hear presentations on issues affecting the global economy in general and the machine vision industry specifically.
300+ Attendees
Frequency: February

5570 **AIIM Annual Expo Conference & Exposition**
Association for Information and Image Management
1100 Wayne Avenue
Suite 1100
Silver Spring, MD 20910

301-587-8202
800-477-2446
Fax: 301-587-2711
E-Mail: aiim@aiim.org
Home Page: www.aiim.org

Jan Andersson, Chair
Robert Zagami, Vice Chair

The largest enterprise content & document management conference and exposition showcasing the technologies and solutions that provide intelligence behind information. For more than 50 years, this annual event attracts business professionals and executive management seeking the latest technologies.
Frequency: May

5571 **AIM Expo**
AIM Global
125 Warrendale Bayne Rd
Suite 100
Warrendale, PA 15086-7570

724-934-4470
Fax: 724-934-4495
E-Mail: info@aimglobal.org
Home Page: www.aimglobal.org

Mary Lou Bosco, President
Linda Young, Business Development Director
900+ Members
Founded in 1972

5572 **AMIA Annual Symposium**
American Medical Informatics Association

4915 St Elmo Avenue
Suite 401
Bethesda, MD 20814

301-657-1291
Fax: 301-657-1296
E-Mail: mail@amia.org
Home Page: www.amia.org

Charles P Friedman, Meeting Chairman
Karen Greenwood, Executive Vice President

Features an outstanding program of scientific papers, posters, tutorials and other educational events that provide information about cutting-edge work in medical informatics.
2000 Attendees
Frequency: Annual/October
Founded in 1977

5573 **ARMA International Conference & Expo**
ARMA International
11880 College Blvd
Suite 450
Overland Park, KS 66215

913-341-3808
800-422-2762
Fax: 913-341-3742
E-Mail: hq@arma.org
Home Page: www.arma.org/conference

Carol Jorgenson, Meetings/Education Coordinator
Wanda Wilson, Senior Manager, Conferences
Elizabeth Zlitni, Exposition Manager

Conference, seminar, workshop, banquet, award ceremony and 175 exhibits of micrographics, optical disk, automated document storage and retrieval systems and more technology of interest to information professionals.
3500 Attendees
Frequency: Annual
Founded in 1956

5574 **ASIS&T Annual Meeting**
American Society for Information Science & Techn.
1320 Fenwick Lane
Suite 510
Silver Spring, MD 20910

301-495-0900
Fax: 301-495-0810
E-Mail: asis@asis.org
Home Page: www.asis.org

Richard B Hill, Executive Director
Nancy Roderer, President

Focus on the diversity of perspectives and insights from all those participating in the information science and technology community, as they generate innovative ideas, define theoretical concepts or work out the nuts and bolts of implementing well-tested ideas in new ways and in new settings.
Frequency: Annual/Oct-Nov

5575 **ASPE Annual Meeting**
American Society for Precision Engineering
PO Box 10826
Raleigh, NC 27605-0826

919-839-8444
Fax: 919-839-8039
Home Page: www.aspe.net

Erika Deutsch Layne, Meetings Manager
Thomas A Dow, Chairman

Offering the latest in precision engineering research through presentations from national and international speakers. Participants in the Annual Meeting have the opportunity to exchange ideas with internationally renowned experts in the field.
Frequency: Annual/Oct-Nov

5576 **AWWA Annual Conference and Exposition**
American Water Works Association
6666 W Quincy Avenue
Denver, CO 80235

303-794-7711
800-926-7337
Fax: 303-347-0804
E-Mail: info@montana-awwa.org
Home Page: www.awwa.org

Nilaksh Kothari, President
Jack W. Hoffbuhr, Executive Director

The source of knowledge and information for water professionals who work to improve the quality and supply of drinking water in North America and beyond. You'll learn from industry experts in the field, hear about cutting edge research and exceptional best practices, and have the opportunity to ask questions, seek advice, and interact with other water professionals regarding both universal topics and items specifically focused to meet your needs.
Frequency: Annual/June

5577 **AWWA Information Management & Technology Conference**
American Water Works Association
6666 W Quincy Avenue
Denver, CO 80235

303-794-7711
800-926-7337
Fax: 303-347-0804
E-Mail: info@montana-awwa.org
Home Page: www.awwa.org

Nilaksh Kothari, President
Jack W. Hoffbuhr, Executive Director

This event is North America's premier conference in the area of water supply information management technology and applications for the water and wastewater industry.
Frequency: March

5578 **Association For Services Management World Conference Expo**
AFSM International
11031 Via Frontera
Suite A
San Diego, CA 92127

239-275-7887
800-333-9786
Fax: 239-275-0794
E-Mail: info@afsmi.org
Home Page: www.afsmi.org

John Schoenewald, Executive Director
Jb Wood, President/Ceo

World's largest gathering of executives in the services and support industry.
Frequency: October

5579 **Association of College Unions International Conference**
Association of College Unions International
120 W 7th Street
One City Centre, Suite 200
Bloomington, IN 47404-3925

812-245-2284
Fax: 812-245-6710
E-Mail: acui@acui.org
Home Page: www.acui.org

Rich Steele, President
Marsha Herman-Betzen, Executive Director

Educational programs, speakers, and exhibits and the opportunity for attendees to connect and network.
Frequency: April
Founded in 1914

5580 **Autodesk Expo**
AEC Systems International/Penton Media
1300 E 9th Street
Cleveland, OH 44114

800-451-1196
Fax: 610-280-7106
E-Mail: sales@acesystems.com
Home Page: www.acesystems.com

Philip McKay, Manager

Highlights AutoCAD and related products from Autodesk and third party developers. 500 exhibits.
20M Attendees
Frequency: May

5581 **Bentley MicroStation Mail**
AEC Systems International/Penton Media
1300 E 9th Street
Cleveland, OH 44114

800-451-1196
Fax: 610-280-7106
E-Mail: sales@acesystems.com
Home Page: www.acesystems.com

Philip McKay, Manager

Showcases a comprehensive line-up of intergrated design, facility management and GIS solutions built around MicroStation software. 500 exhibits.
20M Attendees
Frequency: May

5582 **CALICO Annual Conference**
Computer Assisted Language Instruction Consortium
Southwest Texas State University
116 Centennial Hall
San Marcos, TX 78666

512-245-1417
Fax: 512-245-8298
E-Mail: info@calico.org
Home Page: www.calico.org

Robert Fischer, Executive Director
Esther Horn, Manager

Providing a forum for discussions of state-of-the-art educational technology and its applications to the more effective teaching and learning of languages. The symposia accommodate workshops, papers, demonstrations, panels, and special interest groups for participants at all levels of expertise.
450 Attendees
Frequency: May

5583 **CLA World Computer and Internet Law Congress Conference**
Computer Law Association
3028 Javier Road
Suite 402
Fairfax, VA 22031

703-560-7747
Fax: 703-207-7028
Home Page: www.cla.org

Barbara Fieser, Executive Director

This conference will provide you with proven strategies and best practices that will enable you to effectively address your existing clients' IT-related challenges and problems and seek out clients whom you can assist with knowledge you will gain from the conference.
2000+ Attendees
Frequency: May

5584 **CSI Annual Computer Securtiy Conference & Exhibition**
CMP Media/Computer Security Institute Services
600 Community Drive
Manhasset, NY 11030

516-562-5000
866-271-8529
Fax: 818-487-4550

E-Mail: jstevens@cmp.com
Home Page: www.cmp.com

Jennifer Stevens, Conference Manager
Kimber Heald, Registration Manager
Annette Campo, Manager

The exhibition features 150 security vendors, from the industry leaders to the up-and coming, displaying the latest security technologies.
950 Attendees
Frequency: November

5585 CUMREC
Educause
4772 Walnut Street
Suite 206
Boulder, CO 80301-2538

303-449-4430
Fax: 303-440-0461
E-Mail: info@educause.edu
Home Page: www.educause.edu

Beverly Williams, Director of Conference Activities
Lisa Gesner, Assistant Director of Marketing

Higher education administrative technology conference. The purpose of CUMREC is to provide a forum for higher education professionals to share their expertise and experiences with computer systems in our ever changing world of technology. The CUMREC annual conference, founded in 1956, is devoted to promoting the understanding and use of information technology in higher education.
3M Attendees
Frequency: May
Founded in 1956

5586 Comdex Spring and Fall Shows
MediaLive International
795 Folsom Street
6th Floor
San Francisco, CA 94107-1243

415-905-2300
Fax: 415-905-2FAX
Home Page: www.medialiveinternational.com

Eric Faurot, VP
Marco Pardi, Exhibit Sales

COMDEX is the global marketplace for the IT industry. Buyers and sellers from around the world converge to learn how best to use technology to solve their business challenges and remain competitive. COMDEX is where hardware manufacturers, software vendors and service providers launch new products, where thought-leaders discuss industry trends, and where the media reports on the latest in the IT industry and considers its future.
100M+ Attendees
Frequency: November

5587 CompTIA Annual Breakaway Conference
CompTIA
1815 S Meyers Road
Suite 300
Oakbrook Terrace, IL 60181-5228

630-678-8300
Fax: 630-678-8384
E-Mail: breakaway@comptia.org
Home Page: www.comptia.org

John A Venator, President/CEO
Karen Lukasik, VP Operations
Laurel Chivari, VP Marketing & Communications
Rachel Fabro, Public Relations Specialist
Robert Kramer, VP Public Policy

The annual CompTIA Breakaway conference is the computing industry's premier partnering event. The conference focuses on business-building solutions, networking forums, and the latest industry trends and technologies.
Frequency: Annual/August

5588 Design Automation Conference
Design Automation
5405 Spine Road
Suite 102
Boulder, CO 80301

303-530-4333
Fax: 303-530-4334
E-Mail: feedback@dac.com
Home Page: www.dac.com

Kevin Lepine, Co-President
Lee Wood, Co-President
Nannette Jordan, Registration Coordinator

The premier Electronic Design Automation (EDA) and silicon solution event. DAC features over 50 technical sessions covering the latest in design methodologies and EDA tool developments, and an Exhibition and Demo Suite area with over 250 of the leading EDA, silicon, and IP Providers.
11M+ Attendees
Frequency: June

5589 ESRI Southwest Users Group Conference
Southwest Users Group
18727 Nadal Street
Canyon Country, CA 91351

E-Mail: admin@swug2009.com
Home Page: www.swuggis.org

Interface with ESRI users to learn about the latest technologies and discuss ESRI software-related topics.
Frequency: Annual

5590 Embedded Systems Conference
CMP Media Headquarters
600 Community Drive
Manhasset, NY 11030

516-562-5000
E-Mail: cfahlen@cmp.com
Home Page: www.esconline.com

Christian Fahlen, Senior Conference Manager
Ardis Gough, Conference Manager
Kara Pistochini, Conference Assistant
Annette Campo, Manager

The only conference to focus on the art and science of microcomptroller and microprocessor based development, covering the needs of real-time software engineers.
2.7M Attendees
Frequency: September
Mailing list available for rent

5591 FOSE
Post Newsweek Tech Media
10 G Street NE
Suite 500
Washington, DC 20002-4228

202-772-2500
800-791-FOSE
Fax: 202-772-2511
Home Page: www.ntpshow.com

Lauri Nichols, Trade Show Operations Manager
Melanie Woodfolk, Show Marketing Manager
David Greene, President

Largest information technology exposition serving the government marketplace.
4000 Attendees
Frequency: April

5592 Graph Expo & Convention
Graphic Arts Show Company
1899 Preston White Drive
Reston, VA 20191

703-264-7200
Fax: 703-620-9187
E-Mail: info@gasc.org
Home Page: www.gasc.org

Kelly Kilga, Conference/Show Operations Director
Lilly Kinney, Conference Manager

The largest, most comprehensive prepress, printing, converting and digital equipment trade show and conference in the Americas.
40000 Attendees
Frequency: October

5593 Graphics of the Americas
Printing Association of Florida
6275 Hazeltine National Drive
Orlando, FL 32822

407-240-8009
800-331-0461
Fax: 407-240-8333
Home Page: www.pafgraf.org

Anne Gaither, Convention Director
Michael H Streibig, Staff Executive

We are the second largest Graphic Arts and Converting show in America. We give you two vital markets — southeast US and Latin America: Mexico, South America, Central America and the Caribbean. Our 28 year track record reflects our success with both exhibitors and show visitors.
20000 Attendees
Frequency: Feb

5594 Healthcare Information and Management Systems Society Conference
Healthcare Information and Management Systems
230 E Ohio
Suite 500
Chicago, IL 60611-3269

312-664-4467
Fax: 312-664-6143
E-Mail: kmalone@himss.org
Home Page: www.himss.org

Karen Malone, Director of Meetings
John Daniels, Vice President

An opportunity to learn the latest industry intelligence, find solutions to your most pressing professional challenges, and network with your peers. Pre-conference workshops and education session, see industry newsmakers, explore the latest technologies in more than 600 exhibits and earn continuing education credit and certification.
20000 Attendees
Frequency: February

5595 IAAP International Convention and Education Forum
Int'l Association of Administrative Professionals
10502 NW Ambassador Drive
Kansas City, MO 16415

816-891-6600
Fax: 816-891-9118
E-Mail: tgoodall@iaap-hq.org
Home Page: www.iaap-hq.org

Inge Hafkemeyer, Convention/Meetings/Exhibit Manager
Don Bretthauer, Executive Director

An opportunity to showcase your product or service to this important audience. Office Expo exhibitors include major office product manufacturers, publishers, software vendors, staffing firms, gift suppliers, paper companies, and many more.
2000 Attendees
Frequency: July

5596 IAPP Privacy and Data Security Academy Expo
Internet Alliance

1111 19th Street NW
Suite 1180
Washington, DC 20035-5782

202-284-4380
Fax: 202-955-8081
E-Mail: info@internetalliance.org
Home Page: www.internetalliance.org

Emily T Hackett, Executive Director
Katy Caldwell, California Policy Director

The conference will showcase the latest thinking on important privacy issues in healthcare, financial services, technology and marketing. Attendees will gain a deeper understanding of strategies and tools required to meet today's privacy challenges.
1000 Attendees
Frequency: October
Founded in 1981

5597 IEEE SoutheastCon
IEEE Meeting & Conference Management (MCM)
445 Hoes Lane
Piscataway, NJ 08854

732-562-3878
800-678-4333
Fax: 732-971-1203
E-Mail: conference-services@ieee.org
Home Page. www.ieee.org

A student conference, technical conference, and business meeting.
800 Attendees
Frequency: Annual

5598 IRMA Annual Conference
Information Resources Management Association
701 E Chocolate Avenue
Suite 200
Hershey, PA 17033

717-533-8879
Fax: 717-533-8661
E-Mail: member@irma-international.org
Home Page: www.irma-international.org

Mehdi Khosrow-Pour PhD, President
Sherif Kamel PhD, Communications Director
Gerald Grant PhD, IRMA Doctoral Symposium Director
Lech Janczewski PhD, IRMA World Representative Director
Paul Chalekian, IRMA United States Representative

Provides forums for researchers and practitioners to share leading-edge knowledge in the global resource information management area. Various seminars, conventions and conferences, and other training programs are offered by IRMA throughout the year.
Frequency: May

5599 IS&T/SPIE Annual Symposium Electronic Imaging
International Society for Optical Engineering
1000 20th Street
PO Box 10
Bellingham, WA 98227-6705

360-763-3290
Fax: 360-647-1445
E-Mail: customerservice@spie.org
Home Page: www.spie.org

Giordano B Beretta, Director
Robert L Stevenson, Co-Director
Eugene Arthurs, Executive Director
Amy Nelson, Manager

Electronic Imaging's top-notch technical program gathers the world's prominent experts to discuss and push the forefront of imaging technology and it's applications.
1200 Attendees
Frequency: Annual/January

5600 ISACA International Conference
Information Systems Audit & Control Association
3701 Algonquin Road
Suite 1010
Rolling Meadows, IL 60008

847-253-1545
Fax: 847-253-1443
E-Mail: conference@isaca.org
Home Page: www.isaca.org

Sandy Arens, Registration

The International Conference has long been recognised throughout the world for providing in-depth coverage of the leading-edge technical and managerial issues facing IT governance, control, security and assurance professionals.
Frequency: June

5601 Industrial Virtual Reality
Reed Exhibitions
US Consumer Show Division
225 Wyman Street
Waltham, MA 02451

781-622-8616
Fax: 781-622-8042
E-Mail: inquiry@sport.reedexpo.com
Home Page: www.reedexpo.com

Elizabeth Hitchcock, International Sales

The first trade show focusing on industrial applications of virtual reality and tele-existence.
Frequency: June

5602 Information Technology Week
Information Week/CMP Media
600 Community Drive
Manhasset, NY 11030

516-562-5000
Fax: 516-562-5036
E-Mail: lmonvign@cmp.com
Home Page: www.informationweek.com

Lisa Monvigner, Events Associate Director
Stephanie Iannuzzi, Sr. Marketing Manager
Michael Friedenberg, Publisher

A forum for computer technicians and professionals.
Frequency: May
Mailing list available for rent

5603 International Conference on Methods for Surveying Hard-To-Reach Populations
American Association for Public Opinion Research
111 Deer Lake Road
Suite 100
Deerfield, IL 60015

847-205-2651
Fax: 847-480-9282
E-Mail: aapor-info@goamp.com
Home Page: www.aapor.org
Social Media: Facebook, Twitter, LinkedIn

Paul Lavrakas, President
Rob Santos, VP/President-Elect
Scott Keeter, Secretary-Treasurer

The conference will address both the statistical and survey design aspects of including hard to reach groups. Researchers will report findings from censuses and surveys and other research related to the identification, definition, measurement, and methodologies for surveying and enumerating undercounted populations.
850 Attendees
Frequency: Annual
Mailing list available for rent: 1000 names at $400 per M

5604 International Conference on Software Engineering
Software Engineering Institute
Carnegie Mellon University
Pittsburgh, PA 15213-3890

412-687-7700
Fax: 412-268-6257
E-Mail: customer-relations@sei.cmu.edu
Home Page: www.sei.cmu.edu

Paul Nielsen, CEO
Clyde Chittister, COO
Douglas Schmidt, Deputy Dir Research

ICSE is the premier software engineering conference, providing a forum for researchers, practitioners and educators to present and discuss the most recent innovations, trends, experiences, and concerns in the field of software engineering.
800 Attendees
Frequency: May

5605 International Consumer Electronics Show (C ES)
Consumer Electronics Association
Las Vegas Hotel & Casino
3000 S. Paradise Road
Las Vegas, NV 89109

866-539-8430
Home Page: www.cesweb.org

Tara Dunion, Event Director
Kristen Peifer, Event Manager
Leah Arnold, Exhibitor Coordinator

The largest annual consumer technology tradeshow offering a wealth of opportunity for your business.
140M Attendees
Frequency: Annual/January

5606 International Spectrum MultiValue Conference & Exhibition
International Spectrum
715 J Street
Suite 301
San Diego, CA 92101-2478

619-515-9930
Fax: 619-515-9933
E-Mail: editor@intl-spectrum.com
Home Page: www.intl-spectrum.com

Monica Giobbi, President
Gus Giobbi, Chairman

A conference and exhibition showcasing MultiValue products and services.
6M Attendees
Frequency: March

5607 Interop Conference
Interop
C/O MediaLive International
795 Folsom Street, 6th Floor
San Francisco, CA 94107-1243
415-905-2300
Fax: 415-905-2FAX
E-Mail: jennifer.sioteco@mlii.com
Home Page: www.interop.com

Jennifer Sioteco, Sr. Operations Manager
Lenny Heymann, General Manager

Provides you an overview of the robust conference offerings, workshops and tutorials, and special programs.
60000 Attendees

5608 Java One Conference
Sun Microsystems
4150 Network Circle
Santa Clara, CA 95054

650-960-1300
866-382-7151
Home Page: www.java.sun.com

Jonathan Schwartz, President/CEO
Anil Gadre, Chief Executive Officer

Gain knowledge and Java technology education directly from Sun Microsystems, Inc. and other

industry leaders. Get expert advice on solving the most common Java challenges. Benefit from four full days of content. Choose from hundreds of technical sessions and test drive real-world Java technology solutions.
5000 Attendees
Frequency: June

5609 MacWorld Conference & Expo
MacWorld 2010
PO Box 3221
Boston, MA 02241

805-290-1341
800-645-EXPO
Fax: 805-654-1676
E-Mail: macworld2010@rcsreg.com
Home Page: www.macworldexpo.com

Annual show with hundreds of exhibitors of Mac equipment, supplies and services. Provides education, networking and thought leadership that professionals and consumers alike need to get the most from their technology investment.
65000 Attendees
Frequency: Annual

5610 Marketechnics
Food Marketing Institute
2345 Crystal Drive
Suite 800
Arlington, VA 22202

202-452-8444
Fax: 202-429-4519
Home Page: www.fmi.org

Tim Hammonds, CEO

Provides a once-a-year opportunity to hear, see and discuss new technologies and their impact on the supply chain, store operations and marketing/merchandising strategies.
7000 Attendees
Frequency: Jan-Feb

5611 NACCB Annual Conference
National Association of Computer Consultants
1420 King Street
Suite 610
Alexandria, VA 22314

703-838-2050
Fax: 703-838-3610
E-Mail: susan@naccb.org
Home Page: www.naccb.org

Susan Donohoe, Director of Programs/Public Policy
Beth Berman, Program & Administrative Coord.

The only educational, networking, and leadership event exclusively for the IT Services Industry. The NACCB conference provides a platform where IT services firms connect to address issues and solutions most affecting business today.
Frequency: Annual/November
Founded in 1988

5612 National Ergonomics Conference and Exposition
Continental Exhibitions
370 Lexington Avenue
Suite 1407
New York, NY 10017-6503

212-370-5005
Fax: 212-370-5699
E-Mail: information@ergoexpo.com
Home Page: www.ergoexpo.com

Larry L Elyea, Executive Program Director
Pedro Caceres, Senior VP of Operations

The NECE maximizes your time and effort by providing direct contact with industry leaders that comprise our speaker faculty, direct contact with leading providers of ergonomics products and services, and direct contact with your peers at networking receptions during the exposition.
Frequency: Nov-Dec

5613 Object World Conference
Object Management Group/IDG Management
111 Speen Street
PO Box 9107
Framingham, MA 01701-9514

800-225-4698
Fax: 508-872-8237
Home Page: www.omg.com

Mary DeCristoforo, Conference Director
David Elliott, Exhibit Sales Manager

An annual conference sponsored by the Object Management Group and IDG Management Group to advance object-oriented technology in commercial software development. The event features tutorials and conference sessions.
6.5M Attendees
Frequency: October

5614 Optical Fiber Communications Conference
Optical Society of America
2010 Massachusetts Avenue NW
Washington, DC 20036

202-238-8130
Fax: 202-416-6140
E-Mail: info@ofcconference.org
Home Page: www.ofcnfoec.org

Colleen Morrison, Media Relations Director
Melissa Russell, Exhibit Sales Director
Colleen Morrison, Media Relations Manager
Angela Stark, Director Communications

Provides leading edge, peer reviewed educational programming along with a high powered, commerce driven exhibition. This unique combination attracts the field's most progressive professionals and exhibiting companies.
13111 Attendees
Frequency: March
Founded in 1916

5615 PCB Design Conference West
UP Media Group
2400 Lake Park Dr Se
Suite 440
Smyrna, GA 30080-7695

678-589-8800
Fax: 678-589-8850
E-Mail: askarbek@upmediagroup.com
Home Page: www.pcbwest.com

Alyson Skarbek, Show Operations Manager
Andy Shaughnessy, Conference Chairperson
Brooke Anglin, Exhibit Sales Manager

The first and only conference 100% dedicated to the needs of the PCB designer.
750 Attendees
Frequency: March

5616 PIMA Leadership Conference
Paper Industry Management Association
4700 W Lake Avenue
Glenview, IL 60025-1485

847-375-6860
877-527-5973
Fax: 732-460-7333
E-Mail: info@pimaweb.org
Home Page: www.pima-online.org

Carol Waugh, Meetings Manager
Julie Weir, Account Manager
Mary Cornell, Account Manager

Three-day conference to bring together IT and process control professionals from around the world to share their knowledge of information technology in the pulp and paper industry and to promote systems applications. The only IT conference planned for and by IT professionals.
500 Attendees
Frequency: Annual/June

5617 Pacific Telecommunications Council Conference: PTC Conference
Pacific Telecommunications Council
2454 S Beretania Street
3rd Floor
Honolulu, HI 96826-1596

808-941-3789
Fax: 808-944-4874
E-Mail: snakama@ptc.org
Home Page: www.ptc.org

Sharon Nakama, Conference Director
Dolores Fung, Conference/Seminar Coordinator
Claudine Naruse, Conference/Seminar Coordinator
Justin Riel, Conference/Seminar Assistant

Provides an opportunity to learn and to analyze current issues. Registrants from the ranks of senior corporate officers and management, experts from law and consulting firms, noted analysts and scholars, and technical experts provide a wide diversity of ideas.
1500 Attendees
Frequency: January

5618 SC: High Performance Networking & Computing
Hall-Erickson
98 E Naperville Road
Westmont, IL 60559

630-639-9185
Fax: 630-434-1216
Home Page: www.sc-conference.org

William Kramer, Conference General Chair
Barbara Horner-Miller, Conference Deputy Chair

The world's leading conference on high performance computing, networking and storage. Representatives from many technical communities together to exchange ideas, celebrate past successes and plan for the future.
6000 Attendees
Frequency: Annual/November
Founded in 1988

5619 SCSC: Summer Simulation Multiconference
Society for Modeling and Simulation International
PO Box 17900
San Diego, CA 92177-7900

858-277-3888
Fax: 858-277-3930
E-Mail: scs@scs.org
Home Page: www.scs.org

Steve Branch, Executive Director
Mark Yen, Event Coordinator

Focusing on Innovative Technologies for Simulation this year. Modeling and Simulation is a very critical area for supporting Research and Development as well as competitiveness worldwide; new technologies are enabling new use of M&S and increasing its impact in new areas; SCSC provides an international forum for presenting the state of the art in the international simulation community.
600 Attendees
Frequency: July

5620 SID International Symposium, Seminar and Exhibition
Society for Information Display
610 S 2nd Street
San Jose, CA 95112

408-977-1013
Fax: 408-977-1531

E-Mail: office@sid.org
Home Page: www.sid.org

Mark Goldfab, Conference Coordinator
Bill Klein, Symposium Coordinator
Kate Dickie, Exhibition/Sponsorship Sales Mgr.
Danielle Rocco, Exhibition/Sponsorship Coordinator
Jenny Needham, Manager

The premier international gathering of scientists, engineers, manufacturers and users in the electronic display industry. The event provides access to a wide range of technology and applications from high-definition flat-panel displays using both emissive and liquid-crystal technology to the latest in OLED displays and large-area projection-display systems.
6000 Attendees
Frequency: May
Founded in 1962

5621 SIGGRAPH Conference
Association for Computing Machinery
2 Penn Plaza
Suite 701
New York, NY 10121-0701

212-626-0500
800-342-6626
Fax: 212-944-1318
E-Mail: acmhelp@acm.org
Home Page: www.siggraph.org

Dino Schweitzer, Conference Chief Staff Executive
James Mohler, Conference Chairperson

The annual conference and its year round initiatives provide unique crossroads for a diverse community of researchers, developers, creators, educators and practitioners. Our continuing mission is to be the premier annual conference on leading edge theory and practice of computer graphics and interactive techniques, inspiring progress through education, excellence, and interaction.
50000 Attendees
Frequency: July-August

5622 SMC: Spring Simulation Multiconference
Society for Modeling and Simulation International
PO Box 17900
San Diego, CA 92177-7900

858-277-3888
Fax: 858-277-3930
E-Mail: sbranch@scs.org
Home Page: www.scs.org

Drew Hamilton, Conference General Chair
Steve Branch, Executive Director

Bringing together eight symposia and providing a forum for academia, industry, business and government covering a wide variety of disciplines and domains that utilize modeling and simulation to present their work in a unique setting.
400 Attendees
Frequency: April

5623 Seybold Seminars
MediaLive International
795 Folsom Street
6th Floor
San Francisco, CA 94107-1243
415-905-2300
Fax: 415-905-2FAX
Home Page: www.medialiveinternational.com

Jackie Rees, Program Director
Cynthia Wood, Conference Content Director

Four focused conferences; Chicago, New York, San Francisco, that will deliver new solutions, emerging technologies and real world examples of businesses that have successfully implemented new digital publishing workflow and content management strategies.
21000 Attendees
Frequency: Sept, Oct, Nov

5624 TAWPI Annual Forum & Exposition
Association for Work Process Improvement
185 Devonshire Street
Suite M102
Boston, MA 02110-1407

617-426-1167
800-998-2974
Fax: 617-521-8675
E-Mail: info@tawpi.org
Home Page: www.tawpi.org

Sandra Savage, Conference Planner
Jenny Star, Director Business Development
Tonya Gregoire, Director Business Development

Leading event for technology and management professionals in data capture, mail, imaging, payment/remittance, document and forms processing.
1500 Attendees
Frequency: July

5625 TechNet International
Armed Forces Communications and Electronics Assn
4400 Fair Lakes Court
Fairfax, VA 22033

703-631-6100
800-336-4583
Fax: 703-631-6405
Home Page: www.afcea.org

Kent Schneider, President/CEO
Becky Nolan, Executive VP
John A Dubia, Executive VP

An annual event representing top government, industry and military professionals in the fields of communications, electronics, intelligence, information systems, imaging and multi-media.
Frequency: Annual/June

5626 UNITE Golden Opportunities Annual Technology Conference
UNITE
21523 Harper Avenue
St Clair Shores, MI 48080-2209

586-443-6901
Fax: 586-443-6902
E-Mail: cathmurphy39@hotmail.com
Home Page: www.unite.org

Catherine Murphy, Conference Chair
George Gray, Conference Vice Chair

Held in mid October. Development and use of information technology. Pre-registration for full conference attendees: $1,095; daily attendees: $740.
Frequency: October

5627 Usenix Annual Technical Conference
Usenix
2560 9th Street
Suite 215
Berkeley, CA 94710-2573

510-528-8649
Fax: 510-548-5738
E-Mail: conference@usenix.org
Home Page: www.usenix.org

Jennifer Joost, Conference Manager
Devon Shaw, Administrative Assistant
Andrew Gustafson, Administrative Assistant
Dan Klein, Director
John Arrasjid, Secretary

A 5 day training running alongside a 3 day conference program filled with the latest research, security breakthroughs, sessions devoted to Linux and open source software and practical approaches to the puzzles and problems you wrestle with.
3M Attendees
Frequency: June

5628 Vue/Point Conference
Graphic Arts Show Company
1899 Preston White Drive
Reston, VA 20191
703-264-7200
Fax: 703-620-9187
E-Mail: info@gasc.org
Home Page: www.gasc.org

Kelly Kilga, Conference/Show Operations Director
Lilly Kinney, Administrative Assistant
Erin Omwake, Administrative Assistant
Deborah Vieder, Director of Communications

The only interactive, peer-to-peer conference event in the graphic communications industry.
Frequency: April

5629 WMC: Western Simulation Multiconference
Society for Modeling and Simulation International
PO Box 17900
San Diego, CA 92177-7900

858-277-3888
Fax: 858-277-3930
E-Mail: sbranch@scs.org
Home Page: www.scs.org

Steve Branch, Executive Director
Mark Yen, Events & Publications Coordinator

15 booths of technical and scientific papers.
300+ Attendees
Frequency: January

5630 Westec Exposition
Society of Manufacturing Engineers
One SME Drive
Dearborn, MI 48121

313-425-3000
800-733-4763
Fax: 408-428-9600
E-Mail: service@sme.org
Home Page: www.sme.org

Ana Christiansen, Exposition Marketing
Leslie Schade, Exhibitor Services

The West Coast's definitive manufacturing event, showcasing crucial breakthroughs in machine tools, production methods, materials and management strategies. More than 450 exhibitors.
1500 Attendees
Frequency: Annual

5631 Western Conference & Exposition
Armed Forces Communications and Electronics Assn
4400 Fair Lakes Court
Fairfax, VA 22033

703-631-1397
Fax: 703-818-9177
E-Mail: gmcgovern@afcea.org
Home Page: www.afcea.org

Gina McGovern, Patron/Sponsor Director
Kim Couranz, Senior Vice President
Booz Hamilton, Senior Vice President

Largest event on the West Coast for communications, electronics, intelligence, information systems, imaging, military weapon systems, aviation, shipbuilding, and more. Featuring the people you need to hear from, the products and services you need to do your job, and the critical issues of today and tomorrow.
7000 Attendees
Frequency: January

Directories & Databases

5632 **ACM-SIGGRAPH Computer Graphics Education Directory**
Association for Computing Machinery
1515 Broadway
17th Floor
New York, NY 10036-8901

212-869-7440
800-342-6626
Fax: 212-944-1318
E-Mail: acmhelp@acm.org
Home Page: www.acm.org

Lynn D'Addesio-Kraus, Production Manager
Roma Simon, Associate Director
Robert Okajima, Associate Director
Alain Chesnais, Founder
Liliana Cintron, Administrative Assistant

Compiled to create a unified site where educators, students, and others can find information about computer graphics educational programs, computer graphics curriculum, computer graphics text.
Cost: $20.00
0 Pages
Frequency: Biennial

5633 **ARMA International's Buyers Guide**
ARMA International
11880 College Blvd
Suite 450
Overland Park, KS 66215

913-341-3808
800-422-2762
Fax: 913-341-3742
E-Mail: hq@arma.org
Home Page: www.arma.org/conference

75-100 companies listed. Free.

5634 **AV Market Place**
Information Today
143 Old Marlton Pike
Medford, NJ 08055-8750

609-654-6266
800-300-9868
Fax: 609-654-4309
E-Mail: custserv@infotoday.com
Home Page: www.infotoday.com

Thomas H Hogan, President
Roger R Bilboul, Chairman Of The Board

The complete business directory of audio, audio visual, computer systems, film, video, and programming with industry yellow pages. The only guide needed to find more than 7,500 companies that create, apply or distribute AV equipment and services for business, education, science, and government.
Cost: $199.95
1700 Pages
Frequency: February
ISBN: 1-573871-87-7

5635 **CD-ROM Databases**
Worldwide Videotex
PO Box 3273
Boyton Beach, FL 33424

561-738-2276
E-Mail: markedit@juno.com
Home Page: www.wvpubs.com

Contains information on currently marketed databases available on CD-ROM.
Frequency: Directory

5636 **CD-ROMs in Print**
Thomson Gale
PO Box 09187
Detroit, MI 48209-0187

248-699-4253
800-877-4253
Fax: 248-699-8049
Home Page: www.galegroup.com

Patrick C Sommers, President
Rich Foley, Account Manager
Judy Roberts, Account Manager
Maria Moffre, Product Manager

International guide to CD-ROM, Cdi, 3Do, Mmcd, Cd32, Multimedia, Laserdisc and Electronic Products.
Cost: $205.00
Circulation: 13,000
ISBN: 0-787671-33-9

5637 **Computer Database**
Information Access Company
362 Lakeside Drive
Foster City, CA 94404-1171

650-378-5200
800-227-8431
Fax: 650-378-5368
Home Page: www.iacnet.com

Robert Howells, President

Comprehensive database offering over 500,000 citations, with abstracts, to literature from over 150 trade journals, industry newsletters and platform-specific publications covering the computer, telecommunications and electronics industries.

5638 **Computer Industry Almanac**
Computer Industry Almanac
304 W White Oak
Arlington Heights, IL 60005-3201

847-758-3687
Fax: 847-758-3686
E-Mail: ej@c-i-a.com
Home Page: www.c-i-a.com

Egil Juliussen, Editor
Karen Petska-Juliussen, Editor

A reference book about the computer industry.
Cost: $63.00
800 Pages
Frequency: Annual
ISBN: 0-942107-08-X

5639 **Computer Industry Market Intelligence System**
Hart-Hanks Market Intelligence
9980 Huennekens St
Suite 100
San Diego, CA 92121-2917

858-625-4800
Fax: 858-452-6857
Home Page: www.hartehanksmi.com

Terry Olson, CEO
Randy Ilas, Product Management Director

Database of more than 250,000 business locations with mainframe, mini or micro computer systems.

5640 **Computer Review**
Computer Review
19 Pleasant St
Gloucester, MA 01930-5937

978-283-2100
E-Mail: info@computerreview.com
Home Page: www.computerreview.com

George Luhowy, Owner

Your personal business tool for mining the Knowledge economy. This is a well organized hardcopy directory with a daily online monitor. It shows you what's happening in 12,000 companies from 77 technology sectors.
Cost: $495.00
750 Pages
Frequency: Annual
ISBN: 0-914730-02-9
ISSN: 0093-416X

5641 **DACS Annotated Bibliography**
Data & Analysis Center for Software
775 Daedalian Drive
Rome, NY 13441-4909

315-334-4905
800-214-7921
Fax: 315-334-4964
E-Mail: cust-liasn@dacs.dtic.mil
Home Page: www.iac.dtic.mil/dacs

Thomas McGibbon, Director

Offers citations on over 9,000 technical reports, articles, papers and books concerned with software development and engineering.
Cost: $60.00
400 Pages

5642 **DIALOG Publications**
Dialog, Thomas Business
11000 Regency Parkway
Suite 10
Cary, NC 27511

919-462-8600
800-3DI-ALOG
Fax: 919-468-9890
Home Page: www.dialog.com

Mike Eastwood, VP Finance & Administration
Al Zink, VP Human Resources
Roy Martin, CEO

Offers descriptions of DIALOG system and database publications that are available for purchase.

5643 **DP Directory**
525 Goodale Hill Rd
Glastonbury, CT 06033-4022

860-659-1065
E-Mail: al@dpdirectory.com
Home Page: www.dpdirectory.com

Al Harberg, President

Offers mailing lists for the computer trade as well as information on the value and uses of press releases for marketers.

5644 **Datapro Directory of Microcomputer Hardware**
S. Karger Publishers
26 W Avon Road
PO Box 529
Farmington, CT 06085
860-675-7834
800-828-5479
Fax: 860-675-7302
E-Mail: karger@snet.net
Home Page: www.libri.ch

Martin Buess, Managing Director
Andrea Murdoch, CEO
Monika Augstburger, Account Manager
Marianne Dill, Manager Customer Service

Offers valuable information on over 1,500 manufacturers of microcomputers and peripheral equipment.
Cost: $675.00
1000 Pages
Frequency: Monthly
ISSN: 1074-3308

5645 **Directory of Computer and High Technology Grants**
Research Grant Guides

PO Box 1214
Loxahatchee, FL 33470-1214

561-795-6129

Richard M Eckstein, Author

Offers information on over 750 foundations and corporations that award grants to nonprofit organizations for computers, computer training and software.
Cost: $52.50
200 Pages
Frequency: Biennial
ISBN: 0-945078-07-2

5646 **Directory of Library Automation Software, Systems and Services**
Information Today
143 Old Marlton Pike
Medford, NJ 08055-8750

609-654-6266
800-300-9868
Fax: 609-654-4309
E-Mail: custserv@infotoday.com
Home Page: www.infotoday.com

Thomas H Hogan, President
Roger R Bilboul, Chairman Of The Board

Recognized as the primary reference source for software packages used in automating libraries. This entirely new expanded 2004-2005 edition provides detailed descriptions of hundreds of currently available microcomputer, minicomputer, and mainframe software packages and services.
Cost: $89.00
351 Pages
Frequency: Bi-Annually
Founded in 1983

5647 **Directory of Simulation Software**
Society for Modeling and Simulation International
4838 Ronson Ct
PO Box 17900
San Diego, CA 92177-7900

858-277-3888
Fax: 858-277-3930
E-Mail: info@scs.org
Home Page: www.scs.org

Amy Shapiro, Publications Manager & Editor
Steve Branch, Executive Director

About 200 simulation software packages and their suppliers.
Cost: $40.00
Frequency: Annual
Circulation: 2,000
Mailing list available for rent

5648 **Directory of Top Computer Executives**
Applied Computer Research
PO Box 41730
Phoenix, AZ 85080

602-216-9100
800-234-2227
Fax: 602-548-4800
E-Mail: tara@topitexecs.com
Home Page: www.acrhq.com

Contains the names of more than 52,000 of the most influential information technology managers in the US and Canada. Entrepreneurs and corporate executives have used this data base to build successful businesses for over 30 years.
Cost: $245.00
Frequency: Semi-Annual
Founded in 1972

5649 **Directory of US Government Software for Mainframes and Microcomputers**
US National Technical Information Service
5285 Port Royal Road
Springfield, VA 22161

703-605-6000
800-553-6847
Fax: 703-605-6900
E-Mail: info@ntis.gov
Home Page: www.ntis.gov

Patrik Ekstr"m, Business Development Manager
Reuel Avila, Managing Director

Contains descriptions of some 550 mainframe and microcomputer programs made available from more than 100 federal agencies, or their contractors since 1984. The directory is an essential reference tool for users who wish to tap the wealth of U.S. Government software.
Cost: $65.00
174 Pages
Frequency: Annual
ISBN: 0-934213-37-2

5650 **Electronic Imaging an Image Processing: An Assessment of Technology & Products**
Richard K Mill & Associates
5880 Live Oak Parkway
Suite 270
Norcross, GA 30093-1707

770-416-0006
Fax: 770-416-0052

Richard K Miller, Editor/President
Kelli D Washington, Editor-in-Chief

List of producers and suppliers of electronic imaging computer software and hardware.
Cost: $485.00
ISBN: 0-896711-12-9

5651 **Guide to Free Films, Flimstrips and Slides**
Educators Progress Service
214 Center St
Randolph, WI 53956-1497

920-326-3126
888-951-4469
Fax: 920-326-3127
E-Mail: questions@freeteachingaids.com
Home Page: www.freeteachingaids.com

Kathy Nehmer, President

Offers sources for films, filmstrips, slide sets, audiotapes and videotapes.
Cost: $37.95
135 Pages
Frequency: Annual
ISBN: 0-877083-51-7

5652 **Hoover's Guide to Computer Companies**
Hoover's
5800 Airport Blvd
Austin, TX 78752-3826

512-374-1187
800-486-8666
Fax: 512-374-4501
E-Mail: customersupport@hoovers.com
Home Page: www.hoovers.com

David Mather, President
Paul Pellman, Executive VP Marketing/Products

250 of the largest public and private computer industry companies in in-depth profiles.
Cost: $34.95
737 Pages
Frequency: Annual
ISBN: 1-878753-80-0

5653 **IT Computer Economics Report Journal**
Computer Economics
2082 Business Center Drive
Suite 240
Irvine, CA 92612

949-831-8700
Fax: 949-442-7688
Home Page: www.computereconomics.com

Frank Scavo, President
Dan Husiak, VP

Provides decision makers throughout the world with timely insights into the management of information systems.
Frequency: Monthly
Founded in 1978

5654 **Index to AV Producers & Distributors 10th Edition**
Information Today
143 Old Marlton Pike
Medford, NJ 08055 8750

609-654-6266
800-300-9868
Fax: 609-654-4309
E-Mail: custserv@infotoday.com
Home Page: www.infotoday.com

Thomas H Hogan, President
Roger R Bilboul, Chairman Of The Board

Contains over 23,500 producers and distributors of AV materials of all kinds. This handy softbound volume is an indispensible tool for buyers of audiovisual materials of all kinds.
Cost: $89.00
626 Pages
ISBN: 0-937548-30-8

5655 **Internet & Personal Computing Abstracts Journal**
Information Today
143 Old Marlton Pike
Medford, NJ 08055-8750

609-654-6266
800-300-9868
Fax: 609-654-4309
E-Mail: custserv@infotoday.com
Home Page: www.infotoday.com

Thomas H Hogan, President
Roger R Bilboul, Chairman Of The Board

This comprehensive database contains over 150,000 citations, with abstracts to reviews of commentaries on the use and applications of microcomputers and software packages.
Cost: $235.00
Frequency: Quarterly
Circulation: 10,000
Founded in 1980

5656 **Inventor's Desktop Companion: A Guide to Successfully Marketing Ideas**
Visible Ink Press/Gale Research
PO Box 09187
Detroit, MI 48209-0187

248-699-4253
800-877-GALE
Fax: 248-699-8049

Patrick C Sommers, President

Offers information on agencies and organizations of interest to inventors, including regional and national associations, university innovation research centers and business incubators for the computer and desktop industries.
Cost: $24.95
470 Pages

5657 **Micro Publishing Report's Directory of Desktop Publishing Suppliers**
Cygnus Publishing

PO Box 803
Fort Atkinson, WI 53538-0803

920-000-1111
800-547-7377
Fax: 920-563-1699
E-Mail: rich.reiff@cygnuspub.com
Home Page: www.cygnusb2b.com

John French, CEO
Tom Martin, Director of Public Relations
Kathy Scott, Director of Public Relations
Paul Bonaiuto, CFO

Offers valuable information on over 200 suppliers of microcomputer systems for desktop publishing.
Cost: $35.00
30 Pages
Frequency: Annual

5658 Microcomputer Market Place
Random House
202 E 50th St
New York, NY 10022

212-572-6120

Offers information on manufacturers and suppliers of computer equipment and accessories.
Cost: $29.95
795 Pages

5659 Microprocessor Integrated Circuits
DATA Digest
321 Inverness Drive South
Englewood, CO 80112

303-790-0600
800-525-7052
Home Page: www.ihs.com

Jerre Stead, Chair/CEO
Michael Armstrong, Director

Offers a list of over 185 manufacturers and distributors of microprocessor integrated circuits.
Cost: $205.00
Frequency: SemiAnnual

5660 Microsoft Applications and Systems Forums
Microsoft Corporation
1 Microsoft Way
Redmond, WA 98052-8300

425-882-8080
800-426-9400
Fax: 425-936-7329
Home Page: www.microsoft.com

Steve Ballmer, CEO

This database provides an exchange of information and tips on Microsoft computer systems for participants.

5661 Modern Machine Shop's Handbook for Metalworkingi Industries on CD-ROM
Gardner Publications
6915 Valley Ln
Cincinnati, OH 45244-3153

513-527-8800
800-950-8020
Fax: 513-527-8801
Home Page: www.gardnerweb.com

Rick Kline Sr, CEO
John Campos, Manager
Brian Wertheimer, Account Manager
Eddie Kania, Sales Manager

Provides a balanced blend of traditional and modern topics. In addition to containing a wide range of reference tables covering all aspects of machining, composition of materials, and dimensions of tooling and machine components.
Cost: $55.00
2368 Pages
ISBN: 1-569903-55-7
Founded in 2002

5662 National Directory of Bulletin Board Systems
Penton Media
1300 E 9th St
Suite 316
Cleveland, OH 44114-1503

216-696-7000
Fax: 216-696-6662
E-Mail: information@penton.com
Home Page: www.penton.com

Jane Cooper, Marketing

Computer bulletin board systems that display notices of special events or new products are profiled.
Cost: $45.00
400 Pages
Frequency: Annual

5663 NetWire
Novell
165 Nantasket Beach Avenue
Hull, MA 02045

78- 9-5 17
800-453-2167
Fax: 781-925-6545
E-Mail: john@netwire.com
Home Page: netwire.com

This database concentrates on Novell computer software and hardware information.

5664 Online Networks, Databases & Bulletin Boards on Assistive Technology
ERIC Document Reproduction Service
7420 Fullerton Road
Suite 110
Springfield, VA 22153-2852

703-440-1400
800-443-ERIC
Fax: 703-440-1408

Directory of electronic networks that focus on technology-related services.

5665 Orion Blue Book: Computer
Orion Research Corporation
14555 N Scottsdale Rd
Suite 330
Scottsdale, AZ 85254-3487

480-951-1114
800-844-0759
Fax: 480-951-1117
E-Mail: orion@orionbluebook.com
Home Page: www.orionbluebook.com

Roger Rohrs, Owner

63,053 products listed from 1970's to present. Over 1,000 manufacturers listed.
695 Pages
Frequency: Annual
Founded in 1985

5666 PC-Link
America Online
8619 Westwood Center Drive
Suite 200
Vienna, VA 22182-2238

Home Page: pclink.com.eg

Provides access to a variety of databases and computer services of interest to users of IBM and compatible computers running MS-DOS.
Frequency: Directory

5667 ParaTechnology Directory of Systems and Network Integrators
ParaTechnology
1215 120th Ave NE
Suite 101
Bellevue, WA 98005-2135

425-453-0676
800-377-2021
Fax: 425-453-0338
Home Page: www.eside.org

One thousand computer system and network integrators in North America.
Cost: $495.00
Frequency: Annual

5668 Personal Computing Directory
Resources
PO Box 1067
Cambridge, MA 02238-1067

Directory of services and supplies to the industry.
Cost: $29.95
Frequency: Annual

5669 Pocket Guides to the Internet: Telnetting
Information Today
143 Old Marlton Pike
Medford, NJ 08055-8750

609-654-6266
800-300-9868
Fax: 609-654-4309
E-Mail: custserv@infotoday.com
Home Page: www.infotoday.com

Thomas H Hogan, President
Roger R Bilboul, Chairman Of The Board

Logon information and resources available via telnetting.
Cost: $9.95

5670 Q-Link
America Online
8619 Westwood Center Drive
Suite 200
Vienna, VA 22182-2238

800-227-6364
Fax: 540-265-2135

Anne Botsford

This database consists of several files of general interest news and information for users of Commodore computers.
Frequency: Full-text

5671 Shareware Magazine: PC SIG's Encyclopedia of Shareware Section
Shareware Magazine
1030 E Duane Avenue
Suite D
Sunnyvale, CA 94086-2624

408-733-8900

Offers a variety of software programs for the IBM PC and its compatibles.
Cost: $19.95
Frequency: Bi-Monthly

5672 SoftBase
Information Resources
PO Box 8120
Berkeley, CA 94707-8120

510-525-6220
Fax: 510-525-1568
Home Page: www.searchsoftbase.com

Ruth K Koolish, Editor

It produces software products, services and companies abstracted from more than 200 business, computer, technical, trade and consumer publications.
Frequency: Monthly

5673 Software Encyclopedia
R R Bowker LLC
630 Central Ave
New Providence, NJ 07974-1506

908-286-0288
888-269-5372
Fax: 908-464-3553

E-Mail: info@bowker.com
Home Page: www.bowker.com

R R Bowker

A comprehensive easy to navigate guide filled with detailed information on microcomputer software. Listings of over 44,600 software programs from 4,646 publishers and distributors are fully annotated to facilitate research and acquisition.
Frequency: 2 Volume set
ISBN: 0-835249-69-0

5674 **Software Engineering Bibliography**
Kaman Sciences Corporation
258 Genesse Street
Utica, NY 13502

315-732-1955
Home Page: www.dacs.com

Citation for over 15,000 technical reports, articles, theses, papers and books concerned with software technology.
Cost: $30.00
Frequency: Annual

5675 **Software Life Cycle Tools Directory**
Data & Analysis Center for Software
PO Box 1400
Rome, NY 13442-1400

315-334-4905
800-214-7921
Fax: 315-334-4964
E-Mail: cust-liasn@dacs.dtic.mil
Home Page: www.iac.dtic.mil/dacs

Offers sources of more than 400 software packages for software engineering and maintenance.
Cost: $40.00
500 Pages

5676 **Telecom Internet Directory**
Information Gatekeepers Group
1340 Soldiers Field Rd
Suite 302
Brighton, MA 02135-1000

617-782-5033
800-323-1088
Fax: 617-782-5735
E-Mail: info@igigroup.com
Home Page: www.igigroup.com

Paul Polishuk, CEO
Bev Wilson, Controller
Yesim Taskor, Controller

Developed to help find information in telecommunications efficiently and timely manner. A wide range of researchers, market analysts, information specialists, librarians and others will find the directory useful in finding information about telecommunications on the Internet.
Cost: $195.00

5677 **Top 100 Service Companies**
Coordinated Service
20A Court Street
Groton, MA 01450-4217

978-448-2472

100 of the largest US based independent computer service companies.

5678 **UNISYS World Software Directory**
Publications & Communications
Cypress Creek Road
Suite B
Cedar Park, TX 78613

512-250-9023

Offers valuable information on suppliers of computer software packages compatible with UNISYS Corporation computer systems.
140 Pages
Frequency: SemiAnnual
Circulation: 650

5679 **Uplink Directory**
Virginia A Ostendorf
PO Box 2896
Littleton, CO 80161-2896

303-797-3131

Directory of services and supplies to the industry.

5680 **User's Directory of Computer Networks**
Digital Press
129 Parker Street
Maynard, MA 01754-2199

978-493-1770

Offers a list of hosts, site contacts and administrative domains.
Cost: $35.95
630 Pages

Industry Web Sites

5681 **http://gold.greyhouse.com**
G.O.L.D Grey House OnLine Databases

Grey House Publishing's online database platform, GOLD, offers its Quick Search, Keyword Search and Expert Search for most business sectors including comupter and data processing markets. The GOLD platform makes finding the information you need quick and easy - whether you're a novice searcher or an experienced database user. All of Grey House's directory products are available for subscription on the GOLD platform.

5682 **www.4w.com**
Information Analytics

Dedicated to the non-profit professional development of information systems managers, directors and analysts.

5683 **www.aaai.org**
American Association for Artificial Intelligence

A scientific society devoted to advancing the scientific understanding of the mechanisms underlying thought and intelligent behavior and their embodiment in machines.

5684 **www.aace.org**
Assn for the Advancement of Computing in Education

Promotes the use of computers and the internet in educational settings.

5685 **www.adweek.com**
Adweek

Leading decision makers in the advertising and marketing field go to Adweek.com every day for breaking news, insight, buzz, opinion, analysis, research and classifieds. The resources of all six regional editions of Adweek, as well as the national edition of Brandweek are combined with the knowledge of our online editors and the multimedia-interactive capabilities of the web to deliver vital information quickly and effectively to our target audience.

5686 **www.afsmi.org**
Association for Services Management International

Provides the knowledge, fellowship and career connections that customer services and support managers for technology based products and solutions needed for professional and career development.

5687 **www.aiim.org**
Association for Information and Image Management

The leading international organization focused on helping users to understand the challenges associated with managing documents, content, and business processes.

5688 **www.aimglobal.org**
AIM Global

International trade association representing automatic identification and mobility technology solution providers.

5689 **www.aitp.org**
Association of Information Technology Professional

Comprised of career minded individuals who seek to expand their potential employers, employees, managers, programmers and many others. This organization seeks to provide avenues for all their members to be teachers as well as students and to make contacts with other members in the IS field, all in an effort to become more marketable in rapidly changing technological careers.

5690 **www.apple.com**
Apple

Official web site for Apple; Macintosh computers and software.

5691 **www.asm.com**
Society for Materials Engineers and Scientists

A leading supplier of semiconductor process equipment in both front and back end markets. The Company possesses a strong technological base, state-of-the-art manufacturing facilities, a competent and qualified workforce and a highly trained, strategically distributed support network.

5692 **www.bsa.org**
Business Software Alliance

An organization dedicated to promoting a safe and legal digital world. BSA educates consumers on software management and copyright protection, cyber security, trade, e-commerce and other internet related issues.

5693 **www.bta.org**
Business Technology Association

Serving independent dealers, value added resellers, system integrators, manufacturers and distributors in the business equipment and system industry. BTA helps its members profit through a wide variety of services, including free legal advice and guidance; business benchmarking studies and reports; information on the latest news, trends, and products in the industry.

5694 **www.calico.org**
Computer Assisted Language Instruction Consortium

For language teachers, linguists, courseware developers and governments who are interested in teaching languages with the use of computer assisted instruction.

5695 **www.comptia.org**
CompTIA

Representing the international technology community. The goal is to provide a unified voice, global advocacy and leadership and to advance industry growth through standards, professional competence, education and business solutions.

5696 **www.devx.net**
DevX

The leading provider of technical and services that enable corporate application development teams to efficiently conquer development challenges and keep projects moving.

5697 **www.disa.org**
Data Interchange Standards Association
Many industries are looking to develop and implement eXtensible Markup Language (XML) specifications to eliminate paperwork, improve data accuracy, increase productivity, and reduce operating costs. This effort requires technical and administrative support. DISA can help.

5698 **www.greyhouse.com**
Grey House Publishing
Authoritative reference directories for most business sectors incluidng computer and data processing markets. Users can search the online databases with varied search criteria allowing for custom searches by product category, geographic area, sales volume, keyword, subject and more. Full Grey House catalog and online ordering also available.

5699 **www.guide.sbanetweb.com**
Guide to Computer Vendors
Planning and project management involved in the installation and implementation of client server accounting systems. We provide consulting assitance to a wide range of services such modeling agencies, publishing firms as well as manufacturing and distributors.

5700 **www.icca.org**
Independent Computer Consultants Association
Represents a wide variety of information technology consultants who provide consulting, implementation, support, training, strategic planning, and business analysis services.

5701 **www.internet.com**
Internet.Com/Mecklermedia
A leading source of global Internet news, and analyses. To learn about Internet.com's latest activities

5702 **www.intl-spectrum.com**
International Spectrum
The independent source of information for users and vendors of IBM's UniVerse and UniData; jBASE International's jBASE; Northgate information Solutions Reality; ONgroup's ONware; Raining Data's D3, mvBASE and mvEnterprise; Revelation Software's Opensight and VIA Systems UniVision Databases.

5703 **www.ioma.com**
IOMA
Supports managers involved in building and maintaining state-of-the-art HRIS software, hardware, and Internet/intranet activities. Publishes newsletter.

5704 **www.irga.com**
International Reprographic Association
Provides a framework for the exchange of information and support for the reprographic industry. The IRgA continues to be the only independent association serving the reprographics industry and the AEC community.

5705 **www.iste.org**
International Society for Technology in Education
A worldwide membership of leaders and potential leaders in educational technology. We are dedicated to providing leadership and service to improve teaching and learning by advancing the effective use of technology in K-12 education and teacher education. We provide our members with information, networking opportunities, and guidance as they face the challenge of incorporating computers, the Internet, and other new technologies into their schools.

5706 **www.openapplications.org**
Open Applications Group
A open standards group building process-based XML standards for both B2B and A2A integration.

5707 **www.pcca.org**
Portable Computer and Communications Association
A forum for disparate industries to meet, learn about each other, and collaborate on the interaction of the multiple technologies involved in wireless solutions.

5708 **www.polarmicro.com**
Polar Microsystems
Provides consulting services that enable our clients to advance their businesses through full utilization of the Apple Macintosh hardware and software platform.

5709 **www.sei.cmu.edu**
Software Engineering Institute
Works closely with defense and government organizations, industry, and academia to continually improve software-intensive systems.

5710 **www.sme.org**
Automated Systems Technical Group/SME
This group harnesses the power of information technology for advancing product development and design, manufacturing automation, enterprise integration, and communication throughout the product life cycle and supply chain.

5711 **www.spie.org**
International Society for Optical Engineering
Serves the international technical community as the premier provider of education, information, and resources covering optics, photonics, and their applications.

5712 **www.thinkecs.com**
Enterprise Computing Solutions
A leading provider of IT infrastructure solutions for Fortune 500 and mid-tier companies throughout California. ECS builds sophisticated IT solutions for mission critical applications, provides enterprise storage solutions that ensure data protection and business continuity and delivers state of the art server solutions for optimal computing capacity.

5713 **www.unf.edu/library**
University of North Florida, Carpenter Library
For catalogers of audiovisual materials and electronic resources. Provides information exchange, continuing education, and works toward a common understanding of practices and standards.

5714 **www.vita.com**
VMEbus International Trade Association
For manufacturers of microcomputer boards, hardware, software, military products, controllers, bus interfaces and other accessories compatible with VMEbus architecture. VITA is an incorporated, nonprofit organization of vendors and users having a common market interest.

5715 **www.webdeveloper.com**
Mecklermedia/Internet.Com
Information on maintaining and growing business web sites and intranets.

5716 **www1.hp.com**
Hewlett Packard /Compaq
The official Web site for the Compaq PCs.

Associations

5717 **Aesthetics' International Association**
310 E. Interstate 30
Suite B107
Garland, TX 75043
972-203-8530
877-968-7539
Fax: 972-962-1480
Home Page: www.aestheticsassociation.com
Patricia Strunk, President
Michelle D'Allaird, Vice President
Michelle D'Allaird, VP, Director of Education
Saundra S. Brown, VP, Director of Operations
The association for the advancement of education and public awareness on aesthetics. Paramedical aesthetics and body spa therapy. Professionals from the medical, paramedical and beauty industries working together for the most advanced techniques for the patients and clients.
Founded in 1972

5718 **Allied Beauty Association (ABA)**
145 Traders Blvd. E.
Suites 26&27
Mississauga, ON IL4Z3L3
800-268-6644
Fax: 905-568-1581
Home Page: abacanada.com
Social Media: Facebook, Twitter, LinkedIn
Marc Speir, Executive Director
Manufacturers and distributors of the professional beauty industry that serve Canada.

5719 **American Association for Esthetics Education**
401 N Michigan Avenue
Chicago, IL 60611
312-321-6809
800-883-7808
Home Page: www.aestheticsassociation.com
Social Media: Facebook, Twitter, YouTube
Provides access to educational experts, methods for increasing profits, and infomation on the latest products and techniques.
Cost: $105.00

5720 **American Association of Cosmetology Schools**
9927 E. Bell Road
Suite 110
Scottsdale, AZ 85260
480-810-0431
800-831-1086
Fax: 480-905-0993
E-Mail: jim@beautyschools.org
Home Page: www.beautyschools.org
Social Media: Facebook, Twitter
Jim Cox, Executive Director
Lisa Zarda, General Manager
Association open to all privately owned cosmetology schools.
1100 Members
Founded in 1924

5721 **American Beauty Association**
401 N Michigan Avenue
Chicago, IL 60611
312-245-1595
800-868-4265
Fax: 312-245-1080
Home Page:
www.americanbeautyassociation.com
Pablo Arellano Jr., President
Myriam Clifford, VP
Bruce Selan, First VP
Lydia Sarfati, Second VP
George Schaeffer, Secretary
ABA members are manufacturers, manufacturer reps and consultants in the professional beauty industry. Associate members are made up of trade publications, distributors and salons. The ABA's mission is to expand, serve and protect the interests of the professional beauty industry.
200 Members
Founded in 1985

5722 **American Hair Loss Association**
23679 Calabasas Road
#682
Calabasas, CA 91301
E-Mail: membership@americanhairloss.org
Home Page: www.americanhairloss.org
The American Hair Loss Association is the only national, non-profit membership organization dedicated to educating the public, healthcare professionals, main stream media and legislators about the emotionaally devastating disease of hair loss (alopecia). Committed to the prevention and treatment of hair loss, the ALHA is dedicated to supporting research that will ultimately treat and cure thoses who suffer from this silent epidemic.

5723 **American Hair Loss Council**
30 South Main
Shenandoah, PA 17976
412-765-3666
Fax: 412-765-3669
E-Mail: info@ahlc.org
Home Page: www.ahlc.org
Susan Kettering, Executive Director
The nation's only, unbiased, not for profit agency, dedicated to sorting through this information, discovering what works and what does-n't,a nd presenting our findings to the consumer.

5724 **American Health & Beauty Aids Institute**
PO Box 19510
Chicago, IL 60619-0510
708-633-6328
Fax: 708-633-6329
Home Page: www.ahbai.org
Social Media: Facebook, Twitter
Joe Dudley, Senior President
Jory Luste, President
Nathaniel Bronner, Jr. Executive VP
AHBAI heresents leading, African American-owned companies manufacturing ethnic hair care and beauty products. Members serve African Americans through employment, scholarships and education.

5725 **American Society of Hair Restoration Surgery**
737 North Michigan Avenue
Suite 2100
Chicago, IL 60611
312-981-6760
Fax: 312-981-6787
E-Mail: info@cosmeticsurgery.org
Home Page: www.cosmeticsurgery.org
Social Media: Facebook, Twitter, LinkedIn
Jeffrey P Knezovich, Executive VP
Charlie Baase, Marketing Manager
Comprised of physicians specializing in hair loss, dedicated to promulgating the highest standards of medical practice and medical ethics. Provides continuing education to physicians specializing in hair transplant surgery and gives the public the latest information on medical and surgical treatments for hair loss.
1600 Members

5726 **American Society of Perfumers**
PO Box 1551
West Caldwell, NJ 07004
201-991-0040
Fax: 201-991-0073
E-Mail: info@perfumers.org
Home Page: www.perfumers.org
Social Media: Facebook, Twitter
Marvel Fields, President
Nonprofit organization fosters and encourages the art and science of perfumery in the US while promoting professional exchange and a high standard of professional conduct within the fragrance industry. The ASP holds yearly symposiums in the New York City area where leading members of the fragrance industry are invited to speak and present information on all aspects of the industry.
Founded in 1947

5727 **Association Accredited Cosmetology Schools**
5201 Leesburg Pike
Falls Church, VA 22041-3244
Ronald Smith, Publisher
Association for those concerned with cosmetology.
6 Members

5728 **B-cause**
PO Box 4814
Poughkeepsie, NY 12601
845-431-6670
Home Page: www.bcause.org
Social Media: Facebook
Rudy Sprogis, Founder/President
Non-profit organization that advances charitable causes for salon owners and beauty industry professionals.
Founded in 2000

5729 **BOBSA**
PO Box 25173
San Francisco, CA 94128
650-357-0073
Fax: 858-712-1934
Home Page: bobsaone.org
Social Media: Facebook, Twitter, LinkedIn
Sam Ennon, President
Representing beauty store operators in the ethnic health and beauty-care industry.

5730 **Chain Drug Marketing Association**
43157 W Nine Mile Road
PO Box 995
Novi, MI 48376-0995
248-449-9300
Fax: 248-449-9396
E-Mail: support@chaindrug.com
Home Page: www.chaindrug.com
Social Media: Facebook
Jack Walker, Chairman
Jim Devine, President
Jim Salley, Treasurer
Judy Aspinall, Secretary
Members are regional drug chains from across North ASmerica Association markets over 800 products under the name Quality Choice to its members.
101 Members

5731 **Consumer Healthcare Products Association**
900 19th St Nw
Suite 700
Washington, DC 20006-2105
202-429-9260
Fax: 202-223-6835

E-Mail: eassey@chpa-info.org
Home Page: www.chpa-info.org

Paul L. Sturman, Chair

Promotes industry growth through consumer understanding, appreciation, and acceptance of responsible self-care in America's health care system by developing and sustaining a climate that provides consumers with convenient access to safe and effective nonprescription medicines and other self-care products marketed without undue restrictions.

5732 Cosmetic Executive Women
286 Madison Ave
19th Floor
New York, NY 10017

212-685-5955
Fax: 212-685-3334
E-Mail: ksweeney@cew.org
Home Page: www.cew.org
Social Media: Facebook, Twitter, LinkedIn, YouTube

Carlotta Jacobson, President
Kelly McPhilliamy, Treasurer
Jill Scalamandre, Chairwoman
Barbara Kotlikoff, Vice Chairwomen
Heidi Manheimer, Vice Chairwomen

To advance the professional growth and leadership development of women in the beauty industry.
4000 Members
Founded in 1954

5733 Cosmetic Industry Buyers and Suppliers
36 Lakeville Road
New Hyde Park, NY 11040

516-775-0220
Fax: 516-328-9789
E-Mail: cibsmail@cibsonline.com
Home Page: www.cibsonline.com
Social Media: LinkedIn

Mario Magali, President
Laura Carey, Vice President
Rafael Cruz, Treasurer
Nick LoPrinzi, Director
William F. Standwill, Director

Members are individuals providing and obtaining essential oils, chemicals, packaging and other goods for the cosmetic industry.
800 Members
Founded in 1948

5734 Cosmetologists Chicago
330 North Wabash Ave
Suite 200
Chicago, IL 60611-4255

312-329-0216
800-648-2505
Fax: 312-245-1080
Home Page: www.chicagomidwestbeautyshow.com

Joseph Cartagena, President
Denise Provenzano, First VP
Robert Passage, Secretary
Karen Gordon, Treasurer
Lisa Newman, Director Marketing

A beauty voice and presenter of cosmetology shows.

5735 Cosmetology Advancement Foundation
PO Box 811
FDR Station
New York, NY 10150

212-750-2412
Fax: 212-593-0862
E-Mail: nalcopr@aol.com
Home Page: cosmetology.org

Norma A. Lee, Executive Director

Members represent the professional beauty industry's varied constituencies: cosmetologists, salon owners, cosmetology schools, distributors, manufacturers, associations and professional publications. CAF works through the All-Industry Summit to identify issues that affect the future growth and development of the industry.

5736 Drug, Chemical & Associated Technologies Association
1 Washington Blvd
Suite 7
Robbinsville, NJ 08691-3162

609-448-1000
800-640-3228
Fax: 609-448-1944
E-Mail: mtimony@dcat.org
Home Page: www.dcat.org

Margaret M. Timony, Executive Director
Laura Kuhen, Project Coordinator
Lyra Myers, Finance Officer
George Svokos, Vice President
Jeanne Motola, Administrative Assistent

The premier business development association whose membership is comprised of companies that manufacture, distribute or provide services to the pharmaceutical, chemical, nutritional and related industries.
Founded in 1890

5737 Esthetics Manufacturers and Distributors Alliance
401 N Michigan Avenue
Chicago, IL 60611

312-215-5120
800-868-4265
Fax: 312-245-1080

Paul Dykstra, Executive Director
Paul Scott Premo, President
Charles Mizelle, VP
Mark Lees, Chairman
Julianne Bendel, Manager

A member of the American Beauty Association, whose members are manufacturers of specific products related to the professional beauty industry. EMDA is dedicated to meeting the needs of skin care and body care manufacturers and distributors and the salons they service. The mission of the American Beauty Association and all of its sub-groups is to expand, serve and protect the interests of the professional beauty industry.
40 Members
Founded in 1993

5738 Fragrance Foundation
545 Fifth Avenue
Suite 900
New York, NY 10017

212-725-2755
Fax: 212-779-9058
E-Mail: info@fragrance.org
Home Page: www.fragrance.org
Social Media: Facebook, Twitter, LinkedIn, YouTube

Rochelle R Bloom, President
Mary Ellen Lapsansky, VP

Nonprofit, educational arm of the international fragrance industry. Devotes its energies to creating an atmosphere of understanding and appreciation of the benefits and pleasures of fragrance in all its many forms.
160 Members
Founded in 1949

5739 Fragrance Materials Association of the US
1620 I St NW
Suite 925
Washington, DC 20006-4076

202-293-5800
Fax: 202-463-8998
Home Page: www.fmafragrance.org
Social Media: Facebook, Twitter

Glenn Roberts, Executive Director
Daniel J Carey, VP
Robert Bedoukian, Secretary
Stephen A Block, Treasurer

Manufacturers of fragrance ingredients.
90 Members
Founded in 1927

5740 Fragrance Research Fund
545 Fifth Avenue
Suite 900
New York, NY 10017

212-725-2755
Fax: 212-779-9058
E-Mail: info@fragrance.org
Home Page: www.fragrance.org/
Social Media: Facebook, Twitter, YouTube

Annette Green, Administrator
Mary Lapensky, Vice President
Theresa Molnar, Executive Director
Amy Rubins, Special Projects and Events
Lilia Nicoletti, Director of Office Operations

Offers financial support for doctors and clinical researchers. Bestows awards.
Founded in 1949

5741 Independent Cosmetic Manufacturers and Distributors
1220 W. Northwest Hwy
Palatine, IL 60067

847-991-4499
800-334-2623
Fax: 847-991-8161
E-Mail: info@icmad.org
Home Page: www.icmad.org
Social Media: Facebook, Twitter

Pam Busiek, Chairman of the Board
Sheila Sebor, VP Operations
Vance Seaton, Executive Assistant
Stan Katz, Chairman Emeritus
Karen Acker, Director

Represents cosmetic manufacturers, distributors and suppliers to industry. Mission: to represent, educate and foster the growth and profitability of entrepreneurial companies in the cosmetic and personal care industries worldwide.
540 Members
Founded in 1974

5742 Indoor Tanning Association (ITA)
2025 M St, NW
Suite 800
Washington, DC 20036

888-377-0477
Fax: 202-367-2142
Home Page: www.theita.com

Dan Humiston, President
John Overstreet, Executive Director
Dan Humiston, President
Karen Bentlage, Public Relations

Represents indoor tanning manufacturers, distributors, facility owners and members from other support industries.
1000+ Members
Founded in 1999

5743 **International Aloe Science Council**
Ste 918
8630 Fenton St
Silver Spring, MD 20910-3818

301-588-2420
Fax: 301-588-1174
Home Page: www.iasc.org

Santiago Rodriguez, President
Chris Clarke, President-Elect
Tom Brown, Treasurer
Walt Jones, Director
Chris Clarke, Chairman

Explores the use of aloe in cosmetic industries, hair products, herb preparations, pharmaceuticals and drinks.
300 Members
Founded in 1981

5744 **International Association of Color Manufacturers**
1101 17th Street NW
Suite 700
Washington, DC 20036

202-293-5800
Fax: 202-463-8998
E-Mail: info@iacmcolor.org
Home Page: www.iacmcolor.org

Glenn Roberts, Executive Director
David R. Carpenter, President & Treasurer
Rohit Tibrewala, Secretary

Actively represents the interests of the regulated color industry by demonstrating the safety of color additives and promotes the industry's economic growth by participating in new color approvals, regulatory and legislative issues that affect the industry worldwide.
15 Members
Founded in 1972

5745 **International Perfume Bottle Association**
PO Box 1299
Paradise, CA 95967

E-Mail: paradise@sunset.net
Home Page: www.perfumebottles.org
Social Media: Facebook

Jeffrey Sanfilippo, President
Teri Wirth, Vice President
Peggy Tichenor, Membership Secretary
Shelley Bechtold, Treasurer
Barbara W. Miller, Recording Secretary

Worldwide non-profit organization of people who collect and deal in the variety of perfume containers.
Cost: $45.00
2000+ Members
Founded in 1988

5746 **International SPA Association**
2365 Harrodsburg Road
Suite A325
Lexington, KY 40504

859-226-4445
888-651-4772
Fax: 859-226-4445
E-Mail: ispa@ispastaff.com
Home Page: www.experienceispa.com
Social Media: Facebook, Twitter, LinkedIn, YouTube

Ms. Ella Stimpson, Chair
Mr. Michael Tompkins, Vice Chair
Jennifer Wayland-Smith, Vice Chairman
Ella Stimpson, Secretary/ Treasurer

International community of spa professionals, product manufacturers and service providers.
Cost: $530.00
Founded in 1990

5747 **International SalonSpa Business Network**
207 E. Ohio St.
#361
Chicago, IL 60611

866-444-4272
Fax: 866-444-5139
Home Page: salonspanetwork.org

Jason Volk, President
Jason Volk, Vice President
Paul Brown, Vice President
Larry Walt, Treasurer
Charles Penzone, Secretary

The association strives to unify the industry and drive it to become more politically active. Members share information, conduct roundtables and help each other recruit, train and retain their staffs.
60+ Members

5748 **Nail Manufacturers Council**
Professional Beauty Association
15825 N. 71st Street
Suite 100
Scottsdale, AZ 85254

480-281-0424
800-468-2274
Fax: 480-905-0708
E-Mail: info@probeauty.org
Home Page: www.probeauty.org/nmc
Social Media: Facebook, Twitter, LinkedIn

Reuben Carranza, Chair
Scott Buchanan, Chairman
Bruce Selan, Treasurer

The NMC comprises the leading manufacturers of nail care products sold to, and used in, professional salons. Members cooperate with the association to assure the dissemination of education, training, and technical information concerning nail care products. The NMC has been active in working with international, federal, and state bodies to maintain high professional standards and ensure the safety of industry professionals and their customers, as well as the communities they serve.
50 Members
Founded in 1990

5749 **National Accrediting Commission of Cosmetology Arts & Sciences(NACCAS)**
4401 Ford Avenue
Suite 1300
Arlington, VA 2230

703-600-7600
Fax: 703-379-2200
E-Mail: naccas@naccas.org
Home Page: naccas.org

Tony Mirando, Executive Director
Eddie Broomfield, Assistant to Executive Director

To accredit post-secondary cosmetology schools and programs.
1050 Members

5750 **National Beauty Culturists' League (NBCL)**
25 Logan Circle N.W.
Washington, DC 20005

202-332-2695
Fax: 202-332-0940
Home Page: nbcl.org

Dr. Katie B. Catalon, President

Continuing education and higher learning degree program that serves as a unifying force and a catalyst for professionalism, excellence and growth of the beauty industry.
Founded in 1940

5751 **National Coalition of Estheticians Manufacturers/Distributors Assns.**
484 Spring Avenue
Ridgewood, NJ 07450-4624

201-670-4100
Fax: 201-670-4265
E-Mail: nceaorg@aol.com
Home Page: www.ncea.tv

Susanne S Warfield, Executive Director

Represents and promotes the esthetic and related professions industry by sharing information, building consensus and providing a unified voice on behalf of the industry.
7000+ Members
Founded in 2000

5752 **National Cosmetology Association**
401 N Michigan Ave
22nd Floor
Chicago, IL 60611-4267

312-527-6765
Fax: 480-905-0708
Home Page: www.salonprofessionals.org
Social Media: Facebook, Twitter

Gordon Miller, Executive Director

Nationwide community of salon professionals, connected by a common passion for learning, growing and raising the professionalism of the entire salon industry. As a group we have a storng voice in our communities, our industry and with our government because ithe NCA is for everyone in the professional salon industry. Members have access to education, fashion events, community service and inurance — all the tools needed to build your career.
30000 Members

5753 **National Interstate Council of State Boards of Cosmetology**
7622 Briarwood Cir
Little Rock, AR 72205-4811

501-227-8262
Fax: 501-227-8212
E-Mail: dnorton@nictesting.org
Home Page: www.nictesting.org

Kay Kendrick, President
Betty Leake, Vice President
Wayne Kindle, Secretary/ Treasurer

Merger of National Council of State Boards of Cosmetology and Interstate Council of State Boards of Cosmetology. Persons commissioned by the state governments to administer cosmetology laws and examine applicants for cosmetology licenses.
3200 Members
Founded in 1950

5754 **National Latino Cosmetology Association NLCA**
7925 W Russell Rd
PO Box 401044
Las Vegas, NV 89140

702-448-5020
Fax: 702-448-8993
E-Mail: info@nlcamerican.org
Home Page: nlcamerican.org

Julie Zepeda, President/ CEO
Gustavo Castillo, Executive Producer
Mark Sejvar, Marketing Manager

Unites beauty professionals, including salon/spa owners, licensed cosmetologists, barbers, estheticians, nail technicians, students, distributors and manufacturers representing the interests of the beauty industry on a global level.

5755 **Personal Care Products Council**
1101 17th Street NW
Suite 300
Washington, DC 20036-4702

202-331-1770
Fax: 202-331-1969
Home Page: www.personalcarecouncil.org
Social Media: Twitter, YouTube

Pamela Bailey, President
Mark Pollak, VP
Cheryl Mason, Secretary

The leading national trade association representing the global cosmetic and personal care products industry. Member companies manufacture, distribute, and supply the vast majority of finished personal care products marketed in the U.S.
600 Members
Founded in 1894

5756 **Professional Beauty Association**
15825 N 71st Street
Suite 100
Scottsdale, AZ 85254

480-281-0424
800-468-2274
Fax: 480-905-0708
Home Page: www.probeauty.org
Social Media: Facebook, Twitter, LinkedIn, YouTube

Scott Buchanan, Chair
Reuben Carranza, Vice Chair
Bruce Selan, Treasurer

A non-profit trade association that represents the interests of the professional beauty industry from manufacturers and distributors to salons and spas. Offers business tools, education, advocacy, networking and more to improve individual businesses and the industry as a whole.

5757 **Professional Beauty Foundation**
13034 Saticoy Avenue
N Hollywood, CA 91605

800-211-4872
Home Page: www.probeautyfederation.org

A nonprofit organization made up of professional beauty organizations dedicated to promote and protect the professional beauty industry as it relates to government laws and regulation.

5758 **RIFM: Research Institute for Fragrance Materials**
50 Tice Boulevard
Woodcliff Lake, NJ 07677

201-689-8089
Fax: 201-689-8090
E-Mail: rifm@rifm.org
Home Page: www.rifm.org
Social Media: Facebook, Twitter, LinkedIn

Sean G. Traynor, Ph.D, President (Chair)
Robert H. Bedoukian, Ph.D, President (Vice Chair)
David C. Shipman, Group Vice President (Treasurer)
Steven Hicks, Secretary
Michael Carlos, President (Fragrance Division)

Evaluates and distributes scientific data on the safety of fragrance raw materials found in cosmetics, perfumes, shampoos, acndles, air fresheners and other personal products, to encourage uniform safety standards. Membership is open to all companies that manufacture , sell, distribute or engage in business related to the fragrance industry for at least one year.
Founded in 1966

5759 **Regulatory Affairs Professionals Society**
5635 Fishers Lane
Suite 550
Rockville, MD 20852-3048

301-770-2920
Fax: 301-841-7956
E-Mail: raps@raps.org
Home Page: www.raps.org
Social Media: Facebook, Twitter, LinkedIn, YouTube

Susan E. James, Chairman of the Board
Cecilia Kimberlin, President
Paul Brooks, President-Elect
Leigh M. Vaughan, Secretary/ Treasurer
Linda Bowen, Director

The foremost worldwide member organization creating and upholding standards of ethica, credentialing and education for the regulatory affairs profession within the health product sector.
10000 Members
Founded in 1976

5760 **Scent Marketing Institute**
515 Madison Avenue
New York, NY 10022

646-236-4606
Fax: 914-470-2416
E-Mail: info@scentmarketing.org
Home Page: www.scentmarketing.org
Social Media: Facebook, Twitter, LinkedIn, YouTube

Harald H Vogt, Founder/Chief Marketer
Avery Gilbert PhD, Chief Scientist

Provides networking, educational and marketing support to our member companies and supplies information about scent marketing to the press, marketing, advertising and branding agencies and brand owners.
Founded in 2004

5761 **Sense of Smell Institute**
545 5th Avenue
Suite 900
New York, NY 10017

212-725-2755
Fax: 212-779-9058
Home Page: www.senseofsmell.org

Rochelle Bloom, President

Provides information resources to the public, members of the media, corporate and academic sectors. Also sponsors and conducts educational and public outreach programs to increase awareness of the important role the sense of smell plays in our lives.
Founded in 1949

5762 **Society of Clinical and Medical Hair Removal**
2424 American Lane
Madison, WI 53718

608-443-2470
Fax: 608-443-2474
E-Mail: homeoffice@scmhr.org
Home Page: www.scmhr.org
Social Media: Facebook

William A. Moore, President
Fadia Hoyek, Executive Vice President
Carol Crowley, Vice President
Lisa Birket, Treasurer
Denise MacIsaace, Secretary

An international non profit organization with members in the United States, Canada, Australia, Japan and beyond. Supports all methods of hair removal and is dedicated to the research of new technology that will keep its members at the pinnacle of thier professsion, offering safe, effective hair removal to their clients.
600 Members
Founded in 1985

5763 **Society of Cosmetic Chemists**
120 Wall St
Suite 2400
New York, NY 10005-4088

212-668-1500
Fax: 212-668-1504
E-Mail: scc@scconline.org
Home Page: www.scconline.org
Social Media: Facebook

Guy Padulo, President
Dawn Burke, Vice President
Peter Tsolis, Treasurer
Dawn Burke-Colvin, Secretary
Dawn Thiel Glase, Secretary

Dedicated to the advancement of cosmetic science, the Society strives to increase and disseminate scientific information through meetings and publications. By promoting research in cosmetic science and industry, and by setting high ethical, professional and educational standards, we reach our goal of improving the qualifacations of cosmetic scientists.
3600 Members
Founded in 1945

5764 **The Day Spa Association**
2863 Hedberg Drive
Union City, NJ 07087

877-851-8998
Fax: 855-344-8990
Home Page: dayspaassociation.com
Social Media: Facebook

Hannelore R. Leavy, President & Executive Director

Open to day spas, spa salons, individuals working in the spa industry and companies supplying products and services to the industry. Its aim is to unify and support the spa industry.
900 Members

5765 **Women in Flavor & Fragrance Commerce**
3301 State Route 66
Suite 205
Neptune, NJ 07753-2705

732-922-0500
Fax: 732-922-0560
E-Mail: info@wffc.org
Home Page: www.wffc.org

Allen Share, President
Celine Roche, Vice President
Kathryn Bardsley, Secretary
Anne Marie Api, Treasurer

This organization was borne out of a recognized need for a networking, education and support system for women in our industry. Providing a center of education, camaraderie, support, and networking.
300 Members
Founded in 1982

Newsletters

5766 **American Society of Perfumers Newsletter**
PO Box 1551
West Caldwell, NJ 07004

201-991-0040
Fax: 201-991-0073
E-Mail: info@perfumers.org
Home Page: www.perfumers.org
Social Media: Twitter

Marvel Fields, President

Information on upcoming events, industry news, fragrance related issues and special articles.
Founded in 1947

5767 **FDC Reports: Rose Sheet**
FDC Reports
5550 Friendship Boulevard
Suite 1
Chevy Chase, MD 20815-7256
301-657-9830
800-332-2181
Fax: 301-664-7238
Home Page: www.fdcreports.com
Brooke Mcmanus, Editor
Susan Easton, Publisher
Mike Squires, President
Shaun Smith, Marketing
Nicole Tesschamts, Circulation Manager
For executives in the cosmetics, toiletries, fragrances and skin care industries. Provides, coverage of the regulatory and legal environment for cosmetics, major scientific developments and testing methods product marketing news, new product launches; promotions and advertising, retail weekly trademark listings, mergers and acquisitions and developments in the European community.
Cost: $1050.00
Frequency: Weekly
ISSN: 0279-1110
Founded in 1939

5768 **Perfume Bottle Quarterly**
PO Box 1299
Paradise, CA 95967
E-Mail: paradise@sunset.net
Home Page: www.perfumebottles.org
Ed Lefkowith, President
Anne Conrad, Publications Chair
Features association news bottle photos, people, literature reviews, trade events, and classified ads. Providing a tremendous resource of knowledge about our field, PBQ is essential to staying current on information, events, and people of the field.
24 Pages
Frequency: Quarterly
Founded in 1997
Printed in 4 colors

5769 **Society of Cosmetic Chemists Newsletter**
Society of Cosmetic Chemists
120 Wall St
Suite 2400
New York, NY 10005-4088
212-668-1500
Fax: 212-668-1504
E-Mail: scc@scconline.org
Home Page: www.scconline.org
Randy Wickett, Ph.D, President
Joseph Dallal, Vice President
Guy Padulo, Vice President-Elect
Dawn Burke-Colvin, Secretary
Tony O'Lenick, Treasurer
Issued once a month providing up-to-date information about activities within the SCC and contemporary issues in international arbitration and mediation.
3600 Members
Founded in 1945

5770 **WFFC Newsletter**
Women in Flavor & Fragrance Commerce
3301 State Route 66
Suite 205
Neptune, NJ 07753-2705
732-922-0500
Fax: 732-922-0560
E-Mail: info@wffc.org
Home Page: www.wffc.org
Joanne Kennedy, President
Celine Roche, Vice President
Kathryn Bardsley, Secretary
Anne Marie Api, Treasurer
This organization was borne out of a recognized need for a networking, education and support system for women in our industry. Providing a center of education, camaraderie, support, and networking.
300 Members
Founded in 1982

Magazines & Journals

5771 **Beauty Fashion**
Ledes Group
286 Madison Ave
Suite 200
New York, NY 10017-6407
212-840-8800
Fax: 212-840-7246
Home Page: www.beautyfashion.com
John Ledes, Owner
Michelle Krell Kydd, Marketing
The authoritative magazine in the field of cosmetics, toiletries, fragrances and personal care.
Cost: $25.00
131 Pages
Frequency: Monthly
Circulation: 18672
ISSN: 0005-7487
Printed in 4 colors on glossy stock

5772 **Beauty Fashion: Body/Bath/Sun Issue**
Beauty Fashion
16 E 40th Street
New York, NY 10016
212-328-6789
Fax: 212-840-7246
Home Page: www.beautyfashion.com
Social Media: Facebook
Offers listings of body/bath and sun products as well as manufacturers and US distributors.
Cost: $25.00
Frequency: Annual
Circulation: 17,000

5773 **Beauty Fashion: CTFA Convention Issue**
Beauty Fashion
16 E 40th Street
New York, NY 10016
212-328-6789
Fax: 212-840-7246
Home Page: www.beautyfashion.com
Offers various suppliers of goods and services to the cosmetics industry manufacturers represented at Cosmetic, Toiletry and Fragrance Association convention.
Cost: $25.00
Frequency: Annual
Circulation: 17,000

5774 **Beauty Fashion: Cosmetics Issue**
Beauty Fashion
16 E 40th Street
New York, NY 10016
212-328-6789
Fax: 212-840-7246
Home Page: www.beautyfashion.com
Offers listings of color cosmetics products for women as well as manufacturers and US distributors.
Cost: $25.00
Frequency: Annual
Circulation: 17,000

5775 **Beauty Fashion: Women's Fragrance Issue**
Beauty Fashion
16 E 40th Street
New York, NY 10016-5101
212-328-6789
Fax: 212-840-7246
Home Page: www.beautyfashion.com/
Michelle Kre Kydd, Marketing
Veronica Kelly, Circulation Manager
Adelaide Farah, Editor
Offers listings of women's fragrance products including perfumes, eau de toilettes, and colognes as well as manufacturers and US distributors.
Cost: $25.00
Frequency: Monthly
Circulation: 17000

5776 **Beauty Fashion: Women's Treatment Issue**
Beauty Fashion
Ste 700
286 Madison Ave
New York, NY 10017-6407
212-840-8800
Fax: 212-840-7246
Home Page: www.beautyfashion.com/
Adelaide Farah, Group Editorial Director
Veronica Kelly, Subscription
Michelle Krell Kydd, Marketing
Offers listings of products and manufacturers and US distributors of cosmetics called treatment products.
Cost: $25.00
Frequency: Monthly

5777 **Beauty Forum NAILPRO**
Creative Age Publications
7628 Densmore Ave
Van Nuys, CA 91406-2042
818-782-7560
800-442-5667
Fax: 818-782-7450
E-Mail: dayspa@creativeage.com
Home Page: www.creativeage.com
Linda Lewis, Editor
Linda Kossoff, Marketing Manager
NAILPRO for a number of markets in Europe.
Cost: $22.00
Frequency: Monthly
Founded in 1971

5778 **Beauty Inc.**
Fairchild Publications
7 W 34th St
New York, NY 10001-8100
212-630-3880
800-289-0273
Fax: 212-630-3868
E-Mail: customerservice@fairchildpub.com
Home Page: www.fairchildpub.com
Mary Berner, President
Jenny B. Fine, Editor-in-Chief
Sarah Murphy, Publisher
The ONLY resource for the global beauty supply chain-from the suppliers and manufacturers who develop the products to the retailers who influence purchase. Packed with immediate actionable information and inspiration.
Cost: $ 60.00
Frequency: Monthly
Circulation: 40056

5779 **Beauty Packaging**
Rodman Publishing

70 Hilltop Rd
3rd Floor
Ramsey, NJ 07446-1150

201-825-2552
Fax: 201-825-0553
E-Mail: info@rodpub.com
Home Page: www.nutraceuticalsworld.com

Rodman Zilenziger Jr, President
Matt Montgomery, VP

Covering all types of packaging. Beauty Packaging is published for executives involved in the personal care, cosmetic and fragrance industry.
Cost: $40.00
Circulation: 17387
Founded in 1965

5780 **Beauty Store Business**
Creative Age Publications
7628 Densmore Ave
Van Nuys, CA 91406-2042

818-782-7560
800-442-5667
Fax: 818-782-7450
E-Mail: dayspa@creativeage.com
Home Page: www.creativeage.com

Linda Lewis, Editor
Linda Kossoff, Marketing Manager

Products, news and trends for open-line and professional beauty stores and distributors.
Cost: $22.00
Frequency: Monthly
Founded in 1971

5781 **Cosmetic Ingredient Review**
1101 17th St NW
Suite 310
Washington, DC 20036-4720

202-331-0651
Fax: 202-331-0088
E-Mail: cirinfo@cir-safety.org
Home Page: www.cir-safety.org

Alan Andersen, Executive Director
Wilma F. Bergfeld, Chairman

Assesses the safety of ingredients used in cosmetics in an unbiased manner and publishes the result in open, peer written literature.
Cost: $100.00
Frequency: Annual+
Founded in 1976

5782 **Cosmetic World**
Ledes Group
286 Madison Ave
Suite 200
New York, NY 10017-6407

212-840-8800
Fax: 212-840-7246
Home Page: www.cosmeticworld.com

John Ledes, Owner
Dorene Kaplan, Managing Editor

Current industry events, legislation, management changes and corporate activities, as well as marketing developments and financial analysis.
Cost: $175.00
Frequency: Weekly
Circulation: 5397

5783 **Cosmetics & Toiletries**
Allured Publishing Corporation
336 Gundersen Dr
Suite A
Carol Stream, IL 60188-2403

630-653-2155
Fax: 630-653-2192
E-Mail: customerservice@allured.com
Home Page: www.allured.com

Janet Ludwig, President
Linda Knott, Director Of Operations

This magazine presents a full range of products covering the international cosmetic technology field - including the magazine, a tradeshow, conferences, books and extensive Web sites. The magazine brings the most current technologies in formulating, research, regulations and new ingredients. It also delivers for you a devoted readership base of cosmetic chemists and scientists around the world.
Cost: $98.00
110 Pages
Frequency: Monthly
Circulation: 15,000
ISSN: 0361-4387
Printed in 4 colors on glossy stock

5784 **DaySpa Magazine**
Creative Age Publications
7628 Densmore Ave
Van Nuys, CA 91406-2042

818-782-7560
800-442-5667
Fax: 818-782-7450
E-Mail: dayspa@creativeage.com
Home Page: www.creativeage.com

Linda Lewis, Editor
Linda Kossoff, Marketing Manager

Powerful ideas to build your spa business.
Cost: $22.00
Frequency: Monthly
Founded in 1971

5785 **Delicious Living**
New Hope Natural Media
1401 Pearl St
Suite 200
Boulder, CO 80302-5346

303-939-8440
Fax: 303-939-9886
E-Mail: info@newhope.com
Home Page: www.newhope.com
Social Media: Facebook, Twitter

Fred Linder, President
Pamela Emanoil, Advertising Manager

A trusted health and wellness resource for more than 25 years.
Cost: $12.99
Frequency: Monthly

5786 **Dermascope Magazine**
Aesthetics International Association
2611 N Belt Line Rd
Suite 101
Mesquite, TX 75182-9301

972-203-8530
800-961-3777
Fax: 972-226-2339
Home Page: www.dermascope.com

William Strunk, Publisher
Rachel Valma, Circulation Director
Casey Fore, Editor

The official publication for the advancement of education and public awareness. Variety of articles on skin care, makeup, body spa therapy and paramedical articles where medical and beauty specialists interact.
Cost: $45.00
Frequency: Monthly
Circulation: 80000
Founded in 1972

5787 **Global Cosmetic Industry**
Allured Publishing Corporation
336 Gundelsen Drive
Suite A
Carol Stream, IL 60188-2755
630-653-2155
Fax: 630-597-0118
Home Page: www.gcimagazine.com

Jeff Falk, Editor in Chief
Kim Jednachowski, Sales/Account Manager

The business information resource for marketers, brand managers, manufacturers and executives in the global beauty industry. Industry professionals look to GCI for the strategies, trends, analyses and market data that translate into brand impact.
Circulation: 36,500

5788 **Happi**
Rodman Publishing
70 Hilltop Rd
3rd Floor
Ramsey, NJ 07446-1150

201-825-2552
Fax: 201-825-0553
E-Mail: info@rodpub.com
Home Page: www.nutraceuticalsworld.com

Rodman Zilenziger Jr, President
Matt Montgomery, VP

Serves the manufacturers and fillers of cosmetics, toiletries, fragrances, pharmaceuticals, detergents and chemical specialties inclusing household cleaning products and others product lines allied to the field.
Founded in 1964

5789 **Health Products Business**
Cygnus Publishing
2 Huntington Quad
Suite 301n
Melville, NY 11747-4618

631-845-2700
Fax: 631-845-2723
E-Mail: feedback@magazines.com
Home Page: www.healthproducts.com

Susanne Alberto, Editor/Features
Bruce Leftakels, Publisher

This is a trade magazine that covers news and trends in the natural health products industry vitamins, herbs, dietary supplements and other products. Publishes annual raw materials directory and purchasing guide. Target audience, natural products retail store owners, buyers and managers. Qualified subscription only.
Founded in 1996

5790 **Inside Cosmeceuticals**
Virgo Publishing LLC
3300 N Central Ave
Suite 300
Phoenix, AZ 85012-2532

480-675-9925
Fax: 480-990-0819
E-Mail: peggyj@vpico.com
Home Page: www.vpico.com

Jenny Bolton, President

An online information source exploring emerging product trends and scientific research designed to support the growth and development of the cosmeceuticals market. Visited by manufacturers, marketers and formulators of healthy and innovative cosmetics and personal care products.
Mailing list available for rent: 17000+ names at $var per M

5791 **Inspire**
Creative Age Publications
7628 Densmore Ave
Van Nuys, CA 91406-2042

818-782-7560
800-442-5667
Fax: 818-782-7450
E-Mail: dayspa@creativeage.com
Home Page: www.creativeage.com

Linda Lewis, Editor
Linda Kossoff, Marketing Manager

America's most popular line of hairstyling books.
Cost: $22.00
Frequency: Monthly
Founded in 1971

5792 Journal of Essential Oil Research/JEOR
Allured Publishing Corporation
336 Gundersen Dr
Suite A
Carol Stream, IL 60188-2403

630-653-2155
Fax: 630-653-2192
E-Mail: customerservice@allured.com
Home Page: www.allured.com

Janet Ludwig, President
Linda Knott, Director Of Operations

Forum for the publication of essential oil research and analysis.
Cost: $660.00
Frequency: 6x/Year

5793 Launchpad
Creative Age Publications
7628 Densmore Ave
Van Nuys, CA 91406-2042

818-782-7560
800-442-5667
Fax: 818-782-7450
E-Mail: dayspa@creativeage.com
Home Page: www.creativeage.com

Linda Lewis, Editor
Linda Kossoff, Marketing Manager

News and features about new products for hair, nails, makeup, skincare and tools for beauty professionals.
Cost: $22.00
Frequency: Monthly
Founded in 1971

5794 LiveSpa Magazine
International Spa Association
2365 Harrodsburg Road
Suite A325
Lexington, KY 40504

888-651-4772
Fax: 859-226-4445
E-Mail: ispa@ispastaff.com
Home Page: www.experienceispa.com
Social Media: Facebook, Twitter

Lynne Walker McNees, President
Deborah Waldvogel, Chairman
Jennifer Wayland-Smith, Vice Chairman
Ella Stimpson, Secretary/ Treasurer

ISPA's consumer magazine, explores a variety of fascinating and useful spa topics and answer spa-goer questions. Insights coming straight from the experts, LiveSpa provides consumers with the practical information they need to better embrace this important aspect of their overall wellness routine. (Also available in digital format)
Cost: $530.00

5795 MedEsthetics
Creative Age Publications
7628 Densmore Ave
Van Nuys, CA 91406-2042

818-782-7560
800-442-5667
Fax: 818-782-7450
E-Mail: dayspa@creativeage.com
Home Page: www.creativeage.com

Linda Lewis, Editor
Linda Kossoff, Marketing Manager

News, features and education about noninvasive cosmetic therapies, trends, products and equipment for medical professionals and spa owners/managers in the U.S.
Cost: $22.00
Frequency: Monthly
Founded in 1971

5796 NAILPRO
Creative Age Publications
7628 Densmore Ave
Van Nuys, CA 91406-2042

818-782-7560
800-442-5667
Fax: 818-782-7450
E-Mail: dayspa@creativeage.com
Home Page: www.creativeage.com

Linda Lewis, Editor
Linda Kossoff, Marketing Manager

The magazine for nail professionals.
Cost: $22.00
Frequency: Monthly
Founded in 1971

5797 Nails Magazine
Bobit Business Media
3520 Challenger St
Torrance, CA 90503

310-533-2400
Fax: 310-533-2507
Home Page: www.nailsmag.com

Dedicated to the success of nail professionals.
Cost: $34.50
Frequency: Bi-Monthly
Circulation: 4,500

5798 Perfume 2000 Magazine
Nathalie Publishing Corp
444 Brickell Avenue
Suite 510
Miami, FL 33131

305-669-4602
Fax: 305-669-6116
Home Page: www.perfume2000.com

Bernard Pommier, Circulation Manager
Joseph P Quick, Publisher

Provides an inside look at the American and international prefume industry.
Cost: $18.00
Frequency: Bi-Monthly
ISSN: 1081-7220

5799 Perfumer & Flavorist
Allured Publishing Corporation
336 Gundersen Dr
Suite A
Carol Stream, IL 60188-2403

630-653-2155
Fax: 630-653-2192
E-Mail: customerservice@allured.com
Home Page: www.allured.com

Janet Ludwig, President
Linda Knott, Director Of Operations

Helps readers to analyze global trends, discover new ingredients and innovations, and keep up-to-date with industry news and analysis.
Cost: $135.00
Frequency: 8 Issues + 3 Bonus Issues

5800 Proud Magazine
PO Box 19510
Chicago, IL 60619-0510

708-633-6328
Fax: 708-633-6329
Home Page: www.ahbai.org

Joe Dudley, Senior President
Jory Luste, President
Nathaniel Bronner, Jr. Executive VP

AHBAI reresents leading, African American-owned companies manufacturing ethnic hair care and beauty products. Members serve African Americans through employment, scholarships and education.

5801 Pulse Magazine
International Spa Association
2365 Harrodsburg Road
Suite A325
Lexington, KY 40504

888-651-4772
Fax: 859-226-4445
E-Mail: ispa@ispastaff.com
Home Page: www.experienceispa.com
Social Media: Facebook, Twitter

Lynne Walker McNees, President
Deborah Waldvogel, Chairman
Jennifer Wayland-Smith, Vice Chairman
Ella Stimpson, Secretary/ Treasurer

The magazine for the spa professional. An in-depth look at the latest spa industry trends or tips on balancing your personal and professional life. At Pulse, our goal is to be a source for spa business solutions as well as a medium for personal exploration.
Cost: $530.00

5802 Rite Aid Be Healthy & Beautiful
Drug Store News Consumer Health Publications
425 Park Ave
New York, NY 10022-3526

212-756-5220
800-766-6999
Fax: 212-756-5250
E-Mail: jtanzola@lf.com
Home Page: www.drugstorenews.com

Lebhar Friedman, Publisher

Provides health and beauty tips to millions of women who visit Rite Aid stores.
Frequency: Quarterly
Circulation: 450,000
Founded in 2002

5803 SalonOvation Magazine
Milady Publishing Company
5 Southside Dr
Clifton Park, NY 12065-3870

518-280-9500
800-998-1498
Fax: 518-373-6200
E-Mail: esales@thomsonlearning.com
Home Page: www.delmarlearning.com

Shannon Melldady, Owner
Donna Lewis, Executive Marketing Director
Ron Schlosser, President/CEO

Dedicated to furthering the education of new and established beauty professionals, available by paid subscription to cosmetology students, and practicing massage therapists, cosmetologists, nail technicians, barber-stylists and estheticians.
Cost: $20.00
Frequency: Monthly
Circulation: 80000
Founded in 1945

5804 Scent Marketing Digest
7 Fox Meadow Road
Scarsdale, NY 10583

646-236-4606
Fax: 914-470-2416
E-Mail: info@scentmarketing.org
Home Page: www.scentmarketing.org

Harald H Vogt, Founder/Chief Marketer
Avery Gilbert PhD, Chief Scientist

The essential blog for Scent Marketing resources, industry experts, scent developers and scent solution providers.

5805 The Colorist
Creative Age Publications

7628 Densmore Ave
Van Nuys, CA 91406-2042

818-782-7560
800-442-5667
Fax: 818-782-7450
E-Mail: dayspa@creativeage.com
Home Page: www.creativeage.com

Linda Lewis, Editor
Linda Kossoff, Marketing Manager

The latest in haircolor trends, techniques, products and fashion.
Cost: $22.00
Frequency: Monthly
Founded in 1971

5806 The Link
30 South Main
Shenandoah, PA 17976

412-765-3666
Fax: 412-765-3669
E-Mail: info@ahlc.org
Home Page: www.ahlc.org

Susan Kettering, Executive Director

The voice of the American Hair Loss Council.

5807 WWD Beauty Biz
Fairchild Publications
7 W 34th St
New York, NY 10001-8100

212-630-3880
800-289-0273
Fax: 212-630-3868
E-Mail: customerservice@fairchildpub.com
Home Page: www.fairchildpub.com

Mary Berner, President
Jenny B. Fine, Editor-in-Chief
Sarah Murphy, Publisher

The premier guide to the beauty industry. Provides in-depth coverage and analysis on all aspects of the industry, including trends, brands, retailers, and personalities driving both the general comsumer and insider sides of the business.
Cost: $60.00
Frequency: Monthly
Circulation: 40056

Trade Shows

5808 AACS Annual Convention
9927 E. Bell Road
Suite 110
Scottsdale, AZ 85260

480-810-0431
800-831-1086
Fax: 480-905-0993
E-Mail: jim@beautyschools.org
Home Page: www.beautyschools.org
Social Media: Facebook, Twitter

Jim Cox, Executive Director
Lisa Zarda, General Manager

Association open to all privately owned cosmetology schools.
1100 Members
Founded in 1924

5809 AACS Annual Convention & Expo
American Association of Cosmetology Schools
9927 E. Bell Road
Suite 110
Scottsdale, AZ 85260

480-281-0431
800-831-1086
Fax: 480-905-0993
E-Mail: jim@beautyschools.org
Home Page: www.beautyschools.org

Jim Cox, Executive Director
Lisa Zarda, General Manager

An opportunity to bring your professional team together to lead your school into the future. Education tracks, ckasses, social events, and the expo hall complete the experience.
Frequency: Annual/Fall

5810 AHBAI Mid-Year Conference
American Health & Beauty Aids Institute
PO Box 19510
Chicago, IL 60619-0510

708-633-6328
Fax: 708-633-6329
Home Page: www.ahbai.org

Joe Dudley, Senior President
Jory Luste, President
Nathaniel Bronner, Jr. Executive VP

AHBAI resents leading, African American-owned companies manufacturing ethnic hair care and beauty products. Members serve African Americans through employment, scholarships and education.

5811 Aesthetics' and Spa World Conference
Aesthetics' International Association
2611 N Belt Line Road
Suite 140
Sunnyvale, TX 75182

972-038-8530
800-961-3777
Home Page: www.dermascope.com/aia

Networking, workshops, classes, exhibitors and more for the aesthetics' and spa professionals.
2000 Attendees

5812 America's Beauty Show
America's Beauty Show
401 N Michigan Avenue
Chicago, IL 60611

312-321-6809
800-648-2505
Fax: 312-321-0575
E-Mail: info@americasbeautyshow.com
Home Page: www.americasbeautyshow.com

Pat Dwyer, Tradeshow Logisitics Manager
Ingrid Qualls, Tradeshow Sr Coordinator

Evaluate new products, meet with distributors, continuing education classes on the show floor, and purchase product.
Frequency: Annual/March

5813 America's Expo for Skin Care & Spa
Allured Publishing Corporation
336 Gundersen Drive
Suite A
Carol Stream, IL 60188-2403
630-653-2155
Fax: 630-653-2192
E-Mail: customerservice@allured.com
Home Page: www.allured.com

Janet Ludwig, President
Linda Knott, Director of Operations

Interactive exhibition focuses on professional skin care and spa services. Showcases the newest products, services and technologies from industry manufacturers and suppliers.
Frequency: May

5814 American Society of Perfumers Annual Symposium
PO Box 1551
West Caldwell, NJ 07004

201-991-0040
Fax: 201-991-0073
E-Mail: info@perfumers.org
Home Page: www.perfumers.org
Social Media: Twitter

Marvel Fields, President

All about Perfumery with special guest perfumers speaking about creativity and honors to those who help build our industry.
Founded in 1947

5815 Annual Scientific Meeting and Technology Showcase
Society of Cosmetic Chemists
120 Wall St
Suite 2400
New York, NY 10005-4088

212-668-1500
Fax: 212-668-1504
E-Mail: scc@scconline.org
Home Page: www.scconline.org

Randy Wickett, Ph.D, President
Joseph Dallal, Vice President
Guy Padulo, Vice President-Elect
Dawn Burke-Colvin, Secretary
Tony O'Lenick, Treasurer

Furthering the interest and recognition of cosmetic scientists.
3600 Members
Founded in 1945

5816 Annual Scientific Seminar
Society of Cosmetic Chemists
120 Wall St
Suite 2400
New York, NY 10005-4088

212-668-1500
Fax: 212-668-1504
E-Mail: scc@scconline.org
Home Page: www.scconline.org

Randy Wickett, Ph.D, President
Joseph Dallal, Vice President
Guy Padulo, Vice President-Elect
Dawn Burke-Colvin, Secretary
Tony O'Lenick, Treasurer

Providing information and forums for the exchange of ideas and new developments in cosmetic research and technology.
3600 Members
Founded in 1945

5817 Association of Image Consultants Annual Convention & Exhibitor Showcase
Association of Image Consultants International
910 Charles Street
Fredericksburg, VA 22401

540-370-0311
800-383-8831
Fax: 540-370-0015
Home Page: www.aici.org

Conference and industry related exhibits.
250 Attendees
Founded in 1991

5818 Beacon
Professional Beauty Association
15825 N. 71st Street
Suite 100
Scottsdale, AZ 85254

480-281-0424
800-468-2274
Fax: 480-905-0708
E-Mail: info@probeauty.org
Home Page: www.probeauty.org/nmc

Max Wexler, Chair
Scott Buchanan, Vice Chair
Bruce Selan, Treasurer

Beacon is held annually to provide the nation's top cosmetology students with the guidance to achieve maximum career success. Beacon students attend the most celebrated industry

events during PBA Beauty Week, and benefit from specially designed educational sessions to help them embark on a successful career path.
50 Members
Founded in 1989

5819 **Beauty Exposition USA**
Beauty Expo USA
10725 Midwest Industrial Blvd
Saint Louis, MO 63132
314-426-6333
Fax: 314-426-6335
E-Mail: btexpo@yahoo.com
Home Page: www.beautyexpousa.com
Leon Beatty, Owner
Ann Park, Marketing Director
Hair and beauty supply trade show with a mission of connecting buyers and exhibitors for concentrated business exchanges. Training for retailers in product knowledge and display methods.
2,000 Attendees
Frequency: Annual/Winter

5820 **Beauty Supply Show: West Coast**
West Coast Beauty Supply
5001 Industrial Way
Benicia, CA 94510
707-484-4800
800-233-3141
Fax: 707-748-4623
E-Mail: info@westcoastbeauty.com
Home Page: www.westcoastbeauty.com
Jennifer Coleman, Director
Wayne Clark, President
Jane West, Principal
200 booths of the newest and the best beauty products for the individual and business.
15M Attendees
Frequency: March

5821 **CDMA Education & Trade Show**
Chain Drug Marketing Association
43157 W Nine Mile Road
PO Box 995
Novi, MI 48376-0995
248-499-9300
Fax: 248-449-9396
Home Page: www.chaindrug.com
Social Media: Facebook, Twitter, LinkedIn
James Devine, President
Judy Aspinall, VP
John Devine, VP of Store
Hundreds of exhibitors and thousands of buyers from regional chains, regional wholesalers, and independent pharmacies.
Frequency: Annual
Founded in 1926

5822 **CEA Annual Convention**
Cosmetology Educators of America
9927 E. Bell Road
Suite 110
Scottsdale, AZ 85260
480-810-0431
800-831-1086
Fax: 480-905-0993
E-Mail: jim@beautyschools.org
Home Page: www.beautyschools.org
Social Media: Facebook, Twitter
Jim Cox, Executive Director
Lisa Zarda, General Manager
Chris Cox, Member services Manager
Association open to all privately owned cosmetology schools.
1100 Members
Founded in 1924

5823 **CHPA Annual Executive Conference**
Consumer Health Care Products Association
900 19th St NW
Suite 700
Washington, DC 20006-2105
202-429-9260
Fax: 202-223-6835
E-Mail: eassey@chpa-info.org
Home Page: www.chpa-info.org
Scott Melville, President and CEO
Katie Bernard, State Legislative Analyst
Roman Blazauskas, VP
Chelsea Crutti, Associate Director, State Gov
Join top healthcare executives from across the nation and participate in high-level education sessions focused on the industry's rapidly shifting environment.

5824 **Capitol Hill Visits**
Professional Beauty Association
15825 N. 71st Street
Suite 100
Scottsdale, AZ 85254
480-281-0424
800-468-2274
Fax: 480-905-0708
E-Mail: info@probeauty.org
Home Page: www.probeauty.org/nmc
Max Wexler, Chair
Scott Buchanan, Vice Chair
Bruce Selan, Treasurer
PBA takes Capitol Hill by storm each year. Armed with talking points about issues such as tip-tax reform, association health plans and more, members meet with their Congressional representatives.
50 Members
Founded in 1989

5825 **Circle of Champions**
Premiere Show Group
444 Brickell Avenue
Suite 510
Miami, FL 33131
305-669-4602
Fax: 305-669-6116
E-Mail: magazine@perfume2000.com
Home Page: www.perfume2000.com
Bernard Pommier, Circulation Manager
Joseph P Quick, Publisher
Rewarding the best of the perfume industry.
Frequency: Bi-Monthly

5826 **Cosmetic Science Symposium & Expo**
Personal Care Products Council
1101 17th Street NW
Suite 300
Washington, DC 20036-4702
202-331-1770
Fax: 202-331-1969
Home Page: www.personalcarecouncil.org
Social Media: Facebook, Twitter, LinkedIn, YouTube
Pamela Bailey, President
Mark Pollak, VP
Cheryl Mason, Secretary
Attracts industry leaders and decision-makers and offers personal care products industry staff one-stop shopping for information about Microbiology, Quality Assurance, Safety, and Environmental. The Science Symposium is a great opportunity to learn from the experts and meet colleagues and friends in the industry. Also features the Cosmetic Science Expo.
525 Members
Founded in 1894

5827 **Cosmoprof North America**
Professional Beauty Association
15825 N 71st Street
Suite 100
Scottsdale, AZ 85254
800-468-2274
Fax: 480-905-0708
E-Mail: Cpnainfo@probeauty.org
Home Page: www.cosmoprofnorthamerica.com
Social Media: Facebook, Twitter, LinkedIn
Jen Ingalls, Trade Show Manager
Nathan Miner, Sales Manager
Melissa Coe, Registration Manager
Bonnie Bonadeo, Director Education
Best in hair,cosmetics,packagin and style. Attracted 25,000 professionals from 32 countries with 760 exhibitors.
10M Attendees
Frequency: July
Founded in 2002

5828 **DCAT Western Education Conference**
Drug, Chemical & Associated Technologies
1 Washington Boulevard
Suite 7
Robbinsville, NJ 08691
609-448-1000
800-640-3228
Fax: 609-448-1944
E-Mail: brooke@dcat.org
Home Page: www.dcat.org
Brooke DiGiuseppe, Meeting Services
Margaret Timony, Executive Director
Gain important insights into issues and trends that will affect the future of the nutrition and health industry. Participate in discussion on key business issues with industry experts.

5829 **Elements Showcase**
Skylight West
500 West 36th Street
New York, NY 10018
E-Mail: info@elements-showcase.com
Home Page: www.elements-showcase.com
Social Media: Facebook, Twitter, LinkedIn, YouTube
Showcasing diverse range of cosmetic products. Get to know the latest product range and services that will be displayed by leading and well known companies from every corner of the world.

5830 **Emerging Issues Conference**
Personal Care Products Council
1101 17th Street NW
Suite 300
Washington, DC 20036-4702
202-331-1770
Fax: 202-331-1969
Home Page: www.personalcarecouncil.org
Social Media: Facebook, Twitter, LinkedIn, YouTube
Pamela Bailey, President
Mark Pollak, VP
Cheryl Mason, Secretary
Regulations being considered in California have an impact on every manufacturer and consumer in the United States. Water, waste, air, packaging, ingredients, recycling, new technology, whatever the issue, the discussions often begin in this state. The Council will host an annual Emerging Issues Conference focusing on the many challenges we see on the horizon for our industry.
525 Members
Founded in 1894

5831 **Engredea**
New Hope Natural Media

1401 Pearl St
Suite 200
Boulder, CO 80302-5346

303-939-8440
Fax: 303-939-9886
E-Mail: info@newhope.com
Home Page: www.newhope.com
Social Media: Facebook, Twitter

Fred Linder, President
Pamela Emanoil, Advertising Manager

Encompassing the world of ingredients, Engredea brings together the community of leading suppliers and manufacturers to source new ingredients, packaging, technologies, equipment, and services. Cultivating innovation for tomorrow's best-selling products across food/ beverage, dietary supplement and nutricosmetic categories by offering exhibits, formulation demos, networking events and education opportunities for the industry.
Frequency: Monthly

5832 **Extracts: Essentials for Spa, Home, & Travel**
George Little Management
10 Bank Street
Suite 1200
White Plains, NY 10606

914-486-6070
800-292-4560
Fax: 914-948-6289
E-Mail: laura_woodward@glmshows.com
Home Page: www.extractsny.com/www.glmshows.com

Rita Malek, Show Manager
Laura Anne Woodward, Show Coordinator
George Little II, President
Paula Bertolotti, Sales Manager

EX-TRACTS: Essentials for Spa, Home and Travel is co-located with the International Hotel/Motel Restaurant Show® (IH/MRS). Presenting the finest Apparel & Accessories, Aromatherapy Products & Candles, Baby and Cildren's Spa Products, Bathrobes and Loungewear, Business Services, Cosmetics, Cosmeceuticals, Home Environment Products, Essential Oils, Frangrances, Home Spa Electrics, Massage/Reflexology, Men's Spa Products, Music & Recordings.
10000 Attendees
Frequency: Nov
Founded in 1997

5833 **Extracts: New Discoveries in Beauty and Wellness**
George Little Management
10 Bank Street
Suite 1200
White Plains, NY 10606

914-486-6070
800-292-4560
Fax: 914-948-6289
E-Mail: laura_woodward@glmshows.com
Home Page: www.extractsny.com

Rita Malek, Show Manager
Laura Anne Woodward, Show Coordinator
George Little II, President
Paula Bertolotti, Sales Manager

EXTRACTS® at the NYIGF is a unique, high-quality environment, showcasing the most innovative personal care and wellness products for the gift industry: aromatherapy, bath & bodycare, cosmetics, beauty accessories, candles, home fragrances, massage oils, music & recordings, natural/organic products, perfumes, potpourri and skincare.
43M Attendees
Frequency: Jan/Aug
Founded in 1997

5834 **Face & Body Spa & Healthy Aging**
Allured Publishing
444 Brickell Avenue
Suite 510
Miami, FL 33131

305-669-4602
Fax: 305-669-6116
E-Mail: magazine@perfume2000.com
Home Page: www.perfume2000.com

Bernard Pommier, Circulation Manager
Joseph P Quick, Publisher

Spa professionals gather at Face & Body for practical business solutions, trend information and the latest offerings and insights from leading industry suppliers.
Frequency: Bi-Monthly
ISSN: 1081-7220

5835 **Face & Body Spa Conference & Expo**
Allured Business Media
336 Gundersen Drive
Suite A
Carol Stream, IL 60188-2403

630-653-2155
Fax: 630-653-2192
E-Mail: fbmw@allured.com
Home Page: www.faceandbody.com
Social Media: Facebook

Maureen Nolimal, Account Executive
Sandy Chapin, Group Show Director
Mary Richter, Event Coordinator
Andrew Blood, Exhibits Coordinator

Skin care professionals gather at the Face & Body Midwest for practical business solutions, education, treatments, trends, products and equipment, as well as the latest offerings and insights from leading industry suppliers.
Frequency: Annual

5836 **General Merchandise/Health and Beauty Care Conference**
Food Marketing Institute
2345 Crystal Drive
Suite 800
Arlington, VA 22202-2709

202-452-8444
Fax: 202-429-4519
E-Mail: fmi@fmi.org
Home Page: www.fmi.org
Social Media: Facebook, Twitter, LinkedIn, you Tube

Don McWhirter, Owner

Annual show of 150 exhibitors of health and beauty care products.
3000 Attendees

5837 **HAIRCOLOR USA**
International Beauty Show Group
757 Thrid Ave
5th Floor
New York, NY 10017

212-895-8200
Fax: 212-895-8209
Home Page: www.beautyshows.com
Social Media: Facebook, Twitter, YouTube

Mike Boyce, Show Manager
Rick Rosalina, Operations
Nicole Peck, Media partnerships

0
1500 Attendees
Frequency: June

5838 **Health & Beauty America**
HBA
350 Hudson St
Ste 300
New York, NY 10014

609-759-4700
Fax: 347-962-3889
E-Mail: jgonzalez@cmprinceton.com
Home Page: www.hbaexpo.com
Social Media: Facebook, Twitter, LinkedIn

Jack Gonzalez, Director Health/Beauty Events
Caitlin Carragee, Sales Coordinator

America's largest industry-specific educational conference and exposition for cosmetics, toiletries, fragances and personal care.
16500 Attendees

5839 **ICMAD Annual Meeting**
Independent Cosmetic Manufacturers & Distributors
444 Brickell Avenue
Suite 510
Miami, FL 33131

305-669-4602
Fax: 305-669-6116
E-Mail: magazine@perfume2000.com
Home Page: www.perfume2000.com

Bernard Pommier, Circulation Manager
Joseph P Quick, Publisher

Information about programs and services available to help companies succeed in the beauty and personal care industries.
ISSN: 1081-7220

5840 **ISPA Conference & Expo**
International Spa Association
2365 Harrodsburg Road
Suite A325
Lexington, KY 40504

888-651-4772
Fax: 859-226-4445
E-Mail: ispa@ispastaff.com
Home Page: www.experienceispa.com
Social Media: Facebook, Twitter, LinkedIn, YouTube

Lynne Walker McNees, President
Deborah Waldvogel, Chairman
Jennifer Wayland-Smith, Vice Chairman
Ella Stimpson, Secretary/ Treasurer

The largest ISPA event of the year for spa professionals. The expectation of Conference attendees is to provide spa owners, directors, managers and suppliers with cutting edge tips on where the industry is headed and how to ensure that business is sustainable. Also brings together the leading suppliers in the industry to network with spa decision makers.

5841 **ISSE Long Beach**
Professional Beauty Association
15825 N. 71st Street
Suite 100
Scottsdale, AZ 85254

480-281-0424
800-468-2274
Fax: 480-905-0708
E-Mail: info@probeauty.org
Home Page: www.probeauty.org/nmc

Max Wexler, Chair
Scott Buchanan, Vice Chair
Bruce Selan, Treasurer

The International Salon and Spa Expo is the biggest cash-and-carry beauty show on the West Coast. ISSE Long Beach delivers valuable technical education, quality manufacturers on the exhibit floor and a professionals-only atmosphere.
50 Members
Founded in 1989

5842 **ISSE Midwest**
Professional Beauty Association
15825 N. 71st Street
Suite 100
Scottsdale, AZ 85254

480-281-0424
800-468-2274
Fax: 480-905-0708

E-Mail: info@probeauty.org
Home Page: www.probeauty.org/nmc

Max Wexler, Chair
Scott Buchanan, Vice Chair
Bruce Selan, Treasurer

The International Salon and Spa Expo is the biggest cash-and-carry beauty show. ISSE delivers valuable technical education, quality manufacturers on the exhibit floor and a professionals-only atmosphere.
50 Members
Founded in 1989

5843 Intercoiffure America-Canada
Creative Age Publications
7628 Densmore Ave
Van Nuys, CA 91406-2042

818-782-7560
800-442-5667
Fax: 818-782-7450
E-Mail: dayspa@creativeage.com
Home Page: www.creativeage.com

Deborah Carver, President and CEO
Mindy Rosiejka, VP and COO
Barbara Shepherd, Circulation Director

Creative Age Publications is the association management firm for Intercoiffure America-Canada, the premier organization for salon owners.
Frequency: Monthly
Founded in 1971

5844 International Beauty Show
International Beauty Show Group
757 Third Avenue
5th Floor
New York, NY 10017

212-895-8200
800-736-7170
Fax: 212-895-8209
Home Page: www.ibsnewyork.com
Social Media: Facebook, Twitter, LinkedIn, YouTube

Deborah Carver, Founder
Rick Rosalina, Operations

Annual exposition of hair and skin care products manufacturers and beauty technicians. Held in New York city.
75000 Attendees
Frequency: March

5845 International Congress of Esthetics & Spa
310 E. Interstate 30
Suite B107
Garland, TX 75043

972-203-8530
877-968-7539
Fax: 972-962-1480
E-Mail: AIAtheKey@aol.com
Home Page: www.aestheticsassociation.com

Deborah Carver, Founder
Michelle D'Allaird, VP, Director of Education
Melissa Guillette, Director of Operations

The association for the advancement of education and public awareness on aesthetics. Paramedical aesthetics and body spa therapy. Professionals from the medical, paramedical and beauty industries working together for the most advanced techniques for the patients and clients.
Founded in 1972

5846 International Perfume Bottle Association Annual Convention
PO Box 1299
Paradise, CA 95967

E-Mail: paradise@sunset.net
Home Page: www.perfumebottles.org
Social Media: Facebook

Deborah Carver, Founder
Walter Jones, Vice President
Peggy Tichenor, Membership Secretary
Janet Ziffer, Treasurer
Barbara W. Miller, Recording Secretary

The most exciting event in perfume bottle collecting. A three-day extravaganza featuring the world's premiere exhibition and sale with the field's leading dealers featuring thousands of bottles and an internationally recognized auction. The convention draws together collectors and dealers from around the world.
2000+ Members

5847 Medical Device Submission & Compliance Strategies for the U.S. Market
5635 Fishers Lane
Suite 550
Rockville, MD 20852-3048

301-770-2920
Fax: 301-770-2924
E-Mail: raps@raps.org
Home Page: www.raps.org
Social Media: Facebook, Twitter, LinkedIn, YouTube

Susan E. James, Chairman of the Board
Cecilia Kimberlin, President
Paul Brooks, President-elect
Leigh M. Vaughan, Secretary/ Treasurer
Linda Bowen, Director

Featuring an expert panel of industry professionals and US Food and Drug Administration (FDA) regulators, this RAPS workshop will provide critical information on navigating the medical device submission process and creating compliance strategies for products for the US market.
10000 Members
Founded in 1976

5848 Mid American Beauty Classic
Premiere Show Group
444 Brickell Avenue
Suite 510
Miami, FL 33131

305-669-4602
Fax: 305-669-6116
E-Mail: magazine@perfume2000.com
Home Page: www.perfume2000.com

Bernard Pommier, Circulation Manager
Joseph P Quick, Publisher

Beauty trade show for members of the professional beauty industry. Hair Show, Nail Show, Skincare Show.
Frequency: Bi-Monthly
ISSN: 1081-7220

5849 NAHA
Professional Beauty Association
15825 N. 71st Street
Suite 100
Scottsdale, AZ 85254

480-281-0424
800-468-2274
Fax: 480-905-0708
E-Mail: info@probeauty.org
Home Page: www.probeauty.org/nmc

Max Wexler, Chair
Scott Buchanan, Vice Chair
Bruce Selan, Treasurer

The North American Hairstyling Awards (NAHA) is the most prestigious photographic beauty competition in North America, celebrating the artistry and skill of the professional salon industry. Individuals are recognized in 13 categories of excellence, including the Student Hairstylist of the Year, during a star-studded Awards Ceremony.
50 Members
Founded in 1989

5850 NAILPRO Competitions
Creative Age Publications
7628 Densmore Ave
Van Nuys, CA 91406-2042

818-782-7560
800-442-5667
Fax: 818-782-7450
E-Mail: dayspa@creativeage.com
Home Page: www.creativeage.com

Deborah Carver, President and CEO
Mindy Rosiejka, VP and COO
Barbara Shepherd, Circulation Director

Nail artists from all over the world compete at trade shows all over the U.S. for a chance to be the best and win the coveted annual NAILPRO Cup.
Frequency: Monthly
Founded in 1971

5851 NAILPRO Nail Institute
Creative Age Publications
7628 Densmore Ave
Van Nuys, CA 91406-2042

818-782-7560
800-442-5667
Fax: 818-782-7450
E-Mail: dayspa@creativeage.com
Home Page: www.creativeage.com

Deborah Carver, President and CEO
Mindy Rosiejka, VP and COO
Barbara Shepherd, Circulation Director

Practical marketing education helps nail professionals build their businesses.
Frequency: Monthly
Founded in 1971

5852 NAILPRO Sacramento
Creative Age Publications
7628 Densmore Ave
Van Nuys, CA 91406-2042

818-782-7560
800-442-5667
Fax: 818-782-7450
E-Mail: dayspa@creativeage.com
Home Page: www.creativeage.com

Deborah Carver, President and CEO
Mindy Rosiejka, VP and COO
Barbara Shepherd, Circulation Director

The industry's hottest nails-only trade show spotlights new products and innovative techniques for nail technicians from top manufacturers.
Frequency: Monthly
Founded in 1971

5853 NBCL Annual Convention
National Beauty Culturalists' League
25 Logan Circle NW
Washington, DC 20005-3725

202-332-2695
Fax: 202-332-0940
E-Mail: nbcl@bellsouth.net
Home Page: www.nbcl.org

Dr. Katie B Catalon, President
Dr. William Lindsay, Executive Manager

One hundred booths of beauty industry associates, manufacturing companies and other businesses.
Frequency: July

5854 NBJ Summit
New Hope Natural Media

1401 Pearl St
Suite 200
Boulder, CO 80302-5346

303-939-8440
Fax: 303-939-9886
E-Mail: info@newhope.com
Home Page: www.newhope.com
Social Media: Facebook, Twitter

Fred Linder, President
Pamela Emanoil, Advertising Manager

The premier leadership event for progressive nutrition industry CEOs, investors and thought leaders. It has provided unparalleled education and a tremendous venue for thoughtful leaders to establish strategic relationships and grow the potential of their businesses.
Frequency: Monthly

5855 Natural Products Association MarketPlace
New Hope Natural Media
1401 Pearl St
Suite 200
Boulder, CO 80302-5346

303-939-8440
Fax: 303-939-9886
E-Mail: info@newhope.com
Home Page: www.newhope.com
Social Media: Facebook, Twitter

Fred Linder, President
Pamela Emanoil, Advertising Manager

An intimate trade show for the natural and healthy products industries. Topics cover advocacy, retail training and trends, standards and industry regulation, marketing, sustainability, and other relevant, timely topics direct from industry experts and business leaders.
Frequency: Monthly

5856 Natural Products Expo
New Hope Natural Media
1401 Pearl St
Suite 200
Boulder, CO 80302-5346

303-939-8440
Fax: 303-939-9886
E-Mail: info@newhope.com
Home Page: www.newhope.com
Social Media: Facebook, Twitter

Fred Linder, President
Pamela Emanoil, Advertising Manager

Where new products turn into record profits. Join in an experience with exhibits from different companies showcasing the newest products in natural and specialty foods, organic, health and beauty, natural living, supplements and pet products.
Frequency: Monthly

5857 Nutracon
New Hope Natural Media
1401 Pearl St
Suite 200
Boulder, CO 80302-5346

303-939-8440
Fax: 303-939-9886
E-Mail: info@newhope.com
Home Page: www.newhope.com

Fred Linder, President
Pamela Emanoil, Advertising Manager

The premier education and networking conference for the health and nutrition industry. Provides relevant insights for innovation based on science and technology, case studies and market intelligence. Gain an understanding of the impact of next generation ingredients, emerging markets, consumer trend data and regulatory constraints.
Frequency: Monthly

5858 PBA Beauty Week
Professional Beauty Association
15825 N. 71st Street
Suite 100
Scottsdale, AZ 85254

480-281-0424
800-468-2274
Fax: 480-905-0708
E-Mail: info@probeauty.org
Home Page: www.probeauty.org/nmc

Max Wexler, Chair
Scott Buchanan, Vice Chair
Bruce Selan, Treasurer

PBA Beauty Week is North America's largest, most inclusive beauty event, offering unlimited networking, education, and professional growth opportunities to all sectors of the beauty industry. This week of beauty also features the North American Hairstyling Awards, Best Practice Club, City of Hope and Beacon. PBA Beauty Week is produced by the Professional Beauty Association in cooperation with Cosmoprof North America.
50 Members
Founded in 1989

5859 PBA Symposium
Professional Beauty Association
15825 N. 71st Street
Suite 100
Scottsdale, AZ 85254

480-281-0424
800-468-2274
Fax: 480-905-0708
E-Mail: info@probeauty.org
Home Page: www.probeauty.org/nmc

Max Wexler, Chair
Scott Buchanan, Vice Chair
Bruce Selan, Treasurer

PBA Symposium provides the upper-level business education, unlimited networking and powerful industry research. Held annually during PBA Beauty Week, this three-day educational summit will inspire and educate salon owners and licensed professionals to take their businesses and careers, as well as the entire industry, to the next level.
50 Members
Founded in 1989

5860 Paperboard Packaging Council Annual Convention
Independent Cosmetic Manufacturers & Distributors
444 Brickell Avenue
Suite 510
Miami, FL 33131

305-669-4602
Fax: 305-669-6116
E-Mail: magazine@perfume2000.com
Home Page: www.perfume2000.com

Bernard Pommier, Circulation Manager
Joseph P Quick, Publisher

Industry leaders specializing in sustainability, the economy, and education will come together to impart their knowledge, experience, and business predictions.
Frequency: Bi-Monthly
ISSN: 1081-7220

5861 Perfumers Choice Awards
The American Society of Perfumers
444 Brickell Avenue
Suite 510
Miami, FL 33131

305-669-4602
Fax: 305-669-6116
E-Mail: magazine@perfume2000.com
Home Page: www.perfume2000.com

Bernard Pommier, Circulation Manager
Joseph P Quick, Publisher

Excellence in fragrance creation takes center stage.
Frequency: Bi-Monthly
ISSN: 1081-7220

5862 Personal Care Products Council Annual Meeting
Personal Care Products Council
1101 17th Street NW
Suite 300
Washington, DC 20036-4702

202-331-1770
Fax: 202-331-1969
Home Page: www.personalcarecouncil.org
Social Media: Facebook

Round-tables, R&D, business strategy, and learning panels, along with companies with exhibits of supplies and raw materials for the cosmetic industry.
Frequency: Annual

5863 Personal Care Products Council Legal & Regulatory Conference
Personal Care Products Council
1101 17th Street NW
Suite 300
Washington, DC 20036-4702

202-331-1770
Fax: 202-331-1969
Home Page: www.personalcarecouncil.org
Social Media: Facebook, Twitter, LinkedIn, YouTube

Pamela Bailey, President
Mark Pollak, VP
Cheryl Mason, Secretary

The premier annual meeting for industry general counsel and legal staff, regulatory affairs staff, and outside counsel representing member companies. Held each year exclusively for Council members.
525 Members
Founded in 1894

5864 Professional Beauty Association Annual Convention
Professional Beauty Association
15825 N 71st Street
Suite 100
Scottsdale, AZ 85254

480-281-0424
800-468-2274
Fax: 480-905-0708
E-Mail: cpna@probeauty.org
Home Page: www.probeauty.org

Steven Sleeper, Executive Director
Eric Z Horn, Director Sales/Show Manager

Annual show of 700 exhibitors of industry related equipment, supplies and services.
10M Attendees

5865 Proud Lady Beauty Show
PO Box 19510
Chicago, IL 60619-0510

708-633-6328
Fax: 708-633-6329
E-Mail: ahbail@sbcglobal.net
Home Page: www.ahbai.org

Clyde Hammond, Senior President
Jory Luste, President
Nathaniel Bronner, Jr. Executive VP

The Beauty Professionals Marketplace
Founded in 1981

5866 **RAPS Executive Development Program at the Kellogg School of Management**
5635 Fishers Lane
Suite 550
Rockville, MD 20852-3048
301-770-2920
Fax: 301-770-2924
E-Mail: raps@raps.org
Home Page: www.raps.org
Social Media: Facebook, Twitter, LinkedIn, YouTube
Susan E. James, Chairman of the Board
Cecilia Kimberlin, President
Paul Brooks, President-elect
Leigh M. Vaughan, Secretary/ Treasurer
Linda Bowen, Director
Strong business skills are essential to your success and the ability of your company to survive in a volatile and competitive regulatory environment. This program brings the opportunity to cultivate your business management skills through vigorous discussions with some of the world's best business professors in an intimate learning environment.
10000 Members
Founded in 1976

5867 **RAPS; The Regulatory Convergence**
5635 Fishers Lane
Suite 550
Rockville, MD 20852-3048
301-770-2920
Fax: 301-770-2924
E-Mail: raps@raps.org
Home Page: www.raps.org
Social Media: Facebook, Twitter, LinkedIn, YouTube
Susan E. James, Chairman of the Board
Cecilia Kimberlin, President
Paul Brooks, President-elect
Leigh M. Vaughan, Secretary/ Treasurer
Linda Bowen, Director
Delivers the knowledge, competence development and resources you need to design effective solutions to complex challenges, seize opportunities and lead.
10000 Members
Founded in 1976

5868 **Salon Focus**
Advanstar Communications
641 Lexington Avenue
8th Floor
New York, NY 10022
212-951-6600
Fax: 212-951-6793
E-Mail: info@advanstar.com
Home Page: www.advanstar.com
Joseph Loggia, CEO
Thomas Ehardt, EVP and CFO
Chris Demoulin, EVP
Educational and exhibiting forum for the Southwest professional salon industry. 140 booths.
6.5M Attendees
Frequency: November

5869 **Scent World Expo**
7 Fox Meadow Road
Scarsdale, NY 10583
646-236-4606
Fax: 914-470-2416
E-Mail: info@scentmarketing.org
Home Page: www.scentmarketing.org
Harald H Vogt, Founder/Chief Marketer
Avery Gilbert PhD, Chief Scientist
Learn about the latest scent technology, fragrance trends and success stories. Members of the scent marketing industry, executives from marketing and branding firms as well as consumer goods companies, hotels/ cruise ships, cosmetic companies and other end users of scent. A wonderful lineup of speakers, with top researchers, creative marketing & branding gurus, innovative perfumers and dynamic scent professionals. Take your business to the next level.

5870 **Spring Management and Financial Aid Conference**
9927 E. Bell Road
Suite 110
Scottsdale, AZ 85260
480-810-0431
800-831-1086
Fax: 480-905-0993
E-Mail: jim@beautyschools.org
Home Page: www.beautyschools.org
Social Media: Facebook, Twitter
Jim Cox, Executive Director
Lisa Zarda, General Manager
Chris Cox, Member services Manager
Association open to all privately owned cosmetology schools.
1100 Members
Founded in 1924

5871 **Techniques**
New Dimensions Advertising
47 W Main Street
Mechanicsburg, PA 17055-6262
717-697-4181
800-845-4694
Fax: 717-790-9441
Triennial show of 25 exhibitors of cosmetics and accessories.
1500 Attendees

5872 **The Makeup Show**
E-Mail:
Focuses on and celebrates the art of makeup and networking. Strengthening the working capability and build a professional network for all the people from the makeup artistry community.

5873 **Welcome to Our World**
Professional Beauty Association
15825 N. 71st Street
Suite 100
Scottsdale, AZ 85254
480-281-0424
800-468-2274
Fax: 480-905-0708
E-Mail: info@probeauty.org
Home Page: www.probeauty.org/nmc
Max Wexler, Chair
Scott Buchanan, Vice Chair
Bruce Selan, Treasurer
The professional beauty industry invites Congress for its annual makeover each year. While Congress enjoys the beauty services, members push legislative issues important to the industry.
50 Members
Founded in 1989

5874 **West Coast Spring Style and Beauty Show**
West Coast Beauty Supply
5001 Industrial Way
Benicia, CA 94510
707-484-4800
800-233-3141
Fax: 707-748-4623
E-Mail: info@westcoastbeauty.com
Home Page: www.westcoastbeauty.com
Paul Eggert, Show Director
Wayne Clark, President
John Golliher, Manager
200 booths.
15M Attendees
Frequency: March

5875 **World International Nail and Beauty**
1221 N Lake View Ave
Anaheim, CA 92807
714-779-9892
800-541-9838
Fax: 714-779-9971
E-Mail: dkellenberger@inmnails.com
David Kellenberger
Represents industry, promotes effective use of products, sponsors competition and bestows awards. Also offers world championship competitions for nails, hair and makeup.
13000 Members
Founded in 1981

Directories & Databases

5876 **Beauty Fashion: Men's Issue**
Beauty Fashion
16 E 40th Street
New York, NY 10016
212-328-6789
0
Fax: 212-840-7246
Home Page: www.beautyfashion.com
Social Media: Facebook
Debra Davis, Advertising Director
Adelaide Farah, Editorial Director
Offers listings of men's fragrances, toiletries and related products as well as manufacturers and US distributors.
Cost: $25.00
Frequency: Annual
Circulation: 17,000

5877 **Complete Directory of Cosmetic Specialties**
Sutton Family Communications & Publishing Company
920 State Route 54 East
Elmitch, KY 42343
270-276-9500
E-Mail: jlsutton@apex.net
Theresa Sutton, Editor
Lee Sutton, General Manager
Print-out from database of wholesalers, manufacturers, distributors, importers and close-out houses. Database is updated daily to guarantee the most current and up-to-date sources available.
Cost: $39.50
100+ Pages

5878 **Complete Directory of Personal Care Items**
Sutton Family Communications & Publishing Company
920 State Route 54 East
Elmitch, KY 42343
270-276-9500
E-Mail: jlsutton@apex.net
Theresa Sutton, Editor
Lee Sutton, General Manager
Print-out from database of wholesalers, manufacturers, distributors, importers and close-out houses. Database is updated daily to guarantee the most current and up-to-date sources avail-

able.
Cost: $39.50
100+ Pages

5879 **Cosmetics & Toiletries: Cosmetic Bench Reference**
Allured Publishing Corporation
336 Gundersen Dr
Suite A
Carol Stream, IL 60188-2403
630-653-2155
Fax: 630-653-2192
E-Mail: customerservice@allured.com
Home Page: www.allured.com
Janet Ludwig, President
Linda Knott, Director Of Operations
Offers a full list of cosmetics ingredient suppliers.
Cost: $95.00
Frequency: Biennial

5880 **Cosmetics & Toiletries: Who's Who in R&D Directory Issue**
Allured Publishing Corporation
336 Gundersen Dr
Suite A
Carol Stream, IL 60188-2403
630-653-2155
Fax: 630-653-2192
E-Mail: customerservice@allured.com
Home Page: www.allured.com
Janet Ludwig, President
Linda Knott, Director Of Operations
Offers a list of cosmetic manufacturers and consultants for product development, legal, safety and regulatory assistance.
Cost: $25.00
Frequency: Annual
Circulation: 3,200

5881 **Fragrance Foundation Reference Guide**
Fragrance Foundation
545 5th Ave
Suite 900
New York, NY 10017-3636
212-779-9058
Fax: 212-779-9058
E-Mail: info@fragrance.org
Home Page: www.fragrance.org
Terry Molnar, Executive Director
Mary Lapsansky, VP
Over 1100 fragrances are listed that are available in the US, with dates of introduction and description, alphabetically indexed with company name, address and phone number.
Cost: $60.00
112 Pages
Frequency: Annual

5882 **Fragrance and Olfactory Dictionary**
Fragrance Foundation
545 5th Ave
Suite 900
New York, NY 10017-3636
212-779-9058
Fax: 212-779-9058
E-Mail: info@fragrance.org
Home Page: www.fragrance.org
Terry Molnar, Executive Director
Mary Lapsansky, VP
Definitions of ingredients, techniques, language of fragrance and olfactory references.
Cost: $7.00
32 Pages

5883 **Passion**
Milady Publishing Company
5 Southside Dr
Clifton Park, NY 12065-3870
518-280-9500
800-998-1498
Fax: 518-373-6200
E-Mail: esales@thomsonlearning.com
Home Page: www.delmarlearning.com
Social Media: Twitter
Shannon Mellday, Owner
Donna Lewis, Executive Marketing Director
Ron Schlosser, President/CEO
A Salon Professionals Handbook for Building a Successful Business
Cost: $20.00
Frequency: Monthly
Circulation: 80000
Founded in 1945

5884 **Perfume 2000**
Perfume 2000
444 Brickell Avenue
Suite 510
Miami, FL 33131
305-374-6849
Fax: 305-374-6850
E-Mail: ana@perfume2000.com
Home Page: www.perfume2000.com
Ana Murias, Public Relations
Comprehensive database; services encourage industry networking and integration.

5885 **RIFM Database of Fragrance & Flavor Materials**
50 Tice Boulevard
Woodcliff Lake, NJ 07677
201-689-8089
Fax: 201-689-8090
E-Mail: rifm@rifm.org
Home Page: www.rifm.org/nd
A comprehensive source offering safety evaluations and toxicology data on more than 4,500 fragrance and flavor materials. Operated in full cooperation with Flavor & Extracts Manufacturing Association (FEMA).
Founded in 1966

5886 **Who's Who: Membership Directory of the Cosmetic, Toiletry & Fragrance Assn**
Personal Care Products Council
1101 17th Street NW
Suite 300
Washington, DC 20036-4702
202-331-1770
Fax: 202-331-1969
Home Page: www.personalcarecouncil.org
Gwen Hallill, Director Publications/Comm
Pamela Bailey, President
About 500 member companies of the cosmetics industry.
Cost: $75.00
Frequency: Annual, June

Industry Web Sites

5887 **http://gold.greyhouse.com**
G.O.L.D Grey House OnLine Databases
Grey House Publishing's online database platform, GOLD, offers Quick Search, Keyword Search and Expert Search for most business sectors including beauty, cosmetics, perfumes and personal care markets. The GOLD platform makes finding the information you need quick and easy - whether you're a novice searcher or an experienced database user. All of Grey House's directory products are available for subscription on the GOLD platform.

5888 **www.abbies.org**
American Beauty Association
Works to expand, serve and protect the interests of the professional beauty industry.

5889 **www.ahbai.org**
American Health and Beauty Aids Institute
Trade association representing leading Black-owned companies manufacturing ethnic hair care and beauty products that feature the Proud Lady symbol. Members serve Black America through employment, scholarships and education of consumers on recycling their dollars into the Black community.

5890 **www.bbsi.org**
Beauty and Barber Supply Institute
Our members are wholesaler-distributors, manufacturers and manufacturers' representatives from around the world. Our mission is to maximize the potential of the salon industry.

5891 **www.beautyworks.com/aia**
Aestheticis International Association
For the advancement of education and public awareness on aesthetics. Paramedical aesthetics and body spa therapy. Professionals from the medical, paramedical and beauty industries working together for the most advanced techniques for the patients and clients.

5892 **www.cew.org**
Cosmetic Executive Women
Nonprofit trade organization of approximately 1,500 executives in the beauty, cosmetics, fragrance and related industries. Based in New York City, CEW has associated organizations in France and the United Kingdom. As a leading trade organization in the beauty industry, CEW helps develop the career contacts, knowledge and skills of its members so that they may advance on both professional and personal levels.

5893 **www.cosmeticindex.com**
CosmeticIndex.Com
Home Page: www.cosmeticindex.com
Online source for cosmetics, resources and services.

5894 **www.greyhouse.com**
Grey House Publishing
Authoritative reference directories for most business segments incluidng beauty, cosmetic, perfume and personal care markets. Users can search the online databases with varied search criteria allowing for custom searches by product category, geographic area, sales volume, keyword, subject and more. Full Grey House catalog and online ordering also available.

5895 **www.iacmcolor.org**
International Association of Color Manufacturers
Actively represents the interests of the regulated color industry by demonstrating the safety of color additives and to promote the industry's economic growth by participating in new color approvals, regulatory and legislative issues that affect the industry worldwide.

5896 **www.iasc.org**
International Aloe Science Council
Nonprofit trade organization for the Aloe Vera Industry world-wide. Its membership includes Aloe growers, processors, finished goods manufacturers, marketing companies, insurance companies, equipment suppliers, printers, sales organizations, physicians, scientists and researchers.

5897 **www.icmad.org**
Independent Cosmetic Manufacturers & Distributors

Information on government consumers and the media. Provides group programs for product liability.

5898 **www.inmnails.com**
World International Nail and Beauty Association
Promotes effective use of products, sponsors competition and bestows awards. Also offers world championship competitions for nails, hair and makeup.

5899 **www.isnow.com**
Cosmetologists Chicago
Voice of the salon industry. For over eight decades, we have been a beauty authority and presenter of the Chicago Midwest Beauty Show. We are stylists, estheticians, color technicians, salon owners, educators and nail technicians.

5900 **www.perfumers.org**
American Society of Perfumers
Nonprofit organization fostering and encouraging the art and science of perfumery in the US while promoting professional exchange and a high standard of professional conduct within the fragrance industry. The ASP holds symposiums in the New York City area where leading members of the fragrence community are invited to speak and present information on all aspects of the industry.

5901 **www.personalcarecouncil.org**
Personal Care Products Council
Provides a complete range of services that support the personal care products industry's needs and interests in the scientific, legal, regulatory, legislative and international fields. CTFA strives to ensure that the personal care products industry has the freedom to pursue creative product development and compete in a fair and responsible marketplace.

5902 **www.salonprofessionals.org**
National Cosmetology Association
Nationwide community of 30,000 salon professionals, connected by a common passion for learning, growing and raising the professionalim of the entire salon industry. As a group, we have a strong voice in our communities, our industry and with our government because the NCA is for everyone in the professional community. Members have access to education, fashion events, community service and insurance — all the tools needed to build your career.

Associations

5903 **ACA International**
Association of Credit and Collection Professionals
PO Box 390106
Minneapolis, MN 55439

952-926-6547
Fax: 952-926-1624
E-Mail: aca@acainternational.org
Home Page: www.acainternational.org
Social Media: Facebook, Twitter, LinkedIn, YouTube

Lucia Lebens, director

International trade organization of credit and collection professionals providing a variety of accounts receivable management services to over 1,000,000 credit grantors.
5300 Members
Founded in 1995
Mailing list available for rent

5904 **Advertising Media Credit Executives Association**
PO Box 433
Louisville, KY 40201

502-582-4327
Fax: 502-582-4330
E-Mail: amcea@amcea.org
Home Page: www.amcea.org
Social Media: Facebook

Cheryl E Szluzer, President
Sheila Wroten, VP

A non-profit organization that exists to serve the media credit manager. Directed and managed by professionals just like you, media credit managers who volunteer for various projects to benefit the industry and our association.
Founded in 1953

5905 **Affordable Housing Tax Credit Coalition**
401 9th Street NW
Washington, DC 20004

202-585-8162
Fax: 202-585-8080
E-Mail: info@taxcreditcoalition.org
Home Page: www.taxcreditcoalition.org

Beth Mullen, Treasurer
Alan Cohen, Secretary

Plays a major role in assuring the conitinuance of the low income housing tax credit, with the primary goal of achieving permanent extension of the low income housing tax credit program.
105 Members
Founded in 1988

5906 **American Bankruptcy Institute**
44 Canal Center Plz
Suite 400
Alexandria, VA 22314-1546

703-739-0800
Fax: 703-739-1060
E-Mail: info@abiworld.org
Home Page: www.abiworld.org
Social Media: Facebook, Twitter, LinkedIn, YouTube

Samuel Gerdano, Executive Director
Felicia S Turner, Deputy Executive Director
Hon Wesley W Steen, Chairman

Multidisiplinary, nonpartisan organization dedicated to research and education on matters related to insovency. Engaged in numerous educational and research activities as well as the production of a number of publications both for the insolvency practitioner and the public.
11700 Members
Founded in 1982

5907 **American Financial Services Association**
919 18th Street NW
Suite 300
Washington, DC 20006-5517

202-296-5544
E-Mail: sharrison@afsamail.org
Home Page: www.afsaonline.org
Social Media: Twitter

Chris Steinebert, President/CEO
Gary L. Phillips, Chairman
Nathan D. Benson, Member
Dietmar W. Exler, VP

A national trade association for market funded providers of financial services to consumers and small businesses.
400 Members
Founded in 1916

5908 **American Recovery Association**
5525 N MacArthur Boulevard
Suite 135
Irving, TX 75038

972-755-4755
Fax: 972-870-5755
E-Mail:
homeoffice@americanrecoveryassn.org
Home Page: www.repo.org

Jim Hall, President
Jerry Wilson, VP
David Handschin, Secretary/Treasurer

Approximately 500 offices around the US, Canada and Germany, providing repossesion services around the world.
280 Members
Founded in 1965

5909 **BCCA**
550 W Frontage Rd
Suite 3600
Northfield, IL 60093-1243

847-881-8757
Fax: 847-784-8059
E-Mail: info@bccacredit.com
Home Page: www.bccacredit.com
Social Media: Facebook, Twitter, LinkedIn

Mary Collin, CEO
Jamie Smith, Director of Operations
Cindy Laser, Sales/Membership

BCCA is the media industry's credit association that functions as a central clearing house for credit information on advertisers, agencies and buying services, both locally and nationally. Also provides an Electronic Media Credit Application (EMCAPP.com) to members that helps streamline the application process. One app in one location!
600 Members
Founded in 1972

5910 **Broadcast Cable Credit Association**
550 W Frontage Rd
Suite 3600
Northfield, IL 60093-1243

847-881-8757
Fax: 847-784-8059
E-Mail: info@bccacredit.com
Home Page: www.bccacredit.com
Social Media: Facebook, Twitter, LinkedIn

Mary Collin, CEO
Cheryl Ingram, Chairman
Dalton Lee, Secretary
John Drain, SVP, Finance

Subsidiary of the Media Financial Management Association. BCCA provides industry specific credit reports on individual agencies, advertisers or buying services both national and local. These reports may be obtained upon request online and by phone or fax. Its mission is to provide tools and services that will allow members to perform their functions to the best of their abilities, and help them achieve a profitable bottom line.
600 Members
Founded in 1972

5911 **Business Products Credit Association**
PO Box 75930
St. Paul, 55 63366-2439

651-998-9609
E-Mail: service@bcpa.org
Home Page: www.bcpa.org
Social Media: Facebook, Twitter, LinkedIn

Bob Niebuhr, President
Cherie Taylor, Secretary
Jennifer Cassidy, Treasurer
William Nickel, Program Director
Bob Kunzer, Information Director

Credit Trade Association for manufacturers and wholesalers.
Founded in 1875

5912 **CDC Consumer Debt Counseling**
1300 Hampton Avenue
Saint Louis, MO 63139-3163

314-647-9006
800-820-9232
Fax: 314-647-1359
Home Page: www.consumerdebtcounselors.org

Philip Johnston, President
Melissa Towel, Advisor
Janice Diaz, Customer Care

Nonprofit provider of quality, face-to-face and telephone budget and debt counseling education.

5913 **Capital Markets Credit Analysts Society**
25 N Broadway
Tarrytown, NY 10591

914-332-0040
Fax: 914-332-1541
E-Mail: cmcas@cmcas.org
Home Page: www.cmcas.org
Social Media: Facebook

Stuart Ganes, President
Kelly Byrne, Account Manager
Sherman Wong, Treasurer
Patricia Aquaro, Secretary

A professional society whose membership consists primarily of managers and analysts in credit risk departments that directly support their employers' capital market activities.
500 Members
Founded in 1989
Mailing list available for rent

5914 **Coalition of Higher Education Assistance Organizations**
1101 Vermont Ave NW
Suite 400
Washington, DC 20005-3586

202-289-3910
Fax: 202-371-0197
E-Mail: hwadsworth@wpllc.net
Home Page: www.coheao.com

Maria Livolsi, President
Carl Perry, VP
Robert Frick, Treasurer
Edgar DelosAngeles, Secretary

Focus is on legislative and regulatory advocacy for Federal Perkins and other campus based student loan programs.
365 Members
Founded in 1980

5915 **Commercial Finance Association**
Ste 1801
7 Penn Plz
New York, NY 10001-3979
212-594-3490
Fax: 212-564-6053
E-Mail: info@cfa.com
Home Page: www.cfa.com
Social Media: Facebook, Twitter, LinkedIn, YouTube
Michael Maiorino, President
Bruce H Jones, Executive Director
Andrea Petro, President
Robert Trojan, CEO
Deborah J Monosson, VP
Trade group of the asset-based, financial services industry, with members throughout the US, Canada and around the world. Members include the asset-based lending arms of domestic and foreign commercial banks, small and large independent finance companies, floor plan financing organizations, factoring organizations and financing subsidiaries of major industrial corporations. CFA membership is by organization, not by individual.

5916 **Commercial Mortgage Securities Association**
20 Broad St
7th Floor
New York, NY 10005
212-509-1844
Fax: 646-884-7569
E-Mail: info@crefc.org
Home Page: www.crefc.org
Social Media: Facebook, Twitter, LinkedIn
Stephen Renna, CEO
Ed DeAngelo, VP
Michael Flood, VP
International trade organization for the commercial real estate capital markets. Also represents and promotes an orderly and ethical global institutional secondary market for the sale of commercial mortgage loans and equity investments.
309 Members
Founded in 1994

5917 **Consumer Credit Industry Association**
6300 Powers Ferry Road
Suite 600-286
Atlanta, GA 30339
678-858-4001
E-Mail: webmaster@cciaonline.com
Home Page: www.cciaonline.com
Scott Cipinko, Executive VP
To preserve, promote and enhance the availability, utility and integrity of insurance and related products and services delivered in connection with financial transactions.
140 Members
Founded in 1951

5918 **Consumer Credit Insurance Association**
542 S Dearborn St
Suite 400
Chicago, IL 60605-1599
312-939-4371
Fax: 312-939-8287
E-Mail: webmaster@cciaonline.com
Home Page: www.cciaonline.com
Kris Nelson, President
Tim Kovac, Chairman
Michelle Dicks, General Counsel
To preserve, promote and enhance the availability, utility and integrity of insurance and related products and services delivered in connection with financial transactions.
140 Members
Founded in 1951

5919 **Credit Union National Association**
601 Penn Ave
NW South Building, Suite 600
Washington, DC 20004
202-628-5777
800-356-9655
Fax: 202-638-7729
Home Page: www.cuna.org
Social Media: Facebook, Twitter
Susan Newton, Executive Director
Pat Sowick, VP
Richard Dines, Senior State and League Affairs
Alicia Valencia Erb, League Relations
Shellee Mitchell, Executive Assistant
The premier trade association in the financial services arena. Supports, protects, unifies and advances the credit union movement.

5920 **FCIB**
Finance, Credit, International Business Assoc.
8840 Columbia 100 Pkwy
Columbia, MD 21045-2105
410-423-1840
888-256-3242
Fax: 410-740-5574
E-Mail: fcib_info@fcibglobal.com
Home Page: www.fcibglobal.com
Social Media: Twitter, LinkedIn
Marta Chacon-Martinez, Director
Mike Mino, CCE, Chairman
Ron Shepherd, Director, Membership & Business
FCIB enjoys an international reputation as the premier Association of executives in finance, credit and international business, providing critical export credit and collections insight, practical advice and intelligence to companies of all sizes - from Fortune 500 multi-nationals to medium and small private companies. With international credit management and trade finance professionals in 55 countries around the world, FCIB offers unique networking and educational opportunities
1200 Members
Founded in 1919

5921 **International Association of Commercial Collectors**
4040 W 70th Street
Minneapolis, MN 55435
952-925-0760
Fax: 952-926-1624
E-Mail: iacc@commercialcollector.com
Home Page: www.commercialcollector.com
Patrick Lozano, President
Ted M Smith, Executive Director
International trade association comprised of collection specialists and commercial attorneys, with members throughout the US and 20 international countries. IACC's mission is to promote the commercial collection profession by providing IACC members with the resources to excel in the industry.
350 Members
Founded in 1970

5922 **International Energy Credit Association**
15000 Commerce Parkway
Suite C
Mt. Laurel, NJ 08054
856-380-6854
Fax: 856-439-0525
E-Mail: mbiordi@ahint.com
Home Page: www.ieca.net
Social Media: Facebook, Twitter, LinkedIn
Gary Nicholson, EVP
Michele Biordi, Executive Director
The oldest international industry credit association in the United States. Membership includes companies located in the Uited States, Canada, most Western European countries, Mexico, South America and Asia.
700 Members
Founded in 1923

5923 **Jewelers Board of Trade**
95 Jefferson Blvd
Warwick, RI 02888-1046
401-467-0055
Fax: 401-467-1199
E-Mail: jbtinfo@jewelersboard.com
Home Page: www.jewelersboard.com
Dione Kenyen, President
A not for profit jewelry trade association whose primary function is to compile and disseminate accurate and reliable credit information among its members as to the financial standing, credit history and background of dealers of jewelry and related products.
3200 Members
Founded in 1884

5924 **Mortgage Bankers Association**
1717 Rhode Island Avenue NW
Suite 400
Washington, DC 20036
202-557-2700
E-Mail: membership@mortgagebankers.org
Home Page: www.mortgagebankers.org
Social Media: Facebook, Twitter, LinkedIn, YouTube
Representing the real estate finance industry, MBA serves its membership by representing their legislative and regulatory interests before the US Congress and federal agencies; by meeting their educational needs through programs and a range of periodicals and publications; and by supporting their business interests with a variety of research initiatives and other products and services.
2900 Members
Founded in 1918

5925 **NACUSO**
PMB 3419 Via Lido
#135
Newport Beach, CA 92663
949-645-5296
888-462-2870
Fax: 949-645-5297
E-Mail: info@nacuso.org
Home Page: www.nacuso.org
Jack Antonini, President/CEO
Mark Zook, Chairman
Mike Atkins, Secretary
400 Members
Founded in 1985

5926 **National Association of Consumer Credit**
PO Box 20871
Columbus, OH 43220-871
614-326-1165
Fax: 614-326-1162
E-Mail: nacca2007@sbcglobal.net
Home Page: www.naccaonline.org
Steven O'Shields, President
Kevin Glendening, First VP
James Keiser, Second VP
Mike Larsen, Secretary/treasurer
Improving the supervision of consumer credit agencies; facilitating the administration of laws governing these agencies by providing a forum

for the exchange of information, ideas and experiences among public officials having supervision of such agencies and changes with the administration of such laws; facilitating intercommunication among its members and developing standard information collection concerning consumer credit agencies in each state.
55 Members
Founded in 1935

5927 **National Association of Credit Management**
8840 Columbia 100 Pkwy
Columbia, MD 21045-2100
410-740-5560
Fax: 410-740-5574
E-Mail: robins@nacm.org
Home Page: www.nacm.org
Social Media: Facebook, Twitter, LinkedIn
Toni Drake, Chairperson
Chris Meyers, Chairman/elect
Kevin Quinn, Director
Jay Snyder, Director
NACM and its network of affiliated associations are the leading resource for credit and financial management information and education, delivering products and services which improve the management of business credit and accounts receivable. Our collective voice has influenced legislative results concerning commercial business and trade credit to our nation's policy makers for more than 100 years, and continues to play an active part in legislative issues pertaining to business credit.
18000 Members
Founded in 1896

5928 **National Association of Credit Union Service Organizations**
PMB 3419 Via Lido
Suite 135
Newport Beach, CA 92663
949-645-5296
888-462-2870
Fax: 949-645-5297
E-Mail: info@nacuso.org
Home Page: www.nacuso.org
Jack Antonini, President/CEO
Mark Zook, Chairman
Mike Atkins, Secretary
Leading professional trade association for credit unions and CUSO's seeking to provide a full aray of services, such as mortgages, business lending and business lending depository services, trust services, investments and insurance to their members and non members alike.
412 Members
Founded in 1985

5929 **National Association of Federal Credit Unions**
3138 10th St N
Arlington, VA 22201-2160
703-522-4770
800-336-4644
Fax: 703-524-1082
E-Mail: lcorbin@nafcu.org
Home Page: www.nafcu.org
Social Media: Facebook, Twitter, YouTube
Fred Becker, President
Alicia Hosmer, VP, Marketing
A respected and influential trade association that exclusively represents the interest of federal credit unions before the federal government and the public.
804 Members
Founded in 1967

5930 **National Association of State Credit Union Supervisors**
1655 Fort Myer Dr
Suite 300
Arlington, VA 22209-3108
703-528-8351
800-728-7927
Fax: 703-528-3248
E-Mail: offices@nascus.org
Home Page: www.nascus.org
Social Media: Twitter
Mary Martha Fortney, President
Sandra Troutman, Executive VP
Jennifer Champagne, Director Education
State chartered credit unions and state credit union supervisors.
900 Members
Founded in 1965

5931 **National Chemical Credit Association**
1100 Main Street
Buffalo, NY 14209-2356
716-887-9527
Fax: 716-878-0479
E-Mail: robert.gagliardi@abc-amega.com
Home Page: www.ncca1.org
Robert Gagliardi, Contact
Members are major producers of basic chemicals and allied products.
100 Members
Founded in 1938

5932 **National Council of Postal Credit Unions**
PO Box 160
Del Mar, CA 92014-0160
858-792-3883
Fax: 858-792-3884
E-Mail: ncpcu@ncpcu.org
Home Page: www.ncpcu.org
John King, Chairman
Becca Cuddy, Secretary
Sidney Parfait, Treasurer
Organized to represent the special interests of postal credit unions.
160 Members
Founded in 1984

5933 **National Credit Reporting Association**
701 E. Irving Park Rd
Suite 306
roselle, IL 60712
630-539-1525
Fax: 630-539-1526
E-Mail: tclemans@ncrainc.org
Home Page: www.ncrainc.org
Social Media: Facebook, Twitter, LinkedIn
Terry W Clemans, Executive Director
Purpose is to promote the general welfare of its members. Also provides leadership in education, legislation, ethics and enhanced vendor's relation
150 Members
Founded in 1992

5934 **National Credit Union Administration**
1775 Duke St
Alexandria, VA 22314-6115
703-518-6300
800-755-1030
Fax: 703-518-6539
E-Mail: consumerassistance@ncua.gov
Home Page: www.ncua.gov
Social Media: Facebook, Twitter, YouTube
Debbie Matz, Chairman
Governed by a three member board appointed by the President and confirmed by the US Senate, this independent federal agency charters and supervises federal credit unions. NCUA, with the backing of the full faith and credit of the US government, operates the National Credit Union Share Insurance Fund, insuring the savings of 80 million account holders in all federal credit unions and many state chartered credit unions.
82M Members
Founded in 1970

5935 **National Federation of Community Development Credit Unions**
39 Broadway
Suite 2140
New York, NY 10006-3063
212-809-1850
Fax: 212-809-3274
E-Mail: info@cdcu.coop
Home Page: www.natfed.org
Social Media: Facebook, Twitter, LinkedIn
Cathie Mahon, President
Michael Strange, CFO/ Chief Of Staff
Serve and represent financial cooperatives in low income communities. Members are community based credit unions. Provides training and management support to CDCU's and asists groups in organizing new credit unions.
200 Members
Founded in 1974

5936 **National Foundation for Credit Counseling**
2000 M Street NW
Suite 505
Washington, DC 20036
202-677-4300
800-338-2227
Home Page: www.nfcc.org
Social Media: Facebook, Twitter, YouTube
Susan C Keating, CEO
Paul Weiss, Chief Of Staff/CFO
Lydia Sermons-Ward, Senior VP Marketing
Sets the standard for quality credit counseling, debt reduction services and education for financial wellness.
1200 Members

5937 **New York Media Credit Group**
1100 Main Street
Buffalo, NY 14209
716-887-9547
800-746-9428
Fax: 716-878-0479
E-Mail: robert.gagliardi@abc-amega.com
Home Page: www.ny-media.com
Robert Gagliardi, Director Member Group Services
One of the most active credit association for media credit professionals today. Many of the members are from major media including cable television, sports and news cable TV, and radio.

5938 **Risk Management Association**
One Liberty Place
1801 Market St
Suite 300
Philadelphia, PA 19103-1613
215-446-4000
800-677-7621
Fax: 215-446-4101
E-Mail: customers@rmahq.org
Home Page: www.rmahq.org
Dwight Overturf, CFO
Kevin Blakely, President/CEO
Maurice H Hartigan II, President/CEO
Reid Adamson, Senior VP
William S Aichele, President/CEO
Champions risk management while also monitoring emerging trends. Our strong relationship with members and regulators helps us develop new risk management techniques, innovative

products and education and training programs geared to risk management professionals at different stages of their careers.
3000 Members
Founded in 1914

Newsletters

5939 AHTCC News
Affordable Housing Tax Credit Coalition
401 9th Street NW
Suite 900
Washington, DC 20004
202-585-8162
Fax: 202-585-8080
E-Mail: info@taxcreditcoalition.org
Home Page: www.taxcreditcoalition.org
Joseph Hagan, President
Frequency: Monthly

5940 ARA News & Views
American Recovery Association
5525 N MacArthur Boulevard
Suite 135
Irving, TX 75038
972-755-4755
Fax: 972-870-5755
E-Mail: homeoffice@americanrecoveryassn.org
Home Page: www.repo.org/
Mary Jane Hogan, President
Paul Hallock
Provides news, information and coverage of the recovery industry. Free to members only in print. Available to all others online
28 Pages
Frequency: Quarterly
Founded in 1965

5941 Bankcard Barometer
RAM Research Group
320 E 72nd St
Suite 9C
New York, NY 10021
212-724-7535
Fax: 212-208-4384
E-Mail: info@investmentTechnologies.com
Home Page: www.investmenttechnologies.com
Brian Rom, Owner
Robert B McKinley, Publisher
Reports on the pricing and performance of US bank credit card portfolios. Trendline charts follow deliquency, charge-offs, attrition, payment rates, bankruptcy rates, fraud losses, interest yield, operating expenses, net interest margin and return on assets.
Cost: $1295.00
40 Pages
Frequency: Monthly
Founded in 1986
Printed in 4 colors

5942 Bankcard Dispatch
RAM Research Group
999 Vanderbilt Beach Road
2nd Floor
Naples, FL 34108
239-325-5300
E-Mail: staff@ramresearch.com
Home Page: www.cardweb.com
Robert B McKinley, Editor
Covers the entire payment card industry as it affects the US market. Comprehensive periodical is prepared for payment card executives.
Cost: $1295.00
40 Pages
Frequency: Monthly
Printed in 4 colors

5943 Bankcard Update
RAM Research Group
999 Vanderbilt Beach Road
2nd Floor
Naples, FL 34108
239-325-5300
E-Mail: staff@ramresearch.com
Home Page: www.cardweb.com
Robert B McKinley, Editor/chairman
Updated printed report and CD-ROM on quarterly statistics of the top US issuers. Covers hundreds of portfolios comprising more than 95 percent of the US market. Subscription includes both the printed version and CD-ROM.
Cost: $ 1295.00
40 Pages
Frequency: Monthly
Founded in 1986
Printed in 4 colors

5944 Capitol Watch
National Association of Credit Unions
3138 10th St N
Arlington, VA 22201-2149
703-522-4770
800-336-4644
Fax: 703-524-1082
Home Page: www.nafcu.org
Social Media: Facebook, Twitter, YouTube
Fred Becker, President
Alicia Hosmer, VP, Marketing
This members only electronic format newsletter is NAFCU's monthly communication for credit unions with assets of $50 million or less.

5945 Collection Agency Report
First Detroit Corporation
30033 Paul Ct
Warren, MI 48092-1805
586-573-0045
800-366-5995
Fax: 586-573-9219
E-Mail: ascace@firstdetroit.com
Home Page: www.firstdetroit.com
Albert Scace, President
Patricia Herrick, Marketing Manager
Patricia Herrick, Circulation Manager
Provides financially oriented news on the collection agency and bad debt buying industries worldwide.
Cost: $420.00
8 Pages
Frequency: Monthly
ISSN: 1052-4029
Founded in 1988
Mailing list available for rentat $110 per M

5946 Communicator
Consumer Data Industry Association
1090 Vermont Ave Nw
Suite 200
Washington, DC 20005-4964
202-371-0910
Fax: 202-371-0134
E-Mail: cdia@cdiaonline.org
Home Page: www.cdiaonline.org
Norm Magnuson, VP
Alicia Payne, Contact
Comprehensive online news about the con sumer reporting industry, legislation, member news and schedule of industry events. Members only benefit.
16 Pages
Frequency: Monthly
Circulation: 3000
Founded in 1906

5947 Consumer Bankruptcy News
LRP Publications
Po Box 24668
West Palm Beach, FL 33416-4668
561-622-6520
800-341-7874
Fax: 561-622-2423
E-Mail: custserv@lrp.com
Home Page: www.lrp.com
Kenneth Kahn, President
Keeps readers up-to-date on the latest news and cases involving consumer bankruptcy. A must-have for every bankruptcy professional.
Cost: $290.00
Mailing list available for rent
Printed in 2 colors on matte stock

5948 Covering Credit Newsletter
Covering Credit
13 Calle Larspur
Rancho Santa Margarita, CA 92688
949-460-7609
Fax: 949-460-7609
E-Mail: newsletter@coveringcredit.com
Home Page: www.coveringcredit.com
Social Media: Facebook, LinkedIn
Michael C Dennis, Communications Advisor
Steve Kozack, Financial Consultant
Intended for business professionals dealing with credit risk management and/or commercial debt collection and their advsiors. Free and online.
Frequency: Monthly
Founded in 1989

5949 Credit Union News Watch
Credit Union National Association
601 Penn Ave
NW South Building, Suite 600
Washington, DC 20004
202-628-5777
800-356-9655
Fax: 202-638-7729
Home Page: www.cuna.org
Social Media: Facebook, Twitter
Susan Newton, Executive Director
Pat Sowick, VP
Richard Dines, Senior State and League Affairs Dir
Alicia Valencia Erb, League Relations
Shellee Mitchell, Executive Assistant
Offers news and reports on credit and lending services.
Cost: $50.00
Frequency: Weekly
Founded in 1970

5950 Credit Union Report
Callahan & Associates
1001 Connecticut Ave Nw
Suite 1001
Washington, DC 20036-5523
202-223-3920
800-446-7453
Fax: 202-223-1311
E-Mail: pubs@creditunions.com
Home Page: www.callahan.com
Nader Moghaddam, President/CEO
Keeps an eye on the future, providing stategic vision for every level of credit union management. Each issue includes leading-edge ideas from the industry's top consultants and CEO's, as well as financial trend analysis to help credit unions operate more effectively. Available in print and electronic formats.
Cost: $149.00
Frequency: Monthly

5951 **Credit Union Times**
33-41 Newark Street
2nd Floor
Hoboken, NJ 07030

201-526-1230
800-543-0874
Fax: 201-526-1260
E-Mail: subscriptions@cutimes.com
Home Page: www.cutimes.com
Social Media: Facebook, Twitter, LinkedIn

Sarah Snell Cooke, Editor in Chief
Sarah Snell Cooke, Publisher/Editor in Chief
Donald Shoultz, Managing Editor

Reports on marketing, regulation, technology and developing trends.
Cost: $120.00
Frequency: Weekly
Circulation: 9337
Printed in 4 colors on matte stock

5952 **Inside MBS & ABS**
Inside Mortgage Finance Publishers
7910 Woodmont Ave
Suite 1000
Bethesda, MD 20814-7019

301-951-1240
Fax: 301-656-1709
E-Mail: service@imfpubs.com
Home Page: www.imfpubs.com
Social Media: Twitter, LinkedIn, YouTube

Guy Cecala, Owner
John Bancroft, Managing Editor

If you're involved in issuing, underwriting, investing, research, rating or trading mortgage-backed securities and asset-backed securities, this publication is for you.
Cost: $1699.00
Founded in 1984

5953 **Jumbo Rate News**
Bauer Financial
2655 S Le Jeune Rd
Suite 1A
Coral Gables, FL 33134-5827

305-445-9500
800-388-6686
Fax: 305-445-6775
E-Mail: customerservice@bauerfinancial.com
Home Page: www.bauerfinancial.com

Karen L Dorway, President/CEO

Each issue contains over 1,000 separate Jumbo CD rates in seven categories from over 200 creditworthy banks and thrifts nationwide. Includes star ratings, wire transfer fees, deposit requirements and financial highlights for each institution.
Cost: $4150.00
Frequency: Weekly
Founded in 1986
Printed in 2 colors on matte stock

5954 **MBA Newslink**
Mortgage Bankers Association
1717 Rhode Island Avenue NW
Suite 400
Washington, DC 20036

202-557-2700
E-Mail: mbsnewslink@mortgagebankers.org
Home Page: www.mortgagebankers.org
Social Media: Facebook, Twitter, LinkedIn, YouTube

David H Stevens, President/CEO
Marcia Davies, Chief of Staff/SVP

Learn the latest residential, commercial, and multifamily real estate finance news. Hear what's happening at MBA, read special features that provide vital facts and insight into industry trends, news from Washington, DC and more.
Cost: $69.95
Frequency: Daily
Circulation: 54,000

5955 **NACM E-News**
National Association of Credit Management
8840 Columbia 100 Pkwy
Columbia, MD 21045-2100

410-740-5560
Fax: 410-740-5574
E-Mail: robins@nacm.org
Home Page: www.nacm.org
Social Media: Facebook, Twitter, LinkedIn

Toni Drake, Chairperson
Chris Meyers, Chairman Elect
Kevin Quinn, Director
Jay Snyder, Director

News items of interest to credit and business professionals. Free online.

5956 **National Mortgage News**
Thomson Financial Publishing
1 State St
27th Floor
New York, NY 10004-1481

212-803-8333
800-221-1809
Fax: 800-235-5552
E-Mail: custserv@thomsonmedia.com
Home Page: www.nationalmortgagenews.com
Social Media: Facebook, Twitter, LinkedIn

Timothy Murphy, Group Publisher

Mortgage information, legislation and news.
Cost: $228.00
Frequency: Weekly
Printed in 2 colors on newsprint stock

5957 **Newsbreak**
First Entertainment Credit Union
PO Box 100
Hollywood, CA 90078

323-851-3673
888-800-3328
Fax: 323-874-1397
E-Mail: mail@firstent.org
Home Page: www.firstent.org
Social Media: Facebook, Twitter, You tube

Charles A Bruen, President/CEO

Provides industry, resources and investment news and information for the First Entertainment Credit Union member. Free online.
Frequency: Quarterly

5958 **SNL Daily ThriftWatch**
SNL Financial
212 7th Street NE
Charlottesville, VA 22902
434-977-1600
866-296-3743
Fax: 434-977-4466
E-Mail: CustMerDept@snl.com
Home Page: www.snl.com

Mike Chin, President

Provides the information that thrift executives and investors require to stay on top of the industry. Available in print and electronic formats.
5 Pages
Frequency: Daily
Founded in 1987

5959 **Scope**
International Association of Commercial Collectors
4040 W 70th St
Minneapolis, MN 55435-4104

952-925-0760
800-859-9526
Fax: 952-926-1624
E-Mail: iacc@commercialcollector.com
Home Page: www.commercialcollector.com
Social Media: LinkedIn

Johon Yursha, President
Tammy Schoenberg, Executive Director
Jessica Hartman, Director
Sara Bobrowski, IACC Coordinator
Randy Frazee, Board Treasurer

Provides updates on developments in the industry, important legislative and legal issues, and IACC events and resources. Free to members only.
350 Members
Frequency: Monthly
Circulation: 350
Founded in 1970
Printed in on glossy stock

5960 **Trade Vendor Quarterly**
Blakeley & Blakeley
2 Park Plaza
Suite 400
Irvine, CA 92614

949-260-0611
Fax: 949-260-0613
E-Mail: administrator@vendorland.com
Home Page: www.vendorlaw.com

Scott Blakey, Esq.

Highlights developments in commercial, creditors' rights, e-commerce and bankruptcy law of interest to the credit and financial professional. Free online.
Frequency: Quarterly

Magazines & Journals

5961 **Affordable Housing Finance**
Hanley Wood
300 Montgomery Street
Suite 1060
San Francisco, CA 94104

415-315-1241
Fax: 415-315-1248
E-Mail: ahf@omeda.com
Home Page: www.housingfinance.com
Social Media: Facebook, Twitter

John McManus, Editorial Director
Jerry Ascierto, Editor in Chief

Offers practical information on obtaining debt and equality financing from federal, state, and local governments as well as private resources. In-depth coverage on the federal low-income housing tax credit program, tax-exempt bond financing, corporate tax credit investigation.
Cost: $83.00
88 Pages
Frequency: Monthly
Circulation: 9000
Founded in 1993
Printed in 4 colors on glossy stock

5962 **American Bankruptcy Institute Journal**
American Bankruptcy Institute
44 Canal Center Plz
Suite 404
Alexandria, VA 22314-1546

703-739-0800
Fax: 703-739-1060
E-Mail: Support@abiworld.org
Home Page: www.abiworld.org
Social Media: Facebook, Twitter, LinkedIn

James Markus, President
Patricia Redmond, President-elect
Margaret Howard, VP Research
Brian Shaw, VP Membership

Benefit to ABI members. Written by experts in the insolvency community, the Journal ad-

dresses timely issues involving consumer bankruptcy, the intersection of state laws and the Bankruptcy Code, valuation, turnaround management concerns, recent legislative developments, the US trustee system and more. Available in print or online.
Cost: $225.00
Frequency: 1 Year 10 Issue
Circulation: 10500
Founded in 1982
Printed in 5 colors on matte stock

5963 Apartment Finance Today Magazine
Hanley Wood LLC
One Thomas Circle, NW
Suite 600
Washington, DC 20005
202-452-0800
Fax: 202-785-1974
Home Page: www.hanleywood.com
Peter Goldston, CEO
Frank Anton, Vice Chairman
Provides in-depth and unbiased reporting and insightful analysis for owners, developers and asset managers
80 Pages
ISSN: 1097-4059
Founded in 1995
Printed in 4 colors on glossy stock

5964 Business Credit Magazine
National Association of Credit Management
8840 Columbia 100 Pkwy
Columbia, MD 21045-2100
410-740-5560
Fax: 410-740-5574
E-Mail: robins@nacm.org
Home Page: www.nacm.org
Social Media: Facebook, Twitter, LinkedIn
Toni Drake, Chairperson
Chris Meyers, Chairman/elect
Kevin Quinn, Director
Jay Snyder, Director
Serves those responsible for extending business and trade credit and overseeing risk management for their companies. Keeps individuals up-to-date on cutting-edge trands and important legislative, bankruptcy, business ethics, trade finance, asset protection, benchmarking and scoring issues.
Frequency: 9x/Year
Circulation: 22000

5965 Card Technology
Thomson Financial Publishing
Thomas Reuters
3 Times Square
New York, NY 10036
646-223-4000
E-Mail: general.info@thomsonreuters.com
Home Page: www.tfn.com
Thomas H Glocer, Chief Executive Officer
Store-value cards, optical-memory cards, biometrics, cards on the Internet, cards for electronic data storage, and devices used with these cards in banking, government, telecommunications, transportation and education.
Cost: $ 98.00
Frequency: Monthly
Circulation: 25000
Founded in 1961
Printed in 4 colors on glossy stock

5966 Collections & Credit Risk
Thomson Financial Publishing
1 State St
27th Floor
New York, NY 10004-1481
212-803-8200
800-221-1809
Fax: 800-843-9600
E-Mail: custserv@sourcemedia.com
Home Page: www.creditcollectionsworld.com
Darren Waggoner, Chief Editor
Melissa Buonos, National Sales Manager
Focuses on news and trends of strategic and competitive importance to collections and credit policy executives. Covers the credit risk industry's growth, diversification and technology in both commercial and consumer credit.
Cost: $98.00
66 Pages
Frequency: Monthly
Circulation: 25000
Founded in 1996

5967 Commercial Collection Guidelines for Credit Grantors
International Association of Commercial Collectors
4040 W 70th St
Minneapolis, MN 55435-4104
952-925-0760
800-859-9526
Fax: 952-926-1624
E-Mail: iacc@commercialcollector.com
Home Page: www.commercialcollector.com
Social Media: LinkedIn
John Yursha, President
Tammy M. Schoenberg, Executive Director
Jessica Hartman, Director
Sara Bobrowski, IACC Coordinator
Randy Frazee, Board Treasurer
Helps to assist commercial account credit managers and their staffs in evaluating receivables and collecting accounts. Topics include internal credit control, credit granting and collecting and professional commercial collection service.
Cost: $70.00
350 Members
Frequency: Monthly
Founded in 1970

5968 Commercial Mortgage Insight
Zackin Publications
PO Box 2180
Waterbury, CT 06722-2180
203-755-0158
800-325-6745
Fax: 203-262-4680
E-Mail: info@cmi-online.com
Home Page: www.cmi-online.com
Social Media: Facebook, Twitter
Paul Zackin, Publisher
Phil Hall, Editor
Christina Stanevich, Marketing
For desicion making executives in commercial mortgage banking and brokerage firms, commercial banks and community/savings institutions. Provides professionals with timely and comprehensive market news, trends and know-how needed to make informed decisions and choices.
Cost: $48.00
32 Pages
Frequency: Monthly
Circulation: 18000
ISSN: 1095-0729
Founded in 1997
Printed in 4 colors

5969 Credit & Financial Management Review
Credit Research Foundation
1812 Baltimore Blvd
Suite H
Westminster, MD 21157
443-821-3000
Fax: 443-821-3627
E-Mail: lylew@crfonline.org
Home Page: www.crfonline.org
Lyle Wallis, President
Referred journal that publishes original material concerned with all aspects of credit, accounts receivable and customer financial relationships. It is devoted to the improvement and further development of the theory and practice of credit management.
Cost: $80.00
56 Pages
Frequency: Quarterly
Circulation: 3000
Printed in 2 colors

5970 Credit Card Management
Thomson Financial Publishing
Thomas Reuters
3 Times Square
New York, NY 10036
646-223-4000
800-782-5555
Fax: 646-223-8593
E-Mail: generial.info@thomsonreuters.com
Home Page: www.tfn.com
Thomas H Glocer, Chief Executive Officer
Information on the major developments in the credit card industry.
Cost: $98.00
74 Pages
Frequency: Monthly
Circulation: 19000
Printed in 4 colors on glossy stock

5971 Credit Professional
Credit Professionals International
10726 Manchester Rd
Suite B
St Louis, MO 63122-1320
314-821-9393
Fax: 314-821-7171
E-Mail: creditpro@creditprofessionals.org
Home Page: www.creditprofessionals.org
Sue Heusing, President
Rhonda McKinney, VP
Charlotte Rancilio, Editor
A bi-annual magazine published by Credit Professionals International.
Cost: $15.00
Frequency: Bi-annually
Circulation: 550
Founded in 1989

5972 Credit Union Magazine
Credit Union National Association
601 Penn Ave
NW South Building, Suite 600
Washington, DC 20004
202-628-5777
800-356-9655
Fax: 202-638-7729
E-Mail: webservices@cuna.org
Home Page: www.cuna.org
Social Media: Facebook, Twitter
Daniel A Mica, CEO
Tom Dorety, Vice Chairman
Kathy Kuehn, Manager Periodicals
The role and operations of modern credit unions.
Cost: $50.00
100 Pages
Frequency: Monthly
Circulation: 34401
ISSN: 0011-1066
Printed in 4 colors on glossy stock

5973 Federal Credit Union Magazine
National Association of Federal Credit Unions
3138 10th St N
Arlington, VA 22201-2149
703-522-4770
800-336-4644
Fax: 703-524-1082

E-Mail: fbecker@nafcu.org
Home Page: www.nafcu.org
Social Media: Facebook, Twitter, YouTube

Fred Becker, President
Alicia Hosmer, VP, Marketing

Written for CEO's, senior staff and volunteers of Federal Credit Unions. Offers legislative and regulatory news, as well as technology and operational issues. Call for rates.
50 Pages
Circulation: 1500
ISSN: 1043-7789
Founded in 1967
Printed in 4 colors on glossy stock

5974 **News and Views**
Advertising Media Credit Executives Association
8840 Columbia 100 Parkway
Columbia, MD 21045-2158

410-992-7609
Fax: 410-740-5574
E-Mail: amcea@amcea.org
Home Page: www.amcea.org

Sheila Wroten, President
Mary Younger, VP
Vickie Bolinger, Director

Our magazine reports on current trends and legal issues while offering tips on customer service, time management and collections.
Frequency: Quarterly
Founded in 1953

Trade Shows

5975 **AMCEA Conference**
Advertising Media Credit Executives Association
8840 Columbia 100 Parkway
Columbia, MD 21045-2158

410-992-7609
Fax: 410-740-5574
E-Mail: amcea@amcea.org
Home Page: www.amcea.org

Sheila Wroten, President
Kimberly Riley, VP
Vickie Bolinger, Director

The conference encompasses four days and is a networking extravaganza. Top attorneys discuss bankruptcy and legal issues. We invite advertising agencies to discuss network buying and liability problems.
Frequency: Annual

5976 **Credit Union Executive Society Annual Convention: CUES**
5510 Research Park Drive
Madison, WI 53711-5377

608-712-2664
800-252-2664
Fax: 608-271-2303
E-Mail: cues@cues.org
Home Page: www.cues.org
Social Media: Facebook, Twitter, LinkedIn

Fred Johnson, CEO/President

Offers a rainbow of marketing and technology topics, as well as a supplier showcase, geared toward board members.
Frequency: June
Founded in 1962

5977 **Credit Union National Association Governmental Affairs Conference**
Credit Union National Association
601 Penn Ave
NW South Building, Suite 600
Washington, DC 20004

202-628-5777
800-356-9655
Fax: 202-638-7729
Home Page: www.cuna.org
Social Media: Facebook, Twitter

Susan Newton, Executive Director
Pat Sowick, VP
Richard Dines, Senior State and League Affairs Dir
Alicia Valencia Erb, League Relations
Shellee Mitchell, Executive Assistant

Annual conference held in Washington, DC, with a focus on legislative issues impacting credit unions.
Frequency: February

5978 **Credit Union National Association Future Forum**
601 Penn Ave
NW South Building, Suite 600
Washington, DC 20004

202-628-5777
800-356-9655
Fax: 202-638-7729
Home Page: www.cuna.org
Social Media: Facebook, Twitter

Susan Newton, Executive Director
Pat Sowick, VP
Richard Dines, Senior State and League Affairs Dir
Alicia Valencia Erb, League Relations
Shellee Mitchell, Executive Assistant

Convention and annual general meeting with exhibit hall, educational sessions, and other events.
Frequency: September

5979 **Defense Credit Union's Annual Conference**
Defense Credit Union Council
601 Pennsylvania Avenue NW
South Building, Suite 600
Washington, DC 20004

202-638-3950
Fax: 202-638-3410
E-Mail: admin@dcuc.org
Home Page: www.dcuc.org

Conference and exhibits of equipment, supplies and services for credit unions that serve Department of Defense personnel with problems peculiar to military installations and personnel.
200 Attendees
Frequency: August

5980 **Education Credit Union Council Annual Conference**
Education Credit Union Council
PO Box 7558
Spanish Fort, AL 36577-7558

251-626-3399
Fax: 251-626-3565
E-Mail: l.webster@ecuc.org
Home Page: www.ecuc.org

Lorraine B Zerfas, Executive Director

Any CEOs, directors, committee members and top management active in the operations of any credit union that serves the educational community who want to achieve professional excellence should attend. Interact with peers from across the US serving the fields of education, introduce executive staff and managers to credit union ideas and philosophy on a national level and discuss issues important to your credit union in the coming year.
Frequency: February

5981 **Finance, Credit & International Business Global Conference**
Finance, Credit & International Business
8840 Columbia 100 Parkway
Columbia, MD 21045-2158

410-423-1840
888-256-3242
Fax: 410-423-1845
E-Mail: fcib_info@fciglobal.com
Home Page: www.fcibglobal.com
Social Media: Twitter, LinkedIn

Annual gathering of international credit and finance professionals draws upon the combined expertise of financial executives from all regions of the world to provide attendees with practical insight for managing in a rapidly evolving international environment.
Frequency: November

5982 **Fleet/Lease Remarketing**
S&A Conferences Group
Westview At Weston
301 Cascade Pointe Lane
Cary, NC 27513

800-608-7500
Fax: 919-674-6027
Home Page: www.autoremarketing.com
Social Media: Facebook, Twitter, LinkedIn

Ron Smith, President

Executive conference focused on remarketing strategies for manufacturer, bank, finance, commercial and rental fleet/lease vehicles.
Frequency: February

5983 **International Association of Commercial Collectors Annual Convention**
4040 W 70th Street
Minneapolis, MN 55435

952-925-0760
800-859-9526
Fax: 952-926-1624
E-Mail: iacc@commercialcollector.com
Home Page: www.commercialcollector.com
Social Media: LinkedIn

John Yursha, President
Tammy M. Schoenberg, Executive Director

International trade association comprised of more than 230 collection specialists and 140 commercial attorneys, with members throughout the US and 20 international countries. IACC's mission is to promote the commercial collection profession by providing IACC members with the resources to excel in the industry.
350 Members
Frequency: January
Founded in 1970

5984 **Legal Issues & Regulatory Compliance Conference**
Mortgage Bankers Association
1717 Rhode Island Avenue NW
Suite 400
Washington, DC 20036

202-557-2700
E-Mail: meetings@mortgagebankers.org
Home Page: www.mortgagebankers.org
Social Media: Facebook, Twitter, LinkedIn, YouTube

David H Stevens, President/CEO
Marcia Davies, Chief of Staff/SVP

Learn about all the legal and regulatory developments facing the industry.
Frequency: Annual/May

5985 **NFCC Leaders Conference**
National Foundation for Credit Counseling

2000M Street NW
Suite 505
Washington, DC 20036

202-677-4300
800-388-2227
Home Page: www.nfcc.org
Social Media: Facebook, Twitter, YouTube

Susan C Keating, President/CEO
Paul Weiss, CFO/ Chief Of Staff
William Binzel, Chief Counsel

Three-day conference to discuss credit counceling industry practices, trends and issues.
300 Attendees
Frequency: Annual/Fall
Founded in 1965

5986 **National Association of Credit Management: Annual Credit Congress**
National Association of Credit Management
8840 Columbia 100 Parkway
Columbia, MD 21045

410-740-5560
Fax: 410-740-5574
E-Mail: robins@nacm.org
Home Page: www.nacm.org
Social Media: Facebook, Twitter, LinkedIn

Toni Drake, Chairperson
Chris Meyers, Chairman/elect
Kevin Quinn, Director
Jay Snyder, Director

The event for the business credit and financial professional offering relevant, timely educational offerings, including industry specific programs, over 100 specialized service providers on the expo floor, showcasing the latest products and services, countless networking and relationship-building events to facilitate the sharing of knowlege and expertise.
18000 Members
2000 Attendees
Frequency: May/June

5987 **National Fraud Issues Conference**
Mortgage Bankers Association
1717 Rhode Island Avenue NW
Suite 400
Washington, DC 20036

202-557-2700
E-Mail: meetings@mortgagebankers.org
Home Page: www.mortgagebankers.org
Social Media: Facebook, Twitter, LinkedIn, YouTube

David H Stevens, President/CEO
Marcia Davies, Chief of Staff/SVP

The forum where industry professionals can learn about the issues related to the growing incidence and complexity of mortgage fraud.
Frequency: Annual/March

5988 **National Mortgage Servicing Conference & Expo**
Mortgage Bankers Association
1717 Rhode Island Avenue NW
Suite 400
Washington, DC 20036

202-557-2700
E-Mail: meetings@mortgagebankers.org
Home Page: www.mortgagebankers.org
Social Media: Facebook, Twitter, LinkedIn, YouTube

David H Stevens, President/CEO
Marcia Davies, Chief of Staff/SVP

Provides the opportunity to reach key servicing executives from residential mortgage companies and showcase the product offerings, network with key decision makers, and obtain qualified leads that can help reach goals.
Frequency: Annual/February

5989 **National Policy Conference**
Mortgage Bankers Association
1717 Rhode Island Avenue NW
Suite 400
Washington, DC 20036

202-557-2700
E-Mail: meetings@mortgagebankers.org
Home Page: www.mortgagebankers.org
Social Media: Facebook, Twitter, LinkedIn, YouTube

David H Stevens, President/CEO
Marcia Davies, Chief of Staff/SVP

Brings together key officials, cabinet members and special guest speakers to address these critical issues.
Frequency: Annual/March

5990 **National Technology in Mortgage Banking Conference**
Mortgage Bankers Association
1717 Rhode Island Avenue NW
Suite 400
Washington, DC 20036

202-557-2700
E-Mail: meetings@mortgagebankers.org
Home Page: www.mortgagebankers.org
Social Media: Facebook, Twitter, LinkedIn, YouTube

David H Stevens, President/CEO
Marcia Davies, Chief of Staff/SVP

Forum to learn about the newest industry solutions and how they can increase your company's competitive edge. The conference focuses on relevant topics, including legal / regulatory updates, eMortgages, investor reporting changes and technology advances such as mobile computing.
Frequency: Annual/March

5991 **Risk Management Conference**
Risk Management Association
1801 Market Street
Suite 300
Philadelphia, PA 19103-1628

215-446-4000
800-677-7621
Fax: 215-446-4100
E-Mail: customers@rmahq.org
Home Page: www.rmahq.org

William F Githens, President/CEO
Kathleen M Beans, Public Relations Manager

Educates and helps risk management professionals develop new techniques and learn about new innovative products at different stages of their careers. Mailing list available for exhibitors and sponsors only.
800 Attendees
Frequency: October

Directories & Databases

5992 **AMCEA Member Handbook & Roster**
Advertising Media Credit Executives Association
8840 Columbia 100 Parkway
Columbia, MD 21045-2158

410-992-7609
Fax: 410-740-5574
E-Mail: amcea@amcea.org
Home Page: www.amcea.org

Sheila Wroten, President
Kimberly Riley, VP
Vickie Bolinger, Director

Inside you will find direct telephone numbers to every credit manager in our association along with numbers for credit references and fax inquiries. We also include their e-mail addresses and computer hardware and software information.

5993 **American Recovery Association Directory**
American Recovery Association
5525 N MacArthur Boulevard
Suite 135
Irving, TX 75038

972-755-4755
Fax: 972-870-5755
E-Mail:
homeoffice@americanrecoveryassn.org
Home Page: www.repo.org

Mary Jane Hogan, President
Tom Crosby, Secretary/Treasurer

Contain's listings of ARA's members, offices and services. Available in hardcopy and electronic formats.
308 Pages
Frequency: Annual
Founded in 1965

5994 **Banksearch Book**
Sheshunoff Information Services
2801 Via Fortuna
Suite 600
Austin, TX 78746-7970

512-472-4000
800-477-1772
E-Mail:
editorialqueries.sis@thomsonmedia.com
Home Page: www.smslp.com

Gabrielle Sheshunoff, CEO

Offers information on savings and loans, savings banks and credit unions with assets over 10 million. Customized for your institutution type: bank thrift, bank holding company or credit union. You buy only the data you want — by state, region or nation.
Cost: $295.00
Frequency: Annual

5995 **Business Products Credit Association**
BCPA
607 Westridge Drive
O'Fallon, MO 63366

636-924-5775
Fax: 636-754-0567
E-Mail: service@bpca.org
Home Page: www.bpca.org

BPCA has a database of over 400,000 companies and their payment histories. This is available to members over the Internet.

5996 **Callahan's Credit Union Directory**
Callahan & Associates
1001 Connecticut Ave NW
Suite 1001
Washington, DC 20036-5523

202-223-3920
800-446-7453
Fax: 202-223-1311
Home Page: www.callahan.com

Sean Hession, CEO
Charles Filson, Chairman
Jay Johnson, EVP
Alix Patterson, COO

This directory turns raw data into research, giving you the tools you need to keep up with the credit union industry. Access all the credit union information found in the print edition through the Online Edition on this website. In a special Users Area only for purchasers of the print edition, you can access updated finacials four times a year, conduct searches on key information and save those search results to return to over and over again. Real time updates

directly from our database.
Cost: $135.00
Frequency: Annual

5997 **Collection Agency Directory**
First Detroit Corporation
PO Box 5025
Warren, MI 48090-5025

586-573-0045
800-366-5995
Fax: 586-573-9219
E-Mail: ascace@firstdetroit.com
Home Page: www.firstdetroit.com

Albert W Scace, Publisher

Offers information and statistics on nearly 900 collection agencies throught the world.
Cost: $347.00
301 Pages
Frequency: Annual, Paperback
ISSN: 1058-983X
Founded in 1991
Mailing list available for rent: 11,000 names at $150 per M
Printed in one color on matte stock

5998 **Credit**
American Financial Services Association
919 18th Street NW
Suite 300
Washington, DC 20006-5517

202-296-5544
E-Mail: sharrison@afsamail.org
Home Page: www.afsaonline.org
Social Media: Twitter

Chris Steinebert, President/CEO

Focuses on breaking developments on legislative and regulatory issues on the federal and state levels, as well as consumer education initiatives, industry news, news inside AFSA and information on meetings and conferences. Free online access.
1500 Pages
Frequency: Bi-Monthly

5999 **Credit Card and Check Fraud: A Stop-Loss Manual**
Fraud & Theft Information Bureau
9770 S. Military Trail
Suite 380
Boynton Beach, FL 33436

561-737-8700
Fax: 561-737-5800
E-Mail: sales@fraudandtheftinfo.com
Home Page: www.fraudandtheftinfo.com

Larry Schwartz, Founder and Director
Pearl Sax, Founder and Director

The Fraud And Theft Information Bureau is the leading consultant on credit card and check fraud control and loss prevention — and the publisher of related manuals and fraud-blocker data bases
Cost: $199.95
300 Pages
Founded in 1982

6000 **Credit Union Cooperatives**
Callahan & Associates
1001 Connecticut Ave NW
10th Floor
Washington, DC 20036-5523

202-223-3920
800-446-7453
Fax: 202-223-1311
Home Page: www.callahan.com

Sean Hession, CEO
Charles Filson, Chairman
Jay Johnson, EVP
Alix Patterson, COO

Your source for information on credit union service organizations (CUSOs) and other cooperative providers to the credit industry. The directory has up-to-date contact names, addresses and phone numbers for more than 700 CUSOs and their associated credit unions. Use this publication to compare services offered by CUSOs or if you're looking to start or expand an existing CUSO.
Cost: $165.00

6001 **Credit Union Directory**
National Credit Union Administration
1775 Duke St
Suite 4206
Alexandria, VA 22314-6115

703-518-6300
800-755-1030
Fax: 703-518-6539
E-Mail: consumerassistance@ncua.gov
Home Page: www.ncua.gov
Social Media: Facebook, Twitter, YouTube

Debbie Matz, Chairman

Federal credit and state-chartered credit unions are the focal point of this directory. Free online.
Frequency: Annual

6002 **Credit Union Financial Yearbook**
Callahan & Associates
1001 Connecticut Ave NW
Washington, DC 20036-5523

202-223-3920
800-446-7453
Fax: 202-223-1311
Home Page: www.callahan.com

Sean Hession, CEO
Charles Filson, Chairman
Jay Johnson, EVP
Alix Patterson, COO

Each quarter Callahan publishes a comprehensive study on the state of the industry that includes detailed financials for all credit unions over $50 million. The third quarter edition is published in 3 volumes based on asset size. Fourth quarter edition is based on total assets for the year. Asset sizes considered are $50 to $100 million, $100 - $250 million and over $250 million.
Cost: $565.00
Frequency: Complete Year Price

6003 **Defense Credit Union Directory**
Defense Credit Union Council
601 Pennsylvania Ave NW
Suite 600
Washington, DC 20004-2601
202-638-3950
Fax: 202-638-3410
E-Mail: admin@dcuc.org
Home Page: www.dcuc.org

Roland Arteata, President

Listing of about 360 credit unions with membership consisting wholly or partly of the military and civilian personnel of the United States and worldwide.
Cost: $150.00
60 Pages
Frequency: Biennial
Founded in 1963

6004 **Directory of Venture Capital & Private Equity Firms - Online Database**
Grey House Publishing
4919 Route 22
PO Box 56
Amenia, NY 12501

518-789-8700
800-562-2139
Fax: 845-373-6390
E-Mail: gold@greyhouse.com
Home Page: http://gold.greyhouse.com
Social Media: Facebook, Twitter

Leslie Mackenzie, Publisher
Richard Gottlieb, Editor

Packed with need-to-know information, this database offers immediate access to 2,300 VC firms, over 10,000 managing partners, and over 11,500 VC investments.
Frequency: Annual

6005 **Directory of Venture Capital and Private Equity Firms**
Grey House Publishing
4919 Route 22
PO Box 56
Amenia, NY 12501

518-789-8700
800-562-2139
Fax: 845-373-6390
E-Mail: books@greyhouse.com
Home Page: www.greyhouse.com
Social Media: Facebook, Twitter

Richard Gottlieb, President
Leslie Mackenzie, Publisher

Offers access to over 2,300 domestic and international venture capital and private equity firms, with detailed contact information and extensive data on investment and funds.
Cost: $685.00
1200 Pages
Frequency: Annual
ISBN: 1-592372-72-4

6006 **Dun's Credit Guide**
Dun & Bradstreet Information Service
103 John F Kennedy Pkwy
Short Hills, NJ 07078-2708

973-921-5500
800-234-3867
Fax: 908-665-5803
Home Page: www.dnb.com
Social Media: Facebook, Twitter, LinkedIn, YouTube

Sara Mathew, CEO
James Fernandez, EVP and COO

Providing a dollar-specific credit guideline on manufacturers, wholesalers and retailers, this database is updated continuously for the interested business person.

6007 **National Credit Union Administration Directory**
National Credit Union Administration
1775 Duke St
Suite 4206
Alexandria, VA 22314-6115

703-518-6300
Fax: 703-518-6539
E-Mail: ociomail@ncua.gov
Home Page: www.ncua.gov

Debbie Matz, Chairman

Directory of credit unions governed by a three member board appointed by the President and confirmed by the US Senate, by the independent federal agency that charters and supervises federal credit unions. NCUA, with the backing of the full faith and credit of the US government, operates the National Credit Union Share Insurance Fund, insuring the savings of 80 million account holders in all federal credit unions and many state chartered credit unions.

6008 **Thomson Credit Union Directory**
4709 Golf Road
Skokie, IL 60076-1231
847-676-9600
800-321-3373
Fax: 847-933-8101

E-Mail: custserv@accuitysolutions.com
Home Page: www.accuitysolutions.com

Hugh Johnes IV, President and CEO
Kerry Hewson, EVP
Jay Ryan, Head of Sales

Semi-annual directory that includes valuable industry statistics, a quick telephone lookup index of all credit unions and a resource guide featuring vendors within the credit union marketplace. Includes over 12,500 major credit unions and 5,500 branches, with asset rankings, membership totals and more. Published in partnership with the Credit Union National Association.
Cost: $199.00
Frequency: January/July
ISBN: 1-563103-24-9

6009 **Who's Who in Credit and Financial**
New York Credit and Financial Management Assn
520 8th Avenue
New York, NY 10018-6507

212-695-4807

Directory of services and supplies to the industry.

6010 **World Council of Credit Unions Directory**
World Council of Credit Unions
5710 Mineral Point Road
Madison, WI 53705

608-395-2000
Fax: 608-395-2001
E-Mail: mail@woccu.org
Home Page: www.woccu.org

Pepi Dougherty, Executive
Mike Muckian, Marketing & Communications

Lists over 100 World Council of Credit Union leaders and member organizations in each of seven confederations. African, Asian, Australian, Canadian, Caribbean, Latin-American and the United States.

Industry Web Sites

6011 **http://gold.greyhouse.com**
G.O.L.D Grey House OnLine Databases

Grey House Publishing's online database platform, GOLD, offers Quick Search, Keyword Search and Expert Search for most business sectors including banking, credid and lending service markets. The GOLD platform makes finding the information you need quick and easy - whether you're a novice searcher or an experienced database user. All of Grey House's directory products are available for subscription on the GOLD platform.

6012 **www.aacul.org**
American Association of Credit Union Leagues

Voluntary membership association for credit union leagues that are members of the Credit Union National Association. AACUL provides representation, products, services and programs to its members.

6013 **www.abiworld.org**
American Bankruptcy Institute

ABI is the largest multi-diciplinary, non-partisan organization dedicated to research and education on matters related to insolvency. The ABI membership provides a forum for the exchange of ideas and information. ABI is engaged in numerous educational and research activities, as well as the production of a number of publications both for the insolvency practitioner and the public.

6014 **www.afsaonline.com**
American Financial Services Association

National trade association for market funded providers of financial services to consumers and small businesses. These providers offer an array of finacial services, including unsecured personal loans, automobile loans, home equity loans and credit cards through specialized bank institutions.

6015 **www.amcea.org**
Advertising Media Credit Executives Association

Improving the professionalism, principles, understanding and techniques of media credit management by encouraging the exchange of ideas, methods and procedures within the membership. Providing additional education and training in the business fundamentals of media credit and credit policies and in the related areas of finance, accounting, law and economics for the purpose of enhancing the career development of members.

6016 **www.bccacredit.com**
Broadcast Cable Credit Association

Subsidiary of the Broadcast Cable Financial Management Association. BCCA provides industry specific credit reports on individual agencies, advertisers, or buying services (national and local).

6017 **www.bpca.org**
Business Products Credit Association

Nonprofit trade association for credit personnel of manufacturers, wholesalers and factors. The national credit group consists of discount stores, superstores, commercial stationers, printing and publications, business machines, computer peripherals and software, plus mass merchandisers. In addition, BPCA has groups on school supply, janitorial/sanitary supplies, fine pens/promotional products.

6018 **www.cdiaonline.org**
Consumer Data Industry Association

Trade association representing consumer information companies that provide fraud prevention and risk management products, credit and mortgage reports, tenant and employment screening services, check fraud and verifacation services and collection services. Sets industry standards and provides education for it's members. Provides educational materials for consumers regarding their credit rights and how consumer credit reporting agencies can better serve their needs.

6019 **www.cfa.com**
Commercial Finance Association

Trade group of the asset-based financial services industry, with members throughout the US, Canada and around the world. Members include the asset-based lending arms of domestic and foreign commercial banks, small and large independent finance companies, floor plan financing organizations, factoring organizations and financing subsidiaries of major industrial corporations.

6020 **www.collector.com**
American Collectors Association

International trade organization of credit and collection professionals that provides a variety of accounts recievable management services.

6021 **www.commercialcollector.com**
International Association of Commercial Collectors

International trade association comprised of more than 230 collection specialists and 140 commercial attorneys, with members throughout the US and 20 international countries. IACC's mission is to promote the commercial collection profession by providing IACC members with the resources to excel in the industry.

6022 **www.creditunions.com**
Callahan & Associates

National credit union research and consulting firm specializing in financial publications and analysis software, strategic planning and investment management.

6023 **www.crfonline.org**
Credit Research Foundation

Independent, member run organization, consisting of a dynamic community of like minded business professionals with a vested interest in improving and fostering the field of business credit — more specifically, the practices and technologies of business credit.

6024 **www.cues.org**
Credit Union Executives Society

For credit union executives, we serve to advance the professional development of CEOs, senior management and directors.

6025 **www.cuna.org**
Credit Union National Association

The premier trade association in the financial services arena. Supports, protects, unifies and advances the credit union movement.

6026 **www.ecuc.org**
Education Credit Union Council

Dedicated to providing educational and networking opportunities to credit unions who serve educational communities, industry teachers, administrators, students, support staff and others in the educational community.

6027 **www.electran.org**
Electronic Transaction Association

International trade association serving the needs of organizations offering transaction processing products and services.

6028 **www.fcibglobal.com**
FCIB

Provider of products and services to many small, medium and large size exporters as well as major multinational corporations in 30 countries around the world.

6029 **www.firstent.org**
First Entertainment Credit Union

Nonprofit institution serves as the financial resource for the entertainment community to more than 700 entertainment based companies.

6030 **www.fraudandtheftinfo.com**
Fraud & Theft Information Bureau

Provides problem solving, crime prevention, money saving manuals and fraud blocker databases.

6031 **www.greyhouse.com**
Grey House Publishing

Authoritative reference directories for most business sectors including banking, credit and lending service markets. Users can search the online databases with varied search criteria allowing for custom searches by product category, geographic area, sales volume, keyword, subject and more. Full Grey House catalog and online ordering also available.

6032 **www.mbaa.org**
Mortgage Bankers Association of America

Representing the real estate finance industry, MBA serves its membership by representing their legislative and regulatory interests before the US Congress and federal agencies; by meeting their educational needs through programs and a range of periodicals and publications; and by supporting their business interests with a variety of research initiatives and other products and services.

6033 www.nacm.org
National Association of Credit Management

Promotes honest and fair dealings in credit transactions, fosters and encourages research in the field of credit.

6034 www.ncua.gov
National Credit Union Administration

Governed by a three-member board appointed by the President and confirmed by the US Senate, this is the independent federal agency that charters and supervises the nation's federal credit unions.

6035 www.nfcc.org
National Foundation for Credit Counceling

National nonprofit credit counseling oranization with 1,200 offices helping 1.5 million households annually. Identify NFCC members (Consumer Credit Counseling Service CCCS) by the NFCC member seal representing high standards, free and low-cost confidential services.

6036 www.repo.org
American Recovery Association

Approximately 500 offices throughout the US, Canada and Germany, providing repossesion services around the world.

6037 www.rmahg.org
Risk Management Association

Financial services association that champions best practices in risk management, monitors emerging trends, develops new risk management techniques, innovative products, and education and training programs geared to risk management professionals.

Associations

6038 **ATM Industry Association**

Home Page: www.atmia.com
Social Media: Facebook, LinkedIn, YouTube

Mike Lee, Chief Executive Officer
Sharon Lane, Global Director, Financeÿ
Dana Benson, Dir., Conferences & Sponsorships
Amanda Hardy, Marketing Director, Europe
David Tente, Executive Director, USA

Alliance promoting the proliferation of automated teller machines, ATMs and cash.
5000 Members
Founded in 1997

6039 **Advanced Network & Services**

2600 South Road
Suite 44-193
Poughkeepsie, NY 12601

845-795-2090
Fax: 845-795-2180
E-Mail: contact@advanced.org
Home Page: www.advanced.org

Dr. James McGroddy, Chairman of the Board
Allan Weis, Founder/President/Managing Director
Kristin Mortensen, Secretary/Treasurer

A nonprofit corporation dedicated to advancing education by accelerating the use of computer networking applications and technology.
Mailing list available for rent

6040 **American e-Commerce Association**

Home Page: www.aeaus.com

Computer training, e-commerce education, membership, recognition, endorsement, and evaluation services.

6041 **Armed Forces Communications and Electronics Association (AFCEA)**

4400 Fair Lakes Courtÿ
Fairfax, VA 22033-3899

703-631-6100
800-336-4583
Fax: 703-631-6169
Home Page: www.afcea.org
Social Media: Facebook, Twitter, LinkedIn, Google+, Flickr, YouTube

Linda Gooden, Chair of the Board of Directors
Brig Gen John Meincke, Vice Chair, B.O.D.ÿ
LtGen Robert M. Shea, President, CEO
Pat Miorin, CPA, EVP, CFO, Int. Treasurer
Mike Warlick, Vice President, Defense Operations

A nonprofit international organization that serves its members by providing a forum for the ethical exchange of information and is dedicated to increasing knowledge through the exploration of issues relevant to information technology, communication, and electronics for the defense, homeland security and intelligence communities.

6042 **Business Software Alliance**

20 F Street, NW
Suite 800
Washington, DC 20001

202-872-5500
Fax: 202-872-5501,
E-Mail: info@bsa.org
Home Page: www.bsa.org
Social Media: Facebook, Twitter, You tube

Robert W Holleyman II, CEO
Jodie Kelley, General Counsel and SVP
Matt Reid, SVP, External Affairs
Katherine McGuire, VP, Govt. Relations

An organization dedicated to promoting a safe and legal digital world. BSA educates consumers on software management and copyright protection, cyber security, trade, e-commerce and other internet related issues.
Founded in 1988

6043 **Center for Internet Security**

31 Tech Valley Drive
Suite 2
East Greenbush, NY 12061

518-266-3460
Fax: 518-283-3216
E-Mail: contact@cisecurity.org
Home Page: www.cisecurity.org
Social Media: Facebook, Twitter, LinkedIn, Blog, YouTube

William F. Pelgrin, President, CEO
Thomas Duffy, SVP, Operations and Services
Laura Iwan, SVP, Programs
Julie Evans, Chief Operating Officer
Al Szesnat, Chief Financial Officer

A nonprofit organization that provides products and resources that help partners achieve security goals through expert guidance and cost-effective solutions.

6044 **CompTIA**

3500 Lacey Road
Suite 100
Downers Grove, IL 60515

630-678-8300
Fax: 630-678-8384
E-Mail: techvoice@comptia.org
Home Page: www.comptia.org
Social Media: Facebook, Twitter, LinkedIn, Pinterest, Google+, YouTube

Todd Thibodeaux, President, CEO
Charles Eaton, CEO, Educational Foundation
Ann Batko, SVP, Marketing
Kelly Ricker, SVP, Events and Education
David Sommer, Chief Financial Officer

A nonprofit trade association created by representatives of five microcomputer leaderships and is a provider of professional certifications for theinformation technology (IT) industry.

6045 **Council on CyberSecurity**

1700 North Moore Streetÿ
Suite 2100
Arlington, VA 22209

703-600-1935
E-Mail: info@counciloncybersecurity.org
Home Page: www.counciloncybersecurity.org
Social Media: Facebook, Twitter, LinkedIn

Franklin Reeder, Chairman
Richard Schaeffer, Treasurer
Jane Holl Lute, President, CEO
Maurice Uenuma, Chief Operating Officer
Tony W. Sager, Chief Technologist

Organization that mobilizes a broad community of stakeholders to identify, validate, promote and sustain the adoption of cybersecurity best practice.

6046 **Cyber Security Research Alliance**

401 Edgewater Place
Suite 600
Wakefield, MA 1880

781-876-8860
E-Mail: aobrien@cybersecurityresearch.org
Home Page: www.cybersecurityresearch.org

Julian Warrick, Interim President
Steven Kester, Treasurer
Claire Vishik, Secretary

A nonprofit organization founded by industry stakeholders as a forum develop R & D strategy to address grand challenges in cyber security, and to facilitate public-private partnerships that define a more focused, coordinated, and concerted approach to cyber security research and development.

6047 **Cyber, Space, & Intelligence Association**

703-855-3917
E-Mail: richcoleman1@gmail.com
Home Page: cyberspaceintel.org

Richard Coleman, Chairman, President and Founderÿ
Tidal W. (Ty) McCoy, Senior Executive
Timothy J. Evans, Senior Advisor
Founded in 2011

6048 **Cybersecurity Association**

127 Segre Place
Santa Cruz, CA 95060

831-426-9827
E-Mail: paul.hoffman@cybersecurity.org
Home Page: www.cybersecurity.org

Organization focused on testing the security capabilities and performance of firewalls, intrusion prevention systems and other similar security equipment.

6049 **High Technology Crime Investigation Association**

3288 Goldstone Drive
Roseville, CA 95747

916-408-1751
Fax: 916-384-2232
E-Mail: carol@htcia.org
Home Page: www.htcia.org
Social Media: Facebook, Twitter, LinkedIn

Carol Hutchings, Executive Director
Jimmy Garcia, Public Relations
Elisa Hutchings, Membership Inquiries

A nonprofit professional organization devoted to the prevention, investigation, and prosecution of crimes involving advanced technologies.

6050 **ISACA**

3701 Algonquin Road
Suite 1010
Rolling Meadows, IL 60008ÿ

847-253-1545
Fax: 847-253-1443
Home Page: www.isaca.org
Social Media: Facebook, Twitter, LinkedIn

A nonprofit, independent association that advocates for professionals involved in information security, assurance, risk management and governance.
Founded in 1969

6051 **Information Systems Security Association**

12100 Sunset Hills Road
Suite 130
Reston, VA 20190

866-349-5818
703-234-4077
Fax: 703-435-4390
Home Page: www.issa.org
Social Media: Facebook, Twitter, LinkedIn

Ira Winkler, President
Andrea C. Hoy, Vice President
Kevin D. Spease, Treasurer/CFO
Bill Danigelis, Secretary
Anne Rogers, Director

A nonprofit, international professional organization of informationsecurity professionals and practitioners.

6052 InfraGard

E-Mail: infragardmembership@leo.gov
Home Page: www.infragard.org
Social Media: RSS

A nonprofit organization serving as a public-private partnership between U.S. businesses and the Federal Bureau of Investigation.

6053 Institute for Security, Technology, and Society

7 Maynard Street
Sudikoff Laboratory
Hanover, NH 03755ÿ

603-646-0700
Fax: 603-646-1672
E-Mail: info.ists@dartmouth.edu
Home Page: www.ists.dartmouth.edu
Social Media: Facebook, Twitter, Flickr, YouTube, iTunes

Organization dedicated to pursuing research and education to advance information security and privacy throughout society.
Founded in 2000

6054 Intelligence and National Security Alliance

Ballston Metro Center Office Towers
901 North Stuart Street, Suite 205
Arlington, VA 22203

703-224-4672
Fax: 703-224-4681
Home Page: www.insaonline.org
Social Media: Facebook, Twitter, LinkedIn, Google+, Flickr, YouTube

John Negroponte, Chairman of the Board
Joseph R. DeTrani, President
Charles E. Allen, SeniorÿIntelligenceÿAdvisorÿ
Chuck Alsup, Vice Presidentÿof Policy
Robert Joseph, Senior NationalÿSecurity Advisor

A nonprofit, non-partisan, public-private organization that works to promote and recognize the highest standards within the national security and intelligence communities. Members include current and former high-ranking intelligence, military and government agency leaders, analysts, and experts from industry and academia.

6055 Internet Merchants Association

E-Mail: info@imamerchants.org
Home Page: www.imamerchants.org
Social Media: Facebook

Fred Neff, President
Scott Cole, Vice-President
Doyle Carver, Secretary
Andy Sollofe, Treasurer

Develops, promotes, and protects the economic vitality of internet merchants through a positive business environment and fosters a climate in whichcommerce, industry, and technology will flourish.

6056 Internet Security Alliance

703-907-7090
E-Mail: admin@isalliance.orgÿ
Home Page: www.isalliance.org

Tim McKnight, Board Chairman
Jeff Brown, Board Vice Chairman
Gary McAlum, Board Second Vice Chairman
Larry Clinton, President, CEO
Julie Taylor, Board Member

A nonprofit organization that acts as a forum for information sharing and leadership on information security, and it lobbies for corporate securityinterests.

6057 National Cyber Security Alliance

Home Page: www.staysafeonline.org
Social Media: Facebook, Twitter, LinkedIn, Google+, YouTube

Michael Kaiser, Executive Director, NCSA
Emily Eckland, Director of Digital Strategy
Tiffany Barrett, Data Privacy Day Program Mgr.
Kara Wright, Digital Media Coordinator

A nonprofit, public-private partnership working with the Departmentof Homeland Security (DHS), private sector sponsors, and nonprofit collaboratorsto promote cyber security awareness for home users, small and medium size businesses, and primary and secondary education.

6058 National Cyber-Forensics & Training Alliance

2000 Technology Drive
Suite 450
Pittsburgh, PA 15219

412-802-8000
Fax: 412-802-8510
E-Mail: info@ncfta.net
Home Page: www.ncfta.net

A nonprofit corporation focused on identifying, mitigating, and neutralizing cyber crime threats through strategic alliances and partnerships with Subject Matter Experts (SME) in the public, private, and academic sectors.

6059 National CyberWatch Center

E-Mail: tkepner@nationalcyberwatch.org
Home Page: www.nationalcyberwatch.org
Social Media: Facebook, Twitter, LinkedIn, YouTube

Teri Kepner, Director, Member Services

An organization of higher education institutions, public and private schools, businesses, and government agencies focused on collaborative efforts to advance cybersecurity education and strengthen the national cybersecurity workforce.

6060 National Cybersecurity and Communications Integration Center

245 Murray Lane SW
Building 410
Washington, DC 20598

888-282-0870
E-Mail: info@us-cert.gov
Home Page: www.us-cert.gov/nccic
Social Media: Twitter, RSS

Serves as a central location where a diverse set of partners involved in cybersecurity and communications protection coordinate and synchronize their efforts. Partners include other government agencies, the private sector, and international entities.

6061 National Initiative for Cybersecurity Careers and Studies

E-Mail: NICCS@hq.dhs.gov
Home Page: niccs.us-cert.gov

Robin Williams, Chief

A national resource for cybersecurity awareness, education, careers, and training.

Newsletters

6062 ATM Industry Association Global Newsletter

Home Page: www.atmia.com/media/atmia-global-newsletter
Social Media: Facebook, LinkedIn, YouTube

Mike Lee, Chief Executive Officer
Sharon Lane, Global Director, Financeÿ
Dana Benson, Dir., Conferences & Sponsorships
Amanda Hardy, Marketing Director, Europe
David Tente, Executive Director, USA

Alliance promoting the proliferation of automated teller machines, ATMs and cash.
5000 Members
Founded in 1997

6063 Center for Internet Security

31 Tech Valley Drive
Suite 2
East Greenbush, NY 12061

518-266-3460
Fax: 518-283-3216
E-Mail: contact@cisecurity.org
Home Page: msisac.cisecurity.org/newsletters
Social Media: Facebook, Twitter, LinkedIn, Blog, YouTube

William F. Pelgrin, President, CEO
Thomas Duffy, SVP, Operations and Services
Laura Iwan, SVP, Programs
Julie Evans, Chief Operating Officer
Al Szesnat, Chief Financial Officer

A nonprofit organization that provides products and resources that help partners achieve security goals through expert guidance and cost-effective solutions.

6064 Dot.COM

Business Communications Company
25 Van Zant Street
Suite 13
Norwalk, CT 06855-1713

203-853-4266
Fax: 203-853-0348
E-Mail: sales@bccresearch.com
Home Page: www.bccresearch.com

Louis Naturman, Publisher
C Toenne, Editor

Updates readers on the commercial use of the Internet and related platforms.
Cost: $38.00

6065 E-Healthcare Market Reporter

Health Resources Publishing
1913 Atlantic Ave
Suite 200
Manasquan, NJ 08736-1067

732-292-1100
888-843-6242
Fax: 732-292-1111
E-Mail: info@themcic.com
Home Page: www.healthresourcesonline.com

Robert K Jenkins, Publisher
Judith Granel, Marketing
John Russel, Editor
Brett Powell, Regional Director
Alice Burron, Director

A bi-monthly covering strategies, new products, innovation, privacy issue, business solutions, service available, vendor news and comparative for implementing sales and marketing on the internet.
Cost: $397.00
Frequency: Fortnightly
ISSN: 1098-5654
Founded in 1988

6066 Internet Alliance Cyberbrief
Internet Alliance
1615 L Street NW
Suite 1100
Washington, DC 20036-5624
202-861-2407
E-Mail: tammy@internetalliance.org
Home Page: www.internetalliance.org
Tammy Cota, Executive Director
Coverage of public policy changes in government, enhancing consumer satisfaction in interactive services, and education.
Frequency: Weekly

6067 Internet Business
Information Gatekeepers
1340 Soldiers Field Rd
Suite 3
Brighton, MA 02135-1000
617-782-5033
800-323-1088
Fax: 617-782-5735
E-Mail: info@igigroup.com
Home Page: www.igigroup.com
Paul Polishuk, CEO
Hui Pan, Chief Analyst, Editor in Chief
Bev Wilson, Managing Editor
Covers the rapid developments in the industry.
Cost: $695.00
Frequency: Monthly

6068 Internet World
Mecklermedia Corporation
20 Ketchum Street
Westport, CT 06880
212-260-0758
Fax: 203-454-5840
E-Mail: bbesch@mecklermedia.com
Bill Besch, Publisher
Internet industry news, product reviews and technical reports, with an emphasis on Internet technology, hardware, management and security.
Cost: $160.00
Frequency: Weekly
Circulation: 98,947

6069 Mealey's Litigation Report: Cyber Tech & E -Commerce
LexisNexis Mealey's
555 W 5th Avenue
Los Angeles, CA 90013
213-627-1130
E-Mail: mealeyinfo@lexisnexis.com
Home Page: www.lexisnexis.com/mealeys
Tom Hagy, VP/General Manager
Maureen McGuire, Editorial Director
Mark Rogers, Editor
The Report covers disputes arising from e-commerce. The report tracks emerging legal issues, including: Internet security, data destruction and/or alteration, defamation on the Web, software errors, hardware failure, electronic theft, e-mail trespass, online privacy, government action, shareholder lawsuits, Internet jurisdiction issues, file sharing (copyright) disputes and much more.
Cost: $999.00
100 Pages
Frequency: Monthly
Founded in 1999

6070 Online Reporter
G2 Computer Intelligence
PO Box 7
Glen Head, NY 11545-1616
516-759-7025
Fax: 516-759-7028
E-Mail: news@g2news.com
Home Page: www.g2news.com
Maureen O'Gara, Publisher
Information on recent developments on the Internet through news briefs and a section called Chat Room. Includes information on e-commerce, Java and network security.
Cost: $695.00
Frequency: Weekly

6071 Privacy Journal
PO Box 28577
Providence, RI 02908
401-274-7861
Fax: 401-274-4747
E-Mail: orders@privacyjournal.net
Home Page: www.privacyjournal.net
Robert Ellis Smith, Publisher
An independent monthly on privacy in a computer age.
Cost: $65.00
Frequency: Monthly
ISSN: 0145-7659
Founded in 1974
Printed in one color

6072 The CyberSkeptic's Guide to Internet Research
Information Today
143 Old Marlton Pike
Medford, NJ 08055-8750
609-654-6266
800-300-9868
Fax: 609-654-4309
E-Mail: custserv@infotoday.com
Home Page: www.infotoday.com
Thomas H Hogan, President
Roger R Bilboul, Chairman Of The Board
A monthly subscription newsletter in print, that explores and evaluates free and low cost Web sites and search strategies to help you use the Internet and stay up to date.
Cost: $164.95
ISSN: 1085-2417

Magazines & Journals

6073 Active Server Developer's Journal
ZD Journals
500 Canal View Boulevard
Rochester, NY 14623-2800
585-407-7301
Fax: 585-214-2387
E-Mail: asp@zdjournals.com
Home Page: www.asdj.com
Jon Pyles, Publisher
Taggard Andrews
Addresses such issues as database publishing, creating hack-proof files and getting the most out of server-side components. Special sections focus on client-side solutions, covering the basics and taking an in-depth look at more detailed techniques.
Cost: $149.00
Frequency: Monthly

6074 Electronic Commerce Advisor
Thomson Reuters
195 Broadway # 4
New York, NY 10007-3124
646-822-2000
800-231-1860
Fax: 646-822-2800
E-Mail: trta.lei-support@thomsonreuters.com
Home Page: www.ria.thomsonreuters.com
Elaine Yadlon, Plant Manager
Thomas H Glocer, CEO & Director
Robert D Daleo, Chief Financial Officer
Kelli Crane, Senior Vice President & CIO
Offers the latest in electronic commerce covering what's available and how to select and employ the best technology without costly trial-and-error mistakes. Information on EDI, e-mail, fax gateways, Internet, encryption, VANs, procurement cards, imaging, voice response, remote computering and other related information.
Cost: $155.00
Circulation: 4500
Founded in 1940

6075 ISACA
3701 Algonquin Road
Suite 1010
Rolling Meadows, IL 60008ÿ
847-253-1545
Fax: 847-253-1443
Home Page:
www.isaca.org/journal/pages/default.aspx
Social Media: Facebook, Twitter, LinkedIn
A nonprofit, independent association that advocates for professionals involved in information security, assurance, risk management and governance.
Founded in 1969

6076 Information Security
International Computer Security Association
117 Kendrick Street
Suite 800
Needham, MA 02494
781-657-1000
Fax: 781-657-1100
E-Mail: lwalsh@infosecuritymag.com
Home Page: www.infosecuritymag.com
Andrew Briney, VP
Lawrence Walsh, Editor
Michael S Mimoso, Senior Editor
Gabrielle DeRussy, Advertising Sales
Susan Rastellini Smith, Product Management
Articles and analysis of information-security issues such as media, entwork and virus protection, internet security and encryption reports.
Cost: $100.00
Frequency: Monthly
Circulation: 60000
Founded in 1999

6077 Information Systems Security
Auerbach Publications
2494 Bayshore Boulevard
Suite 201
Dunedin, FL 34698
703-891-6781
800-737-8034
Fax: 703-891-0782
E-Mail: institute@isc2.org
Home Page: www.isc2.org
Social Media: Facebook, Twitter, YouTube
David Shearer, COO
Debra Taylor, CFO
John Colley, Chairman
Debra Taylor, Chief Financial Officer
Hord Tipton, Executive Director
Facts and experience, expert opinion on directions in security, public policy, computer crime and ethics related to the information security field.
Cost: $175.00
Circulation: 1500
Founded in 2003

6078 Internet Security Alliance
703-907-7090
E-Mail: admin@isalliance.orgÿ

Home Page: www.isalliance.org/isa-publications

Tim McKnight, Board Chairman
Jeff Brown, Board Vice Chairman
Gary McAlum, Board Second Vice Chairman
Larry Clinton, President, CEO
Julie Taylor, Board Member

A nonprofit organization that acts as a forum for information sharing and leadership on information security, and it lobbies for corporate securityinterests.

Trade Shows

6079 ATM Industry Association

Home Page: www.atmia.com/conferences/usa
Social Media: Facebook, LinkedIn, YouTube

Mike Lee, Chief Executive Officer
Sharon Lane, Global Director, Financeÿ
Dana Benson, Dir., Conferences & Sponsorships
Amanda Hardy, Marketing Director, Europe
David Tente, Executive Director, USA

Alliance promoting the proliferation of automated teller machines, ATMs and cash.
5000 Members
Founded in 1997

6080 CompTIA

3500 Lacey Road
Suite 100
Downers Grove, IL 60515

630-678-8300
Fax: 630-678-8384
E-Mail: techvoice@comptia.org
Home Page: www.comptia.org/events
Social Media: Facebook, Twitter, LinkedIn, Pinterest, Google+, YouTube

Todd Thibodeaux, President, CEO
Charles Eaton, CEO, Educational Foundation
Ann Batko, SVP, Marketing
Kelly Ricker, SVP, Events and Education
David Sommer, Chief Financial Officer

A nonprofit trade association created by representatives of five microcomputer leaderships and is a provider of professional certifications for theinformation technology (IT) industry.

6081 DMD New York Conference & Expo

Direct Marketing Conferences
20 Academy Street
Norwalk, CT 06850-4032

203-854-9166
800-969-6566
E-Mail: connecticut@dmdays.com
Home Page: www.dmdays.com

Direct Marketing Days New York offers new ideas in media, creative, database, eCommerce and technology. Hundreds of exhibits showcase the newest technologies, products and services. Over 85 sessions and 25 consultation centers led by A level speakers. Network with top-level executives.
Frequency: Annual/June

6082 GovSec

National Trade Productions
313 S Patrick Street
Alexandria, VA 22314

703-838-8500
Fax: 703-836-4486
Home Page: www.govsecinfo.com

Denise Medved, General Manager

Provides a full spectrum of security solutions for federal, state, and local governments tasked with developing comprehensive strategies that address physical security, information security and cyber security needs. Educational programs held in conjunction with displays of a wide variety of security products and services designed specifically for government users.
Frequency: Annual/May

Directories & Databases

6083 ATM Industry Association

Home Page: www.atmia.com/directory-of-atm-services
Social Media: Facebook, LinkedIn, YouTube

Mike Lee, Chief Executive Officer
Sharon Lane, Global Director, Financeÿ
Dana Benson, Dir., Conferences & Sponsorships
Amanda Hardy, Marketing Director, Europe
David Tente, Executive Director, USA

Alliance promoting the proliferation of automated teller machines, ATMs and cash.
5000 Members
Founded in 1997

Industry Web Sites

6084 www.bsa.org

Business Software Alliance

An organization dedicated to promoting a safe and legal digital world. BSA educates consumers on software management and copyright protection, cyber security, trade, e-commerce and other internet related issues.

6085 www.cisecurity.org

Center for Internet Security

Helps organizations around the world effectively manage the risks related to internet security.

Associations

6086 Advertising Mail Marketing Association
Advertising Mail Marketing Association
1333 F Street NW
Suite 710
Washington, DC 20004-1108
202-347-0055
Fax: 202-347-0789
E-Mail: chadr@amma.org
Home Page: www.amma.org
Gene A DelPolito, Publisher
Chad W Robbins, Editor
For those who use mail for fundraising or business purposes.
Founded in 1947

6087 American Marketing Association
311 S Wacker Dr
Suite 5800
Chicago, IL 60606-6629
312-542-9000
800-262-1150
Fax: 312-542-9001
Home Page: www.marketingpower.com
Dennis Dunlap, CEO
A professional association for individuals and organizations involved in the practice, teaching and study of marketing worldwide.
40000 Members

6088 American Teleservices Association
3815 River Crossing Parkway
Suite 20
Indianapolis, IN 46240
317-816-9336
877-779-3974
Fax: 317-218-0323
E-Mail: contact@ataconnect.org
Home Page: www.ataconnect.org
Tim Searcy, CEO
Represents the call centers, trainers, consultants and equipment suppliers that initiate, facilitate and generate telephone, Internet and e-mail sales, service and support.
240 Members

6089 Art Directors Club
106 W 29th St
New York, NY 10001-5301
212-643-1440
Fax: 212-643-4266
E-Mail: info@adcglobal.org
Home Page: www.adcglobal.org
Ami Brophy, CEO
Jon Kamen, VP
Vickie Peslak, Second VP
Thomas Mueller, Secretary
Myrna Davis, Executive Director
An international nonprofit organization of leading creatives in advertising, graphic design, interactive media, broadcast design, typography, packaging, environmental design, photography, illustration and related disciplines.
1200 Members
Founded in 1920
Mailing list available for rent

6090 Association of Direct Marketing Agencies
Cohn & Wells
350 Hudson Street
New York, NY 10014-4504
212-192-2278
Fax: 212-302-6714
E-Mail: jwpgroup@aol.com
Home Page: www.cyberdirect.com/ADMA
John A Greco Jr, President/CEO
Members are direct response advertising agencies.
100 Members

6091 Association of Hispanic Advertising Agencies
8280 Willow Oaks Corporate Drive
Suite 600
Fairfax, VA 22031
703-745-5531
E-Mail: info@ahaa.org
Home Page: www.ahaa.org
Social Media: Facebook, Twitter, LinkedIn, YouTube, Storify
Aldo Quevedo, Chair
Horacio Gavilan, Executive Director
Fulvia Lee, Program Manager
Gabriela Alcantara-Diaz, Treasurer
Carlos Santiago, Secretary
Trade organization for promoting the Hispanic marketing and advertising industry.
Founded in 1996

6092 Association of Teleservices International
222 South Westmonte Drive
Suite 101
Altamonte Springs, FL 32714
866-896-ATSI
Fax: 407-774-6440
E-Mail: admin@atsi.org
Home Page: atsi.org
Social Media: Facebook, Twitter, LinkedIn
Jeff Zindel, President
Doug Robbins, Vice President
Josue Leon, VP- Secretary
JoAnn Fussell, VP- Treasurer
Gary Edwards, Director
An international trade association established by and for entrepreneurs in the TeleServices business. It provides a wide variety of services to businesses, governmental agencies, local emergency respondents and the general public.
35000 Members
Founded in 1942

6093 Business Marketing Association: Atlanta
13 Corporate Square
Suite 100
Atlanta, GA 30329
404-641-9417
800-664-4262
Fax: 312-822-0054
E-Mail: info@bmaatlanta.com
Home Page: www.bmaatlanta.com
Ed King, President-Elect
John Wiley, Marketing & Public Relations
Barry Mirkin, Development & Research
Stacey Krizan, Membership/Education/Certification
Joe Noonan, Programs Co-Chair
The Atlanta chapter of the BMA includes marketing executives from a variety of industries and backgrounds including research, advertising, promotions, events, Web development, printing and more. The BMA offers an information-packed Web site, online skills-building, marketing certification programs, and industry surveys and papers. In addition, members have the opportunity to interact with peers at seminars, participate in chapter training programs and the BMA Annual Conference.

6094 Business Marketing Association: Boston
246 Hampshire Street
Cambridge, MA 02130
617-418-4000
800-664-4262
Fax: 312-822-0054
E-Mail: info@thebmaboston.com
Home Page: www.thebmaboston.com/
Michael Lewis, President
Will Robinson, VP Public Relations
Matthew Mamet, VP Internet Marketing
Larry Perreault, VP Finance
Chris Perkett, VP Programming
BMA Boston helps members improve their ability to manage business-to-business marketing and communications for greater productivity and profitability by providing unique access to information, ideas, and the experience of peers. The BMA offers an information-packed Website, online skills-building, marketing certification programs, and industry surveys and papers. In addition, members have the opportunity to interact with peers at seminars, chapter training programs and the BMA Annual Conference.

6095 Cable & Telecommunications Association for Marketing
120 Waterfront Street
Suite 200
National Harbor, MD 20745
301-485-8900
Fax: 301-560-4964
E-Mail: info@ctam.com
Home Page: www.ctam.com
Social Media: Facebook, Twitter, LinkedIn, YouTube
Mark Greatrex, Chair
Jamia Bigalow, Vice Chairman
John F. Lansing, President/ CEO
Todd Esenwein, Director of Business Services
Zell Murphy, SVP Finance & Administration
Provides marketing knowledge and industry scale to help its membersmanage the future and drive business results. Also provides consumer research, an interactive executive innovation series, conferences and awards.

6096 Color Marketing Group
5904 Richmond Hwy
Alexandria, VA 22303-1864
703-329-8500
Fax: 703-535-3190
E-Mail: cmg@colormarketing.org
Home Page: www.colormarketing.org
Jaime Stephens, Executive Director
Amy Larrabee, Manager/Communications
A nonprofit international association of color designers involved in the use of color as it applies to the profitable marketing of goods and services.
1300 Members
Founded in 1962

6097 Digital Analytics Association
401 Edgewater Place
Suite 600
Wakefield, WA 1880
781-876-8933
Fax: 781-224-1239
Home Page: www.digitalanalyticsassociation.org
Social Media: Facebook, Twitter, LinkedIn, Google+
Jodi McDermott, President
Bob Page, Vice President
Steve Petitpas, Vice President-Marketing
Mike Levin, Executive Director
Jacki Conn, Education Manager

A global organization of practitioners, corporations, vendors, marketing and public relations agencies, consultants, academics, and more involved in the growing digital analytics industry.
Founded in 2004

6098 Digital Concepts for Business
1301 Pyott Road
Suite 102
Lake in the Hills, IL 60156

847-458-5129
Fax: 847-458-5134
E-Mail: info@dcfb.com
Home Page: www.dcfb.com

Mary Owens, Owner

Provides services to companies throughout the US and is dedicated to providing high-quality business communcations solutions using the latest hardware and software for both PC and Macintosh.

6099 Direct International
1501 3rd Avenue
New York, NY 10028-2101

212-861-4188
Fax: 212-986-3757

Alfred Goodloe, President

Offers publications and services for the international direct marketing executive.

6100 Direct Marketing Association
1120 Avenue of the Americas
New York, NY 10036-6700

212-768-7277
Fax: 212-302-6714
Home Page: thedma.org
Social Media: Facebook, Twitter, LinkedIn

Thomas J. Benton, Chief Executive Officer
Bob Greco, SVP of Operations, Finance & Events
Peggy Hudson, SVP, Government Affairs
Linsay Hutter, SVP, Communications
Xenia Boone, JD, SVP, General Counsel

Advances and protects responsible data-driven marketing.

6101 Direct Selling Association
1667 K St NW
Suite 1100
Washington, DC 20006-1660

202-452-8866
Fax: 202-452-9010
E-Mail: info@dsa.org
Home Page: www.wfdsa.org

Neil H Offen, President
Douglas L DeVos, Vice Chairman
Neil H Offen, President
John A Addison Jr, Director
Mark Bosworth, Director

National trade of the leading firms that manufacture and distribute goods and services sold directly to consumers. Members of the association are copanies including many well-known brand names. The association's mission is to protect, serve and promote the effectiveness of member companies and the independent business people they represent.
Founded in 1973

6102 Direct-to-Direct Marketing Association Council for Hispanic Marketing
Direct Marketing Association
1120 Avenue of the Americas
New York, NY 10036-6700

212-768-7277
Fax: 212-768-6714

Allison Longley, Manager

Provides education, information and networking opportunities for direct marketing professionals targeting the Hispanic market.
120 Members
Founded in 1992

6103 EMarketing Association
224 Post Road #129
Westerly, RI 02891

401-315-2194
Fax: 408-884-2461
E-Mail: service@emarketingassociation.com
Home Page: www.emarketingassociation.com

Robert Fleming, President
Todd Daum, VP
John Hastings, VP
Linda Jaffe, VP

An international association of emarketing professionals. Members include government, companies, professionals and students involved with the emarketing arena.

6104 Internet Marketing Association
10 Mar Del Rey
San Clemente, CA 92673

949-443-9300
Fax: 949-443-2215
E-Mail: info@imanetwork.org
Home Page: imanetwork.org
Social Media: Facebook, Twitter, LinkedIn, YouTube, RSS, Google+

Sinan Kanatsiz, CIM, Chairman/ Founder
Matthew Langie, Vice Chairman, Education
Rachel Reenders, CIM, Executive Director
David Steinberg, CIM, VP of Business Alliances
Vince Walden, Finance Director

A professional organization that has gained more than 900,000 members in fields including sales, marketing, business ownership, programming and creative development. It provides a platform where proven Internet marketing strategies are demonstrated and shared to increase members value to their organizations.
90000 Members
Founded in 2001

6105 Life Insurance Direct Marketing Association
3227 S. Cherokee Lane
Suite 1320
Woodstock, GA 30188

770-516-0207
866-890-LEAD
E-Mail: info@lidma.org
Home Page: lidma.org
Social Media: Facebook, Twitter, LinkedIn

Pat Wedeking, Chair
Andy Meehan, President
Jeff McCauley, Vice President
Staci Birk, Director
Cindy Farrow, Secretary/ Treasurer

A nonprofit organization dedicated specifically to supporting businesses and professionals active in direct sales of term life insurance products to consumers.

6106 Mail Advertising Service Association
1421 Prince St
Suite 410
Alexandria, VA 22314-2805

703-836-9200
Fax: 703-548-8204
E-Mail: mfsa-mail@mfsanet.org
Home Page: www.mfsanet.org

David Weaver, President
Charles G Klasek, Vice Chairman
John Rafner, Second Vice Chairman
C Scott Schuh, Treasurer

Supports all those involved in the mailing, addressing, and inserting industries.

6107 Mailing & Fulfillment Service Association
1421 Prince Street
Suite 410
Alexandria, VA 22314-2806

703-836-9200
Fax: 703-548-8204
E-Mail: mfsa-mail@mfsanet.org
Home Page: www.mfsanet.org

Ken Garner, President
Bill Stevenson, Director Marketing

The national trade association for the mailing and fulfillment services industry.
Founded in 1920

6108 Midwest Direct Marketing Association
1821 University Ave W
Suite S256
St Paul, MN 55104-2872

651-999-5351
Fax: 763-753-2240
E-Mail: mdma@mdma.org
Home Page: www.mdma.org

Ed Harrington, Manager
Cidny McCleary, Director

Dedicated to the advancement of professional and ethical practice of direct response marketing by members throughout the Upper Midwest.
600 Members
Founded in 1960

6109 Mobile Marketing Association
770 Broadway
2nd Floor
New York, NY 10003

646-257-4515
E-Mail: northamerica@mmaglobal.com
Home Page: www.mmaglobal.com
Social Media: Facebook, Twitter, LinkedIn, Google+

A global nonprofit trade association comprised of more than 800 member companies that strive to accelerate the transformation and innovation of marketing through mobile, driving business growth with closer and stronger consumerengagement.
800 Members

6110 Mobile Marketing Research Association
216 W. Jackson Blvd.
Suite 625
Chicago, IL 60606

312-252-2502
Home Page: www.mmra-global.org
Social Media: Facebook, Twitter, LinkedIn

Rebecca West, President
Rick West, Vice President
Mark Michelson, Executive Director
Sheila Gidley, Director of Operations
Jan Willem Smulders, Treasurer

A global trade association dedicated to the promotion and development of professional standards and ethics for conducting marketing research on mobile devices.
Founded in 2011

6111 Multi-Level Marketing International Association
119 Stanford Ct
Irvine, CA 92612

949-854-0484
E-Mail: doriswood@mlmia.com
Home Page: www.mlmia.com
Social Media: Facebook, Twitter

Doris Wood, Chairman/ Founder
Carrol Leclerc, President, Canada

Tom Leffler, VP of Support Board
Michael L. Sheffield, Co-Founder
Linda Bruno, Secretary

A nonprofit professional trade organization representing all sectors of the networking marketing industry on a worldwide basis.

6112 North American Farmers' Direct Marketing Association
62 White Loaf Road
Southampton, MA 1073

FAX 413-233-4285
E-Mail: Charlie @ Whiteloafridge.com
Home Page: www.farmersinspired.com
Social Media: Facebook, Twitter, Pinterest, YouTube

Cynthia Chiles, President/ Chair
Charlie Touchette, Executive Director
Becky Walters, VP of Membership
Ben Beaver, VP of Education
Mike Dunn, Treasurer/ Finance Team Chair

A membership association that advances the prosperity of its members and the farm direct marketing industry through networking, participation, education, and innovation.

6113 Professional Association of Customer Engagement
8500 Keystone Crossing
Suite 480
Indianapolis, IN 46240

317-816-9336
E-Mail: tom.chandler@paceassociation.com
Home Page: www.paceassociation.com
Social Media: Facebook, Twitter, LinkedIn, YouTube, RSS

Michael Rauscher, Chair
Barbra Merwin, Vice Chairman
Tom Rocca, Chief Executive Officer
Susan Burt, Finance Director
Angie Brown, Operations Director

A nonprofit trade organization dedicated exclusively to the advancement of companies that utilize contact centers as an integral channel of operations.

6114 Society of Publication Designers
27 Union Square West
Suite 207
New York, NY 10003

212-223-3332
Fax: 212-223-5880
E-Mail: mail@spd.org
Home Page: www.spd.org
Social Media: RSS

Brian Anstey, President
Eric Goeres, Vice President
Tim Leong, Vice President
Keisha Dean, Executive Director
Leah Bailey, Treasurer

An organization dedicated to promoting and encouraging excellence in editorial design. Members include art directors, designers, photo editors, editors, and graphics professionals.
Founded in 1965

Newsletters

6115 Business Owner
Mailing & Fulfillment Service Association
1421 Prince Street
Suite 410
Alexandria, VA 22314-2806

703-836-9200
Fax: 703-548-8204
E-Mail: mfsa-mail@mfsanet.org
Home Page: www.mfsanet.org

David L Perkins Jr, Editor

Developed specifically to communicate with owners and CEOs on issues unique to them. You'll receive a wealth of knowledge on growing your business, tax issues, insurance, estate planning, management, finance and much more.
Frequency: Bi-Monthly

6116 Career News Update
American Marketing Association
311 S Wacker Dr
Suite 5800
Chicago, IL 60606-6629

312-542-9000
800-262-1150
Fax: 312-542-9001
Home Page: www.marketingpower.com

Dennis Dunlap, CEO

You'll receive the latest career and hiring advice as well as useful job resources and employment listings.
Frequency: Monthly

6117 Daily News E-Mail (3D)
Direct Marketing Association
1120 Avenue of the Americas
New York, NY 10036-6700

212-768-7277
Fax: 212-302-6714
E-Mail: customerservice@the-dma.org
Home Page: www.the-dma.org

Lawrence M Kimmel, CEO

Delivers the essential news, research, hot trends, and technological developments from the nations leading newspapers, trade publications, and the government all in an easy-to-read, time-saving format

6118 Direct Response
Direct Marketing Center
21171 S. Western Ave
Suite 260
Torrance, CA 90501

310-212-5727
Fax: 310-212-5773
E-Mail: cdmg@cdmginc.com
Home Page: www.directmarketingcenter.net

Craig Huey, President/Publisher
Kent Komae, Editor

Direct marketing information.
Cost: $79.00
Frequency: Monthly

6119 Direct Selling Association International Bulletin
World Federation of Direct Selling Associations
1667 K St Nw
Suite 1100
Washington, DC 20006-1660

202-452-8866
Fax: 202-452-9010
E-Mail: info@wfdsa.org
Home Page: www.wfdsa.org

Neil H Offen, President

Association activities, legislation affecting direct selling and trends.
Circulation: 1200

6120 Direction
Direct Marketing Consultants
705 Franklin Tpke
Allendale, NJ 07401-1637

201-327-9213

Hugh P Curley, Publisher

How to' information on motivating buying decisions via more creative use of direct mail, sales promotion, newsletters, and other marketing tools.
Cost: $40.00
Circulation: 3800

6121 Empoyment Points
Mailing & Fulfillment Service Association
1421 Prince Street
Suite 410
Alexandria, VA 22314-2806

703-836-9200
Fax: 703-548-8204
E-Mail: mfsa-mail@mfsanet.org
Home Page: www.mfsanet.org

The content is written for business owners and operators who want to stay informed about current employment issues. The editorial is targeted on human resource issues and employment practices in the mailing and fulfillment services industry.
Frequency: 4x/Year
Circulation: 2000

6122 Fred Goss' What's Working in Direct Marketing
United Communications Group
11300 Rockville Pike
Street 1100
Rockville, MD 20852-3030

301-287-2700
Fax: 301-816-8945
E-Mail: webmaster@ucg.com
Home Page: www.ucg.com/

Benny Dicecca, President

Direct response marketing-all forms.
Cost: $242.00
Founded in 1977

6123 Friday Report
Hoke Communications
224 7th Street
Garden City, NY 11530-5771

516-746-6700
800-229-6700
Fax: 516-294-8141
E-Mail: dmmagazine@aol.com
Home Page: www.directmarketingmag.com

Henry R Hoke, Publisher
Joseph D Gatti, Editor
Stuart W Boysen, President
Edson Georges, Mailing Systems Manager

Weekly newsletter of direct marketing.
Cost: $165.00
8 Pages
Frequency: Weekly
Founded in 1951

6124 General Encouragement, Motivation and Inspirational Handbook
Economics Press
12 Daniel Road
Fairfield, NJ 07004-2565

973-227-1224
Fax: 973-227-3558
E-Mail: info@epinc.com
Home Page: www.epinc.com

Allan Yahalen, President
Rob Gilbert, Editor
Cost: $20.00
24 Pages
Frequency: Monthly
Circulation: 200000
Mailing list available for rent: 200,000 names
Printed in 4 colors on matte stock

6125 Inside Mail Order
Mellinger Company

PO Box 956
Santa Clarita, CA 91380-9056

661-259-2303
Fax: 805-257-4840
E-Mail: mell@tradezone.com
Home Page: www.tradezone.com

BL Mellinger III, Publisher

A newsletter offering the latest information to businesses on marketing and advertising through direct mail.

6126 Mail Order Digest & Washington Newsletter
National Mail Order Association
2807 Polk St Ne
Minneapolis, MN 55418-2954

612-788-1673
Fax: 612-788-1147
E-Mail: editor@nmoa.org
Home Page: www.nmoa.org

John Schulte, President
J Bradley, Editor
Paul Muchnick, Founder Director

Contains information of interest to small to midsize mail marketers including new products available, money saving techniques, industry contacts, help for beginners, new concepts for mail order selling, and postal changes and regulations.
Cost: $99.00
Frequency: Monthly
Circulation: 7000
Founded in 1972

6127 Marketing Academics Newsletter
American Marketing Association
311 S Wacker Dr
Suite 5800
Chicago, IL 60606-6629

312-542-9000
800-262-1150
Fax: 312-542-9001
Home Page: www.marketingpower.com

Dennis Dunlap, CEO

This newsletter provides news and information that affect and inform this important constituency. It reviews Academic Council activities, profiles Academic SIGS and highlights upcoming events.

6128 Marketing Matters Newsletter
American Marketing Association
311 S Wacker Dr
Suite 5800
Chicago, IL 60606-6629

312-542-9000
800-262-1150
Fax: 312-542-9001
Home Page: www.marketingpower.com

Dennis Dunlap, CEO

This e-newsletter updates readers on the latest happenings in the marketing profession through news briefs, indepth features and interviews.
Frequency: 2x/Monthly

6129 Marketing Power Newsletter
American Marketing Association
311 S Wacker Dr
Suite 5800
Chicago, IL 60606-6629

312-542-9000
800-262-1150
Fax: 312-542-9001
Home Page: www.marketingpower.com

Dennis Dunlap, CEO

This update of the latest news, research and trends in the marketing industry and allied fields.
Frequency: Weekly

6130 Marketing Researchers Newsletter
American Marketing Association
311 S Wacker Dr
Suite 5800
Chicago, IL 60606-6629

312-542-9000
800-262-1150
Fax: 312-542-9001
Home Page: www.marketingpower.com

Dennis Dunlap, CEO

This e-newsletter provides members with content designed to educate and inform researchers or any member interested in marketing research topics.

6131 Marketing Through Leaders Newsletter
American Marketing Association
311 S Wacker Dr
Suite 5800
Chicago, IL 60606-6629

312-542-9000
800-262-1150
Fax: 312-542-9001
Home Page: www.marketingpower.com

Dennis Dunlap, CEO

These articles focus on the issues and concepts that shape marketing today and tomorrow.
Frequency: Monthly

6132 Memo to Mailers
US Postal Service
475 Lenfant Plz Sw
Room 10523
Washington, DC 20260-1805

202-268-2900
800-275-8777
Fax: 202-268-6436
E-Mail: mmailers@usps.com
Home Page: www.usps.com

Robert F Gardner, Manager

Carries information and news about the Postal Service as well as value added information about using the mail effectively and efficiently. Also offers information to mail center managers on ways to cut costs.
8 Pages
Frequency: Daily
Circulation: 100000

6133 Nonprofit Mailers Foundation
125 Michigan Avenue NE
#239
Washington, DC 20017-1004

202-628-4380

Esther Huggins, Manager

Promotes welfare of groups using nonprofit mail rates for communications and fundraising.
600 Pages
Founded in 1982

6134 PD&D Direct Mail List
Chilton Way
Radnor, PA 19089-0001

973-920-7782
Fax: 973-607-5492
E-Mail: newslettermaterials@advantagemedia.com

Tom Lynch, Group Publisher
Christina Schmidt, Publisher
Don Grennan, Director of Marketing
Jeff Reinke, Editorial Director
David Mantey, Editor

This list is a proven response vehicle for product promotion, seminar announcements and trade show promotions.

6135 PostScripts
Mailing & Fulfillment Service Association
1421 Prince Street
Suite 410
Alexandria, VA 22314-2806

703-836-9200
Fax: 703-548-8204
E-Mail: mfsa-mail@mfsanet.org
Home Page: www.mfsanet.org

Leo Raymond, Editor

Each issue of PostScripts highlights a theme relevant to mailing or fulfillment operations, such as production management or information technology.
Frequency: 18x/Year
Circulation: 2800

6136 Postal Points
Mailing & Fulfillment Service Association
1421 Prince Street
Suite 410
Alexandria, VA 22314-2806

703-836-9200
Fax: 703-548-8204
E-Mail: mfsa-mail@mfsanet.org
Home Page: www.mfsanet.org

Leo Raymond, Editor

Deals exclusively with current and pending postal and delivery issues. Here you will find the facts and analysis of developing postal issues.
Frequency: 18x/Year

6137 Target Market News
Target Market News
228 S Wabash Ave
Suite 210
Chicago, IL 60604-2383

312-408-1867
Fax: 312-408-1867
E-Mail: info@targetmarketnews.com
Home Page: www.targetmarketnews.com

Ken Smikle, President
Hallie Mummert, Editor

News and developments in the areas of black consumer marketing and black-oriented media.
Cost: $40.00
12 Pages
Frequency: Monthly
Founded in 1988

6138 TeleResponse
InfoCision Management
325 Springside Dr
Akron, OH 44333-4504

330-668-1400
Fax: 330-668-1401
Home Page: www.infocision.com

Carl Albright, CEO

Specializes in making outbound sales calls for the infomercial, catalog and direct marketing industries.

6139 Telephone Selling Report
Business By Phone
13254 Stevens Street
Omaha, NE 68137-1728

402-455-1111
800-326-7721
Fax: 402-896-3353
E-Mail: arts@businessbyphone.com
Home Page: www.businessbyphone.com

Art Sobczak, Production Manager

For businesses that use the phone to prospect, service and sell. How-to information on getting through screens; creating interest-grabbing

openings; closes that work; overcoming tough objections; and beating call reluctance. Accepts advertising inserts.
Cost: $109.00
8 Pages
Frequency: Monthly
Mailing list available for rent: 2M names
Printed in 2 colors

6140 **Venture Views & News**
Venture Communications
60 Madison Ave
New York, NY 10010-1600
212-447-5247
Fax: 212-576-1129
E-Mail: sales@ven.com
Home Page: www.venturedirect.com
Rachel Krasny, Editor
Richard Baumer, CEO/President
Neal Mandel, Group Division Sales Manager
Michael Platt, Founder
News and practical advice in the field of direct response marketing.
Frequency: Weekly
Founded in 1983

6141 **What's Working in DM and Fulfillment**
United Communications Group
11300 Rockville Pike
Suite 1100
Rockville, MD 20852-3030
301-816-8950
800-929-4824
Fax: 301-816-8945
E-Mail: webmaster@ucg.com
Home Page: www.ucg.com/
Barbara W Kaplowitz, Publisher
Monica Brown, Circulation Manager
Tested tips, tactics and techniques for direct marketers in all industries, news, legislative updates and winning (and losing) DM ideas including hard costs and how to's.
Cost: $242.00
8 Pages
Founded in 1977
Mailing list available for rentat $125 per M
Printed in 2 colors on matte stock

Magazines & Journals

6142 **BtoB Magazine**
Ad Age Group/ Division of Crain Communications
711 3rd Ave
New York, NY 10017-4014
212-210-0785
Fax: 212-210-0200
E-Mail: info@crain.com
Home Page: www.crain.com
Norm Feldman, Manager
Dedicated to integrated business to business marketing. Every page is packed with substance news, reports, technologies, benchmarks, best practices served up by the most knowledgeable journalists.
Frequency: Monthly
Circulation: 45000

6143 **Chief Marketer**
Penton Media, Inc.
249 W 17th Street
New York, NY 10011
212-204-4200
Home Page: www.penton.com
Social Media: Facebook, Twitter, LinkedIn
Tyler T. Zachehm, Co-CEO
Anup Bagaria, Co-CEO
Nicola Allais, EVP & CFO
Jasmine Alexander, SVP & CIO
Chief Marketer provides fresh, multi-disciplined approaches to direct marketing, events, advertising research, and promotional marketing.
Frequency: Monthly
Founded in 1976

6144 **Customer Interface**
Advanstar Communications
6200 Canoga Avenue
2nd Floor
Woodland Hills, CA 91367
818-593-5000
Fax: 818-593-5020
E-Mail: info@advanstar.com
Home Page: www.advanstar.com
Joseph Loggia, President
Chris DeMoulin, VP
Susannah George, Marketing Director
Magazine for decision-makers actively involved in planning, managing or operating a business call center.
Cost: $39.00
104 Pages
Circulation: 50000
Founded in 1992

6145 **Dateline: DMA**
Direct Marketing Association
11 W 42nd Street
New York, NY 10036-8002
212-391-9683
Fax: 212-768-4546
Offers comprehensive information on the Direct Marketing Association, trends in the industry, technological advances and more for the marketing and advertising professional.

6146 **Direct**
Chief Marketer
249 W 17th Street
New York, NY 10011
212-204-4200
Home Page: www.chiefmarketer.com
Social Media: Facebook, Twitter, LinkedIn
Beth Negus Viveiros, Managing Editor
Brian Quinton, Executive Editor
Patricia Odell, Managing Editor
Richard Levey, Senior Writer
Larry Riggs, Senior Editor
Information Resource for Direct Marketers.
Frequency: Monthly
Founded in 1976

6147 **Direct Marketing**
Haymarket Media
114 W 26th Street
New York, NY 10001
212-625-9251
Fax: 212-925-8752
E-Mail: dmnews@halldata.com
Home Page: www.ibusinessnews.com
Lee Maniscalco, President/CEO
Carol Krol, Editor-in-Chief
Valuable information on the newest trends in direct marketing, catalog statistics and advertising information for persons working in the direct mail industry.
Cost: $49.00
Frequency: Weekly
Founded in 1979

6148 **Journal of Direct Marketing**
John Wiley & Sons
111 River St
Hoboken, NJ 07030-5790
201-748-6000
800-825-7550
Fax: 201-748-6088
E-Mail: info@wiley.com
Home Page: www.wiley.com
William J Pesce, CEO
Richard M Hochhauser, CEO
Publication featuring research articles from some of the best minds in the field of direct marketing. Offers creative ideas for marketing products, analysis of what works, pioneering research from the nation's top universities, articles from other direct marketing publications and special reports on overseas direct marketing.
Cost: $1000.00
Frequency: Quarterly
Founded in 1807

6149 **Journal of International Marketing**
American Marketing Association
311 S Wacker Dr
Suite 5800
Chicago, IL 60606-6629
312-542-9000
800-262-1150
Fax: 312-542-9001
Home Page: www.marketingpower.com
Dennis Dunlap, CEO
Presents scholarly and managerially relevant articles on international marketing.

6150 **Journal of Marketing**
American Marketing Association
311 S Wacker Dr
Suite 5800
Chicago, IL 60606-6629
312-542-9000
800-262-1150
Fax: 312-542-9001
Home Page: www.marketingpower.com
Dennis Dunlap, CEO
The premier broad based scholarly journal of the marketing discipline that focuses on substantive issues in marketing and marketing management.

6151 **Journal of Marketing Research**
American Marketing Association
311 S Wacker Dr
Suite 5800
Chicago, IL 60606-6629
312-542-9000
800-262-1150
Fax: 312-542-9001
Home Page: www.marketingpower.com
Dennis Dunlap, CEO
Covers a wide range of marketing research concepts, methods and applications. You'll read about new techniques, contributions to knowledge based on experimental methods and developments in related fields that have a bearing on marketing research.

6152 **Journal of Public Policy & Marketing**
American Marketing Association
311 S Wacker Dr
Suite 5800
Chicago, IL 60606-6629
312-542-9000
800-262-1150
Fax: 312-542-9001
Home Page: www.marketingpower.com
Dennis Dunlap, CEO
Each issue features a wide ranging forum for the research, findings and discussion of marketing subjects related to business and government.

6153 **Marketing Health Services**
American Marketing Association

311 S Wacker Dr
Suite 5800
Chicago, IL 60606-6629

312-542-9000
800-262-1150
Fax: 312-542-9001
Home Page: www.marketingpower.com

Dennis Dunlap, CEO

Specifically aimed at senior level healthcare marketers and managers, offers targeted information, practical strategies and thought provoking commentary to help achieve your goals and shape your vision.
Frequency: Quarterly

6154 **Marketing Management**
American Marketing Association
311 S Wacker Dr
Suite 5800
Chicago, IL 60606-6629

312-542-9000
800-262-1150
Fax: 312-542-9001
Home Page: www.marketingpower.com

Dennis Dunlap, CEO

Focuses on strategic marketing issues that marketing managers face every day.
Frequency: 6x/Year

6155 **Marketing News**
American Marketing Association
311 S Wacker Dr
Suite 5800
Chicago, IL 60606-6629

312-542-9000
800-262-1150
Fax: 312-542-9001
Home Page: www.marketingpower.com

Dennis Dunlap, CEO

Covers the industry's basics, the core concepts around which winning programs are built.

6156 **Marketing Research**
American Marketing Association
311 S Wacker Dr
Suite 5800
Chicago, IL 60606-6629

312-542-9000
800-262-1150
Fax: 312-542-9001
Home Page: www.marketingpower.com

Dennis Dunlap, CEO

Researchers and managers count on this quarterly resource to help stay on top of current methodologies and issues, management concerns and the latest books and software.
40000 Members
Frequency: Quarterly

6157 **Multichannel Merchant**
Chief Marketer
249 W 17th Street
New York, NY 10011

212-204-4200
Home Page: www.chiefmarketer.com
Social Media: Facebook, Twitter, LinkedIn

Beth Negus Viveiros, Managing Editor
Brian Quinton, Executive Editor
Patricia Odell, Managing Editor
Richard Levey, Senior Writer
Larry Riggs, Senior Editor

Exclusively serves online merchants and catalog companies, as well as retailers, manufacturers and wholesale/distributors.
Frequency: Monthly
Founded in 1976

6158 **Operations & Fulfillment**
Primedia
Po Box 12901
Shawnee Mission, KS 66282-2901

913-341-1300
800-775-3777
Fax: 913-514-6895
E-Mail: rramaswami@primediabusiness.com
Home Page: www.penton.com

Eric Jacobson, Senior VP
Glenn Laudenslager, Marketing Manager
Leslie Bacon, Publisher
Leonard Roberto, Circulation Manager
John French, President

Provides executives information they can't get anywhere else and reach executives and managers with purchasing authority in all areas of operations management. Information on direct to customer fulfillment..
Cost: $36.00
Frequency: Monthly
Founded in 1905

6159 **Politically Direct**
Direct Marketing Association
1120 Avenue of the Americas
New York, NY 10036-6700

212-768-7277
Fax: 212-302-6714
E-Mail: customerservice@the-dma.org
Home Page: www.the-dma.org

Lawrence M Kimmel, CEO

Published both in print and digital, this newsletter on DMA advocacy efforts keeps DMA members informed and involved in the politics and policies that impact them today and ahead of the curve on developments that will affect them tomorrow.
Frequency: Quarterly

6160 **Promo**
Chief Marketer
249 W 17th Street
New York, NY 10011

212-204-4200
Home Page: www.chiefmarketer.com
Social Media: Facebook, Twitter, LinkedIn

Beth Negus Viveiros, Managing Editor
Brian Quinton, Executive Editor
Patricia Odell, Managing Editor
Richard Levey, Senior Writer
Larry Riggs, Senior Editor

Promo Magazine covers the Promotions and the Promotional Marketing Industry.
Frequency: Monthly
Founded in 1976

6161 **Target**
North American Publishing Company
1500 Spring Garden St
Suite 1200
Philadelphia, PA 19130-4094

215-238-5300
Fax: 215-238-5342
E-Mail: editor.tm@napco.com
Home Page: www.targetmarketingmag.com

Ned S Borowsky, CEO
Peggy Hatch, Publisher
Lois Boyle, President

This monthly magazine is the authoritative information source for direct marketers with hands-on, how-to-do-it, ideas you can take to the bank.
Cost: $24.95
Frequency: Monthly
Circulation: 35000
Founded in 1977
Mailing list available for rent
Printed in 4 colors on glossy stock

6162 **Telemarketing Magazine**
Technology Marketing Corporation
1 Technology Plz
Norwalk, CT 06854-1936

203-852-6800
800-243-6002
Fax: 203-853-2845
E-Mail: tmc@tmcnet.com
Home Page: www.tmcnet.com

Rich Tehrani, CEO
Linda Driscoll, Editor/VP
Rich Tehrani, President/Editor-in-Chief

Serves telemarketing, marketing, customer service, sales and telecommunications professionals. Features legislative updates, new product and service releases, techniques and beginner information.
Cost: $49.00
Frequency: Monthly
Founded in 1972

Trade Shows

6163 **Annual Conference and Mailing Fulfillment Expo**
Mailing & Fulfillment Service Association
1421 Prince Street
Suite 410
Alexandria, VA 22314-2806

703-836-9200
Fax: 703-548-8204
E-Mail: mfsa-mail@mfsanet.org
Home Page: www.mfsanet.org

Ken Garner, President
Jennifer Root, Director
Bill Stevenson, Director Marketing

Quality educational sessions, industry specific exhibit hall, networking and more.
Frequency: Annual

6164 **Annual Conference for Catalog and Multichannel Merchants**
PRISM Business Exhibitions
11 River Bend Drive South
Stamford, CT 06907

203-358-9900
800-927-5007
Fax: 203-358-5816
E-Mail: registration@prismb2b.com
Home Page: www.accmshow.com

Ed Berkowitz, Sales Director
Angela Eastin, Group Show Director

Co-presented by the Direct Marketing Association and Multichannel Merchant Magazine, ACCM offers the latest advances, technology and information and solutions for cataloger, retailers and multichannel merchants.
Frequency: May

6165 **Business-to-Business Database Marketing Conference**
Interlect Events
11 Riverbend Drive S
Stamford, CT 06907

203-852-4200
Home Page: http://www.importexporthelp.com/b2b-lists.htm

Robin Altman, Contact

The only database marketing conference that is focused exclusively on business-to-business marketing database strategies and tactics. 40 tabletop exhibits.
500 Attendees
Frequency: Fall

6166 **DMA Annual Conference & Exhibition**
Direct Marketing Association

1120 Avenue of Americas
New York, NY 10036-6700

212-768-7277
Fax: 212-302-6714
E-Mail: dmaconferences@the-dma.org
Home Page: www.the-dma.org

Lawrence M Kimmel, CEO
Julie A Hogan, SVP Conferences/Events

Brings together thousands of practitioners and experts from the entire marketing continuum to discuss solutions and best practices to achieve optimal channel mix and integration that lead to measurable results and increase real-time customer engagement.
12000 Attendees
Frequency: October

6167 **DMD New York Conference & Expo**
Direct Marketing Conferences
20 Academy Street
Norwalk, CT 06850-4032

203-854-9166
800-969-6566
E-Mail: connecticut@dmdays.com
Home Page: www.dmdays.com

Direct Marketing Days New York offers new ideas in media, creative, database, eCommerce and technology. Hundreds of exhibits showcase the newest technologies, products and services. Over 85 sessions and 25 consultation centers led by A level speakers. Network with top-level executives.
Frequency: Annual/June

6168 **Email Evolution Conference**
Direct Marketing Association
1120 Avenue of Americas
New York, NY 10036-6700

212-768-7277
Fax: 212-302-6714
E-Mail: dmaconferences@the-dma.org
Home Page: www.the-dma.org

Julie A Hogan, SVP Conference/Events
Lawrence M Kimmel, CEO

Focuses on the ever-changing and evolving world of email marketing, providing attendees with the best ways to capitalize on the high ROI this low-cost communication tool can provide both on its own, and integrated with social, search, mobile, video and other email enhancers.
10M Attendees
Frequency: Annual/February

6169 **ICSB Annual World Conference**
International Council for Small Business
2201 G Street NW
Suite 315
Washington, DC 20052

202-944-0704
Fax: 202-994-4930
E-Mail: icsb@gwu.edu
Home Page: www.icsb.org

David Smallbone, President
Don B. Bradley, III, President-Elect
Rita Grant, VP/Finance/Control
Ayman El Tarabishy, Executive Director
Michael Battaglia, Operations Manager

Annual business conference attended by entrepreneurs, policy makers, business service providers and researchers.
2000+ Members
Founded in 1956

6170 **Internet Telephony Conference & EXPO (East or West)**
Technology Marketing Corporation (TMCnet)
One Technology Plaza
Norwalk, CT 06854

203-852-6800
800-243-6002
Fax: 203-853-2845
E-Mail: tmc@tmcnet.com
Home Page: www.tmcnet.com

Frank Coppola, Conference Team
Lorna Lyle, Conference Team
Tim Zaccagnini, Conference Team
Kevin Lake, Exhibit Sales
Natasha Barbera, Operations Contact

The world's foremost forum on IP and VoIP, and all things telephony: workshops, training courses, focused tracks, and exhibitors.
Frequency: East/West - Winter/Fall

6171 **MFSA Mailing and Fulfillment Expo**
Mailing & Fulfillment Service Association
1421 Prince Street
Suite 100
Alexandria, VA 22314-2805

703-369-9200
800-333-6272
Fax: 703-548-8204
E-Mail: wecasey@mfsanet.org
Home Page: www.mfsanet.org

Eric Casey, Manager
David Weaver, President

Annual exposition of suppliers to mailing and fulfillment companies. Containing 60 booths and 50 exhibits.
250 Attendees
Frequency: June
Mailing list available for rent

6172 **MFSA Midwinter Executive Conference**
Mailing & Fulfillment Service Association
1421 Prince Street
Suite 410
Alexandria, VA 22314-2806

703-836-9200
Fax: 703-548-8204
E-Mail: mfsa-mail@mfsanet.org
Home Page: www.mfsanet.org

Ken Garner, President
Jennifer Root, Director
Bill Stevenson, Director Marketing

Will address financial operations and business valuation, marketing your own company, the changing world of postal regulations, technology in fulfillment, building a sales team, being strong in digital printing and the landscape of employment law.

6173 **Mailer Strategies Conference**
Mailing & Fulfillment Service Association
1421 Prince Street
Suite 410
Alexandria, VA 22314-2806

703-836-9200
Fax: 703-548-8204
E-Mail: mfsa-mail@mfsanet.org
Home Page: www.mfsanet.org

Ken Garner, President
Jennifer Root, Director
Bill Stevenson, Director Marketing

This conference will focus solely on postal issues that are important to your operations.

6174 **Marketing in the Millennium**
Florida Direct Marketing Association
8851 NW 10th Pl
Plantation, FL 33322-5007
954-472-6374
800-520-FDMA
Fax: 954-472-8165
E-Mail: fdma@juno.org
Home Page: www.fdma.org

Beth Kaufman, Manager

Yearly exhibit of legislative updates and more for members of the direct marketing industry.
Frequency: February
Founded in 1999

6175 **NCDM Conference**
Direct Marketing Association
1120 Avenue of Americas
New York, NY 10036-6700

212-768-7277
Fax: 212-302-6714
E-Mail: dmaconferences@the-dma.org
Home Page: www.the-dma.org

Julie A Hogan, SVP Conference/Events
Lawrence M Kimmel, CEO

Presents industry experts and hard-hitting case studies from a variety of verticles, such as financial services, retail, automotive, publishing, non-profit and many more, who will share the latest strategies and methodologies in gathering, analyzinf, leveraging and protecting the most valuable business asset-the customer database.
10M Attendees
Frequency: Annual/December

6176 **National Catalog Operations Forum**
Primedia
9800 Metcalf Avenue
Overland Park, KS 66212

913-341-1300
Fax: 913-967-1898
Home Page: www.primediabusiness.com

Robin Altman, Contact

The only major national conference devoted exclusively to the sharing of vital catalog operations information. This conference is dedicated to the crucial background of the catalog business, and brings operations management together to meet and learn; 140 booths.
1.2M+ Attendees
Frequency: April/May

6177 **National Conference on Operations & Fulfillment (NCOF)**
Direct Marketing Association
1120 Avenue of Americas
New York, NY 10036-6700

212-768-7277
Fax: 212-302-6714
E-Mail: dmaconferences@the-dma.org
Home Page: www.the-dma.org

Julie A Hogan, SVP Conference/Events
Lawrence M Kimmel, CEO

Focuses on innovative solutions for the warehouse, distribution, operations, and ecommerce needs in the ever-changing world of operations and fulfillment.
10M Attendees
Frequency: Annual/April

6178 **New York Nonprofit Conference**
Direct Marketing Association
1120 Avenue of Americas
New York, NY 10036-6700
212-768-7277
Fax: 212-302-6714
E-Mail: dmaconferences@the-dma.org
Home Page: www.the-dma.org

Julie Hogan, SVP Conference/Events

Discover which acknowledgement programs work best and why, increase revenue with membership options-as well as traditional fund-raising appeals, learn how the Internet and e-mail campaigns can improve fundraising, lower costs and increase advocacy.
10M Attendees

Directories & Databases

6179 **Adweek Directory**
Prometheus Global Media
770 Broadway
New York, NY 10003-9595
212-493-4100
Fax: 646-654-5368
Home Page: www.prometheusgm.com
Richard D. Beckman, CEO
James A. Finkelstein, Chairman
Madeline Krakowsky, Vice President Circulation
Tracy Brater, Executive Director Creative Service
Adweek Directories Online is where you will find searchable databases with comprehensive information on ad agencies, brand marketers and multicultural media.
Frequency: Annual
Circulation: 800
Founded in 1981

6180 **Annual Guide to Telemarketing**
Marketing Logistics
1460 Cloverdale Avenue
Highland Park, IL 60035-2817
847-831-1575
Arnold Fishman, Editor
About 400 telemarketing services bureaus in the United States.
Cost: $475.00
Frequency: Irregular

6181 **Art Directors Annual**
Art Directors Club
106 W 29th St
New York, NY 10001-5301
212-643-1440
Fax: 212-643-4266
E-Mail: info@adcglobal.org
Home Page: www.adcglobal.org
Ami Brophy, CEO
Myrna Davis, Executive Director
Innovative advertising, design, publishing, photography, illustration, film, video, and interactive media.
Cost: $65.00
520 Members
Circulation: 7,000
Mailing list available for rent

6182 **Associations Yellow Book**
Leadership Directories
104 5th Ave
New York, NY 10011-6901
212-627-4140
Fax: 212-645-0931
E-Mail: associations@leadershipdirectories.com
Home Page: www.leadershipdirectories.com
David Hurvitz, CEO
James M Petrie, Associate Publisher
Contact information for over 41,000 officers and board members at 1,000 trade and professional associations, coalitions, PACs, and foundations.
Cost: $245.00
1,300 Pages
Frequency: SemiAnnual
ISSN: 1054-4070
Founded in 1991
Mailing list available for rent: 37,000 names at $125 per M

6183 **Catalog Success**
North American Publishing Company
4001 S Business Park Avenue
Marshfield, WI 54449-9027
715-387-3400
Fax: 715-486-4185
E-Mail: daniel.gust@donnelleymarketing.com
Home Page: www.catalogsuccess.com
Putting marketing management to the test.
Frequency: Monthly
ISSN: 1524-2307
Printed in 4 colors

6184 **Corporate Yellow Book**
Leadership Directories
104 5th Ave
New York, NY 10011-6901
212-627-4140
Fax: 212-645-0931
E-Mail: corporate@leadershipdirectories.com
Home Page: www.leadershipdirectories.com
David Hurvitz, CEO
Contact information for over 48,000 executives at over 1,000 companies and more than 9,000 board members and their outside affiliations.
Cost: $360.00
1,400 Pages
Frequency: Quarterly
ISSN: 1058-2098
Founded in 1986
Mailing list available for rent: 50,000 names at $105 per M

6185 **Customer Interaction Solutions**
Technology Marketing Corporation
1 Technology Plz
Norwalk, CT 06854-1936
203-852-6800
800-243-6002
Fax: 203-853-2845
Home Page: www.tmcnet.com
Rich Tehrani, CEO
Tracy Schelmetic, Editor
Over 1100 domestic and foreign suppliers of equipment products and services to the telecommunications/telemarketing industry.
Cost: $25.00
Frequency: Annual/December/89 Pages
Founded in 1982
Mailing list available for rent: 63,000 names at $25 per M

6186 **D&B Million Dollar Database**
Dun & Bradstreet Information Service
3 Sylvan Way
Parsippany, NJ 07054-3822
973-605-6000
800-526-0651
Fax: 973-605-9630
160,000 public and private businesses with either a net worth of 500,000 or more, 250 emplyees at that location or 25,000,000 or more in sales volume.

6187 **D&B Million Dollar Database: International**
Dun & Bradstreet Information Service
3 Sylvan Way
Parsippany, NJ 07054-3822
973-605-6000
800-526-0651
Fax: 973-605-9630
50,000 top corporations, utilities, transportation companies, bank and trust companies, stock brolers, mutual and stock insurance companies, wholesalers, retailers, and domestic susidiaries of foreign corporations.

6188 **Direct Mail Service**
Information Resource Group
50495 Corporate Drive
Suite 112
Shelby Township, MI 48315-3132
586-726-6237
This database offers over 1,000,000 MIS and corporate professionals at over 150,000 companies throughout the United States.
Cost: $150.00

6189 **Direct Selling World Directory**
World Federation of Direct Selling Association
1776 K St NW
Suite 600
Washington, DC 20006-2304
202-546-5330
Fax: 202-463-4569
Home Page: www.dsa.org
Over 50 direct selling associations and over 1,000 associated member companies are offered in this comprehensive directory.
90 Pages
Frequency: Annual

6190 **Directory of Mail Order Catalogs**
Grey House Publishing
4919 Route 22
PO Box 56
Amenia, NY 12501
518-789-8700
800-562-2139
Fax: 845-373-6390
E-Mail: books@greyhouse.com
Home Page: www.greyhouse.com
Social Media: Facebook, Twitter
Leslie Mackenzie, Publisher
Richard Gottlieb, Editor
The premier source of information on the mail order catalog industry. Covers over 13,000 consumer and business catalog companies with 44 different product chapters from Animals to Toys and Games.
Cost: $395.00
1900 Pages
Frequency: Annual
ISBN: 1-592373-96-8
Founded in 1981

6191 **Directory of Mail Order Catalogs - Online Database**
Grey House Publishing
4919 Route 22
PO Box 56
Amenia, NY 12501
518-789-8700
800-562-2139
Fax: 845-373-6390
E-Mail: gold@greyhouse.com
Home Page: http://gold.greyhouse.com
Social Media: Facebook, Twitter
Leslie Mackenzie, Publisher
Richard Gottlieb, Editor
Reach over 10,000 consumer catalog companies in one easy-to-use source with The Directory of Mail Order Catalogs - Online Database. Filled with business-building detail, each company profile gives you the information you need to access that organization quickly and easily. Listings provide key contacts, sales volume, employee size, printing information, circulation, list data, product descriptions and much more.
Frequency: Annual
Founded in 1981

6192 **Directory of Major Mailers**
North American Publishing Company

1500 Spring Garden St
Suite 1200
Philadelphia, PA 19130-4094

215-238-5300
Fax: 215-238-5342

Ned S Borowsky, CEO

Offers over 7,500 major direct mailers and the key players with their names, addresses, phones and fax numbers, executive contacts, types of business, and the size of the house file. The Directory also contains actual reproductions of these mailings - letters, envelopes, order cards, brochures, etc. You'll see what was mailed, what worked and what didn't.
Cost: $395.00
Frequency: Annual
Founded in 1994
Mailing list available for rent
Printed in one color on matte stock

6193 **International Job Finder: Where the Jobs are Worldwide**
Planning/Communications
7215 Oak Ave
River Forest, IL 60305-1935

708-366-5200
888-366-5200
Fax: 708-366-5280
E-Mail: dl@planningcommunications.com
Home Page: www.planningcommunications.com

Daniel Lauber, President

Describes in detail over 1,200 print and online sources of jobs outside the USA; newsletters, magazines, directories, web sites, online job databases, resume banks, email job alerts, and salary surveys.
Cost: $19.95
384 Pages
Frequency: Every 4 Years
Circulation: 8,000
ISBN: 1-884587-10-0
Founded in 2002
Printed in one color on matte stock

6194 **Nonprofit Sector Yellow Book**
Leadership Directories
104 5th Ave
New York, NY 10011-6901

212-627-4140
Fax: 212-645-0931
E-Mail: info@leadershipdirectories.com
Home Page: www.leadershipdirectories.com

David Hurvitz, CEO
James M Petrie, Associate Publisher

Contact information for over 51,000 nonprofit executives and trustees at over 1,300 nonprofit organizations, including foundations, colleges and universities, museums, performing arts group and centers, medical institutions, library systems, preparatory schools, and charitable service organizations.
Cost: $245.00
1,200 Pages
Frequency: SemiAnnual
ISSN: 1520-9148
Founded in 1999
Mailing list available for rent: 45,000 names at $125 per M

6195 **Nonprofits Job Finder: Where the Jobs are in Charities and Nonprofits**
Planning/Communications
7215 Oak Ave
River Forest, IL 60305-1935

708-366-5200
888-366-5200
Fax: 708-366-5280
E-Mail: dl@planningcommunications.com
Home Page: www.planningcommunications.com

Daniel Lauber, President

Describes in detail over 1,500 sources of jobs in the nonprofit sectors job database online, resume banks, email job alerts, directories, salary surveys, newsletters, and magazines.
Cost: $17.95
300 Pages
Circulation: 6,000
ISBN: 1-884587-06-2
Founded in 2005
Printed in one color on matte stock

6196 **Who's Who: MASA Buyer's Guide to Blue Ribbon Mailing Services**
Mailing & Fulfillment Service Association
1421 Prince Street
Suite 410
Alexandria, VA 22314-2806

703-836-9200
Fax: 703-548-8204
E-Mail: mfsa-mail@mfsanet.org
Home Page: www.mfsanet.org

Ken Garner, President
Bill Stevenson, Director Marketing

Offers a detailed listing of suppliers of equipment, products and services to the direct mail industry, most containing a description of the specific products they provide.
Frequency: Annual

6197 **Yellow Pages & Directory Report**
Simba Information
11200 Rockville Pike
Suite 504
Rockville, MD 20852

240-747-3096
877-352-2021
Fax: 340-747-3004
E-Mail: dgoddard@imslocalsearch.com
Home Page: www.yellowpagesanddirectoryreport.com
Social Media: Facebook, Twitter, LinkedIn

David Goddard, EVP/Senior Analyst/Editor
Kyle Kroll, President

Covers directory publishing, advertising, printing and releases from national yellow pages accounts.
Cost: $695.00

Industry Web Sites

6198 **http://gold.greyhouse.com**
G.O.L.D Grey House OnLine Databases
Grey House Publishing's online database platform, GOLD, offers Quick Search, Keyword Search and Expert Search for most business sectors including direct marketing and public relations markets. The GOLD platform makes finding the information you need quick and easy - whether you're a novice searcher or an experienced database user. All of Grey House's directory products are available for subscription on the GOLD platform.

6199 **www.adweek.com**
Adweek
Leading decision makers in the advertising and marketing field go to Adweek.com everyday for breaking news, insight, buzz, opinion, analysis, research and classifieds. The resources of all six regional editions of Adweek, as well as the national edition of Brandweek are combined with the knowledge of our online editors and the multimedia-interactive capabilities of the web to deliver vital information quickly and effectively to our target audience.

6200 **www.amma.org**
Advertising Mail Marketing Association
Represents the interests of those who use mail for fundraising or business purposes.

6201 **www.ataconnect.org**
American Teleservices Association
Represents the call centers, trainers, consultants and equipment suppliers that initiate, facilitate and generate telephone, Internet and e-mail sales, service and support.

6202 **www.cadm.org**
Chicago Association of Direct Marketing
Promotes the interests of Chicago's direct marketing professionals. Fosters member development through business, educational and social opportunities and provides a high-quality forum for the exchange of ideas by direct marketing professionals.

6203 **www.cyberdirect.com/ADMA**
Cohn & Wells
Members are direct response advertising agencies.

6204 **www.dmad.org**
Direct Marketing Association of Detroit
Not for profit organization dedicated to providing networking and educational opportunities to a dymamic group of direct marketing professionals. It is the premier resource for direct response marketing information, and is committed to recognizing outstanding direct marketing achievements in the Detroit area.

6205 **www.dsa.org**
Direct Selling Association
National trade association of the leading firms that manufacture and distribute goods and services sold directly to consumers. More than 150 companies are members of the association, including many well-known brand names. The association's mission is to protect, serve and promote the effectiveness of member companies and the independent business people they represent.

6206 **www.fraudandtheftinfo.com**
Fraud & Theft Information Bureau
Provides problem solving, crime prevention, money saving manuals and fraud blocker databases.

6207 **www.greyhouse.com**
Grey House Publishing
Authoritative reference directories for most business sectors incluidng direct marketing and public relations markets. Users can search the online databases with varied search criteria allowing for custom searches by product category, geographic area, sales volume, keyword, subject and more. Full Grey House catalog and online ordering also available.

6208 **www.ims-lists.com/links**
IMS Direct Marketing Links
Professional associations links.

6209 **www.marketingpower.com**
American Marketing Association
A professional association for individuals and organizations involved in the practice, teaching and study of marketing worldwide.

6210 **www.mdma.org**
Midwest Direct Marketing Association
Advancing the professional and ethical practice of direct response marketing by members throughout the Upper Midwest. The MDMA seeks to accomplish this by sponsoring educational and professional networking events to share and encourage the best practices in

telemarketing, direct mail and online marketing techniques and strategies.

6211 **www.mfsanet.org**
Mailing & Fulfillment Service Association
The national trade association for the mailing and fulfillment services industry.

6212 **www.nedma.com**
New England Direct Marketing Association

6213 **www.nmoa.org**
National Mail Order Association
Offers the stongest and lowest cost means for people to come together for the purpose of conducting business and creating sales. Small to medium sized organizations come for education, information, ideas, resources and new contacts.

6214 **www.the-dma.org**
Direct Marketing Association
Trade association in the direct marketing field with more than 3,500 member companies from the United States and 54 foreign nations. Included are catalogers, direct marketers from consumer to business-to-business, publishers, retail stores as well as service industries that support them.

Associations

6215 Academy of Managed Care Pharmacy
100 N Pitt St
Suite 400
Alexandria, VA 22314-3141
703-683-8416
800-827-2627
Fax: 703-683-8417
E-Mail: sandres@amcp.org
Home Page: www.amcp.org
Judy Cahill, Executive Director
Elaine Manieri, Director
Cathryn A Carroll, PhD, Treasurer
Promotes the development and application of appropriate and accessible medication therapy. Represents professional pharmacists and associates practicing in managed care settings.
4800 Members
Founded in 1989
Mailing list available for rent

6216 Academy of Managed Care Pharmacy (AMCP)
100 North Pitt Street
Suite 400
Alexandria, VA 22314
703-683-8416
800-827-2627
Fax: 703-683-8417
E-Mail: memberservices@amcp.org
Home Page: www.amcp.org
Social Media: Facebook, Twitter, LinkedIn
Dana Davis McCormick, President
Raulo S Frear, President Elect
Kim A. Caldwell, Past President
Stanley E. Ferrell, Director
H Eric Cannon, Treasurer
6000 Members

6217 Accreditation Council for Pharmacy Education
135 S. LaSalle Street
Suite 4100
Chicago, IL 60603-4810
312-664-3575
Fax: 312-664-4652
E-Mail: ceinfo@acpe-accredit.org
Home Page: www.acpe-accredit.org
Social Media: Facebook
Janet Cline, Chair
Tian Merren Owens, Vice Chair
Stephanie F. Gardner, President
Bruce Canaday, Vice President
Michael A. Mone, Secretary/Treasurer
A nonprofit accreditation national agency.
Founded in 1932

6218 American Association of Colleges of Pharmacy
1727 King St
Alexandria, VA 22314-2700
703-739-2330
Fax: 703-836-8982
Home Page: www.aacp.org
Lucinda Maine, Executive VP
Kenneth W Miller, Senior VP
Daniel J Cassidy, COO
National organization representing the interests of pharmaceutical education and educators. Comprising all 111 US pharmacy colleges and schools including more than 5,000 faculty, 50,000 students enrolled in professional programs and 4,000 individuals pursuing graduate study. AACP is committed to excellence in pharmaceutical education.
3670 Members
Founded in 1900
Mailing list available for rent

6219 American Association of Pharmaceutical Scientists
2107 Wilson Blvd
Suite 700
Arlington, VA 22201-3042
703-243-2800
Fax: 703-243-9650
E-Mail: aaps@aaps.org
Home Page: www.aaps.org
Gene Fiese, President
Patrick Deluca, President Elect
Peter Inchauteguiz, Director Marketing
James Greif, Communcations Specialist
Maureen Downs, Director of Finance
Aims to advance science through the open exchange of scientific knowledge, serve as an information resource and contribute to human health through pharmaceutical research and development.
11000 Members
Founded in 1986
Mailing list available for rent

6220 American Association of Pharmacy Technicians (AAPT)
PO Box 1447
Greensboro, NC 27402
877-368-4771
Fax: 336-333-9068
E-Mail: aapt@pharmacytechnician.com
Home Page: www.pharmacytechnician.com
Sandra Covington, President
Susan Jeffery, VP
Provides leadership and represents the interests of its members to the public as well as health care organizations. Promotes safe efficacious and cost effective dispensing, distribution and use of medications. Provides continuing education programs and services to help technicians update their skills and keep pace with changes in pharmacy services. Promotes pharmacy technicians as an integral part of the patient care team.
850 Members
Founded in 1979

6221 American Association of Pharmacy Technicia
P.O. Box 1447
Greensboro, NC 27402
336-333-9356
877-368-4771
Fax: 336-333-9068
E-Mail: aapt@pharmacytechnician.com
Home Page: www.pharmacytechnician.com
Social Media: Facebook, Twitter
Marci Knorr, President
Judy Neville, Vice President
Ann Barlow Oberg, Immediate Past President
Michelle Porter, Secretary
Bobbie Craddock, Treasurer

6222 American Chemical Society
1155 16th St Nw
Washington, DC 20036-4892
202-872-4600
800-227-5558
Fax: 202-872-4615
E-Mail: service@acs.org
Home Page: www.acs.org
Madeleine Jacobs, CEO
John Crum, Executive Director
C Gordon McCarty, Director
Supports scientists and other professionals working in the field of drug discovery. Publishes monthly magazine.
159K Members
Founded in 1876

6223 American Clinical Laboratory Association
1100 New York Ave Nw
Suite 880
Washington, DC 20005-6172
202-637-9466
Fax: 202-637-2050
E-Mail: info@clinical-labs.org
Home Page: www.clinical-labs.org
Members are clinical laboratories licensed and regulated under medicare and the interstate laboratory program.
Founded in 1971

6224 American College of Apothecaries
2830 Summer Oaks Dr
Bartlett, TN 38134-3811
901-383-8119
Fax: 901-383-8882
E-Mail: aca@acainfo.org
Home Page: www.acainfo.org
D C Huffman, Executive VP
Jeffrey Denton, President
Randall S Myers, VP
Disseminates and translates knowledge, research data and recent developments in professional pharmacy practice for the benefit of pharmacists, pharmacy students and the public. This is achieved through regular distribution of periodicals, development of major publications and continuing education courses on clinical and administrative topics and conducting educational conferences.
1M Members
Founded in 1940

6225 American College of Clinical Pharmacology
21750 Red Rum Drive
Suite 137
Ashburn, VA 20147
571-291-3493
Fax: 571-918-4167
E-Mail: Info@ACCP1.org
Home Page: www.accp1.org
Social Media: Facebook, LinkedIn
Lisa Von Moltke, President
Krista K Levy, Executive Director
Keri J Sperry, Director of Education
Erica Serow, Manager of meetings
A national organization of clinical pharmacology healthcare professionals who seek to advance clinical pharmacology.
Founded in 1969

6226 American College of Clinical Pharmacy
3101 Broadway Street
Suite 650
Kansas City, MO 64111-2416
816-531-2177
Fax: 913-492-0088
Home Page: www.accp.com
Michael Maddux, Executive Director
Professional and scientific society that provides leadership, education, advocacy and resources enabling clinical pharmacists to achieve excellence in practice and research. Membership is composed of practitioners, scientists, educators, administrators, students, residents, fellows and others committed to excellence in clinical pharmacy and patient pharmacotherapy.
Founded in 1979

6227 American College of Medical Quality
4334 Montgomery Ave
Suite B
Bethesda, MD 20814-4415
301-913-9149
800-924-2149

Fax: 301-656-0989
E-Mail: acmq@acmq.org
Home Page: www.acmq.org

Bridget Brodie, Manager

The mission of the American College of Medical Quality is to provide leadership and education in healthcare quality management.
900 Members
Founded in 1972

6228 American Council on Pharmaceutical Education
20 N Clark Street
Suite 2500
Chicago, IL 60602

312-664-3575
Fax: 312-664-4652

Robert Buchman, Executive Director

Promotes the education of pharmaceutical medicine.

6229 American Institute of the History of Pharmacy
777 Highland Ave
Madison, WI 53705-2222

608-262-5378
Fax: 608-262-3397
E-Mail: aihp@mace.wisc.edu
Home Page: www.pharmacy.wisc.edu/aihp

Dr. Gregory Higby, Executive Director
Dr. Elaine C Stroud, Assistant Director
Beth D Fisher, Program Manager
Greg Bond, Project Assistant

Non-profit national organization devoted to advancing knowledge and understanding of the place of pharmacy in history. Contributes to the understanding of the development of civilization by fostering the creation, preservation, and dissemination of knowledge concerning the history and related humanistic aspects of the pharmaceutical field.
900 Members
Founded in 1941

6230 American Pharmacists Association
2215 Constitution Ave NW
Washington, DC 20037-2985

202-628-4410
800-237-2742
Fax: 202-783-2351
E-Mail: infocenter@aphanet.org
Home Page: www.pharmacist.com
Social Media: Facebook, Twitter, LinkedIn, YouTube

Thomas E Menighan, CEO
Elizabeth Keyes, Chief Business Officer
Roger K Browning, CFO

It is the largest association of pharmacists in the United States, whose mission is to provide information, education, and advocacy to empower its members to improve medication use and advance patient care.
60000 Members
Founded in 1852

6231 American Public Health Association
800 I Street NW
Washington, DC 20001-3710

202-777-2742
Fax: 202-777-2534
E-Mail: coments@apha.org
Home Page: www.apha.org

Jay M Bernhardt, Vice Chair
Gene Lutz, President
Georges Benjamin, Executive Director
Jose F Cordero, Member Services
Louise A Anderson, Director Operations

Brings together researchers, health service providers, administrators, teachers and other health workers in a unique, multidisciplinary environment of professional exchange, study and action in the effort to prevent disease and promote health.
50000 Members
Founded in 1872

6232 American Society for Automation in Pharmacy
492 Norristown Road
Suite 160
Blue Bell, PA 19422

610-825-7783
Fax: 610-825-7641
Home Page: www.asapnet.org

WA Lockwood, Executive Director

Assists its members in advancing the application of computer technology in the pharmacist's role as care giver, in the efficient operation of a pharmacy and promoting standards, legislation and guidelines.
350 Members
Founded in 1988

6233 American Society for Clinical Pharmacology and Therapeutics
528 N Washington St
Alexandria, VA 22314

703-836-6981
E-Mail: info@ascpt.org
Home Page: www.ascpt.org

John A Wagner, President
Mario L Rocci, President Elect
Russ B. Altman, Immediate Past President
Gregory L. Kearns, Secretary/Treasurer
Sharon J. Swan, Chief Executive Officer

Focuses on improving the understanding and use of existing drug therapies and developing safe and more effective treatments for the future.
2100 Members
Founded in 1900

6234 American Society for Parenteral & Enteral Nutrition
8630 Fenton Street
Suite 412
Silver Spring, MD 20910

301-587-6315
800-727-4567
Fax: 301-587-2365
E-Mail: aspen@nutr.org
Home Page: www.nutritioncare.org

Marion F Winkler, President
Vincent W Vanek, VP
Robin Kriegel, CAE, Executive Director
Joanne Kieffer, Director Finance

Promotes professional communication among and within professional disciplines in the broad field of clinical nutrition including parenteral and enteral nutrition (tube feeding) through national and regional meetings, local seminars, scientific, clinical and educational exhibits and publications.
6000 Members
Founded in 1979

6235 American Society for Pharmacy Law
1224 Centre West Dr
Suite 400B
Springfield, IL 62704-2184

217-698-6163
Fax: 217-698-6164
Home Page: www.aspl.org

Michael Monson, President
Francis B Paulumbo, Director
Pamela Tolson, CAE, Executive Director
William Fassett, Treasurer

An organization of pharmacists and lawyers who are interested in the law as it applies to the pharmacy industry.

6236 American Society of Consultant Pharmacists
1321 Duke St
Alexandria, VA 22314-3563

703-739-1300
800-355-2727
Fax: 703-739-1321
E-Mail: info@ascp.com
Home Page: www.ascp.com

John Feather, Executive Director
Phylliss M Moret, Associate Executive Director/COO
Linda Williams, Director Communications/Marketing
Claudia Schlosberg, Director, Policy/Advocacy
Trish D'Antonio, Director, Education

The international professional association that provides leadership, education, advocacy and resources to advance the practice of senior care pharmacy.
6500+ Members
Founded in 1969

6237 American Society of Consultant Pharmacists Foundation
1321 Duke Street
Alexandria, VA 22314-3563

703-739-1300
800-355-2727
Fax: 703-739-1500
E-Mail: info@ascpfoundation.org
Home Page: www.ascpfoundation.org

Nancy L Losben, Chairman
Frank Grosso, Executive Director
Jan Allen, Treasurer
Carla McSpadden, Board of Trustees
Ross W. Brickley, Board of Trustees

A charitable organization affiliated with the American Society of Consultant Pharmacists. It sponsors research, administers programs, holds traineeships in pharmacy practice, and performs other educational and outreach functions.
Founded in 1982

6238 American Society of Health-System Pharmacists
7272 Wisconsin Ave
Bethesda, MD 20814-4861

301-657-3000
866-279-0681
Fax: 301-664-8877
Home Page: www.ashp.org

Mark Woods, President
Henri R Manasse Jr, EVP/CEO

An association that brings together health-system pharmacists who practice in hospitals, health maintenance organizations, long-term care facilities, home care, and other components of health care systems. ASHSP has a long history of medication error prevention efforts and believe the mission of pharmacists is to help people make the best use of medicines.
31M Members
Founded in 1942
Mailing list available for rent

6239 American Society of Pharmacognosy

E-Mail: j.porter@usciences.edu
Home Page: www.pharmacognosy.us/
Social Media: Facebook, Twitter, LinkedIn

Brad Moore, Chair
Phil Crews, President
Ed Kennelly, Vice President
William J. Keller, Secretary
Jim McAlpine, Treasurer

A scientific society that promotes the growth and development of pharmacognosy through

presentation of research achievements and publication of meritous research.
1100 Members
Founded in 1959

6240 Aspirin Foundation of America
529 14th St NW
Suite 807
Washington, DC 20045-1801

202-393-0000
800-432-3247
Fax: 202-737-8406
E-Mail: info@aspirin.org
Home Page: www.aspirin.org

A non-profit educational foundation with a membership of companies engaged in the manufacture, preparation, compounding or processing of aspirin and aspirin products. AFA serves as a central source of information on the health benefits of aspirin and aspirin products, when used as directed.
Founded in 1981

6241 Association of Clinical Research Professionals
500 Montgomery Street
Suite 800
Alexandria, VA 22314

703-254-8100
Fax: 703-254-8101
E-Mail: acrp@associationhq.com
Home Page: www.acrpnet.org

Deborah Laser, Chair, Board of Trustees
Thomas L Adams, CAE, President/CEO
James Thomasell, Director Finance

The Academy of Clinical Research Professionals and the Academy of Pharmaceutical Physician and Investigators are affiliates of ACRP. The Academy asministers non-physician certification programs and govermmental affairs activities. APPI represents all physician members of ACRP.
21000 Members
Founded in 1976

6242 Board of Pharmacy Specialties
2215 Constitution Avenue NW
Washington, DC 20037-2985

202-429-7591
Fax: 202-429-6304
Home Page: www.bpsweb.org
Social Media: Facebook, Twitter, YouTube

Sharon M Durfee, Chair
John A Pieper, Chair Elect

A post-licensure certification agency that improves patient care bypromoting the recognition and value of specialized training, knowledge, and skills in pharmacy and specialty board certification of pharmacists.
Founded in 1973

6243 College of Psychiatric and Neurologic Pharmacists
8055 O Street
Suite S113
Lincoln, NE 68510

402-476-1677
Fax: 888-551-7617
E Mail: info@cpnp.org
Home Page: www.cpnp.org
Social Media: Facebook, Twitter, LinkedIn, YouTube, Google+

Steven Burghart, President
Ray Love, President-Elect
Julie Dopheide, Past President
Jennifer Zacher, Secretary
Christopher Thomas, Treasurer

Organization that advances the reach and practice of neuropsychiatric pharmacists.
Founded in 1998

6244 Drug Information Association
800 Enterprise Road
Suite 200
Horsham, PA 19044-3595

215-442-6100
Fax: 215-442-6199
E-Mail: dia@diahome.org
Home Page: www.diahome.org
Social Media: Facebook, Twitter, LinkedIn

Paul Pomerantz BA MBA, Worldwide Executive Director
Lisa Zoks BA, Worldwide Dir Mktg/Communications

Provides a neutral global forum for the exchange and dissemination of information on the discovery, development, evaluation and utilization of medicines and related health care technologies. Through these activities the DIA provides development opportunities for its members.
20000 Members
Founded in 1964

6245 Drug, Chemical & Associated Technologies Association
One Union St
Suite 208
Robbinsville, NJ 8691

609-208-1888
800-640-3228
Fax: 609-208-0599
Home Page: www.dcat.org
Social Media: Facebook, LinkedIn

George Svokos, President
Folker Ruchatz, First Vice President
Milton Boyer, Second Vice President
Margaret M. Timony, Executive Director
David Beattie, Director

A nonprofit, member-supported business development association for the global pharmaceutical manufacturing industry.
Founded in 1890

6246 Drug, Chemical & Associated Technologies
1 Washington Blvd
Suite 7
Robbinsville, NJ 08691-3162

609-448-1000
Fax: 609-448-1944
Home Page: www.dcat.org

Margaret Timony, Executive Director
James K Martin, Senior Vice President
Bob Kanuga, Vice President

The premier business development association whose membership is comprised of companies that manufacture, distribute or provide services to the pharamceutical, chemical, nutritional and related industries.
Founded in 1890

6247 Federation of Pharmacy Networks
30131 Town Center Drive
Suite 100
Laguna Niguel, CA 92677

949-495-5257
Fax: 949-495-1258
E-Mail: info@fpn.org
Home Page: www.fpn.org

Don Anderson, President
Tom Scono, Vice President
Carol Carlson, CEO
Cathi Clark, Secretary
Curtis Woods, Treasurer

An organization of independent pharmacy group purchasing organizations established for the purpose of providing a forum for its members to exchangeideas that promote, advance and ensure the future of independent pharmacy.

6248 Food & Drug Law Institute
1155 15th Street NW
Suite 800
Washington, DC 20005

202-371-1420
800-956-6293
Fax: 202-371-0649
E-Mail: comments@fdli.org
Home Page: www.fdli.org

Susan C. Winckler, President & CEO
Iris V. Stratton CPA, VP Finance & Administration
Michael Sprott, Membership Manager

A nonprofit, educational organization dedicated to improving the understanding of the laws, regulations, and policies affecting health care technologies, food and cosmetics. FDLI is neutral, nonpartisan and does not lobby or advocate positions on any issue.
550+ Members
Founded in 1949

6249 Food and Drug Administration
10903 New Hampshire Avenue
Silver Spring, MD 20993

888-463-6332
Home Page: www.fda.gov
Social Media: Facebook, Twitter, YouTube, Flickr

Margaret A Hamburg, Commissioner of Food and Drugs
Walter S Harris, Deputy Commissioner for Operations
James Tyler, Chief Financial Officer
Denise Esposito, Chief of Staff
Mitch Zeller, Director

A federal agency of the United States Department of Health and Human Services that is responsible for protecting and promoting public health through the regulation and supervision of food safety, tobacco products, dietary supplements, prescription and over-the counter medications, vaccines, animal foods, veterinary products, etc.

6250 Generic Pharmaceutical Association
2300 Clarendon Blvd
Suite 400
Arlington, VA 22201-3367

703-647-2480
Fax: 202-249-7105
E-Mail: info@gphaonline.org
Home Page: www.gphaonline.org

Kathleen Jaeger, President
Charles Kinney, Executive VP

Represents the manufacturers and distributors of finished generic pharmaceutical products, manufacturers and distributors of bulk active pharmaceutical chemicals, and suppliers of other goods and services to the generic pharmaceutical industry.

6251 Healthcare Distribution Management Association
901 N Glebe Rd
Suite 1000
Arlington, VA 22203-1853

703-812-5214
Fax: 703-812-5282
Home Page: www.healthcaredistribution.org

John M Gray, President/CEO
Nancy E Hanagan, Executive VP/COO
Susan Mirvis, Senior VP Marketing/Communications

An organization representing all major constituents of healthcare product distribution management.

6252 **Hematology/Oncology Pharmacy Association**
8735 W. Higgins Road
Suite 300
Chicago, IL 60631

877-467-2791
E-Mail: board@hoparx.org
Home Page: www.hoparx.org

John Kuhn, Chair
Barry Goldspiel, Vice Chair
Michael Vozniak, President
Terri Davidson, Secretary
Susan Goodin, Treasurer

A nonprofit professional organization created to help oncology and hematology.
Founded in 1995

6253 **IAGIM**
4901 Midtown Lane PBG
Florida 33418

561-376-2224
E-Mail: info@iagim.org
Home Page: www.iagim.org

Publishes generic pharmaceutical journals and technical handbooks.

6254 **Independent Pharmacy Cooperative**
1550 Columbus St
Sun Prairie, WI 53590-3901

608-825-9556
800-755-1531
Fax: 608-825-1535
E-Mail: staff@iperx.com
Home Page: www.ipcrx.com

Don Anderson, CEO
Gary Helgerson, COO
Chuck Benjamin, CFO

Provides member pharmacies with the lowest possible contract pricing on quality products and services.
4000 Members
Founded in 1984

6255 **Institute for Safe Medication Practices**
200 Lakeside Drive
Suite 200
Horsham, PA 19044

215-947-7797
Fax: 215-914-1492
Home Page: www.ismp.org
Social Media: Facebook, Twitter

Michael R Cohen, President
Allen J Vaida, Executive Vice President
Judy Smetzer, Vice President
Susan F. Paparella, Vice President
Russell H. Jenkins, Medical Director

A nonprofit organization devoted entirely to medication error prevention and safe medication use.
Founded in 1975

6256 **International Pharmaceutical Excipients Council of the Americas**
1655 North Fort Myer Drive
Suite 700
Arlington, VA 22209

703-875-2127
Fax: 703-525-5157
E-Mail: info@ipecamericas.org
Home Page: www.ipecamericas.org

Alan W Mercill, Secretary/Treasurer
R Christian Moreton PhD, Chairman

Members are companies with an interest in the otherwise inert chemicals used as vehicles for medicines. IPEC is a federation of three independent regional associations headquartered in the US. and Japan. Each association focuses its attention on the applicable laws, regulations, science and business practices of its region to accomplish its members goals.
300 Members
Founded in 1991

6257 **International Pharmaceutical Federation**
2517 JP The Hague
The Netherlands

170-302-1970
Fax: 170-302-1999
Home Page: www.fip.org
Social Media: Facebook, Twitter, LinkedIn

Luc Besancon, Chief Executive Officer
Rachel Van Kesteren, Executive Secretary
Paula Cohen, Secretary
Carola Van der Hoeff, Chief Operating Officer
Lin-Nam Wang, Communication Manager

An international federation of national organizations that represent pharmacists and pharmaceutical scientists.
Founded in 1912

6258 **International Society for Pharmacoepidemiology**
5272 River Road
Suite 630
Bethesda, MD 20816

301-718-6500
Fax: 301-656-0989
E-Mail: ISPE@paimgmt.com
Home Page: www.pharmacoepi.org
Social Media: Facebook, LinkedIn, YouTube

John D Seeger, President
Sonia Hernandez-Diaz, President Elect
Alison Bourke, Vice-President Finance
Mark H. Epstein, Executive Secretary
Andrew Jerdonek, Account Manager

A nonprofit international professional membership organization dedicated to advancing the health of the public by providing a forum for the open exchange of scientific information and for the development of policy, education, and advocacy for pharmacoepidemiology, pharmacovigilance, drug use research, outcomes research, comparative effectiveness research, and therapeutic risk management.

6259 **International Society for Pharmaceutical Engineering (ISPE)**
3109 W Dr Martin Luther King Jr Boulevard
Suite 250
Tampa, FL 33607

813-960-2105
Fax: 813-264-2816
E-Mail: ask@ispe.org
Home Page: www.ispe.org
Social Media: Facebook, Twitter, LinkedIn, MYSPACE

Robert Best, President & CEO
Victoria Smoke, CFO
Kindra Bess, Director, Event Operations
Gloria Hall, Editor & Director of Publications
Karleen Kos, VP of Member Relations

Global society for technical professionals in pharmaceutical manufacturing and drug development sectors.
2000 Members
Founded in 1980

6260 **Joint Commission on the Accreditation of Healthcare Organizations**
601 13th Street, NW
Suite 560
Washington, DC 20005

630-792-5800
Fax: 630-792-5005
Home Page: www.jointcommission.org
Social Media: Facebook, Twitter, LinkedIn, YouTube, Google+

Mark R Chassin, President
Anne Marie Benedicto, Executive Vice President
Ann Jacobson, Executive Director
Amy Panagopoulos, Senior Director
Anita Giuntoli, Director

A nonprofit organization that accredits and certifies more than 20,500 health care organizations and programs in the United States.
Founded in 1951

6261 **Lambda Kappa Sigma (International Professional Pharmacy Fraternity)**
P.O. Box 570
Muskego, WI 53150-0570

800-LKS-1913
Fax: 262-679-4558
E-Mail: ExecutiveDirector@lks.org
Home Page: www.lks.org
Social Media: Facebook, Twitter

Jenny Brandt, President
Patti Lozano, Vice President
Joan Rogala, Executive Director
Kim Hancock, Secretary
Sandy Mullen, Treasurer

An international professional pharmacy fraternity open to undergraduate and graduate pharmacy students and participating pharmacists. It also provides lifelong opportunities for women in pharmacy.
25000 Members
Founded in 1913

6262 **National Alliance of State Pharmacy Associations**
2530 Professional Road
Suite 202
Richmond, VA 23235

804-285-4431
804-612-6555
E-Mail: rsnead@naspa.us
Home Page: www.naspa.us
Social Media: Facebook, LinkedIn

Phil Woodward Oklahoma, President
Mike Larkin Kansas, President-Elect
Pat Epple Pennsylvania, 1st Vice President
Joni Cover Nebraska, 2nd Vice President
Louise Jones Alabama, Secretary/Treasurer

Promotes leadership, sharing, learning, and policy exchange among state pharmacy associations and pharmacy leaders nationwide, and provides education and advocacy to support pharmacists, patients, and communities working together to improve public health.
Founded in 1927

6263 **National Alliance of State Pharmacy Asociations**
2530 Professional Rd
Suite 202
Richmond, VA 23235-3217

804-285-4431
Fax: 804-285-4227
E-Mail: becky@naspa.us
Home Page: www.naspa.us

Rebecca Snead, Executive Director
Baeteena Black, First VP

Represents high level executives in pharmacy and pharmaceutical education.
400 Members
Founded in 1927

6264 **National Association of Boards of Pharmacy**
700 Busse Highway
Park Ridge, IL 60068

847-698-6227
800-774-6227

Fax: 847-391-4502
E-Mail: custserv@nabp.net
Home Page: www.nabp.net

Donna S Wall, Chairperson
Donna M Horn, President
Lawrence H Mokhiber, Treasurer

Serves all American boards of pharmacy in matters of interstate reciprocity of licensure and licensing as well as other matters of mutual concern.

6265 National Association of Chain Drug Stores
413 N Lee Street
PO Box 1417-D49
Alexandria, VA 22313-1480

703-549-3001
Fax: 703-836-4869
Home Page: www.nacds.org

Mary F Sammons, Chairman
Anthony Civello, Vice Chairman
Craig L Fuller, President/CEO
Mark Griffin, Director
David Bernauer, Treasurer

Association for manufacturers or suppliers of chain drug store equipment, supplies and services.
210 Members
Founded in 1933

6266 National Community Pharmacists Association
100 Daingerfield Road
Alexandria, VA 22314

703-683-8200
800-544-7447
Fax: 703-683-3619
E-Mail: info@ncpanet.com
Home Page: www.ncpanet.org

Stephen Giroux PhD, President
Bruce Roberts RPh, Executive VP/CEO

Represents pharmacy owners, managers and employees of nearly 25,000 independent community pharmacies across the US.
60000 Members
Founded in 1898

6267 National Council for Prescription Drug Programs
9240 E Raintree Dr
Scottsdale, AZ 85260-7518

480-477-1000
Fax: 480-767-1042
E-Mail: ncpdp@ncpdp.org
Home Page: www.ncpdp.org

Lee Ann Stember, President
Dennis Kitterman, Director Marketing Communications
Phillip D Scott, SVP Sales/Marketing
Joanne Longie, VP Operations

Members are computer companies, drug manufacturers, drug store chains, drug wholesalers, insurers, mail order prescription drug companies, pharmaceutical claim processors, prescription drug providers, software vendors, service organizations, government agencies and others with a interest in drug program administration standardization.
1350 Members
Founded in 1977

6268 National Institute for Pharmacist Care Outcomes
100 Daingerfield Road
Alexandria, VA 22314

703-481-1518
Fax: 703-683-3619
E-Mail: kathryn.kuhn@ncpanet.org
Home Page: www.ncpanet.org

Kathryn Kuhn, Executive Director, NIPCO Programs
Eleanor Nespica, Coordinator, NIPCO Programs
Mike Clark, Manager

The national accrediting organization for pharmacist care education and training programs leading to the pharmacist care diplomate credential. A leading authority in helping community pharmacists develop new market niches in disease management and wellness.

6269 National Pharmaceutical Alliance
427 King Street
Suite 222
Alexandria, VA 22314

703 836 8816
Fax: 919-469-5858
Home Page: www.npa.org

Cristina Sizemore, Executive Director
Deborah Kline, Manager Communications

Represents the interests of small pharmaceutical companies and allied industries.

6270 National Pharmaceutical Association
107 Kilmayne Drive
Suite C
Cary, NC 27511

877-215-2091
Fax: 919-469-5858
E-Mail: npha@npha.net
Home Page: www.npha.net
Social Media: Facebook

Dr. Carleton Maxwell, President
Erica Hanesworth, President Elect
Cornetta Levi, Immediate Past-President
Gayle Tuckett, Secretary
Joseph T. Lee, Treasurer

A nationwide, professional organization of pharmacists.
Founded in 1950

6271 National Pharmaceutical Council
1894 Preston White Dr
Reston, VA 20191-4313

703-620-6390
Fax: 202-827-0314
E-Mail: info@npcnow.com
Home Page: www.npcnow.org

Daniel Leonard, President
Pat Adams, VP Business Operations
Gary Persinger, VP Health Care Systems
Richard Levy, VP Scientific
Jeffery Warren, Senior Advisor

Represents major, research-intensive, pharmaceutical companies. Conducts national and state studies, holds educational forums and generates publications for consumer and for health care cost containment programs.
31 Members
Founded in 1953

6272 National Pharmacy Purchasing Association
4747 Morena Blvd
Suite 340
San Diego, CA 92117-3468

858-581-6373
888-544-6772
Fax: 858-581-6372
E-Mail: info@pharmacypurchasing.com
Home Page: www.pharmacypurchasing.com
Social Media: Facebook, Twitter

Dale J Kroll, President & CEO
Francine Morgano, Vice President
Michael Thomas, Event & Editorial Assistant
Debby Flannery, Advisory Board
Deb Harden, Advisory Board

An association that promotes the profession of pharmacy purchasing and offers educational opportunities for pharmacy buyers. Members include pharmacy buyers and managers from private, nonprofit, or government-run institutional facilities that work to promote the profession of pharmacy purchasing and offerseducational opportunities for pharmacy buyers.
Founded in 1991

6273 National Pharmacy Technician Association
PO BOX 683148
Houston, TX 77268

888-247-8700
Fax: 888-247-8706
E-Mail: mikej@pharmacytechnician.org
Home Page: www.pharmacytechnician.org

Mike Johnston, Chairman
Robin Luke, President
Wendy Meigs, Board Member
Carol Reyes, Board Member
Rhonda Wilson, Board Member

The world's largest professional organization established specifically for pharmacy technicians.
Founded in 1999

6274 New York State Council of Health-Systems Pharmacists
210 Washington Ave
Albany, NY 12203

518-456-8819
518-456-8819
Fax: 518-456-9319
E-Mail: nyschpweb@nyschp.org
Home Page: www.nyschp.org
Social Media: Facebook, Twitter, LinkedIn

Elizabeth Shlom, President
Stephanie Seyse, President Elect
Chris Jadoch, Vice President
Shaun C. Flynn, Executive Director
Philip Manning, Treasurer

Provides leadership and resources to promote quality pharmaceuticalservices directed at appropriate medication therapy and positive patient outcomes.
2200 Members

6275 Pan American Health Organization
525 Twenty-third Street, N.W.
Washington, DC 20037

202-974-3000
Fax: 202-974-3663
Home Page: www.paho.org
Social Media: Facebook, Twitter, YouTube, Flickr

The world's oldest international public health agency that providestechnical cooperation and mobilizes partnerships to improve health and quality of life in the countries of the Americas.
Founded in 1902

6276 Parenteral Drug Association
3 Bethesda Metro Center
Suite 1500
Bethesda, MD 20814

301-860-0293
Fax: 301 986 0296
E-Mail: info@pda.org
Home Page: www.pda.org

Vince R Anicetti, Chairman
Robert Myers, President
Wanda Neal-Ballard, Director Programs/Meetings
Lance K Hoboy, MBA, VP Finance
Matthew Clark, Director Marketing

A non-profit international association of scientists involved in the development, manufacture, quality control and regulation of

pharmaceuticals/biopharmaceuticals and related products. The association also provides educational opportunities for government and university sectors that have a vocational interest in pharmaceutical/biopharmaceutical sciences and technology.
10500 Members
Founded in 1946

6277 Pediatric Pharmacy Advocacy Group
5865 Ridgeway Center Parkway
Suite 300
Memphis, TN 38120-4014

901-820-4434
Home Page: www.ppag.org
Social Media: Facebook, Twitter, LinkedIn

Kay Kyllonen, President
Jared Cash, President-Elect
Lisa Lubsch, Secretary
Jeffrey Low, Treasurer
Matthew R. Helms, Executive Director

A nonprofit organization that strives to improve the health of children.
800 Members
Founded in 1990

6278 Pennsylvania Pharmacists Association
508 North Third Street
Harrisburg, PA 17101

717-234-6151
E-Mail: ppa@papharmacists.com
Home Page: www.papharmacists.com
Social Media: Facebook, Twitter, LinkedIn, YouTube, Flickr

Eric Esterbrook, President
Donna Hazel, President-Elect
Eric Pusey, First Vice President
Nicholas Leon, Second Vice President
J. Scott Miskovsky, Immediate Past President

A professional membership society of registered pharmacists, student pharmacists, pharmacy technicans, and others who reside, work, attend college,or are interested in pharmacy in Pennsylvania.
Founded in 1878

6279 Pharmaceutical Outsourcing Management Association
8865 W Okeechobee Boulevard
Suite 202
West Palm Beach, FL 33411

561-795-5503
Fax: 561-795-5503
Home Page: www.pomasite.com

Shannon Brome-Ward, President
Linda Wauk, VP
Charles Calvert, Treasurer
Fran Grote, Secretary

Established as a forum to exchange ideas and experiences about outsourcing in the pharmaceutical industry.
Founded in 1995

6280 Pharmaceutical Research and Manufacturers of America
950 F Street, NW
Suite 300
Washington, DC 20004

202-835-3400
E-Mail: newsroom@phrma.org
Home Page: www.phrma.org
Social Media: Facebook, Twitter, YouTube, Flickr, Google+

Ian Read, Chairman
Kenneth C Frazier, Chairman Elect
W. Thomas Amick, President & Chief Executive Officer
George A. Scangos, Treasurer

Mission is to conduct effective advocacy for public policies that encourage discovery of important new medicines for patients by pharmaceutical/biotechnology research companies.
Founded in 1958

6281 Pharmacy Benefit Management Institute, Inc .
2901 N Dallas Pkwy
Ste 420
Plano, TX 75093

480-730-0814
Fax: 480-222-4229
E-Mail: jlutz@pbmi.com
Home Page: www.pbmi.com
Social Media: LinkedIn

Jane Lutz, Executive Director
Kathleen Fairman, Vice President
Linda DeChant, Director of Sales
Julie Blackman, Marketing Manager
Shelly Carey, Research Director

Pharmacy benefit management education, research, and consulting.

6282 Pharmacy Technician Certification Board
2200 C Street NW
Suite 101
Washington, DC 20037

800-363-8012
Fax: 202-888-1699
E-Mail: contact@ptcb.org
Home Page: www.ptcb.org
Social Media: Facebook, Twitter

Scott Meyers, Chair
Paul Abramowitz, Vice Chair
Thomas Menighan, Executive Vice President
Everett B. McAllister, Executive Director & CEO
Larry Wagenknecht, Treasurer

Develops, maintains, promotes, and administers a nationally accredited certification and recertification program for pharmacy technicians to enablethe most effective support of pharmacists to advance patient safety.
Founded in 1995

6283 Pinoy Pharmacy

Home Page: www.pinoypharmacy.com
Social Media: Facebook, Twitter

An online community for Filipino pharmacy professionals around the world.

6284 Professional Compounding Centers of America
9901 South Wilcrest Drive
Houston, TX 77099

281-933-6948
800-331-2498
Fax: 281-933-6627
E-Mail: customerservice@pccarx.com
Home Page: www.pccarx.com
Social Media: Facebook, Twitter, LinkedIn, YouTube, Flickr

Provides independent pharmacists with a complete support system forcompounding unique dosage forms.
3900 Members
Founded in 1981

6285 Regulatory Affairs Professionals Society
5635 Fishers Lane
Suite 550
Rockville, MA 20852

301-770-2920
Fax: 301-770-2924
E-Mail: raps@raps.org
Home Page: www.raps.org
Social Media: Facebook, Twitter, LinkedIn, YouTube, Google+, Flickr

Donald A Middlebrook, Chairman
Rainer Voelksen, President
Martha A. Brumfield, President Elect
Salma Michor, Secretary/Treasurer
Gautam Maitra, Director

The largest global organization of and for those involved with the regulation of healthcare and related products, including medical devices, pharmaceuticals, biologics and nutritional products.
Founded in 1976

6286 Roundtable of Toxicology Consultants
P.O. Box 98224
Raleigh, NC 27624

E-Mail: toxconsultants@earthlink.net
Home Page: www.toxconsultants.com

Dave Hobson, President
Jane Allen, President Elect
Harry Olson, Past President
Peter Korytko, Secretary
Merrill Osheroff, Treasurer

An organization of independently practicing toxicologists dedicatedto solving the problems for clients.
Founded in 1986

6287 Society for Laboratory Automation and Screening
100 Illinois Street
Ste. 242
St. Charles, IL 60174

630-256-7527
877-990-7527
E-Mail: slas@slas.org
Home Page: www.slas.org

Daniel G Sipes, President
Dean Ho, Vice President
Alastair Binnie, Director
Richard Eglen, Secretary
Robyn Rourick, Treasurer

A global community of more than 18,000 scientists from academia, government and industry collectively focused on leveraging the power of technologyto achieve scientific objectives.
18000 Members
Founded in 2009

6288 Society of Critical Care Medicine
500 Midway Drive
Mount Prospect, IL 60056

847-827-6869
Fax: 847-827-6886
E-Mail: info@sccm.org
Home Page: www.sccm.org
Social Media: Twitter, Google+

J. Christopher Farmer, President
David J Martin, Chief Executive Officer
Dorothy Suwanski, Executive Assistant
Ellen Turney, Human Resources Manager
Karen Boman, Business Analyst

The largest multiprofessional organization dedicated to ensuring excellence and consistency in the practice of critical care.

6289 Southeastern Society of Health-System Pharmacists

Home Page: www.smshp.org
Social Media: Facebook, Twitter

A regional association representing pharmacists and related personnel associated with organized health-care settings.

6290 **Student National Pharmaceutical Association**
PO Box 761388ÿ
San Antonio, TX 78245
210-383-7381
Fax: 210-579-1059
E-Mail: contactsnpha@snpha.org
Home Page: www.snpha.org
Social Media: Facebook, Twitter, YouTube, Instagram

Felix Tran, Executive Chairman
Dainielle Fox, President
Jessie Nia Hwang, President Elect
Dr. Carmita Coleman, Executive Director
Joshua Blackwell, Vice President

An educational service association of pharmacy students who are concerned about pharmacy and healthcare related issues, and the poor minority representation in pharmacy and other health-related professions.
Founded in 1972

Newsletters

6291 **AACP News**
American Association of Colleges of Pharmacy
1727 King St
Suite 210
Alexandria, VA 22314-2700
703-739-2330
Fax: 703-836-8982
Home Page: www.aacp.org

Lucinda Maine, Executive VP
Kenneth W Miller, Senior VP
Daniel J Cassidy, COO

Activities and issues in pharmacy education. 12 pages, free to members. Published since 1874.
Cost: $35.00
Frequency: Monthly
Circulation: 300
Founded in 1900
Mailing list available for rent: 300 names
Printed in on newsprint stock

6292 **ACCP Report**
American College of Clinical Pharmacy
13000 W. 87th St Parkway
Lenexa, KS 66215-4530
913-492-3311
Fax: 913-492-0088
E-Mail: accp@accp.com
Home Page: www.accp.com

George Puiges, Publisher
Bruce Mueller, Editor
Micheal Maddux, Executive Director
Jon Poynter, Project Manager, Membership
Kimma Sheldon, Medical Editor

The American College of Clinical Pharmacy (ACCP) is a professional and scientific society that provides leadership, education, advocacy, and resources enabling clinical pharmacists to achieve excellence in practice and research.
Cost: $45.00
Frequency: Monthly
Circulation: 12000

6293 **Alternative Medicine Alert**
American Health Consultants
3525 Piedmont Rd Ne
Building Six, Suite 400
Atlanta, GA 30305-1578
404-467-4243
800-688-2421
Fax: 404-262-7837
Home Page: www.ahcpub.com

Jeff Mac Donald, CEO

Reports on studies of herbs in medicine, reactions in relation to different herbs. Studies that are out and those being done.
Cost: $299.00
Frequency: Monthly
Mailing list available for rent
Printed in 4 colors on matte stock

6294 **Annals of Pharmacotherapy**
Harvey Whitney Books Company
8044 Montgomery Road
PO Box 42696
Cincinnati, OH 45242-0696
513-793-3555
877-742-7631
Fax: 513-793-3600
E-Mail: customer-services@theannals.com
Home Page: www.theannals.com

Tina Whitney, Finance Executive
Eugene Sorkin, Associate Editor
Harvey Whitney, CEO
Greg Johnson, Marketing
Ann Brandwieve, Circulation Manager

For 38 years this independent peer reviewed journal has been dedicated to the advancement of pharmacotherapy. Article categories include; original research, comprehensive reviews, case reports, editorials, and letters. special article features include new drug evaluations, therapeutic controversies, recent theraputic advances, international reports, continuing education articles, and more.
Cost: $158.00
Frequency: Monthly
Circulation: 50000
ISSN: 1060-0280
Founded in 1967
Printed in 4 colors on glossy stock

6295 **Chapter News**
American College of Cardiology
76 S State Street
Concord, NH 03301-3520
603-228-1231
Fax: 603-228-2118
E-Mail: assnrhc@aol.com

Walter Perry, Executive Director

Newsletter for cardiovascular specialists in Maine, New Hampshire and Vermont.
Frequency: Quarterly
Mailing list available for rent

6296 **Clin-Alert-Newsletter**
Technomic Publishing Company
300 S Riverside Plz
Suite 1200
Chicago, IL 60606-6637
312-876-0004
Fax: 312-876-1158
E-Mail: foodinfo@technomic.com
Home Page: www.technomic.com

Ronald Paul, President
Darren Tristano, Executive Vice President
Neil Stern, Senior Partner

This unique adverse drug reaction/interaction reporting service presents-in newsletter format-a summary of adverse clinical events, collected from 103 key medical and research journals from around the world. Approximately 360 abstracts per year.
Cost: $155.00
8 Pages
Frequency: Semimonthly
ISSN: 0069-4770
Printed in 2 colors

6297 **Clinical Investigator News**
CTB International Publishing
PO Box 218
Maplewood, NJ 07040-218
973-966-0997
Fax: 973-966-0242
E-Mail: info@ctbintl.com
Home Page: www.ctbintl.com

FG Racioppi, Marketing Director
William Robison, Circulation Manager

Alerts independent investigators to existing or emerging opportunities to participate in clinical trials of drugs and maintain a steady flow of studies. Covers preclinical development through Phase II/III, approvals and post-marketing surveillance (PMS) studies.
Cost: $647.00
48 Pages
Frequency: Monthly
Founded in 1980
Mailing list available for rent
Printed in one color on newsprint stock

6298 **Clinical Trials Monitor**
CTB International Publishing
PO Box 218
Maplewood, NJ 07040-218
973-966-0997
Fax: 973-379-0242
E-Mail: info@ctbintl.com
Home Page: www.ctbintl.com

Oykue Brogna, Publisher
Christopher Brogna, Editor

Tracks clinical trials planned, underway, completed or abandoned. Lists the drug, the company, the indication, phase or stage, principal investigator, where and when trials will be held, enrollment plans and proposed end points. Reports results at meetings, and in journals.
Cost: $1197.00
64 Pages
Frequency: Monthly
Founded in 1985
Printed in one color on newsprint stock

6299 **Consumer Pharmacist**
Elba Medical Foundation
PO Box 494
Metairie, LA 70004
504-889-7070
Fax: 504-889-7060

John DiMaggio, Publisher

Drug information newsletter.
Cost: $30.00
Frequency: Monthly

6300 **DIA Newsletter**
Drug Information Association
800 Enterprise Rd
Suite 200
Horsham, PA 19044-3595
215-442-6100
Fax: 215-442-6199
E-Mail: dia@diahome.org
Home Page: www.diahome.org
Social Media: Facebook, Twitter, LinkedIn, YouTube

Ling Su, President
John Roberts, Treasurer
Paul Pomerantz,MBA, Worldwide Executive Director

Association activities, technical developments, supplying, and production of drugs.
Cost: $40.00
20 Pages
Frequency: Monthly
Founded in 1964

6301 **Diagnostics Intelligence**
CTB International Publishing

PO Box 218
Maplewood, NJ 07040-218

973-966-0997
Fax: 973-966-0242
E-Mail: info@ctbintl.com
Home Page: www.ctbintl.com

Oyque Brogna, CEO/President
F Racioppi, Marketing Director

Covers the latest in research, development, new product language, regulatory affairs, patents, litigations, opportunities and finance in the invitro diagnostics business.
Cost: $578.00
20 Pages
Frequency: Monthly
Mailing list available for rent
Printed in one color on newsprint stock

6302 **Drug Development Pipeline**
CTB International Publishing
PO Box 218
Maplewood, NJ 07040

973-966-0997
Fax: 973-966-0242
E-Mail: info@ctbintl.com
Home Page: www.ctbintl.com/

FG Racioppi, Marketing Director
Chris Brogna, President
Laszlo Novak, Editor

Newsletter that summarizes the changes in the drug development plans of US and Canadian pharmaceutical companies. Each issue will alert the reader to more than 120 products that are moving through the pipeline.
Cost: $198.00
Frequency: Monthly
Founded in 1982
Mailing list available for rent
Printed in one color on newsprint stock

6303 **Emerging Pharmaceuticals**
CTB International Publishing
PO Box 218
Maplewood, NJ 07040-218

973-966-0997
Fax: 973-966-0242
E-Mail: info@ctbintl.com
Home Page: www.ctbintl.com

FG Racioppi, Marketing Director

Covers the earliest stage of drug development, from discovery through preclinical trials. Alerts readers to news and insights about novel compounds, innovative screening methods and candidates for the R&D pipeline.
Cost: $542.00
14 Pages
Frequency: Monthly
Mailing list available for rent
Printed in one color on newsprint stock

6304 **FDC Reports: Gold Sheet**
FDC Reports
5550 Friendship Boulevard
Suite 1
Chevy Chase, MD 20815-7278

301-657-9830
800-332-2181
Fax: 301-656-3094
E-Mail: fdc.customer.service@elsevier.com
Home Page: www.fdcreports.com

Bill Paulson, Editor
Michael Magoulias, VP Sales/Marketing
Mike Squires, CEO/President
William Paulson, Executive Editor

A specialized publication which focuses each month on important changes in FDA's policies for regulating good manufacturing practices for pharmaceutical companies and their suppliers. Since 1967, this publication has provided quality control professionals with the latest useful information on state-of-the-art production and quality control techniques.
Cost: $595.00
Frequency: Monthly
ISSN: 1530-6194
Founded in 1939
Mailing list available for rent
Printed in 2 colors on matte stock

6305 **FDC Reports: Green Sheet**
FDC Reports
5550 Friendship Boulevard
Suite 1
Chevy Chase, MD 20815-7256

301-657-9830
Fax: 301-656-3094
Home Page: www.fdcreports.com

Mike Squires, President
Michael Koppenhoffer, Editor

For nearly 40 years The Green Sheet has been an independent source of news and information on the pharmacy profession and the pharmaceutical distribution system. This four-page publication provides pharmacists, wholesalers, drugstore managers and trade relations executives with concise coverage of: professional policy; national and state pharmacy association activities; reimbursement issues; new drug introductions and pharmaceutical pricing and deals.
Cost: $65.00
4 Pages
Frequency: Weekly
Founded in 1939

6306 **FDC Reports: Pink Sheet**
FDC Reports
5550 Friendship Boulevard
Suite 1
Chevy Chase, MD 20815-7256

301-657-9830
800-332-2181
Fax: 301-656-3094
E-Mail: PinkEditor@elsevier.com
Home Page: www.fdcreports.com

Wallace Werble Jr, Publisher
Janet Coleman, Editor
Mike Squires, CEO/President
Shawn Smith, Marketing
Emily Brainard, Circulation Manager

Provides in-depth weekly news and analysis about developments affecting the prescription medicines. The publication closely tracks regulatory policies and actions by FDA, FTC, HCFA, Congress, the courts and other key federal and state agencies with jurisdiction over the drug industry. Regular coverage areas include: NDA and Generic Drug approvals, FDA recalls and seizures, mergers, the R&D pipeline, biotechnology start-ups and new product activity.
Cost: $1580.00
35 Pages
Frequency: Weekly
ISSN: 1068-5324
Founded in 1939

6307 **FDC Reports: Tan Sheet**
FDC Reports
5550 Friendship Boulevard
Suite 1
Chevy Chase, MD 20815-7256

301-657-9830
Fax: 301-656-3094
E-Mail: FDC.Customer.Service@Elsevier.com
Home Page: www.fdcreports.com

Mike Squires, CEO/President
Ramsey Baghdadi, Editor
Michael Magoulias, Marketing Manager
Emily Brainard, Circulation Manager

Provides in-depth coverage of nonprescription pharmaceuticals and dietary supplement/nutritionals. Spectrum of coverage includes: regulatory activities of FTC, CPSC and FDA, including monograph and non-monograph decisions, enforcement actions, advisory committee reviews and approvals; Congressional hearings and legislation; business and marketing news such as Rx-to-OTC switches, product development and new product introductions; FDA recalls and seizures and regular listing of product trademarks
Cost: $1285.00
Frequency: Weekly
ISSN: 1068-5316
Founded in 1939

6308 **FDLI Prospectus**
Food & Drug Law Institute
1155 15th Street NW
Suite 800
Washington, DC 20005

202-371-1420
800-956-6293
Fax: 202-371-0649
E-Mail: comments@fdli.org
Home Page: www.fdli.org

Michael D. Levin-Epstein, Vice President, Publications
Abby C. Foster, Managing Editor

weekly e-newsletter
Frequency: Weekly

6309 **Food and Drug Letter**
FDAnews
300 N Washington St
Suite 200
Falls Church, VA 22046-3441

703-538-7600
888-838-5578
Fax: 703-538-7676
E-Mail: customerservice@fdanews.com
Home Page: www.fdanews.com

Cynthia Carter, President
Michael Miven, Editor
Maritva Lizama, Marketing
J T Hrontith, Sales Director

Provides reliable, in-depth analysis of how FDA's regulations and procedures will affect your current decisions and long-term plans and gives you in-depth interpretation to tell you why FDA is making or proposing revisions.
Cost: $1095.00
8 Pages
Frequency: Annual+

6310 **Health News Daily**
FDC Reports
5550 Friendship Boulevard
Suite 1
Chevy Chase, MD 20815-7256

301-657-9830
800-332-2181
Fax: 301-656-3094
Home Page: www.healthnewsdaily.com

Jim Chicca, Editor
Mike Squires, Executive Director

Provides up-to-the-minute coverage on a broad spectrum of health care issues including pharmaceuticals, medical devices and diagnostics, biomedical research, federal health policy and legislation, Medicare-Medicaid, technology reimbursement and cost-containment. Special emphasis is placed on federal regulatory and legislative developments. Published each business day, the publication draws on the expertise of more than 40 F-D-C reports editors and reporters.
Cost: $ 1480.00
Frequency: Daily
Founded in 1939

6311 **International Pharmaceutical Regulatory Monitor**
Omniprint

9700 Philadelphia Ct
Lanham, MD 20706-4405

301-731-7000
800-345-2611
Fax: 301-731-7001
Home Page: www.omniprint.net

Ken Kaufman, President
Stephen Brown, VP

Comprehensive reports on the world's drug and biotechnology regulations for testing and marketing; provides actual regulatory documents (English texts).
Cost: $595.00
60 Pages
Frequency: Monthly
ISSN: 0888-6393
Founded in 1973
Mailing list available for rent
Printed in 2 colors on matte stock

6312 Mealey's Emerging Drugs & Devices
LexisNexis Mealey's
555 W 5th Avenue
Los Angeles, CA 90013

213-627-1130
E-Mail: mealeyinfo@lexisnexis.com
Home Page: www.lexisnexis.com/mealeys

Tom Hagy, VP/General Manager
Maureen McGuire, Editorial Director
Tom Moylan, Editor

The report covers cases involving a variety of prescription drug vaccines, implants and devices. Duract, Parlodel, Accutane, fen-phen, Rezulin, Propulsid, dietary supplements and blood products are among the topics tracked. Medical devices covered include heart catheters, breast implants, heart valves, intraocular lenses, jaw implants, joint replacements, latex gloves, pacemakers, pedicle screws, penile implants, and surgical lasers.
Cost: $1249.00
100 Pages
Frequency: Semi-Monthly
Founded in 1996

6313 Mealey's Litigation Report: Baycol
LexisNexis Mealey's
555 W 5th Avenue
Los Angeles, CA 90013

213-627-1130
E-Mail: mealeyinfo@lexisnexis.com
Home Page: www.lexisnexis.com/mealeys

Tom Hagy, VP/General Manager
Maureen McGuire, Editorial Director
Dylan McGuire, Editor

This report tracks the litigation surrounding Baycol and other statin-based anti-cholesterol drug cases. Since the voluntary withdrawl of Bayer's Baycol and Lipobay brand cerivastatin anti-cholesterol drugs, numerous complaints have been filed. The report will cover hard-to-find filings, new complaints, class actions, MDL developments, trial updates and more.
Cost: $950.00
100 Pages
Frequency: Monthly
Founded in 2002

6314 Mealey's Litigation Report: Fen-Phen/Redux
LexisNexis Mealey's
555 W 5th Avenue
Los Angeles, CA 90013

213-627-1130
E-Mail: mealeyinfo@lexisnexis.com
Home Page: www.lexisnexis.com/mealeys

Tom Hagy, VP/General Manager
Maureen McGuire, Editorial Director
Michael Lefkowitz, Editor

The report provides detailed coverage of the litigation surrounding fen-phen, Redux and other diet drugs. The report covers new filings, class actions, MDL proceedings, trials, settlements, rulings, medical studies, FDA activity and more.
Cost: $995.00
100 Pages
Frequency: Monthly
Founded in 1997

6315 NABP Newsletter
National Association of Boards of Pharmacy
700 Busse Highway
Park Ridge, IL 60068

847-698-6227
800-774-6227
Fax: 847-698-0124
E-Mail: custserv@nabp.net
Home Page: www.nabp.net

Malcom Broussard, Chairperson
Michael Burlson, President
Joseph Adams, Treasurer

Provides coverage of issues important to those who practice pharmacy and those who regulate that practice. Information about NABP's competency assessment and licensure transfer programs, news about the boards of pharmacy, and articles that impact the practice and regulation of pharmacy appear in each issue.
Cost: $35.00
Frequency: 10 Per Year

6316 NCPA Newsletter
National Community Pharmacists Association
100 Daingerfield Road
Alexandria, VA 22314

703-683-8200
800-544-7447
Fax: 703-683-3619
E-Mail: info@ncpanet.com
Home Page: www.ncpanet.org

Mike Conlan, VP Publications
Chris Linville, Managing Editor

Stay up-to-date on the latest developments in legislation, federal regulation, pharmacy news, and other important events with the NCPA Newsletter. Independent pharmacists get the information they need to understand the policies, politics, and government actions that affect independent pharmacy practice. Annual subscription is included in NCPA memership dues.
Cost: $50.00

6317 Nation's Health
American Public Health Association
800 I Street NW
Washington, DC 20001-3710

202-777-2742
Fax: 202-777-2534
E-Mail: membership.mail@apha.org
Home Page: www.apha.org
Social Media: Facebook, Twitter, LinkedIn, YouTube, Blogs

Georges C Benjamin, Executive Director
Mazin Abdelgader, Publication Services
Michele Late, Executive Editor

For the latest news on public health, public health professionals, legislators and decision-makers. This newsletter is part of APHA membership.
Cost: $50.00
Frequency: 10 Per Year

6318 PDA Letter
Parenteral Drug Association
1894 Preston White Drive
Reston, VA 20191-5433

703-620-6390
Fax: 703-476-0904
E-Mail: info@npcnow.org
Home Page: www.npcnow.org

Walter L Morris, III, Senior Editor

Designed to keep members informed of the latest information in the regulatory arena along with scientific happenings within the Association and the industry. It also contains details on upcoming PDA events, as well as worldwide Chapter activities.
Frequency: Monthly
Founded in 1949

6319 Pharmaceutical & Med Packaging News
Canon Communications
11444 W Olympic Blvd
Suite 900
Los Angeles, CA 90064-1555

310-445-4200
Fax: 310-445-4299
E-Mail: feedback@cancom.com
Home Page: www.cancom.com

Klaus Weinmann, CEO
Rudolf Hotter, COO
Frequency: Monthly
Founded in 1992

6320 Pharmaceutical News Daily
CTB International Publishing
PO Box 218
Maplewood, NJ 07040

973-966-0997
Fax: 973-966-0242
E-Mail: info@ctbintl.com
Home Page: www.ctbintl.com

Kris Brogina, CEO/President
Kistine Yanicek, Editor
Oykue Brogina, Publisher
T Tseng, Circulation Manager

This daily electronic newsletter updates the highly competitive pharmaceutical and biotechnology industries. Delivered by e-mail.
Cost: $279.00
Frequency: Daily
Founded in 1984
Mailing list available for rent
Printed in one color on newsprint stock

6321 Pharmacist's Letter
Therapeutic Research
3120 W March Lane
PO Box 8190
Stockton, CA 95208-190

209-472-2240
Fax: 209-472-2249
Home Page: www.pletter.com

Jeff Jellin, Publisher

A newsletter to pharmacists offering coverage of drug development, production, distribution, legislation, safety and other issues concerning the industry.
Cost: $85.00
ISSN: 0883-0371

6322 Pharmacy Practice News
McMahon Group
545 W 45th St
8th Floor
New York, NY 10036-3409

646-557-0966
Fax: 646-957-7230
E-Mail: davidb@mcmahonmed.com
Home Page: www.strategiesinmedicine.com

Raymond Mc Mahon, CEO
Van Velle, President
David Bronstein, Editor-in-Chief
Marsha Radebaugh, Circulation Manager
Michelle McMohan, Creative Director

Created to inform hospital pharmacists of the latest news on drugs, nutrition, research and

trends in the pharmaceutical industry.
Cost: $60.00
Frequency: Monthly
Circulation: 45460
Founded in 1972

6323 **Pharmacy Student**
APLA
2215 Constitution Avenue NW
Washington, DC 20037-2977

202-429-7576

Rick Harding, Publisher

Practical information to help pharmacy students grow.
Cost: $35.00
Frequency: Monthly
Circulation: 100000

6324 **Pharmacy Today**
American Pharmacists Association
2215 Constitution Avenue NW
Washington, DC 20037-2977

202-429-7557
800-237-2742
Fax: 202-783-2351
E-Mail: pt@aphanet.org
Home Page: www.pharmacists.org

Frank Bennicasa, Publisher
L Michael Posey, Editor
Carli Richard, Managing Editor

Offering readers profiles of practices that employ unique MTM techniques to effectively serve their patients. Readers can use these profiles as models to develop and improve their own MTM practice, increase patient adherence, and build patient loyalty.
Cost: $200.00
Frequency: Monthly
ISSN: 1042-0991
Founded in 1962

6325 **Prescriber's Letter**
Therapeutic Research
PO Box 8190
Stockton, CA 95208

209-472-2240
Fax: 209-472-2249
Home Page: www.pletter.com

Jeff Jellin PharmD, Publisher

A newsletter to pharmacists offering coverage of drug development, production, distribution, legislation, safety and other issues concerning the industry.
Cost: $85.00
ISSN: 1073-7219

6326 **Preventive Medicine Update**
HealthComm International
5800 Soundview Drive
PO Box 1729
Gig Harbor, WA 98335-2000

253-858-3315
800-843-9660
Fax: 253-851-9749

Jeffrey Bland, CEO/Contact

6327 **Psoriasis Resource**
National Psoriasis Foundation
6600 Sw 92nd Ave
Suite 300
Portland, OR 97223-7195

503-244-7404
800-723-9166
Fax: 503-245-0626
E-Mail: getinfo@npfusa.org
Home Page: www.psoriasis.org

Pam Field, CEO
Bill Taggart, Managing Editor
Gail Zimmerman, CEO

A newsletter published for members of the National Psoriasis Foundation. Highlights interesting articles on psoriasis products and medications andother health related topics. Contains advertisements for psoriasis-related products and services.
16 Pages
Circulation: 40000
Mailing list available for rent: 28000 names
Printed in 2 colors on matte stock

6328 **Results Newsletter**
American Clinical Laboratory Association
1100 New York Ave Nw
Suite 725
Washington, DC 20005-6172

202-637-9466
Fax: 202-637-2050
E-Mail: info@clinical-labs.org
Home Page: www.clinical-labs.org

Alan Mertz, President
Frequency: Monthly
Mailing list available for rent

6329 **Rx Ipsa Loquitur**
American Society for Pharmacy Law
1224 Centre West Dr
Suite 400
Springfield, IL 62704-2184

217-698-6163
Fax: 217-698-6164
Home Page: www.aspl.org

Michael Monson, Owner
Francis B Palumbo, Director
Pamela Tolson CAE, Executive Director
William Fassett, Treasurer

Featuring recent court decisions, legislative and regulatory news, and other current pharmacy law news and articles.
Frequency: Bi-Monthly

6330 **Washington Drug Letter**
FDAnews
300 N Washington St
Suite 200
Falls Church, VA 22046-3441

703-538-7600
888-838-5578
Fax: 703-538-7676
E-Mail: customerservice@fdanews.com
Home Page: www.fdanews.com
Cynthia Carter, President
Maritza Lizama, Marketing Director

Summaries of FDA regulatory changes and key legislation that affects prescription and over the counter drugs. Each weekly issue brings you up-to-date on pre approval and post approval issues that directly impact your operation.
Cost: $897.00
Frequency: Weekly

Magazines & Journals

6331 **AAPS Newsmagazine**
American Association of Pharmaceutical Scientists
2107 Wilson Blvd
Suite 700
Arlington, VA 22201-3042

703-243-2800
Fax: 703-243-9054
E-Mail: aaps@aaps.org
Home Page: www.aaps.org

John Lisack, Executive Director
Karol Shadle, Associate Director
Maria Nadeau, Member Groups Manager
Me'Gesha Portlock, Administrative Assistant

Exclusive to AAPS members. Features expanded coverage of the industry, complete with expert information on marketplace trends, regulatory matters, and career opportunities.
Mailing list available for rent

6332 **AAPS Online Buyers Guide**
American Association of Pharmaceutical Scientists
2107 Wilson Blvd
Suite 700
Arlington, VA 22201-3042

703-243-2800
Fax: 703-243-9054
E-Mail: aaps@aaps.org
Home Page: www.aaps.org

John Lisack, Executive Director
Karol Shadle, Associate Director
Maria Nadeau, Member Groups Manager
Me'Gesha Portlock, Administrative Assistant
comprehensive sourcebook you need as a pharmaceutical scientist. Research the more than 500 companies providing the products and service you need. You can browse the entire Online Buyers Guide or you can refine your search by Company Name, Region, Business Category, or Keyword.
Mailing list available for rent

6333 **AAPS PharmSciTech Journal**
American Association of Pharmaceutical Scientists
2107 Wilson Blvd
Suite 700
Arlington, VA 22201-3042

703-243-2800
Fax: 703-243-9054
E-Mail: aaps@aaps.org
Home Page: www.aaps.org

John Lisack, Executive Director
Karol Shadle, Associate Director
Maria Nadeau, Member Groups Manager
Me'Gesha Portlock, Administrative Assistant

An online-only journal published and owned by the American Association of Pharmaceutical Scientists. The journal's mission is to disseminate scientific and technical information on drug product design, development, evaluation and processing to the global pharmaceutical research community, taking full advantage of web-based publishing by presenting innovative text with 3-D graphics, interactive figures and databases, video and audio files.
ISSN: 1530-9932
Mailing list available for rent

6334 **America's Pharmacist**
National Community Pharmacists Association
100 Daingerfield Road
Alexandria, VA 22314
703-683-8200
800-544-7447
Fax: 703-683-3619
E-Mail: info@ncpanet.com
Home Page: www.ncpanet.org

Mike Conlan, VP Publications/Editor
Chris Linville, Managing Editor

This informative magazine gives 25,000 independent pharmacists insight into current issues that affect independent pharmacy and NCPA's activities to address those issues. Also; it serves the readers by including monthly articles on clinical topics, a continuing education series for pharmacists who want to earn CE credit, information on how to manage finances, and proven tips on better marketing, as well as profiles of NCPA members from across the country. Annual subscription included in dues.
Cost: $50.00
Frequency: Monthly

6335 **American Institute of the History of Pharmacy**
777 Highland Ave
Madison, WI 53705-2222

608-262-5378
Fax: 608-262-3397
E-Mail: aihp@aihp.org
Home Page: www.aihp.org/

Dr. Gregory Higby, Executive Director
Dr. Elaine Stroud, Assistant Director
Beth Fisher, Assoc. Dir. Curatorial Affairs

Articles on pharmaceutical history and usage.
Cost: $50.00
200 Pages
Frequency: Quarterly
Circulation: 1200
Founded in 1960
Printed in on glossy stock

6336 **American Journal of Health-System Pharmacy**
American Society of Health-System Pharmacists
7272 Wisconsin Ave
Bethesda, MD 20814-4861

301-657-3000
866-279-0681
Fax: 301-664-8877
E-Mail: ajhp@ashp.org
Home Page: www.ashp.org
Social Media: Facebook, Twitter, LinkedIn, YouTube

Kathryn Shultz, President
Paul Abramowitz, CEO
Philip Schneider, Treasurer

The journal for pharmacists practicing in all area's of acute care, ambulatory care, home care, long term care, HMO's, PPO's, and PBM's.
Cost: $165.00
54 Pages
Frequency: Bi-Weekly
Circulation: 42,000
ISSN: 1079-2082
Printed in 2 colors on glossy stock

6337 **American Journal of Medical Quality**
American College of Medical Quality
4334 Montgomery Ave
Suite B
Bethesda, MD 20814-4415

301-913-9149
800-924-2149
Fax: 301-913-9142
E-Mail: acmq@acmq.org
Home Page: www.acmq.org

Bridget Brodie, Manager
Frequency: Bi-Monthly

6338 **American Journal of Pharmaceutical Education**
American Association of Colleges of Pharmacy
1727 King St
Alexandria, VA 22314-2700

703-739-2330
Fax: 703-836-8982
Home Page: www.aacp.org

Lucinda Maine, Executive VP
Kenneth W Miller, Senior VP
Daniel J Cassidy, COO

Official publication of the American Association of Colleges of Pharmacy. Dedicated to all those with interest in professional, graduate, and postgraduate pharmaceutical education. Its purpose is to documnet and advance pharmaceutical education in the United States and Internationally. Features original research articles, editorials, reports on the state of pharmaceutical education, descriptions of teaching innovations, and book reviews.
Cost: $65.00
120 Pages
Frequency: Quarterly
Circulation: 3200
ISSN: 0002-9459
Founded in 1937
Printed in one color on matte stock

6339 **American Journal of Public Health**
American Public Health Association
800 I Street NW
Washington, DC 20001-3710

202-777-2742
Fax: 202-777-2534
Home Page: www.apha.org
Social Media: Facebook, Twitter, LinkedIn, YouTube, Blogs

Mary E Northridge PhD, Editor-in-Chief

Provides in-depth information in the field of public health. Research and program evaluations are accompanied by authoritative editorials, throught-provoking commentary, and timely health policy analysis.
Cost: $419.00
120 Pages
Frequency: Monthly
Founded in 1990

6340 **BioPharm**
Advanstar Communications
6200 Canoga Avenue
2nd Floor
Woodland Hills, CA 91367

818-593-5000
Fax: 818-593-5020
Home Page: biopharminternational.com

Joseph Loggia, President
Chris DeMoulin, VP
Susannah George, Marketing Director

Publication taking a practical approach to the technology and business of developing and manufacturing biotechnology-derived pharmaceutical products. Regular topics include process development, downstream processing, facilities design, emerging technologies and regulatory compliance.
Cost: $64.00
Frequency: Monthly
Circulation: 29,200
ISSN: 1040-8304
Founded in 1987

6341 **Chain Drug Review**
Racher Press
220 5th Avenue
New York, NY 10001

212-213-6000
Fax: 212-725-3961
E-Mail: info@racherpress.com
Home Page: www.racherpress.com

Kevin Burke, VP/Group Advertising
Jeff Woldt, VP/Editorial Director
David Pinto, Editor

Chain Drug Review serves the chain drug industry.
Cost: $185.00
Frequency: Bi-weekly
Circulation: 54000
Founded in 1978
Printed in 4 colors on glossy stock

6342 **Chemistry**
American Chemical Society
1155 16th St Nw
Washington, DC 20036-4892

202-872-4600
800-227-5558
Fax: 202-872-4615
E-Mail: help@acs.org
Home Page: www.acs.org

Madeleine Jacobs, CEO
Judith L Benham, Board Chair

Published for members, student affiliates, and those interested in learning more about the chemical sciences and the American Chemical Society.

6343 **CleanRooms Magazine**
PennWell Publishing Company
98 Spit Brook Rd
Suite 100
Nashua, NH 03062-5737

603-891-0123
Fax: 603-891-9294
E-Mail: georgem@pennwell.com
Home Page: www.pennwell.com

Christine Shaw, VP
James Enos, Publisher
Bob Johnson, Sales & Marketing Manager

Serves the contamination control and ultrapure materials and process industries. Written for readers in the microelectronics, pharmaceutical, biotech, health care, food processing and other user industries. Provides technology and business news and new product listings.
Cost: $97.00
Frequency: Monthly
Circulation: 35031
Founded in 1987

6344 **Community Pharmacist**
ELF Publications
5285 W Louisiana Ave
Lakewood, CO 80232-5976

303-975-0075
800-922-8513
Fax: 303-975-0132
E-Mail: mcasey@elfpublications.com
Home Page: www.elfpublications.com

Judy Lane, Owner
Ronald R Quam, Editor/Publisher

Pharmacy trade journal that meets the professional educational needs of today's practitioner
Cost: $12.00
40 Pages
ISSN: 1096-9179
Founded in 1972
Printed in 4 colors on glossy stock

6345 **Contract Pharma**
Rodman Publishing
70 Hilltop Rd
3rd Floor
Ramsey, NJ 07446-1150

201-825-2552
Fax: 201-825-0553
E-Mail: info@rodpub.com
Home Page: www.nutraceuticalsworld.com

Rodman Zilenziger Jr, President
Matt Montgomery, VP

A global publication providing most up-to-date news, outsourcing information, business trends, commentary, and viewpoints to the Pharmaceutical and Biopharmaceutical outsourcing industry.
Frequency: Monthly
Circulation: 20026
Founded in 1999

6346 **DIA Global Forum**
Drug Information Association
800 Enterprise Road
Suite 200
Horsham, PA 19044-3595

215-442-6100
Fax: 215-442-6199

E-Mail: dia@diahome.org
Home Page: www.diahome.org

Paul Pomerantz BA MBA, Worldwide Executive Director
Lisa Zoks BA, Worldwide Dir Mktg/Communications

Presents important news from DIA conferences and workshops, reports of the Board of Directors and the regional advisory councils that directly impact DIA members, as well as practical tips, regulatory and global updates, upcoming DIA events, program notes, and more.
Frequency: Bi-Monthly
Circulation: 20000
ISSN: 1944-1991
Printed in 4 colors

6347 **DVM News**
Advanstar Communications
8033 Flint St
Lenexa, KS 66214-3335

913-492-4300
800-255-6864
Fax: 913-492-4157
E-Mail: dverdon@advanstar.com
Home Page: www.dvm360.com

Rebecca Turner Chapman, VP

Information from veterinary medicine covering news, features, practice management and new products and services.
Cost: $4.00
Frequency: Monthly
ISSN: 0012-7337
Founded in 1987

6348 **Drug Information Journal**
Drug Information Association
800 Enterprise Road
Suite 200
Horsham, PA 19044-3595

215-442-6100
Fax: 215-442-6199
E-Mail: dia@diahome.org
Home Page: www.diahome.org

Paul Pomerantz BA MBA, Worldwide Executive Director
Lisa Zoks BA, Worldwide Dir Mktg/Communications

Purpose is to disseminate information on manual and automated drug research, development, and information systems; to foster communication between educational, research, industrial and governmental personnel engaged in drug information activities; and to provide a forum for the development of improved methods of presenting research data generated from chemical, toxicologic, pharmacologic, and clinical studies.
Frequency: Bi-Monthly
Circulation: 20000
ISSN: 0092-8615
Founded in 1964

6349 **Drug Store News**
Lebhar-Friedman
425 Park Ave
New York, NY 10022-3526

212-756-5088
Fax: 212-838-9487
E-Mail: editor@drugstorenews.com
Home Page: www.drugstorenews.com

Heather Martin, Manager
J Rodger Friedman, CEO

Publication consists of merchandising trends and pharmacy developments. Provides extensive coverage of every major segment of chain drug retailing and combination stores.
Cost: $119.00
Circulation: 45000
Founded in 1925

6350 **Drug Topics**
Medical Economics Publishing
5 Paragon Dr
Montvale, NJ 07645-1791

973-944-7777
Fax: 973-944-7778
E-Mail: drug.topics@Medec.com
Home Page: www.drugtopics.com
Jim Granto, Publisher
Heather Schlosser, National Account Manager

Information on the distributing and dispensing drug trade.
Cost: $61.00
Printed in 4 colors on glossy stock

6351 **Food & Drug Packaging**
Stagnito Publishing Group
155 Pfingston Road
Suite 205
Deerfield, IL 60015

847-205-5660
Fax: 847-205-5680
E-Mail: gvansomeren@stagnito.com
Home Page: www.fdp.com
Social Media: Facebook, Twitter, LinkedIn, you tube

Lisa McTigue Pierce, Editor-in-Chief
Blayne Long, Senior Marketing Manager
Geneine Van Someren, Circulation Manager
Vince Miconi, Advertising Production Manager
George Misko, Regional Sales Manager

Food and Drug Packaging serves industries engaged in packaging food, beverages, pharmaceuticals, cosmetics and consulting/engineering firms.
Frequency: Monthly
Circulation: 75140
Founded in 1959

6352 **Food and Drug Law Journal**
Food & Drug Law Institute
1155 15th Street NW
Suite 800
Washington, DC 20005

202-371-1420
800-956-6293
Fax: 202-371-0649
E-Mail: comments@fdli.org
Home Page: www.fdli.org

Michael D. Levin-Epstein, Vice President, Publications
Abby C. Foster, Managing Editor

Award-winning journal offering scholarly, in-depth, analytical articles, providing insight into action of the FDA, FTC, and USDA, how the courts interpret these actions, and the reaction of the industry.
Cost: $379.00
Frequency: Quarterly
ISSN: 1064-590x

6353 **Formulary**
Advanstar Communications
6200 Canoga Avenue
2nd Floor
Woodland Hills, CA 91367

818-593-5000
Fax: 818-593-5020
E-Mail: info@advanstar.com
Home Page: www.advanstar.com

Joseph Loggia, President
Chris DeMoulintein, VP
Susannah George, Marketing Director

Peer-reviewed publication providing drug information for physicians, pharmacist, and other health care professionals who influence the selection and use of drugs in hospitals, HMO's, and other managed care settings.
Cost: $61.00
Frequency: Monthly
Circulation: 51402
ISSN: 1082-801X
Founded in 1992
Mailing list available for rent

6354 **HealthCare Distributor**
ELF Publications
5285 W Louisiana Ave
Lakewood, CO 80232-5976

303-975-0075
800-922-8513
Fax: 303-975-0132
E-Mail: elfpub@qwest.net
Home Page: www.elfpublications.com

Judy Lane, Owner
Ronald R Quam, Editor/Publisher
Chuck Austin, Senior Editor
Jerry Lester, Director of Sales

Multi-market publication devoted to the issues and opportunities facing the wholesale drug, chain drug, medical/surgical and home care products distribution industries
Cost: $12.00
80 Pages
Frequency: Bi-annually
Circulation: 12000
ISSN: 1096-9160
Founded in 1972
Printed in 4 colors on glossy stock

6355 **Hospital Pharmacy**
Facts and Comparisons
111 Westport Plz
Suite 300
St Louis, MO 63146-3011

314-216-2100
800-223-0554
Fax: 314-878-5563
E-Mail: service@drugfacts.com
Home Page: www.factsandcomparisons.com

John Pins, VP

Provides pharmacists with peer-reviewed articles and monthly features covering clinical and administrative areas such as drug use, drug distribution systems in hospitals and health-systems, automation, medication errors and adverse events, Joint Commission drug-related material and current FDA drug information.
Cost: $124.95
Frequency: Monthly
ISSN: 0018-5787
Founded in 1965

6356 **Inform**
American Oil Chemists' Society
2710 S Boulder
Urbana, IL 61802-6996

217-359-2344
Fax: 217-351-8091
E-Mail: kheine@aocs.org
Home Page: www.aocs.org
Social Media: Facebook, Twitter, LinkedIn, Blog

Jody Schonfeld, Publications Director
Kimmy Farris, Production Editor
Kathy Heine, Managing Editor

Member benefit pmagazine providing international news on fats, oils, surfactants, detergents, and related materials.
Cost: $175.00
462 Pages
Frequency: Monthly
Circulation: 3700
ISSN: 0897-8026
Founded in 1909
Printed in on glossy stock

6357 **International Pharmaceutical Abstracts**
American Society of Health-System Pharmacists
7272 Wisconsin Ave
Bethesda, MD 20814-4861

301-657-3000
866-279-0681
Fax: 301-664-8877
E-Mail: ipa@ashp.org
Home Page: www.ashp.org

Mark Woods, President

These reports offering the latest in the development of drugs overseas, clinical use, cosmetics and, alternative and herbal medicine. Reports on pharmacy practice are also included.
Cost: $240.00
Frequency: Monthly
Circulation: 31,000
ISSN: 0020-8264
Founded in 1936

6358 **Journal of Managed Care Pharmacy**
Academy of Managed Care Pharmacy
100 N Pitt St
Suite 400
Alexandria, VA 22314-3141

703-683-8416
800-827-2627
Fax: 703-683-8417
E-Mail: sandres@amcp.org
Home Page: www.amcp.org
Social Media: Facebook, Twitter, LinkedIn

Douglas Burgoyne, President
Robert Gregory, Treasurer

Features articles on trends and recent developments in managed care pharmacy, updates from pharmacy educators about the inclusion of managed care topics in cirricula and news and information about the academy and it's activities.
Cost: $60.00
Frequency: Bi-Monthly

6359 **Journal of Parenteral and Enteral Nutrition**
Amer. Society for Parenteral & Enteral Nutrition
8630 Fenton Street
Suite 412
Silver Spring, MD 20910-3803

301-587-6315
800-727-4567
Fax: 301-587-2365
E-Mail: jpen@nutr.org
Home Page: www.nutritioncare.org
Social Media: Facebook, Twitter

Is the premier scientific journal of nutrition and metabolic support. It publishes original, peer-reviewd studies that define the cutting edge of basic and clinical research in the field. It explores the science of optimizing the care of patients receiving enteral or IV therapies. This is included as benefits of membership in ASPEN.
Cost: $90.00
Frequency: Fortnightly
Circulation: 7800
ISSN: 0148-6071
Founded in 1977

6360 **Journal of Pharmaceutical Innovation**
Int'l Society for Pharmaceutical Engineering
3109 W Dr Martin Luther King Jr Boulevard
Suite 250
Tampa, FL 33607

813-960-2105
Fax: 813-264-2816
E-Mail: ask@ispe.org
Home Page: www.ispe.org

Gloria N Hall, Editor & Director of Publications
Lynda Goldbach, Publications Manager
Amy Lecceardone, Publications Coordinator
Valerie Adams, Advertising Sales Coordinator
Frequency: 4/Year
Circulation: 2000

6361 **Journal of Pharmaceutical Marketing and Management**
Taylor & Francis Group LLC
325 Chestnut St
Suite 800
Philadelphia, PA 19106-2614

215-625-8900
800-354-1420
Fax: 215-625-2940
E-Mail: haworthorders@taylorandfrancis.com
Home Page: www.taylorandfrancis.com

Kevin Bradley, President

The journal maintains a vigorous policy of publishing quality research reports of interest to individuals involved in the manufacturing, wholesale, institutional, retail, regulatory, organizational and academic components of the pharmaceutical industry.
Frequency: Quarterly

6362 **Journal of Pharmaceutical Sciences**
Wiley InterScience
350 Main St
Malden, MA 02148-5089

781-388-8250
800-835-6770
Fax: 781-388-8210
E-Mail: cs-journals@wiley.com
Home Page: www.wiley.com

Amy Yodaniss, VP
Julie Fisher, Assistant Editor
Roger Hall, VP
Laurie Beagell, Circulation Manager

A comprehensive look at the world of drugs and pharmaceuticals.
Frequency: Monthly
Circulation: 225

6363 **Journal of Pharmacy Practice**
Technomic Publishing Company
PO Box 3535
Lancaster, PA 17601

717-291-5609
800-233-9936
Fax: 717-295-4538
E-Mail: aflannery@techpub.com
Home Page: www.techpub.com

Amy Flannery, Marketing

The journal provides useful, timely reports on the most challenging issues of pharmacy today and anticipates the unique demands of this rapidly changing field. Each issue's single-topic format and thoughtful, readable analysis gives a better grasp of difficult problems and provides immediately useful information.
Cost: $210.00
80 Pages
ISSN: 0897-1900
Printed in 2 colors on matte stock

6364 **Journal of Pharmacy Technology**
Harvey Whitney Books Company
PO Box 42696
Cincinnati, OH 45242-696

513-793-3555
877-742-7631
Fax: 513-793-3600
E-Mail: customerserv@jpharmtechnol.com
Home Page: www.jpharmtechnol.com

Harvey Whitney, Publisher/Editor
Eugene Sorkin, Associate Editorial
Ann Brandewiede, Circulation Manager

Latest information on drugs, for health professionals. Topics covered include new drug profiles, education and training, legal dilemmas, drug distribution, products and equipment and continuing education.
Cost: $122.00
Circulation: 1000
ISSN: 8755-1225

6365 **Journal of Surfactants and Detergents**
American Oil Chemists' Society
2710 S Boulder
Urbana, IL 61802-6996

217-359-2344
Fax: 217-351-8091
E-Mail: general@aocs.org
Home Page: www.aocs.org
Social Media: Facebook, Twitter, LinkedIn, Blog

Jody Schonfeld, Publications Director
Pam Landman, Journals Coordinator
Kimmy Farris, Production Editor

Dedicated to the practical and theoretical aspects of oleochemical and petrochemical surfactants, soaps and detergents. This growing scientific journal publishes peer-reviewed research papers, and reviews related to surfactants and detergents technologies.
Cost: $457.00
Frequency: Quarterly
Founded in 1998

6366 **Journal of the American Oil Chemists' Society**
American Oil Chemists' Society
2710 S Boulder
Urbana, IL 61802-6966

217-359-2344
Fax: 217-351-8091
E-Mail: general@aocs.org
Home Page: www.aocs.org
Social Media: Facebook, Twitter, LinkedIn, Blog

Jodey Schonfeld, Publications Director
Pam Landman, Journals Coordinator
Kimmy Farris, Production Editor

The leading source for technical papers related to the fats and oils industries. A peer-reviewed journal devoted to fundamental and practical research, production, processing, packaging and distribution in the growing field of fats, oils, proteins and other related substances.
Cost: $619.00
Frequency: Monthly
Founded in 1947

6367 **Journal of the American Pharmacists Association**
American Pharmacists Association
2215 Constitution Ave NW
Washington, DC 20037-2985

202-628-4410
800-237-2742
Fax: 202-783-2351
Home Page: www.pharmacist.com
Social Media: Facebook, Twitter, YouTube

L Michael Posey, Editor
L Douglas Reid, Editor-In-Chief

The official peer-reviewed journal of APhA, provides information on pharmaceutical care, drug therapy, diseases and other health issues, trends in pharmacy practice and therapeutics, informed opinion, and original research.
ISSN: 1544-3191

6368 Lipids
American Oil Chemists' Society
2710 S Boulder
Urbana, IL 61802-6996
217-359-2344
Fax: 217-351-8091
E-Mail: general@aocs.org
Home Page: www.aocs.org
Social Media: Facebook, Twitter, LinkedIn, Blog

Jody Schonfeld, Publications Director
Pam Landman, Journals Coordinator
Kimmy Farris, Production Editor

Scientific journal features full-length original research articles, short communications, methods papers and review articles on timely topics. All papers are meticulously peer-reviewed and edited by some of the foremost experts in their respective fields.
Cost: $461.00
Frequency: Monthly
Founded in 1966

6369 MPMN: Medical Product Manufacturing News
UBM Canon
2901 28th St
Ste. 100
Santa Monica, CA 90045
310-445-4200
Fax: 310-445-4299
E-Mail: john.bethune@cancom.com
Home Page: www.devicelink.com
Social Media: Twitter

Shana Leonard, Editor in Chief
Bob Michaels, Managing Editor

A product tabloid magazine that provides information on the new products and services available to medical device manufacturers.
Frequency: 10x/yr

6370 Med Ad News
Canon Communicaitons Pharmaceutical Media Group
828A Newtown Yardley Road
Newtown, PA 18940
215-944-9800
Fax: 215-867-0053
E-Mail: sandra.baker@cancom.com
Home Page: www.pharmalive.com

Christiane Truelove, Editor

Provides extensive coverage and incisive analyses of issues, events, trends and strategies shaping pharmaceutical business, marketing and sales.
Frequency: Monthly

6371 Modern Drug Discovery
American Chemical Society
1155 16th St Nw
16th Street NW
Washington, DC 20036-4892
202-872-4600
800-227-5558
Fax: 202-872-4615
E-Mail: service@acs.org
Home Page: www.acs.org

Madeleine Jacobs, CEO/Executive Director

Reports matters of interest to scientists and other professionals working in the field of drug discovery.
Frequency: Monthly

6372 Monitor
Association of Clinical Research Professionals
1012 14th Street NW
Suite 108
Washington, DC 20006
202-737-8100
Fax: 202-737-8101
E-Mail: acrp@associationhq.com
Home Page: www.acrpnet.org

Sharada Gilkey, Editor-in-Chief

Features peer-reviewed articles, columns, and home study.
Frequency: Quarterly

6373 Nutrition in Clinical Practice
Amer. Society for Parenteral & Enteral Nutrition
8630 Fenton Street
Suite 412
Silver Spring, MD 20910
301-587-6315
800-727-4567
Fax: 301-587-2365
E-Mail: aspen@nutr.org
Home Page: www.nutritioncare.org
Social Media: Facebook, Twitter

Bridget Hollick, Managing Editor

This compliments the Journal of Parenteral and Enteral Nutrition with practical information and advice. It provides peer-reviewed clinical studies, reviews, techniques and procedures, teaching cases, clinical observations, and nutrition news. Included as benefits of membership is ASPEN.
Cost: $45.00
Frequency: Bi-Monthly
ISSN: 0884-5336

6374 PDA Journal of Pharmaceutical Science and Technology
Parenteral Drug Association
1894 Preston White Drive
Reston, VA 20191-5433
703-620-6390
Fax: 703-476-0904
E-Mail: infoQnpcnow.com
Home Page: www.npcnow.org

Lee Kirsch, Editor

One of the most relevant and outstanding peer-reviewed scientific and technical papers in the pharmaceutical/biopharmaceutical industry. The Journal is distributed to members as a membership benefit.
Frequency: Bi-Monthly

6375 Pharmaceutical & Medical Packaging News
Canon Communications
11444 W Olympic Blvd
Suite 900
Los Angeles, CA 90064-1555
310-445-4200
Fax: 310-445-4299
E-Mail: feedback@cancom.com
Home Page: www.pmpnews.com

Charlie McCurdy, President
Daphne Allen, Editor
Justine Hamilton, Marketing Director
Peter Manfre, Account Executive

Information and news on events, new technology, industry trends, regulatory matters, and health care trade associations for professionals involved in the pharmaceutical and medical product packaging industry.
Cost: $150.00
Frequency: Monthly
Circulation: 20,000
ISSN: 1081-5481
Founded in 1978

6376 Pharmaceutical Engineering
Int'l Society for Pharmaceutical Engineering
3109 W Dr Martin Luther King Jr Boulevard
Suite 250
Tampa, FL 33607
813-960-2105
Fax: 813-264-2816
E-Mail: ask@ispe.org
Home Page: www.ispe.org

Gloria N Hall, Editor & Director of Publications
Lynda Goldbach, Publications Manager
Amy Lecceardone, Publications Coordinator
Valerie Adams, Advertising Sales Coordinator

Journal is published bi-monthly for members only and is considered by ISPE members to be the number one member benefit. Feature articles provide practical application and specification information on the design, construction, supervision and maintenance of process equipment, plant systems, instrumentation and facilities.
Frequency: Bi-monthly
Circulation: 2000

6377 Pharmaceutical Executive
Advanstar Communications
131 W 1st St
Duluth, MN 55802-2065
218-740-7200
800-598-6008
Fax: 218-723-9537
E-Mail: info@advanstar.com
Home Page: www.advanstar.com

Kent Akervik, Manager
Kim Brown, Producation Manager

Publication designed to meet the diverse management and marketing needs of professionals in the pharmaceutical industry worldwide. Editorial provides useful information on marketing, sales and promotion, as well as legal and regulatory issues.
Cost: $70.00
Frequency: Monthly
Circulation: 16237
ISSN: 0279-6570
Founded in 1987
Mailing list available for rent

6378 Pharmaceutical Formulation & Quality
Carpe Diem Communications
208 Floral Vale Boulevard
Yardley, PA 19067
215-860-7800
Fax: 215-860-7900
E-Mail: pharmaeditor@carpediemcomm.com
Home Page: www.pharmaquality.com

Rachel Burley, Publisher
Lisa Dionne, Editorial Director
Paul Juestrich, Creative Director
Karen Devlin, Production Manager

A dynamic magazine written to keep the pharmaceutical and related industries informed about the very latest technologies, techniques and regulations affecting product development and formulation. PFQ's coverage extends throughout the full product lifecycle, from initial development through clinical trials and scale up top manufacturing, focusing on current issues in the competitive business of producing pharmaceuticals and biopharmaceuticals.
Cost: $90.00
100 Pages
Circulation: 20000
ISSN: 1092-7514
Founded in 1998
Mailing list available for rent: 20000 names at $185 per M
Printed in 4 colors on glossy stock

6379 Pharmaceutical Processing
Reed Business Information

100 Enterprise drive
Suite 600
Rockaway, NJ 07866-912

973-920-7000
800-222-0289
Fax: 973-920-7531
Home Page: www.reedbusiness.com

Tim Canny, Publisher
Mike Auerbach, Editor
R Reed, Owner

Contents include news on new products/equipment/services, case history and application articles focusing on equipment, instrumentation, process systems, packaging, validation and outsourcing services offered to the pharmaceutical marketplace.
Frequency: Monthly
Circulation: 31075
Founded in 1984

6380 **Pharmaceutical Research**
Plenum Publishing Corporation
233 Spring St
New York, NY 10013-1522

212-242-1490
Fax: 212-807-1047
E-Mail: info@plenum.com
Home Page: www.plenum.com

Wolfgang Sadee, Editor

Research reports and summaries of the latest in development of certain drugs and pharmaceuticals.
Cost: $49.95
Frequency: Monthly
Founded in 1998

6381 **Pharmaceutical Technology Magazine**
Advanstar Communications
485 Route One South
Building F, First Floor
Iselin, NJ 08830

732-596-0276
Fax: 732-596-0005
E-Mail: mtracey@advanstar.com
Home Page: www.pharmtech.com

Mike Tracey, Publisher
Douglas McCormick, Editor in Chief
Paul Milazzo, Director of Sales
Tria Deibert, Marketing Director

Provides authoritative and timely information covering all aspects of conventional and biotech pharmaceutical manufacturing including: applied research and development, drug delivery, solid dosage, manufacturing machinery and equipment, information technologies, contract services, biotechnology trends, and regulatory issues.
Frequency: Monthly
Circulation: 33691
Founded in 1987

6382 **Pharmacy Times**
Romaine Pierson Publishers
666 Plainsboro Rd
Plainsboro, NJ 08536

609-716-7777
Fax: 609-716-4747
E-Mail: cms@skainfo.com
Home Page: www.pharmacytimes.com
Social Media: Facebook, Twitter, LinkedIn, YouTube

Emilie McCardell, Editor-In-Chief
Cam Bishop, CEO
James Granato, Publisher
James Marshal, Production Director
Margaret P. Roeske, Associate Editor

News, analysis and trends in the pharmaceutical business.
Cost: $65.00
Frequency: Monthly
Circulation: 174,104
Founded in 1897

6383 **Pharmacy West**
Western Communications
Po Box 6020
Bend, OR 97708-6020

541-382-1811
Fax: 541-385-5802

Gordon Black, President

Distributed to pharmacies in the thirteen western states.
Cost: $18.00
Frequency: Monthly

6384 **Profile of Pharmacy Faculty**
American Association of Colleges of Pharmacy
1727 King St
Alexandria, VA 22314-2700

703-739-2330
Fax: 703-836-8982
Home Page: www.aacp.org

Lucinda Maine, Executive VP
Kenneth W Miller, Senior VP
Daniel J Cassidy, COO

Provides statistics describing faculty at U.S. colleges and schools of pharmacy including a summary of the demographics, teaching discipline, rank, highest degree earned, tenure status, type of appointment, and salary of over 3,000 full time faculty members. Updated annually.
Cost: $25.00

6385 **Scrip Magazine**
1775 Broadway
Suite 511
New York, NY 10019

212-262-8230
Fax: 212-262-8234
E-Mail: chonour@ThetaReports.com

An in-depth view of the issues and challenges facing all sectors of the pharmaceutical industry worldwide. Analytical features are written by pharmaceutical experts and opinion leaders as well as specialist journalists.
Frequency: Monthly

6386 **The Consultant Pharmacist**
American Society of Consultant Pharmacists
1321 Duke St
Suite 120
Alexandria, VA 22314-3563

703-739-1300
800-355-2727
Fax: 703-739-1321
E-Mail: info@ascp.com
Home Page: www.ascp.com
Social Media: Facebook, Twitter, LinkedIn, YouTube, Blogs

Patti Thompson, Production Manager
Marlene Bloom, Editor
Debbie Furman, Circulation

Official peer reviewed journal of the American Society of Consultant Pharmacists. Editorial deals with geriatric pharmacotherapy.
Cost: $50.00
6m Members
76 Pages
Circulation: 13000
Founded in 1982
Printed in 4 colors on glossy stock

6387 **Update Magazine**
Food & Drug Law Institute
1155 15th Street NW
Suite 800
Washington, DC 20005

202-371-1420
800-956-6293
Fax: 202-371-0649
E-Mail: comments@fdli.org
Home Page: www.fdli.org
Social Media: Facebook, Twitter, LinkedIn

Michael D. Levin-Epstein, Vice President, Publications
Erin M Jones, Membership and Marketing
Susan C Winckler, President & CEO

Update brings you the latest news from FDLI and the industry, featuring viewpoints on trends, artilces on topics of regulatory concern, changes at the FDA, news about FDLI activities, and recurring columns about current events in the industry. Free to individuals within FDLI member organizations.
Cost: $100.00
Frequency: Bimonthly

Trade Shows

6388 **AACP Annual Meeting and Seminars**
American Association of Colleges of Pharmacy
1727 King Street
Alexandria, VA 22314

703-739-2330
Fax: 703-836-8982
Home Page: www.aacp.org

Lucinda L Maine, Executive VP
Kenneth W Miller, Senior VP
Daniel J Cassidy, COO

A chance to learn and exchange ideas on pharmacy education and recent innovations in health care.
Frequency: July

6389 **AACP Institute**
American Association of Colleges of Pharmacy
1727 King Street
Alexandria, VA 22314

703-739-2330
Fax: 703-836-8982
Home Page: www.aacp.org

Lucinda L Maine, Executive VP
Kenneth W Miller, Senior VP
Daniel J Cassidy, COO
Frequency: May

6390 **AAPS Annual Meeting & Expo**
American AssociationOf Pharmaceutical Scientists
2107 Wilson Boulevard
Suite 700
Arlington, VA 22201-3042

703-243-2800
Fax: 703-243-9650
E-Mail: aaps@aaps.org
Home Page: www.aaps.org

John Lisack, Executive Director
Maureen Downs, Director Finance

925 booths of raw materials, supplies and equipment, research and contract service labs, computer software, packaging and more.
Frequency: Annual November
Mailing list available for rent

6391 **AAPT Annual Convention**
American Association of Pharmacy Technicians

PO Box 1447
Greensboro, NC 27402

877-368-4771
Fax: 336-333-9068
E-Mail: aapt@pharmacytechnician.com
Home Page: www.pharmacytechnician.com

Sandra Covington, President
Susan Jeffery, VP

Education programs and services to help technicians update their skills to keep pace with changes in the pharmacy services.
Frequency: August

6392 **ACLA Annual Meeting**
American Clinical Laboratory Association
1250 H Street NW
Suite 880
Washington, DC 20005

202-637-9466
Fax: 202-637-2050
E-Mail: info@clinical-labs.org
Home Page: www.clinical-labs.org

Aan Mertz, President
JoAnne Glisson, VP
Jason DuBois, VP of Govt. Relations
Francesca O'Reilly, VP of Govt. Affairs

Dedicated to providing the latest information for clinical laboratories.
Frequency: January
Founded in 1971

6393 **ACMP Conference**
Academy of Managed Care Pharmacy
100 N Pitt Street
Suite 400
Alexandria, VA 22314-3134

703-683-8416
800-827-2627
Fax: 703-683-8417
E-Mail: sadres@amcp.org
Home Page: www.amcp.org
Social Media: Facebook, Twitter, LinkedIn

Aimee O'Conner, Assistant Director

Offers an exciting lineup of speakers, workshops, and topical sessions designed to meet the challenges of today's pharmacist practicing in a dynamic and constantly evolving managed care environment.
Frequency: October

6394 **APHA Annual Meeting & Exposition**
American Public Health Association
800 I Street NW
Washington, DC 20001-3710

202-777-2742
Fax: 202-777-2534
E-Mail: diane.lentini@apha.org
Home Page: www.apha.org

Diane Lentini, Meetings Manager
Gene Lutz, President
Georges C Benjamin, Executive Director
Jose F Cordero, Member
Louise A Anderson, Director Operations

The premier platform to share successes and failures, discover exceptional best practices and learn from expert colleagues and the latest reasearch in the field.
13000 Attendees
Frequency: November

6395 **ASHP Summer Meeting**
American Society of Health-System Pharmacists
7272 Wisconsin Avenue
Bethesda, MD 20814-4836

301-657-3000
866-279-0681
Fax: 301-664-8857
E-Mail: info@ascp.com
Home Page: www.ascp.com

Janet A Silvester R.Ph.,MBA, President

Offers a variety of programming, and delivers expertise on subject areas that are crucial to advancing a professional practice. Series programming, learning communities, and updates on hot topics, combined with exhibits and a variety of networking opportunities.
Frequency: June

6396 **ASPL Developments in Pharmacy Law Seminar**
American Society for Pharmacy Law
1224 Centre W
Suite 400B
Springfield, IL 62704

217-391-0219
Fax: 217-793-0041
Home Page: www.aspl.org

Melissa Madigan, President
Francis B Paulumbo, Director
Pamela Tolson, CAE, Executive Director
William Fassett, Treasurer

An annual highlight with nationally renowned speakers and panelists discussing issues pertaining to pharmacy law. This seminar has evolved into an excellent educational opportunity for practicing pharmacists, attorneys, and academicians with the opportunity to gain both pharmacy and legal continuing education credits.
Frequency: Annual

6397 **Academy of Pharmaceutical Research and Science Convention**
American Pharmaceutical Association
2215 Constitution Avenue NW
Washington, DC 20037

202-429-7524
800-237-2742
Fax: 202-628-0443
Home Page: www.aphanet.org

Windy K Christner, Meetings/Expositions

Main exhibits, pharmaceutical equipment supplies and services.
Frequency: Annual

6398 **American Association of College Pharmacies**
1727 King Street
Alexandria, VA 22314

703-739-2330
Fax: 703-836-8982
Home Page: www.aacp.org

Lucinda L Maine, Executive VP
Kenneth W Miller, Senior VP
Daniel J Cassidy, COO

Educational association representing pharmacy scientists, educators and administrators.
2.3M Attendees
Frequency: July

6399 **American College of Medical Quality Annual Meeting**
American College of Medical Quality
4334 Montgomery Avenue
Suite B
Bethesda, MD 20814

301-913-9149
800-924-2149
Fax: 301-656-0989
E-Mail: acmq@aol.com
Home Page: www.acmq.org
Social Media: Facebook, Twitter, LinkedIn

Alan Krumholz, MD, President
James D. Cross, President-elect
Andrew Jerdonek, Executive Director
Donald Casey, Jr MD, Treasurer

Annual show and 10-20 exhibits of computer hardware and software, pharmaceuticals, medical publications and related equipment, supplies and services.
150 Attendees
Founded in 1973

6400 **American Pharmacists Annual Meeting & Expo**
American Pharmacists Association
2215 Constitution Avenue, NW
Washington, DC 20037

202-429-7593
800-237-2742
Fax: 203-737-3211
E-Mail: lmace@aphanet.org
Home Page: www.aphameeting.org

Laura Larson, Exposition & Exchange Information
Todd McDonald, Meeting Schedule Information
Lindsey Mace, General Conference Assistant
Kristen Binaso, Sponsorship Coordinator
Stacy Berkowitz, Educational Coordinator

The APhA Annual Meeting and Exposition provides information on the latest trends and best practices in pharmacy, while providing attendees the opportunity to share experiences and ideas with 7,000 pharmacy professionals from every practice setting; chain, independent, hospital, federal, long-term care, nuclear, and more.
Frequency: Annual/Spring

6401 **Annual NCPA Convention & Trade Exposition**
National Community Pharmacists Associations
100 Daingerfield Road
Alexandria, VA 22314

703-683-8200
800-544-7447
Fax: 703-683-3619
E-Mail: info@ncpanet.com
Home Page: www.ncpanet.org

Litsa Deck, Director Convention/Trade Expos

Workshops and education programs pretaining to Pharmacy industry.
Frequency: October
Mailing list available for rent

6402 **Annual North American Conference and European Annual Conference**
Association of Clinical Research Professionals
1012 14th Street NW
Suite 108
Washington, DC 20006

202-737-8100
Fax: 202-737-8101
E-Mail: acrp@associationhq.com
Home Page: www.acrpnet.org

Robin Newman, Vice Chair
Thomas L Adams, CAE, President/CEO
Larry J Medley, CAE, Director Finance
Alan Armstrong, Director Marketing/COO

The world's leading conferences for clinical research professionals, presenting diverse educational opportunities and face-to-face interactions with industry experts.
Frequency: April, September

6403 **DCAT Western Education Conference**
Drug, Chemical & Associated Technologies
1 Washington Boulevard
Suite 7
Robbinsville, NJ 08691

609-448-1000
800-640-3228
Fax: 609-448-1944
E-Mail: info@dcat.org

Home Page: www.dcat.org
Social Media: Facebook, LinkedIn

Brooke DiGiuseppe, Meeting Services
Margaret Timony, Senior Manager
Jacklyn Vitelli, Deputy Executive Director
Jeanne Motola, Administrative Assistant

Gain important insights into issues and trends that will affect the future of the nutrition and health industry. Participate in discussion on key business issues with industry experts.
Frequency: April

6404 **DIA Annual Meeting**
Drug Information Association
800 Enterprise Road
Suite 200
Horsham, PA 19044-3595

215-442-6100
Fax: 215-442-6199
E-Mail: dia@diahome.org
Home Page: www.diahome.org

Paul Pomerantz BA MBA, Worldwide Executive Director
Lisa Zoks BA, Worldwide Dir Mktg/Communications

6405 **Distribution & Logistics Conference**
National Association of Chain Drug Stores
413 N Lee Street
PO Box 1417 D-49
Alexandria, VA 22313-1480

703-549-3001
Fax: 703-836-4869
Home Page: www.nacds.org
Social Media: Facebook, Twitter, LinkedIn, YouTube

Greg Wasson, Chairman
Bob Narveson, Vice Chairman
John Standley, Treasurer

This unique conference explores and evaluates current systems and emerging technologies, and helps retailers and suppliers forge stronger links through supply chain management. The exhibit hall allows leading industry consultants and vendors to demonstrate their products and services.
Frequency: March

6406 **Distribution Management Conference & Expo**
Healthcare Distribution Management Association
900 N Glebe Road
Suite 1000
Arlington, VA 22203

703-787-0000
Fax: 703-935-3200
E-Mail: lburke@hdmanet.org
Home Page: www.healthcaredistribution.org

John Grey, President and CEO
Ann Bittman, EVP and COO
Patrick Kelly, SVP

Provides the latest information on the most important topics affecting healthcare distribution.
Frequency: June

6407 **FDLI & FDA Annual Conference**
Food and Drug Law Institute
1155 15th Street NW
Suite 800
Washington, DC 20005

202-371-1420
800-956-6293
Fax: 202-371-0649
E-Mail: comments@fdli.org
Home Page: www.fdli.org

Susan C. Winckler, President & CEO
Iris V. Stratton CPA, VP Finance & Administration
Michael Sprott, Membership Manager

Bringing together high-ranking officials from the food and drug industry together with top executives.
550+ Members
Founded in 1949

6408 **HDMA Annual Meeting**
Healthcare Distribution Management Association
900 N Glebe Road
Suite 1000
Arlington, VA 22203

703-787-0000
Fax: 703-935-3200
E-Mail: lburke@hdmanet.org
Home Page: www.healthcaredistribution.org

John Grey, President and CEO
Ann Bittman, EVP and COO
Patrick Kelly, SVP

Provides a unique opportunity for senior-level retailer and supplier member executives to interact and discuss strategic issues.
Frequency: October

6409 **IPC Annual Meeting**
Independent Pharmacy Cooperative
1550 Columbus Street
Sun Prairie, WI 53590

608-259-9556
800-755-1531
Fax: 800-274-5525
E-Mail: staff@ipcrx.com
Home Page: www.ipcrx.com

Mike Flint, President/CEO
Gary Helgerson, COO
Chuck Benjamin, CFO

A venue to provide independent pharmacies vital information to maximize their store's profitability
Frequency: July

6410 **ISPE Annual Meeting**
Int'l Society for Pharmaceutical Engineering
3109 W Dr. Martin Luther King Jr Boulevard
Suite 250
Tampa, FL 33607

813-960-2105
Fax: 813-264-2816
E-Mail: ask@ispe.org
Home Page: www.ispe.org

Education and training on topics pretaining to the pharmaceutical manufacturing industry.
Frequency: Annual

6411 **Midyear Industry & Technology Issues Conference**
American Society for Automation in Pharmacy
492 Norristown Road
Suite 160
Blue Bell, PA 19422

610-825-7783
Fax: 310-825-7641
Home Page: www.asapnet.org

WA Lockwood, Executive Director

Learn about the industry and technology issues facing the pharmacy market today.
Frequency: June

6412 **NABP's Annual Meeting**
National Association of Boards of Pharmacy
700 Busse Highway
Park Ridge, IL 60068

847-698-6227
800-774-6227
Fax: 847-698-0124
E-Mail: custserv@nabp.net
Home Page: www.nabp.net

Carmen A Catizone, Executive Director/Secretary

Building regulatory foundation for patients safety.
Frequency: May

6413 **NABP's Fall Educational Conference**
National Association of Boards of Pharmacy
700 Busse Highway
Park Ridge, IL 60068

847-698-6227
800-774-6227
Fax: 847-698-0124
E-Mail: custserv@nabp.net
Home Page: www.nabp.net

Malcom Broussard, Chairperson
Michael Burlson, President
Joseph Adams, Treasurer
Frequency: December

6414 **NACDS Annual Meeting**
National Association of Chain Drug Stores
413 N Lee Street
Alexandria, VA 22314

703-549-3001
Fax: 703-836-4869
Home Page: www.nacds.org

Jodi Witmer, Executive Director
Terry Arth, VP Meetings/International Programs
Larry Lotridge, VP Conference Exhibits

This meeting provides a stage to meet and discuss strategic issues with key trading partners: Strategic Exchange Appointments in which to do business, participants and sponsors from dozens of relevant companies.
1M Attendees
Frequency: April

6415 **NCPA Annual Conference on National Legislation and Government Affairs**
National Community Pharmacists Associations
100 Daingerfield Road
Alexandria, VA 22314

703-683-8200
800-544-7447
Fax: 703-683-3619
E-Mail: info@ncpanet.com
Home Page: www.ncpanet.org

Litsa Deck, Director Convention/Trade Expos

An opportunity to be an insider to discuss community pharmacy issues on Capitol Hill with the people that can make things happen. It will enhance your understanding of the political process and the many legislative issues that will have a dramatic impact on the way you deliver health care in the coming years.
Frequency: April

6416 **NCPA Annual Meeting**
National Council of State Pharmacy Association
5501 Patterson Avenue
Suite 200
Richmond, VA 23226

804-285-4145
Fax: 804-285-4227
E-Mail: becky@ncspae.org
Home Page: www.ncspae.org

Rebecca P Snead, Executive Vice President
Brad Hall, Executive Director

Offers cutting-edge training for professionals from every facet of the pharmacy industry. Learn the latest about prescription drugs, natural products, and over-the-counter remedies. Discover new products and services from the industry's leading manufacturers, and gain knowledge and insights to better aid patients and advance your career.
Frequency: October

6417 **NCPDP's Annual Conference**
National Council for Prescription Drug Programs
9240 E Raintree Drive
Scottsdale, AZ 85260-7518
480-477-1000
Fax: 480-767-1042
E-Mail: ncpdp@ncpdp.org
Home Page: www.ncpdp.org

Beth Fagan, Meeting Planning
Lee Ann Stember, President

Topic will be Building New Technologies. Offers educational sessions, a trade show, kenote speakers and more.
Frequency: March

6418 **National Clinical Issues Forum: Metabolic Syndrome**
American Pharmaceutical Association Foundation
2215 Constitution Avenue NW
Washington, DC 20037
202-297-7524
800-237-APHA
Fax: 202-429-6300
E-Mail: info@aphafoundation.org
Home Page: www.aphafoundation.org

Carol Bugdalski-Stutrud, Director
Carl Emswiller, Director
Hazel Pipkin, VP
Marie Michnich, Director Health Policy Program
Michael Stewart, Director Public Relations

To provide an opportunity for the exchange of information between leading clinical pharmacists from across the U.S. who are providing innovative patient care services for people afflicted with the co-morbidities of diabetes, hypertension and hyperlipidemia.
Frequency: May

6419 **National Community Pharmacists Association Convention and Exhibition**
National Community Pharmacists Association
100 Daingerfield Road
Alexandria, VA 22314-2833
703-683-8200
800-544-7447
Fax: 703-683-3619
E-Mail: info@ncpanet.com
Home Page: www.ncpanet.org

Litsa Deck, Director Convention/Meetings
Faith James, Coordinator Convention/Meetings
Deleisa Johnson, VP Public Relations

Annual show of 450 exhibitors of pharmaceutical and related equipment, supplies and services.
Frequency: October, Florida

6420 **National Conference on Advances in Perinatal and Pediatric Nutrition**
Amer. Society for Parenteral & Enteral Nutrition
8630 Fenton Street
Suite 412
Silver Spring, MD 20910
301-587-6315
800-727-4567
Fax: 301-587-2365
E-Mail: aspen@nutr.org
Home Page: www.nutritioncare.org
Social Media: Facebook, Twitter

Marion F Winkler, President
Vincent W Vanek, VP
Robin Kriegel, CAE, Executive Director
Joanne Kieffer, Director Finance

The purpose of the conference is to increase knowledge and awareness of the nutritional requirements of these special need patients. Has been planned for dieticians, nurses, obstetricians, neonatologiests, pediatricians, pediatric gastroenterologists, pharmacists, and other health care professionals involved in the care of high risk pregnant mothers, premature infants, and pediatric patients.
Frequency: July

6421 **RX Expo: An Educational Forum and Buying Show**
National Community Pharmacists Association
100 Daingerfield Road
Alexandria, VA 22314-2833
703-683-8200
800-544-7447
Fax: 703-683-3619
E-Mail: info@ncpanet.com
Home Page: www.ncpanet.org

Stephen Giroux PD, President
Bruce Roberts RPh, Executive VP/CEO

Annual show and exhibits of general gifts, sundries and seasonal items, over the counter products, health and beauty aids, electronic products, prescription drug products, personal care products, home health care products, IV products and related products.
1700 Attendees

6422 **Senior Care Pharmacy: ASCP's Annual Meeting**
American Society of Consultant Pharmacists
1321 Duke Street
Alexandria, VA 22314-3563
703-739-1300
800-355-2727
Fax: 703-739-1321
E-Mail: info@ascp.com
Home Page: www.ascp.com

Jackie Hajji, Director Meetings/Conventions

Annual meeting of 300 exhibitors of pharmaceuticals, drug distribution systems, packaging equipment, computers, durable medical equipment and medical supplies.
2000 Attendees
Frequency: November
Founded in 1969

6423 **The Consultant Pharmacist Conference and Exhibition**
American Society of Consultant Pharmacists
1321 Duke St
Suite 120
Alexandria, VA 22314-3563
703-739-1300
800-355-2727
Fax: 703-739-1321
E-Mail: info@ascp.com
Home Page: www.ascp.com
Social Media: Facebook, Twitter, LinkedIn, YouTube, Blogs

Patti Thompson, Production Manager
Marlene Bloom, Editor
Debbie Furman, Circulation

Learn the most up-to-date clinical, business, and regulatory information; discover the latest pharmacy and health information technologies; and establish the professional contacts that are critical for today's consultant and senior care pharmacy practitioners, managers, and business owners.
6m Members
1200 Attendees
Founded in 1982

6424 **USP Annual Scientific Meeting**
United States Pharmacopeial Convention
12601 Twinbrook Parkway
Rockville, MD 20852-1790
301-810-0667
800-227-8772
Fax: 301-816-8148
E-Mail: support@usp.org
Home Page: www.usp.org

Anju K Malhotra, Manager Conferences/Meetings
Roger Williams, Executive Director

Open to the public and serves as an interactive forum where USP and its stakeholders can discuss new direction and standards that affect the pharmaceutical industry. The meeting provides attendees an opportunity to better understand the scope of USP's scientific work and provide input on key standards-setting issues.
Frequency: September

6425 **Western Section Meeting of the Triological Society**
Triological Society
555 N 30th Street
Omaha, NE 68131-2136
402-346-5500
Fax: 402-346-5300
E-Mail: info@triological.org
Home Page: www.triological.org

I Kaufman Arenberg, MD, Executive Director

Annual show of 30 exhibitors of medical services and supplies related to Otolaryngology.
152 Attendees
Frequency: May

Directories & Databases

6426 **American Drug Index**
Lippincott Williams & Wilkins
16522 Hunters Green Pkwy
PO Box 1600
Hagerstown, MD 21740
301-223-2300
800-638-3030
Fax: 301-223-2400
Home Page: www.lww.com
Social Media: Facebook, Twitter

Norman Billups, Editor
Shirley Billups, Editor

Contains more than 22,000 entries. Practical features include: alphabetically listed drug names, extensive cross-indexing, complete information on the distributor's brand name, manufacturer, generic and/or chemical names, chemical strength and much more useful information. Electronic version available.
Cost: $69.95
1088 Pages
Frequency: Annual, Hardcover
ISBN: 1-574391-33-X

6427 **Annual Meeting & Showcase**
Academy of Managed Care Pharmacy
100 N Pitt St
Suite 400
Alexandria, VA 22314-3141
703-683-8416
800-827-2627
Fax: 703-683-8417
E-Mail: sandres@amcp.org
Home Page: www.amcp.org
Social Media: Facebook, Twitter, LinkedIn

Douglas Burgoyne, President
Robert Gregory, Treasurer

Nationally reowned keynote speakers, new research presentations, achievement awards, competitions and Board inaugurations fill the

agenda for managed care pharmacy's premier event.
Frequency: April

6428 **CSO Directory**
Drug Information Association
800 Enterprise Road
Suite 200
Horsham, PA 19044-3595
215-442-6100
Fax: 215-442-6199
E-Mail: dia@diahome.org
Home Page: www.diahome.org
Paul Pomerantz BA MBA, Worldwide Executive Director
Lisa Zoks BA, Worlwide Dir Mktg/Communications
One of the industry's most respected and comprehensive reference guides, compiles company descriptions and contact information from hundreds of companies that provide services for every phase of the clinical trial and drug development process.

6429 **DCAT Digest and Directory of Membership**
Drug, Chemical & Associated Technologies
1 Washington Blvd
Suite 7
Robbinsville, NJ 08691-3162
609-448-1000
800-640-3228
Fax: 609-448-1944
E-Mail: info@dcat.org
Home Page: www.dcat.org
Social Media: Facebook, LinkedIn
Margaret Timony, Executive Director
Lynda M Doyle, Senior Manager
Jacklyn Vitelli, Deputy Executive Director
Jeanne Motola, Administrative Assistant
Keeping members in touch with their colleagues throughout the industry.

6430 **DIOGENES**
FOI Services
704 Quince Orchard Rd
Gaithersburg, MD 20878-1700
301-975-9400
Fax: 301-975-0702
E-Mail: infofoi@foiservices.com
Home Page: www.foiservices.com
John Carey, President
Marlene Bobka, Vice President of Services
This comprehensive database contains citations to more than 1 million unpublished US Food and Drug Administration regulatory documents covering prescription and over-the-counter drugs.
Founded in 1975

6431 **DRUGDEX System**
Thompson Micromedex
6200 South Syracuse Way
Suite 300
Greenwood Village, CO 80111-4740
303-679-9500
800-525-9083
Fax: 303-486-6464
Home Page: www.micromedex.com
Social Media: Facebook
This comprehensive database covers all aspects of drugs and their use, including investigational, FDA-approved, and OTC preparations.
Frequency: Full-text

6432 **DataStat**
NDCHealth
3975 Research Park Drive
Ann Arbor, MI 48108
734-994-0540
800-225-5632
Fax: 734-663-9084
E-Mail: mweindorf@datastat.com
Home Page: www.datastat.com
Marielle Weindorf, Senior Research Director
Ellen Johnson
Randolph Hutto, EVP Business Development
Charles W Miller, EVP Corporate Initiatives
This comprehensive database offers descriptions of drug interactions at the ingredient level for individual drugs and therapeutic classes of drugs.
Frequency: Full-text
Founded in 1967

6433 **Directory of Hospital Personnel**
Grey House Publishing
4919 Route 22
PO Box 56
Amenia, NY 12501
518-789-8700
800-562-2139
Fax: 845-373-6390
E-Mail: books@greyhouse.com
Home Page: www.greyhouse.com
Social Media: Facebook, Twitter
Richard Gottlieb, President
Leslie Mackenzie, Publisher
A Who's Who of the hospital universe that makes it easy to get in touch with over 10,000 key decision makers. Comprehensive data includes listing of US hospitals, detailed contact information, number of physicians and employees, teaching affiliations, accreditation and much more.
Cost: $325.00
2300 Pages
ISBN: 1-592372-86-4
Founded in 1981

6434 **Directory of Hospital Personnel - Online Database**
Grey House Publishing
4919 Route 22
PO Box 56
Amenia, NY 12501
518-789-8700
800-562-2139
Fax: 845-373-6390
E-Mail: gold@greyhouse.com
Home Page: http://gold.greyhouse.com
Social Media: Facebook, Twitter
Richard Gottlieb, President
Leslie Mackenzie, Publisher
The DHP Online Database is the best resource you can have at your fingertips when researching or marketing a product or service to the hospital market. A 'Who's Who' of the hospital universe, this database puts you in touch with over 140,000 key decision-makers at 5,800 hospitals nationwide.
Founded in 1981

6435 **Drug Store and HBC Chains**
Chain Store Guide
3922 Coconut Palm Dr
Tampa, FL 33619-1389
813-627-6700
800-778-9794
Fax: 813-627-7094
E-Mail: info@csgis.com
Home Page: www.csgis.com
Mike Jarvis, Publisher
Chris Leedy, Advertising Sales
Tap into the lucrative drug industry with profiles on more than 1,700 US and Canadian companies operating two or more retail drug stores, deep discount stores, health and beauty care (HBC) stores, cosmetic stores or vitamin stores that have industry sales of at least $250,000. This powerful database empowers you to sell and market your products successfully by reaching more than 8,300 key decision makers.
Cost: $335.00

6436 **Drug and Cosmetic Industry Catalog**
Advanstar Communications
One Park Avenue
New York, NY 10016
212-797-7631
Fax: 212-951-6793
E-Mail: info@advanstar.com
Home Page: www.advanstar.com
Eric Lisman, Executive VP
Over 1,000 manufacturers and suppliers of packaging equipment, private formulas and raw materials used in the drug and cosmetics industries are profiled.
Cost: $25.00
270 Pages
Frequency: Annual
Circulation: 4,000
Mailing list available for rent

6437 **FDC Reports: The NDA Pipeline**
FDC Reports
5550 Friendship Boulevard
Suite 1
Chevy Chase, MD 20815-7278
301-657-9830
Fax: 301-664-7238
E-Mail: fdc.customer.service@elsevier.com
Home Page: www.fdcreports.com
Karl Uhlendo, Executive Editor
Mike Squires, President
The NDA Pipeline is a searchable database available through the Web that contains up-to-date coverage of over 900 companies and more than 7,00 approval records. The NDA Pipeline tracks drug and biological product research, clinical trials and approvals. It also includes a comprehensive listing of products in research, descriptions of phases of development and licensing information and linked articles from The Pink Sheet and other FDC Reports publications.
900 Pages
Frequency: Annual
ISSN: 7012-8630
Founded in 1939

6438 **GAMP Good Practice Guide**
Int'l Society for Pharmaceutical Engineering
3109 W Dr. Martin Luther King Jr Boulevard
Suite 250
Tampa, FL 33607
813-960-2105
Fax: 813-264-2816
E-Mail: ask@ispe.org
Home Page: www.ispe.org
Provides new comprehensive guidance on meeting current regulatory expectations for compliant electronic records and signatures, which includes the need for record integrity, security, and availability throughout the required retention period. This is achieved by well documented, validated systems, and the application of appropriate operational controls.

6439 **ISPE Good Practice Guide**
Int'l Society for Pharmaceutical Engineering
3109 W Dr. Martin Luther King Jr Boulevard
Suite 250
Tampa, FL 33607
813-960-2105
Fax: 813-264-2816

E-Mail: ask@ispe.org
Home Page: www.ispe.org

Provides a standard methodology for use in testing the containment efficiency of solids handling systems used in the pharmaceutical industry under closely defined conditions. It covers the main factors that affect the test results for specific contained solids handling systems, including material handled, room environment, air quality, ventilation and operator technique.

6440 **Ident-A-Drug Reference**
Therapeutic Research
3120 W March Lane
PO Box 8190
Stockton, CA 95219-0190

209-472-2240
Fax: 209-472-2249
Home Page: www.pletter.com

Jeff Jellin, PharmD, Editor

It gives you all the drug identification information found on this web site for more than 30,000 entries.
Cost: $85.00
704 Pages
ISBN: 0-967613-65-5

6441 **InVitro Diagnostics Industry Directory**
CTB International Publishing
PO Box 218
Maplewood, NJ 07040-0218

973-966-0997
Fax: 973-966-0242
E-Mail: info@ctbintl.com
Home Page: www.ctbintl.com

Lists address, phone and fax number of invitro diagnostics companies, suppliers, distributors, regulatory agencies, professional societies and trade associations worldwide and contains over 2,300 entries worldwide-more than 1,200 contact names.
Cost: $277.00
ISBN: 1-887566-17-1
Printed in one color on matte stock

6442 **International Pharmaceutical Abstracts Database**
Thomson Scientific
1500 Spring Garden St
Philadelphia, PA 19130-4067

215-386-0100
800-336-4474
Fax: 215-386-2911
E-Mail: ts.info.na@thomson.com
Home Page: www.thomson.com

Robert C Cullen, President/CEO
Craig Soderstrom, VP Office of CEO
Kristen McCarthy, VP Marketing/Communications
James Smith, Chief Operating Officer

These reports offering the latest in the development of drugs overseas, clinical and inventigotional use, cosmetics and, alternative and herbal medicine. Reports on pharmacy practice are also included.
ISSN: 0020-8264

6443 **NABP Manual**
National Association of Boards of Pharmacy
700 Busse Highway
Park Ridge, IL 60068

847-698-6227
800-774-6227
Fax: 847-698-0124
E-Mail: custserv@nabp.net
Home Page: www.nabp.net

Malcom Broussard, Chairperson
Michael Burlson, President
Joseph Adams, Treasurer

Developed to be read in conjunction with state laws. It presents general information essential to all board of pharmacy members, and serves as a valuable reference for new board members. The manual is ideal for compiling and cross-referencing amendments and other records.
Cost: $25.00

6444 **Natural Medicines Comprehensive Database**
Therapeutic Research
PO Box 8190
Stockton, CA 95208-0190

209-472-2240
Fax: 209-472-2249
Home Page: www.pletter.com

Jeff Jellin, PharmD, Editor

Provides you with monographs on each natural ingredient plus updated helpful charts and tables.
Cost: $85.00
2000 Pages
ISBN: 0-967613-68-X

6445 **Pharma Industry Directory**
CTB International Publishing
PO Box 218
Maplewood, NJ 07040

973-966-0997
Fax: 973-966-0242
E-Mail: info@ctbintl.com
Home Page: www.ctbintl.com

This is divided into 4 sections. The first section contains a complete alphabetical listing of the names, addresses, and phone and fax numbers of over 1,300 companies. The other sections are alphabetical listings of the companies with tables identifying them as to the fields they are involved in. The last section is a business index.
Cost: $250.00
ISBN: 1-887566-21-X
Printed in one color on matte stock

6446 **Pharmaceutical News Index**
UMI/Data Courier
620 S 3rd Street
Suite 400
Louisville, KY 40202-2475

502-583-4111
800-626-2823
Fax: 502-589-5572

Contains the latest US and international information about pharmaceutical, cosmetics, medical devices, and related health industries.

6447 **Physicians' Desk Reference**
Thomson Medical Economics
5 Paragon Drive
Montvale, NJ 07645-1742

201-358-7500
800-442-6657
Fax: 201-573-8999
E-Mail: PDRbookstore@medec.com
Home Page: www.pdr.net

Thomas Eck, Marketing Manager

Physicians have turned to PDR for the latest word in prescription drugs for 57 years. Today, it is considered the standard prescription drug reference and can be found in virtually every phyician's office, hospital and pharmacy in the US.
Cost: $92.95
3,000 Pages
Frequency: Hardcover

6448 **Roster of Faculty and Professional Staff**
American Association of Colleges of Pharmacy
1727 King St
Suite 210
Alexandria, VA 22314-2700

703-739-2330
Fax: 703-836-8982
Home Page: www.aacp.org

Lucinda Maine, Executive VP
Kenneth W Miller, Senior VP
Daniel J Cassidy, COO

A directory of more than 5,000 full and part-time pharmacy faculty members including mailing and e-mail addresses, phone and fax numbers, degrees, and disciplines. Also included is valuable information about AACP such as officers, committee members, staff, and addresses and phone numbers for affiliated associations and corporations. $10 AACP Member.
Cost: $100.00
Frequency: November
Mailing list available for rent

Industry Web Sites

6449 **http://gold.greyhouse.com**
G.O.L.D Grey House OnLine Databases

Grey House Publishing's online database platform, GOLD, offers Quick Search, Keyword Search and Expert Search for most business sectors including drug, pharmaceutical and healthcare markets. The GOLD platform makes finding the information you need quick and easy - whether you're a novice searcher or an experienced database user. All of Grey House's directory products are available for subscription on the GOLD platform.

6450 **www.aacp.org**
American Association of Colleges of Pharmacy

National organization representing the interests of pharmaceutical education and educators. Comprising all 83 US pharmacy colleges and schools including more than 4,000 faculty, 36,000 student enrolled in professional programs and 3,600 individuals pursuing graduate study, AACP is committed to excellence in pharmaceutical education.

6451 **www.aaps.org**
American Association of Pharmaceutical Scientists

Aims to advance science through the open exchange of scientific knowledge, serve as an information resource and contribute to human health through pharmaceutical reseach and development.

6452 **www.accp.com**
American College of Clinical Pharmacy

Professional and scientific society that provides leadership, education, advocacy and resources enabling clinical pharmacists to achieve excellence in practice and research.

6453 **www.acrpnet.org**
Association of Clinical Research Professionals

Provides global leadership for the clinical research profession by promoting and advancing the highest ethical standards and practices.

6454 **www.aihp.org**
American Institute of the History of Pharmacy

Supplies information regarding pharmaceutical history and usage.

6455 **www.apha.org**
American Public Health Association

Brings together researchers, health service providers, administrators, teachers and other health workers in a unique, multidisciplinary environment of professional exchange, study and action on the effort to prevent disease and promote health.

6456 **www.asapnet.org**
American Society for Automation in Pharmacy
Is to assist its members in advancing the application of computer technology in the pharmacists role as caregiver and in the efficient operation and management of a pharmacy.

6457 **www.ashp.org**
American Society of Health-System Pharmacy
An association that brings together health-system pharmacists and addresses their concerns.

6458 **www.aspl.org**
American Society for Pharmacy Law
An organization of pharmacists and lawyers who are interested in the law as it applies to the pharmacy industry.

6459 **www.diahome.org**
Drug Information Association
Association for those interested in technical developments, supply, and production of drugs. Exchanges and disseminates information by continuing to provide a neutral forum, respecting and welcoming all participants and offering quality driven programming.

6460 **www.fdli.org**
Food and Drug Law Institute
Nonprofit educational organization dedicated to improving the understanding of the laws, regulations and policies affecting the food, drug, medical device and biologics industries. A neutral, non-partisan organization that does not lobby.

6461 **www.greyhouse.com**
Grey House Publishing
Authoritative reference directories for most business sectors including drug, pharmaceutical and healthcare markets. Users can search the online databases with varied search criteria allowing for custom searches by product category, geographic area, sales volume, keyword, subject and more. Full Grey House catalog and online ordering also available.

6462 **www.ipecamericas.org**
International Pharmaceutical Excipients Council
Members are companies with an interest in the otherwise inert chemicals used as vehicles for medicines. Federation of three independent regional industry associations headquartered in the US. Each association focuses its attention on the applicable law, regulations, science and business practices of its region. The three associations work together on excipient safety and public health issues, in connection with international trade matters, and to achieve harmonization of regulatory standards.

6463 **www.ncpanet.org**
National Community Pharmacists Association
Represents independent pharmacists, provides support for undergraduate pharmacy education.

6464 **www.npa.org**
National Pharmaceutical Alliance
Represents the interests of small pharmaceutical companies and allied industries.

6465 **www.nutritioncare.org**
American Soc. for Parenteral & Enteral Nutrition
Strives to be a conduit amoung those interested in Nutrition Support.

6466 **www.pda.org**
Parenteral Drug Association
Members are makers of parenteral (injectable) drugs and other pharmaceuticals, as well as suppliers, academia and regulatory bodies. Our mission is to advance the pharmaceutical and biopharmaceutical technology internationally by promoting scientifically sound and practical technical information and education for industry and regulatory issues.

6467 **www.pdr.net**
Thomson Medical Economics
Physicians have turned to PDR for the latest word on prescription drugs for 57 years. Today it is considered the standard prescription drug reference and can be found in virtually every phyician's office, hospital and pharmacy in the US.

6468 **www.pharmacist.com**
American Pharmacists Association
APhA was the first established national professional society of pharmacists, founded in 1852 as the American Pharamceutical Assocation. It is the largest assocation of pharamcists in the US, whose mission is to provide information, education, and advocacy to empower its members to improve medication use and advance patient care.

6469 **www.pharmacytechnician.com**
American Association of Pharmacy Technicians
Provides leadership and represents the interests of its members to the public as well as healthcare organizations. Promotes the safe, effectacious, and cost effective dispensing distribution and use of medications. Provides continuing education programs and services to help technicians update their skills to keep pace with changes in pharmacy services.

6470 **www.thompson.com**
Thompson Scientific and Healthcare
Professionals in business, government, law and academia have reliedon us for the most authorative, timely and practical guidance available.

6471 **www.usp.org**
United States Pharmacopeia
Helps to ensure that consumers recieve quality medicines by establishing state-of-the-art standards that pharmaceutical manufacturers must meet. We provide standards for more than 3,800 medicines, dietary supplements and other health care products.

Associations

6472 **Advanced Network & Services**
2600 South Road
Suite 44-193
Poughkeepsie, NY 12601

845-795-2090
Fax: 845-795-2180
E-Mail: contact@advanced.org
Home Page: www.advanced.org

Dr. James McGroddy, Chairman of the Board
Allan Weis, Founder/President/Managing Director
Kristin Mortensen, Secretary/Treasurer

A nonprofit corporation dedicated to advancing education by accelerating the use of computer networking applications and technology.
Mailing list available for rent

6473 **Advertising Specialty Institute**
4800 Street Rd
Langhorne, PA 19053-6698

215-953-4000
800-546-1350
Fax: 215-953-3045
E-Mail: info@asicentral.com
Home Page: www.asicentral.com
Social Media: Facebook, Twitter, LinkedIn, You tube

Timothy M Andrews, CEO
Susanne Curry, SVP Marketing

Advertising Specialty Institute provides distributors, suppliers and decorators in the advertising specialty industry with catalogs, information directories, newsletters, magazines, web sites and databases, and offers interactive e-commerce, marketing and selling tools.
26000 Members
Founded in 1950

6474 **Alliance for Public Technology**
919 18th St NW
Suite 900
Washington, DC 20006-5512

202-263-2970
Fax: 202-263-2960
Home Page: www.apt.org

Sylvia Rosenthal, Executive Director
Matthew Bennett, Policy Director

A nonprofit membership organization based in Washington, DC.

6475 **American Public Communications Council**
10302 Eaton Place
Suite 340
Fairfax, VA 20030

703-385-5300
800-868-2722
Fax: 703-739-1324
E-Mail: apcc@apcc.net
Home Page: www.apcc.net

Bruce Renard, State Assistant Director
Brad Benge, Additional Director
Michael Bright, At-Large Director
David Cotton, At-Large Director

Aims to protect and expand domestic and foreign markets for public communications and provide business opportunities for members.
Founded in 1988

6476 **American Registry for Internet Numbers**
3635 Concorde Parkway
Suite 200
Chantilly, VA 20151-1130

703-227-9840
Fax: 703-227-0676
E-Mail: hostmaster@arin.net
Home Page: www.arin.net
John Curran, Chairperson
Lee Howard, Treasurer
David Conrad, President

Manage the internet numbering resources for North America focused completely on serving our members and the Internet community at large.

6477 **American e-Commerce Association**
Home Page: www.aeaus.com

Computer training, e-commerce education, membership, recognition, endorsement, and evaluation services.

6478 **Association for the Advancement of Computing in Education**
PO Box 3728
Norfolk, VA 23514

757-623-7588
Fax: 703-997-8760
E-Mail: info@aace.org
Home Page: www.aace.org
International, educational and professional nonprofit organization dedicated to the advancement of the knowledge, theory and quality of learning and teaching at all levels with information technology. Encourages scholarly inquiry related to information technology and research results through publications, conferences, societies and chapters plus inter-organizational projects.

6479 **Association of Internet Researchers**
910 W. Van Buren St.
Suite 142
Chicago, IL 60607-3523

Home Page: www.aoir.org
Social Media: Facebook, Twitter
Lori Kendall, President
Jennifer Stromer-Galley, Vice-President
Michael Zimmer, Treasurer
Andrew Herman, Secretary

A learned society dedicated to the advancement of the transdisciplinary field of Internet Studies.

6480 **Business Marketing Association: Boston**
246 Hampshire Street
Cambridge, MA 02130

617-418-4000
800-664-4262
Fax: 312-822-0054
E-Mail: info@thebmaboston.com
Home Page: www.thebmaboston.com/

Michael Lewis, President
Will Robinson, VP Public Relations
Matthew Mamet, VP Internet Marketing
Larry Perreault, VP Finance
Chris Perkett, VP Programming

BMA Boston helps members improve their ability to manage business-to-business marketing and communications for greater productivity and profitability by providing unique access to information, ideas, and the experience of peers. The BMA offers an information-packed Website, online skills-building, marketing certification programs, and industry surveys and papers. In addition, members have the opportunity to interact with peers at seminars, chapter training programs and the BMA Annual Conference.

6481 **Business Software Alliance**
20 F Street, NW
Suite 800
Washington, DC 20001

202-872-5500
Fax: 202-872-5501
E-Mail: info@bsa.org
Home Page: www.bsa.org
Social Media: Facebook, Twitter, You tube

Robert W Holleyman II, CEO
Jodie Kelley, General Counsel and SVP
Matt Reid, SVP, External Affairs
Katherine McGuire, VP, Govt. Relations

An organization dedicated to promoting a safe and legal digital world. BSA educates consumers on software management and copyright protection, cyber security, trade, e-commerce and other internet related issues.
Founded in 1988

6482 **CTIA-The Wireless Association**
1400 16th Street, NW
Suite 600
Washington, DC 20036

202-785-0081
Home Page: www.ctia.orgy
Social Media: Facebook, Twitter, LinkedIn
Meredith Attwell Baker, President/ CEO
Michael Altschul, Sr. VP, General Counsel
Scott Bergmann, Vice President, Regulatory Affairs
Heather Blanchard, Director, Internet Development
Rocco Carlitti, VP, Finance & Administration
An industry trade group that represents the international wireless telecommunications industry.

6483 **Consumer Electronics Association (CEA)**
1919 S Eads Street
Arlington, VA 22202

703-907-7600
866-858-1555
Fax: 703-907-7675
E-Mail: communications@ce.org
Home Page: www.ce.org
Social Media: Facebook, Twitter, LinkedIn

Gary Shapiro, President/CEO
Pat Lavelle, Chairman
Peter Lesser, Industry Executive Advisor
Jason Oxman, VP Communications
Jenny Pareti, Public Policy Director

Consumer Electronics Association (CEA) provides valuable and innovative member-only resources including: exclusive information and unparalleled market research, networking opportunities with business advocates and leaders, up-to-date educational programs and technical training, exposure in extensive promotional programs, and representation from the voice of the industry.
2000 Members

6484 **EMarketing Association**
224 Post Road #129
Westerly, RI 02891

401-315-2194
Fax: 408-884-2461
E-Mail: service@emarketingassociation.com
Home Page: www.emarketingassociation.com

Robert Fleming, President
Todd Daum, VP
John Hastings, VP
Linda Jaffe, VP

An international association of emarketing professionals. Members include government, companies, professionals and students involved with the emarketing arena.

6485 **Electronic Retailing Association**
2000 14th St N
Suite 300
Arlington, VA 22201-2573

703-841-1751
800-987-6462
Fax: 425-977-1036
E-Mail: contact@retailing.org
Home Page: www.retailing.org

Julie Coons, CEO

To foster growth, development and acceptance of the rapidly growing direct response industry worldwide for the companies who use the power of electronic media to sell goods and services to the public.

6486 **Hispanic Chamber of E-Commerce**
PO Box 9142
La Jolla, CA 92038
858-768-2483
Fax: 858-456-5238
E-Mail: info@hiscec.com
Home Page: www.hiscec.com
Social Media: Facebook, YouTube

Tayde Aburto, Founder
Claudia Garcia, Founder/Chief Education Officer
Lisa Maino, Founder & CEO
German M Bravo, Founder/Chief Technology Officer
Rodrigo Gomez, Founder/Market Intelligence

The Hispanic Chamber of E-Commerce is a B2B membership-based national business association focused on providing tools and solutions to members to increase their presence online.
200 Members
Founded in 2008

6487 **Information Systems Security Association**
12100 Sunset Hills Road.
Suite 130
Reston, VA 20190

703-234-4077
866-349-5818
Fax: 703-435-4390
Home Page: www.issa.org
Social Media: Facebook, Twitter, LinkedIn

Ira Winkler, President
Andrea C. Hoy, Vice President
Bill Danigelis, Secretary/ Director of Operations
Kevin D. Spease, Treasurer/ Chief Financial Officer
Frances Alexander, Director

A nonprofit, international professional organization of information security professionals and practitioners.

6488 **International Society for Technology in Education**
180 W 8th Avenue
Eugene, OR 97401-2916

541-302-3777
800-336-5191
Fax: 541-302-3778
E-Mail: iste@iste.org
Home Page: www.iste.org

Don Knezek, CEO
Leslie Conery, Deputy CEO

A large nonprofit organization serving the technology-using educator.
12M Members
Founded in 1979

6489 **Internet Marketing Association**
10 Mar Del Rey San
Clemente, CA 92673

949-443-9300
Fax: 949-443-2215
E-Mail: info@imanetwork.org
Home Page: www.imanetwork.orgÿ
Social Media: Twitter, LinkedIn

Rachel Reenders, CIM Account Executive
Sinan Kanatsiz, CIM, Chairman and Founder
Matthew Langie, CIM, Vice Chairman of Education
Jeff Marcoux, Director
David Krauss, Director

A professional internet marketing group that provides educational resources on effective internet marketing strategies to business professionals.

6490 **Internet Merchants Association**
E-Mail: info@imamerchants.org
Home Page: www.imamerchants.org
Social Media: Facebook

Fred Neff, President
Scott Cole, Vice-President
Doyle Carver, Secretary
Andy Sollofe, Treasurer

Develops, promotes, and protects the economic vitality of internet merchants through a positive business environment and fosters a climate in whichcommerce, industry, and technology will flourish.

6491 **Internet Society**
1775 Wiehle Ave
Suite 102
Reston, VA 20190-5158
703-326-9880
Fax: 703-326-9881
E-Mail: isoc@isoc.org
Home Page: www.isoc.org

Terry Weigler, Manager
Gregory Kapfer, CFO

Technologists, developers, educators, researchers, government representatives, and business people.
16000 Members
Founded in 1992

6492 **Internet Societyÿ**
1775 Wiehle Avenue
Suite 201
Reston, VA 20190-5108

703-439-2120
E-Mail: isoc@isoc.org
Home Page: www.internetsociety.org
Social Media: Facebook, Twitter, LinkedIn

Kathryn Brown, President/ CEO
Ms. Nicole Armstrong, Senior Events Manager
Howard Baggott, Senior Events Manager
Brenda Boggs, Senior Drupal Developer
Andre Copelin, Chief of Staff

An international, nonprofit organization that provides leadership in Internet related standards, education, and policy.
Founded in 1970

6493 **National E-Commerce Association**
PO Box 2825
Peoria, AZ 85380

Home Page: www.ecommerceassoc.com

The National E-Commerce Association provides an ear and a voice for the E-Commerce industry at the local, state and federal level. In addition to this, we have and will continue to negotiate the most aggressive pricing on goods and services for our members.
Founded in 1980

6494 **NetSuite Ecommerce**
2955 Campus Drive
Suite 100
San Mateo, CA 94403-2511
650-627-1000
Fax: 650-627-1001
E-Mail: info@netsuite.com
Home Page: www.netsuite.com
Social Media: Facebook, Twitter, LinkedIn, YouTube

Evan Goldberg, Co-Founder/Chief Technology Officer
Zach Nelson, President & CEO

NetSuite E-commerce provides you with the tools you need to drive growth in your e-commerce channel and streamline and automate your business operations.
10000 Members
Founded in 1998

6495 **The Entertainment Software Association**
575 7th Street, NW
Suite 300
Washington, DC 20004

E-Mail: esa@theESA.com
Home Page: www.theesa.com
Social Media: Facebook, Twitter

Michael D. Gallagher, President/ CEO

A U.S. association exclusively dedicated to serving the business and public affairs needs of companies that publish computer and video games for video game consoles, handheld devices, personal computers, and the Internet.

6496 **US Internet Industry Association**
PO Box 302
Luray, VA 22835

540-742-1928
Home Page: www.usiia-net.org

Dennis C. Hayes, Chairman
David P. McClure, President/ CEO
Michael McKeehan, Chair Public Policy
Christian Dawson, Chair, Web Hosting Council
Stephen B. May, Chief Technology Officer

A nonprofit North American trade association for Internet commerce, content and connectivity.
Founded in 1994

6497 **Uniform Code Council**
Princeton Pike Corporate Center
1009 Lenox Drive Suite 202
Lawrenceville, NJ 08648

609-620-0200
Fax: 609-620-1200
Home Page: www.uc-council.org

Robert W Carpenter, President
Miguel A Lopera, VP

Barcodes, eCommerce and data synchronization, to EPC/RFID and business process automation standards.
Frequency: Members 280,000
Founded in 1974

6498 **Women in eCommerce**
PO Box 550856
Fort Lauderdale, FL 33355-0856

954-625-6606
877-947-3337
E-Mail: heidi@wecai.org
Home Page: www.wecai.org
Social Media: Facebook, Twitter, LinkedIn

Suzannah Richards, President
Rosana Santos, President Elect
Ellen Sue Burton, VP/Logistics & Hospitality
Racheli Smilovitz, VP/Professional Development

Dalila J. Grohowski, VP/Membership Development

The original business and social networking community for social and professional networking and business development for successful women who want to take their businesses to a new level offline and online. We offer tools, resources and networking opportunities to build a strong foundation for future growth and expansion.
Founded in 2001

6499 **eCommerce Merchants Trade Association**
917-388-1698
Home Page: www.ecmta.org

Brandon Dupsky, Managing Director
Jonathan Garriss, Executive Director

eCommerce Merchants is a trade association founded by a group of online retailers who realized that by working together they could enjoy the premium services and discounted pricing normally available to very large companies.
Founded in 2005

6500 **eMarketing Association**
91 Point Judith Road
Suite 129
Narragansett, RI 02882

800-496-2950
Fax: 408-884-2461
E-Mail: service@eMarketingAssociation.com
Home Page: www.emarketingassociation.com
Social Media: Facebook, Twitter, LinkedIn

Chris Baggott, CEO
Bert DuMars, C-Founder/CEO
Murray Gaylord, VP/Marketing
Jeff Hilmire, President
Simms Jenkins, Founder & Principal

The eMA provides marketing resources, services, research, certifications, educational programs and events to its members and the marketing community. The eMA works with a number of organizations, companies and governments on issues related to e-commerce, multi-channel marketing and legislative issues.~
Founded in 1997

Newsletters

6501 **APT News**
Alliance for Public Technology
919 18th St Nw
Suite 1000
Washington, DC 20006-5512

202-263-2970
Fax: 202-263-2960
Home Page: www.apt.org

Sylvia Rosenthal, Executive Director
Frequency: Bi-Monthly

6502 **Dot.COM**
Business Communications Company
25 Van Zant Street
Suite 13
Norwalk, CT 06855-1713

203-853-4266
Fax: 203-853-0348
E-Mail: sales@bccresearch.com
Home Page: www.bccresearch.com

Louis Naturman, Publisher
C Toenne, Editor

Updates readers on the commercial use of the Internet and related platforms.
Cost: $38.00

6503 **E-Healthcare Market Reporter**
Health Resources Publishing
1913 Atlantic Ave
Suite 200
Manasquan, NJ 08736-1067

732-292-1100
888-843-6242
Fax: 732-292-1111
E-Mail: info@themcic.com
Home Page: www.healthresourcesonline.com

Robert K Jenkins, Publisher
Judith Granel, Marketing
John Russel, Editor
Brett Powell, Regional Director
Alice Burron, Director

A bi-monthly covering strategies, new products, innovation, privacy issue, business solutions, service available, vendor news and comparative for implementing sales and marketing on the internet.
Cost: $397.00
Frequency: Fortnightly
ISSN: 1098-5654
Founded in 1988

6504 **E-News**
Patricia Seybold Group
Po Box 240565
Boston, MA 02129

617-742-5200
800-826-2424
Fax: 617-742-1028
E-Mail: feedback@psgroup.com
Home Page: www.psgroup.com

Patricia Seybold, Founder/CEO

E-mail newsletter includes perspectives on the e-commerce industry, research and upcoming events.

6505 **Ecommerce @lert**
ZD Journals
500 Canal View Boulevard
Rochester, NY 14623-2800

585-407-7301
Fax: 585-214-2387
E-Mail: eca@zd.com
Home Page: www.ecommercealert.com
Social Media: Facebook, Twitter, LinkedIn

Bob Artner, Managing Editor

Explores the emerging digital and online technology used in sales management, as well as the companies in the forefront of this change.
Cost: $495.00

6506 **Electronic Commerce News**
Phillips Publishing
PO Box 60037
Potomac, MD 20859

301-208-6787
Fax: 301-424-2098
E-Mail: htreat@phillips.com
Home Page: www.ectoday.com

Heather Treat, Publisher
Stuart Zipper, Editor
Diane Schwartz, Publisher
Laurie Hofmann, Director of Marketing

Provides business strategies for the extended enterprise with the latest technological development and opportunities.
Cost: $597.00
Frequency: Weekly

6507 **Higher Education Technology News**
Business Publishers
2222 Sedwick Dr
Suite 101
Durham, NC 27713

800-223-8720
Fax: 800-508-2592
E-Mail: custserv@bpinews.com
Home Page: www.bpinews.com

Provides timely, independent coverage of the issues surrounding technology in a higher educational setting. Offers news from federal and state government, the business world and others educators.
Cost: $307.00
8 Pages
Founded in 1963

6508 **International Cyber Centers**
Probe Research
3 Wing Drive
Suite 240
Cedar Knolls, NJ 07927-1000

973-285-1500
Fax: 973-285-1519
E-Mail: probe@proberesearch.com
Home Page: www.proberesearch.com

Strategic positioning and product portfolios of major domestic and international carriers in collocation, Web hosting, applications hosting, e-commerce, IP-centric data, managed services and other value added offerings. Examines the global square footage race in building or upgrading what are variously known as Internet centers, data centers or cyber centers worldwide. Profiles of several key players are included in the bulletin issue.

6509 **Internet Alliance Cyberbrief**
Internet Alliance
1615 L Street NW
Suite 1100
Washington, DC 20036-5624

202-861-2407
E-Mail: tammy@internetalliance.org
Home Page: www.internetalliance.org

Tammy Cota, Executive Director

Coverage of public policy changes in government, enhancing consumer satisfaction in interactive services, and education.
Frequency: Weekly

6510 **Internet Business**
Information Gatekeepers
1340 Soldiers Field Rd
Suite 3
Brighton, MA 02135-1000

617-782-5033
800-323-1088
Fax: 617-782-5735
E-Mail: info@igigroup.com
Home Page: www.igigroup.com

Paul Polishuk, CEO
Hui Pan, Chief Analyst, Editor in Chief
Bev Wilson, Managing Editor

Covers the rapid developments in the industry.
Cost: $695.00
Frequency: Monthly

6511 **Internet Business Advantage**
ZD Journals
500 Canal View Boulevard
Rochester, NY 14623-2800

585-407-7301
Fax: 585-214-2387
E-Mail: iba@zdjournals.com
Home Page: www.zdjournals.com

Bob Artner, Editor-in-Chief

Keeps readers up-to-date of technological advances and new services available on the Internet. Reviews new products and provides tips on businss applications.
Cost: $295.00

6512 **Internet Media Investor**
Kagan World Media

126 Clock Tower Place
Carmel, CA 93923-8746

831-624-1536
800-307-2529
Fax: 831-625-3225
E-Mail: info@kagan.com
Home Page: www.kagan.com
Social Media: Facebook, Twitter, LinkedIn, YouTube

George Niesen, Editor
Tom Johnson, Marketing Manager

Follows public stocks and private deals, analyzes publicly held interactive multimedia companies, tracks key industry subgroups through Kagan stock averages that relate companies by product lines, projects growth of new TV and data networks, programming and technology. Provides economic modeling of new corporate ventures and interprets announcements and events. Three month trial is available.
Cost: $1095.00
Frequency: Monthly
Founded in 1969

6513 **Internet World**
Mecklermedia Corporation
20 Ketchum Street
Westport, CT 06880

212-260-0758
Fax: 203-454-5840
E-Mail: bbesch@mecklermedia.com

Bill Besch, Publisher

Internet industry news, product reviews and technical reports, with an emphasis on Internet technology, hardware, management and security.
Cost: $160.00
Frequency: Weekly
Circulation: 98,947

6514 **Internetweek**
CMP Media
600 Community Drive
Manhasset, NY 11030-3847

516-562-5000
Fax: 516-562-5554
E-Mail: mazzara@cmp.com
Home Page: www.internetweek.com

Mike Azzara, Publisher

News and coverage of the latest trends in electronic commerce and intranet application platforms, the effects of high technology on daily production, changing regulations and operating standards, the best tools and practices, and related business and financial news.
Cost: $143.00
Frequency: Weekly
Circulation: 161264

6515 **Manufacturing Automation**
Vital Information Publications
754 Caravel Lane
Foster City, CA 94404-1712

650-345-7018
Home Page: www.sensauto.com

Peter Adrian, Owner
Gary Kuba, Marketing Director

Provides market research data and vital information about key products, applications, and technologies for a wide range of industrial automation segments, such as CAD/CAM, supply chain management, e-Commerce solutions, enterprise resource planning, automation software, manufacturing technology, industrial controls, and manufacturing systems.

6516 **Mass Storage News**
Corry Publishing
2840 W 21st Street
Erie, PA 16506

814-838-0025
Fax: 814-838-0035
E-Mail: terryp@corrypub.com
Home Page: www.corrypub.com

Terry Peterson, Publisher

News on optical disk based imaging and storage systems, new products, technical developments and industry developments.
Cost: $597.00
Frequency: BiWeekly
Circulation: 1,500

6517 **Mealey's Litigation Report: Class Actions**
LexisNexis Mealey's
555 W 5th Avenue
Los Angeles, CA 90013

213-627-1130
E-Mail: mealeyinfo@lexisnexis.com
Home Page: www.lexisnexis.com/mealeys

Tom Hagy, VP/General Manager
Maureen McGuire, Editorial Director
David Elreth, Editor

This report will provide in-depth coverage of class action litigation involving mass torts and beyond - including consumer law, employment law, securities litigation and e-commerce disputes. Get the latest on: hard-to-find filings, notice plans, fairness hearings, class certification rulings, settlements, trial news and verdicts, attorney fee news, appeals, breaking news stories, new complaints, Supreme Court battles, and much more.
Cost: $1195.00
100 Pages
Frequency: Semi-Monthly
Founded in 1997

6518 **Mealey's Litigation Report: Cyber Tech & E -Commerce**
LexisNexis Mealey's
555 W 5th Avenue
Los Angeles, CA 90013

213-627-1130
E-Mail: mealeyinfo@lexisnexis.com
Home Page: www.lexisnexis.com/mealeys

Tom Hagy, VP/General Manager
Maureen McGuire, Editorial Director
Mark Rogers, Editor

The Report covers disputes arising from e-commerce. The report tracks emerging legal issues, including: Internet security, data destruction and/or alteration, defamation on the Web, software errors, hardware failure, electronic theft, e-mail trespass, online privacy, government action, shareholder lawsuits, Internet jurisdiction issues, file sharing (copyright) disputes and much more.
Cost: $999.00
100 Pages
Frequency: Monthly
Founded in 1999

6519 **Mobile Internet**
Information Gatekeepers
1340 Soldiers Field Rd
Suite 3
Brighton, MA 02135-1000

617-782-5033
800-323-1088
Fax: 617-782-5735
E-Mail: info@igigroup.com
Home Page: www.igigroup.com

Paul Polishuk, CEO
Hui Pan, Chief Analyst, Editor in Chief
Bev Wilson, Managing Editor

Covers worldwide developments in 3G wireless networks, with an emphasis on the worldwide PCS/GSM/CDMA markets.
Cost: $695.00
Frequency: Monthly
Founded in 1977

6520 **Multimedia & Internet Training Newsletter**
Brandon Hall Resources
690 W Fremont Ave
#9C
Sunnyvale, CA 94087-4200

408-736-2335
E-Mail: editor@brandon-hall.com
Home Page: www.brandon-hall.com
Social Media: Facebook, Twitter, LinkedIn

Mike Cooke, CEO
Rachel Ashkin, COO
Michael Rochelle, CSO

The latest in multimedia news, virtual clasroom reports, insight into web-based training, and technology tutorial. Job bank listings, upcoming events, seminars, and tips and techniques.
Cost: $189.00
Frequency: Monthly
Circulation: 900

6521 **Online & CD-ROM Review**
Information Today
1308 W Main
University of Illinois
Urbana, IL 61801

217-333-1074
800-248-8466
Fax: 217-762-3956
E-Mail: custserv@infotoday.com
Home Page: www.infotoday.com/

Martha Williams, Editor
Thomas H Hogan, CEO/President
Heather Rudolph, Marketing
Inge Coffey, Circulation Manager

Covers the use and management of online and CD-ROM services, the training and education of online and CD-ROM users, creation and marketing of databases, and new development in search aids.
Cost: $115.00
Frequency: Monthly
Circulation: 4745

6522 **Online Libraries & Microcomputers**
Information Intelligence
PO Box 31098
Phoenix, AZ 31098

602-996-2283
Home Page: www.infointelligence.com

George Machovec, Managing Editor

Examines new library online and automation applications with reviews of new software and hardware, industry news and trends, and upcoming related events.
Cost: $62.50
9 Pages
Frequency: 10 per year
ISSN: 0737-7770
Founded in 1983

6523 **Online Newsletter**
Information Intelligence
PO Box 31098
Phoenix, AZ 85046-1098

602-996-2283
E-Mail: news@infointelligence.com
Home Page: wwww.infointelligence.com

Richard S Huleatt, Editor

Covers all aspects of online and CD-ROM developments throughout the world. Regular feature sections include news and events, mergers and acquisitions, people in the news, telecommunications, and networks. Editoral reflects product development and its impact on users, and provides listings of upcoming events re-

lated to this industry.
Cost: $62.50
9 Pages
Frequency: 10 per year
ISSN: 0194-0694
Founded in 1983

6524 **Online Reporter**
G2 Computer Intelligence
PO Box 7
Glen Head, NY 11545-1616
516-759-7025
Fax: 516-759-7028
E-Mail: news@g2news.com
Home Page: www.g2news.com
Maureen O'Gara, Publisher
Information on recent developments on the Internet through news briefs and a section called Chat Room. Includes information on e-commerce, Java and network security.
Cost: $695.00
Frequency: Weekly

6525 **Privacy Journal**
PO Box 28577
Providence, RI 02908
401-274-7861
Fax: 401-274-4747
E-Mail: orders@privacyjournal.net
Home Page: www.privacyjournal.net
Robert Ellis Smith, Publisher
An independent monthly on privacy in a computer age.
Cost: $65.00
Frequency: Monthly
ISSN: 0145-7659
Founded in 1974
Printed in one color

6526 **Report on Electronic Commerce**
Telecommunications Reports International
1333 H Street NW
#100 E
Washington, DC 20005-4707
202-842-3022
Fax: 202-842-1875
Home Page: www.tr.com
Jerry Ashworth, Editor
Brian Hammond, Managing Editor
Provides insiths on the latest developments in EDI, EFT, EBT, digital cash, home shopping and baking, value-added networks, and transaction processing. Offers articles, analysis and case studies regarding financial and business transaction over the Internet.
Cost: $745.00
Frequency: BiWeekly

6527 **Sysop News and Cyberworld Report**
BBS Press Service
5610 SW 10th Avenue
Topeka, KS 66604-2104
785-286-4272
Fax: 785-271-0192
E-Mail: alanbenchtold@sysop.com
Home Page: www.sysop.com
Alan R Bechtold, Publisher
Debbie Boos, Owner
Online industry news and updates, Web site reviews, event announcements, Web design basics, Internet-based applicaitons, business solutions and various technical articles of interest.
Cost: $59.95
Frequency: Weekly
Circulation: 18M

6528 **TechTarget**
TechTarget
117 Kendrick St
Suite 800
Needham Heights, MA 02494-2728
781-657-1000
888-274-4111
Fax: 781-657-1100
E-Mail: info@techtarget.com
Home Page: www.techtarget.com
Greg Strakosch, CEO
Don Hawk, President
Lisa Johnson, VP Marketing
Catherine Engelke, Direector Public Relations
IBM iSeries focused media. The IBM e-Server iSeries (formerly the AS/400) is considered to be the world's most often used multi-user business computer. The installed base worldwide is huge and will get bigger, fueled by incresed Web development. The iSeries comes with an integrated Web application server and all the tools needed to build internet, intranet, extranet, and e-commerce sites quickly and will figure prominently into IT strategy and implementation for years to come.
Frequency: Monthly
Founded in 1999

6529 **The CyberSkeptic's Guide to Internet Research**
Information Today
143 Old Marlton Pike
Medford, NJ 08055-8750
609-654-6266
800-300-9868
Fax: 609-654-4309
E-Mail: custserv@infotoday.com
Home Page: www.infotoday.com
Thomas H Hogan, President
Roger R Bilboul, Chairman Of The Board
A monthly subscription newsletter in print, that explores and evaluates free and low cost Web sites and search strategies to help you use the Internet and stay up to date.
Cost: $164.95
ISSN: 1085-2417

6530 **Trade Vendor Quarterly**
Blakeley & Blakeley
2 Park Plaza
Suite 400
Irvine, CA 92614
949-260-0611
Fax: 949-260-0613
E-Mail: administrator@vendorland.com
Home Page: www.vendorlaw.com
Scott Blakey, Esq.
Highlights developments in commercial, creditors' rights, e-commerce and bankruptcy law of interest to the credit and financial professional. Free online.
Frequency: Quarterly

6531 **Web Review**
Miller Freeman Publications
600 Harrison Street
San Francisco, CA 94107
650-573-3210
Veronica Costanza, Publisher
Timely and practical information on the practice of Internet development as well as news on the latest techniques and technologies.
Frequency: BiWeekly
Circulation: 12M

6532 **Webdeveloper.com**
Mecklermedia Corporation
23 Old Kings Hwy S
Darien, CT 06820-4541
203-662-2800
Fax: 203-655-4686
E-Mail: info@WebMediaBrands.com
Home Page: www.webmediabrands.com
Alan M Meckler, CEO
Mike Demiot, Marketing Manager
Product reviews, practical techniques, codes, tools and tips for Internet professionals who design, develop and maintain Web sites and Internet services.
Frequency: Daily

6533 **West Side Leader/Green Leader**
Leader Publications
3075 Smith Rd
Suite 204
Akron, OH 44333-4454
330-665-0909
888-945-9595
Fax: 330-665-9590
E-Mail: webmaster@akron.com
Home Page: www.akron.com
Kathryn Core, Editor
Kathleen Collins, Managing Editor
Maria Lindsay, Assistant Editor
Weekly newspapers.
Cost: $10.00
Circulation: 53000

Magazines & Journals

6534 **Active Server Developer's Journal**
ZD Journals
500 Canal View Boulevard
Rochester, NY 14623-2800
585-407-7301
Fax: 585-214-2387
E-Mail: asp@zdjournals.com
Home Page: www.asdj.com
Jon Pyles, Publisher
Taggard Andrews
Addresses such issues as database publishing, creating hack-proof files and getting the most out of server-side components. Special sections focus on client-side solutions, covering the basics and taking an in-depth look at more detailed techniques.
Cost: $149.00
Frequency: Monthly

6535 **Bio & Software and Internet Report**
Mary Ann Liebert
140 Huguenot St # 3
3rd Floor
New Rochelle, NY 10801-5215
914-740-2100
Fax: 914-740-2101
E-Mail: info@liebertpub.com
Home Page: www.liebertpub.com
Social Media: Facebook, Twitter, LinkedIn
Mary A Liebert, Owner
Gerry Elman, Editor-in-Chief
Robert A Bohrer, Executive Editor
Judith Gunn Bronson, Managing Editor
News and reviews of all areas of scientific computing, including software, hardware and network products.
Cost: $1554.00
ISSN: 1527-9162
Founded in 1980

6536 **Boardwatch Magazine**
Penton Media
1300 E 9th St # 316
Cleveland, OH 44114-1503
216-696-7000
Fax: 216-696-6662

E-Mail: rgoldner@boardwatch.com
Home Page: www.penton.com

Jane Cooper, Marketing
David Icopf, Editorial Director

Editorial coverage for communications service providers.
Cost: $72.00
Frequency: Monthly
Circulation: 50,000
ISSN: 1054-2760
Founded in 1987
Mailing list available for rent: 50,000 names at $250 per M

6537 **BtoB Magazine**
Ad Age Group/ Division of Crain Communications
711 3rd Ave
New York, NY 10017-4014

212-210-0785
Fax: 212-210-0200
E-Mail: info@crain.com
Home Page: www.crain.com

Norm Feldman, Manager

Dedicated to integrated business to business marketing. Every page is packed with substance news, reports, technologies, benchmarks, best practices served up by the most knowledgeable journalists.
Frequency: Monthly
Circulation: 45000

6538 **Card Technology**
Thomson Financial Publishing
1 State St
27th Floor
New York, NY 10004-1481

212-825-8445
800-221-1809
Fax: 212-843-9622
E-Mail: custserv@thomsonmedia.com
Home Page: www.cardtechnology.com

Daniel Wolfe, Editor in Chief
Austin Kilgore, Managing Editor
Ed McKinley, Independent Sales Organizations
Hope Lerman, National Sales Manager

Store-value cards, optical-memory cards, biometrics, cards on the Internet, cards for electronic data storage, and devices used with these cards in banking, government, telecommunications, transportation and education.
Cost: $ 98.00
Frequency: Monthly
Circulation: 25000
Printed in 4 colors on glossy stock

6539 **Computer & Online Industry Litigation Reporter**
Andrews Publications
175 Strafford Avenue
Building 4, Suite 140
Wayne, PA 19087-3331

610-225-0510
800-345-1101
Fax: 610-225-0501
Home Page: www.andrewspub.com

John Backe, Publisher

Editorial covers telecommunications and the Internet for attorneys and professionals in the legal field.
Cost: $850.00

6540 **Computer Gaming World**
Ziff Davis Publishing Company
101 2nd St # 900
8th Floor
San Francisco, CA 94105-3650

415-547-8000
Fax: 415-547-8777
E-Mail: info@ziffdavis.com
Home Page: www.ziffdavis.com

Dale Strang, Manager
Matt Leone, Editor
Paul Fusco, Sales Director
Bobby Markowitz, Marketing Director
Stephen Hicks, General Counsel

Reviews commercially available and on-line games. Features interviews with game designers, as well as strategy tips, contests and news.
Cost: $98.88
Frequency: Monthly
Circulation: 212783

6541 **Computer Journal**
Las Vegas Computer Journal
2232 S Nellis Boulevard
#169
Las Vegas, NV 89104-6213

702-270-4656
Fax: 702-432-6204
E-Mail: info@internetsurfer.com
Home Page: www.internetsurfer.com

Johanna Nezhoda, Publisher

Spotlights Web news, site reviews, interface tools and commentary on the changing face of computing.
Cost: $24.95
Frequency: Monthly
Circulation: 25M

6542 **Computer Music Journal**
MIT Press
3 Cambridge Ctr # 23
Cambridge, MA 02142-1613

617-499-3200
Fax: 617-621-0856
E-Mail: journals-orders@mit.edu
Home Page: www.adoptaboat.org

Miguel Suarez, Manager
Keeril Makan, Managing Editor

Tutorials and research articles, news and reviews of computer music systems, hardware and software for music sound, digital audio, signal processing and multimedia.
Cost: $82.00
120 Pages
Frequency: Quarterly
Circulation: 5000
Founded in 1926

6543 **Computer Service & Repair Magazine**
Searle Publishing Company
5511 Morning Glory Ln
#210-110
Littleton, CO 80123-2701

303-730-3006
810-797-8708
Fax: 303-797-0276
E-Mail: csr@searlepub.com
Home Page: www.independentcable.com

Robert Searle, Publisher
Roderick Robles, Associate Publisher

Information on the maintenance and repair of computer systems. Reviews new products and technology.

6544 **Corporate Help Desk Solutions**
Gartner Group
Po Box 10212
Stamford, CT 06904-2212

203-964-0096
Fax: 203-316-6488
E-Mail: help@gartner.com
Home Page: www.gartner.com
Social Media: Facebook, Twitter, LinkedIn

Jean Hall, CEO
Gene Hall, CEO/President
David Godfrey, Marketing/Circulation
Robin Kranich, SVP Human Resources

Key technologies, management practices and techniques for the most cost-effective help desk solutions.
Cost: $395.00
Frequency: Monthly
Founded in 1979

6545 **Customer Interaction Solutions**
Technology Marketing Corporation
1 Technology Plz
Norwalk, CT 06854-1936

203-852-6800
800-243-6002
Fax: 203-853-2845
E-Mail: tmc@tmcnet.com
Home Page: www.tmcnet.com

Rich Tehrani, CEO
Tracey Schelmetic, Managing Editor
Erik D Lounsbury, Editorial Director

Magazine devoted to teleservices and e-services outsourcing, marketing and consumer management issues.
Frequency: Monthly
Founded in 1982

6546 **Customer Interface**
Advanstar Communications
6200 Canoga Avenue
2nd Floor
Woodland Hills, CA 91367

818-593-5000
Fax: 818-593-5020
E-Mail: info@advanstar.com
Home Page: www.advanstar.com

Joseph Loggia, President
Chris DeMoulin, VP
Susannah George, Marketing Director

Business management resource for senior and mid-level decision makers who are responsible for call centers, customer contact and customer service initiatives. We are stewards for the industry as we prepare it for continued transformation and growth.
Circulation: 50,000
Founded in 1988

6547 **CyberDealer**
Meister Publishing Company
37733 Euclid Ave
Willoughby, OH 44094-5992

440-942-2000
800-572-7740
Fax: 440-975-3447
Home Page: www.meisternet.com

Gary Fitzgerald, President

Helps agricultural dealerships better manage their operations.
Frequency: 6 per year

6548 **Desktop Video Communications**
BCR Enterprises
950 York Road
#203
Hinsdale, IL 60521-8609

630-789-6700
Fax: 630-323-5324
Home Page: www.bcr.com

Fred Knight, Publisher/Editor-in-Chief

Useful information for communications and informations systems managers, line managers, system developers and integrators, value-added resellers, and software vendors.
Frequency: Bi-Monthly
Circulation: 30M

6549 **Digital Travel**
Jupiter Communications Company

627 Broadway
2nd Floor
New York, NY 10012-2612

212-533-8885
Fax: 212-780-6075
Home Page: www.jup.com

Eva Papoutsakis, Editor
Marla Kammer, Managing Director
Ellen Daley, Managing Director
Charles Rutstein, Chief Operating Officer

Editorial includes the latest information and technology in agencies, airlines, lodging, ticketing, mapping, Web advertising, transaction processing, revenue models, demographics, and full-service sites.
Cost: $595.00
Frequency: Monthly

6550 E-Business Advisor
Advisor Media
P.O.Box 503350
San Diego, CA 92150-3350

858-278-5600
800-336-6060
Fax: 858-278-0300
E-Mail: pr@advisor.com
Home Page: www.e-businessadvisor.com

John L Hawkins, Editorial Director
Jane Falla, Senior Editor
Brian Dunning, Technical Editor

E-Business Advisor is the monthly magazine presenting the best innovation, strategies, and practices for e-business leaders. It is an independent guide for the team of business and technical managers within an enterprise responsible for strategic innovation, planning, design, implementation, and management of e-business and e-commerce solutions.
Cost: $49.00
68 Pages
Circulation: 60000
ISSN: 1098-8912
Founded in 1983
Mailing list available for rent: 60000 names at $175 per M

6551 E-Content
Information Today
143 Old Marlton Pike
Medford, NJ 08055-8750

609-654-6266
800-300-9868
Fax: 609-654-4309
E-Mail: custserv@infotoday.com
Home Page: www.infotoday.com

Thomas H Hogan, President
Roger R Bilboul, Chairman Of The Board

Delivers essential research, reporting, news and analysis of content related issues. It is essential reading for executive and professionals involved in content creation, management, acquisition, organization and distribution in both commercial and enterprise environments.
Cost: $115.00
Frequency: 10 issues/yr
Mailing list available for rent: 4M names
Printed in 4 colors on glossy stock

6552 ESchool News
IAQ Publications
7920 Norfolk Ave # 900
Suite 900
Bethesda, MD 20814-2539

301-913-0115
Fax: 301-913-0119
E-Mail: gdowney@eschoolnews.com
Home Page: www.eschoolnews.com

Robert Morrow, Owner

Guide to buying and updating classroom technology for K-12 educators. Product information listings, industry updates and related reports. Covers grant writing and funding, as well as government legislation regarding education.
Cost: $90.00

6553 Electronic Commerce Advisor
Thomson Reuters
195 Broadway # 4
New York, NY 10007-3124
646-822-2000
800-231-1860
Fax: 646-822-2800
E-Mail: trta.lei-support@thomsonreuters.com
Home Page: www.ria.thomsonreuters.com

Elaine Yadlon, Plant Manager
Thomas H Glocer, CEO & Director
Robert D Daleo, Chief Financial Officer
Kelli Crane, Senior Vice President & CIO

Offers the latest in electronic commerce covering what's available and how to select and employ the best technology without costly trial-and-error mistakes. Information on EDI, e-mail, fax gateways, Internet, encryption, VANs, procurement cards, imaging, voice response, remote computering and other related information.
Cost: $155.00
Circulation: 4500
Founded in 1940

6554 Electronic Mail & Messaging Systems
Business Research Publications
1333 H Street NW
Suite 100 East
Washington, DC 20005-4707

202-364-6473
800-822-6338
Fax: 202-842-1875

Rod Kuckro, Editor-in-Chief

Exclusive biweekly intelligence technology applications, products and market trends in electronic mail, computer fax, wireless messaging and the Internet.
Cost: $595.00
Frequency: BiWeekly

6555 Electronic Publishing
PennWell Publishing Company
98 Spit Brook Rd # Ll-1
Nashua, NH 03062-5737

603-891-0123
Fax: 603-891-9294
E-mail: genepri@pennwell.com
Home Page: www.pennwell.com

Christine Shaw, VP
Keith V. Hevenor, Editor

For those who communicate in print, including service bureaus, printers, prepress houses and desktop publishers, it provides latest products, news and related developments.
Cost: $59.00
Frequency: Monthly
Circulation: 68441
Founded in 1910

6556 Electronic Retailer Magazine
Electronic Retailing Association
2000 14th St N # 300
Suite 300
Arlington, VA 22201-2573

703-841-1751
800-987-6462
Fax: 703-841-1860
E-Mail: contact@retailing.org
Home Page: www.retailing.org

Julie Coons, CEO
Vitisia Paynich, Editor-in-Chief
Tom Dellner, Executive Editor

Delivers news updates, exclusives, industry research, educational features and in-depth converage of issues relating to government affairs, legal aspects, concepts and products, production, media-buying as well as all back end services.
Frequency: Monthly
Circulation: 21000

6557 Emediaweekly
Mac Publishing
501 2nd St
San Francisco, CA 94107-1496

415-243-0505
800-288-6848
Fax: 415-442-0766
E-Mail: sitehelp@macworld.com
Home Page: www.macworld.com
Social Media: Facebook, Twitter, YouTube

Mike Kisseberth, CEO

Covers the creation, technologies, applications and hardware for the publishing spectrum, including print, Web, multimedia, CD and digital video. Emphasis on hardware and software products, along with analysis, reviews, and buyer's guides.
Cost: $125.00
Frequency: Weekly

6558 Explore the Net with Internet Explorer
ZD Journals
500 Canal View Boulevard
Rochester, NY 14623-2800

585-407-7301
Fax: 585-214-2386
E-Mail: etn_editor@zdjournals.com
Home Page: www.zdjournals.com

Joelle Martin, Publisher

Informs readers of new features and how they may be used; covering such concepts as browser upgrades, compatibility issues, authoring tools and connection utilities. Regular departments showcase the 'site of the month,' in addition to reviewing other sites that have attractive interfaces and are valauble resources.
Cost: $49.00
Frequency: Monthly

6559 Ezine - WECommerce News
Women in eCommerce
PO Box 550856
Fort Lauderdale, FL 33355-0856

954-625-6606
877-947-3337
E-Mail: heidi@wecai.org
Home Page: www.wecai.org

Suzannah Richards, President
Rosana Santos, President Elect
Ellen Sue Burton, VP/Logistics & Hospitality
Racheli Smilovitz, VP/Professional Development
Dalila J. Grohowski, VP/Membership Development

Helping women do business on the web.
Founded in 2001

6560 GEOWorld
Bel-Av Communciations
359 Galahad Rd
Bolingbrook, IL 60440-2108

E-Mail: tdanielson@geoplace.com
Home Page: www.geoplace.com

Jo Treadwell, VP/Group Publisher
Todd Danielson, Editor

Offers a wealth of knowledge through festures, news and commentary covering the geospatial industry. Covers local and federal government, emergency management, infrastructure, natural resource management, industry trends and in-

novations and more.
Cost: $72.00
Frequency: Monthly
Circulation: 25000

6561 Genealogical Computing
Ancestry
360 W 4800 N
Provo, UT 84604-5675
801-705-7000
800-262-3787
Fax: 801-705-7001
E-Mail: pr@myfamilyinc.com
Home Page: www.myfamily.com
Social Media: Facebook, Twitter
Timothy P Sullivan, CEO
Matthew Wright, Contributing Editor
David C Moon, CEO
Mary-Kay Evans, Director, Public Relations
For readers who use computers and technology to organize and enhance their research into accounts of ancestries and descent.
Cost: $25.00
Frequency: Quarterly

6562 Geospatial Solutions
Advanstar Communications
201 Sandpointe Ave # 600
Suite 500
Santa Ana, CA 92707-8700
714-513-8400
Fax: 714-513-8680
Home Page: www.geospatial-solutions.com
Mike Weldon, Plant Manager
Practical applications of geographic information systems and technologies for planning, developing, preserving, analyzing and managing environments.
Frequency: Monthly
Circulation: 30000
Founded in 1987

6563 Harlow Report: Geographic Information Systems
Advanced Information Management Group
905 Thistledown Lane
Birmingham, AL 35244-3361
334-982-9203
E-Mail: chris@geoint.com
Home Page: www.theharlowreport.com/
Chris Harlow, Publisher/Editor
Key management issues and new software highlights, service providers and users for the geographic information systems industry.
Cost: $190.00
Frequency: Monthly
Founded in 1982

6564 Heller Report on Internet Strategies for Education Markets
Nelson B Heller & Associates
9933 Lawler Avenue
#502
Skokie, IL 60077-3708
800-525-5811
877-435-5373
Fax: 303-209-9444
E-Mail: info@hellerreports.com
Home Page: www.hellerreports.com
Social Media: Facebook, Twitter
Nelson B Heller, President/Publisher
Emily Garner, Sales/Marketing Director
Covers Internet hardware, software and services for educational use. Discusses the funding and deadlines relevant to the products and services offered through the Internet.
Cost: $397.00
12 Pages
Frequency: Monthly
Circulation: 500
Founded in 1981
Printed in 2 colors

6565 IEEE Internet Computing
IEEE Computer Society
PO Box 3014
Los Alamitos, CA 90720-1314
714-821-8380
800-272-6657
Fax: 714-821-4010
E-Mail: volunteer.services@computer.org
Home Page: www.computer.org/internet
Social Media: Facebook, Twitter, LinkedIn, YouTube
Angela Burges, Executive Director
Davis Hennage, CEO/President
Steve Woods, Production Manager
Sandy Brown, Marketing
Steve Woods, Production Manager
Provides a technology roadmap for high-end users and application developers, as well as a venue for standards, case histories, and new ideas. Essays, interview, and roundtable discussions address the Internet's impact on engineering practice. Describes Internet tools, technologies, and application-oriented research.
Cost: $28.00
Frequency: Quarterly
Circulation: 11265
Founded in 1946

6566 IT Cost Management Strategies
Computer Economics
2082 Business Center Dr
Suite 240
Irvine, CA 92612
949-831-8700
Fax: 949-442-7688
Home Page: www.computereconomics.com
Frank Scavo, President
Dan Husiak, VP
Covers budgeting, financial news, computer programming, marketing and management for management information systems directors as a planning assistant.
Frequency: Monthly
Founded in 1978

6567 ITS World
Advanstar Communications
859 Willamette Street
Eugene, OR 97401-2918
541-431-0026
Fax: 541-344-3514
Home Page: www.itsworld.com
Phillip Arndt, Publisher
Articles on industry news, current issues that affect Intelligent Transportation Systems, practical advice, applications, new and existing technology, and new product information.
Cost: $35.00
Frequency: 9 per year
Circulation: 15,124

6568 Information Display
Palisades Institute for Research Services
2 Shadybrook Lane
Norwalk, CT 06854
203-853-7069
Fax: 203-855-9769
E-Mail: office@sid.org
Home Page: www.sid.org
Kenneth I Werner, Editor
Shigeol Mikoshiba, President/CEO
State-of-the-art developments in electronic, electromechanical and hardcopy display equipment; input and output technologies; storage media; human factors and display standards; entrepreneurship, marketing and management; and manufacturing.
Cost: $36.00
Frequency: Monthly
Circulation: 11000
Founded in 1962
Printed in 4 colors

6569 Information Retrieval & Library Automation
Lomond Publications
PO Box 88
Mount Airy, MD 21771-0088
202-362-1361
Fax: 202-362-6156
Thomas Hattery, Publisher
New technology, products and equipment that improve information systems and library services, for science, social, social science, law, medicine, academic institutions and the public.
Cost: $75.00
Frequency: Monthly

6570 Information Security
International Computer Security Association
117 Kendrick Street
Suite 800
Needham, MA 02494
781-657-1000
Fax: 781-657-1100
E-Mail: lwalsh@infosecuritymag.com
Home Page: www.infosecuritymag.com
Andrew Briney, VP
Lawrence Walsh, Editor
Michael S Mimoso, Senior Editor
Gabrielle DeRussy, Advertising Sales
Susan Rastellini Smith, Product Management
Articles and analysis of information-security issues such as media, entwork and virus protection, internet security and encryption reports.
Cost: $100.00
Frequency: Monthly
Circulation: 60000
Founded in 1999

6571 Information Systems Security
Auerbach Publications
2494 Bayshore Boulevard
Suite 201
Dunedin, FL 34698
703-891-6781
800-737-8034
Fax: 703-891-0782
E-Mail: institute@isc2.org
Home Page: www.isc2.org
Social Media: Facebook, Twitter, YouTube
David Shearer, COO
Debra Taylor, CFO
John Colley, Chairman
Debra Taylor, Chief Financial Officer
Hord Tipton, Executive Director
Facts and experience, expert opinion on directions in security, public policy, computer crime and ethics related to the information security field.
Cost: $175.00
Circulation: 1500
Founded in 2003

6572 Inside the Internet
ZD Journals
500 Canal View Boulevard
Rochester, NY 14623-2800
585-407-7301
Fax: 585-214-2387
E-Mail: int@zdjournals.com
Home Page: www.zdjournals.com
Joelle Martin, Publisher
Information and hands-on instruction for applications along with some pictorial explanation.
Cost: $49.00
Frequency: Monthly

6573 **Internet & Intranet Business and Technology Report**
Computer Technology Research Corporation
6 N Atlantic Wharf
Charleston, SC 29401-2115

843-766-5293
Fax: 843-853-7210
Home Page: www.ctrcorp.com

Edward Wagner, Publisher

Reports on international news, historical profiles of the impact of various applications, and developing standards and regulations. Topics covered include domain registration, Webcasting and the market for Internet e-mail.
Cost: $390.00
Frequency: Monthly

6574 **Internet Business**
Ziff Davis Publishing Company
28 E 28th St
New York, NY 10016-7940

212-503-5772
E-Mail: steven_thompson@zd.com

Steve Weitzner, CEO
Adam Gordon, VP

Provides in-depth information and analysis on Internet products, techniques and tools, based on comparative lab testing and real world experience. Feature articles address technology segments that optimize an Internet strategy such as firewalls, authoring tools, etc., and how-to columns look at technical issues surrounding Web site development.
Cost: $24.99
Frequency: Monthly

6575 **Internet Business Strategies**
Gartner Group
Po Box 10212
Stamford, CT 06904-2212

203-964-0096
Fax: 203-316-6488
E-Mail: info@gartner.com
Home Page: www.gartner.com
Social Media: Facebook, Twitter, LinkedIn

Jean Hall, CEO
Eugene Hall, CEO
David Godfrey, Senior Vice President
John Gardner, President
Robin Kranich, SVP Human Resources

Helps readers make informed decisions about how to use the Internet to deploy electronic commerce and interactive initiatives.
Cost: $395.00
Frequency: Weekly
Circulation: 10,000
Founded in 1993

6576 **Internet Reference Service Quarterly**
Taylor & Francis
325 Chestnut Street
Suite 800
Philadelphia, PA 19106

800-354-1420
Fax: 215-625-2940
Home Page: www.tandf.co.uk

Brenda Reeb, Editor

Designed to function as a comprehensive information source librarians can turn to and count on for keeping up-to-date on emerging technological innovations, while emphasizing theoretical, research, and practical applications of Internet-related information services, sources and resources.
Cost: $82.00
Frequency: Quarterly
Circulation: 3000
ISSN: 1087-5301
Founded in 1978

6577 **Internet Shopper**
Mecklermedia Corporation
20 Ketchum Street
Westport, CT 06880-5908

203-662-2800
Fax: 203-454-5840
Home Page: www.internetshopper.com

Susan Leiterstein, Publisher

Edited for consumers who purchas products and services direct from Interet Web sites. Covers online malls, computers and electronics, stocks, books, home furnishings, music and more. Reviews the best sites within their categoreis and includes tips on how to conduct safe and effective online transactions.
Frequency: Daily

6578 **Internet Telephony**
Technology Marketing Corporation
1 Technology Plz
Norwalk, CT 06854-1936

203-852-6800
800-243-6002
Fax: 203-853-2845
E-Mail: tmc@tmcnet.com
Home Page: www.tmcnet.com

Rich Tehrani, CEO
Richard Tehrani, President/Group Publisher
Shirley A. Russo, Circulation Director

News and departments focus on providing readers with information they need to learn about and purchase the equipment, software and services necessary for Internet telephony, through the convergence of voice, video, fax and data.
Frequency: Monthly
Circulation: 28024
Founded in 1972

6579 **Internet World**
Mecklermedia Corporation
20 Ketchum Street
Westport, CT 06880-5908

203-226-6967
Fax: 203-454-5840

Corey Friedman, Publisher
Michael Neubarth, Editor

For noncommercial and commercial uses of Internet and the National Research and Education Network.
Cost: $5.00
Circulation: 256883
Founded in 1971

6580 **Journal of Electronic Imaging**
International Society for Optical Engineering
1000 20th Street
Bellingham, WA 98225-10

360-676-3290
Fax: 360-647-1445
E-Mail: customerservice@spie.org
Home Page: www.spie.org

Kristin Lewotsky, Executive Editor
Winn Hardin, Senior Editor
Michael Brownell, Contributing Editors
Amy Nelson, Manager

Timely information about evolving imaging technologies, including image acquistions, image data storage, image data display, image visualization, image processing, image data communciations, hard copy output and multimedia systems.
Cost: $135.00
Frequency: Quarterly
Circulation: 1500
Founded in 1992

6581 **Journal of Internet Law**
Apen Publishers
400 Hamilton Avenue
Palo Alto, CA 94301-1809

650-328-6561
Fax: 650-327-3699
E-Mail: mailops@gcfw.com
Home Page: www.gcfw.com

Mark F Radcliffe, Editor-in-Chief

Discusses strategies utilized by top intellectual property, computer law and information technology industry experts.
Frequency: Monthly

6582 **Journal of Research on Computing in Education**
International Society for Technology in Education
180 W 8th Avenue
Eugene, OR 97401-2916

541-302-3777
800-336-5191
Fax: 541-302-3778
E-Mail: iste@iste.org
Home Page: www.iste.org

Don Knezek, CEO
Leslie Conery, Deputy CEO

Covers computer research and developments relating to all levels of education. Articles define the state of current and future use of technology in education.
Cost: $79.00
Frequency: Quarterly
Circulation: 4500
Founded in 1989
Mailing list available for rent

6583 **Journal of Technology in Human Services**
Taylor & Francis
325 Chestnut Street
Suite 800
Philadelphia, PA 19106

800-354-1420
Fax: 215-625-2940
Home Page: www.tandf.co.uk

Dick Schoech PhD, Editor

Explores the potentials of computer and telecommunciations technologies in mental health, developmental disability, welfare, addictions, education, and other human services.
Cost: $120.00
Frequency: Quarterly
ISSN: 1522-8835
Founded in 1978
Mailing list available for rent
Printed in one color on matte stock

6584 **KM World**
Information Today
18 Bayview Street
PO Box 1358
Camden, ME 04843-1358

207-236-8524
Fax: 207-236-6452
E-Mail: webmaster@kmworld.com
Home Page: www.kmworld.com
Social Media: Facebook, Twitter, LinkedIn

Hugh McKellar, Editor in Chief
Sandra Haimila, Managing Editor
Michael V Zarrello, Advertising Director
Andy Moore, Publisher
David Panara, Sales Manager

Serves content, document and knowledge of management market to help improve business performance.
Circulation: 56000

6585 **MacTech**
Xplain Corporation

PO Box 5200
Westlake Village, CA 91359-5200

805-494-9797
Fax: 805-494-9798
E-Mail: custservice@mactech.com
Home Page: www.mactech.com
Social Media: Twitter

Neil Ticktin, Publisher
Dave Mark, Executive Editor
Edward Marczak, Executive Editor
David Allen, Production Manager

Provides web developers and network administrators with the most technically advanced information for them to combat the needs of the industry. How to articles, technically oriented product reviews with a Mac focus.
Cost: $19.95
Frequency: Monthly
ISBN: 3-212874-88-7
ISSN: 1067-8360
Founded in 1984
Printed in on glossy stock

6586 On the Internet
Rickard Group
1775 Wiehle Ave
Suite 201
Reston, Va 20190-5108

703-439-2120
E-Mail: editor@isoc.org
Home Page: www.isoc.org
Social Media: Facebook, Twitter, LinkedIn, YouTube

Wendy Rickard Bollentin, Publisher

Internet information for technologists, developers, educators, researchers, government representatives, and business people.
Cost: $22.00
Frequency: Bi-Monthly
Circulation: 9M

6587 Optical Technology 21st Century
Frames Data
PO Box 2141
Skokie, Il 60077

800-739-7555
847-763-9532
E-Mail: customerservice@framesdata.com
Home Page: www.framesdata.com

Skip Johnson, President
Hunter Noell, Business Development Manager

Movement of product electronically; computerization of office functions, lab work, testing procedures and equipment; information on the Internet, optical Web sites, and onlines services.
Cost: $299.00
Frequency: Quarterly
Circulation: 19M

6588 PCAI
Knowledge Technology
PO Box 30130
Phoenix, AZ 85046

602-971-1869
Fax: 602-971-2321
E-Mail: info@pcai.com
Home Page: www.pcai.com/pcai

Terry Hengl, Publisher
Daniel W Rasmus, Editorial Advisor
Don Barker, Senior Editor
Robin Okun, VP of Marketing

Information necessary to help managers, programmers, executives and other professionals understand the unfolding realm of artificial intelligence and intelligent applications.
Cost: $24.00
Founded in 1987

6589 PDN's Pix
VNU Business Media
30 E 23rd St # 5
New York, NY 10010-4442

212-673-1100
Fax: 212-673-7074
E-Mail: bmcomm@vnuinc.com
Home Page: www.vnu.com

Penny Vane, Owner
Rob Ruijter, CFO

Covers the world of electronic digital imaging to help readers use new imaging technology and the Web, digital meda, image capture and transfer.
Cost: $19.94
Circulation: 51753
Founded in 1964

6590 Virus Bulletin
Virus Bulletin
590 Danbury Road
Ridgefield, CT 06877-2722

203-438-7714
Fax: 203-431-8165

Richard Ford, Editor
Victoria Lammer, Production Manager

An international journal addressing computer viruses, Trojan horses and other malicious programs. Emphasis is placed on providing technical and procedural countermeasures for businesses using computers.
Cost: $35.00

6591 WWWiz Magazine
WWWiz Corporation
8840 Warner Avenue
Suite 200
Fountain Valley, CA 92708

714-848-9600
Fax: 714-375-2493
E-Mail: wiz@wwwiz.com
Home Page: www.wwwiz.com

Don Hamilton, Editor-in-Chief
Vivian Hamilton, Managing Editor

WWWiz is a publication focused on the internet with content aimed entrepenuers and business professionals. We interview people who have found success in internet business along with articles pertaining to legal issues, marketing, technology, travel, and other special interest areas.
Cost: $28.00
Frequency: Monthly
Circulation: 120000
Founded in 1995

6592 Wall Street & Technology
Miller Freeman Publications
11 West 19th Street
New York, NY 10011

212-780-0400
Fax: 212-600-3045
E-Mail: mfrieden@cmp.com
Home Page: www.wallstreetandtech.com

Michael Friedenberg, Group Publisher
Richard Rosenblatt, CEO/President
Kerry Massaro, Editor-in-Chief
Anne Marie Miller, Senior VP/Sales & Marketing

Editoral emphasis on the automation of brokerage houses and money management firms.
Frequency: Monthly
Circulation: 21226

6593 Web Builder
Fawcette Technical Publications
2600 S El Camino Real # 300
Suite 300
San Mateo, CA 94403-2381

650-378-7100
800-848-5523
Fax: 650-853-0230
E-Mail: customerservice@fawcette.com
Home Page: www.ftponline.com

James Fawcette, President
Karen Koenen, Sr. Circulation Director
John Sutton, Executive VP
Susan Ogren, Marketing Manager
Henry Allain, President

Highly technical, code-sensitive articles that cover all that goes into designing interfaces for sophisticated Internet/Intranet applications. Features a case-study approach to finding out who is using which Web sites and how.
Cost: $32.96
Frequency: Monthly

6594 Web Content Report
Lawrence Ragan Communications
316 N Michigan Ave # 400
Suite 400
Chicago, IL 60601-3773

312-960-4100
800-493-4867
Fax: 312-960-4106
E-Mail: cservice@ragan.com
Home Page: www.ragan.com

Jim Ylisela, Publisher
Mark Ragan, CEO/President
Kasia Chalko, Marketing Director Events
Frank Bleers, Marketing Director Publisher

Outlines ways to attract visitors to a Web site, and be able to then monitor and evaluate the traffic on the home page. New developments in Web technology, how products can be sold on sites, budgeting matters and communicaiton with management.
Cost: $269.00
Frequency: Monthly
Founded in 1996
Printed in 2 colors on matte stock

6595 Web Guide Monthly
H&S Media
430 Oak Grove Street
Suite 100
Minneapolis, MN 55403-3234

612-990-3203
Fax: 612-879-1082
E-Mail: wdorn@webguidemag.com
Home Page: www.webguidemag.com

Dan Beaver, Publisher

Examines and evaluates useful tools that merge the Internet with everyday life, at work and at home. Sites are sorted into categories, and are referenced in an index.
Cost: $34.95
Frequency: Monthly
Circulation: 120M

6596 Web Techniques
Miller Freeman Publications
411 Borel Avenue
#100
San Mateo, CA 94402-3516

650-573-3210
Fax: 650-655-4250
E-Mail: editors@web-techniques.com
Home Page: www.webtechniques.com

Manny Sawit, Publisher
Deirdre Blake, Managing Editor

Latest information, tips and techniques to Web site developers. Contains information on new products and the latest information about the ever-changing world of Web development.
Cost: $34.95
Frequency: Monthly
Circulation: 100M

6597 Webserver Online Magazine
Computer Publishing Group

1340 Centre Street
Newton Centre, MA 02459-2499

617-641-9101
Fax: 617-641-9102
E-Mail: editor@cpg.com
Home Page: www.cpg.com

S Henry Sacks, CEO/President
Doug Pryor, Editorial Director
Carol Flanagan, Marketing Manager
Tina Jackson, Circulation Manager
S Sacks, Publisher

Source for information Web professionals who need to get the most ot of their Web development and deployment efforts. Technology and industry news, systems and network adminsitration issues, the latest in Web tools, and a guide to new products, services and resources.
Frequency: Monthly
Founded in 1989

6598 WirelessWeek.com
PO Box 266008
Highlands Ranch, CO 80163-6008

303-470-4800
Fax: 303-470-4892
E-Mail: subsmail@reedbusiness.com
Home Page: www.wirelessweek.com

Gerard Van de Aast, CEO
Debby Denton, Publisher
Rhonda Wickham, Editor -in- Chief
Glenn Comar, Marketing Director

Trade Shows

6599 American Public Communications Council Conference & Expo
625 Slaters Lane
Suite 104
Alexandria, VA 22314

703-739-1322
Fax: 703-739-1324
E-Mail: apcc@apcc.net
Home Page: www.apcc.net

Wilard Nichols, President
Deborah Sterman, CFO
Dan Collins, Corporate Counsel

Conference, luncheon and 100 exhibits of public communications equipment and information including, pay phones, internet, atm, multimedia and more.
Founded in 1988

6600 DMD New York Conference & Expo
Direct Marketing Conferences
20 Academy Street
Norwalk, CT 06850-4032

203-854-9166
800-969-6566
E-Mail: connecticut@dmdays.com
Home Page: www.dmdays.com

Direct Marketing Days New York offers new ideas in media, creative, database, eCommerce and technology. Hundreds of exhibits showcase the newest technologies, products and services. Over 85 sessions and 25 consultation centers led by A level speakers. Network with top-level executives.
Frequency: Annual/June

6601 E-Sports & Business Services Show at the Super Show
Communications & Show Management
1450 NE 123rd Street
North Miami, FL 33161

305-893-8771
Fax: 305-893-8783
Home Page: www.bizbash.com
Social Media: Facebook

David Adler, CEO and Founder
Richard Aaron, President
Chad Kaydo

Retailers, distributors, wholesalers, importers/exporters and other buyers of sports related products come for 10,000 exhibits of sports apparel, footwear, accessories and e-commerce products and services.
100k Attendees
Frequency: January

6602 EcomXpo
Wordwide Business Research
535 5th Ave
8th Floor
New York, Ny 10017

888-482-6012
Fax: 646-200-7535
E-Mail: info@ecomxpo.com
Home Page: www.ecomxpo.com

Rick Worden, Chairman and CEO
Steve Goldring, Managing Director

An educationally focused, online virtual trade show designed specifically for search, affiliate and interactive marketers.
Frequency: July

6603 How To Make A Living On-line
Women in eCommerce
PO Box 550856
Fort Lauderdale, FL 33355-0856

954-625-6606
877-947-3337
E-Mail: heidi@wecai.org
Home Page:
www.wecai.org/3909/how-to-make-a-living-on line/

Suzannah Richards, President
Rosana Santos, President Elect
Ellen Sue Burton, VP/Logistics & Hospitality
Racheli Smilovitz, VP/Professional Development
Racheli Smilovitz, VP/Professional Development

An action packed, content-rich luncheon on the topic of internet marketing.
Founded in 2001

6604 Info Today Conference
Information Today
143 Old Marlton Pike
Medford, NJ 08055-8758

609-654-6266
800-300-9868
Fax: 609-654-4309
E-Mail: custserv@infotoday.com
Home Page: www.infotoday.com

Thomas H Hogan, Publisher/President
Roger R Bilboul, Chairman Of The Board

Users of online information services, electronic databases and the Internet. 200 booths.
6M Attendees
Frequency: May
Founded in 1980
Mailing list available for rent: 5000 names

6605 International Consumer Electronics Show (C ES)
Las Vegas Hotel & Casino
3000 S. Paradise Road
Las Vegas, NV 89109

866-539-8430
Home Page: www.ceweb.org
Social Media: Facebook, Twitter, LinkedIn

Gary Shapiro, President/CEO
Pat Lavelle, Chairman
Peter Lesser, Industry Executive Advisor
Jason Oxman, VP Communications
Jenny Pareti, Public Policy Director

The CES reaches across global markets, connects the industry and enables consumer electronics to grow and thrive. International CES is owned and prroduced by the Consumer Electronics Association (CEA).
2000 Members
Frequency: January

6606 Internet Communications Exposition
IDG Expositions
1400 Providence Highway
Norwood, MA 02062
508-879-6700

6607 National Conference on Operations & Fulfillment (NCOF)
Direct Marketing Association
1120 Avenue of Americas
New York, NY 10036-6700

212-768-7277
Fax: 211-302-6714
E-Mail: dmaconferences@the-dma.org
Home Page: www.the-dma.org

Julie A Hogan, SVP Conference/Events
Lawrence M Kimmel, CEO

Focuses on innovative solutions for the warehouse, distribution, operations, and ecommerce needs in the ever-changing world of operations and fulfillment.
10M Attendees

6608 Sporting Goods Manufacturers Markets
1150 17th Street NW
8th Floor
Washington, DC 20036-1604

202-775-1762
Fax: 202-296-7462
E-Mail: info@sgma.com
Home Page: www.sgma.com

Tom Cove, President/CEO
Gregg Harrlety, VP
Kalinda Mathis, Director Marketing

Retailers, distributors, wholesalers, importers/exporters and other buyers of sports related products come for 10,000 exhibits of sports apparel, footwear, accessories and e-commerce products and services.
80000 Attendees
Frequency: Biannual/Spring/Fall

6609 SuiteWorld User Conference
NetSuite Ecommerce
2955 Campus Drive
Suite 100
San Mateo, CA 94403-2511

650-627-1000
Fax: 650-627-1001
E-Mail: info@netsuite.com
Home Page: www.netsuite.com

Evan Goldberg, Co-Founder/Chief Technology Officer
Zach Nelson, President & CEO

SuiteWorld provides customers, users and partners with the opportunity to gain insights, inspiration and hands-on training to run your business smarter and faster on NetSuite.
10000 Members
Founded in 1998

6610 VoIP 2.0
Technology Marketing Corporation
One Technology Plaza
Norwalk, CT 06854

203-852-6800
800-243-6002

Fax: 203-853-2845
Home Page: www.itexpo.com

Frequency: October, San Diego

6611 eM Conference
91 Point Judith Road
Suite 129
Narragansett, RI 02882

800-496-2950
Fax: 408-884-2461
E-Mail: service@eMarketingAssociation.com
Home Page: www.emarketingassociation.com

Chris Baggott, CEO
Bert DuMars, C-Founder/CEO
Murray Gaylord, VP/Marketing
Jeff Hilmire, President
Simms Jenkins, Founder & Principal

The Power of eMarketing Conference offers an unparalleled experience in best practices, case histories and processes for social, email and search marketing.
Frequency: Annual/April
Founded in 1997

Directories & Databases

6612 Adweek Directory
Prometheus Global Media
770 Broadway
New York, NY 10003-9595

212-493-4100
Fax: 646-654-5368
Home Page: www.prometheusgm.com

Richard D. Beckman, CEO
James A. Finkelstein, Chairman
Madeline Krakowsky, Vice President Chairman
Tracy Brater, Executive Director Creative Service

Adweek Directories Online is where you will find searchable databases with comprehensive information on ad agencies, brand marketers and multicultural media.
Frequency: Annual
Circulation: 800
Founded in 1981

6613 America Online
8619 Westwood Center Drive
Suite 200
Vienna, VA 22182-2238

800-227-6364
Fax: 540-265-2135

Jack Daggitt, Director
Anne Botsford

This multi-faceted information service provides complete access to a variety of databases and computer services of interest to users of Macintosh and Apple II computers. Databases included in this systems range from Computing & Software to Lifestyles & Interests.
Frequency: Full-text

6614 Boardwatch Magazine Directory of Internet Service Providers
Penton Media
1300 E 9th St # 316
Cleveland, OH 44114-1503

216-696-7000
Fax: 216-696-6662
E-Mail: rgolden@boardwatch.com
Home Page: www.penton.com

Jane Cooper, Marketing
Bill McCarthy, Editorial Director

Reviews various Internet providers and lists different programs available through their individual companies who operate in the US and Canada.
Cost: $72.00
Frequency: Monthly
Circulation: 70,000

6615 Fulltext Sources Online
Information Today
143 Old Marlton Pike
Medford, NJ 08055-8750

609-654-6266
800-300-9868
Fax: 609-654-4309
E-Mail: custserv@infotoday.com
Home Page: www.infotoday.com

Thomas H Hogan, President
Roger R Bilboul, Chairman Of The Board

A directory of periodicals accessible online in full text through 28 aggregator products. Lists over 22,000 newspapers, journals, newsletters, newswires, and transcripts.
Cost: $145.00
Frequency: Biannually Jan & July
ISBN: 1-573872-23-7

6616 Global Business Directory
Women in eCommerce
PO Box 550856
Fort Lauderdale, FL 33355-0856

954-625-6606
877-947-3337
E-Mail: heidi@wecai.org
Home Page: www.wecai.org

Suzannah Richards, President
Rosana Santos, President Elect
Ellen Sue Burton, VP/Logistics & Hospitality
Racheli Smilovitz, VP/Professional Development
Racheli Smilovitz, VP/Professional Development

30 member institutions; also lists free resources, global network and internet resources.
Founded in 2001

6617 IQ Directory Adweek
Prometheus Global Media
770 Broadway
New York, NY 10003-9595

212-493-4100
Fax: 646-654-5368
Home Page: www.prometheusgm.com

Richard D. Beckman, CEO
James A. Finkelstein, Chairman
Madeine Krakowsky, Vice President Circulation
Tracy Brater, Executive Director Creative Service

Profile of companies at the leading edge of digital marketing, has the specifics you'll need to investigate, launch and/or expand your digital presence. Profiles over 2,200 interactive agencies, web developers, brand marketers, online media, CD-ROM developers, POP/Kiosk designers and multimedia creative companies
Founded in 1981

6618 Internet Blue Pages
Information Today
143 Old Marlton Pike
Medford, NJ 08055-8750

609-654-6266
800-300-9868
Fax: 609-654-4309
E-Mail: custserv@infotoday.com
Home Page: www.infotoday.com

Thomas H Hogan, President
Roger R Bilboul, Chairman Of The Board

The Guide to Federal Government Web Sites is the leading guide to federal government information on the web. Includes over 1,800 annotated agency listings, arranged in the US Government Manual style to help you find the information you need.
Cost: $34.95
464 Pages
ISBN: 0-910965-43-9

6619 Key Guide to Electronic Resources: Language and Literature
Information Today
143 Old Marlton Pike
Medford, NJ 08055-8750

609-654-6266
800-300-9868
Fax: 609-654-4309
E-Mail: custserv@infotoday.com
Home Page: www.infotoday.com

Thomas H Hogan, President
Roger R Bilboul, Chairman Of The Board

Part of the ongoing topic related series of reference guides is an evaluative directory of electronic reference sources in the fields of language and literature.
Cost: $39.50
120 Pages
ISBN: 1-573870-20-x

6620 On-Line Networks, Databases & Bulletin Boards on Assistive Technology
ERIC Document Reproduction Service
7420 Fullerton Road
Suite 110
Springfield, VA 22153-2852

703-440-1400
800-443-ERIC
Fax: 703-440-1408

Directory of electronic networks that focus on technology-related services.

6621 Professional Trade Association Membership
Local Hispanic Chamber of Commerce
1424 K Street NW
Suite 401
Washington, DC 20005

202-715-0494
E-Mail: membership@ushcc.com
Home Page: www.ushcc.com

Javier Palomarez, President & CEO
DeVere Kutscher, Chief of Staff & VP of Strategy

The USHCC is a not-for-profit (501(c)6) organization founded in 1979 to foster Hispanic economic development and to create sustainable prosperity for the benefit of American society.
Founded in 1979

6622 Trade Show News Network
Tarsus Group plc
16985 W Bluemound Road
Suite 210
Brookfield, WI 53005

262-782-1900
Fax: 603-372-5894
E-Mail: rwimberly@tsnn.com
Home Page: www.tsnn.com

Rachel Wimberly, Editor-in-Chief
John Rice, Sales & Business Development
Arlene Shows, Marketing Manager

The world's leading online resource for the trade show, exhibition and event industry since 1996. TSNN.com owns and operates the most widely consulted event database on the internet, containing data about more than 19,500 trade shows, exhibitions, public events and conferences.
13900 Members
Frequency: Bi-Monthly
Founded in 1196

Industry Web Sites

6623 **http://gold.greyhouse.com**
G.O.L.D Grey House OnLine Databases
Grey House Publishing's online database platform, GOLD, offers Quick Search, Keyword Search and Expert Search for most business sectors including e-commerce and internet markets. The GOLD platform makes finding the information you need quick and easy - whether you're a novice searcher or an experienced database user. All of Grey House's directory products are available for subscription on the GOLD platform.

6624 **www.aace.org**
Association for the Advancement of Computing in Ed
Promotes the use of computers and the internet in educational settings.

6625 **www.adsl.com/adsl_forum.html**
Information about ADSL, Asymmetric Digital Subscriber Line, a system that provides high-speed Internet connections

6626 **www.apcc.net**
American Public Communications Council
APCC Proudly offers a wide array of services to the public communications industry, from Perspectives magazine to our annual trade show to our involvement in legal and regulatory issues. This site is a place for the public to find out about our industry and for our members to learn of legal and regulatory developments, to become aware of APCC programs and events and to have a forum for discussion.

6627 **www.bsa.org**
Business Software Alliance
An organization dedicated to promoting a safe and legal digital world. BSA educates consumers on software management and copyright protection, cyber security, trade, e-commerce and other internet related issues.

6628 **www.cabledatacomnews.com/cmic.htm**
Cable modems

6629 **www.computercpa.com**
Accountant's Home Page
Provides information on general accounting for manufacturing, contstruction, service, not-for-profit, e-commerce and more.

6630 **www.conferences.calendar.com/**
Academic conferences, symposia, courses and workshops.

6631 **www.dititalmx.com/wires/**
Integrated Services Digital Network

6632 **www.greyhouse.com**
Grey House Publishing
Authoritative reference directories for most business sectors incluidng e-commerce and internet markets. Users can search the online databases with varied search criteria allowing for custom searches by product category, geographic area, sales volume, keyword, subject and more. Full Grey House catalog and online ordering also available.

6633 **www.hayes.com/prodinfo/adsl/intro.html**
Information about ADSl, Asymmetric Digital Subscriber Line, a system that provides high-speed Internet connections

6634 **www.internets.com**
Internets.com
Searchable database and related industry links.

6635 **www.iste.org**
International Society for Technology in Education
Nonprofit professional organization with a worldwide membership of leaders and potential leaders in educational technology.

6636 **www.sdl.com/en/wcm/**
eMarketing Association
SDL Tridion R5, the core product, provides complete Web content management and content delivery capabilities, focusing on ease-of-use for all content contributors, site managers and power users.

6637 **www.shop.com**
Altura International
CatalogCity.com is a powerful and flexible e-commerce technology. This site includes recognized brand names such as Blair, Bombay, Chef's Catalog, Fisher-Price, Gump's by Mail, Hammacher Schlemmer, Ross-Simmons, The Sharper Image, and many more.

6638 **www.spie.org**
International Society for Optical Engineering
Serves the international technical community as the premier provider of education, information, and resources covering optics, photonics, and their applications.

6639 **www.wecommercenews.com**
Women in eCommerce
A qualified audience of women looking for e-commerce solutions, information and tolls to run their online endeavors.

Associations

6640 **American Automatic Control Council**
3640 Col Glenn Hwy
Dayton, OH 45435

937-775-5062
Fax: 937-775-3936
E-Mail: pmisra@cs.wright.edu
Home Page: www.a2c2.org

R. Russell Reinehart, President
Tariq Samad, President-elect
Jordan Berg, Treasurer
B.Wayne Bequette, Secretary

Supports all those involved in the manufacturer and distribution of automatic controls. Hosts annual trade show.

6641 **Association for High Technology Distributors**
N19 W24400 Riverwood Drive
Waukesha, WI 53188

262-696-3645
800-488-4845
E-Mail: ahtd@ahtd.org
Home Page: www.ahtd.org
Social Media: Twitter, LinkedIn

Neil Montogomery, President
Bryan Roeesler, Executive Director
Neil Montgomery, VP
John Pirner, Secretary/Program Chair
Tom Swenton, Treasurer

Works to increase productivity and profitability of high technology automation solutions, providers and manufacturers.
250 Members
Founded in 1985

6642 **Association of Edison Illuminating**
600 18th Street N
PO Box 2641
Birmingham, AL 35291

205-257-2530
Fax: 205-257-2540
E-Mail: aeicdir@bellsouth.net
Home Page: www.aeic.org

Earl Parsons, Jr, Executive Director/Secretary
Len Holland, Manager AEIC Services
Becky Neel, Administrative Assistant
Cindy McLeod, Administrative Assistant

Association of electric utilities concerned with generating, transmitting and distributing electricity. This organization supplies information and support to the industry.
165 Members
Founded in 1885

6643 **Bioelectromagnetics Society**
2412 Cobblestone Way
Frederick, MD 21702-2626

301-663-4252
Fax: 301-694-4948
E-Mail: office@bems.org
Home Page: www.bems.org

Gloria Parsley, Executive Director
Richard Nuccitelli, VP
Jonna Wilen, Secretary

Nonprofit organization and international resource for excellence in scientific research, knowledge and understanding of the interaction of electromagnetic fields with biological systems. Members are biological and physical scientists, physicians and engineers interested in the interactions of nonionizing radiation with biological systems.
400 Members
Founded in 1978

6644 **Contract Services Association of America**
1000 Wilson Boulevard
Suite 1800
Arlington, VA 22209

703-243-2020
Fax: 703-243-3601
E-Mail: info@csa-dc.org
Home Page: www.csa-dc.org

Barry Cullen, President
Colleen Preston, Senior VP

Represents the government services contracting industry. Membership ranges from small businesses and corporations servicing federal and state government in numerous capacities. CSA acts to foster the effective implementation of the government's policy of reliance on the private sector for support services. Largest DOD association of service contractors.
650 Members
Founded in 1965

6645 **EOS/ESD Association, Inc. (DBA ESD Association)**
Electrostatic Discharge Association
7900 Turin Road
Building 3
Rome, NY 13440-2069

315-339-6937
Fax: 315-339-6793
E-Mail: info@esda.org
Home Page: www.esda.org
Social Media: Facebook, LinkedIn

Leo G. Henry, President
Terry Welsher, Sr. VP
Robert Gauthier, VP
Lisa Pimpinella, Director of Operations

EOS/ESD Association is a professional voluntary association dedicated to advancing the theory and practice of electrical overstress and electrostatice avoidance. The Association expands EOS/ESD awareness through atandards development, educational programs, local chapters, publications, tutorials, certification and symposia.
Cost: $60.00
2000+ Members
Frequency: Bi-Monthly
Founded in 1982

6646 **Edison Electric Institute**
701 Pennsylvania Avenue NW
Washington, DC 20004-2696

202-508-5000
Fax: 202-508 5360
E-Mail: feedback@eei.org
Home Page: www.eei.org
Social Media: Facebook, Twitter, YouTube

Thomas R Kuhn, President
David Owens, Executive VP
Brian Wolff, Senior VP, External Affairs

The association of U.S. Shareholder-owned electric companies.
180 Members
Founded in 1933

6647 **Electric Association**
40 Shuman Blvd
Suite 247
Naperville, IL 60563-8446

630-305-3050
Fax: 630-305-3056
E-Mail: cspaeth@eachicago.org
Home Page: www.eachicago.org
Social Media: Facebook, LinkedIn

Mark Gibson, President
Rick Jamerson, Vice President
Steven Anixter, Treasurer
Thomas Scherzer, Secretary

Provides members of the electrical industry of Chicagoland and their employees with formal educational opportunities, professional development, information exchange, and member services.
Founded in 1926

6648 **Electric Power Research Institute**
3420 Hillview Avenue
Palo Alto, CA 94304

650-855-2121
800-313-3774
Fax: 650-855-2954
E-Mail: askepri@epri.com
Home Page: www.epri.com
Social Media: Facebook, Twitter, LinkedIn, YouTube, Flikr

Nicholas Akins, Chairman
Michael Howard, President/CEO

Nonprofit, energy research consortium for the benefit of utility members, their customers and society. Mission is to provide science and technology-based solutions of indispensable value to our global energy customers by managing a far-reaching program of scientific research, technology development and product implementation.
660 Members
Founded in 1973

6649 **Electrical Apparatus Service Association**
1331 Baur Boulevard
St Louis, MO 63132-1903

314-993-2220
Fax: 314-993-1269
E-Mail: easainfo@easa.com
Home Page: www.easa.com
Social Media: Facebook, Twitter, LinkedIn

Kevin Toor, Chair
Linda J Raynes CAE, President/CEO
Richard Tutka, Finance Manager

An international trade organization of electromechanical sales and service firms in 58 countries. Provides members with a means of keeping up to date on materials, equipment, and state of the art technology.
2100 Members
Founded in 1937
Mailing list available for rent

6650 **Electrical Association**
One Energy Center
40 Shuman Boulevard, Suite 247
Naperville, IL 60563

630-305-3050
Fax: 630-305-3056
E-Mail: cspaeth@eachicago.org
Home Page: www.eachicago.org
Social Media: Facebook, LinkedIn

Mark Gibson, President
Rick Jamerson, Vice President
Steven Anixter, Treasurer
Thomas Scherzer, Secretary

Provides members of the electrical industry of Chicagoland and their employees with formal educational opportunities, professional development, information exchange and member services

6651 **Electrical Equipment Representatives Association**
638 W 39th Street
Kansas City, MO 64111

816-561-5323
800-728-2272
Fax: 816-561-1249
E-Mail: info2005@eera.org
Home Page: www.eera.org

Vince Brown III, President
Brad Cahoon, President Elect

Don Shirk, VP
Kier Cooper, Secretary
Rob Rigsby, Treasurer

Provides technically competent, hands-on, local representation for companies providing products and services to the electric power industry.

6652 Electrical Generating Systems Association
1650 S Dixie Hwy
Suite 400
Boca Raton, FL 33432-7461

561-750-5575
Fax: 561-395-8557
Home Page: www.egsa.org
Social Media: Facebook

Debra Laurentis, President
Edward Murphy, VP
Bob Hafich, Secretary/Treasurer

A trade association made up of companies in the USA and around the world that design, manufacture, sell, distribute, rent, specify, service and use on site power equipment.
600 Members
Founded in 1965

6653 Electrical Safety Foundation International
1300 N 17th Street
Suite 1752
Rosslyn, VA 22209

703-841-3229
Fax: 703-841-3329
E-Mail: info@esfi.org
Home Page: www.esfi.org
Social Media: Facebook, Twitter, YouTube

David Tallman, Chairman
John Engel, Vice Chairman
Evan Gaddis, Treasurer
Barbara Guthrie, Secretary

The mission of the Electrical Safety Foundation International (ESFI) is to advocate electrical safety in the home and in the workplace in order to reduce electrically-related fatalities, injuries and property loss.
Founded in 1994

6654 Electrochemical Society
65 S Main St
Building D
Pennington, NJ 08534-2827

609-737-1902
Fax: 609-737-2743
E-Mail: ecs@electrochem.org
Home Page: www.electrochem.org

Christine Garzon, President
Tetsuya Osaka, Sr. VP
Harikila Deligianni, Secretary
Christina Bock, Treasurer

Members are electrochemists and professionals in related industries.
8000 Members
Founded in 1902

6655 Electronic Industries Association
2214 rock Hill Rd
Suite 170
Herndon, VA 20170

571-323-0294
Fax: 571-323-0245
Home Page: www.eia.org
Social Media: LinkedIn, YouTube

Ronald L Turner, Chairman
Mike Kennedy, Vice Chairman
Dave McCurdy, President
Charles Robinson, Chief Operating Officer
James Shiring, Secretary/Treasurer

Is a national trade organization that includes the full spectrum of U.S. manufacturers.
1300 Members

6656 Electronic Technicians Association
5 Depot St
Greencastle, IN 46135-8024

765-653-8262
800-288-3824
Fax: 765-653-4287
E-Mail: eta@eta-i.org
Home Page: www.eta-i.org
Social Media: Facebook, Twitter, LinkedIn, YouTube

Teresa Maher, President
Chrissy Baker, Marketing Coordinator
John Baldwin, Secretary

Association for electronics technicians worldwide offering over 70 certifications.
5000 Members
Founded in 1978

6657 IPC: Association Connecting Electronics
3000 Lakeside Dr
Suite 309 S
Bannockburn, IL 60015-1249

847-615-7100
Fax: 847-615-7105
E-Mail: webmaster@ipc.org
Home Page: www.ipc.org
Social Media: Facebook, Twitter, LinkedIn, YouTube

Robert Ferguson, Chairman
Stephen Pudles, Vice Chairman
Don Schroeder, Secretary/Treasurer

A trade association for the printed circuit boards and electronics assembly industries, offering programs and resources to board manufacturers and electronic assemblers, designers, industry suppliers and original equipment manufacturers.
2700 Members
Founded in 1957

6658 Independent Electrical Contractors Association
4401 Ford Ave
Suite 1100
Alexandria, VA 22302-1464

703-549-7351
800-456-4324
Fax: 703-549-7448
E-Mail: info@ieci.org
Home Page: www.ieci.org
Social Media: Facebook, Twitter, LinkedIn, you tube

Michael Kallmeyer, National President
Dean Kredit, National Sr. VP
Bobby Tutor, National Secretary/Treasurer

The mission of IEC is to create success among independent electrical contractors by developing a professional workforce, communicating clearly with government, promoting ethical business practices, and providing leadership for the electrical industry.
73000 Members
Founded in 1957

6659 Institute of Electrical/Electronic Engineers
3 Park Ave
17th Floor
New York, NY 10016-5997

212-419-7900
Fax: 212-752-4929
Home Page: www.ieee.org
Social Media: Facebook, Twitter, LinkedIn, YouTube

Moshe Kam, President and CEO
Roger Pollard, Director and Secretary
Dr Mohamed El-Hawary, Director/Secretary

Supports all those involved in the field of electrical engineering. Publishes newsletter and hosts trade show.
365K Members
Founded in 1963

6660 Instrumentation and Measurement Society
3 Park Ave
17th Floor
New York, NY 10016-5997

212-419-7900
Fax: 732-981-0225
E-Mail: webmaster@ieee.org
Home Page: www.ewh.ieee.org

Moshe Kam, President and CEO
Roger Pollard, Director and Secretary
Dr Mohamed El-Hawary, Director/Secretary

A subsidiary of the Institute of Electrical and Electronics Engineers. Provides support to scientists and technicians who design and develop electrical and electronic measuring instruments and equipment.
36000 Members
Founded in 1980

6661 Instrumentation, Systems, and Automation Society
67 Alexander Drive
Box 12277
Research Triangle Park, NC 27709

919-549-8411
Fax: 919-549-8288
E-Mail: info@isa.org
Home Page: www.isa.org
Social Media: Facebook, Twitter, LinkedIn

Ken Baker, President
Patrick Gouhin, Executive Director
Debbie Eby, Executive Assistant
Leo Staples, Treasurer

Nonprofit, educational organization connecting people and ideas in automation. The Society fosters advancement in the theory, design, manufacture, and use of sensors, instruments, computers, and systems for automation in a wide variety of applications.
33000 Members
Founded in 1945

6662 International Electrical Testing Association
3050 Old Centre Ave.
Suite 102
Portage, MI 49024

269-488-6382
888-300-6382
Fax: 269-488-6383
E-Mail: neta@netaworld.org
Home Page: www.netaworld.org
Social Media: Facebook, YouTube

John White, President
Jayne Tanz, Executive Director
Ralph Patterson, 1st VP
Lynn Hamrick, Secretary
Ken Bassett, Treasurer

Defines the standards by which electrical equipment is deemed safe and reliable. Creates specifications, procedures, testing and requirements for commissioning new equipment and testing the reliability and performance of existing equipment.
2000 Members
Founded in 1972

6663 **International Institute of Connector and Interconnection**

3000 Lakeside Drive
Bannockburn, IL 60015

E-Mail: info@iicit.org
Home Page: www.iicit.org

Dale Reed, Content Editor

Dedicated to the spread of technological information throughout the industry. In a time of global competition, success depends on communicating technological breakthroughs, innovations and changes in specifications to engineers, designers, specifiers, consultants and other professionals using your product or services.
2640 Members
Founded in 1958

6664 **International League of Electrical Associations**

P.O. Box 24
Mumford, NY 14511

585-538-6350
Fax: 585-538-6166
E-Mail: inco@ileaweb.org
Home Page: www.ileaweb.org
Social Media: LinkedIn

Chris Price, President
Robert Morris, VP
Kirstie Steves, Secretary
Barbette Cejalvo, Treasurer

An organization of professional electric association and electric league managers from more than thirty US and seven Canadian cities.
Founded in 1936

6665 **International Magnetics Association**

Eight South Michigan Avenue
Suite 1000
Chicago, IL 60603-3310

312-456-5590
Fax: 312-580-0165
E-Mail: ima@gss.net
Home Page: www.intl-magnetics.org

August Sisco, Chair
Lowell Bosley, President
George Orenchak, Secretary/Treasurer

Is the worldwide trade association representing manufacturers of magnetic materials, distributors and fabricators, suppliers to the magnetics industry and others with an interest in magnetics.
35 Members
Founded in 1959

6666 **International Microwave Power Institute**

PO Box 1140
Mechanicsville, VA 23111-5007

804-559-6667
Fax: 804-559-4087
E-Mail: info@impi.org
Home Page: www.impi.org

Bob Schiffman, President
Ben Wilson, Vice President
Dorin Bolder, Secretary
Amy Lawson, Treasurer

To be the global organization that provides a forum for the exchange of information on all aspects of microwave and RF heating technologies.
Founded in 1966

6667 **Laser Institute of America**

13501 Ingenuity Dr
Suite 128
Orlando, FL 32826-3009

407-380-1553
800-345-2737
Fax: 407-380-5588
E-Mail: lia@lia.org
Home Page: www.lia.org
Social Media: Facebook, Twitter, LinkedIn

Klaus Loeffler, President
Stephen Capp, Treasurer
Robert Thomas, Secretary

The Laser Institute of America is the professional membership society dedicated to fostering lasers, laser applications and safety worldwide.
1200 Members
Founded in 1968

6668 **Laser and Electro-Optic Manufacturers**

123 Kent Road
Pacifica, CA 94044-3923

650-738-1492
Fax: 650-738-1769
E-Mail: info@leoma.com
Home Page: www.leoma.com

John Ambroseo, President
Breck Hitz, Executive Director
Lynn Strickland, Treasurer
Brian Lula, Secretary

Is the trade association for North American manufacturers of lasers and associated electro-optics equipment.
Founded in 1986

6669 **National Association of Electrical Distributors**

1181 Corporate Lake Drive
St. Louis, MO 63132

314-991-9000
888-791-2512
Fax: 314-991-3060
E-Mail: customerservice@naed.org
Home Page: www.naed.org
Social Media: Facebook, Twitter, YouTube

Tom Naber, President
Michelle McNamara, VP/Executive Director

Supports manufacturers and distributors of electrical components, supplies and equipment. Publishes directory.
Founded in 1997

6670 **National Electrical Contractors**

3 Bethesda Metro Ctr
Suite 1100
Bethesda, MD 20814-5372

301-657-3110
Fax: 301-215-4500
E-Mail: beth.margulies@necanet.org
Home Page: www.necanet.org
Social Media: Facebook, Twitter, LinkedIn, YouTube

John M Grau, CEO
Russell Alessi, President
Dan Walter, Vice President and COO
J Michael Thompson, Secretary-Treasurer

Represents a segment of the construction market comprised of over 70,000 electrical contracting firms.
65000 Members
Founded in 1901

6671 **National Electrical Manufacturers Representatives Association**

28 Deer Street
Suite 302
Portsmouth, NH 03801

914-524-8650
800-446-3672
Fax: 603-319-1667
E-Mail: nemra@nemra.org
Home Page: www.nemra.org
Social Media: Twitter, LinkedIn

Kenneth Hooper, President
Kirsty Stebbins, Manager of Marketing
Sue Todd, Office Manager

Promotes the function of the independent manufacturer's representative as the most effective way to market electrical products. Increases the income of the rep's firm employees and sales staff by increasing the value of the rep firm to owners and customers. Offers educational opportunities that help representatives strengthen the management, technical and professional capabilities of their firms. Promotes communication between independent electrical representatives and manufacturing partners.

6672 **National Electronics Service Dealers Association**

3608 Pershing Ave
Fort Worth, TX 76107-4527

817-921-9061
800-797-9197
Fax: 817-921-3741
E-Mail: info@nesda.com
Home Page: www.nesda.com
Social Media: Facebook

Ben Fowler, President
Jerrell Helms, Vice President
Wayne Markman, Secretary
George Weiss, Treasurer

Trade association supporting professionals within the electronics business who repair appliances, consumer electronic equipment and computers.
8 Members
Founded in 1950

6673 **National Rural Electric Cooperative Association**

4301 Wilson Blvd
Suite 1
Arlington, VA 22203-1860

703-907-5500
Fax: 703-907-5526
Home Page: www.nreca.org
Social Media: Twitter

Glenn English, CEO

Organized specifically to overcome World War II shortages of electric construction materials, to obtain insurance coverage for newly constructed rural electric cooperatives, and to mitigate wholesale power problems. Since those early days, NRECA has been an advocate for consumer owned cooperatives on energy and operational issues as well as rural community and economic development.
1000 Members
Founded in 1942

6674 **National Systems Contractors Association**

3950 River Ridge Drive NE
Cedar Rapids, IA 52402
319-366-6722
800-446-6722
Fax: 319-366-4164
E-Mail: nsca@nsca.org
Home Page: www.nsca.org
Social Media: Facebook, Twitter, LinkedIn, YouTube

Injolf de Jonh, President
Kelley McCarthy, Vice President
Michael Hester, Treasurer
Ron Bailey, Secretary

Represents the commercial electronic systems industry. Serves as an advocate for all those who work within the low-voltage industry, including systems contractors/integrators, product manufacturers, consultants, sales

representatives and a growing number of architects, specifying engineers and others.
2800 Members
Founded in 1980

6675 North American Electric Reliability Corporation
3353 Peachtree Road, N.E
Suite 600 North Tower
Atlanta, GA 30326
404-446-2560
E-Mail: info@nerc.com
Home Page: www.nerc.com
Gerry Cauley, President/CEO
Mark Rossi, SVP and COO
David R Nevius, Senior Vice President
Joseph K Conner, Jr, Chief Financial Officer
Principal organization for coordinating and promoting North America's electrical supplies, demands and reliability issues.
11 Members
Founded in 1968

6676 North Central Electrical League
2901 Metro Dr
Suite 203
Bloomington, MN 55425-8699
952-854-4405
800-925-4985
Fax: 952-854-7076
E-Mail: dale@ncel.org
Home Page: www.ncel.org
Dale Yohnke, Executive Director
Sarita Woods, Manager
Trade association representing all segments of the electrical industry in the Upper Midwest.
1500 Members
Founded in 1936

6677 Power Sources Manufacturers Association
PO Box 418
Mendham, NJ 07945-0418
973-543-9660
Fax: 973-543-6207
E-Mail: power@psma.com
Home Page: www.psma.com
Social Media: LinkedIn
Dusty Becker, Chairman
Carl Blake, President
Jim Marinos, VP
Michel Grenon, Secretary/Treasurer
The PSMA is a not-for-profit organization incorporated in the state of California. The purpose of the Association shall be to enhance the stature and reputation of its members and their products, improve their knowledge of technological and other developments related to power sources, and to educate the entire electronics industry, plus academia, as well as government and industry agencies as to the importance of, and relevant applications for, all types of power sources and conversion devices.
155 Members
Founded in 1985

6678 Relay and Switch Industry Association
2500 Wilson Boulevard
Arlington, VA 22201
70 -90 -802
Fax: 703-875-8908
E-Mail: narm@ecaus.org
Home Page: http://www.ec-central.org
Robert Willis, President
James Kaplan, Chairman and CEO
Represents the electronics industry sector comprised of companies that manufacturer, produce or market relay and switch technologies and products.
Founded in 1947

6679 SMMA: The Motor & Motion Association
PO Box P182
South Dartmouth, MA 02748
508-979-5935
Fax: 508-979-5845
E-Mail: info@smma.org
Home Page: www.smma.org
Doug Bank, President
Paul Murphy, Vice President
Matt French, Secretary/Treasurer
Trade association for the electric motor and motion control industry in North America. The voice of the motor and motion industry providing a forum for education, communication, research and networking.
110 Members
Founded in 1975

6680 Semiconductor Equipment and Materials International
3081 Zanker Road
San Jose, CA 95134
408-943-6900
Fax: 408-428-9600
E-Mail: semihq@semi.org
Home Page: www.semi.org
Douglas Neugold, Chairman
Andr,-Jacques Auberton-Herv,, Vice Chairman
Global industry association serving the manufacturing supply chains for the microelectronic, display and photovoltaic industries.
2300 Members
Founded in 1970

6681 Semiconductor Industry Association
1101 K Street NW
Suite 450
Washington DC 20005
202-446-1700
866-756-0715
Fax: 202-216-9745
E-Mail: mailbox@sia-online.org
Home Page: www.sia-online.org
George Scalise, President
Brian L Halla, Vice Chairman
Chuck Fraust, Director Environment Health/Safety
Daryl Hatano, VP Public Policy
Trade association representing the US microchip industry. Provides a forum for working collectively to enhance the competitiveness of the US chip industry.
70 Members
Founded in 1977

6682 Society of Manufacturing Engineers
1 SME Drive
Dearborn, MI 48128
313-425-3000
800-733-4763
Fax: 313-425-3400
E-Mail: service@sme.org
Home Page: www.sme.org
Mark Tomlinson, Executive Director/General Manager
Greg Sheremet, Publisher
Bob Harris, Director Finance
Supports all those engineers involved in electrical manufacturing. Hosts trade show.
25K Members
Founded in 1932

6683 Surface Mount Technology Association
5200 Willson Rd
Suite 215
Edina, MN 55424-1316
952-920-7682
Fax: 952-926-1819
E-Mail: joann@smta.org
Home Page: www.smta.org
Social Media: Facebook, Twitter, LinkedIn
Dan Baldwin, President
Roy Starks, VP of Membership
Marie Cole, VP Technical Programs
Tom Forsythe, VP Communications
Kola Akinade, Secretary
Network of professionals building skills, sharing practical experience and developing solutions in electronic assembly technologies and related business operations.
3200 Members
Founded in 1984

Newsletters

6684 Advanced Battery Technology
Seven Mountains Scientific
913 Tressler Street
PO Box 650
Boalsburg, PA 16827
814-466-6559
Fax: 814-466-2777
E-Mail: jo@7ms.com
Home Page: www.7ms.com
E Thomas Chesworth, Technical Editor
Josephine Chesworth, Managing Editor
The oldest, most widely read international newsletter reporting on battery technology, marketing and industry events including new products and financial news. Accepts advertising. Print and online versions available.
Cost: $ 180.00
Circulation: 1000
Printed in 4 colors on matte stock

6685 Cleanroom Markets Newsletter
McIlvaine Company
191 Waukegan Rd
Suite 208
Northfield, IL 60093-2743
847-784-0012
Fax: 847-784-0061
E-Mail: editor@mcilvainecompany.com
Home Page: www.mcilvainecompany.com
Robert McIlvaine, Owner
Robert McIvaine, President
Marilyn McIlvaine, EVP
Information on clean rooms markets worldwide.
Cost: $460.00
8 Pages
Frequency: Monthly
Printed in on newsprint stock

6686 Cleanroom Technology Newsletter
McIlvaine Company
191 Waukegan Rd
Suite 208
Northfield, IL 60093-2743
847-784-0012
Fax: 847-784-0061
Home Page: www.mcilvainecompany.com
Robert McIlvaine, Owner
Robert McIvaine, President
Marilyn McIlvaine, EVP
Information on clean room technology.

6687 **Continuous Improvement**
James Publishing
PO Box 25202
Santa Ana, CA 92799-5202
714-755-5450
800-394-2626
Fax: 714-751-2709
E-Mail: customer-service@jamespublishing.com
Home Page: www.jamespublishing.com
Jim Pawell, Founder and President
Stephen Sicillan, Editor
Tutorial and news on new quality assurance technologies and ISO 9000, QS 9000 and ISO 14000.
Cost: $20.00
Circulation: 2000

6688 **Currents**
Electrical Apparatus Service Association
1331 Baur Boulevard
Saint Louis, MO 63131-1903
314-993-2220
Fax: 314-993-1269
E-Mail: easinfo@easa.com
Home Page: www.easa.com
Kevin Toor, Chairman
William Gray, Vice Chairman
Kenneth Gralow, Secretary Treasurer
Provides information on EASA's programs, seminars, technical articles and industry trends and events. Members receive a copy each month.
Frequency: Monthly
Circulation: 2000+

6689 **Display Technology News**
Business Communications Company
49 Walnut Park
Building 2
Wellesley, MA 02481
781-489-7301
866-285-7215
Fax: 781-253-3933
E-Mail: sales@bccresearch.com
Home Page: www.bccresearch.com
Social Media: Facebook, Twitter
Greg Lindberg, Chairman and CEO
Bridgett Hurley, CMO
Kevin Fitzgerald, Editorial Director
Sharon Blank, Sales Director
Mark McCarthy, Operations Director
Market reports and technology updates of topics such as news materials, news applications, patents, technology transfer, processing and equipment.
Cost: $500.00
Frequency: Monthly
Founded in 1971

6690 **Document Imaging Report**
Corry Publications
5340 Fryling Road
Knowledge Park, Suite 300
Erie, PA 16510
814-897-9000
Fax: 814-899-5583
E-Mail: corrypub@corrypub.com
Home Page: www.corrypub.com
Nicole Hykes, Editor
John Toiston, Publisher
Carry Procious, Marketing
Mindy Sadden, Circulation Manager
Presents the most timely and actionable information on electronic imaging applications, products and user implementation.
Frequency: Monthly
Circulation: 50

6691 **EA Extra**
Electrical Association of Philadelphia
527 Plymouth Road
Suite 408
Plymouth Meeeting, PA 19462-1641
610-825-1600
Fax: 610-825-1603
E-Mail: electric@eap.org
Home Page: www.eap.org
Social Media: Facebook, Twitter, YouTube
Kevin Lane, President
Joe Henry, Vice President
Kim Schneider, Treasurer
Kenneth Hull, Secretary
Carries information on industry trends, events, educational and business opportunities, economic briefings, member happening, mergers, and member benefit updates.
450 Members
Founded in 1917

6692 **Electrical Connection**
Electrical Association of Rochester
PO Box 20219
Rochester, NY 14602-0219
585-538-6350
Fax: 585-538-6166
E-Mail: info@peawny.com
Home Page: www.eawny.com
Joe Lengen, President
Bonnie Curran, First VP
Coreg Merrill, Secretary/Treasurer
Kirstie Steves, Executive Director
Contains information on upcoming events, recaps past events, a message from the President, the current calendar and much more.
Frequency: Quarterly
Founded in 1924

6693 **Electrical Product News**
Business Marketing & Publishing
PO Box 7457
Wilton, CT 06897
203-834-9959
E-Mail: info@epnweb.com
Home Page: www.epnweb.com
Social Media: Facebook
George Young, Editor/Publisher
Accepts advertising.
Cost: $39.50
20 Pages
Frequency: Monthly
Circulation: 3500
Printed in 2 colors on newsprint stock

6694 **Electro Manufacturing**
Worldwide Videotex
PO Box 3273
Boynton Beach, FL 33424-3273
561-738-2276
E-Mail: markedit@juno.com
Home Page: www.wvpubs.com
Computer and electronic technologies used to help improve manufacturing efficiency.
Cost: $165.00

6695 **Executive Newsline**
Electric Power Research Institute
PO Box 10412
Palo Alto, CA 94303-0813
650-855-2000
800-313-3774
Fax: 650-855-2954
E-Mail: askepri@epri.com
Home Page: www.epri.com
Social Media: Facebook, Twitter, LinkedIn, YouTube, Flikr
Steven R Specker, CEO
Jackie Turner, Communications Manager
Don Kintner, Communications Manager
Rick Langley, Director
Contains brief highlights of EPRI science and technology developments and announcements of interest to utility executives.

6696 **Global Electronics**
Pacific Studies Center
222B View Street
Mountain View, CA 94041-1344
650-969-1545
Fax: 650-961-9818
Leonard Siegel, Editor
News items detailing the industry throughout the world and the social, environmental and military implications of production and application.
Cost: $1.00
Circulation: 400

6697 **IEEE Transactions on Applied Superconductivity**
IEEE Instrumentation and Measurement Society
67 Alexander Drive
PO Box 12277
Research Triangle Park, NC 27709
919-549-8411
Fax: 919-549-8288
E-Mail: info@isa.org
Home Page: www.isa.org
Social Media: Facebook, Twitter, LinkedIn
Ken Baker, President
Patrick Gouhin, Executive Director
Jerry Clemons, Department VP
Leo Staples, Treasurer
Concentrates on materials and their applications to electronics and power systems where superconductivity is central to the work.

6698 **IEEE Transactions on Mobile Computing**
IEEE Instrumentation and Measurement Society
67 Alexander Drive
PO Box 12277
Research Triangle Park, NC 27709
919-549-8411
Fax: 919-549-8288
E-Mail: info@isa.org
Home Page: www.isa.org
Social Media: Facebook, Twitter, LinkedIn
Ken Baker, President
Patrick Gouhin, Executive Director
Jerry Clemons, Department VP
Leo Staples, Treasurer
Research papers are presented in this publication dealing with mobile computing, wireless networks, reliability, quality assurance, distributed systems architecture and high-level protocols.
Frequency: Quarterly

6699 **IFAC Newsletter**
American Automatic Control Council
3640 Col Glenn Hwy
Dayton, OH 45435
937-775-5062
Fax: 937-775-3936
E-Mail: pmisra@cs.wright.edu
Home Page: www.a2c2.org
John Watkins, Editor
It contains up-to-date information about forthcoming IFAC events as well as brief announcements of other IFAC related activities. It is sent free of charge to NMO's, IFAC Affiliates and libraries.
Frequency: Bi-Monthly

6700 **Inside FERC**
McGraw Hill

PO Box 182604
Columbus, OH 43272

720-485-5000
877-833-5524
Fax: 614-759-3749
E-Mail: customer.service@mcgraw-hill.com
Home Page: www.mcgraw-hill.com
Social Media: Facebook, Twitter, LinkedIn, YouTube

Harold McGraw, President and CEO
Jack Callahan, Executive VP/CFO
John Berisford, EVP, Human Resources

Provides coverage of the Federal Energy Regulatory Commission's activities and federal regulations.
Cost: $975.00
14 Pages
Frequency: Monthly
Founded in 1884

6701 Inside NRC
McGraw Hill
PO Box 182604
Columbus, OH 43272

614-304-4000
877-833-5524
Fax: 614-759-3749
E-Mail: customer.service@mcgraw-hill.com
Home Page: www.mcgraw-hill.com
Social Media: Facebook, Twitter, LinkedIn, YouTube

Harold McGraw, President and CEO
Jack Callahan, Executive VP/CFO
John Berisford, EVP, Human Resources

Focuses exclusively on the US Nuclear Regulatory Commission.
Cost: $1310.00
13 Pages
Founded in 1800

6702 SMT Trends
New Insights
303 Vallejo Street
Crockett, CA 94525-1237

510-787-2273
Fax: 415-389-8671

Michael New, Publisher/Editor

Marketing and business news for the surface mount industry. Covers component and packaging trends, CAD, CAE, pick and place, robotics and test inspection.
Printed in one color on matte stock

6703 SMTA News
Surface Mount Technology Association
5200 Wilson Road
Suite 215
Minneapolis, MN 55424

952-920-7682
Fax: 952-926-1819
E-Mail: joann@smta.org
Home Page: www.smta.org

Dan Baldwin, President
Marie Cole, VP Tech Programs
Kola Akinade, Secretary
Hal Hendrickson, Treasurer

6704 Seven Mountain Scientific
PO Box 650
Boalsburg, PA 16827-651
814-466-6559
Fax: 814-466-2777
E-Mail: abt@7ms.com
Home Page: www.7ms.com

E Thomas Chesworth, President

Industry news in battery and fuel cell technology, marketing and industry events including new products, electric vehicle, R&D and environmental news.
Cost: $180.00
ISSN: 0001-8627
Founded in 1965

6705 Tech Notes
National Technical Information Service
5301 Shawnee Rd
Alexandria, VA 22312

703-605-6000
Fax: 703-605-6900
E-Mail: info@ntis.gov
Home Page: www.ntis.gov
Social Media: Facebook, Twitter

Bruce Borzino, Director
Patrik Ekstrom, Business Development Manager
Reuel Avila, Managing Director

Describes new processes, equipment, materials and techniques developed by Federal laboratories.
Cost: $8.00

6706 Threshold Newsletter
Electrostatic Discharge Association
7900 Turin Road
Building 3
Rome, NY 13440-2069

315-339-6937
Fax: 315-339-6793
E-Mail: info@esda.org
Home Page: www.esda.org
Social Media: Facebook, LinkedIn, YouTube

Donn Bellmore, President
Leo G. Henry, Sr. VP
Terry Welsher, VP
Lisa Pimpinella, Director of Operations
Donn Pritchard, Treasurer

Benefits of ESD membership include a subscription to the Threshold Newsletter in addition to other Association activities and programs such as educational tutorials and seminars; the EOS/ESD Symposium; participation in local chapters; discounts on Association standards and other publications; extensive networking; membership roster, and participation in standards development.
2000+ Members
Founded in 1982

6707 Transformers for Electronic Circuits
Power Sources Manufacturers Association
PO Box 418
Mendham, NJ 07945-0418

973-543-9660
Fax: 973-543-6207
E-Mail: power@psma.com
Home Page: www.psma.com

Dusty Becker, Chairman
Carl Blake, President
Jim Marinos, VP
Michel Grenon, Secretary/Treasurer

It is a complete, one-stop guide to transformer and inductor design and applications for everyone who designs, builds, or uses power magnetics components. Combines analysis and synthesis, and all theory is related to the solution of real world problems.
Cost: $100.00
155 Members
Founded in 1985

6708 Update
Power Sources Manufacturers Association
PO Box 418
Mendham, NJ 07945-0418

973-543-9660
Fax: 973-543-6207
E-Mail: power@psma.com
Home Page: www.psma.com
Social Media: LinkedIn

Dusty Becker, Chairman
Carl Blake, President
Jim Marinos, VP
Michel Grenon, Secretary/Treasurer

PSMA Update is published and distributed via e-mail quarterly by the Power Sources Manufacturers Association.
Frequency: Quarterly
Circulation: 2700

6709 Vision
Society of Manufacturing Engineers
1 SME Drive
PO Box 930
Dearborn, MI 48128

313-425-3000
800-733-4763
Fax: 313-425-3400
E-Mail: service@sme.org
Home Page: www.sme.org

Paul Bradley, President
Mark Tomlinson, Executive Director/CEO

The newsletter highlights the latest developments in the machine vision industry including applications, techniques and methods.
Cost: $85.00
Frequency: Quarterly
Circulation: 1100
ISSN: 1544-3531

6710 Wafer News Confidential
PennWell Publishing Company
98 Spit Brook Rd
Suite LI-1
Nashua, NH 03062-5737

603-891-0123
800-225-0556
Fax: 603-891-9294
E-Mail: ATD@PennWell.com
Home Page: www.pennwell.com

Christine Shaw, VP
Barbara Pennwell, CEO/President

Provides semiconductor equipment industry executives with information on developments, trends, news and market insights.
Cost: $15.00
Frequency: Monthly
Founded in 1910

Magazines & Journals

6711 Bioelectromagnetics Journal
John Wiley & Sons
2412 Cobblestone Way
Frederick, MD 21702-3519

301-663-4252
Fax: 301-694-4948
E-Mail: office@bems.org
Home Page: www.bems.org

James Lin, Editor in Chief
Carmela Marino, Associate Editor
Andrei Pakhomov, Associate Editor

It is a peer-reviewed, internationally circulated scientific journal that specializes in reporting original data on biological effect and applications of electromagnetic fields that range in frequency from zero hertz static fields) to the terahertz undulations of visible light.
Frequency: 6x yearly

6712 Contact
1000 McKee Street
Batavia, IL 60510-1682

630-879-6000
Fax: 630-879-0867

Steve Wilcox, Editor

Application of electric motor controls to electrically operated machinery and equipment.
Circulation: 4,000

6713 Control Solutions
PennWell Publishing Company
1421 S Sheridan Rd
Tulsa, OK 74112-6619

918-835-3161
800-331-4463
Fax: 918-831-9497
E-Mail: Headquarters@PennWell.com
Home Page: www.pennwell.com

Robert Biolchini, President
Ron Kuhfeld, Editor-in-Chief
Frequency: Monthly

6714 Diesel & Gas Turbine Worldwide
Diesel & Gas Turbine Publications
20855 Watertown Rd
Suite 220
Waukesha, WI 53186-1873

262-754-4100
Fax: 262-754-4175
Home Page: www.dieselspec.com

Michael Osenga, President
Lynne Diefenbach, Advertising Manager

Concentrates its editorial on the design, packaging, operation and maintenance of medium and slow-speed, high output diesel, natural gas and gas turbine engine systems used in the electrical power generation, cogeneration, oil and gas, marine propulsion and railroad markets throughout the world.
Cost: $65.00
Frequency: 10x yearly
Circulation: 22,000
Founded in 1969

6715 ECN Magazine
Reed Business Information
360 Park Ave S
4th Floor
New York, NY 10010-1737

646-746-6400
Fax: 646-756-7583
E-Mail: subsmail@reedbusiness.com
Home Page: www.reedbusiness.com

John Poulin, CEO
Aimee Kalnoskas, Editor
Steve Wirth, Publisher Director
James Reed, Owner

Provides product solutions for designed engineers in the electronics industry.
Cost: $96.19
Frequency: Monthly

6716 EE Product News
Penton Media
1166 Avenue of the Americas/10th Fl
New York, NY 10036

212-204-4200
E-Mail: CorporateCustomerService@penton.com
Home Page: www.penton.com

David Kieselstien, CEO
Nicola Allais, CFO
Jasmine Alexander, CIO

Source of information on new products necessary to successfully design, assemble and test prototypes of commercial, industrial, military and aerospace electronic products.
Frequency: Monthly
Circulation: 111968
Founded in 1892

6717 EE: Evaluation Engineering
Nelson Publishing
2500 Tamiami Trl N
Nokomis, FL 34275-3476
941-966-9521
800-226-6113
Fax: 941-966-2590
E-Mail: pmilo@evaluationengineering.com
Home Page: www.healthmgttech.com
Social Media: Facebook, Twitter

Kristine Russel, President
Phil Colpas, Managing Editor

Magazine devoted exclusively to companies that test, evaluate, design and manufacture electronic products and equipment.
Cost: $43.00
84 Pages
Frequency: Monthly
Founded in 1962
Mailing list available for rent: 65,000 names
Printed in 4 colors on glossy stock

6718 ElectriCITY
Electric Association
40 Shuman Boulevard
Suite 247
Naperville, IL 60563

630-305-3050
Fax: 630-305-3056
E-Mail: cspaeth@eachicago.org
Home Page: www.eachicago.org

Mark Gibson, President
Rick Jamerson, Vice President
Steven Anixter, Treasurer
Thomas Scherzer, Secretary
Founded in 1925

6719 ElectriCITY Magazine
Electric Association
40 Shuman Boulevard
Suite 247
Naperville, IL 60563-8446

630-305-3050
Fax: 630-305-3056
E-Mail: admin@eachicago.org
Home Page: www.eachicago.org
Social Media: Facebook, LinkedIn

Mark Gibson, President
Rick Jamerson, Vice President
Steven Anixter, Treasurer
Thomas Scherzer, Secretary
Bob Porter, Secretary

Corporate news, timely articles, career announcements, product line changes, industry-dates calendars, career placement services, and government legislation updates; circulation across the Midwest.
Frequency: Quarterly

6720 Electric Co-op Today
National Rural Electric Cooperative Association
4301 Wilson Blvd
Suite 1
Arlington, VA 22203-1860

703-907-5500
Fax: 703-907-5526
Home Page: www.nreca.org
Social Media: Twitter

Glenn English, CEO

Devoted to accurate, critical coverage of electric cooperative developments and electric cooperative industry news, unavailable in any other publication. The only weekly publication covering electric cooperative industry news, legislation and regulation, and community and economic development. Each issue highlights what you need to know to understand key industry issues clearly, quickly, and easily.
Cost: $40.00
Frequency: Weekly
Founded in 1994

6721 Electric Light & Power
PennWell Publishing Company
1421 S Sheridan Rd
Tulsa, OK 74112-6619
918-835-3161
800-331-4463
Fax: 918-831-9497
E-Mail: Headquarters@PennWell.com
Home Page: www.pennwell.com

Serves the North American Electric Utility Industry including electric power generation, delivery, and information technology operations in investor-owned electric utilities.
Frequency: Monthly
ISSN: 0013-4120
Founded in 1902

6722 Electric Perspectives
Edison Electric Institute
701 Pennsylvania Avenue NW
Washington, DC 20004-2696

202-508-5000
Fax: 202-508-5360
E-Mail: feedback@eei.org
Home Page: www.eei.org
Social Media: Facebook, Twitter, YouTube

Thomas R Kuhn, President
David Owens, Executive VP Business Operations
Brian Wolff, Senior VP, External Affairs

Written and edited specifically for management-level employees at shareholder-owned electric utilities.
Frequency: Bi-Monthly
Circulation: 15,000
ISSN: 0364-474X

6723 Electrical Apparatus
Barks Publications
400 N Michigan Ave
Suite 900
Chicago, IL 60611-4164

312-321-9440
Fax: 312-321-1288
E-Mail: info@barks.com
Home Page: www.barks.com

Horace Barks, Owner
Elsie Dickson, Associate Publisher
Horace Barks, CEO
Joseph Hoff, Manager

Serves the electromechanical and electronic maintenance and application industries, including manufacturing plants, institutional facilities and service companies.
Cost: $45.00
Frequency: Monthly
Circulation: 15500
Founded in 1969

6724 Electrical Construction & Maintenance
Primedia
1166 Avenue of the Americas/10th Fl
New York, NY 10036

212-204-4200
E-Mail: CorporateCustomerService@penton.com
Home Page: www.penton.com

David Kieselstien, CEO
Nicola Allais, CFO
Jasmine Alexander, CIO

Owners and company officials, engineers, electrical personnel, electrical inspectors, architects

and designers, purchasing and other related personnel.
Circulation: 104344

6725 Electrical Contractor Magazine
National Electrical Contractors Association
3 Bethesda Metro Ctr
Suite 1100
Bethesda, MD 20814-5372
301-657-3110
Fax: 301-215-4500
E-Mail: beth.margulies@necanet.org
Home Page: www.necanet.org
Social Media: Facebook, Twitter, LinkedIn, YouTube
John M Grau, CEO
Dan Walter, VP and COO
Michael Thompson, Secretary/Treasurer
The magazine has been the complete information source for electrical construction professionals. Its goal is to serve all participants in the power and integrated building systems industries. It delivers the latest information in the areas of power, communications and controls in both high voltage and low voltage applications to electrical contractors who compete in residential, commercial, industrial and institutional market segments of the construction arena.
Circulation: 85,000
Founded in 1939

6726 Electrical Distributor Magazine
National Association of Electrical Distributors
1181 Cropporate Lake Drive
St Louis, MO 63132
314-991-9000
888-791-2512
Fax: 314-991-3060
E-Mail: info@naed.org
Home Page: www.naed.org
Social Media: Facebook, Twitter, YouTube
Robert Reynolds, Chairman
Tom Naber, President and CEO
An informative, insightful publication that offers electrical distributors the latest information affecting their business. Subscriptions are free to NAED members.

6727 Electrical Wholesaling
Primedia
1166 Avenue of the Americas/10th Fl
New York, NY 10036
212-204-4200
E-Mail:
CorporateCustomerService@penton.com
Home Page: www.penton.com
David Kieselstien, CEO
Nicola Allais, CFO
Jasmine Alexander, CIO
Offers information on manufacturers, suppliers, prices and marketing of electrical products.
Cost: $25.00
Frequency: Monthly
Circulation: 22,500
Founded in 1905

6728 Electricity Today
1885 Clements Road
Unit 218
Pickering, Canada, ON L1W-3V4
905-686-1040
Fax: 905-686-1078
E-Mail: carol@electricityforum.com
Home Page: www.electricty-today.com
Randy Hurst, Publisher
Electricity Today is a leading electrical transmission and distribution magazine distributed free of charge to North American T&D electric utility engineering, construction and maintenance personnel, and high voltage T&D consulting engineers.

6729 Electronic Design
Penton Media
1166 Avenue of the Americas/10th Fl
New York, NY 10036
212-204-4200
E-Mail:
CorporateCustomerService@penton.com
Home Page: www.penton.com
David Kieselstien, CEO
Nicola Allais, CFO
Jasmine Alexander, CIO
Celebrating 50 years of innovation, this authoritative source provides leading-edge information to electronic and engineering managers around the world.

6730 Fringe Ware Review
Fringe Ware
PO Box 49921
Austin, TX 78765-4858
512-444-2393
Paco Nathan, Co-Founder
Don Lebkowsky, Co-Founder
Monte McCarter, Art Director
Tiffany Lee Brown, Assistant Editor
Stories and review on electronic products made by smaller producers.
Cost: $4.00
Founded in 1992

6731 High Tech News
Electronic Technicians Association International
5 Depot St
Greencastle, IN 46135-8024
765-653-8262
800-288-3824
Fax: 765-653-4287
E-Mail: eta@eta-i.org
Home Page: www.eta-i.org
Social Media: Facebook, Twitter, LinkedIn
Teresa Maher, CSS, President
Cindy Reed, Financial Director
Richard Glass, CETsr, CEO Emeritus
Exclusive bi-monthly publication of ETA International, and a subscription is included with each individual membership. Each issue features information on the changing electronics industry: specialty techniques & technology, trends, qualification opportunities and educational advice.
4500 Members
Frequency: Bi-Monthly
Circulation: 10000
Founded in 1978

6732 IEEE Instrumentation and Measurement Magazine
IEEE Instrumentation and Measurement Society
67 Alexander Drive
PO Box 12277
Research Triangle Park, NC 27709
919-549-8411
Fax: 919-549-8288
E-Mail: info@isa.org
Home Page: www.isa.org
Social Media: Facebook, Twitter, LinkedIn
Kim Fowler, Editor-in-Chief
This publication is included in member dues, it contains applications-oriented articles and news nominations, awards, highlights of conferences, Technical Committee news, book reviews, tutorials and contributions from the membership.
Frequency: Quarterly

6733 IEEE Sensors Journal
IEEE Instrumentation and Measurement Society
67 Alexander Drive
PO Box 12277
Research Triangle Park, NC 27709
919-549-8411
Fax: 919-549-8288
E-Mail: info@isa.org
Home Page: www.isa.org
Social Media: Facebook, Twitter, LinkedIn
Ken Baker, President
Patrick Gouhin, Executive Director
Jerry Clemons, Department VP
Leo Staples, Treasurer
Specializes in the theory, design, fabrication, manufacturing and applications of devices for sensing and transducing physical, chemical and biological phenomena.
Frequency: Bi-Monthly

6734 IEEE Transactions on Intelligent Transportation Systems
IEEE Instrumentation and Measurement Society
67 Alexander Drive
PO Box 12277
Research Triangle Park, NC 27709
919-549-8411
Fax: 919-549-8288
E-Mail: info@isa.org
Home Page: www.isa.org
Social Media: Facebook, Twitter, LinkedIn
Ken Baker, President
Patrick Gouhin, Executive Director
Jerry Clemons, Department VP
Leo Staples, Treasurer
This journal contains basic and applied research to expand the knowledge base on transportation for improved design, management and control of future transportation systems.
Frequency: Quarterly

6735 IEEE Transactions on Nanotechnology
IEEE Instrumentation and Measurement Society
67 Alexander Drive
PO Box 12277
Research Triangle Park, NC 27709
919-549-8411
Fax: 919-549-8288
E-Mail: info@isa.org
Home Page: www.isa.org
Social Media: Facebook, Twitter, LinkedIn
Ken Baker, President
Patrick Gouhin, Executive Director
Jerry Clemons, Department VP
Leo Staples, Treasurer
The journal is devoted to the dissemination of new results and discussions related to understanding the physical basis and engineering applications of phenomena at the nanoscale level.
Frequency: Quarterly

6736 Industrial Laser Solutions
PennWell Publishing Company
98 Spit Brook Rd
Nashua, NH 03062-5737
603-891-0123
80- 2-5 05
Fax: 603-891-9294
Home Page: www.pennwell.com
Christine Shaw, VP
David Belforte, Editor
For all industries that use industrial lasers.
Cost: $260.00
45 Pages
Frequency: Monthly
Circulation: 10,000

ISSN: 1523-4266
Founded in 1986

6737 **Industrial Market Place**
Wineberg Publications
7842 Lincoln Avenue
Skokie, IL 60077

847-676-1900
800-323-1818
Fax: 847-676-0063
E-Mail: info@industrialmktpl.com
Home Page: www.industrialmktpl.com

Eliot Wineberg, President
Jackie Bitensky, Editor

Has advertisements on machinery, industrial and plant equipment, services and industrial auctions in each issue.
Cost: $175.00
60 Pages
Frequency: Bi-Monthly
Circulation: 14,000
Founded in 1951
Printed in 4 colors on glossy stock

6738 **Interface Magazine**
Electrochemical Society
65 S Main St
Building D
Pennington, NJ 08534-2827

609-737-1902
Fax: 609 737-2743
E-Mail: ecs@electrochem.org
Home Page: www.electrochem.org

Christine Garzon, President
Tetsuya Osaka, Sr. VP
Harikila Deligianni, Secretary
Christina Bock, Treasurer

Is an authoritative accessible publication for those in the field of solid-state and electrochemical science and technology which contains technical articles about the latest developments in the field, and presents news and information about and for members of ECS.
Cost: $40.00
Frequency: Quarterly
Circulation: 9000
ISSN: 1064-8208
Founded in 1902
Printed in 4 colors

6739 **Journal of Laser Applications**
Laser Institute of America
13501 Ingenuity Dr
Suite 128
Orlando, FL 32826-3009

407-380-1553
800-345-2737
Fax: 407-380-5588
E-Mail: lia@lia.org
Home Page: www.lia.org
Social Media: Facebook, Twitter, LinkedIn

Klaus Loeffler, President
Stephen Capp, Treasurer
Robert Thomas, Secretary

The official journal of the Laser Institute of America and serves as the major international forum for exchanging ideas and information in disciplines that apply laser technology. Internationally known editors, reviewers, and columnists deliver the latest results of their research worldwide, dealing with the diverse, practical applications of photonic technology.
Cost: $410.00

6740 **Journal of Lightwave Technology**
IEEE Instrumentation and Measurement Society
67 Alexander Drive
PO Box 12277
Research Triangle Park, NC 27709

919-549-8411
Fax: 919-549-8288
E-Mail: info@isa.org
Home Page: www.isa.org
Social Media: Facebook, Twitter, LinkedIn

Ken Baker, President
Patrick Gouhin, Executive Director
Jerry Clemons, Department VP
Leo Staples, Treasurer

The Journal is concerned with research, applications and methods used in all aspects of lightwave technology and fiber optics.
Frequency: Monthly

6741 **Journal of Microwave Power and Electromagnetic Energy**
International Microwave Power Institute
PO Box 1140
Mechanicsville, VA 23111-5007

804-559-6667
Fax: 804-559-4087
E-Mail: info@impi.org
Home Page: www.impi.org

Bob Schiffmann, President
Ben Wilson, Vice President
Dorin Bolder, Secretary
Amy Lawson, Treasurer

The quarterly, technical journal of the Institute published by the Industrial, Scientific, Medical and Instrumentation (ISMI) section. Designed for the information needs of professionals specializing in the research and design of industrial and bio-medical applications, the Journal exemplifies the highest standards of scientific and technical information on the theory and application of electromagnetic power.
Cost: $250.00
Frequency: Quarterly

6742 **Journal of the Electrochemical Society**
Electrochemical Society
65 S Main St
Building D
Pennington, NJ 08534-2827

609-737-1902
Fax: 609-737-2743
E-Mail: ecs@electrochem.org
Home Page: www.electrochem.org

Roque J Calvo, President

This peer reviewed journal publishes 60 articles each month. Articles are posted online, with a monthly paper edition following electronic publication. The ECS membership benefits package includes access to the electronic edition of this journal. Free with membership.
Cost: $110.00
Frequency: Monthly
Circulation: 8300
ISSN: 0013-4651
Founded in 1902

6743 **LIA Today**
Laser Institute of America
13501 Ingenuity Dr
Suite 128
Orlando, FL 32826 3009

407-380-1553
800-345-2737
Fax: 407-380-5588
E-Mail: lia@lia.org
Home Page: www.lia.org
Social Media: Facebook, Twitter, LinkedIn

Klaus Loeffler, President
Stephen Capp, Treasurer
Robert Thomas, Secretary

Includes articles on the latest industry news to keep members and other laser professionals current on important issues that impact the laser community. Readers of LIA TODAY consist of production managers, supervisors, safety professionals, researchers, end-users, laser physicians and nurses.
Frequency: Bi-Monthly
Circulation: 5000

6744 **Laser Tech Briefs**
Associated Business Publications International
317 Madison Avenue
New York, NY 10017

212-490-3999
Fax: 212-986-7864
Home Page: www.abpi.net

Domenic Mucchetti, CEO
Josheph Pramberger, President
Luke Schnirring, Executive VP

For purchasers of laser/optical products.
Circulation: 40,000

6745 **Lighting Dimensions**
Primedia Business
249 W 17th St
New York, NY 10011-5382

212-206-1894
800-827-3322
Fax: 212-514-3719
Home Page: www.lightingdimensions.com
Social Media: Facebook, Twitter

Doug MacDonald, Group Publisher
David Johnson, Associate Publisher
Marian Sandberg-Dierson, Editor
Ellen Lampert-Greaux, Consulting Editor
Jennifer Hirst, Art Director

Trade publication for lighting professionals in film, theatre, television, concerts, clubs, themed environments, architectural, commercial, and industrial lighting. Sponsors of the LDI Trade Show and the Broadway Lighting Master Classes.
Cost: $34.97
Frequency: Monthly
Circulation: 14,177
Founded in 1989

6746 **Market Trends**
Electronic Industries Association
2500 Wilson Boulevard
Arlington, VA 22201-3834

703-907-7500
Fax: 703-907-7767

Statistical information and marketing trends in the electronics industry.
Cost: $195.00
Frequency: Monthly

6747 **Motion Control**
ISA Services
P.O. Box 787
Williamsport, PA 17703

570-567-1982
800-791-8699
Fax: 570-320-2079
E-Mail:
briefingsweborders@publishersserviceasso
Home Page: www.douglaspublications.com

Janine Nunes, Editor
Edward Mueller, Publisher

Information for those who design and maintain motion control systems.
56 Pages
Frequency: Monthly
Circulation: 16,490
ISSN: 1058-4644
Founded in 1985
Printed in 4 colors on glossy stock

6748 **NETA World**
International Electrical Testing Association
Po Box 687
Morrison, CO 80465-0687
303-697-8441
888-300-6382
Fax: 303-697-8431
E-Mail: neta@netaworld.org
Home Page: www.netaworld.org
Social Media: Facebook, YouTube

Mose Ramieh, President
David Huffman, First VP
Ron Widup, Second VP
John White, Treasurer
Walter Cleary, Secretary

Features articles of interest to electrical testing and maintenance companies, consultants, engineers, architects, and plant personnel directly involved in electrical testing and maintenance. Free with membership.
Frequency: Quarterly

6749 **Power Conversion & Intelligent Motion**
Primedia
1166 Avenue of the Americas/10th Fl
New York, NY 10036
212-204-4200
E-Mail:
CorporateCustomerService@penton.com
Home Page: www.penton.com

David Kieselstien, CEO
Nicola Allais, CFO
Jasmine Alexander, CIO

Directed to engineers, designers and manufacturers of power electronic and electronic motion control components, subsystems and systems. Feature articles interpret trends and innovation in these subjects.
Circulation: 31,113

6750 **Power Engineering International**
PennWell Publishing Company
1421 S Sheridan Rd
Tulsa, OK 74112-6619
918-831-9421
800-331-4463
Fax: 918-831-9476
E-Mail: headquarters@pennwell.com
Home Page: www.pennwell.com

Robert Biolchini, President

Serves the global electric power generation and transmission industry.
Frequency: Monthly
Circulation: 34000
ISSN: 1069-4994
Founded in 1896

6751 **Powerline Magazine**
Electrical Generating Systems Association
1650 S Dixie Hwy
Suite 500
Boca Raton, FL 33432-7461
561-750-5575
Fax: 561-395-8557
Home Page: www.egsa.org
Social Media: Facebook

Debra Laurentis, President
Edward Murphy, VP
Bob Hafich, Secretary/Treasurer

Focuses on the entire on-site power generation industry.
Cost: $5.00
Frequency: Bi-Monthly

6752 **ProService Magazine**
National Electronics Service Dealers Association
3608 Pershing Ave
Fort Worth, TX 76107-4527
817-921-9061
800-797-9197
Fax: 817-921-3741
E-Mail: webmaster@nesda.com
Home Page: www.nesda.com
Social Media: Facebook

Ben Fowler, President
Jerrell Helms, Vice President
Wayne Markman, Secretary
George Weiss, Treasurer

Published for members of NESDA/ISCET.
24 Pages
Frequency: Bi-Monthly

6753 **Process Heating**
Business News Publishing Company
155 Pfingsten Road
Suite 205
Deerfield, IL 60015
847-405-4000
Fax: 248-502-1001
E-Mail: PHeditors@bnpmedia.com
Home Page: www.process-heating.com
Social Media: Facebook, Twitter

Anne Armel, Publisher
Linda Becker, Associate Publisher & Editor
Beth McClelland, Production Manager

Magazine covers heat processing at temperatures up to 1000 degrees F at end user and OEM plants in 9 industries. Follow us at twitter.com/ProcessHeating, www.facebook.com/ProcessHeating
Circulation: 25000
Founded in 1994

6754 **RE Magazine**
National Rural Electric Cooperative Association
4301 Wilson Blvd
Suite 1
Arlington, VA 22203-1860
703-907-5500
Fax: 703-907-5526
Home Page: www.nreca.org
Social Media: Twitter

Glenn English, CEO

Editorial content covers utility operations, deployment of the latest industry products and services; a showcase of new products, services, and catalogs; online resources; safety; member(customer) services; business and management trends; marketing tools; community and economic development; local leaders and rural issues; co-op personnel news; and politics and regulatory policies impacting electric co-ops.
Cost: $43.00
Frequency: Monthly
Founded in 1942

6755 **Rural Electrification**
National Rural Electric Cooperative Association
4301 Wilson Blvd
Arlington, VA 22203-1860
703-907-5500
Fax: 703-907-5526
Home Page: www.nreca.org
Social Media: Twitter

Glenn English, CEO

Serves people involved in the rural electric cooperative industry including generation and transmission cooperatives, distribution systems and public utility district members of NRECA; electric equipment manufacturers; US Congress, state and federal regulatory agencies and commissions; and others allied to the field.
Cost: $85.00
Frequency: Monthly
Founded in 1942

6756 **Service Contractor Magazine**
Contract Services Association of America
1000 Wilson Boulevard
Suite 1800
Arlington, VA 22209
703-243-2020
Fax: 703-243-3601
E-Mail: info@csa-dc.org
Home Page: www.csa-dc.org

Barry Cullen, President
Colleen Preston, Senior VP

Focuses on industry developments, regulatory and legislative issues, and any issues encountered in the process of competing for and securing contracts, such as changes in the acquisitions or procurement process. It tailors its content exclusively to government contractors.
Frequency: Bi-Annual

6757 **Standard for Certification of Electrical Testing Technicians**
International Electrical Testing Association
Po Box 687
Morrison, CO 80465-0687
303-697-8441
888-300-6382
Fax: 303-697-8431
E-Mail: neta@netaworld.org
Home Page: www.netaworld.org
Social Media: Facebook, YouTube

Mose Ramieh, President
David Huffman, First VP
Ron Widup, Second VP
John White, Treasurer
Walter Cleary, Secretary

Specifying requisite levels of training, experience, and education for the evaluator of electrical power equipment is an important test procedure itself. The requirements parallel those of the National Skill Standards Board in Washington, DC, which promulgates for various occupations.
Cost: $55.00
36 Pages

6758 **Standard for Electrical Maintenance Testing of Dry-Type Transformers**
International Electrical Testing Assocaition
Po Box 687
Morrison, CO 80465-0687
303-697-8441
888-300-6382
Fax: 303-697-8431
E-Mail: neta@netaworld.org
Home Page: www.netaworld.org
Social Media: Facebook, YouTube

Mose Ramieh, President
David Huffman, First VP
Ron Widup, Second VP
John White, Treasurer
Walter Cleary, Secretary

This Standard has been an individual section within the NETA document entitled Maintenance Testing Specifications for Electrical Power Distribution Equipment and Systems since 1975. The Maintenance Testing Specifications along with NETA's Acceptance Testing Specifications have long been in general use by organizations and individuals involved with testing of electrical apparatus.
Cost: $55.00
18 Pages

6759 **Standard for Electrical Maintenance Testin g of Liquid-Filled Transformers**
International Electrical Testing Association

PO Box 687
Morrison, CO 80465-0687

303-697-8441
888-300-6382
Fax: 303-697-8431
E-Mail: neta@netaworld.org
Home Page: www.netaworld.org
Social Media: Facebook, YouTube

Mose Ramieh, President
David Huffman, First VP
Ron Widup, Second VP
John White, Treasurer
Walter Cleary, Secretary

The Standard has been an individual section within the NETA document entitled Maintenance Testing Specifications for Electrical Power Distribution Equipment and Systems since 1975. The Maintenance Testing Specifications along with NETA's Acceptance Testing Specifications have long been in general use by organizations and individuals involved with testing of electrical apparatus.
Cost: $55.00
21 Pages

Trade Shows

6760 **AHTD Trade Show**
Association for High Technology Distributors
N19 W24400 Riverwood Drive
Waukesha, WI 53188

262-696-3645
800-488-4845
E-Mail: ahtd@ahtd.org
Home Page: www.ahtd.org
Social Media: Twitter, LinkedIn

Neil Montogomery, President
John Pirner, Vice President
Thomas Swenton, Secretary
Brian Lepsis, Treasurer

Works to increase productivity and profitability of high technology automation solutions, providers and manufacturers.
250 Members
Frequency: Annual/September
Founded in 1985

6761 **American Control Conference**
American Automatic Control Council
2145 Sheridan Road
Evanston, IL 60208-3118

847-491-8175
Fax: 847-491-4455
E-Mail: aacc@ece.northwestern.edu
Home Page: www.a2c2.org

R. Russell Reinehart, President
Tariq Samad, President-elect
Jordan Berg, Treasurer
B.Wayne Bequette, Secretary

Covers a broad range of topics relevant to the theory and practice of control and automation, including robotics, manufacturing, guidance and control, power systems, process control, identification and estimation, signal processing, modeling and advanced simulation.
800 Attendees
Frequency: Annual/June

6762 **Annual Connector & Interconnection Technology Symposium and Trade Show**
International Institute of Connector and Intercon
PO Box 20002
Sarasota, FL 34276

941-929-1806
800-854-4248
Fax: 941-929-1807
E-Mail: info@iicit.org
Home Page: www.iicit.org

Dale Reed, Content Editor

Offers the opportunity to meet with other connector/interconnection industry users and vendors to learn about the latest advances in interconnection technology in the areas of radio frequency interconnection, quality, high speed connectors, personal computer interconnections, automotive Interconnections, materials, finishes, and platings, test methods, automation, surface mount technology, fiber optics, spaceflight connector technology, and medical applications.

6763 **Annual Legislative & Regulatory Roundtable**
Electronic Industries Association
2214 rock Hill Rd
Suite 170
Herndon, VA 20170

571-323-0294
Fax: 571-323-0245
Home Page: www.eia.org
Social Media: LinkedIn, YouTube

Gail Tannenbaum, CMP, Manager Meetings

Panel topics in the past have included Broadband, Tax, Trade, Environment, Defense, Space, and the Congressional Leadership Agenda.
Frequency: Annual/August

6764 **Applied Power Electronics Conference & Exposition (APEC)**
Power Sources Manufacturers Association
PO Box 418
Mendham, NJ 07945-0418

973-543-9660
Fax: 973-543-6207
E-Mail: power@psma.com
Home Page: www.psma.com
Social Media: LinkedIn

Dusty Becker, Chairman
Carol Blake, President
Jim Marinos, VP
Michel Grenon, Secretary/Treasurer

APEC continues the long-standing tradition of addressing issues of immediate and long-term interest to the practicing power electronics engineer.
1000 Attendees

6765 **Bioelectromagnetics - Stun Gun Mini Symposium**
Bioelectromagnetics Society
2412 Cobblestone Way
Frederick, MD 21702-3519

301-663-4252
Fax: 301-694-4948
E-Mail: office@bems.org
Home Page: www.bems.org

David Black, President
Gloria Parsley, Executive Director

The focus of this symposium will be the technology, physiology and potential adverse side effects of the use of electronic weapons or stun guns, which are rapidly being deployed in military and police use.
Frequency: Annual/June

6766 **Bioelectromagnetics - U.S. Air Force Workshop**
Bioelectromagnetics Society
2412 Cobblestone Way
Frederick, MD 21702-3519

301-663-4252
Fax: 301-694-4948
E-Mail: office@bems.org
Home Page: www.bems.org

David Black, President
Gloria Parsley, Executive Director

Will focus on the use of molecular biology to identify changes in genes and proteins that may lead to physiological, pathological, or behavioral events.
Frequency: Annual/June

6767 **Bioelectromagnetics Society Meeting**
Bioelectromagnetics Society
2412 Cobblestone Way
Frederick, MD 21702-3519

301-663-4252
Fax: 301-694-4948
E-Mail: office@bems.org
Home Page: www.bems.org

David Black, President
Gloria Parsley, Executive Director
Richard Nuccitelli, VP

This is a joint meeting of The Bioelectromagnetics Society and The European BioElectromagnetics Association. Topics will be: Electric Fields, Human Studies, Exposure Assessment, Dosimetry, In Vitro ELF, Epidemiology, Unique EMF Signals, Medical applications, Mechanisms, Electromagnetic Therapy.
400 Attendees
Frequency: Annual/June

6768 **CSA Winter Meeting**
Contract Services Association of America
1000 Wilson Boulevard
Suite 1800
Arlington, VA 22209

703-243-2020
Fax: 703-243-3601
E-Mail: info@csa-dc.org
Home Page: www.csa-dc.org

Barry Cullen, President
Colleen Preston, Senior VP

This one day workshop is a free flowing exchange of information with real time interaction and information exchange.
Frequency: Annual/January

6769 **Coherence and Electromagnetic Fields in Biological Systems**
Bioelectromagnetics Society
2412 Cobblestone Way
Frederick, MD 21702-3519

301-663-4252
Fax: 301-694-4948
E-Mail: office@bems.org
Home Page: www.bems.org

David Black, President
Gloria Parsley, Executive Director
Richard Nuccitelli, VP

Highlights of the symposium organized by the Institute of Radio Engineering and Electronics, the Academy of Sciences of the Czech Republic and others are expected to include biophysical principles of coherence, role of endogenous EMF in the organization of biological systems, biophysical mechanisms of interaction of biological systems with EMF and more.
Frequency: Annual/July

6770 **Consulting Electrical Engineers(CEE) Technical Forum & Table-Top**
Electric Association
One Energy Center,40 Shuman Boulevard
Suite 247
Naperville, IL 60563

630-305-3050
Fax: 630-305-3056
E-Mail: admin@eachicago.org

Home Page: www.eachicago.org
Social Media: Facebook, LinkedIn

Mark Gibson, President
Rick Jamerson, VP
Steven Anixter, Treasurer
Thomas Scherzer, Secretary

This event will feature a free technical forum for engineers, specifiers, and designers on Short Circuit analysis, Coordination, and Arc Flash Hazard analysis using conventional and computerized methods. The Table Top tradeshow will feature 45 vendors and their latest technology.
Frequency: Annual/May

6771 **EASA Annual Convention**
Electrical Apparatus Services Association
1331 Baur Boulevard
Saint Louis, MO 63131-1903

314-993-2220
Fax: 314-993-1269
E-Mail: easainfo@easa.com
Home Page: www.easa.com

Linda Raynes, President/CEO
Anne Vogel, Executive Secretary

Provides members with a means of keeping up to date on materials, equipment, and state-of-the-art technology. 100+ exhibitor booths.
2500 Attendees
Frequency: Annual/June
Mailing list available for rent

6772 **EDS: Where the Electronics Industry Connects**
Electronics Distributions Show Corporation
2214 Rock Hill Road
Suite 170
Herndon, VA 20170

312-648-1140
Fax: 312-648-4282
E-Mail: eds@edsconnects.com
Home Page: www.edsconnects.com
Social Media: LinkedIn

Gretchen Oie-Weghorst, Director
Gerald M Newman, Executive VP

Attendees are manufacturers of electronic components who sell their products through electronics distributors. Provides networking and meeting opportunities, and opens doors to new business. Hundreds of exhibits, thousands of attendees.
6M Attendees
Frequency: Annual/May
Founded in 1937

6773 **EEI Annual Convention/Expo**
Edison Electric Institute
701 Pennsylvania Avenue NW
Washington, DC 20004-2696

202-508-5000
Fax: 202-508-5360
E-Mail: feedback@eei.org
Home Page: www.eei.org
Social Media: Facebook, Twitter, YouTube

Thomas Kuhn, President
David Owens, Executive VP Business Operations
Brian Wolff, Senior VP, External Affairs
1000 Attendees
Frequency: Annual/June

6774 **EEI Financial Conference**
Edison Electric Institute
701 Pennsylvania Avenue NW
Washington, DC 20004-2696

202-508-5000
Fax: 202-508-5335
E-Mail: feedback@eei.org
Home Page: www.eei.org
Social Media: Facebook, Twitter, YouTube

Thomas Kuhn, President
David Owens, Executive VP Business Operations
Brian Wolff, Senior VP, External Affairs

Provides a unique forum for exchange of ideas and experience; and to give you insight into emerging critical issues.
Frequency: Annual/November

6775 **EERA Annual Meeting**
Electrical Equipment Representation
638 W 39th Street
Kansas City, MO 64111

816-561-5323
800-728-2272
Fax: 816-561-1249
E-Mail: info2005@eera.org
Home Page: www.eera.org

Vince Brown III, President
Brad Cahoon, President Elect
Don Shirk, VP
Kier Cooper, Secretary
Rob Rigsby, Treasurer
Frequency: Annual/April

6776 **EGSA Annual Spring Convention**
Electrical Generating Systems Association
1650 S Dixie Highway
Suite 500
Boca Raton, FL 33432

561-750-5575
Fax: 561-398-8557
Home Page: www.egsa.org
Social Media: Facebook

Cara Clark, Director Conventions/Meetings
Bob Breese, Director of Education

Offers educational sessions covering a broad range of issues effecting the on-site power industry.
Frequency: Annual/March

6777 **EIA's Congressional Technology Forum**
Electronic Industries Association
2214 rock Hill Rd
Suite 170
Herndon, VA 20170

571-323-0294
Fax: 571-323-0245
Home Page: www.eia.org
Social Media: LinkedIn, YouTube

Gail Tannenbaum, CMP, Manager Meetings

Discusses the issues most relevant for the electronics and high-tech industries.
Frequency: Annual/October

6778 **Electri...FYI**
Electrical Association of Rochester
PO Box 20219
Rochester, NY 14602-0219

585-538-6350
Fax: 585-538-6166
E-Mail: info@earoch.com
Home Page: www.eawny.com

Ed Langschwager, President
Joe Lengen, First VP
Rich Monroe, Secretary/Treasurer
Kirstie Steves, Executive Director

Upstate Electrical Show. 120+ exhibitors. Free entry.
2000 Attendees
Frequency: Tri-Annual

6779 **Electric West Conference**
PRIMEDIA Business Exhibitions
11 River Bend Drive S
PO Box 4232
Stamford, CT 06907-0232

203-358-9900
Fax: 203-358-5816
Home Page: www.primediaevents.com

David Small, Show Director
Tara Keating-Magee, Show Coordinator

Educational sessions attract electrical professionals from contracting companies, industrial plants, consulting engineering firms, datacom installers and electricians. Presentations focus on such topics as power quality, lighting, the NEC, project management, claims management and fiber optics. Also provides in-depth coverage of National Electrical Code changes that directly impact the work of electrical professionals. 250 Exhibitors.
6000 Attendees
Frequency: Annual/March

6780 **Energy - Exhibit Promotions Plus**
US Department of Energy/US Dept. of Defense/GSA
11620 Vixens Path
Ellicott City, MD 21042

301-596-3028
Fax: 410-997-0764
Home Page: www.energy2003.ee.doe.gov

Harve Horowitz, President
Kevin Horowitz, Senior Association Manager

Energy is an exclusive Federal Grant sponsored annual educational forum and exhibition.
1000+ Attendees
Frequency: Annual/August

6781 **Fall Technical and Marketing Conference**
Electrical Generating Systems Association
1650 S Dixie Highway
Suite 500
Boca Raton, FL 33432

561-750-5575
Fax: 561-395-8557
Home Page: www.egsa.org
Social Media: Facebook

Cara Clark, Director Conventions/Meetings
Bob Breese, Director of Education

Will focus on technical presentations and marketing efforts.
Frequency: Annual/September

6782 **IETA Annual Technical Conference**
International Electrical Testing Association
106 Stone Street
Morrison, CO 80465

303-697-8441
888-300-6382
Fax: 303-697-8431
E-Mail: neta@netaworld.org
Home Page: www.netaworld.org
Social Media: Facebook, YouTube

Mose Ramieh, President
David Huffman, First VP
Ron Widup, Second VP
John White, Treasurer
Walter Cleary, Secretary

Targets the electrical testing industry.
Frequency: Annual/March

6783 **IFAC World Congress**
American Automatic Control Council
3640 Col Glenn Hwy
Dayton, OH 45435

937-775-5062
Fax: 937-775-3936
E-Mail: pmisra@cs.wright.edu
Home Page: www.a2c2.org

R. Russell Reinehart, President
Tariq Samad, President-elect

Jordan Berg, Treasurer
B.Wayne Bequette, Secretary

You will have the opportunity to take part in the wide spectrum of categories for technical presentations, including plenary lectures, survey papers, regular papers of both lecture and poster session types, panel discussions and case studies.
Frequency: Annual/July

6784 **ILEA Annual Conference**
International League of Electrical Association
12165 West Center Road
Suite 59
Omaha, NE 68144

402-330-7227
Fax: 402-330-7283
E-Mail: info@ileaweb.org
Home Page: www.ileaweb.org
Social Media: LinkedIn

Monique DeBoer, President
Chris Price, VP
Kirstie Steves, Secretary
Barbette Cejalvo, Treasurer

Provides a venue through which information and ideas exchanged and by encouraging all members to attend and share ideas.
Frequency: Annual/July

6785 **IMA Spring Meeting**
International Magnetics Association
8 S Michigan Avenue
Suite 1000
Chicago, IL 60603-3310

312-456-5590
Fax: 312-580-0165
Home Page: www.intl-magnetics.org

August Sisco, Chair
Lowell Bosleyeo, President
George Orenchak, Secretary/Treasurer

Promote the worldwide growth, development, and use of magnetic materials through: collection and dissemination of global trade statistics, publication of industry standards and user and industry education.
Frequency: Annual/May

6786 **IMAPS International Symposium on Microelectronics**
International Microelectronics & Packaging Society
611 2nd Street NE
Washington, DC 20002
202-548-4001
888-464-6277
Fax: 202-548-6115
E-Mail: imaps@imaps.org
Home Page: http://www.imaps.org

Michael O'Donoghue, Executive Director
Ann Bell, Manager Marketing/Communications

Symposium for the microelectronics and electronics packaging industries. Features a powerful technical program, progressive professional development courses and many forums to share the latest developments in microelectronics. Comprehensive exhibition of materials and equipment for the industry.
3000 Attendees
Frequency: Annual/September

6787 **IMPI Annual Symposium**
International Microwave Power Institute
PO Box 1140
Mechanicsville, VA 23111

804-596-6667
Fax: 804-559-4087
E-Mail: info@impi.org
Home Page: www.impi.org

Bob Schiffman, President
Ben Wilson, Vice President
Dorin Bolder, Secretary
Amy Lawson, Treasurer

Brings together researchers from across the globe to share the latest findings related to non-communications uses of microwave energy.
Frequency: Annual/June

6788 **IPC Printed Circuits Expo**
IPC: Association Connecting Electronics
3000 Lakeside Drive
Suite 309 S
Bannockburn, IL 60015

847-615-7100
Fax: 847-615-7105
Home Page: www.ipc.org
Social Media: Facebook, Twitter, LinkedIn, YouTube

Robert Ferguson, Chairman
Stephen Pudles, Vice Chairman
Don Schroeder, Secretary/Treasurer

Meet with everyone who designs, manufactures, and assembles printed circuit boards and electronics assemblies.
Frequency: Annual/February

6789 **ISA Expo**
ISA
67 Alexander Drive
Box 12277
Research Triangle Park, NC 27709

919-549-8411
Fax: 919-549-8288
E-Mail: info@isa.org
Home Page: www.isa.org
Social Media: Facebook, Twitter, LinkedIn

Tracey Berrett-Noble, Event Manager
Rodney Jones, Conference Coordinator
Cyrus Taft, Program Chair
Dale Lee, Director Convention Services
Tracey Berrett, Manager Convention Services

Features the latest and most extensive products and services exhibition, a strategically relevant technical conference, and a prominent continuing education and training program. With practitioners from over 70 countries. Offers the most complete automation and control experience in today's marketplace.
15000 Attendees
Frequency: Annual/October

6790 **ISA Fugitive Emissions LDAR Symposium and Training**
Instrumentation, Systems, and Automation Society
67 Alexander Drive
Box 12277
Research Triangle Park, NC 27709

919-549-8411
Fax: 919-549-8288
E-Mail: info@isa.org
Home Page: www.isa.org
Social Media: Facebook, Twitter, LinkedIn

Dale Lee, Director Convention Services
Tracey Berrett, Manager Convention Services

Covers topics including, but not limited to leak detection repair methods and fugitive emissions management systems. Industry experts in leak detection and repair will discuss implementations and improvements in LDAR programs in plant facilities.
Frequency: Annual/May

6791 **Innovation in Power Generation Measurement & Control Conference**
Instrumentation, Systems, and Automation Society
67 Alexander Drive
Box 12277
Research Triangle Park, NC 27709

919-549-8411
Fax: 919-549-8288
E-Mail: info@isa.org
Home Page: www.isa.org
Social Media: Facebook, Twitter, LinkedIn

Denny Younie, Conference General Chair
Rodney Jones, Conference Coordinator
Cyrus Taft, Program Chair
Dale Lee, Director Convention Services
Tracey Berrett, Manager Convention Services

Dedicated to instrumentation and control in the fossil and nuclear power generation industry. This year's conference includes approximately 50 technical papers presented in 8 sessions over two and a half days, a vendor exhibition area, 5 training courses, several ISA committee meetings, and the EPRI I&C Interest Group meeting and a Sunday evening welcome reception.
Frequency: Annual/June

6792 **International Conference and Exhibition on Device Packaging**
International Microelectronics & Packaging Society
611 2nd Street NE
Washington, DC 20002

202-548-4001
888-464-6277
Fax: 202-548-6115
E-Mail: imaps@imaps.org
Home Page: www.imaps.org

Jim Drehle, President
Michael O'Donoghue, Executive Director
Steve Capp, Treasurer
Lawrence J Rexing, Secretary

Will provide a comprehensive technical program addressing the challenges of applications, and the latest developments in packaging for emerging devices, circuits, MEMS, sensors as well as materials and processes.
Frequency: Annual/March

6793 **International Congress Applications of Lasers and Electro-Optics**
Laser Institute of America
13501 Ingenuity Drive
Suite 128
Orlando, FL 32826-3204

407-380-1553
800-345-2737
Fax: 407-380-5588
E-Mail: icaleo@laserinstitute.org
Home Page: www.laserinstitute.org
Social Media: Facebook, Twitter, LinkedIn

Klaus Loeffler, President
Yongfeng Lu, President Elect
Stephen Capp, Treasurer
Robert Thomas, Secretary

Provides an international forum for the exchange of technical information between the people in the industrial, government and academic communities who apply laser/electro-optic technologies and the scientists, engineers and technicians engaged in developing these technologies. Accepts advertising.
5M Attendees
Frequency: Annual/October

6794 **International Instrumentation Symposium**
Instrumentation, Systems, and Automation Society
67 Alexander Drive
Box 12277
Research Triangle Park, NC 27709

919-549-8411
Fax: 919-549-8288

E-Mail: info@isa.org
Home Page: www.isa.org
Social Media: Facebook, Twitter, LinkedIn

Denny Younie, Conference General Chair
Rodney Jones, Conference Coordinator
Cyrus Taft, Program Chair
Dale Lee, Director Convention Services
Tracey Berrett, Manager Convention Services

Provides an outstanding opportunity to gain valuable technical information and training in the traditional areas of measurements/sensors, instrumentation systems, data and advanced system/sensor technology as well as innovative papers in many other state of the art areas.
Frequency: Annual/May

6795 International Laser Safety Conference
Laser Institute of America
13501 Ingenuity Drive
Suite 128
Orlando, FL 32826

407-380-1553
800-345-2737
Fax: 407-380-5588
E-Mail: lia@laserinstitute.org
Home Page: www.laserinstitute.org
Social Media: Facebook, Twitter, LinkedIn

Klaus Loeffler, President
Yongfeng Lu, President Elect
Stephen Capp, Treasurer
Robert Thomas, Secretary

A comprehensive four-day conference covering all aspects of laser safety practice and hazard control. Technical sessions and workshops will address developments in regulatory, mandatory and voluntary safety standards for laser products and laser use.
Frequency: Annual/March

6796 International Symposium on Bioenergetics and Bioelectrochemistry
Bioelectromagnetics Society
2412 Cobblestone Way
Frederick, MD 21702-3519

301-663-4252
Fax: 301-694-4948
E-Mail: office@bems.org
Home Page: www.bems.org

David Black, President
Gloria Parsley, Executive Director
Richard Nuccitelli, VP
Phil Chadwick, Treasurer
Jonna Wilen, Secretary

Covers analytical chemistry.
Frequency: Annual/June

6797 Joint Conference on Decision and Control & European Control Conference
American Automatic Control Council
3640 Col Glenn Hwy
Dayton, OH 45435

937-775-5062
Fax: 937-775-3936
E-Mail: pmisra@cs.wright.edu
Home Page: www.a2c2.org

R. Russell Reinehart, President
Tariq Samad, President-elect
Jordan Berg, Treasurer
B.Wayne Bequette, Secretary

Dedicated to the advancement of the theory and practice of systems and control. It brings together an international community of experts to discuss the state-of-the-art, new research results, perspectives of future developments, and innovative applications relevant to decision making, control, automation, and related areas.
Frequency: Annual/December

6798 Laser Institute of America
Laser Institute of America
13501 Ingenuity Drive
Suite 128
Orlando, FL 32826

407-380-1553
Fax: 407-380-5588
E-Mail: lia@lia.org
Home Page: www.lia.org
Social Media: Facebook, Twitter, LinkedIn

Klaus Loeffler, President
Stephen Capp, Treasurer
Robert Thomas, Secretary

Devoted to the field of laser applications and laser safety in both medical and industrial fields.

6799 Magnetism Conference: Institute of Electrical/Electronics Engineers
Courtesy Associates
2000 L Street NW
Suite 710
Washington, DC 20036

202-331-2000
Fax: 202-331-0111
E-Mail: magnetism@courtesyassoc.com
Home Page: www.magnetism.org

Paul Crowell, Chair
Yumi Ljiri, Treasurer
Brian Maranville, Publicity

Conference brings together scientists and engineers interested in recent developments in all branches of fundamental and applied magnetism. Emphasis is placed on experimental and theoretical research in magnetism, the properties and synthesis of new magnetic materials and advances in magnetic technology. Program consists of invited and contributed papers.
1.1M Attendees
Frequency: Annual/October

6800 Meeting of the Electrochemical Society
Appliance Manufacturer
65 South Main Street
Building D
Pennington, NJ 08534

609-737-1902
Fax: 609-737-2743
E-Mail: ecs@electrochem.org
Home Page: www.electrochem.org

Christine Garzon, President
Tetsuya Osaka, Sr. VP
Harikila Deligianni, Secretary
Christina Bock, Treasurer

Has become the leading society for solid-state and electrochemical science and technology. ECS has 8000 scientists and engineers in over 75 countries worldwide who hold individual membership, as well as roughly 100 corporations and laboratories who hold corporate membership.
Frequency: Annual/May
Founded in 1902

6801 Mid-Atlantic Electrical Exposition
S&L Productions
1916 Crain Highway S
Suite 16
Glen Burnie, MD 21061-5572

410-863-1180
888-532-3669
Fax: 410-863-1187
E-Mail: slprod@erois.com

Triennial show and 150 exhibits with 200 booths of electrical supplies, hardware and services.
3000 Attendees
Frequency: Annual/October
Founded in 2000

6802 NAED Annual Meeting
National Association of Electrical Distributors
1181 Corporate Lake Drive
St Louis, MO 63132

314-991-9000
888-791-2512
Fax: 314-991-3060
E-Mail: info@naed.org
Home Page: www.naed.org
Social Media: Facebook, Twitter

Tom Naber, President and CEO
Michelle McNamara, Senior VP

The only event to bring the entire industry together in the same place at the same time. In addition to offering strong topical and informational programming, the NAED Annual Meeting provides distributors access to the top management of more than 225 electrical product suppliers.

6803 NECA
National Electrical Contractors Association
3 Bethesda Metro Center
Suite 1100
Bethesda, MD 20814

301-657-3110
Fax: 301-215-4500
E-Mail: beth.margulies@necanet.org
Home Page: www.necanet.org
Social Media: Facebook, Twitter, LinkedIn, YouTube

Russell Alessi, President
John Grau, CEO
Dan Walter, VP and COO
Michael Thompson, Secretary/Treasurer

Brings the largest manufacturers, utilities, contractors, engineers, consultants, plant engineers, and distributors from all over North America and 31 foreign countries.
8000 Attendees
Frequency: Annual/September

6804 NEMA Annual Meeting
National Electrical Manufacturers Association
1300 North 17th Street
Suite 1752
Rosslyn, VA 22209

703-841-3200
Fax: 703-841-5900
Home Page: www.nema.org
Social Media: Facebook, Twitter, LinkedIn, You tube

Evan Gaddis, President

Provides a forum for the standardization of electrical equipment, enabling consumers to select from a range of safe, effective and compatible electrical products.
Frequency: Annual/November
Founded in 1926

6805 NEMRA Annual Conference
Nat'l Electrical Mfgs Representatives Association
28 Deer Street
Suite 302
Portsmouth, NH 03801

914-524-8650
800-446-3672
Fax: 603-319-1667
E-Mail: nemra@nemra.org
Home Page: www.nemra.org
Social Media: Twitter, LinkedIn

Mark Gibson, Chairman
Greg reynolds, Chairman Elect
Greg Baker, Secretary/Treasurer

Provides a forum for the standardization of electrical equipment, enabling consumers to se-

lect from a range of safe, effective, and compatible electrical products.
Frequency: Annual/March

6806 **NORTHCON**
Electronic Conventions
8110 Airport Boulevard
Los Angeles, CA 90045-3119

800-877-2668
Fax: 310-641-5117

Donna Ybarra, Show Manager

400 booths featuring exhibits of components and microelectronics instrumentation.
6057 Attendees
Frequency: Annual/October

6807 **NOx Emissions & Source Monitoring Technical Conference and Training**
Instrumentation, Systems, and Automation Society
67 Alexander Drive
Box 12277
Research Triangle Park, NC 27709

919-549-8411
Fax: 919-549-8288
E-Mail: info@isa.org
Home Page: www.isa.org
Social Media: Facebook, Twitter, LinkedIn

Denny Younie, Conference General Chair
Rodney Jones, Conference Coordinator
Cyrus Taft, Program Chair
Dale Lee, Director Convention Services
Tracey Berrett, Manager Convention Services

Will present experiences with the measurement and control of low level NOx emissions, new concepts for NOx reduction techniques, and innovative monitoring systems. Presenters will participate in Q&A sessions, panel discussions, and be accessible throughout the two days to answer your questions.
Frequency: Annual/August

6808 **NRECA's Annual Meeting**
National Rural Electric Cooperative Association
4301 Wilson Boulevard
Suite 1
Arlington, VA 22203-1860

703-907-5500
Fax: 703-907-5514
Home Page: www.nrcca.coop

Glenn L English, CEO

The national service organization dedicated to representing the national interests of cooperative electric utilities and the consumers they serve. An advocate for consumer-owned cooperatives on energy and operational issues as well as rural community and economic development.
Frequency: Annual/February
Founded in 1942

6809 **NSCA Systems Integration Expo**
National Systems Contractors Assocaition
3950 River Ridge Drive NE
Cedar Rapids, IA 52402

319-366-6722
800-446-6722
Fax: 319-366-4164
E-Mail: nsca@nsca.org
Home Page: www.nsca.org
Social Media: Facebook, Twitter, LinkedIn, YouTube

Injolf de Jonh, President
Kelley McCarthy, Vice President
Michael Hester, Treasurer
Ron Bailey, Secretary

Dedicated to building connections between the people, knowledge and new ideas of the commercial electronic systems industry. A leading not-for-profit association representing the commercial electronic systems industry. A powerful advocate of all who work within the low-voltage industry, including systems contractors/integrators, product manufacturers, consultants, sales representatives, a growing number of architects, engineers and others.
600 exhibitors
11000 Attendees
Frequency: Annual/March

6810 **National Electrical Equipment Show**
Reed Exhibition Companies
255 Washington Street
Suite 275
Newton, MA 02458-1649

617-584-4900
Fax: 617-630-2222

Mike Rusbridge, Chairman/CEO

Serves the electrical and electronic industries.
7.5M Attendees
Frequency: Annual/March

6811 **National Electrical Wire Processing Technology Expo**
Expo Productions
510 Hartbrook Drive
Hartland, WI 53029

262-367-5500
800 367-5520
Fax: 262-367-9956
E-Mail: cheryl@epishows.com
Home Page: www.electricalwireshow.com
Social Media: Facebook

Cheryl L Luck, Sales Manager
Jay Partington, Show Manager

Only trade show tailored expressly to the electrical wire cable processing industry.
2000 Attendees
Frequency: Annual/May

6812 **National Lighting Fair**
Dallas Market Center
2100 N Stemmons Freeway
Suite 1000
Dallas, TX 75207-3009

214-556-6100
Fax: 214-655-6100

Charlie Sullivan, Executive Director
Cindy Morris, Chief Operating Officer

250 booths.
5M Attendees
Frequency: Annual/February

6813 **National Professional Service Convention**
National Electronics Service Dealers Association
3608 Pershing Avenue
Fort Worth, TX 76107

817-921-9061
Fax: 817-921-3741
E-Mail: npsc@nesda.com
Home Page: www.nesda.com
Social Media: Facebook

PAtricia Bohon, Trade Show Manager

Annual show of 55 manufactures, suppliers and distributor of electronics, receivers, recorders, and supplies, software, telecommunications equipment, computers, videocassette recorders, parts and accessories, business forms, warranty companies and magazines/associations. Containing 100 booths and 70 exhibits.
950 Attendees
Frequency: Annual/July
Founded in 1964

6814 **Pacific International Conference on Applications of Lasers and Optics**
Laser Institute of America
13501 Ingenuity Drive
Suite 128
Orlando, FL 32826

407-380-1553
Fax: 407-380-5588
E-Mail: lia@laserinstitute.org
Home Page: www.laserinstitute.org
Social Media: Facebook, Twitter, LinkedIn

Milan Brandt, Conference General Chair

Will focus on growth and application of lasers and optics in the Pacific region.
Frequency: Annual/April

6815 **Power-Gen International Trade Show**
Electrical Generating Systems Association
1650 S Dixie Highway
Suite 500
Boca Raton, FL 33432

561 750 5575
Fax: 561-395-8557
Home Page: www.egsa.org

Cara Clark, Director Conventions/Meetings
Bob Breese, Director of Education

This is a special section of a larger show where we concentrate booths of firms that make, sell, and distribute on-site power products.
Frequency: Annual/December

6816 **Product Safety and Liability Conference**
National Electrical Manufacturers Association
1300 North 17th Street
Suite 1752
Rosslyn, VA 22209

703-841-3200
Fax: 703-841-5900
Home Page: www.nema.org
Social Media: Facebook, Twitter, LinkedIn, YouTube

Evan Gaddis, President
Tom Hixon, Vice President

Provides a forum for the standardization of electrical equipment, enabling consumers to select from a range of safe, effective and compatible electrical products.
Frequency: Annual/September

6817 **Reliability and Maintenance Symposium**
Consulting Services
1768 Lark Lane
Cherry Hill, NJ 08003-3215

856-428-2342
Fax: 856-616-9315
E-Mail: vrmonshaw@ieee.org
Home Page: www.rams.org

V R Monshaw, Administrator
Raymond Sears, Treasurer
Patrick Dallosta, Secretary, Treasurer

The symposium offers the opportunity to explore and learn more about this and other related R&M subjects. 50 booths.
1M Attendees
Frequency: Annual/January

6818 **Rocky Mountain Electronics Expo**
Conference and Management Specialists
138 Garfield St
Denver, CO 80206-5517

303-568-8028
Fax: 303-799-0678

Karen Hone, Executive Director

Annual show and exhibits of products and services related to the hi-tech electronics industry.

6819 **SESHA Annual Symposium**
Semiconductor Environmental, Safety & Health Assn

1313 Dolly Madison Boulevard
Suite 402
McLean, VA 22101

703-790-1745
Fax: 703-790-2672
E-Mail: sesha@burkinc.com
Home Page: seshaonline.org

John D Cox, President
Brett Burk, Co-Founder
Glenn Tom, Co-Founder

For individuals employed within the electronics and related high technology industries with an interest in environmental, health and safety issues.
1235 Attendees
Frequency: Annual/May
Founded in 1978

6820 SMMA: Fall Technical Conference

SMMA: The Motor & Motion Association
PO Box P182
South Dartmouth, MA 02748

508-979-5935
Fax: 508-979-5845
E-Mail: info@smma.org
Home Page: www.smma.org

Elizabeth B Chambers, Executive Director
William Chambers, Operations Director

Provide members and prospective members the opportunity to interact with industry colleagues. Attendees learn about industry trends and technologies, identify new supplier partners and network with other motor and drives professionals.
120 Attendees
Frequency: Annual/November

6821 SMMA: Spring Management Conference

SMMA: The Motor & Motion Association
PO Box P182
S Dartmouth, MA 02748

508-979-5935
Fax: 508-979-5845
E-Mail: info@smma.org
Home Page: www.smma.org

Elizabeth B Chambers, Executive Director
William Chambers, Operations Director

Provide members and prospective members the opportunity to interact with industry colleagues. Attendees learn about industry trends and technologies, identify new supplier partners and network with other motor and drives professionals.
80 Attendees
Frequency: Annual/May

6822 SMTA International

Surface Mount Technology Association
5200 Wilson Road
Suite 215
Minneapolis, MN 55424

952-920-7682
Fax: 952-926-1819
E-Mail: joann@smta.org
Home Page: www.smta.org

Dan Baldwin, President
Marie Cole, VP Technical Programs
Kola Akinade, Secretary
Hal Hendrickson, Treasurer

A network of professionals who build skills, share practical experience and develop solutions in electronics assembly technologies and related business operations.
1200 Attendees
Frequency: Annual/October

6823 SOUTHCON

Electronic Conventions
12340 Rosecrans Avenue
Suite 100
Manhattan Beach, CA 90266

310-524-4100
800-877-2668
Fax: 310-643-7328
Home Page: www.southcon.org

Donna Ybarra, Show Manager

Companies attending represent a major cross-section of the electronics industry including consumer, computer, medical, automotive and others. Offers conference sessions, in-depth technical sessions, product demonstrations and exhibits by vendors.
10M Attendees
Frequency: Annual/March

6824 TechAdvantage Conference

National Rural Electric Cooperative Association
4301 Wilson Boulevard
Suite 1
Arlington, VA 2203-1860

703-907-5500
Fax: 703-907-5514

Glenn L English, CEO

The only utility industry trade show exclusively for electric cooperative network management; engineering and operations; information services and technology; and purchasing employees.

6825 Upper Midwest Electrical Expo

North Central Electrical League
2901 Metro Drive
Suite 203
Bloomington, MN 55425

952-854-4405
800-925-4985
Fax: 952-854-7076
E-Mail: dale@ncel.org
Home Page: www.ncel.org

Jeff Keljik, Chair
Chuck Healy, Vice Chair
Dan Paulson, Treasurer
Dale Yohnke, Secretary

Unites our electrical industry by providing vital industry commerce, educational discussion forums and offering various outlets for peer interaction. NCEL is the bridge between industry sectors and our electrical industry joins together to develop, expand and to protect all stakeholder interests in our Upper MIdwest Electrical Industry.
10213 Attendees
Frequency: Every 2 Years

6826 eastec Exposition

Society of Manufacturing Engineers
Deerborn, MI 48128

313-425-3000
800-763-4763
Home Page: www.sme.org

500 booths of new technologies in equipment, materials and products used in the manufacture of semiconductors and flat panel displays.
8M Attendees
Frequency: Annual/October

Directories & Databases

6827 Buyer's Guide and Member Services Directory

Diesel & Gas Turbine Publications
1650 S Dixie Highway
Suite 500
Boca Raton, FL 33432

561-750-5575
Fax: 561-395-8557
Home Page: www.egsa.org

Donald M Ferreira, Director Publications
George Rowley, Director of Education

It is the ultimate gen-set industry buyer's guide, because the members are listed in one or more of 23 different product categories. Each member's listing also shows whether they sell, rent, and/or service equipment.
Cost: $6.00
Frequency: Annual

6828 Circuits Assembly: Buyers' Guide Issue

Miller Freeman Publications
600 Harrison Street
Suite 400
San Francisco, CA 94107-1391

FAX 415-905-2239

Ron Daniels, Editor-in-Chief

List of suppliers of products and services to the surface mount industry; representatives and distributors.
Cost: $7.00
Frequency: Annual, November
Circulation: 40,500

6829 Compressor Tech Two

Diesel & Gas Turbine Publications
20855 Watertown Rd
Suite 220
Waukesha, WI 53186-1873

262-754-4100
Fax: 262-832-5075
Home Page: www.dieselspec.com

Michael Osenga, President
Phil Burnside, Editor-in-Chief
Brent Haight, Managing Editor
Kara Kane, Advertising Manager
Sheila Lizdas, Circulation Manager

Covers the operation, application and design of gas compression systems, as used in the gas gathering, transportation, storage, processing and related industries worldwide. Featured are new products, new technologies and interesting new applications related to gas compression systems and components.
Cost: $45.00
Frequency: 6 per year
Circulation: 13,000
Founded in 1996

6830 Diesel Progress: International Edition

Diesel & Gas Turbine Publications
20855 Watertown Rd
Suite 220
Waukesha, WI 53186-1873

262-754-4100
Fax: 262-832-5075
Home Page: www.dieselspec.com

Michael Osenga, President
Michael J Brezonick, Editor-in-Chief
Katie Evans, Advertising Sales Manager

Covers the design of engine-powered equipment manufactured outside of North America. This includes various types of mobile on-and-off-highway equipment including construction, mining, forestry, agricultural and turf maintenance vehicles, trucks and buses; specialty vehicles; pleasure boats; and generator, pump and compressor set manufacturers. Editorial focus is on new products and technology for these markets.
Cost: $40.00
Frequency: 6 per year
Circulation: 12,000

ISSN: 1091-3696
Founded in 1981

6831 **Diesel Progress: North American Edition**
Diesel & Gas Turbine Publications
20855 Watertown Rd
Suite 220
Waukesha, WI 53186-1873
262-754-4100
Fax: 262-832-5075
Home Page: www.dieselspec.com
Michael Osenga, President
Patricia May, Advertising Sales Manager
Published for those concerned with the design, distribution and service of equipment powered by diesel, gasoline, or alternatively fueled engines. This includes all types of mobile on-and-off-highway equipment and stationary equipment. Markets covered include: construction, mining, forestry, agricultural and turf maintenance equipment; trucks and buses; pleasure boats; and generator, pump and compressor sets. Editorial focus is on new products and technology for these markets.
Cost: $75.00
Frequency: Monthly
Circulation: 30,000
ISSN: 1091-370X
Founded in 1935

6832 **Directory of Electrical Wholesale Distributors**
Penton
249 W. 17th Street
New York, NY 10011
212-204-4200
Home Page: www.penton.com
Sharon Reynolds, CEO
Features a full search and download capabilities, you can easily assess your current distributor network and look for new distributors for your products. Search by MSA market, location square footage, employee count and many other critical variables. The handy main house and branch cross-reference brings the ever-changing electrical distribution market into focus. Using the simple search functions, you can build and download highly targeted lists in just seconds.
Frequency: Cd-Rom

6833 **EASA Yearbook**
Electrical Apparatus Services Association
1331 Baur Boulevard
Saint Louis, MO 63131-1903
314-993-2220
Fax: 314-993-1269
E-Mail: easainfo@easa.com
Home Page: www.easa.com
Kevin Toor, Chairman
William Gray, Vice Chairman
Kenneth Gralow, Secretary/Treasurer
Cost: $100.00
267 Pages
Mailing list available for rent

6834 **Electrical Construction Materials Directory**
Underwriters Laboratories
2600 N.W. Lake Rd
Camas, WA 98607
877-854-3577
Fax: 360-817-6278
E-Mail: cec@us.ul.com
Home Page: www.UL.com
Keith E Williams, CEO
John Drengenberg, Manager Consumer Affairs
Offers information on companies that have qualified to use the UL listing mark or classification marking with products that have been found to be in compliance with UL regulations.
Cost: $40.00
912 Pages
Frequency: Annual
Printed in on glossy stock

6835 **Electrical Distributor**
National Association of Electrical Distributors
1181 Corporate Lake Drive
St. Louis, MO 63132
314-991-9000
888-791-2512
Fax: 314-991-3060
E-Mail: info@naed.org
Home Page: www.naed.org
Robert Reynolds, Chair
Clarence Martin, Chair Elect
List of manufacturers and distributors of electrical components, supplies and equipment.
Cost: $295.00
Frequency: Biennial
Circulation: 3,500

6836 **Electrical Equipment Representatives Association Membership Directory**
Electrical Equipment Representatives Association
638 W 39th Street
Kansas City, MO 64111
816-561-5323
800-728-2272
Fax: 816-561-1249
Home Page: www.eera.org
Scott Whitehead, President
Vince Brown, President Elect
Brad Cahoon, Vice-President
Don Shirk, Secretary
Kier Cooper, Treasurer
More than 105 manufacturers representatives of electrical equipment companies.
Frequency: Annual, October
Founded in 1948

6837 **Engineers Relay Handbook**
Relay and Switch Industry Association
2500 Wilson Boulevard
Arlington, VA 22201
703-907-8025
Fax: 703-875-8908
E-Mail: narm@ecaus.org
Home Page: www.ec-central.org/RSIA
Dave Baicjaome, Chairman
Jeffrey Boyce, Director Business Development
Rodd Ruland, Director Business Development
Steve Lane, General Manager
In summary, special effort has been made by the editors to cover specification parameters in sufficient detail to provide systems and product design engineers with all the information they need to obtain the correct types of relays for their applications.
Cost: $60.00
Frequency: Annual

6838 **Global Sourcing Guide**
Diesel & Gas Turbine Publications
20855 Watertown Rd
Suite 220
Waukesha, WI 53186-1873
262-754-4100
Fax: 262-832-5075
Home Page: www.dieselspec.com
Michael Osenga, President
Michael J Mercer, Managing Editor
Kara Kane, Publication Manager
Christa Stern, Production Manager
Sheila Lizdas, Circulation Manager
The Global Sourcing Guide is one of the premier references and purchasing guides for the power systems and components industry. Covering products and systems used across the mobile and stationary engine-powered equipment industries, this guide incorporates information in a wide range of classifications.
Cost: $110.00
Frequency: Annual
Founded in 1935

6839 **High-Performance Composites Directory**
Ray Publishing
PO Box 992
Morrison, CO 80465-0992
303-467-1776
Fax: 303-467-1777
Home Page: www.compositesworld.com
Judith Hazen, Publisher
Mike Mussleman, Managing Editor
The publisher of High-Performance Composites and Composites Technology magazines and well as the Sourcebook Industry directory and special design and application guides.
60 Pages
Founded in 1993
Printed in 4 colors on glossy stock

6840 **Indoor Electrical Safety Check Booklet**
Electrical Safety Foundation International
1300 N 17th Street
Suite 1847
Rosslyn, VA 22209
703-413-3209
Fax: 703-841-3329
E-Mail: info@esfi.org
Home Page: www.electrical-safety.org
Grant J Carter, Chair
David Tallman, Vice Chair
Michael Clendenin, Executive Director
Barbara R Guthrie, Secretary
Instructions on running an electrical safety audit of your home and at the same time learn about electrical inspections, circuit maps, power audits, and potential electrical hazards and safety tips from your circuit breaker or fuse panel to your outlets, power cords and extension cords, light bulbs, space heaters, ground fault circuit interrupters (GFCIs), arc fault circuit interrupters (AFCIs), batteries, and much more.

6841 **NEMA Database**
National Electrical Manufacturers Association
1300 17th St N
Suite 1752
Rosslyn, VA 22209-3806
703-841-3200
Fax: 703-841-5900
Home Page: www.nema.org
Evan R Gaddis, CEO
Tom Hixon, VP
This database offers time series on orders, shipments and unfilled orders for 6 major segments of the electrical manufacturing industry.

6842 **National Electrical Manufacturers Representatives Association Locator**
National Electrical Manufacturers Rep Assoc
28 Deer Street
Suite 302
Portsmouth, NH 03801
914-524-8650
800-446-3672
Fax: 603-319-1667

E-Mail: nemra@nemra.org
Home Page: www.nemra.org

Michael Gorin, Chairman
Mark Gibson, Chair Elect
Greg Reynolds, Secretary/Treasurer

Approximately 1,000 electrical manufacturers representative companies.
Cost: $200.00
Frequency: Annual

6843 **National Electronic Distributors Association Membership Directory**
National Electronic Distributors Association
1111 Alderman Dr
Suite 400
Alpharetta, GA 30005-4175

678-393-9990
Fax: 678-393-9998
Home Page: www.nedassoc.org

Brian McNally, President
Michael Knight, President Elect
Robin Gray, Executive VP

Approximately 300 member distributors and 180 member manufacturers of electronics products, plus 1,100 branch offices.

6844 **On-Site Power Generation: A Reference Book**
Electrical Generating Systems Association
1650 S Dixie Hwy
Suite 400
Boca Raton, FL 33432-7461

561-750-5575
Fax: 561-395-8557
Home Page: www.egsa.org

Jalane Kellough, Executive Director
George Rowley, Director of Education

This book contains the most complete and up-to-date technical information covering on-site electrical power generation.
Cost: $95.00
600 Pages

6845 **Outdoor Electrical Safety Check Booklet**
Electrical Safety Foundation International
1300 N 17th Street
Suite 1847
Rosslyn, VA 22209

703-413-3209
Fax: 703-841-3329
E-Mail: info@esfi.org
Home Page: www.electrical-safety.org

Grant J Carter, Chair
David Tallman, Vice Chair
Michael Clendenin, Executive Director
Barbara R Guthrie, Secretary

Use this handy booklet to learn about available electrical safety devices, and the safety rules related to hot tubs, spas and pools, extension cords, electrical lawn and garden products, battery operated products and power tool safety.

6846 **Product and Supplier Information**
Electrical Generating Systems Association
1650 S Dixie Hwy
Suite 400
Boca Raton, FL 33432-7461

561-750-5575
Fax: 561-395-8557
Home Page: www.egsa.org

Jalane Kellough, Executive Director
George Rowley, Director of Education

EGSA publishes a new Buyer's Guide and Member Services Directory listing every member.

6847 **SMMA: Directory**
SMMA: Small Motors & Motion Association
PO Box P182
S Dartmouth, MA 02748

508-979-5935
Fax: 508-979-5845
E-Mail: info@smma.org
Home Page: www.smma.org

Elizabeth Chambers, Executive Director
William Chambers, Operations Director

Manufacturers, suppliers and users of fractional and subfractional horsepower electric motors.
Founded in 1975

6848 **Transmission and Distribution: Specifiers and Buyers Guide Issue**
Penton
249 W. 17th Street
New York, NY 10011

212-204-4200
E-Mail:
CorporateCustomerService@penton.com
Home Page: www.penton.com

Sharon Rowlands, CEO

List of manufacturers and distributors of equipment for electric power transmission and distribution.
Cost: $20.00
Frequency: Annual, September
Circulation: 49,000

6849 **Wholesale Source Directory of Electrical Products, Supplies & Accessories**
Sutton Family Communications & Publishing Company
155 Sutton Lane
Fordsville, KY 42343

270-740-0870
E-Mail: jlsutton@apex.net
Home Page: www.fleamarketeer.net

Theresa Sutton, Editor
Lee Sutton, General Manager

Listings include names, addresses, phone/fax numbers and product descriptions for wholesale distributors, importers, manufacturers, close-out houses and liquidators. Every item needed to become an electrical contractor, open an electrical store or sell this type of merchandise in a hardware store, flea market or other market. Daily updated laser printed copy. Price includes shipping and handling.
Cost: $57.20
100+ Pages
Founded in 1977

Industry Web Sites

6850 **http://gold.greyhouse.com**
G.O.L.D Grey House OnLine Databases

Grey House Publishing's online database platform, GOLD, offers Quick Search, Keyword Search and Expert Search for most business sectors including electrical markets. The GOLD platform makes finding the information you need quick and easy - whether you're a novice searcher or an experienced database user. All of Grey House's directory products are available for subscription on the GOLD platform.

6851 **www.7ms.com**
Seven Mountains Scientific

Industry news in battery technology, marketing and industry events including new products, electric vehicles, R&D and environmental news.

6852 **www.ahtd.org**
Association for High Technology Distributors

Works to increase productivity and profitability of high technology automation solutions, providers and manufacturers.

6853 **www.bioelectromagnetics.org**
Bioelectromagnetics Society

International resource for excellence in scientific research, knowledge and understanding of the interaction of electromagnetic fields with biological systems. Members of the society are biological and physical scientists, physicians and engineers interested in the interactions of nonionizing radiation with biological systems.

6854 **www.construction.com**
McGraw-Hill Construction

McGraw-Hill Construction (MHC), part of The McGraw-Hill Companies, connects people and projects across the design and construction industry, serving owners, architects, engineers, general contractors, subcontractors, building product manufacturers, suppliers, dealers, distributors and adjacent markets.

6855 **www.csa-dc.org**
Contract Services Association of America

Represents the government services contracting industry in Washington, DC. Members range from small businesses to large corporations servicing federal and state government in numerous capacities. CSA acts to foster effective implementation of the government's policy of reliance on the private sector for support services.

6856 **www.eachicago.org**
Electric Association

Its purpose is to serve as the umbrella organization for the various electrical disciplines in the Chicagoland area.

6857 **www.easa.com**
Electrical Apparatus Service Association

An international trade organization of electromechanical sales and service firms in 58 countries. Provides members with a means of keeping up to date on materials, equipment, and state-of-the-art technology

6858 **www.ec-central.org/RSIA**
Relay and Switch Industry Association

The purpose and aims shall be to encourage the advancement of the art and science of making and using those switching devices generally known as relays; to promote and further interest of relay manufacturers consistent with the best interest of relay users; to create a spirit of mutual esteem, respect and recognition among members, and between the members and their customers and suppliers.

6859 **www.eei.org**
Edison Electric Institute

Advocates public policy, expands market opportunities and provides strategic business information for the shareholder-owned electric utility industry. Find out more about EEI's members, upcoming meetings, career opportunities and products and services.

6860 **www.eera.org**
Electrical Equipment Representatives Association

Sales agents for manufacturers of electrical equipment used by utilities. Mission is to advance the quality and increase effectiveness of manufacturer's representatives in the electrical equipment industry.

6861 **www.electric-find.com**
Electric Find
A directory/search engine for the electrical construction industry. Search results have been screened by electrical professionals.

6862 **www.electrochem.org**
Electrochemical Society
The society is an international nonprofit, educational organization concerned with phenomena relating to electrochemical and solid state science and technology. Members are individual scientists and engineers, as well as corporations and laboratories.

6863 **www.epri.com**
Electric Power Research Institute
Research relating to the production, transmission, distribution and utilization of electric power.

6864 **www.esda.org**
Electrostatic Discharge Association
Dedicated to advancing the theory and practice of electrostatic discharge avoidance.

6865 **www.ewh.ieee.org**
Instrumentation and Measurement Society
A subsidiary of the Institute of Electrical and Electronics Engineers. Provides support to scientists and technicians who design and develop electrical and electronic measuring instruments and equipment.

6866 **www.greyhouse.com**
Grey House Publishing
Authoritative reference directories for most business sectors incluidng electrical markets. Users can search the online databases with varied search criteria allowing for custom searches by product category, geographic area, sales volume, keyword, subject and more. Full Grey House catalog and online ordering also available.

6867 **www.icea.net**
Insulated Cable Engineers Association
Professional organization dedicated to developing cable standards for the electric power, control and telecommunications industries. Ensures safe, economical and efficient cable systems utilizing proven state-of-the-art materials and concepts. ICEA documents are of interest to cable manufacturers, architects and engineers, utility and manufacturing plant personnel, telecommunication engineers, consultants and OEMs.

6868 **www.imaps.org**
International Microelectronics & Packaging Society
Dedicated to the advancement and growth of the use of microelectronics and electronic packaging through public and professional education, dissemination of information by means of symposia, workshops and conferences and promotion of the Society's portfolio of technologies.

6869 **www.impi.org**
International Microwave Power Institute
IMPI's members include scientists, researchers, lab technicians, product developers, marketing managers and a variety of other professionals in the microwave industry. The Institute serves the information needs of all specialists working with dielectric (microwave and RF) heating sytems, and was expanded in 1977 to meet the information needs relating to consumer microwave ovens and related products.

6870 **www.ipc.org**
IPC:Association Connecting Electronics
Works to develop standards in circuit board assembly equipment. Brings together all players in the electronic interconnection industry, including designers, board manufacturers, assembly companies, suppliers and original equipment manufacturers. Offers workshops, conferences, meetings and online communications.

6871 **www.ncel.org**
North Central Electrical League
Trade association representing all segments of the electrical industry in the Upper Midwest.

6872 **www.necanet.org**
National Electrical Contractors Association
Represents a segment of the construction market comprised of over 70,000 electrical firms.

6873 **www.nerc.com**
North American Electric Reliability Council
Voluntary organization promoting bulk electric system reliability and security.

6874 **www.netaworld.org**
International Electrical Testing Association
Defines the standards by which electrical equipment is deemed safe and reliable. Creates specifications, procedures, testing and requirements for commissioning new equipment and testing the reliability and performance of existing equipment.

6875 **www.nsca.org**
National Systems Contractors Association
Not-for-profit association representing the commercial electronic systems industry. Serves as an advocate for all those who work within the low-voltage industry including systems contractors/integrators, product manufacturers, consultants, sales representatives and a growing number of architects, specifying engineers and others.

6876 **www.platts.com**
Electrical World
The latest trends in utility engineering and IT, equipment and services, best business practices and critical industry thinking. For managers, engineers and technicians who plan, design, build, maintain and upgrade electric T&D systems around the world.

6877 **www.psma.com**
Power Sources Manufacturers Association
Worldwide membership consists of manufacturers of power sources and conversion equipment. Nonprofit association strives to integrate the resources of the power sources industry to more effectively and profitably serve the needs of the power sources users, providers and PSMA members. Educates the electronics industry and others on the relevant applications for power sources and conversion devices.

6878 **www.semi.org**
Semiconductor Equipment & Materials International
Strengthens the performance of member companies through lobbying, promotion, education and statistical research.

6879 **www.seshaonline.org**
Semiconductor Environmental, Safety & Health Assn
Members are individuals employed within the electronics and related high technology industries with an interest in environmental, health and safety issues.

6880 **www.sia-online.org**
Semiconductor Industry Association
Trade association representing the US microchip industry.

6881 **www.smma.org**
SMMA: Small Motors & Motion Association
Trade association for the electric motor and motion control industry in Northern America. The voice of the motor and motion industry providing a forum for education, communication, research and networking.

6882 **www.smta.org**
Surface Mount Technology Association
A network of professionals building skills, sharing practical experience and developing solutions in electronic assembly technologies and related business operations.

6883 **www.sweets.construction.com**
McGraw Hill Construction
In depth product information that lets you find, compare, select, specify and make purchase decisions in the industrial product marketplace.

Associations

6884 AG Electronic Association
10 S Riverside Plaza
Suite 1220
Chicago, IL 60606-3710

312-321-1470
Fax: 312-321-1480
E-Mail: age@agelectronicsassn.org
Home Page: www.agelectronicsassn.org

Darrin Dollinger, Marketing Manager

Identifies, develops & or facilitates appropriate action aimed at furthering the compatibility & interchangeability of electronics and information systems used in agriculture.

6885 AVS Science & Technology Society
125 Maiden Ln
32nd Floor
New York, NY 10038-4714

212-248-0245
Fax: 212-248-0245
E-Mail: angela@avs.org
Home Page: www.avs.org

Christie R Marrian, President
John Coburn, Treasurer
Joseph E Greene, Clerk/Secretary
Yvonne Towse, Executive Director

Supports all those involved with all aspects of science and technology through research, education, new products, publications and conferences.
5500 Members
Founded in 1953

6886 Aircraft Electronics Association
3570 Ne Ralph Powell Rd
Lees Summit, MO 64064-2360

816-347-8400
Fax: 816-347-8405
E-Mail: info@aea.net
Home Page: www.aea.net

Paula Derks, President
Mark Gibson, VP Administration
Mike Adamson, Information Services Director
Linda Adams, Director Communications

AEA represents aviation businesses, including repair stations that specialize in maintenance, repair and installation of avionics and electronic systems in general aviation aircraft.
1250 Members
Mailing list available for rent

6887 American Electronics Association
5201 Great America Parkway
Santa Clara, CA 95054

408-987-4200
800-284-4232
Fax: 408-987-4298
E-Mail: csc@aeanet.org
Home Page: www.aeanet.org

John V Harker, Chairman
William T Archey, President/CEO
Samuel J Block, VP/Controller
Tim Bennett, COO/EVP

Works to foster a healthy business climate by providing services education and research programs.
3500 Members
Founded in 1943

6888 AmericanÿAssociationÿofÿElectronic Reporters and Transcribers
P.O. Box 9826
Wilmington, DE 19809

302-765-3510
800-233-5306
Fax: 302-241-2177
E-Mail: sherry@aaert.org
Home Page: www.aaert.org
Social Media: Facebook, Twitter, LinkedIn

Buchanan Buck Ewing, President
Raymond Vetter, Vice President
Richard Russell, Treasurer
Geoffrey Hunt, Secretary
Michael Tannen, Executive Director

A national professional association that deals with the electronic court reporting.

6889 Armed Forces Communications and Electronics Association (AFCEA)
4400 Fair Lakes Ct
Fairfax, VA 22033-3899

703-631-1397
800-336-4583
Fax: 703-631-4693
Home Page: www.afcea.org

Kent Schneider, President/CEO
Becky Nolan, Executive VP
John A Dubia, Executive VP

A non-profit membership association serving the military, government, industry, and academia as an ethical forum for advancing professional knowledge and relationships in the fields of communications, IT, intelligence, and global security.
30000 Members
Founded in 1946

6890 Association for Electronics Manufacturing
1 SME Drive
PO Box 930
Dearborn, MI 48121

313-425-3000
800-733-4763
Fax: 313-425-3400
E-Mail: service@sme.org
Home Page: www.sme.org

Mark Tomlinson, Executive Director/General Manager
Greg Sheremet, Publisher
Bob Harris, Director Finance

Represents the electrical manufacturers.
3.6M Members

6891 Association of Progressive Rental Organizations
1540 Robinhood Trail
Austin, TX 78703-2624

512-794-0095
800-204-APRO
Fax: 512-794-0097
E-Mail: cferguson@rtohq.org
Home Page: www.rtohq.org
Social Media: Facebook

Bill Keese, Executive Director
John C Cleek, President
Bill Kelly, Secretary

Members include television, appliance and furniture dealers who rent merchandise with an option to purchase.
2000 Members
Founded in 1980

6892 Consumer Electronics Association (CEA)
1919 S Eads Street
Arlington, VA 22202

703-907-7600
866-858-1555
Fax: 703-907-7675
E-Mail: communications@ce.org
Home Page: www.ce.org

Gary Shapiro, President/CEO
Pat Lavelle, Chairman
Peter Lesser, Industry Executive Advisor
Jason Oxman, VP Communications
Jenny Pareti, Public Policy Director

Consumer Electronics Association (CEA) provides valuable and innovative member-only resources including: exclusive information and unparalleled market research, networking opportunities with business advocates and leaders, up-to-date educational programs and technical training, exposure in extensive promotional programs, and representation from the voice of the industry.
2000 Members

6893 Consumer Electronics Forum
CompuServe Information Service
5000 Arlington Center Boulevard
Columbus, OH 43220

614-457-8600
800-848-8199

Offers valuable information on electronic consumer products, including audio, video and satellite systems and radar detectors.

6894 Custom Electronic Design & Installation Association
7150 Winton Drive
Suite 300
Indianapolis, IN 46268

317-328-4336
800-669-5329
Fax: 317-735-4012
E-Mail: info@cedia.org
Home Page: www.cedia.org
Social Media: Facebook, Twitter, YouTube

Larry Pexton, Chairman
Dennis Erskine, Vice Chairman
Federico Bausone, Immediate Past Chairman
Richard Millson, Secretary
David Humphries, Treasurer

A global authority in the home technology industry that provides access to industry-leading education, certification, research, and consumer awareness.
3500 Members

6895 Electrical Apparatus Service Association
1331 Baur Blvd.
St. Louis, MO 63132

314-993-2220
Fax: 314-993-1269
E-Mail: easainfo@easa.com
Home Page: www.easa.com

Linda J. Raynes, CAE, President & CEO
Anne Vogel, Executive Secretary
Richard Tutka, Finance Manager
Randy D. Joslin, Communications Manager
Tyler Voss, Membership Specialist

An international trade organization of more than 1,900 electromechanical sales and service firms in 62 countries that provides members with a meansof keeping up to date on materials, equipment, and state-of-the-art technology.

6896 Electronic Components Industry Association
1111 Alderman Drive
Suite 400
Alpharetta, GA 30005

678-393-9990
Fax: 678-393-9998
E-Mail: jwood@ecianow.org
Home Page: www.ecianow.org
Social Media: Facebook, Twitter, LinkedIn, YouTube

Michael Knight, Chair
Blair Haas, Chair Elect
John Denslinger, President and CEO
Robert Willis, Chief Technology Officer
Barney Martin, Vice President

Organization made up of electronic component manufacturers, their manufacturer representatives and authorized distributors that provides resources and opportunities for members to improve their business performance while enhancing the industry's overall capacity for growth and profitability.

6897 Electronic Industries Alliance
2500 Wilson Boulevard
Arlington, VA 22201-3834

703-907-7500
Fax: 703-907-7500
Home Page: www.eia.org

Ronald L Turner, Chairman
Mike Kennedy, Vice Chairman
Dave McCurdy, President/CEO
Neal McDonald, Senior Coordinator
James Shiring, Secretary/Treasurer

Trade organization representing the entire spectrum of manufacturers and consumer manufacturers involved in electronic products.
1.5M Members
Founded in 1924

6898 Electronic Retailing Association
2000 14th St N # 300
Suite 300
Arlington, VA 22201-2573

703-841-1751
800-987-6462
Fax: 425-977-1036
E-Mail: contact@retailing.org
Home Page: www.retailing.org

Julie Coons, CEO

The trade association that represents the leaders of direct response: members who maximize revenues through electronic retailing on television, online and on radio. ERA strives to protect the regulatory and legislative climate of direct response while ensuring a favorable landscape that enhances e-retailers' ability to bring quality products and services to the consumer.

6899 Electronic Security Association
6333 North State Highway 161
Suite 350
Irving, TX 75038

972-807-6800
888-447-1689
Fax: 972-807-6883
Home Page: www.esaweb.orgÿ
Social Media: Facebook, Twitter, LinkedIn

Marshall Marinace, President
Roy Pollack, Vice President
Merlin Guilbeau, Executive Director
Jon Sargent, Secretary
Tom Eggebrecht, Treasurer

A nonprofit trade association that represents, promotes, and enhances the growth and professional development of the electronic life safety, security, and integrated sytems industry.
Founded in 1948

6900 Electronic Transactions Association
1101 16th Street NW
Suite 402
Washington, DC 20036

202-828-2635
800-695-5509
Fax: 202-828-2639
Home Page: www.electran.org

Daniel J Neistadt, President
Joe Kaplan, Treasurer
James Baumgartner, Secretary

ETA is the international trade association serving the needs of organizations offering transaction processing products/services.
400M Members
Founded in 1990

6901 Electronics Representatives Association
300 W Adams St
Suite 617
Chicago, IL 60606-5109

312-527-3050
800-776-7377
Fax: 312-559-4566
E-Mail: info@era.org
Home Page: www.era.org

Tom Shanahan, Executive VP
Bob Walsh, President

Provides services and benefits to electronic industry manufacturers and manufacturers' representatives.
Cost: $48.00
450 Members
Founded in 1935

6902 Electronics Technicians Association International
5 Depot Street
Greencastle, IN 46135

765-653-4301
800-288-3824
Fax: 765-653-4287
E-Mail: eta@eta-i.org
Home Page: www.eta-i.org

Teresa Maher, CSS, President
Chrissy Baker, Marketing Coordinator
Richard Glass, CETsr, CEO Emeritus
Lora Roberson, CSS, Certification Admin/Membership
Emily Hatfield, Research & Development

Association for electronic technicians worldwide offering over 70 certifications.
4500 Members
Founded in 1978

6903 ElectronicÿTransactionÿAssociationÿ
1101 16th Street NW
#402
Washington, DC 20036

202-828-2635
800-695-5509
Home Page: www.electran.orgÿ
Social Media: Facebook, Twitter, LinkedIn

Jason Oxman, Chief Executive Officer
Pamela Furneaux, Chief Operating Officer
Scott Talbott, Senior Vice President
Melinda Gray, Member Services Manager
Alicia Howard, Senior Accountant

International trade association for the payment processing industry.
Founded in 1990

6904 Federated Rural Electric
77100 US Highway 71
PO Box 69
Jackson, MN 56143-0069

507-728-8366
800-321-3520
Fax: 507-728-8366
E-Mail: info@federatedrea.coop
Home Page: www.federatedrea.coop

David A. Hansen, President
Dave Meschke, Vice-President
Darvin Voss, Secretary
Bruce Brockmann, Director
Glenn Dicks, Director

A distribution electric utility.
Founded in 1935

6905 IEEE Photonics Society
445 Hoes Lane
Piscataway, NJ 08855-1331

732-562-3926
Fax: 732-562-8434
E-Mail: C.Jannuzzi@ieee.org
Home Page: www.photonicssociety.org

Dalma Novak, President
Hideo Kuwahara, Past President
Peter Smowton, Secretary Treasurer
Christopher Jannuzzi, Executive Director
Douglas Razzano, Associate Executive Director

A leading professional network of 7,000+ members that provide access to technical information.
Founded in 1965

6906 IEEE Power Electronics Society
E-Mail: m.p.kelly@ieee.org
Home Page: www.ieee-pels.org
Social Media: Twitter, LinkedIn

Philip Krein, History Chair
Michael P. Kelly, Executive Director
Donna Florek, Tech Community Program Specialist
Michael Markowycz, Tech Community Program Specialist
Jo-Ellen Snyder, Tech Community Program Specialist

A society of the Institute of Electrical and Electronics (IEEE) that focuses on the developmnet of power electronics technology.

6907 IPC Associationÿ
3000 Lakeside Drive
309 S
Bannockburn, IL 60015

847-615-7100
Fax: 847-615-7105
E-Mail: answers@ipc.org
Home Page: www.ipc.org
Social Media: Facebook, Twitter, LinkedIn, YouTube

Marc Peo, Chairman
Joseph Joe O'Neil, Vice Chairman
Mikel H. Williams, Secretary/ Treasurer
John W. Mitchell, President/ CEO
Stephen Steve Pudles, Immediate Past Chairman

A trade association that standardizes the assembly and production requirements of electronic equipment and assemblies.

6908 IPC: Association Connecting Electronics
2215 Sanders Road
Northbrook, IL 60062-6135

847-509-9700
Fax: 847-615-7105
E-Mail: webmaster@ipc.org
Home Page: www.ipc.org

Denny McGuirk, President
Betty Johnson, Executive Assistant to President
Dick Crowe, Executive Director
Tom McCabe, VP/CFO
Jennifer Sandahl, Controller

A trade association for the printed circuit boards and electronics assembly industries, offering programs and resources to board manufacturers and electronic assemblers, designers, industry suppliers and original equipment manufacturers.
2000 Members
Founded in 1957

6909 Independent Distributors of Electronics Association
P.O. Box 295
West Baden
Springs, IN 47469

714-670-0200
Fax: 714-670-0201
E-Mail: info@IDofEA.org

Home Page: www.idofea.orgÿ
Social Media: Facebook, Twitter, LinkedIn

Paul Romano, President
Dan Ellsworth, Vice President
Homey Shorooghi, Secretary/ Treasurer
Brian Wilson, Executive Board member
Jason Jowers, Executive Board member

A global trade association comprised of organizations for independent distributors to find relevant information and to participate in advancing industry ethics, ensuring customer satisfaction, establishing standards, and promoting education.

6910 **Independent Electrical Contractors**
4401 Ford Avenue
Suite 1100
Alexandria, VA 22302

703-549-7351
800-456-4324
Fax: 703-549-7448
E-Mail: info@ieci.org
Home Page: www.ieci.org
Social Media: Facebook, Twitter, LinkedIn, YouTube, Flickr

Gordon Stewart, President
Bruce Seilhammer, Vice President
Mark Gillespie, Secretary/Treasurer
Thayer Long, Executive Vice President/CEO
Vernice Howard, Chief Financial Officer

A national trade association for merit shop electrical and systems contractors.
Founded in 1957

6911 **Instrumentation & Measurement Society**
Home Page: www.ieee-ims.org
Social Media: Facebook, Twitter, LinkedIn

Reza Zoughi, President
Ruth A Dyer, Executive VP
Frank Reyes, Treasurer
Kim Fowler, Senior Past President
Jorge F Daher, Past President

A professional society of the IEEE whose field of interest is the science, technology, and application of instrumentation and measurement.

6912 **Instrumentation and Measurement Society**
799 N Beverly Glen
Los Angeles, CA 90077

310-446-8280
Fax: 732-981-0225
E-Mail: bob.myers@ieee.org
Home Page: www.ewh.ieee.org

Robert Myers, Executive Director
Lee Myers, Assistant Director
Robert Rassa, President
Barry Oakes, VP Finance

A subsidiary of the Institute of Electrical and Electronics Engineers. Provides support to scientists and technicians who design and develop electrical and electronic measuring instruments and equipment.
6500+ Members
Founded in 1950

6913 **International Electrical Testing Association**
3050 Old Centre Ave.,
Suite 102
Portage, MI 49024

269-488-6382
Fax: 269-488-6383
E-Mail: mrichard@netaworld.org
Home Page: www.netaworld.org
Social Media: Facebook, LinkedIn, YouTube

David Huffman, President
Ron Widup, 1st Vice President
Jim Cialdea, 2nd Vice President
Jayne Tanz, Executive Director
Mose Ramieh, Secretary

Establishes standards, publishes specifications, accredits independent, third-party, electrical testing companies, certifies test technicians, and promotes the services of association members.

6914 **International Microelectronics and Electronic Packaging**
611 2nd Street NE
Washington, DC 20002

202-548-4001
888-464-6277
Fax: 919-287-2339
E-Mail: imaps@imaps.org
Home Page: www.imaps.org

Michael O'Donoghue, Executive Director
Rick Mohn, Operations Manager
Brian Schieman, Director Information Technology
Ann Bell, Manager Marketing/Communications

Promotes interaction among technologies of ceramics, thin and thick films, semiconductor packaging, surface mount technology, multichip modules, semiconductor devices and monolithic circuits. Dedicated to the advancement and growth of the use of microelectronics and electronic packaging through education. Disseminates information through symposia, workshops and conferences.
11000 Members
Founded in 1967

6915 **International SEMATECH**
2706 Montopolis Dr
Austin, TX 78741-6408

512-356-3500
Fax: 512-356-3135
E-Mail: information@ismi.sematech.org
Home Page: www.sematech.org

A global consortium of leading semiconductor manufacturers who engage in cooperative precompetitive efforts to improve semiconductor manufacturing technology through the support of their members.
Founded in 1987

6916 **International Society of Certified Electronic Technicians**
3000-A Landers St.,
Fort Worth, TX 76107-5642

817-921-9101
Fax: 800-946-0201
E-Mail: info@iscet.org
Home Page: www.iscet.org

Pete Rattigan, President
Daniel Champion, Vice President
Dan Mundy, Immediate Past President
Rich Reid, Secretary
John Wilkins, Treasurer

Helps train, prepare, and test technicians in the electronics and appliance service industry.

6917 **International Society of Certified Electronic Technicians**
3608 Pershing Avenue
Fort Worth, TX 76107-4527

817-921-9101
Fax: 817-921-3741
E-Mail: info@iscet.org
Home Page: www.iscetstore.org/about

Mack Blakely, Executive Director
Ed Clingman, Administrator
Sheila Fredrickson, Director Communications

Seeks to provide awareness of and services to certified electronics technicians. Provides educational materials in electronics training to schools, technical institutes and junior colleges. Offers certification programs for electronics technicians in associate and journeyman levels.
46000 Members
Founded in 1965

6918 **Minerals, Metals & Materials Society**
184 Thorn Hill Road
Warrendale, PA 15086-7514

724-776-9000
Fax: 724-776-3770
E-Mail: foundation@tms.org
Home Page: www.tms.org

Tresa Pollock, President
Brajendra Mishra, VP
Alexander Scott, Executive Director
John Parsey, Financial Planning Officer
Marc DeGraef, Director Information Technology

Supports all those in the minerals, metals and materials industries with education, publications, trade shows and conferences.
Founded in 1971

6919 **Mobile Electronics Retailers Associationÿ**
85 Flagship Drive
Suite F
North Andover, MA 1845

800-949-6372
E-Mail: info@merausa.org
Home Page: www.merausa.org

Mike Anderson, Chairman
Chris Cook, President
Mike Bartells, Advisory Board
Tony Dehnke, Advisory Board
Joe Forcella, Advisory Board

Focuses on education and networking opportunities designed to advance the professionalism and profitability of the mobile electronics industry.
Founded in 1992

6920 **National Association of Relay Manufacturers**
2500 Wilson Boulevard
Arlington, VA 22201

703-907-8025
Fax: 703-875-8908
E-Mail: narm@ecaus.org
Home Page: www.ec-central.org/NARM

Dave Bauchaine, Chairman
Jeffrey Boyce, President

NARM is a trade association for the electro-mechanical relay and associated switching devices industry. An affiliate of Electronic Industries Alliance.
32 Members
Founded in 1947

6921 **National Electrical Manufacturers Association**
1300 North 17th Street
Suite 900
Arlington, VI 22209

703-841-3200
Home Page: www.nema.org
Social Media: Facebook, Twitter, LinkedIn, YouTube, Google+, Instagram

Donald J. Hendler, Chairman
Maryrose Sylvester, Vice Chairman
John P. Selldorff, Immediate-Past Chairman
Kevin J. Cosgriff, President
Thomas S. Gross, Treasurer

Develops standards for the electrical manufacturing industry.
Founded in 1926

6922 **National Electronic Distributors Association**
1111 Alderman Drive
Suite 400
Alpharetta, GA 30005-4175

678-393-9990
Fax: 678-393-9998
E-Mail: admin@nedassoc.org
Home Page: www.nedassoc.org

Francis Flynn Jr, President
Robin B Gray Jr, President-Elect
Debbie Conyers, Director Marketing
Barney Martin, VP Industry Practices

Conducts research and offers educational programs for wholesale distributors of electronic components.
Founded in 1939
Mailing list available for rent

6923 **National Electronics Service Dealers Association**
3608 Pershing Ave
Fort Worth, TX 76107-4527

817-921-9061
800-797-9197
Fax: 817-921-3741
E-Mail: info@nesda.com
Home Page: www.nesda.com

Mack Blakely, Executive Director
Sheila Fredrickson, Dir Communications/Info Technology
Patricia Bohon, Membership & Trade Show Coordinator
James Keesler, Associate Editor/Graphic Designer
Margaret Vazquez, Bookkeeper/Administrative Assistant

A national trade association for professionals in the business of repairing consumer electronics equipment, appliances, and computers. NESDA has an e-mail group of members and manufacturers that communicate daily for information sharing. NESDA also has an annual convention and trade show.
600 Members
Founded in 1950

6924 **National Marine Electronics Association**
7 Riggs Ave
Severna Park, MD 21146-3819

410-975-9425
Fax: 410-975-9450
E-Mail: info@nmea.org
Home Page: www.nmea.org

David Hayden, President
Jules Rutstein, Vice Chairman
Beth Kahr, Executive Director
Michael Cerchiaro, Treasurer
Christopher Harley, Secretary

Is the unifying force behind the entire marine electronics industry, bringing together all aspects of the industry for the betterment of all in our business.
400 Members
Founded in 1957

6925 **National Rural Electric Cooperative Association**
4301 Wilson Blvd.
Arlington, VA 22203

703-907-5500
Home Page: www.nreca.coop
Social Media: Facebook, Twitter, LinkedIn, YouTube

Jo Ann Emerson, Chief Executive Officer
Denise Aranoff-Brown, Chief Marketing Officer
Peter Baxter, Senior VP
Marc Breslaw, Executive Director
Jeffrey Connor, Chief of Staff

An organization that represents the interests of over 900 electric cooperatives in the United States to various legislatures.
Founded in 1933

6926 **Optical Society of America**
2010 Massachusetts Ave Nw
Washington, DC 20036-1023

202-223-8130
Fax: 202-223-1096
E-Mail: info@osa.org
Home Page: www.osa.org

Elizabeth Rogan, Executive Director

The Optical Society of America (OSA) was organized to increase and diffuse the knowledge of optics, pure and applied; to promote the common interests of investigators of optical problems, of designers and of users of optical apparatus of all kinds; and to encourage cooperation among them. The purposes of the Society are scientific, technical and educational.
15000 Members
Founded in 1916

6927 **Power Electronics Society**
799 N Beverly Glen
Los Angeles, CA 90077
310-446-8280
Fax: 310-446-8390
E-Mail: bob.myers@ieee.org
Home Page: www.pels.org

Jerry Hudgins, President
Robert Myers, Executive Director
Steven Leeb, Treasurer
Ronald Harley, VP Operations

A subsidiary of the Institute of Electrical & Electronics Engineers. Supports professionals working in the field of power electronics technology.
5000 Members
Founded in 1987

6928 **Power Sources Manufacturers Association**
PO Box 418
Mendham, NJ 07945-0418

973-543-9660
Fax: 973-543-6207
E-Mail: powcr@psma.com
Home Page: www.psma.com
Social Media: LinkedIn

Dusty Becker, Chairman
Carl Blake, President
Jim Marinos, VP

The PSMA is a not-for-profit organization incorporated in the state of California. The purpose of the Association shall be to enhance the stature and reputation of its members and their products, improve their knowledge of technological and other developments related to power sources, and to educate the entire electronics industry, plus academia, as well as government and industry agencies as to the importance of, and relevant applications for, all types of power sources and conversion devices.
155 Members
Founded in 1985

6929 **SPIE**
1000 20th St.
Bellingham, WA 98225-6705

360-676-3290
888-504-8171
Fax: 360-647-1445
E-Mail: CustomerService@SPIE.org
Home Page: www.spie.orgỷ
Social Media: Facebook, Twitter, LinkedIn, YouTube

Dr. H. Philip Stahl, President
Mr. William Arnold, Immediate Past President
Prof Toyohiko Yatagai, President Elect
Dr. Robert A Lieberman, Vice President
Brian Lula, Secretary/ Treasurer

A nonprofit international professional society for optics and photonics technology.
Founded in 1955

6930 **Semiconductor Environmental, Safety & Health Association**
1313 Dolly Madison Boulevard
Suite 420
McLean, VA 22101

703-790-1745
Fax: 703-790-2672
E-Mail: sesha@burkinc.com
Home Page: www.seshaonline.org

Bernie First, President
Brett Burk, Executive Director
Brian Sherin, Treasurer
Karl Albrecht, Secretary

Members are individuals employed within the electronics and related high technology industries with an interest in environmental, health and safety issues.
1500 Members
Founded in 1978

6931 **Semiconductor Equipment and Materials International**
3081 Zanker Road
San Jose, CA 95134

408-943-6900
Fax: 408-428-9600
E-Mail: semihq@semi.org
Home Page: www.semi.org

Scott Smith, Public Relations Manager

An international trade association representing firms supplying equipment, materials and services to the semiconductor industry. Strengthens the performance of members through promotion, lobbying, education and statistical research.
2300 Members
Founded in 1970

6932 **Semiconductor Industry Association**
181 Metro Dr
Suite 450
San Jose, CA 95110-1344

408-436-6600
Fax: 202-216-9745
E-Mail: mailbox@sia-online.org
Home Page: www.sia-online.org

George Scalise, President
Wilfred J Corrigan, Chairman/CEO
John Kelly III, Director

Trade association representing the US microchip industry. Provides a forum for working collectively to enhance the competitiveness of the US chip industry.
70 Members
Founded in 1977

6933 **Society of Manufacturing Engineers**
1 SME Drive
PO Box 930
Dearborn, MI 48121

313-425-3000
800-733-4763
Fax: 313-425-3400
E-Mail: service@sme.org
Home Page: www.sme.org

Mark Tomlinson, Executive Director/General Manager
Greg Sheremet, Publisher
Bob Harris, Director Finance

Supports all engineers in electronics manufacturing. Publishes quarterly newsletter.
70M Members
Founded in 1932

6934 Surface Mount Technology Association
5200 Willson Rd
Suite 215
Minneapolis, MN 55424-1316

952-920-7682
Fax: 952-926-1819
E-Mail: joann@smta.org
Home Page: www.smta.org
Social Media: Facebook, Twitter, LinkedIn

Network of professionals building skills, sharing practical experience and developing solutions in electronic assembly technologies and related business operations.
3200 Members
Founded in 1984

6935 Tobacco Vapor Electronic Cigarette Association
3750 avenue Julien Panchot
Perpignan, BP 66004
E-Mail: info@tveca.com
Home Page: www.tveca.com

Ray Story, CEO
Dac Sprengel, Managing Director
Thomas R. Kiklas, CFO
Chrissy Keheley, Secretary
Christopher Fowler, Web Development

A nonprofit organization dedicated to create a sensible and responsible electronic cigarette market by providing the media, legislative bodies, andconsumers with education, communication, and research.

6936 Universal Association of Computer and Electronics Engineers
42 Broadway
Suite 12-217
New York, NY 10004

212-901-3781
Fax: 212-901-3786
E-Mail: support@uacee.org
Home Page: www.uacee.org

A registered nonprofit society to promote research.

6937 Video Electronics Standards Association
39899 Balentine Dr.
Suite 125
Newark, CA 94560

510-651-5122
Fax: 510-651-5127
E-Mail: moderator@vesa.org
Home Page: www.vesa.org
Social Media: Twitter, YouTube

Alan Kobayashi, Chairman
Syed Athar Hussain, Vice Chairman
Richard Hubbard, Secretary/ Treasurer
Bill Lempesis, Executive Director
Joan White, Membership Services Manager

An international nonprofit corporation standards body for computer graphics.

6938 Wheatland Rural Electric Association
P. O. Box 1209
Wheatland, WY 82201

307-322-2125
800-344-3351
Fax: 307-322-5340
Home Page: www.wheatlandrea.com
Social Media: Facebook

Robert Brockman, President
Bill Teter, Vice-President
Britt Wilson, Secretary/ Treasurer
Gene Schuldies, Director
Jack Finnerty, Director

Home power usage calculations, product and new service information,and youth scholarships.
Founded in 1936

Newsletters

6939 AEA Monthly News
American Electronics Association
5201 Great America Parkway
Santa Clara, CA 95054

408-987-4200
800-284-4232
Fax: 408-987-4298
Home Page: www.aeanet.org

John V Harker, Chairman
William T Archey, President/CEO
Samuel J Block, VP/Controller
Tim Bennett, COO/EVP

AEA Advancing the Business of Technology, Access to Investors, State, Federal & International Lobbying, Insurance Services, Government Procurement, Business Networking, Foreign Market Access, Select Business Services, Executive Education.
Frequency: Monthly

6940 AEA by the Bay
American Electronics Association
5201 Great America Parkway
Santa Clara, CA 95054

408-987-4200
800-284-4232
Fax: 408-987-4298
Home Page: www.aeanet.org

John V Harker, Chairman
William T Archey, President/CEO
Samuel J Block, VP/Controller
Tim Bennett, COO/EVP

Newsletter for the AEA Bay Area Council.
Frequency: Monthly

6941 AEA's Californica Monday Morning Report
American Electronics Association
5201 Great America Parkway
Santa Clara, CA 95054

408-987-4200
800-284-4232
Fax: 408-987-4298
Home Page: www.aeanet.org

John V Harker, Chairman
William T Archey, President/CEO
Samuel J Block, VP/Controller
Tim Bennett, COO/EVP

A weekly report of what is going on in California policy relating to the high-tech industry, and how to change it.
Frequency: Weekly

6942 American Electronics Association Impact
American Electronics Association
5201 Great America Parkway
Santa Clara, CA 95054-1122

408-987-4200
Fax: 408-970-8565
Home Page: www.aeanet.org

William Archey, President

Representing the electronics software and information technology industries. Covers business and management issues for electronics executives.
Frequency: Monthly
Circulation: 25000
Founded in 1945

6943 Consumer Electronic and Appliance News
Kasmar Publications
41905 Boardwalk
Suite L
Palm Desert, CA 92221

800-253-9992
800-253-9992
Fax: 760-723-2876
Home Page: www.kasmarpub.com

Donald Martin, Editor

Home entertainment, consumer electronics and major appliances.
28 Pages
Founded in 1970

6944 Currents
Electrical Apparatus Service Association
1331 Baur Boulevard
Saint Louis, MO 63132-1903

314-993-2220
Fax: 314-993-1269
E-Mail: easainfo@easa.com
Home Page: www.easa.com
Social Media: Facebook, Twitter, LinkedIn

Linda J Raynes, President/CEO
Dale Shuter, Meetings/Expositions Manager

EASA is a trade association recognized internationally as the leader in the electrical and mechanical apparatus sales, service and repair industry.
Frequency: Monthly
Circulation: 2000+
Founded in 1933

6945 Electronic Advertising Marketplace Report
Simba Information
PO Box 4234
Stamford, CT 06907-0234

203-258-8193
Fax: 203-358-5825
E-Mail: simbainfo@simbanet.com
Home Page: www.simbanet.com

Linda Kopp, Editor
Donna Devall, Marketing Director
Joyce Brigish, Circulation Manager

Provides news, analysis and opinion for the emerging business of electronic advertising and shopping and commerce. Discover how publishers, telephone companies, distributors, and retailers are now using information technologies to build the information infrastructure that will reach new customers and match buyers with sellers. Covers electronic marketing, new electronic classified and transactional services, the role of the Internet, electronic yellow pages, etc.
Cost: $499.00
Frequency: BiWeekly

6946 Electronic Education Report
Simba Information
PO Box 4234
Stamford, CT 06907-0234

203-258-8193
Fax: 203-358-5825
E-Mail: simbainfo@simbanet.com
Home Page: www.simbanet.com

Megan St. John, Manager
Patrick Quinn, Editor

Provides information on the multi-billion dollar market for electronic instructional materials. Includes company rankings, financial profiles,

sales and distrbution trends, funding and adoptions, enrollement and demographics, trademark and copyright issues, strategic alliances and mergers.
Cost: $445.00
Frequency: BiWeekly

6947 **Electronic Imaging Report**
Phillips Publishing
7811 Montrose Road
Potomac, MD 20854
301-340-2100
E-Mail: feedback@healthydirections.com
Home Page: www.healthydirections.com
Written for top-level executives interested in learning how imaging technology can streamline their operations, cut their overhead costs and boost their competitiveness. Accepts advertising.
Cost: $397.00
9 Pages
Frequency: BiWeekly

6948 **Electronic Information Report**
Simba Information
PO Box 4234
Stamford, CT 06907-234
203-258-8193
Fax: 203-358-5825
E-Mail: simbainfo@simbanet.com
Home Page: www.simbanet.com
Linda Kopp, Editor
Charlie Friscia, Marketing Director
The original information industry newsletter. Every week, this report monitors, analyzes, and reports on trends and developments in information services. It covers new storage and distribution media, databases, electronic publishing, value-added fax, online, multimedia and voice services. Readers will receive up-to-the-minute news written from a product, financial and marketing viewpoint.
Cost: $685.00
Frequency: 46 Issues Per Y
Founded in 1989

6949 **Electronic Materials Technology News**
Business Communications Company
25 Van Zant Street
Suite 13
Norwalk, CT 06855-1713
203-853-4266
Fax: 203-853-0348
E-Mail: sales@bccresearch.com
Home Page: www.bccresearch.com
Louis Naturman, President
Marc Favrean, Editor
Alan Hall, Editorial Director
Thomas Abraham, VP Research
Marc Favreau, VP Development
Reports on electronic materials and processes, patents, companies involved, trends and business opportunities.
Cost: $35.00
Founded in 1971

6950 **Electronics Manufacturing Engineering**
Society of Manufacturing Engineers
1 SME Drive
PO Box 930
Dearborn, MI 48128
313-425-3000
800-733-4763
Fax: 313-425-3400
E-Mail: service@sme.org
Home Page: www.sme.org
Mark Tomlinson, Executive Director/General Manager
Greg Sheremet, Publisher
Bob Harris, Director Finance
Covers various aspects of electronics manufacturing.
Cost: $60.00
8 Pages
Frequency: Quarterly
Circulation: 2147
Mailing list available for rent: 18190 names at $95 per M
Printed in 2 colors on matte stock

6951 **IEEE All-Society Periodicals Package(ASPP)**
Power Electronics Society
799 N Beverly Glen
Los Angeles, CA 90077
310-446-8280
Fax: 310-446-8390
E-Mail: bob.myers@ieee.org
Home Page: www.pels.org
Jerry Hudgins, President
Robert Myers, Executive Director
Steven Leeb, Treasurer
Ronald Harley, VP Operations
Provides access to our core collection of engineering, electronics, and computer science periodicals.

6952 **ISCET Update**
Int'l Society of Certified Electronics Technicians
3608 Pershing Ave
Fort Worth, TX 76107-4527
817-921-9101
800-946-0201
Fax: 817-921-3741
E-Mail: info@iscet.org
Home Page: www.iset.org
Ed Clingman, Administrator
Sheila Fred, Editor
Brian Gibbson, Circulation Manager
News and information for the electronics community.
Frequency: Monthly
Circulation: 1300

6953 **Integrated Circuit Manufacturing Synopsis**
Semiconductor Equipment & Materials International
3081 Zanker Road
San Jose, CA 95134
408-943-6900
Fax: 408-428-9600
E-Mail: semihq@semi.org
Home Page: www.semi.org
Maggie Hershey, Manager
Anne Miller, Author
Victoria Hadfield, Executive VP/President, N America
An illustrated booklet that provides an excellent introduction to the semiconductor industry and makes a great handout for new employee orientation or as a resource for industry suppliers. It is easy to understand and free of technical terminology.
Cost: $15.75
35 Pages

6954 **Manufacturing Market Insider**
JBT Communications
PO Box 782
Needham Heights, MA 02494-0006
781-444-2154
Fax: 781-455-8409
Home Page: www.mtgmkt.com
John B Tuck, Publisher/Editor
Ann Connors, Circulation Manager
Specializes in contract manufacturing of electronics. Includes acquisitions, expansions, financial results and contract awards announced by contract manufacturers of electronics.
Cost: $420.00
8 Pages
Frequency: Monthly
ISSN: 1072-8651
Founded in 1991
Printed in one color on matte stock

6955 **Military & Aerospace Electronics**
PennWell Publishing Company
98 Spit Brook Rd
Suite Ll-1
Nashua, NH 03062-5737
603-891-0123
Fax: 603-891-9294
E-Mail: ATD@PennWell.com
Home Page: www.pennwell.com
Christine Shaw, VP
Tobias Naegele, Editor
Engineering newspaper written exclusively for military-aeronautical electronic systems designers, buyers and project managers.
Cost: $10.00
Frequency: Monthly
Circulation: 48,100
Founded in 1910

6956 **Optics & Photonics News (OPN)**
Optical Society of America
2010 Massachusetts Ave Nw
Washington, DC 20036-1023
202-223-8130
Fax: 202-223-1096
E-Mail: info@osa.org
Home Page: www.osa.org
Elizabeth Rogan, Executive Director
Optics & Photonics/OPN is a monthly magazine that keeps members up to date on technical innovations, industry news, OSA activities and much more. OPN promotes the generation application, archiving and worldwide dissemination of knowledge in optics and photonics.
Frequency: Monthly
Circulation: 17000
Mailing list available for rent

6957 **SITE**
American Electronics Association
5201 Great America Parkway
Santa Clara, CA 95054
408-987-4200
800-284-4232
Fax: 408-987-4298
Home Page: www.aeanet.org
John V Harker, Chairman
William T Archey, President/CEO
Samuel J Block, VP/Controller
Tim Bennett, COO/EVP
Brings High-Tech HR professionals important information about compensation and benefits, employment law, relevant legislation, education and training.
Frequency: Bi-Monthly

6958 **SouthWest Technology Report**
Communications
PO Box 23899
Tempe, AZ 85285-3899
480-345-1118
Fax: 480-345-1119
Walter J Schuch, Publisher
Focused on business and technology news related to high tech and electronics companies and organizations based in the Southwestern United States.
Cost: $69.00
8 Pages
Frequency: Monthly
Printed in one color on matte stock

6959 **Technician Association News**
Electronic Technicians Association International
5 Depot St
Greencastle, IN 46135-8024

765-653-8262
800-288-3824
Fax: 765-653-4287
E-Mail: eta@eta-i.org
Home Page: www.eta-i.org

Dick Glass, President
Brianna Pinson, Office Manager

A professional and trade journal servicing electronic technicians nationwide. Lists new certified electronics technicians, technical repair services, upcoming seminars and satellite training sessions.
Frequency: Monthly
ISSN: 1092-9592
Founded in 1978
Printed in 2 colors

6960 **Technology News Today**
American Electronics Association
5201 Great America Parkway
Santa Clara, CA 95054

408-987-4200
800-284-4232
Fax: 408-987-4298
Home Page: www.aeanet.org

John V Harker, Chairman
William T Archey, President/CEO
Samuel J Block, VP/Controller
Tim Bennett, COO/EVP
Melissa La vigna, Contact

Aims to benefit investors with exclusive information on high-tech industry trends available only through AEA's extensive research, legislative monitoring and high-leveled networking capabilities.
Frequency: Quarterly

6961 **Twice: This Week in Consumer Electronics**
Reed Business Information
360 Park Ave S
15th Floor
New York, NY 10010-1737

646-746-6400
800-826-6270
Fax: 646-756-7583
E-Mail: mgrand@reedbusiness.com
Home Page: www.reedbusiness.com

John Poulin, CEO
Jeff Greisch, Editor/CEO/President
Stephen F Smith, Editor-in-Chief
James Reed, Owner
Patricia Kennedy, Production Manager

Features include industry news, statistics, financial reports and new product trends and announcements.
Cost: $94.90
Frequency: Monthly
Circulation: 41000

Magazines & Journals

6962 **Advancing Microelectronics**
ISHM-Microelectronics Society
611 2nd street NE
Washington Dc, DC 20002

202-548-4001
888-464-6277
Fax: 202-548-6115
E-Mail: imaps@imaps.org
Home Page: www.imaps.org

For the Microelectronics Society.
Circulation: 4010

6963 **Applied Microwave & Wireless**
Noble Publishing Corporation
1334 Meridian Rd
Thomasville, GA 31792

229-377-0587
Fax: 229-377-0589
E-Mail: randy@noblepub.com
Home Page: www.noblepub.com

Joseph White, Publisher
Randy W Rhea, CEO

Edited for the RF and microwave professional.
Cost: $30.00
Frequency: Monthly
Circulation: 26287
ISSN: 1075-0207
Founded in 1994

6964 **AudioXpress**
Audio Amateur Publications
PO Box 876
Peterborough, NH 03458

603-924-9464
888-924-9465
Fax: 603-924-9467
E-Mail: editorial@audioxpress.com
Home Page: www.audioxpress.com

Edward Dell, Publisher

Focuses on the developments in sound production and enhancements in audio equipment and contains information on the construction of new and modification of existing audio equipment. Projects include schematics, parts lists and instructions necessary for completion aimed at electronic engineers and hobbyists.
Cost: $34.95
72 Pages
Frequency: Monthly
Circulation: 11000
ISSN: 1548-6028
Founded in 2001
Printed in 4 colors on glossy stock

6965 **Avionics News Magazine**
Aircraft Electronics Association
3570 Ne Ralph Powell Rd
Lees Summit, MO 64064-2360

816-347-8400
Fax: 816-478-3100
E-Mail: info@aea.net
Home Page: www.aea.net

Paula Derks, President
Tracy Lykins, Editor
Linda Adams, Managing Editor

This publication is the voice of the general aviation electronics industry. It is recognized as one of the leading publications for the latest information in avionics technology. Subscriptions are complimentary within North America, however, subscribers must be employed within the aviation industry to receive the magazine.
Cost: $132.00
Frequency: Monthly
Mailing list available for rent

6966 **Channel Magazine**
Semiconductor Equipment & Materials International
3081 Zanker Road
San Jose, CA 95134-4080

408-943-6900
Fax: 408-428-9600
E-Mail: semihq@semi.org
Home Page: www.semi.org

Karen Savala, Publisher
Steve Buehler, Editor

A forum for equipment and material suppliers committed to the environment, health and safety as a Global Care member.
Founded in 1970

6967 **Circuits Assembly**
Circuit Assembly
18 Thomas Street
Irvine, CA 92618-2777

949-855-7887
Fax: 949-855-4298
E-Mail: sales@circuitassembly.com
Home Page: www.circuitassembly.com

Laura Brown Sims, Associate Publisher

Devoted to the global electronics assembly industry.
Frequency: Monthly

6968 **CleanRooms Magazine**
PennWell Publishing Company
98 Spit Brook Rd
Nashua, NH 03062-5737

603-891-0123
800-225-0556
Fax: 603-891-9294
E-Mail: jhaystead@pennwell.com
Home Page: www.pennwell.com

Christine Shaw, VP
Angela Godwin, Managing Editor
Heidi Barns, Circulation Manager
Lisa Bergevin, Marketing
James Enos, Publisher

Serves the contamination control and ultrapure materials and process industries. Written for readers in the microelectronics, pharmaceutical, biotech, health care, food processing and other user industries. Provides technology and business news and new product listings.
Frequency: Monthly
Circulation: 35031
Founded in 1987

6969 **CommVerge**
Reed Business Information
2000 Clearwater Dr
Oak Brook, IL 60523-8809

630-574-0825
Fax: 630-288-8781
Home Page: www.reedbusiness.com

Jeff Greisch, President

The world leading publisher and information provider. Provides a range of communication and information channels, magazines, exhibitions, directories, online media, marketing services across five continents. Prestige brands in leading positions in key business sectors we deliver unrivalled access to business professionals across a diverse range of industries.

6970 **Computer Business Review**
ComputerWire
150 Post Street
#520
San Francisco, CA 94108-4707

415-274-8290
Fax: 415-274-8281
E-Mail: cbred@computerwire.com
Home Page: www.computerwire.com/cbr

Tim Langford, Publisher

Company profiles, computer market coverage and technology trends and news for investors and professionals in the computer, communications and microelectronics industries.
Cost: $195.00
Frequency: Monthly
Circulation: 23M

6971 **Computer-Aided Engineering**
Penton Media
1300 E 9th St
Cleveland, OH 44114-1503

216-696-7000
Fax: 216-696-6662

E-Mail: caenetmaster@penton.com
Home Page: www.penton.com

Jane Cooper, Marketing

Applications, news, trends and products for CAD/CAM technology as applied in manufacturing, electronics, architectural and construction industries.
Cost: $50.00
Frequency: Monthly
Circulation: 56,062

6972 Consumer Electronics Vision
Consumer Electronics Association (CEA)
1919 S Eads Street
Arlington, VA 22202

703-907-7600
866-858-1555
Fax: 703-907-7675
E-Mail: cea@ce.org
Home Page: www.ce.org

Cindy Stevens, Publications Director
Jason Oxman, VP Communications
Jenny Pareti, Public Policy Director
Gary Shapiro, President/CEO
Pat Lavelle, Chairman

Provides the latest information on industry standards, public policy, market research, CEA events and training opportunities. Is the premier source of information for the top management of more than 1,000 US corporations that design, develop, manufacture and distribute audio, video, mobile electronics, wireless and landline communications, IT, multimedia, accessory products and related services sold through consumer channels.
Frequency: Monthly
Circulation: 1000
Founded in 1844

6973 Control Solutions
PennWell Publishing Company
1421 S Sheridan Rd
Tulsa, OK 74112-6619

918-831-9421
800-331-4463
Fax: 918-831-9476
E-Mail: headquarters@pennwell.com
Home Page: www.pennwell.com

Robert Biolchini, President
Ron Kuhfeld, Editor-in-Chief
Frequency: Monthly
Founded in 1910

6974 Dealerscope
North American Publishing Company
1500 Spring Garden St
Suite 1200
Philadelphia, PA 19130-4094

215-238-5300
800-627-2689
Fax: 215-238-5342
E-Mail: webmaster@napco.com
Home Page: www.napco.com

Ned S Borowsky, CEO
Rhoda Dixon, Circulation Manager
Eric Schwartz, President/Publishing Dir

Dedicated to delivering peer-based knowledge and experience, Dealerscope is the ultimate vehicle for presenting product and service solutions to the consumer.
Frequency: Monthly
Founded in 1958

6975 ECN Magazine
Reed Business Information
360 Park Ave S
4th Floor
New York, NY 10010-1737

646-746-6400
Fax: 646-756-7583
E-Mail: subsmail@reedbusiness.com
Home Page: www.reedbusiness.com

John Poulin, CEO
James Reed, Owner

Provides product solutions for designed engineers in the electronics industry.
Circulation: 117923
Founded in 1957

6976 EDN Asia
Reed Business Information
45 E 85th St
4th Floor
New York, NY 10028-0957

212-772-8300
Fax: 630-288-8686
E-Mail: mike.pan@rbi-asia.com
Home Page: www.edn.com/

Lawrence S Reed
Mike Pan, Editor
Robin Peter Lange, Managing Editor
Raymond Wong, Publishing Director
Chen Wai Chun, Publisher

A source for all the design features, technology trends, design ideas, hands-on applications and product updates.
Frequency: Monthly
Circulation: 30000
Founded in 1990

6977 EDN China
Reed Business Information
45 E 85th St
4th Floor
New York, NY 10028-0957

212-772-8300
Fax: 630-288-8686
E-Mail: john.dodge@reedbusiness.com
Home Page: www.edninteractive.com

Lawrence S Reed
William Zhang, Publisher Director
John Mu, Executive Editor
Stephen D. Moylan, President

A source for design, development, & applications information foe electronics engineers & managers.
Frequency: Monthly
Circulation: 30018
Founded in 1946

6978 EDN Europe
Reed Business Information
45 E 85th St
4th Floor
New York, NY 10028-0957

212-772-8300
Fax: 630-288-8686
E-Mail: gprophet@reedbusiness.com
Home Page: www.edninteractive.com

Lawrence S Reed
Martin Savery, Publisher
Graham Prophet, Editor

A focused product specific to, and unique in, its own region, that draws on a unique international network of editorial expertise. EDN serves design engineers, providing exactly the information they need to conceive and create tomorrow's electronic products.
Circulation: 35,024

6979 EE Product News
Penton Media
1300 E 9th St
Cleveland, OH 44114-1503

216-696-7000
Fax: 216-696-6662
E-Mail: information@penton.com
Home Page: www.penton.com

Jane Cooper, Marketing
David B. Nussbaum, CEO

Source of information in new products necessary to successfully design, assemble and test prototypes of commerical, industrial, military and aerospace electronic products.
Frequency: Monthly
Circulation: 111968
Founded in 1892

6980 EE: Evaluation Engineering
Nelson Publishing
2500 Tamiami Trl N
Nokomis, FL 34275-3476

941-966-9521
800-226-6113
Fax: 941-966-2590
E-Mail: pmilo@evaluationengineering.com
Home Page: www.healthmgttech.com

A Verner Nelson, Owner
Michael Hughes, Sales

Magazine devoted exclusively to companies that test, evaluate, design and manufacture electronic products and equipment.
Cost: $43.00
84 Pages
Frequency: Monthly
Founded in 1962
Mailing list available for rent: 65,000 names
Printed in 4 colors on glossy stock

6981 Electromagnetic News Report
Seven Mountains Scientific
913 Tressler Street
PO Box 650
Boalsburg, PA 16827

814-466-6559
Fax: 814-466-2777
E-Mail: enr@7ms.com
Home Page: www.7ms.com

Josephine Chesworth, Managing Editor
E Thomas Chesworth, Technical Editor
Patrick D. Elliott, Production Manager

Offers industry news and technical articles of interest to readers as well as a calendar of events, product news and EMI publications.
Cost: $90.00
40 Pages
Circulation: 1000
ISSN: 0270-4935
Founded in 1972
Printed in 4 colors on matte stock

6982 Electronic Business
Reed Business Information
5525 Sierra Rd
Building N
San Jose, CA 95132-3421

408-926-6340
Fax: 408-345-4400
E-Mail: subsmail@reedbusiness.com
Home Page: www.reedbusiness.com

Donald Reed, Owner
Kathleen Doler, Editor-in-Chief
James A Casella, CEO
Shahrokh Rad, Owner
Salina Le Bris, Corporate Communications/PR
Frequency: Monthly
Circulation: 65732
Founded in 1975

6983 Electronic Components
Global Sources
7341 Washington Avenue
Suite C
Whittier, CA 90602

562-945-4612
Fax: 562-945-4192
E-Mail: mktgserv@globalsources.com
Home Page: www.globalsources.com

Anna Maria Anguiano, Account Manager
Mark Sanderson, Publisher

Dan Katz, Managing Director
Cost: $75.00
Frequency: Monthly
Founded in 1971

6984 **Electronic Design**
Penton Media
1300 E 9th St
Cleveland, OH 44114-1503
216-696-7000
Fax: 216-696-6662
E-Mail: information@penton.com
Home Page: www.penton.com
Jane Cooper, Marketing
Mark David, Editor in Chief
Janet Connors, Marketing
Celebrating 50 years of innovation, this authoritative source provides leading-edge technical information to electronic and engineering managers around the world.
Frequency: Monthly
Circulation: 145000
Founded in 1892

6985 **Electronic Packaging & Production**
Reed Business Information
1350 E Touhy Avenue
Des Plaines, IL 60018
630-320-7000
Fax: 630-288-8686
E-Mail: epp@cahners.com
Home Page: www.cahners.com
Vicky Steen, Publisher
Michael Sweeney, Editorial Director
Edited for engineers and managers who are involved in packaging designed, printed circuit board fabrication and assembly, and production testing of electronic circuits, systems, products and equipment.

6986 **Electronic Products**
Hearst Business Communications
645 Stewart Ave
Garden City, NY 11530-4769
516-227-1300
Fax: 516-227-1342
E-Mail: ralphr@electronicproducts.com
Home Page: www.elecprod2.com
Todd Christenson, Publisher
Gail Meyer, Production Manager
R Pell, Editor-in-Chief
News about developments in electronic components and equipment.
Frequency: Monthly
Circulation: 123767
Founded in 1958
Mailing list available for rent: 123767 names
Printed in 4 colors on glossy stock

6987 **Electronics Manufacturing Engineering**
Society of Manufacturing Engineers
1 SME Drive
PO Box 930
Dearborn, MI 48128
313-425-3000
800-733-4763
Fax: 313-425-3400
E-Mail: service@sme.org
Home Page: www.sme.org
Mark Tomlinson, Executive Director/General Manager
Greg Sheremet, Publisher
Bob Harris, Director Finance
For manufacturing engineers and managers involved with electronics manufacturing.
Circulation: 3,300

6988 **High Density Interconnect**
CMP Media
600 Community Drive
Manhasset, NY 11030
516-562-5000
Fax: 415-947-6090
Home Page: www.cmp.com

6989 **High Tech News**
Electronic Technicians Association International
5 Depot St
Greencastle, IN 46135-8024
765-653-8262
800-288-3824
Fax: 765-653-4287
E-Mail: eta@eta-i.org
Home Page: www.eta-i.org
Social Media: Facebook, Twitter, LinkedIn
Teresa Maher, CSS, President
Chrissy Baker, Marketing Coordinator
Richard Glass, CETsr, CEO Emeritus
Exclusive bi-monthly publication of ETA International, and a subscription is included with each individual membership. Each issue features information on the changing electronics industry: specialty techniques & technology, trends, qualification opportunities and educational advice.
4500 Members
Frequency: Bi-Monthly
Circulation: 10000
Founded in 1978

6990 **IEEE Control Systems Magazine**
IEEE Control Systems Society (CSS)
445 Hoes Lane
PO Box 1331
Piscataway, NJ 08854-1331
732-981-0060
Fax: 732-981-1721
E-Mail: society-info@ieee.org
Home Page: www.ieee.org
Dennis S Bernstein, Editor
Susan Schneiderman, Business Development Manager
Focuses on applications of technical knowledge and concentrates on industrial implementations, design tools, technology review, control education and applied research. Geared towards readers with many different responsibilities including applied research, device design, product development and design including software and semiconductor components.
Cost: $210.00
Founded in 1973
Mailing list available for rent

6991 **Journal of Microelectronics & Electronic Packaging**
International Microelectronics & Electronic Pack.
611 2nd Street NE
Washington, DC 20002
202-548-4001
888-464-6277
Fax: 202-548-6115
E-Mail: imaps@imaps.org
Home Page: www.imaps.org
Fred D Barlow III PhD, Editor-in-Chief

6992 **Journal of Microelectronics and Electronic Packaging**
International Microelectronics & Electronics
611 2nd Street NE
Washington, DC 20002
202-548-4001
888-464-6277
Fax: 202-548-6115
E-Mail: impas@imaps.org
Home Page: www.imaps.org
Michael O'Donoghue, Executive Director
Rick Mohn, Operations Manager
Brian Schieman, Director Information Technology
Ann Bell, Manager Marketing/Communications
Dedicated to publishing peer-reviewed papers in microelectronics, multichip module technologies, electronic packaging, electronic materials, surface mount and other related technologies, interconnections, RF and microwaves, wireless communications, manufacturing, design, test, and reliability.
Cost: $35.00

6993 **Journal of Microwave Power and Electromagnetic Energy**
International Microwave Power Institute
PO Box 1140
Mechanicsville, VA 23111-5007
804-559-6667
Fax: 804-559-4087
E-Mail: info@impi.org
Home Page: www.impi.org
Social Media: Facebook, Twitter
Molly Poisant, Executive Director
The quarterly, technical journal of the Institute published by the Industrial, Scientific, Medical and Instrumentation (ISMI) section. Designed for the information needs of professionals specializing in the research and design of industrial and bio-medical applications, the Journal exemplifies the highest standards of scientific and technical information on the theory and application of electromagnetic power.
Cost: $250.00
Frequency: Quarterly

6994 **Laser Focus World**
PennWell Publishing Company
98 Spit Brook Rd
Nashua, NH 03062-5737
603-891-0123
Fax: 603-891-9294
E-Mail: allisono@pennwell.com
Home Page: www.pennwell.com
Christine Shaw, Publisher
Carol Settino, Managing Editor
The world of optoelectronics.
Cost: $150.00
173 Pages
Frequency: Monthly
Circulation: 70004
Founded in 1965
Printed in 4 colors on glossy stock

6995 **Modeling Power Devices and Model Validation**
Power Sources Manufacturers Association
PO Box 418
Mendham, NJ 07945-0418
973-543-9660
Fax: 973-543-6207
E-Mail: power@psma.com
Home Page: www.psma.com
Dusty Becker, Chairman
Carl Blake, President
Jim Marinos, VP
This report consists of two parts, one devoted to modeling, and the other, model validation. The first article in the report reviews commonly used device models used in circuit simulations, and applies these to simulation designed power converters and rectifers. The second article establishes processes by which the features and accuracy of a model are determined by simulating the results of test circuits containing power devices and comparing these

results with the results of actual measurements
Cost: $20.00
155 Members
Founded in 1985

6996 **Optics Letters**
Optical Society of America
2010 Massachusetts Ave Nw
Washington, DC 20036-1023

202-223-8130
Fax: 202-223-1096
E-Mail: info@osa.org
Home Page: www.osa.org

Elizabeth Rogan, Executive Director

Offers rapid dissemination of new results in all areas of optics with short, original, peer-reviewed communications. Optics Letters covers the latest research in optical science, including atmospheric optics, quantum electronics, Fourier optics, integrated optics, and fiber optics.
Frequency: 24 issues per year
ISSN: 0146-9592

6997 **Power Conversion & Intelligent Motion**
Primedia
Po Box 12901
Shawnee Mission, KS 66282-2901

913-341-1300
Fax: 913-514-6895
Home Page: www.penton.com

Eric Jacobson, Senior VP
Sam Davis, Editor

Directed to engineers, designers and manufacturers of power electronic and electronic motion control components, subsystems and systems. Feature articles interpret trends and innovation in these subjects.
Circulation: 31,113

6998 **Power Electronics Technology**
Penton Media, Inc
249 W 17th Street
New York, NY 10011

212-204-4200
E-Mail: bill.baumann@penton.com
Home Page: www.powerelectronics.com

Bill Baumann, Group Publisher
Sam Davis, Editor-in-Chief

Formerly PCIM Power Electronic Systems, delivers timely information to professionals in the power electronic industry.
Frequency: Monthly
Circulation: 36,000
Founded in 1975

6999 **Printed Circuit Fabrication**
CMP Media
600 Community Drive
Manhasset, NY 11030

516-562-5000
Fax: 415-947-6090

7000 **ProService**
Int'l Society of Certified Electronics Technicians
3608 Pershing Ave
Fort Worth, TX 76107-4527

817-921-9101
800-946-0201
Fax: 817-921-3741
E-Mail: info@iscet.org
Home Page: www.iset.org

Ed Clingman, Administrator
Shiela Fredrickson, Publisher

A bi-monthly magazine published by the International Society of Certified Electronics Technicians.
24 Pages
Founded in 1965

7001 **ProService Magazine**
National Electronics Service Dealers Association
3608 Pershing Ave
Fort Worth, TX 76107-4527

817-921-9061
800-797-9197
Fax: 817-921-3741
E-Mail: webmaster@nesda.com
Home Page: www.nesda.com

Brian Gibson, President
Don Cressin, VP
Mack Blakely, Executive Director
Fred Paradis, CSM, Treasurer
Wayne Markman, Secretary

For members of NESDA/ISCET, and a printed magazine is mailed to the membership address on file in April and August.
Frequency: Bi-Monthly

7002 **RTOHQ: The Magazine**
Association of Progressive Rental Merchandise
1540 Robinhood Trail
Austin, TX 78703-2624

512-794-0095
800-204-APRO
Fax: 512-794-0097
E-Mail: cferguson@rtohq.org
Home Page: www.rtohq.org

Bill Keese, Executive Director
John C Cleek, President
Bill Kelly, Secretary
Frequency: Bi-Monthly
Circulation: 11000

7003 **Representor Magazine**
Electronics Representatives Association
300 W Adams St
Suite 617
Chicago, IL 60606-5109

312-527-3050
800-776-7377
Fax: 312-527-3783
E-Mail: info@era.org
Home Page: www.era.org

Tom Shanahan, Executive VP
Bob Walsh, President

Devoted to fulfilling the management, informational, educational and communications needs of representatives and manufacturers in the electronics industry.
Cost: $15.00
450 Members
Frequency: Quarterly
Founded in 1935

7004 **Review of the Electronic and Industrial Distribution Industries**
National Electronic Distributors Association
1111 Alderman Dr
Suite 400
Alpharetta, GA 30005-4175

678-393-9990
Fax: 678-393-9998
E-Mail: admin@nedassoc.org
Home Page: www.nedassoc.org

Robin B Gray Jr, Executive VP
Debbie Conyers, Director Marketing
Barney Martin, VP Industry Practices

Contains academic articles on topics pertinent to our members' business. Leading electronic and industrial distribution academicians provides the content. Offers insightful articles aimed at improving industry practices. $12.00 per volume or $20.00 for an annual subscription.
Cost: $20.00
Frequency: Bi-Annually

7005 **SIGNAL Magazine**
Armed Forces Communications and Electronics Assn
4400 Fair Lakes Ct
Fairfax, VA 22033-3899

703-631-1397
800-336-4583
Fax: 703-631-4693
Home Page: www.afcea.org

Kent Schneider, President/CEO
Becky Nolan, Executive VP
John A Dubia, Executive VP

Is a international news magazine serving the critical information needs of government, military and industry professionals active in the fields of command, control, communications, computers, intelligence, surveillance and reconnaissance (C4ISR); information security; research and development; electronics; and homeland security.
Frequency: Monthly

7006 **Sensors Magazine**
Questex Media
275 Grove St
Suite 2-130
Auburndale, MA 02466-2275

617-219-8300
888-552-4346
Fax: 617-219-8310
E-Mail: jmcmahon@questex.com
Home Page: www.questex.com

Kerry C Gumas, CEO
Stephanie Henkel, Executive Editor

Source among design and production engineers of information on sensor technologies and products, and topic integral to sensor-based systems and applications. Provides practical and in-depth yet accessible information on sensor operation, design, application, and implementation within systems. Covers the effective use of state-of-the-art resources and tools that enable readers to get the maximum benefit from their use of sensors.
Cost: $99.00
Frequency: Monthly
Circulation: 75000
Founded in 1984

7007 **Tech Briefs**
Associated Business Publications International
1466 Broadway
Suite. 910
New York, NY 10036-7309

212-490-3999
Fax: 212-986-7864
E-Mail: alfredo@abpi.net
Home Page: www.techbriefs.com

Dominic Mucchetti, CEO
Hugh Dowling, Circualtion Manager
Linda Bell, Chief Editor

Serves design engineers, managers and scientists in the industries of electronics, industrial equipment, computers, communications, bio-medical, transportation/automotive, power and energy, materials, chemicals and many more related fields.
Cost: $75.00
Frequency: Monthly
Founded in 1958

7008 **Test & Measurement World**
Reed Business Information

275 Washington St
Suite 275
Newton, MA 02458-1611

617-964-3030
Fax: 617-558-4470
E-Mail: tmswales@cahners.com
Home Page: www.designnews.com

Rick Nelson, Chief Editor
Deborah M Sargent, Managing Editor
Russ Pratt, Publisher

The magazine on test, measurement and inspection in the electronics industry.
Frequency: Monthly
Circulation: 65000
Founded in 1981
Mailing list available for rent

7009 The Minerals, Metals & Materials Society/ Journal of Electronic Materials
Minerals, Metals & Materials Society
184 Thorn Hill Road
Warrendale, PA 15086-7528

724-776-9000
800-759-4867
Fax: 724-776-3770
Home Page: www.tms.org

Suzanne Mohney, Editor-In-Chief

Reports on the science and technology of electronic materials, while examining new applications for semiconductors, magnetic alloys, insulators, optical and display materials.
Cost: $131.00
11000 Members
Frequency: Monthly
Circulation: 1400
ISSN: 0361-5235
Founded in 1957
Printed in 2 colors on glossy stock

7010 Wideband
Advanstar Communications
641 Lexington Ave
8th Floor
New York, NY 10022-4503

212-951-6600
Fax: 212-951-6793
E-Mail: info@advanstar.com
Home Page: www.advanstar.com

Joseph Loggia, CEO

Covers accessories, equipment, services, products, and an anlysis of major market trends, industry news, statistics, new products, and personnel changes are featured in every issue.
Frequency: SemiMonthly
Circulation: 26,000

Trade Shows

7011 AEA Annual Convention & Trade Show
Aircraft Electronics Association
4217 S Hocker
Independence, MO 64055

816-373-6565
Fax: 816-478-3100
E-Mail: info@aea.net
Home Page: www.aea.net

Paula Derks, President
Debra McFarland, VP
Tracy Lykins, Director Communications
Mark Gibson, Administration/Meeting Management

Annual show of 131 exhibitors of industry related equipment and supplies.
1500 Attendees
Frequency: Annual
Founded in 1957

7012 AFCEA Sponsored Conferences/Symposia
Armed Forces Communications and Electronics Assn
4400 Fair Lakes Court
Fairfax, VA 22033-3899

703-631-6100
800-336-4583
Fax: 703-631-6405
Home Page: www.afcea.org

Kent Schneider, President/CEO
Becky Nolan, Executive VP
John A Dubia, Executive VP

Offers problem solving and networking opportunities through exhibits, technical panels, and featured speakers. Decision-makers from around the world attend AFCEA conferences for hands-on demonstrations, question-and-answer sessions and system solutions.

7013 AFCEA TechNet Asia-Pacific
Armed Forces Communications and Electronics Assn
4400 Fair Lakes Court
Fairfax, VA 22033-3899

703-631-6200
800-654-4220
Fax: 703-654-6931
E-Mail: technet@jspargo.com
Home Page: www.afcea.org

Paul doCarmo, Assistant Director/Exhibit Sales
Connie Shaw, Exhibit Sales Account Manager

Military, government and industry communications and electronics professionals gather to see exhibits of communications and electronics equipment, supplies and services. Seminar, conference, dinner and luncheon. Co-sponsored by AFCEA International and AFCEA Hawaii.
2000 Attendees
Frequency: Nov 7-9
Founded in 1985

7014 AFCEA TechNet International
Armed Forces Communications and Electronics Assn
4400 Fair Lakes Court
Fairfax, VA 22033-3899
703-631-6200
800-564-4220
Fax: 703-654-6931
E-Mail: technetinternational@jspargo.com
Home Page: www.afcea.org

Paul doCarmo, Sales Manager
Connie Shaw, Sales Manager

This event draws commanders and staff from every branch of the military, including warfighting integration organizations charged with the most critical responsibilities of synthesizing military power on land, at sea, and in the air.
7500 Attendees
Frequency: June

7015 AFCEA/USNI West Conference & Exposition
Armed Forces Communications and Electronics Assn
4400 Fair Lakes Court
Fairfax, VA 22033

703-631-6200
800-564-4220
Fax: 703-654-6931
E-Mail: west@jspargo.org
Home Page: www.afcea.org

Paul doCarmo, Assistant Direct/Exhibit Sales
Connie Shaw, Exhibit Sales Account Manager

Over 350 of the industry's most recognized defense and technology organizations showcase their technology products and services to top decision-makers from the US Pacific Fleet, Naval Station San Diego, Space & Warfare Command, Naval Base Coronado, Camp Pendleton Marine Corps Base and many other west coast military and government facilities.
6000 Attendees
Frequency: January
Founded in 1980

7016 APRO Rent-To-Own Convention & Trade Show
1504 Robin Hood Trail
Austin, TX 78703

512-794-0095
800-204-APRO
Fax: 512-794-0097
E-Mail: cmay@aprovision.org
Home Page: www.rtohq.org

Shannon Strunkec, President
John C Cleek, First VP
Jeannie Hutchison, Program Coordinator
Bill Keese, Manager

Seminar, reception and tours, plus 280 exhibits of products and services of interest to rent to own dealers: stereos, televisions, furniture, fabric protection and more.
1400 Attendees
Frequency: Annual

7017 ASM/TMS Spring Symposium
Minerals, Metals & Materials Society
184 Thorn Hill Road
Warrendale, PA 15086-7514

724-776-9000
Fax: 724-776-3770
E-Mail: foundation@tms.org
Home Page: www.tms.org

Tresa Pollock, President
Brajendra Mishra, VP
Alexander Scott, Executive Director
John Parsey, Financial Planning Officer
Marc DeGraef, Director Information Technology

This symposium, organized by the local chapters of TMS and ASM, will focus on materials for extreme environments, with sessions on materials characterization in three dimensions, structural materials for high temperature, materials for space applications, and materials by design.
Frequency: May

7018 ATE and Instrumentation West
Miller Freeman Publications
600 Harrison Street
Suite 400
San Francisco, CA 94107-1391

415-905-2354
Fax: 415-905-2232

Steve Schulderfrei, Trade Show Director

Geared to the test and measurement of electronics.
5.8M Attendees
Frequency: January

7019 AVS Annual Symposium & Exhibition
AVS Science & Technology Society

125 Maiden Lane
15th Floor
New York, NY 10038

212-248-0200
Fax: 212-248-0245
Home Page: www.avs.org

Christie R Marrian, President
John Coburn, Treasurer
Joseph E Greene, Clerk/Secretary
Yvonne Towse, Executive Director

Promotes communication, dissemination of knowledge, recommended practices, research, and education in the use of vacuum and other controlled environments to develop new materials, process technology, devices, and related understanding of material properties for the betterment of humanity.
Frequency: Annual/February

7020 AVS International Symposium and Exhibition
AVS Science & Technology Society
120 Wall Street
32nd Floor
New York, NY 10005-3993

212-248-0200
Fax: 212-248-0245
E-Mail: angela@avs.org
Home Page: www.avs.org

Christie R Marrian, President
John Coburn, Office Manager
Nancy Schultheis, Office Manager
Joseph E Greene, Clerk/Secretary
Yvonne Towse, Executive Director

This conference has been developed to address cutting edge issues associated with vacuum science and technology in both the research and manufacturing communities. The equipment exhibition is one of the largest in the world and provides an excellent opportunity to view the latest products and services offered by over 200 participating companies.
3000 Attendees

7021 All-Service Convention
Electronic Technicians Association International
5 Depot Street
Greencastle, IN 46135

765-653-4301
800-288-3824
Fax: 765-653-4287
E-Mail: eta@eta-i.org
Home Page: www.eta-i.org

Teresa Maher, President
Chrissy Baker, Marketing Coordinator

Appliances and electronic service products and services. Third party administrators. Certification exams and study materials. Tools and test equipment. Containing 40 booths and 50 exhibits.

7022 Annual Legislative & Regulatory Roundtable
Electronic Industries Alliance
2500 Wilson Boulevard
Arlington, VA 22201-3834

703-907-7500
703-907-7500
Home Page: www.eia.org

Gail Tannenbaum, CMP, Manager Meetings/Industry Relations
Frequency: Annual/August

7023 Asia Card Technology Exhibition
Reed Exhibition Companies
383 Main Avenue Suite 3
PO Box 6059
Norwalk, CT 06851

203-840-4800
Fax: 203-840-9628

Emily Hackett, Executive Director
Peter DiLeo, Marketing Director
Deborah Luongo, Conference Manager

Trade professionals see exhibits on computers and electronics.
Frequency: Annual

7024 Assembly Northeast Exhibition
Reed Exhibition Companies
383 Main Avenue Suite 3
PO Box 6059
Norwalk, CT 06851

203-840-4800
Fax: 203-840-9628

Emily Hackett, Executive Director
Peter DiLeo, Marketing Director
Deborah Luongo, Conference Manager
Gregg Vautrin, CEO

Assembly industry equipment, supplies and services for engineers and managers from electronic and automated assembly operations.
1365 Attendees
Frequency: Annual
Founded in 1999

7025 Assembly Technology Exposition
Reed Exhibition Companies
383 Main Avenue Suite 3
PO Box 6059
Norwalk, CT 06851

203-840-4800
800-267-3796
Fax: 203-840-9686
Home Page: www.atexpo.com

Emily Hackett, Executive Director
Peter DiLeo, Marketing Director
Deborah Luongo, Conference Manager

525 exhibitors with robotics, vision systems, electronics and production machinery of interest to engineers and managers from automated assembly plants.
14000 Attendees
Frequency: Annual
Founded in 1979

7026 Assembly West Exhibition
Reed Exhibition Companies
383 Main Avenue Suite 3
PO Box 6059
Norwalk, CT 06851

203-840-4800
Fax: 203-840-9628

Emily Hackett, Executive Director
Peter DiLeo, Marketing Director
Deborah Luongo, Conference Manager
Gregg Vautrin, CEO

Assembly industry equipment, supplies and services for engineers and managers from electronic and automated assembly operations.
3000 Attendees
Frequency: Annual

7027 Automated Manufacturing Exposition: New England
TEC
2001 Assembly Street
Suite 204
Columbia, SC 29201

803-779-7123
Home Page: www.amexpo.com/newengland

Tony Smith, Founder
Rafael Pastor, Chairman/CEO
Richard Carr, President/Vice Chairman
Jerry Schneider, Chief Financial Officer

In addition to the exhibits, the conference will feature seminars that focus on topics such as continuous improvement and lean manufacturing.

7028 CEA Industry Forum
Consumer Electronics Association (CEA)
1919 S Eads Street
Arlington, VA 22202

703-907-7600
866-858-1555
Fax: 703-907-7675
E-Mail: cea@ce.org
Home Page: www.ce.org/Events/default.asp

Gary Shapiro, President/CEO
Pat Lavelle, Chairman
Peter Lesser, Industry Executive Advisor
Jason Oxman, VP Communications
Jenny Pareti, Public Policy Director

The CEA Industry Forum is a conference designed to inform and connect leaders in the CE industry. The CEA Industry Forum offers a chance to network with the industry's top executives and decision-makers from retailer, manufacturer and service provider companies. It provides needed information on the industry's hottest topics and offers a voice in the direction of the CE industry on future policies, standards and industry initiatives.
Frequency: October

7029 CEA Winter Technology & Standards Forum
Consumer Electronics Association (CEA)
1919 S Eads Street
Arlington, VA 22202

703-907-7600
866-858-1555
Fax: 703-907-7675
E-Mail: cea@ce.org
Home Page: www.ce.org/Events/default.asp

Gary Shapiro, President/CEO
Pat Lavelle, Chairman
Peter Lesser, Industry Executive Advisor
Jason Oxman, VP Communications
Jenny Pareti, Public Policy Director

Attendees can focus on the development of emerging industry standards, contribute their company's viewpoints, and gain networking opportunities. Interface with industry technical leaders as they consider, develop, and finalize crucial CE standards.
Frequency: March, Florida

7030 CEO Summit
Consumer Electronics Association (CEA)
1919 S Eads Street
Arlington, VA 22202

703-907-7600
866-858-1555
Fax: 703-907-7675
E-Mail: cea@ce.org
Home Page: www.ce.org/Events/default.asp

Gary Shapiro, President/CEO
Pat Lavelle, Chairman
Peter Lesser, Industry Executive Advisor
Jason Oxman, VP Communications
Jenny Pareti, Public Policy Director

Presents a rare opportunity to network in a qualified, executive-only environment, to gather insight helpful to your business and to focus on the issues most critical to the industry.
Frequency: June

7031 CLEO/QELS Conference
Optical Society of America
2010 Massachusetts Avenue NW
Washington, DC 20036-1012

202-223-8130
Fax: 202-223-1096

E-Mail: info@osa.org
Home Page: www.osa.org

Elizabeth A Rogan, Executive Director

Is a unique conference that gathers distringuished leaders to discuss the latest research in the fields of optics and photonics. The conference includes application-focused forums, educational sessions and an applications-oriented exhibit.
Frequency: May

7032 **COM Conference of Metallurgists**
Minerals, Metals & Materials Society
184 Thorn Hill Road
Warrendale, PA 15086-7514

724-776-9000
Fax: 724-776-3770
E-Mail: foundation@tms.org
Home Page: www.tms.org

Tresa Polloc, President
Brajendra Mishra, VP
Alexander Scott, Executive Director
John Parsey, Financial Planning Officer
Marc DeGraef, Director Information Technology

Topic: Challenges for the Metals and Materials Industry. This conference will feature symposia on computational analysis in hydrometallurgy; nickel and cobalt; pipelines for the 21st century; materials degradation: innovation, inspection, control, and rehabilitation; light metals; fuel cell and hydrogen technologies; recruitment and early career development programs; and the treatment of gold ores.
Frequency: August

7033 **CONNECTIONS - The Digital Living Conference and Showcase**
Parks Associates
5310 Harvest Hill Road
Suite 235, Lock Box 162
Dallas, TX 75230-5805

972-490-1113
800-727-5711
E-Mail: info@parksassociates.com
Home Page: www.connectionsconference.com

Tricia Parks, Founder and CEO
Stuart Sikes, President
Farhan Abid, Research Analyst
Bill Ablondi, Director, Home Systems Research
John Barrett, Director of Research

This conference attracts over 500 executives focused on innovative consumer technology solutions. The unique conference and showcase highlights consumer and industry research from Parks Associates, showcases key players and new technologies, and delivers insight and recommendations for new business models and opportunities in digital media/content, mobile applications and services, connected consumer electronics, broadband and value-added services, and home systems.
Frequency: Annual
Founded in 1986
Mailing list available for rent

7034 **Ceramic Interconnect and Ceramic Microsystems**
International Microelectronics & Electronics
611 2nd Street
Washington, DC 20002

202-548-4001
888-464-6277
Fax: 202-548-6115
E-Mail: imaps@imaps.org
Home Page: www.imaps.org

Michael O'Donoghue, Executive Director
Rick Mohn, Operations Manager
Brian Schieman, Director Information Technology
Ann Bell, Manager Marketing/Communications
Frequency: April

7035 **DistribuTech Conference**
PennWell Conferences and Exhibitions
350 Post Oak Blouevard
Suite 205
Houston, TX 77056

713-621-8833
Fax: 713-963-6284
Home Page: www.pennwell.com

Bob Biolchini, CEO

Is the leading automation and information technology conference and exhibition in the utility industry; and provides the best resources, tools and networking opportunities relating to electric utility automation and control systems, IT, T&D engineering, power and delivery equipment, and water utility technology.
3000 Attendees
Frequency: January

7036 **EASA Conference**
Electrical Apparatus Service Association
1331 Baur Boulevard
Saint Louis, MO 63132-1903

314-993-2220
Fax: 314-993-1269
E-Mail: easainfo@easa.com
Home Page: www.easa.com
Social Media: Facebook, Twitter, LinkedIn

Linda J Raynes, President/CEO
Dale Shuter, Meetings/Expositions Manager

EASA is a trade association recognized internationally as the leader in the electrical and mechanical apparatus sales, service and repair industry.
2000+ Attendees
Frequency: Annual, June
Founded in 1933

7037 **EIA's Congressional Technology Forum**
Electronic Industries Alliance
2500 Wilson Boulevard
Arlington, VA 22201-3834

703-907-7500
Fax: 703-907-7500
Home Page: www.eia.org

Gail Tannenbaum, CMP, Manager Meetings/Industry Relations
Frequency: October

7038 **EOS/ESD Symposium & Exhibits**
Electrostatic Discharge Association
7900 Turin Road
Building 3
Rome, NY 13440-2069

315-339-6937
Fax: 315-339-6793
E-Mail: info@esda.org
Home Page: www.esda.org
Social Media: Facebook, LinkedIn

Donn Bellmore, President
Leo G. Henry, Sr. VP
Terry Welsher, VP
Lisa Pimpinella, Director of Operations
Donn Pritchard, Treasurer

International technical forum on electrical overstress and electrostatic discharge that features research, technology, and solutions to increase understanding, enhance quality and reliability, reduce and control costs, and improve yields and productivity.
2000+ Members
1M Attendees
Frequency: September
Founded in 1982

7039 **ETA Annual Meeting and Expo**
Electronic Transactions Association
1101 16th Street NW
Suite 402
Washington, DC 20036

202-828-2635
800-695-5509
Fax: 202-828-2639
Home Page: www.electran.org

Jennifer Leo, Meetings Manager
Kurt Strawhecker, Managing Director
Steve Carnevale, Senior Vice President

Featuring valuable networking opportunities, outstanding speakers and educational seminars.
Frequency: April, Las Vegas

7040 **ETA Expo Network**
Electronic Transactions Association
1101 16th Street NW
Suite 402
Washington, DC 20036

202-828-2635
800-695-5509
Fax: 202-828-2639
Home Page: www.electran.org

Jennifer Leo, Meetings Manager
Kurt Strawhecker, Managing Director
Steve Carnevale, Senior Vice President

Offers conference events that focus specifically on delivering need to know education to ISOs and sales agents. ETA created these meetings to increase educational and business development opportunities for the industry. These affordable and easily accessible conferences are the ideal opportunity to increase your knowledge and meet new business partners.

7041 **East Coast Video Show**
Expocon Management Associates
363 Reef Road
PO Box 915
Fairfield, CT 06430-0915

203-882-1300
Fax: 203-256-4730

Diane Stone, Show Director
8000 Attendees

7042 **Electronic Distribution Show and Conference**
Electronic Distribution Show Corporation
222 S Riverside Plaza
Suite 2160
Chicago, IL 60606-6160

312-648-1140
Fax: 312-648-4282
E-Mail: eds@edsc.org
Home Page: www.edsc.org

Gretchen Oie-Weghorst, Show Manager
Gretchen Oie, Manager

Annual conference and exhibits of 500 manufacturers of electronic components who sell through distribution. Containing 700 booths and 500 exhibits.
10M Attendees
Frequency: May

7043 **Electronic Imaging East**
Miller Freeman Publications
600 Harrison Street
Suite 400
San Francisco, CA 94107-1391

415-905-2354
Fax: 415-905-2232

Stephen Schuldenfrei, Trade Show Director

300 booths consisting of electrical equipment and services.
5.3M Attendees
Frequency: October

7044 **Electronic Imaging West**
Miller Freeman Publications
600 Harrison Street
Suite 400
San Francisco, CA 94107-1391

415-905-2534
Fax: 415-905-2232

Stephen Schuldenfrei, Trade Show Director

Exhibits of equipment, supplies and services for the computer and electronics industries.
3M Attendees

7045 **Electronic Materials Conference**
Minerals, Metals & Materials Society
184 Thorn Hill Road
Warrendale, PA 15086-7514

724-776-9000
Fax: 724-776-3770
E-Mail: foundation@tms.org
Home Page: www.tms.org

Tresa Pollock, President
Brajendra Mishra, VP
Alexander Scott, Executive Director
John Parsey, Financial Planning Officer
Marc DeGraef, Director Information Technology

This conference will provide a forum for topics of current interest and significance related to the preparation and characterization of electronic materials. Individuals actively engaged or interested in electronic materials research and development are encouraged to submit an abstract or attend the meeting. A technological exhibition will also be held.
Frequency: June

7046 **Electronic West: Annual Western Electrical Exposition Conference**
Continental Exhibitions
370 Lexington Avenue
Suite 1401
New York, NY 10017

212-370-5005
Fax: 212-370-5699

10000 Attendees

7047 **Embedded Systems Conference - West**
Miller Freeman Publications
600 Harrison Street
Suite 400
San Francisco, CA 94107

415-905-2354
Fax: 415-905-2220
Home Page: www.esconline.com

Lisa Ostrom, Electronics Show Director
Christian Fahlen, CEO

This is an ideal forum to learn relevant new skills, and about the latest technologies and products; to network with industry experts, vendors and your peers; and to discover an exhibits floor featuring leading companies showcasing cutting edge products.
13000 Attendees
Frequency: March

7048 **Executive Leadership Forum & Board of Governors Meeting**
Electronic Industries Alliance
2500 Wilson Boulevard
Arlington, VA 22201-3834

703-907-7500
Fax: 703-907-7500
Home Page: www.eia.org

Gail Tannenbaum, CMP, Manager Meetings/Industry Relations
Frequency: February, California

7049 **IMPI Annual Symposium**
International Microwave Power Institute
7076 Drinkard Way
PO Box 1140
Mechanicsville, VA 23111

804-596-6667
Fax: 804-559-4087
E-Mail: info@impi.org
Home Page: www.impi.org
Social Media: Facebook, Twitter

Bob Schiffmann, President
Ben Wilson, VP
dorin Boldor, Secretary
Amy Lawson, Treasurer
Juan Aguilar, Editor in Chief

Brings together researchers from across the globe to share the latest findings related to non-communications uses of microwave energy.
Frequency: Annual/June

7050 **IS&T/SPIE's Electronic Imaging**
International Society for Optical Engineering
1000 20th Street
PO Box 10
Bellingham, WA 98227-0010

360-763-3290
Fax: 360-647-1445
E-Mail: meetinginfo@spie.org
Home Page: www.spie.org

Electronic Imaging's top-notch technical program gathers the world's most prominent experts to discuss and push the forefront of imaging technology and it's applications.
1200 Attendees
Frequency: Annual/January

7051 **Industry Wide Service and Retail Convention**
Electronic Technicians Association International
5 Depot Street
Greencastle, IN 46135

765-653-4301
800-288-3824
Fax: 765-653-4287
E-Mail: eta@eta-i.org
Home Page: www.eta-i.org

Teresa Maher, President
Brianna Pinson, Office Manager

Three groups united to offer the largest schedule of business management and technical seminars and trade show for educators, servicers and retailers. Thirty booths.
200 Attendees
Frequency: February

7052 **International CES**
Consumer Electronics Association
1919 S Eads Street
Arlington, VA 22202

703-907-7600
866-858-1555
Fax: 703-907-7675
E-Mail: cesreg@ce.org
Home Page: www.cesweb.org

Gary Shapiro, President/CEO
Randy Fry, Chairman
Glenda MacMullin, Treasurer
Karen Chupka, Secretary

Join fellow CEA members and prominent consumer electronics industry leaders at the Las Vegas Convention and World Trade Center for the largest show in the industry. Educates the masses and unites manufacturers, retailers and market movers in addition to offering a glimpse into the digital future.

7053 **International Conference on Trends in Welding Research**
Minerals, Metals & Materials Society
184 Thorn Hill Road
Warrendale, PA 15086-7514

724-776-9000
Fax: 724-776-3770
E-Mail: foundation@tms.org
Home Page: www.tms.org

Tresa Pollock, President
Brajendra Mishra, VP
Alexander Scott, Executive Director
John Parsey, Financial Planning Officer
Marc DeGraef, Director Information Technology

This conference will feature five days of technically intensive programming focusing on both fundamental and applied topics related to welding and joining. Top researchers from industry, government, and academia will present the latest in experimental and modeling developments.
Frequency: May

7054 **International Consumer Electronics Show (C ES)**
Las Vegas Hotel & Casino
3000 S. Paradise Road
Las Vegas, NV 89109

866-539-8430
Home Page: www.ceweb.org
Social Media: Facebook, Twitter, LinkedIn

Gary Shapiro, President/CEO
Pat Lavelle, Chairman
Peter Lesser, Industry Executive Advisor
Jason Oxman, VP Communications
Jenny Pareti, Public Policy Director

The CES reaches across global markets, connects the industry and enables consumer electronics to grow and thrive. International CES is owned and prroduced by the Consumer Electronics Association (CEA).
2000 Members
Frequency: January

7055 **International Symposium for Testing & Failure Analysis**
ASM International
9639 Kinsman Road
Materials Park, OH 44073

440-338-5151
800-336-5152
Fax: 440-338-4634
E-Mail: kim.schaefer@asminternational.org
Home Page: www.asminternational.org

Kim Schaefer, Event Manager
Kelly Thomas, Exposition Account Manager

Annual event focusing on microelectronic and elcetronic device failure analysis, techniques, EOS/ESD testing and descretes aimed at failure analysis engineers and managers, technisians and new failure analysis engineers. 200 exhibitors.
1100 Attendees
Frequency: Annual/November

7056 **Materials, Science & Technology**
Minerals, Metals & Materials Society
184 Thorn Hill Road
Warrendale, PA 15086-7514

724-776-9000
Fax: 724-776-3770
E-Mail: foundaton@tms.org
Home Page: www.tms.org

Tresa Pollock, President
Brajendra Mishra, VP
Alexander Scott, Executive Director
John Parsey, Financial Planning Officer
Marc DeGraef, Director Information Technology

Offers a materials science and applied technology event unlike any other.
Frequency: September

7057 **NCSLI Workshop & Symposium**
NCSL
1800 30th Street
Suite 305 B
Boulder, CO 80301

303-440-3339
Fax: 303-440-3384
E-Mail: info@ncsli.org
Home Page: www.ncsli.org

Harry J Moody, President
William T Pound, Executive Director

Will provide a forum to discuss the impact of these advances have had on metrology, as well as other related issues. Please join us as we reflect on how far and fast metrology has progressed over the past quarter of a century and to discuss its future needs and directions.
1200 Attendees
Frequency: August, Washington

7058 **NEDA Executive Conference**
National Electronic Distributors Association
1111 Alderman Drive
Suite 400
Alpharetta, GA 30005-4175

678-393-9990
Fax: 678-393-9998
E-Mail: admin@nedassoc.org
Home Page: www.nedassoc.org

Francis Flynn Jr, President
Robin B Gray Jr, Executive VP
Debbie Conyers, Director Marketing
Barney Martin, VP Industry Practices
Frequency: November

7059 **NMEA Convention & Expo**
National Marine Electronics Association
Seven Riggs Avenue
Severna Park, MD 21146

410-975-9425
Fax: 410-975-9450
E-Mail: info@nmea.org
Home Page: www.nmea.org

Mark Young, Chairman
Jules Rutstein, Vice Chairman
Beth Kahr, Executive Director
Michael Cerchiaro, Treasurer
Christopher Harley, Secretary
Frequency: October

7060 **NPSC Meeting**
National Electronics Service Dealers Association
3608 Pershing Avenue
Fort Worth, TX 76107-4527

817-921-9061
800-797-9197
Fax: 817-921-3741
E-Mail: webmaster@nesda.com
Home Page: www.nesda.com

Brian Gibson, President
Don Cressin, VP
Mack Blakely, Executive Director
Fred Paradis, CSM, Treasurer
Wayne Markman, Secretary

Featuring Training, Sponsored Meal Events, Meetings, and Opportunities to Network with other service professionals as well as key service industry representatives.
Frequency: July

7061 **Northwest Electronics Technology Conference**
Electronic Conventions Management
8110 Airport Boulevard
Los Angeles, CA 90045-3119

310-215-3976
800-877-2668
Fax: 310-641-5117
E-Mail: northcon@ieee.org
Home Page: www.northcon.org

James Lipman, PhD, Conference Director
Sue Kingston, Trade Show Manager

Offers a concentrated technical conference with complimenting exhibits. It provides a venue where those involved with the design, production and marketing of electronics-related products can converge in a real time, interactive atmosphere.
7000 Attendees
Frequency: May

7062 **OEMBoston**
Canon Communications
11444 W Olympic Boulevard
Suite 900
Los Angeles, CA 90064-1549

310-445-4200
Fax: 310-445-4299
Home Page: www.oemboston,com

William F Cobert, President/CEO
Diane O'Conner, Trade Show Director
Dan Cutrone, Show Marketing Director

The creation of two seperate shows, OEM Electronics and OEMed, the OEMBoston is accessible to thousands of electronics and medical OEMs, who can benefit from the combination of the two shows. The different product classification found at this show include Contract Manufacturing, Electronics Components, Component Fabrication, Production/Assembly Equipment, Packaging Equipment & Supplies, Tubing and more. Held at the Bayside Expo Center in Boston, Massachusetts.
1604 Attendees
Frequency: September

7063 **OFC/NFOEC Conference**
Optical Society of America
2010 Massachusetts Avenue NW
Washington, DC 20036-1012

202-223-8130
Fax: 202-223-1096
E-Mail: info@osa.org
Home Page: www.osa.org

Elizabeth A Rogan, Executive Director

With more than 750 presentations focused on the industry's hottest topics, FTTx and ROADMs at the top of the list, the conference again established itself as the leading technical conference for optical communications. OFC/NFOEC is the show to present new product and corporate announcements.
15000 Attendees
Frequency: March
Founded in 1916

7064 **OSA Technical Conference**
Optical Society of America
2010 Massachusetts Avenue NW
Washington, DC 20036-1012

202-223-8130
Fax: 202-223-1096
E-Mail: info@osa.org
Home Page: www.osa.org

Elizabeth A Rogan, Executive Director

Connect with the most accomplished international scientists, researchers, engineers and business leaders as they shape the future of optics, photonics, and laser science.
Frequency: October

7065 **PhAST Conference**
Optical Society of America
2010 Massachusetts Avenue NW
Washington, DC 20036-1012

202-223-8130
Fax: 202-223-1096
E-Mail: info@osa.org
Home Page: www.osa.org

Elizabeth A Rogan, Executive Director

Will feature previews of new application areas, access to industry innovators and discussions of the engineering ideas behind new products.
Frequency: May

7066 **SEMI Expo CIS**
Semiconductor Equipment & Materials International
3081 Zanker Road
San Jose, CA 95134

408-943-6900
Fax: 408-428-9600
E-Mail: semihq@semi.org
Home Page: www.semi.org

Scott Smith, Public Relations Manager

Will highlight CIS as a region with huge potential and a new developing market for the world semiconductor equipment and materials manufacturers.
Frequency: September

7067 **SESHA Annual Symposium**
Semiconductor Environmental, Safety & Health Assn
1313 Dolly Madison Boulevard
Suite 402
McLean, VA 22101

703-790-1745
Fax: 703-790-2672
E-Mail: sesha@burkinc.com
Home Page: seshaonline.org

Bernie First, President
Brett Burk, Co-Founder
Glenn Tom, Co-Founder
Brian Sherin, Treasurer
Karl Albrecht, Secretary

For individuals employed within the electronics and related high technology industries with an interest in environmental, health and safety issues.
1235 Attendees
Frequency: May
Founded in 1978

7068 **SOUTHCON**
Electronic Conventions
12340 Rosecrans Avenue
Suite 100
Manhattan Beach, CA 90266

310-524-4100
800-877-2668
Fax: 310-643-7328
Home Page: www.southcon.org

Susan Kingston, Show Manager

Companies attending represent a major cross-section of the electronics industry including consumer, computer, medical, automotive and others. Offers conference sessions, in-depth technical sessions, product demonstrations and exhibits by vendors.
10M Attendees
Frequency: March

7069 **Semiconductor**
Semiconductor Equipment & Materials International
3081 Zankeer Road
San Jose, CA 95134

408-943-6900
Fax: 408-428-9600
E-Mail: semihq@semi.org
Home Page: www.semi.org

Scott Smith, Public Relations Manager

The future of the European Semiconductor Industry.
Frequency: June

7070 **Service & Retail Convention**
Electronic Technicians Association International
5 Depot Street
Greencastle, IN 46135

765-653-4301
800-288-3824
Fax: 765-653-4287
E-Mail: eta@eta-i.org
Home Page: www.eta-i.org

Teresa Maher, President
Brianna Pinson, Office Manager

7071 **Southeastern Technology Week**
TEC
2001 Assembly Street
Suite 204
Columbia, SC 29201

803-779-7123
Fax: 803-772-9964
Home Page: www.teconline.com

7072 **Strategic Leadership and Networking Forum**
Electronic Transactions Association
1101 16th Street NW
Suite 402
Washington, DC 20036

202-828-2635
800-695-5509
Fax: 202-828-2639
Home Page: www.electran.org

Jennifer Leo, Meetings Manager
Kurt Strawhecker, Managing Director
Steve Carnevale, Senior Vice President

A unique event designed to help executives thrive in the new payments industry. The Forum goes far beyond fundamental education to tackle the strategic, big-picture issues that today's payment executives and CEOs deal with each day. ETA takes a distinct approach to executive education and has adopted interactive formats conducive to peer-to-peer learning and business-to-business networking.

7073 **Strategic Materials Conference**
Semiconductor Equipment & Materials International
3081 Zanker Road
San Jose, CA 95134

408-943-7805
Fax: 408-428-9600
E-Mail: amorais@semi.org
Home Page: www.semi.org

Anna Morais, Conference Contact

Hear about new business models, emerging players, green requirements and the the diverse partnerships in the semiconductor materials sector; the latest market trends, forecasts, best-practices, and discussions.
12000 Attendees
Frequency: May, Singapore

7074 **Summer Technology & Standards Forum**
Consumer Electronics Association (CEA)
1919 S Eads Street
Arlington, VA 22202

703-907-7600
866-858-1555
Fax: 703-907-7675
E-Mail: cea@ce.org
Home Page: www.ce.org/Events/default.asp

Gary Shapiro, President/CEO
Pat Lavelle, Chairman
Peter Lesser, Industry Executive Advisor
Jason Oxman, VP Communications
Jenny Pareti, Public Policy Director

Focus on development of emerging industry standard, contribute your company's viewpoint, and gain networking opportunities. Take advantage of valuable opportunities to interface with industry technical leaders as they consider, develop, and finalize, crucial CE standards.
Frequency: July

7075 **TABES Technical Business Exhibition & Symposium**
Huntsville Association of Technical Societies
3414 Governors Dr SW
PO Box 1964
Huntsville, AL 35805

256-882-1234
Fax: 205-837-4275
Home Page: www.hats.org/society

J Tardy, Manager
John Young, Treasurer

Brings new business into the community.
10000 Attendees
Founded in 1969

7076 **Tech Advantage Exposition**
National Rural Electric Cooperative Association
4301 Wilson Blouevard
Arlington, VA 22203

703-907-5500
Fax: 703-907-5528
Home Page: www.nreca.org

Gary Pfann, Conference Contact
Barbara Christiana, Expo Contact
11000 Attendees

7077 **westec Exposition**
Society of Manufacturing Engineers
One SME Drive
Dearborn, MI 48121

313-425-3000
800-733-4763
Fax: 408-428-9600
E-Mail: service@sme.org
Home Page: www.sme.org

Ana Christiansen, Exposition Marketing
Leslie Schade, Exhibitor Services

The West Coast's definitive manufacturing event, showcasing crucial breakthroughs in machine tools, production methods, materials and management strategies. More than 450 exhibitors.
1500 Attendees
Frequency: Annual

Directories & Databases

7078 **Antenna Book**
Electronic Technicians Association International
5 Depot St
Greencastle, IN 46135-8024

765-653-8262
800-288-3824
Fax: 765-653-4287
E-Mail: eta@eta-i.org
Home Page: www.eta-i.org

Dick Glass, President
Brianna Pinson, Office Manager

Written by professional technicians who have worked closely with antennas, this two book series is the ultimate study guide for technicians seeking certification through ETA-I's Video Distribution, Certified Satellite Installer and TVRO programs. It can also serve as study materials for electronics classes, employee training, or as a quick reference guide your whole shop can use. Includes shipping & handling.
Cost: $33.00
ISBN: 1-891749-14-5
Printed in on matte stock

7079 **Battery Report**
Power Sources Manufacturers Association
PO Box 418
Mendham, NJ 07945-0418

973-543-9660
Fax: 973-543-6207
E-Mail: power@psma.com
Home Page: www.psma.com

Dusty Becker, Chairman
Carl Blake, President
Jim Marinos, VP

Is a comprehensive report describing the state-of-the-art, current problems and R&D needs for numerous battery systems. The report also includes battery global market trends, status of electric/hybrid vehicle battery development and UN requirements for shipping lithium.
Cost: $125.00
155 Members
Founded in 1985

7080 **ERA Rep Locator**
Electronics Representatives Association
444 N Michigan Avenue
Suite 1960
Chicago, IL 60611

312-527-3050
800-776-7377
Fax: 312-527-3783
E-Mail: info@era.org
Home Page: www.era.org

Mark Motsinger, Chairman
Dave Rossi, Vice Chairman
Mike Kunz, President
Raymond J Hall, EVP/CEO
William R Warfield, Director Finance/Operations

Manufacturers match your products and territories with qualified, professional representatievs firms. The Locator lists ERA member companies with informtion on size of firm, territories covered, type of products represented and customer bases.
Cost: $90.00
Frequency: Annually

7081 **Electronic Buyers News: Specialized and Local/Regional Directory**
CMP Publications
600 Community Dr
Manhasset, NY 11030-3810

516-562-5000
Fax: 516-562-5123

Hailey McKeefry, Editor

List of about 325 distributors of electronic products and supplies operating on less than national scale, or offering only one or a few produst nationwide.

7082 **Electronic Buyers News: Top 50 Distributors Issue**
CMP Publications
600 Community Dr
Manhasset, NY 11030-3810

516-562-5000
Fax: 516-562-5123

David Gabel, Editor

List of electronic distributors ranked by annual gross sales.

7083 **Electronic Distribution Directory**
Electronic Distribution Show Corporation

222 S Riverside Plz
Suite 2160
Chicago, IL 60606-6112

312-648-1140
Fax: 312-648-4282
E-Mail: eds@edsc.org
Home Page: www.edsconnects.com

Gretchen Oie, Manager

7084 **Electronic Industries Association: Trade Directory and Membership List**
Electronic Industries Alliance
2500 Wilson Boulevard
Arlington, VA 22201-3834

703-907-7500
Fax: 703-907-7501
Home Page: www.eia.org

Dave McCurdy, President/CEO
Charles L Robinson, Chief Operating Officer
More than 1,200 member companies in the electronic manufacturing industry.
Frequency: Annual

7085 **Electronic Materials & Process Handbook**
International Microelectronics & Electronics
611 2nd Street NE
Washington, DC 20002

202-548-4001
888-464-6277
Fax: 202-548-6115
E-Mail: imaps@imaps.org
Home Page: www.imaps.org

Charles A Harper, Editor
Ronald M Sampson, Editor
Offers guidance on insulations, conductors, and semiconductor materials, defines critical manufacturing parameters, and shows how these parameters can be combined to create successful electronic devices.
Cost: $80.00
ISBN: 0-070542-99-6

7086 **Electronic Representatives Directory**
Harris Publishing Company
360 B Street
Idaho Falls, ID 83402-1938

208-524-4217
Fax: 208-522-5241
E-Mail: customerservice@harrispublishing.com
Home Page: www.harrispublishing.com

Directory of services and supplies to the industry.
Cost: $25.00
320 Pages
Frequency: Annual
Circulation: 7,500

7087 **Electronics Manufacturers Directory on Diskette**
Harris InfoSource International
2057 E Aurora Rd
Twinsburg, OH 44087-1938

330-425-4481
800-888-5900
Fax: 330-487-5368
Home Page: www.harrisinfo.com

David Wilkof, VP
Diskette. Covers approximately 1,000,000 manufacturers of electronic equipment and products.
Cost: $329.00
Frequency: Annual

7088 **North American Directory of Contract Electronic Manufacturers**
Miller Freeman Publications
600 Harrison Street
Suite 400
San Francisco, CA 94107-1391

FAX 415-905-2239
Home Page: www.cassembly.com

Kimberly Cassidy, Editor
Over 1,350 electronics manufacturers facilities in the United States, Canada, and Mexico.
Cost: $295.00
Frequency: Annual

7089 **ProService Directory and Yearbook**
National Electronics Service Dealers Association
3608 Pershing Ave
Fort Worth, TX 76107-4527

817-921-9061
800-797-9197
Fax: 817-921-3741
E-Mail: webmaster@nesda.com
Home Page: www.nesda.com

Clyde Nabors, Publisher
Wallace Harrison, Editor
Mary Margaret Merill, Production Manager
The yearbook is an annual resource listing for servicers. This directory is sent each January to current members.
Frequency: Annual

7090 **Product Source Guide for Electronic Devices**
Reed Business Information
275 Washington St
Newton, MA 02458-1611

617-964-3030
Fax: 617-558-4470
E-Mail: sales@eb-mag.com
Home Page: www.designnews.com

Donald Swanson, Editor
List of over 4,000 manufacturers and suppliers of equipment and materials used in the production, testing, and packaging of electronic devices and systems.
Cost: $25.00
Frequency: Annual

7091 **Source Book**
Armed Forces Communications and Electronics Assn
4400 Fair Lakes Ct
Suite 100
Fairfax, VA 22033-3899

703-631-1397
800-336-4583
Fax: 703-631-4693
Home Page: www.afcea.org

Kent Schneider, President/CEO
Becky Nolan, Executive VP
John A Dubia, Executive VP
The Source Book published in the January issue, contains the company profiles and contacts of AFCEA's corporate members. It is the who's who of C$ISR and homeland secuity organizations. The annual Security Directory, published in the February issue, focuses on security solutions and the organizations that provide them.
31000 Members
Founded in 1946

7092 **Who's Who in Electronics Buyer's Guide**
Harris Publishing Company
360 B Street
Idaho Falls, ID 83402-1938

208-524-4217
Fax: 208-522-5241
E-Mail: customerservice@harrispublishing.com
Home Page: www.harrispublishing.com

A list of over 15,000 manufacturers and distributors of electronics products in five regional volumes.
Cost: $65.00
Frequency: Annual
Circulation: 60,000

Industry Web Sites

7093 **http://gold.greyhouse.com**
G.O.L.D Grey House OnLine Databases
Grey House Publishing's online database platform, GOLD, offers Quick Search, Keyword Search and Expert Search for most business sectors including electronics markets. The GOLD platform makes finding the information you need quick and easy - whether you're a novice searcher or an experienced database user. All of Grey House's directory products are available for subscription on the GOLD platform.

7094 **www.afcea.org**
Armed Forces Communications and Electronics Assn
An association that represents the professional communications, electronics, intelligence and information systems community.

7095 **www.aprovision.org**
Association of Progressive Rental Organizations
Members include television, appliance and furniture dealers who rent merchandise with an option to purchase.

7096 **www.era.org**
Electronics Representatives Association
Provides services and benefits to electronic industry manufacturers representatives.

7097 **www.eta-i.org**
Electronic Technicians Association International
A worldwide professional association founded by electronics technicians and servicing dealers.

7098 **www.ewh.ieee.org**
Instrumentation and Measurement Society
A subsidiary of the Institute of Electrical and Electronics Engineers. Provides support to scientists and technicians who design and develop electrical and electronic measuring instruments and equipment.

7099 **www.greyhouse.com**
Grey House Publishing
Authoritative reference directories for most business sectors including electronic markets. Users can search the online databases with varied search criteria allowing for custom searches by product category, geographic area, sales volume, keyword, subject and more. Full Grey House catalog and online ordering also available.

7100 **www.imaps.org**
International Microelectronics & Packaging Society
Dedicated to the advancement and growth of the use of microelectronics and electronic packaging through public and professional education, dissemination of information by means of symposia, workshops and conferences and promotion of the Society's portfolio of technologies.

7101 **www.ipc.org**
IPC-Association Connecting Electronics Industries
Works to develop standards in circuit board assembly equipment. Brings together all players in the electronic interconnection industry, including designers, board manufacturers, assembly companies, suppliers and original equipment manufacturers. Offers workshops, conferences, meetings and online communications.

7102 **www.iscet.org**
Int'l Society of Certified Electronics Technicians
Designed to measure the degree of theoretical knowledge and technical proficiency of practicing technicians.

7103 **www.nesda.com**
National Electronics Service Dealers Association
A national trade association for professionals in the business repairing consumer electronics equipment, appliances, and computers. NESDA has an e-mail group of over 600 members and manufacturers that communicate daily for information sharing. NESDA also has an annual convention and trade show.

7104 **www.nmea.org**
National Marine Electronics Association
The unifying force behind the entire marine electronics industry, bringing together all aspects of the industry for the betterment of all in the business.

7105 **www.psma.com**
Power Sources Manufacturers Association
Worldwide membership consists of manufacturers of power sources and conversion equipment. Nonprofit association strives to integrate the resources of the power sources industry to more effectively and profitably serve the needs of the power sources users, providers and PSMA members. Educates the electronics industry and others on the relevant applications for power sources and conversion devices.

7106 **www.semi.org**
Semiconductor Equipment & Materials International
Strengthens the performance of member companies through lobbying, promotion, education and statistical research.

7107 **www.seshaonline.org**
Semiconductor Environmental, Safety & Health Assn
Members are individuals employed within the electronics and related high technology industries with an interest in environmental, health and safety issues.

7108 **www.sia-online.org**
Semiconductor Industry Association
Trade association representing the US microchip industry.

7109 **www.sme.org**
Society of Manufacturing Engineers
Represents the electrical manufacturers.

7110 **www.smta.org**
Surface Mount Technology Association
A network of professionals building skills, sharing practical experience and developing solutions in electronic assembly technologies and related business operations.

Associations

7111 **ASM International/Materials Information Society**
9639 Kinsman Rd
Materials Park, OH 44073

440-338-5151
800-336-5152
Fax: 440-338-4634
Home Page: www.asminternational.org

Jean Deatherage, Administrator
Charles Hayes, Executive Director

The society for materials engineers and scientists, a worldwide network dedicated to advancing industry, technology and applications of metals and materials.
35000 Members
Founded in 1913

7112 **ASME/International Gas Turbine Institute**
Three Park Avenue
New York, NY 10016

973-882-1170
800-843-2763
E-Mail: infocentral@asme.org
Home Page: www.asme.org

Victoria Rockwell, President
Thomas Loughlin, Executive Director
David Soukup, Managing Director Operations

Supports all those involved with engineering and energy technology.
12500 Members
Founded in 1958

7113 **ASTM International**
PO Box C700
W Conshohocken, PA 19428-0700

610-832-9500
Fax: 610-832-9555
E-Mail: service@astm.org
Home Page: www.astm.org
Social Media: Facebook, Twitter

James A Thomas, President
Kenneth Pearson, VP

Not-for-profit organization that provides a global forum for the development and publication of voluntary consensus standards for materials, products, systems and services. Members are users, producers, consumers and representatives of academia and government. Formerly known as the American Society for Testing and Materials.
30000 Members
Founded in 1898

7114 **AVS Science & Technology Society**
125 Maiden Ln
15th Floor
New York, NY 10038-4714

212-248-0200
Fax: 212-248-0245
Home Page: www.avs.org

Angus Rockett, President
Joe Greene, Secretary
Stephen Rossnagel, Treasurer

AVS is a resource for scientists, engineers, industrialists, students and educators.
6000 Members
Founded in 1963

7115 **Abrasive Engineering Society**
144 Moore Rd
Butler, PA 16001-1312

724-282-6210
Fax: 724-234-2376
E-Mail: aes@abrasiveengineering.com
Home Page: www.abrasiveengineering.com

Doug Haynes, President
Ted Giese, Executive Director

Dedicated to promoting technical information about abrasives minerals and their uses including abrasives grains and products such as grinding wheels, coated abrasives and thousands of other related tools and products that serve manufacturing and the consumer.
500 Members
Founded in 1957

7116 **Accreditation Board for Engineering and Technology**
111 Market Place
Suite 1050
Baltimore, MD 21202-4012

410-347-7700
Fax: 410-625-2238
E-Mail: info@abet.org
Home Page: www.abet.org

Phillip Borrowman, President
Larry Kaye, President Elect
Ronald Hinn, Secretary
Bassem Armaly, Treasurer

Accreditation of engineering, technology and applied science educational programs.
31 Members
Founded in 1932

7117 **Acoustical Society of America**
2 Huntington Quad
Suite 1N01
Melville, NY 11747-4505

516-576-2360
Fax: 516-576-2377
E-Mail: asa@aip.org
Home Page: asa.aip.org

Mardi Hastings, President
David Bradley, VP
Brigitte Schulte-Fortkamp, Vice President
David Feit, Treasurer
Charles Schmid, Executive Director

Supports all those involved with the acoustics industry.
7000 Members
Founded in 1929

7118 **Adhesive & Sealant Council**
7101 Wisconsin Ave
Suite 990
Bethesda, MD 20814-4805

301-986-9700
Fax: 301-986-9795
E-Mail: info@ascouncil.org
Home Page: www.ascouncil.org

Matt Croson, President
Kate Zando, Director of Finance
Michael Socha, Marketing

A North American trade association dedicated to representing the adhesive and sealant industry. ASC is bound by the collective efforts of its members, and strives to improve the industry operating environment and strengthen its member companies.
124 Members
Founded in 1958

7119 **Air & Waste Management Association**
420 Fort Duquesne Blvd.
Pittsburgh, PA 15222-1435

412-232-3444
800-270-3444
Fax: 412-232-3450
E-Mail: info@awma.org
Home Page: www.awma.org
Social Media: Facebook, Twitter, LinkedIn

Michael Miller, President
Dallas Baker, President Elect
Sara Head, Immediate Past President
Nancy Meilahn Fowler, Treasurer
Jim Powell, Secretary/ Executive Director

Professional organization that provides training, information, and networking opportunities to environmental professionals.

7120 **Alpha Pi Muÿ**
3005 Lancaster Drive
Blacksburg, VA 24060

E-Mail: office@alphapimu.com
Home Page: www.alphapimu.com

Dr. Wafik H Iskander, President
Sarah Lam, Executive Vice President
Dr. C. Patrick Koelling, Executive Director
Dr. Wafik H Iskander, Vice President
Dr. S. Balachandran, Treasurer

An honor society for Industrial and Systems Engineering students.
Founded in 1949

7121 **American Academy of Environmental Engineers**
130 Holiday Ct
Suite 100
Annapolis, MD 21401-7003

410-266-3311
Fax: 410-266-7653
E-Mail: info@aaee.net
Home Page: www.aaee.net
Social Media: Facebook, LinkedIn

Joseph Cavaretta, CAE, Executive Director
Brian P Flynn, P.E., BGEE, President
Dr. Cecil Lue-Hing, Past President
Joyce Dowen, Executive Assistant
Yolanda Moulden, Production Manager

Periodical for environmental engineers and environmental engineer professionals, as well as environmental engineering services
2500 Members
Founded in 1955

7122 **American Association of Engineering Societies**
1801 Alexander Bell Drive
Reston, VA 20191

202-296-2237
888-400-2237
Fax: 202-296-1151
E-Mail: dbateson@aaes.org
Home Page: www.aaes.org

Carol Bowers, Executive Director
Dan Bateson, Director Engineering Workforce
Connie L Kyle, Office/Accounting Manager

Association for national, U.S. organizations concerned with engineering and related fields.
14 Members
Founded in 1958

7123 **American Automatic Control Council**
Northwestern University
3640 Col Glenn Highway
Dayton, OH 45435

937-775-5062
Fax: 937-775-3936
E-Mail: pmisra@cs.wright.edu
Home Page: www.a2c2.org

Tamer Basar, President
R Russell Rhinehart, President Elect
Jordan Berg, Treasurer
Pradeep Misra, Secretary

Supports industry of automatic controls producers.
1M Members
Founded in 1960

7124 **American Council of Engineering Companies**
1015 15th St
8th floor NW
Washington, DC 20005-2605

202-347-7474
Fax: 202-898-0068
E-Mail: acec@acec.org
Home Page: www.acec.org
Social Media: Facebook, Twitter

Terry Neimeyer, Chairman
David Raymond, President
Sergio Pecori, Treasurer

Membership includes US firms engaged in a range of engineering works. Mission is to contribute to the nation's prosperity through advancing the interests of member firms.
55000 Members
Founded in 1905

7125 **American Crystallographic Association**
Ellicott Station
PO Box 96
Buffalo, NY 14205-0096

716-898-8690
Fax: 716-898-8695
E-Mail: aca@hwi.buffalo.edu
Home Page: www.amercrystalassn.org

Thomas Koetzle, President
George Phillips, Vice President
Carrie Wilmot, Secretary

Supports all those involved with hardware, software, and x-ray equipment for the crystal industry.
2200 Members
Founded in 1949

7126 **American Design Drafting Association**
105 East Main Street
Newbern, TE 38059

731-627-0802
Fax: 731-627-9321
E-Mail: okparker@adda.org
Home Page: www.adda.org
Social Media: Facebook, Twitter, LinkedIn

Rick Frymyer, Chairman
Richard Button, Governor
Alex Devereux, Vice President
Olen K Parker, Executive Director
Donna Brenton, Administrative Manager

An individual membership society for the design drafting community across all industries.
Founded in 1948

7127 **American Engineering Association, Inc.**
533 Waterside Blvd.
Monroe Township, NJ 08831

201-664-6954
E-Mail: aea@aea.org
Home Page: www.aea.org

Richard F. Tax, President
Charles Fischer, Vice President
Jenny Blackford, Marketing Director
Laurie Johnson, Office Assistant

As a national nonprofit professional association the AEA is a voice for engineers. The AEA, Inc. is dedicated to the enhancement of the engineering profession and U.S. Engineering capabilities. AEA is a strong advocate for providing opportunities for US engineers and is involved in issues of utilization, skill enhancement, loss of jobs, offshore manufacturing, layoffs, and many others that affect the lives and professional welfare of our engineers.
Founded in 1979

7128 **American Helicopter Society**
2701 Prosperity Avenue
Suite 210
Fairfax, VA 22031

703-684-6777
855-247-4685
Fax: 703-739-9279
E-Mail: staff@vtol.org
Home Page: www.vtol.org
Social Media: Facebook, Twitter, LinkedIn, YouTube

Edwin Birtwell, Chair
Mick Maurer, President
Leanne Caret, Secretary - Treasurer
David Peters, Technical Director
Michael Hirschberg, Executive Director

The professional society for the advancement of vertical flight technology and its useful application throughout the world.
Founded in 1943

7129 **American Indian Science and Engineering Society**
2305 Renard SE
Suite 200
Albuquerque, NM 87106

505-765-1052
Fax: 505-765-5608
Home Page: www.aises.org
Social Media: Facebook, Twitter, LinkedIn, YouTube

Richard Stephens, Chair
Dr. Twyla Baker-Demaray, Vice-Chair
Marlene Watson, Secretary
Dr. James May, Treasurer
Sarah Echohawk, Chief Executive Officer

A nonprofit professional association with the goal of increasing American Indian and Alaskan Native representation in the fields of engineering, science, and other related technology disciplines.
3000 Members

7130 **American Institute of Chemical Engineers**
3 Park Ave
New York, NY 10016-5991

203-702-7660
800-242-4363
Fax: 203-775-5177
E-Mail: xpress@aiche.org
Home Page: www.aiche.org

Maria Burka, President
Kimberly Ogden, Secretary
Andre Da Costa, Treasurer
June Wispelwey, Executive Director

Professional association providing leadership in advancing the chemical engineering profession. Members are those who develop processes and design and operate manufacturing plants, as well as researchers who assure the safe and environmentally sound manufacture, use and disposal of chemical products.
50000 Members
Founded in 1908

7131 **American Institute of Physics**
1 Physics Ellipse
College Park, MD 20740-3841

301-209-3100
Fax: 301-209-0843
E-Mail: dylla@aip.org
Home Page: www.aip.org

H. Frederick Dylla, CEO and Executive Director
Richard Baccante, Treasurer and CFO
Benjamin Snavely, Secretary

Presents original research in high performance polymer science and technology. Primarily applications-driven, with a major focus on the molecular structure/processability/property relationship with regard to the specified applications.
1931 Members
Founded in 1931

7132 **American Iron and Steel Institute**
25 Massachusetts Avenue, NW
Suite 800
Washington, DC 20001

202-452-7100
Home Page: www.steel.org
Social Media: Facebook, Twitter, YouTube

Michael Rippey, Chairman
Michael T Rehwinkel, Vice Chairman
Thomas J Gibson, President/ CEO
David E Bell, Vice President
Gregory L Crawford, Executive Director

Steel information for consumers, engineers, and other professionals.
125 Members
Founded in 1855

7133 **American Nuclear Society**
555 N Kensington Ave
La Grange Park, IL 60526-5592

708-352-6611
800-323-3044
Fax: 708-352-0499
Home Page: www.ans.org

Eric Loewen, President
Michael Corradini, Vice President
Mikey Brady Raap, Treasurer

Serves its members in their efforts to develop and safely apply nuclear science and technology for public benefit through knowledge exchange, professional development, and enhanced public understanding.
Founded in 1954

7134 **American Oil Chemists Society**
2710 S. Boulder
Urbana, IL 61802

217-359-2344
Fax: 217-351-8091
E-Mail: general@aocs.org
Home Page: www.aocs.org

E. Dumelin, President
D. Myers, VP
T. Kemper, Treasurer
S. Erhan, Secretary
Greg Reed, Manager

A global forum to promote the exchange of ideas, information, and experience, to enhance personal excellence, and to provide high standards of quality among those with a professional interest in the science and technology of fats, oil, surfactants, and related materials.
5400+ Members
Founded in 1909

7135 **American Oil Chemists' Society (AOCS)**
2710 S Boulder Drive
PO Box 17190
Urbana, IL 61803-6996

217-359-2344
Fax: 217-351-8091
E-Mail: general@aocs.org
Home Page: www.aocs.org
Social Media: Facebook, Twitter, LinkedIn

Gloria Cook, Senior Director, Finance
Jeffry L. Newman, Senior Director, Programs

AOCS is a global scientific society open to all individuals and corporations who are interested in fats, oils, surfactants, detergents and related materials. AOCS is a trusted source of information for its members and thousands of

non-members from more than 90 countries worldwide.
4500 Members
Founded in 1909
Mailing list available for rent

7136 **American Society for Engineering Education**
1818 N St NW
Suite 600
Washington, DC 20036-2476
202-331-3500
Fax: 202-265-8504
E-Mail: prism@asee.org
Home Page: www.asee.org
Norman Fortenberry, Executive Director
Sae Park, CFO
Arthur T Murphy, VP/Finance
Supports all those educators in the engineering technology fields.
12000 Members
Founded in 1893

7137 **American Society for Precision Engineering**
PO Box 10826
Raleigh, NC 27605-0826
919-839-8444
Fax: 919-839-8039
Home Page: www.aspe.net
Stephen Ludwick, President
Vivek Badami, Vice President
Members are from academia, industry and government, and include professionals in engineering, materials science, physics, chemistry, mathematics and computer science. Multidisciplinary professional and technical society concerned with precision engineering research and development, design and manufacturing of high accuracy components and systems. Member and nonmember rates for annual meetings, spring and summer topical meetings, books and video tapes. Membership is $65 regular, $30 student.
Founded in 1986

7138 **American Society for Quality**
600 N Plankinton Avenue
PO Box 3005
Milwaukee, WI 53201-3005
414-272-8575
800-248-1946
Fax: 414-272-1734
E-Mail: help@asq.org
Home Page: www.asq.org
James Rooney, Chair
John Timmerman, Chair-Elect
Paul Borawski, CEO
William McBee, Treasurer
ASQ's mission is to facilitate continuous improvement and increase customer satisfaction. Promotes quality principles, concepts and technologies. Provides information, contacts and opportunities to make things better in the workplace, in communities and in people's lives.
100M Members
Founded in 1946

7139 **American Society for the Geoprofessional Business Association (ASFE)**
8811 Colesville Rd
Suite G106
Silver Spring, MD 20910-4343
301-565-2733
Fax: 301-589-2017
E-Mail: info@asfe.org
Home Page: www.asfe.org
David Gaboury, President

Not-for-profit trade association. Supports all employees of engineering companies.
300 Members
Founded in 1969

7140 **American Society of Agricultural and Biological Engineers**
2950 Niles Rd
St Joseph, MI 49085-8607
269-429-0300
800-371-2723
Fax: 269-429-3852
E-Mail: hq@asabe.org
Home Page: www.asabe.org
Mark D Zielke, CEO
Donna Hull, Publication Director
Holds annual meetings and conferences and publishes journals related to agricultural engineering, biological engineering and food process engineering.
8500 Members
Founded in 1907

7141 **American Society of Certified Engineering**
PO Box 1348
Flowery Branch, GA 30542
770-967-9173
Fax: 770-967-8049
Home Page: www.ascet.org
Russell E Freier, Chairman
Leo Saenz, CET, President
Kurt Schuler, Secretary/Treasurer
Strives to obtain recognition of engineering technicians as essential to the engineering scientific team. Provides a forum for discussion of employment issues and improvement of the professional status of engineering technicians.
2000 Members
Founded in 1964

7142 **American Society of Civil Engineers**
1801 Alexander Bell Dr
Reston, VA 20191-4382
703-295-6300
800-548-2723
Fax: 703-295-6222
E-Mail: cybrarian@asce.org
Home Page: www.asce.org/
Kathy Caldwell, President
Professional association of engineers and scientists working in civil and structural engineering, applied mechanics and engineering science, aeronautics and astronautics.

7143 **American Society of Gas Engineers**
PO Box 66
Artesia, CA 90702
562-455-9417
E-Mail: asgecge@aol.com
Home Page: www.asge-national.org
Nancy Wilson, President
Sham Kassab, Vice President
Susan McCarthy, Treasurer
Jerry Moore, Executive Director
Supports all engineers in the gas industry.
250 Members
Founded in 1954

7144 **American Society of Heating, Refrigerating , and Air Conditioning Engineers**
1791 Tullie Circle, N.E.
Atlanta, GA 30329
404-636-8400
Fax: 404-321-5478
E-Mail: ashrae@ashrae.org
Home Page: www.ashrae.org
Social Media: Facebook, Twitter, YouTube
Thomas Phoenix, President
T. David Underwood, President Elect
Darryl K Boyce, Vice President
Timothy G Wentz, Treasurer
Jeff Littleton, Secretary
Global society that focuses on building systems, energy efficiency,indoor air quality, refrigeration, and sustainability.

7145 **American Society of Heating, Refrigeration & Air-Conditioning Engineers**
1791 Tullie Cir Ne
Atlanta, GA 30329-2398
404-636-8400
800-527-4723
Fax: 404-321-5478
E-Mail: ashrae@ashrae.org
Home Page: www.ashrae.org
Ronald Jarnagin, President
Constantinos Balaras, Vice President
William Bahnfleth, Treasurer
An international organization that fulfills its mission of advancing heating, ventilation, air conditioning and refrigeration to serve humanity and promote a sustainable world through research, standards writing, publishing and continuing education.
55000 Members
Founded in 1894

7146 **American Society of Mechanical Engineers**
Three Park Ave
New York, NY 10016-5902
973-882-1170
800-843-2763
Fax: 202-429-9417
E-Mail: infocentral@asme.org
Home Page: www.asme.org
Mark Goldsmith, President
Webb Marner, Secretary/Treasurer
To promote and enhance the technical competency and professional well-being of the members, and through quality programs and activities in mechanical engineering, better enable its practitioners to contribute to the well being of human kind
12000 Members
Founded in 1880

7147 **American Society of Naval Engineers**
1452 Duke Street
Alexandria, VA 22314-3458
703-836-6727
Fax: 703-836-7491
E-Mail: asnehq@navalengineers.org
Home Page: www.navalengineers.org
David Sargent, President
Paul Sullivan, VP
Capt Dennis Krusent, Executive Director
Naval engineering includes all arts construction and sciences as applied in research, development design, construction, operation, maintenance, and logistic support of: surface/sub-surface ships and marine craft.
Founded in 1946

7148 **American Society of Petroleum Operations Engineers**
301 East Culpeper Street
Culpeper, VA 22701
703-768-4159
800-918-8962
Home Page: www.aspoe.org
John B Stanley, President
Gerald Holton, VP
Harry Lyon, Executive VP

Coles Marsh, Treasurer
Cheryl George, Secretary

Works to stimulate interest from the academic world in the qualifications necessary to become a Petroleum Operations Engineer.
Founded in 1976

7149 American Society of Plumbing Engineers
2980 S River Rd
Des Plaines, IL 60018-4203

847-296-0002
Fax: 773-695-9007
E-Mail: info@aspe.org
Home Page: www.aspe.org

Jim Kendzel, CEO and Executive Director

Supports all those engineers in the plumbing industry.
7500 Members
Founded in 1964

7150 American Society of Safety Engineers
1800 E Oakton Street
Des Plaines, IL 60018

847-699-2929
Fax: 847-768-3434
E-Mail: info@asse.org
Home Page: www.asse.org

Terrie Norris, President
Kathy Seabrook, Senior VP
James Smith, VP of Finance
Fred Fortman, Secretary and Executive Director

The oldest and largest professional safety organization. Its members manage, supervise and consult son safety, health, and environmental issues in industry, insurance, government and education.
30000 Members
Founded in 1911

7151 American Society of Sanitary Engineering
901 Canterbury Rd
Suite A
Cleveland, OH 44145-1480

440-835-3040
Fax: 440-835-3488
Home Page: www.asse-plumbing.org

James Bickford, President
Donald Summers, First VP
Steve Silber, Second VP
John Flader, Treasurer

Members are from all segments of the plumbing industry, including contractors, engineers, inspectors, journeymen, apprentices and others who are involved in various segments of the industry. Provides information, an opportunity to exchange ideas, solve problems and offers a forum where all sides can express their views.
300 Members

7152 American Water Works Association
6666 W. Quincy Ave.
Denver, CO 80235

303-794-7711
800-926-7337
Fax: 303-347-0804
Home Page: www.awwa.org
Social Media: Facebook, Twitter, LinkedIn, YouTube

John J Donahue, President
Gene C Koontz, President-Elect
James A Chaffee, Immediate Past-President
Dave E Rager, Treasurer
Michael D Simpson, Vice President

An international nonprofit scientific and educational association founded to improve water quality and supply.
50000 Members
Founded in 1881

7153 Applied Technology Council
201 Redwood Shores Parkway
Suite 240
Redwood City, CA 94065

650-595-1542
Fax: 650-593-2320
E-Mail: atc@atcouncil.org
Home Page: www.atcouncil.org

Bret Lizundia, President
Donald Scott, Vice President
James Amundson, Secretary/Treasurer

Nonprofit, tax-exempt corporation established through the efforts of the Structural Engineers Association of California. ATC's mission is to develop and promote state-of-the-art, user-friendly, engineering resources and applications for use in mitigating the effects of natural and other hazards on the built environment.
300 Members
Founded in 1973

7154 Association for Computing Machinery
2 Penn Plaza
Suite 701
New York, NY 10121-0701

212-626-0500
800 342-6626
Fax: 212-944-1318
E-Mail: acmhelp@acm.org
Home Page: www.acm.org
Social Media: Facebook, Twitter, LinkedIn, YouTube, Google+

Alexander L Wolf, President
Vicki Hanson, Vice President
Vinton Cerf, Past President
Patrick H Madden, Board Chair
Erik R Altman, Secretary/Treasurer

A U.S.-based international learned society for computing.

7155 Association for Facilities Engineering
12801 Worldgate Drive
Suite 500
Herndon, VA 20170

571-203-7171
Fax: 571-766-2142
E-Mail: Info@AFE.org
Home Page: www.afe.org

Thomas Baxter, Chairman
Wayne Carley, Executive Director
Lane T Pierce, CPE, Treasurer
Fred King, VP Marketing/Communications

Provides education, certification, technical information and other relevant information for plant and facility engineering operations and maintenance professionals worldwide.
5000 Members
Founded in 1954

7156 Association for Iron & Steel Technology (AIST)
186 Thorn Hill Rd
Warrendale, PA 15086-7528

724-814-3000
Fax: 724-814-3001
E-Mail: memberservices@aist.org
Home Page: www.aist.org

Ronald E Ashburn, Executive Director
Lori Wharrey, Board Administrator
Chris McKelvey, Assistant Board Administrator
Stacy Vermecky, Membership Services Manager
Penny English, Member Administrator

The Association for Iron & Steel Technology (AIST) is an international technical association representing iron and steel producers, their allied suppliers and related academia. The association is dedicated to advancing the technical development, production, processing and application of iron and steel.
13800 Members
Founded in 2004

7157 Association for the Advancement of Cost Engineering
1265 Suncrest Towne Centre Drive
Suite 100
Morgantown, WV 26505

304-296-8444
800-858-2678
Fax: 304-291-5728
E-Mail: info@aacei.org
Home Page: www.aacei.org

Michael Nosbisch, President
Marlene Hyde, President Elect
Martin Darley, VP of Administration
John Ciccarelli, VP of Finance

Leading-edge society for cost estimators, cost engineers, schedulers project managers, and project control specialists.
7000 Members
Founded in 1956

7158 Association of Building Officials and Code Administrators
500 New Jersey Ave
6th Floor
Washington, DC 20001-2070

202-370-1800
888-422-7233
Fax: 202-783-2348
E-Mail: webmaster@iccsafe.org
Home Page: www.iccsafe.org

James Brothers, President
William Dupler, Vice President
Ronald Piester, Secretary/Treasurer

An independent nonprofit organization which conducts a voluntary program of evaluation of both traditional and innovative building materials, products and systems for compliance with BOCA National Codes.
14000 Members
Founded in 1994

7159 Association of Energy Engineers
4025 Pleasantdale Rd
Suite 420
Atlanta, GA 30340-4264

770-447-5083
Fax: 770-446-3969
E-Mail: info@aeecenter.org
Home Page: www.aeecenter.org

Eric Woodroof, President
Gary Hogsett, President Elect
Bill Younger, Secretary
Paul Goodman, Treasurer

Membership organization of professionals and certification programs in the fields of energy efficiency, utility deregulation, facility management, plant engineering and environmental compliance. Offers seminars, conferences, books to critical buyer-seller, networking trade shows, job listings and certification programs.
8000+ Members
Founded in 1977

7160 Association of Engineering Geologists
3773 Cherry Creek Dr. N
Suite 575
Denver, CO 80246-0518

303-757-2926
Fax: 720-230-4846

E-Mail: aeg@aegweb.org
Home Page: www.aegweb.org

Jennifer Bauer, President
Matthew Morris, Vice President
Gary Luce, Treasurer
Ken Fergason, Secretary

Meets the professional needs of geologists who are applying their scientific training and experience to the broad field of civil and environmental engineering. Mission is to provide leadership in the development and application of geologic principles and knowledge to serve engineering, environmental and public needs.

3000 Members
Founded in 1957
Mailing list available for rent: 3000 names at $100 per M

7161 Association of State Dam Safety Officials
239 S. Limestone
Lexington, KY 40508

859-550-2788
E-Mail: info@damsafety.org
Home Page: www.damsafety.org
Social Media: Facebook, Twitter, LinkedIn, YouTube

Michael Johnson, President
Jim Pawloski, President-Elect
Tom Woosley, Past President
Jon Garton, Secretary
Dusty Myers, Treasurer

Provides outreach programs and a forum for the exchange of information to advance and improve the safety of dams.

Founded in 1998

7162 Audio Engineering Societyÿ
60 East 42nd Street
Room 2520
New York, NY 10165-2520

212-661-8528
Fax: 212-682-0477
Home Page: www.aes.org
Social Media: Facebook, Twitter, LinkedIn, YouTube, Google+

Andres Mayo, President
Sean E Olive, Past President
David W Scheirman, Vice President
Ron Streicher, Secretary
Garry Margolis, Treasurer

Worldwide professional association for professionals and students involved in the audio industry.

7163 Biomedical Engineering Society
8201 Corporate Dr
Suite 1125
Landover, MD 20785-2263

301-459-1999
Fax: 301-459-2444
E-Mail: info@bmes.org
Home Page: www.bmes.org

Edward Schilling, Executive Director
Heather Comstock, Meeting Manager

Supports all those involved in the biomedical engineering industry.

3800 Members
Founded in 1968

7164 Carnegie Mellon University: Information Networking Institute
Carnegie Mellon University
Electrical & Computer Engineering Department
4616 Henry Street
Pittsburgh, PA 15213

412-682-2905
Fax: 412-268-7196
Home Page: www.ini.cmu.edu

Pradeep Khosia, Dean
Mike Niederberger, Business/Finance Administrator
Donald Shields, Director Development
Dean Haritos Tsamitis, Director Information Networking
Sean O'Leary, Manager

Focusing on professional degrees programs combining economics, technologies and global communication networks - information security policies.

Founded in 1989

7165 Cold Regions Research and Engineering Laboratory
US Army Corps of Engineers
72 Lyme Road
Hanover, NH 03755-1290

603-646-4100
Fax: 603-646-4278
E-Mail: info@crrel.usace.army.mil
Home Page:
www.crrel.usace.army.mil/welcome

James L Wuebben, PE, Director
Dr Mary Albert, Research Mechanical Engineer

The mission of this Laboratory is to understand the characteristics of the cold regions of the world and to apply this knowledge to make it easier for people to live and work in those regions. For example, CRREL engineers have conducted a long-term program on the correct design of roofs in heavy snowfall areas.

7166 Cold-Formed Steel Engineers Institute
25 Massachusetts Avenue, N.W.
Suite 800
Washington, DC 20001

202-263-4488
866-465-4732
Fax: 202-452-1039
E-Mail: info@cfsei.org
Home Page: www.cfsei.org

Rahim Zadeh, Chairman
Vincent E. Sagan, Immediate Past Chairman
Jennifer Zabik, Vice Chairman

Produces safe and efficient designs for commercial and residential structures with cold-formed steel.

Founded in 1849

7167 Construction Financial Management Association
100 Village Blvd.
Suite 200
Princeton, NJ 8540

609-452-8000
888-421-9996
Fax: 609-452-0474
E-Mail: info@cfma.org
Home Page: www.cfma.org
Social Media: Facebook, Twitter, LinkedIn, YouTube

Stuart Binstock, President/ CEO
Brian Summers, Vice President
Ariel Sanchirico, Director
Christine Bluestein, Associate Director
Kristy Domboski, Managing Editor

Support and networking for construction financial professionals within the United States.

Founded in 1981

7168 Construction Management Association of America
7926 Jones Branch Drive
Suite 800
McLean, VA 22102-3303

703-356-2622
Fax: 703-356-6388
E-Mail: info@cmaanet.org
Home Page: www.cmaanet.org
Social Media: Facebook, Twitter, LinkedIn, YouTube

Jim Ruddell, Chair
Doug Titzer, Past Chair
Jim Mitchell, Secretary
Mark Cacamis, Vice Chair
Kevin Donnelly, Director

A nonprofit and non-governmental professional association serving the construction management industry.

11000 Members
Founded in 1982

7169 Construction Owners Association of America
5000 Austell Powder Springs Road
Suite 217
Austell, GA 30106

770-433-0820
800-994-2622
Fax: 404-577-3551
E-Mail: coaa@coaa.org
Home Page: www.coaa.org
Social Media: Facebook, Twitter, LinkedIn

Kevin Lewis, President
Dean McCormick, Vice President
Stuart Adler, Director
Gwen Glattes, Secretary/Treasurer
Ted Argyle, Past President

A national organization of public and private owners who manage facilities development and capital improvement projects.

7170 CorrConnectÿ
530 University Ave
Palo Alto, CA 94301

E-Mail: contact@mvesystems.com
Home Page: www.corrconnect.com

Joshua Bane, Project Manager

An online resource center for training modules on corrosion.

Founded in 2007

7171 Council of Engineer and Scientific Specialty Board
PO Box 1448
Annapolis, MD 21401-1448

410-266-3766
Fax: 410-721-1746
E-Mail: academy@aaee.net
Home Page: www.cesb.org

William C Anderson PE DEE, Executive Director

Accredits engineering, science and technology certification programs from professional to technician certificates.

Founded in 1990
Mailing list available for rent

7172 Electric Power Research Institute
3420 Hillview Avenue
Palo Alto, CA 94304

650-855-2121
800-313-3774
E-Mail: orders@epri.com
Home Page: www.epri.com
Social Media: Facebook, Twitter, LinkedIn, YouTube

Denis P O'Brien, Chair
Gil C Quiniones, Vice Chair

Michael W Howard, President/ Chief Executive Officer
Tom Alley, Vice President
John A Bohn, Chief Executive Officer

A nonprofit organization that conducts research on issues related to the electric power industry in the USA.
Founded in 1965

7173 **Engineering Workforce Commission**
1801 Alexander Bell Drive
Reston, VA 20191

202-296-2237
888-400-2237
Fax: 202-296-1151
E-Mail: dbateson@aaes.org
Home Page: www.ewc-online.org

Dan Batson, Director

AAES's Engineering Workforce Commission monitors engineering job stats that help universities, corporations, and government set salary, hiring, enrollment, and degree trends in the marketplace. It publishes three major surveys per year that are regarded as the most accurate, objective and timely reports about the engineering workforce: Degrees, Enrollments, and Salaries.
35 Members
Founded in 1950

7174 **Environmental Information Association**
6935 Wisconsin Ave
Suite 306
Chevy Chase, MD 20815-6112

301-961-4999
888-343-4342
Fax: 301-961-3094
E-Mail: info@eia-usa.org
Home Page: www.eia-usa.org

Brent Kynoch, Managing Director
Kelly Rutt, Development & Communications Mgr
Lisa Mihalik, Membership/Meetings Coordinator
BJ Fungaroli, Board President
Vince Brennan, Board VP

Nonprofit organization dedicated to providing environmental information to individuals, members and industry. Disseminates information on the abatement of asbestos and lead-based paint, indoor air quality, safety and health issues, analytical issues and environmental site assessments.

7175 **Ergosyst Associates**
4840 W 15th Street
Suite 1012
Lawrence, KS 66049

785-842-7334
Fax: 785-842-7348

John Burch, Publisher

Association for those interested in economics/human factors.

7176 **Federation of Materials Societies**
910 17th St NW
Suite 800
Washington, DC 20006-2606

202-296-9282
Fax: 202-833-3014
E-Mail: betsyhou@ix.netcom.com
Home Page: www.materialsocieties.org

Betsy Houston, Executive Director
Petr Vanysek, President

Promotes cooperation among societies concerned with the understanding, development and application of materials and processes.
700K Members
Founded in 1972

7177 **ICC Evaluation Service**
5360 Workman Mill Rd
Whittier, CA 90601-2299

562-699-0541
888-422-7233
Fax: 562-908-5524
E-Mail: es@icc-es.org
Home Page: www.iccsafe.org

James Brothers, President
William Dupler, Vice President
Ronald Piester, Secretary/Treasurer

An independent, nonprofit organization that conducts a voluntary program of evaluation of both traditional and innovative building materials, products and systems for compliance with the three major model codes in the United States.
Founded in 2003

7178 **Illuminating Engineering Society of North America**
120 Wall Street
17th Floor
New York, NY 10005

212-248-5000
Fax: 212-248-5017
E-Mail: ies@ies.org
Home Page: www.ies.org

Dennis Lavoie, President
Chip Israel, Vice President
Shirley Coyle, Treasurer

To advance knowledge and disseminate information for the improvement of the lighted environment to the benefit of society. Publishes a monthly magazine; Lighting Design & Applications.
7000 Members
Founded in 1906

7179 **Industrial Designers Society of America**
45195 Business Ct
Suite 250
Sterling, VA 20166-6717

703-707-6000
Fax: 703-787-8501
E-Mail: idsa@idsa.org
Home Page: www.idsa.org

Clive Roux, CEO
Annette Butler, Executive Assistant
Kaycee Childress, Marketing
Roxann Henze, Press, Media & Public Relations

The IDSA is the world's oldest, largest, member-driven society for product design, industrial design, interaction designs, human factors, ergonomics, design research, design management, university design and related fields.

7180 **Industrial Fabrics Association International**
1801 County Road B W
Roseville, MN 55113-4061

651-222-2508
800-225-4324
Fax: 651-631-9334
E-Mail: generalinfo@ifai.com
Home Page: www.ifai.com

Stephen Warner, CEO
JoAnne Ferris, Marketing Director

A not-for-profit trade association whose member companies represent the international specialty fabrics marketplace, who facilitates the development, application and promotion of products manufactures by the diverse membership.
2000 Members

7181 **Industrial Research Institute**
2200 Clarendon Boulevard
Suite 1102
Arlington, VA 22201

703-647-2580
Fax: 703-647-2581
Home Page: www.iriweb.org

J Stewart Witzeman, Chairman
James Scinta, Chairman-Elect
Edward Bernstein, President

The mission is to enhance the effectiveness of technological innovation industry.
200 Members
Founded in 1938

7182 **Institute of Biological Engineering**
3493 Lansdowne Drive
Suite 2
Lexington, KE 40517

859-977-7450
Fax: 859-271-0607
Home Page: www.ibe.org
Social Media: Facebook, LinkedIn

A nonprofit professional organization which encourages inquiry and interest in the field of biological engineering.

7183 **Institute of Industrial Engineers**
3577 Parkway Lane
Suite 200
Norcross, GA 30092

770-449-0460
800-494-0460
Fax: 770-441-3295
E-Mail: cs@iienet.org
Home Page: www.iienet.org

Don Greene, CEO
Donna Calvert, COO

Supports all industrial engineers with training, education, publications, conferences, etc.
15000 Members
Founded in 1948

7184 **Institute of Noise Control Engineering**
9100 Purdue Road
Suite 200
Indianapolis, IN 46268

317-735-4063
Fax: 317-280-8527
E-Mail: ibo@inceusa.org
Home Page: www.inceusa.org

James Thompson, President
Eric Wood, President Elect
Teik Lim, Vice President
Deane Jaeger, Treasurer
Karl Washburn, Secretary

Supports those involved with hearing protection, modal analysis, and signal processing.
1200 Members

7185 **Institute of Transportation Engineers**
1627 Eye Street, NW
Suite 600
Washington, DC 20006

202-785-0060
Fax: 202-785-0609
E-Mail: ite_staff@ite.org
Home Page: www.ite.org
Social Media: Facebook, Twitter, LinkedIn, YouTube, Instagram, Google+

W. Hibbett Neel, International President
John J Kennedy, International Vice President
Zaki Mustafa, Immediate Past President
Colleen L Hill-Stramsak, International Director
Dean J Kaiser, International Director

An international educational and scientific association of transportation professionals who

are responsible for meeting mobility and safety needs.
13199 Members
Founded in 1930

7186 **Instrument Society of America**
67 T.W. Alexander Drive
PO Box 12277
Research Triangle Park, NC 27709

919-549-8411
Fax: 919-549-8288
E-Mail: info@isa.org
Home Page: www.isa.org
Social Media: Facebook, Twitter, LinkedIn, YouTube, Flickr, Google+

Peggie W Koon, President
Richard W Roop, President Elect
Terrence G Ives, Past President
Patrick J Gouhin, Executive Director/CEO
James W Keaveney, Treasurer

A nonprofit technical society for engineers, technicians, businesspeople, educators and students who work, study or are interested in industrial automation and pursuits related to it, such as instrumentation.
30000 Members
Founded in 1945

7187 **Instrumentation and Measurement Society**
799 N Beverly Glen
Los Angeles, CA 90077

310-446-8280
Fax: 732-981-0225
E-Mail: bob.myers@ieee.org
Home Page: http://sites.ieee.org/

Robert Myers, Executive Director

A subsidiary of the Institute of Electrical and Electronics Engineers. Provides support to scientists and technicians who design and develop electrical and electronic measuring instruments and equipment.
6500 Members
Founded in 1950

7188 **Insulated Cable Engineers Association**
PO Box 1568
Carrollton, GA 30112

770-830-0369
E-Mail: info@icea.net
Home Page: www.icea.net

Lauri J Hiivala, President

Professional organization dedicated to developing cable standards for the electric power, control and telecommunications industries. Ensures safe, economical and efficient cable systems utilizing proven, state-of-the-art materials and concepts. ICEA documents are of interest to cable manufacturers, architects and engineers, utility and manufacturing plant personnel, telecommunication engineers, consultants and OEMs.
Founded in 1925

7189 **International Association for Radio, Telec ommunications and Electromagnets**
600 N. PLANKINTON AVE
Suite 301
Milwaukee, WI 53201

888-722-2440
Fax: 414-765-8661
E-Mail: info@exemplarglobal.org
Home Page: www.narte.org

Adam Ruck, Primary Contact

A worldwide, nonprofit, professional association which certifies qualified engineers and technicians in the fields of Telecommunications, Electromagnetic Compatibility/Interference (EMC/EMI), Product Safety (PS), Electrostatic Discharge control (ESD) and Wireless Systems Installation.

7190 **International Facility Management Association**
800 Gessner Rd.
Ste. 900
Houston, TX 77024-4257

713-623-4362
Fax: 713-623-6124
E-Mail: ifma@ifma.org
Home Page: www.ifma.org
Social Media: Facebook, Twitter, LinkedIn, YouTube, Flickr, Google+

James P Whittaker, Chair
Michael D Feldman, First Vice Chair
Maureen Ehrenberg, Second Vice Chair
Jon Seller, Past Chair
Tony Keane, President & CEO

International association for facility management professionals.
22659 Members
Founded in 1978

7191 **International Reprographic Association**
401 N Michigan Avenue
Chicago, IL 60611

312-245-1026
Fax: 312-527-6705
E-Mail: info@irga.com
Home Page: www.irga.com

Bryan Thomas, President
Dan Stephens, VP

Represents entrepreneurial businesses serving the wide-format imaging needs of graphic arts, architectural, engineering, manufacturing, corporate, legal, retail, and POP industries.
Founded in 1927

7192 **International Society Weighing/Measurement**
9707 Key West Ave
Suite 100
Rockville, MD 20850-3992

301-258-1115
Fax: 301-990-9771
E-Mail: staff@iswm.org
Home Page: www.iswm.org

John Hughes, President
Steven Dishon, Vice President
Jamie Notter, Executive Director

Supports all those involved in the weighing and measurement industry.

7193 **International Society for Optical Engineering**
1000 20th Street
P O Box 10
Bellingham, WA 98225-6705

360-676-3290
888-504-8171
Fax: 360-647-1445
E-Mail: spie@spie.org
Home Page: www.spie.org/

Katerina Svanberg, President
William Arnold, Vice President
Brian Lula, Ssecretary/Treasurer
Eugene Arthurs, CEO

Serves the international, technical community as the premier provider of education, information, and resources covering optics, photonics, and their applications.
16000 Members
Founded in 1955

7194 **Investigative Engineers Association**
10001 W Oakland Park Blvd.
Suite 301
Sunrise, FL 33351

954-530-0715
844-217-6975
Fax: 954-537-4942
E-Mail: jhogge@ienga.net
Home Page: www.ienga.net
Social Media: Facebook, Twitter, LinkedIn

Lewis W Ernest, Advisor
James R Hogge, CEO
Tom Hogge, President
Nancy Pashkoff, Marketing Director
Tammy Lane, National Director

Consists of independent forensic engineering firms nationwide and abroad.

7195 **Materials Research Society**
506 Keystone Dr
Warrendale, PA 15086-7573

724-779-3003
Fax: 724-779-8313
E-Mail: info@mrs.org
Home Page: www.mrs.org

James De Yoreo, President
Bruce Clemens, Vice President
Sean Hearne, Secretary
Michael Fitzsimmons, Treasurer

The Materials Research Society is a not-for-profit organization that brings together scientists, engineers and research managers from industry, government, academia and research laboratories to share findings in the research and development of new materials of technological importance. The Materials Research Society promotes communication for the advancement of interdisciplinary materials research to improve the quality of life.
16000 Members
Founded in 1973

7196 **NACE International**
1440 S Creek Drive
Houston, TX 77084-4906

281-228-6200
800-797-6223
Fax: 281-228-6300
E-Mail: firstservice@nace.org
Home Page: www.nace.org
Social Media: Facebook, Twitter, LinkedIn

Oliver Moghissi, President
Kevin Garrity, Vice President
Jeffrey Didas, Treasurer
Bob Chalker, Executive Director

Advances the knowledge of corrosion engineering and science in all major industries through education, certification, standards, publications, and public awareness.
21000 Members
Founded in 1943

7197 **National Academy of Engineering**
500 5th Street NW
Washington, DC 20001

202-334-3200
Fax: 202-334-2290
Home Page: www.nae.edu

Charles Vest, President
Lance Davis, Executive Officer
Mary Lee Berger-Hughes, Membership Director

Promotes public understanding of the role that engineering plays in the technical fields. Sponsors programs aimed at meeting national needs in the field. Encourages research.
2000 Members
Founded in 1964

7198 National Association of Fire Equipment Distributors
122 S. Michigan Avenue
Suite 1040
Chicago, IL 60603

312-461-9600
Fax: 312-461-0777
E-Mail: dharris@nafed.org
Home Page: www.nafed.org
Social Media: LinkedIn, YouTube

Ed Hugill, President
Ken May, Immediate Past President
Danny Harris, Executive Director
Tamara Matthews, Communications Manager
George Seymour, Treasurer

Improves the economic environment, business performance, and technical competence in the fire protection industry.
Founded in 1963

7199 National Association of Minority Engineers
341 N. Maitland Avenue
Suite 130
Maitland, FL 32751

407-647-8839
Fax: 407-629-2502
E-Mail: namepa@namcpa.org
Home Page: www.namepa.org

Crystal Smith, President
Phil Pyster, Executive VP
Latisha Moore, Assistant Executive Director
Jahi Sauk Simbai, Treasurer
Ivan Favila, Secretary

Provides a communication network among college-level administrators of minority engineering programs.
575 Members

7200 National Board of Boiler and Pressure Vessel Inspectors
1055 Crupper Ave
Columbus, OH 43229-1108

614-888-8320
Fax: 614-888-0750
E-Mail: information@nationalboard.org
Home Page: www.nationalboard.org

Don Tanner, Executive Director
Connie Homer, Senior Executive Secretary

Membership is composed of chief boiler inspectors of states, major US cities and Canadian provinces having boiler laws.
55 Members
Founded in 1919

7201 National Council of Examiners for Engineering and Surveying
280 Seneca Creek Road
Seneca, SC 29678

864-654-6824
800-250-3196
Fax: 864-654-6033
Home Page: www.ncees.org

Martin A Pederson LS, President
Betsy Browne, Executive Director
Jerry Carter, Associate Executive Director
Gregg E Brandow, PhD PE, Treasurer

Promotes uniform standards of registration and coordinates interstate registration of engineers and surveyors.
68 Members
Founded in 1920

7202 National Electrical Contractors Association
3 Bethesda Metro Center
Suite 1100
Bethesda, MD 20814

301-657-3110
Fax: 301-215-4500
Home Page: www.necanet.org
Social Media: Facebook, Twitter, LinkedIn, YouTube, Flickr

John M Grau, Chief Executive Officer
Daniel G Walter, Vice President & COO
Traci Pickus, Secretary/ Treasurer
Russell J Alessi, President
Bill Orgill, Executive Director

A trade association in the United States that represents the electrical industry.
Founded in 1901

7203 National Environmental Balancing Bureau
8575 Grovemont Cir
Gaithersburg, MD 20877-4121

301-977-3698
Fax: 301-977-9589
E-Mail: karen@nebb.org
Home Page: www.nebb.org

William Neudorfer, President
Neil Marshall, President Elect
Stanley Fleischer, Vice President
Bob Linder, Treasurer

NEBB is an international certification association for firms that deliver high performance building systems. Members perform testing, adjusting and balancing (TAB) of heating, ventilating and air-conditioning systems, commission and retro-commission building systems commissioning, execute sound and vibration testing, and test and certify lab fume hoods and electronic and bio clean rooms. NEBB holds the highest standards in certification.
Founded in 1971

7204 National Fire Protection Association
1 Batterymarch Park
Quincy, MA 02169-7471

617-770-3000
800-844-6058
Fax: 617-770-0700
Home Page: www.nfpa.org
Social Media: Facebook, Twitter, LinkedIn, YouTube, Flickr, Google+

Ernest J Grant, Chair
Randolph W Tucker, First Vice Chair
Jim Pauley, President/ CEO
Amy R Acton, Secretary
William J McCammon, Treasurer

Publishes fire and building safety standards including the NationalElectrical Code.
Founded in 1896

7205 National Institute for Certification in Technologies
1420 King St
Alexandria, VA 22314-2750

703-548-1518
888-476-4238
Fax: 703-682-2756
E-Mail: certify@nicet.org
Home Page: www.nicet.org

Michael A Clark, CEO

Issues certification to engineering technicians and technologists who voluntarily apply for certification and satisfy competency criteria through examinations and verification of work experience.
113K Members
Founded in 1961

7206 National Society of Black Engineers
205 Daingerfield Road
Alexandria, VA 22314

703-549-2207
Fax: 703-683-5312
E-Mail: info@nsbe.org
Home Page: www.nsbe.org

Chancee Lundy, Chairperson
Candice M Dixon, Vice Chairperson
Justin Brown, National Parliamentarian
Jennifer Jasper, National Secretary
Carl Mack, Executive Director

Supports all black technical professionals involved in the manufacturing engineering industry.
15000 Members
Founded in 1971

7207 National Society of Professional Engineers
1420 King St
Alexandria, VA 22314-2794

703-684-2800
Fax: 703-836-4875
Home Page: www.nspe.org

Larry Jacobson, President

The mission of the Society is to promote the ethical, competent and licensed practice of engineering and to enhance the professional, social and economic well-being of its members.
60000 Members
Founded in 1934

7208 North American Die Casting Association
241 Holbrook Drive
Wheeling, IL 60090-5809

847-279-0001
Fax: 847-279-0002
E-Mail: nadca@diecasting.org
Home Page: www.diecasting.org

Daniel Twarog, President

The organization serves as the voice of the industry, promoting growth and enhancing member's ability to compete domestically in the global marketplace.
3700 Members
Founded in 1989

7209 North American Manufacturing Research Institute
1 SME Drive
Dearborn, MI 48121

313-425-3000
800-733-4763
Fax: 313-425-3400
E-Mail: service@sme.org
Home Page: www.sme.org

Mark Tomlinson, Executive Director/General Manager
Greg Sheremet, Publisher
Bob Harris, Director Finance

Members are engaged in manufacturing, research and technology development.
180 Members
Founded in 1981

7210 Order Of The Engineer
PO Box 25473
Scottsdale, AZ 85255-0107

866-364-7464
Fax: 480-585-6418
Home Page: www.order-of-the-engineer.org

Paula Ostaff, Executive Director

An association for graduate and professional engineers in the United States that emphasizes pride and responsibility in the engineering profession.

7211 Pi Tau Sigma
Home Page: www.pitausigma.net
Dr. Mun Young Choi, President
Dr. Gloria J Wiens, Vice President
Dr. Alex Moutsoglou, Treasurer
Altaf Khan, Vice President
Dr. Darryl James, Vice President
An International Mechanical Engineering Honor Society.
Founded in 1947

7212 Professional Engineers in Private Practice
1420 King Street
Alexandria, VA 22314-2750
703-684-2800
Fax: 703-836-4875
Home Page: www.nspe.org
Fred Palmerton, PE, Chair
Larry L Britt, PE, Chair-Elect
Steve M Theno, PE, Secretary
Addresses the concerns of individual engineers in private practice, primarily working in design for construction. Offers resources, standard contracts, newsletters and management guidance in the forms of videos, books, and newsletters.
24M Members

7213 Railway Engineering: Maintenance Suppliers Association
500 New Jersey Ave. NW
Suite 400
Washington, DC 20001
202-715-2921
Fax: 202-204-5753
Home Page: www.remsa.org
Philip Homan, President
John Fox, Vice President
Trent Marshall, Secretary/Treasurer
Members are distributors and manufacturers of railway machinery supplies and services.
225 Members
Founded in 1965

7214 Refrigeration Service Engineers Society
1666 Rand Rd
Des Plaines, IL 60016-3552
847-297-6464
800-297-5660
Fax: 847-297-5038
E-Mail: general@rses.org
Home Page: www.rses.org
Social Media: Facebook, Twitter, LinkedIn
Robert Sherman, Intl President
Lawrence Donaldson, Intl Vice President
Wes Maxfield, Intl Secretary/Treasurer
A leading education, training and certification association for heating, ventilation, air conditioning and refrigeration professionals. RSES credentials include the SM/CM/CMS exam series as well as one of the largest EPA Section 608 certification programs in the industry.
15231 Members
Founded in 1933

7215 Reliability Engineering and Management Institute
7340 N La Oesta Ave
Tucson, AZ 85704-3119
520-621-6120
Fax: 520-621-8191
E-Mail: dimitri@u.arizona.edu
Home Page: www.u.arizona.edu
Dr. Dimitri B Kececioglu, Executive Director
Supports all engineers and managers who deal with the issue of Reliability Engineering. Provides publications, training, education, new techniques and product forums and two annual conference.
Founded in 1963
Mailing list available for rent: 44000 names

7216 Research Council on Structural Connections
Sargent & Lundy
55 E Monroe Street
Chicago, IL 60603-5780
312-269-2000
Fax: 312-269-3681
E-Mail: rshaw@steelstructures.com
Home Page: www.boltcouncil.org
Ray Tide, Chairman Executive Committee
Geoff Kulak, Vice Chairman
Charles Carter, Chairman Membership/Funding
Emile Troup, Secretary/Treasurer
Researches the effects of stress on bolted and riveted joints for its member companies and institutions.
45 Members
Founded in 1946

7217 Robotics Industries Association
900 Victors Way
Suite 140
Ann Arbor, MI 48108
734-994-6088
Fax: 734-994-3338
E-Mail: webmaster@robotics.org
Home Page: www.robotics.org
Don Vincent, Executive VP
Brian Huse, Director Marketing/PR
Jim Adams, Marketing Manager
Sharon Adams, Accounting Manager
Jeff Burnstein, Executive Director
Trade group organized specifically to serve the robotics industry. Member companies include leading robot manufacturers, users, system integrators, component suppliers, research groups and consulting firms. Trade show is held every two years.
250+ Members
Founded in 1974

7218 Science and Technology Society
Rm 1501
125 Maiden Ln
New York, NY 10038-4714
212-248-0200
Fax: 212-248-0245
Home Page: www.avs.org
Christie R Marrian, President
John Coburn, Treasurer
Joseph E Greene, Clerk/Secretary
Supports all those in the vacuum industry, especially scientists and engineers.
6000 Members
Founded in 1953

7219 Sigma Phi Delta
438 Smithfield Street
East Liverpool, OH 43920-1723
330-385-5287
E-Mail: webmaster@sigphi.org
Home Page: www.sigphi.org
Derek R Troy, Grand President
Alixandre R Minden, Grand VP
Steven A Weiss, Communications Director
Edward A Hurst, Treasurer
Robert Featheringham, Manager
A professional and social fraternity in engineering.
7200 Members
Founded in 1924

7220 Society for Experimental Mechanics
7 School St
Bethel, CT 06801-1855
203-790-6373
Fax: 203-790-4472
E-Mail: sem@sem1.com
Home Page: www.sem.org
Peter Ifgu, President
Emmanuel Gdoutos, Vice President
Jon Rogers, Treasurer
Tom Proulx, Executive Director
Supports all those involved with general experimental mechanics and the measurement of stresses and strains in metals and other materials.

7221 Society for the Advancement of Material and Process Engineering
1161 Parkview Drive
Suite 200
Covina, CA 91724-3759
626-331-0616
800-562-7360
Fax: 626-332-8929
E-Mail: sampe@sampe.org
Home Page: www.sampe.org
Social Media: Facebook, Twitter, LinkedIn
Gregg Balko, Executive Director
Mike Keilty, Controller
Dr Scott Beckwith, Technical Director
An international professional member society, provides information on new materials and processing technology either via technical forums, journal publications, or books in which professionals in this field can exchange ideas and air their views.
Founded in 1944

7222 Society of Allied Weight Engineers
5734 E. Lucia Walk
Long Beach, CA 90803-4015
562-596-2873
Fax: 562-596-2874
E-Mail: exdirector@sawe.org
Home Page: www.sawe.org
Robert Zimmerman, President
Bill Boze, Executive VP
Anthony Primozich, Senior VP
Errol Oguzhan, VP Training
Ronald Fox, Executive Director
Consists of engineers in the aerospace, shipbuilding, land vehicles, offshore and allied industries.
800 Members
Founded in 1941

7223 Society of American Military Engineers
607 Prince St
Alexandria, VA 22314-3117
703-549-3800
800-336-3097
Fax: 703-684-0231
E-Mail: webmanager@same.org
Home Page: www.same.org
Robert D Wolff, Executive Director
Paul Dinkel, COO
Brings together professional engineers and those in engineering related fields to improve and increase the engineering capabilities of the nation and to exchange and advance the knowledge of engineering technologies, applications and practices.
20000 Members
Founded in 1920

7224 Society of Automotive Engineers
1200 G St., NW
Suite 800
Washington, DC 20005

202-463-7318
Home Page: www.sae.org
Social Media: Facebook, Twitter, LinkedIn, Google+

Daniel M Hancock, President
Robert L Ireland, Vice President
David L Schutt, Chief Executive Officer
George Bradley, Secretary
Dana M Pless, Chief Financial Officer

Advances mobility in land, sea, air, and space.
Founded in 1905

7225 Society of Broadcast Engineers
9102 North Meridian Street
Suite 150
Indianapolis, IN 46260

317-846-9000
Home Page: www.sbe.org

Joseph Snelson, President
Jerry Massey, Vice President
James E Leifer, Secretary
Andrea Cummis, Treasurer
John L Poray, Executive Director

A professional organization for engineers in broadcast radio and television.
5500 Members

7226 Society of Fire Protection Engineers
7315 Wisconsin Avenue
Suite 620E
Bethesda, MD 20814

301-718-2910
Fax: 301-718-2242
E-Mail: foundation@sfpe.org
Home Page: www.sfpe.org
Social Media: Facebook, Twitter, LinkedIn, YouTube

Carl F Baldassarra, President
Daniel Madrzykowski, President Elect
David Barber, Vice President
Michael Madden, Secretary-Treasurer
Nicole Testa Boston, Executive Director

The largest professional society for fire safety engineers.
4500 Members
Founded in 1971

7227 Society of Hispanic Professional Engineers

323-725-3970
703-373-7930
E-Mail: shpenational@shpe.org
Home Page: national.shpe.org
Social Media: Facebook, Twitter, LinkedIn, YouTube, Instagram

Miguel Alemany, Chair
Rodrigo T Garcia, President
Americo Garza, Vice President
Andres SantaMaria, Secretary
Alex Vidaurrazaga, Treasurer

A national organization of professional engineers to serve as rolemodels in the Hispanic community.
Founded in 1974

7228 Society of Manufacturing Engineers
1 SME Drive
Dearborn, MI 48121

313-425-3000
800-733-4763
Fax: 313-425-3400
E-Mail: service@sme.org
Home Page: www.sme.org

Paul Bradley, President
Mark Tomlinson, Executive Driector/CEO

Professional society dedicated to advancing scientific knowledge in the field of manufacturing and to applying its resources for researching, writing, publishing and disseminating information.
70M Members
Founded in 1932

7229 Society of Naval Architects and Marine Engineers
99 Canal Center Plaza
Suite 310
Alexandria, VA 22314

703-997-6701
Fax: 703-997-6702
Home Page: www.sname.org

Peter G Noble, President
Erik W Seither, Executive Director
Jodi Lane, Executive Administrator
Mike Hall, Director of Membership
Lia Vang, Director of Finance

A global professional society that provides a forum for the advancement of the engineering profession as applied to the marine field.
8500 Members
Founded in 1893

7230 Society of Petroleum Engineers
222 Palisades Creek Dr.
Richardson, TX 75080

972-952-9393
800-456-6863
Fax: 972-952-9435
E-Mail: spedal@spe.org
Home Page: www.spe.org

Giovanni Paccaloni, President
Bill Cobb, VP Finance
John E Bethancourt, Director Management/Information
Ian Gorman, Director Production/Operations
Mark Rubin, Executive Director

To provide the means for collection, dissemination and exchange of technical information concerning the development of oil and gas resources, subsurface fluid flow and production of other materials through well bores for the public benefit.
64000 Members
Founded in 1957

7231 Society of Rheology
American Institute of Physics
2 Huntington Quadrangle
Suite 1N01
Meville, NY 11747-4502

516-576-2471
Fax: 516-576-2223
E-Mail: rheology@aip.org
Home Page: www.rheology.org

A.Jeffrey Giacomin, VP
Faith Morrison, President

Composed of physicists, chemists, biologists, engineers, and mathematicians interested in advancing and applying rheology, which is defined as the science of deformation and flow of matter.
1700 Members

7232 Society of Tribologists and Lubrication Engineers
840 Busse Hwy
Park Ridge, IL 60068-2376

847-825-5536
Fax: 847-825-1456
E-Mail: information@stle.org
Home Page: www.stle.org

Michael Dugger, President
Jerry Byers, Vice President
Robert Heverly, Secretary
Maureen Hunter, Treasurer

Strives to advance the science of lubrication tribology and related arts and sciences. Sponsors courses and an annual meeting.
4400 Members
Founded in 1960

7233 Society of Women Engineers
203 N La Salle Street
Suite 1675
Chicago, IL 60601

877-793-4636
E-Mail: membership@swe.org
Home Page: societyofwomenengineers.swe.org
Social Media: Facebook, Twitter, LinkedIn, YouTube, Instagram, Google+

Elizabeth Bierman, President
Colleen M Layman, President Elect
Karen Horting, Executive Director/ CEO
Wendy Schauer Landwe, Secretary
Cindy Hoover, Treasurer

An organization that stimulates women to achieve full potential in careers as engineers.

7234 Tau Beta Pi Association
PO Box 2697
Knoxville, TN 37901-2697

865-546-4578
Fax: 865-546-4579
Home Page: www.tbp.org
Social Media: Facebook, LinkedIn

Larry Simonson, President
Solange Dao, Vice President

The National Engineering honor society recognizes engineering students of superior scholarship and exemplary character and practitioners of engineering. The organization includes 230 collegiate chapters and 16 alumnus chapters.
525K Members
Founded in 1885

7235 The American Association for Wind Engineers
1415 Blue Spruce Drive
Suite 3
Fort Collins, CO 80524

970-498-2334
Fax: 970-221-3124
E-Mail: aawe@aawe.org
Home Page: www.aawe.org

Dr. Partha Sarkar, President
Dr. Greg Kopp, President Elect
Dr. Steve C. S. Cai, Secretary/ Treasurer
Dr. David O Prevatt, Board of Directors
Dr. Anne Cope, Board of Directors

A nonprofit professional organization that promotes and disseminates technical information in the research community.
Founded in 1995

7236 The American Society For Nondestructive Testing
1711 Arlingate Lane
Columbus, OH 43228-0518

614-274-6003
800-222-2768
Fax: 614-274-6899
E-Mail: pwhite@asnt.org
Home Page: www.asnt.org
Social Media: Twitter, LinkedIn, YouTube

Betsy Blazer, Interim Executive Director
Pat White, Membership Coordinator
Matt Monta, Communications Manager
Tim Jones, Senior Manager
Michelle Lindsey, Head Accountant

A technical society for nondestructive testing professionals.
Founded in 1941

7237 **The Associated General Contractors of America**
2300 Wilson Blvd.
Suite 300
Arlington, VA 22201

703-548-3118
800-242-1767
Fax: 703-837-5405
E-Mail: info@agc.org
Home Page: www.agc.org

Alan L Landes, President
Charles L Greco, Senior Vice President
Mark Knight, Vice President
Eric L Wilson, Treasurer
Carolyn McFadden, Executive Director

Trade association for the construction industry.
26000 Members

7238 **Theta Tau**
1011 San Jacinto
Suite 205
Austin, TX 78701

512-482-1904
800-264-1904
Fax: 512-472-4820
E-Mail: central@thetatau.org
Home Page: www.thetatau.org

Michael Livingston, Grand Regent
Justin Wisemen, Grand Vice Regent
Rachael Stensrud, Grand Scribe
J. Matthew Clark, Grand Treasurer

A professional fraternity in engineering. Founded at the University of Minnesota. Purpose of the fraternity is to develop and maintain a high standard of professional interest among its members, and to unite them in a strong bond of fraternal fellowship.
30000 Members
Founded in 1904

7239 **TheÿTire Society**
810 E. 10th St.
Lawrence, KS 66044

785-843-1234
800-627-0326
Fax: 785-843-6153
E-Mail: tst@allenpress.com
Home Page: www.tiresociety.org

Saied Taheri, President
Randy Jenniges, Vice President
Ric Mousseau, Past President
Michell Hoo Fatt, University of Akron
Rusty Adams, Treasurer

A professional engineering society that increases and disseminates knowledge as it pertains to the science and technology of tires.

7240 **United Engineering Foundation**
PO Box 70
Mount Vernon, VA 22121-070

973-244-2328
Fax: 973-882-5155
E-Mail: engfnd@aol.com
Home Page: www.uefoundation.org

Arthur Winston, President
Dr David L Belden, Executive Director

Supports research in engineering science and seeks to advance the profession of engineering.
19 Members
Founded in 1904

7241 **United Engineering Trustees**
3 Park Ave
27th Floor
New York, NY 10016-5902

212-591-7829
Fax: 212-591-7441
E-Mail: engfnd@aol.com
Home Page: www.uefoundation.org

Sidney F Spakie, President
Dr David L Belden, Executive Director
Rosa Landinez, Conference Director
Joel B Snyder, Assistant Treasurer

Aims to advance engineering arts and sciences.
Founded in 1904

Newsletters

7242 **AEG News**
Association of Engineering Geologists
PO Box 460518
Denver, CO 80246

303-757-2926
Fax: 303-757-2969
E-Mail: aeg@aegweb.org
Home Page: www.aegweb.org

Dave Bieber, President
Darrel Schmitz, President-Elect/VP
Becky Roland, Chief Staff Executive
Terry West, Treasurer
Dorian Kuper, Secretary

Includes reports of committee activities, section news, and other news items of interest to the profession.
Frequency: Quarterly

7243 **AIP History Newsletter**
American Institute of Physics
1 Physics Ellipse
College Park, MD 20740-3841

301-209-3100
Fax: 301-209-0843
E-Mail: dylla@aip.org
Home Page: www.aip.org

Marc Brodsky, CEO
Margaret Wiley, Senior Executive Secretary
Benjamin Snavely, AIP Corporate Secretary
Melissa Poleski, Assistant To Corporate Secretary

Our Newsletter reports on work in the history of physics (and allied fields such as astronomy and geophysics), carried out at the American Institute of Physics and elsewhere. It includes lists of recent publications in the history of modern physics, and reports on papers deposited in archives worldwide.

7244 **ASFE Newslog**
ASFE/The Geoprofessional Business Association
8811 Colesville Rd
Suite G106
Silver Spring, MD 20910-4343

301-565-2733
Fax: 301-589-2017
E-Mail: info@asfe.org
Home Page: www.asfe.org

David Gaboury, President

Information on geo professional, environmental, and civil engineering firms. Past issues are available through the online store. Electronic copies are always free to members.

7245 **ASGE Newsletter**
American Society of Gas Engineers
PO Box 66
Artesia, CA 90702

562-455-9417
E-Mail: asgecge@aol.com
Home Page: www.asge-national.org

Nancy Wilson, President
Sham Kassab, VP
Susan McCarthy, Treasurer
Jerry Moore, Executive Director

Keeps members current on events and issues facing the Gas Appliance Industry. Features articles that address new technologies and trends.

7246 **ASTM International Business Link**
ASTM International
PO Box C700
W Conshohocken, PA 19428-0700

610-832-9500
Fax: 610-832-9555
E-Mail: service@astm.org
Home Page: www.astm.org

James A Thomas, President

Provides information on the topics connecting the business and technical communities.
Frequency: Semi-Annual

7247 **Access ASTM International**
ASTM International
PO Box C700
W Conshohocken, PA 19428-0700

610-832-9500
Fax: 610-832-9555
E-Mail: service@astm.org
Home Page: www.astm.org

James A Thomas, President
John Pace, Manager
Jeff Adkins, Manager
Fran Dougherty, Administrative Assistant

Periodic update for ASTM's global customers.
Frequency: Semi-Annual

7248 **American Automatic Control Council Newsletter**
AACC Secretariat
2145 Sheridan Road
Evanston, IL 60208-3118

847-491-8175
Fax: 847-491-4455
E-Mail: aacc@ece.northwestern.edu
Home Page: www.a2c2.org

Bonnie Heck, Publisher
William Levine, President
A Ulsoy, Vice-President

Automatic control council information.
4 Pages
Frequency: Quarterly
Founded in 1961

7249 **BMES Bulletin**
Biomedical Engineering Society
8401 Corporate Dr
Suite 140
Hyattsville, MD 20785-2263

301-459-1999
Fax: 301-459-2444
E-Mail: info@bmes.org
Home Page: www.bmes.org

Barbara Dunlevy, Executive Director
Heather Comstock, Meeting Manager

The Bulletin presents bioengineering science articles, student chapter news, Society and public policy announcements, employment opportunities, and a calendar of conference and events. It is also a forum for member opinions through editorials and letters.
Cost: $30.00
Frequency: Monthly
Circulation: 3500
Founded in 1969
Printed in 2 colors on matte stock

7250 **Bulletin of Tau Beta Pi**
Tau Beta Pi Association
PO Box 2697
Knoxville, TN 37901-2697

865-546-4578
Fax: 865-546-4579
Home Page: www.tbp.org

R E Hawks, Editor

The purpose of The Bulletin is to disseminate news and information about Tau Beta Pi of special interest to the collegiate chapters. It is an important vehicle for the annual repetition of instructions from the Executive Council and national headquarters to the chapters on election and initiation procedures and for the exchange of chapter project ideas and experience.
Frequency: 3x Annually
Founded in 1925

7251 Catalyst Newsletter
Adhesive & Sealant Council
7101 Wisconsin Ave
Suite 990
Bethesda, MD 20814-4805
301-986-9700
Fax: 301-986-9795
E-Mail: info@ascouncil.org
Home Page: www.ascouncil.org
Matt Croson, President

7252 Computer Integrated Manufacture and Engineering
Lionheart Publishing
506 Roswell St Se
Suite 220
Marietta, GA 30060-4101
770-422-3139
Fax: 770-432-6969
E-Mail: lpi@lionhrtpub.com
Home Page: www.lionhrtpub.com/
Marvin Diamond, Advertising Sales Manager
Explores cutting edge developments in manufacturing systems operation management.
Circulation: 24000

7253 Cross Connection Protection Devices
American Society of Sanitary Engineering
901 Canterbury Rd
Suite A
Westlake, OH 44145-1480
440-835-3040
Fax: 440-835-3488
Home Page: www.asse-plumbing.org
James Bickford, President
Donald Summers, First VP
John Flader, Treasurer
Summary of backflow conditions and method of eliminating or minimizing their possible dangers.
Cost: $15.00

7254 Echoes Newsletter
Acoustical Society of America
2 Huntington Quad
Suite 1N01
Melville, NY 11747-4505
516-576-2360
Fax: 516-576-2377
E-Mail: asa@aip.org
Home Page: www.asa.aip.org
Charles E Schmid, President
Covers current and topical happenings of general interest and features articles about current research and personalities. Distributed free to members.
Frequency: Quarterly

7255 Engineering Department Management and Administration Report
Institute of Management and Administration
3 Bethesda Metro Center
Suite 250
Bethesda, MD 20814
703-341-3500
Fax: 800-253-0332
Home Page: www.ioma.com
Focuses on improving efficiency and productivity.
Cost: $245.00
16 Pages
Frequency: Monthly

7256 Engineering Times
National Society of Professional Engineers
1420 King St
Alexandria, VA 22314-2794
703-684-2800
Fax: 703-836-4875
E-Mail: webmaster@nspe.org
Home Page: www.nspe.org
Larry Jacobson, Executive Director/Secretary
Robert Grey, President
Reports on issues affecting the engineering profession; featured monthly series on ethics. Free to members.
Cost: $30.00
24 Pages

7257 High-Tech Materials Alert
Technical Insights
605 3rd Avenue
New York, NY 10158
212-850-6824
800-245-6217
Fax: 212-850-8643
Kenneth Kovaly, Publisher
Opportunities in advanced materials.
Cost: $867.00
12 Pages

7258 Hufact Quarterly: A Current Awareness Resource
Ergosyst Associates
123 W 8th Street
Suite 210
Lawrence, KS 66044-2687
FAX 785-842-7348
John Burch, Publisher
Covers economics/human factors.
Cost: $100.00

7259 IE News: Ergonomics
Institute of Industrial Engineers
3577 Parkway Lane
Suite 200
Norcross, GA 30092
770-449-0460
800-494-0460
Fax: 770-441-3295
E-Mail: cs@iienet.org
Home Page: www.iienet.org
Don Greene, CEO
Donna Calvert, COO
Newsletter for Ergonomics Division.
4 Pages
Frequency: Quarterly
Founded in 1948

7260 IE News: Facilities Planning and Design
Institute of Industrial Engineers
25 Technology Pkwy S
Suite 150
Norcross, GA 30092-2946
770-449-0461
Fax: 770-263-8532
Dona Brown, Publisher
Accepts advertising.
4 Pages

7261 IE News: Operations Research
Institute of Industrial Engineers
25 Technology Pkwy S
Suite 150
Norcross, GA 30092-2946
770-449-0461
Fax: 770-263-8532
Dona Brown, Publisher
News for industrial engineers. Accepts advertising.
4 Pages

7262 IE News: Quality Control and Reliability Engineering
Institute of Industrial Engineers
25 Technology Pkwy S
Suite 150
Norcross, GA 30092-2946
770-449-0461
Fax: 770-263-8532
Dona Brown, Publisher
Association news.
4 Pages

7263 Innovators Digest
InfoTeam
PO Box 15640
Plantation, FL 33318-5640
954-473-9560
Fax: 954-473-0544
Merton Allen, Editor
A multidisciplinary publication covering developments in science, engineering, products, markets, business development, manufacturing and other technological developments having industrial or commercial significance.
Frequency: Bi-Annual

7264 Instrumentation Newsletter
National Instruments
6504 Bridge Point Parkway
Austin, TX 78730-5017
512-389-9119
888-280-7645
Fax: 512-794-8411
E-Mail: info@natinst.com
Home Page: www.natinst.com
Gail Folkins, Managing Editor
John Graff, Vice President of Sales
James Truchard, President
Frequency: Quarterly
Circulation: 150000
Founded in 1976

7265 Last Word
American Council of Engineering Companies
1015 15th St
8th Floor NW
Washington, DC 20005-2605
202-347-7474
Fax: 202-898-0068
E-Mail: acec@acec.org
Home Page: www.acec.org
Social Media: Facebook, Twitter
Dave Raymond, President
Ann Randstapter, Editor
Sheila Mahoutchian, Marketing Manager
Mary Jaffe, Director, Publications
Alan Crockett, Director, Public Relations
Independent private practice engineering companies.
Cost: $90.00
2 Pages
Frequency: Monthly
Circulation: 5800

Founded in 1905
Printed in on glossy stock

7266 **Leadership and Management in Engineering**
American Society of Civil Engineers
1801 Alexander Bell Dr
Suite 100
Reston, VA 20191-4382

703-295-6300
800-548-2723
Fax: 703-295-6222
E-Mail: cybrarian@asce.org
Home Page: www.afce.org

D Wayne Klotz, President

A cutting-edge periodical focusing on the art and practice of management and leadership in the civil engineering community.
Frequency: Quarterly

7267 **Licensure Exchange**
National Council of Examiners for Engineering
280 Seneca Creek Road
PO Box 1686
Clemson, SC 29633

864-654-6824
800-250-3196
Fax: 864-654-6033
Home Page: www.ncees.org

Keri Anderson, Editor
Ashley Cheney, Treasurer
David Widmer, Treasurer
Theodore Sack, Vice President

Provides information, opinion, and ideas regarding the licensure of engineers and land surveyors.
Frequency: Bi-Monthly

7268 **Nuclear News**
American Nuclear Society
555 N Kensington Ave
La Grange Park, IL 60526-5592

708-352-6611
Fax: 708-352-0499
Home Page: www.ans.org

Jack Tuohy, Executive Director

Covers the latest developments in the nuclear field, a large part of which concerns nuclear energy - in particular, the 104 operating U.S. nuclear power plants, and another 334 operating elsewhere around the globe.
Cost: $365.00
Frequency: Monthly
Founded in 2005

7269 **Plumbing Systems & Design**
American Society Of Plumbing Engineers
2980 S River Rd
Des Plaines, IL 60018-4203

773-693-2773
Fax: 773-695-9007
E-Mail: info@psdmagazine.com
Home Page: www.psdmagazine.org/

Tom Govedarica, Executive Publisher
Gretchen Pienta, Managing Editor
Maria Barriga, Circulation Manager
Jill Dirksen, Technical Director
David Ropinski, Graphic Designer

Industry leading technical publication with ASPE news and features. Free to ASPE members and subscribers.
Cost: $150.00
Circulation: 25500
Printed in 4 colors on glossy stock

7270 **Power**
McGraw Hill
PO Box 182604
Columbus, OH 43272-1095

720-485-5000
877-833-5524
Fax: 614-759-3749
Home Page: www.mcgraw-hill.com

Harold McGraw, Chairman and President
Jack Callahan, Executive VP

Published for engineers who design, construct, operate and maintain power operating facilities in cogeneration and independent power plants in electric utilities. Accepts advertising.
Cost: $50.00
Frequency: Monthly
Founded in 1888

7271 **Rheology Bulletin**
Society of Rheology
2 Huntington Quadrangle
Suite 1N01
Meville, NY 11747-4502

516-576-2471
Fax: 516-576-2223
E-Mail: rheology@aip.org
Home Page: www.rheology.org

Faith Morrison, President
Jeffrey Giacomin, Vice President
Albert Co, Secretary
Montgomery Shaw, Treasurer

To inform members of the Society affairs and matters of general interest to rheologists.
Frequency: 2x yearly

7272 **Robotics Today**
Society of Manufacturing Engineers
1 Sme Drive
Dearborn, MI 48128

313-425-3000
800-733-4763
Fax: 343-425-3400
E-Mail: service@sme.org
Home Page: www.sme.org

Paul Bradley, President
Mark Tomlinson, CEO and Executive Director
Dennis Bray, Vice President
Michael Molner, Secretary/Treasurer

Reports on robotics used in manufacturing.
Cost: $60.00
8 Pages
Frequency: Quarterly
Mailing list available for rentat $95 per M
Printed in 2 colors on matte stock

7273 **SAWE Technical Papers**
Society of Allied Weight Engineers
5734 E. Lucia Walk
Long Beach, CA 90803-4015

562-596-2873
Fax: 562-596-2874
E-Mail: exdirector@sawe.org
Home Page: www.sawe.org

Patrick Brown, President
Jeffrey Cerro, Executive VP
Ronald Fox, Executive Director

The Technical Paper Index.
Frequency: Every 3 Years

7274 **Systems**
Institute of Industrial Engineers
25 Technology Pkwy S
Suite 150
Norcross, GA 30092-2946

770-449-0461
Fax: 770-263-8532

SL Browder, Publisher

Newsletter for IIE's society.
4 Pages
Frequency: Quarterly

7275 **The AOCS Newsletter**
American Oil Chemists' Society
2710 S Boulder Drive
P.O. Box 17190
Urbana, IL 61803-6996

217-359-2344
Fax: 217-351-8091
E-Mail: general@aocs.org
Home Page: www.aocs.org
Social Media: Facebook, Twitter, LinkedIn

Gloria Cook, Senior Director, Finance
Jeffry L. Newman, Senior Director, Programs

The AOCS Newsletter is sent electronically each month to approximately 4,200 AOCS members and 10,000 other related industry professionals. It contains the latest AOCS news, including discounted offers, upcoming meeting information and registration details, AOCS press releases, and technical services updates.
4500 Members
Frequency: Annual/April-May
Founded in 1909

7276 **Tribology Letters**
Kluwer Academic/Plenum Publishers
840 Busse Highway
Park Ridge, IL 60068-2376

847-825-5536
Fax: 847-825-1456
E-Mail: information@stle.org
Home Page: www.stle.org

Karl Phipps, Associate Managing Editor

Devoted to the development of the science of Tribology and to its applications. It also serves as the depository for new information on the mechanical properties of surfaces.
Frequency: 95x Yearly

7277 **Velocitus Officers Newsletter**
Theta Tau
815 Brazos
Suite 710
Austin, TX 78701

512-482-1904
800-264-1904
Fax: 512-472-4820
E-Mail: central.office@thetatau.org
Home Page: www.thetatau.org

Michael T Abraham, Executive Director
Dana Wortman, Grand Treasurer
Brandon J Satterwhite, Western Regional Director
Matthew Clark, Treasurer

Available by request via email or calling our 800 number.

Magazines & Journals

7278 **AFE Facilities Engineering Journal**
Association for Facilities Engineering
8160 Corporate Park Drive
#125
Cincinnati, OH 45242-3309

513-489-2473
Fax: 513-247-7422
E-Mail: Info@AFE.org
Home Page: www.afe.org

Gabriella Jacobs, Communications Manager
Bob Kruhm, Advertising Manager
Patrick Janszen, Art Director
Michael Ireland, Executive Director

Information on maintenance management, energy conservation, safety and security, computerized maintenance management systems, environmental compliance, telecommunications

and related issues.
Cost: $225.00
Frequency: Monthly
Circulation: 6000
ISSN: 1088-5900
Founded in 1956
Mailing list available for rent: 10000 names at $100 per M
Printed in 4 colors on glossy stock

7279 ASEE Prism
American Society for Engineering Education
1818 N St NW
#600
Washington, DC 20036-2476

202-331-3500
Fax: 202-265-8504
E-Mail: pubsinfo@asee.org
Home Page: www.asee.org

Frank L Huband, Executive Director
Mary Dalheim, Editor
Sherra E. Kerns, President

Geared towards educators in the engineering technology fields.
Frequency: Monthly
Circulation: 12000
Founded in 1893

7280 ASME News
American Society of Mechanical Engineers
3 Park Ave
New York, NY 10016-5902

212-591-7000
800-843-2763
Fax: 212-591-8676
E-Mail: infocentral@asme.org
Home Page: www.asme.org

Virgil R Carter, CEO
John G Falcioni, Managing Director
David Soukup, Managing Director

News, profiles and more from the American Society of mechanical engineers.
Cost: $125.00
Frequency: Monthly
Circulation: 125000
Founded in 1880
Printed in 4 colors on matte stock

7281 ASTM Standardization News
ASTM International
100 Barr Harbor Drive
PO Box C700
W Conshohocken, PA 19428-2959

610-832-9500
610-832-9500
Fax: 610-832-9555
E-Mail: service@astm.org
Home Page: www.astm.org

James A Thomas, President
Jeff Grove, Vice President

The official magazine of ASTM International, SATM Standardization news reports events in materials research and standardization.
Cost: $18.00
88 Pages
Frequency: Monthly
Circulation: 35000
Founded in 1898

7282 Advanced Materials & Processes
ASM International
9639 Kinsman Rd
Materials Park, OH 44073

440-338-5151
800-336-5152
Fax: 440-338-4634
Home Page: www.asminternational.org

Ed Kubel, Senior Editor
Julie Kalista, Editor
Joanne Miller, Production Manager

AM&P, the monthly technical magazine from ASM International, is designed to keep readers aware of leading-edge developments and trends in engineering materials - metals and alloys, engineering polymers, advanced ceramics, and composites - and the methods used to select, process, fabricate, test, and characterize them.
36000 Members
Frequency: Monthly
Circulation: 32M
Founded in 1977

7283 Aerospace Engineering
400 Commonwealth Drive
Warrendale, PA 15096-1

724-776-4841
Fax: 724-776-9765
Home Page: www.sae.org

JE Robertson PE, President
Robert E Spitzer, VP Aerospace
Raymond Morris, Executive Vice President
Richard Schaum, VP Automotive
Andrew Brown, Treasurer

Serves the international aerospace design and manufacturing field which consists of producers of airliners, helicopters, spacecraft, missiles, and power plants, propulsion systems, avionics, electronic/electrical systems, parts and components.
Cost: $75.00
Circulation: 28440
Founded in 1905

7284 American Consulting Engineer
American Council of Engineering Companies
1015 15th St
8th Floor NW
Washington, DC 20005-2605

202-347-7474
Fax: 202-898-0068
E-Mail: acec@acec.org
Home Page: www.acec.org
Social Media: Facebook, Twitter

David A Raymond, President

American Consulting Engineer serves engineers and surveyors who are employed by Consulting Engineering Firms, Architectural & Engineering Firms, and Surveying Firms.
Cost: $45.00
42 Pages
Frequency: Monthly
Circulation: 15841
ISSN: 1050-2203
Founded in 1905
Printed in 4 colors on glossy stock

7285 Annals of Biomedical Engineering
Biomedical Engineering Society
8201 Corporate Dr
Suite 1125
Landover, MD 20785-2224

301-459-1999
877-871-2637
Fax: 301-459-1999
E-Mail: info@bmes.org
Home Page: www.bmes.org

Edward L. Schilling, Executive Director
Barbara Colburn, Membership Director
Heather Comstock, Meeting Manager

Presents original research in the following areas: tissue and cellular engineering and biotechnology; biomaterials and biological interfaces; biological signal processing and instrumentation; biomechanics, rheology, and molecular motion; dynamical, regulatory, and integrative biology; transport phenomena, systems analysis and electrophysiology; imaging.
Frequency: Monthly

7286 Automotive Engineering International
Society of Automotive Engineers
400 Commonwealth Dr
Warrendale, PA 15086-7511

724-776-4841
877-606-7323
Fax: 724-776-5760
E-Mail: magazines@sae.org
Home Page: www.saesections.org

Richard O Schaum, President
Kevin Jost, Editor
J Robertson, President

For engineers involved in the auto design industry.
Cost: $120.00
125 Pages
Frequency: Monthly
Circulation: 124451
Founded in 1905

7287 Biomedical Engineering Society
8401 Corporate Dr
Suite 140
Hyattsville, MD 20785-2263

301-459-1999
Fax: 301-459-2444
E-Mail: info@bmes.org
Home Page: www.bmes.org

Barbara Dunlevy, Executive Director
Heather Comstock, Meeting Manager

Of interest to those in the biomedical engineering field. To promote the increase of biomedical engineering knowledge and its utilization.
Cost: $175.00
Frequency: Monthly
Founded in 1968
Printed in 8 colors on matte stock

7288 Bridge
National Academy of Engineering
500 5th Street NW
Washington, DC 20001

202-334-3200
Fax: 202-334-2290
Home Page: www.nae.edu

Charles M. Vest, President
Laura Mersky, Senior Executive Assistant

Solicited articles only. News related to the organization
Frequency: Quarterly
Circulation: 6500
Founded in 1954

7289 CET Magazine
American Society of Certified Engineering
PO Box 1348
Flowery Branch, GA 30542-0023

770-967-9173
Fax: 770-967-8049
Home Page: www.ascet.org

Russell E Freier, Chairman
Leo Saenz, CET, President
Kurt Schuler, Secretary/Treasurer

It contains technical, educational, notices of upcoming events, employment opportunities, legislative and informational articles. Also included are national, regional and local society news, reports and activities.
32 Pages
Frequency: Bi-Monthly
Founded in 1964
Printed in one color

7290 Chemical & Engineering News
American Chemical Society
1155 16th St Nw
Suite 600
Washington, DC 20036-4892

202-872-4600
800-227-5558

Fax: 202-872-4615
E-Mail: service@acs.org
Home Page: www.acs.org

Madeleine Jacobs, CEO

Professional magazine which covers all areas of interest to the chemical community, including business, science and government.
Frequency: Weekly
Founded in 1934

7291 **Civil Engineering**
American Society of Civil Engineers
1801 Alexander Bell Dr
Reston, VA 20191-4382

703-295-6300
800-548-2723
703-295-6300
Fax: 703-295-6222
E-Mail: member@asce.org
Home Page: www.asce.org

D Wayne Klotz, President
Virginia Fairweather, Editor-in-Chief
Anne Powell, Editor

Comprised of news, information and updates for the civil engineering industry.
Cost: $180.00
Frequency: Monthly
Circulation: 107,000
Founded in 1855
Printed in 4 colors

7292 **Clientship**
American Council of Engineering Companies
1015 15th St
8th Floor NW
Washington, DC 20005-2605

202-347-7474
Fax: 202-898-0068
E-Mail: acec@acec.org
Home Page: www.acec.org
Social Media: Facebook, Twitter

Dave Raymond, President
Frequency: Monthly

7293 **Community Matters**
Accreditation Board for Engineering & Technology
111 Market Place
Suite 1050
Baltimore, MD 21202-4012

410-347-7700
Fax: 410-625-2238
E-Mail: info@abet.org
Home Page: www.abet.org

Phillip E. Borrowman, President
Larry A. Kaye, President-Elect/VP
Frequency: Monthly
Founded in 1932

7294 **Composites Technology**
Ray Publishing
P.O.Box 992
Morrison, CO 80465-0992

303-467-1776
Fax: 303-467-1777
Home Page: www.raypubs.com

Judith Ray Hazen, Publisher/Editor
Michael Musselman, Managing Editor
Donna K. Dawson, Senior Editor
Susan Rush, Copy Editor
Dirk Weed, Global Sales Manager

To provide comprehensive coverage of the composites industry by focusing on the design, engineering, manufacture and performance of products made from this type of material. Particular attention is given to the transfer of technology from traditional end-use markets into high-volume commercial and industrial arenas.
Cost: $15.00
44 Pages
Circulation: 24000
ISSN: 1083-4117
Founded in 1993
Printed in 4 colors on glossy stock

7295 **Composites in Manufacturing**
Society of Manufacturing Engineers
1 SME Drive
PO Box 930
Dearborn, MI 48121

313-425-3000
800-733-4763
Fax: 313-425-3400
E-Mail: service@sme.org
Home Page: www.sme.org

Mark Tomlinson, Executive Director/General Manager
Greg Sheremet, Publisher
Bob Harris, Director Finance

Covers various aspects of composite materials used in manufacturing.
Frequency: Bi-Annual
Circulation: 20000
Founded in 1932
Mailing list available for rent: 13727 names at $95 per M

7296 **Computer-Aided Engineering**
Penton Media
249 W. 17th Street
New York, NY 10011

216-696-7000
Fax: 216-696-6662
E-Mail: information@penton.com
Home Page: www.penton.com

Sharon Rowlands, CEO

Database applications in design and manufacturing.
Cost: $50.00
96 Pages
Founded in 1982

7297 **Computing in Science & Engineering**
American Institute of Physics
2 Huntington Quad
Suite 1NO1
Melville, NY 11747-4502

516-576-2200
Fax: 516-349-7669
Home Page: www.aip.org

Darlene Walters, Senior VP
Angela Dombroski, CEO
Randolph Nanna, Publisher

Computer science's interdisciplinary juncture with physics, astronomy and engineering.
Cost: $42.00
Frequency: Monthly
Founded in 1931

7298 **Consulting-Specifying Engineer**
Reed Business Information
360 Park Avenue South
New York, NY 10010

646-746-6400
877-422-4637
Fax: 630-288-8781
E-Mail: e-letters@reedbusiness.com
Home Page: www.reedbusiness.com

Jeff Greisch, President
Jim Crockett, Chief Editor
Scott Siddens, Senior Editor

Serves engineering management and engineering personnel who perform mechanical and/or electrical engineering activities.
100 Pages
Frequency: Monthly
Circulation: 46,157
ISSN: 0892-5046
Founded in 1958
Printed in 4 colors on glossy stock

7299 **Control Solutions**
PennWell Publishing Company
1421 S Sheridan Rd
Tulsa, OK 74112-6619

918-831-9421
800-331-4463
Fax: 918-831-9476
Home Page: www.pennwell.com

Robert Biolchini, President
Ron Kuhfeld, Editor-in-Chief

A highly diversified, business-to-business media company providing authoritative print and online publications, conferences and exhibitions, research, databases, online exchanges and information products to strategic global markets.
Founded in 1910

7300 **Corrosion Journal**
NACE International
1440 S Creek Dr
Houston, TX 77084-4906

281-492-0535
Fax: 281-228-6300
Home Page: www.nace.org

Angela Jarrell, Managing Editor
Suzanne Moreno, Editorial Assistant

Recognized internationally as the world's leading research journal devoted exclusively to furthering corrosion science and engineering
Cost: $150.00
Frequency: Monthly
Circulation: 7800

7301 **Cost Engineering Journal**
AACE International
1265 Suncrest Towne Centre Drive
Morgantown, WV 26501-1876

304-296-8444
800-858-2678
Fax: 304-291-5728
E-Mail: info@aacei.org
Home Page: www.aacei.org

Michael R. Nosbisch, President
Marlene Hyde, President-Elect

International journal of cost estimation, cost/schedule control, and project management read by cost professionals around the world to get the most up-to-date information about the profession.
Frequency: Monthly

7302 **Cutting Tool Engineering**
CTE Publications
40 Skokie Blvd
Suite 395
Northbrook, IL 60062-1698

847-498-9100
Fax: 847-559-4444
E-Mail: alanr@jwr.com
Home Page: www.ctemag.com

John W Roberts, CEO
Don Nelson, CEO
Alan Rooks, Director

Serves manufacturing plants in the metal working industries.
Cost: $65.00
72 Pages
Frequency: Monthly
Circulation: 34871
ISSN: 0011-4189
Founded in 1955
Printed in 4 colors on glossy stock

7303 **Design News**
Reed Business Information

225 Wyman St
Waltham, MA 02451-1216

781-734-8000
Fax: 781-290-3178
Home Page: www.reedbusiness.com

Mark Finklestein, President
Karen Auguston Field, CFO
Stuart Whayman, CFO
Tracey Farina, Marketing,
Reck Allis, Circulation Manager

A magazine devoted exclusively to engineering design.
Frequency: Monthly
Circulation: 170114
Founded in 1958
Printed in 4 colors on glossy stock

7304 EE: Evaluation Engineering
Nelson Publishing
2500 Tamiami Trl N
Nokomis, FL 34275-3476

941-966-9521
800-226-6113
Fax: 941-966-2590
Home Page: www.healthmgttech.com

Kristine Russel, President
Phil Colpas, Managing Editor

Magazine devoted exclusively to companies that test, evaluate, design and manufacture electronic products and equipment.
Cost: $43.00
84 Pages
Frequency: Monthly
Circulation: 80000
Founded in 1962
Mailing list available for rent: 65,000 names
Printed in 4 colors on glossy stock

7305 Energy Engineering Journal
The Fairmont Press, Association of Energy Engineer
4025 Pleasantdale Road
Suite 420
Atlanta, GA 30340

770-447-5083
Fax: 770-446-3969
E-Mail: info@aeecenter.org
Home Page: www.aeecenter.org

Jennifer Vendola, Accountant
Ruth Whitlock, Executive Admin

Engineering solutions to cost efficiency problems and mechanical contractors who design, specify, install, maintain, and purchase non-residential heating, ventilating, air conditioning and refrigeration equipment and components.
Cost: $160.00
Circulation: 8000

7306 Energy Services Marketing Institute News
Association of Energy Engineers
4025 Pleasantdale Rd
Suite 420
Atlanta, GA 30340-4264

770-447-5083
Fax: 770-446-3969
E-Mail: info@aeecenter.org
Home Page: www.aeecenter.org

Eric A. Woodroot, President
Gary Hogsett, President-Elect
Paul Goodman, Treasurer
Laurie Wiegand-Jackson, Secretary

Subjects addressed include IPMVP Management and Verification Standard; Performance Contracting; Energy Project Financing and Energy Procurement.
Frequency: 3x Yearly

7307 Engineering Automation Report
Technology Automation Services
PO Box 3593
Englewood, CO 80155-3593

303-689-9099
Fax: 303-770-3660
Home Page: www.eareport.com/eareport

David Weisberg, Publisher
Steve Weisberg, Editor
Dave White, President

Internet/intranet technologies for use in engineering design are covered along with software news.
Cost: $235.00
Frequency: Monthly

7308 Engineering News Record
McGraw Hill
2 Penn Plaza
9th Floor
New York, NY 10121-2298

212-904-3507
Fax: 212-904-2820
E-Mail: scott_lewis@mcgraw-hill.com
Home Page: www.enr.com

Richard Korman, Managing Senior Editor
Ilan Kapla, Senior Manager
Keith Wallace, Production Editor

Provides the news, analysis, commentary and data that construction industry professionals need to do their jobs more effectively. ENR is the national news magazine for the construction industry.
Cost: $82.00
Frequency: Weekly
Circulation: 60000
Founded in 1874

7309 Engineering and Mining Journal
Primedia Business
29 N Wacker Drive
10th Floor
Chicago, IL 60606-2802

312-726-2802
Fax: 312-726-2574
E-Mail: pjohnson@mining-media.com
Home Page: www.mining-media.com

Peter Johnson, Publisher
Steve Fiscor, Managing Editor
Russ Carter, Managing Editor
Victor Matteucci, National Sales Manager

Serves the field of mining including exploration, development, milling, smelting, refining of metals and nonmetallics.
Cost: $79.00
Circulation: 20589
Founded in 1989
Mailing list available for rent
Printed in 4 colors

7310 Engineering in Medicine and Biology
445 Hoes Lane
Piscataway, NJ 08854-1331

732-981-0060
800-678-4333
Fax: 732-981-1721
E-Mail: customer-service@ieee.org
Home Page: www.spectrum.ieee.org/ieeemedia

DesirTe de Myer, Managing Editor
John Enderle, Editor
Susan Schneiderman, Business Development

Focuses on up-to-date biomedical engineering applications for engineers who are at the forefront of electrotechnology innovation.
Cost: $300.00
Circulation: 7983
ISSN: 0739-5175
Founded in 1988

7311 Environmental Engineer
American Academy of Environmental Engineers
130 Holiday Ct
Suite 100
Annapolis, MD 21401-7003

410-266-3311
Fax: 410-266-7653
Home Page: www.aaee.net

Joseph Cavarretta, Executive Director
J. Sammi Olmo, Manager

Articles dealing with environmental engineering practice issues and history.
Cost: $20.00
Frequency: Quarterly
Circulation: 12000
Founded in 1955
Mailing list available for rent

7312 Environmental and Engineering Geosciences
Association of Engineering Geologists
PO Box 460518
Denver, CO 80246

303-757-2926
Fax: 303-757-2969
E-Mail: aeg@aegweb.org
Home Page: www.aegweb.org

Dave Bieber, President
Darrel Schmitz, President-Elect/VP
Becky Roland, Chief Staff Executive
Terry West, Treasurer
Dorian Kuper, Secretary

Presents reviewed technical papers and discussions and book reviews related to the general field of engineering geology.
Frequency: Quarterly

7313 Experimental Mechanics
Society for Experimental Mechanics
2455 Teller Road
Thousand Oaks, CA 91320-1855

800-818-7243
Fax: 805-499-0871
E-Mail: info@sagepub.com
Home Page: www.sagepub.com

Thomas W Proulx, Publisher
N R Sottos, Editor
Hugh Bruck, Associate Tech Editor

Concentrates on advanced research and development. EM is the archival publication of the Society and is recognized as one of the many journals in engineering mechanics. Members receive free electronic access.
Cost: $767.04
Frequency: Quarterly
Circulation: 4500
Founded in 1965

7314 Experimental Techniques
Society for Experimental Mechanics
7 School St
Bethel, CT 06801-1855

203-790-6373
Fax: 203-790-4472
E-Mail: sem@sem1.com
Home Page: www.sem.org

Kathy Ramsey, Manager
Thomas Proulx, Executive Director

Focused on the techniques utilized in experimental mechanics. ET includes Society news, peer-reviewed technical articles and notes, new product information and much more. All members receive a printed copy of the journal and free electronic access.
Cost: $145.00
48 Pages
Circulation: 4000
Founded in 1943
Printed in 4 colors on glossy stock

7315 Exponent
Iowa Engineering Society

100 Court Ave
#102
Des Moines, IA 50309-2257

515-284-7055
Fax: 515-284-7301
E-Mail: ies@iaengr.org
Home Page: www.iaengr.org

David Scott, Executive Director
Brian E Roth, President

Supplies the Iowa engineering society members with vital information on issues and activities such as state legislation, education, ethics.
Cost: $6.00
26 Pages
Frequency: Quarterly
Circulation: 1000

7316 Facilities Engineering Journal
Association for Facilities Engineering
8160 Corporate Park Drive
Suite 125
Cincinnati, OH 45242

513-489-2473
Fax: 513-247-7422
E-Mail: Info@AFE.org
Home Page: www.afe.org

Gabriella Jacobs, Editor/Communications Manager

Provides you with practical, in-depth information on the key issues you face on the job every day.

7317 Fiberoptic Product News
Reed Business Information
100 Enterprise Drive
Suite 600
Rockaway, NJ 07866-912

973-920-7000
Fax: 973-920-7534
Home Page: www.fpnmag.com

Steve Wirth, VP/Group Publisher
Diane Himes, Editor
Kim Potts, Managing Editor
Ernest Worthman, Technical Editorial Director
R Reed, Owner

Edited for designers, engineers, researchers and management personnel who design, install and the buy the products and services that make up the fiberoptic marketplace.
Frequency: Monthly
Circulation: 35000
Founded in 1986
Printed in 4 colors on glossy stock

7318 Fusion Science and Technology
American Nuclear Society
555 N Kensington Ave
La Grange Park, IL 60526-5592

708-352-6611
Fax: 708-352-0499
Home Page: www.ans.org

Jack Tuohy, Executive Director
E James Reinsch, President-Elect/VP
Harry Bradley, Executive Director
William F Naughton, Treasurer

Is the source of information on fusion plasma physics and plasma engineering, fusion plasma enabling science and technology, fusion nuclear technology and material science, fusion applications, fusion design and system studies.
Cost: $1425.00
Frequency: 8x Yearly
Founded in 2005

7319 Geotechnical Fabrics Report
Industrial Fabrics Association International
1801 County Road B W
Roseville, MN 55113-4061

651-222-2508
800-225-4324
Fax: 651-631-9334
E-Mail: generalinfo@ifai.com
Home Page: www.ifai.com

Stephen Warner, CEO
Chris Kelsey, Editor
Susan.B Smeed, Assistant Circulation Manager
Miller Weldmaster, Director
JoAnne Ferris, Director of Marketing

Peer reviewed technical journal for civil engineers using geosynthetics in road construction, erosion control, hazardous waste, drainage, containment and reinforcement.
Cost: $49.00
Circulation: 16000
ISSN: 0882-4983
Founded in 1982
Printed in 4 colors on glossy stock

7320 Geotechnical Testing Journal
ASTM International
PO Box C700
W Conshohocken, PA 19428-0700

610-832-9500
Fax: 610-832-9555
E-Mail: service@astm.org
Home Page: www.astm.org

James A Thomas, President
Jeff Adkins, Manager
Fran Dougherty, Administrative Assistant

Provides a high quality publication that informs the profession of new developments in soil and rock testing and related fields; provides a forum for the exchange of information, particularly that which leads to the development of new test procedures; and to stimulate active participation of the profession in the work of ASTM International Committee D18 on Soil and Rock and related information.
Cost: $229.00
Frequency: Bi-Monthly

7321 Global Design News
Reed Business Information
360 Park Avenue South
New York, NY 10010

646-746-6400
877-422-4637
Fax: 630-288-8781
E-Mail: e-letters@reedbusiness.com
Home Page: www.reedbusiness.com

Jeff Greisch, President
Jim Crockett, Chief Editor
Scott Siddens, Senior Editor

Publication includes articles that cover the key product areas necessary for product development; reports on new technologies in the OEM industries, developments in the field of engineering design; and regular features on European product listings, technique and system updates.
Circulation: 30173
Founded in 1958

7322 Heat Transfer Engineering
Taylor & Francis Group Ltd
2 Park Square
Milton Park
Abingdon Oxford UK OX14 4RN

4.40207E+12
Fax: 4.40207E+12
Home Page: www.tandf.com.uk

James Edward, Publisher
Afshin Ghajar, Editor-in-Chief
Jack Taylor, Owner

Information on refereed papers of original work, state-of-the-art reviews, articles on new developments in equipment and practices and news items on people and companies in the field.

7323 Hispanic Engineer & Information Technology
Career Communications Group
729 E Pratt St
Suite 504
Baltimore, MD 21202-3302

410-244-7101
Fax: 410-752-1837
E-Mail: eaddison@ccgmag.com
Home Page: www.ccgmag.com

Jean Hamilton, Chief Financial Officer
Vishal Thakkar, Director of Marketing
Diane Jones, Director of Marketing
Christy Flemming, Director

Devoted to science and technology and to promoting opportunities in those fields for Hispanic Americans.
Cost: $13.00
56 Pages
ISSN: 1088-3452
Founded in 1982
Printed in 4 colors on glossy stock

7324 Hydraulics & Pneumatics
Penton Media
249 W. 17th Street
New York, NY 10011

212-204-4200
Fax: 216-696-6662
E-Mail: hp@penton.com
Home Page: www.penton.com

Sharon Rowlands, CEO
Nicola Allais, Executive VP

Issues highlight the application of new hydraulic and pneumatic components, new equipment research and listings, new design and literature innovations in fluid power and motion control systems.
Cost: $65.00
Frequency: Monthly
Circulation: 49,878
Founded in 1892

7325 ID International Design
F&W Publications
38 E 29th St
Floor 3
New York, NY 10016-7911

212-447-1400
Fax: 212-447-5231
E-Mail: idedit@fwpubs.com
Home Page: www.printmag.com

Joyce Rutter Kaye, VP
Julie Lasky, Editor - in - chief
Nicole Martin, Circualtion Manager
Barbara Schmitz, VP

The issues include news and features on computers, new technologies, case studies, design management, materials, aesthetics, new components and design trends. They also cover new sources, a calendar of events, personnel news, book reviews and products.
Cost: $30.00
Circulation: 19852
Founded in 1954

7326 IIE Solutions
Institute of Industrial Engineers
3577 Parkway Lane
Suite 200
Norcross, GA 30092

770-449-0460
800-494-0460
Fax: 770-441-3295
E-Mail: cs@iienet.org
Home Page: www.iienet.org

Don Greene, CEO
Donna Calvert, Chief Operating Officer

Listings, literature and news for executive engineers.
Cost: $66.00
Frequency: Monthly
Circulation: 26276
Founded in 1948

7327 InTents
Industrial Fabrics Association International
1801 Country Road BW
Roseville, MN 55113

651-222-2508
800-225-4324
Fax: 651-631-9334
E-Mail: jrwallace@ifai.com
Home Page: www.ifai.com

Peter F. McKernan, Chairman
Kevin Yonce, Vice Chairman

Promotes the use of tents and accessories to the special-event and general rental industries.
Cost: $39.00
Frequency: Bi-Monthly
Circulation: 12,000

7328 Industrial Equipment News
TCC Media Group
90 W Aftan Avenue
#117
Yardley, PA 19067

267-519-1705
800-733-1127
E-Mail: todd@ien.com
Home Page: www.ienonline.com/

Todd Baker, President

Serves the industrial field including manufacturing, mining, utilities, construction, transportation,governmental establishments, and educational services.
Frequency: Monthly
Circulation: 205000
ISSN: 0019-8258
Founded in 1933

7329 Inform
American Oil Chemists' Society
2710 S Boulder Drive
P.O. Box 17190
Urbana, IL 61803-6996

217-359-2344
Fax: 217-351-8091
E-Mail: general@aocs.org
Home Page: www.aocs.org
Social Media: Facebook, Twitter, LinkedIn

Gloria Cook, Senior Director, Finance & Operatio
Jeffry L. Newman, Senior Director, Programs

Inform magazine is an AOCS member benefit providing international news on fats, oils, surfactants, detergents, and related materials.
4500 Members
Frequency: Annual/April-May
Founded in 1909

7330 Innovation
Industrial Designers Society of America
45195 Business Court
Suite 250
Dulles, VA 20166-6717

703-707-6000
Fax: 703-787-8501
E-Mail: idsa@idsa.org
Home Page: www.idsa.org

Clive Roux, CEO
Annette Butler, Executive Assistant
Kaycee Childress, Marketing
Roxann Henze, Press, Media & Public Relations

IDSA is the world's oldest, largest, member-driven society for product design, industrial design, interaction design, human factors, ergonomics, design research, design management, universal design and related design fields. IDSA publishes Innovation, a quarterly on design. IDSA's charitable arm, the Design Foundation, supports the dissemination of undergraduate scholarships annually to further industrial design education.
Cost: $50.00
Frequency: Quarterly
Circulation: 3500
Founded in 1965

7331 Interface Magazine
Electrochemical Society
65 S Main St
Building D
Pennington, NJ 08534-2827

609-737-1902
Fax: 609-737-2743
E-Mail: interface@electrochem.org
Home Page: www.electrochem.org

Roque J Calvo, Executive Director
Mary E. Yess, Deputy Executive Director

Editorial material contains news, reviews, advertisements and articles on technical matters in the fields of electrochemical and solid state science and technology.
Cost: $61.97
Frequency: Quarterly
Circulation: 8000
Founded in 1902

7332 International Dredging Review
PO Box 1487
Fort Collins, CO 80522-1487

970-416-1903
Fax: 970-416-1878
E-Mail: editor@dredgemag.com
Home Page: www.dredgemag.com

Judith Powers, Publisher/Editor
Leonard F Cors, Business Manager
Nelson Spencer, Business Manager
Julia Leach, Production Manager

Targeted to dredging company executives, project managers and dredge crew members, suppliers and service people such as pump manufacturers, hydrographic surveyors, consulting engineers, etc.
Cost: $85.00
Circulation: 3300
ISSN: 0737-8181
Founded in 1981
Mailing list available for rent
Printed in 4 colors on glossy stock

7333 Iron & Steel Technology
Association for Iron & Steel Technolgy (AIST)
186 Thorn Hill Rd
Warrendale, PA 15086-7528

724-814-3000
Fax: 724-814-3001
E-Mail: memberservices@aist.org
Home Page: www.aist.org
Social Media: Facebook, Twitter, LinkedIn

Ron Ashburn, Executive Director
Lori Wharrey, Board Administrator
Chris McKelvey, Assistant Board Administrator

The official monthly publication of AIST, this is the premier technical journal for metallurgical, engineering, operating and maintenance personnel in the global iron and steel industry.
Cost: $20.00
Frequency: Monthly
Circulation: 9500

7334 JSME International Journal
American Society of Mechanical Engineers
3 Park Ave
New York, NY 10016-5902

212-591-7000
800-843-2763
Fax: 212-591-8676
E-Mail: infocentral@asme.org
Home Page: www.asme.org

Victoria Rockwell, President
Marc Goldsmith, President-Elect
David Soukup, Managing Director Operations

Provides advanced scientific and technological information for the mechanical engineering industry to facilitate the international exchange and transfer of technology.
Cost: $200.00
Frequency: Monthly

7335 Journal of Applied Mechanics
American Society of Mechanical Engineers
3 Park Ave
New York, NY 10016-5902

212-591-7000
800-843-2763
Fax: 212-591-8676
E-Mail: infocentral@asme.org
Home Page: www.asme.org

Victoria Rockwell, President
Marc Goldsmith, President-Elect

To serve as a vehicle for the communication of original research results of permanent interest in all branches of mechanics.
Cost: $60.00
Frequency: Bi-Monthly
ISSN: 0021-8936

7336 Journal of Biomechanical Engineering
American Society of Mechanical Engineers
3 Park Ave
New York, NY 10016-5902

212-591-7000
800-843-2763
Fax: 212-591-8676
E-Mail: infocentral@asme.org
Home Page: www.asme.org

Victoria Rockwell, President
Marc Goldsmith, President-Elect

Reports research results involving the application of mechanical engineering and knowledge, skills and principles to the conception, design, development, analysis, and operation of biomechanical systems, including; artificial organs and prostheses; bioinstrumentation and measurements; bio-heat transfer; biomaterials; biomechanics; bioprocess engineering; cellular mechanics; design and control of biological systems, and physiological systems.
Frequency: Bi-Monthly
ISSN: 0148-0731

7337 Journal of Construction Engineering and Management
American Society of Civil Engineers
1801 Alexander Bell Dr
Reston, VA 20191-4382

703-295-6300
800-548-2723
Fax: 703-295-6222
E-Mail: cybrarian@asce.org
Home Page: www.afce.org

D Wayne Klotz, President

Quality papers that aim to advance the science of construction engineering, to harmonize construction practices with design theories, and to further education and research in construction engineering and management.

7338 Journal of Engineering Education
American Society for Engineering Education

1818 N St NW
Suite 600
Washington, DC 20036-2476

202-331-3500
Fax: 202-265-8504
E-Mail: pubsinfo@asee.org
Home Page: www.asee.org

Frank L Huband, Executive Director

It serves as an archival record of scholarly research in engineering education.
Frequency: Quarterly
ISSN: 1069-4730

7339 Journal of Engineering for Industry
American Society of Mechanical Engineers
3 Park Ave
New York, NY 10016-5902

212-591-7000
800-843-2763
Fax: 212-591-8676
E-Mail: infocentral@asme.org
Home Page: www.asme.org

Virgil R Carter, CEO
David Soukup, Managing Director
William T Cousins, President

Covers interfaces of mechanical engineering.
Frequency: Quarterly
Circulation: 2162
Founded in 1880

7340 Journal of Forensic Sciences
ASTM International
PO Box C700
W Conshohocken, PA 19428-0700

610-832-9500
Fax: 610-832-9555
E-Mail: service@astm.org
Home Page: www.astm.org

James A Thomas, President
Jeff Adkins, Manager
Fran Dougherty, Administrative Assistant

Is the official publication of the American Academy of Forensic Sciences (AAFS). It is devoted to the publication of original investigations, observations, scholarly inquiries, and reviews in the various branches of the forensic sciences.
Cost: $249.00
Frequency: Bi-Monthly

7341 Journal of Management in Engineering
American Society of Civil Engineers
1801 Alexander Bell Dr
Reston, VA 20191-4382

703-295-6300
800-548-2723
Fax: 703-295-6222
E-Mail: cybrarian@asce.org
Home Page: www.afce.org

D Wayne Klotz, President

Examines contemporary issues associated with leadership and management for the twenty-first century civil engineer.

7342 Journal of Materials Engineering and Performance
ASM International
9639 Kinsman Road
Materials Park, OH 44073-0002

440-338-5151
800-336-5152
Fax: 440-338-4634
Home Page: www.asminternational.org

Jeane Deatherage, Administrator
Charles Hayes, Executive Director
Virginia Shirk, Executive Assistant

Peer-reviewed journal that publishes contributions on all aspects of materials selection, design, characterization, processing and performance testing. The journal for solving day-to-day engineering challenges - especially those involving components for larger systems.
Cost: $1965.00
Frequency: Bi-Monthly
Circulation: 305
Founded in 1992

7343 Journal of Petroleum Technology
Society of Petroleum Engineers
PO Box 833836
Richardson, TX 75083-3836

972-529-9300
800-456-6863
Fax: 972-952-9435
E-Mail: spedal@spe.org
Home Page: www.spe.org

Giovanni Paccaloni, President
Bill Cobb, VP Finance
John E Bethancourt, Director Management/Information
Ian Gorman, Director Production/Operations
Niki Bradbury, Managing Director

A suite of peer-reviewed, discipline-centered journals; books written by the industry's most honored professionals; and an online, 35,000-paper library.
Cost: $15.00
Frequency: Monthly

7344 Journal of Phase Equilibria
ASM International
9639 Kinsman Rd
Materials Park, OH 44072

440-338-5151
800-336-5152
Fax: 440-338-4634
Home Page: www.asminternational.org

Jeane Deatherage, Administrator
Charles Hayes, Executive Director
Virginia Shirk, Executive Assistant

Peer-reviewed journal that contains basic and applied research results, evaluated phase diagrams, a survey of current literature, and comments or other material pertinent to the previous three areas. The aim is to provide a broad spectrum of information concerning phase equilibria for the materials community.
Cost: $1965.00
Frequency: Bi-Monthly
Circulation: 305

7345 Journal of Process Control
Butterworth Heinemann
313 Washington Street
Suite 302
Newton, MA 02458-1626

617-928-5460
Fax: 617-928-5494

JD Perkins, Editor
T McAvoy, Regional Editor

Covers the application of control theory, operations research, computer science and engineering principles to the solution of process control problems.

7346 Journal of Quality Technology
American Society for Quality
600 N Plankinton Avenue
PO Box 3005
Milwaukee, WI 53201-3005

414-272-8575
800-248-1946
Fax: 414-272-1734
E-Mail: help@asq.org
Home Page: www.asq.org

Roberto M Saco, President
Mike Adams, Director
Erica Gumieny, Sales
Fay Spano, Communications/Media Relations

Published by the American Society for Quality, the JQT is a quarterly, peer-reviewed journal that focuses on the subject of quality control and the related areas of reliability and similar disciplines.
Cost: $30.00
100M Members
Frequency: Quarterly
Founded in 1946

7347 Journal of Rheology
Society of Rheology
2 Huntington Quadrangle
Suite 1N01
Meville, NY 11747-4502

516-576-2471
Fax: 516-576-2223
E-Mail: rheology@aip.org
Home Page: www.rheology.org

Faith A. Morrison, President
A. Jeffrey Giacomin, Vice President
Frequency: Bi-Monthly

7348 Journal of Surfactants and Detergents (JSD)
American Oil Chemists' Society
2710 S Boulder Drive
P.O. Box 17190
Urbana, IL 61803-6996

217-359-2344
Fax: 217-351-8091
E-Mail: general@aocs.org
Home Page: www.aocs.org
Social Media: Facebook, Twitter, LinkedIn

Gloria Cook, Senior Director, Finance
Jeffry L. Newman, Senior Director, Programs

Since 1998, JSD has remained dedicated to the practical and theoretical aspects of oleochemical and petrochemical surfactants, soaps and detergents. This growing quarterly scientific journal publishes peer-reviewed research papers, and reviews related to surfactants and detergents technologies.
4500 Members
Frequency: Annual/April-May
Founded in 1909

7349 Journal of Testing and Evaluation
ASTM International
PO Box C700
W Conshohocken, PA 19428-0700

610-832-9500
Fax: 610-832-9555
E-Mail: service@astm.org
Home Page: www.astm.org

James A Thomas, President
Jeff Adkins, Manager
Fran Dougherty, Administrative Assistant

Provides a multidisciplinary forum for applied sciences and engineering.
Cost: $249.00
Frequency: Bi-Monthly

7350 Journal of Thermal Spray Technology
ASM International
9639 Kinsman Rd
Materials Park, OH 44072-9603

440-338-5151
800-336-5152
Fax: 440-338-4634
Home Page: www.asminternational.org

Jeane Deatherage, Administrator
Charles Hayes, Executive Director
Virginia Shirk, Executive Assistant

Peer-reviewed journal which publishes contributions on all aspects, fundamental and practical, of thermal spray science, including processes, feedstock manufacture, testing and characterization. As the primary vehicle for thermal spray information transfer, its mission is to synergize the rapidly advancing thermal

spray industry and related industries by presenting research and development efforts leading to advancements in implementable engineering applications of the technology.
Cost: $1577.00
Frequency: Bi-Monthly
Circulation: 680
Founded in 1952

7351 **Journal of the Acoustical Society of America**
Acoustical Society of America
2 Huntington Quad
Suite 1N01
Melville, NY 11747-4505
516-576-2360
Fax: 516-576-2377
E-Mail: asa@aip.org
Home Page: www.asa.aip.org
Charles E Schmid, President
Distributed free to members.
Cost: $1545.00
7000 Pages
Frequency: Monthly

7352 **Journal of the American Oil Chemists' Society (JAOCS)**
American Oil Chemists' Society
2710 S Boulder Drive
P.O. Box 17190
Urbana, IL 61803-6996
217-359-2344
Fax: 217-351-8091
E-Mail: general@aocs.org
Home Page: www.aocs.org
Social Media: Facebook, Twitter, LinkedIn
Gloria Cook, Senior Director, Finance
Jeffry L. Newman, Senior Director, Programs
Since 1947, the Journal of the American Oil Chemists' Society has been the leading source for technical papers related to the fats and oils industries. JAOCS is a monthly, peer-reviewed journal devoted to fundamental and practical research, production, processing, packaging and distribution in the growing field of fats, oils, proteins and other related substances.
4500 Members
Frequency: Annual/April-May
Founded in 1909

7353 **Journal of the Electrochemical Society**
Electrochemical Society
65 S Main St
Building D
Pennington, NJ 08534-2827
609-737-1902
Fax: 609-737-2743
E-Mail: ecs@electrochem.org
Home Page: www.electrochem.org
Roque J Calvo, Executive Director
Mary E. Yess, Deputy Executive Director
Roque Calvo, Manager
Contains technical papers covering basic research and technology.
Cost: $63.00
Circulation: 8300
Founded in 1902

7354 **LD&A**
Illuminating Engineering Society of North America
120 Wall Street
17th Floor
New York, NY 10005
212-248-5000
Fax: 212-248-5017
E-Mail: ies@ies.org
Home Page: www.ies.org
Denis Lavoie, President
Chip Israel, Vice President
A magazine for professionals involved in the art, science, study, manufacture, teaching and implementation of lighting. LD&A is designed to enhance and improve the practice of lighting. Free to members.
Cost: $44.00
Frequency: Monthly
Circulation: 7000
ISSN: 0360-6325
Mailing list available for rent: 8000 names

7355 **LEUKOS, The Journal Of IES**
Illuminating Engineering Society of North America
120 Wall Street
17th Floor
New York, NY 10005
212-248-5000
Fax: 212-248-5017
E-Mail: ies@ies.org
Home Page: www.ies.org
Denis Lavoie, President
Chip Israel, Vice President
LEUKOS serves members of the IES, the lighting community, and the public. The journal contains international technical developments of current interest and lasting importance relating to illuminating engineering and lighting design. Free to members, online.
Cost: $250.00
Frequency: Quarterly
ISSN: 1550-2729
Mailing list available for rent: 8000 names

7356 **Lighting Design & Application**
Illuminating Engineering Society of North America
120 Wall St
17th Floor
New York, NY 10005-4001
212-248-5000
Fax: 212-248-5017
E-Mail: iesna@iesna.org
Home Page: www.ies.org
Denis Lavoie, President
Chip Israel, Vice President
Is a magazine for professionals involved in the art, science, study, manufacture, teaching and implementation of lighting. LD+A is designed to enhance and improve the practice of lighting. Every issue of LD+A includes feature articles on design projects, technical articles on the science of illumination, new product developments, industry trends, news of the Illuminating Engineering Society and vital information about the illuminating profession.
Cost: $32.00
Frequency: Monthly
Circulation: 8000
ISSN: 0360-6325

7357 **Lipids**
American Oil Chemists' Society
2710 S Boulder Drive
P.O. Box 17190
Urbana, IL 61803-6996
217-359-2344
Fax: 217-351-8091
E-Mail: general@aocs.org
Home Page: www.aocs.org
Social Media: Facebook, Twitter, LinkedIn
Gloria Cook, Senior Director, Finance
Jeffry L. Newman, Senior Director, Programs
Introduced in 1966, Lipids is a premier journal published in the lipid field today. This monthly scientific journal features full-length original research articles, short communications, methods papers and review articles on timely topics. All papers are meticulously peer-reviewed and edited by some of the foremost experts in their respective fields.
4500 Members
Frequency: Annual/April-May
Founded in 1909

7358 **Low Temperature Physics**
200 Huntington Quadrangle
Suite 1N01
Melville, NY 11747-4502
516-516-2270
Fax: 516-349-9704

7359 **Machine Design**
1300 E 9 Street
Cleveland, OH 44114-2518
216-696-7000
847-763-9670
Fax: 216-696-0177
E-Mail: mdeditor@penton.com
Home Page: www.machinedesign.com
Leland Teschler, Editor
Ken Korane, Managing Editor
Bobbie Macy, Circulation Manager
The only magazine for applied technology for design engineering edited for design engineers and engineering managers. It covers new products and design practices in the fields of mechanical, electromechanical, electronics, motion control and process engineering.
Circulation: 180000
Founded in 1929

7360 **Maintenance Solutions**
Trade Press Publishing Corporation
2100 W Florist Avenue
Milwaukee, WI 53209
414-228-7701
Fax: 414-228-1134
E-Mail: contact@facilitiesnet.com
Home Page: www.facilitiesnet.com/
Dick Yake, Editorial Director
Dan Hounsell, Editor
Brad R. Ehlert, VP
Brian Terry, Publisher
Renee Gryzkewicz, Associate Editor
How to articles and features designed to alleviate reader problems as well as new product information and applications.
Cost: $45.00
42 Pages
Frequency: Monthly
Circulation: 35000
ISSN: 1072-3560
Founded in 1993

7361 **Maintenance Technology**
Applied Technology Publications
1300 S Grove Ave
Suite 105
Barrington, IL 60010-5246
847-382-8100
Fax: 847-304-8603
Home Page: www.mt-online.com
Jane Alexander, Editor-in-Chief
Rick Carter, Executive Editor
Randy Buttstadt, Director of Creative Services
Maintenance Technology magazine serves the business and technical information needs of managers and engineers responsible for assuring availability of plant equipment and systems. It provides readers with articles on advanced technologies, strategies, tools, and services for the life-cycle management of capital assets.
Frequency: Monthly
Circulation: 50,827

Mailing list available for rent: 35,263 names at $$15 per M

7362 **Marine Fabricator**
Industrial Fabrics Association International
1801 County Road B W
Roseville, MN 55113-4061

651-222-2508
800-225-4324
Fax: 651-631-9334
E-Mail: generalinfo@ifai.com
Home Page: www.ifai.com

Peter F. McKernan, Chairman
Kevin Yonce, Vice Chairman

Educates and informs 5,000 marine shop professionals and also provides reportage that reflects the innovations and trends of the industry.
Cost: $34.00
Frequency: Bi-Monthly

7363 **Material Handling Business**
Penton Media
249 W. 17th Street
New York, NY 10011

212-204-4200
Fax: 216-696-6662
E-Mail: information@penton.com
Home Page: www.penton.com

Sharon Rowlands, CEO
Nicola Allais, Executive VP
Antoinette Sanchez Perkins, Circulation Manager

Journal written for design engineering managers, system integrates, material handling distributors and manufacturing sales executives.
86 Pages
Circulation: 92836
Founded in 1892
Printed in 4 colors on glossy stock

7364 **Materials Performance**
NACE International
1440 S Creek Dr
Houston, TX 77084-4906

281-492-0535
800-797-6223
Fax: 281-228-6300
E-Mail: stephanie.garner@nace.org
Home Page: www.nace.org

Oliver Moghissi, President
Kevin Garrity, Vice President

Provides current news and features, practical data, and information on new products and services in the corrosion industry.
Frequency: Monthly
Circulation: 22000
Founded in 1943

7365 **Materials at High Temperatures**
Butterworth Heinemann
313 Washington Street
Newton, MA 02458-1626

617-928-5460
Fax: 781-933-6333

T Suzuki, Co-Editor
TB Gibbons, Co-Editor

Serves the needs of those developing and using materials for high temperature applications in the power, chemical, engine, processing and furnace industries.

7366 **Measurements and Control News**
Measurements and Data Corporation
100 Wallace Avenue
Suite 100
Sarasota, FL 34237

941-954-8405
Fax: 941-366-5743

Ken Kemski, Editor-in-Chief
Kristine Burmester, Associate Editor

Serves engineers, technichians, scientists, and other professionals involved in the recommendation and specification, of instuments and devices for measurement, inspection, testing, analysis, computing, and control.
Frequency: Bi-Monthly

7367 **Medical Equipment Designer**
Adams Business Media
6001 Cuchran Road
Suite 300
Cleveland, OH 44139

216-249-9444
Fax: 440-248-0187
Home Page: www.medicaldesigner.com

Terry Person, Publisher
Steve Wafalosky, Publisher

Published for the design function as it relates specifically to medical manufacturing and design of materials, components and complete systems.
1004 Pages
Frequency: Bi-Monthly
Circulation: 15,000
Founded in 1985
Printed in 4 colors on glossy stock

7368 **Medical Physics**
2 Huntington Quadrangle
Suite 1N01
Melville, NY 11747
516-576-2200
Fax: 516-576-2481
Home Page: www.aip.org

Bill Hendee, Editor
Founded in 1931

7369 **Microwave and RF**
Penton Media
45 Eisenhower Drive
5th Floor
Paramus, NJ 07652
201-452-2400
800-829-9028
Fax: 201-845-2493
Home Page: www.mwrf.com

Jack Browne, Publisher/Editor
Dawn Prior, Editorial Assistant
Dedicated to educating senior level design engineers, engineering managers, both domestic and foreign, who work all types of microwave systems, subsystems and components.
Cost: $81.00
Frequency: Monthly
Circulation: 47000
Founded in 1967
Mailing list available for rent
Printed in on glossy stock

7370 **Modern Materials Handling**
Reed Business Information
275 Washington St
Newton, MA 02458-1611

617-964-3030
Fax: 617-630-3925
E-Mail: support@designnews.com
Home Page: www.designnews.com

Peter Boniface, Publisher
Raymond Kulwiec, Editor
James A Casella, CEO
Jason Cassidy, VP
Greg Flores, Senior Vice President

The magazine for managers and engineers responsible for handling materials and managing inventories in manufacturing, warehousing and distribution.
Frequency: 14x Yearly
Founded in 1977
Printed in 4 colors on glossy stock

7371 **Motion Control**
ISA Services
Po Box 12277
Resrch Trngle P, NC 27709-2277

919-549-8411
Fax: 919-549-8288
E-Mail: info@isa.org
Home Page: www.isa.org

Pat Gouhin, Executive Director

Information for those who design and maintain motion control systems.
Cost: $54.00
56 Pages
Circulation: 41000
ISSN: 1058-4644
Founded in 1945
Printed in 4 colors on glossy stock

7372 **Motion System Distributor**
Penton Media
249 W. 17th Street
New York, NY 10011

212-204-4200
800-249-9365
Fax: 216-696-6662
E-Mail: information@penton.com
Home Page: www.penton.com

Sharon Rowlands, CEO
Nicola Allais, Executive VP
Larry Berardinis, Editor

Provides selling and technical information to individuals and distributors specializing in power transmission, motion control and fluid products.
Cost: $65.00
Frequency: Monthly
Circulation: 54,000
Founded in 1892

7373 **NSBE Magazine**
National Society of Black Engineers
1454 Duke Street
Alexandria, VA 22314-3403

703-549-2207
Fax: 703-683-5312
E-Mail: office@nsbe.org
Home Page: www.nsbe.org

Pamela D Sharif, Publisher
Carl Mack, Manager
George Bowman, Manager

Coverage of all aspects of manufacturing engineering, geared towards black technical professionals.
Cost: $30.00
Circulation: 100000
Printed in 4 colors on glossy stock

7374 **Naval Engineers Journal**
American Society of Naval Engineers
1452 Duke Street
Alexandria, VA 22314-3458

703-836-6727
Fax: 703-836-7491
E-Mail: asnehq@navalengineers.org
Home Page: www.navalengineers.org

Susan King, Editor

It contains technical papers authored by professionals engaged in naval and related engineering fields. Its high quality content is sought by those with an interest in topics of importance to the advancement of naval engineering.
Frequency: Quarterly

7375 **New Equipment Digest**
Penton Media
1300 E 9th St
Cleveland, OH 44114-1503

216-696-7000
Fax: 216-696-1752
E-Mail: information@penton.com
Home Page: www.penton.com

Sharon Rowlands, CEO
Dave Madonia, Publisher
Robert.F King, Editor
Nicola Allais, Executive VP & CEO

New Equipment Digest serves the general industrial field which includes manufacturing, processing, engineering services, construction, transportation, mining, public utilities, wholesale distributors, educational services, libraries and governmental establishments.
Cost: $65.00
Frequency: Monthly
Circulation: 206006
Founded in 1936

7376 **Noise Control Engineering Journal**
Institute of Noise Control Engineering
62 Timberline Drive, Arlington Branch
PO Box 3206
Poughkeepsie, NY 12603-0206

845-462-4006
Fax: 845-463-0201
Home Page: www.ince.org

Alan Marsh, Editor

Includes articles on hearing protection, modal analysis, and signal processing. Information is refereed, authoritative, and technical.
Cost: $110.00
Frequency: Bi-Monthly
Circulation: 2,000
ISSN: 0736-2501

7377 **Noise/News International**
Institute of Noise Control Engineering
9100 Purdue Road
Suite 200
Indianapolis, IN 46268

317-735-4063
E-Mail: ibo@inceusa.org
Home Page: www.inceusa.org

James K Thompson, President
Rich Peppin, Advertising/Expo Manager

Contains not only news items but also feature articles on a wide variety of topics of broad interest in noise control engineering.
Cost: $60.00
Frequency: Quarterly
ISSN: 1021-643X

7378 **Nuclear Science and Engineering**
American Nuclear Society
555 N Kensington Ave
La Grange Park, IL 60526-5592

708-352-6611
Fax: 708-352-0499
Home Page: www.ans.org

Jack Tuohy, Executive Director
E James Reinsch, President-Elect/VP
Harry Bradley, Executive Director
William F Naughton, Treasurer

The journal is widely recognized as an outstanding source of information on research in all scientific areas related to the peaceful use of nuclear energy and radiation. Technical papers, notes, critical reviews, and computer code abstracts are presented.
Cost: $1200.00
Frequency: 9x Yearly
Founded in 1956

7379 **Nuclear Technology**
American Nuclear Society
555 N Kensington Ave
La Grange Park, IL 60526-5592

708-352-6611
Fax: 708-352-0499
Home Page: www.ans.org

Jack Tuohy, Executive Director
E James Reinsch, President-Elect/VP
Harry Bradley, Executive Director
William F Naughton, Treasurer

Leading international publication reporting on new information in all areas of the practical application of nuclear science. Topics include all aspects of reactor technology: operations, safety materials, instrumentation, fuel, and waste management. Also covered are medical uses, radiation detection, production of radiation, health physics, and computer applications,
Cost: $1315.00
Frequency: Monthly
Founded in 2005

7380 **Off-Highway Engineering**
SAE
400 Commonwealth Dr
Warrendale, PA 15086-7511

724-776-4841
Fax: 724-776-5760
Home Page: www.saesections.org

Richard O Schaum, President
Mark Davies, Editor-In-Chief

Off-Highway Engineering serves the international off highway design and manufacturing field which consists of producers of construction, lawn and garden, agricultural equipment, and industrial vehicles. Also served are makers of engines and parts and components and others allied to the field.
Cost: $70.00
66 Pages
Circulation: 16308
ISSN: 1074-6919
Founded in 1905
Printed in 4 colors on glossy stock

7381 **Optics and Spectroscopy**
Optical Society of America
2010 Massachusetts Ave Nw
Washington, DC 20036-1023

202-223-8130
Fax: 202-223-1096
E-Mail: info@osa.org
Home Page: www.osa.org

Elizabeth Rogan, Executive Director
Elizabeth Nolan, Chief Publishing Officer

Optics and Spectroscopy covers such topics as multiphoton spectroscopy, phase conjugation, holography, scattering, and quantum electronics.
Frequency: Monthly
Founded in 1916

7382 **PM Engineer**
Business News Publishing Company
2401 W Big Beaver Road
Suite 700
Troy, MI 48084

248-362-3700
Home Page: www.bnpmedia.com

Katie Rotella, Manager

Provides technical sheets, manufacturer product brochures, news features and analysis of useful industry information on the engineering and design of plumbing, piping, hydronics, cooling/heating, and fire protection/sprinkler systems. Free to trade engineers.
Cost: $64.00
80 Pages
Frequency: Monthly
Circulation: 25000
Founded in 1970
Printed in 4 colors on glossy stock

7383 **PT Design**
Penton Media
1300 E 9th St
Cleveland, OH 44114-1503

216-696-7000
Fax: 216-696-1752
E-Mail: information@penton.com
Home Page: www.penton.com

Sharon Rowlands, CEO
David Madonia, Publisher

Blends state-of-the-art motion system designs with traditional electrical and mechanical technology for the system designer. Also features articles on new products and technology, industry trends and application ideas.
Cost: $ 65.00
Frequency: Monthly
Circulation: 54000
Founded in 1892

7384 **PT Distributor**
Reed Business Information
2000 Clearwater Dr
Oak Brook, IL 60523-8809

630-288-8000
Fax: 630-288-8781
Home Page: www.reedbusiness.com

Mark Kelsey, Global CEO
Jeff DeBalko, President, Media Division

provides information on selling techniques, fiscal and personnel management, purchasing, improving profits, training, and inventory and warehousing control.
Cost: $30.00
Frequency: Bi-Monthly
Circulation: 10,000

7385 **Pharmaceutical Engineering**
Int'l Society for Pharmaceutical Engineering
600 N Westshore Blvd.
Suite 900
Tampa, FL 33609

813-960-2105
Fax: 813-264-2816
E-Mail: ask@ispe.org
Home Page: www.ispe.org

Charles DiMarco, Director of Marketing
Danielle Hould, Communications Manager
Angie Brumley, Publications Coordinator
Valerie Adams, Advertising Sales Coordinator

Journal is published bi monthly for members only and is considered by ISPE members to be the number one member benefit. Feature articles provide practical application and specification information on the design, construction, supervision and maintenance of process equipment, plant systems, instrumentation and facilities.
Circulation: 13138

7386 **Plant Engineering**
Reed Business Information
8878 Barrons Blvd
Littleton, CO 80129-2345

303-470-4000
800-446-6551
Fax: 303-470-4691
E-Mail: subsmail@reedbusiness.com
Home Page: www.reedbusiness.com

Tim Myers, Executive
Bobbie Wisniewski, Advertising Production Manager
Rick Ellis, Circulation Manager
Rick Dunn, Editor
Jim Silvestri, Managing Editor

Provides a constant reminder of engineering products and services and helps keep your company at the top of your customers' minds.
Frequency: Monthly
Circulation: 100034
Founded in 1947

7387 **Plant Services**
Putman Media
555 W Pierce Rd
Suite 301
Itasca, IL 60143-2626

630-467-1301
800-984-7644
Fax: 630-467-0197
Home Page: www.putman.net

John Cappelletti, CEO
Mike Bacidore, Editor-in-Chief
Mike Brenner, Group Publisher
Keith Larson, VP Content

The newsletters reach a monthly world wide audience of more than 150,000 professionals responsible for optimizing the productivity and insuring the reliability of manufacturing plants, facilities and utilities in North America and across the globe.
Cost: $96.00
Frequency: Monthly
Circulation: 80100
ISSN: 0199-8013
Founded in 1938
Mailing list available for rent: 10,000 names
Printed in 4 colors on glossy stock

7388 **Plastics Engineering**
Society of Plastics Engineers
13 Church Hill Rd
Newtown, CT 06470

203-775-0471
Fax: 203-775-8490
E-Mail: info@4spe.org
Home Page: www.4spe.org

Susan Oderwald, Executive Director

A communication to SPE's global audience of plastics professionals about current developments in the industry, technology, and activities of the Society.
Frequency: Monthly

7389 **Plumbing Engineer**
Delta Communications
1167 W Bluemound Road
Wauwatosa, WI 53226

262-542-8820
Fax: 262-542-9111
E-Mail: delta@deltacommunications.com
Home Page: www.deltacommunications.com

Edwin Scott, Editor

Offers news and updates to plumbing engineers and manufacturers.
Cost: $35.00
Frequency: Monthly
Founded in 1973

7390 **Plumbing Standard Magazine**
American Society of Sanitary Engineering
901 Canterbury Rd
Suite A
Cleveland, OH 44145-1480

440-835-3040
Fax: 440-835-3488
Home Page: www.asse-plumbing.org

Ken Van Wagnen, Manager
Donald Summers, First VP
Steve Silber, Second VP
Scott Hamilton, Third VP
Shannon Corcoran, Executive Director

This magazine includes technical articles, current information on codes, standards, and other developments in the plumbing industry and related fields. Free with membership.
Cost: $12.00
Frequency: Quarterly

7391 **Powder Diffraction**
International Center for Diffraction Data
12 Campus Boulevard
Newton Square, PA 19073-3200

610-325-9814
Fax: 610-325-9823
E-Mail: info@icdd.com
Home Page: www.icdd.com

Timothy Fawcett, Executive Director
Cathyann Colaiezzi, Managing Editor
Theresa Kahmer, Publication Manager

A quarterly journal devoted to the use of the powder method for material characterization is available on annual subscription. The journal focus is on materials. Characterization employing x-ray powder diffraction and related techniques.
Cost: $90.00
Frequency: Quarterly
Founded in 1941

7392 **Powder and Bulk Engineering**
CSC Publishing
1155 Northland Dr
St Paul, MN 55120-1288

651-287-5600
Fax: 651-287-5650
Home Page: www.cscpublishinginc.com

Richard R Cress, Publisher
Terry O' Neill, Editor

Featured editorial includes technical articles, case histories, test centers, product news and literature, and industry news items.
Cost: $100.00
Frequency: Monthly

7393 **Power Engineering International**
PennWell Publishing Company
1421 S Sheridan Rd
Tulsa, OK 74112-6619

918-835-3161
800-331-4463
Fax: 918-831-9497
E-Mail: candiced@pennwell.com
Home Page: www.pennwell.com

Robert Biolchini, President
Brian Schimmoller, Managing Editor

Serves the global electric power generation and transmission industry.
Cost: $180.00
Frequency: Monthly
ISSN: 1069-4994
Founded in 1896

7394 **Precision Engineering**
Elsevier Science
PO Box 10826
Raleigh, NC 27605-0826

919-839-8444
Fax: 919-839-8039
Home Page: www.aspe.net

W T Estler, Editor-in-Chief

Is the foremost international journal devoted to the study of ultra-high precision engineering and metrology.

7395 **Printed Circuit Design**
CMP Media
240 West 35th Street
New York, NY 10001

516-562-5000
Fax: 415-947-6090
Home Page: www.cmp.com

David Levin, CEO

7396 **Process Heating**
Business News Publishing Company
155 Pfingsten Road
Suite 205
Deerfield, IL 60015

847-405-4000
Fax: 248-502-1001
E-Mail: PHeditors@bnpmedia.com
Home Page: www.process-heating.com
Social Media: Facebook, Twitter

Anne Armel, Publisher
Linda Becker, Associate Publisher & Editor
Beth McClelland, Production Manager

Magazine covers heat processing at temperatures up to 1000 degrees F at end user and OEM plants in 9 industries. Follow us at twitter.com/ProcessHeating, www.facebook.com/ProcessHeating
Circulation: 25000
Founded in 1994

7397 **Processing**
Putman Media
PO Box 698
Birmingham, AL 35243

888-431-2877
Fax: 205-408-3797
E-Mail: webmaster@grandviewmedia.com
Home Page: www.grandviewmedia.com

Dennis Van Milligen, Editor in Chief
Mike Wasson, Publisher

Offers information on printing, publishing and processing. Information is given on the latest technology in these and other desktop industries.
Cost: $15.00
53 Pages
Frequency: Monthly
Founded in 1960

7398 **Product Design and Development**
Reed Business Information
301 Gibraltar Drive
Box 650
Morris Plains, NJ 07950

973-292-5100
Fax: 630-288-8686
Home Page: www.reedbusiness.com

Stuart Whayman, CFO

7399 **Product Development Best Practices Report**
Management Roundtable
92 Crescent St
Waltham, MA 02453-4315

781-891-8080
Fax: 781-398-1889
Home Page: www.pharmcentric.com

Stewart Maws, Owner

The goal of this publication is to help firms market, manufacture and design better products at a lower rate.
Cost: $219.00
Frequency: Monthly

7400 **Professional Safety Journal**
American Society of Safety Engineering
1800 E Oakton Street
Des Plaines, IL 60018

847-699-2929
Fax: 847-768-3434
E-Mail: customerservice@asse.org
Home Page: www.asse.org
Social Media: Facebook, Twitter, LinkedIn

Fred Fortman, Executive Director
Bruce Sufranski, Finance/Controller Director
Diane Hurns, Manager Public Relations Department
Sally Madden, Human Resources Manager

The American Society of Safety Engineers (ASSE) is the oldest professional safety society committed to protecting people, property and

the environment. ASSE has more than 32,000 occupational safety, health and environmental (SH&E) professional members who manage, supervise, research and consult on safety, health, transportation and the environment in all industries, government, labor and education.
34000 Members
Frequency: Monthly
Circulation: 40,000
Founded in 1911

7401 **Quality Engineering**
American Society for Quality
600 N Plankinton Avenue
PO Box 3005
Milwaukee, WI 53201-3005

414-272-8575
800-248-1946
Fax: 414-272-1734
E-Mail: help@asq.org
Home Page: www.asq.org

Roberto M Saco, President
Paul E Borawski, CEO
Erica Gumieny, Sales
Fay Spano, Communications/Media Relations

Co-published with Taylor and Francis, this journal is for professional practitioners and researchers whose goal is quality engineering improvements and solutions.
Cost: $34.75
100M Members
Frequency: Quarterly/Members Price
Founded in 1946

7402 **Quality Management Journal**
American Society for Quality
600 N Plankinton Avenue
PO Box 3005
Milwaukee, WI 53201-3005

414-272-8575
800-248-1946
Fax: 414-272-1734
E-Mail: help@asq.org
Home Page: www.asq.org

Roberto M Saco, President
Paul E Borawski, CEO
Erica Gumieny, Sales
Fay Spano, Communications/Media Relations

Published by the American Society for Quality, the QMT is a quarterly, peer-reviewed journal that focuses on the subject of quality management practice and provides a discussion forum for both practitioners and academics in the area of research.
Cost: $50.00
100M Members
Frequency: Quarterly
Founded in 1946

7403 **Quality Progress**
American Society for Quality
600 N Plankinton Avenue
PO Box 3005
Milwaukee, WI 53201-3005

414-272-8575
800-248-1946
Fax: 414-272-1734
E-Mail: help@asq.org
Home Page: www.asq.org

Roberto M Saco, President
Paul E Borawski, CEO
Erica Gumieny, Sales
Fay Spano, Communications/Media Relations

Published by the American Society for Quality, the QP is a peer-reviewed journal that focuses on the subject of quality control, discussing the usage and implementation of quality principles including the subject areas of organizational behavior, knowledge management and process improvement.
Cost: $55.00
100M Members
Founded in 1946

7404 **RSES Journal**
Refrigeration Service Engineers Society
1666 Rand Rd
Des Plaines, IL 60016-3552

847-297-6464
800-297-5660
Fax: 847-297-5038
E-Mail: general@rses.org
Home Page: www.rses.org
Social Media: Facebook, Twitter, LinkedIn

Robert Sherman, President
Lawrence Donaldson, Vice President
Wes Maxfield, Secretary Treasurer

Providing quality technical content in digital and printed forms that can be applied on the job site.
Frequency: Monthly
Circulation: 15231

7405 **Radwaste Solutions**
American Nuclear Society
555 N Kensington Ave
La Grange Park, IL 60526-5592

708-352-6611
Fax: 708-352-0499
Home Page: www.asn.org

Jack Tuohy, Executive Director
E James Reinsch, President-Elect/VP
Harry Bradley, Executive Director
William F Naughton, Treasurer
Cal Poly, Vice President

Containing articles that discuss practical approaches and solutions to everyday problems and issues in all fields of radioactive waste management and environmental restoration.
Cost: $455.00
Frequency: Bi-Monhtly
Founded in 2005

7406 **Reliability Engineering and Management Proceedings**
7340 N La Oesta Ave
Tucson, AZ 85704-3119

520-621-6120
Fax: 520-621-8191
E-Mail: dimitri@u.arizona.edu
Home Page: www.u.arizona.edu

Dimitri B Kececioglu, Owner

Proceedings where over 15 leading corporations present their latest techniques in this field.
Cost: $50.00
Frequency: Annual+
Circulation: 50
Founded in 1963
Mailing list available for rent: 43000 names at $152 per M

7407 **Repro Report**
International Reprographic Association
401 N Michigan Avenue
Chicago, IL 60611

312-245-1026
Fax: 312-527-6705
E-Mail: info@irga.com
Home Page: www.irga.com

Bryan Thomas, President
Dan Stephens, Executive Director
Steve Bova, Executive Director
Ben Barclay, Director of Operations

Articles on blueprint service companies, engineering equipment manufacturers and suppliers.
Cost: $150.00
Circulation: 1000
Founded in 1927

7408 **Research-Technology Management**
Industrial Research Institute
2300 Clarendon Boulevard
Suite 400
Arlington, VA 22201-3331

703-647-2580
Fax: 703-647-2581
E-Mail: information@iriweb.org
Home Page: www.iriweb.org

Martha Collins, Chairman
Daniel Abramowicz, Chairman-Elect
Edward Bernstein, President
James Euchner, Editor-in-Chief
Maryanne Gobble, Managing Editor

As the official journal of IRI, Research-Technology Management, is the bi-monthly, peer-reviewed journal, providing authoritative, practitioner-oriented articles for technology leaders.
200 Members
Frequency: 6x Yearly
Circulation: 1800
ISSN: 0895-6308
Founded in 1938

7409 **Resource**
American Society of Agricultural Engineers
2950 Niles Rd
St Joseph, MI 49085-8607

269-429-0300
800-371-2723
Fax: 269-429-3852
E-Mail: hq@asabe.org
Home Page: www.asabe.org

Ronald McAllister, President
Donna Hull, Publication Director

Accepts advertising.
Cost: $75.00
Circulation: 9000
ISSN: 1076-3333
Founded in 1907
Printed in on matte stock

7410 **Review of Scientific Instruments**
American Institute of Physics
2 Huntington Quadrangle
Melville, NY 11747-4502

516-576-2200
Fax: 516-349-7669
E-Mail: rsi@aip.org
Home Page: www.aip.org

Darlene Walters, Senior VP
Douglas LaFrenier, Marketing Director

Presents original articles on new principles, devices and techniques in scientific instrumentation.
Cost: $90.00
Frequency: Monthly
Circulation: 3100
Founded in 1931

7411 **Robotics and Computer-Intergrated Manufacturing**
Elsevier Science
PO Box 945
New York, NY 10159

212-895-5800
Fax: 212-633-3680
E-Mail: usinfo-f@elsevier.com
Home Page: www.elsevier.com

Nam P Sata, Editor
A. Sharon, Chief Executive Officer
Bill Godfrey, Chief Information Officer
David Clark, Senior Vice President

Contains original papers on theoretical, applied and experimental robotics and computer-integrated manufacturing, with emphasis on flexi-

ble manufacturing systems.
Cost: $1156.00
Circulation: 2500
Founded in 1880

7412 SAMPE Journal
Society for the Advancement of Material & Process
1161 Park View Drive
Suite 200
Covina, CA 91724-3751
626-331-0616
800-562-7360
Fax: 626-332-8929
E-Mail: sampeibo@sampe.org
Home Page: www.sampe.org
Social Media: Facebook, LinkedIn
Dr Scott Beckwith, Technical Editor
Jennifer Stephens, Production Manager
Patty Hunt, Advertising Rep
An informative and acclaimed publication provides a steady stream of technical articles, industry and international technical news, product and new literature announcements, book reviews, technical events calendars, and local SAMPE information. This publication is mailed complimentary to all SAMPE members.
Cost: $82.00
Frequency: Bi-Monthly

7413 SAWE Weight Engineers Handbook
Society of Allied Weight Engineers
5734 E. Lucia Walk
Long Beach, CA 90803-4015
562-596-2873
Fax: 562-596-2874
E-Mail: exdirector@sawe.org
Home Page: www.sawe.org
Patrick Brown, President
Jeffery Cerro, Executive VP
Ronald Fox, Executive Director
Robert Ridenour, VP Publications
Clint Bower, Executive VP
Contains technical information on materials, engineering formulas as well as other reference materials.
Cost: $100.00
348 Pages
Frequency: Periodic

7414 SPE Drilling & Completion
Society of Petroleum Engineers
PO Box 833836
Richardson, TX 75083-3836
972-529-9300
800-456-6863
Fax: 972-952-9435
E-Mail: spedal@spe.org
Home Page: www.spe.org
Giovanni Paccaloni, President
Bill Cobb, VP Finance
John E Bethancourt, Director Management/Information
Ian Gorman, Director Production/Operations
Niki Bradbury, Managing Director
Features papers covering bit technology, completions, drilling fluids and operations, equipment and instrumentation, perforation and sand control, simulations tubulars, well control, and work over well construction related topics.
Cost: $30.00
Frequency: Quarterly

7415 SPE Journal
Society of Petroleum Engineers
PO Box 833836
Richardson, TX 75083-3836
972-529-9300
800-456-6863
Fax: 972-952-9435
E-Mail: spedal@spe.org
Home Page: www.spe.org
Giovanni Paccaloni, President
Bill Cobb, VP Finance
John E Bethancourt, Director Management/Inforamtion
Ian Gorman, Director Production/Operations
Niki Bradbury, Managing Director
Includes full length technical papers covering all aspects of petroleum technology. SPE Journal covers the theories and emerging concepts that will become the new technologies of tomorrow.
Cost: $60.00
Frequency: Quarterly

7416 SPE Production & Facilities
Society of Petroleum Engineers
PO Box 833836
Richardson, TX 75083-3836
972-529-9300
800-456-6863
Fax: 972-952-9435
E-Mail: spedal@spe.org
Home Page: www.spe.org
Giovanni Paccaloni, President
Bill Cobb, VP Finance
John E Bethancourt, Director Management/Information
Ian Gorman, Director Production/Operations
Niki Bradbury, Managing Director
It includes papers on artificial lift, chemical treatments, design and operation of surface facilities and downhole equipment, formation damage control, fracturing, gas production and storage, offshore operations, production logging and optimization systems, sand control, separation and processing, and work over-production improvement.
Cost: $30.00
Frequency: Quarterly

7417 SPE Reservoir Evaluation & Engineering
Society of Petroleum Engineers
PO Box 833836
Richardson, TX 75083-3836
972-529-9300
800-456-6863
Fax: 972-952-9435
E-Mail: spedal@spe.org
Home Page: www.spe.org
Giovanni Paccaloni, President
Bill Cobb, VP Finance
John E Bethancourt, Director Management/Information
Ian Gorman, Director Production/Operations
Niki Bradbury, Managing Director
The journal covers a wide range of topics, including the following: Reservoir Engineering.
Cost: $40.00
Frequency: Bi-Monthly

7418 Sea Technology Magazine
Compass Publications, Inc.
1501 Wilson Blvd
Suite 1001
Arlington, VA 22209-2403
703-524-3136
Fax: 703-841-0852
E-Mail: seatechads@sea-technology.com
Home Page: www.sea-technology.com
Social Media: Facebook, Twitter
Amos Bussmann, President/Publisher
Joy Carter, Circulation Manager
Meghan Ventura, Managing Editor
Worldwide information leader for marine/offshore business, science and engineering. Read in more than 110 countries by management, engineers, scientists and technical personnel working in industry, government and education.
Cost: $40.00
Frequency: Monthly
Circulation: 16304
ISSN: 0093-3651
Founded in 1960
Mailing list available for rentat $80 per M
Printed in 4 colors

7419 Software Quality Professional
American Society for Quality
600 N Plankinton Avenue
PO Box 3005
Milwaukee, WI 53201-3005
414-272-8575
800-248-1946
Fax: 414-272-1734
E-Mail: help@asq.org
Home Page: www.asq.org
Roberto M Saco, President
Paul E Borawski, CEO
Erica Gumieny, Sales
Fay Spano, Communications/Media Relations
Published by the American Society for Quality, the SQP is a quarterly, peer-reviewed journal for software development professionals that focuses on the subject of quality practice principles in the implementation of software and the development of software systems.
Cost: $45.00
100M Members
Frequency: Quarterly
Founded in 1946

7420 TEST Engineering & Management
Mattingley Publishing Company
3756 Grand Ave
#205
Oakland, CA 94610-1545
510-839-0909
Fax: 510-839-2950
Home Page: www.mattingley-publ.com
Eve Mattingley, Owner
Nora Archambeau, Advertising Sales Manager
Includes mechanical testing, environmental simulation, and related technologies in industry, government, testing labs, and universities.
Cost: $45.00
Frequency: Monthly
Circulation: 9500
ISSN: 0193-4120
Founded in 1959
Printed in 4 colors on glossy stock

7421 The Bent
Tau Beta Pi Association
PO Box 2697
Knoxville, TN 37901-2697
865-546-4578
800-250-3196
Fax: 865-546-4579
Home Page: www.tbp.org
Social Media: Facebook
James D Froula, Executive Director/Editor
Dr. Larry Simonson, President
The official publication of the Tau Beta Pi Association - the engineering honor society and the world's largest engineering organization.
Cost: $10.00
Frequency: Quarterly
Circulation: 87000
ISSN: 0005-884x

7422 Tribology & Lubrication Technology
Society of Tribologists & Lubrication
840 Busse Hwy
Park Ridge, IL 60068-2376
847-825-5536
Fax: 847-825-1456

E-Mail: information@stle.org
Home Page: www.stle.org

Ed Salek, Executive Director
Karl Phipps, Associate Editor
Dr Neil Canter, Contributing Editor

Technical magazine that serves an audience of interdisciplinary professionals from industry, academic institutions and government. Included in this group are scientists, engineers, corporate leaders, researchers and product developers, plant managers and maintenance professionals, sales and marketing people and more.
Frequency: Monthly
Circulation: 7,000

7423 **Tribology Transaction**
Society of Tribologists & Lubrication
840 Busse Hwy
Park Ridge, IL 60068-2376

847-825-5536
Fax: 847-825-1456
E-Mail: information@stle.org
Home Page: www.stle.org

Ed Salek, Executive Director

Provides you with new and useful reports and analysis of every aspect of tribology and lubrication presented by renowned authors from around the globe. Available online as well.
Frequency: Quarterly

7424 **US Black Engineer & Information Technology**
Career Communications Group
729 E Pratt St
Suite 504
Baltimore, MD 21202-3302

410-244-7101
Fax: 410-752-1837
E-Mail: customer_service@ccgmag.com
Home Page: www.ccgmag.com

Jean Hamilton, Chief Financial Officer
Lango Deen, Technology Editor
Antonio Watson, VP Sales
Guy Madison, Publisher
Diane Jones, Director of Marketing

Devoted to engineering, science, and technology and to promoting opportunities in those fields for Black Americans.
Cost: $26.00
84 Pages
Frequency: Quarterly
Circulation: 100,000
ISSN: 1088-3444
Printed in 4 colors on glossy stock

7425 **VXI Journal**
30233 Jefferson Avenue
Saint Clair Shores, MI 48282

586-415-6500
Fax: 586-415-4882

Magazine is geared towards test engineers who are using or considering VXI bus systems and equipment.
Frequency: Quarterly
Circulation: 8000

7426 **Way Ahead Magazine**
Society of Petroleum Engineers
PO Box 833836
Richardson, TX 75083-3836

972-529-9300
800-456-6863
Fax: 972-952-9435
E-Mail: spedal@spe.org
Home Page: www.spe.org

Giovanni Paccaloni, President
Bill Cobb, VP Finance
John E Bethancourt, Director Management/Information
Ian Gorman, Director Production/Operations
Niki Bradbury, Managing Director

Designed for and written by young professionals in the oil and gas industry. In it, you will find items of particular interest to the younger members of our industry, including articles on the current state of the job market, how to improve communication skills, and what SPE young professionals are doing will be.
Frequency: 3x Yearly

7427 **Weighing & Measurement**
Key Markets Publishing Company
4729 Charles Street
PO Box 5867
Rockford, IL 61125-0867

815-636-7739

David M Mathieu, Publisher

Articles on new products, industry news, previews and reviews of events, and technical approaches to measurement.
Frequency: Bi-Monthly
Circulation: 12,000

7428 **Wireless Design & Development**
Reed Business Information
301 Gibraltar Drive
PO Box 650
Morris Plains, NJ 07950-0650

973-292-5100
Fax: 973 292-0783
Home Page: www.wirelessdesignmag.com

Wayne Curtis, Group Publisher
Kim Stokes, Editor

Edited for wireless component and system design engineers in the commercial RF and microwave market.
Frequency: Monthly

Trade Shows

7429 **AACE Annual Meeting**
Association of Cost Engineering
1265 Suncrest Towne Centre Drive
Morgantown, WV 26505-1876

304-296-8444
800-858-2678
Fax: 304-291-5728
E-Mail: info@aacei.org
Home Page: www.aacei.org

Jennie Amos, Marketing/Meetings Manager

See and hear outstanding technical presentations, panel discussions, workshops, tours, and guest speakers
Frequency: Annual/June

7430 **ACA Annual Meeting & Exhibition**
American Crystallographic Association
Ellicott Station
PO Box 96
Buffalo, NY 14205-0096

716-898-8690
Fax: 716-898-8695
E-Mail: aca@hwi.buffalo.edu
Home Page: www.AmerCrystalAssn.org

Thomas Koetzle, President
George Philip, Vice President

75 manufacturers exhibits of commercial hardware and software, and x-ray equipment. In addition to the exhibition, take advantage of workshops, and scientific and poster sessions.
1000 Attendees
Frequency: Annual
Founded in 1955

7431 **AEE Globacon**
Association of Energy Engineers
4025 Pleasantdale Road
Suite 420
Atlanta, GA 30340

770-447-5083
Fax: 770-446-3969
E-Mail: ashley@aeecenter.org
Home Page: www.aeecenter.org

Ashley Clark, Exhibits Manager
Patricia Ardavin, Conference Registration Director
Michelle Oxner, Conference Speakers Director
Lauren Lake, Event & Marketing Director
Bill Kent, Sponsorship Programs

Decision makers from business, industry and government coming together to seek integrated solutions to assure secure and affordable power supplies, effective management practices of both energy and overall operations costs, and exploring new technologies. The multi-track conference offer opportunity to learn about in novative and cost-conscious strategies, compare energy supply options, network, and workshops. Expo includes the Northeast Green Showcase by Energy Star.
8.2M Attendees
Mailing list available for rent

7432 **AHR Expo**
Refrigeration Service Engineers Society
1666 Rand Road
Des Plaines, IL 60016-3552

847-297-6464
800-297-5660
E-Mail: webmaster@rses.org
Home Page: www.rses.org

Robert Sherman, Intl President
Lawrence Donaldson, Intl Vice President

Attracts thousands of attendees from all facets of the industry, including contractors, engineers, dealers, distributors, wholesalers, OEM's, architects and builders, industrial plant operators, facility owners and managers, agents and reps.
Frequency: Annual/January

7433 **AISTech Conference & Exposition**
Association for Iron & Steel Technology
186 Thorn Hill Rd
Warrendale, PA 15086-7528

724-814-3000
Fax: 724-814-3001
E-Mail: info@aist.org
Home Page: www.aist.org

Ronald E Ashburn, Executive Director
Brian Bliss, Technology Programs Manager
Karen Hickey, Publications Manager/Editor
Mark Didiano, Finance & Administration Manager
Stacy Varmecky, Membership Services Manager

Featuring technologies from across the globe, allowing steel producers to compete in today's global market. Submit technical papers for presentation at the event. 300 exhibitors. Registration starts at $425.
7000 Attendees
Frequency: Annual/Spring

7434 **AMSE International Manufacturing Science & Engineering Conference**
American Society of Mechanical Engineers
Three Park Avenue
New York, NY 10016-5990

973-882-1167
800-843-2763
E-Mail: infocentral@asme.org
Home Page: www.asme.org

Victoria Rockwell, President

The MSEC highlights cutting edge manufacturing research in technical paper, poster and panel sessions.
3200 Attendees
Frequency: Annual/Fall
Mailing list available for rentat $125 per M

7435 **ANS Annual Meeting**
American Nuclear Society
555 North Kensington Avenue
La Grange Park, IL 60526

708-352-6611
Fax: 708-352-0499
Home Page: www.ans.org

Dr Lawrence Papay, General Chair
Dr Atambir Rao, Technical Program Chair
Harry Bradley, Executive Director
Frequency: Annual/June

7436 **AOCS Annual Meeting & Expo**
American Oil Chemists Society
2710 S Boulder
Urbana, IL 61802-6996

217-359-2344
Fax: 217-351-8091
E-Mail: general@aocs.org
Home Page: www.aocs.org

Joy McClaugherty, Conference Contact
Jodey Schonfeld, Publications
Frequency: Annual/April-May

7437 **APPA Annual Conference & Exposition**
Association of Higher Education Facilities
1643 Prince Street
Alexandria, VA 22314-2818

703-684-1446
Fax: 703-549-2772
E-Mail: katy@appa.org
Home Page: www.appa.org

E. Lander Medlin, Executive VP
Anita Dosik, Publications Manager
Ted Weidner, CAPPA Event Contact

Discussions and programs centered around today's educational facilities professionals: gain insight on current trends and conditions, identify challenges and solutions being implemented by industry experts, CEU and networking opportunities, and the innovative showcase of exhibitors.
Frequency: Annual

7438 **ASA Annual Meeting & Noise-Con**
Acoustical Society of America
2 Huntington Quadrable
Suite 1NO1
Melville, NY 11747

516-576-2360
Fax: 516-576-2377
E-Mail: asa@aip.org
Home Page: asa.aip.org

Charles E Schmid, Executive Director
Elaine Moran, ASA Office Manager
Mardi Hastings, President
700 Attendees
Frequency: Annual/Spring

7439 **ASA: Drive Systems-Control Units-Automation**
Stygar Associates
1202 Allanson Road
Mundelein, IL 60060

847-566-4566
Fax: 847-566-4580
E-Mail: estygariii@aol.com
Home Page: www.stygarassociates.com

376 exhibitors of hydraulic and pneumatic elements, compressed air systems, automation components, openloop and measuring controls.
40000 Attendees
Frequency: Biennial

7440 **ASCE Annual Civil Engineering Conference & Exposition**
American Society of Civil Engineers
1801 Alexander Bell Drive
Reston, VA 20191-4400

703-295-6000
800-548-2723
Fax: 703-295-6144
E-Mail: conf@asce.org
Home Page: www.asce.org

Mark Geiger, Sr Coor, Exhibits & Meeting Svcs
Heather Doughlin, Sr Mgr, Conferences & Meeting Svcs
Kathy Caldwell, President

175 exhibits of industry related products and services, seminars, workshops and banquet plus continuing education classes.
3000 Attendees
Frequency: Annual/Fall
Founded in 1879

7441 **ASCE Annual Meeting**
American Society of Certified Engineering
PO Box 1348
Flowery Branch, GA 30542-0023

770-967-9173
Fax: 770-967-8049
Home Page: www.ascet.org

Russell E Freier, Chairman
Leo Saenz, CET, President
Kurt Schuler, Secretary/Treasurer
Frequency: Annual/June

7442 **ASCE's Annual Civil Engineers Conference**
American Society of Civil Engineers
1801 Alexander Bell Drive
Reston, VA 20191-4400

703-295-6000
800-548-2723
Fax: 703-295-6144
Home Page: www.asce.org

Phil Gaughan, President

Focus on the challenges faced by companies and agencies already implementing the next generation of infrastructure in Water (e.g. dams, desalination, and recycling) and Transportation (e.g. seaports, rail, and roads). 100 booths.
24M Attendees
Frequency: Annual/October

7443 **ASEE Annual Conference & Exposition**
American Society for Engineering Education
1818 N Street NW
Suite 600
Washington, DC 20036-2476

202-331-3500
Fax: 202-265-8504
E-Mail: pubsinfo@asee.org
Home Page: www.asee.org

Patti Greenawalt, Director Meetings/Conventions
Frank Huband, Executive Director
Frequency: Annual/June

7444 **ASFE Fall Meeting**
ASFE/The Geoprofessional Business Association
8811 Colesville Road
Suite G106
Silver Springs, MD 20910

301-565-2733
Fax: 301-589-2017
E-Mail: info@asfe.org
Home Page: www.asfe.org

John P Bachner, Executive VP
David Gaboury, President
Frequency: Annual/Fall

7445 **ASFE Spring Meeting**
ASFE/The Geoprofessional Business Association
8811 Colesville Road
Suite G106
Silver Springs, MD 20910

301-565-2733
Fax: 301-589-2017
E-Mail: info@asfe.org
Home Page: www.asfe.org

John P Bachner, Executive VP
David Gaboury, President
Frequency: Annual/Spring

7446 **ASFE Winter Leadership Conference**
ASFE/The Geoprofessional Business Association
8811 Colesville Road
Suite G106
Silver Springs, MD 20910

301-565-2733
Fax: 301-589-2017
E-Mail: info@asfe.org
Home Page: www.asfe.org

John Bachner, Executive VP
David Gaboury, President
Frequency: Annual/January

7447 **ASGE National Conference**
American Society of Gas Engineers
PO Box 66
Artesia, CA 90702

562-455-9417
E-Mail: asgecge@aol.com
Home Page: www.asge-national.org

Nancy Wilson, President
Sham Kassab, VP
Jerry Moore, Executive Director

Where members meet to discuss the most current events and issues facing the Gas Appliance industry. Allows individuals to learn about new technology and to network with other Gas Industry Professionals.
Frequency: Annual

7448 **ASM Heat Treating Society Conference & Exposition**
ASM International/Materials Information
9639 Kinsman Road
Materials Park, OH 44073

440-338-5151
800-336-5152
Fax: 440-338-4634
E-Mail: pamela.kleinman@asminternational.org
Home Page: www.asminternational.org

Pamela Kleinma, Senior Manager, Events
Kellye Thomas, Exposition Account Manager
Dr. Mark Smith, President

Conference and exhibits of heat treating equipment and supplies plus information of interest to metallurgists, manufacturing, research and design technical professionals. 300 exhibitors.
3500 Attendees
Frequency: Bi-Annual
Founded in 1974

7449 **ASM Materials Science & Technology (MS&T)**
ASM International
9639 Kinsman Road
Materials Park, OH 44073-0002

440-338-5151
800-336-5152
Fax: 440-338-4634
E-Mail: pamela.kleinman@asminternational.org
Home Page: www.asminternational.org

Pamela Kleinman, Senior Manager, Events
Kelly Thomas, Exposition Account Manager
Dr. Mark Smith, President

Annual event focusing on testing, analysis, characterization and research of materials such as engineered materials, high performance metals, powdered metals, metal forming, surface modification, welding and joining. 350 exhibitors.
4,000 Attendees
Frequency: Annual/October
Founded in 2005

7450 **ASME Annual Meeting**
American Society of Mechanical Engineers
Three Park Avenue
New York, NY 10016

973-882-1170
800-843-2763
Fax: 212-591-7856
E-Mail: infocentral@asme.org
Home Page: www.asme.org

Melissa Torres, Meetings Manager
Mary Jakubowski, Meetings Manager
Marc Goldsmith, President
Frequency: Annual/June

7451 **ASME Gas Turbine Users Symposium (GTUS)**
American Society of Mechanical Engineers/IGTI
6525 The Corners Pkwy
Suite 115
Norcross, GA 30092

404-847-0072
Fax: 404-847-0151
E-Mail: igtiprogram@asme.org
Home Page: www.asme.org/igti

Smita Solanki, Coordinator, IGTI Conferences
Kristen Barranger, Manager, IGTI Conferences & Expos
Michael Ireland, Managing Director

A show focused on the role gas turbines will play in meeting the nation's future energy demands, provides the information related to gas turbine operations, maintenance, advances, and design.
2000 Attendees
Frequency: Annual

7452 **ASNT Fall Conference & Quality Testing Show**
American Society for Nondestructive Testing
1711 Arlingate Lane
PO Box 28518
Columbus, OH 43228-0518

614-274-6003
800-222-2768
Fax: 614-274-6899
Home Page: www.asnt.org

Michael O'Toole, Sernior Manager, Conferences
Jacquie Guinta, Meeting Coordinator
Ruth Staat, Exhibit/Event Supervisor

Seminar, conference and 150 exhibits of nondestructive testing equipment, services, supplies and laboratory representatives. Holds a smaller conference in the spring.
3000 Attendees
Frequency: Annual/Fall

7453 **ASPE Technical Symposium**
American Society of Plumbing Engineers
8614 Catalpa Avenue
Suite 1007
Chicago, IL 60656-1116

773-693-2773
Fax: 773-695-9007
E-Mail: info@aspe.org
Home Page: www.aspe.org

Pat Delaney, Convention/Symposium Information
Stan Wolson, Executive Director

For professional plumbing engineers, designers and contractors to improve their skills, learn original design concepts and make important networking contacts to help them stay abreast of current trends, codes and technologies.
Frequency: Annual/October

7454 **ASPE's Annual Meeting**
American Society for Precision Engineering
PO Box 10826
Raleigh, NC 27605-0826

919-839-8444
Fax: 919-839-8039
Home Page: www.aspe.net

Erika Deutsch-Layne, Meetings Manager

Offers the latest in precision engineering research through presentations from national and international.
Frequency: Annual/October

7455 **ATCE**
Society of Petroleum Engineers
PO Box 833836
Richardson, TX 75083-3836

972-529-9300
800-456-6863
Fax: 972-952-9435
E-Mail: spedal@spe.org
Home Page: www.spe.org

Giovanni Paccaloni, President
Bill Cobb, VP Finance
John E Bethancourt, Director Management/Information
Ian Gorman, Director Production/Operations
Niki Bradbury, Managing Director
40482 Attendees
Frequency: Annual/October

7456 **AVS International Symposium & Exhibition**
American Vacuum Society
125 Maiden Lane
15th Floor
New York, NY 10038

212-248-0200
Fax: 212-248-0245
E-Mail: jeannette@avs.org
Home Page: www.avs.org

Jeannette DeGennaro, Exhibition & Sales Coordinator
Angela Klink, Membership Services Coordinator
Heather Korff, Events/Office Coordinator AVS West
Yvonne Towse, Managing Director
Angus Rockett, President

The Symposium and Exhibition has been developed to address cutting-edge issues associated with the vacuum science and technology in both the research and manufacturing communities. It offers a week long forum for exchange, topical conferences, courses, training, career workshops and networking. Over 200 booths of the latest products and services around vacuum science and technology.
3000 Attendees
Frequency: Annual

7457 **AVS International Symposium and Exhibition**
AVS Science & Technology Society
120 Wall Street
32nd Floor
New York, NY 10005-3993

212-248-0200
Fax: 212-248-0245
E-Mail: david_aspnes@avs.org
Home Page: www.avs.org

David E Aspnes, President
Christie R Marrian, President-Elect
John Coburn, Treasurer
Joseph J Greene, Clerk/Secretary
Yvonne Towse, Executive Director

This has been developed to address cutting-edge issues associated with vacuum science and technology in both the research and manufacturing communities. The Symposium is a week long forum for science and technology exchange featuring papers from technical divisions and technology groups, and topical conferences on emerging technologies.
3000 Attendees
Founded in 1953

7458 **AVS New Mexico Chapter Annual Symposium Short Courses/Vendor Show**
AVS Science & Technology Society
120 Wall Street
32nd Floor
New York, NY 10005-3993

212-248-0200
Fax: 212-248-0245
E-Mail: david_aspnes@avs.org
Home Page: www.avs.org

David E Aspnes, President
Christie R Marrian, President-Elect
John Coburn, Treasurer
Joseph J Greene, Clerk/Secretary
Yvonne Towse, Executive Director
Frequency: Annual/May

7459 **Adhesion Society Annual Meeting**
Adhesion Society
2 Davidson Hall-0201
Blacksburg, VA 24061

540-231-7257
Fax: 540-231-3971
E-Mail: adhesoc@vt.edu
Home Page: www.adhesionsociety.org

Ken Shull, Program Chair
Leonardo Lopez, Exhibition Chair
Esther Brann, Office Manager

Engineers, chemists, biologists, mathematicians, physicists, physicians and dentists visit exhibits relating to the study of adhesion's role in coatings, composite materials, the function of biological tissues, and the performance of bonded structures.
400 Attendees
Frequency: Annual/February

7460 **Adhesive & Sealant Fall Convention**
Adhesive & Sealant Council
7101 Wisconsin Avenue
Suite 990
Bethesda, MD 20814

301-986-9700
Fax: 301-986-9795

E-Mail: info@ascouncil.org
Home Page: www.ascouncil.org

Malinda Armstrong, Senior Manager Conventions/Meetings
Matt Croson, President
400 Attendees
Frequency: Annual/October

7461 **AeroMat Conference and Exposition**
ASM International
9639 Kinsman Road
Materials Park, OH 44073-0002

440-338-5151
800-336-5152
Fax: 440-338-4634
Home Page: www.asminternational.org

Kim Schaefer, Event Manager
Kelly Thomas, Exposition Account Manager
Mark F Smith, President
Stanley Theobald, Managing Director

Conference for Aerospace Materials Engineers, Structural Engineers and Designers. The annual event focuses on affordable structures and low-cost manufacturing, titanium alloy technology, advanced intermetallics and refractory metal alloys, materials and processes for space applications, aging systems, high strength steel, NDT evaluation, light alloy technology, welding and joining, and engineering technology. 150 exhibitors.
1500 Attendees
Frequency: Annual/June
Founded in 1984

7462 **Airlines Engineering Committee**
Aeronautical Radio
2551 Riva Road
Annapolis, MD 21401-7435

410-266-4000
Fax: 410-266-4040

Daniel Martinec, Director Avionics

Commercial airline and other transport aircraft avionics engineers.
800 Attendees
Frequency: October

7463 **American Society for Engineering Education Conference and Exposition**
American Society for Engineering Education
1818 N State Street
Suite 600
Washington, DC 20036

202-331-3500
Fax: 202-265-8504
E-Mail: conferences@asee.org
Home Page: www.asee.org

Patti Greenawalt, Director Conventions/Meetings
Jennifer Atkinson, Meetings Assistant
Kathi J Springer, Manager Exhibits/Sponsorships
Frank Huband, Executive Director

Annual conference of 150 publishers, manufacturers, producers, suppliers, designers of scientific instrumentation and distributors. Exhibits include publications, engineering supplies and equipment, computers, software and research companies all products and services related to engineering education.
1700 Attendees
Frequency: Annual/June

7464 **American Society of Plumbing Engineers Meeting**
American Society of Plumbing Engineers
2980 S River Road
Des Plaines, IL 60018

847-296-0002
Fax: 773-695-9007
E-Mail: info@aspe.org
Home Page: www.aspe.org

Cliff Reis, Managing Director of Education
Jim Kendzel, Executive Director

Biennial meeting and exhibits for the plumbing engineering industry. 600 booths.
7000 Attendees
Founded in 1964

7465 **American Society of Safety Engineers Professional Development Conference**
American Society of Safety Engineers
1800 E Oakton Street
Des Plaines, IL 60018

847-699-2929
Fax: 847-768-3434
E-Mail: customerservice@asse.org
Home Page: www.asse.org

Terri Norris, President
James Smith, Vice President/ Finance
Diane Hurns, Manager Public Relations Department

Annual conference and expo of 250 manufacturers and suppliers of safety equipment and health products.
3500 Attendees
Frequency: Annual/June

7466 **Annual Applied Reliability Engineering and Product Assurance**
The University of Arizona
Aerospace and Mechanical Engineering Department
Building 119, PO Box 210119
Tucson, AZ 85721-0119

520-215-5511
Fax: 520-621-8191
E-Mail: dimitri@u.arizona.edu
Home Page: www.u.arizona.edu/~dimitri

Dimitri B Kececioglu PE, Professor Aerospace/Mechanical Eng.
Frequency: Annual/July

7467 **Annual Canadian Conference on Intelligent Systems**
Robotics Industris Association
900 Victors Way
PO Box 3724
Ann Arbor, MI 48106

734-994-6088
Fax: 734-994-3338
E-Mail: webmaster@robotics.org
Home Page: www.robotics.org

Don Vincent, Executive VP
Brian Huse, Director Marketing/PR
Jim Adams, Manager of Public Relations
Sharon Adams, Accounting Manager

Canada's leading showcase of research excellence and breakthroughs in robotics and intelligent systems, featuring technology displays, demonstrations, presentations and workshops.
Frequency: Annual/June

7468 **Annual Lean Management Solutions Conference**
Institute of Industrial Engineers
3577 Parkway Lane
Suite 200
Norcross, GA 30092

770-449-0460
800-494-0460
Fax: 770-441-3295
E-Mail: cs@iienet.org
Home Page: www.iienet.org

Gregg Griffith, Marketing Director
Don Greene, CEO

Will enable you to significantly improve performance, reduce costs, and increase customer satisfaction. With over 60 presentations and new tracks in MRO, Food Processing, Aviation, Healthcare, and Product Design, you will find what you need.
Frequency: Annual/December

7469 **Annual Lean Six Sigma Conference**
American Society for Quality
600 N Plankinton Avenue
PO Box 3005
Milwaukee, WI 53201-3005

414-272-8575
800-248-1946
Fax: 414-272-1734
E-Mail: help@asq.org
Home Page: www.asq.org

Paul Borawski, CEO
James Rooney, Chair
Erica Gumieny, Sales
Fay Spano, Communications/Media Relations

An exclusive two-day briefing and networking event designed by and for the top practitioners in the Six Sigma community.
100M Members
Frequency: Annual/February
Founded in 1946

7470 **Annual Meeting of the Society of Rheology**
Socieety of Rheology
2 Huntington Quadrangle
Suite 1N01
Meville, NY 11747-4502

516-576-2471
Fax: 516-576-2223
E-Mail: rheology@aip.org
Home Page: www.rheology.org

A. Jeffrey Giacomin, VP
Faith Morrison, President
Frequency: Annual/October

7471 **Annual Physical Electronics Conference**
AVS Science & Technology Society
120 Wall Street
32nd Floor
New York, NY 10005-3993

212-248-0200
Fax: 212-248-0245
E-Mail: david_aspnes@avs.org
Home Page: www.avs.org

David E Aspnes, President
Christie R Marrian, President-Elect
John Coburn, Treasurer
Joseph J Greene, Clerk/Secretary
Nancy Schultheis, Office Manager

Will provide a forum for the dissemination and discussion of new research results in the physics and chemistry of surfaces and interfaces. The conference will continue to emphasize fundamental science in materials systems, including metals, semiconductors, insulators and biomaterials.
Frequency: Annual/June

7472 **Annual Quality Audit Conference**
American Society for Quality
600 N Plankinton Avenue
PO Box 3005
Milwaukee, WI 53201-3005

414-272-8575
800-248-1946
Fax: 414-272-1734
E-Mail: help@asq.org
Home Page: www.asq.org

Paul Borawski, President
James Rooney, Chair

Topics of interest include: new innovating audit/process approaches, value added involvement, corporate expectations, corporate/social

responsibility, auditing in the overall corporate scheme.
100M Members
Frequency: Annual/October
Founded in 1946

7473 **Annual RSES Conference & Expo**
Refrigeration Service Engineers Society
1666 Rand Road
Des Plaines, IL 60016-3552

847-297-6464
800-297-5660
E-Mail: webmaster@rses.org
Home Page: www.rses.org

Robert Sherman, Intl President
Lawrence Donaldson, Intl Vice President
Frequency: Annual/September

7474 **Annual Service Quality Conference**
American Society for Quality
600 N Plankinton Avenue
PO Box 3005
Milwaukee, WI 53201-3005

414-272-8575
800-248-1946
Fax: 414-272-1734
E-Mail: help@asq.org
Home Page: www.asq.org

James Rooney, President
Paul E Borawski, CEO
Erica Gumieny, Sales
Fay Spano, Communications/Media Relations

The sessions we plan will help you to navigate through unpredictable consumer behavior and increasing competition to build a strong foundation for reaching superior levels of quality service.
100M Members
Frequency: Annual/September
Founded in 1946

7475 **Annual Simulation Solutions Conference**
Institute of Industrial Engineers
3577 Parkway Lane
Suite 200
Norcross, GA 30092

770-449-0460
800-494-0460
Fax: 770-441-3295
E-Mail: cs@iienet.org
Home Page: www.iienet.org

Greg Griffith, Marketing Director
Don Greene, CEO

You will have a rich menu of over forty presentations by successful practitioners of simulation in transportation and military applications; management strategies; manufacturing; lean scheduling and operations; healthcare; simulation skills; supply chain, material handling, and distribution; and service and business processes.
Frequency: Annual/May

7476 **Annual World Conference on Quality and Improvement**
American Society for Quality
600 N Plankinton Avenue
PO Box 3005
Milwaukee, WI 53201-3005

414-272-8575
800-248-1946
Fax: 414-272-1734
E-Mail: help@asq.org
Home Page: www.asq.org

James Rooney, President
Paul E Borawski, CEO
Erica Gumieny, Sales
Fay Spano, Communications/Media Relations

Conference focuses on quality and improvement with more than 2,000 exhibits and attendees. Keynote speakers and sessions discuss quality tools, techniques and methodologies. Provides the opportunity for members to meet and network with colleagues in the industry.
100M Members
Frequency: Annual/May
Founded in 1946

7477 **Atlantic Design & Manufacturing**
Canon Communications
11444 W Olympic Boulevard
Suite 900
Los Angeles, CA 90064-1549

310-445-4200
Fax: 310-445-4299
Home Page: www.cancom.com

Diane O'Conner, Trade Show Director
Dan Cutrone, Show Marketing Manager

Serves the East Coast's dynamic design, process, and manufacturing marketplace. This exposition, recently acquired by Canon Communications, is now co-located with Medical Design and Manufacturing East. Product classifications include: Coatings and Finishes, Composites, Computer Aided Design/Computer Aided Manufacturing, Electrical/Electronic, Electric Optical Components and Equipment, Engineered Safety Products, Engineering Management and Tools, Fasteners, Fluid Media, Fluid Power and Control.
Frequency: Annual/May

7478 **Atomic Layer Deposition**
AVS Science & Technology Society
120 Wall Street
32nd Street
New York, NY 10005-3993

212-248-0200
Fax: 212-248-0245
E-Mail: david_aspnes@avs.org
Home Page: www.avs.org

David E Aspnes, President
Chrisitie R Marrian, President-Elect
John Coburn, Treasurer
Joseph J Greene, Clerk/Secretary
Nancy Schultheis, Office Manager

Conference will be a three-day meeting, dedicated to the science and technology of atomic layer controlled deposition of thin films, in particular atomic layer deposition.
Frequency: Annual/August

7479 **BMES Annual Fall Meeting**
Biomedical Engineering Society
8201Corporate Drive
Suite 1125
Landover, MD 20785-2224

301-459-1999
877-871-BMES
Fax: 301-459-2444
E-Mail: info@bmes.org
Home Page: www.bmes.org

Richard Waugh, President
Edward Schilling, Executive Director
Debra Tucker, Meetings Director
Frequency: Annual/September

7480 **Design Part Show**
Job Shop Company
16 Waterbury Road
Prospect, CT 06712-1215

800-317-0474
Home Page: www.jobshoptechnology.com

Gerald Schmidt, President
Jennifer Bryda, Production Manager

The show is designed to attract the highest caliber engineers and buyers from your major DEM product manufacturers.
2000 Attendees
Frequency: Annual/April
Founded in 1999

7481 **ESTECH, IEST's Annual Technical Meeting and Exposition**
American Institute of Physics
One Physics Ellipse
College Park, MD 20740-3843

301-209-3100
E-Mail: dylla@aip.org
Home Page: www.aip.org

H. Frederick Dylia, Executive Director/CEO
John Haynes, Vice President Publishing
Benjamin Snavely, AIP Corporate Secretary
Melissa Poleski, Assistant To Corporate Secretary

Will feature a cutting-edge technical program, hot-topic tutorials, must attend Working Group meetings, and a state-of-the-art exposition.
Frequency: Annual/May

7482 **Earth and Space**
American Society of Civil Engineers
1801 Alexander Bell Drive
Reston, VA 20191

703-295-6000
800-548-2723
Fax: 703-295-6222
E-Mail: webmaster@asce.org
Home Page: www.asce.org

Patricia Galloway, President
Lawrence Roth, Deputy Executive Director
Patrick Natale, Secretary/Treasurer

You will be among experts from a variety of disciplines and have ample, enjoyable opportunities to discuss exploration, engineering, construction, and operations in challenging environments on Planet Earth, in Space, and on other planetary bodies such as the Moon and Mars.
Frequency: Annual/March

7483 **Electric West**
PRIMEDIA Business Exhibitions
11 River Bend Drive S
PO Box 4949
Stamford, CT 06907-0949

203-358-9900
Fax: 203-358-5816
Home Page: www.primediaevents.com

Liza Wylie, Show Director
Mandy Ferreira-Nunez, Operations Manager

Educational sessions attract electrical professionals from contracting companics, industrial plants, consulting engineering firms, datacom installers and electricians. Presentations focus on such topics as power quality, lighting, the NEC, project management, claims management and fiber optics. Also provides in-depth coverage of National Electrical Code changes that directly impact the work of electrical professionals.
Frequency: Annual/March

7484 **European Symposium of the Protein Society**
American Institute of Physics
One Physics Ellipse
College Park, MD 20740-3843

301-209-3100
E-Mail: dylla@aip.org
Home Page: www.aip.org

H. Frederick Dylla, Executive Director/CEO
John Haynes, Vice President Publishing
Benjamin Snavely, AIP Corporate Secretary
Melissa Poleski, Assistant To Corporate Secretary

The meeting features sessions on nanotechnology, biosensors and proteins as materials, proteomics, protein networks and systems biology. membrane proteins and diseases,

protein folding and diseases, protein flexibility, and molecular recognition.
Frequency: Annual/May

7485 Finishing Expo
Society of Manufacturing Engineers
1 SME Drive
PO Box 930
Dearborn, MI 48121

313-425-3000
800-733-4763
Fax: 313-425-3400
E-Mail: service@sme.org
Home Page: www.sme.org

Mark Tomlinson, Executive Director/General Manager
Paul Bradley, President
Bob Harris, Director Finance

The conference will include workshops, tutorials, and technical sessions. 200 booths.
25M Attendees

7486 General Convention
Sigma Phi Delta
438 Smithfield Street
East Liverpool, OH 43920-1723

330-385-5287
E-Mail: webmaster@sigphi.org
Home Page: www.sigphi.org

Derek R Troy, Grand President
Alixandre R Minden, Grand VP
Steven A Weiss, Communications Director
Edward A Hurst, Treasurer
Levon Haig Barsoumian, Executive Secretary

Includes a tentative schedule of business sessions, symposiums and events.
Frequency: Annual/July

7487 GeoFlorida
Geo-Institute, American Society of Civil Engineers
1801 Alexander Bell Drive
Reston, VA 20191-4400

703-295-6350
Fax: 703-295-6351
E-Mail: stacey.gardiner@tggroup.com
Home Page: content.geoinstitute.org

Stacey Gardiner, Conference Director
Greory DiLoreto, President- Elect
Mark Rusnica, Deputy Executive Director

The annual geo-conference of the Geo-Institute of ASCE. Presents developments in geotechnical engineering analysis, modeling and design; opportunities to share knowledge, learn about innovations and emerging technologies; panel discussions, technical sessions, lectures, short courses, workshops and student competition; and an extensive exhibit hall.
Frequency: Annual

7488 Geoline Expo
Association of Engineering Geologists
PO Box 460518
Denver, CO 80246

303-757-2926
Fax: 720-230-4846
E-Mail: aeg@aegweb.org
Home Page: www.aegweb.org

Becky Roland, Chief Staff Executive

The symposium will cover three major topics. Session 1 Field investigations: Strategy, Organization, Methods, and Uncertainties, Session 2 Inserting the Structure in its Environment, Session 3 Construction, Monitoring, Evolution and Maintenance.
400 Attendees
Frequency: Annual/December

7489 GlobalCon Conference & Expo
Association of Energy Engineers
4025 Pleasantdale Rd
Suite 420
Atlanta, GA 30340-4264

770-447-5083
Fax: 770-446-3969
E-Mail: info@aeecenter.org
Home Page: www.aeecenter.org
Social Media: Facebook, Twitter, LinkedIn, YouTube

Eric A. Woodroof, President
Gary Hogsett, President Elect
Bill Younger, Secretary
Paul Goodman, C.P.A., Treasurer

Designed specifically to facilitate those seeking to expand their knowledge of fast-moving developments in the energy field, explore promising new technologies, compare energy supply options, and learn about innovative and cost-conscious project implementation strategies.
8.2M Members
Founded in 1977

7490 Government Affairs Briefing
North American Die Casting Association
241 Holbrook Drive
Wheeling, IL 60090-5809

847-279-0001
Fax: 847-279-0002
E-Mail: twarog@diecasting.org
Home Page: www.diecasting.org

Daniel Twarog, President

Will provide you with important information in the following informative sessions, state of US manufacturing, trade and global competition, metalcasting research programs, health care & other worker issues, new air standards & other environmental issues.
Frequency: Annual/June

7491 IDSA National Conference
Industrial Designers Society of America
45195 Business Court
Suite 250
Sterling, VA 20166-6717

703-707-6000
Fax: 703-787-8501
E-Mail: idsa@idsa.org
Home Page: www.idsa.org

Clive Roux, CEO
Bob Swartz, Executive Director
Kaycee Childress, Marketing
Roxann Henze, Press, Media & Public Relations

IDSA is the world's oldest, largest, member-driven society for product design, industrial design, interaction design, human factors, ergonomics, design research, design management, universal design and related design fields. IDSA organizes the renowned International Design Excellence Award competition annually; hosts the International Design Conference and five regional conferences each year.
800 Attendees
Frequency: Annual/August

7492 IES Annual Meeting
Illuminating Engineering Society of North America
120 Wall Street
17th Floor
New York, NY 10005

212-248-5000
Fax: 212-248-5018
E-Mail: ies@ies.org
Home Page: www.ies.org

William Hanley, Executive VP
Marianne Conrad, Director Member Services
400 Attendees
Frequency: Annual

7493 IFAI Annual Expo
Industrial Fabrics Association International
1801 Country Road BW
Roseville, MN 55113

651-222-2508
800-225-4324
Fax: 651-631-9334
E-Mail: generalinfo@ifai.com
Home Page: www.ifai.com

Todd Lindemann, VP Conference Manger
Stephen Warner, President

A trade event in the Americas for the technical textiles and specialty fabrics industry.
Frequency: Annual/September

7494 IFAI Outlook
Industrial Fabrics Association International
1801 Country Road BW
Roseville, MN 55113

651-222-2508
800-225-4324
Fax: 651-631-9334
E-Mail: generalinfo@ifai.com
Home Page: www.usifi.com

Todd Lindemann, VP Conference Manger
Stephen Warner, President

Will bring industry leaders together to discuss important issues and challenges faced by the United States textile industry.
Frequency: Annual/May

7495 IIE Annual Conference
Institute of Industrial Engineers
3577 Parkway Lane
Suite 200
Norcross, GA 30092

770-449-0460
800-494-0460
Fax: 770-441-3295
E-Mail: cs@iienet.org
Home Page: www.iienet.org

Greg Griffith, Marketing Director
Don Greene, CEO

With over 600 content filled presentations and expert speakers, it is the productivity event of the year. Discover the latest tools, techniques and solutions from top professionals in the field. Network with peers, decision makers, and leaders during the conference.
1,100 Attendees
Frequency: Annual/May

7496 IPTC
Society of Petroleum Engineers
PO Box 833836
Richardson, TX 75083-3836

972-529-9300
800-456-6863
Fax: 972-952-9435
E-Mail: spedal@spe.org
Home Page: www.spe.org

Giovanni Paccaloni, President
Bill Cobbs, VP Finance
John E Berthancourt, Director Management/Information
Ian Gorman, Director Production/Operations
Niki Bradbury, Managing Director

The theme for the conference is Sustaining World Growth - Technology and People. A new meeting brought to you by four leading industry societies (AAPG, EAGE, SEG, and SPE). Natural gas will be a major focus of this meeting.
Frequency: Annual/November

7497 IRI Annual Meeting
Industrial Research Institute

2200 Clarendon Boulevard
Suite 1102
Arlington, VA 22201

703-647-2580
Fax: 703-647-2581
Home Page: www.iriweb.org

Robert Kumpf, Chairman
Ryan Dirkx, Chairman-Elect
Edward Bernstein, President
Frequency: Annual/May

7498 IRgA Annual Convention and Trade Show
International Reprographic Association
401 N Michigan Avenue
Chicago, IL 60611

312-673-4805
Fax: 312-321-5150
E-Mail: info@irga.com
Home Page: www.irga.com

Robert Roperti, President
Dan Mulrooney, VP
Steve Bova, Executive Director

You will gain first hand knowledge and experience from technical sessions presented by experts in their field, access to the latest products and services available to enhance your company's performance at the trade show, re-establish contacts and connections as you interact with peers to find out how they are handling the latest challenges.
Frequency: Annual/May

7499 ISWM Annual Conference & Expo
International Society of Weighing & Measurement
1801 Alexander Bell Avenue
Reston, VA 20191

703-295-6350
Fax: 703-295-6351
E-Mail: staff@iswm.org
Home Page: content.geoinstitute.org

Kate Fitzgerald CMP, Director of Meetings

150 booths; presentations from industry leaders; workshops, panels, and discussions.
1.8M Attendees

7500 International Code Council Annual Conference
BOCA Evaluation Services
500 New Jersey Avenue
6th Fl
Washington, DC 20001-2070

888-422-7233
Fax: 202-783-2348
E-Mail: webmaster@iccsafe.org
Home Page: www.iccsafe.org

James Brothers, President
William Dupler, Vice President

The conference features the Final Action Hearings, the Education Program, the Annual Business Meeting, the International Code Council Expo and networking opportunities with your peers in the building safety and fire prevention fields.
Frequency: Annual/September

7501 International Conference on Construction Engineering/Management
American Society for Civil Engineers
1801 Alexander Bell Drive
Reston, VA 20191

703-295-6000
800-548-2723
Fax: 703-295-6222
E-Mail: webmaster@asce.org
Home Page: www.asce.org

Patricia Galloway, President
Lawrence Roth, Deputy Executive Director
Patrick Natale, Secretary/Treasurer
Frequency: Annual/October

7502 International Conference on Deburring and Surface Finishing
Abrasive Engineering Society
144 Moore Road
Butler, PA 16001

724-282-6210
Fax: 724-234-2376
E-Mail: aes@abrasiveengineering.com
Home Page: www.abrasiveengineering.com

Doug Haynes, President
Ted Giese, Executive Director

The program, which is part of series of international conferences, is scheduled for June. This conference will include a Technical Exhibition and Tours. A special course on deburring and surface finishing will be taught following the conference.
Frequency: Annual/June

7503 International Conference on Metallurgical Coatings and Thin Films
AVS Science & Technology Society
120 Wall Street
32nd Floor
New York, NY 10005-3993

212-248-0200
Fax: 212-248-0245
E-Mail: david_aspnes@avs.org
Home Page: www.avs.com

David E Aspnes, President
Christie R Marrian, President-Elect
John Coburn, Treasurer
Joseph J Greene, Clerk/Secretary
Steve Sukman, Executive Vice President

Internationally recognized as a vibrant technical conference that integrates fundamentals and applied research focused on thin film deposition, characterization, and advanced surface modification techniques leading-edge technology.
Frequency: Annual/May

7504 International Symposium for Testing & Failure Analysis
ASM International
9639 Kinsman Road
Materials Park, OH 44073

440-338-5151
800-336-5152
Fax: 440-338-4634
Home Page: www.asminternational.org

Jaime Creighton, Event Manager
Kelly Thomas, Exposition Account Manager

Annual event focusing on microelectronic and electronic device failure analysis, techniques, EOS/ESD testing and desecrates aimed at failure analysis engineers and managers, technicians and new failure analysis engineers. 200 exhibitors.
1100 Attendees
Frequency: Annual/November

7505 International Symposium on Advances in Abrasives Technology
Abrasive Engineering Society
141 Moore Road
Butler, PA 16001

724-826-6210
Fax: 742-234-2376
E-Mail: aes@abrasiveengineering.com
Home Page: www.abrasiveengineering.com

Doug Haynes, President
Ted Giese, Executive Director

Jointly sponsored by the International Committee for Abrasives Technology and the Japan Society for Abrasive Technology, which has conducted eight international conferences on abrasives technologies. Topics including abrasive machining, finishing, assessment of grinding performance, machine tools and systems, coolant and other topics.
Frequency: Annual/November

7506 International Thermal Spray Conference & Exposition
ASM International
9639 Kinsman Road
Materials Park, OH 44073

440-338-5151
800-336-5152
Fax: 440-338-4634
E-Mail: natalie.nemec@asminternational.org
Home Page: www.asminternational.org

Pamela Kleinman, Event Manager
Kelly Thomas, Exposition Account Manager

Global annual event attracting professional interested in thermal spray technology focusing on advances in HVOF, plasma and detonation gun, flame spray and wire arc spray processes, performance of coatings, and future trends. 150 exhibitors.
1000 Attendees
Frequency: Annual/May

7507 International Workshop on Deep Inelastic Scattering - DIS05
American Institute of Physics
One Physics Ellipse
College Park, MD 20740-3843

301-209-3100
E-Mail: dylla@aip.org
Home Page: www.aip.org

H. Frederick Dylla, Executive Director/CEO
Benjamin Snavely, Senior Executive Secretary
Benjamin Snavely, AIP Corporate Secretary
Melissa Poleski, Assistant to Corporate Secretary

The aim of these workshops is to review the progress in the field of DIS and QCD and to discuss and lay the groundwork for the future. DIS 2005 will bring together about 250 experimentalists and theorists. The workshop format will involve plenary sessions with review talks and parallel working group sessions with shorter contributions.
Frequency: Annual/April

7508 LIGHTFAIR International Trade Show
Illuminating Engineering Society of North America
120 Wall Street
17th Floor
New York, NY 10005

212-248-5000
Fax: 212-248-5018
E-Mail: ies@ies.org
Home Page: www.ies.org

William Hanley, Executive VP
Marianne Conrad, Director Member Services
Denis Lavoie, President
23000 Attendees
Frequency: Annual

7509 MCAA Annual Conference
Mechanical Contractors Association of America

1385 Piccard Drive
Rockville, MD 20850-4340

301-869-5800
Fax: 301-990-9690
Home Page: www.mcaa.org

Lonnie Coleman, MCAA President

Containing 100 booths and 95 exhibits. Education sessions, leadership and keynote presentations, exhibitions.

7510 **MIACON Construction, Mining & Waste Management Show**
Finocchiaro Enterprises
2921 Coral Way
Miami, FL 33145

305-441-2865
Fax: 305-529-9217
Home Page: www.miacon.com

Michael Finocchiaro, President
Jose Garcia, VP
Justine Finocchiaro, Chief Operations

Annual show of 650 manufacturers, suppliers, distributors and exporters of equipment, machinery, supplies and services for the construction, mining and waste managment industries. There will be 600 booths.
10M Attendees
Frequency: Annual/October
Founded in 1994

7511 **Meeting of the Acoustical Society of America**
Acoustical Society of America
2 Huntington Quandrangle
Suite 1N01
Melville, NY 11747-4502

516-576-2360
Fax: 516-576-2377
E-Mail: asa@aip.org
Home Page: www.asa.aip.org

William A Kuperman, President
William A Yost, President-Elect
Mark F Hamilton, VP
Donna L Neff, VP Elect
Charles E Schmid, Executive Director
Frequency: Annual/May

7512 **Metalcasting Congress**
North American Die Casting Association
241 Holbrook Drive
Wheeling, IL 60090-5809

847-279-0001
Fax: 847-279-0002
E-Mail: twarog@diecasting.org
Home Page: www.diecasting.org

Daniel Twarog, President

With the wide range of opportunities for technology transfer, it promises to be the industry's premier show. The American Foundry Society and the North American Die Casting Association are joining together.
Frequency: Annual/April

7513 **Mid-Atlantic Job Shop Show**
Edward Publishing
16 Waterbury Road
Prospect, CT 06712-1215

203-758-6658
Fax: 203-758-4476
Home Page: www.jobshoptechnology.com

Jennifer Bryda, Production Manager

The show is designed to attract the highest caliber engineers and buyers from your major DEM product manufacturers. There will be 260 exhibitors and booths.
2500 Attendees
Frequency: Annual/May
Founded in 1999

7514 **NACE International Annual Conference & Expo (CORROSION)**
NACE International
1440 S Creek Drive
Houston, TX 77084-4906

281-228-6200
800-797-6223
Fax: 281-228-6300
E-Mail: firstservice@nace.org
Home Page: www.nace.org

Oliver Moghissi, President
Bob Chalker, Executive Director

World's largest conference dedicated to Corrosion control and prevention
5000 Attendees
Frequency: Annual

7515 **NADCA Sales Training**
North American Die Casting Association
241 Holbrook Drive
Wheeling, IL 60090-5809

847-279-0001
Fax: 847-279-0002
E-Mail: twarog@diecasting.org
Home Page: www.diecasting.org

Daniel Twarog, President

NADCA will be providing a one day seminar to address the challenges we face in today's marketplace.
Frequency: Annual/June

7516 **NSPE Annual Convention and Expo**
National Society of Professional Engineers
1420 King Street
Alexandria, VA 22314-2794

703-684-2800
888-285-2853
Fax: 703-836-4875
E-Mail: webmaster@nspe.org
Home Page: www.nspe.org

Katrina Robinson, Marketing Manager

The National Society of Professional Engineers is the only engineering society that represents individual engineering professionals and licensed engineers across all disciplines. Founded in 1934, NSPE serves some 60,000 members and the public through 53 state and territorial societies and more than 500 chapters nationally and internationally. The conference brings together the decision makers of engineering companies and business owners nationwide to network and discuss issues of importance.
700 Attendees
Frequency: Annual/July
Mailing list available for rent: 50,000+ names at $130 per M

7517 **National Industrial Automation, Integration & Control Show**
Reed Exhibition Companies
383 Main Avenue Suite 3
PO Box 6059
Norwalk, CT 06851-1543

203-840-4800
Fax: 203-840-5805
E-Mail: inquiry@reedexpo.com
Home Page: www.reedexpo.com

Peter DiLeo, Marketing Director
Mike Rusbridge, CEO
Domonic Shine, Chief Information Officer

Annual show of 200 exhibitors of chemical engineering and processing, electronics, machinery equipment, supplies and services.
19M Attendees

7518 **National Quality Education Conference**
American Society for Quality
600 N Plankinton Avenue
PO Box 3005
Milwaukee, WI 53201-3005

414-272-8575
800-248-1946
Fax: 414-272-1734
E-Mail: help@asq.org
Home Page: www.asq.org

James Rooney, Chair
Paul E Borawski, CEO
Erica Gumieny, Sales
Fay Spano, Communications/Media Relations

Provides teachers, administrators, and support personnel opportunities to examine continuous improvement principles used in education. It provides resources and best practices to help you address requirements of No Child Left Behind, while helping you increase student achievement and improve overall performance.
100M Members
Frequency: Annual/November
Founded in 1946

7519 **Northern American Material Handling Show & Forum**
Appliance Manufacturer
5900 Harper Road
Suite 105
Solon, OH 44139-1935

440-349-3060
800-345-1815
Fax: 440-498-9121
E-Mail: cmiller@mhia.org
Home Page: www.mhia.com

Carol Miller, Senior Director Marketing
Frequency: Bi-Annual

7520 **Northwest Plant Engineering & Maintenance Show and Conference (NWPE)**
Cygnus Expositions
3167 Skyway Court
Fremont, CA 94539

510-543-3131
Fax: 510-354-3159
E-Mail: showinfo@proshows.com
Home Page: proshows.com

Erin Sparks, Marketing Manager
Paul Bonaiuto, CFO
Kathy Scott, Director of Public Relations

Annual show of 233 exhibitors of low-tech cleaning systems, high-tech computerized maintenance management systems, diagnostic problem software, indoor air quality controllers and related products and services.
5000 Attendees
Frequency: Annual/May

7521 **Nuclear and Emerging Technologies for Space**
555 N Kensington Ave
La Grange Park, IL 60526-5592

708-352-6611
800-323-3044
Fax: 708-352-0499
E-Mail: advertising@ans.org
Home Page: www.ans.org
Social Media: Facebook, Twitter, LinkedIn

Jack Tuohy, Executive Director
James S Tulenko, VP
William F Naughton, Treasurer

Positive collaborative environment and series of discussion forums and technical showcasing.
10500 Members
Founded in 1954

7522 **OTC Expo**
Society of Petroleum Engineers

PO Box 833836
Richardson, TX 75083-3836

972-529-9300
800-456-6863
Fax: 972-952-9435
E-Mail: spedal@spe.org
Home Page: www.spe.org

Giovanni Paccaloni, President
Bill Cobbs, VP Finance
John E Bethancourt, Director Management/Information
Ian Gorman, Director Production/Operations
Niki Bradbury, Managing Director
51300 Attendees

7523 Pacific Design & Manufacturing
Canon Communications
11444 W Olympic Boulevard
Suite 900
Los Angeles, CA 90064-1549

310-445-4200
Fax: 310-445-4299
Home Page: www.pacdesignshow.com

Diane O'Conner, Trade Show Director
Dan Cutrone, Show Marketing Manager

The Pacific Design Engineering show is the most comprehensive event serving the West Coast's design, process and manufacturing marketplace. Product classifications include Coatings & Finishes, Composites, Computer Aided Design/Computer Aided Manufacturing, Electrical/Electronic, ElectroOptical Components & Equipment, Engineered Safety products, Engineering Management & Tools and more. Held at the Anaheim Convention Center in Anaheim, California.
35970 Attendees
Frequency: Annual/January

7524 Plant & Facilities Expo (PFE)
Association of Energy Engineers
4025 Pleasantdale Road
Suite 420
Atlanta, GA 30340

770-447-5083
Fax: 770-446-3969
E-Mail: info@aeecenter.org
Home Page: www.aeecenter.org

Ruth Whitlock, Executive Director
Jennifer Vendola, Accountant

Seek solutions for plant and facility needs. Vendors have an opportunity to meet prospective customers, reacquaint themselves with existing customers, and network with other vendors.
5000 Attendees
Frequency: October

7525 ProMat
Material Handling Industry of America
8720 Red Oak Blvd
Suite 201
Charlotte, NC 28217

704-676-1190
800-345-1815
Fax: 704-676-1199
Home Page: www.mhia.org

Tom Carbott, Exhibiting Information
Terri Heisey, Educational Conference & Seminar

You can compare the latest solutions essential to the productivity of your manufacturing, warehousing, and distribution operations. The material handling & logistics solutions you discover at ProMat will help you differentiate your product, improve customer service and increase overall corporate profitability. 700 exhibits.
Frequency: Annual

7526 Professional Development Conference & Exposition
1800 E Oakton Street
Des Plaines, IL 60018

847-699-2929
Fax: 847-768-3434
E-Mail: customerservice@asse.org
Home Page: www.asse.org
Social Media: Facebook, Twitter, LinkedIn

Fred Fortman, Executive Director
Bruce Sufranski, Finance/Controller Director
Diane Hurns, Manager Public Relations Department
Sally Madden, Human Resources Manager

The American Society of Safety Engineers (ASSE) is the oldest professional safety society committed to protecting people, property and the environment. ASSE has more than 32,000 occupational safety, health and environmental (SH&E) professional members who manage, supervise, research and consult on safety, health, transportation and the environment in all industries, government, labor and education.
34000 Members
4,000 Attendees
Founded in 1911

7527 REMSA and AREMA Meeting
Railway Engineering: Maintenance Supplies Assn
500 New Jersey Avenue
Suite 400
Washington, DC 20001

202-715-2921
Fax: 202-204-5753
E-Mail: home@remsa.org
Home Page: www.remsa.org

Philip Hoffman, President
John Fox, VP
David Soule, Executive Director
Ronald C Olds, Secretary/Treasurer

Holding the exhibits and technical conference simultaneously in Louisville give added benefit to REMSA members.
Frequency: Annual/September

7528 REMSA and NRC: Synergy in Action
Railway Engineering: Maintenance Supplies Assn
500 New Jersey Avenue
Suite 400
Washington, DC 20001

202-715-2921
Fax: 202-204-5753
E-Mail: home@remsa.org
Home Page: www.remsa.org

Philip Hoffman, President
John Fox, VP
David Soule, Executive Director
Ronald C Olds, Secretary/Treasurer

Members and other industry suppliers discuss their products, services and equipment with attendees representing a broad spectrum of railroaders: transits, short lines, commuter and Class I railroads. There were 56 exhibiting companies.
Frequency: Annual/January

7529 RSES Annual Conference and HVAC Technology Expo
Refrigeration Service Engineers Society
1666 Rand Road
Des Plaines, IL 60016-3552

847-297-6464
800-297-5660
E-Mail: general@rses.org
Home Page: www.rses.org
Social Media: Facebook, Twitter, LinkedIn

Lawrence Donaldson, Intl. Executive Vice President
Josh Flaim, Operations Manager
Jean Birch, Conference & Seminar Manager

80 booths consisting primarily of products and services.

7530 RoboBusiness Conference and Exposition
American Institute of Physics
One Physics Ellipse
College Park, MD 20740-3843

301-209-3100
E-Mail: dylla@aip.org
Home Page: www.aip.org

H. Frederick Dylla, Executive Director/CEO
John Haynes, Vice President Publishing
Benjamin Snavely, AIP Corporate Secretary
Melissa Poleski, Assistant To Corporate Secretary

Focuses on the business development and technical issues involved with the commercial application of mobile robotics and intelligent systems technology to develop entirely new markets and product categories, open additional lines of business and enhance existing product lines.
Frequency: Annual/May

7531 SAFETY Expo
American Society of Safety Engineers
1800 E Oakton Street
Des Plaines, IL 60018

847-699-2929
Fax: 847-768-3434
E-Mail: info@asse.org
Home Page: www.asse.org

Terri Norris, President
Kathy Seabrook, Senior Vice President
Diane Hurns, Manager Public Relations Department

A full 3-day conference featuring more than 200 sessions, an exposition with 300 exhibitors, special pre- and post-conference seminars, conference proceedings on CD, numerous networking events and more.
Frequency: Annual/July

7532 SAMPE Tech Conference
Society for the Advancement of Material & Process
1161 Park View Drive
Suite 200
Covina, CA 91724-3751

626-331-0616
800-562-7360
Fax: 626-332-8929
E-Mail: sampeibo@sampe.org
Home Page: www.sampe.org
Social Media: Facebook, LinkedIn

Gregg Balko, Executive Director
Rosemary Loggia, Conference/Exhibits Manager
Priscilla Heredia, Conference/Symposia Assistant Mgr

Known for its excellent conference programs. Featuring expert speakers and industry insiders, the information take-away from this event is invaluable to M&P professionals.
Frequency: Annual/October

7533 SME Annual Meeting
Society of Manufacturing Engineers
1 SME Drive
PO Box 930
Dearborn, MI 48121

313-425-3000
800-733-4763
Fax: 313-425-3400
E-Mail: service@sme.org
Home Page: www.sme.org

Mark Tomlinson, Executive Director/General Manager

Greg Sheremet, Publisher
Bob Harris, Director Finance

Bringing together hundreds of SME members to interact and exchange ideas with their fellow practitioners. This yearly forum offers technical training, special sessions for members, and a celebration of the best that manufacturing has to offer through our International Honor Awards Banquet.
Frequency: Annual/June

7534 STL Annual Meeting
Society of Tribologists & Lubrication
840 Busse Highway
Park Ridge, IL 60068-2376
847-825-5536
Fax: 847-825-1456
E-Mail: information@stle.org
Home Page: www.stle.org
Merle Hedland, Meetings Manager
Expect more than 300 technical and practical presentations will be selected for the Calgary program.
Frequency: Annual/May

7535 Street & Area Lighting Conference
Illuminating Engineering Society of North America
120 Wall Street
17th Floor
New York, NY 10005
212-248-5000
Fax: 212-248-5018
E-Mail: ies@ies.org
Home Page: www.ies.org
William Hanley, Executive VP
Valerie Landers, Director Member Services
500 Attendees
Frequency: Annual

7536 TBP Annual Convention
Tau Beta Pi Association
PO Box 2697
Knoxville, TN 37904-2697
865-546-4578
Fax: 865-546-4579
Home Page: www.tbp.org
Social Media: Facebook, LinkedIn
James D Froula, Executive Director
Larry Simonson, President
James Froula, Executive Director
A convention at which members conduct the official business of the Association, network with engineers from around the country, and participate in a recruiting fair.
500+ Attendees

7537 Texoma Regional Education & Training Conference
Society of American Military Engineers
607 Prince Street
Alexandria, VA 22314-3117
703-549-3800
800-336-3097
Fax: 703-684-0231
E-Mail: webmanager@same.org
Home Page: www.same.org
Dr Robert D Wolff, Executive Director
Ann McLeod, Director of Meetings
Jenni Ford, CPA, Director Finance/Accounting
Will provide opportunities to attend SAME sponsored sessions as well as TSPE sponsored training sessions. This diversity of training venues is intended to provide the attendee with exposure to a wide variety of topics and will provide a beneficial learning experience.
Frequency: Annual/June

7538 Total Product Development
American Supplier Institute
17333 Federal Drive
Suite 220
Allen Park, MI 48101-3614
313-336-8877
800-462-4500
Fax: 313-336-3187
Home Page: www.amsup.com
Dr Genichi Taguchi, Executive Director
Annual show and exhibits relating to the encouragement of change in US industry through development and implementation of advanced manufacturing and engineering technologies.
200 Attendees

7539 UNYVAC's Co-Sponsored Symposium
AVS Science & Technology Society
120 Wall Street
32nd Floor
New York, NY 10005-3993
212-248-0200
Fax: 212-248-0245
E-Mail: david_aspnes@avs.org
Home Page: www.avs.org
David E Aspnes, President
Christie R Marrian, President-Elect
John Coburn, Treasurer
Joseph J Greene, Clerk/Secretary
Nancy Schultheis, Office Manager
Topic: Functional Coatings and Surface Engineering. Will provide a forum for training and discussion of the physics and chemistry of functional coatings and surfaces.
Frequency: Bi-Annual

7540 West Coast Energy Management Congress EMC
Association of Energy Engineers
4025 Pleasantdale Road
Suite 420
Atlanta, GA 30340
770-447-5083
Fax: 770-446-3969
E-Mail: info@aeecenter.org
Home Page: www.aeecenter.org
Jennifer Vendola, Accountant
Ruth Whitlock, Executive Admin
Specifically for business, industrial and institutional energy users. It brings together the top experts in all areas of the field to help you set a clear, optimum path to both energy cost control and energy supply security.
Frequency: Annual/June

7541 Winter Meeting and Nuclear Technology Expo
American Nuclear Society
555 North Kensington Avenue
La Grange Park, IL 60526
708-352-6611
Fax: 708-352-0499
Home Page: www.ans.org
Thomas A Christopher, General Co-Chair
Michael Wallac, General Co-Chair
Topic: Talk About Nuclear Differently: A Good Story Untold.
Frequency: Annual/November

7542 World Energy Engineering Congress
Association of Energy Engineers
4025 Pleasantdale Road
Suite 420
Atlanta, GA 30340
770-447-5083
Fax: 770-446-3969
E-Mail: info@aeecenter.org
Home Page: www.aeecenter.org
Jennifer Vendola, Accountant
Ruth Whitlock, Executive Admin
A comprehensive forum where participants can fully assess the big picture and see exactly how the economic and market forces, new technologies, regulatory developments and industry trends all merge to shape their critical decisions on their organizations' energy and economic future.
Frequency: Annual/September

Directories & Databases

7543 AEG Annual Directory
Association of Engineering Geologists
300 S Jackson Street, Suite 100
PO Box 460518
Denver, CO 80246
303-757-2926
Fax: 303-757-2969
E-Mail: webeditor@aegweb.org
Home Page: www.aegweb.org
Dave Bieber, President
Darrel Schmitz, President-Elect/VP
Becky Roland, Chief Staff Executive
Terry West, Treasurer
Dorian Kuper, Secretary
Contains member and Association information.

7544 ANS Buyers Guide
American Nuclear Society
555 N Kensington Ave
La Grange Park, IL 60526-5592
708-352-6611
Fax: 708-352-0499
Home Page: www.ans.org
Jack Tuohy, Executive Director
E James Reinsch, President-Elect/VP
Harry Bradley, Executive Director
William F Naughton, Treasurer
Buyer's Guide Directory lists approximately 1150 suppliers of products and services to the nuclear industry. This comprehensive listing contains approximately 500 categories representing the wide range of nuclear components and services available today.
Cost: $110.00
Frequency: Annual
Founded in 2005

7545 ASME Database
American Society of Mechnical Engineers
3 Park Ave
Suite 21
New York, NY 10016-5990
212-591-7000
800-843-2763
Fax: 212-591-7674
E-Mail: infocentral@asme.org
Home Page: www.asme.org
Victoria Rockwell, President
Warren Leonard, Managing Director Operations
Virgil Carter, Executive Director
Provides proven direct mail buyers and selection options that enable you to customize lists to achieve your objective.

7546 AWWA Buyer's Guide
American Water Works Association
6666 W Quincy Ave
Denver, CO 80235-3098
303-794-7711
800-926-7337
Fax: 303-347-0804
Home Page: www.awwa.org
Jerry Stevens, President
David LaFrance, Executive Director
The official resource guide to water industry products and services.

7547 Advanced Energy Design Guide for Small Office Buildings
Illuminating Engineering Society of North America
120 Wall St
17th Floor
New York, NY 10005-4001
212-248-5000
Fax: 212-248-5017
E-Mail: ies@ies.org
Home Page: www.ies.org
William Hanley, Executive VP
Valerie Landers, Director Member Services
Provides a sensible approach by including practical products and readily-available, off-the-shelf technology. The Guide offers you all the tools you need to create an energy-efficient building where the owners will see a 30 percent energy savings compared to buildings that only meet the minimum requirements of Standard 90.1.
Cost: $47.00
390 Pages
Founded in 2004

7548 American Association of Cost Engineers Membership Directory
Association for Total Cost Management
209 Prairie Avenue
#100
Morgantown, WV 26501-5949
FAX 304-291-5728
Andy Dowd, Executive Director
Member directory.
Cost: $35.00
100 Pages
Frequency: Annual

7549 American Society for Engineering Education Membership Directory
1818 N St NW
Suite 600
Washington, DC 20036-2476
202-331-3500
Fax: 202-265-8504
E-Mail: f.huband@asee.org
Home Page: www.asee.org
Frank L Huband, Executive Director
Offers information on over 10,000 colleges and university engineering professors and personnel, practicing engineers and industry executives who are members of the ASEE.
200 Pages
Frequency: Annual
Circulation: 10,000

7550 American Society of Civil Engineers Official Register
1801 Alexander Bell Dr
Suite 100
Reston, VA 20191-4382
703-295-6300
800-548-2723
Fax: 703-295-6222
E-Mail: conf@asce.org
Home Page: http://www.asce.org
D Wayne Klotz, President
Provides ready access to governing documents, statistics, and general information about ASCE for leadership, members, and staff.
Cost: $24.00
640 Pages
Frequency: Annual
ISBN: 0-784407-73-8
Founded in 2005

7551 BMES Membership Directory
Biomedical Engineering Society
8201 Corporate Dr
Suite 1125
Landover, MD 20785-2224
301-459-1999
888-871-BMES
Fax: 301-459-2444
E-Mail: info@bmes.org
Home Page: www.bmes.org
Richard Waugh, President
Debra Tucker, Meeting Manager
Edward Schilling, Executive Director
A directory listing members' names, mailing addresses, telephone numbers, e-mail addresses, areas of specialization, as well as indexes of professional interest and geographic location.
Frequency: Annual

7552 Basics of Code Division Multiple Access (CDMA)
International Society for Optical Engineering
PO Box 10
Bellingham, WA 98227-0010
360-676-3290
Fax: 360-647-1445
E-Mail: customerservice@spie.org
Home Page: www.spie.org
Raghuveer Rao, Editor
Sohail Dianat, President
Amy Nelson, Manager
This text, aimed at the reader with a basic background in electrical or optical engineering, covers CDMA fundamentals: from the basics of the communication process and digital data transmission, to the concepts of code division multiplexing, direct sequence spreading, diversity techniques, the near-far effect, and the IS-95 CDMA standard form.
Cost: $35.00
120 Pages
ISBN: 0-819458-69-4

7553 CED Directory of Engineering and Engineering Technology Programs
Mississippi State University
PO Box 6046
Mississippi State, MS 39762-6046
662-258-8122
Fax: 662-325-8733
Mike Mathews, Editor
Over 150 colleges and universities with cooperative education programs in engineering and engineering technology are listed.
Cost: $50.00
250 Pages
Frequency: Biennial

7554 CRC Press
2000 NW Corporate Boulevard
Boca Raton, FL 33431
561-994-0555
800-272-7737
Fax: 772-998-0876
E-Mail: techsupport@crcpress.com
Home Page: www.crcpress.com
Eleanor Riemer, Publisher
Emmett Dages, CEO
Publisher in science, medicine, environmental science, forensic, engineering, business, technology, mathematics, and statistics. Our food science and nutrition books and our journal, Critical Reviews in Food and Nutrition, are well established and respected publications in the food science industry.

7555 CSA Engineering
Cambridge Scientific Abstracts
7200 Wisconsin Ave
Suite 601
Bethesda, MD 20814-4890
301-961-6700
Fax: 301-961-6790
E-Mail: service@csa.com
Home Page: www.csa.com
Andrew M Snyder, President
Martin Nowicki, Editor, Engineering
This database offers information on more than 500,000 citations, with abstracts, to international periodical and other research literature covering all fields of engineering and science.
Cost: $945.00
Frequency: Monthly

7556 Coolant Filtration-Additional Technologies
Society of Tribologists & Lubrication
840 Busse Hwy
Park Ridge, IL 60068-2376
847-825-5536
Fax: 847-825-1456
E-Mail: information@stle.org
Home Page: www.stle.org
Ed Salek, Executive Director
The text covers coolant cleaning and handling for metalworking operations where coolants are used as part of the process. The publication also provides the latest thinking on specific metalworking applications with some comprehensive guidelines. 76 illustrations.
Cost: $56.00
223 Pages

7557 Design-Build Project Delivery (ACEC)
American Council of Engineering Companies
1015 15th St
8th Floor NW
Washington, DC 20005-2605
202-347-7474
Fax: 202-898-0068
E-Mail: acec@acec.org
Home Page: www.acec.org
Social Media: Facebook, Twitter
Dave Raymond, President
Howard Messner, Executive Director
Guide for firms considering design/build projects. Analyzes risks, steps and milestones necessary for successful completion of design/build projects.

7558 Directory of Accredited Engineering & Technology Certification Programs
Council of Engineer and Scientific Specialty Board
PO Box 1448
Annapolis, MD 21404-1488
410-266-3766
Fax: 410-721-1746
E-Mail: academy@aaee.net
Home Page: www.cesb.org
Ronald Council, Owner
William C Anderson PE DEE, Executive Director
Provides a description of existing programs for persons interested in being certified and for those seeking an objective assessment of an expert's capability and competence.

7559 Directory of Engineering Document Sources
Global Engineering Documents
15 Inverness Way E
Englewood, CO 80112-5710
303-900-0600
800-854-7179

Fax: 303-397-2740
E-Mail: CustomerCare@ihs.com
Home Page: www.global.ihs.com

Charles Picasso, CEO

Offers over 10,000 document initialisms and acronyms for governmental, military and industry specifications and related publications.
Cost: $145.00
274 Pages
Frequency: Annual

7560 Directory of Engineers in Private Practice
National Society of Professional Engineers
1420 King St
Suite 500
Alexandria, VA 22314-2794

703-684-2800
Fax: 703-836-4875
E-Mail: webmaster@nspe.org
Home Page: www.nspe.org

Larry Jacobson, Executive Director

Consulting engineering firms and individuals who are members of the Society's Professional Engineers in Private Practice division.
Cost: $85.00
260 Pages
Frequency: Annual

7561 Directory of Iron and Steel Plants
186 Thorn Hill Rd
Warrendale, PA 15086-7528

724-814-3000
Fax: 724-814-3001
E-Mail: memberservices@aist.org
Home Page: www.aist.org

Ronald E Ashburn, Executive Director
William A Albaugh, Technology Programs Manager
Joann Cantrell, Publications Manager/Editor
Mark Didiano, Finance & Administration Manager
Stacy Varmecky, Membership Communications Manager

The Directory lists more than 2,000 companies and 17,500 individuals. Featuring data on essentially ever steel producer in the USA, Canada and Mexico, including names and titles of executive, engineering, maintenance and operating personnel. Also includes an alpha listing of all major equipment, product and service providers to the international iron and steel industry, and a listing of associations affiliated with the industry, with complete geo-indexing. Softbound book with CD.
Cost: $95.00
ISBN: 1-935117-00-1

7562 EI Page One
Engineering Information
1 Castle Point Ter
Hoboken, NJ 07030-5906

201-356-6800
800-221-1044
Fax: 201-356-6801
E-Mail: eicustomersupport@elsevier.com
Home Page: www.ei.org

This database contains a table of contents listing citations to more than 350,000 journal articles and conference papers and proceedings in all fields of engineering.

7563 ENR: Top International Design Firms Issue
McGraw Hill
1221 Avenue of the Americas
47th Floor
New York, NY 10020-1095

212-512-2000
Fax: 212-512-3840
E-Mail: webmaster@mcgraw-hill.com
Home Page: www.mcgraw-hill.com

Harold W McGraw III, CEO

Offers a list of over 200 design firms competing outside their own national borders who received largest dollar volumes in foreign contracts.
Cost: $270.00
Frequency: Annual
Circulation: 900,000

7564 Energy Engineering: Directory of Software for Energy Managers and Engineers
Fairmont Press
700 Indian Trail Lilburn Rd NW
Lilburn, GA 30047-6862

770-925-9388
Fax: 770-381-9865
Home Page: www.fairmontpress.com

Brian Douglas, President

Directory of services and supplies to the industry.
Cost: $15.00
Circulation: 8,500
ISSN: 0199-8895

7565 Manufacturer and Repair Directory
National Board of Boiler & Pressure Vessel
1055 Crupper Ave
Columbus, OH 43229-1108

614-888-0750
Fax: 614-888-0750
E-Mail: information@nationalboard.org
Home Page: www.nationalboard.org

Don Tanner, Manager
Connie Homer, Senior Executive Secretary

Manufacturers of boilers, pressure vessels, or other pressure-retaining items who are authorized to register these items with the National Board, Repair organizations holding National Board certificates of authorization for use of either the R, VR, or NR stamps.

7566 Mechanical Contractor Directory Marketing
Mechanical Contractors Association America
1385 Piccard Dr
Rockville, MD 20850-4329
301-869-5800
Fax: 301-990-9690
E-Mail: webmaster@mcaa.org
Home Page: www.mcaa.org

John Gentille, Executive VP
John Gentille, Executive VP

7567 Plumbing Directory
American Society of Sanitary Engineering
901 Canterbury Rd
Suite A
Cleveland, OH 44145-1480

440-835-3040
Fax: 440-835-3488
Home Page: www.asse-plumbing.org

Ken Van Wagnen, Manager
Sara Marxen, Compliance Coordinator
Steven Hazzard, Staff Engineer

Contains more than 4,000 plumbing words and terms, abbreviations, cross references, helpful charts and illustrations, solar energy terms. A great teaching tool for plumbing and related fields.
Cost: $21.00

7568 Research, Training, Test, and Production Reactor Directory
American Nuclear Society
555 N Kensington Ave
La Grange Park, IL 60526-5592

708-352-6611
Fax: 708-352-0499
Home Page: www.asn.org

Jack Tuohy, Executive Director
E James Reinsch, President-Elect/VP
Harry Bradley, Executive Director
William F Naughton, Treasurer
Cal Poly, Vice President

This comprehensive directory includes administrative, operational, and technical data for all nonpower reactors in the United States.
Cost: $400.00
876 Pages
ISBN: 0-894485-12-1
Founded in 1988

7569 Tau Beta Pi Information Book
Tau Beta Pi Association
PO Box 2697
Knoxville, TN 37901-2697

865-546-4578
Fax: 865-546-4579
Home Page: www.tbp.org
Social Media: Facebook, LinkedIn

Larry Simonson, President
Solange Dao, VP
Curtis D. Gomulinski, Executive Director/Treasurer

The book also serves as a reference to membership and alumni giving statistics as well as names of past and present officers, fellows, scholars, and other award winners.
Frequency: Yearly

7570 US Abrasives Industry Directory
Abrasive Engineering Society
144 Moore Rd
Butler, PA 16001-1312

724-282-6210
Fax: 724-234-2376
E-Mail: aes@abrasiveengineering.com
Home Page: www.abrasiveengineering.com

Ted Giese, Owner

Though the scene for industrial abrasive manufacturers has changed significantly over the last decade, the US continues as one of the world's largest manufacturers of abrasive products developing new abrasive grains and products that set international standards for quality and performance.

7571 Wage & Benefit Survey
North American Die Casting Association
241 Holbrook Drive
Wheeling, IL 60090-5809

847-279-0001
Fax: 847-279-0002
E-Mail: twarog@diecasting.org
Home Page: www.diecasting.org

Daniel Twarog, President

This survey provides a comprehensive look at 13 different job classifications of hourly wage earners, how they are compensated, what benefits they receive and how practices vary by company size and location.
Cost: $200.00
42 Pages
Founded in 2004

7572 Who's Who in Environmental Engineering
American Academy of Environmental Engineers
130 Holiday Ct
Suite 100
Annapolis, MD 21401-7003

410-266-3311
Fax: 410-266-7653

E-Mail: info@aaee.net
Home Page: www.aaee.net

Brian P. Flynn, President
Pasquale S. Canzano, Vice President
Joseph S. Cavarretta, Executive Director
Howard B. LaFever, Treasurer

A recognized reference for industry, consultants, recruiters, attorneys and health professionals who need to identify and locate experts in the environmental engineering profession.
Frequency: Annual
Mailing list available for rent

7573 **World Directory of Nuclear Utility Management**
American Nuclear Society
555 N Kensington Ave
La Grange Park, IL 60526-5592

708-352-6611
Fax: 708-352-0499
Home Page: www.ans.org

Jack Tuohy, Executive Director
F. James Reinsch, President-Elect/VP
Harry Bradley, Executive Director
William F Naughton, Treasurer

Is a handy desk reference listing key personnel at nuclear utility headquarters and nuclear plant sites, including plant managers, maintenance superintendents, radwaste managers, contacts for purchasing and public relations, and more.
Cost: $850.00
249 Pages
Founded in 2005

Industry Web Sites

7574 **http://gold.greyhouse.com**
G.O.L.D Grey House OnLine Databases
Grey House Publishing's online database platform, GOLD, offers Quick Search, Keyword Search and Expert Search for most business sectorc incluidng engineering markets. The GOLD platform makes finding the information you need quick and easy - whether you're a novice searcher or an experienced database user. All of Grey House's directory products are available for subscription on the GOLD platform.

7575 **www.aacei.org**
Association for Advancement of Cost Engineering
Individuals interested in applying scientific principals to the solution of problems.

7576 **www.aaee.net**
American Academy of Environmental Engineers
Improves the standards of environmental engineering. Certifies those with the special knowledge of environmental engineering and supplies a list of certified engineers to the public. Publishes reference books and other matters of interest for the profession.

7577 **www.aaee.org**
American Association for Employment in Education
Provides information and other resources to assist colleges and universities in the employment of education.

7578 **www.aaes.org**
American Association of Engineering Societies
A multidisciplinary organization dedicated to advancing the knowledge, understanding and practice of engineering in the public interest.

7579 **www.abet.org**
Accreditation Board for Engineering and Technology
Accreditation of engineering, technology and applied science educational programs.

7580 **www.abrasiveengineering.org**
Abrasive Engineering Society
Dedicated to promoting technical information about abrasives minerals and their uses including abrasives grains and products such as grinding wheels, coated abrasives and thousands of other related tools and products that serve manufacturing and the consumer.

7581 **www.acec.org**
American Council of Engineering
Membership includes more than 5,800 US firms engaged in a range of engineering works. Mission is to contribute to the nation's prosperity through advancement of the business interests of member firms.

7582 **www.acesystems.com**
AEC Systems International/Penton Media
Focuses on Internet/Intranet for the design, engineering and construction industries.

7583 **www.aea.org**
American Engineering Association, Inc.
Dedicated to the enhancement of the engineering profession and U.S. Engineering capabilities.

7584 **www.aeecenter.org**
Association of Energy Engineers
Source of information on the field of energy efficiency, utility deregulation, plant engineering, facility management and environmental compliance. Membership includes more than 8,000 professionals and certification programs. Offers seminars, conferences, job listings and certification programs.

7585 **www.aegweb.org**
Association of Engineering Geologists
Meets the professional needs of geologists who are applying their scientific training and experience to the broad field of civil and environmental engineering. Mission is to provide leadership in the development and application of geologic principles and knowledge to serve engineering, environmental and public needs.

7586 **www.aes.org**
Audio Engineering Society
Professional society devoted to audio technology. Membership includes leading engineers, scientists and other authorities in the field. Serves its members, the industry and the public by stimulating and facilitating advances in the constantly changing field of audio.

7587 **www.aiche.org**
American Institute of Chemical Engineers
Professional association of more than 50,000 members, providing leadership in advancing the chemical engineering profession. Members are those who develop processes and design and operate manufacturing plants, as well as researchers who assure the safe and environmentally sound manufacture, use and disposal of chemical products.

7588 **www.akropolis.net**
Akropolis
Directory of architects, engineers, designers, construction professionals and others in related fields. Web portal to showcase modules and applications developed by our company.

7589 **www.aocs.org**
American Oil Chemists Society
Largest international society focused on the science and technology of fats, oils, lipids, and related substances.

7590 **www.ascet.org**
American Society of Certified Engineering
Strives to obtain recognition of engineering technicians as essential to the engineering scientific team. Provides a forum for discussion of employment issues and improvement of the professional status of engineering technicians.

7591 **www.asem.org**
American Society for Engineering Management
Strives to promote the profession of engineering management as well as assisting its members in developing and improving their skills as practicing managers of engineering and technology. Members are from academic, field, industrial and governmental organizations.

7592 **www.asfe.org**
ASFE
Not-for-profit trade association. Helps geoprofessional, environmental and civil engineering firms profit through professionalism.

7593 **www.asnt.org**
American Society for Nondestructive Testing
Helps create a safer world by serving the nondestructive testing professions and promoting NDT technologies through publishing, certification, research and conferencing.

7594 **www.aspe.net**
American Society for Precision Engineering
Technical society emphasizing research, design, development, manufacture and measurement of high accuracy components and systems. Members come from the fields of engineering, materials science, physics, chemistry, mathematics and computer science, and work in industry, academia and national labs.

7595 **www.asq.org**
American Society for Quality
ASQ's mission is to facilitate continuous improvement and increase customer satisfaction. Promotes quality principles concepts and technologies. Provides information, contacts and opportunities to make things better in the workplace, in communities and in people's lives.

7596 **www.asse-plumbing.org**
American Society of Sanitary Engineering
Members are from all segments of the plumbing industry, including contractors, engineers, inspectors, journeymen, apprentices and others involved in the industry. Provides information, the opportunity to exchange ideas, solve problems and offers forum where all sides can express their views.

7597 **www.astm.org**
ASTM International
Not-for-profit organization providing a global forum for development and publication of voluntary consensus standards for materials, products, systems and services. Over 30,000 members from 100 nations include producers, users, consumers and representatives of academia and government. Formerly known as the American Society for Testing and Materials.

7598 **www.atcouncil.org**
Applied Technology Council
A nonprofit, tax-exempt corporation established through the efforts of the Structural Engineers Association of California. ATC's mission is to develop and promote state-of-the-art, user-friendly engineering re-

sources and applications for use in mitigating the effects of natural and other hazards on the built environment.

7599 **www.construction.com**
McGraw-Hill Construction

McGraw-Hill Construction (MHC), part of The McGraw-Hill Companies, connects people and projects across the design and construction industry, serving owners, architects, engineers, general contractors, subcontractors, building product manufacturers, suppliers, dealers, distributors and adjacent markets.

7600 **www.eia-usa.org**
Environmental Information Association

Nonprofit organization dedicated to providing environmental information to individuals, members and the industry. Disseminates information on the abatement of asbestos and lead-based paint, indoor air quality, safety and health issues, analytical issues and environmental site assessments.

7601 **www.electrochem.org**
Electrochemical Society

The society is an international nonprofit, educational organization concerned with phenomena relating to electrochemical and solid state science and technology. Members are individual scientists and engineers, as well as corporations and laboratories.

7602 **www.ewh.ieee.org**
Instrumentation and Measurement Society

A subsidiary of the Institute of Electrical and Electronics Engineers. Provides support to scientists and technicians who design and develop electrical and electronic measuring instruments and equipment.

7603 **www.greyhouse.com**
Grey House Publishing

Authoritative reference directories for most business sectors incluidng engineering markets. Users can search the online databases with varied search criteria allowing for custom searches by product category, geographic area, sales volume, keyword, subject and more. Full Grey House catalog and online ordering also available.

7604 **www.icc-es.org**
ICC Evaluation Service

An independent, nonprofit organization that conducts a voluntary program of evaluation of both traditional and innovative building materials, products and systems for compliance with the three major model codes in the United States.

7605 **www.iccsafe.org**
International Code Council

Nonprofit membership association with more than 16,000 members who span the building community, from code enforcement officials to materials manufacturers. Dedicated to preserving the public health, safety and welfare in the built environment through the effective use and enforcement of model codes.

7606 **www.icea.net**
Insulated Cable Engineers Association

Professional organization dedicated to developing cable standards for the electric power, control and telecommunications industries. Ensures safe, economical and efficient cable systems utilizing proven state-of-the-art materials and concepts. ICEA documents are of interest to cable manufacturers, architects and engineers, utility and manufacturing plant personnel, telecommunication engineers, consultants and OEMs.

7607 **www.iienet.org**
Institute of Industrial Engineers

Founded in Columbus, Ohio as the American Institute of Industrial Engineers.

7608 **www.irga.com**
International Reprographic Association

Represents entrepreneurial businesses serving the wide-format imaging needs of graphic arts, architectural, engineering, manufacturing, corporate, legal, retail, and POP industries.

7609 **www.manufacturing.net**
Manufacturing Marketplace

Manufacturing industry news and resources for the engineering, design, purchasing, logistics and distribution professional.

7610 **www.materialsocieties.org**
Federation of Materials Societies

Promotes cooperation among societies concerned with the understanding, development and application of materials and processes.

7611 **www.mt-online.com**
Applied Technology Publications

MT-online.com is the premier source of capacity assurance and best practice solutions for manufacturing, process and service operations worldwide. Online home of Maintenance Technology magazie, the dynamic MT-online.com portal serves the critical technical, business and professional-development needs of engineers, managers and technicians from across all industrial, institutional and commercial sectors.

7612 **www.nace.org**
National Association of Corrosion Engineers

Conducts research on corrosion control. Sponsors short courses annually at universities.

7613 **www.nationalboard.org**
National Board of Boiler & Pressure Vessel Inspec.

Membership is composed of chief boiler inspectors of states, major US cities and Canadian provinces having boiler laws.

7614 **www.naval.org**
American Society of Naval Engineers

Includes all arts construction and sciences as applied in research, development design, construction, operation, maintenance, and logistic support of surface/sub-surface ships and marine craft.

7615 **www.ncees.org**
Natl Council of Examiners for Engineering & Survey

Promotes uniform standards of registration and to coordinate interstate registration of engineers and surveyors.

7616 **www.nspe.org**
National Society of Professional Engineers

The mission of the Society is to promote the ethical, competent and licensed practice of engineering and to enhance the professional, social and economic well-being of its members.

7617 **www.remsa.org**
Railway Engineering-Maintenance Suppliers Assn

Members are distributors and manufacturers of railway track machinery supplies and services.

7618 **www.reta.com**
Refrigerating Engineers & Technicians Association

Seeks to upgrade the skills and knowledge of experienced members. Offers home-study courses on refrigeration and air conditioning.

7619 **www.rses.org**
Refrigeration Service Engineers Society

RSES is the leading training and education association for heating, ventilation, air conditioning and refrigeration professionals. It is a non-profit organization of 25,000 members in 421 chapters in the US and Canada, as well as affiliate organizations in other countries.

7620 **www.same.org**
Society of American Military Engineers

Brings together professional engineers and those in engineering-related fields to improve and increase the engineering capabilities of the nation, and to exchange and advance the knowledge of engineering technologies, applications, and practices.

7621 **www.sawe.org**
Society of Allied Weight Engineers

Consists of engineers in the aerospace industry.

7622 **www.sme.org**
Society of Manufacturing Engineers

Members are engaged in manufacturing, research and technology development.

7623 **www.spe.org**
Society of Petroleum Engineers

To provide the means for collection, dissemination and exchange of technical information concerning the development of oil and gas resources, subsurface fluid flow and production of other materials through well bores for the public benefit. To provide opportunities through its programs for interested individuals to maintain and upgrade their individual technical competence in the aforementioned areas for the public benefit.

7624 **www.steelnews.com**
Association for Iron and Steel Technology (AIST)

SteelNews.com is a publication created by the Association for Iron and Steel Technology (AIST) for the steel community. The site features daily updates of the latest global headlines.

7625 **www.sweets.construction.com**
McGraw Hill Construction

In depth product information that lets you find, compare, select, specify and make purchase decisions in the industrial product marketplace.

7626 **www.tbp.org**
Tau Beta Pi Association

The National Engineering honor society recognizes engineering students of superior scholarship and exemplary character and practitioners of engineering. Founded in 1885, the world's largest engineering organization includes 218 collegiate chapters and 220 alumnus chapters.

7627 **www.thetatau.org**
Theta Tau

A professional fraternity in engineering. Founded at the Univerity of Minnesota. Purpose of the fraternity is to develop and maintain a high standard of professional interest among its members, and to unite them in a strong bond of fraternal fellowship.

7628 **www.u.arizona.edu/n aimitril**
Reliability Engineering and Management Institute

This is an annual conference on Reliability Engineering and Management of all types of products. Over 15 leading corporations present their latest techniques in this field, and the proceedings thereof are published.

7629 **www.uefoundation.org**
United Engineering Foundation
Aims to advance engineering arts and sciences.

7630 **www.usace.army.mil**
US Army Corps of Engineers
Information on flood control, environmental protection, disaster response, military construction and support of others through the sharing of engineering expertise with other agencies, state and local governments, academia and foreign nations.

Associations

7631 **ASFE/The Geoprofessional Business Association**
8811 Colesville Rd
Suite G106
Silver Springs, MD 20910-4343
301-565-2733
Fax: 301-589-2017
E-Mail: info@asfe.org
Home Page: www.asfe.org
John P Bachner, Executive VP
Not-for-profit trade association. Supports all employess of engineering companies.
300 Members
Founded in 1969

7632 **Academy for Educational Development**
1875 Connecticut Ave Nw
Washington, DC 20009-5728
202-884-8000
Fax: 202-884-8400
E-Mail: web@aed.org
Home Page: www.aed.org
Social Media: Facebook, Twitter, YouTube
Edward W. Russell, Chairman of the Board
Roberta N. Clarke, Vice Chairman of the Board
Rebecca Logan, President and CEO
A nonprofit organization working globally to improve education, health, civil society and economic development-the foundation of thriving societies.
Founded in 1961

7633 **Adirondack Council**
103 Hand Ave, Suite 3
PO Box D-2
Elizabethtown, NY 12932-0640
877-873-2240
Fax: 518-873-6675
E-Mail: info@adirondackcouncil.org
Home Page: www.adirondackcouncil.org
Brian Ruder, Chair
Ann E. Carmel, Vice-Chair
Robert Kafin, Vice-Chair
David Heidecorn, Treasurer
Curtis R. Welling, Secretary
Research, education and advocacy to protect the natural character and communities of the Adirondack Park. Also publishes an annual State of Park Report and quarterly newsletters.
Founded in 1975
Mailing list available for rent

7634 **African American Environmentalist Association**
1629 K Street, NW
Suite 300
Washington, DC 20006
443-569-5102
E-Mail:
africanamericanenvironmentalist@msn.com
Home Page: aaenvironment.Blogspot.com
Social Media: Facebook, Twitter, LinkedIn, YouTube, RSS
Dedicated to providing energy and environmental information and educating the African American community.

7635 **Agricultural Research Institute**
1034 Miner Farm Road
PO Box 90
Chazy, NY 12921
518-846-7121
Fax: 518-846-8445
Home Page: www.whminer.com
Social Media: Facebook
Institutions concerned with environmental issues, pest control, agricultural meteorology, biotechnology, food irradiation, agricultural policy, research and development, food safety, technology transfer and remote sensing.
125 Members

7636 **Air & Waste Management Association**
420 Fort Duquesne Boulevard
One Gateway Center, 3rd Floor
Pittsburgh, PA 15222-1435
412-652-2458
Fax: 412-232-3450
E-Mail: info@awma.org
Home Page: www.awma.org
Social Media: Facebook, Twitter, LinkedIn
Jeffry Muffat, President
Merlyn L. Hough, President Elect
Mike Kelly, Secretary/ Executive Director
Amy Gilligan, Treasurer
Dallas Baker, Vice President
Supports all those involved with the environment, specifically the air and waste management industry. Publishes a magazine.
9000 Members
Founded in 1907

7637 **Air Pollution Control Association**
420 Fort Duquesne Boulevard
One Gateway Center, 3rd Floor
Pittsburgh, PA 15222
412-232-3444
Fax: 412-232-3450
E-Mail: info@awma.org
Home Page: www.awma.org
Jeffry Muffat, President
Merlyn L. Hough, President Elect
Mike Kelly, Secretary/ Executive Director
Amy Gilligan, Treasurer
Dallas Baker, Vice President
Association for the environment and conservation industry.
9000 Members
Founded in 1907

7638 **Alliance for Bio-Integrity**
2040 Pearl Lane
#2
Fairfield, IA 52556
206-888-4852
E-Mail: info@biointegrity.org
Home Page: www.biointegrity.org
Steven M Druker, Executive Director
A nonprofit organization dedicated to the advancement of human and environmental health through sustainable and safe technologies.

7639 **Alliance to Save Energy**
1850 M Street, NW
Suite 610
Washington, DC 20036
202-857-0666
Home Page: www.ase.org
Social Media: Facebook, Twitter, LinkedIn, RSS, Google+, Flickr, YouTube
Mark Warner, Honorary Chair
Jorge Carrasco, Co-Chair
Iain Campbell, 1st Vice-Chair
William Von Hoene, 2nd Vice-Chair
Carolyn Green, Treasurer
Promotes energy efficiency to achieve a healthier economy, a cleaner environment, and greater energy security.

7640 **America the Beautiful Fund**
725 15th St NW
Suite 605
Washington, DC 20005-6093
202-638-1649
Fax: 202-638-2175
E-Mail: katie@america-the-beautiful.org
Home Page: www.freeseeds.us
Nanine Bilski, President
Kathleen Rehicaldt, Program Director
Daniel Schneider, Secretary
Groups and private citizens that improve the quality of the environment.
1M Members
Founded in 1965

7641 **American Association for Aerosol Research (AAAR)**
15000 Commerce Parkway
Suite C
Mount Laurel, NJ 08054
856-439-9080
877-777-6753
Fax: 856-439-0525
E-Mail: info@aaar.org
Home Page: www.aaar.org
William Nazaroff, President
Barbara Turpin, Vice President
Barbara Wyslouzil, Vice President Elect
Murray Johnston, Treasurer
CY Wu, Secretary
AAAR is a nonprofit professional organization for scientists and engineers who wish to promote and communicate technical advances in the field of aerosol research. The Association fosters the exchange of information among members and with other disciplines through conferences, symposia and publication of a professional journal. Committed to the development of aerosol and its application to important social issues, AAAR offers an international forum for education, communication and networking.
1000 Members
Founded in 1982

7642 **American Bird Conservancy**
4249 Loudoun Ave.
P.O. Box 249
The Plains, VA 20198-2237
540-253-5780
888-247-3624
Fax: 540-253-5782ÿ
Home Page: www.abcbirds.org
George H. Fenwick, President
Rita Fenwick, VP, Development
Merrie Morrison, VP, Operations
Bob Johns, Dir., Public Relations
Anne Law, Dir., Govt. Relations
A nonprofit membership organization dedicated to the conservation of wild birds and their habitats in the Americas.
Founded in 1980

7643 **American Council on Science and Health**
1995 Broadway
Suite 202
New York, NY 10023-5882
212-362-7044
866-905-2694
Fax: 212-362-4919
E-Mail: acsh@acsh.org
Home Page: www.acsh.org
Social Media: Facebook, Twitter, LinkedIn
Dr. Elizabeth Whelan, Sc.D., M.P.H., President
Cheryl Martin, Associate Director
Dr. Gilbert Ross, M.D., Medical Director
A consumer education organization providing the public with scientifically accurate evalua-

tions of food, chemicals, the environment and health.
Founded in 1978

7644 American Farmland Trust
1150 Connecticut Avenue
Suite 600
The Plains, VA 20036
202-331-7300
Fax: 202-659-8339
Home Page: www.farmland.org
Social Media: Facebook, Twitter, WordPress
Barton Thompson, Jr., Chair
John Hardin, Vice Chair
William Cohan, Treasurer
Andrew McElwaine, President, CEO
Jimmy Daukas, VP, Programs
An organization that protects farmland and ranch land in the UnitedStates, promotes environmentally sound farming practices and keeps farmers on the land.
Founded in 1980

7645 American Fisheries Society
5410 Grosvenor Ln
Suite 110
Bethesda, MD 20814-2199
301-897-8616
Fax: 301-897-8096
Home Page: www.fisheries.org
Social Media: Facebook, Twitter
Bill Fisher, President
John Boreman, President-Elect
Bob Hughes, First Vice President
Donna Parrish, Second Vice President
Supports all those involved in the fishing industry, specifically environmental issues that the profession addresses.
9000 Members
Founded in 1870

7646 American Forests
1220 L Street NW
Suite 750
Washington, DC 20005
202-737-1944
E-Mail: info@americanforests.org
Home Page: www.americanforests.org
Social Media: Facebook, Twitter, YouTube
Ann Nichols, Chair
Bruce Lisman, Vice Chair
Roderick DeArment, Treasurer
Scott Steen, President & CEO
Peter Hutchins, Vice President/ COO
The oldest national nonprofit conservation organization in the U.S.that advocates for the protection and expansion of forests.
Founded in 1990

7647 American Institute of Hydrology
1230 Lincoln Drive
Carbondale, IL 62901
618-453-7809
E-Mail: aih@engr.siu.edu
Home Page: www.aihydrology.org
Emitt C. Witt, III, President
Marzi Sharfaei, Secretary
T. Allen J. Gookin, Treasurer
Registers and certifies hydrologists and hydrogeologists, provides a forum to discuss national and international issues, and provides educational courses.
1000 Members
Founded in 1981

7648 American Nuclear Society
555 N Kensington Ave
La Grange Park, IL 60526-5592
708-352-6611
800-323-3044
Fax: 708-352-0499
E-Mail: advertising@ans.org
Home Page: www.ans.org
Social Media: Facebook, Twitter, LinkedIn
Jack Tuohy, Executive Director
James S Tulenko, VP
William F Naughton, Treasurer
Supports all those involved in the fields of radioactive waste management, removal, handling, disposal, treatment, cleanup and environmental restoration.
10500 Members
Founded in 1954

7649 American Phytopathological Society
3340 Pilot Knob Road
Saint Paul, MN 55121-2097
651-454-7250
800-328-7560
Fax: 651-454-0766
E-Mail: aps@scisoc.org
Home Page: www.apsnet.org
Carol A. Ishimaru, President
Michael J. Boehm, President-Elect
George S. Abawi, Vice President
Randall C. Rowe, Treasurer
David M. Gadoury, Internal Communications Officer
Scientific organization that studies plant diseases and their control.
4500 Members
Founded in 1908

7650 American Public Works Association
2345 Grand Blvd
Suite 700
Kansas City, MO 64108-2625
816-472-6100
800-848-2792
Fax: 816-472-1610
Home Page: www.apwa.net
Social Media: Facebook, Twitter, YouTube
Diane M. Linderman, President
Elizabeth Treadway, President Elect
Richard F. Stinson, Director, Region I
Edward A. Gottko, Director, Region II
William Barney Mills, Jr., Director, Region III
International educational and professional association of public agencies, private sector companies, and individuals dedicated to providing high quality public works, goods and services. APWA provides a forum brings important public works-related topics to public attention in local, state, and federal areas. Mailing list for members only.
Cost: $100.00
26000 Members
Founded in 1937

7651 American Shore and Beach Preservation Association
5460 Beaujolais Lane
Fort Myers, FL 33919
239-489-2616
Fax: 239-362-9771
E-Mail: exdir@asbpa.org
Home Page: www.asbpa.org
Social Media: Facebook, Twitter
Harry Simmons, President
Nicole Elko, Secretary
Brad Pickel, Treasurer
Thomas Campbell, VP
Federal, state and local government agencies and individuals interested in conservation, development and restoration of beaches and shorefronts.
1M Members
Founded in 1926

7652 American Society for Environmental History
UW Interdisciplinary Arts and Sciences Program
1900 Commerce Street
Tacoma, WA 98402
206-343-0226
Fax: 206-343-0249
E-Mail: director@aseh.net
Home Page: www.aseh.net
John McNeill, President
Gregg Mitman, Vice President/ President Elect
Ellen Stroud, Secretary
Mark Madison, Treasurer
ASEH members are techers and researchers with an interest in human ecology and environmental history.
1200 Members
Founded in 1976

7653 American Society for Photogammetry and Remote Sensing (ASPRS)
5410 Grosvenor Lane
Suite 210
Bethesda, MD 20814-2160
301-493-0290
Fax: 301-493-0208
E-Mail: asprs@asprs.org
Home Page: www.asprs.org
Jaws Plasker, Exec. Director
Supports all those involved in mapping, photogrammetry, environmental management, remote sensing, geographic infromation, and natural resources.
6000 Members
Founded in 1934

7654 American Society of Agronomy
5585 Guilford Rd.
Madison, WI 53711-1086
608-273-8080
Fax: 608-273-2021
E-Mail: headquarters@sciencesocieties.org
Home Page: www.agronomy.org
Social Media: Facebook, Twitter, LinkedIn
Newell Kitchen, President
Kenneth Barbarick, President-Elect
Supports educators and scientists interested in the impacts of environmental perturbations on the biological and physical sciences.
10000 Members
Founded in 1907

7655 American Society of Mining and Reclamation
American Society of Mining and Reclamation
3134 Montevesta Road
Lexington, KY 40502-3548
859-351-9032
Fax: 859-335-6529
E-Mail: asmr@insightbb.com
Home Page: www.asmr.us
Social Media: Facebook
Eddie Bearden, President
Bruce Buchanan, President Elect
Richard Barnhisel, Executive Secretary
Dissemination of technical information relating to the reclamation of lands disturbed by mineral extraction. Members yearly issue is paid out of proceeding. Membership dues $50 regular $10 students.
500 Members
Founded in 1983

7656 **American Society of Safety Engineers**
1800 E Oakton Street
Des Plaines, IL 60018

847-699-2929
Fax: 847-768-3434
E-Mail: customerservice@asse.org
Home Page: www.asse.org
Social Media: Facebook

Terrie S. Norris, President
Richard A. Pollock, President Elect
Kathy Seabrook, Senior Vice President
Fred J. Fortman, Jr., Secretary & Executive Director
James D. Smith, Vice President, Finance

The oldest and largest professional safety organization. Its members manage, supervise and consult on safety, health, and environmental issues in industry, insurance, government and education.
30000 Members
Founded in 1911

7657 **Animal Protection and Rescue League**
302 Washington St.
#404
San Diego, CA 92103

858-541-0240
E-Mail: info@aprl.org
Home Page: www.aprl.org
Social Media: Facebook, Twitter, YouTube

A nonprofit organization that influences animal protection legislation, conducts rescues of abused factory farmed animals and educates people abouthumane eating.
Founded in 2003

7658 **Aquatic Plant Management Society**
PO Box 821265
Vicksburg, MS 39182-1265

FAX 601-634-5502
E-Mail: dpetty@ndrsite.com
Home Page: www.apms.org
Social Media: Facebook, LinkedIn

Tyler Koschnick, President
Terry Goldsby, President-Elect
Mike Netherland, Vice-President
Sherry Whitaker, Treasurer
Rob Richardson, Editor

An international organization of scientists, educators, students, commercial pesticide applicators, administrators, and concerned individuals interested in the management and study of aquatic plants.
Founded in 1961

7659 **Association for Environmental Health and Sciences (AEHS) Foundation, Inc.**
150 Fearing Street
Amherst, MA 01002

413-549-5170
Fax: 413-549-0579
Home Page: www.aehsfoundation.org

Paul T Kostecki, PhD, Executive Director

AEHS Foundation is a multi-disciplinary association providing a forum for individual professionals concerned with soil protection and cleanup. Fields represented include chemistry, geology, hydrogeology, law, engineering, modeling, toxicology, regulatory science, public health and public policy.
600 Members
Founded in 1989

7660 **Association for Population/Family Planning Libraries & Information Conference**
Family Health International Library
PO Box 13950
Research Triangle Park, NC 27709

919-447-7040
Home Page: www.aplici.org

Claire Twose, President
Lori Rosman, Vice-President
Joann Donatiello, Treasurer

Offers support for all those involved in issues concerning population and family planning, including publications, training and conferences.
Frequency: Annual

7661 **Association of Engineering Geologists**
PO Box 460518
Denver, CO 80246-0518

303-757-2926
Fax: 720-230-4846
E-Mail: aeg@aegweb.org
Home Page: www.aegweb.org
Social Media: Facebook, Twitter

Jennifer Bauer, President
Matthew B. Morris, Vice President/ President Elect
Gary Lice, Treasurer
Ken Fergason, Secretary

Meets the professional needs of geologists who are applying their scientific training and experience to the broad field of civil and environmental engineering. Mission is to provide leadership in the development and application of geologic principles and knowledge to serve engineering, environmental and public needs.
3000 Members
Founded in 1957
Mailing list available for rent: 3000 names at $100 per M

7662 **Association of Environmental Engineering and Science Professors**
2303 Naples Court
Champaign, IL 61822

217-398-6969
Fax: 217-355-9232
Home Page: www.aeesp.org

Joel G. Burken, President
Mark Weisner, President Elect
Jennifer Becker, Vice President
Steve K. Dentel, Secretary
Margaret Lang, Treasurer

Individuals working or teaching in the field of environmental engineering, including water quality and treatment, air quality, air pollution control and solid and hazardous waste management.
700 Members
Founded in 1963

7663 **Association of Environmental and Resource Economists**
13006 Peaceful Terrace
Silver Spring, MD 20904

202-559-8998
Fax: 202-559-8998
E-Mail: info@aere.org
Home Page: www.aere.org

Catherine L. Kling, President
Sarah L. Stafford, Secretary
Juha Siikamaki, Treasurer
Wiktor L. Adamowicz, Vice President

AERE serves as an information resource for economists involved in natural resources policy planning and research. It was estabilshed as a way to exchange ideas, stimulate research, and promote graducate research in environmental economics.
900 Members
Founded in 1979

7664 **Association of Fish & Wildlife Agencies**
444 N Capitol St NW
Suite 725
Washington, DC 20001-1553

202-624-7890
Fax: 202-624-7891
E-Mail: info@fishwildlife.org
Home Page: www.fishwildlife.org
Social Media: Facebook, Twitter

Jon Gassett, President
Jeff Vonk, Vice President
Dave Chanda, Secretary/ Treasurer
Curtis Taylor, Past President

The organization that represents all of North America's fish and wildlife agencies that promotes sound management and conservation, and speaks with a unified voice on important fish and wildlife issues.
Founded in 1902

7665 **Association of State Floodplain Managers**
2809 Fish Hatchery Rd
Suite 204
Madison, WI 53713-5020

608-274-0123
Fax: 608-828-6319
E-Mail: Larry@floods.org
Home Page: www.floods.org
Social Media: Facebook

Sally McConkey, Chair
William Nechamen, Vice Chair
Alan J. Giles, Secretary
John V. Crofts, Treasurer

Promotes common interest in flood damage abatement, supports environmental protection for floodplain areas, provides education on floodplain management practices and policy and urges incorporating multi-objective management approaches to solve local flooding problems.
6500 Members
Founded in 1977

7666 **Association of Zoos and Aquariums**
8403 Colesville Rd
Suite 710
Silver Spring, MD 20910-6331

301-562-0777
Fax: 301-562-0888
Home Page: www.aza.org
Social Media: Facebook, Twitter

L. Patricia Simmons, Chair
Tom Schmid, Chair-Elect
Jackie Ogden, PhD, Vice-Chair

A nonprofit organization dedicated to the advancement of accredited zoos and aquariums in the areas of animal care, wildlife conservation, education and science.
200 Members
Founded in 1924

7667 **Center for Biological Diversity**
P.O. Box 710ÿ
Tucson, AZ 85702-0710

520-623-5252
866-357-3349
Fax: 520-623-9797
E-Mail: center@biologicaldiversity.org
Home Page: www.biologicaldiversity.org
Social Media: Facebook, Twitter, YouTube, Instagram

Marcey Olajos, Board Chair
Stephanie Zill, Treasurer
Mary Brell, Chief Financial Officer
Paula Simmonds, Director, Development
Mike Stark, Communications Director

National U.S. group using science, law, and creative media to protect the lands, waters, and climate that species need to survive.

7668 Center for Environmental Philosophy
1155 Union Circleÿ
#310980
Denton, TX 76203-5017

940-565-2727
Fax: 940-565-4439
E-Mail: cep@unt.edu
Home Page: www.cep.unt.edu

Graduate program in environmental ethics at the University of NorthTexas.

7669 Center for Food Safety
660 Pennsylvania Ave, SE
#302
Washington, DC 20003

202-547-9359
Fax: 202-547-9429
E-Mail: office@centerforfoodsafety.org
Home Page: www.centerforfoodsafety.org
Social Media: Facebook, Twitter, Pinterest, YouTube

Andrew Kimbrell, Executive Director
Rebecca Spector, West Coast Director
Donna Solen, Senior Attorney
Cristina Stella, Staff Attorney
Elisabeth Holmes, Consulting Attorney

A U.S. environmental, nonprofit organization based in Washington, D.C.

7670 Center for a New American Dream
POÿBoxÿ797
Charlottesville, VA 22902

301-891-3683
E-Mail: newdream@newdream.org
Home Page: www.newdream.org
Social Media: Facebook, Twitter, YouTube, Pinterest

Wendy Philleo, Executive Director
Sarah Baird, Dir., Outreach & Comm.
Guinevere Higgins, Dir., Development
Edna Rienzi, Program Coordinator
Lisa Mastny, Sr. Editor & Dir. - Publications

A nonprofit organization that helps Americans reduce and shift their consumption to improve quality of life, protect the environment, and promote social justice.
Founded in 1997

7671 Citizens Campaign for the Environment
225-A Main Street
Farmingdale, NY 11735

516-390-7150
Fax: 516-390-7160
E-Mail: farmingdale@citizenscampaign.org
Home Page: www.citizenscampaign.org
Social Media: Facebook, Twitter, YouTube, RSS, Blog

Adrienne Esposito, Executive Director
Brian Smith, Associate Exe. Dir.
Mary Ellen Dour, Financial Director
Sarah Eckel, Policy Director
Jacob McCaffery, Outreach Dir.

Works to protect the environment and public health with the supportof members in New York and Connecticut.
Founded in 1985

7672 Citizens' Climate Lobbyÿ
1330 Orange Ave
#300
Coronado, CA 92118

619-437-7142
E-Mail: ccl@citizensclimatelobby.org
Home Page: citizensclimatelobby.org
Social Media: Facebook, Twitter, Instagram

Marshall Saunders, Founder/ President
Mark Reynolds, Executive Director
Steve Valk, Communications Director
Amy Bennett, Director, Operations
Danny Richter, Legislative Director

An international grassroots environmental group that trains and supports volunteers to build relationships with their Members of Congress in order to influence climate policy.

7673 Coastal Conservation Association
6919 Portwest Dr
Suite 100
Houston, TX 77024-8049

713-626-4234
800-201-FISH
Fax: 713-626-5852
E-Mail: ccantl@joincca.org
Home Page: www.joincca.org
Social Media: Twitter

David Cummins, President

Seeks to advance protection and conservation of all marine life. Conducts seminars and bestows awards.
85000 Members
Founded in 1977

7674 Committee for a Constructive Tomorrow
P.O. Box 65722
Washington, DC 20035

202-429-2737
Home Page: www.cfact.org
Social Media: Facebook, Twitter, RSS, YouTube

David Rothbard, President/ Co-Founder
Craig Rucker, Executive Director, Co-Founder
Marc Morano, Director of Communications
Duggan Flanakin, Director of Policy Research
Christina Wilson Norman, Development Officer

A conservative Washington, D.C.-based nonprofit organization that promotes a positive voice on environment and development issues.

7675 Community Alliance with Family Farmers
PO Box 363
Davis, CA 95617-363

530-756-8518
Fax: 530-756-7857
E-Mail: info@caff.org
Home Page: www.caff.org
Social Media: Facebook, Twitter, YouTube

Carol Presley, Board Chair
Pete Price, Vice President
Judith Redmond, Secretary
Vicki Williams, Treasurer

Non-profit organization that advocates for California's family farmers and sustainable agriculture. Strives to build on shared values around food and agriculture, and work together in practical, on-the-ground programs. Parterships create locally based economic vitality, improved human and environmental health, and long-term sustainability of family farms.
Cost: $47.95

7676 Conservation Education Association
Department of Conservation
PO Box 180
Jefferson City, MO 65102-0180

573-751-4115
Fax: 573-751-4467
Home Page: www.conservation.state.mo.us

John Hoskins, Director
Lorna Domke, Outreach/Education
Tom Cwyner, Editor

Focuses on conservation and the importance of protecting the environment.
Founded in 1937

7677 Conservation Fund
1655 N. Fort Myer Drive
Suite 1300
Arlington, VA 22209-3199

703-525-6300
Fax: 703-525-4610
E-Mail: postmaster@conservationfund.org
Home Page: www.conservationfund.org
Social Media: Facebook

J. Rutherford Seydel II, Chairman
R. Michael Leonard, Vice Chairman
Lawrence A. Selzer, President and CEO
Richard L. Erdmann, Executive VP and General Counsel
David K. Phillips, Jr., Treasurer, Executive VP & CFO

Works with private and public agencies and organizations to protect wildlife habitats, historic sites and parks.
Founded in 1985

7678 Conservation International
2011 Crystal Dr
Suite 500
Arlington, VA 22202-3787

703-341-2400
800-429-5660
Home Page: www.conservation.org
Social Media: Facebook, Twitter

Peter Seligmann, Chairman of the Board & CEO
Niels Crone, COO
Russell Mittermeier, Ph.D, President
Amelia Smith, Senior Vice President

Mission is to conserve the Earth's living heritage-our global biodiversity-and to demonstrate that human societies are able to live harmoniously with nature.
60M Members
Founded in 1987

7679 Conservation Law Foundation
62 Summer Street
Boston, MA 02110-1016

617-350-0990
E-Mail: e-info@clf.org
Home Page: www.clf.org
Social Media: Facebook, Twitter, LinkedIn, RSS, Instagram

John Kassel, President
William Coleman, SVP, CLF Ventures
Kate Saunders, VP, Development
Mack Davidson, VP, Finance & Admin.
Carol Gregory, VP, Marketing & Comm.

An environmental advocacy organization based in New England that advocates on behalf of the region's environment and its communities.
Founded in 1966

7680 Conservation Treaty Support Fund
3705 Cardiff Road
Chevy Chase, MD 20815

301-654-3150
800-654-3150
Fax: 301-652-6390
E-Mail: ctsf@conservationtreaty.org
Home Page: www.conservationtreaty.org

George A Furness Jr, President
Frederick E. Morris
John C. Goldsmith

Promotes awareness, understanding and support of conservation treaties and their goals. Through the International Endangered Species Treaty, the Wetlands Convention, and other conservation agreements, more than 150 nations are committed to work together to pre-

serve the wildlife and habitats that are our shared natural heritage.
Founded in 1986

7681 **Conservation and Preservation Charities of America**
1100 Larkspur Landing Circle
Suite 340
Larkspur, CA 94939

800-626-6685
Home Page: www.conservenow.org

Patrick Mcguire, President

CPCA is a consortium of environmental stewardship organizations. CPCA acts as a central focus for charitable giving dedicated to the protection of the natural habitat and historic treasures. Sponsors workplace giving campaigns in support of its member organizations.

7682 **Defenders of Wildlifeÿ**
1130 17th Street, NW
Washington, DC 20036

202-682-9400
800-385-9712
E-Mail: defenders@mail.defenders.org
Home Page: www.defenders.org
Social Media: Facebook, Twitter, RSS, YouTube, Flickr

Winsome Dunn McIntosh, Chair
Susan Wallace, Vice Chair
Richard Kopcho, Treasurer
Caroline Gabel, Secretary
Jamie Rappaport Clark, President, CEO

A nonprofit conservation organization based in the United States that protects all animals and plants native to North America in their natural communities.
Founded in 1947

7683 **Earth Island Institute**
2150 Allston Way
Suite 460
Berkeley, CA 94704-1375

510-859-9100
Fax: 510-859-9091
E-Mail: arch@earthisland.org
Home Page: www.earthisland.org
Social Media: Facebook, Twitter, YouTube

Martha Davis, President
Kenneth Brower, Vice President
Michael Hathaway, Vice President
Jennifer Snyder, Secretary
Alex Giedt, Treasurer

Seeks to prevent destruction of environment and sponsors fund drives and activist projects to protect wildlife.
33M Members
Founded in 1985

7684 **Earth Policy Institute**
1350 Connecticut Avenue NW
Suite 403
Washington, DC 20036

202-496-9290
Fax: 202-496-9325
E-Mail: epi@earthpolicy.org
Home Page: www.earth-policy.org
Social Media: Facebook, Twitter, RSS

Judith Gradwohl, Chairman
Lester R. Brown, Founder, President
Reah JaniseÿKauffman, Co-Founder, VP
Janet Larsen, Director of Research
J. Matthew Roney, Research Associate

An independent nonprofit environmental organization based in Washington D.C. in the United States.
Founded in 2001

7685 **Earth Regeneration Society**
1442A Walnut Street
#57
Berkeley, CA 94709-1405

510-527-9716
Fax: 510-559-8410
E-Mail: alden@earthregenerationsociety.org
Home Page: www.earthregenerationsociety.org

Alden Bryant, President
Cynthia Johnson, Secretary
Glen A. Frendel, Executive Director

Organized to develop and study scientific and practical solutions to environmental issues.

7686 **Earth Society Foundation**
238 East 58th Street
Suite 2400
New York, NY 10022

212-832-3659
800-3EA-THDA
E-Mail: earthsociety1@hotmail.com
Home Page: www.earthsocietyfoundation.org
Social Media: Facebook

Monica Getz, Chairperson
Stan Cohen, President
Tom Dowd, VP

News of interest in environmental and sociological issues. Purpose is to promote Earth Day and the Earth Trustee agenda; Every individual and institution should seek choices in ecology, economics, and ethics that will eliminate pollution, poverty, and violence.

7687 **Earth's Birthday Project**
PO Box 1536
Santa Fe, MN 87504-1536

505-986-6040
800-698-4438
Fax: 505-984-9176
E-Mail: info@earthsbirthday.org
Home Page: www.earthsbirthday.org
Social Media: Facebook, Twitter

Albert Scharfÿ, President
Richard Murray, Treasurer
Mary Hofstedt, Secretary
Clifford Ross, Executive Director
Alia Munn, National Program Director

A U.S. based educational nonprofit organization that inspires wonder, learning, and care of the natural world in children, teachers, and parents.
Founded in 1989

7688 **Ecological and Toxicological Association of Dyes**
1850 M St NW
Suite 700
Washington, DC 20036-5810

202-721-4154
Fax: 202-296-8120
Home Page: www.etad.com

Jill Aker, President

Represents the interests of manufacturers and formulators of dyes in the region with regard to environmental and health hazards in the manufacture, processing, shipment, use and disposal of thier products.
Founded in 1982

7689 **Energy Action Coalition**

Home Page: www.energyactioncoalition.org
Social Media: Facebook, Twitter, RSS, Flickr, YouTube, Vimeo

Maura Cowley, Executive Director
Kristina Banks, Operations Coordinator
Whit Jones, Campaign Director
Tina Johnson, Senior Director
Joe Solomon, Social Media Coordinatorÿ

A North American nonprofit organization made up of 50 partner organizations in the U.S. and Canada that runs campaigns to build the youth and student clean energy movement and advocate for changes on local, state, national, andinternational levels in North America.

7690 **Environmental & Energy Study Institute**
122 C Street NW
Suite 630
Washington, DC 20001

202-628-1400
Fax: 202-204-5244
E-Mail: eesi@eesi.org
Home Page: www.eesi.org
Social Media: Facebook, Twitter, YouTube

Jared Blum, Board Chair
Shelley Fidler, Board Treasurer
Richard L. Ottinger, Board Chair Emeritus

A non-profit organization dedicated to promoting environmentally sustainable societies.
Founded in 1984

7691 **Environmental Alliance for Senior Involvement**
5615 26th St N
Arlington, VA 22207-1407

703-241-4927
Fax: 203-779-0025
Home Page: www.easi.org

Thomas Benjamin, President
Roy Geiger, VP Administration
Peggy Knight, VP Programs

Engaging senior volunteers to use their experience in the restoration and maintenance of environmentally sound environments.
International network.
Founded in 1990

7692 **Environmental Assessment Association**
810 N. Farrell Drive
PO Box 879
Palm Springs, CA 92263

760-327-5284
877-810-5643
Fax: 760-327-5631
E-Mail: info@eaa-assoc.org
Home Page: www.eaa-assoc.org
Social Media: LinkedIn

Robert Johnson, Executive Director

Supports all those involved in environmental assessment, including training and education, publications, conferences and research resources.

7693 **Environmental Bankers Association**
510 King St
Suite 410
Alexandria, VA 22314-3212

703-549-0977
800-966-7475
Fax: 703-548-5945
E-Mail: eba@envirobank.org
Home Page: www.envirobank.org

Rich Ferguson, President
Sharon Valverde, Vice President
Scott Beckerman, Treasurer
Stephen Richardson, Secretary
D. Jeffrey Telego, Executive Co-Director

EBA voting members are banks, trust companies, credit unions, savings and loan associations, and other financial services organizations with an interest in environmental risk management and related issues. Active participants are bankers from Trust or Credit offices with responsibility for environmental liability, and financial services officers with environmental

interests. Affiliate members are from law firms, consulting and insurance organizations.
Founded in 1994

7694 **Environmental Business Association**
991 Broadway
Suite 207
Albany, NY 12204
518-432-6400
Fax: 518-432-1383
Home Page: www.eba-nys.org
Suzanne Maloney, Executive Director
Deidre Murphy, Program Director
EBA members represent all segments of the environmental industry—consultants, labaoratories, remediation companies, disposal firms, recyclers and technology innovators. EBA facilitates arrangements and information exchange among members to develop business opportunities. Services include sponsoring seminars, monthly meetings, industry trends, changes in technology and legislation.
Founded in 1989

7695 **Environmental Compliance Institute**
165 Sherwood Ave
Farmingdale, NY 11735
631-414-7757
Fax: 631-843-6331
E-Mail: pbany@c2g.us
Home Page: www.c2g.us
Attorneys and corporations interested in environmental law and federal regulations governing waste disposal and other matters related to the environment.

7696 **Environmental Council of the States(ECOS)**
50 F Street NW
Suite 350
Washington, DC 20001
202-266-4920
Fax: 202-266-4937
Home Page: www.ecos.org
R. Steven Brown, Executive Director
Carolyn Hanson, Deputy Executive Director
Jim Blizzard, Senior Counselor
Improving the capability of State environmental agencies and their leaders to protect and improve human health and the environment of the United States of America.

7697 **Environmental Design Research Association**
1760 Old Meadow Road
Suite 500
McLean, VA 22102
703-506-2895
Fax: 703-506-3266
E-Mail: edra@telepath.com
Home Page: www.edra.org
Social Media: Facebook, Twitter, LinkedIn
Nick Watkins, Chair
Mallika Bose, Chair-Elect
Vikki Chanse, Secretary
Shauna Mallory-Hill, Treasurer
Kate O'Donnell, Executive Director(ex-officio)
Is to advance the art and science of environmental design research, to improve understanding of the interrelationships between people and their built and natural surroundings, and to help create environments responsive to human needs. EDRA members are designers and other professionals with an interest in environmental design research.
700 Members
Founded in 1968

7698 **Environmental Industry Association**
4301 Connecticut Ave Nw
Suite 300
Washington, DC 20008-2304
202-244-4700
800-424-2869
Fax: 202-966-4824
E-Mail: wa@envasns.org
Home Page: www.envasns.org
Social Media: Facebook
Bruce Parker, President
Supports all those involved with technology of recycling, resource recovery and sanitary landfills. Publishes magazine.

7699 **Environmental Information Association**
6935 Wisconsin Ave
Suite 306
Chevy Chase, MD 20815-6112
301-961-4999
888-343-4342
Fax: 301-961-3094
E-Mail: info@eia-usa.org
Home Page: www.eia-usa.org
Dana Hudson, President
Mike Schrum, President Elect
Kevin Cannan, Vice President
Joy Finch, Secretary
Chris Gates, Treasurer
Nonprofit organization dedicated to providing environmental information to individuals, members and industry. Disseminates information on the abatement of asbestos and lead-based paint, indoor air quality, safety and health issues, analytical issues and environmental site assessments.

7700 **Environmental Law Institute**
2000 L St NW
Suite 620
Washington, DC 20036-4919
202-939-3800
800-433-5120
Fax: 202-939-3868
E-Mail: law@eli.org
Home Page: www.eli.org
John Cruden, President
Martin Dickinson, VP Development
Chandra Middleton, Director Associates Programs
Melodie DeMulling, Director, Associates Programs
Supports all those involved in environmental issues from a legal perspective, fostering the exchange of ideas and solutions for pressing environmental issues.

7701 **Environmental Mutagen Society**
1821 Michael Faraday Drive
Suite 300
Reston, VA 20190
703-438-8220
Fax: 703-438-3113
E-Mail: emshq@ems-us.org
Home Page: www.ems-us.org
Catherine B. Klein, President
Mats Ljungman, President-Elect
Suzanne M. Morris, Secretary
Barbara S. Shane, Treasurer
Tonia Masson, Executive Director
Members are scientists of diverse backgrounds and varied interests working in the field of molecular genetics and mutagenesis, whether in academia, industry or government. Focus is to encourage the study mutagens in the human environment particularly as they affect public health.
1500 Members
Founded in 1969

7702 **Environmental and Energy Study Instituteÿ**
1112 16th Street, NW
Suite 300
Washington, DC 20036
202-628-1400
Fax: 202-204-5244
E-Mail: info@eesi.org
Home Page: www.eesi.org
Social Media: Facebook, Twitter, YouTube, Google+
Carol Werner, Executive Director
Alison Alford, Program & Administrative Assistant
John Michael Cross, Policy Associate
Amaury Laporte, Communications Director
David Robison, Director of Finance
Educating Congress on energy efficiency and renewable energy; advancing innovative policy solutions.
Founded in 1984

7703 **Federation of Environmental Technologists**
W175 N11081 Stonewood Dr.
Ste 203
Germantown, WI 53022-4771
262-437-1700
Fax: 262-437-1702
E-Mail: info@fetinc.org
Home Page: www.fetinc.org
Dan Brady, Board Chair
Mark Steinberg, President
Dave Seitz, Vice President
Anthony Montemurro, Treasurer
Jeffrey Nettesheim, Secretary
FET assists members in interpretation of and compliance with environmental regulations.
700 Members
Founded in 1981

7704 **Floodplain Management Association**
PO Box 712080
Santee, CA 92072-2080
619-204-4380
Fax: 619-749-9524
E-Mail: admin@floodplain.org
Home Page: www.floodplain.org
Lovanka Todt, Manager
A nonprofit educational association established to promote the reduction of flood losses and to encourage the protection and enhancement of nautral floodplain values through the use of effective wetland management strategies and engineering technolgies.
Founded in 1990

7705 **Forest History Society**
701 William Vickers Ave
Durham, NC 27701-3162
919-682-9319
Fax: 919-682-2349
E-Mail: recluce2@duke.edu
Home Page: www.foresthistory.org
Social Media: Facebook, Twitter
L. Michael Kelly, Chairman
Robert Healy, Co-Vice Chairman
Mark Wilde, Co-Vice Chairman
Henry I. Barclay III, Treasurer
Steven Anderson, Secretary & President
Nonprofit, educational institution that explores the history of the environment, forestry and conservation.
2000 Members
Founded in 1946

7706 **Forestry, Conservation Communications Association**
PO Box 162655
Miami, FL 33116-2655
717-338-1505
Fax: 717-334-5656
E-Mail: ed@fcca-usa.org
Home Page: www.fcca.info
Lloyd M. Mitchell, President
Roy Mott, Vice President
John McIntosh, Secretary/Treasurer
Ralph Haller, Executive Director
Association for manufacturers or suppliers of forestry and conservation communications equipment, systems and procedures.

7707 **Friends of the Trees Society**
PO Box 826
Tonasket, WA 98855
509-486-4056
E-Mail: friendsofthetrees@yahoo.com
Home Page: www.friendsofthetrees.net
Michael Pilarski, Director
Nonprofit organization helping tree lovers worldwide.
Founded in 1978

7708 **GREENGUARD Environmental Institute**
2211 Newmarket Parkway
Suite 110
Marietta, GA 30067
888-485-4733
Fax: 770-980-0072
E-Mail: environment@ul.com
Home Page: www.greenguard.org
An industry-independent organization that aims to protect human health and improve quality of life by enhancing indoor air quality and reducing people's exposure to chemicals and other pollutants.

7709 **Global Water Policy Project**
E-Mail: info@globalwaterpolicy.org
Home Page: www.globalwaterpolicy.org
Promotes the preservation and sustainable use of Earth's fresh water through research, writing, outreach, and public speaking.

7710 **Great Lakes United**
4380 Main St
Amherst, NY 14226-3592
716-886-0142
Fax: 716-204-9521
E-Mail: glu@glu.org
Home Page: www.glu.org
Catherine Gillespie, President
Julie O'Leary, VP
Robert Miller, Treasurer
An international, environmental coaltion working to preserve and protect the Great Lakes and St. Lawrence River. Memberships are as follows: $100 organizational members, $25 organizational members w/bugdets below $15,000, $25 individuals, and $50 family members.
1.1M Members
Founded in 1982

7711 **Green Zionist Alliance**
PO Box 30006
New York, NY 10011
347-559-4492
E-Mail: info@greenzionism.org
Home Page: www.aytzim.org
Rabbi Michael Cohen, Co-founder
David Krantz, Board of Director
Susan Levine, Board of Director
Netta Schmeidler, Board of Director
Pesach Stadlin, Board of Director
A North America-based nonprofit organization that works to educate and mobilize people around the world for Israel's environment, to protect Israel's environment and support its environmental movement.
Founded in 2001

7712 **Greenpeace USA**
702 H St NW
Suite 300
Washington, DC 20001-3876
202-737-2336
Fax: 202-462-4507
E-Mail: goa@wdc.greenpeace.org
Home Page: www.greenpeaceusa.org
Social Media: Facebook
John Passacantando, CEO
Ellen McPeake, COO
Leading independent campaigning organization that uses non-violent direct action and creative communication to expose global environmental problems and to promote solutions that are essential to a green and peaceful future.
2.5M Members
Founded in 1971

7713 **Honor The Earth**
Home Page: www.honorearth.org
Social Media: Facebook, Twitter
A nonprofit organization founded to raise awareness and financial support for Indigenous environmental justice.
Founded in 1993

7714 **Institute for Energy and Environmental Research**
6935 Laurel Ave.
Suite 201
Takoma Park, MD 20912ÿ
301-270-5500
Fax: 301-270-3029
E-Mail: info@ieer.org
Home Page: ieer.org
Social Media: Facebook, Twitter, RSS
Arjun Makhijani, President, Senior Engineer
Sadaf Rassoul Cameron, Vice President
David Close, Ph.D., Treasurer, Secretary
Annie Makhijani, Project Scientist
Christina Mills, Staff Scientist
Focuses on the environmental safety of nuclear weapons production, ozone layer depletion, and other issues relating to energy.
Founded in 1987

7715 **Institute for Environmental Auditing**
St. Nicholas House 70 Newport
Lincoln LN1 3DP
152-540-90
E-Mail: info@iema.net
Home Page: www.iema.net
Jam Chimel, Chief Executive
Matrin Baxter, Executive Director
Allison Hall, Marketing Director
Claire Lea, Director of Membership Services
Bea Walshaw, Operations Manager
A professional organization of environmental auditors.
100 Members

7716 **Institute for World Resource Research**
PO Box 50303
Palo Alto, CA 94303-0303
630-910-1551
Fax: 202-729-7610
Home Page: www.globalwarming.net
BJ Jefferson, Advertising/Sales
Supports those involved in all phases of developments in forestry and reforestation of northern nations including the US, Canada, Russia, Sweden, Finland, Norway, China, Japan and others. Its goal is to increase the worldwide understanding of the ecological and economic roles of the northern forest regions of the world.

7717 **Institute of Environmental Sciences and Technology**
5005 Newport Drive
Suite 506
Rolling Meadows, IL 60008-3841
847-255-1561
Fax: 847-981-4130
Home Page: www.iest.org
Social Media: Facebook, Twitter, LinkedIn
Julie Kendrick, Executive Director
Robert Burrows, Director Communications Services
Corrie Roesslein, Director Programs/Administration
Is an international professional society that serves members and the industries they represent through education and the development of recommended practices and standards.
1600 Members
Founded in 1953

7718 **Institute of Gas Technology**
1700 S Mount Prospect Rd
Des Plaines, IL 60018-1804
847-768-0664
Fax: 847-768-0669
Home Page: www.gastechnology.org
Social Media: Facebook, Twitter, LinkedIn, YouTube
David Carroll, President & CEO
Ronald Snedic, Vice President/ Corporate Devel.
Paul Chromek, General Counsel & Secretary
Supports all those involved in the gas industry worldwide, including energy industry production, consumption, reserves, imports and prices.

7719 **Institute of Scrap Recycling Industries**
1615 L St NW
Suite 600
Washington, DC 20036-5664
202-662-8500
Fax: 202-626-0900
E-Mail: isri@isri.org
Home Page: www.isri.org
John Sacco, Chairman
Jerry I. Simms, Chair Elect
Douglas Kramer, Vice Chair
Mark R. Lewon, Secretary Treasurer
Supports all those involved in the scrap processing and recycling industry.
165 Members
1987 Attendees

7720 **International Association for Food Protection**
6200 Aurora Ave
Suite 200W
Des Moines, IA 50322-2864
515-276-3344
800-369-6337
Fax: 515-276-8655
E-Mail: info@foodprotection.org
Home Page: www.foodprotection.org
Social Media: Facebook, Twitter, LinkedIn
Isabel Walls, President
Katherine M.J. Swanson, President-Elect
Don Schaffner, Vice President
Don Zink, Secretary
David W. Tharp, Executive Director
Nonprofit, educational association of food protection professionals. The association is dedi-

cated to the education and service of its members, specifically, as well as industry personnel.
3400 Members
Founded in 1911

7721 **International Association of Wildland Fire**
1418 Washburn Street
Missoula, MT 59801

406-531-8264
888-440-4293
E-Mail: iawf@iawfonline.org
Home Page: www.iawfonline.org
Social Media: Facebook, Twitter

Chuck Bushey, President
Kris Johnson, VP
Mikel Robinson, Executive Director
Kevin Ryan, Secretary
Daniel Bailey, Treasurer

IWAF members are academics and professionals with an interest in wildland fires.
800 Members
Founded in 1990

7722 **International Council on Nanotechnology - ICON**

214-494-2071
Home Page: icon.rice.edu

Vicki Colvin, Executive Director
Kristen Kulinowski, Director

A portal for information about the environmental, health, and safety aspects of nanotechnology.

7723 **International Ecotourism Society**
PO Box 96503 #34145
Washington, DC 20090-6503

202-506-5033
Fax: 202-789-7279
E-Mail: info@ecotourism.org
Home Page: www.ecotourism.org
Social Media: Facebook, Twitter, YouTube

Kelly Bricker, Chair
Tony Charters, Vice Chair
Neal Inamdar, Director Finance/Administration

Society members include park managers, tour operators, conservation professionals, and others with an interest in the development of ecology-centered tourism.
900 Members
Founded in 1990

7724 **International Lead Zinc Research Organization**
1822 NC Highway 54 East
Suite 120
Durham, NC 27713

919-361-4647
Fax: 919-361-1957
E-Mail: rputnam@ilzro.org
Home Page: www.ilzro.org

Stephen Wilkinson, President
Frank Goodwin, VP Materials Sciences
Scott Mooneyham, Treasurer
Rob Putnam, Director Communications

ILZRO members are miners and refiners of lead and zinc. Trade association of the lead and zinc industry worldwide. Focus on research and development to detect new uses for the metals and refine existing uses.
Founded in 1958

7725 **International Society for Ecological Economics**
15 River Street
#204
Boston, MA 02108

703-790-1745
Fax: 703-790-2672
E-Mail: secretariat@ecoeco.org
Home Page: www.ecoeco.org
Social Media: Facebook, Twitter

John Gowdy, President
Bina Agarwal, President-Elect
Anne Aitken, Treasurer

Members are researchers, academics, and other professionals who study the impact of economic models and policies on the environment.
750 Members
Founded in 1989

7726 **Isaak Walton League**
707 Conservation Lane
Gaithersburg, MD 20878

301-548-0150
800-453-5463
Fax: 301-548-0146
E-Mail: general@iwla.org
Home Page: www.iwla.org
Social Media: Facebook, Twitter

Jim A. Madsen, President
Robert Chapman, Vice President
Marj Striegel, Secretary
Walter Lynn Jr., Treasurer

Protects America's outdoors through education, community-based conservation, and promoting outdoor recreation.
37000 Members
Founded in 1922

7727 **Keep America Beautiful**
1010 Washington Boulevard
Stamford, CT 6901

203-659-3000
Fax: 203-659-3001
E-Mail: info@kab.org
Home Page: www.kab.org
Social Media: Facebook, Twitter, Tumblr, YouTube, Pinterest

Timothy Gardner, Chairman
Jennifer M. Jehn, President/ CEO
Lynn Markley, SVP, Brand Development
Becky Lyons, Chief Operating Officer
Kathleen Quinn, Director, Finance

Nonprofit organization that builds and sustains vibrant communities.
Founded in 1953

7728 **League of Conservation Votersÿ**
1920 L Street, NW
Suite 800
Washington, DC 20036

202-785-8683
Fax: 202-835-0491
E-Mail: jeff_gohringer@lcv.org
Home Page: www.lcv.org
Social Media: Facebook, Twitter, YouTube, Flickr

Carol Browner, Chair
Sherwood Boehlert, Vice Chair
Tom Kiernan, Treasurer
Marcia Bystryn, Secretary
Gene Karpinski, President

A political advocacy organization that advocates for sound environmental policies and elects pro-environmental candidates who will adopt and implement such policies.

7729 **Marine Technology Society**
1100 H St., Nw
Suite LL-100
Washington, DC 20005

202-717-8705
Fax: 202-347-4302
E-Mail: membership@mtsociety.org
Home Page: www.mtsociety.org
Social Media: Facebook, Twitter, LinkedIn

Jerry Boatman, President
Drew Michel, President-Elect
Jerry Wilson, VP of Industry and Technology
Jill Zande, VP of Education and Research
Justin Manley, VP of Gov. & Public Affairs

Addresses coastal zone management, marine, mineral and energy resources, marine environmental protection, and ocean engineering issues.
2M Members
Founded in 1963

7730 **Midwest for Environmental Science and Public Policy**
1845 N Farwell Avenue
Suite 100
Milwaukee, WI 53202

414-271-7280
Fax: 414-273-7293
Home Page: www.mcespp.org

Patrice Ann Morrow, Chair
Jeffery A Foran, President/CEO

For citizens concerned with environmental protection.

7731 **NORA: Association of Responsible Recyclers**
5965 Amber Ridge Rd
Haymarket, VA 20169-2623

703-753-4277
Fax: 703-753-2445
E-Mail: sparker@noranews.org
Home Page: www.noranews.org

Chris Ricci, President
Brandon Velek, Executive Vice President
Bill Hinton, Vice President
Don Littlefield, Vice President, Finance

Is a trade association representing the interests of companies in the United States engaged in the safe recycling of used oil, antifreeze, waste water and oil filters.
Founded in 1984

7732 **National Association for Environmental Management**
1612 K St NW
Suite 1102
Washington, DC 20006-2830

202-986-6616
800-391-6236
Fax: 202-530-4408
E-Mail: programs@naem.org
Home Page: www.naem.org
Social Media: Facebook, Twitter, LinkedIn

Kelvin Roth, President
Stephen Evanoff, 1st Vice President
Debbie Hammond, 2nd Vice President
Frank Macielak, Secretary and Treasurer

Dedicated to advancing the profession of environmental management and supports the professional corporate and facility environmental manager.
1000+ Members
Founded in 1990

7733 **National Association for PET Containers**
Po Box 1327
Sonoma, CA 95476

707-996-4207
Fax: 707-935-1998
E-Mail: information@napcor.com
Home Page: www.napcor.com
Social Media: Facebook

Dennis Sabourin, Executive Director
Kate Eagles, Communications
Don Kneass, Director
Sandi Childs, Director

National association for the PET plastic industry. Promotes the use of PET plastic packaging and facilitates the recycling of PET containers.
Frequency: Bi-Monthly
Founded in 1987

7734 National Association of Environmental Professionals
PO Box 460
Collingswood, NJ 08108
856-283-7816
Fax: 856-210-1619
E-Mail: naep@bowermanagementservices.com
Home Page: www.naep.org
Social Media: Facebook, LinkedIn

Paul Looney, President
Harold Draper, Vice President
Joseph F. Musil Jr., Treasurer
Robert P. Morris Jr., Secretary

Our mission is to be the interdisciplinary organization dedicated to developing the highest standards of ethics and proficiency in the environmental professions. Our members are public and private sector professionals who promote excellence in decision-making in light of the environmental, social, and economic impacts of those decisions.

7735 National Association of Local Government Environmental Professionals
1333 New Hampshire Ave NW
Second Floor
Washington, DC 20036-1532
202-879-4014
Fax: 202-393-2866
E-Mail: nalgep@spiegelmcd.com
Home Page: www.nalgep.org
Social Media: Facebook

Is a national organization representing local government professionals responsible for environmental compliance and the development of local environmental policy. NALGEP brings together local environmental officials to share information on practices, conduct policy projects, promote environmental training and education, and communicate the view of local officials on national environmental issues.
150 Members
Founded in 1993

7736 National Audubon Society
225 Varick Street
New York, NY 10014
212-979-3000
E-Mail: webmaster@audubon.org
Home Page: www.audubon.org
Social Media: Facebook, Twitter, YouTube

Conserves and restores natural ecosystems, focusing on birds, other wildlife, and their habitats for the benefit of humanity and the earth's biological diversity.
50000 Members
Founded in 1992

7737 National Center for Appropriate Technology
3040 Continental Drive
PO Box 3838
Butte, MT 59702
406-494-4572
800-275-6228
Fax: 406-494-2905
Home Page: www.ncat.org
Social Media: Facebook, Twitter, LinkedIn

Gene Brady, Chairman
Randall Chapman, Vice Chairman
George Ortiz, Chairman Emeritus
Jeannie Jertson, Secretary
Brian Castelli, Treasurer

Their mission is to help people by championing small-scale, local, and sustainable solutions to reduce poverty, promote healthy communities, and protect natural resources.
Founded in 1976

7738 National Conference of Local Environmental Health Administrators
1010 South Third Street
Dayton, WA 99328
509-382-2181
Fax: 360-382-2942
E-Mail: David_Riggs@co.columbia.wa.us
Home Page: www.ncleha.org

A professional association for supervisors, administrators and managers of environmental health programs in local agencies.

7739 National Council for Science and the Environment
1101 17th Street NW
Suite 250
Washington, DC 20036ÿ
202-530-5810
Fax: 202-628-4311
E-Mail: NCSE@NCSEonline.org
Home Page: www.ncseonline.org
Social Media: Facebook, Twitter, LinkedIn, YouTube, Flickr

Peter Saundry, Ph.D., Executive Director
Andi Glashow, Director, Finance
Sudeep Vyapari, Ph.D., Associate Executive Director
Jessica Soule, Director, EnvironMentors
David Blockstein, Ph.D., Senior Scientist, Dr. Education

A U.S. based nonprofit organization that improves the scientific basis for environmental decision-making.

7740 National Environmental Balancing Bureau
8575 Grovemont Cir
Gaithersburg, MD 20877-4121
301-977-3698
866-497-4447
Fax: 301-977-9589
E-Mail: karen@nebb.org
Home Page: www.nebb.org

Neil J. Marshall, President
Stanley J. Fleischer, President-Elect
Bob Linder, Vice President
James Huber, Treasurer

NEBB is an international certification assocaition for firms that deliver high performance building systems. Members perform testing, adjusting and balancing (TAB) of heating, ventilating and air-conditioning systems, commission and retro-commission building systems commissioning, execute sound and vibration testing, and test and certify lab fume hoods and electronic and bio clean rooms. NEBB holds the highest standards in certification.
Founded in 1971

7741 National Environmental Development Association
One Thomas Circle NW
10th Floor
Washington, DC 20006
202-332-2933
Fax: 202-530-0659

Phil Clapp, President
Steve Hellem, Executive Director

NEDA members are companies and other organizations concerned with balancing environmental and economic interests to obtain both a clean environment and a strong economy.
Founded in 1973

7742 National Environmental, Safety and Health Training Association
2700 N. Central Avenue
Suite 900
Phoenix, AZ 85004-1147
602-956-6099
Fax: 602-234-1867
E-Mail: neshta@neshta.org
Home Page: www.neshta.org

A non-profit educational society for environmental, safety, health and other technical training and adult education professionals. Mission is to promote trainer competency through trainer skills training, continuing education, voluntary certification, peer networking and the adoption of national and international training and trainer standards.
Founded in 1977

7743 National Institutes for Water Resources
47 Harkness Road
Pelham, MA 10002
413-253-5686
Fax: 413-253-1309
E-Mail: tracy@uidaho.edu
Home Page: niwr.net

Jeffery Allen, President
Reagan Waskom, President-Elect
John Tracy, Secretary-Treasurer

NIWRD represents state and territorial Water Research Institutes and Centers in collective activities to implement the provisions of the Water Resources Act of 1984, and subsequesnt federal legislation. NIWR networks these separate institutes into a coordinated unit, represented by 8 regional groupings, and facilitates the response of the Water Research Institutes and its membership to other mutual concerns and interests in water resources.
54 Members
Founded in 1974

7744 National Registry of Environmental Professionals
PO Box 2099
Glenview, IL 60025
847-724-6631
Fax: 847-724-4223
E-Mail: nrep@nrep.org
Home Page: www.nrep.org
Social Media: Facebook, Twitter, LinkedIn, YouTube

Richard A Young, PhD, Executive Director
Edward Beck, PhD, Senior Director
Carol Schellinger, Director

To promote legal and professional recognition of individuals possessing education, training and experience as environmental managers, engineers, technologists, scientists and technicians-and to consolidate that recognition in one centralized source-so that the public, government, employers and insurers can justify the importance and acceptance of such individuals to carry out operations and management of environmental activities.
17000 Members
Founded in 1983
Mailing list available for rent

7745 **National Society of Environmental Consultants**
PO Box 12528
San Antonio, TX 78212-0528

210-271-0781
800-486-3676
Fax: 210-225-8450

Supports all activities of environmental consultants.
600 Members
Founded in 1992

7746 **National Solid Wastes Management Association**
4301 Connecticut Ave NW
Suite 300
Washington, DC 20008-2304

202-244-4700
800-424-2869
Fax: 202-966-4824
E-Mail: wa@envasns.org
Home Page: www.envasns.org
Social Media: Facebook, Twitter, YouTube

Bruce Parker, President
Chaz Miller, Director, State Programs
David Biderman, General Counsel & Director
Christine Hutcherson, Director, Member Services
Alice Jacobsohn, Director, Education

Supports all those involved in the environment industry, especially the handling, transportation and disposal of infectious wastes.

7747 **National Wildlife Federation**
11100 Wildlife Center Dr
Reston, VA 20190-5362

703-438-6000
Fax: 703-438-3570
Home Page: www.nwf.org

Mark Van Putten, CEO

Encourages management of natural resources. Gives financial aid to local groups and graduate studies. Conducts guided nature trail tours, produces programs and sponsors competitions.
4.5MM Members
Founded in 1936

7748 **National Wildlife Refuge Associationÿ**
1001 Connecticut Ave. NW
Suite 905
Washington, DC 20036

202-417-3803
E-Mail: nwra@refugeassociation.org
Home Page: refugeassociation.org
Social Media: Facebook, Twitter, LinkedIn, RSS

David Houghton, President
Anne Truslow, VP, Chief Operating Officer
Desiree Sorenson-Groves, VP, Government Affairs
Christine McGowan, Dir., Strategic Communications
Debbie Harwood, Office Manager

An independent membership organization that works to conserve American wildlife.

7749 **National Woodland Owners Association**
374 Maple Ave E
Suite 310
Vienna, VA 22180-4718

703-255-2300
800-470-8733
E-Mail: argow@nwoa.net
Home Page: www.nationalforestry.net

Keith A Argow, President
Bert Udell, Executive Committee Chair
Gerald A Rose, Midwest Regional VP

Provides timely information about forestry and forest practices with news from Washington,DC and state capitals. Written for non-industrial land owners. Includes state landowner association news.
39M Members
Founded in 1983

7750 **Native Forest Councilÿ**
PO Box 2190
Eugene, OR 97402

541-688-2600
Fax: 541-461-2156
E-Mail: info@forestcouncil.org
Home Page: forestcouncil.org
Social Media: Facebook, Twitter, Vimeo, YouTube

Bill Barton, Board of Director
Allan Branscomb, Board of Director
Calvin Hececta, Board of Director
Timothy Hermach, Board of Director
Timothy Moxley, Board of Director

Provides news and resources for the protection of publicly owned lands from logging, mining, grazing, drilling, and off-road vehicles.
Founded in 1987

7751 **Natural Resources Defense Council**
40 W 20th St
New York, NY 10011-4231

212-727-2700
Fax: 212-727-1773
E-Mail: nrdcinfo@nrdc.org
Home Page: www.nrdc.org
Social Media: Facebook, Twitter, YouTube

Frances Beinecke, President
Daniel R. Tishman, Chair
Frederick A.O. Schwarz Jr., Chair Emeritus
Adam Albright, Vice Chair
Patricia Bauman, Vice Chair

Dedicated to the wise management of natural resources through research, public education and the development of effective public policies.
50000 Members
Founded in 1970

7752 **Nature's Classroom**
19 Harrington Rd.
Charlton, MA 1507

508-248-2741
800-433-8375
Fax: 508-248-2745
E-Mail: info@naturesclassroom.org
Home Page: www.naturesclassroom.org
Social Media: Facebook

A nonprofit outdoor environmental education program.

7753 **NatureServe**
4600 N. Fairfax Dr.
7th Floor
Arlington, VA 22203
703-908-1800
Fax: 703-229-1670
Home Page: www.natureserve.org
Social Media: Facebook, Twitter, LinkedIn, YouTube, Vimeo, Flickr, RSS

Mary Klein, President/ CEO
Lori Scott, Chief Information Officer
Ravi Shankar, CFO/ COO
Leslie Honey, VP, Conservation Services
Don Kent, Director of Network Relations

A nonprofit organization that provides proprietary wildlife conservation-related data, tools, and services to private and government clients, partner organizations, and the public.
Founded in 1974

7754 **Negative Population Growth**
2861 Duke St.
Suite 36
Alexandria, VA 22314

703-370-9510
Fax: 703-370-9514
Home Page: www.npg.org
Social Media: Facebook, Twitter, RSS, YouTube

Donald Mann, President
Craig Lewis, Executive Vice President
Tracy Canada, Deputy Director
Dianeÿ Saco, Board of Director
Sharon Marks, Board of Director

A membership organization in the United States that works on overpopulation issues and advocates a gradual reduction in U.S. and world population.
Founded in 1972

7755 **North American Association for Environmental Education**
2000 P Street NW
Suite 540
Washington, DC 20036

202-419-0412
Fax: 202-419-0415
E-Mail: info@naaee.org
Home Page: www.naaee.org
Social Media: Facebook

Brian Day, Executive Director
Bridget Chisholm, Conference Manager
Sue Bumpous, Communications Manager

Purpose is to assist and support the work of individuals and groups engaged in environmental education, research and service.
1500 Members
Founded in 1971

7756 **North American Chapter - International Society for Ecological Modelling**
550 M Ritchie Highway
PMB 255
Severna Park, MD 21146

Home Page: www.isemna.org

Sven E. Jorgensen, President
Tarzan Legovic, Secretary-General
David A. Mauriello, Treasurer

Promotes the international exchange of general knowledge, ideas and scientific results in the area of the application of systems analysis and simulation to ecology, environmental science and natural resource management using mathematical and computer modelling of ecological systems.
150 Members
Founded in 1983

7757 **North American Lake Management Society**
4513 Vernon Boulevard, Suite 100
PO Box 5443
Madison, WI 53705-443

608-233-2836
Fax: 608-233-3186
E-Mail: info@nalms.org
Home Page: www.nalms.org
Social Media: Facebook, LinkedIn

Bev Clark, President
Al Sosiak, President-Elect
Reesa Evans, Secretary
Linda Green, Treasurer

Members are academics, lake managers and others interested in furthering the understanding of lake ecology. The North American Lake Management Society's mission is to forge partnerships among citizens, scientists and professionals to foster the management and

protection of lakes and reservoirs for today and tomorrow. Please call for rate information.
1700 Members
Founded in 1980

7758 Organic Seed Alliance
PO Box 772
Port Townsend, WA 98368-0772

360-385-7192
Fax: 360-385-7455
E-Mail: info@seedalliance.org
Home Page: www.seedalliance.org
Social Media: Facebook, Twitter

Stephen Harris, President
Tony Kleese, Secretary
Zea Sonnabend, Treasurer

Organic Seed Alliance suppports the ethical development and stewardship of the genetic resources of agricultural seed.
25M Members
Founded in 1975

7759 Plant Growth Regulation Society of America
Rhone-Poulenc, Ag Company
1018 Duke Street
Alexandria, VA 22314

703-836-4606
Fax: 706-883-8215
E-Mail: dmancini@ashs.org
Social Media: Facebook, Twitter

Dr Eric A Curry, President
Dr Louise Ferguson, VP
Dr Ed Stover, Secretary

Functions as a nonprofit educational and scientific organization.
325 Members
Founded in 1973

7760 Rachel Carson Council
PO Box 10779
Silver Springs, MD 20914

301-593-7507
E-Mail: rccouncil@aol.com
Home Page: rachelcarsoncouncil.org
Social Media: Twitter

Diana Post, Executive Director
David B McGrath, Treasurer
Dr Diana Post, Secretary

Library and clearinghouse on pesticide toxicity, lower risk alternatives for pest control, and Rachel Carson. Produces publications and sponsors conventions/meetings on these topics, issues newsletter. Nonprofit.
Founded in 1965

7761 Renewable Fuels Association
425 Third Street, SW
Suite 1150
Washington, DC 20024

202-289-3835
Fax: 202-289-7519
E-Mail: info@ethanolrfa.org
Home Page: www.ethanolrfa.org
Social Media: Facebook, Twitter

Chuck Woodside, Chairman
Neill McKinstray, Vice Chairman
Randall Doyal, Treasurer
Walter Wendland, Secretary

Members are companies and individuals involved in the production and use of ethanol.
55 Members
Founded in 1981

7762 Renewable Natural Resources Foundation
5430 Grosvenor Ln
Bethesda, MD 20814-2193

301-493-9101
Fax: 301-493-6148
E-Mail: info@rnrf.org
Home Page: www.rnrf.org

Howard N. Rosen, Chairman
Richard A. Engberg, Vice-Chairman
Robert D. Day, Executive Director

A consortium of professional and scientific societies whose members are concerned with the advancement of research, education, scientific practice and policy formulation for the conservation, replenishment and use of the earth's renewable natural resources.
14 Members
Founded in 1972

7763 Resource Policy Institute
1525 Selby Avenue
Ste. 304
Los Angeles, CA 90024-5796

310-470-9711

Dr Arthur Purcell, Director/Founder

Education, and consulting research group concerned with environmental policies, technologies, and management strategies..
Founded in 1975

7764 Safe Buildings Alliance
Metropolitan Square
655 15th Street NW
Suite 1200
Washington, DC 20005-5701

202-879-5120
Fax: 202-638-2103
Home Page: sba.lfpc.org

Association of building products companies that formerly manufactured asbestos-containing materials for building construction. Its main focus is to provide public information on issues relating to asbestos in building. SBA promotes a reasonable, safe response to the problem of asbestos in buildings, including the development of uniform, objective Federal and State standards for asbestos identification and abatement, nonremoval alternatives and the regulation of inspectors.
Founded in 1984

7765 Sagamore Institute of the Adirondacks Inc
Great Camp Sagamore
PO Box 40
Raquette Lake, NY 13436-0040

315-354-5311
Fax: 315-354-5851
E-Mail: info@greatcampsagamore.org
Home Page: www.greatcampsagamore.org
Social Media: Facebook, YouTube

Beverly Bridge, Executive Director

Non-profit 501c3 National Historic Landmark, former retreat of the Vanderbilts, offering educational programs on history, ecology and culture of the Adirondack Park.

7766 Silicones Environmental Health and Safety
2325 Dulles Corner Boulevard
Suite 500
Herndon, VA 20171

703-788-6570
Fax: 703-788-6545
E-Mail: sehsc@sehsc.com
Home Page: www.sehsc.com

Karluss Thomas, Executive Director

A not-for-profit trade association comprised of North American silicone chemical producers and importers.
6 Members
Founded in 1971

7767 Society for Ecological Restoration International
1017 O Street NW
Washington, DC 20001

202-299-9518
Fax: 270-626-5485
E-Mail: info@ser.org
Home Page: www.ser.org
Social Media: Facebook

Steve Whisenant, Chair
Cara R. Nelson, Vice Chair
Mary Travaglini, Treasurer
Alan Unwin, Secretary

SER members are academics, scientists, environmental consultants, government agencies and others with an interest in ecological restoration.
2300 Members
Founded in 1988

7768 Society for Environmental Geochemistry and Health
4698 S Forrest Avenue
Springfield, MO 65810

417-851-1166
Fax: 417-881-6920
E-Mail: DRBGWIXSON@aol.com
Home Page: www.segh.net

Prof. Xiangdong Li, President
Prof. Andrew Hursthouse, European Chair
Kyoung-Woong Kim, Asia/Pacific Chair
Anthea Brown, Membership Secretary/Treasurer
Malcolm Brown, Secretary

Promotes a multi-disciplinary approach to research in fields of geochemistry and health to facilitate and expand communication among scientists within these disciplines and to advance knowledge in the area.
400 Members
Founded in 1971

7769 Society for Human Ecology
College of the Atlantic
105 Eden Street
Bar Harbor, ME 04609-0180

207-288-5015
Fax: 207-288-3780
E-Mail: carter@coa.edu
Home Page: www.societyforhumanecology.org
Social Media: Facebook, Twitter

Zachary Smith, President
Rob Dyball, Vice President
Lee Cerveny, Second Vice President
Chiho Watanabe, Third Vice President-International
Rob Lilieholm, Treasurer

SHE members are academics, scientists, health professionals and others with an interest in studying the interrelationship of man's actions and his environment.
150 Members
Founded in 1981

7770 Society for Occupational and Environmental Health
111 North Bridge Road
#21-01 Peninsula Plaza
Singapore 179098

Home Page: www.oehs.org.sg

Gregory Chan, President
Ang Boon Tian, Vice President
Kam Wai Kuen, Honorary Secretary
Kenneth Choy, Honorary Treasurer

Members include physicians, hygienists, economists, laboratory scientists, academicians, labor and industry representatives, or anyone interested in occupational and/or environmental health. Serves as a forum for the presentation of scientific data and the exchange of informa-

tion among members; sponsors conferences and meetings which address specific problem areas and policy questions.
300 Members
Founded in 1972

7771 **Society of Environmental Journalists**
PO Box 2492
Jenkintown, PA 19046

215-884-8174
Fax: 215-884-8175
Home Page: www.sej.org
Social Media: Facebook, Twitter

Carolyn Whetzel, President
Peter Fairley, 1st Vice Pres
Jeff Burnside, 2nd Vice Pres
Don Hopey, Treasurer

To advance public understanding of environmental isues by improving the quality, accuracy, and visibility of environmental reporting.
Founded in 1990

7772 **Society of Environmental Toxicology and Chemistry**
1013 N 12th Ave
Pensacola, FL 32501-3306

850-437-1901
Fax: 850-469-9778
E-Mail: setac@setac.org
Home Page: www.setac.org
Social Media: Facebook, Twitter, LinkedIn

Paul van den Brink, President
Tim Canfield, Vice President
Fred Heimbach, Treasurer

Is a professional society established to promote the use of multidisciplinary approaches to solving problems of the impact of chemicals and technology on the environment. SETA members are professionals in the fields of chemistry, toxicology, biology, ecology, atmospheric sciences, health sciences, earth sciences, and environmental engineering.
4000 Members
Founded in 1979

7773 **Society of Exploration Geophysicists**
8801 South Yale
Suite 500
Tulsa, OK 74137-3575

918-497-5500
Fax: 918-497-5557
E-Mail: web@seg.org
Home Page: www.seg.org
Social Media: Facebook, Twitter, LinkedIn

Mary Fleming, Executive Director
Vladimir Grechka, Editor

The Society of Exploration Geophysicists/SEG is a not-for-profit organization that promotes the science of geophysics and the education of applied geophysicists. SEG fosters the expert and ethical practice of geophysics in the exploration and development of natural resources, in characterizing the near surface, and in mitigating earth hazards.
Founded in 1930

7774 **Soil and Plant Analysis Council**
347 North Shores Circle
Windsor, CO 80550

970-686-5702
E-Mail: rmiller@lamar.colostate.edu
Home Page: www.spcouncil.com

Rigas Karamanos, President
Robert Miller, Secretary/ Treasurer
Rao Mylavarapu, Vice President

Supports all those involved in the analysis of soil and plants.

7775 **Soil and Water Conservation Society**
945 SW Ankeny Rd
Ankeny, IA 50023-9764

515-289-2331
800-843-7645
Fax: 515-289-1227
E-Mail: swcs@swcs.org
Home Page: www.swcs.org

Bill Boyer, President
Dan Towery, Vice-President
Clark Gantzer, Secretary
Jerry Pearce, Treasurer

SWCS is a nonprofit scientific and educational organization that serves as an advocate for conservation professionals and for science-based conservation practice, programs, and policy.
5000+ Members
Founded in 1943

7776 **Southeastern Association of Fish and Wildlife Agencies**
8005 Freshwater Farms Road
Tallahassee, FL 32309-9009

850-770-0007
Fax: 850-893-6204
E-Mail: seafwa@aol.com
Home Page: www.seafwa.org

Robert Cook, President
Robert M Brantly, Executive Secretary
Kenneth Haddad, VP
John D Hoskins, Secretary/Treasurer
Darrell Smith, Manager

An organization whose members are the state agencies with primary responsibility for management and protection of the fish and wildlife resources in 16 states, Puerto Rico and the US Virgin Islands.
18 Members
Founded in 1947

7777 **Steel Recycling Institute**
680 Andersen Drive
Pittsburgh, PA 15220-2700

412-922-2772
800-876-7274
Fax: 412-922-3213
Home Page: www.recycle-steel.org
Social Media: Facebook, Twitter, YouTube

William H Heenan Jr, President

Promotes steel recycling and works to forge a coalition of steelmakers, can manufacturers, legislators, government officials, solid waste managers, business and consumer groups.
Founded in 1988

7778 **Student Conservation Association**
689 River Road
PO Box 550
Charlestown, NH 03603-0550

603-543-1700
Fax: 603-543-1828
E-Mail: jcota@thesca.org
Home Page: www.sca-inc.org
Social Media: Facebook, Twitter, YouTube

Dale Penny, President and CEO
Valerie Bailey, Vice President

To build the next generation of conservation leaders and inspire lifelong stewardship of our environment and communities by engaging young people in hands-on service to the land.
35000 Members
Founded in 1957

7779 **Surfaces in Biomaterials Foundation**
1000 Westgate Drive
Suite 252
St Paul, MN 55114-8679

651-290-6267
Fax: 651-290-2266
E-Mail: memberservices@surfaces.org
Home Page: www.surfaces.org
Social Media: LinkedIn

Andy Shelp, Executive Director
Ashley Crunstedt, Events/Meetings Planner
Janey Duntley, Web Coor/Newsletter Managing Editor

Dedicated to exploring creative solutions to technical challenges at the BioInterface by fostering education and multidisciplinary cooperation among industrial, academic, clinical and regulatory communities.
250 Members

7780 **Test Boring Association**
Five Mapleton Road
Suite 200
Princeton, NJ 08540

609-514-2600
Fax: 609-514-2660
Home Page: www.testboring.com

Patrizia Zita, Management Executive

Contractors engaged in test boring and core drilling.
Founded in 1941

7781 **The African Wild Dog Conservancyÿ**

E-Mail: lycaonpictus@awdconservancy.org
Home Page: www.awdconservancy.org

A nonprofit, non-governmental organization working with local communities, and national and international stakeholders to conserve the African wilddog through scientific research and education.
Founded in 2001

7782 **The Center for International Environmental Law**
1350 Connecticut Avenue NW
Suite #1100
Washington, DC 20036

202-785-8700
Fax: 202-785-8701
E-Mail: info@ciel.org
Home Page: www.ciel.org

Carroll Muffett, President/ CEO
Jeffrey Wanha, Dir., Finance & Admin.
Marcos A. Orellana, Director, Human Rights
Cameron Aishton, Administrator
Kevin Parker, Development Directorÿ

Nonprofit organization that provides environmental legal services in international and comparative environmental law.

7783 **The Indoor Air Institute**
2548 Empire Grade
Santa Cruz, CA 95060

831-426-0148
Fax: 831-426-6522
E-Mail: info@IndAir.org
Home Page: indair.org

Hal Levin, President
William Fisk, Vice President
William Nazaroff, Vice President

Supports all those involved with indoor air quality and climate with training, education, resource materials and an annual conference.

7784 **The Marine Mammal Center**
2000 Bunker Road
Fort Cronkhite
Sausalito, CA 94965-2619

415-289-7325
Home Page: www.marinemammalcenter.org
Social Media: Facebook, Twitter, RSS, Pinterest, YouTube

Marci Davis, Chief Financial Officer
Dr. Jeff Boehm, Executive Director
Nancy Sackson, Dir., Marketing & Development

Rachel Bergren, Education Director
Heather Groninger, Human Resources Director

A private, nonprofit U.S. organization established for the purpose of rescuing, rehabilitating, and releasing marine mammals who are injured, ill, or abandoned.
Founded in 1975

7785 The Nature Conservancy
4245 North Fairfax Drive
Suite 100
Arlington, VA 22203-1606

703-841-5300
Home Page: www.nature.org
Social Media: Facebook, Twitter

Teresa Beck, Co-Chairman of the Board
Steven A. Denning, Co-Chairman of the Board
Mark R. Tercek, President and CEO
Gordon Crawford, Vice Chair
Roberto Hernandez Ramirez, Vice Chair

The leading conservation organization working around the world to protect ecologically important lands and waters for nature and people. Addresses the most pressing conservation threats at the largest scale.
Founded in 1984

7786 The School for Field Studies
100 Cummings Center
Suite 534-G
Beverly, MA 1915

978-741-3567
Fax: 978-922-3835
E-Mail: jcramer@fieldstudies.org
Home Page: www.fieldstudies.org
Social Media: Facebook, Twitter, LinkedIn, YouTube, Google+, Flickr

James A. Cramer, President
Carrie Camp, BS, Chief Financial Officer
Amanda Freeman, Center Director
Dave Ware, Center Director
Holly Border, MA, Student Affairs Manager

Creates transformative study abroad experiences through field-basedlearning and research.
Founded in 1980

7787 The Wilderness Society
1615 M Street, NW
Washington, DC 20036

202-833-2300
800-843-9453
Home Page: wilderness.org
Social Media: Facebook, Twitter, LinkedIn, YouTube, Instagram, Pinterest

Jamie Williams, President
Thomas Tepper, Vice President
Kitty Thomas, Vice President
Ame Hellman, Vice President
Melyssa Watson, Vice President

An American nonprofit organization that is dedicated to protecting wilderness areas as national public lands in the United States.
Founded in 1935

7788 Union of Concerned Scientists
Two Brattle Sq.
Cambridge, MA 02138-3780

617-547-5552
Fax: 617-864-9405
Home Page: www.ucsusa.org
Social Media: Facebook, Twitter, Google+

James J. McCarthyÿ, Chair
Peter A. Bradford, Vice Chair
James S. Hoyte, Treasurer
Thomas H. Stone, Secretary
Kenneth Kimmell, President

A nonprofit science advocacy organization based in the United States.

7789 United Association of Used Oil Services
318 Newman Road
Sebring, FL 33870-6702

941-655-3880
800-877-4356

Established to be an effective presence in dealing with regulations and to provide a network for those with an interest in the collection and proper disposition of used lubricating oils.
Founded in 1987

7790 Water Environment Federation
601 Wythe St
Alexandria, VA 22314-1994

703-684-2400
800-666-0206
Fax: 703-684-2492
Home Page: www.wef.org
Social Media: Facebook, Twitter

Matt Bond, President
Cordell Samuels, President-Elect
Sandra Ralston, Vice President
Chris Browning, Treasurer
Jeff Eger, Secretary and Executive Director

Supports those involved in issues that affect the international water environment.
79 Members
ISSN: 1044-9943
Founded in 1928

7791 Water Quality Association
4151 Naperville Rd
Lisle, IL 60532-3696

630-505-0160
Fax: 630-505-9637
E-Mail: info@wqa.org
Home Page: www.wqa.org
Social Media: Facebook, Twitter, YouTube

Dave Haataja, Executive Director
Margit Fotre, Director of Membership & Marketing
Lynn Mathers, Operations Coordinator

An international, nonprofit trade association representing retail/dealers and manufacturer/suppliers in the point of use/entry water quality improvement industry. Membership benefits and services include technical and scientific information, educational seminars and home correspondence course books, professional certification and discount services.
2.5M Members
Founded in 1974

7792 Wilderness Society
1615 M St NW
Washington, DC 20036-3258

202-833-2300
800-843-9453
Fax: 202-429-3945
E-Mail: member@tws.org
Home Page: www.wilderness.org
Social Media: Facebook, Twitter

Douglas W. Walker, Chair
Molly McUsic, Vice Chair
William J. Cronon, Vice Chair
Marcia Kunstel, Secretary
Kevin Luzak, Treasurer

Establishes the land ethic as a basic element of the American culture and educates people on the importance of wilderness preservation and land protection.
200M Members
Founded in 1935
Mailing list available for rent: 178000 names at $90 per M

7793 Wildlife Conservation Society
2300 Southern Boulevard
Bronx, NY 10460

718-220-5100
Fax: 718-584-2625
E-Mail: membership@wcs.org
Home Page: www.wcs.org
Social Media: Facebook, YouTube

Ward W. Woods, Chair
Edith McBean, Vice Chair
Gordon B. Pattee, Vice Chair
Brian J. Heidtke, Treasurer
Andrew H. Tisch, Secretary

Supports all those involved in the conservation of wildlife, especially the most rare and endangered species.

7794 Wildlife Habitat Council
8737 Colesville Road
Suite 800
Silver Spring, MD 20910

301-588-8994
Fax: 301-588-4629
E-Mail: whc@wildlifehc.org
Home Page: www.wildlifehc.org
Social Media: Facebook, YouTube

Greg Cekander, Chairman
Lawrence A Selzer, Vice Chairman
Kevin Butt, Secretary-Treasurer

Supports corporate, government and conservation leaders from around the globe involved in environmental stewardship.
120+ Members
Founded in 1988

7795 Wildlife Management Institute
4426 VT Route 215N
Cabot, VT 05647

802-563-2087
Fax: 802-563-2157
E-Mail: wmisw@together.net
Home Page: www.wildlifemanagementinstitute.org

Richard E McCabe, Executive VP
Scot J Williamson, VP
Carol J Peddicord, Finance Manager
Robert L Byrne, Wildlife Program Coordinator
Ronald R Helinski, Conservation Policy Specialist

Supports all those involved with the challenges of modern conservation.

7796 Wildlife Society
5410 Grosvenor Ln
Suite 200
Bethesda, MD 20814-2144

301-897-9770
Fax: 301-530-2471
E-Mail: tws@wildlife.org
Home Page: www.wildlife.org
Social Media: Facebook, Twitter, LinkedIn

Michael Hutchins, Executive Director
Laura Bies, Director, Government Affairs
Jane Jorgensen, Office and Finance Manager
Yanin Walker, Operations Manager

Supports all those involved in wildlife conservation, including wildlife artists, environmental consultants, conservation groups, scientific associations and natural resource companies, industry groups and government agencies.
9000 Members
Founded in 1937

7797 Women's Council on Energy and the Environment
PO Box 33211
Washington, DC 20033-0211

202-997-4512
Fax: 202-478-2098

Home Page: www.wcee.org
Social Media: Facebook, Twitter

Ronke Luke, President
Mary Brosnan-Sell, Secretary
Robin Cantor, Vice President
Alice Grabowski, Treasurer
Joyce Chandran, Executive Director

Supports women involved in the environmental community with education, research, new trend information and several publications.

7798 **World Research Foundation**
41 Bell Rock Plaza
Sedona, AZ 86351-8804

928-284-3300
Fax: 928-284-3530
E-Mail: info@wrf.org
Home Page: www.wrf.org

Steven A Ross, President

A unique, international, health information network, so that people could be informed of all available treatments around the world, and so that they could have the freedom to choose, based on complete and in-depth information.
41000 Members
Founded in 1984

7799 **World Resources Institute**
10 G St NE
Suite 800
Washington, DC 20002-4252

202-729-7600
Fax: 202-729-7610
E-Mail: front@wri.org
Home Page: wri.org
Social Media: Facebook, Twitter, LinkedIn, YouTube

Andrew Steer, President/CEO
Manish Bapna, Executive VP/Managing Director
Steve Barker, CFO/VP Finance & Administration
Jennifer Morgan, Director, Climate & Energy Program

Compiles information, conducts research, publishes the Environmental Almanac and more.
Founded in 1982

7800 **World Society for the Protection of Animals**
Lincoln Plaza
89 South Street #201
Boston, MA 02111

800-883-9772
Fax: 212-564-4250
Home Page: www.wspa-usa.org
Social Media: Facebook, Twitter, YouTube

Robert S. Cummings, President
John Bowen, Secretary
Carter Luke, Treasurer

International animal protection news reports. Lobbies for effective animal welfare laws and provides educational material.
12 Members

7801 **World Wildlife Fund**
1250 24th Street, NW
PO Box 97180
Washington, DC 20090-7180

202-293-4800
Fax: 202-293-9211
Home Page: www.worldwildlife.org
Social Media: Facebook, Twitter, YouTube

Carter Roberts, President
Lawrence H. Linden, Chairman
Neville Isdell, Vice-Chair
Pamela Matson, Vice-Chair
Brenda S. Davis, Treasurer

Supports all those involved in maintaining wildlife and their environment. Monitors human development, and seeks to influence public opinion and policy makers in favor of ecologically sound practices.
4M Members
Founded in 1961

7802 **Worldwatch Institute**
1400 16th Street NW
Suite 430
Washington, DC 20036

202-745-8092
Fax: 202-478-2534
E-Mail: worldwatch@worldwatch.org
Home Page: www.worldwatch.org
Social Media: Facebook, Twitter, LinkedIn, RSS, YouTube, Flickr

Ed Groarkÿ, Chair
Robert Charles Friese, Vice Chair
John Robbins, Treasurer
Nancy Hitzÿ, Secretary
Barbara Fallin, Dir., Finance & Administration

Analyzes interdisciplinary environmental data from around the world, providing information on how to build a sustainable society.
Founded in 1974

Newsletters

7803 **AEESP Newsletter**
2303 Naples Court
Champaign, IL 61822

217-398-6969
Fax: 217-355-9232
Home Page: www.aeesp.org

Joanne Fetzner, Business Secretary

Official newsletter of the Association of Environmental Engineering and Science Professors. Topics cover the scope and diversity of challenges faced in environmental engineering and science.
Frequency: Quarterly

7804 **AEG News**
Association of Engineering Geologists
PO Box 460518
Denver, CO 80246-0518

303-757-2926
Fax: 720-230-4846
E-Mail: aeg@aegweb.org
Home Page: www.aegweb.org
Social Media: Facebook, Twitter

Jennifer Bauer, President
Matthew B. Morris, Vice President/ President Elect
Gary Lice, Treasurer
Ken Fergason, Secretary

Connecting Professionals, Practice and the Public.
3000 Members
Founded in 1957
Mailing list available for rent: 3000 names at $100 per M

7805 **AERE Newsletter**
Association of Environmental and Resource
1616 P St Nw
Suite 400
Washington, DC 20036-1434

202-328-5157
Fax: 202-939-3460
E-Mail: voigt@rff.org
Home Page: www.aere.org

Marilyn Voigt, Executive Secretary
Ralph Metts, President

Includes policy essays, meeting announcements, calls for papers, new publications, research reports, position announcements and other information of interest to AERE members and environmental economists in general.
Frequency: Semi-Annual

7806 **AIH Bulletin**
American Institute of Hydrology
1230 Lincold Drive
Carbondale, IL 62901

618-453-7809
E-Mail: aih@engr.siu.edu
Home Page: www.aihydrology.org

Cathy Lipsett, Owner
Cathryn Seaburn, Manager

Newsletter for the American Institute of Hydrology, providing information designed to improve professional skills and abilities of its members, the professional community and the public at large.
Frequency: Quarterly

7807 **APLIC Communicator**
Family Health International Library
PO Box 13950
Research Triangle Park, NC 27709

919-447-7040
Home Page: www.aplici.org

Claire Twose, President
Lori Rosman, Vice-President
Joann Donatiello, Treasurer

Read by population and reproductive health information specialists, librarians, and documentalists.
Frequency: Annual

7808 **ASBPA Newsletter**
American Shore & Beach Preservation Association
5460 Beaujolais ch Road
Fort Myers, FL 33919

239-489-2616
Fax: 239-362-9771
E-Mail: exdir@asbpa.org
Home Page: www.asbpa.org
Social Media: Facebook, Twitter

Harry Simmons, President
Nicole Elko, Secretary
Brad Pickel, Treasurer
Kate Gooderham, Editor

Federal, state and local government agencies and individuals interested in conservation, development and restoration of beaches and shorefronts.
1M Members
Founded in 1926

7809 **ASEH News**
American Society for Environmental History
UW Interdisciplinary Arts and Sciences Program
1900 Commerce Street
Tacoma, WA 98402

206-343-0226
Fax: 206-343-0249
E-Mail: director@aseh.net
Home Page: www.aseh.net

John McNeill, President
Gregg Mitman, Vice President/ President Elect
Ellen Stroud, Secretary
Mark Madison, Treasurer

Updated and timely information on current environmental issues and their historical background, as well as Society news and events.
1200 Members
Founded in 1976

7810 **ASFE Newslog**
ASFE/The Geoprofessional Business Association

8811 Colesville Rd
Suite G106
Silver Springs, MD 20910-4343

301-565-2733
Fax: 301-589-2017
E-Mail: info@asfe.org
Home Page: www.asfe.org

John P Bachner, Executive VP

Information on geo professional, environmental, and civil engineering firms. Past issues are available through the online store. Electronic copies are always free to members.
Cost: $240.00
16 Pages
Frequency: 6/Year
Circulation: 5000

7811 ASMR Newsletter
American Society of Mining and Reclamation
3134 Montavesta Road
Lexington, KY 40502

859-335-6529
E-Mail: asmr@insightbb.com
Home Page: www.ca.uky.edu/assmr

Richard I Barnhisel, Executive Secretary

Promotes the advancement of basic and applied reclamation science.
Frequency: 10/year

7812 ATTRAnews
National Center for Appropriate Technology
3040 Continental Drive
PO Box 3838
Butte, MT 59702

406-494-4572
800-275-6228
Fax: 406-494-2905
Home Page: www.ncat.org
Social Media: Facebook, Twitter, LinkedIn

Eugene Brady, Chairman
Kathleen Hadley, Executive Director

ATTRAnews brings you up to date on the latest developments in sustainable agriculture, what's happening at the USDA and with Sustainable Agriculture Working Groups around the country. ATTRAnews features events and opportunities in sustainable agriculture, information on funding and financing, and it keeps you current on programs and policies that can affect your future.
Frequency: 6x/Year
Founded in 1976

7813 Advisor
Great Lakes Commission
2805 S Industrial Hwy
Suite 100
Ann Arbor, MI 48104-6791

734-971-9135
Fax: 734-971-9150
Home Page: www.glc.org

Tim Eder, Executive Director
Cook Havtrkamp, Author

Covers economic and environmental issues of the Great Lakes region with a special focus on activities of the Great Lakes Commission.
12 Pages
Frequency: Quarterly
Founded in 1955
Printed in one color on matte stock

7814 Air Water Pollution Report's Environment Week
Business Publishers
8737 Colesville Road
Suite 1100
Silver Spring, MD 20910-3928

301-876-6300
800-274-6737
Fax: 301-589-8493
E-Mail: custserv@bpinews.com
Home Page: www.bpinews.com

Leonard A Eiserer, Publisher
Beth Early, Operations Director
David Goeller, Editor

Provides a balanced, insightful update on the week's most important environmental news from Washington, D.C.
Cost: $595.00
Frequency: Weekly
Founded in 1963

7815 Annual Research Program Report
National Institutes for Water Resources

Home Page: niwr.net

Paul Joseph Godfrey, PhD, Executive Director

7816 Aquatic Plant News
Aquatic Plant Management Society
PO Box 821265
Vicksburg, MS 39182-1265

FAX 601-634-5502
E-Mail: dpetty@ndrsite.com
Home Page: www.apms.org
Social Media: Facebook, LinkedIn

Linda Nelson, President
Terry Goldsby, VP
Sherry Whitaker, Treasurer

Aquatic Plant News is produced 3 times each year, and is distributed primarily by email.
Frequency: 3x/Year
Founded in 1961

7817 Asbestos & Lead Abatement Report
Business Publishers
8737 Colesville Road
Suite 1100
Silver Spring, MD 20910-3928

301-876-6300
800-274-6737
Fax: 301-589-8493
E-Mail: custserv@bpinews.com
Home Page: www.bpinews.com

Leonard Eiserer, Publisher

Contains articles on regulation compliance, environmental trends, and business opportunities.
Cost: $382.00
Frequency: Monthly
Founded in 1963

7818 BNA's Environmental Compliance Bulletin
Bureau of National Affairs
1801 S Bell St
Arlington, VA 22202-4501

703-341-3000
800-372-1033
Fax: 800-253-0332
E-Mail: customercare@bna.com
Home Page: www.bnabooks.com

Paul N Wojcik, CEO
Gregory C McCaffery, President

Water and air pollution, waste management and regulatory updates, as well as a summary of selected regulatory actions and a list of key environmental compliance dates.
Cost: $649.00
Frequency: Annual+
Founded in 1929

7819 BankNotes
Environmental Bankers Association
510 King St
Suite 410
Alexandria, VA 22314-3212

703-549-0977
Fax: 703-548-5945
E-Mail: eba@envirobank.org
Home Page: www.envirobank.org

Rick Ferguson, President
Sharon Valverde, Vice President
Scott Beckerman, Treasurer
Stephen Richardson, Secretary

Timely information on the EBA, read by bank and non-bank financial institutions, insurers, asset management firms and those who provide services to them. Covers environmental risk issues, risk management, development, and due diligence policies and procedures.
Frequency: Bi-Monthly

7820 Biosolids Technical Bulletin
Water Environment Federation
601 Wythe St
Alexandria, VA 22314-1994

800-666-0206
Fax: 703-684-2492
Home Page: www.wef.org
Social Media: Facebook, Twitter

Matt Bond, President
Cordell Samuels, President-Elect
Sandra Ralston, Vice President
Chris Browning, Treasurer
Jeff Eger, Secretary and Executive Director

A must have for anyone involved in residuals and biosolids management. The latest treatment processes, odor management, beneficial use options, environmental management systems, or public outreach approaches.
79 Members
ISSN: 1044-9943
Founded in 1928

7821 Bulletins
World Research Foundation
41 Bell Rock Plz
Sedona, AZ 86351-8804

928-284-3300
Fax: 928-284-3530
E-Mail: laverne@wrf.org
Home Page: www.wrf.org

Steven A Ross, President

Updates on recent research including topics involving health information pertinent to the World Research Foundation.
Frequency: Quarterly

7822 CCA Newsletter
Coastal Conservation Association
6919 Portwest Dr
Suite 100
Houston, TX 77024-8049

713-626-4234
800-201-FISH
Fax: 713-626-5852
E-Mail: ccantl@joincca.org
Home Page: www.joincca.org
Social Media: Twitter

David Cummins, President

Contains timely updates from CCA state chapters and bulletins on developing fisheries issues.
85000 Members
Founded in 1977

7823 CCHEST Newsletter
Council on Certification of Health, Environmental
2301 W. Bradley Avenue
Champaign, IL 61821

217-359-9263
Fax: 217-359-0055
E-Mail: cchest@cchest.org

Home Page: www.cchest.org
Social Media: Facebook, Twitter, LinkedIn

Margaret M. Carroll, President
Carl W. Heinlein, Vice President
Emory E. Knowles III, Treasurer

Keeps members up to date on events, OSHA news and the latest safety courses.
Frequency: Annual
Mailing list available for rent: 20,000 names

7824 **Capitol Connect**
Society of Chemical Manufacturers & Affiliates
1850 M St Nw
Suite 700
Washington, DC 20036-5803

202-721-4100
Fax: 202-296-8120
E-Mail: info@socma.org
Home Page: www.socma.org

Larry Brotherton, Ph.D., Chair
Dave Hurder, Vice Chair
Davide DeCuir, Treasurer
J. Steel Hutchinson, Secretary

Government relations newsletter covering a range of environmental, safety, security, chemicals management and trade topics.
10 Pages
Frequency: Bi-Weekly

7825 **ChemStewards**
Society of Chemical Manufacturers & Affiliates
1850 M St Nw
Suite 700
Washington, DC 20036-5803

202-721-4100
Fax: 202-296-8120
E-Mail: info@socma.org
Home Page: www.socma.org

Larry Brotherton, Ph.D., Chair
Dave Hurder, Vice Chair
Davide DeCuir, Treasurer
J. Steel Hutchinson, Secretary

e-Newsletter focusing on ChemStewards Training Opportunities, upcoming events, and the latest program news.
10 Pages
Frequency: Bi-Weekly

7826 **Clean Water Report**
CJE Associates
Silver Spring, MD 20910-3928
301-589-5103
800-274-6737
Fax: 301-589-8493
E-Mail: custserv@bpinews.com
Home Page: www.bpinews.com

Follows the latest news from the EPA, Congress, the states, the courts, and private industry. A key information source for environmental professionals, covering the important issues of ground and drinking water, wastewater treatment, wetlands, drought, coastal protection, non-point source pollution, agrichemical contamination and more.
8 Pages

7827 **Climate Change News**
Environmental & Energy Study Institute
122 C Street NW
Suite 630
Washington, DC 20001

202-628-1400
Fax: 202-628-1825
E-Mail: eesi@eesi.org
Home Page: www.eesi.org
Social Media: Facebook, Twitter, YouTube

Jared Blum, Board Chair
Shelley Fidler, Board Treasurer
Richard L. Ottinger, Board Chair Emeritus

Recounts the top climate science, business, and politics stories of the week and includes a list of upcoming events and pending federal legislation.
Founded in 1984

7828 **Composting News**
McEntee Media Corporation
9815 Hazelwood Ave
Strongsville, OH 44149-2305

440-238-6603
Fax: 440-238-6712
E-Mail: ken@recycle.cc
Home Page: www.recycle.cc

Ken Mc Entee, Owner

The latest in composting, wood waste recycling and organics management in a monthly newsletter.
Cost: $83.00
Frequency: Monthly
Circulation: 2000
Founded in 1990

7829 **Conservation Commission News**
New Hampshire Association of Conservation Comm.
54 Portsmouth Street
Concord, NH 03301-5486

603-225-3431
Fax: 603-228-0423

Marjory Swope, Publisher

Encourage conservation and appropriate use of New Hampshire's natural resources by providing assistance to New Hampshire's municipal conservation commissions and by facilitating communication among commissions and between commissions and other public and private agencies involved in conservation.
Cost: $5.00
8 Pages
Frequency: Quarterly
Circulation: 1,650
Printed in one color on matte stock

7830 **Convention Proceedings**
Society for Human Ecology
College of the Atlantic
105 Eden Street
Bar Harbor, ME 04609-0180

207-288-5015
Fax: 207-288-3780
E-Mail: carter@ecology.coa.edu
Home Page: www.societyforhumanecology.org

Barbara Carter, Assistant to Executive Director

7831 **Cosecha Mensual**
National Center for Appropriate Technology
3040 Continental Drive
PO Box 3838
Butte, MT 59702

406-494-4572
800-275-6228
Fax: 406-494-2905
Home Page: www.ncat.org
Social Media: Facebook, Twitter, LinkedIn

Eugene Brady, Chairman
Kathleen Hadley, Executive Director

NCAT's Spanish-language electronic newsletter on sustainable agriculture. Subscribers enjoy news items and reviews of Spanish-language resources.
Frequency: Monthly
Founded in 1976

7832 **Council on Women in Energy and Environmental Leadership Newsletter**
Association of Energy Engineers
4025 Pleasantdale Rd
Suite 420
Atlanta, GA 30340-4264

770-447-5083
Fax: 770-446-3969
E-Mail: info@aeecenter.org
Home Page: www.aeecenter.org
Social Media: Facebook, Twitter, LinkedIn, YouTube

Eric A. Woodroof, President
Gary Hogsett, President Elect
Bill Younger, Secretary
Paul Goodman, C.P.A., Treasurer

Addressing the high cost of energy, present and future sources of energy, and the impact of energy on the environment.
8.2M Members
Founded in 1977

7833 **Daily Environment Report**
Bureau of National Affairs
1801 S Bell St
Arlington, VA 22202-4501

703-341-3000
800-372-1033
Fax: 800-253-0332
E-Mail: customercare@bna.com
Home Page: www.bnabooks.com

Paul N Wojcik, CEO
Gregory C McCaffery, President

A 40-page daily report providing comprehensive, in-depth coverage of national and international environmental news. Each issue contains summaries of the top news stories, articles, and in-brief items, and a journal of meetings, agency activities, hearings and legal proceedings. Coverage includes air and water pollution, hazardous substances, and hazardous waste, solid waste, oil spills, gas drilling, pollution prevention, impact statements and budget matters.
Cost: $ 3537.00
40 Pages
Frequency: Daily
ISSN: 1060-2976

7834 **Digital Traveler**
International Ecotourism Society
733 15th Street NW
Suite 1000
Washington, DC 20005

202-547-9203
Fax: 202-387-7915
Home Page: www.ecotourism.org

Martha Honey, Executive Director
Amos Bien, Director International Programs
Neal Inamdar, Director Finance/Administration

Regular updates about TIES work and programs.
Frequency: Monthly

7835 **E&P Environment**
Pasha Publications
1616 N Fort Myer Dr
Suite 1000
Arlington, VA 22209-3107

703-528-1244
800-424-2908
Fax: 703-528-1253
Home Page: www.newsletteraccess.com

Harry Baisden, Group Publisher
Jerry Grisham, Editor

Reports on environmental regulations, advances in technology and litigation aimed specifically at the exploration and production segments of the oil and gas industry.
Cost: $395.00

7836 **E-Scrap News**
Resource Recycling

PO Box 42270
Portland, OR 97242-270

503-233-1305
Fax: 503-233-1356
E-Mail: info@resource-recycling.com
Home Page: www.resource-recycling.com

Jerry Powell, Publisher/Editor
Andrew Santosusso, Managing Editor
Betsy Loncar, Circulation Director

Monthly newsletter covering all aspects of recovering, recycling, and managing electronics scrap. Coverage includes market prices and trends, collection events, product stewardship developments and global trends.
Cost: $99.00
6 Pages
Frequency: Monthly
Circulation: 1000
ISSN: 1536-3856
Founded in 1983
Mailing list available for rent: 40,000 names at $100 per M
Printed in 2 colors on matte stock

7837 ECOMOD Newsletter
International Society for Ecological Modelling
University of California, Animal Sciences Dept
One Shields Avenue
Davis, CA 95616-8521

530-752-5362
Fax: 530-752-0175
Home Page: www.isemna.org

Wolfgang Pittroff, Secretary-General

Information on conferences, workshops and symposia that promote the systems philosophy in ecological research and teaching. Members frequently contribute articles.
Frequency: Quarterly

7838 EH&S Software News Online
Donley Technology
PO Box 152
Colonial Beach, VA 22443-152

804-224-9427
800-201-1595
Fax: 804-224-7958
Home Page: www.ehssoftwarenews.com

John Donley, Editor

Reports on news and upgraded software products, database, and on-line systems from commercial developers and government resources.
Cost: $125.00
Founded in 1988

7839 EMS Newsletter
Environmental Mutagen Society
1821 Michael Faraday Drive
Suite 300
Reston, VA 20190

703-438-8220
Fax: 703-438-3113
E-Mail: emshq@ems-us.org
Home Page: www.ems-us.org

Kathleen Hill, Editor
Barbara Parsons, Editor
Cathy Klein, Editor

Current scientific research, policies, and guidelines for the causes and consequences of damage to the genome and epigenome.
Frequency: Bi-Annual

7840 Economic Opportunity Report
Business Publishers
2222 Sedwick Dr
Suite 101
Durham, NC 27713

800-223-8720
Fax: 800-508-2592
E-Mail: custserv@bpinews.com
Home Page: www.bpinews.com

Antipoverty news coverage and analysis which gives insight into developments that affect social programs.
Cost: $383.00
Frequency: Weekly

7841 Environment Reporter
Bureau of National Affairs
1801 S Bell St
Arlington, VA 22202-4501

703-341-3000
800-372-1033
Fax: 800-253-0332
E-Mail: customercare@bna.com
Home Page: www.bnabooks.com

Paul N Wojcik, CEO
Gregory C McCaffery, President

A weekly notification and reference service covering the full-spectrum of legislative, administrative, judicial, industrial and technological developments affecting pollution control and environmental protection.
Cost: $3776.00
Frequency: Weekly
ISSN: 0013-9211
Founded in 1929

7842 Environmental Design Research Association Newsletter
Environmental Design Research Association
PO Box 7146
Edmond, OK 73083-7146

405-330-4863
Fax: 405-330-4150
E-Mail: edra@telepath.com
Home Page: www.edra.org

Janet Singer, Executive Director

Document collection includes pdfs of full papers that have appeared in the annual EDRA conference proceedings.
Frequency: Annual

7843 Environmental Engineers and Managers Institute Newsletter
Association of Energy Engineers
4025 Pleasantdale Rd
Suite 420
Atlanta, GA 30340-4264

770-447-5083
Fax: 770-446-3969
E-Mail: info@aeecenter.org
Home Page: www.aeecenter.org
Social Media: Facebook, Twitter, LinkedIn, YouTube

Eric A. Woodroof, President
Gary Hogsett, President Elect
Bill Younger, Secretary
Paul Goodman, C.P.A., Treasurer

Keeps members ahead on trends, upcoming conferences, industry leaders, jobs, relevant publications and more.
8.2M Members
Founded in 1977

7844 Environmental Health Newsletter
International Lead Zinc Research Organization
2525 Meridian Parkway, Suite 100
PO Box 12036
Durham, NC 27713

919-361-4647
Fax: 919-361-1957
Home Page: www.ilzro.org

Stephen Wilkinson, President
Frank Goodwin, VP Materials Sciences
Scott Mooneyham, Treasurer
Rob Putnam, Director Communications

Information on environmental health sciences, use of technology, rules, and public education.
Frequency: Quarterly

7845 Environmental Nutrition
52 Riverside Drive
Suite 15A
New York, NY 10024

212-362-0424
800-424-7887
Fax: 212-362-2066
E-Mail: betty@environmentalnutrition.com
Home Page: www.environmentalnutrition.com

Betty Goldblatt, Publisher
Susan Male Smith, Editor

Monthly nutrition newsletter on nutrition and health. Written and edited by registered dietitians.
Cost: $24.00
Frequency: Monthly
Circulation: 50000
Founded in 1977
Printed in 2 colors on matte stock

7846 Environmental Policy Alert
Inside Washington Publishers
1919 S Eads St
Suite 201
Arlington, VA 22202-3028

703-418-3981
800-424-9068
Fax: 703-416-8543
E-Mail: iwp@sprintmail.com
Home Page: www.iwpnews.com

Alan Sosenko, Owner

Adresses the legislative news and provides reports on the federal environmental policy process.
Cost: $560.00
Founded in 1980

7847 Environmental Problems & Remediation
InfoTeam
PO Box 15640
Plantation, FL 33318-5640

954-473-9560
Fax: 954-473-0544
E-Mail: infoteamma@aol.com

Merton Allen, Editor

Concerned with environmental problems and effects, the methods and approaches for mitigation and remediation. Covers air pollution; surface and ground water pollution; wastewater; soil contamination; waste recycling; medical wastes; landfills and waste sites; stack gases; combustion and incineration; earth warming and more.

7848 Environmental Regulatory Advisor
JJ Keller
3003 W Breezewood Lane
Neenah, WI 54956-368

920-722-2848
800-327-6868
Fax: 800-727-7516
E-Mail: sales@jjkeller.com
Home Page: www.jjkeller.com

Webb Shaw, Editor
Robert Keller, CEO

Covers developments at the EPA.
Founded in 1953

7849 Environotes Newsletter
Federation of Environmental Technologists
PO Box 624
Slinger, WI 53086-0624

414-540-0070
Fax: 262-644-7106

E-Mail: info@fetinc.org
Home Page: www.fetinc.org

Triese Haase, Administrator

Educating and Developing Excellence in Environmental Professionals
Frequency: Monthly

7850 Facility Managers Institute Newsletter
Association of Energy Engineers
4025 Pleasantdale Rd
Suite 420
Atlanta, GA 30340-4264

770-447-5083
Fax: 770-446-3969
E-Mail: info@aeecenter.org
Home Page: www.aeecenter.org
Social Media: Facebook, Twitter, LinkedIn, YouTube

Eric A. Woodroof, President
Gary Hogsett, President Elect
Bill Younger, Secretary
Paul Goodman, C.P.A., Treasurer

Online newsletter addresses subjects such as the Integrated Approach to plant management, security and safety issues, and overall facility management.
8.2M Members
Founded in 1977

7851 Fibre Market News
GIE Media
4012 Bridge Avenue
Cleveland, OH 44113-3320

216-961-4130
800-456-0707
Fax: 216-961-0364

Richard Foster, Publisher
Daniel Sandoval, Editor

Covers the international paper recycling industry. Trends, markets, expansions, economics covered in an in-depth fashion. Also have weekly fax update covering late-breaking news.
Cost: $115.00
16 Pages
Frequency: BiWeekly

7852 ForeFront
National Registry of Environmental Professionals
PO Box 2099
Glenview, IL 60025

847-724-6631
Fax: 847-724-4223
E-Mail: nrep@nrep.org
Home Page: www.nrep.org
Social Media: Facebook, Twitter, LinkedIn

Richard A Young, PhD, Executive Director
Edward Beck, PhD, Senior Director
Carol Schellinger, Director
Christopher Young, Director of Operation
Marie Hunter, Director

Information on continuing education, certification, and recognition for the professionals who help understand and study the environment.
20000 Members
Frequency: Bi-Monthly
Founded in 1987

7853 Forest History Society
Forest History Society
701 William Vickers Ave
Durham, NC 27701-3162

919-682-9319
Fax: 919-682-2349
E-Mail: recluce2@duke.edu
Home Page: www.foresthistory.org

Steven Anderson, President
R Scott Wallinger, Chairman
Yvan Hardy, Co-Vice Chairman
Mark Wilde, Co Vice-Chairman

Nonprofit educational institution that explores the history of the environment, forestry and conservation.

7854 From the Ground Up
Ecology Center
117 Division Street
Ann Arbor, MI 48104-1523

734-761-3186
Fax: 734-663-2414
Home Page: www.ecocenter.org

Ted Sylvester, Editor
Mike Wallad, President
Michael Garfield, Director

Progressive environmental news from southeast Michigan.
Cost. $30.00
32 Pages
Frequency: Monthly
Circulation: 5000
Founded in 1970
Printed in 4 colors on newsprint stock

7855 GRAS Flavoring Substances 25
Flavor & Extract Manufacturers Association
1620 I Street NW
Suite 925
Washington, DC 20006

202-293-5800
Fax: 202-462-8998
Home Page: www.femaflavor.org
Social Media: YouTube, RSS Feed

Ed R. Hays, Ph.D., President
George C. Robinson, III, President Elect
Mark Scott, Treasurer
Arthur Schick, VP & Secretary
John Cox, Executive Director

The 25th publication by the Expert Panel of the Flavor and Extract Manufacturers Association provides an update on recent progress in the consideration of flavoring ingredients generally recognized as safe under the Food Additive Amendment.
123 Members
Frequency: Biennial
Founded in 1909

7856 Global Environmental Change Report
Aspen Publishers
76 Ninth Avenue
7th Floor
New York, NY 10011

212-771-0600
800-638-8437
Home Page: www.aspenpublishers.com

Mark Dorman, CEO
Gustavo Dobles, VP Operations

News and analysis of policy, science and industry developments in the areas of global warming and acid rain.
Cost: $447.00
Frequency: BiWeekly

7857 HazTECH News
Haztech News
14120 Huckleberry Lane
Silver Spring, MD 20906

301-871-3289
Fax: 301-460-5859
E-Mail: HazTECH@ix.netcom.com

Cathy Dombrowski, Editor/Publisher

Describes technologies for hazardous waste management, site remediation, industrial wastewater treatment and VOC control.
Cost: $385.00
8 Pages
Frequency: Bi-Weekly
Printed in one color

7858 Hazardous Materials Intelligence Report
World Information Systems
PO Box 535
Cambridge, MA 02238-535

617-492-3312
Fax: 617-492-3312
Home Page: members.aol.com/socejp/hmir.html

Richard S Golob, Publisher
Roger B Wilson Jr, Editor

Provides news analysis on environmental business, hazardous materials, waste management, pollution prevention and control. Covers regulations, legislation and court decisions, new technology, contract opportunities and awards and conference notices.
Cost: $375.00
Frequency: Weekly
Circulation: 50000

7859 Hazardous Materials Transportation
Bureau of National Affairs
1801 S Bell St
Arlington, VA 22202-4501

703-341-3000
800-372-1033
E-Mail: customercare@bna.com
Home Page: www.bnabooks.com

Gregory C McCaffery, President
Paul N Wojcik, Chairman

A two-binder service containing the full-text of rules and regulations governing shipment of hazardous material by rail, air, ship, highway and pipeline, including DOT's Hazardous Materials Tables and EPA's rules for its hazardous waste tracking system.
Cost: $933.00
Frequency: Monthly

7860 Hazardous Waste Report
Aspen Publishers
7201 McKinney Cir
Frederick, MD 21704-8356

301-698-7100
800-638-8437
Fax: 212-597-0335
Home Page: www.aspenpublishers.com

Paul Gibson, Publisher
Sally Almeria, Editor
Bruce Becker, CEO/President
Tom Ceodi, Marketing

Provides information on industry news.
Cost: $875.00
8 Pages
Founded in 1958

7861 Health Facts and Fears.com
American Council on Science and Health
1995 Broadway
2nd Floor
New York, NY 10023-5882

212-362-7044
Fax: 212-362-4919
E-Mail: acsh@acsh.org
Home Page: www.acsh.org

Dr Elizabeth Whelan, President
Jeff Stier, Associate Director

Daily e mail blast on the latest public health news and junk science scares.
Frequency: Weekly

7862 IES Quarterly Newsletter
International Ecotourism Society

733 15th Street NW
Suite 1000
Washington, DC 20005

202-547-9203
Fax: 202-387-7915
Home Page: www.ecotourism.org

Martha Honey, Executive Director
Amos Bien, Director International Programs
Neal Inamdar, Director Finance/Administration

Offering information on advocacy uniting communities, conservation, and sustainable travel.
Frequency: Quarterly

7863 **Industrial Health & Hazards Update**
InfoTeam
PO Box 15640
Plantation, FL 33318-5640

954-473-9560
Fax: 954-473-0544
E-Mail: infoteamma@aol.com

Merton Allen, Editor

Covers occupational safety, health, hazards, and disease, mitigatioin and control of hazardous situations; waste recycling and treatment; environmental pollution and control; product safety and liability; fires and explosions; plant and computer security,; air pollution; surface and ground water; wastewater; soil gases; combustion and incineration; earth warming; ozone layer depletion; electromagnetic radiation; toxic materials; and many other related topics.

7864 **Infectious Wastes News**
National Solid Wastes Management Association
4301 Connecticut Ave Nw
Suite 300
Washington, DC 20008-2304

202-966-4701
Fax: 202-966-4818
E-Mail: wa@envasns.org
Home Page: www.envasns.org

Bruce Parker, President

A publication by the Environmental industry association geared toward providing readers with timely news and information about the handling, transportation and disposal of infectious wastes.
Frequency: BiWeekly

7865 **Integrated Environmental Assessment and Management**
Society of Environmental Toxicology and Chemistry
1013 N 12th Ave
Pensacola, FL 32501-3306

850-437-1901
Fax: 850-469-9778
E-Mail: rparrish@setac.org
Home Page: www.edwardjones.com

Rodney Parrish, Executive Director

Focuses on the application of science in environmental decision-making, regulation, and management, including aspects of policy and law, and the development of scientifically sound approaches to environmental problem solving.
Frequency: Quarterly

7866 **Integrated Waste Management**
1801 S Bell Street
Arlington, VA 22202

212-512-3916
800-372-1033
Fax: 212-512-2723
Home Page: www.bna.com

Gregory C McCaffery, President
Paul N Wojcik, Chairman

Articles geared toward integration of solid waste management.
Cost: $745.00
8 Pages
Frequency: BiWeekly

7867 **Interface Newsletter**
Society for Environmental Geochemistry and Health
4698 S Forrest Avenue
Springfield, MO 65810

417-885-1166
Fax: 417-881-6920
E-Mail: drbgwixson@wixson.com
Home Page: www.segh.net

Bobby Wixson, Director Membership

7868 **International Environment Reporter**
Bureau of National Affairs
1801 S Bell St
Arlington, VA 22202-4501

703-341-3000
800-372-1033
Fax: 800-253-0332
E-Mail: customercare@bna.com
Home Page: www.bnabooks.com

Gregory C McCaffrey, President
Paul N Wojcik, Chairman

A four-binder information and reference service covering international environmental law and developing policy in the major industrial nations.
Cost: $2555.00

7869 **Journal of Science and Sustainability**
National Registry of Environmental Professionals
PO Box 2099
Glenview, IL 60025

847-724-6631
Fax: 847-724-4223
E-Mail: nrep@nrep.org
Home Page: www.nrep.org
Social Media: Facebook, Twitter, LinkedIn

Richard A Young, PhD, Executive Director
Edward Beck, PhD, Senior Director
Carol Schellinger, Director
Christopher Young, Director of Operation
Marie Hunter, Director

Digital journal serving sustainability professionals worldwide.
20000 Members
Frequency: Semi-Annual
Circulation: 50,000
Founded in 1987

7870 **Marine Conservation News**
Center for Marine Conservation
2029 K Street
Washington, NW 20006

202-750-0574
800-519-1541
Fax: 202-872-0619
Home Page: www.cmc-ocean.org

Rose Bierce, Publisher
Roger Rufe, President
Stephanie Drea, VP Commun
Matt Schatzle, VP Membership & Development
Wanda Cantrell, Manager

Updates members of CMC on the organization projects and activities.
24 Pages
Frequency: Quarterly
Circulation: 100000
Printed in 2 colors on matte stock

7871 **McCoy's Hazardous Waste Regulatory Update**
McCoy & Associates
25107 Genesee Trail Road
Suite 200
Golden, CO 80228-4173

303-526-2674
Fax: 303-526-5471
E-Mail: info@mccoyseminars.com
Home Page:
www.mccoyseminars.com/contact.cfm

Offers a complete text of the federal hazardous waste regulations, summaries, interpretations and indexes.
Founded in 1983

7872 **McCoy's Regulatory Analysis Service**
McCoy & Associates
25107 Genesee Trail Road
Golden, CO 80401-5708

303-526-2674
Fax: 303-526-5471
E-Mail: info@mccoyseminars.com
Home Page: www.mccoyseminars.com

Provides timely, in-depth analyses of hazardous waste regulations within 10 working days after their publication in the Federal Register.
Cost: $550.00
Founded in 1983

7873 **Mealey's Litigation Report: Insurance**
LexisNexis Mealey's
555 W 5th Avenue
Los Angeles, CA 90013

213-627-1130
E-Mail: mealeyinfo@lexisnexis.com
Home Page: www.lexisnexis.com/mealeys

Tom Hagy, VP/General Manager
Maureen McGuire, Editorial Director
Vivi Gorman, Editor
Shawn Rice, Co-Editor

The report tracks declaratory judgment actions regarding coverage for litigation arising from long-tail claims, including environmental contamination and latent damage and injury allegedly caused by asbestos, tox chemicals and fumes, lead, breast implants, medical devices, construction defects, and more. Key issues: allocation, occurrence, policy exclusion, choice of law, discovery, duty to defend, notice, trigger of coverage and known loss.
Founded in 1984

7874 **Montana Green Power Update**
National Center for Appropriate Technology
3040 Continental Drive
PO Box 3838
Butte, MT 59702

406-494-4572
800-275-6228
Fax: 406-494-2905
Home Page: www.ncat.org
Social Media: Facebook, Twitter, LinkedIn

Eugene Brady, Chairman
Kathleen Hadley, Executive Director

This free monthly electronic newsletter contains the latest success stories in renewable energy development in the state of Montana, hot tips, information on financing and tax incentives, upcoming events, and links to stories from regional and national sources as featured on the Montana Green Power web site.
Frequency: Monthly
Founded in 1976

7875 **Motor Carrier Safety Report, HAZMAT Transp ortation Report**
J.J. Keller & Associates, Inc.
3003 Breezewood Lane
PO Box 368
Neenah, WI 54957-0368

920-722-2848
800-327-6868

Fax: 800-727-7516
E-Mail: sales@jjkeller.com
Home Page: www.jjkeller.com

Stephanie Hallman, Business Development

The nation's leader in risk and regulatory management solutions, including printed publications, videos, and online training for workplace safety, hazardous materials, transportation, human resources, and environmental safety.
Cost: $90.00
12 Pages
Frequency: Monthly
ISSN: 1056-3164
Founded in 1953

7876 NAESCO Newsletter
National Association of Energy Service Companies
1615 M St NW
Suite 800
Washington, DC 20036-3213
202-822-0950
Fax: 202-822-0955
E-Mail: info@naesco.org
Home Page: www.naesco.org

Terry E Singer, Executive Editor
Michael Hamilton, Marketing Manager
Mary Lee Berger-Hughes, Publisher

Targets energy service companies, electric and gas utilities amd other energy providers. Highlights industry news and features energy conservation.
Circulation: 200
Founded in 1985

7877 NCAT Action
National Center for Appropriate Technology
3040 Continental Drive
PO Box 3838
Butte, MT 59702
406-494-4572
800-275-6228
Fax: 406-494-2905
Home Page: www.ncat.org
Social Media: Facebook, Twitter, LinkedIn

Eugene Brady, Chairman
Kathleen Hadley, Executive Director

Action is a quarterly newsletter featuring local solutions for a sustainable future. Each issue focuses on a different topic, providing information that will help you move toward a more sustainable lifesytle in your home and in your community. Action features thought-provoking commentary, informative news stories, and extensive resource lists compiled by NCAT's expert professional staff.
Frequency: Quarterly
Founded in 1976

7878 NORA News
NORA: an Association of Responsible Recyclers
5965 Amber Ridge Rd
Haymarket, VA 20169-2623
703-753-4277
Fax: 703-753-2445
E-Mail: sparker@noranews.org
Home Page: www.noranews.org

Scott Parker, Executive Director

7879 National Association of Conservation Districts
National Association of Conservation Districts
509 Capitol Ct. NE
Washington, DC 20002-4937
202-547-6223
Fax: 202-547-6450
Home Page: www.nacdnet.org

Krysta Harden, CEO
Bob Cordova, Second Vice President

Highlights forestry issues of importance to districts and to showcase district-related forestry projects and success stories. Funded through a cooperative agreement between NACD and the U.S. Forest Service.
Cost: $35.00
12 Pages
Frequency: Monthly
Circulation: 25000
Founded in 1937

7880 Nature's Voice
National Resources Defense Council
40 W 20th St
New York, NY 10011-4231
212-727-2700
Fax: 212-727-1773
E-Mail: nrdcinfo@nrdc.org
Home Page: www.nrdc.org
Social Media: Facebook, Twitter, YouTube

Frances Beinecke, President
Daniel R. Tishman, Chair
Frederick A.O. Schwarz Jr., Chair Emeritus
Adam Albright, Vice Chair
Patricia Bauman, Vice Chair

Environmental news and activism, using law, science and the support of more than 1 million members and online activists to protect the plante's wildlife and wild places and to ensure a healthy environment for all living things.
50000 Members
Founded in 1970

7881 Networker
National Center for Appropriate Technology
3040 Continental Drive
PO Box 3838
Butte, MT 59702
406-494-4572
800-275-6228
Fax: 406-494-2905
Home Page: www.ncat.org
Social Media: Facebook, Twitter, LinkedIn

Eugene Brady, Chairman
Kathleen Hadley, Executive Director

The newsletter is compiled by the LIHEAP Clearinghouse, and NCAT project. Stories highlight state energy assistance program and low-income energy news.
Frequency: Quarterly
Founded in 1976

7882 News Flash
National Association of Local Government
1333 New Hampshire Ave Nw
Suite 400
Washington, DC 20036-1532
202-887-4107
Fax: 202-393-2866
E-Mail: nalgep@spiegelmcd.com
Home Page: www.nalgep.org

Kenneth E Brown, Executive Director
David Dickson, Projects Manager

Brings together noteworthy funding opportunities, conferences, legislative tracking on climate change and highlights projects completed on the federal or local level.
Frequency: Bi-Weekly

7883 Noise Regulation Report
Business Publishers
2222 Sedwick Dr
Suite 101
Durham, NC 27713
800-223-8720
Fax: 800-508-2592
E-Mail: custserv@bpinews.com
Home Page: www.bpinews.com

Exclusive coverage of airport, highway, occupational and open space noise, noise control and mitigation issues.
Cost: $511.00
10 Pages
Frequency: 12 per year
Printed in on matte stock

7884 Nuclear Monitor
Nuclear Information & Resource Services
1424 16th Street NW
Suite 404
Washington, DC 20036-2239
202-328-0002
Fax: 202-462-2183
E-Mail: nirsnet@nirs.org
Home Page: www.nirs.org
Social Media: Twitter, YouTube

Michael Mariotte, Editor
Linda Gunder, Media Manager

NIRS and WISE merged the Nuclear Monitor and WISE News Communique into a new Nuclear Monitor. Now available as an international edition.
Cost: $250.00
12 Pages
Frequency: 18 issues per y
Circulation: 1200
Founded in 1978
Printed in one color on matte stock

7885 Nuclear Waste News
Business Publishers
2222 Sedwick Dr
Suite 101
Durham, NC 27713
800-223-8720
Fax: 800-508-2592
E-Mail: custserv@bpinews.com
Home Page: www.bpinews.com

Worldwide coverage of the nuclear waste management industry including waste generation, packaging, transport, processing and disposal.
Cost: $697.00
10 Pages
Frequency: 25 per year
Mailing list available for rent
Printed in 2 colors on matte stock

7886 Outdoor News Bulletin
Wildlife Management Institute
4426 VT Route 215N
Cabot, VT 05647
802-563-2087
Fax: 802-563-2157
E-Mail: wmisw@together.net
Home Page: www.wildlifemanagementinstitute.org

Richard E McCabe, Executive VP
Scot J Williamson, VP
Carol J Peddicord, Finance Manager
Robert L Byrne, Wildlife Program Coordinator
Ronald R Helinski, Conservation Policy Specialist

Reports on select, significant issues, circumstances and other information that bear on the professional management of wildlife and related natural resources.

7887 RESTORE
Society for Ecological Restoration

1017 O Street NW
Washington, DC 20001

202-299-9518
Fax: 270-626-5485
E-Mail: info@ser.org
Home Page: www.ser.org

Steve Whisenant, Chair
Cara R. Nelson, Vice Chair
Mary Travaglini, Treasurer
Alan Unwin, Secretary

Weekly e-bulletin. Contains articles of interest to people in the field of restoration ecology, and is an indispensable way to keep up with what's happening in the world of ecological restoration, rounding up all the latest, breaking news from around the world on a wide variety of restoration-related issues. Available in electronic form only.
Frequency: Semi-Annual

7888 Reclamation Matters
American Society of Mining and Reclamation
3134 Montevesta Road
Lexington, KY 40502-3548

859-351-9032
Fax: 859-335-6529
E-Mail: asmr@insightbb.com
Home Page: www.asmr.us

Eddie Bearden, President
Bruce Buchanen, President Elect
Richard Barnhisel, Executive Secretary

Newsletter of the ASMR. Free to members or $10/year.
500 Members
Founded in 1983

7889 Recycling Markets
NV Business Publishers Corporation
43 Main St
Avon By the Sea, NJ 07717-1051

732-502-0500
Fax: 732-502-9606
E-Mail: nvrecycle@aol.com
Home Page: www.nvpublications.com

Ted Vilardi, Owner
Anna Dutko, Managing Editor
Tom Vilardi, President/Publisher
Ted Vilardi Jr., Co-Publisher

Contains profiles on recycling mills, as well as large users and generators of recycled materials for the broker, dealers and processors of paper stock, scrap metal, plastics and glass.
Cost: $180.00
Frequency: Weekly
Circulation: 3315
Printed in 4 colors on newsprint stock

7890 Resource Conservation & Recovery Act: A Guide to Compliance
McCoy & Associates
13701 W Jewell Avenue
Suite 202
Lakewood, CO 80228-4173

303-870-0835
Fax: 303-989-7917

Drew McCoy, Publisher
Deborah McCoy, President

Land disposal restrictions for hazardous waste.
300 Pages
Frequency: Annual

7891 Resource Development Newsletter
University of Tennessee
PO Box 1071
Knoxville, TN 37996-1071

865-974-1000
Fax: 865-974-7448
E-Mail: rpdavis@utk.edu

Alan Barefield, Publisher

Community development information.
4 Pages
Frequency: Quarterly
Circulation: 2000
Founded in 1794
Printed in one color on matte stock

7892 Resource Recovery Report
PO Box 3356
Warrenton, VA 20188-1956

540-347-4500
800-627-8913
Fax: 540-349-4540
E-Mail: rwill@coordgrp.com
Home Page: www.coordgrp.com

Richard Will, Production Manager

Covers all alternatives to landfills, i.e., recycling, energy recovery, composting in North America, Government, industry, associations, universities, etc. are included.
Cost: $227.00
12 Pages
Frequency: Monthly
Mailing list available for rent: 12M names
Printed in one color on matte stock

7893 SEG Extra
Society of Exploration Geophysicists
8801 South Yale
Suite 500
Tulsa, OK 74137-3575

918-497-5500
Fax: 918-497-5557
E-Mail: web@seg.org
Home Page: www.seg.org
Social Media: Facebook, Twitter, LinkedIn

Mary Fleming, Executive Director
Vladimir Grechka, Editor

eNewsletter, delivering the most relevant, up-to-date information pertaining directly to SEG members and stakeholders.
Founded in 1930

7894 SEJournal
Society of Environmental Journalists
PO Box 2492
Jenkintown, PA 19046

215-884-8174
Fax: 215-884-8175
Home Page: www.sej.org
Social Media: Facebook, Twitter

Carolyn Whetzel, President
Peter Fairley, 1st Vice Pres
Jeff Burnside, 2nd Vice Pres
Don Hopey, Treasurer

In-depth stories on hot topics on the environment beat.
Founded in 1990

7895 SOCMA Newsletter
Society of Chemical Manufacturers & Affiliates
1850 M St Nw
Suite 700
Washington, DC 20036-5803

202-721-4100
Fax: 202-296-8120
E-Mail: info@socma.org
Home Page: www.socma.org

Larry Brotherton, Ph.D., Chair
Dave Hurder, Vice Chair
Davide DeCuir, Treasurer
J. Steel Hutchinson, Secretary

Provides the specialty, batch and custom chemical industry with the latest regulatory, legislative and commerce news in a convenient newsletter exclusively compiled for members.
10 Pages
Frequency: Bi-Weekly

7896 Salt & Highway Deicing Newsletter
Salt Institute
700 N Fairfax St
Suite 600
Alexandria, VA 22314-2085

703-549-4648
Fax: 703-548-2194
E-Mail: info@saltinstitute.org
Home Page: www.saltinstitute.org

Richard L Hanneman, President
Tammy Goodwin, Director
Mark OKeefe, Director of Communications

A quarterly e-newsletter published by the Salt Institute that focuses on highway uses of salt.
Frequency: Quarterly
Circulation: 77000
Founded in 1914
Printed in on glossy stock

7897 Salt and Trace Minerals Newsletter
Salt Institute
700 N Fairfax St
Suite 600
Alexandria, VA 22314-2085

703-549-4648
Fax: 703-548-2194
E-Mail: info@saltinstitute.org
Home Page: www.saltinstitute.org

Richard L Hanneman, President

E-Newsletter containing information on animal nutrition.
Frequency: Quarterly
Circulation: 77000
Founded in 1914
Printed in on glossy stock

7898 SmartBrief
American Wind Energy Association
1501 M Street NW
Suite 1000
Washington, DC 20005

202-383-2500
Fax: 202-383-2505
E-Mail: windmail@awea.org
Home Page: www.awea.org
Social Media: Facebook, Twitter, YouTube

Ned Hall, Chair
Thomas Carnahan, Chair-Elect
Gabriel Alonso, Secretary
Don Furman, Treasurer
Vic Abate, Past Chair

Delivers quickly digestible summaries of the day's wind energy-related stories from across the media, keeps readers informed about the industry, and allows readers to stay on top of what's being said about it.
2400 Members

7899 Society Update
American Society of Safety Engineers
1800 E Oakton Street
Des Plaines, IL 60018

847-699-2929
Fax: 847-768-3434
E-Mail: customerservice@asse.org
Home Page: www.asse.org
Social Media: Facebook

Terrie S. Norris, President
Richard A. Pollock, President Elect
Kathy Seabrook, Senior Vice President
Fred J. Fortman, Jr., Secretary & Executive Director
James D. Smith, Vice President, Finance

Highlights the latest Society news, activities, upcoming events and notable member achievements.
30000 Members
Founded in 1911

7900 **Society of Chemical Manufacturers & Affiliates Newsletter**
1850 M St NW
Suite 700
Washington, DC 20036-5803

202-721-4100
Fax: 202-296-8120
E-Mail: info@socma.org
Home Page: www.socma.org

Larry Brotherton, Ph.D., Chair
Dave Hurder, Vice Chair
Davide DeCuir, Treasurer
J. Steel Hutchinson, Secretary

Newsletter tailored to provide industry executives with the most up-to-date information on events hosted or sponsored by SOCMA.
10 Pages
Frequency: Bi-Weekly

7901 **State Recycling Laws Update**
Raymond Communications
5111 Berwin Road
Suite no#115
College Park, MD 20740

301-345-4237
Fax: 301-345-4768
Home Page: www.raymond.com

Lorah utter, Editor
Bruce Popka, Vice President of Communications
Allyn Weet, Circulation Manager

Contains analysis and reports, provides coverage of recycling legislation affecting business, as well as the outlook on future legislation across the states and Canada. Also publishes special reports on related topics, for example, Transportation Packaging and the Environment.
Cost: $367.00
Frequency: Monthly
Circulation: 200
Founded in 1991

7902 **Superfund Week**
Pasha Publications
8737 Colesville Road
Suite 1100
Silver Spring, MD 20910-3928

301-589-5103
800-274-6737
Fax: 301-589-8493
E-Mail: custserv@bpinews.com
Home Page: www.bpinews.com

Harry Baisden, Group Publisher
Michael Hopps, Editor

Reporting the most recent developments in Congress, the EPA, and other government offices affecting hazardous waste investigations and cleanups in the federal Superfund and RCRA programs. Contains progress reports on specific cleanup sites in federal and state programs.
Cost: $525.00
Frequency: Weekly
Founded in 1963

7903 **SurFACTS in Biomaterials**
Surfaces in Biomaterials Foundation
1000 Westgate Drive
Suite 252
St Paul, MN 55114-8679

651-290-7487
Fax: 651-290-2266
E-Mail: memberservices@surfaces.org
Home Page: www.surfaces.org

Steven Goodman, Executive Editor
Janeyy Duntley, Managing Editor

Dedicated to exploring creative solutions to technical challenges at the BioInterface by fostering education and multidisciplinary cooperation among industrial, academic, clinical and regulatory communities.
Frequency: Bimonthly

7904 **The Current**
Women's Council on Energy and the Environment
PO Box 33211
Washington, DC 20033-0211

202-997-4512
Fax: 202-478-2098
Home Page: www.wcee.org
Social Media: Facebook, Twitter

Ronke Luke, President
Mary Brosnan-Sell, Secretary
Robin Cantor, Vice President
Alice Grabowski, Treasurer
Joyce Chandran, Executive Director

Keeps members up to date on energy and environmental issues to foster the professional development.

7905 **The Dirt**
Land and Water
Po Box 1197
Fort Dodge, IA 50501-1197

515-576-3191
Fax: 515-576-2606
Home Page: www.landandwater.com
Social Media: Facebook

Amy Dencklau, Publisher
Shanza Dencklau, Assistant Editor
Rasch M. Kenneth, President

eNewsletter including information relating to the erosion control and water management industry such as: feature stories, industry news, conferences, expert tips and video clips, new products and more. Striving to keep readers up-to-date on all current happenings and relevant information beyond the pages of Land and Water Magazine.
Cost: $20.00
72 Pages
Circulation: 20000
Founded in 1959
Mailing list available for rent: 20M names
Printed in 4 colors on glossy stock

7906 **The Forest Timeline**
Forest History Society
701 William Vickers Ave
Durham, NC 27701-3162

919-682-9319
Fax: 919-682-2349
E-Mail: recluce2@duke.edu
Home Page: www.foresthistory.org
Social Media: Facebook, Twitter

L. Michael Kelly, Chairman
Robert Healy, Co-Vice Chairman
Mark Wilde, Co-Vice Chairman
Henry I. Barclay III, Treasurer
Steven Anderson, Secretary & President

E-newsletter to keep the public informed of FHS news and activities.
2000 Members
Founded in 1946

7907 **The Networker**
National Center for Appropriate Technology
3040 Continental Drive
PO Box 3838
Butte, MT 59702

406-494-4572
800-275-6228
Fax: 406-494-2905
Home Page: www.ncat.org
Social Media: Facebook, Twitter, LinkedIn

Gene Brady, Chairman
Randall Chapman, Vice Chairman
George Ortiz, Chairman Emeritus
Jeannie Jertson, Secretary
Brian Castelli, Treasurer

Compiled by the LIHEAP Clearinghouse, an NCAT project. Stories highlight state energy assistanc program and low-income energy news.
Founded in 1976

7908 **The Resource**
National Association of Conservation Districts
509 Capitol Ct. NE
Washington, DC 20002-4937
202-547-6223
Fax: 202-547-6450
Home Page: www.nacdnet.org

Krysta Harden, CEO
Bob Cordova, Second Vice President

NACD's print publication provides in depth coverage of the association's recent activities and features columns by the NACD CEO and President, in addition to guest and partnership columns.
Cost: $35.00
12 Pages
Frequency: Monthly
Circulation: 25000
Founded in 1937

7909 **The Soil Plant Analyst**
Soil and Plant Analysis Council
347 North Shores Circle
Windsor, CO 80550

970-686-5702
E-Mail: rmiller@lamar.colostate.edu
Home Page: www.spcouncil.com/

Rigas Karamanos, President
Robert Miller, Secretary/Treasurer
Rao Mylavarapu, Vice President

Quarterly newsletter dedicated to the Agricultural Laboratory Industry.
Cost: $80.00
Circulation: 250

7910 **TipSheet**
Society of Environmental Journalists
PO Box 2492
Jenkintown, PA 19046

215-884-8174
Fax: 215-884-8175
Home Page: www.sej.org
Social Media: Facebook, Twitter

Carolyn Whetzel, President
Peter Fairley, 1st Vice Pres
Jeff Burnside, 2nd VP
Don Hopey, Treasurer

News tips to notify journalists of potential environmental stories and sources.
Founded in 1990

7911 **WEF Highlights**
Water Environment Federation
601 Wythe St
Alexandria, VA 22314-1994

800-666-0206
Fax: 703-684-2492
Home Page: www.wef.org
Social Media: Facebook, Twitter

Matt Bond, President
Cordell Samuels, President-Elect
Sandra Ralston, Vice President
Chris Browning, Treasurer
Jeff Eger, Secretary and Executive Director

Covers current Federation activities, Member Association news, and items of concern to the water quality field.
79 Members
ISSN: 1044-9943
Founded in 1928

7912 **Washington Environmental Protection Report**
Callahan Publications
PO Box 1173
Mc Lean, VA 22101-1173

703-356-1925
Fax: 703-356-9614
E-Mail: sue@newsletteraccess.com
Home Page: www.newsletteraccess.com

Vincent Callahan, Editor

Twice-monthly letter on contracting opportunities, legislation, research and development, and rules and regulations for the nation's environmental programs. The war on pollution, in all its forms, is coming to the forefront of federal priorities and could be the answer to the many economic problems facing America.
Cost: $190.00
8 Pages
Frequency: Bi-monthly
Founded in 1990
Printed in one color

7913 **Waste Handling Equipment News**
Lee Publications
6113 Strate Highway 5
PO Box 121
Palatine Bridge, NY 13428

518-673-3237
800-218-5586
Fax: 518-673-2381
E-Mail: mstanley@leepub.com
Home Page: www.wastehandling.com

Fred Lee, Publisher
Matt Stanley, Sales Manager
Holly Rieser, Editor

Addresses equipment needs of owners and operating managers involved in construction demolition, asphalt/concrete recycling, wood waste recycling, scrap metal recycling and composting. Every issue features editorial on new equipment, equipment adaptations, site stories, and news focused on our targeted segment of the recycling industry.
Frequency: Monthly
Circulation: 14000
Founded in 1993
Printed in on newsprint stock

7914 **Waste News**
Crain Communications
1155 Gratiot Ave.
Detroit, MI 48207-2997

313-446-6000
E-Mail: info@wastenews.com
Home Page: www.crain.com

Keith Crain, Chairman
Rance Crain, President
Mary Kay Crain, Treasurer/Assistant Secretary
Merrilee P. Crain, Secretary/Assistant Treasurer

Trade publication covering the solid waste industry.
Frequency: Bi-Weekly
Circulation: 52838
Founded in 1995

7915 **Waste Recovery Report**
Icon: Information Concepts
211 S 45th St
Philadelphia, PA 19104-2995

215-349-6500
Fax: 215-349-6502
E-Mail: wasterec@aol.com
Home Page: www.wrr.icodat.com

Alan Krigman, Publisher/Editor

Contains information on waste-to-energy, recycling, composting and other technologies.
Cost: $60.00
6 Pages
Frequency: Monthly
Circulation: 500
ISSN: 0889-0072
Founded in 1975

7916 **Water Environment Laboratory Solutions**
Water Environment Federation
601 Wythe St
Alexandria, VA 22314-1994

800-666-0206
Fax: 703-684-2492
Home Page: www.wef.org
Social Media: Facebook, Twitter

Matt Bond, President
Cordell Samuels, President-Elect
Sandra Ralston, Vice President
Chris Browning, Treasurer
Jeff Eger, Secretary and Executive Director

Focuses on day-to-day concerns regarding equipment use, sample tracking, and quality control, as well as discussing certification issues, staff management approaches, and new and revised analytical methods.
79 Members
ISSN: 1044-9943
Founded in 1928

7917 **Water Environment Regulation Watch**
Water Environment Federation
601 Wythe St
Alexandria, VA 22314-1994

800-666-0206
Fax: 703-684-2492
Home Page: www.wef.org
Social Media: Facebook, Twitter

Matt Bond, President
Cordell Samuels, President-Elect
Sandra Ralston, Vice President
Chris Browning, Treasurer
Jeff Eger, Secretary and Executive Director

Monthly snapshot of Washington's water quality activities. Provides concise reports of related bills, regulations, legal decisions, congressional hearings, and other federal government actions, following key issues from introduction to final determination.
79 Members
ISSN: 1044-9943
Founded in 1928

7918 **Weather & Climate Report**
Nautilus Press
1056 National Press Building
Washington, DC 20045-2001

202-347-6643

John R Botzum, Editor

Reports on federal actions which impact weather, climate research and global changes in climate.

7919 **Weekly Harvest**
National Center for Appropriate Technology
3040 Continental Drive
PO Box 3838
Butte, MT 59702

406-494-4572
800-275-6228
Fax: 406-494-2905
Home Page: www.ncat.org
Social Media: Facebook, Twitter, LinkedIn

Eugene Brady, Chairman
Kathleen Hadley, Executive Director

This e-newsletter is a Web digest of sustainable agriculture news, resources, events and funding opportunities gleaned from the Internet and featured on the website.
Frequency: Weekly
Founded in 1976

7920 **World Research News**
World Research Foundation
41 Bell Rock Plz
Sedona, AZ 86351-8804

928-284-3300
Fax: 928-284-3530
E-Mail: laverne@wrf.org
Home Page: www.wrf.org

LaVerne Boeckman, Co-Founder
Steven Ross, Co-Founder

Health information that is collected, categorized and disseminated in an independent and unbiased manner. Including allopathic medicine alongside complementary and alternative medicine... ancient and traditional techniques and healing therapies as well as the latest medical technology.
Frequency: Quarterly

7921 **World Wildlife Fund: Focus**
World Wildlife
PO Box 97180
Washington, DC 20090-7180

202-293-4800
Fax: 202-293-9211
Home Page: www.worldwildlife.org

Kathryn S Fuller, CEO
Jennifer Seeger, Chief Financial Officer
Michael Bauer, Chief Financial Officer
Marcia Marsh, Chief Operating Officer

WWF projects are highlighted around the world in 450 national parks and nature reserves, with emphasis on coverage of programs and activities in the US.
8 Pages
Frequency: Monthly
Founded in 1960

7922 **eNotes**
National Association of Conservation Districts
509 Capitol Ct. NE
Washington, DC 20002-4937

202-547-6223
Fax: 202-547-6450
Home Page: www.nacdnet.org

Krysta Harden, CEO
Bob Cordova, Second Vice President

NACD's weekly news briefs.
Cost: $35.00
12 Pages
Frequency: Monthly
Circulation: 25000
Founded in 1937

Magazines & Journals

7923 **ACCA Insider**
Air Conditioning Contractors of America
2800 Shirlington Rd
Suite 300
Arlington, VA 22206-3607

703-575-4477
E-Mail: info@acca.org
Home Page: www.acca.org
Social Media: Facebook, Twitter, LinkedIn, YouTube

Paul Stalknecht, President & CEO

Offering targeted news to ACCA members.

7924 **ASNT Annual Fall Conference**
American Society for Nondestructive Testing

1711 Arlingate Lane
PO Box 28518
Columbus, OH 43228

614-274-6003
800-222-2768
Fax: 614-274-6899
Home Page: www.asnt.org

Tim Jones, Senior Manager, Publications
Wayne Holliday, Executive Director

Research, reviews and information of nondestructive testing materials. Provides members and subscribers the latest news and technical information concerning this industry.
Cost: $75.00
12000 Members
90 Pages
Frequency: Monthly
Circulation: 13000
ISSN: 0025-5327
Founded in 1942
Printed in 4 colors on glossy stock

7925 Aerosol Science and Technology (AS&T)
American Association for Aerosol Research
15000 Commerce Parkway
Suite C
Mount Laurel, NJ 08054

856-439-9080
Fax: 856-439-0525
E-Mail: info@aaar.org
Home Page: www.aaar.org

Peter McMurry, Editor-In-Chief
Tami C Bond, Editor
Warren H Finlay, Editor

AS&T is the offficial journal of AAAR. It publishes the results of theoretical and experimental investigations into aerosol phenomena and closely related material as well as high-quality reports on fundamental and applied topics.
Cost: $1214.00

7926 Agronomy Journal
American Society of Agronomy
5585 Guilford Rd.
Madison, WI 53711-1086

608-273-8080
Fax: 608-273-2021
E-Mail: headquarters@sciencesocieties.org
Home Page: www.agronomy.org
Social Media: Facebook, Twitter, LinkedIn

Newell Kitchen, President
Kenneth Barbarick, President-Elect

Journal of agriculture and natural resource sciences. Articles convey original research in soil science, crop science, agroclimatology, agronomic modeling, production agriculture, instrumentation, and more.
10000 Members
Founded in 1907

7927 American Environmental Laboratory
International Scientific Communications
30 Controls Drive
PO Box 870
Shelton, CT 06484-0870

203-926-9300
Home Page: www.iscpubs.com

Brian Howard, Editor
Robert G Sweeny, Publisher

Laboratory activities, new equipment, and analysis and collection of samples are the main topics.
Cost: $282.42
Frequency: Monthly
Circulation: 185000

7928 American Forests
Po Box 2000
Suite 800
Washington, DC 20013-2000

202-737-1944
Fax: 202-955-4588
E-Mail: info@amfor.org
Home Page: www.americanforests.org

Deborah Gangloff, Executive Director

A publication that offers our members the best in conservation news. Articles include different perspectives on current environmental issues, stories on wildlife restoration projects, updates on forest management practices, and ways to engage the conservation movement in your community.
Cost: $25.00
Frequency: Quarterly
Founded in 1875

7929 American Waste Digest
Charles G Moody
226 King St
Pottstown, PA 19464-9105

610-326-9480
800-442-4215
Fax: 610-326-9752
E-Mail: awd@americanwastedigest.com
Home Page: www.americanwastedigest.com

Carasue Moody, Publisher
Shannon Costa, Circulation Manager
J. Robert Tagert, Sales Manager

Provides reviews on new products, profiles on sucessful waste removal businesses, and provides discussion on legislation on municipal regulations on recycling.
Cost: $24.00
86 Pages
Frequency: Monthly
Circulation: 33000
Printed in 4 colors on glossy stock

7930 Archives of Environmental Health
Society for Occupational and Environmental Health
111 North Bridge Road #21-01
Peninsula Plaza
Singapore 179098

703-556-9222
Fax: 703-556-8729
Home Page: www.oehs.org

Laura Degnon, Manager

Publishing new research based on the most rigorous methods and discussion to put this work in perspective for public health, public policy, and sustainability, the Archives addresses such topics of current concern as health significance of chemical exposure, toxic waste, new and old energy technologies, industrial processes, and the environmental causation of disease.
Frequency: Bi-Monthly

7931 Bio-Mineral Times
Allen C Forter & Son
3450 W Central Avenue
#328
Toledo, OH 43606-1418

419-535-6374
Fax: 419-535-7008
E-Mail: info@nviro.com
Home Page: www.nviro.com

Bonnie Hunter, Publisher
James McHugh, Chief Financial Officer

Issues focus on environmental legislation efforts, regulation compliance, and finding answers to the mechanics and practical applications of the distribution and management of biosolids derived products.
Frequency: Quarterly
Circulation: 25,000

7932 CONNECT Magazine
Association of Zoos and Aquariums
8403 Colesville Rd
Suite 710
Silver Spring, MD 20910-6331

301-562-0777
Fax: 301-562-0888
Home Page: www.aza.org
Social Media: Facebook, Twitter

L. Patricia Simmons, Chair
Tom Schmid, Chair-Elect
Jackie Ogden, PhD, Vice-Chair

Window to the professional zoo and aquarium world. Magazine features fascinating stories that explore trends, educational initiatives, member achievements and conservation efforts.
200 Members
Founded in 1924

7933 CSA News
American Society of Agronomy
5585 Guilford Rd.
Madison, WI 53711-1086

608-273-8080
Fax: 608-273-2021
E-Mail: headquarters@sciencesocieties.org
Home Page: www.agronomy.org
Social Media: Facebook, Twitter, LinkedIn

Newell Kitchen, President
Kenneth Barbarick, President-Elect

The official magazine for members of the American Society of Agronomy, Crop Science Society of America, and Soil Science Society of America.
10000 Members
Founded in 1907

7934 Crop Science
American Society of Agronomy
5585 Guilford Rd.
Madison, WI 53711-1086

608-273-8080
Fax: 608-273-2021
E-Mail: headquarters@sciencesocieties.org
Home Page: www.agronomy.org
Social Media: Facebook, Twitter, LinkedIn

Newell Kitchen, President
Kenneth Barbarick, President-Elect

Publishes original research in crops and turfgrass science.
10000 Members
Founded in 1907

7935 Crops & Soils
American Society of Agronomy
5585 Guilford Rd.
Madison, WI 53711-1086

608-273-8080
Fax: 608-273-2021
E-Mail: headquarters@sciencesocieties.org
Home Page: www.agronomy.org
Social Media: Facebook, Twitter, LinkedIn

Newell Kitchen, President
Kenneth Barbarick, President-Elect

The magazine for certified crop advisors, agronomists, and soil scientists. Focuses on solutions to the daily challenges facing those working in the field and features information on new technology and products, company strategies, CEU articles and quizzes, and regulatory and industry news.
10000 Members
Founded in 1907

7936 E/Environmental Magazine
28 Knight St
Norwalk, CT 06851-4719

203-854-5559
800-967-6572
Fax: 203-866-0602

E-Mail: info@emagazine.com
Home Page: www.emagazine.com

Jim Motavalli, Editor
Karen Soucy, Associate Publisher
Doug Moss, Publisher & Executive Dir
Brita Belli, Director
Trudy Hodenfield, Operations Manager

Providing information about environmental issues and sharing ideas and resources so that readers can live more sustainable lives and connect with ongoing efforts for change. Covers everything environmental, from big issues like climate change, renewable energy and toxins and health, to the topics that directly impact our readers' daily lives; how to eat right and stay healthy, where to invest responsibly and how to save energy at home.
Cost: $19.95
Circulation: 185,000
Founded in 1988

7937 **EI Digest: Hazardous Waste Marketplace**
Environmental Information
PO Box 390266
Minneapolis, MN 55439

952-831-2473
Fax: 952-831-6550
Home Page: www.envirobiz.com

Cary Perket, President

Focused on serving the market information needs of the commercial hazardous waste management sector. Included those involved in recycling and re-use, energy recovery, waste treatment, and waste disposal. Provides compilations and analysis of the commercial markets for hazardous waste energy recovery, fuel blending, incineration, landfill and solvent recovery. Also undertakes special reports on chemical distributors, RCRA metal recyclers and wastewater treatment.
ISSN: 1042-251X
Founded in 1983
Printed in 2 colors

7938 **EM**
Air & Waste Management Association
420 Fort Duquesne Boulevard
One Gateway Center, 3rd Floor
Pittsburgh, PA 15222-1435

412-652-2458
Fax: 412-232-3450
E-Mail: info@awma.org
Home Page: www.awma.org
Social Media: Facebook, Twitter, LinkedIn

Jeffry Muffat, President
Merlyn L. Hough, President Elect
Mike Kelly, Secretary/ Executive Director
Amy Gilligan, Treasurer
Dallas Baker, Vice President

A&WMA's magazine for environmental managers, explores a range of issues affecting the industry with timely, provocative articles and regular columns written by leaders in the field. Keeps readers informed of coverage of regulatory changes, EPA research, new technologies, market analyses, environment, health, and safety issues, new products, professional development opportunities, and more.
9000 Members
Founded in 1907

7939 **Earth Island Journal**
2150 Allston Way
Suite 460
Berkeley, CA 94704-1375

510-859-9100
Fax: 510-859-9091
E-Mail: arch@earthisland.org
Home Page: www.earthisland.org
Social Media: Facebook, Twitter, YouTube

Martha Davis, President
Kenneth Brower, Vice President
Michael Hathaway, Vice President
Jennifer Snyder, Secretary
Alex Giedt, Treasurer

Combines investigative journalism and thought-provoking essays that make the subtle but profound connections between the environment and other contemporary issues. The Journal's unique brand of environmental journalism is a key resource for anyone eager to help protect our shared planet.
33M Members
Founded in 1985

7940 **Ecological Economics, The ISEE Journal**
International Society for Ecological Economics
15 River Street
#204
Boston, MA 02108

703-790-1745
Fax: 703-790-2672
E-Mail: secretariat@ecoeco.org
Home Page: www.ecoeco.org
Social Media: Facebook, Twitter

John Gowdy, President
Bina Agarwal, President-Elect
Anne Aitken, Managing Editor

Concerned with extending and integrating the study and management of ecology and economics. This integration is necessary because conceptual and professional isolation have led to economic and environmental policies which are mutually destructive rather than reinforcing in the long term.
750 Members
Founded in 1989

7941 **Ecological Management & Restoration**
Society for Ecological Restoration International
1017 O Street NW
Washington, DC 20001

202-299-9518
Fax: 270-626-5485
E-Mail: info@ser.org
Home Page: www.ser.org
Social Media: Facebook

Steve Whisenant, Chair
Cara R. Nelson, Vice Chair
Mary Travaglini, Treasurer
Alan Unwin, Secretary

Aims to bridge the gap between the ecologist's perspective and field manager's experience. Answers the growing need among land managers for reliable, relevant information and acknowledges the need for two-way communication in devising new hypotheses, sound experimentation, effective treatments and reliable monitoring.
2300 Members
Frequency: Quarterly
Founded in 1988

7942 **Economics of Energy and Environmental Policy (EEEP)**
International Association for Energy Economics
28790 Chagrin Blvd
Suite 350
Cleveland, OH 44122-4642

216-464-5365
Fax: 216-464-2737
E-Mail: iaee@iaee.org
Home Page: www.iaee.org
Social Media: Facebook, LinkedIn

Mine Yucel, President
Lars Bergman, President-Elect
David L. Williams, Executive Director

Policy oriented, focusing on all policy issues in the interface between energy and environmental economics. Provides a research-based, scholarly, yet easily read and accessible source of information on contemporary economic thinking and analysis of energy and environmental policy.
3400 Members
Founded in 1977

7943 **Energy Engineering**
Association of Energy Engineers
4025 Pleasantdale Rd
Suite 420
Atlanta, GA 30340-4264

770-447-5083
Fax: 770-446-3969
E-Mail: info@aeecenter.org
Home Page: www.aeecenter.org

Albert Thumann, Executive Director
Ruth Whitlock, Executive Admin
Albert Thumann, Executive Director
Ruth Marie, Managing Editor

Engineering solutions to cost efficiency problems and mechanical contractors who design, specify, install, maintain, and purchase non-residential heating, ventilating, air conditioning and refrigeration equipment and components.
Circulation: 8000
Founded in 1976

7944 **Environ: A Magazine for Ecologic Living and Health**
Environ
1616 Seventeenth Street
Suite 468
Denver, CO 80202

303-285-5543
Fax: 303-628-5597
Home Page: www.environcorp.com

Suzanne Randegger, Publisher/Editor
Ed Randegger, Co-Publisher/Ad Director
John Haasbeek, Senior Manager
Chris Keller, Managing Director

Designed to keep health and ecology conscious readers aware of circumstances hazardous to human health, and provide alternatives - practical, political, and global. Coverage of environmental legislation, ecologic food-growing practices and certification, geographically and climatically safe and hazardous locations, and a view of today's health problems with active solutions. Supported by screened advertisers.
Cost: $15.00
40 Pages
Frequency: Quarterly

7945 **Environment**
Helen Dwight Reid Educational Foundation
1319 18th Street NW
Washington, DC 20036-1802

202-296-6267
Fax: 202-296-5149
E-Mail: brichman@heldref.org
Home Page: www.heldref.org

Douglas Kirkpatrick, Publisher
Barbara Richman, Editor
Fred Huber, Circulation Manager
Emily Tawlowski, Marketing Manager
Steve Hellem, Executive Director

Analyzes the problems, places, and people where environment and development come together, illuminating concerns from the local to the global. Articles and commentaries from researchers and practitioners who provide a broad range of international perspectives. Also

features in-depth reviews of major policy reports, conferences, and environmental education initiatives, as well as guides to the best Web sites, journal articles, and books.
Cost: $51.00
Frequency: Monthly
Circulation: 11,408
Founded in 1956

7946 **Environmental & Engineering Geoscience Journal**
Association of Engineering Geologists
PO Box 460518
Denver, CO 80246-0518
303-757-2926
Fax: 720-230-4846
E-Mail: aeg@aegweb.org
Home Page: www.aegweb.org
Social Media: Facebook, Twitter
Jennifer Bauer, President
Matthew B. Morris, Vice President/ President Elect
Gary Lice, Treasurer
Ken Fergason, Secretary
Publishes peer reviewed manuscripts that address issues relating to the interaction of people with hydrologic and geologic systems. Theoretical and applied contributions are appropriate, and the primary criteria for acceptance are scientific and technical merit.
3000 Members
Founded in 1957
Mailing list available for rent: 3000 names at $100 per M

7947 **Environmental Business Journal**
Environmental Business International
4452 Park Boulevard Suite 306
PO Box 371769
San Diego, CA 92116-1769
619-295-7685
Fax: 619-295-5743
E-Mail: ebi@ebiusa.com
Home Page: www.ebiusa.com
Grant Ferrier, Publisher
Dan Johnson, Manager
An overview piece, segment analysis by country, profiles of domestic and foreign firms, financial data on listed environmental companies in the region, the latest developments on government initiatives and regulations, company news and projects are included in the features of this publications.
Cost: $495.00
Founded in 1988
Printed in 2 colors

7948 **Environmental Communicator**
North American Association for Environmental
2000 P St NW
Suite 540
Washington, DC 20036-6921
202-419-0412
Fax: 202-419-0415
E-Mail: email@naaee.org
Home Page: www.naaee.org
Brian Day, Executive Director
A publication of the North American Association for EE. Feature articles, association news, affiliate news, op-ed pieces, announcements on new EE resources, available jobs, and future events and opportunities.
Frequency: Bi-Monthly

7949 **Environmental Engineering Science**
Mary Ann Liebert
140 Huguenot St
New Rochelle, NY 10801-5215
914-740-2100
Fax: 914-740-2101
E-Mail: info@liebertpub.com
Home Page: www.liebertpub.com
Mary A Liebert, Owner
Dumpnico Grosso, Editor-in-Chief
Stephanie Paul, Production Editor
Lisa Cohen, Associate Editors
Publishing studies of innovative solutions to problems in air, wter, and land contamination and waste disposal. Features applications of environmental engineering and scientific discoveries, policy issues, environmental economics, and sustainable development.
Cost: $330.00
Frequency: Monthly
Circulation: 1800
ISSN: 1092-8758
Founded in 1980

7950 **Environmental Forensics**
AEHS Foundation Inc
150 Fearing Street
Amherst, MA 01002
413-549-5170
Fax: 413-549-0579
Home Page: www.aehsfoundation.org
Paul T Kostecki, PhD, Executive Director
An international publication offering scientific studies that explore source, fate, transport and ecological effects of environmental contamination, with contamination being delineated in terms of chemical characterization, biological influence, responsible parties and legal consequences.
600 Members
Founded in 1989

7951 **Environmental Geochemistry and Health**
Society for Environmental Geochemistry and Health
4698 S Forrest Avenue
Springfield, MO 65810
417-885-1166
Fax: 417-881-6920
Home Page: www.segh.net
Bobby Wixson, Director Membership
Publishes original research papers, short communications, reviews and topical special issues across the broad field of environmental geochemistry. Coverage includes papers that directly link health and the environment.
Frequency: Quarterly

7952 **Environmental History (EH)**
UW Interdisciplinary Arts and Sciences Program
1900 Commerce Street
Tacoma, WA 98402
206-343-0226
Fax: 206-343-0249
E-Mail: director@aseh.net
Home Page: www.aseh.net
John McNeill, President
Gregg Mitman, Vice President/ President Elect
Ellen Stroud, Secretary
Mark Madison, Treasurer
The world's leading scholarly journal in environmental history. Brings together scholars, scientists, and practitioners from a wide array of disciplines to explore changing relationships between humans and the environment over time.
1200 Members
Founded in 1976

7953 **Environmental Practice**
National Association of Environmental Professional
PO Box 2086
Bowie, MD 20718-2086
888-251-9902
Fax: 301-860-1141
Home Page: www.naep.org
John Perkins, Editor
Incorporates original research articles, news of issues and of the NAEP, and opinion pieces. Of interest to private consultants, academics, and professionals in federal, state, local, and tribal governments, as well as in corporations and non-governmental organizations. Reports on historic and contemporary environmental issues that help inform current practices.
Frequency: Quarterly

7954 **Environmental Protection**
Stevens Publishing Corporation
5151 Belt Line Rd
10th Floor
Dallas, TX 75254-7507
972-687-6700
Fax: 972-687-6767
Home Page: www.eponline.com
Craig S Stevens, President
Dana Cornett, President/COO
Randy Dye, Publisher
Sherleen Mahoney, Editor
Margaret Perry, Circulation Director
The comprehensive online information resource for environmental professionals.
Circulation: 63000
Founded in 1925

7955 **Environmental Science and Technology**
American Chemical Society
1155 16th St Nw
Washington, DC 20036-4892
202-872-4600
800-227-5558
Fax: 202-872-4615
E-Mail: service@acs.org
Home Page: www.acs.org
Madeleine Jacobs, CEO/Executive Director
Publishes news and research in diverse areas of environmental science and engineering.
Cost: $156.00
110 Pages
Frequency: Monthly
Circulation: 13000
Founded in 1966

7956 **Environmental Times**
Environmental Assessment Association
1224 N Nokomis NE
Alexandria, MN 56308
320-763-4320
E-Mail: info@eaa-assoc.org
Home Page: www.iami.org/eaa.html
Robert Johnson, Executive Director
This publications contents contain environment conferences and expos, industry trends, federal regulations related to the environment and industry assessments.
Cost: $19.95
24 Pages
Circulation: 7000
Founded in 1972
Printed in 4 colors on newsprint stock

7957 **Environmental Toxicology and Chemistry**
Society of Environmental Toxicology and Chemistry
1013 N 12th Ave
Pensacola, FL 32501-3306
850-437-1901
Fax: 850-469-9778

E-Mail: rparrish@setac.org
Home Page: www.edwardjones.com

Chad Stacy, Manager

Dedicated to furthering scientific knowledge and disseminating information on environmental toxicology and chemistry, including the application of these sciences to risk management. Provides a forum for professionals in academia, business, and government.

7958 **Environmental and Molecular Mutagenesis**
Environmental Mutagen Society
1821 Michael Faraday Drive
Suite 300
Reston, VA 20190

703-438-8220
Fax: 703-438-3113
E-Mail: emshq@ems-us.org
Home Page: www.ems-us.org

Publishes original research articles on environmental mutangenesis. Manuscripts published in the six general areas of mechanisms of mutagenesis, genomics, DNA damage, replication, recombination and repair, public health, and DNA technology.
Frequency: 8/year

7959 **ExecutiveBrief**
Synthetic Organic Chemical Manufacturers Assn
1850 M St Nw
Suite 700
Washington, DC 20036-5803

202-721-4100
Fax: 202-296-8120
E-Mail: info@socma.org
Home Page: www.socma.org

Joseph Acker, President
Vivian Diko, Executive Assistant & CEO
Charlene Patterson, Editor

Provides quality content on software development, outsourcing, project and risk management.

7960 **Fisheries**
American Fisheries Society
5410 Grosvenor Ln
Suite 110
Bethesda, MD 20814-2199

301-897-8616
Fax: 301-897-8096
Home Page: www.fisheries.org

Gus Rassam, Executive Director
Charles Moseley, Journals Manager

Peer reviewed articles that address contemporary issues and problems, techniques, philosophies and other areas of interest to the general fisheries profession. Monthly features include letters, meeting notices, book listings and reviews, environmental essays and organization profiles.
Cost: $76.00
50 Pages
Frequency: Monthly
Founded in 1870
Mailing list available for rent: 8500 names at $250 per M

7961 **Forest History Today**
Forest History Society
701 William Vickers Ave
Durham, NC 27701-3162

919-682-9319
Fax: 919-682-2349
E-Mail: recluce2@duke.edu
Home Page: www.foresthistory.org
Social Media: Facebook, Twitter

L. Michael Kelly, Chairman
Robert Healy, Co-Vice Chairman
Mark Wilde, Co-Vice Chairman
Henry I. Barclay III, Treasurer
Steven Anderson, Secretary & President

Providing members of FHS with engaging writings in forest history and staying updated with current FHS activities.
2000 Members
Founded in 1946

7962 **Fusion Science and Technology**
American Nuclear Society
555 N Kensington Ave
La Grange Park, IL 60526-5592

708-352-6611
800-323-3044
Fax: 708-352-0499
E-Mail: advertising@ans.org
Home Page: www.ans.org
Social Media: Facebook, Twitter, LinkedIn

Jack Tuohy, Executive Director
James S Tulenko, VP
William F Naughton, Treasurer

Information on fusion plasma physics and plasma engineering, fusion plasma enabling science and technology, fusion nuclear technology and material science, fusion applications, fusion design and system studies. Plasma and fusion energy physics, tokamak experiments, stellarators, next step burning plasma experiments, target fabrications and technology for inertial confinement fusion, inertial fusion science and applications, tritium science and technology, and more.
10500 Members
Founded in 1954

7963 **Geophysics**
Society of Exploration Geophysicists
8801 South Yale
Suite 500
Tulsa, OK 74137-3575

918-497-5500
Fax: 918-497-5557
E-Mail: web@seg.org
Home Page: www.seg.org
Social Media: Facebook, Twitter, LinkedIn

Mary Fleming, Executive Director
Vladimir Grechka, Editor

An archival journal encompassing all aspects of research, exploration, and education in applied geophysics.
Founded in 1930

7964 **Hauler**
Hauler Magazine
166 S Main Street
PO Box 508
New Hope, PA 18938

800-220-6029
800-220-6029
Fax: 215-862-3455
E-Mail: mag@thehauler.com
Home Page: www.thehauler.com

Thomas N Smith, Publisher/Editor
Barbara Gibney, Circulation Manager
Leslie T Smith, Marketing Director

Dedicated to the refuse and solid waste industry. It is the acknowledged leader in the new and used refuse truck and equipment marketplace, and now lists hundreds of new and used trash trucks, trailers, containers, services, plus parts and accessories from the best suppliers in the industry.
Cost: $12.00
Frequency: Monthly
Circulation: 18630
Founded in 1978

7965 **Hazardous Management**
Ecolog
1450 Don Mills Road
Don Mills, Ontario M3B-2X7

416-442-2292
888-702-1111
Fax: 416-442-2204
Home Page: www.hazmatmag.com

Lynda Reilly, Publisher

The latest environmental regulations and programs as well as the evolving technology and equipment needed to achieve compliance.
Cost: $39.50
Frequency: Bi-Monthly
Circulation: 16,000
ISSN: 0843-9303
Founded in 1989
Mailing list available for rental $250 per M
Printed in 4 colors on glossy stock

7966 **Hazardous Waste Consultant**
Aspen Publishers
8400 east cresent parkway
6 floor greenwood village
Lakewood, CO 80111

720-528-4270
800-638-8437
Fax: 212-597-0335

A unique approach to hazardous waste issues. It is written by engineers and regulatory specialists who have an extensive background in the field and understand the problems that industry, consultants, and regulators face.
Cost: $475.00

7967 **Human Ecology Review**
Society for Human Ecology
College of the Atlantic
105 Eden Street
Bar Harbor, ME 04609-0180

207-288-5015
Fax: 207-288-3780
E-Mail: carter@ecology.coa.edu
Home Page: www.societyforhumanecology.org

Barbara Carter, Assistant to Executive Director

Publishes peer-reviewed research and theory on the interaction between humans and the environment and other links between culture and nature, essays and applications relevant to human ecology, book reviews, and relevant commentary, announcements, and awards.
Frequency: Semi-Annual

7968 **Human and Ecological Risk Assessment**
AEHS Foundation Inc
150 Fearing Street
Amherst, MA 01002
413-549-5170
Fax: 413-549-0579
Home Page: www.aehsfoundation.org

Paul T Kostecki, PhD, Executive Director

Devoted to providing a framework for professionals researching and assessing developments in both human and ecological risk assessment.
600 Members
Founded in 1989

7969 **Hydrological Science and Technology**
American Institute Of Hydrology
300 Village Green Circle
Suite 201
Smyrna, GA 30080

770-269-9388
Home Page: www.aihydro.org

Cathy Lipsett, Owner
Cathryn Seaburn, Manager

Peer-reviewed international journal covering research and practical studies on hydrological science, technology, water resources and related topics including water, air and soil pollution and hazardous waste issues.

Communicating ideas, findings, methods, techniques and summaries of interesting projects or investigations in the area of hydrology.
Frequency: Quarterly

7970 IEEE Power and Energy Magazine
IEEE
PO Box 1331
Piscataway, NJ 08855

732-981-0061
Fax: 732-981-9667
E-Mail: society-info@ieee.org
Home Page: www.ieee.org

Mel Olken, Editor
Susan Schneiderman, Business Development

Dedicated to disseminating information on all matters of interest to electric power engineers and other professionals involved in the electric power industry. Feature articles focus on advanced concepts, technologies, and practices associated with all aspects of electric power from a technical perspective in synergy with nontechnical areas such as business, environmental, and social concerns.
Cost: $260.00
82 Pages
Frequency: Monthly
Circulation: 23000
ISSN: 1540-7977
Founded in 2003
Mailing list available for rent
Printed in on glossy stock

7971 Identifying Business Risks & Opportunities
World Resources Institute
10 G St NE
Suite 800
Washington, DC 20002-4252

202-729-7600
Fax: 202-729-7610
E-Mail: front@wri.org
Home Page: www.wcdassessment.org

Jonathan Lash, President

7972 Indoor Air Journal
The Indoor Air Institute
2548 Empire Grade
Santa Cruz, CA 95060

831-426-0148
Fax: 831-426-6522
E-Mail: info@IndAir.org
Home Page: indair.org

Hal Levin, President
William Fisk, Vice President
William Nazaroff, Vice President

Providing a location for reporting original research results in the broad area defined by the indoor environment of non-industrial buildings. The results will provide the information to allow designers, builders, owners and operators to provide a healthy and comfortable environment for building occupants. Health effects, monitoring and modelling, source characterization, ventilation and other environmental control techniques, thermal comfort, and public policy.

7973 Indoor Environment Review
IAQ Publications
7920 Norfolk Ave
#900
Bethesda, MD 20814-2539

301-913-0115
Fax: 301-913-0119
Home Page: www.eschoolnews.com

Robert Morrow, Owner

New technology, research and legislation concerning all indoor air and water quality issues.
Frequency: Monthly
Circulation: 10000

7974 Industrial Safety & Hygiene
Business News Publishing Company
2401 W. Big Beaver Road
Suite 700
Troy, MI 48084

847-763-9534
Fax: 847-763-9538
E-Mail: ishn@halldata.com
Home Page: www.ishn.com

Randy Green, Publisher/ West Coast Manager
Dave Johnsen, Editor
Maureen Brady, Managing Editor/Project Editor
Vince Miconi, Production Manager
Lydia Stewart, Inside Sales/Classifides

A business-to-business trade publication targeted at key safety, health and industrial hygiene buying influencers at manufacturing facilities of all sizes. Designed for the busy professionals with early mail dates and short articles backed by dynamite graphics. Each issue is packed with vital editorial on OSHA and EPA regulations, ho-to features, safety and health management topics, and the latest product news. For safety and health managers at high-hazard worksites.

7975 Industrial Wastewater
Water Environment Federation
601 Wythe St
Alexandria, VA 22314-1994

800-666-0206
Fax: 703-684-2492
Home Page: www.wef.org
Social Media: Facebook, Twitter

Matt Bond, President
Cordell Samuels, President-Elect
Sandra Ralston, Vice President
Chris Browning, Treasurer
Jeff Eger, Secretary and Executive Director

Discusses relevant regulatory and legal issues, provides examples of real-world treatment options, and offers suggestions on minimizing waste and preventing pollution.
79 Members
ISSN: 1044-9943
Founded in 1928

7976 Inside EPA
Inside Washington Publishers
1919 S Eads St
Arlington, VA 22202-3028

703-418-3981
800-424-9068
Fax: 703-416-8543
E-Mail: support@iwpnews.com
Home Page: www.iwpnews.com

Alan Sosenko, Owner

Gives timely information on all facets of waste, water, air, and other environmental regulatory programs.
Frequency: Weekly
Founded in 1980

7977 Inside Waste
John Cupps Associates
2757 13th Street
Sacramento, CA 95818-2907

916-448-5272
Fax: 916-448-7862

John A Cupps, Publisher/Editor

The waste trade spans a diverse range of activities, from waste collection to resource recovery to landfilling. The operating environment varies from state to state, between urban and rural areas, and even among different councils. Inside Waste brings this all together, covering all the news, projects, contracts and issues that matter to the waste trade.
Frequency: Monthly

7978 Integrated Environmenal Assessment and Management
SETAC
1013 N 12th Ave
Pensacola, FL 32501-3306

850-437-1901
Fax: 850-469-9778
E-Mail: setac@setac.org
Home Page: www.setac.org
Social Media: Facebook, Twitter, LinkedIn

Paul van den Brink, President
Tim Canfield, Vice President
Fred Heimbach, Treasurer

Bridges the gap between scientific research and its application in environmental decision-making, regulation, and management.
4000 Members
Founded in 1979

7979 International Dredging Review
PO Box 1487
Fort Collins, CO 80522-1487

970-416-1903
Fax: 970-416-1878
E-Mail: editor@dredgemag.com
Home Page: www.dredgemag.com

Judith Powers, Publisher
Julia Leach, Business Manager
Nelson Spencer, Business Manager

Targeted to dredging company executives, project managers and dredge crew members, suppliers and service people such as pump manufacturers, hydrographic surveyors, consulting engineers, etc.
Cost: $85.00
Frequency: Monthly
Circulation: 3300
ISSN: 0737-8181
Founded in 1967

7980 International Environmental Systems Update
CEEM
3975 University Drive
Suite 230
Fairfax, VA 22030-3223

703-437-9000
800-745-5565
Fax: 703-437-9001
Home Page: www.qsuonline.com

Paul Scicchitano, Publisher
Suzanne Leonard, Senior Editor

Provides information covering the emerging environmental issues that affect business and industry around the globe including competitive advantages, global updates, strategies, management systems and company profiles.
Cost: $ 390.00
24 Pages
Frequency: Monthly
Circulation: 50000
ISSN: 1079-0837
Founded in 1994
Mailing list available for rent
Printed in 2 colors on matte stock

7981 International Journal of Phytoremediation
AEHS Foundation Inc.
150 Fearing Street
Amherst, MA 01002

413-549-5170
888-540-2347
Home Page: www.aehsfoundation.org

Paul T Kostecki, PhD, Executive Director

Devoted to the publication of current laboratory and field research describing the use of plant systems to remediate contaminated environments. Designed to link professionals in the many environmental disciplines involved in the

development, application, management, and regulation of emerging phytoremediation technologies.
600 Members
Frequency: Quarterly
Founded in 1989

7982 International Journal of Wildland Fire
International Association of Wildland Fire
4025 Fair Ridge Drive
Fairfax, VA 22033

785-423-1818
Fax: 785-542-3511
E-Mail: sandy@iawfonline.org
Home Page: www.iawfonline.org
Social Media: Facebook, Twitter

Sacha Dick, Programs Manager
Mikel Robinson, Executive Director

Online journal publishing new and significant papers that advance basic and applied research concerning wildland fire. Aims to publish quality papers on a broad range of wildland fire issues, and has an international perspective, since wildland fire plays a major social, economic, and ecological role around the globe.
Frequency: Quarterly

7983 Journal of Air & Waste Management Association
Air & Waste Management Association
1 Gateway Center
3rd Floor
Pittsburgh, PA 15222-1435

412-652-2458
800-270-3444
Fax: 412-232-3450
E-Mail: info@awma.org
Home Page: www.awma.org
Social Media: Facebook, Twitter, LinkedIn

Andy Knopes, Production Manager/Editor
Richard Sherr, Execetive Director

Intended to serve those occupationally involved in air pollution control and waste management through the publication of timely and reliable information. Descriptions of contemporary advances in air quality and waste management science and technology for use in improving environmental protection.
Cost: $330.00
Frequency: Monthly
Circulation: 3500
ISSN: 1047-3289
Founded in 1907

7984 Journal of Environmental Economics and Management
Association of Environmental and Resource
1616 P St Nw
Suite 400
Washington, DC 20036-1434

202-328-5125
Fax: 202-939-3460
E-Mail: info@aere.org
Home Page: www.aere.org

Devoted to the publication of theoretical and empirical papers concerned with the linkage between economic systems and environmental and natural resources systems. The top journal in natural resources and environmental economics, it concentrates on the management and/or social control of the economy in its relationship with the management and use of natural resources and the natural environment.
Frequency: Bi-Monthly

7985 Journal of Environmental Education
Heldref Publications
1319 18th St Nw
Washington, DC 20036-1802

202-296-6267
Fax: 202-296-5149
E-Mail: jee@heldref.org
Home Page: www.heldref.org

James Denton, Executive Director
J. Heldref, Editor

Details how best to present environmental issues and how to evaluate programs already in place for primary through university level and adult students. Publishes material that advances the instruction, theory, methods, and practice of environmental education and communication. Subject areas include the sciences, social sciences, and humanities.
Cost: $58.00
Frequency: Quarterly
Circulation: 1250
Founded in 1970

7986 Journal of Environmental Engineering
American Society of Civil Engineers
1801 Alexander Bell Dr
Reston, VA 20191-4382

703-295-6300
800-548-2723
703-295-6300
Fax: 703-295-6222
E-Mail: webmaster@asce.org
Home Page: www.asce.org

D Wayne Klotz, President
M. Kathy Banks, Editor

Emphasizes on the implementaion of effective and safe methods for handling, transporting, and treating waste materials.
Cost: $308.00
Frequency: Monthly
Circulation: 2,500
Founded in 1852

7987 Journal of Environmental Geochemistry and Health
Society for Environmental Geochemistry & Health
4698 S Forrest Avenue
Springfield, MO 65810

417-851-1166
Fax: 417-881-6920
E-Mail: DRBGWIXSON@aol.com
Home Page: www.segh.net

Prof. Xiangdong Li, President
Prof. Andrew Hursthouse, European Chair
Kyoung-Woong Kim, Asia/Pacific Chair
Anthea Brown, Membership Secretary/Treasurer
Malcolm Brown, Secretary

Publishes original research papers, research notes and reviews across the broad field of environmental geochemistry.
400 Members
Founded in 1971

7988 Journal of Environmental Health
National Environmental Health Association
720 S Colorado Blvd
Suite 970S
Denver, CO 80246-1926

303-756-9090
Fax: 303-691-9490
E-Mail: staff@neha.org
Home Page: www.neha.org
Social Media: Facebook, Twitter, LinkedIn

Nelson Fabian, Executive Director
Julie Collins, Research
Kim Brandow, Marketing/Sales Manager
Larry Marcum, Managing Director
Bob Custard, Manager

A practical journal containing information on a variety of environmental health issues.
Cost: $90.00
5000 Members
70 Pages
Frequency: 10 per year
Circulation: 20,000
ISSN: 0022-0892
Founded in 1937
Printed in 4 colors on glossy stock

7989 Journal of Environmental Quality
American Society of Agronomy
5585 Guilford Rd.
Madison, WI 53711-1086

608-273-8080
Fax: 608-273-2021
E-Mail: headquarters@sciencesocieties.org
Home Page: www.agronomy.org
Social Media: Facebook, Twitter, LinkedIn

Newell Kitchen, President
Kenneth Barbarick, President-Elect

Papers are grouped by subject matter and cover water, soil, and atmospheric research as it relates to agriculture and the environment.
10000 Members
Founded in 1907

7990 Journal of Food Protection
International Association for Food Protection
6200 Aurora Ave
Suite 200W
Des Moines, IA 50322-2864

515-276-3344
800-369-6337
Fax: 515-276-8655
E-Mail: info@foodprotection.org
Home Page: www.foodprotection.org
Social Media: Facebook, Twitter, LinkedIn

Isabel Walls, President
Katherine M.J. Swanson, President-Elect
Don Schaffner, Vice President
Don Zink, Secretary
David W. Tharp, Executive Director

Each issue contains scientific research and authoritative review articles reporting on a variety of topics in food science pertaining to food safety and quality.
3400 Members
Founded in 1911

7991 Journal of Intelligent Material Systems and Structures
Sage Journals Online
Home Page: www.jim.sagepub.com

Dan Inman, Editor-In-Chief

An international peer reviewed journal that publishes the highest quality original research. JIMSS reports on the results of experimental or theoretical work on any aspect of intelligent materials systems and/or structures research also called smart structure, smart materials, active materials, adaptive structures and adaptive materials.
Cost: $995.00
80 Pages
Frequency: Monthly
ISSN: 1045-389X
Printed in 2 colors on matte stock

7992 Journal of Natural Resources & Life Sciences Education
American Society of Agronomy
5585 Guilford Rd.
Madison, WI 53711-1086

608-273-8080
Fax: 608-273-2021
E-Mail: headquarters@sciencesocieties.org

Home Page: www.agronomy.org
Social Media: Facebook, Twitter, LinkedIn

Newell Kitchen, President
Kenneth Barbarick, President-Elect

Today's educators look here for the latest teaching ideas in the life sciences, natural resources, and agriculture.
10000 Members
Founded in 1907

7993 Journal of Plant Registrations
American Society of Agronomy
5585 Guilford Rd.
Madison, WI 53711-1086

608-273-8080
Fax: 608-273-2021
E-Mail: headquarters@sciencesocieties.org
Home Page: www.agronomy.org
Social Media: Facebook, Twitter, LinkedIn

Newell Kitchen, President
Kenneth Barbarick, President-Elect

Publishes cultivar, germplasm, parental line, genetic stock, and mapping population registration manuscripts.
10000 Members
Founded in 1907

7994 Journal of Soil and Water Conservation
Soil and Water Conservation Society
945 SW Ankeny Rd
Ankeny, IA 50023-9764

515-289-2331
800-843-7645
Fax: 515-289-1227
E-Mail: pubs@swcs.org
Home Page: www.swcs.org

Oksana Gieseman, Director of Publications

The JSWC is a multidisciplinary journal of natural resource conservation research, practice, policy, and perspectives. The journal has two sections: the A Section containing various departments and features and the Research Section containing peer-reviewed research papers.
Cost: $99.00
Frequency: Bimonthly
Circulation: 2000
ISSN: 0022-4561
Founded in 1945

7995 Journal of Wildlife Management
Wildlife Society
5410 Grosvenor Ln
Suite 200
Bethesda, MD 20814-2197

301-897-9770
Fax: 301-530-2471
E-Mail: tws@wildlife.org
Home Page: www.wildlife.org
Social Media: Facebook, Twitter, LinkedIn

Michael Hutchins, Executive Director

One of the world's leading scientific journals covering wildlife science, management and conservation.
Founded in 1937

7996 Journal of the Air Pollution Control Association
Air Pollution Control Association
1 Gateway Center 3rd Floor
420 Fort Duquesne Blvd.
Pittsburgh, PA 15222-1435

412-232-3444
800-270-3444
Fax: 412-232-3450
E-Mail: info@awma.org
Home Page: www.awma.org/
Social Media: Facebook, Twitter, LinkedIn

Tim Keener, Technical Editor-in-Chief
George Hidy, Co-Editor
Jeffrey Brook, Associate Editor

A comprehensive journal offering information to the environment and conservation industry.
Cost: $95.00
Frequency: Monthly
Circulation: 700
Founded in 1907

7997 Journal of the IEST
Institute of Environmental Sciences and Technology
5005 Newport Drive
Suite 506
Rolling Meadows, IL 60008-3841

847-255-1561
Fax: 847-255-1699
Home Page: www.iest.org
Social Media: Facebook, Twitter, LinkedIn

Julie Kendrick, Executive Director
Robert Burrows, Director Communications Services
Corrie Roesslein, Director Programs/Administration

The official publication of the IEST. Contains technical articles and reports on simulation, testing, modeling, control, current research, covering contamination control, environmental laboratory and field-testing and evaluation, reliability assessment and evaluation methods, and others. To support the pursuit of knowledge, the advancement of technology, and the creation of pathways of communication in the environmental sciences.
1600 Members
Founded in 1953

7998 Journal of the Institute of Environmental Sciences and Technology
Institute of Environmental Sciences and Technology
5005 Newport Drive
Suite 506
Rolling Meadows, IL 60008-3841

847-255-1561
Fax: 847-255-1699
E-Mail: information@iest.org
Home Page: www.iest.org

Julie Kendrick, Executive Director
Robert Burrows, Director Communications Services
Corrie Roesslein, Director Programs/Administration

Contains technical articles and reports on simulation, testing, modeling, control, current research, and the teaching of the enrionmental sciences and technologies. The content covers contamination control, environmental laboratory and field-testing and evaluation, reliability assessment and evaluation methods, environmental instrumentation and measurements, envrionmental effects, environmental and safety standards, computer applications, and many other topics.
Frequency: Annual

7999 Journal of the U.S. SJWP
Water Environment Federation
601 Wythe St
Alexandria, VA 22314-1994

800-666-0206
Fax: 703-684-2492
Home Page: www.wef.org
Social Media: Facebook, Twitter

Matt Bond, President
Cordell Samuels, President-Elect
Sandra Ralston, Vice President
Chris Browning, Treasurer
Jeff Eger, Secretary and Executive Director

Electronic publication. Purpose is to share the fresh thinking of today's young scientists with the entire water quality community. In addition to the benefit of research exchange, students are mentored in scientific writing and publication.
79 Members
ISSN: 1044-9943
Founded in 1928

8000 Lake & Reservoir Management
North American Lake Management Society
PO Box 5443
Madison, WI 53705

608-233-2836
Fax: 608-233-3186
E-Mail: info@nalms.org
Home Page: www.nalms.org
Social Media: Facebook, LinkedIn, Flickr

Bev Clark, President
Reesa Evans, Secretary

Publishes original studies relevant to lake and reservoir management. Papers address the management of lakes and reservoirs, their watersheds and tributaries, along with limnology and ecology needed for sound supervision of these systems.
Frequency: Quarterly

8001 LakeLine Magazine
North American Lake Management Society
PO Box 5443
Madison, WI 53705-443

608-233-2836
Fax: 608-233-3186
E-Mail: info@nalms.org
Home Page: www.nalms.org

Bev Clark, President
Reesa Evans, Secretary
Linda Green, Treasurer

Contains news, commentary and articles on topics affecting lakes, reservoirs and watersheds. Organized around a theme, like control of invasive species or resolving recreational conflicts, each issue becomes a valued resource for lake users and advocates.
Frequency: Quarterly

8002 Land and Water Magazine
Land and Water
Po Box 1197
Fort Dodge, IA 50501-1197

515-576-3191
Fax: 515-576-2606
Home Page: www.landandwater.com
Social Media: Facebook

Amy Dencklau, Publisher
Shanza Dencklau, Assistant Editor
Rasch M. Kenneth, President

Edited for contractors, engineers, architects, government officials and those working in the field of natural resource management and restoration from idea stage through project completion and maintenance.
Cost: $20.00
72 Pages
Circulation: 20000
Founded in 1959
Mailing list available for rent: 20M names
Printed in 4 colors on glossy stock

8003 MSW Management
Forester Communications
2946 De La Vina street
Santa Barbara, CA 93105

805-682-1300
Fax: 805-682-0200

E-Mail: customerservice@forester.net
Home Page: www.foresterpress.com

Daniel Waldman, Publisher/President
John Trotti, Group Editor

Provides municipal solid waste professionals with general news on facility construction, financing, new equipment and revenue issues.
Cost: $94.95
Circulation: 25000
Founded in 1990

8004 Marine Technology Society Journal
Marine Technology Society
1100 H St., Nw
Suite LL-100
Washington, DC 20005

202-717-8705
Fax: 202-347-4302
E-Mail: membership@mtsociety.org
Home Page: www.mtsociety.org
Social Media: Facebook, Twitter, LinkedIn

Jerry Boatman, President
Drew Michel, President-Elect
Jerry Wilson, VP of Industry and Technology
Jill Zande, VP of Education and Research
Justin Manley, VP of Gov. & Public Affairs

Publishes the highest caliber, peer-reviewed papers on subjects of interest to the society; marine technology, ocean science, marine policy and education. Dedicated to publishing timely special issues on emerging ocean community concers while also showcasing general interest and student-authored works.
2M Members
Founded in 1963

8005 Natural History Magazine
American Museum of Natural History
79th St & Central Park W
New York, NY 10024

212-769-5400
Fax: 212-769-5009
E-Mail: communications@amnh.org
Home Page: www.library.amnh.org

Michael J Novacek, CEO
Victor W Fazio, Editor

Chronicled the major expeditions and research findings by curators at the American Museum of Natural History and at other natural history museums and science centers. Mission of this magazine is to promote public understanding and appreciation of nature and science.
Cost: $55.00

8006 Natural Resources & Environment
American Bar Association
321 N Clark St
Chicago, IL 60654-7598

312-988-5000
800-285-2221
Fax: 312-988-5280
E-Mail: askaba@abanet.org
Home Page: www.abanet.org
Social Media: Facebook, Twitter

Lori Lyons, Staff Editor
Christine LeBel, Executive Editor

Practical magazine on the latest developments in the field of natural resources law for the ABA Section of Environment, Energy, and Resources.
Cost: $80.00
64 Pages
Frequency: Quarterly
ISSN: 0822-3812
Printed in 4 colors

8007 North American Elk: Ecology & Management
Wildlife Management Institute
1146 19th St NW
Suite 700
Washington, DC 20036-3727

202-973-7710
Fax: 202-785-1348
Home Page:
www.wildlifemanagementinstitute.org

Dale E Toweill, Editor

8008 Northeast Sun
NE Sustainable Energy Association
50 Miles St
Greenfield, MA 01301-3255

413-774-6051
Fax: 413-774-6053
E-Mail: nesea@nesea.org
Home Page: www.nesea.org

David Barclay, Executive Director
Paul Horowitz, Chairman

Includes articles by leading authorities on sustainable energy practices, energy efficiency and renewable energy.
Frequency: Quarterly
Circulation: 5000
Founded in 1974

8009 Nuclear News
American Nuclear Society
555 N Kensington Ave
La Grange Park, IL 60526-5592

708-352-6611
800-323-3044
Fax: 708-352-0499
E-Mail: advertising@ans.org
Home Page: www.ans.org
Social Media: Facebook, Twitter, LinkedIn

Jack Tuohy, Executive Director
James S Tulenko, VP
William F Naughton, Treasurer

The flagship membership publication of the American Nuclear Society, the recognized credible advocate for advancing and promoting nuclear science and technology.
10500 Members
Founded in 1954

8010 Nuclear Science and Engineering
American Nuclear Society
555 N Kensington Ave
La Grange Park, IL 60526-5592

708-352-6611
800-323-3044
Fax: 708-352-0499
E-Mail: advertising@ans.org
Home Page: www.ans.org
Social Media: Facebook, Twitter, LinkedIn

Jack Tuohy, Executive Director
James S Tulenko, VP
William F Naughton, Treasurer

The research journal of the American Nuclear Society, widel recognized as an outstanding source of information on research in all scientific areas related to the peaceful use of nuclear energy and radiation. Technical papers, notes, critical reviews, and computer code abstracts are presented.
10500 Members
Founded in 1954

8011 Nuclear Technology
American Nuclear Society
555 N Kensington Ave
La Grange Park, IL 60526-5592

708-352-6611
800-323-3044
Fax: 708-352-0499
E-Mail: advertising@ans.org
Home Page: www.ans.org
Social Media: Facebook, Twitter, LinkedIn

Jack Tuohy, Executive Director
James S Tulenko, VP
William F Naughton, Treasurer

The leading international publication reporting on new information in all areas of the practical application of nuclear science. Topics include all aspects of reactor technology; operations, safety materials, instrumentation, fuel, and waste management. Also covered are medical uses, radiation detection, production of radiation, health physics, and computer applications.
10500 Members
Founded in 1954

8012 Occupational Health and Safety
Stevens Publishing Corporation
5151 Belt Line Rd
10th Floor
Dallas, TX 75254-7507

972-687-6700
Fax: 972-687-6767
Home Page: www.ohsonline.com

Craig S Stevens, President
Dana Cornett, President/COO
Randy Dye, Publisher
Jerry Laws, Editor
Margaret Perry, Circulation Director

Practical advice on how to keep the workplace safe from hazards and in full compliance with ever-changing laws and regulations. Delivering the most up-to-date info for professionals in the health, safety, industrial hygiene, environmental, security and fire protection fields with in-depth features, new product releases and more!
Circulation: 63000
Founded in 1925

8013 OnEarth
National Resources Defense Council
40 W 20th St
New York, NY 10011-4231

212-727-2700
Fax: 212-727-1773
E-Mail: nrdcinfo@nrdc.org
Home Page: www.nrdc.org
Social Media: Facebook, Twitter, YouTube

Frances Beinecke, President
Daniel R. Tishman, Chair
Frederick A.O. Schwarz Jr., Chair Emeritus
Adam Albright, Vice Chair
Patricia Bauman, Vice Chair

Publication exploring the challenges that confront our world, the solutions that promise to heal it, and the way we can use those solutions to improve our homes, our health, our communities, and our future.
50000 Members
Founded in 1970

8014 Outdoor America
Isaak Walton League
707 Conservation Lane
Gaithersburg, MD 20878

301-548-0150
Fax: 301-548-0146
E-Mail: general@iwla.org
Home Page: www.iwla.org

David Hoskins, Executive Director

Entertaining and educational articles about the conservation work of IWLA members. Also provides in-depth coverage of broader conservation issues such as national energy policy, urban sprawl, and wetland loss.
Cost: $36.00
Frequency: Quarterly
Circulation: 37000
ISSN: 0021-3314

8015 **Photogrammetric Engineering & Remote Sensing (PE&RS)**
ASPRS
5410 Grosvenor Lane
Suite 210
Bethesda, MD 20814-2160
301-493-0290
Fax: 301-493-0208
E-Mail: asprs@asprs.org
Home Page: www.asprs.org
Social Media: Facebook, Twitter
Jaws Plasker, Exec. Director
The official journal for imaging and geospation information science and technology.
6000 Members
Founded in 1934

8016 **Phytopathology**
American Phytopatholgical Society
3340 Pilot Knob Road
Saint Paul, MN 55121-2097
651-454-7250
800-328-7560
Fax: 651-454-0766
E-Mail: aps@scisoc.org
Home Page: www.apsnet.org
Greg Grahek, Director of Marketing
The premier international journal for publication of articles on fundamental research that advances understanding of the nature of plant diseases, the agents that cause them, their spread, the losses they cause, and measures that can be used to control them.
Frequency: Monthly
Circulation: 1200
ISSN: 0031-949X
Printed in 4 colors

8017 **Plant Disease**
American Phytopatholgical Society
3340 Pilot Knob Road
Saint Paul, MN 55121-2097
651-454-7250
800-328-7560
Fax: 651-454-0766
E-Mail: aps@scisoc.org
Home Page: www.apsnet.org
Greg Grahek, Director of Marketing
Leading international journal for rapid reporting of research on new diseases, epidemics, and methods of disease control. Covers basic and applied research, which focuses on practical aspects of disease diagnosis and treatment.The popular Disease Notes section contains brief and timely reports of new diseases, new disease outbreaks, new hosts, and pertinent new observations of plant diseases and pathogens worldwide.
Frequency: Monthly
Circulation: 1200
ISSN: 0191-2917

8018 **Plastics Recycling Update**
Resource Recycling
PO Box 42270
Portland, OR 97242-270
503-233-1305
Fax: 503-233-1356
E Mail: pru@resource-recycling.com
Home Page: www.resource-recycling.com
Jerry Powell, Publisher
The only magazine in North America focusing exclusively on polymer recovery efforts. A superb source for marketing recycling equipment and services and offers an excellent means of sourcing new suppliers of recovered plastics. The authority in plastic recycling market analysis, coverage of the latest legislation, industry news and views, and technical specs on the latest equipment.
Cost: $59.00
6 Pages
Frequency: Monthly
Circulation: 1000
ISSN: 1052-4908
Founded in 1981
Mailing list available for rent: 40,000 names at $100 per M
Printed in one color on matte stock

8019 **Pollution Engineering**
Business News Publishing Company
2401 W Big Beaver Rd
Suite 700
Troy, MI 48084-3333
248-362-3700
Fax: 248-362-0317
E-Mail: Roy@PollutionEngineering.com
Home Page: www.bnpmedia.com
Social Media: Facebook, Twitter
Mitchell Henderson, CEO
Roy Bigham, Managing Editor
Seth Fisher, Products Editor
Providing must read information for today's Engineers and Consulting Engineers in Pollution Control for; Air, Wastewater, and Remediation Hazardous Solid Waste. Up-to-date information on regulatory requirements, coverage of economic benefits of environmental control techniques, and up-to-date information on innovative and cost effective environmental equipment, products, technology and services.
Frequency: Monthly
ISSN: 0032-3640
Founded in 1969

8020 **Pollution Equipment News**
Rimbach Publishing
8650 Babcock Blvd
Suite 1
Pittsburgh, PA 15237-5010
412-364-5366
800-245-3182
Fax: 412-369-9720
E-Mail: info@rimbach.com
Home Page: www.rimbach.com
Social Media: Facebook, Twitter
Norberta Rimbach, President
Karen Galante, Circulation Manager
Paul Henderson, VP of Sales and Marketing
Provides information to those responsible for selecting products and services for air, water, wastewater and hazardous waste pollution abatement.
Frequency: Bi-Annually
Circulation: 91000
Founded in 1968

8021 **Pollution Prevention Northwest**
US EPA
Ariel Rios Building
1200 Pennsylvania Avenue NW
Washington, DC 20460
202-272-0167
Home Page: www.epa.gov
Bob Zachariasiewicz, Acting Director
Articles include recent information on source reduction and sustainable technologies in industry, transportation, consumer, agriculture, energy, and the international sector.
Frequency: Monthly
Circulation: 12000
Founded in 1970

8022 **Popular Science**
2 Park Ave
9th Floor
New York, NY 10016-5614
212-779-5000
Fax: 212-986-2656
E-Mail: letters@popsci.com
Home Page: www.popsci.com
Greg Hano, Publisher
Robert Novick, General Manager
A leading source of science and technology news, with insightful commentary on the new innovations, and even scientific takes on the hottest Hollywood stories.
Cost: $48.00
Frequency: Monthly
Founded in 1964

8023 **Pumper**
COLE Publishing
PO Box 220
Three Lakes, WI 54562-220
715-546-3346
Fax: 715-546-3786
E-Mail: info@pumper.com
Home Page: www.pumper.com
Social Media: Facebook, Twitter, YouTube
Ted Rulseh, Editor
Jeff Bruss, President
Emphasis on companies, individuals and industry events while focusing on customer service, environmental issues and employment trends.
Cost: $16.00
Frequency: Monthly
Circulation: 20,740
Founded in 1978

8024 **Radwaste Solutions**
American Nuclear Society
555 N Kensington Ave
La Grange Park, IL 60526-5592
708-352-6611
800-323-044
Fax: 708-352-0499
E-Mail: advertising@ans.org
Home Page: www.ans.org/advertising
Jack Tuohy, Executive Director
Sarah Wells, Editor
Harry Bradley, Executive Director
Gloria Naurocki, Membership & Marketing
Mary Beth Gardner, Scientific Publications
The magazine of radioactive waste management and facility remediation. Serving the nuclear waste management and cleanup business segments of the industry. Also included are articles on radwaste management programs and practices outside the US, as well as guest editorials and letters to the editor, shorter thought-pieces, and articles on recent academic/technical advances detailing their immediate or planned practical applications.
Cost: $455.00
Frequency: Fortnightly
Circulation: 2000
Founded in 1954
Printed in on matte stock

8025 **Recharger Magazine**
1050 E Flamingo Rd
Suite 237
Las Vegas, NV 89119-7427
702-438-5557
Fax: 702-873-9671
E-Mail: info@rechargermag.com
Home Page: www.rechargermag.com
Social Media: Facebook, Twitter
Phyllis Gurgeview, Publisher
Amy Turner, Managing Editor
Brenda Potts, Circulation Manager
Becky Fenton, Manager
Amy Weiss, Director

Information on remanufacturing imaging supplies including articles that cover business and marketing, technical updates, association and industry news, and company profiles. Related features focus on supply sales and equipment service.
Cost: $45.00
250 Pages
Frequency: Monthly
Circulation: 8000
ISSN: 1053-7503
Printed in 4 colors

8026 Reclamation Matters
American Society of Mining and Reclamation
3134 Montevesta Road
Lexington, KY 40502-3548

859-351-9032
Fax: 859-335-6529
E-Mail: asmr@insightbb.com
Home Page: www.asmr.us
Social Media: Facebook

Eddie Bearden, President
Bruce Buchanan, President Elect
Richard Barnhisel, Executive Secretary

The official magazine of ASMR.
500 Members
Founded in 1983

8027 Recycling Laws International
Raymond Communications
P.O.Box 4311
Silver Spring, MD 20914-4311

301-345-4237
Fax: 301-345-4768
E-Mail: circulation@raymond.com
Home Page: www.raymond.com

Lorah Utter, Editor
Allyn Sweet, Circulation Manager
Michele Raymond, President

Covers recycling, takeback, green labeling policy for business in 35 countries. Also contains a country page document that is updated annually.
Cost: $485.00
200 Pages
Circulation: 150
Founded in 1991

8028 Recycling Product News
Baum Publications
2323 Boundary Road
#201
Vancouver, BC 0

604-291-9900
Fax: 604-291-1906
E-Mail: webadmin@baumpub.com
Home Page: www.baumpub.com

Engelbert J Baum, Publisher
Keith Barker, Editor

Published for the recycling center operators and other waste mangers, articles discuss technology and new products.
Circulation: 14000

8029 Recycling Today
GIE Media
4012 Bridge Avenue
Cleveland, OH 44113-3320

216-961-4130
800-456-0707
Fax: 216-961-0364
E-Mail: info@recyclingtoday.com
Home Page: www.recyclingtoday.com/
Social Media: Facebook, Twitter

James R Keefe, Group Publisher
Brian Taylor, Editor
Richard Foster, CEO
Debbie Kean, Manager

Published for the secondary commodity processing/recycling market.
Cost: $30.00
Frequency: Monthly
Circulation: 15000

8030 Renewable Resources Journal
Renewable Natural Resources Foundation
5430 Grosvenor Ln
Suite 220
Bethesda, MD 20814-2193

301-493-9101
Fax: 301-493-6148
E-Mail: info@rnrf.org
Home Page: www.rnrf.org

Robert D Day, Executive Director
Ryan M Colker, Programs Director
Chandru Krishna, Circulation

Provides information of general interest concerning public policy issues related to natural resources management. Comprised of contributed and solicited articles on a wide range of natural resource issues, news items about RNRF's members, notices of significant meetings, editorials, and commentaries.
Cost: $25.00
32 Pages
Frequency: Quarterly
Circulation: 1800
ISSN: 0738-6532
Founded in 1975
Printed in 2 colors on matte stock

8031 Resource Recycling
Resource Recycling
PO Box 42270
Portland, OR 97242-270

503-233-1305
Fax: 503-233-1356
E-Mail: info@resource-recycling.com
Home Page: www.resource-recycling.com

Jerry Powell, Editor/Publisher
Rick Downing, Graphic Designer
Suzette Ducharme, Graphic Designer
Mary Lynch, Executive Editor

The nation's leading recycling and composting magazine. This monthly journal focuses on efforts in the US and Canada to recover materials from homes and businesses for recycling. Accepts advertising.
Cost: $52.00
64 Pages
Frequency: Monthly
Circulation: 14000+
ISSN: 0744-4710
Founded in 1982
Printed in 4 colors on glossy stock

8032 Restoration Ecology
Blackwell Science
350 Main St
Malden, MA 02148-5089

781-388-8250
Fax: 781-388-8210
E-Mail:
subscrip@bos.blackwellpublishing.com
Home Page: www.blackwellpublishing.com

Amy Yodaniss, VP
Richard Hobbs, Editor

Provides the most recent developments in the ecological and biological restoration field for both the fundamental and practical implications of restorations.
Cost: $200.00
Frequency: Quarterly
Circulation: 2000
Founded in 1897

8033 Restoration Ecology Journal
Society for Ecological Restoration International
1017 O Street NW
Washington, DC 20001

202-299-9518
Fax: 270-626-5485
E-Mail: info@ser.org
Home Page: www.ser.org
Social Media: Facebook

Steve Whisenant, Chair
Cara R. Nelson, Vice Chair
Mary Travaglini, Treasurer
Alan Unwin, Secretary

Primary emphases are: research on restoration and ecological principles that help explain restoration processes, descriptions of techniques that the authors have pioneered and that are likely to be of use to other practicing restorationists, desriptions of setbacks and surprises encountered during restoration and the lessons learnt, analytical opinions, and reviews of articles that summarize literature on specialized aspects of restoration.
2300 Members
Frequency: Bi-Monthly
Founded in 1988

8034 Review of Environmental Economics and Policy (REEP)
Association of Environmental and Resource Economis
13006 Peaceful Terrace
Silver Spring, MD 20904

202-559-8998
Fax: 202-559-8998
E-Mail: info@aere.org
Home Page: www.aere.org

Catherine L. Kling, President
Sarah L. Stafford, Secretary
Juha Siikamaki, Treasurer
Wiktor L. Adamowicz, Vice President

Designed for broad appeal to economists and others in academia, government, the private sector, and the advocacy world who share a common interest in environmental and natural resource policy. Rather than focusing on technical and methodological aspects of research, articles will focus on the broad lessons that can be learned, for environmental and resource economics or for public policy, from broader lines of research.
900 Members
Founded in 1979

8035 Risk Policy Report
Inside Washington Publishers
1919 S Eads St
Suite 1400
Arlington, VA 22202-3028

703-418-3981
Fax: 703-415-8543
E-Mail: support@iwpnews.com
Home Page: www.iwpnews.com

Alan Sosenko, Owner
David Clarke, Editor

Contains analysis, great perspectives, industry news, policymaking profiles and a calendar of events.
Cost: $295.00
Frequency: Monthly
Founded in 1980

8036 SETAC Globe
Society of Environmental Toxicology and Chemistry
1013 N 12th Ave
Pensacola, FL 32501-3306

850-437-1901
Fax: 850-469-9778
E-Mail: rparrish@setac.org
Home Page: www.edwardjones.com

Chad Stacy, Manager
Greg Schifer, Manager

Stay up to date on the latest firm news, and learn about the companies followed with Edward Jones.
Frequency: Bi-Monthly

8037 SOLAR TODAY
American Solar Energy Society
4760 Walnut Street
Suite 106
Boulder, CO 80301-2843

303-443-3130
Fax: 303-443-3212
E-Mail: ases@ases.org
Home Page: www.ases.org
Social Media: Facebook, Twitter, LinkedIn

David G. Hill, Chair
Bill Poulin, Treasurer
Jason Keyes, Secretary
Jeff Lyng, Immediate Past Chair

Trusted source for the latest technology, policy advances and analysis. Brings together ASES' professional members as contributors and readers, amid the community of ASES chapters nationwide, to publish industry-leading editorial.
ISSN: 1042-0630

8038 Science Magazine
American Assn for the Advancement of Science
1200 New York Avenue NW
Washington, DC 20005-3941

202-266-6721
Fax: 202-371-9227
E-Mail: membership@aaas.org
Home Page: www.aaas.org
Social Media: Facebook, Twitter

Kathy Fishback, Publication Services Director

The world's leading outlet for scientific news, commentary, and cutting-edge research. Available online and in print, Science Magazine continues to publish the very best in scientific research, news, and opinion.

8039 Scrap Magazine
Institute of Scrap Recycling Industries
1615 L St NW
Suite 600
Washington, DC 20036-5664

202-662-8500
Fax: 202-626-0900
E-Mail: isri@isri.org
Home Page: www.isri.org

John Sacco, Chairman
Jerry I. Simms, Chair Elect
Douglas Kramer, Vice Chair
Mark R. Lewon, Secretary Treasurer

Providing practical and useful information to scrap professionals through articles and columns that will increase the profitability of their businesses. The editorial content is designed to stimulate- to help scrap professionals manage all aspects of their businesses more successfully.
165 Members
1987 Attendees

8040 Security Products
Stevens Publishing Corporation
5151 Belt Line Rd
10th Floor
Dallas, TX 75254-7507

972-687-6700
Fax: 972-687-6767
Home Page: www.secprodonline.com

Craig S Stevens, President
Dana Cornett, President/COO
Randy Dye, Publisher
Ralph Jensen, Editor-In-Chief
Margaret Perry, Circulation Director

Leading new product and technology resource for security dealers, integrators and end users seeking comprehensive product-related information.
Circulation: 63000
Founded in 1925

8041 Shore & Beach
American Shore and Beach Preservation Association
5460 Beaujolais Lane
Fort Myers, FL 33919

239-489-2616
Fax: 239-362-9771
E-Mail: exdir@asbpa.org
Home Page: www.asbpa.org
Social Media: Facebook, Twitter

Harry Simmons, President
Kate Gooderham, Executive Director
Lesley Ewing, Editor
Beth Sciaudone, Managing Editor
Ken Gooderham, Production

Information and articles regarding management of shores and beaches.
1M Members
Founded in 1926

8042 Soil Science Society of America Journal
American Society of Agronomy
5585 Guilford Rd.
Madison, WI 53711-1086

608-273-8080
Fax: 608-273-2021
E-Mail: headquarters@sciencesocieties.org
Home Page: www.agronomy.org
Social Media: Facebook, Twitter, LinkedIn

Newell Kitchen, President
Kenneth Barbarick, President-Elect

Publishes basic and applied soil research in agricultural, forest, wetlands, urban settings and more.
10000 Members
Founded in 1907

8043 Soil Survey Horizons
American Society of Agronomy
5585 Guilford Rd.
Madison, WI 53711-1086

608-273-8080
Fax: 608-273-2021
E-Mail: headquarters@sciencesocieties.org
Home Page: www.agronomy.org
Social Media: Facebook, Twitter, LinkedIn

Newell Kitchen, President
Kenneth Barbarick, President-Elect

Informs and entertains with research updates, soil problems and solutions, history of soil survey, and personal essays from the lives of soil scientists in the field.
10000 Members
Founded in 1907

8044 Soil and Sediment Contamination
AEHS Foundation Inc.
150 Fearing Street
Suite 21
Amherst, MA 01002

413-549-5170
888-540-2347
Home Page: www.aehs.com

Paul T Kostecki, PhD, Executive Director

Focuses on soil and sediment contamination from; sludges, petroleum, petrochemicals, chlorinated hydrocarbons, pesticides, and lead and other heavy metals. Offers detailed descriptions of all the latest and most efficient offsite and in situ remediation techniques, strategies for assessing health effects and hazards, and tips for dealing with everyday regulatory and legal issues. Assess, mitigate, and solve rural and urban soil contamination problems.
Frequency: Bi-Monthly

8045 Solid Waste & Recycling
Southam Environment Group
1450 Don Mills Road
Don Mills, ON 0

905-305-6155
888-702-1111
Fax: 416-442-2026
E-Mail: bobrien@solidwastemag.com
Home Page: www.solidwastemag.com

Brad O'Brien, Publisher
Bibi Khan, Circualtion Manager
Guy Crittenden, Editor-in-Chief

Emphasizes municipal and commercial aspects of collection, handling, transportation, hauling, disposal and treatment of solid waste , including incineration, recycling and landfill technology.
Cost: $29.95
Frequency: Weekly
Circulation: 10000

8046 Solid Waste Report
Business Publishers
2222 Sedwick Dr
Suite 101
Durham, NC 27713

800-223-8720
Fax: 800-508-2592
E-Mail: custserv@bpinews.com
Home Page: www.bpinews.com

Comprehensive news and analysis of legislation, regulation and litigation in solid waste management including resource recovery, recycling, collection and disposal. Regularly features international news, state updates and business trends.
Cost: $567.00
Founded in 1963

8047 TIDE
Coastal Conservation Association
6919 Portwest Dr
Suite 100
Houston, TX 77024-8049

713-626-4234
800-201-FISH
Fax: 713-626-5852
E-Mail: ccantl@joincca.org
Home Page: www.joincca.org
Social Media: Twitter

David Cummins, President

The official magazine of the CCA.
85000 Members
Founded in 1977

8048 The Leading Edge
Society of Exploration Geophysicists
8801 South Yale
Suite 500
Tulsa, OK 74137-3575

918-497-5500
Fax: 918-497-5557
E-Mail: web@seg.org
Home Page: www.seg.org
Social Media: Facebook, Twitter, LinkedIn

Mary Fleming, Executive Director
Vladimir Grechka, Editor

A gateway publication, introducing new geophysical theory, instrumentation, and established practices to scientists in a wide range of geoscience disciplines. Most material is presented in a semitechnical manner that minimizes mathematical theory and emphasizes practical application. Also serves as SEG's publication venue for official society business.

8049 The Plant Genome
American Society of Agronomy

5585 Guilford Rd.
Madison, WI 53711-1086

608-273-8080
Fax: 608-273-2021
E-Mail: headquarters@sciencesocieties.org
Home Page: www.agronomy.org
Social Media: Facebook, Twitter, LinkedIn

Newell Kitchen, President
Kenneth Barbarick, President-Elect

Electronic journal providing leadership of the latest advances and breakthroughs in plant genomics research.
10000 Members
Founded in 1907

8050 Tree Farmer Magazine, the Guide to Sustaining America's Family Forests
American Forest Foundation
1111 19th St NW
Suite 780
Washington, DC 20036

202-463-2700
Fax: 202-463-2785
E-Mail: info@forestfoundation.org
Home Page: www.forestfoundation.org

Tom Martin, President & CEO
Brigitte Johnson APR, Director Communications, Editor

The official magazine of ATFS, this periodical provides practical, how-to and hands-on information and techniques, and services to help private fore landowners to become better stewards, save money and time, and add to the enjoyment of their land.

8051 Vadose Zone Journal
American Society of Agronomy
5585 Guilford Rd.
Madison, WI 53711-1086

608-273-8080
Fax: 608-273-2021
E-Mail: headquarters@sciencesocieties.org
Home Page: www.agronomy.org
Social Media: Facebook, Twitter, LinkedIn

Newell Kitchen, President
Kenneth Barbarick, President-Elect

Focuses on multidisciplinary research in the unsaturated zone appealing to a diverse group of scientists and engineers.
10000 Members
Founded in 1907

8052 Washington Environmental Compliance Update
M Lee Smith Publishers
PO Box 5094
Bentwood, TN 37024-5094

615-737-7517
800-274-6774

F Lee Smith, Publisher
Douglas S Little, Editor

Review of environmental laws.
Cost: $225.00
8 Pages
Frequency: Daily
Mailing list available for rent
Printed in 2 colors on matte stock

8053 Waste Age
Environmental Industry Association
4301 Connecticut Ave NW
#300
Washington, DC 20008-2304

202-966-4701
Fax: 202-966-4818
E-Mail: contact@envasns.org
Home Page: www.envasns.org
Social Media: Facebook, Twitter, YouTube

Bruce Parker, President
Patricia-Ann Tom, Editor
Laura Magliola, Marketing Manager
Christine Hutcherson, Director Member Services
Alice Jacobsohn, Director Education

Contents focus on new system technologies, recycling, resource recovery and sanitary landfills with regular features on updates in the status of government regulations, new products, guides, company profiles, exclusive survey information, legislative implications and news.
Frequency: Monthly
Circulation: 38000

8054 Waste Age's Recycling Times
Environmental Industry Association
4301 Connecticut Ave NW
#300
Washington, DC 20008-2304

202-966-4701
Fax: 202-966-4818
E-Mail: rct@envasns.org
Home Page: www.wasteage.com

Bruce Parker, President
Wendy Angel, Assistant Editor
Gregg Herring, Group Publisher

Features municipalities, recycling goals and rates, program innovations, waste habits, and new materials being recycled.
Cost: $99.00
Frequency: Monthly
Circulation: 5000

8055 Water & Wastes Digest
Scranton Gillette Communications
3030 W Salt Creek Lane
Suite 201
Arlington Heights, IL 60005-5025

847-391-1000
Fax: 847-390-0408
E-Mail: nsimeonova@sgcmail.com
Home Page: www.scrantongillette.com
Social Media: Facebook, Twitter, LinkedIn

Neda Simeonova, Editorial Director
Caitlin Cunningham, Managing Editor

Serves readers in the water and/or wastewater industries. These people work for municipalities, in industry, or as engineers. They design, specify, buy, operate and maintain equipment, chemicals, software and wastewater treatment services.
Cost: $40.00
128 Pages
Frequency: Monthly
Circulation: 101000
ISSN: 0043-1181
Founded in 1961

8056 Water Environment & Technology (WE&T)
Water Environment Federation
601 Wythe St
Alexandria, VA 22314-1994

800-666-0206
Fax: 703-684-2492
Home Page: www.wef.org
Social Media: Facebook, Twitter

Matt Bond, President
Cordell Samuels, President-Elect
Sandra Ralston, Vice President
Chris Browning, Treasurer
Jeff Eger, Secretary and Executive Director

Premier magazine for the water quality field. Provides information on what professionals demand; cutting-edge technologies, innovative solutions, regulatory and legislative impacts, and professional development.
79 Members
ISSN: 1044-9943
Founded in 1928

8057 Water Environment Research (WER)
Water Environment Federation
601 Wythe St
Alexandria, VA 22314-1994

800-666-0206
Fax: 703-684-2492
Home Page: www.wef.org
Social Media: Facebook, Twitter

Matt Bond, President
Cordell Samuels, President-Elect
Sandra Ralston, Vice President
Chris Browning, Treasurer
Jeff Eger, Secretary and Executive Director

Original, fundamental and applied research in all scientific and technical areas related to water quality, pollution contro, and management.
79 Members
ISSN: 1044-9943
Founded in 1928

8058 Water Quality Products
Scranton Gillette Communications
3030 W Salt Creek Lane
Suite 201
Arlington Heights, IL 60005

847-391-1000
Fax: 847-390-0408
E-Mail: nsimeonova@sgcmail.com
Home Page: www.wqpmag.com
Social Media: Facebook, Twitter

Neda Simeonova, Editorial Director
Dennis Martyka, VP/Group Publisher
Kate Cline, Managing Editor

Provides balanced editorial content including developments in water conditioning, filtration and disinfection for residential, commercial and industrial systeme.
Cost: $40.00
68 Pages
Frequency: Monthly
Circulation: 19000
ISSN: 1092-0978
Founded in 1995

8059 Wildfire Magazine
International Association of Wildland Fire
4025 Fair Ridge Drive
Fairfax, VA 22033

785-423-1818
Fax: 785-542-3511
E-Mail: sandy@iawfonline.org
Home Page: www.iawfonline.org

Sacha Dick, Programs Manager
Mikel Robinson, Executive Director

Addresses the needs of chiefs and wildland forestry managers by providing a unique international prospective. Each issue focuses on the demand of leaders responsible for managing and controlling wildland fires. Readers are the top decision makers and leaders who have influence over purchasing equipment, supplies and contracted services. Readership includes fire chiefs, governmental agencies, private sector professionals, consultants and contractors.
Frequency: Monthly

8060 Wildlife Conservation Magazine
2300 S Boulevard
Bronx, NY 10460

718-220-5121
800-786-8226
Fax: 718-584-2625

E-Mail: magazine@wcs.org
Home Page: www.wildlifeconservation.org/

Debby Bahler, Editor
Diana Warren, Advertising Director
4teve Sanderson, President

A national nature and science magazine. Contains stunning photography, conservation news and special updates on endangered species. Learn how to help protect local wildlife, and the secrets of the world's rarest and most mysterious animals.
Cost: $19.95
96 Pages
Circulation: 150000
Founded in 1895

8061 **World Resource Review**
SUPCON International
International Headquarters 2W381
75th Street
Naperville, IL 60565-9245

630-910-1551
Fax: 630-910-1561
E-Mail: syshen@megsinet.net
Home Page: www.globalwarming.net

Dr. Sinyan Shen, Production Manager

For business and government readers, provides expert worldwide reviews of global warming and extreme events in relation to the management of natural, mineral and material resources. Subjects include global warming impacts on agriculture, energy, and infrastructure, monitoring of changes in resources using remote sensing, actions of national and international bodies, global carbon budget, greenhouse budget and more.
Cost: $72.00
Frequency: Quarterly
Circulation: 12000
ISSN: 1042-8011

8062 **World Wastes: The Independent Voice**
Communication Channels
6151 Powers Ferry Road NW
Atlanta, GA 30339-2959

770-953-4805
Fax: 770-618-0348

Bill Wolpin, Editor
Jerrold France, President Argus Business

Reaches individuals and firms engaged in the removal and disposal of solid wastes.
Cost: $48.00
Frequency: Monthly
Circulation: 36,000

8063 **World Water**
Water Environment Federation
601 Wythe St
Alexandria, VA 22314-1994

800-666-0206
Fax: 703-684-2492
Home Page: www.wef.org
Social Media: Facebook, Twitter

Matt Bond, President
Cordell Samuels, President-Elect
Sandra Ralston, Vice President
Chris Browning, Treasurer
Jeff Eger, Secretary and Executive Director

International magazine for the water quality industry. Provides the most cutting-edge and helpful information on global water issues.
79 Members
ISSN: 1044-9943
Founded in 1928

8064 **World Water Reuse & Desalination**
Water Environment Federation
601 Wythe St
Alexandria, VA 22314-1994

800-666-0206
Fax: 703-684-2492
Home Page: www.wef.org
Social Media: Facebook, Twitter

Matt Bond, President
Cordell Samuels, President-Elect
Sandra Ralston, Vice President
Chris Browning, Treasurer
Jeff Eger, Secretary and Executive Director

Becoming the global news and information resource for the water reuse and quality industries. Provides the most up-to-date and innovative information on all facets of global water reuse and desalination issues.
79 Members
ISSN: 1044-9943
Founded in 1928

Trade Shows

8065 **AAAR Annual Conference**
American Association for Aerosol Research
15000 Commerce Parkway
Suite C
Mount Laurel, NJ 08054

856-439-9080
877-777-6753
Fax: 856-439-0525
E-Mail: info@aaar.org
Home Page: www.aaar.org

William Nazaroff, President
Barbara Turpin, Vice President
Barbara Wyslouzil, Vice President Elect
Murray Johnston, Treasurer
CY Wu, Secretary

Benefit from learning about the latest advances across the full frontier of aerosol science and technology. An excellent opportunity to renew old acquaintances and to meet new colleagues.
1000 Members
Founded in 1982

8066 **AAAR Annual Meeting**
American Association for Aerosol Research
15000 Commerce Parkway
Suite C
Mount Laurel, NJ 08054

856-439-9080
Fax: 856-439-0525
E-Mail: dbright@ahint.com
Home Page: www.aaar.org

Lynn Russell, Program Chair
Melissa Baldwin, Executive Director

Exibits related to aerosol research in areas including industrial process, air pollution, and industrial hygiene. Over 600 professionals attend.
600 Attendees
Frequency: Annual, October

8067 **AAAS Annual Meeting**
Renewable Natural Resources Foundation
5430 Grosvenor Ln
Bethesda, MD 20814-2193

301-493-9101
Fax: 301-493-6148
E-Mail: info@rnrf.org
Home Page: www.rnrf.org

Howard N. Rosen, Chairman
Richard A. Engberg, Vice-Chairman
Robert D. Day, Executive Director

The most important general science venue for a growing segment of scientists and engineers.
14 Members
Founded in 1972

8068 **ACCA Annual Meetings**
Air Conditioning Contractors of America
2800 Shirlington Rd
Suite 300
Arlington, VA 22206

703-575-4477
E-Mail: info@acca.org
Home Page: www.acca.org
Social Media: Facebook, Twitter, LinkedIn, YouTube

Paul T Stalknecht, President & CEO

Where America's most successful HVACR, building services, and energy professionals come together to share, learn, and collaborate. Options for learning how to take your business to the next levels of profitability and success.
Frequency: February/March

8069 **ACE Annual Conference**
Air & Waste Management Association
420 Fort Duquesne Boulevard
One Gateway Center, 3rd Floor
Pittsburgh, PA 15222-1435

412-652-2458
Fax: 412-232-3450
E-Mail: info@awma.org
Home Page: www.awma.org
Social Media: Facebook, Twitter, LinkedIn

Jeffry Muffat, President
Merlyn L. Hough, President Elect
Mike Kelly, Secretary/ Executive Director
Amy Gilligan, Treasurer
Dallas Baker, Vice President

Environmental professionals from around the world to the outstanding technical program, exhibits of the latest products and services, and networking and professional development opportunities.
9000 Members
Founded in 1907

8070 **AEESP Annual Meeting**
Association of Environmental Engineering and
2303 Naples Court
Champaign, IL 61822

217-398-6969
Fax: 217-355-9232
E-Mail: joanne@aeesp.org
Home Page: www.aeesp.org

Joanne Fetzner, Business Secretary

With the Water Environment Federation
Frequency: Fall

8071 **AERE Summer Conference**
Association of Environmental and Resource
1616 P Street NW
Suite 600
Washington, DC 20036

202-328-5125
Fax: 202-939-3460
E-Mail: voigt@rff.org
Home Page: www.aere.org

Marilyn Voigt, Executive Director

nonprofit international professional association for economists working on the environment and natural resources.
850 Members
350 Attendees
Frequency: January
Founded in 1979

8072 **APLIC Annual Conference**
Family Health International Library

PO Box 13950
Research Triangle Park, NC 27709

919-447-7040
Home Page: www.aplici.org

Claire Twose, President
Lori Rosman, Vice-President
Joann Donatiello, Treasurer

Focuses on current issues in communication, information, and resource technology and management.
Frequency: Annual

8073 APWA International Public Works Congress & Expo
American Public Works Association
2345 Grand Boulevard
Suite 700
Kansas City, MO 64108-2625

816-472-6100
800-848-2792
Fax: 816-472-1610
E-Mail: ddancy@apwa.net
Home Page: www.apwa.net

Peter King, Executive Director
David Dancy, Director Of Marketing

Offers the benefit of a variety of educational sessions, depth of the exhibit program and endless opportunities for networking. The latest cutting-edge technologies, managerial techniques and regulatory trends designed to keep you focused on the right solutions at the right time.
6500 Attendees
Frequency: Annual/September
ISSN: 0092-4873
Founded in 1894

8074 ASAS Annual Meeting
American Society of Animal Science
1111 N Dunlap Avenue
Savoy, IL 61874

217-356-9050
Fax: 217-398-4119
Home Page: www.asas.org

Paula Schultz, Meetings Coordinator
Lorena Nicholas, General Meeting Information
Kim Surles, Exhibits/Advertising
Jerry Baker, Executive Director

This meeting serves as an international forum to gather vital information for the future of the animal agriculture industry. A cutting-edge scientific program in food science, animal health, dairy production, beef nutrition, swine nutrition, reproduction, companion animals, and many other diverse interests.
3500 Attendees
Frequency: July/Non-Members Fee
Founded in 1908

8075 ASEH Annual Meeting
American Society for Environmental History
119 Pine Street
Suite 301
Seattle, WA 98101

206-343-0226
Fax: 206-343-0249
Home Page: www.aseh.net

Lisa Mighetto, Acting Executive Director

Individuals and groups all over the world will attend to collaborate on ways to live better with nature, and to make a better world for all outside of traditional political structures and older models of environmentalism.
Frequency: Spring, Texas

8076 ASES National Solar Conference
American Solar Energy Society
4760 Walnut Street
Suite 106
Boulder, CO 80301-2843

303-443-3130
Fax: 303-443-3212
E-Mail: ases@ases.org
Home Page: www.ases.org
Social Media: Facebook, Twitter, LinkedIn

David G. Hill, Chair
Bill Poulin, Treasurer
Jason Keyes, Secretary
Jeff Lyng, Immediate Past Chair

America's premier educational event for solar energy professionals. The conference introduces you to the leaders, innovators and technologies moving the industry forward.
ISSN: 1042-0630

8077 ASES National Solar Tour
American Solar Energy Society
4760 Walnut Street
Suite 106
Boulder, CO 80301-2843

303-443-3130
Fax: 303-443-3212
E-Mail: ases@ases.org
Home Page: www.ases.org
Social Media: Facebook, Twitter, LinkedIn

David G. Hill, Chair
Bill Poulin, Treasurer
Jason Keyes, Secretary
Jeff Lyng, Immediate Past Chair

The largest grassroots solar event in history. Offers participants the opportunity to tour homes and buildings to see how neighbors are using solar energy, energy efficiency and other sustainable technologies to reduce their monthly utility bills and help tackle climate change.
ISSN: 1042-0630

8078 ASFE Fall Meeting
ASFE/The Geoprofessional Business Association
8811 Colesville Road
Suite G106
Silver Springs, MD 20910

301-565-2733
Fax: 301-589-2017
E-Mail: info@asfe.org
Home Page: www.asfe.org

John P Bachner, Executive VP

Providing geotechnical, geologic, environmental, construction materials engineering and testing, and related professional services information and education.
Frequency: Annual/Fall

8079 ASFE Spring Meeting
ASFE
8811 Colesville Road
Suite G106
Silver Springs, MD 20910

301-565-2733
Fax: 301-589-2017
E-Mail: info@asfe.org
Home Page: www.asfe.org

John P Bachner, Executive VP

Provides geotechnical, geologic, environmental, construction materials engineering and testing, and related professional services information and education.
Frequency: Annual/Spring

8080 ASFE Winter Leadership Conference
ASFE/The Geoprofessional Business Association
8811 Colesville Road
Suite G106
Silver Springs, MD 20910

301-565-2733
Fax: 301-589-2014
E-Mail: info@asfe.org
Home Page: www.asfe.org

John Bachner, Executive VP

ASFE's leaders meet to finish priorities for the current year and determine the direction of ASFE for the coming year.
Frequency: Annual/January

8081 ASFPM Annual Conference
Association of State Floodplain Managers
2809 Fish Hatchery Road
Suite 204
Madison, WI 53713

608-274-0123
Fax: 608-274-0696
E-Mail: memberhelp@floods.org
Home Page: www.floods.org

Larry Larson, Executive Director
Alison Stierli, Manager
Diane Brown, Manager

Focus on floodproofing techniques, materials, floodproofing and elevation contractors, current issues and programs, new federal tax impications and the various means of funding floodproofing projects. implications.
Frequency: Annual

8082 ASFPM Annual National Conference
Association of State Floodplain Managers
2809 Fish Hatchery Rd
Suite 204
Madison, WI 53713-5020

608-274-0123
Fax: 608-274-0696
E-Mail: Larry@floods.org
Home Page: www.floods.org
Social Media: Facebook

Sally McConkey, Chair
William Nechamen, Vice Chair
Alan J. Giles, Secretary
John V. Crofts, Treasurer

The national conferences all community, state and federal floodplain managers plan to attend. Many of the most important consulting firms and product vendors associated with floodplain management attend.
6500 Members
Founded in 1977

8083 ASMA Annual Meeting
American Society of Mining and Reclamation
3134 Montevesta Road
Lexington, KY 40502-3548

859-351-9032
Fax: 859-335-6529
E-Mail: asmr@insightbb.com
Home Page: www.asmr.us

Dennis Neuman, President
Richard Bamhisel, Executive Secretary

Approximately 30 exhibitors.
300 Attendees
Frequency: Annual

8084 ASMR Meeting & Conference
American Society of Mining and Reclamation
3134 Montavesta Road
Lexington, KY 40502

859-335-6529
E-Mail: asmr@insightbb.com
Home Page: www.ca.uky.edu/assmr

Richard I Barnhisel, Executive Secretary

Promoting the advancement of basic and applied reclamation science through research and technology transfer.
Frequency: June

8085 ASPRS Annual Conference
American Society for Photogammetry/Remote Sensing
5410 Grosvenor Lane
Suite 210
Bethesda, MD 20814-2160

301-493-0290
Fax: 301-493-0208
E-Mail: asprs@asprs.org
Home Page: www.asprs.org

Dr. Carolyn J. Merry, Ph.D., President
Roberta Lenczowski, VP
Dr. Donald Laurer, Treasurer
James Plasker, Executive Director

One hundred exhibits of mapping, photogrammetry, environmental management, remote sensing, geographic information, natural resources and much more.
6000 Members
2000 Attendees
Founded in 1934

8086 AWEA Offshore Windpower Conference Exhibition
American Wind Energy Association
1501 M Street NW
Suite 1000
Washington, DC 20005

202-383-2500
Fax: 202-383-2505
E-Mail: windmail@awea.org
Home Page: www.awea.org
Social Media: Facebook, Twitter, YouTube

Ned Hall, Chair
Thomas Carnahan, Chair-Elect
Gabriel Alonso, Secretary
Don Furman, Treasurer
Vic Abate, Past Chair

Brings together exhibitors and attendees from all over the world who are interested in becoming players in this new and highly promising market.
2400 Members

8087 Aerosol/ Atmospheric Optics: Visibility and Air Pollution
A&WMA
420 Fort Duquesne Boulevard
One Gateway Center, 3rd Floor
Pittsburgh, PA 15222-1435

412-652-2458
Fax: 412-232-3450
E-Mail: info@awma.org
Home Page: www.awma.org
Social Media: Facebook, Twitter, LinkedIn

Jeffry Muffat, President
Merlyn L. Hough, President Elect
Mike Kelly, Secretary/ Executive Director
Amy Gilligan, Treasurer
Dallas Baker, Vice President

Provide a technical forum on advances in the scientific understanding of the effects of aerosols.
9000 Members
Founded in 1907

8088 Air Quality Measurement Methods and Technology
A&WMA
420 Fort Duquesne Boulevard
One Gateway Center, 3rd Floor
Pittsburgh, PA 15222-1435

412-652-2458
Fax: 412-232-3450
E-Mail: info@awma.org
Home Page: www.awma.org
Social Media: Facebook, Twitter, LinkedIn

Jeffry Muffat, President
Merlyn L. Hough, President Elect
Mike Kelly, Secretary/ Executive Director
Amy Gilligan, Treasurer
Dallas Baker, Vice President

Explore advances in measurement technology, data quality assurance, and data uses.
9000 Members
Founded in 1907

8089 Air and Waste Management Association Annual Conference and Exhibition
Air and Waste Management Association
1 Gateway Center
3rd Floor
Pittsburgh, PA 15222-1435

412-652-2458
800-270-3444
Fax: 412-232-3450
E-Mail: info@awma.org
Home Page: www.awma.org

Deborah Hilfman, Show Manager
Robert Greenbaum, Exhibit Manager

Environmental professionals from all sectors of the economy including colleges, universities, natural resource manufacturing and process industries, consultants, local state, provincial, regional and federal governments, construction, utilities industries. Over 300 exhibits of envirnomental control products.
6000 Attendees

8090 Alternative Clean Transportation Expo(ACT)
Society of Environmental Journalists
PO Box 2492
Jenkintown, PA 19046

215-884-8174
Fax: 215-884-8175
Home Page: www.sej.org
Social Media: Facebook, Twitter

Carolyn Whetzel, President
Peter Fairley, 1st Vice Pres
Jeff Burnside, 2nd Vice Pres
Don Hopey, Treasurer

The largest alternative fuels and clean vehicle technologies show in North America.
Founded in 1990

8091 American Meteorological Society Annual Meeting
Renewable Natural Resources Foundation
5430 Grosvenor Ln
Bethesda, MD 20814-2193

301-493-9101
Fax: 301-493-6148
E-Mail: info@rnrf.org
Home Page: www.rnrf.org

Howard N. Rosen, Chairman
Richard A. Engberg, Vice-Chairman
Robert D. Day, Executive Director

Technology in research and operations, how we got here and where we're going.
14 Members
Founded in 1972

8092 American Occupational Health Conference & Exhibits
Slack
4930 Del Ray Avenue
Bethesda, MD 20814

301-654-2055
Fax: 301-654-5920
E-Mail: member@gastro.org
Home Page: www.gastro.org

Robert Greenberg, Executive Vp
Michael Stolar, Senior Vp

400 exhibits of pharmaceuticals, equipment, software and supplies for health professionals, offices and labs.
4500 Attendees

8093 American Society for Environmental History Annual Conference
Society of Environmental Journalists
PO Box 2492
Jenkintown, PA 19046

215-884-8174
Fax: 215-884-8175
Home Page: www.sej.org
Social Media: Facebook, Twitter

Carolyn Whetzel, President
Peter Fairley, 1st Vice Pres
Jeff Burnside, 2nd VP
Don Hopey, Treasurer

Join for an intellectual and collegial journey, from the local to the global; ethics, environmentalism, and environmental history in an interdependent world.
Founded in 1990

8094 American Society of Safety Engineers Professional Development Conference
American Society of Safety Engineers
1800 E Oakton Street
Des Plaines, IL 60018

847-699-2929
Fax: 847-768-3434
E-Mail: customerservice@asse.org
Home Page: www.asse.org

Fred Fortman, Executive Director
Jim Drzewiecki, Finance/Controller Director
Diane Hurns, Manager Public Relations Department

Annual conference and expo of 250 manufacturers and suppliers of safety equipment and health products.
3500 Attendees
Frequency: June

8095 American Water Resources Association Annual Water Resource Conference
Renewable Natural Resources Foundation
5430 Grosvenor Ln
Bethesda, MD 20814-2193

301-493-9101
Fax: 301-493-6148
E-Mail: info@rnrf.org
Home Page: www.rnrf.org

Howard N. Rosen, Chairman
Richard A. Engberg, Vice-Chairman
Robert D. Day, Executive Director

Brings together a diverse group of water resource professionals from across the state. Presenting a unique opportunity for water resource practitioners from diverse disciplines to gether and interact together.
14 Members
Founded in 1972

8096 Annual EcoFarm Conference
Community Alliance with Family Farmers
PO Box 363
Davis, CA 95617-363

530-756-8518
Fax: 530-756-7857
E-Mail: info@caff.org
Home Page: www.caff.org
Social Media: Facebook, Twitter, YouTube

Carol Presley, Board Chair
Pete Price, Vice President
Judith Redmond, Secretary
Vicki Williams, Treasurer

Oldest and largest ecological agricultural gathering in the West, meets every year to create, maintain, and promote healthy, safe, and just food farming systems. Myriad opportunities for networking with colleagues, discovering the newest ecological agricultural delvelopment and techniques, and building skills for individuals and together as a community.

8097 Annual International Conference on Soil, Water, Energy, and Air
AEHS Foundation Inc
150 Fearing Street
Amherst, MA 01002

413-549-5170
Fax: 413-549-0579
Home Page: www.aehsfoundation.org

Paul T Kostecki, PhD, Executive Director

Live equipment demonstrations augment the exhibition hall, bringing real world application to the technical theory presented in the sessions. An exciting opportunity for all those concerned with the challenge of developing creative, cost-effective assessments and solutions that can withstand the demands of regulatory requirements.
600 Members
Founded in 1989

8098 Annual International Conference on Soils, Sediments, Water and Energy
AEHS Foundation Inc
150 Fearing Street
Amherst, MA 01002

413-549-5170
Fax: 413-549-0579
Home Page: www.aehsfoundation.org

Paul T Kostecki, PhD, Executive Director

Live equipment demonstrations augment the exhibition hall, bringing real world application to the technical theory presented in the sessions. An exciting opportunity for all those concerned with the challenge of developing creative, cost-effective assessments and solutions that can withstand the demands of regulatory requirements.
600 Members
Founded in 1989

8099 Annual National Ethanol Conference
Renewable Fuels Association
425 Third Street, SW
Suite 1150
Washington, DC 20024

202-289-3835
Fax: 202-289-7519
E-Mail: info@ethanolrfa.org
Home Page: www.ethanolrfa.org
Social Media: Facebook, Twitter

Chuck Woodside, Chairman
Neill McKinstray, Vice Chairman
Randall Doyal, Treasurer
Walter Wendland, Secretary

Delivers accurate, timely information on marketing, legislative and regulatory issues facing the ethanol industry. Industry leaders and experts address accelerating innovation in technology, marketing, logistics and feedstocks for the production of advanced ethanol.
55 Members
Founded in 1981

8100 Annual Odors and Air Pollutants Conference
Water Environment Federation
601 Wythe St
Alexandria, VA 22314-1994

800-666-0206
Fax: 703-684-2492
Home Page: www.wef.org
Social Media: Facebook, Twitter

Matt Bond, President
Cordell Samuels, President-Elect
Sandra Ralston, Vice President
Chris Browning, Treasurer
Jeff Eger, Secretary and Executive Director

Topics covered include; odor and emission Control Systems, Biological odor control, innovative technologies, design of odor control systems, collection systems tunnel ventilation, emission from biosolids, fate and odor modeling, and many more.
79 Members
ISSN: 1044-9943
Founded in 1928

8101 Annual SWCS International Conference
Soil and Water Conservation Society
945 SW Ankeny Rd
Ankeny, IA 50023-9764

515-289-2331
800-843-7645
Fax: 515-289-1227
E-Mail: swcs@swcs.org
Home Page: www.swcs.org

Bill Boyer, President
Dan Towery, Vice-President
Clark Gantzer, Secretary
Jerry Pearce, Treasurer

Considering Ecology, Economics and Ethics.
5000+ Members
Founded in 1943

8102 Aquatic Plant Management Society Annual Meeting
Aquatic Plant Management Society
PO Box 821265
Vicksburg, MS 39182-1265

FAX 601-634-2398
E-Mail: dpetty@ndrsite.com
Home Page: www.apms.org
Social Media: Facebook, LinkedIn

Linda Nelson, President
Terry Goldsby, VP
Sherry Whitaker, Treasurer
Jeff Schardt, Secretary
Greg Aguillard, Director

An international organization of educators, scientists, commercial pesticide applicators, administrators and individuals interested in aquatic plant species and plant management.
Founded in 1961

8103 Biennial International Conference on Petroleum Geophysics
Society of Exploration Geophysicists
8801 South Yale
Suite 500
Tulsa, OK 74137-3575

918-497-5500
Fax: 918-497-5557
E-Mail: web@seg.org
Home Page: www.seg.org
Social Media: Facebook, Twitter, LinkedIn

Mary Fleming, Executive Director
Vladimir Grechka, Editor

Continuing education courses, exhibitions and networking.
Founded in 1930

8104 BioInterface
Surfaces in Biomaterials Foundation
1000 Westgate Drive
Suite 252
Saint Paul, MN 55114

651-290-6295
Fax: 651-290-2266
E-Mail: memberservices@surfaces.org
Home Page: www.surfaces.org

Bill Monn, Executive Director
Larry Salvati, President

One of the best technical and most stimulating conferences in the field of biomaterials science. Connect, share and learn by relaxed contact with fellow attendees. Be enriched by the science, and the high quality of interaction that is fostered by the unique blend of industry, academic, regulatory and clinical attendees.
150 Attendees
Frequency: Annual/Fall

8105 CONTE Conference on Nuclear Training and Education
555 N Kensington Ave
La Grange Park, IL 60526-5592

708-352-6611
800-323-3044
Fax: 708-352-0499
E-Mail: advertising@ans.org
Home Page: www.ans.org
Social Media: Facebook, Twitter, LinkedIn

Jack Tuohy, Executive Director
James S Tulenko, VP
William F Naughton, Treasurer

Topics of interest include knowledge retention, industry training practices, workforce development, government support, partnerships with colleges and universities, applications of technology to training, and training for next generation of nuclear plants.
10500 Members
Founded in 1954

8106 Coastal Summit
American Shore & Beach Preservation Association
5460 Beaujolais Lane
Fort Myers, FL 33919

239-489-2616
Fax: 239-362-9771
E-Mail: exdir@asbpa.org
Home Page: www.asbpa.org
Social Media: Facebook, Twitter

Harry Simmons, President
Nicole Elko, Secretary
Brad Pickel, Treasurer
Anthony Pratt, Chair

Federal, state and local government agencies and individuals interested in conservation, development and restoration of beaches and shorefronts.
1M Members
Founded in 1926

8107 Conference of the Brazilian Association for Aerosol Research
American Association for Aerosol Research
15000 Commerce Parkway
Suite C
Mount Laurel, NJ 08054

856-439-9080
877-777-6753
Fax: 856-439-0525
E-Mail: info@aaar.org
Home Page: www.aaar.org

William Nazaroff, President
Barbara Turpin, Vice President
Barbara Wyslouzil, Vice President Elect
Murray Johnston, Treasurer
CY Wu, Secretary

Opportunity to meet with other aerosol scientists and learn of the latest advances in all frontiers of aerosol science and technology. Meet new colleagues, and network with academia, government, and industry researchers.
1000 Members
Founded in 1982

8108 Conference on the Applications of Air Pollution Meteorology
A&WMA

420 Fort Duquesne Boulevard
One Gateway Center, 3rd Floor
Pittsburgh, PA 15222-1435

412-652-2458
Fax: 412-232-3450
E-Mail: info@awma.org
Home Page: www.awma.org
Social Media: Facebook, Twitter, LinkedIn

Jeffry Muffat, President
Merlyn L. Hough, President Elect
Mike Kelly, Secretary/ Executive Director
Amy Gilligan, Treasurer
Dallas Baker, Vice President

Topics dealing with ALL aspects of air pollution meteorology ranging from the microscale to the global scale and including field and laboratory measurements, instrumentation, theoretical studies, numerical modeling, evaluation studies and applications. Also on transport and dispersion modeling systems, urban meteorology and dispersion, and regional to global scale transport and dispersion.
9000 Members
Founded in 1907

8109 Department of Defense Fire & Emergency Services Conference
International Association of Fire Chiefs
4025 Fair Ridge Dr
Fairfax, VA 22033-2868

703-273-0911
Fax: 703-273-9363
Home Page: www.iafc.org
Social Media: Facebook, LinkedIn

Al H. Gillespie, President & Chairman of the Board
Hank Clemmensen, First Vice President
William R. Metcalf, Second Vice President
Richard Carrizzo, Treasurer
Luther L. Fincher, Jr., Director-At-Large

Official conference for the military fire and emergency service, including Army, DLA, Navy, Marine Corp, Air Force and Coast Guard fire service personnel.
12000 Members
Founded in 1873

8110 Downscaling Climate Models for Planning
A&WMA
420 Fort Duquesne Boulevard
One Gateway Center, 3rd Floor
Pittsburgh, PA 15222-1435
412-652-2458
Fax: 412-232-3450
E-Mail: info@awma.org
Home Page: www.awma.org
Social Media: Facebook, Twitter, LinkedIn

Jeffry Muffat, President
Merlyn L. Hough, President Elect
Mike Kelly, Secretary/ Executive Director
Amy Gilligan, Treasurer
Dallas Baker, Vice President
9000 Members
Founded in 1907

8111 EBA Annual Meeting
Environmental Business Association
1150 Connecticut Avenue NW
9th Floor
Washington, DC 20036-4129

202-624-4363
Fax: 202-828-4130
E-Mail: wbode@bode.com

William H Bode, President

Learn more about the research, development and demonstration activities in fuel cells, hydrogen production delivery and storage technologies.
Frequency: June

8112 EBA Semi-Annual Meeting
Environmental Bankers Association
510 King Street
Suite 410
Alexandria, VA 22314

703-549-0977
800-966-7475
Fax: 703-548-5945
Home Page: www.environbank.org

D J Telego, Executive Co-Director

Network with peers in the bank and non-bank financial institutions, insurers, asset management firms and those who provide services to them. Learn more about environmental risk management, sustainable development, and due diligence policies and procedures in financial institutions.
Frequency: January, June

8113 ECOS Annual Meeting
Society of Environmental Journalists
PO Box 2492
Jenkintown, PA 19046

215-884-8174
Fax: 215-884-8175
Home Page: www.sej.org
Social Media: Facebook, Twitter

Carolyn Whetzel, President
Peter Fairley, 1st Vice Pres
Jeff Burnside, 2nd Vice Pres
Don Hopey, Treasurer

Members of the Environmental Council of the States, the national association of state and territorial environmental agency leaders, will confer on matters of importance to the states such as air, water, waste, compliance, cross-media, and planning.
Founded in 1990

8114 EDRA Annual Meeting
Environmental Design Research Association
PO Box 7146
Edmond, OK 73083-7146

405-304-4863
Fax: 403-330-4150
E-Mail: edra@telepath.com
Home Page: www.edra.org

Janet Singer, Executive Director

Providing information about the advancement and dissemination of environmental design research, improving understanding of the interrelationships between people, their built and natural surroundings, and creating environments responsive to human needs.
Frequency: Spring-Summer

8115 EHS Management Forum
National Assoc. for Environmental Management
1612 K St NW
Suite 1102
Washington, DC 20006-2830

202-986-6616
800-391-6236
Fax: 202-530-4408
E-Mail: programs@naem.org
Home Page: www.naem.org
Social Media: Facebook, Twitter, LinkedIn

Kelvin Roth, President
Stephen Evanoff, 1st Vice President
Debbie Hammond, 2nd Vice President
Frank Macielak, Secretary and Treasurer

The largest annual gathering of EHS and sustainability decision-makers. Three days of interactive breakout sessions and keynote presentations, the Forum is the best opportunity for professional networking, benchmarking, and best-practice sharing available to EHS and sustainability practitioners today.
1000+ Members
Founded in 1990

8116 EIA's National Conference & Exposition
Environmental Information Association
6935 Wisconsin Ave
Suite 306
Chevy Chase, MD 20815-6112

301-961-4999
888-343-4342
Fax: 301-961-3094
E-Mail: info@eia-usa.org
Home Page: www.eia-usa.org

Dana Hudson, President
Mike Schrum, President Elect
Kevin Cannan, Vice President
Joy Finch, Secretary
Chris Gates, Treasurer

Providing the environmental industry with the information needed to remain knowledgeable, responsible, and compctitive in the environmental health and safety industry.

8117 EMS Annual Meeting
Environmental Mutagen Society
1821 Michael Faraday Drive
Suite 300
Reston, VA 20190

703-438-8220
Fax: 703-438-3113
E-Mail: emshq@ems-us.org
Home Page: www.ems-us.org

Tonia Masson, Executive Director
Suzanne Morris, Secretary
Barbara Shane, Treasurer

Environmental Impacts on the Genome and Epigenome; Mechanisms and Risks.
Frequency: Spring

8118 EPRI-A&WMA Workshop on Future Air Quality Model Development Needs
American Association for Aerosol Research
15000 Commerce Parkway
Suite C
Mount Laurel, NJ 08054
856-439-9080
877-777-6753
Fax: 856-439-0525
E-Mail: info@aaar.org
Home Page: www.aaar.org

William Nazaroff, President
Barbara Turpin, Vice President
Barbara Wyslouzil, Vice President Elect
Murray Johnston, Treasurer
CY Wu, Secretary

Designed to bring together researchers from academia, government and private institutions, industry, and other stakeholders to brainstorm on various air quality model development needs and to develop a comprehensive research agenda that can be used by the community to help guide research plans and to promote collaboration amongst researchers.
1000 Members
Founded in 1982

8119 ESTC Annual Convention
International Ecotourism Society
PO Box 96503 #34145
Washington, DC 20090-6503

202-506-5033
Fax: 202-789-7279
E-Mail: info@ecotourism.org

Home Page: www.ecotourism.org
Social Media: Facebook, Twitter, YouTube

Kelly Bricker, Chair
Tony Charters, Vice Chair
Neal Inamdar, Director Finance/Administration

Highlighting global challenges and local opportunities, supporting sustainable development of tourism and promoting solutions that balance conservation, communities and sustainable travel.
900 Members
Founded in 1990

8120 **ESTECH Annual Technical Meeting and Exposition of IEST**
Institute of Environmental Sciences and Technology
5005 Newport Drive
Suite 506
Rolling Meadows, IL 60008-3841

847-255-1561
Fax: 847-255-1699
Home Page: www.iest.org

Heather Dvorak, Marketing Associate

IEST's annual technical meeting and exposition presents the finest educational program with tutorials, technical sessions, and working group meeting, as well as displays in the tabletop exhibition for design, test and evaluation.
300 Attendees
Frequency: May

8121 **ETAD Annual Meeting**
Ecological and Toxicological Association of Dyes
1850 M Street NW
Suite 700
Washington, DC 20036

202-721-4154
Fax: 202-296-8120
Home Page: www.etad.com

Dr C Tucker Helmes, Executive Director

Cooperate with ETAD member companies and value chain for the benefit of health and the environment. Learn more about environmental regulations.
Frequency: Spring

8122 **Effective Cover Cropping in the Midwest**
Soil and Water Conservation Society
945 SW Ankeny Rd
Ankeny, IA 50023-9764

515-289-2331
800-843-7645
Fax: 515-289-1227
E-Mail: swcs@swcs.org
Home Page: www.swcs.org

Bill Boyer, President
Dan Towery, Vice-President
Clark Gantzer, Secretary
Jerry Pearce, Treasurer

Targeted to farmers and cover crop service providers. Provides a forum for farmers to exchange information, discuss opportunities for collaboration, and learn about new and successful practices related to cover crops. Goal of this conference is to get farmers together to learn how to effectively manage cover crops in a way that enhances soil quality, keeps nutrients in the fields, and increases the bottom line.
5000+ Members
Founded in 1943

8123 **Enviro Expo**
Industrial Shows Northeast
333 Trapelo Road
Belmont, MA 02478-1856

617-489-2302
800-543-5259
Fax: 781-489-5534
Home Page: www.enviroexpo.com
Social Media: Facebook, Twitter, LinkedIn

Russ Ryan, President
Diane Fisher, Show Manager

A single stop responsible family-oriented event, designed to educate and entertain. Variety of products and services that specialize in; health & wellness, transportation, home & garden, renewable energy, and Eco fashions.
5,000 Attendees
Frequency: May
Founded in 1987

8124 **Environmental Technology Expo**
Association of Energy Engineers
4025 Pleasantdale Road
Suite 420
Atlanta, GA 30340

770-447-5083
Fax: 770-446-3969
E-Mail: info@aeecenter.org
Home Page: www.aeecenter.org

Ruth Whitlock, Executive Admin
Jennifer Vendola, Accountant

Annual show and exhibits of air and water pollution contrasts, waste-to-energy services information, asbestos abatement and monitoring instruments and equipment.
Frequency: October

8125 **Executive Edge**
International Association of Fire Chiefs
4025 Fair Ridge Dr
Fairfax, VA 22033-2868

703-273-0911
Fax: 703-273-9363
Home Page: www.iafc.org
Social Media: Facebook, LinkedIn

Al H. Gillespie, President & Chairman of the Board
Hank Clemmensen, First Vice President
William R. Metcalf, Second Vice President
Richard Carrizzo, Treasurer
Luther L. Fincher, Jr., Director-At-Large

Fire service experts take participants through an intensive program that teaches lessons not taught in any school. Executive leadership program is designed for newly appointed fire chiefs and those preparing to become fire chiefs.
12000 Members
Founded in 1873

8126 **FET Annual Meeting**
Federation of Environmental Technologists
PO Box 624
Slinger, WI 53086-0624

414-540-0070
Fax: 262-644-7106
E-Mail: info@fetinc.org
Home Page: www.fetinc.org

Triese Haase, Administrator

Attend the program, visit the exhibitions and hear from keynote speakers on relevant environmental topics.
Frequency: March

8127 **FET's Environment Annual Conference & Exhibition**
Federation of Environmental Technologists
W175 N11081 Stonewood Dr.
Ste 203
Germantown, WI 53022-4771

262-437-1700
Fax: 262-437-1702
E-Mail: info@fetinc.org
Home Page: www.fetinc.org

Dan Brady, Board Chair
Mark Steinberg, President
Dave Seitz, Vice President
Anthony Montemurro, Treasurer
Jeffrey Nettesheim, Secretary

Courses on Air Pollution Control, Emergency Preparedness and Business Continuity, Managing Contaminated Sediments and an Environmental, Health & Safety Primer.
700 Members
Founded in 1981

8128 **Fish Wildlife Agencies Association Southeast**
8005 Freshwater Farms Road
Tallahassee, FL 32309

850-893-1204
Fax: 850-893-6204
E-Mail: seafwa@aol.com
Home Page: www.seafwa.org

Robert Brently, Executive Secretary

Fifteen booths.
1,000 Attendees
Frequency: October

8129 **Forestry, Conservation Communications Association Annual Meeting**
Forestry, Conservation Communications Association
Hall of the States
444 N Capitol
Washington, DC 20001

202-624-5416
Fax: 202-751-9099

Joe Friend, Executive Director

Annual meeting and exhibits of forestry and conservation communications equipment, systems and procedures.

8130 **Global Warming International Conference & Expo**
SUPCON International
PO Box 5275
Woodridge, IL 60517-0275

630-910-1551
Fax: 630-910-1561
E-Mail: syshen@megsinet.net
Home Page: www.globalwarming.net

Environmental and energy technology, global warming mitigation, journals, publications and software, greenhouse gas measurements, alternative vehicles and alternative energy. Containing 100 booths and exhibits.
2000 Attendees
Frequency: April Boston

8131 **GlobalCon Conference & Expo**
Association of Energy Engineers
4025 Pleasantdale Rd
Suite 420
Atlanta, GA 30340-4264

770-447-5083
Fax: 770-446-3969
E-Mail: info@aeecenter.org
Home Page: www.aeecenter.org
Social Media: Facebook, Twitter, LinkedIn, YouTube

Eric A. Woodroof, President
Gary Hogsett, President Elect
Bill Younger, Secretary
Paul Goodman, C.P.A., Treasurer

Designed specifically to facilitate those seeking to expand their knowledge of fast-moving developments in the energy field, explore promising new technologies, compare energy supply options, and learn about innovative and cost-conscious project implementation strategies.
8.2M Members
Founded in 1977

8132 **Green Industry Conference - GIC**
Professional Lawncare Network, Inc (PLANET)
950 Herndon Parkway
Suite 450
Herndon, VA 20170

703-736-9666
800-395-2522
Fax: 703-736-9668
E-Mail: info@gie-expo.com
Home Page: www.landcarenetwork.or/cmc/gic.html

Held in conjunction with the GIE+EXPO, the conference offers leadership series, workshops, educational opportunities, events, and new member orientation.
Frequency: Annual

8133 **Healthy Buildings Conference & Exhibition**
The Indoor Air Institute
2548 Empire Grade
Santa Cruz, CA 95060

831-426-0148
Fax: 831-426-6522
E-Mail: info@IndAir.org
Home Page: indair.org

Hal Levin, President
William Fisk, Vice President
William Nazaroff, Vice President

Issues addressed relate to indoor air quality and its impact on health. The main focus is on buildings as confined spaces where we spend around 90% of our life.

8134 **Heating with Biomass;**
Environmental & Energy Study Institute
122 C Street NW
Suite 630
Washington, DC 20001

202-628-1400
Fax: 202-628-1825
E-Mail: eesi@eesi.org
Home Page: www.eesi.org
Social Media: Facebook, Twitter, YouTube

Jared Blum, Board Chair
Shelley Fidler, Board Treasurer
Richard L. Ottinger, Board Chair Emeritus

Win-Win for Households, Economic Development, Energy Security. Learn about how clean, renewable, efficient biomass heating can contribute to job creation, economic development, and energy security in communities across the country, as well as ways in which policies can help overcome some of the existing challenges and barriers to biomass use in the residential, commercial, and institutional sectors.
Founded in 1984

8135 **HydroVision**
HCI Publications
410 Archibald Street
Kansas City, MO 64111-3001

816-931-1311
Fax: 816-931-2015
Home Page: www.hcipub.com

Leslie Eden, Manager

Focusing on asset management, civil works and dam safety, new development, ocean/ tidal/ stream power, operations and maintenance, policies and regulations, and water resources.
1,600 Attendees
Frequency: July-August

8136 **IAWF Annual Meetings**
International Association of Wildland Fire
4025 Fair Ridge Drive
Fairfax, VA 22033

785-423-1818
Fax: 785-542-3511
E-Mail: sandy@iawfonline.org
Home Page: www.iawfonline.org
Social Media: Facebook, Twitter

Sacha Dick, Programs Manager
Mikel Robinson, Executive Director

Participants represent a wide range of organizations, disciplines, and countries. Conference program includes workshops, invited speakers, oral and poster presentations, panels, and vendor displays.

8137 **IEST Annual Meeting**
Institute of Environmental Sciences and Technology
5005 Newport Drive
Suite 506
Rolling Meadows, IL 60008-3841

847-255-1561
Fax: 847-255-1699
E-Mail: information@iest.org
Home Page: www.iest.org

Julie Kendrick, Executive Director

Single source of contamination control knowledge for the industry. Participate in exceptional continuing education training courses and interactive working group meetings.
Frequency: Spring

8138 **ILZRO Annual Meeting**
International Lead Zinc Research Organization
2525 Meridian Parkway, Suite 100
PO Box 12036
Durham, NC 27713-2036

919-361-4647
Fax: 919-361-1957
Home Page: www.ilzro.org

Stephen Wilkinson, President
Frank Goodwin, VP Materials Sciences
Scott Mooneyham, Treasurer
Rob Putnam, Director Communications

Focused on new technology and its role in managing risks in the production and use of lead, the drivers for health and environmental legislation and their likely future direction, trends, threats and opportunities in the global lead/zinc market, in particular those arising from the increasing desire for more low emission vehicles. Enabling delegates to meet a wide cross-section of key players in the lead producing and consuming countries.
Frequency: November

8139 **ISEE Annual Meetings**
International Society for Ecological Economics
1313 Dolley Madison Boulevard
Suite 402
McLean, VA 22101
703-790-1745
Fax: 703-790-2672
Home Page: www.ecologicaleconomics.org
Social Media: Facebook, Twitter, LinkedIn

Heide Scheiter-Rohland, Director Membership

Provides an excellent opportunity for members to meet other ecological economists, test their ideas by presenting papers, and participate in the governance of the Society.
Frequency: Summer or Fall

8140 **ISEMNA Annual Meeting**
International Society for Ecological Modelling
University of California, Animal Sciences Dept
One Shields Avenue
Davis, CA 95616-8521

530-752-5362
Fax: 530-752-0175
E-Mail: webmaster@isemna.org
Home Page: www.isemna.org

Wolfgang Pittroff, Secretary-General
David Mauriello, Treasurer

Providing a forum for scientists from around the world to exchange ideas, theories, concepts, methodologies, and results from ecological modelling that address these important issues.
Frequency: August

8141 **IWA-WEF Wastewater Treatment Modelling Seminar**
Water Environment Federation
601 Wythe St
Alexandria, VA 22314-1994
800-666-0206
Fax: 703-684-2492
Home Page: www.wef.org
Social Media: Facebook, Twitter

Matt Bond, President
Cordell Samuels, President-Elect
Sandra Ralston, Vice President
Chris Browning, Treasurer
Jeff Eger, Secretary and Executive Director

With stricter effluent limits for nutrients and other contaminants, and concerns about plant efficiency, climate change, and emerging contaminants, there is a drive for new, more sophisticated application of modeling. Objective is to present recent findings and successful case studies with the aim of bringing together different approaches.
79 Members
ISSN: 1044-9943
Founded in 1928

8142 **IWLA National Convention**
Izaak Walton League
707 Conservation Lane
Gaithersburg, MD 20878

301-548-0150
800-453-5463
Fax: 301-548-0146
E-Mail: general@iwla.org
Home Page: www.iwla.org
Social Media: Facebook, Twitter

Jim A. Madsen, President
Robert Chapman, Vice President
Marj Striegel, Secretary
Walter Lynn Jr., Treasurer

Explore how Izaak Walton League members can make a difference for the future of America's great rivers, and the people and wildlife that depend on them.
37000 Members
Founded in 1922

8143 **Instructional Technology for Occupational Safety and Health Professionals**
Nat. Environmental, Safety & Health Training Assoc
2700 N. Central Avenue
Suite 900
Phoenix, AZ 85004-1147

602-956-6099
Fax: 602-956-6399
E-Mail: neshta@neshta.org
Home Page: www.neshta.org

Design, develop, deliver, evaluate and manage workplace safety and health training programs. Prepare and give a 15-minute presentation on a relevant workplace health and safety topic. The presentation will include skills and techniques learned in the course; however you will be encouraged to also bring materials that you are currently working on to use as a reference.
Founded in 1977

8144 **Int'l Conference on Southern Hemisphere Meteorology & Oceanography**
Renewable Natural Resources Foundation
5430 Grosvenor Ln
Bethesda, MD 20814-2193
301-493-9101
Fax: 301-493-6148
E-Mail: info@rnrf.org
Home Page: www.rnrf.org

Howard N. Rosen, Chairman
Richard A. Engberg, Vice-Chairman
Robert D. Day, Executive Director

An interdisciplinary forum for presentations of our current state of knowledge, as well as motivating new research and applications within the variety of disciplines related to weather and climate of the ocean and atmosphere.
14 Members
Founded in 1972

8145 **Inter-American Dialogue on Water Management**
Water Environment Federation
601 Wythe St
Alexandria, VA 22314-1994
800-666-0206
Fax: 703-684-2492
Home Page: www.wef.org
Social Media: Facebook, Twitter

Matt Bond, President
Cordell Samuels, President-Elect
Sandra Ralston, Vice President
Chris Browning, Treasurer
Jeff Eger, Secretary and Executive Director

The most prominent water encounter in the region. Gathering a wide myriad of sectors, government officials, national and international cooperation agency representatives, stakeholders, and practitioners in water management in the Americas. Address the need to evolve towards an inter-generation dialogue to embrace water management challenges beyond sectoral barriers that we have built in recent generations.
79 Members
ISSN: 1044-9943
Founded in 1928

8146 **International Association for Energy Economics Conference**
International Association for Energy Economics
28790 Chagrin Boulevard
Suite 350
Cleveland, OH 44122-4630
216-464-5365
Fax: 216-464-2737
E-Mail: iaee@iaee.org
Home Page: www.iaee.org

David Williams, Executive Director
John Jimison, Managing Director

Semi-annual conference and exhibits relating to energy economics including publications, consultants, energy database software.
325 Attendees

8147 **International Conference & Exhibition on Liquefied Natural Gas (LNG)**
Institute of Gas Technology
1700 S Mount Prospect Rd
Des Plaines, IL 60018-1804
847-768-0664
Fax: 847-768-0669
Home Page: www.gastechnology.org
Social Media: Facebook, Twitter, LinkedIn, YouTube

David Carroll, President & CEO
Ronald Snedic, Vice President/ Corporate Dev
Paul Chromek, General Counsel & Secretary

A landmark strategic, technical and commercial event for leaders, experts and committed professionals of the worldwide LNG Industry.

8148 **International Conference On Air Quality- Science and Application**
A&WMA
420 Fort Duquesne Boulevard
One Gateway Center, 3rd Floor
Pittsburgh, PA 15222-1435
412-652-2458
Fax: 412-232-3450
E-Mail: info@awma.org
Home Page: www.awma.org
Social Media: Facebook, Twitter, LinkedIn

Jeffry Muffat, President
Merlyn L. Hough, President Elect
Mike Kelly, Secretary/ Executive Director
Amy Gilligan, Treasurer
Dallas Baker, Vice President

One of the most prominent forums for discussing the latest scientific developments, applications and implications for policy and other uses. An important feature it that it brings together scientists and other stakeholders from the air pollution, climate change, policy and health communities.
9000 Members
Founded in 1907

8149 **International Conference on Facility Operations-Safeguards Interface**
555 N Kensington Ave
La Grange Park, IL 60526-5592
708-352-6611
800-323-3044
Fax: 708-352-0499
E-Mail: advertising@ans.org
Home Page: www.ans.org
Social Media: Facebook, Twitter, LinkedIn

Jack Tuohy, Executive Director
James S Tulenko, VP
William F Naughton, Treasurer

New methods, products, instructions and ideas for the nuclear science and technology safety field.
10500 Members
Founded in 1954

8150 **International Conference on Ground Penetrating Rador GPR**
Society of Exploration Geophysicists
8801 South Yale
Suite 500
Tulsa, OK 74137-3575
918-497-5500
Fax: 918-497-5557
E-Mail: web@seg.org
Home Page: www.seg.org
Social Media: Facebook, Twitter, LinkedIn

Mary Fleming, Executive Director
Vladimir Grechka, Editor

Devoted to the development of ground penetrating radar. Presents the most recent technical information and case studies on ground penetrating radar for engineers, scientists, and end users.
Founded in 1930

8151 **International Conference on Indoor Air Quality and Climate**
International Academy of Indoor Air Sciences
343 Soquel Avenue
PMB 312
Santa Cruz, CA 95062
831-426-0148
Fax: 831-426-6522
Home Page: www.indoorair2002.org

Multidisciplinary event involving participants from medicine, engineering, architecture and related fields. The conference will cover all aspects of Indoor Air Quality and Climate and the effects on human health, comfort and productivity. Cutting-edge research results will be presented, including ways to achieve an optimal indoor environment in a sustainable manner. Will address a variety of indoor environments, residential, office, school, industrial, commercial and transport.
Frequency: June-July

8152 **International Hazardous Materials Response Teams Conference**
International Association of Fire Chiefs
4025 Fair Ridge Drive
Fairfax, VA 22033
703-273-0911
Fax: 703-273-9363

One of the largest gatherings of hazmat responders, facilitating new ideas. Dedicated exhibit hours and events, and indoor and outdoor exhibits.

8153 **International High-Level Radioactive Waste Management**
555 N Kensington Ave
La Grange Park, IL 60526-5592
708-352-6611
800-323-3044
Fax: 708-352-0499
E-Mail: advertising@ans.org
Home Page: www.ans.org
Social Media: Facebook, Twitter, LinkedIn

Jack Tuohy, Executive Director
James S Tulenko, VP
William F Naughton, Treasurer

Subject coverage includes site characterization, analogue studies, geochemical studies, disruptive events, spent fuel and high-level-waste transportation, engineered barrier systems, design and testing, disposal containers, and waste form. Performance assessment and regulatory issues are also addressed.
10500 Members
Founded in 1954

8154 **International Society for Environmental Epidemiology Meeting**
American Association for Aerosol Research
15000 Commerce Parkway
Suite C
Mount Laurel, NJ 08054
856-439-9080
877-777-6753
Fax: 856-439-0525
E-Mail: info@aaar.org
Home Page: www.aaar.org

William Nazaroff, President
Barbara Turpin, Vice President
Barbara Wyslouzil, Vice President Elect
Murray Johnston, Treasurer
CY Wu, Secretary

Discussion of problems unique to the study of health and the environment.
1000 Members
Founded in 1982

8155 **International Symposium on Environmental Geochemistry**
Society for Environmental Geochemistry & Health

4698 S Forrest Avenue
Springfield, MO 65810

417-851-1166
Fax: 417-881-6920
E-Mail: DRBGWIXSON@aol.com
Home Page: www.segh.net

Prof. Xiangdong Li, President
Prof. Andrew Hursthouse, European Chair
Kyoung-Woong Kim, Asia/Pacific Chair
Anthea Brown, Membership Secretary/ Treasurer
Malcolm Brown, Secretary

Convey expertise in a range of scientific fields, such as geochemistry, biology, engineering, geology, hydrology, epidemiology, chemistry, medicine, nutrition and toxicology.
400 Members
Founded in 1971

8156 **International Topical Meeting on Nuclear Plant Instrumentation**
555 N Kensington Ave
La Grange Park, IL 60526-5592

708-352-6611
800-323-3044
Fax: 708-352-0499
E-Mail: advertising@ans.org
Home Page: www.ans.org
Social Media: Facebook, Twitter, LinkedIn

Jack Tuohy, Executive Director
James S Tulenko, VP
William F Naughton, Treasurer

Control and Human Machine Interface Technologies
10500 Members
Founded in 1954

8157 **International Workshop on Seismic Anisotropy**
Society of Exploration Geophysicists
8801 South Yale
Suite 500
Tulsa, OK 74137-3575

918-497-5500
Fax: 918-497-5557
E-Mail: web@seg.org
Home Page: www.seg.org
Social Media: Facebook, Twitter, LinkedIn

Mary Fleming, Executive Director
Vladimir Grechka, Editor

Cover both theoretical and applied aspects of seismic anisotropy in earth sciences. Focusing on applications of anisotropic models and methods in exploration & development of both conventional and unconventional Oil & Gas reservoirs, earthquake seismology, and reservoir monitoring using seismic anisotropy and microseismic.
Founded in 1930

8158 **Joint International Conference PBC/ SEGH**
Society for Environmental Geochemistry & Health
4698 S Forrest Avenue
Springfield, MO 65810

417-851-1166
Fax: 417-881-6920
E-Mail: DRBGWIXSON@aol.com
Home Page: www.segh.net

Prof. Xiangdong Li, President
Prof. Andrew Hursthouse, European Chair
Kyoung-Woong Kim, Asia/Pacific Chair
Anthea Brown, Membership Secretary/ Treasurer
Malcolm Brown, Secretary

On behalf of the Pacific Basin Consortium and the Society for Environmental Geochemistry and Health (Asia/ Pacific region)
400 Members
Founded in 1971

8159 **MEGA Symposium**
A&WMA
420 Fort Duquesne Boulevard
One Gateway Center, 3rd Floor
Pittsburgh, PA 15222-1435

412-652-2458
Fax: 412-232-3450
E-Mail: info@awma.org
Home Page: www.awma.org
Social Media: Facebook, Twitter, LinkedIn

Jeffry Muffat, President
Merlyn L. Hough, President Elect
Mike Kelly, Secretary/ Executive Director
Amy Gilligan, Treasurer
Dallas Baker, Vice President

Addresses issues related to power plant air emissions through the combined efforts of four key industry payers. Update seasoned professionals and provide an excellent learning experience for early career engineers.
9000 Members
Founded in 1907

8160 **MTS TechSurge, Oceans in Action**
Marine Technology Society
1100 H St., Nw
Suite LL-100
Washington, DC 20005

202-717-8705
Fax: 202-347-4302
E-Mail: membership@mtsociety.org
Home Page: www.mtsociety.org
Social Media: Facebook, Twitter, LinkedIn

Jerry Boatman, President
Drew Michel, President-Elect
Jerry Wilson, VP of Industry and Technology
Jill Zande, VP of Education and Research
Justin Manley, VP of Gov. & Public Affairs

Learn how government agencies and universities are supporting both current and emerging oceanographic operations worldwide. Discover how marine science, technology, engineering, products and services come together to support real-world issues around the globe, including piracy, disaster monitoring and recovery, prediction and forecast of ocean properties, coastal restoration, hypoxia, harmful algal blooms, fisheries and much more.
2M Members
Founded in 1963

8161 **Middle East Geosciences Conference & Exhibition**
Society of Exploration Geophysicists
8801 South Yale
Suite 500
Tulsa, OK 74137-3575

918-497-5500
Fax: 918-497-5557
E-Mail: web@seg.org
Home Page: www.seg.org
Social Media: Facebook, Twitter, LinkedIn

Mary Fleming, Executive Director
Vladimir Grechka, Editor
Founded in 1930

8162 **NAAEE Annual Meeting**
North American Association for Environmental
2000 P Street NW
Suite 540
Washington, DC 20036

202-419-0412
Fax: 202-419-0415
E-Mail: email@naaee.org
Home Page: www.naaee.org

William H Dent, Jr, Executive Director
Barbara Eager, Conference Coordinator
Paul Werth, Owner

Concurrent sessions, plenary sessions and networking, as well as workshops, field experiences and special events.
Frequency: Fall

8163 **NAEP Annual Meeting**
National Association of Environmental Professional
PO Box 2086
Bowie, MD 20718-2086

301-860-1140
888-251-9902
Fax: 301-860-1141
Home Page: www.naep.org

Sandi Worthman, Administrator

Learn unbiased information on environmental practices.
Frequency: Spring

8164 **NALGEP Annual Meetings**
National Association of Local Government
1333 New Hampshire Avenue NW
Washington, DC 20036

202-638-6254
Fax: 202-393-2866
E-Mail: nalgep@spiegelmcd.com
Home Page: www.nalgep.org

Kenneth Brown, Executive Director
David Dickson, Project Manager

Discussion of congressional issues
Frequency: Regional Workshops

8165 **NALMS Symposium**
North American Lake Management Society
4513 Vernon Boulevard, Suite 100
PO Box 5443
Madison, WI 53705-443

608-233-2836
Fax: 608-233-3186
E-Mail: nalms@nalms.org
Home Page: www.nalms.org

Bev Clark, President
Reesa Evans, Secretary
Linda Green, Treasurer

A collection of professional presentations, general workshops and non-stop discussions on managing lakes and reservoirs. Vendors are present with the latest lake management tools displayed. Scientific and environmental minds will offer a variety of relevant topical subject matter to be covered in breakout educational sessions, and networking opportunities will allow for collaboration with lake property association members and other interested parties.
1700 Members
Frequency: Annual/October
Founded in 1980

8166 **NAPE**
Society of Exploration Geophysicists
8801 South Yale
Suite 500
Tulsa, OK 74137-3575

918-497-5500
Fax: 918-497-5557
Home Page: www.napeexpo.com
Social Media: Facebook, Twitter, LinkedIn

Mary Fleming, Executive Director
Vladimir Grechka, Editor

Provides a marketplace for the buying, selling and trading of oil and gas products and producing properties via exhibit booths. Brings prospects and producing properties, capital formation, services and technologies all to-

gether in one location, creating an environment to establish strategic alliances for doing business and initiating purchases and trades.
Founded in 1930

8167 **NEHA Annual Educational Conference and Exhibition**
National Environmental Health Association
720 S Colorado Boulevard
Suite 970-S
Denver, CO 80246-1925

303-756-9090
Fax: 303-691-9490
E-Mail: staff@neha.org
Home Page: www.neha.org

Toni Roland, Conference Coordinator
Kim Brandow, Managing Director
Larry Marcum, Managing Director
Bob Custard, Manager
Jill Cruickshank, Communications Manager

The National Environmental Health Association (NEHA) is a unique organization representing all professionals in environmental health. NEHA offers credentials, publications, training, Journal of Environmental Health, and discounts for members. Each year NEHA conducts the Annual Educational Conference and Exhibition, this year it will be at the Minneapolis Hilton in Minneapolis, MN.
2000 Attendees
Frequency: June-July

8168 **NEHA Annual Meeting**
National Conference of Local Environmental Health
c/o NEHA, 720 S Colorado Boulevard
South Tower, Suite 970
Denver, CO 80246-1925

303-756-9090
Fax: 303-691-9490
E-Mail: nfabian@neha.org
Home Page: http://www.neha.org

Nelson E Fabian, Executive Director

Held with the National Environmental Health Association.
Frequency: June

8169 **NESHTA Annual Meetings**
National Environmental, Safety and Health Training
PO Box 10321
Phoenix, AZ 85064-0321

602-956-6099
Fax: 602-956-6399
E-Mail: info@neshta.org
Home Page: www.neshta.org

Charles L Richardson, Executive Director
Joan J Jennings, Manager Association Services
Suzanne Lanctot, Manager Certification/Membership

The network for academic, government, industrial, utility and consulting trainers and training managers responsible for protecting public health, workers, and our physical environment.
Frequency: June

8170 **NGWA Ground Water Summit & GWPC Spring Meeting**
Renewable Natural Resources Foundation
5430 Grosvenor Ln
Bethesda, MD 20814-2193

301-493-9101
Fax: 301-493-6148
E-Mail: info@rnrf.org
Home Page: www.rnrf.org

Howard N. Rosen, Chairman
Richard A. Engberg, Vice-Chairman
Robert D. Day, Executive Director

Innovate and Integrate.
14 Members
Founded in 1972

8171 **NIWR Annual Conference**
National Institutes for Water Resources
47 Harkness Road
Pelham, MA 10002

413-253-5686
Fax: 413-253-1309
E-Mail: tracy@uidaho.edu
Home Page: niwr.net

Jeffery Allen, President
Reagan Waskom, President-Elect
John Tracy, Secretary-Treasurer

Water Resource Institute directors and associate directors are invited to join for the annual meeting.
54 Members
Founded in 1974

8172 **NORA Semi-Annual Meetings**
NORA: Association of Responsible Recyclers
5965 Amber Ridge Road
Haymarket, VA 20169

703-753-4277
Fax: 703-753-2445
E-Mail: sparker@noranews.org
Home Page: www.noranews.org

Scott D Parker, Executive Director
Jim Letteney, Vice President

The liquid recycling industry's premier networking and education event.
Frequency: May, November

8173 **NREP Annual Meetings**
National Registry of Environmental Professionals
PO Box 2099
Glenview, IL 60025

847-724-6631
Fax: 847-724-4223
E-Mail: nrep@nrep.org
Home Page: www.nrep.org

Richard A Young, PhD, Executive Director

Certification preparatory workshops, technical papers and special seminars.
1000 Attendees
Frequency: Semi-Annual
Mailing list available for rent

8174 **National Coastal Conference**
American Shore and Beach Preservation Association
5460 Beaujolais Lane
Fort Myers, FL 33919

239-489-2616
Fax: 239-362-9771
E-Mail: exdir@asbpa.org
Home Page: www.asbpa.org
Social Media: Facebook, Twitter

Harry Simmons, President
Kate Gooderham, Executive Director
Nicole Elko, Secretary
Russell Boudreau, VP
Brad Pickel, Treasurer

Federal, state and local coastal policy and legal issues, shoreline processes and coastal management, shoreline projects and global coastal issues are discussed.
1M Members
Founded in 1926

8175 **National Environmental Balancing Bureau Meeting**
National Environmental Balancing Bureau
8575 Grovemont Circle
Gaithersburg, MD 20877-4121

301-977-3698
Fax: 301-977-9589

Michael Dolim, VP

Annual meeting and exhibits of testing and balancing equipment, supplies and services.

8176 **National Fish & Wildlife Conservation Congress**
Association of Fish & Wildlife Agencies
444 N Capitol St NW
Suite 725
Washington, DC 20001-1553

202-624-7890
Fax: 202-624-7891
E-Mail: info@fishwildlife.org
Home Page: www.fishwildlife.org
Social Media: Facebook, Twitter

Jon Gassett, President
Jeff Vonk, Vice President
Dave Chanda, Secretary/ Treasurer
Curtis Taylor, Past President

Bring together leading fish and wildlife scientists, government leaders, federal, provincial, state and local fish and wildlife agencies, conservation organizations and anglers and hunters to participate in discussions and debates about the future of fish and wildlife resources in North America.
Founded in 1902

8177 **National Flood Risk Management; Flood Risk Summit**
Association of State Floodplain Managers
2809 Fish Hatchery Rd
Suite 204
Madison, WI 53713-5020

608-274-0123
Fax: 608-274-0696
E-Mail: Larry@floods.org
Home Page: www.floods.org
Social Media: Facebook

Sally McConkey, Chair
William Nechamen, Vice Chair
Alan J. Giles, Secretary
John V. Crofts, Treasurer

Invitation-only. Soliciting feedback and providing updates to local, state, regional, and federal officials and the private sector on vital national policies currently under construction at the Federal level.
6500 Members
Founded in 1977

8178 **National FloodProofing Conference and Exposition Levees and Beyond**
Association of State Floodplain Managers
2809 Fish Hatchery Rd
Suite 204
Madison, WI 53713-5020

608-274-0123
Fax: 608-274-0696
E-Mail: Larry@floods.org
Home Page: www.floods.org
Social Media: Facebook

Sally McConkey, Chair
William Nechamen, Vice Chair
Alan J. Giles, Secretary
John V. Crofts, Treasurer

Making Wise Choices Highlighting the various floodproofing methods, products, techniques, programs, funding sources, and issues that have developed. Showcasing the state-of-the-art in materials, services, equipment, accessories and techniques.
6500 Members
Founded in 1977

8179 National Planning Conference
Renewable Natural Resources Foundation
5430 Grosvenor Ln
Bethesda, MD 20814-2193

301-493-9101
Fax: 301-493-6148
E-Mail: info@rnrf.org
Home Page: www.rnrf.org

Howard N. Rosen, Chairman
Richard A. Engberg, Vice-Chairman
Robert D. Day, Executive Director

Hosted by the American Planning Association.
14 Members
Founded in 1972

8180 National Quail Symposium
Wildlife Habitat Council
8737 Colesville Road
Suite 800
Silver Spring, MD 20910

301-588-8994
Fax: 301-588-4629
E-Mail: whc@wildlifehc.org
Home Page: www.wildlifehc.org
Social Media: Facebook, YouTube

Greg Cekander, Chairman
Lawrence A Selzer, Vice Chairman
Kevin Butt, Secretary-Treasurer

Highlight the diversity in conservation of quails. Serve as an excellent venue to publish current research and advance quail conservation.
120+ Members
Founded in 1988

8181 National Real Estate Environmental Conference
National Society of Environmental Consultants
PO Box 12528
San Antonio, TX 78212-0528

210-225-2897
800-486-3676
Fax: 956-225-8450

Annual conference and exhibits related to the environmentally responsible use of real estate.

8182 National Water Monitoring Conference
Renewable Natural Resources Foundation
5430 Grosvenor Ln
Bethesda, MD 20814-2193

301-493-9101
Fax: 301-493-6148
E-Mail: info@rnrf.org
Home Page: www.rnrf.org

Howard N. Rosen, Chairman
Richard A. Engberg, Vice-Chairman
Robert D. Day, Executive Director

National forum provides an exceptional opportunity for federal, state, local, tribal, volunteer, academic, private, and other water stakeholders to exchange information and technology related to water monitoring, assessment, research, protection, restoration, and management, as well as to develop new skills and professional networks.
14 Members
Founded in 1972

8183 North American Environmental Field Conferences & Expositions
1230 Lincoln Drive
Carbondale, IL 62901

618-453-7809
E-Mail: aih@engr.siu.edu
Home Page: www.aihydrology.org

Emitt C. Witt, III, President
Marzi Sharfaei, Secretary
T. Allen J. Gookin, Treasurer

Interactive indoor workshops, presented by some of the world's foremost authorities in the field, discussing cutting-edge field-based technologies and methods for environmental site characterization, sampling monitoring and remediation. Hands-on interactive outdoor workshops and equipment demos featuring the latest environmental field methods and equipment.
1000 Members
Founded in 1981

8184 North American Wildlife and Natural Resources Conference
Wildlife Management Institute
1101 14th Street NW
Suite 801
Washington, DC 20005

202-371-1808
Fax: 202-408-5059
Home Page:
www.wildlifemanagementinstitute.org

Meeting the challenges of modern conservation. Industry leaders dedicated to the conservation, enhancement and management of North America's wildlife and other natural resources.

8185 Ocean Sciences Meeting
Renewable Natural Resources Foundation
5430 Grosvenor Ln
Bethesda, MD 20814-2193

301-493-9101
Fax: 301-493-6148
E-Mail: info@rnrf.org
Home Page: www.rnrf.org

Howard N. Rosen, Chairman
Richard A. Engberg, Vice-Chairman
Robert D. Day, Executive Director

Largest worldwide conference in the geophysical sciences, attracting Earth and space scientists, educators, students and policy makers. Meeting showcases current scientific theory focused on discoveries that will benefit humanity and ensure a sustainable future for our planet.
14 Members
Founded in 1972

8186 Oceans MTS/IEEE Conference
Marine Technology Society
1100 H St., Nw
Suite LL-100
Washington, DC 20005

202-717-8705
Fax: 202-347-4302
E-Mail: membership@mtsociety.org
Home Page: www.mtsociety.org
Social Media: Facebook, Twitter, LinkedIn

Jerry Boatman, President
Drew Michel, President-Elect
Jerry Wilson, VP of Industry and Technology
Jill Zande, VP of Education and Research
Justin Manley, VP of Gov. & Public Affairs

The major international forum for scientists, engineers, and responsible ocean users to present the latest research results, ideas, developments, and applications in Oceanic Engineering and Marine Technology.
2M Members
Founded in 1963

8187 Offshore Technology Conference
Marine Technology Society
1100 H St., Nw
Suite LL-100
Washington, DC 20005

202-717-8705
Fax: 202-347-4302
E-Mail: membership@mtsociety.org
Home Page: www.mtsociety.org
Social Media: Facebook, Twitter, LinkedIn

Jerry Boatman, President
Drew Michel, President-Elect
Jerry Wilson, VP of Industry and Technology
Jill Zande, VP of Education and Research
Justin Manley, VP of Gov. & Public Affairs

The world's foremost event for the development of offshore resources in the fields of drilling, exploration, production and environmental protection. A worldwide forum for the exchange of technical information vital to exploration and development of ocean resources.
2M Members
Founded in 1963

8188 Plant Growth Regulation Society of America Annual Conference
Rhone-Poulenc, Ag Company
1018 Duke Street
Alexandria, VA 22314

703-836-4606
Fax: 706-883-8215
E-Mail: dmancini@ashs.org
Social Media: Facebook, Twitter

Dr Eric A Curry, President
Dr Louise Ferguson, VP
Dr Ed Stover, Secretary

Highlights the latest in basic and applied research in plant growth regulation including hormone binding, stress physiology and plant growth regulator application.
325 Members
Founded in 1973

8189 Residuals and Biosolids Conference
Water Environment Federation
601 Wythe St
Alexandria, VA 22314-1994

800-666-0206
Fax: 703-684-2492
Home Page: www.wef.org
Social Media: Facebook, Twitter

Matt Bond, President
Cordell Samuels, President-Elect
Sandra Ralston, Vice President
Chris Browning, Treasurer
Jeff Eger, Secretary and Executive Director

Highlights beneficial reuse options, science, and technologies currently available to leverage biosolids as a valuable resource.
79 Members
ISSN: 1044-9943
Founded in 1928

8190 SEG Annual Meeting
Society of Exploration Geophysicists
PO Box 702740
Tulsa, OK 74170-2740

918-497-5500
Fax: 918-497-5557
E Mail: web@seg.org
Home Page: www.seg.org/index.shtml

Mary Fleming, Executive Director
Vladimir Grechka, Editor

The world's largest oil, energy and mineral exposition showcasing cutting-edge technology for use in exploration and associated industries. It is the premier venue for individuals to meet

and discuss new geophysical technologies and their uses.
9300 Attendees
Frequency: October

8191 SEGH Annual Meetings
Society for Environmental Geochemistry and Health
4698 S Forrest Avenue
Springfield, MO 65810

417-885-1166
Fax: 417-881-6920
Home Page: www.segh.net

Bobby Wixson, Director Membership
Environmental determinants of quality of life, including water resources, sediments and soil pollution and climate change, engineered solutions to hazardous waste including treatment of hazardous substances and regulatory solutions and approaches to hazardous substances, and all other environmental quality and human health issues.
Frequency: Summer-Fall

8192 SEJ Annual Meeting
Society of Environmental Journalists
PO Box 2492
Jenkintown, PA 19046

215-884-8174
Fax: 215-884-8175
E-Mail: jletto@sej.org
Home Page: www.sej.org

Jay Letto, Annual Conference Coordinator
Organized by journalists for journalists who cover environment and related issues.
Co-hosted by the University of Vermont and Vermont Law School.
Frequency: September

8193 SER Annual Meeting
Society for Ecological Restoration
285 West 18th Street #1
Tucson, AZ 85701

520-622-5485
Fax: 520-622-5491
E-Mail: info@ser.org
Home Page: www.ser.org

Mary Kay C LeFevour, Executive Director
Jane Cripps, Membership
Julie St John, Communications
Dennis Martinez, Founder
Val Schaefer, Secretary
Provides members (and non-members) with the opportunity to exchange ideas and information, participate in activities such as workshops and field trips, reconnect with friends and colleagues, and make new acquaintances.
Frequency: Fall

8194 SER World Conference on Ecological Restoration
Society for Ecological Restoration
1017 O Street NW
Washington, DC 20001

202-299-9518
Fax: 270-626-5485
E-Mail: info@ser.org
Home Page: www.ser.org

Steve Whisenant, Chair
Cara R. Nelson, Vice Chair
Mary Travaglini, Treasurer
Alan Unwin, Secretary
Provide members and non-members with the opportunity to exchange ideas and information, participate in activities such as workshops and field trips, reconnect with friends and colleeagues, and make new acquaintances.
Frequency: Semi-Annual

8195 SETAC Annual Meeting
Society of Environmental Toxicology and Chemistry
1010 N 12th Street
Pensacola, FL 32501-3367

850-469-1500
Fax: 850-469-9778
E-Mail: rparrish@setac.org
Home Page: www.setac.org

Rodney Parrish, Executive Director
Greg Schifer, Manager
Information and collaboration on environmental toxicology and chemistry.
Frequency: Fall

8196 SHE Bi-Ennial Meetings
Society for Human Ecology
College of the Atlantic
105 Eden Street
Bar Harbor, ME 04609-0180

207-288-5015
Fax: 207-288-3780
E-Mail: carter@ecology.coa.edu
Home Page: www.societyforhumanecology.org

Barbara Carter, Assistant to Executive Director
Brings together scholars and practitioners associated with the study and practice of human ecology because of the importance of the disciplines' philosophy and applications in developing mutually beneficial solutions for society and the environment. A platform for sharing knowledge on present status and approaches for sustainable development.

8197 SOCMA Annual Meeting
Synthetic Organic Chemical Manufacturers Assn
1850 M Street NW
Suite 700
Washington, DC 20036

202-721-4100
Fax: 202-296-8120
E-Mail: info@socma.com
Home Page: www.socma.com

Joseph Acker, President
Vivian Diko, Executive Assistant & CEO
Charlene Patterson, Director Human Resources
Industry leaders come together.
Frequency: Early Spring

8198 SOEH Annual Meeting
Society for Occupational and Environmental Health
6728 Old McLean Village Drive
McLean, VA 22101

703-556-9222
Fax: 703-556-8729
E-Mail: soeh@degnon.org
Home Page: www.soeh.org

George K Degnon, CAE, Executive Director
Topic will be international aspects of pesticide exposure and health, and key interest areas for presentations and posters will be; chronic health effects from pesticide exposure, agricultural worker surveillance and biomonitoring studies, good models of integrated pesticide management and involvement of community members, and much more.
Frequency: Spring

8199 Science, Politics, and Policy: Environmental Nexus
National Association of Environmental Professional
PO Box 460
Collingswood, NJ 08108

856-283-7816
Fax: 856-210-1619
E-Mail: naep@bowermanagementservices.com
Home Page: www.naep.org
Social Media: Facebook, LinkedIn

Paul Looney, President
Harold Draper, Vice President
Joseph F. Musil Jr., Treasurer
Robert P. Morris Jr., Secretary
NEPA and Decision Making, program on what happens after NEPA documents are prepared, and how that information is useful to their preparation. Also a program on Advance Topics in Visual Resource Impact Assessment.

8200 SeminarFest
American Society of Safety Engineers
1800 E Oakton Street
Des Plaines, IL 60018

847-699-2929
Fax: 847-768-3434
E-Mail: customerservice@asse.org
Home Page: www.asse.org
Social Media: Facebook

Terrie S. Norris, President
Richard A. Pollock, President Elect
Kathy Seabrook, Senior Vice President
Fred J. Fortman, Jr., Secretary & Executive Director
James D. Smith, Vice President, Finance
Pass your ASP, CSP, OHST and CHST exams with confidence by taking our certification preparation workshops. Earn a certificate of completion in Safety Management & the Executive Program in Safety Management. Develop business acument, leadership and training skills. Measure safety effectiveness and review safety management approaches. Also participate in technical and topical seminars.
30000 Members
Founded in 1911

8201 Sino-European Symposium on Environment and Health (SESH)
Society for Environmental Geochemistry & Health
4698 S Forrest Avenue
Springfield, MO 65810

417-851-1166
Fax: 417-881-6920
E-Mail: DRBGWIXSON@aol.com
Home Page: www.segh.net

Prof. Xiangdong Li, President
Prof. Andrew Hursthouse, European Chair
Kyoung-Woong Kim, Asia/Pacific Chair
Anthea Brown, Membership Secretary/ Treasurer
Malcolm Brown, Secretary
Provides an opportunity for a direct communication between experts from China and the rest of the world.
400 Members
Founded in 1971

8202 Smart Energy Summit
Parks Associates
5310 Harvest Hill Road
Suite 235, Lock Box 162
Dallas, TX 75230-5805

972-490-1113
800-727-5711
E-Mail: info@parksassociates.com
Home Page: www.parksassociates.com

Tricia Parks, Founder and CEO
Stuart Sikes, President
Farhan Abid, Research Analyst
Bill Ablondi, Director, Home Systems Research
John Barrett, Director of Research
Smart Energy Summit is an annual three-day event that examines the opportunities and technical business requirements inherent in the consumer programs and advanced systems and

services made possible by Smart Grids and Residential Energy Management solutions.
Frequency: Annual
Founded in 1986

8203 Soil and Water Conservation Society Annual International Conference
Soil and Water Conservation Society
945 SW Ankeny Road
Ankeny, IA 50021-9764
515-289-2331
800-843-7645
Fax: 515-289-1227
Home Page: www.swsc.org
Craig A Cox, Executive VP
Explores ways to improve the linkages among conservation science, policy and application at local, national, and international scales. The conference will provide participants an opportunity to teach skills, learn techniques, compare successes, and improve understanding.
1200 Attendees
Frequency: Annual

8204 Spatial Cognition for Architectural Design Symposium
Environmental Design Research Association
1760 Old Meadow Road
Suite 500
McLean, VA 22102
703-506-2895
Fax: 703-506-3266
E-Mail: edra@telepath.com
Home Page: www.edra.org
Social Media: Facebook, Twitter, LinkedIn
Nick Watkins, Chair
Mallika Bose, Chair-Elect
Vikki Chanse, Secretary
Shauna Mallory-Hill, Treasurer
Kate O'Donnell, Executive Director(ex-officio)
Addresses the theoretical and methodological achievements of the cognitive and computational disciplines in the domain of architectural design. A dialogue between scientists from design research and educational disciplines is sought with the aim to identify how such application of knowledge may provide real benefit for the theory and professional practice of architectural design.
700 Members
Founded in 1968

8205 Sustainability in Public Works Conference
2345 Grand Blvd
Suite 700
Kansas City, MO 64108-2625
816-472-6100
800-848-2792
Fax: 816-472-1610
Home Page: www.apwa.net
Social Media: Facebook, Twitter, YouTube
Diane M. Linderman, President
Elizabeth Treadway, President Elect
Richard F. Stinson, Director, Region I
Edward A. Gottko, Director, Region II
William Barney Mills, Jr., Director, Region III
International educational and professional association of public agencies, private sector companies, and individuals dedicated to providing high quality public works, goods and services. APWA provides a forum brings important public works-related topics to public attention in local, state, and federal areas. Mailing list for members only.
26000 Members
Founded in 1937

8206 Sustainable Water Management Conference
Water Environment Federation
601 Wythe St
Alexandria, VA 22314-1994
800-666-0206
Fax: 703-684-2492
Home Page: www.wef.org
Social Media: Facebook, Twitter
Matt Bond, President
Cordell Samuels, President-Elect
Sandra Ralston, Vice President
Chris Browning, Treasurer
Jeff Eger, Secretary and Executive Director
Will focus on large-scall sustainability issues related to water supply and management topics such as water conservation, urban planning and design, and sustainable utilities, infrastructure, and communities.
79 Members
ISSN: 1044-9943
Founded in 1928

8207 Take It Back
Raymond Communications
5111 Berwin Road
#115
College Park, MD 20740
301-345-4237
Fax: 301-345-4768
Home Page: www.raymond.com
Michele Raymond, Publisher/Editor
The conference brings in the top recycling policy experts from around the world to brief customers. We also have practical sessions with case histories on such issues as packaging design, design for environment in electronics, and lifecycle issues.
150 Attendees
Frequency: March
Founded in 1996

8208 Teaming With Wildlife Fly-In Day
Association of Fish & Wildlife Agencies
444 N Capitol St NW
Suite 725
Washington, DC 20001-1553
202-624-7890
Fax: 202-624-7891
E-Mail: info@fishwildlife.org
Home Page: www.fishwildlife.org
Social Media: Facebook, Twitter
Jon Gassett, President
Jeff Vonk, Vice President
Dave Chanda, Secretary/ Treasurer
Curtis Taylor, Past President
Join in supporting funding for the State & Tribal Wildlife Grants Program, the nation's CORE program for preventing fish and wildlife from becoming endangered in every state and territory.
Founded in 1902

8209 The Utility Management Conference
Water Environment Federation
601 Wythe St
Alexandria, VA 22314-1994
800-666-0206
Fax: 703-684-2492
Home Page: www.wef.org
Social Media: Facebook, Twitter
Matt Bond, President
Cordell Samuels, President-Elect
Sandra Ralston, Vice President
Chris Browning, Treasurer
Jeff Eger, Secretary and Executive Director
Water and wastewater managers and professionals will gather to be part of the latest approaches, practices, and techniques in all aspects of utility management.
79 Members
ISSN: 1044-9943
Founded in 1928

8210 Thermal Treatment Technologies/ Hazardous Waste Combustors
A&WMA
420 Fort Duquesne Boulevard
One Gateway Center, 3rd Floor
Pittsburgh, PA 15222-1435
412-652-2458
Fax: 412-232-3450
E-Mail: info@awma.org
Home Page: www.awma.org
Social Media: Facebook, Twitter, LinkedIn
Jeffry Muffat, President
Merlyn L. Hough, President Elect
Mike Kelly, Secretary/ Executive Director
Amy Gilligan, Treasurer
Dallas Baker, Vice President
Brings together industry experts from around the world to share experiences, lessons learned and new ideas on how to best operate thermal treatment facilities.
9000 Members
Founded in 1907

8211 Topical Meeting on the Technology of Fusion Energy (TOFE)
555 N Kensington Ave
La Grange Park, IL 60526-5592
708-352-6611
800-323-3044
Fax: 708-352-0499
E-Mail: advertising@ans.org
Home Page: www.ans.org
Social Media: Facebook, Twitter, LinkedIn
Jack Tuohy, Executive Director
James S Tulenko, VP
William F Naughton, Treasurer
Providing a forum for sharing the exciting new progress that has been made in fusion research as well as presenting the future of national and worldwide fusion programs. Draws together scientists, engineers, and students from various countries.
10500 Members
Founded in 1954

8212 Underwater Intervention Conference
Marine Technology Society
1100 H St., Nw
Suite LL-100
Washington, DC 20005
202-717-8705
Fax: 202-347-4302
E-Mail: membership@mtsociety.org
Home Page: www.mtsociety.org
Social Media: Facebook, Twitter, LinkedIn
Jerry Boatman, President
Drew Michel, President-Elect
Jerry Wilson, VP of Industry and Technology
Jill Zande, VP of Education and Research
Justin Manley, VP of Gov. & Public Affairs
The conference is of interest to a number of diverse marine industries, including offshore oil and gas, marine construction, shipwreck exploration, ocean mining and marine salvage. Presentation tracks include cable, remote intervention, commercial diving, and shipwreck salvage, among others.
2M Members
Founded in 1963

8213 Utility Working Conference and Vendor Technology Expo
555 N Kensington Ave
La Grange Park, IL 60526-5592
708-352-6611
800-323-3044
Fax: 708-352-0499
E-Mail: advertising@ans.org

Home Page: www.ans.org
Social Media: Facebook, Twitter, LinkedIn

Jack Tuohy, Executive Director
James S Tulenko, VP
William F Naughton, Treasurer

Dedicated to identifying innovations in all areas of nuclear power plant operations. The functional area tracks/ sessions bring together professionals with different perspectives focusing on current issues and innovations.
10500 Members
Founded in 1954

8214 WINDPOWER Conference and Exhibition
American Wind Energy Association (AWEA)
1501 M Street NW
Suite 1000
Washington, DC 20005

202-383-2500
Fax: 202-383-2505
E-Mail: windmail@awea.org
Home Page: www.windpowerexpo.org

Denise Bode, Chief Executive Officer
Pam Poisson, Chief Financial Officer
Britt Theismann, Chief Operating Officer
Rob Gramlich, Senior VP, Public Policy
Peter Kelley, VP, Public Affairs

The WINDPOWER Conference & Exhibition is produced by the American Wind Energy Association to provide a venue for the wind industry to network, do business, and solve problems. Recognized as one of the fastest-growing trade shows in the U.S., WINDPOWER includes nearly 1,400 exhibiting companies, thousands of qualified wind energy professionals, engaging educational information and unmatched networking opportunities and special events.
2500 Members
20000 Attendees
Frequency: Annual

8215 WSSA Annual Meeting
Weed Science Society of America
PO Box 7050
Lawrence, KS 66044

785-429-9622
800-627-0629
Fax: 785-843-1274
Home Page: www.wssa.net

Rhonda Green, Registration Coordinator

Usually held during the first full week of February in the United States or Canada. These Meetings provide a venue for the exchange of research and educational ideas and for discussion and activity on society business.
1M Attendees
Frequency: February
Founded in 1956

8216 Waterpower XIII
HCI Publications
410 Archibald Street
Kansas City, MO 64111-3001

816-931-1311
Fax: 816-931-2015
Home Page: www.hcipub.com

Leslie Eden, Manager

The conference offers industry professionals a forum in which to share new ideas and approaches to move hydropower forward as the world's leading source of renewable energy. Containing 120 booths.
1,000 Attendees
Frequency: July-August

8217 Wildlife Habitat Council Annual Symposium
Wildlife Habitat Council
8737 Colesville Road
Suite 800
Silver Spring, MD 20910

301-588-8994
Fax: 301-588-4629
E-Mail: whc@wildlifehc.org
Home Page: www.wildlifehc.org

Bill Howard, President
Martha Gruelle, Program Manager
Linda Duvall, Accounting Manager
Tiffany Msonthi, Executive Assistant

The annual symposium brings together corporate, government and conservation leaders from around the globe for informative sessions, exhibits and field trips on environmental stewardship.
400 Attendees
Frequency: November

8218 Wildlife Society Annual Conference
Wildlife Society
5410 Grosvenor Lane
Suite 200
Bethesda, MD 20814-2144

301-897-9770
Fax: 301-530-2471
E-Mail: tws@wildlife.org
Home Page: www.wildlife.org

Lisa Moll, Program Assistant/Membership

Hear from industry leaders to discuss new and evolving trends and innovations in wildlife management and conservation, learn about the latest research from original research and techniques presented by wildlife professionals, connect with colleagues at the largest gathering of wildlife professionals in North America.
1200 Attendees
Frequency: September
Founded in 1994

8219 Windpower Conference
American Wind Energy Association
1501 M Street NW
Suite 1000
Washington, DC 20005

202-383-2500
Fax: 202-383-2505
E-Mail: windmail@awea.org
Home Page: www.awea.org
Social Media: Facebook, Twitter, YouTube

Ned Hall, Chair
Thomas Carnahan, Chair-Elect
Gabriel Alonso, Secretary
Don Furman, Treasurer
Vic Abate, Past Chair
2400 Members

8220 World Future Energy Summit
Society of Environmental Journalists
PO Box 2492
Jenkintown, PA 19046

215-884-8174
Fax: 215-884-8175
Home Page: www.sej.org
Social Media: Facebook, Twitter

Carolyn Whetzel, President
Peter Fairley, 1st Vice Pres
Jeff Burnside, 2nd Vice Pres
Don Hopey, Treasurer

World leaders, international policy makers, industry leaders, investors, experts, academia, intellectuals and journalists to find practical and sustainable solutions for today's energy security, climate change challenges and the advancement of clean technology.
Founded in 1990

Directories & Databases

8221 A Guide to Internet Resources
American Assoc for the Advancement of Science
1200 New York Avenue NW
Washington, DC 20005-3941

202-266-6721
Fax: 202-371-9227
E-Mail: membership@aaas.org
Home Page: www.aaas.org

Nathan E Bell, Editor

Free online document provides a starting point for finding internet resources. Topics include internet resources for math, science, health, english, software, grants, shareware, and much more.

8222 ACCA Membership Directory
Air Conditioning Contractors of America
2800 Shirlington Rd
Suite 300
Arlington, VA 22206-3607

703-575-4477
E-Mail: info@acca.org
Home Page: www.acca.org
Social Media: Facebook, Twitter, LinkedIn, YouTube

Paul Stalknecht, President & CEO

8223 ACSH Media Update
American Council on Science and Health
1995 Broadway
2nd Floor
New York, NY 10023-5882

212-362-7044
Fax: 212-362-4919
E-Mail: acsh@acsh.org
Home Page: www.acsh.org

Elizabeth Whelan, President
Jeff Stier, Director of Publications
Alyssa Pelish, Director of Publications
Gilbert Ross, Executive Director
Frequency: Semi-Annual

8224 ASMR Membership Directory
American Society of Mining and Reclamation
3134 Montavesta Road
Lexington, KY 40502

859-335-6529
E-Mail: asmr@insightbb.com
Home Page: www.ca.uky.edu/assmr

Richard I Barnhisel, Executive Secretary
Frequency: Annual

8225 Aboveground Storage Tank Management and SP CC Guide
ABS Group
PO Box 846304
Dallas, TX 75284-6304

FAX301-921-0264

8226 Acid Rain
Watts, Franklin
90 Sherman Turnpike
Danbury, CT 06816

203-797-3500
800-621-1115
Fax: 203-797-3657

Lists over 4,000 citations, with abstracts, to the worldwide literature on the sources of acid rain and its effects on the environment.

8227 Alternative Energy Network Online
Environmental Information Networks
119 S Fairfax Street
Alexandria, VA 22314-3301
703-548-1202
Reports on news of all energy sources designed as alternatives to conventional fossil fuels, including wind, solar and alcohol fuels.
Frequency: Full-text

8228 American Recycling Market: Directory/Reference Manual
Recycling Data Management Corporation
PO Box 577
Ogdensburg, NY 13669-0577
315-785-9072
Offers information, in three volumes, encompassing over 15,000 recycling companies and centers.
Cost: $175.00
1000 Pages
Frequency: Annual
ISSN: 0885-2537

8229 Business and the Environment: A Resource Guide
Island Press
1718 Connecticut Ave NW
Suite 300
Washington, DC 20009-1148
202-232-7933
Fax: 202-234-1328
E-Mail: info@islandpress.org
Home Page: www.islandpress.org
Chuck Savitt, President
Allison Pennell, Editor
List of approximately 185 business and environmental educators working to integrate environmental issues into management, research, education and practices.
Cost: $60.00

8230 Canadian Environmental Directory
Grey House Publishing
4919 Route 22
PO Box 56
Amenia, NY 12501
518-789-8700
800-562-2139
Fax: 845-373-6390
E-Mail: books@greyhouse.com
Home Page: www.greyhouse.com
Social Media: Facebook, Twitter
Leslie Mackenzie, Publisher
Tannys Williams, Managing Editor
Canada's most complete national listing of environmental associations and organizations, government regulators and purchasing groups, product and service companies, special libraries, and more.
Cost: $315.00
900 Pages
ISBN: 1-592372-24-9
Founded in 1981

8231 Carcinogenicity Information Database of Environmental Substances
Technical Database Services
10 Columbus Circle
New York, NY 10019-1203
212-556-0001
Fax: 212-556-0036
This database contains test results on the carcinogenic and mutagenic effects of approximately 1000 substances of environmental or health concerns.

8232 Conservation Directory
National Wildlife Federation
11100 Wildlife Center Dr
Reston, VA 20190-5362
703-438-6000
800-822-9919
Fax: 703-438-3570
E-Mail: info@nwf.org
Home Page: www.nwf.org
Mark Van Putten, CEO
Federal agencies, national and international organizations and state government agencies.
Cost: $20.00
500 Pages
Frequency: Annual

8233 Department of Energy Annual Procurement and Financial Assistance Report
US Department of Energy
1000 Independence Ave SW
Washington, DC 20585-0001
202-586-5000
Fax: 202-586-0573
Home Page: www.energy.gov
Mary Lein, Manager
Offers a list of universities, research centers and laboratories that represent the Department of Energy.
Frequency: Annual

8234 Directory of Environmental Websites: Online Micro Edition
US Environmental Directories
PO Box 65156
Saint Paul, MN 55165-0156
612-331-6050
Home Page: www.geocities.com/usenvironmentaldirectories
Roger N McGrath, Publisher
John C Brainard, Editor
The Directory is a complete guide to the environmental movement on the Internet, provides a concise, practical listing of over 190 of the major Internet addresses of the Environmental Movement. A clear, understandable and comprehensive guide to national and international environmental organizations, directories, networks and services on the Internet.
Cost: $25.75
48 Pages
ISSN: 1096-3316
Founded in 1998

8235 Directory of International Periodicals & Newsletters on Built Environments
Division of Mineral Resources
PO Box 3667
Charlottesville, VA 22903-0667
434-951-6341
Fax: 434-951-6365
Home Page: www.mme.state.va.us
Scott Richeson, Programs Director
More than 1,400 international periodicals and newsletters that cover architectural design and the building industry, and the aspects of the environment that deal with the industry are covered.
Cost: $6.00
29 Pages

8236 EDOCKET
Environmental Protection Agency
1200 Pennsylvania Avenue NW
Mail Code 3213A
Washington, DC 20460
202-260-2090
Fax: 202-566-0545
E-Mail: r9.info@epa.gov
Home Page: www.epa.gov
An electronic public docket and on-line comment system designed to expand access to documents in EPA's major dockets.
Frequency: Full-text

8237 EH&S Compliance Auditing & Teaching Software Report
Donley Technology
PO Box 152
Colonial Beach, VA 22443-0152
804-224-9427
800-201-1595
Fax: 804-224-7958
E-Mail: donleytech@donleytech.com
Home Page: www.donleytech.com
Elizabeth Donley, Editor
Profiles 25 software packages for achieving and maintaining compliance, including detailed product descriptions, tables comparing system features, and contact information.
Cost: $195.00
240 Pages
Frequency: Every 2 Years
ISBN: 1-891682-08-3
Founded in 1997
Printed in on matte stock

8238 EMS Membership Roster
Environmental Mutagen Society
1821 Michael Faraday Drive
Suite 300
Reston, VA 20190
703-438-8220
Fax: 703-438-3113
E-Mail: emshq@ems-us.org
Home Page: www.ems-us.org
Tonia Masson, Executive Director
Suzanne Morris, Secretary
Barbara Shane, Treasurer
Frequency: Irregular

8239 Ecology Abstracts
Cambridge Scientific Abstracts
7200 Wisconsin Ave
Suite 601
Bethesda, MD 20814-4890
301-961-6700
800-843-7751
Fax: 301-961-6790
E-Mail: service@csa.com
Home Page: www.csa.com
Andrew M Snyder, President
Theodore Caris, Publisher
Robert Hilton, Editor
Mark Furneaux, VP Marketing
Angela Hitti, Production Manager
This large database updated continuously, offers over 150,000 citations, with abstracts, to the worldwide literature available on ecology and the environment.
Cost: $945.00
Frequency: Monthly

8240 Education for the Earth: A Guide to Top Environmental Studies Programs
Peterson's Guides
202 Carnegie Center
#2123
Princeton, NJ 08540-6239
800-338-3282
Fax: 609-869-4531
Colleges and universities that offer programs in environment and conservation are listed.
Cost: $10.95
192 Pages

8241 Educational Communications
Educational Communications

PO Box 351419
Los Angeles, CA 90035-9119

310-559-9160
Fax: 310-559-9160
E-Mail: ECNP@aol.com
Home Page: www.ecoprojects.org

Nancy Pearlman, Editor/Executive Director

Directory of over 6,500 environmental organizations worldwide are the focus of this comprehensive directory. Over 400 1/2 hour television shows on the environment. Environmental directions - radio has over 1,500 interviews with ecological experts. Monthly newsletter, TV and radio series about ecological problems and solutions; promotion of ecotourem. Audo/video cassettes available.
Cost: $20.00
244 Pages
Frequency: Annual Paperback
Founded in 1957
Mailing list available for rent

8242 **El Environmental Services Directory**
Environmental Information Networks
7301 Ohms Lane
Suite 460
Eding, MN 55439

952-831-2473
Fax: 952-831-6550
E-Mail: customerservice@envirobiz.com
Home Page: www.envirobiz.com

Cary Perket
James Rue, Secretary
Marshall Sanders, Manager
Bruce McGranahan, Director

Waste-handling facilities, transportation and spill response firms, laboratories and the broad scope of environmental services. Online versions are also available.
Cost: $1250.00
Frequency: Biennial
ISSN: 1053-475N
Founded in 1984

8243 **Emergency Response Directory for Hazardous Materials Accidents**
Odin Press
PO Box 536
New York, NY 10021-0011

212-605-0338

Pamela Lawrence, Editor

Over 1,000 federal, state and local governmental agencies, chemical manufacturers and transporters, hotlines and strike teams, burn care centers, civil defense and disaster centers and other organizations concerned with the containment and cleanup of chemical spills and other hazardous materials accidents.
Cost: $36.00
Frequency: Biennial

8244 **Energy Statistics Spreadsheets**
Institute of Gas Technology
1700 S Mount Prospect Rd
Des Plaines, IL 60018-1804

847-768-0664
Fax: 847-768-0669
Home Page: www.gastechnology.org

Carol L Worster, Manager
Edward Johnston, Managing Director

The coverage of this database encompasses worldwide energy industry statistics, including production, consumption, reserves, imports and prices.

8245 **Energy User News: Energy Technology Buyers Guide**
Chilton Company
300 Park Ave
Suite 19
New York, NY 10022-7409

212-751-3596
Fax: 212-443-7701
Home Page: www.chiltonfunds.com

Richard L Chilton Jr, Owner
Lisa Czachor, Director
Mary Morse, Senior Vice President

A list of about 1,500 manufacturers, dealers and distributors of energy conservation and used equipment.
Cost: $10.00
Frequency: Annual
Circulation: 40,000

8246 **Environmental Bibliography**
International Academy at Santa Barbara
5385 Hollister Avenue
#210
Santa Barbara, CA 93111

805-683-8889
Fax: 805-965-6071
E-Mail: info@iasb.org
Home Page: www.iasb.org

Gloria Lindfield, Executive Assistant
Hilary Eastman, Manager
Tom Seidenstein, Chief Operating Officer

Over 615,000 citations are offered in this database, aimed at scientific, technical and popular periodical literature dealing with the environment.
Cost: $1750.00
ISSN: 1053-1440
Founded in 1972

8247 **Environmental Cost Estimating Software Report**
Donley Technology
PO Box 152
Colonial Beach, VA 22443-0152

804-224-9427
800-201-1595
Fax: 804-224-7958
E-Mail: donleytech@donleytech.com
Home Page: www.donleytech.com

Elizabeth Donley, Editor
John Donley, Editor

Profiles 20 software packages for estimating the cost of environmental projects, including detailed product descriptions, tables comparing system features, and contact information.
Cost: $195.00
162 Pages
ISBN: 1-891682-05-9
Founded in 1996
Printed in on matte stock

8248 **Environmental Health & Safety Dictionary**
ABS Group
PO Box 846304
Dallas, TX 75284-6304

FAX 301-921-0264

Lydia Simpson, Manager

8249 **Environmental Law Handbook**
ABS Group
PO Box 846304
Dallas, TX 75284-6304

FAX 301-921-0264

8250 **Environmental Protection Agency Headquarters Telephone Directory**
Environmental Protection Agency
1200 Pennsylvania Avenue NW
Pittsburgh, PA 15250-7954

412-442-4000
Fax: 202-512-2250
Home Page:
www.epa.gov/customerservice/phonebook

Ken Bowman, Executive Director

Directory of services and supplies to the industry.
Cost: $15.00
400 Pages

8251 **Environmental Resource Handbook**
Grey House Publishing
4919 Route 22
PO Box 56
Amenia, NY 12501

518-789-8700
800-562-2139
Fax: 845-373-6390
E-Mail: books@greyhouse.com
Home Page: www.greyhouse.com
Social Media: Facebook, Twitter

Leslie Mackenzie, Publisher
Richard Gottlieb, Editor

The most up-to-date and comprehensive source for Environmental Resources and Statistics. Included is contact information for resource listings in addition to statistics and rankings on hundreds of important topics such as recycling, air and water quality, climate, toxic chemicals and more.
Cost: $155.00
1200 Pages
ISBN: 1-592371-95-7
Founded in 1981

8252 **Environmental Resource Handbook - Online Database**
Grey House Publishing
4919 Route 22
PO Box 56
Amenia, NY 12501

518-789-8700
800-562-2139
Fax: 845-373-6390
E-Mail: gold@greyhouse.com
Home Page: http://gold.greyhouse.com
Social Media: Facebook, Twitter

Leslie Mackenzie, Publisher
Richard Gottlieb, Editor

With a subscription to Environmental Resource Handbook - Online Database, you'll have immediate access to over 7,000 associations, organizations & government agencies, awards & honors, conferences & trade shows, foundations & charities, national parks & wildlife refuges, research centers & educational programs, legal resources and much more.
Founded in 1981

8253 **Environmental Statutes**
Government Institutes
4 Research Place
Suite 200
Rockville, MD 20850-3226

301-921-2323
Fax: 301-921-0264
Home Page: www.govinst.com

Two-volume set. Complete and exact text of the statues and amendments made by Congress concerning environmental law.
Cost: $125.00
1678 Pages
Frequency: Paperback
ISBN: 0-865879-33-8

8254 **Fibre Market News: Paper Recycling Markets Directory**
Recycling Media Group GIE Publishers

4012 Bridge Avenue
Cleveland, OH 44113-3320

216-961-4130
800-456-0707
Fax: 216-961-0364
Home Page: www.giemedia.com

Dan Moreland, Executive Vice President

A list of over 2,000 dealers, brokers, packers and graders of paper stock in the United States and Canada.
Cost: $28.00
Frequency: Annual
Circulation: 3,000

8255 Floodplain Management: State & Local Programs
Association of State Floodplain Managers
2809 Fish Hatchery Rd
Suite 204
Fitchburg, WI 53713-5020

608-274-0123
Fax: 608-274-0696
E-Mail: memberhelp@floods.org
Home Page: www.floods.org

Larry A Larson, Executive Director
Alison Stierli, Member Services Coordinator
Anita Larson, Member Services
Mark Riebau, Project Manager
Diane Brown, Manager

The most comprehensive source assembled to date, this report summarizes and analyzes various state and local programs and activities.
Cost: $25.00

8256 Geothermal Progress Monitor
Office of Geothermal Technologies EE-12
1000 Independence Avenue SW
Washington, DC 20585-0001

202-586-1361
Fax: 202-586-8185

Allan J Jelacic, Director

Lists of operating, planned and under construction geothermal electric generating plants; geothermal articles and publications; federal and state government employees active in geothermal energy development.
Frequency: Annual

8257 Grey House Safety & Security Directory
Grey House Publishing
4919 Route 22
PO Box 56
Amenia, NY 12501

518-789-8700
800-562-2139
Fax: 845-373-6390
E-Mail: books@greyhouse.com
Home Page: www.greyhouse.com
Social Media: Facebook, Twitter

Leslie Mackenzie, Publisher
Richard Gottlieb, Editor
Kristen Thatcher, Production Manager

Comprehensive guide to the safety and security industry, including articles, checklists, OSHA regulations and product listings. Focuses on creating and maintaing a safe and secure enviroment, and dealing specifically with hazardous materials, noise and vibration, workplace preparation and maintenance, electrical and lighting safety, fire and rescue and more.
Cost: $165.00
1600 Pages
ISBN: 1-592373-75-5
Founded in 1981

8258 Handling Dyes Safely - A Guide for the Protection of Workers Handling Dyes
ETAD North America
1850 M St NW
Suite 700
Washington, DC 20036-5810

202-721-4100
Fax: 202-296-8120
Home Page: www.etad.com

Jill Aker, President

8259 Hazardous Materials Guide
JJ Keller
PO Box 368
Neenah, WI 54957-0368

920-722-2848
800-327-6868
Fax: 800-727-7516
E-Mail: contactus@jjkeller.com
Home Page: www.jjkeller.com

Webb Shaw, Editor

A complete reference guide of hazardous materials regulations.

8260 Hazardous Materials Information Resource System
One Church Street
Suite 200
Rockville, MD 20850

301-577-1842
Fax: 301-738-2330

CAPT Michael J. Macinski, Commanding Officer
CAPT Robert W. Farr, Executive Officer
HMCM Robert E. Searles, II, Command Master Chief

The Hazardous Materials Information Resource System is a Department of Defense (DOD) automated system developed and maintained by the Defense Logistics Agency. HMIRS is the central repository for Material Safety Data Sheets (MSDS) for the United States Government military services and civil agencies.

8261 Hazardous Waste Guide
JJ Keller
PO Box 368
Neenah, WI 54957-0368

920-722-2848
800-327-6868
Fax: 800-727-7516
E-Mail: contactus@jjkeller.com
Home Page: www.jjkeller.com

Webb Shaw, Editor

Contains word-for-word regulations.

8262 Hydro Review: Industry Sourcebook Issue
HCI Publications
410 Archibald St
Kansas City, MO 64111-3288

816-931-1311
Fax: 816-931-2015
E-Mail: hci@aol.com
Home Page: www.hcipub.com

Leslie Eden, President

List of over 800 manufacturers and suppliers of products and services to the hydroelectric industry in the US and Canada.
Cost: $20.00
180 Pages
Frequency: Annual December
Circulation: 5000
Founded in 1984
Printed in 4 colors on glossy stock

8263 IES Membership Directory
International Ecotourism Society
733 15th Street NW
Suite 1000
Washington, DC 20005

202-547-9203
Fax: 202-387-7915
Home Page: www.ecotourism.org

Martha Honey, Executive Director
Amos Bien, Director International Programs
Neal Inamdar, Director Finance/Administration
Frequency: Annual

8264 International Directory of Human Ecologists
Society for Human Ecology
College of the Atlantic
105 Eden Street
Bar Harbor, ME 04609-0180

207-288-5015
Fax: 207 288 3780
E-Mail: carter@ecology.coa.edu
Home Page: www.societyforhumanecology.org

Barbara Carter, Assistant to Executive Director
Frequency: Irregular

8265 LEXIS Environmental Law Library
Mead Data Central
9443 Springboro Pike
Dayton, OH 45401

888-223-6337
Fax: 518-487-3584
Home Page: www.lexis-nexis.com

Andrew Prozes, CEO
Rebecca Schmitt, Chief Financial Officer

This database contains decisions related to environmental law from the Supreme Court and other legislative bodies.
Frequency: Full-text

8266 NIWR Member Directory
National Institutes for Water Resources
47 Harkness Road
Pelham, MA 10002

413-253-5686
Fax: 413-253-1309
E-Mail: godfrey@tei.umass.edu
Home Page: snr.unl.edu/NIWR

Paul Joseph Godfrey, PhD, Executive Director

8267 National Directory of Conservation Land Trusts
Land Trust Alliance
1319 F Street NW
Suite 501
Washington, DC 20004-1106

202-638-4725
Fax: 202-638-4730
E-Mail: info@lta.org
Home Page: www.lta.org

More than 1,200 nonprofit land conservation organizations at the local and regional levels are profiled.
Cost: $12.00
210 Pages
Frequency: Biennial

8268 National Environmental Data Referral Service
US National Environmental Data Referral Service
1825 Connecticut Avenue NW
Washington, DC 20235-0003

202-606-4089

More than 22,200 data resources that have available data on climatology and meteorology, ecology and pollution, geography, geophysics and geology, hydrology and limnology, oceanography and transmissions from remote sensing satellites.
Frequency: Quarterly

8269 **National Organic Directory**
Community Alliance with Family Farmers
PO Box 363
Davis, CA 95617-0363
530-756-8518
800-892-3832
Fax: 530-756-7857
E-Mail: info@caff.org
Home Page: www.caff.org
Wriiten for all sectors of the booming organic food and fiber industry. Offers international listing with full contact information and extensive, cross-referenced index - Also provides regulatory updates, essays by industry leaders and other ressources.
Cost: $47.95
324 Pages
Frequency: Annual
Circulation: 2,500
ISBN: 1-891894-04-8
Founded in 1983

8270 **POWER**
US Department of Energy
Forrestal Building
5H - 021
Washington, DC 20585-0001
202-646-5095
Fax: 202-586-1605
Home Page: www.eren.doe.gov
Timothy Unruh, Program Manager
A large database offersing information on all forms of energy, including fossil, nuclear, solar, geothermal and electrical.

8271 **Pollution Abstracts**
Cambridge Scientific Abstracts
7200 Wisconsin Ave
Suite 601
Bethesda, MD 20814-4890
301-961-6700
Fax: 301-961-6790
E-Mail: service@csa.com
Home Page: www.csa.com
Andrew M Snyder, President
Ted Caris, Publisher
Evelyn Beck, Editor
Mark Furneaux, VP Marketing
Angela Hitti, Production Manager
This database offers information on environmental pollution research and related engineering studies.
Cost: $985.00
Frequency: Monthly

8272 **Public Citizen Organizations**
Public Citizen
215 Pennsylvania Ave SE
Suite 3
Washington, DC 20003-1188
202-544-4985
Fax: 202-547-7392
E-Mail: cmep@citizen.org
Bob Ritter, Manager
Patricia Lovera, Organizer
Ronald Taylor, Manager
We provide many publications regarding nuclear safety, nuclear waste, water, food, and energy deregulation.
Frequency: Annual

8273 **RIFM/FEMA Fragrance and Flavor Database**
Flavor & Extract Manufacturers Association
1620 I Street NW
Suite 925
Washington, DC 20006
202-293-5800
Fax: 202-462-8998
Home Page: www.femaflavor.org
Social Media: YouTube, RSS Feed
Ed R. Hays, Ph.D., President
George C. Robinson, III, President Elect
Mark Scott, Treasurer
Arthur Schick, VP & Secretary
John Cox, Executive Director
The Database currently contains over 50,000 references and more than 103,000 human health and environmental studies.
Frequency: Annual
Founded in 1909

8274 **Recycling Today: Recycling Products & Services Buyers Guide**
Recycling Today GIE Publishers
4012 Bridge Avenue
Cleveland, OH 44113-3320
216-961-4130
Fax: 216-961-0364
Home Page: http://www.recyclingtoday.com
Richard Foster, President
James Keefe, Publisher
Mark Phillips, Editor
Rosalie Slusher, Circulation Director
Jami Childs, Production Manager
Directory of services and supplies to the industry.
Cost: $19.95
Frequency: Annual
Circulation: 22,000

8275 **Using Multiobjective Management to Reduce Flood Losses in Your Watershed**
Association of State Floodplain Managers
2809 Fish Hatchery Rd
Suite 204
Fitchburg, WI 53713-5020
608-274-0123
Fax: 608-274-0696
E-Mail: memberhelp@floods.org
Home Page: www.floods.org
Larry A Larson, Executive Director
Alison Stierli, Manager
Diane Brown, Manager
Introduction to multiobjective management and planning process that helps a community select suitable flood loss reduction measures.
Cost: $15.00

8276 **Waste Manifest Software Report**
Donley Technology
PO Box 152
Colonial Beach, VA 22443-0152
804-224-9427
800-201-1595
Fax: 804-224-7958
E-Mail: donleytech@donleytech.com
Home Page: www.donleytech.com
Elizabeth Donley, Editor
Profiles 30 software packages for solid and hazardous waste management, including detailed product descriptions, tables comparing system features, and contact information.
Cost: $97.50
118 Pages
ISBN: 1-891682-01-6
Founded in 1996
Printed in on matte stock

8277 **Water Environment and Technology Buyers Guide/Yearbook**
Water Environment Federation
601 Wythe St
Alexandria, VA 22314-1994
703-684-2400
800-666-0206
Fax: 703-684-2492
E-Mail: confinfo@wef.org
Home Page: www.wef.org
Bill Bertera, Executive Director
Offers listings of the Water Environment Federation and consultant members.
Cost: $28.00
Frequency: Annual
ISSN: 1044-9943

8278 **Weather America**
Grey House Publishing
4919 Route 22
PO Box 56
Amenia, NY 12501
518-789-8700
800-562-2139
Fax: 845-373-6390
E-Mail: books@greyhouse.com
Home Page: www.greyhouse.com
Social Media: Facebook, Twitter
Leslie Mackenzie, Publisher
Richard Gottlieb, Editor
Provides extensive climatological data for over 4,000 places throughout the United States - states, counties, cities, and towns. Included are rankings across the US for precipitation, snowfall, fog, humidity, wind speed and more.
Cost: $175.00
2020 Pages
ISBN: 1-891482-29-7
Founded in 1981

8279 **Who's Who in Training**
National Environmental, Safety and Health Training
5320 N 16th Street
Suite 114
Phoenix, AZ 85016-3241
602-956-6099
Fax: 602-956-6399
E-Mail: info@neshta.org
Home Page: www.neshta.org
Charles L Richardson, Executive Director
Joan J Jennings, Manager Association Services
Suzanne Lanctot, Manager Certification/Membership
Frequency: Annual

8280 **Wilderness Preservation: A Reference Handbook**
ABC-CLIO
PO Box 1911
Santa Barbara, CA 93116-1911
805-705-9339
Offers a list of agencies and organizations concerned with wilderness preservation.

8281 **World Directory of Environmental Organizations**
California Institute of Public Affairs
PO Box 189040
Sacramento, CA 95818-9040
916-442-2472
Fax: 916-442-2478
Home Page: www.interenvironment.org
Over 2,500 governmental, intergovernmental and United Nations organizations are covered.
Cost: $47.00
232 Pages

8282 **Your Resource Guide to Environmental Organizations**
Smiling Dolphin Press
4 Segura
Irvine, CA 92612-1726
Information is offered, in three separate sections, on non-governmental organizations, federal agencies and state agencies that address

environmental concerns.
Cost: $15.95
514 Pages

Industry Web Sites

8283 **http://gold.greyhouse.com**
G.O.L.D Grey House OnLine Databases
Grey House Publishing's online database platform, GOLD, offers Quick Search, Keyword Search and Expert Search for most business sectors including environment and conservation markets. The GOLD platform makes finding the information you need quick and easy - whether you're a novice searcher or an experienced database user. All of Grey House's directory products are available for subscription on the GOLD platform.

8284 **www.adirondackcouncil.org**
Adirondack Council
Research, education and advocacy to protect the natural character and communities of the Adirondack Park. Also publishes an annual State of Park Report and quarterly newsletters.

8285 **www.aeecenter.org**
Association of Energy Engineers
Source of information on the field of energy efficiency, utility deregulation, plant engineering, facility management and environmental compliance. Membership includes more than 8,000 professionals and certification programs. Offers seminars, conferences, job listings and certification programs.

8286 **www.aga.org**
American Gas Association
Association for the natural gas industry.

8287 **www.america-the-beautiful-fund.org**
America the Beautiful Fund
Groups and private citizens that improve the quality of the environment.

8288 **www.apwa.net**
American Public Works Association
The American Public Works Association is an international educational and professional association of public agencies, private sector companies, and individuals dedicated to providing high quality public works goods and services. APWA provides a forum in which public works professionals competency, increase the performance of their agencies and companies, and bring important public works-related topics to public attention in local, state, and federal areas. Mailing list for members only.

8289 **www.asbpa.org**
American Shore and Beach Preservation Association
Federal, state and local government agencies and individuals interested in conservation, development and restoration of beaches and shorefronts.

8290 **www.ases.org**
American Solar Energy Society
Individuals and professionals working in the field of solar energy and conservation.

8291 **www.asfe.org**
ASFE
Not-for-profit trade association. Helps geoprofessional, environmental and civil engineering firms profit through professionalism.

8292 **www.audbon.org**
National Audubon Society
Conserves and restores natural ecosystems, focusing on birds, other wildlife, and thier habitats for the benefit of humanity and the earth's biological diversity.

8293 **www.bisoncentral.com**
National Bison Association
The National Bison Association was formed to promote the production, marketing, and preservation of bison.

8294 **www.blr.com**
Business & Legal Reports
Provides essential tools for safety and environmental compliance and training needs

8295 **www.cbemw.org**
Citizens for a Better Environment
For citizens concerned with environmental protection. Maintains library.

8296 **www.cnie.org/nle**
National Library for the Environment
Environment-related information: daily environment and congressional news, upcoming conferences, education resources and congressional research reports.

8297 **www.conservation.state.mo.us**
Department of Conservation
Focuses on conservation and the importance of protecting the environment.

8298 **www.conservationfund.org**
Conservation Fund
Works with private and public agencies and organizations to protect wildlife habitats, historic sites and parks.

8299 **www.conservationtreaty.org**
Conservation Treaty Support Fund
Promotes awareness, understanding and support of conservation treaties and their goals.

8300 **www.construction.com**
McGraw-Hill Construction
McGraw-Hill Construction (MHC), part of The McGraw-Hill Companies, connects people and projects across the design and construction industry, serving owners, architects, engineers, general contractors, subcontractors, building product manufacturers, suppliers, dealers, distributors and adjacent markets.

8301 **www.earthisland.org/ei**
Earth Island Institute
Seeks to prevent destruction of environment and sponsors fund drives and activist projects to protect wildlife.

8302 **www.earthsite.org**
Earth Society Foundation
News of interest in environmental and sociological issues. Purpose is to promote Earth Day and the Earth Trustee agenda.

8303 **www.eia-usa.org**
Environmental Information Association
Nonprofit organization dedicated to providing environmental information to individuals, members and the industry. Disseminates information on the abatement of asbestos and lead-based paint, indoor air quality, safety and health issues, analytical issues and environmental site assessments.

8304 **www.epa.gov**
US Environmental Protection Agency

8305 **www.ethenolrfa.org**
Renewable Fuels Association
Members are companies and individuals involved in the production and use of ethanol.

8306 **www.femaflavor.org**
Flavor & Extract Manufacturers Assn of the US
1620 I Street NW
Suite 925
Washington, DC 210006

202-293-5800
Fax: 202-463-8998

Ed R. Hayes, President
George C. Robinson III, President Elect
Mark Scott, Treasurer
Arthur Schick, Vice President & Secretary
FEMA is comprised of flavor manufacturers, flavor users, flavor ingredient suppliers, and others with an interest in the U.S. flavor industry. FEMA works with legislators and regulators to assure that the needs of members and consuemr are continuously addressed and is committed to assuring a substantial supply of safe flavoring substances.

8307 **www.floods.org**
Association of State Floodplain Managers
Promotes common interest in flood damage abatement, supports environmental protection for floodplain areas, provides education on floodplain management practices and policy, and urges incorporating multi-objective management, approaches to solve local flooding problems.

8308 **www.greyhouse.com**
Grey House Publishing
Authoritative reference directories for most business sectors including environment and conservation markets. Users can search the online databases with varied search criteria allowing for custom searches by product category, geographic area, sales volume, keyword, subject and more. Full Grey House catalog and online ordering also available.

8309 **www.ia-usa.org**
National BioEnergy Industries Association

8310 **www.iaee.org**
International Association for Energy Economics
Association for those involved in energy economics including publications, consultants, energy database software.

8311 **www.iaia.org**
International Association for Impact Assessment
IAIA provides a forum for the exchange of the ideas and experiences to stimulate innovation in assessing, managing and mitigating the consequences of development.

8312 **www.iwla.org**
Isaak Walton League
Conducts research and education on river ecosystems and healthy fisheries.

8313 **www.joincca.org**
Coastal Conservation Association
Seeks to advance protection and conservation of all marine life. Conducts seminars and bestows awards.

8314 **www.lib.duke.edu/forest/**
Forest History Society
Non-profit educational institution that explores the history of the environment, forestry, and conservation.

8315 **www.members.aol.com/rccouncil**
Rachael Carson Council
Seeks to promote awareness of the problems of environmental contamination and by serving as

an information clearing house on chemical contaminates, especially pesticides.

8316 **www.mtsociety.org**
Marine Technology Society

Addresses coastal zone management, marine mineral and energy resources, marine environmental protection, and ocean engineering issues.

8317 **www.nacdnet.org**
National Association of Conservation Districts

Association for those interested in the environment.

8318 **www.naem.org**
National Association for Environmental Management

Dedicated to advancing the profession of environmental management and supports the professional corporate and facility environmental manager.

8319 **www.nalms.org**
North American Lake Management Society

Members are academics, lake managers and others interested in furthering the understanding of lake ecology.

8320 **www.napcor.com**
National Association for Pet Container Resources

National trade association which promotes the recycling of food containers made from PET plastic (containers with recycle code #1).

8321 **www.nationalwoodlands.org**
National Woodland Owners Association

Provides timely information about forestry and forest practices with news from washington,Dc and state capitals. written for non-industrial land owners. Includes state landowner association news.

8322 **www.ncat.org**
National Center for Appropriate Technology

A resource center for information and expertise on methods of promoting conservation and energy self sufficiency. The term, appropriate technology, is defined as a small-scale, environmentally sound, low-cost, locally based approach to problems with an emphasis on self help.

8323 **www.neha.org**
National Environmental Health Association

Association for suppliers of environmental educational materials.

8324 **www.noaa.gov**
National Oceanic and Atmospheric Administration

National weather forecasts, statistics, searchable databases, agency directory and links to related agencies and sites.

8325 **www.pollutiononline.com**
Pollution Online

For vendors and professionals in pollution equipment and control industries. News, product information, links to related web sites and business information.

8326 **www.purezone.com**
PureZone

Devoted to indoor air quality. Discussion forum moderated by industry experts on topics such as sensors and transducers technology.

8327 **www.recycle-steel.srs**
Steel Recycling Institute

Promotes steel recycling and works to forge a coalition of steelmakers, can manufacturers, legislators, government officials, solid waste managers, business and consumer groups.

8328 **www.rnrf.org**
Renewable Natural Resources Foundation

A consortium of professional and scientific societies whose members are concerned with the advancement of research, education, scientific practice and policy formulation for the conservation, replenishment and use of the earth's renewable natural resources.

8329 **www.sca-inc.org**
Student Conservation Association

8330 **www.socma.com**
Silicone Health Council

Coordinates health, environmental and safety programs. Conveys scientifically sound information about silicones.

8331 **www.sweets.construction.com**
McGraw Hill Construction

In depth product information that lets you find, compare, select, specify and make purchase decisions in the industrial product marketplace.

8332 **www.techknow.org**
TechKnow

Lists environmentally friendly remediation and ozone-depleting substance management resources.

8333 **www.terrassa.pnl.gov:2080/hydrology**
Hydrology Web

Lists of related internet resource lists.

8334 **www.usace.army.mil**
US Army Corps of Engineers

Information on flood control, environmental protection, disaster response, military construction and support of others through the sharing of engineering expertise with other agencies, state and local governments, academia and foreign nations.

8335 **www.woodlandowners.org**
National Woodland Owners Association

Provides timely information about forestry and forest practices with news from washington,Dc and state capitals. written for non-industrial land owners. Includes state landowner association news.

8336 **www.wqa.org**
Water Quality Association

An international nonprofit trade association representing retail/dealers and manufacturer/suppliers in the point of use/entry water quality improvement industry. Membership benefits and services include technical and scientific information, educational seminars and home correspondence course books, professional certification and discount services.

Associations

8337 **AMC Institute**
100 North 20th Street
4th Floor
Philadelphia, PA 19103
215-564-3484
Fax: 215-963-9785
E-Mail: info@amcinstitute.org
Home Page: www.amcinstitute.org

Andrew Bower, MBA, Executive Director
Jennifer Miller, Associate Director
Mike Mirabella, Administrative Director

AMCs are professional service firms that provide executive, administrative, and financial management; strategic counsel planning; membership development; public affairs and lobbying, education and professional development; statistical research; meetings management; and marketing and communication services.
175 Members
Founded in 2006

8338 **American Business Media**
375 Third Avenue
7th Floor
New York, NY 10017-5704
212-661-6360
Fax: 212-370-0736
E-Mail: info@abmmail.com
Home Page: www.americanbusinessmedia.com

Clark Pettit, President/CEO
Michael Burns, VP, Events
Todd Hittle, Chief Financial Officer
Claudia Flowers, VP, Recruitment & Retention
Marie Griffin, VP, Content & Programming

An association for business-to-business information providers, including producers of print publications, Web sites, trade shows and other media.
200+ Members
Founded in 1906

8339 **American Society of Association Executives**
1575 I St NW
Washington, DC 20005-1103
202-371-0940
888-950-2723
Flickr
Fax: 202-371-8315
E-Mail: service@asaenet.org
Home Page: www.asaenet.org
Social Media: Facebook, Twitter, LinkedIn

Peter J O'Neil, CAE, Chairman
Joseph M McGuire, CAE, Chairman-Elect
Arlene A Pietranton, CAE, Secretary-Treasurer
Karen L Hackett, FACHE, CAE, Immediate Past Chairman

ASAE is the premier source of learning, knowledge and future-oriented research for the association and nonprofit profession, and provides resources, education, ideas and advocacy to enhance the power and performance of the association and nonprofit community.
21M Members
Founded in 1920

8340 **Association of Collegiate Conference and Special Events**
Colorado State University
8037 Campus Delivery
Fort Collins, CO 80523-8037
877-502-2233
Fax: 970-449-4965
E-Mail: acced@colostate.edu
Home Page: www.acced-i.colostate.edu

Deborah Blom, Executive Director
Monica Nesbit Schultz, Marketing/Sales Manager
Lori Everhart, Electronic Communications

Members are college and university conference and special events directors, professionals and others who design, market and coordinate conferences and special events.
1400 Members
Founded in 1980

8341 **Association of International Meeting Planners**
2547 Monroe Street
Dearborn, MI 48124-3013
313-563-0360
Fax: 972-702-3070

Meeting planners.
40 Members
Founded in 1986

8342 **Association of Science-Technology Centers**
1025 Vermont Ave NW
Suite 500
Washington, DC 20005-6310
202-783-7200
Fax: 202-783-7207
E-Mail: info@astc.org
Home Page: www.astc.org

Bonnie Van Dorn, Executive Director
Lesley Lewis, President
Wit Ostrenko, Secretary/Treasurer
William Booth, Member at Large

Organization of science centers and museums dedicated to futhering the public understanding of science among increasingly diverse audiences. Encourges excellence and innovation in informal science learning by serving and linking its members worldwide and advancing their common goals.
550 Members
Founded in 1973

8343 **CEMA**
1512 Weiskopf Loop
Round Rock, TX 78664-6128
512-310-8330
Fax: 510-682-0555
E-Mail: ebrunke@cemaonline.com
Home Page: www.cemaonline.com

Erika Brunke, Executive Director
Olga Rosenbrook, Member Services
Alexia Henrie, Secretary
Trinette R Cunningham, Executive Staff

Professionals from the event, trade show and marketing communications industry. Striving to be the definitive resource for event marketing professionals in the information technology industry.
250 Members
Founded in 1990

8344 **Center for Exhibition Industry Research**
12700 Park Central Dr
Suite 750
Dallas, TX 75251-1526
972-687-9230
Fax: 972-458-8119
E-Mail: info@ceir.com
Home Page: www.iaee.com

Steven Hacker, President
David A Korse, Secretary/Treasurer
Thomas Ackert, Executive Director

The Center for Exhibition Industry Research is an apolitical, nonprofit orgnization with the dual mission of producing research that supports the unique features and value of exhibitors; then, using that research and other tools to promote the image and growth of the exhibition industry

8345 **Connected International Meeting**
9200 Bayard Place
Fairfax, VA 22032
512-684-0889
Fax: 267-390-5193
E-Mail: susan2@cimpa.org
Home Page: www.cimpa.org

Andrea Sigler, President/CEO

Members are conference and convention planners with a certificate in convention management. Specializes in planning meetings events, incentives, using the internet.
8000 Members
Founded in 1982

8346 **Convention Industry Council**
1620 Eye St NW
Suite 615
Washington, DC 20006
202-429-8634
877-429-8634
Fax: 571-527-3105
Home Page: www.conventionindustry.org

Thomas M Mobley Jr, Chair
John H Graham, Vice Chair
Mary Power, President/CEO
Amy Hawthorne, Project Coordinator

An organization that represents individuals as well as 15,000 firms and properties involved in the meetings, conventions and exhibitions industries.
98000 Members
Founded in 1949

8347 **Convention Liaison Council**
10200 W 44th Avenue
Suite 310
Wheat Ridge, CO 80033-2840
303-420-2902
Fax: 303-422-8894
E-Mail: clc@resourcenter.com
Home Page: www.clc.org

Francine Butler, Executive VP

Members are associations which are directly involved in the convention, exposition, trade show and meeting industry.

8348 **Display Distributors Association**
Modern Display
424 S 700 E
Salt Lake City, UT 84102-2864
801-355-7427
Fax: 801-521-3040

Members are distributors of display equipment.
16 Members
Founded in 1950

8349 **Event Service Professionals Association**
191 Clarksville Road
Princeton Junction, NJ 08550
609-799-3712
Fax: 609-799-7032
E-Mail: info@espaonline.org
Home Page: www.acomonline.org
Social Media: Facebook, Twitter, LinkedIn

Lynn McCullough, Executive Director
Diane Galante, Manager, Member Service/Mtg Planner
Elizabeth Roe, Association Coordinator
Meghan Higgins, Public Relations Manager

Dedicated to elevating the event and convention service profession and to preparing members, through education and networking, for their pivotal role in innovating and successful event execution.
400 Members
Founded in 1988

8350 **Exhibit Designers & Producers Association**
10 Norden Place
Norwalk, CT 06855

203-852-5698
Fax: 203-854-6735
E-Mail: kwilson@edpa.com
Home Page: www.edpa.com

Dan Cantor, President
John Rose, VP, Finance & Administration
Cam Stevens, VP, Education
Justin Hersh, VP, Member Communications
Jeff Provost, Executive Director

Internationally recognized, national trade association with corporate members from 18 countries that are engaged in the design, manufacture, transport, installation and service of displays and exhibits primarily for the trade show industry. EDPA's purpose is to champion the prosperity of member businesses.
400+ Members
Founded in 1956

8351 **Exhibit and Event Marketers Association**
2214 NW 5th St.
Bend, OR 97701

541-317-8768
Fax: 541-317-8749
E-Mail: tsea@tsea.org
Home Page: www.tsea.org

Amanda Helgemoe, President
Michael Mulry, Vice President
Glenda Brundgardt, Treasurer
Chris Griffin, Secretary
Jim Wurm, Executive Director

Supports marketing and management professionals.

8352 **Exposition Service Contractors Association**
2340 E Trinity Mills Road
Suite 100
Carrollton, TX 75006

469-574-0698
877-792-3722
Fax: 469-574-0697
Home Page: www.esca.org

Aaron Bludworth, President
Tim McGill, Secretary

Annual guide to exposition service is distributed annually and lists safety regulations and building rules in major US convention centers.
120 Members
Founded in 1970

8353 **Healthcare Convention & Exhibitors Association**
1100 Johnson Ferry Rd NE
Suite 300
Atlanta, GA 30342-1733

404-252-3663
Fax: 404-252-0774
E-Mail: hcea@kellencompany.com
Home Page: www.hcea.org
Social Media: Facebook, Twitter, LinkedIn

Eric Allen, Executive Vice President
Jackie Beaulieu, Associate Director

Trade association of organizations involved in health care exhibiting or providing services to health care conventions, exhibitions, and/or meetings.
600 Members
Founded in 1930

8354 **Hospitality Sales & Marketing Association International**
1760 Old Meadow Road
Suite 500
McLean, VA 22102

703-506-3280
Fax: 703-506-3266
E-Mail: info@hsmai.org
Home Page: www.hsmai.org

Fran Brasseux, Executive VP
Kathleen Tindell, Program Director

The hospitality industry's source for knowledge, community, and recognition for leaders committed to professional development, sales growth, revenue optimization, marketing and branding.
7000 Members
Founded in 1927

8355 **International Association for Exhibition Management**
811 LBJ Freeway
Suite 750
Dallas, TX 75251-1313

972-458-8002
Fax: 972-458-8119
E-Mail: iaem@iaem.org
Home Page: www.iaem.org

Steven G Hacker, CAE, President
Cathy Breden, CAE, SVP
Susan Brower, Director Marketing/Communications

Members are managers of shows, exhibits and expositions; associate members are industry suppliers.
3500 Members
Founded in 1928

8356 **International Association for Modular Exhibitry**
155 W Street
Suite 3
Wilmington, MA 01887-3064

978-988-1200

Irving Sacks, Executive Director

Members are companies that promote the use of modular exhibits for trade shows and museums.
47 Members
Founded in 1987

8357 **International Association of Assembly Management**
635 Fritz Dr
Suite 100
Coppell, TX 75019-4462

972-906-7441
800-935-4226
Fax: 972-906-7418
E-Mail: mike.meyers@iaam.org
Home Page: www.iaam.org

Dexter King, Executive Director
Robyn Williams, First Vice President

Members are managers of auditoriums, arenas, convention centers, stadiums and performing arts centers.
400 Members
Founded in 1924

8358 **International Association of Conference Centers**
243 N Lindbergh Boulevard
Saint Louis, MO 63141

314-993-8575
Fax: 314-993-8919
E-Mail: info@iacconline.org
Home Page: www.iaccnorthamerica.org
Social Media: Facebook, Twitter, LinkedIn

Tom Bolman, Executive VP
James Mahon, Director Marketing
Jerry White, Director of Education

Facilities-based organization which advances the understanding and awareness of conference centers as distinct within the training, education, hospitality and travel fields.
377 Members
Founded in 1981

8359 **International Association of Fairs and Expositions**
3043 E Cairo
PO Box 985
Springfield, MO 65802

417-862-5771
800-516-0313
Fax: 417-862-0156
E-Mail: iafe@fairsandexpos.com
Home Page: www.fairsandexpos.com

Jim Tucker, President
Steve Siever, Director

The International Association of Fairs and Expositions (IAFE) is a voluntary, non-profit corporation whose members provide services and products that promote the overall development and improvement of fairs, shows, expositions, and allied fields.
Founded in 1885

8360 **International Festivals and Events Association**
2603 W Eastover Ter
Boise, ID 83706-2800

208-433-0950
Fax: 208-433-9812
E-Mail: nia@ifea.com
Home Page: www.ifea.com

Steven Schmader, President
Nia Forster, VP/Marketing

A voluntary association of events, event producers, event suppliers, and related professionals and organizations whose common purpose is the production and presentation of festivals, events, and civic and private celebrations.
2000 Members
Founded in 1956

8361 **International Laser Display Association**
7062 Edgeworth Drive
Orlando, FL 32819

407-797-7654
Fax: 503-344-3770
E-Mail: president@laserist.org
Home Page: www.laserist.org

Tim Walsh, President
Patrick Murphy, Executive Director

ILDA members are individuals involved in the laser entertainment and display industry.
Founded in 1986

8362 **International Special Events Society**
401 N Michigan Avenue
Chicago, IL 60611-4267

312-321-6853
800-688-4737
Fax: 312-673-6953
E-Mail: info@ises.com
Home Page: www.ises.com

Kevin Hacke, Executive Director
Kristin Prine, Operations Director
Cassie Lapekas, Operations Coordinator
Kristin Kindsvater, Membership Coordinator

Professionals in over a dozen countries representing special event producers, caterers, decorators, florists, destination management companies, rental companies, special effects

experts, tent suppliers, audio-visual technicians, party and convention coordinators, ballon artists, educators, journalists, hotel sales managers, specialty entertainers, convention center managers and more.
4000 Members
Founded in 1987

8363 Meeting Professionals International
3030 LBJ Fwy
Suite 1700
Dallas, TX 75234-2759

972-702-3000
Fax: 972-702-3070
E-Mail: feedback@mpiweb.org
Home Page: www.mpiweb.org

Bruce Mac Millan, President

MPI members manage meetings and related activities for association, corporations, and educational institutions, or provide goods and services to the meetings industry.
1900 Members
Founded in 1972

8364 National Association for Campus Activities
13 Harbison Way
Columbia, SC 29212

803-732-6222
800-845-2338
Fax: 803-749-1047
E-Mail: info@naca.org
Home Page: www.naca.org

Steve Westbrook, Director Student Affairs
Alan Davis, Executive Director
Gordon Schell, Manager/Member Services
Dawn Thomas, Director/Educational/Events
Erin Wilson, Manager Communications

Largest collegiate organization for campus activities. Purpose is to assist in marketing entertainment services to educational institutions and providing student leadership development programs and services.
1100 Members
Founded in 1960

8365 National Association of Agricultural Fair Agencies
MI State Department of Agriculture
PO Box 30017
Lansing, MI 48909

517-373-9766
Fax: 517-373-9146

Carol Carlson, Secretary/Treasurer

U.S. and Canadian representatives of state/provincial agencies that are responsible for the support of education and agricultural fairs.
Founded in 1966

8366 National Association of Consumer Shows
147 Se 102nd Ave
Portland, OR 97216-2703

503-253-0832
800-728-6227
Fax: 503-253-9172
E-Mail: info@publicshows.com
Home Page: www.publicshows.com

Mike Fisher, Manager
Nelson Ligori, Director

Nonprofit organization dedicated to furthering the interests of consumer show producers and suppliers.
265 Members
Founded in 1987

8367 National Association of Display Industries
4651 Sheridan Street
Suite 200
Hollywood, FL 33021

954-893-7300
Fax: 954-893-7500
E-Mail: nadi@nadi-global.com
Home Page: www.nadi-global.com

Klein Merriman, Executive Director
Tracy Dillon, Director Communications

Sponsors seminars and annual contests. Conducts research programs and maintains placement services.
400 Members
Founded in 1937

8368 National Association of Professional Organizers
15000 Commerce Parkway
Suite C
Mount Laurel, NJ 08054-2212

847-375-4746
Fax: 856-439-0525
E-Mail: hq@napo.net
Home Page: www.napo.net

Standolyn Robertson, President
Sandy Stelter, Secretary

Members are time, productivity and organization management consultants.
1800 Members
Founded in 1985

8369 National Catholic Educational Exhibitors
2621 Dryden Road
Suite 300
Dayton, OH 45439

937-293-1415
888-555-8512
Fax: 937-293-1310
E-Mail: cynpleg@aol.com
Home Page: www.nceeonline.org

Peter Li, Executive Director

A group for companies that provide products or services for Catholoc education.
500 Members
Founded in 1950

8370 National Coalition of Black Meeting Planners
441 Huntchase Drive
Bowe, MD 20720

301-860-0200
Fax: 301-860-0500
E-Mail: ncbmp@compuserve.com
Home Page: www.ncbmp.com

Ozzie Jenkins, Manager
Ana Aponte Curtis, President

Nonprofit organization dedicated to the training needs of African American meeting planners.
Founded in 1983

8371 North American Farm Show Council
590 Woody Hayes Drive
Room 232
Columbus, OH 43210

614-292-4278
Fax: 614-292-9448
E-Mail: gamble.19@osu.edu
Home Page: www.farmshows.org

Dennis Alford, President
Chuck Gamble, Secretary-Treasurer
Chip Blalock, 1st Vice President
David Zimmerman, 2nd Vice President
Doug Wagner, Immediate Past-President

Strives to improve the value of its member shows through education, communication and evaluation. The overall goal is to provide the beest possible marketing showcase for exhibitors for agricultural equipment and related products to the farmer/rancher/producer customer.
37 Members
Founded in 1972

8372 Professional Convention Management Association
35 East Wacker Drive
Suite 500
Chicago, IL 60601-2105

312-423-7262
877-827-7262
Fax: 312-423-7262
E-Mail: communications@pcma.org
Home Page: www.pcma.org
Social Media: Facebook, Twitter, LinkedIn

Johnnie White, CMP, Chair
Christopher Wehking, CMP, Chair-Elect
Ray Kopcinski, CMP, Secretary-Treasurer
Kent Allaway, CEM, CMP, Immediate Past Chair
Martin Balogh, Director

PCMA delivers superior and innovative education, to promote the value of professional convention management.
6100 Members
Founded in 1957

8373 Professional Show Managers Association
One Regency Drive
PO Box 30
Bloomfield, CT 06002

860-243-3977
Fax: 860-286-0787
E-Mail: msorensen@ssmgt.com
Home Page: www.psmashows.org
Social Media: Facebook, LinkedIn

Dordy Fontinel, President
Christine Palmer, Vice President
Steven Wesler, Secretary/Treasurer
Nancy Johnson, Immediate Past President
Frank Gaglio, Director
Founded in 1987

8374 Religious Conference Management Assocation
7702 Woodland Drive
Suite 120
Indianapolis, IN 46278

317-632-1888
Fax: 317-632-7909
E-Mail: rcma@rcmaweb.org
Home Page: www.rcmaweb.org
Social Media: Facebook, LinkedIn, YouTube

Harry R. Schmidt, Executive Director/CEO
Dean
Dean Jones, Director of Conferenec & Events
Judy Valenta, Special Projects Cooordinator
Debbie Hochstetler, Director of Finance

Provides members with a wealth of resources designed specifically to enhance their professionalism and overall effectiveness as religious leaders.
3200 Members
Founded in 1972

8375 **Society of Government Meeting Professionals**
908 King Street
Suite 200
Alexandria, VA 22314

703-549-0892
Fax: 703-549-0708
E-Mail: headquarters@sgmp.org
Home Page: www.sgmp.org
Social Media: Facebook

Rob Coffman, CGMP, President
Maggie McGowan, CGMP, CMP, First Vice President
Debra Kilpatrick, CGMP, Secretary
James Lynton, CGMP, Treasurer
Rob Bergeron, CAE, CGMP, Executive Director & CEO

Trade association for government meeting planners and exhibitors.
3100 Members
Founded in 1981

8376 **Society of Independent Show Organizers**
2601 Ocean Park Blvd
Suite 200
Santa Monica, CA 90405-5250

310-450-8831
877-937-7476
Fax: 310-450-9305
Home Page: www.shomex.com
Social Media: Facebook, Twitter, LinkedIn

David Audrain, Chairman
Rick McConnell, Vice Chair
Charles McCurdy, Treasurer
Tony Calanca, Secretary
Lewis R. Shomer, Executive Director
200 Members
Founded in 1990

8377 **Visitor Studies Association**
2885 Sanford Ave SW
Suite 18100
Grandville, MI 49418

740-872-0566
Fax: 301-637-3312
E-Mail: info@visitorstudies.org
Home Page: www.visitorstudies.org
Social Media: Facebook, Twitter

Joe Heimlich, President
Kimberly Kiehl, President-elect
Dave Ucko, Vice President
Bob Breck, Vice President, Outreach
Jessica Luke, Vice President, Professional Dev

Members are professionals at various institutions interested in studying audience experiences at museums, zoos, parks, etc. Promotes research in visitor participation and application of such research to programming and policy.
365 Members
Founded in 1990

Newsletters

8378 **ACOMmodate**
Association for Convention Operations Management
191 Clarksville Road
Princeton Junction, NJ 08550

609-799-3712
Fax: 609-799-7032
E-Mail: info@acomonline.org
Home Page: www.acomonline.org

Lynn McCullough, Executive Director

Includes news, networking ideas, and articles of professional interest.
Frequency: Quarterly

8379 **Affiliate Connection**
International Festivals and Events Association
2603 W Eastover Ter
Boise, ID 83706-2800

208-433-0950
Fax: 208-433-9812
E-Mail: craig@ifea.com
Home Page: www.ifea.com

Steven Schmader, President
Nia Forster, VP/Marketing
Craig Sarton, Director

The IFEA newsletter provides information and news 24 hours a day, 7 days a week, keeping members, suppliers and affaliates up-to-date and current.
2000 Members
Frequency: Monthly
Founded in 1956

8380 **Annual Conference Abstracts**
Visitor Studies Association
8175-A Sheridan Boulevard
Suite 362
Arvada, CO 80003-1928

303-467-2200
Fax: 303-467-0064
E-Mail: info@visitorstudies.org
Home Page: www.visitorstudies.org

Alan Friedman, President
Ellen Cox, Treasurer
Jessica Luke, Treasurer
Frequency: Annual

8381 **Aviso**
American Association of Museums
1575 Eye Street NW
Suite 400
Washington, DC 20005-1113

202-289-1818
Fax: 202-289-6578
E-Mail: membership@aam-us.org
Home Page: www.aam-us.org

Ford Bell, President
Kim Igone, VP Policy & Program

Reports on musuems in the news, federal legislation affecting museums, upcoming seminars and workshops, fedel grant deadlines and AAM activities and services.
Frequency: Monthly
Mailing list available for rent

8382 **CEMA Communicator**
Computer Event Marketing Association
1512 Weiskopf Loop
Round Rock, TX 78664-6128

512-310-8330
Fax: 978-443-4715
Home Page: www.cemaonline.com

Mitch Ahiers, President

Newsletter posted directly on the Internet.
Frequency: Monthly
Founded in 1990

8383 **ESCA Voice Newsletter**
Exhibition Services and Contractors Association
2260 Corporate Circle
Suite 400
Henderson, NV 80914

702-319-9561
877-792-3722
Fax: 702-450-7732
E-Mail: askus@esca.org
Home Page: www.esca.org

Susan L Schwartz, Director Communications
Cynthia Kelly, Accounting Manager
Frequency: Quarterly

8384 **Exhibition Perspectives**
American Academy of Equine Art
c/o Kentucky Horse Park
4089 Iron Works Parkway
Lexington, KY 40511

859-281-6031
Fax: 859-281-6043
Home Page: www.aaea.net

Julie Buchanan, Director
Frequency: Annual

8385 **HCEA Edge**
Healthcare Convention & Exhibitors Association
5775 Peachtree Dnwdy Rd
Building G, Suite 500
Atlanta, GA 30342-1556

404-252-3663
Fax: 404-252-0774
E-Mail: hcea@kellencompany.com
Home Page: www.hcea.org

Eric Allen, Executive Vice President

News and events of the trade association of over 600 organizations involved in healthcare exhibiting or providing services to healthcare conventions, exhibitions and/or meetings.
Frequency: Monthly, Members Only

8386 **IEG Endorsement Insider**
IEG
640 N La Salle Dr
Suite 600
Chicago, IL 60654-3186

312-944-1727
800-834-4850
Fax: 312-944-1897
E-Mail: valuationservices@sponsorship.com
Home Page: www.sponsorship.com

Lesa Ukman, CEO
John Ukman, Publisher

A newsletter covering the use of sports and entertainment personalities for endorsements, appearances and other marketing purposes.
Cost: $295.00
Frequency: Monthly

8387 **IEG Sponsorship Report**
IEG
640 N La Salle Dr
Suite 600
Chicago, IL 60654-3186

312-944-1727
800-834-4850
Fax: 312-944-1897
E-Mail: ieg@sponsorship.com
Home Page: www.sponsorship.com

Lesa Ukman, CEO
John Ukman, Publisher
Bart Zautcke, CEO
Brad Smith, Marketing

Newsletter on sports, arts, event, entertainment and cause marketing.
Cost: $415.00
8 Pages
Frequency: Biweekly
Circulation: 15000
Founded in 1982

8388 **NAAFA Newsletter**
National Association of Agricultural Fair Agencies
MI State Department of Agriculture
PO Box 30017
Lansing, MI 48909

517-373-9766
Fax: 517-373-9146

Carol Carlson, Secretary/Treasurer
Frequency: Annual

8389 **NAFSC Brochure**
North American Farm Show Council
590 Woody Hayes Drive
Columbus, OH 43210-6131

614-292-4278
Fax: 614-292-9448
E-Mail: gamble19@osu.edu
Home Page: www.farmshows.org

Dennis Alford, First VP
Chuck Gamble, Secretary-Treasurer

The North American Farm Show Council strives to improve the value of its member shows through education, communication and evaluation. The goal of the Council is to provide the best possible marketing showcase for the exhibitors of agricultural equipment & related products.
Frequency: Bi-Ennial
Founded in 1972

8390 **NCEE News**
National Catholic Educational Exhibitors
2621 Dryden Road
Suite 300
Dayton, OH 45439

937-293-1415
888-555-8512
Fax: 937-293-1310
E-Mail: cynpleg@aol.com
Home Page: www.nceeonline.org

Peter Li, Executive Director

A regular newsletter for the exclusive use of NCEE members. Each issue brings messages from the NCEE president and the NCEA Convention and Exposition Director; market and association updates, and the Exhibition Planning Calendar

8391 **Newsbytes**
Meeting Professionals International
3030 Lbj Fwy
Suite 1700
Dallas, TX 75234-2759

972-702-3000
Fax: 972-702-3070
E-Mail: feedback@mpiweb.org
Home Page: www.mpiweb.org

Bruce Mac Millan, President
Frequency: Weekly

8392 **Newsletter**
American Academy of Equine Art
c/o Kentucky Horse Park
4089 Iron Works Parkway
Lexington, KY 40511

859-281-6031
Fax: 859-281-6043
Home Page: www.aaea.net

Julie Buchanan, Director
Frequency: Semi-Annual

8393 **Workshop Brochure**
American Academy of Equine Art
c/o Kentucky Horse Park
4089 Iron Works Parkway
Lexington, KY 40511

859-281-6031
Fax: 859-281-6043
Home Page: www.aaca.net

Julie Buchanan, Director
Frequency: Annual

Magazines & Journals

8394 **American Speaker**
Briefings Publishing Group
1101 King St
Suite 110
Alexandria, VA 22314-2944

703-548-3800
800-722-9221
Fax: 703-684-2136
Home Page: www.briefings.com

Aram Bakshian Jr, Editor-in-Chief
Alan Douglas, President

An updateable loose leaf product geared to amateur and polished public speakers. The product has tips on speaking, model speeches, and filler material for all speaking needs.
Cost: $395.00
Frequency: Monthly
Founded in 1992
Mailing list available for rent: 14000 names at $125 per M
Printed in 2 colors on matte stock

8395 **Association Conventions & Facilities**
Coastal Communications Corporation
2700 N Military Trail
Suite 120
Boca Raton, FL 33431

561-989-0600
Fax: 561-989-9509
E-Mail: ccceditor@att.net
Home Page: www.themeetingmagazines.com

Harvey Grotsky, Publisher/Editor-In-Chief
Susan Wycoff Fell, Managing Editor
Susan Gregg, Managing Editor

Edited for association meeting planners with the responsibility for staging and planning meetings, conferences and conventions, for site selection, specifying accommodations and transportation. Issues provide in-depth focus on sites and transportation, current legislation, seminar and training oprtions, budget and cost controls, and destination reports.
Cost: $60.00
Frequency: BiMonthly
Circulation: 20,500
ISSN: 2162-8831
Founded in 2008

8396 **Association Meetings**
Primedia
Po Box 12901
Shawnee Mission, KS 66282-2901

913-341-1300
Fax: 913-514-6895
E-Mail: bblair@primediabusiness.com
Home Page: www.penton.com

Eric Jacobson, Senior VP
Larry Keltto, Editor

Directed to association executive directors and meeting planners with the objective of aiding the planning, site selection, and organization of meetings and conventions.
Cost: $223.65
Circulation: 20065
Printed in 4 colors

8397 **Convene Magazine**
Professional Convention Management Association
2301 S Lake Shore Dr
Suite 1001
Chicago, IL 60616-1419

312-423-7262
877-827-7262
Fax: 312-423-7222
E-Mail: communications@pcma.org
Home Page: www.pcma.org

Deborah Sexton, President/CEO
Kati S Quigley CMP, Chairman of Board
Barry L Smith, Chair Board of Trustees

The leading meetings industry trade publication for education content and timely, relevant information from the Professional Convention Management Association
Frequency: Monthly
Circulation: 35000

8398 **Convention South**
2001 W First Street
2001 West First Street
Gulf Shores, AL 36542

251-968-5300
Fax: 251-968-4532
E-Mail: info@conventionsouth.com
Home Page: www.conventionsouth.com

J Talty O'Connor, Editor/Publisher
Kristen S McIntosh, VP/Executive Editor
Pamela Redden, Marketing Services Manager
Suzanne Kellams, Manager, Circulation Development

For planners of meetings, conferences, seminars and similar events that are held in the South
Frequency: Monthly
Circulation: 18000
ISSN: 1074-0627
Founded in 1983
Printed in 4 colors on glossy stock

8399 **Corporate & Incentive Travel**
Coastal Communications Corporation
2700 N Military Trail
Suite 120
Boca Raton, FL 33431

561-989-0600
Fax: 561-989-9509
E-Mail: ccceditor1@att.net
Home Page: www.themeetingmagazines.com

Harvey Grotsky, Publisher/Editor-In-Chief
Susan Wyckoff Fell, Managing Editor
Susan Gregg, Managing Editor

The magazine for corporate meetings and incentive travel planners. In-depth editorial focus on site selection, accommodations and transportation, current legislation, conference, seminar and training facilities, budget and cost controls and destination reports. Regular features highlight industry news and developments, trends and personalities, meeting values, facilities, and destinations.
Frequency: Monthly
Circulation: 40,000
Founded in 1983

8400 **Corporate Meetings & Incentives**
Primedia
Po Box 12901
Shawnee Mission, KS 66282-2901

913-341-1300
Fax: 913-514-6895
E-Mail: bbair@primediabusiness.com
Home Page: www.penton.com

Eric Jacobson, Senior VP
Melissa Fromento, Publisher

Senior executives guide to decision-making.
138 Pages
Frequency: Monthly
Circulation: 34246
Founded in 1980
Printed in 4 colors on glossy stock

8401 **ESCA Extra Magazine**
Exhibition Services and Contractors Association
2260 Corporate Circle
Suite 400
Henderson, NV 80914

702-319-9561
877-792-3722
Fax: 702-450-7732

E-Mail: askus@esca.org
Home Page: www.esca.org

Susan L Schwartz, CEM, Executive Director
Heather Geldner, Accounting Manager
Cynthia Kelly, Accounting Manager
Frequency: Monthly

8402 **EXPO Magazine**
Expo Magazine
7015 College Blvd
Overland Park, KS 66211-1579

913-469-1185
800-444-4388
Fax: 913-469-0806
E-Mail: expo@halldata.com
Home Page: www.expoweb.com

Cam Bishop, President
Donna Sanford, Publisher
Danica Tormohlen, Editor-in-Chief
Magazine for exposition managment.
Cost: $48.00
134 Pages
Circulation: 7500
ISSN: 1046-3925
Founded in 1989
Printed in 4 colors on glossy stock

8403 **Event Solutions**
Virgo Publishing LLC
3300 N Central Ave
Suite 300
Phoenix, AZ 85012-2532

480-675-9925
Fax: 480-990-0819
E-Mail: mikes@vpico.com
Home Page: www.vpico.com

Jenny Bolton, President
Topics featured include decor, themes, high tech support, indoor facility equipment, food and beverage ideas, special effects, new products, and financial issues and regulations. Provides corporate, product and even profiles with suggestions from experts in the field.
Cost: $45.00
Frequency: Monthly
Circulation: 25,000

8404 **Events World**
International Special Events Society: Indiana
401 North Michigan Avenue
Chicago, IL 60611-4267

312-321-6853
800-688-4737
Fax: 312-673-6953
E-Mail: info@ises.com
Home Page: www.ises.com

Kevin Hacke, Executive Director
Kristin Prine, Operations Director
Editorial contents include practical information on each of the seven disciplines, news on promotions, job banks, people in the industry, ISES activities and events, technology trends, and global vision information about environmental, legal and political issues relating to the special events industry.
Frequency: Monthly
Circulation: 20000
Founded in 1987

8405 **Exhibit Builder**
Exhibit Builder
22900 Ventura Boulevard #245
PO Box 4144
Woodland Hills, CA 91365

818-225-0100
800-356-4451
Fax: 818-225-0138
Home Page: www.exhibitbuilder.net

Jill Brookman, CEO/President
Judy Pomerantz, Managing Editor
Jollen Ryan, Circulation Manager
Scott Gray, Editors
Devoted to the business and technical interest of the designers and fabricators of exhibits for trade shows, museums and point of purchase displays, includes application articles, new products, and new technology for creating booths.
Cost: $40.00
72 Pages
Frequency: Annual+
Circulation: 15000
ISSN: 0887-6878
Founded in 1983
Printed in 4 colors on glossy stock

8406 **Exhibit Marketing Magazine**
Eaton Hall Publishing
256 Columbia Turnpike
Florham Park, NJ 07932-1231

973-514-5900
800-746-9646
Fax: 973-514-5977
E-Mail: info@eatonhall.com
Home Page: www.eatonhall.com

Scott Goldman, Publisher
Eaton Hall is a publishing and trade show firm which specializes in bringing buyers and sellers together.
Cost: $5.00
52 Pages
Frequency: Quarterly
Circulation: 31000
Founded in 1990
Printed in 4 colors on glossy stock

8407 **Exhibitor**
Exhibitor Magazine Group
Po Box 368
Suite 745
Rochester, MN 55903-0368

507-289-6556
888-235-6155
Fax: 507-289-5253
E-Mail: webmaster@exhibitoronline.com
Home Page: www.exhibitoronline.com

Lee Knight, Owner
John Pavek, VP Publishing
Cara Schulz, National Sales Manager
Nicole Brudos Ferrara, Managing Editor
Whitney Archibald, Editor
The magazine for trade show and event marketing management.
Cost: $78.00
122 Pages
Frequency: Monthly
Circulation: 30000
ISSN: 0739-6821
Founded in 1982
Printed in 4 colors on glossy stock

8408 **Facilities & Destinations**
Bedrock Communications
650 1st Ave
7th Floor
New York, NY 10016-3240

212-532-7088
Fax: 212-213-6382
E-Mail: mikecaffin@aol.com
Home Page: www.facilitiesonline.com

Stella Johnson, Senior Executive Editor
Timothy Herrick, Director
Serves the association meeting industry defined as finance, banking, health, education,religious, trade, labor, fraternal, manufacturing, civic, social, professional, government/military, association management companies, independent meeting planners, destination management companies, trade show/event production companies and other groups who use the facilities industry for meetings, conferences, exhibitions, trade shows and conventions.
45 Pages
Circulation: 34000+
Founded in 1988

8409 **Facilities & Event Management**
Bedrock Communications
650 1st Ave
7th Floor
New York, NY 10016-3240

212-532-7088
Fax: 212-213-6382
E-Mail: mikecaffin@aol.com
Home Page: www.facilitiesonline.com/

Michael Caffin, Managing Editor
Glen O'Grady, Director
Timothy Herrick, Director
Editorial articles solve problems based on industry facts and statistics and coverage encompasses various segments of the facilities industry, including: convention centers, exhibition halls, hotel/conference centers, civic centers, arenas, stadiums, arts centers, etc. Monthly features detail facility business activity and provide coverage of the products and services available. Subscription, $48.00
Cost: $4.95
52 Pages
Frequency: Monthly
Circulation: 30000
ISSN: 1524-0258

8410 **Fairs and Expositions**
International Association of Fairs & Expositions
3043 E Cairo
PO Box 985
Springfield, MO 65802

417-862-5771
800-516-0313
Fax: 417-862-0156
E-Mail: iafe@fairsandexpos.ocm
Home Page: www.fairsandexpos.com

Jim Tucker, President
Steve Siever, Director
Max Willis, Editor
The source of information for fair trends, innovative ideas and association activities.
Frequency: 10/year
Founded in 1885

8411 **Feed and Grain**
Cygnus Business Media
1233 Janesville Avenue
Fort Atkinson, WI 53538

920-563-6388
Fax: 920-563-1702
Home Page: www.feedandgrain.com

Arlette Sambs, Publisher
Jackie Roembke, Editor
Committed to providing targeted editorial that addresses the specific needs of its readers. Subscribers consist of feed manufacturers, integrated livestock operators, pet food manufacturers, soybean processors, builders, designers and millwrights, as well as businesses such as rice mills, country and terminal elevators, flour mills, breweries and distilleries.
Cost: $48.00
Frequency: Bi-Monthly
Circulation: 15700
Founded in 1966
Mailing list available for rent: 16,505 names at $100 per M
Printed in 4 colors on glossy stock

8412 **IE - Business of International Events Magazine**
International Festivals and Events Association

2603 W Eastover Ter
Boise, ID 83706-2800

208-433-0950
Fax: 208-433-9812
E-Mail: craig@ifea.com
Home Page: www.ifea.com

Steven Schmader, President
Nia Forster, VP/Marketing
Craig Sarton, Director

IFEA'S quarterly magazine that provides members with the latest news and features focusing on current trends and topics, events, resources and more.
2000 Members
Founded in 1956

8413 Inside Events
Trio Communications
8899 Beverly Boulevard
#408
Los Angeles, CA 90048-2431

310-888-8566
Fax: 310-888-1866

Elisabeth Familian, Publisher

Articles include area listings of sites and vendors for any type of gathering. Profiles the creative ideas of industry professionals.
Frequency: Quarterly
Circulation: 20,000

8414 Insurance & Financial Meetings Management
Coastal Communications Corporation
2700 N Military Trail
Suite 120
Boca Raton, FL 33431-6394

561-989-0600
Fax: 561-989-9509
E-Mail: ccceditor@att.net
Home Page: www.themeetingmagazines.com

Harvey Grotsky, Publisher/Editor-In-Chief
Susan Wyckoff Fell, Managing Editor
Susan Gregg, Managing Editor

The executive source for planning meetings and incentives for the financial and insurance sectors. With regular features and special focus on site selection, destinations, industry-related studies and activities, motivational and incentive programs, program and event planning.
Frequency: Monthly
Circulation: 40,000
Founded in 1983

8415 Insurance Conference Planner
Primedia
Po Box 12901
Shawnee Mission, KS 66282-2901

913-341-1300
866-505-7173
Fax: 913-514-6895
Home Page: www.penton.com

Eric Jacobson, Senior VP
Melissa Fromento, Publisher

Meeting and incentive strategies for the financial services industry.
148 Pages
Frequency: Monthly
Circulation: 8005
Founded in 1965
Printed in 4 colors on glossy stock

8416 Laserist
International Laser Display Association
7062 Edgeworth Drive
Orlando, FL 32819

407-797-7654
Fax: 503-344-3770
E-Mail: president@laserist.org
Home Page: www.laserist.org

Tim Walsh, President
Patrick Murphy, Executive Director

Providing the latest news about the art and technology of laser displays
Frequency: Quarterly
Founded in 1986

8417 Medical Meetings
Primedia
11 Riverbend Dr S
Stamford, CT 06907-2524

203-316-8178
Fax: 203-358-5812
Home Page: www.meetingsnet.com

Betsy Bair, Editor Director
Melissa Framento, Publisher

International guide for health care and meeting planners.
106 Pages
Frequency: Monthly
Circulation: 10,823
Founded in 1973
Printed in 4 colors on glossy stock

8418 Meeting Professionals
Meeting Professionals International
3030 LBJ Fwy
Suite 1700
Dallas, TX 75234-2759

972-702-3000
Fax: 972-702-3070
E-Mail: feedback@mpiweb.org
Home Page: www.mpiweb.org

Bruce MacMillan, President
Eric Rozenberg CMP,CMM, Vice Chairman Administration

Furthers the professional development and education of all those who participate in the meetings industry.
Cost: $99.00
Frequency: Monthly
Circulation: 28,000
Founded in 1972

8419 Meetings & Conventions
Reed Business Information
500 Plaza Drive
Secaucus, NJ 07094
201-021-1960
Fax: 201-902-2053
E-Mail: lcioffi@ntmllc.com
Home Page: www.meetings-conventions.com

Bernard Lynch, Associate Editor
Lori Cioffi, Editor in Chief
Loren G. Edelstein, Executive Editor
Allen Sheinman, Managing Editor
Lisa Grimaldi, Senior Editor

Serves the corporate and independent travel and meeting planner with features on meeting facilities, hotels/airports/car rental, incentive travel options, trade show coverage, entertainment/leisure options and industry news.
Cost: $70.00
Frequency: Monthly
Circulation: 70013
Founded in 1965

8420 Meetings Industry
Dunn Enterprises
513 Commerce Dr
Upper Marlboro, MD 20774-7434
301-249-4600
Fax: 301-249-9100
Home Page: www.jtdunn.com

Barbara Cox, Owner
Robert Lantang, Graphic Designer

Profiles meetings sites and accomodations for meetings of all sizes. Includes personnel appointments of other meeting planners.
Circulation: 35000

8421 Programming Magazine
National Association for Campus Activities
13 Harbison Way
Columbia, SC 29212-3401

803-732-6222
800-845-2338
Fax: 803-749-1047
E-Mail: info@naca.org
Home Page: www.naca.org

Glenn Farr, Editor
Erin Wilson, Circulation

Features cover facilities and financial management, promotions, and student development to help plan a wide range of events.
Cost: $70.00
Circulation: 4300
Founded in 1960

8422 Religious Conference Manager
Religious Conference Management Association
7702 Woodland Drive
Suite 120
Indianapolis, IN 46228-6150

317-632-1888
Fax: 317-632-7909
E-Mail: rcma@rcmaweb.org
Home Page: www.rcmaweb.org

Eric Allen, Executive Director

Presents timely information for the meeting professional. Content focuses on current trends and features educational articles and news within this specialized field.
Frequency: Bi-Monthly

8423 Resorts, Hotels, Meetings & Incentives
Publishing Group
PO Box 318
Trumbull, CT 06611-0318

860-279-0149

John Mortimer, Publisher

Editorial contents include in-depth articles on industry trends, budgeting, planning tips, and profiles of the top meeting facilities in the world.
Frequency: Monthly
Circulation: 58,601

8424 Special Events Magazine
Primedia Publication
17383 W Sunset Blvd
Suite A220
Pacific Plsds, CA 90272-4187

310-230-7160
800-543-4116
Fax: 310-230-7168
E-Mail: lhurley@specialevents.com
Home Page: www.specialevents.com

Lisa Hurley, Editor
Lisa Perrin, President, Chief Executive Officer
Wanda McKnight, Sales Manager

Resource for event professionals who design and produce special events (including social, corporate and public events) in hotels, resorts, banquet facilities and other venues.
Cost: $48.43
Frequency: Monthly
Circulation: 2000+
Founded in 1982

8425 Tradeshow & Exhibit Manager
Goldstein & Associates

2117 Highland Avenue
Louisville, KY 40204

502-548-3188
Fax: 502-742-8749
Home Page: www.goldsteinandassociates.com

Steve Goldstein, Publisher

Featured articles focus on the issues, trends and products of interest connected to the tradeshow industry. Topics include security, boothmanship, legislation and shipping.
Cost: $80.00
Circulation: 14600

8426 **Tradeshow Week**
Reed Business Information
5700 Wilshire Boulevard
Suite 120
Los Angeles, CA 90036-5804

323-576-6600
Fax: 323-965-2407
Home Page: www.tradeshowweek.com

Amy Lacey, Marketing Director
Adam Schaffer, Publisher
Michael Hart, Editor-in-Chief
Carlos Lopez, Production Director
Heidi Genoist, Senior Associate Editor

For corporate exhibit managers, independent show managers, special event and meeting planners, association show managers and industry suppliers. Focuses on changing trends, new ideas and issues shaping the exposition industry in the US/Canada and abroad. Each issue contains a national and international show calendar.
Cost: $439.00
Frequency: Weekly
Circulation: 2394
Founded in 1971
Printed in 4 colors on matte stock

8427 **Visitor Studies Today**
Visitor Studies Association
8175-A Sheridan Boulevard
Suite 362
Arvada, CO 80003-1928

303-467-2200
Fax: 303-467-0064
E-Mail: info@visitorstudies.org
Home Page: www.visitorstudies.org

Alan Friedman, President
Ellen Cox, Treasurer
Jessica Luke, Treasurer
Frequency: 3/year

Trade Shows

8428 **AAEA Annual Meetings**
American Academy of Equine Art
c/o Kentucky Horse Park
4089 Iron Works Parkway
Lexington, KY 40511

859-281-6031
Fax: 859-281-6043
Home Page: www.aaea.net

Shelley Hunter, Executive Director
Julie Buchanan, President
Frequency: April, September

8429 **AAM Meeting & MuseumExpo**
American Association of Museums
1575 Eye Street NW
Suite 400
Washington, DC 20005-1113

202-289-1818
Fax: 202-289-6578
E-Mail: membership@aam-us.org
Home Page: www.aam-us.org

Dean Phelus, Meetings Director
Malena Malone, Senior Manager Meetings
4500 Attendees
Frequency: Annual/May

8430 **ASTC Annual Conference & Exhibit Hall**
Association of Science/Technology Centers
1025 Vermont Avenue NW
Suite 500
Washington, DC 20005-6310

202-783-7200
Fax: 202-783-7207
E-Mail: conference@astc.org
Home Page: www.astc.org

Cindy Kong, Director, Meetings & Conferences
Wendy Pollock, Dir, Research, Pubs, Exhibitions
Sheryl Thorpe, Manager, Conference & Exhibit Hall

Provides science center professionals from across the world a forum to exchange ideas and discuss the field's leading issues. With over 100 conference sessions, participants are challenged to explore ways of making science centers more essential to their communities.
1500 Attendees
Founded in 1973

8431 **Affordable Meetings Exposition and Conference**
George Little Management
10 Bank Street
Suite 1200
White Plains, NY 10606-1954

914-486-6070
800-272-7469
Fax: 914-948-6180
E-Mail: customer_relations@glmshows.com
Home Page: www.glmshows.com

Susan Sloan, Show Manager
George Little II, President

Focuses on the needs of meeting planners from all types and sizes of organizations who are responsible for producing successful yet cost effective meetings. 430 booths.
3M Attendees
Frequency: September

8432 **Association of Collegiate Conference & Events Directors Conference**
Assn of Collegiate Conference & Events Directors
1301 S College Avenue
Fort Collins, CO 80523-8037

877-502-2233
Fax: 970-491-0667
E-Mail: acced@colostate.edu
Home Page: acced-i.colostate.edu

Deborah Blom, Executive Director
Monica Nesbit Schultz, Marketing/Sales Manager

Workshop, conference, banquet and luncheon plus exhibits of conference and special event planning supplies, equipment and service information.
1300 Attendees
Frequency: March
Founded in 1980

8433 **Business to Business Exposition**
Trade Shows West
2880 S Main
Suite 110
Salt Lake City, UT 84115

801-485-0176
Fax: 801-485-0241
16000 Attendees

8434 **Conventions and Expositions**
American Society of Association Executives
1575 I Street NW
Washington, DC 20005-1105
202-262-2723
Fax: 202-626-8825

Judy Comeaux, Advertising
John Young, Production

Exposition planners trade show; 500-700 booths.
2-5M Attendees
Frequency: March

8435 **ESC Semi-Annual Meetings**
Exhibition Services and Contractors Association
2260 Corporate Circle
Suite 400
Henderson, NV 80914

702-319-9561
877-792-3722
Fax: 702-450-7732
E-Mail: askus@esca.org
Home Page: www.esca.org

Susan L Schwartz, CEM, Executive Director
Heather Geldner, Accounting Manager
Cynthia Kelly, Accounting Manager

December Meeting with International Association for Exposition Management and Summer Educational Conference.
Frequency: December, Summer

8436 **ESCA's Summer Educational Conference**
Exhibition Services & Contractors Association
2340 E Trinity Mills Road
Suite 100
Carrollton, TX 75006

469-574-0698
877-792-ESCA
Fax: 469-574-0697
Home Page: www.esca.org

Designed to give attendees the opportunity to advance their knowledge and to have an impact on the shape of the exhibition industry's future, as well as to network. Three session tracks, interactive forums and roundtables, speakers, and exhibits.
Frequency: Annual

8437 **ESPA Annual Conference**
Event Service Professionals Association
191 Clarksville Road
Princeton Junction, NJ 08550

609-799-3712
Fax: 609-799-7032
E-Mail: info@espaonline.org
Home Page: www.acomonline.org
Social Media: Facebook, Twitter, LinkedIn

Lynn McCullough, Executive Director
Diane Galante, Meeting Planner
Elizabeth Roe, Association Coordinator
Meghan Higgins, Public Relations Manager

Conference geared specifically to the event and convention services industry.
Frequency: Annual

8438 **Exhibit Ideas Show**
Exhibit Builder

1600 Golf Road
Suite 550
Rolling Meadows, IL 60008-4273

800-638-6396
Fax: 847-280-0771

Russ Eisenhardt, Show Manager
Jill Brookman, Publisher

Marketplace for products, services and technologies for exhibit builders and buyers. Elements included in trade show, museum and point of purchase booth construction are displayed, as are portable, modular and custom exhibit systems. 700 booths.
20M Attendees
Frequency: April

8439 **Exhibit Industry Conference & Exposition**
Trade Show Exhibitors Association
McCormick Place, 2301 S Lake Shore Drive
Suite 1005
Chicago, IL 60616

312-842-8732
Fax: 312-842-8744
E-Mail: tsea@tsea.org
Home Page: www.tsea.org

Stephen Schuldenfrei, President
Emily Burger, Sales Manager
Frequency: July

8440 **Exhibitor Conference**
Exhibitor Magazine Group
98 E Naperville Road
Westmont, IL 60559

630-434-7779
800-752-6312
Fax: 630-434-1216
E-Mail: exhibitorshow@heiexpo.com
Home Page: www.exhibitorshow.com

Carol Fojtik, Managing Director/Sr VP

Conference program combined with exhibit hall featuring latest products and resources shaping the future of exhibiting and corporate event programs. Anyone responsible for planning, managing or implementing trade show or corporate event marketing functions should attend. Conference is held annually in Las Vegas, NV.
5M Attendees
Frequency: March
Founded in 1989

8441 **HCEA Annual Meeting**
Healthcare Convention & Exhibitors Association
1100 Johnson Ferry Rd NE
Suite 300
Atlanta, GA 30342-1733

404-252-3663
Fax: 404-252-0774
E-Mail: hcea@kellencompany.com
Home Page: www.hcea.org

Eric Allen, Executive Vice President
Jackie Beaulieu, Associate Director

Cost varies; approximately 50 booths; 800 attendees.
200 Attendees
Frequency: Annual

8442 **HCEA Marketing Summit**
Healthcare Convention & Exhibitors Association
1100 Johnson Ferry Rd NE
Suite 300
Atlanta, GA 30342-1733

404-252-3663
Fax: 404-252-0774
E-Mail: hcea@kellencompany.com
Home Page: www.hcea.org

Eric Allen, Executive Vice President
Jackie Beaulieu, Associate Director

Cost varies; no exhibits; 200-250 attendees.
200 Attendees
Frequency: Annual

8443 **IAAM Annual Conference & Trade Show**
International Association of Assembly Managers
635 Fritz Drive
Suite 100
Coppell, TX 75019-4442

972-906-7441
800-935-4226
Fax: 972-906-7418
E-Mail: kristie.todd@iaam.org
Home Page: www.iaam.org

Kristie Todd, Membership & Exposition Coordinator
JoAnn Ramsey, Exhibition Manager

Members are managers of auditoriums, arenas, convention centers, stadiums and performing arts centers, coming together for education and networking opportunities, expert speakers, and exhibits.
3000 Attendees
Frequency: Annual/
Founded in 1925
Mailing list available for rent: 2800 names at $300 per M

8444 **IAEE Expo! Expo!**
International Assn of Exhibitions and Events
12700 Park Central Drive
Suite 308
Dallas, TX 75251

972-458-8002
Fax: 972-458-8119
E-Mail: news@iaee.com
Home Page: www.iaee.com

Annual show of 250 exhibitors of conventions and visitor bureaus, hotels, travel airlines, car rental, shippers, insurance, computer hardware and software, service contractors, printing products, specialty advertisement products, photography equipment and audio-visual equipment.
2500 Attendees
Frequency: Annual/December
Founded in 1928

8445 **IAEM Semi-Annual Meetings**
International Association for Exhibition Mgmt
8111 LBJ Freeway, Suite 750
PO Box 802425
Dallas, TX 75251-1313

972-458-8002
Fax: 972-458-8119
E-Mail: iaem@iaem.org
Home Page: www.iaem.org

Steven G Hacker, CAE, President
Cathy Breden, CAE CMP, SVP
Susan Brower, Director Marketing/Communications

Annual show of 250 exhibitors of conventions and visitor bureaus, hotels, travel airlines, car rental, shippers, insurance, computer hardware and software, service contractors, printing products, specialty advertisement products, photography equipment and audio-visual equipment.
2200 Attendees
Frequency: June, December

8446 **IAFE Annual Meeting**
International Association of Fairs & Expositions
3043 E Cairo
PO Box 985
Springfield, MO 65802

417-862-5771
800-516-0313
Fax: 417-862-0156
E-Mail: iafe@fairsandexpos.com
Home Page: www.fairsandexpos.com

Jim Tucker, President
Steve Siever, Director

Many branch divisions of the IAFE within the United States and Canada have their own annual meetings where members can meet, have access to resources, programs and workshops.
5000 Attendees
Frequency: Fall, Neveda
Founded in 1885

8447 **IFEA Annual Convention and Expo**
International Festivals and Events Associations
2603 W Eastover Terrace
Boise, ID 83706

208-433-0950
Fax: 208-433-9812
E-Mail: shauna@ifea.com
Home Page: www.ifea.com

Steve Wood Schmader, President
Nia Forster, VP/Marketing
Shauna Spencer, Director

Unites hundreds of the world's leading festivals and events, suppliers, media, sponsors and related industry professionals to share information on every aspect of event production through in-depth workshops, round-table discussions and networking.
2000 Members
800 Attendees
Frequency: Fall
Founded in 1956

8448 **ILDA Conference**
International Laser Display Association
7062 Edgeworth Drive
Orlando, FL 32819

407-797-7654
Fax: 503-344-3770
E-Mail: president@laserist.org
Home Page: www.laserist.org

Tim Walsh, President
Patrick Murphy, Executive Director

One of the world's largest exhibitions of entertainment technology. Features international exhibitors from the fields of lighting, lasers, audio, video and staging.
70000 Attendees
Founded in 1986

8449 **International Technology Meetings & Incentives Conference**
Techno-Savvy Meeting Professional
9200 Bayard Place
Fairfax, VA 22032-2103

703-978-6287
Fax: 703-978-5524
E-Mail: cimpa@cimpa.org
Home Page: www.cimpa.org

Andrea Sigler, President

Containing 100 booths and 100 exhibits.
Frequency: November

8450 **MPI Semi-Annual Meetings**
Meeting Professionals International
3030 LBJ Freeway
Suite 1700
Dallas, TX 75234

972-023-3000
Fax: 972-702-3070

E-Mail: feedback@mpiweb.org
Home Page: www.mpiweb.org

Colin C Rorrie, Jr PhD CAE, President/CEO
Frequency: Summer, Winter

8451 **NAAFA Semi-Annual Meetings**
National Association of Agricultural Fair Agencies
MI State Department of Agriculture
PO Box 30017
Lansing, MI 48909

517-373-9766
Fax: 517-373-9146

Carol Carlson, Secretary/Treasurer
Frequency: Summer, Winter

8452 **NAFSC Annual Meeting**
North American Farm Show Council
590 Woody Hayes Drive
Columbus, OH 43210-6131

614-292-4278
Fax: 614-292-9448
E-Mail: gamble19@osu.edu
Home Page: www.farmshows.org

Dennis Alford, First VP
Chuck Gamble, Secretary/Treasurer
Frequency: May
Founded in 1972

8453 **NCEE Annual Meeting**
National Catholic Educational Exhibitors
2621 Dryden Road
Suite 300
Dayton, OH 45439

937-293-1415
888-555-8512
Fax: 937-293-1310
E-Mail: bthomas@peterli.com

Bret Thomas, Executive Director

In conjunction with the National Catholic Educational Association.
Frequency: March

8454 **PCMA Annual Meeting**
Professional Convention Management Association
2301 S Lake Shore Dr
Suite 1001
Chicago, IL 60616-1419

312-423-7262
877-827-7262
Fax: 312-423-7222
E-Mail: communications@pcma.org
Home Page: www.pcma.org

Deborah Sexton, President/CEO
Kati S Quigley CMP, Chairman of Board
Barry L Smith, Chair Board of Trustees
3000 Members

8455 **RCMA Conference & Exposition**
Religious Conference Management Association
7702 Woodland Drive
Suite 120
Indianapolis, IN 46228-6150

317-632-1888
Fax: 317-632-7909
E-Mail: rcma@rcmaweb.org
Home Page: www.rcmaweb.org

Eric Allen, Executive Director
Frequency: Annual

8456 **The Special Event Annual Conference & Exhibition**
Special Event Magazine
PO Box 8987
Malibu, CA 90265-8987

708-486-0731
866-486-0731
Fax: 310-317-0264
E-Mail: registration@penton.com
Home Page: www.specialevents.com

Sharon Morabito, Group Show Director
Tara Melingonis, Conference Manager
Kim Romano, Special Events Manager
Wanda McKnight, Sales Manager
Dacia Coppola, Show Coordinator

Brings together those in the special events industry for new product displays, education, networking and learning. 275 booths.
3M Attendees
Frequency: Annual/January

8457 **VSA Annual Meeting**
Visitor Studies Association
8175-A Sheridan Boulevard
Suite 362
Arvada, CO 80003-1928

303-467-2200
Fax: 303-467-0064
E-Mail: info@visitorstudies.org
Home Page: www.visitorstudies.org

Alan Friedman, President
Ellen Cox, Treasurer
Jessica Luke, Treasurer
Frequency: Summer

Directories & Databases

8458 **Association Management: Convention Bureau and Convention Hall Issue**
American Society of Association Executives
1575 Eye St NW
Washington, DC 20005-1103

202-626-2700
Fax: 202-371-8825
E-Mail: publicpolicy@asaenet.org
Home Page: www.asaenet.org

A list of halls, centers, auditoriums, arenas and visitors bureaus in the United States and Canada.
Cost: $4.00
Circulation: 20,000

8459 **Audarena International Guide & Facility Buyers Guide**
VNU Business Publications
49 Music Sq W
4th Floor
Nashville, TN 37203-3213

615-321-4251
Fax: 615-320-0454
E-Mail: Research@billboard.com
Home Page: www.billboard.com

Ken Schlager, Executive Editor
Mitch Tebo, Directory Marketing Director
George Van, President
Monica Herrera, Manager
Bill Werde, Director
Cost: $99.00
310 Pages
Frequency: October

8460 **CEMA Member Directory and Meeting Planner**
Computer Event Marketing Association
1512 Weiskopf Loop
Round Rock, TX 78664-6128

512-310-8330
Fax: 510-682-0555
Home Page: www.cemaonline.com

Erika Brunke, Executive Director
Olga Rosenbrook, Member Services

All event managers and primary IA members.
500 Pages
Founded in 1990

8461 **Constitution and Membership Roster**
National Association of Agricultural Fair Agencies
MI State Department of Agriculture
PO Box 30017
Lansing, MI 48909

517-373-9766
Fax: 517-373-9146

Carol Carlson, Secretary/Treasurer
Frequency: Annual

8462 **Corporate and Incentive Travel: Official**
2700 N Military Trl
Suite 120
Boca Raton, FL 33431-6394

561-989-0600
Fax: 561-989-9509
Home Page: www.corporate-inc-travel.com

Harvey Grotsky, President

8463 **HCEA Directory of Healthcare Meetings and Conventions**
Healthcare Convention & Exhibitors Association
5775 Peachtree Dnwdy Rd
Building G, Suite 500
Atlanta, GA 30342-1556

404-252-3663
Fax: 404-252-0774
E-Mail: hcea@kellencompany.com
Home Page: www.hcea.org

Eric Allen, Executive Director
Carol Wilson, Director Meetings

Information on 6,000 health care meetings, available to members only.
500 Pages
Founded in 1930

8464 **IAFE Directory**
International Association of Fairs & Expositions
3043 E Cairo
PO Box 985
Springfield, MO 65802

417-862-5771
800-516-0313
Fax: 417-862-0156
E-Mail: iafe@fairsandexpos.com
Home Page: www.fairsandexpos.com

Jim Tucker, President
Steve Siever, Director

A annual reference guide giving members access to their associate members' products, services, and business activities.
1300 Members
Frequency: Annual
Founded in 1885

8465 **IEG Sponsorship Sourcebook**
IEG
640 N La Salle Dr
Suite 450
Chicago, IL 60654-3186

312-944-1727
800-834-4850
Fax: 312-944-1897
E-Mail: ieg@sponsorship.com
Home Page: www.sponsorship.com

Lesa Ukman, CEO
John Ukman, Publisher
Alicia Fidler, Product Manager

A directory of sponsors, properties, agencies and suppliers from th most active sponsors to the hottest sponsorship opportunities. Contains the critical data you need to make smart spon-

sorship connections.
Cost: $299.00
468 Pages
Frequency: Annual
ISBN: 0-944807-43-7
Printed in on glossy stock

8466 **MPI Membership Directory**
Meeting Professionals International
3030 Lbj Fwy
Suite 1700
Dallas, TX 75234-2759

972-702-3000
Fax: 972-702-3070
E-Mail: feedback@mpiweb.org
Home Page: www.mpiweb.org

Bruce Mac Millan, President
Frequency: Annual

8467 **Meetings and Conventions: Gavel International Directory Issue**
Reed Travel Group
500 Plaza Dr
Suite C
Secaucus, NJ 07094-3619

201-902-1800
Fax: 207-319-1628

Alina Dalmau, Editor
Lori Cioffi, Manager

Lists over 4,000 convention halls and hotels in the United States, suitable for meetings.
Cost: $35.00
Frequency: Annual
Circulation: 80,000

8468 **NCEE Membership Directory**
National Catholic Educational Exhibitors
2621 Dryden Road
Suite 300
Dayton, OH 45439

937-293-1415
888-555-8512
Fax: 937-293-1310
E-Mail: bthomas@peterli.com

Bret Thomas, Executive Director
Frequency: Annual

8469 **Nationwide Directory of Corporate Meeting Planners**
Reed Reference Publishing RR Bowker
121 Chanlon Road
New Providence, NJ 07974-1541

908-665-2834
Fax: 908-464-3553
E-Mail: info@bowker.com
Home Page: www.bowker

Offers valuable information on over 12,000 corporations that hold regular, off-site meetings arranged by over 18,000 corporate meeting planners.
Cost: $297.00
1140 Pages
Frequency: Annual

8470 **Official Meeting Facilities Guide**
Reed Travel Group
500 Plaza Dr
Suite C
Secaucus, NJ 07094-3619

201-902-1800
Fax: 201-902-2053

Virginia Nonneman, Editor
Lori Cioffi, Manager

One thousand national and international meeting facilities, primarily hotels in the US.
Cost: $45.00
Frequency: SemiAnnual
Circulation: 18,500

8471 **Protocol**
Protocol Directory
101 W 12th St
Suite PH-H
New York, NY 10011-8142

212-633-6934
Fax: 212-633-6934
E-Mail:
noemail@councilofprotocolexecutives.org
Home Page:
www.councilofprotocolexecutives.org

Edna Greenbaum, Editor

Approximately 4,000 suppliers of products and services used by planners of executive meetings, special events and other entertainment.
Cost: $60.00
Frequency: 1 issue
Founded in 1989
Printed in on matte stock

8472 **Sports Market Place Directory - Online Database**
Grey House Publishing
4919 Route 22
PO Box 56
Amenia, NY 12501

518-789-8700
800-562-2139
Fax: 845-373-6390
E-Mail: gold@greyhouse.com
Home Page: http://gold.greyhouse.com
Social Media: Facebook, Twitter

Leslie Mackenzie, Publisher
Richard Gottlieb, Editor

For over 20 years, this comprehensive, up-to-date directory provides current key information about the people, organizations and events involving the sports industry including, contact information and key executives for single sports organizations, multi-sport organizations, media, sponsors, college sports, manufacturers, trade shows and more.
Founded in 1981

8473 **Trade Show Exhibitors Association: Membership Directory**
Trade Show Exhibitors Association
2301 S Lake Shore Dr
Suite 1005
Chicago, IL 60616-1419

312-842-8732
Fax: 541-317-8749
E-Mail: tsea@tsea.org
Home Page: www.tsea.org

Steve Schuldenfrei, President
Emily Burger, Sales Manager

About 1,900 members of the Trade Show Exhibitors Association.
Cost: $55.00
Frequency: Annual February

8474 **Trade Show News Network**
Tarsus Group plc
16985 W Bluemound Road
Suite 210
Brookfield, WI 53005

262-782-1900
Fax: 603-372-5894
E-Mail: rwimberly@tsnn.com
Home Page: www.tsnn.com

Rachel Wimberly, Editor-in-Chief
John Rice, Sales & Business Development
Arlene Shows, Marketing Manager

The world's leading online resource for the trade show, exhibition and event industry since 1996. TSNN.com owns and operates the most widely consulted event database on the internet, containing data about more than 19,500 trade shows, exhibitions, public events and conferences.
13900 Members
Frequency: Bi-Monthly
Founded in 1196

8475 **TradeShow & Exhibit Manager's Buyer's Guide**
2117 Highland Avenue
Louisville, KY 40204

502-548-3188
Fax: 502-742-8749
Home Page: www.goldsteinandassociates.com

Steve Goldstein, Publisher

Over 1,000 suppliers of products and services to the trade show industry are profiled.
Cost: $60.00
150 Pages
Frequency: Annual
Circulation: 12,000

8476 **Tradeshow Week Exhibit Manager**
Goldstein & Associates
2117 Highland Avenue
Louisville, KY 40204

502-548-3188
Fax: 502-742-8749
Home Page: www.goldsteinandassociates.com

Steve Goldstein, Publisher

For exhibit managers.
Cost: $80.00
Frequency: Bi-Monthly
Founded in 1983

8477 **Tradeshow Week's Tradeshow Services Directory**
Business Information Publication
5700 Wilshire Blvd
Suite 120
Los Angeles, CA 90036-7209

323-549-4100
Fax: 323-965-2407
Home Page: www.tradeshowweek.com

Tina George-Reyes, Editor
Adam Schaffer, Publisher

Offers information on designers, builders, carriers and decorators involved in tradeshow and convention industries.
Cost: $95.00
300 Pages
Frequency: Annual

8478 **VSA Membership Directory**
Visitor Studies Association
8175-A Sheridan Boulevard
Suite 362
Arvada, CO 80003-1928

303-467-2200
Fax: 303-467-0064
E-Mail: info@visitorstudies.org
Home Page: www.visitorstudies.org

Alan Friedman, President
Ellen Cox, Treasurer
Jessica Luke, Treasurer
Frequency: Annual

8479 **Who's Who in Exposition Management**
International Assn for Exhibition Management
PO Box 802425
Dallas, TX 75380-2425

972-216-1511
Fax: 972-458-8119

Over 1,500 show manager members and 1,500 associate members.
Cost: $225.00
Frequency: Annual June

8480 **Worldwide Tradeshow Schedule**
1700 K Street NW
Suite 403
Washington, DC 20006-3810

202-463-4088

Over 110 international trade fairs are listed in all major industrial sectors.
10 Pages

Industry Web Sites

8481 **http://gold.greyhouse.com**
G.O.L.D Grey House OnLine Databases

Grey House Publishing's online database platform, GOLD, offers Quick Search, Keyword Search and Expert Search for most business sectors including exhibit and meeting planning markets. The GOLD platform makes finding the information you need quick and easy - whether you're a novice searcher or an experienced database user. All of Grey House's directory products are available for subscription on the GOLD platform.

8482 **www.aacei.org**
Association for Advancement of Cost Engineering

Association for Advancement of Cost Engineering provides its members with the resources they need to enhance their performance and ensure continued grouth and success. Serves cost management professionals: cost management and engineers, project managers, planners and schedulers, estimators and bidders, and value engineers.

8483 **www.acced-i.colostate.edu**
Colorado State University

Members are college and university conference and special events directors, profesionals and others who design, market and coordinate conferences and special events.

8484 **www.acmenet.org**
Association for Convention Marketing Executives

Annual meetings for marketing and sales executives.

8485 **www.acomonline.org**
Association for Convention Operations Management

Dedicated to advancing the practice of convention services management in the meetings industry, and to preparing CSM professionals for their critical role in the growth and success of their organizations.

8486 **www.cimpa.org**
Connected Int'l Meeting Professionals Association

Members are conference and convention planners with a certificate in convention management. Specializes in planning meetings events, incentives, using the internet.

8487 **www.clc.org**
Convention Liaison Council

Members are associations which are directly involved in the convention, exposition, trade show and meeting industry.

8488 **www.edpa.com**
Exhibit Designers & Producers Association

Exhibit Designers and Producers Association is an internationally recognized national trade association with more than 370 corporate members from 18 countries that are engaged in the design, manufacture, transport, installation and service of display and exhibits primarily for the trade show industry

8489 **www.edsc.org**
Electronic Distribution Show Corporation

Attendees are manufacturers of electronic components who sell their products through electronics distributors.

8490 **www.esca.org**
Exposition Service Contractors Association

Guide to exposition service is distributed annually and lists safety regulations and building rules in major US convention centers.

8491 **www.greyhouse.com**
Grey House Publishing

Authoritative reference directories for most business sectors including exhibit and meeting planning markets. Users can search the online databases with varied search criteria allowing for custom searches by product category, geographic area, sales volume, keyword, subject and more. Full Grey House catalog and online ordering also available.

8492 **www.hcea.org**
Healthcare Convention & Exhibitors Association

Trade association of over 700 organizations involved in health care exhibiting or providing services to health care conventions, exhibitions and/or meetings.

8493 **www.iaam.org**
International Association of Assembly Managers

Members are managers of auditoriums, arenas, convention centers, stadiums and performing arts centers.

8494 **www.iacc.online.org**
International Association of Conference Centers

A facilities-based organization which advances the understanding and awareness of conference centers as distinct within the training, education, hospitality and travel fields.

8495 **www.iaem.org**
Int'l Association for Exposition Management

Members are managers of shows, exhibits and expositions; associate members are industry suppliers.

8496 **www.moderndisplay.com**
Modern Display

Members are distributors of display equipment.

8497 **www.mpiweb.org**
Meeting Planners International

Meeting industry professionals who plan and/or manage meetings, trade shows and conferences for corporations, educational institutions and associations.

8498 **www.naca.org**
National Association for Campus Activities

Largest collegiate organization for campus activities.

8499 **www.nceeonline.org**
National Catholic Educational Exhibitors

A group for companies that provide products or services for Catholoc education.

8500 **www.pcma.org**
Professional Convention Management Association

Features emphasize solutions of practical and logistical problems concerning business travel, the hospitality/hotel industry, and related event planning topics

8501 **www.publicshows.com**
National Association of Consumer Shows

Non-profit organization dedicated to furthering the interests of consumer show producers and suppliers.

8502 **www.rcmaweb.org**
Religious Conference Management Association

Provides members with a wealth of resources designed specifically to enhance their professionalism and overall effectiveness as religious leaders.

8503 **www.sgmp.org**
Society of Government Meeting Planners

Trade association for government meeting planners and exhibitors.

8504 **www.tsea.org**
Trade Show Exhibitors Association

Provides knowledge to marketing and management professionals.

Associations

8505 ACA International
Association of Credit and Collection Professionals
PO Box 390106
Minneapolis, MN 55439-0106

952-926-6547
Fax: 952-926-1624
E-Mail: aca@acainternational.org
Home Page: www.acainternational.org
Social Media: Facebook, Twitter, LinkedIn, YouTube, The Hub

Mark Neeb, President

International trade organization of over 5,300 credit and collection professionals providing a variety of accounts receivable management services to over 1,000,000 credit grantors.

8506 About US Association for Financial Counseling and Planning Education
1940 Duke Street
Suite 200
Alexandria, VA 22314
703-684-4484
Fax: 703-684-4485
E Mail: rwiggins@afcpe.org
Home Page: www.afcpe.org
Social Media: Facebook, LinkedIn

Rebecca Wiggins, Executive Director
Michelle Starkey, Certification Program Coordinator
Kathryn Strine, Post Certification Program
Katie Tornow, Operations Officer
Frances C. Lawrence, Ph.D, Journal Editor

AFCPE is a non-profit professional organization created to promote the education and training of the professional in financial management.
810 Members
Founded in 1983

8507 Alliance of Merger & Acquisition Advisors
200 E Randolph St
24th Floor
Chicago, IL 60601-6435

312-856-9590
877-844-2535
Fax: 312-729-9800
E-Mail: info@amaaonline.com
Home Page: www.amaaonline.com
Social Media: Facebook, Twitter, LinkedIn

Michael Nall, CM&AA, CGMA, Founder and Managing Director
Diane Niederman, VP Business Development
?Amie Schneider, Director of Operations
Dylan Whitcher, CM&AA, Business Development Manager
Maxie Gallegos, Social Media & Marketing Specialist

AM&AA is the premier International Organization serving the educational and resource needs of the middle market M&A profession.
Founded in 1998

8508 Alliance of Merger and Acquisition Advisors
200 E Randolph Street
24th Floor
Chicago, IL 60601

312-856-9590
877-844-2535
Fax: 312-729-9800
Home Page: www.amaaonline.com
Social Media: Facebook, Twitter, LinkedIn

Michael Nall, CM&AA, CGMA, Founder and Managing Director
Diane Niederman, VP Business Development
?Amie Schneider, Director of Operations
Dylan Whitcher, CM&AA, Business Development Manager
Maxie Gallegos, Social Media & Marketing Specialist

A national organization serving the educational and resource needs of the M&A profession.
200 Members
Founded in 1999

8509 Allied Financial Adjusters Conference
956 S. Bartlett Road
Suite 321
Bartlett, IL 60103

800-843-1232
Fax: 888-949-8520
E-Mail: alliedfinanceadjusters@gmail.com
Home Page: www.alliedfinanceadjusters.com
Social Media: Facebook, LinkedIn, YouTube

George Badeen, President
David Sullivan, First Vice President
James Osselburn, Second Vice President
Stephanie Findley, Executive Secretary
Dan Cody, Treasurer

Membership is composed of professsional liquidators, repossessors and skip tracers. Membership fee varies with size of populations of the city served.
200 Members
Founded in 1936

8510 American Association of Individual Investors
625 N Michigan Ave
Suite 1900
Chicago, IL 60611-3151

312-280-0170
800-428-2244
Fax: 312-280-9883
E-Mail: members@aaii.com
Home Page: www.aaii.com

James B Cloonan, Ph.D., CEO

An independent, nonprofit corporation formed in 1978 for the purpose of assisting individuals in becoming effective managers of their own assets through programs of education, information and research.
13000 Members
Founded in 1978

8511 American Association of Residential Mortgage Regulators
1025 Thomas Jefferson Street NW
Suite 500 East
Washington, DC 20007

202-521-3999
Fax: 202-833-3636
E-Mail: efreundel@aarmr.org
Home Page: www.aarmr.org

Cindy Begin, President
Charlie Fields, Vice President
Don DeBastiani, Treasurer
Louisa Broudy, Secretary
David A. Saunders, Executive Director

Members are state employees responsible for administration or residential mortgage oversight. Primary members include model legislation and best practics.
100 Members
Founded in 1989

8512 American Bankers Association
1120 Connecticut Avenue NW
Washington, DC 20036-3902

202-663-5000
800-226-5377
Fax: 202-828-4540
E-Mail: custserv@aba.com
Home Page: www.aba.com
Social Media: Facebook, Twitter, LinkedIn, YouTube

Jeff L. Plagge, Chairman
John A. Ikard, Chairman-Elect
R. Daniel Blanton, Vice Chairman
Gary D. Hemmer, Treasurer
Frank Keeting, President and CEO

Brings together all categories of banking institutions to best represent the interests of this rapidly changing industry. It's membership — which includes community, regional and money center banks and holding companies, as well as savings associations, trust companies and savings banks, makes ABA one of the largest banking trade associations in the country.
Founded in 1875

8513 American Bankruptcy Institute
66 Canal Center Plaza
Suito 600
Alexandria, VA 22314-1546

703-739-0800
Fax: 703-739-1060
E-Mail: support@abiworld.org
Home Page: www.abiworld.org
Social Media: Facebook, Twitter, LinkedIn

Geoffrey L. Berman, Chairman
Patricia A. Redmond, President
James T. Markus, Immediate Past President
Brian L. Shaw, President Elect
Prof. Nancy B. Rapoport, Vice President-Research / Grants

Multidisiplinary, nonpartisan organization dedicated to research and education on matters related to insovency. Engaged in numerous educational and research activities as well as the production of a number of publications both for the insolvency practitioner and the public.
11700 Members
Founded in 1982

8514 American Cash Flow Association
255 S Orange Avenue
#600
Orlando, FL 32801

407-206-6523
800-253-1294
E-Mail: info@americancashflow.com
Home Page: www.acfa.org

Fred Rewey, President

8515 American Council of Life Insurance
101 Constitution Ave NW
Suite 700
Washington, DC 20001-2133

202-624-2000
877-674-4659
E-Mail: contact@acli.com
Home Page: www.acli.com
Social Media: Facebook, Twitter

Dirk Kempthorne, President & Chief Executive Officer
Kimberly Olson Dorgan, Senior Executive Vice President
Brian Waidmann, Chief of Staff
Gary E. Hughes, Executive Vice President
David C. Turner, Executive Vice President

Works to advance the interests of the life insurance industry and to provide effective government relations. Conducts investment and social research programs.
631 Members
Founded in 1976

8516 **American Education Finance Association**
8365 S Armadillo Trail
Evergreen, CO 80439

303-674-0857
Fax: 303-670-8986
Home Page: www.aefa.cc

Ed Steinbecher, Executive Director

AEFA encourages communications among groups and individuals in the education finance field, including academicians, researchers, policy makers and practitioners. Serving as a forum for a broad range of issues and concerns, AEFA concerns include traditional school finance concepts, issues of public policy, and teaching school finance.
650 Members
Founded in 1975
Mailing list available for rent

8517 **American Finance Association**
Haas School of Business
University Of California
Berkley, CA 94729-1900

800-835-6770
Fax: 781-388-8232
Home Page: www.afajof.org
Social Media: Facebook, Twitter

Robert Stambaugh, President
Luigi Zingales, President Elect
Patrick Bolton, Vice President
James (Jim) Schallheim, Executive Secretary and Treasurer
Kenneth J. Singleton, Editor of the Journal of Finance

Seeks to improve public understanding of financial problems and to provide for exchange of ideas.
11500 Members
Founded in 1939

8518 **American Financial Services Association**
919 18th Street NW
Suite 300
Washington, DC 20006-5517

202-296-5544
E-Mail: info@afsamail.org
Home Page: www.afsaonline.org
Social Media: Facebook, Twitter, LinkedIn, Google+

Gary L. Phillips, Chair
Danielle Fagre Arlowe, Senior Vice President
Michele Battaline, CMP, Director of Conferences
Jenny Bengtson, Associate Director, Membership
Dan Bucherer, State Government Affairs

The American Financial Services Association is the national trade association for market funded providers of financial services to consumers and small business. These providers offer an array of financial services, including unsecured personal loans, automotive loans, home equity loans and credit cards through specialized bank institutions
400 Members
Founded in 1916

8519 **American Society of Appraisers**
11107 Sunset Hills Rd
Suite 310
Reston, VA 20190

703-478-2228
800-272-8258
Fax: 703-742-8471
E-Mail: asainfo@appraisers.org
Home Page: www.appraisers.org
Social Media: Facebook, Twitter, YouTube

J. Mark Penny, ASA, International President
Gary L. Smith, ASA, MGA, International Vice President
Linda B. Trugman, ASA, International Secretary/Treasurer
Daniel R. Van Vleet, ASA, International Past President
Susan Golashovsky, ASA, Region 1 Governor

Professional association of appraisers of all kinds.
6500 Members
Founded in 1936

8520 **American Society of Military Comptrollers**
415 N Alfred St
Alexandria, VA 22314-2269

703-549-0360
800-462-5637
Fax: 703-549-3181
Home Page: www.asmconline.org
Social Media: Facebook, Twitter, LinkedIn

Marilyn M. Thomas, President
Gretchen Anderson, Vice President
Art Hagler, Vice President
Joseph Marshall, Vice President
Ann-Cecile M. McDermott, Vice President

ASMC is the successor to the Society of Military Accountants and Statisticians.
18000 Members
Founded in 1948

8521 **American Trucking Associations**
950 North Glebe Road
Suite 210
Arlington, VA 22203-4181

703-838-1700
Fax: 70- 8-8 17
E-Mail: nafc@trucking.org
Home Page: www.truckline.com
Social Media: Facebook, Twitter, YouTube

Bill Graves, President & CEO
Duane Long, First Vice Chairman
Pat Thomas, Second Vice Chairman
John M. Smith, Secretary
Douglas W. Stotlar, Treasurer

ATA's mission is to serve and represent the trucking industry with a single, united voice to influence policies beneficial to the industry; promote safety on America's highways; improve the industry's image, efficiency, and competitiveness; educate the public about the critical role trucking plays in the economy
1000 Members
Founded in 1933

8522 **Association for Financial Professionals**
4520 East West Hwy
Suite 750
Bethesda, MD 20814-3319

301-907-2862
Fax: 301-907-2864
E-Mail: customerservice@afponline.org
Home Page: www.afponline.org
Social Media: Facebook, Twitter, LinkedIn

Susan Glass, CTP, Chairman
Anita Patterson, CTP, Vice Chairman
Jeff Johnson, CTP, CPA, Vice Chairman

Association of 12,000 financial professionals. Please call for our publication listings or visit us online.
14000 Members
Founded in 1979

8523 **Association for Financial Technology**
34 North High Street
New Albany, OH 43054-8057

614-895-1208
Fax: 614-895-3466
E-Mail: aft@aftweb.com
Home Page: www.aftweb.com
Social Media: Twitter, LinkedIn

David Culbertson, President
Kelli Schultz, Immediate Past President & Scholars
Russ Bernthal, Vice President & Program Committee
James R. Bannister, Executive Director
Erin Thomas, Managing Director

Trade association for companies providing services to the financial industry. Our members provide systems, applications and outsourcing services to 90% of America's banks. Vendors of computer hardware, software and ancillary products and services are also welcome.
52 Members
Founded in 1975

8524 **Association for Management Information in Financial Services**
14247 Saffron Circle
Carmel, IN 46032

317-815-5857
Fax: 317-815-5877
E-Mail: ami2@amifs.org
Home Page: www.amifs.org
Social Media: LinkedIn

Jeff Nathasingh, President
Robert McDonald, SVP
Rita Bostick, Treasurer
Andy Streiff, Immediate Past President
Kevin W. Link, Executive Director

The Association for Management Information in Financial Services is the preeminent organization for management information professionals in the financial services industry.
300 Members
Founded in 1980

8525 **Association for the Advancement of Cost Engineering**
1265 Suncrest Towne Centre Drive
Morgantown, WV 26505-1876

304-296-8444
Fax: 304-291-5728
E-Mail: info@aacei.org
Home Page: www.aacei.org
Social Media: Facebook, LinkedIn

John J Ciccarelli, PE CCP PSP, President
Martin R Darley, FRICS CCP, President-Elect
Nicholas L Kellar CCP EVP PSP, VP - Administration
John C Livengood CFCC PSP, VP - Finance
Donald F McDonald, Jr PE CCP PS, VP -TEC

The leading-edge professional society for cost estimators, cost engineers, schedulers project managers, and project control specialists.
7000 Members
Founded in 1956

8526 **Association of Commercial Finance Attorneys**
Kennedy Covington Lobdell & Hickman, LLP
214 N Tryon St
22nd Floor
Charlotte, NC 28202-2367

704-350-7721
E-Mail: acfa@acfalaw.org
Home Page: www.acfalaw.org

Gary Scharmett, President
R. Marshall Grodner, Vice President
Alison Manzer, Vice President

Paul Ricotta, Treasurer
Janet Nadile, Secretary

ACF members are attorneys specializing in commercial finance and bankruptcy law. ACFA provides continuing education and publishes material relevant to the field for its members.
350 Members
Founded in 1958

8527 Association of Finance and Insurance Professionals
4104 Felps Drive
Suite H
Colleyville, TX 76034-5868

817-428-2434
Fax: 817-428-2534
E-Mail: info@afip.com
Home Page: www.afip.com
Social Media: Facebook, Twitter, LinkedIn

Deb Hankins, Manager
Linda J Robertson, Senior Vice President

A nonprofit educational foundation that serves the needs of in-dealership finance and insurance personnel for the automobile, RV, commercial truck and equipment, motorcycle, and motorized sports industries while assisting the lenders, vendors and independent general agents who support the F&I function.
Founded in 1989
Mailing list available for rent

8528 Association of Government Accountants
2208 Mount Vernon Avenue
Alexandria, VA 22301-1314

703-684-6931
800-AGA-7211
Fax: 703-548-9367
E-Mail: agacgfm@agacgfm.org
Home Page: www.agacgfm.org
Social Media: LinkedIn

Relmond P. Van Daniker, DBA, CPA, Executive Director
Mary E. Peterman, CGFM, CPA, 2013-2014 National President
Cristina Barbudo, MS, CPA, Director of Finance
Katya Silver, Director of Professionals
Maryann Malesardi, Director of Communications/Journal

AGA is an educational association dedicated to enhancing public financial management by serving the professional interests of governmental managers and public accounting firms.
15000 Members
Founded in 1950

8529 Association of Mortgage Professionals
2701 W. 15th Street
Suite 536
Plano, TX 75075

972-758-1151
Fax: 530-484-2906
E-Mail: membership@namb.org
Home Page: www.namb.org
Social Media: Facebook, Twitter, LinkedIn, YouTube

Donald J.ÿ Frommeyer, CRMS, President
Rocke Andrews, CMC, CRMS, Vice President
Kay A Cleland, CMC, CRMS, Secretary
Andy W. Harris, CRMS, Treasurer
Fred Kreger, CMC, Director

The only national trade association representing the mortgage broker industry. Promotes the industry through programs and services such as education, professional certification and government affairs representation.
25000 Members
Founded in 1973

8530 BCCA
550 W Frontage Rd
Suite 3600
Northfield, IL 60093-1243

847-881-8757
Fax: 847-784-8059
E-Mail: info@bccacredit.com
Home Page: www.bccacredit.com

Mary Collin, CEO
Jamie Smith, Director of Operations
Cindy Laser, Sales/Membership

BCCA is the media industry's credit association that functions as a central clearing house for credit information on advertisers, agencies and buying services, both locally and nationally. Also provides an Electronic Media Credit Applicationi (EMCAPP.com) to members that helps streamline the application process. One app in one location
600 Members
Founded in 1972

8531 Bond Market Foundation
360 Madison Avenue
New York, NY 10017-7111

646-637-9067
Fax: 646-637-9120

Micah Green

The Bond Market Foundation is a charitable and educational not for profit (501-c-3) association. The Foundation develops and enhances the public's access to quality saving and investor education in addition to providing credible non-proprietary research capacity and expert discussion on public issues relevant to the bond markets. The Bond Market Foundation is partner to the Securities Industry and Financial Markets Association (SIFMA).

8532 Broadcast Cable Credit Association
550 W Frontage Rd
Suite 3600
Northfield, IL 60093-1243

847-881-8757
Fax: 847-784-8059
E-Mail: info@bccacredit.com
Home Page: www.bccacredit.com
Social Media: Twitter

Mary Collin, President & CEO
Jamie Smith, Director of Operations
Cindy Laser, Sales/Membership
Susan Graves, Credit Investigators
Tracey Harris, Credit Investigators

Subsidiary of the Media Financial Management Association. BCCA provides credit information, education, and netwroking opportunities which enables members to efficiently manage credit risk and increase profitability.
600 Members
Founded in 1972

8533 CFA Institute
560 Ray C. Hunt Drive
PO Box 3668
Charlottesville, VA 22903

434-951-5499
800-247-8132
Fax: 434-951-5262
E-Mail: info@cfainstitute.org
Home Page: www.cfainstitute.org
Social Media: Facebook, Twitter, LinkedIn, Sina Weibo

Charles J. Yang, CFA, Chair, Board of Governors
Aaron Low, CFA, Vice Chair
Alan M. Meder, CFA, Immediate Past Chair
Giuseppe Ballocchi, CFA, Audit and Risk Committee Chair
John Rogers, CFA, President and CEO, CFA Institute

CFA Institute is the global, non-profit professional association that administers the Chartered Financial Analyst curriculum and examination program worldwide and sets voluntary, ethics-based professional and performance-reporting standards for the investment industry.
70000 Members
Founded in 1990

8534 CRE Finance Council
20 Broad St
7th Ffloor
New York, NY 10005

FAX 646-884-7569
E-Mail: info@crefc.org
Home Page: www.cmbs.org
Social Media: Facebook, Twitter, LinkedIn

Keith A. Gollenberg, Chairman
Daniel E. Bober, Treasurer
Stephen M. Renna, President & Chief Executive Officer
Erin Liberatore, Director of Meetings & Members
Ed DeAngelo, Vice President, Technology

International trade organization for the commercial real estate capital markets. Also represents and promotes an orderly ans ethical global institutional secondary market for the sale of commercial mortgage loans and equity investments.
309 Members
Founded in 1994

8535 Coalition of Higher Education Assistance Organizations
1101 Vermont Ave NW
Suite 400
Washington, DC 20005-3586

202-289-3910
Fax: 202-371-0197
E-Mail: hwadsworth@wpllc.net
Home Page: www.coheao.com

Maria Livolsi, President
Carl Perry, Vice President
Tom Schmidt, Secretary
Bob Frick, Treasurer
Robert Perrin, Past President

Focus is on legislative and regulatory advocacy for Federal Perkins and other campus based student loan programs.
365 Members
Founded in 1981

8536 Commercial Finance Association
370 7th Avenue
Suite 1801
New York, NY 10001

212-792-9390
Fax: 212-564-6053
E-Mail: info@cfa.com
Home Page: www.cfa.com
Social Media: Facebook, Twitter, LinkedIn, YouTube

Michael Haddad, Chairman of the Board
Michael Maiorino, President
Michael Coiley, First Vice President
Patrick Trammell, Vice President - Finance
Andrea Petro, Vice President

Trade group of the asset based financial services industry, with members throughout the US, Canada and around the world. Members include the asset based lending arms of domestic and foreign commercial banks, small and large independent finance companies, floor plan financing organizations, factoring organizations and financing subsidiaries of major industrial corporations. CFA membership is by organization, not by individual.
300 Members
Founded in 1944

8537 **Defense Credit Union Council**
601 Pennsylvania Ave NW
South Building, Suite 600
Washington, DC 20004-2601
202-638-3950
Fax: 202-638-3410
E-Mail: admin@dcuc.org
Home Page: www.dcuc.org
Social Media: Facebook, Twitter
Roland Arteata, President
Organizations of credit unions whose membership consists wholly or in part of personnel of the US Department of Defense, both military and civilians.
14 m Members
Founded in 1963

8538 **EMTA - Emerging Markets Trade Association**
360 Madison Avenue
17th Floor
New York, NY 10017
646-289-5410
Fax: 646-289-5429
E-Mail: awerner@emta.org
Home Page: www.emta.org
Mark L. Coombs, Co-Chair
Robert H. Milam, J.P, Co-Chair
Jonathan R. Murno, Managing Director
Michael M Chamberlin, Executive Director
Aviva Werner, General Counsel
EMTA is the principal trade group for the Emerging Markets trading and investment community and is dedicated to promoting the orderly development of fair, efficient, and transparent trading markets for Emerging Markets into the global capital markets.
Founded in 1990

8539 **Evangelical Council for Financial Accountability**
440 W Jubal Early Dr
Suite 130
Winchester, VA 22601-6319
540-535-0103
800-323-9473
Fax: 540-535-0533
E-Mail: info@ecfa.org
Home Page: www.ecfa.org
Social Media: Facebook, Twitter, LinkedIn, YouTube
David Wills, Chair
Michael Little, Vice Chair
Dan Busby, President
John Van Drunen, Vice President and Legal Counsel
Kim Sandretzky, Director of Communications
Helps organizations earn the public's trust through developing and maintaining standards of accountability that convey ethical practices.
1500 Members
Founded in 1979

8540 **FSC/DISC Tax Association**
PO Box 1012
White Plains, NY 10602
914-328-5656
800-207-4432
Fax: 914-328-5757
E-Mail: info@citeusa.org
Home Page: www.citeusa.org
Michele Harris, Principal
Joan Fisher, Vice President
Sri Rajan, Manager
The only organization operating on a national level devoted to educational interests of companies that have set up a foreign sales corporation.
300 Members
Founded in 1982

8541 **Financial & Security Products Association (FSPA)**
1024 Mebane Oaks Road
Suite 273
Mebane, NC 27302
919-648-0664
800-843-6082
Fax: 919-648-0670
E-Mail: info@fspa1.com
Home Page: www.fspa1.com
Mark Thatcher, Chairman
Bill Mercer, President
John M Vrabec, Executive Director
Independent dealers, manufacturers and associates whose outstanding products and services give financial institutions a crucial edge in performance, efficiency and economy.
Founded in 1973

8542 **Financial Executives International**
1250 Headquarters Plaza
West Tower, 7th Floor
Morristown, NJ 07960
973-765-1000
Fax: 973-765-1018
E-Mail: membership@financialexecutives.org
Home Page: www.financialexecutives.org
Social Media: Facebook, Twitter, LinkedIn, YouTube
Taylor Hawes, Sr., Chair
Donald Robillard, Jr., Vice Chair
Gregory Ulferts, National Secretary
Ann Flatz, National Treasurer
Marie N. Hollein, CTP, President and CEO
A professional organization of individuals performing the duties of CFO, Controller, Treasurer or VP of Finance. Has an annual budget of $6.5 million.
15M Members
Founded in 1931

8543 **Financial Management Association International**
University of South Florida
4202 E Fowler Ave
BSN 3331
Tampa, FL 33620-5500
813-974-2084
Fax: 813-974-3318
E-Mail: fma@coba.usf.edu
Home Page: www.fma.org
Jack S Rader, Executive Director
Jacqueline Garner, Vice President Financial Education
Kenneth Eades, Vice President Global Services
Rawley Thomas, VP Practitioner Services
Anthony Saunders, Vice President Annual Meeting
The mission of the FMA is to broaden the common interests between academicians and practitioners, provide opportunities for professional interaction between and among academicians, practitioners and students, promote the development and understanding of basic and applied research and of sound financial practices, and to enhance the quality of education in finance.
3000 Members
Founded in 1970

8544 **Financial Managers Society**
1 North LaSalle Street
Suite 3100
Chicago, IL 60602-4003
312-578-1300
800-275-4367
Fax: 312-578-1308
E-Mail: info@fmsinc.org
Home Page: www.fmsinc.org/cms
William J. Kline, Jr, CPA, Chairman
Alan Renfroe, Vice Chairman
Dick Yingst, President
Is the only individual membership society exclusively serving the technical and professional needs of today's bank, thrift and credit union financial officers.
1600 Members
Founded in 1948

8545 **Financial Markets Association**
PO Box 156
Parlin, NJ 08859
732-316-0384
E-Mail: info@fma-usa.org
Home Page: www.fma-usa.org
Peter Wadkins, President
Geoffrey Gowey, Vice President
Robert J Tum-Suden, Treasurer
Carlene Crnkovich, Secretary
A world-class organization of Foreign Exchange, Money Market, and Derivative traders, salespersons, brokers, vendors, and corporate participants organized for the purpose of education, promotion, fellowship, and advancement of the wholesale market within the United States.
300 Members
Founded in 1958

8546 **Financial Planning Association**
7535 E. Hampden Avenue
Suite 600
Denver, CO 80231
303-759-4900
800-322-4237
Fax: 303-759-0749
E-Mail: Member.Services@FPAnet.org
Home Page: www.fpanet.org
Marv Tuttle, Executive Director
Ian McKenzie, Managing Director/Publishing
Lauren Schadle CAE, Associate Executive Director/COO
FPA is the professional membership association that represents the financial planning community.
29000 Members
Founded in 2000

8547 **Financial Services Technology Consortium**
44 Wall St
12th Floor
New York, NY 10005-2413
212-461-7116
Fax: 646-349-3629
E-Mail: fstcadmin@fstc.org
Home Page: www.fstc.org
Michael Gifford, President
Zachary Turnin, Executive Director
Deb Karl, Business Manager
Association of leading North American-based financial institutions, technology vendors, independent research organizations and government agencies. Goal is to promote interoperable, open-standard technologies that provide critical infrastructures for the finacial services industry.

8548 **Financial Services Roundtable**
1001 Pennsylvania Ave NW
Suite 500 South
Washington, DC 20004-2508
202-289-4322
Fax: 202-628-2507

E-Mail: info@fsround.org
Home Page: www.fsround.org

Tim Pawlenty, President and CEO
Richard Whiting, Executive Director
John Dalton, President, Housing Policy Council
Paul N. Smocer, BITS, President
Scott Talbott, Senior Vice President

Mission is to be the premier executive forum for the leaders of the financial services industry; to provide powerful legislative and regulatory advocacy; to enhance the industry's public reputation; and led by BITS, to promote best practices and a strong infrastrucutre in technology.
Founded in 1993

8549 **Financial Services Technology Consortium**
44 Wall St
12th Floor
New York, NY 10005-2413

212-461-7116
Fax: 646-349-3629
E-Mail: fstcadmin@fstc.org
Home Page: www.fstc.org

J Andrew Spindler, President
Zachary Tumin, Executive Director

FSTC sponsors product testing, development programs, and other projects to ensure the continued viability of new technologies in the financial sector.
Founded in 1993

8550 **Financial Services Technology Network**
8 S Michigan Avenue
Chicago, IL 60603

312-782-4951
Fax: 312-580-0165
E-Mail: fstn@gss.net

Kathleen Luleasile, Executive Director
Dale Smith, President
Kathy Johnson, Secretary/Treasurer

8551 **Financial Women International**
1027 W Roselawn Avenue
Roseville, MN 55113

651-487-7632
866-807-6081
Fax: 651-489-1322
E-Mail: info@fwi.org
Home Page: www.fwi.org

Melissa Curzon, President
Cindy Hass, VP
Carleen DeSisto, Secretary

FWI is dedicated to developing leaders, accelerating careers, and generating results for professionals in the banking and financial services industry.
1000 Members
Founded in 1921

8552 **Fraud & Theft Information Bureau**
9770 S Military Trail
Suite 380
Boynton Beach, FL 33436

561-737-8700
Fax: 561-737-5800
E-Mail: sales@fraudandtheftinfo.com
Home Page: www.fraudandtheftinfo.com

Larry Schwartz, Founder/Director
Pearl Sax, Founder/Director

A leading consultant on credit card and check fraud control and loss prevention, and the publisher of related manuals and fraud-blocker data bases.
Founded in 1982

8553 **Futures Industry Association**
2001 Pennsylvania Ave NW
Suite 600
Washington, DC 20006-1823

202-446-5460
Fax: 202-296-3184
E-Mail: info@futuresindustry.org
Home Page: www.futuresindustry.org
Social Media: Twitter

Walter L. Lukken, President and CEO
Barbara Wierzynski, Executive Vice President
Mary Ann Burns, Executive Vice President
Will Acworth, Senior Vice President
Allison Lurton, Senior Vice President

Representative of all organizations that have an interest in the futures market.
180 Members
Founded in 1955

8554 **Global Association of Risk Professionals**
100 Town Square Pl
Suite 1215
Jersey City, NJ 07310-2778

201-719-7210
Fax: 201-222-5022
E-Mail: rich.apostolik@garp.com
Home Page: www.garp.com
Social Media: Facebook, Twitter, LinkedIn

Richard Apostolik, President and CEO
Carolin Statman, Sales/Marketing

GARP's international membership includes a varity of professionals from the finance industry who share a common interest in financial risk management practice and research.
52330 Members
Founded in 2000

8555 **Government Finance Officers Association**
203 N La Salle St
Suite 2700
Chicago, IL 60601-1216

312-977-9700
Fax: 312-977-4806
E-Mail: inquiry@gfoa.org
Home Page: www.gfoa.org

Timothy L. Firestine, President
Stephen Gauthier, Director, Technical Services
Anne Spray Kinney, Director Research & Consulting
John Jurkash, CFO Financial Administration
Barrie Tabin Berger, Assistant Director, Federal Liaison

The purpose of the Government Finance Officers Association is to enhance and promote the professional management of governments for the public benefit by identifying and developing financial policies and practices and promoting them through education, training and leadership.
17300 Members
Founded in 1906

8556 **Healthcare Billing and Management Association**
1540 South Coast Highway
Suite 203
Laguna Beach, CA 92651

877-640-4262
877-640-4262
Fax: 949-376-3456
E-Mail: info@hbma.org
Home Page: www.hbma.org
Social Media: Facebook, Twitter, LinkedIn, YouTube

Bradley J Lund, Executive Director
Paul Myers, Director of Education
Cindy Rounds, Associate Director Finance
Michelle Botana, Director of Communication
Sherri Dumford, Director of External Affairs

Members are companies providing third-party medical billing services.
500 Members
Founded in 1993
Mailing list available for rent

8557 **Healthcare Financial Management Association**
3 Westbrook Corporate Center
Suite 600
Westchester, IL 60154

708-531-9600
800-252-4362
Fax: 708-531-0032
E-Mail: webmaster@hfma.org
Home Page: www.hfma.org
Social Media: Facebook, Twitter, LinkedIn, YouTube

Joseph J. Fifer, FHFMA, CPA, CEO & President
Edwin P. Czopek, FHFMA, CPA, CA, Senior Vice President
Susan Brenkus, Vice President, Human Resources
ÿRichard L Gundling, Vice President, Healthcare
Leeÿ Guthrieÿ, Vice President, Marketing

Brings perspective and clarity to the industry's complex issues for the purpose of preparing our members to succeed. Through our programs, publications and partnerships we enhance the capabilities that strengthen not only individual careers, but also the organizations from which our members come.
40000 Members

8558 **Initiatives of Change, USA**
2201 West Broad Street
Suite 200
Richmond, VA 23220-2022

804-305- 176
Fax: 804-358-1769
E-Mail: support@web.iofc.org
Home Page: www.us.iofc.org
Social Media: Facebook, Twitter

H. Alexander Wise, Chaiman
Patrick T. Mcnamara, Executive Vice Chairman
William S. Elliott, Executive Director
Valerie Lemmie, Treasurer
Anjum A. Ali, Secretary

Is the national voice for lenders and investors engaged in the reverse mortgage business.
Founded in 1997
Mailing list available for rent

8559 **Institute for Divorce Financial Analysts**
2224 Sedwick Road
Suite 102
Durham, NC 27713

989-631-3605
800-875-1760
Fax: 888-527-7657
E-Mail: info@institutedfa.com
Home Page: www.institutedfa.com
Social Media: Facebook, Twitter, LinkedIn

The Institute for Divorce Financial Analysts (IDFAT) is the premier national organization dedicated to the certification, education and promotion of the use of financial professionals in the divorce arena.
Founded in 1993

8560 **Institute of Internal Auditors**
247 Maitland Ave
Altamonte Springs, FL 32701-4201

407-937-1111
Fax: 407-937-1101
E-Mail: customerrelations@theiia.org

Home Page: www.theiia.org
Social Media: Facebook, Twitter, LinkedIn

Paul J. Sobel, CIA, CRMA, Chairman of the Board
Carolyn D. Saint, CIA, CRMA, CPA, Chairman of North American Board
Richard F. Chambers, CIA, CGAP, C, President and CEO

Independent, objective assurance and consulting activity designed to add value to an organization's operations. It helps an organization accomplish its objectives by bringing a systematic, disciplined approach to evaluate and improve the effectiveness of risk management, control and governance processes. Representation from more than 100 countries.
10000 Members
Founded in 1941

8561 Institute of International Finance

1333 H St NW
Suite 800 E
Washington, DC 20005-4770

202-857-3600
Fax: 202-775-1430
E-Mail: info@iif.com
Home Page: www.iif.com

Douglas J. Flint, Chairman
Roberto E Setubal, Vice Chairman
Walter Kielholz, Vice Chairman
Marcus Wallenberg, Vice Chairman and Treasurer
Timothy D. Adams, President and CEO

Members are primarily international, commercial banks that focus on middle-income countries by communicating with the debtor countries, international financial institutions and regulatory agencies in order to improve the process of international lending.
450 Members
Founded in 1983

8562 Institute of Management & Administration

3 Bethesda Metro Center
Suite 250
Bethesda, MD 20814-5377

800-372-1033
703-341-3500
Fax: 800-253-0332
Home Page: www.ioma.com

An independent source of exclusive business management information for experienced senior and middle management professionals.

8563 Institute of Management Accountants

10 Paragon Drive
Suite 1
Montvale, NJ 07645-1760

201-573-9000
800-638-4427
Fax: 201-474-1600
E-Mail: ima@imanet.org
Home Page: www.imanet.org
Social Media: Facebook, Twitter, LinkedIn, YouTube

Jeffrey C Thomson, President & CEO

To provide a dynamic forum for management accounting and finance professionals to develop and advance their careers through certification, research and practice development, education, networking, and the advocacy of the highest ethical and professional practices.
65000 Members
Founded in 1919

8564 Institutional Shareholder Services

101 Federal St.
Suite 2105
Boston, MA 02110

617-768-3000
Fax: 301-556-0491
Home Page: www.issgovernance.com

Gary Retelny, President
Stephen Harvey, Chief Revenue Officer
Nancy Adler, Head of Marketing
J. Scott Berniker, Head of Securities
Mark Brockway, Head of the ISS Corporate Services

Leading provider of independent and impartial research on coporations and their shareholders.
500 Members
Founded in 1972

8565 Interactive & Newsmedia Financial

MFM, 550 W. Frontage Road
Ste. 3600
Northfield, IL 60093

847-716-7000
Fax: 847-716-7004
E-Mail: info@mediafinance.org
Home Page: www.infe.org
Social Media: Twitter, LinkedIn

Mary M. Collins, President & CEO
Chad Richardsonÿ, Chairman
Dalton A. Lee, Vice Chairman
Jamie L. Smith, MFM/BCCA Director of Operations
Arcelia Pimentel, MFM Membership Manager & Sales

Focuses on newspaper financial management, with members representing most North American newspaper companies, as well as many offshore. INFE's activities include publishing, conferences, workshops, industry surveys and studies, and offers members networking opportunities.
1200 Members
Founded in 1961

8566 International Association of Financial Engineers

555 Eight Avenue
Suite 1902
New York, NY 10018
646-736-0705
Fax: 646-417-6378
E-Mail: main@iafe.org
Home Page: www.iaqf.org

David Jaffe, Executive Director

The IAFE is a not-for-profit, professional society dedicated to fostering the profession of quantitative finance by providing platforms to discuss cutting-edge and pivotal issues in the field. Its composed of individual academic and practioners from banks, broker dealers, hedge funds, pension funds, asset managers, technology firms, regulators, accounting, consulting and law firms and universities worldwide.
Founded in 1992

8567 International Association of Purchasing

45 Woodside W
Patchogue, NY 11772

631-654-2384
Fax: 516-475-2754

A professional organization dedicated to the advancement of world trade. Membership is open to buyers, purchasing managers, executives and all individuals that may be involved or have an interest in the important function of buying goods and services on the global market. A nonprofit organization.
1600 Members
Founded in 1985

8568 International Society of Financiers

64 Brookside Drive
Hendersonville, NC 28792-9207

828-698-7805
Fax: 828-698-7806
Home Page: www.insofin.com

Ronald I Gershen, Chairman/President

A professional society of brokers, consultants, investors and corporate lenders active in financial projects and transactions. ISF provides an exclusive and confidential forum for member-to-member exchange and business networking.
300 Members
Founded in 1979

8569 International Swaps and Derivatives Association

360 Madison Ave
16th Floor
New York, NY 10017

212-901-6000
Fax: 212-901-6001
E-Mail: isda@isda.org
Home Page: www.isda.org

Stephen O Connor, Chairman
Robert G. Pickel, CEO
George Handjinicolaou, Deputy CEO
Mary Cunningham, Chief Operating Officer
Katherine Tew Darras, General Counsel, Americas

Represents firms, primarily financial institutions, corporations and government entities who deal in privately-negoiated derivatives, as well as firms who provide services to such institutions. ISDA's, mission is to encourage the productive development of interest rate, currency, commodity, and equity swaps as financial products.
Founded in 1985

8570 International Union of Housing Finance

Rue Jacques de Lalaing 28
B-1040 Brussels
Belgium

322-231-0371
Fax: 322-230-8245
E-Mail: info@housingfinance.org
Home Page: www.housingfinance.org

Dale Bottom, Secretary General

Disseminates information in housing finance policies and techniques worldwide.
107 Members
Founded in 1914

8571 Investment Company Institute

1401 H St NW
Suite 1200
Washington, DC 20005
202-326-5800
E-Mail: webmaster@ici.org
Home Page: www.ici.org
Social Media: Facebook, Twitter, LinkedIn, vimeo.com

F.William McNabb III, Chairman
Gregory E. Johnson, Vice Chairman
Paul Schott Stevens, President & CEO
Peter H Gallary, Chief Operating Officer
Donald C Auerbach, Chief Government Affairs Officer

Acts to represent members in matters of legislation, taxation, regulation, economic research and marketing and public information regarding investments and mutual funds.
9400+ Members
Founded in 1940

8572 Investment Recovery Association
638 W 39th Street
Kansas City, MO 64111

816-561-5323
800-728-2272
Fax: 816-561-1991
E-Mail: jmale@swassn.com
Home Page: www.invrecovery.org

Jane Male CAE, Executive Director

Helps fulfill an important role by bringing people together from disparate industries...all focused on sharing best IR practices and improving the knowledge and skills necessary to properly perform the wide-ranging responsibilities required of investment recovery practitioners.

8573 Media Financial Management Association
550 W. Frontage Road
Suite 3600
Northfield, IL 60093

847-716-7000
Fax: 847-716-7004
E-Mail: info@mediafinance.org
Home Page: www.mediafinance.org
Social Media: Twitter, LinkedIn

Mary M. Collins, President & CEO
Chad Richardsonÿ, Chairman
Dalton A. Lee, Vice Chairman
Jamie L. Smith, MFM/BCCA Director of Operations
Arcelia Pimentel, MFM Membership Manager & Sales

Professional society of more than 1,300 of media's top financial, MIS Credit and HR executives, plus associates in auditing, data processing, software development, law, tax and credit and collections.
1200 Members
Founded in 1961

8574 Mortgage Bankers Association of America
1919 M Street NW
5th Floor
Washington, DC 20036

202-557-2700
E-Mail: membership@mortgagebankers.org
Home Page: www.mortgagebankers.org

David H Stevens, President & CEO
Marcia Davies, Chief of Staff and Senior VP
Jay Brinkmann, Chief Economist and SVP
Gail Cardwell, Senior Vice President
Margaret A Colon, Chief Administrative Officer

Association for all state and local MBA officers.
2200 Members

8575 Mutual Fund Education Alliance
100 NW Englewood Rd
Suite 130
Kansas City, MO 64118-4076

816-454-9422
Fax: 816-454-9322
E-Mail: mfea@mfea.com
Home Page: www.mfea.com
Social Media: Facebook, Twitter

Michelle Smith, Executive Director

Conducts public education and public relation activities in an effort to acquaint investors, industry organizations and government agencies with direct market funds.
Founded in 1971

8576 Mutual Fund Investors Association
85 Wells Avenue
Suite 109
Newton, MA 02459

617-321-2200
800-492-6868
Fax: ÿ61- 32- 221
E-Mail: info@adviserinvestments.com
Home Page: www.kobren.com

Lewis C. Frost, Portfolio Executive
Christopher M. Hagan, Director of Executive Services
Suzzane M. Irwin, Portfolio Administrator
Joshua W. Jones, Portfolio Review Committee
John Kennedy, Account Executive

Association for those interested in information and rates for mutual funds, investments, stocks and bonds.
Founded in 1994

8577 NACHA - Electronic Payments Association
13450 Sunrise Valley Drive
Suite 100
Herndon, VA 20171

703-561-1100
Fax: 703-787-0996
E-Mail: abuse@nacha.org.
Home Page: www.nacha.org
Social Media: Facebook, Twitter, LinkedIn

Janet O Estep, CEO
Deb Evans-Doyle, Sr Director Conference Marketing
Julie Hedlund, Sr Director Electronic Commerce
Michael Herd, Director Public Relations

NACHA is a trade association that forms the cooperative foundation for the automated clearing house (ACH) payments system through a network of 21 ACH associations nationwide. It also provides marketing and educational members through direct memberships and a network of regional payment associations.
Founded in 1974

8578 Nat'l Institute of Pension Administrators
330 N Wabash Ave
Suite 2000
Chicago, IL 60611-7621

800-999-6472
800-999-6272
Fax: 312-673-6609
E-Mail: nipa@nipa.org
Home Page: www.nipa.org
Social Media: LinkedIn

Ralph Delsesto, APR, President
Ann Slotwinski, APR, President Elect and CFO
James Eberhardt, , APA, Immediate Past President
Laura Rudzinski, Executive Director
Alexis Bauer-Kolak, Director of Operations

The Institute is responsible for the formation Of professional standards, an ongoing education program consisting of workshops and home study courses, and awards of the APA and the APR designations by examination and experience.
1000 Members
Founded in 1983

8579 National Aircraft Finance Association
PO Box 1570
Edgewater, MD 21037

410-571-1740
Fax: 410-571-1780
E-Mail: info@nafa.aero
Home Page: www.nafa.aero
Social Media: Facebook, Twitter, LinkedIn

David Jarvis, President
Chris Miller, Vice President
Ford Von Weise, Vice President
Karen Griggs, Executive Director
Anthony Kioussis, Secretary

A non-profit corporation dedicated to promoting the general welfare of individual and organization providing aircraft financing and loans secured by aircraft; to improve the industry's service to the public; to work with government agencies to foster a greater understanding of our member's needs.
95 Members
Founded in 1969

8580 National Association of Affordable Housing Lenders
1667 K St NW
Suite 210
Washington, DC 20006

202-293-9850
Fax: 202-293-9852
E-Mail: naahl@naahl.org
Home Page: www.naahl.org

Judith Kennedy, President & CEO
Paul Haaland, Chief Operating Officer
Sara Olson, Administrative Assistant

Is the only association devoted to increasing private capital lending and investment in low and moderate income communities.
800 Members
Founded in 1977

8581 National Association of Bankruptcy Trustees
One Windsor Cove
Suite 305
Columbia, SC 29223

803-252-5646
800-445-8629
Fax: 803-765-0860
E-Mail: info@nabt.com
Home Page: www.nabt.com

Christina Hicks, Executive Director
Nancy H. Cooper, Executive Liasion

The majority of the members of the NABT are Chapter 7 trustees who primarily liquidate non-exempt assets for the benefit of creditors.
1200 Members
Founded in 1982

8582 National Association of Certified Valuators and Analysts
5217 South State Street
Suite 400
Salt Lake City, UT 84107

801-486-0600
800-677-2009
Fax: 801-486-7500
E-Mail: nacva1@nacva.com
Home Page: www.nacva.com

Pamela Bailey, Executive Advisory Board
Melissa Bizyak, Executive Advisory Board
Parnell Black, Executive Advisory Board
Rod Burket, Executive Advisory Board
Mark Hanson, Executive Advisory Board

Global, professional association that supports the business valuation and litigation consulting disciplines within the CPA and professional communities. Along with its training and certification programs, NACVA offers a range of support services, reference materials, software, and customized databases to enhance the professional capabilities and capacities of its members.
6500 Members
Founded in 1990

8583 National Association of Corporate Treasurers
12100 Sunset Hills Road
Suite 130
Reston, VA 20190-3221

703-437-4377
Fax: 703-435-4390
E-Mail: nact@nact.org
Home Page: www.nact.org
Social Media: LinkedIn

Ramon Yi, Chairman
Mary Dean Hall, President
Joseph C. Sullivan, Vice-President
Ruud Roggekamp, Secretary/Treasurer
Thomas C. Deas, Immediate Past Chairman

Members are corporate chief financial officers, treasurers or assistant treasurers.
825 Members
Founded in 1982

8584 National Association of Development Companies
1100 H Street NW
Suite 1030
Washington, DC 20005

202-349-0070
Fax: 202-349-0071
E-Mail: info@nadco.org
Home Page: www.nadco.org
Social Media: Facebook, Twitter, Stumbleupon

Beth Solomon, President & CEO
Rhonda Pointon, Vice President
Denise Ripley, Associate Manager of Programs
Karen Szulgit, Senior Manager of Administration
Mandy Robertson, Vice President Conferences

Provides long term, fixed asset financing to small businesses.
135 Members
Founded in 1981

8585 National Association of Division Order Analysts
PO Box 746327
Arvada, CO 80006-6327

972-715-4489
E-Mail: administrator@nadoa.org
Home Page: www.nadoa.org
Social Media: Facebook, Twitter, LinkedIn

Lisa Buffaloe, CDOA, President
Mary Sons, Vice President
Nancy Cemino, CDOA, 2nd Vice President
Angela Korthauer, Treasurer
Kim Henderson, CDOA, Corresponding Secretary

Division order analysts are petroleum and gas company employees or independent consultants responsible for royalty working interest and overiding royalty payments. Offers a certification program providing education, training and testing for qualified applicants desiring to attain Certified Divison Order Analyst credentials.
900 Members
Frequency: 4
Founded in 1974

8586 National Association of Equipment Leasing Brokers
455 South Fourth Street
Suite 650
Louisville, KY 40202

800-996-2352
Fax: 877-875-4750
E-Mail: info@naelb.org
Home Page: www.naelb.org
Social Media: Facebook, Twitter, LinkedIn, YouTube

Monica Harper, Executive Administrator
Leah Woods, Membership Coordinator

Broker-oriented association.
500 Members
Founded in 1990

8587 National Association of Federal Credit Unions
3138 10th St N
Arlington, VA 22201-2149

703-522-4770
800-336-4644
Fax: 703-524-1082
E-Mail: msc@nafcu.org.
Home Page: www.nafcu.org
Social Media: Facebook, Twitter

Michael J. Parsons, Chair/Region I Director
Ed Templeton, Vice Chair/Director-at-Large
Richard L. Harris, Treasurer/Region Director
Jeanne Kucey, Secretary/Region III Director
Martin Breland, Region II Director

Trade association exclusively represents the interests of federal credit unions before the federal government and the public. Provides members with representation, information, education and assistance to meet the challenges that cooperative financial institutions face in today's economic environment. Stands as a national forum for the federal credit union community where new ideas, issues, concerns and trends can be identified, discussed and resolved.
Founded in 1967

8588 National Association of Independent Public Finance Advisors
PO Box 304
Montgomery, IL 60538-0304

630-896-1292
800-624-7321
Fax: 209-633-6265
E-Mail: rhoban@naipfa.com
Home Page: www.naipfa.com

Jeanine Rogers Caruso, President
Terri Heaton, Vice President
Bruce A. Kimmel, CIPFA, Secretary
Micheal Sudsina, CIPFA, Treasurer
Shelly Aronson,CIPFA, Director at large

A professional organization limited to firms that specialize in providing financial advice on bond sales and financial planning on public projects of public agencies. Promotes the common interests of independent advisory firm members.
48 Members
Founded in 1989

8589 National Association of Investors Corporation
711 W 13mile Road
Suite 900
Madison Heights, MI 48071

248-583-6242
877-275-6242
Fax: 248-583-4880
E-Mail: service@betterinvesting.org
Home Page: www.betterinvesting.org
Social Media: Facebook, Twitter

Roger H Ganser, Chairman
Kamie Zaracki, CEO
Stephen Sanborn, Treasurer
Gary Ball, Director
Robert Brooker, Director

Strives to counsel and teach investing techniques and sound investment procedures to interested people.
23000 Members
Founded in 1951

8590 National Association of Local Housing Finance Agencies
2025 M St NW
Suite 800
Washington, DC 20036

202-367-1197
Fax: 202-367-2197
E-Mail: info@nalhfa.org
Home Page: www.nalhfa.org

John C Murphy, Executive Director
Ernestine Garey, President
Marc Jahr, Vice President
Ron Williams, Treasurer
Paula Sampson, Secretary

The National Association of Local Housing Finance Agencies, founded in 1982, is the national association of professionals working to finance affordable housing in the broader community development context at the local level. As a non-profit association, NALHFA is an advocate before Congress and federal agencies on legislative and regulatory issues affecting affordable housing and provides technical assistance and educational opportunities to its members and the public.
Founded in 1982

8591 National Association of Personal Financial Advisors
3250 N Arlington Heights Road
Suite 109
Arlington Heights, IL 60004

847-483-5400
888-333-6659
Fax: 847-483-5415
E-Mail: info@napfa.org
Home Page: www.napfa.org

Linda Leitz, Chairman
Giles Almond, Treasurer
Robert Gerstemeier, Vice Chairman & Secretary
Tony Ogorek, Operating Manager

Members are financial planners who are compensated only by fees. NAPFA members are prohibited from receiving any type of product-related compensation, such as sales commissions. Members do not sell products nor do they direct sales to parties with whom they have financial interests.
2400 Members
Founded in 1983

8592 National Association of Publicly Traded Partnerships
1200 19th Street, NW
Suite 700
Washington, DC 20036

202-973-2400
800-621-8390
Fax: 202-973-2401
E-Mail: inquiries@navigant.com
Home Page: www.navigantconsulting.com
Social Media: LinkedIn, YouTube

William M Goodyear, Chairman And CEO
Thomas A. Glidehaus, Director
Cynthia A. Glassman, Phd, Director
Julie M. Howard, Director & Navigant CEO
Stephan A. James, Director

A trade association representing publicly traded limited partnerships (and publicly traded LLCs taxed partnerships) and those who work with them.
Founded in 1983
Mailing list available for rent

8593 National Association of Review Appraisers & Mortgage Underwriters
810 N Farrell Drive
Palm Springs, CA 92262

760-327-5284
877-743-6805
Fax: 760-327-5631
E-Mail: support@assoc-hdqts.org
Home Page: www.naramu.org
Social Media: LinkedIn

Robert G Johnson, Executive Director

Association for professionals who review real estate appraisals and underwrite real estate mortgages. The association offers the CRA, Certified Review Appraiser and RMU, Registered Mortgage Underwriter, professional designation.
2852 Members
Founded in 1975
Mailing list available for rent: 3500 names at $75 per M

8594 National Association of Sales Professionals
555 Friendly Street
Bloomfield Hills, MI 48341

480-596-6634
866-365-1520
Fax: 248-254-6757
E-Mail: info@nasp.com
Home Page: www.nasp.com
Social Media: Facebook, Twitter, LinkedIn

Rod Hairston, CEO & Chairman
Idris Grant, President and COO
Tonia Revere, Director
Sabine Grant, Vice President
Amanda Ritz, Membership, director & advisor

Members are companies who purchase structured settlements, lottery annuities, and similar periodic payment plans from their beneficiaries.
Founded in 1991

8595 National Association of State Budget Officers
444 N Capitol St NW
Suite 642
Washington, DC 20001

202-624-5382
Fax: 202-624-7745
E-Mail: spattison@nasbo.org
Home Page: www.nasbo.org
Social Media: Facebook, Twitter, LinkedIn

Scott D. Pattison, Executive Director
Stacy Mazer, Senior Staff Associate
Brian Sigritz, Director of State Fiscal Studies
Michael Streepey, Fiscal Policy Analyst
Kathryn Vesey White, Director, Member Relations

Membership limited to three budget officers per state. Affiliated with the National Governors Association.
160 Members
Founded in 1945

8596 National Association of Tax Professionals
PO Box 8002
Appleton, WI 54912 8002

920-749-1040
800-558-3402
Fax: 800-747-0001
E-Mail: natp@natptax.com
Home Page: www.natptax.com

Jo Ann Schoen, EA, President
Jean Millerchip,EA,CPF, Vice-President
Gerard F. Cannito CPA,CPF, Treasurer
Praticia(Ann) Mcneer EA, Secretary
Dorothy Atchison, EA, Director

The National Association of Tax Professionals (NATP) is a nonprofit professional association founded in 1979 and is committed to excellence in the tax profession. Our national headquarters is located in Appleton, Wisconsin and employs 42 professionals and 25 instructors. NATP was formed to serve professionals who work in all areas of tax practice and has more than 19,500 members nationwide.
24000 Members
Founded in 1979

8597 National Association of Trade Exchanges
10151 IH35 North
San Antonio, TX 78233

617-763-3311
E-Mail: bartertrainer@aol.com
Home Page: www.natebarter.com
Social Media: Facebook, LinkedIn

Ric Zampatti, President
Sharon Connelly, Vice-President
Rachel Taylor Hooper, Director
Maurya Lane, Director
Kim Ames, Secretary

NATE offers their members additional benefits such national and regional meetings and accreditation opportunities.
80 Members
Founded in 1984

8598 National Automotive Finance Association
7250 Parkway Dr
Suite 510
Hanover, MD 21076-1343

410-712-4036
800-463-8955
Fax: 410-712-4038
E-Mail: information@nafassociation.com
Home Page: www.nafassociation.com
Social Media: LinkedIn

Jack Tracey, CAE, Executive Director

NAF Association serves companies and professionals in the non-prime auto lending industry.
85 Members
Founded in 1996

8599 National Bankers Association
1513 P St Nw
Washington, DC 20005

202-588-5432
Fax: 202-588-5443
E-Mail: eholliday@nationalbankers.org
Home Page: www.nationalbankers.org

B. Doyle Mitchell, Jr., Chairman
Robert P. Cooper, Immediate Past Chairman
Michael A. Grant, President
Cynthia N. Day, Secretary
Neil W. Wright, Treasurer

Association for banks owned or controlled by minority group persons or women.
15000 Members
Founded in 1927

8600 National Community Capital Association
Public Ledger Building, 620 Chestnut Street
Suite 572
Philadelphia, PA 19106

215-923-4754
Fax: 215-923-4755
E-Mail: info@opportunityfinance.net
Home Page: www.ofn.org
Social Media: Facebook, Twitter, LinkedIn, www.vimeo.com

Trinita Logue, Chair President
Eric Belsky, Executive Director
John Berdes, President/CEO
Keith Bisson, Program Management & Development
Donald Bowen, Sr. Vice President

Provides support for nonprofit, revolving loan funds that lend capital and offer technical assistance in distressed and disenfranchised communities.
52 Members
Founded in 1986

8601 National Credit Union Administration
1775 Duke St
Alexandria, VA 22314-6115

703-518-6300
Fax: 703-518-6539
E-Mail: ociomail@ncua.gov
Home Page: www.ncua.gov

Michael Fryzel, Manager

Governed by a three member board appointed by the President and confirmed by the US Senate, this independent federal agency charters and supervises federal credit unions. NCUA, with the backing of the full faith and credit of the US government, operates the National Credit Union Share Insurance Fund, insuring the savings of 80 million account holders in all federal credit unions and many state chartered credit unions.

8602 National Defined Contribution Council
307 Waverley Oaks Rd.
Waltham, MA 02452

781-693-7500
Fax: 866-904-9666
Home Page: www.zoominfo.com
Social Media: Facebook, Twitter, LinkedIn

Yonaton Stern, CEO & Chief Scientist
Eugenia Gillan, Vice President of Engineering
Mark Ruthfield, Vice President of Sales
Santosh Sharan, Vice President of Production Mgt.
Don Wynns, Vice President of Business Dev

NDCC is dedicated to the promotion and protection of the defined contribution industry and the public it serves. The Council specifically addresses the legislative needs of the defined contribution industry's plan service providers.
300 Members
Founded in 1995

8603 National Federation of Municipal Analysts
PO Box 14893
Pittsburgh, PA 15234

412-341-4898
Fax: 412-341-4894
E-Mail: lgood@nfma.org
Home Page: www.nfma.org
Social Media: Twitter, LinkedIn

Jeffery Burger, Chairman
Susan Dushock, Vice Chairman
Jennifer Johnston, Treasurer
Lisa Washburn, Secretary
Lisa Good, Executive Director

Promotes the profession of municipal credit analysts through educational programs, industry, communications and related programming.
1000 Members
Founded in 1997

8604 National Finance Adjusters
8075 E. Morgan Trail
Suite 4
Scottsdale, AZ 85258

623-516-1018
Fax: 410-728-2528
E-Mail: info@nfacoop.com
Home Page: www.nfacoop.com

Burton Greenwood Jr, Secretary/Treasurer
Jack S Barnes, Executive Director

Members are collateral recovery specialists.

8605 National Futures Association
300 S. Riverside Plaza
#1800
Chicago, IL 60606-6615

312-781-1300
Fax: 312-781-1467
E-Mail: information@nfa.futures.org
Home Page: www.nfa.futures.org

Daniel J. Roth, President and President
Kenneth F. Haase, Senior Vice President, Information
Regina G. Thoele, Senior Vice President, Compliance
Edward Dasso, III, Vice President of Market Regulation
Jamila Piracci, Vice President of OTC Derivatives

Association for corporations and firms that are registered with the Commodity Futures Trading Commission.

8606 National Home Equity Mortgage Association
42484 Bellagio Drive
Bermuda Dunes, CA 92203

760-772-5806

Jeffrey Zeltzer, Principal

Mission is to promote the growth and recognition of the home equity lending industry.
300 Members
Founded in 1974

8607 National Institute of Pension Administrators
330 N Wabash Ave
Suite 2000
Chicago, IL 60611-7621

800-999-6472
Fax: 312-673-6609
E-Mail: nipa@nipa.org
Home Page: www.nipa.org
Social Media: LinkedIn

Ralph Delsesto, APR, President
Ann Slotwinski, APR, President Elect and CFO
James Eberhardt, , APA, Immediate Past President
Laura Rudzinski, Executive Director
Alexis Bauer-Kolak, Director of Operations

The mission is to enhance professionalism in the retirement plan industry
1000 Members
Founded in 1983

8608 National Investment Company Service Association
8400 Westpark Drive
2nd Floor
McLean, VA 22102

508-485-1500
Fax: 508-488-1560
E-Mail: info@nicsa.org
Home Page: www.nicsa.org
Social Media: Facebook, Twitter, LinkedIn, Google+

Fred J. Naddaff, Chairman
Maureen Leary Jago, Vice Chairman
Barry Benjamin, Treasurer
Theresa Hamacher, CFA, President
Michele Liston, CMP, Deputy Executive Director

NICSA works to facilitate and promote leadership and innovation within the operations sector of the mutual fund industry.
10000 Members
Founded in 1962

8609 National Pawnbrokers Association
P.O.Box 508
Keller, TX 76244
817-337-8830
Fax: 817-337-8875
E-Mail: info@nationalpawnbrokers.org
Home Page: www.nationalpawnbrokers.org
Social Media: Facebook, Twitter, Youtube

Dana Meinecke, Executive Director
Margie Swoyer, Director of Membership
Lindsay Wilson, Director of Meetings and Events
Chris Pearcey, Communications Specialist
Mathew Church, Govt. Relations Administrator

NPA was founded to unite all pawnbrokers in their common efforts to improve the image of the industry, educate the public, adn disseminate professional information and assistance.
2000 Members
Founded in 1987

8610 National Vehicle Leasing Association
7250 Prakway Drive
Suite 510
Hanover, MD 21076

410-782-2342
800-225-6852
Fax: 410-712-4038
E-Mail: info@nvla.org
Home Page: www.nvla.org
Social Media: LinkedIn

Ben Carfrae, CVLE, Past President
PJ McMahon, CVLE, President/Treasurer
Scott Crawford, CVLE, Director
Jack Tracey, CAE, Executive Director
Michael Cardello, III, NY/NJ/CT Chapter Chair

Fosters education, publishing, conferences, legal services, advancement and industry relations certification.
500 Members
Founded in 1968

8611 National Venture Capital Association
1655 Fort Myer Dr
Suite 850
Arlington, VA 22209

703-524-2549
Fax: 703-524-3940
E-Mail: mheesen@nvca.org
Home Page: www.nvca.org
Social Media: Facebook, Twitter, LinkedIn, Youtube

Bobby Franklin, President & CEO
Kelly Slone, Vice President
Mark G. Heseen, President Emeritus
John S. Taylor, Head of Research
Roberta Catucci, Vice President of Administration

National trade association that represents venture capital firms. Activities include advocacy, professional development, networking and research.
450 Members
Founded in 1973

8612 Neighborhood Reinvestment Corporation
5111 North Scottsdale Road
Suite 201
Scottsdale, AZ 85250

800-808-3372
Fax: 480-994-4456
E-Mail: sales@federalregister.com
Home Page: www.federalregister.com

Supplies training, grants, developmental assistance, and a range of other technical services designed to help the local partnerships achieve substantially self-reliant neighborhoods. The goal is to improve a neighborhood's housing and physical conditions, build a positive community image, and establish a healthy real estate market and a core of neighbors capable of managing the continued health of their neighborhood.
Founded in 1978

8613 Partnership for Philanthropic Planning
233 S McCrea St
Suite 300
Indianapolis, IN 46225

317-269-6274
Fax: 317-269-6268
E-Mail: info@pppnet.org
Home Page: www.pppnet.org
Social Media: Facebook, Twitter, LinkedIn, YouTube, flickr

Jeffrey Lydenberg, Chair
Jay Steenhuysen, Chair-elect
Melanie J. Norton, Treasurer
Laura Hansen Dean, Secretary
Michael Kenyon, President and CEO

Members are professionals involved in the process of planning and cultivating charitable gifts.
11500 Members
Founded in 1988

8614 RMA - Risk Management Association
1801 Market Street
Suite 300
Philadelphia, PA 19103-1628

215-446-4000
800-677-7621
Fax: 215-446-4101
E-Mail: customers@rmahq.org
Home Page: www.rmahq.org

Michael J. Loughlin, Chairman
Nancy J. Foster, Vice Chairman
M. Robert Rose, Immediate Past Chair
William F Githens, President & CEO
J. Tol Broome, Jr., CRC, Director

Seeks to improve the risk management capabilities and principles of commercial lending and credit functions, loan administration and asset management in commercial banks and other financial industries.
17500 Members
Founded in 1914

8615 Retirement Industry Trust Association
424 Montgomery Avenue
Suite 102
Bethesda, MD 20814

301-652-5066
Fax: 301-577-6476
E-Mail: obryonco@aol.com

David S O'Bryon, CAE, Executive Director

8616 Securities Industry and Financial Markets Association (SIFMA)
1101 New York Ave NW
8th Floor
Washington, DC 20005

202-962-7300
Fax: 202-962-7305
E-Mail: webmaster@sifma.org
Home Page: www.sifma.org
Social Media: Twitter, LinkedIn, Youtube, Google+

Judd Gregg, CEO
Kenneth E. Bentsen, Jr., President
Cheryl Crispen, Executive Vice President
Ira D. Hammerman, Executive VP & CEO General Counsel
David Krasner, Chief Financial Officer

SIFMA's mission is to champion policies and practices that benefit investors and issuers, expand and perfect global capital markets, and foster the development of new products and services. SIFMA provides an enhanced member network of access and forward-looking services, as well as premiere educational resources for the professionals within the industry and the investors whom they serve.

8617 Security Traders Association
1115 Broadway
Suite 1110
New York, NY 10010

855-603-1348
Fax: 212-321-3449
E-Mail: jwippern@securitytraders.org
Home Page: www.securitytraders.org
Social Media: Facebook, Twitter, LinkedIn

Jim Toes, President & CEO
Kerry E. Flynn, Vice President
Michele Lindenberger, Director of Marketing

Members involved in the securities industry.
7000 Members
Founded in 1934

8618 Small Business Investor Alliance
1100 H Street NW
Suite 610
Washington, DC 20005

202-628-5055
Fax: 202-628-5080
E-Mail: info@sbia.org
Home Page: www.sbia.org
Social Media: Twitter, LinkedIn

Charles McCusker, Chairman
Mike Blackburn, Chair-Elect
JD White, Vice Chairman
Carolyn Galiette, Treasurer
Brett Palmer, President

Trade association representing federally licensed venture capital firms and small private equity firms.
400 Members
Founded in 1958

8619 Society for Information Management
15000 Commerce Pkwy.
Suite C
Mount Laurel, NJ 08054

856-380-6807
800-387-9746
Fax: 856-439-0525
E-Mail: sim@simnet.org
Home Page: www.simnet.org
Social Media: Facebook, Twitter, LinkedIn, www.multiview.com

Jim Knight, Chairman
Eric Gorham, Vice Chairman
Caren Shiozaki, Treasurer/Secretary
Patricia A. Coffey, Chair Emeritus
Kevin More, Director, Chapter Representative

SIM was formed to enhance international recognition of information as a basic organizational resource and to promote the effective utilization and management of this resource towards the improvement of management performance. It attempts to enhance communications between IS executives and the senior executives responsible for management of the business enterprise.
3000 Members
Founded in 1969

8620 Society of Financial Examiners
12100 Sunset Hills Rd
Suite 130
Reston, VA 20190-3221

703-234-4140
800-787-7633
Fax: 888-436-8686
E-Mail: sofe@sofe.org
Home Page: www.sofe.org
Social Media: Facebook, LinkedIn

L Brackett, Executive Director
Judy Estus, Administrator
Richard Foster, President
Rick Nelson, Treasurer
Annette Knief, Secretary

Is a professional society for examiners of insurance companies, banks, savings and loans, and credit unions.
1600 Members
Founded in 1973

8621 Society of Quantitative Analysts
PO Box 6
Rutledge, MO 63563

800-918-7930
E-Mail: sqa@sqa-us.org
Home Page: www.sqa-us.org
Social Media: Facebook, LinkedIn

Sergei Polevikov, CFA, President
Indrani De, CFA, Vice President
Peg DiOrio, Secretary
Inna Okounkova, Secretary
Irina Bogacheva, Past President

SQA is concerned with the application of new and innovative techniques for finance, with particular emphasis on the use of quantitative techniques in investment management.
350 Members
Founded in 1989

8622 Stable Value Investment Association
1025 Connecticut Avenue NW
Suite 1000
Washington, DC 20036

202-580-7620
800-327-2270
Fax: 202-580-7621
E-Mail: info@StableValue.org
Home Page: www.stablevalue.org
Social Media: Twitter, LinkedIn

Marc Magnoli, Chair

Members are firms and individuals with a professional interest in savings for retirement.
Founded in 1990

8623 State Debt Management Networking
2760 Research Park Drive
Lexington, KY 40511

859-244-8175
Fax: 859-244-8053
E-Mail: nast@csg.org
Home Page: www.sdmn.org

Hon. Richard K Ellis, Chair
Robert Coalter, Vice-chair
Laura Lockwood-Mccall, Director, Debt Management
Robert L. Watson, Assistant Director
Colin Macnaught, Assistant Treasurer

SDMN members are state officials concerned with the insurance or management of state debt. The purpose is to enhance debt management practices throough training, development of educational materials, and data collection and dissemination
50 Members
Founded in 1991

8624 State Risk and Insurance Management Association
PO Box 13777
Austin, TX 78711

512-936-1502
Home Page: www.strima.org

Jonathan Bow, President

STRIMA members are state government risk and insurance managers.
50 Members
Founded in 1974

8625 Tax Executives Institute
1200 G St NW
Suite 300
Washington, DC 20005

202-638-5601
Fax: 202-638-5607
Home Page: www.tei.org

Timothy Mc Cormally, Executive Director
Deborah K Gaffney, Director Conference Planning
Deborah C Giesey, Director Administration

A professional organization of corporate tax executives. Membership is open to corporate officers and employees chargesd with administering their company's tax affairs.
7000 Members
Founded in 1944

8626 The Fiduciary & Investment Risk Management Association
P.O.Box 507
Stockbridge, GA 30281-0507

678-565-6211
Fax: 678-565-8788
E-Mail: info@thefirma.org
Home Page: www.thefirma.org
Social Media: Facebook, Twitter, LinkedIn

Bruce K Goldberg, CTA, CPA, President
Jennifer De Vries, CTA, Vice President
Jeffrey S. Kropschot, CTCP, IACCP, Secretary

Members are audit and compliance professionals.
820 Members
Founded in 1989

8627 The Resource Centre for Religious Institutes
8824 Cameron Street
Silver Spring, MD 20910

301-589-8143
Fax: 301-589-2897
E-Mail: trcri@trcri.org
Home Page: www.trcri.org
Social Media: Facebook, Twitter, www.blogspot.com

Fr. Thomas Carkhuff, OSC, President
Sr. Lynn McKenzie, OSB, Vice-President
Daniel J. Ward, OSB, JCL, JD, Executive Director
Sr. Margaret Ma Cosgrove, BVM, Treasurer
Sr. Margaret Perron, RJM, Secretary

The leading resource and provider of education, services, and information to meet the current and emerging stewardship needs of all religious institutes throughout the United States.
Founded in 1981

8628 Urban Homesteading Assistance Board
120 Wall St
20th Floor
New York, NY 10005

212-479-3300
Fax: 212-344-6457
E-Mail: webmaster@uhab.org
Home Page: www.uhab.org
Social Media: Facebook, Twitter, Youtube

Andrew Reicher, Executive Director
Richard Heitler, Chief Operations Officer
Janice Lancaster, Office Manager
Julie Harris, Chief Financial Officer
Christine Heeg, Director

The oldest provider of technical assistance to homesteading and sweat equity groups in the country. Promotes homesteading as an important component of comprehensive self-help housing programs. Provides technical assistance and training in self-help housing rehabili-

tation and managment to low income tenants, cooperative shareholders and homesteaders.
8 Members
Founded in 1973

8629 Wall Street Technology Association
620 Shrewsbury Ave
Suite C
Tinton Falls, NJ 07701

732-530-8808
Fax: 732-530-0020
E-Mail: info@wsta.org
Home Page: www.wsta.org
Social Media: Facebook, Twitter, LinkedIn

John Killeen, President
Michael Maffattone, 1st Vice President
Joseph Weitekamp, 2nd Vice President
Phyllis Lampell, Executive Director
JoAnn Cooper, Executive Director

Nonprofit educational organization that focuses on technologies, operational approaches, and business issues for the global financial community.
2600+ Members
Founded in 1967

8630 Wall Street Technology Association (WSTA)
620 Shrewsbury Ave
Suite C
Tinton Falls, NJ 07701

732-530-8808
Fax: 732-530-0020
E-Mail: info@wsta.org
Home Page: www.wsta.org
Social Media: Facebook, Twitter, LinkedIn

John Killeen, President
Phyllis Lampell, Executive Director
JoAnn Cooper, Executive Director

Nonprofit educational organization that focuses on technologies, operational approaches, and business issues for the global financial community.
2800+ Members
Founded in 1967

8631 Washington Municipal Treasurers Associaion
2601 Fourth Avenue
Suite 800
Seattle, WA 98121-1280

206-625-1300
E-Mail: hstewart@mrsc.org
Home Page: www.wmta-online.com

Deborah Booher, President
Michael Olson, President-Elect
Stephanie McKenzie, Secretary
Elizabeth Alba, Treasurer

Mission is to promote the profession of municipal treasurers through education, mutual support, professional recognition, and legislative advocacy.
Founded in Was

Newsletters

8632 AARMR Newsletter
American Association of Residential Mortgage
1025 Thomas Jefferson Street NW
Suite 500 East
Washington, DC 20007

202-521-3999
Fax: 202-833-3636
E-Mail: efreundel@aarmr.org
Home Page: www.aarmr.org

David A Saunders, Executive Director
Erika Freundel, Manager Of Member Services
Frequency: Quarterly

8633 AEFA Newsletter
American Education Finance Association
8365 S Armadillo Trail
Evergreen, CO 80439

303-674-0857
Fax: 303-670-8986
Home Page: www.aefa.cc

Ed Steinbacher, Executive Director
Frequency: Quarterly

8634 AFCPE Newsletter
Association for Financial Counseling and Planning
2112 Arlington Avenue
Suite H
Upper Arlington, OH 43221

614-485-9650
Fax: 614-485-9621
Home Page: www.afcpe.org

Sharon Burns, PhD, Executive Director
Frequency: Quarterly

8635 AMI Bulletin
Assn for Management Information in Financial Svcs
14247 Saffron Circle
Carmel, IN 46032

317-518-5857
Fax: 317-518-5877
E-Mail: ami2@amifs.org
Home Page: www.amifs.org

Adam Schabes, President

News, calendars, events, and industry articles.
Frequency: Quarterly

8636 Airline Financial News
PBI Media
1201 Seven Locks Road
Suite 300
Potomac, MD 20854-2931

301-354-1400
800-777-5006
Fax: 301-309-3847
Home Page: www.aviationtoday.com

Richard Koulbanis, Publisher

Provides information for CEO's financial directors, operations managers, engine aircraft manufacturers and suppliers on financial, market development, buying, leasing and aircraft transactions.
Cost: $697.00
Frequency: Weekly
Circulation: 1850

8637 Annual Statement Studies
RMA - Risk Management Association
6147 Ridge Ave
Suite 2300
Philadelphia, PA 19128-2627

215-482-3222
800-677-7621
Fax: 215-446-4101
E-Mail: customers@rmahq.org
Home Page: www.rmahq.org

Angelo Roma, Owner
William F Githens, Director Member Relations
Dwight Overturf, CFO/Information Technology Officer
Florence J Wetzel, COO/Administrative Officer
John Rumm, Executive Director
Frequency: Annual

8638 Asset-Backed Alert
Harrison Scott Publications
5 Marine View Plz
Suite 301
Hoboken, NJ 07030-5722

201-386-1491
Fax: 201-659-4141
E-Mail: info@hspnews.com
Home Page: www.hspnews.com

Andy Albert, Owner
Tom Ferris, Editor
Daniel Cowles, CEO/President
Barbara Bannace, Marketing
Joan Tassie, Operations Director

A weekly newsletter on the securitization of consumer and corporate receivables.
Cost: $2297.00
10 Pages
Frequency: Weekly
Circulation: 2178
ISSN: 1520-3700
Founded in 1988
Printed in 4 colors on matte stock

8639 BNA Pension & Benefits Reporter
Bureau of National Affairs
1801 S Bell St
Arlington, VA 22202-4501

703-341-3000
800-372-1033
Fax: 800-253-0332
E-Mail: customercare@bna.com
Home Page: www.bnabooks.com

Gregory C McCaffrey, President
Paul N Wojcik, Chairman

Covers latest pension developments stemming from the passage of ERISA and its amendments, plus pension and welfare benefit regulations, standards, enforcement actions, court decisions, legislative and administrative actions, agency options, and employee benefit trust fund requirements.
Cost: $1448.00
Frequency: Weekly
Founded in 1929
Printed in on matte stock

8640 Back-Office Bulletin
United Communications Group
Two Washingtonian Center
9737 Washingtonian Blvd Suite 100
Gaithersburg, MD 20878-7364

301-287-2700
Fax: 301-287-2039
Home Page: www.ucg.com

Daniel Brown, Publisher

For financial operations professionals.
Founded in 1970

8641 Bandwidth Investor
Kagan World Media
1 Lower Ragsdale Dr
Building 1, Suite 130
Monterey, CA 93940-5749

831-624-1536
Fax: 831-625-3225
E-Mail: info@kagan.com
Home Page: www.kagan.com

Tim Baskerville, President/CEO
Harvey Kraft, Circulation/Marketing Manager
Cost: $1195.00
Frequency: Monthly
Founded in 1969

8642 Bank 13D Dictionary
SNL Securities
PO Box 2124
Charlottesvle, VA 22902-2124

434-977-1600
Fax: 434-977-4466

E-Mail: isales@snl.com
Home Page: www.snl.com

Todd Davenport, Editor
Reid Nagle, Chief Operating Officer
Nick Cafferillo, Chief Operating Officer
Adam Hall, Managing Director

For banks, thrifts, investors, investment bankers, law firms, consultants and regulatory agencies. Contains all active 13D filings and related filings for every public traded bank in the country, including those which trade on the 'pink sheets.'
Frequency: Quarterly
Founded in 1987

8643 Benefax
SNL Securities
PO Box 2124
Charlottesvle, VA 22902-2124

434-977-1600
Fax: 434-977-4466
E-Mail: isales@snl.com
Home Page: www.snl.com

Keith Davis, Editor
Reid Nagle, Chief Operating Officer
Nick Cafferillo, Chief Operating Officer
Adam Hall, Managing Director

For bank and thrift executives. Contains only summaries of available information.
1 Pages
Frequency: Monthly
Founded in 1987

8644 Bondweek
Institutional Investor
225 Park Ave S
7th Floor
New York, NY 10003-1605

212-224-3300
Fax: 212-224-3197
E-Mail: iieditor@institutionalinvestor.com
Home Page: www.institutionalinvestor.com

Christopher Brown, CEO
Erik Kolk, Publisher
Deirdre Brennan, Managing Editor
Nick Ferris, Group Marketing Director

Coverage of stocks, bonds and investments for the financial professional and consumer, information includes rates.
Cost: $2245.00
Frequency: 51 issues per y
Founded in 1967

8645 Broadcast Banker/Broker
Kagan World Media
1 Lower Ragsdale Dr
Building One,Suite 130
Monterey, CA 93940-5749

831-624-1536
800-307-2529
Fax: 831-625-3225
E-Mail: info@kagan.com
Home Page: www.kagan.com

Tim Baskerville, President
Tom Johnson, Marketing Manager

A readers guide to equity deals and debt financing for radio and TV Station buying and selling analyzed. Key details on station trades with critical yardsticks of value. Three month trial is available.
Cost: $925.00
Frequency: Monthly

8646 Broadcast Investor
Kagan World Media
126 Clock Tower Place
Carmel, CA 93923-8746

831-624-1536
Fax: 831-624-5882
E-Mail: info@kagan.com
Home Page: www.kagan.com

George Niesen, Editor
Tom Johnson, Marketing Manager

The newsletter on investments in radio and TV stations and publicly held companies. Comprehensive analysis of cash flow multiples and trends that impact value. Three month trial available.
Cost: $895.00
Frequency: Monthly

8647 Broker Magazine
Thomson Media
1 State St
27th Floor
New York, NY 10004-1481

212-825-8445
800-221-1809
Fax: 800-235-5552
Home Page: www.sourcemedia.com

Timothy Murphy, Publisher
James Malkin, Director of Sales
Melissa Sefic, Director of Sales

Features on training, motivation, technology, legislation and marketing
Frequency: Monthly
Circulation: 750000

8648 Budget Processors in the States
National Association of State Budge Officers
444 N Capitol St NW
Suite 642
Washington, DC 20001-1512

202-624-5382
Fax: 202-624-7745
E-Mail: spattison@nasbo.org
Home Page: www.nasbo.org

Frequency: Bi-Ennial

8649 Bull & Bear Financial Report
PO Bo 917179
Longwood, FL 32791

954-781-3455
800-336-2855
Fax: 954-781-5865
Home Page: www.thebullandbear.com

David J Robinson, Publisher/Editor

Dozens of original articles by leading investment pros with investment information on precious metals, commodities, mutual funds, currencies, economic trends and monetary survival.
Circulation: 55000

8650 Bulletin Newsletter
EMTA - Trade Association for the Emerging Markets
360 Madison Avenue
17th Floor
New York, NY 10017

646-289-5410
Fax: 646-289-5429
E-Mail: awerner@emta.org
Home Page: www.emta.org

Michael M Chamberlin, Executive Director
Aviva Werner, General Counsel
Jonathan Murno, Managing Director
Suzette Ortiz, Office Manager
Monika Forbes, Administrative Assistant
Frequency: Quarterly

8651 CFMA Building Profits
Construction Financial Management Association
29 Emmons Drive
Princeton, NJ 08540

609-452-8000
Fax: 609-452-0474
E-Mail: pwristen@cfma.org
Home Page: www.cfma.org

Paula Wristen, Editor
Sarah Patt, Sales/Advertising Director
William Schwab, President

The leading source of education and information about financial management within the construction industry. The only magazine dedicated to helping financial managers in the construction business find practical solutions to emerging issues in the industry. Accepts advertising.
32 Pages
Circulation: 6500

8652 CIPFA Newsletter
National Association of Independent Public Finance
PO Box 304
Montgomery, IL 60538-0304

630-896-1292
800-624-7321
Fax: 209-633-6265
E-Mail: rhoban@naipfa.com
Home Page: www.naipfa.com

Roseanne M Hoban, Executive Director
Frequency: Quarterly

8653 CRA/HMDA Update
Inside Mortgage Finance Publishers
7910 Woodmont Ave
Suite 1000
Bethesda, MD 20814-7019

301-951-1240
Fax: 301-656-1709
E-Mail: service@imfpubs.com
Home Page: www.imfpubs.com

Guy Cecala, Owner
John Lewis, President

Complete coverage of Community Reinvestment Act and Home Mortgage Disclosure Act developments and other affordable housing and community development issues.
Cost: $395.00
Frequency: Monthly
Circulation: 450

8654 Cable Program Investor
Kagan World Media
126 Clock Tower Place
Carmel, CA 93923-8746

831-624-1536
Fax: 831-624-5882
E-Mail: info@kagan.com
Home Page: www.kagan.com

George Niesen, Editor
Tom Johnson, Marketing Manager

Covers the economics of basic cable programming networks. Numbers, perspective unavailable from any other source. Programmers applaud its accuracy. Three month trial available.
Cost: $845.00
Frequency: Monthly

8655 Cable TV Finance
Kagan World Media
126 Clock Tower Place
Carmel, CA 93923-8746

831-624-1536
800-307-2529
Fax: 831-624-5882
E-Mail: info@kagan.com
Home Page: www.kagan.com

George Niesen, Editor
Tom Johnson, Marketing Manager
Tim Baskerville, CEO/President

Cable's financial bible. Analyzes sources of funding for cable TV. Selling and buying of cable systems. Financing strategies and trends.

Exclusive surveys of capital sources. Three month trial available.
Cost: $995.00
Frequency: Monthly
Founded in 1969

8656 Cable TV Investor
Kagan World Media
1 Lower Ragsdale Dr
Building One, Suite 130
Monterey, CA 93940-5749

831-624-1536
800-307-2529
Fax: 831-625-3225
E-Mail: info@kagan.com
Home Page: www.kagan.com

Tim Baskerville, President
Tom Johnson, Marketing Manager

Readers road map to cable stock trends. Chart service tracking stock price movements of 37 publicly held cable TV companies. Each graph shows two years of stock price activity. Three month trial available.
Cost: $945.00
Frequency: Monthly

8657 Card News
Phillips Publishing
7811 Montrose Road
Potomac, MD 20854

301-340-2100
E-Mail: feedback@healthydirections.com
Home Page: www.healthydirections.com

Covering the financial card marketplace.

8658 Client Information Bulletin
WPI Communications
55 Morris Ave
Suite 300
Springfield, NJ 07081-1422

973-467-8700
Fax: 973-467-0368
E-Mail: info@wpicomm.com
Home Page: www.wpicomm.com

Steve Klinghoffer, Owner
Marilyn Lang, Chairman

Bulletin for lawyers and CPAs to distribute to clients to keep them informed on tax matters. This original publication which has been helping accountants build their practices since 1952, has been redesigned. Covers important new tax developments, general business principals, financial planning, estate planning and other related topics.

8659 Collection Agency Report
First Detroit Corporation
PO Box 5025
Warren, MI 48090-5025

586-573-0045
800-366-5995
Fax: 586-573-9219
E-Mail: info@firstdetroit.com
Home Page: www.firstdetroit.com

Albert Scace, President
Petricia Herrick, Marketing Manager

Provides financially oriented news on the collection agency and bad debt buying industries worldwide.
Cost: $289.00
8 Pages
Frequency: Monthly
ISSN: 1052-4029
Mailing list available for rent: 5000 names at $110 per M

8660 Commercial Mortgage Alert
Harrison Scott Publications
5 Marine View Plz
Suite 301
Hoboken, NJ 07030-5722

201-386-1491
Fax: 201-659-4141
E-Mail: info@hspnews.com
Home Page: www.hspnews.com

Andy Albert, Owner
Tom Ferris, Director
Michelle Lebowitz, Director

A weekly newsletter on the securitization of consumer and corporate receivables.
Cost: $1497.00
10 Pages
Frequency: Weekly
Circulation: 500
ISSN: 1520-3700
Printed in 4 colors on matte stock

8661 Conference Executive Summaries
Society for Information Management
401 N Michigan Avenue
Chicago, IL 60611

312-215-5190
Fax: 312-245-1081
Home Page: www.simnet.org

Jim Luisi, Executive Director
Frequency: Semi-Annual

8662 Conversion Candidates List
SNL Securities
PO Box 2124
Charlottesvle, VA 22902-2124

434-977-1600
Fax: 434-977-4466
E-Mail: isales@snl.com
Home Page: www.snl.com

Chris Smith, Editor
Reid Nagle, Chief Operating Officer
Nick Cafferillo, Chief Operating Officer
Adam Hall, Managing Director

For thrift executives, individual investors and institutional investors. Lists mutual thrifts that are in a position to convert to stock ownership by offering shares for sale.
Frequency: Monthly
Founded in 1987

8663 Conversion Watch
SNL Securities
PO Box 2124
Charlottesvle, VA 22902-2124

434-977-1600
Fax: 434-977-4466
E-Mail: isales@snl.com
Home Page: www.snl.com

Chris Smith, Editor
Nick Cafferillo, Chief Operating Officer
Adam Hall, Managing Director

Delivered via fax whenever new activity is announced, including rumored, pending, announced and completed activity. Provides relevant data from conversion-related filings, including eligible record dates, offering size, Pro Formas, opening and closing dates for the subscription, asset size, net worth and rating of the thrift.
Cost: $1200.00
5 Pages
Frequency: Annual+
Founded in 1987

8664 Cost Control News
Siefer Consultants
PO Box 1384
Storm Lake, IA 50588-1384

712-732-7340
Fax: 712-732-7906
E-Mail: info@siefer.com
Home Page: www.siefer.com/

Dan Siefer, Publisher

Cost cutting opportunities for financial institutions.
Cost: $297.00
8 Pages
Founded in 1981

8665 Credit Collections News
SourceMedia
550 W Van Buren
Suite 1100
Chicago, IL 60607-6680

312-913-1334
Fax: 312-913-1340
Home Page: www.sourcemedia.com

John Stewart, Publisher
Melissa Sefic, Director of Sales

Analysis of the global economy, current industry trends and policies, as well as problems commonly encountered in credit collections.
Frequency: Monthly

8666 Credit Union Journal
SourceMedia
224 Datura Street
Suite 615
West Palm Beach, FL 33401

561-832-2929
Fax: 561-832-2939
Home Page: www.cujournal.com

Frank J Dierkmann, Publisher/Editor
Tim O'Hara, Co-Publisher

JournalScan to review recent credit union developments, industry news articles, an agenda of upcoming meetings, deadlines and events and Washington Watch covering the latest news in Washington DC.
Frequency: Weekly
Circulation: 5300

8667 Credit Union Management
Credit Union Executives Society
PO Box 14167
Madison, WI 53714-167

608-271-2664
800-252-2664
Fax: 608-271-2303
E-Mail: cues@cues.org
Home Page: www.cues.org

Mary Arnold, Publisher
Theresa Sweeney, Editor
Fred Johnson, CEO/President
Cost: $93.00
Frequency: Monthly
Printed in 4 colors on glossy stock

8668 Credit and Collection Manager's Letter
Bureau of Business Practice
76 Ninth Avenue
7th Floor
New York, NY 10011

212-771-0600
Fax: 212-771-0885
Home Page: www.aspenpublishers.com
Social Media: Facebook, Twitter, LinkedIn

Mark Dorman, CEO
Gustavo Dobles, VP Operations

Hands-on information for improving the credit and collection departments in both commercial and consumer markets.
Frequency: SemiMonthly
Circulation: 9380

8669 Daily Tax Report
Bureau of National Affairs

1801 S Bell St
Arlington, VA 22202-4501

703-341-3000
800-372-1033
Fax: 800-253-0332
E-Mail: customercare@bna.com
Home Page: www.bnabooks.com

Paul N Wojcik, CEO

A daily tax notification service that covers legislative, regulatory, judicial and policy developments on a national basis, designed to give tax professionals rapid notification and comprehensive coverage of those developments.
Cost: $3215.00
Frequency: Daily
ISSN: 0092-6884

8670 **Debit Card News**
SourceMedia
224 Datura Street
Suite 615
West Palm Beach, FL 33401

561-832-2929
Fax: 561-832-2939
Home Page: www.cujournal.com

Don Davis, Editor

Marketing, pricing, different card applications, smart cards, point-of-sale and other electronic banking activities.
Frequency: SemiMonthly

8671 **Declined Contribution Market Insights**
National Defined Contribution Council
9101 E Kenyon
Suite 300
Denver, CO 80237-0467

303-770-5353
Fax: 303-770-1812
Home Page: www.ndcconline.org

Al Brust, Executive VP
Frequency: Annual

8672 **Equipment Leasing & Finance**
Equipment Leasing And Finance Association
1825 K Street NW
Suite 900
Washington, DC 20006

202-238-3400
Fax: 202-238-3401
E-Mail: EL&F@elfaonline.org
Home Page: www.elfaonline.org

Amy Vogt, Managing Editor

As the flagship publication of the Equipment Leasing and Finance Association, Equipment Leasing & Finance is the trusted leader, bringing readers unrivaled coverage of the people, trends and issues that have an impact on the $628 billion equipment finance industry. Information of funding sources, portfolio management, sales and marketing strategy, large ticket leasing, transportation leasing, the computer leasing market, remarketing equipment, and the role of the equipment manager.
Frequency: 6x/Year
Circulation: 10000
Founded in 1961
Printed in 4 colors on glossy stock

8673 **Executive Brief**
Society for Information Management
401 N Michigan Avenue
Chicago, IL 60611

312-215-5190
Fax: 312-245-1081
Home Page: www.simnet.org

Jim Luisi, Executive Director
Frequency: Quarterly

8674 **Executive Compensation Review for Commercial Banks**
SNL Securities
PO Box 2124
Charlottesvle, VA 22902-2124

434-977-1600
Fax: 434-977-4466
Home Page: www.snlnet.com

Keith Davis, Editor
Nick Cafferillo, Chief Operating Officer
Reid Nagle, Publisher
Mark Outlaw, Advertising Director
Adam Hall, Managing Director

For banks, regulatory agencies and executive recruiters. Includes detailed compensation and benefit information for the top 5 officers of all publicly traded banks, thrifts, REITs and insurance companies.
550 Pages
Frequency: Annual
Founded in 1988

8675 **Executive Compensation Review for Insurance Companies**
SNL Securities
PO Box 2124
Charlottesvle, VA 22902-2124

434-977-1600
Fax: 434-977-4466
Home Page: www.snlnet.com

Keith Davis, Editor
Nick Cafferillo, Chief Operating Officer
Reid Nagle, Publisher
Mark Outlaw, Advertising Director
Pat LaBua, Subscription Manager

For insurance companies, investment analysts, service providers to the insurance industry and regulators. Includes detailed compensation and benefit information for the top 5 officers of all publicly traded banks, thrifts, REITs and insurance companies.
200 Pages
Frequency: Annual
Founded in 1997

8676 **Executive Compensation Review for REITs**
SNL Securities
PO Box 2124
Charlottesvle, VA 22902-2124

434-977-1600
Fax: 434-977-4466
E-Mail: isales@snl.com
Home Page: www.snl.com

Keith Davis, Editor
Chandler Spears, Chief Operating Officer
Nick Cafferillo, Chief Operating Officer
Adam Hall, Managing Director

For REITs, REIT service providers, investment companies, executive recruiters and regulators. Annual data digests that include detailed compensation and benefit information for the top 5 officers of all publicly traded banks, thrifts, REITs and insurance companies.
Cost: $495.00
Frequency: Monthly
Founded in 1987

8677 **Executive Compensation Review for Thrift Institutions**
SNL Securities
PO Box 2124
Charlottesvle, VA 22902-2124

434-977-1600
Fax: 434-977-4466
E-Mail: isales@snl.com
Home Page: www.snl.com

Keith Davis, Editor
Nick Cafferillo, Chief Operating Officer
Adam Hall, Managing Director

For thrifts, regulatory agencies and executive recruiters. Annual data digests that include detailed compensation and benefit information for the top 5 officers of all publicly traded banks, thrifts, REITs and insurance companies.
Cost: $495.00
Frequency: Monthly
Founded in 1987

8678 **Export Finance Letter**
International Business Affairs Corporation
5523 Brite Dr
#346
Bethesda, MD 20817-6304

301-907-8647
Fax: 301-907-8650
E-Mail: editor@exportsourcebook.com
Home Page: www.exportsourcebook.com

Richard Barovick, Owner

A report on government and private resources in US Export & Import Finance, Payments and Risk Management.
Founded in 1979

8679 **FEI Briefing**
Financial Executives Institute
200 Campus Drive
PO Box 674
Forham Park, NJ 07932

973-360-0177
Fax: 973-765-1023
Home Page: www.fei.org

P Norman Roy, Publisher
Christopher Allen, Editor
Colleen Sayther Cunningham, CEO/President
Christopher Allen, Marketing
Lucinda Arsenio, Secretary

Up-to-date news for treasurers and controllers of large corporations.
Circulation: 14000
Founded in 1931

8680 **FSR Newsletter**
Financial Services Roundtable
1001 Pennsylvania Ave Nw
Suite 500 S
Washington, DC 20004-2508

202-628-2455
Fax: 202-289-1903
E-Mail: info@fsround.org
Home Page: www.fsround.org

Steve Bartlett, CEO
Frequency: Monthly

8681 **Federal Securities Act**
Matthew Bender and Company
744 Broad St
Newark, NJ 07102-3885

973-820-2000
800-227-9597
Fax: 937-865-1284
E-Mail: info.in@lexisnexis.com
Home Page: www.lexisnexis.com

Kent Frankstone, Manager
Rebecca Schmitt, Chief Financial Officer

A comprehensive, up-to-date treatise on the Securities Act of 1933 and all amendments thereto, as well as the application of the Trust Indenture Act of 1939.

8682 **Fee Income Report**
Siefer Consultants
PO Box 1384
Storm Lake, IA 50588-1384

712-732-7340
Fax: 712-732-7906
E-Mail: info@siefer.com
Home Page: www.siefer.com

Dan Siefer, Publisher

Fee income news and opportunities for financial institutions.
Cost: $297.00
8 Pages
Frequency: Monthly
Founded in 1981

8683 Fidelity Insight
Mutual Fund Investors Association
20 William St
Suite 200
Wellesley, MA 02481-4138

781-235-1560
800-586-4727
Home Page: www.kobren.com

Eric Kobren, President
Chris Keith, Senior Vice President
Todd Peters, Senior Vice President

Offers information and rates for mutual funds, investments, stocks and bonds.
Cost: $127.00
8 Pages
Frequency: Monthly
Founded in 1985

8684 Finance Company Weekly
SNL Securities
PO Box 2124
Charlottesvle, VA 22902-2124

434-977-1600
Fax: 434-977-4466
E-Mail: isales@snl.com
Home Page: www.snl.com

David Meadors, Editor
Nick Cafferillo, Chief Operating Officer
Adam Hall, Managing Director

Weekly news on publicly and privately traded finance companies. Includes consumer, commercial, credit card companies, pawn shops and leasing companies. Summarizes recent industry earnings announcement, trends, registration statements and performance rankings.
Cost: $396.00
10 Pages
Frequency: Weekly
Founded in 1987

8685 Financial Management Association International (FMA)
University of South Florida
4202 E Fowler Ave
Tampa, FL 33620-9951

813-974-2011
Fax: 813-974-5530
E-Mail: fma@coba.usf.edu OR info@fma.org
Home Page: www.usf.edu

Judy L Genshaft, President
William Christie, Financial Management Editor
Keith M Howe, Journal of Applied Finance Editor
James Schallheim, FMA Survey Synthesis Series Editor
John Finnerty, Editor FMA Online

Financial books, textbooks, databases, newspapers, research services, software and related products and services.
Frequency: Quarterly
Founded in 1970

8686 Financial Managers Update
Financial Managers Society
100 W Monroe
Suite 810
Chicago, IL 60603

312-578-1300
800-275-4367
Fax: 312-578-1308
E-Mail: info@fmsinc.org
Home Page: www.fmsinc.org/cms

Dick Yingst, President/CEO
Jennifer Vimarco, Professional Development Director
Jennifer Doak, Director of Marketing

The latest accounting and regulatory information related to financial institutions, as well as news and trends. Includes a regulatory check list.
8 Pages
Circulation: 1400
Mailing list available for rent
Printed in one color

8687 Financial NetNews
Institutional Investor
488 Madison Ave
15th Floor
New York, NY 10022-5701

212-303-3100
800-115-9196
Fax: 212-224-3491
E-Mail: iieditor@institutionalinvestor.com
Home Page: www.institutionalinvestor.com

Dahlia Weinman, Publisher
Deirdre Brennan, Editor
Nick Ferris, Marketing Manager
Chris Brown, CEO/President

Businesses and their Web sites, providing up-to-date information on networkings and assessment of industry trends and mistakes.
Frequency: Weekly

8688 Financial News
Financial News Corporation
PO Box 1769
Jacksonville, FL 32201-1769

904-356-2466
Fax: 904-353-2628
E-Mail: editorial@jaxdailyrecord.com
Home Page: www.jaxdailyrecord.com

James F Bailey Jr, Publisher
Angie Campbell, Business Manager
Karen Mathis, Managing Editor

Business and legal information for financial institutions.
Cost: $89.00
Frequency: Daily

8689 Financial Planning Advisory
WPI Communications
55 Morris Ave
Suite 300
Springfield, NJ 07081-1422

973-467-8700
800-323-4995
Fax: 973-467-0368
E-Mail: info@wpicomm.com
Home Page: www.wpicomm.com

Steve Klinghoffer, Owner
Marilyn Lang, Chairman

Offers institutions and businesses information on financial planning and campaigns.
Founded in 1952

8690 Financial Services
8180 Corporate Park Drive
Suite 305
Cincinnati, OH 45242-3309

513-591-0149
Fax: 513-527-3141

Linda Niesz, Publisher

National and regional news for members.
Cost: $7.00
6 Pages
Frequency: Monthly

8691 Financial Services Daily
SNL Securities
PO Box 2124
Charlottesvle, VA 22902-2124

434-977-1600
Fax: 434-977-4466
E-Mail: isales@snl.com
Home Page: www.snl.com

David Meadors, Editor
Nick Cafferillo, Chief Operating Officer
Adam Hall, Managing Director

Daily fax of news headlines on finance companies, mortgage banks, investment advisors and brokers/dealers, plus divident and earnings announcements, stock highlights and index values, registration statements and ownership filings.
6 Pages
Frequency: Daily
Founded in 1987

8692 Financial Services M&A Insider
SNL Securities
PO Box 2124
Charlottesvle, VA 22902-2124

434-977-1600
Fax: 434-977-4466
E-Mail: isales@snl.com
Home Page: www.snl.com

L Vencil, Editor
Reid Nagle, Chief Operating Officer
Nick Cafferillo, Chief Operating Officer
Adam Hall, Managing Director

Fax newsletter featuring in-depth articles and the latest financial information on financial services M&A activity. Covers mortgage banks, finance companies, investment advisors and broker/dealers. Analyzes industry trends and specific market and ownership changes to identify potential consolidation activity.
Cost: $695.00
10 Pages
Frequency: Monthly
Founded in 1987

8693 Financial Women Today
Financial Women International
1027 W Roselawn Avenue
Roseville, MN 55113

651-487-7632
866-807-6081
Fax: 651-489-1322
E-Mail: info@fwi.org
Home Page: www.fwi.org

Melissa Curzon, President
Cindy Hass, VP
Carleen DeSisto, Secretary

Covers financial services industry trends, as well as women's issues and association news.
1000 Members
Circulation: 10,000
Founded in 1921

8694 First Friday
ASCU
PO Box 5488
Madison, WI 53705-0488

608-238-2646
Fax: 608-238-2646

C Barle, Publisher

Market research and statistics.
Cost: $35.00
6 Pages
Frequency: Monthly
Founded in 1973
Mailing list available for rent: 11,000 names at $60 per M
Printed in on matte stock

8695 Fiscal Survey of the States
National Association of State Budget Officers
444 N Capitol St Nw
Suite 642
Washington, DC 20001-1556

202-624-8020
Fax: 202-624-7745

E-Mail: spattison@nasbo.org
Home Page: www.nasbo.org

Scott Pattison, Executive Director
Frequency: Semi-Annual

8696 **Focus on Accountability**
Evangelical Council for Financial Accountability
440 W Jubal Early Dr
Suite 130
Winchester, VA 22601

540-535-0103
800-323-9473
Fax: 540-535-0533
E-Mail: info@ecfa.org
Home Page: www.ecfa.org

Dan Busby, President
Frequency: Quarterly
Circulation: 30000

8697 **Forecaster**
Forecaster Publishing Company
19623 Ventura Blvd
Tarzana, CA 91356-2918

818-345-4421
Fax: 818-345-0468

John Kamin, Owner
Brian Kamin, CEO/President

Analyzes lucrative speculations in unusual areas. Researches gold, silver, coins, gems, property, antiques, interest rates, business cycles, economic advice, tax strategies, wine, guns, collector cars and more.
Cost: $180.00
8 Pages
Frequency: Weekly
ISSN: 0095-294X
Founded in 1962
Mailing list available for rentat $170 per M
Printed in 2 colors on matte stock

8698 **Fund Directions**
Financial Communications Company
225 Park Avenue S
New York, NY 10003

212-953-3500
800-715-9195
Fax: 212-224-3699
E-Mail: customerservice@iinews.com
Home Page: www.funddirections.com

Colin Minnihan, Publisher
Wendy Connett, Executive Editor
Amy Cohen, Managing Editor
Kevin Francella, Plant Manager
Kim Lemmonds, Marketing Director

Trends in the rapidly changing fund environment and analysis of key issues in fund governance.
Frequency: Monthly
Circulation: 2500

8699 **Futures Market Alert**
Robbins Trading Company
8700 W Bryn Mawr Ave
Seventh Floor, S Tower
Chicago, IL 60631-3530

773-380-9700
800-453-4444
Fax: 773-380-9701
E-Mail: info@robbinstrading.com
Home Page: www.rabjohnsnef.com

Reginold Rabjohns, Partner

Covers futures trading.

8700 **Genomics Investing**
Asset Alternatives
170 Linden Street
Wellesley, MA 02482

781-304-1400
Fax: 781-304-1440
Home Page: www.assetnews.com

Tom Salemi, Senior Editor
Brian Gormley, Editor
Lisa Hughes, Circulation Manager
Barbara Bissonnette, VP Marketing/Sales

The genomics market offers a wealth of public and private investment opportunities. Genomics Investing helps you determine which are likely to be winners by identifying the most attractive companies and industry sub-sectors, and uncovering hot trends in genomics investing. Every monthly issue puts you intouch with the investment analysts, mutual fund managers, venture capitalists, and industry executives who are shaping the marketplace.
Cost: $1195.00
Frequency: Monthly
Printed in on matte stock

8701 **Global Money Management**
Institutional Investor
225 Park Ave S
7th Floor
New York, NY 10003-1605

212-224-3300
800-543-4444
Fax: 212-224-3197
E-Mail: iieditor@institutionalinvestor.com
Home Page: www.institutionalinvestor.com

Christopher Brown, President/CEO
Deirdre Brennan, Managing Editor
Stuart Wise, Senior Editor
Nick t Ferris, Group Marketing Director

Money management news. Accepts advertising.
Cost: $11.95
Frequency: Fortnightly
Founded in 1967

8702 **Gold Newsletter**
Blanchard and Company
2400 Jefferson Hwy
Suite 600
New Orleans, LA 70121-3838

504-835-0029
800-877-8847
Fax: 504-837-4884
E-Mail: gnlmail@jeffersoncompanies.com
Home Page: www.neworleansconference.com

James Blanchard, President
Brien Lundin, CEO

Offers information and news for the financial community on stocks, bonds and investment opportunities.
Cost: $198.00
Frequency: Monthly
Founded in 1971

8703 **Government Affairs Bulletin**
Financial Services Roundtable
1001 Pennsylvania Ave Nw
Suite 500 S
Washington, DC 20004-2508

202-628-2455
Fax: 202-289-1903
E-Mail: info@fsround.org
Home Page: www.fsround.org

Steve Bartlett, CEO
Frequency: Monthly

8704 **Government Finance Officers Association Newsletter**
Government Finance Officers Association
203 N La Salle St
Suite 2700
Chicago, IL 60601-1216

312-977-9700
Fax: 312-977-4806
E-Mail: inquiry@gfoa.org
Home Page: www.gfoa.org

Jeffrey L Esser, Executive Director
Karen Utterback, Editor/Research & Consulting
Rebecca Russum, Senior Editor Technical Services
Barbara Mollo, Director Operations & Marketing
John Jurkash, CFO/Financial Administration

The purpose of the Government Finance Officers Association is to enhance and promote the professional management of governments for the public benefit by identifying and developing financial policies and practices and promoting them through education, training and leadership. Membership includes a twice-monthly newsletter in addition to specialty newsletters on cash management, accounting, auditing, and financial reporting.
17300 Pages
Founded in 1906

8705 **HBMA Newsletter**
Healthcare Billing and Management Association
1540 South Coast Highway
Suite 203
Laguna Beach, CA 92651

877-640-4262
Home Page: http://www.hbma.org

Bradley Lund, Executive Director
Paul Myers, Director of Education
Frequency: Monthly

8706 **HFMA's Leadership E-Newsletter**
Healthcare Financial Management Association
Two Westbrook Corporate Center
Suite 700
Westchester, IL 60154-5700

708-319-9600
800-252-4362
Fax: 708-531-0032
Home Page: www.hfma.org/leadership

Robert Fromberg, Editor-in-Chief
Maggie Van Dyke, Product Manager & Editor
Chris Burke, Advertising Manager
Kurt Belisle, Sponsorhip Manager

Showcases examples of how leading healthcare organizations are driving down costs, enhancing quality, and collaborating across disciplines and care sites. The initiative highlightes innovative providers. Subscription includes a twice-yearly print publication, monthly e-newsletter, webcasts, and exclusive invites.
Frequency: Monthly
Circulation: 32900

8707 **HFMA's The Business of Caring**
Healthcare Financial Management Association
Two Westbrook Corporate Center
Suite 700
Westchester, IL 60154-5700

708-319-9600
800-252-4362
Fax: 708-531-0032
Home Page: www.hfma.org/boc

Robert Fromberg, Editor-in-Chief
Maggie Van Dyke, Product Manager & Editor
Chris Burke, Advertising Manager
Kurt Belisle, Sponsorhip Manager

Helps nurse managers navigate the business side of health care to become successful hospital leaders. Topics discussed include: budget-

ing, workforce management, cost containment, and IT implementation. Available Free Online.
Frequency: Quarterly

8708 Hedge Fund Alert
Harrison Scott Publications
5 Marine View Plz
Suite 301
Hoboken, NJ 07030-5722
201-386-1491
Fax: 201-659-4141
E-Mail: info@hspnews.com
Home Page: www.hspnews.com
Andy Albert, Owner
Tom Ferris, Editor
Howard Kapiloff, Managing Editor
Barbara Eannace, Advertising Director
Michelle Lebowitz, Director
A weekly newsletter on the securitization of consumer and corporate receivables.
Cost: $2097.00
10 Pages
Frequency: Weekly
Circulation: 500
ISSN: 1520-3700
Printed in 4 colors on matte stock

8709 High Yield Report
American Banker-Bond Buyer
1 State St
27th Floor
New York, NY 10004-1561
212-803-8450
800-367-3989
Fax: 212-843-9624
Home Page: www.sourcemedia.com
Jim Malkin, CEO
Mario DiUbaldi, Director of Sales
Melissa Sefic, Director of Sales
The only financial publication dealing exclusively with high yield corporate debt and distressed bank debt.
Cost: $795.00
Frequency: Weekly
Circulation: 350

8710 Housing Finance Report
National Assn. of Local Housing Finance Agencies
2025 M St Nw
Suite 800
Washington, DC 20036-2422
202-367-1197
Fax: 202-367-2197
Home Page: www.noca.org
Greg Brown, Editor
Karen Thompson, Production Manager
This newsletter covers major developments in housing finance in the Congress, federal agencies and private sector. It also gives highlights new and innovative activities of ALHFA members.
Circulation: 450
Founded in 1982

8711 IBC's Money Fund Report
IBC Financial Data
1 Research Dr
Westborough, MA 01581-3922
508-616-5567
Fax: 508-616-5511
E-Mail: info@imoneynet.com
Home Page: www.imoneynet.com/
Kenneth Bohlin, Publisher
Peter Crane, Editor
Randy Wood, CEO
Claudia Missert, marketin
Compiles yield, average maturity and portfolio data for each money fund along with summary information for more than a dozen categories.
Cost: $3125.00
Frequency: Weekly
Circulation: 200
Founded in 1975
Printed in 2 colors on matte stock

8712 IE News: Financial Services
Institute of Industrial Engineers
25 Technology Pkwy S
Suite 150
Norcross, GA 30092-2946
770-449-0461
Fax: 770-263-8532
Offers full coverage of the financial community pertaining to engineering and industrial corporations.

8713 IHS Haystack Standard Standards
Information Handling Services
15 Inverness Way E
Englewood, CO 80112-5710
303-790-0600
800-525-7052
Fax: 303-754-3940
Home Page: www.ihs.com
Jerre L Stead, CEO
Michael Armstrong, Director
Frequency: Daily

8714 IPO Reporter
Securities Data Publishing
1290 6th Avenue
36th Floor
New York, NY 10104-0101
212-765-5311
Fax: 212-957-0420
Ted Weissberg, Group Publisher
Reliable news, data and analysis. Provides the most comprehensive coverage available, including a detailed calendar of upcoming deals; new IPOs filled with the SEC; valuation information; comaparison data; company name and locationas well as names of underwriters, auditors and counsels.
Frequency: Weekly

8715 IRA Reporter
Universal Pensions
PO Box 979
Brainerd, MN 56401-0979
218-855-0565
800-346-3860
Fax: 218-829-4814
Thomas G Anderson, President
Jennifer M Norquist, Editor
Discusses IRS rulings, regulations, legislation and other industry news and trends relating to IRA's.
Cost: $115.00
8 Pages
Frequency: Monthly
Printed in on glossy stock

8716 ISDA Newsletter
International Swaps and Derivatives Association
360 Madison Ave
16th Floor
New York, NY 10017-7126
212-901-6000
Fax: 212-901-6001
E-Mail: isda@isda.org
Home Page: www.isda.org
Robert Pickel, CEO
Ruth Ainslie, Director Communications
Corrine Gerasley, Director Administration
Frequency: 5/year

8717 Inside Mortgage Technology
Inside Mortgage Finance Publishers
7910 Woodmont Ave
Suite 1000
Bethesda, MD 20814-7019
301-951-1240
Fax: 301-656-1709
E-Mail: service@imfpubs.com
Home Page: http://www.insidemortgagefinance.com
Guy Cecala, Owner
Francis Solomon, President
Focuses on the evolving technology developments that are changing the mortgage business. Covers internet strategies, what's new and whats working, automated systems and e-commerce businesses.
Cost: $556.00
13 Pages
ISSN: 1093-4049

8718 Insurance M&A Newsletter
SNL Securities
One SNL Plaza
PO Box 2124
Charlottesville, VA 22902
434-977-1600
Fax: 434-977-4466
E-Mail: subscriptions@snl.com
Home Page: www.snl.com
L Todd Vencil, Editor
Reid Nagle, Chief Operating Officer
Nick Cafferillo, Chief Operating Officer
Adam Hall, Managing Director
For investment bankers, analysts, insurance investors, insurance company executives and insurance regulators. Features in-depth articles and the latest financial information on insurance mergers and acquisitions activity.
Cost: $998.00
15 Pages
Frequency: Fortnightly
Founded in 1987

8719 Interactive Mobile Investor
Kagan World Media
126 Clock Tower Place
Carmel, CA 93923-8746
831-624-1536
Fax: 831-625-3225
E-Mail: info@kagan.com
Home Page: www.kagan.com
George Niesen, Editor
Tom Johnson, Marketing Manager
Cost: $945.00
Frequency: Monthly

8720 Interactive TV Investor
Kagan World Media
126 Clock Tower Place
Carmel, CA 93923-8746
831-624-1536
Fax: 831-625-3225
E-Mail: info@kagan.com
Home Page: www.kagan.com
George Niesen, Editor
Tom Johnson, Marketing Manager
Cost: $895.00
Frequency: Monthly

8721 International Financier Newsletter
International Society of Financiers
PO Box 398
Naples, NC 28760
828-698-7805
Fax: 828-698-7806
Home Page: www.insofin.com
Ronald I Gershen, Chairman/President
Frequency: Monthly

8722 International Securitization & Structured Finance
WorldTrade Executive
2250 Main Street Suite 100
PO Box 761
Concord, MA 01742-761

978-287-0301
Fax: 978-287-0302
E-Mail: info@wtexec.com
Home Page: www.wtexec.com

Jill McKenna, Production Manager
Gary Brown, CEO
Scott stutbar, Editor
John Margel, Marketing
Heather Margel, Circulation Manager

A twice monthly report devoted exclusively to asset-backed securities in international markets. Covers all aspects of international asset-backed securitization, including innovative product trends, issuer considerations, regulatory matters, and tax and accounting considerations. Examines what is working in emerging markets and spotlights unique US transactions.
Cost: $1333.00

8723 International Wealth Success
PO Box 1866
Merrick, NY 11566

516-378-3922
800-323-0548
Fax: 516-766-5919

Tyler G Hicks, Publisher

Monthly newsletter giving sources and techniques for financing a variety of small businesses - import-export, mail order, real estate, home-based activities, etc. Gives specific, hands-on methods for beginners to start and own a successful business of their own.
Cost: $24.00
16 Pages
Frequency: Monthly
Mailing list available for rent: 100 M names at $75 per M
Printed in 2 colors on matte stock

8724 Internet Media Investor
Kagan World Media
126 Clock Tower Place
Carmel, CA 93923-8746

831-624-1536
Fax: 831-625-3225
E-Mail: info@kagan.com
Home Page: www.kagan.com

George Niesen, Editor
Tom Johnson, Marketing Manager
Cost: $945.00
Frequency: Monthly

8725 Investing in Crisis
KCI Communications
1750 Old Meadow Road
Suite 301
McLean, VA 22102

703-905-8000
800-832-2330
Fax: 703-905-8100
E-Mail: service@kci-com.com
Home Page: www.2.kci-com.com

Allie Ash Jr, Publisher

Offers information on investments, low-risk bonds, stocks and campaigns for businesses in times of economic survival.
Cost: $195.00
80 Pages

8726 Investment Dealers' Digest
Thomson Financial Publishing
195 Broadway
Suite 4
New York, NY 10007-3124

646-822-2000
Fax: 646-822-2800
Home Page: www.thomson.com

Elaine Yadlon, Plant Manager
James Smith, Chief Operating Officer

Corporation financing, market conditions, financial techniques and organizational strategies.
Frequency: Weekly
Circulation: 6255

8727 Investment News
Crain Communications Inc
711 3rd Ave
Suite 3
New York, NY 10017-9214

212-210-0171
Fax: 212-210-0237
E-Mail: info@crain.com
Home Page: www.investmentnews.com

Rance Crain, President

Provides news vital to their businesses, including news affecting their clients investments and reports about the growing financial advisory industry and the companies that serve it.
Frequency: Weekly
Circulation: 61000
Founded in 1916

8728 Investment Quality Trends
IQ Trends
2888 Loker Avenue East
Suite 116
Carlsbad, CA 92010

866-927-5250
Fax: 866-927-5251
E-Mail: info@iqtrends.com
Home Page: www.iqtrends.com

Michael Minney, Publisher
Kelley Wright, Managing Editor
Geraldine Weiss, Publisher Emeritus

Investment newsletter specializing in high-quality, divident-paying blue chip stocks, macro-economics, and market outlook.
Cost: $310.00
12 Pages
Frequency: Bi-monthly
Founded in 1966

8729 Investment Recovery Association
638 W 39th Street
Kansas City, MO 64111

816-561-5323
800-728-2272
Fax: 816-561-1991
E-Mail: ira@invrecovery.org
Home Page: www.invrecovery.org

David Rupert CMIR, President
Al Kidney CMIR, VP

Helps fulfill an important role by bringing people together from disparate industries...all focused on sharing best IR practices and improving the knowledge and skills necessary to properly perform the wide-ranging responsibilities required of investment recovery practitioners.
Cost: $300.00
16 Pages
Frequency: Monthly
Circulation: 900

8730 Investor Relations Newsletter
Kennedy Information
1 Pheonix Mill Lane
Floor 3
Petersborough, NH 03458

603-924-1006
800-531-0007
E-Mail: bookstore@kennedyinfo.com
Home Page: www.kennedyinfo.com

Gerald Murray, Editor

Provides practical, hands on strategy and tactics for the investor relations professional.
Cost: $295.00
Frequency: Monthly
ISSN: 1535-5802
Founded in 1970

8731 John Bollinger's Capital Growth Letter
Bollinger Capital Management
Po Box 3358
Manhattan Beach, CA 90266-1358

310-798-8855
800-888-8400
Fax: 310-798-8858
E-Mail: bbands@bollingerbands.com
Home Page: www.bollingerbands.com

John Bollinger, Owner

Covers stocks, bonds, precious metals, commodities, the dollar and the international markets. Utilizes a technically driven asset allocation approach and investment recommendations. A free twice-a-week hotline is available to all subscribers. Online or by mail.
Cost: $300.00
12 Pages
Frequency: Monthly
Circulation: 500
Founded in 1980
Printed in 2 colors

8732 John Bollinger's Group Power
Bollinger Capital Management
Po Box 3358
Manhattan Beach, CA 90266-1358

310-798-8855
800-888-8400
Fax: 310-798-8855
E-Mail: BBands@BollingerBands.com
Home Page: www.bollingerbands.com

John Bollinger, Owner
Dorit Kehr, Contact

Electronic daily newsletter available everyday via email or on Bollinger's home page. Provides group analysis using a group structure, provides a wide array of marketing statistics designed to assist the investor in making market timing and investment decisions.
Frequency: Daily

8733 Jumbo Rate News
Bauer Financial
Gables International Plaza
PO Box 143520
Coral Gables, FL 33114

800-388-6686
Fax: 800-230-9569
E-Mail: customerservice@bauerfinancial.com
Home Page: www.bauerfinancial.com

Karen L Dorway, President/CEO
Caroline Jervey, Editor

Each issue contains over 1,000 separate Jumbo CD rates in seven categories from over 200 creditworthy banks and thrifts nationwide. Includes star ratings, wire transfer fees, deposit requirements and financial highlights for each institution.
Cost: $445.00
Frequency: Weekly
Founded in 1983
Printed in 2 colors on matte stock

8734 **Kagan Media Investor**
Kagan World Media
126 Clock Tower Place
Carmel, CA 93923-8746

831-624-1536
800-307-2529
Fax: 831-625-3225
E-Mail: info@kagan.com
Home Page: www.kagan.com

George Niesen, Editor
Tom Johnson, Marketing Manager
Robin Flynn, Senior VP

News of the Kagan Media Investor. Three month trial available.
Cost: $1195.00
Frequency: Monthly
Founded in 1969

8735 **Kagan Media Money**
Kagan World Media
1 Lower Ragsdale Dr
Bldg 1 Suite 130
Monterey, CA 93940-5749

831-624-1536
Fax: 831-625-3225
E-Mail: info@kagan.com
Home Page: www.kagan.com

George Niesen, Editor
Harvey Kraft, Marketing Manager
Tim Baskerville, CEO
Harvey Kraft, Circulation Manager
Sandy Borthwick, Communications Manager

Analysts dissect deals, anticipate trends, project revenues, track financings and value the debt and equity of hundreds of privately held and publicly traded advertising, broadcasting, cable TV, digital TV, home video, Internet media, motion picture, newspaper, pay TV, professional sports and wireless telecommunications companies in the US and abroad.
Cost: $1245.00
Frequency: Monthly
Founded in 1969

8736 **Kagan Music Investor**
Kagan World Media
126 Clock Tower Place
Carmel, CA 93923-8746

831-624-1536
Fax: 831-625-3225
E-Mail: info@kagan.com
Home Page: www.kagan.com

George Niesen, Editor
Tom Johnson, Marketing Manager

News and analysis for investors in the music industry.
Cost: $945.00
Frequency: Monthly

8737 **Kiplinger Tax Letter**
Kiplinger Washington Editors
1729 H St Nw
Washington, DC 20006-3924

202-887-6400
800-544-0155
Fax: 202-778-8976
E-Mail: sub.services@kiplinger.com
Home Page: www.kiplinger.com

Knight Kiplinger, VP
Steven D Ivins, Editor

Biweekly tax letter for investors, business owners and managers. Covers current developments in Congress, IRS and the courts.
Cost: $54.00
4 Pages
Circulation: 125000
Mailing list available for rent
Printed in one color

8738 **Latin American Finance & Capital Markets**
WorldTrade Executive
PO Box 761
Concord, MA 01742-0761

978-287-0301
Fax: 978-287-0302
E-Mail: info@wtexec.com
Home Page: www.wtexec.com

Alison French, Production Manager

An action-oriented report on treasury management, tax, legal, accounting and other operational issues that impact doing business in Latin America. Provides an independent assessment of local capital markets.
Cost: $595.00
Frequency: Twice monthly

8739 **Limelight eNewsletter**
Wall Street Teechnology Association
521 Newman Springs Road
Suite 12
Lincroft, NJ 07738

732-530-8808
Fax: 732-530-0020
E-Mail: info@wsta.org
Home Page: www.wsta.org

Phyllis Lampell, Executive Director
JoAnn Cooper, Executive Director
Frequency: Monthly
Circulation: 14000

8740 **Long Term Investing**
Concept Publishing
5202 Humphreys Road
Lake Park, GA 31636

229-257-0367
Fax: 229-219-1097
Home Page: www.newconceptspublishing.com

Jim Dovan, Publisher
David Coleman, Editor
Madris Gutierrez, Editor-in-Chief
Andrea DePasture, Senior Editor

Offers full coverage of long term stocks, bonds and investments.
Cost: $98.00
12 Pages
Frequency: Monthly
Circulation: 600
Founded in 1998
Printed in one color on matte stock

8741 **MAR/Hedge**
Managed Account Reports
1250 Broadway
26th Floor
New York, NY 10001

212-213-6202
800-638-2525
Fax: 212-213-1870
E-Mail: subs@marhedge.com
Home Page: www.marhedge.com

Greg Newton, Publisher
Randall Devere, Editor-in-Chief
Lisa McErlane, Director of Marketing
Gary Lynch, President/Publisher

The first newsletter to cover the field of hedge funds in its entirety with industry news, in-depth articles and reviews of hedge fund managers and fund of funds and rankings of these managers and fund of funds.
Cost: $1195.00
16 Pages
Frequency: Monthly
Circulation: 300
Founded in 1994
Printed in 2 colors on matte stock

8742 **Managing 401(k) Plans**
Institute of Management and Administration
1 Washington Park
Suite 1300
Newark, NJ 07102

212-244-0360
Fax: 973-622-0595
Home Page: www.ioma.com

The definitive resource for HR and Financial Department managers looking to run the best plan for their company.
Cost: $429.00

8743 **Managing Credit, Receivable & Collections**
Institute of Management and Administration
1 Washington Park
Suite 1300
Newark, NJ 07102

212-244-0360
Fax: 973-622-0595
Home Page: www.ioma.com

Accelerate receivables and learn what technology and techniques are working best.
Cost: $269.00
Frequency: Monthly

8744 **Media Mergers & Acquisitions**
Kagan World Media
126 Clock Tower Place
Carmel, CA 93923-8746

831-624-1536
Fax: 831-624-5882
E-Mail: info@kagan.com
Home Page: www.kagan.com

George Niesen, Editor
Tom Johnson, Marketing Manager

Where it all comes together. Exclusive scorecard of deals done by media companies. Dollar amounts, multiples paid, trends captured in succinct summaries of complex transactions. Three month trial available.
Cost: $795.00
Frequency: Monthly

8745 **Merger Strategy Report**
SNL Securities
PO Box 2124
Charlottesvle, VA 22902-2124

434-977-1600
Fax: 434-977-4466
Home Page: www.snlnet.com

Erik Winthrow, Editor
John Minor, Editor
Reid Nagle, Publisher
Mark Outlaw, Advertising Director
Nick Cafferillo, Chief Operating Officer

For bank and thrift executives, with a regional M&A recap; list of deals; ranking of advisors and lawyers.
5 Pages
Frequency: Quarterly
Founded in 1995

8746 **Mergers & Acquisitions Executive Compensation Review**
SNL Securities
One SNL Plaza
PO Box 2124
Charlottesvle, VA 22902-2124

434-977-1600
Fax: 434-977-4466
E-Mail: isales@snl.com
Home Page: www.snl.com

John Minor, Editor
Michael Spears, Advertising
Mike Scott, Mergers/Acquisitions
Nick Cafferillo, Chief Operating Officer
Adam Hall, Managing Director

For banks, thrifts, investment banks, law firms that advise on mergers, executives at banks expecting to merge and personnel and compensa-

tion specialists. Provides compensation information on the executives of banks that have entered into agreements to be acquired.
Cost: $495.00
10 Pages
Frequency: Monthly
Founded in 1987

8747 Micro Ticker Report
Waters Information Services
PO Box 2248
Binghamton, NY 13902-2248
607-770-8535
Fax: 607-723-7151
Dennis Waters, Publisher
Andrew Delaney, Editor
Covers the financial quotation industry.

8748 Money Management Letter
Institutional Investor
225 Park Ave S
12th Floor
New York, NY 10003-1605
212-224-3300
Fax: 212-224-3197
E-Mail: iieditor@institutionalinvestor.com
Home Page: www.institutionalinvestor.com
Christopher Brown, CEO
Tom Lamont, Editor
This newsletter offers businesses information on investments, stocks, bonds, low-risk campaigns and financial planning opportunities.

8749 Mortgaged Backed Securities Letter
American Banker-Bond Buyer
1 State St
26th Floor
New York, NY 10004-1483
212-803-8350
Fax: 212-843-9600
Home Page: www.securitiesindustry.com
John Del Mauro, VP
Tom Steinert-Threlkeld, Director
Provides coverage of structured finance and includes comprehensive listings of asset backed securities.
Frequency: Weekly
Circulation: 4200

8750 Motion Picture Investor
Kagan World Media
126 Clock Tower Place
Carmel, CA 93923-8746
831-624-1536
Fax: 831-625-3225
E-Mail: info@kagan.com
Home Page: www.kagan.com/
George Niesen, Editor
Tom Johnson, Marketing Manager
Cost: $845.00
Frequency: Monthly
Founded in 1969

8751 NACHA Operating Rules & Guidelines
NACHA: The Electronic Payments Association
13450 Sunrise Valley Drive
Suite 100
Herndon, VA 20171
703-561-1100
Fax: 703-787-0996
E-Mail: info@nacha.org
Home Page: www.nacha.org
Janet O Estep, CEO
Marcie Haitema, Chairperson
Reflects the results of the Rules Simplification initiative. PReviously organized around major topics, the simplified Rules framework is structured around the rights and responsibilities of participants in the ACH Network.
Cost: $78.00
Frequency: Annual

8752 NADOA Newsletter
National Association of Division Order Analysts
2805 Oak Trail Court
Suite 6312
Arlington, TX 76016
972-715-4489
E-Mail: administrator@nadoa.org
Home Page: www.nadoa.org
Lynn S McCord, Administrator
Frequency: Bi-Monthly

8753 NALHFA Newsletter
National Association of Local Housing Finance
2025 M St Nw
Suite 800
Washington, DC 20036-2422
202-367-1197
Fax: 202-367-2197
E-Mail: john_murphy@nalhfa.org
Home Page: www.noca.org
John C Murphy, Executive Director
Scott Lynch, Association Manager
Kim McKinon, Coordinator Membership
Frequency: Bi-Monthly

8754 NAPFA Newslink
National Association of Personal Financial Advisor
3250 N Arlington Heights Road
Suite 109
Arlington Heights, IL 60004
847-483-5400
800-366-2732
Fax: 847-483-5415
E-Mail: info@napfa.org
Home Page: www.napfa.org
Ellen Turf, CEO
Margery Wasserman, Director Conference
Frequency: Quarterly

8755 NASDAQ Subscriber Bulletin
National Association of Securities Dealers
1212newyork anenue
suite950
Washington, DC 20005-1516
202-371-5535
Fax: 202-371-5536
Margo Porter, Publisher
Richard DeLouise, Editor
Pamela Anderson, Executive
Developments in the NASDAQ market.

8756 NATRI Newsletter
National Association for Treasurers of Religious
8824 Cameron Street
Silver Springs, MD 20910
301-587-7776
Fax: 301-589-2897
Home Page: www.natri.org
Laura Reicks, Publisher
Lorelle Elcock, Associate Director Finance
Frequency: Bi Monthly

8757 NICSA News
National Investment Company Service Association
36 Washington Street
Suite 70
Wellesley Hills, MA 02481
781-416-7200
Fax: 781-416-7065
E-Mail: info@nicsa.org
Home Page: www.nicsa.org
Barbara V Weidlich, President
Keith Dropkin, Director Operations
Doris Jaimes, Registrar
Sheila Kobaly, Events Manager
Chris Ludent, IT Manager
Frequency: Quarterly

8758 National Mortgage News
Thomson Financial Publishing
1 State St
27th Floor
New York, NY 10004-1481
212-825-8445
800-235-5552
Fax: 212-292-5216
Home Page: www.nationalmortgagenews.com/
Timothy Murphy, Group Publisher
Mark Fogarty, Editorial Director
Paul Muolo, M&A/Data Editor
Timothy Reifschneider, Advertising Director
Jose Thomas, Manager
Mortgage information, legislation and news.
Cost: $228.00
Frequency: Weekly
Circulation: 5000
Printed in 2 colors on newsprint stock

8759 Network Newsletter
Society for Information Management
401 N Michigan Avenue
Chicago, IL 60611
312-215-5190
Fax: 312-245-1081
Home Page: www.simnet.org
Jim Luisi, Executive Director
Frequency: Bi-Monthly

8760 Newspaper Investor
Kagan World Media
1 Lower Ragsdale Dr
Building One, Suite 130
Monterey, CA 93940-5749
831-624-1536
831-625-3225
Fax: 831-625-3225
E-Mail: info@kagan.com
Home Page: www.kagan.com
Tim Baskerville, President
Tom Johnson, Marketing Manager
Cost: $845.00
Frequency: Monthly
Founded in 1969

8761 OTC Chart Manual
Standard & Poor's Corporation
55 Water St
New York, NY 10041-0003
212-438-1000
Fax: 212-438-0299
Home Page: www.standardandpoors.com
Deven Sharma, President
Charts on over 800 OTC stocks.

8762 Origination News
4709 Golf Road
Skokie, IL 60076
847-676-9600
800-321-3373
Fax: 847 933 8101
E-Mail: custserv@accuitysolutions.com
Home Page: www.accuitysolutions.com
Timothy Murphy, Group Publisher
Mark Fogarty, Editorial Director
Jose Thomas, Manager
Malcolm Taylor, Managing Director
Information for mortgage industry executives on mortgage brokers, mortgage bankers and mortgage executives in commercial banks, sav-

ings banks, savings and loan associations and credit unions.
Cost: $78.00
Frequency: Monthly

8763 **Pawnbroker News**
National Pawnbrokers Association
P.O.Box 508
Keller, TX 76244-0508
817-491-4554
Fax: 817-491-8770
E-Mail: info@NationalPawnbrokers.org
Home Page: www.nationalpawnbrokers.org
Bob Benedict, CAE, Executive Director
Emmett Murphy, Director
Teresa Congleton, Administrative Assistant
Frequency: 8/year

8764 **Pink Comparison Report**
SNL Securities
PO Box 2124
Charlottesvle, VA 22902-2124
434-977-1600
Fax: 434-977-4466
Home Page: www.snlnet.com
Maria Moyer, Editor
Reid Nagle, Publisher
Mark LaBua, Subscription Manager
Mark Outlaw, Advertising Director
Nick Cafferillo, Chief Operating Officer
For CEOs, CFOs and IRCs of banks. Compares a subscribing bank or thrift's consolidated financial and market performance to other banks and thrifts chosen by the subscriber and banks and thrifts of similar asset size and location.
40 Pages
Frequency: Quarterly

8765 **Private Equity Week**
Securities Data Publishing
40 W 57th St
New York, NY 10019-4001
212-484-4701
Fax: 212-956-0112
Home Page: www.sdponline.com
Jennifer Reed, Editor-in-Chief
Edward Cortese, Marketing Executive
News of the past week and forecast of the weeks to come for investors.
Cost: $780.00
Frequency: Weekly

8766 **Private Placement Letter**
Securities Data Publishing
1290 6th Avenue
36th Floor
New York, NY 10104-101
212-765-5311
Fax: 212-957-0420
E-Mail: custserv@sourcemedia.com
Home Page: www.privateplacementletter.com/
John Toth, Publisher
Ronald Cooper, Editor-in-Chief
Lauren Klopacs, Marketing Manager
Mark Cialdella, Circulation Manager
David Harkey, Advertising Manager
Highly sophisticated information on the debt private placement market including senior and mezzanine level debt.
Cost: $1395.00

8767 **Proceedings of the National Conference on Planned Giving**
National Committee on Planned Giving
233 S McCrea St
Suite 400
Indianapolis, IN 46225-1068
317-269-6274
Fax: 317-269-6276
Home Page: www.ncpg.org
Tanya Howe Johnson, President
Sandra Kerr, Director Government Education
Barbara Owens, Director Membership
Kathryn J Ramsey, Director Meetings
Kurt Reusze, Manager Education/Technology
Frequency: Annual

8768 **Quality Performance Report**
Managed Account Reports
220 5th Avenue
19th Floor
New York, NY 10001-7708
212-213-6202
800-638-2525
Fax: 212-213-6273
Home Page: www.marhedge.com
Randall Devere, Editor-in-Chief
Lois Peltz, Editor
Gary Lynch, President
Lisa McErlane, Marketing
The pre-eminent source of qualitative and quantitative information on global managed derivatives. Delivers in-depth analysis on the performance of the trading advisors in MAR's qualified database. Now covering over 500 trading advisors and programs.
Cost: $299.00
Frequency: Quarterly
Circulation: 400
Founded in 1913
Printed in 2 colors on matte stock

8769 **REIT Daily Fax**
SNL Securities
One SNL Plaza
PO Box 2124
Charlottesvle, VA 22902-2124
434-977-1600
Fax: 434-293-0407
E-Mail: isales@snl.com
Home Page: www.snl.com
Amy Woolard, Editor
Nick Cafferillo, Chief Operating Officer
Alan Zimmerman, Publisher
Pat LaBua, Customer Service Director
Adam Hall, Managing Director
Newsletter designed specifically for REIT industry professionals and investors. Features important industry events, condensed news stories, recent capital offerings and the latest market information.
4 Pages
Frequency: Daily
Founded in 1987

8770 **REIT Performance Graph**
SNL Securities
One SNL Plaza
PO Box 2124
Charlottesvle, VA 22902-2124
434-977-1600
Fax: 434-977-4466
E-Mail: subscriptions@snl.com
Home Page: www.snl.com
Steve Arnold, Vice Chairman, CFO
Chandler Spears, Editor
Keven Lindemann, Real Estate
Gregg Amonette, General Media
Nick Cafferillo, Chief Operating Officer
For publicly traded REITs and REIT service providers. Compares the investment performance of a publicly traded REIT to a specific SNL index or to a selected peer group and the appropriate broad multi-industry index. Covers a 5-year period or the period beginning with the IPO date.
Cost: $399.00
1 Pages
Founded in 1987

8771 **Real Estate Alert**
Harrison Scott Publications
5 Marine View Plz
#301
Hoboken, NJ 07030-5722
201-386-1491
Fax: 201-659-4141
E-Mail: info@hspnews.com
Home Page: www.hspnews.com
Andy Albert, Owner
Bob Mura, Editor
Barbara Eannaci, Marketing Manager
Michelle Lebowitz, Director
Information on investment opportunities in institutional grade commercial real estate, includes sales acquisitions and personnel changes.
Cost: $1597.00
Frequency: Weekly
Circulation: 650
Founded in 1989

8772 **Real Estate Finance Today**
Mortgage Bankers Association of America
1919 Pennsylvania Avenue NW
Washington, DC 20006-3404
202-557-2700
E-Mail: info@mortgagebankers.org
Home Page: www.mortgagebankers.org
Information on anticipating industry trends, regulatory changes, economic outlook, federal and state legislation and trends in the secondary mortgage industry.
Cost: $100.00
Frequency: Monthly
Circulation: 1500
Founded in 1939

8773 **Real-Estate Alert**
Harrison Scott Publications
5 Marine View Plz
Suite 301
Hoboken, NJ 07030-5722
201-386-1491
Fax: 201-659-4141
E-Mail: info@hspnews.com
Home Page: www.hspnews.com
Andy Albert, Owner
Tom Ferris, Director
Michelle Lebowitz, Director
A weekly newsletter on the securitization of consumer and corporate receivables.
Cost: $1497.00
10 Pages
Frequency: Weekly
Circulation: 600
ISSN: 1520-3700
Printed in 4 colors on matte stock

8774 **Reducing Benefits Costs**
Institute of Management and Administration
1 Washington Park
Suite 1300
Newark, NJ 07102
212-244-0360
Fax: 973-622-0595
Home Page: www.ioma.com
Provides information on controlling benefit costs.
Cost: $245.00
16 Pages
Frequency: Monthly

8775 **Regional Economic Digest**
Federal Reserve Bank of Kansas City

925 Grand Avenue
Kansas City, MO 64198-0001

816-881-2970
800-333-1010
Fax: 816-881-2569
Home Page: http://ideas.repec.org

Thomas Davis, Publisher
Bob Regan, Editor

A review of financial and economic conditions in the Tenth District. Includes articles of regional interest, statistics on District commercial banks and the area economy and results of a survey of agricultural credit conditions.
32 Pages

8776 Regulatory Risk Monitor
United Communications Group
11300 Rockville Pike
Street 1100
Rockville, MD 20852-3030

301-287-2700
Fax: 301-816-8945
E-Mail: webmaster@ucg.com
Home Page: www.ucg.com

Benny Dicecca, President

Updates banking officials, credit union, compliance officers, attorneys and auditors with current independent news and guidance.
Founded in 1970

8777 Report on Financial Analysis, Planning & Reporting
Institute of Management and Administration
1 Washington Park
Suite 1300
Newark, NJ 07102

212-244-0360
Fax: 973-622-0595
Home Page: www.ioma.com

FARP regularly covers performance measurements effective use of new FASB, IRS and SEC financial and accounting requirements for all industries, shows managers the best way to evaluate business opportunities, how to read and evaluate capital budgets, earbug reports and analysts see the big picture through the use of new financial tools such as Economic Value Assets and Shareholder Valuations models.
Cost: $269.00
Frequency: Monthly

8778 Retirement Plans Bulletin
Universal Pensions
PO Box 979
Brainerd, MN 56401

218-855-0565
800-346-3860
Fax: 218-829-4814

Thomas G Anderson, President
Jennifer M Norquist, Editor

Digests IRS technical jargon on IRA's and qualified plans and translates it into understandable articles and advice for financial organizations.
Cost: $89.00
10 Pages
Frequency: Monthly
Printed in 2 colors on glossy stock

8779 SNL Bank M&A DataSource
SNL Securities
One SNL Plaza
PO Box 2124
Charlottesvle, VA 22902-2124

434-977-1600
Fax: 434-977-4466
E-Mail: subscriptions@snl.com
Home Page: www.snl.com

John Minor, Publisher
Eric Hoffer, Editor
John McCune, Banks/Thrifts Manager
Michael Spears, Advertising
Nick Cafferillo, Chief Operating Officer

For investment bankers, investment companies, banks, thrifts, consultants and broker/dealers. Includes all merger and acquisition activity involving a bank or thrift as a buyer or seller.
Founded in 1987

8780 SNL Branch Migration DataSource
SNL Securities
PO Box 2124
Charlottesvle, VA 22902-2124

434-977-1600
Fax: 434-977-4466
Home Page: www.snlnet.com

Melissa Hobson, Editor
John Minor, Editor
Reid Nagle, Publisher
Mark Outlaw, Advertising Director
Nick Cafferillo, Chief Operating Officer

For investment bankers, investment companies, banks, thrifts, consultants and regulatory agencies. Re-assigns bank and thrift branch deposits to account for all M&A activity that has occurred since the last regulatory release.
Frequency: Annual
Founded in 1991

8781 SNL Corporate Performance Graphs for Banks
SNL Securities
One SNL Plaza
PO Box 2124
Charlottesvle, VA 22902-2124

434-977-1600
Fax: 434-977-4466
E-Mail: subscriptions@snl.com
Home Page: www.snl.com

Will Wick, Editor
James Record, Editor
John McCune, Banks/Thrifts Manager
Michael Spears, Advertising
Nick Cafferillo, Chief Operating Officer

For publicly traded banks, law firms, accountants and consulting firms. Includes a 5-year comparison of an institution's stock to both a selected peer group index and a broad multi-industry index.
1 Pages
Founded in 1987

8782 SNL Financial DataSource
SNL Securities
One SNL Plaza
PO Box 2124
Charlottesvle, VA 22902-2124

434-977-1600
Fax: 434-977-4466
E-Mail: subscriptions@snl.com
Home Page: www.snl.com

Steve Tomasi, Editor
Steve Ferguson, Editor
Edward Metz, Financial
Michael Spears, Advertising
Nick Cafferillo, Chief Operating Officer

For investment bankers, investment companies, banks, thrifts, institutional investors, consultants and broker/dealers. Available in six separate interactive modules that contain data for equity research, industry trend analysis, peer group comparisons and identification of investment and acquisition opportunities.
Founded in 1987

8783 SNL Mutual Thrift Conversion Investors Kit
SNL Securities
One SNL Plaza
PO Box 2124
Charlottesvle, VA 22902-2124

434-977-1600
Fax: 434-977-4466
E-Mail: subscriptions@snl.com
Home Page: www.snl.com

Chris Smith, Editor
Reid Nagle, Publisher
John McCune, Banks/Thrifts Manager
Michael Spears, Advertising
Nick Cafferillo, Chief Operating Officer

For thrift executives, individual investors and institutional investors. Contains a set of articles explaining the mechanics of mutual-to-stock conversion and the 'how-to' of investing, reviewing profitability of conversion investments and outlining regulatory issues that affect conversions.
Cost: $495.00
100 Pages
Frequency: Monthly
Founded in 1987

8784 SNL Pink Quarterly
SNL Securities
PO Box 2124
Charlottesvle, VA 22902-2124

434-977-1600
Fax: 434-977-4466
Home Page: www.snlnet.com

Maria Moyer, Editor
Reid Nagle, Publisher
Mark Outlaw, Advertising Director
Pat LaBua, Subscription Manager
Nick Cafferillo, Chief Operating Officer

For investment companies, banks and thrifts, broker/dealers and individual investors. Contains detailed financial and market information on all banks and thrifts traded on the OTC bulletin boards and by market makers, as well as in-depth analysis of this sector.
240 Pages
Frequency: Quarterly
Founded in 1995

8785 SNL Securities Thrift Performance Graph
SNL Financial
PO Box 2124
Charlottesvle, VA 22902-2124

434-977-1600
Fax: 434-977-4466
Home Page: www.snlnet.com

Reid Nagle, Publisher
John Racine, Editor
Mark Outlaw, Advertising Director
Pat Labua, Subscription Manager
Jeff Sternberg, Production Editor

SNL Securities is a research and publishing company that focuses on banks, thrifts, REITs insurance companies, and specialized, financial service companies. Founded in 1987, SNL securities has become the authority for information on financial institutions.

8786 SNL Securities Bank Comparison Report
SNL Securities
PO Box 2124
Charlottesvle, VA 22902-2124

434-977-1600
Fax: 434-977-4466
Home Page: www.snlnet.com

Mona Thompson, Editor
Dan Oakey, Editor
Keith Davis, Editor
Reid Nagle, Publisher
Nick Cafferillo, Chief Operating Officer

For CEOs, CFOs and IRCs of banks. Compares a subscribing bank's consolidated financial and market performance to that of banks and thrifts of similar asset size and location.
40 Pages
Frequency: Quarterly
Founded in 1987

8787 SNL Securities Thrift Comparison Report
SNL Securities
PO Box 2124
Charlottesvle, VA 22902-2124
434-977-1600
Fax: 434-977-4466
Home Page: www.snlnet.com
Dave Spence, Editor
Reid Nagle, Publisher
Mark Outlaw, Advertising Director
Pat LaBua, Subscripton Manager
Nick Cafferillo, Chief Operating Officer
Report for CEOs, CFOs and IRCs of thrifts and major corporate stockholders. Illustrates and compares a subscribing thrift's consolidated financial and market performance to thrifts of similar asset size and location.
40 Pages
Frequency: Quarterly
Founded in 1988

8788 Secured Leader
Commercial Finance Association
Ste 1801
7 Penn Plz
New York, NY 10001-3979
212-594-3490
Fax: 212-564-6053
E-Mail: info@cfa.com
Home Page: www.cfa.com
Bruce H Jones, Executive Director
Theodore Kompa, President
Only publication devoted exclusively to the asset-based financial services industry. Editorial matter is directed toward practitioners of asset-based financing. Accepts advertising.
Cost: $56.00
76 Pages
Circulation: 5000
Founded in 1944

8789 Securities Industry News
Source Media
1 State St
27th floor
New York, NY 10004-1561
212-803-8200
800-221-1809
Fax: 212-843-9608
E-Mail: custserv@sourcemedia.com
Home Page: www.sourcemedia.com
James M Malkin, CEO
Michael Eggebrecht, Managing Director
Edward Hanasik, Marketing Director
Omar Asmar, Art Director
David Greenough, VP/Business Technology Group
Securities Industry News is a weekly newspaper in the global securities and financial markets that delivers original, time-critical news and analysis to senior decision-makers in charge of operations, technology, processing services, and compliance in the global securities and financial markets.
Cost: $575.00
Frequency: 42 Issues Annually

8790 Securities Week
McGraw Hill
PO Box 182604
Columbus, OH 43272
614-304-4000
877-833-5524
Fax: 614-759-3759
E-Mail: customer.service@mcgraw-hill.com
Home Page: www.mcgraw-hill.com
Michael Ocrant, Managing Editor
Harold McGraw, CEO
Information on firms and exchanges strategy plans, new hires, events and issues, as well as legislation and legal rulings impacting the securities industry.
Frequency: Weekly
Founded in 1884

8791 Seller/Service Update
Inside Mortgage Finance Publishers
7910 Woodmont Ave
Suite 1000
Bethesda, MD 20814-7019
301-951-1240
Fax: 301-656-1709
E-Mail: service@imfpubs.com
Home Page: www.imfpubs.com
Guy Cecala, Owner
John Bancroft, Managing Editor
Mary Lou Probka, Director of Marketing
Mary Lou Probka, Director of Circulation
Complete coverage of underwriting and servicing, changes occurring in the mortgage market. Focuses on Fannie Mae, Freddie Mac, HUD, FHA, VA, private mortgage insurers and private conduits.
Cost: $395.00
Frequency: Monthly
Circulation: 500
Founded in 1984

8792 Shareholder Satisfaction Survey
National Investment Company Service
36 Washington Avenue
Suite 70
Wellesley Hills, MA 02481
781-416-7200
Fax: 781-416-7065
E-Mail: info@nicsa.org
Home Page: www.nicsa.org
Barbara V Weidlich, President
Keith Dropkin, Director Operations
Doris Jaimes, Registrar
Sheila Kobaly, Events Manager
Chris Ludent, IT Manager
Frequency: Annual

8793 Special Stock Report
Wall Street Transcript
67 Wall Street
9th Floor
New York, NY 10005-3701
212-952-7400
800-246-7673
Fax: 212-668-9842
E-Mail: twsteditor@twst.com
Home Page: www.twst.com
Andrew Pickup, President/CEO
Doug Estadt, Online Editor
Andrew Pickup, Publisher
Jason Flatt, Marketing
Monthly stock pick based on research, interviews, and data contained in the wall st. transcript.
Cost: $399.00
Frequency: Monthly
Circulation: 7274
Founded in 1963

8794 Specialty Lender
SNL Securities
PO Box 2124
Charlottesvle, VA 22902-2124
434-977-1600
Fax: 434-977-4466
Home Page: www.snlnet.com
Dave Meadors, Editor
Jim Allen, Editor
L Todd Vencil, Editor
Reid Nagle, Publisher
Nick Cafferillo, Chief Operating Officer
For executives of specialty lending companies, banks and thrifts which have specialty lending operations, heads of captive finance companies, investors, investment bankers and equity analysts. Provides news, analysis and financial and market information about specialty lenders, focusing on credit management and access to capital.
40 Pages
Frequency: Monthly
Founded in 1996

8795 Specialty Lender Performance Graph
SNL Securities
PO Box 2124
Charlottesvle, VA 22902-2124
434-977-1600
Fax: 434-977-4466
Home Page: www.snlnet.com
David Meadors, Editor
Reid Nagle, Publisher
Mark Outlaw, Advertising Director
Pat LaBua, Subscription Manager
Nick Cafferillo, Chief Operating Officer
For publicly traded specialty lenders and specialty lender service providers. Compares the investment performance of a specialty lender to a specific SNL index or to a selected peer group and the appropriate broad multi-industry index. Covers a 5-year period or the period beginning with the IPO date.
Frequency: By request
Founded in 1997

8796 Streaming Media Investor
Kagan World Media
126 Clock Tower Place
Carmel, CA 93923-8746
831-624-1536
Fax: 831-624-5882
E-Mail: info@kagan.com
Home Page: www.kagan.com
George Niesen, Editor
Tom Johnson, Marketing Manager
News of the Streaming Media Investor. Three month trial available.
Cost: $895.00
Frequency: Monthly

8797 TV Program Investor
Kagan World Media
126 Clock Tower Place
Carmel, CA 93923-8746
831-624-1536
800-307-2529
Fax: 831-625-3225
E-Mail: info@kagan.com
Home Page: www.kagan.com
George Niesen, Editor
Harvy Kraft, Marketing Manager
Tim Baerville, CEO/President
Robert Naylor, Circulation Manager
Cost: $895.00
Frequency: Monthly
Founded in 1969

8798 **Tax Management Compensation Planning**
1250 23rd Street NW
Washington, DC 20037-1164

202-337-7240
800-223-7270
Fax: 202-496-6013

David McFarland, President
Glenn Davis, Managing Editor

Nearly 40 portfolios, each focusing on specific tax, labor and other aspects of qualified and non-qualified retirement plans, employee welfare benefit plans, executive compensation, employment taxes and accounting for deferred compensation. Offers practitioner-authored articles, analysis of recent developments and decisions, and insightful comments from leading practitioners on the latest planning strategies.
Cost: $837.00
Frequency: Monthly

8799 **Taxpractice**
Tax Analysts
6830 North
Fairfax Drive
Arlington, VA 22213-1001

703-533-4400
800-955-2444
Fax: 703-533-4444
E-Mail: webmaster@tax.org
Home Page: www.tax.org

Thomas F Field, Publisher
Jill Biden, Vice President

Contains comprehensive coverage of IRS rulings, court decisions, tax law changes and other topics of interest.
Cost: $749.00
Frequency: Weekly
Circulation: 2200
Founded in 1970

8800 **TheStreet Ratings, Inc.**
14 Wall Street
15th Floor
New York, NY 10005

212-321-5000
800-289-9222
Fax: 212-321-5016
E-Mail: letters@thestreet.com
Home Page: www.thestreet.com

Dave Kansas, Editor-in-Chief

Information on what is happening on Wall Street, along with mutual fund and economic news, stock quotes, market summaries, and analyses of key indicators.
Cost: $69.95
Frequency: Daily

8801 **Thrift 13D Dictionary**
SNL Securities
PO Box 2124
Charlottesvle, VA 22902-2124

434-977-1600
Fax: 434-977-4466
Home Page: www.snlnet.com

Todd L Davenport, Editor
Reid Nagle, Publisher
Mark Outlaw, Advertising Director
Pat LaBua, Subscription Manager
Nick Cafferillo, Chief Operating Officer

Contains all active 13D filings and related filings for every publicly traded bank in the country, including those which trade on the pink sheets.
250 Pages
Frequency: Quarterly

8802 **Thrift Performance Graph**
SNL Securities
One SNL Plaza
PO Box 2124
Charlottesvle, VA 22902-2124

434-977-1600
Fax: 434-977-4466
E-Mail: subscriptions@snl.com
Home Page: www.snl.com

Will Wick, Editor
James Record, Editor
John McCune, Banks/Thrifts Manager
Michael Spears, Advertising
Nick Cafferillo, Chief Operating Officer

Compares investment performance of a publicly traded Thrift company to a specific SNL index or to a selected peer group and the appropriate broad multi-industry index. Graph covers a 5-year period or the period beginning with the IPO date. For publicly traded thrifts, law firms, accountants and consulting firms.
1 Pages
Founded in 1987

8803 **Trading Technology Week**
Waters Information Services
270 Lafayette St
Suite 700
New York, NY 10012-3311

212-925-6990
Fax: 212-925-7585
E-Mail: eugene.grygo@incisivemedia.com
Home Page: www.dealingwithtechnology.com

Tim Weller, CEO
Eugene Grygo, Editor
Adrian Goulbourn, Publisher
Lillian Lopez, Production Manager
Melissa Jao, Business Development Manager

Information covering the latest applications, platforms and strategies in trading room systems and proprietary execution.
Cost: $2025.00
Frequency: Weekly
Founded in 2000

8804 **Transactions**
AACE International
209 Prairie Ave
Suite 100
Morgantown, WV 26501-5934

304-296-8444
800-858-2678
Fax: 304-291-5728
E-Mail: info@aacei.org
Home Page: www.aacei.org

Andrew Dowd, Executive Director
Megan McCulla, Asst Manager
Jenny Alms, Marketing Manager
Cost: $65.00
Frequency: Monthly
Circulation: 5000
Founded in 1956

8805 **Turning Points**
Concept Publishing
PO Box 500
York, NY 14592-500

800-836-4575
800-836-4575
Fax: 585-243-3148
E-Mail: publishing@conceptpub.com
Home Page: www.conceptpub.com

Jim Dovan, Publisher
David Coleman, Editor

Economic news.
Cost: $198.00
2 Pages
Circulation: 600
Founded in 1974
Printed in one color on matte stock

8806 **VOD Investor**
Kagan World Media
126 Clock Tower Place
Carmel, CA 93923-8746

831-624-1536
800-307-2529
Fax: 831-625-3225
E-Mail: info@kagan.com
Home Page: www.kagan.com

George Niesen, Editor
Tom Johnson, Marketing Manager
Robin Flynn, Senior VP

News of the VOD Investor. Three month trial available.
Cost: $1045.00
Frequency: Monthly
Founded in 1969

8807 **Venture Capital & Health Care**
Asset Alternatives
170 Linden Street
Wellesley, MA 02482-7919

781-304-1400
Fax: 781-304-1440
Home Page: www.assetnews.com

Tom Salemi, Senior Editor
Lisa Hughes, Circulation Manager

Explores the business of health care investing in the trillion dollar health care market. Provides insight into the deals, deal makers, and portfolio companies in all sectors of health care, including services, biotechnology, medical devices, and 'infomedics.'
Cost: $795.00
Frequency: Monthly

8808 **Venture Capital Information Technology**
Asset Alternatives
170 Linden Street
Wellesley, MA 02482-7919

781-304-1400
Fax: 781-304-1440
E-Mail: info@PrivateEquityAnalyst.com
Home Page: www.assetnews.com

Lisa Hughes, Circulation Manager
Barbara Bissonnette, Vice President
Marketing/Sales

Delivers information an insight into the fast-moving world of venture investing in technology. Every month, it brings readers the IT deals, fund formations, exits, and personnel news at the venture firms and corporate venturing groups they need to stay abreast of venture investing in IT.
Cost: $795.00
Frequency: Monthly

8809 **Video Investor**
Kagan World Media
126 Clock Tower Place
Carmel, CA 93923-8746

831-624-1536
Fax: 831-624-5882
E-Mail: info@kagan.com
Home Page: www.kagan.com

George Niesen, Editor
Tom Johnson, Marketing Manager

Authoritative look inside the business of renting and selling video cassettes. Exclusive estimates of retail and wholesale transactions and inventories. Tracking movies into the home. Three month trial is available.
Cost: $ 795.00
Frequency: Monthly

8810 **Wall Street Technology Association Enewsletter**
620 Shrewsbury Ave
Suite C2
Tinton Falls, NJ 07701

732-530-8808
Fax: 732-530-0020
E-Mail: info@wsta.org
Home Page: www.wsta.org
Social Media: Facebook, Twitter, LinkedIn

John Killeen, President
Phyllis Lampell, Executive Director
JoAnn Cooper, Executive Director

Nonprofit educational organization that focuses on technologies, operational approaches, and business issues for the global financial community.
2000+ Members
Frequency: Monthly
Circulation: 14000+
Founded in 1967

8811 **Water Investment Newsletter**
US Water News
230 Main St
Halstead, KS 67056-1913

316-835-2222
800-251-0046
Fax: 316-835-2223
Home Page: www.uswaternews.com

Thomas Bell, Owner
Toni Young, Chairman

News, features and profiles of shareholder owned water supply and treatment companies. General news on water-related investment opportunities with stock portfolio.
Cost: $140.00
8 Pages
Frequency: Monthly
ISSN: 1049-443X
Printed in one color on matte stock

8812 **Wireless Market Stats**
Kagan World Media
1 Lower Ragsdale Dr
Building One, Suite 130
Monterey, CA 93940-5749

831-624-1536
800-307-2529
Fax: 831-625-3225
E-Mail: info@kagan.com
Home Page: www.kagan.com

Tim Baskerville, President
Tom Johnson, Marketing Manager

News of the Wireless Market Stats. Three month trial available.
Cost: $1095.00
Frequency: Monthly
Founded in 1969

8813 **Wireless Telecom Investor**
Kagan World Media
1 Lower Ragsdale Dr
Bldg 1, Suite 130
Monterey, CA 93940-5749

831-624-1536
800-307-2529
Fax: 831-625-3225
E-Mail: info@kagan.com
Home Page: www.kagan.com

Tim Baskerville, President
Harvey Kraft, Director of Marketing
George Niesen, Editor
Robert Naylor, Circulation Manager
Sandie Borthwick, Publisher

Exclusive analysis of private and public values of wireless telecommunications companies, including cellular telephone, ESMR and PCS. Exclusive databases of subscribers, market penetrations, market potential, industry growth. Catching super-fast growth in a capsule. Three month trial available.
Cost: $1095.00
Frequency: Monthly
Founded in 1970

8814 **Wireless/Private Cable Investor**
Kagan World Media
126 Clock Tower Place
Carmel, CA 93923-8746

831-624-1536
Fax: 831-624-5882
E-Mail: info@kagan.com
Home Page: www.kagan.com

George Niesen, Editor
Tom Johnson, Marketing Manager

The original bible of the wireless cable, multipoint distribution pay TV industry. Published continuously since 1972, this newsletter is the window on cable competition. Three month trial available.

Magazines & Journals

8815 **AAII Journal**
American Association of Individual Investors
625 N Michigan Avenue
Chicago, IL 60611

312-280-0170
800-428-2244
Fax: 312-280-9883
E-Mail: members@aaii.com
Home Page: www.aaii.com

James Cloonan, Chairman
James Cloonan, Founder

Journal focusing on personal finance, specifically investing in stocks and mutual funds and portfolio management.
Cost: $29.00
40 Pages
Circulation: 170000
ISSN: 0192-3315
Founded in 1978

8816 **AG Lender**
Food 360/Vance Media
10901 W 84th Ter
Lenexa, KS 66214-1631

913-438-5721
800-808-2623
Fax: 913-438-0697
E-Mail: rkeller@vancepublishing.com
Home Page: www.vancepublishing.com

Cliff Becker, VP

AG Lender magazine reaches key agricultural financial leaders with editorial material geared to their business success.
Frequency: Monthly
Circulation: 1700
Founded in 1923

8817 **AGA Today**
Association of Government Accountants
2208 Mount Vernon Ave
Alexandria, VA 22301-1314

703-562-0900
800-242-7211
Fax: 703-548-9367
E-Mail: agacgfm@agacgfm.org
Home Page: www.agacgfm.org

Relmond Van Daniker, Executive Director

This publication acts as a clearinghouse for current government financial management information.
Frequency: Bi-Weekly
Circulation: 12,000

8818 **Accounting and Business Review World**
Scientific Publishing Company
1060 Main Street
River Edge, NJ 07661-2013

201-487-9655
Fax: 201-487-9656

Ed Yang Hoong Pang

Aims to provide a forum for the publication of accounting and business research papers which are of interest to educators, students and practitioners.
Cost: $60.00

8819 **Affiliate Forum**
NACHA: Electronic Payments Association
13665 Dulles Technology Dr
Suite 300
Herndon, VA 20171-4607

703-561-1100
Fax: 703-787-0996
E-Mail: info@nacha.org
Home Page: www.nacha.org

Janet O Estep, CEO

8820 **Alert**
Defense Credit Union Council
601 Pennsylvania Ave NW
South Building, Suite 600
Washington, DC 20004-2601

202-638-3950
Fax: 202-638-3410
Home Page: www.dcuc.org

Roland Arteata, President
Frequency: Monthly

8821 **American Cash Flow Journal**
American Cash Flow Association
255 S Orange Avenue
#600
Orlando, FL 32801

407-206-6523
800-253-1294
E-Mail: info@americancashflow.com
Home Page: www.acfa.org

Fred Rewey, President

Issues cover factoring accounts receivable and dealing with privatly held mortgages, along with thirty income streams. Offering updates on the legal and regulatory aspects of handling debt instruments and reports on new technology.
Frequency: Monthly
Circulation: 25,000

8822 **Annual Institute Journal**
National Association of Division Order Analysts
2805 Oak Trail Court
Suite 6312
Arlington, TX 76016

972-715-4489
E-Mail: administrator@nadoa.org
Home Page: www.nadoa.org

Lynn S McCord, Administrator
Frequency: Annual

8823 **Armed Forces Comptroller**
American Society of Military Comptrollers
415 N Alfred St
Alexandria, VA 22314-2269

703-549-0360
800-462-5637
Fax: 703-549-3181
Home Page: www.asmconline.org

Robert Hale, Executive Director
Frequency: Quarterly

8824 **Asset Management**
ASMC
170 Avenue at the Common
PO Box 7930
Shrewsbury, NJ 07702-4803

732-389-8700
Fax: 732-389-8701
Home Page: www.djassetmanagement.com

Barry Vinocur, Publisher

Departments include a mutual fund snapshot, a variable annuity databank, asset allocation, a journal watch and much more. Also offering topical features of interest to industry professionals.
Frequency: Bi-Monthly
Circulation: 30,000

8825 **Asset Protection: Offshore Tax Reports**
Offshore Press
4500 W 72nd Ter
Shawnee Mission, KS 66208-2824

913-362-9667
Fax: 913-432-7174
E-Mail: jacobs@offshorepress.com
Home Page: www.offshorepress.com

Vernon K Jacobs, President
Cost: $120.00
Frequency: Weekly
Founded in 1981

8826 **Barter News**
PO Box 3024
Mission Viejo, CA 92690-1024

949-831-0607
Fax: 949-831-9378
E-Mail: bmeyer@barternews.com
Home Page: www.barternews.com

Bob Meyer, Publisher/Editor
Michael Mercier, VP
Fredrick Fuest, COO
Julia Homer, CFO

Industry news is covered including listings of CEO's and CFO's and editorials. An in-depth look into the changes and evolution of barter, and shows how-to profitability use barter to increase the bottom line.
Cost: $40.00
96 Pages
Frequency: Quarterly
Circulation: 30,000
Founded in 1980
Printed in 4 colors on glossy stock

8827 **Business Credit**
National Association of Credit Management
8840 Columbia 100 Pkwy
Columbia, MD 21045-2100

410-740-5560
Fax: 410-740-5574
E-Mail: robins@nacm.org
Home Page: www.nacm.org

Robin Schauseil, President
Jim Vanghel, Vice President

For professionals responsible for extending credit and collecting receivables. Topics include business law, lein law, technology, credit management, collections, deductions, fraud, credit risk, credit scoring, outsourcing, information services, trade finance and more.
Cost: $54.00
72 Pages
Circulation: 32000
Founded in 1896
Printed in 4 colors on matte stock

8828 **Business Finance**
Duke Communications International
221 E 29th Street
PO Box 3438
Loveland, CO 80539-3438

970-634-4700
Fax: 970-593-1050
E-Mail: info@businessfinancemag.com
Home Page: www.businessfinancemag.com

David Blansfield, Publisher
Laurie Brannen, Editor-in-Chief
Meg Waters, Managing Editor
Matthew Weiner, Associate Publisher
Bruce Lynn, Managing Partner

Articles cover a broad range of topics from accounting to the Internet, from benchmarking to best practices, and cost management to career management.
Frequency: Monthly
Circulation: 50000

8829 **CEIR - Quarterly National Economic Reports**
National Association of Certified Valuation
1111 Brickyard Road
Suite 200
Salt Lake City, UT 84106-5401

303-698-1883
800-677-2009
E-Mail: sherril@nacva.com
Home Page: www.navca.com

Pamela R Bailey, Executive Director
Parnell Black, MBA CPA CVA, CEO
Roberto Castro, Director Business Development
Dean Dinas, Director Economic Research
Brien K Jones, General Manager Conferences
Frequency: Quarterly

8830 **CMBA World**
Commerical Mortgage Securities Association
30 Broad St
28th Floor
New York, NY 10004-4119

212-509-1844
Fax: 212-509-1895
E-Mail: info1@cmbs.org
Home Page: www.cmbs.org

Dottie Cunningham, CEO
Frequency: Quarterly

8831 **Capitol Comment**
National Association of Mortgage Brokers
8201 Greensboro Drive
Suite 300
McLean, VA 22102

703-610-9009
Fax: 703-610-9005
E-Mail: rdeloach@namb.org
Home Page: www.namb.org

Frequency: Monthly

8832 **Collections & Credit Risk**
Thomson Financial Publishing
1 State St
27th Floor
New York, NY 10004-1481

212-825-8445
800-221-1809
Fax: 212-803-1592
Home Page: www.creditcollectionsworld.com

Sharon Rowlands, President/CEO
Louis Eccleston, Marketing Director
Catherine Ladwig, Editor
Darren Waggoner, Executive Editor
Jose Thomas, Manager

Focuses on news and trends of strategic and competitive importance to collections and credit policy executives. Covers the credit risk industry's growth, diversification and technology in both commercial and consumer credit.
Cost: $98.00
66 Pages
Frequency: Monthly
Circulation: 25000
ISSN: 1093-1260
Founded in 1961
Printed in 4 colors on glossy stock

8833 **Collector Magazine**
ACA International
PO Box 390106
Minneapolis, MN 55439-106

952-926-6547
Fax: 952-926-1624
E-Mail: aca@acainternational.org
Home Page: www.acainternational.org

Timothy Dressen, Editor/Director Comm
Gary Rippentrop, CEO
Anne Rosso, Associate Editor

Brings you vital, up to the minute information on industry trends, regulations and legislation each month.
Cost: $70.00
Frequency: Monthly
Circulation: 6000
Founded in 1939

8834 **Commercial Mortgage Insight**
Zackin Publications
PO Box 2180
Waterbury, CT 06722-2180

203-755-0158
800-325-6745
Fax: 203-755-3480
E-Mail: info@cmi-online.com
Home Page: www.cmi-online.com

Joe Caton, Editor
Paul Zackin, Publisher
June Han, Marketing

For desicion making executives in commercial mortgage banking and brokerage firms, commercial banks and community/savings institutions. Provides professionals with timely and comprehensive market news, trends and know-how needed to make informed decisions and choices.
Cost: $48.00
32 Pages
Frequency: Monthly
Circulation: 18000
ISSN: 1095-0729
Founded in 1969
Printed in 4 colors

8835 **Computerized Investing**
American Association of Individual Investors
625 N Michigan Avenue
Chicago, IL 60611

312-280-0170
800-428-2244
Fax: 312-280-9883
E-Mail: mambers@aaii.com
Home Page: www.aaii.com

James Cloonan, Chairman

Offers information on computed investing, stocks and bonds.
Cost: $40.00
Founded in 1978

8836 **Consumer Finance Law Quarterly Report**
Conference on Consumer Finance Law
Oklahoma City University School of Law
2501 N Blackwelder
Oklahoma City, OK 73106

405-208-5363
Fax: 405-208-5089

E-Mail: ccflqr@lec.okcu.edu
Home Page: www.ccfonline.org

Alvin C Harrell, Executive Director
Frequency: Quarterly

8837 Contingency Planning & Management
Witter Publishing Corporation
84 Park Avenue
Flemington, NJ 08822

908-788-0343
Fax: 908-788-3782
Home Page: www.WitterPublishing.com

Steve Biggers, Publisher
Andy Hagg, Editor
Andrew Witter, President

Serves the fields of financial/banking, manufacturing industrial, transportation, utilities, telecommunications, health care, government, insurance and other allied fields.
Founded in 1996

8838 Controller's Quarterly
Institute of Management Accountants
10 Paragon Dr
Suite 1
Montvale, NJ 07645-1774

201-573-9000
800-638-4427
Fax: 201-474-1600
E-Mail: ima@imanet.org
Home Page: www.imanet.org

Paul Sharman, President
Sandra Richtermeyer, Chair
Frequency: Monthly

8839 Corporate Controller
Thomson Reuters
195 Broadway
New York, NY 10007-3124

646-822-2000
800-231-1860
Fax: 646-822-2800
E-Mail: trta.lei-support@thomsonreuters.com
Home Page: www.ria.thomsonreuters.com

Elaine Yadlon, Plant Manager
Thomas H Glocer, CEO & Director
Robert D Daleo, Chief Financial Officer
Kelli Crane, Senior Vice President & CIO

Includes health care costs, cash management, executive compensation and environmental insurance as well as regular columns on tax planning, technology advances, and innovative business trends.
Frequency: Bi-Monthly
Circulation: 3500

8840 Corporate Risk Management
Oster Communications
219 Main St
Cedar Falls, IA 50613-2742

319-277-1271
Fax: 319-277-7481

Merrill Oster, President

Written for financial decision makers.
48 Pages
Frequency: Monthly
Founded in 1989

8841 Cost Engineering Journal
AACE International
209 Prairie Avenue
Suite 100
Morgantown, WV 26501-5934

304-296-8444
800-858-2678
Fax: 304-291-5728
E-Mail: info@aacei.org
Home Page: www.aacei.org

Marvin Gelhausen, Managing Editor
Noah Kinderknecht, Editor

International journal of cost estimation, cost/schedule control, and project management read by cost professionals around the world to get the most up-to-date information about the profession.
Frequency: Monthly

8842 Cost Management Update
Institute of Management Accountants
10 Paragon Dr
Suite 1
Montvale, NJ 07645-1774

201-573-9000
800-638-4427
Fax: 201-474-1600
E-Mail: ima@imanet.org
Home Page: www.imanet.org

Paul Sharman, President
Sandra Richtermeyer, Chair
Frequency: Monthly

8843 Credit Card Management
Thomson Financial Publishing
1 State St
27th Floor
New York, NY 10004-1481

212-825-8445
800-535-8403
Fax: 800-235-5552
E-Mail: custserv@sourcemedia.com
Home Page: www.cardforum.com

James Daly, Editor
Sharon Rowlands, President/CEO
Louis Eccleston, Marketing Director
Jose Thomas, Manager

Information on the major developments in the credit card industry.
Cost: $98.00
74 Pages
Frequency: Monthly
Circulation: 19000
Founded in 1962
Printed in 4 colors on glossy stock

8844 Credit Scoring
Credit Research Foundation
8840 Columbia 100 Pkwy
Suite 100
Columbia, MD 21045-2100

410-740-5499
Fax: 410-740-4620
E-Mail: crf_info@crfonline.org
Home Page: www.crfonline.org

Terry Callahan, President
Michael Durant, Vice-Chairman

8845 Credit Union Executive Journal
Credit Union National Association
Po Box 431
Madison, WI 53701-0431

608-231-4000
800-356-9655
Fax: 608-231-1869
E-Mail: dorothy@cuna.org
Home Page: www.cuna.org

Daniel A Mica, CEO

Techniques and concepts available in management, finance, marketing, lending, human resources and technology for credit unions.
Cost: $202.00
Circulation: 2400
Founded in 1930

8846 Credit Union Magazine
Credit Union National Association
5710 Mineral Point Road
Madison, WI 53705-4454

800-356-9655
Fax: 608-231-4263
E-Mail: dorothy@cuna.org
Home Page: www.cuna.org

Daniel A Mica, CEO
Tom Dorety, Vice Chairman
Bill Merrick, Managing Editor

The role and operations of modern credit unions.
Cost: $50.00
100 Pages
Frequency: Monthly
Circulation: 32776
ISSN: 0011-1066
Founded in 1981
Printed in 4 colors on glossy stock

8847 Credit Union Technology
Credit Union Technology
110-64 Queens Boulevard
#106
Forest Hills, NY 11375-6347

718-793-9400
Fax: 718-793-9414
Home Page: www.cutmag.com

Andrew Mallon, Publisher

Information on improving customer service through technological advances.
Cost: $36.00
24 Pages
Frequency: Bi-Monthly
Circulation: 6000
ISSN: 1054-7304
Founded in 1991
Printed in 4 colors on glossy stock

8848 Credit and Collection Survey
Broadcast Cable Credit Association
550 W Frontage Rd
Suite 3600
Northfield, IL 60093-1243

847-881-8757
Fax: 847-784-8059
E-Mail: info@bccacredit.com
Home Page: www.bccacredit.com

Mary Collin, CEO
Jamie Smith, Director of Operations
Rachelle Brooks, BCCA Sales
Frequency: Bi-Ennial

8849 DC Advocate
National Defined Contribution Council
9101 E Kenyon
Suite 300
Denver, CO 80237-0467

303-770-5353
Fax: 303-770-1812
Home Page: www.ndcconline.org

Al Brust, Executive VP
Frequency: Quarterly

8850 Disclosure Record
Newsfeatures
8511 249th Street
Jamaica, NY 11426-2105
Jack Lotto, Editor

Full texts of corporate and financial news reports.
Cost: $50.00
8 Pages
Frequency: Monthly
Founded in 1973

8851 Economic Outlook
America's Community Bankers

900 19th Street NW
Suite 400
Washington, DC 20006

202-857-3100
888-872-0275
Fax: 202-296-8716
E-Mail: info@acbankers.org
Home Page:
www.americascommunitybankers.com

Nancy Feig, Editor
Debra Cope, Publisher
Diane Casey-Landry, President/CEO

A first rate resource for strategically countering the hanging economic winds of the financial world.
Cost: $315.00
4 Pages
Frequency: Monthly
Founded in 1992

8852 **Electronics Payment Journal**
NACHA: Electronic Payments Association
13665 Dulles Technology Dr
Suite 300
Herndon, VA 20171-4607

703-561-1100
Fax: 703-787-0996
E-Mail: info@nacha.org
Home Page: www.nacha.org

Janet O Estep, CEO
Deb Evans-Doyle, Senior Director Conference Mktg
Julie Hedlund, Senior Director Electronic Commerce
Michael Herd, Director Public Relations
Priscilla Holland, AAP, Senior Director Corporate Pymts

8853 **Estate Planning Review**
2700 Lake Cook Road
Riverwoods, IL 60015-3867

847-267-7000
800-224-8299
Fax: 800-224-8299
Home Page: www.support.cch.com

Robert Becker, President and CEO
Cost: $275.00
Frequency: Monthly
Founded in 1913

8854 **Examiner**
Society of Financial Examiners
174 Grace Blvd
Altamonte Spgs, FL 32714-3210

407-682-4930
800-787-7633
Fax: 407-382-3175
Home Page: www.sofe.org

Pauline Keyes, Owner
Stephen J Szypula, Financial Administrator
Frequency: Quarterly

8855 **F & I Management Technology**
Association of Finance and Insurance Professionals
4112 Southwood E
Colleyville, TX 76034

817-428-2434
Fax: 817-428-2534
Home Page: www.afip.com

David N Robertson, Executive Director

8856 **Federal Credit Union Magazine**
National Association of Federal Credit Unions
3138 10th St N
Arlington, VA 22201-2160

703-522-4770
800-336-4644
Fax: 703-524-1082
E-Mail: fbecker@nafcu.org
Home Page: www.nafcu.org

Fred Becker, President

Written for CEO's, senior staff and volunteers of Federal Credit Unions. Offers legislative and regulatory news, as well as technology and operational issues. Call for rates.
50 Pages
Circulation: 1500
ISSN: 1043-7789
Founded in 1967
Printed in 4 colors on glossy stock

8857 **Financial Analysts Journal**
CFA Institute
Po Box 3668
Charlottesville, VA 22903-0668

434-951-5499
800-247-8132
Fax: 434-951-5262
E-Mail: info@cfainstitute.org
Home Page: www.cfainstitute.org

John Rogers, CEO
Rodney N Sullivan, Associate Editor

To advance the knowledge and understanding of the practice of investment management through the publication of high-quality, practitioner-relevant research
Founded in 1945

8858 **Financial Executive**
Financial Executives International
200 Campus Dr
Suite 8
Florham Park, NJ 07932-1007

973-236-0177
800-336-0773
Fax: 973-765-1018
Home Page: www.financialexecutives.com

Jim Abel, President
Ellen Heffes, Managing Editor
Colleen S Cunningham, President
Maria O'Grady, Marketing Manager

Addresses accounting and treasury subjects, as well as overall strategies in corporate financial mangement.
Cost: $74.39
72 Pages
Frequency: Monthly
Circulation: 16500
ISSN: 0895-4186
Founded in 1931
Printed in 4 colors on glossy stock

8859 **Financial Management Journal**
Financial Management Association International
4202 E Fowler Ave
BSN 3331
Tampa, FL 33620-9951

813-974-2084
Fax: 813-974-3318
E-Mail: info@fma.org
Home Page: www.fma.org

Jack S Rader, Executive Director
Jeffrey Coles, Advisory Editor
John Graham, Advisory Editor
Michael Lemmon, Advisory Editor
Jay Ritter, Advisory Editor

Financial Management serves both academicians and practitioners who are concerned with the financial management of non-financial businesses, financial institutions, and public and private not-for-profit organizations. The journal serves the profession by publishing significant new scholarly research in finance that is of the highest quality.
Frequency: Quarterly

8860 **Financial Manager**
Broadcast Cable Financial Management Association
550 W Frontage Rd
Suite 3600
Northfield, IL 60093-1243

847-716-7000
Fax: 847-784-8059
E-Mail: info@bccacredit.com
Home Page: www.bcfm.com

Mary Collins, President
Jamie Smith, Director of Operations
Rachelle Brooks, BCCA Sales

A bi-monthly magazine published by the Broadcast Cable Financial Management Association.
Cost: $69.00
36 Pages
Circulation: 300
Mailing list available for rent: 1100 names at $495 per M

8861 **Financial Manager/Credit Topics**
Broadcast Cable Credit Association
550 W Frontage Rd
Suite 3600
Northfield, IL 60093-1243

847-881-8757
Fax: 847-784-8059
E-Mail: info@bccacredit.com
Home Page: www.bccacredit.com

Mary Collin, CEO
Jamie Smith, Director of Operations
Rachelle Brooks, BCCA Sales
Frequency: Bi-Monthly

8862 **Financial Planning & Counseling Journal**
Association for Financial Counseling and Planning
2112 Arlington Avenue
Suite H
Upper Arlington, OH 43221

614-485-9650
Fax: 614-485-9621
Home Page: www.afcpe.org

Sharon Burns, PhD, Executive Director
Frequency: Semi-Annual

8863 **Financial Planning Digest**
Harcourt Brace Professional Publishing
6277 Sea Harbor Drive
Orlando, FL 32887

407-345-2000
Fax: 407-345-3016
Home Page: www.harcourt.com

Angelita Streeter, Editor
Paul Amidei, Managing Editor

Estate, retirement, insurance planning tips and strategies, practice management insight, book reviews and legislation updates.
Cost: $99.00
Frequency: Monthly

8864 **Financial Review Magazine**
NFR Communications
4948 Washburn Avenue S
Minneapolis, MN 55410

612-929-8110
Fax: 612-929-8146
Home Page: www.nfrcom.com

Tom Bengtson, Editor
Jackie Hilgert, Production Manager

Trade publication covering the commercial banking industry in the upper midwest. Designed for the decision-maker in the bank.
Frequency: 25 per year

8865 **Financial Services Quarterly**
SNL Securities

One SNL Plaza
PO Box 2124
Charlottesvle, VA 22902-2124

434-977-1600
Fax: 434-977-4466
E-Mail: subscriptions@snl.com
Home Page: www.snl.com

Pam Askea, Editor
Dan Oakey, Editor
Michael Spears, Advertising
Edward Metz, Financial Services
Nick Cafferillo, Chief Operating Officer

Comprehensive reference guide available on finance companies, mortgage banks, investment advisors and securities brokers/dealers. In-depth company profiles and financial data on these publicly traded companies and summary financials on thousands of non-public financial services companies.
Cost: $696.00
400 Pages
Frequency: Quarterly
Founded in 1987

8866 Financier
Bank Administration Institute
1 N Franklin St
Chicago, IL 60606-3598

312-553-4600
Fax: 312-683-2373
E-Mail: info@bai.org
Home Page: www.bai.org

Deborah Bianucci, CEO
Willard Rappleye Jr, Executive Vice President
Ann Barcroft, Executive Vice President
Anne Matsumoto, Managing Director

Forum of ideas for the private sector.
Cost: $5.00
Circulation: 32,000

8867 Forbes Global
Forbes Media LLC.
60 5th Ave
New York, NY 10011-8868

212-620-2200
Fax: 212-620-1857
E-Mail: readers@forbes.com
Home Page: www.forbes.com

Malcolm S Forbes Jr, CEO
Bruce Rogers, VP Marketing
Paul Maidment, Executive Editor
Michael Smith Maidment, VP, GM Operations

A magazine giving detailed information about business and finance.
Frequency: Monthly

8868 Forbes Magazine
Forbes Media LLC.
60 5th Ave
11th Floor
New York, NY 10011-8868

212-620-2200
Fax: 212-620-1857
E-Mail: customerservice@forbes.com
Home Page: www.forbes.com

Malcolm S Forbes Jr, CEO
Bruce Rogers, VP Marketing
Paul Maidment, Executive Director
Micheal Smith Maidment, VP, GM Operations

A magazine giving detailed information about business and finance.
Cost: $4.95
304 Pages
Founded in 1917

8869 Futures Industry
Futures Industry Association
2001 Pennsylvania Ave NW
#600
Washington, DC 20006-1823

202-223-1528
Fax: 202-296-3184
E-Mail: info@futuresindustry.org
Home Page: www.futuresindustry.org

John Damgard, President/CEO
Erin Kairys, Manager
Will Acworth, Editor
Roselia Marmolejos, Administrative Assistant

Front and back office operations, marketing, research, money management, regulatory and brokerage issues from a domestic and international perspective.
Circulation: 15000
Founded in 1955

8870 Futures Magazine
Oster Communications
219 Main St
Suite 6
Cedar Falls, IA 50613-2742

319-277-1271
Fax: 319-277-7481
Home Page: www.futuresmag.com

Merrill Oster, President
Ginger Szala, Publisher

News, analysis, and strategies for futures, options and derivatives traders. Descriptions include annual sourcebook directory of exchange, contract, company and product information.
Cost: $39.00
Frequency: Monthly
Circulation: 60000
Founded in 1972

8871 Global Custodian
Asset International
125 Greenwich Avenue
Greenwich, CT 06830

203-295-5015
Fax: 203-629-5024
E-Mail: office@assetpub.com
Home Page: www.globalcustodian.com

Dominic Hobson, Editor-in-Chief
Charles Ruffel, Executive Editor
Meredith Hughes, Publisher
Alix Hughes, Sales Director

An in-depth perspective on the business of international investing, custody and clearing, and directory-type data on industry participants and trends. Provides investment professionals with an analysis of the strength and weaknessed of the players and systems that underlie international investing.
Cost: $185.00
Circulation: 30,488
Founded in 1989

8872 Global Investment Magazine
Global Investment Technology
820 2nd Ave
4th Floor
New York, NY 10017-4504

212-370-3700
Fax: 212-370-4606
E-Mail: info@globalinv.com
Home Page: www.globalinv.com

Micheal Horton, Publisher
Pierre-Yves Sacchi, Managing Director

Portfolio management, trading and global asset services, and a wide range of issues pertaining to institutional portfolio management strategies and decision making in the US and cross-border markets.
Frequency: Quarterly
Circulation: 15000

8873 Global Investment Technology
Global Investment Technology
820 2nd Ave
4th Floor
New York, NY 10017-4504

212-370-3700
Fax: 212-370-4606
E-Mail: info@globalinv.com
Home Page: www.globalinv.com

Micheal Horton, Publisher
Pavan Sehgal, Managing Director
Pierre-Yves Sacchi, Managing Director

The strategic business interests of top-level decision makers as well as their operations and systems professionals.
Cost: $695.00
Circulation: 1800
Founded in 1990

8874 Healthcare Financial Management
2 Westbrook Corporate Ctr #700
Westchester, IL 60154-5723

708-531-9614
Fax: 708-531-0032
Home Page: www.hfma.org

Richard L Clarke, President

8875 IBIS Review
Charles D Spencer
250 S Wacker Drive
#600
Chicago, IL 60606-5800

312-993-7900
Fax: 312-993-7910
E-Mail: ibisnet@mindspring.com
Home Page: www.ibisnews.com

Charles D Spencer, Publisher
Celia Cruz, Owner

For the individual responsible for the compensation and benefits of employees working abroad. Topics include pensions and profit-sharing plans, stock purchase and savings plans, death and disability benefits, health care coverage, termination indemnities, executive renumeration plans, investments, and expatriate plans.
Frequency: Monthly
Circulation: 1500

8876 IMA Focus
Institute of Management Accountants
10 Paragon Dr
Suite 1
Montvale, NJ 07645-1774

201-573-9000
800-638-4427
Fax: 201-474-1600
E-Mail: ima@imanet.org
Home Page: www.imanet.org

Paul Sharman, President
Frequency: Bi-Monthly

8877 INSIGHT
Society of Financial Examiners
174 Grace Blvd
Altamonte Spgs, FL 32714-3210

407-682-4930
800-787-7633
Fax: 407-682-3175
Home Page: www.sofe.org

Pauline Keyes, Owner
Stephen J Szypula, Financial Administrator
Frequency: Monthly

8878 ISM Info Edge
Institute for Supply Management

2055 E Centennial Circle
PO Box 22160
Tempe, AZ 85285-2160

480-752-6276
800-888-6276
Fax: 480-752-7890
E-Mail: infocenter@ism.ws
Home Page: www.ism.ws

Paul Novak, CPM, CEO
Holly LaCroix Johnson, Senior Vice President
Deborah Webber, SVP
Jean McHale, Manager
Frequency: Quarterly

8879 **Inside Mortgage Finance**
Inside Mortgage Finance Publishers
7910 Woodmont Ave
Suite 1010
Bethesda, MD 20814-7019

301-951-1240
Fax: 301-656-1709
E-Mail: service@imfpubs.com
Home Page:
http://www.insidemortgagefinance.com

Industry news and related trade literature. Includes extensive market data, from rankings of top originators to the leading private mortgage insurers.
Cost: $889.00
12 Pages
ISSN: 8756 0003
Founded in 1984
Printed in 2 colors on matte stock

8880 **Inside Mortgage Update**
Inside Mortgage Finance Publishers
7910 Woodmont Ave
Suite 1010
Bethesda, MD 20814-7019

301-951-1240
Fax: 301-656-1709
E-Mail: service@imfpubs.com
Home Page:
http://www.insidemortgagefinance.com

Guy Cecala, Owner
John Bancroft, President

Covers this dynamic market of lending to borrowers with less than perfect credit with news, analysis and truly useful market intelligence.
Cost: $659.00
14 Pages
Circulation: 1000
ISSN: 1093-4030
Founded in 1996
Printed in 2 colors on matte stock

8881 **Inside Supply Management**
Insitute for Supply Management
2055 E Centennial Circle
PO Box 22160
Tempe, AZ 85285-2160

480-752-6276
800-888-6276
Fax: 480-752-7890
E-Mail: infocenter@ism.ws
Home Page: www.ism.ws

Paul Novak, CPM, CEO
Holly LaCroix Johnson, Senior Vice President
Deborah Webber, SVP
Jean McHale, Manager
Frequency: Monthly

8882 **Institute of Management & Administration Newsletter**
Institute of Management and Administration
1 Washington Park
Suite 1300
Newark, NJ 07102

212-244-0360
Fax: 973-622-0595
Home Page: www.ioma.com

Information for those involved in international sales. Regular monthly features.

8883 **Insurance & Financial Meetings Managment**
Coastal Communications Corporation
2700 N Military Trail
Suite 120
Boca Raton, FL 33431

561-989-0600
Fax: 561-989-9509
E-Mail: ccceditor@att.net
Home Page: www.themeetingmagazines.com

Harvey Grotsky, Publisher/Editor-In-Chief
Susan Wycoff Fell, Managing Editor
Susan Gregg, Managing Editor

The executive source for planning meetings and incentives for the financial and insurance sectors. With regular features and special focus on site selection, destinations, industry-related studies and activities, motivational and incentive programs, program and event planning.
Frequency: Monthly
Circulation: 40,000
Founded in 1983

8884 **International Journal of Supply Chain Management**
Institute for Supply Management
2055 E Centennial Circle
PO Box 22160
Tempe, AZ 85285-2160

480-752-6276
800-888-6276
Fax: 480-752-7890
E-Mail: infocenter@ism.ws
Home Page: www.ism.ws

Paul Nocak, CPM, CEO
Holly LaCroix Johnson, Senior Vice President
Deborah Webber, SVP
Jean McHale, Manager
Frequency: Quarterly

8885 **Investor Relations Business**
Securities Data Publishing
40 W 57th St
New York, NY 10019-4001

212-484-4701
Fax: 212-956-0112
E-Mail: sdp@tfn.com

Matthew Greco, Editor
Edward Cortese, Marketing Executive

News updates, career opportunities and personnel announcements for CEO's, CFO's, treasurers and directors of corporations.
Cost: $415.00
Frequency: Bi-Monthly

8886 **Journal of Applied Finance**
Financial Management Association International
4202 E Fowler Ave
BSN 3331
Tampa, FL 33620-9951

813-974-2084
Fax: 813-974-3318
E-Mail: info@fma.org
Home Page: www.fma.org

Jack S Rader, Executive Director
Ali Fatemi, Editor
Reena Aggarwal, Associate Editor
James S Ang, Associate Editor
Robert F Bruner, Associate Editor

Launched in 2001, JAF publishes easy-to-read pieces that focus on financial practice and education - a standard reference for those seeking knowledge on the new developments in applied finance.
Frequency: Bi-Annual

8887 **Journal of Asset Protection**
Thomson Reuters
195 Broadway
New York, NY 10007-3124

646-822-2000
800-231-1860
Fax: 646-822-2800
E-Mail: trta.lei-support@thomsonreuters.com
Home Page: www.ria.thomsonreuters.com

Elaine Yadlon, Plant Manager
Thomas H Glocer, CEO & Director
Robert D Daleo, Chief Financial Officer
Kelli Crane, Senior Vice President & CIO

Information on shielding personal and business assets from creditors, third party attachments and government claims.
Cost: $195.00
Frequency: Bi-Monthly
Circulation: 2,000

8888 **Journal of Cost Management**
Thomson Reuters
195 Broadway
New York, NY 10007-3124

646-822-2000
800-231-1860
Fax: 646-822-2800
E-Mail: trta.lei-support@thomsonreuters.com
Home Page: www.ria.thomsonreuters.com

Elaine Yadlon, Plant Manager
Thomas H Glocer, CEO & Director
Robert D Daleo, Chief Financial Officer
Kelli Crane, Senior Vice President & CIO

Information on cost management techniques and manufacturing technology. Provides essays and or research papers by professionals and educators.
Cost: $210.00
Frequency: Monthly
Circulation: 5000
Founded in 1940

8889 **Journal of Education Finance**
American Education Finance Association
5249 Cape Leyte Drive
Sarasota, FL 34242-1805

941-349-7580

Information and news to educational organizations on financial investing and prospecting.
150 Pages
Frequency: Quarterly
Circulation: 700
Founded in 1978

8890 **Journal of Finance**
American Finance Association
Haas School of Business
Berkley, CA 94720-1900

510-642-2397
Fax: 510-525-6246
E-Mail: pyle@haas.berkley.edu
Home Page: www.afajof.org

Robert F Stambaugh, Editor
Anat R Admati, Associate Editors
Wendy Washburn, Editorial Assistant
David H Pyle, Business Manager

Covers theory and practice in the field of finance.
Frequency: Bi-Monthly
Circulation: 10000+
Founded in 1939

8891 **Journal of Financial Planning**
4100 E Mississippi Avenue
Suite 400
Denver, CO 80246

303-759-4900
800-322-4237
Fax: 303-759-0749
E-Mail: journal@fpanet.org
Home Page: www.fpanet.org

Marvin W Tuttle CAE, Executive Director/CEO
Ian McKenzie, Managing Director/Publishing

A comprehensive financial publication offering information and news on financial planning, investing and prospecting.
Cost: $90.00
Frequency: Monthly
Circulation: 50,000
Founded in 1979

8892 **Journal of Fixed Income**
Institutional Investor
488 Madison Ave
16th Floor
New York, NY 10022-5701

212-303-3100
800-945-2034
Fax: 212-224-3491
E-Mail: iieditor@institutionalinvestor.com
Home Page: www.institutionalinvestor.com/

Allison Adams, Publisher
Brian Bruce, Editor
Anne O'Brien, Marketing

Reporting on analysis of theories and ideas involving fixed income.
Cost: $370.00
Frequency: Quarterly
Circulation: 2500
Founded in 1967

8893 **Journal of Gift Planning**
National Committee on Planned Giving
233 S McCrea St
Suite 400
Indianapolis, IN 46225-1068

317-269-6274
Fax: 317-269-6276
Home Page: www.ncpg.org

Tanya Howe Johnson, President
Sandra Kerr, Director Government Education
Barbara Owens, Director Membership Manager
Kathryn J Ramsey, Director Meetings
Kurt Reusze, Manager Education/Technology
Frequency: Quarterly

8894 **Journal of Government Financial Management**
Association of Government Accountants
2208 Mount Vernon Ave
Alexandria, VA 22301-1314

703-562-0900
800-242-7211
Fax: 703-548-9367
E-Mail: agacgfm@agacgfm.org
Home Page: www.agacgfm.org

Relmond Van Daniker, Executive Director

Provides valuable information for governmental decision makers. Examines budgeting, accounting, auditing and date process developments.
Frequency: Quarterly
Circulation: 14,769

8895 **Journal of Healthcare Administrative Management**
American Association of Healthcare Administrative
11240 Waples Mill Rd
Suite 200
Fairfax, VA 22030-6078

703-934-0164
Fax: 703-359-7562
E-Mail: moayad@aaham.org
Home Page: www.aaham.org

Sharon Geller, Executive Director
Linda Sheaffer, Chair
Frequency: Quarterly

8896 **Journal of Investing**
Institutional Investor
1900 Preston Road
#267-310
Plano, TX 75093-5175

214-495-9533
Fax: 212-224-3491
E-Mail: info@iijournals.com
Home Page: www.iijournals.com

Brian Bruce, Editor-in-Chief
Allison Adams, Publisher
Anne O'Brien, Director of Marketing

Features equity investments, fixed income investing, security valuation and related investment vehicles.
Cost: $360.00
Frequency: Quarterly
Circulation: 2500
Founded in 1967

8897 **Journal of Mutual Fund Services**
Securities Data Publishing
600 Atlantic Avenue
Boston, MA 02210-2211

617-723-6400
Fax: 617-624-7200
Home Page: www.dalbar.com

Ken Heath, Publisher
Kathleen Whalen, Managing Director

Focuses on backroom operations of the mutual fund industry, with directories featuring transfer assets, fund accountants, custodians, attorneys and other service personnel.
Cost: $795.00
Frequency: 8 per year

8898 **Journal of Performance Management**
Assn for Management Information in Financial Svcs
14247 Saffron Circle
Carmel, IN 46032

317-815-5857
Fax: 317-815-5877
E-Mail: ami2@amifs.org
Home Page: www.amifs.org

Adam Schabes, President
Cost: $200.00
Frequency: 3/year
Circulation: 350

8899 **Journal of Portfolio Management**
Institutional Investor
488 Madison Ave
16th Floor
New York, NY 10022-5701

212-303-3100
800-437-9997
Fax: 212-224-3491
E-Mail: iieditor@institutionalinvestor.com
Home Page: www.institutionalinvestor.com/

Allison Adams, Publisher
Peter Bernstein, Editor
Anne O'Brien, Marketing Manager

Ideas and concepts in the practice and theory of portfolio management.
Cost: $430.00
Frequency: Quarterly
Circulation: 5000
Founded in 1975

8900 **Journal of Taxation**
Thomson Reuters
195 Broadway
New York, NY 10007-3124

646-822-2000
800-231-1860
Fax: 646-822-2800
E-Mail: trta.lei-support@thomsonreuters.com
Home Page: www.ria.thomsonreuters.com

Elaine Yadlon, Plant Manager
Thomas H Glocer, CEO & Director
Robert D Daleo, Chief Financial Officer
Kelli Crane, Senior Vice President & CIO

Information on tax developments and trends, revenue rulings, court decisions and legislative and administrative actions of significance to the sophisticated tax professional.
Cost: $315.00
Frequency: Monthly
Circulation: 12000
ISSN: 0022-4863
Founded in 1984
Printed in on glossy stock

8901 **Legislative Currents**
American Association of Healthcare Administrative
11240 Waples Mill Rd
Suite 200
Fairfax, VA 22030-6078

703-934-0164
Fax: 703-359-7562
E-Mail: moayad@aaham.org
Home Page: www.aaham.org

Sharon Geller, Executive Director
Linda Sheaffer, Chair
Frequency: Bi-Monthly

8902 **MS Quarterly Journal**
Society for Information Management
401 N Michigan Avenue
Chicago, IL 60611

312-215-5190
Fax: 312-245-1081
Home Page: www.simnet.org

Jim Luisi, Executive Director
Frequency: Quarterly

8903 **Management and Technology**
Association of Finance and Insurance Professionals
412 Southwood E
Colleyville, TX 76034

817-428-2434
Fax: 817-428-2534
Home Page: www.afip.com

David N Robertson, Executive Director

8904 **Market Survey**
International Swaps and Derivatives Association
360 Madison Ave
16th Floor
New York, NY 10017-7126

212-901-6000
Fax: 212-901-6001
E-Mail: isda@isda.org
Home Page: www.isda.org

Robert Pickel, CEO
Ruth Ainslie, Director Communications
Corrine Greasley, Director Administration
Frequency: Semi-Annual

8905 **Money**
1271 Avenue of the Americas
32nd Floor
New York, NY 10020-1300

212-759-4094
Fax: 212-522-0773

8906 **Mortgage Originator**
Pfingsten Publishing
3990 Oldtown Avenue
Suite A203
San Diego, CA 92110

619-223-9989
800-995-2090
Fax: 619-223-9943
Home Page: www.mortgageoriginator.com

Chuck Hirsch, Publisher
David Robinson, Editor
Andy Strasser, Marketing Manager
Sue Burns, Circulation Director

Information on sales and marketing issues, correspondent management, retail mortgage, bankers and wholesale originators.
Cost: $58.00
Circulation: 19,500
ISSN: 1070-5708
Founded in 1998
Printed in 4 colors on glossy stock

8907 **Mortgage Servicing News**
Thomson Financial Publishing
1 State St
27th floor
New York, NY 10004-1481

212-825-8445
800-221-1809
Fax: 212-292-5216
Home Page: www.mortgageservicingnews.com

Timothy Murphy, Publisher
Mark Fogarty, Editorial Director
Robert Cullen, CEO

Information on cross serving techniques, legislative decisions, management strategies, and professional profiles.
Cost: $98.00
Frequency: Monthly
Circulation: 20000

8908 **NABTalk**
National Association of Bankruptcy Trustees
One Windsor Cove
Suite 305
Columbia, SC 29233

803-252-5646
800-445-8629
Fax: 803-765-0860
E-Mail: info@nabt.com
Home Page: www.nabt.com

Carol H Webber, Executive Director
Frequency: Quarterly

8909 **NAPFA Advisor Magazine**
National Association of Personal Financial Advisor
3250 N Arlington Heights Road
Suite 109
Arlington Heights, IL 60004

847-483-5400
800-366-2732
Fax: 847-483-5415
E-Mail: info@napfa.org
Home Page: www.napfa.org

Ellen Turf, CEO
Margery Wasserman, Director Conferences
Frequency: Monthly

8910 **NATE Update**
National Association of Trade Exchange
8836 Tyler Road
Mentor, OH 44060

440-205-5378
Fax: 440-205-5379
Home Page: www.nate.org

Thomas H McDowell, Executive Director

8911 **Natinal Pawnbroker Magazine**
National Pawnbrokers Association
P.O.Box 508
Keller, TX 76244-0508

817-491-4554
Fax: 817-481-8770
E-Mail: info@NationalPawnbrokers.org
Home Page: www.nationalpawnbrokers.org

Bob Benedict, CAE, Executive Director
Emmett Murphy, Director
Teresa Congleton, Administrative Assistant
Frequency: Quarterly

8912 **National Association of Investors Corporation**
Po Box 220
Royal Oak, MI 48068-0220

248-583-6242
887-ASK-NAIC
Fax: 248-583-4880

Kathleen Zaracki, CEO
Adam Ritt, Editor

Articles on counseling and teaching investing techniques. Magazine is included with membership.
100 Pages
Frequency: Monthly
Circulation: 250,000
Founded in 1951
Printed in 4 colors on glossy stock

8913 **National Mortgage Broker**
National Association of Mortgage Brokers
23425 N 39th Drive
104-193
Glendale, AZ 85310

623-516-2723
Fax: 623-516-7738
Home Page: www.namb.org

Jon Ruzan, Publisher/Editorial Director
Mollie Regan, Editor
Michael Nizankiewicz, Executive Vice President/CEO

Information on the National Association of mortgage Brokers including regulatory activities, education and certification, and building consumer awareness.
Cost: $59.95
Frequency: Monthly
Circulation: 7500
Founded in 1973

8914 **Nelson's World's Best Money Managers**
Nelson Publishing
2500 Tamiami Trl N
Nokomis, FL 34275-3476

941-966-9521
Fax: 941-966-2590
E-Mail: webmaster@nelsonpub.com
Home Page: www.healthmgttech.com

A Verner Nelson, Owner
George G Lindsey, COO
Kevin T Black, VP Database

A special quarterly report extracted from the Nelson Investment Manager Database which ranks the top investment managers by performance results in each of 200 categories.
Cost: $245.00
200 Pages
Frequency: Quarterly

8915 **Newspaper Financial Executive Journal**
Interactive & Newsmedia Financial Executives
14237 Bookcliff Court
Suite 200
Purcellville, VA 20132

703-421-4060
Fax: 703-421-4068
Home Page: www.infe.org

Jeff Hood, President

Trade publication for financial management of newspapers. More than 800 members.
Frequency: Weekly
Circulation: 1000
Founded in 1947

8916 **OCC Quarterly Journal**
Comptroller of the Currency
250 E St Sw
250 E Street SW
Washington, DC 20219-0001

202-874-5000
800-613-6743
Fax: 202-874-4490
E-Mail: Webmaster@occ.treas.gov
Home Page: www.occ.treas.gov

John C Dugan, CEO
Nancy K Jones, Administrative Assistant
Ruth Montgomery, Administrative Assistant
Teri Pote, Program Manager

Significant actions and policies of the Office of Comptroller of the Currency, the agency that regulates national banks. Legal interpretations, merger decisions, speeches and testimony and statistical and structural data on national banks are included.
Cost: $100.00
132 Pages
Frequency: Quarterly
Circulation: 6500
Founded in 1863

8917 **Pensions & Investments**
Crain Communications
360 N Michigan Ave
Chicago, IL 60601-3800

312-649-5200
Fax: 312-649-7937
E-Mail: info@crain.com
Home Page: www.crain.com

Keith Crain, CEO

Delivers critical financial news to executives responsible for the investment of large institutional assets such as pension funds, endowments and foundations.
Frequency: Monthly
Circulation: 52000

8918 **Plan Horizons**
National Institute of Pension Administrators
401 N Michigan Avenue
Suite 2200
Chicago, IL 60611-4267

800-999-6472
E-Mail: nipa@nipa.org
Home Page: www.nipa.org

Laura J Rudzinski, Executive Director
Frequency: Quarterly

8919 **Private Equity Analyst**
Asset Alternatives
888 Worcester Street
3rd Floor
Wellesley, MA 02482

781-304-1400
800-257-2947
Fax: 781-304-1440
E-Mail:

CustomerService@PrivateEquityAnalyst.com
Home Page: www.assetnews.com

David Toll, Managing Editor
Lisa Hughes, Circulation Manager

Insider contacts and timely reports on the latest in venture capital, mezzanine, LBO and turn around financing. Original research and in-depth feature articles helps you understand critical trends and issues in the market.
Cost: $1495.00
Frequency: Monthly

8920 Professional Collector
Pohly & Partners
27 Melcher Street
2nd Floor
Boston, MA 02210

617-451-1700
Fax: 617-338-7767
Home Page: www.pohlypartners.com

Karen English, Editor
Piania Pohly, CEO/President
Annie Swearingven, Marketing Manager

Information on the latest technology, legislation and other issues affecting the debt collections industry.
Cost: $24.95
Frequency: Quarterly
Circulation: 148000
Printed in 4 colors

8921 Purchasing
Reed Business Information
225 Wyman St
Waltham, MA 02451-1216

781-734-8000
800-446-6551
Fax: 781-290-3201
E-Mail: subsmail@reedbusiness.com
Home Page: www.reedbusiness.com

Mark Finklestein, President
Kathy Doyle, CFO
Stuart Whayman, CFO

Information for purchasing personnel in industry.
Frequency: bi-monthly
Circulation: 95,078
Founded in 1915
Printed in 4 colors on glossy stock

8922 REIT Securities Monthly
SNL Securities
PO Box 2124
Charlottesvle, VA 22902-2124

434-977-1600
Fax: 434-977-4466
Home Page: www.snlnet.com

Eden Rood, Editor
Reid Naglews, Chief Operating Officer
Nick Cafferillo, Chief Operating Officer
Adam Hall, Managing Director

Features sector analysis and interviews with industry leaders, as well as coverage of REIT investing and capital raising. The source for REIT and real estate investors, analysts and executives.
50 Pages
Frequency: Monthly

8923 RMA Journal
RMA - Risk Management Association
6147 Ridge Ave
Suite 2300
Philadelphia, PA 19128-2627

215-482-3222
800-677-7621
Fax: 215-446-4101
E-Mail: customers@rmahq.org
Home Page: www.rmahq.org

Angelo Roma, Owner
William F Githens, Director Member Relations
Dwightce J Overturf, CFO/Information Technology Officer
Florence J Wetzel, COO/Administrative Officer
Dom DiBernardi, Associate Director
Frequency: Monthly

8924 Regional Review
Federal Reserve Bank of Boston
600 Atlantic Ave
Boston, MA 02210-2204

617-973-3397
800-248-0168
Fax: 617-973-4292
E-Mail: boston.library@bos.frb.org
Home Page: www.bos.frb.org

Joyce Hannan, Manager
Cathy E Minehan, President/CEO
Jane Katz, Editor

Reliable and balanced discussions of economic issues. It is addressed to the opinion leaders of New England's business and government community.
Frequency: Quarterly
Circulation: 21000
Founded in 1913

8925 Registered Representative
Primedia
Po Box 12901
Shawnee Mission, KS 66282-2901

913-341-1300
866-505-7173
Fax: 913-514-6895
E-Mail: rgcs@pbsub.com
Home Page: www.penton.com

Eric Jacobson, Senior VP
Rich Santos, Group Publisher

Magazine for retail stockbrokers that presents highly focused career-oriented editorials. Accepts advertising.
Cost: $59.00
Frequency: Monthly
Circulation: 108067
Founded in 1976
Printed in 4 colors on glossy stock

8926 Report on Business
Institute for Supply Management
2055 E Centennial Circle
PO Box 22160
Tempe, AZ 85285-2160

480-752-6276
800-888-6276
Fax: 480-752-7890
E-Mail: infocenter@ism.ws
Home Page: www.ism.ws

Paul Novak, CFM, CEO
Holly LaCroix Johnson, Senior Vice President
Deborah Webber, SVP
Jean McHale, Manager
Frequency: Monthly

8927 Research
Financial Communications Company
PO Box 7588
San Francisco, CA 94120

415-621-0220
Fax: 415-621-0735
Home Page: www.researchmag.com

Robert Tyndall, Publisher
Bill Nieder, Managing Director
Joseph Geraci, Managing Director

Corporate profiles, investment information, and reports on building and keeping client base.
Cost: $35.00
Frequency: Monthly
Circulation: 65,227

8928 Responsible Owner
Institute for Responsible Housing Preservation
401 9th St NW
Suite 900
Washington, DC 20004-2145

202-585-8000
Fax: 202-457-5355
E-Mail: info@housingpreservation.org

Kathryn Holmes, VP
Frequency: Monthly

8929 Reverse Mortgage Advisor
National Reverse Mortgage Lenders Association
1625 Massachusetts Ave Nw
Suite 601
Washington, DC 20036-2212

202-939-1780
Fax: 202-265-4435
Home Page: www.afjs.org

Peter H Bell, Executive Director
Glenn Petherick, Director Communications
Frequency: Quarterly

8930 Secondary Marketing Executive
LDJ Corporation
PO Box 2180
Waterbury, CT 06722-2330

203-755-0158
800-325-6745
Fax: 203-755-3480
E-Mail: info@sme-online.com
Home Page: www.sme-online.com

Paul Zackin, Publisher
Mike Kling, Editor
June Han, Marketing

Delivers news, analysis and how-to advice to people involved in the buying and selling of mortgage loans and servicing rights nationwide.
Cost: $48.00
44 Pages
Frequency: Monthly
Circulation: 21000
Founded in 1986

8931 Secured Lender
Commercial Finance Association
Ste 1801
7 Penn Plz
New York, NY 10001-3979

212-594-3490
Fax: 212-564-6053
E-Mail: info@cfa.com
Home Page: www.cfa.com

Bruce H Jones, Executive Director
Theodore Kompa, President
Eileen M. Wubbe, Assistant Editor
Edward R. Fallon, Editorial Consultant
Linda C. Mohr, Production Manager

Provides in-depth reporting on federal and state legislation affecting the industry, legal notes on a wide range of issues, a full caladar year of industry workshops, meetings and seminars, personnel shifts, industry news and reviews of publications covering the industry. Discouted subscription rates for members.
Cost: $56.00
Frequency: 6 issues per ye
Circulation: 27000
Founded in 1944
Printed in 4 colors on glossy stock

8932 Small Business Update
Institute of Management Accountants

10 Paragon Dr
Suite 1
Montvale, NJ 07645-1774

201-573-9000
800-638-4427
Fax: 201-474-1600
E-Mail: ima@imanet.org
Home Page: www.imanet.org

Paul Sharman, President
Frequency: Monthly

8933 Stable Times
Stable Value Investment Association
2121 K St Nw
Suite 800
Washington, DC 20037-1801

202-261-6530
800-327-2270
Fax: 202-261-6527
E-Mail: info@StableValue.org
Home Page: www.stablevalue.org

Andrew Cohen, Editor
Frequency: Quarterly

8934 Strategic Finance
Institute of Management Accountants
10 Paragon Dr
Suite 1
Montvale, NJ 07645-1774

201-573-9000
800-638-4427
Fax: 201-474-1600
E-Mail: ima@imanet.org
Home Page: www.imanet.org

Paul Sharman, President
Frederick Schea, Chair-Emeritus
Sandra Richtermeyer, Chair-Elect
Jeffrey Thomson, President & CEO

IMA's award winning magazine that provides the latest information about practices and trends in finance, accounting, and information management that will impact members and their jobs.
Cost: $195.00
Frequency: Monthly
Printed in 4 colors on glossy stock

8935 Tax Executive
Tax Executives Institute
1200 G St NW
Suite 300
Washington, DC 20005-3833

202-638-5601
Fax: 202-638-5607
Home Page: www.tei.org

Timothy Mc Cormally, Executive Director
Deborah K Gaffney, Director Conference Planning
Deborah C Giesey, Director Administration
Karina Horesky, Coordinator Membership
Fred F Murray, General Counsel
Frequency: Bi-Monthly

8936 Tax Lawyer
American Bar Association Section of Taxation
321 N Clark St
Chicago, IL 60654-7598

312-988-5000
800-285-2221
Fax: 312-988-6281
E-Mail: askaba@abanet.org
Home Page: www.abanet.org

Louis A. Mezzullo, Editor-in-Chief
William H. Lyons, Managing Editor

Journal of scholarly articles written by highly respected tax attorneys and professors. It provides key reports by Section committees and task forces, and student notes and comments on timely topics.
Frequency: Quarterly

8937 Taxes: the Tax Magazine
CCH
2700 Lake Cook Rd
Riverwoods, IL 60015-3867

847-940-4600
800-835-5224
Fax: 773-866-3095
E-Mail: taxes@cch.com
Home Page: www.cch.com

Mike Sabbatis, President
Douglas M Winterrose, Vice President & CFO
Jim Bryant, EVP Software Products

Information on legal, accounting and economic aspects of federal and state taxes.
Cost: $245.00
Frequency: Monthly
Circulation: 10000
Founded in 1913

8938 ThriftInvestor
SNL Securities
One SNL Plaza
PO Box 2124
Charlottesvle, VA 22902

434-977-1600
Fax: 434-977-4466
E-Mail: isales@snl.com
Home Page: www.snl.com

Mark Saunders, Editor
Pat LaBua, Customer Service
Michael Spears, Advertising Director
Nick Cafferillo, Chief Operating Officer
Adam Hall, Managing Director

Timely articles by industry experts on topics such as conversions, investment opportunities and government regulations. Source for important financial news, investor filings, conversion data and current financial and market information on all publicly traded thrifts.
Cost: $495.00
80 Pages
Frequency: Monthly
Founded in 1987

8939 Ticker Magazine
Wall Street Teechnology Association
521 Newman Springs Road
Suite 12
Lincroft, NJ 07738

732-530-8808
Fax: 732-530-0020
E-Mail: info@wsta.org
Home Page: www.wsta.org

JoAnn Cooper, Managing Editor

Features articles that provide practical suggestions for technology professionals in the financial community, evaluate costs and benefits of alternate technologies, and disseminate news about the association
Frequency: Quarterly
Circulation: 14000

8940 Trader's World Magazine
Halliker's
2508 W Grayrock St
Springfield, MO 65810-2165

417-882-9697
Fax: 417-886-5180
E-Mail: publisher@tradersworld.com
Home Page: www.tradersworld.com

Lawrence Jacobs, Owner

Information on stock indexes, techniques of trading, exchange activities and current developments.
Cost: $19.95
64 Pages
Frequency: Quarterly
Circulation: 12000
ISSN: 1045-7690
Founded in 1989
Printed in 4 colors on glossy stock

8941 Traders Magazine
Securities Data Publishing
40 W 57th St
11th Floor
New York, NY 10019-4001

212-484-4701
Fax: 212-956-0112

Ken Heath, Publisher
Edward Cortese, Marketing Executive

Focuses on industry news, market and regulatory trends and the firms and individuals who shape the equities market.
Frequency: Monthly
Circulation: 6,000

8942 Trusts and Estates
PRIMEDIA Intertec-Marketing & Professional Service
Po Box 12901
Shawnee Mission, KS 66282-2901

913-341-1300
Fax: 913-514-6895
E-Mail: treddy@primediabusiness.com
Home Page: www.penton.com

Eric Jacobson, Senior VP
Rorie Sherman, Editor in Chief
Thrupthi Reddy, Editor
Rich Santos, Group Publisher

Features updates on trust department operations, estates and life insurance, wills, federal tax notes and current literature.
Cost: $199.00
Frequency: Monthly
Circulation: 14730
Founded in 1886

8943 Value Examiner
National Association of Certified Valuation
1111 Brickyard Road
Suite 200
Salt Lake City, UT 84106-5401

801-486-0600
800-677-2009
Fax: 801-486-7500
E-Mail: nacva1@nacva.com
Home Page: www.nacva.com

Parnell Black, CEO
Frequency: Bi-Monthly

8944 Venture Capital Journal
Securities Data Publishing
40 W 57th St
New York, NY 10019-4001

212-484-4701
Fax: 212-956-0112
E-Mail: sdp@tfn.com

Merry Logan, Associate Publisher
Edward Cortese, Marketing Executive

Provides information on recent issues, monitors current companies and looks at companies who have recently gone public.
Cost: $1025.00
Frequency: Monthly
Circulation: 1500

8945 Wall Street Computer Review
Miller Freeman Publications
1199 S Belt Line Rd
Suite 100
Coppell, TX 75019-4666

972-906-6500
Fax: 972-419-7825

Elizabeth Katz, Publisher
Pavan Sahgal, Editor

For financial and investment professionals and individual investors.
Cost: $5.00
Circulation: 34,000

8946 **Washington Alert**
Institute for Responsible Housing Preservation
401 9th St NW
Suite 900
Washington, DC 20004-2145
202-585-8000
Fax: 202-457-5355
E-Mail: info@housingpreservation.org
Home Page: www.nixonpeabody.com
Kathryn Holmes, VP
Brian Moynihan, Communications Manager
Frequency: Irregular

8947 **Washington Update**
National Association of Affordable Housing Lenders
1667 K St NW
Suite 905
Washington, DC 20006-1612
202-293-9850
Fax: 202-293-9852
E-Mail: naahl@naahl.org
Home Page: www.naahl.org
Judy Kennedy, President
Frequency: Monthly

Trade Shows

8948 **AACE Annual Meeting**
AACE International
209 Prairie Avenue
Suite 100
Morgantown, WV 26501-5934
304-296-8444
800-858-2678
Fax: 304-291-5728
E-Mail: info@aacei.org
Home Page: www.aacei.org
Andrew S Dowd Jr, Executive Director
Jennie Amos la, Marketing/Meetings Manager
Frequency: June

8949 **AAHAM Annual Meeting**
American Association of Healthcare Administrative
11240 Waples Mill Road
Suite 200
Fairfax, VA 22030
703-281-4043
Fax: 703-359-7562
E-Mail: moayad@aaham.org
Home Page: www.aaham.org
Robert Debiase, National President
Linda Sheaffer, Chair
Frequency: October

8950 **AARMR Annual Meeting**
American Association of Residential Mortgage
1255 23rd Street NW
Suite 200
Washington, DC 20037
202-521-3999
Fax: 202-883-3636
Home Page: www.aarmr.org
Christopher Murphy, Executive Director
Frequency: Fall

8951 **ABA Annual Convention, Business Expo & Director' Forum**
American Bankers Association
1120 Connecticut Avenue NW
Washington, DC 20036
202-635-5000
800-BAN-KERS
E-Mail: custserv@aba.com
Home Page: www.aba.com
Gail Kolakowski, VP Bus Development & Show Manager
Event for CEOs, presidents and other C-level executives from financial services firms across the nation, offering a products and services showcases, lanches and announcements, sessions focused on strategies and tactics for success, regulatory updates, effective leadership, and more.
Frequency: Annual

8952 **ACA Annual International Convention & Exposition**
American Credit Association International
PO Box 390106
Minneapolis, MN 55439
952-926-6547
Fax: 952-926-1624
E-Mail: aca@acainternational.org
Home Page: www.acainternational.com
Gary D Rippentorp CAE, CEO
Cathy Berg, Director Meetings
Annual international convention and exposition for credit and collection professionals.
Frequency: July

8953 **AEFA Annual Meeting**
American Education Finance Association
8365 S Armadillo Trail
Evergreen, CO 80439
303-674-0857
Fax: 303-670-8986
Home Page: www.aefa.cc
Ed Steinbecher, Executive Director
Frequency: March

8954 **AGA Annual Meeting**
Association of Government Accountants
2208 Mount Vernon Avenue
Alexandria, VA 22301
703-684-6931
800-242-7211
Fax: 703-548-9367
Home Page: www.agacgfm.org
Relmond P Van Daniker, Executive Director
Marie S Force, Director Communications
Susan Fritzlen, Deputy Exeucutive Director
Brian Watkins, Manager
Pamella Shaw, Accounting Manager
Frequency: July

8955 **AMIFS Annual Meeting**
Association for Management Information
3895 Fairfax Court
Atlanta, GA 30339
770-444-3557
Fax: 770-444-9084
E-Mail: webmaster@amifs.org
Home Page: www.amifs.org
Kevin Link, Executive Director
Frequency: May

8956 **AMIFS Annual Profitability & Performance Measurement Conference**
Assn for Management Information in Financial Svcs
14247 Saffron Circle
Carmel, IN 46032
317-815-5857
Fax: 317-815-5877
E-Mail: ami2@amifs.org
Home Page: www.amifs.org
Charles Stockton, Chairman Conference/EVP
Jane Blake, Conference Committee
Kevin W Link, Executive Director
3-day conference consisting of one day of workshops, and two days of educational sessions. 10 exhibitors.
Frequency: April

8957 **ASMC Annual Meeting**
American Society of Military Comptrollers
415 N Alfred Street
Alexandria, VA 22314-4650
703-549-0360
800-462-5637
Fax: 703-549-3181
Home Page: www.asmconline.org
James F McCall, Executive Director
Frequency: May

8958 **American Bankers Association Annual Convention & Banking Industry Forum**
American Bankers Association
1120 Connecticut Avenue NW
Washington, DC 20036-3902
202-635-5000
Fax: 202-663-5210
Home Page: http://www.aba.com
Edward Yingling, President/CEO
Annual convention and 200 exhibitors of systems and products for the banking industry.
5000 Attendees

8959 **American Bankers Association National Agricultural Bankers Conference**
1120 Connecticut Avenue NW
Washington, DC 20036-3902
800-226-5377
E-Mail: custserv@aba.com
Home Page: www.aba.com
Edward Yingling, President/CEO
Diane M Casey-Landry, COO/Senior Executive VP
1M Attendees
Frequency: Novembe

8960 **American Bankers Association: Bank Operations & Technology Conference**
American Bankers Association
1120 Connecticut Avenue NW
Washington, DC 20036-3902
202-635-5000
Fax: 202-663-5210
Edward Yingling, President/CEO
Diane M Casey-Landry, COO/Senior Executive VP
Designed to address hot topics for bank operations professinals, covers critical issues and provides insights into the practical applications of bank technology
2600 Attendees
Frequency: April

8961 **American Bankers Association: National Bank Card Conference**
American Bankers Association
1120 Connecticut Avenue NW
Washington, DC 20036-3902
202-635-5000
Fax: 202-663-5210
Home Page: http://www.aba.com
Edward Yingling

8962 **Appraisers Association of America National Conference**
Appraisers Association of America

386 Park Avenue S
Suite 2000
New York, NY 10016-8804

212-889-5404
Fax: 212-889-5503
E-Mail: twniem@appraisersassoc.org
Home Page: www.appraisersassoc.org

Beth Weingast, President

Exhibits of interest to appraisers, workshops, and presentations.

8963 **Association for Financial Professionals Annual Conference**
Association for Financial Professionals
4520 East West Highway
Suite 750
Bethesda, MD 20814

301-907-2862
Fax: 301-907-2864
E-Mail: AFP@AFPonline.org
Home Page: www.AFPonline.org

Loren Starr, Chairman
James Gilligan, Vice Chairman
Karen E Ball, Marketing Director

Workshop and 642 exhibits of lockboxes, check processing systems, computers, investments, pensions, foreign exchange, consulting, mergers, aquistions and more information of interest to finacial professionals.
6000 Attendees
Frequency: November
Founded in 1979

8964 **BCCA Annual Meeting**
Broadcast Cable Credit Association
550 Frontage Road
Suite 3600
Northfield, IL 60093

847-881-8757
Fax: 847-784-8059
E-Mail: info@bccacredit.com
Home Page: www.bccacredit.com

Mary Collins, President/CEO
Jamie Smith, Director of Operations
Rachelle Brooks, BCCA Sales
Frequency: May

8965 **CCFL Semi-Annual Meetings**
Conference on Consumer Finance Law
Oklahoma City University School of Law
2501 N Blackwelder
Oklahoma City, OK 73106

405-521-5363
Fax: 405-521-5089
E-Mail: ccflqr@lec.okcu.edu
Home Page: www.theccfl.com

Alvin C Harrell, Executive Director

Held with American Bar Association.
Frequency: Spring, Summer

8966 **CDFA Annual Meeting**
Council of Development Finance Agencies
301 NW 63rd Avenue
Suite 500
Oklahoma City, OK 73116

405-848-6059
Fax: 405-842-3299
E-Mail: info@cdfa.net
Home Page: www.cdfa.net

Stan Provus, Training Director
Don Conkle, Manager
Frequency: Fall

8967 **CDVCA Annual Conference**
Community Development Venture Capital Alliance
330 Seventh Avenue
19th Floor
New York, NY 10001

212-594-6747
Fax: 212-594-6717
E-Mail: info@cdvca.org
Home Page: www.cdvca.org

Kerwin Tesdell, President
Gary Brooks, Managing Director

Attended by management of social venture capital funds; those thinking of starting funds; investors in social venture capital funds; economic development professionals; banking and investment professionals; foundation representatives and policy makers and government professionals.
Frequency: March

8968 **CFA Institute Annual Conference**
CFA Institute
560 Ray C Hunt Drive
Charlottesville, VA

434-951-5499
800-247-8132
Fax: 434-951-5262
E-Mail: info@cfainstitute.org
Home Page: www.cfainstitute.org

Jeffrey Diermeier, President/CEO

Provides an unparalleled look at the trends and investment issues critical to success in today's global marketplace
Frequency: April

8969 **CIFA Semi-Annual Meetings**
Council of Infrastructure Financing Authorities
805 15th Street NW
Suite 500
Washington, DC 20005

202-371-9694
Fax: 202-371-6601
Home Page: www.cifanet.org

Richard T Farrell, Executive Director
Richard T Farrell, Executive Director
Letitia Chambers, Owner

Legislative Conference, Spring & Workshop, Fall

8970 **CMSA Annual Meeting**
Commercial Mortgage Securities Association
30 Broad Street
28th Floor
New York, NY 10004

212-509-1844
Fax: 212-509-1895
E-Mail: info1@cmbs.org
Home Page: www.cmbs.org

Dottie Cunningham, CEO
Frequency: Winter

8971 **CORFAC Semi-Annual Meetings**
Corporate Facility Advisors
2000 N 15th Street
Suite 101
Arlington, VA 22201

703-528-3500
Fax: 703-528-0113
E-Mail: info@corfac.com
Home Page: www.corfac.com

Thomas P Bennett, Executive Director
Bill Hawkins, Treasurer
Robert Tillsley, Secretary
Frequency: February, September

8972 **CRF Annual Meeting**
Credit Research Foundation
8840 Columbia Parkway
Suite 100
Columbia, MD 21045-2117

410-740-5499
Fax: 410-740-4620
E-Mail: crf_info@crfonline.org
Home Page: www.crfonline.org

Alex Behm, Chairman
Michael Durant, Vice-Chairman
Frequency: May

8973 **California Accounting & Business Show**
Flagg Management
353 Lexington Avenue
New York, NY 10016

212-286-0333
Fax: 212-286-0086
E-Mail: flaggmgmnt@msn.com
Home Page: www.flaggmgmt.com

Russell Flagg, President

150 exhibitors of investment management systems, databases, real-time and on-line systems. Global and US markets, Windows, PC and client/server systems. New income opportunities for CPAs in California with the change to commissionable financial services. The show is free; the conference is $40 per day and offers CPE sessions. Sponsored by the California CPA Education Foundation.
Frequency: Annual

8974 **Credit Union Executives Expo**
Credit Union Executives Society
Po Box 14167
Madison, WI 53708-0167

608-712-2664
800-252-2664
Fax: 608-271-2303
E-Mail: fred@cues.org
Home Page: www.cues.org

Fred Johnson, President/CEO

Expo is held in conjunction with CUES Marketing, Operations and Technology Conference, where the top marketers and operations professionals in the industry gather.
500 Attendees
Frequency: May
Founded in 1962

8975 **DCUC Annual Meeting**
Defense Credit Union Council
601 Pennsylvania Avenue NW
South Building, Suite 600
Washington, DC 20004-2601

202-638-3950
Fax: 202-638-3410
Home Page: www.dcuc.org

Frequency: August

8976 **EMTA Annual Meeting**
EMTA - Trade Association for the Emerging Markets
360 Madison Avenue
18th Floor
New York, NY 10017

646-637-9100
Fax: 646-637-9128
E-Mail: awerner@emta.org
Home Page: www.emta.org

Michael M Chamberlin, President
Aviva Werner, Managing Director
Jonathan Murno, Managing Director
Suzette Ortiz, Office Manager
Monika Forbes, Administrative Assistant
Frequency: December

8977 **FMS Annual Meeting**
Financial Managers Society

100 W Monroe Street
Suite 810
Chicago, IL 60603-1959

312-781-1300
800-275-4367
Fax: 312-578-1308
E-Mail: diane@fmsinc.org
Home Page: www.fmsinc.org

Richard A Yingst, President/CEO
Jennifer Doak, Director Marketing
Diane Walter, VP/Director Professional Dev
Frequency: June

8978 FPA Annual Meeting
Financial Planning Association
4100 E Mississippi Avenue
Suite 400
Denver, CO 80246

303-759-4900
800-322-4237
Fax: 303-759-0749
E-Mail: info@fpanet.org
Home Page: www.fpanet.org

Martin W Tuttle CAE, Executive Director/CEO
Ian McKenzie, Managing Director Publishing
Frequency: Fall

8979 FPA Experience: The Annual Conference of the Financial Planning Community
Financial Planning Association
7535 East Hampden Avenue
Suite 600
Denver, CO 80231

303-759-4900
800-322-4237
Fax: 303-759-0749
Home Page: www.fpaannualconference.org
Social Media: Facebook, Twitter, LinkedIn, FPA Connect

The event provides networking and professional development opportunities, as well as exhibits.
24000 Members
3000 Attendees
Frequency: Annual/Fall
Founded in 2000

8980 FSR Semi-Annual Meetings
Financial Services Roundtable
1001 Pennsylvania Avenue NW
Suite 500 S
Washington, DC 20004

202-289-4322
Fax: 202-628-2507
E-Mail: info@fsround.org
Home Page: www.fsround.org

Steve Bartlett, President/CEO
Frequency: Spring, Fall

8981 FSTC Annual Meeting
Financial Services Technology
44 Wall Street
12th Floor
New York, NY 10005

212-711-1400
Fax: 646-349-3629
E-Mail: fstcadmin@fstc.org
Home Page: www.fstc.org

Zachary Tumin, Executive Director
Frequency: Spring

8982 Fiduciary and Risk Management Association Annual Meeting
Fiduciary and Risk Management Association
PO Box 48297
Athens, GA 30604

706-354-0083
Fax: 706-353-3994
E-Mail: info@thefirma.org
Home Page: www.thefirma.org

Hale Mast, Executive Director
Deborah A Austin, VP

To educate, support and promote risk management professionals and improve the effectiveness of risk management for the fiduciary and investment service industry.
Frequency: Spring

8983 FinEXPO
Miller Freeman Publications
1975 W El Camino Real
Suite 307
Mountain View, CA 94040-2218

FAX 650-966-8934

Sixty exhibitors of full range of systems, software, service and solutions that financial and information system decision makers need to meet the challenges of today and the future.
2000 Attendees

8984 Financial Management Association International Annual Meeting
University of South Florida
College of Business Administration/BSN 3331
4202 E Fowler Avenue
Tampa, FL 33620-5500

813-974-2084
Fax: 813-974-3318
E-Mail: fma@coba.usf.edu OR info@fma.org
Home Page: www.fma.org/

Jonathan Karpoff, President Director
Jacqueline Garner, Vice President Financial Education
Rawley Thomas, VP Practitioner Services
Kenneth Eades, Vice President Global Services
Anthony Saunders, Vice President Annual Meeting

Annual meeting and exhibits of financial management related equipment, supplies and services.
Frequency: October

8985 Financial Women International Annual Conference
Financial Women International
1027 W Roselawn Avenue
Roseville, MN 55113

651-487-7632
866-807-6081
Fax: 651-489-1322
E-Mail: info@fwi.org
Home Page: www.fwi.org

Melissa Curzon, President
Cindy Hass, VP
Carleen DeSisto, Secretary
Frequency: September

8986 HBMA Annual Meeting
Healthcare Billing and Management Association
1540 South Coast Highway
Suite 203
Laguna Beach, CA 92651

877-640-4262
Home Page: http://www.hbma.org

Bradley Lund, Executive Director
Paul Myers, Director of Education
Frequency: March

8987 HMFA's ANI: The Healthcare Finance Conference
Healthcare Finance Management Association
100 W Monroe Street
Suite 1001
Chicago, IL 60603

312-541-0567
Fax: 312-541-0573
Home Page: www.hfma.org/events/ani

Access to education programs, speaker sessions and hundreds of vendors, as well as networking and best practices sharing opportunities.

8988 HMFA's Virtual Healthcare Finance Conference & Career Fair
Healthcare Finance Management Association
100 W Monroe Street
Suite 1001
Chicago, IL 60603

312-541-0567
Fax: 312-541-0573
E-Mail: virtualhcfc@hfma.org
Home Page: www.hfma.org

Access live education programs and on-demand sessions from your office. Keynote speakers and presenters, and a virtual exhibit hall and career fair.

8989 IMA Annual Meeting
Institute of Management Accountants
10 Paragon Drive
Suite 1
Montvale, NJ 07645-1718

201-573-9000
800-638-4427
Fax: 201-474-1600
E-Mail: ima@imanet.org
Home Page: www.imanet.org

John Brausch, Chair
Frederick Schea, Chair-Emeritus
Sandra Richtermeyer, Chair-Elect
Jeffrey Thomson, President & CEO
1500 Attendees
Frequency: July

8990 IRHP Meeting/Conference
Institute for Responsible Housing Preservation
401 Ninth Street NW
Suite 900
Washington, DC 20004

202-858-8000
Fax: 202-585-8080
E-Mail: info@housingpreservation.org
Home Page: www.housingpreservation.org

Linda D Kirk, Executive Director
Frequency: January

8991 ISM Annual Meeting
Institute for Supply Management
2055 E Centennial Circle
PO Box 22160
Tempe, AZ 85285-2160

480-752-6276
800-888-6276
Fax: 480-752-7890
E-Mail: infocenter@ism.ws
Home Page: www.ism.ws

Paul Novak, CPM, CEO
Holly LaCroix Johnson, Senior Vice President
Deborah Webber, SVP
Jean McHale, Manager
3000 Attendees
Frequency: May

8992 NAAHL Annual Meetings
National Association of Affordable Housing Lenders

1300 Connecticut Avenue NW
Suite 905
Washington, DC 20036

202-293-9850
Fax: 202-293-9852
E-Mail: naahl@naahl.org

Judith A Kennedy, President/CEO
Frequency: Winter, Spring

8993 **NABT Semi-Annual Meetings**
National Association of Bankruptcy Trustees
One Windsor Cove
Suite 305
Columbia, SC 29233

803-252-5646
800-445-8629
Fax: 803-765-0860
E-Mail: info@nabt.com
Home Page: www.nabt.com

Carol H Webster, Executive Director
Frequency: August

8994 **NACM's Credit Congress and Exposition**
National Association of Credit Management
8840 Columbia 100 Parkway
Columbia, MD 21045-2282

410-740-5560
Fax: 410-740-5574
E-Mail: robins@nacm.org
Home Page: www.nacm.org

Jim Vanghel, Vice President
Robin Schauseil, President

Annual exhibits of relevance to credit and financial executives.
2500 Attendees
Frequency: June

8995 **NACVA Annual Consultants' Conference**
Nat'l Association of Certified Valuation Analysts
1111 Brickyard Road
Suite 200
Salt Lake City, UT 84106-5401

801-486-0600
800-677-2009
Fax: 801-486-7500
E-Mail: nacva1@nacva.com
Home Page: www.nacva.com

Parnell Black, CEO
750 Attendees
Frequency: June

8996 **NADOA Annual Meeting**
National Association of Division Order Analyst
2805 Oak Trail Court
Suite 6312
Arlington, TX 76016

972-715-4489
E-Mail: administrator@nadoa.org
Home Page: www.nadoa.org

Lynn S McCord, Administrator
Frequency: September

8997 **NAELB Annual Meeting**
National Association of Equipment Leasing Brokers
304 W Liberty Street
Suite 201
Louisville, KY 40202

800-996-2352
Home Page: www.naelb.org

Carol Davis, Administrator
Frequency: May

8998 **NAFC Annual Meeting**
National Accounting and Finance Council
2200 Mill Road
Alexandria, VA 22314

703-838-1915
E-Mail: nafc@trucking.org
Home Page: www.truckline.com

David Hershey, Executive Director
500 Attendees
Frequency: June

8999 **NAFCU Annual Conference and Exhibition**
National Association of Federal Credit Unions
3138 10th Street N
Suite 300
Arlington, VA 22201-2149

703-224-4770
800-336-4644
Fax: 703-524-1082
Home Page: http://www.nafcu.org

Jerome Bruce, Exhibits/Advertising Manager
Fred Becker, President

Annual show of 150 manufacturers and suppliers of complete range of financial products and services. 175 booths.

9000 **NALHFA Semi-Annual Meetings**
National Association of Local Housing Finance
2025 M Street NW
Suite 800
Washington, DC 20036-3309

202-367-1197
Fax: 202-367-2197
E-Mail: john_murphy@nalhfa.org
Home Page: www.nalhfa.org

John C Murphy, Executive Director
Scott Lynch, Association Manager
Kim McKinon, Coordinator Membership
Frequency: Spring, Fall

9001 **NAMB Annual Meeting**
National Association of Mortgage Brokers
8201 Greensboro Drive
Suite 300
McLean, VA 22102

703-610-9009
Fax: 703-610-9005
E-Mail: rdeloach@namb.org
Home Page: www.namb.org

Michael J Nizankiewicz, PhD CAE, Executive VP/CEO
Roy DeLoach, Executive Vice President
Rebecca Dopkin, VP Meetings
Frequency: June

9002 **NAPFA Annual Meeting**
National Association of Personal Financial Advisor
3250 N Arlington Heights Road
Suite 109
Arlington Heights, IL 60004

847-483-5400
800-366-2732
Fax: 847-483-5415
E-Mail: info@napfa.org
Home Page: www.napfa.org

Ellen Turf, CEO
Margery Wasserman, Director Conferences
800 Attendees
Frequency: May

9003 **NAPTP Meeting/Conference**
Nat'l Assoc of Publicly Traded Partnerships
805 15th Street NW
Suite 500
Washington, DC 20005

202-973-4515
Fax: 202-973-3101
Home Page: www.ptpcoalition.org

Mary Lyman, Executive Director
Frequency: February

9004 **NASBO Annual Meeting**
National Association of State Budget Officers
444 North Capitol Street NW
Suite 642
Washington, DC 20001

202-624-5382
Fax: 202-624-7745
E-Mail: spattison@nasbo.org
Home Page: www.nasbo.org

Scott Pattison, Executive Director
Lauren Cummings, Manager Member Relations
Frequency: Summer

9005 **NATP National Conference & Expo**
National Association of Tax Professionals
PO Box 8002
Appleton, WI 54912

920-749-1040
800 558-3402
Fax: 800-747-0001
E Mail: natp@natptax.com
Home Page: www.natptax.com

Annual conference and exhibits of computer hardware, tax accounting and planning software, tax research information, tax forms, one-write accounting, financial planning information, office products and business equipment.
Frequency: Annual

9006 **NATRI National Conference**
National Association for Treasurers of Religious
8824 Cameron Street
Silver Springs, MD 20910

301-587-7776
Fax: 301-589-2897
E-Mail: natri@natri.org
Home Page: www.natri.org

Barbara Matteson, Executive Director
Helen Burke, Associate Director
Frequency: November

9007 **NCPG Annual Meeting**
National Committee on Planned Giving
233 McCre Street
Suite 400
Indianapolis, IN 46225-1030

317-269-6274
Fax: 317-269-6276
Home Page: www.ncpg.org

Tanya Howe Johnson, President/CEO
Sandra Kerr, Director Government Education
Barbara Owens, Director Membership/Manager HR
Kathryn J Ramsey, Director Meetings
Kurt Reusze, Manager Education/Technology
1700 Attendees

9008 **NDCC Semi-Annual Meetings**
National Defined Contribution Council
9101 E Kenyon
Suite 300
Denver, CO 80237-0467

303-770-5353
Fax: 303-770-1812
Home Page: www.ndcconline.org

Al Brust, Executive VP
Frequency: Spring, Fall

9009 NICSA Annual Meeting
National Investment Company Service Association
36 Washingtn Street
Suite 70
Wessesley Hills, MA 02481

781-416-7200
Fax: 781-416-7065
E-Mail: info@nisca.org
Home Page: www.nisca.org

Barbara V Weidlich, President
Keith Dropkin, Director Operations
Doris Jaimes, Registrar
Sheila Kobaly, Events Manager
Chris Ludent, IT Manager
Frequency: February

9010 NIPA Semi-Annual Meetings
National Institute of Pension Administrators
401 N Michigan Avenue
Suite 2200
Chicago, IL 60611-4267

800-999-6472
E-Mail: nipa@nipa.org
Home Page: www.nipa.org

Laura J Rudzinski, Executive Director
Frequency: Winter, Spring

9011 NPA Annual Meeting
National Pawnbrokers Association
PO Box 1040
Roanoke, TX 76262

817-491-4554
Fax: 817-491-8770
E-Mail: info@NationalPawnbrokers.org
Home Page: www.nationalpawnbrokers.org

Bob Benedict, CAE, Executive Director
Emmett Murphy, Director
Teresa Congleton, Administrative Assistant
1000 Attendees
Frequency: Summer

9012 National Association of Review Appraisers & Mortgage Underwriters Convention
National Assn of Review Appraisers/Mortgage Under.
1224 N Nokomis NE
Alexandria, MN 56308

320-763-7626
Fax: 320-763-9290
E-Mail: nara@iami.org
Home Page: www.iami.org

Robert G Johnson, Executive Director

Annual convention of real estate related information and services. Containing 50-75 booths, as well as environmental, home inspection, and construction inspection.
450 Attendees
Frequency: October
Founded in 1962
Mailing list available for rent: 2500 names at $75 per M

9013 Payments
NACHA: Electronic Payments Association
13450 Sunrise Valley Drive
Suite 100
Herndon, VA 20171

703-561-1100
Fax: 703-787-0996
E-Mail: info@nacha.org
Home Page: www.nacha.org

Marcie Haitema, Chairperson
Janet O Estep, CEO

The premier source for payments professionals from across industries and around the globe to get the most vital and actionable information needed to help address the myraid of issues and opportunities in today's rapidly changing environment.
1000 Attendees
Frequency: Annual/April-May

9014 Private Equity Analyst Conference
Asset Alternatives
170 Linden Street
2nd Floor
Wellesley, MA 02482-7919

781-304-1400
Fax: 781-304-1440
Home Page: www.assetnews.com

Lisa Hughs, Production Manager

The industry's premiere gathering of more than 1000 institutional investors, venture capitalists, buyout specialists, deal originators, and senior and mezzanine lenders. Three specialized tracks focus on institutional, venture capital, and LBO investing.

9015 Private Equity Analyst Global Investing Conference
Asset Alternatives
170 Linden Street
2nd Floor
Wellesley, MA 02482-7919

781-235-4565
Fax: 781-304-1440
Home Page: www.assetalt.com

Lisa Hughs, Production Manager

Hundreds of institutional investors, private equity managers, and deal sources to debate the merits of funds of funds and regional funds for investing in Western and Eastern Europe, Latin America, Asia, the Middle East, and elsewhere.

9016 Risk Management Association's Annual Conference
Risk Management Association
1801 Market St
Suite 300
Philadelphia, PA 19103-1628

215-446-4000
800-677-7621
Fax: 215-446-4100
E-Mail: customers@rmahq.org
Home Page: www.rmahq.org

Kevin Blakely, President/CEO
Sonny Lyles, Vice Chair

Educates and helps risk management professionals develop new techniques and learn about new innovative products at different stages of their careers.
800 Attendees
Frequency: September/October

9017 SFE Annual Meeting
Society of Financial Examiners
174 Grace Boulevard
Altamonte Springs, FL 32714

407-682-4930
800-787-7633
Fax: 407-682-3175
Home Page: www.sofe.org

Paula Keyes, Executive Director
Stephen J Szypula, Financial Administrator
500 Attendees

9018 SIM Annual Meeting
Society for Information Management
401 N Michigan Avenue
Chicago, IL

312-215-5190
Fax: 312-245-1081
Home Page: www.simnet.org

Jim Luisi, Executive Director
Frequency: Fall

9019 SQA Annual Meeting
Society of Quantitative Analysts
25 North Broadway
Tarry Town, NY 10591

914-332-0040
Fax: 914-332-1541
E-Mail: cmcas@cmcas.org
Home Page: www.cmcas.org

Stuart Ganes, President
Frequency: May

9020 STA's Annual Conference & Business Meeting
Security Traders Association
777 Post Road
Suite 200
Darien, CT 06820

203-202-7680
Fax: 203-202-7681
E-Mail: traders@securitytraders.org
Home Page: www.securitytraders.org

John C Giesea, President & CEO

Keynote speakers, discussions on trading issues, regulatory updates, exchange topics, and exhibits.
1700 Attendees
Frequency: Annual

9021 Securities Industry and Financial Markets Association (SIFMA) Annual Meeting
1101 New York Avenue NW
8th Floor
Washington, DC 20005

202-962-7300
Fax: 202-962-7305
Home Page: www.sifma.org

T Timothy Ryan Jr, President/CEO
Randy Snook, Senior Managing Director/EVP
Donald D Kittell, CFO

The Securities Industry and Financial Markets Association/SIFMA Annual Meeting and Conference program addresses a variety of topics that may include competitiveness of the U.S. capital markets, global exchange consolidation, regulatory and legal initiatives, and trends in the fixed-income and capital markets.

9022 Southern Finance Association
University of Florida
Mowry Road, Building 116
PO Box 110811
Gainesville, FL 32611-0811

352-392-5930
Fax: 352-392-7902
Home Page: www.aceweb.org

Dr. Robert Radcliffe, Show Manager

Twenty five ooths.
1.4M Attendees
Frequency: November

9023 Success Forum
International Association for Financial Planning
2 Concourse Parkway NE
Suite 800
Atlanta, GA 30328-5588

770-351-9600
800-945-IAFP
Fax: 770-668-7758

J Patrick Tinley, CEO

Annual show and exhibits of financial services equipment, supplies and services.
2500 Attendees

9024 TEI Annual Meeting
Tax Executives Institute

1200 G Street NW
Suite 300
Washington, DC 20005-3814

202-638-5601
Fax: 202-638-5607
E-Mail: dgaffney@tei.org
Home Page: www.tei.org

Timothy J McNormally, Executive Director
Deborah K Gaffney, Director Conference Planning
Deborah C Giesey, Director Administration
Karina Horesky, Coordinator Membership
Fred F Murray, General Counsel/Dir Tax Affairs
Frequency: April

9025 **Venture Capital & Health Care Conference**
Asset Alternatives
170 Linden Street
2nd Floor
Wellesley, MA 02482-7919

781-235-4565
Fax: 781-304-1440
Home Page: www.assetalt.com

Lisa Hughs, Production Manager

This annual gathering of top investors, deal sources, entrepreneurs, Wall Street analysts, and senior health care executives explores the latest trends in health care services, devices, and medical information systems.
Circulation: 0

Directories & Databases

9026 **AACE Directory**
Assoc. for the Advancement of Cost Engineering
209 Prairie Ave
Suite 100
Morgantown, WV 26501-5934

304-296-8444
800-858-2678
Fax: 304-291-5728
E-Mail: info@aacei.org
Home Page: www.aacei.org

Andrew Dowd, Executive Director
Megan McCulla, Asst Manager
Charla Miller, Staff Director Education
Carol S Rogers, Manager Finance
Frequency: Annual

9027 **AEFA Membership Directory**
American Education Finance Association
8365 S Armadillo Trail
Evergreen, CO 80439

303-674-0857
Fax: 303-670-8986
Home Page: www.afea.cc

Ed Steinbecher, Executive Director
Frequency: Annual

9028 **ALERT**
AuTex Systems
11 Farnsworth Street
Boston, MA 02210-1210

617-345-2000

A database offering all available information on securities and securities trading information.

9029 **ATLAS**
Technical Data
11 Farnsworth Street
Boston, MA 02210-1210

617-345-2000

Contains a variety of financial data and analyses of 7 major government bond markets.

9030 **All-Quotes**
545 Madison Avenue
Suite 1400
New York, NY 10022-4219

FAX 212-425-6895

Offers real-time and delayed quotes, and price and volume history for about 100,000 stocks, options and commodities.

9031 **Almanac of Business and Industrial Financial Ratios**
Pearson Education
1 Lake St
Upper Saddle Rv, NJ 07458-1813

201-236-7000
800-947-7700
Fax: 201-236-7696
Home Page: www.prenhall.com

Will Ethridge, President

Profiles corporate performance in two analytical tables for a variety of industries.
Cost: $69.95
Frequency: Annual

9032 **American Banker On-Line**
American Banker-Bond Buyer
1 State St
27th Floor
New York, NY 10004-1561

212-803-8450
207-581-3042
Fax: 207-581-3015
Home Page: www.sourcemedia.com

Jim Malkin, CEO
Mario DiUbaldi, Publisher
Phil Roosevelt, Editor
Carole Lambert, Sales/Marketing Director
Stacy Weinstein, Production Director

World wide web edition of daily financial services newspaper. Journal available.

9033 **American Financial Directory**
4709 Golf Road
Skokie, IL 60076

847-676-9600
800-321-3373
Fax: 847-933-8101
E-Mail: custserv@accuitysolutions.com
Home Page: www.accuitysolutions.com

Marideth Johnson, Manager, Marketing/Communications
Malcolm Taylor, Managing Director
Cost: $523.00
Frequency: January/July
Circulation: 41300
ISBN: 1-563103-47-8

9034 **American Society of Appraisers Directory**
American Society of Appraisers
11107 Sunset Hills Rd
Suite 310
Reston, VA 20190

703-478-2228
800-272-8258
Fax: 703-742-8471
E-Mail: asainfo@appraisers.org
Home Page: www.appraisers.org
Social Media: Facebook, Twitter, LinkedIn, YouTube

Jane Grimm, Executive VP
Susan Fischer, Governance Manager
Jack Washbourn, President

Directory of association members who are accredited appraisers.
Cost: $12.50
5000 Members
Circulation: 8,000
Founded in 1936
Mailing list available for rent: 5,000 names at $200 per M

9035 **American Stock Exchange Fact Book**
Publications Department
86 Trinity Pl
New York, NY 10006-1817

212-308-0046
Fax: 212-306-2160

Neal Wolkoff, CEO

Lists addresses, telephone and fax numbers and ticker symbols of every listed company. Historical statistics and all-time trading records for equities, with a list of every stock option, index option and derivative security traded on the American Stock Exchange.
Cost: $20.00
Frequency: Annual
Circulation: 10,000
Founded in 1994

9036 **American Stock Exchange Guide**
CCH
2700 Lake Cook Rd
Riverwoods, IL 60015-3867

847-940-4600
800-835-5224
Fax: 773-866-3095
Home Page: www.cch.com

Mike Sabbatis, President
Douglas M Winterrose, Vice President & CFO
Jim Bryant, EVP Software Products

Volume 1 lists a directory of officials, members, organizations and securities; Volume 2 lists by-laws and rules of the exchange.
Cost: $570.00

9037 **Asia Pacific Securities Handbook**
Reference Press
6448 E Highway 290
Suite E104
Austin, TX 78723-1041

512-331-1815
Fax: 512-374-4501

Dan Capper, President

Offers stock information on the exchanges in Australia, Bangladesh, China, Hong Kong, India, Indonesia, Japan, Malaysia, Nepal, New Zealand, Pakistan, Taiwan, Sri Lanka, and Thailand.
Cost: $99.95
250 Pages
Founded in 1993

9038 **Bank Mergers & Acquisitions Yearbook**
SNL Securities
PO Box 2124
Charlottesvle, VA 22902-2124

434-977-1600
Fax: 434-977-4466
Home Page: www.snlnet.com

John Minor, Editor
Nick Cafferillo, Chief Operating Officer
Christie Atkinson, Editor
Reid Nagle, Publisher
Mark Outlaw, Advertising Director

For bank and thrift CEOs, CFOs, investment banks, merger and acquisition advisors, law firms, accounting firms and individual investors. Covers all bank and thrift merger activity from the previous year, state-by-state reviews of all private sector whole-bank and whole-thrift transactions, branch sales, merger

conversions and government-assisted transactions announced in that year.
150 Pages
Frequency: Annual
Founded in 1994

9039 **Bank Securities Monthly**
SNL Securities
212 7th Street NE
Charlottesville, VA 22902
434-977-1600
Fax: 434-977-4466
E-Mail: subscriptions@snlnet.com
Home Page: www.snlnet.com
Mike Chinn, President
Steve Tomasi, Editor
Reid Nagle, Publisher
Mark Outlaw, Senior Vice President
Provides current financial, market and merger information on publicly traded banks. News highlights of the past month and comprehensive industry articles addressing topics such as bank investment opportunities, capital structure and earnings prospects.
70 Pages
Frequency: Monthly

9040 **Bloomberg Business News**
499 Park Ave
New York, NY 10022-1240
212-893-5555
Fax: 212-369-5966
Home Page: www.bloomberg.com
Kim Bang, Manager
Matthew Winkler, Editor
A 24-hour global news service available exclusively on The Bloomberg. All stories are fully integrated into The Bloomberg's newsminder which instantly alerts you to developments in all stock and bond markets.

9041 **Bloomberg Financial Markets Commodities News**
PO Box 888
Princeton, NJ 08542-0888
609-279-3000
Fax: 609-279-2028
Michael Bloomberg, Publisher
Matthew Winkler, Editor
Beth Mazzeo, Global Products
A leading multimedia distributor of news, information, data and analysis, providing information on everything from capital markets and airline schedules to employment opportunities and luxury goods.
Cost: $795.00
Frequency: Monthly

9042 **Bond Buyer's Municipal Marketplace**
Thomson Financial Publishing
4709 Golf Road
6th Floor
Skokie, IL 60076-1231
847-778-8037
James L Nowell, Editor
Offers information on firms and personnel in the municipal bond industry, including municipal bond dealers, chief finance officers of municipalities which issue bonds, and attorneys specializing in the field of municipal finance.
Cost: $185.00
937 Pages
Frequency: Semiannual

9043 **Bonds Data Base**
ADP Data Services
42 Broadway
Suite 1730
New York, NY 10004-1617
212-406-2820
This database, update daily, contains historical prices and trading volumes for more than 33,000 corporate, government and agency bonds.

9044 **Bowser Directory of Small Stocks**
Bowser Report
PO Box 6278
Newport News, VA 23606-0278
757-877-5979
Fax: 757-595-0622
E-Mail: Ministocks@aol.com
Home Page: www.thebowsersreport.com
Cindy Bowser, Editor
Lists 14 fields of information on over 700 low-priced stocks.
Cost: $89.00
35 Pages
Frequency: Monthly
ISSN: 1053-0908

9045 **Bridge Information System**
717 Office Parkway
Saint Louis, MO 63141-7115
314-567-8100
800-325-3282
Fax: 314-432-5391
Tony Bridge, Manager
This large database contains real-time, last sale and quote data on all listed and unlisted stocks, options, futures and foreign securities.

9046 **Bull and Bear's Directory of Investment Advisory Newsletters**
Bull & Bear Financial Report
PO Box 917179
Longwood, FL 32791-7179
407-682-6170
Home Page: www.thebullandbear.com
David J Robinson, President
Advice from investment advisory newsletters on various investment areas, small-cap stocks, global and domestic stock markets, mutual funds, precious metals and economy.
Cost: $29.00
48 Pages
Frequency: Annual
Circulation: 55,000
Founded in 1974

9047 **Business and Financial News Media**
Larriston Communications
PO Box 20229
New York, NY 10025-1518
310-871-0563
Sheila Gordon, Editor
Lists over 300 daily newspapers with at least 50,000 in circulation and a business or finance correspondent; television stations and all-news radio stations in the largest 40 markets.
Cost: $89.00
175 Pages
Frequency: Annual

9048 **CDA/Wiesenberger Investment Companies Service**
CDA Investment
1355 Piccard Drive
Suite 200
Rockville, MD 20850-4300
Jay Nadler, Editor
Lists 5,000 open and closed mutual funds, unit trusts and investment companies listing policies and objectives, history, and statistical information of the company.
1500 Pages
Frequency: Annual

9049 **CIN: Corporation Index System**
Office of Applications & Reports Services
450 5th Street NW
Washington, DC 20001-2739
202-942-0020
David Weiss, Manager
Lists 1,580 active companies registered under the Investment Company Act of 1940. Information is extend to include related underwriters and advisers and 800 number.
Cost: $90.00
Frequency: Monthly

9050 **CISCO**
CISCO
170 W Tasman Dr
San Jose, CA 95134-1706
408-526-4000
805-553-6387
Fax: 408-853-3683
E-Mail: dljones@cisco-futures.com
Home Page: www.cisco-futures.com
Frank A Calderoni, Executive VP
Contains technical analyses and prices of commodities futures, and currencies.

9051 **CUSIP Master Directory**
Standard & Poor's Corporation
55 Water St
New York, NY 10041-0003
212-438-1000
Fax: 212-438-0299
Deven Sharma, President
Official listings of numbers and descriptions for more than 1,500,000 stocks, bonds and warrants of 100,000 issuers, including corporations and municipalities of the United States and Canada.
Cost: $1900.00
Frequency: Annual

9052 **Commodity Futures Trading Commission Geographic Directory**
Three Lafayette Centre
1155 21st Street NW
Washington, DC 20581
202-418-5000
Fax: 202-418-5521
E-Mail: opa@cftc.org
Home Page: www.cftc.org
Offers information on corporations and firms that are registered with the Commodity Futures Trading Commission.
Cost: $25.00

9053 **Corporate Finance Sourcebook**
Reed Reference Publishing RR Bowker
121 Chanlon Road
New Providence, NJ 07974-1541
908-665-2834
Fax: 908-464-3553
E-Mail: info@bowker.com
Home Page: www.bowker.com
Tom Bachmann, Editor
Christine Kerwin, Editor
Contains a variety of information on the financial services industry. Listings include securities research analysts, major private lenders, mergers and acquisitions, commercial finance firms, pension managers and leasing companies.
Cost: $425.00
1600 Pages
Frequency: Annual

9054 **Corporate Venturing Directory & Yearbook**
Asset Alternatives
170 Linden Street
Wellesley, MA 02482

781-304-1400
Fax: 781-304-1440
Home Page: www.corporateventuring.com

Dave Barry, Senior Editor
Barbara Bissonnette, VP Marketink/Sales

Features the most comprehensive data ever essembled on corporations participating in venture-backet deals, and the young companies they're financing.
Cost: $495.00
Frequency: Annual
Printed in on matte stock

9055 **Cost Engineers Notebook**
AACE International
209 Prairie Ave
Suite 100
Morgantown, WV 26501-5934

304-296-8444
800-858-2678
Fax: 304-291-5728
E-Mail: info@aacei.org
Home Page: www.aacei.org

Andrew Dowd, Executive Director
Megan McCulla, Asst Manager
Charla Miller, Staff Director Education
Carol S Rogers, Manager Finance
Frequency: Irregular

9056 **Credit Decisioning Study**
Credit Research Foundation
8840 Columbia Pkwy
Suite 100
Columbia, MD 21045-2100

410-740-5499
Fax: 410-740-4620
E-Mail: crf_info@crfonline.org
Home Page: www.crfonline.org

Terry Callahan, President
Michael Durant, Vice-Chairman

9057 **Current Market Snapshot**
CompuServe Information Service
5000 Arlington Centre Blvd
Columbus, OH 43220-5439

614-326-1002
800-848-8199

Offers information on up-to-date stock prices foreign currency data, and general market statistics.

9058 **DIAL/DATA**
Track Data Corporation
95 Rockwell Pl
Brooklyn, NY 11217-1105

718-522-7373
Fax: 718-260-4324
E-Mail: info@trackdata.com
Home Page: www.trackdata.com

Martin Kaye, CEO
Stan Stern, Senior Vice President

This database contains current and historical data on securities, options and commodities.

9059 **DRI Commodities**
DRI/McGraw-Hill
11000 Regency Parkway
Suite 400
Cary, NC 27511

919-462-8600
Fax: 919-468-9890
Home Page: www.profound.com

This database contains more than 51,000 daily time series of price and trading data for major commodities traded on makrets in the US, Canada, London and Singapore.

9060 **DRI Transportation**
DRI/McGraw-Hill
11000 Regency Parkway
Suite 400
Cary, NC 27511

919-462-8600
Fax: 919-468-9890
Home Page: www.profound.com

This large database contains over 15,000 weekly, monthly, and annual time series on commodity traffic by mode, carrier operations and financial data.

9061 **DRI US Bonds**
DRI/McGraw-Hill
11000 Regency Parkway
Suite 400
Cary, NC 27511

919-462-8600
Fax: 919-468-9890
Home Page: www.profound.com

This financial database contains daily time series of current and historical prices, yields and fundamental financial information for more than 60,000 dealer-priced debt issues.

9062 **Daily Foreign Exchange Analysis & Updates**
Technical Data
11 Farnsworth Street
Boston, MA 02210-1210

617-345-2000

This database offers daily reports from major world financial centers including, currency forecasts, analysis of the US bond and money markets, currency reports and the trends of the New York foreign exchange market.
Frequency: Full-text

9063 **Dick Davis Digest**
Dick Davis Publishing
P.O.Box 2049
Salem, MA 01970-6249

954-733-3996
Fax: 954-733-8559
E-Mail: editorial@dickdavis.com
Home Page: www.dickdavis.com

Steven Halpern, Publisher/Editor
Lorianne Kiesl, Marketing Director
Donald Hanrahan, Owner

The digest excerpts over 400 newsletters and the research reports from leading Wall Street analysts and compiles this information into a 12 page compendium of what leading financial advisors currently recommend.
Cost: $165.00
Frequency: BiWeekly

9064 **Directory of Alternative Investment Programs**
Asset Alternatives
170 Linden Street
2nd Floor
Wellesley, MA 02482-7919

781-304-1400
Fax: 781-304-1440
Home Page: www.assetnews.com

David Toll, Managing Editor

The private equity programs of more than 500 leading pension funds, endowments and other institutions, plus their advisors.
Cost: $595.00

9065 **Directory of Buyout Financing Sources**
Securities Data Publishing
40 W 57th St
New York, NY 10019-4001

212-484-4701
Fax: 212-956-0112
E-Mail: sdp@tfn.com
Home Page: www.sdponline.com

Ted Weissberg, Editor-in-Chief
Deborah Chieglis, Advertising Manager
Edward Cortese, Marketing Executive

Over 700 sources of financing, including senior lenders, equity and mezzanine providers in the United States and international avenues, with detailed information on industry, geographic and invetment size preferances and recent activity for each firm.

9066 **Directory of Defense Credit Union**
Defense Credit Union Council
601 Pennsylvania Ave NW
Suite 600
Washington, DC 20004-2601

202-638-3950
Fax: 202-638-3410
E-Mail: dcucl@cuna.com
Home Page: www.dcuc.org

Roland Arteata, President
Frequency: Bi-Ennial

9067 **Directory of Manufacturers' Sales**
Manufacturers' Agents National Association
PO Box 3467
Laguna Hills, CA 92654-3467

949-859-4040
Fax: 949-855-2973
Home Page: www.manaonline.org

Joseph Miller, President
Susan Strouse, Secretary, Treasurer
Alane LaPlante, Director

Association for independent agents and firms representing manufacturers and other businesses in specified territories on a commission basis, including consultants and associate member firms interested in the manufacturer/agency method of marketing.
Cost: $129.00
Frequency: Annual
Circulation: 25,000

9068 **Directory of Mastercard and Visa Credit Cards**
Todd Publications
PO Box 635
Nyack, NY 10960-0635

845-358-6213
Fax: 845-358-1059
E-Mail: toodpub@aol.com
Home Page: toddpublications.com

Barry Klein, Editor

Offers information on 500 credit cards from 200 banks across the country.
Cost: $50.00
1000 Pages
Frequency: Biennial
Circulation: 5,000
Founded in 1994
Mailing list available for rent: 200 names at $50 per M

9069 **Directory of Mutual Funds**
Investment Company Institute
100 F Street
Washington, DC 20549

202-942-8088

Sue Duncan, Editor
Cost: $5.00
247 Pages
Frequency: Annual

9070 Directory of Venture Capital & Private Equity Firms - Online Database
Grey House Publishing
4919 Route 22
PO Box 56
Amenia, NY 12501

518-789-8700
800-562-2139
Fax: 845-373-6390
E-Mail: gold@greyhouse.com
Home Page: http://gold.greyhouse.com
Social Media: Facebook, Twitter

Leslie Mackenzie, Publisher
Richard Gottlieb, Editor

Packed with need-to-know information, this database offers immediate access to 2,300 VC firms, over 10,000 managing partners, and over 11,500 VC investments.
Frequency: Annual

9071 Directory of Venture Capital and Private Equity Firms
Grey House Publishing
4919 Route 22
PO Box 56
Amenia, NY 12501

518-789-8700
800-562-2139
Fax: 845-373-6390
E-Mail: books@greyhouse.com
Home Page: www.greyhouse.com
Social Media: Facebook, Twitter

Leslie Mackenzie, Publisher
Richard Gottlieb, Editor

Offers access to over 2,300 domestic and international venture capital and private equity firms, including detailed contact information and extensive data on investments and funds.
Cost: $685.00
1200 Pages
Frequency: Annual
ISBN: 1-592372-72-4

9072 Dow Jones Business and Finance Report
Dow Jones & Company
PO Box 300
Princeton, NJ 08543-0300

609-520-4000
Home Page: http://www.dowjones.com

This large database offers financial news and information on developments in business and industry, domestic and international economies, and the stock market.
Frequency: Full-text

9073 Dow Jones Futures and Index Quotes
Dow Jones & Company
PO Box 300
Princeton, NJ 08543-0300

609-520-4000

This database, updated continuously, offers current and historical stock quotations for more than 80 contracts from major North American stock exchanges.

9074 Dow Jones Text Library
Dow Jones & Company
PO Box 300
Princeton, NJ 08543-0300

609-520-4000
Home Page: http://www.dowjones.com

This large database offers business and financial news covering more than 6,000 US companies, 700 Canadian companies and 50 industries.
Frequency: Full-text

9075 E-Z Telephone Directory of Brokers and Banks
106 7th Street
Garden City, NY 11530-5796

516-294-0350
Fax: 516-294-0356

MJ Gentile, Editor

Security brokers, banks, and financial organizations in the New York area are listed in this directory.
Cost: $90.00
200 Pages
Frequency: SemiAnnual
Circulation: 10,000
Printed in on matte stock

9076 ECFA Member List
Evangelical Council for Financial Accountability
440 W Jubal Early Dr
Suite 130
Winchester, VA 22601

540-535-0103
800-323-9473
Fax: 540-535-0533
E-Mail: dan@ecfa.org
Home Page: www.ecfa.org

Dan Busby, President
Frequency: Annual

9077 EMARKET
International Financial Corporation
1818 H St NW
Washington, DC 20433-0001

202-473-1000
Fax: 202-974-4384
Home Page: www.ifc.org

Robert Zoellich, President

This database offers over 1,000 weekly, annual and monthly time series on company stocks from over 18 developing countries.

9078 Evans Economics Analysis and Commentary
Evans Economics
1660 L Street NW
Suite 207
Washington, DC 20036-5603

This database reports on changes in economic activity to all major financial markets. Over 20 files are listed that provide the forecasts and reports on the effect of economic variables on debt and equity markets.
Frequency: Full-text

9079 Financial Ratios for Manufacturing Corporations Database
US Department of Commerce
Herbert Rm 4885
Washington, DC 20230-0001

202-690-7650
Fax: 202-482-0325
Home Page: www.access.gpo.gov

Pam Nacci

This database provides 20 quarterly seasonally adjusted financial and operating ratios for selected two- and three-digit SIC groups in the manufacturing sector.
Cost: $85.00
Frequency: Series

9080 Financial Services Canada
Grey House Publishing
4919 Route 22
PO Box 56
Amenia, NY 12501

518-789-8700
800-562-2139
Fax: 845-373-6390
E-Mail: books@greyhouse.com
Home Page: www.greyhouse.com
Social Media: Facebook, Twitter

Leslie Mackenzie, Publisher
Richard Gottlieb, Editor

With over 18,000 organizations and hard-to-find business information, Financial Services Canada is the most up-to-date source for names and contact information of industry professionals, senior executives, portfolio managers, financial advisors, agency bureaucrats and elected representatives.
Cost: $325.00
900 Pages
ISBN: 1-592372-78-3
Founded in 1981

9081 Financial Yellow Book
Leadership Directories
104 5th Ave
New York, NY 10011-6901

212-627-4140
Fax: 212-645-0931
E-Mail: financial@leadershipdirectories.com
Home Page: www.leadershipdirectories.com

David Hurvitz, CEO
James M Petrie, Associate Publisher

Contact information for over 26,000 executives at public and private financial institutions, and over 5,000 board members and their outside affiliations.
Cost: $245.00
900 Pages
Frequency: Semiannual
ISSN: 1058-2878
Founded in 1987
Mailing list available for rent: 20,000 names at $95 per M

9082 Financing Your Business in Eastern Europe
WorldTrade Executive
PO Box 761
Concord, MA 01742-0761

978-287-0301
Fax: 978-287-0302
E-Mail: info@wtexec.com
Home Page: www.wtexec.com

Alison French, Production Manager

Provides reliable information on financing sources, including local and international banks, capital markets, venture capital funds, and government sources
Cost: $135.00

9083 FirstList
Vision Quest Publishing
37308 12th Street
Phoenix, AZ 86086

928-451-4445
E-Mail: mergers@firstlist.com
Home Page: http://www.firstlist.com

A Robert Weicherding, President

Information is offered in this directory covering companies that are candidates for merger or acquisition, buyers seeking acquisitions, sources of financinf, equity or debt financing and joint venture and licensing opportunities. Also available on-line and the Internet.
Cost: $350.00
120 Pages
Frequency: 8 per year

9084 Ford Data Base
Ford Investor Services
11722 Sorrento Valley Rd
Suite 1
San Diego, CA 92121-1021

858-755-1327
Fax: 858-455-6316

E-Mail: info@fordequity.com
Home Page: www.fordequity.com

Tim Alward, President

This database offers 80 financial data items for each of 2,000 leading common stocks.

9085 Futures Magazine Sourcebook
Oster Communications
5081 Olympic Boulevard
Erlanger, KT 41018

319-277-1271
E-Mail: gszala@futuresmag.com
Home Page: www.futuresmag.com

Ginger Szala, Group Publisher/Editorial Director
Daniel P Collins, Managing Editor
Christine Birkner, Associate Editor

This issue deals with exchanges in futures and options contracts, including commodities, foreign currencies, stock indexes and international financial coverage.
Cost: $22.00
130 Pages
Frequency: Annual
Circulation: 60,000

9086 Galante's Venture Capital & Private Equity Directory
Asset Alternatives
170 Linden Street
Wellesley, MA 02482-7919

781-304-1400
Fax: 781-304-1440
Home Page: www.assetnews.com

David Toll, Managing Editor

Complete investment criteria of venture capital, buyout, and mezzanine firms into one complete reference.

9087 Hulbert Guide to Financial Newsletters
Dearborn Financial Publishing
155 Wacker Avenue
Chicago, IL 60606

312-836-4400

Matt Schiff, Owner
Kathleen A Welton, VP

Lists over 100 financial newsletters offering descriptions and evaluation of model portfolios.
Cost: $27.95
574 Pages
Frequency: Biennial

9088 IBC/Donoghue's Money Fund Report/ Electronic
290 Eliot Street
#9104
Ashland, MA 01721-2351

This valuable database offers information and analyses of trends and developments in the money market mutual funds industry.
Frequency: Full-text

9089 IBC/Donoghue's Mutual Funds Almanac
290 Eliot Street
#9104
Ashland, MA 01721-2351
Ann V Needle, Editor

Over 2,400 load and no load mutual funds, including equity, bond and municipal funds.
Cost: $39.95
Circulation: 25,000

9090 Insider Trading Monitor Database
CDA Investment
3265 Meridian Parkway
Suite 130
Fort Lauderdale, FL 33331-3506

954-384-1500

More than 12,500 companies and all insider security transactions reported to the US Securities and Exchange Commission, FDIC, Toronto Stock Exchange and OTS.
Frequency: Daily

9091 Insiders' Chronicle
CDA Investment
3265 Meridian Parkway
Suite 130
Fort Lauderdale, FL 33331-3506

954-384-1500

Robert Gabele, Editor

Publicly held companies in whose securities there has been significant buying or selling by executive officers, directors, and those who hold 10% or more of its shares.
15 Pages

9092 International Financial Statistics
International Monetary Fund
700 19th St NW
Washington, DC 20431-0002

202-623-7000
Fax: 202-623-4661
E-Mail: publications@imf.org
Home Page: www.imf.org

Masood Ahmed, VP
Kathleen Tilmans, Secretary
Olivier Blanchard, Secretary
Christine Lagarde, Managing Director

Offers informaiton on more than 23,000 annual, quarterly and monthly time series of economic and dinancial statistics on over 200 countries.

9093 International Investor's Directory
Asset International
125 Greenwich Avenue
Suite 5
Greenwich, CT 06830-5512

203-629-5015
Fax: 203-629-5024

Eric Laursen, Editor

Directory of services and supplies to the industry.
Cost: $235.00
735 Pages
Frequency: Annual

9094 Investment Blue Book
Securities Investigations
PO Box 888
Woodstock, NY 12498-0888

845-679-2300

Lists over 6,000 brokers and dealers in tax shelter plans; 2,000 sponsors of tax shelter products and suppliers of service to the industry and mutual funds information.
Cost: $145.00
350 Pages
Frequency: Irergular
Circulation: 10,000

9095 Investment Recovery Association Directory
Investment Recovery Association
5800 Foxridge Drive
Suite 115
Mission, KS 66202-2338

913-624-4597
Fax: 913-262-0174

Jane Male, Editor

Directory of services and supplies to the industry.
Cost: $250.00
Frequency: Annual
Circulation: 400

9096 Investor Relations Resource Guide
National Investor Relations Institute
8045 Leesburg Pike
Suite 600
Vienna, VA 22182

571-633-0532
Fax: 703-506-3571
E-Mail: info@niri.org
Home Page: www.niri.org

Melissa Jones, Editor
Ariel Finno, Director Research

Lists about 110 investment counseling firms, 50 financial investment associations and 40 financial investment service firms such as publishers of magazines and newsletters.
Cost: $50.00
83 Pages
Frequency: Annual

9097 Japanese Investment in the Midwest
Japan-America Society of Greater Cincinnati
441 Vine Street
Cincinnati, OH 45202-2821

513-579-3114
Fax: 513-579-3101
Home Page: www.patent-pros.com

Jack Adams, Executive Director

A list of more than 400 Japanese manufacturing firms in the states of Illinois, Indiana, Kentucky, Michigan, Ohio, and Tennessee.
Cost: $40.00
30 Pages
Frequency: Annual

9098 Lipper Marketplace
Lipper, A Thomson Reuters Company
3 Times Square
New York, NY 10036

646-223-4000
800-782-5555
E-Mail: salesinquiries@thomsonreuters.com
Home Page: www.lippermarketplace.com

James C Smith, Chief Executive Officer
Stephane Bello, Chief Financial Officer
David W Craig, President, Finance
Robert D Daleo, Vice Chairman
Susan Taylor Martin, President, Reuters Media

This powerful web-based solution opens the door to highly targeted prospects by putting the tools to identify your market at your fingertips. Designed with the input of institutional investment professionals, MarketPlace not only helps you qualify your prospects, it also gives you the cutting-edge competitive intelligence you need to transform your prospects into clients.

9099 Loan Broker: Annual Directory
Ben Campbell, Publisher
917 S Park Street
Owosso, MI 48867-4422

Lists approximately 800 loan brokers, private funding sources and business financing services operating in the continental United States.
Cost: $59.95
Frequency: Annual
Circulation: 3,000

9100 MJK Commodities Database
MJK Associates

1289 S Park Victoria Drive
Suite 205
Milpitas, CA 95035-6974

FAX 408-941-3404

Offers information on United States and Canadian commodities; international monetary markets; futures indexes and stock index futures.

9101 Mentor Support Group Directory
National Association of Certified Valuation
1111 Brickyard Road
Suite 200
Salt Lake City, UT 84106-5401

801-486-0600
800-677-2009
Fax: 801-486-7500
E-Mail: nacva1@nacva.com
Home Page: www.nacva.com

Parnell Black, CEO
Frequency: Annual

9102 Merger & Acquisition Sourcebook Edition
Quality Services Company
5290 Overpass Road
Suite 126
Santa Barbara, CA 93111-3009

805-964-7841
Fax: 805-964-1073

Walter Jurek, Editor
Nancy Rothlein, Production Manager

Contains complete information on the previous years' merger and acquisitions actuary.
Cost: $350.00

9103 Merger Yearbook
Securities Data Publishing
40 W 57th St
11th Floor
New York, NY 10019-4001

212-484-4701
Fax: 212-956-0112
E-Mail: sdp@tfn.com
Home Page: www.sdponline.com

Ted Weissberg, Editor-in-Chief
Deborah Chieglis, Advertising Manager
Edward Cortese, Marketing Executive

Information on tens of thousands of announces and completed deals plus charts giving awards information on industry rankings and transactions.

9104 Merger and Corporate Transactions Database
Securities Data Publishing
1180 Raymond Boulevard
Suite 5
Newark, NJ 07102-4107

This database contains more than 85,000 records on transactions involving mergers, acquisitions, divestitures leveraged buyouts and stock repurchases.
Frequency: Full-text

9105 Mergers & Acquisitions Yearbook
American Banker-Bond Buyer
1 State St
27th Floor
New York, NY 10004-1561

212-803-8450
800-367-3989
Fax: 212-843-9624
Home Page: www.sourcemedia.com

Jim Malkin, CEO
Mario DiUbaldi, Publisher
Phil Roosevelt, Editor
Carole Lambert, Sales/Marketing Director
Stacy Weinstein, Production Director

Annual yearbook detailing all bank merger and acquisition activity for the previous year. Includes sale price, financial and legal advisors and governmental information.
Cost: $175.00
Frequency: Annual

9106 Mergers and Acquisitions Handbook
National Association of Division Order Analysts
2805 Oak Trail Court
Suite 6312
Arlington, TX 76016

972-715-4489
E-Mail: administrator@nadoa.org
Home Page: www.nadoa.org

Lynn S McCord, Administrator
Frequency: Annual

9107 Money Market Directory of Pension Funds and their Investment Managers
Money Market Directories
PO Box 1608
Charlottesville, VA 22902-1608
434-977-1450
800-446-2810
Fax: 434-979-9962
Home Page: www.mmdaccess.com

Tom Lupo, Manager
John Martin, Production Manager
Dennis Thurston, Publications

Over 44,000 tax-exempt funds with over $1,000,000 in assets, and about 1,800 investment management services including bank trust departments and insurance companies, each handling at least $25,000,000 in tax-exempt funds.
Cost: $1150.00
2000 Pages
Frequency: Annual January
Circulation: 8,500
ISBN: 0-939712-31-8
ISSN: 0736-6051
Founded in 1970

9108 Money Source Book
Business Information Network
15851 Dallas Parkway
Suite 600
Dallas, TX 75248
972-982-8686

Over 1,500 traditional and non-traditional sources of business capital with an emphasis on the south-central United States.
Cost: $24.95
200 Pages
Frequency: Annual
Circulation: 20,000

9109 MoneyData
Technical Data
11 Farnsworth Street
Boston, MA 02210-1210

617-345-2000

This database offers a full line of information on money markets.

9110 MoneyWatch
McCarthy, Crisanti & Maffei
71 Broadway
New York, NY 10006-2601

212-675-5880
Fax: 212-509-7389

This database offers valuable information on the money market, including economic indicators.
Frequency: Full-text

9111 Morningstar
Morningstar
225 W Washington Street
Chicago, IL 60602

312-384-4000
Fax: 312-696-6001
E-Mail: productinfo@morningstar.com
Home Page: www.morningstar.com

Joe Mansueto, Chairman & CEO
Chris Boruff, President, Software Division
Peng Chen, President, Global Investment Div.
Bevin Desmond, President, International Operations
Scott Cooley, Chief Financial Officer

Morningstar provides data on approximately 330,000 investment offerings, including stocks, mutual funds, and similar vehicles, along with real-time global market data on more than 5 million equities, indexes, futures, options, commodities, and precious metals, in addition to foreign exchange and Treasury markets. Morningstar also offers investment management services and has more than $167 billion in assets under advisement and management.

9112 Mutual Fund Encyclopedia
Dearborn Financial Publishing
155 Wacker Drive
Chicago, IL 60606

312-836-4400

Gerald W Perritt, Author

Directory of services and supplies to the industry.
Cost: $35.95
600 Pages
Frequency: Annual

9113 Mutual Fund/Municipal Bond
Interactive Data Corporation
10 Post Office Sq
39th Floor
Boston, MA 02109-4695

617-428-1600
E-Mail: info@interactivedata.com
Home Page: www.interactivedata.com

James Murawski, Manager

This database contains over 3,000 time series of price data for municipal bonds held in the portfolios of selected mutual funds.

9114 NADOA Directory
National Association of Division Order Analysts
2805 Oak Trail Court
Suite 6312
Arlington, TX 76016

972-715-4489
E-Mail: administrator@nadoa.org
Home Page: www.nadoa.org

Lynn S McCord, Administrator
Frequency: Annual

9115 NALHFA Membership Directory
National Associatin of Local Housing Finance
2025 M St NW
Suite 800
Washington, DC 20036-2422

202-367-1197
Fax: 202-367-2197
E-Mail: john_murphy@nalhfa.org
Home Page: www.noca.org

John C Murphy, Executive Director
Scott Lynch, Association Manager
Kim McKinon, Coordinator Membership
Frequency: Annual

9116 NASBO Newsletter
National Association of State Budget Officers

444 N Capitol St NW
Suite 642
Washington, DC 20001-1556

202-624-8020
Fax: 202-624-7745
E-Mail: spattison@nasbo.org
Home Page: www.nasbo.org

Scott Pattison, Executive Director
Lauren Cummings, Manager Member Relations

9117 NASD Manual
CCH
2700 Lake Cook Rd
Riverwoods, IL 60015-3867

847-940-4600
800-835-5224
Fax: 773-866-3095
Home Page: www.cch.com

Mike Sabbatis, President
Douglas M Winterrose, Vice President & CFO
Jim Bryant, EVP Software Products

Officials, members, by-laws and rules of NASD.
Founded in 1913

9118 NATRI Membership Directory
National Association for Treasurers of Religious
8824 Cameron Street
Silver Springs, MD 20910

301-587-7776
Fax: 301-589-2897
Home Page: www.natri.org

Laura Reicks, Executive Director
Lorelle Elcock, Associate Director Finance
Frequency: Annual

9119 National Bankers Association: Roster of Minority Banking Institutions
National Bankers Association
1513 P St NW
Washington, DC 20005-1909

202-588-5432
Fax: 202-588-5443
E-Mail: webmaster@nationalbankers.org
Home Page: www.nationalbankers.org

Michael Grant, President
Floyd Weekes, Chairman

About 140 banks owned or controlled by minority group persons or women.
Cost: $5.00
Frequency: Annual October

9120 National Credit Union Administration Directory
National Credit Union Administration
1775 Duke St
Suite 4206
Alexandria, VA 22314-6115

703-518-6300
Fax: 703-518-6539
E-Mail: ociomail@ncua.gov
Home Page: www.ncua.gov

Michael Fryzel, Chairman
Sarah Vega, Executive Director

Directory of credit unions governed by a three member board appointed by the President and confirmed by the US Senate, by the independent federal agency that charters and supervises federal credit unions. NCUA, with the backing of the full faith and credit of the US government, operates the National Credit Union Share Insurance Fund, insuring the savings of 80 million account holders in all federal credit unions and many state chartered credit unions.

9121 National Directory of Investment Newsletters
GPS
PO Box 372
Morrisville, PA 19067-8372

215-295-8700
Home Page: www.investmentnewsletterdirectory.com

George T Scilieber, Editor

Lists over 800 newsletters dealing with investments and financial planning and their publishers.
Cost: $49.95
60 Pages
Frequency: Biennial

9122 North American Financial Institutions Directory
4709 Golf Road
Skokie, IL 60076

847-676-9600
800-321-3373
Fax: 847-933-8101
E-Mail: custserv@accuitysolutions.com
Home Page: www.accuitysolutions.com

Marideth Johnson, Manager, Marketing/Communications
Malcolm Taylor, Managing Director
Cost: $460.00
Circulation: 31850

9123 PC Bridge
Bridge Information Systems
717 Office Parkway
Saint Louis, MO 63141-7115

314-567-8100
Fax: 314-432-5391

Tony Bridge, Manager

This database delivers real-time market information, monitoring up to 100 symbols per page on 10 available pages.

9124 Pacific Stock Exchange Guide
CCH
2700 Lake Cook Rd
Riverwoods, IL 60015-3867

847-940-4600
800-835-5224
Fax: 773-866-3095
Home Page: www.cch.com

Mike Sabbatis, President
Douglas M Winterrose, Vice President & CFO
Jim Bryant, EVP Software Products

Lists officials, members, member organizations; by-laws and rules of the Pacific Stock Exchange.
Cost: $405.00

9125 Pensions & Investments: Investment Managers
Crain Communications
711 3rd Ave
New York, NY 10017-4014

212-210-0785
Fax: 212-210-0465
E-Mail: jmurphy@crain.com

Norm Feldman, Manager
Chris Battaglia, Publisher

List of over 1,050 banks, insurance companies, investment advisors and other investment management organizations.
Cost: $40.00
Frequency: Annual May
Circulation: 41,000

9126 Pensions & Investments: Master Trust, Custody and Global Custody Banks
Crain Communications
711 3rd Ave
New York, NY 10017-4014

212-210-0785
Fax: 212-210-0465
E-Mail: jmurphy@crain.com

Norm Feldman, Manager
Chris Battaglia, Publisher

List of banks with master trust/master custodial assets and global custody assets.
Cost: $10.00
Frequency: Annual October
Circulation: 41,000

9127 Philadelphia Stock Exchange Guide
CCH
2700 Lake Cook Rd
Riverwoods, IL 60015-3867

847-940-4600
800-835-5224
Fax: 773-866-3095
Home Page: www.cch.com

Mike Sabbatis, President
Douglas M Winterrose, Vice President & CFO
Jim Bryant, EVP Software Products

Lists officials, members, member organizations, securities, by-laws and rules of the Exchange.
Cost: $350.00
Frequency: Monthly

9128 Pratt's Guide to Private Equity & Venture Capital Sources
Thomson Reuters
3 Times Square
New York, NY 10036

646-223-4431
800-782-5555
E-Mail: rpp.americas@thomsonreuters.com
Home Page: www.thomsonreuters.com

James C Smith, Chief Executive Officer
Stephane Bello, Chief Financial Officer
David W Craig, President, Finance
Robert D Daleo, Vice Chairman
Susan Taylor Martin, President, Reuters Media

This is the definitive reference source to actively investing private equity and venture capital firms operating around the world. Pratt's Guide is available in both hard copy and online format - the latter being continually updated with new fund-raising data, new investment and exit data and new contact information.

9129 Professional Investor Report
Dow Jones & Company
PO Box 300
Princeton, NJ 08543-0300

609-520-4000

Offers information on unusual stock trading activity taking place on the New York and American stock exchanges and the National Market System portion of the OTC market.

9130 Quarterly Financial Report
GE Information Services
401 N Washington Street
Rockville, MD 20850-1707

301-388-8284
Fax: 301-294-5501

Cathy Ge, Owner

This unique database offers information on financial estimates for US enterprises within 31 industry classifications.

9131 RSP Funding for Nursing Students and Nurses
Reference Service Press

5000 Windplay Dr
Suite 4
El Dorado Hills, CA 95762-9319

916-939-9620
Fax: 916-939-9626
E-Mail: info@rspfunding.com
Home Page: www.rspfunding.com

Gail Schlachter, Owner
R David Weber, Manager
Martin Sklar, Manager

You can find out about the more than 600 scholarships, fellowships, loans, loan repayment programs, forgivable loans, grants, awards, prizes and interships set aside specifically to support study, research, creative activities, past accomplishments, future projects, professional development and traineeships. This is more than twice the number of nursing related funding programs covered in any other source.
Cost: $30.00
210 Pages
Frequency: Biennial
ISBN: 1-588410-95-1
Founded in 1998

9132 Registry of Financial Planning Practitioners
International Association for Financial Planning
1580 W. El Camino Real
Suite 10
Mountain View, CA 94040

877-794-9511
650-390-6400
Fax: 650-989-2131
E-Mail: customer.service@trademarkia.com
Home Page: www.trademarkia.com

J Patrick Tinley, CEO
Alexander Esq, Owner

Directory of services and supplies to the industry.
80 Pages
Frequency: Annual

9133 Research Reports
National Committee on Planned Giving
233 S McCrea St
Suite 400
Indianapolis, IN 46225-1068

317-269-6274
Fax: 317-269-6276
Home Page: www.ncpg.org

Tanya Howe Johnson, President
Sandra Kerr, Director Government Education
Barbara Owens, Director Membership/Manager HR
Kathryn J Ramsey, Director Meetings
Kurt Reusze, Manager Education/Technology
Frequency: Irregular

9134 Roster of Minority Financial Institutions
US Department of the Treasury
401 14th Street SW
Room 523C
Washington, DC 20024-2106

202-874-5740
Fax: 202-874-6907

Robert Jones, Editor

About 170 commercial, minority-owned and controlled financial institutions participating in the Department of the Treasury's Minority Bank Deposit program.
Frequency: Biennial

9135 S&P MarketScope Database
Standard & Poor's Corporation
55 Water St
New York, NY 10041-0003

212-438-1000
Fax: 212-438-0299

Deven Sharma, President

Over 5,000 companies are listed in the Reference Section of Standard and Poors database offering names, addresses, background information and current and historical financial information.

9136 Secondary Marketing Executive Directory of Mortgage Technology
LDJ Corporation
P.O.Box 2180
Waterbury, CT 06722-2180

203-755-0158
Fax: 203-755-3480

David Zackin, Publisher
John Florian, Editor

A who's who directory of technology products and services to the real estate finance industry.
Cost: $5.00
Frequency: Annual
Circulation: 21,000

9137 Service Directory
National Association for Treasurers of Religious
8824 Cameron Street
Silver Springs, MD 20910

301-587-7776
Fax: 301-589-2897
Home Page: www.natri.org

Laura Reicks, Executive Director
Lorelle Elcock, Associate Director Finance
Frequency: Annual

9138 Sheshunoff Bank & S&L Quarterly
Sheshunoff Information Services
2801 Via Fortuna
Suite 600
Austin, TX 78746-7970

512-472-4000
800-477-1772
Fax: 512-305-6575
E-Mail: sales@smslp.com
Home Page: www.smslp.com

Gabrielle Sheshunoff, CEO

Overview of the financial health of the banking industry and of every bank and S&L in the nation. Information includes CAMEL, fachois, asset quality, earnings, and rotation.
Cost: $543.00
Frequency: Quarterly

9139 Sheshunoff Banking Organization Quarterly
Sheshunoff Information Services
2801 Via Fortuna
Suite 600
Austin, TX 78746-7970

512-472-4000
800-456-2340
Fax: 512-305-6575
E-Mail: gsheshunoff@smslp.com
Home Page: www.smslp.com

Gabrielle Sheshunoff, CEO

Offers ownership structure for all bank holding companies and overview and ratings for bank holding companies and their brinking subs.
Cost: $499.00
Frequency: Quarterly

9140 Small Business Investment Company Directory and Handbook
International Wealth Success
PO Box 186
Merrick, NY 11566-0186

516-766-5850
800-323-0548
Fax: 516-766-5919
E-Mail: admin@iwsmoney.com
Home Page: www.iwsmoney.com
Social Media: Facebook, LinkedIn

Tyler G Hicks, President

Lists more than 400 small business investment companies that invest in small businesses to help them prosper. Also gives tips on financial management in business.
Cost: $20.00
135 Pages
Frequency: Annual
ISBN: 1-561503-12-6
Founded in 1975

9141 Speakers Bureau Directory
National Association of Certified Valuation
1111 Brickyard Road
Suite 200
Salt Lake City, UT 84106-5401

801-486-0600
800-677-2009
Fax: 801-486-7500
E-Mail: nacva1@nacva.com
Home Page: www.nacva.com

Parnell Black, CEO
Frequency: Annual

9142 Standard & Poor's Directory of Bond Agents
Standard & Poor's Corporation
55 Water St
New York, NY 10041-0003

212-438-1000
Fax: 212-438-0299

Deven Sharma, President

A list of paying agents, registrars, co-registrars and conversion agents for 30,000 corporate and municipal bonds are included.
Cost: $1250.00

9143 Standard & Poor's Security Dealers of North America
Standard & Poor's Financial Services, LLC
401 East Market Street
PO Box 1608
Charlottesville, VA 22902

434-977-1450
800-446-2810
Fax: 434-979-9962
Home Page: www.mmdwebaccess.com

Deven Sharma, President

The most comprehensive guide to brokerage and investment banking firms in the US and Canada. The directory contains all the facts you need for conveniently locating firms and facilitating transactions.
Cost: $498.00
Frequency: 2x/Year

9144 State Expenditure Report
National Association of State Budget Officers
444 N Capitol St NW
Suite 642
Washington, DC 20001-1556

202-624-8020
Fax: 202-624-7745
E-Mail: spattison@nasbo.org
Home Page: www.nasbo.org

Scott Pattison, Executive Director
Lauren Cummings, Manager Member Relations
Frequency: Annual

9145 TA Guide & Checklist
National Investment Company Service Association
36 Washington Street
Suite 70
Wellesley Hills, MA 02481
781-416-7200
Fax: 781-416-7065
E-Mail: info@nisca.org
Home Page: www.nisca.org
Barbara V Weidlich, President
Keith Dropkin, Director Operations
Doris Jaimes, Registrar
Sheila Kobaly, Events Manager
Chris Ludent, IT Manager
Frequency: Annual

9146 TRW Trade Payment Guide
TRW Business Credit Services
500 City Pkwy W
Orange, CA 92868-2913
714-385-7000
800-344-0603
Fax: 714-938-2586
Approximately 2,500,000 credit active business locations.
Frequency: Quarterly

9147 Tax Directory
Tax Analysts
6830 N Fairfax Drive
Arlington, VA 22213-1001
703-533-4400
800-955-3444
Fax: 703-533-4664
E-Mail: taxdir@tax.org
Home Page: www.tax.org
Amie Chant, Editor
Thomas F Field, Vice President
Jill Biden, Vice President
A reference tool that provides users with comprehensive listings of federal, state and private sector tax professionals. Now in three sections - Government Officials, Corporate Tax Managers and International Officials.
Cost: $ 399.00
960 Pages
Frequency: Quarterly
Circulation: 2,000
ISSN: 0888-1243

9148 Tax Free Trade Zones of the World
Matthew Bender and Company
11 Penn Plz
Suite 5101
New York, NY 10001-2006
212-000-1111
Eric Blood, Data Processing
Covers over 450 free trade zones, transit zones, free perimeters and free ports. The emphasis is placed on tax advantages of each.
Cost: $280.00
1000 Pages

9149 Technical Resources Handbook
National Association of Certified Valuation
1111 Brickyard Road
Suite 200
Salt Lake City, UT 84106-5401
801-486-0600
800-677-2009
Fax: 801-486-7500
E-Mail: nacva1@nacva.com
Home Page: www.nacva.com
Parnell Black, CEO
Frequency: Annual

9150 TheStreet Ratings Guide to Bond & Money Market Mutual Funds
Grey House Publishing
4919 Route 22
PO Box 56
Amenia, NY 12501
518-789-8700
800-562-2139
Fax: 845-373-6390
E-Mail: books@greyhouse.com
Home Page: www.greyhouse.com
Social Media: Facebook, Twitter
Leslie Mackenzie, Publisher
Richard Gottlieb, Editor
Each quarterly edition provides ratings and analyses of more than 4,200 fixed income funds, more than any other publication, including corporate bond funds, municipal bond funds, mortgage security funds, money market funds, global bond funds, and government bond funds.
Cost: $249.00
600 Pages
Frequency: Quarterly
Founded in 1981

9151 TheStreet Ratings Guide to Common Stocks
Grey House Publishing
4919 Route 22
PO Box 56
Amenia, NY 12501
518-789-8700
800-562-2139
Fax: 845-373-6390
E-Mail: books@greyhouse.com
Home Page: www.greyhouse.com
Social Media: Facebook, Twitter
Leslie Mackenzie, Publisher
Richard Gottlieb, Editor
Each quarterly edition provides reliable insight into the risk-adjusted performance of over 7,500 common stocks listed on the NYSE, AMEX, and NASDAQ, more than any other publication. This user-friendly guide offers step-by-step guidance for users to find out which type of stocks are best for them, and quickly and easily points the user to the best performing stocks in that category.
Cost: $249.00
600 Pages
Frequency: Quarterly
Founded in 1981

9152 TheStreet Ratings Guide to Exchange-Traded Funds
Grey House Publishing
4919 Route 22
PO Box 56
Amenia, NY 12501
518-789-8700
800-562-2139
Fax: 845-373-6390
E-Mail: books@greyhouse.com
Home Page: www.greyhouse.com
Social Media: Facebook, Twitter
Leslie Mackenzie, Publisher
Richard Gottlieb, Editor
The intuitive, consumer-friendly ratings allow investors to instantly identify those funds that have historically done well and those that have under-performed the market. Identifies top-performing exchange-traded funds based on risk category, type of fund, and overall risk-adjusted performance.
Cost: $249.00
600 Pages
Frequency: Quarterly
Founded in 1981

9153 TheStreet Ratings Guide to Stock Mutual Funds
Grey House Publishing
4919 Route 22
PO Box 56
Amenia, NY 12501
518-789-8700
800-562-2139
Fax: 845-373-6390
E-Mail: books@greyhouse.com
Home Page: www.greyhouse.com
Social Media: Facebook, Twitter
Leslie Mackenzie, Publisher
Richard Gottlieb, Editor
Offers ratings and analyses on more than 8,000 equity mutual funds, including growth funds, index funds, balanced funds and sector or international funds - more than any other publication.
Cost: $249.00
600 Pages
Frequency: Quarterly
Founded in 1981

9154 TheStreet Ratings Ultimate Guided Tour of Stock Investing
Grey House Publishing
4919 Route 22
PO Box 56
Amenia, NY 12501
518-789-8700
800-562-2139
Fax: 845-373-6390
E-Mail: books@greyhouse.com
Home Page: www.greyhouse.com
Social Media: Facebook, Twitter
Leslie Mackenzie, Publisher
Richard Gottlieb, Editor
This user-friendly guide provides a step-by-step introduction to stock investing designed for the beginning to intermediate investor. Starting with the basics of stock investing and ending with an evaluation of the user's risk tolerance and the identification of the types of stocks that best match their needs, this easy-to-navigate guide pulls together all of the information necessary to educate the consumer on how to get the best start in investing.
Cost: $249.00
600 Pages
Frequency: Quarterly
Founded in 1981

9155 Top Mortgage Market Players Directory
Inside Mortgage Finance Publishers
7910 Woodmont Ave
Suite 1000
Bethesda, MD 20814-7019
301-951-1240
Fax: 301-656-1709
E-Mail: service@imfpubs.com
Home Page: www.imfpubs.com
Guy Cecala, Owner
John Bancroft, Managing Editor
Didi Parks, Marketing/Advertising
Listing of over 4,500 residential mortgage lenders.
Cost: $375.00
Frequency: Annual

9156 Trading Volume Survey
EMTA - Trade Association for the Emerging Markets
360 Madison Avenue
18th Floor
New York, NY 10017
646-637-9100
Fax: 646-637-9128
E-Mail: awerner@emta.org
Home Page: www.emta.org
Michael M Chamberlin, Executive Director
Aviva Werner, Managing Director
Jonathan Murno, Managing Director

Suzette Ortiz, Office Manager
Monika Forbes, Administrative Assistant
Frequency: Quarterly

9157 Trusts & Estates: Directory of Trust Institutions Issue
Primedia
PO Box 12901
Shawnee Mission, KS 66282-2901
913-341-1300
Fax: 913-514-6895
Home Page: www.penton.com
Eric Jacobson, Senior VP
Offers a list of about 5,000 trust departments in the United States and Canadian banks.
Cost: $82.00
Frequency: Annual January
Circulation: 12,200

9158 Valuation Compilation
National Association of Certified Valuation
1111 Brickyard Road
Suite 200
Salt Lake City, UT 84106-5401
801-486-0600
800-677-2009
Fax: 801-486-7500
E-Mail: nacva1@nacva.com
Home Page: www.nacva.com
Parnell Black, CEO
Frequency: Bi-Ennial

9159 Venture Capital: Where to Find it
National Association of Small Business Investment
1199 N Fairfax Street
Suite 200
Alexandria, VA 22314-1437
703-549-2100
Jeanette D Smith, Editor
Directory of services and supplies to the industry.
Frequency: Annual

9160 Weiss Ratings Consumer Box Set
Grey House Publishing
4919 Route 22
PO Box 56
Amenia, NY 12501
518-789-8700
800-562-2139
Fax: 845-373-6390
E-Mail: books@greyhouse.com
Home Page: www.greyhouse.com
Social Media: Facebook, Twitter
Leslie Mackenzie, Publisher
Richard Gottlieb, Editor
Each guide in the Weiss Ratings Consumer Box Set is packed with accurate, unbiased information, including helpful, step-by-step Worksheets & Planners. The set consists of Consumer Guides to Variable Annuities, Elder Care Choices, Medicare Supplement Insurance, Medicare Prescription Drug Coverage, Homeowners Insurance, Automobile Insurance, Long-Term Care Insurance, and Term Life Insurance.
Cost: $249.00
600 Pages
Frequency: Quarterly
Founded in 1981

9161 Weiss Ratings Guide to Banks & Thrifts
Grey House Publishing
4919 Route 22
PO Box 56
Amenia, NY 12501
518-789-8700
800-562-2139
Fax: 845-373-6390
E-Mail: books@greyhouse.com
Home Page: www.greyhouse.com
Social Media: Facebook, Twitter
Leslie Mackenzie, Publisher
Richard Gottlieb, Editor
Offers accurate, intuitive safety ratings your patrons can trust; supporting ratios and analyses that show an institution's strong & weak points; identification of the Weiss Recommended Companies with branches in your area and more.
Cost: $249.00
600 Pages
Frequency: Quarterly
Founded in 1981

9162 Weiss Ratings Guide to Credit Unions
Grey House Publishing
4919 Route 22
PO Box 56
Amenia, NY 12501
518-789-8700
800-562-2139
Fax: 845-373-6390
E-Mail: books@greyhouse.com
Home Page: www.greyhouse.com
Social Media: Facebook, Twitter
Leslie Mackenzie, Publisher
Richard Gottlieb, Editor
This new reference tool provides accurate financial strength ratings of the 7,800 credit unions in the United States.
Cost: $249.00
600 Pages
Frequency: Quarterly
Founded in 1981

9163 Weiss Ratings Guide to Health Insurers
Grey House Publishing
4919 Route 22
PO Box 56
Amenia, NY 12501
518-789-8700
800-562-2139
Fax: 845-373-6390
E-Mail: books@greyhouse.com
Home Page: www.greyhouse.com
Social Media: Facebook, Twitter
Leslie Mackenzie, Publisher
Richard Gottlieb, Editor
Weiss Ratings Guide to Health Insurers is the first and only source to cover the financial stability of the nation's health care system, rating the financial safety of more than 6,000 health maintenance organizations (HMOs) and all of the Blue Cross Blue Shield plans - updated quarterly to ensure the most accurate, up-to-date informations.
Cost: $249.00
600 Pages
Frequency: Quarterly
Founded in 1981

9164 Weiss Ratings Guide to Life & Annuity Insurers
Grey House Publishing
4919 Route 22
PO Box 56
Amenia, NY 12501
518-789-8700
800-562-2139
Fax: 845-373-6390
E-Mail: books@greyhouse.com
Home Page: www.greyhouse.com
Social Media: Facebook, Twitter
Leslie Mackenzie, Publisher
Richard Gottlieb, Edtior
Each easy-to-use edition provides independent, unbiased ratings on the financial strength of 1,000 life and annuity insurers, including companies providing life insurance, annuities, guaranteed investment contracts (GICs) and other pension products.
Cost: $249.00
600 Pages
Frequency: Quarterly
Founded in 1981

9165 Weiss Ratings Guide to Property & Casualty Insurers
Grey House Publishing
4919 Route 22
PO Box 56
Amenia, NY 12501
518-789-8700
800-562-2139
Fax: 845-373-6390
E-Mail: books@greyhouse.com
Home Page: www.greyhouse.com
Social Media: Facebook, Twitter
Leslie Mackenzie, Publisher
Richard Gottlieb, Editor
Updated quarterly, this publication is the only resource that provides independent, unbiased ratings and analyses on the 2,400 insurers offering auto & homeowners, business, worker's compensation, product liability, medical malpractice and other professional liability insurance in the United States.
Cost: $249.00
600 Pages
Frequency: Quarterly
Founded in 1981

9166 Who's Who in Economic Development Directory
International Economic Development Council (IEDC)
734 15th St NW
Suite 900
Washington, DC 20005-1013
202-223-7800
Fax: 202-223-4745
Home Page: www.iedconline.org
Jeffrey Finkle, CEO
Jon Roberts, Managing Director
Jackie Gibson, Project Manager
Charles Stein, Founder
A listing of over 2,500 Council members and other certified individuals. Directory is limited to international coverage.
200 Pages
Frequency: Annual

9167 Who's Who in Venture Capital
Grey House Publishing
4919 Route 22
PO Box 56
Amenia, NY 12501
518-789-8700
800-562-2139
Fax: 845-373-6390
E-Mail: books@greyhouse.com
Home Page: www.greyhouse.com
Social Media: Facebook, Twitter
Leslie Mackenzie, Publisher
Richard Gottlieb, Editor
Provides immediate access to nearly 10,000 principals, partners and managing directors heading the world's Venture Capital and Private Equity firms. The listings contain comprehensive profile information including partner and firm names, titles, education, professional background, directorships and full contact information.
Cost: $295.00
643 Pages
Founded in 1981

9168 World Emerging Stock Markets
Probus Publishing Company

1333 Burbridge Parkway
Burbridge, IL 60521

Directories of stock markets in Central and South America, Middle East and Europe.
Cost: $59.95

9169 **Yearbook of Education Finance**
American Education Finance Association
8365 S Armadillo Trail
Evergreen, CO 80439

303-674-0857
Fax: 303-670-8986
Home Page: www.aefa.cc

Ed Steinbecher, Executive Director

Information and updates for educational institutions and organizations regarding financial investing, prospecting and fundraising.
Frequency: Annual

Industry Web Sites

9170 **http://gold.greyhouse.com**
G.O.L.D Grey House OnLine Databases
Grey House Publishing's online database platform, GOLD, offers Quick Search, Keyword Search and Expert Search for most business sectors including financial services and banking markets. The GOLD platform makes finding the information you need quick and easy - whether you're a novice searcher or an experienced database user. All of Grey House's directory products are available for subscription on the GOLD platform.

9171 **www.aacei.org**
Association for Advancement of Cost Engineering
Association for those interested in the financial aspects of engineering all aspects of cost management.

9172 **www.aaii.com**
American Association of Individual Investors
An independent nonprofit corporation formed in 1978 for the purpose of assisting individuals in becoming effective managers of their own assets through programs of education, information and research.

9173 **www.abiworld.org**
American Bankruptcy Institute
Provides a multi-disiplinary, non-partisan organization dedicated to research and education on matters related to insolvency. Provides a forum for the exchange of ideas and information. ABI is engaged in numerous educational and research activities, as well as the production of a number of publications both for the insolvency practitioner and the public.

9174 **www.acainternational.org**
ACA International
Formerly know as the American Collectors Association, is the association of credit and collection professionals. Founded in 1939, it has over 5,300 members, including third party collection agencies, attorneys, credit grantors and vendor affiliates. Headquartered in Minneapolis, ACA serves members in the US and Canada plus 58 other countries worldwide.

9175 **www.aefa.org**
American Education Finance Association
Encourages communications among groups and individuals in education financial fields.

9176 **www.afponline.org**
Association for Financial Professionals
Association of 12,000 financial professionals.

9177 **www.afsaonline.com**
American Financial Services Association
National trade association for market funded providers of financial services to consumers and small businesses. These providers offer an array of finacial services, including unsecured personal loans, automobile loans, home equity loans and credit cards through specialized bank institutions.

9178 **www.agacgfm.org**
Association of Government Accountants
AGA is an educational association dedicated to enhancing public financial management by serving the professional interests of governmental managers and public accounting firms.

9179 **www.appraisalinstitute.org**
Appraisal Institute
Promotes a code of ethics and uniform standards of the real estate appraisal practice. Publishes periodicals, books and appraisal-related materials, and sponsors courses and seminars.

9180 **www.appraisers.org**
American Society of Appraisers
Professional association of appraisers of all kinds.

9181 **www.bcfm.com**
Broadcast Cable Financial Management Association
Professional association for TV, radio and cable CEOs, bueinss managers, HR, MIS controllers and financial personnel, as well as associate members in legal, audit and related fields.

9182 **www.bma.net.org**
Bank Marketing Association
Association for suppliers of industry related products and services.

9183 **www.communitycapital.org**
National Community Capital Association
Provides support for non-profit revolving loan funds that lend capital and offer technical assistance in distressed and disenfranchised communities.

9184 **www.dbcams.com**
FCSI Industry Web Sites
A resource for the financial industry, including stock exchanges, news, pricing services, research, information and more.

9185 **www.ecfa.org**
Evangelical Council for Financial Accountability
Helps Christ-centered organizations earn the public's trust through developing and maintaining standards of accountability that convey God-honoring ethical practices.

9186 **www.federalregister.com**
Neighborhood Reinvestment Corporation
Supplies training, grants, developmental assistance, and a range of other technical services designed to help the local partnerships achieve substantially self-reliant neighborhoods. The goal is to improve a neighborhood's housing and physical conditions, build a positive community image, and establish a healthy real estate market and a core of neighbors capable of managing the continued health of their neighborhood.

9187 **www.fei.org**
Financial Executives International
A professional organization of individuals performing the duties of C.F.O., Controller, Treasurer or Vice President of Finance.

9188 **www.financialratingsseries.com**
Grey House Publishing
Financial Ratings Series Online combines the strength of Weiss Ratings and TheStreet Ratings to offer the library community with a single source for financial strength ratings and financial planning tools covering Banks, Insurers, Mutual Funds and Stocks. This powerful database will provide the accurate, independent information consumers need to make informed decisions about their financial planning.

9189 **www.fma.org**
Financial Management Association
Strives to facilitate exchanges of ideas among persons in financial management.

9190 **www.fmsinc.org**
Financial Managers Society
Provides technical information and education to financial officers in banks, thrifts and credit unions.

9191 **www.globalpurchasing.org**
International Association of Purchasing Managers
A professional organization dedicated to the advancement of world trade, membership is open to buyers, purchasing managers, executives and all individuals that may be involved or have an interest in the important function of buying goods and services on the global market. A NON-PROFIT organization..

9192 **www.greenwood.com**
Greenwood Publishing Group
Business and professional publishing, academic books in Business, Finance, Business Law, and Applied Economics management.

9193 **www.greyhouse.com**
Grey House Publishing
Authoritative reference directories for most business sectors including financial services and banking markets. Users can search the online databases with varied search criteria allowing for custom searches by product category, geographic area, sales volume, keyword, subject and more. Full Grey House catalog and online ordering also available.

9194 **www.houisingfinance.org**
Int'l Union of Housing Finance Institutions
Disseminates information in housing finance policies and techniques worldwide.

9195 **www.iami.org**
National Association of Review Appraisers
Association for professionals who review real estate appraisals and underwrite real estate mortgagers. The association offers the CRA, Certified Review Appraiser and RMU, Registered Mortgage Underwriter, professional designation.

9196 **www.ici.org**
Investment Company Institute
Acts to represent members in matters of legislation, taxation, regulation, economic research and marketing and public information regarding investments and mutual funds.

9197 **www.investavenue.com**
Invest Avenue
Online magazine featuring articles from leading professionals in the finacial world, current news and analysis. Newsletter can be e-mailed on request.

9198 **www.invrecovery.org**
Investment Recovery Association
Association for manufacturers of services and supplies to the industry.

9199 **www.irrc.org**
Investor Responsibility Research Center
Acts to publish reports and analyses of social issues and public policy affecting corporation and investors.

9200 **www.kobren.com**
Mutual Fund Investors Association
Association for those interested in information and rates for mutual funds, investments, stocks and bonds.

9201 **www.marketresearch.com**
Research Reports
Search financial services reports from over 350 sources. Updated daily.

9202 **www.mfea.com**
Mutual Fund Education Alliance
Conducts public education and public relation activities in an effort to acquaint industry, organizations and government agencies with direct market funds.

9203 **www.mortgagepress.com**
National Mortgage Professional
Information on new products, industry news, personnel announcements and calendar of events.

9204 **www.nact.org**
National Association of Corporate Treasurers
Members are corporate chief financial officers, treasurers or assistant treasurers.

9205 **www.nadco.org**
National Association of Development Companies
Provides long-term fixed asset financing to small businesses.

9206 **www.nafa-us.org**
National Aircraft Finance Association
Members are lending institutions involved in aircraft financing.

9207 **www.nafcunet.org**
National Association of Federal Credit Unions
Association for manufacturers and suppliers of complete range of financial products and services.

9208 **www.nasbic.org**
Nat'l Assn of Small Business Investment Companies
Trade Association representing federally licensed ventures capital firms, Email, and business investment companies.

9209 **www.natptax.com**
National Association of Tax Professionals
The National Association of Tax Professionals (NATP) is a nonprofit association dedicated to excellence in taxation and related financial services. NATP was formed to serve professionals who work in all areas of tax practice. Members include Enrolled Agents, Certified Public Accountants, individual practitioners, accountants, attorneys, and financial planners.

9210 **www.nchffa.com**
National Council of Health Facilities Finance
To serve the common interests and enhance the effectiveness of member Authorities through communication, education and advocacy.

9211 **www.nfa.future.org**
National Futures Association
Association for corporations and firms that are registered with the Commodity Futures Trading Commission.

9212 **www.nfa.org**
National Finance Adjusters
Serves collateral recovery specialists.

9213 **www.nfma.org**
National Federation of Municipal Analysts
Promotes the profession of municipal credit analysts through educational programs, industry, communications and related programming.

9214 **www.nibesa.com**
National Independent Bank Equipment & Systems Assn
Association of financial security equipment nationwide. Annual convention and showcase and monthly newsletter.

9215 **www.nipa.org**
National Institute of Pension Administrators
Enhancing professionalism in the retirement plan industry through education.

9216 **www.nvca.org**
National Venture Capital Association
Corporations, corporate financiers and private individuals who invest private capital in young companies on a professional basis.

9217 **www.nvla.org**
National Vehicle Leasing Association
Fosters education, publishing, conferences, legal services, advancement and industry relations certification.

9218 **www.plunkettresearch.com/finance/index.htm**
Plunkett Research
Free section of company web site provides an synopsis of trends in the finacial industry and a glossary of terms.

9219 **www.securitytraders.org**
Security Traders Association
Serves the securities industry.

9220 **www.snl.com**
SNL Securities
News articles on banks and thrifts, insurance and other financial services. Also features vital company information.

9221 **www.theiia.org**
Institute of Internal Auditors
International organization composed of internal auditors, corporate executives and board members. Contact and current development information.

9222 **www.thestreet.com**
TheStreet Ratings, Inc.
Publisher of ratings guides.

9223 **www.uhab.org**
Urban Homesteading Assistance Board
Information on affordable housing and self reliance. Activities include advocacy, organizing, classroom and on-site training, direct technical assistance, development consulting, development and sponsorship of new co-ops and services to member co-ops that include bookkeeping, insurance, legal services, bulk purchasing, newsletters and IT services.

9224 **www.wsta.org**
Wall Street Technology Association
White papers on the latest in technology for IT professionals working in the finacial field. Resource guide for industry products and services and information on seminars and conferences included.

Associations

9225 **American Crappie Association**
125 Ruth Avenue
Benton, KY 42025

270-395-4204
Fax: 270-395-4381
E-Mail: office@crappieusa.com
Home Page: www.crappieusa.com
Social Media: Facebook

Darrell VanVactor, President
Charles Rogers, VP
Larry Crecelius, Public Relations Director
Jim Perry, Secretary/Treasurer
Dan Wagoner, Member

For all crappie anglers, from weekend fishermen to tournament pros. Influencing national manufacturers to produce more and better crappie fishing products, establishing a voice and lobby for crappie anglers everywhere and elevating the sport of crappie fishing to its rightful place in the limelight.
Cost: $20.00
Frequency: Individual Membership

9226 **American Fisheries Society**
5410 Grosvenor Ln
Suite 110
Bethesda, MD 20814

301-897-8616
Fax: 301-897-8096
E-Mail: sjohnston@fisheries.org
Home Page: www.fisheries.org
Social Media: Facebook, Twitter, vimeo, flickr

Bob Hughes, President
Donna L. Parrish, President-Elect
Ronald J. Essig, First Vice President
Joe Margraf, Second Vice President
John Boreman, Past President

AFS promotes scientific research and enlightened management of resources for optimum use and enjoyment by the public. It also encourages a comprehensive education for fisheries scientists and continuing on-the-job training
Cost: $100.00
8500 Members
Frequency: Membership Fee
Founded in 1870
Mailing list available for rent: 8500 names

9227 **American Fly Fishing Trade Association**
321 East Main St.
Suite 300
Bozeman, MO 59715

406-522-1556
Fax: 406-522-1557
Home Page: www.affta.com
Social Media: Facebook

Ben Bulis, President
Tucker Ladd, Chairman

A sole trade organization for the fly fishing industry. The mission is to promote the sustained growth of the fly fishing industry.
400 Members
Founded in 2003
Mailing list available for rent

9228 **American Institute of Fishery Research Biologists**
205 Blades Road
Havelock, NC 28532

Home Page: www.aifrb.org
Social Media: Facebook, Twitter, LinkedIn, Stumbleupon, www.digg.com

Steve Cadrin, President
Allen Shimada, Treasurer
Kathy Dickson, Secretary
Richard Beamish, Past President
Linda Jones, Past President

A professional organization founded to promote conservation and proper utilization of fishery resources through application of fishery science and related sciences.
1000 Members
Founded in 1956

9229 **American Littoral Society**
18 Hartshorne Drive
Suite #1
Highlands, NJ 7732

732-291-0055
Fax: 732-291-3551
E-Mail: driepe@nyc.rr.com
Home Page: www.littoralsociety.org
Social Media: Facebook, Twitter, Stumbleupon

Tim Dillingham, Executive Director
Eileen Kennedy, Deputy Director
Stevie Thorson, Education & Outreach Coordinator
Bill Shadel, Habitat Restoration Director
Jeff Dement, Fish Tagging Director

Dedicated to the environmental well-being of coastal habitat.
5000+ Members
Frequency: Membership Fee: $30-$35
Founded in 1961
Mailing list available for rent

9230 **American Shrimp Processors Association**
PO Box 4867
EIN #72-6029637
Biloxi, MS 39535

857-445-4165
Fax: 228-385-2565
E-Mail: info@fundraise.com
Home Page: www.fundraise.com
Social Media: Facebook, Twitter

Nate Drouin, CEO
Kurt Schneider, Chief Operating Officer
Kevin Bedell, Chief Technical Officer
Ivan Sifrim, UX Developer
Nick Alekhine, Developer

A non-profit trade organization designed to represent U.S. shrimp processors in all aspects of business. Allowing processors and related industries to work together to foster a business and technological climate in which its members can prosper while providing the highest quality product to its customers.
Founded in 1964

9231 **Association of Fish and Wildlife Agencies**
444 N Capitol St NW
Suite 725
Washington, DC 20001

202-624-7890
Fax: 202-624-7891
E-Mail: info@fishwildlife.org
Home Page: www.fishwildlife.org
Social Media: Facebook, Twitter

Carter Smith, Chairman
Dave Chanda, Vice Chairman
Dan Forster, President
Larry Voyles, Vice President
Glenn Normandeau, Secretary/Treasurer

The organization that represents all of North America's fish and wildlife agencies that promotes sound management ans conservation, and speaks with a unified voice on important fish and wildlife issues.
Founded in 1902

9232 **Association of Smoked Fish Processors**
c/o Shuster Labs
85 John Road
Canton, MA 02120

781-821-2200
800-444-8705
Fax: 781-821-9266
E-Mail: info@shusterlabs.com
Home Page: www.shusterlabs.com

Members are food processors with an interest in smoked fish.
Founded in 1963

9233 **Association of Zoos and Aquariums**
8403 Colesville Rd
Suite 710
Silver Spring, MD 20910-3314

301-562-0777
Fax: 301-562-0888
E-Mail: membership@aza.org
Home Page: www.aza.org
Social Media: Facebook, Twitter

Jackie Ogden, Chair
Dennis E. Pate, Chair-Elect
Steve Burns, Vice-Chair
Jim Breheny, Director
Lynn Clements, Director

A nonprofit organization dedicated to the advancement of accredited zoos and aquariums in the areas of animal care, wildlife conservation, education and science.
200 Members
Founded in 1924

9234 **At-Sea Processors Association**
4039 21st Ave W
Suite 400
Seattle, WA 98199

206-285-5139
Fax: 206-285-1841
Home Page: www.atsea.org

Stephanie Madsen, Executive Director
Paul MacGregor, General Counsel
Jim Gilmore, Public Affairs Director

A trade association representing seven copmanies that own and operate 19 U.S. flag cathcer/processor vessels that participate principally in the Alaska pollack fishery and west coast Pacific whiting fishery.
Cost: $500.00
7 Members
Frequency: Membership Fees Vary
Founded in 1985

9235 **Atlantic States Marine Fisheries Commission**
1050 N. Highland St.
Suite 200 A-N
Arlington, VA 22201

703-842-0740
Fax: 703-842-0741
E-Mail: info@asmfc.org
Home Page: www.asmfc.org
Social Media: Facebook, Twitter

Robert E. Beal, Executive Director
Tina L. Berger, Director of Communications
Deke Tompkins, Legislative Executive Assistant
Laura C. Leach, Director
Cecelia Butler, Human Resources Administrator

The commission was formed by the fifteen Atlantic coast states. It serves as a deliberative body, coordinating the conservation and management of the states shared near shore fishery resources.
45 Members
Founded in 1942

9236 **Bass Anglers Sportsman Society**
3500 Blue Lake Drive
Suite 330
Birmingham, AL 35243
334-272-9530
877-227-7872
Fax: 334-279-7148
E-Mail: bassmaster@emailcustomerservice.com
Home Page: www.bassmaster.com
Social Media: Facebook, Twitter
Dean Kassel, President
Chris Horton, Associate Director
A service organization for bass fishermen. It protecs and preserves the fishing environment, reports on the newest products and techniques, and provides an arena for professional and amateur fishing competitions.
Cost: $14.95
600M Members
Frequency: Annual Membership Fee
Founded in 1972

9237 **Blue Water Fishermen's Association**
PO Box 398
910 Bayview Avenue
Barnegat Light, NJ 08006
609-361-9229
Fax: 609-494-7210
E-Mail: bwfa@usa.net
Home Page: www.bwfa-usa.org
Social Media: Facebook, Twitter, LinkedIn, Stumbleupon
Nelson R Beideman, Executive Director
Non-profit organization of companies and individuals representing fishermen, Captains, vessel owners, docks, dealers, suppliers and related service businesses.
Founded in 1990

9238 **California Fisheries & Seafood Institute**
1521 I St
Sacramento, CA 95814
916-441-5560
Fax: 916-446-1063
E-Mail: fishead123@aol.com
Home Page: www.calseafood.net
Kevin Joyce, President
Dave Rudie, 1st Vice President
Steve Foltz, Treasurer
Sal Balestrieri, Vice President-Legislative
Kathleen Halson, Vice Presdient-Promotion
Regional trade organization representing members of the consumer seafood supply industry.
130+ Members
Founded in 1954

9239 **California Salmon Council**
PO Box 2255
Folsom, CA 95763-2255
916-933-7050
Fax: 916-933-7055
E-Mail: info@calkingsalmon.org
Home Page: www.calkingsalmon.org
Mike Stiller, Chairman
Jack Carlson, Vice-Chairman
Represents the marketing interests of California's commercial salmon fishermen. It creates consumer awareness and demand for California King Salmon.
Founded in 1989

9240 **Catfish Farmers of America**
1100 Highway 82 E
Suite 202
Indianola, MS 38751
662-887-2699
Fax: 662-887-6857
Home Page: www.catfishfarmersofamerica.org
Social Media: Facebook, Twitter
Hugh Warren, President
Represents the largest aquaculture industry in the United States. Represents the interests of farm-raised catfish industry of farmers, processors, feed mills, researchers and supplier industries.
Cost: $40.00
Frequency: Membership Fee
Founded in 1968

9241 **FishAmerica Foundation**
1001 North Fairfax St.
Suite 501
Alexandria, VA 22314
703-519-9691
Fax: 703-519-1872
E-Mail: fafgrants@asafishing.org
Home Page: www.fishamerica.org
Social Media: Facebook, Twitter, Youtube
Gregg Walner, Chairman
Dave Bulthuis, Vice Chairman
Donn Schaible, Secretary
Jim Hubbard, Treasurer
Jeff Marble, Immediate Past President
The sportfishing industry's trade association, committed to looking out for the interests of the entire sportfishing community.
650+ Members
Founded in 1962

9242 **Fishermen's Marketing Association**
1585 Heartwood Drive
Suite E
McKinleyville, CA 95519
707-840-0182
Fax: 707-840-0539
E-Mail: fma@trawl.org
Home Page: www.trawl.org
Peter Leipzig, Executive Director
Represents commercial groundfish and shrimp fishermen from San Pedro, California to Bellingham, Washington. The mission is to engage in activities which promote stable prices and an orderly flow of wholesome seafood to the consumer
60 Members
Founded in 1952

9243 **Fishing Vessel Owners Association**
4005 20th Ave W
Room 232
Seattle, WA 98199
206-284-4720
Fax: 206-283-3341
Home Page: www.fvoa.org
Eric Olsen, President
Per Odegaard, Vice-President
John Crowley, Secretary/Treasurer
Robert D. Alverson, Manager
Carol M. Batten, Executive Assistant
Trade association of longline vessel operators which promotes safety at sea, habitat-friendly gear with minimum bycatch and ensures competitive pricing.
Founded in 1914

9244 **Garden State Seafood Association**
212 W State St
Trenton, NJ 08608
609-898-1100
Fax: 609-898-6070
E-Mail: gregdidomenico@gardenstateseafood.org
Home Page: www.gardenstateseafoodassociation.com
Social Media: Facebook, Twitter
Ernie Panacek, President
Jeffrey Reichel, Vice-President
Greg DiDomenico, Executive Director
Dedicated to assure that New Jersey's marine resources are managed responsibly and are able to be enjoyed by anglers and seafood consumers for generations.
Founded in 1999

9245 **Great Lakes Fishery Commission**
2100 Commonwealth Blvd
Suite 100
Ann Arbor, MI 48105
734-662-3209
Fax: 734-741-2010
E-Mail: info@glfc.org
Home Page: www.glfc.int
Social Media: Facebook, Twitter
Michael Hansen, Chairman
Dale Burkett, Director
Steve Domeracki, Manager
Robert (Bob) Lambe, Executive Secretary
Ted Treska, Information Manager
The commission has two major responsibilities; to develop coordinated programs of research on the Great Lakes and to formulate and implement a program to eradicate or minimize sea lamprey populations in the Great Lakes.
Founded in 1955
Mailing list available for rent

9246 **Gulf and Caribbean Fisheries Institute (GCFI)**
2796 Overseas Highway
Suite 119
Marathon, FL 33050
305-289-2330
Fax: 305-289-2334
E-Mail: webmaster@gcfi.com
Home Page: www.gcfi.org
Social Media: Facebook
Bob Glazer, Chairman
LeRoy Creswell, Secretariat
Mel Goodwin, PhD, Treasurer
Provides information exchange among governmental, non-governmental, academic and commerical users of marine resources in the Gulf and Carribean Region
950 Members
Founded in 1947

9247 **Gulf of Mexico Fishery Management Council**
2203 N Lois Avenue
Suite 1100
Tampa, FL 33607
813-348-1630
888-833-1844
Fax: 813-348-1711
E-Mail: info@gulfcouncil.org
Home Page: www.gulfcouncil.org
Social Media: Facebook
Doug Gregory, Executive Director
Carrie Simons, Deputy Executive Director
Charlene Ponce, Public Information Officer
Cathy Readinger, Administrative Officer
Beth Hager, Financial Assistant
The council preserves fishery plans which are designed to manage fishery resources from where state waters end out to the 200 mile limit of the Gulf of Mexico.
Founded in 1976

9248 **International Institute of Fisheries Economics and Trade**
Dept of Agricultural & Resource Economic
Oregon State University
Corvallis, OR 97331-3601

541-737-1416
Fax: 541-737-2563
E-Mail: iifet@oregonstate.edu
Home Page: www.oregonstate.edu/dept/iifet

Ann L Shriver, Executive Director
Dr. Rebecca Metzner, President
Dr. Ralph Townsend, President-Elect
Kara Keenan, Assistant

An international group of economists, government managers, private industry members, and others interested in the exchange of research and information on marine resource issues. Founded to promote interaction and exchange between people from all countries and professional disciplines about marine resource economics and trade issues.
Founded in 1982

9249 **National Fisheries Institute**
7918 Jones Branch Dr
Suite 700
Mc Lean, VA 22102-3319

703-752-8890
Fax: 703-752-7583
E-Mail: admin@SIRFonline.org
Home Page: www.sirfonline.org
Social Media: Facebook, Twitter, LinkedIn

Russ Mentzer, Chairman
Eric Bloom, Director
Jim Bonnvie, Director
Pete Cardone, Director
Dan DiDonato, Director

Members are farmers, food processors and food distributors with an interest in aquaculture.
Founded in 1964

9250 **National Seafood Educators**
PO Box 6006
Richmond Beach, WA 98160

206-546-6410
Fax: 206-546-6411
E-Mail: Information@SeafoodEducators.com
Home Page: www.seafoodeducators.com

Evie Hansen, Founder

The goal is to educate and inform the public about the many health benefits of a seafood diet. National Seafood Educators has also consulted with many seafood retail businesses on how to sell, store and prepare wholesome seafood.
Founded in 1977

9251 **National Shellfisheries Association**
c/o US EPA, Atlantic Ecology Division
27 Tazewell Drive
Narragansett, RI 02880

631-653-6327
Fax: 631-653-6327
E-Mail: webmaster@shellfish.org
Home Page: www.shellfish.org

Christopher V. Davis, President
Karolyn Mueller Hansen, President-Elect
Marta Gomez-Chiarri, Vice-President
Steven Allen, Secretary
John Scarpa, Treasurer

An international organization of scientists, management officials and members of industry, all deeply concerned with the biology, ecology, production, economics and management of shellfish resources-clams, oysters, mussels, scallops, snails, shrimp, lobsters, crabs, among many other species of commercial importance.
Cost: $85.00
1000 Members
Frequency: Membership Fee
Founded in 1908

9252 **North Carolina Fisheries Association**
PO Box 335
Bayboro, NC 28515-0335

252-745-0225
Fax: 252-745-0258
E-Mail: peggy@ncfish.org
Home Page: www.ncfish.org

Billy Carl Tillett, Chairman
Sherrill Styron, Vice Chairman
Sean McKeon, President
Leslie Daniels, Treasurer

Non-profit trade organization created to facilitate the promotion of North Carolina families, heritage and seafood through accessible data about the commercial fishing industry. NCFA lobbies Local, State, and Federal legislators and engages in a wide scope of public awareness projects.
Founded in 1952

9253 **Pacific Coast Federation of Fishermen's Association**
Building 991, Marine Drive
PO Box 29370
San Francisco, CA 94129-0370

415-561-5080
Fax: 415-561-5464
E-Mail: fish1ifr@aol.com
Home Page: www.pcffa.org

Zeke Grader, Executive Director
David Bitts, President
Vivian Helliwell, Watershed Conservation Director

Commercial fishermen's organizations from California to Alaska. Works to prevent and improve the resources of the commercial fishing industry, protect rivers from herbicide and pesticide applications that may threaten salmon populations, maintain activity within the industry, regain local control over fisheries management.
22 Members
Founded in 1976

9254 **Pacific Seafood Processors Association**
1900 West Emerson Place
Suite 205
Seattle, WA 98119

206-281-1667
Fax: 206-283-2387
E-Mail: info@pspafish.net
Home Page: www.pspafish.net

Glenn Reed, President
Nancy Diaz, Administrative Assistant

Trade association to foster a better public understanding of the seafood industry and its value to the regional and national economies.
25 Members
Founded in 1914

9255 **Recreational Fishing Alliance**
Po Box 3080
New Gretna, NJ 08224

609-404-1060
888-564-6732
Fax: 609-294-3812
Home Page: www.joinrfa.org

Jim Donofrio, Executive Director
Jim Hutchinson Jr, Managing Director
Kim Forgach, Administrative Assistant
Gary Caputi, Corporate Relations Director

An organization that supports and fights back against federal government state legislatures impose unreasonable restrictions on our ability to enjoy recreational fishing.
Frequency: $35/Membership

9256 **Southeastern Fisheries Association**
1118-B Thomasville Rd.
Tallahassee, FL 32303

850-224-0612
Fax: 850-222-3663
Home Page: www.seafoodsustainability.us

Bob Jones, Executive Director

To defend, preserve and enhance the commercial fishing industry in the southeastern United States for present participants as well as future generations through all legal means.
Founded in 1952

9257 **West Coast Seafood Processors Association**
1618 SW 1st Ave
Suite 318
Portland, OR 97201

503-227-5076
Fax: 503-296-2824
E-Mail: wcseafood@comcast.net
Home Page: www.wcspa.com

Rod Moore, Executive Director

Serves the needs of the shore-based seafood processors in California, Oregon and Washington, helping them to face and survive economic, environmental and regulatory challenges.
13 Members

9258 **Women's Fisheries Network**
2442 NW Market Street
#243
Seattle, WA 98107

206-789-1987
Fax: 206-789-1987
Home Page: www.fis.com/wfn

Stephanie Madsen, President

Men and women dedicated to education of issues confronting the fishing and seafood industry.
2000 Members
Founded in 1993

Newsletters

9259 **American Sportfishing**
American Sportfishing Association
1001 North Fairfax Street
Suite 501
Alexandria, VA 22314

703-519-9691
Fax: 703-519-1872
E-Mail: info@asafishing.org
Home Page: www.asafishing.org
Social Media: Facebook

Mike Nussman, President/CEO
Joyce Anderson-Logan, Executive Assistant
Gordon Robertson, Vice President
Diane Carpenter, Chief Financial Officer

Provides a broader view of the activities of ASA and our partners. Includes information about industry news, events, perspectives and trends that affect the sportfishing community.
Frequency: Bi-Monthly

9260 **Aquaculture North America**
Capamara Communications
815 1st Ave
#301
Seattle, WA 98104

250-474-3982
800-936-2266

Fax: 250-478-3979
E-Mail: jeremy@capamara.com
Home Page: www.naqua.com

Peter Chetteburgh, Editor-in-Chief
Jeremy Thain, Sales Manager
James Lewis, Production Department

Follows the trends, issues, people and events that have set the pace for the fastest growing agribusiness sector on the continent. Coverage is relevant to all finfish and shellfish species grown in North America plus special reports from other regions around the world.
Cost: $27.95
Frequency: Bi-monthly
Circulation: 4000
Founded in 1985

9261 Briefs
American Institute of Fishery Research Biologists
205 Blades Road
Havelock, NC 28532

Home Page: www.aifrb.org

John Butler, Editor
John Merriner, Production Editor

It is intended to communicate the professional activities and accomplishments of the Institute, its District, and Members; the results of research; the effects of management; unusual biological events; matters affecting the profession; political problems and other matters of importance to the fishery community.
Frequency: Bi-Monthly

9262 Commercial Fisheries News
Compass Publications
Deer Isle, ME

800-989-5253
Fax: 207-348-1059
E-Mail: comfish@fish-news.com
Home Page: www.fish-news.com

Richard W Martin, Publisher
Susan Jones, Editor

Provides the latest waterfront news along with coverage of the state and federal rules and regulations affecting the harvest of all the region's major species. Regular features include lobster and fish market reports, a safety column, new boats, the enforcement report, and the popular and effective classifieds section.
Cost: $21.95
72 Pages
Frequency: Monthly
Circulation: 9223
ISSN: 0273-6713
Founded in 1978
Printed in 4 colors on n stock

9263 Crow's Nest
Casamar Group/Holdings
8082 Firethorn Lane
Las Vegas, NV 89123

702-792-6868
Fax: 702-792-6668
E-Mail: casamarholdings@casamarintl.com
Home Page:
www.casamarintl.com/CrowsNest/CrowsNest.html

Malu Marigomen, Executive Director

An in-depth report on the status of the Tuna Industry
Frequency: Monthly

9264 Currents
Women's Fisheries Network
2422 NW Market Square
Seattle, WA 98107

206-789-1987
Fax: 206-789-1987
Home Page: www.fis.com/wfn

Debbie Slotivg, Editor
Ron Gawith, Owner

Features current topics in fisheries, members'activities, upcoming events and chapter reports.
Frequency: Monthly

9265 Fish Farming News
Compass Publications
Deer Isle, ME

800-989-5253
Fax: 207-348-1059
E-Mail: comfish@fish-news.com
Home Page: www.fish-news.com

Richard W Martin, Publisher
Susan Jones, Editor

The business newspaper for the U.S. aquaculture industry. Readers are aquaculture professionals who are directly or indirectly involved in the business of growing fish and seafood products. Encompassing all major farm raised species (finfish, shellfish and aquatic plants) both marine (saltwater) and fresh water aquaculture.
Cost: $21.95
72 Pages
Frequency: Monthly
Circulation: 9223
ISSN: 0273-6713
Founded in 1978
Printed in 4 colors on n stock

9266 Fishermen's News
PCFFA
Building 991, Marine Drive
PO Box 29370
San Francisco, CA 94129-0370

415-561-5080
Fax: 415-561-5464
E-Mail: fish1ifr@aol.com
Home Page: www.pcffa.org

Zeke Grader, Executive Director
Chuck Wise, President

Oldest publication in the west coast commercial fishing industry. Deals with resource protection and policy issues of great importance to the fishing industry, as well as with critical Congressional issues which affect us all.
22 Members
Founded in 1976

9267 IIFET Newsletter
International Institute of Fisheries Economics
Dept of Agricultural & Resource Economic
Oregon State University
Corvallis, OR 97331-3601

541-737-1439
Fax: 541-737-2563
E-Mail: iifet@oregonstate.edu
Home Page: www.oregonstate.edu/dept/iifet

Provides conference listings, news items, and information on new publications and the activities of members.
20 Pages
Frequency: Semi-Annual
ISSN: 1048-9509

9268 Littorally Speaking
American Littoral Society Northeast Chapter
28 W 9th Rd
Broad Channel, NY 11693-1112

718-318-9344
Fax: 718-318-9345
E-Mail: driepe@nyc.rr.com
Home Page: www.alsnyc.org

Don Riepe, Executive Director

A digest of environmental concerns

9269 Makin' Waves Quarterly Newsletter
Recreational Fishing Alliance
PO Box 3080
New Gretna, NJ 08224

609-404-1060
888-564-6732
Fax: 609-294-3812
Home Page: www.joinrfa.org

James Donofrio, Executive Director
Gary Caputi, Corporate Relations Director
Courtney Howell Thompson, Marketing Coordinator/PR

This RFA paper has proven that fish and fishermen are not the only variables in the equation of fisheries management.
Frequency: $35/Membership

9270 NSA Newsletter
National Shellfisheries Association
c/o US EPA, Atlantic Ecology Division
27 Tazewell Drive
Narragansett, RI 02880

401-782-3155
Fax: 401-782-3030
E-Mail: news@shellfish.org
Home Page: www.shellfish.org

Dr Evan Ward, Editor

Current issues and concerns in shellfish research and in the shellfish industry, including details regarding upcoming meetings, employment listings, and gossip items for our Metamorphoses column.

9271 National Shellfisheries Association Quarterly Newsletter
National Shellfisheries Association
C/O US EPA, Atlantic Ecology Division
27 Tazewell Drive
Narragansett, RI 02880

631-653-6327
Fax: 631-653-6327
Home Page: www.shellfish.org

R. LeRoy Creswell, President
Christopher V. Davis, President-Elect
George E. Flimlin, VP & Program Chair
Marta Gomez-Chiarri, Secretary

An informative newsletter for the shellfish industry, shellfish managers and shellfish researchers.
Cost: $85.00
1000 Members
Frequency: Membership Fee
Founded in 1908

9272 PSPA Update
Pacific Seafood Processors Association
1900 W Emerson Pl
Suite 205
Seattle, WA 98119-1649

206-281-1667
Fax: 206-283-2387
E-Mail: info@pspafish.net
Home Page: www.pspafish.net

Glenn Reed, President

Daily news update for major seafood processing companies with operations in Alaska and Washington.
25 Members
Founded in 1914

9273 Tradewinds
North Carolina Fisheries Association

PO Box 12303
New Bern, NC 28561

252-633-2288
Fax: 252-633-9616
E-Mail: peggy@ncfish.org
Home Page: www.ncfish.org

Sean McKeon, President
Peggy C Page, Bookkeeper

Members only newspaper, which includes special bulletins regarding legislative issues and various articles concerning fisheries issues.
24 Pages
Frequency: Bi-Monthly

9274 **Wheel Watch**
Fishing Vessel Owners Association
4005 20th Ave W
Room 232, West Wall Bldg
Seattle, WA 98199-1273

206-284-4720
Fax: 206-283-3341
Home Page: www.fvoa.org

Robert D. Alverson, Manager
Carol M. Batteen, Executive Assistant

Brings you up-to-date with regards to action of the Halibut Commission, North Pacific Council, Pacific Council, and market information.
Frequency: Quarterly

Magazines & Journals

9275 **Aquaculture North America**
Capamara Communications
PO Box 1409
Arden, NC 28704

250-474-3982
877-687-0011
Fax: 250-478-3979
Home Page: aquaculturenorthamerica.com

Gregory J Gallagher, Editor/Publisher
Rebekah Craig, Circulation Manager
Brenda Jo McManama, Advertising/Sales

Earning the respect of aquaculture industry professionals throughout the world who hold its trade publications in high regard.
Cost: $24.00
96 Pages
Frequency: Annually/Summer
Circulation: 5000
ISSN: 0199-1388
Founded in 1968

9276 **Atlantic Fisherman**
Advocate Media Publishing
181 Brown's Point Road
Nova Scotia B0K-1H0

902-485-1990
800-236-9526
Fax: 902-485-6353
Home Page: www.atlanticfisherman.com
Social Media: Twitter

Susan Purdy, Publications Manager

Provides news for the commercial fisherman in the four Atlantic provinces of Canada. Includes prespectives from the unions, the government and the fishermen themselves.
Cost: $16.00
Frequency: Monthly
Circulation: 9950

9277 **Bass Times**
Bass Anglers Sportsman Society
3500 Blue Lake Drive
Suite 330
Birmingham, AL 35243

334-272-9530
877-227-7872
Fax: 334-279-7148
Home Page: www.bassmaster.com
Social Media: Facebook, Twitter

Dean Kassel, President
Chris Horton, Associate Director

Each issue includes; detailed, in-depth tips & techniques, bass biology, conservation news, BASS Federation Nation news, Bassmaster Tournament Trail coverage, and Legislation coverage.
Cost: $14.95
600M Members
Frequency: Annual Membership Fee
Founded in 1972

9278 **Catfish Journal**
Catfish Farmers of America
6311 Ridgewood Road
Suite W404
Jackson, MS 39211

601-977-9559
Fax: 601-977-9632
E-Mail: info@catfishinstitute.com
Home Page: www.uscatfish.com
Social Media: Facebook, Twitter

Mike McCall, Editor
Sandra Goff, Production Manager

News on catfish production, processing, feed manufacturing and research.
Frequency: Monthly

9279 **Connect Magazine**
American Zoo and Aquarium Association
8403 Colesville Rd
Suite 710
Silver Spring, MD 20910-6331

301-562-0777
Fax: 301-562-0888
Home Page: www.aza.org

Jim Maddy, Executive Director
Kris Vehrs, Executive Director
Muri Dueppen, Marketing

For the professional zoo and aquarium world. This magazine features fascinating stories that explore trends, educational initiatives, member achievements and conservation efforts.
200 Members
Frequency: Monthly
Circulation: 6000

9280 **Esox Angler**
Esox Angler
PO Box 895
Hayward, WI 54843

715-638-2311
E-Mail: info@esoxangler.com
Home Page: www.esoxangler.com

Jack Burns, Senior Editor
Rob Kimm, Editor

A muskie and pike magazine for the world's muskie and pike anglers. Articles focusing on proven techniques and new ideas from top name anglers, as well as regular guys who are catching lots of fish.

9281 **Fish Sniffer**
3201 Eastwood Road
Sacramento, CA 95821

916-685-2245
Fax: 916 685-1498
E-Mail: danielbacher@fishsniffer.com
Home Page: www.fishsniffer.com
Social Media: Facebook

Dan Bacher, Editor
Cal Kellogg, Associate Editor

Current fishing reports, weather conditions, fishing news, photos, boats for sale, what and where to fish and much more.
Cost: $29.00
Frequency: Bi-Weekly

9282 **Fisheries**
American Fisheries Society
5410 Grosvenor Ln
Suite 110
Bethesda, MD 20814-2199

301-897-8616
Fax: 301-897-8096
Home Page: www.fisheries.org
Social Media: Facebook, Twitter

Gus Rassam, Executive Director
Myra Merritt, Office Administrator

Peer reviewed articles that address contemporary issues and problems, techniques, philosophies and other areas of interest to the general fisheries profession. Monthly features include letters, meeting notices, book listings and reviews, environmental essays and organization profiles.
Cost: $106.00
50 Pages
Frequency: Monthly
Circulation: 9800
Founded in 1870
Mailing list available for rent: 8500 names at $250 per M

9283 **Fishermen's News**
Philips Publishing Group
2201 W Commodore Way
Seattle, WA 98199-1298

206-284-8285
Fax: 206-284-0391
E-Mail: circulation@rhppublishing.com
Home Page: www.pacmar.com

Peter Philips, Publisher
Lisa Albers, Editor
Maggie Cheung, Circulatiom Manager

Covers commercial fishing activity, market trends, gear and boat building news, political news and financial matters related to the industry.
Founded in 1945

9284 **Fly Fisherman**
InterMedia Outdoors Inc
PO Box 420235
Palm Coast, FL 32142-0235

212-852-6600
Home Page: www.flyfisherman.com
Social Media: Facebook, Twitter

Jeff Paro, President

From the deepest bass ponds, wildest rivers or abundant saltwater flats, America's fishing sportsmen rely on this magazine to provide them with the newest techniques, tools and tips whenever and wherever they need this information.
Cost: $19.95
Frequency: Annually
Founded in 1969

9285 **IAFWA Proceedings**
International Association of Fish and Wildlife
444 N Capitol St NW
Suite 725
Washington, DC 20001-1553

202-638-7999
Fax: 202-638-7291
E-Mail: info@iafwa.org
Home Page: www.statenet.com

Wayne Muhlstein, VP
Eric Schwaab, Resource Director

Reports on the business transacted by the Association at its March meeting held in conjunction with the North American Wildlife and Natural Resources Conference and at its September annual conference.

9286 **In-Fisherman**
InterMedia Outdoors Inc

PO Box 420235
Palm Coast, FL 420235

218-829-1648
E-Mail: ross.purnell@imoutdoors.com
Home Page: www.in-fisherman.com
Social Media: Facebook, Twitter

Ross Purnell, Editor

Written for the avid freshwater angler. In each issue, you'll find detailed instructions and demonstrations on catching, cleaning, and eating your favorite species of fish, and reports on the latest scientific studies concerning fish and habitat conservation.
Cost: $12.00
Frequency: 8x/year
Founded in 1975

9287 **Island Fisherman**
610 Azalea Place
Campbell River
BC Canada V9W 7H2

250-923-0939
E-Mail: ifmm@shaw.ca
Home Page:
www.islandfishermanmagazine.com

Larry E Stefanyk, Founder/Publisher
Bob Jones, Editor

Covering the west coast of British Columbia from the Queen Charlottes to Victoria on Vancouver Island. Covering saltwater and freshwater fishing with how to and where to tips to help you find the big one or just experience what the west coast of British Columbia has to offer.
Cost: $40.00
Frequency: Monthly
Founded in 2001

9288 **Journal of Aquatic Animal Health**
American Fisheries Society
5410 Grosvenor Ln
Suite 110
Bethesda, MD 20814-2199

301-897-8616
Fax: 301-897-8096
Home Page: www.fisheries.org
Social Media: Facebook, Twitter

Bill Fisher, President
John Boreman, President-Elect
Bob Hughes, First Vice President
Donna Parrish, Second Vice President

International journal publishing original research on diseases affecting aquatic life, including effects, treatments and prevention.
Cost: $100.00
8500 Members
Frequency: Membership Fee
Founded in 1870

9289 **Marine and Coastal Fisheries: Dynamics, Management, and Ecosystem Science**
American Fisheries Society
5410 Grosvenor Ln
Suite 110
Bethesda, MD 20814-2199

301-897-8616
Fax: 301-897-8096
Home Page: www.fisheries.org
Social Media: Facebook, Twitter

Bill Fisher, President
John Boreman, President-Elect
Bob Hughes, First Vice President
Donna Parrish, Second Vice President

Online publication focusing on marine, coastal, and estuarine fisheries.
Cost: $100.00
8500 Members
Frequency: Membership Fee
Founded in 1870

9290 **Marlin**
World Publications
460 N Orlando Avenue
Suite 200
Winter Park, FL 32789

407-628-4802
Fax: 407-628-7061
Home Page:
www.marlinmag.com/www.worldpub.net

Dave Ferrell, Editor
Glen Hughes, Group Publisher
Terry Snow, Owner

The bible for big-game fishermen. It is written for the most affluent anglers who need to know what is happening around the world regarding offshore fishing. It is the who's who of the sport, written in the voice of the sportfisherman, one-on-one to a peer, as a member of this elite fraternity. Marlin magazine will continue to be the No. 1 buy in big-game fishing by delivering the best targeted edit to the wealthiest boat-owning saltwater fishermen in the world.
Cost: $24.95
Frequency: 8x/year
Circulation: 40,000

9291 **National Fisherman**
Diversified Business Communications
Po Box 7437
Portland, ME 04112-7437

207-842-5600
Fax: 207-842-5503
E-Mail: editor@nationalfisherman.com
Home Page: www.nationalfisherman.com
Social Media: Facebook, Twitter

Nancy Hasselback, President/CEO
Lincoln Bedrosian, Senior Editor

Regional coverage of boats, fishing gear, environmental developments, technology, new products, and fishery resource information
Cost: $19.95
Frequency: Monthly
Circulation: 38,000
Founded in 1903

9292 **North American Journal of Aquaculture**
American Fisheries Society
5410 Grosvenor Ln
Suite 110
Bethesda, MD 20814-2199

301-897-8616
Fax: 301-897-8096
Home Page: www.fisheries.org
Social Media: Facebook, Twitter

Gus Rassam, Executive Director
Myra Merritt, Office Administrator

Publishes research in all areas of fish culture.
Cost: $38.00
Frequency: Quarterly
ISSN: 1548-8454

9293 **North American Journal of Fisheries Management**
American Fisheries Society
5410 Grosvenor Ln
Suite 110
Bethesda, MD 20814-2199

301-897-8616
Fax: 301-897-8096
Home Page: www.fisheries.org
Social Media: Facebook, Twitter

Bill Fisher, President
John Boreman, President-Elect
Bob Hughes, First Vice President
Donna Parrish, Second Vice President

Promotes communication among managers. Published with a focus on maintenance, enhancement, and allocation of resources.
Cost: $100.00
8500 Members
Frequency: Membership Fee
Founded in 1870

9294 **Outdoor Journal**
American Crappie Association
125 Ruth Avenue
Benton, KY 42025

270-395-4204
Fax: 270-395-4381
E-Mail: office@crappieusa.com
Home Page: www.crappieusa.com

Darrell VanVactor, President
Larry Crecelius, Public Relations Director

Features news and updates on memberships, events, tournaments, and more for crappie anglers from amateurs to professionals.
Frequency: Annually
Circulation: 60000

9295 **Pacific Fishing**
Pacific Fishing
1000 Andover Park E
Seattle, WA 98188-7632

206-324-5644
Fax: 206-324-8939
Home Page: www.pacificfishing.com

Michael Daigle, Owner
Jon Holland, Editor
Duane Brady, es & Marketing Manager

Serving owners and operators of commercial fishing boats throughout the world's most productive ocean, from Alaska to the tropical Pacific. Our readers also include crew members, processors, fisheries managers, suppliers, seafood brokers and distributors, educators, and others who want serious information about the business of hauling up food from the Pacific.
Cost: $15.00
Frequency: Monthly
Circulation: 7160
Founded in 1980

9296 **SaltWater**
Time, Inc.
2 Park Avenue
New York, NY 10016

212-221-1212
Fax: 212-779-5999
E-Mail: editor@saltwatersportsman.com
Home Page: www.saltwatersportsman.com

David DiBenedetto, Editor
Gerald Bethge, Executive Editor
Jason Y Wood, Managing Editor
Karl Anderson, Senior Editor

A publication on salt-water sport fishing. Each monthly issue contains exciting feature stories, columns, award-winning color photos covering both big- and small-game fishing, the newest techniques, tackle, boats and equipment, and the latest developments in conservation and fishery management.
Founded in 1939

9297 **Saltwater Sportsman**
World Publications
460 N Orlando Avenue
Suite 200
Winter Park, FL 32789

407-628-4802
Fax: 407-628-7061
Home Page:
www.marlinmag.com/www.worldpub.net
Social Media: Facebook, Twitter

Dave Ferrell, Editor
Glen Hughes, Group Publisher
Terry Snow, Owner

Designed for serious recreational salt water fishermen who demand the most accurate and

detailed information available on inshore and offshore fishing from boats. Articles cover the entire spectrum of boat and tackle rigging, tactics and methods for catching game fish, travel, boat and equipment reviews, U.S. regional/ local coverage, and fisheries management and conservation.
Cost: $24.95
Frequency: 8x/year
Circulation: 40,000

9298 **Sea Technology Magazine**
Compass Publications, Inc.
1501 Wilson Blvd
Suite 1001
Arlington, VA 22209-2403

703-524-3136
Fax: 703-841-0852
E-Mail: oceanbiz@sea-technology.com
Home Page: www.sea-technology.com
Social Media: Twitter

Amos Bussmann, President/Publisher
Joy Carter, Circulation Manager
Meghan Ventura, Managing Editor

Worldwide information leader for marine/offshore business, science and engineering. Read in more than 110 countries by management, engineers, scientists and technical personnel working in industry, government and education.
Cost: $40.00
Frequency: Monthly
Circulation: 16304
ISSN: 0093-3651
Founded in 1960
Mailing list available for rentat $80 per M
Printed in 4 colors

9299 **Seafood Business**
Diversified Business Communications
121 Free Street
PO Box 7438
Portland, ME 04112-7437

207-842-5542
E-Mail: mlarkin@divcom.com
Home Page: www.seafoodbusiness.com
Social Media: Facebook, Twitter, LinkedIn

Mary Larkin, Publisher
Fiona Robinson, Associate Publisher, Editor
James Wright, Associate Editor
Melissa Wood, Assistant Editor

Focuses on the business of buying and selling seafood and provides seafood buyers with the tools and analysis they need to make educated safood buying decisions.
Frequency: Monthly
Circulation: 15,000
Founded in 1982

9300 **Sport Fishing**
World Publications
460 N Orlando Avenue
Winter Park, FL 32789

407-628-4802
Fax: 407-628-7061
E-Mail: editor@sportfishingmag.com
Home Page: www.sportfishingmag.com
Social Media: Facebook, Twitter

Glenn Hughes, Group Publisher
Bruce Miller, Circulation VP
Terry Snow, Owner

Written for the passionate angler who must have in-depth, cutting-edge information on the latest techniques, the hottest locations and the newest equipment to maximize his day on the water, Sport Fishing magazine is the source for saltwater fishing information.
Cost: $19.97
Frequency: 10x/year
Circulation: 150,000
Founded in 2001

9301 **The Fisherman**
326 12th Street
1st Floor
New Westminster, BC V3M-4H6

604-669-5569
Fax: 604-688-1142
E-Mail: fisherman@ufawu.org
Home Page: www.thefisherman.ca
Social Media: Facebook, Twitter, YouTube

Sean Griffin, Editor
Suzanne Thomson, Advertising Manager

Covering saltwater and freshwater fishing from Maine through Delaware Bay. Local fishing reports.
Frequency: Monthly
Circulation: 8000

9302 **Transactions of the American Fisheries Society**
American Fisheries Society
5410 Grosvenor Ln
Suite 110
Bethesda, MD 20814-2199

301-897-8616
Fax: 301-897-8096
Home Page: www.fisheries.org

Gus Rassam, Executive Director
Myra Merritt, Office Administrator

The Society's highly regarded international journal of fisheries science features results of basic and applied research in genetics, physiology, biology, ecology, population dynamics, economics, health, culture, and other topics germane to marine and freshwater finfish and shellfish and their respective fisheries and environments
Cost: $43.00
Frequency: Bi-Monthly
ISSN: 0002-8487
Founded in 1872

Trade Shows

9303 **ASA Sportfishing Summit**
American Sportfishing Association
225 Reinekers Lane
Suite 420
Alexandria, VA 22314

703-519-9691
Fax: 703-519-1872
E-Mail: info@asafishing.org
Home Page: www.asafishing.org

Mary Jane Williamson, Communications Director
Amy Yohanes, Administrative Services Manager

Membership meeting and premier networking event. From special sessions, to busiess workshops to association committee meeting, the Summit provides a wide-range of opportunities to gain information on the most relevant issues facing the sportfishing industry.
Frequency: October

9304 **ASA/Eastern Fishing & Outdoor Exposition**
American Sportfishing Association
1001 North Fairfax Street
Suite 501
Alexandria, VA 22314

703-519-9691
Fax: 703-519-1872
E-Mail: info@asafishing.org
Home Page: www.asafishing.org
Social Media: Facebook

Mike Nussman, President/CEO
Joyce Anderson-Logan, Executive Assistant
Gordon Robertson, Vice President
Diane Carpenter, Chief Financial Officer

The finest sportsmen's expos on the East Coast. The best outdoor gear, accessories and resources for fishing, boating, hunting, adventure and travel are available at these shows. The only sport shows where 100 percent of the proceeds go to safeguarding and promoting the enduring social, economic and conservation values of America's outdoor heritage.
Frequency: Bi-Monthly

9305 **AZA Regional Conference**
American Zoo and Aquarium Association
8403 Colesville Road
Suite 710
Silver Spring, MD 20910-3314

301-562-0777
Fax: 301-562-0888
Home Page: www.aza.org

Jim Maddy, President
Kris Vehrs, Executive Director
Jill Nicoll, Marketing

Exhibits, workshops and discussions about the industry.
200 Members
Founded in 1924

9306 **Annual Fish Baron's Ball**
North Carolina Fisheries Association
PO Box 12303
New Bern, NC 28561

252-745-0225
Fax: 252-633-9616
E-Mail: peggy@ncfish.org
Home Page: www.ncfish.org

Billy Carl Tillett, Chairman
Sherrill Styron, Vice Chairman
Sean McKeon, President
Janice Smith, Treasurer

Attendees getting together for an evening of great seafood and fun, and participate in the silent auction. Program proceeds go toward Association-related activities.
Founded in 1952

9307 **CFA Fish Farming Trade Show**
Catfish Farmers of America
1100 Highway 82 E
Suite 202
Indianola, MS 38751

662-887-2699
Fax: 662-887-6857
Home Page: www.catfishfarmersamerica.org

America's largest fish farming equipment expo.
Frequency: February

9308 **Catfish Farmers of America Annual Convention & Research Symposium**
Catfish Farmers of America
1100 Highway 82 E
Suite 202
Indianola, MS 38751-2251

662-887-2699
Fax: 662-887-6857
Home Page: www.catfishfarmersofamerica.org

Hugh Warren, President

Opportunity to launch new products, meet new buyers, learn emerging trends and access the North American seafood market.
Frequency: Membership Fee
Founded in 1968

9309 **Eastern Fishing & Outdoor Expo**
Eastern Fishing & Outdoor Expositions
PO Box 4720
Portsmouth, NH 00380

603-431-4315
Fax: 603-431-1971

E-Mail: info@sportshows.com
Home Page: www.sportshows.com

Paul Fuller, President/Show Director
Judy L Chapman, Assistant Show Director

Partnership with American Sportfishing Association. Exhibitors representing the entire spectrum of saltwater sportfishing. This includes inshore to offshore, light tackle to big-game tackle, and everything in between. Fishermen will see and touch the latest from major tackle manufacturers and buy the latest tackle from local retailers at special show prices.

9310 **Fish Expo Workboat Atlantic**
National Fisherman/Diversified Bus. Communications
121 Free Street
PO Box 7437
Portland, ME 04112

207-425-5608
Fax: 207-842-5509
E-Mail: fewa@divcom.com
Home Page: www.fishexpoatlantic.com

Bob Callahan, Show Director
Heather Palmeter, Show Coordinator

Newest products and technology, attend free seminars and workshops, talk to technical experts, and find the best deals on equipment and gear.
6,000 Attendees
Frequency: April

9311 **Fly-Fishing Retailer World Trade Expo**
VNU Expositions/Business Media
770 Broadway
New York, NY 10003

646-545-5100
Home Page:
www.fly-fishing-retailer.com/www.vnubusinessmedia.com

Andy Tompkins, Show Director
Peter Devin, Group Show Director

Where brands are launched, innovations are unveiled and connections are made. Designed for the specialty fly-fishing industry, Fly-Fishing Retailer World Trade Expo connects a targeted audience to conduct business in a professional yet friendly atmosphere.
Frequency: August
Founded in 1998

9312 **IAFWA Annual Meeting**
International Association of Fish and Wildlife
444 North Capitol Street NW
Suite 725
Washington, DC 20001

202-624-7890
Fax: 202-624-7891
Home Page: www.fishwildlife.org

Gary T Myers, Executive Director
Cindy Delaney, Meetings Coordinator
Wayne Muhlstein, VP

Providing many opportunities to hear from our nation's wildlife conservation leaders, partners, and management experts. The meeting is our response to the need for national consensus on state-by-state fish and wildlife management issues.
250 Attendees
Frequency: September

9313 **ICAST**
American Sportfishing Association
225 Reinekers Lane
Suite 420
Alexandria, VA 22314

703-519-9691
Fax: 703-519-1872
E-Mail: mdelvalle@asafishing.org
Home Page: www.asafishing.org

Maria del Valle, ICAST Director
Kenneth Andres, ICAST Associate

The sportfishing industry's largest trade event is a major catalyst for sales and a terrific networking opportunity for the sportfishing community.

9314 **IIFET Biennial International Conference**
IIFET
Dept of Agricultural & Resource Economic
Oregon State University
Corvallis, OR 97331-3601

541-737-1416
Fax: 541-737-2563
E-Mail: iifet@oregonstate.edu
Home Page: www.oregonstate.edu/dept/iifet

Ann L Shriver, Executive Director
Dr. Rebecca Metzner, President
Dr. Ralph Townsend, President-Elect

An important forum for members and others to learn about important research developments in seafood trade, aquaculture, and fisheries management issues. Attended by fisheries social scientists, managers, and industry members from all of the world's fishing areas. Provides participants with unparalleled opportunities to interact with the world's foremost fisheries economists in both formal and informal settings. Learn more about fishing and aquaculture activities across the globe.
Founded in 1982

9315 **IPHC Annual Meeting**
Pacific Seafood Processors Association
1900 West Emerson Place
Suite 205
Seattle, WA 98119-1649

206-281-1667
Fax: 206-283-2387
E-Mail: nancy@pspafish.net
Home Page: www.pspafish.net

Glenn Reed, President

Annual members meeting to discuss catch limits each year.
25 Members
Founded in 1914

9316 **International Boston Seafood Show**
Diversified Business Communications
PO Box 7437
Portland, ME 04112-7437

207-842-5504
Fax: 207-842-5505
E-Mail: customerservice@divcom.com
Home Page: www.bostonseafood.com

Diane Vassar, Promotions Director
David Lowell, President

This event attracts top-tier buyers and sellers of seafood. You will find exhibit categories representing every aspect of seafood including; seafood, seafood equipment, services and organizations and seafood packaging.
20M Attendees
Frequency: March/Silver Pkg $250

9317 **International Convention of Allied Sportfishing Trades (ICAST)**
American Sportfishing Association
1001 North Fairfax Street
Suite 501
Alexandria, VA 22314

703-519-9691
Fax: 703-519-1872
E-Mail: info@asafishing.org
Home Page: www.asafishing.org
Social Media: Facebook

Mike Nussman, President/CEO
Joyce Anderson-Logan, Executive Assistant
Gordon Robertson, Vice President
Diane Carpenter, Chief Financial Officer

World's largest sportfishing trade show, representing the cornerstone of the sportfishing industry, driving sportfishing companies' product sales year round and is the showcase for the latest innovations in gear and accessories.
Frequency: Bi-Monthly

9318 **International Fly Tackle Dealer Show**
American Fly Fishing Trade Association
901 Front St.
Suite B-125
Louisville, CO 80027

303-604-6132
Fax: 303-604-6162
Home Page: www.affta.com

Randi Swisher, President
Gary Berlin, Business Manager
Jim Klug, Chairman

The largest international gathering of fly fishing manufacturers, retailers, sales reps, media and fly fishing organizations in the world. Best venue to meet with the industry, people, products, innovations, emerging trends and the leading brand presentations, latest gear, equipment, waders, fly like, tippet and accessories for the upcoming season.
400 Members
Founded in 2003

9319 **International West Coast Seafood Show**
Diversified Business Communications
PO Box 7437
Portland, ME 04112-7437

207-842-5500
Fax: 207-842-5503
E-Mail: mlarkin@divcom.com
Home Page: www.westcoastseafood.com

Mary Larkin, VP Seafood Expositions

A total resource for seafood industry leaders; showcases the latest seafood products and equipment from the US, Pacific Rim and beyond.
Frequency: October
Founded in 1996

9320 **NSA Annual Meeting**
National Shellfisheries Association
c/o US EPA, Atlantic Ecology Division
27 Tazewell Drive
Narragansett, RI 02880

401-782-3155
Fax: 401-782-3030
E-Mail: news@shellfish.org
Home Page: www.shellfish.org

Dr Lou D'Abramo, President
Christopher Davis, Treasurer

A time and place to interact with other associations and industry people.
Frequency: Spring

9321 **National River Rally**
American Sportfishing Association
225 Reinekers Ln
Suite 420
Alexandria, VA 22314-2875

703-519-9691
Fax: 703-519-1872
E-Mail: info@asafishing.org
Home Page: www.fishamerica.org

Mike Nussman, President/CEO
Diane Carpenter, CFO
Gordon Robertson, Vice President

The premier national event to come together to learn, inspire and celebrate the passionate work of all things rivers and watersheds. Trainings, field trips and a deeply moving River Heroes awards banquet honoring incredible River leaders.
650+ Members
Founded in 1962

9322 Pacific Marine Expo
Diversified Business Communications
121 Free Street
PO Box 7437
Portland, ME 04112

207-425-5608
Fax: 207-842-5509
E-Mail: pme@divcom.com
Home Page: www.pacificmarineexpo.com

Bob Callahan, Show Director
Heather Palmeter, Show Coordinator

A trade show dedicated to the pacific maritime industry that provides a gathering of marine products and services. With nearly 500 manufacturers and distributors showcasing the latest technologies and thousands of products for all commercial vessels, tugs, barges, boat building, marine construction, passenger vessels, seafood processing plants and more, PME is the best source for all marine business needs.
6,000 Attendees
Frequency: November

9323 Seafood Processing America
Catfish Farmers of America
1100 Highway 82 E
Suite 202
Indianola, MS 38751-2251

662-887-2699
Fax: 662-887-6857
Home Page: www.catfishfarmersofamerica.org

Hugh Warren, President

Opportunity to launch new products, meet new buyers, learn emerging trends and access the North American seafood market.
Frequency: Membership Fee
Founded in 1968

9324 Sportfishing Summit
American Sportfishing Association
1001 North Fairfax Street
Suite 501
Alexandria, VA 22314

703-519-9691
Fax: 703-519-1872
E-Mail: info@asafishing.org
Home Page: www.asafishing.org
Social Media: Facebook

Mike Nussman, President/CEO
Joyce Anderson-Logan, Executive Assistant
Gordon Robertson, Vice President
Diane Carpenter, Chief Financial Officer

Where industry leaders met to discuss the issues impacting recreational fishing.
Frequency: Bi-Monthly

Directories & Databases

9325 AZA Membership Directory
American Zoo and Aquarium Association
8403 Colesville Rd
Suite 710
Silver Spring, MD 20910-3314

301-562-0777
Fax: 301-562-0888
E-Mail: membership@aza.org
Home Page: www.aza.org
Social Media: Facebook, Twitter

L. Patricia Simmons, Chair
Tom Schmid, Chair-Elect
Jackie Ogden, Ph.D, Vice-Chair

Accredited institutions, professional affiliates, professional fellows, commercial members, related facilities and conservation partners receive one complimentary copy as a membership benefit.
Cost: $50.00
200 Members
Frequency: Annual
Founded in 1924

9326 Angling America Database
PO Box 22567
Alexandria, VA 22304

E-Mail: info@anglingamerica.com
Home Page: www.anglingamerica.com

Stephen Aaron, Director
Austin Ducworth, Director

The most searchable database for fishing charters and guides across America.

9327 Commercial Marine Directory & Fish Farmers Phone Book/ Directory
Compass Publications
Deer Isle, ME

800-989-5253
Fax: 207-348-1059
E-Mail: comfish@fish-news.com
Home Page: www.fish-news.com

Richard W Martin, Publisher
Susan Jones, Editor

Go-to-reference tools for commercial fishermen and fish farmers. Comprehensive listing of suppliers providing essential goods and services and convenient industry yellow pages.
Cost: $21.95
72 Pages
Frequency: Monthly
Circulation: 9223
ISSN: 0273-6713
Founded in 1978
Printed in 4 colors on n stock

9328 IIFET Membership Directory
International Institute of Fisheries Economics
Dept of Agricultural & Resource Economic
Oregon State University
Corvallis, OR 97331-3601

541-737-1416
Fax: 541-737-2563
E-Mail: iifet@oregonstate.edu
Home Page: www.orst.edu/dept/iifet
Social Media: Facebook, Twitter, LinkedIn, YouTube, Flickr

Ann L Shriver, Executive Director
Kara Kennan, Assistant Executive Director

This handbook lists all members with complete contact information, including an e-mail directory, plus areas of interest. Regular updates are provided with the newsletter.
Frequency: Biennial

9329 Who's Who in the Fish Industry
Urner Barry Publications
PO Box 389
Toms River, NJ 08754-0389

732-240-5330
800-932-0617
Fax: 732-341-0891
E-Mail: sales@urnerbarry.com
Home Page: www.urnerbarry.com

Jay Bailey, Sales Manager
Janice Brown, Advertising Manager

The source for buying and selling contacts in the North American Seafood Industry. This 2006-2007 edition is fully updated and verified, boasting over 6,000 listings of seafood companies in the US and Canada. The directory boasts detailed information about each company listed such as products handled, contact names, product forms, product origin, sales volume, company website and much more.
Cost: $199.00
800 Pages
Frequency: Annual
ISSN: 0270-1600
Founded in 1979

Industry Web Sites

9330 http://gold.greyhouse.com
G.O.L.D Grey House OnLine Databases

Grey House Publishing's online database platform, GOLD, offers Quick Search, Keyword Search and Expert Search for most business sectors including fishing and food markets. The GOLD platform makes finding the information you need quick and easy - whether you're a novice searcher or an experienced database user. All of Grey House's directory products are available for subscription on the GOLD platform.

9331 www.asafishing.org
American Sportfishing Association

Manufacturers and importers of fishing tackle and allied products. Promotes fishing for children and adults. Compiles statistics. Sponsors National Fishing Week.

9332 www.fish307.com/links.htm

This site provides links to Lake George Regional Web Sites, Fishing Charters, International Web Sites related to fishing.

9333 www.fishhoo.com

Fishhoo search Index for Fishermen. The internet's best fishing resources. There are 2991 links to choose from and translate to: French, German and Spanish.

9334 www.greyhouse.com
Grey House Publishing

Authoritative reference directories for most businsee sectors including fishing and food markets. Users can search the online databases with varied search criteria allowing for custom searches by product category, geographic area, sales volume, keyword, subject and more. Full Grey House catalog and online ordering also available.

9335 www.internets.com/sfishing.htm

Fishing Databases Search Engines.

9336 www.nauticalworld.com

Dedicated to bringing all related web sites within easy access to watersports enthusiasts. This search engine has been designed to locate advertiser's information within Nautical World but will also offer access to other watersport related web sites as well. Offers sections on marine electronics and hardware, sailing, boats, dock supplies, fishing accessories, diving accessories, industry news, watersports, weather forecasting and more.

9337 www.nfi.org
National Fishing Institute

Promotes the shipping and production of fishery products in international trade.

9338 www.ospafish.net
Pacific Seafood Processors Association

Trade association for the onshore processors in Oregon, Washington and Alaska.

9339 **www.pcffa.org**
Pacific Coast Federation of Fishermen's Assoc
Commercial fishermen's organizations from California to Alaska. Works to prevent and improve the resources of the commercial fishing industry, protect rivers from herbicide and pesticide applications that may threaten salmon populations, maintain activity within the industry, regain local control over fisheries management.

9340 **www.web.mit.edu/seagrant/www/wfn.html**
Women's Fisheries Network
Men and women dedicated to education of issues confronting the fishing and seafood industry. Conducts educational programs.

Associations

9341 **AACC International**
3340 Pilot Knob Road
St. Paul, MN 55121

651-454-7250
800-328-7560
Fax: 651-454-0766
E-Mail: aacc@scisoc.org
Home Page: www.aaccnet.org
Social Media: Facebook, Twitter, LinkedIn

Jan A. Delcour, President
David H. Hahn, Chairman
Gerard Downey, President-Elect
Dave L. Braun, Treasurer
Marta S. Izydorczyk, Director

Formerly the American Association of Cereal Chemists, a non-profit organization of members who are specialists in the use of cereal grains in foods.
Founded in 1915

9342 **ASI Food Safety Consultants**
7625 Page Avenue
St. Louis, MO 63133

314-725-2555
800-477-0778
Fax: 314-727-2563
E-Mail: kristah@asifood.com
Home Page: www.asifood.com
Social Media: Facebook, Twitter, LinkedIn

Tom Huge, President
Gary Huge, Vice President
Jane Griffith, Technical Director
Jeff Capell, GMP, Technical Director
Jeanette Huge, Director

A full service provider of food safety audits, GMP audits, seminars and HACCP setups, as well as HACCP verification. Thoroughly addresses every vital concern of your valuable facility including food safety, pest control, employee practices and facility conditions.
Founded in 1930

9343 **Academy of Nutrition and Dietics**
120 S Riverside Plaza
Suite 2000
Chicago, IL 60606-6995

312-899-0040
800-877-1600
E-Mail: info@eatright.org
Home Page: www.eatright.org
Social Media: Facebook, Twitter, LinkedIn, Pinterest, Youtube

The American Dieteric Association is the World's largest organization of food and nutrition professionals. ADA is committed to improving the nation's health and advancing the profession of dietetics through research, education and advocacy.
75000 Members
Founded in 1917
Mailing list available for rent

9344 **Agribusiness Council**
PO Box 5565
Washington, DC 20016

202-296-4563
Fax: 202-887-9178
E-Mail: info@agribusinesscouncil.org
Home Page: www.agribusinesscouncil.org

Lyndon B. Jhonson, President

Organization dedicated to strengthening US agro-industrial competitiveness through programs which highlight international trade and development potentials as well as broad issues which encompass several individual agribusiness sectors and require a food systems approach.
Founded in 1967

9345 **Agricultural & Applied Economics Association**
555 E. Wells St.
Suite 1100
Milwaukee, WI 53202

414-918-3190
Fax: 414-276-3349
E-Mail: Info@aaea.org
Home Page: www.aaea.org
Social Media: Facebook, Twitter, LinkedIn

Julie Caswell, President
Barry Goodwin, President-Elect
Michael Boland, Director
Hayley Chouinard, Director
Keith H. Koble, Director

A not for profit association serving the professional interests of members working in agricultural and broadly related fields of applied economics. Will be the leading organization for professional advancement in, knowledge about agricultural, development, environmental, food and consumer, natural resource, regional, rural, and associated areas of applied economics and business.
Cost: $150.00
4M Members
Frequency: Regular Membership Fee
Founded in 1910

9346 **Agricultural Education National HQ**
National FFA Organization
6060 FFA Drive
PO Box 68960
Indianapolis, IN 46268-0960

317-802-6060
888-332-2668
E-Mail: membership@ffa.org
Home Page: www.ffa.org
Social Media: Facebook, Twitter

Steve A. Brown, National FFA Advisor, Board Chair
Sherene R. Donaldson, National FFA Executive Secretary
Marion D. Fletcher, National FFA Organization Treasurer
Mike Womochil, State Supervisor

Headquarters of the National FFA Organization, the organization's mission is to prepare students for successful careers and a lifetime of informed choices in the global agriculture, food, fiber and natural resources systems.
507M Members
Founded in 1928

9347 **Agricultural Retailers Association**
1156 15th St NW
Suite 500
Washington, DC 20005

202-457-0825
800-844-4900
Fax: 202-457-0864
E-Mail: ara@aradc.org
Home Page: www.aradc.org
Social Media: Facebook, Twitter

Johnny Council, Chairman
Gary Farell, Chairman-Elect
Dave Dufault, Vice-Chairman
Mark Sharitz, Secretary/Treasurer
Billy Pirkle, Immediate Past Chairman

Nonprofit trade organization representing the interests of retailers across the United States on legislative and regulatory issues on Capitol Hill.
1200 Members
Frequency: Membership Dues Vary
Founded in 1993

9348 **Allied Purchasing**
PO Box 1249
Mason City, IA 50402-1249
800-247-5956
Fax: 800-635-3775
E-Mail: kbamrick@alliedpurchasing.com
Home Page: www.alliedpurchasing.com
Social Media: Facebook, LinkedIn

Brian Janssen, President/CFO
Steve Husome, Executive Vice President
Kari Mondt, Senior Account Manager
Nicole Reisdorfer, Senior Account Manager
Kim Bamrick, Account Manager

A member owned not-for-profit buying organization established to negotiate favorable purchasing programs in part because we offer quantity purchases and prompt payment to suppliers. Purchases equipment, supplies, ingredients, and services for, dairy, soft drink, bottled water, water treatment and brewery industries.
Cost: $50.00
1200 Members
Frequency: Membership: 1 Share Stock
Founded in 1937

9349 **Allied Trades of the Baking Industry**
c/o Cereal Food Processors
2001 Shawnee Mission Parkway
Mission Woods, KS 66205

913-890-6300
E-Mail: t.miller@cerealfood.com
Home Page: www.atbi.org

Rick McGrath, President
Tom McCurry, First Vice President
John Hellman, Second Vice President
Tom McCurry, Secretary/Treasurer

An organization which exists to serve the grain-based food industry through cooperation between a large cross-section of suppliers to the wholesale manufacturers that each day provide our country with bread, rolls, cereals, cakes, cookies, crackers, tortillas and any number of other items that incorporate grains as their base. Values the relationships which have been built between the supplier and the manufacturer over the nearly 90 years since its inception.
Cost: $50.00
Frequency: Annual Dues
Founded in 1920

9350 **Aluminum Foil Container Manufacturers Association**
10 Vecilla Lane
Hot Springs Village, AR 71909

440-781-5819
Fax: 440-247-9053
E-Mail: info@afcma.org
Home Page: www.afcma.org

Coke Williams, Executive Secretary

Represents leading manufacturers of aluminum foil containers in the United States and Canada. The Association has worked to promote aluminum foil as a superior packaging material since the beginning.
13 Members
Founded in 1955

9351 **American Agricultural Law Association**
American Agricultural Economics Association
127 Young Rd.
Kelso, WA 98626

360-200-5699
Fax: 360-423-2287
E-Mail: RobertA@aglaw-assn.org
Home Page: www.aglaw-assn.org

Robert Achenbach, Executive Director

The only national professional organization focusing on the legal needs of the agricultural community. Crossing traditional barriers, it offers an independent forum for investigation of innovative and workable solutions to complex agricultural law problems. This role has taken on greater importance in the midst of the current international and environmental issues reshaping agriculture and the impending technological advances which promise equally dramatic changes.
600 Members
Founded in 1980

9352 **American Angus Association**
3201 Frederick Ave
St Joseph, MO 64506

816-383-5100
Fax: 816-233-9703
E-Mail: angus@angus.org
Home Page: www.angus.org
Social Media: Facebook, Twitter

Gordon Stucky, President
Cathy Watkins, Vice President
Bryce Schumann, CEO
Jim Sitz, Treasurer

To provide programs, services, technology and leadership to enhance the genetics of the Angus breed, broaden its influence within the beef industry, and expand the market for superior tasting, high-quality Angus beef worldwide. Achieve Angus excellence through information, increase beef demand with Angus equity, identify and implement relevant technologies, optimize resources, and create opportunities.
Cost: $80.00
30+M Members
Frequency: Membership Fees Vary
Founded in 1883

9353 **American Association of Candy Technologist**
711 W Water St.
PO Box 266
Princeton, WI 54968

920-295-6959
Fax: 920-295-6843
E-Mail: aactinfo@gomc.com
Home Page: www.aactcandy.org

Randy Hofberger, President
Judy Cooley, First Vice President
Adam Lechter, Second Vice President
Patrick Hurley, Secretary
Michael Allured, Treasurer

A premier professional group of individual technologists, operations personnel, educators, students, business staff and others dedicated to the advancement of the confectionery industry.
Cost: $60.00
Frequency: Membership Fee
Founded in 1947

9354 **American Association of Crop Insurers**
1 Massachusetts Ave NW
Suite 800
Washington, DC 20001

202-789-4100
Fax: 202-408-7763
E-Mail: aaci@mwmlaw.com
Home Page: www.cropinsurers.com

Mike Mc Leod, Executive Director
David Graves, Manager/Secretary

AACI is widely recognized on Capitol Hill as the leading source of crop insurance information and advice on legislative and administrative proposals. AACI is a member of a coalition of groups in Washington working together to improve the risk management options for America's farmers.
15 Members
Frequency: Membership Fee

9355 **American Association of Grain Inspection and Weighing Agencies**
PO Box 26426
Kansas City, MO 64196

816-569-4020
Fax: 816-221-8189
E-Mail: info@aagiwa.org
Home Page: www.aagiwa.org

David Ayers, President
Tom Dahl, Vice President
Dave Reeder, Secretary/ Treasurer

Established to provide a liaison between the Federal Grain Inspection Service and designated agencies.
50 Members
Founded in 1964

9356 **American Association of Meat Processors**
One Meating Place
Elizabethtown, PA 17022

717-367-1168
Fax: 717-367-9096
E-Mail: aamp@aamp.com
Home Page: www.aamp.com

Tim J. Hean, President
Erica Hering, 1st Vice President
Doug Hankes, 2nd Vice President
Louis Muench, 3rd Vice President
Kevin Western, Treasurer

Membership consists of small to medium sized meat, poultry and food businesses including, slaughterers, processors, wholesalers, home food service businesses, deli and catering operators and suppliers to the industry. AAMP is affiliated with 32 state, regional and provincial associations.
1400 Members
Founded in 1939

9357 **American Association of Nutritional Consultants**
220 Parker St.
Warsaw, IN 46580

574-269-6165
888-828-2262
Fax: 574-268-2120
E-Mail: registrar@aanc.net
Home Page: www.aanc.net
Social Media: Facebook, Twitter, Pinterest

Wendell Whitman, Owner

Promotes ethical standards in the field of nutrition consultants, and those who hold bachelor's degrees in the health related fields.
Cost: $60.00
Frequency: Annual Membership Fee
Founded in 1985

9358 **American Bakers Association**
1300 I St NW
Suite 700 West
Washington, DC 20005

202-789-0300
Fax: 202-898-1164
E-Mail: info@americanbakers.org
Home Page: www.americanbakers.org
Social Media: Twitter, LinkedIn, Youtube, Stationerswidows

Robb Mackie, President & CEO
Howard R. Alton, III, Chairman of the Board
Fred Penny, First Vice Chairman
Rich Scalise, Second Vice Chairman
Lee Sanders, Secretary

A long and dedicated history of representing the interests of the wholesale baking industry before the U.S. Congress, federal agencies, state legislatures and agencies, and international regulatory authorities.
300 Members
Frequency: Membership Dues Vary
Founded in 1897

9359 **American Beekeeping Federation**
3525 Piedmont Rd
Bldg 5 Suite 300
Atlanta, GA 30305

404-760-2875
Fax: 404-240-0998
E-Mail: info@abfnet.org
Home Page: www.abfnet.org

George Hansen, President
Tim Tucker, Vice President
Regina Robuck, Executive Director

A national organization that continually works in the interest of all beekeepers, large or small, and those associated with the industry to ensure the future of the honey bee. Members share a common interest to work toward better education and information for all segments of the industry in the hope of increasing chances for survival in today's competitive world.
Cost: $35.00
1200 Members
Frequency: Membership Fees Vary
Founded in 1943

9360 **American Berkshire Association**
2637 Yeager Road
West Lafayette, IN 47906

765-497-3618
Fax: 765-497-2959
E-Mail: berkshire@nationalswine.com
Home Page: www.americanberkshire.com
Social Media: Facebook

Lorraine Hoffman, President
John Baker, Vice President
Merrill Smith, Secretary
Steve Brown, Treasurer

The official national registry for the Berkshire breed of pigs. The ABA promotes the Berkshire breed of hogs, and maintains breed purity through registration of purebred Berkshires. Dedicated Berkshire breeders focus on delivering the superior meat quality that drives the popularity of Berkshire pork among discerning culinary experts.
300+ Members
Founded in 1998

9361 **American Beverage Association**
1101 Sixteenth Street NW
Washington, DC 20036

202-463-6732
Fax: 202-659-5349
E-Mail: info@ameribev.org
Home Page: www.ameribev.org
Social Media: Facebook, Twitter, YouTUBE

Claude B. Nielson, Chair
Rodger L. Collins, Vice Chair
Susan Neely, President
Amy E. Hancock, Secretary
Ralph D. Crowley Jr., Treasurer

The national voice for the non-alcoholic refreshment beverage industry, providing a neutral forum in which members convene to discuss common issues while maintaining their tradition of spirited competition in the American marketplace. Also serving as liaison between the industry, government and the public, and providing a unified voice in legislative and regulatory matters.
Founded in 1919

9362 **American Beverage Licensees Association**
5101 River Rd
Suite 108
Bethesda, MD 20816-1560

301-656-1494
Fax: 301-656-7539
E-Mail: info@ablusa.org
Home Page: www.ablusa.org
Social Media: Facebook, Twitter

Harry Klock, President
Steve Morris, Vice President
Warren Scheidt, Vice President
Paul Santelle, Vice President
Don Diserens, Vice President

An association representing off-premise licensees in the open or license states and on-premise proprietors in markets across the nation. ABL was created after the merger of the National Association of Beverage Retailers (NABR) and the National Licensed Beverage Association (NLBA).
17000 Members
Founded in 2002

9363 **American Brahman Breeders Association**
3003 S Loop W
Suite 520
Houston, TX 77054

713-349-0854
Fax: 713-349-9795
E-Mail: abba@brahman.org
Home Page: www.brahman.org
Social Media: Facebook, Twitter

Ricky Hughes, President
Chris Shivers, Executive Vice President
J.D. Sartwelle, Jr., Vice President
George Kempfer, Secretary/ Treasurer

American Brahman is a beef crossbreeding organization that plays a big role in the United States and beyond.
Founded in 1924

9364 **American Center for Wine, Food & the Arts**
500 First Street
Napa, CA 94559

707-259-1600
888-512-6742
Fax: 707-257-8601
E-Mail: info@copia.org
Home Page: www.copia.org

Arthur Jacobus, President
Kurt Nystrom, COO
Larry Tsai, Chief Marketing Officer

A non-profit discovery center whose mission is to explore and celebrate the cultural significance of wine, food and the arts.

9365 **American Cheese Society**
2696 S. Colorado Blvd
Suite 570
Denver, CO 80222-5954

720-328-2788
Fax: 720-328-2786
E-Mail: info@cheesesociety.org
Home Page: www.cheesesociety.org
Social Media: Facebook, Twitter, LinkedIn, YouTube

Greg O Neil, President
Peggy Smith, Vice President
Christine Hyatt, Chair
Sasha Davies, Secretary
Jeff Jirik, Treasurer

The Society's membership includes farmstead, artisanal and specialty cheesemakers; academicians and enthusiasts; marketing and distribution specialists; food writers and cookbook authors and specialty foods retailers from the United States, Canada and Europe.
800 Members
Founded in 1983

9366 **American Council on Science and Health**
1995 Broadway
Suite 202
New York, NY 10023-5882

212-362-7044
866-905-2694
Fax: 212-362-4919
E-Mail: acsh@acsh.org
Home Page: www.acsh.org
Social Media: Facebook, Twitter, Youtube

Elizabeth M. Whelan, President
Judith A. D Agostino, Executive Assistant
Josh Bloom, Director of Chemical Science
Gilbert Ross, Executive Director
Ana Simovska, Director of Video Production

A consumer education organization providing the public with scientifically accurate evaluations of food, chemicals, the environment and health.
Founded in 1978

9367 **American Culinary Federation**
180 Center Place Way
St Augustine, FL 32095

904-824-4468
800-624-9458
Fax: 904-825-4758
E-Mail: acf@acfchefs.net
Home Page: www.acfchefs.org
Social Media: Facebook, Twitter, Flickr

Thomas J. Macrina, President
James Taylor, Secretary
William Tillinghast, Treasurer

A professional, not-for-profit organization for chefs and cooks. The principal goal of the founding chefs remains true to ACF today_to promote the professional image of American chefs worldwide through education among culinarians at all levels, from apprentices to the most accomplished certified master chefs.
19000 Members
Founded in 1929

9368 **American Dairy Association Mideast**
5950 Sharon Woods Blvd
Columbus, OH 43229

614-890-1800
800-292-MILK
Fax: 614-890-1636
E-Mail: info@drink-milk.com
Home Page: www.drink-milk.com
Social Media: Facebook, Twitter, Youtube, Pinterest

Scott Higgins, CEO
Jenny Hubble, Vice President of Communication

We represent dairy farmers and serve as the local affiliate for the American Dairy Association and the National Dairy Council. We work closely with Dairy Management Inc. and the Milk Processors Education Program to extend national dairy promotion programs to the local level.
3800 Members

9369 **American Dairy Council**
Interstate Place II
100 Elwood Davis Road
North Syracuse, NY 13212

315-472-9143
Fax: 315-472-0506
E-Mail: dairyinfo@adadc.com
Home Page: www.adadc.com
Social Media: Facebook, Twitter

Richard Naczi, Director

To economically benefit diary farmers by encouraging the consumption of milk and diary products through advertising, education and promotion, to reach consumers with product benefits and advantages.
Founded in 1915
Mailing list available for rent

9370 **American Dairy Products Institute**
126 N. Addison Avenue
Elmhurst, IL 60126

630-530-8700
Fax: 630-530-8707
E-Mail: info@adpi.org
Home Page: www.adpi.org

David Thomas, CEO
Steve Griffin, Director of Finance
Carl Roode, Director of Board Member Services
Dan Meyer, Director of Technical Services
Beth Holcomb, Director of Member Communications

An association for manufactured dairy products, including dry milks, whey, lactose, evaporated and condensed milk. ADPI's main purpose is to effectively communicate the many positive attributes and benefits of our members' products. Additionally, we serve our membership by offering the most current industry information available and by collaborating with dairy associations to represent members' interests before state and federal regulatory agencies.
150 Members
Founded in 1986

9371 **American Dairy Science Association**
1800 S. Oak Street
Suite 100
Champaign, IL 61820-6974

217-356-5146
Fax: 217-398-4119
E-Mail: adsa@assochq.org
Home Page: www.adsa.org/foundation.asp

Scott Rankin, President
Al Kertz, Vice President
Mike Schutz, Treasurer
Peter Studney, Executive Director
Roger Shanks, Editor-In-Chief

Organization of professional researchers. Publishes journals and holds annual member meetings.
4000 Members
Founded in 1896

9372 **American Dry Bean Boardÿ**
Home Page: www.americanbean.org

Health benefits of beans, bean salad recipes, healthy bean soup recipes, and bean facts.

9373 **American Egg Board**
1460 Renaissance Drive - Ste 301
PO Box 738
Park Ridge, IL 60068

847-296-7043
Fax: 847-296-7007
E-Mail: aeb@aeb.org
Home Page: www.aeb.org

Joanne Ivy, CEO
Elisa Maloberti, Consumer Information Coordinator

U.S. egg producer's link to the consumer in communicating the value of the incredible egg. As the egg industry's promotion arm, AEB's foremost challenge is to convince the American public that the egg is still one of nature's most nearly perfect foods. AEB's basic task is to improve the demand for shell eggs, egg products,

as well as spent fowl throughout the United States.
300 Members
Founded in 1976

9374 American Emu Association
121 W Main St
Suite 2
Ottawa, IL 61350

541-332-0675
E-Mail: info@aea-emu.org
Home Page: www.aea-emu.org
Social Media: Facebook

Tony Citrhyn, President
Betty Lou Couffman, Vice President
Matt Gulick, Secretary
Susan Wright, Treasurer
Richard Merrow, Parliamentarian

A national, member driven, non-profit agricultural association dedicated to the emu industry. AEA promotes public awareness of emu products, fosters research and publishes a bi-monthly newsletter and several industry brochures. Represents an alternative agricultural industry, dominated by the small farmer, who is committed to humane and environmentally positive practices that produce high quality, beneficial products.
Cost: $100.00
1,700 Members
Frequency: Membership Fee
Founded in 1989

9375 American Farm Bureau Federation
600 Maryland Ave SW
Suite 1000W
Washington, DC 20024

202-484-3600
Fax: 202-484-3604
E-Mail: webmaster@fb.org
Home Page: www.fb.org
Social Media: Facebook, Twitter, YouTube, Googleplus

Bob Stallman, President
Julie Anna Potts, Executive VP & Treasurer
Lynne Finnerty, Director
Jean Bennis, Executive Assistant

An independent, non-governmental, voluntary organization governed by and representing farm and ranch families united for the purpose of analyzing their problems and formulating action to achieve educational improvement, economic opportunity and social advancement and, thereby, to promote the national well-being. The voice of agricultural producers at all levels.
3MM Members
Founded in 1919
Mailing list available for rent

9376 American Forage and Grassland Council
PO Box 867
Berea, KY 40403

800-944-2342
Fax: 859-623-8694
E-Mail: info@afgc.org
Home Page: www.afgc.org

Jerald Bush, President
Jerry Hall, Vice President
Shelby Filley, Secretary
Don Wirth, Treasurer

An international organization with the primary objective to promote the profitable production and sustainable utilization of quality forage and grasslands.
Cost: $30.00
3,000 Members
Frequency: Annual Dues
Mailing list available for rent: 2400+ names

9377 American Frozen Food Institute
2000 Corporate Ridge, Blvd.
Suite 1000
McLean, VA 22102

703-821-0770
Fax: 703-821-1350
E-Mail: info@affi.com
Home Page: www.affi.com

Jeff Varcoe, Chairman
Dave Yanda, First Vice Chairman
Paul Bakus, Second Vice Chairman

AFFI is the national trade association the promotes and represents the interests of all segments of the frozen food industry.
500 Members
Founded in 1942

9378 American Guernsey Association
1224 Alton Darby Creek Road
Suite G
Columbus, OH 43228

614-864-2409
Fax: 614-864-5614
E-Mail: info@usguernsey.com
Home Page: www.usguernsey.com
Social Media: Facebook

David Trotter, President
Emily Hartmann, First Vice President
Duane Schuler, Second Vice President
David Trotter, Interim Executive Secretary
Lee Kohler, Treasurer

Promotes programs and services to the dairy industry.
36 Members
Founded in 1877

9379 American Herb Association
PO Box 1673
Nevada City, CA 95959

530-265-9552
Fax: 530-274-3140
Home Page: www.ahaherb.com

Kathi Keville, Director
Robert Brucia, Co-Director
Marion Wyckoff, Secretary

An association of Medical Herbalists. Membership is open to anyone interested in herbs and includes the AHA Quarterly. The goals of the AHA are to promote the understanding, acceptance and ecological use of herbs.
Cost: $20.00
Frequency: Membership Fee
Founded in 1981

9380 American Herbal Products Association
8630 Fenton St
Suite 918
Silver Spring, MD 20910

301-588-1171
Fax: 301-588-1174
E-Mail: ahpa@ahpa.org
Home Page: www.ahpa.org

Michael McGuffin, President
Marc Allen, Chair
Travis Borchardt, Vice Chair
Wilson Lau, Secretary
Mitch Coven, Treasurer

The national trade association which represents manufacturers, importers and distributors of herbs and herbal products. AHPA seeks self-regulation, establishment of standards and rules of ethical conduct, member enrichment and public outreach.
Cost: $1000.00
300 Members
Frequency: Membership Fees Vary
Founded in 1983

9381 American Hereford Association
PO Box 014059
Kansas City, MO 64101

816-842-3757
Fax: 816-842-6931
E-Mail: aha@hereford.org
Home Page: www.hereford.org
Social Media: Facebook

Craig Huffhines, Executive VP
Jack Ward, Chief Operating Officer
Leslie Mathews, Chief Financial Officer
Angie Stump Denton, Director of Communications
Stacy Sanders, Director of Records Department

Association for people in the Hereford cattle industry.
8M Members
Founded in 1986

9382 American Honey Producers Association
PO Box 435
Mendon, UT 84325

281-900-9740
Fax: 403-463-2583
E-Mail: cassie@AHPAnet.com
Home Page: www.americanhoneyproducers.org

Randy Verhoek, President
Darren Cox, VP
Cassie Cox, Executive Secretary
Kelvin Adee, Treasurer

Represents the interests of major US honey producers and pollinators.
Cost: $150.00
700 Members
Frequency: Membership Fees Vary
Founded in 1969

9383 American Institute for Cancer Research
1759 R Street, NW
Washington, DC 20009

202-328-7744
800-843-8114
Fax: 202-328-7226
E-Mail: aicrweb@aicr.org
Home Page: www.aicr.org
Social Media: Facebook, Twitter, Pinterest

Melvin Hutson, Chairman
Lawrence Pratt, Vice Chairman
Marilyn Gentry, President
Kelly B. Browning, Chief Executive Officer
Susan Pepper, Secretary/Treasurer

First organization to focus research on the link between diet and cancer and translating the results into practical information for the public. AICR helps people make choices that reduce their chances of developing cancer.
Founded in 1982

9384 American Institute of Bakingÿ
PO Box 3999
Manhattan, KS 66505-3999

785-537-4750
800-633-5137
Fax: 785-537-1493
E-Mail: sales@aibonline.org
Home Page: www.aibonline.org
Social Media: Facebook, Twitter, LinkedIn

Andre Biane, President/ CEO
Maureen Olewnik, SVP, Food Safety Services
Susan Hancock, VP, Learning and Communications
William Gambe, VP, Client Development
Brian Strouts, Vice President, Baking

A nonprofit corporation founded by the North American wholesale andretail baking industries

as a technology transfer center for bakers and food processors.
Founded in 1919

9385 American Institute of Food Distribution
10 Mountain View Road
Suite S125
Upper Saddle River, NJ 07458
201-791-5570
Fax: 201-791-5222
E-Mail: questions@foodinstitute.com
Home Page: www.foodinstitute.com
Social Media: Facebook, Twitter, LinkedIn
Dean Erstad, Chairman
Michael Sansolo, Vice Chairman
Donna L. George, President and COO
Susan T. Borra, Senior Vice President
Peter R. Lavoy, Former President & CEO
The best source for timely, current, and relevant information about the food industry. A nonprofit organization for providing information on the hottest topics and latest trends, reports and studies, and industry analysts to answer member inquiries.
Cost: $725.00
2700 Members
Frequency: Annual Membership Fee
Founded in 1928

9386 American Institute of Wine & Food
26384 Carmel Rancho Lane
Suite 200E
Carmel, CA 93923
831-250-7595
800-274-2493
Fax: 831-250-7641
E-Mail: info@aiwf.org
Home Page: www.aiwf.org
Social Media: Facebook
Frank Giaimo, National Chair
Mary Chamberlin, National Vice Chair
Drew Jaglom, National Secretary
George Linn, National Treasurer
Robert Evans, Chapter Relations Chair
The American Institute of Wine & Food is one of the few national organizations with the unique combination membership of dedicated wine and food enthusiasts and professionals. Wine and food enthusiasts get to meet and learn from reowned chefs, winemakers, authors, culinary historians, and food producers, while industry professionals have the opportunity to know and understand their core consumers
Cost: $75.00
6000+ Members
Frequency: Memberships Vary
Founded in 1981

9387 American International Charolais Association
11700 NW Plaza Circle
Kansas City, MO 64153
816-464-5977
Fax: 816-464-5759
E-Mail: north@charolaisusa.com
Home Page: www.charolaisusa.com
Larry Lehman, President
Bill Nottke, Vice President
Robb Creasey, Treasurer
John Chism, Secretary
J. Neil Orth, Executive VP
The official registry of Charolais and Charbray cattle in the United States.
2,900 Members

9388 American Jersey Cattle Association
6486 E Main Street
Reynoldsburg, OH 43068-2362
614-861-3636
Fax: 614-861-8040
Home Page: www.usjersey.com
Social Media: Facebook, Twitter
Neal Smith, Executive Secretary & CEO
Whittney Smith, Admisitrative Assistant
Vickie White, Treasurer and Office Manager
Cindy Watson, Assistant to the Treasurer
They improve and promote the Jersey cattle breed.
Founded in 1868

9389 American Livestock Conservancy
PO Box 477
Pittsboro, NC 27312
919-542-5704
Fax: 919-545-0022
E-Mail: albc@albc-usa.org
Home Page: www.livestock.org
Social Media: Facebook, Blogger, Youtube
Charles R Bassett, Executive Director
Don T Schrider, Communications Director
Jeannette Beranger, Research/Technical Program Manager
Anneke Jakes, Breed Registry Manager
Ensuring the future of agriculture through genetic conservation and the promotion of endangered breeds of livestock and poultry. A non profit membership organization working to protect over 180 breeds of livestock and poultry from extinction.
Cost: $30.00
Frequency: Membership Fee
ISSN: 1064-1599
Founded in 1977

9390 American Meat Institute
1150 Connecticut Ave NW
12th Floor
Washington, DC 20036
202-587-4200
Fax: 202-587-4300
Home Page: www.meatami.com
Social Media: Facebook, Twitter, LinkedIn
J. Patrick Boyle, President & CEO
Christl McCarthy, Exec. Assistant to the President
James Hodges, Executive Vice President
Scott Goltry, Vice President
Susan Backus, Executive Director
AMI keeps its fingers on the pulse of legislation, regulation and media activity that impacts the meat and poultry industry and provides rapid updates and analyses to its members to help them stay informed. Also conducts scientific research through its Foundation designed to help meat and poultry companies improve their plants and their products.
300 Members
Frequency: Membership Fees Vary
Founded in 1906

9391 American Meat Science Association
PO Box 2187
Champaign, IL 61825
800-517-AMSA
Fax: 888-205-5834
Fax: 217-356-5370
E-Mail: information@meatscience.org
Home Page: www.meatscience.org
Robert J. Delmore, President
Brad Morgan, President Elect
Betsy L. Booren, Chair
Thomas Powell, Executive Director
Casey B. Frye, Treasurer
AMSA fosters community and professional development among individuals who create and apply science to efficiently provide safe and high quality meat.

9392 American Mushroom Institute
1 Massachusetts Ave NW
Suite 800
Washington, DC 20001
202-842-4344
Fax: 202-408-7763
E-Mail: ami@mwmlaw.com
Home Page: www.americanmushroom.org
Joseph G. Poppiti, Chairman
Don Needham, Chairman Elect
Curtis Jurgensmeyer, Vice Chair/ Treasurer
Stephen Anania, Secretary
Laura Phelps, President
This organization is comprised of mushroom growers, associate businesses and suppliers who represent growers and coordinate industry research.
Founded in 1955

9393 American Oil Chemists' Society
2710 S. Boulder
Urbana, IL 61802-6996
217-359-2344
Fax: 217-351-8091
E-Mail: general@aocs.org
Home Page: www.aocs.org
Social Media: Facebook, Twitter, LinkedIn
T. Kemper, President
S. Hill, Vice President
N. Widlak, Secretary
B. Hendrik, Treasurer
P. Donnelly, Chief Executive Officer
Largest international society focused on the science and technology of fats, oils, lipids and related substances.
Cost: $10.00
5400 Members
Frequency: Membership Dues Vary
Founded in 1909

9394 American Ostrich Association
PO Box 166
Ranger, TX 76470
936-333-6142
Fax: 936-333-6142
E-Mail: aoa@ostriches.org
Home Page: www.ostriches.org
Dianna Westmoreland, President
Larry Moore, Vice President
Sharon Birmingham, Secretary/ Treasurer
Carol Garnett, Director at large
Organization that provides leadership for the ostrich industry and its future through the promotion of ostrich products.
Cost: $150.00
Frequency: Membership Fee
Founded in 1988

9395 American Peanut Council
1500 King St
Suite 301
Alexandria, VA 22314
703-838-9500
Fax: 703-838-9508
E-Mail: info@peanutsusa.com
Home Page: www.peanutsusa.com
Social Media: Facebook, Twitter
Patrick Archer, President
The council was formed through a merger of the National Peanut Council and the National Peanut Council of America. Serving as a forum for all segments of the peanut industry to discuss issues which impact the production, utilization and marketing of peanuts and peanut products worldwide.
Founded in 1997

9396 **American Peanut Research and Education Society**
PO Box 15825
College Station, TX 77841-5026
979-845-8278
Fax: 979-845-6483
E-Mail: peanuts@nationalpeanutboard.org
Home Page: www.aprensic.org

Tim Brenneman, President
Naveen Bubala, President-elect
Kimberly J. Cutchins, Executive Officer
Jeffrey Pope, Board Representative
Howard Valentine, Director of Science & Technology

The purpose of this Society is to instruct and educate the public on the properties, production, and use of the peanut through the organization and promotion of public discussion groups, forums, lectures, and other programs or presentations to the interested public.
Cost: $80.00
550 Members
Frequency: Organizational Fee: $100
Founded in 1968

9397 **American Pomological Society**
102 Tyson Building
University Park, PA 16802
814-863-6163
Fax: 814-237-3407
E-Mail: aps@psu.edu
Home Page: www.americanpomological.org

Kirk Pomper, President
Peter Hirst, Vice President
Michele Warmund, Vice President
Richard Marini, Secretary
Robert Crassweller, Treasurer/ Business Manager

The oldest fruit organization in North America, to foster the science and practice of fruit growing and variety development.
Cost: $40.00
1000 Members
Frequency: Annual Membership Fee
Founded in 1848

9398 **American Poultry Association**
PO Box 306
Burgettstown, PA 15021
724-729-3459
E-Mail: AmPoultryAssoc@yahoo.com
Home Page: www.amerpoultryassn.com

Sam Brush, President
Airling Gunderson, Vice President
Pat Horstman, Secretary/Treasurer
Dave Anderson, Director at large

The mission of the association is to promote and protect the standard bred poultry industry in all its phases. To encourage and protect poultry shows as being the show window of the industry, an education for both breeders and the public and a means of interesting young future breeders.
Cost: $25.00
Frequency: Annual Membership

9399 **American Seafood Institute**
25 Fairway Circle
Hope Valley, RI 02832
401-491-9017
Fax: 401-491-9024
Home Page: www.americanseafood.org

Colleen Coyne, Director

9400 **American Seed Trade Association**
1701 Duke Street
Suite 275
Alexandria, VA 22314
703-837-8140
Fax: 703-837-9365
E-Mail: infi@amseed.org
Home Page: www.amseed.com
Social Media: Facebook, Twitter, Youtube, Googleplus

Andy Lavigna, President & CEO
Bernice Slutsky, Senior Vice President
Jane Demarchi, Vice President
Rick Dunkle, Senior Director
Michelle Kohn, Director

Producers of seeds for planting purposes. Consists of companies involved in seed production and distribution, plant breeding and related industries in North America.
850 Members
Frequency: Membership Fees Vary
Founded in 1883

9401 **American Sheep Industry Association**
9785 Maroon Circle
Suite 360
Englewood, CO 80112
303-771-3500
Fax: 303-771-8200
E-Mail: eatlamb@wildblue.net
Home Page: www.sheepusa.org
Social Media: Facebook, Twitter

Clint Krebs, President
Burton Pfliger, Vice President
Mike Corn, Secretary/Treasurer
Peter Orwick, Executive Director
Paul Rodgers, Deputy Director of Policy

A federation of state associations dedicated to the welfare and profitability of the sheep industry.
8000+ Members
Founded in 1865

9402 **American Shrimp Processors Association**
PO Box 4867
EIN #72-6029637
Biloxi, MS 39535
857-445-4165
Fax: 228-385-2565
E-Mail: info@fundraise.com
Home Page: www.fundraise.com
Social Media: Facebook, Twitter

Nate Drouin, CEO
Kurt Schneider, Chief Operating Officer
Kevin Bedell, Chief Technical Officer
Ivan Sifrim, UX Developer
Nick Alekhine, Developer

A non-profit trade organization designed to represent U.S. shrimp processors in all aspects of business. Allowing processors and related industries to work together to foster a business and technological climate in which its members can prosper while providing the highest quality product to its customers.
Founded in 1964

9403 **American Society for Enology and Viticulture**
PO Box 1855
Davis, CA 95617-1855
530-753-3142
Fax: 530-753-3318
E-Mail: society@asev.org
Home Page: www.asev.org
Social Media: Twitter, LinkedIn

James Kennedy, President
Lise Asimont, First Vice President
Mark Greenspan, Second Vice President
Dr. James Harbertson, Secretary/ Treasurer
Linda Bisson, AJEV Science Editor

A tax exempt professional society dedicated to the interests of enologists, viticulturists, and others in the fields of wine and grape research and production throughout the world.
2400+ Members
Founded in 1950

9404 **American Society for Horticultural Science**
1018 Duke Street
Alexandria, VA 22314
703-836-4606
Fax: 703-836-2024
E-Mail: webmaster@ashs.org
Home Page: www.ashs.org
Social Media: Facebook, Twitter, LinkedIn, Pinterest

Paul Bosland, Chair
Mary Hokenberry Meyer, President
Michael A. Arnold, President-elect
Sandra B. Wilson, Education Division Vice President
Jeffery P. Norrie, Industry Division Vice President

A cornerstone of research and education in horticulture and an agent for active promotion of horticultural science.
Frequency: Membership Fees Vary
ISSN: 0018-5345
Founded in 1903

9405 **American Society for Parenteral and Enteral Nutrition**
8630 Fenton Street
Suite 412
Silver Spring, MD 20910
301-587-6315
Fax: 301-587-2365
E-Mail: aspen@nutr.org
Home Page: www.nutritioncare.org
Social Media: Facebook, Twitter

Ainsley Malone, President
Daniel Teitelbaum, President-Elect
Gordon Sacks, Vice President
Lawrence A. Robinson, Secretary/Treasurer
Deborah A. Andris, Director

Advancing the science and practice of clinical nutrition and metabolism. An interdisciplinary organization whose members are involved in the provision of clinical nutrition therapies, including parenteral and enteral nutrition.
5000+ Members
Founded in 1976

9406 **American Society of Agricultural Consultants**
N78W14573 Appleton Avenue
Suite 287
Menomonee Falls, WI 53051
262-253-6902
Fax: 262-253-6903
E-Mail: cmerry@agconsultants.org
Home Page: www.agconsultants.org
Social Media: Facebook, LinkedIn

Russell Morgan, CAC, Principal
Norman Brown, President-Elect
Robert Mehrle, Vice President
Erin Pirro, Chief Financial Officer
Roy Ferguson, Director

An association representing the full range of agricultural consultants which serves as an information, resource, and networking base for its members.
181 Members
Founded in 1963

9407 **American Society of Agronomy**
5585 Guilford Road
Madison, WI 53711-5801
608-273-8080
Fax: 608-273-2021
E-Mail: headquarters@agronomy.org
Home Page: www.agronomy.org
Social Media: Facebook, Twitter, LinkedIn

Sharon Clay, President
David B. Mengel, President-elect
Ellen G.M. Bergfeld, Chief Executive Officer

Society members are dedicated to the conservation and wise use of natural resources to produce food, feed, and fiber crops while maintaining and improving the environment. Membership is tax deductible. ASA is seen as a progressive, scientific society.
11000 Members
Founded in 1907

9408 American Society of Animal Science
PO Box 7410
Champaign, IL 61826-7410
217-356-9050
Fax: 217-689-2436
E-Mail: asas@asas.org
Home Page: www.asas.org
Social Media: Facebook, Twitter, Youtube

Dr. Gregory P. Lardy, President
Dr. Debra K. Aaron, President-Elect
Dr. David P. Casper, Foundation Trustee Chair
Dr. Greg S. Lewis, Editor-in-chief
Dr. Elizabeth B Kegley, Recording Secretary

A professional organization for animal scientists designed to help members provide effective leadership through research, extension, teaching and service for the dynamic and rapidly changing livestock and meat industries.
ISSN: 0021-8812
Founded in 1908

9409 American Society of Baking
PO Box 336
Swedesboro, NJ 08085
800-713-0462
Fax: 888-315-2612
E-Mail: info@asbe.org
Home Page: www.asbe.org
Social Media: Facebook, Twitter, LinkedIn, Googleplus

Dave Hipenbecker, Chairman
Anthony Turano, 1st Vice Chairman
Mike Saulsberry, 2nd Vice Chairman
Ramon Rivera, 3rd Vice Chairman
Dr. Lin Carson, Secretary/ Treasurer

Formerly known as the American Society of Bakery Engineers, a professional society comprised of members in either engaged in, involved with, or interested in wholesale or large scale bakery production. The purpose is to promoted the advancement of baking science technology through the exchange of information and interaction among baking industry professionals.
Cost: $135.00
2900 Members
Frequency: Membership Fee
Founded in 1924

9410 American Society of Brewing Chemists
3340 Pilot Knob Rd
St. Paul, MN 55121
651-454-7250
Fax: 651-454-0766
E-Mail: asbc@scisoc.org
Home Page: www.asbcnet.org
Social Media: Facebook, LinkedIn

Jeffery L. Cornell, President
Thomas H. Shellhammer, President-Elect
Christina Schoenberger, Vice President
Kelly A. Tretter, Secretary
Charles Benedict, Treasurer

ASBC is dedicated to ensuring the highest quality, consistency and safety of malt-based beverages and their ingredients. Analytical, scientific process control methods, problem solving on industry-wide issues, scientific support to evaluate raw materials for optimum performance, and professional development opportunities.
Cost: $233.00
750+ Members
Frequency: Membership Fee
Founded in 1934

9411 American Society of Farm Managers and Rural Appraisers
950 S Cherry St
Suite 508
Denver, CO 80246-2664
303-758-3513
Fax: 303-758-0190
E-Mail: hevans@asfmra.org
Home Page: www.asfmra.org
Social Media: Facebook, Twitter, LinkedIn

Jim Rickert, President
Fred L. Hepler, President-Elect
Merrill E. Swanson, First Vice President
LeeAnn E. Moss, Academic Vice President

Protects and promotes the interest of members before government, regulatory bodies, and other organizations, enhances member opportunities for professional development and interation with peers, improves ethics, standards and quality of service offered by members, promotes awareness and confidence, and recruits and maintains a highly qualified, professional membership.
Cost: $175.00
Frequency: Membership Fees Vary
Founded in 1929

9412 American Soybean Association
12125 Woodcrest Executive Drive
Suite 100
Saint Louis, MO 63141
314-576-1770
800-688-7692
Fax: 314-576-2786
E-Mail: membership@soy.org
Home Page: www.soygrowers.com
Social Media: Facebook, Twitter, Youtube, Feedburner

Danny Murphy, President
Steve Wellman, Chairman
Ray Gaesser, 1st Vice President
Randy Mann, Secretary
Richard Wilkins, Treasurer

A primary focus of the American Association is policy development and implementation and to improve US soybean farmer profitability.
22000 Members
Founded in 1920

9413 American Spice Trade Association
1101 17th St NW
Suite 700
Washington, DC 20036
ÿ20- 33- 246
Fax: 202-463-8998
E-Mail: info@astaspice.org
Home Page: www.astaspice.org

Gaspare Colletti, President
Kirk Bewley, Vice President/ Secretary
Greg Lightfood, Treasurer
Martin Michelle, Associate Group Director
Dan Crabbe, Director

ASTA, The voice of the US spice industry, works to ensure the supply of clean, safe spice, shape public policy on behalf of the global industry and advance the business interests of its members.
Frequency: Membership Dues Vary
Founded in 1907

9414 American Sugar Alliance
2111 Wilson Blvd
Suite 600
Arlington, VA 22201
703-351-5055
Fax: 703-351-6698
E-Mail: info@sugaralliance.org
Home Page: www.sugaralliance.org
Social Media: Facebook, Twitter

Ryan Weston, ASA Chairman
Vickie Rideout Meyer, Executive Director
Jack Roney, Director of Economy and Policy
Phillip W. Hayes, Director of Media Relations
Laura Gouge, Staff Assistant

The American Sugar Aliance is a national coalition of sugarcane and sugarbett farmers, processors, refiners, suppliers, workers and others dedicated to preserving a strong domestic sugar industry.
Frequency: Membership Fee
Founded in 1983

9415 American Sugar Beet Growers Association
1156 15th St NW
Suite 1101
Washington, DC 20005
202-833-2398
Fax: 240-235-4291
E-Mail: info@americansugarbeet.org
Home Page: www.americansugarbeet.org

Kelly Erickson, President
John Snyder, Vice President
Luther Markwart, Executive Vice President
Ruthan Geib, Vice President
Don Steinbeisser Jr., Treasurer

The purpose of the organization is to unite sugarbeet growers in the United States and promote the common interest of state and regional beet grower associations, which include legislative and international representation and public relations.
10000 Members

9416 American Veal Association
2900 NE Brooktree Lane
Suite 200
Gladstone, MO 64119
717-823-6995
E-Mail: info@americanveal.com
Home Page: www.americanveal.com
Social Media: Facebook, Twitter, Digg, Stumbleupon,Reddit

Jurian Bartelse, President
Dr. Adnan Aydin, Vice President
Chris Landwehr, Treasurer
Dale Bakke, Secretary

Provides information on veal production practices, industry facts, a tour of a modern veal barn and educational materials. Promoting the American veal industry, and encouraging communications and distributing information pertinent to the veal industry.
1300 Members
Founded in 1984

9417 American Wholesale Marketers Association
2750 Prosperity Ave
Suite 530
Fairfax, VA 22031
703-208-3358
800-482-2962
Fax: 703-573-5738
E-Mail: info@awmanet.org
Home Page: www.awmanet.org
Social Media: Facebook, Twitter

Scott Ramminger, President & CEO
Robert Pignato, IOM, Senior Vice President & COO

Anne Holloway, Vice President Government Affairs
Jane Berzan, Vice President of Strategy
Bob Gatty, Vice President, Communications

International trade organization working on behalf of convenience distributors in the U.S. Associate members include manufacturers, brokers, retailers and others allied to the convenience product industry. Typical products purchased and sold by convenience distributors include candy, tobacco, snacks, beverages, health and beauty care items, general merchandise, foodservice and groceries.
530 Members
Frequency: Membership Dues
Founded in 1942

9418 American Wine Society
PO Box 279
Englewood, OH 45322

888-297-9070
E-Mail: executivedirector@americanwinesociety.or
Home Page: www.americanwinesociety.com
Social Media: Facebook, Twitter, LinkedIn

Willis L. Parker, President
Jane M. Duralia, Vice President
John W. Hames, Executive Director
Samuel D. Streiff, Treasurer

The oldest and largest consumer based wine education organization in North America. A non-profit, educational, consumer-oriented organization for those interested in learning more about all aspects of wine.
Cost: $52.00
5000 Members
Frequency: Membership Dues Vary
Founded in 1967

9419 Animal Agriculture Alliance
2101 Wilson Blvd
Suite 916-B
Arlington, VA 22201

703-562-5160
Fax: 703-524-1921
E-Mail: info@animalagalliance.org
Home Page: www.animalagalliance.org
Social Media: Facebook, Twitter

Kay Johnson Smith, President & CEO
Morgan Hawley, Executive Assistant to President
Emily Metz Meredith, Communications Director
Shakera Daley, Administrative Assistant

The animal Agriculture Alliance is a 501 (c)(3) education foundation. The alliance's mission is to support and promote animal agricultural practices that provide for farm animal well-being through sound science and public education.
3000 Members
Founded in 1987

9420 Apple Processors Association
1701 K Street, NW
Suite 650
Washington, DC 20006

202-785-6715
Fax: 202-331-4212
E-Mail: pweller@agriwashington.org
Home Page: www.appleprocessors.org
Social Media: Facebook

Paul S. Weller Jr., President
Andrea Ball, Sr. Director of Mtgs & Admin
Nancy Chapman, VP, Food & Nutrition Policy

A national association of companies that manufacture quality apple products from whole apples. Members are either apple grower/processor cooperatives, or proprietary firms.
25 Members
Founded in 1987

9421 Apple Products Research & Education Council
1100 Johnson Ferry Road
Suite 300
Atlanta, GA 30342

404-252-3663
Fax: 404-252-0774
E-Mail: info@appleproducts.org
Home Page: www.appleproducts.org

Formerly known as The Processed Apples Institute. We are producers of processed apple products; suppliers of equipment, packaging or ingredients to the industry and brokers and concentrate manufacturers.
80 Members
Founded in 1951

9422 Association for Dressings & Sauces
1100 Johnson Ferry Road
Suite 300
Atlanta, GA 30342

678-298-1181
Fax: 404-252-0774
E-Mail: ads@kellencompany.com
Home Page: www.dressings-sauces.org
Social Media: Facebook, Youtube

Pam Chumley, President
Jeannie Milewski, Executive Director
Jacque Knight, Membership/Administration Manager

This association is comprised of manufacturers of mayonnaise, salad dressings and condiment sauces, as well as industry suppliers. Its purpose is to serve the best interests of industry members, its customers, and consumers of its products.
184 Members
Founded in 1926
Mailing list available for rent

9423 Association for Packaging and Processing Technologies
Packaging Machinery Manufacturers Institute
11911 Freedom Drive
Suite 600
Reston, VA 20190

703-243-8555
888-275-7664
Fax: 703-243-8556
E-Mail: pmmiwebhelp@pmmi.org
Home Page: www.pmmi.org
Social Media: Facebook, Twitter, LinkedIn, YouTube

Charles D. Yuska, President
Katie Bergmann, Vice President, Administration

Members manufacture packaging and packaging-related converting machinery in the United States and Canada. PMMI's vision is to be the leading global resource for packaging. Its mission is to improve and promote members' abilities to meet the needs of their customers.
500+ Members
Founded in 1933

9424 Association of American Feed Control Officials
Purdue University
1800 S. Oak Street
Suite 100
Champaign, IL 61820-6974

217-356-4221
Fax: 217-398-4119
E-Mail: aafco@aafco.org
Home Page: www.aafco.org
Social Media: Facebook

Tim Darden, President
Doug Lueders, President-Elect
Ali Kashani, Secretary/Treasurer
Mark LeBlanc, Sr. Director
Richard Teneyck, Sr. Director

A voluntary membership association of local, state and federal agencies charged by law to regulate the sale and distribution of animal feeds and animal drug remedies.
54 Members
Founded in 1909

9425 Association of American Seed Control Officials
Utah Department of Agriculture and Food
350 N Redwood Road
PO Box 146500
Salt Lake City, UT 84114-6500

801-538-7182
Fax: 801-538-7189
E-Mail: walshm@purdue.edu
Home Page: www.seedcontrol.org

John Heaton, President
Steve Malone, 1st Vice President
Jim Drews, 2nd Vice President
Greg Helmbrecht, Treasurer
Larry Nees, Secretary

The AASCO's purpose is to promote and establish basic requirements of a state seed law which shall serve as guidelines for member states, to promote and foster uniformity of procedures and policies by member states, to exchange problems and solutions or ideas and suggestions, to coordinate action and cooperate, and to impress and create a sense of mutual understanding between members and other organizations that are concerned with orderly legal merchandising of high quality seed.
Founded in 1949

9426 Association of Correctional Food Service Affiliates
210 N Glenoaks Blvd
Suite C
Burbank, CA 91502

818-843-6608
Fax: 818-843-7423
E-Mail: philip.atkinson@co.hennepin.mn.us
Home Page: www.acfsa.org
Social Media: Facebook, Twitter, Shutterfly

Phil Atkinson, President
Robin Sherman, CCFP, CFSM, Vice President
Laurie Maurino, Vice President Elect/Treasurer
Karen Candito, CCFP, CFSM, Secretary

An international non-profit organization dedicated to the professional growth of our many nation's correctional foodservice employees. Association members are foodservice professionals employed in correctional facilities and agencies within federal, state and municipal prison/jail systems. Members are employed within government and commercially operated facilities within the United States, Canada, and an expanding international market.
Cost: $50.00
1300 Members
Frequency: Dues up to $150
Founded in 1969

9427 Association of Food Industries
3301 State Route 66
Building C, Suite 205
Neptune, NJ 07753

732-922-3008
Fax: 732-922-3590
E-Mail: info@afius.org
Home Page: www.afius.org
Social Media: Facebook

Andy Gellert, Chair
Jill Bush, 1st Vice Chair
Fred Mortati, 2nd Vice Chair
Stephen O'Mara, Treasurer
James Libby, Secretary

Promotes free trade and commerce in the food industry. Offers information and education on customs and usage of trade in the food markets and represents member interests in government.
Cost: $1040.00
800 Members
Frequency: Membership Dues Vary
Founded in 1906

9428 **Association of Food and Drug Officials**
2550 Kingston Rd
Suite 311
York, PA 17402
717-757-2888
Fax: 717-650-3650
E-Mail: afdo@afdo.org
Home Page: www.afdo.org
Social Media: Twitter
David Read, President
Stephen Stich, President-elect
Stan Stromberg, Vice-President
Steven Moris, Secretary/Treasurer
Joseph Corby, Executive Director
Promotes the enforcement of laws and regulations at all levels of government. Fosters understanding and cooperation between industry and regulators. Develops model laws and regulations and seeks their adoption.
800 Members
Frequency: Membership Dues Vary
Founded in 1896

9429 **Association of Seafood Importers**
Empress International
10 Harbor Park Drive
Port Washington, NY 11050-4681
516-621-5900
800-645-6244
Fax: 516-621-8318
Burt C Faure
Membership is comprised of seafood importers focusing on problems facing the industry.

9430 **Association of Smoked Fish Processors**
85 John Road
Canton, MA 02021
781-821-2200
800-444-8705
Fax: 781-821-9266
E-Mail: info@shusterlabs.com
Home Page: www.shusterlabs.com
This association provides technical consulation and services to the smoked fish and seafood industry. Services include recall manuals, plant audits, product evaluations, process evaluation, process evaluation, microbiological testing, analytical testing. HACCP plan development and plan ventilation.

9431 **At-Sea Processors Association**
4039 21st Ave W
Suite 400
Seattle, WA 98199
206-285-5139
Fax: 206-285-1841
Home Page: www.atsea.org
Stephanie Madsen, Executive Director
Paul MacGregor, General Counsel
Jim Gilmore, Public Affairs Director
A trade association representing seven copmanies that own and operate 19 U.S. flag cathcer/processor vessels that participate principally in the Alaska pollack fishery and west coast Pacific whiting fishery.
Cost: $500.00
7 Members
Frequency: Membership Varies
Founded in 1985

9432 **Bakery Equipment Manufacturers and Allieds (BEMA)**
10740 Nall Avenue
Suite 230
Overland Park, KS 66211
913-338-1300
Fax: 913-338-1327
E-Mail: info@bema.org
Home Page: www.bema.org
Social Media: Facebook, Twitter
Troy Henry, President & CEO
Rick Hoskins, President
Bruce Campbell, Vice President Technology
Bob Miller, Vice President & Director
Through the exchange of information, active involvement on committees and participation in educational seminars, BEMA members are continually able to increase the efficiency and sophistication of their equipment while keeping design in adherence with Baking Industry Standarts Committee (BISSC) codes. Continually improving the efficiency of production and establishing sanitation standards.
208 Members
Frequency: Annual Membership Dues
Founded in 1918

9433 **Baking Industry Sanitation Standards Committee**
PO Box 3999
Manhattan, KS 66505-3999
866-342-4772
785-537-4750
Fax: 785-537-1493
E-Mail: bissc@bissc.org
Home Page: www.bissc.org
James Munyon, President
Jon Anderson, Board Member
Develops and promotes sanitation standards for the design and construction of bakery equipment. Offers certification and third party verification programs for the member companies whose equipment conforms to the BISSC standards.
125 Members
Founded in 1949

9434 **Beef Industry Food Safety Council**
Attn: Deb Cole
9110 E. Nichols Ave
Centennial, CO 80112
303-850-3320
Fax: 303-770-6921
E-Mail: dcole@beef.org
Home Page: www.bifsco.org
Deborah Cole, Administrative Coordinator
Gary Voogt, President
Forrest Roberts, CEO
Luisa Munsee, Treasurer
Bill Donald, VP
BIFSCo brings together representatives from all segments of the beef industry to develop industry-wide, science-based strategies to solve the problem of food borne pathogens.

9435 **Beef and Lamb New Zealand**
PO Box 121
Wellington, NZ 6140
644-473-9150
800-233-352
Fax: 644-474-0800
E-Mail: enquiries@beeflambnz.com
Home Page: www.beeflambnz.com
Social Media: Facebook, Twitter, LinkedIn, Youtube, Pinterest
Dr. Scott Champion, Chief Executive Officer
Cros Spooner, Chief Operating Officer
Andy Fox, Director
Anne Munro, Director
Craig Hickson, Director
Funded by livestock producers through levies on all beef, sheep and goats slaughtered and on all wool sold. This income is used primarily to market New Zealand wool and meat worldwide, to maintain and extend trade access for New Zealand wool and meat, to provide solutions that will help improve New Zealand farm returns, and to provide technology to the wool industry.

9436 **Beer Institute**
Beer Institute
122 C St NW
Suite 350
Washington, DC 20001
202-737-2337
800-379-2739
Fax: 202-737-7004
E-Mail: info@beerinstitute.org
Home Page: www.beerinstitute.org
Social Media: Facebook, Twitter
Joe McClain, President
Mary Jane Saunders, VP & General Counsel
The national trade association for the brewing industry. Representing both big and small brewers as well as importers and industry suppliers.
Founded in 1986

9437 **Beet Sugar Development Foundation**
800 Grant Street
Suite 300
Denver, CO 80203
303-832-4460
Fax: 303-832-4468
E-Mail: Tom@bsdf-assbt.org
Home Page: www.bsdf-assbt.org
J.W. Schorr, President
T.D. Knudsen, First Vice President
J. Dean, Second VP
T.K. Schwartz, Executive Vice President/Secretary
Association specializing in beet sugar research and the advertisement of seed companies.
Cost: $100.00
13 Members
Frequency: Membership Fee/Max. $450

9438 **Biodynamic Farming & Gardening Association**
1661 N Water Streetÿ
Suite 307
Milwaukeeÿ, WI 53202
262-649-9212
Fax: 262-649-9213
E-Mail: info@biodynamics.com
Home Page: www.biodynamics.com
Social Media: Facebook
Robert Karp, Executive Director
Thea Maria Calson, Director of Programs
Jessica St. John, Director of Operations
Rebecca Briggs, Communications Coordinator
Ken Keffer, Program Assistant
A non-profit, membership organization open to the public with a purpose to foster knowledge of the practices and principles of the biodynamic method of agriculture, horticulture, and forestry in the North American continent and to advance the applications of this method through educational activities such as research, lectures, conferences; publishing literature on the biodynamic methods, and supporting consultation and extension services to farmers, gardeners, and foresters.
Cost: $45.00
Frequency: 6 per year
Circulation: 1000+

9439 Biscuit & Cracker Manufacturers' Association
6325 Woodside Court
Suite 125
Columbia, MD 21046

443-545-1645
Fax: 410-290-8585
E-Mail: dvanlaar@thebcma.org
Home Page: www.thebcma.org
Social Media: Facebook, Twitter

Dave Van Laar, President
Vanessa Vial, Comm. & eLearning Manager
Kathy Kinter Phelps, Member & Edu. Services Mgr

An international trade organization representing the entire spectrum of companies in the manufacturing of cookies and crackers and suppliers to theindustry.

9440 Blue Diamond Growers
1701 C Street
Sacramento, CA 95811

916-442-0771
800-987-2329
Fax: 916-446-8461
E-Mail: feedback@bdgrowers.com
Home Page: www.bluediamondgrowers.com
Social Media: Facebook, Twitter, Youtube, Pinterest

Clinton Shick (McFarland), Chairman of the Board
Dale Van Groningen, Vice Chairman
Mark Jansen, President & CEO
Don Yee, Director-at-large
David Baker, Director, Member relations

The world's largest tree nut processing and marketing company. Building markets and creating new products, uses, and opportunities for members.

9441 Board of Trade of Wholesale Seafood
7 Dey Street
Room 801
New York, NY 10007-3223

212-732-4340
Fax: 212-732-6644
Home Page: www.aboutseafood.com
Social Media: Facebook, Twitter, Googelplus

Albert Altesnan, President/Administrator

Credit exchange and collection agency for wholesale seafood merchants and producers, in the US and Canada.
Founded in 1931

9442 Bread Bakers Guild of America
670 West Napa Street
Suite B
Sonoma, CA 95476

707-935-1468
Fax: 707-935-1672
E-Mail: info@bbga.org
Home Page: www.bbga.org
Social Media: Facebook, Twitter

Jeff Yankellow, Board Chair
Phyllis Enloe, Board Vice Chair
Neale Creamer, Treasurer

Well known in the baking community as the go-to educational resource for substantive, accurate information on the craft of making bread. The definitive resource on all aspects of artisan baking in America, supporting and fostering the growth of the artisan baking community. Defining and upholding the highest professional standarts, and celebrating the craft and the passion of the artisan baker.
1300 Members
Founded in 1993

9443 Brewers Association
736 Pearl Street
Boulder, CO 80302

303-447-0816
888-822-6273
Fax: 303-447-2825
E-Mail: info@brewersassociation.org
Home Page: www.beertown.org
Social Media: Facebook, Twitter

Sam Calagione, Chair
Gary Fish, Vice Chair
Mark Edelson, Treasurer/Secretary

The goal of the BA is to promote and protect small and independent American brewers, their craft beers and the community of brewing enthusiasts.
1900 Members
Founded in 1978

9444 Brown Swiss Association
800 Pleasant St
Beloit, WI 53511-5456

608-365-4474
Fax: 608-365-5577
E-Mail: info@brownswissusa.com
Home Page: www.brownswissusa.com
Social Media: Facebook

Lee Barber, President
Bill Nolan, Vice President
David Wallace, Executive Secretary
Dieter Bradley, Director
Tome Portner, Director

Membership is comprised of key dairy industry leaders and dairy producers who are on the cutting edge of the world's latest agricultural technology.
800 Members
Founded in 1880

9445 Brown Swiss Cattle Breeder's Association
800 Pleasant Street
Beloit, WI 53511

608-365-4474
Fax: 608-365-5577
E-Mail: info@brownswissusa.com
Home Page: www.brownswissusa.com
Social Media: Facebook

Lee Barber, President
Tom Portner, Vice President
David Wallace, Exec. Secretary
Bill Nolan, Board of Director
Jeffrey Kennedy, Board of Director

Registers about 10,000 animals per year and promotes and expands the Brown Swiss breed with programs that assist the membership and industry to compete favorably in the market place.

9446 CCFMA Annual Convention
Conference Caterers & Food Manufacturers Assoc.
1205 Spartan Drive
Madison Heights, MI 48071

248-982-5379
E-Mail: ccfma@ymail.com
Home Page: www.mobilecaterers.com

See the changes in the industry, learn tools to help business succeed and grow, and network with peers.
Frequency: Annual/October
Founded in 1964

9447 Calaveras Winegrape Alliance
P.O. Box 2492
Murphys, CA

209-728-9467
866-806-9463
E-Mail: calaveraswines@att.net
Home Page: www.calaveraswines.org
Social Media: Facebook, Twitter, Pinterest

Dedicated to increasing the awareness of all wines produced in Calaveras County and/or produced from Calaveras grapes.

9448 California Walnuts
101 Parkshore Dr.
Ste. 2503
Folsom, CA 95630

916-932-7070
Fax: 916-932-7071
E-Mail: info@walnuts.org
Home Page: www.walnuts.org
Social Media: Facebook, Twitter, YouTube, Pinterest

Dennis A. Balint, Executive Director

Established to represent walnut growers and handlers. The board promotes usage of walnuts in the U.S. through publicity, product promotions and production research and education programs.
Founded in 1948
Mailing list available for rent

9449 Calorie Control Council
2611 Winslow Dr Ne
Atlanta, GA 30305-3777

678-608-3200
Fax: 404-252-0774
E-Mail: webmaster@caloriecontrol.org
Home Page: www.caloriecontrol.org

An international non-profit association representing the low-calorie food and beverage industry. The Council seeks to provide an effective channel of communication among its members, the public and government officials, and to assure that scientific, medical and other pertinent research and information is developed and made available to all interested parties.
60 Members
Founded in 1966

9450 Can Manufacturers Institute
1730 Rhode Island Ave NW
Suite 1000
Washington, DC 20036

202-232-4677
Fax: 202-232-5756
Home Page: www.cancentral.com
Social Media: Facebook, Twitter, LinkedIn

Robert Budway, President

Serves as the voice of the metal can making industry, providing a forum for members to advocate common industry problems to legislative and regulatory agencies whose activities impact the metal can market, to address issues of common concern, and to promote cost-effectively the benefits of the can to protect and grow the market.
35 Members
Founded in 1939

9451 Canned Foods
PO Box 5258
Madison, WI 53705-0000

608-231-2250
Fax: 608-231-6952
E-Mail: webmaster@cannedveggies.org
Home Page: www.cannedveggies.org

Gene Kroupa, Executive Director

An educational and promotional organization of vegetable canners whose goals are to raise the awareness of consumer and food service buyers regarding canned vegetables.
80 Members
Founded in 1977

9452 Canola Council of Canada
167 Lombard Avenue Suite 400
Winnipeg, Manitoba
Canada R3B 0T6

204-982-2100
866-834-4378
Fax: 204-942-1841
E-Mail: admin@canola-council.org
Home Page: www.canola-council.org

Patti Miller, President
Jim Everson, Vice President, Gov Relations
Bruce Jowett, Vice President, Market Development
Curtis Rempel, Vice President, Crop Production
Cari Mell, Comptroller

Representing canola growers, input suppliers, researchers, processors and marketers of canola and its products.

9453 Cape Cod Cranberry Growers Association
1 Carver Square Boulevard
PO Box 97
Carver, MA 02330

508-866-7678
Fax: 508-866-4220
E-Mail: info@cranberries.org
Home Page: www.cranberries.org

Brad Morse, President
Gary Garretson, 1st Vice President
Keith Mann, 2nd Vice President
Carolyn DeMoranville, Secretary/ Treasurer

Established to standardize the measure with which cranberries are sold, the CCCGA is one of the country's oldest farmers' organizations. Giving growers both a single voice and a collective strength in promoting the cranberry industry, and working to ensure that cranberry farming can survive urbanization and the open space and clean water, vital to growing, will be preserved.

9454 Carneros Wine Alliance
PO Box 189
Vineburg, CA 95487

707-812-1919
E-Mail: info@carneros.com
Home Page: www.carneros.com
Social Media: Facebook, Twitter

T. J. Evans, Chair
Anne Moller-Racke, Vice Chair
Scott Bauer, Treasurer
Alison Crowe, Board of Director
Mitch Davis, Board of Director

A nonprofit association of wineries and grape-owners in the Carneros American Viticultural Area (AVA).

9455 Center for Food Safety & Applied Nutrition
5100 Paint Branch Parkway
College Park, MD 20740

888-723-3366
E-Mail: consumer@fda.gov
Home Page: www.cfsan.fda.gov

Provides services to consumers, domestic and foreign industry and other outside groups regarding field programs; agency administrative tasks; scientific analysis and support; and policy, planning and handling of critical issues related to food and cosmetics.

9456 Cheese Importers Association of America
204 E Street NE
Washington, DC 20002

202-547-0899
Fax: 202-547-6348
E-Mail: info@theciaa.org
Home Page: www.theciaa.org

Thomas Gellert, President
Dominique Delugeau, First Vice President
Ken Olsson, 2nd Vice President
Philip Marfuggi, Treasurer
Daniel Schnyder, Secretary

Helps facilitate the efficient import of dairy products from around thw world into the United States. The CIAA endeavors to support dairy trade, within the context of compliance with international trade agreements and all applicable US regulations, and maintains active contacts with government officials worldwide in order to further the objectives of the organization and its members.
150 Members
Founded in 1942

9457 Cherry Marketing Institute
PO Box 30285
Lansing, MI 48909
925-838-5454
Fax: 925-838-2311
E-Mail: info@choosecherries.com
Home Page: www.choosecherries.com
Social Media: Facebook, Twitter

Philip Korson II, President
Fred Tubbs, Chairman
Chris Dunkel, Manager

Association representing the cherry industry. Provides promotional material to food service operators, brokers, retailers and manufacturers.
Founded in 1988
Mailing list available for rent

9458 Chocolate Manufacturers Association
1101 30th Street NW
Suite 200
Washington, DC 20007

202-534-1440
Fax: 202-337-0637
E-Mail: info@candyUSA.com
Home Page: www.chocolateusa.org

Lynn Bragg, President
Carly Zoerb, Executive Assistant

The trade group for manufacturers and distributors of cocoa and chocolate products in the United States. The association was founded to fund and administer research, promote chocolate to the general public and serve as an advocate of the industry before Congress and government agencies.
9 Members
Founded in 1884

9459 Citrus Industry Magazine
5053 NW Hwy 225-A
Ocala, FL 34482

352-671-1909
Fax: 888-943-2224
E-Mail: office@southeastagent.com
Home Page: www.citrusindustry.net

Ernie Ness, Editor

Association for citrus grower organizations and other trade associations within the industry.
Mailing list available for rent

9460 Coca-Cola Bottlers Association
3282 Northside Parkway
Suite 200
Atlanta, GA 30327

404-872-2258
Fax: 404-872-2869
Home Page: www.ccbanet.com

Michael Faber, President
Hank Flint, Vice President
M. Trevor Messinger, Treasurer
Ann Burton, CFO
John Gould, Executive Director & CEO

Assisting members in reducing costs and improving efficiency, the Association acts as a servicing arm and agent on behalf of participating Bottlers to meet their needs in numerous areas, including procurement, employee benefits, insurance programs and retirement plans. Also serves as a primary mechanism for fostering the exchange of ideas and information within the Coca-Cola system.

9461 Coffee, Sugar and Cocoa Exchange
New York Board of Trade
1 N End Avenue
New York, NY 10282-1101

212-748-4000
Fax: 212-748-4039
Home Page: www.csce.com

Acts as a financial exchange where futures and options are traded, the CSCE provides hedging and investing, opportunities in the coffee, sugar, cocoa and dairy markets.

9462 Colombia Coffee Federation
140 E 57th Street
New York, NY 10022

212-421-8300
Fax: 212-758-3816
E-Mail: judyb@juynvald.com

John Boden, Manager
Founded in 1964

9463 Commercial Food Equipment Service Association
PO BOX 77139
Greensboro, NC 27417

336-346-4700
Fax: 336-346-4745
E-Mail: asidders@cfesa.com
Home Page: www.cfesa.com
Social Media: Facebook, LinkedIn, MySpace, YouTube

Joe Pierce, President
Brock Coleman, Vice President
Paul Toukatly, Vice President
Wayne Stoutner, Treasurer
David Hahn, Secretary

The trade association of professional service and parts distributors. Helps members meet the challenges of the industry and ensure customer satisfaction.
450 Members
Founded in 1963
Mailing list available for rent

9464 Communicating for America
112 E Lincoln Avenue
Fergus Falls, MN 56537

218-739-3241
800-432-3276
Fax: 218-739-3832
E-Mail: memberbenefits@cainc.org
Home Page: www.communicatingforamerica.org

Milt Smedsrud, Chairman
Patty Strickland, President & COO
Wayne Nelson, President
Stephen Rufer, Vice President & General Counsel
Roger Gussiaas, Vice President

Strives to promote health, well being and advancement of people in agriculture and agribusiness.
40M Members
Founded in 1972

9465 Communication and Agricultural Education
Oklahoma State University

301 Umberger Hall
Manhattan, KS 66506

785-532-5804
Fax: 785-532-5633
E-Mail: commdept@ksu.edu
Home Page: www.communications.ksu.edu
Social Media: Facebook, Twitter, Youtube, Foursquare

Beth Holz, President
Wyatt Betchel, First VP
Megan Brouk, Second VP
Amanda Spoo, Secretary
Brittney Machado, Treasurer

The Mission of National ACT is to build relationships among agricultural communication professionals and college students and faculty, to provide professional and academic development for members and to promote agriculture through communications efforts.
Founded in 1970

9466 Composite Can and Tube Institute

50 S Pickett Street
Suite 110
Alexandria, VA 22304-7206

703-823-7234
Fax: 703-823-7237
E-Mail: ccti@cctiwdc.org
Home Page: www.cctiwdc.org

Kristine Garland, Executive VP
Janine Marczak, Associate Manager, Events
Wayne Vance, Association Counsel

CCTI is an international nonprofit trade association representing the interests of manufacturers of composite paperboard cans, containers, canisters, tubes, cores, edgeboard and related or similar composite products and suppliers to those manufacturers of such items as paper, machinery, adhesives, labels and other services and materials.
Founded in 1933

9467 Concord Grape Association

112 N, Portage Street
PO Box 399
Westfield, NY 14787

716-326-3161
E-Mail: info@concordgrape.org
Home Page: www.concordgrape.org

Pam Chumley, Executive Director
Linda Whitley, Contact

The Concord Grape Association represents processors of Concord grapes and manufacturers of products derived from them. The organization operates as the Concord Grape Section under the umbrella of the Juice Products Association (JPA), which represents the juice and juice products industry in the U.S. and overseas. Members handle more than the majority of the Concord grapes processed annually in the United States.

9468 Consultants Association for the Natural Products Industry (CANI)

PO Box 4014
Clovis, CA 93613

559-325-7192
Fax: 559-325-7195
E-Mail: info@cani-consultants.org
Home Page: www.cani-consultants.org
Social Media: LinkedIn

Karena K. Dillon, President
Robert Forbes, Vice President
Ginni Garner, Treasurer
Sheldon Baker, Director

Committed to working individually and collectively, to enhance the growth and integrity of the natural products industry by providing professional expertise and objective counsel to our clients. These specialized services contribute to the prosperity and values of the individual business as well as the industry as a whole.
Founded in 1991

9469 Convenience Caterers & Food Manufacturers Association

1205 Spartan Drive
Madison Heights, MI 48071

248-982-5379
E-Mail: ccfma@ymail.com
Home Page: www.mobilecaterers.com

Dedicated to the best interests of the growing industrial catering industry and to a commitment of excellence in service to catering truck operators, the food service industry, and the public. An international association representing food service professionals who are anxious to improve mobile catering operations.
Founded in 1964

9470 Cookware Manufacturers Association

PO Box 531335
Birminghan, AL 35253-1335

205-592-0389
Fax: 205-599-5598
E-Mail: hrushing@usit.net
Home Page: www.cookware.org

Jay Zilinskas, President
Gene Karlson, VP
Hugh J Rushing, Executive VP

Represents manufactures of cookware and bakeware in the US and Canada. Publishes consumer guides to cookware and engineering standards for industry.
21 Members
Founded in 1922

9471 Corn Refiners Association

1701 Pennsylvania Avenue N.W.
Suite 950
Washington, DC 20006

202-331-1634
Fax: 202-331-2054
E-Mail: comments@corn.org
Home Page: www.corn.org
Social Media: Facebook, Twitter, Stumbleupon, Digg

Audrae Erickson, President
Shannon Weiner, Executive Assistant
Bob Adams, Director Public Affairs
Pat Saks, Assistant Director

Supports carbohydrate research programs through grants to colleges, government laboratories and private research centers.
8 Members
Founded in 1913

9472 Council for Agricultural Science and Technology

4420 West Lincoln Way
Ames, IA 50014-3447

515-292-2125
Fax: 515-292-4512
E-Mail: cast@cast-science.org
Home Page: www.cast-science.org
Social Media: Facebook, Twitter, LinkedIn, YouTube, Schooltube

Lowell Midla, President
David Songstad, President-Elect
Linda M. Chimenti, Executive Vice President
Gerald Weigel, Treasurer

Assembles, interprets and communicates science based information regionally, nationally and internationally on food, fiber, agriculture, natural resources, and related societal and environmental issues.
2000+ Members
Founded in 1972

9473 Council for Responsible Nutrition

1828 L St NW
Suite 510
Washington, DC 20036-5114

202-204-7700
Fax: 202-204-7701
E-Mail: webmaster@crnusa.org
Home Page: www.crnusa.org
Social Media: Twitter, Googleplus

Steve Mister, President & CEO
Judy Blatman, Senior Vice President
Mike Greene, Vice President, Gov Relations
James C. Griffiths, Vice President, Scientific
Douglas Mackay, Vice President, Science

The leading trade association representing dietary supplement manufacturers and ingredient suppliers. Member companies manufacture popular national brands as well as the store brands marketed by major supermarkets, drug store and discount chains. All members also agree to adhere to voluntary guidelines for manufacturing, marketing and CRN's Code of Ethics.
70 Members
Founded in 1973

9474 Council of Supply Chain Management Professionals

333 E Butterfield Rd
Suite 140
Lombard, IL 60148

630-574-0985
Fax: 630-574-0989
E-Mail: cscmpadmin@cscmp.org
Home Page: www.cscmp.org
Social Media: Facebook, Twitter, LinkedIn, YouTube

Heather Sheehan, Chair
Theodore Stank, Chair-Elect
Kevin Smith, Vice Chair
Mary Long, Secretary & Treasurer

CSCMP's mission is to lead the evolving supply chain management profession by developing, advancing, and disseminating supply chain knowledge and research.
10000 Members
Founded in 1963

9475 Crop Insurance and Reinsurance Bureau

201 Massachusetts Avenue, NE
Suite C5
Washington, DC 20002

202-544-0067
Fax: 202-330-5255
E-Mail: mtorrey@cropinsurance.org
Home Page: www.cropinsurance.org

Greg Mills, Chairman
Sheri Bane, Vice-Chairwoman
Mike Torrey, Executive Vice President
Tara Smith, Federal Affairs Vice President
Ron Rutledge, Treasurer

National trade association made up of insurance providers and related organizations that provide a variety of insurance products for our nation's farmers.
Founded in 1964

9476 Crop Life America

1156 15th St NW
Washington, DC 20005

202-296-1585
Fax: 202-463-0474
E-Mail: webmaster@croplifeamerica.org
Home Page: www.croplifeamerica.org
Social Media: Facebook, Twitter, LinkedIn, YouTube

Jay Vroom, President
Bill Kuckuck, Executive VP & COO
Dr. Barbara Glenn, Senior Vice President

Rachel Lattimore, Senior Vice President
Doug Nelson, Senior Advisor

A trade association of manufacturers and distributors of agriculture crop protection and pest control products.
74 Members
Founded in 1933

9477 **Crop Science Society of America**
5585 Guilford Rd.
Madison, WI 53711-5801

608-273-8080
Fax: 608-273-2021
E-Mail: membership@sciencesocieties.org
Home Page: www.crops.org
Social Media: Facebook, Twitter, LinkedIn

Mark Brick, President
David Baltensperger, President-Elect
Ellen G.M. Bergfeld, CEO

Dedicated to the conservation and wise use of natural resources to produce food, feed, and fiber crops while maintaining and improving the environment. Continuously evolving and modifying it's educational offerings to support the changing needs of its members.
4700 Members
Founded in 1955

9478 **Dairy Farmers of America**
10220 N Ambassador Dr
Kansas City, MO 64153

816-801-6455
888-332-6455
Fax: 816-801-6456
E-Mail: webmail@dfamilk.com
Home Page: www.dfamilk.com
Social Media: Facebook, Twitter, LinkedIn, YouTube

Rick Smith, President & CEO
John McDaniel, Senior Vice President
Alex Bachelor, Senior Vice President
Randy McGinnis, Senior Vice President & COO
David Meyer, Senior Vice President, Finance

A milk marketing cooperative and dairy food processor dedicated to delivering value to members through secure markets, competitive pricing and increasing value throughout the entire diary chain.
Founded in 1998

9479 **Dairy Management, Inc.**
O'Hare International Center
10255 W Higgins Rd
Suite 900
Rosemont, IL 60018-5616

847-803-2000
800-853-2479
Fax: 847-803-2077
Home Page: www.dairy.org

James Ahlem, Chair
Skip Hardie, Secretary

This association aims to provide the sale and consumption of milk and milk products in the US.
Founded in 1980

9480 **Dairy and Food Industries Supply Association**
1451 Dolley Madison Boulevard
McLean, VA 22101-3879

703-883-0515
Fax: 703-761-4334

John Martin, President
Burce D'Agostino, Vice President
Mary O'Dea, Communications Manager

Trade association of almost 800 suppliers to the food, beverage, dairy, pharmaceutical and related sanitary processing industries.

9481 **Diamond of California**
1050 S Diamond Street
Stockton, CA 95205

209-467-6000
Fax: 209-467-6788
Home Page: www.diamondnuts.com

Brian J. Discoll, President & CEO
Ray Silcock, Executive Vice President & CFO
Lloyd J. Jhonson, Executive Vice President
David Colo, Executive Vice President & COO
Stephen Kim, Senior Vice President

Walnut growers' association with Diamond guarantees a market for their crops and provides the company with high quality walnuts. Diamond provides information and resources to help growers to produce the best nuts in the world.
1900 Members
Founded in 1912

9482 **Distillers Grains Technology Council**
University of Louisville
Lutz Hall
Room 435
Louisville, KY 40292

502-852-1575
800-759-3448
Fax: 502-852-1577
E-Mail: chstaf01@louisville.edu
Home Page: www.distillersgrains.org

Charles Staff, Executive Director/CEO

A non-profit organization that stresses the importance of utilization of distillers co-products in animal feeds. We address the production and product quality issues that are known to impact the market acceptability and production costs of these products.
7 Members
Founded in 1945

9483 **Dr. Pepper Bottlers Association**
PO Box 906
Rowlett, TX 75030-0906

972-475-7397
Fax: 972-475-5290
Social Media: Facebook, Twitter, Googleplus

Bill Elmore Jr, President
James Lee, Vice President
Scott Chase, Secretary/ Director
Bill Yarbrough, Treasurer/ Director

Represents 430 bottlers for the Dr. Pepper Company.

9484 **Drug, Chemical & Associated Technologies Association**
1 Washington Blvd
Suite 7
Robbinsville, NJ 08691

609-448-1000
800-640-3228
Fax: 609-448-1944
E-Mail: mtimony@dcat.org
Home Page: www.dcat.org

Lyra Myers, President
George Svokos, Sr. Vice President
Milton Boyer, Vice President
Christopher Rayfield, VP-Pharmaceutical Services Industry
David Beattie, VP-Biotechnology

The premier business development association whose membership is comprised of companies that manufacture, distribute or provide services to the pharamceutical, chemical, nutritional and related industries.
Founded in 1890

9485 **Eastern Frosted and Refrigerated Foods Association**
17 Park St
Wanaque, NJ 07465

973-835-1710
Fax: 973-835-1708
E-Mail: efra@efraweb.org
Home Page: www.efraweb.org

Bob Bollbach, President
Paul Raguso, 1st Vice President
Pat Longo, 2nd Vice President
Sue Brooks, 3rd Vice President
Hans Ketel, Secretary

Brings together all related segments of the frozen food industry; brokers, warehousing, manufacturers, transportation, distributors, packaging/labeling and retailers. Constantly gathering information for members from authoritative national and regional sources, other members, and publication editorials affecting the industry.
65 Members
Founded in 1937

9486 **Eastern Perishable Products Association**
61 Woodhollow Road
PO Box 478
Colts Neck, NJ 07722

973-831-4100
Fax: 973-831-8100
Home Page: www.eppainc.org
Social Media: Facebook

Fred D'Agostino, President
Barry Kahn, Chairman
Robert Carley, Vice President
Stan Futoran, Vice President
Tom Tracy, Secretary

Regional association with national and international recognition. The EPPA keeps the industry current with the trends, new products, packaging, programs, changes and technical advances that are so dynamic in todays marketplace through projects, publications and activities.
130 Members

9487 **Electric Foodservice Council**
180 Raymond Court
PO Box 142156
Fayetteville, GA 30214

770-461-3870
Fax: 770-461-7799
E-Mail: krhutchinson1@msn.com
Home Page: www.foodservicecouncil.org

Billy Griffis, President
Jim Wixson, Senior Vice President
Roshena Ham, Secretary
Mitzi Shanks, Treasurer

Unique organization designed to bring together utilities, equipment manufacturers, trade allies, and foodservice operators who are committed to the advancement of the foodservice industry.
Founded in 1987

9488 **Farmer Direct Foods Inc.**
511 Commercial
PO Box 326
Atchison, KS 66002

913-367-4422
800-372-4422
Fax: 913-367-4443
E-Mail: orders@farmerdirectfoods.org
Home Page: www.farmerdirectfoods.com

Kent Symns, Chief Executive Officer
Marcia Walters, Director Of Operations

A producer owned cooperative marketing corporation formed in 1988 with the mission to

develop white wheat markets for wheat producers.
125 Members
Founded in 1988

9489 Fermenters International Trade Association
PO Box 1373
Valrico, FL 33595
813-685-4261
Fax: 813-681-5625
Home Page: www.hwbta.org
Social Media: Facebook, Twitter
Dee Roberson, Executive Director
Bill Metzger, Editor
Manufacturers, wholesalers, retailers, authors and editors having a commercial interest in the beer and wine trade. Offers publications to members only.
200+ Members
Founded in 1976

9490 Fertilizer Institute
425 Third Street, SW
Suite 950
Washington, DC 20024
202-962-0490
Fax: 202-962-0577
E-Mail: information@tfi.org
Home Page: www.tfi.org
Social Media: Facebook, Twitter, LinkedIn
Chris Jahn, President
Pamela Guffain, Vice President, Member Services
Kathy Mathers, Vice President, Public affairs
Monica Conway, Executive Assistant to Secretary
Carol Dorrough, Director, Administration & Finance
Members include brokers, producers, importers, dealers and manufacturers of fertilizer and fertilizer-related equipment.
325 Members
Founded in 1969

9491 Fishermens Marketing Association
1585 Heartwood Drive
Suite E
McKinleyville, CA 95519
707-840-0182
Fax: 707-840-0539
E-Mail: fma@trawl.org
Home Page: trawl.org
Peter Leipzig, Executive Director
An organization made up of fishermen which promotes stable prices and an orderly flow of wholesome seafood to the consumer.

9492 Flavor & Extract Manufacturers Association (FEMA)
1101 17th St NW
Suite 700
Washington, DC 20036
202-293-5800
Fax: 202-463-8998
Home Page: www.femaflavor.org
Social Media: YouTube, RSS Feed
Arthur Schick, President
Christopher E. Gibson, President Elect & Treasurer
Kevin Renskers, Vice President & Secretary
John Cox, Executive Director
Comprised of flavor manufacturers, flavor users, flavor ingredient suppliers, and others with an interest in the U.S. flavor industry. Working with legislators and regulators to assure that the needs of members and consumers are continuously addressed. FEMA is committed to assuring a substantial supply of safe flavoring substances.
123 Members
Founded in 1909

9493 Food & Nutrition Service
3101 Park Center Drive
Alexandria, VA 22302
703-305-2062
Fax: 703-305-2312
Home Page: www.fns.usda.gov
Social Media: Facebook, Twitter, Flickr, YouTube
Audrey Rowe, Administrator
Kevin Concannon, Under Secretary
Dr. Janey Thronton, Deputy under Secretary
Provides children and needy families better access to food and a more healthful diet through its food assistance programs and comprehensive nutrition education efforts. FNS also works to empower program participants with knowledge of the link between diet and health.
Founded in 1969
Mailing list available for rent

9494 Food Allergy Research & Education
7925 Jones Branch Dr.
Suite 1100
McLean, VA 22102
703-691-3179
800-924-4040
Fax: 703-691-2713
E-Mail: faan@foodallergy.org
Home Page: www.foodallergy.org
Social Media: Facebook, Twitter, Youtube, Flickr, Pinterest
Todd J. Slotkin, Chairman
Elliot S. Jaffe, Chairman Emeritus
Janet Atwater, Vice Chair & Secretary
John L Lehr, Chief Executive Officer
David R. Jaffe, Treasurer
The only nonprofit organization in the United States devoted solelyto patient education for food allergies. Mission is to create public awareness about food allergies and anaphylaxis, to provide education, and to advance research on behalf of all those affected by food allergy.
Cost: $30.00
22000 Members
Frequency: 6 per year
Founded in 1991

9495 Food Distribution Research Society
PO Box 441110
Fort Washington, MD 20749-1110
301-292-1970
Fax: 706-542-0739
E-Mail: Jonathan_baros@ncsu.edu
Home Page: fdrs.tamu.edu
Timothy A. Woods, President
Dawn Thilmany, President-Elect
Randall D. Little, Vice President Communication
Deacue Fields, Vice President Education
Mike Schroder, Vice President Logistics & Outreach
Food distribution research society encourages research, serves as an information clearinghouse and encourages implementation of research. The Society organizes conferences and meetings for industry, academic and government leaders within the food industry sector.
Founded in 1967

9496 Food Export Association of the Midwest USA
309 West Washington
Suite 600
Chicago, IL 60606
312-334-9200
Fax: 312-334-9230
E-Mail: info@foodexportusa.org
Home Page: www.foodexportusa.org
Social Media: Facebook
Tim F Hamilton, Executive Director
Lauren Swartz, Deputy Director
John Belmont, Communications Manager
Suzanne Milshaw, International Marketing Program
A non-profit organization that promotes the export of food and agricultural products from the northeast region of the United States. The organization has been helping exporters of northeast food and agricultural products sell their products overseas since it was first organized.
Founded in 1973

9497 Food Industry Association Executives
5657 W. 10770 North
Highland, UT 84003
801-599-1095
Fax: 815-550-1731
E-Mail: jolsen@fiae.net
Home Page: www.fiae.net
Jamie Pfhul, Chairwoman
Jarron Springer, CAE, Vice Chairman
Jim Olsen, President
Pat Davis, Vice President, State Government
Ellie Taylor, Secretary/Treasurer
Sponsors meetings, activities, publications and services to advance the knowledge and professionalism of the food industry association executive, and serves as a vehicle for the advancement of the food industry's agenda.
125 Members
Founded in 1927

9498 Food Industry Suppliers Association
1207 Sunset Drive
Greensboro, NC 27408
336-274-6311
Fax: 336-691-1839
E-Mail: stella@fisanet.org
Home Page: www.fisanet.org
Bob Morava, President
Brad Myers, Vice President
Rob Clark, Director
Jeff Heerema, Director
Andrew Hider, Director
Trade association dedicated to promoting distribution in serving high purity industries. Membership includes independent distributors and manufacturers who go to market through distribution. Members serve customers in food, beverage, personal care, pharmaceutical, Bio-Pharm and other high purity industries.
245 Members
Founded in 1968
Mailing list available for rent

9499 Food Information Service Center
21050 SW 93rd Lane Road
Dunnellon, FL 34431
352-489-8919
800-443-5820
Fax: 352-489-8919
E-Mail: fcsgroup@artdc.net
James Allen Mixon, President
Publishes technical assistance manuals for operating congregate feeding food service programs. Reaches market through direct mail and publicity.
Founded in 1957

9500 Food Marketing Institute
2345 Crystal Drive
Suite 800
Arlington, VA 22202

202-452-8444
Fax: 202-429-4519
Home Page: www.fmi.org
Social Media: Facebook, Twitter, LinkedIn, YouTube

Frederick J. Morganthall II, Chair
Leslie G. Sarasin Esq., CAE, President & CEO
Rob Bartels, Vice-Chair
Jerry Garland, Vice-Chair
Henry Jhonson, Vice-Chair

Food Marketing Institute (FMI) conducts programs in public affairs, food safety, research, education and industry relations on behalf of food retailers and wholesalers in the United States and around the world. FMI's U.S. members operate approximately 26,000 retail food stores and 14,000 pharmacies. Their combined annual sales volume of $680 billion represents three-quarters of all retail food store sales in the United States.
1500 Members
Founded in 1977
Mailing list available for rent

9501 Food Processing Suppliers Association
1451 Dolley Madison Blvd
Suite 101
Mc Lean, VA 22101-3850

703-761-2600
Fax: 703-761-4334
E-Mail: info@fpsa.org
Home Page: www.fpsa.org
Social Media: Facebook, Twitter, LinkedIn

Jeff Dahl, Chairman
Gil Williams, Vice Chair
David Seckman, President
Andy Drennan, Senior Vice President
Adam Finney, VP of Membership & Communications

FPSA members are organized in vertical industry councils which focus association programs on specific concerns and needs that are unique to that industry sector. Membership permits companies to participate in as many industry councils as appropriate at no additional cost.
510 Members
Founded in 2005

9502 Food Processors Suppliers Association
1451 Dolly Madison Boulevard
Suite 101
McLean, VA 22101-3850

703-761-2600
Fax: 703-761-4334
E-Mail: info@fpsa.org
Home Page: www.fpsa.org
Social Media: Facebook, Twitter, LinkedIn

Jeff Dahl, Chairman
Gil Williams, Vice Chair
David Seckman, President & CEO
Robyn Roche, CFO
Scott Gregory, Treasurer

MISA offers its members an opportunity to project a common and uniform stance on important industry issues, particularly in the regulatory and machinery safety and hygienic standards area.
500+ Members
Founded in 1983

9503 Foodservice & Packaging Institute
201 Park Washington Court
Falls Church, VA 22046

703-538-3550
Fax: 703-241-5603
E-Mail: ldyer@fpi.org
Home Page: www.fpi.org
Social Media: Facebook, Twitter, LinkedIn

Lynn Dyer, President
Natha Dempsey, Vice President
Jennifer Goldman, Membership & Meetings Manager

A national association comprised of manufacturers and suppliers of single-use foodservice packaging products.
25 Members
Founded in 1933

9504 Foodservice Consultants Society International
PO Box 4961
Louisville, KY 40204

502-379-4122
Fax: 519-856-0648
E-Mail: info@fcsi.org
Home Page: www.fcsi.org
Social Media: Facebook, Twitter

Ed Norman, President
Jonathan Doughty, Secretary/Treasurer

Professional organization offering design and management consulting services, specialized in the foodservice and hospitality industry across the world.
Founded in 1955

9505 Foodservice Sales and Marketing Association
Grocery Manufactures Association
1801-J York Road
Suite 384
Lutherville, MD 21093

410-715-4084
800-617-1170
Fax: 888-668-7496
E-Mail: info@fsmaonline.com
Home Page: www.fsmaonline.com
Social Media: Facebook, Twitter, LinkedIn, Youtube

Rick Abraham, President & CEO
Sharon Boyle, Vice President
Stuart Wolff, Chairman
Dan Cassidy, CEO of Key Imapact Sales
Jessica Muffoletto, Manager, Membership & Meetings

Advances the interests of the food, beverage and consumer products industry on key issues that effect the ability of brand manufacturers their products profitably and deliver superior value to the consumer.
250 Members
Founded in 2003

9506 Fresh Mushrooms - Nature's Hidden Treasure
2880 Zanker Road
Suite 203
San Jose, CA 95134

408-432-7210
Fax: 408-432-7213
E-Mail: info@mushroominfo.com
Home Page: www.mushroomcouncil.com
Social Media: Facebook, Twitter, Youtube, Pinterest, Googleplus

Carla Blackwell-Mckinney, Vice Chair
Robert Crouch, Secretary

Plays an important role in the national promotion of fresh mushrooms through consumer public relations, foodservice communications and retail communications.
Founded in 1993
Mailing list available for rent

9507 Fresh Produce Association of the Americas
590 East Frontage Road
PO Box 848
Nogales, AZ 85621

520-287-2707
Fax: 520-287-2948
E-Mail: info@freshfrommexico.com
Home Page: www.freshfrommexico.com

Alejandro Canelos, Chairman
Matt Mandel, Chairman Elect

Represents more than 125 member companies involved in growing, harvesting, marketing and importing of Mexican produce entering the US at Nogales, Arizona.
125 Members
Founded in 1944

9508 Fresh Produce and Floral Council
16700 Valley View Ave
Suite 130
La Mirada, CA 90638

714-739-0177
Fax: 714-739-0226
E-Mail: info@fpfc.org
Home Page: www.fpfc.org

Mike Casazza, Chairman
Rich Van Valkenburg, Chair Elect
Carissa Mace, President
Brad Martin, Treasurer/Secretary

Provides unique networking and business growth opportunities for professionals in the produce and floral industries in California. Members include growers, snippers, wholesalers, brokers, distributors and retailers of produce and/or floral items.
500 Members
Founded in 1965

9509 Frozen & Refrigerated Association of the North East
PO Box 6377
Wolcott, CT 06716-0377

203-597-7215
Fax: 203-879-0594
E-Mail: frane@frane.org
Home Page: www.frane.org
Social Media: Facebook

Maureen Ray, Chair
Jim Wright, Co-Chair
Donna Maglio, President
Sal Marrocco, Vice-President

Non-profit regional trade association, representing the ever changing frozen and refrigerated industries throughout the Northeast. It remains one of the largest and most active associations in the United States and is affiliated with the National Frozen & Refrigerated Association (NFRA).
135 Members
Founded in 1955

9510 Future Food
101 Finsbury Pavement
London, UK EC2A 1RS

203-002-3002
Fax: 203-003-3003
E-Mail: prteam@marcusevans.com
Home Page: www.marcusevans.com
Social Media: Facebook, Twitter, LinkedIn, Googleplus,vimeo

European events and publications for food industry.
Founded in 1983

9511 **Ginseng Board of Wisconsin**
668 Maratech Avenue
Suite E
Marathon, WI 54448

715-443-2444
Fax: 715-443-2444
E-Mail: ginseng@ginsengboard.com
Home Page: www.ginsengboard.com

Joe Heil, President

Representing Wisconsin Ginseng producers as the worldwide leader of the American Ginseng industry, committed to the advertising, promotion and the sale of Wisconsin Ginseng, the purest ginseng in the world. Working to improve the health and wellness of consumers while suporting the sustainability of the industry and the rural economy associated with it.
Founded in 1986

9512 **Glass Packaging Institute**
1001 N. Fairfax St
Suite 301A
Alexandria, VA 22314

703-684-6359
Fax: 703-546-0588
E-Mail: info@gpi.org
Home Page: www.gpi.org
Social Media: Facebook, Twitter

Arnaud De Weert, Chairman
Lynn M. Bragg, President

Represents the North American glass container industry. Through GPI, glass container manufacturers speak with one voice to advocate industry standards, promote sound environmental policies and educate packaging professionals. Member companies manufacture glass containers for food, beverage, cosmetic and many other products.
Founded in 1919

9513 **Global Cold Chain Alliance**
1500 King Street
Suite 201
Alexandria, VA 22314-2730

703-373-4300
Fax: 703-373-4301
E-Mail: email@gcca.org
Home Page: www.gcca.org
Social Media: Facebook, Twitter, LinkedIn

Corey Rosenbuch, President & COO
Megan Costello, Vice President of Member & Industry
J. William Hudson, CEO
Richard Tracy, Vice President

The Global Cold Chain Alliance (GCCA) is committed to building and strengthening the temperature-controlled supply chain around the world. As part of that mission, GCCA provides specialized cold chain advisory services to government agencies, organizations, and associations through its core partner, the World Food Logistics Organization (WFLO)
900 Members
Frequency: Membership Dues Vary
Founded in 1891

9514 **Glutamate Association: US**
1010 Wiconsin Ave. NW
Ste. 350
Washington, DC 20007

202-384-1840
Fax: 202-384-1850
E-Mail: info@watsongreenllc.com
Home Page: www.msgfacts.com
Social Media: Facebook, Twitter, LinkedIn

Lisa Watson, Executive Director

(TGA) is an association of manufacturers,national marketers,and processed food users of glutamic acid and its salts, principally the flavor enhancer, monosodium glutamat (MSG). TGA seeks to povide an effective channel of communcation among its members, the public,the media,the scientific community, foof professionals and government officials about the use and safety of glutamates.
12 Members
Founded in 1977

9515 **Golden Gold Chain Alliance**
1500 King Street
Suite 201
Alexandria, VA 22314-2730

703-373-4300
Fax: 703-373-4301
E-Mail: email@gcca.org
Home Page: www.gcca.org
Social Media: Facebook, Twitter, LinkedIn

Corey Rosenbuch, President & COO
Megan Costello, Vice President of Member & Industry
J. William Hudson, CEO
Richard Tracy, Vice President

The Global Cold Chain Alliance (GCCA) is committed to building and strengthening the temperature-controlled supply chain around the world. As part of that mission, GCCA provides specialized cold chain advisory services to government agencies, organizations, and associations through its core partner, the World Food Logistics Organization (WFLO)
900 Members
Founded in 1891

9516 **Grocery Manufacturers Association**
1350 Eye (I) Street NW
Suite 300
Washington, DC 20005

202-639-5900
Fax: 202-639-5932
E-Mail: info@gmaonline.org
Home Page: www.gmaonline.org
Social Media: Facebook, Twitter, RSS

Advances the interests of the food, beverage and consumer products industry on key issues that affect the ability of brand manufacturers to market their products profitably and deliver superior value to the consumer.
Frequency: Membership Dues Vary
Founded in 1908

9517 **Hand in Hand Foundation**
PO Box 67351
Scott's Valley, CA 95067

831-438-3736
Fax: 831-535-6331
E-Mail: adoptions@handinhand.us
Home Page: www.handinhandfoundation.com

David Boschen, Director
Melissa Thomas, Case Worker
April Pao, Office Manager
Kari Gale, Admin Assistant

Not for profit that solicits food and donations for the needy.
Founded in 1971

9518 **Hazelnut Council**
424 2nd Avenue W
Seattle, WA 98119

206-270-4321
Fax: 206-270-4656
E-Mail: info@hazelnutcouncil.org
Home Page: www.hazelnutcouncil.org

The Hazenut Council represents the world's leading hazelnut producers, importers and distributors.

9519 **Healthy Water Association**
PO Box 1417
Patterson, CA 95363

408-897-3023
Fax: 408-897-3028
E-Mail: paulmason@mgwater.com
Home Page: www.mgwater.com/hwa.shtml

Paul Mason, President

Serves the bottled water industry.

9520 **Herb Growing and Marketing Network**
PO Box 245
Silver Spring, PA 17575-0245

717-393-3295
Fax: 717-393-9261
E-Mail: herbworld@aol.com
Home Page: www.herbworld.com

Maureen Rogers, Director

The largest trade association for the herb industry.
Cost: $48.00
1000+ Members
Founded in 1990

9521 **Herb Research Foundation**
5589 Arapahoe Ave
Suite 205
Boulder, CO 80303

303-449-2265
Fax: 303-449-7849
E-Mail: info@herbs.org
Home Page: www.herbs.org

Rob McCaleb, President

Provides scientific based and traditional information about use and safety of herbs for health. Fee based hotline, information packs and literature are available to all.
Founded in 1983
Mailing list available for rent

9522 **Herb Society of America**
9019 Kirtland Chardon Rd
Kirtland, OH 44094

440-256-0514
Fax: 440-256-0541
E-Mail: herbs@herbsociety.org
Home Page: www.herbsociety.org

Katrinka Morgan, Executive Director
Robin Siktberg, Editor/Horticulturist

An organization that focuses on educating its members and the public on the cultivation of herbs and the study of their history and uses, both past and present.
Founded in 1933

9523 **Holstein Association USA**
1 Holstein Place
PO Box 808
Brattleboro, VT 05302-0808

802-254-4551
800-952-5200
Fax: 802-254-8251
Home Page: www.holsteinusa.com
Social Media: Facebook, Twitter, YouTube

Glen E. Brown, President
Gordie Cook, Vice President
Barbara Casna, Treasurer
John M. Meyer, Executive Secretary
John S. Burket, Board of Directors

The world's largest dairy cattle breed organization offering information services to all dairy producers.
Founded in 1903

9524 **Home Baking Association**
10841 S Crossroads Drive
Suite 105
Parker, CO 80138

785-478-3283
Fax: 785-478-3024

Home Page: www.homebaking.org
Social Media: Facebook, Twitter, Flickr

Kent Symms, President
Sam Garlow, First Vice President
Eric Wall, Second Vice President

Promoting home baking by providing educators tools and knowledge to perpetuate future generations of home bakers.
Founded in 1951
Mailing list available for rent

9525 **Hospitality Link**
866 SE 14th Terrace
Suite 128
Deerfield Beach, FL 33441

954-579-1802
Fax: 954-421-1046
E-Mail: info@hospitalitylink.com
Home Page: www.hospitalitylink.com
Social Media: LinkedIn

Provides consulting for food technology.

9526 **Hydroponic Society of America**
PO Box 1183
El Cerrito, CA 94530

510-926-2908
Home Page: www.lisarein.com/hydroponics

Joseph O Brien, President

The scientific and educational arm of the hydroponic community. The H.S.A. is rooted in science and physics, plant physiology and photo-biology and the other 16 disciplines required to understand the complexity of the science known as hydroponics. The H.S.A. separates the fiction from the fact, and the truth from the mythology.
Founded in 1976

9527 **Independent Bakers Association**
PO Box 3731
Washington, DC 20027-0231

202-333-8190
Fax: 202-337-3809
E-Mail: independentbaker@yahoo.com
Home Page: www.independentbaker.net
Social Media: Twitter, LinkedIn

Ron Cardey, Chairman
Joe Davis, First Vice Chair
Scott Barth, Second Vice Chair
Brian Stevenson, Secretary
Heidi Brenner, Treasurer

National trade association of mostly family owned wholesale bakeries and allied industry trades. Protects the interests of independent wholesale bakers from antitrust and anti-competitive mergers and acquisitions; pressures Congress to support market-oriented farm commodity programs, seeking representation to consider federal labor, tax and environmental law.
400 Members
Founded in 1968

9528 **Indian River Citrus League**
7925 20th Street
Vero Beach, FL 32966

772-562-2728
Fax: 772-562-2577
E-Mail: info@ircitrusleague.org
Home Page: ircitrusleague.org

Rusty Varn, Board of Director
Trey Smith, Board of Director
Scott Lambeth, Board of Director
Daniel R. Richey, Board of Director
Daniel Scott, Board of Directors

Organization of growers in the area. Newsletters, links and contactinformation.
Founded in 1807

9529 **Institute of Food Science and Engineering**
2650 North Young Avenue
Fayetteville, AR 72704

479-575-4040
Fax: 479-575-2165
Home Page: www.uark.edu/depts/ifse

Steve Brooks, President & CEO
Dr. Jean Francois Meullent, Director

Serves as the primary entity in Arkansas for research, graduate education and extension to help ensure that; food supply is high quality, wholesome, safe and nutritious, value is added to raw agricultural products to enhance economic development of the state, region and nation, and the nutritional needs of society are understood, communicated and met.

9530 **Institute of Food Technologists**
525 W Van Buren
Suite 1000
Chicago, IL 60607

312-782-8424
800-438-3663
Fax: 312-782-8348
E-Mail: info@ift.org
Home Page: www.ift.org
Social Media: Facebook, Twitter, LinkedIn, Youtube

Robert Gravani, Chairman
Janet Collins, President
Mary Ellen Camire, President-Elect
Barbara Byrd Keenan, Executive Vice President
Bruce Stillings, Treasurer

A nonprofit scientific society working in food science, food technology, and related professions in industry, academia and government.
18000 Members
Founded in 1939

9531 **Institute of Food and Agricultural Sciences (IFAS)**
University of Florida
PO Box 110180
Gainesville, FL 32611-0180

352-392-1971
Home Page: www.ifas.ufl.edu
Social Media: Facebook, Twitter

Ruth Borger, Assistant Vice President
Jenny Mooney, Manager

A federal-state-county partnership throughout Florida, dedicated to improving your life by developing and providing knowledge in agriculture, natural resources, and life sciences.
Founded in 1906

9532 **Institute of Packaging Professionals**
1833 Centre Point Circle
Suite 123
Naperville, IL 60563
630-544-5050
800-432-4085
Fax: 630-544-5055
E-Mail: info@iopp.org
Home Page: www.iopp.org
Social Media: Facebook, Twitter, LinkedIn, YouTube

Ralph Brandt, Chair
Bret Carlson, President
Dan Alexander, Executive VP, Finance & Operations
Robert Meisner, EVP - Education & Certification
Ukachi Anonyuo, Executive VP-Membership

Information regarding the packaging industry internationally.

9533 **Institute of Shortening & Edible Oils**
1319 F Street NW
Suite 600
Washington, DC 20004

202-783-7960
Fax: 202-393-1367
E-Mail: contactus@iseo.org
Home Page: www.iseo.org

Robert L. Collette, President
Diana L. Stare, Office Administrator

A trade association representing the refiners of edible fats and oils in the United States. Members represent approximately 90-95 percent of the edible fats and oils produced domestically that are used in baking and frying fats (shortening), cooking and salad oils, margarines, spreads, confections and toppings, and ingredients in a wide variety of foods.
Founded in 1936

9534 **International Dairy-Deli-Bakery Association (IDDBA)**
636 Science Drive
Madison, WI 53711-1073

608-310-5000
Fax: 608-238-6330
E-Mail: iddba@iddba.orgÿ
Home Page: www.iddba.org

A nonprofit trade association providing education, training, and marketing resources for food retailers, manufacturers, brokers, distributors, and other interested professionals.
Founded in 1964

9535 **International Association for Color Manufacturers**
1101 17th Street NW
Suite 700
Washington, DC 20036

202-293-5800
Fax: 202-463-8998
E-Mail: info@iacmcolor.org
Home Page: www.iacmcolor.org
Social Media: LinkedIn

David R Carpenter, President & Treasurer
Rohit Tibrewala, President-Elect & Secretary

The IACM is a trade association that represents the manufacturers and end-users of coloring substances that are used in foods. Members include producers and users of both certified and exempt colors.
Founded in 1972

9536 **International Association of Culinary Professionals**
1221 Avenue of the Americas
42nd Floor
New York, NY 10020

646-358-4957
866-358-4951
Fax: 866-358-2524
E-Mail: info@iacp.com
Home Page: www.iacp.com
Social Media: Facebook, Twitter, Youtube, Vimeo

Julia M. Usher, President
Raghavan Iyer, Vice President
Margaret Bradley-Foley, Secretary/ Treasurer

IACP connects culinary professionals with the people, places, and knowledge they need to succeed. IACP is a worldwide forum for the development and exchange of information, knowledge, and inspiration within the professional food and beverage community. This organization of creative and talented professionals is engaged in and committed to excellence in the food industry.
3000+ Members
Founded in 1978

9537 **International Association of Ice Cream and Vendors**
3601 East Joppa Road
Baltimore, MD 21234

410-931-8100
Fax: 410-931-8111
E-Mail: info@iaicdv.org
Home Page: www.iaicdv.org
Social Media: Facebook, Twitter, Stumbleupon, Gmail

Chris Long, President
Hoss Rafaty, President-elect
Michelle Franklin, Vice President
Nick Nikbakht, Secretary-Treasurer

Members are manufacturers and distributors of ice cream novelties and street vendors.
Founded in 1969

9538 **International Association of Milk Control Agencies**
Department of Agriculture
Division of Dairy Industry Services
Albany, NY 12235-0001

518-457-3880
Fax: 518-485-5816
E-Mail: charlie.huff@agmkt.state.ny.us
Home Page: www.nasda.org/cms

Charles Huff, Secretary/Treasurer

Founded to improve the effectiveness and uniformity of regulation among the economic regulatory agencies and to provide a forum for exchange of information.
Founded in 1935

9539 **International Association of Operative Millers**
10100 West 87th Street
Suite 306
Overland Park, KS 66212

913-338-3377
Fax: 913-338-3553
E-Mail: info@iaom.info
Home Page: www.iaom.info/about/
Social Media: Facebook, Twitter, LinkedIn

Joel Hoffa, President
Damon Sidles, Vice President
Melinda Farris, Executive Vice President
Roy Loepp, Treasurer

An international organization, comprised of flour millers, cereal grain and seed processors and allied trades representatives and companies devoted to the advancement of technology in the flour milling, cereal grain processing industries.
1500 Members
Founded in 1896

9540 **International Banana Society**
1901 Pennsylvania Ave NW
Suite 1100
Washington, DC 20006-3412

202-303-3400
Fax: 202-303-3433
E-Mail: info@eatmorebananas.com
Home Page: www.bananas.org
Social Media: Facebook, LinkedIn, Youtube

A trade organizatoin consisting of members engaged in teh business of importing bananas into the United States. Provides a forum for members to discuss common and technical issues pertaining to banana production, distribution, and marketing.
Founded in 1982

9541 **International Beverage Dispensing Equipment Association**
PO Box 248
Reisterstown, MD 21136

410-602-0616
877-404-2332
Fax: 410-486-6799
E-Mail: ibdea@cornerstoneassoc.com
Home Page: www.ibdea.org
Social Media: Facebook, LinkedIn, Youtube

An international non-profit trade association representing companies that sell, lease, rent, manufacture and service beverage dispensing equipment and supplies. Members are companies that provide equipment, related products and services to restaurants, bars, taverns, hospitals, schools and other institutions.
250+ Members
Founded in 1971

9542 **International Bottled Water Association**
1700 Diagonal Rd
Suite 650
Alexandria, VA 22314

703-683-5213
800-928-3711
Fax: 703-683-4074
E-Mail: info@bottledwater.org
Home Page: www.bottledwater.org
Social Media: Facebook, Twitter, YouTube

Breck Speed, Chairman
David Muscato, Vice Chairman
Joseph Doss, President
Robert R. Hirst, Vice President
Bryan Shinn, Treasurer

The leading voice of the bottled water industry and serves to protect the interests of bottled water bottlers, distributors and suppliers.
Founded in 1958

9543 **International Chewing Gum Association**
1001 G Street NW
Suite 500 West
Washington, DC 20001

E-Mail: information@gumassociation.org
Home Page: www.gumassociation.org

Andy Pharoah, President

The leading voice of the chewing gum industry. ICGA continues to gain recognition and credibility among decision-makers across the globe.

9544 **International Council on Hotel, Restaurant and Institutional Education**
2810 N Parham Road
Suite 230
Richmond, VA 23294

804-346-4800
Fax: 804-346-5009
E-Mail: info@chrie.org
Home Page: www.chrie.org
Social Media: Facebook, Twitter, LinkedIn

Dennis Reynolds, President
Martin O Neill, Vice President
Kathy McCarty, Chief Executive Officer
Chris Roberts, Secretary
Stephanie Hein, Treasurer

A marketplace for facilitating exchanges of information, ideas, research, products and services related to education, training and resource development for the hospitality and tourism industry (food, lodging, recreation and travel services). Serving as the hospitality and tourism education network, striving to unite educators, industry executives and associations.
1400 Members
Founded in 1946

9545 **International Dairy Foods Association**
1250 H Street NW
Suite 900
Washington, DC 20005

202-737-4332
Fax: 202-331-7820
E-Mail: membership@idfa.org
Home Page: www.idfa.org
Social Media: Facebook, Twitter, YouTube, Blog, Smartbrief

Patricia Stroup, Chair
Jeffery Kaneb, Vice Chair
Michael Walls, Secretary
Mike Reidy, Treasurer

Represents the nation's dairy manufacturing and marketing industries and their suppliers. IDFA is composed of three constituent organizations; Milk Industry Foundation, National Cheese Institute, and the International Ice Cream Association.
550 Members

9546 **International Dairy-Deli-Bakery Association**
636 Science Drive
PO Box 5528
Madison, WI 53705-0528

608-310-5000
Fax: 608-238-6330
E-Mail: iddba@iddba.org
Home Page: www.iddbanet.org

William J. Klump, Chairman
David Leonhardi, Executive Vice Chairman
John Cheesman, Vice Chairman
Jewel Hunt, Treasurer

IDDBA members meet the challenges of today's business world by exchanging information and ideas, participating in educational programs and networking.
Founded in 1964

9547 **International Flight Services Association**
1100 Johnson Ferry Road
Suite 300
Atlanta, GA 30342

404-252-3663
Fax: 404-252-0774
E-Mail: ifsa@kellencompany.com
Home Page: www.ifsanet.com
Social Media: Facebook, Twitter, LinkedIn, YouTube

David Loft, Chairperson
Pam Suder Smith, President
Jane Bernier -Tran, Vice President
Paul Platamone, Treasurer
Peter Wilander, Secretary

Represents the $14 billion inflight and travel catering industry. Activities include annual conferences, trade shows, seminars and training events around the world.
400 Members
Founded in 1965

9548 **International Food Additives Council**
1100 Johnson Ferry Road
Suite 300
Atlanta, GA 30342

404-252-3663
Fax: 404-252-0774
E-Mail: jrogers@kellencompany.com
Home Page: www.foodadditives.org

An international trade association of food additives manufacturers and businesses having interest in food additives.

9549 **International Food Information Council Foundation**
1100 Connecticut Ave NW
Suite 430
Washington, DC 20036

202-296-6540
Fax: 202-296-6547
E-Mail: info@foodinsight.org

Home Page: www.foodinsight.org
Social Media: Facebook, Twitter, LinkedIn

David B. Schmidt, President & CEO
Geraldine McCann, COO
Marianne Smith Edge, Senior VP, Nutrition & Food Safety
Andy Benson, Senior Vice President
Kimberly Reed, Executive Director

Dedicated to the mission of effectively communicating science-based information on health, nutrition and food safety for the public good. Independent and non-profit, bringing together, working with, and providing information to consumers, health and nutrition professionals, educators, government officials, and food, beverage, and agricultural industry professionals.
33 Members
Founded in 1985

9550 International Food Processors Association
200 Daingerfield Road
Suite 100
Alexandria, VA 22314-2884

703-684-1080
Fax: 703-548-6563

9551 International Food Service Brokers Association
1101 Pennsylvania Avenue
Washington, DC 20004

Home Page: www.foodbrokers.org
1500 Members
ISSN: 0884-7185
Founded in 1956

9552 International Food Service Editorial Council
7 Point Place
PO Box 491
Hyde Park, NY 12538

845-229-6973
Fax: 845-229-6973
E-Mail: ifec@ifeconline.com
Home Page: www.ifeconline.com
Social Media: Facebook, Twitter

Jeffrey Yarbrough, President
Alexei Rudolf, Vice President
Jody Shee, Secretary
John Scroggins, Treasurer

A networking association that fosters the open exchange of information and the building of productive working relationships among foodservice editor and publicist members. Conferences and other activities offer professional development as well as opportunities to make new contacts and gain hands-on-experience of the food cultures and personalities in cities where conferences are held.
265 Members
Founded in 1956

9553 International Food Service Executives Association
4955 Miller Street
Suite 107
Wheat Ridge, CO 80033

800-893-5499
E-Mail: ifseahqoffice@gmail.com
Home Page: www.ifsea.com
Social Media: Facebook

David Orosz, Chairman

Professional association with members from the food service and hospitality profession. IFSEA's mission is to enhance the careers of its members through food service certification, education seminars, networking, student mentorships and community service. Members inclued executive chefs, restaurant owners, catering directors, equipment manufacturers, food suppliers, military, professionals new to the industry and students.
3000 Members
Founded in 1901

9554 International FoodService Manufacturers Association
180 North Stetson Avenue
Suite 850
Chicago, IL 60601

312-540-4400
Fax: 312-540-4401
E-Mail: ifma@ifmaworld.com
Home Page: www.ifmaworld.com
Social Media: Facebook, LinkedIn, YouTube

Lyons Magnus, Chairman
Loren Kimura, First Vice Chairman
Richard Ferranti, Vice Chairman
Joe Bybel, Vice Chairman
Kevin Delahunt, Treasurer

Member companies of the IFMA can capitalize on opportunities, tackle challenges, as well as gain new customer contact and networking opportunities, education and training that helps company sales force build market share, and leadership roles in such initiatives as GS1.
650 Members
Founded in 1952

9555 International Foodservice Distributors Association
1410 Spring Hill Road
Suite 210
McLean, VA 22102

703-532-9400
Fax: 703-538-4673
Home Page: www.ifdaonline.org
Social Media: Twitter, LinkedIn

Thomas A. Zatina, Chairman
James Crawford, Vice Chairman
Mark S. Allen, President & CEO
Jonathan Eisen, Senior Vice President
Andrew Mercier, Treasurer

Trade association comprised of food distribution companies that supply independent grocers and food service operations throughout the US, Canada and 19 other countries.
135 Members
Founded in 2003

9556 International Foodservice Distributors Ass
1410 Spring HIll Road
Suite 210
McLean, VA 22102

703-532-9400
Fax: 703-538-4673
Home Page: www.ifdaonline.org
Social Media: Twitter, LinkedIn

Thomas A. Zatina, Chairman
James Crawford, Vice Chairman
Mark S. Allen, Jr., President/ CEO
Andy Mercier, Treasurer
Jonathan Eisen, SVP, Government Relations

9557 International Glutamate Technical Committee
5775 Peachtree Dunwoody Rd NE
Atlanta, GA 30342

404-252-3663
Fax: 404-252-3663
E-Mail: info@aspartame.org
Home Page: www.aspartame.org

Andrew Ebert PhD, Chairman
Judy Rogers, Contact

Members are associations that are engaged in the manufacture, sale and commercial use of glutamates.
8 Members
Founded in 1965

9558 International HACCP Alliance
120 Rosenthal Center
2471 TAMU
College Station, TX 77843-2471

979-862-3643
Fax: 979-862-3075
E-Mail: kharris@tamu.edu
Home Page: www.haccpalliance.org

Ranzell Nickelson, Chairman
Rosemary Mucklow, Vice Chairman
Robert Hibbert, Treasurer/ Secretary
Alling Yancy, Past Chairman
Rena Pietrami, Board of Directors

Provides a uniform program to assure safer meat and poultry products.
Founded in 1994

9559 International Herb Association
PO Box 5667
Jacksonville, FL 32247-5667

904-399-3241
Fax: 904-396-9467
Home Page: www.iherb.org

Nancy Momsen, President
Kathryn Clayton, Vice President
Karen O'Brien, Secretary
Marge Powell, Treasurer

Supports herb businesses and educates the public.
Founded in 1986

9560 International Institute of Fisheries Economics & Trade
213 Ballard Hall
Corvallis, OR 97331-3601

541-737-2942
Fax: 541-737-2563
E-Mail: osuweb@lists.orst.edu
Home Page: www.oregonstate.edu/dept/IIFET

Dr. Ralph Townsend, President
Dr. Dan Holland, President-elect
Ann L. Shriver, Executive Director
Kara Keenan, Assistant

Promotes discussion, research projects and sponsors educational courses. Publications available.
400 Members
Founded in 1982

9561 International Maple Syrup Institute
5072 Rock St. RR#4
Spencerville, ON K0E 1X0

613-658-2329
Fax: 877-683-7241
E-Mail: agrofor@ripnet.com
Home Page:
www.internationalmaplesyrupinstitute.com

Richard Norman, President
Yvon Poitras, Vice President
Steve Selby, Treasurer
Dave Chapeskie, Executive Director

Members are producers, processors, industry suppliers and others interested in promoting the industry.
15M Members
Founded in 1975

9562 International Natural Sausage Casing Association
12100 Sunset Hills Road
Suite 130
Reston, VA 20190

703-234-4112
Fax: 703-435-4390
Home Page: www.insca.kdgp.me

David Blanga, Chairman
Elliot Simon, Vice Chairman
Michael Mayo, Treasurer

The only international association for the natural sausage casing industry. Members include producers, suppliers and brokers of natural casing products.
265+ Members
Founded in 1965

9563 International Olive Council
Principe de Vergara
154
Spain, MD 28002

491-590-3638
Fax: 491-563-1263
E-Mail: iooc@internationaloliveoil.org
Home Page: www.internationaloliveoil.org

Jean Louis Barjol, Executive Director

The world's only international intergovernmental organization in the field of olive oil and table olives. The Council is a decisive player in contributing to the sustainable and responsible development of olive growing and serves as a world forum for discussing policymaking issues and tackling present and future challenges.
Founded in 1959

9564 International Organization of the Flavor Industry (IOFI)
Flavor & Extract Manufacturers Association
1101, 17th Street NW
Suite 700
Washington, DC 20036

202-293-5800
Fax: 202-462-8998
Home Page: www.femaflavor.org

Arthur Schick, President
Christopher E. Gibson, President Elect & Treasurer
Kevin Renskers, Vice President & Secretary
John Cox, Executive Director

FEMA staff monitors regulations that impact flavor and extracts all around the world.
Frequency: Annual
Founded in 1909
Mailing list available for rent

9565 International Packaged Ice Association
238 East Davis Blvd.
Suite 213
Tampa, FL 33606

813-258-1690
800-742-0627
Fax: 919-251-2783
E-Mail: jane@packagedice.com
Home Page: www.packagedice.com

Bob Morse, Chairman
Bo Russell, Vice Chairman/ Treasurer
John Smibert, Secretary/ Assistant Treasurer
Mike Ringstaff, Conference Chairman

A trade association representing manufacturers and distributors of packaged ice and manufacturers of ice making equipment.
400 Members
Frequency: Call For Membership Info
Founded in 1917

9566 International Society of Beverage Technologists(ISBT)
14070 Proton Rd
Suite 100, LB 9
Dallas, TX 75244-3601

972-233-9107
Fax: 972-490-4219
E-Mail: office@bevtech.org
Home Page: www.bevtech.org

Sally Potter, President
Ron Puvak, 1st Vice President
Brian Stegmann, 2nd Vice President
Larry Hobbs, Executive Director

Enhance promotione, development and dissemination of knowledge relating to art and science of beverage technology. Focus ares include beverage formulation, production, packaging and more. We provide forums, stimulate the uise of science in the industry, encourage and foster research.

9567 International Warehouse Logistics Association
2800 S River Rd
Suite 260
Des Plaines, IL 60018

847-813-4699
Fax: 847-813-0115
E-Mail: email@iwla.com
Home Page: www.iwla.com

Paul Verst, Chairman
Tom Herche, Vice Chairman
Steve DeHaan, President & CEO
Rob Doyle, Treasurer
Mark DeFabis, Secretary

A trade association of warehouse logistics providers that helps members run high-quality, profitable businesses. IWLA focuses on the warehouse logistics business, providing ideas and information that make it easier for member companies to succeed.
Founded in 1891

9568 Interstate Professional Applicators Association
PO Box 1420
Milton, WA 98354-1420

253-922-9437
Fax: 253-922-3788

Provides education and information for the professional horticultural applicator. Legislative work involves the states of Washington, Oregon, Idaho in the area of laws and regulations.

9569 Iowa Meat Processors Association
PO Box 334
Clarence, IA 52216

563-452-3329
Fax: 563-452-2141
E-Mail: execdirector@iowameatprocessors.org
Home Page: www.iowameatprocessors.org

Andy Thesing, President
Kerry Kraft, 1st Vice President
Tom Taylor, 2nd Vice President
Merrill Angell, 3rd Vice President

An organization comprised of beef, pork, wild game, and poultry processors and allied businesses from throughout the state of Iowa. Members include slaughterers, food service companies, packers, locker operators, butcher shops, ham manufacturers, smokehouse owners, wholesalers, custom operations, retail operations, and companies that supply goods and services to the meat industry.

9570 Islamic Food and Nutrition Council of America (IFANCA)
777 Busse Hwy
Park Ridge, IL 60068
847-993-0034
Fax: 847-993-0038
E-Mail: m.masood@ifanca.org; z.sadek@ifanca.org
Home Page: www.ifanca.org
Social Media: Facebook, Twitter, LinkedIn, Youtube,stumbleupon,digg,frien

Zeshan Sadek, Director International Services
Mujahid Masood, Ph.D., Senior Food Scientist

A non-profit Islamic organization dedicated to promote halel food and the institution of halel.
Founded in 1982

9571 Italian Trade Agency
Italian Trade Commission
33 E 67th St
New York, NY 10065-5949

212-980-1500
Fax: 212-758-1050
E-Mail: newyork@ice.it
Home Page: www.italtrade.com

Pace Marisa, Executive Secretary
Augusta Smargiassi, Senior Deputy Trade Commissioner
Antonio Lucarelli, Senior Trade Commission

The Italian government agency entrusted with the promotion of trade, business opportunities and industrial cooperation between Italian and foreign companies. It supports the internationalisation of Italian firms and their consolidation in foreign markets.

9572 Italian Wine and Food Institute
One Grand Central Place
60 East 42nd St. Suite 2214
New York, NY 10165

212-867-4111
Fax: 212-867-4114
E-Mail: iwfi@aol.com
Home Page: www.italianwineandfoodinstitute.com

Lucio Caputo, President
Vincent Giampaolo, VP

Members are producers, distributors and marketers of Italian wines and foods.
Founded in 1983

9573 Juice Products Association
750 National Press Building
529 14th Street NW
Washington, DC 20045

202-785-3232
Fax: 202-223-9741
E-Mail: jpa@kellencompany.com
Home Page: www.juiceproducts.org

Richard E Cristol, President
Carol Freysinger, Executive Director

The trade association for the fruit and juice products industry, including juice processors, packers, extractors, brokers as well as marketers of fruit juices and vegetable juices, juice beverages, fruit jams, jellies and preserves and similar products. JPA also represents juice industry suppliers and food testing laboratories and includes firms engaged in the trading of frozen concentrated orange juice futures and/or options on behalf of JPA processor members.
135 Members
Founded in 1957

9574 LaSalle Food Processing Association
108 S Broadway
PO Box 97
La Salle, MN 56056-0097

507-375-3408
Fax: 507-642-3077

Pat Thiner, Manager

A meat packers trade association.

9575 Leafy Greens Council
33 Pheasant Lane
Saint Paul, MN 55127

651-484-7270
Home Page: www.leafy-greens.org

Ray Clark, Executive Director
Robert Strube, President

Purpose is to improve the marketing and increase consumption through national promotions, to educate consumers about the nutritional values of leafy greens through media campaigns, to represent member interests to government, and to provide networking opportunities for members. Members represent growers, shippers, brokers, terminal market operators, and suppliers.
117 Members
Founded in 1974

9576 Les Amis d'Escoffier Society of New York, Inc.
787 Ridgewood Road
Millburn, NJ 07041

212-414-5820
Fax: 973-379-3117
Home Page: www.escoffier-society.com

Mark Arnao, President
George McNeill, First Vice President
Jay Jones, Secretary
Kurt Keller, Executive Director

Providing opportunitites for members' delight and edification and also generate gains in the perfection of the art of fine dining. Membership consists of chefs de cuisine, hotel executives, restaurateurs and business executives.
Founded in 1936

9577 Livestock Marketing Association
10510 NW Ambassador Drive
Kansas City, MO 64153

816-891-0502
800-821-2048
Fax: 816-891-0552
E-Mail: lmainfo@lmaweb.com
Home Page: www.lmaweb.com
Social Media: Facebook, Twitter

David Macedo, Chairman
Tim Starks, President
Dan Harris, Vice President
Mark Mackey, Chief Executive Officer
Vincent Nowal, Chief Financial Officer

Committed to the support and protection of the local livestock auction markets. LMA is the voice for the auction markets on legislative and regulatory issues and in providing member services to maintain successful, viable marketing businesses and better service to all of the livestock producers who sell at auction.

9578 Machalek Communications, Inc.
Machalek Communications
12550 W Frontage Road
Suite 220
Burnsville, MN 55337

952-736-8000
800-846-5520
Fax: 866-490-8834
E-Mail: info@machalek.com
Home Page: www.machalek.com
Social Media: Facebook, LinkedIn

Andrea McChalek, President/CEO
Deanna Morin, Vice Pres. of Business Development
Krista Gardner, Office Manager

Includes over 20 employees and publishes seven nationwide postcard advertising decks. Distributes more then 100 million postcards per year to over 800,000 qualified buyers. Company has furthermore evolved to include additional sales lead generation services including list rental, mail, and internet marketing.
25 Members
Founded in 1987
Mailing list available for rent

9579 Maraschino Cherry and Glace Fruit Processors
3301 State Route 66
Neptune, NJ 07753

732-922-3008

Richard Sullivan, Executive VP

9580 Material Handling Industry of America
8720 Red Oak Blvd
Suite 201
Charlotte, NC 28217-3996

704-676-1190
Fax: 704-676-1199
E-Mail: gbaer@mhia.org
Home Page: www.mhia.org
Social Media: Facebook, Twitter, LinkedIn, YouTube

E. Larry Strayhorn, Executive Chairman
Dave Young, Executive Vice Chairman
John Paxton, Vice Chairman

The complexity of managing supply chains that span continents and dominate markets demands strategies, equipment and systems that are agile, adaptable, and aligned. With product lifescycles shortening and worldwide competition increasing, success depends on effective material handling and logistics solutions for the global supply chain. Being able to deliver the right product to the right market at the right time.

9581 Meat & Livestock Australia
Level 1, 40 Mount Street
Locked Bag 991
North Sydney, NS 2060

294-639-333
Fax: 294-639-393
E-Mail: info@mla.com.au
Home Page: www.mla.com.au
Social Media: Facebook, Twitter, YouTube

Michele Allan, Chairman
Scott Hansen, Managing Director
Lucinda Corrigan, Director
Greg Harper, Director
Christine Gilbertson, Director

Providing marketing and research and development services to cattle, sheep and goat producer members and the broader red meat industry to help them meet community and consumer expectations. MLA is committed to fostering world leadership for the Australian red meat and livestock industry for creating op portunities for its stakeholders, the environment, red meat consumers and the community.
30000 Members
Founded in 1998

9582 Meat & Livestock Australia, North American Region
1401 K Street NW
Suite 602
Washington, DC 20005

202-521-2551
Fax: 202-521-2699
E-Mail: info@mlana.com
Home Page: www.australian-meat.com
Social Media: Facebook, Twitter, YouTube

David Pietsch, Regional Manager, North America
Scott Hansen, Managing Director

Providing marketing and research and development services to cattle, sheep and goat producer members and the broader red meat industry to help them meet community and consumer expectations. MLA is committed to fostering world leadership for thc Australian red meat and livestock industry for creating opportunities for its stakeholders, the environment, red meat consumers and the community.
30000 Members
Founded in 1998

9583 Meat Import Council of America
1901 Fort Myer Dr
Suite 1110
Arlington, VA 22209

703-522-1910
800-522-1910
Fax: 703-524-6039
E-Mail: lauriebryant@micausa.org
Home Page: www.micausa.org

Kim Holzner, Chairman
David Rind, Vice Chairman
Donald E. Stewart, Treasurer
Laurie I. Bryant, Executive Director & Secretary

To foster the trade, commerce and interests of importers and exporters of fresh and/or frozen and/or cured and/or cooked and/or canned meats.
130 Members
Founded in 1962

9584 Meat Trade Institute
213 South Avenue East
Spencer Savings Bank Building
Cranford, NJ 07016

908-276-5111
Fax: 212-279-4016
E-Mail: sflannagan@sprintmail.com
Home Page: www.spcnetwork.com/mti/

John J. Calcaguno, President

A full-time fully-staffed trade association serving meat and poultry industries in the northeast. The Institute seeks to build and strengthen the relationships of its members with government, labor, and all other segments of the meat and poultry industry.

9585 Mid-Atlantic Canners Association
316 S Front Street
Hamburg, PA 19526

610-562-3061
Fax: 610-562-0281

Robert Crosswell, Crosswell
D Seibert, VP Finance

Mid Atlantic Canners Association is a cooperative soft drink canning facility for the Coca-Cola system. All of the national Coca-Cola Company brands are canned, packaged and shipped by truck to various Coca-Cola franchised distributors located throughout the northeast United States.

9586 **Mid-Atlantic Dairy Association**
325 Chestnut St
Suite 600
Philadelphia, PA 19106
215-627-8800
Fax: 215-627-8887
E-Mail: dairyspot@milk4u.org
Home Page: www.dairyspot.com
Social Media: Facebook, Twitter, LinkedIn, Youtube, Pinterest, Googleplus
Patty Purcell, CEO
Mid-Atlantic Dairy Association is one of 19 state and regional promotion organizations working under the umbrella of the United Dairy Industry Association. Working to bring a fully integrated national promotion program to the Mid-Atlantic region.
Mailing list available for rent

9587 **Mid-States Meat Association**
1335 Dublin Rd
Suite 10
Columbus, OH 43215-1000
614-459-5188
Fax: 614-442-5516
E-Mail: kristin@ohiogrowers.org
Kristin Mullins, Executive Director
100 Members

9588 **Midwest Dairy Association**
2015 Rice St
St Paul, MN 55113
651-488-0261
800-642-3895
Fax: 651-488-0265
E-Mail: snewell@midwestdairy.com
Home Page: www.midwestdairy.com
Social Media: Facebook, Twitter, Youtube, Pinterest
Mike Kruger, CEO
Works on behalf of dairy farmers to increase dairy sales, foster innovation and inspire consumer confidence in dairy products and practices.
210M Members
Founded in 1940

9589 **Midwest Food Processors Association**
4600 American Pkwy
Suite 210
Madison, WI 53718-8334
608-255-9946
Fax: 608-255-9838
E-Mail: info@mwfpa.org
Home Page: www.mwfpa.org
Social Media: Facebook, Twitter, LinkedIn
Nick George, President
Brian Elliot, Director of Communications
Robin Fanshaw, Manager
Trade association that advocates on behalf of food processing companies and affiliated industries in Illinois, Minnesota, and Wisconsin. Influencing public policy and making the Midwest a great place for food processors to do business. Advocating, educating, communicating, and facilitating.
Founded in 1905

9590 **Missouri Grocers Association**
315 North Ken Avenue
Springfield, MO 65802
417-831-6667
Fax: 417-831-3907
E-Mail: cmcmillian@missourigrocers.com
Home Page: www.missourigrocers.com
Social Media: Facebook
Lynda Ryan, Chairman
Erick Taylor, President
John Porter, Vice President
Mike Beal, Treasurer
Committed to the growth and profitability of its members by providing proactive state and federal legislative and regulatory representation, effective communication, beneficial member services, and education of industry innovations.

9591 **Mushroom Council**
2880 Zanker Road
Suite 203
San Jose, CA 95134
408-432-7210
Fax: 408-432-7213
E-Mail: info@mushroomcouncil.org
Home Page: mushroomcouncil.org
Social Media: Facebook, Twitter, YouTube, Pinterest, RSS
Plays an important role in the national promotion of fresh mushrooms through consumer public relations, foodservice communications and retail communications.

9592 **National Advisory Group**
19111 Detroit Road
Suite 201
Rocky River, OH 44116
440-250-1583
E-Mail: info@nagconvenience.com
Home Page: www.nag-net.com
Social Media: Facebook
Ben Jatlow, Chairman
Mary Banmiller, President
Mission is to provide industry retail leaders a peer-to-peer forum for the exchange of ideas to improve their business performance.
Founded in 1992

9593 **National Agri-Marketing Association**
11020 King Street
Suite 205
Overland Park, KS 66210
913-491-6500
Fax: 913-491-6502
E-Mail: agrimktg@nama.org
Home Page: www.nama.org
Social Media: Facebook, Twitter, LinkedIn, YouTube, Flickr
Paul Redhage, President
Kenna Rathai, 1st Vice President
Sally Behringer, Vice President
Amy Bradford, Vice President
Marvin Kokes, Secretary/Treasurer
The nation's largest association for professionals in marketing and agribusiness.
Cost: $170.00
3500 Members
Frequency: Membership Dues
Founded in 1957

9594 **National Agriculture Day**
11020 King St
Suite 205
Overland Park, KS 66210
913-491-1895
Fax: 913-491-6502
E-Mail: info@agday.org
Home Page: www.agday.org
Social Media: Facebook, Twitter, YouTube, Flickr
Tres Bailey, Chair
Colin Woodall, Vice Chair
Curt Blades, Secretary/ Treasurer
An organization uniquely composed of leaders in the agriculture, food and fiber communities dedicated to increasing the public awareness of agriculture's vital role in our society.
Founded in 1973

9595 **National Alcohol Beverage Control Association**
4401 Ford Avenue
Suite 700
Alexandria, VA 22302-1433
703-578-4200
Fax: 703-820-3551
E-Mail: nabca.info@nabca.org
Home Page: www.nabca.org
Social Media: Facebook, Twitter, Youtube, Google
J. Neal Insley, Chairman
Jeffery R. Anderson, Chairman-Elect
James M. Sgueo, President & CEO
Jerome J. Janicki, Sr. Vice President of Operations
Patricia Kelly, Sr. Vice President
It is the mission of the National Alcohol Beverage Control Association to support and benefit alcohol control systems by providing research, fostering relationships, and managing resources to address policy for the responsible sale and consumption of alcohol beverages. Members include control jurisdictions, supplier members and industry trade associations.
175 Members
Frequency: Membership Dues Vary
Founded in 1938

9596 **National Association for the Specialty Food Trade**
Home Page: www.specialtyfood.com
Social Media: Facebook, Twitter, LinkedIn, YouTube, Pinterest
Nonprofit business trade association established to foster trade, commerce, and interest in the specialty food industry.
Founded in 1952

9597 **National Association of Agricultural Educators**
University of Kentucky
300 Garrigus Building
Lexington, KY 40546-0215
859-257-2224
800-509-0204
Fax: 859-323-3919
E-Mail: naae@uky.edu
Home Page: www.naae.org
Social Media: Facebook, Twitter
Farrah Johnson, President
Kevin Stacy, President-Elect
Jay Jackman, Executive Director
Alissa Smith, Associate Executive Director
A federation of 50 affiliated state vocational agricultural teacher associations. The mission is to provide agricultural education for the global community through visionary leadership, advocacy and service.
7600 Members
Founded in 1948

9598 **National Association of Animal Breeders**
PO Box 1033
Columbia, MO 65205
573-445-4406
Fax: 573-446-2279
E-Mail: naab-css@naab-css.org
Home Page: www.naab-css.org
Keith Heikes, Chairman
Charles Sattler, Vice-Chairman
Gordon A. Doak, President
Gordon A. Doak, Secretary/Treasurer
Unite those individuals and organizations engaged in the artificial insemination of cattle and other livestock into an affiliated federation operating under self-imposed standards of performance and to conduct and promote the mutual interest and ideals of its members.

Members are farmer co-ops and others interested in livestock improvement.
Founded in 1946

9599 National Association of Beverage Importers Inc.
529 14th St NW
Suite 1183
Washington, DC 20045
202-393-6224
Fax: 202-393-6595
Home Page: www.bevimporters.org
John F. Beaudette, Chairman
Michael J. Rudy, Chairman of the Committee
Stacey M. Tank, Vice Chairman
William T. Earle, President
Marc P. Goodrich, Treasurer
Trade association representing US importers of alcohol beverages, representing the interests of importers of alcohol beverages on issues that have a principal impact on importers, and cooperating with other trade associations on issues that impact all alcohol beverages whether imported or domestic.
Founded in 1934

9600 National Association of Concessionaires
180 N. MICHIGAN AVENUE
Suite 2215
Chicago, IL 60601
312-236-3858
Fax: 312-236-7809
E-Mail: info@naconline.org
Home Page: www.naconline.org
Social Media: Facebook, LinkedIn
John Evans Jr., Chairman
Jeff Scudillo, Presdient
Terry Conlon, President-Elect
Dan Borschke, Executive Vice President
Andrew Cretors, Treasurer
Trade association for the recreation and leisure-time food and beverage concessions industry. Providing members with information and services that maintain and enhance the standards of excellence and professionalism within the recreation and leisure time food, beverage and related services industry.
800 Members
Founded in 1944

9601 National Association of Convenience Stores
1600 Duke St
7th Floor
Alexandria, VA 22314
703-684-3600
800-684-3600
Fax: 703-836-4564
E-Mail: nacs@nacsonline.com
Home Page: www.nacsonline.com
Social Media: Facebook, Twitter, LinkedIn, YouTube
Henry Armour, President & CEO
Lyle Beckwith, Sr. VP, Government Relations
Michael Davis, V.P., Member Services
Shirley Jaffe, V.P.,Business Operations
Bob Hughes, V.P., Supplier Relations
Providing news, information and resources to the convenience and petroleum retail stores.
4000 Members
Founded in 1961

9602 National Association of Flavors and Food Ingredient Systems
3301 State Route 66
Building C, Suite 205
Neptune, NJ 07753
732-922-3218
Fax: 732-922-3590
E-Mail: info@naffs.org
Home Page: www.naffs.org
Arthur Curran, Chair
Dave Adams, President
Christine Daley, President-Elect
Pia Henzi, Vice President
Chris Williams, Vice President
A broad-based trade association of manufacturers, processors and suppliers of fruits, flavors, syrups, stabilizers, emulsifiers, colors, sweeteners, cocoa and related food ingredients. Its associate membership is open to all companies that provide products and services to the food industry.
120 Members

9603 National Association of Margarine Manufacturers
E-Mail: NAMM@kellencompany.com
Home Page: www.iheartbutterytaste.com
Social Media: Facebook, Twitter, Pinterest
Information and recipes about buttery soft spread margarines.

9604 National Association of Pizzeria Operators
909 S 8th Street
Suite 200
Louisville, KY 40203
502-736-9532
Fax: 502-736-9502
E-Mail: dwyatt@pizzatoday.com
Home Page: www.napo.com
Social Media: Facebook, Twitter, Youtube
Joe Straughan, President
Mary Sullivan, Membership Coordinator
Mission is to create and foster a community of independent and small chain pizzeria operators and their industry suppliers where doing business with another is mutually beneficial.
1100+ Members
Founded in 1984
Mailing list available for rent: 25000 names

9605 National Association of State Departments of Agriculture
4350 North Fairfax Drive
Suite 910
Arlington, VA 22203
202-296-9680
Fax: 703-880-0509
E-Mail: nasda@nasda.org
Home Page: www.nasda.org
Social Media: Facebook, Twitter
Chuck Ross, President
Russell Kokubun, 1st Vice President
Greg Ibach, 2nd Vice President
Michael Strain, Secretary/Treasurer
Mission is to represent the state departments of agriculture in the development, implementation, and communication of sound public policy and programs which support and promote the American agricultural industry, while protecting consumers and the environment.
Founded in 1915

9606 National Association of Wheat Growers
415 Second Street NE
Suite 300
Washington, DC 20002-4993
202-547-7800
Fax: 202-546-2638
E-Mail: wheatworld@wheatworld.org
Home Page: www.wheatworld.org
Social Media: Facebook, Twitter, YouTube
Wayne Hurst, President
Erik Younggren, 1st Vice President
Bing Von Bergen, 2nd Vice President
Paul Penner, Secretary/ Treasurer
Dana Peterson, CEO
A nonprofit partnership of US wheat growers who, by combining their strengths, voices and ideas, are working to ensure a better future for themselfves, their industry and the general public. Focusing on the policies of the US government that affect the livelihoods of US wheat producers.
Founded in 1950

9607 National Association of Wholesalers - Distributors
1325 G Street NW
Suite 1000
Washington, DC 20005-3100
202-872-0885
Fax: 202-785-0586
E-Mail: naw@naw.org
Home Page: www.naw.org
Social Media: Facebook, Twitter, YouTube
Dirk Van Dongen, President
Jade West, Senior Vice President
James A. Anderson, Junior Vice President
Joy Goldman, Vice President-Administrative
Representing the wholesale distributor industry. NAW is active in these areas: government relations and political action; research and education; and group purchasing. In addition the association operates the Wholesaler-Distributor Political Action Committee, the Distribution Research & Education Foundation, and the NAW Service Corporation.

9608 National Bar and Restaurant Association
307 W Jackson Avenue
Oxford, MS 38655
662-236-5510
Fax: 202-331-2429
Home Page: www.bar-restaurant.com
Jennifer Robinson, COO
Laura Speakes, Financial Affairs VP
Founded by Nightclub and Bar magazine, the association's mission is to provide discounts, services and networking opportunities enabling restaurant, bar and hospitality professionals to increase revenues and profits through innovative promotions, marketing and management.
Founded in 1924

9609 National Barbecue Association
455 S 4th Street
Suite 650
Louisville, KY 40202
888-909-2121
Fax: 502-589-3602
Home Page: www.nbbqa.org
Social Media: Facebook, Twitter, LinkedIn, Youtube
Roy Slicker, President
Linda Orrison, President-Elect
Mark Lambert, Treasurer
Bonnie Gomez, Secretary
Jeff Allen, Executive Director
Mission is to provide the barbeque community with a visionary, beneficial, and responsive association. NBBQA's goals are to promote the art and enjoyment of barbecue, facilitate the effective networking of industry resources and to foster new business opportunities.
Founded in 1991

9610 National Beer Wholesalers Association
1101 King Street
Suite 600
Alexandria, VA 22314-2944
703-683-4300
Fax: 703-683-8965
E-Mail: info@nbwa.org

Home Page: www.nbwa.org
Social Media: Facebook, Twitter, YouTube, Flickr

Greg LaMantia, Chair
Craig A Purser, President & CEO

NBWA represents the interests of America's 2,850 independent, licensed beer distributors which service every congressional district and media market in the country.
Founded in 1938
Mailing list available for rent

9611 **National Bison Association**
8690 Wolff Ct
200
Westminster, CO 80031

303-292-2833
Fax: 303-845-9081
E-Mail: david@bisoncentral.com
Home Page: www.bisoncentral.com
Social Media: Facebook

Peter Cook, President
Bruce Anderson, Vice-President
Amil Kleinert, Secretary/Treasurer
Dave Carter, Executive Director

Bringing together stakeholders to celebrate the heritage of American bison/buffalo, educating, and creating a sustainable future for our industry.
900 Members
Founded in 1975

9612 **National Bulk Vendors Association**
1202 East Maryland Avenue
Suite 1k
Phoenix, AZ 85014

888-628-2872
Home Page: www.nbva.org
Social Media: Facebook

Steve Schnecher, President
Carl Morcate, Vice President
Judi Heston, Treasurer
Shawn Dumphy, Secretary

A national, not-for-profit trade association comprised of the manufacturers, distributors and operators of bulk vending machines and products.
Founded in 1950

9613 **National Cattlemen's Beef Association**
9110 E. Nichols Ave.
#300
ÿCentennial, CO 80112

303-694-0305
Fax: 303-694-2851
E-Mail: customerservice@beef.org
Home Page: www.beef.org
Social Media: Facebook, Twitter

Forrest Roberts, CEO
John Queen III, President
Thad Larson, Director

Consumer focused, producer directed organization representing the largest segment of the nation's food and fiber industry.
28000 Members
Founded in 1898
Mailing list available for rent

9614 **National Cherry Growers and Industries Foundation (NCGIF)**
2667 Reed Road
Hood River, OR 97031

541-386-5761
Fax: 541-386-3191
E-Mail: osweetcherry@gmail.com
Home Page: www.nationalcherries.com

B J Thurlby, President
Idell Dunn, Assessment Supervisor
Andrew Willis, Promotion Director
Cheryl Kroupa, Marketing Director

Formed for the purpose of having a unified effort from the processed cherry industry to lobby against excessive cherry imports. The foundation compiles and distributes to members a yearly statistical publication of information regarding cherry production, utilization, and sales, both import and export.
Founded in 1948

9615 **National Coffee Association**
45 Broadway
Suite 1140
New York, NY 10006

212-766-4007
Fax: 212-766-5815
E-Mail: info@ncausa.org
Home Page: www.ncausa.org
Social Media: Facebook, Twitter, LinkedIn

John E. Boyle, Chairman
Bruce Goldsmith, Vice Chairman
Robert F. Nelson, President & CEO
Dan Dwyer, Secretary

Established on the behalf of the coffee companies in the United States. Respond to external issues and represent the coffee industry before the legislative and executive branches of government.
200 Members
Founded in 1911

9616 **National Confectioners Association**
1101 30th Street NW
Suite 200
Washington, DC 20007

202-534-1440
Fax: 202-337-0637
E-Mail: info@candyUSA.com
Home Page: www.candyusa.com

Robert M. Simpson, Chairman
Peter W. Blommer, Vice Chairman
Lawrence T. Graham, President
Eugene M. Dunkin, Jr., Vice President
Joseph Vittoria, Treasurer

Representing the entire confection industry, offering education and leadership in manufacturing, technical research, public relations, retailing practices, government relations, and statistical analyses.
Founded in 1884

9617 **National Confectionery Sales Association**
Spitfire House
3135 Berea Road
Cleveland, OH 44111

216-631-8200
Fax: 216-631-8210
E-Mail: info@candyhalloffame.org
Home Page: www.candyhalloffame.com/NCSA
Social Media: Facebook, Twitter

Alastair Northway, Chairman
Mark Antonucci, President
Joe Muck, 1st Vice President
John A. Leipold Jr., 2nd Vice President
Morton B. Gleit, Treasurer

Dedicated to furthering positive growth and acceptance of confectionery and allied products by education, open and frank dialogue, and recognition of peers' notable accomplishments. The Associations' responsibility to principals, customers, members and the community is to represent their products and services professionally and ethically in all relationships.
375 Members
Founded in 1899

9618 **National Conference of State Liquor Administrators**
543 Long Hill Road
Gurnee, IL 60031

847-721-6410
E-Mail: pamsalario@cox.net
Home Page: www.ncsla.org

Anne Hutchison, President
Robert S. Hill, 1st Vice President
W. Curtis Coleburn, 2nd Vice President
Matthew D. Botting, 3rd Vice President

Promoting the enactment of the most effective and equitable types of state alcoholic beverage control laws, to devise and promote the use of methods which provide the best enforcement of the particular alcoholic beverage control laws in each state, to work for the adoption of uniform laws, and to promote harmony with the federal government in its administration.

9619 **National Conference on Interstate Milk Shipments**
PO Box 108
Monticello, IL 61856

217-762-2656
E-Mail: ncims.bordson@gmail.com
Home Page: www.ncims.org

Dr. Stephen Beam, Chair
David E. Latten, Vice Chair
Marlena G. Bordson, Executive Secretary

The goal is to assure the safest possible milk supply for all the people. The NCIMS is governed by an executive board comprised of representatives from state and local regulatory agencies from three geographical regions; FDA, USDA, industry and laboratories and academia.
Founded in 1940

9620 **National Corn Growers Association**
632 Cepi Drive
Chesterfield, MO 63005

636-733-9004
Fax: 636-733-9005
E-Mail: corninfo@ncga.com
Home Page: www.ncga.com
Social Media: Facebook, Twitter, Pinterest

Pam Jhonson, Chairwoman
Martin O Barbre, President
Chip Bowling, First Vice President
Rick Tolman, Chief Executive Officer
Kathy Baker, Executive Assistant

Mission is to create and increase opportunities for corn growers. The Association will continue to be the recognized leader working in cooperation with its suppliers and customers to maintain sustainability and to achieve new business and profit opportunities for those it represents.
32300 Members
Founded in 1957
Mailing list available for rent

9621 **National Council of Chain Restaurants**
325 7th St NW
Suite 1100
Washington, DC 20004

202-783-7971
800-673-4692
Fax: 202-737-2849
E-Mail: info@nrf.com
Home Page: www.nccr.net

Chip Kunde, Chairman
Mary Schell, Vice Chairman
Cicely Simpson, Treasurer
Lynn Liddle, Secretary

The leading trade association exclusively representing chain restaurant companies. Working to advance sound public policy that best serves

the interests of restaurant businesses and the millions of people they employ.
Founded in 1965

9622 **National Council of Farmer Cooperatives**
50 F Street NW
Suite 900
Washington, DC 20001

202-626-8700
Fax: 202-626-8722
Home Page: www.ncfc.org
Social Media: Facebook, Twitter, Flickr

Charles Conner, President/ CEO
Marlis Carson, SVP, Legal, Tax
Justin Darisse, Vice President, Communications
Lisa Van Doren, Vice President & Chief of Staff
Kevin Natz, Vice President

Regional and national farmer cooperatives.

9623 **National Country Ham Association**
PO Box 948
Conover, NC 28616

828-466-2760
800-820-4426
Fax: 828-466-2770
E-Mail: eatham@countryham.org
Home Page: www.countryham.org

Allan Benton, President

Encourages promotion, development and improvement of the businesses of country ham carvers and encourages the use of country carved meats through co-operative methods of production, promotion, education and advertisement.
53 Members
Founded in 1992

9624 **National Dairy Council**
Interstate Place II
100 Elwood Davis Road
North Syracuse, NY 13212

315-472-9143
Fax: 315-472-0506
E-Mail: ndc@dairyinformation.com
Home Page: www.nationaldairycouncil.org
Social Media: Facebook, Twitter, Pinterest

This association operates under the auspices of the United Dairy Industry Association. NDC provides timely, scientifically sound nutrition information to the media, physicians, dietitians, nurses, educators, consumers and others concerned about fostering a healthier society.
Founded in 1915
Mailing list available for rent

9625 **National Farmers Organization**
528 Billy Sunday Road
Suite 100, P.O. Box 2508
Ames, IA 50010ÿ

800-247-2110
E-Mail: nfo@nfo.org
Home Page: www.nfo.org
Social Media: Facebook, YouTube

Members represent a cross-section of both conventional and organic production—grain growers, cattle and hog producers and dairymen and women.

9626 **National Farmers Unionÿ**
20 F Street NW
Suite 300
Washington, DC 20001

202-554-1600
Fax: 202-554-1654
Home Page: www.nfu.org
Social Media: Facebook, Twitter, LinkedIn, YouTube, Flickr

Roger Johnson, President
Jeff Knudson, Senior VP, Operations
Chandler Goule, SVP, Programs
Donn Teske, Vice President
Maria Miller, Executive Director

A national federation of state Farmers Union organizations in the United States.
Founded in 1902

9627 **National Federation of Coffee Growers of Colombia**
140 E 57th St
New York, NY 10022-2765

212-271-8802
Home Page: www.friendsofjuan.com

This organization is comprised of coffee growers from Colombia whose goal is to promote Colombian coffee in the US.

9628 **National Frozen & Refrigerated Foods Association Inc.**
4755 Linglestown Road Suite 300
PO Box 6069
Harrisburg, PA 17112

717-657-8601
Fax: 717-657-9862
E-Mail: info@nfraweb.org
Home Page: www.nfraweb.org
Social Media: Facebook, Twitter, LinkedIn

H V Skip Shaw Jr, President/CEO
Jeff Rumachik, Executive Vice President/COO
Julie W. Henderson, Vice President of Communications
Jessica Kurtz, Vice President of Finance
Dayna Jackson, Director of Membership

NFRA is a non-profit trade association representing all segments of the frozen the frozen and refrigerated foods industry. Heaquartered in Harrisburg, PA, NFRA is the sponsor of March National Frozen Food Month, June Dairy Month, and the Summer Favorites Ice Cream novelties promotion as well as the October Cool Food for Kids educational outreach program. NFRA holds the annual National Frozen & Refrigerated Foods Convention in October.
400 Members
Founded in 1945

9629 **National Frozen Dessert and Fast Food Association**
9614 Tomstown Road
Waynesboro, PA 17268

800-535-7748

This association is made up of small, independent owners and operators of ice cream and fast food establishments.

9630 **National Grape Growers Association**
2 South Portage Street
Westfield, NY 14787

716-326-5200
Fax: 716-326-5494
E-Mail: nationalinfo@welchs.com
Home Page: www.nationalgrape.com

Joseph C Falcone, President

More than just an organization of grape growers, stringent quality growing and harvesting standards, viticultural research, and aggressively funding new product development, manufacturing and marketing programs of Welch's.
Founded in 1897

9631 **National Honey Board**
11409 Business Park Circle
Suite 210
Firestone, CO 80504-9200

303-776-2337
Fax: 303-776-1177
E-Mail: honey@nhb.org
Home Page: www.honey.com
Social Media: Facebook, Twitter, Youtube,Pinterest,Googleplus

Brent Barkman, Chairperson
Mark Mammen, Vice Chairperson
Bruce Boynton, Chief Executive Officer
Nancy J. Gamber-Olcott, Secretary/Treasurer

Conducts research, advertising and promotion programs to help maintain and expand domestic and foreign markets for honey.
Founded in 1987
Mailing list available for rent

9632 **National Honey Packers & Dealers Association**
3301 Route 66
Suite 205, Building C
Neptune, NJ 07753

732-922-3008
Fax: 732-922-3590
E-Mail: info@nhpda.org
Home Page: www.nhpda.org

Bob Bauer, Executive Vice President

Comprised of US packers, importers and foreign exporters.

9633 **National Hot Dog and Sausage Council**
1150 Connecticut Avenue, NW
12th Floor
Washington, DC

202-587-4200
Home Page: www.hot-dog.org
Social Media: Facebook, YouTube, Pinterest

Janet Riley, President
Eric Mittenthal, Vice President, Public Affairs

Conducts scientific research to benefit hot dog and sausage manufacturers.
Founded in 1994

9634 **National Hot Pepper Association**
400 NW 20th Street
Fort Lauderdale, FL 33311-3818

954-565-4972
Fax: 954-566-2208
E-Mail: peppergal@mindspring.com

Networking among industry and private members. Education and information sharing.

9635 **National Ice Cream Mix Association**
2101 Wilson Blvd
Suite 400
Arlington, VA 22201

703-243-5630
Fax: 703-841-9328
E-Mail: nicma@nmpf.org
Home Page: www.icecreammix.org

Craig Colonno, President
Joe Duscher, Vice President
Jamie Jonker, Vice President, Scientific Regs
Pat Galloway, Treasurer
Tom Balmer, Executive Director

This group is made up of manufacturers of soft-serve ice cream, ice milk, shakes and other dessert mixes.
Founded in 1926

9636 **National Ice Cream Retailers Association**
1028 W Devon Avenue
Elk Grove Village, IL 60007

847-301-7500
866-303-6960
Fax: 847-301-8402
E-Mail: info@nicra.org
Home Page: www.nicra.org
Social Media: Facebook

Nanette Frey, President
Carl Chaney, President Elect
Jim Oden, Vice President
Lynda Utterback, Executive Director

NICRA is a trade organization whose members are in the retail ice cream and frozen dessert business. NICRA will associate with similar associations dedicated to the same interests, facilitate communication and education that both newcomers and veterans in the industry desire to be successful.
500 Members
Founded in 1933
Mailing list available for rent

9637 **National Mango Board**
3101 Maguire Blvd
Suite 111
Orlando, FL 32803

407-629-7318
877-MAN-OS 1
Home Page: www.mango.org
Social Media: Facebook, Twitter, Pinterest, YouTube

Bethany Ellis, Consumer and Trade Media
Susan Hughes, Foodservice
Kristine Concepcion, Mango Industry Contact

A national promotion and research organization which is supported by assessments from domestic and imported mangos.

9638 **National Meat Canners Association**
1150 Connecticut Avenue, NW
12th Floor
Washington, DC 20036

202-587-4200
Fax: 202-587-4300
E-Mail: webmaster@meatami.com
Home Page: www.meatami.org
Social Media: Facebook, Twitter, LinkedIn

Nick Merigolli, Chairman
Greg Benedict, Vice-Chairman
J.Patrick Boyle, President & CEO
Gary Jacobson, Treasurer
Dave McDonald, Secretary

AMI is the national trade association representing companies that process 70 percent of U.S. meat and their suppliers throughout America.

9639 **National Milk Producers Federation**
2101 Wilson Blvd
Suite 400
Arlington, VA 22201

703-243-6111
Fax: 703-841-9328
E-Mail: info@nmpf.org
Home Page: www.nmpf.org
Social Media: Facebook, Twitter, Flickr, YouTube

Randy Mooney, Chairman
Ken Nobis, 1st Vice Chairman
Cornell Kasbergen, 2nd Vice Chairman
Mike McCloskey, 3rd Vice Chairman
Pete Kappelman, Treasurer

Develops and carries out policies that advance the well being of dairy producers and the cooperatives they own. Provides a forum through which dairy farmers and their cooperatives formulate policy on national issues that affect milk production and marketing.
Founded in 1916
Mailing list available for rent

9640 **National Oilseed Processors Association**
1300 L St NW
Suite 1020
Washington, DC 20005

202-842-0463
Fax: 202-842-9126
E-Mail: nopa@nopa.org
Home Page: www.nopa.org

Thomas A. Hammer, President
David J. Hovermale, Executive Vice President
David C. Ailor, Executive Vice President
Kathleen A. Pennington, Office Administrator

Represents firms engaged in the actual processing of oilseeds, and associate firms who are consumers of vegetable oil or oilseed meal, including some refiners and mixed feed manufacturers.
Founded in 1929

9641 **National Onion Association**
822 7th St
Suite 510
Greeley, CO 80631

970-353-5895
Fax: 970-353-5897
Home Page: www.onions-usa.org
Social Media: Twitter, Pinterest

Gary Mayfield, President
Shawn Hartley, Vice President
John Rietveld, 2nd Vice President
Wayne Mininger, Executive Vice President
Monna Canaday, Administrative Assistant

Represents interests of US onion producers. Informational lobbying and generic promotional headquarters for fresh dry bulb onion growers. Provides connections for networking and education exchange.
600 Members
Founded in 1913
Mailing list available for rent

9642 **National Pasta Association**
750 National Press Building
529 14th Street NW
Washington, DC 20045

202-591-2459
Fax: 202-591-2445
E-Mail: info@ilovepasta.org
Home Page: www.ilovepasta.org

Patrick Regan, Chairman
Peter Bisaccia, Vice Chairman
Jim Meyer, Treasurer

To increase the consumption of pasta, to promote the development of sound public policy and, act as a center of knowledge for the industry.
Founded in 1904

9643 **National Peanut Board**
3350 Riverwood Parkway
Suite 1150
Atlanta, GA 30339

678-424-5750
866-825-7946
Fax: 678-424-5751
E-Mail: peanuts@nationalpeanutboard.org
Home Page: www.nationalpeanutboard.org
Social Media: Facebook, Twitter, Pinterest

Vic Jordan III, Chairman
John C. Harell, Vice Chairman
Bob H. White, Treasurer
Monty Rast, Secretary

A farmer-funded national research, promotion and education check-off program. Through NPB, growers from across the United States come together to contribute to the research and promotion of USA-grown peanuts.

9644 **National Pecan Shellers Association**
1100 Johnson Ferry Road
Suite 300
Atlanta, GA 30342

678-298-1189
Fax: 404-591-6811
E-Mail: npsa@kellencompany.com
Home Page: www.ilovepecans.org
Social Media: Facebook, Twitter, Pinterest

The NPSA is the trade association for the pecan shelling and processing industry. The association is dedicated to educating culinary and health professionals, food technologists, educators and the general public about the health benefits, nutritional value, variety of uses and all-around great taste of pecans.

9645 **National Pork Producers Council**
122 C Street NW
Suite 875
Washington, DC 20001

202-347-3600
Fax: 202-347-5265
E-Mail: warnerd@nppc.org
Home Page: www.nppc.org
Social Media: Facebook, Twitter, LinkedIn, Swinecast, Pinterest, Flickr

Randy Spronk, President
Howard Hill, President-Elect
Ron Prestage, Vice President
Neil Dierks, Chief Executive Officer

Conducts public-policy outreach on behalf of its 43 affiliated state associations, enhancing opportunities for the success of US pork producers and other industry stakeholders by establishing the US pork industry as a consistent and responsible supplier of high-quality pork to the domestic and world markets.

9646 **National Potato Council**
1300 L St NW
Suite 910
Washington, DC 20005

202-682-9456
Fax: 202-682-0333
E-Mail: spudinfo@nationalpotatocouncil.org
Home Page: www.nationalpotatocouncil.org
Social Media: Facebook, Twitter, Youtube

Randy Mullen, President
Randy Hardy, First Vice President
Nels Iverson, Vice President, Finance
Jim Tiede, Vice President, Government Affairs
Dwayne Weyers, Vice President, Growers

Represents US potato growers on federal legislative and regulatory issues.
6000 Members
Founded in 1948

9647 **National Poultry & Food Distributors Association**
2014 Osborne Road
Saint Marys, GA 31558

770-535-9901
Fax: 770-535-7385
E-Mail: kkm@npfda.org
Home Page: www.npfda.org
Social Media: Facebook, Twitter, LinkedIn

Marc Miro, President
Ted Rueger, Vice President
Lee Wilson, Treasurer
Kristin McWhorter, Executive Director

To promote the poultry and food distributors, processors and allied industries by bringing them together and providing a forum to foster long term business relationships.
210 Members
Founded in 1967

9648 **National Renderers Association**
500 Montgomery Street
Suite 310
Alexandria, VA 22314

703-683-0155
Fax: 571-970-2279
E-Mail: renderers@nationalrenderers.com
Home Page: www.nationalrenderers.org
Social Media: Twitter

Gerald F. Smith Jr., Chairman
Ross Hamilton, First Vice Chairman
Tim Guzek, Second Vice Chairman
Tom Cook, President

Representing members' interests to regulatory and other governmental agencies, promoting the greater use of animal by-products and fostering the opening and expansion of trade between foreign buyers and North American exporters.

9649 **National Restaurant Association Educational Foundation**
2056 L. St. NW
Washington, DC 20036

202-315-4102
800-424-5156
E-Mail: wsafstrom@nraef.org
Home Page: www.nraef.org
Social Media: Facebook, Twitter, Youtube

Denise Marie Fugo, Chair
Mike Gibbons, Vice Chair
Dawn Sweeney, President & CEO
Rob Gifford, Executive Vice President
Michael Hickey, Treasurer

NRAEF is the philanthropic foundation of the National Restaurant Association. Committed to enhancing the restaurant industry's service to the public through education, community engagement and promotion of career opportunities.
Founded in 1987

9650 **National Restaurant Association**
2055 L. St. NW
Suite 700
Washington, DC 20036

202-331-5900
800-424-5156
Fax: 202-331-2429
Home Page: www.restaurant.org
Social Media: Facebook, Twitter, YouTube

Phil Hickey, Chair
Ken Concard, Vice Chair
Dawn Sweeney, President & CEO
Jack Crawford, Treasurer

Striving to help members build customer loyalty, find financial success and provide rewarding careers in foodservice.
60000 Members
Founded in 1919

9651 **National Seafood Educators**
PO Box 60006
Richmond Beach, WA 98160

206-546-6410
Fax: 206-546-6411
E-Mail: information@seafoodeducators.com
Home Page: www.seafoodeducators.com

Evie Hansen, Founder

Goal is to educate and inform the public about the many health benefits of a seafood diet. Also has consulted with many seafood retail businesses on how to sell, store, and prepare wholesome seafood.
Founded in 1977

9652 **National Seasoning Manufacturers Association Inc**
8905 Maxwell Dr
Suite 200
Potomac, MD 20854

301-765-9675
Fax: 301-299-7523
E-Mail: alsmeyerfood@isp.com

Dick Alsmeyer PhD, Executive Director

Food seasoning manufacturers, producers of meat curing compounds, flavors, supplies, services, and equipment used for the seasoning and preserving of food.
23 Members
Founded in 1972

9653 **National Shellfisheries Association**
National Marine Fisheries Service Laboratory
Oxford, MD 21654

631-653-6327
Fax: 631-653-6327
E-Mail: webmaster@shellfish.org
Home Page: www.shellfish.org

Christopher Davis, President
Karolyn Mueller Hansen, President-Elect
Marta Gomez-Chiarri, Vice President
Steven Allen, Secretary
John Scarpa, Treasurer

Organization comprised of scientists, public health workers, shellfish producers and fishery administrators to promote and advance shellfisheries research and the application of results to the shellfish industry.
1M Members
Founded in 1908

9654 **National Society on Healthcare Foodservice**
455 S. 4th Street
Suite 650
Louisville, KY 40202

888-528-9552
Fax: 502-589-3602
E-Mail: info@healthcarefoodservice.org
Home Page: www.healthcarefoodservice.org
Social Media: Facebook, Twitter, LinkedIn, YouTube

Laura Watson, President
Lisette Coston, President-Elect
Jacqueline Sikoski, Secretary
Robert Darrah, Treasurer
Julie Jones, Treasurer-Elect

The only professional society dedicated to professionals and suppliers in the self-operated healthcare foodservice industry- those facilities who choose to keep their foodservice departments on staff, instead of outsourcing them to third-party contractors.

9655 **National Sunflower Association**
2401 46th Avenue SE
Suite 206
Mandan, ND 58554-4829

701-328-5100
888-718-7033
Fax: 701-328-5101
E-Mail: larryk@sunflowernsa.com
Home Page: www.sunflowernsa.com
Social Media: Facebook, YouTube

John Sandbakken, Executive Director
Tina Mittlesteadt, Manager

A non-profit commodity organization working on problems and opportunities for the improvement of all members. Members include growers and the support industry.
20000 Members
Founded in 1981

9656 **National Turkey Federation**
1225 New York Avenue NW
Suite 400
Washington, DC 20005

202-898-0100
Fax: 202-898-0203
E-Mail: info@turkeyfed.org
Home Page: www.eatturkey.com
Social Media: Facebook, Twitter, Youtube, Pinterest

John Burkel, Chairman
Gary Cooper, Vice Chairman
Joel Brandenberger, President
Damon Wells, Vice President
Jihad Douglas, Secretary-Treasurer

(NTF) is the national Advocate for all segments of the $8 billion turkey industry, providing services and conducting activities that increase demand for its members' products. The federation also protects and enhances its members' ability to effectively and profitably provide wholesome, high quality, nutritious turkey products.
264 Members
Founded in 1939

9657 **National WIC Association**
2001 S St NW
Suite 580
Washington, DC 20009

202-232-5492
Fax: 202-387-5281
E-Mail: douglasg@nwica.org
Home Page: www.nwica.org
Social Media: Facebook, Twitter, Pinterest

Douglas Greenaway, President & CEO

Members are geographic state, Native American state and local agency directors of the Special Supplement nutrition program for women, infants and children.
900 Members
Founded in 1983

9658 **National Watermelon Promotion Board**
1321 Sundial Point
Winter Springs, FL 32708

407-657-0261
877-599-9595
Fax: 407-657-2213
E-Mail: info@watermelon.org
Home Page: www.watermelon.org
Social Media: Facebook, Twitter, RSS, YouTube, Instagram

Mark Arney, Executive Director
Rebekah Dossett, Director of Operationsÿ
Gordon Hunt, Dir., Marketing & Comm.
Stephanie Barlow, Director of Public Relations
Andrea Smith, Industry Affairs Manager

Increase consumer demand for fresh watermelon through promotion, research, and educational programs.
Founded in 1989

9659 **Natural Marketing Institute**
272 Ruth Road
Harleysville, PA 19438

215-513-7300
Fax: 215-513-1713
E-Mail: Nancy.White@NMIsolutions.com
Home Page: www.NMIsolutions.com
Social Media: Facebook, Twitter, LinkedIn

Maryellen Molyneaux, President
George Ward, Vice President Strategic Consulting
John Devries, Vice President Strategic Consulting
Diane Ray, Vice President of Strategy

NMI is an international strategic marketing consultancy specializing in health, wellness,

sustainability and healthy aging with full-service consulting and market research services.
Founded in 1989

9660 Natural Products Association
1773 T Street, NW
Washington, DC 20009

202-223-0101
800-966-6632
Fax: 202-223-0250
E-Mail: natural@NPAinfo.org
Home Page: www.npainfo.org
Social Media: Facebook, Twitter, LinkedIn, Pinterest, Googleplus

Jon Fiume, Chair
Jain Drinkwalter, Chair
Jeffery Wright, President
Roxanne Green, President-Elect
John Shaw, Executive Director & CEO

The nation's largest and oldest non-profit organization dedicated to the natural products industry. NPA unites a diverse membership, from the smallest health food store to the largest dietary supplement manufacturer.
1900+ Members
Founded in 1936

9661 New York Apple Association
7645 Main Street
PO Box 350
Fishers, NY 14453-0350

585-924-2171
Fax: 585-924-1629
Home Page: www.nyapplecountry.com
Social Media: Facebook, Twitter

Jim Allen, President
Julia Stewart, Communications
Molly Golden, Director of Marketing
Linda Quinn, Media Representative

The New York Apple Association is a non-profit trade association representing over 600 commercial apple growers in New York State. The apple industry produces about 25 million bushels each year at a value of approximately $137 million, making it one of the largest sectors in New York agriculture.
600 Members
Founded in 1950

9662 North American Association of Food Equipment Manufacturers
161 N Clark Street
Suite 2020
Chicago, IL 60601

312-821-0201
Fax: 312-821-0202
E-Mail: info@nafem.org
Home Page: www.nafem.org

Thomas R. Campion, President
Michael L. Whiteley, President-Elect
Kevin Fink, Secretary/Treasurer
Deirdre Flynn, Executive Vice President

The North American Association of Food Equipment Manactures (NAFEM) is a trade association of more than 625 foodservice equipment and supplies manufacturers that provide products for food preparation, cooking, storage and table service providers. NAFEM's biennial trade show attracts approximately 20,000 foodservice professionals and features more than 600 North American manufacturers.
625 Members

9663 North American Blueberry Council
80 Iron Point Circle
Suite 114
Folsom, CA 95630

916-983-2279
Fax: 916-983-9370
E-Mail: info@nabcblues.org
Home Page: www.nabcblues.org

Neil Moore, President
Bob Carini, First Vice President
Tom Bodtke, Second Vice President
Art Galletta, Treasurer
Tom Avinelis, Secretary

A non-profit association with the important role of acting as a voice for the highbush blueberry industry.
Founded in 1965

9664 North American Farm Show Council
590 Woody Hayes Drive
Columbus, OH 43210

614-292-4278
Fax: 614-292-9448
E-Mail: gamble.19@osu.edu
Home Page: www.farmshows.org

Dennis Alford, President
Chip Blalock, 1st Vice President
David Zimmerman, 2nd Vice President
Chuck Gamble, Secretary/Treasurer

Strives to improve the value of its member shows through education, communication and evaluation. The overall goal is to provide the best possible marketing showcase for exhibitors of agricultural equipment and related products to the farmer/rancher/producer customer.
Founded in 1972

9665 North American Limousin Foundation
6 Inverness Court East
Suite 260
Englewood, CO 80112-5595

303-220-1693
Fax: 303-220-1884
E-Mail: limousin@nalf.org
Home Page: www.nalf.org
Social Media: Facebook, Twitter

Bob Mitchell, President
Mat Lewis, Vice President
Mike Hall, Secretary
Chad Settje, Treasurer
Mark Anderson, Executive Director

Register, promote and research on Limousin beef cattle.
4000 Members
Founded in 1968

9666 North American Meat Association
1150 Connecticut Avenue, NW
12th Floor
Washington, DC 20036
202-640-5333
800-368-3043
Fax: 202-318-4078
E-Mail: info@meatassociation.com
Home Page: www.meatassociation.com
Social Media: Twitter, LinkedIn

Mike Hesse, Co-Chairman
Brian Coelho, Co-President
Barry Carpenter, Chief Executive Officer
Phil Kimball, CAE, Executive Director
Sabrina Moore, Director, Meetings

Provides its members unique one-on-one assistance resolving regulatory issues. Mission is to be proactive and responsive in serving members both individually and collectively.
Founded in 2012

9667 North American Millers' Association
600 Maryland Ave SW
Suite 825 West
Washington, DC 20024

202-484-2200
Fax: 202-488-7416
E-Mail: generalinfo@namamillers.org
Home Page: www.namamillers.org
Social Media: Facebook

James M. Meyer, Chairman
Dan Dye, Vice Chairman
James A. McCarthy, President & CEO
James A. Bair, Vice President
Sherri Lehman, Director of Government Relations

Trade association representing the wheat, corn, oat and rye milling industry. NAMA members operate one hundred and seventy mills in thrirty-eight states and Canada. Their aggregate production of more than one hundred and sixty million pounds per day is approximately ninety-five percent of the industry capacity in the U.S.
Founded in 1902

9668 North American Natural Casing Association
494 Eighth Avenue
Suite 805
New York, NY 10001

212-695-4980
Fax: 212-695-7153
E-Mail: nanca18hq@yahoo.com
Home Page: www.nanca.org

Barbara Negron, President
Phil Schwartz, Vice President
Mike Wallace, Secretary
Eric Svendsen, Treasurer

To obtain legislation favorable to the industry's interests and prevent or change legislation deemed harmful at the local, state and federal levels, including protection from unfair trade practices by foreign countries, and working with member governments to ease trade. Also addresses common industry problems encountered by management in the production, distribution and financial function of the naturasl casing industry.

9669 North American Olive Oil Association
3301 Route 66
Suite 205, Building C
Neptune, NJ 07753

732-922-3008
Fax: 732-922-3590
E-Mail: info@naooa.org
Home Page: www.naooa.org
Social Media: Facebook, Twitter

Eryn Balch, Executive Vice President

Committed to supplying North American consumers with quality products in a fair and competitive environment; to fostering a clear understanding of the different grades of olive oil; and to expounding the benefits of olive oil in nutrition, health, and the culinary arts.
Founded in 1989

9670 Northeast Fresh Foods Alliance
1189R N Main Street
Randolph, MA 02368

781-963-9726
Fax: 781-963-5829

Brian Long, President
Bob Ogan, Executive VP
Chris Bruhn, First VP
Paul Sullivan, Secretary
Paul Palumbo, Treasurer
350 Members
Founded in 1979

9671 Northwest Cherry Briners Association Inc.
2667 Reed Rd
Hood River, OR 97031

E-Mail: director.orgcouncil@gmail.com
Home Page: www.orgcouncil.com

Carl Payne, VP Tech Services

Association of briners of sweet cherries in the northwestern US. The organization works to inform briners of regulatory decisions and current practices affecting brining operations.
8 Members
Founded in 1936

9672 **Northwest Food Processors Association**
8338 NE. Alderwood Road
Suite 160
Portland, OR 97220

503-327-2200
Fax: 503-327-2201
E-Mail: info@nwfpa.org
Home Page: www.nwfpa.org
Social Media: Facebook, Twitter, LinkedIn

Mark Dunn, Chair
Jim Robbins, Chair Elect
Steven Rowe, Vice Chair
David Zepponi, President
Pam Barrow, Director

NWFPA is an advocate for members interests and a resource for enhancing the food processing industry in Oregon, Washington and Idaho.
350 Members
Founded in 1914

9673 **Northwest Meat Processors Association**
2380 NW Roosevelt St
Portland, OR 97210-2323

503-226-2758
Fax: 503-224-0947
E-Mail: haysmgmt@pipeline.com

Dennis Hays, Executive Director
250 Members
Founded in 1962

9674 **Organic Alliance**
Organic Alliance International
Asheville, NC 28804

828-337-6114
Home Page: www.organicalliance.org

An alliance of people, businesses and organizations working together to promote the goodness of organics and help to make it available to all.

9675 **Organic Crop Improvement Association International (OCIA)**
1340 North Cotner Boulevard
Lincoln, NR 68505-1838

402-477-2323
Fax: 402-477-4325
E-Mail: info@ocia.org
Home Page: www.ocia.org

Kevin Koester, President
Jack Geiger, 1st Vice President
Lyle Hamann, 2nd Vice President
Demetria Stephens, Secretary
Terence Sheehan, Treasurer

An accredited world leader in the certified organic industry, provides certification, education and research services to thousands of organic farmers, processors and handlers from 20 countries in North, Central and South America and Asia.
3500 Members
Founded in 1985

9676 **Organic Trade Association**
28 Vernon St
Suite 413
Brattleboro, VT 05301

802-275-3800
Fax: 802-275-3801
E-Mail: info@ota.com
Home Page: www.ota.com
Social Media: Facebook, Twitter, LinkedIn

Melody Meyer, President
Sarah Bird, Vice President
Tony Bedard, Treasurer
Leslie Zuck, Secretary

A business association for the organic industry in North America. OTA's mission is to encourage global sustainability through promoting and protecting the growth of diverse organic trade.
1400 Members
Founded in 1985
Mailing list available for rent

9677 **Ozark Food Processors Association**
2650 N Young Avenue
Fayetteville, AR 72704

479-575-4607
Fax: 479-575-2165
E-Mail: ofpa@uark.edu
Home Page: ofpa.uark.edu

Susan Shivas, President
Jason Hayward, Vice President
Dr. Renee Threlfall, Secretary

This association is comprised of regional food processors and national suppliers for the food service industry.
90 Members
Founded in 1906

9678 **Pacific Coast Shellfish Growers Association**
120 State Ave NE
#142
Olympia, WA 98501

360-754-2744
Fax: 360-754-2743
E-Mail: pcsga@pcsga.net
Home Page: www.pcsga.net
Social Media: Facebook, Flickr

Margaret Pilaro Barrette, Executive Director
Connie Smith, Projects Manager
Mary Middleton, Executive Assistant

Members grow a wide variety of healthy, sustainable shellfish including oysters, clams, mussels, scallops and geoduck. PCSGA works on behalf of its members on a broad spectrum of issues, including environmental protection, shellfish safety, regulations, technology, and marketing.
Founded in 1930

9679 **Paperboard Packaging Council**
1350 Main Street
Suite 1508
Springfield, MA 01103-1670

413-686-9191
Fax: 413-747-7777
E-Mail: paperboardpackaging@ppcnet.org
Home Page: www.ppcnet.org
Social Media: Facebook, Twitter, LinkedIn, YouTube

Stephen Scherger, Chair
Kyle Eldred, Vice Chair
Ben Markens, President
Lou Kornet, Vice President
Steven Levkoff, Treasurer

Trade association serving converters and suppliers of all forms of paperboard packaging, including folding cartons, rigid boxes, paper cylinders, and laminated small flute containers.
Founded in 1929

9680 **Peanut and Tree Nut Processors Association**
PO Box 2660
Alexandria, VA 22301

301-365-2521
Fax: 301-365-7705
Home Page: ptnpa.org

William P. Elam, Chairman
Brian Ezell, Vice Chairman
Michael J. Valentine, Secretary/Treasurer

Representing the owners and operators of companies (large and small) who shell, process, salt and/or roast peanuts and tree nuts. In addition, our members also supply equipment and services that are critical to our industry.
Founded in 1939

9681 **Pear Bureau Northwest**
4382 SE International Way
Suite A
Milwaukie, OR 97222-4635

503-652-9720
Fax: 503-652-9721
E-Mail: info@usapears.com
Home Page: www.usapears.com
Social Media: Facebook, Twitter, YouTube, Pinterest

Kevin D. Moffitt, President & CEO
Linda Bailey, VP of Operations

A non-profit marketing organization that promotes, advertises and develops markets for fresh pears grown in Oregon and Washington. Through professional representatives in the U.S. and around the world, the Bureau coordinates activities designed to increase awareness and consumption of fresh USA Pears, facilitating research on behalf of the Northwest pear industry relative to consumer awareness and preferences, nutritional benefits and emerging global markets.
1600 Members
Founded in 1931

9682 **Pickle Packers International Inc.**
1620 I Street NW
Suite 925
Washington, DC 20006-4076

202-331-2465
Fax: 202-463-8998
Home Page: www.ilovepickles.org
Social Media: Facebook

Sponsors research, represents industry before government agencies, produces educational materials, and provides superior networking opportunities to members. Members inlude processors, salters, green shippers, brokers, growers, seed companies, ingredient and equipment manufacturers, packaging suppliers, and those providing goods and services to the industry.
Founded in 1896

9683 **Popcorn Board**
330 N Wabash Avenue
Suite 2000
Chicago, IL 60611

312-644-6610
Fax: 312-527-6783
E-Mail: info@popcorn.org
Home Page: www.popcorn.org
Social Media: Facebook, Twitter, Blog

A non-profit organization funded by US popcorn processors to raise awareness of popcorn as a versatile, whole-grain snack.
Founded in 1943

9684 **Printing Industries of America**
200 Deer Run Road
Sewickley, PA 15143

412-741-6860
800-910-4283

Fax: 412-741-2311
E-Mail: printing@printing.org
Home Page: www.gain.net
Social Media: Facebook, Twitter, LinkedIn, Pinterest, Googleplus

Jeff Ekstein, Chairman
David A. Olberding, 1st Vice Chairman
Bradley L. Thompson II, 2nd Vice Chairman
Michael L. Wurst, Treasurer
Kurt Kriesler, Secretary

Members are companies printing labels for food or consumer products.
40 Members

9685 Produce Marketing Association
1500 Casho Mill Road
PO Box 6036
Newark, DE 19711

302-738-7100
Fax: 302-731-2409
E-Mail: solutionctr@pma.com
Home Page: www.pma.com
Social Media: Facebook, Twitter, Flickr, YouTube, Xchange

Cathy Burns, President
Bryan Silbermann, CEO
Tony Parassio, Chief Operating Officer
Yvonne Bull, CFO

Providing business solutions that strengthen and lead the global produce community, PMA has set the standard for quality events with the annual convention and continues to revolutionize one of the world's most vibrant industries.
100 Members
Founded in 1949

9686 Professional Farmers of America
6612 Chancellor Dr.
Cedar Falls, IA 50613

319-277-1278
800-772-0023
Fax: 319-827-1792

Mike Walsten, VP
Merrill Oster, Executive Director

Provides farmers with marketing strategies and market-trend data, as well as seminars and home study courses.
25M Members
Founded in 1972

9687 Quality Bakers of America Cooperative
1275 Glenlivet Drive
Suite 100
Allentown, PA 18106-3107

973-263-6970
Fax: 973-263-0937
E-Mail: info@qba.com
Home Page: www.qba.com

Providing members with access to sources of appropriate services in order to maintain the highest product quality and sanitation standards.
Founded in 1922

9688 Quality Chekd Dairies
901 Warrenville Rd
Suite 405
Lisle, IL 60532

800-222-6455
Fax: 630-717-1126
E-Mail: qchekd@qchekd.com
Home Page: www.qchekd.com

Peter Horvath, President

A cooperative of dairy foods processors who use the Quality Checked trademark on their products and engage in group purchasing of ingredients and supplies.
Founded in 1944

9689 Raisin Administration Committee
2445 Capitol Street
Suite 200
Fresno, CA 93721-2236

559-225-0520
Fax: 559-225-0652
E-Mail: info@raisins.org
Home Page: www.raisins.org

Gary Schulz, President
Debbie Powell, Sr. Vice President of Operations
Larry Blagg, Sr. Vice President of Marketing
Ron Degiuli, Vice President of Accounting

Administrative board of growers and packers of raisins.

9690 Red Angus Association of America
4201 N Interstate 35
Denton, TX 76207-3415

940-387-3502
Fax: 888-829-6069
E-Mail: info@redangus.org
Home Page: www.redangus.org
Social Media: Facebook

Tim Whitley, President
Myron Edelman, Interim Co-CEO
Larry Keenan, Interim Co-CEO

Dedicated to providing its members with excellence and innovation in leadership, service, information and education. An association for breeders of Red Angus cattle.
2000 Members
Founded in 1954

9691 Refrigerated Foods Association
1640 Powers Ferry Road
Bldg. 2, Suite 200A
Marietta, GA 30067

770-303-9905
Fax: 770-303-9906
E-Mail: info@refrigeratedfoods.org
Home Page: www.refrigeratedfoods.org

George Bradford, President
Steve Loehndorf, Vice President
Wes Thaller, Secretary
Kenneth Funger, Treasurer

An organization of manufacturers and suppliers of refrigerated prepared foods united by a common interest; to advance and safeguard the industry. Members include manufacturers and suppliers of wet salads, refrigerated entrees and side dishes, dips, desserts, soups, and ethnic foods, as well as companies engaged in business operations related to the refrigerated foods industry.
200+ Members
Founded in 1980

9692 Research and Development Associates for Military Food and Packaging Systems
16607 Blanco Rd
Suite 501
San Antonio, TX 78232

210-493-8024
Fax: 210-493-8036
E-Mail: hqs@militaryfood.org
Home Page: www.militaryfood.org

Tim Zimmerman, Chairman
Bill McCreary, Vice Chairman
John Simmons, President
Daniel Weil, Executive Vice President
John Knapp, Treasurer

To provide the safest and highest food service to the US Armed Forces by linking industry, government and academics.
700 Members
Founded in 1946

9693 Retail Bakers of America
15941 Harlem Avenue
#347
Tinley Park, IL 60477

800-638-0924
Fax: 800-638-0924
E-Mail: Info@retailbakersofamerica.org
Home Page: www.retailbankersofamerica.org
Social Media: Facebook

Richard Reinwald, Chairman
Paul Sapienza, Secretary
Dale A. Biles, Treasurer

Comprised of retail bakeries, allied suppliers and other industry members. The purpose is to offer our members knowledge and resources to enhance business operations through learning opportunities, shared best practices, networking and industry communication.
2000 Members
Founded in 1918

9694 Retail Confectioners International
2053 S. Waverly
Ste. C
Springfield, MO 65804

417-883-2775
800-545-5381
Fax: 417-883-1108
E-Mail: van@retailconfectioners.org
Home Page: www.retailconfectioners.org
Social Media: Facebook, Twitter, YouTube

Doug Dressman, President
Virginia Whetstone, 1st Vice President
Brian Pelletier, 2nd Vice President
Judith Hilliard McCarthy, 3rd Vice President
Angie Burlison, Secretary/Treasurer

Providing education, promotion and legislative services to our members who are manufacturing retailers of quality boxed chocolate and other confectionery products throughout the U.S., Canada and overseas.
600 Members
Founded in 1917

9695 Rocky Mountain Bean Dealers Association
PO Box 1285
Elizabeth, CO 80107

303-646-8883
Fax: 720-306-2878
E-Mail: rmbean@revealmail.com

Vickie Root, Executive Director

This organization is dedicated to advancing the general interest of its members and the industry.

9696 Rocky Mountain Food Industry Association
PO Box 1083
Arvada, CO 80001-1083

303-830-7001
Fax: 303-424-7114
Home Page: www.rmfia.org

Mary Lou Chapman, President/CEO

The trade organization for the Colorado and Wyoming grocery industry, representing retail grocers, convenience stores, and their wholesale suppliers. The association serves as a voice for its members with state legislatures, US Congress and the various governmental agencies that regulate the food industry.
500 Members
Founded in 1917

9697 Roundtable of Food Professionals
4363 Larwin Avenue
Cypress, CA 90630

714-562-5088
Fax: 714-670-2965

E-Mail: info@rfporg.org
Home Page: www.rfporg.org

Barb Colucci, President
Jenny Rosoff, President-Emeritus
David Stennes, VP
Stephany Rosenthal, Membership Co-Chair

Provide opportunities for development and career expansion within the whole spectrum of the food industry.
50 Members
Founded in 2002

9698 Royal Crown Bottlers Association
515 Eline Ave
St Matthews, KY 40207-3655

502-896-0861
Fax: 502-896-0861

Stephanie Garling, Executive Director

Represents franchised Royal Crown bottlers.
100 Members
Founded in 1964

9699 Salt Institute
700 N Fairfax St
Suite 600
Alexandria, VA 22314-2040

703-549-4648
Fax: 703-548-2194
E-Mail: info@saltinstitute.org
Home Page: www.saltinstitute.org
Social Media: Facebook, Twitter, YouTube

Lori Roman, President
Morton Satin, Vice President
Jorge Amselle, Director of Communication

A source of authoritative information about salt and its more than 14,000 known users. Provides public information and advocates on behalf of its members, including use of the website.
Founded in 1914

9700 Santa Gertrudis Breeders International
PO Box 1257
Kingsville, TX 78364

361-592-9357
Fax: 361-592-8572
E-Mail: sgbi@sbcglobal.net
Home Page: www.santagertrudis.com
Social Media: Facebook, Twitter, Googleplus

Curtis Salter, President
Deanna Parker, Secretary/Treasurer
John E. Ford, Executive Director

The original American beef breed. Custom built for the range and market, these cattle have proven themselves worldwide to be a hardy and profitable breed from the mountains of Montana and Mexico to the tropics and deserts of Argentina and Australia. Worldwide, cattlemen are getting results using Santa Gertrudis genetics.
Founded in 1950

9701 School Nutrition Association
120 Waterfront St
Suite 300
National Harbor, MD 20745

301-686-3100
800-877-8822
Fax: 301-686-3115
E-Mail: servicecenter@schoolnutrition.org
Home Page: www.schoolnutrition.org
Social Media: Digg

Leah Schmidt, President
Julia Bauscher, President-Elect
Jean Ronnei, Vice President
Melanie Konarik, Secretary/Treasurer

This is a national, nonprofit professional organization representing members who provide high quality, low-cost meals to students across the country.
55000 Members
Founded in 1946

9702 Sioux Honey Association
301 Lewis Boulevard
PO Box 388
Sioux City, IA 51101

712-258-0638
Fax: 712-258-1332
Home Page: www.suebeehoney.com
Social Media: Facebook, Twitter, YouTube, Pinterest

David Allibone, President/CEO

Established by five beekeepers so that they could market their honey at greater profit through sharing services and equipment, processing and packing facilities and complete marketing and sales organizations.
315 Members
Founded in 1921

9703 Small Farm Resource
Home Page: www.farminfo.org

Contains a wide variety of information useful to those with small farms and rural property.

9704 Snack Food Association
1600 Wilson Blvd
Suite 650
Arlington, VA 22209

703-836-4500
800-628-1334
Fax: 703-836-8262
E-Mail: sfa@sfa.org
Home Page: www.sfa.org
Social Media: Facebook, Twitter, LinkedIn, Youtube, Flickr

Tom Dempsy, CEO
Liz Wells, Vice President, Meetings & Events

Representing snack manufacturers and suppliers worldwide. Serving as the voice for the snack industry before government, researches and compiles annual snack sales and consumer data, educates manufacturers on technological advances in equipment and raw ingredients and provides technical support to its members through direct assistance, videos, seminars and publications.
800 Members
Founded in 1937

9705 Society for Laboratory Automatic and Screening
100 Illinois Street
Suite 242
St. Charles, IL 60174

630-256-7527
877-990-7527
Fax: 203-748-7557
E-Mail: slas@slas.org
Home Page: www.slas.org
Social Media: Facebook, Twitter, LinkedIn, YouTube

Jeff Paslay, President
Daniel G. Sipes, Vice President
Robyn Rourick, Treasurer
Dean Ho, Secretary

Supports research and discovery in pharmaceutical biotechnology and the agrichemical industry that utilize biomolecular screening procedures.
2000+ Members
Founded in 1994

9706 Society of Commercial Seed Technologists
1601 52nd Avenue
Suite 1
Moline, IL 61265

309-736-0119
Fax: 607-273-1638
E-Mail: scst@seedtechnology.net
Home Page: www.seedtechnology.net

Neal Foster, President
Barbara Cleave, VP

A organization comprised of commercial, independent and government seed technologists. Developed over the years into a progressive organization that trains and provides accreditation of technologists, conducts research studies and proposes rule changes, and serves as an important resource to the seed industry.
Founded in 1922

9707 Southeast United Dairy Industry Association
5340 W Fayetteville Rd
Atlanta, GA 30349-5416

678-833-0580
800-343-4693
Fax: 770-996-6925
E-Mail: info@sudiainc.com
Home Page: www.southeastdairy.org
Social Media: Facebook, Twitter, YouTube, Pinterest

Amanda Trice, Director of IR & Communications
Rebecca Egseiker, Assistant Director of Communication

Provides a wealth of information for milk and dairy consumers, media, school and health professionals and dairy farmers.
6000 Members
Founded in 1971
Mailing list available for rent

9708 Southeastern Dairy Foods Research Center
NCSU Department of Food Science
PO Box 7624
Raleigh, NC 27695

919-515-4197
Fax: 919-513-0014
E-Mail: bernard_eckhardt@ncsu.edu
Home Page: www.cals.ncsu.edu/food_science/
Social Media: Facebook, Twitter, YouTube

One of six National Centers funded and managed by Dairy Management Incorporated. The mission is to conduct research to develop and apply new technologies for value-added processing of fluid milk and its components into dairy products and ingredients with improved safety, quality or expanded functionalities.
Founded in 1988

9709 Southern Peanut Farmers Federation
1025 Sugar Pike Way
Canton, GA 30115

770-751-6615
E-Mail: lpwagner@comcast.net
Home Page: www.southernpeanutfarmers.org

Formed to educate American consumers about the US peanut industry and its products.
Founded in 1998

9710 Southern Peanut Growers
1025 Sugar Pike Way
Canton, GA 30115

770-751-6615
E-Mail: lpwagner@comcast.net
Home Page: www.peanutbutterlovers.com
Social Media: Facebook, Twitter, YouTube, Pinterest

Leslie Wagner, Executive Director

A nonprofit trade association representing peanut farmers in Georgia, Alabama, Florida and Mississippi. Formed to educate American consumers about the US peanut industry and its products.
6000 Members
Founded in 1980
Mailing list available for rent

9711 Southern US Trade Association
701 Poydras St
Suite 3725
New Orleans, LA 70139
504-568-5986
Fax: 504-568-6010
E-Mail: susta@susta.org
Home Page: www.susta.org
Social Media: Facebook
Jerry Hingle, Executive Director
Penny Lawrence, Manager
Troy Rosamond, Financial Director
A non-profit agricultural export trade development association comprised of the Departments of Agriculture of the 15 southern states and the Commonwealth of Puerto Rico.
Founded in 1973

9712 Soy Protein Council
1255 23rd Street NW
Washington, DC 20037
202-467-6610
Fax: 202-833-3636
Home Page: www.spcouncil.org
Social Media: Facebook, Twitter
David A Saunders, Executive VP
Elroy Wolff, General Counsel
Primary purpose is to promote the growth and interests of the soy protein industry and broaden the acceptance of soy products as key components of the worldwide food system.
Founded in 1971

9713 Soyfoods Association of North America
1050 17th Street, NW
Suite 600
Washington, DC 20036
202-659-3520
E-Mail: info@soyfoods.org
Home Page: www.soyfoods.org
Social Media: Facebook, Twitter, YouTube, Pinterest
Kate Leavltt, President
Katy Raneri, Vice President
Rebecca Zimmerman, Treasurer
Nancy Chapman, Executive Director
A trusted advocate in providing information about the health benefits and nutritional advantages of soy consumption. Encouraging sustainability, integrity and growth of the soyfoods industry through members.
50+ Members
Founded in 1978

9714 Specialty Coffee Association of America
330 Golden Shore
Long Beach, CA 90802
562-624-4100
Fax: 562-624-4101
E-Mail: info@scaa.org
Home Page: www.scaa.org
Social Media: Facebook, Twitter, YouTube
Paul Thornton, President
Sawn Hamilton, Vice President
Tracy Allen, 2nd Vice President
Ben Pitts, Secretary/Treasurer
One of the primary functions is to set the industry's standards for growing, roasting and brewing. Members of the SCAA include coffee retailers, roasters, producers, exporters and importers, as well as manufacturers of coffee equipment and related products.
2500+ Members
Founded in 1982
Mailing list available for rent

9715 Specialty Food Association and Fancy Food Show
136 Madison Avenue
12th Floor
New York, NY 10016
212-482-6440
Fax: 212-482-6459
Home Page: www.specialtyfood.com
Social Media: Facebook, Twitter, LinkedIn, YouTube
Mike Silver, Chair
Shawn McBride, Vice Chair
Ann Daw, President
Becky Renfro Borbolla, Treasurer
Matt Neilsen, Secretary
A business trade association to foster trade, commerce and interest in the specialty food industry. Composed of domestic and foreign manufacturers, importers, distributors, brokers, retailers, restaurateurs, caterers and others in the specialty foods business.
2100 Members
Founded in 1952

9716 Sugar Association
1300 L Street NW
Suite 1001
Washington, DC 20005
202-785-1122
Fax: 202-785-5019
E-Mail: sugar@sugar.org
Home Page: www.sugar.org
Social Media: Facebook, Twitter, Pinterest
Andrew Briscoe, President/CEO
Charles W Baker, Executive VP/Chief Science Officer
Cheryl Digges, VP Public Policy & Education
Lisa Swanson, Administrative Assistant
Promoting the consumption of sugar through sound scientific principles while maintaining an understanding of the benefits that sugar contributes to the quality of wholesome foods and beverages.
Founded in 1943

9717 Switzerland Cheese Association
704 Executive Blvd
Suite I
Valley Cottage, NY 10989-2010
845-268-2460
Fax: 845-268-9991
Paul U Schilt, CEO

9718 Tea Association of the USA
362 Fifth Avenue
Suite 801
New York, NY 10001
212-986-9415
Fax: 212-697-8658
E-Mail: info@teausa.com
Home Page: www.teausa.com
Social Media: Facebook, Twitter
Joe Simrany, President
Association of companies dedicated to the interests and growth of the US tea industry.
100 Members
Founded in 1899
Mailing list available for rent

9719 Tea Board of India
14 B.T.M. Sarani
Kolkata, KO 700001
332-235-1331
Fax: 332-221-5715
Home Page: www.teaboard.gov.in
M.G.V.K. Bhanu, Chairman
Neelam Meena, Deputy Chairman
Sumita Lahiri, Personal Secretary to Chairman
This association promotes Indian tea and develops new markets for tea in the US and Canada.
Founded in 1953

9720 The American Dairy Association Indiana, Inc.
9360 Castlegate Dr
Indianapolis, IN 46256
317-842-3060
800-225-6455
Fax: 317-842-3065
E-Mail: osza@winnersdrinkmilk.comÿ
Home Page: www.indianadairycouncil.org
Social Media: Facebook, Twitter, LinkedIn, YouTube
Donald Gurtner, President
Paul Mills, Vice President
Steve Phares, Treasurer
Anita Schmitt, Secretary
A not-for-profit organization which promotes the sale and consumption of diary foods.

9721 The Biscuit & Cracker Manufacturers' Association
6325 Woodside Court
Suite 125
Columbia, MD 21046
443-545-1645
Fax: 410-290-8585
E-Mail: info@thebcma.org
Home Page: www.thebcma.org
Social Media: Facebook, LinkedIn
David Van Laar, Chair
Miquel Moreno, Vice Chair
Stacey S. Sharpless, President
Todd Wallin, Treasurer
Kathy Kinter Phelps, Secretary
International trade organization representing the entire spectrum of companies involved in the manufacturing of biscuits and crackers and the suppliers to the baking industry. Our mission is to bring unparalled educational training programs and networking opportunities to members of the cookie and cracker industry.
250 Members
Founded in 1901

9722 The Catfish Institute
6311 Ridgewood Road
Suite W404
Jackson, MS 39211
601-977-9559
Fax: 662-887-6857
E-Mail: info@catfishinstitute.com
Home Page: www.uscatfish.com
Social Media: Facebook, Twitter, Youtube, Pinterest
Butch Wilson, President
Roger Barlow, Executive Vice-President
Represents the largest aquaculture industry in the United States. Represents the interests of the farm-raised catfish industry of farmers, processors, feed mills, researchers, and supplier industries. Promotes the many healthy, great tasting uses for genuine U.S. Farm-Raised Catfish.
Cost: $40.00
Frequency: Membership Fees
Founded in 1986
Mailing list available for rent

9723 **The Food and Beverage Association of America**
111 East 14th Street
Suite 390
New York, NY 10003

212-344-8252
Fax: 212-504-9536
E-Mail: office@fbassoc.com
Home Page: www.fbassoc.com
Social Media: LinkedIn

Gladys Mouton Di Stefano, Chairperson
Steven V. Gattullo, President
Sean Cassidy, First Vice President
Gus Montesantos, Second Vice President
Claudia Nieto, Executive Director

A nonprofit, philanthropic, trade organization for executives of the food and beverage industries of the New York metropolitan area.
Founded in 1956

9724 **The Industry Council for Research on Packaging and the Environment**
SoanePoint, 6-8 Market Place
Reading
Berkshire RG1 2EG

118-925-5991
Fax: 202-833-3636
E-Mail: info@incpen.org
Home Page: www.incpen.org
Social Media: Facebook, Twitter

Steve Young, President

A research organization, which draws together an influential group of companies who share a vision of the future where all production, distribution, and consumption are sustainable. Aiming to ensure policies on packaging makes a positive contribution to sustainability, encourages the industry to minimize the environmental impact of packaging and continuously improve packaging, and explain the role of packaging in society.
Founded in 1974

9725 **The National Chicken Council**
1152 15th Street NW
Suite 430
Washington, DC 20005-2622

202-296-2622
Fax: 202-293-4005
E-Mail: ncc@chickenusa.org
Home Page: www.nationalchickencouncil.org
Social Media: Facebook, Twitter

Michael J. Brown, President
William P. Roenigk, Senior Vice President
Mary M. Colville, VP of Government Affairs
Ashley Peterson, VP of Science & Regulatory Affairs
Tom Super, Vice President of Communications

National, non-profit trade association representing the US chicken industry. Promoting and protecting the interests of the chicken industry and acts as the industry's voice before Congress and federal agencies. Members include chicken producer/processors, poultry distributors, and allied industry firms.
150+ Members
Founded in 1954

9726 **The National Confectioners' Association**
1101 30th Street, NW
Suite 200
Washington, DC 20007

202-534-1440
Fax: 202-337-0637
E-Mail: info@CandyUSA.com
Home Page: www.candyusa.com
Social Media: Facebook, Twitter, LinkedIn, Flickr, Pinterest, YouTube

Robert M. Simpson, Jr., Chairman
Peter W. Blommer, Vice Chairman
John H. Downs, Jr., President/ CEO
Joseph Vittoria, Treasurer
Martino Caretto, Vice President

Advances, protects, and promotes the confectionery industry.
Founded in 1884

9727 **Today's Market Prices**
Home Page: www.todaymarket.com

A user friendly information center that provides within its market prices service, daily price information on more than 200 fruit, vegetables, and herbs from the most important wholesale markets of the USA, Canada, Mexico, and Europe.
Founded in 1996

9728 **Tortilla Industry Association**
1600 Wlison Blvd
Suite 650
Arlington, VA 22209

800-944-6099
Fax: 800-944-6177
E-Mail: info@tortilla-info.com
Home Page: www.tortilla-info.com

Ezequiel Montemayor Jr., Chairman
Jim Kabbani, Chief Executive Officer
Dana Beall, Secretary

Members include companies engaged in manufacturing tortillas and suppliers, food brokers and Mexican restaurant owners.
175 Members
Founded in 1990

9729 **U.S. Meat Export Federationy̌**
1855 Blake Street
Suite 200
Denver, CO 80202

303-623-MEAT
Fax: 303-623-0297
E-Mail: migoe@usmef.org
Home Page: www.usmef.org
Social Media: Facebook, Twitter, YouTube

Leann Saunders, Chair
Roel Andriessen, Chair-elect
Bruce Schmoll, Vice Chair
Dennis Stiffler, Treasurer/ Secretary
Philip M. Seng, President, CEO

A nonprofit trade association working to create new opportunities and develop existing international markets for U.S. beef, pork, lamb, and veal.

9730 **U.S. Poultry & Egg Associationy̌**
1530 Cooledge Road
Tucker, GA 30084-7303

770-493-9401
Fax: 770-493-9257
E-Mail: info@uspoultry.org
Home Page: www.uspoultry.org
Social Media: Facebook, Twitter, LinkedIn, Google+, YouTube

John Starkey, President
Charles Olentine, PhD, Executive Vice President
Gwen Venable, Vice President of Communications
Jason Rivera, Vice President, IT
Barbara Jenkins, Vice President - Education Programs

Represents producers and processors of broilers, turkeys, eggs and breeding stock, as well as allied companies.
Founded in 1947

9731 **U.S. Wheat Associates**
3103 10th Street, North
Suite 300
Arlington, VA 22201

202-463-0999
Fax: 703-524-4399
E-Mail: info@uswheat.org
Home Page: www.uswheat.org
Social Media: Facebook, Twitter, YouTube, Flickr

Roy Motter, Chairman
Brian O'Toole, Vice Chairman
Dan Hughes, Past Chairman
Alan Tracy, President
Jason Scott, Secretary-Treasurer

Supports the sale of wheat by offering education for overseas buyers, onsite training services, promotes trade policies, and consumer promotion.

9732 **US Animal Health Association**
4221 Mitchelle Ave.
Saint Joseph, MO 64507

816-671-1144
Fax: 816-671-1201
E-Mail: usaha@usaha.org
Home Page: www.usaha.org
Social Media: Facebook, Twitter

Dr. Stephen Crawford, President
Dr. Bruce King, President-Elect
Dr. David Schmitt, First Vice President
Dr. Boyd Parr, Second Vice President
Mrs. Barbara Determan, 3rd Vice President

Seeks to prevent, control and eliminate livestock diseases.
1400 Members
Founded in 1897

9733 **US Apple Association**
8233 Old Courthouse Rd
Suite 200
Vienna, VA 22182

703-442-8850
Fax: 703-790-0845
E-Mail: info@usapple.org
Home Page: www.usapple.org
Social Media: Facebook, Twitter, Youtube

Diane Kurrle, Vice President of Public Affairs
Mark Seetin, Director, Regulatory Affairs
Jessa Allen, Director,Membership&Communicatons
Wendy Brannen, Director,Consumer Health

Providing all segments of the US apple industry the means to profitably produce and market apples and apple products. Committed to serving the entire US apple industry by representing the industry on national issues, increasing the demand for apples and apple products, and providing information on matters pertaining to the apple industry.
440 Members
Founded in 1970

9734 **US Beet Sugar Association**
1156 15th St NW
Suite 1019
Washington, DC 20005

202-296-4820
Fax: 202-331-2065
Home Page: www.beetsugar.org

James Johnson, President
Elin Peltz, VP
Claudia Tidwell, Administration Director
Hillary Fabrico, Government Affairs Assistant

Beet sugar processing companies make up the membership of this association.
Founded in 1911

9735 **US Canola Association**
600 Pennsylvania Ave SE
Suite 320
Washington, DC 20003

202-969-8113
Fax: 202-969-7036
Home Page: www.uscanola.com
Social Media: Facebook

Ryan Pederson, President
Jeff Scott, First VP
Robert Rynning, Second Vice President

Works to support and advance US canola production, marketing, processing and use through government and industry relations. Striving to develop and implement agricultural policies, promote efficient production of the crop, and develop markets for US canola products.
Founded in 1989

9736 **US Grains Council**
20 F Street, NW
Suite 600
Washington, DC 20001

202-789-0789
Fax: 202-898-0522
E-Mail: grains@grains.org
Home Page: www.grains.org
Social Media: Facebook, Twitter, Youtube, Flickr

Julius Schaaf, Chairman
Ron Gray, Vice Chairman
Thomas Sleight, President & CEO
Alan Tiemann, Secretary

Develops export markets for US barley, corn, grain sorghum and related products. Members include producer organizations and agribusinesses with a common interest in developing export markets.
100 Members
Founded in 1960

9737 **US Meat Export Federation**
1855 Blake St
Suite 200
Denver, CO 80202

303-623-6328
Fax: 303-623-0297
E-Mail: migoe@usmef.org
Home Page: www.usmef.org

Mark Jagels, Chairman
Leann Saunders, Chair-Elect
Roel Andriessen, Vice-Chair
Philip M. Seng, President & CEO
Bruce Schmoll, Secretary/Treasurer

A trade association working to create new opportunities and develop existing international markets for U.S. beef, pork, lamb and veal.
160 Members
Founded in 1996

9738 **US Poultry & Egg Association**
1530 Cooledge Rd
Tucker, GA 30084-7303

770-938-6915
Fax: 770-493-9257
E-Mail: chanson@poultryegg.org
Home Page: www.poultryegg.org
Social Media: Facebook

Gary Cooper, Chairman
John Starkey, President
Carol 9anson, Executive Assistant

Representing the entire industry as an All Feather association. Membership includes producers and processors of broilers, turkeys, ducks, eggs, and breeding stock, as well as allied companies.
Cost: $300.00
600 Members
Frequency: Membership Dues
Founded in 1947

9739 **USA Rice Federation**
2101 Wilson Boulevard
Suite 610
Arlington, VA 22201ÿÿ

703-236-2300
Fax: 703-236-2301
E-Mail: riceinfo@usarice.com
Home Page: www.usarice.com
Social Media: Facebook, Twitter, RSS, YouTube, Pinterest

A national association representing producers, millers and allied businesses advancing the use and consumption of U.S. grown rice.

9740 **United Agribusiness League**
54 Corporate Park
Irvine, CA 92606

800-223-4590
Fax: 949-975-1671
E-Mail: membership@unitedag.org
Home Page: www.unitedag.org
Social Media: Facebook

Brian Edmonds, Chairman
Anthony Vollering, Vice Chairman
A.J. Cisney, Treasurer
Kirti Mutatkar, CEO
Clare Marie Einsmann, Executive Vice President

Creating a community for agribusiness—networking and education.

9741 **United Braford Breeders**
Home Page: www.brafords.org

Organization that registers Braford cattle in the United States.

9742 **United Egg Producers**
1720 Windward Concourse
Alpharetta, GA 30005

770-360-9220
Fax: 770-360-7058
Home Page: www.unitedegg.org
Social Media: Facebook, Twitter

Chad Gregory, President & CEO
David Inall, Senior Vice President
Sherry Shedd, Vice President of Finance
Oscar Garrison, Director of Food Safety
Derreck Nassar, Director of Operations

UEP is a Capper-Volstead cooperative of egg farmers from all across the United States and representing the ownership of all the nation's egg-laying hens.
Founded in 1968

9743 **United Food and Commercial Workers International Union**
1775 K St Nw
Washington, DC 20006

202-223-3111
Fax: 202-466-1562
E-Mail: ssmith@ufcw.org
Home Page: www.ufcw.org
Social Media: Facebook, Twitter

Joseph T. Hansen, President
Anthony M Perrone, Secretary/Treasurer
William T McDonough, Executive VP
Patrick J. O'Neill, Executive VP
Wayne E. Hanley, Executive VP

UFCW is North America's neighborhood union, members standing together to improve the lives and livelihoods of workers, families and communities.
1.4 M Members
Founded in 1979

9744 **United Fresh Produce Association**
1901 Pennsylvania Ave NW
Suite 1100
Washington, DC 20006

202-303-3400
Fax: 202-303-3433
E-Mail: united@unitedfresh.org
Home Page: www.unitedfresh.org
Social Media: Facebook, Twitter, LinkedIn

Tom Stenzel, President/CEO
Dan Hilleary, Chief Finacial Officer
Victoria Backer, Senior Vice President
Miriam Wolk, Vice President of Membership
Jeff Oberman, Vice President, Trade Relations

A trade association committed to driving the growth and success of produce companies ans their partners. Represents the interests of member companies throughout the global, fresh produce supply chain, including family-owned, private and publicly trade businesses as well as regional, national and international companies.
Founded in 1987

9745 **United Soybean Board**
16305 Swingley Ridge Rd
Suite 150
Chesterfield, MO 63017

636-530-1777
800-989-8721
Fax: 636-530-1560
E-Mail: ydock@unitedsoybean.com
Home Page: www.unitedsoybean.org
Social Media: Facebook, Twitter, YouTube

Jim Stillman, Chairman
Jim Call, Vice Chair
John Becherer, CEO
Lewis Brainbridge, Secretary
Bob Haselwood, Treasurer

Mission is to ensure that US soy is of the highest quality and the most competitive in a global marketplace.
Founded in 1972
Mailing list available for rent

9746 **United States Cane Sugar Refiners**
1730 Rhode Island Ave NW
#608
Washington, DC 20036-3101

202-331-1458

Joseph Cox, President

9747 **United States Potato Board**
4949 S. Syracuse St.
#400
Denver, CO 80237

303-369-7783
Fax: 303-369-7718
E-Mail: info@uspotatoes.com
Home Page: www.uspotatoes.com

Rob Davis, Chairman
Blair Richardson, President & CEO
Diana LeDoux, VP,Finance/Information Technology
David Fraser, VP, Industry Communciations
John Toaspern, Vice President, International

The nation's potato marketing organization. The central organizing force in implementing programs that will increase demand for potatoes, providing the ideas, information, tools and inspiration for the industry to unite in achieving common goals.
Founded in 1971

9748 **United States Tuna Foundation**
1101 17th St NW
Suite 609
Washington, DC 20036-4718

202-857-0610
Home Page: www.tunafacts.com

Desiree Filippone, Manager

Serves as an umbrella organization representing the various interests of the U.S. canned tuna industry. Representing the internationaln and domestic interests to federal and state regulations, to national legislation, to domestic marketing.
Founded in 1976

9749 **Vegetarian Awareness Network/VEGANET**
PO Box 3545
Washington, DC 20027-0045

800-872-8343
Fax: 877-329-8343
Home Page: www.wholefoodsmagazine.com

Howard V. Wainer, President

Networks to promote healthful living, environmental healing, and respect for all life; to advance public awareness of the advantages of the increasingly popular vegetarian lifestyle; to enhance the visibility and accessibility of vegetarian products and services; and to facilitate the formation and expansion of local vegetarian organizations.
Founded in 1980

9750 **Vegetarian Resource Group**
PO Box 1463
Baltimore, MD 21203

410-366-8343
Fax: 410-366-8804
E-Mail: vrg@vrg.org
Home Page: www.vrg.org
Social Media: Facebook, Twitter

Debra Wasserman, Director

An organization dedicated to educating the public on vegetarianism and the interrelated issues of health, nutrition, ecology, ethics, and world hunger.
15000 Members
Founded in 1982
Mailing list available for rent

9751 **Vidalia Onion Committee**
100 Vidalia Sweet Onion Drive
PO Box 1609
Vidalia, GA 30474

912-537-1918
Fax: 912-537-2166
E-Mail: info@vidaliaonion.org
Home Page: www.vidaliaonion.org
Social Media: Facebook, Twitter, YouTube, Pinterest

Aries Haygood, Chairman
Michael E. Hively, Vice Chairman
Myrtle S. Jones, Secretary

Promote growth, distribution and awareness of this one of a kind crop.
225 Members
Founded in 1931

9752 **Vinegar Institute**
1100 Johnson Ferry Road
Suite 300
Atlanta, GA 30342

404-252-3663
Fax: 404-252-0774
E-Mail: vidsmith@kellencompany.com
Home Page: www.versatilevinegar.org
Social Media: Facebook

Pamela A Chumley, President
Jeannie Milewski, Executive Director

Manufacturers and bottlers of vinegar and suppliers to the industry are the members of this association. Publications available only to members.
Founded in 1967

9753 **Walnut Council**
1011 N 725 W
West Lafayette, IN 47906-9431

765-583-3501
Fax: 765-583-3512
E-Mail: walnutcouncil@walnutcouncil.org
Home Page: www.walnutcouncil.org

Donald Greene, President
Jerry Van Sambeek, Vice President
Liz Jackson, Executive Director
Bill Hoover, Treasurer

Representing woodland owners, foresters, forest scientists and wood producing industry representatives. The purpose is to assist in the technical transfer of forest research to field applications, help build and maintain bettermarkets for wood products and nut crops.
1000 Members
Founded in 1970

9754 **Western Dairy Association**
12000 Washington
Suite 175
Thornton, CO 80241

303-451-7711
800-274-6455
Fax: 303-451-0411
E-Mail: info@westerndairyassociation.org
Home Page: www.westerndairyassociation.org
Social Media: Facebook, Twitter, YouTube

Arley George, Chairman
Rick Podtburg, Vice-Chairman
Ron Shelton, Secretary
Jim Webb, Treasurer
Cindy Haren, Chief Executive Officer

Leading dairy farmer members and the industry in a world class direction of partnerships and business resulting in economic viability, new innovations in dairy products and building stronger community commitment to dairy farms and dairy families.

9755 **Western Growers Association**
17620 Fitch Street
Irvine, CA 92614

949-863-1000
800-333-4942
Fax: 949-863-9028
Home Page: www.wga.com

Stephen J. Barnard, Chairman
Bruce C. Taylor, Senior Vice Chairman
Victor Smith, Vice Chairman
John S. Manfre, Secretary
Mark J. Teixeria, Treasurer

Association for growers, shippers, packers, brokers and distributors of fruits and vegetables in California and Arizona.
3000 Members
Founded in 1926

9756 **Western U.S. Agricultural Trade Association**
4601 NE 77th Ave
Suite 240
Vancouver, WA 98662

360-693-3373
Fax: 360-693-3464
E-Mail: export@wusata.org
Home Page: www.wusata.org

Andy Anderson, Executive Directorÿ
Janet Kenefsky, Deputy Director
Tricia Walker, Branded Program Managerÿÿÿ
Betsy Green, Branded Coordinator
Robin Koss, Branded Coordinator

Exporting resource for agribusinesses based in the Western United States.

9757 **Western United States Agricultural Trade Association**
4601 NE 77th Avenue
Suite 240
Vancouver, WA 98662

360-693-3373
Fax: 360-693-3464
E-Mail: export@wusata.org
Home Page: www.wusata.org

Andy Anderson, Executive Director
Diane McAllister, Executive Assistant

This organization offers information and support to increase exports of US agricultural products.
200 Members
Founded in 1980

9758 **Wheat Foods Council**
51 Red Fox Lane
Unit D
Ridgway, CO 81432

970-626-9828
Fax: 303-840-6877
E-Mail: wfc@wheatfoods.org
Home Page: www.wheatfoods.org
Social Media: Facebook, Twitter

Erica Olson, Chair
Cindy Falk, Vice Chair
Judi Adams, President
Gayle Veum, Vice President
Don Brown, Treasurer/Secretary

An industry-wide partnership dedicated to increasing wheat and other grain foods consumption through nutrition information, education, research and promotional programs.
Founded in 1972

9759 **Wild Blueberry Association of North America**
PO Box 100
Old Town, ME 04468

207-570-3535
Fax: 207-581-3499
E-Mail: wildblueberries@gwi.net
Home Page: www.wildblueberries.com
Social Media: Facebook, Twitter, Youtube, Pinterest, Googleplus

Ragnar Kamp, President
Mike Collins, Marketing Manager

Represents processors and growers of wild blueberries in Eastern Canada and Maine. The Association is focused on the generic promotion of wild blueberries around the world. It offers promotional materials, joint funding, product development, assistance, seminars, newsletters, supplier lists and ongoing support to users of wild blueberries in all retail, manufacturing, food service and bakery trade segments.
Founded in 1981

9760 **Wine & Spirits Wholesalers of America, Inc**
805 15th Street NW
Suite 430
Washington, DC 20005

202-371-9792
Fax: 202-789-2405
Home Page: www.wswa.org

Craig Wolf, President and CEO
Jim Rowland, Senior VP, Government Affairs
Dawson Hobbs, Vice President, State Affairs
Reilly O Connor, Vice President, Government Affairs
Catherine McDaniel, Vice President, Government Affairs

Wine & Spirits Wholesalers of America, inc.(WSWA) is the national trade organization representing the wholesale tier of the wine and spirits industry. It is dedicated to advancing the

interests and independence of wholesale distributors and brokers of wine and spirits.
450 Members
Founded in 1943

9761 Wine Appreciation Guild
360 Swift Ave
Unit 30-40
S San Francisco, CA 94080

650-866-3020
800-239-9463
Fax: 650-866-3029
E-Mail: info@wineappreciation.com
Home Page: www.wineappreciation.com

James Mackey, Manager
Jason Simon, Manager

Formed as the official successor in the distribution of wine accessories, and the publication and distribution of books and educational materials.
1500 Members
Founded in 1973

9762 Wine Institute
425 Market St
Suite 1000
San Francisco, CA 94105

415-512-0151
Fax: 415-356-7569
E-Mail: info@wineinstitute.org
Home Page: www.wineinstitute.org

Robert Koch, President/CEO
Kaye Clement, Executive Assistant

Dedicated to initiating and advocating state, federal and international public policy to enhance the environment for the responsible consumption and enjoyment of wine.
887 Members
Founded in 1934

9763 Wine and Spirits Shippers Association
11800 Sunrise Valley Dr
Suite 332
Reston, VA 20191

703-860-2300
800-368-3167
Fax: 703-860-2422
E-Mail: info@wssa.com
Home Page: www.wssa.com
Social Media: Facebook, Twitter, LinkedIn

V. James Andretta, Jr., Chairman
Louis Healey, President
Howard Jacobs, Vice President

A non-profit shippers association composed of importers and exporters of beverages and allied products. Provides members, importers and exporters with efficient and economical ocean transportation and other logestic services.
400 Members
Founded in 1976

9764 Wine and Spirits Wholesalers of America, Inc.
805 15th Street, NW
Suite 430
Washington, DC 20036

202-371-9792
Fax: 202-789-2405
E-Mail: Info@wswa.org
Home Page: www.wswa.org
Social Media: Facebook, Twitter, YouTube, RSS

Alan Dreeben, Chairman
Douglas Hertz, Immediate Past Chairman
Brien Fox, Vice Chairman
Doug Epstein, Senior VP
Sydney Ross, Treasurer

National trade organization representing the wholesale branch of the wine and spirits industry.

9765 Women in Flavor & Fragrance Commerce
Association of Food Industries
3301 Route 66
Suite 205, Building C
Neptune, NJ 07753

732-922-0500
Fax: 732-922-0560
E-Mail: info@wffc.org
Home Page: www.wffc.org
Social Media: Facebook, LinkedIn

Celine Roche, President
Amy Marks-Mcgee, Vice President
Kay Bardsley-Murano, Secretary
June Buckhardt, Treasurer

Provides a center of education, camaraderie, support and networking opportunities for women in our industry. Our membership encompasses women involved is sales, purchasing, customer service as well as technical and laboratory careers. WFFC has timely seminars as well as social and networking opportunities for our members and the industry as a whole.
300 Members
Founded in 1982

Newsletters

9766 AAMPlifier Bulletin
American Association of Meat Processors
One Meating Place
Elizabethtown, PA 17022

717-367-1168
Fax: 717-367-9096
E-Mail: aamp@aamp.com
Home Page: www.aamp.com

Contains a wealth of information on industry trends, important national news, Association activities, and operational information to keep members fully informed about events affecting their business.
Frequency: Bi-Monthly
Founded in 1939

9767 ABF Newsletter
American Beekeeping Federation
3525 Piedmont Rd
Bldg 5 Suite 300
Atlanta, GA 30305-1509

404-760-2875
Fax: 404-240-0998
E-Mail: info@abfnet.org
Home Page: www.abfnet.org

Robin Dahlen, President
David Mendes, VP

A member benefit published to inform members about ABF activities and happenings in the beekeeping industry.
Cost: $35.00
1200 Members
Frequency: Membership Fees Vary
Founded in 1943

9768 ABL Insider
American Beverage Licensees Association
5101 River Rd
Suite 108
Bethesda, MD 20816-1560

301-656-1494
Fax: 301-656-7539
E-Mail: info@ablusa.org
Home Page: www.ablusa.org

Lyle Fitzsimmons, Editor

The voice of America's beer, wine & spirits retailers.
Frequency: Monthly

9769 ADPI Weekly Newsletter
American Dairy Products Institute
116 N York Street
Suite 200
Elmhurst, IL 60126

630-530-8700
Fax: 630-530-8707
E-Mail: info@adpi.org
Home Page: www.adpi.org

Electronic communication of industry news, regulatory developments, and association matters.
Frequency: Weekly
Circulation: 1000

9770 AFFI Newsletter
American Frozen Food Institute
2000 Corporate Ridge
Suite 1000
McLean, VA 22102-7862

703-821-0770
Fax: 703-821-1350
E-Mail: info@affi.com
Home Page: www.affi.com

Kraig R Naasz, President/CEO
Jason Bassett, Director Legislative Affairs
Chuck Fuqua, VP Communications
Robert L Garfield, SVP Public Policy/Intl Affairs
Frequency: Weekly

9771 AHA Quarterly
American Herb Association
PO Box 1673
Nevada City, CA 95959-1673

530-265-9552
Fax: 530-274-3140
Home Page: www.ahaherb.com

Kathi Keville, Director
Robert Brucia, Co-Director
Marion Wyckoff, Secretary

Reports on the latest scientific studies, new herb, aromatherapy, cooking and gardening books, international herb news, legal and environmental issues, herb-related events and conferences.
Cost: $20.00
20 Pages
Frequency: w/Membership
Founded in 1981

9772 AICR Newsletter
American Institute for Cancer Research
1759 R St NW
Washington, DC 20009-2570

202-328-7744
800-843-8114
Fax: 202-328-7226
E-Mail: aicrweb@aicr.org
Home Page: www.aicr.org

Marilyn Gentry, President

Explains current cancer research, provides recipes and menu ideas for healthy eating, and offers practical advice to lower cancer risk.
Frequency: Quarterly
Circulation: 1.6MM
Founded in 1982

9773 ALBC News
American Livestock Breeds Conservancy
15 Hillsboro Street
PO Box 477
Pittsboro, NC 27312
919-542-5704
Fax: 919-545-0022
E-Mail: albc@albc-usa.org
Home Page: www.albc-usa.org

Marjorie Bender, Prog. Coord./Research
Don Schrider, Communication Director
Charles Bassett, Executive Director

Angelique Thompson, Operations Manager
Jennifer Kendall, Communications Director

Breeders directory; annual conference; catalog of publications available.
Cost: $30.00
20 Pages
Circulation: 3000
ISSN: 1064-1599
Founded in 1977
Printed in one color on matte stock

9774 AMSA eNews
American Meat Science Association
2441 Village Green Pl
Champaign, IL 61822-7676

800-517-AMSA
Fax: 888-205-5834
Fax: 217-356-5370
E-Mail: information@meatscience.org
Home Page: www.meatscience.org

William Mikel, President
Scott J. Eilert, President Elect
Casey B. Frye, Treasurer

Published for all AMSA members every other week, including member news and meat science information updates.

9775 APIS
CITA International
3464 W Earll Drive
Suites E & F
Phoenix, AZ 85017

602-447-0480
Fax: 602-447-0305
E-Mail: esam@citainternational.com
Home Page: www.citainternational.com

EM Morsy, Editor
PE Pederson, Advertising/Sales

The international bulletin for specialty livestock, pet animal and ag-chem product developments.
Frequency: Quarterly
Founded in 1988

9776 ASBC Newsletter
American Society of Brewing Chemists
3340 Pilot Knob Rd
Eagan, MN 55121-2055

651-454-7250
Fax: 651-454-0766
E-Mail: asbc@scisoc.org
Home Page: www.asbcnet.org

Steven C Nelson, VP

Contains the annual meeting program, lists of ASBC committees and reports, and local section news.
Frequency: Quarterly
Circulation: 800+
Founded in 1934

9777 ASTA Advocate
American Spice Trade Association
2025 M St NW
Suite 800
Washington, DC 20036-2422

202-367-1127
Fax: 202-367-2127
E-Mail: info@astaspice.org
Home Page: www.astaspice.org

Donna Tainter, President
Roger Clarke, Vice President/ Secretary
Gaspare Colletti, Treasurer
David Howe, Associate Group Director

Electronic newsletter designed to keep members informed about the spice industry, events impacting the industry and ASTA activities. ASTA Advocate is ASTA's regulatory newsletter.
Frequency: Membership Dues Vary
Founded in 1907

9778 Agri Times Northwest
Sterling Ag
PO Box 189
Pendleton, OR 97801

541-276-7845
Fax: 541-276-7964
Home Page: www.agritimes.com/

Virgil Rupp, CEO/President
Sterling Allen, Publisher/Marketing Director

Regional agricultural newspaper.
Cost: $20.00
16 Pages
Circulation: 3700
Printed in 4 colors on newsprint stock

9779 Agri-Pulse
International Dairy Foods Association
1250 H Street NW
Suite 900
Washington, DC 20005

202-737-4332
Fax: 202-331-7820
E-Mail: membership@idfa.org
Home Page: www.idfa.org
Social Media: Facebook, Twitter, YouTube, Blog

Connie Tipton, President & CEO
Mike Nosewicz, Chair
Brian Perry, Vice Chair
Jon Davis, Secretary
Ed Mullins, Treasurer

The latest information and news in agricultural information. Investigating several aspects of the food, fuel, feed and fiber industries, looking at the economic, statistical and financial trends and evaluate the changes impacting businesses.
550 Members
Frequency: Weekly

9780 Alcoholic Beverage Control Fast: From the State Capitals
Wakeman Walworth
PO Box 7376
Alexandria, VA 22307-7376

703-768-9600
Fax: 703-768-9690
Home Page:
www.statecapitals.com/alcoholbev.html

Keyes Walworth, Publisher

Covers binge drinking laws, internet sales, advertising, taxes, bottle bills, Sunday sales laws, license regulation, drunk driving laws, under-age drinking, mini-bottles and other state laws affecting beer, liquor and wine distribution.
4 Pages
Frequency: Weekly
Founded in 1962
Printed in one color on matte stock

9781 Alcoholic Beverage Executives' Newsletter International
Patricia Kennedy
PO Box 3188
Omaha, NE 68103-1088

402-397-5514
Fax: 402-397-3843

Patricia Kennedy, Editor

Current news of the wine, beer, and distilled spirits marketplace, and provides information and ideas for the marketing and advertising campaigns of these beverages.
Cost: $275.00
Frequency: Weekly
ISSN: 0889-3510

9782 American Agriculturist
Farm Progress Companies
255 38th Avenue
Suite P
St Charles, IL 60174-5410

630-462-2224
800-441-1410
E-Mail: jvogel@farmprogress.com
Home Page:
www.farmprogress.com/american-agriculturist/

John Vogel, Editor
Willie Vogt, Cororate Editorial Director
Dan Crummett, Executive Editor

Serves Northeast producers with information to help them maximize their productivity and profitability. Each issue is packed with information, ideas, news and analysis.
Cost: $29.65
Frequency: Monthly
Founded in 1842

9783 American Bakers Association Bulletin
American Bakers Association
1350 I Street NW
Suite 1290
Washington, DC 20005-3305

202-789-0300
Fax: 202-898-1164
E-Mail: kkotche@americanbakers.org
Home Page: www.americanbakers.org

Kelly Kotche, Communications/Membership Manager
Paul Abenante, President/CEO

The association's newsletter that covers the conventions.
Frequency: Semi-Annual

9784 American Beekeeping Federation Newsletter
American Beekeeping Federation
3525 Piedmont Rd
Bldg 5 Suite 300
Atlanta, GA 30305-1509

404-760-2875
Fax: 404-240-0998
E-Mail: info@abfnet.org
Home Page: www.abfnet.org

Raymond Payne, President

ABF-member benefit to inform members about ABF activities and happenings in the beekeeping industry.
24 Pages
Frequency: Bi-Monthly
Circulation: 1,200
Founded in 1943

9785 American Herb Association Quarterly Newsletter
American Herb Association
PO Box 1673
Nevada City, CA 95959-1673

530-265-9552
Fax: 530-274-3140
Home Page: www.ahaherb.com

Kathi Keville, Director
Robert Brucia, Co-Director
Marion Wyckoff, Secretary

Updates and news on the herbal industry, such as; new scientific herbal and aromatherapy studies, plants interaction with ecology, reports on legal issues about herbs, a calendar of herbal and aromatherapy events, and a media report listing the herbal stories in the media.
Cost: $20.00
Frequency: Membership Fee
Founded in 1981

9786 American Institute of Baking Technical Bulletin
American Institute of Baking

PO Box 3999
Manhattan, KS 66505-3999
785-537-4750
866-342-4772
Fax: 785-565-6060
E-Mail: bissc@bissc.org
Home Page: www.bissc.org
James Munyon, President
Developed to keep the baking and allied trades apprised of current trends in ingredients, products, equipment, processing, packaging, nutrition and research.
Frequency: Monthly

9787 **American Meat Institute: Newsletter**
American Meat Institute
1150 Connecticut Ave Nw
Suite 1200
Washington, DC 20036-4126
202-587-4200
Fax: 202-587-4300
Home Page: www.meatami.com
J Patrick Boyle, CEO
Janet Riley, Editor
Ayoka Blandford, Marketing Manager
Subscription includes news of legislative and government regulations and actions relevant to the meat industry.
Frequency: Quarterly
Circulation: 3000
Founded in 1906

9788 **American Society of Agricultural Consultants News**
American Society of Agricultural Consultants
950 S Cherry Street
Suite 508
Denver, CO 80246-2664
303-758-3514
Fax: 303-758-0190
Home Page: www.agconsultants.org
Deborah Wiig, Editor
Informs ASAC members of news regarding members, events, education and government issues.
8-12 Pages
Frequency: Quarterly
Circulation: 200
Founded in 1963
Printed in on newsprint stock

9789 **American Soybean Association Newsletter**
American Soybean Association
12125 Woodcrest Executive
Suite 100
Creve Coeur, MO 63141-5009
314-576-1770
800-688-7692
Fax: 314-576-2786
E-Mail: bcallanan@soy.org
Home Page: www.soygrowers.com
Steve Censky, CEO
Neal Bredehoeft, President
Bob Metz, VP
Mission is to improve US soybean farmer profitability.
Frequency: Monthly
Founded in 1920
Printed in 4 colors on glossy stock

9790 **Angus Beef Bulletin**
American Angus Association
3201 Frederick Ave
St Joseph, MO 64506-2997
816-383-5100
Fax: 816-233-9703
E-Mail: angus@angus.org
Home Page: www.angus.org
Social Media: Facebook, Twitter
Joe Hampton, Chair
Jarold Callahan, Vice Chair
Phil Trowbridge, Treasurer
To provide programs, services, technology and leadership to enhance the genetics of the Angus breed, broaden its influence within the beef industry, and expand the market for superior tasting, high-quality Angus beef worldwide. Achieve Angus excellence through information.
Cost: $80.00
30+M Members
Frequency: Membership Fees Vary
Founded in 1883

9791 **Association of American Seed Control Officials Bulletin**
Utah Department of Agriculture
801 Summit Crossing Place
Suite C
Gastonia, NC 28054
704-810-8877
Fax: 704-853-4109
E-Mail: richard.payne2@usda.com
Home Page: www.seedcontrol.org
Ron Pence, President
John Heaton, Services Director
Brenda Ball, Second VP
Brenda Ball, Second VP
Greg Helmbrecht, Treasurer
Seed laws in the US and Canada.
Frequency: Annual

9792 **Association of Food Industries Newsletter**
Association of Food Industries
3301 State Route 66
Suite 205, Building C
Neptune, NJ 07753-2705
732-922-3008
Fax: 732-922-3590
E-Mail: info@naooa.org
Home Page: www.naooa.org
Robert Bauer, President
Offers information & education on customs and usage of trade in the food industry and current events in the business.
Founded in 1906

9793 **BEMA Newsletter**
Bakery Equipment Manufacturers Association
10740 Nall Avenue
Suite 230
Overland Park, KS 66211
913-338-1300
Fax: 913-338-1327
E-Mail: info@bema.org
Home Page: www.bema.org
Published by BEMA, to keep members informed about the latest baking and food industry news.
Frequency: Quarterly

9794 **Bakers Band Together to Demand Relief-ABA Calls for March on Washington**
American Bakers Association
1120 Connecticut Avenue NW
Washington, DC 200036
800-226-5377
Home Page: www.aba.com
Robb Mac Kie, President
Frequency: Monthly

9795 **Beer Marketer's Insights Newsletter**
Beer Marketer's Insights
49 E Maple Ave
Suffern, NY 10901-5507
845-624-2337
Fax: 845-624-2340
Home Page: www.beerinsights.com
Benj Steinman, President
Reports on the competitive battle among brewers for a share of the beer market. Analyzes recent legislation and factors that affect the industry.
Frequency: Monthly

9796 **Beer Perspectives**
National Beer Wholesalers Association
1101 King Street
Suite 600
Alexandria, VA 22314-2965
703-683-4300
Fax: 703-683-8965
E-Mail: info@nbwa.org
Home Page: www.nbwa.org
Social Media: Facebook, Twitter
Craig A Purser, President & CEO
Michael Johnson, EVP
Rebecca Spicer, VP Public Affairs/Chief
Paul Pisano, SVP Industry Affairs/Gen. Counsel
NBWA's newsletter reporting legislative, regulatory and industry news of importance to beer distributors.
Frequency: Bi-Weekly

9797 **Beer Statistics News**
Beer Marketer's Insights
49 E Maple Ave
Suffern, NY 10901-5507
845-624-2337
Fax: 845-624-2340
Home Page: www.beerinsights.com
Benj Steinnan, CEO/President
Jerry Curley, Circulation Manager
Supplies data for major brewers' shipments in 39 reporting states.
Cost: $450.00
Frequency: Annual+

9798 **Beverage Digest**
Beverage Digest
PO Box 621
Bedford Hills, NY 10507-0621
914-244-0700
Fax: 914-244-0774
E-Mail: order@beverage-digest.com
Home Page: www.beverage-digest.com
John Sicher, Editor/Publisher
Tom Fine, Managing Editor
Authoritative publication covering the non-alcoholic beverages industry.
Cost: $675.00
Frequency: 22 issues per y
Founded in 1982

9799 **Beverage World Periscope**
Keller International Publishing Corporation
150 Great Neck Rd
Suite 400
Great Neck, NY 11021-3309
516-829-9722
Fax: 516-829-9306
Home Page: www.supplychainbrain.com
Terry Beirne, Publisher
Bryan DeLuca, Editor
Jerry Keller, President
Mary Chavez, Director of Sales
Analysis of developments as they occur in the beverage marketplace, presented in a tightly-written, four-color tabloid format, makes this a unique newsletter. This publica-

tion limits advertising to tabloid or standard pages.
Frequency: Monthly
Circulation: 33000
Founded in 1882

9800 **Bottled Water Reporter**
Bottled Water Association
1700 Diagonal Road
Suite 650
Alexandria, VA 22314-2844

703-683-5213
Fax: 703-683-4074
E-Mail: mbusetti@bottledwater.org
Home Page: www.bottledwater.org

Sabrina Hicks, Editor

Trade news.

9801 **Brewers Bulletin**
PO Box 677
Thiensville, WI 53092

262-242-6105
Fax: 262-242-5133
E-Mail: bulletindigest@milwpc.com

Thomas Volke, President

Brewing industry newspaper.
Cost: $53.00
Circulation: 550
Founded in 1907

9802 **Brown Swiss Bulletin**
Brown Swiss Cattle Breeder's Assoc of the USA
800 Pleasant St
Beloit, WI 53511-5456

608-365-4474
Fax: 608-365-5577
E-Mail: info@brownswissusa.com
Home Page: www.brownswissusa.com

David Wallace, Executive Secretary
Charlotte Muenzenberg, Sup't of Records
Leonard Johnson, Genetic Programs/Show Manager
Cost: $25.00
Frequency: Monthly
ISSN: 0007-2516

9803 **Bu$Iness of Herbs**
Herb Growing and Marketing Network
PO Box 245
Silver Spring, PA 17575-0245

717-393-3295
Fax: 717-393-9261
E-Mail: herbworld@aol.com
Home Page: www.herbworld.com

Finds a wide variety of articles that will help with marketing, growing and genergal business issues. Has profiles of herb businesses and how they've created a business that allows them to support themselves with their passion.
Cost: $48.00
Frequency: Monthly

9804 **Business of Herbs**
Northwind Farm Publications
439 Ponderosa Way
Jemez Springs, NM 87025-8036

505-829-3448
Fax: 505-829-3449
Home Page: www.herb-biz.com

David Oliver, Publisher
Paula Oliver, Editor

News of interest for herb growers and marketers. Covers all aspects of the herb industry and offers book reviews, events calendar, new products, business profiles, sources, resources, networking and more. Geared to small businesses.
Cost: $24.00
48 Pages
Frequency: Bi-Monthly
Circulation: 2,500
Printed in one color on matte stock

9805 **CPA Connection Newsletter**
Contract Packaging Association
1833 Centre Point Circle
Suite 123
Naperville, IL 60563-4848

630-544-5053
Fax: 630-544-5055
E-Mail: info@contractpackaging.org
Home Page: www.contractpackaging.org

Joe Jaruszewski, President
Chris Nutley, Vice President
Vicky Smitley, Treasurer

Providing news that impacts the contract packaging industry.
155 Members
Founded in 1992

9806 **Calorie Control Commentary**
Calorie Control Council
2611 Winslow Dr Ne
Atlanta, GA 30305-3777

678-608-3200
Fax: 404-252-0774
E-Mail: webmaster@caloriecontrol.org
Home Page: www.caloriecontrol.org

Timely information on low-calorie and reduced-fat foods and beverages, weight management, physical activity and healthy eating.
60 Members
Founded in 1966

9807 **Cameron's Foodservice Marketing Reporter**
Cameron's Publications
5423 Sheridan Drive
PO Box 676
Williamsville, NY 14231

519-586-8785
Fax: 519-586-8816
E-Mail: mail@cameronpub.com
Home Page: www.cameronpub.com

Successful promotion and advertising case histories for the restaurant and hotel industry.

9808 **Can Shipments Report**
Can Manufacturers Institute
1730 Rhode Island Ave Nw
Suite 1000
Washington, DC 20036-3112

202-232-4677
Fax: 202-232-5756
Home Page: www.cancentral.com

Robert Budway, President
Shawn Relly, Editor/Publisher

Provides a summary of the past year's accomplishments, as well as a look at the strategy to fulfill goals in the coming year.
Frequency: Annual
Founded in 1938

9809 **Capitol Line-Up**
American Association of Meat Processors
PO Box 269
Elizabethtown, PA 17022

717-367-1168
Fax: 717-367-9096
E-Mail: aamp@aamp.com
Home Page: www.aamp.com

Tom K Inboden, President
Jon Frohling, First VP
Daniel T Weber, Second VP

Deals strictly with governmental affairs in the industry. Keeps AAMP members up to date with the latest news about government affairs from Congress and key agencies in Washington, as well as state legislatures and state regulatory bodies.
Frequency: 26x Yearly

9810 **Catering Service Idea Newsletter**
Prosperity & Profits Unlimited
PO Box 416
Denver, CO 80201

303-573-5564

A Doyle, Editor

Catering service business ideas and possibilities.

9811 **Center of the Plate**
American Culinary Federation
180 Center Place Way
St Augustine, FL 32095-8859

904-824-4468
800-624-9458
Fax: 904-825-4758
E-Mail: acf@acfchefs.net
Home Page: www.acfchefs.org

Heidi Cramb, Executive Director
Kay Orde, Editor
Joachim Buchner, CEO
Michael Feierstein, Administrative Assistant
Bryan Hunt, Graphic Designer

Official membership newsletter of the American Culinary Federation.
Cost: $50.00
Frequency: Monthly
Circulation: 25,000
Founded in 1956

9812 **Cereal Foods World**
AACC International
3340 Pilot Knob Rd
Eagan, MN 55121-2055

651-454-7250
800-328-7560
Fax: 651-454-0766
E-Mail: aacc@scisoc.org
Home Page: www.aaccnet.org

Steven Nelson, Publisher
Susan Kohn, Executive Editor
Amanda Aranowski, Managing Editor
Patti Ek, Production Manager

Covers grain-based food science, technology, and new product development. Includes articles that focus on advances in grain-based food science and the application of these advances to product development and food production practices.
Frequency: Bimonthly
ISSN: 0146-6283

9813 **Champagne Wines Information Bureau**
KCSA
800 2nd Avenue
5th Floor
New York, NY 10017-4709

212-682-6300
800-642-4267
Fax: 212-697-0910
E-Mail: info@champagnes.com
Home Page: www.champagnes.com

Jean Louis Carbonnier, Editor
Herbert L Corbin, President/CEO

Representative of Comite Interprofessionnel duVinde Champagne, Epernay, France.
4 Pages
Circulation: 10000
Printed in one color on matte stock

9814 **Cheese Reporter**
Cheese Reporter Publishing Company

2810 Crossroads Dr
Suite 3000
Madison, WI 53718-7972

608-246-8430
Fax: 608-246-8431
E-Mail: info@cheesereporter.com
Home Page: www.cheesereporter.com

Dick Groves, Publisher/Editor
Kevin Thome, Marketing Director
Betty Mertes, Circulation Manager

Leading weekly publication serving manufacturers and marketers of cheese, butter, ice cream, yogurt and other fermented milk foods, whey and other dairy processors.
Cost: $150.00
16 Pages
Frequency: Weekly
Circulation: 2000
ISSN: 0009-2142
Founded in 1876
Printed in 4 colors on n stock

9815 **Coffee Reporter**
National Coffee Association
15 Maiden Ln
Suite 1405
New York, NY 10038-5113

212-766-4007
Fax: 212-766-5815
E-Mail: info@ncausa.org
Home Page: www.ncausa.org

Robert F Nelson, President
Joseph F DeRupo, Communications/PR Director

Contains news of NCA activities and programs, new product development and market trends in both the U.S. and global coffee industry, regulatory action affecting the U.S. coffee industry and statistical data on ICO prices and U.S. retail prices. A single copy subscription is supplied free of charge to members, non-eligible parties for membership the cost is $40.00
Cost: $65.00
Frequency: Quarterly

9816 **Coffee, Sugar and Cocoa Exchange Daily Market Report**
New York Board of Trade
1 North End Avenue
New York, NY 10282-1101
212-748-4000
877-877-8890
Fax: 212-748-4039
E-Mail: webmaster@nybot.com
Home Page: www.nybot.com

Leonel Fern ndez, President

Offers market reports on the stock market exchange covering foods and specific food investing.

9817 **Communique**
CHRIE
2810 N Parham Road
Suite 230
Richmond, VA 23294

804-346-4800
Fax: 804-346-5009
E-Mail: info@chrie.org
Home Page: www.chrie.org
Social Media: Facebook, Twitter, LinkedIn

Susan Fournier, President
Josette Katz, Vice President
Chris Roberts, Secretary
John Drysdale, Treasurer
Kathy McCarty, CEO

Council on Hotel, Restaurant, and Institutional Educations informational newsletter.
Cost: $45.00
Frequency: Monthly

9818 **Concessionworks Newsletter**
National Association of Concessionaires
35 E Wacker Dr
Suite 1816
Chicago, IL 60601-2270

312-236-3858
Fax: 312-236-7809
E-Mail: scross@naconline.org
Home Page: www.naconline.org

Charles A Winans, Executive Director

For members with updates on association happenings, feature articles, new member listings, product news and industry updates.
Founded in 1944

9819 **Country World Newspaper**
Echo Publishing Company
401 Church Street
PO Box 596
Sulphur Springs, TX 75483

903-885-8663
800-245-2149
Fax: 903-885-8768
E-Mail: lori@countryworldnews.com
Home Page: www.countryworldnews.com

Scott Keys, Publisher
Lori Cope, Editor
Jim Horton, Advertising Manager

A newspaper offering agricultural information to farmers, ranchers, dairyfarmers, and agribusinesses.
Cost: $24.00
36 Pages
Frequency: Weekly
Circulation: 16200
Founded in 1981
Printed in 4 colors on newsprint stock

9820 **Crop Protection Management**
2892 Crescent Avenue
Eugene, OR 97408

541-343-5641
800-874-3276
Fax: 541-686-0248

Jeff Powell, Publisher

This newsletter covers all aspects of crop management and protection, including pesticides, agricultural chemicals and legislation.
Frequency: 5 per year

9821 **Daily Advocate**
Thomson Newspapers
PO Box 220
Greenville, OH 45331-220

937-548-3151
Fax: 937-548-3913
E-Mail: webmaster@dailyadvocate.com
Home Page: www.dailyadvocate.com

Gary Lamberg, Publisher
Bob Robinson, Editor
Ken Bowen, Circulation Manager
Ashley Fritz, Graphic Designer
Barb Wilson, Business Manager

Farming interests, grain, livestock. Sections on senior citizens, farmers, builders, religion, sports, as well as special sections on agriculture and home improvement.
Cost: $117.00
Frequency: Daily
Founded in 1883

9822 **Dairy Council Digest**
National Dairy Council
Interstate Place II
100 Elwood Davis Road
North Syracuse, NY 13212

315-472-9143
Fax: 315-472-0506
E-Mail: ndc@dairyinformation.com
Home Page: www.nationaldairycouncil.org
Social Media: Facebook, Twitter

Provides a comprehensive review of research on topics ranging from the benefits of dairy foods in child nutrition, to dairy's potential protective role for metabolic syndrome and type 2 diabetes.
Frequency: Bi-Monthly
Founded in 1915

9823 **Dairy Industry Newsletter**
Eden Publishing Company
10255 W Higgins Road
Suite 900
Rosemont, IL 60018-4924

312-240-2880
Home Page: www.dairyindustrynewsletter.com

Resource serving all sectors of the dairy industry. Reports on commercial, trade, political and market information.
8 Pages
Frequency: 25x Yearly
Printed in 2 colors on glossy stock

9824 **Dairy Market Report**
American Butter Institute
2101 Wilson Boulevard
Suite 400
Arlington, VA 22201

703-243-5630
Fax: 703-841-9328
E-Mail: AMiner@nmpf.org
Home Page: www.nmpf.org/ABI

Peter Vitaliano, Editor

9825 **Dairy Profit Weekly**
DairyBusiness Communications
6437 Collamer Road
East Syracuse, NY 13057-1031

315-703-7979
800-334-1904
Fax: 315-703-7988
Home Page: www.dairybusiness.com

Dave Natzke, Editorial Director
Joel Hastings, Publisher
Eleanor Jacobs, Regional Editor

Latest information, tips, and trends.
Cost: $179.00
4 Pages
Frequency: Weekly
Circulation: 1700
Printed in 2 colors on newsprint stock

9826 **Dairy-Deli-Bake Digest**
International Dairy-Deli-Bakery Association
636 Science Drive
PO Box 5528
Madison, WI 53705-0528
608-310-5000
Fax: 608-238-6330
E-Mail: IDDBA@iddba.org
Home Page: www.iddbanet.org

Carol Christison, Executive Director

Packed with practical how-to information to help readers run a successful business. Features new management trends, new products, reports, reviews, association news, features, and consumer attitudes and trends.
Frequency: Monthly
Founded in 1964

9827 **Dairy-Deli-Bake Wrap-Up**
International Dairy-Deli-Bakery Association
636 Science Drive
PO Box 5528
Madison, WI 53705-0528

608-310-5000
Fax: 608-238-6330

E-Mail: IDDBA@iddba.org
Home Page: www.iddbanet.org

Carol Christison, Executive Director

Covers IDDBA's seminars, expositions, member news, awards, and programs and services.
Frequency: Quarterly
Founded in 1964

9828 Distributor News
Food Industry Suppliers Association
1207 Sunset Drive
Greensboro, NC 27408

336-274-6311
Fax: 336-691-1839
E-Mail: stella@fisanet.org
Home Page: www.fisanet.org

David Brink, President
Bob Morava, Vice President

FISA's official newsletter, publishing industry happenings and business management information.
245 Members
Frequency: Quarterly
Founded in 1968

9829 Doane's Agricultural Report
Doane Agricultural Services
77 Westport Plz
Suite 250
St Louis, MO 63146-3121

314-569-2700
866-647-0918
Fax: 314-569-1083
Home Page: www.doane.com

Dan Manternach, Editor

Provides information to US farmers and agricultural professionals. Doane keeps you up to date on factors affecting your farm program benefits and production costs too.
Frequency: Weekly

9830 FDRS Newsletter
Food Distribution Research Society
PO Box 441110
Fort Washington, MD 20749

301-292-1970
Fax: 301-292-1787
E-Mail: Jonathan_baros@ncsu.edu
Home Page: fdrs.tamu.edu

John Park, President
Ron Rainey, President-Elect
Kellie Raper, Secretary/ Treasurer
Jennifer Dennis, Director
Stan Ernst, Director

Reports on Society events and happenings as well as related news from the industry and abroad.
Frequency: Quarterly

9831 FPA Update
Flexible Packaging Association
971 Corporate Blvd
Suite 403
Linthicum, MD 21090-2253

410-694-0800
Fax: 410-694-0900
E-Mail: fpa@flexpack.org
Home Page: www.flexpack.org

Marla Donahue, President

Updating membership as well as the industry on FPA activities, events and accomplishments throughthe FPA Update, which is included within Flexible Packaging magazine.
Frequency: Monthly

9832 FSC Newsletter
Food Safety Consortium
110 Agriculture Building
University of Arkansas
Fayetteville, AR 72701

479-575-5647
Fax: 479-575-7531
E-Mail: fsc@cavern.uark.edu
Home Page: www.fsconsortium.net

Dave Edmark, Communications Manager

A production of the three member schools of the consortium; University of Arkansas, Iowa State University and Kansas State University.
Frequency: Monthly
Founded in 1988

9833 FYI ASTA
American Spice Trade Association
2025 M St NW
Suite 800
Washington, DC 20036-2422

202-367-1127
Fax: 202-367-2127
E-Mail: info@astaspice.org
Home Page: www.astaspice.org

Donna Tainter, President
Roger Clarke, Vice President/ Secretary
Gaspare Colletti, Treasurer
David Howe, Associate Group Director

Electronic newsletter designed to keep members informed about the spice industry, events impacting the industry and ASTA activities. The resource for members looking for information about ASTA, our programs and services.
Frequency: Membership Dues Vary
Founded in 1907

9834 Federal Focus
Natural Products Association
2112 E 4th St
Suite 200
Santa Ana, CA 92705-3816

714-460-7732
800-966-6632
Fax: 714-460-7444
Home Page: www.npainfo.org
Social Media: Facebook, Twitter, LinkedIn

John F. Gay, Executive Director & CEO
Jeffrey Wright, President

Provides information and alerts from the federal and state agencies that affect the industry.
1900+ Members
Frequency: Monthly
Founded in 1936

9835 Fence Post
423 Main Street
Windsor, CO 80550-5129

970-686-5691
800-275-5646
Fax: 970-686-5694
Home Page: www.thefencepost.com

Jim Eisberry, President
Gary Sweeney, Publisher
Luke Gonzales, Business Manager
Tom Vilsack, Secretary

Farming news and reports.
Cost: $39.00
Frequency: Weekly

9836 Food Allergy News
Food Allergy & Anaphlaxis Network
11781 Lee Jackson Mem Hwy
Suite 160
Fairfax, VA 22033-3309

703-691-3179
800-929-4040
Fax: 703-691-2713
E-Mail: faan@foodallergy.org
Home Page: www.foodallergy.org

Anne Munoz-Furlong, President
Andreia Miller, Editor

Allergy newsletter with two pages of allergy-free recipes, coping strategies, research and studies.
Cost: $30.00
12 Pages
Circulation: 28000
ISSN: 1075-4318
Founded in 1991
Printed in 2 colors on glossy stock

9837 Food Industry Futures: A Strategy Service
CRS
PO Box 430
Fayetteville, NC 28302

910-486-9059
Fax: 910-486-9058

Ian Cuthill, Publisher, Editor

Includes new developments concerning management or marketing practices, mergers and acquisitions, economics, trade policies, etc. It covers the industry from farm and retail stores, mostly in the US but also internationally. Accepts advertising.
Cost: $150.00
4 Pages

9838 Food Industry Newsletter
Newsletters
PO Box 342730
Bethesda, MD 20827-2730

301-469-8507
Fax: 301-469-7271
E-Mail: foodltr@aol.com

Ellis Meredith, Publisher
Ray Marsili, Editor
Alice Corcoran, Circulation Manager

Concise, objective report for busy food executives, covering major food industry developments, including mergers and acquisitions, new trends and products, corporate and marketing strategies, etc. In addition to 22 regular issues a year, subscription also includes Special Food Marketing Reports on timely matters.
Cost: $245.00
Frequency: twice monthly except Aug.
Founded in 1972

9839 Food Insight
International Food Information Council
1100 Connecticut Ave Nw
Suite 430
Washington, DC 20036-4120

202-296-6540
Fax: 202-296-6547
E-Mail: foodinfo@ific.org
Home Page: www.ific.org

Dave Schmidt, President
Nick Alexander, Associate Editor
Michael Hayes, Copy Editor
8 Pages
Frequency: 6 issues per ye
Circulation: 45000
Printed in 4 colors on glossy stock

9840 Food Institute Report
American Institute of Food Distribution
1 Broadway
2nd Floor
Elmwood Park, NJ 07407-1844

201-791-5570
Fax: 201-791-5222
Home Page: www.foodinstitute.com

Brian Todd, President
Mike Slattery, Chairman
Michael Sansolo, Senior Vice President
Joe Crocker, Vice Chairman
Donna George, Treasurer

Membership includes a subscription to The Food Institute Report, an in-depth weekly digest that delivers insights on new products,

crop markets, legislation, customer demographics, mergers, food industry statistics, competitors and market trends.
Frequency: Weekly
Circulation: 3000
Founded in 1928

9841 Food Merchants Advocate
New York State Food Merchant
130 Washington Ave
Albany, NY 12210-2220

518-463-0300
Fax: 518-462-5474
Home Page: www.nyscar.org

Christopher Pellnat, Editor

A tabloid newspaper for food retailers.
Cost: $10.00
Frequency: Monthly

9842 Food Safety Professional
Carpe Diem
208 Floral Vale Boulevard
Yardley, PA 19067

215-860-7800
Fax: 215-860-7900
Home Page: www.foodquality.com

Paul Juestrich, Production Manager
Ken Potuznik, Director
Lisa Dionne, Creative Director

The Food Safety Professional is a quarterly publication of The antional Registry of Food Safety Professionals. Practical hands on article and advice form the experts will keep you informed of the latest technique an technologies in food safety.'
Cost: $20.00
Frequency: Quarterly
Circulation: 30,000

9843 Food Trade News
Best-Met Publishing
5537 Twin Knolls Rd
Suite 438
Columbia, MD 21045-3270

410-730-5013
Fax: 410-740-4680
E-Mail: office@best-met.com
Home Page: www.best-met.com

Jeff Metzger, Publisher
Terri Maloney, Editor
Beth Pripstein, Office Manager
Cost: $63.00
Frequency: Monthly
Printed in one color on matte stock

9844 Food World Information Services
Best-Met Publishing Company
5537 Twin Knolls Rd
Suite 438
Columbia, MD 21045-3270

410-730-5013
Fax: 410-740-4680
E-Mail: tmaloney@best-met.com
Home Page: www.best-met.com

Jeff Metzger, Publisher
Terri Maloney, Editor
Beth Pripstein, Office Manager
Richard J. Bestany, President

Provides market data for Baltimore, Washington, Central Pennsylvania and Philadelphia
Frequency: Monthly
Printed in on newsprint stock

9845 Food for Thought
D/FW Grocers Association
3044 Old Denton Rd
Suite 111, PMB 323
Carrollton, TX 75007

214-731-3132
800-791-6590
Fax: 469-574-5252
E-Mail: info@dfwga.net
Home Page: www.dfwga.net

Offers information on grocery retailing and items of interest to members of the Grocers Association.
Frequency: Quarterly
Circulation: 1,000
Founded in 1947

9846 FoodTalk
Pike & Fischer
PO Box 25277
Alexandria, VA 22313

703-548-3146
Fax: 703-548-3017
E-Mail: info@setantapublishing.com
Home Page: www.setantapublishing.com

Declan Couroy, Editor/Publisher

Sanitation tips for food workers.
Cost: $120.00
Frequency: Quarterly
Circulation: 5000
Founded in 1987
Printed in 2 colors on matte stock

9847 Friday Notes
Council for Agricultural Science and Technology
4420 West Lincold Way
Ames, IA 50014-3447

515-292-2125
Fax: 515-292-4512
E-Mail: cast@cast-science.org
Home Page: www.cast-science.org

John Bonner, Executive VP
Lynette Allen, Assistant Editor

Electronic newsletter featuring lead articles on current topics being discussed in agriculture, congressional updates, and advance announcements of upcoming CAST publications and activities.
Frequency: 48x Yearly
Founded in 1972

9848 GRAS Flavoring Substances 25
Flavor & Extract Manufacturers Association
1620 I Street NW
Suite 925
Washington, DC 20006

202-293-5800
Fax: 202-462-8998
Home Page: www.femaflavor.org
Social Media: YouTube, RSS Feed

Ed R. Hays, Ph.D., President
George C. Robinson, III, President Elect
Mark Scott, Treasurer
Arthur Schick, VP & Secretary
John Cox, Executive Director

The 25th publication by the Expert Panel of the Flavor and Extract Manufacturers Association provides an update on recent progress in the consideration of flavoring ingredients generally recognized as safe under the Food Additive Amendment.
Frequency: Biennial
Founded in 1909

9849 Global Food Marketer
Food Export USA
309 West Washington
Suite 600
Chicago, IL 60606

312-334-9200
Fax: 312-334-9230
E-Mail: info@foodexportusa.org
Home Page: www.foodexportusa.org

Tim F Hamilton, Executive Director
Daleen D Richmond, Deputy Director

Newsletter for US exporters, containing useful articles, updates on overseas market conditions and trends, marketing tips, a column by a food export helpline counselor, and calendar of upcoming events.
Frequency: Bi-Monthly
Founded in 1973

9850 Gourmet News
Oser Communications Group
1877 N Kolb Road
Tuscon, AZ 85715

520-721-1300
Home Page: www.gourmetnews.com

Rocelle Aragon, Editor
Kate Seymour, Senior Associate Publisher

The authoritative voice, and publication of choice for thousands of professionals in the gourmet and specialty food business. Reports timely and trustworty stories about events, issues, trends and other happenings within the trade.
Cost: $65.00
Frequency: Monthly
Circulation: 23100
Founded in 1991

9851 Grayson Report
Grayson Associates
30728 Paseo Elegancia
San Juan Cpstrn, CA 92675-5426

949-487-9970
Fax: 949-487-9975
Home Page: www.graysonassociates.com

Suzanne Grayson, President
Robert Grayson, Director

Marketing analysis of the packaged goods industry.
Founded in 1970

9852 Grocery Manufacturers of America:
Grocery Manufacturers Association of America
1350 I St Nw
Suite 300
Washington, DC 20005-3377

202-337-9400
Fax: 202-639-5932
E-Mail: info@gmaonline.org
Home Page: www.gmabrands.com

Pamela G Bailey, CEO
Jeff Nedelman, VP Communications

Focuses on the productivity and public policy issues affecting our industry.
Founded in 1908

9853 Herd on the Hill
National Meat Association
1970 Broadway
Suite 825
Oakland, CA 94612

510-763-1533
Fax: 510-763-6186
E-Mail: staff@nmaonline.org
Home Page: www.nmaonline.org

Robert Rebholtz, Chairman
Larry Vad, President
Marty Evanson, Vice President
Mike Hesse, Secretary
Brian Coelho, Treasurer

Provides up-to-date information on what's happening in Washington in relation to the meat and poultry industry.
600 Members
Frequency: Weekly
Founded in 1946

9854 Home Baking Association Newsletter
Home Baking Association

10841 S Crossroads Drive
Suite 105
Parker, CO 80135

785-478-3283
Fax: 785-478-3024
Home Page: www.homebaking.org
Social Media: Facebook, Twitter, Flickr

Striving to bring a wide variety of educational materials that benefit the community of Bakers and Baking Educators worldwide. Newsletter includes the latest tips, recipes and baking resources.
Frequency: Monthly

9855 **Hot Sheet**
Fresh-Cut Produce Association
1600 Duke Street
Suite 440
Alexandria, VA 22314

530-756-8900
Fax: 530-756-8901
Home Page: www.fresh-cuts.org

Jerry Gorny, President
Sean Handerhan, Marketing Director

A newsletter containing technical information, marketing news and exhibit information on the produce trade. Serves over 500 members.
Cost: $35.00
Frequency: Monthly
Circulation: 23,000
Founded in 1987

9856 **Hotel, Restaurant, Institutional Buyers Guide**
Urner Barry Publications
PO Box 389
Toms River, NJ 08754

732-240-5330
800-932-0617
Fax: 732-341-0891
E-Mail: help@urnerbarry.com
Home Page: www.urnerbarry.com/

Paul B Brown Jr, President
Sheila M Deane, Marketing Manager
Richard A. Brown, VP

Reports on perishable food prices, meat, seafood, fruits, vegetables and others compiled for the metropolitan New York, New Jersey and Connecticut markets.
Cost: $86.00
4 Pages
Frequency: Weekly
Circulation: 120
ISSN: 0270-4161
Founded in 1858

9857 **Hotel, Restaurant, Institutional Meat Price Report**
Urner Barry Publications
PO Box 389
Toms River, NJ 08754-2741

732-240-5330
800-932-0617
Fax: 732-341-0891
E-Mail: help@urnerbarry.com
Home Page: www.urnerbarry.com

Paul B Brown Jr, President
Karen Mick, Circulation Director

Current meat and poultry pricing for the hotel, restaurant and institutional buyers.
Cost: $174.00
Frequency: Weekly
Circulation: 200
ISSN: 1067-3962
Founded in 1858

9858 **IAFIS Global Food MegaTrends**
International Assn of Food Industry Suppliers
1451 Dolley Madison Boulevard
Suite 101
McLean, VA 22101

703-761-2600
Fax: 703-761-4334
E-Mail: info@fpsa.org
Home Page: www.fpsa.org

George Melnykovich, President
Andrew Drennan, VP

A quarterly bulletin covering international news and its effect on the food processing and packaging industries.

9859 **IBDEA Report**
International Beverage Dispensing Association
3837 Naylors Lane
Baltimore, MD 21208

410-602-0616
877-404-2332
Fax: 410-486-6799
E-Mail: ibdea@cornerstoneassoc.com
Home Page: www.ibdea.org

Official newsletter of the International Beverage Dispensing Association, offering the latest news and technologies in the industry.
Frequency: Quarterly

9860 **IDDBA & YOU**
International Dairy-Deli-Bakery Association
636 Science Drive
PO Box 5528
Madison, WI 53705-0528

608-310-5000
Fax: 608-238-6330
E-Mail: IDDBA@iddba.org
Home Page: www.iddbanet.org

Carol Christison, Executive Director

E-Newsletter designed for deli and bakery supermarket management and in-store staff teams. A fact-filled relevant resource on deli and bakery trends, timely sales data, merchandising ideas, training, new products, seminars, experts, news, and programs.
Frequency: Monthly
Founded in 1964

9861 **IDDBA Legis-Letter**
International Dairy-Deli-Bakery Association
636 Science Drive
PO Box 5528
Madison, WI 53705-0528

608-310-5000
Fax: 608-238-6330
E-Mail: IDDBA@iddba.org
Home Page: www.iddbanet.org

Carol Christison, Executive Director

Formerly IDDA UPDATE, a membership benefit. Highlights recent legislative bills and reports, FDA activities, and topical issues such as state action on bst, NLEA, and HACCP.
Frequency: Monthly
Founded in 1964

9862 **IFSEA Infusion**
International Food Service Executives
4955 Miller Street
Suite 107
Wheat Ridge, CO 80033

800-893-5499
E-Mail: hq@ifsea.com
Home Page: www.ifsea.com
Social Media: Facebook

Barbara Sadler, Chairwoman
Fred Wright, Chair-Elect
David Orosz, Treasurer

Official newsletter of the IFSEA focusing on the happenings and news, as well as industry tips and recipes.
Frequency: Monthly

9863 **INsight**
Southern US Trade Association
701 Poydras St
Suite 3725
New Orleans, LA 70139-4596

504-568-5986
Fax: 504-568-6010
E-Mail: susta@susta.org
Home Page: www.susta.org

Troy Rosamond, Financial Director
Bernadette Wiltz, Deputy Director

Providing the latest exporting information.
Frequency: Quarterly
Founded in 1973

9864 **Ice Cream Reporter**
Ice Cream Reporter
Hilton Terrace
Willsboro, NY 12996

518-963-4333
Fax: 518-963-4999

Howard Waxman, Publisher/Editor

News for ice cream executives.
Cost: $395.00
Frequency: Monthly
Founded in 1987

9865 **Independent Bakers Association Newsletter**
Independent Bakers Association
Georgetown Station
PO Box 3731
Washington, DC 20027-0231

202-333-8190
Fax: 202-337-3809
E-Mail: independentbaker@yahoo.com
Home Page: www.independentbaker.net

Updating Washington legislative and regulatory actions and analyzing pro-business positions impacting on wholesale baking, allied industry operations.
Frequency: Monthly

9866 **Insight**
Retailer's Bakery Association
14239 Park Central Drive
Laurel, MD 20707-5261

301-725-2149
800-638-0924
Fax: 301-725-2187
E-Mail: Info@RBAnet.com
Home Page: www.rbanet.com

Bernard Reynolds, Publisher
Stewart Taylor, Convention Director
Katrina Cooley, Marketing & Communications Director

Member newsletter for baking industry professionals.
8 Pages
Frequency: Monthly
Founded in 1918
Printed in 2 colors on matte stock

9867 **International Association of Food**
1451 Dolley Madison Boulevard
Suite 101
McLean, VA 22101

703-761-2600
Fax: 703-761-4334
E-Mail: info@fpsa.org
Home Page: www.fpsa.org

George Melnykovich, President
Andrew Drennan, VP

Dairy food and beverage industries, and related sanitary processing industries addressing the marketing and business information needs of the food supply channel.
Founded in 1983
Mailing list available for rent

9868 **IoPP update**
Institute of Packaging Professionals
Ste 123
1833 Centre Point Cir
Naperville, IL 60563-4848

630-544-5050
800-432-4085
Fax: 630-544-5005
E-Mail: info@iopp.org
Home Page: www.iopp.org
Social Media: Facebook, Twitter, LinkedIn, YouTube

Edwin Landon, Executive Director
Patrick Farrey, General Manager
Stan Zelesnik, Director Education
Robert DePauw, Finance Manager
Kelly Staley, Member Services Manager

Emailed newsletter of the Institute of Packaging Professionals.
Frequency: Bi-Weekly

9869 **Kane's Beverage Week**
Whitaker Newsletters
313 S Avenue
#340
Fanwood, NJ 07023-1364

800-359-6049
Fax: 908-889-6339

Joel Whitaker, Publisher

News on marketing, economic and regulatory factors affecting the alcohol beverage industry.
Cost: $499.00
6 Pages
Frequency: Quarterly
ISSN: 0882-2573

9870 **Kashrus Magazine**
Yeshiva Birkas Revuen
PO Box 204
Brooklyn, NY 11230

718-336-8544
Fax: 718-336-8550
E-Mail: webmaster@kashrusmagazine.com
Home Page: www.kashrusmagazine.com

Rabbi Yosef Wikler, Editor
Vaad Hakashrut, Director
Rabbi Levin, Executive Director

Regular, complete update on Kosher food mislabelings, dairy/nondairy status, kosher supervision standards, newly certified products and food technology, travel and Jewish life.
Cost: $18.00
88 Pages
Circulation: 10000
Founded in 1980
Printed in 4 colors on glossy stock

9871 **Kettle Talk**
Retail Confectioners International
2053 S Waverly Ave
Suite 204
Springfield, MO 65804-2414

417-883-2775
800-545-5381
Fax: 847-724-2719
E-Mail: info@retailconfectioners.org
Home Page: www.retailconfectioners.org

Terry Craft, President
Terry Hickling, Chairman of Marketing
Dan Malley, VP

Membership newsletter, including confection recipes. Also regional meetings.
Frequency: Monthly
Circulation: 550
Founded in 1917
Printed in on matte stock

9872 **Kiplinger Agricultural Letter**
Kiplinger Washington Editors
1729 H St Nw
Washington, DC 20006-3924

202-887-6400
800-544-0155
Fax: 202-778-8976
E-Mail: sub.services@kiplinger.com
Home Page: www.kiplinger.com

Knight Kiplinger, VP
Kevin McCormally, Editorial Director
Fred Frailey, Editor
David Harrison, Manager

Forecasts and judgments on wages, income, food packaging, processing and marketing techniques.
Cost: $56.00
Founded in 1923

9873 **Kitchen Times**
Howard Wilson and Company
PO Box 290
Waukegan, IL 60079-0290

708-339-5111
800-245-7224
Fax: 708-210-2069
Home Page: www.hwilson.com

Howard Wilson, Publisher/Editor

News on food and cooking.
Cost: $33.00
8 Pages
Frequency: Monthly
Founded in 1959

9874 **Lean Trimmings**
National Meat Association
1970 Broadway
Suite 825
Oakland, CA 94612-2299

510-763-1533
Fax: 510-763-6186
E-Mail: staff@nmaonline.org
Home Page: www.nmaonline.org

Barry Carpenter, CEO
Jen Kempis, Operations Manager

Covers industry regulations, new technology and export news, as well as labor issues and business strategy.
Frequency: Weekly
Founded in 1946
Printed in one color on matte stock

9875 **Legislative Onion Outlet**
Legislative Onion Outlet
822 7th St
Suite 510
Greeley, CO 80631-3941

970-353-5895
Fax: 970-353-5897
E-Mail: info@onions-usa.org
Home Page: www.onions-usa.org

Wayne Mininger, Executive VP
Tanya Fell, Public/Industry Relations

An annual bulletin published by the National Onion Association.
Circulation: 600
Founded in 1913
Mailing list available for rent: 600 names

9876 **Legislative Update**
Independent Bakers Association
2 S Portage Street
Westfield, NY 14787

716-326-5200
E-Mail: nationalinfo@welchs.com
Home Page: www.nationalgrape.com

Nicholas Pyle, Manager

Updating Washington legislative and regulatory actions and analyzing pro-business positions impacting on wholesale baking, allied industry operations.
Frequency: Monthly

9877 **Link Newsletter**
R&D Associates
16607 Blanco Road
Suite 1506
San Antonio, TX 78232-1940

210-493-8024
Fax: 210-493-8036
E-Mail: hqs@militaryfood.org
Home Page: www.militaryfood.or

David Dee, Editor

Food packaging, food processing and foodservice industry.
300 Pages
Frequency: Quarterly

9878 **Loan Trimmings & Herd on the Hill**
1970 Broadway Avenue
Suite 825
Oakland, CA 94612-2299

510-763-1533
Fax: 510-763-6186
E-Mail: staff@amaonline.org
Home Page: www.nmaonline.org

Barry Carpenter, Executive Director
Jen Kempis, Associate Director
Frequency: Weekly
Circulation: 600

9879 **Make It Tasty**
Prosperity & Profits Unlimited
PO Box 416
Denver, CO 80201-0416

303-573-5564

AC Doyle, Publisher

Spice company blends food business newsletter with salt-free, herb and spice blend recipes.
Founded in 1996

9880 **Making a Difference**
National FFA Organization
6060 FFA Drive
PO Box 68960
Indianapolis, IN 46268-0960

317-802-6060
888-332-2668
E-Mail: membership@ffa.org
Home Page: www.ffa.org

Steve A. Brown, National FFA Advisor
Marion D. Fletcher, National FFA Organization Treasurer

Resource for Agriculture teachers. It features news from FFA and Team Ag Ed, teaching resources, ideas, inspiration and more.
507M Members
Founded in 1928

9881 **Market News**
Meat & Livestock Australia
1401 K Street NW
Suite 602
Washington, DC 20005

202-521-2551
Fax: 202-521-2699
E-Mail: info@mla.com.au
Home Page: www.mla.com.au
Social Media: Facebook, Twitter, YouTube

Don Heatley, Chairman
David Palmer, Managing Director
Bernie Bindon, Director
Chris Hudson, Director

eNewsletter presents the latest market news from Australia and key international markets.
30000 Members
Frequency: Weekly
Founded in 1998

9882 **Meat & Poultry**
Meat Trade Institute

213 South Avenue East
Spencer Savings Bank Building
Cranford, NJ 07016

908-276-5111
Fax: 212-279-4016
E-Mail: sflannagan@sprintmail.com
Home Page: www.spcnetwork.com/mti/

John Calcangno, President

A respected newsletter which keeps readers abreast of membership information and all news pertinent to Institute members. Available online.
Frequency: Monthly

9883 **Meat and Livestock Weekly**
Meat & Livestock Australia
1401 K Street NW
Suite 602
Washington, DC 20005

202-521-2551
Fax: 202-521-2699
E-Mail: info@mla.com.au
Home Page: www.mla.com.au
Social Media: Facebook, Twitter, YouTube

Don Heatley, Chairman
David Palmer, Managing Director
Bernie Bindon, Director
Chris Hudson, Director

eNewsletter providing the latest news, analysis and trends for domestic and export markets, including information on buyer and competitor activity and trends.
30000 Members
Frequency: Weekly
Founded in 1998

9884 **More Beef from Pastures**
Meat & Livestock Australia
1401 K Street NW
Suite 602
Washington, DC 20005

202-521-2551
Fax: 202-521-2699
E-Mail: info@mla.com.au
Home Page: www.mla.com.au
Social Media: Facebook, Twitter, YouTube

Don Heatley, Chairman
David Palmer, Managing Director
Bernie Bindon, Director
Chris Hudson, Director

eNewsletter designed to keep readers up-to-date with the latest developments in the MLA More Beef from Pastures program.
30000 Members
Frequency: Quarterly
Founded in 1998

9885 **NAFEM online**
N. American Assn. of Food Equipment Manufacturing
161 N Clark Street
Suite 2020
Chicago, IL 60601

312-821-0201
Fax: 312-821-0202
E-Mail: info@nafem.org
Home Page: www.nafem.org

Steven R. Follett, President
Thomas R. Campion, President-Elect
Michael L. Whiteley, Secretary/Treasurer
Deirdre Flynn, Executive Vice President

The latest and greatest NAFEM and industry news to all NAFEM members. e-Newsletter.
Frequency: Monthly

9886 **NAMA Newsletter**
North American Millers' Association
600 Maryland Ave SW
Suite 825 W
Washington, DC 20024

202-484-2200
Fax: 202-488-7416
E-Mail: generalinfo@namamillers.org
Home Page: www.namamillers.org

Betsy Faga, President
James Bair, VP

Trade association representing the wheat, corn, oat and rye milling industry. NAMA members operate one hundred and seventy mills in thirty-eight states and Canada. Their aggregate production of more than one hundred and sixty million pounds per day is approximately ninety-five percent of the industry capacity in the U.S.
Frequency: Monthly
Circulation: 250

9887 **NCA Annual Convention**
National Coffee Association
15 Maiden Ln
Suite 1405
New York, NY 10038-5113

212-766-4007
Fax: 212-766-5815
E-Mail: info@ncausa.org
Home Page: www.ncausa.org

Robert F Nelson, President
Steven M Wolfe, Membership/Marketing Director

The coffee event of the year, industry executives from all over the world get together to learn from the most current educational sessions, see old friends and meet new ones.
Frequency: Annual/March
Founded in 1911

9888 **NFRA Update**
National Frozen & Refrigerated Foods Association
4755 Linglestown Road Suite 300
PO Box 6069
Harrisburg, PA 17112

717-657-8601
Fax: 717-657-9862
E-Mail: info@nfraweb.org
Home Page: www.nfraweb.org

H V Skip Shaw Jr, President/CEO
Jeff Romachik, Executive VP/COO
Marlene Barr, VP Membership

NFRA's main communication tool in keeping members informed of upcoming frozen and refrigerated food promotions and Association meetings and resources. Also covers local associations, members' personnel changes and member news such as the introduction of new products and facility expansions.
Frequency: Monthly
Circulation: 2300

9889 **NICRA Bulletin**
National Ice Cream Retailers Association
1028 W Devon Avenue
Elk Grove Village, IL 60007

847-301-7500
866-303-6960
Fax: 847-301-8402
E-Mail: info@nicra.org
Home Page: www.nicra.org

Lynn Dudek, President
Dan Messer, VP

Information to assist you with Practical Advice on Daily Operations, Industry Trends, Tax Related Articles, Legislative Issues, Association News, Labeling Information, and more.
Frequency: Monthly
Circulation: 500

9890 **NPA Fact of the Week**
Natural Products Association
2112 E 4th St
Suite 200
Santa Ana, CA 92705-3816

714-460-7732
800-966-6632
Fax: 714-460-7444
Home Page: www.npainfo.org
Social Media: Facebook, Twitter, LinkedIn

John F. Gay, Executive Director & CEO
Jeffrey Wright, President

Emailed to Congressional staffers who handle health issues for their representative or senator. Highlights the latest news, research and trends in dietary supplements and the natural products industry.
1900+ Members
Frequency: Weekly
Founded in 1936

9891 **NPA NOW**
Natural Products Association
2112 E 4th St
Suite 200
Santa Ana, CA 92705-3816

714-460-7732
800-966-6632
Fax: 714-460-7444
Home Page: www.npainfo.org
Social Media: Facebook, Twitter, LinkedIn

John F. Gay, Executive Director & CEO
Jeffrey Wright, President

Provides members with important association and industry news on a timely basis.
1900+ Members
Frequency: 6x Yearly
Founded in 1936

9892 **NPFDA NEWS**
National Poultry & Food Distributors
2014 Osborne Road
Saint Marys, GA 31558

770-535-9901
Fax: 770-535-7385
E-Mail: kkm@npfda.org
Home Page: www.npfda.org

Chris Sharp, President
Al Acunto, Vice President
Marc Miro, Treasurer
Kristin McWhorter, Executive Director

Brings the latest information about NPFDA members- featuring Member Spotlights, government regulations and upcoming industry events.
Frequency: Monthly
Founded in 1967

9893 **NSA Newsletter**
National Shellfisheries Association
National Marine Fisheries Service Laboratory
Oxford, MD 21654

631-653-6327
Fax: 631-653-6327
E-Mail: webmaster@shellfish.org
Home Page: www.shellfish.org

R. LeRoy Creswell, President
Christopher V. Davis, President-Elect
George E. Flimlin, VP & Program Chair
Marta Gomez-Chiarri, Secretary
Sandra E. Shumway, Editor

Current issues and concerns in shellfish research and in the shellfish industry, including details regarding upcoming meetings, employment listings, and column.
1M Members
Frequency: Quarterly
Founded in 1908

9894 **National Automatic Merchandising**
National Automatic Merchandising Association
20 N Wacker Dr
Suite 3500
Chicago, IL 60606-3102

312-346-0370
800-331-8816
Fax: 312-704-4140
E-Mail: dmathews@vending.org
Home Page: www.vending.org

Richard Geerdes, President
Craig Hesch NCE, Senior Vice Chairman
Brad Ellis NCE, Vice Chairman

Serves food and refreshment, vending, contract foodservice management and office coffee service industries.
2500 Members
Founded in 1936

9895 **National Conference on Interstate Milk Shipments**
National Conference on Interstate Milk
123 Buena Vista Drive
Frankfort, KY 40601-8770

502-695-0253
Fax: 502-695-0253
Home Page: www.ncims.org

Leon Townsend, Executive Secretary
Marlena Bordson, Chair
Founded in 1946

9896 **National Fertilizer Solutions Association Newsletter**
339 Consort Drive
Manchester, MO 63011-4439

636-256-6650
Fax: 636-256-4901

Kelly O'Brien-Wray, Publisher
Fred Speckmann, Editor

Accepts advertising.
90 Pages

9897 **National Honey Market News**
US Department of Agriculture
21 N 1st Avenue
#224
Yakima, WA 98902-2663

509-575-2494
Fax: 509-457-7132
E-Mail: FVInfo@ams.usda.gov
Home Page: www.ams.usda.gov/fv/mncs

Linda Verstrate, Publisher
Michael Jarvis, Director

Current honey market information and colony conditions in the US.
Cost: $24.00
10-12 Pages
Frequency: Monthly

9898 **National Hot Pepper Association**
400 NW 20th Street
Fort Lauderdale, FL 33311-3818

954-565-4972
Fax: 954-566-2208
E-Mail: pcppergal@mindspring.com
Home Page: www.inter-linked.com/org/nhpa

Robert J Payton, Publisher
Betty Payton, Editor

Networking among industry and private members. Education and information sharing.
Cost: $20.00
28 Pages
Frequency: Quarterly
Printed in on matte stock

9899 **National Nutritional Foods Association Today**
National Nutritional Foods Association
2112 E 4th St
Suite 200
Santa Ana, CA 92705-3816

949-622-6272
800-966-6632
Fax: 949-622-6266
Home Page: www.nnfa.org

Amanda Thomason, Editor/Publications Manager
Paul Bennett, CEO/President

Nonprofit trade organization dedicated to protecting and advancing the natural products industry for both retailers and suppliers.
Cost: $48.00
Frequency: Monthly
Circulation: 8000
Founded in 1936

9900 **National Onion Association Newsletter**
National Onion Association
822 7th St
Suite 510
Greeley, CO 80631-3941

970-353-5895
Fax: 970-353-5897
E-Mail: info@onions-usa.org
Home Page: www.onions-usa.org

Wayne Mininger, Executive VP
Kim Reddin, Public/Industry Relation

Newsletter published by and only for the National Onion Association.
Frequency: Monthly
Circulation: 600
Founded in 1913
Mailing list available for rent: 600 names

9901 **National Seasoning Manufacturers Newsletter**
National Seasoning Manufacturers Association
2527 Mill Race Road
Frederick, MD 21701-6812

301-694-0419
Fax: 301-299-7523
E-Mail: alsmeyerfood@isp.com

Dick Alsmeyer PhD, Executive Director
Frequency: Quarterly

9902 **National Shellfisheries Association News**
Long Island University/Southampton College
Natural Sciences Division
Southampton, NY 11968

631-283-4000
Fax: 631-287-8054

Sandra Shumway, Production Manager
Eric Lang, Owner

Newsletter focusing on information for public health workers, shellfish producers and fishery administrators.
Cost: $125.00
Circulation: 1000
Mailing list available for rent: 1M names
Printed in one color on matte stock

9903 **National Young Farmer Educational News**
National FFA Organization
PO Box 68960
6060 FFA Drive
Alexandria, VA 22309-160

317-802-6060
888-332-2668
Fax: 800-366-6556
E-Mail: aboutffa@ffa.org
Home Page: www.ffa.org

Wayne Sprick, Publisher
Larry Case, CEO

Tabloid which receives articles and information from state associations as well as information from the National Association.
12 Pages
Founded in 1928

9904 **Natural News Update**
Natural Products Association
2112 E 4th St
Suite 200
Santa Ana, CA 92705-3816

714-460-7732
800-966-6632
Fax: 714-460-7444
Home Page: www.npainfo.org
Social Media: Facebook, Twitter, LinkedIn

John F. Gay, Executive Director & CEO
Jeffrey Wright, President

A weekly news and information resource, offering the latest news, federal activity, association announcements and research.
1900+ Members
Frequency: Weekly
Founded in 1936

9905 **Nebraska Alfalfa Dehydrators Bulletin**
Nebraska Alfalfa Dehydrators Association
8810 Craig Dr
Shawnee Mission, KS 66212-2916

913-648-6800
Fax: 913-648-2648
Home Page: www.nebada.org

Wanda L Cobb, Executive VP

Market Information on Alfalfa Pellets, Meal, Cubes, and Hay.
Frequency: Weekly
Founded in 1941

9906 **News in a Nutshell**
National Peanut Board
2839 Paces Ferry Road
Suite 210
Atlanta, GA 30339-5769

678-424-5750
866-825-7946
Fax: 678-424-5751
E-Mail: peanuts@nationalpeanutboard.org
Home Page: www.nationalpeanutboard.org
Social Media: Facebook, Twitter, YouTube, Flickr

George Jeffcoat, Chairman
Cindy Belch, Vice Chairman
John Harrell, Secretary
Vic Jordan, Treasurer

e-Newlsetter from the National Peanut Board with news about everything peanut.
Frequency: Bi-Weekly

9907 **No-Till Farmer**
Lessiter Publications
PO Box 624
Brookfield, WI 53008-0624

262-782-4480
800-645-8455
Fax: 262-782-1252
E-Mail: info@lesspub.com
Home Page: www.lesspub.com

Donna Schwierske, Manager
Frank Lessiter, Accounting Manager
Michael Storts, Accounting Manager

Management information for farmers interested in conservation tillage.
Cost: $37.95
16 Pages
Frequency: Monthly

he National FFA's newsletter for State Staff nd Advisors. Find important news, information and program updates.
507M Members
Founded in 1928

Urner Barry's Price-Current
Urner Barry Publications
PO Box 389
Toms River, NJ 08754-0389
732-240-5330
800-932-0617
Fax: 732-341-0891
E-Mail: help@urnerbarry.com
Home Page: www.urnerbarry.com
Paul B Brown Jr, President
Sheila M Deane, Marketing Manager
Daily market price report serving the poultry and egg industries.
Cost: $415.00
8 Pages
Frequency: Daily
Circulation: 3,000
ISSN: 0273-9992

9948 **Urner Barry's Price-Current West Coast Edition**
Urner Barry Publications
PO Box 389
Toms River, NJ 08754
732-240-5330
800-932-0617
Fax: 732-341-0891
E-Mail: help@urnerbarry.com
Home Page: www.urnerbarry.com/
Paul Brown Jr, President
Sheila M Deane, Marketing Manager
Richard A. Brown, VP
Reports changes in price and market conditions of poultry and eggs on the West Coast.
Cost: $444.00
8 Pages
Frequency: Daily
Circulation: 3000
ISSN: 0273-5016
Founded in 1858

9949 **Urner Barry's Yellow Sheet**
Urner Barry Publications
PO Box 389
Toms River, NJ 08754
732-240-5330
800-932-0617
Fax: 732-341-0891
E-Mail: help@urnerbarry.com
Home Page: www.urnerbarry.com
Paul B Brown Jr, President
Richard A Brown, VP/Treasurer
Market price report of timely unbiased meat quotes to help pinpoint the latest trading levels of beef, pork, lamb, veal, meat by-products, carcasses and boxed cuts.
Cost: $559.00
8 Pages
Frequency: Daily
Circulation: 1500
ISSN: 1066-8195
Founded in 1858

9950 **Vegetarian Times**
Active Interest Media
300 Continental Blvd
Suite 650
El Segundo, CA 90245-5067
310-356-4100
Fax: 310-356-4110
E-Mail: editor@vegetariantimes.com
Home Page: www.amedia.com
Efrem Zymbalist III, CEO
John Robles, Marketing Manager
Inspiring everyone to eat healthier, live greener, and be happier.
Cost: $19.95
Frequency: Monthly
Founded in 1999

9951 **Vinotizie Italian Wine Newsletter**
Italian Trade Commission
499 Park Ave
6th Floor
New York, NY 10022-1240
212-980-1500
Fax: 212-758-1050
Home Page: www.italtrade.com/ice
Michelle Jones, Editor
This newsletter discusses developments in the Italian wine industry and market, as well as reviews of imported wines from Italy.
Frequency: Bi-Monthly

9952 **WSSA Newsletter**
Weed Science Society of America
P.O.Box 7065
Lawrence, KS 66044-7065
785-429-9622
800-627-0629
Fax: 785-843-1274
E-Mail: wssa@allenpress.com
Home Page: www.wssa.net
David Shaw, Editor
Michael E Foley, Publications Director
Subscription is included in the annual dues.
Cost: $5.00
Frequency: Quarterly/Non-Member Fee

9953 **Washington Association of Wine Grape Growers**
PO Box 716
Cashmere, WA 98815
509-782-8234
Fax: 509-782-1203
E-Mail: info@wawgg.org
Home Page: www.wawgg.org
Vicky Scharlau, Executive Director
Paul Champoux, Business Manager
Debbie Sands, Business Manager
Janet Heath, Office Manager
Julie Lindholm, Director
Guidance in research and education, and maintaining leadership in local, state and national wine grape issues.
Cost: $115.00
Founded in 1983

9954 **Washington Report Newsletter**
National Chicken Council
1015 15th Street NW
Suite 930
Washington, DC 20005-2622
202-081-1339
Fax: 202-293-4005
E-Mail: ncc@chickenusa.org
Home Page: www.nationalchickencouncil.com
George Watts, President
William P Roenigk, Senior VP
Richard L Lobb, Communications Director
Margaret Ernst, Director Meetings/Membership Comm.
NCC's weekly, member's only newsletter provides information on current statistics, as well as information on economic, trade, and marketing developments, updates on regulatory, legislative, technology, and other industry issues and news
Frequency: Weekly
Circulation: 5000
Founded in 1954

9955 **Webster Agricultural Letter**
Webster Communications Corporation
1530 Key Blvd
Suite 401W
Arlington, VA 22209-1531
703-525-4512
Fax: 703-852-3534
Home Page: www.agletter.com
James C Webster, Editor/CEO
Agricultural politics and policy issues.
Cost: $397.00
6 Pages
Frequency: Fortnightly
ISSN: 1073-4813
Founded in 1980
Printed in one color on matte stock

9956 **Weekly Insiders Dairy & Egg Letter**
Urner Barry Publications
PO Box 389
Toms River, NJ 08754
732-240-5330
800-932-0617
Fax: 732-341-0891
E-Mail: help@urnerbarry.com
Home Page: www.urnerbarry.com
Paul B Brown Jr, President
Randy Pesciotta, Editor
Janice Brown, Advertising
Statistical newsletter of storage stocks of whole, liquid and dried eggs, slaughter and consumption figures and retail selling prices as well as critical data on butter, margarine and cheese.
Cost: $24.00
4 Pages
Frequency: Weekly
Circulation: 10000
ISSN: 0270-4153
Founded in 1858

9957 **Weekly Insiders Poultry Report**
Urner Barry Publications
PO Box 389
Toms River, NJ 08754-389
732-240-5330
800-932-0617
Fax: 732-341-0891
E-Mail: help@urnerbarry.com
Home Page: www.urnerbarry.com
Paul B Brown Jr, President
Sheila M Deane, Marketing Manager
Statistical news of broiler eggs set and hatched, current chicken and fowl slaughter, storage holdings and competing red meat availability.
Cost: $190.00
4 Pages
Frequency: Weekly
Circulation: 230
ISSN: 0160-4910
Founded in 1858

9958 **Weekly Insiders Turkey Report**
Urner Barry Publications
PO Box 389
Toms River, NJ 08754-389
732-240-5330
800-932-0617
Fax: 732-341-0891
E-Mail: help@urnerbarry.com
Home Page: www.urnerbarry.com
Paul B Brown Jr, President
Sheila M Deane, Marketing Manager
Richard A. Brown, VP Treasurer
Michael W. O'Shaughnessy, Secretary
Statistical report containing slaughter figures, consumption patterns, US Storage Stock Estimates and comparative weekly prices.
Cost: $173.00
4 Pages
Frequency: Weekly
Circulation: 230

Circulation: 5500
ISSN: 0091-9993
Founded in 1984
Mailing list available for rent: 5,000 names at $90m per M
Printed in 2 colors on glossy stock

9908 **Organic Business News**
Hotline Printing & Publishing
PO Box 161132
Atamonte Springs, FL 32716-1132
407-628-1377
Fax: 407-628-9935
Home Page:
www.hotlineprinting.com/obn.html
Dennis Blank, Publisher/Editor
Christine Blank, Senior Editor
Leading industry publication that tracks the latest government actions, policy trends and financial development in development in the organic food business.
Cost: $110.00
12 Pages
Printed in 2 colors

9909 **Organic Trade Association Newsletter**
Organic Trade Association
60 Wells Street
PO Box 547
Greenfield, MA 01302
413-774-7511
Fax: 413-774-6432
E-Mail: info@ota.com
Home Page: www.ota.com
Christine Bushway, Executive Director/CEO
Linda Lutz, Membership Manager
Laura Batcha, Marketing/Public Relations Director
Members are businesses involved in the organic agriculture and products industry. Seeks to promote the industry and establish production and marketing standards. Also publishes The Organic Page: North American Resource Directory

9910 **Packer**
Vance Publishing
400 Knightsbridge Parkway
Lincolnshire, IL 60069
847-634-2600
Fax: 847-634-4379
E-Mail: info@vancepublishing.com
Home Page: www.vancepublishing.com
William C Vance, Chairman
Peggy Walker, President
News and information on fresh fruit and vegetable marketing.

9911 **Pear Newsletter**
Pear Bureau Northwest
4382 SE International Way
Suite A
Milwaukie, OR 97222-4627
503-652-9720
Fax: 503-652-9721
E-Mail: info@usapears.com
Home Page: www.usapears.com
Kevin Moffitt, President/CEO
Cristie Mather, Communciations Manager
Frequency: Monthly

9912 **Peterson Patriot**
Peterson Patriot Printers-Publishers
202 Main Street
Peterson, IA 51047
712-295-7711
Fax: 712-295-7711
E-Mail: patriot@iowatelecom.net
Roger Stoner, Publisher
Jane Stoner, Editor
Agricultural news.
Cost: $18.00
12 Pages
Frequency: Weekly
Circulation: 549

9913 **Practical Gourmet**
Linick Group
Gourmet Building 7 Putter Lane
PO Box 102
Middle Island, NY 11953-0102
631-924-3888
E-Mail: roger@practicalgourmet.com
Home Page: www.practicalgourmet.com
Gaylen Andrews, Publisher/Editor
Roger Dextor, VP/Director of PR
Barbara Deal, Marketing Manager
Andrew Linick, Manager
Bill Bruzy, Contributing Editor
Since 1982, the focus of this upscale monthly publication is on providing 'healthy dining trends for the affluent traveler' 45 plus; includes feature articles and in-depth interviews with award winning chefs, wineries/tastings, honoring 2-5 star restaurants with PG's Gold Taste Dining Awards, upscale hotels, properties, resorts, spas, cruises/yachting, airlines, ground operators, food festivals/contests, cooking schools and worldwide culinary events.
Cost: $48.00
36 Pages
Frequency: Monthly
Circulation: 210,000
Founded in 1975
Mailing list available for rent: 210 M names at $110 per M
Printed in 4 colors on glossy stock

9914 **Produce Merchandiser**
United Fresh Fruit & Vegetable Association
1901 Pennsylvania Ave Nw
Suite 1100
Washington, DC 20006-3412
202-862-4989
Fax: 202-303-3433
E-Mail: united@uffva.org
Home Page: www.uffva.org
Thomas E Stenzel, CEO
Information on promotion and consumer issues.

9915 **Product Alert**
Marketing Intelligence Service
482 N Main St
Canandaigua, NY 14424-1049
585-374-6326
800-836-5710
Fax: 585-374-5217
Home Page: www.productscan.com
Christine Dengler, Marketing/Sales Manager
A twice-monthly briefing on new packaged goods introduced in North America. Featuring product pictures and descriptions with indexing provided in two convenient formats. Also available in a twice monthly, international version.
Cost: $795.00
Frequency: Fortnightly

9916 **RBA Newsbrief**
Retail Bakers of America
202 Village Circle
Suite 1
Slidell, LA 70458
985-643-6504
800-638-0924
Fax: 985-643-6929
E-Mail: Info@RBAnet.com
Home Page: www.rbanet.com
Social Media: Facebook
Felix Sherman, Sr., President
Kenneth Downey, Sr., 1st Vice President
Marlene Goetzeler, 2nd Vice President
Dale A. Biles, Treasurer
Susan Nicolais, CAE, Secretary
Distributed electronically to RBA members, containing articles gathered from an expansive list of sources.
2000 Members
Frequency: Weekly
Founded in 1918

9917 **Regulatory Register**
American Butter Institute
2101 Wilson Boulevard
Suite 400
Arlington, VA 22201
703-243-5630
Fax: 703-841-9328
E-Mail: AMiner@nmpf.org
Home Page: www.nmpf.org/ABI
Randy Mooney, Chairman
Dave Fuhrmann, Secretary
Clyde Rutherford, 1st Vice Chairman
Cornell Kasbergen, 2nd Vice Chairman
Ken Nobis, Treasurer
A publication for dairy cooperatives and producers which details recent regulatory activity directly impacting the operation of their farms and manufacturing facilities. Highlights the following areas of regulatory affairs; animal health, food safety, nutrition, standards and labeling, and environment and energy.
31 Members
Founded in 1908

9918 **Research Report for Foodservice**
1 Bridge St
Irvington, NY 10533-1550
914-591-4297
E-Mail: info@restaurantchains.net
Home Page: www.restaurantchains.net
James Santo, President
Market research company that provides contact information for companies in the foodservice industry. Our two primary brands are RestaurantChains.net, a directory of company profiles and sales leads for US restaurant chains, and FoodserviceReport.com; a weekly bulletin on new US restaurant openings and changes of ownership.
3600 Members
Founded in 1996
Mailing list available for rent: 80000 names

9919 **Restaurant Chain Growth**
Research Report for Foodservice
1 Bridge St
Irvington, NY 10533-1550
914-591-4297
E-Mail: info@restaurantchains.net
Home Page: www.restaurantchains.net
James Santo, President
Providing the reader with proprietary information.
3600 Members
Frequency: Weekly
Founded in 1996
Mailing list available for rent: 80000 names

9920 **Restaurants and Institutions**
Reed Business Information

125 Park Avenue
23rd Floor
New York, NY 10017

212-309-8100
Fax: 212-309-8187
Home Page: www.rimag.com

A magazine for restaurant professionals faced with fast-paced consumer demands, government regulations, health concerns and evolving food trends in a variety of market segments. R&I keeps these professionals informed and offers menu advice to prepare for new customers and business growth.

9921 Salad Special
Refrigerated Foods Association
2971 Flowers Rd S
Suite 266
Chamblee, GA 30341-5403

770-452-0660
Fax: 770-455-3879
E-Mail: info@refrigeratedfoods.org
Home Page: www.refrigeratedfoods.org

Terry Dougherty, Executive Director

A newsletters covering technical and marketing aspects of the industry, including news of projects, conventions and expositions.
Frequency: Monthly
Founded in 1980

9922 Salt & Trace Mineral Newsletter
Salt Institute
700 N Fairfax St
Suite 600
Alexandria, VA 22314-2085

703-549-4648
Fax: 703-548-2194
E-Mail: info@saltinstitute.org
Home Page: www.saltinstitute.org

Richard L Hanneman, President
Martina Moran, Director
Tammy Goodwin, Director
Mark OKeefe, Director of Communications

Information on animal nutrition.
Circulation: 3000
Founded in 1940
Printed in on glossy stock

9923 Seafood Price-Current
Urner Barry Publications
PO Box 389
Toms River, NJ 08754-389

732-240-5330
800-932-0617
Fax: 732-341-0891
E-Mail: help@urnerbarry.com
Home Page: www.urnerbarry.com

Paul B Brown Jr, President
Karen Mick, Circulation Director

Spot market prices of the most widely traded fresh and frozen fin and shellfish items.
Cost: $383.00
8 Pages
Frequency: Weekly
Circulation: 1500
ISSN: 0270-4170
Founded in 1858

9924 Seafood Trend Newsletter
Seafood Trend
8227 Ashworth Ave N
Seattle, WA 98103-4434

206-523-2280
Fax: 206-526-8719
E-Mail: seafoodtrend@aol.com

Ken Talley, Editor/Publisher

Provides information, statistics and economic facts and figures pertaining to the seafood market.
Cost: $235.00
4 Pages
Circulation: 400
ISSN: 1057-2708
Founded in 1984
Printed in 2 colors on matte stock

9925 Shelby Report of the Southeast
Shelby Publishing Company
517 Green St Nw
Gainesville, GA 30501-3300

770-534-8380
Fax: 770-535-0110
E-Mail: shelbpub@bellsouth.net
Home Page: www.shelbypublishing.com

Ron Johnston, President
Chuck Gilmer, Editor
Carol Tomaseski, Circulation Manager
Ileen Bloch, VP Publishing

A newsletter offering information on the retail and wholesale food trade.
Cost: $36.00
Frequency: Monthly
Circulation: 25,201
Founded in 1966
Printed in on newsprint stock

9926 Shrimp News International
Aquaculture Digest
9450 Mira Mesa Boulevard
#B562
San Diego, CA 92126-4850

FAX 858-271-0324

Robert Rosenberry, Editor

Publishes reports and directories on the world's shrimp industry.
Cost: $95.00
24 Pages
Frequency: Biweekly
Mailing list available for rent
Printed in one color on matte stock

9927 Signals Newsletter
Association for Communications Excellence
University of Florida
PO Box 110811
Gainesville, FL 32611-0811

FAX 352-392-8583
E-Mail: ace@ifas.ufl.edu
Home Page: www.aceweb.org

Features news of interest to members. Includes articles with a professional development focus; updates from special interest groups, states and regions; announcements about upcoming workshops and conferences; and write-ups about members' awards and accomplishments, job changes and more.

9928 Soft Drink Letter
Whitaker Newsletters
313 S Avenue
#203
Fanwood, NJ 07023-1364

908-889-6336
800-359-6049
Fax: 908-889-6339
E-Mail: bevnews@att.net
Home Page: www.att.net

Joel Whitaker, Editor

For managers and owners of bottling and soft drink and water companies.
Cost: $349.00
Printed in one color

9929 Speedy Bee
Fore's Honey Farms
PO Box 998
Jesup, GA 31598

912-427-4018
Fax: 912-427-8447

Troy Fore, Editor

Honey and beekeeping industry news.
Cost: $17.25
16 Pages
Frequency: Monthly
Circulation: 4000
ISSN: 0190-6798
Founded in 1972
Printed in on newsprint stock

9930 Spiceletter
American Spice Trade Association
2025 M St Nw
Suite 800
Washington, DC 20036-2422

202-367-1127
Fax: 202-367-2127
Home Page: www.iamss.org

Cheryl Deem, Executive Director
Frequency: Bi-Monthly

9931 Spirited Living: Dave Steadman's Restaurant Scene
5301 Towne Woods Rd
Coram, NY 11727-2808

631-736-0436
Fax: 631-736-0436

Dave Steadman, Editor

Newsletter published biweekly except January, July, and August.
Cost: $75.00

9932 Sunflower Week in Review
National Sunflower Association
2401 46th Avenue SE
Suite 206
Mandan, ND 58554-4829

701-328-5100
888-718-7033
Fax: 701-328-5101
E-Mail: larryk@sunflowernsa.com
Home Page: www.sunflowernsa.com
Social Media: Facebook, YouTube

Larry Kleingartner, Executive Director

Provides the latest news regarding sunflower information, conveniently summarized with highlights and data to keep you informed.
Frequency: Weekly
Founded in 1981

9933 Supermarket News
Fairchild Publications
750 3rd Ave
New York, NY 10017-2703

212-630-4000
877-652-5295
Fax: 212-630-3563
Home Page: www.fairchildpub.com

Mary G Berner, CEO
David Merrefield, VP, Editorial Director
David Orgel, Editor-in-Chief
Dan Bagan, Publishing Director

A weekly guide aimed at retailers, wholesalers, manufacturers and others in the food industry.
Cost: $23.00
Frequency: Weekly
Circulation: 36346
Founded in 1892

9934 THE LINK
R & D Associates for Military Food & Packaging
16607 Blanco Rd
Suite 501
San Antonio, TX 78232-1940

210-493-8024
Fax: 210-493-8036
E-Mail: rda50@flash.net
Home Page: www.militaryfood.org

Barney Guarino, Chairman
Jim Merryman, Vice Chairman
Tim Zimmerman, President
Bill McCreary, Executive Vice President
Jim Fagan, Executive Director

Provides pertinent data available and will keep readers informed of the activities of major government agencies.
Frequency: Quarterly
Founded in 1946

9935 TecAgri News
Clark Consulting International
PO Box 68
Park Ridge, IL 60068-0068

847-836-5100
Fax: 847-792-7565
E-Mail: warren.clark@ccimarketing.com
Home Page: www.tecagrinews.com

Warren E Clark, President

News on new technology in agriculture reaching large computerized family farmers.
Cost: $1200.00
Frequency: Weekly
Circulation: 100,000
Founded in 1986
Mailing list available for rent: 2.1M names at $250 per M

9936 Technical E-News
Refrigerated Foods Association
1640 Powers Ferry Road
Bldg. 2, Suite 200A
Marietta, GA 30067

770-303-9905
Fax: 770-303-9906
E-Mail: info@refrigeratedfoods.org
Home Page: www.refrigeratedfoods.org

Brian Edmonds, President
George Bradford, Vice President
Steve Loehndorf, Secretary
Wes Thaller, Treasurer

Contains the latest technical and regulatory news affecting the industry.
200+ Members
Frequency: Bi-Monthly
Founded in 1980

9937 The Business Owner
Retail Bakers of America
202 Village Circle
Suite 1
Slidell, LA 70458

985-643-6504
800-638-0924
Fax: 985-643-6929
E-Mail: Info@RBAnet.com
Home Page: www.rbanet.com
Social Media: Facebook

Felix Sherman, Sr., President
Kenneth Downey, Sr., 1st Vice President
Marlene Goetzeler, 2nd Vice President
Dale A. Biles, Treasurer
Susan Nicolais, CAE, Secretary

Publication delivering basic business advice and know-how for today's small and mid-size business proprietor. Each issue delivers knowledge in the areas of business strategy, profit and cash flow maximization, risk reduction and avoidance, insurance, sales and marketing, advertising and branding.
2000 Members
Frequency: 6x Yearly
Founded in 1918

9938 The Business of Herbs
Herb Growing and Marketing Network
PO Box 245
Silver Spring, PA 17575-0245

FAX 717-393-9261
E-Mail: herbworld@aol.com
Home Page: www.herbnet.com, www.herbworld.com

Maureena Rogers, Editor

Information on commercial cultivation of herbs and marketing. Also regulatory information, calender of events, business notes.
40 Pages
Frequency: Monthly
Circulation: 2,000
Founded in 1990

9939 The Coffee Reporter
National Coffee Association
45 Broadway
Suite 1140
New York, NY 10006

212-766-4007
Fax: 212-766-5815
E-Mail: info@ncausa.org
Home Page: www.ncausa.org
Social Media: Facebook, Twitter, LinkedIn

Dub Hay, Chairman
John E. Boyle, Vice Chairman
Richard Emanuele, Secretary
Robert F. Nelson, President & CEO

National Coffee Association's official online newsletter.
Frequency: Weekly

9940 The Culinary Insider
American Culinary Federation
180 Center Place Way
St Augustine, FL 32095-8859

904-824-4468
800-624-9458
Fax: 904-825-4758
E-Mail: acf@acfchefs.net
Home Page: www.acfchefs.org
Social Media: Facebook, Twitter

Michael Ty, President
Thomas J. Macrina, Secretary
James Taylor, Treasurer

ACF's electronic newsletter featuring the latest culinary news, events, continuing education opportunities and more.
19000 Members
Founded in 1929

9941 The Exchange
Agricultural & Applied Economics Association
555 E. Wells St.
Suite 1100
Milwaukee, WI 53202-6600

414-918-3190
E-Mail: Info@aaea.org
Home Page: www.aaea.org

Robert P. King, President
Richard Sexton, President-Elect
Bruce A. Babcock, Director
Jayson Lusk, Director
Lori Lynch, Director

Bi-monthly electronic newsletter published by AAEA for members only. The content of the newsletter includes association announcements, membership news, and updates from the profession.
Cost: $150.00
4M Members
Frequency: Regular Membership Fee
Founded in 1910

9942 Today's Grocer
Florida Grocer Publications
PO Box 430760
S Miami, FL 3324

305-661-0792
800-440-3067
Fax: 305-661-6720
E-Mail: todaysgr@bells
Home Page: www.todays

Jack Nobles, Publisher
Dennis Kane, Editor

Provides the latest food indu trends to Florida, Georgia, A Mississippi and the Carolinas.
Cost: $29.00
24 Pages
Frequency: Monthly
Circulation: 19500
ISSN: 1529-4420
Founded in 1968
Printed in 4 colors on newsprint sto

9943 US Beer Market
Business Trend Analysts/Industry R
2171 Jericho Tpke
Suite 200
Commack, NY 11725-2937

631-462-5454
800-866-4648
Fax: 631-462-1842
Home Page: www.bta-ler.com

Charles J Ritchie, Executive VP
Donna Priani, Marketing Director

Profiles markets for premium, superpremium, popular and light beers.
Cost: $1495.00
Founded in 1978

9944 USA Rice Daily
USA Rice Federation
4301 N Fairfax Drive
Suite 425
Arlington, VA 22203

703-226-2300
Fax: 703-236-2301
E-Mail: riceinfo@usarice.com
Home Page: www.usarice.com

Jamie Warshaw, Chairman

The latest news on issues and activities for the U.S. rice industry.

9945 Uncorked
California Wine Club
2175 Goodyear Ave Suite 102
PO Box 3699
Ventura, CA 93006-3699

805-504-4330
800-777-4443
Fax: 800-700-1599
E-Mail: info@cawineclub.com
Home Page: www.cawineclub.com

Bruce Boring, Publisher
Judy Reynolds, Editor

8 page newsletter that describes featured winery. It provides an upclose and personal look at a small boutique California winery.
Circulation: 10000
Founded in 1990

9946 Update
National FFA Organization
6060 FFA Drive
PO Box 68960
Indianapolis, IN 46268-0960

317-802-6060
888-332-2668
E-Mail: membership@ffa.org
Home Page: www.ffa.org

Steve A. Brown, National FFA Advisor
Marion D. Fletcher, National FFA Organization Treasurer

ISSN: 0160-4910
Founded in 1858

9959 Weekly Livestock Reporter
Weekly Livestock
PO Box 7655
Fort Worth, TX 76111-0655

817-838-0106
Fax: 817-831-3117
E-Mail: service@weeklylivestock.com
Home Page: www.weeklylivestock.com

Ted Gouldy, Publisher
Phil Stoll, Editor

Offers comprehensive weekly information for cattle farmers and livestock agricultural professionals.
Cost: $18.00
Frequency: Weekly
Circulation: 10000
Founded in 1897

9960 Weekly Weather and Crop Bulletin
NOAA/USDA Joint Agricultural Weather Facility
1400 Independence Ave SW
Washington, DC 20250

202-720-2791
E-Mail: jawfweb@oce.usda.gov
Home Page: www.noaa.gov

Robert Keeney, Administrator
David Miscus, Managing Editor

Provides a vital source of information on weather, climate and agricultural developments worldwide, along with detailed charts and tables of agrometeorological information that is appropriate for the season.
Frequency: Weekly
Circulation: 1500
Founded in 1807

9961 Western Hemisphere Agriculture and Trade Report
US Department of Agriculture
Room 112-A
US Department of Agriculture
Washington, DC 20250-3810

202-012-2000
Fax: 202-690-4915
E-Mail: webmaster@usda.gov
Home Page: www.usda.gov

Miriam Stuart, Publisher
Abraham Lincoln, Chief Information Officer
Chris Smith, Chief Information Officer
Matt Paul, Director of Communications
Ramona Romero, General Counsel

Information on current and projected agricultural production and trade trends for North, Central, South America and the Caribbean. Includes information on trade agreements and blocks in the Hemisphere.
Founded in 1862

9962 What's News in Organic
Organic Trade Association
60 Wells Street
PO Box 547
Greenfield, MA 01302

413-774-7511
Fax: 413-774-6432
E-Mail: info@ota.com
Home Page: www.ota.com
Social Media: Facebook, Twitter, LinkedIn

Matt McLean, President
Sarah Bird, Vice President
Todd Linsky, Secretary
Kristen Holt, Treasurer

Includes a feature focusing on a hot topic for the industry, a pertinent quotation, and a world of news section outlining brief news related to the industry. Electronic publication.
Frequency: Quarterly
Founded in 1985

9963 Wine on Line Food and Wine Review
Enterprise Publishing
PO Box 328
Blair, NE 68008-0328

402-426-2121
Fax: 402-426-2227
E-Mail: mrhoades@enterprisepub.com
Home Page: www.enterprisepub.com

Mark Rhoades, President
Dave Smith, Production Manager
Tracy Prettyman, Business Manager

Reviews, feature articles and information on all areas of food and wine, including restaurants, hotels, trains and airlines. Accepts advertising.
Cost: $100.00
10 Pages
Frequency: Monthly

9964 fridayfeedback
Meat & Livestock Australia
1401 K Street NW
Suite 602
Washington, DC 20005

202-521-2551
Fax: 202-521-2699
E-Mail: info@mla.com.au
Home Page: www.mla.com.au
Social Media: Facebook, Twitter, YouTube

Don Heatley, Chairman
David Palmer, Managing Director
Bernie Bindon, Director
Chris Hudson, Director

Providing a weekly wrap-up of market information, industry news and updates, and on-farm information including tools and calculators, and producer case studies.
30000 Members
Frequency: Weekly
Founded in 1998

Magazines & Journals

9965 ABF E-Buzz
American Beekeeping Federation
3525 Piedmont Rd
Bldg 5 Suite 300
Atlanta, GA 30305-1509

404-760-2875
Fax: 404-240-0998
E-Mail: info@abfnet.org
Home Page: www.abfnet.org

Robin Dahlen, President
David Mendes, VP

A member benefit published electronically to inform members about ABF activities and happenings in the beekeeping industry.
Cost: $35.00
1200 Members
Frequency: Membership Fees Vary
Founded in 1943

9966 ABL Insider
American Beverage Licensees Association
5101 River Rd
Suite 108
Bethesda, MD 20816-1512

301-656-1494
Fax: 301-656-7539
E-Mail: rogers@ablusa.org
Home Page: www.ablusa.org
Social Media: Facebook, Twitter

Chuck Ferrar, President
Ray Cox, Vice President
Harry Klock, Vice President
Victor Pittman, Vice President
Robert Sprenger, Vice President

A publication of the American Beverage Licensees, the voice of America's beer, wine, and spirits retailers.
17000 Members
Founded in 2002

9967 AHA Quarterly
American Herb Association
PO Box 1673
Nevada City, CA 9595-1673

530-265-9552
Fax: 530-274-3140
Home Page: www.ahaherb.com

Kathi Keville, Editor/Director
Mindy Green, Associate Editor

Contains news bulletins, scientific studies, book reviews, research in the field and networking between members. Also offers directories of herb education and mail order sources of herbs.
Cost: $20.00
20 Pages
Frequency: Quarterly
Circulation: 1000
Founded in 1981
Printed in on matte stock

9968 ASMC Sales & Marketing Magazine
Association of Sales & Marketing Companies
1010 Wisconsin Avenue NW, #900
9th Floor
Washington, DC 20007

202-337-9351
Fax: 202-337-4508
E-Mail: info@asmc.org
Home Page: www.asmc.org

Jamie DeSimone, Dir, Marketing/Member Services

Reports on the progress and change in the food broker profession.
Cost: $25.00
450 Pages
Frequency: Bi-Annual
ISSN: 0884-7185
Founded in 1904
Printed in 4 colors

9969 AWS Wine Journal
American Wine Society
PO Box 279
Englewood, OH 45322-0279

888-297-9070
Fax: 937-529-7888
Home Page: www.americanwinesociety.org

John Hames, Executive Director

Contains articles on all aspects of wine appreciation, wine making, wine destinations, and wine & food. Articles provide a wide range of exciting stories and educational information.
Frequency: Quarterly
Founded in 1967

9970 AgProfessional Magazine
Agricultural Retailers Association
1156 15th St NW
Suite 500
Washington, DC 20005-1745

202-457-0825
800-844-4900
Fax: 202-457-0864
Home Page: www.agprofessional.com
Social Media: Twitter, YouTube

Provides editorial and advertising for agronomic and business management solutions specifically to agricultural retailers/distributors,

professional farm managers and crop consultants.
1200 Members
Frequency: Membership Dues Vary
Founded in 1993

9971 Agri Marketing Magazine
Henderson Communications LLC
1422 Elbridge Payne Rd
Suite 250
Chesterfield, MO 63017-8544
636-728-1428
Fax: 636-777-4178
E-Mail: info@agrimarketing.com
Home Page: www.agrimarketing.com
Lynn Henderson, Owner
Covers the unique interests of corporate agribusiness executives, their marketing communications agencies, the agricultural media, ag trade associations and other ag related professionals.
Frequency: Monthly
Circulation: 8000
Founded in 1962

9972 Agribusiness Fieldman
Western Agricultural Publishing Company
4969 E Clinton Way
Suite 104
Fresno, CA 93727-1549
559-252-7000
888-382-9772
Fax: 559-252-7387
E-Mail: westag@psnw.com
Home Page: www.westagpubco.com
Paul Baltimore, Publisher
Randy Bailey, Editor
Robert Fujimoto, Assistant Director
For the professional agricultural consultant, featuring the latest information on chemical regulation, pest control techniques and feature stories on PCA and PCO community.

9973 Agribusiness Fresh Fruit and Business News
Agribusiness Publications
PO Box 669
Sanger, CA 93657-669
559-875-4585
800-364-4894
Fax: 559-875-4587
Home Page: www.agribusinesspublisher.com
John Van Nortwick, Publisher
Michelle Cox, Editor
Keeps subscribers abreast of business news for the fruit growing and producing industry.
Cost: $36.00
Frequency: Monthly
Circulation: 10000
Founded in 1980

9974 Airline Catering International
International Inflight Food Service Association
5775 Peachtree-Dunwoody Road, Building G
Suite 500
Atlanta, GA 30342
404-252-3663
Fax: 404-252-0774
E-Mail: ifsa@kellencompany.com
Home Page: www.ifsanet.com
Social Media: Facebook, Twitter, LinkedIn, YouTube
Sandra Pineau, President
Ken Samara, VP
A review of inflight catering and galley equipment. Provides expert coverage and analysis of next-generation galley technology through to the latest menu development trends and eco-friendly food packaging initiatives. Offers a fresh take on the fast-moving and specialized inflight catering market.
400 Members
Frequency: Bi-Annually
Founded in 1965

9975 Alaska Fisherman's Journal
Diversified Business Communications
PO Box 7437
Portland, ME 04112-7437
207-842-5600
Fax: 207-842-5503
Home Page: www.divbusiness.com
Nancy Hasselback, CEO
Randy Le Shane, Production Manager
Mike Lodato, Publisher
Neil Casey, Advertising Coordinator
Stephanie Wendel, Audience Development Manager
Primary publication serving the North Pacific commercial fishing fleet in the world's healthiest and most lucrative commercial fishing region.
Cost: $21.00
Frequency: Monthly
Circulation: 10,000
ISSN: 0164-8330

9976 Alimentos Balanceados Para Animales
WATT Publishing Company
122 S Wesley Ave
Mt Morris, IL 61054-1451
815-734-7937
Fax: 815-734-4201
E-Mail: gill@wattmm.com
Home Page: www.wattnet.com
Clayton Gill, Editorial Director
James Watt, Owner
For feed industry professionals in Latin America.
Cost: $42.00
Circulation: 9471
ISSN: 0274-5571
Founded in 1917
Printed in 4 colors on glossy stock

9977 All About Beer
501 Washington St
Suite H
Durham, NC 27701-2169
919-530-8150
800-999-9718
Fax: 919-530-8160
E-Mail: editor@allaboutbeer.com
Home Page: www.allaboutbeer.com
Julie Bradford, Publisher
Natalie Abernethy, Circulation Manager
Quality beers, breweries and restaurants.
Cost: $19.99

9978 Allied Tradesman
Allied Trades of the Baking Industry
2001 Shawnee Mission Pkwy
Mission Woods, KS 62205
707-935-0103
Fax: 707-935-0174
Home Page: www.atbi.org
Gary Cain, President
Tim Miller, Secretary, Treasurer
Brad Hahn, Secretary, Treasurer
Matt Ungashick, Secretary
Bruce Criss, Vice President
Frequency: Monthly
Circulation: 500
Founded in 1920

9979 Almond Facts
Blue Diamond Growers
1802 C Street
PO Box 1768
Sacramento, CA 95811
916-442-0771
Fax: 916-325-2880
E-Mail: feedback@bdgrowers.com
Home Page: www.bluediamond.com
Robert Donovan, CFO
Douglas D Youngdahl, CEO/President
The latest news affecting Blue Diamond and the almond industry with Almond Facts magazine. Service to Blue Diamond's grower-owners, also available online.
Cost: $25.00
Frequency: Bi-Monthly
Founded in 1910
Printed in 4 colors

9980 American Beefalo World Registry
30 Stevenson Road
#5
Laramie, WY 82070
307-745-3505
866-374-2297
Fax: 307-745-3505
Home Page: www.abwr.org
Offers information for beef and cattle farmers.

9981 American Brewer
1049 B Street
PO Box 510
Hayward, CA 94543-510
510-886-7418
Fax: 510-538-7644
E-Mail: info@ambrew.com
Home Page: www.ambrew.com
Bill Owens, Publisher
Greg Kitsock, Editor
A magazine covering the business of beer.
Cost: $50.00
Frequency: Quarterly
Founded in 1979

9982 American Fruit Grower
Meister Publishing Company
37733 Euclid Ave
Willoughby, OH 44094-5992
440-942-2000
800-572-7740
Fax: 440-975-3447
E-Mail: afg.circ@meistermedia.com
Home Page: www.meisternet.com
Gary Fitzgerald, President
Joe Monahan, Group Publisher
Fran Mihalik, Circulation Manager
Specialized production and marketing information and industry-wide support for fruit growers.
Cost: $19.95
66 Pages
Frequency: Monthly
Circulation: 37,000
Founded in 1931

9983 American Journal of Enology and Viticulture
American Society for Enology and Vinticulture
1784 Picasso Avenue Suite D
PO Box 2160
Davis, CA 95617-2160
530-753-3142
Fax: 530-753-3318
Home Page: www.ajevonline.org
Judith McKibben, Managing Editor
Full-length research papers, literature reviews, research notes and technical briefs on various aspects of enology and viticulture, including wine chemistry, sensory science, process engineering, wine quality assessments, microbiol-

ogy, methods development, plant pathogenesis, diseases and pests of grape, rootstock and clonal evaluation, effect of field practices and grape genetics and breeding.
Frequency: Quarterly
Mailing list available for rent

9984 **American Red Angus Magazine**
Red Angus Association of America
4201 N Interstate 35
Denton, TX 76207-3415
940-387-3502
Fax: 888-829-5573
E-Mail: info@redangus.org
Home Page: www.redangus.org
Social Media: Facebook
Joe Mushrush, President
Greg Comstock, CEO
The most comprehensive resource guide to the Red Angus breed. Keep informed about a breed that is focused on economic value, efficiency and quality.
2000 Members
Founded in 1954

9985 **American Small Farm Magazine**
560 Sunbury Rd
Suite 6
Delaware, OH 43015-8692
740-363-2395
Fax: 740-369-9526
E-Mail: sales@smallfarm.com
Home Page: www.smallfarm.com
Marti Smith, Information
Andy Stevens, Editor
Published for the owner/operator of farms from five to three hundred acres. Focuses on production agriculture including alternative and sustainable farming ideas and technology, case studies, small farm lifestyle and tradition.
Cost: $18.00
ISSN: 1064-7473

9986 **American Vegetable Grower**
Meister Media Worldwide
37733 Euclid Ave
Willoughby, OH 44094-5992
440-942-2000
800-572-7740
Fax: 440-975-3447
E-Mail: avg.circ@meistermedia.com
Home Page: www.meisternet.com
Gary Fitzgerald, President
Ken Hall, Communications Manager
Josep W Monahan, Publisher
Fran Mihalik, Circulation manager
Information source for commercial vegetable growers.
Cost: $19.95
Frequency: Monthly
Circulation: 34772
Founded in 1931

9987 **American Wholesale Marketers Association/ Convenience Distribution**
American Wholesale Marketers Association
2750 Prosperity Ave
Suite 530
Fairfax, VA 22031-4338
703-208-3358
800-482-2962
Fax: 703-573-5738
E-Mail: info@awmanet.org
Home Page: www.awmanet.org; www.conveniencedistributionmagazine.com
Scott Ramminger, Publisher Executive Editor
Joan Fay, Editor + Associate Publisher
A magazine specifically targeted toward convenience distributors. Our readers are involved in the purchase and sale of candy, tobacco, snacks, beverages, health and beauty care items, general merchandise, foodservice, groceries and more.
Cost: $36.00
Frequency: Monthly/Non-Members Fee
Circulation: 11,000
ISSN: 1083-9313
Printed in 4 colors on glossy stock

9988 **Angus Journal**
American Angus Association
3201 Frederick Ave
St Joseph, MO 64506-2997
816-383-5100
Fax: 816-233-9703
E-Mail: angus@angus.org
Home Page: www.angus.org
Social Media: Facebook, Twitter
Joe Hampton, Chair
Jarold Callahan, Vice Chair
Phil Trowbridge, Treasurer
To provide programs, services, technology and leadership to enhance the genetics of the Angus breed, broaden its influence within the beef industry, and expand the market for superior tasting, high-quality Angus beef worldwide. Achieve Angus excellence through information.
Cost: $80.00
30+M Members
Frequency: Membership Fees Vary
Founded in 1883

9989 **Applied Economic Perspectives and Policy**
Agricultural & Applied Economics Association
555 E. Wells St.
Suite 1100
Milwaukee, WI 53202-6600
414-918-3190
E-Mail: Info@aaea.org
Home Page: www.aaea.org
Robert P. King, President
Richard Sexton, President-Elect
Bruce A. Babcock, Director
Jayson Lusk, Director
Lori Lynch, Director
Publishes articles that synthsize, integrate, and analyze areas of current applied economic research within the mission of the AAEA as well as stimulate linkages between sub-fields of agricultural and applied economics.
Cost: $ 150.00
4M Members
Frequency: Regular Membership Fee
Founded in 1910

9990 **Applied Engineering in Agriculture**
American Society of Agricultural Engineers
2950 Niles Rd
St Joseph, MI 49085-8607
269-429-0300
800-371-2723
Fax: 269-429-3852
E-Mail: hq@asabe.org
Home Page: www.asabe.org
Mark D Zielke, CEO
Donna Hull, Pubilcation Director
Focus is on agricultural equipment, farm buildings, electrification, soil conservation, irrigation and food engineering.
26 Pages
Frequency: Monthly
Circulation: 9000
Founded in 1907

9991 **Aquaculture Magazine**
Achill River Corporation
PO Box 2329
Asheville, NC 28802-2329
828-687-0011
Fax: 828-681-0601
E-Mail: info@aquaculturemag.com
Home Page: www.aquaculturemag.com
Gregory J Gallagher, Editor/Publisher
Doinita Cociovei, Circulation Manager
Joseth Strickland, Advertisement Manager
Focus emphasizes the production, processing, and marketing of aquatic organisms and plant life.
Founded in 1968

9992 **Arbor Age**
Green Media
1030 W Higgins Road
Suite 230
Park Ridge, IL 60068
847-720-5600
Fax: 847-720-5601
Home Page: www.arborage.com
John Kmitta, Senior Editor
Targets arborists in the commercial, municipal and utility sectors. Content is provided by a wide range of green industry experts, including professional arborists, academicians, instructors, consultants, government bodies and research organizations.
43 Pages
Frequency: 9x Yearly
Circulation: 16,500
Founded in 1981
Printed in 4 colors on glossy stock

9993 **Atlantic Control States Beverage Journal**
Club & Tavern
3 12th Street
Wheeling, WV 26003-3276
304-232-7620
Fax: 304-233-1236
Arnold Lazarus, Editor
A magazine for the alcoholic beverage industry. Serving bars, restaurants, clubs and industry personnel with West Virginia, Virginia, and North Carolina state editions. Includes states' liquor price lists.

9994 **Automatic Merchandiser**
Cygnus Business Media
1233 Janesville Avenue
Fort Atkinson, WI 53538
800-547-7377
E-Mail: gary.thom@vendingmarketwatch.com
Home Page: www.vendingmarketwatch.com
Gary Thom, Publisher
Serves the business management, marketing, technology and product information needs of its readers.
Cost: $66.00
84 Pages
Frequency: Monthly
Circulation: 14000
Founded in 1937
Mailing list available for rent: 16004 names at $150 per M
Printed in 4 colors on newsprint stock

9995 **Bagel Bits**
Independent Bakers Association
2 S Portage Street
Westfield, NY 14787
716-326-5200
E-Mail: nationalinfo@welchs.com
Home Page: www.nationalgrape.com
Nicholas Pyle, Manager
Founded in 1965

9996 **Baker's Rack**
Retail Bakers of America
202 Village Circle
Suite 1
Slidell, LA 70458

985-643-6504
800-638-0924
Fax: 985-643-6929
E-Mail: Info@RBAnet.com
Home Page: www.rbanet.com
Social Media: Facebook

Felix Sherman, Sr., President
Kenneth Downey, Sr., 1st Vice President
Marlene Goetzeler, 2nd Vice President
Dale A. Biles, Treasurer
Susan Nicolais, CAE, Secretary

Reaching retail baking professionals and the baking industry as a whole. Articles are submitted from industry experts who understand the unique interests and needs of today's retail baker.
2000 Members
Frequency: Quarterly
Founded in 1918

9997 **Bakery Production and Marketing**
245 W 17th Street
1350 E Toughy Avenue
New York, NY 10011

212-414-1160
Fax: 212-337-7198
Home Page: www.cahners.com

Doug Krumrei, Editor
Stuart Whayman, CFO

Dedicated to delivering sensible ideas for profitable baking with editorial that addresses solutions and opportunities found within retail, instore, food service and intermediate wholesale bakeries.
Cost: $70.00
Frequency: Monthly
Circulation: 31,000

9998 **Baking Buyer**
Sosland Publishing Company
4800 Main St
Suite 100
Kansas City, MO 64112-2513

816-756-1000
Fax: 816-756-0494
E-Mail: web@sosland.com
Home Page: www.sosland.com

Gordon Davidson, President
John Unrein, Editor
Tarre Beach, Managing Editor

This publication offers information on state-of-the-art baked foods and ingredients.
Circulation: 31000
Founded in 1922

9999 **Baking and Snack**
Paul Lattan
4800 Main Street
Suite 100
Kansas City, MO 64112-2504

816-756-1000
Fax: 816-756-0494
E-Mail: bbcservice@sosland.com
Home Page: www.bakingbusiness.com

Steve Barne, Editor
Laurie Gorton, Executive Editor

A magazine offering information on baking equipment and ingredients for the commercial baker.
Frequency: Monthly
Circulation: 12,494
Founded in 1922

10000 **Bar & Beverage Business Magazine**
Mercury Publications
1839 Inkster Boulevard
Winnipeg, Ma 0

204-954-2085
Fax: 204-954-2057
E-Mail: webmaster@mercury.mb.ca
Home Page: www.mercury.mb.ca/

Frank Yeo, Publisher
Robert Thompson, National Account Manager
Kelly Gray, Editor
Angie Finnbogason, Circulation Manager
Carly Peters, Editorial Production Manager

The buying and selling of beverages, operator profiles, new products, product merchandising and trends.
Cost: $35.00
Frequency: Quarterly
Circulation: 16923
Founded in 1948
Mailing list available for rent

10001 **Bartender Magazine**
Foley Publishing Corporation
PO Box 157
Spring Lake, NJ 07762

732-449-4499
Fax: 732-974-8289
E-Mail: barmag@aol.com
Home Page: www.bartender.com
Social Media: Facebook, Twitter

Raymond Foley, Publisher
Jaclyn Wilson Foley, Editor

Serves all full-service drinking establishments, including individual restaurants, hotels, motels, bars, taverns, lounges and all other full service on premise licenses.
76 Pages
Frequency: Quarterly
Circulation: 104000
Founded in 1979
Printed in 4 colors on glossy stock

10002 **Bee Culture**
AI Root Company
PO Box 706
Medina, OH 44258-0706

330-725-6677
800-289-7668
Fax: 330-725-5624
E-Mail: weboptout@rootcandles.com
Home Page: www.rootcandles.com

John Root, President
Kathy Summers, Production Manager

Honey bees and their keeping for beginners and experienced apiculturists. Accepts advertising, press releases, new products, and book reviews.
Cost: $21.50
64 Pages
Circulation: 12000
ISSN: 1071-3190
Founded in 1863
Printed in 4 colors on matte stock

10003 **Beer, Wine & Spirits Beverage Retailer**
Oxford Publishing
Ste 1
1903b University Ave
Oxford, MS 38655-4150

662-236-5510
800-247-3881
Fax: 662-236-5541
E-Mail: ncb@nightclub.com
Home Page: www.nightclub.com

Ed Meek, Publisher
Michael Harrelson, Editor
Jennifer Parsons, Marketing
Jennifer Robinson, COO
Adam Alson, Founder

Beverage Retailer serves retail establishments in the beer, wine and spirits industries, including liquor, package and wine stores and others allied to the field.
Cost: $30.00
52 Pages
Frequency: Monthly
Circulation: 19985
Founded in 1997
Printed in 4 colors on glossy stock

10004 **Beverage Dynamics**
The Beverage Information Group
17 High Street
2nd Floor
Norwalk, CT 06851

203-855-8499
E-Mail: lzimmerman@m2media360.com
Home Page: www.bevinfogroup.com

Liza Zimmerman, Editor-in-Chief
Jeremy Nedelka, Managing Editor

Provides a unique and essential communciations link between suppliers and chain and independent retailers in the off-premise market (liquor stores, supermarkets, beverage outlets, etc)
Cost: $35.00
Frequency: Bi-Monthly
Founded in 1934

10005 **Beverage Industry**
Stagnito Communications
2401 W Big Beaver Road
Suite 700
Troy, MI 48084

847-763-9534
Fax: 847-763-9538
E-Mail: bi@halldata.com
Home Page: www.bevindustry.com
Social Media: Facebook, Twitter, LinkedIn

Steve Pintarelli, Publisher
Jessica Jacobsen, Editor
Stephanie Cernivec, Managing Editor

Provides the most in-depth information about the beverage market including production, technology and distribution. The changing industry demands a change leader and BI fills that role by reporting behind the scenes of the gigantic 65 billion market.
Cost: $40.00
Frequency: Monthly
Circulation: 28000
Founded in 1946

10006 **Beverage Journal**
Michigan Licensed Beverage Association
920 N Fairview Ave
Lansing, MI 48912-3238

517-374-9611
877-292-2896
Fax: 517-374-1165
E-Mail: info@mlba.org
Home Page: www.mlba.org

Lou Adado, CEO
Catherine Pavick, Executive Director

Offers information on the alcoholic beverage industry/retail sales
Cost: $52.00
Frequency: Monthly
ISSN: 1050-4427
Printed in on glossy stock

10007 **Beverage Media**
Beverage Media Group
152 Madison Avenue
Suite 600
New York, NY 10016
212-571-3232
Fax: 212-571-4443
Home Page: www.bevnetwork.com

Journal offering information on the liquor, wine and beer trade. New products & promo-

tions, industry news and current trends.
Cost: $119.00
Frequency: Monthly

10008 Beverage Network
4437 Concord Lane
Skokie, IL 60076-2605

617-497-0062
Fax: 617-812-7740
E-Mail: sales@bevnet.com
Home Page: www.bevnet.com

Organization of beverage distributors dealing with specialty, nonalcoholic products.

10009 Beverage Retailer Magazine
Oxford Publishing
Ste 1
1903b University Ave
Oxford, MS 38655-4150

662-236-5510
800-247-3881
Fax: 662-236-5541
E-Mail: br@beverage.retailer.com
Home Page: www.beverage-retailer.com

Ed Meek, Publisher
Brenda Owen, Editor
Ruth Ann Wolfe, Circualtion Manager

A magazine covering the off-premise market for retailers in the wine, beer and spirits business.
Cost: $30.00
Frequency: Monthly
Circulation: 25000
Founded in 1920
Printed in 4 colors on glossy stock

10010 Biodynamics
Biodynamic Farming & Gardening Association
PO Box 944
East Troy, WI 53120-0944

262-649-9212
E-Mail: info@biodynamics.com
Home Page: www.biodynamics.com
Social Media: Facebook

Charles Beedy, Contact

A membership publication providing a thoughtful collection of original articles centered on a theme of interest to the biodynamic community. Voices from the community, discussion of the biodynamic preparations, regional, national, and international news and updates, event overviews, book and film reviews, organizational updates, seasonal recipes, columns and more.
Cost: $45.00
Frequency: 6 per year
Circulation: 1000+

10011 Bison World Magazine
National Bison Association
8690 Wolff Ct
200
Westminster, CO 80234

303-292-2833
Fax: 303-845-9081
E-Mail: david@bisoncentral.com
Home Page: www.bisoncentral.com

Jim Matheson, Assistant Director
Dave Carter, Executive Director

Featured articles and regular departments cover all aspects of raising bison and what's happening in this exciting industry. Available with all levels of membership with the association.
Frequency: Quarterly
Circulation: 1000

10012 Body, Mind & Spirit Magazine
PO Box 95
Dogsland, SK

306-356-4634
Fax: 306-356-4634
Home Page: www.saskworld.com/bodymindspirit

Jeni Mayer, Publisher
Adele Azar-Rucquoi, Contributing Writers
Frequency: Quarterly

10013 Bottled Water Reporter
International Bottled Water Association
1700 Diagonal Rd
Suite 650
Alexandria, VA 22314-2870

703-683-5213
817-719-6197
Fax: 703-683-4074
E-Mail: ibwainfo@bottledwater.org
Home Page: www.bottledwater.org

Joseph Doss, Publisher/President

Covers IBWA events and programs while highlighting new technologies and equipment within the industry, taking notice of personnel changes and reporting on the latest industry statistical data. It also features useful articles on management, operations and marketing specific to the bottled water industry.
Cost: $50.00
74 Pages
Circulation: 2500
Founded in 1958
Printed in 4 colors on glossy stock

10014 Brahman Journal
American Brahman Breeders Association
915 12th Street
Suite 520
Houston, TX 77054

979-826-4347
Fax: 979-826-2007
E-Mail: info@brahmanjournal.com
Home Page: www.brahmanjournal.com
Social Media: Facebook

Victoria Lambert, Editor
Brandy Barnes, Field Representative
Mandy Chambers, Assistant Editor

Provides timely, useful information about one of the largest. most dynamic and most influential breeds of beef cattle in the world. Each issue reports on American Brahman and International Brahman shows, American Brahman and international Brahman events, Brahman sales and Brahman history, as well as pertinent cattle industry news, technical articles and the latest research as it pertains to the Brahman Breed and its followers.
Cost: $25.00
Frequency: Monthly
Circulation: 7000
Founded in 1971

10015 Brandpackaging
Independent Publishing Company
P.O.Box 3116
Saint George, UT 84771-3116

435-656-1555
800-808-7449
Fax: 435-656-1511
Home Page: www.independentpublishing.com

Josh Warburton, President/Publisher
Circulation: 5500
Founded in 1996

10016 Brewers Digest
Siebel Publishing Company
Business Office
PO Box 677
Thiensville, WI 53092-6026

915-877-3319
Fax: 915-877-3319

Thomas Volke, Publisher
Dori Whitney, Editor

The gamut of operational, production, buying, engineering, and packaging issues affecting brewing companies and enterprises.
Cost: $20.00
70 Pages
Frequency: Monthly
Circulation: 3000
ISSN: 0006-971X
Founded in 1926
Printed in 4 colors on glossy stock

10017 Business of Herbs
Northwind Farm Publications
439 Ponderosa Way
Jemez Springs, NM 87025-8036

505-829-3448
Fax: 505-829-3449
Home Page: www.herb-biz.com

Paula Oliver, Publisher
David Oliver, Editor

Primarily for herb businesses and those keenly interested in herbs and botanicals.
Cost: $4.00

10018 Calf News (Cattle Feeder Magazine)
1531 Kensington Boulevard
Garden City, KS 67846

620-276-7844
Fax: 620-275-7333
E-Mail: steve@calfnews.com
Home Page: www.calfnews.com

Betty Jo Gigot, Editor & Publisher
Patti Wilson, Sales Manager
Larisa Willrett, Copy Editor/Circulation
Kathie Bedolli, Director

This magazine offers the latest information to cattle breeders and feeders.
Cost: $33.00
Circulation: 6,352
Founded in 1964

10019 Candy Industry
Stagnito Communications
155 Pfingsten Road
Suite 205
Deerfield, IL 60015

847-205-5660
Fax: 847-205-5680
Home Page: www.stagnito.com

Harry Stagnito, President
Korry Stagnito, Publishing Director
Sue Ravenscraft, VP Circulation

Magazine serving chocolate and confectionary manufacturers.
Cost: $59.00
Frequency: Monthly
Founded in 1944
Printed in 4 colors on glossy stock

10020 Capital Press
Press Publishing Company
PO Box 2048
Salem, OR 97308-2048

503-364-4431
800-882-6789
Fax: 503-370-4383
E-Mail: eshein@capitalpress.com
Home Page: www.capitalpress.com

Carl Sampson, Managing Editor
Elaine Shein, Editor/Publisher
Mike O'Brien, Circulation/General Manager

For the agricultural and forest community of the Pacific Northwest.
Cost: $44.00
60 Pages
Frequency: Weekly
Circulation: 37000
Founded in 1928
Printed in 4 colors on newsprint stock

10021 Carnetec
1415 N Dayton
Chicago, IL 60622

312-266-3311
Fax: 312-266-3363
E-Mail: annica@meatingplace.com
Home Page: www.carnetec.com

Ryan Pfister, Product Manager

Spanish language magazine reaching executives in the Latin American meat and poultry processing industry. Helps improve the manufacturing process, equipment, sanitation, safety and technology.

10022 Carrot Country
Columbia Publishing
8405 Ahtanum Rd
Yakima, WA 98903-9432

509-248-2452
800-900-2452
Fax: 509-248-4056
Home Page: www.carrotcountry.com

Brent Clement, Editor/Publisher
Mike Stoker, Publisher

Includes information on carrot production, grower and shipper feature stories, carrot research, new varieties, market reports, spot reports on overseas production and marketing and other key issues and trends of interest to US and Canadian carrot growers.
Cost: $10.00
Frequency: Quarterly
Circulation: 2700
Founded in 1975
Printed in 4 colors on glossy stock

10023 Cereal Chemistry
AACC International
3340 Pilot Knob Rd
Eagan, MN 55121-2055

651-454-7250
800-328-7560
Fax: 651-454-0766
Home Page: www.scientificsocieties.org

Steven Nelson, VP
Bernie Bruinsma, Chair of Board
Laura Hansen, Treasurer

The premier international archival journal in cereal science. No other journal surpasses it in the quantity and quality of juried, original research. Research presented explores raw materials, processes, products utilizing cereal, oilseeds, and pulses, as well as analytical procedures, technological tests and fundamental research in the cereals area.
Cost: $79.00
Frequency: Bi-Monthly
Circulation: 3539
Founded in 1915

10024 Cereal Foods World
AACC International
3340 Pilot Knob Rd
Eagan, MN 55121-2055

651-454-7250
800-328-7560
Fax: 651-454-0766
Home Page: www.scientificsocieties.org

Steven Nelson, VP
Bernie Bruinsma, Chair of Board
Laura Hansen, Treasurer

A leading source of information on grain-based food science, technology, and new product development. Includes articles that focus on advances in grain-based food science and the application of these advances to product development and current food production practices.
Cost: $48.00
Frequency: Bi-Monthly
Circulation: 4500
ISSN: 0146-6283
Founded in 1956

10025 Cheers
Jobson Publishing Corporation
100 Avenue of the Americas
Suite 9
New York, NY 10013-1678

212-274-7000
Fax: 212-431-0500
Home Page: www.jobson.com

Michael J Tansey, CEO

Every issue is designed to help on-premise operators enhance the profitability of their beverage operations.

10026 Cheese Market News
Quarne Publishing
PO Box 620244
Middleton, WI 53562

608-831-6002
Fax: 608-831-1004
E-Mail: squarne@cheesemarketnews.com
Home Page: www.cheesemarketnews.com

Susan Quarne, Publisher
Kate Sander, Editorial Director

Weekly trade news for the nation's cheese and dairy/deli business
Cost: $105.00
16 Pages
Frequency: Weekly
Circulation: 2200
ISSN: 0891-1509
Founded in 1981
Mailing list available for rent: 2200 names at $500 per M
Printed in 4 colors on newsprint stock

10027 Chef
Talcott Communications Corporation
20 W Kinzie St
Suite 1200
Chicago, IL 60654-5827

312-849-2220
800-229-1967
Fax: 312-849-2174
Home Page: www.talcott.com

Daniel Von Rabenau, Executive Director
Robert S Benes, Senior Editor

Information on food production and presentation, includes chef profiles, trend studies, marketing information and restaurant profiles.
Cost: $32.00
Circulation: 40,000
ISSN: 1087-061X
Founded in 1956
Printed in 4 colors on glossy stock

10028 Chemical and Pharmaceutical Press
C&P Press
90 william strret
5th Floor
New York, NY 10106-2899

212-326-6760
800-544-7377
Fax: 646-733-6010
Home Page: www.cppress.com

Dr. Mary Conway, Executive Editor
Bron Zienkiewicz, Sales/Marketing
Sonia Tighe, Publisher

Supplies chemical information to professionals involved with the sale, application, storage or regulations of agricultural or ornamental and turf pesticides. Information is available in either reference book form or on computer disc. Complete product labels, MSDS's and indexes are included.
Founded in 1984

10029 Choices
Agricultural & Applied Economics Association
555 E Wells Street
Suite 1100
Milwaukee, WI 53202

414-918-3190
Fax: 414-276-3349
E-Mail: info@aaea.org
Home Page: www.choicesmagazine.org

Walter J Armbruster, Editor
James Novak, Associate Editor

Provides current coverage regarding economic implications of food, farm, resource, or rural community issues directed toward a broad audience. Publishes thematic groupings of papers and individual papers.
Frequency: Quarterly
ISSN: 0886-5558
Founded in 1910
Printed in 4 colors on glossy stock

10030 Citograph
Western Agricultural Publishing Company
4969 E Clinton Way
#104
Fresno, CA 93727-1549

559-252-7000
Fax: 559-252-7387
E-Mail: westag@psn.com
Home Page: www.westapub.com

Paul Baltimore, Publisher

The oldest continuous citrus-specific publication in the world. Stories centering on all aspects of citrus production from planting to harvest and all maintenance in between. Lemons, limes, oranges, avocados — all citrus is included.

10031 Citrus & Vegetable Magazine
Vance Publishing
400 Knightsbridge Parkway
Lincolnshire, IL 60069

847-634-2600
Fax: 847-634-4379
E-Mail: info@vancepublishing.com
Home Page: www.vancepublishing.com

William C Vance, Chairman
Peggy Walker, President

Delivers profitable production and management strategies to commerical citrus and vegetable growers in Florida.
Cost: $45.00
Frequency: Monthly
Circulation: 12004

10032 CleanRooms Magazine
PennWell Publishing Company
98 Spit Brook Rd
Suite 100
Nashua, NH 03062-5737

603-891-0123
Fax: 603-891-9294
E-Mail: info@pennwell.com
Home Page: www.pennwell.com

Christine Shaw, VP
James Enos, Publisher
Adam Japker, CEO

Serves the contamination control and ultrapure materials and process industries. Written for readers in the microelectronics, pharmaceutical, biotech, health care, food processing and other

user industries. Provides technology and business news and new product listings.
Founded in 1987

10033 Communications in Soil Science and Plant Analysis
Marcel Dekker
270 Madison Avenue
New York, NY 10016
212-696-9000
800-228-1160
Fax: 212-685-4540
Home Page: www.dekker.com
Harry A Mills, Editor
Marcel Dekker, President
All aspects of soil science and crop production in all climates.
Cost: $567.00
120 Pages
Circulation: 23500
ISSN: 0010-3624
Founded in 1963

10034 Concession Profession
National Association of Concessoinaires
35 East Wacker Drive
Suite 1816
Chicago, IL 60601-2270
312-236-3858
Fax: 312-236-7809
E-Mail: info@naconline.org
Home Page: www.naconline.org
Social Media: Facebook, LinkedIn
Charles A Winans, Executive Director
Susan M Cross, Communications Director
Barbara Aslan, Membership Services Manager
The NAC member magazine devoted to the recreational and leisuretime food and beverage concessions industry, featuring news briefs, feature articles, association news and advertising opportunities.
800 Members
Founded in 1944

10035 Concession Professsion
National Association of Concessionaires
35 E Wacker Dr
Suite 1816
Chicago, IL 60601-2270
312-236-3858
Fax: 312-236-7809
E-Mail: scross@NAConline.org
Home Page: www.naconline.org
Social Media: Facebook, LinkedIn
John Evans, Jr., President
Jeff Scudillo, President-Elect
Ron Krueger II, Board Chairman
Devoted to the recreational and leisuretime food and beverage concessions industry, featuring news briefs, feature articles, association news and advertising opportunities.
Frequency: Bi-Annual
Printed in 4 colors

10036 Convenience Store Decisions
Harbor Communications
19111 Detroit Road
Suite 201
Rocky River, OH 44116
440-250-1538
Fax: 440-333-1892
Home Page: www.csdecisions.com
Jeff Donohoe, Owner
Jay Gordon, Editor
For buyers, directors, field managers, owners and executives in the convenience store business. Free to qualified subscribers.
180 Pages
Frequency: Monthly
Circulation: 40000+
Founded in 1892

10037 Cooking for Profit
CP Publishing
PO Box 267
Fond du Lac, WI 54936
920-923-3700
Fax: 920-923-6805
E-Mail: comments@cookingforprofit.com
Home Page: www.cookingforprofit.com
Colleen Phalen, Editor-in-Chief/Publisher
Paid subscription trade magazine targeted to foodservice owners, managers and chefs. Each month features current trends in food preparation with step-by-step recipes and photographs; effective management techniques; and the latest in foodservice equipment — all written by industry experts. Also features in-depth profiles of a successful foodservice operation.
Cost: $26.00
28 Pages
Frequency: Monthly
Circulation: 75000
Founded in 1932
Printed in 4 colors on glossy stock

10038 Cooperative Grocer
361 East College Street
Iowa City, IA 52240-267
319-466-9029
Fax: 866-600-4588
E-Mail: dave@cooperativegrocer.com
Home Page: cooperativegrocer.coop
Dave Gutknecht, Editor
Dan Nordley, Publisher
Don McLemore, CEO
Trade magazine by and for people working with consumer cooperative grocery stores.
Founded in 1999

10039 Cotton Farming
One Grower Publishing
5118 Park Avenue
Suite 111
Memphis, TN 38117-5710
901-767-4020
Fax: 901-767-4026
E-Mail: throton@onegrower.com
Home Page: www.cottonfarming.com
Social Media: Twitter, Flickr
Lia Guthrie, Publisher/VP
Tommy Horton, Editor
Serving the industry, providing the latest news and technology information.
Frequency: Monthly
Founded in 1937

10040 Country Folks
Lee Publications
6113 State Highway 5
PO Box 121
Palatine Bridge, NY 13428-121
518-673-2269
800-218-5586
Fax: 518-673-3245
E-Mail: subscriptions@leepub.com
Home Page: www.countryfolks.com
Frederick Lee, Publisher
Marjorie Struckle, Editor
Bruce Button, President
Janet Button, Marketing Manager
Tom Mahoney, Sales Manager
Agricultural news from national, state and local levels. Some features on farm and agricultural industry, rural interest, etc.
Cost: $12.00
75 Pages
Frequency: Weekly
Circulation: 27000

10041 Country Living
Arens Corporation
PO Box 69
Covington, OH 45318-0069
937-473-2020
Fax: 937-473-2500
E-Mail: garyg@arenspub.com
Home Page: www.arenspub.com
Gary Godfrey, Publisher/President
Don Selanders, Sales Manager
Connie Didier, Circulation Manager
Current news and features devoted to the agricultural industry.
Cost: $1395.00
Frequency: Monthly
Circulation: 17500
Founded in 1950

10042 Country Woman
Reiman Publications
5400 S 60th St
Greendale, WI 53129-1404
414-423-0100
800-344-6913
Fax: 414-423-1143
E-Mail: editors@countrywomanmagazine.com
Home Page: www.countrywomanmagazine.com
Barbara Newton, President
Ann Kaiser, Editor
Offers recipes, stories, profiles and articles pertaining to the country woman.
Cost: $14.98
68 Pages
Founded in 1965

10043 Critical Reviews in Food and Nutrition
CRC Press
6000 Broken Sound Pkwy NW
Suite 300
Boca Raton, FL 33487-5704
561-994-0555
800-272-7737
Fax: 561-989-9732
E-Mail: techsupport@crcpress.com
Home Page: www.crcpress.com
Emmett Dages, CEO
Susan Lee, Editor
Founded in 1913

10044 Culinary Trends
Culinary Trends Publications
6285 Spring St
Number 107
Long Beach, CA 90808
714-826-9188
Fax: 714-826-0333
E-Mail: Editor@culinarytrends.net
Home Page: www.culinarytrends.net
Fred Mensigna, Publisher
Jean Hutchins, Director
Information for food and beverage managers along with managers of hotels and restaurants.
Cost: $21.00
Frequency: Quarterly
Circulation: 10000
Founded in 1993

10045 DDBC News
Dairy, Deli, Bakery Council of Southern California
PO Box 1872
Whittier, CA 90609
562-947-7016
Fax: 562-947-7872
E-Mail: delicouncil@earthlink.net
Home Page: www.ddbcsc.com
Bob Dreffler, CEO
Dave Daniel, Editor
Susan Steele, Circulation Manager

Serves the deli, dairy, bakery and meat industry.
Cost: $25.00
Frequency: Monthly
Circulation: 5000
ISSN: 0011-7862
Founded in 1960
Printed in 4 colors on glossy stock

10046 DFA Leader
Dairy Farmers of America
10220 N Ambassador Dr
Kansas City, MO 64153-1367

816-801-6455
888-332-6455
Fax: 816-801-6456
E-Mail: webmail@dfamilk.com
Home Page: www.dfamilk.com
Social Media: Facebook, Twitter, LinkedIn, YouTube

Randy Mooney, Chairman of the Board
George Mertens, Vice Chairman
Tom Croner, Secretary/ Treasurer

Provides members with information about DFA and the dairy industry, along with features on members whose innovative ideas are worth emulating.
Frequency: Quarterly
Founded in 1998

10047 Dairy Foods Magazine
Business News Publishing
1050 IL Route 83
Suite 200
Bensenville, IL 60106-1096

630-377-5909
Fax: 630-227-0527
Home Page: www.dairyfoods.com

Katie Rotella, Manager
David Phillips, Executive Editor
Marina Mayer, Executive Editor
Scott Wolters, Director
Barb Szatko, Regional Sales Manager

Dairy Foods serves the dairy industry by analyzing and reporting on technologies trends and issues and how they affest North America's processors of milk, cheese, frozen deserts and cultured products. Current issues and qualification forms for free subsciptions will be available to attendees. Dairy Foods is part of BNP Food Group.
Frequency: Weekly
Circulation: 20000
Founded in 1926
Printed in 4 colors on glossy stock

10048 Dairy Today
AgWeb
30 S 15th Street
Suite 900
Philadelphia, PA 19102-4826

215-557-8900
Fax: 215-568-4436
E-Mail: jdickrell@farmjournal.com
Home Page: www.agweb.com

Bill Newham, Publisher
Jim Dickrell, Editor

A trusted source of dairy information for its subscriber base of US dairy producers.
Frequency: Monthly
Circulation: 65000
Founded in 1989

10049 Dairy, Food and Environmental Sanitation
International Association for Food Protection
6200 Aurora Ave
Suite 200W
Urbandale, IA 50322-2864

515-276-3344
800-369-6337
Fax: 515-276-8655
E-Mail: info@foodprotection.org
Home Page: www.foodprotection.org

David W Tharp, Executive Director
Vickie Lewandowski, VP
Isabel Walls, Secretary

Published as the general membership publication by the International Association for Food Protection, each issue contains referred articles on applied research, applications of current technology and general interest subjects for food safety professionals. Regular features include industry and association news, an industry related product section and a calendar of meetings, seminars and workshops.Updates of government regulations and sanitary design is also featured. All members receive DFES.
Cost: $227.00
Frequency: Monthly
Circulation: 3000
ISSN: 1043-3546
Mailing list available for rent: 3000+ names at $150 per M
Printed in 4 colors

10050 Dietitian's Edge
Rodman Publishing
70 Hilltop Rd
3rd Floor
Ramsey, NJ 07446-1150

201-825-2552
Fax: 201-825-0553
E-Mail: info@rodpub.com
Home Page: www.nutraceuticalsworld.com

Bob Rodman Zilenziger Jr, President
Matt Montgomery, VP

10051 Drovers Journal
Vance Publishing
400 Knightsbridge Parkway
Lincolnshire, IL 60069

847-634-2600
Fax: 847-634-4379
E-Mail: info@vancepublishing.com
Home Page: www.vancepublishing.com

William C Vance, Chairman
Peggy Walker, President

Recognized as the beef industry leader for more than 30 years, valued for its management, production and marketing information.
Cost: $60.00
Frequency: Monthly
Circulation: 91715
Founded in 1937

10052 Eastern Milk Producer
Eastern Milk Producers Cooperative Association
PO Box 6966
Syracuse, NY 13217-6966

315-437-1225

Bob Stronach, Editor
Trish Stokes, Production Manager

Communicates to members of the association dairy issues, farm issues, association events and policy.
Cost: $13.00
20 Pages
Frequency: Monthly

10053 Egg Industry
WATT Publishing Company
303 N Main Street
Suite 500
Rockford, IL 61101

815-966-5400
Fax: 815-966-6416
E-Mail: tokeefe@wattnet.net
Home Page: www.wattnet.com

James Watt, Chairman/CEO
Greg Watt, President/COO
Terrence O'Keefe, Editor

Reports on trends, production practices, processing, marketing and economics, and is regarded as the standard for information on current issues, personalities and emerging technology. A pivotal source of news, data and information for innovators and decision-makers in the buying centers of companies producing eggs and further-processed products.
Cost: $36.00
Frequency: Monthly
Circulation: 1553
Founded in 1917

10054 El Restaurante Mexicano
Maiden Name Press
PO Box 2249
Oak Park, IL 60303

708-267-0023
E-Mail: kfurore@restmex.com
Home Page: www.restmex.com
Social Media: Facebook

A quarterly magazine featuring industry specific food news, features restaurant profiles and new product information for personnel of restaurants serving mexican/southwestern menu items nationwide.
Cost: $108.00
Circulation: 27000
ISSN: 1091-5885
Founded in 1997
Printed in 4 colors on glossy stock

10055 Europe Agriculture and Trade Report
USDA Economic Research Service
1800 M Street NW
Washington, DC 20036-5831

202-203-3935
800-999-6779
E-Mail: service@ers.usda.gov
Home Page: www.ers.usda.gov

Susan Offutt, Administrator
Leslee Lowstuter, Central Operations Staff Director
Thomas McDonald, Publishing/Communications
Suchada Langley, Global Agricultural Markets Branch
Ron Bianchi, Associate Director

An important resource for agribusiness and researchers.
Circulation: 2000

10056 Executive Guide to World Poultry Trends
WATT Publishing Company
303 N Main Street
Suite 500
Rockford, IL 61101

815-966-5400
Fax: 815-966-6416
Home Page: www.wattnet.com

James Watt, Chairman/CEO
Greg Watt, President/COO
Jeff Swanson, Publishing Director

Packed with facts and figures that give a full overview of the world poultry market.
Frequency: Annual

10057 FEDA News & Views
Foodservice Equipment Distributors Association

2250 Point Boulevard
Suite 200
Elgin, IL 60123

224-293-6500
Fax: 224-293-6505
E-Mail: feda@feda.com
Home Page: www.feda.com

Ray Herrick, EVP/Publisher/Editor-in-Chief
Stacy Ward, Editor

Keep updated with the latest issues within the dealer community. Well-read among the FEDA membership, and includes stories on dealers, letters to the editor on industry issues, the President's message, and other items of interes to both dealers and manufacturer.
Cost: $160.00
Frequency: Bi-Monthly
Founded in 1933

10058 FFA New Horizons
National FFA Organization
6060 FFA Drive
Indianapolis, IN 46268

317-802-4235
800-772-0939
E-Mail: newhorizons@ffa.org
Home Page: www.ffanewhorizons.org

Jessy Yancey, Association Editor
Christina Carden, Associate Production Director
Julie Woodard, FFA Publications Manager

The official member magazine of the FFA is published bimonthly and mailed to more than 525,000 readers. Each issue contains information about agricultural education, career possibilities, chapter and individual accomplishments and news on FFA. Now available online.
100 Pages
ISSN: 1069-806x
Founded in 1928
Printed in 4 colors

10059 Fancy Foods & Culinary Products
Talcott Communications Corporation
20 W Kinzie St
12th Floor
Chicago, IL 60654-5827

312-849-2220
888-545-3676
Fax: 312-849-2174
E-Mail: fancyfood@talcott.com
Home Page: www.talcott.com

Daniel Von Rabenau, Executive Director
Natalie Hamm Noblitt, Editor

Specialty food stores, department store specialty food departments, gift departments, confection stores, independent groceries and supermarket chains, gift basket retailers, cookware and kitchen stores, cooking school gift stores, cheese stores, coffee and tea stores brokers/represenatives/manufacturers/importers/wholesalers/distributors and others allied to the field.
Cost: $26.00
Frequency: Monthly
Circulation: 23,000
ISSN: 1521-5156
Founded in 1983

10060 Fastline Productions
PO Box 248
Buckner, KY 40010-0248

502-222-0146
800-626-6409
Fax: 502-222-0615
E-Mail: custcare@fastline.com
Home Page: www.fastlinepub.com

William G Howard, President
Crysten Minzenberger, Marketing Director

Nationwide and regional picture buying guides for the farming industry.
Cost: $144.00
Frequency: Monthly
Founded in 1978

10061 Feedback
Meat & Livestock Australia
1401 K Street NW
Suite 602
Washington, DC 20005

202-521-2551
Fax: 202-521-2699
E-Mail: info@mla.com.au
Home Page: www.mla.com.au
Social Media: Facebook, Twitter, YouTube

Don Heatley, Chairman
David Palmer, Managing Director
Bernie Bindon, Director
Chris Hudson, Director

The red meat and livestock industry journal, featuring on-farm updates and market information for the north, south-east and south-west areas of Australia.
30000 Members
Frequency: 9x Yearly
Founded in 1998

10062 Fine Foods Magazine
Griffin Publishing Group
201 Oak Street
Suite A
Pembroke, MA 02359

781-294-4700
Fax: 781-829-0134
E-Mail: griffinbooks@earthlink.com
Home Page: www.griffenpublishing.com

Stephen Griffin, President

A magazine offering information on the Northeast specialty, ethnic and prepared foods business.
Frequency: Monthly

10063 Fisheries
American Fisheries Society
5410 Grosvenor Ln
Suite 110
Bethesda, MD 20814-2199

301-897-8616
Fax: 301-897-8096
Home Page: www.fisheries.org

Gus Rassam, Executive Director
Myra Merritt, Office Administrator

Peer reviewed articles that address contemporary issues and problems, techniques, philosophies and other areas of interest to the general fisheries profession. Monthly features include letters, meeting notices, book listings and reviews, environmental essays and organization profiles.
Cost: $106.00
50 Pages
Frequency: Monthly
Circulation: 9800
Founded in 1870
Mailing list available for rent: 8500 names at $250 per M

10064 Food & Drug Packaging
Stagnito Communications
210 S 5th Street
Suite 202
Saint Charles, IL 60174

847-205-5660
Fax: 630-377-1678
Home Page: www.fdp.com

Edwin Landon, Publisher
Vince Miconi, Advertising Production Manager
George Misko, Regional Sales Manager
Catherine Wynn, Sales Manager

Food and Drug Packaging serves industries engaged in packaging food, beverages, pharmaceuticals, cosmetics and consulting/engineering firms.
Frequency: Monthly
Circulation: 75140
Founded in 1959

10065 Food Aid Needs Assessment
US Department of Agriculture
200 Independence Ave SW
Washington, DC 20201-0007

202-690-7650
Fax: 202-219-0942

Gene Mathia, Branch Chief

This annual report assesses the food situation in 60 developing countries. Most of the data are presented by region; crisis countries are covered individually.

10066 Food Arts Magazine
M Shanken Communications
387 Park Ave S
8th Floor
New York, NY 10016-8872

212-684-4224
Fax: 212-684-5424
Home Page: www.cigaraficionado.com

Marvin Shanken, Publisher
Julie Mautner, President

A publication serving the fine food service industry is edited for restauranteurs, chefs, food and beverage directors and caterers.
Frequency: Monthly
Circulation: 50000
Founded in 1972
Printed in 4 colors on glossy stock

10067 Food Channel Trend Wire
Noble & Associates
2155 W Chesterfield Blvd
Springfield, MO 65807-8650

417-875-5000
800-545-4087
Fax: 417-875-5051
Home Page: www.noble.net

Robert Noble, CEO

Designed to make the food industry professionals food trend experts. Encapsulates trend information from more than 125 food and consumer publications each month. Provides insights into emerging food trends.
Cost: $195.00
Circulation: 2000

10068 Food Distribution Research Society News
Silesia Companies
PO Box 441110
Fort Washington, MD 20749-1110

301-292-1970
Fax: 706-542-0739
Home Page: www.fdrs.ag.utk.edu

John Strovinsky, Publisher
Wojciech Florkowski, Editor

Food distribution research society encourages research, serves as an information clearinghouse and encourages implementation of research. The Society organizes conferences, and meetings for industry, academic and government leaders within the food industry sector.
Cost: $65.00
16 Pages
Circulation: 150
Founded in 1960
Mailing list available for rent: 150 names

10069 Food Engineering
Business News Publishing Company

1050 IL Route 83
Suite 200
Bensenville, IL 60106-1096

630-377-5909
Fax: 947-763-9538
Home Page: www.foodengineering.com
Social Media: Facebook, Twitter

Patrick Young, Publisher & District Sales Manager
Paul Kelly, District Sales Manager
Brian Gronowski, District Sales Manager
Wayne Wiggins Jr, District Sales Manager
Carolyn Dress, Inside & Online Sales Manager

A publication offering information on all facets of the food industry, from ingredients to food packaging and processing.
Cost: $64.00
Frequency: Monthly
Circulation: 15000
Founded in 1926

10070 Food Management
Penton Publishing Company
1300 E 9th St
Suite 1020
Cleveland, OH 44114-1514

216-861-0360
Fax: 216-696-0836
E-Mail: information@penton.com
Home Page: www.food-management.com

Preston L Vice, CFO
Adrian Meredith, CFO
David Brodowski, General Manager
Denise Walde, Senior Production Manager

Combines the industry's most comprehensive circulation package with an editorial mix that emphasizes business management strategies and ideas, food trends and recipes and in-depth news analysis in a contemporary feature magazine.
90 Pages
Frequency: Monthly
Circulation: 47899
ISSN: 0091-018X
Founded in 1892
Printed in 4 colors on glossy stock

10071 Food Processing
555 W Pierce Road
Suite 301
Itasca, IL 60143

630-467-1300
Fax: 630-467-1124
Home Page: www.foodprocessing.com

Lily Modjeski, Sales Manager
Patricia Donatiu, Circulation Manager
Dave Fusaro, Editor-in-Chief
Steve Slankis, Group Publisher
Anetta Gauthier, Production Manager

Information on food equipment, packaging material and other supplies and services.
Frequency: Monthly
Circulation: 65000
Founded in 1938

10072 Food Product Design
Virgo Publishing LLC
3300 N Central Ave
Suite 300
Phoenix, AZ 85012-2532

480-675-9925
Fax: 480-990-0819
E-Mail: peggyj@vpico.com
Home Page: www.foodproductdesign.com

Jenny Bolton, President

Publication distributed to product development professionals and corporate management executives at food and beverage manufacturing and foodservice companies.
Circulation: 20000
Founded in 1986
Printed in on glossy stock

10073 Food Production/Management Magazine
CTI Publications
2823 Benson Mill Rd
Sparks Glencoe, MD 21152-9575

410-308-2080
Fax: 410-308-2079
Home Page: www.ctipubs.com

Randy Gerstmyer, Publisher/Editor

Serves those in the canning, glasspacking, freezing and aseptic packaged food industries. Readers include corporate executives and staff personnel responsible for direction of management, operations, production, engineering, packaging, research and development. Accepts advertising.
Cost: $40.00
32 Pages
Frequency: Monthly
Circulation: 4482
ISSN: 0191-6181
Founded in 1878
Mailing list available for rent: 4500 names at $675 per M
Printed in 4 colors on glossy stock

10074 Food Protection Trends
International Association for Food Protection
6200 Aurora Ave
Suite 200W
Urbandale, IA 50322-2864

515-276-3344
800-369-6337
Fax: 515-276-8655
E-Mail: info@foodprotection.org
Home Page: www.foodprotection.org

David W Tharp, Executive Director
Vickie Lewandowski, VP
Isabel Walls, Secretary

Each issue contains articles on applied research, applications of current technology and general interest subjects for food safety professionals. Regular features include industry and association news, and industy-related products section and a calendar of meetings, seminars and workshops. Updates of government regulations and sanitary design are also featured.
Cost: $227.00
Frequency: Monthly
Circulation: 9000
ISBN: 0-362028-X -
Founded in 1911
Mailing list available for rent
Printed in 4 colors on glossy stock

10075 Food Quality
Wiley-Blackwell
111 River Street
Hoboken, NJ 07030-5774

856-380-4117
800-322-9373
E-Mail: custsrvd@starrcorp.com
Home Page: www.foodquality.com

The established authority in the market as the science-based news magazinw focused on quality, assurance, safety, and security in the food and beverage industry.
Cost: $195.00
66 Pages
Frequency: Monthly
Circulation: 21000
ISSN: 1092-7514
Founded in 1994
Mailing list available for rent: 15,000 names at $195 per M
Printed in 4 colors on glossy stock

10076 Food Safety Magazine
Target Group
1945 W Mountain St
Glendale, CA 91201-1258

818-842-4777
Fax: 818-769-2939
E-Mail: info@foodsafetymagazine.com
Home Page: www.foodsafetymagazine.com
Social Media: Facebook, Twitter, LinkedIn

Don Meeker, Owner/CEO
Andrea Karges, Circulation Manager
Barbara VanRenterghem, Editorial Director

Publicaton is for food safety and quality assurance/control professionals at food and beverage processors, food service companies and agri-food laboratories worldwide. These decision makers implement science-based food safety strategies and systems to prevent, control, test and verify that chemical, microbiological and physical hazards do not enter the food supply.
Cost: $19.00
Frequency: Monthly
Circulation: 20,000
Founded in 1980

10077 Food Service Equipment & Supplies Specialist
Reed Business Information
2000 Clearwater Dr
Oak Brook, IL 60523-8809
630-574-0825
Fax: 630-288-8781
Home Page: www.reedbusiness.com

Jeff Greisch, President
Maureen Slocum, Publisher
Judy Erickson, Group Circulation Manager
Stuart Whayman, CFO

Magazine for professionals who specify, sell and distribute food service equipment, supplies and furnishings.
Cost: $69.95
Frequency: Monthly
Circulation: 22,740
Founded in 1948
Printed in 4 colors on glossy stock

10078 Food Technology
Institute of Food Technologists
525 W Van Buren
Suite 1000
Chicago, IL 60607-3842

312-782-8424
Fax: 312-782-8348
E-Mail: info@ift.org
Home Page: www.ift.org

Bob Swientek, Editor-in-Chief

The leading publication addressing all facets of food science and technology. Its in-depth and balance coverage includes the latest research developments, industry news, consumer product innovations, and professional opportunities.
Cost: $190.00
Frequency: Monthly
Circulation: 18000
ISSN: 0015-6639

10079 Food Trade News
Best-Met Publishing
5537 Twin Knolls Rd
Suite 438
Columbia, MD 21045-3270

410-730-5013
Fax: 410-740-4680
E-Mail: jmetzger@best-met.com
Home Page: www.best-met.com

Jeff Metzger, Publisher
Terri Maloney, Editor

Nina Weiland, VP
Beth Pripstein, Office Manager
Richard J Bestany, Advertising Director

A magazine aimed at the players in the food distribution industry.

10080 Food World
Best-Met Publishing Company
5537 Twin Knolls Rd
Suite 438
Columbia, MD 21045-3270

410-730-5013
Fax: 410-740-4680
E-Mail: jmetzger@best-met.com
Home Page: www.best-met.com

Jeff Metzger, Publisher
Jeffrey W. Metzger, Publisher
Beth Pripstein, Office Manager
Richard J. Bestany, President

Regional food trade newspaper covering the Mid-Atlantic market
Frequency: Monthly
Printed in on newsprint stock

10081 FoodService and Hospitality
Kostuch Publications
Two City Place Drive
Suite 200 PMB 2004
Saint Louis ario, MO 63141-3P6

314-812-2565
Fax: 314-835-0044
E-Mail: wgilchri@ix.netcom.com
Home Page: www.foodserviceworld.com

Mitch Kostuch, President
Rosanna Caira, Publisher/Editor
Wendy Gilchrist, Director Business Development
Phoebe Fung, Owner
Owen Knowlton, Director

Canada's only national specialty business magazine reaching owners,managers and buyers in all sections of the foodservice industry.
Cost: $50.00
Frequency: Monthly
Circulation: 25,000
Printed in on glossy stock

10082 FoodTalk
Pike & Fischer
PO Box 25277
Alexandria, VA 22313

703-548-3146
Fax: 703-548-3017
E-Mail: info@setantapublishing.com
Home Page: www.setantapublishing.com

Declan Couroy, Editor/Publisher

Sanitation tips for food workers.
Cost: $120.00
Frequency: Quarterly
Circulation: 5000
Founded in 1987
Printed in 2 colors

10083 Foodservice Equipment & Supplies
Reed Europe
2000 Clearwter Drive
Oak Brook, IL 60523

630-320-7000
800-446-6551
Fax: 630-288-8282
Home Page: www.fesmag.com

Maureen Slocum, Publisher
Mitchell Schechter, Editor-in-Chief

Edited for readers outside the US who are employed in firms that manufacture food and beverage products.
Frequency: Monthly
Founded in 1948

10084 For Fish Farmers
Mississippi Cooperative Extension Service
PO Box 9690
Mississippi State, MS 39762-9690

662-325-3174
Fax: 601-857-2358

Martin W Bunson, Editor

A magazine offering information that addresses the concerns of fish farmers.
Frequency: Quarterly

10085 Fresh Cup Magazine
Fresh Cup Publishing Company
537 SE Ash Street Suite 300
PO Box 14827
Portland, OR 97293

503-236-2587
800-868-5866
Fax: 503-236-3165
E-Mail: freshcup@freshcup.com
Home Page: www.freshcup.com

Ward Barbee, Publisher
Jan Weigel, President
Julie Beals, Marketing
Bill Berninger, Circulation Manager
Natalie Caceres, Marketing Coordinator
Cost: $60.00
80 Pages
Frequency: Monthly
Circulation: 15000
Founded in 1992
Printed in 4 colors on glossy stock

10086 Fresh Cut Magazine
Great American Publishing
75 Applewood Drive, Suite A
PO Box 128
Sparta, MI 49345

616-887-9008
Fax: 616-887-2666
Home Page: www.freshcut.com

Matt McCallum, Publisher
Scott Christie, Managing Editor

The only publication covering all sectors of the international value-added produce industry. Growers, processors, retailers and foodservice professionals all find information relating to their day-to-day operations in the pages of Fresh Cut magazine.
Cost: $15.00
40 Pages
Frequency: Monthly
ISSN: 1072-2831
Founded in 1993
Printed in 4 colors on glossy stock

10087 Frozen Food Digest, Inc.
271 Madison Ave
Suite 1402-A
New York, NY 10016-1014

212-557-8600
Fax: 212-986-9868
E-Mail: saulbeckffdqffaol.com

Saul Beck, President/Hall of Fame Member
Cost: $45.00
Circulation: 16000
Founded in 1985

10088 Fruit Country
Clintron Publishing
PO Box 30998
Spokane, WA 99223-3016

509-248-2452
800-869-7923
Fax: 509-458-3547
Home Page: www.agpowermag.com

Clintke Withers, Publisher
John M Dahlin, Editor
Tyson Graff, Circualtion Manager

Written for and about growers, their operations and their needs. Stories on growers and shippers, developments and trends in the fruit industry, human interest stories and politics, new products, chemicals and supplies, avant garde management techniques, cultural practices and tips on profitability. Advertising equipment and services to the fruit industry and distribution system.
Cost: $12.00
Frequency: Monthly
Circulation: 11500
Founded in 1976

10089 Futures Magazine
Futures Magazine
111 W Jackson Blvd
7th Floor
Chicago, IL 60604-4139

312-977-0999
Fax: 312-846-4638
E-Mail: dcollins@futuresmag.com
Home Page: www.aip.com

Steve Lown, Manager
Daniel P Collins, Editor
Gabby Mouizerh, Production Manager
Steve Lown, Manager

Agriculture commodities charted by various technical studies, plus analysis.
Cost: $39.00
24 Pages
Frequency: Monthly
Circulation: 60,000
Founded in 1972

10090 Game Bird Gazette
Allen Publishing
970 East
3300 South
Salt Lake City, UT 84106

801-485-1299
E-Mail: memberservices@gamebird.com
Home Page: www.gamebird.com

George Allen, Editor

All about keeping, breeding and raising pheasants, quails, partridges, peacocks, doves, pigeons, waterfowl and gamebirds of all kinds.
Cost: $23.95
45 Pages
Frequency: Monthly
Founded in 1940

10091 Gourmet Retailer Magazine
3301 Ponce De Leon Blvd
Suite 300
Coral Gables, FL 33134-7273

305-273-0437
800-765-9797
Fax: 305-446-2868
E-Mail: info@gourmetretailer.com
Home Page: www.gourmetretailer.com

Edward Loeb, Publisher
Michael Keighley, Editorial Director
Laura Everage, Managing Editor
Shari Levenson, Marketing Manager
Kathy Colwell, Advertising Production Manager
Frequency: Monthly
Circulation: 25000
Founded in 1979

10092 Grape Grower
Western Agricultural Publishing Company
4969 E Clinton Way
#104
Fresno, CA 93727-1549

559-252-7000
888-382-9772
Fax: 559-252-7387
E-Mail: westag@westagpubco.com
Home Page: www.westagpubco.com

Paul Baltimore, Publisher
Randy Bailey, Editor
Robert Fujimoto, Assistant Editor

The West's most widely read authority on the cultivation of table grapes, raising grapes and wine grapes. All aspects of production are covered with the most current university, government and private research.
Mailing list available for rent

10093 Greenhouse Product News

Scranton Gillette Communications
3030 W Salt Creek Lane
Suite 201
Arlington Heights, IL 60005-5025

847-391-1000
Fax: 847-390-0408
E-Mail: bbellew@sgcmail.com
Home Page: www.gpnmag.com

Bob Bellew, VP/Group Publisher
Tim Hodson, Editorial Director
Jasmina Radjevic, Managing Editor

Features the industry's leading Buyer's Guide directory, the PGR table and the bookstore are just a few of the reasons the industry's buyers keep coming back.
Cost: $30.00
Frequency: Monthly
Circulation: 19000
Mailing list available for rent: 19,000 names

10094 Griffin Report: Market Studies

Griffin Publishing Company
201 Oak Street
Pembroke, MA 02359

781-829-4700
Fax: 781-829-0134
Home Page: www.griffinreport.com

Mike Berger, Editor
Kevin Griffin, Vice President
Karen Harty, Vice President
Julie Mignosa, Office Manager

This report offers statistics on the leading chain and multi-store independent grocers in the northeast.
Cost: $42.00
Frequency: Monthly
Founded in 1966
Mailing list available for rent: 10,000 names at $350 per M
Printed in on newsprint stock

10095 Grocers Report

Super Markets Productions
PO Box 6124
San Rafael, CA 94903-124

415-479-0211
Fax: 415-479-0211

Lori Abrams, CEO
JM Adlman, Publisher
Joan Adams, Circulation Manager

Offers information on the retail grocery industry.
Cost: $10.00
Frequency: Quarterly
Circulation: 18000
Founded in 1978
Printed in 4 colors on glossy stock

10096 Growertalks Magazine

Ball Publishing
622 Town Road
PO Box 1660
West Chicago, IL 60186

630-231-3675
888-888-0013
Fax: 630-231-5254
E-Mail: info@ballpublishing.com
Home Page: www.growertalks.com

Chris Beytes, Editor/Publisher
Jennifer Zurko, Associate Editor

Specializes in the publishing of horticulture information, primarily related to floriculture production and marketing.
Frequency: Monthly
Circulation: 12000
Founded in 1937

10097 Growing for Market

Fairplain Publications
PO Box 3747
Lawrence, KS 66046

785-748-0605
800-307-8949
Fax: 785-748-0609
E-Mail: growing4market@earthlink.net
Home Page: www.growingformarket.com

Lynn Byczynski, Editor/Publisher
Roger Yepsen, Author

A monthly periodical for small-scale farmers, market gardeners, and grower of vegetables, fruits, herbs and flowers. Offers news and ideas about organic production, pest control, tools and equipment and direct marketing.
Cost: $ 30.00
20 Pages
Frequency: Monthly
Circulation: 4000
ISSN: 1060-9296
Founded in 1992

10098 Guernsey Breeders' Journal

Purebred Publishing Inc
7616 Slate Ridge Blvd
Reynoldsburg, OH 43068-3126

614-575-4620
Fax: 614-864-5614
E-Mail: khenson@usguernsey.com
Home Page: www.usguernsey.com

Katie Henson, Editor

The oldest dairy breed magazine published by a US breed organization. Contents range across current management trends, breeder stories and events withing the Guernsey industry in the US and worldwide.
Cost: $20.00
Frequency: 10x Yearly

10099 Health Products Business

Cygnus Publishing
445 Braod Hollow Road
Melville, NY 11747-3669

631-845-2700
800-308-6397
Fax: 631-845-2723
E-Mail: micheal.schiavitz@cygnuspub.com
Home Page: www.healthproducts.com

Bruce Ceftakes, Publisher/Sales
Micheal Schiavetta, Editor
Christian Biscuiti, Assistant Editor

This is a trade magazine that covers news and trends in the natural health products industry including vitamins, herbs, dietary supplements and other products. Publishes annual raw materials directory and purchasing guide, as well as other speciality issues. Targets natural products retail store owners, buyers and managers. Qualified subsciption only.
ISSN: 0149-9602

10100 Herb Quarterly

EGW Publishing Company
4075 Papazian Way
Suite 204
Fremont, CA 94538-4372

510-668-0268
Fax: 510-668-0280
E-Mail: info@egw.com
Home Page: www.herbquarterly.com

Chris Slaughter, VP
Jennifer Barrett, Editor

Each issue introduces readers to new herbs and fascinating herbal lore; provides tips on hard to grow varieties and medicinals; showcases gardens from around the world; and tempts the palate with seasonal menus and tantalizing recipes built around herbs and edible flowers.
Cost: $19.97
68 Pages
Frequency: Quarterly
Circulation: 36753
Founded in 1978
Printed in 4 colors on matte stock

10101 Hereford World

American Hereford Association
PO Box 014059
Kansas City, MO 64101

816-842-3757
Fax: 816-842-6931
E-Mail: aha@hereford.org
Home Page: www.hereford.org

Craig Huffhines, Executive VP

Trade magazine for breeders of registered Hereford cattle. Articles and columns provide in-depth information about the beef industry.
Frequency: Monthly
Circulation: 9500
Founded in 1742

10102 Honey Producer

American Honey Producers Association
PO Box 162
Power, MT 59468

406-463-2227
Fax: 406-463-2583
E-Mail: beeguy4jensen@yahoo.com
Home Page: www.americanhoneyproducers.org

Lyle Johnston, Editor

Highlights current industry news, publishes submitted articles from the scientific community, informs of legal battles being fought in Washington,'DC, provides cmoplete AHPA convention schedules.
Cost: $20.00
Frequency: Quarterly
ISSN: 1091-3394

10103 Hospitality News Featuring Coffee Talk

PO Box 21027
Salem, OR 97307-1027

503-390-8343
800-685-1932
Fax: 503-390-8344
E-Mail: eds@hospnews.com
Home Page: www.hospnews.com

Kerri R Goodman-Small, Publisher
Miles Small, Editor-in-Chief

Serves restaurants, lodges, health care facilities, schools, clubs,casinos, caterers, and culinary and beverage marketplaces nationally.
Circulation: 30000
ISSN: 1084-2551
Founded in 1988
Printed in on newsprint stock

10104 Hotline Magazine

International Food Service Executives
4955 Miller Street
Suite 107
Wheat Ridge, CO 80033

800-893-5499
E-Mail: hq@ifsea.com
Home Page: www.ifsea.com
Social Media: Facebook

Barbara Sadler, Chairwoman
Fred Wright, Chair-Elect
David Orosz, Treasurer

IFSEA's membership magazine that focuses on all things IFSEA and food service. Also available electronically.
Frequency: Bi-Annually

10105 IAFIS Reporter
International Assn of Food Industry Suppliers
1451 Dolley Madison Boulevard
Suite 101
McLean, VA 22101
703-761-2600
Fax: 703-761-4334
E-Mail: info@fpsa.org
Home Page: www.fpsa.org
George Melnykovich, President
Andrew Drennan, VP
Happenings and trends in the food and dairy industry.
Founded in 1983

10106 IGA Grocergram
Pace Communications
PO Box 13607
Greensboro, NC 27415-3607
336-378-6065
Fax. 336-275-2864
E-Mail: info@pacecommunications.com
Home Page: www.pacecommunications.com
Bonnie McElveen, CEO
Wes Isley, Chief Financial Officer
Leigh Klee, Chief Financial Officer
Ed Calfo, Executive Vice President
Edited for IGA retailers and wholesalers throughout the US. Focuses on training, merchandising, display, promotion, and advertising and marketing techniques. Also addresses financial and personnel management and innovations in store engineering and development.
Cost: $24.00
Frequency: Monthly

10107 Import Statistics
Association of Food Industries
3301 State Route 66
Suite 205, Building C
Neptune, NJ 07753-2705
732-922-3008
Fax: 732-922-3590
E-Mail: info@afius.org
Home Page: www.naooa.org
Robert Bauer, President
Cost: $40.00
Frequency: Annual+
Circulation: 1200
Founded in 1906

10108 In Good Taste
Specialty Coffee Association of America
302 5th Avenue
5th Floor
New York, NY 10001
646-733-6000
800-544-7377
Fax: 646-733-6010
Home Page: www.cppress.com
Ted R Lingle, Editor
This periodical offers business, promotional and educational advice in the areas of cultivation, processing, preparation and marketing of specialty coffee.
Frequency: Monthly

10109 Industria Alimenticia
Stagnito Communications
155 Pfingster Road
Suite 205
Deerfield, IL 60015
847-205-5660
Fax: 847-205-5680
Home Page: www.stagnito.com
Harry Stagnito, President
Elsa Rico, Director/Editor
Mary Mazur, Circulation
Information source for Latin American food and beverage processors
Cost: $85.00
Printed in 4 colors on glossy stock

10110 Inform
American Oil Chemists' Society
2710 S. Boulder
PO Box 17190
Urbana, IL 61802-6996
217-359-2344
Fax: 217-351-8091
E-Mail: general@aocs.org
Home Page: www.aocs.org
Social Media: Facebook, Twitter
E. Dumelin, President
D. Myers, Vice President
S. Erhan, Secretary
T. Kemper, Treasurer
The monthly business and scientific magazine of AOCS, providing international news on fats, oils, surfactants, detergents, and related materials.
Cost: $10.00
5400 Members
Frequency: Membership Dues Vary
Founded in 1909

10111 Insider Magazine
American Correctional Food Service Affiliates
210 N Glenoaks Blvd
Suite C
Burbank, CA 91502
818-843-6608
Fax: 818-843-7423
Home Page: www.acfsa.org
Jon Nichols, Executive Director
Contains news pertaining to correctional foodservice activities of the Association and fellow members, as well as industry-specific educational articles.
56 Pages
Frequency: Quarterly
Circulation: 1500
Founded in 1969
Printed in 4 colors on glossy stock

10112 Institute of Food and Nutrition
HealthComm International
9770 44th Avenue
N.W. Suite 100
Gig Harbor, WA 98332
253-851-3943
800-692-9400
Fax: 253-851-9749
E-Mail: info@metagenics.com
Home Page: www.metagenics.com
Jeffrey Bland, President/Chief Science Officer
Jeffrey Katke, Chairman of the Board/CEO
Carl Mickey Moore, Co-Chief Operating Officer
Janice Moore, Co-Chief Operating Officer
Matthew Tripp, VP of Research & Development
Founded in 1983

10113 Intermountain Retailer
Utah Food Industry Association
1578 W 1700 S
Suite 100
Salt Lake City, UT 84104-3489
801-973-9517
800-423-6636
Fax: 801-972-8712
Home Page: www.utfood.com
James Olsen, President
Meik Rapp, Editor
This annual guide offers information on brokers in Utah that are serving the retail food industry.
Cost: $25.00
48 Pages
Frequency: Annual+
Circulation: 1200
Founded in 1896

10114 International Journal of Food Engineering
Reed Business Information
360 Park Ave S
New York, NY 10010-1737
646-746-6400
Fax: 646-756-7583
E-Mail: corporatecommunications@reedbusiness.com
Home Page: www.reedbusiness.com
John Poulin, CEO
Peter Havens, Publisher
James Reed, Owner
Devoted to engineering disciplines related to processing foods. The areas of interest include heat, mass transfer and fluid flow in food processing; food microstructure development and characterization; application of artificial intelligence in food research; food biotechnology, and more.
Frequency: Annual
Circulation: 15,000

10115 International Product Alert
Marketing Intelligence Service
482 N Main St
Canandaigua, NY 14424-1049
585-374-6326
800-836-5710
Fax: 585-374-5217
Home Page: www.productscan.com
Tom Vierhile, Executive Editor
Sherry Meeker-Barton, Editor-in-Chief
Reports the introduction of new food, beverage, health & beauty aides, household & pet products outside of North America. Reports include full product descriptions and selected illustrations of products and advertising backup.
Cost: $700.00

10116 Italian Cooking and Living
Italian Culinary Institute
302 5th Avenue
9th Floor
New York, NY 10001
212-899-9057
888-742-2373
Fax: 212-889-3907
E-Mail: irene@italiancookingandliving.com
Home Page: www.italiancookingandliving.com
Paolo Villoresi, Publisher
Irene De Gasparis, Associate Publisher
Charles Pennino, Owner
American magazine devoted to Italian cuisine/culture/travel
Founded in 2001

10117 JAOCS
American Oil Chemists' Society

2710 S. Boulder
PO Box 17190
Urbana, IL 61802-6996

217-359-2344
Fax: 217-351-8091
E-Mail: general@aocs.org
Home Page: www.aocs.org
Social Media: Facebook, Twitter

E. Dumelin, President
D. Myers, Vice President
S. Erhan, Secretary
T. Kemper, Treasurer

The leading source for technical papers related to the fats and oils industries. A peer-reviewed journal devoted to fundamental and practical research, production, processing, packaging and distribution in the growing field of fats, oils, proteins and other related substances.
Cost: $10.00
5400 Members
Frequency: Membership Dues Vary
Founded in 1909

10118 Journal of Animal Science
American Society of Animal Science
2441 Village Green Pl
Champaign, IL 61822-7676

217-356-9050
Fax: 217-398-4119
E-Mail: susanp@assochq.org
Home Page: www.asas.org

Meghan Wulster-Radcli, Executive Director
Susan Pollack, Managing Editor/Editorial Director

The official journal of the American Society of Animal Science, JAS publishes results of original research in Genetics, Growth and Physiology, Nutrition, Production, Products, and Special Topics. JAS consistently ranks in the top tier in the category of Agriculture, Dairy, and Animal Sciences
Frequency: Monthly
Circulation: 3500
ISSN: 0021-8812
Founded in 1908
Printed in on glossy stock

10119 Journal of Business Logistics
Council of Supply Chain Management Professionals
333 E Butterfield Rd
Suite 140
Lombard, IL 60148-5617

630-574-0985
Fax: 630-574-0989
E-Mail: cscmpadmin@cscmp.org
Home Page: www.cscmp.org
Social Media: Facebook, Twitter, LinkedIn, YouTube

Rick Blasgen, President & CEO
Sue Paulson, Executive Assistant
Nancy Nix, Chair
Rick J. Jackson, Chair-Elect
Theodore Stank, Secretary & Treasurer

Provides a forum for the dissemination of original thoughts, research, and best practices within the logistics and supply chain arenas. Provides readers with new and helpful information, new supply chain management theory or techniques, research generalizations, creative views and sytheses of dispersed concepts, and articles in subject areas which have significant current impact on thought and practice in logistics and supply chain management.
10000 Members
Founded in 1963

10120 Journal of Child Nutrition & Management
School Nutrition Association
120 Waterfront St
Suite 300
National Harbor, MD 20745-1142

301-686-3100
800-877-8822
Fax: 301-686-3115
E-Mail: servicecenter@schoolnutrition.org
Home Page: www.schoolnutrition.org

Helen Phillips, President
Sandy Ford, President-Elect
Leah Schmidt, Vice President
Beth Taylor, Secretary/Treasurer

Features up-to-date research articles on significant issues affecting child nutrition and school foodservice management. Provides timely and relevant insights into the many challenges and opportunities surrounding child nutrition programs. Information facilitates decision-making and serves as evidence of how effective child nutrition programs are.
55000 Members
Frequency: Monthly
Founded in 1946

10121 Journal of Dairy Science
American Dairy Science Association
2441 Village Green Pl
Champaign, IL 61822-7676

217-356-5146
Fax: 217-398-4119
E-Mail: adsa@assochq.org
Home Page: www.adsa.org

Michael Mangino, Senior Editor
Sharon Frick, Secretary
Diane Hekken, Secretary
Richard Pursley, Secretary, Treasurer

Research in dairy cattle production and dairy food products.
Cost: $110.00
Frequency: Monthly
Founded in 1990

10122 Journal of Environmental Quality
American Society of Agronomy
5585 Guilford Road
Madison, WI 53711-1086

608-273-8080
Fax: 608-273-2021
E-Mail: headquarters@agronomy.org
Home Page: www.agronomy.org
Social Media: Facebook, Twitter, LinkedIn

Newell Kitchen, President
Kenneth Barbarick, President-Elect

Papers are grouped by subject matter and cover water, soil, and atmospheric research as it relates to agriculture and the environment.
11000 Members
Founded in 1907

10123 Journal of Food Distribution Research
Food Distribution Research Society
PO Box 441110
Fort Washington, MD 20749

301-292-1970
Fax: 301-292-1787
E-Mail: Jonathan_baros@ncsu.edu
Home Page: fdrs.tamu.edu

John Park, President
Ron Rainey, President-Elect
Kellie Raper, Secretary/ Treasurer
Jennifer Dennis, Director
Stan Ernst, Director

Publishes articles that cover every aspect of our modern food system. JFDR is a peer reviewed journal published exlusively online.
Frequency: 3x Yearly

10124 Journal of Food Protection
International Association for Food Protection
6200 Aurora Ave
Suite 200W
Des Moines, IA 50322-2864

515-276-3344
800-369-6337
Fax: 515-276-8655
E-Mail: info@foodprotection.org
Home Page: www.foodprotection.org
Social Media: Facebook, Twitter, LinkedIn

Isabel Walls, President
Katherine M.J. Swanson, President-Elect
Don Schaffner, Vice President
Don Zink, Secretary
David W. Tharp, Executive Director

Each issue contains scientific research and authoritative review articles reporting on a variety of topics in food science pertaining to food safety and quality.
3400 Members
Founded in 1911

10125 Journal of Food Science
Institute of Food Technologists
525 W Van Buren St
Suite 1000
Chicago, IL 60607-3842

312-782-8424
Fax: 312-782-8348
E-Mail: info@ift.org
Home Page: www.ift.org

Barbara Byrd Keenan, Executive VP
Daryl B Lund, Editor-in-Chief

IFT's premier science journal, containing peer-reviewed reports of original research and critical reviews of all aspects of food science.
Frequency: 9x Yearly
Founded in 1936

10126 Journal of Foodservice Business Research
Taylor & Francis Group LLC
325 Chestnut St
Suite 800
Philadelphia, PA 19106-2614

215-625-8900
800-354-1420
Fax: 215-625-2940
Home Page: www.taylorandfrancis.com

Kevin Bradley, President

Features articles from international experts in various disciplines, including management, marketing, finance, law, food technology, nutrition, psychology, information systems, anthropology, human resources, and more.
Frequency: Quarterly

10127 Journal of Hospitality & Tourism Research
CHRIE
2810 N Parham Road
Suite 230
Richmond, VA 23294

804-346-4800
Fax: 804-346-5009
E-Mail: info@chrie.org
Home Page: www.chrie.org
Social Media: Facebook, Twitter, LinkedIn

Susan Fournier, President
Josette Katz, Vice President
Chris Roberts, Secretary
John Drysdale, Treasurer
Kathy McCarty, CEO

Offers high quality refereed articles which advance the knowledge base of the hospitality field. Articles on empirical research, theoretical developments and innovative methodologies are guided by an editor and a review board consisting of leading hospitality and tourism researchers.
Frequency: Quarterly

10128 Journal of Hospitality and Tourism Education
CHRIE
2810 N Parham Road
Suite 230
Richmond, VA 23294

804-346-4800
Fax: 804-346-5009
E-Mail: info@chrie.org
Home Page: www.chrie.org
Social Media: Facebook, Twitter, LinkedIn

Susan Fournier, President
Josette Katz, Vice President
Chris Roberts, Secretary
John Drysdale, Treasurer
Kathy McCarty, CEO

A refereed, interdisciplinary quarterly magazine designed to serve the needs of all levels of hospitality and tourism education through the presentation of issues and opinions pertinent to the field.
Frequency: Quarterly

10129 Journal of Natural Resources & Life Sciences Education
American Society of Agronomy
5585 Guilford Road
Madison, WI 53711-1086

608-273-8080
Fax: 608-273-2021
E-Mail: headquarters@agronomy.org
Home Page: www.agronomy.org
Social Media: Facebook, Twitter, LinkedIn

Newell Kitchen, President
Kenneth Barbarick, President-Elect

Today's educators look here for the latest teaching ideas in the life sciences, natural resources, and agriculture. Articles are written by and for educators in extension, universities, industry, administration, and grades k-12.
11000 Members
Founded in 1907

10130 Journal of Packaging
Institute of Packaging Professionals
Ste 123
1833 Centre Point Cir
Naperville, IL 60563-4848

630-544-5050
800-432-4085
Fax: 630-544-5005
E-Mail: info@iopp.org
Home Page: www.iopp.org
Social Media: Facebook, Twitter, LinkedIn, YouTube

Edwin Landon, Executive Director
Patrick Farrey, General Manager
Stan Zelesnik, Director Education
Robert DePauw, Finance Manager
Kelly Staley, Member Services Manager

Serves the entire packaging community's educational needs. The Journal is a resource for professional analysis of all packaging issues. Available online only, it is a forum that covers issues in depth.
Frequency: Daily ,

10131 Journal of Plant Registrations
Crop Science Society of America
5585 Guilford Rd.
Madison, WI 53711-1086

608-273-8080
Fax: 608-273-2021
Home Page: www.crops.org
Social Media: Facebook, Twitter, LinkedIn

Maria Gallo, President
Jeffrey Volenec, President-Elect
Ellen G.M. Bergfeld, CEO

Publishes cultivar, germplasm, parental line, genetic stock, and mapping population registration manuscripts.
4700 Members
Frequency: Monthly
Founded in 1955

10132 Journal of Shellfish Research
National Shellfisheries Association
National Marine Fisheries Service Laboratory
Oxford, MD 21654

631-653-6327
Fax: 631-653-6327
E-Mail: webmaster@shellfish.org
Home Page: www.shellfish.org

R. LeRoy Creswell, President
Christopher V. Davis, President-Elect
George E. Flimlin, VP & Program Chair
Marta Gomez-Chiarri, Secretary
Sandra E. Shumway, Editor

The international journal promoting all aspects of shellfish research.
1M Members
Frequency: Monthly
Founded in 1908

10133 Journal of Sugar Beet Research
Beet Sugar Development Foundation
800 Grant Street
Suite 300
Denver, CO 80203

303-832-4460
Fax: 303-832-4468
E-Mail: aa@bsdf-assbt.org
Home Page: www.bsdf-assbt.org

Fosters all phases of sugarbeet and beet sugar research, promotes the dissemination of relevant scientific knowledge, and strives to maintain high standards of ethics, and to cooperate with other organizations having objectives beneficial to the beet sugar industry.
Frequency: Quarterly
ISSN: 0899-1502

10134 Journal of Surfactants and Detergents (JSD)
American Oil Chemists' Society
2710 S. Boulder
PO Box 17190
Urbana, IL 61802-6996

217-359-2344
Fax: 217-351-8091
E-Mail: general@aocs.org
Home Page: www.aocs.org
Social Media: Facebook, Twitter

E. Dumelin, President
D. Myers, Vice President
S. Erhan, Secretary
T. Kemper, Treasurer

A scientific journal dedicated to the practical and theoretical aspects of oleochemical and petrochemical surfactants, soaps, and detergents.
Cost: $10.00
5400 Members
Frequency: Membership Dues Vary
Founded in 1909

10135 Journal of the American Dietetic Association
Elsevier Health Publishing
1600 John F Kennedy Blvd
Suite 1800
Philadelphia, PA 19103-2398

215-239-3900
Fax: 215-239-3990
E-Mail:
journal@eatright.org/elspcs@elsevier.com
Home Page: www.elsevier.com

Michael Hansen, CEO
Jason Swift, Editor
Ryan Lipscomb, Department Editor
Linda Van Horn, Editor-in-Chief

A premier source for the practice and science of food, nutrition, and dietetics. The Journal focuses on advancing professional knowledge across the range of research and practice issues such as: nutritional science, medical nutrition therapy, public health nutrition, food science and biotechnology, foodservice systems, leadership and management and dietetics education.
Cost: $229.00
Frequency: Monthly/Subscription
ISSN: 0002-8223

10136 Journal of the American Oil Chemists' Society
American Oil Chemists' Society
2710 S Boulder
Urbana, IL 61802-6996

217-359-2344
Fax: 217-351-8091
E-Mail: general@aocs.org
Home Page: www.aocs.org

Jody Schonfeld, Publications Director
Pam Landman, Journals Coordinator
Kimmy Farris, Production Editor

The leading source for technical papers related to the fats and oils industries. A peer-reviewed journal devoted to fundamental and practical research, production, processing, packaging and distribution in the growing field of fats, oils, proteins and other related substances
Frequency: Monthly
Founded in 1947

10137 Journal of the American Pomological Society
103 Tyson Building
University Park, PA 16802-4200

814-863-6163
Fax: 814-237-3407
E-Mail: bardenja@vt.edu
Home Page: www.americanpomological.org

Dr John Barden, Editor

The Journal contains refereed technical articles and a wide variety of applied articles relating to fruit varieties.
Frequency: Quarterly/Free to Members

10138 Journal of the American Society for Horticultural Science
American Society for Horticultural Science
113 S West St
Suite 200
Alexandria, VA 22314-2851

703-836-4606
Fax: 703-836-2024
E-Mail: journal@ashs.org
Home Page: www.ashs.org

Michael Neff, Publisher/Executive Director
Katharine J Lewis, Managing Editor

A peer-reviewed publication of results of orginal research on horticultural plants and their products or directly related research areas. Its prime function is communication of mission-oriented, fundamental research to other researchers.
Cost: $55.00
Frequency: Bi-Monthly/Members Rate
ISSN: 0003-1062
Founded in 1903
Mailing list available for rent: 2500 names at $100 per M

10139 Journal of the Association of Food and Dru g Officials
Association of Food and Drug Officials

2550 Kingston Rd
Suite 311
York, PA 17402-3734

717-757-2888
Fax: 717-755-8089
E-Mail: afdo@afdo.org
Home Page: www.afdo.org

Denise Rooney, Executive Director

News and the latest legislation for the Food and Drug Association.
Founded in 1937

10140 Kosher Today
1428 36th street
219
Brooklyn, NY 11218

718-854-4460
Fax: 718-854-4474
E-Mail: info@koshertoday.com
Home Page: www.koshertoday.com/

Menachem Lubinsky, CEO
Bill Springer, Account Executive
Christine Salmon, Account Executive
Karyn Gilbert, Marketing Manager

Covers the kosher food industry.
28 Pages
Frequency: Weekly
Circulation: 20000
Founded in 1984
Printed in 4 colors on newsprint stock

10141 Lean Trimmings Prime
National Meat Association
1970 Broadway
Suite 825
Oakland, CA 94612

510-763-1533
Fax: 510-763-6186
E-Mail: staff@nmaonline.org
Home Page: www.nmaonline.org

Robert Rebholtz, Chairman
Larry Vad, President
Marty Evanson, Vice President
Mike Hesse, Secretary
Brian Coelho, Treasurer

Brings a broad range of topics and essential association information to the membership and beyond.
600 Members
Frequency: Weekly
Founded in 1946

10142 Lipids
American Oil Chemists' Society
2710 S. Boulder
PO Box 17190
Urbana, IL 61802-6996

217-359-2344
Fax: 217-351-8091
E-Mail: general@aocs.org
Home Page: www.aocs.org
Social Media: Facebook, Twitter

E. Dumelin, President
D. Myers, Vice President
S. Erhan, Secretary
T. Kemper, Treasurer

A premier journal in the lipid field, published monthly, featuring full-length original research articles, short communications, methods papers, and review articles on timely topics.
Cost: $10.00
5400 Members
Frequency: Membership Dues Vary
Founded in 1909

10143 Logistics Journal
Transportation Intermediaries Association
1625 Prince St
Suite 200
Alexandria, VA 22314-2883

703-299-5700
Fax: 703-836-0123
E-Mail: info@tianet.org
Home Page: www.tianet.org

Robert Voltmann, President
Nancy King, Marketing Manager

Education and policy organization for North American transportation intermediaries. The only national association representing the interests of all third party transportation service providers. Members include logistics management firms, property brokers, perishable commodities brokers, freight forwarders, intermodal marketers and ocean and air forwarders.
Frequency: Monthly
Circulation: 1000
Founded in 1978

10144 Manufacturing Confectioner
MC Publishing
711 W Water Street
PO Box 266
Princeton, WI 54968

920-295-6969
Fax: 920-295-6843
E-Mail: mcinfo@gomc.com
Home Page: www.gomc.com

Eric Schmoyer, President
Michael Allured, Publisher/Editor-in-Chief

The worldwide business, marketing and technology journal of the candy, chocolate, confectionery, cough drop, and sweet baked goods industry. Provides in-depth coverage of news, industry statistics, sales and marketing, ingredients, equipment and services.
Cost: $65.00
Frequency: Monthly
Founded in 1921

10145 Meat Marketing and Technology
Marketing & Technology Group
1415 N Dayton St
Suite 115
Chicago, IL 60642-7033

312-266-3311
Fax: 312-266-3363
E-Mail: webinars@meatingplace.com
Home Page: www.meatingplace.com

Mark Lefens, Owner
Dan Allen, Editor-at-Large
Jim Goldberg, VP Sales/Marketing
John Gregerson, Editor
Deborah Silver, Managing Editor

Provides information on meat processing, retail, slaughtering and fabricating and rendering.
Cost: $40.00
Frequency: Monthly
Circulation: 20,009
Founded in 1993
Printed in 4 colors on glossy stock

10146 Meat Science
American Meat Science Association
2441 Village Green Pl
Champaign, IL 61822-7676

800-517-AMSA
Fax: 888-205-5834
Fax: 217-356-5370
E-Mail: information@meatscience.org
Home Page: www.meatscience.org

William Mikel, President
Scott J. Eilert, President Elect
Casey B. Frye, Treasurer

The official journal of AMSA. Peer-reviewed resource is the best way to stay current on the latest research in meat science across all meat products and in all aspects of meat production and processing. Available online or in print.

10147 Meat and Poultry
Sosland Publishing Company
4800 Main St
Suite 100
Kansas City, MO 64112-2513

816-756-1000
Fax: 816-756-0494
E-Mail: web@sosland.com
Home Page: www.sosland.com

Gordon Davidson, President
Mark Sabo, President
Joel Crews, Editor

Serves meat, poultry and seafood processors, wholesalers-distrubuters, slaughterers, fabricators, cutters, meat buyers, and rendering and pet food manufacturers.
Cost: $42.00
Frequency: Monthly
Circulation: 21,000
Founded in 1955
Printed in 4 colors on glossy stock

10148 Midwest Food Service News
Pinnacle Publishing
316 N Michigan Avenue
Suite 300
Chicago, IL 60601

312-272-2401
800-493-4867
Fax: 312-960-4106
E-Mail: pinpub@ragan.com
Home Page:
www.midwestfoodservicenews.com

Keith Hadley, Publisher
Joanne Cooper, Editor

Communicates directly and exclusively with restaurant and food service operations in Indiana, Kentucky, Michigan, Ohio, Pennsylvania and West Virginia.
52 Pages
Frequency: Bi-Monthly
Circulation: 40,000
Founded in 1982
Printed in 4 colors on newsprint stock

10149 Military Grocer
Downey Communications
4800 Montgomery Lane
Suite 710
Bethesda, MD 20814-3461

301-718-7600
Fax: 301-718-7604

Richard T Carroll, Publisher
Loretta M Downey, CEO

Serves defense commissary employees worldwide.
Frequency: 5 per year
ISSN: 1058-8620
Printed in 4 colors on glossy stock

10150 Milk and Liquid Food Transporter
Glen Street Publications
W4652 Glen Street
Appletone, WI 54913

920-749-4880
Fax: 920-749-4877
Home Page: www.glenstreet.com

Jane Plout, Publisher

Information for owners, operators and managers of companies that haul milk or other liquid foods in sanitary or food grade tankers. Publication covers maintenance, association news, state of the industry, business management, and activities of independent haulers.
16 Pages
Frequency: Monthly
Circulation: 4768
Founded in 1960
Printed in 4 colors on glossy stock

10151 Milling Journal
3065 Pershing Court
Decatur, IL 62526

217-877-9660
800-728-7511
Fax: 217-877-6647
E-Mail: webmaster@grainnet.com
Home Page: www.grainnet.com

Jim Camillo, Editor
Mark Avery, Publisher
Kay Merryfield, Circulation Manager
Jody Sexton, Editorial Assistant
Deb Coontz, Sales Manager

Mailed to all active AOM members in the US, Canada, and internationally, including wheat flour/corn mills and corn/oilseed processors in US and Canada.
Frequency: Quarterly
Circulation: 1217

10152 Milling and Baking News
Sosland Publishing Company
4800 Main St
Suite 100
Kansas City, MO 64112-2513

816-756-1000
Fax: 816-756-0494
E-Mail: web@sosland.com
Home Page: www.sosland.com

Gordon Davidson, President
Joshua Sosland, Editor
Neil N Sosland, Executive Editor
Eric Schroeder, Managing Editor
Jeff Gelski, Associate Editor

This magazine is aimed at baking, milling and food processing industries.
Cost: $52.00
Frequency: Monthly
Circulation: 4032

10153 Missouri Grocer
Missouri Grocers Association
315 North Ken Avenue
Springfield, MO 65802-6213

417-831-6667
Fax: 417-831-3907
E-Mail: cmcmillian@missourigrocers.com
Home Page: www.missourigrocers.com
Social Media: Facebook

Erick Taylor, President
John Porter, Vice President
Mike Beal, Treasurer
Linda Ryan, Chairperson

Referred to as the pre-convention issue. Highlights the exhibitors, sponsors, awardees and events that will be taking place during the Annual Convention and Merchandising Show.

10154 Modern Baking
Penton Media
330 N Wabash
Suite 2300
Chicago, IL 60611

E-Mail: katie.martin@penton.com
Home Page: modern-baking.com

Jerry Rymont, VP Penton Food Group
Katie Martin, Chief Editor
Matt Reynolds, Group Managing Editor

Provides the latest product and service information to the $20 billion in-store and $14.9 billion retail baking and toodservice markets.
Cost: $75.00
112 Pages
Frequency: Monthly
Circulation: 27000
ISSN: 0897-6201
Founded in 1987
Mailing list available for rent: 27,000 names
Printed in 4 colors on glossy stock

10155 Modern Brewery Age
Business Journals
50 Day Street
S Norwalk, CT 06854-3100

203-853-6015
Fax: 203-852-8175
E-Mail: pete@breweryage.com
Home Page: www.breweryage.com

Peter VK Reid, Editor
Britton Jones, President
Arthur Heilman, Circulation Manager

A magazine for the wholesale and brewing industry.
Cost: $95.00
Frequency: Quarterly
Founded in 1933

10156 Modern Brewery Age: Tabloid Edition
Business Journals
50 Day Street
#5550
Norwalk, CT 06854-3100

203-853-6015
Fax: 203-852-8175

Peter VK Reid, Editor

Brewery industry tabloid.
Cost: $85.00
Frequency: Weekly

10157 Monthly Price Review
Urner Barry Publications
PO Box 389
Toms River, NJ 08754

732-240-5330
800-932-0617
Fax: 732-341-0891
E-Mail: help@urnerbarry.com
Home Page: www.urnerbarry.com

Paul B Brown Jr, President
Karen Mick, Circulation Director

Lists price of eggs, turkeys, chickens, fowl, butter, margarine, cheese and concentrated milk products for the month and compares the monthly average to the previous year.
Cost: $149.00
Frequency: Monthly
Circulation: 310
ISSN: 0566-3628
Founded in 1858

10158 Mushroom News
American Mushroom Institute
1284 Gap Newport Pike
Suite 2
Avondale, PA 19311-9503

610-268-7483
Fax: 610-268-8015
E-Mail: mushroomnews@kennett.net
Home Page: www.americanmushroom.org

Sara Manning, Manager
Mark Wach, Chairman
Laura Phelps, President
Bill Barber, Publisher

For growers and scientists in mushroom production.
Cost: $275.00
Frequency: Monthly
Founded in 1956

10159 NACS Magazine
National Association of Convenience Stores
1600 Duke St
Suite 700
Alexandria, VA 22314-3436

703-684-3600
Fax: 703-836-4564
E-Mail: bmoyer@nacsonline.com
Home Page: www.nacsonline.com

Hank Armour, President
Ben Moyer, Advertising Manager

Delivered to all members, this magazine reaches a majority of the convenience and petroleum marketing channel of trade.
Frequency: Monthly
Circulation: 27,632

10160 NAEDA Equipment Dealer
North American Equipment Dealers Association
1195 Smizer Mill Rd
Fenton, MO 63026-3480

636-349-5000
Fax: 636-349-5443
E-Mail: naeda@naeda.com
Home Page: www.naeda.com
Social Media: Twitter, LinkedIn

Paul Kindinger, President/CEO
Michael Williams, VP, Government Relations/Treasurer
Terry Leath, Executive Assistant
Roger Gjellstad, First Vice Chair
Lester Killebrew, Chairman

Featuring articles about successful dealers, new products, new technology, industry news, insurance loss control solutions and top management tips.
Cost: $40.00
5000 Members
Frequency: Monthly
Circulation: 9,500
Founded in 1900
Printed in 4 colors on glossy stock

10161 NWAC News: Thad Cochran National Warmwater Aquaculture Center
127 Experiment Station Road
Stoneville, MS 38776-197

662-686-3273
Fax: 662-686-3320
E-Mail: javery@drec.msstate.edu
Home Page: www.msstate.edu/dept/tcnwac

Jimmy Avery, Editor
J Lee, CEO/President
Frequency: Monthly
Circulation: 1200
Founded in 1998
Printed in 3 colors on matte stock

10162 Nation's Restaurant News
Lebhar-Friedman
425 Park Ave
Suite 6
New York, NY 10022-3526

212-756-5088
Fax: 212-838-9487
E-Mail: info@lf.com
Home Page: www.lf.com

Heather Martin, Manager
Michael Cardillo, VP Sales

Serves commercial and onsite food service and lodging establishments including restaurants, schools, universities, hospitals, nursing homes and other health and welfare facilities, hotels and motels with food service, government installations, clubs and other related firms.
Cost: $44.95
Circulation: 85999
Founded in 1925
Mailing list available for rent: 100,000 names at $100 per M
Printed in 4 colors on matte stock

10163 National Confectionery Sales Association Annual Journal
Teresa Tarantino
10225 Berea Road, Suite B
Cleveland, OH 44102
216-631-8200
Fax: 216-631-8210
E-Mail: ttarantino@mail.propressinc.com
Home Page: www.candyhalloffame.com
Tony Rufrano, President
Steve Foster, Executive Director
Annual membership listing and biographies of Candy Hall of Fame industees.
Cost: $25.00
76 Pages
Founded in 1997
Printed in 4 colors on matte stock

10164 National Culinary Review
American Culinary Federation
180 Center Place Way
St Augustine, FL 32095-8859
904-824-4468
800-624-9458
Fax: 904-825-4758
E-Mail: acf@acfchefs.net
Home Page: www.acfchefs.org
Heidi Cramb, Executive Director
A monthly magazine that is circulated by paid subscription. ACF members receive this publication as a benefit of membership in the American Culinary Federation. The National Culinary Review contains chef-tested recipes, industry news, and culinary techniques and is an educational resource for everyone interested in food preparation.
Cost: $50.00
Frequency: 10x Yearly
Circulation: 25,000
Founded in 1932

10165 National Farmers Union News
National Farmers Union
11900 E Cornell Ave
Aurora, CO 80014-6201
303-368-7300
800-347-1961
Fax: 303-368-1390
Home Page: www.nfu.org
David Frederickson, President
Rae Price, Publications Editor
A grass roots structure in which policy positions are initiated locally. The goal is to sustain and strengthen family farm and ranch agriculture.
Cost: $30.00
Frequency: Monthly
Founded in 1902

10166 National Fisherman
Diversified Business Communications
PO Box 7437
Portland, ME 04112-7437
207-842-5600
Fax: 207-842-5503
E-Mail: info@divcom.com
Home Page: www.divbusiness.com
Nancy Hasselback, President/CEO
Randy Le Shane, VP Operations
Nancy Gelette, VP Operations
Stephnie Wendel, Circulation Manager
The most widely read commercial fishing magazine and the only commercial fishing publication providing national coverage and national circulation.
Cost: $22.95
Frequency: Monthly
Circulation: 38000
ISSN: 0027-9250
Founded in 1949

10167 National Food Processors Association State Legislative Report
National Food Processors Association
1350 Eye St NW
Suite 300
Washington, DC 20005-3377
202-393-0890
800-355-0983
Fax: 202-639-5932
Home Page: www.nfpa-food.org
Cal Dooley, CEO
Lisa Weddig, Executive Director
Tammy Morgan, Contact
Frequency: Monthly
Circulation: 345
Founded in 1901

10168 National Grocer
National Grocers Association
1005 N Glebe Rd
Suite 250
Arlington, VA 22201-5758
703-516-0700
Fax: 703-516-0115
Home Page: www.ngacampus.com
Thomas A Zaucha, President
Frank Dipasquale, Senior Vice President
Source of information on all aspects of the retail/wholesale grocery industry.
Cost: $5.00
Frequency: Quarterly
Circulation: 7000
Founded in 1992

10169 National Hog Farmer
7900 International Dr
Suite 300
Minneapolis, MN 55425-2562
952-851-4710
Fax: 952-851-4601
Home Page: nationalhogfarmer.com/
Dale Miller, Editor
Tom Vilsack, Secretary
JoAnn DeSmet, Marketing
Robert Moraczewski, Senior Vice President
Offers production information for hog farming business managers.
Frequency: Monthly
Circulation: 84000
Founded in 1960
Mailing list available for rent: 84M names
Printed in 4 colors on glossy stock

10170 National Provisioner
Stagnito Communications
155 Pfingster Road
Suite 205
Deerfield, IL 60015
847-205-5660
Fax: 847-205-5680
Home Page: www.nationalprovisioner.com
Ned Bardic, Publisher
Barbara Young, Editor
Tommy Howell, Marketing
Vito Laudati, Business Development Manager
Diana Rotman, Sales Manager
Magazine for meat, poultry, prepared food processors.
Cost: $85.00
Frequency: Monthly
Circulation: 25000
Founded in 1912

10171 Natural Foods Merchandiser
New Hope Natural Media
1401 Pearl St
Suite 200
Boulder, CO 80302-5346
303-939-8440
800-431-1255
Fax: 303-939-9886
E-Mail: info@newhope.com
Home Page: www.newhope.com
Fred Linder, President
Marty Traynor, Editor
Lynne Brenner, Human Resources Executive
Natural Foods Merchandiser features a comprehensive overview of the industry, the latest reports on new ingredients and formulations, market news, new product releases and many other features specifically designed for the retailmarket. It offers the information and the products retailers require to succeed in the competitive natural products marketplace.
65 Pages
Frequency: Monthly
Circulation: 15,000
ISSN: 0164-335x
Founded in 1979
Printed in 4 colors on glossy stock

10172 Natural Products INSIDER
Virgo Publishing LLC
3300 N Central Ave
Suite 300
Phoenix, AZ 85012-2532
480-675-9925
Fax: 480-990-0819
Home Page: www.naturalproductsinsider.com
Jenny Bolton, President
Official magazine for SupplySide. Provides timely information and news for marketers, manufacturers and formulators of dietary supplements, functional foods and personal care. The website also offers exclusive resources and offers, free weekly e-newsletters and a searchable news archive.
Mailing list available for rent: 15000+ names at $var per M

10173 Natural Products Marketplace
Virgo Publishing LLC
3300 N Central Ave
Suite 300
Phoenix, AZ 85012-2532
480-675-9925
Fax: 480-990-0819
E-Mail: peggyj@vpico.com
Home Page: www.vpico.com
Jenny Bolton, President
Publication discussing the dietary supplement, food and personal care industries, focusing on the latest news, products and trend analysis to keep retailers informed and ahead of the competition.
Mailing list available for rent: 15000+ names at $var per M

10174 Nightclub & Bar Magazine
Oxford Publishing
Ste 1
1903b University Ave
Oxford, MS 38655-4150
662-236-5510
800-247-3881
Fax: 662-236-5541
E-Mail: ed@oxpub.com
Home Page: www.nightclub.com
Ed Meek, Publisher
Taylor Rau, Editor
Jennifer Parsons, Marketing
Jennifer Robinson, CEO/President
Adam Alson, Founder
A monthly publication covering the nightclub and bar hospitality industry.
Cost: $30.00
Frequency: Monthly
Circulation: 30000
Printed in 4 colors on glossy stock

10175 **North Africa and Middle East International Agricultural and Trade Report**
US Department of Agriculture
1301 New York Avenue NW
#612
Washington, DC 20005-4701
202-219-0724
Fax: 202-219-0942
Michael Kurrzig, Editor
Information on current and projected agriculture production and trade in North Africa and the Middle East. Reports include trade and production data and highlight US and European trade with the region.
Frequency: Annual

10176 **North American Deer Farmers Magazine**
North American Deer Farmers Association
104 S Lakeshore Dr
Lake City, MN 55041-1641
651-345-5600
Fax: 651-345-5603
E-Mail: info@nadefa.org
Home Page: www.nadefa.org
Shawn Schafer, Executive Director
Dave McQuaig, First VP
Glenn Dice Jr, Second VP
National association of deer farming and ranching. Membership dues are $75-195 which include this quarterly magazine.
Frequency: Quarterly
Circulation: 1000
ISSN: 1084-0583
Founded in 1983
Mailing list available for rent
Printed in on glossy stock

10177 **North American Journal of Aquaculture**
American Fisheries Society
5410 Grosvenor Ln
Suite 110
Bethesda, MD 20814-2199
301-897-8616
Fax: 301-897-8096
Home Page: www.fisheries.org
Gus Rassam, Executive Director
Myra Merritt, Office Administrator
Formerly published as The Progressive Fish-Culturist. The focus is on culture of all aquatic organisms that are of importance to North American culturists. Topics include, but are not limited to, nutrition and feeding, broodstock selection and spawning, drugs and chemicals, health and water quality, and testing new techniques and equipment for the management and rearing of aquatic species
Cost: $38.00
Frequency: Quarterly
ISSN: 1548-8454

10178 **Northeast DairyBusiness**
DairyBusiness Communications
6437 Collamer Road
East Syracuse, NY 13057-1031
315-703-7979
800-334-1904
Fax: 315-703-7988
Home Page: www.dairybusiness.com
Eleanor Jacobs, Editor
Susan Harlow, Managing Editor
Business resource for successful milk producers. Devoted exclusively to the business and dairy management needs of milk producers in the 12 northeastern states.
Cost: $38.95
51 Pages
Frequency: Monthly
Circulation: 17,500
ISSN: 1523-7095
Founded in 1904
Printed in 4 colors on glossy stock

10179 **Northwest Palate Magazine**
Pacifica Publishing
PO Box 10860
Portland, OR 97296
503-224-6039
800-398-7842
Fax: 503-222-5312
E-Mail: editorial@nwpalate.com
Home Page: http://www.northwestpalate.com
Cameron Nagel, Publisher/Editor
Angie Jabine, Owner
Ericka Burke, Owner
Regional magazine that focuses on food, wine and travel. Coverage includes restaurants, destinations and the wines of the Pacific Northwest states and British Columbia.
Cost: $15.00
56 Pages
Frequency: 6 issues per ye
Circulation: 45000
ISSN: 0892-8363
Founded in 1987
Printed in 4 colors on glossy stock

10180 **Nut Grower**
Western Agricultural Publishing Company
4969 E Clinton Way
Suite 104
Fresno, CA 93727-1549
559-252-7000
888-382-9772
Fax: 559-252-7387
E-Mail: editorial@westgpubco.com
Home Page: www.westagpubco.com
Paul Baltimore, Publisher
Randy Bailey, Editor
Robert Fujimoto, Assistant Editor
Covers production topics, the latest in research developments, and crop news on almonds, walnuts, pistachios, pecans and chestnuts.

10181 **Nutraceuticals World**
Rodman Publishing
70 Hilltop Rd
3rd Floor
Ramsey, NJ 07446-1150
201-825-2552
Fax: 201-825-0553
E-Mail: info@rodpub.com
Home Page: www.nutraceuticalsworld.com
Rodman Zilenziger Jr, President
Matt Montgomery, VP
Articles about many aspects of the market, from dietary supplements to functional foods to nutritional beverages, and everything in between.
Frequency: Monthly
Circulation: 12010

10182 **Nutrition Action Healthletter**
Center for Science in the Public Interest
1875 Connecticut Avenue NW
Suite 300
Washington, DC 20009
202-332-9110
Fax: 202-265-4954
E-Mail: cspi@cspinet.org
Home Page: www.cspinet.org
Stephen B Schmidt, Editor-in-Chief
Chris Schmidt, Customer Service Manager
Michael Jacobson, Executive Director
Jamie Jonker, Director Regulatory Affairs
A magazine covering food and nutrition, the food industry, and relevant government regulations.
Cost: $32.00
16 Pages
Circulation: 800000
Founded in 1971
Mailing list available for rent: 700,000 names at $90 per M
Printed in 4 colors on matte stock

10183 **On-Campus Hospitality**
Executive Business Media
825 Old Country Road
PO Box 1500
Westbury, NY 11590
516-334-3030
Fax: 516-334-8959
E-Mail: ebm-mail@ebmpubs.com
Home Page: www.ebmpubs.com
Murry H Greenwald, President/Publisher
Paul Ragusa, Managing Editor
College and university food service operations and outlets and related purchasing and administrative offices.
Cost: $30.00
Circulation: 9,445
ISSN: 0887-431X
Founded in 1979
Printed in 4 colors

10184 **Onboard Services**
International Publishing Company of America
664 La Villa Dr
Miami Springs, FL 33166-6030
305-887-1700
800-525-2015
Fax: 305-885-1923
Home Page: www.onboard-services.com
Alexander Morton, Owner
George Hulcher, Contributing Editor
Keeps airline, cruise ships, railroad, and terminal concessions management and purchasing departments up-to-date on all phases of passenger services.
Cost: $25.00
24 Pages
ISSN: 0892-4236
Founded in 1968
Printed in 4 colors on glossy stock

10185 **Organic WORLD**
John Pappenheimer
3939 Leary Way NW
Seattle, WA 98107-5043
206-781-3347
Fax: 206-632-7055
Covers the news of organic gardening.
Cost: $15.00
Frequency: Quarterly

10186 **PMT Magazine**
Packaging Machinery Manufacturers Institute
11911 Freedom Drive
Suite 600
Reston, VA 20190
703-243-8555
888-275-7664
Fax: 703-243-8556
E-Mail: pmmi@pmmi.org
Home Page: www.pmmi.org
Social Media: Facebook, Twitter, LinkedIn, YouTube
Chuck Yuska, President
The only publication dedicated to the packaging machinery end user. The magazine features articles on mechatronics, sustainability and the packaging professional. Regular features bring news about trends, automation solutions, processing and more.
500+ Members

10187 Pacific Farmer-Stockman
999 West Riverside Avenue
PO Box 2160
Spokane, WA 99201-1006

509-595-5385
800-624-6618
Fax: 509-459-3929
E-Mail: information@spokane.net
Home Page: www.nmv.pointshop.com

Barry Roach, Ad Director
Shaun Higgins, President
Colleen Striegel, Operations Manager
Mike Craigen, Marketing Executive

Offers farming news and information for farmers and herdsmen located in the Pacific states.
Cost: $29.95
Frequency: Monthly

10188 Packer
Vance Publishing
400 Knightsbridge Parkway
Lincolnshire, IL 60069

847-634-2600
Fax: 847-634-4379
E-Mail: info@vancepublishing.com
Home Page: www.vancepublishing.com

William C Vance, Chairman
Peggy Walker, President

Leading source of news and information on fresh fruit and vegetable marketing.
Frequency: Weekly
Circulation: 12434
Founded in 1937
Printed in on glossy stock

10189 Peanut Farmer
Specialized Agricultural Publications
5808 Faringdon Place
Suite 200
Raleigh, NC 27609

919-872-5040
Fax: 919-876-6531
E-Mail: publisher@peanutfarmer.com
Home Page: www.peanutfarmer.com

Dayton H Matlick, President
Mary Evans, Publisher
Mary Cornwall, Chief Copy Editor
Jeanne Sherman, Director of Circulation

Offers peanut farmers profitable methods of raising, marketing and promoting peanuts, plus key related issues.
Cost: $15.00
24 Pages
Frequency: Monthly
Circulation: 18500
Founded in 1965
Printed in 4 colors on glossy stock

10190 Peanut Grower
Vance Publishing
38 Peace Drive
Bronson, FL 32621

352-486-7006
Fax: 352-486-7009
E-Mail: ahuber@svic.net
Home Page: www.peanutgrower.com

Amanda Huber, Editor
Lia Guthrie, Sales

Written for the largest 24,000 US peanut farmers. Covers disease, weed and insect control, legislation, farm equipment, marketing and new research.
Founded in 1937

10191 Peanut Science
American Peanut Research and Education Society
Oklahoma State University
376 Ag Hall
Stillwater, OK 74078-6025

405-372-3052
Fax: 405-624-6718
Home Page: www.peanutscience.com

Dr J Ronald Sholar, Executive Officer

A professional journal with current research results.
Cost: $9.00
Frequency: Bi-Annual
Founded in 1979

10192 Pig International
WATT Publishing Company
303 N Main Street
Suite 500
Rockford, IL 61101

815-966-5400
Fax: 815-966-6416
E-Mail: rabbott@wattnet.net
Home Page: www.wattnet.com

James Watt, Chairman/CEO
Greg Watt, President/COO
Roger Abbott, Editor

Covers nutrition, animal health issues, feed procurement, and how producers can be profitable in the world pork market.
Cost: $50.00
Frequency: Monthly
Circulation: 17642
ISSN: 0191-8834
Founded in 1971
Printed in 4 colors on glossy stock

10193 Pizza Today
National Association of Pizzeria Operators
908 S 8th Street
Suite 200
Louisville, KY 40203

502-736-9500
800-489-8324
Fax: 502-736-9502
E-Mail: plachapelle@pizzatoday.com
Home Page: www.pizzatoday.com
Social Media: Facebook, Twitter

Pete Lachapelle, Publisher/President
Jeremy White, Editor-in-Chief
Mandy Detwiler, Managing Editor
Pat Cravens, Editorial Coordinator

Up-to-date information on pizza restaurant management, pizza equipment for sale, a vendor directory and more.
130 Pages
Frequency: Monthly
Circulation: 47,000
Founded in 1983
Printed in 4 colors on glossy stock

10194 Pork
10901 W 84th Ter
Suite 200
Lenexa, KS 66214-1631

913-438-8700
800-255-5113
Fax: 913-438-0695
E-Mail: info@vancepublishing.com
Home Page: www.vancepublishing.com

Cliff Becker, Publisher
Jane Messenger, Chief Financial Officer
Lori Eppel, Chief Financial Officer
Bill Raufer, Contributing Editor

A magazine specifically designed for the professional pork producer.
Cost: $59.88
Frequency: Monthly
Circulation: 21,464
Founded in 1981
Mailing list available for rent

10195 Potato Country
Columbia Publishing
8405 Ahtanum Rd
Yakima, WA 98903-9432

509-248-2452
800-900-2452
Fax: 509-248-4056
Home Page: www.potatocountry.com

Brent Clement, Editor/Publisher
Mike Stoker, Publisher

Edited for potato growers and allied industry people throughout the Western fall-production states. Editorial material covers production, seed, disease forecast, equipment, fertilizer, irrigation, pest/weed management, crop reports and annual buyers guide.
Cost: $18.00
32 Pages
Circulation: 6300
ISSN: 0886-4780
Founded in 1975
Printed in 4 colors on glossy stock

10196 Potato Grower
Harris Publishing Company
360 B Street
Idaho Falls, ID 83402

208-524-4217
Fax: 208-522-5241
Home Page: www.potatogrower.com

Jason Harris, Publisher
Gary Rawlings, Editor
Nancy Butler, Staff Writer
Rob Erickson, Marketing
Eula Endecott, Circulation

Current news on growing potatoes, market trends, technology.
Cost: $20.95
48 Pages
Frequency: Monthly
ISBN: m-ountai-n -w
Founded in 1965
Printed in 4 colors on glossy stock

10197 Poultry
Marketing and Technology Group
1415 N Dayton St
Suite 115
Chicago, IL 60642-7033

312-266-3311
Fax: 312-266-3363
E-Mail: webinars@meatingplace.com
Home Page: www.meatingplace.com

Mark Lefens, Owner
Tom Cosgrove, Editor

Serves companies who deal with poultry slaughter, rendering or processing.
Frequency: Monthly
Circulation: 20,000
Founded in 1993
Printed in 4 colors on glossy stock

10198 Poultry Digest
WATT Publishing Company
122 S Wesley Ave
Mt Morris, IL 61054-1451

815-734-7937
Fax: 815-734-4201
E-Mail: olentine@wattmm.com
Home Page: www.wattnet.com

James W Watt, President
Charles G Olentine Jr, PhD, Publisher

A magazine serving the production side of the entire poultry industry.
Founded in 1917

10199 Poultry International
WATT Publishing Company

303 N Main Street
Suite 500
Rockford, IL 61101

815-966-5400
Fax: 815-966-6416
E-Mail: mclements@wattnet.net
Home Page: www.wattnet.com

James Watt, Chairman/CEO
Greg Watt, President/COO
Mark Clements, Editor

Viewed by commercial poultry integrators as the leading international source of news, data and information for their businesses. Serves commercial broiler, turkey, duck and egg producers.
Cost: $63.00
68 Pages
Frequency: Monthly
Circulation: 20000
ISSN: 0032-5767
Founded in 1962
Printed in 4 colors

10200 Poultry Times
Poultry & Egg News
PO Box 1338
Gainesville, GA 30503-1338

770-536-2476
Fax: 770-532-4894
Home Page: www.poultrytimes.net
Social Media: Facebook

Cindy Wellborn, Manager
Chris Hill, CEO
Barbara L Olejnik, Associate Editor
Kyle Hatcher, National Sales Representative

The only newspaper in the poultry industry. Provides the most up to date news for the poultry industry.
Cost: $12.00
Frequency: 26 X a year
Circulation: 13000
ISSN: 0885-3371
Founded in 1954
Printed in on glossy stock

10201 Poultry USA
WATT Publishing Company
303 N Main Street
Suite 500
Rockford, IL 61101

815-966-5400
Fax: 815-966-6416
Home Page: www.wattnet.com

James Watt, Chairman/CEO
Greg Watt, President/COO
Jeff Swanson, Publishing Director

Poultry USA serves individuals and firms engaged in the production, processing and marketing of broilers.
60 Pages
Frequency: Monthly
Circulation: 15,092
ISSN: 0007-2176
Founded in 1917
Printed in 4 colors on glossy stock

10202 Practical Winery & Vineyard
58 Paul Dr
Suite D
San Rafael, CA 94903-2054

415-479-5819
Fax: 415-492-9325
E-Mail: Office@practicalwinery.com
Home Page: www.practicalwinery.com

Don Neel, Owner
Tina L Vierra, Associate Publisher

Journal of grape grown and wine production in North America.
Cost: $33.86
Frequency: 6 issues per ye
Circulation: 7,500
Founded in 1985

10203 Prepared Foods
Business News Publishing
2401 W Big Beaver Rd
Suite 700
Troy, MI 48084-3333

248-362-3700
Fax: 248-362-0317
Home Page: www.bnpmedia.com

Mitchell Henderson, CEO
Kathy Travis, Art Director

About 600 food and beverage companies.
Cost: $95.00
109 Pages
Circulation: 70100
Founded in 1926
Printed in 4 colors on glossy stock

10204 Private Label Buyer
Stagnito Communications
155 Pfingsten Road
Suite 205
Deerfield, IL 60015

847-205-5660
Fax: 847-205-5680
Home Page: www.stagnito.com

Steven T Lichtenstein, Publisher
Jill Bruss, Editor

Serves the private label industry, including retailers, voluntaries, wholesalers, manufacturers and others allied to the field.
Frequency: Monthly
Circulation: 30021
Founded in 1986

10205 Process Cooling & Equipment
BNP Publications
1050 IL Route 83
Suite 200
Bensenville, IL 60106-1096

630-377-5909
Fax: 630-694-4002
E-Mail: GlennD@bnpmedia.com
Home Page: www.process-cooling.com

Katie Rotella, Manager
Doug Glenn, Publishing Director

Written for manufacturing engineers who use cooling equipment, components, materials and supplies. refrigerated engineers and technicians assoc

10206 Prograzier
Meat & Livestock Australia
1401 K Street NW
Suite 602
Washington, DC 20005

202-521-2551
Fax: 202-521-2699
E-Mail: info@mla.com.au
Home Page: www.mla.com.au
Social Media: Facebook, Twitter, YouTube

Don Heatley, Chairman
David Palmer, Managing Director
Bernie Bindon, Director
Chris Hudson, Director

Companion publication to feedback magazine. Highlights how individual producers have succesfully introduced best management practices into their farming enterprise and the benefits that have been achieved.
30000 Members
Frequency: Quarterly
Founded in 1998

10207 Progressive Farmer
2100 Lakeshore Drive
Birmingham, AL 35209-6721

205-877-6333
800-357-4466
Fax: 205-877-6860
E-Mail: ProgressiveFarmer@timeinc.com
Home Page: www.progressivefarmer.com

Ed Dickinsen, Publisher
Jack Odle, Editor

Farming news with regional focus on the midwest, midsouth and southwest.
Cost: $84.00
106 Pages
Frequency: Monthly
Circulation: 610000
ISSN: 0033-0760

10208 Progressive Grocer's Marketing Guidebook
Trade Dimensions
770 Broadway
New York, NY 10003

847-763-9050
Fax: 203-563-3131
E-Mail: info@progressivegrocer.com
Home Page: www.progressivegrocer.com

Jenny McTaggart, Senior Editor
Olivia Wilson, Publisher

Over 800 retailer chains and wholesalers in the US and Canada. Also includes over 20,000 key executives. Plus, over 1,700 speciality distributors including C-Store and smaller food store wholesalers, food brokers, and candy, tobacco, and media distributors.
Cost: $380.00
Founded in 1970

10209 QSR Magazine
101 Europa Drive
Suite 150
Chapel Hill, NC 27517

919-945-0705
Fax: 919-945-0701
Home Page: www.qsrmagazine.com

Sam Oches, Editor
Eugene Drezner, National Sales Director
Webb Howell, President
Frequency: Monthly
Founded in 1997

10210 RCI Magazine
Retail Confectioners International
2053 S Waverly Ave
Suite 204
Springfield, MO 65804-2414

417-883-2775
800-545-5381
Fax: 847-724-2719
E-Mail: info@retailconfectioners.org
Home Page: www.retailconfectioners.org

Evans Billington, Executive Director

Covers the retail confection industry.
Frequency: Monthly
Circulation: 800
Founded in 1917

10211 RF Design
131 E Main Street
Bellevue, OH 44811 1449

419- 48- 741
Fax: 419-483-3617
Home Page: www.rfdesign.com/

David Morrison, Editor
Pete May, President

Comprehensive source of rural agricultural news and information for farmers and the general public.
Frequency: Monthly
Founded in 2000

10212 Reciprocation
American Meat Science Association
2441 Village Green Pl
Champaign, IL 61822-7676
800-517-AMSA
Fax: 888-205-5834
Fax: 217-356-5370
E-Mail: information@meatscience.org
Home Page: www.meatscience.org
William Mikel, President
Scott J. Eilert, President Elect
Casey B. Frye, Treasurer
Published twice a year for all AMSA members, this magazine features articles on current meat science issues facing the industry.

10213 Refrigerated & Frozen Foods
Stagnito Communications
155 Pfingsten Road
Suite 205
Deerfield, IL 60015
847-205-5660
Fax: 847-205-5680
Home Page: www.refrigeratedfrozenfood.com
Jeff Plaster, Publisher
Geneine Esquibel, Marketing Manager
Katie Gutierrez, Marketing Manager
Features on leading refrigerated and frozen food processors. Current and future trends in processing, packaging, new product development, food safety and logistics. Serves the dairy, meat, vegetable, fruit, bakery, deli, ingredient, snack, ethnic and other food industry related organizations. Free to qualified subscribers.
Cost: $65.00
64 Pages
Frequency: Monthly
Circulation: 20500
ISSN: 1061-6152
Founded in 1919
Printed in 4 colors on glossy stock

10214 Render
National Renderers Association
801 N Fairfax St
Suite 205
Alexandria, VA 22314-1776
703-683-0155
Fax: 703-683-2626
Home Page: www.nationalrenderers.org
Thomas M Cook, President
Keeping members abreast of advancements and trends taking place within the industry.
Frequency: Monthly

10215 Restaurant Business
National Council of Chain Restaurants
325 7th St NW
Suite 1100
Washington, DC 20004
202-783-7971
800-673-4692
Fax: 202-737-2849
E-Mail: info@nrf.com
Home Page: www.nccr.net
Mike Starnes, Chairman
Rob Green, Executive Director
Scott Vinson, Vice President
Chip Kunde, Treasurer
Mary Schell, Secretary
The only publication that is all about and only about the restaurant entrepreneur, serving regional and emerging chains, multi-concept operators and high-volume independents with ideas to innovate and grow. Features include growth strategies, innovations, the restaurant life, and more.
Frequency: Monthly
Founded in 1965

10216 Restaurant Digest
Panagos Publishing
7913 Westpark Drive
Suite 305
McLean, VA 22102
703-917-6420
Fax: 703-917-6408
Home Page: www.restaurantdigest.com
Bruce Panagos, Publisher
Developments and news of interest to owners, managers, and operators of dining and entertainment establishments in the region.

10217 Restaurant Hospitality
Penton Media
1300 E 9th St
Suite 316
Cleveland, OH 44114-1503
216-696-7000
Fax: 216-696-6662
E-Mail: information@penton.com
Home Page: www.penton.com
Jane Cooper, Marketing
Mike Sanson, Editor-in-Chief
A national trade publication that covers the full-service restaurant industry. It offers cover story features, an extensive food section with recipes, a multi-page news section and a variety of one page profiles on rising stars, equipment, food safety, beverages, design and more.
Cost: $70.00
130 Pages
Frequency: Monthly
Circulation: 117,721
ISSN: 0147-9989
Founded in 1892
Mailing list available for rentat $165 per M
Printed in 4 colors on glossy stock

10218 Restaurant Marketing
Oxford Publishing
Ste 1
1903b University Ave
Oxford, MS 38655-4150
662-236-5510
800-247-3881
Fax: 662-236-5541
E-Mail: ed@oxpub.com
Home Page: www.nightclub.com
Ed Meek, Publisher
Taylor Rau, Editor
Jennifer Parsons, Marketing Director
Amy Dierks, VP Advertising
Michael Harrelson, Executive Editor
A trade magazine providing marketing information and promotional ideas for restaurant owners, hotel and casino operators and caterers.
Cost: $30.00
Frequency: Monthly
Circulation: 30000
Founded in 1985

10219 Restaurant Wine
Wine Profits
PO Box 222
Napa, CA 94559-222
707-224-4777
Fax: 707-224-6740
Home Page: www.restaurantwine.com
Zelma Long, President
Ronn R Wiegand, Publisher
Sandy Flanders, Director of Marketing
Paul Grieco, Co-Owner
Information on the marketing of wine in restaurants, hotels and clubs, wine and food pairing ideas and review of wines.
Cost: $99.00
Circulation: 3000
ISSN: 1040-7030
Printed in 2 colors on matte stock

10220 Restaurants & Institutions
Reed Business Information
2000 Clearwater Dr
Oak Brook, IL 60523-8809
630-574-0825
800-446-6551
Fax: 630-288-8781
Home Page: www.rimag.com
Jeff Greisch, President
Scott Hume, Managing Editor
For restaurant professionals faced with fast-paced consumer demands, government regulations, health concerns and evolving food trends in a variety of market segments.
Frequency: Monthly
Circulation: 154110
Founded in 1937
Printed in 4 colors on glossy stock

10221 Restaurants USA
National Restaurant Association
1200 17th St Nw
Washington, DC 20036-3006
202-331-5900
800-424-5156
Fax: 202-331-2429
Home Page: www.restaurant.org
Dawn M Sweeney, CEO
Sarah Smith-Hamaker, Treasurer
Phil Hickey, Treasurer
A trade magazine offering information for restaurant owners and managers, including industry trends, operational pointers, management principles and association activities.
Cost: $125.00
48 Pages
Frequency: Monthly
Circulation: 44,000
Founded in 1980
Printed in 4 colors

10222 Rice Farming
Vance Publishing
5050 Poplar Avenue
Suite 200
Memphis, TN 38157-2099
901-767-4020
800-888-9784
Fax: 901-767-4026
E-Mail: vlboyd@worldnet.att.net
Home Page: www.ricefarming.com
John Sowell, Publisher
Marci Deshores, Editor
Barbara Johnson, Manager
Profitable production strategies for commercial rice growers.
Founded in 1937

10223 Rice Journal
Specialized Agricultural Publications
3000 Highwoods Boulevard
Suite 300
Raleigh, NC 27604-1029
919-878-0540
Fax: 919-876-6531
Home Page: www.ricejournal.com
Dayton H Matlick, President
Mary Evans, Publisher
Offers rice growers profitable methods of producing, marketing and promoting rice, plus key related issues.
Cost: $15.00
24 Pages
Frequency: Monthly January-July
Circulation: 11,600

Founded in 1897
Printed in 4 colors on glossy stock

10224 Ristorante|
1010 Lake St
Suite 604
Oak Park, IL 60301-1136

708-848-3200
Fax: 708-445-9477
Home Page: www.ristorantemag.com

Joe Madden, Owner

10225 Rural Heritage
Allan Damerow
281 Dean Ridge Ln
Gainesboro, TN 38562-5039

931-268-0655
Fax: 931-268-5884
E-Mail: info@ruralheritage.com
Home Page: www.ruralheritage.com

Gail Damerow, Owner
Allan Damerow, Publisher

Publication for people who farm and log with horses and other draft animals.
Cost: $28.00
100 Pages
ISSN: 0889-2970
Founded in 1976
Printed in 4 colors on glossy stock

10226 Rural Living
Michigan Farm Bureau
7373 W Saginaw Highway
PO Box 30960
Lansing, MI 48909-8460

517-237-7000
800-292-2680
Fax: 517-323-6793
Home Page: www.michiganfarmbureau.com

Dennis Rudat, Editor
Sue Snyder, President
Brigette Leach, Director
Earl Butz, Secretary

Editorial emphasis on consumer food news, travel information and issue analysis.
24 Pages
Frequency: Quarterly

10227 S.O. Connected
National Society on Healthcare Foodservice
455 S. 4th Street
Suite 650
Louisville, KY 40202

888-528-9552
Fax: 502-589-3602
E-Mail: info@healthcarefoodservice.org
Home Page: www.healthcarefoodservice.org
Social Media: Facebook, LinkedIn, YouTube

Patti Oliver, President
Beth Yesford, President-Elect
Laura Watson, Secretary
Randy Sparrow, Treasurer
Robert Darrah, Treasurer-Elect

An important resource for news and recognition.

10228 School Foodservice & Nutrition
School Nutrition Association
120 Waterfront St
Suite 300
Oxon Hill, MD 20745 1142

301-749-1481
800-877-8822
Fax: 301-739-3915
E-Mail: servicecenter@schoolnutrition.org
Home Page: www.schoolnutrition.org

Mary Hill, Director
Dora Rivas SNS, President-Elect
Nancy Rice SNS, VP

This is the official publication of the School Nutrition Association which contains the latest information on a host of items that affect the successful operation of a school foodservice program.
Cost: $75.00
Frequency: Monthly
Circulation: 57,000

10229 School Nutrition Magazine
School Nutrition Association
120 Waterfront St
Suite 300
National Harbor, MD 20745-1142

301-686-3100
800-877-8822
Fax: 301-686-3115
E-Mail: servicecenter@schoolnutrition.org
Home Page: www.schoolnutrition.org

Helen Phillips, President
Sandy Ford, President-Elect
Leah Schmidt, Vice President
Beth Taylor, Secretary/Treasurer

The latest information on a host of items that affect the successful operation of a school foodservice program.
55000 Members
Frequency: Monthly
Founded in 1946

10230 Science Matters
Natural Products Association
2112 E 4th St
Suite 200
Santa Ana, CA 92705-3816

714-460-7732
800-966-6632
Fax: 714-460-7444
Home Page: www.npainfo.org
Social Media: Facebook, Twitter, LinkedIn

John F. Gay, Executive Director & CEO
Jeffrey Wright, President

Dedicated to providing timely information and advancing the understanding of natural products from a scientific perspective.
1900+ Members
Frequency: Monthly
Founded in 1936

10231 Seafood Business
Diversified Business Communications
121 Free Street
PO Box 7437
Portland, ME 04112-7437

207-842-5500
Fax: 207-842-5503
E-Mail: bspringer@divcom.com
Home Page: www.seafoodbusiness.com

Fiona Robinson, Editor
Bill Springer, Publisher
Nancy Hasselback, CEO
Linda Skinner, Managing Editor
Wendy Jalbert, Production Director

Current, comprehensive news on the rapidly expanding seafood industry.
Frequency: Monthly
Circulation: 15,000
Founded in 1949

10232 Sheep!
145 Industrial Drive
Medford, WI 54451

715-785-7979
800-551-5691
Fax: 715-785-7414
E-Mail: sheepmag@tds.net
Home Page: www.sheepmagazine.com

Dave Belanger, Publisher
Nathan Griffith, Editor

Explores a wide range of sheep-related topics of interest to sheep growers and sheep product marketers at all levels of experience.
Cost: $21.00
Frequency: 6x Yearly

10233 Shorthorn Country
Durham Management Company
5830 S 142nd St
Suite A
Omaha, NE 68137-2894

402-827-8003
Fax: 402-827-8006
Home Page:
www.durhamstaffingsolutions.com

Machael Durham, President
Pat Cloutier, Production Manager

Magazine published for cattle producers who breed and sell registered Shorthorn and Polled Shorthorn cattle.
Cost: $24.00
Frequency: 11 per year
Circulation: 3,000
ISSN: 0149-9319

10234 Simply Seafood
Sea Fare Group
2360 W Commodore Way
Suite 210
Seattle, WA 98199

206-829-2323
Fax: 206-789-0504
E-Mail: peter@seafare.com
Home Page: www.simplyseafood.com

Peter Redmayne, Editor

Articles on today's seafood, with cooking ideas, tips & techniques and recipes for healthy meal. Editor's Letter provides all the latest news and insights on seafood products and consumer issues as well as a Market Report with each seasons best buys.
Frequency: Quarterly
Circulation: 131,257

10235 Sizzle
American Culinary Federation
180 Center Place Way
St Augustine, FL 32095-8859

904-824-4468
800-624-9458
Fax: 904-825-4758
E-Mail: acf@acfchefs.net
Home Page: www.acfchefs.org
Social Media: Facebook, Twitter

Michael Ty, President
Thomas J. Macrina, Secretary
James Taylor, Treasurer

The American Culinary Federation quarterly for students of cooking. The only magazine in the United States exclusively targeting culinary, baking, and pastry students. Includes articles on emerging job markets, mentoring, continuing education, culinary trends and product application, as well as scholarship information and culinary/ pastry techniques. Digital publication.
19000 Members
Founded in 1929

10236 Snack Food & Wholesale Bakery
Stagnito Communications
155 Pfingster Road
Suite 205
Deerfield, IL 60015

847-205-5660
Fax: 847-205-5680
Home Page: www.stagnito.com

Ron Bean, Publisher
Harry Stagnito, Publishing Director
Dan Malovany, Editor
Bernard Pacyniak, Editorial Director
Andy Hanacek, Managing Editor

Covers topics and products in the snack and wholesale bakery market
Cost: $85.00
Frequency: Monthly
Circulation: 14,854
Founded in 1912
Printed in 4 colors on glossy stock

10237 **Snack World**
Snack Food Association
1233 Janesville Avenue
Fort Atkinson, WI 53538-2738

703-836-4500
800-547-7377
Fax: 920-563-1702

Gloria Cosby, Publisher
Tracey McMahon, Editor

The official international publication of the Snack Food Association covering trends in the snack food industry, including new products and services, industry news and supplier services.
Frequency: 10 per year
Circulation: 14,000

10238 **Southeastern Peanut Farmer**
Southern Peanut Farmer's Federation
110 E 4th Street
PO Box 706
Tifton, GA 31794

229-386-3470
Fax: 229-386-3501
E-Mail: info@gapeanuts.com
Home Page: www.gapeanuts.com/

Joy Carter, Editor

Offers information to peanut farmers.
Cost: $25.00
20 Pages
Frequency: 5x/Year
Circulation: 9000
ISSN: 0038-3694
Founded in 1961
Printed in 4 colors on glossy stock

10239 **Southern Beverage Journal**
14337 Sw 119th Ave
Miami, FL 33186-6006

305-233-7230
Fax: 305-252-2580
E-Mail: info@bevmedia.com
Home Page: www.bevmedia.com

Sharon Mijares, Manager
William Slone, Publisher

A magazine for the alcoholic beverage industry.
Cost: $35.00
Frequency: Monthly
Circulation: 10000

10240 **Soybean Digest**
Primedia Business
7900 International Dr
Suite 300
Minneapolis, MN 55425-2562

952-851-9329
800-722-5334
Fax: 952-851-4601
E-Mail:
CorporateCustomerService@penton.com
Home Page: www.penton.com

Robert Moraczewski, Executive VP
Ron Sorensen, Chairman
Kelly Conlin Conlin, President/CEO

Leading publication in the soybean market. Offers in-depth coverage for wise management decisions dealing with production of soybeans, corn, wheat, sorghum and cotton.
Cost: $25.00
Frequency: Monthly
Circulation: 147000
Founded in 1940

10241 **Soybean South**
6263 Poplar Avenue
Suite 540
Memphis, TN 38119-4736

901-385-0595
Fax: 901-767-4026

John Sowell, Publisher
Jeff Kehl, Circulation Director

Profitable prediction strategies for soybean farmers.
Frequency: 5 per year
Printed in 4 colors on glossy stock

10242 **Specialty Food Magazine**
National Association for the Specialty Food Trade
120 Wall St
27th Floor
New York, NY 10005-4011

212-482-6440
Fax: 212-482-6459
Home Page: www.fancyfoodshows.com

Ann Daw, President

Provides comprehensive planning information for each Show and aggressive on-site bonus distribution, as well as the industry's most in-depth pre-Show, on-site, and post-Show coverage.
Cost: $30.00
Frequency: Monthly
Circulation: 30100
Founded in 1952

10243 **Spudman Magazine**
75 Applewood Drive
Sparta, MI 49435

616-887-9008
Fax: 616-887-2666
Home Page: www.spudman.com

Matt McCallum, Publisher
Greg Brown, Managing Editor
Erica Bernard, Circulation Manager
Marnie Draper, Advertising Manager
Jill Peck, Creative Director

Information for potato farming and marketing.
Frequency: 9 issues per ye
Circulation: 15500
Founded in 1964

10244 **StateWays**
The Beverage Information Group
17 High St
2nd Floor
Norwalk, CT 06851

203-855-8499
E-Mail: lzimmerman@m2media360.com
Home Page: www.bevinfogroup.com

Liza Zimmerman, Editor-in-Chief
Jeremy Nedelka, Managing Editor

Written for commissioners, board members, headquarters personnel, and retail store managers responsible for buying beverage alcohol in the eighteen control states. Covered editorial product knowledge, market trends, store operations, merchandising, warehousing, comoputerization, administration, training and other topics.
Cost: $20.00
Frequency: Bi-Monthly
Circulation: 8500

10245 **Stores Magazine**
National Council of Chain Restaurants
325 7th St NW
Suite 1100
Washington, DC 20004

202-783-7971
800-673-4692
Fax: 202-737-2849
E-Mail: info@nrf.com
Home Page: www.nccr.net

Mike Starnes, Chairman
Rob Green, Executive Director
Scott Vinson, Vice President
Chip Kunde, Treasurer
Mary Schell, Secretary

Offers an insider's view of the entire retail industry by featuring the latest trends, hottest ideas, current technologies and consumer attitudes.
Frequency: Monthly
Founded in 1965

10246 **Sugar: The Sugar Producer Magazine**
Idaho Golf Harris Publishing
520 Park Avenue
Idaho Falls, ID 83402

208-523-1500
800-638-0135
Fax: 208-522-5241
E-Mail:
customerservice@harrispublishing.com
Home Page: www.sugarproducer.com

Jason Harris, Publisher
David FairBourn, Editor
Eula Endecott, Circulation Manager
Rob Erickson, Marketing Manager

Sugar beet industry information.
Cost: $15.95
Frequency: Monthly
Circulation: 16000
Founded in 1975

10247 **Sunbelt Food Service**
Shelby Publishing Company
517 Green St Nw
Gainesville, GA 30501-3300

770-534-8380
Fax: 770-535-0110
E-Mail: shelbyfs@bellsouth.net
Home Page: www.shelbypublishing.com

Ron Johnston, President
Penny Smith, Account Manager

Sales and promotion of products and services sold through food service establishments across the sunbelt.
Cost: $36.00
Frequency: Monthly
Circulation: 30090
Founded in 1965
Printed in on newsprint stock

10248 **Sunflower Magazine**
National Sunflower Association
Ste 206
2401 46th Ave SE
Mandan, ND 58554-4829

701-328-5100
888-718-7033
Fax: 701-328-5101
Home Page: www.sunflowernsa.com

Larry Kleingartner, Executive Director
John Sanbakken, Marketing Director

Magazine geared to sunflower products.
Cost: $9.00
Frequency: Monthly
Circulation: 29,300
Founded in 1981
Printed in 4 colors

10249 **Sunflower and Grain Marketing Magazine**
Sunflower World Publishers
3307 Northland Drive
Suite 130
Austin, TX 78731-4964

512-407-3434
Fax: 512-323-5118

Ed Randall Allen

Offers news and information on the sunflower and grain industries.
Circulation: 15,000

10250 Supermarket News: Center Store
Penton Media Inc
249 W 17th St
Suite 6
New York, NY 10011-5390

212-204-4200
Fax: 212-206-3622
E-Mail: julie.gallagher@penton.com
Home Page: www.penton.com

Sharon Rowlands, CEO
Jerry Rymont, Publisher

A nationally circulated weekly trade magazine for the food distribution industry.

10251 Supermarket News: Retail/Financial
Penton Media Inc
249 W 17th St
Suite 6
New York, NY 10011-5390

212-204-4200
Fax: 212-206-3622
E-Mail: mark.hamstra@penton.com
Home Page: www.penton.com

Sharon Rowlands, CEO

A nationally circulated weekly trade magazine for the food distribution industry
Frequency: Monthly
Circulation: 36346
ISSN: 0039-5803
Founded in 1892

10252 Supermarket News: Technology & Logistics
Penton Media Inc
249 W 17th St
Suite 6
New York, NY 10011-5390

212-204-4200
Fax: 212-206-3622
E-Mail: michael.garry@penton.com
Home Page: www.penton.com

Sharon Rowlands, CEO

A nationally circulated weekly trade magazine for the food distribution industry
Cost: $45.00
ISSN: 0039-5803
Founded in 1892

10253 Swine Practitioner
Vance Publishing
10901 W 84th Terrace
3 Pine Ridge Plaza
Lenexa, KS 66214-1649

913-438-8700
800-255-5113
Fax: 913-438-0695
E-Mail: cbecker@vancepublishing.com
Home Page: www.vancepublishing.com

Jim Carlton, Editor
Cliff Becker, Group Publisher
William C Vance, Chairman

Offers technical information, primarily on swine health and related production areas, to veterinarians and related industry professionals.
Founded in 1937
Mailing list available for rent

10254 THE SUNFLOWER
National Sunflower Association
2401 46th Avenue SE
Suite 206
Mandan, ND 58554-4829

701-328-5100
888-718-7033
Fax: 701-328-5101
E-Mail: larryk@sunflowernsa.com
Home Page: www.sunflowernsa.com
Social Media: Facebook, YouTube

Larry Kleingartner, Executive Director

Contains fresh, current and important articles on production strategies, ongoing research and market information.
Frequency: 6x Yearly
Founded in 1981

10255 Tea & Coffee Trade Journal
Lockwood Publications
26 Broadway
Floor 9M
New York, NY 10004-1704

212-391-2060
845-267-3489
Fax: 212-391-2060
Home Page: www.lockwoodpublications.com

Robert Lockwood Sr, President

Premiere magazine for tea and coffee industry.
Cost: $49.00
Frequency: Monthly
Circulation: 12
Founded in 1901
Printed in 4 colors on glossy stock

10256 The County Agent
National Association of County Agricultural Agents
6584 W Duroc Road
Maroa, IL 61756

217-794-3700
Fax: 217-794-5901
E-Mail: exec-dir@nacaa.com
Home Page: www.nacaa.com

Rick Gibson, President

Members receive professional improvement, news of association activities, shared education efforts from other states and reports from NACAA leadership and member states.
Frequency: Monthly
Circulation: 5000
Founded in 1916

10257 The New Brewer
Brewers Association
736 Pearl Street
Boulder, CO 80302

303-447-0816
888-822-6273
Fax: 303-447-2825
E-Mail: webmaster@brewersassociation.org
Home Page: www.beertown.org
Social Media: Facebook, Twitter

Chris P. Frey, Chair
Jake Keeler, Vice Chair
Roxanne Westendorf, Secretary

Offers practical insights and advice for breweries of all sizes. Features on topics like brewing technology and problem solving, pub and restaurant management, and packaged beer sales and distribution. Also important industry news, sales charts and market share performance. The annual Industry Review tallies production for every craft brewery in America, producing both regional and national lists of the biggest players in every sector.
1900 Members
Founded in 1978

10258 TheConsultant
Food Service Consultants Society International
144 Parkedge Street
Rockwood, ON, Canada N0B 2K0

519-856-0783
Fax: 519-856-0648
E-Mail: liz@fcsi.org
Home Page: www.fcsi.org

Liz Campbell, Editor

Professional publication for FCSI members and the food service industry.
Cost: $40.00
150 Pages
Frequency: Quarterly
Circulation: 4500
Printed in 4 colors on glossy stock

10259 Today's Grocers
Florida Grocer Publications
PO Box 430760
S Miami, FL 33246

305-661-0792
800-440-3067
Fax: 305-661-6720

Jack Nobles, Publisher
Dennis Kane, Editor

Provides the latest food industry news and trends to Florida, Georgia, Alabama, Louisiana, Mississippi and the Carolinas.
Cost: $29.00
24 Pages
Frequency: Monthly
Circulation: 19,000
ISSN: 1529-4420
Founded in 1956
Printed in on newsprint stock

10260 Tomato Country
Columbia Publishing
8405 Ahtanum Rd
Yakima, WA 98903-9432

509-248-2452
800-900-2452
Fax: 509-248-4056
Home Page: www.tomatomagazine.com

Brent Clement, Editor/Publisher
Mike Stoker, Publisher

Includes information on tomato production and marketing, grower and shipper feature stories, tomato research, from herbicide and pesticide studies to new varieties, market reports, feedback from major tomato meetings and conventions, along with other key issues and points of interest for US and Canada tomato growers.
Cost: $12.00
Frequency: Annually
Founded in 1993

10261 Trading Rules
National Oilseed Processors Association
1300 L St NW
Suite 1020
Washington, DC 20005-4168

202-842-0463
Fax: 202-842-9126
E-Mail: nopa@nopa.org
Home Page: www.nopa.org

Kathy Pennington, Manager
David J Hovermale, Executive VP
Karri L Moore, Project Manager
Julia Kinnaird, Manager
Cost: $50.00
Founded in 1929

10262 Transactions of the American Fisheries Society
American Fisheries Society
5410 Grosvenor Ln
Suite 110
Bethesda, MD 20814-2199

301-897-8616
Fax: 301-897-8096
Home Page: www.fisheries.org

Gus Rassam, Executive Director
Myra Merritt, Office Administrator

The Society's highly regarded international journal of fisheries science features results of basic and applied research in genetics, physiology, biology, ecology, population dynamics, economics, health, culture, and other topics germane to marine and freshwater finfish and shellfish and their respective fisheries and environments
Cost: $43.00
Frequency: Bi-Monthly
ISSN: 0002-8487
Founded in 1872

10263 Tree Fruit
Western Agricultural Publishing Company
4969 E Clinton Way
#104
Fresno, CA 93727-1546
559-252-7000
888-382-9772
Fax: 559-252-7387
E-Mail: westag@westagpubco.com
Paul Baltimore, Publisher
Randy Bailey, Editor
Robert Fujimoto, Assistant Editor
For tree fruit growers in California.

10264 Truth About Organic Foods
Henderson Communications LLC
1422 Elbridge Payne Rd
Suite 250
Chesterfield, MO 63017-8544
636-728-1428
Fax: 636-777-4178
E-Mail: info@agrimarketing.com
Home Page: www.agrimarketing.com
Lynn Henderson, Owner
This 231-page book provides a fair and balanced look from a scientific standpoint about the heritage, production and nutritive value of organic foods.

10265 US Beer Market: Impact Databank Review and Forecast
M Shanken Communications
387 Park Ave S
8th Floor
New York, NY 10016-8872
212-684-4224
Fax: 212-684-5424
E-Mail: impact@mshanken.com
Home Page: www.cigaraficionado.com
Marvin Shanken, Publisher
Cost: $895.00
Frequency: Annual+
Founded in 1972

10266 US Fast Food and Multi-Unit Restaurants
Business Trend Analysts/Industry Reports
2171 Jericho Tpke
Suite 200
Commack, NY 11725-2937
631-462-5454
800-866-4648
Fax: 631-462-1842
Home Page: www.businesstrendanalysts.com
Charles J Ritchie, Executive VP
Donna Priani, General Manager
This survey offers information on the fast food industry, including chains and franchises.
Cost: $1995.00
Founded in 1986

10267 US Liquor Industry
Business Trend Analysts/Industry Reports
2171 Jericho Tpke
Suite 200
Commack, NY 11725-2937
631-462-5454
Fax: 631-462-1842
Home Page: www.businesstrendanalysts.com
Charles J Ritchie, Executive VP
Donna Priani, Marketing Director
A survey summarizing the past, current and future markets and trends in the liquor industry.
Cost: $1495.00
Founded in 1999

10268 US Market for Bakery Products
Business Trend Analysts/Industry Reports
2171 Jericho Tpke
Suite 200
Commack, NY 11725-2937
631-462-5454
800-866-4648
Fax: 631-462-1842
Home Page: www.businesstrendanalysts.com/
Charles J Ritchie, Executive VP
Donna Priani, General Manager
Profiles markets for bread, rolls, cakes, pies, cookies, crackers, other sweets and pretzels; provides information on consumption patterns, distribution trends, pricing, new products, and advertising strategies.
Cost: $1495.00
Frequency: Annual+
Founded in 1978

10269 Valley Potato Grower
Ola Highway 2 E
East Grand Forks, MN 56721
218-773-7783
Fax: 218-773-6227
E-Mail: communication@nppga.org
Home Page: www.rrvpotatoes.org
Duane W Maatz, President
Ted Kreis, Marketing
Information on potato farming.
Cost: $17.95
Frequency: Monthly
Founded in 1946

10270 Vegetable
US Department of Agriculture
PO Box 1258
Sacramento, CA 95812-1258
Home Page: www.usda.gov
Chris Smith, Chief Information Officer
Matt Paul, Director of Communications
Ramona Romero, General Counsel
Historic information relating to various types of vegetable crops.

10271 Vegetable Growers News
Great American Publishing
75 Applewood Drive Suite A
PO Box 128
Sparta, MI 49345-1531
616-887-9008
Fax: 616-887-2666
Home Page: www.vegetablegrowersnews.com
Kimberly Warren, Managing Editor
Matt McCallum, Executive Publisher
Erica Bernard, Circulation Manager
Jill Peck, Creative Director
Greg Ryan, Graphic Designer
Market and marketing news.
Cost: $12.00
Frequency: Monthly
Circulation: 14000
Founded in 1970

10272 Vegetables
Western Agricultural Publishing Company
4969 E Clinton Way
#104
Fresno, CA 93727-1549
559-252-7000
888-382-9772
Fax: 559-252-7387
E-Mail: editorial@westapubco.com
Paul Baltimore, Publisher
Randy Bailey, Editor
Robert Fujimoto, Assistant Editor
The definitive source for information on all aspects of western vegetable production.

10273 Vegetarian Journal
Vegetarian Resource Group
PO Box 1463
Baltimore, MD 21203
410-366-8343
Fax: 410-366-8804
E-Mail: vrg@vrg.org
Home Page: www.vrg.org
Debra Wasserman, Director
The practical magazine for those interested in Vegetarian Health, Ecology, and Ethics.
Frequency: Quarterly
Circulation: 15000
Mailing list available for rent

10274 Veggie Life Magazine
EGW
4075 Papazian Way
Suite 204
Fremont, CA 94538-4372
510-668-0268
Fax: 510-668-0280
E-Mail: info@egw.com
Home Page: www.veggielife.com
Chris Slaughter, VP
Shanna Masters, Editor
The modem voice on seasonal vegetarian cooking, optimum nutrition, and natural healing for today's health-conscious consumer features vaulable tips techniques, recipes, and remedies from dieticians, herbalists, doctors and other health experts on new ways to prpare creative plant-based cuisine, implement diet programs, and use natural remedies for an improved and vibrant lifestyle.
Cost: $19.96
68 Pages
Frequency: Quarterly
Circulation: 80000
Founded in 1980

10275 Vending Times
Vending Times
1375 Broadway
6th Floor
New York, NY 10018
516-442-1850
Fax: 516-442-1849
E-Mail: subscriptions@vendingtimes.net
Home Page: www.vendingtimes.com
Alicia Lavay-Kertes, President/Publisher
Nick Montano, VP/Executive Editor
Tim Sanford, Editor-in-Chief
Vending Times serves the automatic merchandising and coffee service industries. This includes music and game operations, vending operations, mobile catering operations, consultants and associations.
Cost: $40.00
Frequency: Monthly
Circulation: 16,000
Founded in 1962

10276 Vineyard and Winery Management
Vineyard & Winery Management

421 E Street
P.O. Box 14459
Santa Rosa, CA 95404

707-577-7700
800-535-5670
Fax: 707-577-7705
Home Page: www.vwmmedia.com

Robert Merletti, CEO/Publisher
Jason Thomas, Business Manager
Tina Caputo, Editor-in-Chief
Ethan Simon, Director of Sales
Suzanne Webb, Marketing Director

Leading independent and award-winning wine trade magazine serving all of North America.
Cost: $37.00
100 Pages
Frequency: Bi-monthly
Circulation: 6900
ISSN: 1047-4951
Founded in 1975
Printed in 4 colors on glossy stock

10277 WATT Poultry Magazine
WATT Poultry USA
122 S Wesley Ave
Mt Morris, IL 61054-1451

815-734-7937
Fax: 815-734-4201
E-Mail: watt@wattmm.com
Home Page: www.wattnet.com

James Watt, President
Charles Olentine, Publisher
Gary Thornton, Editor

Dedicated to supporting every phase of the turkey industry by providing information for decision-makers on breeding, production, management, processing and marketing.

10278 WD Hoard and Sons Company
Po Box 801
Fort Atkinson, WI 53538-0801

920-563-5551
Fax: 920-563-7298
E-Mail: hoards@hoards.com
Home Page: www.hoards.com
Social Media: Facebook, Twitter

Brian V Knox, CEO
Gary L Vorpahl, Marketing Director

News aimed at the dairy farmer.
Cost: $18.00
Frequency: 20x/Year
Circulation: 63317
Founded in 1871
Printed in 4 colors on glossy stock

10279 Wallaces Farmer
Farm Progress Companies
255 38th Avenue
Suite P
St Charles, IL 60174-5410

630-462-2224
800-441-1410
E-Mail: rswoboda@farmprogress.com
Home Page: www.farmprogress.com

Rod Swoboda, Editor
Willie Vogt, Corporate Editorial Director
Frank Holdmeyer, Executive Editor

Serves Iowa farmers and ranchers with information to help them maximize their productivity and profitability. Each issue is packed with information, ideas, news and analysis.
Cost: $26.95
Frequency: Monthly
Founded in 1855

10280 Western Dairy Business
DairyBusiness Communications
6437 Collamer Road
East Syracuse, NY 13057-1031

315-703-7979
866-520-2880
Fax: 315-703-7988
E-Mail: circ@dairybusiness.com
Home Page: www.dairybusiness.com

Ron Goble, Associate Publisher
Cecilia Parsons, Associate Editor
Scott A Smith, CEO

Business resource for successful milk producers. Covers 13 Western states. Provides information and news that is helpful in the daily operations of dairymen.
Cost: $38.95
67 Pages
Frequency: Monthly
Circulation: 14000
ISSN: 1528-4360
Founded in 1904
Printed in 4 colors on glossy stock

10281 Western Farm Press
Primedia
2104 Harvell Circle
Bellevue, NE 68005

913-341-1300
866-505-7173
Fax: 913-967-1898
E-Mail: wfcs@pbsub.com
Home Page: www.westernfarmpress.com
Social Media: Facebook, Twitter

Robert Fraser, Managing Editor
Harry Cline, Editor
Greg Frey, Publisher
Darrah Parker, Marketing Director

Timely reliable information for western agriculture.
Circulation: 16,000
Founded in 1989

10282 Western Fruit Grower
Meister Media Worldwide
37733 Euclid Ave
Willoughby, OH 44094-5992

440-942-2000
800-572-7740
Fax: 440-975-3447
E-Mail: afg.edit@meistermedia.com
Home Page: www.meisternet.com

Gary Fitzgerald, President
Brian Sparks, Editor
Terry Doak, Circulation Manager

Edited for commercial growers of deciduous crops and citrus fruit, nut grape crops in the Western US.
Cost: $20.00
66 Pages
Frequency: Monthly
Circulation: 36,000

10283 Western Grocery News
80 Willow Road
Menlo Park, CA 94025-3661

650-321-3600
800-227-7346
Fax: 650-327-7537
Frequency: Bi-Monthly
Circulation: 9,187

10284 Western Growers & Shippers
Western Growers Association
PO Box 2130
Newport Beach, CA 92658-8944

949-863-1000
Fax: 949-863-9028
Home Page: www.wga.com

Tom Nassif, President
Tim Linden, Editor

Listing over 3,000 growers, shippers, packers, brokers and distributors of fruits and vegetables in California and Arizona.
32 Pages
Frequency: Monthly
Circulation: 5000
ISSN: 0043-3799
Founded in 1926
Printed in 4 colors on glossy stock

10285 Western Livestock Journal
Crow Publications
7355 E Orchard Road
Suite 300
Greenwood Village, CO 80111

303-722-7600
800-850-2769
Fax: 303-722-0155
E-Mail: editorial@wlj.net
Home Page: www.wlj.net

Pete Crow, Publisher

Offers its readers the best coverage of timely, necessary news and information that affects the livestock industry, particularly cattle.
Cost: $45.00
Frequency: Weekly
Founded in 1922

10286 Whole Foods Magazine
WFC
4041g Hadley Rd
Suite 101
South Plainfiel, NJ 07080-1120

908-769-1160
Fax: 908-769-1171
E-Mail: info@wfcinc.com
Home Page: www.wfcinc.com
Social Media: Facebook, Twitter, LinkedIn

Howard Wainer, President
Kaylynn Ebner, Editor
Ronda Collins, Circulation Manager
Tim Person, Assistant Editor

Serves the natural/health products industry.
Cost: $70.00
Frequency: Monthly
Founded in 1979
Printed in on glossy stock

10287 Wine Advocate
Robert M Parker Jr
PO Box 311
Monkton, MD 21111

410-329-6477
Fax: 410-357-4504
E-Mail: wineadvocate@erobertparker.com
Home Page: www.erobertparker.com

Robert M Parker Jr, Editor/CEO
Daniel Thomases, Partner

An independent magazine covering reviews of wine.
Cost: $60.00
64 Pages
Frequency: Bi-monthly
Circulation: 40000
Founded in 1978

10288 Wine World
Wine World Publishing
6433 Topanga Canyon Boulevard
#412
Canoga Park, CA 91303 2621
Dee Snidt, Editor

For the wine consumer and industry.
Cost: $16.00
48 Pages
Frequency: Monthly
Founded in 1971

10289 Wines & Vines
1800 Lincoln Ave
San Rafael, CA 94901-1298

415-453-9700
Fax: 415-453-2517
E-Mail: info@winesandvines.com
Home Page: www.winesandvines.com

Chet Klingensmith, Publisher
Kendra Campbell, Director of Sales and Marketing
Tina Caputo, Editor
Jacques Brix, Vice President

Voice of the grape and wine industry.
Cost: $32.50
Frequency: Monthly
Circulation: 3200
Founded in 1919
Printed in 4 colors on matte stock

10290 Yankee Food Service
201 Oak Street
Suite A
Pembroke, MA 02359

781-829-4700
866-677-4700
Fax: 781-829-0134
E-Mail: info@griffinpublishing.net
Home Page: www.griffinpublishing.net

Stephen M Griffin, President
Jack Walsh, Vice President
Karen Harty, Vice President
Julie Mignosa, Office Manager

Reports news and happenings of the food service industry in New England.
Cost: $47.00
48 Pages
Frequency: Monthly
Circulation: 22,111
Founded in 1970

Trade Shows

10291 A Year of Enchantment
Int'l Council on Hotel, Restaurant Institute Edu.
1200 17th Street NW
Washington, DC 20036-3006

202-467-6300
E-Mail: publications@chrie.org
Home Page: www.chrie.org

Susan Gould, Manager
Joseph Bradley, Treasurer

Containing over 70 booths and over 50 exhibits.
750 Attendees
Frequency: August
Founded in 1946

10292 AACC International Annual Meeting
3340 Pilot Knob Road
St. Paul, MN 55121-2055

651-454-7250
800-328-7560
Fax: 651-454-0766
E-Mail: aacc@scisoc.org
Home Page: www.aaccnet.org
Social Media: Facebook, Twitter, LinkedIn

Betty Ford, Meetings Director
Rhonda Wilkie, Meetings Coordinator
Deborah Rogers, Chair
David Hahn, President
Steven C. Nelson, Executive Vice President

Formerly the American Association of Cereal Chemists, the AACC meeting offers the chance to come together, network with peers, discuss critical issues in the science and discover the methods of others.
1200 Attendees
Frequency: October

10293 AACT Technical Conference
American Association of Candy Technologists
711 W. Water St.
PO Box 266
Princeton, WI 54968

920-295-6969
Fax: 920-295-6843
E-Mail: aactinfo@gomc.com
Home Page: www.aactcandy.org

Bob Huzinec, President
Bill Dyer, First VP

Approximately 20 papers are presented to an audience of technologists in the sweet goods industry. These talks range from basics to innovations, provising the industry with practical information to help in understanding processes and ingredients used by their companies.
300 Attendees
Frequency: Annual/October

10294 AAEA Annual Meeting
American Agricultural Economics Association
1110 Buckeye Avenue
Ames, IA 50010-8063

515-233-9087
Fax: 575-233-3101

Nancy Knight, Manager Meetings

Annual meeting and trade show of 25 exhibitors.
1700 Attendees

10295 AAW Annual Convention
American Agri-Women
2103 Zeandale Road
Manhattan, KS 66502

785-537-6171
Fax: 785-537-9727
E-Mail: info@americanagriwomen.org
Home Page: www.americanagriwomen.org

Marcie Williams, President

Tradeshow consisting of products of interest to women in agriculture.
350 Attendees
Frequency: Annual/November

10296 ABI/ADPI Joint Annual Meeting
American Butter Institute
2101 Wilson Boulevard
Suite 400
Arlington, VA 22201

703-243-6111
Fax: 703-841-9328
E-Mail: AMiner@nmpf.org
Home Page: www.butterinstitute.org

Jerome J Kozak, Executive Director
Chris Galen, Communications VP

This event is co-sponsored by The American Dairy Products Institute for manufacturers, marketers and suppliers of manufactured dairy products. 35 exhibitors.
700 Attendees
Frequency: Annual

10297 ACF National Convention
American Culinary Federation
180 Center Place Way
St Augustine, FL 32095-8859

904-824-4468
800-624-9458
Fax: 904-825-4758
E-Mail: acf@acfchefs.net
Home Page: www.acfchefs.org
Social Media: Facebook, Twitter

Michael Ty, President
Thomas J. Macrina, Secretary
James Taylor, Treasurer

Learn the latest culinary trends during educational seminars and demonstrations and enjoy spectacular meal events. Competitions, exhibits and more.
19000 Members
Founded in 1929

10298 ACF National Convention & Trade Show
American Culinary Federation
180 Center Place Way
Saint Augustine, FL 32095

904-824-4468
800-624-9458
Fax: 904-825-4758
E-Mail: acf@acfchefs.net
Home Page: www.acfchefs.org
Social Media: Facebook, Twitter, Flickr

Kevin Brune, Director, Events & Operations Mgmt
Jennifer Keith, Event & Sales Specialist
Claudia More, Events Management Coordinator

Two-hundred booths of products and foodstuffs for the food service industry. Seminars, workshops, cooking demos, more.
2000 Attendees
Frequency: Annual/July

10299 ACF Regional Conference
American Culinary Federation
180 Center Place Way
St Augustine, FL 32095-8859

904-824-4468
800-624-9458
Fax: 904-825-4758
E-Mail: acf@acfchefs.net
Home Page: www.acfchefs.org
Social Media: Facebook, Twitter

Michael Ty, President
Thomas J. Macrina, Secretary
James Taylor, Treasurer

Catch up on the latest culinary trends and watch cooking demonstrations from expert chefs. This events series is a great way to earn continuing education hours and meet other professionals in the culinary industry.
19000 Members
Founded in 1929

10300 ACS Annual Conference and Competition
American Cheese Society
304 W Liberty Street
Suite 201
Louisville, KY 40202

502-583-3783
Fax: 502-589-3602
E-Mail: mwilson@hqtrs.com
Home Page: www.cheesesociety.org

Marci Wilson, Executive Director
Carlos Scrivener, Manager

This Conference and Competition offers a unique opportunity to learn the latest about cheese in America and indulge your cheese fantasies by tasting more than 700 American artisan and specialty cheeses.
Frequency: Associate Fee

10301 ADPI/ABI Annual Conference
American Dairy Products Institute
126 N Addison St
Elmhurst, IL 60126

630-530-8700
Fax: 630-530-8707

E-Mail: info@adpi.org
Home Page: www.adpi.org

Dale Kleber, CEO

Held in Chicago, this event attracts programs, the annual meeting, and the exhibition hall. Fifty exhibits of equipment and supplies for condensed milk, dry and evaporated milk and whey products, plus conference, seminar, workshop and banquet.
650 Attendees
Frequency: Annual/April

10302 AEA National Convention
American Emu Association
PO Box 2502
San Angelo, TX 76902

541-332-0675
E-Mail: info@aea-emu.org
Home Page: www.aea-emu.org

Charles Ramey, President
Martha Hendricks, VP

This convention provides a chance for the AEA Board of Directors (AEA-BOD) to meet, face to face, during the week prior to the actual convention. It is a place for members to gather to learn the latest information and research about the emu industry, see the latest new products and network with other emu growers from across the U.S. and around the world.
Frequency: July/Non-Member $230

10303 AFFI Frozen Food Convention
American Frozen Food Institute
2000 Corporate Ridge, Blvd.
Suite 1000
McLean, VA 22102-7862

703-821-0770
Fax: 703-821-1350
E-Mail: info@affi.com
Home Page: www.affi.com

Kraig R Naasz, President/CEO
Thomas Bradshaw, Manager Legislative Affairs
Corey Henry, VP Communications
Robert L Garfield, SVP Public Policy/Intl Affairs

Learn more about the frozen food industry, network with peers, see new research, and get higher education.
500 Members
Founded in 1942

10304 AFFI-Con
American Frozen Food Institute
2000 Corporate Ridge Blvd
Suite 1000
McLean, VA 22102

703-821-0770
Fax: 703-821-1350
E-Mail: info@affi.com
Home Page: www.affi.com

Mary Becton, Conference Director

Helping you make connections and helping you be better informed about industry issues.
1500 Attendees
Frequency: Annual/February

10305 AFS Annual Meeting
American Fisheries Society
5410 Grosvenor Lane
Bethesda, MD 20814

301-897-8616
Fax: 301-897-8096
Home Page: www.fisheries.org
Social Media: Facebook, Twitter, Flickr

Gus Rassa,, Executive Director
Myra Merritt, Office Administrator

Held in conjunction with American Institute of Fishery Research Biologists. Explore the interrelation between fish, aquatic habitats and man; highlight challenges facing aquatic resource professionals and the methods that have been employed to resolve conflicts between those that use or have an interest in our aquatic resources.
Frequency: Annual/September

10306 AMI International Meat, Poultry & Seafood Convention and Exposition
Convention Mangement Group
10472 Armstrong Street
Fairfax, VA 22031

703-934-4700
Fax: 703-934-4899
Home Page: www.amiexpo.com
Social Media: Facebook, Twitter, LinkedIn

Anne Halal, Convention/Member Services VP
Anne Nuttall, Convention/Members Director
Katie Brannan, Convention/Members Sr. Manager

Sponsored by the American Meat Institute it features exhibits featuring the latest innovations in processing and packaging equipment, business and processing software systems, supplies, services and formulations.
25000 Attendees
Frequency: Annual/April

10307 AMSA Reciprocal Meat Conference
American Meat Science Association
2441 Village Green Place
Champaign, IL 61822

217-356-5370
800-517-AMSA
Fax: 888-205-5834
Fax: 217-356-5370
E-Mail: information@meatscience.org
Home Page: www.meatscience.org\rmc

Thomas Powell, Executive Director
Diedrea Mabry, Program Director
Kathy Ruff, Meetings & Member Svcs Director

RMC is the annual meeting for AMSA, featuring an interactive program tailored to bring attendees the very best and inspiring educational experience. Attendees are professionals in academia, government and industry, as well as students in the meat, food and animal science fields.
Frequency: Annual

10308 AOCS Annual Meeting & Exposition
American Oil Chemists' Society
2710 S Boulder
Urbana, IL 61802-6996

217-359-2344
Fax: 217-359-8091
E-Mail: meetings@aocs.org
Home Page: www.aocs.org

Nurhan Dunford, General Chairperson
Mindy Cain, Meetings Specialist

The premier global science and business forum on fats, oils, surfactants, lipids, and related materials. Includes oral and poster presentations, short courses, and exhibit, and networking with more than 1,600 colleagues from 60 countries.
2000 Attendees
Frequency: Annual/April

10309 APA Annual Meeting
Apple Processors Association
1666 K Street NW
Suite 260
Washington, DC 20006

202-785-6710
Fax: 202-331-4212
E-Mail: pweller@agriwashington.org
Home Page: www.appleprocessors.org

Paul S Weller Jr, President
Andrea Ball, Sr Director Meetings/Administration

A three-day meeting which brings top industry and consumer experts together for a dialogue on timely issues. These include marketing tips, packaging trends, consumer research, and media reports and reaction to industry initiatives.
Frequency: Annual/June

10310 APS/CPS/MSA Annual Joint Meeting
American Phytopathological Society
3340 Pilot Knob Road
Saint Paul, MN 55121-2097

651-454-7250
800-328-7560
Fax: 651-454-0766
E-Mail: aps@scisoc.org
Home Page: www.meeting.apsnet.org
Social Media: Facebook, Twitter, LinkedIn, YouTube

Betty Ford, Director of Meetings

Featuring over 18 state-of-the-art education sessions daily, over 700 poster presentations, one-of-a-kind preconvention tours and workshops and exhibits from leading suppliers.
Frequency: Annual/Summer

10311 ASA/CSSA/SSSA International Annual Meeting
American Society of Agronomy
677 S Segoe Road
Madison, WI 53711

608-273-8080
Fax: 608-273-2021
Home Page: www.agronomy.org

Keith R Schlesinger, Meetings/Convention Director
Stacey Phelps, Exhibit/Meetings Assistant
Linda Nelson, Meetings Specialist
Ellen Bergfeld, Executive Vice President

Co-sponsored with Crop Science Society of America and with the Soil Science Society of America. This event is a unique convergence of the leading agronomy, crops, soils and environmental sciences professionals from around the world. A blend of technical sessions, poster sessions, social functions, career networking and exhibits draw a growing number of prominent professionals and students.
3,500 Attendees
Frequency: November
Founded in 1907

10312 ASABE Annual International Meeting
American Society of Agricultural & Biological Eng.
950 S Cherry Street
Suite 508
Denver, CO 80246-2664

303-759-5091
Fax: 303-758-0190
E-Mail: chesser@asabe.org
Home Page: www.asabe.org

Michael Chesser, Meetings/Conference Director
Sharon McKnight, Meetings Support Staff

100 and more diverse technical sessions, 11 continuing professional development sessions, 5 technical tours, an industry exhibit hall and a keynote address from Dr. Lowell B. Catlett; this year's meeting is full of must attend events.
Frequency: July

10313 ASBC Annual Meeting
American Society of Brewing Chemists
3340 Pilot Knob Road
Saint Paul, MN 55121-2055

651-454-7250
Fax: 651-454-0766

E-Mail: bford@scisoc.org
Home Page: www.meeting.asbcnet.org

Betty Ford, Meetings Director
Sue Casey, Meetings Coordinator
Steven Nelson, VP

Network with peers and learn about the latest technologies available to brewers.
300 Attendees
Frequency: Annual/June

10314 ASHS Annual Conference
American Society for Horticultural Science
1018 Duke Street
Alexandria, VA 22314

703-836-4606
Fax: 703-836-2024
Home Page: www.ashs.org
Social Media: Facebook

Michael W Neff, Executive Director
Tracy Shawn, Assistant Executive Director

A place to meet with colleagues, talk with exhibitors and view over 400 posters.
1,200 Attendees
Frequency: Annual/July

10315 ASME Business Forum & Expo
Associaton of Sales and Marketing Companies
2100 Reston Parkway
Suite 400
Reston, VA 20191

703-758-7790
Fax: 703-758-7787
E-Mail: info@asmc.org
Home Page: www.asmc.org

Julie Casson, Sales Manager

Seminar and 75 exhibits of food manufacturers, computer equipment and services, food product services, foreign trade, incentive displays, shelf space management and related information.
7000 Attendees
Frequency: Annual
Founded in 1985

10316 ASTA/CSTA Joint Annual Convention
American Seed Trade Association
225 Reinekers Lane
Suite 650
Alexandria, VA 22314-2875

703-837-8140
Fax: 703-837-9365
Home Page: www.amseed.com

Jennifer Lord, Meetings Director
Jason Laney, Meetings Associate Director

Includes meetings of all divisions of ASTA and CSTA and several joint meetings of both organizations, exhibits, prominent keynote speakers relevant to both associations, sessions that include representatives discussing how seed moves through the pipelines of our industry to the end user and those whose roles affect the regulation and administration of the framework.
800 Attendees
Frequency: July/Fee $129-$799

10317 AWMA Real Deal Expo
American Wholesale Marketers Association
2750 Prosperity Avenue
Suite 530
Fairfax, VA 22031

703-208-3358
Fax: 703-573-5738
E-Mail: info@awmanet.org
Home Page: www.awmanet.org

Marcia Barker, Public Affairs Manager
Nate Wills, Exhibit Information

The only trade show geared to convenience distributors. Exhibitors include purveyors of tobacco products, candy, beverages, snacks, foodservice, health and beauty care items, general merchandise, warehouse equipment, computer systems and much more.
2,500 Attendees
Frequency: Annual/February

10318 AWS National Conference
American Wine Society
PO Box 279
Englewood, OH 45322

888-297-9070
Fax: 937-529-7888
Home Page: www.americanwinesociety.org

John Hames, Executive Director

The annual conference brings professional, serious amateurs and novices together to discover what is new in wine. Seminars and lectures on all aspects of wine appreciation, wine production, grape growing and cuisine. Attendees must be a member of the society.
Frequency: Annual/November

10319 Ag Progress Days
Penn State University Agricultural Sciences
420 Agricultural Administration Building
University Park, PA 16802

814-865-2081
Fax: 814-865-1677
E-Mail: agprogressdays@psu.edu
Home Page: www.apd.cas.psu.edu

Bob Oberheim, Manager

Agricultural trade show focusing on the innovations and progress made in the agricultural industry.
50M Attendees
Frequency: Annual/August

10320 Agri News Farm Show
Agri News
18 1st Avenue SE
Rochester, MN 55904-3722

507-857-7707
800-633-1727
Fax: 507-281-7474
E-Mail: rallen@agrinews.com
Home Page: www.agrinews.com

Rosie Allen, Advertising Manager
John Losness, President
Todd Heroff, Manager

Annual show of 160 exhibitors of farming equipment, supplies and services.
8000 Attendees
Frequency: March

10321 Agri-Marketing Conference
National Agri-Marketing Association
11020 King Street
Suite 205
Overland Park, KS 66210-1201

913-491-6500
Fax: 913-491-6502
E-Mail: agrimktg@nama.org
Home Page: www.nama.org
Social Media: Facebook, Twitter, LinkedIn, YouTube, Flickr

Vicki Henrickson, President
Beth Burgy, President Elect
Paul Redhage, Secretary/Treasurer

Learn more about customer behaviors, market shares, and other top industry tips.
3500 Members
Frequency: Annual/April
Founded in 1957

10322 Agricultural Retailers Association Convention and Expo
Agricultural Retailers Association
1156 15th Street
Suite 500
Washington, DC 20005

202-457-0825
800-844-4900
Fax: 314-567-6888
E-Mail: kellyaradc.org
Home Page: www.aradc.org

Daren Coppock, President/CEO
Richard Gupton, Sr. VP., Public Policy
Michelle Hummel, VP
Marketing/Communications

Annual show of 120 manufacturers, suppliers and distributors of agricultural chemicals and fertilizers. Seminar, conference and banquet.
1200 Attendees
Frequency: December, St. Louis

10323 Agro-International Trade Fair for Agricultural Machinery & Equipment
Glahe International
PO Box 2460
Germantown, MD 20875-2460

301-515-0012
Fax: 301-515-0016

Biennial show of agricultural machinery and equipment.

10324 All Candy Expo
National Confectioners Association
110 30th Street NW
Suite 200
Washington, DC 20007

202-534-1440
E-Mail: AllCandyExpo@CandyUSA.com
Home Page: allcandyexpo.com

Theresa Delaney, Expo/Membership Director
Daria Moore, Exhibits Manager

A trade show offering exhibits of confectionery industry supplies.
5000+ Attendees
Frequency: Annual/June

10325 All Things Organic Conference and Trade Show
Organic Trade Association
28 Vernon St.
Suite 413
Brattleboro, VT 05301

802-275-3800
Fax: 802-275-3801
E-Mail: info@ota.com
Home Page: www.ota.com

Christine Bushway, Executive Director
Linda Lutz, Membership Manager
Laura Batcha, Marketing/Public Relations Director

Join OTA members, Board and staff for association business, member meetings, and social and networking events.
Frequency: Annual/June

10326 America's Supermarket Showcase
National Grocer's Association
1825 Samuel Morse Drive
Reston, VA 20190

703-437-5300
Fax: 703-437-7768

Dan Rudt

350 exhibits of food and non food consumer goods and services, fixtures and equipment for supermarket operations. Workshop, conference, banquet, luncheon and tours.
5000 Attendees
Frequency: Annual
Founded in 1983

10327 **American Bakery Expo**
5 Executive Court
Suite 2
South Barrington, IL 60010

610-667-9600
Fax: 610-667-1475
E-Mail: info@americanbakeryexpo.com
Home Page: www.americanbakeryexpo.com
Social Media: Facebook, Twitter

Mark Gedris, Membership Manager

Sponsored by Retail Bakers of America and New York/New Jersey Bakers Association. A trade show, creative decorating competition, bakery arts and cakes display, industry chats, tips and trends demonstrations and seminars.
8000 Attendees
Frequency: Annual/October

10328 **American Beverage Licensees Annual Convention & Trade Show**
American Beverage Licensees
5101 River Road
Suite 108
Bethesda, MD 20816-1560

301-656-1494
Fax: 301-656-7539
Home Page: www.nabronline.org

Harry Wiles, Executive Director
Susan Day Pirieda, Office Manager

Annual show of 75 manufacturers, suppliers and distributors of alcoholic beverages.
700 Attendees
Frequency: March

10329 **American Butter Institute Annual Conference**
American Butter Institute
2101 Wilson Boulevard
Suite 400
Arlington, VA 22201

703-243-5630
Fax: 703-841-9328
E-Mail: AMiner@nmpf.org
Home Page: www.butterinstitute.org

The annual conference and meeting is a joint project between the American Butter Institute and the American Diary Products Institute. Over 600 manufacturers, marketers and suppliers of butter and dairy products are represented at the convention which offers the opportunity to network with industry professionals.
Frequency: Annual/November

10330 **American Convention of Meat Processors**
American Association of Meat Processors
One Meating Place
Elizabethtown, PA 17022

717-367-1168
Fax: 717-367-9096
E-Mail: aamp@aamp.com
Home Page: www.aamp.com

Tom K Inboden, President
Jon Frohling, First VP
Daniel T Weber, Second VP

Features a serious educational program for operators, sparkling entertainment, fun and fellowship...plus exhibits and displays by leading industry manufacturers and suppliers.
Frequency: Annual

10331 **American Convention of Meat Processors & Suppliers' Exhibition**
American Association of Meat Processors
One Meating Place
Elizabethtown, PA 17022

717-367-1168
Fax: 717-367-9096
E-Mail: aamp@aamp.com
Home Page: www.aamp.com

Jon Frohling, President
Tim J. Haen, 1st Vice President
Kevin Western, 2nd Vice President
Gary Bardine, 3rd Vice President
Michael D. Sloan, Treasurer

Geared toward U.S., Canadian, and Foreign operators of small and very small firms in the meat, poultry & food business: packers, processors, wholesalers, HRI, retailers, caterers, deli operators, home food service dealers, and catalog marketers. Both members and non-members of the Association attend this event looking for a vast array of ideas, supplies, and services.
1400 Members
Founded in 1939

10332 **American Correctional Food Service Association Conference**
ACFSA
4248 Park Glen Road
Minneapolis, MN 55416-4758

952-928-4658
Fax: 952-929-1318
E-Mail: webmaster@acfsa.org
Home Page: www.acfsa.org

Karen Wesloh, Executive Director
Hope Cook, Assistant Director Exhibits
Gloria Grove, Assistant Director Atendees

Annual exhibit of 200 exhibitors of food prod ucts, kitchen equipment, food processing equipment, dining facility equipment, tableware and related food service equipment.
450 Attendees
Frequency: August
Founded in 1999

10333 **American Craft Beer Week**
Brewers Association
736 Pearl Street
Boulder, CO 80302

303-447-0816
888-822-6273
Fax: 303-447-2825
E-Mail: webmaster@brewersassociation.org
Home Page: www.beertown.org
Social Media: Facebook, Twitter

Chris P. Frey, Chair
Jake Keeler, Vice Chair
Roxanne Westendorf, Secretary

Celebrates craft brewers and craft beer culture in the US.
1900 Members
Founded in 1978

10334 **American Cured Meat Championships, Cured Meat Competition**
American Association of Meat Processors
One Meating Place
Elizabethtown, PA 17022

717-367-1168
Fax: 717-367-9096
E-Mail: aamp@aamp.com
Home Page: www.aamp.com

Jon Frohling, President
Tim J. Haen, 1st Vice President
Kevin Western, 2nd Vice President
Gary Bardine, 3rd Vice President
Michael D. Sloan, Treasurer

This competition is the only national event of its kind in North America. Meat processors enter their products for evaluation by judges who are meat scientists and specialists in the meat industry. This evaluation provides information for product enhancement that could result in greater sales and business opportunities.
1400 Members
Founded in 1939

10335 **American Farm Bureau Federation Annual Convention**
600 Maryland Avenue SW
Suite 1000
Washington, DC 20024

202-406-3600
Fax: 202-406-3602
E-Mail: bstallman@fb.org
Home Page: www.fb.org

Bob Stallman, President
Kathleen Early, Director
Julie Anna Potts, Secretary

Exhibits of farm equipment, chemical fertilizers and agricultural equipment and supplies.
6M Attendees
Frequency: Annual/January

10336 **American Mushroom Institute**
North American Mushroom Conference
1 Massachusetts Avenue, Suite 800
Washington, DC 20001

202-842-4344
Fax: 202-408-7763

Laura Phelps, President

10337 **American Peanut Research and Education Society Annual Meeting**
American Peanut Research and Education Society
Oklahoma State University
376 Ag Hall
Stillwater, OK 74078

405-372-3052
Fax: 405-624-6718
Home Page: www.apres.okstate.edu

Ron Sholar, Executive Officer

Annual meetings of the Society are held for the presentation of papers and/or discussion, and for the transaction of business. At least one general business session will be held during regular annual meetings at which reports from the executive officer and all standing committees will be given to such other matters as the Board of Directors may determine.
Frequency: Annual/July

10338 **American Society for Enology and Vinticulture Annual Meeting**
American Society for Enology and Vinticulture
PO Box 1855
Davis, CA 95617

530-753-3142
Fax: 530-753-3318
E-Mail: society@asev.org
Home Page: www.asev.org

Bill Mead, Event/Tradeshow Coordinator

With technical sessions, research forums, symposia and a supplier shocasw.
Frequency: June
Founded in 1951
Mailing list available for rent

10339 **American Spice Trade Association Annual Meeting**
2025 M Street NW
Washington, DC 20036

202-367-1127
Fax: 202-367-2127
E-Mail: info@astaspice.org
Home Page: www.astaspice.org

Cheryl Deem, Executive Director

10340 **American Sugarbeet Growers Asscociation Annual Meeting**
American SugarBeet

1156 15th Street NW
Suite 101
Washington, DC 20005-1704

202-833-2398
Fax: 202-833-2962
E-Mail: RGeib@americansugarbeet.org
Home Page: www.americansugarbeet.org

Ruthann Geib, Meetings Director/VP
Luther Markwart, Executive VP
James Creek, Executive Assistant
Pam Alther, Office/Financial Manager

Attendees are primarily the officers and board members of these local associations and their spouses, as well as representatives of seed, chemical, and other supplier companies. The purpose of the Annual Meeting is to bring members up-to-date on legislative and international issues that affect the domestic sugar industry, and to determine future policy and strategies.
350 Attendees
Frequency: July/November
Founded in 1983

10341 American Wine Society
3006 Latta Road
Rochester, NY 14612-3298

585-225-7613
Fax: 585-225-7613
E-Mail: angel910@aol.com
Home Page: americanwinesociety.com

Angel E Nardone, Executive Director

Twelve booths.
600 Attendees
Frequency: November
Founded in 1967

10342 Animal Transportation Association
PO Box 797095
Dallas, TX 75379-7095

FAX 214-769-2867

Cherie Derouin, Administrator
Sherry Lynne Boone, Administrative Assistant

An international association promoting the humane handling and transportation of animals.
10-15 booths.
150 Attendees
Frequency: Spring

10343 Annual Chicken Marketing Seminar
National Poultry & Food Distributors
2014 Osborne Road
Saint Marys, GA 31558

770-535-9901
Fax: 770-535-7385
E-Mail: kkm@npfda.org
Home Page: www.npfda.org

Chris Sharp, President
Al Acunto, Vice President
Marc Miro, Treasurer
Kristin McWhorter, Executive Director

Features a very informative program, great networking opportunities, and golf. Learn new techniques for greater marketing success.
Frequency: Annual/July
Founded in 1967

10344 Annual Conference of the Food Distribution Research Society
Food Distribution Research Society
PO Box 441110
Fort Washington, MD 20749

301-292-1970
Fax: 301-292-1787
E-Mail: Jonathan_baros@ncsu.edu
Home Page: fdrs.tamu.edu

John Park, President
Ron Rainey, President-Elect
Kellie Raper, Secretary/ Treasurer
Jennifer Dennis, Director
Stan Ernst, Director

Meeting the quality demands of food buyers. Discuss how the industry is meeting these specific aspects of quality demands, and how these factors impact trade success, how members of the food chain are incorporating them in food production and handling, and how sensory examination is incorporated into food quality assurance, design and product development.
Frequency: Annual/October

10345 Annual Food Manufacturing & Packaging Expo and Conference
The Foodservice Group, Inc
PO Box 681864
Marietta, GA 30068-0032

770-971-8116
Fax: 770-971-1094
E-Mail: kreynolds@fsgroup.com
Home Page: www.fsgroup.com

Chris Bresler, President
Brad Johnson, Vice President
Bob Sheridan, Secretary
Bryan Lewis, Treasurer

This event attracts a diverse range of professionals including CEO's, plant managers, puchasing managers, production and quality assurance managers, engineers, and sales/marketing managers as well as mechanics on the production floor. See and experience the latest technology, systems and related information to improve business operations.
Frequency: Annual/January

10346 Annual Hotel, Motel and Restaurant Supply Show of the Southeast
Leisure Time Unlimited
PO Box 332
Myrtle Beach, SC 29577

843-448-9483
800-261-5991
Fax: 843-626-1513
E-Mail: hmrss@sc.rr.com
Home Page: www.hmrsss.com
Social Media: Facebook, Twitter

Trade show for the hospitality industry.
23000 Attendees
Frequency: Annual/January

10347 Annual Meat Conference
American Meat Institute
1150 Connecticut Ave NW
12th Floor
Washington, DC 20036-4126

202-587-4200
Fax: 202-587-4300
Home Page: www.meatami.com
Social Media: Facebook, Twitter

Dennis Vignieri, Chairman
Larry Odom, Vice Chairman
Nick Meriggioli, Treasurer
Greg Benedict, Secretary
J. Patrick Boyle, President & CEO

The educational format of this conference includes a variety of ways to explore the latest developments in meat retailing today. Gain tools, insights, inspiration and new ideas to differentiate unique products and services, fortify marketing ROI, increase sales, and build customer loyalty.
300 Members
Frequency: Membership Fees Vary
Founded in 1906

10348 Annual Sugar Outlook
1300 L Street NW
Suite 1001
Washington, DC 20005

202-785-1122
Fax: 202-785-5019
E-Mail: sugar@sugar.org
Home Page: www.sugar.org
Social Media: Facebook, Twitter

Andrew Briscoe, President/CEO
Charles W Baker, Executive VP/Chief Science Officer
Melanie Miller, VP Public Relations
Cheryl Digges, VP Public Publicy & Education

To discuss sugar consumption and demand issues and initiatives.
Frequency: Annual/April

10349 Asia Food Processing & Packaging Technology Exhibition
Reed Exhibition Companies
383 Main Avenue
PO Box 6059
Norwalk, CT 06851

203-840-4800
Fax: 203-840-9628

One hundred and seventy four exhibitors for an audience of manufacturers, packaging design and development professionals.
Frequency: Biennial

10350 Associated Food Dealers Annual Trade Show
Associated Food Dealers of Michigan
18470 W Ten Mile
Southfield, MI 48075

248-557-9600
Fax: 248-557-9610
Home Page: www.afdom.org

Ginny Bennett, Show Manager
Frequency: September

10351 Association for Dressing and Sauces Annual Meeting
1100 Johnson Ferry Road
Atlanta, GA 30342

404-252-3663
Fax: 404-252-0774
E-Mail: ads@kellencompany.com
Home Page: www.dressings-sauces.org
Social Media: Facebook

Pam Chumley, President
Jeannie Milewski, Executive Director
Jacque Knight, Membership/Administration Manager

Learn about the most up-to-date technologies and guidelines for packaging, food safety, emulsions and quality.
Frequency: Annual/October

10352 Association of College Unions International Conference
One City Centre, 120 W. 7th St.
Suite 200
Bloomington, IN 47404

812-245-2284
Fax: 812-245-6710
E-Mail: acui@acui.org
Home Page: www.acui.org

Rich Steele, President
Marsha Herman-Betzen, Executive Director
Andrea Langeveld, Marketing

International conference with 100 exhibits of graphic supplies, recreation equipment, computer hardware & software, furnishings, entertainment and speaker bureau information, food service equipment, and more related information and supplies.
1000 Attendees
Frequency: Annual

10353 Atlantic Bakery Expo
Retail Bakers of America

202 Village Circle
Suite 1
Slidell, LA 70458

985-643-6504
800-638-0924
Fax: 985-643-6929
E-Mail: Info@RBAnet.com
Home Page: www.rbanet.com
Social Media: Facebook

Felix Sherman, Sr., President
Kenneth Downey, Sr., 1st Vice President
Marlene Goetzeler, 2nd Vice President
Dale A. Biles, Treasurer
Susan Nicolais, CAE, Secretary

A complete educational program with demonstrations, seminars and hands-on classes to go along with a trade show floor packed with all the exhibitors.
2000 Members
Frequency: Annual
Founded in 1918

10354 Atlantic Coast Exposition: Showcasing the Vending and Food Service Industry
InfoMarketing
2501 Aerial Center Parkway
Suite 103
Morrisville, NC 27560

919-459-2070
Fax: 919-459-2075
Home Page: www.atlanticcoastexpo.com
Social Media: Facebook

Sarah Gillian, Executive Director

This convention offers exhibits of vending machines, office coffee service products, commissary equipment, food and beverage products for the institutional market, as well as accountability systems and security devices.
3M Attendees
Frequency: Annual/May

10355 B&CMA Convention
Biscuit & Cracker Manufacturer's Association
6325 Woodside Court
Suite 125
Columbia, MD 21046

443-545-1645
Fax: 410-290-8585
E-Mail: kkurowski@thebcma.org
Home Page: www.thebcma.org

Stacey Sharpless, President
Kerry Kurowski, Education/Meetings Manager

Provides members an invaluable opportunity to network with fellow executives.
Founded in 1901

10356 BIF Annual Meeting and Research Symposium
Red Angus Association of America
4201 N Interstate 35
Denton, TX 76207-3415

940-387-3502
Fax: 888-829-5573
E-Mail: info@redangus.org
Home Page: www.redangus.org
Social Media: Facebook

Joe Mushrush, President
Greg Comstock, CEO

Seedstock and commercial cow-calf producers, university specialists and breed association leaders will gather to explore innovative technologies and management practices to improve beef production for the benefit of seedstock and commercial producers.
2000 Members
Founded in 1954

10357 BakingTech
American Society of Baking
PO Box 336
Swedesboro, NJ 08085

800-713-0462
Fax: 888-315-2612
E-Mail: info@asbe.org
Home Page: www.asbe.org

Technical sessions, receptions, luncheons, meetings, speakers, and ceremonies with industry experts sharing their knowledge, ideas and experience.
Frequency: Annual/March

10358 Beer, Wine & Spirits Industry Trade Show
Indiana Association of Beverage
200 S Meridian Street
Suite 350
Indianapolis, IN 46225

317-684-7580
Fax: 317-673-4210

Teresa Koch, Show Manager

Annual show of 125 exhibitors of alcohol beverage distillers brewers that are recognized primary sources in the state of Indiana as supplies for retailers.
2500 Attendees

10359 Beltwide Cotton Conference
National Cotton Council of America
7193 Goodlett Farms Parkway
Cordova, TN 38016

901-274-9030
Fax: 901-725-0510
Home Page: www.cotton.org/beltwide/

Mark Lange, President/CEO
A. John Maguire, Senior Vice President

Offers a forum for agricultural professionals.
Frequency: Annual/January

10360 Big Iron Farm Show and Exhibition
Red River Valley Fair Association
PO Box 797
West Fargo, ND 58058-0797

701-282-2200
800-456-6408
Fax: 701-282-6909
E-Mail: bryan@redrivervalleyfair.com
Home Page: www.bigironfarmshow.com

Bryan Schulz, Manager

Connects agricultural exhibitors and attendees who all come together for one purpose, to advance agriculture.
80M Attendees
Frequency: Annual/September

10361 Branding ID: Strategies to Drive Sales
Association of Sales & Marketing Companies
1010 Wisconsin Avenue NW #900
Washington, DC 20007

202-337-9351
Fax: 202-337-4508
E-Mail: info@asmc.org

Mark Baum, President
Karen Connell, Executive VP
Rick Abraham, VP/COO Foodservice
Jamie DeSimone, Director Marketing/Member Services
Frequency: March

10362 CFESA Conference
Commercial Food Equipment Service Association
2216 W Meadowview Road
Suite 100
Greensboro, NC 27407

336-346-4700
Fax: 336-346-4745
E-Mail: asidders@cfesa.com
Home Page: www.cfesa.com
Social Media: Facebook, LinkedIn, MySpace, YouTube

Scott Hester, President

Held twice yearly, members benefit from networking within the foodservice industry, viewing high quality presentations and speeches, visiting interactive workshops, and learning from group meetings to create awareness of new development.
450 Members
Frequency: Bi-Annual
Founded in 1963

10363 CMAA's World Conference on Club Management & Club Business Expo
Club Managers Association of America
1733 King Street
Alexandria, VA 22314

703-739-9500
Fax: 703-739-0124
E-Mail: cmaa@cmaa.org
Home Page: www.cmaa.org

Guy Doria, Show Manager
Jim Singerling, Executive VP

Provides a variety of unique education opportunities that reflect the latest trends in the club industry.
5000 Attendees
Frequency: Annual/February

10364 California League of Food Processors Expo & Showcase of Processed Foods
980 Ninth Street
Sacremento, CA 95814

916-444-9260
Fax: 916-444-2746
Home Page: www.clfp.com

Robert Graf, President/CEO
Ed Yates, Senior VP
Nora Basrai, Meetings/Members Services
Rob Neenan, Senior Vice President
Amy Alcorn, Marketing Manager

Information, networking and displays of processed food from apricots to zucchini in every package type imaginable.
Frequency: January
Founded in 1905

10365 Candy Hall of Fame
National Confectionery Sales Association
Spitfire House
3135 Berea Road
Cleveland, OH 44111

216-631-8200
Fax: 216-631-8210
E-Mail: info@candyhalloffame.org
Home Page: www.candyhalloffame.com/NCSA
Social Media: Facebook, Twitter

Michael F. Gilmore, Chairman
Alastair Northway, President
Mark Antonucci, 1st Vice President
Joe Muck, 2nd Vice President
Morton B. Gleit, Treasurer

Recognizes the achievements of industry leaders drawn from across the world. Inductees are selected from numerous nominations of candy brokers, sales personnel, manufacturers, retail buyers, wholesalers, industry suppliers, retail confectioners and others allied to the industry.
375 Members
Founded in 1899

10366 CaterSource
PO Box 14776
Chicago, IL 60614

773-525-6800
800-932-3632
Fax: 800-387-4744
E-Mail: info@catersource.com
Home Page: www.catersource.com

Micheal Roman, President
Jean Blackmer, Creative Director
Laurie Scheel, Advertising Director

10367 Cattle Industry Convention
Red Angus Association of America
4201 N Interstate 35
Denton, TX 76207-3415

940-387-3502
Fax: 888-829-5573
E-Mail: info@redangus.org
Home Page: www.redangus.org
Social Media: Facebook

Joe Mushrush, President
Greg Comstock, CEO

The oldest and largest convention for the cattle business. The convention and trade show create a unique, fun environment for cattle industry members to come together to network, create policy for the industry and to have some fun.
2000 Members
Founded in 1954

10368 Chicken Marketing Seminar
National Chicken Council
1015 15th Street NW
Suite 930
Washington, DC 20005-2622

202-296-2622
Fax: 202-293-4005
E-Mail: ncc@chickenusa.org
Home Page: www.nationalchickencouncil.org
Social Media: Facebook

Michael J. Brown, President
William P. Roenigk, Senior Vice President
Mary M. Colville, VP of Government Affairs
Dr. Ashley Peterson, VP of Science & Technology

Brings together poultry marketing and sales managers, distributors, supermarket and foodservice buyers, further processors, traders and brokers, and other executives working in the chicken industry. Informative general sessions, social networking events, and recreational opportunities.
Frequency: Annual/July
Founded in 1954

10369 Commodity Classic
American Soybean Association
12125 Woodcrest Executive Drive
Suite 100
Saint Louis, MO 63141-5009

314-576-1770
800-688-7692
Fax: 314-576-2786
E-Mail: registration@commodityclassic.com
Home Page: www.commodityclassic.com

Meeting and exhibits of soybean industry related equipment and information.
4000 Attendees
Frequency: Annual/March

10370 Conference on New Food & Beverage Concepts Innovators
NorthStar Conferences
1211 Avenue of the Americas
New York, NY 10036

212-596-6006
Fax: 212-596-6092
E-Mail: cservice@northstarconferences.com
Home Page: www.northstarconferences.com

Cheryl Callahan, Marketing Director

10371 Council of Food Processors Association Annual Convention
1401 New York Avenue NW
Suite 400
Washington, DC 20005-2124

202-471-1835
Fax: 202-639-5932

John Cady, President
Barbara Arnwine, Executive Director

10372 Craft Brewers Conference and Brew Expo America
Brewers Association
736 Pearl Street
Boulder, CO 80302

303-447-0816
888-822-6273
Fax: 303-447-2825
Home Page: www.craftbrewersconference.com

Charlie Papazian, President
Bob Pease, VP
Cindy Jones, Sales/Marketing Director

For professional brewers, CBC is the number one environment in North America for concentrated, affordable brewing education and idea sharing to improve brewery quality and performance.
2600 Attendees
Frequency: Annual/May

10373 Crop Life America & RISE Spring Conference
Crop Life America
1156 15th St NW
Washington, DC 20005-1752

202-296-1585
Fax: 202-463-0474
E-Mail: webmaster@croplifeamerica.org
Home Page: www.croplifeamerica.org
Social Media: Facebook, Twitter, LinkedIn, YouTube

Jay Vroom, President
Rich Nolan, VP

Discuss the most up-to-date science and regulatory issues impacting the crop protection and specialty pesticide industries.
Frequency: Annual/April

10374 Crop Science Society of America Meeting and Exhibits
Crop Science Society of America
677 S Segoe Road
Madison, WI 53711-1048

608-273-8086
Fax: 608-273-2021
E-Mail: tmoeller@agronomy.org
Home Page: www.crops.org

John Nicholiadis, Managing Editor
David M Kral, Associate Executive VP
Ellen Bergfeld, Executive VP

Annual exhibits of agricultural equipment, supplies and services.
Frequency: October

10375 Dairy-Deli-Bake Seminar & Expo
International Dairy-Deli-Bakery Association
636 Science Drive
Madison, WI 53711-1073

608-310-5000
Fax: 608-238-6330
E-Mail: iddba@iddba.org
Home Page: www.iddba.org

Judy Valaskey, Membership Coordinator

The largest show in the world serving these categories. Also the most focused show because it only targets the serious buyers, merchandisers, and executives who have a shared passion for food.
7000 Attendees
Frequency: Annual/June

10376 Distribution Solutions Conference
International Foodservice Distributors Association
1410 Spring Hill Road
Suite 210
McLean, VA 22102-3035

703-532-9400
Fax: 703-538-4673
Home Page: www.ifdaonline.org

Mark Allen, President & CEO
Jonathan Eisen, Senior VP/ Government Relations

Includes a robust operations agenda that incorporates warehouse and transportation issues, plus a powerful executive track, people issues in an HR track, and special sessions on convenience distribution and supply chain issues.
Frequency: Annual/October

10377 Dixie Classic Fair
City of Winston-Salem
PO Box 7525
Winston-Salem, NC 27109

336-727-2236
Fax: 336-727-2236

David Sparks, Executive Director

10378 EMDA Industry Showcase
Equipment Marketing & Distribution Association
PO Box 1347
Iowa City, IA 52244

319-354-5156
Fax: 319-354-5157
E-Mail: pat@emda.net
Home Page: www.emda.net

Patricia A Collins, Executive VP

Annual convention and 130 exhibits of equipments, supplies and services for wholesaler-distributor and independent manufacturer's representatives of shortline and specialty farm equipment, light industrial, lawn and garden, turf care equipment, eestate and park maintenance equipment.
600 Attendees
Frequency: Annual/November

10379 EastPack
Cannon Communications
11444 W Olympic Boulevard
Los Angeles, CA 90064-1549

323-755-7646
Fax: 310-996-9499
Home Page: www.eastpackshow.com

10380 Eastern Perishable Products Association Trade Show
Eastern Perishable Products Association
17 Park Street
Wanaque, NJ 07465

973-831-4100
Fax: 973-831-8100
Home Page: www.eppainc.org

Barry Kahn, President
Steve Migliara, Administrative Vice President

For the perishable food industry, including dairy, deli, bakery, seafood, food service, meat ect. Exhibitors are manufacturers and services of perishable food products. Attendees are buyers, executives, managers and supervisors

of supermarket chains, independents and specialty stores. 400 Booths
8M Attendees
Frequency: April
Founded in 1971

10381 El Foro
WATT Publishing Company
122 S Wesley Avenue
Mount Morris, IL 61054-1497

815-734-4171
Fax: 815-734-7727
E-Mail: olentine@wattmm.com
Home Page: www.wattnet.com

James Watt, Owner

A trade show and technical symposium for the Latin American poultry, pig and feed industries. Containing 50 booths and 150 exhibits.
275 Attendees
Frequency: July

10382 Executive Conference
Association of Sales & Marketing Companies
1010 Wisconsin Avenue NW
#900
Washington, DC 20007

202-337-9351
Fax: 202-337-4508
E-Mail: info@asmc.org

Mark Baum, President
Karen Connell, Executive VP
Rick Abraham, VP/COO Foodservice
Jamie DeSimone, Director Marketing/Member Services
Frequency: July

10383 Executive Leadership Forum
Snack Food Association
1600 Wilson Blvd
Suite 650
Arlington, VA 22209-2510

703-836-4500
800-628-1334
Fax: 703-836-8262
E-Mail: sfa@sfa.org
Home Page: www.sfa.org

James A McCarthy, President/CEO

An invitation only event for CEO's and senior level executives in the international snack food industry.
800 Members
Frequency: Annual/September
Founded in 1937

10384 Expo Carnes
Consejo Mexicano de la Carne
Ave. Parque Fundidora
#505 Loc. 88, P.N. Col. Obrera
Monterrey N.L. Mexico

52(81)8369 6660
Fax: 52(81)8369 6732
E-Mail: lsierra@apex.org.mx
Home Page: www.expocarnes.com

The every other year Meat Industry International Exposition and Convention that brings together meat suppliers, meat packers and other sectors of the meat industry, facilitating meat specialists from around the world to do business in Latin America. This event takes place in February 2011.
150 Members

10385 Expo of the Americas
EJ Krause & Associates
6550 Rock Spring Drive
Suite 500
Bethesda, MD 20817-1126

301-493-5500
Fax: 301-493-5705
Home Page: www.ejkrause.com

Ned Krause, President

Annual show and exhibits of hotel and restaurant food and beverages.

10386 FEMA Annual Convention
FEMA
1620 I Street NW
Suite 925
Washington, DC 20006

202-293-5800
Fax: 202-462-8998
Home Page: www.femaflavor.org
Social Media: YouTube

Ed R. Hays, Ph.D., President
George C. Robinson, III, President Elect
Mark Scott, Treasurer
Arthur Schick, VP & Secretary
John Cox, Executive Director

FEMA is comprised of flavor manufacturers, flavor users, flavor ingredient suppliers and others with an interest in the U.S. flavor industry.
Founded in 1909

10387 FEMA Winter Committee Meetings
FEMA
1620 I Street NW
Suite 925
Washington, DC 20006

202-293-5800
Fax: 202-462-8998
Home Page: www.femaflavor.org
Social Media: YouTube

Ed R. Hays, Ph.D., President
George C. Robinson, III, President Elect
Mark Scott, Treasurer
Arthur Schick, VP & Secretary
John Cox, Executive Director

FEMA is comprised of flavor manufacturers, flavor users, flavor ingredient suppliers and others with an interest in the U.S. flavor industry.
Founded in 1909

10388 FFA National Agricultural Career Show
5632 Mount Vernon Memorial Highway
Alexandria, VA 22309-1502

888-332-2668
Fax: 800-366-6556
E-Mail: jack-pitzer@ffa.org
Home Page: www.ffa.org

Jack Pitzer, Show Manager

Eight hundred and fifty booths encouraging high school youth to select careers in the agricultural industry.
45M Attendees
Frequency: November

10389 FIAE Annual Convention
Food Industry Association Executives
5657 W. 10770 North
Highland, UT 84003-2711

801-599-1095
Fax: 815-550-1731
E-Mail: jolsen@fiae.net
Home Page: www.fiae.net
Jim Olsen, President

Format of the convention continues to provide valuable information and networking opportunities.
125 Members
Frequency: Annual/November
Founded in 1927

10390 FMI/AMI Annual Meat Conference
American Meat Institute
1150 Connecticut Avenue NW
Washington, DC 20036

202-587-4200
Fax: 202-587-4223
Home Page: www.meatconference.com

Eric Zito, Manager, Convention & Member Svcs

400 booths for equipment, supplies and services to the meat-packaging industry.
12M Attendees
Frequency: Annual/Spring

10391 FPSA Annual Conference
Food Processing Suppliers Association
1451 Dolley Madison Blvd
Suite 101
Mc Lean, VA 22101-3850

703-761-2600
Fax: 703-761-4334
E-Mail: info@fpsa.org
Home Page: www.fpsa.org
Social Media: Facebook, Twitter, LinkedIn

David Seckman, President
George Melnykovich, Senior Advisor
Robyn Roche, CFO

Where suppliers to the food and beverage industry connet and network. Ample opportunity is given to network with peers as participants expand their industry knowledge through educational business sessions and research roundtables.
510 Members
Frequency: Annual/November
Founded in 2005

10392 Farm Progress Show
Farm Progress Companies
255 38th Avenue
Suite P
St Charles, IL 60174-5410

630-462-2224
800-441-1410
E-Mail: drovner@farmprogress.com
Home Page: www.farmprogressshow.com
Social Media: Facebook, Twitter

Matt Jungmann, National Shows Manager

Annual farm show of 400 exhibitors representing various types of agricultural products and services for farmers and agribusiness, including small operations to top producers.
Frequency: Annual/August

10393 Farm Science Review
Ohio State University
590 Woody Hayes Drive
Agricultural Engr. Building- Rm 232
Columbus, OH 43210

614-292-3671
800-644-6377
Fax: 614-292-9448
E-Mail: fendrick.1@osu.edu
Home Page: fsr.osu.edu
Social Media: Facebook, Twitter, YouTube, Flickr

Craig Fendrick, Manager

Annual show of 625 exhibitors of agricultural equipment, supplies and services.
140M Attendees
Frequency: Annual/September

10394 Farmfest
Farm Fairs

PO Box 731
Lake Crystal, MN 56055-0731

507-726-6863
800-347-5863
Fax: 507-726-6750

Annual show of 450 manufacturers, suppliers and distributors of farm equipment and machinery, computers and software products, chemicals, seeds and crops, and techniques of planting, tillage and harvesting.
50M Attendees

10395 Fertilizer Outlook and Technology Conference
Fertilizer Institute
425 Third Street, SW
Suite 950
Washington, DC 20024

202-962-0490
Fax: 202-962-0577
E-Mail: information@tfi.org
Home Page: www.tfi.org
Social Media: Facebook, Twitter, LinkedIn

Ford West, President

Geared towards industry members, financial analysts, business consultants, trade press representatives, agricultural retailers, agronomists, engineers and government economists. Key topics of discussion include new technology and issues that impact plant nutrition.
Frequency: Annual/November

10396 Fish Expo Workboat Northwest
National Fisherman Magazine
121 Free Street
PO Box 7437
Portland, ME 04112

207-842-5608
Fax: 207-842-5509
E-Mail: cmmarketing@divcom.com
Home Page: www.fishexposeattle.com

Jane Bogual, Director

West Coast trade show attracting thousands of visitors from the fields of commercial fishing, workboat, port/harbor, boatbuilding, seafood processing, and other marine industries.
6,000 Attendees
Frequency: November

10397 Food & Nutrition Conference & Expo
American Dietetic Association
120 South Riverside Plaza
Suite 2000
Chicago, IL 60606

312-899-0040
800-877-1600
E-Mail: info@eatright.org
Home Page: www.eatright.org
Social Media: Facebook, Twitter

Katie Roski, Exhibits Manager

The premiere event for food and nutrition professionals. Features the latest nutrition science information, foodservice trends and access to the top experts.
Frequency: Annual/October

10398 Food Marketing Institute Conferences
2345 Crystal Drive
Suite 800
Arlington, VA 22202

202-452-8444
Fax: 202-429-4519
E-Mail: fmi@fmi.org
Home Page: www.fmi.org

Laurel Kelly, Manager Education
Beth Watt, Contact
Tim Hammonds, CEO

Hosts shows that cover a number of different topics.

10399 Food Processing Suppliers Association Annual Conference
1451 Dolley Madison Boulevard
Suite 101
McLean, VA 22101

703-761-2600
Fax: 703-761-4334
E-Mail: info@fpsa.org
Home Page: www.fpsa.org

George Melnykovich, President/CEO
Andrew Drennan, VP

Gain insights into the business of food processing and production.
Frequency: Annual/ March

10400 Food Product Design
Virgo Publishing LLC
3300 N Central Avenue
Suite 300
Phoenix, AZ 85012

480-990-1101
Fax: 480-675-8154
E-Mail: peggyj@vpico.com
Home Page: www.foodproductdesign.com

Peggy Jackson, Publishing Director

Publication distributed to product development professionals and corporate management executives at food and beverage manufacturing and foodservice companies.

10401 Food Safety Summit
ASI Food Safety Consultants
7625 Page Boulevard
St. Louis, MO 63133

314-725-2555
800-477-0778
Fax: 314-727-2563
E-Mail: kristah@asifood.com
Home Page: www.asifood.com
Social Media: Facebook, Twitter, LinkedIn

Dr. W. Ernest McCullough, Vice President of Operations
Tom Huge, President, Food Safety Consultant
Gary Huge, VP, Food Safety Consultants

Provides useful food safety information and solutions to those responsible for assuring food safety across the food supply chain thereby keeping the food safety platform current and relevant for today and tomorrow.
Founded in 1930

10402 Food Safety Summit: Chicago
Eaton Hall Exhibitions
256 Columbia Turnpike
Florham Park, NJ 07932

973-514-5900
800-746-9646
Fax: 973-514-5977
E-Mail: sgoldman@eatonhall.com
Home Page: www.foodsafetysummit.com

Scott Goldman, President
Michael Pesick, Exhibits/Sponsors
Amy Reimer, Registration

Food safety, quality assurance, microbiology and plant sanitation.
1500 Attendees
Frequency: October

10403 Food Safety Summit: Washington
Eaton Hall Exhibitions
256 Columbia Turnpike
Florham Park, NJ 07932

973-514-5900
800-746-9646
Fax: 973-514-5977
E-Mail: sgoldman@eatonhall.com
Home Page: www.foodsafetysummit.com

Scott Goldman, President
Michael Pesick, Exhibits/Sponsors
Amy Reimer, Registration

Held in Washington DC. Food safety, quality assurance, microbiology and plant sanitation.
1500 Attendees
Frequency: March

10404 Food System Summit: Food Choices, Challenges and Realities
Crop Life America
1156 15th St NW
Washington, DC 20005-1752

202-296-1585
Fax: 202-463-0474
E-Mail: webmaster@croplifeamerica.org
Home Page: www.croplifeamerica.org
Social Media: Facebook, Twitter, LinkedIn, YouTube

Jay Vroom, President
Rich Nolan, VP

Hosts speakers sharing a wide range of perspectives on key food and health issues focusing on four significant topic areas: food animal well-being, nutrition and health, food safety, and technology and innovation.
Frequency: Annual/October

10405 Food Tech
Glahe International
PO Box 6009
Sun City Center, FL 33571

813-633-6335
Fax: 813-633-6355

Iye Boyd, President

Annual exhibits of food technology.

10406 Fresh Summit International Convention & Exposition
Produce Marketing Association
1500 Casho Mill Road
PO Box 6036
Newark, DE 19711

302-738-7100
Fax: 302-731-2409
E-Mail: solutionctr@pma.com
Home Page: www.pma.com
Social Media: Twitter, Flickr, YouTube, Xchange

Bryan Silbermann, President & CEO
Lorna D. Christie, Vice President & COO
Duane Eaton, Senior VP, Administration
Yvonne Bull, CFO

Where participants throughout the global fresh produce and floral supply chains come together as a community to learn, network, build relationships and do business.
18500 Attendees
Frequency: Annual/October

10407 Global Minor Use Summit
Crop Life America
1156 15th St NW
Washington, DC 20005-1752

202-296-1585
Fax: 202-463-0474
E-Mail: webmaster@croplifeamerica.org
Home Page: www.croplifeamerica.org
Social Media: Facebook, Twitter, LinkedIn, YouTube

Jay Vroom, President
Rich Nolan, VP

Brings regulators, growers, and representatives of the crop protection industry from around the world together to explore options and incentives for improving the availability of crop protection tools for production of minor crops.
Frequency: Annual/December

10408 Gourmet Products Show
George Little Management
577 Airport Boulevard
Suite 440
Burlingame, CA 94010

650-344-5171
800-272-SHOW
Fax: 650-344-5270
Home Page: www.thegourmetshow.com

Susan Corwin, VP

Cookware, tabletop, gadgets, cutlery, specialtry electric appliances, home textiles, contemporary lifestyle, furnishings, garden and travel accessories, home storage items, personal care, coffee and teas and specialty foods. Contains 950 exhibitors. 2700 booths
9000 Attendees
Frequency: April

10409 Government Action Summit
American Frozen Food Institute
2000 Corporate Ridge Blvd.
Suite 1000
McLean, VA 22102-7844

703-821-0770
Fax: 703-821-1350
E-Mail: info@affi.com
Home Page: www.affi.com

Kraig R. Naasz, President & CEO

National trade association representing the interests of the frozen food industry for more than 60 years. Its 540 corporate members account for more than 90 percent of the frozen food production in the US.
Frequency: Annual/September

10410 Government Affairs Conference
USA Rice Federation
4301 N Fairfax Drive
Suite 425
Arlington, VA 22203

703-226-2300
Fax: 703-236-2301
E-Mail: riceinfo@usarice.com
Home Page: www.usarice.com

Jamie Warshaw, Chairman

Discuss issues and activities for the U.S. rice industry, legislation, training, and seminars.
Frequency: Annual

10411 Grape Grower Magazine Farm Show
Western Agricultural Publishing Company
4974 E Clinton Way
Suite 123
Fresno, CA 93727-1520

559-261-0396
Fax: 559-252-7387

Phill Rhoads, Manager

Seminars, exhibits and prizes for grape growers. Contianing 80 booths and exhibits.

10412 Great American Beer Festival
Brewers Association
736 Pearl Street
Boulder, CO 80302

303-447-0816
888-822-6273
Fax: 303-447-2825
Home Page:
www.greatamericanbeerfestival.com
Social Media: Facebook, Twitter

Charlie Papazian, President
Bob Pease, VP
Cindy Jones, Sales/Marketing Director

Don't miss the largest gathering of beer enthusiasts.
Frequency: Annual/September

10413 GrowerExpo
Ball Publishing
PO Box 9
Batavia, IL 60510-0009

630-208-9080
800-456-5380
Fax: 630-456-0132

John Martens, President

A trade show devoted to horticulture and floriculture production and marketing. 175 booths.
2M Attendees
Frequency: January

10414 HMAA Food & New Products Show
Pacific Expositions
1580 Makaola Street
Suite 1200
Honolulu, HI 92814

808-945-3594
Fax: 808-946-6399

Pat Shine, General Sales Manager
Kimalar K Carroll, Show Director/Coordinator

This popular event, featuring the Food Show in the arena and New Products Show in the exhibition hall, is the original new products expo. Local and mainland exhibitors gather each year to present electronic, household, recreational and food products and service— often unvailed for the first time in Hawaii.
96000 Attendees

10415 Hawkeye Farm Show
Midwest Shows
PO Box 737
Austin, MN 55912

507-437-7969
Fax: 507-437-7752
E-Mail: salesfsu@farmshowsusa.com
Home Page: www.farmshowsusa.com

Penny Swank, Show Manager
18000 Attendees
Frequency: March

10416 Health & Nutrition Product Development Start to Finish
New Hope Natural Media
1401 Pearl Street
Suite 200
Boulder, CO 80302

303-998-9399
E-Mail: rdebarros@newhope.com

Rob DeBarros, Marketing Manager
Frequency: March, Anaheim

10417 Heart of America Hospitality Expo
Bartle Hall Convention & Entertainment Center
301 W 13th Street, Suite 100
Kansas City, MO 64105

816-513-5000
800-821-7060
Fax: 816-513-5001
Home Page: www.kcconvention.com

Charles Hart II, President
Pat Bergaur, Regional Director

10418 Home Baking Association Annual Conference
10841 S Crossroads Drive
Suite 105
Parker, CO 80135

303-840-8787
Fax: 303-840-6877
Home Page: www.homebaking.org

Sharon Davis, Show Manager

Learn the newest techniques and technologies available to the home bakers of America!
Frequency: Annual

10419 Hospitality Food Service Expo
Reed Business Information
275 Washington Street
Boston, MA 02458

617-261-1166
Fax: 630-288-8686
Home Page: www.reedbusiness.com

Patrick Paleno, Show Manager
Barry Reed Jr, CFO
Stuart Whayman, CFO

Four hundred booths featuring educational seminars, culinary salon, and exhibits of products and services.
12M Attendees
Frequency: October

10420 Hydroponic Society of America
PO Box 6067
Concord, CA 94524-1067

FAX 510-232-2323

Gene Brisbon, Executive Director

Thirty five booths featuring the latest in hydroponic equipment.
500 Attendees
Frequency: April

10421 IACP Annual Conference
International Association of Culinary Professional
1100 Johnson Ferry Road
Suite 300
Atlanta, GA 30342

404-252-3663
800-928-4227
Fax: 404-252-0774
E-Mail: info@iacp.com
Home Page: www.iacp.com
Social Media: Facebook, LinkedIn, Flickr

Cynthia Nims, President
Doug Duda, VP & President-Elect
Julia Usher, Secretary/ Treasurer

Go behind the scenes with key industry players, getting access to the style-makers, tasting the latest culinary trends.
3000+ Members
Frequency: Annual/March
Founded in 1978

10422 IAOM Conferences and Expos
International Association of Operative Millers
10100 West 87th Street
Suite 306
Overland Park, KS 66212

913-338-3377
Fax: 913-338-3553
E-Mail: info@iaom.info
Home Page: www.aomillers.org
Social Media: Facebook, LinkedIn

Bart Hahlweg, President
Joe Woodard, Executive VP
Aaron Black, Treasurer

Premier educational events for grain milling and seed processing professionals. The annual events gather milling and allied trade professionals from around the world for several days of education, networking and fellowship.
Frequency: Annual/May
Founded in 1896

10423 IBA Messe Duesseldorf North America
150 N Michigan Avenue
Suite 2920
Chicago, IL 60601

312-621-5800
Fax: 312-781-5188

E-Mail: info@mdna.com
Home Page: www.mdna.com

Frank Thorwirth, President
Pyon Klemon, Vice President
Eva Rowe, Vice President
Justin Kesselring, Project Manager
100 T Attendees
Frequency: October

10424 IBIE Bakery Expo
BEMA: Baking Industry Suppliers Association
7101 College Boulevard
Suite 1505
Overland Park, KS 66210

913-338-1300
Fax: 913-338-1327
E-Mail: info@bema.org
Home Page: www.ibie2007.org

Matt Zielsdorf, Convention Chairman

Co-sponsored with the American Bakers Association. event that offers complete equipment, ingredient and supply solutions to serious baking professionals. Directors and managers from every segment of the grain-based food industry count on IBIE for the new technology, products, strategies and information they need to stay competitive in all aspects of their operation.
20000 Attendees
Frequency: October

10425 IBWA Convention & Trade Show International Bottled Water Assn
International Bottled Water Association
1700 Diagonal Road
Suite 650
Alexandria, VA 22314

703-683-5213
800-WAT-ER11
Fax: 703-683-4074
E-Mail: ibwainfo@bottledwater.org
Home Page: www.bottledwater.org

Trade association representing the bottled water industry. IBWA's member companies produce and distribute 80 percent of the bottled water sold in the US. Our membership includes US and international bottlers, distributors and suppliers.
3250 Attendees
Frequency: Annual/October

10426 IFDA Sales & Marketing Conference
International Foodservice Distributors Association
1410 Spring Hill Road
Suite 210
McLean, VA 22102-3035

703-532-9400
Fax: 703-538-4673
Home Page: www.ifdaonline.org

Mark Allen, President & CEO
Jonathan Eisen, Senior VP/ Government Relations

Newest technologies and marketing ideas for the foodservice distributors industry.
Frequency: Annual/July

10427 IFDA Supply Chain Connect
International Foodservice Distributors Association
1410 Spring Hill Road
Suite 210
McLean, VA 22102-3035

703-532-9400
Fax: 703-538-4673
Home Page: www.ifdaonline.org

Mark Allen, President & CEO
Jonathan Eisen, Senior VP/ Government Relations

Designed to connect distributor and manufacturer counterparts involved in distributor inbound to help drive efficiencies.
Frequency: Annual/July

10428 IFEC Annual Conference
International Food Service Editorial Council
7 Point Place
PO Box 491
Hyde Park, NY 12538-491

845-229-6973
Fax: 845-229-6973
E-Mail: ifec@ifeconline.com
Home Page: www.ifeconline.com
Social Media: Facebook, Twitter

Megan McKenna, President
Jeffrey Yarbrough, Vice President
Amelia Levin, Secretary
John Scroggins, Treasurer

Sessions with government and industry leaders, top chefs, and food tour hosts, gain new insights into the complex role that government plays in shaping America's diet, the growing impact that food environmentalism is having on foodservice, and the confluence of the two.
Frequency: Annual/November

10429 IFT Annual Meeting & Food Expo
Institute of Food Technologists
525 W Van Buren St
Suite 1000
Chicago, IL 60607-3842

312-782-8424
Fax: 312-782-8348
Home Page: www.ift.org

Barbara Byrd Keenan, EVP
Marianne Gillette, President

Brings together the most repected food professionals in industry, government and academia.
20000 Attendees
Frequency: June

10430 IHA Educational Conference & Meeting of Members
International Herb Association
PO Box 5667
Jacksonville, FL 32247-5667

904-399-3241
Fax: 904-396-9467
Home Page: www.iherb.org

Nancy Momsen, President
Kathryn Clayton, Vice President
Karen O'Brien, Secretary
Marge Powell, Treasurer

Conference offers tours, herb information and recipes, as well as leading industry news.
Frequency: Annual/July
Founded in 1986

10431 IMPA Convention & Trade Show
Iowa Meat Processors Association
PO Box 334
Clarence, IA 52216-0334

563-452-3329
Fax: 563-452-2141
E-Mail: execdirector@iowameatprocessors.org
Home Page: www.iowameatprocessors.org

David L. Walter, President
Kent Stricker, 1st Vice President
Kevin Hastings, 2nd Vice President
Andy Thesing, 3rd Vice President

IMPA, leading the way in innovations, marketing, profits and adaptations. Also featuring a cured meat competition and product show.

10432 IS/LD Conference
1350 I Street NW
Suite 300
Washington, DC 20005

202-639-5900
Fax: 202-639-5932
E-Mail: info@gmaonline.org
Home Page: www.gmabrands.com

Cindy Baker, Meetings/Conference Sr. Manager

A place where senior logistics and information technology executives from CPG manufacturers and leading retailers come together to study and seek solutions to the pressing issues affecting today's global supply chain.
Frequency: Annual/April

10433 IWLA Convention & Expo
International Warehouse Logistics Association
2800 S River Rd
Suite 260
Des Plaines, IL 60018-6003

847-813-4699
Fax: 847-813-0115
E-Mail: email@iwla.com
Home Page: www.iwla.com

Joel Anderson, President & CEO
Linda Hothem, Chairman
Paul Verst, Treasurer
Tom Herche, Secretary

Promoting professional development and expose attendees to newer and better ways of doing business.
Founded in 1891

10434 Independent Bakers Association Annual Convention
Independent Bakers Association
Georgetown Station
PO Box 3731
Washington, DC 20027-0231

202-333-8190
Fax: 202-337-3809
E-Mail: independentbaker@yahoo.com
Home Page: www.independentbaker.net

Enables bakers and allied industry representatives to tackle vital issues and develop strategies to enhance industry interests.
Frequency: Annual/June

10435 Institute of Food Technologists Annual Meeting & Food Expo
Institute of Food Technologists
525 W Van Buren
Suite 1000
Chicago, IL 60607-3814

312-782-8424
Fax: 312-782-8348
E-Mail: info@ift.org
Home Page: www.ift.org

Roger Clemens, President
John Ruff, President-Elect
Bruce Stillings, Treasurer
Barbara Byrd Keenan, Executive VP

Technical exposition directed to the $302 billion food industry. Offering person-to-person marketplace and technical forum for suppliers of food ingredients. 2,400 booths.
24M Attendees
Frequency: Annual/June

10436 International Air Conditioning, Heating & Refrigerating Expo
ASHRAE
1791 Tullie Circle NE
Atlanta, GA 30329

404-636-8400
800-527-4723
Fax: 404-321-5478

E-Mail: ashrae@ashrae.org
Home Page: www.ashrae.org

William A Harrison, President
Jeff H Littleton, Executive VP

The largest HVAC&R event in America featuring over 1,600 exhibiting companies. Held in conjunction with the ASHRAE Winter Meeting
30000 Attendees
Frequency: Annual/January

10437 International Assoc of Operative Millers Technical Conference/Trade Show
International Association of Operative Millers
10100 W 87th Street
Suite 306
Overland Park, KS 66212

913-338-3377
Fax: 913-338-3553
E-Mail: info@iaom,info
Home Page: www.aomillers.org
Social Media: Facebook, LinkedIn

Joe Woodard, President
Aaron Black, Vice President
Joel Hoffa, Treasurer
Melinda Farris, Executive VP

Conference, banquet and over 100 exhibits of cereal milling equipment, ancillary equipment, supplics and information.
Frequency: Annual/May

10438 International Baking Industry Exposition
Retail Bakers of America
202 Village Circle
Suite 1
Slidell, LA 70458

985-643-6504
800-638-0924
Fax: 985-643-6929
E-Mail: Info@RBAnet.com
Home Page: www.rbanet.com
Social Media: Facebook

Felix Sherman, Sr., President
Kenneth Downey, Sr., 1st Vice President
Marlene Goetzeler, 2nd Vice President
Dale A. Biles, Treasurer
Susan Nicolais, CAE, Secretary

Thousands of industry professionals unite for the world's largest, most comprehensive Baking Expo of the year. More than 700 exhibiting companies will showcase cutting-edge technologies, equipment and new products to help attendees from the grain-based foods industry strengthen their competitive position, uncover new opportunities and maximize profits.
2000 Members
Frequency: Annual/September
Founded in 1918

10439 International Beverage Industry Exposition
1101 16th Street NW
Washington, DC 20036-4803

202-857-4722

Lisa Feldman, Show Manager

450 booths.
16M Attendees
Frequency: October

10440 International Boston Seafood Show
National Fishermans Expositions
PO Box 7437
Portland, ME 04112-7437

207-842-5500
Fax: 207-842-5505

Diane Vassar, Promotions Director
David Lowell, President

Nine hundred and seventy booths. Annual trade show for the seafood industry.
20M Attendees
Frequency: March

10441 International Dairy Foods Show
International Dairy Foods Association
1250 H St NW
Suite 900
Washington, DC 20005-5902

202-737-4332
Fax: 202-331-7820
E-Mail: membership@idfa.org
Home Page: www.idfa.org

Constance Tipton, President
Neil Moran, Sr. VP, Finance/Tradeshow/Admin.
Peggy Armstrong, VP, Communications
Diana Carmenates, VP, Meetings & Educational Services
Cindy Cavallo, Director, Membership

The International Dairy Foods Association, the Milk Industry Foundation and the International Ice Cream Association work to represent the best interests of manufacturers, distributors and marketers of ice cream, frozen yogurt, frozen desserts, fluid milk, cultured dairy products, dips and other milk products.
Frequency: Annual

10442 International Exposition for Food Processors
Food Processing Machinery Association
1451 Dolly Madison Boulevard
Suite 200
McLean, VA 22101

703-761-2600
800-331-8816
Fax: 703-548-6563
Home Page: www.foodprocessingmachinery.com

Nancy Janssen, Show Manager

Show with more than 1,600 exhibitors, up-to-the-minute technology, fast-track educational sessions. Great source for solutions and networking with industry peers. Colocated with Pack Expo International. McCormick Place, Chicago, IL.
50M Attendees
Frequency: Annual/September

10443 International Food Processors Association Expo
200 Daingerfield Road
Suite 100
Alexandria, VA 22314-2884

703-299-5001
Fax: 703-299-5100

George Melnykozich, Show Manager

Four hundred and twenty five booths of food processing and supplies.
16M Attendees
Frequency: January

10444 International Food Service Exposition
Florida Restaurant Association
230 S Adams Street
Tallahassee, FL 32301

850-224-2250
Fax: 850-224-9213
Home Page: www.flra.com

Hosting the third largest food service show in the country with over 1,200 booths and over 23,000 qualified buyers and attendees.
22000 Attendees

10445 International Foodservice Distributors: Productivity Convention & Expo
201 Park Washington Court
Falls Church, VA 22046-4521

703-532-9400
Fax: 703-538-4673
Home Page: www.ifdaonline.org

Mark Allen, President/CEO
Jonathan Eisen, Senior VP Of Government Relations

Workshops, assemblies, facility tours and an exposition are featured. Educational programming features many practitioners who sahre knowledge to be applied to various operations. Practical information for transportation, information technology, human resources and more.
Frequency: October
Founded in 2003

10446 International Institute of Foods and Family Living Annual Meeting
225 W Ohio Street
Chicago, IL 60610-4198

312-527-3860
Fax: 312-670-0824

Phyllis Favelman, President

10447 International Marketing Conference & Annual Membership Meeting
US Grains Council
1400 K St NW
Suite 1200
Washington, DC 20005-2449

202-789-0789
Fax: 202-898-0522
E-Mail: grains@grains.org
Home Page: www.grains.org

Thomas C. Dorr, President/CEO
Wendell Shauman, Chairman
Don Fast, Vice Chairman
Julius Schaaf, Treasurer
Ron Gray, Secretary

Join Council members and guests to kick off this special meeting with a welcome reception. Great opportunity to network with industry colleagues, get acquainted with new Council members and talk with the Council's international directors and staff.
Frequency: Annual/February
Founded in 1960

10448 International Pizza Expo
MacFadden Protech
137 E Market Street
New Albany, IN 47150
812-949-0909
800-489-8324
Fax: 812-949-1867
E-Mail: boakley@pizzatoday.com
Home Page: www.pizzaexpo.com

William T Oakley, Senior VP Expositions
Linda Keith, Manager
Patty Crone, Manager

One thousand booths featuring exhibits of equipment for pizza industry and restaurants.
6000 Attendees
Frequency: February/March

10449 International Poultry Expo
US Poultry & Egg Association/American Feed Assoc.
1530 Cooledge Road
Tucker, GA 30084-7303

770-493-9401
Fax: 770-493-9257
E-Mail: colentine@poultryegg.org
Home Page:

www.internationalpoultryexposition.com
Social Media: Facebook, Twitter, LinkedIn

Charles Olentine, Executive VP
Pennie Stathes, Logistics Manager

A world large trade show for the poultry and feed sectors.
15000 Attendees
Frequency: January

10450 International Whey Conference
American Dairy Products Institute
126 N Addison St
Elmhurst, IL 60126

630-530-8700
Fax: 630-530-8707
Home Page: www.iwc-2011.org

Dale Kleber, CEO

Offers an unparalleled opportunity to learn about the latest research, cutting-edge product innovations, technical developments and marketing strategies relating to this intriguing, value-added ingredient.
500 Attendees
Frequency: September

10451 Interpack
150 N Michigan Avenue
Suite 2920
Chicago, IL 60601
312-781-5180
Fax: 312-781-5188
E-Mail: info@mdna.com
Home Page: www.mdna.com

Ryan Klemm, Senior Project Manager
Eva Rowe, Vice President
Justin Kesselring, Project Manager
Frequency: April

10452 JPA Annual Meeting
Juice Products Association
750 National Press Building
529 14th Street NW
Washington, DC 20045

202-785-3232
Fax: 202-223-9741
E-Mail: jpa@kellencompany.com
Home Page: www.juiceproducts.org

Richard E Cristol, President
Carol Freysinger, Executive Director

Includes presentations of current interest, such as crop estimates and conditions, transportation and export problems, packaging and marketing concepts, advertising trends and government and regulatory reporting.
Frequency: Annual/Spring

10453 KFYR Radio Agri International Stock & Trade Show
KFYR Radio
PO Box 1658
Bismarck, ND 58502-1738

701-224-9393
800-472-2170
Fax: 701-255-8155
E-Mail: mwall@clearchannel.com
Home Page: www.kfyr.com

Syd Stewart, General Manager
Michelle J Wall, Manager
Jim Lowe, Manager

Annual show of 250 exhibitors of agricultural equipment, supplies, livestock and services.
15000 Attendees
Frequency: February

10454 Keystone Farm Show
Lee Publications
PO Box 121
Palatine Bridge, NY 13428-0121

518-673-2269
Fax: 518-673-2699
E-Mail: info@leepub.com
Home Page: www.leepub.com

Ken Maning, Show Manager
Tom Mahoney, Sales Manager

10455 MEATXPO
National Meat Association
1970 Broadway
Suite 825
Oakland, CA 94612

510-763-1533
Fax: 510-763-6186
E-Mail: info@meatxpo.org
Home Page: www.meatxpo.org

Barry Carpenter, CEO
Jen Kempis, Operations Manager

Biennial suppliers' exposition that brings together consultants, equipment manufacturers and other professionals in the industry, to give a first-hand view of the newest industry equipment, packaging and related services.
Frequency: Annual/February
Founded in 1948

10456 MWR Expo
American Logistics Association
1133 15th Street NW
Suite 640
Washington, DC 20005-2708

202-466-2520
Fax: 202-296-4419
E-Mail: membership@ala-national.org
Home Page: www.ala-national.org

Cologne Hunter, Meetings/Expo Director
Maurice Branch, Operations VP

A gathering of MWR professionals and brings together the many components of the Morale, Welfare and Recreation industry. The event features products and services that are sold to military and government agencies for use in community support activities on military installations throughout the world.
Frequency: Biennial/August
Founded in 1972

10457 Maraschino Cherry and Glace Fruit Processors Annual Convention
5 Ravine Drive
#776
Matawan, NJ 07747-3106

FAX 732-583-0798

Richard Sullivan, Executive VP
Frequency: April/May

10458 Marketechnics
Food Marketing Institute
800 Connecticut Avenue NW
Washington, DC 20006

202-220-0600
Fax: 202-429-4519

Beth Watt, Contact
6000 Attendees

10459 Meat Industry Research Conference
American Meat Science Association
2441 Village Green Pl
Champaign, IL 61822-7676

800-517-AMSA
Fax: 888-205-5834
Fax: 217-356-5370
E-Mail: information@meatscience.org
Home Page: www.meatscience.org

William Mikel, President
Scott J. Eilert, President Elect
Casey B. Frye, Treasurer

Cosponsored by the American Meat Institute Foundation and the American Meat Science Association. A forum for presenting the latest research in terms of direct application for the meat industry.

10460 Mid-America Farm Show
Salina Area Chamber of Commerce
120 W Ash Street
PO Box 586
Salina, KS 67401

785-827-9301
Fax: 785-827-9758
Home Page: www.salinakansas.org

Don Weiser, Show Manager

Annual show of 325 exhibitors of agricultural equipment, supplies and services, including irrigation equipment, fertilizer, farm implements, hybrid seed, agricultural chemicals, tractors, feed, farrowing crates and equipment, silos and bins, storage equipment and farm buildings.
13M Attendees
Frequency: Annual/March

10461 Mid-America Horticultural Trade Show
1000 N Rand Road
Suite 214
Wauconda, IL 60084-1188

847-526-2010
Fax: 847-526-3993
E-Mail: mail@midam.org
Home Page: www.midam.org

Rand A Baldwin CAE, Managing Director
Suzanne Spohr, President
Jim Melka, Secretary

Mid-Am is the premier event featuring more than 650 leading suppliers offering countless products, equipment, and services for the horticulture industry. Mid-Am also offers a variety of educational seminars featuring the best and the brightest in the horticultural and business communities to help keep you informed of the latest trends.
Frequency: January

10462 Mid-America Resturant, Soft Serve & Pizza Exposition
Exhibition Productions
PO Box 81845
Wellesley, MA 02481

800-909-7469
Fax: 617-431-2662

17000 Attendees

10463 Mid-Atlantic Food, Beverage & Lodging Expo
Restaurant Association of Maryland
6301 Hillside Court
Columbia, MD 21046

410-290-6800
800-874-1313
Fax: 410-290-7898
E-Mail: dimbessi@marylandrestaurants.com
Home Page: www.midatlanticexpo.com

Dennis Imbessi, Director Expo/Membership Sales
Licia Spinelli, Director Marketing/Special Events
Valerie Maione, Owner

Annual Mid-Atlantic regional trade show of products and services for the restaurant and hospitality industry. Exhibitors include food manufacturers, equipment, beverages and services providers. Open to food service professionals, taking place annually during the month of September with 500 exhibitors and 600 booths.
15M Attendees
Frequency: Annual/October

10464 Midway USA Food Service and Hospitality Exposition
Kansas Restaurant and Hospitality Association

359 S Hydraulic Street
Wichita, KS 67211-1908

316-267-8383
Fax: 316-267-8400

Dennis Carpenter, CEO

Annual show of 35 food service, beverage, suppliers.
6000 Attendees

10465 Midwest Expo: IL
Illinois Fertilizer & Chemical Association
130 W Dixie Highway
PO Box 186
Saint Anne, IL 60964-0186

815-939-1566
800-892-7122
Fax: 815-427-6573

Jean Trobec, President

Annual show of 130 manufacturers, suppliers and distributors of agricultural chemical and fertilizer application equipment, supplies and services.
2500 Attendees
Frequency: August, Danville

10466 Midwest Farm Show
North Country Enterprises
5322 250th Street
Cadott, WI 54727

715-289-4632
E-Mail: nceinfo@yahoo.com
Home Page: www.northcoutnryentreprises.com

Steve Henry, President

Top farm show exhibiting dairy and Wisconsin's tillage equipment, feed and seed. 20 booths.
11M+ Attendees
Frequency: January
Founded in 1975

10467 Midwest Food Processors Association Convention/Trade Show
4600 American Pkwy
Suite 110
Madison, WI 53718-8334

608-255-9946
Fax: 608-255-9838
E-Mail: info@mwfpa.org
Home Page: www.mwfpa.org

Nick George, President
Robin Fanshaw, Office Manager/Event Planner
Brian Elliott, Director of Communications
Bruce Jacobson, Chair

Processing industry members come together at the convention to learn, network and gain insight to improve their company's course.
1M Attendees
Frequency: Annual/November
Founded in 1905

10468 Midwest Gourmet Exposition
Fairchild Urban Expositions
1395 S Marietta Parkway
Building 400, Suite 210
Marietta, GA 30067

678-901-1700
Fax: 770-956-9644

Robert Collins, President

10469 Midwest Leadership Conference
Indiana Retail Grocers Association
115 W Washington Street
Suite 1364
Indianapolis, IN 46204

317-220-0033
Fax: 317-231-7858

10470 Midwest Regional Grape & Wine Conference
Missouri Grape and Wine Board
1616 Missouri Boulevard
Jefferson City, MO 65109-0630

573-751-3374
800-392-WINE
Fax: 573-751-2868
E-Mail: sue.berendzen@mda.mo.gov
Home Page: www.missouriwine.org
Social Media: Facebook, Twitter, YouTube, Flickr

Jim Anderson, Executive Director
Denise Kottwitz, Assistant

A major national conference for hundreds of vintners, growers and wine industry executives throughout the US Conference includes speakers, trade show, workshops and wine dinners. Over 45 booths.
400+ Attendees
Frequency: Annual/February
Founded in 1985

10471 Midwestern Food Service and Equipment Exposition
Missouri Restaurant Association
9233 Ward Parkway
Suite 123
Kansas City, MO 64114

816-753-5222
Fax: 816-753-6993
Home Page: www.morestaurants.org

Chad Treaster, President

Annual show of 200 suppliers of food service and hospitality industries equipment, supplies and services.
12M Attendees

10472 NAAB Annual Convention
National Association of Animal Breeders
PO Box 1033
Columbia, MO 65205

573-445-4406
Fax: 573-446-2279
E-Mail: naab-css@naab-css.org
Home Page: www.naab-css.org

Gordon Doak, President
Jere Mitchell, Technical Director

A welcomer reception, election of directors, consideration of Bylaw Amendments, resolutions and other association business and a award recognitions presentation.
Frequency: Annual/September

10473 NAAE Annual Convention
National Association of Agricultural Educators
University of Kentucky
300 Garrigus Building
Lexington, KY 40546-215

859-257-2224
800-509-0204
Fax: 859-323-3919
E-Mail: JJackman.NAAE@uky.edu
Home Page: www.naae.org

Wm Jay Jackman, Executive Director
Samantha Alvis, Associate Executive Director

Featuring a meet and greet, professional development workshops, meetings, tours and a career tech expo.
Frequency: Nov/Fees Vary
Founded in 1948
Mailing list available for rent

10474 NABCA Annual Conference
National Alcohol Beverage Control Association
4401 Ford Avenue
Suite 700
Alexandria, VA 22302

703-784-4200
Fax: 703-820-3551
E-Mail: jsgueo@nabca.org
Home Page: www.nabca.org
Social Media: Facebook, Twitter

James M Sgueo, President/CEO

An event to provides its members opportunities to interact and conduct business. Featuring nationally known speakers, informative seminars, interact workshops and suppliers and vendors demonstrating their products.
Frequency: Annual

10475 NABR Tasting & Display Event Annual Convention
American Beverage Licensees
5101 River Road
Suite 108
Bethesda, MD 20816-1560

301-656-1494
Fax: 301-656-7539
Home Page: www.nabronline.org

Harry Wiles, Executive Director
Shawn Ross, Office Manager

Offers exhibits on spirits, beer and wine industry supplies, equipment, bar accessories and computers. The NABR Annual Convention is a gathering of alcohol beverage retailers and proprietors for networking and educational opportunities. An exclusive trade display and tasting event is held to promote brands and services of use to retailers and proprietors. There are 25-75 booths.
500+ Attendees
Frequency: March

10476 NAC Annual Convention & Trade Show
35 E Wacker Drive
Suite 1816
Chicago, IL 60601-2103

312-236-3858
Fax: 312-236-7809
Home Page: www.naconline.org
Social Media: Facebook, LinkedIn

John Evans Jr., President
Ron Krueger II, Board Chairman
Jeff Scudillo, President-Elect
Andrew Cretors, Treasurer

Bringing together the top food and beverage concession leaders in the recreation and leisure-time industry at this annual event.
3M Attendees
Frequency: Annual/August
Founded in 1982

10477 NACD Annual Meeting
National Association of Conservation Districts
509 Capitol Court NE
Washington, DC 20002-4937

202-547-6223
Fax: 202-547-6450
Home Page: www.nacdnet.org
Social Media: Facebook, Flickr

Krysta Harden, CEO
Bob Cordova, Second Vice President

Discussions with agency leaders on priorities for the coming years, training sessions, key leaders in agricultural, conservation and wildlife discussing their perspectives on the future Farm Bill, highlighted challenges and addressing areas of common interest.
Frequency: Annual/February
Founded in 1946

10478 NACS Show
National Association of Convenience Stores
1600 Duke Street
Alexandria, VA 22314

703-684-3600
Fax: 703-836-4564
E-Mail: sromello@nacsonline.com
Home Page: www.nacsshow.com
Social Media: Facebook, Twitter, LinkedIn, YouTube

Sherri Romello, Conventions/Meeting Director
Bob Hughes, Expo/Advertising Director

Access thousands of new profit centers on the expo floor, discover insights on issues facing convenience and petroleum retailers in educational sessions and network with industry peers.
24M Attendees
Frequency: Annual/October

10479 NAFEM Annual Meeting & Management Workshop
NAFEM
161 N Clark Street
Suite 2020
Chicago, IL 60601

312-821-0201
Fax: 312-821-0202
E-Mail: info@nafem.org
Home Page: www.nafem.org

Steven R. Follett, President
Thomas R. Campion, President-Elect
Michael L. Whiteley, Secretary/Treasurer
Deirdre Flynn, Executive Vice President

Workshop geared toward CEOs, CFOs, COOs and directors of member companies. Education is offered on a wide range of topics designed to inspire you personally and professionally. Plenty of networking time with industry peers is built in to encourage the exchange of ideas and expertise.
625 Members
Frequency: Biennial/February

10480 NAFEM Show
North American Assoc of Food Equipment Manufacture
161 N Clark Street
Suite 2020
Chicago, IL 60601

312-245-1054
Fax: 312-821-0202
E-Mail: thenafemshow@nafem.org
Home Page: www.nafem.org

Deirdre Flynn, Executive VP

Attracts approximately 20,000 foodservice professionals and features 500+ exhibitors displaying products for food preparation, cooking, storage and table service.
Frequency: Biennial/February

10481 NAG Conference
National Convenience Store Advisory Group
3331 Street Road
Suite 410
Bensalem, PA 19020

215-245-4555
Fax: 215-245-4060
E-Mail: jhowton@nag-net.com
Home Page: www.nag-net.com

Joseph Howton, Executive VP/COO

Promoting relationships, networking, and executable ideas and takeaways.
Frequency: Annual/September

10482 NAMA National Expo
National Automatic Merchandising Association
20 N Wacker Drive
Suite 3500
Chicago, IL 60606-3102

312-346-0370
800-331-8816
Fax: 312-704-4140
E-Mail: dmathews@vending.org
Home Page: www.vending.org
Social Media: Facebook, Twitter, YouTube

Brad Ellis, Chairman
Mark Dieffenbach, Chairman-Elect
Pete Tullio, Vice Chairman
Dennis Hogan, Secretary/Treasurer

This event features an impressive array of the industry's newest products and hottest technology, educational sessions and unmatched networking opportunities.
5000+ Attendees
Frequency: Annual/October

10483 NAMP PROCESS EXPO
NAMP
1910 Association Drive
Reston, VA 20191-1545

703-758-1900
800-368-3043
Fax: 703-758-8001
E-Mail: smoore@namp.com
Home Page: www.namp.com

Sabrina Moore, Accounting/Meeting Manager
Philip Kimball, Executive Director

Delivering the most valuable tradeshow experience to food industry suppliers and processors at the lowest possible cost.
250 Attendees
Frequency: Annual/November

10484 NAPO International Pizza Expo
National Association of Pizzeria Operators
908 S 8th Street
Suite 200
Louisville, KY 40203

502-736-9500
800-489-8324
Fax: 502-736-9501
E-Mail: bmacintosh@pizzatoday.com
Home Page: www.pizzatoday.com

Bobbie MacIntosh, Booth/Sponsorship Sales Director

The trade show for the pizza industry that includes; pizzeria owners, operators, managers, distributors and food brokers. Workshops, seminars and exhibits.
5400 Attendees
Frequency: March

10485 NASFT Fancy Food Shows
National Association for the Specialty Food Trade
136 Madison Avenue
12th Floor
New York, NY 10016

212-482-6440
Fax: 212-482-6459
Home Page: www.fancyfoodshows.com
Social Media: Facebook

Dennis Deschaine, Chairman
Mike Silver, Vice Chairman
Shawn McBride, Treasurer
Becky Renfro Borbolla, Secretary

Held three times a year; winter, spring and summer time. Over 350 domestic exhibitors from around the country, presentations of exotic new specialty foods from all over the world, tastings, seminars and workshops. These shows are a chance to learn about each product first-hand and do business directly with the decision makers onsite.
30M Attendees
Frequency: 3x Yearly

10486 NBBQA Annual Convention
National Barbecue Association
455 S. 4th Street
Suite 650
Louisville, KY 40202

888-909-2121
Fax: 502-589-3602
E-Mail: nbbqa@hqtrs.com
Home Page: www.nbbqa.org

Kell Phelps, President
Roy Slicker, President-Elect
Marc Farris, Treasurer
Bonnie Gomez, Secretary

Learn and network with a group of BBQ folks on how to better prepare and utilize grills, smokers, fuels, sauces, marinades, rubs and all the necessary utensils. Barbeque presentations, programming, demonstrations, contests, sampling and contacts and leads.
Frequency: Annual/February

10487 NBVA Annual Convention
National Bulk Vendors Association
1202 East Maryland Avenue
Suite 1K
Phoenix, AZ 85014

888-628-2872
Home Page: www.nbva.org
Social Media: Facebook

Bernie Schwarzli, President
Lauri Logue, Vice President
Steve Schnecher, Secretary
Andy Belsky, Treasurer & CPA

Each spring the leading manufacturers and suppliers of bulk vending machines and products display their merchandise. Featuring workshops and seminars to discuss current industry problems and interchange ideas.
530 Attendees
Frequency: Annual/Spring

10488 NBVA Conference
National Bulk Vendors Association
1202 East Maryland Avenue
Suite 1k
Phoenix, AZ 85014

888-628-2872
Home Page: www.nbva.org
Social Media: Facebook

Bernie Schwarzli, President
Lauri Logue, Vice President
Steve Schnecher, Secretary
Andy Belsky, Treasurer & CPA

Brings together suppliers, manufacturers, distributors and operators to see the newest products and innovations. Seminars are created to familiarize attendees with the latest bulk vending innovations and legal issues.
Frequency: Annual/April
Founded in 1950

10489 NBWA Annual Convention
National Beer Wholesalers Association
1101 King Street
Suite 600
Alexandria, VA 22314

703-683-4300
Fax: 703-683-8965
E-Mail: info@nbwa.org
Home Page: www.nbwa.org
Social Media: Facebook, Twitter

Craig A Purser, President & CEO
Michael Johnson, EVP/Chief Advisory Officer
Rebecca Spicer, VP Public Affairs/Chief
Paul Pisano, SVP Industry Affairs & Gen. Counsel

Designed to provide valuable education programs and important networking opportunities for the beer industry. Featuring speakers and

seminars on a number of topics of importance to beer distributors.
2500 Attendees
Frequency: Annual/Fall

10490 NBWA Legislative Conference
National Beer Wholesalers Association
1101 King Street
Suite 600
Alexandria, VA 22314-2944

703-683-4300
Fax: 703-683-8965
E-Mail: info@nbwa.org
Home Page: www.nbwa.org
Social Media: Facebook, Twitter, YouTube, Flickr

Craig A Purser, President & CEO

Industry leaders meet in Washington, D.C. to discuss the industry's legislative goals and priorities with members of Congress and their staffs.
Frequency: Annual/April
Founded in 1938

10491 NBWA Trade Show
National Beer Wholesalers Association
1101 King Street
Suite 600
Alexandria, VA 22314-2944

703-683-4300
Fax: 703-683-8965
E-Mail: info@nbwa.org
Home Page: www.nbwa.org
Social Media: Facebook, Twitter, YouTube, Flickr

Craig A Purser, President & CEO

Gives beer distributors an opportunity to interact with brewers and vendors and make valuable contacts for future business needs. Introduces distributors to new brewers as well as new products, innovative technologies and vendors who supply the materials needed to run their operations.
Frequency: Biennial
Founded in 1938

10492 NCA Annual Convention
National Coffee Association
45 Broadway
Suite 1140
New York, NY 10006

212-766-4007
Fax: 212-766-5815
E-Mail: info@ncausa.org
Home Page: www.ncausa.org
Social Media: Facebook, Twitter, LinkedIn

Dub Hay, Chairman
John E. Boyle, Vice Chairman
Richard Emanuele, Secretary
Robert F. Nelson, President & CEO

Meet a worldwide mix of leadership in the industry in one location, get educational as well as social interaction that cannot be matched at any other convention.
Frequency: Annual/March

10493 NCA Coffee Summit
National Coffee Association
45 Broadway
Suite 1140
New York, NY 10006

212-766-4007
Fax: 212-766-5815
E-Mail: info@ncausa.org
Home Page: www.ncausa.org
Social Media: Facebook, Twitter, LinkedIn

Dub Hay, Chairman
John E. Boyle, Vice Chairman
Richard Emanuele, Secretary
Robert F. Nelson, President & CEO

Bringing together industry knowledge and expertise, for the best available education, networking and product knowledge.
Frequency: Annual/March

10494 NCBA Annual Convention & Trade Show
National Cattlemen's Beef Association
9110 E Nichols Avenue
Suite 300
Centennial, CO 80112

303-694-0305
Fax: 303-694-2851
E-Mail: dkaylor@beef.org
Home Page: www.beefusa.org
Social Media: Facebook, Twitter

Debbie Kaylor, Convention/Meetings Executive Dir.
Valerie Proni, Registration Manager
Kristin Torres, Trade Show Coordinator
Forest Roberts, CEO

The meeting features joint and individual meetings by five industry organizations. Over 250 companies will offer attendees a chance to see the latest products and services while networking with other cattle producers.
28000 Members
6000 Attendees
Frequency: Annual
Founded in 1898

10495 NCC's Annual Conference
National Chicken Council
1015 15th Street NW
Suite 930
Washington, DC 20005-2622

202-296-2622
Fax: 202-293-4005
E-Mail: ncc@chickenusa.org
Home Page: www.nationalchickencouncil.org
Social Media: Facebook

Michael J. Brown, President
William P. Roenigk, Senior Vice President
Mary M. Colville, VP of Government Affairs
Dr. Ashley Peterson, VP of Science & Technology

Brings together senior executives from US chicken processing companies and allied industries to address current agricultural, public affiars, legislative, regulatory, political, economic, and world trade issues affecting the chicken industry.
Frequency: Annual/October
Founded in 1954

10496 NCIMS Conference
National Conference on Interstate Milk Shipments
585 County Farm Road
Monticello, IL 61856

217-762-2656
E-Mail: ncims.bordson@gmail.com
Home Page: www.ncims.org

Leon Townsend, Executive Secretary

Bringing together the people in the dairy industry to discuss laws that directly involve the dairy industry.
Frequency: Biennially/May
Founded in 1950

10497 NCPA's Annual Convention
National Cottonseed Products Association
866 Willow Tree Circle
Cordova, TN 38018-6376

901-682-0800
Fax: 901-682-2856
E-Mail: info@cottonseed.com
Home Page: www.cottonseed.com
Social Media: Twitter, Flickr, YouTube

Ben Morgan, Executive VP & Secretary
Sandi Stine, Treasurer

Featuring a board of directors meeting, committee meeting, luncheons, and discussion on the latest trends in the industry.
Founded in 1897

10498 NCSLA Annual Conference
National Conference of State Liquor Administrators
C/O Massachusetts ABCC
239 Causeway Street, 1st Floor
Boston, MA 02114

617-727-3040
Fax: 617-727-1510
E-Mail: cmarshall@tre.state.ma.us
Home Page: www.ncsla.org

Cheryl Marshall, Conference Coordinator

Provide opportunities for state-licensed administrators to meet and exchange ideas and information and to formulate uniform regulations, statue and laws affecting the sales of alcholic beverages.
Frequency: June/Fee Varies

10499 NICRA Annual Meeting
National Ice Cream Retailers Association
1028 W Devon Avenue
Elk Grove Village, IL 60007

847-301-7500
866-303-6960
Fax: 847-301-8402
E-Mail: info@nicra.org
Home Page: www.nicra.org

Offers educational seminars, exhibits, networking and social opportunities
325 Attendees
Frequency: Annual/November
Founded in 1933

10500 NPFDA Annual Convention
National Poultry & Food Distributors
2014 Osborne Road
Saint Marys, GA 31558

770-535-9901
Fax: 770-535-7385
E-Mail: kkm@npfda.org
Home Page: www.npfda.org

Chris Sharp, President
Al Acunto, Vice President
Marc Miro, Treasurer
Kristin McWhorter, Executive Director

Features the Poultry Suppliers Showcase and many opportunities to network with other industry representatives. Participating in this convention provides access to the latest industry trends, presents ways to improve business operations, and increases number of industry contacts.
Frequency: Annual/January
Founded in 1967

10501 NW Food Manufacturing & Packaging Expo
Northwest Food Processors Association
9700 SW Capitol Highway
Suuite 250
Portland, OR 97219

503-327-2200
Fax: 503-327-2201
E-Mail: nwfpa@nwfpa.org
Home Page: www.nwfpa.org

Teonna Embelton, Events Coordinator
Stephanie Kennedy, Events Consultant

Provides comprehensive programs encompassing topics ranging from food sciences and technologies to energy efficiencies.
Frequency: Jan Oregon

10502 NW Food Manufacturing and Packaging Expo
8338 NE. Alderwood Road
Suite 160
Portland, OR 97220

503-327-2200
Fax: 503-327-2201
E-Mail: nwfpa@nwfpa.org
Home Page: www.nwfpa.org
Social Media: Facebook, Twitter, LinkedIn

David Zepponi, President
David C Klick, Cluster Outreach Executive
Craig Smith, VP
Connie Kirby, Scientific & Technical Director
Pam Barrow, Energy Affairs Manager

NWFPA is an advocate for members interests and a resource for enhancing the food processing industry in Oregon, Washington and Idaho.
350 Members
4000 Attendees
Founded in 1914

10503 NWA Annual Education and Networking Conference & Exhibits
National WIC Association
2001 S St NW
Suite 580
Washington, DC 20009-1165

202-232-5492
Fax: 202-387-5281
Home Page: www.nwica.org
Social Media: Facebook, Twitter

Douglas Greenaway, President & CEO

Offers a terrific opportunity to learn new skills and to network with more than 1200 colleagues and peers, public health professionals, technical experts and nationally recognized speakers from a variety of fields who will engage participants during plenary and concurrent sessions.
900 Members
Frequency: Annual/May
Founded in 1983

10504 NWA Technology Conference
National WIC Association
2001 S St NW
Suite 580
Washington, DC 20009-1165

202-232-5492
Fax: 202-387-5281
Home Page: www.nwica.org
Social Media: Facebook, Twitter

Douglas Greenaway, President & CEO

The future is now! Learn about the latest technologies available and used in all the WIC programs.
900 Members
Frequency: Annual/September
Founded in 1983

10505 NWA Washington Leadership Conference
National WIC Association
2001 S St NW
Suite 580
Washington, DC 20009-1165

202-232-5492
Fax: 202-387-5281
Home Page: www.nwica.org
Social Media: Facebook, Twitter

Douglas Greenaway, President & CEO

The conference will provide a forum to discuss Federal initiatives affecting the health and nutritional wellbeing of WIC mothers and young children, WIC's role as a preventative public health nutrition program, as well as service delivery and the effective management of the Program.
900 Members
Frequency: Annual/March
Founded in 1983

10506 National Agri-Marketing Association Conference
National Agri-Marketing Association
11020 King Street
Suite 205
Overland Park, KS 66210-1201

913-491-6500
Fax: 913-492-6502
E-Mail: agrimktg@nama.org
Home Page: www.nama.org
Social Media: Facebook, Twitter, LinkedIn, YouTube, Flickr

Stephanie Gable, National President
Vicki Henrickson, Vice President

Annual show of 60 exhibitors of marketing and communication suppliers, including trade publications, radio and television broadcast sales organizations, premium/incentive manufacturers, printers, marketing research firms and photographers.
1100 Attendees
Frequency: Annual

10507 National Agricultural Plastics Congress
American Society for Plasticulture
526 Brittany Drive
State College, PA 16803-1420

814-238-7045
Fax: 814-238-7051
E-Mail: contact@plasticulture.org
Home Page: www.plasticulture.org

Patricia Heuser, Executive Director

Congress of research presentations, with exhibit area of equipment, supplies and services relating to greenhouse production and mulch film production of agricultural and horticultural crops.
225 Attendees
Frequency: September

10508 National Association Extension 4-H Agents Convention
University of Georgia
Hoke Smith Annex
Athens, GA 30602

706-542-3000
Fax: 706-542-2115

Peggy Adkins, Show Manager

Fifty booths for young people, youth staff and volunteers involved in 4-H.
1.2M Attendees
Frequency: November

10509 National Association of College and University Food Services Convention
Michigan State University-Manly Miles Building
1405 S Harrison Road
Suite 305
East Lansing, MI 48823-5245

517-332-2494
Fax: 517-332-8144
E-Mail: jspina@nacufs.org
Home Page: www.nacufs.org/nacufs

Joseph Spina, Executive Director
Donna Addy, Administrative Assistant
Nancy Lane, Director

Annual convention and exhibits of equipment, supplies and services for food preparation and service on college and university campuses.

10510 National Association of County Agricultural Agents Conference
National Association of County Agricultural Agents
Courthouse-Room 217
5th & Main Street
Ellensburg, WA 98926

FAX 509-627-74

Annual conference and exhibits for county agricultural agents and extension workers.

10511 National Association of Fruits, Flavors and Syrups Annual Convention
5 Ravine Drive
#776
Matawan, NJ 07747-3106

732-988-4800
Fax: 732-583-0798

Bob Bauer, Director
Frequency: September

10512 National Chicken Council Conference
1015 15th Street NW
Suite 930
Washington, DC 20005-2622

202-296-2622
Fax: 202-293-4005
Home Page: www.nationalchickencouncil.com

Michael J. Brown, President
William P. Roenigk, Senior VP

NCC's Annual Conference brings together senior executives from U.S. chicken processing companies and allied industries to address current agricultural, public affairs, legislative, regulatory, political, economic, and world trade issues affecting the chicken industry.
Frequency: Annual
Founded in 1954

10513 National Confectioners Association Education Exposition
National Confectioners Association
7900 Westpar Drive
Suite A-320
McLean, VA 22102

703-790-5750
Fax: 730-790-5752

Linda Jamie, Finance Executive
600 Attendees

10514 National Confectioners Association Expo
8320 Old Courthouse Road
Suite 300
Vienna, VA 22182

703-790-5750
Fax: 703-790-5752
E-Mail: info@candyusa.org
Home Page: www.allcandyexpo.com

Larry Graham, President
Libby Taylor, VP

Confectionery trade show featuring more chocolate, candy and gum than one can imagine. Held annually in June at Chicago's McCormick Place. 1200 booths.
15 M Attendees
Frequency: June

10515 National Conservation Association District Annual Convention
9150 W Jewell Avenue
Suite 113
Lakewood, CO 80232-6469

303-839-1852

Robert Raschke, Regional Representative

Eighty booths including companies who manufacture, service or who are otherwise involved with equipment used in agricultural production.
2M Attendees
Frequency: February

10516 National Convenience Store Advisory Group Convention

2063 Oak Street
Jacksonville, FL 32204

904-845-5989
Fax: 904-387-3362
E-Mail: jhowton@nag-net.com
Home Page: www.nag-net.com

Joseph Howton, Executive VP/COO

One-hundred booths.
500 Attendees
Frequency: January

10517 National Corn Growers Association

1000 Executive Parkway Drive
Suite 105
Creve Cocur, MO 63141-6397

314-275-9915
Fax: 314-275-7061

Peggy Findley, Director of Conventions

Five hundred and fifty booths of equipment, seed and chemicals.
4000 Attendees
Frequency: February

10518 National Country Ham Association Annual Meeting

PO Box 948
Conover, NC 28613

828-466-2760
800-820-4426
Fax: 828-466-2770
E-Mail: eatham@countryham.org
Home Page: www.countryham.org

Candace Cansler, Executive Director

Providing an array of speakers, discussion topics and activities.
Frequency: Non-Members:$300

10519 National Farm Machinery Show and Championship Tractor Pull

Kentucky Fair and Exposition Center
PO Box 37130
Louisville, KY 40233

502-367-5000
Fax: 502-367-5299
Home Page: www.farmmachineryshow.org

Harold Workman, Show Manager

Annual show of 800 plus exhibitors of agricultural products, equipment, supplies and services.
280M Attendees
Frequency: February

10520 National Food Processors Association Convention

National Food Processors Association
1350 I Street NW
Suite 300
Washington, DC 20005-3377

202-930-0890
Fax: 202-639-5932

John Cady, President
Lisa Weddig, Executive Director

Annual convention and exhibits of equipment, supplies and services for food processing quality control measures, spoilage prevention, frozen food technology, sanitation techniques and waste treatment techniques.

10521 National Frozen and Refrigerated Foods Convention

National Frozen & Refrigerated Foods Association
4755 Linglestown Road Suite 300
PO Box 6069
Harrisburg, PA 17112

717-657-8601
Fax: 717-657-9862
E-Mail: info@nfraweb.org
Home Page: www.nfraweb.org

Dayna Jackson, Admin Asst, Meetings/Member Service

The National Frozen and Refrigerated Foods Convention is an opportunity for you to meet with hundreds of frozen and refrigerated food decision-makers. This premier business event brings representatives from all segments of our industry together to conduct business and build relationships. it is structured around one-on-one business appointments, with ample opportunity to network.
1,200 Attendees
Frequency: Annual/October

10522 National Grange Annual Meeting

1616 H Street NW
Washington, DC 20006

202-628-3507
888 447 2643
Fax: 503-622-0343
E-Mail: info@nationalgrange.org
Home Page: www.nationalgrange.org

William Steel, President
Jennifer Dugent, Secretary
Phil Prelli, Secretary
Judy Sherrod, National Secretary

Agricultural forum.
3M Attendees
Frequency: November

10523 National Grocers Association Annual Convenience & Supermarket Showcase

National Grocers Association
1825 Samuel Morse Drive
Reston, VA 22090

703-437-5300
Fax: 703-437-7768
2800 Attendees

10524 National Homebrewers Conference and National Homebrew Competition

Brewers Association
736 Pearl Street
Boulder, CO 80302

303-447-0816
888-822-6273
Fax: 303-447-2825
E-Mail: webmaster@brewersassociation.org
Home Page: www.beertown.org
Social Media: Facebook, Twitter

Chris P. Frey, Chair
Jake Keeler, Vice Chair
Roxanne Westendorf, Secretary

Education and fun combine for a great experience at the national conference for amateur brewers.
1900 Members
Founded in 1978

10525 National Ice Cream Retailers Association Annual Convention

1028 West Devon Avenue
Elk Grove Village, IL 60007

847-301-7500
866-303-6960
Fax: 847-301-8402
E-Mail: info@nicra.org
Home Page: www.nicra.org

Dan Messer, President
David Zimmerman, President-Elect
Nanette Frey, Vice President
Carl Chaney, Secretary/Treasurer
Lynda Utterback, Executive Director

A major national convention for those in the retail ice ceam and frozen dessert business. Attendees are mostly independent operators/owners and vendors that sell to the retail/wholesale trade. Thirty-five to forty booths.
Frequency: Annual/November

10526 National Nutritional Foods Association

1773 T Street, NW
Washington, DC 20009

202-223-0101
800-966-6632
Fax: 202-223-0250
E-Mail: natural@NPAinfo.org
Home Page: www.npainfo.org
Social Media: Facebook, Twitter, LinkedIn

John F. Gay, Executive Director & CEO
Jeffrey Wright, President

Six hundred booths including educational seminars and exhibits of health and natural foods.
7.5M Attendees
Frequency: Annual/June

10527 National Orange Show

PO Box 5749
San Bernardino, CA 92412-5749

909-888-6788
Fax: 909-889-7666

Esther Armstrong, Executive Director
Brad Randall, Manager

Agricultural forum.
262M Attendees
Frequency: May

10528 National Pest Management Association Annual Eastern Conference

10460 North Street
Fairfax, VA 22030

703-352-6762
800-678-6722
Fax: 703-352-3031
Home Page: www.npmapestworld.org
Social Media: Facebook, Twitter

Robert Lederer, Executive VP

Two hundred forty booths.
7000 Members
3500 Attendees
Frequency: Annual/October
Founded in 1933

10529 National Policy Conference

Crop Life America
1156 15th St NW
Washington, DC 20005-1752

202-296-1585
Fax: 202-463-0474
E-Mail: webmaster@croplifeamerica.org
Home Page: www.croplifeamerica.org
Social Media: Facebook, Twitter, LinkedIn, YouTube

Jay Vroom, President
Rich Nolan, VP

Brings together leading experts, academics and politicos to engage in a debate on the development of the Farm Bill. How does Congress design a Farm Bill that addresses human, social, economic, research and environmental needs while taking into account farmers, consumers

and the natural systems that give us the food and fiber we need to live?
Frequency: Annual/May

10530 **National Potato Council's Annual Meeting**
National Potato Council
5690 Dtc Boulevard
Greenwood Village, CO 80111-3232
303-773-9295
Fax: 303-773-9296
E-Mail: npcspud@ix.netcom.com
Home Page: www.npcspod.com
Annual meeting and exhibits of potato growing equipment, supplies and services.

10531 **National ProStart Invitational**
NRAEF
175 W Jackson Boulevard
Suite 1500
Chicago, IL 60604-2814
312-715-1010
800-765-2122
Fax: 312-583-9767
Home Page: www.nraef.org
Culinary and management competition attracts top high school ProStart students from around the country. Winning teams secure scholarships from the NRAEF and The Coca-Cola Company, along with colleges and universities.
Frequency: Annual/April
Founded in 1987

10532 **National Restaurant Association Convention**
National Restaurant Association
150 N Michigan Avenue
Suite 2000
Chicago, IL 60601
312-853-2525
Fax: 312-853-2548
Mary Heftman, Senior VP
80000 Attendees
Frequency: May

10533 **National Soft Drink Association Show**
1101 16th Street NW
Suite 700
Washington, DC 20036-4877
202-463-6732
Fax: 202-463-8178
Susan K Neely, President
Patricia M Vaughan, Secretary
Jim L Turner, Treasurer
Annual show of 300 members of soft drink makers and their suppliers.
25M Attendees
Frequency: Annual Fall
Founded in 1919

10534 **National Turkey Federation Annual Meeting**
National Turkey Federation
1225 New York Avenue NW
Suite 400
Washington, DC 20005-6404
202-898-0100
Fax: 202-898-0203
E-Mail: info@turkeyfed.org
Home Page: www.eatturkey.com
Social Media: Facebook, Twitter, YouTube
Joel Brandenberger, President
Jennifer Zukowski, Meetings & Membership
Advocates for all segments of the US turkey industry, providing services and conducting activities that increase demand for its members' products. The federation also protects and enhances its members' ability to effectively and profitably provide wholesome, high quality, nutritious turkey products.
Frequency: Annual

10535 **National Watermelon Association**
Annual Meeting
406 Railroad Street
Morven, GA 31638
229-775-2130
Fax: 229-775-2344
Nacy Childers, Contact

10536 **National Wheat Growers Association Convention**
415 2nd Street NE
Suite 300
Washington, DC 20002-4900
202-547-7800
Fax: 202-546-2638
E-Mail: wheatworld@wheatworld.org
Home Page: www.wheatworld.org
Social Media: Facebook, Twitter, YouTube
Wayne Hurst, President
Erik Younggren, 1st Vice President
Bing Von Bergen, 2nd Vice President
Paul Penner, Secretary-Treasurer
Major agri business exhibits including farm equipment and services. 100 booths.
Frequency: Annual/January

10537 **Natural Products Exposition East**
New Hope Natural Media
1301 Spruce Street
Boulder, CO 80302
303-939-8440
Fax: 303-939-9559
20000 Attendees

10538 **Natural Products Exposition West**
New Hope Communications
1301 Spruce Street
Boulder, CO 80302
303-939-8440
Fax: 303-939-9559
31000 Attendees

10539 **New England Equipment Dealers Association**
PO Box 895
Concord, NH 03302-0895
603-225-5510
Fax: 603-225-5510
George M Becker, Managing Director
Annual convention and trade show held the first weekend in December for farm, industrial and outdoor equipment dealers in the six New England states. 95 booths.
300 Attendees
Frequency: December

10540 **Nightclub & Bar Beverage Retailer Beverage & Food Convention and Trade Show**
Oxford Publishing
307 West Jackson Avenue
Oxford, MS 38655
662-236-5510
888-966-2727
Fax: 662-513-3990
E-Mail: registration@oxpub.com
Home Page: www.nightclub.com

10541 **Nightclub & Bar/Beverage Retailer Food & Beverage Trade Show**
Oxford Publishing
307 W Jackson Avenue
Oxford, MS 38655-2154
662-236-5510
888-966-2727
Fax: 662-513-3990
E-Mail: jrobinson@oxpub.com
Home Page: www.nightclub.com
Jennifer Robinson, Show Manager
Adam Alson, Founder
Yosi Benvenisti, Owner
Fastest growing food, beverage and hospitality show in the US. This show is for both on-premise and off-premise.
20M Attendees
Frequency: March/July/November

10542 **Nightclub and Bar/Beverage Retailer Convention and Trade Show**
National Bar and Restaurant Association
307 Jackson Avenue W
Oxford, MS 38655
662-236-5510
800-247-3881
Fax: 662-236-5541
Home Page: www.beverage-retailer.com
Jennifer Robinson, Senior VP
Hollis Green, Trade Show Director
Kaytee Hazlewood, VP Marketing
The industry's first national conference and trade show devoted to business basics, promotions and marketing for liquor stores, nightclubs and bars. More than 2,500 exhibits.
38800 Attendees
Frequency: March

10543 **North American Deer Farmers Association Annual Conference & Exhibit**
North American Deer Farmers Association
104 S Lakeshore Drive
Lake City, MN 55041-1266
651-345-5600
Fax: 651-345-5603
E-Mail: info@nadefa.org
Home Page: www.nadefa.org
Social Media: Facebook
Carolyn Laughlin, President
R.Ray Burdette, First VP
Will Ainsworth, Second VP
Bill Pittenger, Third VP
Dr. Hank Dimuzio, Treasurer
Annual show of more than 30 exhibitors of deer farming equipment, supplies and services.
550+ Attendees
Frequency: Annual/Summer
Founded in 1984

10544 **North American Farm and Power Show**
Tradexpos
811 W Oakland Avenue
PO Box 1067
Austin, MN 55912
507-437-4697
800-949-3976
Fax: 507-437-8917
E-Mail: steve@tradexpos.com
Home Page: www.tradexpos.com
Steve Guenthner, Show Director
Agri-business farm show for the 5-state region. Free admission and parking.
32M Attendees
Frequency: Annual/March

10545 **North American Fertilizer Transportation Conference**
Fertilizer Institute

425 Third Street, SW
Suite 950
Washington, DC 20024

202-962-0490
Fax: 202-962-0577
E-Mail: information@tfi.org
Home Page: www.tfi.org
Social Media: Facebook, Twitter, LinkedIn

Ford West, President

Provides an opportunity for shippers and carriers to discuss issues of concern and work to reach mutually-beneficial solutions to logistical problems.
Frequency: Annual/October

10546 North American Olive Oil Association Mid- Year Meeting
North American Olive Oil Association
3301 Route 66
Suite 205, Building C
Neptune, NJ 07753

732-922-0500
Fax: 732-922-3590
Home Page: www.aboutoliveoil.org

Bob Bauer, President

Olive growers and oil processors group for legislative advocacy and trade networking.

10547 North American Specialty Coffee Retailers' Expo
PO Box 14827
Portland, OR 97293

503-236-2587
800-548-0551
Fax: 503-236-3165
Home Page: www.nascore.net

Jan Weigel, Director
Founded in 1995

10548 Northeast Food Service and Lodging Expo and Conference
Reed Exhibition Companies
383 Main Avenue
Norwalk, CT 06851

203-840-4800
Fax: 203-840-4824

Linda Karpowich, Customer Service Manager

Annual show of 600 exhibitors of food services, operating equipment and services for the hospitality and institutional foodservice industry.
29000 Attendees

10549 Northeast Pizza Expo
MacFadden Protech
137 E Market Street
New Albany, IN 47150

812-949-0909
800-489-8324
Fax: 812-949-1867
E-Mail: lkeith@pizzatoday.com
Home Page: www.pizzaexpo.com

William T Oakley, Senior VP Expositions
Linda F Keith, Manager
Patty Crone, Manager

Manufacturers, food purveyors and service representatives from pizza or related industries.

10550 Northwest Agricultural Congress
4991 Drift Creek Rd SE
Sublimity, OR 97385-9764

503-769-8940
Fax: 503-769-8946
Home Page: www.nwagshow.com

Jim Heater, Show Manager

Second largest agricultural show on the west coast. Show is produced by the Northwest Horticultural Congress which is a partnership between Oregon Horticultural Society, the Oregon Association of Nurseries and Northwest Nut Growers Association. Show held in conjunction with annual meetings and seminars by all three of the horticultural groups.
21000 Members

10551 Northwest Food Manufacturing & Packaging Association
Northwest Food Processors Association
6950 SW Hampton Street
Suite 340
Portland, OR 98223-8332

503-639-7676
Fax: 503-639-7007
Home Page: www.nwpfa@nwpfa.org

Stephanie Green, Show Manager
Mindy Todd, Marketing Coordinator

Containing 450 booths.
3000 Attendees
Frequency: Janurary

10552 Nut Grower Magazine Farm Show
Western Agricultural Publishing Company
4974 E Clinton Way
Suite 123
Fresno, CA 93727-1520

559-261-0396
Fax: 559-252-7387

Phill Rhoads, Manager

Productions seminars, guest speakers, prizes and exhibits for nut growers. Containing 80 booths and exhibits.

10553 OFPA Annual Convention and Exposition
Ozark Food Processors Association
2650 N Young Avenue
Fayetteville, AR 72704

479-575-4607
Fax: 479-575-2165
E-Mail: ofpa@uark.edu
Home Page: ofpa.uark.edu

Cindy Stricklaw, President
Roure Threfall, Director

OFPA members and registered guests learn about new trends in the food industry during technical sessions and the exposition. The location for the 2012 meeting is Springfield, AR.
500 Attendees
Frequency: Annual/ April
Founded in 1906

10554 Oklahoma Restaurant Convention & Expo
Oklahoma Restaurant Association
3800 N Portland Avenue
Oklahoma City, OK 73112-2948

405-942-8181
800-375-8181
Fax: 405-942-0541
Home Page: www.okrestaurants.com

Lori Culver, Convention Manager

Annual show of 450 manufacturers, suppliers and distributors. Exhibits of providers of food service and hospitality products, services and equipment. Held at the Myriad Convention Center in Oklahoma City, Oklahoma.
9M Attendees
Frequency: April
Founded in 1938

10555 PACK International Expo
Packaging Machinery Manufacturers Institute
4350 N Fairfax Drive
Suite 600
Arlington, VA 22203

703-243-8555
Fax: 703-243-8556
E-Mail: expo@pmmi.org
Home Page: www.pei2006.packexpo.com

Jim Pittas, Trade Show VP
Dinah Sprouse, Trade Show Operations Director
Kim Beaulieu, Exhibitor Services Manager

Browse more than 2,000 packaging and processing exhibitors covering virtually the entire packaging supply chain. Network with others in the industry, attend specialized education sessions led by industry experts and evaluate the latest advances while experiencing hands on demonstrations of the latest technologies in the industry.
1600 Attendees
Frequency: Oct-Nov

10556 PACex International
Packaging, Food Process and Logistics Exhibition
2255 Sheppard Avenue E
Suite E330
Toronto Ontario M2J-4YI

416-490-7860
Fax: 416-490-7844
Home Page: www.pacexinternational.com

Maria Tavares, Expositions Manager
15000 Attendees
Frequency: September-October

10557 PLMA Trade Show
Private Label Manufacturers Association
630 Third Avenue
New York, NY 10017-6506

212-972-3131
Fax: 212-983-1382
E-Mail: info@plma.com
Home Page: www.plma.com

Brian Sharoff, President
Myra Rosen, VP
Tom Prendergast, Director, Research Services

The best place for private label networking.
3200+ Members
10000 Attendees
Frequency: Annual/November
Founded in 1979

10558 PMA Foodservice Conference & Exposition
Produce Marketing Association
1500 Casho Mill Road
Newark, DE 19711-3547

302-738-7100
Fax: 302-731-2409
E-Mail: showmanagement@pma.com
Home Page: www.pma.com
Social Media: Twitter, YouTube, Flickr

Jamie Hillegas, Show Manager
Susan Eller, Trade Show Planner

Join the who's-who of chefs, menu developers, restaurant operators, grower-shippers, distributors and foodservice suppliers to see and sample the newest products and services, learn about the latest consumer trends and tastes, see old colleagues or make new contacts.
Frequency: Annual/July
Founded in 1981

10559 PMA Fresh Summit International Convention & Exposition
Produce Marketing Association
1500 Casho Mill Road
PO Box 6036
Newark, DE 19711-3547

302-387-7100
Fax: 302-731-2409
E-Mail: showmanagement@pma.com

Home Page: www.pma.com/freshsummit
Social Media: Facebook, Twitter, YouTube

Don Harris, Summit Chairman
Jamie Hillegas, Show Manager
Susan Eller, Trade Show Planner
Sheli Parlier, Exhibits Sales Manager
Bryan Silbermann, President

An event that attracts buyers and suppliers from the produce and floral industries; from the retail and foodservice channels and from more than 70 counties.
17M Attendees
Frequency: Annual/October

10560 PTNPA Annual Convention
Peanut & Tree Nut Processors Association
PO Box 2660
Alexandria, VA 22301
301-365-2521
Fax: 301-365-7705
E-Mail: ptnpa@mindspring.com
Home Page: www.ptnpa.org

General meeting sessions, keynote speakers, exhibitors from the industry.
400 Attendees
Frequency: Annual/January

10561 Pan-American International Livestock Exposition
State Fair of Texas
PO Box 150009
Dallas, TX 75315-0009
214-565-9931
Fax: 214-421-8792
E-Mail: livestock@greatstatefair.com
Home Page: www.bigtex.com

Benny Clark, Director
Elvis Presley, Vice President

Annual show and exhibits of livestock, livestock equipment, agricultural technology and consumer products.
3.5M Attendees
Frequency: September/October

10562 Pickle Packers International Pickle Fair
1620 i St Nw
Suite 925
Washington, DC 20006-4035
202-312-2859
Fax: 630-584-0759
E-Mail: staff@ppii.org

Richard Hentschell, Executive VP

Fifty booths, seminars and programs held in odd numbered years.
300+ Attendees
Frequency: October

10563 Poultry Supplier Showcase
National Poultry & Food Distributors
2014 Osborne Rd
Saint Marys, GA 31558
770-535-9901
877-845-1545
Fax: 770-535-7385
E-Mail: info@npfda.org
Home Page: www.npfda.org

Chris Sharp, President
Al Acunto, Vice President
Marc Miro, Treasurer
Kristin McWhorter, Executive Director

Annual convention and poultry suppliers showcase. Three day convention and trade show.
900 Attendees
Frequency: Annual/January
Founded in 1967

10564 Pre-Harvest Food Safety Conference
North American Meat Processors Association
1910 Association Drive
Reston, VA 20191-1500
703-758-1900
800-368-3043
Fax: 703-758-8001
Home Page: www.namp.com

Philip Kimball, Executive Director
Sabrina Moore, Accounting/Meetings Manager
Ann Wells, Director Scientific Affairs
Jane Jacobs, Communications Director

Brings regulators and researchers together with experts from the poultry industry, and the allied industries that serve them, to discuss the known and unknown issues associated with the control of food borne pathogens in pre-harvest operations. Conference will be one of the most thorough explorations into the poultry pre-harvest arena that has ever been conducted.
Frequency: Annual/January

10565 Presidents Conference
International Foodservice Distributors Association
1410 Spring Hill Road
Suite 210
McLean, VA 22102-3035
703-532-9400
Fax: 703-538-4673
Home Page: www.ifdaonline.org

Mark Allen, President & CEO
Jonathan Eisen, Senior VP/ Government Relations

Gain breakthrough insights and take away high value solutions. Collaborate with fellow leaders in an information rich learning environment with plenty of networking opportunities. All-industry forum addressing issues impacting the foodservice supply chain.
Frequency: Annual/October

10566 Private Label Manufacturers Association Trade Show
630 Third Avenue
New York, NY 10017
212-972-3131
Fax: 212-983-1382
E-Mail: info@plma.com
Home Page: www.plma.com

Brian Sharoff, President
Myra Rosen, Vice President

A private label trade show.
3200+ Members
Frequency: Annual/November
Founded in 1979

10567 ProMat
Material Handling Industry of America
8720 Red Oak Boulevard
Suite 201
Charlotte, NC 28217-3992
704-676-1190
Fax: 704-676-1199
E-Mail: gbaer@mhia.org
Home Page: www.mhia.org

Greg Baer, Senior Sales Associate
Jennifer Breadling, Manager Of Communications

The premier showcase of material handling and logistics solutions in North America. The show is designed to offer productivity solutions and information by showcasing the products and services of over 700 leading material handling and logistics providers.
Frequency: Annual

10568 Process Expo
Food Processing Suppliers Association
1451 Dolley Madison Blvd
Suite 101
Mc Lean, VA 22101-3850
703-761-2600
Fax: 703-761-4334
E-Mail: info@fpsa.org
Home Page: www.fpsa.org
Social Media: Facebook, Twitter, LinkedIn

David Seckman, President
George Melnykovich, Senior Advisor
Robyn Roche, CFO

Tradeshow where qualified buyers representing every market of the food industry meet face to face with suppliers showcasing the newest developments in processing technology. Exhibitors are able to demonstrate state-of-the-art food processing equipment in baking, beverage, dairy, fruit and vegetable, and meat/poultry industries.
510 Members
Frequency: Annual/November
Founded in 2005

10569 Produce Marketing Association
1500 Casho Mill Road
PO Box 6036
Newark, DE 19711-3547
302-738-7100
Fax: 302-731-2409
E-Mail: bsilbermann@mail.pma.com
Home Page: www.pma.com

Bryan Silbermann, President
Dan Henderaon, Marketing

Largest convention and exposition for the fresh fruit, vegetable and floral industries. More than 12,000 people and 1,500 booths.
12M Attendees
Frequency: October

10570 Productivity Conference and Distribution/ Transportation Exposition
Food Distributors International
1410 Spring Hill Road
Suite 210
McLean, VA 22102
703-532-9400
Fax: 703-538-4673
Home Page: www.ifdaonline.org

Mark S. Allen, President/CEO
Malcolm Sullivan, Jr., Chairman
Thomas Zatina, Vice Chairman
James Crawford, Treasurer

A conference exhibiting services and supplies geared toward the grocery industry. Containing 200 booths and 200 exhibits.
2400 Attendees
Frequency: Annual/October

10571 R&DA Annual Spring & Fall Meeting and Exhibition
R&D Associates
16607 Blanco Road
Suite 305
San Antonio, TX 78232-1940
210-682-4302
Fax: 830-493-8036
E-Mail: jfagan@militaryfood.org

Jim Fagan, Meeting Coordinator

Hear presentations by key officials, network with decision makers, get updates on key issues and gain a competitive edge within the industry.
300 Attendees
Frequency: Apr/Oct/Non-Members:$1099

10572 RFA Annual Conference
Refrigerated Foods Association

1640 Powers Ferry Road
Bldg. 2, Suite 200A
Marietta, GA 30067

770-303-9905
Fax: 770-303-9906
E-Mail: info@refrigeratedfoods.org
Home Page: www.refrigeratedfoods.org

Brian Edmonds, President
George Bradford, Vice President
Steve Loehndorf, Secretary
Wes Thaller, Treasurer

The RFA Conference is a great way to network and gain important new information affecting the industry, including technical innovations, sales and marketing tips, consumer trends, distribution solutions, new product and package development, and food safety issues.
200+ Members
Frequency: Annual/February
Founded in 1980

10573 RFA Annual Conference & Exhibition
Refrigerated Foods Association
2971 Flowers Road S
Suite 266
Atlanta, GA 30341-5403

770-452-0660
Fax: 770-455-3879
E-Mail: info@refrigeratedfoods.org
Home Page: www.refrigeratedfoods.org

Brian Edmonds, President
George Bradford, Vice President
Steve Loehndorf, Secretary
Wes Thaller, Treasurer

Suppliers displaying the latest offerings in equipment, packaging, ingredients and services for the industry. A great way to network and gain important new information affecting the industry, including technical innovations, sales and marketing tips, consumer trends, distribution solutions, new product and packaging development and food safety issues.
Frequency: Annual/April

10574 Restaurants Rock
NRAEF
175 W Jackson Boulevard
Suite 1500
Chicago, IL 60604-2814

312-715-1010
800-765-2122
Fax: 312-583-9767
Home Page: www.nraef.org

The only official party of the NRA Show, Restaurants Rock brings together the restaurant and hospitality industry in a night of networking and celebration.
Frequency: Annual/May
Founded in 1987

10575 Retail Confectioners International Annual Convention and Exposition
Retail Confectioners International
1807 Glenview Road
Suite 204
Glenview, IL 60025-2968

847-724-6120
Fax: 847-724-2719

Van Billington, Director
Michelle May, Contact

Annual exhibition offering exhibits of confectionery equipment, supplies, finished products and packaging materials.
1.5M Attendees
Frequency: Annual

10576 SANA/USB Annual Soy Symposium
Soyfoods Association of North America
1001 Connecticut Avenue NW
Suite 1120
Washington, DC 20036

202-659-3520
E-Mail: info@soyfoods.org
Home Page: www.soyfoods.org

Nancy Chapman, Executive Director
Anne Chambers, Membership Coordinator

Co-sponsored with United Soybean Board, see the latest innovative designs and products from industry representatives.
Frequency: Apr/Non-Members:$995
Founded in 1978

10577 SAVOR, An American Craft Beer & Food Experience
Brewers Association
736 Pearl Street
Boulder, CO 80302

303-447-0816
888-822-6273
Fax: 303-447-2825
E-Mail: webmaster@brewersassociation.org
Home Page: www.beertown.org
Social Media: Facebook, Twitter

Chris P. Frey, Chair
Jake Keeler, Vice Chair
Roxanne Westendorf, Secretary

The main beer and food pairing event in the US. Where beer enthusiasts and foodies can interact directly with some of the greatest brewers and brewery owners in the world.
1900 Members
Founded in 1978

10578 SBS Annual Conference & Exhibition
Society for Biomolecular Sciences
36 Tamarack Avenue
Suite 348
Danbury, CT 06811

203-788-8828
Fax: 203-748-7557
E-Mail: email@sbsonline.org
Home Page: www.sbsonline.org

Agnes Amos, Exhibitions/Meetings Director
Marietta Manoni, Exhibitions/Meetings Manager

This event brings together leaders in the pharmaceutical, biotech and agrochemical industries from around the world. Highlighting the impact of screening and technology applications on drug discovery.
Frequency: Sept/Non-Members $1,445
Founded in 1995

10579 SCAA Annual Conference & Exhibition
Specialty Coffee Association of America
330 Golden Shore
Suite 50
Long Beach, CA 90802

562-624-4100
Fax: 562-624-4101
E-Mail: coffee@scaa.org
Home Page: www.scaa.org

Ted Lingle, Executive Director
Scott Welker, Administrative Director

The country's premier coffee event, attracting coffee professionals from more than 40 countries. Attendees include coffee producers, exporters and importers, roasters, manufacturers, brew masters, and consumer enthusiasts.
8000 Attendees
Frequency: April/Non-Members:$585
Founded in 1982

10580 SCAA Annual Exposition
Specialty Coffee Association of America
330 Golden Shore
Suite 50
Long Beach, CA 90802-4246

562-624-4100
Fax: 562-624-4101
E-Mail: info@scaa.org
Home Page: www.scaa.org
Social Media: Facebook, Twitter, YouTube

Ric Rhinehart, Executive Director
Tracy Ging, Deputy Executive Director
Ted Lingle, Senior Advisor

Roasters & retailers attend and have the opportunity to exhibit products on the show floor, network with industry's decision makers, and further their professional careers by participating in the SCAA's numerous lectures, labs or certification programs.
2500+ Members
Frequency: Annual/April
Founded in 1982

10581 SCST Annual Meeting
Society of Commerical Seed Technologists
101 E State Street
Suite 214
Ithaca, NY 14850

607-256-3313
Fax: 607-256-3313
E-Mail: scst@twcny.rr.com
Home Page: www.seedtechnology.net

Anita Hall, Executive Director

A joint meeting with the Association of Official Seed Analysts and the Association of Official Seed Certifying Agencies. Workshops, Exhibits, speakers and more regarding the seed industry.
Frequency: June
Founded in 1922

10582 SEAFWA Annual Convention
Southeast Association of Fish & Wildlife Agencies
8005 Freshwater Farms Road
Tallahassee, FL 32309-9009

850-893-1204
Fax: 850-893-6204
E-Mail: SEAFWA2006@dgif.virginia.gov
Home Page: www.seafwa2006.org/www.seafwa.org

Robert M Brantly, Executive Secretary
Dianne Waller, Conference Coordinator

Providing a forum for presentation of information and exchange of ideas regarding the management and protection of fish and wildlife resources throughout the nation but emphasis on the southeast.
Frequency: Oct/Nov
Founded in 1947

10583 SFA's Legislative Summit
Snack Food Association
1600 Wilson Blvd
Suite 650
Arlington, VA 22209-2510

703-836-4500
800-628-1334
Fax: 703-836-8262
E-Mail: sfa@sfa.org
Home Page: www.sfa.org

James A McCarthy, President/CEO

Discuss many of the most important legislative issues which will impact the snack food industry.
800 Members
Frequency: Annual/May
Founded in 1937

10584 SNAXPO
Snack Food Association

1600 Wilson Blvd
Suite 650
Arlington, VA 22209-2510

703-836-4500
800-628-1334
Fax: 703-836-8262
E-Mail: sfa@sfa.org
Home Page: www.sfa.org

James A McCarthy, President/CEO

The world's largest, most comprehensive trade show devoted exclusively to the international snack food industry. Owners, executives and buyers from every segment of the industry around the globe come together for this premier event.
800 Members
Frequency: Annual/March
Founded in 1937

10585 SNAXPO: Snack Food Association
1600 Wilson Boulevard
Suite 650
Arlington, VA 22209-2510

703-836-4500
800-628-1334
Fax: 703-836-8262
E-Mail: sfa@sfa.org
Home Page: www.sfa.org

Judi Barth, VP Marketing
Ann Wilkes, VP Communications
2000 Attendees
Frequency: February/March
Founded in 1938

10586 School Nutrition Association Annual National Conference
School Nutrition Association
120 Waterfront Street
Suite 300
National Harbor, MD 20745

301-686-3100
800-877-8822
Fax: 301-686-3115
E-Mail: servicecenter@schoolnutrition.org
Home Page: www.schoolnutrition.org

Helen Phillips, President
Sandy Ford, President-Elect
Leah Schmidt, VP
Beth Taylor, Secretary/Treasurer

Learn, grow and exchange ideas with others committed to the healthful feeding of our children. With over 400 exhibitors and more than 90 quality education sessions, ANC gives you the opportunity to learn about the top trends and issues in school nutrition.
Frequency: Annual/July

10587 Southern Convenience Store & Petroleum Show
GA Ass'n of Convenience Stores/Petroleum Retailers
168 North Johnston Street
Suite 209
Dallas, GA 30132-4744

770-736-9723
877-294-1885
Fax: 770-736-9725
E-Mail: jtudor@aol.com
Home Page: www.gacs.com
Social Media: Facebook

Jim Tudor, President
Angela Holland, Vice President

Targeted to reach key individuals in the convenience store and petroleum industry from throughout the South. Attendees will include board members and key representatives from the Georgia Association of Convenience Stores and will be open to retailers from throughout the southern US.
2000 Attendees
Frequency: Annual/October

10588 Southwest Foodservice Exposition
Texas Restaurant Association
PO Box 1429
Austin, TX 78767

512-472-8990
Fax: 512-472-2777

31000 Attendees

10589 Special Event
Special Event Corporation
PO Box 8987
Malibu, CA 90265-8987

310-317-4522
Fax: 310-317-9644

4300 Attendees

10590 Sunbelt Agricultural Exposition
PO Box 28
Tifton, GA 31793-0028

229-985-1968
Fax: 229-387-7503
E-Mail: sunexpo@surfsouth.com

Dr. Edward White, Director

The latest agricultural technology in products and equipment plus harvesting and tillage demonstrations in the field. Largest farm show in North America. 4,000 booths.
Frequency: October

10591 Supermarket Industry Convention and Educational Exposition
Food Marketing Institute
2345 Crystal Drive
Suite 800
Arlington, VA 22202

202-452-8444
Fax: 202-429-4519
Home Page: www.fmi.org
Social Media: Facebook, Twitter, LinkedIn, YouTube

Brian Tully, Show Manager
Matt Olmsted, Consumer Goods Exhibiting
Allyson Samuel, Technolgy and Packaging Exhibits
Carrie Anderson, Attending

Features over 1,500 exhibitors, over 30 educational workshops and unique pavilions as well as the presentation of the Food Marketing Institute's annual state of the industry research. Attended by a worldwide audience of professionals with an interest in the food distribution industry from CEOs through store level management.
36000 Attendees
Frequency: Annual/May

10592 SupplySide East
Virgo Publishing LLC
3300 N Central Avenue
Suite 300
Phoenix, AZ 85012

480-990-1101
Fax: 480-675-8154
E-Mail: peggyj@vpico.com
Home Page: www.supplysideshow.com
Social Media: Facebook, Twitter, LinkedIn

Tradeshow that brings global dietary supplement, food and personal care companies together with healthy and innovative ingredient suppliers. Meadowlands Exposition Center, Secaucus New Jersey. More than 340 booths.
Frequency: Annual/May

10593 SupplySide West
Virgo Publishing LLC
3300 N Central Avenue
Suite 300
Phoenix, AZ 85012

480-990-1101
Fax: 480-675-8154
E-Mail: peggyj@vpico.com
Home Page: www.supplysideshow.com

Tradeshow that brings global dietary supplement, food and personal care companies together with healthy and innovative ingredient supplier. More than 1100 booths.
Frequency: Annual/October

10594 TFI Fertilizer Marketing & Business Meeting
Fertilizer Institute
425 Third Street, SW
Suite 950
Washington, DC 20024

202-962-0490
Fax: 202-962-0577
E-Mail: information@tfi.org
Home Page: www.tfi.org
Social Media: Facebook, Twitter, LinkedIn

Ford West, President

Brings together members from each sector of the fertilizer industry for two days of networking and conducting business leading up the the spring planting season.
Frequency: Annual/February

10595 TFI World Fertilizer Conference
Fertilizer Institute
425 Third Street, SW
Suite 950
Washington, DC 20024

202-962-0490
Fax: 202-962-0577
E-Mail: information@tfi.org
Home Page: www.tfi.org
Social Media: Facebook, Twitter, LinkedIn

Ford West, President

Providing two days of networking and conducting business with industry leaders. Agenda includes two breakfast sessions with high profile speakers focusing on the global challenges facing the fertilizer industry.
Frequency: Annual/September

10596 The NAFEM Show
NAFEM
161 N Clark Street
Suite 2020
Chicago, IL 60601

312-821-0201
Fax: 312-821-0202
E-Mail: info@nafem.org
Home Page: www.nafem.org

Steven R. Follett, President
Thomas R. Campion, President-Elect
Michael L. Whiteley, Secretary/Treasurer
Deirdre Flynn, Executive Vice President

Attracts foodservice professionals and features exhibitors displaying products for food preparation, cooking, storage and table service. Connecting buyers and sellers of foodservice equipment and supplies, The NAFEM Show provides a showcase for the hottest and coolest products available and features education sessions and social events with big-name entertainment.
625 Members
Frequency: Biennial/February

10597 The NGA Show
National Grocers Association

1005 N Glebe Rd
Suite 250
Arlington, VA 22201-5758

703-516-0700
Fax: 703-516-0115
E-Mail: info@nationalgrocers.org
Home Page: www.nationalgrocers.org
Social Media: Facebook, Twitter, LinkedIn, YouTube

Peter J. Larkin, President & CEO
Charlie Bray, Executive VP & COO
Tom Wenning, Executive VP & General Counsel

Providing an unparalleled opportunity to network, learn, and advance business. Guaranteed a convention experience that is informational, motivational, and enjoyable.
Frequency: Annual/February

10598 Top-to-Top Conference
Association of Sales & Marketing Companies
1010 Wisconsin Avenue NW
#900
Washington, DC 20007

202-337-9351
Fax: 202-337-4508
E-Mail: info@asmc.org

Mark Baum, President
Karen Connell, Executive VP
Rick Abraham, VP/COO Foodservice
Jamie DeSimone, Director Marketing/Member Services
Frequency: February

10599 Top2Top
Grocery Manufactures Association
1801-J York Road
Suite 384
Lutherville, MD 21093

410-715-4084
800-617-1170
Fax: 888-668-7496
E-Mail: info@fsmaonline.com
Home Page: www.fsmaonline.com
Social Media: Facebook

Rick Abraham, President & CEO
Sharon Boyle, Vice President
Jessica Muffoletto, Manager, Membership & Meetings

Learn, share, and be inspired. Network with industry peers and hear from extraordinary speakers.
250 Members
Founded in 1995

10600 Tortilla Industry Annual Convention and Trade Exposition
Tortilla Industry Association
1600 Wilson Blvd
Suite 650
Arlington, VA 22209

800-944-6099
Fax: 800-944-6177
E-Mail: info@tortilla-info.com
Home Page: www.tortilla-info.com

Nathan W. Fisher, Chairman
Joseph F. Riley, Chairman-Elect
Nick Scheurer, 2nd Vice President
Sam Tamayo, Treasurer

A growing event for tortilla producers and suppliers that provides the only annual trade show featuring materials, equipment, and services exclusively for the Tortilla industry, plus business lectures to assist in improving your business and personal knowledge.
900 Attendees
Frequency: Annual/September

10601 Tree Fruit Expo
Western Agricultural Publishing Company
4974 E Clinton Way
Suite 123
Fresno, CA 93727-1520

559-261-0396
Fax: 559-252-7387

Phill Rhoads, Manager

Productions seminars, dessert contest, guest speakers, prizes and exhibits for tree fruit growers. Containing 80 booths and exhibits.

10602 US Apple Association Annual Apple Crop Outlook & Marketing Conference
8233 Old Courthouse Road
Suite 200
Vienna, VA 22182

703-442-8850
Fax: 703-790-0845
E-Mail: info@usapplc.org
Home Page: www.usapple.org
Social Media: Facebook, Twitter, YouTube

Provides up to the minute apple market analysis and premier networking opportunities.
300+ Attendees
Frequency: Annual/April

10603 US Meat Export Federation
1050 17th Street
Suite 2200
Denver, CO 80265-2077

303-623-6328
Fax: 303-623-0297
E-Mail: info@usmef.org
Home Page: www.usmef.org

Jackie Boubin, Director of Services
Phil Seng, President

A convention of meat packers, grain, cattle and hog producers, trade officials and agribusiness and a trade show offering exhibits of beef, pork, veal, lamb products and more for foreign buyers. Trade show in May, convention in November.
300 Attendees

10604 USA Rice Millers' Association Convention
USA Rice Millers Association/Federation
4301 N Fairfax Drive
Suite 425
Arlington, VA 22203-1616

703-226-2300
Fax: 703-236-2301
E-Mail: riceinfo@usarice.com
Home Page: www.usarice.com/industry/meetings/hotel_annual.html
Social Media: Facebook, Twitter, YouTube

Jeanette Davis, Convention Coordinator
Betsy Ward, President/CEO
Linda Sieh, Vice President Finance
Johnny Broussard, Legislative Affairs Director
Lauren Echols, Government Affairs Coordinator

Exhibits, seminars on the advances in products, technologies and services, keynote speakers from the industry. The convention is recognized as the annual gathering for the U.S. rice milling industry. It is an opportunity to strengthen business ties and make new connections.
Frequency: Annual/June
Founded in 1900

10605 Unified Wine and Grape Symposium
PO Box 1855
Davis, CA 95617-1855

530-753-3142
Fax: 530-753-3318
E-Mail: info@unifiedsymposium.org
Home Page: unifiedsymposium.org

Bill Mead, Event/Tradeshow Coordinator

One of the industry's premier gatherings, presents a vital platform to focus on the issues shaping today, while interfacing the topics and trends shaping the future of grapegrowing and winemaking.
Frequency: Annual/January

10606 Unipro Food Service Companies Association
Unipro Food Service
PO Box 724945
Atlanta, GA 31139-1945

770-952-0871
Fax: 770-952-0872

Donna Campbell, Show Manager
Roger Toomey, CEO

250 tables.
1.3M Attendees

10607 United Produce Show
United Fresh Fruit & Vegetable Association
1901 Pennsylvania Avenue NW
Suite 1100
Washington, DC 20006

202-303-3400
Fax: 202-303-3433
E-Mail: united@unitedfresh.org
Home Page: www.uffva.org
Social Media: Facebook, Twitter, YouTube

Access to the best and newest products from the entire retail supply continuum, make new contacts, learn what your competition is bringing to the table and much more.
30M Attendees
Frequency: Annual/May

10608 Upper Midwest Hospitality Restaurant & Lodging Show
Corcoran Expositions
100 W. Monroe
Suite 1001
Chicago, IL 60603

312-541-0567
Fax: 312-541-0573
Home Page: www.corcexpo.com

Tom Corcoran, President
33000 Attendees
Founded in 1990

10609 Vinegar Institute Annual Meeting
1100 Johnson Ferry Road
Suite 300
Atlanta, GA 30342

404-252-3663
Fax: 404-252-0774
E-Mail: vi@kellencompany.com
Home Page: www.versatilevinegar.org

Pamela A Chumley, President
Jeannie Milewski, Executive Director

Presentations regarding possible health claims for vinegar, an economic update and a world wine and grape supply update. Other topics include from green to greenwashing; how food companies are succeeding (and failing) at market sustainability and best practices in energy & carbon management. Also numerous networking opportunities available for all attendees.
Frequency: Annual/March

10610 WFLO/IARW Annual Convention & Trade Show
World Food Logistics Organization

1500 King Street
Suite 201
Alexandria, VA 22314

703-373-4300
Fax: 707-373-4301
E-Mail: mkalaski@iarw.org
Home Page: www.wflo.org

Megan Kalaski, Trade Show Coordinator
Lorien Onderdonk, Member Services Coordinator

offers a singular opportunity to present product and service information to the largest concentration of public refrigerated warehouse executives in the world.
Frequency: Annual/April

10611 WSWA Annual Convention
Wine and Spirits Wholesalers of America
805 15th Street NW
Suite 430
Washington, DC 20005

202-719-9792
Fax: 202-789-2405
E-Mail: Kari.Mazanec@wswa.org
Home Page: www.wswa.org

Rae Ann Bevington, Convention Manager
Kari Mazanec, Exhibit Manager
Juanita Duggan, CEO

Get the latest information for wholesale wine distributors, exhibits and speakers from the industry.
Frequency: April-May
Founded in 1943

10612 WSWA Convention & Exposition
Wine and Spirits Wholesalers of America
805 15th Street NW
Suite 430
Washington, DC 20005

202-371-9792
Fax: 202-789-2405
Home Page: www.wswa.org

Robert Harmelin, Chairman
Charles Merinoff, Vice Chairman
Douglas Hertz, Senior Vice President
Alan Dreeben, Vice President
Brien Fox, Secretary

Where distributors seek out new and exciting beverage products for US consumers, meet with existing portfolio partners and look for services to enhance internal operations. Providing the opportunities needed to introduce new products or grow brands, products, or services in the US marketplace.
450 Members
Frequency: Annual/April
Founded in 1943

10613 WSWA Executive Committee Meeting
Wine and Spirits Wholesalers of America
805 15th Street NW
Suite 430
Washington, DC 20005

202-371-9792
Fax: 202-789-2405
Home Page: www.wswa.org

Robert Harmelin, Chairman
Charles Merinoff, Vice Chairman
Douglas Hertz, Senior Vice President
Alan Dreeben, Vice President
Brien Fox, Secretary

The Executive Committee, Committee Chairs and Vice Chairs and past chairmen are invited to attend.
450 Members
Frequency: Annual/January
Founded in 1943

10614 Waldbaum International Food Nutrition Show
80 Town Line Road
Rocky Hill, CT 06067-1249

860-529-1416
Fax: 860-721-6258

John Masterson, Manager

A wide variety of new and existing food products and services. 225 booths.
25M Attendees
Frequency: March

10615 Walnut Council Annual Meeting
Walnut Council
Wright Forestry Center
1011 N 725 West
West Lafayette, IN 47906-9431

765-583-3501
Fax: 765-583-3512
E-Mail: walnutcouncil@walnutcouncil.org
Home Page: www.walnutcouncil.org

Liz Jackson, Exhibits Coordinator

Exhibits of equipment, supplies and services for walnut growing.
Frequency: Annual/July

10616 Washington Insight & Advocacy Conference
International Foodservice Distributors Association
1410 Spring Hill Road
Suite 210
McLean, VA 22102-3035

703-532-9400
Fax: 703-538-4673
Home Page: www.ifdaonline.org

Mark Allen, President & CEO
Jonathan Eisen, Senior VP/ Government Relations

IFDA members from coast-to-coast converge on the capitol to gain insight from congressional leaders and federal regulators and let them know how their decisions affect the foodservice distribution idustry.
Frequency: Annual/April

10617 West Coast Seafood Show
Diversified Expositions
121 Free Street
Portland, ME 04112

207-842-5500
Fax: 207-842-5505
E-Mail: food@divcom.com
Home Page: www.westcoastseafood.com

Karen Butland, Show Manager
Brian Perkins, Executive Director
Frequency: November

10618 Western Farm Show
Southwestern Association
638 W 39th Street
Kansas City, MO 64111

816-561-5323
800-728-2272
Fax: 816-561-1991

Annual show of 700 manufacturers, suppliers and distributors of equipment, supplies and services relating to the agricultural industry.
35M Attendees
Frequency: February

10619 Western Food Industry Exposition
555 Capitol Mall
Suite 235
Sacramento, CA 95814-4557

FAX 703-876-0904
E-Mail: cga@cmgexpo.com

Keith Biersner, Account Executive

Retailers from 13 western states and suppliers from around the world. Relevant education sessions, vibrant exhibits and excellent social events are all designed to create the best form to enhance your companies bottom line. 400 booths.
3500 Attendees
Frequency: October
Founded in 1998

10620 Western Food Service and Hospitality Expo
California Restaurant Association
383 Main Avenue
PO Box 6059
Norwalk, CT 06851
203-840-5612
800-840-5612
Fax: 203-840-9612
Home Page: www.westernfoodexpo.com

Chris Tatulli, Sales Manager
Steve Kalman, Industry VP

Showcases food products, food service equipment and allied services for the restaurant, food service and hospitality industries, as well as gourmet and prepared foods. Located on the West Coast, the show alternates annually between the Moscone Center in San Francisco and the LA Convention Center.
20M Attendees
Frequency: August

10621 Western Restaurant Show
California Restaurant Association
1011 10th St
Sacramento, CA 95814-3501
916-447-5793
Fax: 213-384-1723

A trade show of food service equipment, supplies and services. 2,000 booths.
35M Attendees
Frequency: August

10622 Wine and Spirits Wholesalers of America
805 15th Street NW
Suite 430
Washington, DC 20005

202-371-9792
Fax: 202-789-2405
E-Mail: wswa@wswa.org
Home Page: www.wswa.org

Craig Wolf, President/CEO
Megan McIntire, Director Convention/Meetings
Karen Gravois, VP Public Relations/Communications

Suppliers of alcoholic beverages from around the world. 300 booths plus educational sessions.
3M Attendees
Frequency: April

10623 Wineries Unlimited
Vineyard & Winery Management
3883 Airway Drive
Suite 250
Santa Rosa, CA 95403

707-577-7700
Fax: 707-577-7705
Home Page: www.wineriesunlimited.com
Social Media: Facebook, Twitter

The largest, longest running, and most powerful wine industry event in the eastern US.
2000 Attendees
Frequency: Annual/February

10624 Winter State Policy Conference
Wine and Spirits Wholesalers of America

805 15th Street NW
Suite 430
Washington, DC 20005

202-371-9792
Fax: 202-789-2405
Home Page: www.wswa.org

Robert Harmelin, Chairman
Charles Merinoff, Vice Chairman
Douglas Hertz, Senior Vice President
Alan Dreeben, Vice President
Brien Fox, Secretary

Provides an opportunity for wholesaler state association leaders to discuss the political and legal issues facing wholesalers across the country.
450 Members
Frequency: Annual/December
Founded in 1943

10625 Wisconsin Restaurant Expo
Wisconsin Restaurant Association
2801 Fish Hatchery Road
Madison, WI 53703-3197

608-270-9950
800-589-3211
Fax: 608-270-9960
E-Mail: dfaris@wirestaurant.org
Home Page: www.wirestaurant.org

Dawn Renz-Faris, Exposition Director
Carrie Douglas, Executive Assistant
Gail Parr, Executive|Vice President

Comprehensive foodservice trade show featuring hundreds of exhibits, free educational seminars and exciting floor show events.
10000 Attendees
Frequency: March
Founded in 1933
Mailing list available for rent

10626 World Conference & Exhibition on Oil Seed and Vegetable Oil Utilization
American Oil Chemists Society
2710 S. Boulder
Urbana, IL 61802-6996

217-359-2344
Fax: 217-351-8091
E-Mail: general@aocs.org
Home Page: www.aocs.org
Social Media: Facebook, Twitter

Sevim Erhan, Committee Chairperson

Attendees are interested in learning the latest information on currint and emerging technologies from all areas in oilseed and vegetable oil utilization.
Frequency: Annual/August

10627 World Dairy Expo
3310 Latham
Madison, WI 53713

608-224-6455
Fax: 608-224-0300
E-Mail: wde@wdexpo.com
Home Page: www.worlddairyexpo.com

Tom McKittrick, Manager
Lisa Behnke, Marketing Manager
65M Attendees
Frequency: October, Annually
Founded in 1966

10628 World Pork Exposition
National Pork Producers Council
PO Box 10383
Des Moines, IA 50306-9960

515-788-8012
Fax: 847-838-1941
E-Mail: wrigleyj@nppc.org
Home Page: www.worldpork.org

John Wrigley, General Manager
Alice Vinsand, Trade Show Manager

More than 450 companies show the newest technology, information, products and services for pork producers. Activities include breed shows and sales, business district, environmental education center, pork product showcase, big grill, pork 101, educational seminars and activities.
40000 Attendees
Frequency: June

10629 World Wine Market
775 E Blithedale Avenue
#370
Mill Valley, CA 94941

415-383-1226
Fax: 415-383-0858
E-Mail: sclarke@world-wine-market.com
Home Page: www.world-wine-market.com

Stephanie Clarke, VP Sales/Marketing

10630 World of Food and Fuel EXPO
Tennessee Grocers Association
1838 Elm Hill Pike
Suite 136
Nashville, TN 37210-3726

615-889-0136
800-238-8742
Fax: 615-889-2877
Home Page: www.tngrocer.org

Jarron Springer, President
Cyndi Randle, Chairman
John Wampler, Treasurer
8000 Attendees
Frequency: April

10631 Worldwide Food Expo
Dairy and Food Industries Supply Association
1451 Dolley Madison Boulevard
Suite 101
McLean, VA 22101

703-761-2600
Fax: 703-761-4334
Home Page: www.worldwidefoodexpo.com

Trade show and education forum for the food, dairy, beverage and technologically related industries, featuring equipment, services and ingredients that highlight new development and technologies in processing and packaging. 350,000 square feet.
Frequency: Annual/October

Directories & Databases

10632 ACFSA Directory
American Correctional Food Service Affiliates
210 N Glenoaks Blvd
Suite C
Burbank, CA 91502

818-843-6608
Fax: 818-843-7423
Home Page: www.acfsa.org

Jon Nichols, Executive Director

Directory of ACFSA members and the services provided by vender members.
Cost: $5.00
235 Pages
Frequency: Annually
Circulation: 1,500
Printed in 4 colors on glossy stock

10633 AGRICOLA
US National Agricultural Library
10301 Baltimore Ave
Room 13
Beltsville, MD 20705-2351

301-504-5755
Fax: 301-504-5675
Home Page: www.nal.usda.gov

Gary K McCone, Associate Director

A database containing more than 3.2 million citations to journal literature, government reports, proceedings, books, periodicals, theses, patents, audiovisuals, electronic information, and other materials related to agriculture and its allied sciences.

10634 ARI Network
330 E Kilbourn Ave
Suite 565
Milwaukee, WI 53202-3144

414-220-9100
800-558-9044
Fax: 414-283-4357
Home Page: www.aris-corporation.com

Lawrence Shindell, Owner
John Kermath, Director

Offers current information on agricultural business, financial and weather information as well as statistical information for farmers.

10635 Ag Ed Network
ARI Network Services
330 E Kilbourn Ave
Suite 565
Milwaukee, WI 53202-3144

414-220-9100
800-558-9044
Fax: 414-283-4357
Home Page: www.aris-corporation.com

Lawrence Shindell, Owner
John Kermath, Director

Offers access to more than 1,500 educational agriculture lessons covering farm business management and farm production.
Frequency: Full-text

10636 AgriMarketing Services Guide
Henderson Communications LLC
1422 Elbridge Payne Rd
Suite 250
Chesterfield, MO 63017-8544

636-728-1428
Fax: 636-777-4178
Home Page: www.agrimarketing.com

Lynn Henderson, Owner

AgriMarketing Services Guide is published each December and is commonly referred to as the Who's Who in the North American ag industry sector.
Frequency: Annual

10637 Agribusiness Worldwide International Buyer's Guide Issue
Keller International Publishing Corporation
150 Great Neck Rd
Great Neck, NY 11021-3309

516-829-9722
Fax: 516-829-9306
Home Page: www.supplychainbrain.com

Jerry Keller, President
Mary Chavez, Director of Sales

A list of companies that supply, manufacture or distribute agricultural products and services.
Cost: $42.00
Frequency: Annual

10638 Agricultural Research Institute: Membership Directory
Agricultural Research Institute

9650 Rockville Pike
Bethesda, MD 20814-3998

301-530-7122
Fax: 301-530-7007

Richard A Herrett, Executive Director

One hundred and twenty-five member institutions; also lists study panels and committees interested in environmental issues, pest control, agricultural meteorology, biotechnology, food irradiation, agricultural policy, research and development, food safety, technology transfer and remote sensing.
Cost: $50.00
Frequency: Annual

10639 **Airline, Ship & Catering: Onboard Service Buyer's Guide & Directory**
International Publishing Company of America
664 La Villa Dr
Miami Springs, FL 33166-6030

305-887-1700
Fax: 305-885-1923

Alexander Morton, Owner

Offers information on over 6,000 airlines, railroads, ship lines and terminal restaurants.
Cost: $125.00
Frequency: Annual
Circulation: 6,000

10640 **Almanac of Food Regulations and Statistical Information**
Edward E Judge & Sons
PO Box 866
Westminster, MD 21158-0866

410-876-2052
800-729-5517
Fax: 410-848-2034
Home Page: www.eejudge.com

Includes labeling law and FDA regulations, HACCP requirements for seafood, FDA current good manufacturing practice regulations, USDA canning regulations, frozen food handling code, FDA standards of identity, quality and fill of container, USDA quality grade standards, frozen fruit and vegetable pack statistics, agricultural statistics, and census of manufacturing.
Cost: $71.00
824 Pages
Frequency: Annual
Circulation: 3,000
ISBN: 1-880821-19-2
Founded in 1916

10641 **American Butter Institute: Membership Directory**
American Butter Institute
2101 Wilson Boulevard
Suite 400
Arlington, VA 22201

703-243-5630
Fax: 703-841-9328
Home Page: www.butterinstitute.org

Cindy Cazallo, Editor

This directory offers a comprehensive list of over 35 processors, distributors and packagers of butter in the US and suppliers to the industry. Members only.
Cost: $250.00
25 Pages
Frequency: Annual

10642 **American Fruit Grower**
Meister Media Worldwide
37733 Euclid Ave
Willoughby, OH 44094-5992

440-942-2000
800-572-7740
Fax: 440-975-3447
E-Mail: jwmonahan@meistermedia.com
Home Page: www.meisternet.com

Gary Fitzgerald, President
Sue Stearns, Assistant Circulation Manager
JoAnne Mauer, Sales Assistant

Offers a list of manufacturers and distributors of equipment and supplies for the commercial fruit growing industry.
Cost: $19.95
66 Pages
Frequency: 10x
Circulation: 35,849
Founded in 1880

10643 **American Meat Science Association Directory of Members**
American Meat Science Association
2441 Village Green Pl
Champaign, IL 61822-7676

217-356-5370
800-517-AMSA
Fax: 888-205-5834
Fax: 217-356-5370
E-Mail: information@meatscience.org
Home Page: www.meatscience.org

Thomas Powell, Executive Director
Randy Huffman, President-Elect
Kathy Ruff, Meetings & Member Services Director

Directory for American Meat Science members only.
Cost: $20.00
230 Pages
Frequency: Biennial

10644 **American Red Angus: Breeders Directory**
Red Angus Association of America
4201 N Interstate 35
Denton, TX 76207-3415

940-387-3502
Fax: 940-383-4036
E-Mail: info@redangus.org
Home Page: www.redangus.org
Social Media: Facebook

Judy Edwards, Manager
Betty Grimshaw, Association Admin Director
Clint Berry, Commercial Marketing Director

This directory is a list of over 1,800 breeders of Red Angus cattle.
Frequency: Annual
Circulation: 8,000

10645 **American Society of Consulting Arborists: Membership Directory**
American Society of Consulting Arborists
15245 Shady Grove Road
Rockville, MD 20850-3222

301-947-0483

Beth Palys, Executive Director
Steven Geist, President

About 270 persons specializing in the growth and care of urban shade and ornamental trees; includes expert witnesses and monetary appraisals.
Frequency: Annual March

10646 **American Spice Trade Association Membership Roster**
American Spice Trade Association
2025 M St NW
Suite 800
Washington, DC 20036-2422

202-367-1127
Fax: 202-367-2127
Home Page: www.iamss.org

Cheryl Deem, Executive Director
Frequency: Annual

10647 **Automatic Merchandiser Blue Book Buyer's Guide Issue**
Cygnus Publishing
PO Box 803
Fort Atkinson, WI 53538-0803

920-000-1111
800-547-7377
Fax: 920-563-1699
Home Page: www.cygnusb2b.com

John French, CEO
Kathy Scott, Director of Public Relations
Paul Bonaiuto, CFO

Thousands of suppliers are profiled that offer products, services and equipment to the merchandise vending, food service and office coffee service industries.
Cost: $35.00
Frequency: Annual

10648 **BEMA Equipment & Suppliers Datebase**
BEMA
10740 Nall Avenue
Suite 230
Overland Park, KS 66211

913-338-1300
Fax: 913-338-1327
E-Mail: info@bema.org
Home Page: www.bema.org

Find the baking industry's leading suppliers.
220 Pages
Founded in 1918

10649 **Bakery Materials and Methods**
Elsevier Science
655 Avenue of the Americas
New York, NY 10010-5107

212-633-3800
Fax: 212-633-3850
Home Page: www.elsevier.com

Young Suk Chi, Chairman
Bill Godfrey, Chief Information Officer
David Clark, Senior Vice President
Cost: $41.50
Founded in 1978

10650 **Bakery Production and Marketing Buyers Guide Issue**
Delta Communications
11617 W Bluemound Road
Wauwatosa, WI 53226

414-774-7270
Fax: 414-777-7277
Home Page: delta@deltacommunications.com

Pat Reynolds, Editor

This publication offers a list of over 1,800 manufacturers of equipment, ingredients, and supplies for bakeries. Enteries offer company names, addresses, phones, faxes and name and title of contract.

10651 **Bakery Production and Marketing Red Book Issue**
Delta Communications
Ste 300
20900 Swenson Dr
Waukesha, WI 53186-4050

262-542-9111
Fax: 262-542-8820
E-Mail: delta@deltacommunications.com
Home Page: www.deltacommunications.com

Offers a list of over 2,500 wholesale, multi-unit retail, grocery chain and co-op bakery companies and plants in the US and Canada that manufacture bread, cakes, cookies, crackers, pretzels, snack foods, and frozen bakery products.
Cost: $255.00
Frequency: Annual

10652 Baking Buyer Yearbook Issue
Sosland Publishing Company
4800 Main St
Suite 100
Kansas City, MO 64112-2513
816-756-1000
Fax: 816-756-0494
E-Mail: web@sosland.com
Home Page: www.sosland.com
Gordon Davidson, President
Over 1,000 distributors and manufacturers of products and equipment for the baking industry are profiled in this comprehensive directory.
Cost: $75.00
Frequency: Annual

10653 Baking/Snack Directory and Buyer's Guide
Sosland Publishing Company
4800 Main St
Suite 100
Kansas City, MO 64112-2513
816-756-1000
Fax: 816-756-0494
E-Mail: web@sosland.com
Home Page: www.sosland.com
Gordon Davidson, President
Wholesalers of bread and baked goods, as well as snacks and frozen dough are listed in this directory.
Cost: $90.00
Frequency: Annual
Circulation: 8,000

10654 Beef Sire Directory
American Breeders Service/Customer Service
PO Box 459
De Forest, WI 53532-0459
608-846-3721
Fax: 608-846-6392
E-Mail: custserv_dept@absglobal.com
Home Page: www.absglobal.com
Ian Biggs, CEO
A directory listing beef cattle associations in the US and Canada.
Frequency: Annual

10655 Beverage Digest Fact Book
Beverage Digest
PO Box 621
Bedford Hills, NY 10507-0621
914-244-0700
Fax: 914-244-0774
E-Mail: order@beverage-digest.com
Home Page: www.beverage-digest.com
John Sicher, Owner
This book is a complete portrait of the global non-alcoholic beverage business.

10656 Beverage Digest Soft Drink Atlas
Beverage Digest
PO Box 621
Bedford Hills, NY 10507-0621
914-244-0700
Fax: 914-244-0774
E-Mail: order@beverage-digest.com
Home Page: www.beverage-digest.com
John Sicher, Owner
Book of US maps related to soft drink bottler territories. This book offers a geographic portrait of the US carbonated beverage bottling business.

10657 Beverage Marketing Directory
Beverage Marketing Corporation
2670 Commercial Ave
Mingo Junction, OH 43938-1613
740-598-4133
800-332-6222
Fax: 740-598-3977
Home Page: www.beveragemarketing.com
Andrew Standardi III, Director of Operations
Kathy Smurthwaite, Editor
Publication is available in Print Copy (Price-$1,465), PDF Format (Price-$1,465), CD-ROM Format (For pricing, call number listed for details or visit website), and Online.
1196 Pages

10658 Biological & Agricultural Index
HW Wilson Company
950 Dr Martin L King Jr Blvd
Bronx, NY 10452-4297
718-588-8405
800-367-6770
Fax: 718-590-1617
Home Page: www.hwwilson.com
Harold Regan, CEO
Kathleen McEvoy, Director of Public Relations
Provides fast access to core literature. In addition to citations to research and feature articles, users finding indexing of reports of symposia and conferences, and citations to current book reviews. Available on Web and disc.

10659 Blue Book Buyer's Guide
Food Processing Machinery Association
1451 Dolley Madison Blvd
Suite 101
McLean, VA 22101-3850
703-761-2600
Fax: 703-761-4334
E-Mail: info@fpsa.org
Home Page: www.fpsa.org
A buyers guide offering information on over 500 member food and beverage industry firms. Entries are cross-referenced with both a product and commodity locator.
Cost: $50.00
200 Pages
Circulation: 30,000

10660 Blue Book: Fruit and Vegetable Credit and Marketing Service
Produce Reporter Company
845 E Geneva Rd
Carol Stream, IL 60188-3520
630-668-3500
Fax: 630-668-0303
E-Mail: sales@bluebookprco.com
Home Page: www.bluebookprco.com
C James Carr, President
A directory offering information on over 15,000 produce growers, wholesalers, shippers and retailers in the US.
Cost: $575.00
1275 Pages
Frequency: Semiannual
Founded in 1901

10661 Bottled Water Market
MarketResearch.com
641 Avenue of the Americas
3rd Floor
New York, NY 10011
212-807-2629
800-298-6699
Fax: 212-807-2676
The report provides descriptions and coverage of market size and growth, market comppsition, leading marketers, the competitive situation, new product trends, advertising and promotion, and more.
Cost: $2750.00
139 Pages

10662 Brand Directory
Vance Publishing
10901 W 84th Ter
Suite 200
Lenexa, KS 66214-1631
913-438-5721
800-255-5113
Fax: 913-438-0697
E-Mail: info@vancepublishing.com
Home Page: www.vancepublishing.com
Cliff Becker, Vice President, Director
Dan Woods, Chief Financial Officer
Lori Eppel, Chief Financial Officer
A composite of major fresh fruit and vegetable brands and suppliers. It is divided into three sections and contains 66 commodities.
Cost: $10.00

10663 Brewers Digest: Buyers Guide and Brewery Directory
Ammark Publishing
4049 W Peterson Avenue
Chicago, IL 60646-6001
Lists all breweries in the Western Hemisphere, suppliers, associations and importers.
Cost: $30.00
Frequency: Annual
Circulation: 3,000

10664 Brewers Resource Directory
Brewers Association
736 Pearl Street
Boulder, CO 80302
303-447-0816
888-822-6273
Fax: 303-447-2825
E-Mail: webmaster@brewerassociation.org
Home Page: www.beertown.org
Social Media: Facebook, Twitter
Various categories of listees are included that have a direct relation to the beer and liquor industry.
Mailing list available for rent

10665 Brown Swiss Cattle Breeders' Association Directory
Brown Swiss Cattle Breeders' Association
800 Pleasant St
Beloit, WI 53511-5456
608-365-4474
Fax: 608-365-5577
E-Mail: info@brownswissusa.com
Home Page: www.brownswissusa.com
Roger Neitzel, Manager
David Kendall, Secretary

10666 CID Service
US Department of Agriculture
200 Independence Ave SW
Washington, DC 20201-0007
202-690-7650
This database contains 467 categories of information prepared by the US Department of Agriculture and its agencies.
Frequency: Full-text

10667 CRC Press
2000 NW Corporate Boulevard
Boca Raton, FL 33431
561-994-0555
800-272-7737
Fax: 561-998-0876
E-Mail: techsupport@crcpress.com
Home Page: www.crcpress.com
Eleanor Riemer, Publisher
Emmett Dages, CEO
Publisher in science, medicine, environmental science, forensic, engineering, business, technology, mathematics, and statistics. Our food

science and nutrition books and our journal, Critical Reviews in Food and Nutrition, are well established and respected publications in the food science industry.

10668 CRIS/USDA Database
Current Research Information System
1400 Independence Avenue SW
Suite 2270
Washington, DC 20250

202-690-0119
Fax: 202-690-0634
E-Mail: cris@csrees.usda.gov
Home Page: cris.csrees.usda.gov

Ellen A Terpstra, CEO
Don Tilmon, Director

Offers over 35,000 ongoing and recently completed agricultural, food and nutrition and forestry research projects sponsored by the US Department of Agriculture.

10669 California League of Food Processors Annual Directory of Members
980 Ninth Street
Sacremento, CA 95814

916-444-9260
Fax: 916-444-2746
Home Page: www.clfp.com

Robert Graf, President/CEO
Ed Yates, Senior VP
Nora Basrai, Meetings/Members Services
Rob Neenan, Senior Vice President
Amy Alcorn, Marketing Manager

Contains listings of all members, including plant locations and products produced. Over 800 industry leaders are listed.
200 Pages
Founded in 1905

10670 Candy Marketer: Candy, Snack and Tobacco Buyers' Guide
Stagnito Communications
155 Pfingster Road
Suite 205
Deerfield, IL 60015

847-205-5660
Fax: 847-205-5680

Linda Stagnito, President

A publication that includes a list of suppliers to the confectionery, snack and tobacco products industries. Entries include company names, addresses, key personnel, warehouse locations and firms represented.
Cost: $25.00
Frequency: Annual

10671 Chain Restaurant Operators Directory
Chain Store Guide
3922 Coconut Palm Dr
Suite 300
Tampa, FL 33619-1389

813-627-6700
800-972-9202
Fax: 813-627-7094
E-Mail: info@csgis.com
Home Page: www.csgis.com

Mike Jarvis, Publisher
Chris Leedy, Advertising Sales

Discover more than 5,600 listings and more than 26,000 unique personnel within the Restaurant Chain, Foodservice Management, and Hotel/Motel Operator markets in the U.S. and Canada. Each company must have at least $1 million in annual sales either system wide or industry and have two or more units/accounts.
Cost: $335.00
Frequency: Annual

10672 Cheese Market News: Annual
Quarne Publishing
PO 628254
Middleton, WI 53562

608-831-6002
Fax: 608-831-1004
E-Mail: squarne@cheesemarketnews.com
Home Page: www.cheesemarketnews.com

Susan Quarne, Publisher

Comprehensive listings include the companies that manufacture the latest styles and varieties of cheese as well as the industry's key suppliers of cheese equipment, packaging equipment, materials and supplies and services.
Cost: $30.00
Frequency: Annual
Circulation: 3,000

10673 Citrus & Vegetable Magazine: Farm Equipment Directory Issue
Vance Publishing
10901 W 84th Ter
Suite 200
Lenexa, KS 66214-1631

913-438-5721
Fax: 913-438-0697
E-Mail: info@vancepublishing.com
Home Page: www.vancepublishing.com

Cliff Becker, Vice President, Director
Lori Eppel, Chief Financial Officer

Offers information on a list of manufacturers of produce and citrus growing, handling, picking and packaging equipment.
Cost: $25.00
48 Pages
Frequency: Annual
Circulation: 12,000
ISSN: 0009-7586
Founded in 1938

10674 Coffee Anyone???
9616 Thunderbird Drive
Suite 215
San Ramon, CA 94583

925-829-4022
800-347-9687
Fax: 925-829-4025
E-Mail: coffee@coffee-anyone.com
Home Page: http://www.coffeeanyone.com

This database contains descriptions of gourmet, regular, decaffenated and flavored coffees, including a chart summarizing the strength and taste of each coffee.

10675 Coffee, Sugar and Cocoa Exchange Guide
Commerce Clearing House
2700 Lake Cook Rd
Riverwoods, IL 60015-3867

847-940-4600
Fax: 847-779-1535
E-Mail: mediahelp@cch.com
Home Page: www.cch.com

Mike Sabbatis, President

Offers information on member and member organizations of the Exchange.
Cost: $240.00
170 Pages
Frequency: Monthly

10676 Commercial Food Equipment Service Association Directory
Commercial Food Equipment Service Association
2216 W Meadowview Road
Suite 100
Greensboro, NC 27407

336-346-4700
Fax: 336-346-4745
E-Mail: cstrickland@cfesa.com
Home Page: www.cfesa.com

Carla Strickland, Executive Director
Lauri Smith, Treasurer
Wayne Stoutner, Treasurer
David Hahn, Secretary

Independent food service companies that repair commercial food equipment.
Frequency: Annual

10677 Complete Directory of Concessions & Equipment
Sutton Family Communications & Publishing Company
920 State Route 54 East
Elmitch, KY 42343

270-276-9500
E-Mail: jlsutton@apex.net

Theresa Sutton, Editor
Lee Sutton, General Manager

Printout from database of wholesalers, manufacturers, distributors, importers and close-out houses; updated daily to guarantee the most current and up-to-date sources available.
Cost: $27.90
100+ Pages

10678 Complete Directory of Food Products
Sutton Family Communications & Publishing Company
920 State Route 54 East
Elmitch, KY 42343

270-276-9500
E-Mail: jlsutton@apex.net

Theresa Sutton, Editor
Lee Sutton, General Manager

Printout from database of wholesalers, manufacturers, distributors, importers and close-out houses. Database is updated daily to guarantee the most current and up-to-date sources available.
Cost: $27.90
100+ Pages

10679 Consumer's Guide to Fruits & Vegetables & Other Farm Fresh Products
Missouri Cooperative Extension Service
PO Box 29
Jefferson City, MO 65102-0029

573-681-5301
Fax: 573-635-2314

David N Sasseville, Editor

A directory covering over 400 fruit and vegetable farm markets in Missouri.
124 Pages
Frequency: Annual

10680 Contemporary World Issues: Agricultural Crisis in America
ABC-CLIO
PO Box 1911
Santa Barbara, CA 93116-1911

805-705-9339
800-422-2546
Fax: 805-685-9685

Barbara McEwan, Editor

List of agencies and organizations in the US concerned with agricultural issues.
Cost: $39.50

10681 Convenience Store Decisions Sales Tracking Study
Harbor Communications

19111 Detroit Road
Suite 201
Rocky River, OH 44116

440-250-1583
Fax: 440-333-1892
Home Page: www.csdecisions.com

Joseph Howton, Executive VP/COO

Survey of convenience store chain buyers that tracks the effectiveness of supplier promotional programs. It reports on how manufacturers call on retail chains and how those chains are responding to suppliers' merchandising efforts.
Frequency: Annual

10682 Cookies Market
MarketResearch.com
641 Avenue of the Americas
3rd Floor
New York, NY 10011

212-807-2629
800-298-6699
Fax: 212-807-2676

This report uncovers trends in its in-depth investigation of US retail sales of packaged and fresh-baked cookies. The analysis covers packaged cookie retail sales by distribution channel, marketer, and product line. The leading marketers are profiled in order to review growth-and-profit-oriented strategies. The data information is analyzed in order for users to uncover growing product lines, target key demographics, pinpoint distribution channel sales opportunities, and profitable strategies.
Cost: $2250.00
169 Pages

10683 Corn Annual
Corn Refiners Association
1701 Pennsylvania Ave NW
Suite 950
Washington, DC 20006-5806

202-331-1634
Fax: 202-331-2054
Home Page: www.corn.org

Report featuring articles on the state of the industry. Includes statistical report on corn shipments, supply and consumption in the US and abroad.
Frequency: Annually
Circulation: 8,000

10684 Crop Protection Reference
C&P Press
565 5th Ave
5th Floor
New York, NY 10017-2413

212-587-8620
Fax: 646-733-6010
Home Page: www.cppress.com

A single comprehensive source of up-to-date label information of crop protection products marketed in the US by basic manufacturers and formulators. Extensive product indexing helps to locate products by brand name, manufacturer, crop site, mode of action, disease, insect, week, product category, common name and tank mix.
Cost: $170.00
Frequency: Annual

10685 Culinary Collection Directory
International Association/Culinary Professionals
304 W Liberty Street
Suite 201
Louisville, KY 40202

502-587-7953
800-928-4227
Fax: 502-589-3602
E-Mail: info@iacp.com
Home Page: www.iacp.com

Kerry Edwards, Sr Member Services Representative
Trina Gribbins, Manager

Teachers, cooking school owners, caterers, writers, chefs, media cooking personalities, editors, publishers, food stylists, food photographers, restauranteurs, leaders of major food corporations and vintners. Literally a who's who of the food world.

10686 Dairy Foods Market Guide
Delta Communications
455 N Cityfront Plaza Drive
Chicago, IL 60611-5503

312-836-2000
Fax: 312-222-2026

A guide including a list of 1,600 manufacturers of dairy processing equipment and over 900 distributors of dairy processing equipment.
Cost: $99.00
Frequency: Annual

10687 Developing Successful New Products for Foodservice Markets
International Food Service Manufacturers
180 North Stetson Avenue
Suite 4400
Chicago, IL 60601-6766

312-540-4400
Fax: 312-540-4401
E-Mail: ifma@ifmaworld.com
Home Page: www.ifmaworld.com
Social Media: Facebook, LinkedIn, YouTube

Larry Oberkfell, President & CEO
Jennifer Tarulis, CFO
Michael Hickey, Chairman
Mark Bendix, 1st Vice Chairman
Loren Kimura, Treasurer

Handbook on new product development offers sound advice on the critical success factors confronting new product managers. Up-to-date information on new products and practices and an expanded section on market research.
Cost: $ 495.00
Frequency: Annual

10688 Directory & Products Guide
Vineyard & Winery Services
PO Box 2358
Windsor, CA 95492

707-836-6820
800-535-5670
Fax: 707-836-6825
Home Page: vwm-online.com

Jennifer Merietti, Sales/Marketing Manager
Dennis Black, General Manager
Suzanne Webb, Marketing Director

A must have reference book that belongs on the desk of every wine professional. Whether it's tracking down a particular vendor, shopping for the best deal on oak barrels or searching for out-of-state winery contacts, the DPG is a powerhouse of information. Over 2,300 supplier listings and 2,700 winery/vineyard listings, it is a reliable resource that saves time and money.
Cost: $95.00
450+ Pages
Frequency: Annually

10689 Directory of AFFI Member Companies
American Frozen Food Institute
2000 Corporate Ridge
Suite 1000
McLean, VA 22102-7862

703-821-0770
Fax: 703-821-1350
E-Mail: info@affi.com
Home Page: www.knowitsyogurt.com

Robert L Garfield, President
Jason Bassett, Director Legislative Affairs
Chuck Fuqua, VP Communications
Cost: $100.00
Frequency: Annual
Circulation: 5000

10690 Directory of American Agriculture
Agricultural Resources & Communications
301 Broadway
Belvue, KS 66407

785-456-9705
Fax: 785-456-1654
E-Mail: chris@agresources.com
Home Page: www.agresources.com

Christina Wilson, President

This directory lists over 7,000 state and national associations involved in providing products and services related to food and fiber industries, in 27 categories. There are categorical indexes as well. Includes guide to Washington, DC offices, USDA listings, and guide to ag commodity commissions. Available on CD for $99.
Cost: $64.95
350 Pages
ISSN: 0897-1919
Founded in 1988
Printed in on matte stock

10691 Directory of Convenience Stores
Trade Dimensions
45 Danbury Rd
Wilton, CT 06897-4445

203-563-3000
Fax: 860-563-3131
Home Page: www.tradedimensions.com

Jennifer Gillbert, Editor
Lynda Guticulez, Managing Editor

The directory comprises nearly 1,500 detailed profiles on the companies you need to do business with. Extensive dependable information on the grocery industry's most volatile segment.
Cost: $245.00
Frequency: Annual

10692 Directory of Custom Food Processors and Formulators
Delphi Marketing Services
400 E 89th Street
Apartment 2J
New York, NY 10128-6728

Covers formulators and processors of custom food products.
Cost: $260.00
Frequency: Annual

10693 Directory of State Departments of Agriculture
US Department of Agriculture
200 Independence Ave SW
Room 3964
Washington, DC 20201-0007

202-690-7650
Home Page: www.usda.gov

Chris Smith, Chief Information Officer
Matt Paul, Director of Communications
Ramona Romero, General Counsel

Offer valuable information on all the state departments of agriculture, including their officials.
73 Pages
Frequency: Biennial

10694 Directory of the Canning, Freezing, Preserving Industries
Edward E Judge & Sons

PO Box 866
Westminster, MD 21158-0866

410-876-2052
Fax: 410-848-2034
Home Page: www.eejudge.com

Daniel P Judge, Publisher

This directory offers extensive company profiles including over 10,000 managers, over 3,000 North American Food plants that are involved in canning, freezing and preserving fruits, vegetables, dinners, specialties and more. Published in standard edition, 768 pages, and special deluxe edition 1,408 pages.
Cost: $175.00
768 Pages
Frequency: Biennial
ISBN: 1-880821-20-6
Founded in 1966

10695 Diversified Business Communications
PO Box 7437
Portland, ME 04112-7437

207-842-5600
Fax: 207-842-5503
Home Page: www.divbusiness.com

Nancy Hasselback, CEO
Nancy Gelette, VP Operations

A producer of international trade expositions for the seafood and commercial marine industries.

10696 EMDA Membership Directory
Equipment Marketing & Distribution Association
PO Box 1347
Iowa City, IA 52244-1347

319-354-5156
Fax: 319-354-5157
E-Mail: pat@emda.net
Home Page: www.emda.net

Patricia A Collins, Executive VP

Annual directory of Association members, includes address, phone, fax, web, e-mail, territory covered (with map) product descriptions, key personnel and a descriptive paragraph.
Cost: $50.00

10697 Electronic Pesticide Reference: EPR II
C&P Press
New York, NY 10001

212-326-6760
Fax: 646-733-6010
Home Page: www.cppress.com

Complete electronic reference to our 1,500 crop protection products; a full range of product information: full text labels and supplemental labels, full text MSDS's, product summaries, list of labeled tank mixes, worker protection information, DOT shipping information, SARA Title III reporting information. Search by brand name, manufacturer, common name crop, plant, site, weed, disease, insect plus much more. All versions of EPR II are provided on CD-ROM for windows.

10698 Essential Rendering
National Renderers Association
801 N Fairfax St
Suite 205
Alexandria, VA 22314-1776

703-683-0155
Fax: 703-683-2626
Home Page: www.nationalrenderers.org

Thomas M Cook, President

An in-depth guide that covers the various aspects of rendering.
Frequency: Monthly

10699 Feed Additive Compendium
The Miller Publishing Company
12400 Whitewater Dr
Suite 160
Hopkins, MN 55343-4590

952-931-0211
Fax: 952-938-1832
Home Page: www.feedcompendium.com

Sarah Muirhead, Publisher

Provides the latest information on which medicated additives can be used at what inclusion levels for what puposes. Also provides information on regulation, compliance and quality control, product specimen labels, and a directory of state and FDA contacts.
Cost: $52.00
Frequency: Weekly
Founded in 1931

10700 Food & Beverage Marketplace Directory
Grey House Publishing
4919 Route 22
PO Box 56
Amenia, NY 12501

518-789-8700
800-562-2139
Fax: 845-373-6390
E-Mail: books@greyhouse.com
Home Page: www.greyhouse.com
Social Media: Facebook, Twitter

Richard Gottlieb, President
Leslie Mackenzie, Publisher

A three-volume set that is the most comprehensive resource in the food and beverage industry. Available in print, a subscription-based online database, as well as a mailing list and database formats.
Cost: $595.00
2000 Pages
Frequency: Annual

10701 Food & Beverage Marketplace: Online Database
Grey House Publishing
4919 Route 22
PO Box 56
Amenia, NY 12501

518-789-8700
800-562-2139
Fax: 845-373-6390
E-Mail: gold@greyhouse.com
Home Page: http://gold.greyhouse.com
Social Media: Facebook, Twitter

Richard Gottlieb, President
Leslie Mackenzie, Publisher

This complete updated Food & Beverage Market Place: Online Database is the go-to source for the food and beverage industry. Anyone involved in the food and beverage industry needs this 'industry bible' and the important contacts to develop critical research data that can make for successful business growth.
Frequency: Annual
Founded in 1981

10702 Food Businesses: Snack Shops, Specialty Food Restaurants & Other Ideas
Prosperity & Profits Unlimited
PO Box 416
Denver, CO 80201

303-573-5564

A Doyle, Editor

Ideas and possibilities for food businesses, snack shops, restaurants.
Cost: $29.95
82 Pages
Circulation: 8000
ISBN: 0-911569-69-3
Founded in 1990
Printed in on matte stock

10703 Food Channel Database
Noble Communications
500 N Michigan Avenue
Chicago, IL 60611-3764

312-670-4470
Fax: 312-670-7410

This database reports industry news and developments of interest to decision-makers in food processing, grocery, and c-store retailing distribution.

10704 Food Engineering Directory
Business News Publishing
3817 Timothy Lane
Bethlehem, PA 18020

610-317-6180
Fax: 610-317-0378

George Misko

Hardbound reference book listing of all food and beverage companies with 20 or more employees throughout the US.
Cost: $395.00

10705 Food Master
BNP Media
45 Beacon St
Sommerville, MA 02143

617-660-1322
Home Page: www.foodmasterinc.com

Bob Iannaccone, Manager
Founded in 1947

10706 Food Processing Guide & Directory
555 W Pierce Road
Suite 301
Itasca, IL 60143

773-252-7891
Fax: 630-467-1108

Lily Modjeski, Sales Manager

Presents advertising opportunities that will generate quality sales leads, incerase market share, identify market opportunities and increase exposure through our website.
Frequency: Annual

10707 Food Production Management: Advertisers Buyers Guide Issue
CTI Publications
2823 Benson Mill Rd
Sparks Glencoe, MD 21152-9575

410-308-2080
Fax: 410-308-2079
Home Page: www.ctipubs.com

W Randall Gerstmyer, Publisher
Cost: $15.00
48 Pages
Frequency: Annual
Circulation: 5,000
ISSN: 0191-6181
Founded in 1878

10708 Food Service Industry
MarketResearch.com
641 Avenue of the Americas
3rd Floor
New York, NY 10011

212-807-2629
800-298-6699
Fax: 212-807-2676

The report analyzes sales and profit trends of full-service restaurants, limited-service restaurants, cafeterias, snack bars, in-plant contractors, caterers, mobile food services and drinking places.
Cost: $2250.00
240 Pages

10709 Food and Agricultural Export Directory
US Department of Agriculture
PO Box 2022
Washington, DC 20250-0001

202-690-7650
Fax: 202-512-2250
Home Page: www.access.gpo.gov

Offers valuable information on federal and state agencies, trade associations and others willing to assist the US firms that wish to export food and agricultural products overseas.
100 Pages
Frequency: Annual

10710 Food, Beverages & Tobacco in US Industrial Outlook
Superintendent of Documents
US Government Printing Office
Washington, DC 20402-0001

FAX 202-512-2250

Contains industry reviews and forecasts; coverage includes bakery products.
Cost: $34.00
Frequency: Annual

10711 Food, Hunger, Agribusiness: A Directory of Resources
Third World Resources
218 E 21st Street
Oakland, CA 94606

510-533-7583
Fax: 510-533-0923

Offers information on organizations and publishers of books and other materials on food, hunger and agribusiness overseas.
Cost: $12.95
160 Pages

10712 FoodService Distributors Database
Chain Store Guide
3922 Coconut Palm Dr
Suite 300
Tampa, FL 33619-1389

813-627-6700
800-778-9794
Fax: 813-627-7094
E-Mail: info@csgis.com
Home Page: www.csgis.com

Mike Jarvis, Publisher
Shami Choon, Manager

Over 4,900 distributors of food, equipment and supplies to restaurants and institutions are reviewed in this directory for the food service industry. The names of more than 23,000 key executives are included, along with each company's distribution centers.
Cost: $335.00
800 Pages

10713 Foods ADLIBRA
Foods ADLIBRA Publications
9000 Plymouth Avenue N
Minneapolis, MN 55427-3870

763-764-4759
Fax: 763-764-3166

Judith O'Connell, Editor

This database offers over 287,000 citations, with abstracts to journal literature on research and development in food technology and packaging. Seafood, food service, snacks and beverage monthly current awareness are also available.
Cost: $200.00
ISSN: 0146-9304

10714 Foodservice Yearbook International/Global Foodservice
150 Great Neck Road
Great Neck, NY 11021

516-829-9210
Fax: 516-829-5414

10715 Foreign Countries and Plants Certified to Export Meat and Poultry to the US
US Department of Agriculture
Food Safety & Inspection Services
Washington, DC 20250-0001

202-690-7650
800-535-4555

A comprehensive list of over 1,000 meat and poultry plants in foreign countries.
150 Pages
Frequency: Annual

10716 Fortified Foods Market
MarketResearch.com
641 Avenue of the Americas
3rd Floor
New York, NY 10011

212-807-2629
800-298-6699
Fax. 212-807-2676

This new study examines the regulatory environment, analyzes the growth and product trends shaping the fortified foods market and inspects the changing retail picture. It also unveils the marketing and promotional strategies of major players such as Kellogg's, General Mills, PepsiCo, Coca-Cola, Novartis, Heinz and many others. Finally, the study takes a look at differences and commonalities among consumers of fortified cereals, breads, juice drinks, baby foods and snacks.
Cost: $2750.00
234 Pages

10717 Frozen Dinners and Entrees
Leading Edge Reports/Industry Reports
2171 Jericho Turnpike
Suite 200
Commack, NY 11725-2937

631-462-5454
Fax: 631-462-1842
E-Mail: bta@li.net
Home Page: www.businesstrendanalysts.com

Charles J Ritchie, Executive VP
Donna Priani, Marketing Director
Linda Sherman, Production Manager
Jennifer Wichert, Research Director

A product-by-product analysis of the markets for frozen dinners and entrees, including traditional as well as low-calorie and health oriented products.
Cost: $1995.00
170 Pages
Founded in 1996

10718 Getaways for Gourmets in the Northeast
Wood Pond Press
365 Ridgewood Rd
West Hartford, CT 06107-3517

860-521-0389
Fax: 860-313-0185
Home Page: www.green-cuisine.com

Richard M Woodworth, Owner

Directory of services and supplies to the industry.
Cost: $14.95
514 Pages

10719 Gold Book: AAMP
American Association of Meat Processors
1 Meating Pl
Elizabethtown, PA 17022-2883

717-367-1168
Fax: 717-367-9096
E-Mail: aamp@aamp.com
Home Page: www.aamp.com

Jay Wenther, Executive Director
Daniel W Flier, First VP
Jon Frohling, Second VP

Consists of AAMP members, including: honorary members, associates, operators/wholesalers, home food service companies, suppliers, distributors, allied and affiliated state/regional/provincial associations. A powerful source for meat business buyers seeking products/services.
Cost: $300.00
170 Pages
Frequency: Every 2 Years
Circulation: 2,000

10720 Grain & Milling Annual
Sosland Publishing Company
4800 Main St
Suite 100
Kansas City, MO 64112-2513

816-756-1000
Fax: 816-756-0494
E-Mail: web@sosland.com
Home Page: www.sosland.com

Gordon Davidson, President

Offers a list of milling companies, mills, grain companies and cooperatives.
Cost: $90.00
Frequency: Annual
Circulation: 6,000

10721 Grain Journal
Country Journal Publishing Company
2490 N Water Street
Decatur, IL 62526-4251

217-877-9660
800-728 7511
Fax: 217-877-6647
E-Mail: webmaster@grainnet.com
Home Page: www.grainnet.com

Mark Avery, Publisher
Ed Zdrojewski, Editor
Deb Coontz, Advertising Sales
Jeff Miller, Advertising Sales

Provides a list of over 700 equipment manufacturers, suppliers and system designers, as well as offering useful information on governmental agencies relevant to the grain industry.
Cost: $40.00
254 Pages
Frequency: Bi-Monthly
Circulation: 13,000
ISSN: 0274-7138
Founded in 1972
Mailing list available for rent: 10,000 names at $600 per M
Printed in 4 colors on glossy stock

10722 Great Lakes Vegetable Growers News
PO Box 128
Sparta, MI 49345-0128

616-887-9008
Fax: 616-887-2666

Barry Brand, Editor

10723 Guernsey Breeders' Journal: Convention Directory Issue
Purebred Publishing Inc
7616 Slate Ridge Blvd
Reynoldsburg, OH 43068-3126

614-575-4620
Fax: 614-864-5614

E-Mail: sjohnson@usguernsey.com
Home Page: www.usguernsey.com

Seth Johnson, Manager
Dale Jensen, President
Tom Ripley, VP

A convention directory offering a list of officers and national members of the American Guernsey Cattle Association.
Cost: $15.00
Frequency: Annual

10724 **Guide to Poultry Associations**
Poultry & Egg News
PO Box 1338
Gainesville, GA 30503-1338

770-536-2476
Fax: 770-532-4894
E-Mail: ptedit@mindspring.com

Randall Smalladod, Publisher
Chris Hill, Editor

This directory offers information on national, regional and state poultry associations.
Cost: $25.00
24 Pages
Frequency: Annual
Circulation: 11,500

10725 **Health and Natural Foods Market**
MarketResearch.com
641 Avenue of the Americas
3rd Floor
New York, NY 10011

212-807-2629
800-298-6699
Fax: 212-807-2676

The report covers six product categories: packaged groceries, bulk groceries, frozen, refrigerated, produce and other/miscellaneous. The major players in the market are profiled, including Gardenburger, Hain Food Group, Horizon Organic Dairy, Small Planet Foods and others. The report details which types of new products have been recently introduced and reports on consumer attitudes and behavior.
Cost: $2750.00
289 Pages

10726 **Health and Natural Foods Market: Past Performance, Current Trends & More**
Business Trend Analysts/Industry Reports
2171 Jericho Tpke
Suite 200
Commack, NY 11725-2937

631-462-5454
Fax: 631-462-1842
Home Page: www.businesstrendanalysts.com

Charles J Ritchie, Executive VP
Vincent Seeno, Editor
Donna Priani, General Manager
Linda Holm, Production Manager

A statistical summary and analysis offering historical, current and projected sales data for the natural foods market.
Cost: $2195.00
335 Pages
Founded in 1986

10727 **Herbal Green Pages**
Herb Growing and Marketing Network
PO Box 245
Silver Spring, PA 17575-0245

FAX 717-393-9261
E-Mail: herbworld@aol.com
Home Page: www.herbnet.com

Maureen Rogers, Editor

This annual guide offers information on 5,000 companies involved in herbal marketing and growing.
Cost: $25.00
Frequency: Annual
Printed in one color on matte stock

10728 **High Volume Independent Restaurants Database**
Chain Store Guide
3922 Coconut Palm Dr
Suite 300
Tampa, FL 33619-1389

813-627-6700
800-778-9794
Fax: 813-627-7094
E-Mail: info@csgis.com
Home Page: www.csgis.com

Mike Jarvis, Publisher
Shami Choon, Manager

Covers this growing niche through its nearly 5,900 listings featuring casual dining, family restaurants and fine dining establishments. Plus, access to over 15,000 key personnel names puts you in contact with key decision makers.
Cost: $335.00
1,000 Pages
Frequency: Annual

10729 **Hort Expo Northwest**
Mt Adams Publishing and Design
14161 Fort Road
White Swan, WA 98552-9786

509-948-2706
800-554-0860
Fax: 509-848-3896
Home Page: www.hortexponw.com

Vee Graves, Editor
Julie LaForge, Advertising Manager

Besides being mailed to it's family of subscribers it is also available complimentary at horticulture shows in the Northwest.
32 Pages
Frequency: Annually
Circulation: 11,000
Founded in 1989
Printed in 4 colors on glossy stock

10730 **IGWB Buyer's Guide**
BNP Media
PO Box 1080
Skokie, IL 60076-9785

847-763-9534
Fax: 847-763-9538
E-Mail: igwb@halldata.com
Home Page: www.igwb.com

James Rutherford, Editor
Lynn Davidson, Marketing
Nikki Smith, Director

A comprehensive resource listing over 1000 gaming products and services suppliers.
Frequency: Annual
ISSN: 0 -

10731 **Ice Cream and Frozen Desserts**
Business Trend Analysts/Industry Reports
2171 Jericho Tpke
Commack, NY 11725-2937

631-462-5454
Fax: 631-462-1842
E-Mail: bta@li.net
Home Page: www.businesstrendanalysts.com

Charles J Ritchie, Executive VP
Donna Priani, Marketing Director
Linda Sherman, Production Manager
Jennifer Wichert, Research Director

A survey of the ice cream and frozen dessert market, including low-calorie, low-fat and gourmet ice creams and frozen desserts.
Cost: $1295.00
Founded in 2000

10732 **Illinois Beverage Guide**
Indiana Beverage Life, Inc
7379 Fox Hollow Ridge
PO Box 5067
Zionsville, IN 46077

317-733-0527
Fax: 317-733-0528
E-Mail: ibjzstew@indy.rr.com

Stewart Baxter, Publisher/Editor

10733 **Impact International Directory: Leading Spirits, Wine and Beer Companies**
M Shanken Communications
387 Park Ave S
8th Floor
New York, NY 10016-8872

212-684-4224
Fax: 212-684-5424
Home Page: www.cigaraficionado.com

Marvin Shanken, Publisher

A directory offering information on the major players of the alcoholic beverage industry.
Cost: $295.00

10734 **Impact Yearbook: Directory of the US Wine, Spirits & Beer Industry**
M Shanken Communications
387 Park Ave S
8th Floor
New York, NY 10016-8872

212-684-4224
Fax: 212-684-5424
Home Page: www.cigaraficionado.com

Marvin Shanken, Publisher

A directory offering information on the top 40 American distributors and profiles of companies.
Cost: $170.00
Frequency: Annual

10735 **International Association of Food Industry Suppliers**
1451 Dolley Madison Boulevard
Suite 101
McLean, VA 22101

703-761-2600
Fax: 703-761-4334
E-Mail: info@fpsa.org
Home Page: www.fpsa.org

George Melnykovich, President/CEO

A directory offering information on member manufacturers and suppliers of equipment, ingredients and services to the food and dairy industry.
700 Pages
Founded in 1911

10736 **International Dairy Foods Association: IDFA Membership Directory**
IDFA Membership Directory
1250 H St NW
Suite 900
Washington, DC 20005-5902

202-737-4332
Fax: 202-331-7820
E-Mail: membership@idfa.org
Home Page: www.idfa.org

Constance Tipton, President
Miriam Brown, Advisory Committee

The directory provides a complete listing of IDFA's members— over 500 companies— representing approximately 83 percent of all dairy foods processed in the US, as well as the industry's leading supplier companies. Information about locations, products and contacts is in-

cluded.
Cost: $495.00
250 Pages

10737 **International Directory of Refrigerated Warehouse & Distribution Centers**
Int'l Association of Refrigerated Warehouses
1500 King Street
Suite 201
Alexandria, VA 22314

301-652-5674
Fax: 703-373-4301
E-Mail: email@iarw.org
Home Page: www.iarw.org

Corey Rosenbusch, Vice President
Nikki Duncan, Programs Manager
Margot Dersal, Controller

A complete listing of public refrigerated warehouses available to the food industry.
Cost: $18.00

10738 **International Green Front Report**
Friends of the Trees
PO Box 1064
Tonasket, WA 98855-1064

FAX 509-485-2705
E-Mail: michael@friendsofthetrees.net

Michael Pilarski, Editor

Organizations and periodicals concerned with sustainable forestry and agriculture and related fields.
Cost: $7.00
Frequency: Irregular

10739 **International Soil Tillage Research Organization**
International Soil Tillage Research
1680 Madison Avenue
Wooster, OH 44691-4114

330-263-3700
Fax: 330-263-3658

More than 750 individuals and institutions in 72 countries involved in the research or application of soil tilage and related subjects.
Cost: $100.00
Frequency: Semiannual

10740 **Kosher Directory: Directory of Kosher Products & Services**
Union of Orthodox Jewish Congregations of America
333 7th Avenue
18th Floor
New York, NY 10001-5004

212-563-4122
Fax: 212-564-9058

Shelly Sharf, Editor

A directory covering over 10,000 consumer, institutional and industrial products and services.

10741 **Landscape & Irrigation: Product Source Guide**
Adams Business Media
Suite J
Cathedral City, CA 92234

760-322-9878
Fax: 312-846-4638
Home Page: www.americanbusinessmedia.com

Leslee Adams, Owner

Offers information on suppliers, distributors and manufacturers serving the professional agriculture and landscaping community.
Cost: $6.00
Circulation: 37,000

10742 **LifeWise Ingredients**
350 Telser Rd
Lake Zurich, IL 60047-6701

847-550-8270
Fax: 847-550-8272
E-Mail: info@lifewise1.com
Home Page: www.lifewise1.com

Millie Galey, Manager
Carol Bender, Manager
Richard Share, Owner

Manufacture industrial food ingredients.

10743 **MISA Buyer's Guide on CD**
Meat Industry Suppliers Alliance
1451 Dolly Madison Boulevard
McLean, VA 22101

703-761-2600
800-331-8816
Fax: 703-548-6563
E-Mail: info@fpsa.org
Home Page: www.foodprocessingmachinery.com

George O Melnkovich, PhD, President
Cheryl Clark, Director Member Services
Frequency: Annual

10744 **Manufacturing Confectioner: Directory of Ingredients, Equipment & Packaging**
Manufacturing Confectioner Publishing Company
P.O.Box 2249
New Preston Marble Dale, CT 06777-0249

201-652-2655
Fax: 201-652-3419
E-Mail: mcinfo@gomc.com
Home Page: www.gomc.com

Kate Allured, Editor

Publication offers suppliers of machinery, equipment, raw materials, and supplies to the confectionery industry.
Cost: $25.00
Frequency: Annual

10745 **Market for Nutraceutical Foods & Beverages**
Frost & Sullivan Market Intelligence
2525 Charleston Road
Mountain View, CA 94043-1626

650-961-1000
Fax: 650-961-5042

Analyzes the nutraceutical market and offers information on ongoing laboratory research and forecasts for this particular industry.
Cost: $1850.00

10746 **Material Safety Data Sheet Reference**
C&P Press
565 5th Ave
5th Floor
New York, NY 10017-2413

212-587-8620
Fax: 646-733-6010
Home Page: www.cppress.com

Regulatory and product safety requirements. Contains full text MSDS's for products listed in the 1999 15th Edition Crop Protection Reference plus additional safety information such as DOT shipping information, SARA Title III regulations, Hazardous Chemical inventory reporting information plus much more.

10747 **Meat Buyer's Guide**
North American Meat Processors Association
1920 Association Dr
Suite 400
Reston, VA 20191-1500

703-758-8001
800-368-3043
Fax: 703-758-8001
E-Mail: smoore@namp.com
Home Page: www.namp.com

Sabrina Moore, Accounting/Meeting Manager
Philip Kimball, Executive Director

A pictorial directory depicting the food service cuts of beef, lamb, pork, and veal, along with their corresponding IMPS numbers (Institutional Meat Purchase Specification) numbers, instituted by USDA. The Guide is used by chefs, meat processors, and purveyors, food service personnel in institutions, hotels and restaurants.

10748 **Meat Price Book**
Urner Barry Publications
PO Box 389
Toms River, NJ 08754-0389

732-240-5330
800-932-0617
Fax: 732-341-0891
E-Mail: help@urnerbarry.com
Home Page: www.urnerbarry.com

Paul B Brown Jr, President
Sheila M Deane, Marketing Manager

Seven year price history of selected beef, lamb and veal cuts as quoted in Urner Barry's Yellow Sheet.
Cost: $95.00
Frequency: Annual
Circulation: 400

10749 **Meat and Poultry Inspection Directory**
US Department of Agriculture
Administration Building
Room 344
Washington, DC 20250-0001

202-690-7650
Fax: 202-512-2250
Home Page: www.access.gpo.gov

Offers valuable information on all meat and poultry plants that ship meat interstate and therefore come under the US Department of Agriculture inspection.
Cost: $16.00
600 Pages
Frequency: Semiannual

10750 **Membership Directory of the Retail Confectioners International**
1807 Glenview Rd
Suite 104
Glenview, IL 60025-2961

847-657-7400
Fax: 847-724-2719
Home Page: www.mdtechnical.com

Frequency: Annual

10751 **Mid-Atlantic Retail Food Industry Buyers' Guide**
Mid-Atlantic Food Dealers Services
19 Hamill Rd # E
Baltimore, MD 21210-1754

410-522-6924
Fax: 410-377-7137

Robert Mead, Executive Director

Offers extensive coverage of retail food stores and suppliers to the food industry in the states of Delaware, Maryland, New Jersey, Virginia and Washington, DC.
Cost: $15.00
130 Pages
Frequency: Annual
Circulation: 5,000

10752 **Missouri Grocers Association Annual Convention & Food Trade Show**
Missouri Grocers Association
PO Box 10223
Springfield, MO 65808
417-831-6667
Fax: 417-831-3907
Home Page: http://www.missourigrocers.com
1300 Pages

10753 **NAMA Directory of Members**
National Automatic Merchandising Association
20 N Wacker Dr
Suite 3500
Chicago, IL 60606-3102
312-346-0370
800-331-8816
Fax: 312-704-4140
E-Mail: dmathews@vending.org
Home Page: www.vending.org
Richard Geerdes, President
Craig Hesch NCE, Senior Vice Chairman
Brad Ellis NCE, Vice Chairman
Listings of over 2,200 vending, coffee service and foodservice management firms that are NAMA members, including independent firms and branches of national operating companies. Listed by state and city, identifies products vending by each firm and other services provided. Includes listing of machine manufacturer and product supplier firms that are members as well as brokers and distributors and sustaining.
Cost: $25.00
Frequency: Annual
Founded in 1936

10754 **NASDA Directory**
National Association of State Dept of Agriculture
1156 15th St NW
Suite 1020
Washington, DC 20005-1711
202-296-9680
Fax: 202-296-9686
E-Mail: nasda@patriot.net
Home Page: www.nasda.org
Stephen Haterius, Executive Director
Top agricultural officials in 50 states and four territories.
Cost: $100.00
Frequency: Annual

10755 **National Agri-Marketing Association Directory**
11020 King St
Suite 205
Overland Park, KS 66210-1201
913-491-6500
Fax: 913-491-6502
E-Mail: agrimktg@nama.org
Home Page: www.nama.org
Jennifer Pickett, CEO
Vicki Henrickson, Vice President
Cost: $150.00
2500 Pages
Frequency: Annual Spring
Founded in 1956

10756 **National Association of Specialty Food and Confection Brokers**
11004 Wood Elves Way
Columbia, MD 21044-1085
410-969-3663
Fax: 410-740-2958
Judi Epstein, Secretary
Lists members by state of residence and by states covered. Code of ethics and articles describing the function of a 'specialty' food broker in the marketplace.
86 Pages

10757 **National Coffee Service Association: Membership Directory**
8201 Greensboro Drive
Suite 300
McLean, VA 22102-3814
703-610-9000
800-221-3196
Fax: 703-273-9011
A directory covering over 800 member operators and suppliers of office coffee service products.
Frequency: Annual

10758 **National Meat Association: Membership Directory**
1970 Broadway
Suite 825
Oakland, CA 94612-2299
510-763-1533
Fax: 510-763-6186
E-Mail: staff@nmaonline.org
Home Page: www.nmaonline.org
Barry Carpenter, CEO
Jen Kempis, Associate Director
This annual guide offers information on over 250 meat packers, processors and jobbers in 19 western states.
100 Pages
Frequency: Annual

10759 **National Organic Directory**
Community Alliance with Family Farmers
PO Box 464
Davis, CA 95617-0464
916-786-5155
800-852-3832
Fax: 530-756-7857
Annual directory offering information on over 1,000 growers and wholesalers of organically grown produce and organic products. The new edition includes information on regulations and resources for the industry.
Cost: $34.95
288 Pages
Frequency: Annual
Circulation: 2,500

10760 **New Product News**
Avtex
N6w23673 Bluemound Rd
Waukesha, WI 53188-1741
262-542-9111
Fax: 262-542-8820
E-Mail: info@avtex.com
Home Page: www.avtex.com
Spencer Thomason, President
Martin Friedman, Editor
Diane McBride, Circulation Manager
Chris Kumsher, Chief Financial Officer
Offers food and drug manufacturers up-to-date information on products sold in supermarkets, drug stores, gourmet stores and natural food stores. Includes in-depth analysis of new product trends.
Cost: $359.00
65 Pages
Frequency: Monthly
Mailing list available for rentat $300 per M
Printed in one color on matte stock

10761 **Organic Food Mail Order Suppliers**
Center for Science in the Public Interest
1875 Connecticut Avenue NW
Suite 300
Washington, DC 20009-5736
202-332-9110
Fax: 202-265-4954
Home Page: www.cspinet.org
Michael Jacobson, Executive Director
Jamie Jonker, Director Regulatory Affairs
A directory of organic-food growers and suppliers who make their products available by mail-order.
Founded in 1992

10762 **Organic Pages Online**
Organic Trade Association
60 Wells Street
PO Box 547
Greenfield, MA 01302
413-774-7511
Fax: 413-774-6432
Home Page: www.theorganicpages.com
Christine Bushway, Executive Director/CEO
Linda Lutz, Membership Manager
Laura Batcha, Marketing/Public Relations Manager
Online searchable directory
Founded in 1984

10763 **PMMI Packaging Machinery Directory**
Packaging Machinery Manufacturers Institute (PMMI)
4350 Fairfax Dr
Suite 600
Arlington, VA 22203-1632
703-243-8555
Fax: 703-243-8556
E-Mail: maria@pmmi.org
Home Page: www.pmmi.org
Chuck Yuska, President
Alaina Sacramo, Services Coordinator
Contains information on all 500+ member companies, who are committed to producing quality products and providing world class service to their customers.
Cost: $5.00
Frequency: Non-Members Fee

10764 **Packer: Produce Availability and Merchandising Guide**
Vance Publishing
10901 W 84th Ter
Suite 200
Lenexa, KS 66214-1631
913-438-5721
800-255-5113
Fax: 913-438-0697
E-Mail: info@vancepublishing.com
Home Page: www.vancepublishing.com
Cliff Becker, Vice President, Director
Ben Wood, Editor
Lance Jungmeyer, Managing Editor
Leanne Ball, Manager
Lori Eppel, Chief Financial Officer
Publication of about 6,000 fruit and vegetable suppliers and sales agents.
Cost: $35.00
Frequency: Annual

10765 **Parity Corp**
11812 N Creek Pkwy N
Suite 204
Bothell, WA 98011-8202
425-487-0997
Fax: 425-487-2317
E-Mail: info@paritycorp.com
Home Page: www.paritycorp.com
Arvid Tellevik, Owner

Integrated business information system and services designed specifically for the food industry.
Founded in 1985

10766 Pasta Industry Directory
National Pasta Association
1156 15th St NW
Suite 900
Washington, DC 20005-1717
202-367-1861
Fax: 202-367-1865
E-Mail: info@ilovepasta.org
Home Page: www.civilwar.org
Jim Lighthizer, President
Lists by category pasta manufacturers and industry suppliers, including contact names.
Cost: $25.00
Frequency: Annual
Circulation: 1,000

10767 Pickle Packers International Directory
1620 Eye St NW
Suite 925
Washington, DC 20006-4076
202-293-5800
Fax: 202-463-8998
Home Page: www.hazmatshippers.org
Glenn Roberts, President
Frequency: Annual

10768 Pioneers of the Hospitality Industry
CHRIE
2810 N Parham Road
Suite 230
Richmond, VA 23294
804-346-4800
Fax: 804-346-5009
E-Mail: info@chrie.org
Home Page: www.chrie.org
Social Media: Facebook, Twitter, LinkedIn
Susan Fournier, President
Josette Katz, Vice President
Chris Roberts, Secretary
John Drysdale, Treasurer
Kathy McCarty, CEO
Lessons from Leaders, Innovators and Visionaries. A tribute to those dedicated individuals who have shaped the hospitality industry through their colorful lives, their foresight, and their leadership. These profiles offer readers the opportunity to analyze successful leadership and entrepreneurial characteristics, and to evaluate the significance of their contributions.
Cost: $45.00

10769 Pizza Today: Pizza Industry Buyer's Guide
National Association of Pizzeria Operators (NAPO)
908 S 8th Street
Suite 200
Louisville, KY 40203
502-736-9530
800-489-8324
Fax: 502-736-9531
Home Page: www.pizzatoday.com
Pete Lachapelle, Publisher
Joe Straughan, Association Executive Director
A directory listing over 3,000 manufacturers and suppliers of products, equipment and services to the pizza industry.
Cost: $25.00
Frequency: Annual
Circulation: 40000
Founded in 1984

10770 Pork Guide to Hero Health Issue
Vance Publishing
10901 W 84th Ter
Suite 200
Lenexa, KS 66214-1631
913-438-5721
Fax: 913-438-0697
E-Mail: info@vancepublishing.com
Home Page: www.vancepublishing.com
Cliff Becker, Vice President, Director
Lori Eppel, Chief Financial Officer
This comprehensive directory offers a list of manufacturers of swine health products.
Cost: $25.00
Frequency: Annual
Circulation: 77,000

10771 Poultry Digest: Buyer's Guide Issue
WATT Publishing Company
122 S Wesley Ave
Mt Morris, IL 61054-1451
815-734-7937
Fax: 815-734-4201
E-Mail: olentine@wattmm.com
Home Page: www.wattnet.com
Charles Perry, Editor
James Watt, Owner
A list of suppliers to the poultry industry of the US and Canada are listed.
Cost: $6.00
Frequency: Annual
Circulation: 20,000

10772 Poultry International: Who's Who International
WATT Publishing Company
303 N Main Street
Suite 500
Rockford, IL 61101
815-966-5400
Fax: 815-966-6416
Home Page: www.wattnet.com
James Watt, Chairman/CEO
Greg Watt, President/COO
Jeff Swanson, Publishing Director
A guide offering information on over 2,500 manufacturers and suppliers of poultry equipment, services and products.
Cost: $15.00
Frequency: Annual
Circulation: 20,000
ISSN: 0032-5767

10773 Poultry Price Book
Urner Barry Publications
PO Box 389
Toms River, NJ 08754-0389
732-240-5330
800-932-0617
Fax: 732-341-0891
E-Mail: help@urnerbarry.com
Home Page: www.urnerbarry.com
Paul B Brown Jr, President
Sheila M Deane, Marketing Manager
Seven year price history of selected turkey and chicken items as quoted in Urner Barry's Price— Current.
Cost: $55.00
Frequency: Annual
Circulation: 400

10774 Poultry Processing: Buyer's Guide Issue
WATT Publishing Company
122 S Wesley Ave
Mt Morris, IL 61054-1451
815-734-7937
Fax: 815-734-4201
E-Mail: olentine@wattmm.com
Home Page: www.wattnet.com
Virginia Lazar, Editor
James Watt, Owner
Annual reference offering information on over 800 manufacturers and suppliers of equipment, machinery and raw materials for the poultry packing industry.

10775 Prepared Foods
Delta Communications
455 N Cityfront Plaza Drive
Chicago, IL 60611-5503
312-836-2000
Fax: 312-222-2026
This database offers information of interest to the processed food industry.
Frequency: Full-text

10776 Proceedings
Flavor & Extract Manufacturers Assn of the US
1620 Eye St NW
Suite 925
Washington, DC 20006-4076
202-293-5800
Fax: 202-463-8998
Home Page: www.hazmatshippers.org
Glenn Roberts, President
Kim Earle, Contact
Updates and reports on the proceedings of the association.
Frequency: Annual

10777 Produce Marketing Association Membership Directory & Buyer's Guide
Produce Marketing Association
1500 Casho Mill Road
PO Box 6036
Newark, DE 19711-3547
302-738-7100
Fax: 302-731-2409
Kathy Means, VP Membership
Dan Henderson, Marketing
Bryan Silbermann, President
A directory offering information on over 2,000 members involved in retail grocery and food service marketing.
Cost: $70.00
280 Pages
Frequency: Annual

10778 Produce Services Sourcebook
Vance Publishing
10901 W 84th Ter
Suite 200
Lenexa, KS 66214-1631
913-438-5721
800-255-5113
Fax: 913-438-0697
E-Mail: info@vancepublishing.com
Home Page: www.vancepublishing.com
Cliff Becker, Vice President, Director
Lori Eppel, Chief Financial Officer
The produce industry's directory of allied services and products. Content is a balance between practical reference information, allied trends and supplier or source listings.
Cost: $20.00

10779 Professional Workers in State Agricultural Experiment Stations
US Department of Agriculture

PO Box 2022
Washington, DC 20250-0001

202-690-7650
Fax: 202-512-2250
Home Page: www.access.gpo.gov

This directory offers information on academic and research personnel in all agricultural, forestry, aquaculture and home economics industries.
Cost: $15.00
289 Pages
Frequency: Annual

10780 Purebred Picture: Breeders Directory Issue
American Berkshire Association
PO Box 2346
W Lafayette, IN 47996-2346

765-497-3618
Fax: 765-497-2959

Lois Wall, Managing Editor

Annual guide offering information on cattle and hog breeders in the US.
Cost: $12.00
Frequency: Annual
Circulation: 4,000

10781 Quick Frozen Foods Annual Processors Directory & Buyer's Guide
Frozen Food Digest, Saul Beck Publications
271 Madison Ave
Suite 1402a
New York, NY 10016-1014

212-557-8600
Fax: 212-986-9868

Saul Beck, Owner
Audrey Beck, General Manager

A buyer's guide listing over 10,000 frozen food processors, associations, equipment manufacturers and suppliers, and public refrigerated warehouses, transportation, freezing & refrigerated equipment, manufacturers, packagers and railroad lines, brokers, etc.
Cost: $140.00
400 Pages
Frequency: Annual
Circulation: 5,000

10782 RIFM/FEMA Fragrance and Flavor Database
Flavor & Extract Manufacturers Association
1620 I Street NW
Suite 925
Washington, DC 20006

202-293-5800
Fax: 202-462-8998
Home Page: www.femaflavor.org
Social Media: YouTube, RSS Feed

Ed R. Hays, Ph.D., President
George C. Robinson, III, President Elect
Mark Scott, Treasurer
Arthur Schick, VP & Secretary
John Cox, Executive Director

The Database currently contains over 50,000 references and more than 103,000 human health and environmental studies.
Frequency: Annual
Founded in 1909

10783 Refrigerated Transporter: Warehouse Directory Issue
Tunnell Publications
PO Box 66010
Houston, TX 77266

713-523-8124
Fax: 713-523-8384
Home Page: http://www.refrigeratedtrans.com

Gary Macklin, Editor

Listing of approximately 265 refrigerated warehouses in the US and Canada.

10784 Restaurant Hospitality: Hospitality 500 Issue
Penton Media
1300 E 9th St
Suite 316
Cleveland, OH 44114-1503

216-696-7000
Fax: 216-696-6662
E-Mail: information@penton.com
Home Page: www.penton.com

Jane Cooper, Marketing

500 independent restaurants selected on basis of sales.
Cost: $25.00
Frequency: Annual June
Circulation: 123,000

10785 Restaurant TrendMapper
National Restaurant Association
1200 17th St Nw
Washington, DC 20036-3006

202-331-5900
800-424-5156
Fax: 202-331-2429
Home Page: www.restaurant.org
Social Media: Facebook, Twitter, LinkedIn, YouTube, Flickr

Sally Smith, Chair
Rosalyn Mallet, Vice Chair
Phil Hickey, Treasurer
Dawn Sweeney, President & CEO

Contains detailed analysis of the economic trends that impact the restaurant industry, as well as forecasts of key industry indicators on the national and state levels.
60000 Members
Founded in 1919

10786 Restaurants and Institutions: Annual Issue
Reed Business Information
1350 E Touhy Avenue
Suite 200E
Des Plaines, IL 60018-3358

847-962-2200
Fax: 630-288-8686
Home Page: www.reedbusiness.com

Roland Dietz, CEO
Stuart Whayman, CFO
Cost: $25.00
Frequency: Annual
Circulation: 16,000

10787 Santa Gertrudis Breeders International Membership Directory
PO Box 1257
Kingsville, TX 78364-1257

361-592-9357
Fax: 361-592-8572
Home Page: http://www.santagertrudis.com

Ervin Kaatz, Executive Director

Annual guide offering information on over 4,5000 producers of Santa Gertrudis beef and cattle throughout the world.

10788 Santa Gertrudis USA
Santa Gertrudis Breeders International
PO Box 1257
Kingsville, TX 78364-1257

361-592-9357
Fax: 361-592-8572
Home Page: http://www.santagertrudis.com

Ervin Kaatz, Executive Director

Monthly publication offering information on over 1,000 producers of Santa Gertrudis beef cattle throughout the United States.
Cost: $30.00
125 Pages
Frequency: Monthly
Circulation: 2,500
Founded in 1998
Printed in on glossy stock

10789 Sauces and Gravies
MarketResearch.com
641 Avenue of the Americas
3rd Floor
New York, NY 10011

212-807-2629
800-298-6699
Fax: 212-807-2676

This market profile analyzes US shipments, retail sales, consumer demographics, and food service and food processor purchases for 22 product lines. Also analyzes the sauce and gravy product line, retail sales, brand share, and customer demographics for 16 major marketers.
Cost: $2250.00
250 Pages

10790 Seafood Buyer's Handbook
Diversified Business Communications
PO Box 7438
Portland, ME 04112-7438

207-842-5500
Fax: 207-842-5505
Home Page: www.divbusiness.com

Nancy Gelette, VP Operations

This comprehensive directory lists about 1,200 North American fish and shellfish suppliers, distributors and suppliers of related services and equipment to the seafood industry.
Cost: $18.00
250 Pages
Frequency: Annual
Circulation: 15,000

10791 Seafood Price Book
Urner Barry Publications
PO Box 389
Toms River, NJ 08754-0389

732-240-5330
800-932-0617
Fax: 732-341-0891
E-Mail: help@urnerbarry.com
Home Page: www.urnerbarry.com

Paul B Brown Jr, President
Sheila M Deane, Marketing Manager

Seven year price history of selected fresh/frozen seafood items as quoted in Urner Barry's Seafood Price— Current.
Cost: $95.00
Frequency: Annual
Circulation: 400

10792 Seafood Shippers' Guide
American Seafood Institute
25 Fairway Circle
Hope Valley, RI 02832

401-491-9017
Fax: 401-491-9024
Home Page: www.americanseafood.org

Trucking, freight and cold storage companies that directly affect the seafood packing and shipping industry.
Cost: $29.95
100 Pages
Circulation: 2,000

10793 Seed Technologist Training Manual
Society of Commercial Seed Technologists

101 E State Street
Suite 214
Ithaca, NY 14850

607-256-3313
Fax: 607-256-3313
E-Mail: scst@twcny.rr.com
Home Page: www.seedtechnology.net

Anita Hall, Executive Director
Dr Wayne Guerke, Editor

This manual represents the most comprehensive treatment of seed testing technology anywhere.
Cost: $175.00
450 Pages
Frequency: Bi-Annually
Circulation: 500
Founded in 1922

10794 Single Unit Supermarkets Operators Directory
Chain Store Guide
3922 Coconut Palm Dr
Suite 300
Tampa, FL 33619-1389

813-627-6700
800-778-9794
Fax: 813-627-7094
E-Mail: info@csgis.com
Home Page: www.csgis.com

Mike Jarvis, Publisher
Shami Choon, Manager

Discover more than 7,100 single-unit supermarkets with annual sales topping $500,000 dollars. This comprehensive desktop reference makes it easy to reach our compiled list of 21,000 key executives and buyers, plus their primary wholesalers.
Cost: $335.00
725 Pages
Frequency: Annual

10795 Soya & Oilseed Bluebook
Soyatech Inc
P.O.Box 1307
Southwest Harbor, ME 04679-1307

207-288-4969
800-424-7692
Fax: 207-288-5264
E-Mail: subscribe@soyatech.com
Home Page: www.soyatech.com

Provides the world with information on the processing industry that supports development and value creation along each step of the supply chain.

10796 Supermarket News Distribution Study of Grocery Store Sales
Fairchild Publications
7 W 34th St
3rd Floor
New York, NY 10001-8100

212-630-3880
Fax: 212-630-3868

Directory of services and supplies to the industry.
Cost: $75.00
Frequency: Annual

10797 Supermarket News Retailers & Wholesalers Directory
Fairchild Publications
7 W 34th St
New York, NY 10001-8100

212-630-3880
800-360-1700
Fax: 212-630-3868

Over 2,200 US and Canadian retailers, including supermarkets, discount department stores, membership clubs, drug stores, plus voluntary, cooperative and nonsponsoring wholesalers.

10798 Supermarket, Grocery & Convenience Store Chains
Lebhar-Friedman
425 Park Ave
New York, NY 10022-3526

212-756-5088
Fax: 212-838-9487
E-Mail: info@lf.com
Home Page: www.lf.com

Heather Martin, Manager

Directory of US and Canadian supermarket chains.
Cost: $335.00

10799 Supermarket, Grocery & Convenience Stores
Chain Store Guide
3922 Coconut Palm Dr
Suite 300
Tampa, FL 33619-1389

813-627-6700
800-778-9794
Fax: 813-627-7094
E-Mail: info@csgis.com
Home Page: www.csgis.com

Mike Jarvis, Publisher
Shami Choon, Manager

Contains information on close to 3,400 U.S. and Canadian supermarket chains, each with at least $2 million in annual sales - one of the most profitable segments in this sector of the economy. The companies in this database operate over 41,000 individual supermarket, superstore, club store, gourmet supermarkets and combo-store units. A special convenience store section profiles 1,700 convenience store chains operating over 85,000 stores.
Cost: $335.00
Frequency: Annual

10800 Technomic Top 500 Chain Restaurant Report
International Food Service Manufacturers
180 North Stetson Avenue
Suite 4400
Chicago, IL 60601-6766

312-540-4400
Fax: 312-540-4401
E-Mail: ifma@ifmaworld.com
Home Page: www.ifmaworld.com
Social Media: Facebook, LinkedIn, YouTube

Larry Oberkfell, President & CEO
Jennifer Tarulis, CFO
Michael Hickey, Chairman
Mark Bendix, 1st Vice Chairman
Loren Kimura, Treasurer

Provides a comprehensive ranking, analysis and overview of the US chain resaurant industry, helping readers develop sales and marketing strategies, identify growth opportunities, and monitor performance. All data is compiled for US operations and adjusted to calendar-year basis, making it an accurate and easy-to-use resource.
Cost: $850.00
Frequency: Annual

10801 Top 100 Fast Casual Chain Restaurant Report
International Food Service Manufacturers
180 North Stetson Avenue
Suite 4400
Chicago, IL 60601-6766

312-540-4400
Fax: 312-540-4401
E-Mail: ifma@ifmaworld.com
Home Page: www.ifmaworld.com
Social Media: Facebook, LinkedIn, YouTube

Larry Oberkfell, President & CEO
Jennifer Tarulis, CFO
Michael Hickey, Chairman
Mark Bendix, 1st Vice Chairman
Loren Kimura, Treasurer

Provides rankings, analysis and profiles of the leading Fast Casual chain restaurants and gives manufacturers a handle on the evolving trends. Also featuring an in-depth industry overview, a segment performance review and update on emerging chains, performance report, key trends, and individual profiles and sales rankings.
Cost: $850.00
Frequency: Annual

10802 Trade Dimensions
45 Danbury Rd
Wilton, CT 06897-4445

203-563-3000
Fax: 203-563-3131
Home Page: www.tradedimensions.com

Hal Clark, Owner

Trade Dimensions has over 30 years of experience and innovation in developing some of the most sophisticated, reliable and widely used directories and retail site data bases available.

10803 US Agriculture
WEFA Group
800 Baldwin Tower Boulevard
Eddystone, PA 19022-1368

610-490-4000
Fax: 610-490-2770
E-Mail: info@wefa.com
Home Page: www.wefa.com

Harry Baumes

This large database offers information on US macroeconomic farm crop and related agricultural data.

10804 US Alcohol Beverage Industry Category CD
Beverage Marketing Corporation
2670 Commercial Ave
Mingo Junction, OH 43938-1613

740-598-4133
800-332-6222
Fax: 740-598-3977
Home Page: www.beveragemarketing.com

Andrew Standardi III, Director of Operations
Kathy Smurthwaite, Editor

Contains information on approximately 3,030 companies including breweries, microbreweries, wineries, distilleries, wholesalers and importers.
Cost: $3010.00
Frequency: Annual

10805 US Bagel Industry
Leading Edge Reports/Industry Reports
2171 Jericho Turnpike
Suite 200
Commack, NY 11725-2937

631-462-5454
Fax: 631-462-1842
E-Mail: bta@li.net
Home Page: www.businesstrendanalysts.com

Charles J Ritchie, Executive VP
Donna Priani, Marketing Director
Linda Sherman, Production Manager
Vincent Seeno, Research Director

A comprehensive investigation of the dynamics of the US Bagel Industry. Both historical and current market data is presented.
Cost: $1995.00
150 Pages
Founded in 2000

10806 US Beer Industry Category CD
Beverage Marketing Corporation

2670 Commercial Ave
Mingo Junction, OH 43938-1613

740-598-4133
800-332-6222
Fax: 740-598-3977
Home Page: www.beveragemarketing.com

Andrew Standardi III, Director of Operations
Kathy Smurthwaite, Editor

Contains information on approximately 2,084 companies including breweries, microbreweries, beer wholesalers and beer importers.
Cost: $2070.00
Frequency: Annual

10807 US Beverage Distribution Landscape Category CD
Beverage Marketing Corporation
2670 Commercial Ave
Mingo Junction, OH 43938-1613

740-598-4133
800-332-6222
Fax: 740-598-3977
Home Page: www.beveragemarketing.com

Andrew Standardi III, Director of Operations
Kathy Smurthwaite, Editor

Contains information on approximately 3,340 companies distributing soft drinks, bottled water, beer, wine and spirits.
Cost: $3320.00
Frequency: Annual

10808 US Beverage Manufacturers and Filling Locations Category CD
Beverage Marketing Corporation
2670 Commercial Ave
Mingo Junction, OH 43938-1613

740-598-4133
800-332-6222
Fax: 740-598-3977
Home Page: www.beveragemarketing.com

Andrew Standardi III, Director of Operations
Kathy Smurthwaite, Editor

Contains information on approximately 2,402 companies including breweries, microbreweries, wineries, distillieries, soft drink fillers and franchise companies, bottled water fillers, juice, sports beverages and energy drinks, soy, coffee, tea, and milk manufacturers.
Cost: $2390.00
Frequency: Annual

10809 US Bottled Water Industry
Business Trend Analysts/Industry Reports
2171 Jericho Tpke
Suite 200
Commack, NY 11725-2937

631-462-5454
Fax: 631-462-1842
E-Mail: bta@li.net
Home Page: www.businesstrendanalysts.com

Charles J Ritchie, Executive VP
Donna Priani, Marketing Director
Linda Sherman, Production Manager
Vincent Seeno, Research Director

BTA continues its pioneering coverage of the bottled water industry with this updated and dramatically expanded edition.
Cost: $1550.00
Founded in 1997

10810 US Bottled Water Operations Category CD
Beverage Marketing Corporation
2670 Commercial Ave
Mingo Junction, OH 43938-1613

740-598-4133
800-332-6222
Fax: 740-598-3977
Home Page: www.beveragemarketing.com

Andrew Standardi III, Director of Operations
Kathy Smurthwaite, Editor

Contains information on approximately 3,010 companies including bottled water fillers and distributors.
Cost: $2995.00
Frequency: Annual

10811 US Bread Market
MarketResearch.com
641 Avenue of the Americas
3rd Floor
New York, NY 10011

212-807-2629
800-298-6699
Fax: 212-807-2676

This study covers packaged, fresh and frozen bread products, including a growing number of specialty bread products. Major marketing, retailing and demographic trends are all explored in-depth. Special attention is given to the in-store bakery phenomenon.
Cost: $2750.00
197 Pages

10812 US Candy and Gum Market
MarketResearch.com
641 Avenue of the Americas
3rd Floor
New York, NY 10011
212-807-2629
800-298-6699
Fax: 212-807-2676

This report dissects the 23.5 billion market for chocolate candy, hard candy, soft candy, mints and gum, covering both the mass-market and gourmet levels. Market size, growth and composition are tabulated, with sales projections through 2004. Competition at the retail level as a major impetus to market growth is covered in full, as are consumer demographics by product type, brand and usage levels.
Cost: $2750.00
351 Pages

10813 US Carbonated Soft Drink Operations Category CD
Beverage Marketing Corporation
2670 Commercial Ave
Mingo Junction, OH 43938-1613

740-598-4133
800-332-6222
Fax: 740-598-3977
Home Page: www.beveragemarketing.com

Andrew Standardi III, Director of Operations
Kathy Smurthwaite, Editor

Contains information on approximately 2,713 companies including CSD bottlers, canners, franchise companies and distributors.
Cost: $2700.00
Frequency: Annual

10814 US Cheese Market
Business Trend Analysts/Industry Reports
2171 Jericho Tpke
Suite 200
Commack, NY 11725-2937

631-462-5454
800-866-4648
Fax: 631-462-1842
Home Page: www.bta-ler.com

Charles J Ritchie, Executive VP
Donna Priani, Marketing Director
Linda Holm, Production Manager
Jennifer Wichert, Research Director

Survey offering the size and growth of markets for natural, process, cottage and substitute cheeses.
Cost: $1395.00
480 Pages
Founded in 2001

10815 US Confectionary Market
Business Trend Analysts/Industry Reports
2171 Jericho Tpke
Suite 200
Commack, NY 11725-2937

631-462-5454
Fax: 631-462-1842
E-Mail: bta@li.net
Home Page: www.businesstrendanalysts.com

Charles J Ritchie, Executive VP
Donna Priani, Marketing Director
Linda Sherman, Production Manager
Vincent Seeno, Research Director

Profiles markets for chocolate and nonchocolate candies, gum, snack nuts, and seeds, as well as providing information on distribution, trends and future opportunities.
Cost: $1250.00
760 Pages
Founded in 1996

10816 US Date Code Directory for Product Labeling
Danis Research
1 Gothic Plaza
Fairfield, NJ 07004-2411

973-575-3509
Fax: 973-575-5366

Over 500 companies using date code labeling on their food products; over 500 quality control managers and consumer affairs managers from companies that produce snack foods, baked goods, confectioneries and other food products.
Cost: $295.00

10817 US Ethnic Foods Market
Business Trend Analysts/Industry Reports
2171 Jericho Tpke
Suite 200
Commack, NY 11725-2937

631-462-5454
Fax: 631-462-1842
E-Mail: bta@li.net
Home Page: www.businesstrendanalysts.com

Charles J Ritchie, Executive VP
Donna Priani, Marketing Director
Linda Sherman, Production Manager
Vincent Seeno, Research Director

A detailed analysis of the expanding US markets for Italian, Hispanic/Mexican, Oriental, Indian and Kosher foods.
Cost: $995.00
Founded in 1995

10818 US Hot Beverage Market
Business Trend Analysts/Industry Reports
2171 Jericho Tpke
Suite 200
Commack, NY 11725-2937

631-462-5454
Fax: 631-462-1842
E-Mail: bta@li.net
Home Page: www.businesstrendanalysts.com

Charles J Ritchie, Executive VP
Donna Priani, Marketing Director
Linda Sherman, Production Manager
Vincent Seeno, Research Director

A survey offering profiles of the coffee, tea and cocoa products market.
Cost: $1995.00
330 Pages
Founded in 1998

10819 US Market for Cereal & Other Breakfast Foods
Business Trend Analysts/Industry Reports

2171 Jericho Tpke
Suite 200
Commack, NY 11725-2937

631-462-5454
800-866-4648
Fax: 631-462-1842
Home Page: www.businesstrendanalysts.com

Charles J Ritchie, Executive VP
Donna Praini, General Manager
Linda Sherman, Production Manager
Jennifer Wichert, Research Director

Provides up-to-date information on consumer attitudes and buying patterns, new product development, marketing strategies and current and projected sales trends for all types of hot and cold cereals, baked breakfast foods and frozen breakfast products.
Cost: $1495.00
396 Pages
Founded in 1986

10820 US Market for Fats & Oils
Business Trend Analysts/Industry Reports
2171 Jericho Tpke
Suite 200
Commack, NY 11725-2937

631-462-5454
Fax: 631-462-1842
E-Mail: bta@li.net
Home Page: www.businesstrendanalysts.com

Charles J Ritchie, Executive VP
Donna Priani, Marketing Director
Linda Sherman, Production Manager
Vincent Seeno, Research Director

Analyzes the markets for different oils (corn, soybean, peanut, canola, linseed, cottonseed, fish and others), edible and inedible tallow, grease and lard.
Cost: $1295.00
540 Pages
Founded in 1998

10821 US Market for Fruit and Vegetable Based Beverages
MarketResearch.com
641 Avenue of the Americas
3rd Floor
New York, NY 10011

212-807-2629
800-298-6699
Fax: 212-807-2676

This new study covers refrigerated juices and juice drinks, aseptic juices, frozen and unfrozen concentrates, shelf-stable juices and juice drinks in bottles and cans. It provides the latest available sales and volume by category and retail outlet, as well as detailed marketer/brand shares. The report unveils the competitive strategies, advertising and promotional campaigns and new product launches of major players; tracks trends in packaging, flavor-blending, health drinks, and other niches.
Cost: $2750.00
258 Pages

10822 US Market for Juices, Aides & Noncarbonated Drinks
Business Trend Analysts/Industry Reports
2171 Jericho Tpke
Suite 200
Commack, NY 11725-2937

631-462-5454
Fax: 631-462-1842
E-Mail: bta@li.net
Home Page: www.businesstrendanalysts.com

Charles J Ritchie, Executive VP
Donna Priani, Marketing Director
Linda Sherman, Production Manager
Vincent Seeno, Research Director

A comprehensive market analysis covering all types of fresh and frozen fruit juices, fruit drinks, vegetable juices and canned ades.
Cost: $1195.00
810 Pages
Founded in 1998

10823 US Market for Pizza
Leading Edge Reports/Industry Reports
2171 Jericho Turnpike
Suite 200
Commack, NY 11725-2937

631-462-5454
Fax: 631-462-1842
E-Mail: bta@li.net
Home Page: www.businesstrendanalysts.com

Charles J Ritchie, Executive VP
Donna Priani, Marketing Director
Linda Sherman, Production Manager
Vincent Seeno, Research Director

This report examines the size and growth of the US Pizza market through all channels.
Cost: $1995.00
225 Pages
Founded in 1999

10824 US Market for Salted Snacks
MarketResearch.com
641 Avenue of the Americas
3rd Floor
New York, NY 10011

212-807-2629
800-298-6699
Fax: 212-807-2676

This new study provides a coherent view of the market as well as its individual segments: potato chips, tortilla chips, corn chips, pretzels, popcorn, snack nuts and extruded snacks. It explains not only what the industry does, but how it works: how shelf life shapes the entire industry; how hundreds of smaller companies manage to thrive in a market dominated by Frito-Lay. This study profiles the giant companies and regional players.
Cost: $2750.00
263 Pages

10825 US Non-Alcoholic Beverage Industry Category CD
Beverage Marketing Corporation
2670 Commercial Ave
Mingo Junction, OH 43938-1613

740-598-4133
800-332-6222
Fax: 740-598-3977
Home Page: www.beveragemarketing.com

Andrew Standardi III, Director of Operations
Kathy Smurthwaite, Editor

Contains information on approximately 4,206 companies including CSD and bottled water operations, sports beverages and energy drinks, juice, soy, coffee, tea, and milk manufacturers.
Cost: $4185.00
Frequency: Annual

10826 US Organic Food Market
MarketResearch.com
641 Avenue of the Americas
3rd Floor
New York, NY 10011

212-807-2629
800-298-6699
Fax: 212-807-2676

This report covers the booming organic market as it expands into mainstream and gains increased public awareness. The report covers the market size and composition, important trends, and projections for future growth. The information contained in this report will help players in the organic arena make informed decisions to complete successfully in this exciting market.
Cost: $2750.00
275 Pages

10827 US Pasta Market
Business Trend Analysts/Industry Reports
2171 Jericho Tpke
Suite 200
Commack, NY 11725-2937

631-462-5454
Fax: 631-462-1842
E-Mail: bta@li.net
Home Page: www.businesstrendanalysts.com

Charles J Ritchie, Executive VP
Donna Priani, Marketing Director
Linda Sherman, Production Manager
Vincent Seeno, Research Director

Quantifies historial, current and projected sales trends in the ever-expanding market for pasta products. Covers all typed of dry, canned, frozen and fresh pasta, as well as shelf-stable noodle dishes and pasta meals.
Cost: $ 1395.00
380 Pages
Founded in 2000

10828 US Poultry and Small Game Market
Business Trend Analysts/Industry Reports
2171 Jericho Tpke
Suite 200
Commack, NY 11725-2937

631-462-5454
Fax: 631-462-1842
E-Mail: bta@li.net
Home Page: www.businesstrendanalysts.com

Charles J Ritchie, Executive VP
Donna Priani, Marketing Director
Linda Sherman, Production Manager
Vincent Seeno, Research Director

Profiles market for poultry and small game products and provides information on pricing, foreign trade, and advertising and promotion.
Cost: $1995.00
280 Pages
Founded in 1999

10829 US Processed Fruits & Vegetables Market
Business Trend Analysts/Industry Reports
2171 Jericho Tpke
Suite 200
Commack, NY 11725-2937
631-462-5454
Fax: 631-462-1842
E-Mail: bta@li.net
Home Page: www.businesstrendanalysts.com

Charles J Ritchie, Executive VP
Donna Priani, Marketing Director
Linda Sherman, Production Manager
Vincent Seeno, Research Director

A comprehensive marketing, economic and financial analysis of the processed fruits and vegetables industry, covering all types of canned, frozen, dried and dehydrated fruits and vegetables.
Cost: $1195.00
815 Pages
Founded in 1997

10830 US Processed Meat Market
Business Trend Analysts/Industry Reports
2171 Jericho Tpke
Suite 200
Commack, NY 11725-2937

631-462-5454
Fax: 631-462-1842
E-Mail: bta@li.net
Home Page: www.businesstrendanalysts.com

Charles J Ritchie, Executive VP
Donna Priani, Marketing Director
Linda Sherman, Production Manager
Vincent Seeno, Research Director

Profiles markets for processed meat products, including sausage, processed pork products,

canned meats, and meat snacks.
Cost: $1295.00
800 Pages
Founded in 2000

10831 US Snack Food Market
Business Trend Analysts/Industry Reports
2171 Jericho Tpke
Suite 200
Commack, NY 11725-2937

631-462-5454
Fax: 631-462-1842
Home Page: www.businesstrendanalysts.com

Charles J Ritchie, Executive VP
Donna Priani, Marketing Director
Linda Sherman, Production Manager
Vincent Seeno, Research Director

A product-by-product analysis of the intensely competitive US snack food industry.
Cost: $1495.00
860 Pages
Founded in 1999

10832 US Soyfoods Market
MarketResearch.com
641 Avenue of the Americas
3rd Floor
New York, NY 10011

212-807-2629
800-298-6699
Fax: 212-807-2676

This report covers five product categories: meat alternatives, dairy alternatives, snacks, cereals, breads, bulk soybeans, meal replacements/protein powders and other soyfoods including soy sauce and miso. It profiles leading soyfoods producers such as Kellog's, White Wave and Lightlife Foods. The report projects sales trends through 2005 and provides insight into the factors shaping this market. Distributor trends and consumer attitudes and behaviors are also covered in detail.
Cost: $2750.00
150 Pages

10833 US Sweeteners Market
Business Trend Analysts/Industry Reports
2171 Jericho Tpke
Suite 200
Commack, NY 11725-2937
631-462-5454
Fax: 631-462-1842
E-Mail: bta@li.net
Home Page: www.businesstrendanalysts.com

Charles J Ritchie, Executive VP
Donna Priani, Marketing Director
Linda Sherman, Production Manager
Vincent Seeno, Research Director

In-depth coverage of the continually evolving sweetener industry, providing up-to-date information on the latest product developments.
Cost: $1995.00
375 Pages
Founded in 1998

10834 US Vitamins & Nutrients Market
Business Trend Analysts/Industry Reports
2171 Jericho Tpke
Suite 200
Commack, NY 11725-2937

631-462-5454
Fax: 631-462-1842
E-Mail: bta@li.net
Home Page: www.businesstrendanalysts.com

Charles J Ritchie, Executive VP
Donna Priani, Marketing Director
Linda Sherman, Production Manager
Vincent Seeno, Research Director

Statistical report on the vitamin and health food industries.
Cost: $1995.00
410 Pages
Founded in 1999

10835 US Wine & Spirits Industry Category CD
Beverage Marketing Corporation
2670 Commercial Ave
Mingo Junction, OH 43938-1613

740-598-4133
800-332-6222
Fax: 740-598-3977
Home Page: www.beveragemarketing.com

Andrew Standardi III, Director of Operations
Kathy Smurthwaite, Editor

Contains information on approximately 1,484 companies including wineries, distilleries, wine & spirit wholesalers, and wine & spirit importers.
Cost: $1475.00
Frequency: Annual

10836 US Wine Market
Business Trend Analysts/Industry Reports
2171 Jericho Tpke
Suite 200
Commack, NY 11725-2937

631-462-5454
Fax: 631-462-1842
Home Page: www.businesstrendanalysts.com

Charles J Ritchie, Executive VP
Donna Priani, Marketing Director
Linda Sherman, Production Manager
Jennifer Wichert, Research Director

An analysis of the wine industry, domestic and imported.
Cost: $1295.00
470 Pages
Founded in 1996

10837 Uker's International Tea and Coffee Buyer's Guide & Directory
Lockwood Trade Journal
26 Broadway
Suite 1050
New York, NY 10004-1777

212-269-7053
Fax: 212-827-0945
E-Mail: teacof@aol.com
Home Page: www.lockwoodpublications.com

Robert Lockwood, CEO
Jane McCabe, Editor

A directory covering firms that are involved in importing and exporting coffee and tea; manufacturers, suppliers and retailers to the industry; and specialty roasters and their suppliers.
Cost: $48.00
Frequency: Annual
Printed in 4 colors on glossy stock

10838 Urner Barry's Meat & Poultry Directory
Urner Barry Publications
PO Box 389
Toms River, NJ 08754-0389

732-240-5330
800-932-0617
Fax: 732-341-0891
E-Mail: help@urnerbarry.com
Home Page: www.urnerbarry.com

Paul B Brown Jr, President
Karen Mick, Circulation Director

National business directory of traders in the meat and poultry industry.
Cost: $95.00
760 Pages
Frequency: Annual
Circulation: 2,000
ISSN: 0738-6745

10839 Vinegar Institute Directory
1100 Johnson Ferry Road
Suite 300
Atlanta, GA 30342

404-252-3663
Fax: 404-252-0774
E-Mail: vi@kellencompany.com
Home Page: www.versatilevinegar.org

Pamela A Chumley, President
Jeannie Milewski, Executive Director

Online membership directory for members only

10840 Vinegar Institute: Basic Reference Manual
Vinegar Institute
1100 Johnson Ferry Road
Suite 300
Atlanta, GA 30342

404-252-3663
Fax: 404-252-0774
E-Mail: vi@kellencompany.com
Home Page: www.verstailevinegar.org

Looseleaf service guide to vinegar products for technical personnel such as shop foremen and production managers.
Cost: $250.00

10841 Vineyard & Winery Management Magazine
Vineyard & Winery Services
PO Box 2358
Windsor, CA 95492

707-836-6820
800-535-5670
Fax: 707-836-6825
Home Page: vwm-online.com

Robert Merletti, President
Jennifer Merletti, Sales/Marketing Manager

A leading technical trade publication serving the North American Wine Industry and designed for today's serious wine business professional.
Founded in 1975

10842 Warehouses Licensed Under US Warehouse Act
Farm Service Agency-US Dept. of Agriculture
PO Box 2415
Washington, DC 20013-2415

FAX 202-690-0014

Agricultural warehouses voluntarily licensed under the US Warehouse Act governing public storage facilities.
Frequency: Annual

10843 Western Fruit Grower: Source Book Issue Agriculture
Meister Publishing Company
37733 Euclid Ave
Willoughby, OH 44094-5992

440-942-2000
800-572-7740
Fax: 440-975-3447
Home Page: www.meisternet.com

Gary Fitzgerald, President

This annual resource offers information on manufacturers and distributors of suppliers and supplies for the fruit growing industry.
Cost: $5.00
Frequency: Annual
Circulation: 57,000

10844 Western Growers Export Dirctory
Western Growers Association

PO Box 2130
Newport Beach, CA 92658-8944

949-863-1000
Fax: 949-863-9028
Home Page: www.wga.com

Heather Flower, Editor

A directory offering information on shippers of fresh produce and fruit in the states of California and Arizona.
32 Pages
Frequency: Annual

10845 Who is Who: A Directory of Agricultural Engineers Available for Work

American Society of Agricultural Engineers
2950 Niles Rd
St Joseph, MI 49085-8607

269-429-0300
800-371-2723
Fax: 269-429-3852
Home Page: www.asabe.org

Mark D Zielke, CEO
Donna Hukk, Publication Director

This directory pertains to the availability of agricultural engineers to work in developing countries. The directory lists over 650 individuals from 60 countries, primarily engineers, available for work in land or water management, farm structures and other aspects of the field.
Cost: $27.50
210 Pages

10846 Who's Who International

WATT Publishing Company
303 N Main Street
Suite 500
Rockford, IL 61101
815-966-5400
Fax: 815-966-6416
Home Page: www.wattnet.com

James Watt, Chairman/CEO
Greg Watt, President/COO
Jeff Swanson, Publishing Director
Founded in 1917

10847 Who's Who in Beer Wholesaling Directory

National Beer Wholesalers Association
1101 King Street
Suite 600
Alexandria, VA 22314-8965

703-683-4300
Fax: 703-683-8965
E-Mail: info@nbwa.org
Home Page: www.nbwa.org
Social Media: Facebook, Twitter

Craig A Purser, President & CEO
Michael Johnson, EVP/Chief Advisory Officer
Rebecca Spicer, VP Public Affairs/Chief
Paul Pisano, SVP Industry Affairs & Gen. Counsel

A listing of more than 3,000 beer distributors and suppliers in the industry.
Cost: $50.00

10848 Who's Who in the Egg & Poultry Industries in the USA & Canada

WATT Publishing Company
303 N Main Street
Suite 500
Rockford, IL 61101

815-966-5400
Fax: 815-966-6416
Home Page: www.wattnet.com

James Watt, Chairman/CEO
Greg Watt, President/COO
Jeff Swanson, Publishing Director

Annual directory offering information on producers, processors, and distributors of poultry meat and eggs in the US and Canada.
Cost: $75.00
170 Pages
Frequency: Annual
Circulation: 10,000

10849 Who's Who in the Egg & Poultry Industry

WATT Publishing Company
303 N Main Street
Suite 500
Rockford, IL 61101
815-966-5400
Fax: 815-966-6416
Home Page: www.wattnet.com

James Watt, Chairman/CEO
Greg Watt, President/COO
Jeff Swanson, Publishing Director

10850 Who's Who in the Fish Industry

Urner Barry Publications
PO Box 389
Toms River, NJ 08754-0389

732-240-5330
800-932-0617
Fax: 732-341-0891
E-Mail: help@urnerbarry.com
Home Page: www.urnerbarry.com

Paul B Brown Jr, President
Sheila M Deane, Marketing Manager

A business directory of Canadian traders in the seafood industry.
Cost: $125.00
Frequency: Annual
Circulation: 2,000

10851 Whole Foods Annual Source Book

Wainer Finest Communications
3000 Hadley Road
2nd Floor
South Plainfield, NJ 07080-1183

908-769-1160
Fax: 908-769-1171
E-Mail: info@wfcinc.com
Home Page: www.wfcinc.com

Howard Wainer, Publisher
Alan Richman, Editor
Heather Wainer, Associate Publisher
Cost: $75.00
135 Pages
Frequency: Monthly
Circulation: 16,000
Founded in 1979
Mailing list available for rent: 16000 names at $125 per M

10852 Wholesale Beer Association Executives of America Directory

Wholesale Beer Association Executives of America
2805 E Washington Avenue
Madison, WI 53704-5165

608-255-6464
Fax: 608-255-6466

7 Pages
Frequency: Annual

10853 Wholesale Grocers Directory

Chain Store Guide
3922 Coconut Palm Dr
Suite 300
Tampa, FL 33619-1389

813-627-6700
800-972-0292
Fax: 813-627-7094
E-Mail: info@csgis.com
Home Page: www.csgis.com

Mike Jarvis, Publisher
Shami Choon, Manager

We have uncovered the facts on more than 1,900 grocery suppliers in the U.S. and Canada in this database. This targeted database allows you to reach food wholesalers, cooperatives and voluntary group wholesalers, non-sponsoring wholesalers, and cash and carry operators who serve grocery, convenience, discount and drug stores. You will also find information regarding company headquarters, divisions, branches, and over 11,000 key executives and buyers.
Cost: $335.00
Frequency: Annual

10854 Wine & Spirits Industry Marketing

Jobson Publishing Corporation
100 Avenue of the Americas
9th Floor
New York, NY 10013-1678

212-274-7000
Fax: 212-431-0500

Michael J Tansey, CEO

List of about 300 wine and liquor firms including wineries, producers, distillers and importers.
Cost: $150.00
Frequency: Annual April

10855 Wines and Vines Directory of the Wine Industry in North America Issue

Hiaring Company
1800 Lincoln Avenue
San Rafael, CA 94901-1221

415-453-9700
Fax: 415-453-2517
E-Mail: info@winesandvines.com
Home Page: www.winesandvines.com

Dorthy Kubota-Cordery, Editor
Phil Hiaring, Publisher
Debbie Hennessy, Editor
Renee Skiadas, Circulation Director
Chet Klingensmith, Owner

Annual guide offering listings of wineries and wine industry suppliers in the US, Canada and Mexico.
Cost: $85.00
505 Pages
Frequency: Annual
Circulation: 5000

10856 World Databases in Agriculture

National Register Publishing
121 Chanlon Road
New Providence, NJ 07974-1541

908-464-6800
800-473-7020
Fax: 908-464-3553
Home Page: www.nationalregisterpub.com

CJ Armstrong, Editor

Agricultural information on databases, including CD-ROM, magnetic tape, diskette, online, fax or databroadcast worldwide.
Cost: $165.00

10857 Yogurt Market

MarketResearch.com
641 Avenue of the Americas
3rd Floor
New York, NY 10011
212-807-2629
800-298-6699
Fax: 212-807-2676

Brand share and brand consumer profiles are supplemented with profiles of major US manufacturers and new product information in order

to provide the reader with competitor intelligence.
Cost: $2250.00
140 Pages

10858 Zagat.Com Restaurant Guides
Zagat Survey
4 Columbus Cir
3rd Floor
New York, NY 10019-1180

212-977-6000
Fax: 212-977-9760
E-Mail: customerservice@zagat.com
Home Page: www.zagat.com

Tim Zagat, CEO

Zagat.com was launched in May of 1999 and contains the most trusted and authoritive dining information online for over 20,000 restaurants in dozens of cities worldwide. Based in New York City, the Zagat survey was founded in 1979 by Tim and Nina Zagat.

Industry Web Sites

10859 http://gold.greyhouse.com
G.O.L.D Grey House OnLine Databases
Grey House Publishing's online database platform, GOLD, offers Quick Search, Keyword Search and Expert Search for most business sectors including food, beverage and agriculture markets. The GOLD platform makes finding the information you need quick and easy - whether you're a novice searcher or an experienced database user. All of Grey House's directory products are available for subscription on the GOLD platform.

10860 www.aaccnet.org
American Association of Cereal Chemists
Non profit international organization of nearly 4,000 members who are specialists in the use of cereal grains in foods. AACC has been an innovative leader in gathering and disseminating scientific and technical information to professionals in the grain-based foods indusrty wordwide for over 85 years. We know it's hard to keep up with the latest technology, that's why AACC is here to help you. We're a tool unlike any other in your lab or office. Industry leaders turn to and trust AACC.

10861 www.aaea.org
American Agricultural Economics Association
The professional association for agricultural economists and related fields.

10862 www.aaicc.org
National Alliance of Independent Crop Consultants
Represents individual crop consultants and contract researchers.

10863 www.aaminc.org
American Agriculture Movement
An umbrella organization composed of state organizations representing family farm producers.

10864 www.aamp.com
American Association of Meat Processors
Membership consists of small to medium sized meat, poultry and food businesses including: packers, processors, wholesalers, home food service businesses, retailers, deli and catering operators and suppliers to the industry. AAMP is also affiliated with 34 states, regional and provincial organizations which represent meat and poultry businesses.

10865 www.aanc.net
American Association of Nutritional Consultants
An association combating public ignorance and adverse legislation.

10866 www.aapausa.org
American Alfalfa Processors Association
Information for the processors and suppliers in the alfalfa industry.

10867 www.abfnet.org
American Beekeeping Federation
For honey producers, packers, suppliers and shippers of honey products.

10868 www.aceweb.org
Agricultural Communicators in Education
For writers, editors, broadcasters and communicators who are involved in the dissemination of agricultural, food sciences and natural resource information in land-grant colleges, federal and state agencies, international agencies and other private communications work.

10869 www.acfsa.org
American Correctional Food Service Affiliates
International, professional association created to serve the needs and interests of food service personnel in the correctional environments. The association brings together highly skilled food service workers and their vendors who are interested in the common goal of providing nutritious, cost-efficient meal service for confined populations.

10870 www.acsh.org
American Council on Science and Health
A nonprofit, consumer education organization concerned with issues related to food, nutrition, chemicals, pharmaceuticals, lifestyles, the environment and health.

10871 www.adpi.org
American Dairy Products Institute
An association for manufactured dairy products, including dry milks, whey, lactose, evaporated and condensed milk. ADPI's main purpose is to effectively communicate the many positive attributes and benefits of our members' products. Additionally, we serve our membership by offering the most current industry information available and by collaborating with dairy associations to represent members' interests before state and federal regulatory agencies.

10872 www.adsa.uiuc.edu
American Dairy Science Association
Publications, information, etc.

10873 www.aeb.org
American Egg Board
Facts, recipes, industry and nutrition information.

10874 www.afco.org
Association of American Feed Control Officials
Officials of government agencies at the state and federal levels engaged in the regulation and distribution of products, animal feeds and livestock remedies.

10875 www.affi.com
American Frozen Food Institute
News and events, facts, tips, and recipes, etc.

10876 www.afia.org
Animal Industry Foundation
Works to improve animal production practices in the US, to dispel misconceptions that a diet containing meat, milk and eggs is unhealthy and that animals raised for foods in the US are mistreated.

10877 www.afius.org
Association of Food Industries
The association is a trade association serving the food import trade.

10878 www.ag.ohio-state.edu/~farmshow
North American Farm Show Council
Agriculture trade shows and suppliers of services to these shows. Strives to improve education, communication and evaluation and provide the best possible marketing showcase for exhibitors and related products to the farmer/rancher/producer customer.

10879 www.agnic.org/
Access to experts in various fields of agriculture as well as links to agricultural databases. Find out about conferences, meetings and seminars in your area.

10880 www.agribsuiness.com
National Agri-Marketing Association
Industry information, member directory and links to member sites.

10881 www.agriwashington.org
Apple Processors Association
Organization consisting of processors and suppliers which provides a forum for discussion regarding legislation, regulations and new technology.

10882 www.agriwashington.org/aagiwa.html
American Association of Grain Inspection
Established to provide a liaison between the Federal Grain Inspection Service and designated agencies.

10883 www.agview.com/
All aspects of agriculture: Usenet groups, Web resources, archives, mailing lists, etc.

10884 www.ahpa.org
American Herbal Products Association
For manufacturers, importers and distributors of herbs and herbal products. AHPA seeks self-regulation, establishment of standards and rules of ethical conduct, member enrichment and public outreach.

10885 www.aibonline.org
American Institute of Baking Technical Bulletin
This organization provides research, education, training and consulting for the baking and food industries worldwide.

10886 www.aiccbox.org
International Corrugated Packaging Foundation
Videos, promotional materials, demonstrating support of the corrugated packaging industry worldwide. Place corrugated equipment into universities and technical colleges to provide students with corrugated industry skills.

10887 www.aicr.org
American Institute for Cancer Research
Third largest cancer charity in the US, focusing exclusively on research and education in regard to diet and cancer.

10888 www.aiwf.org
American Institute of Wine & Food
A non-profit educational organization devoted to improving the appreciation, understanding and accessibility of food and drink.

10889 **www.ala-national.org**
American Logistics Association
A nonprofit trade organization supporting the Military Resale and Morale, Welfare & Recreation industry.

10890 **www.alaskaseafood.org**
Alaska Seafood Marketing Institute
Organization of private industry and government fishing. Markets only Alaskan seafood. This association also offers educational and promotional materials on fresh and frozen seafood.

10891 **www.allied-purchasing.com**
Allied Purchasing
A group of ice cream plants, soft drink bottlers, dairies, brewries and water companies collaborating to obtain group purchasing rates on equipment, services, ingredients and supplies.

10892 **www.almond-growers.com**
California Independent Almond Growers
Association for almond growers, processors, packers and shippers

10893 **www.almondsarein.com**
Almond Board of California
This association provides production research, mandatory inspection and marketing promotion statistics for the almond/nut industry.

10894 **www.americanbakers.org**
American Bakers Association
Association comprised of wholesale bakers.

10895 **www.americanberkshire.com**
American Berkshire Association
Association for cattle and hog breeders in the US.

10896 **www.americandairyproducts.com**
American Dairy Products Institute
A national trade association representing the processed dairy products industry.

10897 **www.americanhoneyproducers.org**
American Honey Producers Association
Represents the interests of major USA honey producers and pollinators.

10898 **www.americanwineries.org**
American Vintners Association

10899 **www.amif.org**
American Meat Institute Foundation

10900 **www.amseed.com**
American Seed Trade Association
Producers of seeds for planting purposes.

10901 **www.amsey.org**
American Soybean Association
To improve US soybean farmer profitability. Publishes a monthly newsletter

10902 **www.angus.org**
American Angus Association
Industry and member links, information, etc.

10903 **www.animalagriculture.org**
National Institute for Animal Agriculture

10904 **www.aob.org**
Association of Brewers
Membership, publications, news, events, etc.

10905 **www.aomillers.org**
International Association of Operative Millers
An international organization, comprised of flour millers, cereal grain and seed processors and allied trades representatives and companies devoted to the advancement of technology in the flour milling and cereal grain processing industries.

10906 **www.apics.org**
APICS Association for Operations Management
The primary purpose of this specific industry group is to educate food and beverage manufacturers on effective marketing strategies, market trends and material management.

10907 **www.applejuice.org**
Processed Apples Institute
Producers of processed apple products; suppliers of equipment, packaging or ingredients to the industry and brokers and concentrate manufacturers.

10908 **www.appleprocessors.org**
Apple Processors Association
A national association of companies that manufacture quality apple products from whole apples. Members are either apple grower/processor cooperatives, or proprietary firms.

10909 **www.appleproducts.org**
Processed Apples Institute
Links to related industry sites.

10910 **www.apricotproducers.com**
Apricot Producers of California

10911 **www.ari.org/crm**
Commercial Refrigerator Manufacturers Division
Provides information, instruction, education to members in technical and business areas; also specializes in solving common problems and stimulating growth within the industry.

10912 **www.asac.org**
American Society of Agricultural Consultants
For agricultural consultants acting as an information base for members.

10913 **www.asae.org**
American Society of Agricultural Engineers
Information on agricultural engineering, biological engineering and food process engineering.

10914 **www.asas.org**
American Society of Animal Society
For professional researchers, publishes journals and holds seminars in the Animal Science field.

10915 **www.asbe.org**
American Society of Baking
Research and development of machinery for baking applications.

10916 **www.asfsa.org**
American School Food Service Association
An association focused on good nutrition for all children.

10917 **www.ashrae.org**
American Society of Heating, Refrigerating and
Air Conditioning
An international membership organization of engineers who create the worlds we live in.

10918 **www.asifood.com**
ASI Food Safety Consultants
ASI Food Safety Consultants is a full service provider of food safety audits, seminars and HACCP programs.

10919 **www.asmc.org**
Association of Sales & Marketing Companies
Members are representatives for producers of food, packaged goods, and other consumer products.

10920 **www.astaspice.org**
American Spice Trade Association
United States based organization whose worldwide membership is comprised of the leading firms in the spice industry.

10921 **www.atsea.org**
AT-SEA Processors Association
The At-sea Association represents US flag catcher/processor vessels that participate in the healthy and abundant ground fish fisheries of the Bering Sea.

10922 **www.australian-beef.com**
Meat & Livestock Australia
Promotes comsumption of Australian beef, lamb, mutton and goat in Canada, US and Mexico. The company is funded by Australian producers. They key focus is to increase access for Australian meat producers to the North American market and to raise awareness of its nutritional value, quality and safety.

10923 **www.australian-lamb.com**
Meat & Livestock Australia
Promotes comsumption of Australian beef, lamb, mutton and goat in Canada, US and Mexico. The company is funded by Australian producers. They key focus is to increase access for Australian meat producers to the North American market and to raise awareness of its nutritional value, quality and safety.

10924 **www.australianmeatsafety.com**
Meat & Livestock Australia
Promotes comsumption of Australian beef, lamb, mutton and goat in Canada, US and Mexico. The company is funded by Australian producers. They key focus is to increase access for Australian meat producers to the North American market and to raise awareness of its nutritional value, quality and safety.

10925 **www.avocado.org**
California Avacado Commission
A resource for the California avocado industry.

10926 **www.awmanet.org**
American Wholesale Marketers Association
An international trade organization working on behalf of convenience distributors in the United States.

10927 **www.awwpa.com**
American White Wheat Producers Association
Organization of white wheat producers promoting and introducing new white wheat products.

10928 **www.bakeryonline.com**
Bakery Online
A database for bakers, food scientists, food engineers, process engineers, plant managers, business managers, executives and other professionals involved in the bakery industry. Features a comprehensive buyer's guide, interactive discussion forums and daily news updates and reports on business, regulatory and technology trends vital to the industry.

10929 **www.bbga.org**
Bread Bakers Guild of America

Links to member sites.

10930 **www.beef.org**
National Cattlemen's Beef Association
Related industry information.

10931 **www.beerinstitute.org**
Beer Institute
National trade association for the malt beverage industry. Represents the diversity of brewers and suppliers.

10932 **www.beertown.org**
American Homebrewers Association
Devoted to the education of home-brewed beer. Publishes magazine devoted exclusively to education, art and science of homebrewing. Services include: Beer Judge Certification Program, Sanctioned Competitions, World's Largest Homebrew Competition.

10933 **www.bema.org**
Bakery Equipment Manufacturers Association
An international nonprofit association representing leading bakery and food equipment manufacturers and suppliers whose combined efforts in research and development have led to the continual improvement of the baking and food industries.

10934 **www.bestapples.com**
Washington Apple Commission
Marketing professionals promote apples through retail marketing, advertising, public relations, health and food communications.

10935 **www.beverageonline.com**
Beverage Online
A database for beverage chemists, food scientists, food technologists, process engineers, plant managers, business managers, executives and other professionals involved in the beverage processing industry.

10936 **www.biodynamics.com**
Bio-Dynamic Farming and Gardening Association
Supporting biodynamic growers and processors in North America and acts to safeguard and promote the biodynamic method of agriculture.

10937 **www.bisoncentral.com**
National Bison Association
The National Bison Association was formed to promote the production, marketing and preservation of bison.

10938 **www.bissc.org**
Baking Industry Sanitation Standards Committee
Develops and promotes sanitation standards for the design and construction of bakery equipment. Offers self certification and third party certification programs for member companies whose equipment conforms to the BISSC standards.

10939 **www.blueberry.org**
North American Blueberry Council
History, crop information, products, international markets and berry sites.

10940 **www.bottledwater.org**
Bottled Water Association

10941 **www.brownswissusa.com**
Brown Swiss Cattle Breeders Associ of the USA

10942 **www.bsdf-assbt.org**
Beet Sugar Development Foundation
Association specializing in beet sugar research and the advertisement of seed companies.

10943 **www.butterinstitute.org**
American Butter Institute
Represents butter manufacturers and conducts research.

10944 **www.ca-seafood.org**
California Seafood Council

10945 **www.caa-aqua.org**
California Aquaculture Association

10946 **www.cacheeseandbutter.org**
California Cheese & Butter Association
Membership directory along with links.

10947 **www.calbeef.org**
California Beef Council

10948 **www.californiadates.org**
California Date Commission

10949 **www.californiafigs.com**
California Fig Advisory Board
History and facts, nutritional information, recipes and contests.

10950 **www.calolive.org**
California Olive Committee

10951 **www.caloriecontrol.org**
Calorie Control Council

10952 **www.calpear.com**
California Pear Association
Consumer information, research reports, marketing and promo information.

10953 **www.calstrawberry.com**
California Strawberry Commission
Health and nutrition, contests, recipes, news, etc.

10954 **www.cancentral.com**
Can Manufacturers Institute
Serves can manufacturers and can industry suppliers

10955 **www.candyhalloffame.com**
National Confectionery Sales Association
Association of salespersons, brokers, sales managers, wholesalers and manufacturers in the confectionery industry.

10956 **www.candyusa.org**
National Confectioners Association
Association news, candy stats, health information, and candy history.

10957 **www.cannedveggies.org**
Canned Vegetable Council
An educational and promotional organization of vegetable canners whose goals are to raise the awareness of consumer and food service buyers regarding canned vegetables.

10958 **www.canonline.org**
Composite Can & Tube Institute
Serving the composite cans and tube industry.

10959 **www.cast-science.org**
Council for Agricultural Science and Technology
Identifies food, fiber, environmental and other agricultural issues for all stake holders.

10960 **www.cawineclub.com**
California Wine Club
A wine of the month club that features only California's small boutique wineries. Each month members receive two bottles of award-winning wine.

10961 **www.ccpgab.com**
California Cling Peach Advisory Board

10962 **www.cdfa.ca.gov**
North American Agricultural Marketing
For state and provincial officials responsible for agricultural products marketing programs in the US, Canada and ultimately Mexico.

10963 **www.cemanet.org**
Conveyor Equipment Manufacturers Association

10964 **www.cheesesociety.org**
American Cheese Society
Promotes cheese industry. Holds cheese tasting and workshops on cheesemaking. Sponsors competition.

10965 **www.chicagomidwestmeatasso.com**
Chicago-Midwest Meat Association
The CMMA conducts its activities as a not-for-profit trade association for meat companies in the midwest. Its purpose is to support and promote the meat industry

10966 **www.chocolateandcocoa.org**
American Cocoa Research Institute

10967 **www.choosecherries.org**
Cherry Marketing Institute
Association representing the cherry industry. Provides promotional material to food service operators, brokers, retailers and manufacturers.

10968 **www.chowbaby.com**
This web site is a search engine for restaurants. Provides help in finding the perfect eatery close to your home or travel destination. Online reservations, maps, menus and more. Can be searched by International Location, US Location, US Map or Cuisine type.

10969 **www.chrie.org**
Int'l Council on Hotel, Restaurant Institute Edu.
To enhance professionalism at all levels of the hospitality and tourism industry through education and training.

10970 **www.christree.org**
National Christmas Tree Association
Provides industry leaders a chance to work directly with their suppliers and distributors.

10971 **www.ciachef.edu**
Culinary Institute of America

10972 **www.clm1.org**
Council of Logistics Management

10973 **www.coffeeindustry.org**
Specialty Coffee Association of America
Association offering business, professional, promotional and educational assistance in the areas of cultivation, processing, and marketing of specialty coffees. The association also hosts the largest event in the world dedicated to coffee, the SCAA Annual Conference and exhibition.

10974 **www.colborne.com/apc/home.htm**
American Pie Council
Membership, recipes, coupons, etc.

10975 **www.corn.org**
Corn Refiners Association
Stats, career opportunities, publications and newsbriefs.

10976 **www.cosmos.com.mx:80**
Index of Food
Manufacturers indexed by industry, company name, products and brands.

10977 **www.cottonseed.com**
National Cottonseed Products Association
National association of cottonseed products.

10978 **www.countryham.org**
National Country Ham Association
The NCHA encourages promotion, development, and improvement at the businesses of country ham carvers and encourages the use of country carved meats through cooperative methods of production, promotion, education and advertisement.

10979 **www.cpif.org**
California Poultry Industry Federation
Links to other associations.

10980 **www.cpma.ca**
Canadian Produce Marketing Association
Profile and services, links, technical resources, etc.

10981 **www.cranberries.org**
Cranberry Institute
Association which gathers and disseminates information about cranberry growing, horticultural and environmental issues to cranberry growers and handlers in the US and Canada.

10982 **www.crnusa.org**
Council for Responsible Nutrition
Vitamin manufacturers.

10983 **www.cropinsurance.org**
Crop Insurance Research Bureau
Crop insurance trade organization.

10984 **www.croplifeamerica.org**
CropLife America
Information on protecting crops and environmentally fragile agriculture.

10985 **www.crops.org**
Crop Science Society of America
Seeks to advance research, extension and teaching of all basic and applied phases of the crop sciences.

10986 **www.csce.com**
Coffee, Sugar and Cocoa Exchange
Acts as a financial exchange where futures and options are traded, the CSCE provides hedging and investing, opportunities in the coffee, sugar, cocoa and dairy markets.

10987 **www.css.orst.edu/weeds/iwss**
International Weed Science Society
For institutions and individuals concerned with the study of weeds and their control.

10988 **www.culinary.com**
Louisiana Sweet Potato Commission
Links to member sites.

10989 **www.dairyinfo.com**
Dairy Management
Links to related associations.

10990 **www.dairynetwork.com**
Dairy Network
Searchable database of food industry related items.

10991 **www.delianet.com**
Deli Associates
Association for manufacturers or suppliers of confectionary, candy and bakery products.

10992 **www.delicouncil.com**
Dairy, Deli-Bakery Council of Southern California

10993 **www.dhia.org**
National Dairy Herd Improvement Association
Sets policies, holds meetings and offers seminars for dairymen.

10994 **www.diamondwalnut.com**
Diamond Walnut Growers

10995 **www.doitwithdairy.com**
Dairy Management — American Dairy Association, National Dairy Council, US Dairy Export Council

10996 **www.dressings-sauces.org**
Association for Dressings and Sauces
This association is comprised of manufacturers of mayonnaise, salad dressings and condiment sauces, as well as industry suppliers.

10997 **www.drink-milk.com**
American Dairy Association Mideast
We represent dairy farmers and serve as the local affiliate for the American Dairy Association and the National Dairy Council. We work closely with Dairy Management Inc. and the Milk Processors Education Program to extend national dairy promotion programs to the local level.

10998 **www.duckling.org**
Duckling Council
Consortium of duckling producers located coast-to-coast, whose goal is to increase consumption of duckling nationwide and increase awareness of duckling's nutritionally improved profile.

10999 **www.eatchicken.com**
National Broiler Council
Recipes, industry information and statistics.

11000 **www.eatright.org**
American Dietetic Association
Nutrition resources, hot topics, FAQ's.

11001 **www.eatturkey.com**
National Turkey Federation
Advocate for all segments of the US turkey industry, providing services and conducting activities that increase demand for its members' products. The federation also protects and enhances its members' ability to effectively and profitably provide wholesome, high quality, nutritious turkey products.

11002 **www.eddal.com**
Eastern Dairy Deli Bakery Association
This association encourages growth and education regarding dairy, deli and bakery industries. It promotes the sales of Dairy, Deli and Bakery products through supermarkets and specialty stores and acts as a resource and information center for the industry.

11003 **www.eggs.org**
Egg Clearing House
Links to related members and associations.

11004 **www.ejkrause.com**
EJ Krause & Associates
Association for suppliers of hotel and restaurant food and beverages.

11005 **www.elettric80.com**
Electric 80
Supports automated material handling systems, robotic palletizers and laser-guided vehicles.

11006 **www.eppainc.org**
Eastern Dairy Perishable Products Association
This association encourages growth and education regarding perishable products. It promotes the sales of perishable products through supermarkets and specialty stores and acts as a resource and information center for the industry.

11007 **www.fancyfoodshows.com**
Nat'l Association for the Specialty Food Trade
Members are manufacturers, importers, distributors and retailers of specialty gourmet and fancy foods. Has an annual budget of approximately $15 million.

11008 **www.fb.com**
American Farm Bureau Federation
For state Farm Bureaus in the 50 states and Puerto Rico.

11009 **www.fbminet.ca/agnews.htm**
Agricultural news releases.

11010 **www.fcsi.org**
Food Service Consultants Society International
Membership, publications, industry links etc.

11011 **www.fda.gov**
Food and Drug Administration
The official website of FDA.

11012 **www.fdi.org**
Food Service Distributors International

11013 **www.fdrs.ag.utk.edu/**
Food Distribution Research Society
Investigates how food is distributed and traded.

11014 **www.feda.com**
Food Service Equipment Distributors Association
Dealers and distributors of foodservice equipment and supplies.

11015 **www.femaflavor.org**
Flavor & Extract Manufacturers Assn of the US
1620 I Street NW
Suite 925
Washington, DC 210006
202-293-5800
Fax: 202-463-8998
Ed R. Hayes, President
George C. Robinson III, President Elect
Mark Scott, Treasurer
Arthur Schick, Vice President & Secretary
FEMA is comprised of flavor manufacturers, flavor users, flavor ingredient suppliers, and others with an interest in the U.S. flavor industry. FEMA workds with legislators and regulators to assure that the needs of members and consumers are continuously addressed and is committed to assuring a substantial supply of safe flavoring substances.

11016 **www.fewa.org**
Farm Equipment Wholesalers Association
For wholesale/distributors of ag equipment and related products.

11017 **www.ffane.org**
Frozen Food Association of New England
Promotes the frozen food industry.

11018 **www.fiae.com**
Food Industry Association Executives

11019 **www.fightbac.org**
Fight Bac

Sound advice for better food safety.

11020 **www.fl-citrus-mutual.com**
Florida Citrus Mutual
History and mission, member information.

11021 **www.foodallergy.org**
Food Allergy & Anaphylaxis Network
The only nonprofit organization in the US devoted solely to patient education for food allergies. Mission is to create public awareness about food allergies and anaphylaxis to provide education, and to advance research on behalf of all those affected by food allergy.

11022 **www.foodcontact.com**
Food Contact
Searchable directory of food and beverage processors and exporters.

11023 **www.foodexplorer.com**
Food Explorer
Database of industry related materials.

11024 **www.foodfront.com**
Internet Foodfront
Searchable database of food industry related items and resources.

11025 **www.foodindustry.com**
Industry Guides.net
Link directory for related industry.

11026 **www.foodingredientsonline.com**
Food Ingredients Online
International forum where buyers and sellers connect. Highly targeted and focused site offers original material, daily news updates, a product showcase, projects for bid, employment opportunities, downloadbale software, and a free interactive buyers guide which produces instant leads.

11027 **www.foodinstitute.com**
American Institute of Food Distribution
Serves as a central information service for food trades. Issues, reports, studies and statistical data and maintains a library. Member companies throughout the US and over 40 foreign countries.

11028 **www.foodnet.gr**
FoodNet
Searchable database of food industry related items and resources.

11029 **www.foodonline.com**
Food Online
Searchable database of food industry related items.

11030 **www.foodproductdesign.com**
Food product design magazine

11031 **www.foodprotection.org**
International Association for Food Protection
The International Association for Food Protection, founded in 1911, is a nonprofit educational association with a mission to provide food safety professional worldwide with a forum to exchange information on protecting the food supply. The Association is comprised of over 3,000 members from 50 nations. Affiliate chapters are located in the US, Canada, Mexico and South Korea.

11032 **www.foodservice.com/doorway.htm**
Foodservice.com
Database of information and resources for food industry buyers and sellers.

11033 **www.foodserviceworld.com**
Food Service World
Food associations, suppliers and events.

11034 **www.foodshow.com**
Foodshow
Electronic food show with booths for manufacturers.

11035 **www.foodweb.com**
Foodweb
Links to suppliers of food and equipment, distributors, unions, etc.

11036 **www.foodwine.com/digest**
Netfood Directory (The BLUE Directory)
List of relevant food and food service internet sites.

11037 **www.fourhcouncil.edu**
National 4-H Council
Focuses on diverse groups of young people in a variety of urban and suburban locales while continuing to serve youth in rural areas. Helps provide hands-on co-educational programs and activities to young people nationwide.

11038 **www.fpaota.org**
Fresh Produce Association of the Americas
Trade association for Mexican produce. Formerly known as West Mexico Vegetable Distributors Association.

11039 **www.fpfc.org**
Fresh Produce and Floral Council
Promotes through communication and education, fresh fruit, vegetable and floral products.

11040 **www.fpi.org**
Food Service & Packaging Institute
A national association comprised of manufacturers and suppliers of disposables for the food service industry.

11041 **www.fpmsa.org (or www.iefp.org)**
Food Processing Machinery Association
List of exhibitors from IEFP (links included).

11042 **www.fresh-cuts.org**
International Fresh-Cut Produce Association
IFPA advances the fresh-cut produce industry by supporting members with technical information, representation, and knowledge to provide convenient safe and wholesome food. Members are processor companies, suppliers and researchers.

11043 **www.freshcut.com**
Columbia Publishing
Information on carrot production, growers and shippers.

11044 **www.frozenfoodcouncil.com**
Frozen Food Council of Northern California
Coupons, promotions, contests, member information and events.

11045 **www.fsgroup.com**
Food Service Group
This organization is comprised of food service brokerage companies meeting the needs and offering a national exchange of ideas and information of food service sales professionals.

11046 **www.fspronet.com**
Food Service Professionals Network
Database of food industry related items including directories, etc.

11047 **www.georgiapecans.org**
Georgia Pecan Commission

11048 **www.gmabrands.com**
Grocery Manufacturers of America
Government affairs, industry regulations, news, etc.

11049 **www.gpi.org**
Glass Packaging Institute
Serves the glass container suppliers for the beer, juice, RTD tea, liquor, wine and dairy businesses.

11050 **www.grains.org**
US Feed Grains Council
For grain sorghum, barley and corn producer associations and representatives of the agricultural community. Provides commodity export market development.

11051 **www.greyhouse.com**
Grey House Publishing
Authoritative reference directories for most business sectors including food, beverage and agriculture markets. Users can search the online databases with varied search criteria allowing for custom searches by product category, geographic area, sales volume, keyword, subject and more. Full Grey House catalog and online ordering also available.

11052 **www.hazelnut.com**
Hazelnut Growers of Oregon
Recipes, health and ingredient information, etc.

11053 **www.hazelnutcouncil.org**
Hazelnut Council
Promotion to commercial information exhibiting ingredient users and recipies, formulas and food service

11054 **www.healthfinder.gov**
Association of Food and Drug Officials
Promotes the enforcement of laws and regulations at all levels of government. Fosters understanding and cooperation between industry and regulators. Develops model laws and regulations and seeks their adoption.

11055 **www.herbnet.com/, www.herbworld.com**
Herb Growing and Marketing Network
Trade association information services for herb related businesses. Hosts national conference for those in the herb industry with seminars covering commercial production, medicinal herbs and general business topics.

11056 **www.herbs.org**
Herb Research Foundation
Provides scientific-based and traditional information about use and safety of herbs for health. Fee-based hotline, information packs and literature are available to members.

11057 **www.herbsociety.org**
Herb Society of America
Educates its members and the public on the cultivation of herbs, as well as the history and uses of herbs.

11058 **www.hereford.org**
American Hereford Association
For people in the Hereford cattle industry.

11059 **www.holsteinusa.com**
Holstein Association
For people with strong interests in breeding, raising and milking Holstein cattle.

11060 **www.iacp.com**
International Association of Culinary
A not-for-profit organization whose members represent virtually every profession in the culi-

nary universe: teachers, cooking school owners, caterers, writers, chefs, media cooking personalities, editors, publishers, food stylists, food photographers, restauranteurs, leaders of major food corporations and vintners. Literally a who's who of the food world. Founded in 1978.

11061 www.iacsc.org
International Association of Cold Storage

11062 www.iafenet.org
International Association of Fairs & Expositions
Membership consists of individual agricultural fairs and regional associations of agricultural fairs.

11063 www.iaff.ttu.edu/aals
Association for Arid Land Studies

11064 www.iafis.org
Int'l Association of Food Industry Suppliers
Serves the dairy food and beverage industries, and related sanitary processing industries addressing the marketing and business information needs of the food supply channel.

11065 www.iaicv.org
International Association of Ice Cream Vendors
Members are manufacturers and distributors of ice cream novelties and street vendors.

11066 www.iarw.org
International Association of Refrigerated
Trade association of public refrigerated warehouse storing of all types of perishable products.

11067 www.ibdea.org
International Beverage Dispensing Equipment
Serves independent purveyors of equipment, service and products for the food and beverage industry.

11068 www.iddanet.org
International Dairy-Deli-Bakery Association
Newsletter, training information, publications, member list and FQA's.

11069 www.iddba.org
International Dairy-Deli-Bakery Association
Furthers relationship between manufacturing, production, marketing used in delivery of goods to marketplace. Presents awards and maintains a hall of fame.

11070 www.idfa.org
International Dairy Foods Association
IDFA represents the best interests of the U.S. dairy processing and marketing industry, as well as its supplier members and industry's leading suppliers companies.

11071 www.ifas.ufl.edu
Agricultural Communicators of Tomorrow
For college students professionally interested in communications related to agriculture, food, natural resources and allied fields.

11072 www.ific.org
International Food Information Council
Food safety and nutritional information, press releases and publications.

11073 www.ifmaworld.com
International Foodservice Manufacturers
Trade association for food, beverage, equipment and supply manufacturers and ancillary service companies serving the food service industry.

11074 www.ifse.tamu.edu/sma.html
Southwest Meat Association
Newsletter, member information and links.

11075 www.ifsea.org
International Food Service Executives
Provides education and community service to the foodservice industry.

11076 www.ift.org
Institute of Food Technologists
Member information, publications, calender of expos and meetings.

11077 www.iherb.org
International Herb Association
Supports the herb businesses and educates the public.

11078 www.iiar.org
International Institute of Ammonia Refrigeration
Promotes the safe use of ammonia as a refrigerant. Offers educational, promotional and standards development programs and legislative/regulatory support to manufacturers, contractors, consulting engineers, wholesalers and end users.

11079 www.ilovepasta.org
National Pasta Association
List of members, FAQ's, pasta nutrition and recipes.

11080 www.ilovepickles.org
Pickle Packers International
Addresses the concerns of pickle packers, shippers and manufacturers.

11081 www.ilsi.org
International Life Sciences Institute
Scientific institution that supports research on nutrition, food safety and toxicology.

11082 www.independentbaker.org
Independent Bakers Association
Organization of member bakers.

11083 www.insca.org
International Natural Sausage Casing Association

11084 www.iopp.org
Institute of Packaging Professionals

11085 www.ipmwww.ncsu.edu/cernag/
All aspects of agriculture: Usenet groups, Web resources, archives, mailing lists, etc.

11086 www.irrigation.org
Irrigation Association
Irrigation industry information.

11087 www.iseo.org
Institute of Shortening & Edible Oils

11088 www.jps.net/ahaherb
American Herb Association
Membership is comprised of professional herablists and herbal enthusiasts. The goal is to increase knowledge and offer updated scientific information on herbs.

11089 www.juanvaldez.com
National Federation of Coffee Growers of Colombia
This organization is comprised of coffee growers from Colombia whose goal is to promote Colombian coffee in the US.

11090 www.kab.org
Keep America Beautiful
National nonprofit education organization whose corporate members include packagers, retailers, bottlers, and makers of chemical, steel, glass, paper and aluminum products.

11091 www.kiwifruit.org
California Kiwifruit Commission
News, recipes, export information, etc.

11092 www.kla.org
Kansas Livestock Association

11093 www.lambchef.com
American Lamb Council

11094 www.larw.org
Refrigeration Research and Education Foundation
Sponsors graduate-level scientific research on the refrigeration of perishable commodities. Offers annual training institute for public refrigerated warehouse personnel.

11095 www.leafy-greens.org
Leafy Greens Council
Made up of growers and shippers. This association promotes the consumption of leafy greens and vegetables for battling diseases like cancer.

11096 www.llovepecans.org
National Pecan Shellers Association
An association aimed at promoting the pecan shelling and processing industry.

11097 www.mainelobsterpromo.com
Maine Lobster Promotion Council

11098 www.mainpotatoes.com
Maine Potato Board

11099 www.meatami.com
American Meat Institute
A leading trade association for the meat processing industry.

11100 www.meatandpoultryonline.com
Meat and Poultry Online
Searchable database of food industry related items.

11101 www.meatnz.co.nz
Meat New Zealnd

11102 www.meatpoultry.com
Meat and poultry magazine

11103 www.mhia.org
Material Handling Industry

11104 www.micausa.org
Meat Importers Council of America

11105 www.michiganapples.dcom
Michigan Apple Committee

11106 www.militaryfood.org
Research and Development Associates for Military
Founded as a forum for the interchange of technical data on food products, feeding systems, food and feeding equipment and food packaging between industry and professors of Food Science and Technology and the US Armed Forces and Government.

11107 www.mindspring.com/~independentbaker
Independent Bakers Association
Links, issue papers, etc.

11108 www.msgfacts.com
Glutamate Association— US

Members are manufacturers, distributors and processed food users of glutamate, glutamate acid and its salts in the food industry.

11109 **www.mtgplace.com**
Source of information for food product developers

11110 **www.mushroomcouncil.com**
Mushroom Council

11111 **www.mwfpa.org**
Midwest Food Processors Association
This association offers member companies information on legislation and industry matters.

11112 **www.naab-css.org**
National Association of Animal Breeders
For farmer co-ops and others interested in livestock improvement.

11113 **www.nabi-inc.gpg.com**
National Association of Beverage Importers
Members hold a Federal Basic Importer's permit.

11114 **www.nabronline.org**
National Association of Beverage Retailers
Represents over 15,000 off-premise licensees in the 'open' or 'license' states and on-premise proprietors in markets across the nation. Offers members information on legislation and industry matters.

11115 **www.nacaa.com**
National Association County Agricultural Agents
For agents focusing on educational programs for the youth of the community.

11116 **www.naconline.org**
National Association of Concessionaires
This association works to professionalize the concession industry by providing information services and training programs for concession managers and employees. Holds conventions, seminars, trade shows, and certification programs for the leisure time food and beverage industry. Produces newsletters and magazines for its international membership.

11117 **www.nacufs.org**
National Assn of College & University Food Service
Educational programs, conferences, publications, etc.

11118 **www.nadefa.org**
North American Deer Farmers Association
A nonprofit organization that offers representation of US and Canadian breeders and producers of venison. Velvet and trophy stock.

11119 **www.nafem.org**
Food Equipment Manufacturers Association
A trade association of foodservice equipment and supplies manufacturers, that provide products for food preparation, cooking, storage and table service.

11120 **www.naffs.org**
National Association of Fruits, Flavors & Syrups
Industry information, member directory and links to member sites.

11121 **www.nama.org**
National Agri-Marketing Association
Marketing and communication suppliers, including trade publications, radio and television broadcast sales organizations, premium/incentive manufacturers, printers, marketing research firms, photographers and related professionals.

11122 **www.namamillers.org**
North American Millers' Association

11123 **www.namp.com**
North American Meat Processors Association
Represents processors and distributors of meat, poultry, seafood and game to the food service industry.

11124 **www.nanca.org**
North American Natural Casing Association
The NANCA responds to issues and service needs that are unique to the North American segment of the industry.

11125 **www.nas.edu**
National Research Council/National Academy

11126 **www.nasda-hq.org**
National Association of State Departments of
Agriculture

11127 **www.nationalgrange.org**
National Grange
Promotes general welfare and agriculture through local organizations. Presides over the advancement and promotion of the farming and agriculture industry.

11128 **www.nationalgrocers.org**
National Grocers of America
This association services as the information network to the National Grocers Association. Purposes of this organization: handling government affairs regarding the operation of retail groceries; developing educational programs and literature regarding the industry; and supports women in the retail distribution industry.

11129 **www.navigator.tufts.edu**
Tufts University Nutrition Navigator
A rating guide for more than 300 nutrition websites.

11130 **www.nbva.org**
National Bulk Vendors Association
An organization comprised of manufacturers, distributors and operators of bulk vending merchandise and equipment.

11131 **www.nbwa.org**
National Beer Wholesalers Association
Research and development, quality control and ingredients.

11132 **www.nca-cna.org**
National Confectioners Association
Manufacturers of confectionary products and services.

11133 **www.ncausa.org and www.coffeescience.org**
National Coffee Association of USA
This association promotes business relations among members of the trade. Also collects and publishes information on the coffee industry, maintaining a library of 1000 science and medical books and literature about coffee and caffeine.

11134 **www.ncga.com**
National Corn Growers Association

11135 **www.neffa.com**
Northeast Fresh Foods Alliance

11136 **www.nfdffa.org**
National Frozen Dessert and Fast Food Association
This association is made up of small, independent owners and operators of ice cream and fast food establishments.

11137 **www.nffa.org**
National Frozen Food Association
Training, research, networking services, etc.

11138 **www.nfi.org**
National Aquaculture Council
For farmers, food processors and food distributors with an interest in aquaculture.

11139 **www.nfo.org**
National Farmers Union
Promotes educational, cooperative and legislative activities of farm families in 44 states.

11140 **www.nfpa-food.org**
National Food Processors Association
A leading food industry trade association.

11141 **www.nfraweb.org**
National Frozen & Refrigerated Foods Association
Nonprofit trade association comprised of 650 member companies representing all segments of the frozen and refrigerated food industry. NFRA has been serving the frozen food industry since 1945 and just recently in 2001 began serving the refrigerated foods industry. The mission of NFRA is to promote the sales and consumption of frozen and refrigerated foods through: educations, training, research, sales planning and menu development and providing a forum for industry dialogue.

11142 **www.nhb.org**
National Honey Board
This organization offers information and support to members in the honey producing industry.

11143 **www.nicra.org**
National Ice Cream Retailers Association
A trade organization whose members are in the retail ice cream; frozen custard; gelato; frozen yogurt and water ice business. Members are located all across the United States, Canada and several other countries.

11144 **www.nims.com**
Network of Ingredient Marketing Specialists
This organization has established a network of ingredient manufacturers' representatives that offers ingredient manufacturers the most cost effective access to US, Canadian and European markets.

11145 **www.njpa.com**
National Juice Products Association

11146 **www.nmaonline.org**
National Meat Association
Provides it members unique one-on-one assistance resolving regulatory issues. Mission is to be proactive and responsive in serving members both individually and collectively.

11147 **www.nmpf.org**
National Milk Producers Federation

11148 **www.noble.net**
Noble & Associates
Advertising agency for food industry professionals.

11149 **www.nopa.org**
National Oilseed Processors Association

11150 **www.npcspud.com**
National Potato Council
Represents US potato growers on federal legislative and regulatory issues.

11151 **www.nppc.org**
National Pork Producers Council
Nutrition information, educational resources and research results.

11152 **www.nsda.org**
National Soft Drink Association
Industry, product and recycling information, issues and events.

11153 **www.nwcherries.com**
Northwest Cherry Growers

11154 **www.nwfpa.com**
Northwest Food Processors Association
Conventions and exhibits, member listings and links.

11155 **www.nwfpa.org**
Northwest Food Processors Association
An organization that aims to develop and promote the food processing industry located in Oregon, Idaho, and Washington.

11156 **www.nyapplecounty.com**
New York Apple/New York Cherry Growers

11157 **www.oamp.org**
Ohio Association of Meat Processors

11158 **www.ocia.org**
Organic Crop Improvement Association
For farmers, processors, manufacturers and traders of organic crops.

11159 **www.oilseeds.org**
American Soybean Association
Consumption statistics, related associations.

11160 **www.onions-usa.org**
National Onion Association
Recipes, member information and allied industry and export information.

11161 **www.opensecrets.org**
Cheese Association of America
The Center for Responsive Politics is a nonpartisan, nonprofit research group based in Washington, DC that tracks money in politics, and its effect on campaign finance issues for the news media, academics, activists and the public at large.

11162 **www.oregon-berries.com**
Oregon Rasberry & Blackberry Commission
Supports the rasberries, blackberries, marionberries and boysenberries industries.

11163 **www.oregonhazelnuts.org**
Hazelnut Marketing Board
This organization was established to promote and provide for the Oregon hazelnut industry.

11164 **www.organic.org**
Organic Alliance

11165 **www.ostriches.org**
American Ostrich Association
Organization that provides leadership for the ostrich industry and its future through the promotion of ostrich products.

11166 **www.osu.orst.edu/dept/iifet**
International Institute of Fisheries Economics
Promotes discussion, research projects and sponsors educational courses. Publications available.

11167 **www.ota.org**
Organic Trade Association
For businesses involved in the organic agriculture and products industry. Seeks to promote the industry and establish production and marketing standards.

11168 **www.ou.org**
Orthodox Union

11169 **www.pabeef.org**
Pennsylvania Cattlemen's Association

11170 **www.packagingeducation.org**
Packaging Education Forum
A membership organization through which industry guides the development of, establishes quality standards for, and provides financial assistance to packaging education programs, curricula and students at the university.

11171 **www.packagingnetwork.com**
Packaging Network
Searchable database of food industry related items.

11172 **www.packexpo.com**
Packging Machinery Manufacturers Institute
Members are manufacturers of packaging and packaging related coconverting machinery in the US and Canada. PMMI offers meetings, an inquiry service, statistics and surveys and a business to business service on it's website. PMMI also sponsors several Pack Expos (packaging related tradeshows).

11173 **www.packinfo-world.com**
World Packaging Organization
Information regarding the packaging industry internationally.

11174 **www.packinfo-world.org**
Contract Packaging and Manufacturing Association
Information on major packaging associations.

11175 **www.peanutbutterlovers.com**
Peanut Advisory Board
This organization conducts the marketing and promotion of peanut and peanut butter products.

11176 **www.peanutsusa.com**
American Peanut Council
Association members include growers and manufacturers of peanuts and peanut products.

11177 **www.pigglywiggly.com**
National Piggly Wiggly Operators Association
An association of independent grocers operating under Piggly Wiggly franchises in 24 states. Includes both small operators of one to five supermarkets as well as multiple store organizations of as many as 90 or more supermarkets.

11178 **www.pistachios.org**
California Pistachio Commission
Commodity board representing California pistachio growers.

11179 **www.pizzatoday.com**
National Association of Pizza Operators
The membership of this organization is independent and franchised pizza operators, manufacturers and suppliers of pizza equipment.

11180 **www.plma.com**
Private Label Manufacturers Association (PLMA)
Trade Association promoting the private label industry.

11181 **www.pma.com**
Produce Marketing Association
For those who market fresh fruits, vegetables, and floral products worldwide; involved in the production, distribution, retail, and food service sectors of the industry.

11182 **www.popcorn.org**
Popcorn Institute
A trade association representing the popcorn industry. Institute activites include projects to improve popcorn growing and processing technology, serving as a liasion with several government regulatory agencies and a generic marketing program to promote product awareness and consumption.

11183 **www.poultryegg.org**
US Poultry & Egg Association

11184 **www.ppws.vt.edu/newss/society.htm**
Northeastern Weed Science Society

11185 **www.processfood.com**
Food Processing Machinery & Supplies Association

11186 **www.prunes.org**
California Prune Board

11187 **www.ptnpa.org**
Peanut and Tree Nut Processors Association

11188 **www.qba.com**
Quality Bakers of America Cooperative
Members are independent wholesale bakeries and their suppliers.

11189 **www.qchekd.com**
Quality Checked Dairies
A cooperative of Dairy foods processors who use the Quality Checked trademark on their products and engage in group purchasing of ingredients and supplies.

11190 **www.raisins.org**
California Raisin Marketing Food Tech. Program

11191 **www.rbanet.com**
Retail Bakers Association
Links to other associations.

11192 **www.realbutter.com**
American Dairy Association
Recipes, media information, celebrity chefs and industry news.

11193 **www.redangus1.org**
Red Angus Association of America
Association for breeders of Red Angus cattle.

11194 **www.redraspberry.com**
Washington Red Raspberry Commisson

11195 **www.refrigeratedfoods.com**
Refrigerated Foods Association
Formerly called the Salad Manufacturers Association, the Refrigerated Foods Association is an international organization comprised of manufacturers and suppliers of prepared, refrigerated, ready-to-eat food products.

11196 **www.register.com/food**
Food Institute
Member and industry links.

11197 **www.renderers.org**
National Renderers Association
Members recycle animal by-products only, also provide services to renderers.

11198 **www.restaurant.org**
National Restaurant Association
Trends, government affairs, training, research, dining guides and links.

11199 **www.reta.com**
Refrigerating Engineers & Technicians Association

11200 **www.retailconfectioners.org**
Retail Confectioners International
Provides education, promotion and legislative services. Holds courses and bestows awards.

11201 **www.saltinstitute.org**
Salt Institute
Industry information and member businesses.

11202 **www.sbsonline.org**
Society for Biomolecular Screening
Supports research and discovery in pharmaceutical biotechnology and the agrichemical industry that utilize biomolecular screening procedures.

11203 **www.scaa.com**
Specialty Coffee Association of America
Training programs, newsletter, member websites, etc.

11204 **www.scisoc.org/asbc**
American Society of Brewing Chemists
Annual scientific meeting for professionals in the brewing industry.

11205 **www.seafwa.org**
Southeastern Association of Fish and Wildlife
The Southeastern Association of Fish and Wildlife Agencies is an organization whose members are the state agencies with primary responsibility for management and protection of the fish and wildlife resources in 16 states, Puerto Rico and the US Virgin Islands.

11206 **www.seedtechnology.net**
Society of Commercial Seed Technologists
Professionals involved in the testing and analysis of seeds, including research, production and handling based on botanical and agricultural sciences.

11207 **www.sheepusa.org**
American Sheep Industry Association
For state associations dedicated to the welfare and profitability of the sheep industry.

11208 **www.shellfish.org**
National Shellfisheries Association
Organization comprised of scientists, public health workers, shellfish producers and fishery administrators. To promote and advance shellfisheries research and the application of results to the shellfish industry

11209 **www.snax.com**
Snack Food Association
Facts, stats and trivia about snack food industry.

11210 **www.southeastdairy.org**
Southeast United Dairy Industry Association
Promotes milk and milk products in the southeastern states.

11211 **www.southerncottonginners.org**
Southern Cotton Ginners Association
Operates in a five state area as an information center covering safety and governmental regulations.

11212 **www.soyfoods.com**
US Soy Food Directory
Searchable database of soy food processors, suppliers, and industry information.

11213 **www.soyfoods.org**
Soyfoods Association of North America
Sponsors April as soy foods month. Conducts annual seminar on soy foods in fall.

11214 **www.spcouncil.org**
Soy Protein Council
Members of this association include persons, firms and corporations regularly engaged within the US in the processing and sale of vegetable proteins or vegetable protein products derived from agricultural services.

11215 **www.specialityfoods.org**
Speciality Food Distributors & Manufacturers

11216 **www.state.id.us/bean**
Idaho Bean Commission
Directory of dealers, recipes, nutritional values and research.

11217 **www.steel.org**
American Iron and Steel Institute
Develops and implements market development programs for appropriate food and beverage packaging applications.

11218 **www.suebeehoney.com**
Sioux Honey Association

11219 **www.sugar.org**
Sugar Association
Represents processors and refiners of beet and cane sugar in nutrition and health matters.

11220 **www.sugaralliance.org**
American Sugar Alliance
For domestic producers, processors, suppliers and labor organizations in the sugar and sugarcane industry.

11221 **www.sunflowernsa.com**
National Sunflower Association
For companies associated with sunflower products.

11222 **www.sunmaid.com**
Sun-Maid Growers of California

11223 **www.susta.org**
Southern US Trade Association
A non-profit agricultural export trade development association comprised of the Departments of Agriculture of the 15 southern states and the Commonwealth of Puerto Rico.

11224 **www.teausa.com**
Tea Council of the USA
International companies and governments interested in cultivating and expanding the demand for the sale and consumption of tea in the US.

11225 **www.teleport.com/~hazelnut**
Hazelnut Marketing Board
This organization was established to promote and provide for the Oregon hazelnut industry.

11226 **www.tfi.org**
Fertilizer Institute
For brokers, producers, importers, dealers and manufacturers of fertilizer and fertilizer-related equipment.

11227 **www.theamericancenter.org**
American Center for Wine, Food & the Arts

11228 **www.thebcma.org**
Biscuit & Cracker Manufacturers Association
An organization that represents and promotes the cookie and cracker manufacturing industry.

11229 **www.therestaurantfinder.com**
This search engine help to find restaurants by type or location.

11230 **www.tianet.org**
Transportation Intermediaries Association
Education and policy organization for North American transportation intermediaries representing the interests of all third party transportation service providers. Members include logistics management firms, property brokers, perishable commodities brokers, freight forwarders, intermodal marketers, ocean and air forwarders, and NVOCC's.

11231 **www.tortilla-info.com**
Tortilla Industry Association
News, trade information, 'where to buy' and recipes.

11232 **www.turkeyfed.org**
National Turkey Federation
Member site links and industry information.

11233 **www.txbeef.com**
Texas Beef Council
Recipes, ranching information, tips and links.

11234 **www.uark.edu/depts/ifse/ofpa**
Ozark Food Processors Association
This association is comprised of regional food processors and national suppliers for the food service industry. Hosts an annual convention in the spring which includes at attendence of over 700 and over 100 exhibitors.

11235 **www.uffva.org**
United Fresh Fruit & Vegetable Association
Equipment, supplies, cartons, packaging machinery, computers, sorting and sizing equipment, harvesting equipment, film wrap manufacturing and commodity organizations.

11236 **www.usapears.com**
Pear Bureau Northwest
Promotes fresh pears grown in the Pacific Northwest area.

11237 **www.usapple.org**
US Apple Association
Members are US and foreign firms, other than retailers, that handle apples.

11238 **www.usarice.com**
USA Rice Federation

11239 **www.usda.gov**
US Department of Agriculture
The official website of USDA.

11240 **www.usda.gov/fcs/fcs.html**
Food & Nutrition Service

11241 **www.usguernsey.com**
American Guernsey Association
Register and deliver guernsey cattle throughout the US.

11242 **www.usmef.org**
US Meat Export Federation

11243 **www.uspastry.org**
US Pastry Alliance

11244 **www.uspotatoes.com**
National Potato Promotion Board
Also known as the potato board. Organized to operate a national promotion plan to position potatoes as low calorie, nutritious vegetables and to facilitate market expansion into domestic and export sales.

11245 **www.vealfarm.com**
American Veal Association
For veal producers and processors.

11246 **www.vending.org**
National Automatic Merchandising Association
Serves merchandising, vending, contract foodservice management and office coffee service industries.

11247 **www.versatilevinegar.org**
Vinegar Institute
Manufacturers and bottlers of vinegar and suppliers to the industry are the members of this association. Publications available only to members.

11248 **www.vrg.org**
Vegetarian Resource Group

11249 **www.vtcheese.com**
Vermont Cheese Council

11250 **www.walnut.org**
Walnut Marketing Board
History, statistics, supplier listings, etc.

11251 **www.warehouselogistics.org**
American Warehouse Association

11252 **www.watermelon.org**
National Watermelon Promotional Board

11253 **www.wawgg.org**
Washington Association of Wine Grape Growers
Guidance in research and education, and maintaining leadership in local, state and national wine grape issues.

11254 **www.wdairycouncil.com**
Western Dairyfarmers' Promotion Association
Promotes dairy products for the dairy farmer.

11255 **www.westernassn.com**
Western Retail Implement and Hardware Association
For manufacturers, suppliers and distributors of equipment, supplies and services relating to the agricultural industry.

11256 **www.wflo.com**
World Food Logistics Organization
The activities of the WFLO include improving the application of refrigeration technology for the preservation and distribution of food and other commodities, stimulating and supporting research in the science of food refrigeration through grants, training and educating industry personnel, growing its bank of scientific information on the storage and distribution of perishable goods, and developing and supporting national associations.

11257 **www.wga.com**
Western Growers Association
Links and news, safety and legal information.

11258 **www.wheatfoods.org**
Wheat Foods Council
Links, nutrition and product information, news and tips.

11259 **www.wheatworld.org**
National Association of Wheat Growers
Member information, government agencies, research information, etc.

11260 **www.whybiotech.com**
Council for Biotechnology Information
Our vision and mission is to improve understanding and acceptance of biotechnology by collecting balanced, credible and science based information, then communicating this information through a variety of channels. Plant biotechnology has the potential to provide more and better food for a growing world population while helping steward the environment.

11261 **www.wicdirectors.org**
National Association of WIC Directors
Members are geographic state, Native American state and local agency directors of the special supplement nutrition program for women, infants and children.

11262 **www.wildblueberries.com**
Wild Blueberry Association of North America
Sources, recipes, news and product ideas.

11263 **www.wineinstitute.org**
Wine Institute
Organization that represents the wine and spirit industry to state and federal lawmaking bodies.

11264 **www.wislink.org**
Wisconsin Milk Marketing Board

11265 **www.worldfoodnet.com**
Source of information for food product developers

11266 **www.wssa.com**
Wine and Spirits Shippers Association
Provides members, importers and exporters with efficient and economical ocean transportation and other logistic services.

11267 **www.wusata.org**
Western US Agricultural Trade Association
This organization offers information and support to increase exports of US agricultural products.

Associations

11268 A Philanthropic Partnership for Black Communities
333 Seventh Avenue
14th Floor
New York, NY 10001
646-230-0306
Fax: 646-230-0310
E-Mail: info@abfe.org
Home Page: www.abfe.org
Social Media: Facebook

Toya Randall, Chair
Gary Cunningham, Vice Chair
Kenneth Jones, Treasurer
Towalame Austin, Secretary
Ivye L. Allen, President

Encourages blacks in the grantmaking field and helps members improve their job effectiveness.
Founded in 1971

11269 American Society of Association Executives
1575 I St NW
Washington, DC 20005
202-371-0940
888-950-2723
Fax: 202-371-8315
E-Mail: service@asaenet.org
Home Page: www.asaenet.org
Social Media: Facebook, Twitter, LinkedIn

Arlene A Pietranton, CAE, Chairman
Susan K. Neely, CAE, Chairman-Elect
Abe Eshkenazi, Secretary-Treasurer

ASAE is the premier source of learning, knowledge and future-oriented research for the association and nonprofit profession, and provides resources, education, ideas and advocacy to enhance the power and performance of the association and nonprofit community.
21M Members
Founded in 1920

11270 Association for Healthcare Philanthropy
313 Park Avenue
Suite 400
Falls Church, VA 22046
703-532-6243
Fax: 703-532-7170
E-Mail: ahp@ahp.org
Home Page: www.ahp.org
Social Media: Facebook, LinkedIn

William S. Littlejohn, Chair
David L. Flood, Chair Elect
William C. McGinly, President & CEO
Randy A. Varju, Secretary/Treasurer

Represents health care fundraising professionals through education and eventually bestows the credentials upon them.
4100 Members
Founded in 1967

11271 Association of Fund-Raising Professionals
4300 Wilson Blvd.
Suite 300
Arlington, VA 22203
703-684-0410
800-666-3863
Fax: 703-684-0540
E-Mail: mbrship@afpnet.org
Home Page: www.afpnet.org
Social Media: Facebook, Twitter, LinkedIn, YouTube, Pinterest, Instagram

Bob E. Carter, Chair
Patrick J. Feeley, Chair-Elect
Kevin J. Foyle, Vice Chair,Resource Dev.
Ann M. Hale, Secretary
Catherine M. Connolly, Treasurer

Supports all involved in the fundraising profession. Publishes monthly newsletter.
26000 Members
Founded in 1965

11272 Association of Small Foundations/ASF
1720 N St NW
Washington, DC 20036
202-580-6560
888-212-9922
Fax: 202-580-6579
E-Mail: asf@smallfoundations.org
Home Page: www.smallfoundations.org
Social Media: Twitter

Anne Gunsteens, Chair
Shirish Dayal, Vice Chair
Henry L. Berman, Chief Executive Officer
Floyd S. Keene, Secretary
Christopher Petermann, Treasurer

ASF enhances the power of small foundation giving by providing the donors, trustees, and staff of member foundations with peer learning opportunities, targeted tools and resources, and a collective voice in and beyond the philanthropic community.
3000 Members

11273 BoardSource
750 9th Street, NW
Suite 650
Washington, DC 20001-4793
202-349-2500
877-892-6873
Fax: 202-349-2599
E-Mail: mail@boardsource.org
Home Page: www.boardsource.org

John Griswold, Chair
Philip Henderson, Vice Chair
Anne Wallestad, President & CEO
Dawn McNally, Treasurer
Kimberly Roberson, Secretary

Formerly the National Center for Nonprofit Boards, is the premier resource for practical information, tools and best practices, training, and leadership development for board members of nonprofit organizations worldwide.
7000 Members
Founded in 1988

11274 Bond Market Foundation
360 Madison Avenue
New York, NY 10017-7111
646-637-9200
Fax: 646-637-9120
E-Mail: kedmundson@bondmarkets.com
Home Page: www.bondmarkets.org/default.shtml

Michael D McCarthy, Chairman
Kathryn L Edmundon, Executive Director
Robert E Foran, Vice Chairman
Hugh Moore, Treasurer
Brian Macwilliams, Assistant Secretary

The Bond Market Foundation is a charitable and educational not for profit (501-c-3) association. The Foundation develops and enhances the public's access to quality saving and investor education in addition to providing credible non-proprietary research capacity and expert discussion on public issues relevant to the bond markets. The Bond Market Foundation is partner to the Securities Industry and Financial Markets Association (SIFMA).

11275 Center for Effective Philanthropy
675 Massachusetts Avenue
7th Floor
Cambridge, MA 02139
617-492-0800
Fax: 617-492-0888
E-Mail: addya@effectivephilanthropy.org
Home Page: www.effectivephilanthropy.org
Social Media: Facebook, Twitter, LinkedIn, Youtube, Flickr

Phil Buchanan, President
Latia King, Executive Assistant to President
Ellie Beteau, Vice President, Research
Kevin Bolduc, Vice President, Assessment Tools

To provide management and governance tools to define, assess, and improve overall foundation performance
Mailing list available for rent

11276 Council for Advancement & Support of Education
1307 New York Ave NW
Suite 1000
Washington, DC 20005
202-328-2273
Fax: 202-387-4973
E-Mail: memberservicecenter@case.org
Home Page: www.case.org
Social Media: Facebook, Twitter, LinkedIn, Blog

John Lippincott, President/CEO
Brett Chambers, Executive Director of Volunteers

Supports all those involved in campus fund raising, public relations,and alumni administration. Publishes monthly magazine.

11277 Council on Foundations
2121 Crystal Drive
Suite 700
Arlington, VA 22202
800-673-9036
E-Mail: info@cof.org
Home Page: www.cof.org
Social Media: Facebook, Twitter

Kevin K. Murphy, Chair
Sherry P. Magill, Vice Chair
Vikki Spruill, President & CEO
Akhtar Badshah, Secretary
William W. Ginsberg, Treasurer

Supports all those involved in the foundation business. Publishes monthly magazine. We provide leadership expertise, legal services and networking opportunities among other services to our members and to the general public.
2000 Members

11278 Foundation Center
79 5th Ave
New York, NY 10003
212-620-4230
800-424-9836
Fax: 212-807-3677
E-Mail: feedback@foundationcenter.org
Home Page: www.foundationcenter.org
Social Media: Facebook, Twitter, YouTube, Flickr,Googleplus, Fo

Bradford K. Smith, President
Lisa Philip, VP for Strategic Philantropy
Lawrence T. McGill, VP for Research
Jeffery Falkenstein, VP for Data Architecture
Anjula Duggal, VP for Marketing & Communications

A national association for those interested in fund raising related to government agencies. The leading source on philanthropy worldwide.
Founded in 1956

11279 Giving Institute
303 W Madison St.
Suite 2650
Chicago, IL 60606-3396

312-981-6794
800-462-2372
Fax: 312-265-2908
E-Mail: info@givinginstitute.org
Home Page: www.aafrc.org
Social Media: Facebook, Twitter

David H. King, Chair
Jeffrey D. Byrne, 1st Vice Chair
Rachel Hutchison, 2nd Vice Chair
Michelle D. Cramer, Secretary
Sarah J. Howard, Treasurer

Formerly the American Association of Fund-raising Counsel (AAFRC). Mission is to educate and engage members in the ethical delivery of counsel and related services to non-profits through research, advocacy, and best practices.
Founded in 1935
Mailing list available for rent

11280 Independent Sector
1602 L St NW
Suite 900
Washington, DC 20036

202-467-6100
888-860-8118
Fax: 202-467-6101
E-Mail: info@independentsector.org
Home Page: www.independentsector.org
Social Media: Facebook, Twitter

Stephen B. Heintz, Chair
Ralph B. Everett, Vice Chair
Diana Aviv, President & CEO
Lorie A. Slutsky, Treasurer
Kelvin H. Taketa, Secretary

The leadership forum for charities, foundations, and corporate giving programs committed to advancing the common good in America and around the world.
700 Members
Founded in 1980

11281 MacArthur Foundation
140 S Dearborn Street
Chicago, IL 60603-5285

312-726-8000
Fax: 312-920-6258
E-Mail: 4answers@macfound.org
Home Page: www.macfound.org/site/htm
Social Media: Facebook, Twitter

Majorie M. Scardino, Chair
Robert Gallucci, President
Marc P. Yanchura, Vice President & CFO
Elizabeth Kane, Secretary

Private, independent grant-making institution dedicated to helping groups and individuals foster lasting improvement in the human condition. Through the support it provides, the Foundation fosters the development of knowledge, nurtures individual creativity, strengthens institutions, helps improve public policy, and provides information to the public, primarily through support for public interest media.
Founded in 1978

11282 Music Performance Trust Fund
1501 Broadway
Suite 600
New York, NY 10036

212-391-3950
Fax: 212-221-2604
E-Mail: lwilliamson@musicpf.org
Home Page: www.musicpf.org
Social Media: Facebook

Dan Beck, Trustee

Foundation allocates money for the promotion of live music for the general public. The concerts must be free of charge and have no admittance restrictions.
Founded in 1948

11283 National Catholic Development Conference Inc.
86 Front St
Hempstead, NY 11550-3667

516-481-6000
888-879-6232
Fax: 516-489-9287
E-Mail: glehmuth@ncdcusa.org
Home Page: www.ncdc.org
Social Media: Facebook, Twitter, LinkedIn

Paulette M. Karas, Chair
Donald M. Demers, Vice-Chair
Georgette Lehmuth, President & CEO
Keith Zekind, Treasurer
Diane Brondyke, Secretary

Members include development officers and key fund raisers of charitable institutions and agencies.
400 Members
Founded in 1968
Mailing list available for rent

11284 National Committee for Responsive Philanthropy
1331 H Street NW
Suite 200
Washington, DC 20005

202-387-9177
Fax: 202-332-5084
E-Mail: info@ncrp.org
Home Page: www.ncrp.org
Social Media: Facebook, Twitter

Sherece Y. West-Scantlebury, Chair
Gara LaMarche, Vice Chair
Judy Hatcher, Treasurer
Priscilla Hung, Secretary
Aaron Dorfman, Executive Director

Supports all those involved in the philanthropy field. Publishes quarterly newsletter.
Founded in 1976

11285 National School Foundation Association (NSFA)
2130 Grand Avenue
Des Moines, IA 50312

516-971-2324
866-824-8513
Fax: 813-280-4820
E-Mail: bill@billhoffmanandassociates.com
Home Page: www.schoolfoundations.org
Social Media: Facebook, Twitter

Lynne Grasz, Board Chair
Bill Hoffman, Executive Director

The mission of the National School Foundation Association is to encourage K-12 school and school foundation personnel in the very rewarding and important process of establishing, developing and maintaining school foundations.

11286 Northwest Development Officers Association
2150 N 107th Street
Suite 205
Seattle, WA 98133-9009

206-367-8704
Fax: 206-367-8777
E-Mail: office@ndoa.org
Home Page: www.ndoa.org
Social Media: Facebook, Twitter, LinkedIn

Rebecca Zanatta, President
Jodie Miner, President Elect
Rebecca Stephens, Secretary
Michael Cheever, Treasurer

To provide its members and other fundraising professionals with collegial peer support, networking, and comprehensive training opportunities to advance philanthropy and strengthen community. Provides fellowship,. targeted training, and a sounding board for development officers, volunteers, board members, students, nonprofit managers and others who are committed to fundraising and philanthropy.
800+ Members
Founded in 1978

11287 Partnership for Philanthropic Planning
233 S McCrea St
Suite 300
Indianapolis, IN 46225

317-269-6274
Fax: 317-269-6268
E-Mail: info@pppnet.org
Home Page: www.pppnet.org
Social Media: Facebook, Twitter, LinkedIn, YouTube, Flickr,Googleplus

Jeffery Lydenberg, Chair
Jay Steenhuysen, Chair Elect
Michael Kenyon, President
Melanie J. Norton, Treasurer
Laura Hansen Dean, Secretary

Serving people and organizations that work together to make charitable giving most meaningful.
112 Members
Founded in 1988

11288 Society for Non-Profits
P.O.Box 510354
Livonia, MI 48151

734-451-3582
Fax: 734-451-5935
E-Mail: submit@feedbackform
Home Page: www.snpo.org
Social Media: Facebook, Twitter, LinkedIn, Yahoo

Katie Burnham Laverty, President

Provides busy nonprofit leaders with concise and practical articles whose advice can be easily implemented .
Cost: $69.00
Frequency: Bi-Monthly
Circulation: 7000
ISSN: 8755-7614

11289 Society for Nonprofit Organizations
PO Box 510354
Livonia, MI 48151

734-451-3582
Fax: 734-451-5935
E-Mail: submit@feedbackform
Home Page: www.snpo.org
Social Media: Facebook, Twitter, LinkedIn, Yahoo

Katie Burnham Laverty, President

Dedicated to bringing together those who serve in the nonprofit world in order to build a strong network of professionals throughout the country. Publishes Nonprofit World Magazine and has an on-line certificate in Nonprofit Management in partnership with Michigan State University.
7000 Members
Founded in 1983

11290 The Association of Fund-Raising Distributors & Suppliers
1100 Johnson Ferry Rd
Suite 300
Atlanta, GA 30342

404-252-3663
Fax: 404-252-0774
E-Mail: afrds@kellencompany.com

Home Page: www.afrds.org
Social Media: Facebook

Kurt Koehler, President
Russ Colombo, Vice President Distributor Affairs
Carol Gentry-Brewer, Vice President Supplier Affairs
Paul Mahler, Treasurer
Kim Hodous, Secretary

Association for manufacturers or suppliers of fundraising products, supplies and services. Its members manufacturer, supply or distribute products that are resold by not-for-profit organizations for fundraising purposes.
700+ Members

11291 **The Grantsmanship Center**
350 South Bixel St., Suite 110
PO Box 17220
Los Angeles, CA 90017

213-482-9860
800-421-9512
Fax: 213-482-9863
E-Mail: info@tgci.com
Home Page: www.tgci.com
Social Media: Facebook, Twitter, YouTube,Pinterest,Googleplus

Cathleen Kiritz, President & Publisher
Barbara Floersch, Director
Susan Andres, Editor

Provides training and publications about obtaining funidng for nonprofit and government agencies. Free e-magazine, Centerd, offers a digest of useful articles for grant proposal writers, as well as expert advice from The Grantsmanship Center's trainers.
Founded in 1972

Newsletters

11292 **AFP eWire**
Association of Fund-Raising Professionals
4300 Wilson Blvd.
Suite 300
Arlington, VA 22203

703-684-0410
800-666-3863
Fax: 703-684-0540
E-Mail: mbrship@afpnet.org
Home Page: www.afpnet.org
Social Media: Facebook, Twitter, LinkedIn, YouTube

Andrew Watt, President & CEO
Tom Clark, COO
Rebecca A. Knight, Director
Mike Eason, CFO

Delivers the latest fundraising news and information.
26000 Members
Frequency: Weekly
Founded in 1965

11293 **AHP E-Connect**
Association for Healthcare Philanthropy
313 Park Avenue
Suite 400
Falls Church, VA 22046

703-532-6243
Fax: 703-532-7170
E-Mail: ahp@ahp.org
Home Page: www.ahp.org
Social Media: Facebook, LinkedIn

Susan J. Doliner, Chair
William S. Littlejohn, Chair Elect
Merv D. Webb, Secretary/Treasurer

Provides updates on industry news and research, educational and professional opportunities, book reviews and articles related to health care philanthropy.
Cost: $60.00
4100 Members
Frequency: 8x Yearly
Founded in 1967

11294 **AID for Education**
CD Publications
8204 Fenton St
Silver Spring, MD 20910-4571

301-588-6380
800-666-6380
Fax: 301-588-6385
E-Mail: info@cdpublications.com
Home Page: www.cdpublications.com

Michael Gerecht, President
Frank Kalimko, Editor

Private and federal funding opportunities and news for all levels of education including grants for bilingual education, special education, literacy, minorities and more.
Cost: $419.00
18 Pages
Founded in 1991
Mailing list available for rent: 2,000 names at $160 per M

11295 **Board Source**
Board Source
1828 L St Nw
Suite 900
Washington, DC 20036-5114

202-452-6262
800-883-6262
Fax: 202-452-6299
E-Mail: mail@boardsource.org
Home Page: www.boardsource.org

Linda Crompton, CEO
Betsy Rosenblatt, Senior Editor

National newsletter for board members and staff leaders of nonprofit organizations includes strategies for building effective nonprofit boards. Comentaries from nonprofit leaders, case studies, and nonprofit governance news.
Cost: $139.00
Founded in 1988

11296 **BoardSource E-Newsletter**
BoardSource
750 9th Street, NW
Suite 650
Washington, DC 20001-4590

202-349-2500
877-892-6873
Fax: 202-349-2599
E-Mail: mail@boardsource.org
Home Page: www.boardsource.org

Linda C. Crompton, President & CEO
Fred Sherman, CFO
Anne Wallestad, COO
David J. Nygren, Ph.D, Chair
Roxanne Spillett, Vice Chair

Members-only benefit, offering timely news and information on nonprofit governance issues and trends affecting nonprofit boards.
7000 Members
Frequency: Monthly
Founded in 1988

11297 **CEO Connection**
Association for Healthcare Philanthropy
313 Park Avenue
Suite 400
Falls Church, VA 22046

703-532-6243
Fax: 703-532-7170
E-Mail: ahp@ahp.org
Home Page: www.ahp.org
Social Media: Facebook, LinkedIn

Susan J. Doliner, Chair
William S. Littlejohn, Chair Elect
Merv D. Webb, Secretary/Treasurer

From AHP President to health care organization CEOs discussing issues affecting health care philanthropy.
4100 Members
Frequency: Quarterly
Founded in 1967

11298 **Centered**
The Grantsmanship Center
1125 W 6th Street 5th Floor
PO Box 17220
Los Angeles, CA 90017

213-482-9860
800-421-9512
Fax: 213-482-9863
E-Mail: centered@tgci.com
Home Page: www.tgci.com

Susan Andres, Editor
Cathleen Kiritz, Publisher

Provides a digest of useful articles for grantseekers and proposal writers, as well as expert advice from The Grantsmanship Center's trainers. Our goal is to deliver practical information that will help you sharpen your grant research, proposal-writing, evaluation, and team-building skills.
Frequency: Monthly
Circulation: 35000

11299 **Chronicle of Philanthropy**
1255 23rd St Nw
Suite 700
Washington, DC 20037-1146

202-466-1200
800-728-2819
Fax: 202-452-1033
E-Mail: press@philanthropy.com
Home Page: www.philanthropy.com

Robin Ross, Publisher
Phil Semas, Editor
Michael Solomon, Manager of External Communications

A newspaper providing news and information for executives of nonprofit, tax-exempt organizations in health, education, religion, the arts, social services and other fields, as well as fund raisers, professional employees of foundation, and corporate grant makers. Features news, lists of grants, fundraising ideas and techniques, statistics, updates on regulations, reports on tax and court rulings, book summaries, calendar of events.
Cost: $72.00
Frequency: Fortnightly
Circulation: 100000
Founded in 1997

11300 **Community Health Funding Report**
CD Publications
8204 Fenton St
Silver Spring, MD 20910-4571
301-588-6380
800-666-6380
Fax: 301-588-6385
E-Mail: info@cdpublications.com
Home Page: www.cdpublications.com

Michael Gerecht, President
Amy Bernstein, Editor
Jessica Cha, Owner

Highlights sources of funding for healthcare ranging from AIDS education to teen pregnancy to minority health care. Plus national and local community health news.
Cost: $339.00
Mailing list available for rent: 2,000 names at $160 per M

11301 Connections
Foundation Center
79 5th Ave
New York, NY 10003-3076

212-620-4230
800-424-9836
Fax: 212-807-3677
E-Mail: feedback@foundationcenter.org
Home Page: www.foundationcenter.org
Social Media: Facebook, Twitter, YouTube, Flickr

Melissa Berman, President & CEO

The best philanthropy-related content the Web has to offer.
Frequency: Bi-Weekly
Founded in 1956

11302 Contributions
Contributions
28 Park St
Suite A
Medfield, MA 02052-2518

508-359-0019
Fax: 508-359-2703
E-Mail: kbrennan@contributionsmagazine.com
Home Page: www.contributionsmagazine.com

Jerry Cianciolo, Editor
Kathleen Brennan, Director of Communications
Robert Riordan, Director of Communications

Offers full coverage of fund raising campaigns.
Cost: $40.00
Circulation: 22,000
Founded in 1987

11303 Corporate Giving Directory
Information Today Inc
143 Old Marlton Pike
Medford, NJ 08055-8750

609-654-6266
Fax: 609-654-4309
E-Mail: custserv@infotoday.com
Home Page: www.infotoday.com

Thomas H Hogan, President

Delivers the latest information on program priorities, giving preferences, evaluation criteria, corporate and foundation officers and directors, and all the other data you need to help your nonprofit organization gain a crucial edge as corporate philanthropy budgets tighten.

11304 Corporate Philanthropy Report
LRP Publications
PO Box 24668
West Palm Beach, FL 33416-4668

561-622-6520
Fax: 561-622-0757
E-Mail: webmaster@lrp.com
Home Page: www.lrp.com

Kenneth Kahn, President
Eileen Banashek, Editor

A report for both the corporate and nonprofit communities, spotlighting a different field or industry in each issue.
Cost: $235.00
Frequency: Monthly
Founded in 1977

11305 Development and Alumni Relations Report
LRP Publications
747 Dresher Road Suite 500
PO Box 980
Horsham, PA 19044-980

215-784-0912
800-341-7874
Fax: 215-784-9639
E-Mail: webmaster@lrp.com
Home Page: www.lrp.com

Anne Checkosky, Editor
Dionne Ellis, Marketing

Gives innovative ideas for improving annual giving, endowment and capital campaigns, planned giving, and alumni relations. Offers suggestions on new ways to spur participation and increase total contributions from alumni, corporate donors and foundations.
Cost: $185.00
Frequency: Monthly
Founded in 1977

11306 Dimensions
National Catholic Development Conference
86 Front St
Hempstead, NY 11550-3667

516-481-6000
888-879-6232
Fax: 516-489-9287
E-Mail: glehmuth@ncdcusa.org
Home Page: www.ncdc.org

Rachel Donofrio, Editor
Richard Reale, Director Membership
Georgette Lehmuth, CEO
Patricia Newman, Manager

Offers information on development and fund raising including direct mail, planned giving and major gifts and capitol campaigns.
Cost: $1000.00
16 Pages
Circulation: 550
Founded in 1968
Printed in 2 colors on matte stock

11307 Disability Funding News
CD Publications
8204 Fenton St
Silver Spring, MD 20910-4571

301-588-6380
800-666-6380
Fax: 301-588-6385
E-Mail: info@cdpublications.com
Home Page: www.cdpublications.com

Michael Gerecht, President
Martha McPartlin, Editor

Alerts the reader to funding for programs for the disabled, including housing, transportation, rehabilitation, research and special education. Plus advice on successful grantseeking and news updated on national and local developments.
Cost: $419.00
Founded in 1993
Mailing list available for rent: 2,000 names at $160 per M

11308 E-ssentials
National Catholic Development Conference
86 Front St
Hempstead, NY 11550-3667
516-481-6000
888-879-6232
Fax: 516-489-9287
E-Mail: glehmuth@ncdcusa.org
Home Page: www.ncdc.org

Mark Melia, Chair
Curtis Yarlott, Vice-Chair
Keith Zekind, Treasurer

Connects NCDC members together by providing news about upcoming NCDC events, workshops, and webinars; membership committee news; member success stories; award notifications; fundraising white papers and quick tips; and CFRE exam information.
400 Members
Frequency: Weekly
Founded in 1968

11309 Funding Alert Newsletter
Society for Nonprofit Organizations
PO Box 510354
Livonia, MI 48151

734-451-3582
Fax: 734-451-5935
Home Page: www.snpo.org
Social Media: Facebook, Twitter, LinkedIn

Katherine Burnham Leverty, Co-Founder/President/CEO

The leading e-newsletter for current grant and funding opportunities.
7000 Members
Founded in 1983

11310 Giving USA Update
American Association of Fund-Raising Counsel
4700 W Lake Avenue
Glenview, IL 60025

847-375-4709
800-462-2372
Fax: 866-263-2491
E-Mail: info@aafrc.org
Home Page: www.aafrc.org

Ann Kaplan, Publisher
John J Glier, Chair

Contains analysis, data and comments on charitable giving.
Cost: $125.00
Frequency: Quarterly
Founded in 1935

11311 Health Grants Funding Alert
Health Resources Publishing
1913 Atlantic Ave
Suite 200
Manasquan, NJ 08736-1067

732-292-1100
888-843-6242
Fax: 732-292-1111
E-Mail: info@healthresourcesonline.com
Home Page: www.healthresourcesonline.com

Robert K Jenkins, Publisher
Barbara Brown, Regional Director
Brett Powell, Regional Director
Alice Burron, Director

Monthly report sharing news of critical federal and foundation funding opportunities and trends, read by development directors and grants officers.
Cost: $495.00
8 Pages
Frequency: Monthly
ISSN: 0193-7928
Founded in 1978

11312 Kaleidoscope
Association of Fund-Raising Professionals
4300 Wilson Blvd.
Suite 300
Arlington, VA 22203

703-684-0410
800-666-3863
Fax: 703-684-0540
E-Mail: mbrship@afpnet.org
Home Page: www.afpnet.org
Social Media: Facebook, Twitter, LinkedIn, YouTube

Andrew Watt, President & CEO
Tom Clark, COO
Rebecca A. Knight, Director
Mike Eason, CFO

Supports AFP's strategic goal of connecting communities around the world by promoting diversity to donors, boards and fundraisers.
26000 Members
Frequency: Quarterly
Founded in 1965

11313 **National Center for Nonprofit Boards: Board Member Newsletter**
1828 L Street NW
Washington, DC 20036

202-452-6262
800-883-6262
Fax: 202-452-6299
Home Page: www.ncnb.org

Monthly newsletter for board members and staff leaders of nonprofit organizations includes news updates, case studies, checklists, interviews and opinion pieces to increase the effectiveness of nonprofit boards.
Cost: $99.00
Frequency: Monthly
Circulation: 6800
Printed in 2 colors on matte stock

11314 **Philanthropy News Digest**
Foundation Center
79 5th Ave
New York, NY 10003-3076

212-620-4230
800-424-9836
Fax: 212-807-3677
E-Mail: feedback@foundationcenter.org
Home Page: www.foundationcenter.org
Social Media: Facebook, Twitter, YouTube, Flickr

Melissa Berman, President & CEO

Long-running, award-winning news digest of the Foundation Center.
Frequency: Weekly
Founded in 1956

11315 **RFP Bulletin**
Foundation Center
79 5th Ave
New York, NY 10003-3076

212-620-4230
800-424-9836
Fax: 212-807-3677
E-Mail: feedback@foundationcenter.org
Home Page: www.foundationcenter.org
Social Media: Facebook, Twitter, YouTube, Flickr

Melissa Berman, President & CEO

A roundup of recently announced Requests for Proposals (RFPs) from private, corporate, and government funding sources.
Frequency: Weekly
Founded in 1956

11316 **Responsive Philanthropy**
National Committee for Responsive Philanthropy
2001 S St Nw
Suite 620
Washington, DC 20009-1165

202-387-9177
Fax: 202-332-5084
E-Mail: info@ncrp.org
Home Page: www.ncrp.org

Aaron Dorfman, Executive Director
Naomi Tacuyan, Editor

With news and feature articles about philanthropy, fund raising and social justice, covering issues often unreported in mainstream philanthropic publications.
Cost: $25.00
16 Pages
Frequency: Quarterly
Circulation: 5000
Founded in 1976
Mailing list available for rent: 10000 names
Printed in 2 colors on matte stock

11317 **Smith Funding Report**
SFR
20 O'Neill Circle
Monroe, NY 10950-3210

914-774-4449

Melanie Smith, President

Quarterly guide to private foundation research/project grant opportunities for education and health institutions.
Cost: $195.00
40 Pages
Frequency: Quarterly
Printed in one color on matte stock

11318 **Substance Abuse Funding News**
CD Publications
8204 Fenton St
Silver Spring, MD 20910-4571

301-588-6380
800-666-6380
Fax: 301-588-6385
E-Mail: info@cdpublications.com
Home Page: www.cdpublications.com

Michael Gerecht, President
Joseph Smith, Editor

Detailed coverage of private and federal funding opportunities nationwide for alcohol and substance abuse programs. Advice on successful grantmaking strategies and roundup of national news.
Cost: $419.00
Founded in 1992
Mailing list available for rent: 2,000 names at $160 per M

11319 **Te Informa**
Association of Fund-Raising Professionals
4300 Wilson Blvd.
Suite 300
Arlington, VA 22203

703-684-0410
800-666-3863
Fax: 703-684-0540
E-Mail: mbrship@afpnet.org
Home Page: www.afpnet.org
Social Media: Facebook, Twitter, LinkedIn, YouTube

Andrew Watt, President & CEO
Tom Clark, COO
Rebecca A. Knight, Director
Mike Eason, CFO

AFP's Spanish-language e-newsletter covering issues of fundraising pertinent to Mexico and other Latin American countries.
26000 Members
Frequency: Quarterly
Founded in 1965

Magazines & Journals

11320 **Advancing Philanthropy**
Association of Fund-Raising Professionals
4300 Wilson Blvd.
Suite 300
Arlington, VA 22203

703-684-0410
800-666-3863
Fax: 703-684-0540
E-Mail: mbrship@afpnet.org
Home Page: www.afpnet.org
Social Media: Facebook, Twitter, LinkedIn, YouTube

Andrew Watt, President & CEO
Tom Clark, COO
Rebecca A. Knight, Director
Mike Eason, CFO

Provides practical information, useful tools and other resources to help members succeed and advance.
26000 Members
Frequency: Bi-Monthly
Founded in 1965

11321 **Association Management**
American Society of Association Executives
1575 I St NW
Washington, DC 20005-1103

202-626-2700
Fax: 202-408-9635
E-Mail: publicpolicy@asaenet.org
Home Page: www.asaenet.org

Keith C Skillman, Editor
Karl Ely, Publisher

Association Management strives to provide timely, practical information to help association executives succeed in their dual role as manager and visionary.
Cost: $50.00
106 Pages
Frequency: Monthly
Circulation: 24678
ISSN: 0004-5578
Founded in 1920
Printed in 4 colors on glossy stock

11322 **Association for Healthcare Philanthropy**
313 Park Avenue
Suite 400
Falls Church, VA 22046-3303

703-532-6243
Fax: 703-532-7170
E-Mail: ahp@ahp.org
Home Page: www.ahp.org

Kathy Renzetti, Marketing Manager/Editor
William C McGinly, CEO/President
Yvette Banks, Membership Manager
Alison Shaffer, Administrative Assistant

Written for development professionals, fundraisers, trustees, public relations professionals and executives in health care fundraising. Provides timely information on fundraising, career enhancement, planned giving, donor relations, organizational strategies and the effect of health care reform on philanthropy.
Founded in 1967
Mailing list available for rent: 3000 names at $200 per M

11323 **BBB Wise Giving Guide**
BBB Wise Giving Alliance
4200 Wilson Boulevard
Suite 800
Arlington, VA 22203-1838

703-276-0100
Fax: 703-525-8277
Home Page: www.bbb.org

Margery Heitbrink, Editor

Includes a summary of the latest results of the Alliance's national charity evaluations along with a cover story about giving tips and or charity accountability issues.
Frequency: 3x Yearly
Circulation: 35000

11324 **Centered**
The Grantsmanship Center
350 South Bixel St., Suite 110
PO Box 17220
Los Angeles, CA 90017

213-482-9860
800-421-9512
Fax: 213-482-9863
E-Mail: info@tgci.com

Home Page: www.tgci.com
Social Media: Facebook, Twitter, MySpace

Cathleen Kiritz, President
Barbara Floersch, Director
Susan Andres, Editor
Cathleen Kiritz, Publisher

Provides a digest of useful articles for grantseekers and proposal writers, as well as expert advice from the Center's trainers.
Frequency: Monthly
Founded in 1972

11325 **Currents**
Council for Advancement & Support of Education
1307 New York Ave NW
Suite 1000
Washington, DC 20005-4726

202-393-1301
Fax: 202-387-4973
E-Mail: memberservicecenter@case.org
Home Page: www.case.org

John Lippincott, President
Deborah Bangiorno, Editor-in-Chief
Andrea Gabrick, Senior Editor
Toni Lewis-Bennett, Director of Membership
Anne Brown, Executive Director

Offers information on campus fund raising, public relations,and alumni administration.
Cost: $115.00
Circulation: 15,000
Founded in 1994

11326 **Essentials**
Association of Small Foundations/ASF
1720 N St NW
Washington, DC 20036-2907

202-580-6560
888-212-9922
Fax: 202-580-6579
E-Mail: asf@smallfoundations.org
Home Page: www.smallfoundations.org
Social Media: Twitter

Henry L. Berman, CEO
Floyd S. Keene, Chair

Provides practical articles on a range of information in one easy read.
3000 Members
Frequency: Quarterly

11327 **Foundation News & Commentary**
Council on Foundations
2121 Crystal Drive
Suite 700
Arlington, VA 22202

8006739036
Home Page: www.foundationnews.org

Offers news and information for foundations, legislation news and fundraising campaign reviews.
Cost: $24.00
Frequency: Monthly

11328 **Fundraising EDGE**
Association of Fund-Raising Distributors
1100 Johnson Ferry Rd
Suite 300
Atlanta, GA 30342-1733

404-252-3663
Fax: 404-252-0774
E-Mail: atrds@kellencompany.com
Home Page: www.afrds.org
Social Media: Facebook

Kurt Koehler, President
Leslie Lawrence, Secretary
Steve Wienkers, Treasurer

Published by the Association of Fund-Raising distributors and suppliers, offers the latest information about product fundraising.
700+ Members

11329 **Fundraising: Hands on Tactics for Nonprofit Groups**
McGraw-Hill Trade
2 Penn Plz
New York, NY 10121-0101

212-904-4450
877-833-5524
Fax: 212-904-2348
E-Mail: Philip_Ruppel@mcgraw-hill.com
Home Page: www.aviationdaily.com

L Peter Edles, Editor
Philip Ruppel, VP & Group Publisher
Jeffrey Krames, Publisher & Editor-in-Chief
William Garvey, Managing Editor
Iain Blackhall, Managing Director

This hands-on operations manual remedies the funding crisis by showing nonprofit professionals and volunteers how to design and run successful fundraising campaigns for their organizations. Combines sound, cost-effective strategies for building better organizational, management, sales, and marketing practices.
Cost: $19.95
288 Pages
ISBN: 0-070189-28-5
Founded in 1992

11330 **Giving USA**
American Association of Fund-Raising Counsel
4700 W Lake Avenue
Glenview, IL 60025-7406

847-375-4709
800-462-2372
Fax: 866-263-2491
E-Mail: info@aafrc.org
Home Page: www.aafrc.org/

Ann Kaplan, Editor

An annual report on charitable giving in the United States, tracking total charitable giving from four categories of sources to seven kinds of organizations.
Cost: $125.00
Frequency: Quarterly
Circulation: 9000
Founded in 1935

11331 **Grant Funding for Elderly Health Services**
Health Resources Publishing
1913 Atlantic Ave
Suite 200
Manasquan, NJ 08736-1067

732-292-1100
888-843-6242
Fax: 732-292-1111
E-Mail: info@healthresourcesonline.com
Home Page: www.healthresourcesonline.com

Robert K Jenkins, Publisher
Lisa Mansfield, Marketing Assistant
Caroline Pense, Editor
Brett Powell, Regional Director
Alice Burron, Director

This report will give insight into which proposals will get funds for which organization. Lists the organizations that will recieve the most funds from grantmakers during this decade and beyond. Also studies different case histories of successful grant proposals.
Cost: $95.00
Frequency: Monthly
ISBN: 1-882364-46-5
Founded in 1978

11332 **Grants Magazine**
Plenum Publishing Corporation
233 Spring St
New York, NY 10013-1522

212-242-1490
Fax: 212-463-0742
E-Mail: info@plenum.com
Home Page: www.plenum.com

Ricot Paillent, Manager

A magazine listing sources for grants, offering legislative news for the fundraising community, and foundation listings.
Founded in 1946

11333 **Healthcare Philanthropy**
Association for Healthcare Philanthropy
313 Park Avenue
Suite 400
Falls Church, VA 22046

703-532-6243
Fax: 703-532-7170
E-Mail: ahp@ahp.org
Home Page: www.ahp.org
Social Media: Facebook, LinkedIn

Susan J. Doliner, Chair
William S. Littlejohn, Chair Elect
Merv D. Webb, Secretary/Treasurer

Previously called the AHP Journal. Contains articles on health care fundraising and development, including ideas and methods for creating successful development programs, analyses of the current health care environment and projec tions of future trends.
Cost: $50.00
4100 Members
Frequency: Bi-Annually
Founded in 1967

11334 **International Journal of Educational Advancement**
Association of Fundraising Professionals
Henry Stewart Publications
PO Box 10812
Birmingham, AL 35202-0812

205-995-1567
800-633-4931
Fax: 205-995-1588
E-Mail: brenda@hspublications.co.uk
Home Page: www.afpnet.org / www.henrystewart.com

Joyce O'Brien, VP of Communications & Marketing
Brenda Rouse, Publisher

Features new ideas, shares examples of best practices and develops a body of knowledge in educational advancement.
Cost: $250.00
Frequency: 4x/year

11335 **Journal of Gift Planning**
National Committee on Planned Giving
233 S McCrea St
Suite 400
Indianapolis, IN 46225-1068

317-269-6274
Fax: 317-269-6276
Home Page: www.ncpg.org

Tanya Howe Johnson, President

Provides in-depth analysis of issues of daily concern to both nonprofit planners and for-profit donor advisors. Each issue provides an orientation to national issues and trends affecting the profession, such as the release of major research related to planned gift fundraising or the debate over professional certification for gift planners.
Cost: $45.00
Frequency: Quarterly

11336 **Nonprofit World**
Society for Nonprofit Organizations
PO Box 510354
Livonia, MI 48151

734-451-3582
Fax: 734-451-5935
E-Mail: info@snpo.org

Home Page: www.snpo.org
Social Media: Facebook, Twitter, LinkedIn

Katherine Burnham Laverty, President
Jason Chmura, Membership Director
Jill Muehrcke, Editor

Contains original articles and departments on all aspects of running an effective nonprofit organization. Accepts advertising. Now includes the Directory of Service and Product Providers and the Resource Center Catalog with discounted resources for nonprofit organizations.
Cost: $79.00
40 Pages
Frequency: Bi-Monthly
Circulation: 4000
ISSN: 8755-7614
Founded in 1983
Printed in 2 colors

11337 **Philanthropy Monthly**
Non-Profit Report
PO Box 989
New Milford, CT 06776

860-354-7132
860-354-7132
Fax: 860-354-7132

Henry Suhrke, Publisher

Editorial range covers concerns of nonprofits; legislative, economic, fund raising, nonprofit accounting, litigation, etc.
Cost: $84.00
Circulation: 6208

11338 **Responsive Philanthropy**
National Committee for Responsive Philanthropy
1331 H Street NW
Suite 200
Washington, DC 20005

202-387-9177
Fax: 202-332-5084
E-Mail: info@ncrp.org
Home Page: www.ncrp.org
Social Media: Facebook, Twitter

Diane Feeney, Chair
Dave Beckwith, Vice Chair
Cynthia Guyer, Secretary
Robert Edgar, Treasurer

Looks at ending homelessness, funding direct services, supporting re0enfranchisement efforts and more.
Frequency: Quarterly
Founded in 1976

Trade Shows

11339 **AFP International Conference on Fundraising**
Association of Fundraising Professionals
1101 King Street
Suite 700
Alexandria, VA 22314-2944

703-684-0410
800-666-3863
Fax: 703-684-0540
E-Mail: webmaster@afpnet.org
Home Page: www.afpnet.org

Shannon Watson, Director Meetings & Expositions
Myrlin Young, Conferences Coordinator
Paulette Maehara, President
Michael Nilsen, senior Director public affairs

The largest gathering of fundraisers in the profession. The Conference has become the premier resource for fundraisers to network, learn, and discover new products and services.
Frequency: April
Founded in 1962

11340 **ASF Annual National Conference**
Association of Small Foundations/ASF
1720 N St NW
Washington, DC 20036-2907

202-580-6560
888-212-9922
Fax: 202-580-6579
E-Mail: asf@smallfoundations.org
Home Page: www.smallfoundations.org
Social Media: Twitter

Henry L. Berman, CEO
Floyd S. Keene, Chair

Dozens of educational sessions, preconference workshops, networking opportunities, and inspiring site visits and service projects.
3000 Members
Frequency: Biennial

11341 **Annual AFRDS Convention & Trade Show**
Association of Fund-Raising Distributors
1100 Johnson Ferry Rd
Suite 300
Atlanta, GA 30342-1733

404-252-3663
Fax: 404-252-0774
E-Mail: afrds@kellencompany.com
Home Page: www.afrds.org
Social Media: Facebook

Kurt Koehler, President
Leslie Lawrence, Secretary
Steve Wienkers, Treasurer

The biggest event in product fundraising.
700+ Members
1000+ Attendees
Frequency: Annual/January

11342 **Annual NCDC Conference and Exposition**
National Catholic Development Conference
86 Front St
Hempstead, NY 11550-3667

516-481-6000
888-879-6232
Fax: 516-489-9287
E-Mail: glehmuth@ncdcusa.org
Home Page: www.ncdc.org

Mark Melia, Chair
Curtis Yarlott, Vice-Chair
Keith Zekind, Treasurer

Network, learn and be inspired by the amazing community gathered in the spirit of the ministry of fundraising.
400 Members
Frequency: Weekly
Founded in 1968

11343 **Annual Winter & Spring Conferences**
Northwest Development Officers Association
2150 N 107th Street
Suite 205
Seattle, WA 98133

206-367-8704
Fax: 206-367-8777
E-Mail: office@ndoa.org
Home Page: www.ndoa.org

Lara Littlefield, President
Louise S. Miller, Executive Director
Jenny Poast, Secretary

Educational meetings focusing on fundraising issues, skills, and best practices. 30 exhibitiors.
400 Attendees
Frequency: Annual Winter & Spring

11344 **CEP Bi-Annual Conference**
Center for Effective Philanthropy
675 Massachusetts Avenue
7th Floor
Cambridge, MA 02139

617-492-0800
Fax: 617-492-0888
E-Mail: addya@effectivephilanthropy.org
Home Page: www.effectivephilanthropy.org

Phil Buchanan, President

To provide management and governance tools to define, assess, and improve overall foundation performance.
Frequency: Bi-Annual

11345 **Council on Foundations Annual Conference**
Council on Foundations
1828 L Street NW
Washington, DC 20036-5104

202-466-6512
Fax: 202-785-3926
E-Mail: jonee@cof.org
Home Page: www.cof.org

Edward Jones, Program Director
Heidi Lyn Capati, Conference Logistics
Michelle Dunston, Registration
Dorothy Ridings, President

Annual conference and exhibits relating to trends and legislation in the field of philanthropy.
Frequency: April

11346 **Fall Conference for Community Foundations**
Council on Foundations
2121 Crystal Drive
Suite 700
Arlington, VA 22202

800-673-9036
E-Mail: info@cof.org
Home Page: www.cof.org
Social Media: Facebook, Twitter

Carol Larson, Chair
Kevin Murphy, Vice Chair
Sherece West, Secretary
Will Ginsberg, Treasurer

Three days of bold steps, original ideas, and new solutions for community foundations.
2000 Members
Frequency: Annual/September

11347 **Independent Sector Annual Conference**
Independent Sector
1602 L Street NW
Suite 900
Washington, DC 20036

202-467-6100
888-860-8118
Fax: 202-467-6101
E-Mail: info@independentsector.org
Home Page: www.independentsector.org
Social Media: Facebook, Twitter

Stephen B. Heintz, Chair
Ralph B. Everett, Vice Chair
Kelvin H. Taketa, Treasurer
Lorie A. Slutsky

The conference focuses on the social compact of the charitable community's role.
1000 Attendees
Frequency: Annual/November

11348 **National Conference on Planned Giving**
National Committee on Planned Giving

233 McCrea Street
Suite 400
Indianapolis, IN 46225-1030

317-269-6274
Fax: 317-269-6276
Home Page: www.ncpg.org

Shana McMahon, Meetings Manager
Kathryn J Ramsey, Meetings Director
Tanya Howe Johnson, President

Annual conference and exhibits of fundraising equipment, supplies and services.
Frequency: September-October

11349 **Rural Philanthropy Conference**
Council on Foundations
2121 Crystal Drive
Suite 700
Arlington, VA 22202

800-673-9036
E-Mail: info@cof.org
Home Page: www.cof.org
Social Media: Facebook, Twitter

Carol Larson, Chair
Kevin Murphy, Vice Chair
Sherece West, Secretary
Will Ginsberg, Treasurer

Each session encourages defining rural philanthropy's role, focusing on successful case studies, providing the tools needed to replicate them in the communities.
2000 Members
Frequency: Annual/July

11350 **Windows Annual Conference**
Council on Foundations
2121 Crystal Drive
Suite 700
Arlington, VA 22202

800-673-9036
E-Mail: info@cof.org
Home Page: www.cof.org
Social Media: Facebook, Twitter

Carol Larson, Chair
Kevin Murphy, Vice Chair
Sherece West, Secretary
Will Ginsberg, Treasurer

Features three days of transparency, honesty, and candor in the field of philanthropy.
2000 Members
Frequency: Annual/April

Directories & Databases

11351 **Annual Register of Grant Support: A Directory of Funding Services**
Information Today
143 Old Marlton Pike
Medford, NJ 08055-8750

609-654-6266
800-300-9868
Fax: 609-654-4309
E-Mail: custserv@infotoday.com
Home Page: www.infotoday.com

Beverley McDonough, Editor
Daniel Bazikian, Editor

Contains more that 3,500 grant giving organziations. IS also the definitive resource for researching and uncovering a full range of available grant sources.Also directs you to traditional corporate, private, and public funding programs, it also shows you the way to little known, nontraditional grant sources such as educational associations and unions.
Cost: $240.00
1476 Pages
Frequency: Annual
ISBN: 1-573872-04-0

11352 **Charitable Trust Directory**
Office of the Secretary of State
Charitable Trust Program
801 Capitol Way South
Olympia, WA 98504-0234

360-753-0863
800-332-GIVE
Home Page: www.secstate.wa.gov/charities

Sam Reed, Chairman/Secretary of State
Linda Vallegos Bremer, Director of General Administration

Directory of charitable trusts regulations in the State of Washington.
Cost: $27.00
290 Pages
Frequency: CD-ROM Available

11353 **Corporate Giving Directory**
Information Today Inc
143 Old Marlton Pike
Medford, NJ 08055-8750

609-654-6266
Fax: 609-654-4309
E-Mail: custserv@infotoday.com
Home Page: www.infotoday.com

Thomas H Hogan, President

Delivers the latest information on program priorities, giving preferences, evaluation criteria, corporate and foundation officers and directors, and all the other data you need to help your nonprofit organization gain a crucial edge as corporate philanthropy budgets tighten.
1610 Pages
Frequency: Biennial
ISBN: 1-573872-93-5

11354 **Directory of Research Grants**
Greenwood Publishing Group
130 Cremona Drive
PO Box 1911
Santa Barbara, CA 93117

800-368-6868
Fax: 866-270-3856
E-Mail: CustomerService@abc-clio.com
Home Page: www.abc-clio.com

Directory containing information for more than 5,100 programs being offered through 1,880 sponsors. Includes contact info for grants and examples of past grants awarded, all of which is divided by subject, program, location, and sponsoring organization.
Cost: $151.95
1208 Pages
ISBN: 9-780897-74-9

11355 **Environmental Grantmaking Foundations Directory**
Resources for Global Sustainability
PO Box 3665
Cary North, NC 27519-3665

800-724-1857
Fax: 919-363-9841
Home Page: www.environmentalgrants.com

Corrine Szymko, President

Over 900 private foundations, community foundations and corporate giving programs that provide funding for environmental interests.
Cost: $115.00
Frequency: Annual
ISBN: 0-976788-00-4

11356 **Financial Aid for African Americans**
Reference Service Press
5000 Windplay Dr
Suite 4
El Dorado Hills, CA 95762-9319

916-939-9620
Fax: 916-939-9626
E-Mail: info@rspfunding.com
Home Page: www.rspfunding.com

Gail Schlachter, Editor
Martin Sklar, Manager

This directory describes nearly 1,450 scholarships, fellowships, loans, grants, awards and internships for African Americans
Cost: $40.00
522 Pages
Frequency: Biennial
ISBN: 1-588410-68-5
Founded in 1997

11357 **Financial Aid for Asian Americans**
Reference Service Press
5000 Windplay Dr
Suite4
El Dorado Hills, CA 95762-9319

916-939-9620
Fax: 916-939-9626
E-Mail: info@rspfunding.com
Home Page: www.rspfunding.com

Gail Schlachter, Editor
Martin Sklar, Manager

Use this source to find funding for Americans of Chinese, Japanese, Korean, Vietnamese, Filipino, or other Asian origins. Nearly 1,000 funding opportunities are described.
Cost: $37.50
346 Pages
Frequency: Biennial
ISBN: 1-588410-69-2
Founded in 1997
Printed in on matte stock

11358 **Financial Aid for Hispanic Americans**
Reference Service Press
5000 Windplay Dr
Suite 4
El Dorado Hills, CA 95762-9319

916-939-9620
Fax: 916-939-9626
E-Mail: info@rspfunding.com
Home Page: www.rspfunding.com

Gail Schlachter, Editor
Martin Sklar, Manager

This directory describes nearly 1,300 funding opportunities open to Americans of Mexican, Puerto Rican, Central American, or other Latin American heritage.
Cost: $30.00
402 Pages
Frequency: Biennial
ISBN: 1-588410-70-6
Founded in 1997
Printed in on matte stock

11359 **Financial Aid for Native Americans**
Reference Service Press
5000 Windplay Dr
Suite 4
El Dorado Hills, CA 95762-9319

916-939-9620
Fax: 916-939-9626
E-Mail: info@rspfunding.com
Home Page: www.rspfunding.com

Gail Schlachter, Editor
Martin Sklar, Manager

In this directory you will find 1,500 funding opportunities set aside just for American Indians, Native Alaskans, and Native Pacific Islanders.
Cost: $40.00
546 Pages
ISBN: 1-588410-71-4
Founded in 1997

11360 **Financial Aid for Veterans, Military Personnel and their Dependents**
Reference Service Press

5000 Windplay Dr
Suite 4
El Dorado Hills, CA 95762-9319

916-939-9620
Fax: 916-939-9626
E-Mail: info@rspfunding.com
Home Page: www.rspfunding.com

Gail Schlachter, Editor
Martin Sklar, Manager

This one-stop directory identifies 1,200 scholarships, fellowships, loans, awards, grants and internships.
Cost: $40.00
418 Pages
Frequency: Biennial
ISBN: 1-588410-97-8
Founded in 1988
Printed in on matte stock

11361 Financial Aid for the Disabled and their Families

Reference Service Press
5000 Windplay Dr
Suite 4
El Dorado Hills, CA 95762-9319

916-939-9620
Fax: 916-939-9626
E-Mail: info@rspfunding.com
Home Page: www.rspfunding.com

Gail Schlachter, Editor
Martin Sklar, Manager

A comprehensive directory identifies 1,200 scholarships, fellowships, loans, internships, awards, and grants for these groups.
Cost: $40.00
502 Pages
Frequency: Biennial
ISBN: 0-918276-65-9

11362 Foundation Directory

Foundation Center
79 5th Ave
New York, NY 10003-3076

212-620-4230
800-424-9836
Fax: 212-807-3677
E-Mail: feedback@foundationcenter.org
Home Page: www.foundationcenter.org

Bradford K Smith, President
Laura Cascio, Chief Information Officer
Patrick Collins, Chief Information Officer
Nancy Kami, Executive Director

Key facts on the nation's top 10,000 foundations by total giving. And, with over 46,000 descriptions of selected grants, the Directory provides fundraisers with unique insight into foundation giving priorities.
Cost: $215.00
2,533 Pages
ISBN: 1-595420-18-5

11363 Foundation Directory Online Database

Foundation Center
79 5th Ave
New York, NY 10003-3076

212-620-4230
800-424-9836
Fax: 212-807-3677
E-Mail: feedback@foundationcenter.org
Home Page: www.foundationcenter.org

Bradford K Smith, President
Laura Cascio, Chief Information Officer
Patrick Collins, Chief Information Officer
Nancy Kami, Executive Director

Search our databases online to get detailed information on up to nearly 80,000 foundations, links to current foundation 990-PF returns, crucial facts on more than half a million grants, including the purpose of grants.
Cost: $ 19.95
Frequency: Monthly

11364 Foundation Directory Supplement

Foundation Center
79 5th Ave
New York, NY 10003-3076

212-620-4230
800-424-9836
Fax: 212-807-3677
E-Mail: feedback@foundationcenter.org
Home Page: www.foundationcenter.org

Bradford K Smith, President
Laura Cascio, Chief Information Officer
Patrick Collins, Chief Information Officer
Nancy Kami, Executive Director

Provides revised entries for hundreds of foundations in The Foundation Directory and The Foundation Directory Part 2. Any alterations in giving interests, or updates on staff, financial data, contact information, and more, will be reflected in the Supplement.
Cost: $125.00
1000 Pages
ISBN: 1-931923-89-2

11365 Foundation Grants Index

Foundation Center
79 5th Ave
New York, NY 10003-3076

212-620-4230
800-424-9836
Fax: 212-807-3677
E-Mail: feedback@foundationcenter.org
Home Page: www.foundationcenter.org

Bradford K Smith, President
Laura Cascio, Fulfillment Manager
Michael Seltver, President
Patrick Collins, Chief Information Officer
Nancy Kami, Executive Director

Covers the grants of over 1,000 of the largest independent, corporate, and community foundations in the U.S. and features approximately 125,000 grant descriptions in all.
Cost: $175.00
Frequency: CD-ROM
ISBN: 1-595420-09-6

11366 Foundation Grants to Individuals

Foundation Center
79 5th Ave
New York, NY 10003-3076

212-620-4230
800-424-9836
Fax: 212-807-3677
E-Mail: feedback@foundationcenter.org
Home Page: www.foundationcenter.org

Bradford K Smith, President
Laura Cascio, Fulfillment Manager
Michael Seltver, President
Patrick Collins, Chief Information Officer
Nancy Kami, Executive Director

Featuring over 6,200 entries packed with current information for individual grantseekers.
Cost: $65.00
1,117 Pages
Frequency: Biennial
ISBN: 1-595420-42-8

11367 Foundation Operations and Management Report

Association of Small Foundations/ASF
1720 N St NW
Washington, DC 20036-2907

202-580-6560
888-212-9922
Fax: 202-580-6579
E-Mail: asf@smallfoundations.org
Home Page: www.smallfoundations.org
Social Media: Twitter

Henry L. Berman, CEO
Floyd S. Keene, Chair

The tool for small foundation benchmarking. Easy-to-read data and commentary on small foundation administration, boards, grantmaking and investments.
3000 Members
50+ Pages
Frequency: Annual

11368 Foundation Salary & Benefits Report

Association of Small Foundations/ASF
1720 N St NW
Washington, DC 20036-2907

202-580-6560
888-212-9922
Fax: 202-580-6579
E-Mail: asf@smallfoundations.org
Home Page: www.smallfoundations.org
Social Media: Twitter

Henry L. Berman, CEO
Floyd S. Keene, Chair

Small foundations use this annual report to benchmark base salaries by region, gender, experience, asset size, and more. Data includes information on health insurance premiums, retirement contributions, paid leave, and more.
3000 Members
50+ Pages
Frequency: Annual

11369 Funding for Persons with Visual Impairments

Reference Service Press
5000 Windplay Dr
Suite 4
El Dorado Hills, CA 95762-9319

916-939-9620
Fax: 916-939-9626
E-Mail: info@rspfunding.com
Home Page: www.rspfunding.com

Gail Schlachter, Editor
Martin Sklar, Manager

For low-vision readers, we have prepared a large-print listing of the scholarships, fellowships, loans, grants-in-aid, awards, and internships that are set aside just for persons with visual impairments (from high school seniors through professionals and others). Nearly 270 funding opportunities are described in detail here.
Cost: $30.00
274 Pages
Frequency: Annual
ISBN: 1-588411-29-X
Founded in 1997

11370 Grants for Foreign and International Programs

Foundation Center
79 5th Ave
New York, NY 10003-3076

212-620-4230
800-424-9836
Fax: 212-807-3677
E-Mail: feedback@foundationcenter.org
Home Page: www.foundationcenter.org

Bradford K Smith, President
Michael Seltver, Chief Information Officer
Patrick Collins, Chief Information Officer
Nancy Kami, Executive Director

A customized list of thousands of recent grants of $10,000 or more that have been awarded to organizations in foreign countries and to domestic recipients for international activities in such areas as: development and relief, peace and security, arms control, human rights, con-

ferences and research, and more.
Cost: $75.00
436 Pages
ISBN: 1-595420-23-1

11371 **Guide to Funding for International and Foreign Programs**
Foundation Center
79 5th Ave
New York, NY 10003-3076
212-620-4230
800-424-9836
Fax: 212-807-3677
E-Mail: feedback@foundationcenter.org
Home Page: www.foundationcenter.org
Bradford K Smith, President
Patrick Collins, Chief Information Officer
Nancy Kami, Executive Director
Includes up-to-date information on over 1,000 foundations and corporate givers that have supported a wide range of projects with an international focus both in the U.S. and in foreign countries.
Cost: $125.00
358 Pages
ISBN: 1-931923-95-7

11372 **Guide to US Foundations, Their Trustees, Officers and Donors**
Foundation Center
79 5th Ave
New York, NY 10003-3076
212-620-4230
800-424-9836
Fax: 212-807-3677
E-Mail: feedback@foundationcenter.org
Home Page: www.foundationcenter.org
Bradford K Smith, President
Patrick Collins, Chief Information Officer
Nancy Kami, Executive Director
The only published source of data on all active grantmaking foundations and the individuals who run them, provides current information on over 68,000 foundations. Featuring a master list of the decision-makers who direct America's foundations, the Guide is a powerful fundraising reference tool.
Cost: $350.00
4,235 Pages
Frequency: Annual
ISBN: 1-595420-35-5

11373 **Matching Gift Details**
Council for Advancement & Support of Education
1307 New York Ave NW
Suite 1000
Washington, DC 20005-4726
202-393-1301
Fax: 202-387-4973
E-Mail: memberservicecenter@case.org
Home Page: www.case.org
Silvia France, Matching Gifts Coordinator
Compiled and maintained by the Matching Gifts Clearinghouse, a comprehensive annual directory of more than 8,600 companies that match employee charitable gifts.
Cost: $100.00
286 Pages
ISBN: 0-899643-83-3

11374 **National Directory of Corporate Giving**
Foundation Center
79 5th Ave
New York, NY 10003-3076
212-620-4230
800-424-9836
Fax: 212-807-3677
E-Mail: feedback@foundationcenter.org
Home Page: www.foundationcenter.org
Bradford K Smith, President
Patrick Collins, Chief Information Officer
Nancy Kami, Executive Director
This comprehensive directory features up-to-date information that helps fundraisers tap into their share of grant money earmarked by companies for nonprofit support. Detailed portraits of close to 2,500 corporate foundations and some 1,400 direct giving programs feature essential information.
Cost: $195.00
1,165 Pages
Frequency: Annual
ISBN: 1-595420-04-5

11375 **New Foundation Guidebook**
Association of Small Foundation
4905 Del Ray Avenue
Suite 200
Bethesda, MD 20814
301-073-3337
888-212-9922
Fax: 301-907-0980
E-Mail: asf@smallfoundations.org
Home Page: www.smallfoundations.org
Carmen Wong, Director of Communications
Deborah Brody Hamilton, CEO
Hanh Le, Director Member Services
Kathryn Petrillo Smith, Managing Director
Contains articles and advice from over 40 foundation respresentatives and experts included in the Association of Small Foundations' newsletters and publications.
Cost: $40.00
86 Pages

11376 **New Nonprofit Almanac & Desk Reference**
Independent Sector
1602 L St NW
Suite 900
Washington, DC 20036-5682
202-467-6100
888-860-8118
Fax: 202-467-6101
E-Mail: info@independentsector.org
Home Page: www.independentsector.org
Provides managers, researchers, volunteers, and the press with the essential facts and figures needed to understand the size, scope, and nature of the nonprofit sector and its contributions to American society.
Cost: $42.00
288 Pages
ISBN: 9-780787-95-7

11377 **The Complete Guide to Grantmaking Basics: A Field Guide for Funders**
Council on Foundations
2121 Crystal Drive
Suite 700
Arlington, VA 22202
800-673-9036
E-Mail: info@cof.org
Home Page: www.cof.org
Social Media: Facebook, Twitter
Carol Larson, Chair
Kevin Murphy, Vice Chair
Sherece West, Secretary
Will Ginsberg, Treasurer
A practical guide to honing your grantmaking effectiveness and adapting to the changing nonprofit world.
Cost: $65.00
2000 Members

11378 **The Foundation Guidebook**
Association of Small Foundations/ASF
1720 N St NW
Washington, DC 20036-2907
202-580-6560
888-212-9922
Fax: 202-580-6579
E-Mail: asf@smallfoundations.org
Home Page: www.smallfoundations.org
Social Media: Twitter
Henry L. Berman, CEO
Floyd S. Keene, Chair
Gain the baseline knowledge to operate your foundation smoothly and effectively.
Cost: $69.00
3000 Members

Industry Web Sites

11379 **http://gold.greyhouse.com**
G.O.L.D Grey House OnLine Databases
Grey House Publishing's online database platform, GOLD, offers Quick Search, Keyword Search and Expert Search for most business sectors including foundation and fund raising markets. The GOLD platform makes finding the information you need quick and easy - whether you're a novice searcher or an experienced database user. All of Grey House's directory products are available for subscription on the GOLD platform.

11380 **www.aafrc.org**
American Association of Fund-Raising Counsel
To promote ethical practice and professional standards in the fund-raising consultant field.

11381 **www.ahp.org**
Association for Healthcare Philanthropy
Represents health care fundraising professionals through education and eventually bestows the credentials upon them.

11382 **www.boardsource.org**
BoardSource
Formerly the National Center for Nonprofit Boards, is the premier resource for practical information, tools and best practices, training, and leadership development for board members of nonprofit organizations worldwide.

11383 **www.cof.org**
Council on Foundations
Supports all those involved in the foundation business. Publishes monthly magazine. We provide leadership expertise, legal services and networking opportunities among other services to our members and to the general public.

11384 **www.grantsmart.org**
Grantsmart
An online resource database that contains 96,337 private foundations and charitable trusts.

11385 **www.greyhouse.com**
Grey House Publishing
Authoritative reference directories for most business sectors including foundation and fund raising markets. Users can search the online databases with varied search criteria allowing for custom searches by product category, geographic area, sales volume, keyword, subject and more. Full Grey House catalog and online ordering also available.

11386 **www.guidestar.org**
GuideStar
A database of more than 1 million nonprofit organizations in the United States. It's the

world's most comprehensive source of information about American nonprofit organizations.

11387 **www.idealist.org**
Action Without Borders
Over 45,000 nonprofit and community organizations in 165 countries, which you can search or browse by name, location or mission.

11388 **www.independentsector.org**
Independent Sector
The leadership forum for charities, foundations, and corporate giving programs committed to advancing the common good in America and around the world.

11389 **www.naspl.org**
North American Assn of State & Provincial Lottery
Represents 47 lottery organizations throughout North America. Provides information and benefits of state and provincial lottery organizations.

11390 **www.ncdcusa.org**
National Catholic Development Conference
Members include development officers and key fund raisers of charitable institutions and agencies.

11391 **www.philathropy.org**
A Philanthropic Partnership for Black Communities
Providing information on innovative vehicles for the black communities.

11392 **www.snpo.orgorg/snpo**
Society for Nonprofit Organizations
Dedicated to bringing together those who serve in the nonprofit world in order to build a strong network of professional throughout the country.

11393 **www.tgci.com**
The Grantsmanship Center
Launched the world's first training program for grantseekers in 1972 and continues to set the standard in the field.

11394 **www.uwex.edu/li**
Learning Institute
The Center provides you with a number of resources on the web that could provide you with assistance in a variety of nonprofit management and leadership issues. In the nonprofit web sites section you will find a number of useful annotated resources organized by topic.

Associations

11395 American Chemistry Council
700 Second St, NE
Washington, DC 20002

202-249-7000
Fax: 202-249-6100
Home Page: www.americanchemistry.com/pfpg
Social Media: Facebook, Twitter

Calvin M. Dooley, President
Raymond J. O Bryan, CFO & Chief Administrative Officer
Roger D. Bernstein, Vice President, State Affairs
Walter Moore, Vice President of Federal Affairs
Anne Womack Kolton, Vice President of Communications

Promotes effective use of recycling of polystyrene. Works to provide effective information about waste disposal and offers technical assistance.
Founded in 1988

11396 American Trucking Associations
950 North Glebe Road
Suite 210
Arlington, VA 22203-4181

703-838-1700
E-Mail: nafc@trucking.org
Home Page: www.trucking.org

Philip L. Byrd Sr., Chairman
Bill Graves, President & CEO
Duane Long, First Vice Chairman
John M Smith, Secretary
Douglas W. Stotlar, Treasurer

Largest national trade association for the trucking industry.
1000 Members
Founded in 1933

11397 Association of Independent Corrugated Converters
113 S. West Street
3rd Floor
Alexandria, VA 22314

703-836-2422
877-836-2422
Fax: 703-836-2795
E-Mail: info@aiccbox.org
Home Page: www.aiccbox.org
Social Media: Facebook, Twitter, LinkedIn, YouTube

Mark Mathes, Chairman
Greg Tucker, First Vice Chairman
Tyler Howland, Vice Chairman
Mark Williams, Vice Chairman
Jim Nelson, Vice Chairman

Provides a forum for discussion of problems and offers educational programs and seminars.
1100 Members
Founded in 1974

11398 Composite Can and Tube Institute
50 S Pickett Street
Suite 110
Alexandria, VA 22304-7206

703-823-7234
Fax: 703-823-7237
E-Mail: ccti@cctiwdc.org
Home Page: www.cctiwdc.org

Kristine Garland, Executive Vice President
Janine Marczak, Associate Manager, Events
Wayne Vance, Association Counsel

CCTI is an international nonprofit trade association representing the interests of manufacturers of composite paperboard cans, containers, canisters, tubes, cores, edgeboard and related or similar composite products and suppliers to those manufacturers of such items as paper, machinery, adhesives, labels and other services and materials.
Founded in 1934

11399 Containerization & Intermodal Institute
960 Holmdel Road
Bldg 2, Suite 201
Holmdel, NJ 07733

732-817-9131
Fax: 732-817-9133
E-Mail: connie@containerization.org
Home Page: www.containerization.org
Social Media: LinkedIn

Brendan McCahill, Sr., Chairman
Allen Clifford, Vice Chairman
Michael DiVirgilio, President
Steven Blust, Vice President
Anne Kappel, Secretary

Provides educational opportunities through existing programs and initiatives, including educational outreach, scholarships, and award programs.
Founded in 1960

11400 Contract Packaging Association
1833 Centre Point Circle
Suite 123
Naperville, IL 60563

630-544-5053
Fax: 630-544-5055
E-Mail: info@contractpackaging.org
Home Page: www.contractpackaging.org
Social Media: Twitter, LinkedIn

Chris Nutley, President
Vicky Smitley, Vice President
Tim Koers, Treasurer

A national, not-for-profit trade association that includes dynamic and growing companies offering contract packaging services.
155 Members
Founded in 1992

11401 Corrugated Packaging Alliance
25 Northwest Point Blvd
Suite 510
Elk Grove Village, IL 60007

847-364-9600
Fax: 847-364-9739
E-Mail: inquiries@corrugated.org
Home Page: www.corrugated.org
Social Media: LinkedIn

Rachel K Kenyon, Vice President
Dennis Colley, Executive Director

Develops and coordinates industry-wide programs to address corrugated packaging issues. The Council's mission is to inform consumers, manufacturers, retailers and government officials of corrugated packaging's performance and environmental attributes.
Founded in 1994

11402 Express Carriers Association
9532 Liberia Avenue
Suite 752
Manassas, VA 20110

703-361-1058
866-322-7447
Fax: 703-361-5274
E-Mail: eca@expresscarriers.org
Home Page: www.expresscarriers.org

John DiTucci, President
Paul Steffes, Vice President
Jim Luciani, 2nd Vice President
MJ Hill, Treasurer
Mike Coyle, Secretary

Trade association representing regional carriers. Presents annual marketplace to bring together carriers and shippers

11403 Fibre Box Association
25 Northwest Point Blvd
Suite 510
Elk Grove Village, IL 60007

847-364-9600
Fax: 847-364-9639
E-Mail: fba@fibrebox.org
Home Page: www.fibrebox.org
Social Media: LinkedIn

John Davis, Chairman
Mike Waite, First Vice Chairman
Bill Hoel, Second Vice Chairman
Dennis Colley, President
Rachel Kenyon, Vice President1

Represents 90 percent of the US corrugated paper board, packaging, manufacturing industry.
141 Members
Founded in 1940

11404 Flexible Intermediate Bulk Container Association
PO Box 241894
Saint Paul, MN 55124-7019

952-412-8867
Fax: 661-339-0023
E-Mail: info@fibca.com
Home Page: www.fibca.com
Social Media: Facebook, Twitter, LinkedIn, Youtube, Googleplus, blogspot

Lewis Anderson, Executive Director

Works to develop minimum standards of testing and performance for FIBC. Acts as a forum through seminars and other programs and serves as an advocate for the industry.
50 Members
Founded in 1983

11405 Flexible Packaging Association
971 Corporate Blvd
Suite 403
Linthicum, MD 21090
410-694-0800
Fax: 410-694-0900
E-Mail: fpa@flexpack.org
Home Page: www.flexpack.org

Marla Donahue, President

One of the leading trade associations for converters of flexible packaging and suppliers to the industry. Also provides a wealth of information to its members through focused services and benefits of membership.

11406 Foodservice & Packaging Institute
201 Park Washington Ct
Falls Church, VA 22046
703-538-3550
Fax: 703-241-5603
E-Mail: fpi@fpi.org
Home Page: www.fpi.org
Social Media: Facebook, Twitter, LinkedIn

Lynn Dyer, President
Natha Freiburg, Vice President
Rob Kittredge, Chair
Michael Evans, 1st Vice Chair
Tracy Pearson, 2nd Vice Chair

Manufacturers, suppliers and distributors of one-time use products used for food service, as well as packaging products made from paper, plastic, aluminum and other materials.
37 Members
Founded in 1933

11407 Gemini Shippers Group
137 West 25th Street
3rd Floor
New York, NY 10001

212-947-3424
Fax: 212-629-0361

E-Mail: info@geminishippers.com
Home Page: www.geminishippers.com

Shippers association with global contracts for all commodities.
200 Members
Founded in 1916

11408 Glass Packaging Institute
1001 North Fairfax St
Suite 301A
Alexandria, VA 22314

703-684-6359
Fax: 703-546-0583
E-Mail: info@gpi.org
Home Page: www.gpi.org
Social Media: Facebook, Twitter

Arnaud De Weert, Chairman
Lynn M. Bragg, President

Develops and evaluates testing procedures and equipment, conducts advertising campaigns for generic products.
Founded in 1945

11409 Healthcare Compliance Packaging Council
2711 Buford Road
#268
Bon Air, VA 23235-2423

804-338-5778
Fax: 888-812-4272
Home Page: www.hcponline.org
Social Media: Facebook, LinkedIn

Walt Berghahn, Executive Director

Promotes the many benefits of unit dose blister and strip packaging, especially its ability to be designed in compliance, promoting formats that help people take their medications properly.
Founded in 1990

11410 Institute of International Container Lessors
1120 Connecticut Avenue
Suite 440
Washington, DC 20036-3946

202-223-9800
Fax: 202-223-9810
E-Mail: info@iicl.org
Home Page: www.iicl.org

Jeremy Matthew, Chairman
Steven Blust, President & Secretary
Celine Wei, 1st Vice President
Philip Brewer, 2nd Vice President
George Elkas, Treasurer

Represents international container and chassis leasing industry in technical, governmental and legal matters. Publishes leading worldwide manuals on inspection and repair of containers and inspector and maintenance of chassis. Sponsors container and chassis inspection examination once a year in over 40 countries and chassis examination in North America.
Founded in 1971

11411 Institute of Packaging Professionals
1833 Centre Point Circle
Suite 123
Naperville, IL 60563

630-544-5050
Fax: 630-544-5055
E-Mail: info@iopp.org
Home Page: www.iopp.org
Social Media: Facebook, Twitter, LinkedIn, YouTube

Ralph Brandt, Chair
Bret Carlson, President
Dana Alexander, Executive VP- Finance & Operations
Robert Meisner, Executive VP- Education
Ukachi Anonyuo, Executive VP- Membership

Dedicated to creating networking and educational opportunities that help packaging professionals succeed.

11412 International Air Transport Association
703 Waterford Way
Suite 600
Miami, FL 33126

305-779-9860
Fax: 305-264-8088
Home Page: www.iata.org/
Social Media: Twitter, LinkedIn, YouTube

Tony Tyler, Director General & CEO

Seeks to improve understanding of the industry among decision makers and increase awareness of the benefits that aviation brings to national and global economies. It fights for the interests of airlines across the globe, challenging unreasonable rules and charges, holding regulators and governments to account, and strivign for sensible regulation.
240+ Members

11413 International Molded Fiber Association
1425 W Mequon Rd
Suite C-D
Mequon, WI 53092

262-241-0522
Fax: 262-241-3766
E-Mail: info@imfa.org
Home Page: www.imfa.org
Social Media: Facebook, Twitter, LinkedIn

Cassandra Niesing, Asst. Director
Joseph Grygny, Chairman

Acts as an information center for the molded fiber industry with worldwide membership of users and manufacturers of molded fiber producs. Promotes use of natural and recycled fibers.
Founded in 1997

11414 Keep America Beautiful
1010 Washington Blvd
Stamford, CT 06901

203-659-3000
Fax: 203-659-3001
E-Mail: info@kab.org
Home Page: www.kab.org
Social Media: Facebook, Twitter, Youtube

Timothy Gardner, Chairman
Drew Becher, President
Barry H. Caldwell, Vice President
Kathy Caso, Vice President, Corporate
Al Carey, Chief Executive Officer

National, nonprofit, education organization whose corporate members include packagers, retailers, bottlers, and makers of chemical, steel, glass, paper and aluminum products.
Founded in 1953

11415 Lake Carriers Association
20325 Center Ridge Road
Suite 720
Rocky River, OH 44116

440-333-4444
Fax: 440-333-9993
E-Mail: info@lcaships.com
Home Page: www.lcaships.com

James H I Weakley, President
Glen Nekvasil, Vice President
Harold W. Henderson, General Counsel
Katie Gumeny, Administrative Assistant

Members are US-Flag Great Lakes vessel operators engaged in transporting iron ore, coal, grain, limestone, cement and petroleum products.
Founded in 1880

11416 National Customs Brokers and Forwarders Association of America, Inc.
1200 18th St NW
Suite 901
Washington, DC 20036

202-466-0222
Fax: 202-466-0226
E-Mail: staff@ncbfaa.org
Home Page: www.ncbfaa.org

Jeffery C. Coopersmith, Chairman
Darrell Sekin, Jr., President
Geoffrey Powell, Vice President
William S. App. Jr., Treasurer
Amy Magnus, Secretary

Learn about new business leads, stay on top of Customs Service and other agency regulations that will impact your operations and provide invaluable professional development resources for your employees.
600+ Members

11417 National Institute of Packaging, Handling, and Logistics Engineers
5903 Ridgeway Drive
Grand Prairie, TX 75052

817-466-7490
866-464-7490
E-Mail: admin@niphle.com
Home Page: www.niphle.com
Social Media: Facebook, Twitter, LinkedIn

Sean Kernis, President

An assemblage of professionals whose interest in the complex and diverse practice of distribution and logistics is a common bond.
600 Members
Founded in 1956

11418 Paperboard Packaging Council
1350 Main Street
Suite 1508
Springfield, MA 01103-1670

413-686-9191
Fax: 413-747-7777
E-Mail: paperboardpackaging@ppcnet.org
Home Page: www.ppcnet.org
Social Media: Facebook, Twitter, LinkedIn, Youtube

Ben Markens, President
Lou Kornet, VP & Chief of Staff

The leading industry association serving suppliers and converters of all forms of paperboard packaging, works to grow, promote, and protect the paperboard packaging industry while providing its members with resources and tools to compete effectively and successfully in the marketplace.
Founded in 1967

11419 Petroleum Packaging Council
ATD Management Inc.
1519 Via Tulipan
San Clemente, CA 92673

949-369-7102
Fax: 949-366-1057
E-Mail: PPC@ATDmanagement.com
Home Page: www.ppcouncil.org
Social Media: LinkedIn

David Taylor, President
John Ressler, Vice President
James Overheul, Secretary/ Treasurer
Ron Sarto, Assistant Treasurer

Provides technical leadership and education to the petroleum packaging industry.
400 Members
Founded in 1950

11420 **Pressure Sensitive Tape Council**
1833 Centre Point Circle
Suite 123
Naperville, IL 60563
630-544-5048
Fax: 630-544-5055
E-Mail: info@pstc.org
Home Page: www.pstc.org
Social Media: Twitter, LinkedIn, Flickr
Wayne Helton, President
Greg Yull, Vice President
Michael Merkx, Treasurer
Patrick M. Farrey, Executive Vice President
Trade association for tape manufacturers and affiliate suppliers, dedicated to helping the industry produce quality pressure sensitive adhesive tape products in the global marketplace. PSTC provides education and training, works with ASTM and global trade organizations to harmonize test methods and monitors legislative and regulatory activities.

11421 **Recycled Paperboard Technical Association**
P.O. Box 5774
Elgin, IL 60121-5774
847-622-2544
Fax: 847-622-2546
E-Mail: rpta@rpta.org
Home Page: www.rpta.org
Mark Maley, President
Louis Lemaire, Vice President
Peter Traeger, Treasurer
An association of US, Canadian and overseas companies interested in cooperative research and development in the industry.
33 Members
Founded in 1953

11422 **Retail Packaging Association**
2205 Warwick Way
Suite 110
Marriottsville, MD 21104
410-925-9809
Fax: 410-741-3004
E-Mail: info@retailpackaging.org
Home Page: www.retailpackaging.org
Joel Zaas, President
Serves its members and the entire retail packaging industry. Also organizes the largest trade show and conference of its kind in the US. A self-governed not-for-profit organization comprised of professionals involved in all facets of production and distribution of retail packaging products.
Founded in 1989
Mailing list available for rent

11423 **Reusable Industrial Packaging Association**
51 Monroe Street
Suite 812
Rockville, MD 20850
301-577-3786
Fax: 301-577-6476
Home Page: www.reusablepackaging.org
Social Media: Facebook, Twitter
Spencer Walker, Chair
Ricky Buckner, Vice Chair
Paul W. Rankin, President
Jerry Butler, Treasurer
Jeff Bey, Secretary
Founded in 1942

11424 **Technical Association of the Pulp & Paper Industry**
15 Technology Parkway South
Suite 115
Peachtree Corners, GA 30092
770-446-1400
800-322-8686
Fax: 770-446-6947
E-Mail: webmaster@tappi.org
Home Page: www.tappi.org
Social Media: Facebook, Twitter, LinkedIn
Thomas J. Garland, Chair
Chris Luettgen, Vice Chair
Larry N. Montague, President & CEO
To engage the people and resources of our association in providing technically sound solutions to the workplace problems and opportunities that challenge our current and future members.
12000 Members
Founded in 1915

11425 **The Adhesive and Sealant Council, Inc.**
7101 Wisconsin Avenue
Suite 990
Bethesda, MD 20814
301-986-9700
Fax: 301-986-9795
E-Mail: info@ascouncil.org
Home Page: www.ascouncil.org
Social Media: Twitter, LinkedIn
C. Russell Thompson, Jr., Chair
Matt Croson, President
Andrew Johnston, Treasurer
ASC is a North American trade association dedicated to representing the adhesive and sealant industry. ASC is bound by the collective efforts of its members, and strives to improve the industry operating environment and strengthen its member companies.

11426 **Transportation Intermediaries Association**
1625 Prince St
Suite 200
Alexandria, VA 22314-2883
703-299-5700
Fax: 703-836-0123
E-Mail: voltmann@tianet.org
Home Page: www.tianet.org
Robert Voltmann, President
Alec Gizzi, Chair
Geoff Turner, Vice Chair
Jeff Tucker, Treasurer
Barcy Vidt, Secretary
Education and policy organization for North American transportation intermediaries. The only national association representing the interests of all third party transportation service providers. Members include logistics management firms, property brokers, perishable commodities brokers, freight forwarders, intermodal marketers and ocean and air forwarders.
700 Members
Founded in 1977

11427 **Transportation Marketing Communications Association (TMCA)**
9382 Oak Avenue
Waconia, MN 55387
952-442-5638
Fax: 952-442-3941
E-Mail: brian07@tmcatoday.org
Home Page: www.tmcatoday.org
John Ferguson, President
Tom Nightingale, VP
Tracy Robinson, Treasurer
Edward Moritz, Secretary
Brian Everett, Executive Director
The only association serving transportation marketing, sales and communications pros in all modes and market segments of the North American transportation industry.
225 Members
Founded in 1924

Newsletters

11428 **ASC e-Catalyst**
The Adhesive and Sealant Council, Inc.
7101 Wisconsin Avenue
Suite 990
Bethesda, MD 20814
301-986-9700
Fax: 301-986-9795
E-Mail: info@ascouncil.org
Home Page: www.ascouncil.org
Glenn E. Frommer, Chair
C. Russell Thompson, Jr., Treasurer
Matthew E. Croson, President
Delivers the latest ASC news, industry information and end-user trends.
Frequency: Monthly

11429 **Air Cargo Report**
Phillips Publishing
1201 Seven Locks Road
Potomac, MD 20854-2931
301-541-1400
Fax: 301-424-2098
E-Mail: info@accessintel.com
Home Page: www.accessintel.com
Richard Koulbanis, Publisher
Donald Pazour, CEO/President
Reports on emerging trends and business strategies for airline cargo, integrator, freight forwarding and all-cargo carrier operations.
Circulation: 1430

11430 **CanTube Bulletin**
Composite Can and Tube Institute
50 S Pickett Street
Suite 110
Alexandria, VA 22304-7206
703-823-7234
Fax: 703-823-7237
E-Mail: ccti@cctiwdc.org
Home Page: www.cctiwdc.org
Excellent source of information about issues affecting this industry, as well as updates on CCTI activities.
Frequency: Bi-Monthly
Circulation: 800+

11431 **Mail Center Management Report**
Institute of Management and Administration
3 Bethesda Metro Center
Suite 250
Bethesda, MD 20814-5377
800-372-1033
Fax: 800-253-0332
Home Page: www.ioma.com
Shows you how to improve mail center productivity, reduce costs, and get you the recognition you deserve through buying and leasing new equipment, negotiating rates with carriers, and much more. Shows proven techniques to improve relations with the USPS and other service vendors. You'll find tactics for improving your dealing with senior management, purchasing, marketing and logistics.

11432 **Packaging Strategies**
Packaging Strategies

600 Willowbrook Lane
Suite 610
West Chester, PA 19382

610-436-4220
800-524-7225
Fax: 610-436-6277
E-Mail: packinfo@packstrat.com
Home Page: www.packstrat.com
Social Media: Facebook, Twitter, LinkedIn

Joe Pryweller, Editor/Conference Director
Janet Martinelli, Conference/Study Support Manager
Randy Green, Publisher
Karen Vaillancourt, Sales Manager
Karen Close, Senior Events Manager

A subscription newsletter focusing on news and analysis of technology and business issues in the packaging industry. Also producer of 4 conferences per year: structural packagingsummit, food packaging technologies summit, global pouch firum, sustainable packaging forum and multi-client industry studies.
Cost: $497.00
8 Pages
ISSN: 8755-6189
Founded in 1983
Printed in 2 colors on matte stock

11433 Transportation Intermediaries Update
Transportation Intermediaries Association
1625 Prince St
Suite 200
Alexandria, VA 22314-2883

703-299-5700
Fax: 703-836-0123
E-Mail: voltmann@tianet.org
Home Page: www.tianet.org

Robert Voltmann, President

Education and policy organization for North American transportation intermediaries. TIA is the only national association representing the interests of all third party transportation service providers. The members of TIA include logistics management firms, property brokers, perishable commodities brokers, freight forwarders, intermodal marketers, ocean and air forwarders, and NVOCC's.
700 Pages
Frequency: Monthly

Magazines & Journals

11434 Advanced Packaging
PennWell Publishing Company
98 Spit Brook Rd
Suite L11
Nashua, NH 03062-5737

603-891-0123
Fax: 603-891-9294
E-Mail: lwilliam@pennwell.com
Home Page: www.pennwell.com

Christine Shaw, VP
Gail Flower, Editor

Focuses on materials, assembly, design and reliability issues facing the global packaging community.
Cost: $88.00
Frequency: Monthly
Circulation: 22,000
Founded in 1910

11435 Air Cargo Focus
Cargo Network Services Corporation
703 Waterford Way
Suite 680
Miami, FL 33126-4677

786-413-1000
Fax: 786-413-1005
E-Mail: cns@cnsc.us
Home Page: www.cnsc.net

Fernando Garcia, VP
Anthony P Calabrese, President

A forum for professionals involved in the sale , marketing, services and movement of air cargo.
Frequency: Quarterly
Circulation: 8000
Founded in 1986

11436 Air Cargo News
PO Box 98
Portage, MI 49081-98

718-479-0716
Fax: 718-740-0761
E-Mail: judy@aircargonews.com
Home Page: www.aircargonews.com

Geoffrey Arend, Publisher

CAB regulations, and other news of interest to those in the air cargo industry.
Cost: $39.95
Frequency: Monthly
Circulation: 100,000
Founded in 1975

11437 American Shipper
Howard Publications
300 W Adams Street Suite 600
PO Box 4728
Jacksonville, FL 32201-4728

904-355-2601
800-874-6422
Fax: 904-791-8836
Home Page: www.americanshipper.com

Hayes H Howard, Publisher
Gary G. Burrows, Managing Editor

Provides those involved in domestic and global supply chain management with news and information of a strategic nature, useful in the formation of logistics polices and partnerships.
Cost: $30.00
100 Pages
Frequency: Monthly
Circulation: 13487
ISSN: 1074-8350
Founded in 1951
Printed in 4 colors on glossy stock

11438 Cargo Facts
Air Cargo Managment Group
520 Pike St
Suite 1010
Seattle, WA 98101-4058

206-587-6537
Fax: 206-587-6540
E-Mail: news@cargofacts.com
Home Page: www.cargofacts.com

Edwin Laird, Manager
David Harris, Editor
Jackie Edinger, Circulation Manager

Includes fiscal reports, freighter aircraft transactions, short segments, international perspectives, and industry updates.
Cost: $395.00
24 Pages
Frequency: Monthly
Circulation: 7500
ISSN: 0278-0801
Founded in 1980

11439 Contract Packaging
Contract Packaging Association
1833 Centre Point Circle
Suite 123
Naperville, IL 60563-4848

630-544-5053
Fax: 630-544-5055
E-Mail: info@contractpackaging.org
Home Page: www.contractpackaging.org

Joe Jaruszewski, President
Chris Nutley, Vice President
Vicky Smitley, Treasurer

Covers conract packaging issues and news, and is an excellent source of CPA news and industry developments, trends, analysis, and information for buyers and sellers of contract packaging.
155 Members
Founded in 1992

11440 Cosmetic Personal Care Packaging
O&B Communications
11444 W Olympic Boulevard
Los Angeles, CA 90064-1303

310-445-4200
Fax: 310-445-4299
E-Mail: info@cpcpkg.com
Home Page: www.cpcpkg.com

Patricia Spinner, Publisher
John Bethune, Editorial Director
Jennifer Kwok, Managing Editor

Provides information on new packaging containers, materials, equipment and services that are involved with the cosmetic industry.
Cost: $60.00
Frequency: Monthly
Circulation: 12,500
Founded in 1996

11441 Courier Times
Courier Times
27-16 168th Street
Flushing, NY 11358-1130

718-291-1253
Fax: 718-359-1959
Home Page: www.couriertimes.com

Bill Goodman, Editor
C Tsamis, Owner

New products vital to the industry, discusses insurance and technology updates, also offers customer service guidelines.
Cost: $39.00
Frequency: Monthly
Circulation: 1100

11442 Electronic Packaging & Production
Reed Business Information
360 Park Ave S
New York, NY 10010-1737

646-746-6400
Fax: 646-756-7583
E-Mail: corporatecommunications@reedbusiness.com
Home Page: www.reedbusiness.com

John Poulin, CEO
Michael Sweeney, Editorial Director
James Reed, Owner

Edited for engineers and managers who are involved in packaging design, printed circuit board fabrication and assembly, and production testing of electronic circuits, systems, products and equipment.
Founded in 1960

11443 Flexible Packaging
Flexible Packaging Association
971 Corporate Blvd
Suite 403
Linthicum, MD 21090-2253

410-694-0800
Fax: 410-694-0900

E-Mail: fpa@flexpack.org
Home Page: www.flexpack.org

Marla Donahue, President

Offering subscribers up-to-the-minute information on industry news and trends, material and substrate developments, innovations in equipment, and the latest in business management. The only magazine in the market that dedicates 100 percent of its editorial content and circulation to flexible packaging converters.
Frequency: Monthly

11444 Food & Beverage Packaging
155 Pfingsten Road
Suite 205
Deerfield, IL 60015

847-405-4000
Fax: 847-405-4100
Home Page: www.foodandbeveragepackaging.com

Randy Green, Publisher

Identifies and analyzes the market trends and packaging solutions that matter to food and beverage processors.
Frequency: Monthly
Circulation: 75140
Founded in 1959

11445 Harbour & Shipping
Progress Publishing Company, Ltd
1489 Marine Drive
Suite 510
West Vancouver, BC V7 T1

604-922-6717
Fax: 604-922-1739

Allison Smith, Editor
Murray McLellan, Publisher/Marketing

Serves the deep sea and coastal shipping, and ship building, repair and supply industries of Canada and worldwide. Accepts advertising.
Cost: $60.00
Frequency: Monthly
Circulation: 2200
ISSN: 0017-7637
Printed in 4 colors on glossy stock

11446 International Paper Board Industry
Brunton Publications & NV Public
43 Main Street
Avon By The Sea, NJ 07717-1051

732-502-0500
Fax: 732-502-9606
E-Mail: jcurley@NVPublications.com
Home Page: nvpublications.com

Mike Brunton, Publisher
Jim Curley, Editor
Tom Vilardi, President

Information on corrugated paper and converting industry, encompassing news and production worldwide.
Cost: $60.00
Frequency: Monthly
Circulation: 6500

11447 Journal of HazMat Transportation
Packaging Research International
404 Price St
West Chester, PA 19382-3531

610-436-8292
877-429-7447
Fax: 610-436-9422
Home Page: www.hazmatship.com

Vincent A Vitollo, Owner

A professionally prepared technical reporting system, focused exlusively on explaining changes to the hazardous materials transportation regulations. Thoroughly covers and provides technical reviews of the US 49CFR, International Civil Aviation Organization Technical Instructions, the International Maritime Dangerous Goods Code, and the European Road and Rail Regulations.
Cost: $209.00
Circulation: 1000
Founded in 1990
Printed in 4 colors on matte stock

11448 MAIL: The Journal of Communication Distribution
1 Elmcoft Road
Stamford, CT 06926-700

203-356-5000
800-672-6937
Fax: 203-739-3488
Home Page: www.pb.com

Meg Reiley, President
Ina Steiner, Publisher

Manages change and positions customers for both tactical and long-term success with innovative, cost-effective, end-to-end messaging solutions.

11449 Modern Bulk Transporter
Tunnell Publications
PO Box 66010
Houston, TX 77266

713-523-8124
Fax: 713-523-8384
Home Page: www.bulktransporter.com/
Social Media: Facebook, Twitter

Charles Wilson, Editor
Martine Ewing, Advertising Director
Mary Davis, Associate Editor

Serves the truck industry that transports petroleum and petroleum products. Accepts advertising.
Frequency: Monthly
Circulation: 15000

11450 PARCEL
RB Publishing
2901 International Lane
Madison, WI 53704-3102

608-778-8785
800-536-1992
Fax: 608-241-8666
Home Page: www.parcelindustry.com
Social Media: LinkedIn

Marll Thiede, CEO
Chad Griepentrog, President
Mike Beacom, Editor

Brings the insights needed to improve parcel operations and keep costs under control. PARCEL gives you access to experts who look at the entire process, from order entry to the shipping dock to customer delivery, to give you information you can use.
Circulation: 30000
Founded in 1988

11451 Packaging Digest Magazine
UBM Canon
1200 Jorie Blvd.
Suite 230
Oak Brook, IL 60523-2260

630-990-2371
Fax: 630-990-8894
E-Mail: packagingdigest@ubm.com
Home Page: www.packagingdigest.com

John Kalkowski, Editorial Director
Lisa McTigue Pierce, Editor
Jenni Spinner, Senior Editor

Serves the manufacturing, wholesale and service industries.
Cost: $75.00
Frequency: Monthly
Founded in 1963

11452 Packaging Technology & Engineering
North American Publishing Company
1500 Spring Garden St
12th Floor
Philadelphia, PA 19130-4094

215-238-5300
800-777-8074
Fax: 215-238-5342
E-Mail: customerservice@napco.com
Home Page: www.napco.com

Ned S Borowsky, CEO
Richard Soloway, CEO/President
Glen Reynolds, Circulation Manager
Nolle Skodzinski, Editor

Reports on evironmental concerns, legislation and regulation, product design, material availability, and economic trends.
Cost: $69.00
Frequency: Monthly
Circulation: 20271
Founded in 1958

11453 Packaging World
Summit Publishing Company
330 N Wabash Ave
Suite 2401
Chicago, IL 60611-7618

312-222-1010
Fax: 312-222-1310
E-Mail: reynolds@packworld.com
Home Page: www.packworld.com

Lloyd Ferguson, Owner
Joseph Angel, Vice President
Patrick Reynolds, VP/Editor
Timothy Hammack, Circulation Director
Jim George, Marketing & Design Editor

Serves the manufacturing, wholesaling, and service industries.
Frequency: Monthly
Circulation: 92547
ISSN: 1073-7367
Founded in 1994
Printed in 4 colors on matte stock

11454 Paperboard Packaging
2835 North Sheffield Avenue
Suite 226
Chicago, IL 60657

773-880-2234
Fax: 773-880-2244
Home Page: www.packaging-online.com
Social Media: Facebook, Twitter

Marisa Palmieri, Editor

Publication edited for management and other key personnel involved in the manufacturing and marketing segments of the paperboard packaging industry.
Cost: $39.00
Frequency: Monthly
ISSN: 0031-1227

11455 Pharmaceutical & Medical Packaging News
Canon Communications
11444 W Olympic Blvd
Suite 900
Los Angeles, CA 90064-1555

310-445-4200
Fax: 310-445-4299
E-Mail: sales@devicelink.com
Home Page: www.devicelink.com

Charlie Mc Curdy, President
Daphne Allen, Managing Editor
Bob Michaels, Managing Editor
Nicole Welter, Account Executive

Information and news on events, new technology, industry trends, regulatory matters, and health care trade associations for professionals involved in the pharmaceutical and medical

product packaging industry.
Cost: $150.00
Frequency: Monthly
Circulation: 20000
ISSN: 1081-5481
Founded in 1978

11456 **Refrigerated Transporter**
4200 S. Shepherd Dr.
Suite 200
Houston, TX 77098-2901

713-523-8124
800-880-0368
Fax: 713-523-8384
E-Mail: jay.miller@penton.com
Home Page: www.refrigeratedtrans.com

The information source for those involved in the transportation and distribution of refrigerated products ranging from food to pharmaceuticals, from film and cosmetics to chemicals. Provides practical information derived from the experience of businesses in the field as well as up-to-the-minute news on developments and equipment for the industry.
Frequency: Monthly
Circulation: 15023
Founded in 1905

11457 **TAPPI Journal**
Technical Association of the Pulp & Paper Industry
15 Technology Parkway South
Norcross, GA 30092

770-446-1400
800-322-8686
Fax: 770-446-6947
E-Mail: webmaster@tappi.org
Home Page: www.tappi.org

Larry N. Montague, President & CEO

Serves domestic and international pulp, paper, paperboard, packaging and converting industries; manufacturers and suppliers of machinery, equipment, chemicals and other material.
Cost: $350.00
130 Pages
Frequency: Monthly
Circulation: 5300
ISSN: 0734-1415
Founded in 1949
Printed in 4 colors on glossy stock

11458 **Trucker's Connection**
Megan Cullingford
5960 Crooked Creek Road
Suite 15
Norcross, GA 30092

770-416-0927
Fax: 770-416-1734
Home Page: www.truckersconnection.com

Megan Cullingford, General Manager
Dan Barnhill, Editor
Reid Ramsay, Production Manager

Published for the use of long haul, over-the-road truck drivers, owner operators, small trucking company fleet owners, safety and recruiting of personnel for trucking companies in the US and Canada.
Frequency: Monthly
Circulation: 165000
Founded in 1986
Printed in 4 colors on glossy stock

11459 **World Wide Shipping (WWS)**
World Wide Shipping Guide
16302 Byrnwyck Ln
Odessa, FL 33556-2807

813-920-4788
Fax: 813-920-8268
E-Mail: info@wwship.com
Home Page: www.wwship.com

Lee Di Paci, Publisher
Barbara Edwards, Marketing Manager
Bob Susor, Marketing Manager

Dedicated to the interests of North American exporters, importers, distributors, freight forwarders, NVOCC's and customs brokers requiring freight tranportation services and equipment.
Cost: $32.00
32 Pages
Frequency: Fortnightly
Circulation: 9000
ISSN: 1060-7900
Founded in 1919
Printed in 4 colors on glossy stock

Trade Shows

11460 **Contract Packaging Association Annual Meeting**
Contract Packaging Association
1833 Centre Point Circle
Suite 123
Naperville, IL 60563-4848

630-544-5053
Fax: 630-544-5055
E-Mail: info@contractpackaging.org
Home Page: www.contractpackaging.org

Joe Jaruszewski, President
Chris Nutley, Vice President
Vicky Smitley, Treasurer

Includes experts discussing success patterns that work, uncovering winning and learning attitudes and methods that will guide your business toward lasting results.
155 Members
Founded in 1992

11461 **International Molded Fiber Packaging Seminar**
International Molded Fiber Association
1425 W Mequon Rd
Suite C
Mequon, WI 53092-3262

262-241-0522
Fax: 262-241-3766
E-Mail: info@imfa.org
Home Page: www.imfa.org
Social Media: Facebook, Twitter, LinkedIn

Cassandra Niesing, Asst. Director
Joseph Grygny, Chairman

Opportunity to network, learn, and grow in the molded fiber industry.
Founded in 1996

11462 **LabelExpo**
Tarsus Group
9501 W Devon Avenue
Rosemont, IL 60018-4811

847-292-3700
Fax: 847-318-1506
Home Page: www.labelresource.com

Steve Krogulski, Manager

The largest event for the lable, web printing, product decoration, converting and packaging industry in the Americas.
13700 Attendees
Frequency: Annual/September

11463 **Outlook & Strategies Conference**
Paperboard Packaging Council
1350 Main Street
Suite 1508
Springfield, MA 01103-1670

413-686-9191
Fax: 413-747-7777
Home Page: www.ppcnet.org

Ben Markens, President
Lou Kornet, Vice President/Chief of Staff

Industry leaders specializing in sustainability, the economy, and education will come together to impart their knowledge, experience, and business predictions.
325 Attendees
Frequency: Annual/March

11464 **PROPAK Asia**
Reed Exhibition Companies
383 Main Avenue
PO Box 6059
Norwalk, CT 06851

203-840-4800
Fax: 203-840-9628

One hundred and seventy four exhibitors for an audience of manufacturers, packaging design and development professionals. International food processing and packaging technology exhibition.
Frequency: Annual

11465 **Shipper/Carrier Marketplace**
Express Carriers Association
9532 Liberia Ave
Suite 752
Manassas, VA 20110-1719

703-361-1058
866-322-7447
Fax: 703-361-5274
Home Page: www.expresscarriers.org

Stuart Hyden, President
Lance Adams, First VP
Fiona Morgan, Executive Director

Brings about 500 representatives from regional and national companies together to explore business relationships through face-to-face interviews
500 Attendees
Frequency: Annual

11466 **Transportation Intermediaries Annual Convention & Trade Show**
Transportation Intermediaries Association
1625 Prince Street
Suite 200
Alexandria, VA 22314

703-299-5700
Fax: 703-836-0123
E-Mail: voltmann@tianet.org
Home Page: www.tianet.org
Social Media: Facebook, Twitter, LinkedIn

Robert Voltmann, President/CEO

The only meeting for third-party logistics providers. A once a year opportunity to interact with representatives from throughout North America and abroad. Key decision makers with buying authority attend this meeting.
700 Attendees
Frequency: Annual/March
Founded in 1978

11467 **World Packaging Conference**
Reed Business Information
2000 Clearwater Drive
Oak Brook, IL 60523

630-740-0825
Fax: 630-288-8686
Home Page: www.reedbusiness.com

Jay Singh, Conference Chair
Bruce Harte, Consultant

One thousand three hundred and fourteen booths.
500 Attendees
Frequency: Annual/June

Directories & Databases

11468 **ABS International Directory of Offices**
American Bureau of Shipping
16855 Northchase Dr
Houston, TX 77060-6006

281-673-2800
Fax: 281-877-5801
Home Page: www.abs-group.com

Tony Nassif, CEO

Over 175 operations offices of the bureau worldwide are listed.
122 Pages
Frequency: Semiannual

11469 **Air Freight Directory**
Air Cargo
1819 Bay Ridge Avenue
Suite 1
Annapolis, MD 21403-2899

410-805-5578
800-747-6505
Fax: 410-268-3154

Debbi Mayes

Gives contact details for 35,000 global air cargo companies including 24,000 freight forwarders and 1700 airports. Track and trace shipments, locate airfreight personnel, or just follow the latest air cargo industry news.
Cost: $84.00
Frequency: Bi-Monthly

11470 **American Drop-Shippers Directory**
World Wide Trade Service
PO Box 283
Medina, WA 98039-0283

206-236-4795

Over 200 firms are listed that are willing to drop ship single item orders at wholesale prices for mail order and other direct marketers.
Cost: $15.00
36 Pages
Frequency: Biennial
Circulation: 5,000

11471 **Commercial Carrier Journal: Buyers' Guide Issue**
Reed Business Information
1 Chilton Way
Wayne, PA 19089-0002

646-746-6400
Fax: 646-746-7433
Home Page: www.reedbusiness.com
Social Media: Facebook, Twitter, LinkedIn

Gerald F Standley, Editor
Stuart Whayman, CFO

List of vehicles, components and accessories suppliers for the truck and bus fleet markets.
Cost: $10.00
Frequency: Annual/October
Circulation: 85,000

11472 **Commercial Carrier Journal: Top 100 Issue**
Reed Business Information
360 Park Avenue
New York, NY 10010

212-450-0067
Fax: 646-746-7433
Home Page: www.ccjdigital.com

List of top 100 for-hire motor carriers, ranked by gross revenues; also the next 200 carriers in gross revenue.
Cost: $10.00
Frequency: Annual/August
Circulation: 85,000

11473 **Directory of Contract Packagers and their Facilities**
Institute of Packaging Professionals
Ste 123
1833 Centre Point Cir
Naperville, IL 60563-4848

630-544-5050
800-432-4085
Fax: 630-544-5055
E-Mail: info@iopp.org
Home Page: www.iopp.org

Edwin Landon, Executive Director
Patrick Farrey, General Manager

More than 400 contract packagers in the US and abroad.
Frequency: Biennial

11474 **Directory of Corrugated Plants**
Fibre Box Association
25 Northwest Point Blvd
Suite 510
Elk Grove Village, IL 60007

847-364-9600
Fax: 847-364-9639
E-Mail: fba@fibrebox.org
Home Page: www.fibrebox.org
Social Media: LinkedIn

Over 1,600 manufacturing facilities in the North American corrugated and solid fibre industry. Distributed in microsoft excel spreadsheet.
Cost: $200.00

11475 **Directory of Freight Forwarders and Custom House Brokers**
International Wealth Success
PO Box 186
Merrick, NY 11566-0186

516-766-5850
800-323-0548
Fax: 516-766-5919
E-Mail: admin@iwsmoney.com
Home Page: www.iwsmoney.com
Social Media: Facebook, LinkedIn

Tyler G Hicks, President

Lists hundreds of these firms throughout the U.S. who help in the export/import business.
Cost: $20.00
106 Pages
Frequency: Annual
ISBN: 1-561503-46-0
Founded in 1980

11476 **Directory of Packaging Consultants**
Institute of Packaging Professionals
Ste 123
1833 Centre Point Cir
Naperville, IL 60563-4848

630-544-5050
800-432-4085
Fax: 630-544-5055
E-Mail: info@iopp.org
Home Page: www.iopp.org
Social Media: Facebook, Twitter, LinkedIn

Edwin Landon, Executive Director
Patrick Farrey, General Manager

Packaging consultants in the US.
Cost: $25.00
Frequency: Annual

11477 **Directory of US Flexographic Packaging Sources**
JPC Directories
PO Box 488
Plainview, NY 11803-0488

516-822-6861

Joel J Shulman, Editor

Offers information on narrow web and wide web printer/converters and suppliers to the printing industry.
125 Pages
Frequency: Annual
Circulation: 50,000

11478 **Flexible Packaging Association Membership Directory**
Flexible Packaging Association
971 Corporate Boulevard
Suite 403
Linthicum, MD 21090-4769

410-694-0800
Fax: 410-694-0900
E-Mail: fpa@flexpack.org

Over 200 member companies that manufacture flexible packaging and supplies used in this industry are profiled.
Frequency: Annual
Circulation: 20,000

11479 **Food & Beverage Market Place**
Grey House Publishing
4919 Route 22
PO Box 56
Amenia, NY 12501

518-789-8700
800-562-2139
Fax: 845-373-6390
E-Mail: books@greyhouse.com
Home Page: www.greyhouse.com
Social Media: Facebook, Twitter

Leslie Mackenzie, Publisher
Richard Gottlieb, Editor

This information packed three-volume set is the most powerful buying and marketing guide for the US food and beverage industry. Includes thousands of industry and transportation listings. Contains a significant chapter on food and beverage transportation.
Cost: $595.00
2000 Pages
Frequency: Annual
ISBN: 1-592373-61-5
Founded in 1981

11480 **Food & Beverage Marketplace: Online Database**
Grey House Publishing
4919 Route 22
PO Box 56
Amenia, NY 12501

518-789-8700
800-562-2139
Fax: 845-373-6390
E-Mail: gold@greyhouse.com
Home Page: http://gold.greyhouse.com
Social Media: Facebook, Twitter

Richard Gottlieb, President
Leslie Mackenzie, Publisher

This complete updated Food & Beverage Market Place: Online Database is the go-to source for the food and beverage industry. Anyone involved in the food and beverage industry needs this 'industry bible' and the important contacts

to develop critical research data that can make for successful business growth.
Frequency: Annual
Founded in 1981

11481 **Modern Bulk Transporter: Buyers Guide**
Tunnell Publications
PO Box 66010
Houston, TX 77266
713-523-8124
Fax: 713-523-8384
Charles Wilson, Editor
Directory of suppliers of products or services for companies operating tank trucks.
Frequency: Annual/October
Circulation: 16,000

11482 **NCBFAA Membership Directory**
National Customs Brokers & Forwarders Association
1200 18th St NW
Suite 901
Washington, DC 20036-2572
202-466-0222
Fax: 202-466-0226
E-Mail: staff@ncbfaa.org
Home Page: www.ncbfaa.org
About 600 customs brokers, international air cargo agents, and freight forwarders in the United States.
Cost: $24.00
Frequency: Annual

11483 **National Highway and Airway Carriers Directory**
National Highway Carriers Directory
PO Box 6099
Buffalo Grove, IL 60089-6099
847-634-0606
Fax: 847-634-1026
Home Page: www.national-highway.com
Pam W Ferreira, President/Editor
Provides information on: LTL motor freight carriers - with over 250,000 detailed routing points and terminals for US and Canada, contract carriers (truckload), airline cargo companies, transportation brokers, intermodel trucking companies, freight forwarders, warehousing companies, Canadian carriers, refrigerated carriers, railroads and ocean carriers.
Cost: $195.00
1400 Pages
Frequency: Biannually
Circulation: 5000
Founded in 1942
Printed in 2 colors on newsprint stock

11484 **National Motor Carrier Directory and Additional Products**
Transportation Technical Services
500 Lafayette Boulevard
Fredericksburg, VA 22401-6070
540-899-9872
888-665-9887
Fax: 540-899-1948
E-Mail: truckinfo@ttstrucks.com
Home Page: www.ttstrucks.com/www.fleetseek.com
Ronald D Roth, Executive VP
Over 46,000 motor carriers with revenues of $100,000 or more.
Cost: $495.00
1781 Pages
Frequency: Annual/November
Founded in 1989

11485 **Official Container Directory**
Advanstar Communications
641 Lexington Ave
8th Floor
New York, NY 10022-4503
212-951-6600
Fax: 212-951-6793
E-Mail: info@advanstar.com
Home Page: www.advanstar.com
Joseph Loggia, CEO
Directory of services and supplies to the industry.
200 Pages
Circulation: 5,000

11486 **Official Freight Shippers Guide**
Official Motor Freight Guides
1700 W Cortland Street
Chicago, IL 60622-1121
773-342-1000
800-621-4650
Fax: 773-489-0482
E Koch, Editor
Eric J Robison, Editor
Major air, rail, water and motor carriers published in three local editions covering Chicago, New York and St. Louis.
Cost: $55.00
516 Pages
Frequency: Annual

11487 **Official Motor Carrier Directory**
Official Motor Freight Guides
1700 W Cortland Street
Chicago, IL 60622-1121
773-342-1000
800-621-4650
Fax: 773-489-0482
Edward K Koch, Editor
Approximately 2,100 general and specialized motor carriers and air cargo carriers; federal and state agencies concerned with the trucking industry; tariff publishing bureaus, US and Canadian port authorities; state associations.
Cost: $59.50
Frequency: SemiAnnual
Circulation: 6,000

11488 **Official Motor Freight Guide**
C&C Publishing Company
1700 W Cortland Street
Chicago, IL 60622-1121
773-536-2050
This directory is published in over 21 regional editions that list air and water freight transportation, motor carriers and warehouse facilities for the metropolitan areas of Baltimore, Boston, Chicago, Cincinnati, Cleveland, Denver, Detroit, Evansville, Ft. Wayne, Indianapolis, Kansas City, Philadelphia, Pittsburgh, Quad Cities and Toledo.
Cost: $45.00
500 Pages
Frequency: Semiannual

11489 **PMMI Packaging Machinery Directory**
Packaging Machinery Manufacturers Institute (PMMI)
4350 Fairfax Dr
Suite 600
Arlington, VA 22203-1632
703-243-8555
Fax: 703-243-8556
E-Mail: pmmiwebhelp@pmmi.org
Home Page: www.pmmi.org
Chuck Yuska, President
Sara Kryder, Manager Communications
Contains information on all 500+ member companies, who are committed to producing quality products and providing world class service to their customers.

11490 **Packaging Digest: Machinery Materials Guide Issue**
Delta Communications
Ste 300
20900 Swenson Dr
Waukesha, WI 53186-4050
262-429-9111
Fax: 262-546-8820
E-Mail: delta@deltacommunications.com
Home Page: www.deltacommunicatons.com
Barbara McDonough, Editor
List of more than 3,100 manufacturers of machinery and materials for the packaging industry, and about 260 contract packagers.
Frequency: Annual

11491 **Rauch Guide to the US Packaging Industry**
Impact Marketing Consultants
PO Box 1226
Manchester Center, VT 05255
802-362-2325
802-362-3693
E-Mail: comments@impactmarket.com
Home Page: www.impactmarket.com
Donald R Dykes, Editor
C Verbanic, Editor
Analyzes the US packaging industry, with data on industry economics, raw materials, major products, and unique profiles of 50% producers.
Cost: $495.00
Frequency: Triennial

11492 **Transportation Telephone Tickler**
Commonwealth Business Media
50 Millstone Rd
Building 400, Suite 200
East Windsor, NJ 08520-1418
609-371-7700
800-215-6084
Fax: 609-371-7879
Home Page: www.cbizmedia.com
Alan Glass, CEO
Edith Chaudoin-Stahlberger, Editor
Provides vital contact information for 24,000 suppliers of 160 types of transportation services in the US, Canada, Caribbean and parts of Latin America.
Cost: $124.95
2425 Pages
Frequency: Annual
Founded in 1949

11493 **Who's Who & What's What in Packaging**
481 Carlisle Drive
Herndon, VA 20170-4830
703-471-8922
Offers information on members of the Institute of Packaging Professionals, including placement firms, colleges that offer packaging curricula, and related organizations.
Cost: $125.00
240 Pages
Frequency: Annual

Industry Web Sites

11494 **http://gold.greyhouse.com**
G.O.L.D Grey House OnLine Databases
Grey House Publishing's online database platform, GOLD, offers Quick Search, Keyword Search and Expert Search for most business sectors including freight, packaging and transportation markets. The GOLD platform makes finding the information you need quick and

easy - whether you're a novice searcher or an experienced database user. All of Grey House's directory products are available for subscription on the GOLD platform.

11495 **plastics.americanchemistry.com**
Polystyrene Packaging Council
Links to other associations.

11496 **www.adhesives.org**
Adhesive and Sealant Council, Inc.
Association for the packaging industry.

11497 **www.aiccbox.org**
Association of Independent Corrugated Converters
Provides a forum for discussion of problems and offers educational programs and seminars.

11498 **www.corrugated.org**
Corrugated Packaging Council
Develops and coordinates industry-wide programs to address corrugated packaging issues. The Council's mission is to inform consumers, manufacturers, retailers and government officials of corrugated packaging's performance and environmental attributes.

11499 **www.fibca.com**
Flexible Intermediate Bulk Container Association

Social Media: Facebook, Twitter

11500 **www.fibrebox.org**
Fibre Box Association
Represents 90 percent of the US corrugated paper board, packaging, manufacturing industry.

11501 **www.flexpack.org**
Flexible Packaging Association
Trade association of manufacturers, converters and suppliers of paper, metal foil and plastic or cellulose film.

11502 **www.fpi.org**
Foodservice & Packaging Institute
Sanitation and environmental information, plus programs and services.

11503 **www.ftd.com**
Florists' Transworld Delivery Association
Has an annual budget of approximately $140 million.

11504 **www.geminishippers.com**
Gemini Shippers Group
Shippers association with global contracts for all commodities.

11505 **www.graysonassociates.com**
Grayson Associates
Association for those interested in marketing analysis of the package goods industry.

11506 **www.greyhouse.com**
Grey House Publishing
Authoritative reference directories for most business sectors including freight, packaging, and transportation markets. Users can search the online databases with varied search criteria allowing for custom searches by product category, geographic area, sales volume, keyword, subject and more. Full Grey House catalog and online ordering also available.

11507 **www.homefair.com**
Offers comprehensive content and services for people moving to a new home or relocating to another community.

11508 **www.iicl.org**
Institute of International Container Lessors
Represents international container and chassis leasing industry in technical, governmental and legal matters. Publishes leading worldwide manuals on inspection and repair of containers and inspector and maintenance of chassis. Sponsors container and chassis inspection examination once a year in over 40 countries and chassis examination in North America.

11509 **www.lcaships.com**
Lake Carriers Association
Members are US- Flag Great Lakes vessel operators engaged in transporting iron ore, coal, grain, limestone, cement and petroleum products.

11510 **www.mfsanet.org/**
Mailing & Fulfillment Service Association
For over 80 years, this national trade association has been serving the mailing and fulfillment services industry by providing opportunities for learning and professional development of the managers of these companies.

11511 **www.niphle.com**
National Institute of Packaging, Handling and
Logistics

Originally the DC chapter of the Society of Packaging and Handling engineers, the Institute became independent in an effort to give more emphasis on the governmental responsibilities of its members.

11512 **www.nmaonline.org**
National Meat Association
Association for meat packers, processors and jobbers through out the USA.

11513 **www.packagingnetwork.com**
Packaging Network
Searchable database of food industry related items.

11514 **www.palletcentral.com**
National Wooden Pallet & Container Association
Membership roster, tech talk, publications and industry watch.

11515 **www.pmmi.org**
Packaging Machinery Manufacturers Institute (PMMI)
For manufacturers of packaging and packaging-related converting equipment.

11516 **www.polysort.com**
Polysort LLC
Links to related companies.

11517 **www.ppcnet.org**
Paperboard Packaging Council
Represents industry before legislative and regulatory bodies. Conducts technical seminars on sales, marketing, costs and management methods. Publishes a quarterly newsletter

11518 **www.ppcouncil.org**
Petroleum Packaging Council
Provides technical leadership and education to the petroleum packaging industry.

11519 **www.tianet.org**
Transportation Intermediaries Association
Education and policy organization for North American transportation intermediaries. TIA is the only national association representing the interests of all third party transportation service providers. The members of TIA include logistics management firms, property brokers, perishable commodities brokers, freight forwarders, intermodal marketers, ocean and air forwarders, and NVOCC's.

11520 **www.unitdose.org**
Healthcare Compliance Packaging Council
A not-for-profit trade association that was established in 1990 to promote the many benefits of unit dose blister and ship packaging - especially its ability to be designed in compliance-promoting formats that help people take their medications properly.

11521 **www.unitedfresh.org**
United Fresh Fruit & Vegetable Association
Equipment, supplies, cartons, packaging machinery, computers, sorting and sizing equipment, harvesting equipment, film wrap manufacturing and commodity organizations.

Associations

11522 American Innerspring Manufacturers Association
1918 N Parkway
Memphis, TN 38112
901-749-9030
800-882-5604
E-Mail: aimy@aiminfo.org
Home Page: www.aiminfo.org

Members make and sell innerspring units and box springs to mattress manufacturers. Also conducts year round public relations program directed at consumers, encouraging purchase of innerspring mattresses.
Founded in 1966

11523 American Society of Furniture Designers
144 Woodland Drive
New London, NC 28127
910-576-1273
Fax: 910-576-1573
E-Mail: info@asfd.com
Home Page: www.asfd.com

John Conrad, President
Christine Evans, Executive Director
Jena Hall, Editor-in-Chief

An international non-profit professional organization dedicated to advancing, improving, and supporting the profession of furniture design and its positive impact in the marketplace.
Founded in 1981

11524 Association of Progressive Rental Organizations
1504 Robin Hood Trail
Austin, TX 78703
800-204-2776
Fax: 512-794-0097
E-Mail: cferguson@rtohq.org
Home Page: www.rtohq.org
Social Media: Facebook, Twitter, Youtube, Flickr

David P. David, President
Gary Ferriman, 1st Vice President
Sidney Burton, 2nd Vice President
Richard Rose, Secretary
Gopal Reddy, Treasurer

Members include television, appliance and furniture dealers who rent merchandise with an option to purchase.
2000 Members
Founded in 1980
Mailing list available for rent

11525 Authentic Home Furnishings Association
PO Box 520
Spofford, NH 03462
518-832-7939
800-487-8321
Fax: 518-824-5719
E-Mail: ufa@unfinishedfurniture.org
Home Page: www.unfinishedfurniture.org

Fred Moriarty, Executive Director
Tim Case, President
Lara Lindner, Secretary
Steve Cavanaugh, Treasurer
Anthony Sabatino, Vice President

Our mission is to promote the common business interests of the unfinished furniture industry, encourage the most efficient and professional organization and administration of firms in the unfinished furniture industry; and to conduct meetings and educational programs, and to collect and publish information about the unfinished furniture industry.
600 Members
Founded in 1990

11526 Business and Institutional Furniture Manufacturers Association
678 Front Ave NW
Suite 150
Grand Rapids, MI 49504-5368
616-285-3963
Fax: 616-285-3765
E-Mail: email@bifma.org
Home Page: www.bifma.org
Social Media: Twitter, LinkedIn

Chuck Saylor, President
Lynn Utter, President-Elect
Franco Bianchi, Treasurer
Tom Reardon, Executive Director

BIFMA is a not-for-profit trade association of furniture manufacturers and suppliers, addressing issues of common concern.
245+ Members
Founded in 1973

11527 Futon Association International
PO Box 593730
Orlando, FL 32859
800-327-3262

Members are retailers, manufacturers, distributors, associates, sales representatives of their country in the industry.
400 Members
Founded in 1984

11528 Illuminating Engineering Society of North America
120 Wall St
Floor 17
New York, NY 10005-4001
212-248-5000
Fax: 212-248-5017
E-Mail: ies@ies.org
Home Page: www.ies.org
Social Media: Facebook, Twitter, LinkedIn

Daniel Salinas, President
Paul Mercier, President-Elect
William Hanley, Executive Vice President
Nick Bleeker, Treasurer

To advance knowledge and disseminate information for the improvement of the lighted environment to the benefit of society. Publishes a monthly magazine.

11529 International Furniture Rental Association
5008 Pine Creek Drive
#6
Westerville, OH 43081-4848
614-755-3910
800-367-7368

A non-profit trade organization devoted exclusively to furniture rental and leasing.
Founded in 1967

11530 International Furniture Transportation and Logistics Council
PO Box 889
Gardner, MA 01440-0889
978-632-1913
Fax: 978-630-2917
E-Mail: jsears@iftlc.org
Home Page: www.iftlc.org

Raynard F Bohman Jr, Managing Director

Members are furniture manufacturers, retailers, carriers, wholesalers and warehouses of allied products.
150 Members

11531 International Home Furnishings Center
210 E Commerce Ave
High Point, NC 27260
336-888-3700
336-801-6102
Fax: 336-882-1873
Home Page: www.ifsa-info.com

Nonprofit trade association of wholesale distributors, importers and manufacturers of finished goods. Supports furniture retailers by continuous improvement of the industry through advocacy, research and the exchange of ideas. Membership is open to any legitimate furniture wholesaler, importer, manufacturer, agent or any other firm operating within the supply chain of finished goods.
150 Members
Founded in 1928

11532 International Housewares Association
6400 Shafer Ct
Suite 650
Rosemont, IL 60018
847-292-4200
Fax: 847-292-4211
E-Mail: pbrandl@housewares.org
Home Page: www.housewares.org
Social Media: Facebook, Twitter, LinkedIn, YouTube

Keith Jaffee, Chairman
Michael L. Magerman, Vice Chairman
Philip J. Brandl, President/CEO
David Elliott, Treasurer
Dean Kurtis, Vice President, Finance

A full-service trade association dedicated to promoting the sales and marketing of housewares.
Founded in 1938

11533 International Sleep Products Association
501 Wythe Street
Alexandria, VA 22314-1917
703-683-8371
Fax: 703-683-4503
E-Mail: info@sleepproducts.org
Home Page: www.sleepproducts.org
Social Media: Facebook, Twitter, LinkedIn, Googleplus,Pinterest,Youtube

Ryan Trainer, President

Maintains a strong organization to influence government actions, inform and educate the membership and act on industry issues to enhance the growth, profitability and stature of the sleep products industry. Provides members with information and services to manage their business more effectively and efficiently. Publishes a magazine devoted exclusively to the mattress industry, BEDtimes covers a broad range of issue and news important to the industry.
Cost: $65.00
650 Members
Frequency: Monthly
Circulation: 3,500
Founded in 1915

11534 Juvenile Products Manufacturers Association
15000 Commerce Parkway
Suite C
Mt. Laurel, NJ 08054
856-638-0420
Fax: 856-439-0525
E-Mail: jpma@jpma.org
Home Page: www.jpma.org/
Social Media: Facebook, Twitter, LinkedIn

Andy Keimach, Chairman
Luanne Lager, Vice Chairman

Robert Waller Jr.-CAE, President
Mark Messner, Treasurer
Michael Dwyer-CAE, Executive Director

The Juvenile Products Manufacturers Association exists to advance the interests, growth and well-being of the juvenile products industry through advocacy,public relations, information sharing and business devrlopment opportunities.
Founded in 1962

11535 National Association of Display Industries
4651 Sheridan Street
Suite 200
Hollywood, FL 33021

954-893-7300
Fax: 954-893-7500
E-Mail: nadi@nadi-global.com
Home Page: www.nadi-global.com

Klein Merriman, Executive Director
Tracy Dillon, Director Communications

Sponsors seminars and annual contests. Conducts research programs and maintains placement services.
400 Members
Founded in 1937

11536 National Cotton Batting Institute
4322 Bloombury St
Southaven, MS 38672

901-218-2393
Fax: 662-449-0046
E-Mail: info@natbat.com
Home Page: www.natbat.com

Weston Arnall, President
Greg Windsperger, VP
Fred Middleton, Executive Secretary-Treasurer

NCBI respresents U.S. companies that manufacture and sell batting for use in mattresses, futons, home furnishing, and upholstered products. It provides a range of services to assist its members in expanding markets, monitoring and contributing to legislative and regulatory decisions that affect the industry, and conducting consumer education and information programs.
27 Members
Founded in 1954

11537 National Unfinished Furniture Institute
1850 Oak Street
Northfield, IL 60093-3042

847-784-1225
Fax: 847-446-3523

Ray Passis, Executive Director

Provides publicity and insurance for industry, offers educational seminars and bestows awards.
1.2M Members
Founded in 1979

11538 National Waterbed Retailers Association
2 Greentree Center
Suit 225
Marlton, NJ 08053-3102

312-236-6662
800-832-3553
Fax: 312-236-1140

Promotes industry through educational seminars, sells educational materials on waterbeds, health care and conducts surveys.
500 Members
Founded in 1972

11539 North America Home Furnishings Association
2050 N Stemmons Fwy
Suite 292
Dallas, TX 75207

800-942-4663
Fax: 214-742-9103
E-Mail: info@hfia.com
Home Page: www.nahfa.org
Social Media: Facebook, Twitter, LinkedIn

Howard Haimsohn, Chairman
Richard Howard, President
Marty Cramer, President-Elect
Mary Frye, Executive Vice President
Steve Kidder, Vice President

Committed to strengthening the home furnishing industry trhough collective support, services, and leadership.
Founded in 1923

11540 Paint & Decorating Retailers Association
1401 Triad Center Dr
St Peters, MO 63376

636-326-2636
Fax: 636-326-1823
E-Mail: info@pdra.org
Home Page: www.pdra.org
Social Media: Facebook, Twitter, LinkedIn

Jeff Baggaley, President
Dan Simon, Executive Vice President
Phil Merlo, VP/Treasurer

Provides members with the tools they need and prosper such as information, sales training, and business operations programs.
1500 Members
Founded in 1947

11541 Quarters Furniture Manufacturers Association
1211 Popes Head Drive
Fairfax, VA 22030

240-215-9700
Fax: 276-632-7894
E-Mail: matt.yanson@cma-gsa.com
Home Page: www.qfma.net

Michael Gittinger, President
Chris Arndt, Vice President
Malcolm Wilson, Secretary
Allyn Richert, Treasurer

Represents companies who produce furniture for military markets. Monitors federal procurement policy as it relates to prison industries.
20 Members
Founded in 1995

11542 Society of Glass & Ceramic Decorated Products
PO Box 2489
Zanesville, OH 43702

740-588-9882
Fax: 740-588-0245
E-Mail: info@sgcd.org
Home Page: www.sgcd.org

Chad Yaw, President
Jan Weyrich, Vice President
Mike Gervais, Treasurer
David Stanton, Secretary
Myra Warne, Executive Director

Provides designers, decorators and marketers of glass, ceramic and related products with resources for maximizing profitability, technical applications and regulatory compliance.
525 Members

11543 Summer and Casual Furniture Manufacturers Association
317 W High Avenue
High Point, NC 27260

336-884-5000
Fax: 336-884-5303
E-Mail: jlogan@ahfa.us
Home Page: http://www.ahfa.us/divisions/scfma.asp
Social Media: Facebook, LinkedIn

Merv Conn, Chairman
Rory Rehmert, President
Ken Burrows, 1st Vice President
Dean Engelage, 2nd Vice President
Joseph P. Logan, Executive Director

Sponsors the International Casual Furniture and Accessories Market in Chicago, the Apollo Awards, recognizing excellence in casual furniture retailing and the Casual Furniture Design Excellence Awards.
500+ Members
Founded in 1959

11544 The American Home Furnishings Alliance
317 West High Avenue
10th Floor
High Point, NC 27260

336-884-5000
Fax: 336-884-5303
E-Mail: pbowling@ahfa.us
Home Page: www.ahfa.us
Social Media: Facebook, LinkedIn

Andy Counts, CEO

The world's largest and most influential trade organization serving the home furnishings industry. AHFA is dedicated to fostering the growth and global well being of its member companies.
450 Members
Founded in 1905

11545 The Association of Woodworking & Furnishings Suppliers
2400 E Katella Ave
Suite 340
Anaheim, CA 92806

323-838-9440
800-946-2937
Fax: 323-838-9443
Home Page: www.awfs.org
Social Media: Facebook, Twitter, LinkedIn

Wade Gregory, President
Archie Thompson, Vice President
Philip Martin, Secretary/Treasurer

The largest national trade association in the US representing the interests of the broad array of companies that supply the home and commercial furnishings industry. Members include manufacturers and distributors of machinery, hardware, lumber, upholstery materials, bedding components, wood products and other supplies to furnishings and wood products manufacturers.
Founded in 1979

11546 Upholstered Furniture Action Council
PO Box 2436
High Point, NC 27261

336-885-5065
Fax: 336-885-5072
E-Mail: info@ufac.org
Home Page: www.ufac.org

Joseph Ziolkowski, Executive Director

Conducts research and disseminates information about adoption of guidelines for cigarette-resistant furniture. Educates public about safe use of smoking materials.
Founded in 1972

11547 World Floor Covering Association
2211 E Howell Ave
Anaheim, CA 92806
714-978-6440
800-624-6880
Fax: 714-978-6066
E-Mail: wfca@wfca.org
Home Page: www.wfca.org
Social Media: Facebook, Twitter
Scott Humphrey, CEO
Terry Hearne, Director of Operations
Cammie Weitzel, Director of Finance/Administration
Donna Archambault, Membership Operations Manager
Shapes and defines public policy through agressive, national legislative advocacy on behalf of our members. Provides continuing professional educational programming through educational forums and the Regional Installation and Training Education (RITE) program.
45 Members
Founded in 1973

Newsletters

11548 AWFS Suppliers' Edge
Association of Woodworking & Furnishings Suppliers
500 Citadel Drive
Suite 200
Commerce, CA 90040
323-838-9440
800-946-2937
Fax: 323-838-9443
Home Page: www.awfs.org
Social Media: Facebook, Twitter, LinkedIn
Joan Kemp, President
Wade Gregory, Vice President
Archie Thompson, Secretary/Treasurer
Industry events, manufacturing news, AWFS Fair news, member news and more.
Frequency: Tri-Annually
Founded in 1979

11549 At The Table
American Home Furnishings Alliance
317 High Avenue
10th Floor
High Point, NC 27260
336-884-5000
Fax: 336-884-5303
E-Mail: pbowling@ahfa.us
Home Page: www.ahfa.us
Social Media: Facebook, LinkedIn
Andy Counts, CEO
News from legislative and regulatory forums where AHRA is at the table, serving as the voice of the home furnishings industry.
450 Members
Frequency: Quarterly
Founded in 1905

11550 Focus on Benefits
American Furniture Manufacturers Association
PO Box Hp7
High Point, NC 27261
336-884-5000
Fax: 336-884-5303
E-Mail: pbowling@ahfa.us
Home Page: www.ahfa.us
Patricia Bowling, VP Communications
Adresses timely benefits subjects along with developing trends.
Frequency: Quarterly

11551 Furniture Executive
American Furniture Manufacturers Association
PO Box Hp7
High Point, NC 27261
336-884-5000
Fax: 336-884-5303
E-Mail: pbowling@ahfa.us
Home Page: www.ahfa.us
Patricia Bowling, VP Communications
Includes news on all upcoming programs and events, a message from the AHFA President, news from Washington, updates on the AHFA public relations program, and updates on AHFA member benefits and programs.
Frequency: Monthly

11552 Human Resources Close-Up
American Home Furnishings Alliance
317 High Avenue
10th Floor
High Point, NC 27260
336-884-5000
Fax: 336-884-5303
E-Mail: pbowling@ahfa.us
Home Page: www.ahfa.us
Social Media: Facebook, LinkedIn
Andy Counts, CEO
Online newsletter, addresses pertinent legal subjects in the employment/labor relations arena, along with relevant court and National Labor Relations Board cases.
450 Members
Frequency: Monthly
Founded in 1905

11553 National Association of Display Industries Newsletter
4651 Sheridan Street
Suite 470
Hollywood, FL 33021
954-893-7300
Fax: 954-893-7500
E-Mail: nadi@nadi-global.com
Home Page: www.nadi-global.com
Klein Merriman, Executive Director
Tracy Dillon, Director Communications
Accepts advertising.
Cost: $45.00
16 Pages
Circulation: 8000
Founded in 1956

11554 Square Yard
American Floorcovering Association
2211 E Howell Avenue
Anaheim, CA 92806-6009
714-572-8370
Fax: 714-780-0488
Edward Korczak, Publisher
Offers full coverage of interior design in association with floor coverings, carpets and rug manufacturers.
8 Pages
Frequency: Monthly

11555 Suppliers on Demand
American Home Furnishings Alliance
317 High Avenue
10th Floor
High Point, NC 27260
336-884-5000
Fax: 336-884-5303
E-Mail: pbowling@ahfa.us
Home Page: www.ahfa.us
Social Media: Facebook, LinkedIn
Andy Counts, CEO
Online newsletter designed to help manufacturer members find the product and service suppliers they need, when they need them.
450 Members
Frequency: Quarterly
Founded in 1905

Magazines & Journals

11556 Architectural Lighting
One Thomas Circle, NW
Suite 600
Washington, DC 20005
202-452-0800
Fax: 202-785-1974
Social Media: Twitter
Ned Cramer, Editor-in-Chief
Elizabeth Donoff, Editor
Covers design specifications and application of electrical lighting and daylighting systems.
Frequency: Monthly
Circulation: 54,000

11557 BEDtimes Magazine
International Sleep Products Association
501 Wythe Street
Alexandria, VA 22314-1917
703-683-8371
Fax: 703-683-4503
E-Mail: info@sleepproducts.org
Home Page: www.sleepproducts.org
Julie Palm, Editor
Kerri Bellias, Administrative Assistant
Dana Jackson, Administrative Assistant
Mary Best, Managing Editor
A magazine covering the bedding industry. Target audience as mattress suppliers and manufacturers.
Cost: $50.00
Frequency: Monthly
Circulation: 3000
ISSN: 0893-5556
Founded in 1915
Printed in 4 colors on glossy stock

11558 Designer
HDC Publications
429 Montague Ave
Caro, MI 48723-1921
989-673-4121
800-843-6394
Fax: 989-673-2031
E-Mail: info@hdc-caro.org
Home Page: www.hdc-caro.org
Maryann Vandemark, Executive Director
A magazine offering information on interior design.
Frequency: Monthly

11559 Draperies and Window Coverings
840 US Highway One
Suite 330
North Palm Beach, FL 33408
561-627-3393
847-548-3900
Fax: 561-694-6578
Home Page: www.dwcdesignet.com
Carolyn Silberman, Publisher
Howard Shingle, Editor
Sarah Christy, Associate Editor
Covers trends and specific industry topics.
Cost: $33.00
160 Pages
Frequency: Monthly
Circulation: 28,000
Founded in 1981

11560 **Eastern Floors Magazine**
Specialist Publications
22801 Ventura Boulevard
Suite 115
Woodland Hills, CA 91364-1230

818-224-8035
800-835-4398
Fax: 818-224-8042
Home Page: www.icsmag.com
Social Media: Facebook, Twitter

Howard Olansky, Editor
Phil Johnson, Group Publisher
Evan Kessler, Publisher
Amy Levin, Production Manager

Serving the floor covering and tile industry.
Cost: $140.00
Frequency: Monthly
Founded in 1990

11561 **Furniture Today**
Reed Business Information
PO Box 2754
High Point, NC 27261-2754

336-605-1000
800-395-2329
Fax: 336-605-1143
Home Page: www.reedbusiness.com
Social Media: Facebook, Twitter

Kevin Castellani, President
Ray Allegeeza, Editor-in-Chief
Helene Checinski, Circulation Manager
Kim Bashford, Production Manager
Delaney Rudd, Ower

Business and fashion newspaper of the furniture industry, edited for retail furniture executives in furniture stores, department stores, mass merchants, furniture specialty stores and catalog showrooms, as well as manufacturing executives at all levels. Focus is on the business and fashion news that these executives need at key decision times in their merchandising and marketing cycles.
Cost: $159.97
Frequency: Weekly
Circulation: 21212
Founded in 1976
Printed in on glossy stock

11562 **Home Accents Today**
Reed Business Information
360 Park Ave S
New York, NY 10010-1737

646-746-6400
Fax: 646-756-7583
Home Page: www.homeaccentstoday.com
Social Media: Facebook, Twitter

John Poulin, CEO
Marion Kelly, Publisher
Gerard Van de Aast, CEO
Becky Boswell Smith, Editor-in-Chief
James Reed, Owner

Enables home furnishing retailers to develop merchandising programs, define new style statements, make buying decisions, and create retail strategies. Editorially covers the broad fashion mix of home accent products.
Cost: $24.94
Frequency: Monthly
Circulation: 21300

11563 **Home Furnishing Retailer**
National Home Furnishings Association
3910 Tinsley Drive
Suite 101
Highpoint, NC 27265-3610

336-886-6100
800-888-9590
Fax: 336-801-6102
E-Mail: info@nhfa.org
Home Page: www.nhfa.org
Social Media: Facebook, Twitter, LinkedIn, YouTube

Provides the latest information specifically for industry retailers; current trends and strategies to keep business profitable.
Cost: $70.00
Frequency: Monthly
Circulation: 10000
ISSN: 1073-5585

11564 **Home Lighting & Accessories**
Doctorow Communications
1011 Clifton Ave
Suite 1
Clifton, NJ 07013-3518

973-779-1600
Fax: 973-779-3242
E-Mail: email@homelighting.com
Home Page: www.homelighting.com

Jeffrey Doctorow, President
Jon Doctorow, Circulation Director

Home Lighting & Accessories is a magazine of lamps, lighting fixtures, shades and decorative home accessories. Articles cover marketing and retailing aspects applied to portable lamps, lamps shades, residential lighting fixtures and decorative home accessories - customer relations, sales training, trends, lighting showroom layout, design and operations. Plus industry and company news, new promotions, appointments, literature, patents
Cost: $15.00
Founded in 1953

11565 **ICS Cleaning Specialist**
Business News Publishing Company
22801 Ventura Blvd
Suite 115
Woodland Hills, CA 91364-1230

818-224-8035
800-835-4398
Fax: 818-224-8042
Home Page: www.bnpmedia.com

Phil Johnson, Publisher
Evan Kessler, Publisher
Jeffrey Stouffer, Editor
Amy Levin, Production Manager

For carpet cleaning, restoration and floor care service providers.
68 Pages
Frequency: Monthly
Circulation: 24250
ISSN: 1522-4708
Founded in 1963
Printed in 4 colors on glossy stock

11566 **Journal of Family & Consumer Sciences**
American Association of Family & Consumer Sciences
400 N Columbus St
Suite 202
Alexandria, VA 22314-2264

703-706-4600
800-424-8080
Fax: 703-706-4663
E-Mail: pr@aafcs.org
Home Page: www.aafcs.org
Social Media: Facebook, Twitter, LinkedIn, Flickr

Carolyn Jackson, Executive Director

Contains scholarly peer-reviewed articles, practical information geared toward family and consumer sciences professionals, and news and information about AAFCS.
Frequency: Quarterly

11567 **Metropolis**
Bellerophon Publications
61 W 23rd St
Floor 4
New York, NY 10010-4246

212-627-9977
Fax: 212-627-9988
E-Mail: edit@metropolismag.com
Home Page: www.metropolismag.com

Horace Havemeyer, Publisher
Susan Szenasy, Editor in Chief
Julie Taraska, Editor
Denise Csaky, Marketing Director

The only magazine that covers all facets of design: architecture, interiors, furniture, preservation, urban design, graphics and crafts.
Cost: $27.95
Circulation: 51000
Founded in 1981

11568 **NHFA Trade Show**
National Home Furnishings Association
3910 Tinsley Drive
Suite 101
Highpoint, NC 27265-3610

336-886-6100
800-888-9590
Fax: 336-801-6102
E-Mail: info@nhfa.org
Home Page: www.nhfa.org

Steve DeHaan, Executive VP
Karin Mayfield, Senior Director for Membership
Frequency: Annual

11569 **Panel World**
Hatton-Brown Publishers
PO Box 2268
Montgomery, AL 36102-2268

334-834-1170
800-669-5613
Fax: 334-834-4525
E-Mail: mail@hattonbrown.com
Home Page: www.hattonbrown.com/

D K Knight, Editor-in-chief
Rich Donnell, Editor
David Ramsey, President
Rhonda Thomas, Marketing

A magazine covering the interior design community.
Cost: $40.00
Frequency: Monthly
Circulation: 12000
Printed in 4 colors on matte stock

11570 **RTOHQ: The Magazine**
Association of Progressive Rental Merchandise
1540 Robinhood Trail
Austin, TX 78703-2624

512-794-0095
800-204-APRO
Fax: 512-794-0097
E-Mail: cferguson@rtohq.org
Home Page: www.rtohq.org

Bill Keese, Executive Director
John C Cleek, President
Bill Kelly, Secretary

Emphasis on larger issues facing it players in the rent-to-own industry. Readers are rent-to-own dealers, owners, managers, employees, manufacturers and suppliers to the industry.
Frequency: Bi-Monthly
Circulation: 11000

Trade Shows

11571 **AAFCS Annual Conference & Exposition**
American Association of Family & Consumer Sciences
400 N Columbus Street
Suite 202
Alexandria, VA 22314

703-706-4600
Fax: 703-706-4663
E-Mail: connect@aafcs.org
Home Page: www.aafcs.org
Social Media: Facebook, Twitter, LinkedIn, Flickr

Johnny Reynolds, Project Manager
Roxana Ayona, Manager

Informative speakers, cutting-edge workshops, and a panel discussion.
Frequency: Annual/June

11572 **APRO Rent-To-Own Convention & Trade Show**
Association of Progressive Rental Organizations
1504 Robin Hood Trail
Austin, TX 78703

512-794-0095
800-204-APRO
Fax: 512-794-0097
Home Page: www.rtohq.org

Shannon Strunkec, President
John C Cleek, First VP
Jeannie Hutchison, Program Coordinator
Bill Keese, Manager

Seminar, reception and tours, plus 280 exhibits of products and services of interest to rent to own dealers: stereos, televisions, furniture, fabric protection and more.
1400 Attendees
Frequency: Annual

11573 **Association of College Unions International Conference**
120 W. Seventh St.
Suite 200
Bloomington, IN 47404

812-245-2284
Fax: 812-245-6710
Home Page: www.acui.org

Rich Steele, President
Marsha Herman-Betzen, Executive Director
Andrea Langeveld, Marketing

One hundred exhibits of graphic supplies, recreation equipment, computer hardware and software, furnishings, entertainment and speaker bureau information, food service equipment, and more related information and supplies.
1000 Attendees
Frequency: Annual

11574 **Canyon County Home & Garden Show**
Spectra Productions
837 E State Street
PO Box 333
Eagle, ID 83616

208-939-6426
Fax: 208-939-6437
E-Mail: david@spectraproductions.com
Home Page: www.spectraproductions.com

David Beale, Show Manager

Features exhibitors displaying building materials, contractors, decorators, doors and windows, pools and spas, heating and cooling systems and much more.
150 Attendees
Frequency: April

11575 **Denver Home Show**
Industrial Expositions
PO Box 480084
Denver, CO 80248-0084

303-892-6800
800-457-2434
Fax: 303-892-6322
E-Mail: info@iei-expos.com
Home Page: www.bigasalloutdoors.com

Formerly the Spring Home & Patio Show.
23000 Attendees
Frequency: Annual/March

11576 **Evergreen Home Show**
Westlake Promotions
6020 Seaview Avenue NW
Seattle, WA 98107

206-783-5957
Fax: 206-782-6250
Home Page: www.westlakepromo.com

Bill Bradley, VP

See what's new and what you can do for your home. Fresh ideas and practical advice from our remodeling and construction specialists. See demonstrations on how to make dramatic improvements to your home.
7500 Attendees

11577 **Fall Home and Garden Expo**
Mid-America Expositions, Inc
7015 Spring Street
Omaha, NE 68106

402-346-8003
800-475-7469
Fax: 402-346-5412
E-Mail: info@showofficeonline.com
Home Page: www.showofficeonline.com

Robert P Mancuso, CEO
Mike Mancuso, VP/Manager

Displays on everything for the home including kitchens, room additions, bathrooms, interior decorating, fireplaces, outdoor equipment, heating and air conditioning, remodeling contractors, security, siding, appliances, windows, doors, fencing, roofing, fitness equipment, spas and much more.
Frequency: Annual/October

11578 **Furniture Expo**
Glahe International
PO Box 2460
Germantown, MD 20875-2460

301-515-0012
Fax: 301-515-0016

Annual show and exhibits of furniture making.

11579 **Glass & Ceramic Decorators Annual Seminar & Exposition**
Society of Glass & Ceramic Decorators
47 N 4th Street
PO Box 2489
Zanesville, OH 43702

202-298-8660
Fax: 740-588-0245
Home Page: www.sgcd.org

Myra Warne, Exhibit

The SGCD show attracts major suppliers to the decorating industry, including several firms from overseas. With a full seminar program and first step program that attracts attendees on their own merits.
525 Attendees

11580 **Great Northeast Home Show**
Osborne/Jenks Productions
936 Silas Deane Highway
Wethersfield, CT 06109-4273

860-563-2111
800-955-7469
Fax: 860-563-3472

Two hundred and fifty booths.
25M Attendees
Frequency: Annual/February

11581 **Home World Home & Garden Show**
Show Biz Productions
16520 Harbor Blouevard
Fountain Valley, CA 92708

714-418-2000
Fax: 714-418-2009
E-Mail: marlene@sbhomeshow.com
Home Page: www.sbhomeshow.com

Marlene Thorne, VP

Featuring vendors of window, doors, painting, heating, air conditioning, kitchens and baths, flooring, furniture, remodeling services and more.
40000 Attendees
Frequency: Annual/May
Founded in 1991

11582 **Home and Outdoor Living Expo**
Tower Show Productions
800 Roosevelt Road
Building A, Suite 109
Glen Ellyn, IL 60137

630-469-4611
800-946-4611
Fax: 630-469-4811
E-Mail: jaylake20@towershow.com
Home Page: www.towershow.com

J Lake, VP Home Shows

The largest and longest running home improvement show.
15000 Attendees
Frequency: January
Founded in 1977

11583 **ICFF International Contemporary Furniture**
George Little Management
10 Bank Street
White Plains, NY 10606-1933

914-486-6070
800-272-7469
Fax: 914-948-6180
E-Mail: info@icff.com
Home Page: www.icff.com
Social Media: Facebook, Twitter

Troy Hansen, Show Manager
Alex Cabat, Show Coordinator
George Little II, President
Tony Orlando, Operations Manager

More than 500 exhibitors will display contemporary furniture, seating, lighting, carpet and flooring, wall coverings, textiles, accessories, kitchen and bath, outdoor furniture, and materials for residential and commercial interiors. The combination of domestic and international exhibitors provides easy access to the best and hippest home and contract products.
12000 Attendees
Frequency: Annual/December

11584 **International Bedding Exposition**
International Sleep Products Association
501 Wythe Street
Alexandria, VA 22314-1917

703-683-8371
Fax: 703-683-4503
E-Mail: info@sleepproducts.org
Home Page: www.sleepproducts.org

Susan Perry, Executive VP, Business Development

Dana Jackson, Administrative Assistant
Mary Best, Managing Editor

200 booths, net 120,000 square feet with 200 exhibitors participating.
4M Attendees
Frequency: Annual/March

11585 International Home Furnishings Market
International Home Furnishings Market Authority
101 S Main Street
High Point, NC 27262

336-691-1000
Fax: 336-889-6999
Home Page: www.highpointmarket.org

Judy Mendenhall, President
Jan Wellmon, Executive Assistant
Shannon Kennedy, Director of Marketing

Large home furnishings trade show with a variety of new opportunities to make your visit easy, cost effective and productive. Ten million square seet of exhibition space with 2,500 manufacturers represented.
75000 Attendees
Frequency: Bi-Annual
Founded in 1921

11586 International Housewares Show
National Housewares Manufacturers Association
6400 Shafer Court
Suite 650
Rosemont, IL 60018

708-292-4200
Fax: 847-292-4211
Home Page: www.housewares.org

Mia Rampersad, VP Trade Show & Meetings

See first-hand consumer lifestyle and product trends for all areas of the home, both inside and out, under one roof.
60000 Attendees

11587 International Woodworking Machinery and Furniture Supply Fair: USA
Reed Exhibition Companies
1350 E Touhy Avenue
Des Plaines, IL 60018-3303

847-294-0300
Fax: 847-635-1571

Paul Pajor, National Marketing Manager

The largest woodworking machinery and furniture supply manufacturing exposition held in the Western Hemisphere. Exhibitors interface with North American furniture, cabinet, and woodworking manufacturers. One thousand booths.
37M Attendees
Frequency: Biennial/August

11588 Juvenile Products Manufacturers Association Trade Show
PO Box 955
Marlton, NJ 08053-0955

856-231-8500
Fax: 856-985-2878

William Macmillan, Show Manager

Home acessories and products for children's rooms.
2.5M Attendees
Frequency: Annual/October

11589 Kitchen & Bath Industry Show
National Kitchen & Bath Association
687 Willow Grove Street
Hackettstown, NJ 07840

908-520-0033
800-843-6522
Fax: 908-852-1695
Home Page: www.kbis.com

Lee Hershberg, Sales Manager
Grayson Lutz, Operations Manager

Targeting dealers, designers, distributors, retailers, consumers, home centers and many other high-quality kitchen and bath professionals. Showcasing the latest products and cutting-edge design ideas of the kitchen and bath industry.
40000 Attendees
Frequency: Annual/April

11590 Kitchen/Bath Industry Show & Multi-Housing World Conference
VNU Expositions
1145 Sanctuary Parkway
Suite 355
Alpharetta, GA 30004

770-691-1540
800-933-8735
Fax: 770-777-8700

Lee Hershberg, Sales Manager

The latest products and technologies, industry and consumer trends, design and business tools and more to stay ahead of your competitors.
35000 Attendees

11591 LightFair
AMC
120 Wall Street
17th Floor
New York, NY 10005

212-843-8358
Fax: 212-248-5017
Home Page: www.iesna.org

Pamela R Weess, Circulation Director
Nini Schwenk, Manager

A major lighting trade show in North America featuring architectural lighting products from all spectrons of the industry. Containing 600 booths and 400 exhibits.
17M Attendees
Frequency: June
Mailing list available for rent: 10M names at $100 per M
Printed in 4 colors on glossy stock

11592 Mid-Atlantic Industrial Woodworking Expo Supply Show
Trade Shows
PO Box 2000
Claremont, NC 28610-2000

828-459-9894
Fax: 828-459-1312
E-Mail: tsi@tsishows.com
Home Page: www.tsishows.com

Keith Eidson, Show Manager

Annual show of 300 manufacturers of woodworking and furniture industry equipment, supplies and services.
4500 Attendees
Frequency: Annual/April

11593 National City Home & Garden Show
Expositions
PO Box 550
Edgewater Branch
Cleveland, OH 44107-0550

216-529-1300
Fax: 216-529-0311
E-Mail: showinfo@expoinc.com
Home Page: www.expoinc.com

Featuring showcases on how to make your dream home a reality. Create the garden oasis, backyard retreat or a relaxing sanctuary.
35000 Attendees
Frequency: Annual/February

11594 National Hardware Show
Reed Exhibition Companies
383 Main Avenue
Norwalk, CT 06851

203-840-4800
Fax: 203-840-4824

The prime time and place for face to face sourcing, trading and learning for the US home improvement and DIY markets.
70000 Attendees

11595 Old House New House Home Show
Kennedy Productions
1208 Lisle Place
Lisle, IL 60532-2262

630-515-1160
Fax: 630-515-1165
Home Page: www.kennedyproductions.com

Laura McNamara, Event Producer

Over 300 home improvement exhibitors displaying cutting-edge home enhancements for kitchens, baths, home and garden including landscape, interior remodeling, pools, spas, floors, doors and more.
8000 Attendees
Frequency: Biannual
Founded in 1984

11596 PDRA Paint & Decorating Show
Paint & Decorating Retailers Association
403 Axminister Drive
Fenton, MO 63026

636-326-2636
800-737-0107
Fax: 636-326-1823
E-Mail: tina@pdra.org
Home Page: www.pdra.org

Dan Simon, Executive Vice President

Retailers from the paint and decorating products industry to discuss a variety of business topics. Gain insight from retailers who face the same problems that you do everyday.
1000 Attendees
Frequency: Annual/May

11597 Remodeling and Decorating Expo
893 N Jan Mar Ct
Olathe, KS 66061-3693

913-768-8148
Fax: 785-780-4777

Tom Reno, VP
Mary Jo Doherty, Executive Director

Four hundred booths of the latest products and services related to remodeling and decorating. Also a presentation of How-To stage presentations on remodeling, decorating and home repair.
40M Attendees
Frequency: Annual/February

11598 Southern Home & Garden Show
Home Builders Association
702 E McBee Avenue
Greensville, SC 29601

864-229-7722
Fax: 864-232-3541

Exhibitors include professional landscapers, nurseryment, interior designers and home and garden experts.
40000 Attendees
Frequency: Biannual

11599 Spring Home Show
Osborne/Jenks Productions

936 Silas Deane Highway
Wethersfield, CT 06109

860-563-2111
Fax: 860-563-3472

Exhibitors include remodelers, homebuilders, custom cabinets, kitchens & baths, chimneys, wood stoves, sunrooms, awnings & decks, duct & vent maintenance, storage buildings, heating & cooling services, windows, doors & siding, water treatment systems, banks & mortgage companies, home theatre systems, security systems, financial planners, building supplies, insulation, energy management companies and so much more.
Frequency: Annual/March

11600 Surfaces Conference
World Floor Covering Association
2211 E Howell Avenue
Anaheim, CA 92806

714-978-6440
800-624-6880
Fax: 714-978-6066
E-Mail: wfca@wfca.org
Home Page: www.wfca.org

Casey Voorhees, Executive Director
Tina Krulich, Administrative Assistant

The event for the floor covering industry with the latest trends to keep your business competitive, proven strategies to increase sales and profitability and all the critical industry information you need to make the right decisions.
40000 Attendees
Frequency: Annual/January

11601 West Week
Pacific Design Center
8687 Melrose Avenue
West Hollywood, CA 90069

310-652-6992
Fax: 310-652-9576

Show featuring the top interior designers and decorators.
Frequency: Annual/March

11602 Woodworking and Furniture Expo
Glahe International
PO Box 2460
Germantown, MD 20875-2460

301-515-0012
Fax: 301-515-0016

Annual show and exhibits of woodworking and furniture making.

Directories & Databases

11603 AHFA's Industry Resource Guide
American Home Furnishing Alliance
PO Box HP-7
High Point, NC 27261

336-884-5000
Fax: 336-884-5303
Home Page: www.ahfa.us

Andy Counts, Executive VP

A who's who in the furniture industry, supplying information on over 500 furniture manufacturers and their suppliers.
80 Pages
Founded in 1966

11604 Casual Living: Casual Outdoor Furniture and Accessory Directory Issue
Reed Business Information
360 Park Ave S
New York, NY 10010-1737

646-746-6400
Fax: 646-756-7583
Home Page: www.reedbusiness.com

John Poulin, CEO
Toni Agpar, Editor

List of manufacturers, manufacturers' trepresentatives, and suppliers of outdoor furniture, wicker and rattan furniture, and backyard accessories such as barbecue grills, picnic accessories, outdoor lighting cushions, pads, patio umbrellas, vinyl refinishing, and maintenance, products.
Cost: $10.00
Frequency: Annual
Circulation: 13,000

11605 Complete Directory of Discount & Catalog Merchandisers
Sutton Family Communications & Publishing Company
920 State Route 54 East
Elmitch, KY 42343

270-276-9500
E-Mail: jlsutton@apex.net

Theresa Sutton, Publisher
Lee Sutton, Editor

Print-out from database of wholesalers, manufacturers, distributors, importers and close-out houses. Database is updated daily to guarantee the most current and up-to-date sources available.
Cost: $125.00
100 Pages

11606 Complete Directory of Home Furnishings
Sutton Family Communications & Publishing Company
920 State Route 54 East
Elmitch, KY 42343

270-276-9500
E-Mail: jlsutton@apex.net

Theresa Sutton, Publisher
Lee Sutton, Editor

Print-out from database of wholesalers, manufacturers, distributors, importers and close-out houses. Database is updated daily to guarantee the most current and up-to-date sources available.
Cost: $44.50
100 Pages

11607 Complete Directory of Kitchen Accessories
Sutton Family Communications & Publishing Company
920 State Route 54 East
Elmitch, KY 42343

270-276-9500
E-Mail: jlsutton@apex.net

Theresa Sutton, Editor
Lee Sutton, General Manager

Print-out from database of wholesalers, manufacturers, distributors, importers and close-out houses. Database is updated daily to guarantee the most current and up-to-date sources available.
Cost: $49.50
100+ Pages

11608 Complete Directory of Lamps, Lamp Shades & Lamp Parts
Sutton Family Communications & Publishing Company
955 Sutton Lane
20 State Route 54 East
Elmitch, KY 42343

270-276-9500
E-Mail: jlsutton@apex.net

Theresa Sutton, Editor
Lee Sutton, General Manager

Print-out from database of wholesalers, manufacturers, distributors, importers and close-out houses. Database is updated daily to guarantee the most current and up-to-date sources available.
Cost: $39.50
100+ Pages

11609 Complete Directory of Serving Ware
Sutton Family Communications & Publishing Company
920 State Route 54 East
Elmitch, KY 42343

270-276-9500
E-Mail: jlsutton@apex.net

Theresa Sutton, Editor
Lee Sutton, General Manager

Print-out from database of wholesalers, manufacturers, distributors, importers and close-out houses. Database is updated daily to guarantee the most current and up-to-date sources available.
Cost: $39.50
100+ Pages

11610 Complete Directory of Showroom Fixtures and Equipment
Sutton Family Communications & Publishing Company
920 State Route 54 East
Elmitch, KY 42343

270-276-9500
E-Mail: jlsutton@apex.net

Theresa Sutton, Publisher
Lee Sutton, Editor

Print-out from database of wholesalers, manufacturers, distributors, importers and close-out houses. Database is updated daily to guarantee the most current and up-to-date sources available.
Cost: $39.50
100 Pages

11611 Complete Directory of Small Furniture
Sutton Family Communications & Publishing Company
920 State Route 54 East
Elmitch, KY 42343

270-276-9500
E-Mail: jlsutton@apex.net

Theresa Sutton, Publisher
Lee Sutton, Editor

Print-out from database of wholesalers, manufacturers, distributors, importers and close-out houses. Database is updated daily to guarantee the most current and up-to-date sources available.
Cost: $39.50
100 Pages

11612 Complete Directory of Upholstery Materials Supplies and Equipment
Sutton Family Communications & Publishing Company
920 State Route 54 East
Elmitch, KY 42343

270-276-9500
E-Mail: jlsutton@apex.net

Theresa Sutton, Publisher
Lee Sutton, Editor

Print-out from database of wholesalers, manufacturers, distributors, importers and close-out houses. Database is updated daily to guarantee the most current and up-to-date sources available. Over 600 American wholesale direct supplies in 3-ring binder.
Cost: $67.50
100 Pages

11613 Furniture Retailer Resource Guide
Pace Communications
PO Box 13607
Suite 100
Greensboro, NC 27415-3607
336-378-6065
Fax: 336-275-2864
Home Page: www.pacecommunications.com
Bonnie McElveen, CEO
Directory of services and supplies to the industry.
Cost: $20.00
Frequency: Annual;
Circulation: 16,000

11614 Hearth & Home: Furnishings Issue
Village West Publishing
PO Box 1288
Laconia, NH 03247-2008
603-528-4285
800-258-3772
Fax: 603-524-0643
E-Mail: avignone@villagewest.com
Richard Wright, Publisher/Editor
Jackie Avignone, Advertising Director
Karen Dipietro, Owner
Trade journal for hearth, barbecue and patio retailing. July issue is Buyer's Guide for the three industries, available separately for $15.
Cost: $6.00
Frequency: Annual
Circulation: 17,000
ISSN: 0273-5695

11615 Home Furnishing Retailers
Chain Store Guide
3922 Coconut Palm Dr
Suite 300
Tampa, FL 33619-1389
813-627-6700
800-972-0292
Fax: 813-627-7094
E-Mail: info@csgis.com
Home Page: www.csgis.com
Mike Jarvis, Publisher
Shami Choon, Manager
This database features detailed information on over 2700 companies in the U.S. and Canada, with contact information for over 8600 key executives and buyers.
Cost: $275.00
Frequency: Annual

11616 IFRA Member Directory
International Furniture Rental Association
5008 Pine Creek Drive
#6
Westerville, OH 43081-4848
614-755-3910
800-367-7368
Home Page: www.ifra.org
About 100 member furniture rental companies.

11617 Market Resource Guide
International Home Furnishings Center
PO Box 828
High Point, NC 27261-0828
336-888-3700
Fax: 336-882-1873
E-Mail: marketing@ihfc.com
Home Page: www.ihfc.com
Bruce Miller, CEO
Two-volume directory offers over 1,500 manufacturers and distributors in the furniture industry with exhibits at the International Home Furnishings Market.
Cost: $25.00
624 Pages
Frequency: Semiannual
Founded in 1974
Printed in 4 colors on glossy stock

11618 Specialized Furniture Carriers Directory
National Furniture Traffic Conference
PO Box 889
Gardner, MA 01440-0889
978-632-1913
Fax: 978-630-2917
Ray Bohman, Editor
Nearly 200 trucking firms specializing in transportation of new furniture, not including household moving firms.
Cost: $39.95

Industry Web Sites

11619 http://gold.greyhouse.com
G.O.L.D Grey House OnLine Databases
Grey House Publishing's online database platform, GOLD, offers Quick Search, Keyword Search and Expert Search for most business sectors including furnishing, fixure and decorating markets. The GOLD platform makes finding the information you need quick and easy - whether you're a novice searcher or an experienced database user. All of Grey House's directory products are available for subscription on the GOLD platform.

11620 www.ahfa.us
American Home Furnishings Alliance
The largest and most influential trade organization serving the home furnishings industry. Dedicated to fostering the growth and global well being of its member companies.

11621 www.ahfa.us/divisions/scfma.asp
Summer & Casual Furniture Manufacturers Assn
Sponsors the International Casual Furniture and Accessories Market in Chicago, the Apollo Awards recognizing excellence in casual furniture retailing and the Casual Furniture Design Excellence Awards.

11622 www.awfs.org
Association of Woodworking & Furnishings Suppliers
Organization for furniture and accessories manufacturers and suppliers that are covered in this comprehensive journal.

11623 www.bifma.org
Business and Institutional Furniture Manufacturers
The voice of the office furniture industry, BIFMA members are manufacturers and suppliers of goods and services to the industry.

11624 www.greyhouse.com
Grey House Publishing
Authoritative reference directories for most business sectors including furnishings, fixtures and decorating marekts. Users can search the online databases with varied search criteria allowing for custom searches by product category, geographic area, sales volume, keyword, subject and more. Full Grey House catalog and online ordering also available.

11625 www.hfia.com/
Home Furnishings International Association
Product categories include residential casegoods, upholstery, gift and decorative accessories, lighting and area floor coverings and beddings.

11626 www.natbat.com
National Cotton Batting Institute
Association representing members of the cotton batting industry.

11627 www.nhfa.org
National Home Furnishings Association
Trade association of furniture retailers which works to improve retailer's business opportunities and management practices.

11628 www.ofdanet.org
Office Furniture Dealers Association
Explores the effect of office environment on productivity and uses contract sales staff to anticipate changes in market.

11629 www.rtohq.org/
Association of Progressive Rental Organizations
Members include television, appliance and furniture dealers who rent merchandise with an option to purchase.

11630 www.unfinishedfurniture.org
Unfinished Furniture Association

Associations

11631 American Herbal Products Association
8630 Fenton St
Suite 918
Silver Spring, MD 20910

301-588-1171
Fax: 301-588-1174
E-Mail: ahpa@ahpa.com
Home Page: www.ahpa.org

Marc Allen, Chair
Travis Borchardt, Vice Chair
Michael McGuffin, President
Wilson Lau, Secretary
Mitch Coven, Treasurer

A organization that only focuses on herbs and herbal products.
200 Members
Founded in 1982

11632 American Horticultural Society
7931 E Boulevard Dr
Alexandria, VA 22308

703-768-5700
800-777-7931
Fax: 703-768-8700
E-Mail: dhundley@ahs.org
Home Page: www.ahs.org
Social Media: Facebook, Twitter, Flickr

Harry Rissetto, Chair
Jane Diamantis, 1st Vice Chair
Mary Pat Matheson, 2nd Vice Chair
Leslie Ariail, Secretary
J. Landon Reeve, Treasurer

Educates and inspires people of all ages to become successful and environmentally responsible gardeners by advancing the art and science of hoticulture. It is an education, nonprofit, 501 organization that recognizes and promotes best practices in American horticulture. AHS is known for its educational programs and the dissemination of horticultural information.
27M Members
Founded in 1922
Mailing list available for rent

11633 American Horticultural Therapy Association
610 Freedom Business Centre
#110
King of Prussia, PA 19406

610-992-0020
800-634-1603
Fax: 610-225-2364
Home Page: www.ahta.org
Social Media: Facebook, Twitter, LinkedIn, Youtube, Pinterest

MaryAnne McMillan, President
Leigh Anne Starling, Vice President
Rene Malone, Treasurer
Natasha Etherington, Secretary

Advancing the practice of horticulture as therapy to improve human well-being.
Founded in 1973

11634 American Institute of Floral Designers
720 Light Street
Baltimore, MD 21230

410-752-3318
Fax: 410-752-8295
E-Mail: aifd@assnhqtrs.com
Home Page: www.aifd.org
Social Media: Facebook, Twitter, LinkedIn, YouTube

John Kittinger, President
Tim Farrell, President-Elect
Joyce Mason-Monheim, Vice President
Suzie Kostick, Secretary
Tom Simmons, Treasurer

Nonprofit association to support the floral design industry.
1300 Members
Founded in 1962

11635 American Nursery & Landscape Association
1200 G Street NW
Suite 800
Washington, DC 20005

202-789-2900
Fax: 202-789-1893
E-Mail: info@anla.org
Home Page: www.anla.org
Social Media: Facebook

Bob Terry, President
Dale Deppe, President Elect
Michael V. Geary, Executive Vice President

The American Nursery and Landscape Association serves firms who grow, sell or use plants. ANLA advocates the industry's interests before government and provides its members with unique business knowledge essential to long-term growth and profitability.
2000 Members
Founded in 1876

11636 American Rose Society
8877 Jefferson Paige Road
PO Box 30000
Shreveport, LA 71130

318-938-5402
800-637-6534
Fax: 318-938-5405
E-Mail: ars@ars-hq.org
Home Page: www.ars.org
Social Media: Facebook, Twitter, Flickr,Pinterest,Youtube

Steve Jones, President
Jeff Wycoff, VP
Jeff Ware, Executive Director
Carol Spiers, Assistant to Executive Director

Striving to provide educational services to encourage the greater use of our national flower in private and public gardens throughout the country.
24000 Members
ISSN: 1078-5833
Founded in 1892

11637 American Society for Horticultural Science
1018 Duke Street
Alexandria, VA 22314
703-836-4606
Fax: 703-836-2024
E-Mail: webmaster@ashs.org
Home Page: www.ashs.org
Social Media: Facebook, Twitter, LinkedIn, Pinterest

Paul Bosland, Chair
Mary Hockenberry Meyer, President
Michael A Arnold, President-Elect
David Hensley, Treasurer

A cornerstone of research and education in horticulture and an agent for active promotion of horticultural science.
1200 Members
Founded in 1908

11638 American Society of Consulting Arborists
9707 Key West Avenue
Suite 100
Rockville, MD 20850-3222
301-947-0483
Fax: 301-990-9771
E-Mail: asca@mgmtsol.com
Home Page: www.asca-consultants.org
Social Media: Facebook, Twitter, LinkedIn, Pinterest

Gordon Mann, President
Patrick B Brewer, President Elect
Jan C Scow, Treasurer
Beth W Palys, Executive Director

The industry's premier professional association focusing solely on arboricultural consulting. Consulting Arborists are authoritative experts on trees, consulting property owners, municipalitites, attorneys, insurance professionals and others on tree disease, placement, preservation and dispute resolution in addition to providing consulting and experto testimony in the legal, insurance and environmental arenas.

11639 American Society of Irrigation Consultants
4660 S Hagadorn
Suite 110F
East Lansing, MI 48823

508-763-8140
866-828-5174
Fax: 508-763-8102
E-Mail: info@asic.org
Home Page: www.asic.org

Carol Colein, Executive Director
Jeffrey L. Bruce, President
Steven L. Sisler, Vice President
Steven M. Hohl, Secretary
Michael Krones, Treasurer

Provides a forum wherein irrigation design professionals can meet to exchange information and advance skills and techniques in irrigation design, installation and product application.

11640 American Society of Landscape Architects
636 Eye Street, NW
Washington, DC 20001-3736

202-898-2444
800-787-2752
Fax: 202-898-1185
E-Mail: info@asla.org
Home Page: www.asla.org
Social Media: Facebook, Twitter, LinkedIn, Pinterest, Instagram, RSS

Thomas R Tavella, President
Mark A Focht, President Elect
Mark H Hough, VP, Communications
David L Lycke, VP, Finance
K Richard Zweifel, VP, Education

Residential and commercial real estate developers, federal and state agencies, city planning commissions and individual property owners are all among the thousands of people and organizations in America and Canada that will retain the services of landscape architect this year.
13500 Members
Founded in 1899

11641 Association of Specialty Cut Flower Growers
17 1/2 W. College St.
MPO Box 268
Oberlin, OH 44074

440-774-2887
Fax: 440-774-2435
E-Mail: ascfg@oberlin.net
Home Page: www.ascfg.org

Judy Laushman, Executive Director
Vicki Stamback, President
Leah Cook, Vice-President
Andrea Gagnon, Treasurer
Carolyn Tschetter, Secretary

Trade association that provides cultural and marketing information to specialty cut flower growers.
700 Members
Founded in 1988

11642 **Floral Trade Council**
101 N Main Street
Ovid, MI 48866

989-341-1322
Fax: 517-339-1393

Will Carlson, Executive Director

Association of US fresh cut flower growers.
70 Members
Founded in 1988

11643 **Garden Writers Association of America**
7809 FM 179
Shallowater, TX 79363

806-832-1870
Fax: 806-832-5244
E-Mail: webtech@gardenwriters.org
Home Page: www.gwaa.org
Social Media: Facebook, Twitter

Larry Hodgson, President
Kirk Brown, Vice President
Becky Health, Treasurer
Jo Ellen Meyers Sharp, Secretary
Robert LaGasse, Executive Director

A organization with materials of interest to garden writers and news on members of the Association.

11644 **Illinois Landscape Contractors Association**
Illinois Landscape Contractors Association
2625 Butterfield Road
Suite 204W
Oak Brook, IL 60523

630-472-2851
Fax: 630-472-3150
E-Mail: information@ilca.net
Home Page: www.ilca.net

Joe Hobson, President
Charlie Keppel, Secretary/Treasurer
Tim Caldwell, Vice President

ILCA's mission is to enhance the professionalism and capabilities of members by providing leadership, education and valued services while promoting environmental awareness within the landscape industry. Sponsor or Mid-Am Horticulture Trade Show.
Founded in 1959

11645 **International Society of Arboriculture**
1400 W Anthony Drive
PO Box 3129
Champaign, IL 61826

217-355-9411
888-472-8733
Fax: 217-355-9516
E-Mail: isa@isa-arbor.com
Home Page: www.isa-arbor.com
Social Media: Facebook, Twitter, LinkedIn, YouTube, RSS

Jim Skiera, Executive Director
Jerri Moorman, Executive Assistant
Mark Bluhm, Director, Finance & Operations
Keely Roy, Director, Marketing
Sharon Lilly, Director, Educational Goods

A worldwide professional organization dedicated to fostering a greater appreciation for trees and to promoting research, technology, and the professional practice of arboriculture.

11646 **Los Angeles Community Garden Council**
4470 W Sunset Blvd
#381
Los Angeles, CA 90027

847-864-5781
Fax: 847-448-8805
Home Page: www.lagardencouncil.org
Social Media: Facebook

Connect people with community garden space in their neighborhoods.

11647 **Mailorder Gardening Association**
PO Box 429
LaGrange, GA 30241

706-298-0022
Fax: 706-883-8215
E-Mail: consumer@mailordergardening.com
Home Page: www.mailordergardening.com
Social Media: Facebook, Twitter, LinkedIn

Greg Brown, President
Frank DiPaolo, 1st VP
Mike Zuckermandel, 2nd VP
Clare Liberis, Secretary
Polly Welch, Treasurer

Mail-order suppliers of gardening and nursery stock and supplies.
210 Members
Founded in 1934

11648 **National Council of Commercial Plant Breeders**
1701 Duke Street
Suite 275
Alexandria, VA 22314

703-299-6633
E-Mail: ajorss@amseed.org
Home Page: www.nccpb.org

Stephen Smith, President
Andrew LaVigne, Executive Vice President
Tom Koch, 1st Vice President
Marcelo Queijo, 2nd Vice President
Ann Jorss, Secretary/Treasurer

A non-profit organization to promote the achievement and interest of American plant breeders both in the United States and abroad.

11649 **National Pest Management Association**
10460 North Street
Fairfax, VA 22030

703-352-6762
800-678-6722
Fax: 703-352-3031
Home Page: www.npmapestworld.org
Social Media: Facebook, Twitter, Flickr

Gary McKenzie, CFO
Bob Rosenberg, EVP
Jean Baum, Executive Assistant
Gene Harrington, VP, Govt. Affairs
Dominique Stumpf, VP, Conventions & Professional Dev

Represents the interests of its members and the structural pest control industry.
7000 Members
3500 Attendees
Founded in 1933

11650 **North American Horticultural Supply Association**
100 North 20th Street
Suite 400
Philadelphia, PA 19103-3572

215-320-3877
Fax: 215-564-2175
E-Mail: nahsa@fernley.com
Home Page: www.nahsa.org

Neal Farnham, President
Richard Smith, Vice President
Charles Germano, Treasurer

Promotes full service distributors in the greenhouse and nursery hard good supply market.
120 Members
Founded in 1988

11651 **Professional Grounds Management Society**
720 Light St
Baltimore, MD 21230-3850

410-223-2861
800-609-7467
Fax: 410-752-8295
E-Mail: pgms@assnhqtrs.com
Home Page: www.pgms.org
Social Media: Facebook, Twitter, LinkedIn, YouTube, RSS

Walter Bonvell, President
John Burns, President-Elect
John Doiron, Vice President
Marion Bolick, Treasurer/Secretary

Members are professionals involved in the care and maintenance of public and private sites.
1400 Members
Founded in 1911

11652 **Professional Landcare Network**
950 Herndon Parkway
Suite 450
Herndona, GA 20170

703-736-9666
800-395-2522
Fax: 703-736-9668
E-Mail: webmaster@landcarenetwork.org
Home Page: www.landcarenetwork.org
Social Media: Facebook, Twitter, LinkedIn, YouTube

Glenn Jacobson, President
Jim McCutcheon, President-Elect

PLANET emerged from the joining of the PLCAA and the ALCA in 2005. It is an educational, professional resource for landcare, exterior maintenance and interiorscape professionals and the lawn and landscape industry.
1200 Members
Founded in 1979

11653 **Society of American Florists**
1601 Duke St
Alexandria, VA 22314-3406

703-836-8700
800-336-4743
Fax: 703-836-8705
E-Mail: webmaster@safnow.org
Home Page: www.safnow.org
Social Media: Facebook, Twitter, LinkedIn

Robert Williams, Chairman
Shirley Lyons, President
Martin Meskers, President-Elect
Dwight Larimer, Treasurer
Peter J Moran, EVP/CEO

Represents all segments of the U.S. floral industry.
12K Members
Founded in 1884

11654 **Turf Grass Producers International**
2 East Main Street
East Dundee, IL 60118

847-649-5555
800-405-8873
Fax: 847-649-5678
E-Mail: info@turfgrasssod.org

Home Page: www.turfgrasssod.org
Social Media: Facebook

Den Gardner, Editor
Lynn Grooms, Managing Editor
Veronica Iwanski, Membership & Marketing Manager
Jim Novak, Public Relations Manager
Geri Hannah, Accounting & Office Manager

An organization featuring business news and updates on legislation and agronomics concerning the turf industry.
1000 Members
Founded in 1967

Newsletters

11655 **Bulletin**
Garden Club of America
590 Madison Ave
Suite 19
New York, NY 10022-2544

212-872-1000
Fax: 212-872-1002
Home Page: www.akingump.com

Daniel H Golden, Partner

GCA's oldest publication, articles include news from GCA member clubs around the country, with reports from national committees, zones, and GCA conferences and meetings.
Cost: $8.00
Frequency: Bi-Monthly

11656 **Front Page News**
Professional Landcare Network, Inc
950 Herndon Parkway
Suite 450
Herndon, VA 20170

703-736-9666
800-395-2522
Fax: 703-736-9668
Home Page: www.landcarenetwork.org

Dan Foley, Publisher

E-newsletter with timely association and industry news and topics.
16 Pages
Frequency: Monthly

11657 **Landscape Architect and Specifier News**
George Schmok
14771 Plaza Dr
Suite M
Tustin, CA 92780-8012

714-979-5276
Fax: 714-979-3543
E-Mail: webmaster@landscapeonline.com
Home Page: www.landscapeonline.com

George Schmok, Publisher
Jim Lipot, Circulation Manager
Leslie McGuire, Managing Editor

A photographically oriented professional journal featuring topics of concern and state of the art projects designed or influenced by registered landscape architects worldwide.
Frequency: Monthly
Circulation: 29162
Printed in 4 colors on glossy stock

11658 **PLANET News Magazine**
Professional Landcare Network, Inc
950 Herndon Parkway
Suite 450
Herndon, VA 20170

703-736-9666
800-395-2522
Fax: 703-736-9668
E-Mail: info@actionletter.com
Home Page: www.landcarenetwork.org

News and information of the gardening and landscaping industries.
Frequency: Monthly

11659 **Quill and Trowel**
Garden Writers Association of America
10210 Leatherleaf Ct
Manassas, VA 20111-4245

703-257-1032
Fax: 703-257-0213
E-Mail: webmaster@gardenwriters.org
Home Page: www.gwaa.org

Robert C La Gasse, Executive Director
Ann Marie Van Nest, Vice President
Seymour Jordan, Publisher

Material of interest to garden writers and news of members of the Association.
12 Pages
Frequency: Monthly
Circulation: 1800
Founded in 1848

11660 **The Cut Flower Quarterly**
Association of Specialty Cut Flower Growers
17 1/2 W. College St.
MPO Box 268
Oberlin, OH 44074

440-774-2887
Fax: 440-774-2435
E-Mail: ascfg@oberlin.net
Home Page: www.ascfg.org

Newsletter
Cost: $175.00
Frequency: Quarterly
Circulation: 1200
ISSN: 1068-8013

11661 **The Dirt**
American Society of Landscape Architects
636 Eye Street, NW
Washington, DC 20001-3736

202-898-2444
800-787-2752
Fax: 202-898-1185
E-Mail: info@asla.org
Home Page: www.dirt.asla.org

Covers the latest news on the build and natural environments and features stories on landscape architecture.
13500 Members
Frequency: Weekly
Founded in 1899

Magazines & Journals

11662 **American Nurseryman**
American Nurseryman Publishing Company
223 W Jackson Blvd
Suite 500
Chicago, IL 60606-6911

312-427-7318
800-621-5727
Fax: 312-427-7346
E-Mail: editors@amerinursery.com
Home Page: www.amerinursery.com
Social Media: Facebook, Twitter

Allen Seidel, President
Sally Benson, Editor

Focuses on topics relevant to professional growers, landscapers and retail garden center operators.
Cost: $48.00
100 Pages
Frequency: Fortnightly
Circulation: 16000
ISSN: 0003-0198
Founded in 1904
Printed in 4 colors on glossy stock

11663 **American Rose Magazine**
American Rose Society
PO Box 30000
Shreveport, LA 71130

318-221-5026
800-637-6534
Fax: 318-938-5405
Home Page: www.ars.org

Mike Kromer, Executive Director
Beth Smiley, Editor
Benny Ellerbe, Executive Director
Marny Fife, Marketing Director

Publication focusing on rose growing, culture and enjoyment. Accepts advertising.
Cost: $37.00
Frequency: Monthly
Circulation: 21000
ISSN: 1078-5833
Founded in 1894

11664 **Casual Living**
Reed Business Information
PO Box 2754
Suite 200
High Point, NC 27261-2754

336-605-1000
800-652-2948
Fax: 336-605-1143
Home Page: www.reedbusiness.com

Kevin Castellani, President
Becky B Smith, Editor-in-Chief
Delaney Rudd, Owner
Stuart Whayman, CFO

Content includes industry lifestyle features, business analysis and product trend information.
Frequency: Monthly
Circulation: 10000
Founded in 1958

11665 **Fine Gardening**
Taunton Press
63 South Main St
PO Box 5506
Newtown, CT 06470-5506

203-706-6206
800-888-8286
Fax: 203-426-3434
E-Mail: fg@taunton.com
Home Page: www.taunton.com

LeeAnne White, Editor
Cathy Austermann, Advertising Manager
Todd Meier, Publisher
John Lagan, National Account Manager

Landscaping and ornamental gardening are the magazine's primary editorial focus. Step-by-step in-depth information for the country. Articles written by gardening experts and enthusiasts.
Cost: $29.95
83 Pages
Circulation: 202163
Founded in 1988

11666 **Florists' Review**
PO Box 4368
Topeka, KS 66604

785-266-0888
800-367-4708
Fax: 785-266-0333
E-Mail: mail@floristsreview.com
Home Page: www.floristsreview.com
Social Media: Facebook

Frances Dudley, President / Publisher
David L Coake, Editorial Director
Heather Kline, Circulation Coordinator

Lisa Strydom, Advertising Sales Director
Sue Lafferty, Account Executive

For wholesalers and retailers and desingers of fresh and dried flowers.
Cost: $42.00
Frequency: Monthly
Circulation: 28000
Founded in 1897

11667 Flowers&
Richard Salvaggio
11444 W Olympic Boulevard
Los Angeles, CA 90064-1549

310-966-3518
800-321-2665
Fax: 310-966-3610
E-Mail: flowersand@teleflora.com
Home Page: www.flowersandmagazine.com

Bruce Wright, Editor
Jill Fox, Circulation Manager
Richard Salvaggio, Publisher

Business information and tips for the retail florist.
Cost: $54.00
Frequency: Monthly
Circulation: 30,000
Founded in 1985
Printed in 4 colors on glossy stock

11668 Garden Center Magazine
GIE Media
801 Cherry St.
Suite 960 Unit 2
Fort Worth, TX 76102

817-882-4110
800-456-0707
Fax: 817-882-4121
E-Mail: greenbeam@branchsmith.com
Home Page: www.gardencentermagazine.com
Social Media: Facebook

Yale Youngblood, Publisher
Sarah Martinez, Managing Editor

Garden Center magazine has made the business decision to be the voice to serve the total market with the content to serve common needs; the business of buying, merchandising and selling of trees, ornamentals, bedding plants and related garden materials and accessories to homeowner consumers.
Cost: $90.00
Frequency: Monthly
Circulation: 16249

11669 Garden Center Merchandising & Management
Branch-Smith Publishing
120 St. Louis Avenue
PO Box 1868
Fort Worth, TX 76101

817-882-4120
800-433-5612
Fax: 817-882-4121
E-Mail: kneal@branchsmith.com
Home Page: www.greenbeam.com

Carol Miller, Editor
Patricia Kuhl, Publisher
Tiffany O'Kelley, Media Manager
Mike Branch, President
Frequency: Monthly

11670 Green Industry PRO
Cygnus Publishing
1233 Janesville Avenue
Fort Atkinson, WI 53538-0803

920-000-1111
800-547-7377
Fax: 920-563-1699
E-Mail: Grant.Dunham@cygnuspub.com
Home Page: www.cygnusb2b.com

Rick Monogue, Publisher
Gregg Wartgow, Associate Publisher
Lisa Danes, Associate Editor

A national trade publication providing the critical business information landscape contractors need for success. Readership includes the leaders of companies performing landscape management, installation, lawn care, irrigation and maintenance. Covers how to topics such as surviving and thriving through the pinch-points of growth, maximizing productivity, matching the right tools and equipment to the appliation at ahnd, and taking innovative approaches to the marketplace.
Frequency: Monthly
Circulation: 55000
Founded in 1937

11671 Greenhouse Management
GIE Media
4020 Kinross Lakes Pkwy
Richfield, OH 44286

800-456-0707
Home Page:
www.greenhousemanagementonline.com

Richard Foster, Publisher
Todd Davis, Editorial Director
Kristy O'Hara, Editor
Kelli Rodda, Managing Editor

National magazine for commercial greenhouse growers. Accepts advertising.
Frequency: Monthly

11672 Grounds Maintenance
Penton Media
249 W. 17th Street
New York, NY 10011

212-204-4200
Home Page: www.grounds-mag.com

Keeping readers informed on the latest techniques and products for gounds care. The most popular source of information for grounds maintenance professionals. Readership includes golf course superintendants, corporate/municipal groundskeepers and landscape professionals, providing them with content they trust and creating a deep source of reference and how-to information.
Frequency: Monthly
Circulation: 70000
Founded in 1966

11673 Hearth & Home
Village West Publishing
PO Box 1288
Laconia, NH 03247

603-284-4285
800-258-3772
Fax: 603-524-0643

Richard Wright, Editor
Jackie Avignone, Advertising Director

Magazine for retailers, including specialty, hardware, patio and barbecue.
Frequency: Monthly
Circulation: 17,000
Founded in 1980

11674 HortScience
American Society for Horticultural Science
1018 Duke Street
Alexandria, VA 22314-2851

703-836-4606
Fax: 703-836-2024
E-Mail: webmaster@ashs.org
Home Page: www.ashs.org
Social Media: Facebook

Michael W. Neff, Executive Director
Ruth Gaumond, Managing Editor
Tecola Forbes, Publications Coordinator

Journal of interest to a broad array of horticultural scientists and others interested in horticulture. Goals are to provide information on significant research, education, extension findings and methods, and developments and trends that affect the profession.
Frequency: Monthly
ISSN: 0018-5345
Founded in 1903

11675 HortTechnology
American Society for Horticultural Science
1018 Duke Street
Alexandria, VA 22314-2851

703-836-4606
Fax: 703-836-2024
E-Mail: webmaster@ashs.org
Home Page: www.ashs.org
Social Media: Facebook

Michael W. Neff, Executive Director
Ruth Gaumond, Managing Editor
Tecola Forbes, Publications Coordinator

Brings reliable, current, peer-reviewed technical information to help solve problems and deal with current challenges in production, education, and extension.
Frequency: Bi-Monthly
Founded in 1903

11676 Horticulture Magazine
F+W Media
10151 Carver Road
Suite 200
Cincinnati, OH 45242

513-531-2690
Fax: 513-891-7153
E-Mail: edit@hortmag.com
Home Page: www.hortmag.com
Social Media: Facebook, Twitter

Dedicated to celebrating the passion of avid gardeners, who take delight not just in gardens but in garden-making. Our informative, engaging writing and brilliant photography enables gardeners to create spaces that make them proud, beautify their hometowns and provide a gathering place for family and friends.
Frequency: Monthly

11677 Journal of Arboriculture
International Society of Arboriculture
1400 W Anthony Drive
PO Box 3129
Champaign, IL 61826

217-355-9411
888-472-8733
Fax: 217-355-9516
E-Mail: isa@isa-arbor.com
Home Page: www.isa-arbor.com

Jim Skiera, Executive Director
Jerri Moorman, Executive Assistant

Refereed journal devoted to the dissemination of knowledge in the science and art of planting and caring for trees in the urban environment. Published by the International Society of Arboriculture, whose mission is to foster a greater appreciation for trees and to promote the research, technology, and practice of professional arboriculture.
Cost: $105.00
Frequency: Bi-Monthly
Circulation: 17000
ISSN: 0278-5226
Founded in 1924

11678 Journal of the American Society for Horticultural Science
American Society for Horticultural Science

113 S West St
Suite 200
Alexandria, VA 22314-2851

703-836-4606
Fax: 703-836-2024
E-Mail: journal@ashs.org
Home Page: journal.ashspublications.org/

Neal D. De Vos, Editor in Chief
Michael W. Neff, Publisher
Ruth Gaumond, Managing Editor

Publishes papers on the results of original research on horticultural plants and their products or directly related research areas. Its prime function is to communicate mission-oriented, fundamental research to other researchers. The journal includes detailed reports of original research results on various aspects of horticultural science and directly related subjects.
Frequency: Bi-Monthly
ISSN: 0003-1062
Founded in 1903
Mailing list available for rent: 2500 names at $100 per M

11679 Landscape & Irrigation
Adams Business Media
111 W Jackson Blvd
7th Floor
Chicago, IL 60604-3589

312-846-4600
Fax: 312-977-1042
Home Page: www.adamsbusinessmedia.com

John Kmitta, Editor
Steve Brackett, VP/Group Publisher
Joanne Juda, Circulation Manager

Targets decision-makers throughout the landscape industry, from residential contractors to commercial grounds managers, to public works professionals and irrigation and water management professionals. Information includes advice from industry professionals, coverage of specific projects, details on the latest products and innovations, and news from around the world.
Cost: $57.50
Frequency: 9x Yearly
ISSN: 0745-3795

11680 Landscape Illinois
Illinois Landscape Contractors Association
2625 Butterfield Road
Suite 204W
Oak Brook, IL 60523

630-472-2851
Fax: 630-472-3150
E-Mail: information@ilca.net
Home Page: www.ilca.net

Scott Grams, Executive Director

An annual publication geared toward homeowners, business owners and consumers
36 Pages
Frequency: Monthly
Circulation: 40,000
Printed in 4 colors on glossy stock

11681 Landscape Management
Advanstar Landscape Group
7500 Old Oak Blvd
Cleveland, OH 44130-3343

440-243-8100
800-225-4569
Fax: 440-891-2740
Home Page: www.act-europe.org
Social Media: Facebook, Twitter

Tony D Avino, General Manager
Kevin Stoltman, Publisher
Michael Harris, Sales Manager
Stephanie Ricca, Managing Editor
Ron Hall, Editor In Chief

Covers news, market trends, business and operations management, technical information on horticulture and agronomy for 51,000 professional landscape contractors, lawncare operators and inhouse grounds managers.
Cost: $46.00
Frequency: Monthly
Circulation: 60,000
Founded in 1965
Printed in 4 colors on glossy stock

11682 Lawn & Landscape
Gie Publishing
4012 Bridge Avenue
Cleveland, OH 44113

216-961-4130
800-456-0707
Fax: 216-961-0364
Home Page: www.gie.net

Ron Lowy, Publisher
Dan Moreland, Executive Vice President

National trade magazine for the landscape professional. Accepts advertising.
120 Pages
Frequency: Monthly
Circulation: 73000
Founded in 1980

11683 Nursery Management
GIE Media
4020 Kinross Lakes Pkwy
Richfield, OH 44286

800-456-0707
Home Page:
www.nurserymanagementonline.com

Todd Davis, Publisher
Kelli Rodda, Editor

Nurserymen, landscapers and garden centers. Accepts advertising.
Cost: $24.00
136 Pages
Frequency: Monthly
Founded in 1910

11684 Nursery Retailer
Brentwood Publications
3023 Eastland Boulevard
Clearwater, FL 33761-4106

727-724-0200
Fax: 727-724-0021
Home Page: www.nurseryretailer.com

Jeff Morey, President & Publisher
Cheryl Morey, Vice President & Publisher

News of retail growers.
Cost: $15.00
Frequency: Bi-Monthly
Founded in 1955

11685 Power Equipment Trade
Hatton-Brown Publishers
225 Hanrick Street
PO Box 2268
Montgomery, AL 36102-2268

334-834-1170
800-669-5613
Fax: 334-834-4525
E-Mail: rich@hattonbrown.com
Home Page: www.poweret.com

David H Ramsey, Co-Publisher
DK Knight, CEO
Rich Donnell, Editor

Leading publication in the power equipment community. Articles include profiles on successful power equipment retailers (dealers) and manufacturers and accounts pertaining to technology, market trends and timely issues.
Frequency: 10x Yearly
Circulation: 21788
ISSN: 0163-0414
Founded in 1952

11686 Southern Nursery Digest
Betrock Information Systems
7770 Davie Road Ext
Hollywood, FL 33024-2516

954-810-0300
Fax: 954-438-2632

Irv Betrock, Editor
Sean Patrick, Manager

This comprehensive magazine covers the gardening and nursery business in the south.
Frequency: Monthly

11687 The American Gardener
Amerian Horticultural Society
7931 E Boulevard Dr
Alexandria, VA 22308-1300

703-768-5700
800-777-7931
Fax: 703-768-8700
E-Mail: dhundley@ahs.org
Home Page: www.ahs.org

Tom Underwood, Executive Director
Harry Rissetto, Chair
Mary Pat Matheson, 1st Vice Chair
Leslie Ariail, Secretary
J. Landon Reeve, Treasurer

Features inspiring color photographs and in-depth articles on new and native plants, influetial garden personalities, garden history, and earth friendly gardening techniques and products. Also regular departments on design, children's gardening, conservation issues, and reviews of the latest gardening books, as well as a calendar of gardening events nationwide.
27M Members
Founded in 1922

11688 The Cut Flower Quarterly
Association of Specialty Cut Flower Growers
17 1/2 W. College St.
MPO Box 268
Oberlin, OH 44074

440-774-2887
Fax: 440-774-2435
E-Mail: ascfg@oberlin.net
Home Page: www.ascfg.org

Judy Laushman, Executive Director
Vicki Stamback, President
Leah Cook, Vice-President
Andrea Gagnon, Treasurer
Carolyn Tschetter, Secretary

The only regular publication dedicated to information about the production, postharvest care and marketing of cut flowers.
700 Members
Frequency: Quarterly
Founded in 1988

11689 The Landscape Contractor
Illinois Landscape Contractors Association
2625 Butterfield Road
Suite 204W
Oak Brook, IL 60523

630-472-2851
Fax: 630-472-3150
E-Mail: information@ilca.net
Home Page: www.ilca.net

Scott Grams, Executive Director

Providing readers with news and developments in the industry with emphasis on regional concerns. Read by ILCA members and nonmembers who own, manage or supervise exterior and interior design/guild and maintenance firms, nurseries and garden centers, landscape architectural firms, as well as the staffs of parks and recreation districts and landscape industry professionals throughout the Midwest.
Cost: $75.00
Frequency: Monthly
Founded in 1959

11690 **Tomato Country**
Columbia Publishing
8405 Ahtanum Rd
Yakima, WA 98903-9432

509-248-2452
800-900-2452
Fax: 509-248-4056
Home Page: www.tomatomagazine.com

Brent Clement, Editor/Publisher
Mike Stoker, Publisher

Includes information on tomato production and marketing, grower and shipper feature stories, tomato research, from herbicide and pesticide studies to new varieties, market reports, feedback from major tomato meetings and conventions, along with other key issues and points of interest for USA and Canada tomato growers.
Cost: $12.00

11691 **Turf News**
Turf Grass Producers International
2 East Main Street
East Dundee, IL 60118

847-649-5555
800-405-8873
Fax: 847-649-5678
E-Mail: info@turfgrasssod.org
Home Page: www.turfgrasssod.org

Kirk T Hunter, Executive Director

The only magazine devoted exclusively to turfgrass sod production. focuses on the business of turfgrass by targeting farm owners and managers. A valuable tool for suppliers and manufacturers, featuring industry trends, product news, technical information, marketing, research, government issues, human resources, seed & planting stock, equipment/machinery, farm profiles, as well as vital industry and association news.
Frequency: Bi-Monthly
Circulation: 1600
Founded in 1977

11692 **Yard and Garden**
Cygnus Publishing
PO Box 803
Fort Atkinson, WI 53538-0803

920-000-1111
800-547-7377
Fax: 920-563-1699
E-Mail: noel.brown@cygnuspub.com
Home Page: www.cygnusb2b.com

John French, CEO
Dan Newman, Director of Public Relations
Kathy Scott, Director of Public Relations
Paul Bonaiuto, CFO

A national trade publication providing the critical business information independent outdoor power equipment servicing dealers need for success. Readership includes the owners and managers of full-service outdoor power equipment dealerships serving both commercial and residential customers. Focuses on retail trends, management strategies, dealer best practices, supplier news, and the latest products and services to hit the lawn and garden marketplace.
Frequency: 8x Yearl
Circulation: 17504
Founded in 1977

Trade Shows

11693 **ASCA's Annual Conference**
American Society of Consulting Arborists
9707 Key West Avenue
Suite 100
Rockville, MD 20850-3222

301-947-0483
Fax: 301-990-9771
E-Mail: asca@mgmtsol.com
Home Page: www.asca-consultants.org

James R. Clark, Ph.D, President
Gordon Mann, President Elect

Recognized as a high quality, in depth conference with cutting edge speakers. Combining the best forum for discussion of current and relevant arboricultural issues, as well as consulting practice management issues and key consulting topics such as the role of the expert witness, risk assessment and tree appraisal.

11694 **ASHS Annual Conference**
American Society for Horticultural Science
1018 Duke Street
Alexandria, VA 22314-2851

703-836-4606
Fax: 703-836-2024
E-Mail: webmaster@ashs.org
Home Page: www.ashs.org
Social Media: Faccbook

Fred T. Davies, Chair
Dewayne Ingram, President
Paul Bosland, President-Elect

Attracts US and international horticulturists who attend to learn about research and new developments in horticulture.
Frequency: Annual/August

11695 **American Nursery & Landscape Association Convention**
American Nursery & Landscape Association
1200 G Street NW
Suite 800
Washington, DC 20005

202-789-2900
Fax: 202-789-1893
Home Page: www.anla.org
Social Media: Facebook

Robert S. Lyons, President
Robert Terry, President-Elect

Serves firms who grow, sell or use plants. ANLA advocates the industry's interests before government and provides its members with unique business knowledge essential to long-term growth and profitability.
Frequency: Annual/July

11696 **American Society of Irrigation Consultants Conference**
PO Box 426
Byron, CA 94514-0426

925-516-1124
Fax: 925-516-1301

Wanda M Sarsfield, Secretary

Addressing major industry issues and learn from each other and leading experts in irrigation, water management and related fields. Member participate in the conference to showcase the latest in irrigation solution technology and services.
Frequency: Annual
Founded in 1970

11697 **American Society of Landscape Architects Annual Meeting & Educational Expo**
636 Eye Street NW
Washington, DC 20001-3736

202-898-2444
800-787-2752
Fax: 202-898-1185
E-Mail: info@asla.org
Home Page: www.asla.org

Nancy Somerville, Executive Vice President
Gerald Beaulieu, CFO/Director Business Operations

Landscape architect ecucational session and workshop plus 500 exibits of outdoor lighting, playground and park equipment, landscape maintanence equipment, computer hardware and software and much more.
4700 Attendees

11698 **Annual Convention of the International Lilac Society**
9500 Sperry Road
Kirtland, OH 44094

440-946-4400
Fax: 216-256-1655

Exhibits on lilacs, including innovative cultivation and the use of lilacs in public and private landscaping.
Frequency: Annual
Founded in 1974

11699 **Annual Fort Worth Home & Garden Show**
International Exhibitions
1635 W Alabama
Houston, TX 77006

713-295-5366
Fax: 713-529-0936

The place to experience what's new in home, gardening, remodeling, home decor, and much more. Meet over 400 experts and experience thousands of products and services.
40000 Attendees

11700 **Annual Gulf Coast Home & Garden Expo**
Exposition Enterprises of Alabama
PO Box 430
Pinson, AL 35126

205-680-0234
Fax: 205-680-0615

Like a well tended garden, the show keeps growing and growing.
12000 Attendees

11701 **Central Environmental Nursery Trade Show (CENTS)**
Ohio Nursery & Landscape Association
72 Dorchester Square
Westerville, OH 43081-3350

614-991-1195
800-825-5062
Fax: 614-899-9489
E-Mail: info@onla.org
Home Page: www.onla.org/cents
Social Media: Facebook, LinkedIn

Jay Daley, President
Andy Harding, President-Elect
Kevin Thompson, Executive Director
Tracie Zody, Trade Show/Even Manager

Innovations and ideas in an expanded market.
Frequency: Annual/January

11702 **Farwest**
2780 SE Harrison Street
Suite 102
Milwaukie, OR 97222-7574

FAX 503-653-1528

Clayton Hannon, Executive Director

775 booths promoting the sale and exchange of nursery/landscape products and services.
13M Attendees
Frequency: August

11703 GIE+EXPO - Green Industry & Equipment Expo
Professional Lawncare Network, Inc
222 Pearl Street
Suite 300
New Albany, IN 47150
812-949-9200
800-558-8767
Fax: 812-949-9600
E-Mail: info@gie-expo.com
Home Page: www.gie-expo.com
Anna Demoret, Trade Show Coordinator
Annual show of 400 manufacturers, suppliers and distributors of lawn care equipment, supplies and services, including fertilizers, weed control materials, insurance information and power equipment. Take advantage of the education sessions and presentations and demos, as well as six-hundred and fifty booths.
Frequency: Annual

11704 Green Industry Conference - GIC
Professional Lawncare Network, Inc (PLANET)
950 Herndon Parkway
Suite 450
Herndon, VA 20170
703-736-9666
800-395-2522
Fax: 703-736-9668
E-Mail: info@gie-expo.com
Home Page: www.landcarenetwork.or/cmc/gic.html
Keep current as a green industry professional. Stay tuned in to the new technology, products and services hitting the market every year. Hone your skills with applicable education that you can practice immediately. Green industry firms in all market segments including landscape management, lawn care, design, build and installation, irrigation and water management should attend.
Frequency: Annual

11705 Green Industry Great Escape
Professional Landcare Network
950 Herndon Parkway
Suite 450
Herndona, GA 20170
703-736-9666
800-395-2522
Fax: 703-736-9668
E-Mail: webmaster@landcarenetwork.org
Home Page: www.landcarenetwork.org
Social Media: Facebook, Twitter, LinkedIn, YouTube
Gerald J. Grossi, President
Norman Goldenberg, President-Elect
An annual destination meeting for upper-level management, owners, and key personnel.
1200 Members
Founded in 1979

11706 Green Profit's Retail Experience
Green Profit Magazine
335 N River Street
Batavia, IL 60510
630-208-9080
888-888-0013
Fax: 630-208-9350
E-Mail: info@ballpublishing.com
Home Page: www.ballpublishing.com/conferences
Michelle Mazza, Show Manager
Educational event and tradeshow dedicated exclusively to garden center retailing. Covers topics from store layout and design to merchandising strategies and business management. 20 booths
300 Attendees
Frequency: Annual/September
Founded in 2006

11707 Interior Plantscape Symopsium
Professional Landcare Network
950 Herndon Parkway
Suite 450
Herndon, VA 20170
703-736-9666
800-395-2522
Fax: 703-736-9668
E-Mail: webmaster@landcarenetwork.org
Home Page: www.plcaa.org/conference
Social Media: Facebook, Twitter, LinkedIn, YouTube
Education will offer practical training for the front line with opportunities to earn CEUs toward Landscape Industry Certified Technician recertification as well as pesticide credits. Attendees will walk away with knowledge on how to run their businesses more effectively and keep customers happy. Technicians will learn cutting-edge techniques to make their jobs easier.
Frequency: Annual/April

11708 International Floriculture Expo
207-842-5508
Fax: 207-842-5509
E-Mail: floriexpo@divcom.com
Home Page: www.floriexpo.com
Where buyers and suppliers from each stage of the floriculture production cycle come together to network, teach and learn from one another. With the live products, equipment, technology and education necessary for cultivating and retailing, find the ideas, new products, suppliers, trends and tools to flourish in the US market. Open to all buyers within the floriculture industry.
Frequency: Annual

11709 International Floriculture Trade Fair (IFTF)
Trade Show Bookings
PO Box 499
Fresh Meadows, NY 11365-0499
George Birne, Show Manager
The industry wide event serving all segments of the floriculture chain, from breeders, propagators, growers to the fresh flower trade.
40M Attendees
Frequency: Annual/November

11710 International Lawn Garden & Power Equipment Expo
Andry Montgomery and Associates
550 S 4th Avenue
#200
Louisville, KY 40202-2504
FAX 502-473-1999
Warren Sellers, Show Manager
The dream trade show for those interested in the concept of more power. The show is filled with outdoor lawn equipment that could do more faster, more quietly, more efficiently, and with the least amount of emissions.
25M Attendees
Frequency: Annual/July

11711 International Symposium on Orchids and Ornamental Plants
Home Page: www.orchidsociety.com
There are 75 booths and 50 exhibits that include bonsai trees, pots, tools and supplies, orchids, live plants and supplies for orchids and more.
Frequency: Annual/January

11712 Lawn & Garden Marketing & Distribution Summit Conference
2105 Laurel Bush Road
Suite 200
Bel Air, MD 21015
443-640-1080
Fax: 443-640-1031
Home Page: www.lgmda.org
Steven T King, Executive VP
Marci L Hickey, Director Meetings/Member Services
Amy Chetelat, Financial Manager
Lawn and garden products. 120 booths.
500 Attendees
Frequency: Bi-Annual

11713 Lawn, Flower and Patio Show
Mid-America Expositions, Inc
7015 Spring Street
Omaha, NE 68106-3518
402-346-8003
800-475-7469
Fax: 402-346-5412
E-Mail: info@showofficeonline.com
Home Page: www.showofficeonline.com
Robert P Mancuso, CEO
Mike Mancuso, VP/Manager
Annual show and exhibits of equipment, supplies and services for the lawn, flower and patio.
Frequency: Annual/February

11714 Mid Atlantic Nursery Trade Show
PO Box 11739
Baltimore, MD 21206-0339
410-882-5300
Carville Akehurst, Executive VP
Landscaping materials and horticultural tools. 750 booths, nursery stock, garden center and greenhouse supplies. 750 booths.
7.1M Attendees
Frequency: Annual/January

11715 Mid-Atlantic Nursery Trade Show
Mid Atlantic Nurserymen's Trade Shows
PO Box 818
Brooklandville, MD 21022
800-431-0066
Fax: 410-296-8288
Widely known as the masterpiece of trade shows.
11M Attendees
Founded in 1970

11716 Midwest Herb and Garden Show
PO Box 3434
Omaha, NE 68103-0434
Jane Booth, Show Manager
With vendors from throughout the midwest and nationally known speakers, this event is geared for everyone from the novice to master gardeners. Exhibitors display a variety of items including fresh herbs, herbs for culinary, medicinal, and decorative use, bulbs, seeds, books on birds, herbs and gardening, plans, herbal cookbooks, gardening magazines, bird feeders, houses and baths, antiques, china, spices, trellises, gourds, orchids, fudge, and much more.
15M Attendees
Frequency: Annual/February

11717 National City Home & Garden Show
Expositions
PO Box 550
Edgewater Branch
Cleveland, OH 44107-0550
216-529-1300
Fax: 216-529-0311

E-Mail: showinfo@expoinc.com
Home Page: www.expoinc.com

Featuring showcases on how to make your dream home a reality. Create the garden oasis, backyard retreat or a relaxing sanctuary.
35000 Attendees
Frequency: Annual/February

11718 **National Lawn & Garden Trade Show**
Great American Exhibitions
112 Main Street
Norwalk, CT 06851

203-498-8735
Fax: 203-845-9183

Ronald Gratt, Manager

Sole mission has been to provide an affordable, efficient, alternative to traditional tradeshows which assures buyer/vendor introductions in preset scheduled appointments.
5000 Attendees
Frequency: Annual

11719 **National Lawn and Garden Show**
Controlled Marketing Conferences
PO Box 1771
Monument, CO 80132

719-488-0226
888-316-0226
Fax: 719-488-8168
Home Page: www.nlgshow.com
Social Media: Facebook, Twitter, LinkedIn

Bob Mikulas, President

This is the lawn and gardens premier headlines event and features both a pre-set scheduled appointment division and a traditional booth division.
300 Attendees
Frequency: June
Founded in 1995

11720 **National Pest Management Association Annual Eastern Conference**
10460 North Street
Fairfax, VA 22030

703-352-6762
Fax: 703-352-3031
E-Mail: info@pestworld.com
Home Page: www.npmapestworld.org
Social Media: Facebook, Twitter

Robert Lederer, Executive VP
7000 Members
3500 Attendees
Frequency: January
Foundod in 1933

11721 **Novi Expo Backyard, Pool and Spa Show**
Show Span
1400 28th Street SW
Grand Rapids, MI 48509

616-530-1919
800-328-6550
Fax: 616-530-2122
E-Mail: events@showspan.com
Home Page: www.showspan.com

Melissa Moore
Mike Wilbraham, President
Adam Starr, Manager
Molly Harrison, Administrative Assistant

Held at the Novi Expo Center in Novi, Michigan.

11722 **Nursery/Landscape Expo**
Texas Nursery & Landscape Association
7730 S IH-35
Austin, TX 78745-6698

512-280-5182
800-880-0343
Fax: 512-280-3012
E-Mail: info@txnla.org
Home Page: www.txnla.org

Ed Edmonson, Show Manager
Amy Prenger, President
Nancy Sollohub, Executive Assistant
Darlene Lanham, Communications Manager

Learn about industry trends, experience the breadth and depth of the green industry all under one roof, network, hear about industry best practices from peers and industry experts, and find the best deals from the best dealers in the southwest and beyond.
11M Attendees
Frequency: Annual/August

11723 **Old House New House Home Show**
Kennedy Productions
1208 Lisle Place
Lisle, IL 60532

630-515-1160
Fax: 630-515-1165
E-Mail: info@kennedyproductions.com
Home Page: www.kennedyproductions.com
Social Media: Facebook

Laura McNamara, Event Producer

Over 300 home improvement exhibitors displaying cutting-edge home enhancements for kitchens, baths, home and garden including landscape, interior remodeling, pools, spas, floors, doors and more.
8000 Attendees
Frequency: Bi-Annual
Founded in 1984

11724 **Perennial Production Conference**
335 N River Street
Batavia, IL 60510

630-208-9080
888-888-0013
Fax: 630-208-9350
Home Page: ofaconferences.org

Michelle Mazza, Show Manager

Perennial producers of all levels are urged to attend this unique event, which offers an educational and networking experience focused 100 percent on perennials. Learn everything about perennial production and retailing through workshops, seminars, tours, and a trade show.
600 Attendees
Frequency: Annual/September
Founded in 2003

11725 **Tropical Plant Industry Exhibition**
Florida Nursery Growers Landscape Association
1533 Park Center Drive
Orlando, FL 32835

407-295-7994
800-375-3642
Fax: 407-295-1619
E-Mail: info@fngla.org
Home Page: www.fngla.org/tpie/
Social Media: Facebook, Twitter, LinkedIn

Linda Adams, Show Manager
Sabrina Haines, Trade Show Coordinator

The trade event showcasing the latest trends in foliage, floral and tropicals. More than an exhibit area, it's 200,000 square feet of living and vibrant plants creating a virtual indoor garden of showstopping displays.
8,000 Attendees
Frequency: Annual/January

Directories & Databases

11726 **Complete Directory of Home Gardening Products**
Sutton Family Communications & Publishing Company
920 State Route 54 East
Elmitch, KY 42343

270-276-9500
E-Mail: jlsutton@apex.net

Theresa Sutton, Editor
Lee Sutton, General Manager

Print-out from database of wholesalers, manufacturers, distributors, importers and close-out houses. Database is updated daily to guarantee the most current and up-to-date sources available.
Cost: $39.50
100+ Pages

11727 **Complete Directory of Horticulture**
Sutton Family Communications & Publishing Company
920 State Route 54 East
Elmitch, KY 42343

270-276-9500
E-Mail: jlsutton@apex.net

Theresa Sutton, Editor
Lee Sutton, General Manager

Print-out from database of wholesalers, manufacturers, distributors, importers and close-out houses. Database is updated daily to guarantee the most current and up-to-date sources available.
Cost: $39.50
100+ Pages

11728 **DGA Membership Directory**
Mailorder Gardening Association
5836 Rockburn Woods Way
Elkridge, MD 21075-7302

410-540-9830
Fax: 410-540-9827
Home Page: www.mailordergardening.com

Camille Cimino, Executive Director

Member catalogers who sell gardening and nursery stock and supplies to consumers.
Cost: $2.00
Frequency: Annual

Industry Web Sites

11729 **http://gold.greyhouse.com**
G.O.L.D Grey House OnLine Databases

Grey House Publishing's online database platform, GOLD, offers Quick Search, Keyword Search and Expert Search for most business sectors including garden and lawncare markets. The GOLD platform makes finding the information you need quick and easy - whether you're a novice searcher or an experienced database user. All of Grey House's directory products are available for subscription on the GOLD platform.

11730 **www.ahs.org**
American Horticultural Society

Individuals, institutions and businesses interested in a wide range of horticultural concerns.

11731 **www.ahta.org**
American Horticultural Therapy Association

Professional therapists, rehabilitation specialists and others using horticulture as a medium of rehabilitation.

11732 **www.aifd.org**
American Institute of Floral Designers
Non-profit association to support the floral design industry.

11733 **www.anla.org**
American Nursery & Landscape Association
The American Nursery and Landscape Association serves firms who grow, sell or use plants. ANLA advocates the industry's interests before government and provides its members with unique business knowledge essential to long-term growth and profitability.

11734 **www.ascfg.org**
Association of Specialty Cut Flower Growers
Trade association that provides cultural and marketing information to specialty cut flower growers.

11735 **www.asla.org**
American Society of Landscape Architects
Landscape architects.

11736 **www.emda.net**
Farm Equipment Wholesalers Association
International trade association of wholesale/distributors of ag equipment and related products.

11737 **www.gardenwriters.org**
Garden Writers Association of America
A organization with materials of interest to garden writers and news on members of the Association.

11738 **www.greyhouse.com**
Grey House Publishing
Authoritative reference directories for most business sectors including garden and lawncare markets. Users can search the online databases with varied search criteria allowing for custom searches by product category, geographic area, sales volume, keyword, subject and more. Full Grey House catalog and online ordering also available.

11739 **www.landcarenetwork.org**
Professional Landcare Network
Lawn care companies, manufacturers/suppliers, ground managers and university personnel comprise membership of PLCAA. PLCAA is an educational, professional resource for the lawn and landscape industry.

11740 **www.mailordergardening.com**
Mailorder Gardening Association
Mail-order suppliers of gardening and nursery stock and supplies.

11741 **www.nahsa.org**
North American Horticultural Supply Association
Promotes full service distributors in the greenhouse and nursery hard good supply market.

11742 **www.pgms.org/**
Professional Grounds Management Society
Members are professionals involved in the care and maintenance of public and private sites.

11743 **www.safnow.org**
Society of American Florists
Represents all segments of the U.S. floral industry.

11744 **www.turfgrasssod.org**
Turf Grass Producers International
An organization featuring business news and updates on legislation and agronomics concerning the turf industry.

11745 **www.turfzone.com**
Turf Zone
Includes, commerical lawn care, consumer lawn care, irrigation equipment, fertilizer and other turf products.

11746 **www2.gcamerica.org**
Garden Club of America
Bestows awards, maintains a library and more.

Associations

11747 **American Craft Council**
1224 Marshall St. NW
Suite 200
Minneapolis, MN 55413

612-206-3100
800-836-3470
Fax: 612-355-2330
E-Mail: council@craftcouncil.org
Home Page: www.craftcouncil.org
Social Media: Facebook, Twitter, Flickr, YouTube, RSS

Chris Amundsen, Executive Director
Alanna Nissen, Office Coordinator
Greg Allen, Director, Finance & Administration
Claudia Cackler, Director, Development
Pamela Diamond, Director, Marketing & Communication

The American Craft Council is a national, non-profit educational organization to champion craft.
Founded in 1943

11748 **Gift & Home Trade Association**
2550 Sandy Plains Road
Suite 225, PO Box 214
Marietta, GA 30066

877-600-4872
E-Mail: info@giftandhome.org
Home Page: www.giftandhome.org
Social Media: Facebook, Twitter, LinkedIn

John Keiser, Chairman
Todd Litzman, President
Bob Ricciardi, Vice President
Joe Harris, Treasurer
Cindy Henry, Secretary

The association was designed to help and encourage vendors, sales agencies, industry affiliates and retailers to work together, improving relationships and making business better by providing members with the opportunity to exchange ideas and network with industry leaders.
Founded in 2000

11749 **Gift Association of America**
115 Rolling Hills Road
Johnstown, PA 15905-5225

814-288-3893

Michael Russo, President

Gift association comprised of retailers and wholesalers in the gift industry.
Founded in 1592

11750 **Museum Store Association**
3773 E Cherry Creek North Drive
#755
Denver, CO 80246-3055

303-504-9223
Fax: 303-504-9585
E-Mail: info@museumstoreassociation.org
Home Page: www.museumstoreassociation.org
Social Media: Facebook, Twitter, LinkedIn, Pinterest

Jama Rice, CEO/Executive Director
Andrea Miller, Manager Of Learning
Kathy Cisar, Communications Manager
Jennifer Anderson, Meetings & Conference Manager

Providing member representatives with the professional opportunities and educational resources they need to operate effectively and ethically.
2500 Members
Founded in 1955

11751 **National Gift Organization**
332 Hurst Mill N
Bremen, GA 30110

505-798-0375
800-446-2533
Home Page: www.naled.org

Ken Shirley, President

Trade association for the gift and collectibles industry. Offers once yearly expositions, a newsletter, software, low cost credit card processing, telephone service discounts and more to help you run your business profitably.
350 Members

11752 **National Specialty Gift Association**
PO Box 843
Norman, OK 73070

405-329-7847

Joni Damico, Executive Director

Specialty gift resource center for retailers, wholesale vendors and related professionals.
Cost: $29.95
400 Members
Founded in 1998

11753 **Organization of Associated Salespeople in the Southwest/OASIS**
15591 W Yucatan Drive
Surprise, AZ 85379

602-952-2050
800-424-9519
Fax: 602-952-2244
E-Mail: information@oasis.org
Home Page: www.oasis.org
Social Media: Facebook

Kristi Thomas, Media Relations

A gift trade association which represents the manufacturing, sales and distribution side of the giftware industry. OASIS exhibitors offer trend setting general merchandise, world imports, home d,cor, jewelry, Native American art and crafts, western flair and southwestern gifts.
Founded in 1976

Magazines & Journals

11754 **American Craft Magazine**
American Craft Council
1224 Marshall St. NW
Suite 200
Minneapolis, MN 55413

612-206-3100
800-836-3470
Fax: 612-355-2330
E-Mail: council@craftcouncil.org
Home Page: www.craftcouncil.org

Chris Amundsen, Executive Director
Alanna Nissen, Office Coordinator
Greg Allen, Director, Finance & Administration
Claudia Cackler, Director, Development
Pamela Diamond, Director, Marketing & Communication

Official magazine of the American Craft Council containing contemporary craft art and happenings of the Council.
Cost: $25.00
Frequency: 6x/Year
Founded in 1943

11755 **Gift Basket Review**
Festivities Publications
815 Haines Street
Jacksonville, FL 32206-6025

904-634-1902
800-729-6338
Fax: 904-633-8764
Home Page: www.festivities-pub.com

Debra Paulk, Publisher
Kathy Horak, Managing Editor

Magazine devoted to issues relating to the gift basket and gift packing industries.
Cost: $29.94
Frequency: Monthly
Circulation: 15000
Founded in 1990

11756 **Gifts & Decorative Accessories**
Reed Business Information
360 Park Ave S
4th Floor
New York, NY 10010-1737

646-805-0234
Fax: 646-756-7583
E-Mail: corporatecommunications@reedbusiness.com
Home Page: www.giftsanddec.com

Caroline Kennedy, Editor in Chief
Kathy Krassner, Editor at Large
Pamela Brill, Editor at Large

Serves retailers of stationery, greeting cards, collectibles, china, glass, lamps, and accessories.
Cost: $49.95
Frequency: Monthly
Circulation: 23737
ISSN: 0016-9889
Founded in 1946
Printed in 4 colors on glossy stock

11757 **Giftware News**
Talcott Communications Corporation
20 W Kinzie St
12th Floor
Chicago, IL 60654-5827

312-849-2220
800-229-1967
Fax: 312-849-2174
Home Page: www.talcott.com
Social Media: Twitter

Daniel Von Rabenau, Executive Director
Claire Weingarden, Associate Editor
John Saxtan, Editor in Chief

Edited for gift, stationery and department stores.
Cost: $39.00
Frequency: 18x Yearly
Circulation: 60000
Founded in 1982

11758 **Museum Store**
Museum Store Association
4100 E Mississippi Ave
Suite 800
Denver, CO 80246-3055

303-504-9223
Fax: 303-504-9585
E-Mail: info@museumstoreassociation.org
Home Page: www.museumstoreassociation.org
Social Media: Facebook, Twitter, LinkedIn

Beverly J Barsook, Executive Director
Valerie Troyansky, President
Beth Ricker, 1st Vice President
Stacey Stachow, 2nd Vice President

Providing ideas, tips, insights and unique product sources for nonprofit retailers.
2500 Members
Frequency: Quarterly
Founded in 1955

11759 **Souvenirs, Gifts & Novelties Magazine**
Kane Communications

7000 Terminal Square
Suite 210
Upper Darby, PA 19082-2330

610-734-2420
Fax: 610-734-2423
Home Page: www.souvmag.com

Scott Borowsky, President
Mary Anne Peacocti, Director Circulation
Caroline Burns, Managing Editor
Larry White, VP Marketing

Serves the general gift and trend marketplace with a core readership in the tourism and resorts gift and apparel stores.
Cost: $30.00
140 Pages
Frequency: 8x Yearly
Circulation: 43085
Founded in 1962
Printed in 4 colors on glossy stock

Trade Shows

11760 **ASD/AMD National Trade Show**
ASD/AMD Merchandise Group
2950 31st Street
Suite 100
Santa Monica, CA 90405

310-255-4633
Fax: 310-396-8476

The nation's largest, most comprehensive merchandise trade show. Featuring thousands of exhibitors, carrying products in more than 100 catebories, from jewelry and home decor to fashion accessories and general discount merchandise items.
10000 Attendees
Frequency: Annual/March

11761 **ASD/AMD's Gift Expo**
ASD/AMD Merchandise Group
2950 31st Street
Suite 100
Santa Monica, CA 90405

310-396-6006
800-421-4511
Fax: 310-399-2662
Home Page: www.merchandisegroup.com

Julie Ichiba, Show Director

A general merchandise event which attracts over 50,000 buyers to Las Vegas. Tens of thousands of unique products in hundreds of popular consumer product categories are on display at this event.
55000 Attendees
Frequency: Bi-Annual

11762 **Accent on Design**
George Little Management
10 Bank Street
Suite 1200
White Plains, NY 10606-1954

914-486-6070
800-272-7469
Fax: 914-948-2867
Home Page: www.nyigf.com

Elizabeth Murphy, Manager
George Little II, President

370 booths of the latest and most innovative gift lines such as decorative accessories and home furnishings.
50M Attendees
Frequency: Annual/August
Founded in 1999

11763 **American Craft Council Show**
American Craft Council
1224 Marshall St. NW
Suite 200
Minneapolis, MN 55413

612-206-3100
800-836-3470
Fax: 612-355-2330
E-Mail: council@craftcouncil.org
Home Page: www.craftcouncil.org

Chris Amundsen, Executive Director
Alanna Nissen, Office Coordinator
Greg Allen, Director, Finance & Administration
Claudia Cackler, Director, Development
Pamela Diamond, Director, Marketing & Communication

The American Craft Council Show presents outstanding works by America's leading craftspeople for purchase by the public and to the trade
Founded in 1943

11764 **Annual Dickens Christmas Show and Festival**
Leisure Time Unlimited
2101 N. Oak Street
Myrtle Beach, SC 29577

843-448-9483
800-261-5991
Fax: 843-626-1513
E-Mail: dickensshow@sc.rr.com
Home Page: www.dickenschristmasshow.com
Social Media: Facebook, Twitter

Linda Cremer, Show Director

Victorian craft and gift show.
28000 Attendees
Frequency: Annual/November
Founded in 1981

11765 **Annual Spring New Products Show**
Pacific Expositions
1580 Makaola Street
Suite 1200
Honnolulu, HI 96814-3801

808-945-3594
Fax: 808-946-6399

Pat Shine, General Sales Manager
Kimalar K Carrol, Show Director/Coordinator

Over 200 New Products Booth Displays featuring for the entire family. All categories of consumer products and service are presented: roofing, siding, jewerly, cosmetics, cars, boats, home improvement products. Over 75 Food & Crafts displays, Sportscards & memorabilia displays.
18000 Attendees
Frequency: Annual/April
Founded in 1974

11766 **GHTA Annual Conference**
Gift & Home Trade Association
4380 Brockton Drive SE
Suite 1
Grand Rapids, MI 49512

877-600-4872
E-Mail: info@giftandhome.org
Home Page: www.giftandhome.org

Marc Rice, Chairman of the Board
Julie Dix, President
John Keiser, Vice President
Todd Litzman, Treasurer
Denny King, Secretary

GHTA has partnered with the Gift Associates Interchange Network, Inc. (GAIN) to form a new credit reporting interchange. The interchange will give GHTA members access to retailer payment experiences, flash notices, predictive payment scoring, educational resources and more.
Frequency: Annual
Founded in 2000

11767 **General Gifts: A Division of the New York International Gift Fair**
George Little Management
10 Bank Street
White Plains, NY 10606-1954

914-486-6070
800-272-7469
Fax: 914-948-6180
Home Page: www.nyigf.com

George Little II, President

Featuring stationary, collectibles, ceramic giftware, toys, pet items, party lines, trend merchandise, premiums, trim-a-tree, souvenirs and novelties, specialty foods, home office, floral & garden accessories, Judaica, and general items.
Frequency: Biennial

11768 **Grand Strand Gift and Resort Merchandise Show**
Fairchild Urban Expositions
5500 Interstate N Parkway
Suite 520
Atlanta, GA 30328

770-952-6444
Fax: 770-956-9644
Social Media: Facebook

Bringing the nation's retailers an unrivaled selection of themed merchandise, resort apparel, gifts and souvenirs.
300 Attendees
Frequency: Annual/December

11769 **Gulf Coast Gift Show**
Fairchild Urban Expositions
5500 Interstate N Parkway
Suite 520
Atlanta, GA

770-952-6444
Fax: 770-956-9644
Home Page: www.urban-expo.com
Social Media: Facebook

Offering retailers from the Florida Panhandle and surrounding Gulf Coast areas to New Orleans an opportunigy to buy last minute holiday merchandise and get a jump on their spring/summer resort buying.
4000 Attendees
Frequency: Annual/October

11770 **Holiday Market**
Gilmore Enterprises
3514 Drawbridge Pkwy
Suite A
Greensboro, NC 27410-8584

336-282-5550
Fax: 336-282-0555
E-Mail: contact@gilmoreshows.com
Home Page: www.gilmoreshows.com
Social Media: Facebook

Tami Gilmore, Show Manager
Clyde Gilmore, Executive Director
Jan Donovon, Marketing Manager

There are two Holiday Market Shows, one in Greensboro, NC and the others in N. Cahrleston, SC. celebrate the season at Holiday Market. Children visit with santa and you will come away with ideas, recipes, samples, beauty makeovers and treats and holiday gifts.
35000 Attendees
Frequency: Annual/November
Founded in 1989

11771 **Immediate Delivery Show: Fall**
AMC Trade Shows/DMC Expositions
240 Peachtree Street NW
Suite 2200
Atlanta, GA 30303

404-220-3000
Fax: 404-220-3030

Mary Ellen Jackson, Show Manger

A trade show that allows you to move discontinued merchandise, overstocked inventory, samples and one of a kind items.
9000 Attendees
Frequency: Annual/November

11772 **Indoor/Outdoor Home Show**
True Value
PO Box 17
Bethel Park, PA 15102
412-276-6292
Fax: 412-851-6975
E-Mail: EllenDiOrio@aol.com
Home Page: www.pitthomeshow.com
Plenty of exhibits and vendors, and the ultimate displays for the home office, garage, backyard and patio, dream windows, home flooring, and bathroom.
61000 Attendees
Frequency: Annual/January

11773 **International Jewelry Fair/General Merchandise Show**
Helen Brett Enterprises
5111 Academy Drive
Lisle, IL 60532
630-241-9865
800-541-8171
Fax: 630-241-9870
E-Mail: dharrington@helenbrett.com
Home Page: www.gift2jewelry.com
Dave Harrington, Show Manager
Containing 1500 booths during the fall show and 800 booths during the spring show. Tradeshow open to wholesale buyers only (credentials required to attend).
44000 Attendees
Frequency: Bi-Annual

11774 **Licensing International Expo**
310-857-7544
888-644-2022
Home Page: www.licensingexpo.com
Talia Loggia, Marketing Manager
Annual show of 220 exhibitors of logos, corporate trademarks, characters, designs and other advertising techniques that require licensing.
7000 Attendees
Frequency: Annual/July

11775 **Memphis Gift & Jewelry Show-Fall**
Helen Brett Enterprises
5111 Academy Drive
Lisle, IL 60532
630-241-9865
800-541-8171
Fax: 630-241-9870
E-Mail: dharrington@helenbrett.com
Home Page: www.gift2jewelry.com
Dave Harrington, Show Manager
Containing over 350 booths during the fall show and 350 booths during the spring show. Tradeshow open to wholesale buyers only (credentials required to attend).
9000 Attendees
Frequency: Annual/August

11776 **Memphis Gift & Jewelry Show-Spring**
Helen Brett Enterprises
5111 Academy Drive
Lisle, IL 60532
630-241-9865
800-541-8171
Fax: 630-241-9870
E-Mail: dharrington@helenbrett.com
Home Page: www.gift2jewelry.com
Dave Harrington, Show Manager
Containing over 350 booths during the spring show and 350 booths during the fall show. Tradeshow open to wholesale buyers only (credentials required to attend).
9000 Attendees
Frequency: Annual/February

11777 **Mid-South Jewelry & Accessories Fair -Spring**
Helen Brett Enterprises
5111 Academy Drive
Lisle, IL 60532
630-241-9865
800-541-8171
Fax: 630-241-9870
E-Mail: dharrington@helenbrett.com
Home Page: www.gift2jewelry.com
Dave Harrington, Show Manager
Containing over 300 booths during the spring show and 500 booths during the fall show. Tradeshow open to wholesale buyers only (credentials required to attend).
8500 Attendees
Frequency: Annual/May

11778 **Mid-South Jewelry & Accessories Fair-Fall**
Helen Brett Enterprises
5111 Academy Drive
Lisle, IL 60532
630-241-9865
800-541-8171
Fax: 630-241-9870
E-Mail: dharrington@helenbrett.com
Home Page: www.gift2jewelry.com
Dave Harrington, Show Manager
Containing 500 booths during the fall show and over 300 booths during the spring show. Tradeshow open to wholesale buyers only (credentials required to attend).
16000 Attendees
Frequency: Annual/November

11779 **Motivation Show**
Hall-Erickson
98 E Naperville Road
Westmont, IL 60559
630-963-9185
800-752-6312
Fax: 630-434-1216
E-Mail: moti@heiexpo.com
Home Page: www.motivationshow.com
Nancy A Petitti, Show Director
Connecting engagement, loyalty, and financial results, learn from professional seminars on the latest trends, topics and best practices from some of America's leading organizations.
24000 Attendees
Frequency: Annual/September
Founded in 1929

11780 **Museum Source**
George Little Management
10 Bank Street
Suite 1200
White Plains, NY 10606-2867
914-486-6070
800-272-7469
Fax: 914-948-6180
E-Mail: customer_relations@glmshows.com
Home Page: www.glmshows.com/nyigf
Chelsea A Weinert, Divisional Manager
George Little II, President
Semi-annual show devoted to manufacturers, importers and publishers whose products are appropriate for museum gift shops, bookshores, specialty shops, zoos, aquariums and galleries. Items displayed include calendars, novelties, ethnic and craft items, historical interpretational products, art objects, children's educational items and posters.
Frequency: SemiAnnual

11781 **Museum Source: West**
George Little Management
10 Bank Street
Suite 1200
White Plains, NY 10606-1954
914-486-6070
800-272-7469
Fax: 914-948-6180
E-Mail: customer_relations@glmshows.com
Home Page: www.glmshows.com/sfig
Elizabeth Murphy, Division Manager
George Little II, President
Semi-annual show devoted to manufacturers, importers and publishers whose products are appropriate for museum gift shops, bookshores, specialty shops, zoos, aquariums and galleries. Items displayed include calendars, novelties, ethnic and craft items, historical interpretational products, art objects, children's educational items and posters.
Frequency: SemiAnnual

11782 **Museum Store Association Trade Show**
Museum Store Association
4100 E Mississippi Avenue
Suite 800
Denver, CO 80246
303-504-9223
Fax: 303-504-8585
Home Page: www.museumdistrict.com
Beverly Barsook, Executive Director
Stacey Woldt, Assistant Director Programs
Identify new sales leads, enhance your image and visibility in this niche market, reach your target audience, personally meet your customers, introduce a new product or service, generate sales, and network.
2500 Attendees
Frequency: Annual/April
Founded in 1955

11783 **National Halloween Convention**
Transworld Exhibits
1850 Oak Street
Northfield, IL 60093
847-784-6905
800-323-5462
Fax: 847-446-3523
Home Page: www.nationalhalloweenconvention.com
This once a year event is where over 10,000 attendees will converge on Chicago from all across the US and over 50 foreign countries to see what over 700 manufacturers and distributors are showcasing as new and exciting for parties, shops and haunted houses. Free educational seminars and workshops.
Frequency: Annual/May

11784 **National Stationery Show**
Gerorge Little Management
10 Bank Street
Suite 1200
White Plains, NY 10606
741-421-3200
800-272-7469
Fax: 914-948-2918
E-Mail: nationalstationeryshow@gmshows.com
Home Page: www.nationalstationeryshow.com
Lori Robinson, Show Manager
The National Stationery Show is the premiere market for stationery resources in the Unite States. The National Stationery Show presents more than 1,400 exhibitors and product in five distinctive sections; Presents, Celebrate, Take Note, HomeWork, and Indulgences. The show draws 15,000 domestic and international retailers representing department, chain and specialty stores, museum shops, galler and craft

retailers, boutiques, stationery, greeting card and gift shops, bookstores, bridal shops
15000 Attendees
Frequency: Annual/May

11785 **New Orleans Gift & Jewelry Show-Fall**
Helen Brett Enterprises
5111 Academy Drive
Lisle, IL 60532

630-241-9865
800-541-8171
Fax: 630-241-9870
E-Mail: dharrington@helenbrett.com
Home Page: www.gift2jewelry.com
Social Media: Facebook

Dave Harrington, Show Manager

Containing 850 booths during the fall show and 750 booths during the spring show. Tradeshow open to wholesale buyers only (credentials required to attend).
27000 Attendees
Frequency: Annual/August

11786 **New Orleans Gift & Jewelry Show-Spring**
Helen Brett Enterprises
5111 Academy Drive
Lisle, IL 60532

630-241-9865
800-541-8171
Fax: 630-241-9870
E-Mail: dharrington@helenbrett.com
Home Page: www.gift2jewelry.com

Dave Harrington, Show Manager

Containing 750 booths during the spring show and 850 booths during the fall show. Tradeshow open to wholesale buyers only (credentials required to attend).
20000 Attendees
Frequency: Annual/January

11787 **New Yorks Newest: A Division of the New York International Gift Fair**
George Little Management
10 Bank Street
White Plains, NY 10606-1954

914-486-6070
800-272-7469
Fax: 914-948-6180
Home Page: www.nyigf.com

George Little II, President

Showcasing 250 exhibitors new to the NYIGF spanning all categories and featuring fresh and innovative lines.
Frequency: SemiAnnual

11788 **OASIS Gift Show**
Organization of Assn Salespeople in the Southwest
1250 E Missouri Avenue
Phoenix, AZ 85014

602-952-2050
800-424-9519
Fax: 602-952-2244
E-Mail: information@oasis.org
Home Page: www.oasis.org

Brings success, opportunity, and convenience to buyers and exhibitors. Each show features an expansive product selection on the main floor, the jury-chosen artisans' showcase, and the gifts 2 go cash and carry area. Exhibitors offer trend setting general merchandise, world imports, home decor, jewelry, native american arts and crafts, western flair and southwestern gifts. OASIS is dedicated to providing a wholesale gift marketplace.
6000+ Attendees
Frequency: Annual/January

11789 **Offinger's Handcrafted Martketplace**
Offinger Management Company
1100-H Brandywine Boulevard
Zanesville, OH 43701-7303

888-878-4438
Fax: 740-452-2552
E-Mail: gift@offinger.com
Home Page: www.offingershandcrafted.com

Providing safe, convenient and inexpensive trade shows with rich collections of handmades, limited-production creations, traditional crafts and gifts, home furnishings, furniture and home accents. Meet the country's top producers of folk art, rustic primitives, museum quality replicas, handmade country collectibles, as well as one-of-a-kind, contemporary works of art.
3300 Attendees
Frequency: Triannual

11790 **San Francisco International Gift Fair**
San Francisco, CA

Home Page: sfigf.com

Top name manufacturers, innovative newcomers, and cutting edge designs.
2500 Attendees

11791 **Smoky Mountain Gift Show: Fall**
Smoky Mountain Gift Show
PO Box 50
Gatlinburg, TN 37738

865-436-4418
800-441-7889
Fax: 865-436-2878
Home Page:
www.smokymountaingiftshow.com

Eva Havlicek, Owner

The most beloved, most popular trade shows for the souvenir, resort and gift industry. Brings the top-name product selection, buyer base, service levels, and spirit of fun and hospitality that defined the show at its prime.
3000 Attendees
Frequency: Annual/November
Founded in 1966

11792 **Smoky Mountain Gift Show: Spring**
Smoky Mountain Gift Show
PO Box 50
Gatlinburg, TN 37738

865-436-4418
800-441-7889
Fax: 865-436-2878
Home Page:
www.smokymountaingiftshow.com

Eva Havlicek, Owner

Geared to the gift and souvenier market. Wholesale trade show open only to buyers in the retail industry. Buyers must present credentials upon registration.
12000 Attendees
Frequency: Annual/March

11793 **Southern Christmas Show**
Southern Shows
PO Box 36859
Charlotte, NC 28236

704-566-1898
Fax: 703-376-6345

Check out the holiday trees, mantels and doors, stroll the Christmas Village, munch on tasty treats and sway with yuletide entertainment.
13200 Attendees

11794 **Southern Ideal Home Show: Fall**
Southern Shows
PO Box 36859
Charlotte, NC 28236

704-566-1898
800-849-0248
Fax: 704-676-6345
E-Mail: dzimmerman@southernshows.com
Home Page: www.southershows.com

David Zimmerman, Show Manager
Brenda Crofts, Assistant Show Manager

Gardens, designer rooms, seminars, exhibitors, and experts on remodeling, decorating, home improvement and landscaping
20000 Attendees
Frequency: Annual/September

11795 **Toy Fair**
Toy Industry Association
1115 Broadway
Suite 400
New York, NY 10010

212-675-1141
Fax: 212-645-3246
E-Mail: toyfairs@toy-tia.org
Home Page: www.toy-tia.org

Thomas Conley, President
Diane Cardinale, Public Information Manager

Products include: games, toys, puzzles, dolls, science and hobby craft kits, books, bicycles and ride-ons, computer and video games and software, playground and sporting equipment, costumes and holiday decorations.
22000 Attendees
Frequency: Annual/February

11796 **Variety Merchandise Show**
Miller Freeman Publications
One Penn Plaza
PO Box 2549
New York, NY 10116

212-714-1300
Fax: 212-714-1313

An emphasis on customer service, community building forums and practical business education seminars.
20000 Attendees

11797 **Western States Toy and Hobby Show**
Western Toy and Hobby Representative Association
9397 Reserve Drive
Corona, CA 92883

951-771-1598
Fax: 909-277-1599
Home Page: www.wthra.com

Phylis St. John, Manager

The biggest assortment of toys, games, hobbies and educational fun.
3000 Attendees
Frequency: March

Directories & Databases

11798 **AR100 Award Show Guide**
Black Book Marketing Group
10 Aston Place
6th Floor
New York, NY 10003

212-956-1425
Fax: 212-539-9801

H Huntington Stehli, President/Publisher

Lists of winners at the AR100 Award Show, which recognizes excellence in the field of annual reports; includes photographers, design firms, illustrators, printers and paper companies; includes listings and ads for winners of past shows.
Cost: $60.00
Frequency: Annual
Circulation: 10,000

11799 **Complete Directory of Giftware Items**
Sutton Family Communications & Publishing Company
920 State Route 54 East
Elmitch, KY 42343
270-276-9500
E-Mail: jlsutton@apex.net
Theresa Sutton, Publisher
Lee Sutton, Editor
Print-out from database of wholesalers, manufacturers, distributors, importers and close-out houses. Database is updated daily to guarantee the most current and up-to-date sources available. Approximately 1,500 American direct wholesale sources in a three-ring binder.
Cost: $107.50
100 Pages

11800 **Complete Directory of Tabletop Items**
Sutton Family Communications & Publishing Company
920 State Route 54 East
Elmitch, KY 42343
270-276-9500
E-Mail: jlsutton@apex.net
Theresa Sutton, Editor
Lee Sutton, General Manager
Print-out from database of wholesalers, manufacturers, distributors, importers and close-out houses. Database is updated daily to guarantee the most current and up-to-date sources available.
Cost: $54.50
100+ Pages

11801 **Gift Associates Interchange Database**
1100 Main Street
Buffalo, NY 14209
716-885-4444
Fax: 716-878-2866
J Warren Wright, Secretary
An online credit interchange database.
240 Pages
Founded in 1974

11802 **Gift Associates Interchange Network**
716-887-9508
800-746-9428
E-Mail: info@gaingroup.com
Home Page: www.gaingroup.com
Donna Mosteller, Director, Member Group Services
Rosanne Battaglia, Member, Development Representative
GAIN is an online credit interchange database designed by and for credit managers in giftware, greeting card, silk floral, and related industries.
200 Members

11803 **Giftware Manufacturers Credit Interchange**
1100 Main Street
Buffalo, NY 14209-2356
716-885-4444
Fax: 716-878-2866
Home Page: www.gaingroup.com
J Warren Wright, Executive Secretary
Manufacturers and importers of giftware and china.
60 Pages

Industry Web Sites

11804 **http://gold.greyhouse.com**
G.O.L.D Grey House OnLine Databases
Grey House Publishing's online database platform, GOLD, offers Quick Search, Keyword Search and Expert Search for most business sectors including home and corporate gift markets. The GOLD platform makes finding the information you need quick and easy - whether you're a novice searcher or an experienced database user. All of Grey House's directory products are available for subscription on the GOLD platform.

11805 **www.greyhouse.com**
Grey House Publishing
Authoritative reference directories for most business sectors including home and corporate gift markets. Users can search the online databases with varied search criteria allowing for custom searches by product category, geographic area, sales volume, keyword, subject and more. Full Grey House catalog and online ordering also available.

11806 **www.museumstoreassociation.org**
Museum Store Association
Providing member representatives with the professional opportunities and educational resources they need to operate effectively and ethically.

11807 **www.naled.org**
National Gift Organization
Trade association for the gift and collectibles industry. Offers once yearly expositions, a newsletter, software, low cost credit card processing, telephone service discounts and more to help you run your business profitably.
350 Pages

11808 **www.oasis.org**
Organization of Associated Salespeople Southwest
A gift trade association which represents the manufacturing, sales and distribution side of the giftware industry.

11809 **www.shop.com**
Altura International
CatalogCity.com is a powerful and flexible e-commerce technology. This site includes recognized brand names such as Blair, Bombay, Chef's Catalog, Fisher-Price, Gump's by Mail, Hammacher Schlemmer, Ross-Simmons, The Sharper Image, and many more.

Associations

11810 **ASM International Everything Material**
Materials Information Society
9639 Kinsman Rd
Materials Park, OH 44073-0002

440-338-5151
800-336-5152
Fax: 440-338-4634
Home Page: www.asminternational.org

Charles Hayes, Executive Director

The society for materials engineers and scientists, a worldwide network dedicated to advancing industry, technology and applications of metals and materials.
35000 Members
Founded in 1913

11811 **American Ceramic Society**
600 N. Cleveland Ave.
Suite 210
Westerville, OH 43082

240-646-7054
866-721-3322
Fax: 301-206-9789
E-Mail: customerservice@ceramics.org
Home Page: www.ceramics.org
Social Media: Facebook, Twitter, LinkedIn, RSS

Charles Spahr, Executive Director

The National Institute of Ceramic Engineers, the Ceramic Manufacturing Council and the Ceramic Education Council are affiliated groups. All are leading organizations dedicated to the advancement of ceramics.
10000 Members
Founded in 1898

11812 **American Cut Glass Association**
PO Box 482
Ramona, CA 92065

760-789-2715
Fax: 760-789-7112
E-Mail: acgakathy@aol.com
Home Page: www.cutglass.org
Social Media: Facebook, YouTube

Kathy Emmerson, Executive Secretary
Judy Northrop, President

A non-profit organization devoted to the study and research of American Brilliant Cut Glass.
1500 Members
Founded in 1978

11813 **American Flint Glass Workers Union**
1440 S Byrne Road
Toledo, OH 43614-2363

419-385-6687
Fax: 419-385-8839
E-Mail: ljs@primenet.com

Timothy Tuttle, President

Organized as the United Flint Glass Workers.
21.7M Members
Founded in 1878

11814 **American Scientific Glassblowers Society**
PO Box 453
Machias, NY 14101

716-353-8062
Fax: 716-353-4259
E-Mail: natl-office@asgs-glass.org
Home Page: www.asgs-glass.org
Social Media: Facebook

Patrick DeFlorio, President
Frank Meints, President-Elect
Steven Moder, Secretary
Victor Mathews, Treasurer
Jerry Cloninger, Executive Secretary

A not for profit organization that is dedicated to sharing the knowedge,techniques, and skills of scientific glassblowing to its worldwide membership.
650 Members
Founded in 1952

11815 **Art Glass Association**
5610 Pleasant View Dr.
Nashport, OH 43830

740-450-6547
866-301-2421
Fax: 661-264-5277
E-Mail: bbird@artglassassociation.com
Home Page: www.artglassassociation.com

Steve Shupper, Chairman
Jennifer Urbaniak, Vice Chair
Bill Bird, Treasurer
Craig Bradley, Secretary
Vickie Gillespie, Membership

International, nonprofit organization whose purpose is to create awareness, knowledge and involvement for the growth and prosperity of the art glass industry. Programs include an annual conference, group health insurance, marchant listings on our website and more.
Founded in 1986

11816 **Ceramic Tile Distributors Association**
800 Roosevelt Rd
Building C, Suite 312
Glen Ellyn, IL 60137-5899

630-545-9415
800-938-2832
Fax: 630-790-3095
E-Mail: info@ctdahome.org
Home Page: www.ctdahome.org

Frank Donahue, President
Tom Kotel, VP
Robert DeAngelis, Treasurer
Bill Ives, Legal Counsel
Rick Church, Executive Director

An international association of distributors, manufacturers and allied professionals of ceramic tile and related products. Mission is to provide educational and networking opportunities for distributors of ceramic tile and their suppliers to further the consumption of ceramic tile.
500 Members
Founded in 1978

11817 **Ceramic Tile Institute of America**
12061 Jefferson Blvd.
Culver City, CA 90230-6219

310-574-7800
Fax: 310-821-4655
E-Mail: ctioa@earthlink.net
Home Page: www.ctioa.org

Promoting excellence in tile installation and encouraging greater consumption of tile through education, public relations and liaison with all facets of the construction industry as well as the general public.
Founded in 1992

11818 **China Clay Producers Association-CCPA**
113 Arkwright Landing
Macon, GA 31210

478-757-1211
Fax: 478-757-1949
E-Mail: info@georgiamining.org
Home Page: www.kaolin.com/

Lee Lemke, Executive VP

Organized to advance and encourage the development and production of kaolin-based products, and to work together with the people of Georgia in the communities where the mineral is mined and products manufactured.
Founded in 1978

11819 **Glass Art Society**
6512 23rd Ave. NW
Suite 329
Seattle, WA 98117

206-382-1305
Fax: 206-382-2630
E-Mail: info@glassart.org
Home Page: www.glassart.org
Social Media: Facebook, Twitter, LinkedIn, Pinterest

Jutta Annette Page, President
Jay MacDonnell, Vice President
Roger MacPherson, VP
Ed Kirshner, Treasurer

International nonprofit organization encouraging excellence, advancing education, promoting appreciation and development of the glass arts, and supporting the worldwide community of artists who work with glass. Members are artists, students, educators, collectors, gallery and museum personnel, writers and critics.
3100 Members
Founded in 1971

11820 **Glass Association of North America**
800 SW Jackson St.
Suite 1500
Topeka, KS 66612-1200

785-271-0208
Fax: 785-271-0166
Home Page: www.glasswebsite.com

William M Yanek, Executive VP
Ashley M Charest, Account Executive
Urmilla Sowell, Technical Director

Offers education on blueprint reading, labor and glass estimating and analysis; manuals on glazing guidelines, sealant compatibility and labor hours and a quarterly newsletter. Serves distributors, installers and fabricators of glass for use in the construction automotive and industrial industries.
250 Members
Founded in 1994

11821 **Insulating Glass Certification Council**
PO Box 730
Sackets Harbor, NY 13685

315-646-2234
Fax: 315-646-2297
E-Mail: staff@amscert.com
Home Page: www.igcc.org

Erin Ackley, Administrative Staff
John G Kent, Administrative Staff

IGCC sponsors and directs an independent, true third-party certification program. Periodic accelerated laboratory tests, per American Society for Testing and Materials specifications, and unannounced plant quality audits and inspections assure the quality and performance of sealed insulating glass products.
48 Members
Founded in 1977

11822 **National Glass Association**
1945 Old Gallows Rd
Suite 750
Vienna, VA 22182

703-442-4890
866-342-5642
Fax: 703-442-0630
E-Mail: nga@glass.org
Home Page: www.glass.org
Social Media: Facebook, Twitter, LinkedIn

Philip J. James, President & CEO
Nicole Harris, Vice President & Publisher
Denise M Sheehan, VP, Industry Events
James Gandorf, VP, Association Services

Pamela S Paroline, Director, Administration & Finance

The National Glass Association is the largest trade association representing the flat (architectural and automotive) glass industry. Member companies and locations reflect the entire vertical flat glass market. To support this ever changing industry, NGA produces products and services specifically for the industry.
4900 Members
Founded in 1948

11823 National Industrial Sand Association
2011 Pennsylvania Avenue, NW
Suite 301
Washington, DC 20006

202-457-0200
Fax: 202-457-0287
E-Mail: info@sand.org
Home Page: www.sand.org

Mark Ellis, President
Darrell K. Smith, Ph.D, Executive Vice President
Chris Greissing, VP Government Affairs
Paige Huggins, Financial Assistant

Trade association representing major manufacturers of industrial sand in North America. Committed to the safe use of industrial sand products and to advancing research and maintaining a dialogue with industry, legislators, regulatory agencies and the scientific community in support of the safety of empoyees and customers.
Founded in 1936

11824 Porcelain Enamel Institute
PO Box 920220
Norcross, GA 30010

770-676-9366
Fax: 770-409-7280
E-Mail: penamel@aol.com
Home Page: www.porcelainenamel.com
Social Media: Twitter, LinkedIn, RSS

Cullen Hackler, Executive Director

Dedicated to advancing the common interests of porcelain enameling plants and suppliers of porcelain enameling materials and equipment.
85 Members
Founded in 1930

11825 Refractory Ceramic Fiber Coalition
2300 N Street, NW
Room 3187
Washington, DC 20037

202-663-9188
Fax: 202-354-5230
E-Mail: info@htiwcoalition.org
Home Page: www.htiwcoalition.org

An association of the leading US producers of refractory ceramic fibers(RCFs). The RCF Coalition develops and promotes proper work practices and standards for the RCF industry, conducts RCF health research and disseminates information on the proper handling and use of refractory ceramic fiber.
Founded in 1992

11826 Safety Glazing Certification Council
100 West Main Street
PO Box 730
Sackets Harbor, NY 13685

315-646-2234
Fax: 315-646-2297
E-Mail: staff@amscert.com
Home Page: www.sgcc.org

Bill Nugent, President
Bernie Herron, Vice President
June Willcott, Secretary
Elaine S. Rodman, Treasurer

A nonprofit corporation that provides for the certification of safety glazing materials. Comprised of safety glazing manufacturers and other parties concerned with public safety.
105 Members
Founded in 1971

11827 Society of Glass and Ceramic Decorated Products (SGCDpro)
47 N 4th Street
PO Box 2489
Zanesville, OH 43702

740-588-9882
Fax: 740-588-0245
E-Mail: info@sgcd.org
Home Page: www.sgcd.org

Ed Weiner, President

Membership gives decorators and marketers of glass, ceramic and related products the confidence that they are part of a network of professionals who have shared knowledge and resources for nearly 50 years. Helps industry professionals identify new and profitable technology, keeps members abreast of the latest regulatory mandates and works with government and industry to provide reasonable solutions to regulatory compliance.
525 Members

11828 Stained Glass Association of America
9313 East 63rd Street
Raytown, MO 64133

816-737-2090
800-438-9581
Fax: 816-737-2801
E-Mail: headquarters@sgaaonline.com
Home Page: www.stainedglass.org
Social Media: Facebook, Twitter

Membership consists of the finest architectural stained and decorative art glass artists and studios in the US and around the world. Actively works for the betterment of the craft of stained glass and architectural art glass through various programs that are designed to benefit the members of the SGAA and the clients whom we serve.
Founded in 1903

11829 Technical Ceramics Manufacturers Association
25 N Broadway
Tarrytown, NY 10591-3221

914-332-0040
Fax: 914-332-1541
E-Mail: webmaster@tecma.org

A organization of manufacturers of custom and standard technical ceramic products for use in commercial, residential or industrial applications.

11830 United States Advanced Ceramics Association
1020 19th St NW
Suite 375
Washington, DC 20036-6118

202-467-5459
Fax: 202-467-5469
E-Mail: usaca@strategicmi.com
Home Page: www.advancedceramics.org

Jay E Lane, Chairman
Todd E Steyer, Vice Chair
Tom Foltz, Treasurer
Kent W Buesking, Secretary

The premier association that champions the common business interests of the advanced ceramic producer and end user industries.
Founded in 1985

Newsletters

11831 American Ceramic Society Bulletin
The American Ceramic Society
600 N. Cleveland Ave.
Suite 210
Westerville, OH 43082

866-720-3322
Fax: 301-206-9789
E-Mail: customerservice@ceramics.org
Home Page: www.ceramics.org

L David Pye, President
Scott Steen, Executive Director

The undisputed authority on news and new developments in the Ceramics and Glass industries, focuses on five end-use industries: transportation, electronics, defense, energy and construction.
Cost: $75.00
Frequency: 9x Yearly
Circulation: 10,000
ISSN: 0002-7812
Founded in 1898
Printed in 4 colors on glossy stock

11832 The Hobstar
American Cut Glass Association
PO Box 482
Ramona, CA 92065

760-789-2715
Fax: 760-789-7112
E-Mail: acgakathy@aol.com
Home Page: www.cutglass.org

ACGA's highly educational journal.
Frequency: 10x Yearly
Founded in 1876
Printed in 2 colors on glossy stock

11833 WDweekly
National Glass Association
1945 Old Gallows Rd
Suite 750
Vienna, VA 22182

703-442-4890
866-342-5642
Fax: 703-442-0630
E-Mail: nga@glass.org
Home Page: www.glass.org
Social Media: Facebook, Twitter, LinkedIn

Philip J. James, President & CEO
Nicole Harris, Vice President & Publisher
John Swanson, Editor & Associate Publisher

E-newsletter for manufacturers, distributors and dealers. The most thorough, convenient source for the latest industry news and insights on market, design, technology and economic trends.
4900 Members
Frequency: Weekly
Circulation: 30000
Founded in 1948

Magazines & Journals

11834 AGRR Magazine
Key Communications
PO Box 569
Garrisonville, VA 22463

540-577-7174
Fax: 540-720-5687
E-Mail: info@agrrmag.com

Home Page: www.agrrmag.com
Social Media: Facebook, Twitter, LinkedIn

Debra Levy, Publisher
Megan Headley, President

Source of unbiased, accurate information about auto glass repair and replacement industry.
Cost: $49.95
Frequency: 6x Yearly
Circulation: 10000+
Founded in 1993

11835 Advanced Materials & Processes
ASM International
9639 Kinsman Rd
Materials Park, OH 44073

440-338-5151
800-336-5152
Fax: 440-338-4634
Home Page: www.asminternational.org

Joseph M Zion, Publisher
Joanne Miller, Managing Editor
Margaret Hunt, Editor-in-Chief

Covers the latest developments in materials technology.
Frequency: Monthly
Circulation: 32M
Founded in 1977

11836 American Flint Magazine
American Flint Glass Workers Union
1440 S Byrne Road
Toledo, OH 43614-2363

419-385-6687
Fax: 419-385-8839

Timothy Tuttle, President

Union news and information for the glass industry.
Frequency: Monthly

11837 Ceramic Bulletin
American Ceramic Society
600 N. Cleveland Avenue
Suite 210
Westerville, OH 43082

240-646-7054
866-721-3322
Fax: 240-396-5637
E-Mail: customerservice@ceramics.org
Home Page: www.ceramics.org

L David Pye, President
Scott Steen, Executive Director

Written for ceramic and materials engineers and production management teams involved in industrial ceramics manufacturing. Topics covered include government relations, environmental issues, developing technology, industry statistics, cutting-edge manufacturing processes and technology.
Cost: $75.00
Frequency: Monthly
Circulation: 50000
ISSN: 0027-812
Founded in 1953
Printed in 4 colors on glossy stock

11838 Ceramic Industry
Business News Publishing Company
6075 B Glick Rd
Powell, OH 43065

281-550-5855
Fax: 248-244-6439
E-Mail: ci@halldata.com
Home Page: www.ceramicindustry.com

Amy Vallance, Publisher
Susan Sutton, Editor in Chief/Integrated Media
Teresa Mcpherson, Managing Editor
Cory Emery, Art Director
Karen Telan, Production Manager

Serves manufacturers of advanced ceramics, glass, whitewares, refractories and other ceramic businesses. CI's offerings include practical, real-world solutions to manufacturing problems, information on the latest technological advancements, and up-to-date coverage of news, issues and trends.
Frequency: Monthly
Circulation: 10000
Founded in 1926

11839 Ceramics Monthly
American Ceramic Society
735 Ceramic Pl
Suite 100
Westerville, OH 43081-8728

614-895-4213
Fax: 614-891-8960
E-Mail: editorial@ceramicsmonthly.org
Home Page: www.ceramicsmonthly.org

Sherman Hall, Editor
Rich Guerrein, Publisher
Jennifer Poellot, Assistant editor
Susan Enderle, Marketing Manager
Erin Pfeifer, Advertising Manager

An internationally distributed magazine covering ceramic arts and crafts. Includes lists of conferences, exhibitions, festivals, fairs, sales and workshops for crafts people.
Cost: $32.00
Frequency: Monthly
Circulation: 35000
ISSN: 0009-0328
Founded in 1953
Printed in on glossy stock

11840 Fired Arts and Crafts
Jones Publishing
N7450 Aanstad Road
PO Box 5000
Iola, WI 54945-5000

715-445-5000
800-331-0038
Fax: 715-445-4053
E-Mail: jonespub@jonespublishing.com
Home Page: www.jonespublishing.com

Joe Jones, CEO/President
Mick Harbridge, Editor
Branden Hardy, Marketing

Features on projects and patterns, celebrity clips, new products, show listings, industry news and book reviews.
Cost: $32.95
Frequency: Monthly
Circulation: 15000

11841 Fusion
American Scientific Glassblowers Society
PO Box 778
Madison, NC 27025

336-427-2406
Fax: 336-427-2496
E-Mail: natl-office@asgs-glass.org
Home Page: www.asgs-glass.org

Marylin Brown, Editor

Contains technical articles, references and abstracts from other publications, book reviews, new product information, local section reports and announcements, committee reports, and information about health and safety concerns. An excellent source for vendor information with ads of goods and services.
Cost: $40.00
Frequency: Quarterly
Circulation: 850
Founded in 1954

11842 Glass Craftsman
Arts & Media
10 Canal Street
Suite 300
Bristol, PA 19007

215-826-1799
Fax: 215-826-1788
E-Mail: webmaster@artglassworld.com
Home Page: www.artglassworld.com

Joe Porcelli, Publisher

Providing the best professionally produced, technical, aesthetic and practical information to its readers and a strong, committed audience of glass enthusiasts and professionals to its family of advertisers.
Cost: $25.00
Circulation: 12000
ISSN: 1079-199X

11843 Glass Magazine
National Glass Association
1945 Old Gallows Rd
Suite 750
Vienna, VA 22182

703-448-1319
Fax: 703-442-0630
Home Page: www.glassmagazine.com

Nicole Harris, VP
Nancy Davis, Editor-in-Chief

Provides subscribers informative coverage of glass industry news, trends and analysis, product introductions, and best business practices, in addition to glass industry statistics and supplier resource guides.
Cost: $34.95
Frequency: 11x Yearly
Circulation: 27098
Founded in 1948

11844 Journal of Materials Engineering and Performance
ASM International
9639 Kinsman Road
Materials Park, OH 44073-0002

440-338-5151
800-336-5152
Fax: 440-338-4634
Home Page: www.asminternational.org

Jeffrey A. Hawk, Editor
Rajiv Asthana, Associate Editor
Narandra Dahotre, Associate Editor
Omar S. Es-Said, Associate Editor

Covers all aspects of materials selection, design, processing, characterization and evaluation, including how to improve materials properties through processes and process control of casting, forming, heat treating, surface modification and coating, and fabrication.
Cost: $1965.00
Frequency: Bimonthly
Circulation: 305
Founded in 1992

11845 Journal of Phase Equilibria and Diffusion
ASM International
9639 Kinsman Rd
Materials Park, OH 44072

440-338-5151
800-336-5152
Fax: 440-338-4634
Home Page: www.asminternational.org

J.F. Smith, Editor
John Morral, Deputy Editor
H. Okamoto, Supplemental Lit. Review Editor

Covers the significance of diagrams as well as new research techniques, equipment, data evaluation, nomenclature, presentation and other aspects of phase diagram preparation and use. Content includes information on phenomena such as kinetic control of equilibrium, coher-

ency effects, impurity effects, and thermodynamic and crystallographic characteristics.
Frequency: Bimonthly
Circulation: 305

11846 Journal of the American Ceramic Society
American Ceramic Society
735 Ceramic Pl
Suite 100
Westerville, OH 43081

866-721-3322
Fax: 301-206-9789
E-Mail: customerservice@ceramics.org
Home Page: www.ceramics.org

David J. Green, Associate Editor
David W. Johnson, Jr., Associate Editor
Lisa Klein, Associate Editor
John Halloran, Associate Editor

Contains records of original research that provide or lead to fundamental principles in the science of ceramics and ceramic-based composites. These papers include reports of the discovery of new phases, phase relationships, processing approaches and microstructures that relate to ceramic materials and processes.
Cost: $1190.00
Frequency: Monthly
ISSN: 0002-7820
Founded in 1905

11847 Pottery Making Illustrated
Ceramic Publications Company
735 Ceramic Pl
Suite 100
Westerville, OH 43081

866-721-3322
Fax: 301-206-9789
E-Mail: customerservice@ceramics.org
Home Page: www.ceramics.org

Charlie Spahr, Publisher
Bill Jones, Editor
Mona Thiel, Advertising Manager
Steve Hecker, Marketing Manager
Erin Pfeifer, Editorial Assistant

Provides intermediate to advanced potters with practical techniques, tips and information for the studio in a well-illustrated format. With articles on throwing, handbuilding, sculpture, decorating and firing, PMI covers every aspect of the studio ceramic process. In addition, PMI provides up-to-date information on tools, supplies and materials for the ceramic studio.
Cost: $22.00
Frequency: Bi-Monthly
Circulation: 20000
Founded in 1905

11848 Stained Glass
Stained Glass Association of America
9313 East 63rd Street
Raytown, MO 64133

816-737-2090
800-438-9581
Fax: 816-737-2801
E-Mail: headquarters@sgaonline.com
Home Page: www.stainedglass.org
Social Media: Facebook, Twitter

Features articles about historical and contemporary installations that will show you what others in the field are doing.
Frequency: Quarterly
Founded in 1903

11849 The Hobstar
American Cut Glass Association
PO Box 482
Ramona, CA 92065

760-789-2715
Fax: 760-789-7112
E-Mail: acgakathy@aol.com
Home Page: www.cutglass.org
Social Media: Facebook, YouTube

Kathy Emmerson, Executive Secretary
Karen Parker, President

ACGA's highly educational journal.
1500 Members
Frequency: 10x Yearly
Founded in 1978

11850 US Glass, Metal & Glazing
Key Communications
PO Box 569
Garrisonville, VA 22463

540-577-7174
Fax: 540-720-5687
E-Mail: scarpenter@glass.com
Home Page: www.usglassmag.com
Social Media: Facebook, Twitter, LinkedIn

Penny Stacey, Advertising Coordinator
Ellen Giard Chilcoat, Editor
Debra Levy, President

Serves manufactures/fabricators, contract glaziers, distributors and wholesalers, retailors/dealers of glass/metal and/or glass/metal products and others allied to the field.
Frequency: Monthly
Circulation: 25572
ISSN: 0041-7661
Founded in 1965
Printed in 4 colors on glossy stock

11851 Window & Door
National Glass Association
1945 Old Gallows Rd
Suite 750
Vienna, VA 22182

703-442-4890
866-342-5642
Fax: 703-442-0630
E-Mail: nga@glass.org
Home Page: www.glass.org
Social Media: Facebook, Twitter, LinkedIn

Philip J. James, President & CEO
Nicole Harris, Vice President & Publisher
John Swanson, Editor & Associate Publisher

Serves the entire fenestration industry, including manufacturers, distributors, and dealers. Offers readers focused news coverage, insightful articles on market and design trends, regular columns on codes, legal issues, and marketing ideas, full coverage of new products, expert articles on operations and technology, and much more.
4900 Members
Frequency: 8x Yearly
Founded in 1948

Trade Shows

11852 ACGA Annual Convention
PO Box 482
Ramona, CA 92065-0482

760-789-2715
Fax: 760-789-7112
E-Mail: acgakathy@aol.com
Home Page: www.cutglass.org

Kathy Emmerson, Executive Secretary
Karen Parker, President

Opportunity to learn about cut glass.
Frequency: Annual/July

11853 ASM Heat Treating Society Conference & Exposition
ASM International
9639 Kinsman Road
Materials Park, OH 44073-0002

440-338-5151
800-336-5152
Fax: 440-338-4634
E-Mail:
pamela.kleinman@asminternational.org
Home Page: www.asminternational.org

Pamela Kleinma, Senior Manager, Events
Kellye Thomas, Exposition Account Manager

The ASM Heat Treating Society and the American Gear Manufacturers Association partner to create a mix of education, technology, networking and exposition opportunities.
3500 Attendees
Frequency: Bi-Annual
Founded in 1974

11854 AeroMat Conference and Exposition
ASM International
9639 Kinsman Road
Materials Park, OH 44073-0002

440-338-5151
800-336-5152
Fax: 440-338-4634
Home Page: www.asminternational.org

Kim Schaefer, Event Manager
Kelly Thomas, Exposition Account Manager

Brings together hundreds of delegates and exhibiting companies to discuss and display the latest advances in materials and processes for aerospace applications. AeroMat is the world's leading aerospace conference devoted entirely to materials and processes used in the fabrication of flight vehicles. Learn the latest technologies in aerospace materials, research and processes.
1500 Attendees
Frequency: Annual/June
Founded in 1984

11855 American Ceramic Society Annual Meeting and Expo
600 N. Cleveland Ave.
Suite 210
Westerville, OH 43082

866-721-3322
Fax: 240-396-5637
E-Mail: customerservice@ceramics.org
Home Page: www.ceramics.org

George Wicks, President
Richard Brow, President-Elect
Ted Day, Treasurer
Charlie Spahr, Executive Director

Three-hundred booths of ceramic materials, products manufacturing, testing, processing, research, components and software. Technical conference on ceramic materials research and development with over 1000 papers presented in more than 25 topical areas.
2,500 Attendees
Frequency: Annual/April

11856 American Scientific Glassblowers Exhibition
American Scientific Glassblowers Society
PO Box 453
Machias, NY 14101

716-353-8062
Fax: 716-353-4259
E-Mail: natl-office@asgs-glass.org
Home Page: www.asgs-glass.org

Patrick DeFlorio, President
Frank Meints, President-Elect
Steven Moder, Secretary
Victor Mathews, Treasurer
Jerry Cloninger, Executive Secretary

Great opportunity to expand glassblowing knowledge through seminars, demonstrations, technical papers and posters.
650 Members
Frequency: Annual/June
Founded in 1952

11857 BEC Conference
Glass Association of North America
800 SW Jackson St.
Suite 1500
Topeka, KS 66612-1200
785-271-0208
Fax: 785-271-0166
Home Page: www.glasswebsite.com
William M Yanek, Executive VP
Ashley M Charest, Account Executive
Urmilla Sowell, Technical Director
Features educational seminars for glazing contractors and executives in contracting companies.
Frequency: Annual/March

11858 DECO
Society of Glass & Ceramic Decorators
4340 E West Highway
Suite 200
Bethesda, MD 20814
301-986-9800
Fax: 301-951-3801
Home Page: www.sgcd.org
Focusing on technical and regulatory issues affecting glass and ceramic decorators.

11859 Dealers Show of the American Cut Glass Association
American Cut Glass Association
PO Box 482
Ramona, CA 92065-0482
760-789-2715
Fax: 760-789-7112
E-Mail: acgakathy@aol.com
Home Page: www.cutglass.org
Kathy Emmerson, Executive Secretary
Annual show and exhibits of American brilliant period cut glass and related articles.

11860 Electronic Materials and Applications
American Ceramic Society
600 N. Cleveland Ave.
Suite 210
Westerville, OH 43082
240-646-7054
866-721-3322
Fax: 301-206-9789
E-Mail: customerservice@ceramics.org
Home Page: www.ceramics.org
Charles Spahr, Executive Director
Focuses on electronic materials for energy generation, conversion and storage applications.
10000 Members
Frequency: Annual/January
Founded in 1898

11861 GANA Annual Conference
Glass Association of North America
800 SW Jackson St.
Suite 1500
Topeka, KS 66612-1200
785-271-0208
Fax: 785-271-0166
Home Page: www.glasswebsite.com
William M Yanek, Executive VP
Ashley M Charest, Account Executive
Urmilla Sowell, Technical Director
Seven Divisions of GANA have meetings planned at this event, along with the non-Division Committees including Fire-Rated Glazing, Glazing Industry Code Committee, Marketing, and Protective Glazing.
250 Members
Founded in 1994

11862 Glass & Optical Materials Division Annual Meeting
American Ceramic Society
600 N. Cleveland Ave.
Suite 210
Westerville, OH 43082
240-646-7054
866-721-3322
Fax: 301-206-9789
E-Mail: customerservice@ceramics.org
Home Page: www.ceramics.org
Charles Spahr, Executive Director
Involving the physical properties and technological processes important to glasses, amorphous solids and optical materials.
10000 Members
Frequency: Annual/May
Founded in 1898

11863 Glass Art Society Conference
Glass Art Society
6512 23rd Ave. NW
Suite 329
Seattle, WA 98117
206-382-1305
Fax: 206-382-2630
E-Mail: info@glassart.org
Home Page: www.glassart.org
Jeremy Lepisto, President
Jutta-Annette Page, Vice-President
Caroline Madden, Secretary
Lance Friedman, Treasurer
Annual conference and exhibits for those who make, collect, exhibit and appreciate objects made with glass.
2000 Attendees
Frequency: Annual/June

11864 Glass Craft Exposition
Las Vegas Management
2408 Chapman Drive
Las Vegas, NV 89104
702-734-0070
800-217-4527
Fax: 702-734-0636
Home Page: www.glasscraftexpo.com
Shirley Harvey, Director
Learn new techniques and create new things.
3500 Attendees
Frequency: Annual/March

11865 Glass Expo Midwest
US Glass Magazine
PO Box 569
Garrisonville, VA 22463
540-720-5584
Fax: 540-720-5687
E-Mail: expos@glass.com
Home Page: www.glassexpos.com/
Patrick Smith, Marketing Manager
Annual show and exhibits of flat, container, heavy insulated and tempered glass, architectural sealants and hardware, mirror products and windows and doors.
800 Attendees
Frequency: Annual/August

11866 Glass TEXpo
Key Communications, Inc.
PO Box 569
Garrisonville, VA 22463-0569
540-720-5584
Fax: 540-720-5687
E-Mail: expos@glass.com
Home Page: www.glassexpos.com
Patrick Smith, Marketing Manager
Annual show and exhibits of flat, container, heavy insulated and tempered glass, architectural sealants and hardware, mirror products and windows and doors. Hosted in Dallas, TX.
700 Attendees
Frequency: Annual/October

11867 International Conference and Expo on Advanced Ceramics and Composites
American Ceramic Society
600 N. Cleveland Ave.
Suite 210
Westerville, OH 43082
240-646-7054
866-721-3322
Fax: 301-206-9789
E-Mail: customerservice@ceramics.org
Home Page: www.ceramics.org
George Wicks, President
Richard Brow, President-Elect
Ted Day, Treasurer
Charlie Spahr, Executive Director
Showcases cutting-edge research and product developments in advanced ceramics, armor ceramics, solid oxide fuel cells, ceramic coating, bioceramics and more.
Frequency: Annual/January

11868 International Conference and Exposition on Advanced Ceramics & Composites
American Ceramic Society
600 N. Cleveland Ave.
Suite 210
Westerville, OH 43082
240-646-7054
866-721-3322
Fax: 301-206-9789
E-Mail: customerservice@ceramics.org
Home Page: www.ceramics.org
Charles Spahr, Executive Director
Showcases cutting-edge research and product developments in advanced ceramics, armor ceramics, solid oxide fuel cells, ceramic coatings, bioceramics and more.
10000 Members
Frequency: Annual/January
Founded in 1898

11869 International Glass Show
Dame Associates
100 Lincoln Street
Boston, MA 02135
617-783-4777
800-843-3263
Fax: 617-783-4787
Home Page: www.dameassoc.com
Annual show of 115 manufacturers and suppliers of windows, doors, sun enclosures, windshields and mirrors, glass, machinery, hardware and insulating units, sealants, adhesives, mastic, security glazing and thermal barriers, aluminum, curtain wall computers and trucks.
2500 Attendees
Frequency: Annual/May

11870 International Symposium for Testing and Failure Analysis
ASM International
9639 Kinsman Road
Materials Park, OH 44073-0002
440-338-5151
800-336-5152
Fax: 440-338-4634
E-Mail:

pamela.kleinman@asminternational.org
Home Page: www.asminternational.org

Pamela Kleinman, Senior Manager, Events
Kelly Thomas, Exposition Account Manager

Annual event focusing on testing, analysis, characterization and research of materials such as engineered materials, high performance metals, powdered metals, metal forming, surface modification, welding and joining.
4,000 Attendees
Frequency: Annual/October
Founded in 2005

11871 **International Thermal Spray Conference & Exposition**
ASM International
9639 Kinsman Road
Materials Park, OH 44073

440-338-5151
800-336-5152
Fax: 440-338-4634
E-Mail: natalie.nemec@asminternational.org
Home Page: www.asminternational.org

Natalie Neme, Event Manager
Kelly Thomas, Exposition Account Manager

Global annual event attracting professional interested in thermal spray technology focusing on advances in HVOF, plasma and detonation gun, flame spray and wire arc spray processes, performance of coatings, and future trends. 150 exhibitors.
1000 Attendees
Frequency: Annual/May

11872 **International Window Film Conference and Expo**
Window Film Magazine
PO Box 569
Garrisonville, VA 22463-0569

540-720-5584
Fax: 540-720-5687
E-Mail: expos@glass.com
Home Page: www.glassexpos.com

Patrick Smith, Marketing Manager

Numerous opportunities to network, socialize, and learn from others in the window film industry.
Frequency: Annual/March

11873 **MCARE: Materials Challenges in Alternative & Renewable Energy**
American Ceramic Society
600 N. Cleveland Ave.
Suite 210
Westerville, OH 43082

240-646-7054
866-721-3322
Fax: 301-206-9789
E-Mail: customerservice@ceramics.org
Home Page: www.ceramics.org

Charles Spahr, Executive Director

Facilitates information sharing on the latest developments involving materials for alternative and renewable energy systems. Emphasis will be on materials challenges and innovations in areas of solar energy, wind power, hydro, geothermal, biomass, nuclear, hydrogen, electric grid, materials availability, nanocomposites/manomaterials, and battery and energy storage.
10000 Members
Frequency: Annual/February
Founded in 1898

11874 **Porcelain Enamel Institute Technical Forum & Suppliers Mart**
4004 Hillsboro Pike
Suite B224
Nashville, TN 37215-2722

615-385-5357
Fax: 615-385-5463
E-Mail: penamel@aol.com
Home Page: www.porcelainenamel.com

Cullen Hackler, Executive VP
Patricia Melton, Executive Secretary

Members include suppliers and makers of porcelain enamel products and raw materials. Attendees of the PEI conference and workshops attend this show. There will be 20 booths.
250 Attendees
Frequency: Annual/May
Founded in 1989

11875 **Seattle Gift Show**
George Little Management
10 Bank Street
Suite 1200
White Plains, NY 10606

914-486-6070
800-272-7469
Fax: 914-948-2918
Home Page: www.washingtongiftshow.com

Louise Seeber, Show Manager
Laura Scott, Exhibit Sales Manager
George Little II, President

See new products and proven bestsellers that cater to the eclectic tastes of the discerning Pacific Northwest consumer.
6000 Attendees
Frequency: Annual/January

Directories & Databases

11876 **Ceramic Abstracts**
American Ceramic Society
600 N. Cleveland Ave.
Suite 210
Westerville, OH 43081

240-646-7054
866-721-3322
Fax: 240-396-5637
E-Mail: customerservice@ceramics.org
Home Page: www.ceramics.org

Charles Spahr, Executive Director

Abstracting/indexing publication covering ceramic materials-related literature. 15,000 entries published annually.
Frequency: Bi-Monthly
Circulation: 2,500

11877 **CeramicSOURCE**
American Ceramic Society
735 Ceramic Pl
Suite 100
Westerville, OH 43081-8728

614-904-4700
Fax: 614-794-5892
Home Page: www.ceramicsource.org

Patricia Janeway, Editor
Marc Bailey, Director Global Marketing

Annual buyer's guide/directory of equipment and materials' suppliers to the industrial ceramic manufacturing market.
Cost: $25.00
Frequency: 1 issue
Circulation: 14,500
ISSN: 0002-7812
Founded in 1985
Printed in 4 colors on glossy stock

11878 **Complete Directory of Glassware & Glass Items**
Sutton Family Communications & Publishing Company
920 State Route 54 East
Elmitch, KY 42343

270-276-9500
E-Mail: jlsutton@apex.net

Theresa Sutton, Publisher
Lee Sutton, Editor

Print-out from database of wholesalers, manufacturers, distributors, importers and close-out houses. Database is updated daily to guarantee the most current and up-to-date sources available. Over 800 American firms which sell direct to small retailers, in three-ring binder format.
Cost: $94.50
100 Pages

11879 **Complete Guide: US Advanced Ceramic Industry**
Business Communications Company
49 Walnut Park
Building 2
Wellesley, MA 02481-1713

866-285-7215
Fax: 781-489-7308
E-Mail: sales@bccresearch.com
Home Page: www.bccresearch.com

David Nydam, President
Kevin R. Fitzgerald, Editorial Director
Andrew Hunt, Marketing Director

Approximately 450 companies and institutions involved in the advanced ceramic industry in the US.

11880 **Data Book and Buyers' Guide**
Ceramic Industry
2540 Billingsley Road
Business News Publishing Company
Columbus, OH 43235-1990

FAX 440-498-9121

List of over 1300 suppliers of equipment and materials for the advanced and traditional ceramics and heavy clay products.
Cost: $25.00
Frequency: Biennially

11881 **Glass Factory Directory of North America**
Glass News
Box 2267
Hempstead, NY 11551-2267

516-481-2188
Home Page: www.glassfactorydir.com

Liz Scott, Editor

Over 600 glass manufacturers and plants in the US, Canada and Mexico.
Cost: $25.00
Frequency: Annually
Circulation: 1,500

11882 **Porcelain Enamel Institute Source List**
4004 Hillsboro Pike
Suite B224
Nashville, TN 37215-2722

615 385 5357
Fax: 615-385-5463
E-Mail: penamel@aol.com
Home Page: www.porcelainenamel.com

Tom Sanford, Executive VP
Patricia Melton, Executive Secretary
Frequency: Annual/Fall
Founded in 1930

11883 **Society of Glass & Ceramic Decorating Products Directory**
Society of Glass & Ceramic Decorating Products
PO Box 2489
Zanesville, OH 43702

740-588-9882
Fax: 740-588-0245
E-Mail: info@sgcd.org
Home Page: www.sgcd.org

Directory of more than 700 member manufacturers, suppliers, decorators and designers of glass and ceramics; international coverage indexed by product type and decorating technology.
Cost: $250.00
172 Pages
Frequency: Annual
Circulation: 800
Founded in 1964

11884 **US Glass, Metal & Glazing: Buyers Guide**
Key Communications
PO Box 569
Garrisonville, VA 22463-0569

540-577-7174
Fax: 540-720-5687
Home Page: www.usglass.com

Debra A Levy, Publisher

About 3,000 suppliers of glass and glazing supplies for the glass, metal and glazing industry.
Cost: $20.00
Frequency: Annual
Circulation: 21,000

Industry Web Sites

11885 **http://gold.greyhouse.com**
G.O.L.D Grey House OnLine Databases

Grey House Publishing's online database platform, GOLD, offers Quick Search, Keyword Search and Expert Search for most business sectors including glass and ceramic markets. The GOLD platform makes finding the information you need quick and easy - whether you're a novice searcher or an experienced database user. All of Grey House's directory products are available for subscription on the GOLD platform.

11886 **www.acers.org**
American Ceramic Society

The National Institute of Ceramic Engineers, the Ceramic Manufacturing Council and the Ceramic Education Council are affiliated classes.

11887 **www.advancedceramics.org**
United States Advanced Ceramics Association

Promotes the use of advanced ceramic materials in industrial applications.

11888 **www.asgs-glass.org**
American Scientific Glassblowers Society

Encourages the free exchange of knowledge and the broadening of scientific glassblowing skills to assist scientists, educators and the industry by designing and constructing glass components and scientific apparatus.

11889 **www.ceramics.org**
American Ceramic Society

The National Institute of Ceramic Engineers, the Ceramic Manufacturing Council and the Ceramic Education Council are affiliated groups.

11890 **www.ctdahome.org**
Ceramic Tile Distributors Association

Promotes the sales of ceramic tile and similar products.

11891 **www.ctioa.org**
Ceramic Tile Institute of America

This organization has over 500 member manufacturers of ceramic tile in the western United States.

11892 **www.cutglass.org**
American Cut Glass Association

A non-profit organization devoted to the study and research of Americal Brilliant Cut Glass.

11893 **www.dameassoc.com**
Dame Associates

An organization with a biennial show w/250 manufacturers and suppliers of windows, doors, sun enclosures, windshields, mirrors, glass machinery, hardware, insulating units, sealants, adhesives, mastic, security glazing, thermal barriers, aluminum, curtain wall computers and trucks.

11894 **www.glass.org**
National Glass Association

An organization with an annual show of 325 manufacturers, suppliers and distributors of glass and glass-related products, supplies, equipment, tools and machinery, automotive glazing, equipment/machinery, curtain wall, store front systems, doors/hardware, windows, mirrors, shower/tub enclosures and tools.

11895 **www.glasswebsite.com**
Glass Association of North America

Offers educational on blueprint reading, labor, and glass estimating and analysis; manuals on glazing guidelines, sealant compatibility and labor hours; and a quarterly newsletter. Serves distributors, installers, fabricators of glass for use in the construction automotive and industrial industries.

11896 **www.glasswebsite.com/gicc**
Glazing Industry Code Committee

Protects the glass and glazing interests by monitoring, testifying and developing code proposals at the model building and energy codes.

11897 **www.greyhouse.com**
Grey House Publishing

Authoritative reference directories for most business sectors including glass and ceramic markets. Users can search the online databases with varied search criteria allowing for custom searches by product category, geographic area, sales volume, keyword, subject and more. Full Grey House catalog and online ordering also available.

11898 **www.igcc.org**
Insulating Glass Certification Council

Sponsors and directs a program of laboratory testing and unannounced plant inspection to ensure continuing product information.

11899 **www.igmaonline.org**
Insulating Glass Manufacturers Alliance

11900 **www.porcelainenamel.com**
Porcelain Enamel Institute

Members include suppliers and makers of porcelain enamel products and raw materials.

11901 **www.sgcc.org**
Safety Glazing Certification Council

Information center for this nonprofit corporation that provides for the certification of safety glazing materials.

Associations

11902 **Academy for State and Local Government**
444 N Capitol St NW
Washington, DC 20001-1512

202-434-4850
Fax: 202-434-4851

The policy center for the national organizations for the chief elected and appointed officials for state and local governments, functioning as their joint technical assistance, training and research organization. Its mission is to promote cooperation among federal, state and local governments.

11903 **American Association of State Highway and Transportation Officials**
444 N Capitol St NW
Suite 249
Washington, DC 20001-1539
202-624-5800
Fax: 202-624-5806
E-Mail: info@aashto.org
Home Page: www.transportation.org
Social Media: Facebook, Twitter

Mike Hancock, President
John Cox, Vice-President
Carlos Braceras, Secretary/ Treasurer
Frederick G Wright, Executive Director

Membership is composed of highway and transportation departments in the 50 states, the District of Columbia, and Puerto Rico.
52 Members

11904 **American Conference of Governmental Industrial Hygienists (NCGIH)**
1330 Kemper Meadow Drive
Cincinnati, OH 45240

513-742-2020
Fax: 513-742-3355
E-Mail: mail@acgih.org
Home Page: www.acgih.org

Robert F Herrick, Chair
J Torey Nalbone, Vice Chair
Heather D Borman, Secretary/Treasurer
A Anthony Rizzuto, Executive Director

A professional society of government and university employees engaged in a full program of industrial hygiene.
Founded in 1938

11905 **American Correctional Association**
206 N Washington St
Alexandria, VA 22314-2528

703-224-0000
800-222-5646
Fax: 703-224-0179
E-Mail: jeffw@aca.org
Home Page: www.aca.org
Social Media: Facebook, Twitter

Jeff Washington, Deputy Executive Director
James Gondles Jr, Executive Director

For individuals involved in the correctional field.
20000 Members
Founded in 1870

11906 **American Federation of Government Employees**
80 F St NW
Washington, DC 20001-1528

202-737-8700
Fax: 202-639-6490
E-Mail: comments@afge.org
Home Page: www.afge.com
Social Media: Facebook, Twitter, Youtube, Flickr, RSS

J David Cox Sr., President
Eugene Hudson, Secretary/Treasurer
Augusta Thomas, VP for Women's & Fair Practices

The largest federal employee union representing workers nationwide and overseas. Workers in virtually all functions of government at every federal agency depend upon AFGE for legal representation, legislative advocacy, technical expertise and informational services.
600K Members
Founded in 1932

11907 **American Federation of State, County & Municipal Employees**
1625 L Street NW
Washington, DC 20036-5687

202-429-1000
Fax: 202-429-1293
E-Mail: afsa@afsaadmin.org
Home Page: www.afscme.org
Social Media: Facebook, Twitter, YouTube, RSS

Lee Saunders, President
Laura Reyes, Secretary/ Treasurer

With members in hundreds of different occupations, AFSCME advocates for fairness in the workplace, excellence in public services and prosperity and opportunity for all working families.

11908 **American Foreign Service Association**
2101 E St Nw
Washington, DC 20037-2990
202-338-4045
Fax: 202-338-6820
E-Mail: member@afsa.org
Home Page: www.afsa.org
Social Media: Facebook, Twitter, Youtube, RSS

Robert J Silverman, President
Hon. Charles A Ford, Treasurer
Angela Dickey, Secretary

Missions are to enhance the effectiveness of the Foreign Service, to protect the professional interests of its members, to ensure the maintenance of high professional standards for both career diplomats and political appointeese, and to promote understanding of the critical role of the Foreign service in promoting America's national security and economic prosperity.
11M Members
Founded in 1924

11909 **American Judges Association**
300 Newport Ave
Williamsburg, VA 23185-4147

757-259-1841
Fax: 757-259-1520
E-Mail: aia@ncsc.dni.us
Home Page: aja.ncsc.dni.us

Judge Elliot L Zide, President
Judge Brian MacKenzie, President-Elect
Judge John E Conery, Vice President
Justice Russell Otter, Secretary
Jugde Kevin S Burke, Treasurer

The objective and purpose of the Association is: to promote and improve the effective administration of justice; to maintain the status and independance of the judiciary; to provide a forum for the continuing education of its members and the general public; and for the exchange of new ideas among all judges.
2500 Members
Founded in 1959

11910 **American League of Lobbyists**
300 North Washington Street
Suite 205
Alexandria, VA 22314

703-960-3011
888-712-1357
E-Mail: info@alldc.org
Home Page: www.alldc.org
Social Media: Facebook, Twitter, LinkedIn

Monte Ward, President
James Hickey, 1st Vice President
Paul T Kelly, 2nd Vice President
Wright Andrews, Secretary
Paul Kangas, Treasurer

National association dedicated to serving government relations and public affairs professionals. Provides programs and conferences of interest to lobbyists.
600+ Members
Founded in 1979

11911 **American Logistics Association**
1101 Vermont Ave NW
Suite 1002
Washington, DC 20005-2710

202-466-7636
Fax: 202-296-4419
E-Mail: membership@ala-national.org
Home Page: www.ala-national.org

Patrick B Nixon, President
Russ Moffett, VP, Member Relations
Maurice Branch, VP, Operations
Tracey Durand, Director, Meetings & Expositions

Organization that represents the private industry to promote food sales to commissaries on military bases.
Cost: $828.00
400 Members
***Frequency:* Membership Dues Vary**
Founded in 1972

11912 **American National Standards Institute**
1889 L Street NW
11th Floor
Washington, DC 20036-3864

202-293-8020
Fax: 202-293-9287
E-Mail: info@ansi.org
Home Page: www.ansi.org
Social Media: Facebook, Twitter, LinkedIn, Youtube, Google+

James T Pauley, Chairman
Joe Bhatia, President & CEO

Promotes the knowledge for approved standards for industry, engineering and safety design.
1000 Members
Founded in 1918

11913 **American Public Human Services Association**
1133 19th Street NW
Suite 400
Washington, DC 20036-3623

202-682-0100
Fax: 202-289-6555
Home Page: www.aphsa.org
Social Media: Facebook, Twitter, LinkedIn

Reggie Bicha, President
Uma Ahluwalia, Treasurer
Tracy Wareing, Secretary

APHSA pusues excellence in health and human services by supporting state and local agencies, informing policymakers, and working with partners to drive innovative, integrated and efficient solutions in policy and practice.
Founded in 1930

11914 American Society for Public Administration
1301 Pennsylvania Avenue NW
Suite 700
Washington, DC 20004

202-393-7878
Fax: 202-638-4952
E-Mail: info@aspanet.org
Home Page: www.aspanet.org
Social Media: Facebook, Twitter, LinkedIn

Stephen E Condrey, President
Allan Rosenbaum, President Elect
Maria Aristigueta, VP

Offers a wide range of services and membership options for individuals in public administration careers. Sponsors 127 local chapters and 16 sections on specific areas of governments, such as the Section of Natural Resources and Environmental Administration and the Section on Human Resource Administration.
15M Members
Founded in 1939

11915 American Society of Access Professionals
1444 I(Eye) St. NW
Suite 700
Washington, DC 20005-6542

202-712-9054
Fax: 202-216-9646
E-Mail: asap@bostrom.com
Home Page: www.accesspro.org
Social Media: Facebook, Twitter

Scott Hodes, President
Joel D Miller, Vice President
Karen Finnegan, Treasurer
Amy Bennett, Secretary

Members are government employees, lawyers, journalists and others concerned with access to government data under current personal privacy and public informaiton statues.
Founded in 1980

11916 Americans for Democratic Action
1625 K St NW
Suite 300
Washington, DC 20006-1611

202-785-5980
Fax: 202-204-8637
E-Mail: info@adaction.org
Home Page: www.adaction.org
Social Media: Facebook, Twitter, Flickr, YouTube

Lynn Woolsey, President
David Card, Treasurer
Mary Von Euler, Secretary

Liberal lobbying group.

11917 Association for Federal Information Resources Management
400 North Washington St.
Suite 300
Alexandria, VA 22314

703-778-4646
Fax: 703-683-5480
E-Mail: info@affirm.org
Home Page: www.affirm.org
Social Media: Facebook, Twitter, LinkedIn, Flickr

Eric Won, President
Barry West, Vice President
Onelia Codrington, VP, Industry
Brian Moran, VP
Stacy Riggs, VP

A non-profit, volunteer, educational organization whose overall purpose is to improve the management of information, and related systems and resources, within the Federal government. Members include information resource management professionals from the Federal, academic, and industry sectors.
350 Members
Founded in 1979

11918 Association for Postal Commerce
1800 Diagonal Rd.
Suite 320
Alexandria, VA 22314-2862

703-524-0096
Fax: 703-997-2414
Home Page: www.postcom.org
Social Media: Facebook

National organization representing those who use, or who support, the use of mail as a medium for communication and commerce. Publishes a weekly newsletter covering postal policy and operational issues.
Founded in 1947

11919 Association of Boards of Certification
2805 SW Snyder Blvd.
Suite 535
Ankeny, IA 50023

515-232-3623
Fax: 515-965-6827
E-Mail: abc@abccert.org
Home Page: www.abccert.org

Brent Herring, President
Brian Thorburn, President-Elect
Ray Olson, Vice President

The Association of Boards of Certification is dedicated to protecting public health and the environment by advancing the quality and integrity of environmental certification programs through innovative technical support services, effective information exchange, professional and cost-effective examination services, and other progressive services for certifying members.
Founded in 1972

11920 Association of Civilian Technicians (ACT)
12620 Lake Ridge Dr
Lake Ridge, VA 22192-2335

703-494-4845
Fax: 703-494-0961
E-Mail: actnational@actnat.com
Home Page: www.actnat.com
Social Media: Facebook

Terry Garnett, President
Raul Toro, Treasurer

Labor organization of civilian employees of Air Force, Army, National Guard and Reserves.
12M Members

11921 Association of Fish and Wildlife Agencies
444 N Capitol St NW
Suite 725
Washington, DC 20001-1553

202-624-7890
Fax: 202-624-7891
E-Mail: info@fishwildlife.org
Home Page: www.fishwildlife.org
Social Media: Facebook, Twitter, Blogger

Ron Regan, Executive Director
Carol Bambery, Association Counsel
Kathy Boydston, Wildlife & Energy Liasion
John Bloom, Accounting Manager
Arpita Choudhury, Science & Research Liasion

The organization that represents all of North America's fish and wildlife agencies that promotes sound management and conservation, and speaks with a unified voice on important fish and wildlife issues.
Founded in 1902

11922 Association of Food and Drug Officials
2550 Kingston Rd
Suite 311
York, PA 17402-3734

717-757-2888
Fax: 717-650-3650
E-Mail: afdo@afdo.org
Home Page: www.afdo.org

Joseph Korby, Executive Director
Denise Rooney, Association Manager
Pat Smith, Support Staff
Randy Young, IT Administrator
Krystal Reed, Admin/Special Projects Assistant

Promotes the enforcement of laws and regulations at all levels of government. Fosters understanding and cooperation between industry and regulators. Develops model laws and regulations and seeks their adoption.
800 Members
Founded in 1986

11923 Association of Former Agents of the US Secret Service
525 SW 5th Street
Suite A
Des Moines, IW 50309-0848

515-282-8192
Fax: 515-282-9117
Home Page: www.oldstar.org

Founded to bring together former and current employees of the Secret Service for comradeship, friendship and support in time of need. Members include Special Agents, Technical Specialists and other support personnel who carried out the investigative and protective responsibilities of the United States Secret Service.
950 Members
Founded in 1971

11924 Association of Labor Relations Agencies
38 Wolcott Hill Road
Wethersfield, CT 06109

860-263-6860
Fax: 860-263-6875
Home Page: www.alra.org

Kevin Flanigan, President
Tim Noonan, President-Elect
Gilles Grenier, VP, Administration
Scot Beckenbaugh, VP, Finance
Ginette Brazeau, VP, Professional Development

An association of impartial government agencies in the US and Canada responsible for administering labor-management relations laws or services. Promotes cooperation among these agencies, high professional standards, public interest in labor relations, improved employer-employee relationships, peaceful resolution of employment and labor disputes, and the exchange of information regarding the administration and improvement of agency services.

11925 Center for Neighborhood Enterprise
1625 K. Street NW
Suite 1200
Washington, DC 20006

202-518-6500
Fax: 202-588-0314
Home Page: www.cneonline.org
Social Media: Facebook, Twitter, YouTube, Flickr

Robert L Woodson Sr, President
Clifford Ehrlich, Chair

Founded to help the residents of low-income neighborhoods address the problems of their communities. Mission is to transform lives,

schools, and troubled neighborhoods, from the inside out. Current programs are the Violence-Free Zone youth violence reduction program; Training and Technical Assistance for Community-Based Organizations; and Adult Financial Literacy.
Founded in 1981

11926 **Center for the Study of the Presidency and Congress (CSPC)**
1020 19th St NW
Suite 250
Washington, DC 20036-6120
202-872-9800
Fax: 202-872-9811
E-Mail: email@thepresidency.org
Home Page: www.thepresidency.org
Social Media: Facebook, Twitter, YouTube
David M Abshire, Vice Chair
Maxmillian Angerholzer III, President/CEO
Dan Mahaffee, Director, Policy & Board Relations
Jonathan Murphy, Director, External Affairs
Elizabeth Perch, COO & CFO
CSPC strives to: promote leadership in the Presidency and Congress to generate innovative solutions to current national challenges; preserve the historic memory of the Presidency by identifying lessons from successes and failures of such leadership; draw on a wide range of talent to offer ways to better organize an increasingly compartmentalized Federal Government; educate and inspire the next generation of America's leaders to incorporate civility, inclusiveness, and character into their lives.

11927 **Citizens Against Government Waste**
1301 Pennsylvania Ave
Suite 1075
Washington, DC 20004
202-467-5300
Fax: 202-467-4253
E-Mail: membership@cagw.org
Home Page: www.cagw.org
Social Media: Facebook, Twitter, Youtube
Thomas A Schatz, President
Ariane E Sweeney, VP, Membership & Development
Leslie K Paige, VP Policy & Communications
Robert J Tedeschi, Treasurer/CFO
Public advocacy, non-partisan organization committed to eliminate government waste, fraud, abuse, mismanagement and inefficiency.
1MM+ Members
Founded in 1984
Mailing list available for rent

11928 **Citizens for Global Solutions**
418 7th St Se
Washington, DC 20003-2707
202-546-3950
Fax: 202-546-3749
E-Mail: info@globalsolutions.org
Home Page: www.globalsolutions.org
Social Media: Facebook, Twitter, YouTube
Don Kraus, CEO
Marvin Perry, Office Manager
Daniel Watson, Director, IT
Valerie Schrock, Creative Director
Nonprofit, tax deductible memebership organization of 50 chapters and groups throghout the United States. We work to educate policy-makers and the American public on issues of global governance, international law and grassroots activism.
11000 Members
Founded in 1978

11929 **Coalition for Government Procurement**
1990 M St NW
Suite 450
Washington, DC 20036-3466
202-331-0975
Fax: 202-822-9788
E-Mail: info@thecgp.org
Home Page: www.thecgp.org
Social Media: Facebook, Twitter, LinkedIn, Flickr, RSS
Roger Waldron, President
Carolyn Alston, EVP & General Counsel
Robert Rendely, CFO
Denise Meliski, Director, Business Development
Matt Cahill, VP, Membership & Marketing
Representing commercial contractors in the Federal market. Advocating for common sense policies that improve the acquisition environment for government, industry and ultimately the American taxpayer. Focusing outreach efforts on the General Services Administration, Department of Veterans Affairs, Office of Management and Budget, Department of Defense, and Capitol Hill.
350 Members
Founded in 1979

11930 **Commissioned Officers Association of the United States Public Health Service**
8201 Corporate Dr
Suite 200
Landover, MD 20785-2230
301-731-9080
866-366-9593
Fax: 301-731-9084
E-Mail: gfarrell@coausphs.org
Home Page: www.coausphs.org
Social Media: Facebook
Protects the interests of the Commissioned Corps officers of the US Public Health Service, who are leaders in the realms of public and global health. Dedicated to improving and protecting the public health of the US by addressing unmet health needs and providing support.
7M Members

11931 **Community Leadership Association**
1240 S Lumpkin Street
Athens, GA 30602
706-542-0301
Fax: 706-542-7007
E-Mail: sheena@claweb.org
Home Page: www.claweb.org
Gene A Honn, Executive Director
Organization dedicated to nurturing leadership in communities throughout the US and internationally. Members include hundreds of diverse community leadership organizations at local, state and national levels, thousands of individual graduates of these organizations and others interested in community leadership development.
2M Members
Founded in 1979

11932 **Conference of Minority Public Administrators**
PO Box 1552
Norfolk, VA 23510
301-333-5282
Fax: 202-638-4952
E-Mail: info@compahr.org
Home Page: www.compahr.org
Social Media: Facebook
Stanley Skinner, President
Linda A. Harmon, President-Elect
Pamela Alexxander, Treasurer
Tiffany L. Smith, Recording Secretary
Lynn Cherry-Miller, Corresponding Secretary
COMPA is one of America's leading national organizations committed to excellence in public service and public administration in city, county, state and federal government.
500 Members
Founded in 1977

11933 **Contract Services Association of America**
1000 Wilson Boulevard
Suite 1800
Arlington, VA 22209-3920
703-243-2020
Fax: 703-243-3601
Christopher Jahn, President
Represents the government services contracting industry. Membership ranges from small businesses and corporations servicing federal and state government in numerous capacities. CSA acts to foster the effective implementation of the government's policy of reliance on the private sector for support services.
650 Members
Founded in 1965

11934 **Council of State Community Development Agencies**
1825 K St NW
Suite 515
Washington, DC 20006-1261
202-293-5820
Fax: 202-293-2820
E-Mail: info@coscda.org
Home Page: www.coscda.org
John Greiner, President
Steve Charleston, VP
Kathleen Wiessenberger, Secretary
Keith Heaton, Treasurer
Dianne E Taylor, Executive DIrector
The premier national association advocating and enhancing the leadership role of states in community development through innovative policy development and implementation, customer-driven technical assistance, education, and collaborative efforts.

11935 **Council of State Governments**
2760 Research Park Drive
PO Box 11910
Lexington, KY 40578-1910
859-244-8000
800-800-1910
Fax: 859-244-8001
Home Page: www.csg.org
Social Media: Facebook, Twitter, YouTube
David Adkins, Executive Director & CEO
Brian Schweitzer, President
Luis Fortuno, President-Elect
Bob Godfrey, Chair
Jay Emler, Chair-Elect
Members include every elected and appointed state and territorial official in the US. A nonpartisan organization that brings state leaders together to share capitol ideas, providing them the chance to learn valuable lessons from each other. Also foster innovation in state government and shine a spotlight on examples of how ingenuity and leadership are transforming the way state government serves residents of the states and territories.
Founded in 1933

11936 **Council of State Housing Agencies**
Hall of States
444 N Capitol St NW
Suite 438
Washington, DC 20001-1505
202-624-7710
Fax: 202-624-5899

E-Mail: bthompson@ncsha.org
Home Page: www.ncsha.org
Social Media: Facebook, Twitter

Brian A Hudson, President
Thomas R Gleason, Vice President
Grant S Whitaker, Secretary/Treasurer
Barbara J. Thompson, Executive Director
Cary D Knox, Executive Office Admin

A nonprofit, nonpartisan organization created to represent members in Washingtong before Congress, the Administration, and the several federal agencies concerned with housing, including the Department of Housing and Urban Development, the Department of Agriculture, and the Treasury, and with other advocates for affordable housing.

11937 Council on Licensure, Enforcement and Regulation
403 Marquis Ave
Suite 200
Lexington, KY 40502-2104

859-269-1289
Fax: 859-231-1943
E-Mail: jhorne@clearhq.org
Home Page: www.clearhq.org
Social Media: Facebook, Twitter, LinkedIn

Darrell S Crimmins, President
Marc Seale, President-Elect
Adam Parfitt, Executive Director
Janet Horne, Office Manager
Rosa Brown, Administrative Associate

Members include occupational and professional licensing boards and agencies and private interests in the 50 states, territories and Canada.
380 Members
Founded in 1980

11938 Digital Government Institute
1934 Old Gallows Road
Suite 350
Vienna, VA 22182

703-752-6243
Fax: 703-752-6201
E-Mail: info@digitalgovernment.com
Home Page: www.digitalgovernment.com
Social Media: Facebook, Twitter, LinkedIn, Flickr

Specializes in the design and production of leading edge educational programs on emerging trends and technologies for government IT management professionals. A trusted source for education, networking and results.
Founded in 1998

11939 Energy Bar Association
1990 M St NW
Suite 350
Washington, DC 20036-3429

202-223-5625
Fax: 202-833-5596
E-Mail: admin@eba-net.org
Home Page: www.eba-net.org
Social Media: Facebook

Adrienne E Clair, President
Jason F Leif, President-Elect
Richard Meyer, Vice President
Katy M Gottsponer, Secretary
Jane E Rueger, Treasurer

An international, nonprofit association of attorneys and non-attorney professionals active in all areas of energy law. EBA's voluntary membership is comprised of government, corporate and private attorneys, as well as non-attorney professionals from across the globe, and includes law students interested in energy law.
2600 Members
Founded in 1946

11940 Federal Bar Association
1220 North Fillmore St.
Suite 444
Arlington, VA 22201

571-481-9100
Fax: 571-481-9090
E-Mail: fba@fedbar.org
Home Page: www.fedbar.org
Social Media: Facebook, Twitter, LinkedIn

Karen Silberman, Executive Director
Stacy King, Executive Deputy Director
Heather Gaskins, Director, Development
Steve Smith, Director, Membership & Marketing

Members are attorneys in the Federal Government or who have interest in federal law.
16000 Members
Founded in 1920

11941 Federal Criminal Investigators Association
12427 Hedges Run Drive
Suite 104
Lake Ridge, VA 22192

630-969-8537
800-403-3374
E-Mail: info@fedcia.org
Home Page: www.fedcia.org

Mission of FCIA is to ensure that Federal Law Enforcement Professionals have the tools and the support network to meet the challenges of future criminal investigations while becoming more community oriented.
1500 Members
Founded in 1953

11942 Federal Facilities Council
500 Fifth St. NW
Washington, DC 20001

202-334-3374
Fax: 202-334-3370
Home Page: sites.nationalacademies.org/DEPS/FFC/
Social Media: Facebook, Twitter

Operating under the auspices of the BICE, the FFC's mission is to identify and advance technologies, processes, and management practices that improve the performance of federal facilities over their entire life-cycle, from planning to disposal.
130 Members
Founded in 1953

11943 Federal Managers Association
1641 Prince St
Alexandria, VA 22314-2818

703-683-8700
Fax: 703-683-8707
E-Mail: info@fedmanagers.org
Home Page: www.fedmanagers.org

Patricia A Niehaus, President
George J Smith, VP
Richard J Oppedisano, Secretary
Katie L Smith, Treasurer
Todd V Wells, Executive Director

Advocates excellence in public service through effective management and professionalism, as well as the active representation of its members' interests and concerns.
15M Members
Founded in 1913

11944 Federal Physicians Association
12427 Hedges Run Drive
Suite 104
Lake Ridge, VA 22192

703-426-8400
877-333-7497
Fax: 703-426-8400
E-Mail: info@fedphy.org
Home Page: www.fedphy.com

Brian J Ribiero, MD, President
Indira Jevaji, MD, VP
Michael Nesemann, MD, Treasurer
Michael Borecky, MD, Secretary

Represents and advocates for Physicians employed by the Federal Government.
400 Members
Founded in 1979

11945 Federation of Tax Administrators
444 N Capitol St NW
Suite 348
Washington, DC 20001-1538

202-624-5890
Fax: 202-624-7888
Home Page: www.taxadmin.org

James R Eads, Executive Director

Members are the tax agencies of the 50 state governments, the District of Columbia & New York City.
53 Members

11946 Fund for Constitutional Government
122 Maryland Ave NE
Washington, DC 20002-5610

202-546-3799
Fax: 202-543-3156
E-Mail: info@fcgonline.org
Home Page: www.fcgonline.org

Anne B. Zill, President
Russell Hemenway, Chairperson
Conrad Martin, Executive Director
Kat Saunders, Secretary

Seeks to expose and correct illegal activities, corruption, and lack of accountability in the federal government.
Founded in 1974

11947 Government Finance Officers Association
203 N La Salle St
Suite 2700
Chicago, IL 60601-1210

312-977-9700
Fax: 312-977-4806
E-Mail: inquiry@gfoa.org
Home Page: www.gfoa.org

Timothy L Firestine, President
Robert W Eichem, President Elect
Joseph G Costello, Executive Director
Ade' A Ariwoola, Finance Director
Linda B Cramer, Finance Director

The purpose of the Government Finance Officers Association is to enhance and promote the professional management of governments for the public benefit by identifying and developing financial policies and practices and promoting them through education, training and leadership.
17300 Members
Founded in 1906

11948 Hispanic Elected Local Officials
National League of Cities
1301 Pennsylvania Ave NW
Suite 550
Washington, DC 20004-1747
202-626-3169
Fax: 202-626-3103
Social Media: Facebook, Twitter, LinkedIn, Youtube, RSS, Google+

Chris Coleman, President
Ralph Becker, 1st Vice President
Melodee Colbert Kean, 2nd Vice President
Clarence E Anthony, Executive Director

Serves as a forum for communication and exchange among Hispanic local government offi-

cials within the framework of the National League of Cities.
100+ Members
Founded in 1976

11949 Housing Assistance Council
1025 Vermont Ave NW
Suite 606
Washington, DC 20005-3516
202-842-8600
Fax: 202-347-3441
E-Mail: hac@ruralhome.org
Home Page: www.ruralhome.org
Social Media: Facebook, Twitter, LinkedIn
Moises Loza, Executive Director
Joe Belden, Deputy Executive Director
Lilla Sutton, Executive Coordinator
Leslie Strauss, Senior Policy Analyst
Expands the pool of decent housing available to the rural poor. Creates and sustains interest and action from all levels of government concerning rural housing for low-income people and helps rural housing organizations become more productive and professional.
30 Members
Founded in 1971

11950 Industry Coalition on Technology Transfer
1400 L St NW
Suite 800
Washington, DC 20005-3502
202-371-5994
Fax: 202-371-5950
Coalition of major high technology trade associations concerned with the US Government export controls. Monitors and addresses federal regulations on technology transfer.
4 Members
Founded in 1983

11951 International Association of Correctional Training Personnel
PO Box 81826
Lincoln, NE 68501
312-341-6340
Home Page: www.iactp.org
James Clark, President
Correctional officers and juvenile administrators.
9.5M Members

11952 International Association of Fire Chiefs
4025 Fair Ridge Drive
Fairfax, VA 22033-2868
703-273-0911
Fax: 703-273-9363
Home Page: www.iafc.org
Social Media: Facebook, LinkedIn
William R Metcalf, President & Chairman
G Keith Bryant, 1st Vice President
Stephen Dean, 2nd Vice President
Richard R. Carrizzo, Treasurer
Represents the leadership of firefighters and emergency responders worldwide; members are the world's leading experts in firefighting, emergency medical services, terrorism response, hazardous materials spills, natural disasters, search and rescue, and public safety policy.
12000 Members
Founded in 1873

11953 International Association of Official Human Rights Agencies
444 N Capitol Street NW
Suite 536
Washington, DC 20001
202-624-5410
Fax: 202-624-8185
E-Mail: iaohra@sso.org
Home Page: www.iaohra.org
Shawn Martel Moore, Esq., President
Jean Kelleher Niebauer, 2nd Vice President
Paula Haley, Secretary
Lonnie L. Douglas, Treasurer
Private non-profit corporation consisting of human rights agencies in the US and Canada. Provides opportunities and forums for the exchange of ideas and information among human rights advocates. Also provides training opportunities for members and other concerned groups and organizations.
200 Members

11954 International Code Council
500 New Jersey Ave NW
6th Floor
Washington, DC 20001-2005
888-422-7233
Fax: 202-783-2348
E-Mail: webmaster@iccsafe.org
Home Page: www.iccsafe.org
Social Media: Facebook
Stephen D Jones, President
Guy Tomberlin, Vice President
Alex Olszowy III, Secretary/Treasurer
A nonprofit membership association dedicated to preserving the public health, safety and welfare in the built environment through the promulgation of model codes suitable for adoption by governmental entities and assisting code enforcement officials, design professionals, builders, manufacturers and others involved in the design, construction and regulatory processes.
16M Members
Founded in 1915

11955 International Downtown Association
1025 Thomas Jefferson Street, NW
Sutie 500W
Washington, DC 20007
202-393-6801
Fax: 202-393-6869
E-Mail: question@ida-downtown.org
Home Page: www.ida-downtown.org
Social Media: Facebook, Twitter, LinkedIn
David Downey, President & CEO
Kevin Moran, Communications & IT Manager
Rebecca Bishophall, Manager, Membership Services
Tracie Clemmer, Development & Exhibits Director
Patricia Stephenson, Director, Finance & Administration
The International Downtown Association has member organizations worldwide in North America, Europe, Asia and Africa. Through a network of committed individuals, a rich body of knowledge and unique capacity to nurture community-building partnerships, IDA is a guiding force in creating healthy and dynamic centers that anchor the well being of towns, cities and regions of the world.
650+ Members
Founded in 1954

11956 International Economic Development Council
734 15th Street NW
Suite 900
Washington, DC 20005
202-223-7800
Fax: 202-223-4745
Home Page: www.iedconline.org/
Social Media: Facebook, Twitter, LinkedIn
Dyan Lingle Brasington, CEc, Chair
Jeff Finkle, CEcD, President/CEO
Katelyn Palomo, Executive Assistant
Swati Ghosh, Director, Research
Carrie Mulcaire, Director, Federal Grants
Nonprofit membership organization dedicated to helping economic developmers do their job more effectively and raising the profile of the profession. Members create more high-quality jobs, develop more vibrant communities, and generally improve the quality of life in their regions.
1.8M Members
Founded in 1967

11957 Interstate Council on Water Policy
505 North Ivy Street
Arlington, VA 22220-1707
703-243-7383
Fax: 301-984-5841
E-Mail: phe@riverswork.com
Home Page: www.icwp.org
Social Media: Facebook, Twitter
Ryan Mueller, Chairman
Peter Evans, Executive Director
Bob Tudor, Secretary & Treasurer
Jerry Schulte, 1st Vice Chairman
Edward Swaim, 2nd Vice Chairman
The ICWP is the national organization of state and regional water resources management agencies. It provides a means for members to exchange information, ideas and experience to work with federal agencies which share water management responsibilities.
70 Members
Founded in 1959

11958 Interstate Oil and Gas Compact Commission
900 NE 23rd Street
Oklahoma City, OK 73105
405-525-3556
800-822-4015
Fax: 405-525-3592
E-Mail: iogcc@iogcc.state.ok.us
Home Page: www.iogcc.state.ok.us
Mike Smith, Executive Director
Gerry Baker, Associate Executive Director
Laurel Baird, Member Services Coordinator
Amy Childers, Federal Projects Manager
Carol Booth, CommunicationsÿManager
A multi-state government agency that champions the conservation and efficient recovery of domestic oil and natural gas resources.
700 Members
Founded in 1935

11959 National Academy of Public Administration
900 7th St NW
Suite 600
Washington, DC 20001-3815
202-347-3190
Fax: 202-393-0993
Home Page: www.napawash.org
Social Media: Facebook, Twitter, LinkedIn, Vimeo
Robert J. Shea, Chair
Nancy R. Kingsbury, Vice Chair
Dan G. Blair, President and CEO
Tom Reidy, Chief Financial Officer
Lisa Trahan, Director of Fellow Relations
Through its trusted and experienced leaders, the Academy improves the quality, performance, and accountability of governments in the nation and the world.
500 Members
Founded in 1967

11960 National Affordable Housing Management Association
400 N Columbus Street
Suite 203
Alexandria, VA 22314

703-683-8630
Fax: 703-683-8634
Home Page: www.nahma.org

Kris Cook, Executive Director
Michelle L. Kitchen, Director, Government Affairs
Rajni Agarwal, Director, Finance
Brenda Moser, Director, Meetings & Membership
Scott McMillen, Coordinator, Government Affairs

The leading voice for affordable housing, advocating on behalf of multifamily property managers and owners whose mission is to provide quality affordable housing. Membership includes the industry's most distinguished multifamily managers, owners, and industry stakeholders.
3000 Members
Founded in 1990

11961 National Alliance of State and Territorial AIDS Directors
444 N Capitol St NW
Suite 339
Washington, DC 20001

202-434-8090
Fax: 202-434-8092
E-Mail: nastad@nastad.org
Home Page: www.nastad.org
Social Media: Facebook, Twitter, LinkedIn, Blogger, Youtube

Julie Scofield, Executive Director

NASTAD strengthens state and territory-based leadership, expertise, and advocacy and brings them to bear in reducing the incidence of HIV and viral hepatitis infections and on providing care and support to all who live with HIV/AIDS and viral hepatitis. NASTAD's vision is a world free of HIV/AIDS and viral hepatitis.
59 Members
Founded in 1992

11962 National Assembly of State Arts Agencies
1029 Vermont Ave NW
2nd Floor
Washington, DC 20005-3517

202-347-6352
Fax: 202-737-0526
E-Mail: nasaa@nasaa-arts.org
Home Page: www.nasaa-arts.org

Pam Breaux, President
Jonathan Katz, Chief Executive Officer
Kelly J. Barsdate, Chief Program and Planning Officer
Laura S. Smith, CFRE, Chief Advancement Officer
Sharon Gee, Director of Meetings and Events

Unites, represents and serves the nation's state and jurisdictional arts agencies. Representing state arts agencies by empowering their work through knowledge, and advance the arts as an essential public benefit.
56 Members
Founded in 1968

11963 National Association for County Community and Economic Development
2025 M St NW
Suite 800
Washington, DC 20036-3309

202-367-1149
Fax: 202-367-2149
Home Page: www.nacced.org

John Murphy, Executive Director
Brian Paulson, President
Jack Exler, Vice President
Tony Agliata, Secretary/Treasurer
Bill J. Lake, Director

Purpose is to develop the technical capacity of county government practitioners to professionally administer federally-funded affordable housing, community development, and economic development programs that benefit their low- and moderate-income households.
120+ Members
Founded in 1989

11964 National Association for Search and Rescue
PO Box 232020
Centreville, VA 20120-2020

703-222-6277
877-893-0702
Fax: 703-222-6277
E-Mail: meganr@nasar.org
Home Page: www.nasar.org

Dan Hourihan, President
Megan Bartlett, Executive Director
Ross Robinson, Chief Financial Officer
Ellen Wingerd, Customer Care Manager

A not-for-profit membership association dedicated to advancing professional, literary, and scientific knowledge in fields related to search and rescue.
3M Members

11965 National Association of Clean Air Agencies
444 N Capitol Street NW
Suite 307
Washington, DC 20001-1506

202-624-7864
Fax: 202-624-7863
E-Mail: 4cleanair@4cleanair.org
Home Page: www.4cleanair.org

George S Aburn Jr., Co-President
Merlyn Hough, Co-President
Bill Becker, Executive Director
Nancy Kruger, Deputy Director
Stu A Clark, Co-Vice President

Represents state and local air pollution control officers from over 150 major metropolitan areas and 53 states and territories.

11966 National Association of Conservation Districts (NACD)
509 Capitol Court, NE
Washington, DC 20002-4937
202-547-6223
Fax: 202-547-6450
Home Page: www.nacdnet.org
Social Media: Facebook, Twitter, LinkedIn, Vimeo, Google Plus, Flickr

Earl Garber, President
Lee McDaniel, First Vice President
Brent Van Dyke, Second Vice President
John Larson, Chief Executive Officer
Laura Wood Peterson, Director of Government Affairs

NACD develops national conservation policies, influences lawmakers and builds partnerships with other agencies and organizations. NACD also provides services to its districts to help them share ideas in order to better serve their local communities.
17000 Members
Founded in 1946

11967 National Association of Counties
25 Massachusetts Ave NW
Suite 500
Washington, DC 20001-1450

202-393-6226
888-407-6226
Fax: 202-393-2630
E-Mail: nacomeetings@naco.org
Home Page: www.naco.org/
Social Media: Facebook, Twitter, LinkedIn, YouTube

Linda ?? Langston, President
Riki Hokama, 1st Vice President
Sallie Clark, 2nd Vice President
Matthew D. Chase, Executive Director
Karen McRunnel, Executive Assistant to the CEO

The National Association of Counties (NACo) is an organization that represents county governments in the United States. NACo advances issues with a unified voice before the federal government, improves the public's understanding of county government, and assists counties in finding and sharing innovative solutions through education and research. NACo's membership totals more than 2,000 counties, representing over 80 percent of the nation's population.
Founded in 1935

11968 National Association of County Engineers
25 Mass. Ave, NW
Suite 580
Washington, DC 20001-1454

202-393-5041
Fax: 202-393-2630
E-Mail: nace@naco.org
Home Page: www.countyengineers.org

Brian C Roberts, Executive Director
Rebecca Page, Director of Marketing & Membership
Constantine Connie Radoulovitch, Office Manager

Members are county engineering professionals or road management authorities.
1900 Members
Founded in 1956

11969 National Association of Development Organizations (NADO)
400 N Capitol St NW
Suite 390
Washington, DC 20001-6505

202-624-7806
Fax: 202-624-8813
E-Mail: info@nado.org
Home Page: www.nado.org
Social Media: Facebook, Twitter, RSS

Peter Gregory, President
Vicki Glass, Director of Meetings and Membership
Susan Howard, Director of Government Relations
Brian Kelsey, Director of Economic Development
Carrie Kissel, Associate Director

The National Association of Development Organizations (NADO) serves as the national voice for regional development organizations. NADO helps its members achieve their goals by providing effective advocacy and lobbying services at the federal level, producing timely information and research, and offering opportunities for professional and organizational growth.

11970 National Association of Government Archives & Records Administrators
1450 Western Avenue
Suite 101
Albany, NY 12203
518-694-8472
Fax: 518-463-8656
E-Mail: nagara@caphill.com
Home Page: www.nagara.org

Daphne DeLeon, President
Pari Swift, Vice President
Jannette Goodall, Secretary
Galen R. Wilson, Treasurer
Steve Grandin, Membership Services & Publications

Professional association dedicated to the improvement of federal, state, and local government records and information management and the professional development of government records administrators and archivists. Members include county, municipal, and special district governments, state agencies, the National Archives and Records Administration; individual federal employees; the General Archives of Puerto Rico; and a number of provincial and institutional programs.

11971 National Association of Housing and Redevelopment Officials
630 Eye Street, NW
Washington, DC 20001-3736
202-289-3500
877-866-2476
Fax: 202-289-8181
E-Mail: nahro@nahro.org
Home Page: www.nahro.org

Saul Ramirez, Executive Director
Donald J Cameron, Senior VP
Joseph E Gray Jr, VP
Elizabeth C Morris, VP Housing
Saul Ramirez, Manager

A professional membership association representing local housing authorities, community development agencies and individual professionals in the housing, community development and redevelopment fields.
700 Members
Founded in 1933

11972 National Association of Local Housing Finance Agencies
2025 M St NW
Suite 800
Washington, DC 20036-2422
202-367-1197
Fax: 202-367-2197
E-Mail: info@nalhfa.org
Home Page: www.nalhfa.org

Ernestine Garey, President
Marc Jahr, Vice President
Ron Williams, Treasurer
Paula Sampson, Secretary

The national association of professionals working to finance affordable housing in the broader community development context at the local level. Nonprofit association working as an advocate before Congress and federal agencies on legislative and regulatory issues affecting affordable housing and provides technical assistance and educational opportunities to its members and the public.
Founded in 1982

11973 National Association of Neighborhoods
1300 Pennsylvania Ave NW
Suite 700
Washington, DC 20004-3024
202-332-7766
Fax: 202-588-5881
E-Mail: info@nanworld.org
Home Page: www.nanworld.org

Mission is to improve the quality of life in the nation's most important communities- its neighborhoods. Remains an organization of neighborhood coalitions, block clubs, community councils, and individuals, united by a love of neighborhoods and a strong determination to make them better.
2500+ Members
Founded in 1975

11974 National Association of Postmasters of the United States
8 Herbert St
Alexandria, VA 22305-2600
703-683-9027
Fax: 703-683-6820
E-Mail: napusinfo@napus.org
Home Page: www.napus.org

Robert J. Rapoza, President
Michael E. Quinn, Secretary/ Treasurer

Mission is to represent, promote, and protect postmasters. To foster a favorable image of public service and to assure users of the mail the best possible service. To be an advocate with the Congress of the United States. And to work closely with the United States Postal Service in the development of strategies for the enhancement of Postmasters and the Postal Service.
41M Members
Founded in 1898

11975 National Association of Regional Councils
777 North Caoitol Street NE
Suite 305
Washington, DC 20002
202-618-5696
Fax: 202-986-1038
E-Mail: lindsey@narc.org
Home Page: www.narc.org

Fred Abousleman, Executive Director
Lindsey Riley, Deputy of Communications

State of regional repositories of instructional materials or services.
250 Members

11976 National Association of Regulatory Utility Commissioners (NARUC)
1101 Vermont Ave NW
Suite 200
Washington, DC 20005-3553
202-898-2200
Fax: 202-898-2213
E-Mail: admin@naruc.org
Home Page: www.naruc.org

Colette D. Honorable, President
Lisa Polak Edgar, 1st Vice President
Susan K. Ackerman, 2nd Vice President
Charles D. Gray, Executive Director
David E. Ziegner, Treasurer

Representing the State Public Service Commissioners who regulate essential utility services, including energy, telecommunications, and water. Members are responsible for assuring reliable utility service at fair, just, and reasonable rates. The Association is an invaluable resource for members and the regulatory community, providing a venue to set and influence public policy, share best practices, and foster innovative solutions to improve regulation.
Founded in 1889

11977 National Association of State Development
12884 Harbor Drive
Woodbridge, VA 22192
703-490-6777
Fax: 703-880-0509

Miles Friedman, President/CEO
Sally Pope, Director Finance
Pofen Salem, Project Manager

Established to provide a forum for directors of state economic development agencies to exchange information, compare programs, and establish an organizational base to approach the Federal Government on issues of mutual interest.
250 Members
Founded in 1946

11978 National Association of State Facilities
2760 Research Park Drive
PO Box 11910
Lexington, KY 40578-1910
859-244-8000
800-800-1910
Fax: 859-244-8001
Home Page: www.csg.org
Social Media: Facebook, Twitter, YouTube

Gary Stevens, Chair
Gov. Jay Nixon, President
Carl Marcellino, Vice Chair
Mark Norris, Chair-Elect
David Adkins, Executive Director/CEO

Brings state leaders together to share capitol ideas, providing them the chance to learn valuable lessons from each other. Fosters innovation in state government and shining a spotlight on examples of how ingenuity and leaderhsip are transforming the way state government serves residents of the states and territories.
Founded in 1933

11979 National Association of Towns and Townships
1130 Connecticut Ave NW
Suite 300
Washington, DC 20036-3981
202-454-3950
866-830-0008
Fax: 202-331-1598
Home Page: www.natat.org

Larry Merrill, President
Matthew DeTemple, Vice President
Jennifer Imo, Federal Director
Bill Hanka, Deputy Federal Director
Mark Limbaugh, Senior Advisor

Seeks flexible and alternative approaches to federal policies to ensure that small communities can meet federal requirements. Advocates for fair share funding, technical assistance, and other affirmative steps to address the inherent disadvantages that small governments face in our present intergovernmental system.
13M Members

11980 National Border Patrol Council
2445 Fifth Ave.
Suite 350
San Diego, CA 92101
520-219-5152
800-620-1613
Fax: 520-219-5154
Home Page: www.nbpc1613.org
Social Media: Facebook

James Harlan, President
Dan Mais, 1st Vice President
Terence Shigg, 2nd Vice President
Robert Lopez, 3rd Vice President
Victor Cantu, Treasurer

Exlusive representative for non-supervisory Border Patrol Agents and support personnel as-

signed to the San Diego Sector of the United States Border Parol.
69000 Members
Founded in 1965

11981 **National Community Development Association**
522 21st St NW
#120
Washington, DC 20006-5012

202-293-7587
Fax: 202-887-5546
Home Page: www.ncdaonline.org
Social Media: LinkedIn

Cardell Cooper, Executive Director
Vicki Watson, Assistant Director
Karen Parker, Operations Manager

National nonprofit organization at the forefront in securing effective and responsive housing and community development programs for local governments. Provides timely, direct information and technical support to its members on federal housing and community development programs.
550+ Members

11982 **National Conference of State Legislatures**
National Conference of State Legislatures
7700 E 1st Pl
Denver, CO 80230-7143

303-364-7700
Fax: 303-364-7800
E-Mail: ncslnet-admin@ncsl.org.
Home Page: www.ncsl.org
Social Media: Facebook, Twitter, LinkedIn, Youtube

Terie Norelli, President
Jean Cantrell, Vice President
Patsy Spaw, Secretary/Treasurer

A bipartisan organization that serves the legislators and staffs of the nation's 50 states, its commonwealths and territories.
Cost: $49.00
15000 Members
Circulation: 18000
ISSN: 0147-0644
Founded in 1975
Printed in 4 colors

11983 **National Council of State EMS Training Coordinators**
201 Park Washington Court
Falls Church, VA 22046

888-240-4696
Fax: 703-241-5603
Home Page: www.nscemstc.org

Members are supervisors or coordinators of state EMS training programs, and limited to three from each state.

11984 **National Council of State Housing Agencies**
Hall of States
444 N Capitol St NW
Suite 438
Washington, DC 20001-1505

202-624-7710
Fax: 202-624-5899
E-Mail: bthompson@ncsha.org
Home Page: www.ncsha.org
Social Media: Facebook, Twitter

Brian A. Hudson, President
Thomas R. Gleason, Vice President
Barbara J. Thompson, Executive Director
Maury L. Edwards, Director of Meetings
Kevin B. Burke, CPA, Director of Finance and Operations

NCSHA represents its members in Washington before Congress, the Administration, and the several federal agencies concerned with housing, including the Department of Housing and Urban Development, the Department of Agriculture, and the Treasury, and with other advocates for affordable housing.
350 Members
Founded in 1974

11985 **National District Attorneys Association**
99 Canal Center Plaza
Suite 330
Alexandria, VA 22314-1548

703-549-9222
Fax: 703-836-3195
Home Page: www.ndaa.org
Social Media: Facebook

Scott Burns, Executive Director
Rick Hasey, CFO
Richard Hanes, Chief of Staff
Joanne Thomka, Director, Traffic Program
Allie Phillips, Deputy Director

Serves as a nationwide, interdisciplinary resource center for training, research, technical assistance, and publications reflecting the highest standards and cutting-edge practices of the prosecutorial profession.
7000 Members
Founded in 1950

11986 **National Emergency Management Association**
PO Box 11910
Lexington, KY 40578

859-244-8000
Fax: 859-244-8239
E-Mail: nemaadmin@csg.org
Home Page: www.nemaweb.org
Social Media: Facebook

Charley English, President
Bryan Koon, Vice President
Trina R. Sheets, NEMA Executive Director
Beverly Bell, Senior Policy Analyst
Karen Cobuluis, Meeting & Marketing Coordinator

A nonpartisan, nonprofit association dedicated to enhancing public safety by improving the nation's ability to prepare for, respond to, and recover from all emergencies, disasters, and threats to our nation's security. Provides national leadership and expertise in comprehensive emergency management, serves as a vital emergency management information and assistance resource, and advances continuous improvement in emergency management.
263 Members
Founded in 1970

11987 **National Forum for Black Public Administrators**
777 N Capitol St NE
Suite 807
Washington, DC 20002-4291

202-408-9300
Fax: 202-408-8558
E-Mail: webmaster@nfbpa.org
Home Page: www.nfbpa.org
Social Media: Facebook, YouTube

Verdenia C. Baker, President
Bruce T. Moore, 1st Vice President
Regina V. K. Williams, Interim Executive Director
Malick Diagne, Fiscal Director
Yvette Harris, Membership Coordinator

Committed to strengthening the position of Blacks within the field of public administration; increasing the number of Blacks appointed to executive positions in public service organizations; and, to groom and prepare younger, aspiring administrators for senior public management posts in the years ahead.
2.8M Members
Founded in 1983

11988 **National Governors' Association**
Hall of States
444 N Capitol St
Suite 267
Washington, DC 20001-1512

202-624-5300
Fax: 202-624-5313
E-Mail: webmaster@nga.org
Home Page: www.nga.org
Social Media: Facebook, Twitter

Governor Mary Fallin, Chair
Governor John Hickenlooper, Vice Chair
Dan Crippen, Executive Director
Barry Anderson, Deputy Director
David Quam, Deputy Director, Policy

Coordinates the formulation of state policies by governors, and works to ensure consideration of these positions in the development of national policies and programs. The governors belong to seven standing committees: agriculture; community and economic development; justice and public protection; energy and environment; human resources; international trade; and foreign relations.
Founded in 1908

11989 **National Housing Law Project**
703 Market Street
Suite 2000
San Francisco, CA 94103

415-546-7000
Fax: 415-546-7007
E-Mail: nhlp@nhlp.org
Home Page: www.nhlp.org

Robert C. Pearman, Jr., Chairperson
John Relman, Vice Chair
Gideon Anders, Senior Staff Attorney
Catherine M. Bishop, Senior Staff Attorney
James R. Grow, Deputy Director

A nonprofit corporation that provides assistance on public and private housing and community development matters to Legal Services attorneys and housing specialists throughout the country. The project's goals are to produce, maintain and conserve low and moderate income housing and protect and expand the rights of lower income persons to decent and affordable housing.
Founded in 1968

11990 **National Institute of Governmental Purchasing/NIGP**
151 Spring Street
Herndon, VA 20170-5223

703-736-8900
800-367-6447
Fax: 703-736-9639
E-Mail: grante@co.cape-may.nj.us
Home Page: www.nigp.org
Social Media: Facebook, Twitter, LinkedIn

Marcheta E. Gillespie, CPPO, CPPB,, President
Rick Grimm, CPPO, CPPB, Chief Executive Officer
Brent Maas, Executive Director, Business
Catherine Patin, Communications Manager
Carol Hodes, CAE, Executive Director

An international not-for-profit educational and technical organization of public purchasing agencies. NIGP develops, supports and promotes the public procurement profession through premier educational and research programs, professional support, and advocacy initiatives that benefit members and constituents.
2600+ Members
Founded in 1944

11991 **National League of Cities**
1301 Pennsylvania Ave NW
Suite 550
Washington, DC 20004-1747

202-626-3180
877-827-2385
Fax: 202-626-3043
E-Mail: info@nlc.org
Home Page: www.nlc.org
Social Media: Facebook, Twitter, LinkedIn, RSS, Youtube, Google Plus

Chris Coleman, President
Ralph Becker, 1st Vice President
Melodee Colbert Kean, 2nd Vice President
Clarence Anthony, Executive Director
David DeLorenzo, Chief Digital Officer

Dedicated to helping city leaders build better communities. The NLC advocates for cities and towns, provides programs and services, provides opportunities for involvement and networking, keeps leaders informed, strengthens leadership skills, recognizes municipal achievements, partners with state leagues, and promotes cities and towns.
1700 Members
Founded in 1924

11992 **National Public Employer Labor Relations Association**
1012 South Coast Highway
Suite M
Oceanside, CA 92054

760-433-1686
877-673-5721
Fax: 760-433-1687
E-Mail: mike@npelra.org
Home Page: www.npelra.org
Social Media: Facebook, Twitter, LinkedIn

Michael T. Kolb, Executive Director
Yvonne Gillengerten, Operations Manager
Janessa Stephens, Association Specialist
Allison Wittwer, Administrative Assistant
Stephanie Biggs, Administrative Assistant

Provides Professional Development, Networking, and Advocacy Services to Labor Relations & Human Resources professionals, so that public sector employers may deliver the most efficient and effective services to citizens & taxpayers.
2000+ Members
Founded in 1971

11993 **National Rural Housing Coalition**
1331 G St NW
10th FL
Washington, DC 20002

202-393-5229
Fax: 202-393-3034
Home Page: www.nrhcweb.org
Social Media: Facebook, Twitter

Tom Carew, President
Karen Speakman, 1st Vice President
Greg Sparks, 2nd Vice President
Marty Miller, Secretary
Kathleen Tyler, Treasurer

Works to focus policy makers on the needs of rural areas by direct advocacy and by coordinating a network of rural housing advocates around the nation. National Rural Housing Coalition is supported entirely by donations, contributions and subscriptions.
300 Members
Founded in 1969

11994 **National WIC Association**
2001 S Street NW
Suite 580
Washington, DC 20009-1165

202-232-5492
Fax: 202-387-5281
E-Mail: crichardson@nwica.org
Home Page: www.nwica.org
Social Media: Facebook, Twitter, Pinterest

Jacqueline Marlette-Boras, Chair
Douglas Greenaway, President & CEO
Cecilia Richardson, Staff/Nutrition Programs Director
Robert A. Lee, Membership Coordinator
Samantha Lee, Communications, Media and Marketing

NWA is the proactive voice supporting, inspiring and empowering the WIC Community through creativity, teamwork and leadership to serve America's low-income, high-risk women, infants and children.
900 Members
Founded in 1979

11995 **North American Gaming Regulators Association**
1000 Westgate Drive
Suite 252
St Paul, MN 55114-8612

651-203-7244
Fax: 651-290-2266
E-Mail: info@nagra.org
Home Page: www.nagra.org

Lisa M. Christiansen, President
Andres Alvarez, Vice President
Debbie Parpounas, CPA, Treasurer
Gary A. Vigneault, Secretary

A nonprofit professional association of gaming regulators throughout North America. The organization brings together agencies that regulate gaming activities and provides them a forum for the mutual exchange of regulatory information and techniques. Collecting and disseminating regulatory and enforcement information, procedures, and experiences from all jurisdictions provides on-going gaming education and training for all members.
120 Members
Founded in 1984

11996 **North American Securities Administrators Association, Inc.**
750 First Street NE
Suite 1140
Washington, DC 20002-8034

202-737-0900
Fax: 202-783-3571
Home Page: www.nasaa.org
Social Media: Facebook, RSS

Andrea Seidt, President
Russ Iuculano, Executive Director
John H. Lynch, Deputy Executive Director
Joseph Brady, General Counsel
Michael Canning, Director of Policy

NASAA is the international organization representing securities administrators from all 50 states, the District of Columbia, Canada, Mexico and Puerto Rico, and is responsible for investor protection and education. NASAA recommends national policies in the securities industry and provides model legislation for state securities agencies to adopt affecting the regulation of broker/dealers and investment advisers. Consumers can contact NASAA to get phone numbers of state securities regulators.
66 Members
Founded in 1919

11997 **Patent and Trademark Office Society**
PO Box 2089
Arlington, VA 22202-0089

703-305-8340
Home Page: www.ptos.org

Matthew Troutman, President
Brandon Rosati, Vice President
David Sosnowski, Secretary
Fred Guillermety, Administrator
Tsung-Yin Tsai, Treasurer

Internationally recognized for its activities in the patent and trademark fields. The Society has actively influenced the patent and trademark systems- promoting the systems' growth and well-being.
1800 Members
Founded in 1917
Mailing list available for rent

11998 **Procurement Round Table**
1464 Nieman Road
Shady Side, MD 20764

301-261-9918
Home Page: www.procurementroundtable.org

Allan V. Burman, Chairman
Bill Gormley, Vice Chair
Kenneth J. Oscar, Treasurer

Chartered by former federal acquisition officials concerned about the economy, efficiency and effectiveness of the federal acquisition system. Its Directors and Officers are private citizens who serve pro bono with the objective of advising and assisting the government in making improvements in federal acquisition.
40 Members
Founded in 1984

11999 **Public Employees Roundtable**
PO Box 75248
Washington, DC 20013-5248
202-927-4926
Fax: 202-927-4920
Home Page: www.theroundtable.org

Committed to helping future public servants reach their goals. Supporting young people planning careers in public service through the scholarship, fellowship and internship programs of its members.

12000 **Public Housing Authorities Directors Association**
511 Capitol Court NE
Washington, DC 20002-4947
202-546-5445
Fax: 202-546-2280
Home Page: www.phada.org

Timothy Kaiser, Executive Director
Ted Van Dyke, Director of Government Affairs
Yaniv Goury, Director of Communications
Jim Armstrong, Policy Analyst
Kathleen Whalen, Policy Analyst

Represents and serves the needs of executive directors of housing authorities of all sizes, in all regions of the nation. In pursuing the Association's goal of improving assisted housing, the corporation works with Congress and federal agencies as well as with all interested groups to improve the nation's housing programs.
1.6M Members
Founded in 1979

12001 **Republican Communications Association**
Longworth House Office Building
1317 Longworth
PO Box 550
Washington, DC 20515-0001

E-Mail: RCA@mail.house.gov
Home Page: www.rcaweb.org

Neal Patel, President
Tom Wilbur, Vice-President
Shea Snider, Treasurer
Michael Marinaccio, Digital Director
John Cummins, Professional Development Director

Sponsors professional development and networking programs. Conducts seminars, briefings, and tours.
165 Members
Founded in 1970

12002 **Society of Government Economists**
PO Box 77082
Washington, DC 20013
202-643-1743
E-Mail: sge@sge-econ.org
Home Page: www.sge-econ.org

Robert Lerman, President
Julia Lane, Vice-President
Marvin Ward, Executive Director
Andrew Felton, Website Director
Brian Sloboda, Outreach Director and Event Planner

Supports the professional development of government economists, and those who are interested in public policy economics, by providing them with research, publications, and professional communication opportunities.
500 Members
Founded in 1970

12003 **State Government Affairs Council**
515 King Street
Suite 325
Alexandria, VA 22314
703-684-0967
Fax: 703-684-0968
E-Mail: eloudy@sgac.org
Home Page: www.sgac.org
Social Media: Facebook, Twitter, LinkedIn

Katrina Iserman, President
Elizabeth A. Loudy, Executive Director
Jennifer Mendez, Vice President
Crislyn Lumia, Director, Education & Training
Kate Necaise, Manager, Communications

The premier national association for multi-state government affairs professionals, providing opportunities for networking and professional development.
260 Members
Founded in 1981

12004 **State Higher Education Executive Officers Association**
3035 Center Green Drive
Suite 100
Boulder, CO 80301-2205
303-541-1600
Fax: 303-541-1639
E-Mail: sheeo@sheeo.org
Home Page: www.sheeo.org
Social Media: Twitter

Teresa Lubbers, Chair
George Pernsteiner, President
Julie Carnahan, Senior Associate
Glady Kerns, Director of Administration
Andy Tompkins, Treasurer

A nonprofit, nationwide association of the chief executive officers serving statewide coordinating boards and governing boards of postsecondary education.
56 Members
Founded in 1954

12005 **The National Association for State Community Services Programs**
111 K Street NE
Suite 300
Washington, DC 20002
202-624-5866
Fax: 202-624-8472
E-Mail: nascsp@nascsp.org
Home Page: www.nascsp.org
Social Media: Facebook, Twitter

Timothy R. Warfield, Executive Director
Joan Harris, Director
Brad Penney, General Counsel
Gretchen Knowlton, Policy Director
Tabitha Beck, Research Director

The premier national association charged with advocating and enhancing the leadership role of states in preventing and reducing poverty.
100 Members
Founded in 1968

12006 **Trust for Public Land**
101 Montgomery Street
Suite 900
San Francisco, CA 94104
415-495-4014
Fax: 415-495-4103
E-Mail: info@tpl.org
Home Page: www.tpl.org
Social Media: Facebook, Twitter, Youtube

Stephen W. Baird, President & CEO
Brian Beitner, Chief Investment Officer
Sean Connolly, Chief Marketing Officer
Ernest Cook, Senior Vice President
Kathy DeCoster, Vice President

A nonprofit land acquisition and conservation organization, working with community groups, landowners, public land management agencies and rural groups to preserve open space lands and to pioneer methods of community ownership of land. Through its Investment Lands Program, the Trust for Public Land also acquires underutilized properties by gift or bargain sales.
Founded in 1972

12007 **U.S. Chamber of Commerce**
1615 H St Nw
Washington, DC 20062-2000
202-659-6000
800-638-6582
Fax: 202-463-5836
E-Mail: press@uschamber.com
Home Page: www.uschamber.org
Social Media: Facebook, Twitter

Thomas J Donohue, President & CEO
David C. Chavern, Executive Vice President
Myron Brilliant, Executive Vice President
Lily Fu Claffee, Senior Vice President
Shannon DiBari, Senior Vice President

The mission of the Chamber of Commerce is to advance human progress through an economic, political and social system based on individual freedom, incentive, initiative, opportunity, and responsibility. The Chamber of Commerce provides a voice of experience and influence in Washington, D.C., and around the globe, fighting for business and free enterprise before Congress, the White House, regulatory agencies, and the courts.

12008 **United States Conference of Mayors**
1620 Eye Street, NW
Washington, DC 20006-4033
202-293-7330
Fax: 202-293-2352
E-Mail: info@usmayors.org
Home Page: www.usmayors.org
Social Media: Facebook, Twitter

Mayor Scott Smith, President
Mayor Kevin Johnson, Vice President
Mayor Stephanie Rawlings-Blake, 2nd Vice President
Tom Cochran, CEO and Executive Director

Primary roles are to promote development of policies, strengthen federal-city relationships, ensure federal policy meets urban needs, provide mayors with leadership and management tools, and create a forum in which mayors can share ideas and information.
30000 Members
Founded in 1987

12009 **United States Interagency Council on Homelessness**
Federal Center SW
409 Third St. SW Suite 310
Washington, DC 20024
202-708-4663
Fax: 202-708-1216
E-Mail: usich@usich.gov
Home Page: www.ich.gov
Social Media: Facebook, Twitter

Barbara Poppe, Executive Director

Mission is to coordinate the federal response to homelessness and to create a national partnership at every level of government and with the private sector to reduce and end homelessness in the nation while maximizing the effectiveness of the Federal Government in contributing to the end of homelessness.
Founded in 1987

12010 **Urban Land Institute**
1025 Thomas Jefferson St NW
Suite 500 West
Washington, DC 20007-5230
202-624-7000
Fax: 202-624-7140
E-Mail: ulifoundation@uli.org
Home Page: www.uli.org
Social Media: Facebook, Twitter, LinkedIn, YouTube, Flickr, Google Plus

Lynn Thurber, Chairman
Patrick L. Phillips, Chief Executive Officer
Michael Terseck, CFO
Kathleen B. Carey, Chief Content Officer
Jason Ray, Chief Technology Officer

Founded to provide a land-use information resource for both the professionals and the public. ULI conducts seminars, workshops, semiannual meetings, research programs and publishes books on all aspects of land use and development issues. ULI offers an advisory service, and gives annual Awards for Excellence.
14M Members
Founded in 1936

12011 **Urban and Regional Information Systems Association**
701 Lee Street
Suite 680
Des Plaines, IL 60016-4508
847-824-6300
Fax: 847-824-6363
E-Mail: info@urisa.org
Home Page: www.urisa.org
Social Media: Facebook, Twitter, LinkedIn

Allen Ibaugh AICP, GISP, President
Wendy Nelson, Executive Director
Keri Brennan, GISP, Education Manager
Patricia Francis, Meeting Coordinator
Verlanda McBride, Registrar & Database Manager

Concerned with the effective use of information systems technology at the state, regional and local levels. Members informed of current developments in the information systems field. Its goal is to stimulate and encourage the advancement of an interdisciplinary professional approach to planning, designing and operating information systems.
3000 Members
Founded in 1963

Newsletters

12012 **ADA Today**
Americans for Democratic Action

1625 K St NW
Suite 102
Washington, DC 20006-1611

202-785-5980
Fax: 202-785-5969
E-Mail: info@adaction.org
Home Page: www.adaction.org

David Card, Editor

The nation's oldest liberal lobbying group. This newsletter describes national and local chapter activities and updates federal legislative action.
Cost: $20.00
Frequency: Quarterly
Circulation: 65000
Mailing list available for rent: 65000 names
Printed in 2 colors on matte stock

12013 ADAction News and Notes
Americans for Democratic Action
1625 K St NW
Suite 210
Washington, DC 20006-1611

202-785-5980
Fax: 202-785-5969
E-Mail: info@adaction.org
Home Page: www.adaction.org

Allen Kukovich, Executive Committee Chair
Jim McDermott, CEO
Don Kufler, Circulation Manager

Offers information on legislative issues and lobbying.
Cost: $20.00
Frequency: Weekly
Circulation: 3000
Founded in 1948
Mailing list available for rent: 3000 names
Printed in one color on matte stock

12014 AJA Benchmark
American Judges Association
300 Newport Ave
Williamsburg, VA 23185-4147

757-259-1841
Fax: 757-259-1520
Home Page: aja.ncsc.dni.us

Judge Kevin S. Burke, President
Judge Toni Manning Higginbotham, President-Elect
Judge Elliott L. Zide, Vice President
Judge Brian MacKenzie, Secretary
Judge Harold V. Froehlich, Treasurer

Latest news from the American Judges Association.
2500 Members
Frequency: Quarterly
Founded in 1959

12015 ANSI Congressional Standards Update
American National Standards Institute
1819 L St NW
11th Floor
Washington, DC 20036-3864

202-293-8020
Fax: 202-293-9287
E-Mail: info@ansi.org
Home Page: www.ansi.org

Arthur E. Cote, Chairman
Joe Bhatia, President & CEO

Designed to provide members of Congress and their staff with timely information on key standards and conformity assessment issues that impact the global competitiveness of US business and the US quality of life.
1000 Members
Frequency: Monthly
Founded in 1918

12016 ASAP Newsletter
American Society of Access Professionals
1444 I St Nw
Suite 700
Washington, DC 20005-6542

202-712-9054
Fax: 202-216-9646
E-Mail: asap@bostrom.com
Home Page: www.accesspro.org

Claire Shanley, Executive Director

Provides information about upcoming and recent ASAP events, insights, and information about changes in the laws, and court decisions.
Frequency: Yearly

12017 Advocate
PHADA
511 Capitol Court NE
Washington, DC 20002-4947

202-546-5445
Fax: 202-546-2280
Home Page: www.phada.org

Timothy Kaiser, Executive Director

Provides members with insights into HUD and Congressional actions, funding opportunities, job vacancies, and major developments in the public housing field.
1.6M Members
Frequency: Bi-Weekly
Founded in 1979

12018 American Planning Association
American Planning Association
1030 15th St.
Suite 750 W
Washington, DC 20005

202-872-0611
Fax: 202-872-0643
E-Mail: CustomerService@planning.org
Home Page: www.planning.org/
Social Media: Facebook, Twitter, LinkedIn

Paul Farmer, CEO
Ann Simms, CFO/EOO

The American Planning Association(APA) brings together thousands of people- practicing planners, citizens, elected officials-committed to making great communities.
Cost: $645.00
40000 Members
Frequency: Monthly
Founded in 1917

12019 Assisted Housing Accounts & Audits Insider
Brownstone Publishers
149 5th Ave
16th Floor
New York, NY 10010-6832

212-473-8200
800-643-8095
Fax: 212-473-8786
E-Mail: info@vendomegrp.com
Home Page: www.vendomegrp.com

David B Klein, Editor
John M Striker, Publisher

Explains how to comply with regulatory STET requirements for accounting and auditing for HUD-assisted housing. Includes accounting control policies, audit preparation checklists, model accounting book entries, forms, staff memos and model letters.
Cost: $195.00
Frequency: Monthly
Founded in 1980
Printed in 2 colors on matte stock

12020 Assisted Housing Management Insider
Brownstone Publishers
149 5th Ave
16th Floor
New York, NY 10010-6832

212-473-8200
800-643-8095
Fax: 212-473-8786
E-Mail: info@hcmarketplace.com
Home Page: www.hcmarketplace.com

John Striker, Publisher

Explains HUD regulatory requirements for federally-assisted housing, and gives advice on how to stay in compliance. Includes sample copies of model leases, clauses, letters, eviction notices, authorization forms, checklists and signs.
Printed in 2 colors on matte stock

12021 BNA's Eastern Europe Reporter
Bureau of National Affairs
1801 S Bell St
Arlington, VA 22202-4501

703-341-3000
800-372-1033
Fax: 800-253-0332
E-Mail: customercare@bna.com
Home Page: www.bnabooks.com

Paul N Wojcik, CEO
William A. Beltz

This is just one of many biweekly notification services covering legislative, regulatory and legal developments affecting business, trade and investment in Eastern Europe and the former Soviet Union.
Cost: $1750.00
Frequency: Bi-annually

12022 CQ Congressional Quarterly
Congressional Quarterly
1414 22nd Street NW
Washington, DC 20037-1003

202-887-8500

Offers information on House and Senate committee hearings scheduled for up to two months from publication date.
Cost: $1299.00

12023 CQ Schedules
Congressional Quarterly
77 K Street NE
Washington, DC 20002-4681

202-650-6500
800-432-2250
E-Mail: customerservice@cqrollcall.com
Home Page: www.cq.com

Susan Benkelman, Executive Editor
Randy Wynn, Deputy Executive Editor
Anne Q Hoy, Managing Editor, Spec. Publications
Caitlin Hendel, Managing Editor, CQ Today
Melanie Starkey, Editor, Daily News

A daily guide to what's happening in Washington.

12024 CQ Today
Congressional Quarterly
77 K Street NE
Washington, DC 20002-4681

202-650-6500
800-432-2250
E-Mail: customerservice@cqrollcall.com
Home Page: www.cq.com

Susan Benkelman, Executive Editor
Randy Wynn, Deputy Executive Editor
Anne Q Hoy, Managing Editor, Spec. Publications
Caitlin Hendel, Managing Editor, CQ Today
Melanie Starkey, Editor, Daily News

CQ Today, available in print and online, delivers unparalleled coverage and analysis from the floor, committee markups, hearings and more.

Subscribers receive updates throughout the day as news breaks on Capitol Hill.

12025 Census and You
Census Bureau
4700 Silver Hill Rd
Washington, DC 20233-0001
301-763-3030
Fax: 301-457-3670
E-Mail: NPC.Call.Center.Info@census.gov
Home Page: www.census.gov
Thomas E Zebelsky, Plant Manager
Highlights data products and program of the US Census Bureau. Shows which reports, CD-ROMs, tapes, etc. to choose and also highlights releases on the Internet.
Cost: $21.00
12 Pages
Frequency: Monthly
Circulation: 11000
Founded in 1790
Printed in 2 colors on matte stock

12026 Civil Rights: From the State Capitals
Wakeman Walworth
PO Box 7376
Alexandria, VA 22307-7376
703-768-9600
Fax: 703-768-9690
Home Page: www.statecapitals.com/civilrights.html
Keyes Walworth, Publisher
Covers ethnic, race and gender discrimination; including hate crime legislation, racial profiling, the current battle over affirmative action plus gay rights, domestic partner issues, rights of the disabled, rights of minors, women in the workforce, Hispanic issues. Includes legislation, judicial and administrative decisions across the country, as well as federal actions that affect the states.
Cost: $245.00
4 Pages
Frequency: Weekly
Founded in 1962
Printed in one color on matte stock

12027 Clearinghouse
NAGARA
1450 Western Avenue
Suite 101
Albany, NY 12203
518-694-8472
Fax: 518-463-8656
E-Mail: nagara@caphill.com
Home Page: www.nagara.org
Paul R. Bergeron, President
Daphne DeLeon, Vice President
Caryn Wojcik, Secretary
Nancy Fortna, Treasurer
Illustrated newsletter of NAGARA. Features lively articles, informative announcements, a wide variety of news, and a column by the Archivist of the United States. Provides a forum for archivists to share information and learn from each other. Electronic publication only.
Frequency: Quarterly

12028 Connections
National Public Employer Labor Relations Assoc
1012 South Coast Highway
Suite M
Oceanside, CA 92054
760-433-1686
877-673-5721
Fax: 760-433-1687
E-Mail: mike@npelra.org
Home Page: www.npelra.org
The outstanding monthly e-newsletter, your connection to national, regional and local developments. For members only
Frequency: Monthly
Circulation: 2000

12029 Cooperative Housing Bulletin
National Association of Housing Cooperatives
1444 I St Nw
Suite 700
Washington, DC 20005-6542
202-737-0797
Fax: 202-216-9646
E-Mail: info@nahc.coop
Home Page: www.coophousing.org
Provides up-to-date information on issues of interest to the cooperative housing community. Accepts advertising.
Frequency: Monthly
Circulation: 2500
Printed in 2 colors on matte stock

12030 Divisions Digest
Federal Bar Association
1220 North Fillmore St.
Suite 444
Arlington, VA 22201
571-481-9100
Fax: 571-481-9090
E-Mail: fba@fedbar.org
Home Page: www.fedbar.org
Social Media: Facebook, Twitter, LinkedIn
Fern C. Bomchill, President
Robert J. DeSousa, President-Elect
Hon. Gustavo Gelpi, Jr., Treasurer
Serves the Corporate and Association Counsel, Federal Career Service, Senior Lawyers, and the Younger Lawyers Divisions of the FBA.
16000 Members
Frequency: Bi-Annually
Founded in 1920

12031 Downtown Idea Exchange
Alexander Communications Group
1916 Park Ave
8th Floor
New York, NY 10037-3733
212-281-6099
800-232-4317
Fax: 212-283-7269
E-Mail: info@downtowndevelopment.com
Home Page: www.downtowndevelopment.com
Laurence Alexander, Owner
Nadine Harris, Marketing Manager
News of downtown revitalization for downtown leaders and officials in local and state government.
Cost: $167.00
8 Pages
Frequency: Monthly
ISSN: 0012-5822

12032 Downtown Promotion Reporter
Alexander Communications Group
1916 Park Ave
8th Floor
New York, NY 10037-3733
212-281-6099
800-232-4317
Fax: 212-283-7269
E-Mail: info@downtowndevelopment.com
Home Page: www.downtowndevelopment.com
Romauld Alexander, Owner
Laurence Alexander, CEO
Sarah Benardos, Production Manager
Paul Felt, Editor
Proven promotion ideas and methods to bring shoppers to downtown stores.
Cost: $189.00
12 Pages
Frequency: Monthly
Circulation: 1000
ISSN: 0363-2830
Founded in 1954

12033 EBA UPDATE
Energy Bar Association
1990 M St NW
Suite 350
Washington, DC 20036-3429
202-223-5625
Fax: 202-833-5596
E-Mail: admin@eba-net.org
Home Page: www.eba-net.org
Social Media: Facebook
Derek A. Dyson, President
Susan A. Olenchuk, President-Elect
Jason F. Leif, Vice President
Emma F. Hand, Secretary
Hugh E. Hilliard, Treasurer
Providing members with the latest news regarding the energy industry.
2600 Members
Frequency: Quarterly
Founded in 1946

12034 EENR Pursuits
Federal Bar Association
1220 North Fillmore St.
Suite 444
Arlington, VA 22201
571-481-9100
Fax: 571-481-9090
E-Mail: fba@fedbar.org
Home Page: www.fedbar.org
Social Media: Facebook, Twitter, LinkedIn
Fern C. Bomchill, President
Robert J. DeSousa, President-Elect
Hon. Gustavo Gelpi, Jr., Treasurer
EENR Section newsletter.
16000 Members
Frequency: Bi-Annually
Founded in 1920

12035 Economic Development Now
International Economic Development Council
734 15th Street NW
Suite 900
Washington, DC 20005
202-223-7800
Fax: 202-223-4745
Home Page: www.iedc.org
Jeff Finkle, President & CEO
Dennis G. Coleman, Chair
Jay C. Moon, Vice Chair
Paul Krutko, Secretary/ Treasurer
Member publication providing a survey of current economic development news, original reports examining best practices, and updates concerning federal funding and activity.
1.8M Members
Frequency: Bi-Monthly
Founded in 1967

12036 Economic Development: From the State Capitals
Wakeman Walworth
PO BOX 7376
Alexandria, VA 22307-7376
703-768-9600
Fax: 703-768-9690
Home Page: www.statecapitals.com/
Keyes Walworth, Publisher
Covers environmental requirements, land use regulation, mass transportation, highway construction plans, utility rates, changes in labor

laws, tax policies, enterprise zones, parkland development, taxes, licensing and fees. Includes vital urban development programs: growth control legislation, state construction programs involving airports, stadiums, and building codes.
Cost: $245.00
8 Pages
Frequency: Weekly
Founded in 1963
Printed in one color on Y stock

12037 **Employee Policy for the Public and Private Sector: From the State Capitals**
Wakeman Walworth
PO Box 7376
Alexandria, VA 22307-7376
703-768-9600
Fax: 703-549-1372
Home Page: www.statecapitals.com/employeepolicy.html
Keyes Walworth, Publisher
Provides a nationwide perspective on employee health insurance programs, sexual harassment policies, unemployment and workers' compensation, retirement policies, family medical leave, new ergonomic rules, pay equity programs, collective bargaining, dismissal practices, minimum wages, drug testing, background checks, day care centers, domestic partner rules.
Cost: $245.00
4 Pages
Frequency: Weekly
Printed in one color on matte stock

12038 **EuroWatch**
WorldTrade Executive
PO Box 761
Concord, MA 01742
978-287-0301
Fax: 978-287-0302
E-Mail: info@wtexec.com
Home Page: www.wtexec.com
Alison French, Production Manager
Analyzes the most recent EU judicial and legislative developments. Covers EU trade issues, labor issues, single market and currency issues, EU and individual country business law, trademark issues.
Cost: $797.00

12039 **Federal Action Affecting the States: From the State Capitals**
Wakeman Walworth
PO Box 7376
Alexandria, VA 22307-7376
703-768-9600
Fax: 703-768-9690
Home Page: www.statecapitals.com/fedaction.html
Keyes Walworth, Publisher
Gives a state perspective on Federal court rulings, overseer programs, changes in state jurisdiction, federal funds for state programs, highway, drug abuse control, disaster, environmental and other programs that involve both the states and the Feds.
Cost: $245.00
4 Pages
Frequency: Weekly
Founded in 1955
Printed in one color on matte stock

12040 **Federal Assistance Monitor**
CD Publications
8204 Fenton St
Silver Spring, MD 20910-4571
301-588-6380
800-666-6380
Fax: 301-588-6385
Home Page: www.cdpublications.com
Michael Gerecht, President
Dave Kittross, Editor
Comprehensive review of federal funding announcements, private grants, rule changes and legislative actions affecting the community programs.
Cost: $419.00
Frequency: Monthly
Founded in 1961
Mailing list available for rent: 2,000 names at $160 per M

12041 **Federal Employees News Digest**
1850 Centennial Park Drive
Suite 520
Reston, VA 20191
703-648-9551
800-989-3363
Fax: 703-648-0265
Publishes weekly newsletter and self-help books for federal and postal employees on retirement and pay, as well as other benefit-related topics. Accepts advertising.
Cost: $49.00
4 Pages
Frequency: 5x Yearly
Founded in 1951

12042 **Federal Times**
6883 Commercial Dr
Springfield, VA 22159
800-368-5718
E-Mail: armylct@atpco.com
Home Page: www.defensenews.com
Mark Winans, VP
Elaine Howard, President/CEO
Alex Neill, Managing Editor
Jim Tice, Senior Writer
David Smith, Marketing
Timely news and information on the rapid changes impacting today's federal managers, managing staff, the latest technology, and financial and career decisions.
Cost: $55.00
Frequency: Weekly
Circulation: 1MM

12043 **Friday Flash**
Coalition for Government Procurement
1990 M St Nw
Suite 450
Washington, DC 20036-3466
202-331-0975
Fax: 202-822-9788
E-Mail: info@thecgp.org
Home Page: www.thecgp.org
A weekly newsletter published by the Coalition for Government Procurement.
38387 Pages
Frequency: Weekly
Circulation: 1200
Founded in 1979

12044 **From the State Capitals**
Wakeman Walworth
PO BOX 7376
Alexandria, VA 22307-7376
703-768-9600
Fax: 703-768-9690
Home Page: statecapitals.com/
Keyes Walworth, Publisher
Keeps readers informed of national trends in domestic lawmaking. Issues dealing with taxes, the environment, economic development, drug abuse, abortion and education.
Founded in 1955

12045 **GovManagement Daily**
American Society for Public Administration
1301 Pennsylvania Avenue NW
Suite 700
Washington, DC 20004
202-393-7878
Fax: 202-638-4952
E-Mail: info@aspanet.org
Home Page: www.aspanet.org
Social Media: Facebook, Twitter, LinkedIn
Erik O. Bergrud, President
Stephen E. Condrey, Vice-President
Kuotsai Tom Liou, President-Elect
Presenting headlines and brief summaries of news and other information and analysis on public-sector management at all levels of government.
15M Members
Frequency: Daily
Founded in 1939

12046 **Government Employee Relations Report**
Bureau of National Affairs
1801 S Bell St
Arlington, VA 22202-4501
703-341-3000
800-372-1033
Fax: 800-253-0332
E-Mail: customercare@bna.com
Home Page: www.bnabooks.com
Paul N Wojcik, CEO
A notification service that covers federal, state and municipal government employee relations.
Cost: $1479.00
Frequency: Weekly

12047 **Government PROcurement**
Penton Media
1300 E 9th St
Suite 316
Cleveland, OH 44114-1503
216-696-7000
Fax: 216-696-6662
Home Page: www.govpro.com
Jane Cooper, Marketing
Kristin M Atwater, Managing Editor
Kay Ross Baker, Publisher
Specifically for the public sector purchasing professional.
58 Pages
Circulation: 20000
ISSN: 1078-0769
Founded in 1892
Printed in 4 colors on glossy stock

12048 **Government Waste Watch Newspaper**
Citizens Against Government Waste
1301 Pennsylvania Ave NW
Suite 1075
Washington, DC 20004-1707
202-467-5300
Fax: 202-467-4253
E-Mail: membership@cagw.org
Home Page: www.cagw.org
Thomas A. Schatz, President
Robert J. Tedeschi, Treasurer & CFO
A quarterly newspaper published by Citizens Against Government Waste.
Cost: $25.00
Frequency: Quarterly
Circulation: 108000
Founded in 1984
Mailing list available for rent

12049 **HAC News**
Housing Assistance Council
1025 Vermont Ave NW
Suite 606
Washington, DC 20005-3516
202-842-8600
Fax: 202-347-3441

E-Mail: hac@ruralhome.org
Home Page: www.ruralhome.org

Moises Loza, Executive Director
Janice Clark, Editor

Newsletter publishing issues of rural and low-income housing. Free.
ISSN: 1093-8036

12050 HOTLINE
National Journal
The Watergate
600 New Hampshire Ave., NW
Washington, DC 20037

202-739-8400
800-207-8001
Fax: 202-833-8069
E-Mail: webmaster@asahq.org
Home Page: www.nationaljournal.com

Julie Abramson, Associate Production Editor
Tim Alberta, Sr Editor, National Journal Hotline
Ronald Brownstein, Editorial Director

Online daily newsletter offers information on US national, state and local political campaigns and issues.
Frequency: Weekly
Founded in 1987

12051 Health Officer News
US Conference of Local Health Officers
1620 I Street NW
Washington, DC 20006-4005

202-887-6120
Fax: 202-293-2352

Alan Campbell, Publisher
Stephen Horn, Editor

The official publication of the US conference of local health officers. Accepts advertising.
Cost: $35.00
12 Pages
Frequency: BiWeekly

12052 Housing Law Bulletin
National Housing Law Project
703 Market Street
Suite 2000
San Francisco, CA 94103

415-546-7000
Fax: 415-546-7007
E-Mail: nhlp@nhlp.org
Home Page: www.nhlp.org

Marcia Rosen, Executive Director
James Grow, Deputy Director
Susan Stern, Deputy Director, Administration

Updates in housing law information for use by legal services organizations.
Cost: $175.00
Frequency: Monthly
Circulation: 400

12053 ICBA NewsWatch Today
Independent Community Bankers of America
1615 L Street NW
Suite 900
Washington, DC 20036

800-422-8439
Fax: 202-659-3604
E-Mail: info@icba.org
Home Page: www.icba.org

Salvatore Marranca, Chairman
Jeffrey L. Gerhart, Chairman-Elect
William A. Loving, Jr., Vice Chairman
Steven R. Gardner, Secretary
Jack Hartings, Treasurer

Free electronic news bulletin highlighting breaking industry news and information.
Frequency: Daily

12054 In Hot Pursuit
Federal Bar Association
1220 North Fillmore St.
Suite 444
Arlington, VA 22201

571-481-9100
Fax: 571-481-9090
E-Mail: fba@fedbar.org
Home Page: www.fedbar.org
Social Media: Facebook, Twitter, LinkedIn

Fern C. Bomchill, President
Robert J. DeSousa, President-Elect
Hon. Gustavo Gelpi, Jr., Treasurer

Criminal Law Section newsletter.
16000 Members
Frequency: Bi-Annually
Founded in 1920

12055 Inside Energy
Platts, McGraw Hill Companies
1221 Avenue of the Americas
New York, NY 10020-1001

212-512-2000
Fax: 212-512-3840
E-Mail: support@platts.com
Home Page: www.mcgraw-hill.com

Glenn S Goldberg, President
Georgia Safos, Circulation Director

Covers the Department of Energy including energy, science/technology, and environmental management programs as well as energy programs at the Interior Department.
Cost: $1395.00
16 Pages
Frequency: Weekly
Founded in 1884

12056 International Association of Emergency Managers
201 Park Washington Court
Falls Church, VA 22046-4513

703-538-1795
Fax: 703-241-5603
E-Mail: info@iaem.com
Home Page: www.iaem.com

Elizabeth B Armstrong, Executive Director
Sharon L Kelly, Member Director
Elizabeth B Armstrong, CEO
Karen Thompson, Editor
Dawn Shiley, Communication Manager

Representatives of city and county government departments responsible for emergency management and disaster preparedness.
Cost: $160.00
20 Pages
Frequency: Monthly
Circulation: 2700
Founded in 1952
Printed in 2 colors on matte stock

12057 Lottery, Parimutuel & Casino Regulation: From the State Capitals
Wakeman Walworth
PO BOX 7376
Alexandria, VA 22307-7376

703-768-9600
Fax: 703-768-9690
Home Page:
www.statecapitals.com/lotterypari.html

Keyes Walworth, Publisher

Covers regulation, or attempts to regulate every form of gambling from internet gambling to cockfighting. It covers state lottery prize structures, ticket marketing policies, distribution of revenues, new games and equipment; Indian gaming, gambling compacts with tribes and revenue sharing; regulation and taxation of casinos, pari-mutuel wagering operations plus horse racing, dog racing, jai alai, riverboat gambling, bingo and other forms of gaming.
Cost: $345.00
4 Pages
Frequency: Weekly
Founded in 1962
Printed in one color on matte stock

12058 Managing Today's Federal Employees
LRP Publications
PO Box 980
Horsham, PA 19044-0980

215-784-0912
800-341-7874
Fax: 215-784-9639
E-Mail: webmaster@lrp.com
Home Page: www.lrp.com

Todd Lutz, CFO
Patrick Byrne, Editor
Chris Donohue, Legal Editor

Keeping supervisors informed of their personnel management responsibilities has always been one of the most difficult tasks facing federal agency personnel officers. This newsletter is a working resource as well as a comprehensive training tool. Gives sensible solutions to common management challenges and covers controversial issues such as sexual harassment, contracting out of federal jobs, alternative dispute resolutions and more.
Cost: $155.00
8 Pages
Frequency: Monthly
Founded in 1977
Printed in 2 colors on matte stock

12059 Mediaite
584 Broadway
Suite 510
New York, NY 10012

E-Mail: info@mediaite.com
Home Page: www.mediaite.com

Dan Abrams, Founder
Jon Nicosia, Senior Editor & Video Director
Nando Di Fino, Senior Editor & TV Reporter
Tommy Christopher, Political Editor & WH Correspondent
Colby Hall, Editor at Large

Mediaite is the site for news, information and smart opinions about print, online and broadcast media, offering original and immediate assessments of the latest news as it breaks.

12060 Motor Vehicle Regulation: From the State Capitals
Wakeman Walworth
PO Box 7376
Alexandria, VA 22307-7376

703-768-9600
Fax: 703-768-9690
Home Page:
www.statecapitals.com/motorreg.html

Keyes Walworth, Publisher

Covers all fifty states regarding inspections, tags, fees and taxes, emissions standards, drunken driving laws, motorist licensing, insurance and education . We report on helmet , seat belt, and child restraint seat laws; regulation of all motor vehicles including autos, trucks, motorcycles, school buses, electric vehicles, watercraft. We also cover motor vehicle department administrative changes.
Cost: $245.00
4 Pages
Frequency: Weekly
Founded in 1962
Printed in one color on matte stock

12061 NACCED Alerts
Nat'l Assoc. for County & Economic Development

2025 M St NW
Suite 800
Washington, DC 20036-3309

202-367-1163
Fax: 202-367-2149
Home Page: www.nacced.org

John Murphy, Executive Director
Brian Paulson, President
Jack Exler, Vice President
Tony Agliata, Secretary/Treasurer
Bill J. Lake, Director

Analyze federal legislation and regulations, highlight innovative county activities, report on current developments in the field, and provide updates on association activities.
120+ Members
Frequency: Bi-Weekly
Founded in 1989

12062 NADC News
National Association of Development Companies
6764 Old McLean Village Dr
Mc Lean, VA 22101-3906

703-748-2575
Fax: 703-748-2582
E-Mail: merril@nadco.org
Home Page: www.nadco.org

Chris Crawford, President

Provides long-term fixed asset financing to small businesses. Publishes newsletter.
Frequency: Monthly
Circulation: 244
Founded in 1981

12063 NAHMA News
National Affordable Housing Management Association
400 N Columbus Street
Suite 203
Alexandria, VA 22314

703-683-8630
Fax: 703-683-8634
Home Page: www.nahma.org

Trade association for professional property managers of federally assisted housing. Publishes a newsletter.
Cost: $95.00
Frequency: Bimonthly
Circulation: 3000

12064 NASAA Insight
NA Securities Administrators Association
750 First Street NE
Suite 1140
Washington, DC 20002-8034

202-737-0900
Fax: 202-783-3571
Home Page: www.nasaa.org
Social Media: Facebook

Jack Herstein, President
Preston DuFauchard, President-Elect
Rick Hancox, Secretary
Fred J. Joseph, Treasurer

Designed to keep readers informed of recent NASAA activities.
Frequency: Quarterly
Founded in 1919

12065 NASCSP Newsletter
Nat'l Assoc. for State Community Service Programs
444 N Capitol St NW
Suite 846
Washington, DC 20001-1556

202-624-5866
Fax: 202-624-7745
E-Mail: nascsp@nascsp.org
Home Page: www.nascsp.org
Social Media: Facebook, Twitter

Steve Payne, President
William Brand, Vice President
Jennifer Sexson, Treasurer
Ditzah Wooden-Wade, Secretary

Updates the Community Action Network on pertinent legislation, best practices, CSBG and WAP program highlights, and the latest events.
100 Members
Founded in 1968

12066 NASFA News
Natl' Assoc. of State Facilities Administrators
2760 Research Park Drive
PO Box 11910
Lexington, KY 40578-1910

859-311-1877
800-800-1910
Fax: 859-244-8001
E-Mail: nasfa@nasfa.net
Home Page: www.nasfa.net/

Marcia Stone, Executive Director

State administrators of facilities and property. A newsletter is published for members.
Cost: $1800.00
Frequency: Quarterly
Circulation: 2000
Founded in 1987

12067 NATAT's Reporter
National Association of Towns and Townships
444 N Capitol St Nw
Suite 397
Washington, DC 20001-1512

202-624-8195
Fax: 202-624-3554
E-Mail: natat@sso.org
Home Page: www.natat.org

Kelly Aylward, Manager
Larry Merrill, Vice President
Matthew DeTemple, Secretary, Treasurer

Covers federal legislation and regulation that pertain to local governments, with emphasis on compact or small towns (under 50,000; many under 1,000); also includes case studies of exemplary, creative local government, programs and association news from the National Association of Towns & Townships.
Cost: $36.00
24 Pages
Frequency: BiWeekly
Circulation: 15,200
Mailing list available for rent: 11700 names at $85 per M
Printed in 2 colors on newsprint stock

12068 NCDA News
National Community Development Association
522 21st St NW
Suite 120
Washington, DC 20006-5012

202-293-7587
Fax: 202-887-5546
Home Page: www.ncdaonline.org

Shandra Western, Editor

A national nonprofit membership organization representing local governments that implement community development programs. The members administer federally supported community development, housing and human services programs. NCDA provides counsel at the federal level on new program design and current program implementation and advocates on behalf of responsive community development.
13 Pages

12069 Nation's Cities Weekly
National League of Cities
1301 Pennsylvania Ave NwW
Suite 550
Washington, DC 20004-1747

202-626-3180
Fax: 202-626-3043
E-Mail: info@nlc.org
Home Page: www.nlc.org

Donald J Borut, Executive Director

News for and about cities.
Cost: $96.00
Frequency: Weekly
Circulation: 30000
ISSN: 0164-5935

12070 National Association of Conservation Districts
NACD
509 Capitol Court, NE
Washington, DC 20002-4937

202-547-6223
Fax: 202-547-6450
Home Page: www.nacdnet.org

John Larson, CEO

Highlights forestry issues of importance to districts and to showcase district-related forestry projects and success stories.
17000 Members
Frequency: Monthly
Founded in 1946

12071 National Association of Regional Councils
National Association of Regional Councils
1666 Connecticut Ave NW
Suite 305
Washington, DC 20002

202-986-1032
Fax: 202-986-1038
E-Mail: lindsey@narc.org
Home Page: www.narc.org

Fred Abousleman, Executive Director
Lindsey Riley, Deputy of Communications
Frequency: Weekly
Circulation: 2000

12072 Navy Times
Gannett Government Media
6883 Commercial Drive
Springfield, VA 22159-500

703-750-7400
800-368-5718
Fax: 703-750-8622
E-Mail: tnaegele@atpco.com
Home Page: www.navytimes.com

Elaine Howard, President
Judy McCoy, Associate Publisher
David Smith, VP Marketing/Business Dev
Dick Howlett, AVP Circulation Operations
Tobias Naegele, Executive Editor

The trusted, independent source for news and information of the Navy community. Breaking news, personal finance information, healthcare, recreational resources, exclusive videos and photos, Guard and Reserve information, and an expanded community area connecting service members, military families and veterans.
Cost: $143.00
Frequency: Weekly

12073 Outlook: From the State Capitals
Wakeman Walworth
PO Box 7376
Alexandria, VA 22307-7376

703-768-9600
Fax: 703-549-1372

Home Page: www.statecapitals.com/theoutlook.html

Keyes Walworth, Publisher

Gives an excellent perspective of trend- setting topics in state lawmaking: internet taxes, school choice, economic development, abortion, environmental issues, gambling laws. Each week is devoted to a different subject. In addition, a special feature called In the Works Around The Nation provides current highlights from other State Capitals newsletters.
Cost: $245.00
4 Pages
Frequency: Weekly
Printed in one color on matte stock

12074 PA TIMES
American Society for Public Administration
1301 Pennsylvania Avenue NW
Suite 700
Washington, DC 20004

202-393-7878
Fax: 202-638-4952
E-Mail: info@aspanet.org
Home Page: www.aspanet.org
Social Media: Facebook, Twitter, LinkedIn

Erik O. Bergrud, President
Stephen E. Condrey, Vice-President
Kuotsai Tom Liou, President-Elect

ASPA's newspaper covering developments in the professional field of public administration. Article topics include successful local state and federal government programs, PA trends and new PA methods. Focuses on the issues that face public managers today. Also highlights best practices in the field and updates members on how ASPA plays a role in the support of the public sector.
15M Members
Frequency: Monthly
Founded in 1939

12075 Politico
Capitol News Company
1100 Wilson Blvd
Suite 610
Arlington, VA 22209

703-647-7999
E-Mail: newsrelease@politico.com
Home Page: www.politico.com

Robert L Allbritton, Publisher
Frederick J Ryan Jr, President & CEO
Kim Kingsley, Chief Operating Officer
John F Harris, Editor-In-Chief
Jim VandeHei, Executive Editor

Provides insider-like access to Washington and the latest from the world of politics.

12076 Public Health: From the State Capitals
Wakeman Walworth
PO Box 7376
Alexandria, VA 22307-7376

703-768-9600
Fax: 703-768-9690
Home Page: www.statecapitals.com

Keyes Walworth, Publisher

Reports on a wide range of health care legislation such as AIDS disclosure and testing, drug programs, abortion rulings, cancer prevention including smoking restrictions in public places, mental health and disability programs, disease control, regulation of hospitals and nursing homes, clinics, food inspection policies, organ donor management and Medicare. It covers such current issues as mail order through pharmacies on the internet.
Cost: $245.00
4 Pages
Frequency: Weekly
Printed in one color on matte stock

12077 Public Safety and Justice Policies: From the State Capitals
Wakeman Walworth
PO Box 7376
Alexandria, VA 22307-7376

703-768-9600
Fax: 703-768-9690
Home Page:
www.statecapitals.com/publicsafety.html

Keyes Walworth, Publisher

Covers gun control on school grounds, buy-back programs, gunmaker lawsuits, law enforcement, arrest procedures, drug law enforcement and penalties; financing and administration of substance-abuse counseling, school violence , police administration, truth in sentencing , prison administration, prisoner drug testing and AIDS testing, new evidence such as DNA, inmate work programs, gender bias in the courtroom, family and juvenile justice, victim compensation laws, inmate living conditions
Cost: $245.00
4 Pages
Frequency: Weekly
Printed in one color on matte stock

12078 Roads and Bridges
Scranton Gillette Communications
3030 W Salt Creek Lane
Suite 201
Arlington Heights, IL 60005-5025

847-391-1000
Fax: 847-390-0408
E-Mail: bwilson@sgcmail.com
Home Page: www.roadbridges.com

Bill Wildon, Editorial Director
Allen Zeyher, Managing Editor
Rick Schwer, Publisher

Provides engineers, contractors and government officials with the latest advancements in the road and bridge industry, timely news coverage and important information on products beneficial to the job site of office.
Cost: $40.00
92 Pages
Frequency: Monthly
Circulation: 70000
ISSN: 8750-9229
Founded in 1905

12079 SideBAR
Federal Bar Association
1220 North Fillmore St.
Suite 444
Arlington, VA 22201

571-481-9100
Fax: 571-481-9090
E-Mail: fba@fedbar.org
Home Page: www.fedbar.org
Social Media: Facebook, Twitter, LinkedIn

Fern C. Bomchill, President
Robert J. DeSousa, President-Elect
Hon. Gustavo Gelpi, Jr., Treasurer

Federal Litigation Section Newsletter
16000 Members
Frequency: Quarterly
Founded in 1920

12080 Standards Action
American National Standards Institute
1819 L St NW
11th Floor
Washington, DC 20036-3864

202-293-8020
Fax: 202-293-9287
E-Mail: info@ansi.org
Home Page: www.ansi.org

Arthur E. Cote, Chairman
Joe Bhatia, President & CEO

Published to assure a complete consensus of ANSI members and the general public by facilitating review of proposed standards. Also included is information on draft American National Standards, governmental and other foreign standards and conformity assessment activities.
1000 Members
Frequency: Weekly
Founded in 1918

12081 Tax Administrators News
Federation of Tax Administrators
444 N Capitol St NW
Suite 348
Washington, DC 20001-1538

202-624-5890
Fax: 202-624-7888
Home Page: www.taxadmin.org

Harley Duncan, Executive Director
Rian Turruss, Editor

Covers state and federal legislation, US Supreme Court and state court cases, and developments relating to state tax administration.
Cost: $40.00
12 Pages
Frequency: Monthly
Circulation: 2000
Founded in 1930
Printed in one color on matte stock

12082 Taxes-Property: From State Capitals
Wakeman Walworth
PO Box 7376
Alexandria, VA 22307-7376

703-689-9600
Fax: 703-768-9690
Home Page:
www.statecapitals.com/taxprop.html

Keyes Walworth, Publisher

Covers new property tax legislation, initiatives, referenda, property assessment programs, tax exemptions, tax incentives, and tax collection methods. This newsletter emphasizes the use of property taxes for school financing including state aid formulas, alternative school financing methods, budget issues related to teacher pay and class sizes.
Cost: $345.00
4 Pages
Frequency: Weekly
Printed in one color on matte stock

12083 The Certifier
Association of Boards of Certification
2805 SW Snyder Blvd.
Suite 535
Ankeny, IA 50023

515-232-3623
Fax: 515-965-6827
E-Mail: abc@abccert.org
Home Page: www.abccert.org

Paul Bishop, Executive Director
Bob Hoyt, Vice President
Cheryl Bergener, President
Kathy Cook, VP

The newsletter for environmental certification authorities, filled with news and updates on the latest in certification and focuses on state and provincial certification programs, certification issues, and association events.
Frequency: Monthly
Founded in 1972

12084 The Government Standard
American Federation of Government Employees
80 F St NW
Washington, DC 20001-1528

202-737-8700
Fax: 202-639-6490

E-Mail: comments@afge.org
Home Page: www.afge.com

John Gage, President
J. David Cox, Secretary/Treasurer
Augusta Thomas, VP for Women's & Fair Practices

AFGE's official membership publication keeping members up to date on what their local government is up to.
Frequency: Quarterly
Founded in 1932

12085 **The Resolver**
Federal Bar Association
1220 North Fillmore St.
Suite 444
Arlington, VA 22201

571-481-9100
Fax: 571-481-9090
E-Mail: fba@fedbar.org
Home Page: www.fedbar.org
Social Media: Facebook, Twitter, LinkedIn

Fern C. Bomchill, President
Robert J. DeSousa, President-Elect
Hon. Gustavo Gelpi, Jr., Treasurer

Turning conflict into resolution, Alternative Dispute Resolution Section newsletter.
16000 Members
Frequency: Bi-Annually
Founded in 1920

12086 **The Resource**
National Association of Conservation Districts
509 Capitol Ct. NE
Washington, DC 20002-4937

202-547-6223
Fax: 202-547-6450
Home Page: www.nacdnet.org

Krysta Harden, CEO
Bob Cordova, Second Vice President

NACD's print publication provides in depth coverage of the association's recent activities and features columns by the NACD CEO and President, in addition to guest and partnership columns.
Cost: $35.00
12 Pages
Frequency: Monthly
Circulation: 25000
Founded in 1937

12087 **This Week in Washington**
American Public Human Services Association
1133 19th Street NW
Suite 400
Washington, DC 20036-3623

202-682-0100
Fax: 202-289-6555
Home Page: www.aphsa.org

Tracy Wareing, Executive Director

Gives readers concise updates on initiatives of the administration, legislative action in human service programs, the latest information on federal regulations, and state agency personnel changes- everything the human service administrator needs to know from the nation's capital.
Frequency: Weekly
Founded in 1930

12088 **URISA Newsletter**
Association for GIS Professionals
701 Lee St.
Suite 680
Des Plaines, IL 60016-4508

847-824-6300
Fax: 847-824-6363
E-Mail: info@urisa.org
Home Page: www.urisa.org

Susan Johnson, President
Wendy Nelson, Executive Director

Effective use of information systems technology at the state, regional and local levels Newsletter is published.
Frequency: Monthly
Founded in 1963

12089 **US Mayor**
US Conference of Mayors
1620 I St Nw
Suite 40
Washington, DC 20006-4034

202-464-0790
Fax: 202-293-2352
E-Mail: info@usmayors.org
Home Page: www.usmayors.org

Don Plusquellic, President
Tom Cochan, Editor
Guy Smith, Managing Editor
Michael Guido, Chair Advisory Board
J Thomas Cochran, CEO

Federal government and congressional activities.
Cost: $35.00
16 Pages
Circulation: 6000
Founded in 1933

12090 **USNC News and Notes**
American National Standards Institute
1819 L St NW
11th Floor
Washington, DC 20036-3864

202-293-8020
Fax: 202-293-9287
E-Mail: info@ansi.org
Home Page: www.ansi.org

Arthur E. Cote, Chairman
Joe Bhatia, President & CEO

For the electrotechnology community summarizing activities, events, and items of interest for the US National Committee of the International Electrotechnical Commission, keeping US stakeholders informed about the latest standards and conformity assessment updates in the domestic, regional and global arenas.
1000 Members
Frequency: Quarterly
Founded in 1918

12091 **United Nations Jobs Newsletter**
Thomas F Burola & Associates
6477 Telephone Road
Suite 7R
Ventura, CA 93003-4459

805- 64- 725
Fax: 805-654-1708

Thomas F Burola, Publisher

Focus of this newsletter is employment conditions within the United Nations System and vacancy notices.
Cost: $145.00
Circulation: 3,500
Founded in 1994
Printed in 2 colors on matte stock

12092 **United States Conference of Mayors News**
United States Conference of Mayors
1620 Eye Street, NW
Washington, DC 20006-4005

202-293-7330
Fax: 202-293-2352
E-Mail: info@usmayors.org
Home Page: www.usmayors.org/uscm/

J Thomas Cochran, President
William Fay, CEO

City government officials. Newsletter is available for members.
Circulation: 30000
Founded in 1932

12093 **Washington Report**
Federal Managers Association
1641 Prince St
Alexandria, VA 22314-2818

703-683-8700
Fax: 703-683-8707
E-Mail: info@fedmanagers.org
Home Page: www.fedmanagers.org

Todd Wells, Manager
Darryl A Perkinson, President

News bulletin detailing the latest developments on Capitol Hill and in the nation's capital.
15M Members
Frequency: Quarterly
Founded in 1913

12094 **Washington Spectator**
Public Concern Foundation
PO Box 20065
New York, NY 10011

212 741 2365
E-Mail: subscriptions@washingtonspectator.com
Home Page: www.washingtonspectator.com/

Kevin Walter, Publisher
Ben A Franklin, Editor
Lisa Vandepaer, Associate Editor
Marvin Shanken, Owner
Ruth Shikes, Co-Founder

News, comment and analysis on current national and international affairs; politics, economics, environment and social issues.
Cost: $15.00
4 Pages
Circulation: 60,000
Founded in 1974
Mailing list available for rent: 60000 names at $75 per M
Printed in one color on matte stock

12095 **Washington Trade Daily**
Trade Reports International Group
PO Box 1802
Wheaton, MD 20915-1802

301-946-0817
Fax: 301-946-2631
E-Mail: trigtrig@aol.com
Home Page: www.washingtontradedaily.com/
Social Media: Twitter

Jim Berger, CEO
D Kanth, Editor

The only faxed daily newsletters of its kind that covers the goings-on in the nation's Capital related to imports, exports and foreign investment. It reports daily to readers on the Executive Branch - including the US Trade Representative's office and the Commerce Department - as well as Congress. Readers can gain insight every morning on what are likely to be new laws and regulations governing international business tomorrow.
Cost: $650.00
16 Pages
Frequency: Daily
Founded in 1991
Printed in one color

12096 **What's New?**
American National Standards Institute
1819 L St NW
11th Floor
Washington, DC 20036-3864

202-293-8020
Fax: 202-293-9287

E-Mail: info@ansi.org
Home Page: www.ansi.org

Arthur E. Cote, Chairman
Joe Bhatia, President & CEO

Electronic newsletter distributed to members and constituents free of charge. Includes synopses and links to the most recent news, events and publications available from ANSI Online.
1000 Members
Frequency: Weekly
Founded in 1918

12097 Worldwide Government Report
Worldwide Government Directories
7979 Old Georgetown Road
Suite 900
Bethesda, MD 20814-2429

301-258-2677
800-332-3535
Fax: 301-718-8494

Jonathan Hixon, Publisher

Each issue provides detailed reports of elections, government and military turnover. Events covered include ousted heads of state, reshuffled governments, changes in ruling majorities, analyses of recent elections, outlooks for upcoming elections, and senior military appointments.
Cost: $247.00
Frequency: Monthly

12098 eNotes
National Association of Conservation Districts
509 Capitol Ct. NE
Washington, DC 20002-4937

202-547-6223
Fax: 202-547-6450
Home Page: www.nacdnet.org

Krysta Harden, CEO
Bob Cordova, Second Vice President

NACD's weekly news briefs.
Cost: $35.00
12 Pages
Frequency: Monthly
Circulation: 25000
Founded in 1937

Magazines & Journals

12099 AASHTO Daily Transportation Update
Amer. Assoc. of State Highway & Trans. Officials
444 N Capitol St NW
Suite 249
Washington, DC 20001-1539

202-624-5800
Fax: 202-624-5806
E-Mail: info@aashto.org
Home Page: www.transportation.org
Social Media: Facebook, Twitter

Kirk T. Steudle, President
Michael P. Lewis, Vice-President
Carlos Braceras, Secretary/ Treasurer
John Horsley, Executive Director

To help members and other transportation professionals stay informed about critical industry happenings and events.
52 Members
Frequency: Daily

12100 AASHTO Journal
Amer. Assoc. of State Highway & Trans. Officials
444 N Capitol St NW
Suite 249
Washington, DC 20001-1539

202-624-5800
Fax: 202-624-5806
E-Mail: info@aashto.org
Home Page: www.transportation.org
Social Media: Facebook, Twitter

Kirk T. Steudle, President
Michael P. Lewis, Vice-President
Carlos Braceras, Secretary/ Treasurer
John Horsley, Executive Director

Electronic journal to help members and other transportation professionals stay informed about critical industry happenings and events.
52 Members

12101 ANSI's Annual Report
American National Standards Institute
1819 L St NW
11th Floor
Washington, DC 20036-3864

202-293-8020
Fax: 202-293-9287
E-Mail: info@ansi.org
Home Page: www.ansi.org

Arthur E. Cote, Chairman
Joe Bhatia, President & CEO

Designed to inform members of the standards community of the Institute's accomplishments and financial activities of the past year, while also laying out goals for the future as presented by the chairman and president.
1000 Members
Frequency: Annually
Founded in 1918

12102 APWA Reporter
American Public Works Association
1275 K Street NW
Suite 750
Washington, DC 20005

202-408-9541
800-848-2792
Fax: 202-408-9542
E-Mail: ddancy@apwa.net
Home Page: www.apwa.net

Peter King, Executive Director
David Dancy, Director Of Marketing
Connie Hartline, Publisher

Prime communication link uniting the community of public works professionals that make up APWA.
Cost: $100.00
Frequency: Monthly
Circulation: 25000
ISSN: 0092-4873
Founded in 1937
Mailing list available for rent

12103 American Public Human Services Association Public Human Services Directory
American Public Human Services Association
1133 19th St NW
Suite 400
Washington, DC 20036-3623

202-682-0100
Fax: 202-204-0071
E-Mail: memberservice@aphsa.org
Home Page: www.aphsa.org

Tracy L. Wareing, Executive Director

A must-have for all human service professionals. Backed by APHSA, the Directory has consistently help steer people to the right contacts. Program contacts for such programs as Temporary Assistance for Needy Families, Child Welfare, Medicaid, Nutrition Assistance, Long-Term Care, Mental Health, Workforce Investment Act, and the Social Services Block Grant are available at a glance.
Cost: $115.00
Founded in 1930

12104 Armed Forces Journal
6883 Commercial Dr
Springfield, VA 22159

800-368-5718
E-Mail: armylet@atpco.com
Home Page: www.defensenews.com

Mark Winans, VP
Elaine Howard, President/CEO
Alex Neill, Managing Editor
Jim Tice, Senior Writer
David Smith, Marketing

The leading joint service monthly magazine for officers and leaders in the US military community. AFJ has been providing essential review and analysis on key defense issues for more than 140 years. Offers in-depth coverage of military technology, procurement, logistics, strategy, doctrine and tactics. Also covers special operations, US Coast Guard and US National Guard developments.
Cost: $55.00
Frequency: Monthly
Circulation: 1MM

12105 Army Magazine
2425 Wison Boulevard
Arlington, VA 22201-3326

703-841-4300
800-336-4570
Fax: 703-525-9039
E-Mail: membersupport@ausa.org
Home Page: www.ausa.org

Gen. Gordon Sullivan, President
Mary Blake French, Editor
Millie Hurlbut, Director of Marketing
Founded in 1950

12106 Army Times
Army Times Publishing Company
6883 Commercial Dr
Springfield, VA 22151-4202

703-750-9000
800-368-5718
Fax: 703-750-8622
E-Mail: jmccoy@atpco.com
Home Page: www.armytimes.com

Elaine Howard, CEO
Judy McCoy, Associate Publisher
Tobias Naegele, Executive Editor
David Smith, Marketing Manager

Magazine soldiers and their families rely on as trusted, independent sources for news and information on the most important issues affecting their careers and personal lives. A single source for breaking news; personal finance information; healthcare; recreational resources; exclusive videos and photos; Guard and Reserve information; and an expanded community area connecting service members, military families and veterans.
Cost: $52.00
Frequency: Weekly

12107 C41SR Journal
Defense News
6883 Commercial Dr
Springfield, VA 22159

800-368-5718
E-Mail: armylet@atpco.com
Home Page: www.defensenews.com

Mark Winans, VP
Elaine Howard, President/CEO
Alex Neill, Managing Editor
Jim Tice, Senior Writer
David Smith, Marketing

Dedicated to the rapidly advancing, high-tech realm of military intelligence, surveillance and reconnaissance. It was the first major periodical to specifically serve this key area of military growth and development, and has a strong following in the world's network-centric warfare community.
Cost: $55.00
Frequency: Monthly
Circulation: 1MM

12108 **CQ Weekly**
Congressional Quarterly
77 K Street NE
Washington, DC 20002-4681

202-650-6500
800-432-2250
E-Mail: customerservice@cqrollcall.com
Home Page: www.cq.com

Susan Benkelman, Executive Editor
Randy Wynn, Deputy Executive Editor
Anne Q Hoy, Managing Editor, Spec. Publications
Caitlin Hendel, Managing Editor, CQ Today
Melanie Starkey, Editor, Daily News

This award-winning publication provides a clear perspective on how legislation is shaped, who is shaping it and how the process could affect your interests.

12109 **Capitol Ideas**
National Association of State Facilities
2760 Research Park Drive
PO Box 11910
Lexington, KY 40578-1910

859-244-8000
800-800-1910
Fax: 859-244-8001
Home Page: www.csg.org
Social Media: Facebook, Twitter, YouTube

Gov. Brian Schweitzer, President
Gov. Luis Fortuno, President-Elect
Bob Godfrey, Chair
Jay Emler, Chair-Elect
Gary Stevens, Vice Chair

Includes member-driven content, including a targeted focus for each issue, news from each region and association news, focusing on what is going on in the states that might be of interest to other states.

12110 **Code Official**
International Code Council
4051 Flossmoor Rd
Country Club Hl, IL 60478-5771

708-799-2300
800-214-4321
202-783-2348
Fax: 708-799-4981
Home Page: www.bocai.org

Paul K Myers, CEO
Margaret M Leddin, Managing Editor

Serves a wide-ranging readership of professionals who are interested in the development, maintenance and enforcement of progressive and reponsive building regulations.
Cost: $30.00
Frequency: Monthly
Circulation: 16000
Founded in 1994
Printed in on glossy stock

12111 **Congressional Digest**
Congressional Digest Corporation
4416 East-West Highway
Suite 400
Bethesda, DC 20814-3389

301-634-3113
800-638-8380
Fax: 301-634-3189
Home Page: www.congestionaldigest.com

Griff Thomas, President
Page Robinson, Publisher
Kathy Thorne, Circulation Manager
Sarah Orrick, Editor

The only publication about Congress that concentrates each month on a single legislative issue in a unique Pro and Con format. It is an indispensable education tool for students of national and world affairs.
Cost: $62.00
36 Pages
ISSN: 0010-5899
Founded in 1921
Printed in 2 colors on glossy stock

12112 **Contract Management**
National Contract Management Association
8260 Greensboro Drive
Suite 200
McLean, VA 22102-3728

571-382-0082
800-344-8096
Fax: 703-448-0939
E-Mail: cm@ncmahq.org
Home Page: www.ncmahg.org

Neal J Couture, Executive Director
Kathryn Mullan, Assistant Editor

It covers the myriad aspects of government and commercial contract management. News and features provide information on such topics as procurement policy, on-the-job techniques, regulations, case law, ethics, contract administration, electronic commerce, international and small business matters, education and career development.
Cost: $178.00
80 Pages
Frequency: Monthly
Circulation: 22000
Founded in 1959
Printed in 4 colors on glossy stock

12113 **Cooperative Housing Bulletin**
National Association of Housing Cooperatives
1444 I Street, NW
Suite 700
Washington, DC 20005-6542

202-737-0797
Fax: 202-216-9646
E-Mail: info@nahc.coop
Home Page: www.coophousing.org

Member benefit conatining articles for co-op board members and professionals, up-to-date news on legislative issues that NAHC is monitoring, and practical information on issues facing housing cooperatives.
Frequency: Quarterly
Printed in 2 colors on matte stock

12114 **Correctional Health Today**
American Correctional Association
206 N Washington St
Suite 200
Alexandria, VA 22314-2528

703-224-0000
800-222-5646
Fax: 703-224-0179
E-Mail: jeffw@aca.org
Home Page: www.aca.org

Jeff Washington, Deputy Executive Director
James Gondles Jr, Executive Director

An interdisciplinary, peer-reviewed, academic publication devoted to examining all areas of health care within corrections. Available in print and electronically.
20000 Members
Frequency: Monthly
Founded in 1870

12115 **Corrections Compendium**
American Correctional Association
206 N Washington St
Suite 200
Alexandria, VA 22314-2528

703-224-0000
800-222-5646
Fax: 703-224-0179
E-Mail: jeffw@aca.org
Home Page: www.aca.org

Jeff Washington, Deputy Executive Director
James Gondles Jr, Executive Director

The peer-reviewed, research-based journal of the American Correctional Association. Presents research findings and trends and examines events in corrections and criminal justice.
20000 Members
Frequency: Quarterly
Founded in 1870

12116 **Corrections Today**
American Correctional Association
206 N Washington St
Suite 200
Alexandria, VA 22314-2528

703-224-0000
Fax: 703-224-0179
E-Mail: execoffice@aca.org
Home Page: www.aca.org
Social Media: Facebook, Twitter

James Gondles, Executive Director

The professional membership publication of the ACA. Its international readership includes individuals involved in every sector of the corrections and criminal justice fields.
Frequency: 6x Yearly

12117 **Court Review**
American Judges Association
300 Newport Ave
Williamsburg, VA 23185-4147

757-259-1841
Fax: 757-259-1520
Home Page: aja.ncsc.dni.us

Judge Kevin S. Burke, President
Judge Toni Manning Higginbotham, President-Elect
Judge Elliott L. Zide, Vice President
Judge Brian MacKenzie, Secretary
Judge Harold V. Froehlich, Treasurer

Court technology, managing your staff, controlling your docket-a bench's eye view of information you won't find anywhere else.
2500 Members
Frequency: Quarterly
Founded in 1959

12118 **Defense News**
6883 Commercial Dr
Springfield, VA 22151-4202

703-750-9000
800-424-9335
Fax: 703-658-8412
E-Mail: armylet@atpco.com
Home Page: www.defensenews.com

Mark Winans, VP
Elaine Howard, President/CEO
Alex Neill, Managing Editor
Jim Tice, Senior Writer
David Smith, Marketing

Provides the global defense community with the latest news and analysis on defense programs, policy, business and technology. With bureaus and reporters around the world, Defense News sets the standard for accuracy, credibility and timeliness in defense reporting. Circulates to top leaders and decisionmakers in North America and in Europe, Asia and the

Middle East.
Cost: $55.00
Frequency: Weekly
Circulation: 1MM

12119 **Democratic Communique**
Union for Democratic Communications
777 Glades Rd
Boca Raton, FL 33431

Home Page:
www.democraticcommunications.net

Janet Wasko, Publisher

News of Democratic and grassroots communications projects, issues and publications.
Cost: $20.00
12 Pages
Frequency: BiWeekly

12120 **Economic Development Journal**
International Economic Development Council
734 15th Street NW
Suite 900
Washington, DC 20005

202-223-7800
Fax: 202-223-4745
Home Page: www.iedc.org

Jeff Finkle, President & CEO
Dennis G. Coleman, Chair
Jay C. Moon, Vice Chair
Paul Krutko, Secretary/ Treasurer

Premier publication of IEDC's diverse and dynamic discipline, featuring in-depth accounts of important programs, projects, and trends from the US and around the world.
1.8M Members
Frequency: Quarterly
Founded in 1967

12121 **Energy Law Journal**
Energy Bar Association
1990 M St NW
Suite 350
Washington, DC 20036-3429

202-223-5625
Fax: 202-833-5596
E-Mail: admin@eba-net.org
Home Page: www.eba-net.org
Social Media: Facebook

Derek A. Dyson, President
Susan A. Olenchuk, President-Elect
Jason F. Leif, Vice President
Emma F. Hand, Secretary
Hugh E. Hilliard, Treasurer

Providing members with the latest news regarding the energy industry.
2600 Members
Frequency: Bi-Annually
Founded in 1946

12122 **Federal Criminal Investigator**
P.O. Box 23400
Washington, DC 20026

800-403-3374
630-969-8537
Fax: 800-528-3492
E-Mail: fcianat@aol.com
Home Page: www.fedcia.org

Richard Zehme, President
William Paulin, Vice President
Rich Ahern, National Treasurer/Secretary

This comprehensive publication covers legislation and federal information for the police official and officer.
Frequency: Quarterly
Founded in 1956

12123 **Federal Manager**
Federal Managers Association
1641 Prince St
Alexandria, VA 22314-2818

703-683-8700
Fax: 703-683-8707
E-Mail: info@fedmanagers.org
Home Page: www.fedmanagers.org

Todd Wells, Manager
Darryl A Perkinson, President

Magazine focusing on current management issues.
15M Members
Frequency: Quarterly
Founded in 1913

12124 **Foreign Service Journal**
American Foreign Service Association
2101 E St NW
Washington, DC 20037-2990

202-338-4045
800-704-2572
Fax: 202-338-6820
E-Mail: member@afsa.org
Home Page: www.afsa.org

Susan R. Johnson, President
Andrew Winter, Treasurer

Each issue covers foreign affairs from an insider's perspective, providing thoughtful articles on international issues, the practice of diplomacy and the US Foreign Service.
Cost: $40.00
68 Pages
Frequency: Monthly
Circulation: 12500
ISSN: 0146-3543
Founded in 1924
Printed in on glossy stock

12125 **Government Executive**
National Journal
600 New Hampshire Ave NW
Suite 4
Washington, DC 20037-2403

202-739-8400
Fax: 202-833-8069
E-Mail: webmaster@govexec.com
Home Page: www.govexec.com
Social Media: Facebook, Twitter

John Fox Sullivan, President
Shane Harris, Editor

Serving senior executives and managers in the federal government's departments and agencies. Subscribers are high-ranking civilian and military officials who are responsible for defending the nation and carrying out the many laws that define the government's role in our economy and society. Covers the business of the federal government and its huge departments and agencies.
Cost: $48.00
72 Pages
Frequency: Monthly
Circulation: 75,000
Founded in 1970

12126 **Government Product News**
Penton Media
1300 E 9th St
Suite 316
Cleveland, OH 44114-1503

216-696-7000
Fax: 216-696-6662
Home Page: www.penton.com

Jane Cooper, Marketing
Kristin M Atwater, Managing Editor
Vaughn Rockhold, Group Publisher
Kay Ross-Baker, Publisher
Sarah Arnold, Marketing Director

Serves officials in the executive, legislative, administrative, engineering, purchasing, financial and other operational departments, within government agencies.
40 Pages
Frequency: Monthly
Circulation: 85000
ISSN: 0017-2642
Founded in 1962
Printed in 4 colors on glossy stock

12127 **Government Recreation & Fitness**
Executive Business Media
825 Old Country Road
PO Box 1500
Westbury, NY 11590

516-334-3030
Fax: 516-334-3059
E-Mail: mail@ebmpubs.com
Home Page: www.ebmpubs.com

Murry Greenwald, Publisher
Paul Ragnoz, Managing Editor

Government Recreation and Fitness reaches recreation and fitness professionals in every department and agency of the federal government, goes directly to the people who purchase your products, with deep market penetration, and covers both appropriated and nonappropriated fund budgets.
Cost: $35.00
42 Pages
Frequency: 10x Yearly
Circulation: 8521
ISSN: 1086-7899
Founded in 1996
Printed in 4 colors on glossy stock

12128 **Government Technology**
GT Publications
150 Almaden Blvd
Suite 600
San Jose, CA 95113-2016

408-275-9000
Fax: 408-275-0582
Home Page: www.grantthornton.com
Social Media: Facebook

Jeffrey S Pera, Managing Partner
Sherese Graves, Advertising Director
Dennis McKenna, Publisher
Micki Gerardi, Manager

Covering information technology's role in state and local governments. Through in-depth coverage of IT case studies, emerging technologies, and the implications of digital technology on the policies and management of public sector organizations, Government Technology chronicles the dynamics of governing in the information age. Readers include managers, elected officials, CIOs and technology staff at all levels of government.
56 Pages
Frequency: Monthly

12129 **ICBA Independent Banker**
Independent Community Bankers of America
1615 L Street NW
Suite 900
Washington, DC 20036

800-422-8439
Fax: 202-659-3604
E-Mail: info@icba.org
Home Page: www.independantbanker.org

Salvatore Marranca, Chairman
Jeffrey L. Gerhart, Chairman-Elect
William A. Loving, Jr., Vice Chairman
Steven R. Gardner, Secretary
Jack Hartings, Treasurer

Covers the news topics and trends that are important to the nation's community bank senior executives. Keeping members informed about and connected with their national association and its activities; and providing them with timely, relevant information on developments

to growth their business franchise within the rapidly evolving financial services industry.
Frequency: Monthly

12130 **International Debates**
Congressional Digest Corporation
4416 E West Hwy
Suite 400
Bethesda, MD 20814-4568

301-634-3113
800-637-9915
Fax: 301-634-3189
E-Mail: info@congressionaldigest.com
Home Page: www.pro-and-con.org/

Griff Thomas, President
Page Robinson, Publisher

Independent journal featuring controversies before the United Nations and other international forums. Each issue covers an important and timely international issue and includes in-depth background information, key documents, and diverse global perspectives.
Frequency: 9x Yearly
Founded in 1921

12131 **Journal of Food Protection**
International Association for Food Protection
6200 Aurora Ave
Suite 200W
Urbandale, IA 50322-2864

515-276-3344
800-369-6337
Fax: 515-276-8655
E-Mail: info@foodprotection.org
Home Page: www.foodprotection.org
Social Media: Facebook, Twitter, LinkedIn

Lisa Hovey, Managing Editor
Didi Loynachan, Administrative Editor

Internationally recognized as the leading publication in the field of food microbiology, each issue contains scientific research and authoritative review articles reporting on a variety of topics in food science pertaining to food safety and quality.
Cost: $335.00
Frequency: Monthly
Circulation: 11000+
ISBN: 0-362028-X-
Founded in 1911
Mailing list available for rent: 3000+ names at $150 per M
Printed in 4 colors on glossy stock

12132 **Journal of Housing Economics**
630 Eye St NW
Washington, DC 20001-3736

202-289-3500
877-866-2476
Fax: 202-289-8181
Home Page: www.journals.elsevier.com

Saul Ramirez, Executive Director
Donald J Cameron, CEO

Provides a focal point for the publication of economic research related to housing and encourages papers that bring to bear careful analytical technique on important housing-related questions. The journal covers the broad spectrum of topics and approaches that constitute housing economics, including analysis of important public policy issues.
Cost: $33.00
Founded in 1933

12133 **Journal of Medical Regulation**
Federation of State Medical Boards
400 Fuller Wiser Rd
Suite 300
Euless, TX 76039-3856

817-868-4043
Fax: 817-868-4099
E-Mail: dcarlson@fsmb.org
Home Page: www.fsmb.org

Rhonda Olsobrook, Manager

Peer-reviewed scholarly publication that helps raise awareness of important trends and challenging issues in the regulatory community.
Frequency: Monthly

12134 **Journal of Occupational and Environmental Hygiene (JOEH)**
ACGIH
1330 Kemper Meadow Drive
Cincinnati, OH 45240

513-742-2020
Fax: 513-742-3355
E-Mail: mail@acgih.org
Home Page: www.acgih.org

Lisa M. Brosseau, Chair
Bill R. McArthur, Vice Chair
Robert F. Herrick, Vice Chair-Elect
Heather D. Borman, Secretary/ Treasurer
A. Anthony Rizzuto, Executive Director

Focuses on publishing information that practicing professionals can apply in their day-to-day activities.
Founded in 1938

12135 **Journal of the Association of Food and Drug Officials**
2550 Kingston Road
Suite 311
York, PA 17402

717-757-2888
Fax: 717-755-8089
E-Mail: afdo@afdo.org
Home Page: www.afdo.org

News and the latest legislation for the Food and Drug Association.
Cost: $80.00
Frequency: Quarterly
Founded in 1896

12136 **Legislative Update**
1250 Eye St NW
Suite 902
Washington, DC 20005-3947

202-393-5225
Fax: 202-393-3034
Home Page: www.nrhcweb.org

Robert A Rapoza, Publisher/Executive Director

Published by the National Rural Housing Coalition.
Cost: $250.00
Frequency: 25x Yearly
Circulation: 300
Founded in 1969

12137 **McGraw-Hill's Federal Technology Report**
McGraw Hill
1200 G St Nw
Suite 900
Washington, DC 20005-3821

202-383-2377
800-223-6180
Fax: 202-383-2438
Home Page: www.aviationnow.com

Jennifer Michels, Manager
Georgia Safos, Circulation Director

Brings readers inside those areas of the federal government where federal technology policy and legislation is made; also identifies commercial opportunities at federal labs.
Cost: $1015.00
16 Pages
Frequency: Weekly

12138 **NCOA Journal**
Todays NCOA
10635 N 35th
San Antonio, TX 78233-6627

210-653-6161
800-662-2620
Fax: 210-637-3337
E-Mail: membsvc@ncoausa.org
Home Page: www.uag-inc.com

Gene Overstreet, President/CEO
Cathy John, Advertising Manager

The official magazine for the Non Commissioned Officers Association.
Frequency: Quarterly
Circulation: 60000
Founded in 1960

12139 **NIST Tech Beat**
National Institute of Standards & Technology
Public & Business Affairs
100 Bureau Drive, Stop 1070
Gaithersburg, MD 20899-1070

800-877-8339
Fax: 301-926-1630
E-Mail: media@nist.gov
Home Page: www.nist.gov
Social Media: Facebook, Twitter, YouTube, Flickr

Michael Baum, Segments Editor
Ben Stein, Segments Editor
Michael E Newman, Segments Editor
Evelyn Brown, Segments Editor
Laura Ost, Segments Editor

A biweekly lay-language newsletter of recent research results and other news from the National Institute of Standards and Technology. NIST is the nation's physical sciences and engineering measurement laboratory. Archives available online.
Frequency: Biweekly

12140 **Nation's Cities Weekly**
National League of Cities
1301 Pennsylvania Ave NW
6th Floor, Suite 550
Washington, DC 20004-1747

202-626-3180
Fax: 202-626-3043
E-Mail: memberservices@nlc.org
Home Page: www.nlc.org

Donald J Borut, Executive Director
Cyndy Hogan, Managing Editor

Delivers top stories about advocacy activities, successful and innovative city programs, new research and networking opportunities for local elected officials and city employees.
Cost: $96.00
12 Pages
Frequency: Weekly
Circulation: 27000
Founded in 1978

12141 **National Journal**
National Journal
600 New Hampshire Ave NW
Suite 4
Washington, DC 20037-2403

202-739-8400
800-207-8001
Fax: 202-833-8069
Home Page: nationaljournal.com
Social Media: Facebook, Twitter

John Fox Sullivan, President

Delivers highly engaged consumers with all of the information and insights that they need to know to conduct business successfully in Washington. Trusted professional resource for Members of Congress and their senior staffs, the Executive branch, federal agency executives, government affairs professionals, corporate and association leaders, and the political

news media.
Cost: $1799.00
Founded in 1969

12142 **Navy News and Undersea Technology**
Pasha Publications
1616 N Fort Myer Drive
Suite 1000
Arlington, VA 22209-3107

703-528-1244
800-424-2908
Fax: 703-528-1253

Harry Baisden, Group Publisher
Thomas Jandl, Editor
Tod Sedgwick, Publisher

This report on the Navy, as well as the Marine Corps and naval developments overseas. Frequently cited by experts in the field as the source for breaking developments in submarine and anti-submarine warfare technology, this newsletter sets the standard for Navy reporting.
Cost: $545.00
Frequency: Weekly

12143 **Off the Shelf**
Coalition for Government Procurement
1990 M St NW
Suite 450
Washington, DC 20036-3466

202-331-0975
Fax: 202-822-9788
E-Mail: info@thecgp.org
Home Page: www.thecgp.org

Larry Allen, Executive VP

Providing vital updates on rules, regulations, and GSA Schedule developments that may impact your business.
Frequency: Monthly
Founded in 1979

12144 **Parameters**
US Army War College
122 Forbes Ave
Suite C34
Carlisle, PA 17013-5220

717-245-3131
Fax: 717-245-3323
Home Page: www.carlisle.army.mil

Robert J Ivany, Manager

Refereed journal of ideas and issues. Provides a forum for mature thought on the art and science of land warfare, joint and combined matters, national and international security affairs, military strategy, military leadership and management, military history, ethics, and other topics of significant and current interest to the US Army and the Department of Defense.
Cost: $26.00
Frequency: Quarterly
Circulation: 1300

12145 **Policy & Practice**
American Public Human Services Association
1133 19th Street NW
Suite 400
Washington, DC 20036-3623

202-682-0100
Fax: 202-289-6555
Home Page: www.aphsa.org

Tracy Wareing, Executive Director

Presents a lively and comprehensive look at key human service issues. Its aim is to highlight the experiences of those who administer public assistance programs and services; to examine cutting-edge public human service research and demonstration projects; and to provide readers with a variety of resources to guide them in their challenging roles in the human service arena.
Frequency: Bi-Monthly
Founded in 1930

12146 **Presidential Studies Quarterly**
Center for the Study of the Presidency & Congress
1020 19th St NW
Suite 250
Washington, DC 20036-6120

202-872-9800
Fax: 202-872-9811
E-Mail: email@thepresidency.org
Home Page: www.thepresidency.org
Social Media: Facebook, Twitter, YouTube

George C Edwards III, Editor

Available in print and online, PSQ is widely viewed by scholars and professionals as an indispensable resource for understanding the Presidency. The only scholarly journal that focuses on the most powerful political figure in the world - the President of the United States. Offers articles, features, review essays, and book reviews covering Presidential decision making, the operations of the White House, and much more.
Frequency: Quarterly
Circulation: 6000
ISSN: 0360-4918

12147 **Prosecutor**
National District Attorneys Association
44 Canal Center Plaza
Suite 110
Alexandria, VA 22314-1548

703-549-9222
Fax: 703-836-3195
Home Page: www.ndaa.org

Jean Hemphill, Publications Director/Editor

Fascinating articles, names in the news, upcoming conferences, capital perspective, profiles, course announcements, message from the President, message from the Executive Director, and much more.
Frequency: Quarterly
Circulation: 7000

12148 **Public Administration Review (PAR)**
American Society for Public Administration
1301 Pennsylvania Avenue NW
Suite 700
Washington, DC 20004

202-393-7878
Fax: 202-638-4952
E-Mail: info@aspanet.org
Home Page: www.aspanet.org
Social Media: Facebook, Twitter, LinkedIn

Erik O. Bergrud, President
Stephen E. Condrey, Vice-President
Kuotsai Tom Liou, President-Elect

The preeminent journal in the field of public administration research and theory.
15M Members
Frequency: Bi-Monthly
Founded in 1939

12149 **Public Integrity**
American Society for Public Administration
1301 Pennsylvania Avenue NW
Suite 700
Washington, DC 20004

202-393-7878
Fax: 202-638-4952
E-Mail: info@aspanet.org
Home Page: www.aspanet.org
Social Media: Facebook, Twitter, LinkedIn

Erik O. Bergrud, President
Stephen E. Condrey, Vice-President
Kuotsai Tom Liou, President-Elect

Furthering the understanding of ethics in government by publishing articles of interest to practitioners and scholars.
15M Members
Frequency: Monthly
Founded in 1939

12150 **Public Risk**
Public Risk Management Association
500 Montgomery St
Suite 750
Alexandria, VA 22314-1565

703-647-6244
Fax: 703-739-0200
E-Mail: info@primacentral.org
Home Page: www.primacentral.org
Social Media: Facebook, LinkedIn

Jim Hirt, Executive Director
Jon Ruzan, Manager
Kerry Langley, Manager

Provides risk managers in the public sector with timely, focused information in an easy-to-read format. Features articles from risk management practitioners as well as industry experts.
Frequency: 10x Yearly
Circulation: 8000+
Founded in 1978

12151 **Pull Together**
1306 Dahlgren Avenue SE
Washington Navy Yard, DC 20374-5055

202-678-4333
Fax: 202-889-3565
E-Mail: nhfwny@navyhistory.org
Home Page: www.navyhistory.org

Captain Charles Creekman, Executive Director
Robert F Dunn, President
Cost: $25.00
Founded in 1926

12152 **Rural Housing Reporter**
1250 Eye St NW
Suite 902
Washington, DC 20005-3947

202-393-5225
Fax: 202-393-3034
Home Page: www.nrhcweb.org

Robert A Rapoza, Publisher/Executive Director

Published by the National Rural Housing Coalition.
Cost: $250.00
Frequency: Monthly
Founded in 1969

12153 **Rural Voices**
Housing Assistance Council
1025 Vermont Ave NW
Suite 606
Washington, DC 20005-3516

202-842-8600
Fax: 202-347-3441
E-Mail: hac@ruralhome.org
Home Page: www.ruralhome.org
Social Media: Twitter, LinkedIn

Moises Loza, Executive Director

Written in non-technical language for a general audience.
Frequency: Quarterly
Founded in 1971

12154 **Society of Cost Estimating and Analysis Journal**
Society of Cost Estimating and Analysis
527 Maple Ave E
Suite 301
Vienna, VA 22180-4753

703-938-5090
Fax: 703-938-5091

E-Mail: scea@sceaonline.org
Home Page: www.sceaonline.net

Elmer Cleg, Executive Director
Joseph Dean, National VP

Subscribers are professionals engaged primarily in the field of government contract estimating and pricing.
Cost: $40.00
Frequency: Annual+
Circulation: 4500
ISSN: 0882-3871
Founded in 1984

12155 **State Legislatures**
National Conference of State Legislatures
7700 E 1st Pl
Denver, CO 80230-7143

303-364-7700
Fax: 303-364-7800
E-Mail: pubs-info@ncsl.org
Home Page: www.ncsl.org
Social Media: Twitter, LinkedIn

William Pound, Executive Director
Edward Smith, Managing Editor
LeAnn Hoff, Director, Revenue & Sales

The national magazine of state government and policy.
Cost: $49.00
15000 Members
Circulation: 18000
ISSN: 0147-0644
Founded in 1975
Printed in 4 colors

12156 **Supreme Court Debates**
Congressional Digest Corporation
4416 E West Hwy
Suite 400
Bethesda, MD 20814-4568

301-634-3113
800-637-9915
Fax: 301-634-3189
E-Mail: info@congressionaldigest.com
Home Page: www.pro-and-con.org/

Griff Thomas, President
Page Robinson, Publisher

Independent journal featuring controversies before the US Supreme Court. Each issue covers a current prominent case, along with in-depth historical and legal background and excerpts from lawyers' arguments before the Court. Each issue also lists cases expected to be considered by the High Court during the current term.
Frequency: 9x Yearly
Founded in 1921

12157 **The Federal Lawyer**
Federal Bar Association
1220 North Fillmore St.
Suite 444
Arlington, VA 22201

571-481-9100
Fax: 571-481-9090
E-Mail: fba@fedbar.org
Home Page: www.fedbar.org
Social Media: Facebook, Twitter, LinkedIn

Fern C. Bomchill, President
Robert J. DeSousa, President-Elect
Hon. Gustavo Gelpi, Jr., Treasurer

The only magazine written and edited for lawyers who practice in federal courts or have an interest in federal law as well as judges who sit on the federal bench. Editorial content covers immigration, Indian, antitrust, labor and employment, bankruptcy, criminal, intellectual property, environmental, and other types of law that fall within federal jurisdiction.
Cost: $35.00
16000 Members
Frequency: Monthly
Founded in 1920

12158 **The Forum**
National Forum for Black Public Administrators
777 N Capitol St NE
Suite 807
Washington, DC 20002-4291

202-408-9300
Fax: 202-408-8558
E-Mail: webmaster@nfbpa.org
Home Page: www.nfbpa.org
Social Media: Facebook, YouTube

Aretha R. Ferrell-Benavides, President
Verdenia C. Baker, 1st Vice President
Bruce T. Moore, 2nd Vice President
Jelynne LeBlanc Burley, Secretary/Treasurer
John E. Saunders, III, Executive Director

Has been used as a means of polishing and honing the skills of capable and experienced administrators by providing practical advice on professional development and insight on social and economic concerns impacting the Black community. Strives to present timely, factual, and comprehensive information on subjects of critical importance to its readers who share a common commitment to excellence in public service.
2.8M Members
Frequency: Quarterly
Founded in 1983

12159 **Training & Simulation Journal**
6883 Commercial Dr
Springfield, VA 22159

800-368-5718
E-Mail: armylet@atpco.com
Home Page: www.defensenews.com

Mark Winans, VP
Elaine Howard, President/CEO
Alex Neill, Managing Editor
Jim Tice, Senior Writer
David Smith, Marketing

About trends in the global military training and simulation market, and a forum for market leaders to obtain and exchange information on emerging issues, new technologies, and new products.
Cost: $55.00
Frequency: Bi-Monthly
Circulation: 1MM

12160 **Translog**
200 Stovall Street
Hoffman Building Room 11N57
Alexandria, VA 22332-5000

703-428-3207
Fax: 703-428-3312

An authorized online publication for members of the Department of Defense, published under supervision of the SDDC Director of Command Affairs to provide timely, relevant information concerning SDDC people, missions, policies, operations, technical developments, trends, and ideas of and about SDDC and the US Army.

12161 **Urban Land**
Urban Land Institute
1025 Thomas Jefferson St NW
Suite 500 West
Washington, DC 20007-5230

202-624-7000
Fax: 202-624-7140
E-Mail: ulifoundation@uli.org
Home Page: www.uli.org
Social Media: Facebook, Twitter, LinkedIn, YouTube

Patrick Phillips, CEO
Richard Rosan, President
Michael Terseck, CFO

Focuses on the information needs of land use and development professionals worldwide, providing them with timely, objective, practical, and accessible articles on a wide variety of subjects related to their professional interests.
14M Members
Frequency: Monthly
Founded in 1936

12162 **Washington Law & Politics**
100 W Harrison St
Suite 340
Seattle, WA 98119-4196

206-282-9527
Fax: 206-282-9601
Home Page: www.superlawyers.com

Keith Goben, Publisher
Beth Taylor, Editor
Paul Englund, Circulation Manager
Tina Justison, Production Manager

A magazine for those who care about, or have a stake in, the public policy debate that is the basis of our editorial. Readers consist of those in positions of power in media, government, politics, law and business. Attracts a curious blend of readers ranging from corporate CEOs to political junkies.
48 Pages
Frequency: 6x Yearly
Circulation: 18000
Founded in 1977
Printed in 4 colors on glossy stock

12163 **Washington Remote Sensing Letter**
Dr. Murray Felsher
1057B National Press Building
Washington, DC 20045-2001

202-393-3640

Dr. Murray Felsher, Publisher
Murray Felsher, Editor
Dr. Murray Felsher, Publisher
Dr. Murray Felsher, Marketing
Dr. Murray Felsher, Circulation Manager

The recognized leader in reporting and analysis of US and international news dealing with all phases and applications of satellite remote sensing of the earth and global analyses research, including imagery, photography, surveillance and monitoring the Earth from space.
Cost: $1100.00
4 Pages
ISSN: 0739-6538
Founded in 1980
Printed in 2 colors on matte stock

12164 **Western City Magazine**
League of California Cities
1400 K St
4th Floor
Sacramento, CA 95814-3971

916-658-8200
800-262-1801
Fax: 916-658-8289
E-Mail: info@westerncity.com
Home Page: www.cacities.org
Social Media: Facebook

Pam Blodgett, Ad Manager
Eva Spiegel, Managing Editor
Chris McKenzie, Executive Director

The magazine of the League of California Cities.
Cost: $39.00
Frequency: Monthly
Circulation: 10500
Founded in 1924
Printed in 4 colors on glossy stock

Trade Shows

12165 **ACAP National Training Conference**
American Society of Access Professionals
1444 I(Eye) St. NW
Suite 700
Washington, DC 20005-6542

202-712-9054
Fax: 202-216-9646
E-Mail: asap@bostrom.com
Home Page: www.accesspro.org

Anne Weismann, President
Will Kammer, Vice President
Karen Finnegan, Treasurer
Carmen L. Mallon, Secretary

Created to bring educational opportunities beyond the Washington, D.C. area. Combines training topics with the thought-provoking and practical issues associated with FOIA and Privacy Act processing and requesting.
Frequency: Annual/March
Founded in 1980

12166 **ASPA Annual Conference**
American Society for Public Administration
1301 Pennsylvania Avenue NW
Suite 840
Washington, DC 20004

202-393-7878
Fax: 202-638-4952
E-Mail: info@aspanet.org
Home Page: www.aspanet.org

Antoinette Samuel, Executive Director
Lyric Jonze, Administration Assistant

Offers cuttin-edge educational programming at this year's conference. There are over 150 educational options to choose from - Panel Sessions, Best Practice Workshops, and Roundtable Discussions.
550 Attendees
Frequency: Annual/May

12167 **AURP International Conference**
Association of University Research Parks
6262 N. Swan Road
Suite 100
Tucson, AZ 85718-8936

520-529-2521
Fax: 520-529-2499
E-Mail: info@aurp.net
Home Page: www.aurp.net
Social Media: Facebook, Twitter

Eileen Walker, CEO
Victoria Palmer, Events Manager
Chelsea Simpson, Membership & Marketing Manager

Bringing together the world's leaders in high-tech economic development, this conference features professional development for university research park professionals.
Frequency: Annual/September

12168 **America's Town Meeting**
National Association of Towns and Townships
1130 Connecticut Ave NW
Suite 300
Washington, DC 20036-3981

202-454-3954
866-830-0008
Fax: 202-331-1598
Home Page: www.natat.org

NATaT's national conference is the largest national conference for grassroots government leaders. Educational workshops and legislative workshops help officials be more effective representatives for the citizens they serve. The conference provides a time for attendees to lobby members of Congress on issues important to their towns.
13M Members
Frequency: Annual

12169 **American Association of Port Authorities Annual Convention**
1010 Duke Street
Alexandria, VA 22314-3589

703-684-5700
Fax: 703-684-6321
E-Mail: info@aapa-ports.org
Home Page: www.aapa-ports.org

Kurt Nagle, President/CEO

AAPA's largest membership meeting of the year. It includes technical and policy committee meetings, business sessions and social networking opportunities for port professionals and others in the marine transportation industry.
700 Attendees
Frequency: Annual/September
Founded in 1912

12170 **American Industrial Hygiene Conference and Exposition**
ACGIH
1330 Kemper Meadow Drive
Cincinnati, OH 45240

513-742-2020
Fax: 513-742-3355
E-Mail: mail@acgih.org
Home Page: www.acgih.org

Lisa M. Brosseau, Chair
Bill R. McArthur, Vice Chair
Robert F. Herrick, Vice Chair-Elect
Heather D. Borman, Secretary/ Treasurer
A. Anthony Rizzuto, Executive Director

One of the world's premier conferences for occupational and environmental safety and health professionals. Committees and individual members contribute their expertise in professional development courses, technical sessions, and poster sessions.
8000 Attendees
Founded in 1938

12171 **American Political Science Association Annual Meeting**
1527 New Hampshire Avenue NW
Washington, DC 20036-1206

202-483-2512
Fax: 202-483-2657
E-Mail: apsa@apsanet.org
Home Page: www.apsanet.org

G. Bingham Powell, Jr., President
Jane Mansbridge, President-Elect
Jonathan Benjamin-Alvarado, Treasurer
Lisa L. Martin, Secretary
Michael A. Brintnall, Executive Director

Workshop, luncheon and 150 plus exhibits of publications and software relating to political science.
6500 Attendees
Frequency: Annual
Founded in 1903

12172 **CLEAR Annual Educational Conference**
Council on Legislative Enforcement & Regulation
403 Marquis Ave
Suite 200
Lexington, KY 40502-2104

859-269-1289
Fax: 859-231-1943
E-Mail: jhorne@clearhq.org
Home Page: www.clearhq.org
Social Media: Facebook

Bruce Matthews, President
Michelle Pedersen, President-Elect

Conference content focuses on compliance and discipline, credentialing and licensing, examination issues, and legislative and policy issues/ reulatory administration.
380 Members
400+ Attendees
Frequency: Annual/September
Founded in 1980

12173 **CSG National Conference & North American Summit**
Council of State Governments
2760 Research Park Drive
PO Box 11910
Lexington, KY 40578-1910

859-244-8000
800-800-1910
Fax: 859-244-8001
Home Page: www.csg.org
Social Media: Facebook, Twitter

Key officials that shape and make today's economic decisions.
1000+ Attendees
Frequency: Annual/October

12174 **Congress of Cities & Exposition**
National League of Cities
1301 Pennsylvania Avenue NW
Suite 550
Washington, DC 20004

202-626-3100
800-564-4220
Fax: 202-626-3043
Home Page: www.nlc.org

Ted Ellis, President
Marie Lopez Rogers, 1st Vice President
Chris Coleman, 2nd Vice President
Don Borut, Executive Director

Provides educational content on the most pressing challenges facing city leaders. Conference attendees hear from prominent speakers and issue experts, participate in leadership training sessions, attend issue-specific workshops, visit best practices keynote speakers, issue workshops, mobile workshops, and leadership training sessions.
4200 Attendees
Frequency: Annual/December
Founded in 1924

12175 **EANGUS National Conference**
Exhibit Promotions Plus
11620 Vixens Path
Ellicott City, MD 21042

301-596-3028
Fax: 410-997-0764
Home Page: www.eangus.org

Kevin Horowitz, Exhibit Mgmt.

General conference and exhibition for the Enlisted Association of the National Guard of the United States. All attendees are either National Guard members, retirees or their families.
2000+ Attendees
Frequency: Annual/August
Founded in 1971

12176 **Energy - Exhibit Promotions Plus**
US Dept. of Energy/US Dept. of Defense/GSA
11620 Vixens Path
Ellicott City, MD 21042

301-596-3028
Fax: 410-997-0764
Home Page: www.energy2003.ee.doe.gov

Harve Horowitz, President
Kevin Horowitz, Senior Association Manager

Energy is an exclusive Federal Grant sponsored annual educational forum and exhibition.
1000+ Attendees
Frequency: Annual/August

12177 **FOSE**
Contingency Planning & Management Conference
3141 Fairview Park Drive
Suite 777
Falls Church, VA 22042
703-876-5100
800-638-8510
Home Page: www.fose.com
Social Media: Facebook, Twitter, LinkedIn
Sylvia Griffiths, Customer Supervisor
Vendors in different marketplaces & pavilions, providing the opportunity to source effective & actionable IT solutions, in-depth conferences, workshops, camps, keynote & theater education designed to help achieve sucess with government IT mandates & initiatives. Association meetings, CIO Summits and peer networking opportunities, bringing the government IT community together.
80M Attendees
Frequency: April

12178 **Government Finance Officers Association Annual Conference**
203 N LaSalle Street
Suite 2700
Chicago, IL 60601-1210
312-977-9700
Fax: 312-977-4806
E-Mail: inquiry@gfoa.org
Home Page: www.gfoa.org
Jeffrey Esser, Executive Director/CEO
Barbara Mollo, Director Operations & Marketing
Anne Spray Kinney, Director Research & Consulting
John Jurkash, CFO/Financial Administration
Barrie Tabin Berger, Federal Liaison Coordinator
The Government Finance Officers Association's Annual Conference provides training and networking opportunities for public sector finance professionals from across the United States and Canada. 250 booths with 200 exhibitors.
4000 Attendees
Frequency: June

12179 **HFA Institute**
National Council of State Housing Agencies
444 N Capitol St NW
Suite 438
Washington, DC 20001-1505
202-624-7710
Fax: 202-624-5899
E-Mail: bthompson@ncsha.org
Home Page: www.ncsha.org
Social Media: Facebook, Twitter
Gerald M. Hunter, President
Brian A. Hudson, Vice President
Thomas R. Gleason, Secretary/ Treasurer
Barbara J. Thompson, Executive Director
Premier training event providing an unprecedented chance to network with peers and receive top-notch education and invaluable advice from key federal officials, leading trainers and consultants, noted industry professionals, and experienced HFA practitioners.
350 Members
Frequency: Annual/December
Founded in 1974

12180 **Housing Credit Conference & Marketplace**
National Council of State Housing Agencies
444 N Capitol St NW
Suite 438
Washington, DC 20001-1505
202-624-7710
Fax: 202-624-5899
E-Mail: bthompson@ncsha.org
Home Page: www.ncsha.org
Social Media: Facebook, Twitter
Gerald M. Hunter, President
Brian A. Hudson, Vice President
Thomas R. Gleason, Secretary/ Treasurer
Barbara J. Thompson, Executive Director
The industry event of the year. Only NCSHA brings leaders and top development and compliance staff from the state Housing Credit allocating agencies together with government officials, developers, lenders syndicators, investors, attorneys, accountants, property managers, compliance experts, owners, and nonprofits.
350 Members
Frequency: Annual/June
Founded in 1974

12181 **IAEM Annual Conference**
International Association of Emergency Managers
201 Park Washington Court
Falls Church, VA 22046
703-538-1795
Fax: 703-241-5603
E-Mail: info@iaem.com
Home Page: www.iaem.com
Provides a forum for current trends and topics, information about the latest tools and technology in emergency management and homeland security, and advances IAEM-USA committee work. Sessions encourage stakeholders at all levels of government, the private sector, public health and related professions to exchange ideas on collaborating to protect lives and property from disaster.
1000 Attendees
Frequency: Annual/November

12182 **ICMA Annual Conference**
International City/County Management Association
777 N Capitol Street NE
Suite 500
Washington, DC 20002
202-624-4600
800-745-8780
Fax: 202-962-3500
E-Mail: amahoney@icma.org
Home Page: www.icma.org
Pat Phillips, Show Manager
Bill Hansell, Executive Director
The largest annual event in the world for local government managers and staff.
3.5M Attendees
Frequency: Annual/October

12183 **ICMA Regional Summit**
International City/County Management Association
777 N Capitol Street NE
Suite 500
Washington, DC 20002-4239
202-289-4262
800-745-8780
Fax: 202-962-3500
E-Mail: customerservices@icma.org
Home Page: www.icma.org
Social Media: Facebook, Twitter, LinkedIn, YouTube, Flickr
Barry Sacks, Show Manager
Robert J. O'Neill, Executive Director
A networking and professional development opportunity for members and state officers in the four regions.
3.5M Attendees
Frequency: Annual/September

12184 **Legislative Conference**
National Council of State Housing Agencies
444 N Capitol St NW
Suite 438
Washington, DC 20001-1505
202-624-7710
Fax: 202-624-5899
E-Mail: bthompson@ncsha.org
Home Page: www.ncsha.org
Social Media: Facebook, Twitter
Gerald M. Hunter, President
Brian A. Hudson, Vice President
Thomas R. Gleason, Secretary/ Treasurer
Barbara J. Thompson, Executive Director
Join HFA leaders and their board members and stakeholders in Washington to learn about NCSHA's legislative priorities and strategize the best way to communicate our message to Congress with one unified voice. Hear from key Congressional staff and industry leaders about the issues of the day.
350 Members
Frequency: Annual/March
Founded in 1974

12185 **MMA Annual Meeting and Trade Show**
Massachusetts Municipal Association
One Winthrop Square
Boston, MA 02110
617-426-7272
Fax: 617-695-1314
Home Page: www.mma.org
The largest regular gathering of Massachusetts local government officials. Features educational workshops, nationally recognized speakers, awards programs, a large trade show, and an opportunity to network with municipal officials from across the state.
1000 Attendees
Frequency: Annual/January

12186 **Marine West Military Expo**
Nielsen Business Media, USA
1145 Sanctuary Parkway
Suite 355
Alpharetta
703-488-2762
Ron Bates, Event Organizer
This event is fully dedicated to the defense industry. The event will showcase the latest products and equipments used for marine and related industry at one place. The visitors will be the military professionals, equipment buyers, decision makers and the other people related to the field of defense.
Frequency: Annual/February

12187 **NACE Annual Conference**
National Association County Engineers
25 Mass. Avenue NW
Suite 580
Washington, DC 20001
202-393-5041
Fax: 202-393-2630
E-Mail: nace@naco.org
Home Page: www.countyengineers.org
Mark A. Craft, President
Richie Beyer, President-Elect
Mark K. Servi, Secretary/ Treasurer
Attendees will have many opportunities to meet road and bridge professionals and their counterparts from other counties around the country, to exchange ideas and have some fun. The exhibit show offers a friendly environment for

delegates to learn about the latest products and services.
450 Attendees
Frequency: Annual/April

12188 NACo Annual Conference and Exposition
National Association of Counties
25 Massachusetts Avenue, NW
Suite 500
Washington, DC 20001
202-393-6226
888-407-6226
Fax: 202-393-2630
E-Mail: nacomeetings@naco.org
Home Page: admin.naco.org
Larry E. Naake, Executive Director
Provides an opportunity for all county leaders and staff to learn, network and guide the direction of the association. Provides county officials with a great opportunity to vote on NACo's policies related to federal legislation and regulation; elect officers; network with colleagues; learn about innovative county programs; find out about issues impacting counties across the country; and view products and services from participating companies and exhibitors.
Frequency: Annual/July

12189 NACo's Annual Conference and Exposition
National Association of Counties
440 1st Street NW
Washington, DC 20001-2028
202-393-6226
Fax: 202-393-2630
E-Mail: webmaster@naco.org
Home Page: www.naco.org
Amanda Clark, Conference & Meetings Associate
Kim Struble, Conference & Meetings Director
Larry Naake, CEO
The place for elected and appointed county officials to network, attend educational sessions and meet with companies that sell products to counties. It includes a variety of activities designed to meet the needs of all delegates. In addition to strong educational sessions, the conference includes affiliate, steering and subcommittee meetings, state association meetings and social events.
4000 Attendees
Frequency: Annual

12190 NAHRO National Conference
Nat'l Assn of Housing & Redevelopment Officials
630 Eye Street NW
Washington, DC 20001-3736
202-289-3500
877-866-2476
Fax: 202-289-8181
E-Mail: nahro@nahro.org
Home Page: www.nahro.org
A wide array of products and services needed by the housing and community development field.
3M Attendees
Frequency: Annual/October

12191 NARC Conference and Exhibition
National Association of Regional Councils
1666 Connecticut Ave NW
Suite 305
Washington, DC 20002
202-986-1032
Fax: 202-986-1038
E-Mail: lindsey@narc.org
Home Page: www.narc.org
Fred Abousleman, Executive Director
Lindsey Riley, Deputy of Communications
500+ Attendees
Frequency: Annual/June

12192 NASTAD Annual Conference
Nat'l Alliance of State/Territoral AIDS Directors
444 N Capitol St NW
Suite 339
Washington, DC 20001
202-434-8090
Fax: 202-434-8092
E-Mail: nastad@nastad.org
Home Page: www.nastad.org
Julie Scofield, Executive Director
Apprenticeship directors from around the nation come together to problem solve, share innovative ideas to the Registered Apprenticeship model as well as to bring the association up to date on each state's activities.
Frequency: Annual/May

12193 NCBM Annual Convention
National Conference of Black Mayors
191 Peachtree Street, NE
Suite 849
Atlanta, GA 30303
404-765-6444
Fax: 404-765-6430
E-Mail: info@ncbm.org
Home Page: www.ncbm.org
Vanessa R. Williams, Executive Director
Robert L. Bowser, President
Jamie Mayo, Treasurer
Johnny L. DuPree, Ph.D, Secretary
John White, Sergeant-at-Arms
Serving as a catalyst for bringing together mayors and municipal leaders, including several international delegations, state and federal officials, as well as leaders in the public and private sectors for the purpose of networking and obtaining information on the latest policies and strategies for enhancing municipal government.
542 Members
Founded in 1974

12194 NCSHA Housing Credit Conference & Marketplace
444 N Capitol Street NW
Suite 438
Washington, DC 20001-1512
202-624-7710
Fax: 202-624-5899
Home Page: www.ncsha.org
Louise Moors, Membership Coordinator
William Pound, Executive Director
Brings leaders and top development and compliance staff from the state Housing Credit allocating agencies together with government officials, developers, lenders, syndicators, investors, attorneys, accountants, property managers, compliance experts, owners, and nonprofits. Heavy hitters of the industry and their partners will deliver the latest news on how to make the housing Credit work in these unprecedented times.
700 Attendees
Frequency: Annual/June

12195 NCSL Fall Forum
National Conference of State Legislatures
7700 East First Place
Denver, CO 80230
303-364-7700
Fax: 303-364-7800
Home Page: www.ncsi.org
Peg Coniglio, Manager
Deana Blackwood, Circulation Director
Focuses on how best to advance the States' Agenda and tackle the difficult policy issues of our time, including budget gaps, health care coverage, education affordability, transportation funding, energy costs and many others.
6700 Attendees
Frequency: Annual/November

12196 NCSL Legislative Summit
National Conference of State Legislatures
444 North Capitol Street NW
Suite 515
Washington, DC 20001
202-624-5400
Fax: 202-737-1069
E-Mail: deana.blackwood@ncsl.org
Home Page: www.ncsl.org
William T Pound, Executive Director
Leticia Van de Putte, President
Steven Rauschenberger, VP
Max Arinder, Staff Chair
Four days of 150 policy sessions on the most pressing issues facing state legislatures. Some of the topics include budget conditions, education reform, health care implementation and renewable energy.
13M+ Members
4800+ Attendees
Frequency: Annual/August
Founded in 1975

12197 NCWM Annual Meeting
National Conference on Weights and Measures
1135 M Street
Suite 110
Lincoln, NE 68508
402-434-4880
Fax: 402-434-4878
E-Mail: info@ncwm.net
Home Page: www.ncwm.net
Don Onwiler, Executive Director
Technical presentations are a way to stay on the cutting edge of new developments in the weights and measures community. Complete the business of the conference through open hearings and voting on national standards.

12198 NEMA Mid-Year Conference
National Emergency Management Association
PO Box 11910
Lexington, KY 40578
859-244-8000
Fax: 859-244-8239
E-Mail: nemaadmin@csg.org
Home Page: www.nemaweb.org
Jim Mullen, President
John Madden, Vice President
Charley English, Treasurer
Tom Sands, Secretary
Brenda Bergeron, Legal Counsel
Gives the opportunity to discuss important issues in the field of emergency management and homeland security. Also hear from respected leaders working on many of these issues. Opportunities to meet and network with peers are invaluable in these times of rapid change and economic challenges.
Frequency: Annual/March

12199 NFBPA FORUM
National Forum for Black Public Administrators

777 N Capitol Street NE
Suite 807
Washington, DC 20002-4239

202-289-5851
800-745-8780
Fax: 202-962-3500
E-Mail: webmaster@nfbpa.org
Home Page: www.nfbpa.org

Aretha R. Ferrell-Benavides, President
Verdenia C. Baker, 1st Vice President
Bruce T. Moore, 2nd Vice President
Jelynn LeBlanc Burley, Secretary/ Treasurer

Waves of change, oceans of opportunity repositioning our communities for the future. Plenary sessions and luncheons, public policy forum, workshops, banquet and brunch, corporate exhibit, vendor showcase, artist's gallery and more.
1.4M Attendees
Frequency: Annual/April

12200 **NPELRA Annual Training Conference**
National Public Employer Labor Relations Assoc.
1620 I Street NW
4th Floor
Washington, DC 20006-4005

202-591-1190
Fax: 202-293-2352
Home Page: www.npelra.org
Social Media: Facebook, Twitter, LinkedIn

Sam Penrod, President
Michael S. Bates, Executive Vice President
Christa Ballowe, Vice President
Walt Pellegrini, Vice President
Joel Kuhl, Secretary/ Treasurer

Attend the best training available for public sector Labor Relations & Human Resources professionals with over 30 program sessions; in addition the conference provides credit hours for CLE and HRCI recertification. Interact with colleagues representing public sector labor relations professionals from across the country.
350 Attendees
Frequency: Annual

12201 **NPELRA Training Conference**
National Public Employer Labor Relations Assoc
1012 South Coast Highway
Suite M
Oceanside, CA 92054

760-433-1686
877-673-5721
Fax: 760-433-1687
E-Mail: mike@npelra.org
Home Page: www.npelra.org
Social Media: Facebook, Twitter, LinkedIn

Michael T Kolb, Executive Director
Janessa Stephens, Association Specialist
Yvonne Gillengerten, Operation Manager
Stephanie Biggs, Administrative Assistant
Allison Wittwer, Administrative Assistant

Attend the best training available for public sector Labor Relations and Human Resources professionals with over 30 program sessions; in addition the conference provides credit hours for CLE and HRCI recertification. Interact wth colleagues representing public sector labor relations professionals from across the country.
Frequency: Annual

12202 **NSCL Legislative Summit**
National Conference of State Legislatures
7700 E 1st Pl
Denver, CO 80230-7143

303-364-7700
Fax: 303-364-7800
E-Mail: pubs-info@ncsl.org
Home Page: www.ncsl.org
Social Media: Twitter, LinkedIn

William Pound, Executive Director
Edward Smith, Managing Editor
LeAnn Hoff, Director, Revenue & Sales

A bipartisan organization that serves the legislators and staffs of the nation's 50 states, its commonwealths and territories.
15000 Members
5500 Attendees
Founded in 1975

12203 **National Association Regional Councils**
1666 Conneticut Ave NW
Suite 305
Washington, DC 20002

202-986-1032
Fax: 202-986-1038
Home Page: www.narc.org

Shawn Sample, Show Manager

80 booths.
1.2M Attendees
Frequency: June
Founded in 1965

12204 **National Council of State Housing Agencies Conference**
444 N Capitol St NW
Suite 438
Washington, DC 20001-1505

202-624-7710
Fax: 202-624-5899
E-Mail: bthompson@ncsha.org
Home Page: www.ncsha.org
Social Media: Facebook, Twitter

Gerald M. Hunter, President
Brian A. Hudson, Vice President
Thomas R. Gleason, Secretary/ Treasurer
Barbara J. Thompson, Executive Director

The premier gathering of state HFAs and NCSHA affiliate members. It is the main networking event of the year for HFAs and the partners who work with them to increase housing opportunities through the financing, developemnt, and preservation of affordable housing.
350 Members
Frequency: Annual/October
Founded in 1974

12205 **National Electricity Forum**
NARUC
1101 Vermont Ave NW
Suite 200
Washington, DC 20005-3553

202-898-2200
Fax: 202-898-2213
E-Mail: admin@naruc.org
Home Page: www.naruc.org

David A. Wright, Chairman & President
Philip B. Jones, 1st Vice President
Colette D. Honorable, 2nd Vice President
David E. Ziegner, Treasurer
Charles D. Gray, Executive Director

Addressing cutting-edge issues and discuss how collaboration can successfully modernize the nation's electricity infrastructure. The forum will feature national thought leaders from all sectors of the electric power industry, academia, policymakers, equipment manufacturers, consumers, and other affected parties.
Frequency: Annual/February
Founded in 1889

12206 **National League of Postmasters Annual National Convention**
National League of Postmasters
5904 Richmond Highway
Suite 500
Alexandria, VA 22303-1864

703-329-4550
Fax: 703-329-0466
E-Mail: exhibit@epponline.com
Home Page: www.epponline.com

Mark W. Strong, President

Extensive training and educational opportunities.
1400 Attendees
Frequency: Annual/August
Founded in 1903

12207 **National Postal Forum**
3998 Fair Ridge Drive
Suite 300
Fairfax, VA 22033

703-218-5015
Fax: 703-218-5020
E-Mail: info@npf.org
Home Page: www.npf.org
Social Media: Facebook, Twitter, LinkedIn, Flickr

Mary Guthrie, Director, Marketing & Exhibits
Laurie Woodhams, Exhibits Assistant

The premier educational event and tradeshow available to mail professionals today. Attend the National Postal Forum to get a complete education in the Business of Mail.
Frequency: Annual/April

12208 **Norfolk NATO Festival**
440 Bank Street
Norfolk, VA 23510

757-282-2800
Fax: 757-282-2787
Home Page: www.azaleafestival.org

Kelly Harlan, General Manager

A salute to the NATO's Allied Command Atlantic forces in order to create new friendships, provide a basis for cultural exchange, recognize the military's role in maintaining peace in the world and pursue new lines of trade between Norfolk and the world.
5M Attendees
Frequency: Canada
Founded in 1953

12209 **PHADA Annual Convention and Exhibition**
Public Housing Authorities Directors Association
511 Capitol Court NE
Washington, DC 20002-4937

202-546-5445
Fax: 202-546-2280
Home Page: www.phada.org

Timothy G. Kaiser, Executive Director
Stephanie White, Director of Meetings

Provides the latest information and tools housing authorities need to run their agencies in these changing times. Also, many exciting housing suppliers and vendors will be on-hand to showcase their services. There are many sessions to provide attendees with important information emanating from Congress and HUD headquarters.
800 Attendees
Frequency: Annual/May

12210 **Transforming Local Government Conference**
Mid-America Regional Council
6604 Harney Road, Suite L
PO Box 16645
Tampa, FL 33687-6645

813-622-8484
Fax: 813-664-0051
Home Page: www.tlgconference.org

Social Media: Facebook, Twitter, Flickr, YouTube

Mary Laird, Executive Assistant
David Warm, Executive Director

Through innovative case study sessions, conference attendees will take an in-depth look at the ingenuity and creativity of successful government programs. TLG attracts participation from local governments that are deliberately seeking new and innovative ways to connect people, information and ideas that support their efforts to be the best communities in which to live, work, and prosper.

800 Attendees
Frequency: Annual
Printed in one color on matte stock

12211 **UDT: Undersea Defense Technology Conference and Exhibition**
Reed Exhibition Companies
255 Washington Street
Newton, MA 02458-1637

617-584-4900
Fax: 617-630-2222
Social Media: Facebook, Twitter, LinkedIn

Elizabeth Hitchcock, International Sales

The world's leading exhibition and conference for undersea defence and security. Gain access to the latest technologies, connect with existing suppliers and create new business relationships. Gives the invaluable opportunity to network across the global maritime community. Suppliers exhibiting; UUVs and components, acoustic technologies, maritime surveillance solutions, harbour and port security products, mine detection systems, and submarine hardware and electronics.
Frequency: Annual/May

12212 **UNA-USA Annual Meeting**
United Nations Association of the USA
1800 Massachusetts Avenue NW
Suite 400
Washington, DC 20036

202-887-9040
Fax: 202-887-9021
E-Mail: inquiries@un.org
Home Page: www.unausa.org

Patrick Madden, Executive Director

Brings together UNA-USA's constituencies for a variety of skills trainings, issue briefings, networking opportunities and capacity-building.
400 Attendees
Frequency: Annual/November

12213 **Western Legislative Conference**
1107 9th Street
Suite 730
Sacramento, CA 95814

916-553-4423
Fax: 916-446-5760
E-Mail: csgw@csg.org
Home Page: www.csgwest.org

Rosie Berger, Chair
Kelvin Atkinson, Chair-Elect
Craig Johnson, Vice Chair

Brings together legislators from western states to learn from each other and collaborate on issues of regional concern such as water, public lands, energy and transportation. Also offers training and professional development opportunities for all legislators.
500 Attendees
Frequency: Annual/July
Founded in 1933

Directories & Databases

12214 **Almanac of American Politics**
National Journal
1730 M St NW
Suite 800
Washington, DC 20036-4551

202-828-0300
Fax: 202-457-5160

Marcia Coyle, Manager

The definitive guide to understanding the forces that shape American politics. Has been established as a Washington institution in its own right and an indispensable resource for anyone involved or interested in the American political scene.
Cost: $59.95
1500 Pages
Frequency: Biennial

12215 **Almanac of the Federal Judiciary**
Prentice Hall Law & Business
270 Sylvan Avenue
Englewood Cliffs, NJ 07632-2521

201-569-0006

Providing balanced, responsible judicial profiles of every federal judge and all the key bankruptcy judges and magistrate judges- profiles that include reliable inside information based on interviews with lawyers who have argued cases before the federal judiciary.
Cost: $1715.00
2130 Pages
Frequency: Annual
ISBN: 9-780735-56-8

12216 **American Bench**
Forster-Long
3280 Ramos Cir
Sacramento, CA 95827-2513
916-362-3276
800-328-5091
Fax: 916-362-5643
Home Page: www.forster-long.com

Jay Long, Vice President, Marketing

Over 19,000 judges who sit in local, state and federal courts are profiled. The definitive biographical reference to the American judiciary.
Cost: $595.00
Frequency: Daily
Founded in 1977

12217 **BRB Publications**
BRB Publications
PO Box 27869
Tempe, AZ 85285-7869

480-829-7475
800-929-3811
Fax: 800-929-4981
E-Mail: mike@brbpublications.com
Home Page: www.BRBpublications.com

Mike Sankey, President

Comprehensive listing of government agencies that have placed public records online, both free and fee based.
Founded in 1988

12218 **Billcast Archive**
George Mason University, Public Choice Center
4400 University Dr
Fairfax, VA 22030-4444

703-993-1120

Clayton Austin, Manager

This database contains information on public bills introduced in the US House of Representatives and Senate during the preceding session of Congress.

12219 **Book of the States**
Council of State Governments
2760 Research Park Drive
PO Box 11910
Lexington, KY 40578-1910

859-244-8000
800-800-1910
Fax: 859-244-8001
E-Mail: research@csg.org
Home Page: www.csg.org

Jodi Rell, President
Carol Juett, Director of Development
Roger Werholtz, Secretary

A reference tool of choice and includes comparative information on everything from highway miles to state government employment and everything in between.
Cost: $99.00
Frequency: Annually
Founded in 1935

12220 **CSG State Directories**
Council of State Governments
2760 Research Park Drive
PO Box 11910
Lexington, KY 40578-1910

859-244-8000
800-800-1910
Fax: 859-244-8001
E-Mail: research@csg.org
Home Page: www.csg.org

Jodi Rell, President
Carol Juett, Director of Development
Roger Werholtz, Secretary

Includes the names and contact information for key state government officials.
Frequency: Annually

12221 **Canadian Almanac & Directory**
Grey House Publishing Canada
555 Richmond Street West
Suite 301
Toronto, ON M5V 3B1

416-644-6479
866-433-4739
Fax: 416-644-1904
E-Mail: info@greyhouse.ca
Home Page: www.greyhouse.ca
Social Media: Facebook, Twitter, LinkedIn

Richard Gottlieb, President
Leslie Mackenzie, Publisher

A combination of textual material, charts, colour photographs and directory listings, the Canadian Almanac & Directory provides the most comprehensive picture of Canada, from physical attributes to economic and business summaries to leisure and recreation.
Cost: $360.00
1936 Pages
Frequency: Annual
ISBN: 1-592377-69-5

12222 **Canadian Parliamentary Guide**
Grey House Publishing Canada
555 Richmond Street West
Suite 301
Toronto, ON M5V 3B1
416-644-6479
866-433-4739
Fax: 416-644-1904
E-Mail: info@greyhouse.ca
Home Page: www.greyhouse.ca
Social Media: Facebook, Twitter, LinkedIn

Richard Gottlieb, President
Leslie Mackenzie, Publisher

Canadian Parliamentary Guide provides the most complete and comprehensive information on elected and appointed members in federal

and provincial government.
Cost: $229.00
1152 Pages
Frequency: Annual
ISBN: 1-592377-65-7

12223 **Capital Source**
National Journal
600 New Hampshire Ave NW
Suite 4
Washington, DC 20037-2403
202-739-8400
Fax: 202-833-8069
E-Mail: capitalsource@nationaljournal.com
John Fox Sullivan, President
Directory brimming with key information on the most important players and institutions Inside-the-Beltway, The Capital Source is the place for essential and current contact information all year round. A must-have resource for anyone in the business of politics, policy, government relations or the media.
Cost: $29.95
160 Pages
Frequency: Monthly

12224 **Carroll's County Directory**
Carroll Publishing
4701 Sangamore Rd
Suite S-155
Bethesda, MD 20816-2532
301-263-9800
800-336-4240
Fax: 301-263-9805
E-Mail: customersvc@carrollpub.com
Home Page: www.carrollpub.com
Social Media: Twitter, LinkedIn
Bill Wade, President/COO
Kathleen Undegraff, VP Marketing
Cost: $350.00
Founded in 1973

12225 **Carroll's Federal Directory**
Carroll Publishing
4701 Sangamore Rd
Suite 155S
Bethesda, MD 20816-2532
301-263-9800
800-336-4240
Fax: 301-263-9805
E-Mail: info@carrollpub.com
Home Page: www.carrollpub.com
Tom Carroll, President
Offers complete coverage of the headquarter offices of the Executive, Legislative, and Judicial branches of government. Includes over 38,000 positions offering direct contact information for all Executive departments, independent agencies, Congressional Agencies and US Federal Courts.
Cost: $500.00
450 Pages
Frequency: Annual

12226 **Carroll's Federal Regional Directory**
Carroll Publishing
4701 Sangamore Rd
Suite 155S
Bethesda, MD 20816-2532
301-263-9800
800-336-4240
Fax: 301-263-9805
E-Mail: info@carrollpub.com
Home Page: www.carrollpub.com
Tom Carroll, President
The one regional resource that has it all. Covering regional and field offices of Federal government departments, home-state offices for members of Congress, federal district courts and more. Reach over 32,000 government people located outside of Washington.
Cost: $170.00
370 Pages
Frequency: Bi-Annually

12227 **Carroll's Municipal Directory**
Carroll Publishing
4701 Sangamore Rd
Suite 155S
Bethesda, MD 20816-2532
301-263-9800
800-336-4240
Fax: 301-263-9805
E-Mail: info@carrollpub.com
Home Page: www.carrollpub.com
Tom Carroll, President
The most comprehensive municipal directory available anywhere. It includes more than 60,000 appointed officials, career officials and local authorities across the US. Covering more cities than any other source, this has nearly 8,000 cities, towns and villages.
Cost: $170.00
550 Pages
Frequency: Bi-Annually

12228 **Carroll's State Directory**
Carroll Publishing
4701 Sangamore Rd
Suite 155S
Bethesda, MD 20816-2532
301-263-9800
800-336-4240
Fax: 301-263-9805
Home Page: www.carrollpub.com
Social Media: Twitter, LinkedIn
Bill Wade, President/COO
Kathleen Updegraff, VP Marketing
Provides complete contact information for over 68,000 key officials in all 50 states, plus the District of Columbia, Puerto Rico and the American Territories.
Cost: $210.00
530 Pages
Frequency: TriAnnual

12229 **Congress at Your Fingertips: Congressional Directory**
Capitol Advantage
1255 22nd St NW
Washington, DC 20037-1217
703-899-9636
800-659-8708
Fax: 703-289-4678
E-Mail: sales@capitoladvantage.com
Home Page: www.capitoladvantage.com
Dr. John Hansan, Production Manager
Comprehensive directory lists members of the US Senate and House of Representatives, complete with color photos and a fold-out map of Capitol Hill.
Cost: $13.95
Frequency: Annual

12230 **Congressional Staff Directory**
Leadership Directories, Inc.
1167 K Street NW
Suite 801
Washington, DC 20006
202-628-7757
Fax: 202-628-3430
E-Mail: infoleadershipdirectories.com
Home Page: www.leadershipdirectories.com
Gretchen Teichgraeber, CEO
William Cressey, Chairman
Locate key decision-makers and support staff that work behind the scenes on important legislative issues. Pinpoint key contacts on committees who work day-to-day on legislation that's most important.
Cost: $69.00
1200 Pages
Frequency: SemiAnnual

12231 **Daily Defense News Capsules**
United Communications Group
11300 Rockville Pike
Suite 1100
Rockville, MD 20852-3030
301-816-8950
Fax: 301-816-8945
Greg Beaudoin, Editor
This database offers the complete text of Periscope - Daily Defense News Capsules, that provide abstracts of international press coverage of military and defense news.

12232 **Defense Industry Charts**
Carroll Publishing
4701 Sangamore Rd
Suite 155S
Bethesda, MD 20816-2532
301-263-9800
800-336-4240
Fax: 301-263-9805
E-Mail: info@carrollpub.com
Home Page: www.carrollpub.com
Tom Carroll, President
19000 key personnel in top US defense contractors, including major aerospace, electronic, military hardware, information technology and systems integration companies. Serves as a road map to the critical players in this important industry.
Cost: $2050.00
Frequency: Quarterly

12233 **Defense Programs**
Carroll Publishing
4701 Sangamore Rd
Suite 155S
Bethesda, MD 20816-2532
301-263-9800
800-336-4240
Fax: 301-263-9805
E-Mail: info@carrollpub.com
Home Page: www.carrollpub.com
Tom Carroll, President
Detailed description of more than 2,000 military research, development, test and evaluation programs and projects.
Cost: $1060.00
Frequency: Quarterly

12234 **Defense and Foreign Affairs Handbook**
International Strategic Studies Association
PO Box 19289
Alexandria, VA 22320-0289
703-548-1070
Fax: 703-684-7476
E-Mail: dfa@strategicstudies.org
Home Page: www.strategicstudies.org
Gregory Copley, Editor
Important global reference encyclopedia for most world leaders .Comprehensive chapters on 238 countries and territories worldwide, with each chapter giving full cabinet and leadership listings, history, recent developments, demographics, economic statistics, political and constitutional data, news media,defense overview, defense structure.
Cost: $297.00
2500 Pages
Frequency: Monthly
Circulation: 4,000
ISBN: 1-892998-06-8
Founded in 1976

12235 **Directory of Congressional Voting Scores and Interest Group Ratings**
1414 22nd Street NW
Washington, DC 20037-1003

202-887-8500
800-432-2250
Fax: 800-380-3810
Home Page: www.cqpress.com

Complete compilation of CQ voting studies and interest group rating data for every legislator who has served in Congress since 1947. This resource is perfect for quick or in-depth research and provides the easiest, most accurate way to gauge the political orientation of members of Congress over time. This is the best source for understanding the political preferences of US senators and representatives, and what it means about their choices on future votes.
Cost: $450.00
1700 Pages
Frequency: Triennial

12236 **Encyclopedia of Governmental Advisory Organizations**
Gale/Cengage Learning
PO Box 6904
Florence, KY 41022-6904

800-354-9706
Fax: 800-487-8488
E-Mail: gale.galeord@cengage.com
Home Page: www.gale.com

Patrick C Sommers, President

Contains entries which describe the activities and personnel of groups and committees that function to advise the President of the United States and various departments and bureaus of the federal government, as well as detailed information about historically significant committees.
Frequency: Annual

12237 **Federal Benefits for Veterans, Dependents and Survivors**
US Department of Veterans Affairs
810 Vermont Ave NW
Washington, DC 20420-0002

202-273-5400
Fax: 202-273-4880

John R Gingirch, CEO

Health care benefits, disability benefits, pensions, home loan, insurance, and much more.
Cost: $3.25
Frequency: Annual

12238 **Federal Buyers Guide**
Gold Crest
650 Ward Dr # A
Santa Barbara, CA 93111-2395

805-683-9000
800-922-3233
Fax: 805-683-7661
Home Page: www.goldcrestinc.com

Roger Edgar, CEO
Gunnar Sundstrom, OPS Manager

Companies that serve or wish to serve as vendors to the federal government. Reading specialty lights, giftware, manufacturer, distributor, Mighty Bright brand.
170 Pages
Frequency: Quarterly
ISSN: 1043-7568
Founded in 1979

12239 **Federal Directory of Contract Administration Services Components**
Contract Mgmt. Command/Defense Logistics Agency
Caremon Station
Alexandria, VA 22304

703-781-9807

Lists the names and telephone numbers of those DCMA and other agency offices that offer contract administration services within designated geographic areas and at specified contractor plants.
110 Pages
Frequency: Annually

12240 **Federal Government Certification Programs**
US National Institute of Standards & Technology
Administration Building
Room 629
Gaithersburg, MD 20899-0001

301-975-2281
Fax: 301-963-2871

A directory available certification programs.
Cost: $18.95
229 Pages

12241 **Federal Staff Direcotry**
1414 22nd Street NW
Washington, DC 20037-1003

202-887-8500
800-432-2250
Fax: 800-380-3810
Home Page: www.cqpress.com

Penny Perry, Editor

Pinpoint senior officials and top aides working directly with the President and Vice President using the most well-researched information available. Find all the information needed to locate high-ranking policy-makers, their deputies, bureau chiefs, and division heads. Connect with top-level officials at agencies ranging from the American Red Cross to the Environmental Protection Agency.
Cost: $450.00
1700 Pages
Frequency: Monthly

12242 **Federal Technology Source**
Government Executive- National Journal Group
600 New Hampshire Ave NW
Suite 4
Washington, DC 20037-2403

202-739-8500
800-356-4838
Fax: 202-739-8511
E-Mail: webmaster@govexec.com
Home Page: www.govexec.com

Matt Dunie, President
Sue Fourney, Managing Editor

A directory of most important people and organizations in the federal technology community.
Cost: $9.95
168 Pages
Frequency: Annual
Circulation: 73,500
ISSN: 0017-2626
Printed in 4 colors on glossy stock

12243 **Foreign Consular Offices in the United States**
Bureau of Public Affairs/US Department of State
2201 C Street NW
Washington, DC 20520-0001

202-647-6141

A complete and official listing of the foreign consular offices in the US, and recognized consular officers. Compiled by the US Department of State, with the full cooperation of the foreign missions in Washington, it is offered as a convenience to organizations and persons who must deal with consular government agencies, state tax officials, international trade organizations, chamber of commerce, and judicial authorities.
Cost: $4.00
290 Pages
Frequency: Annual

12244 **Getting Started in Federal Contracting: A Guide Through the Federal Maze**
Panoptic Enterprises
PO Box 11220
Burke, VA 22009-1220

703-451-5953
800-594-4766
Fax: 703-451-5953
Home Page: www.fedgovcontracts.com

Vivina Mcvay, President
Barry L McVay, Editor

Information is given on over 65 government procurement offices, Department of Labor offices, General Services Administration business services and Small Business Administration regional and branch offices.
Cost: $39.95
395 Pages
ISBN: 0-912481-24-2
Founded in 1984

12245 **Government Assistance Almanac: Guide to all Federal Financial Programs**
Omnigraphics
615 Griswold
Detroit, MI 48226

313-961-1340
800-234-1340
Fax: 313-961-1383
E-Mail: editorial@omnigraphics.com
Home Page: www.omnigraphics.com

Robert Dumouchel, Editor

Provides updated information on all 1,613 federal domestic assistance programs available. These programs represent $1.675 trillion worth of federal assistance earmarked for distribution to consumers, children, parents, veterans, senior citizens, students, businesses, civic groups, state and local agencies, and others.
Cost: $240.00
1,000 Pages
Frequency: Annual
ISBN: 0-780807-00-6

12246 **Government Phone Book USA**
Omnigraphics
615 Griswold Street
Detroit, MI 48226

313-961-1340
800-234-1340
Fax: 313-961-1383
E-Mail: editorial@omnigraphics.com
Home Page: www.omnigraphics.com

David Bianco, Marketing Director

Key federal, state and local government offices in the US are profiled. More than 270,000 listings with complete contact data.
Cost: $275.00
2,700 Pages
Frequency: Annual
ISBN: 0-780806-93-X
Founded in 1992

12247 **Government Research Directory**
Gale/Cengage Learning
PO Box 09187
Detroit, MI 48209-0187

248-699-4253
800-877-4253
Fax: 248-699-8049

E-Mail: gale.galeord@cengage.com
Home Page: www.gale.com

Patrick C Sommers, President

In this vital resource you'll find research facilities and programs of the US and Canadian federal governments. Listings include e-mail addresses, information on patents available for licensing and expanded coverage of key personal contact.
ISBN: 1-414420-23-4

12248 Governments Canada
Grey House Publishing Canada
555 Richmond Street West
Suite 301
Toronto, ON M5V 3B1

416-644-6479
866-433-4739
Fax: 416-644-1904
E-Mail: info@greyhouse.ca
Home Page: www.greyhouse.ca
Social Media: Facebook, Twitter, LinkedIn

Richard Gottlieb, President
Leslie Mackenzie, Publisher

Governments Canada is the most complete and comprehensive tool for locating people and programs in Canada. It provides regularly updated listings on federal, provincial and territorial government departments, offices and agencies across Canada. Branch and regional offices are also included, along with all associated agencies, boards, commissions and crown corporations. Listings include contact names, full address, telephone and fax numbers, as well as e-mail addresses.
Cost: $299.00
600 Pages
Frequency: 2x/Year
ISBN: 1-592379-85-9

12249 Grey House Safety & Security Directory
Grey House Publishing
4919 Route 22
PO Box 56
Amenia, NY 12501

518-789-8700
800-562-2139
Fax: 845-373-6390
E-Mail: books@greyhouse.com
Home Page: www.greyhouse.com
Social Media: Facebook, Twitter

Leslie Mackenzie, Publisher
Richard Gottlieb, Editor

Comprehensive guide to the safety and security industry, including articles, checklists, OSHA regulations and product listings. Focuses on creating and maintaining a safe and secure enviroment, and dealing specifically with hazardous materials, noise and vibration, workplace preparation and maintenance, electrical and lighting safety, fire and rescue and more.
Cost: $165.00
1600 Pages
ISBN: 1-592373-75-5
Founded in 1981

12250 Guide to Management Improvement Projects in Local Government
ICMA Publications
777 N Capitol St NE
Suite 600
Washington, DC 20002-4240

202-216-9408
800-745-8780
Fax: 202-962-3500
Home Page: www,icma.org

Joan Mc Callen, President

Projects conducted by municipal governments that have resulted in improvements in efficiency or cost reductions are listed.
Cost: $65.00
50 Pages
Frequency: Quarterly

12251 Hudson's Washington News Media Contacts Directory
Grey House Publishing
4919 Route 22
PO Box 56
Amenia, NY 12501

518-789-8700
800-562-2139
Fax: 845-373-6390
E-Mail: books@greyhouse.com
Home Page: www.greyhouse.com
Social Media: Facebook, Twitter

Leslie Mackenzie, Publisher
Richard Gottlieb, President

A comprehensive guide to the entire Washington, D.C. press corps, broken down into categories.
Cost: $289.00
350 Pages
ISBN: 1-592378-53-6
Printed in one color on matte stock

12252 Hudson's Washington News Media Contacts - Online Database
Grey House Publishing
4919 Route 22
PO Box 56
Amenia, NY 12501

518-789-8700
800-562-2139
Fax: 845-373-6390
E-Mail: gold@greyhouse.com
Home Page: http://gold.greyhouse.com
Social Media: Facebook, Twitter

Leslie Mackenzie, Publisher
Richard Gottlieb, President

With 100% verification of data, Hudson's is the most accurate, most up-to-date source for media contacts in our nation's capital. With the largest concentration of news media in the world, having access to Washington's news media will get your message heard by these key media outlets.

12253 IAEM Directory
International Association of Emergency Managers
111 Park Pl
Falls Church, VA 22046-4513

703-538-1795
Fax: 703-241-5603
E-Mail: info@iaem.com
Home Page: www.iaem.com

Shan Coffin, Editor
Sharon L Kelly, Circulation Director
Cost: $100.00
Circulation: 8,000

12254 Immediate Need Resource Directory
Gold Crest
650 Ward Dr
Suite A
Santa Barbara, CA 93111-2395

805-683-9000
800-922-3233
Fax: 805-683-7661
Home Page: www.goldcrestinc.com

Roger Edgar, CEO
Gunnar Sundstrom, OPS Manager

A directory catering to the immediate needs of Federal government purchasing agents. Reading and speciality lights, giftware, manufacturer, distributor, Mighty Bright brand.
Cost: $20.00
50 Pages
Frequency: Monthly
Founded in 1990

12255 Judicial Yellow Book
Leadership Directories
104 5th Ave
New York, NY 10011-6901

212-627-4140
Fax: 212-645-0931
E-Mail: judicial@leadershipdirectories.com
Home Page: www.leadershipdirectories.com

David Hurvitz, CEO
James M Petrie, Associate Publisher

Contact information for over 3,250 federal and state judges in federal and state appellate courts, including staff and law clerks, and the law schools they attended.
Cost: $245.00
1,100 Pages
Frequency: SemiAnnual
ISSN: 1082-3298
Founded in 1995
Mailing list available for rent: 13,000 names at $125 per M

12256 Kaleidoscope: Current World Data
ABC-CLIO
PO Box 1911
Santa Barbara, CA 93102-1911

805-968-1911
Fax: 805-685-9685
E-Mail: CustomerService@abc-clio.com
Home Page: www.abc-clio.com

Ron Boehm, CEO

This comprehensive database takes a look at all aspects of the American culture. Listings of information include statistics and factual information on the population, culture, economy, military forces, government, and political systems of countries around the world, the US States and Canadian provinces.
Frequency: Full-text

12257 Leadership Directories
104 5th Ave
New York, NY 10011-6901

212-627-4140
Fax: 212-645-0931
E-Mail: info@leadershipdirectories.com
Home Page: www.leadershipdirectories.com

David Hurvitz, CEO
Barry Graubart, Executive VP/CMO

The mission of Leadership Directories is to compile, produce and offer subscribers, in all media and in easily usable form, the most current and accurate directories of leaders in the major categories of American activity, including government, business, the professions, and the nonprofits.
Founded in 1969

12258 Leadership Library in Print
Leadership Directories
104 5th Ave
New York, NY 10011-6901

212-627-4140
Fax: 212-645-0931
E-Mail: info@leadershipdirectories.com
Home Page: www.leadershipdirectories.com

David Hurvitz, CEO

Complete set of all 14 leadership directories. Provides subscribers with complete contact information for the 400,000 individuals who constitute the institutional leadership of the US.
Cost: $2300.00
Frequency: Semiannually
Founded in 1996

12259 Leadership Library on Internet and CD-ROM
Leadership Directories
104 5th Ave
New York, NY 10011-6901
212-627-4140
Fax: 212-645-0931
E-Mail: info@leadershipdirectories.com
Home Page: www.leadershipdirectories.com
David Hurvitz, CEO
Makes all 14 leadership directories available over the Internet and on CD-ROM in one integrated directory. They provide subscribers with complete contact information, in one database. Subscription includes Internet access and four CD-ROM editions quarterly.
Cost: $3065.00
Frequency: Updated Daily
ISSN: 1075-3869
Founded in 1999
Mailing list available for rent
Printed in A colors on B stock

12260 Local Court & County Record Retrievers
BRB Publications
PO Box 27869
Tempe, AZ 85285
480-677-7200
800-929-3811
Fax: 480-829-8505
Home Page: www.brbpub.com
Mark Sankey, President
Who's who of the public record retrieval industry. Over 2,700 companies profiled and indexed, can search alphabetically and by location.
Cost: $39.95
632 Pages
Frequency: Annual
ISBN: 1-879792-76-1
Founded in 1994

12261 Member Data Disk
CQ Staff Directories
815 Slaters Lane
Alexandria, VA 22314-1219
800-252-1722
Fax: 703-739-0234
Bruce B Brownson, Editor
Covers all members of the US Congress and their key staff members in Washington, DC and principal district offices.
Cost: $395.00
Frequency: Quarterly

12262 Military Biographical Profiles
CTB/McGraw Hill
20 Ryan Ranch Rd
Monterey, CA 93940-5770
831-393-0700
800-538-9547
Fax: 831-393-6528
E-Mail: CTBTechnicalSupport@CTB.com
Home Page: www.ctb.com
Ellen Haley, President
Sandor Nagy, Chief Operating Officer
Offers valuable information on US military officers and Department of Defense officials.
Frequency: Full-text

12263 Municipal Year Book
ICMA Publications
777 N Capitol St NE
Suite 600
Washington, DC 20002-4240
202-216-9408
800-745-8780
Fax: 202-962-3500
E-Mail: cpmmail@icma.org
Home Page: www.icma.org
Joan Mc Callen, President
Gary Huff, Founder
Directory of services and supplies to the industry.
Cost: $79.95
416 Pages
Frequency: Annual

12264 Municipal Yellow Book
Leadership Directories
104 5th Ave
New York, NY 10011-6901
212-627-4140
Fax: 212-645-0931
E-Mail: municipal@leadershipdirectories.com
Home Page: www.leadershipdirectories.com
David Hurvitz, CEO
James M Petrie, Associate Publisher
Contact information for over 33,000 elected and administrative officials of US cities, counties, and local authorities.
Cost: $245.00
1,200 Pages
Frequency: SemiAnnual
ISSN: 1054-4062
Founded in 1991
Mailing list available for rent: 30,000 names at $125 per M

12265 National Directory of Corporate Public Affairs
Columbia Books
PO Box 251
Annapolis Junction, MD 20701-0251
888-265-0600
Fax: 240-646-7020
E-Mail: info@columbiabooks.com
Home Page: www.columbiabooks.com
J Valerie Steele, Senior Editor
Tracks the public/government affairs programs of about 1,900 major US corporations and lists the 14,00 people who run them, Also lists: Washington area offices, corporate PACs, federal and state lobbyists, outside contract lobbyists. Indexed by subject and geographic area. Includes membership directory of the Public Affairs Council.
Cost: $109.00
Frequency: Annual January

12266 National Directory of Women Elected Officials
National Women's Political Caucus
1630 Connecticut Avenue NW
Suite 201
Washington, DC 20009
202-785-1100
Fax: 202-785-3605
E-Mail: info@nwpc.org
Home Page: www.nwpc.org
Directory of services and supplies to the industry.
230 Pages
Frequency: Biennial

12267 National and Federal Employment Report
Federal Reports
1010 Vermont Ave NW
Suite 408
Washington, DC 20005-4945
202-393-1552
Fax: 202-393-1553
Home Page: www.attorneyjobs.com
Richard L Hermann, Owner
Over 600 current attorney and law-related job opportunities with the US government are listed.
Cost: $111.20
Frequency: Monthly

12268 New York State Directory
Grey House Publishing
4919 Route 22
PO Box 56
Amenia, NY 12501
518-789-8700
800-562-2139
Fax: 845-373-6390
E-Mail: books@greyhouse.com
Home Page: www.greyhouse.com
Social Media: Facebook, Twitter
Leslie Mackenzie, Publisher
Richard Gottlieb, Editor
A comprehensive and easy-to-use guide to accessing public officials and private sector organizations and individuals who influence public policy in the state of New York. Includes important information on all New York state legislators and congressional representatives, including biographies and key committee assignments.
Cost: $145.00
800 Pages
ISBN: 1-592373-58-5
Founded in 1981

12269 New York State Directory - Online Database
Grey House Publishing
4919 Route 22
PO Box 56
Amenia, NY 12501
518-789-8700
800-562-2139
Fax: 845-373-6390
E-Mail: gold@greyhouse.com
Home Page: http://gold.greyhouse.com
Social Media: Facebook, Twitter
Leslie Mackenzie, Publisher
Richard Gottlieb, Editor
A comprehensive and easy-to-use guide to accessing public officials and private sector organizations and individuals who influence public policy in the state of New York. Includes important information on all New York state legislators and congressional representatives, including biographies and key committee assignments. With a subscription to the online database, you'll have immediate access to this wealth of contact information.
Founded in 1981

12270 Organization Charts
Carroll Publishing
4701 Sangamore Rd
Suite 155S
Bethesda, MD 20816-2532
301-263-9800
800-336-4240
Fax: 301-263-9805
Home Page: www.carrollpub.com
Tom Carroll, President
Provide a unique graphic visualization of the personnel relationships in Federal, Defense and Defense Industry organizations. Traditionally used to display report relationships between individuals, these charts are the #1 authoritative source for getting an up-to-date picture of the hierarchy within government, defense and defense contractors, including major aerospace, military hardware and IT companies.
Cost: $1160.00
185 Pages
Frequency: 8x Yearly

12271 Politics in America
Congressional Digest

4416 East West Highway
Suite 400
Bethesda, MD 20814-4568
301-634-3113
800-637-9915
Fax: 301-634-3189
Home Page: www.pro-and-con.org

Offers information on United States senators and representatives.
Cost: $89.95
1700 Pages
Frequency: Biennial

12272 **Profiles of Worldwide Government Leaders**
Worldwide Government Directories
7979 Old Georgetown Road
Suite 900
Bethesda, MD 20814-2429
301-258-2677
800-332-3535
Fax: 301-718-8494

Jonathan Hixon, Publisher

Spanning 195 countries, includes comprehensive biographical snapshots of as many as 30 or more ministers from each country. The material is obtained from primary and secondary sources including embassies, government ministries, offices of the United States government and proprietary global network of correspondents.
Cost: $297.00
850+ Pages
Frequency: Annual

12273 **Public Human Services Directory**
American Public Human Services Association
1133 19th Street NW
Suite 400
Washington, DC 20036-3623
202-682-0100
Fax: 202-289-6555
Home Page: www.aphsa.org

Tracy Wareing, Executive Director

State-by-state guide to people, programs and a must-have for all human service professionals.
Frequency: Annual
Founded in 1930

12274 **Public Record Research System**
BRB Publications
PO Box 27869
Tempe, AZ 85285
480-677-7200
800-929-3811
Fax: 480-829-8505
E-Mail: brb@brbpub.com
Home Page: www.publicrecordsources.com

Mark Sankey, President

Comprehensive public records locator, over 26,000 government agencies and institutions profiled.
Cost: $119.00

12275 **Public Records Online**
BRB Publications
PO Box 27869
Tempe, AZ 85285-7869
480-677-7200
800-929-3811
Fax: 800-929-4981
Home Page: www.brbpub.com

Mark Sankey, President

Comprehensive listing of government agencies that have placed public records online, both free and fee based.
Cost: $20.95
520 Pages
ISBN: 1-889150-21-5
Founded in 2000

12276 **Public Risk Management Association Membership Directory**
500 Montgomery Street
Suite 750
Alexandria, VA 22314
703-528-7701
Fax: 703-739-0200
E-Mail: info@primacentral.org
Home Page: www.primacentral.org

Jim Hirt, Executive Director
Jon Ruzan, Manager
Kerry Langley, Manager

Lists all members alphabetically; by state/country; by category; government; private; associate. Yellow pages give vender and service provider 50-wind thumbnail descriptions. Advertising sold.
Circulation: 2,000

12277 **The Guide to County Court Records**
BRB Publications
PO Box 27869
Tempe, AZ 85285-7869
480-829-7475
800-929-3811
Fax: 800-929-4981
E-Mail: mike@brbpublications.com
Home Page: www.BRBpublications.com

Mike Sankey, President
Founded in 1988

12278 **The MVR Access and Decoder Digest**
BRB Publications
PO Box 27869
Tempe, AZ 85285-7869
480-829-7475
800-929-3811
Fax: 800-929-4981
E-Mail: mike@brbpublications.com
Home Page: www.BRBpublications.com

Mike Sankey, President
Founded in 1988

12279 **The Manual to Online Public Records**
BRB Publications
PO Box 27869
Tempe, AZ 85285-7869
480-829-7475
800-929-3811
Fax: 800-929-4981
E-Mail: mike@brbpublications.com
Home Page: www.BRBpublications.com

Mike Sankey, President
Founded in 1988

12280 **US Congress Handbook**
8120 Woodmont Ave.
Suite 110
Bethesda, MD 20814

E-Mail: info@uscongresshandbook.com
Home Page: www.uscongresshandbook.com
Social Media: Facebook, Twitter

Washington's most trusted source for information on Congressional offices and their staff. The most comprehensive Congressional directory available.
Frequency: Annually
Founded in 1974

12281 **United States Government Manual**
Office of the Federal Register
National Archives Administration
Washington, DC 20408-0001
202-564-2480
Fax: 202-501-0599

The official handbook of the United States government; includes descriptions and lists of principal personnel of agencies and government bodies.
Cost: $30.00
935 Pages
Frequency: Annual

12282 **Washington Information Directory**
Congressional Quarterly
1414 22nd Street NW
Washington, DC 20037-1003
202-887-8500
Fax: 202-822-6583

Paul McClure, Editor
Will Gardner, Associate Editor

5,000 governmental agencies, congressional committees and non-governmental associations considered competent sources of specialized information.
Cost: $105.00
Frequency: Annual June

12283 **Washington: Comprehensive Directory of the Key Institutions and Leaders**
Columbia Books
1212 New York Avenue NW
Suite 330
Washington, DC 20005-3969
202-641-1662
888-265-0600
Fax: 202-898-0775
E-Mail: info@columbiabooks.com
Home Page: www.columbiabooks.com

Buck Downs, Senior Editor

Over 5,000 federal and district government offices, businesses, associations, publications, radio and television stations, labor organizations, religious and cultural institutions, health care facilities and community organizations in the District of Columbia area.
Cost: $75.00
Frequency: Annual May

12284 **Worldwide Directory of Defense Attorneys**
Worldwide Government Directories
7979 Old Georgetown Road
Suite 900
Bethesda, MD 20814-2429
301-258-2677
800-332-3535
Fax: 301-718-8494

Jonathan Hixon, Publisher

One-of-a-kind resource covering military and civilian defense and national security agencies from the ministry of defense down to service branches in 195 countries worldwide.
Cost: $647.00
1,100 Pages
Frequency: Annual

12285 **Worldwide Government Directory**
Worldwide Government Directories
7979 Old Georgetown Road
Suite 900
Bethesda, MD 20814-2429
301-258-2677
800-332-3535
Fax: 301-718-8494

Jonathan Hixon, Publisher

Offers valuable information on every senior government official in the executive, legislative, and judicial branches as well as the diplo-

matic and defense communities of 195 countries worldwide. Plus senior officials in over 100 international organizations. Each entry includes name, address, title, telephone, telex, facsimile number, and more. Also included are current state agencies and corporations, official forms of address, international dialing codes and central bank information.
Cost: $347.00
1,400 Pages
Frequency: Annual

12286 **Worldwide Government Directory with International Organizations**
1414 22nd Street NW
Washington, DC 20037-1003
202-887-8500
800-432-2250
Fax: 800-380-3810
Home Page: www.cqpress.com
Linda Dziobek, Editor
Coverage includes over 1800 pages of executive, legislative and political branches; heads of state, ministers, deputies, secretaries and spokespersons as well as state agencies, diplomats and senior level defense officials. Also covers the leadership of more than 100 international organizations.
Cost: $450.00
1700 Pages
Frequency: Annually

Industry Web Sites

12287 **http://gold.greyhouse.com**
G.O.L.D Grey House OnLine Databases
Grey House Publishing's online database platform, GOLD, offers Quick Search, Keyword Search and Expert Search for most business sectors including govenment markets. The GOLD platform makes finding the information you need quick and easy - whether you're a novice searcher or an experienced database user. All of Grey House's directory products are available for subscription on the GOLD platform.

12288 **www.aashto.org**
American Association of State Highway and Transportation
Membership is composed of highway and transportation departments in the 50 states, the District of Columbia, and Puerto Rico.

12289 **www.abccert.org**
Association of Boards of Certification
The Association of Boards of Certification is dedicated to protecting public health and the environment by advancing the quality and integrity of environmental certification programs through innovative technical support services, effective information exchange, professional and cost-effective examination services, and other progressive services for certifying members.

12290 **www.access.digex.net/fedbar**
Federal Bar Association
Members are attorneys in the Federal Government or who have interest in federal law.

12291 **www.accesspro.org**
American Society of Access Professionals
Members are government employees, lawyers, journalists and others concerned with access to government data under current personal privacy and public informaiton statues.

12292 **www.acsp.uic.edu/iaco**
International Association of Correctional Officers
Correctional officers and juvenile administrators.

12293 **www.actnat.com**
Association of Civilian Technicians
Union of civilian employees of the Army and National Guard and Air Reserve.

12294 **www.admin.org**
American Federation of School Administrators
Established in 1971 as the school administrators and supervisors organizing committee. Information of interest to those in public education.

12295 **www.affirm.org**
Associ for Federal Information Resources Mngt
Seeks to improve the management of information systems and resources of the Federal Government.

12296 **www.afge.org**
American Federation of Government Employees
The largest federal employee union representing 700,000 workers nationwide and overseas.

12297 **www.afscase.org**
American Federation of State, County and Municipal Employees
Sponsors their own Political Action Committee.

12298 **www.aglf.org/**
Association for Governmental Leasing and Finance
Provides an exchange of information among tax-exempt issuers, investment banking firms and party lease brokers.

12299 **www.aja.ncsc.dni.cs**
American Judges Association
An independent organization of judges in all jurisdictions in Canada, Mexico and the United States.

12300 **www.alexandriagroup.com**
National Association of Government Communicators
A merger of Federal Editors association, the Government Information Organization, and the Armed Forces Writers League.

12301 **www.alldc.org**
American League of Lobbyists
National association dedicated to serving government relations and public affairs professionals. Provides programs and conferences of interest to lobbyists.

12302 **www.ansi.org**
American National Standards Institute
Promotes the knowledge for approved standards for industry, engineering and safety design.

12303 **www.aphf.org**
American Federation of Police & Concerned Citizens
Operates the American police Academy as its educational arm. Maintains the American Police Hall of Fame & Museum in Miami, Florida.

12304 **www.aspanet.org**
American Society for Public Administration
Offers a wide range of services and membership options for individuals in public administration careers. Sponsors 127 local chapters and 16 sections on specific areas of governments, such as the Section of Natural Resources and Environmental Administration and the Section on Human Resource Administration.

12305 **www.aspehhs.gov**
Interagency Council on the Homeless
Seeks to evaluate and monitor federal activities for the homeless, collect information, study problems related to homelessness and disseminate information. Provides technical and professional assistance to the State and local governments and other public and private organizations to maximize resources and develop innovative programs to help the homeless.

12306 **www.brbpub.com**
BRB Publications
Over 700 reviewers are indexed and profiled by county of expertise. Includes the membership of The Public Record Retriever Network, links to hundreds of sites with free public records and you may order research books online.

12307 **www.cagw.com**
Citizens Against Government Waste
Public advocacy, non-partisan organization committed to eliminate government waste, fraud, abuse, mismanagement and inefficiency.

12308 **www.clearhq.org**
Council on Licensure, Enforcement and Regulation
Members include occupational and professional licensing boards and agencies and private interests in the 50 states, territories and Canada.

12309 **www.communityleadership.org**
Community Leadership Association
Founded by 40 community leadership organizations.

12310 **www.coscda.org**
Council for State Community Development Agencies
Employees of state community affairs agencies.

12311 **www.csa-dc.org**
Contract Services Association of America
Represents the government services contracting industry in Washington, DC. Members range from small businesses to large corporations servicing federal and state government in numerous capacities. CSA acts to foster effective implementation of the government's policy of reliance on the private sector for support services.

12312 **www.cued.org**
National Council for Urban Economic Development
National membership organization serving public and private participants in economic development across the United States and in international settings. CUED provides information to its members who build local economies through the tools used for job creation, attraction and retention. Members include public economic development directors, chamber of commerce staff, utility executives and academicians, plus the many other professionals who help design and implement development programs.

12313 **www.eba-net.org**
Energy Bar Association
Lawyers engaged in promoting proper administration of federal laws relating to the production, development and economic regulation of energy.

12314 www.epic.org
Fund for Constitutional Government
Seeks to expose and correct illegal activities, corruption, and lack of accountability in the federal government.

12315 www.fbi.gov
Federal Investigators Association
Formerly the United States Treasury Agents.

12316 www.fedphy.org
Federal Physicians Association
The purpose of the Federal Physicians Association is to improve the practice of medicine within the federal government; and to improve the working conditions and benefits of Federal Civil Service Physicians.

12317 www.foodprotection.org
International Association for Food Protection
The International Association for Food Protection founded in 1911, is a nonprofit educational association with a mission to provide food safety professional worldwide with a forum to exchange information on protecting the food supply. The Association is comprised of a cross-section of over 3,000 members from 50 nations. Affiliate chapters are located in the United States, Canada and South Korea.

12318 www.ginniemae.gov/about/contract.htm
Government National Mortgage Association - Ginnie Mae
Supports government housing objectives by establishing secondary markets for residential mortgages. Through its mortgage-backed securities programs, Ginnie Mae creates a vehicle for channeling funds from the securities markets into the mortgage market and helps to increase the supply of credit available for housing.

12319 www.govexec.com
National Journal
The website of Government Executive Magazine.

12320 www.greyhouse.com
Grey House Publishing
Authoritative reference directories for most business sectors including government markets. Users can search the online databases with varied search criteria allowing for custom searches by product category, geographic area, sales volume, keyword, subject and more. Full Grey House catalog and online ordering also available.

12321 www.healthfinder.gov
Association of Food and Drug Officials
Promotes the enforcement of laws and regulations at all levels of government. Fosters understanding and cooperation between industry and regulators. Develops model laws and regulations and seeks their adoption.

12322 www.ida-downtown.org
International Downtown Association
Represents organizations and individuals involved in downtown development. Members include city center redevelopment organizations and local officials, businesses, property owners, financiers, planners, university and foundation representatives, and legal and accounting professionals. Offers conferences, technical assistance, consulting services and extensive information services.

12323 www.ihs.com
International Code Council
Nonprofit membership association with more than 16,000 members who span the building community, from code enforcement officials to materials manufacturers. Dedicated to preserving the public health, safety and welfare in the built environment through the effective use and enforcement of model codes.

12324 www.imsasafety.org
International Municipal Signal Association
International resource for information, education and certification for public safety.

12325 www.iogcc.state.ok.us
Interstate Oil and Gas Compact Commission
Represents the governors of 37 states that produce virtually all the domestic oil and natural gas in the United States.

12326 www.leadershipdirectories.com
Leadership Directories
Offers free online directory of Presidential Transition Team, free online roster of newly elected congressman and subscription information.

12327 www.liberty.uc.wlu.edu
Journalism Resources
Lists of newspapers, film resources, jobs and internships and political advocacy groups.

12328 www.nacced.org
National Association for County Community and Economic Development
Members are directors and staff members of county, community and economic development agencies.

12329 www.naco.org
Nat'l Assn of County Information Technology Admin

12330 www.nagra.org
North American Gaming Regulators Association
Members are government entities involved in local, state, federal and provincial regulation of gambling activities.

12331 www.nahma.org
National Affordable Housing Management Association
Trade association representing companies and individuals involved in the management of affordable multifamily housing.

12332 www.nahro.org
Ntl Assoc of Housing & Redevelopment Officials
A professional membership association representing local housing authorities, community development agencies, and individual professionals in the housing, community development, and redevelopment fields.

12333 www.nalhfa.org
National Assn. of Local Housing Finance Agencies
County and city agencies which finance affordable housing using tax-exempt annual tools such as the low income housing tax credit and private activity bonds.

12334 www.napawash.org
National Academy of Public Administration
An independent, non-profit organization chartered by Congress to improve governance at all levels- local, regional, state, national and international.

12335 www.napus.org
National Association of Postmasters of the US
Sponsors and supports the Political Education for Postmasters Political Action Committee.

12336 www.narc.org
National Association of Regional Councils
State of regional repositories of instructional materials or services.

12337 www.nasaa-arts.org
National Assembly of State Arts Agencies
NASAA's mission is to advance and promote a meaningful role for the arts in the lives of individuals, families and communities throughout the United States. We empower state art agencies through strategic assistance that fosters leadership, enhances planning and decision making, and increases resources. TTD 202-347-5948.

12338 www.nasaa.org
North American Securities Administrators Assoc
NASAA is the international organization representing 66 securities administrators from all 50 states, the District of Columbia, Canada, Mexico and Puerto Rico, and is responsible for investor protection and education. NASAA recommends national policies in the securities industry and provides model legislation for state securities agencies to adopt affecting the regulation of broker/dealers and investment advisers. Consumers can contact NASAA to get phone numbers of state securities regulators.

12339 www.nasar.org
National Association for Search and Rescue
Members belong to various emergency medical, fire or survival rescue services.

12340 www.nasda.com
National Association of State Development Agencies
Established to provide a forum for directors of state economic development agencies to exchange information, compare programs, and establish an organizational base to approach the Federal Government on issues of mutual interest.

12341 www.nast.net
Ntl Assoc of State Facilities Administrators
State administrators of facilities and property.

12342 www.nastad.org
Nat'l Alliance of State/Territorial AIDS Directors
NASTAD strengthens state and territory-based leadership, expertise, and advocacy and brings them to bear in reducing the incidence of HIV and viral hepatitis infections and on providing care and support to all who live with HIV/AIDS and viral hepatitis. NASTAD's vision is a world free of HIV/AIDS and viral hepatitis.

12343 www.natat.org
National Association of Towns and Townships
A nonprofit membership organization offering technical assistance, educational services and public policy support to local officials from more than 13,000 town and township governments across the country. The purpose is to strengthen the effectiveness of town and township governments and promote their interests in the public and private sectors.

12344 **www.nbpc.net**
National Border Patrol Council
A labor union representing employees of the US border patrol.

12345 **www.ncne.com**
National Center for Neighborhood Enterprise
A research demonstration and development organization providing support and technical assistance to grassroots organizations who are working toward revitalization of urban communities. The Center accomplishes this goal by promoting, and explaining alternative approaches to community development; identifies successful transferable program principles, strategies and techniques; and encouraging policy recommendations to assist neighborhood revitalization.

12346 **www.ncsha.org**
National Council of State Housing Agencies
Represents the views of state housing finance agencies in 48 states. A high priority for the Council is promoting the views of state housing agencies on the issue of delivery of housing financing for low and moderate income people. Other priorities include increasing the stock of affordable rental units and generating innovative approaches to providing public housing acceptable to residents and communities.

12347 **www.ncsl.org**
National Conference of State Legislatures
A bipartisan organization dedicated to serving the lawmakers and staffs of the nations 50 states, its commonwealths and territories.

12348 **www.ndaa-apri.org**
Prosecutor
To be the voice of America's prosecutors and to support their efforts to protect the rights and safety of the people.

12349 **www.ndaa.org**
National District Attorneys Association
Voice of America's prosecutors and to support their efforts to protect the rights and safety of the people.

12350 **www.nedaonline.org**
National Community Development Association
A national nonprofit membership organization representing local governments that implement community development programs. The members administer federally supported community development, housing and human services programs. NCDA provides counsel at the federal level on new program design and current program implementation and advocates on behalf of responsive community development.

12351 **www.nemaweb.org**
National Emergency Management Association
Members include federal agencies, local emergency management representatives and interested individuals, associations and corporations.

12352 **www.nfbpa.org**
National Forum for Black Public Administrators
An association for public administrators.

12353 **www.nhlp.org**
National Housing Law Project
A nonprofit corporation that provides assistance on public and private housing and community development matters to Legal Services attorneys and housing specialists throughout the country. The project's goals are to produce, maintain and conserve low and moderate income housing and protect and expand the rights of lower income persons to decent and affordable housing.

12354 **www.nlc.org**
National League of Cities
Advocates on behalf of cities and regularly monitors all three branches of the federal government. Promotes the National Municipal Policy developed and adopted by member cities at the annual Congress of Cities.

12355 **www.npelra.org**
National Labor Relations Board of Professionals
Represents members in contract negotiations and grievance laws.

12356 **www.nrhcweb.org**
National Rural Housing Coalition
A national membership organization that advocates improved housing for low-income rural families and works to increase public awareness of rural housing problems. The Coalition works with a network of state coalitions and nonprofit organizations to promote federal housing policy that benefits both rural housing and community development programs.

12357 **www.patriot.net/users/permail**
Public Employees Roundtable
Demonstrates the value of government employees. Develop an 'espirit de corps' among public service employees and encourages public service careers.

12358 **www.phada.org**
Public Housing Authorities Directors Association
Represents and serves the needs of executive directors of housing authorities of all sizes, in all regions of the nation. In pursuing the Association's goal of improving assisted housing, the corporation works with Congress and federal agencies as well as with all interested groups to improve the nation's housing programs.

12359 **www.postcom.org**
Association for Postal Commerce
National Organization representing those who use, or support the use, of mail as a medium for communication and commerce. Postcom publishes a weekly newsletter covering postal policy and operational issues.

12360 **www.ptos.org**
Patent and Trademark Office Society
Members are examiners in the US Patent & Trademark Office, registered patent attorneys and agents, agencies, judges and other patent professionals.

12361 **www.publicrecordsources.com**
BRB Publications
The BRB Public Record Vendor search tool indexes and categorizes: Over 450 search firms, gateways, proprietary database managers and online public record vendors, over 250 pre employment and tenant screening companies, has links to free public sites, and locates industry trade associations.

12362 **www.ruralhome.org**
Housing Assistance Council
Expands the pool of decent housing available to the rural poor. Creates and sustains interest and action from all levels of government concerning rural housing for low-income people and helps rural housing organizatins become more productive and professional.

12363 **www.sgac.org**
State Government Affairs Council
Seeks to improve the state legislative process through interaction with major state governmental conferences. Conducts educational programs on public policies to further understanding between private sector businesses and state legislations.

12364 **www.sge-econ.org**
Society of Government Economists
Membership benefits economists employed in the public sector or who are interested in the economic aspects of government policies.

12365 **www.sheeo.org**
State Higher Education Executive Officers
Members are the full-time chief executive officers serving statewide coordinating or governing boards of postsecondary education.

12366 **www.sso.org**
Intl Assoc of Official Human Rights Agencies
Members are state and local government human rights and human relations agencies.

12367 **www.sso.org/iafwa**
Intl Assoc of Fish and Wildlife Agencies
Established as the National Association of Game Commissioners.

12368 **www.statenews.org**
Council of State Governments
Research and service agency for state governments and state officials.

12369 **www.theiacp.org**
International Association of Chiefs of Police
Has an annual budget of approximately $7 million.

12370 **www.urisa.org**
Urban & Regional Information Systems Association
Concerned with the effective use of information systems technology at the state, regional and local levels. Members informed of current developments in the information systems field. Its goal is to stimulate and encourage the advancement of an interdisciplinary professional approach to planning, designing and operating information systems.

12371 **www.usmayors.org/uscm/**
United States Conference of Mayors
An organization of city government officials.

12372 **www.water.dnr.state.sc.us/water/icwp**
Interstate Council on Water Policy
Members are state and regional agencies concerned with conservation and environmental issues.

12373 **www.wicdirectors.org**
National Association of WIC Directors
Members are geographic state, Native American state and local agency directors of the Special Supplement nutrition program for woman,infants and children.

Associations

12374 **ACM SIGGRAPH**
Association for Computing Machinery

Home Page: www.siggraph.org
Social Media: Facebook, Twitter, LinkedIn, YouTube, Google Plus, RSS

Jeff Jortner, President
Paul Debevec, VP
Tony Baylis, Treasurer

The Association for Computing Machinery's Special Interest Group on Computer Graphics and Interactive Techniques promotes the generation and dissemination of information on computer graphics and interactive techniques. Fostering a membership community whose core values help them to catalyze the innovation and application of computer graphics and interactive techniques.
8300+ Members
Founded in 1974

12375 **American Institute of Graphic Arts**
164 Fifth Avenue
New York, NY 10010-5989

212-807-1990
Fax: 212-807-1799
Home Page: www.aiga.org
Social Media: Facebook, Twitter, LinkedIn

Richard Grefe, Executive Director
Katie Baker, Director of chapter development
Jennifer Bender, Director of Communications
Elaine Bowen, Director of strategic partnerships
Kathleen Bundy, Program director

To further excellence in design as a broadly defined discipline, strategic tool for business and cultural force. A professional association committed to stimulating thinking about design through the exchange of ideas and information, the encouragement of critical analysis and research and the advancement of education and ethical practice.
18575 Members
Founded in 1922

12376 **Association of Graphic Communications**
330 7th Ave
9th Floor
New York, NY 10001-5010

212-279-2100
Fax: 212-279-5381
Home Page: www.agcomm.org

Serves as a provider of graphic arts education and training, a network for industry information and idea exchange, an advocate for legislative and regulatory/environmental issues, and a vehicle for industry promotion.
560 Members
Founded in 1865

12377 **Graphic Artists Guild**
32 Broadway
Suite 1114
New York, NY 10004-1612

212-791-3400
Fax: 212-791-0333
E-Mail: admin@gag.org
Home Page: www.graphicartistsguild.org
Social Media: Facebook, Twitter, LinkedIn, Google Plus

Haydn Adams, President
Chuck Schultz, Vice President
Lauren Rabinowitz, Treasurer
Lara Kisielewska, Secretary
Patricia McKiernan, Executive Director

Promotes and protects the economic interests of member artists and is committed to improving conditions for all ceators of graphic arts and raising standards for the enitre industry.
1400 Members
Founded in 1967

12378 **Graphic Arts Association**
1210 Northbrook Dr
Suite 200
Trevose, PA 19053-8406

215-396-2300
Fax: 215-396-9890
E-Mail: gaa@gaaonline.org
Home Page: www.gaa1900.com/
Social Media: Facebook, Twitter

Melissa Jones, President
Bill Scotese, Director of Credit and Collections
Stephen Stankavage, Environmental, Health
Rita Donlan, Bookkeeper/Office Manager
Patti Rose, Administrative Assistant

Mission is to be the leading resource for the printing and graphic communications industry in advocacy, education, and information to enhance the strength and profitability of its members.
400 Members
Founded in 1886

12379 **Guild of Natural Science Illustrators**
Guild of Natural Science Illustrators
PO Box 652
Ben Franklin Station
Washington, DC 20044-0652

301-309-1514
Fax: 301-309-1514
E-Mail: gnsihome@his.com
Home Page: www.gnsi.org

Scott Rawlins, President
Britt Griswold, Vice President
Gail Guth, Membership Secretary
Ikumi Kayama, Secretary
Marjorie Leggitt, Treasurer

A nonprofit organization of persons employed or genuinely interested in the field of natural science illustration. It maintains and encourages high standards of competence and professional ethics by increasing communication among its members. Provides opportunities for professional and scholarly development, and seeks to promote better understanding of the profession among the general public and potential clients requiring the services of natural science illustrators.
1.1M Members
Founded in 1968

12380 **International Digital Enterprise Alliance**
1600 Duke Street
Suite 420
Alexandria, VA 22314-2805

703-837-1070
Fax: 703-837-1072
E-Mail: dsteinhardt@idealliance.org
Home Page: www.idealliance.org
Social Media: Facebook, Twitter, LinkedIn

Laura C Reid, Board Chair
David J Steinhardt, President & CEO
Joe Duncan, Board Vice Chair
Debbie Cooper, Treasurer
Penny Sullivan, Secretary

A global community of content and media creators, and their service providers, material suppliers, and technology partners. Association identifies best practices for efficient end-to-end digital media workflows, from content creation through distribution. Providing members the forum for the exchange of information that results in the creation of the industry's most valued standards.
300+ Members
Founded in 1966

12381 **National Association for Printing Leadership (NAPL)**
One Meadowlands Plaza
Suite 1511
East Rutherford, NJ 07073

201-634-9600
800-642-6275
Fax: 201-634-0324
E-Mail: webmaster@napl.org
Home Page: www.napl.org
Social Media: Facebook, Twitter, LinkedIn, YouTube, Google Plus, Pinteres

Nigel Worme, Chairman
Niels Winther, Vice Chairman
Joseph P. Truncale, Ph.D., CAE., President & CEO
Mike Philie, Senior Vice President
Mark R. Hahn, Senior Vice President

A not-for-profit national trade association serving companies in the $100 billion+ graphic communications industry. NAPL offers a comprehensive slate of business and building solutions that provides company leaders with the strategies, insights, and guidance they can use to make informed business decisions, minimize risk, anticipate change, and profitably grow their business.
2000 Members
Founded in 1933

12382 **Pacific Printing & Imaging Association**
6825 SW Sandburg Street
Portland, OR 97223

877-762-7742
Fax: 503-221-5691
E-Mail: info@ppiassociation.org
Home Page: www.ppiassociation.org
Social Media: Facebook, Twitter, LinkedIn, YouTube

Dedicated to promoting members and their industries while providing a variety of benefits and money saving programs to Visual & Graphic Communications Companies and individuals in six states. Purpose is to deliver what it takes to help members become more successful and profitable in their businesses.
200 Members
Founded in 1948

12383 **Printing Industries of America**
200 Deer Run Rd
Sewickley, PA 15143-2600

412-741-6860
800-910-4283
Fax: 412-741-2311
E-Mail: info@printing.org
Home Page: www.printing.org
Social Media: Facebook, Twitter, LinkedIn, Pinterest

Michael F. Makin, President & CEO
Mary Garnett, Executive Vice President
Nicholas Stratigos, CFO
Ronnie Davis Senior, Vice President & Chief Economist
Lisbeth Lyons, Vice President, Government Affairs

A graphic arts trade association representing our members in this industry. Printing Industries of America, along with its affiliates, delivers products and services that enhance the growth, efficiency and profitability of its members and the industry through advocacy, education, research and technical information
10000 Members
Founded in 1887

12384 Society for Environmental Graphic Design
1000 Vermont Ave NW
Suite 400
Washington, DC 20005-4921

202-638-5555
Fax: 202-478-2286
E-Mail: segd@segd.org
Home Page: www.segd.org
Social Media: Facebook, Twitter, LinkedIn, RSS

Jessica London, CEO
Ann Makowski, COO

Members work in the planning, design, fabrication, and implementation of communications in the built environment. SEGD is the global community of people working at the intersection of communication design and the built environment.
1600+ Members
Founded in 1974

12385 Society of Publication Designers
27 Union Square West
Suite 207
New York, NY 10003

212-223-3332
Fax: 212-223-5880
E-Mail: mail@spd.org
Home Page: www.spd.org
Social Media: Twitter, RSS

Francesca Messina, President
Brian Anstey, Vice President
Todd Weinberger, Vice President
Leah Bailey, Secretary
Courtney Murphy, Treasurer

The only organication specifically addressing the visual concerns of print and online editorial professionals. Activities promote the role of members as journalists and partners in the editorial process, as well as fostering new generations of publication designers through educational outreach and scholarship opportunities.
550 Members
Founded in 1965

12386 Technical Association of the Graphic Arts
200 Deer Run Road
Sewickley, PA 15143

412-259-1706
800-910-4283
Fax: 412-741-2311
Home Page: www.printing.org/taga
Social Media: Facebook, Twitter, LinkedIn, Pinterest, Google Plus

Michael F. Makin, President & CEO
Mary Garnett, Executive Vice President
Nicholas Stratigos, CFO
Ronnie Davis Senior, Vice President & Chief Economist
Lisbeth Lyons, Vice President, Government Affairs

Provides a worldwide forum for sharing and disseminating theoretical,functional and practical information on current and emerging technologies for Graphic Arts print production and related processes
900+ Members
Founded in 1948

Newsletters

12387 Graphic News
Printing Industry of Minnesota
2829 University Avenue SE
Suite 750
Minneappolis, MN 55414-3222

612-379-3360
800-448-756
Fax: 618-379-6030
E-Mail: davidr@pimn.org
Home Page: www.pimn.org

David Radziej, President
Arlene Roth, Director Public Relations
John Connelly, Director of Membership
Carla Steuck, Director of Education Services
Patricia Barnum, CFO

For the printing and graphic arts industries.
16 Pages
Frequency: Bi-Monthly
Circulation: 12000
Founded in 1955

12388 Graphics Update
Printing Association of Florida
6095 NW 167 Street
Suite D-7
Miami, FL 33015

305-558-4855
800-331-0461
Fax: 305-823-8965
E-Mail: printpaf@ix.netcom.com
Home Page: www.pafgraf.org
Social Media: Facebook, Twitter, LinkedIn, Flickr, YouTube

Gene Strul, Editor
Michael H Streibig, Staff Executive
Ron Davis, Chief Economist

A monthly newsletter to the members of the Printing Association of Florida. Full color publication with attractive advertising purchases and a focused buying circulation.
Cost: $200.00
Frequency: Monthly

12389 Guild News
Graphic Artists Guild
32 Broadway
Suite 1114
New York, NY 10004-1612

212-791-3400
Fax: 212-791-0333
Home Page: www.graphicartistsguild.org

Patricia McKiernan, Executive Director
Haydn Adams, President
Chuck Schultz, Vice President
Lauren Rabinowitz, Treasurer
Lara Kisielewska, Secretary

Designed to keep individuals abreast of what's going on with the Guild, the industry, and in the area.
Frequency: Bimonthly

12390 Holography News
Reconnaissance International Consulting
PO Box 40976
Denver, CO 80204

303-628-5568
Fax: 303-628-5594
Home Page: www.reconnaissance-intl.com

Ian Lancaster, Director
Jon Senft, VP
Lewis Kontnik, Publisher

Leading global source of business intelligence on holography and authentication for document security, personal identification and brand protection. Unique knowledge and experience of these highly-specialized and rapidly-changing industries, this newsletter is offering invaluable insight into and authoritative information on markets, strategic management and technical issues through reports, newsleters, conferences, executive briefings and consultancy.
Cost: $774.00
Frequency: Monthly
Founded in 1987

12391 Messages
Society of Environmental Graphic Designers
1000 Vermont Ave Nw
Suite 400
Washington, DC 20005-4903

202-638-0891
Fax: 202-638-0891
E-Mail: segd@segd.org
Home Page: www.segd.org
Social Media: Facebook, Twitter, LinkedIn

Be the first to hear about new SEGD initiatives, events, and educational resources. Also learn about new contracts, new products, personnel changes, and other news from SEGD member companies. Messages is also the conduit for special SEGD publications and resources such as the ADA White Papers, the SEGD Green Paper, and other valuable educational materials.
Frequency: Monthly

Magazines & Journals

12392 Animation Magazine
Animation Magazine
30941 Agoura Rd
suite 102
Westlake Villag, CA 91361-4637

818-991-2884
Fax: 818-991-3773
E-Mail: info@animationmagazine.net
Home Page: www.animationmagazine.net

Jean Thoren, President

Covers the animation industry trends, technology, new products, historical perspectives coverage of current animated programming and features, and general news.
Cost: $65.07
Frequency: Monthly
Founded in 1985
Printed in 4 colors on glossy stock

12393 Before & After: How to Design Cool Stuff
Pagelab
323 Lincoln Street
Roseville, CA 95678-2229

956-78 -229
800-266-5783
Fax: 916-784-3995
E-Mail: contact@bamagazine.com
Home Page: www.bamagazine.com
Social Media: Facebook, Twitter, YouTube

John McWade, Publisher
Gaye McWade, Editor

Practical approach to graphic design. Dedicated to making graphic design understandable, useful and even fun for everyone.
Cost: $36.00
Circulation: 26000
Founded in 1990

12394 Bulletin Magazine
International Digital Enterprise Alliance
1421 Prince St
Suite 230
Alexandria, VA 22314-2805

703-837-1070
Fax: 703-837-1072
Home Page: www.idealliance.org
Social Media: Facebook, Twitter, LinkedIn

David Steinhardt, President & CEO
Lisa Bos, Chair
Chip Harding, Vice Chair

Paul Clancy, Treasurer
Jim Mikol, Secretary
The voice of IDEAlliance+IPA, keeping members abreast of business challenges and opportunities, assuring workflows are state-of-the-art, speeding information across the end-to-end digital media supply chain, from content creation through delivery. Since its founding, the Bulletin has played a significant role in the dissemination of information for the graphic communications industry.
300+ Members
Frequency: Bi-Monthly
Founded in 1966

12395 **Cadalyst**
Longitude Media
Home Page: www.cadalyst.com
Social Media: Facebook, Twitter

Nancy Spurling Johnson, Editor-in-Chief
Cyrena Respini-Irwin, Senior Editor
The most complete source of essential information about computer-aided design and related software and hardware technologies for the fields of AEC, manufacturing, and GIS. Delivers timely, objective, and practical product reviews and updates, tips, tutorials, insight, and advice to help CAD managers and users make informed decisions about technology, get productive, and get the job done.
Cost: $39.95
100 Pages
Frequency: Monthly
Circulation: 90000
ISSN: 0360-3520
Founded in 1987
Printed in 4 colors

12396 **Communication Arts**
Coyne & Blanchard
110 Constitution Dr
Menlo Park, CA 94025-1107

650-326-6040
Fax: 650-326-1648
E-Mail: editorial@commarts.com
Home Page: www.commarts.com

Patrick Coyne, Publisher
Ernie Schenck, Creative Director
Mike Krigel, Marketing Executive
Features profile individuals, studios and agencies with examples of their work. Includes reviews of software, books and products, as well as discussing the latest in digital and broadcast design.
Cost: $53.00
Frequency: 8 issues per ye
Circulation: 71927
ISSN: 0010-3519
Founded in 1959
Printed in 4 colors

12397 **Computer Graphics World**
COP Communications, Inc.
620 W. Elk Ave
Glendale, CA 91204

603-432-7568
E-Mail: karen@cgw.com
Home Page: www.cgw.com

Karen Moltenbrey, Chief Editor
William R. Rittwage, Publisher, President & CEO
Kelly Ryan, Marketing Coordinator
Michael Viggiano, Art Director
Covers specific applications of computer graphics, written by users and vendors of equipment and services to the industry. The magazine of 3D computer graphics for engineering and animation professionals.
Cost: $55.00
Frequency: Monthly
Circulation: 40597
Founded in 1977
Printed in 4 colors on glossy stock

12398 **Critique**
Neumeier Design Team
120 Hawthorne Avenue
#102
Palo Alto, CA 94301-1000

650-326-4396
Fax: 650-323-3298
Home Page: www.critiquemag.com

Marty Neumeier, Editor
Features include methods and products to increase the creativity and technological advance of graphic artwork.
Cost: $60.00
Frequency: Quarterly
Circulation: 10000

12399 **Desktop Publishers Journal**
Desktop Publishing Institute
462 Boston Street
Topsfield, MA 01983-1200

FAX 978 887-9245

Thomas Tetreault, Publisher
Barry Harrigan, Editor
Desktop publishing topics and issues and association information.
Frequency: Weekly
Circulation: 60000

12400 **Digital Imaging**
Cygnus Publishing
3 Huntington Quadrangle
Suite 301N
Melville, NY 11747

631-845-2700
800-308-6397
Fax: 631-845-2798
Home Page: www.cygnuspub.com

Laureen Delaney, Associate Publisher
Kathy Schneider, Group Publisher
Andrew Darlow, Editorial Director
Liz Vickers, Advertising Sales Manager
Paul Bonaiuto, CFO
For the imaging professional. Dedicated to bridging the digital imaging gap between graphics and photography while providing in-depth solutions.
Circulation: 30,000
Founded in 1966

12401 **Dynamic Graphics**
Dynamic Graphics
6000 N Forest Park Drive
Peoria, IL 61614-3592

309-888-8851
888-698-8542
Fax: 800-488-3492
Home Page: www.dynamicgraphics.com

Alan Meckler, President, JupiterMedia
David Moffly, President/CEO
Marcy Slane, Managing Editor
Encourages users to take their electronic tools to the next level of productivity and creativity. Emphasizes practical and real-world solutions.
Cost: $36.00
72 Pages
Frequency: 6
Circulation: 66143
ISSN: 1094-2548
Founded in 1964
Printed in on glossy stock

12402 **GATFWORLD Magazine**
Graphic Arts Technical Foundation Association
200 Deer Run Road
Sewickley, PA 15143-2324

412-741-6860
800-910-4283
Fax: 412-741-2311
E-Mail: gain@piagatf.org
Home Page: www.gain.net

George Ryan, Executive VP/COO
Michael Makin, President/CEO
Deanna Gentile, Editor
A bi-monthly magazine for GATF members and subscribers that reports on research and technical trends in the graphic arts (printing) industry, environmental and safety news, developments in graphic communications education and news of emerging products, programs and services.
Cost: $75.00
Circulation: 18000
Founded in 1924

12403 **Gasp Report**
GASP Engineering
234 Benjamin W Avenue
Swarthmore, PA 19081-1421

610-543-5194
800-256-4282
Fax: 610-328-1358
Home Page: www.gaspnet.com

Steve Hannaford, Publisher
Covers new technology, financing, marketing and other business concerns of the printing, graphics and publishing industries. In-depth articles highlight strategies for industry professionals.
Cost: $195.00
Frequency: Monthly
Circulation: 400

12404 **Graphic Arts Monthly**
360 Park Avenue S
New York, NY 10010

212-636-6834
800-217-7874
Fax: 646-746-7422
Home Page: www.worldleadersinprint.com

Phil Saran, Publisher
Roger Ynostroza, Editorial Director
The magazine of the printing industry including commercial, in-plant and related operations, such as color separations, composition, binding and pre-press service bureaus.
Frequency: Monthly
Circulation: 75,000

12405 **Graphic Design: USA**
Kaye Publishing Corporation
641 Lexington Ave
Suite 1202
New York, NY 10022-4503

212-259-0400
Fax: 212-489-4736
E-Mail: gkaye@gdusa.com
Home Page: www.gdusa.com

M Kaye, Owner
Maria Mohamed, Circualtion Manager
Gordon D. Kaye, Publisher
A publication for the graphic designer, offering information and news of the industry.
Cost: $60.00
120 Pages
Frequency: Monthly
ISSN: 0274-7499
Founded in 1965

12406 **Graphic Impressions**
Pioneer Communications

218 6th Ave
Fleming Building, Suite 610
Des Moines, IA 50309-4009

515-246-0402
Fax: 515-282-0125
Home Page: www.pioneercommunicationsinc.com

Rick Thomas, President

Provides providing industry news and information including in-depth coverage of PIM, and PIAMS association news and events. Features cover technology, legal, environmental, niche printing, education, new products, marketing, distribution, finance and insurance.
Cost: $20.00
32 Pages
Frequency: 10 per year
Circulation: 7,000
Founded in 1995
Printed in 4 colors on glossy stock

12407 **Graphics Pro**
Graphic Products Association
4709 N El Capitan Avenue
Suite 103
Fresno, CA 93722

559-276-8494
800-276-8428
Fax: 559-276-8496
E-Mail: info@graphicspro.org
Home Page: www.graphicspro.org

Michael R Neer, Publisher
Steven V Neer, Associate Publisher
Damara Torres, Owner

A bi-monthly journal published by the Graphic Products Association.
Cost: $55.00
Circulation: 7500
Founded in 1994
Printed in on glossy stock

12408 **Graphis**
Graphis Press
307 5th Ave
10th Floor
New York, NY 10016-6517

212-532-9387
866-648-2915
Fax: 212-213-3229
E-Mail: info@graphis.com
Home Page: www.graphis.com

Martin Pederson, Owner
Walter Herdeg, Editor

Graphis is an international journal of design and visual communication, covering graphic arts, design, photography, architecture and related topics. The targeted readership includes professionals in these disciplines as well as all creative visual communicators.
Cost: $90.00
Circulation: 22000
Founded in 1944

12409 **HOW Magazine**
F&W Publications
4700 E Galbraith Rd
Cincinnati, OH 45236-2726

513-531-2690
Fax: 513-531-1843
E-Mail: editorial@howdesign.com
Home Page: www.fwpublications.com

David Nussbaum, CEO
Bryn Mooth, Editor
William R. Reed, President
Jim Ogle, Chief Financial Officer
Kate Rados, Marketing Director

Business and creative resource for graphic designers. Latest business, technological and creative information.
Cost: $49.00
194 Pages
Circulation: 39946
ISSN: 0886-0483
Founded in 1900
Printed in 4 colors on glossy stock

12410 **ID Magazine**
38 East 29th Street
Floor 3
New York, NY 10016

212-447-1400
800-258-929
Fax: 212-447-5231
E-Mail: gary.lynch@id-mag.com
Home Page: www.id-mag.com

Kelly N Kofron, Executive Editor
Dave Richmond, Executive Editor

Leading critical magazine covering the art, business and culture of design.
Frequency: 8 per year

12411 **PC Graphics & Video**
Advanstar Communications
Ste 300
17770 Cartwright Rd
Irvine, CA 92614-5815

714-513-8400
Fax: 714-513-8481
E-Mail: info@advanstar.com
Home Page: www.advanstar.com

Michael Forcillo, Publisher
Gene Smarte, Chief Executive Officer

Covers graphics and video for personal computers.
Cost: $5.00
Circulation: 10,699

12412 **Print Magazine**
RC Publications
38 E 29th Street
3rd Floor
New York, NY 10016

212-447-1400
Fax: 212-447-5231
E-Mail: info@printmag.com
Home Page: www.printmag.com

Joyce Rutter Kay, Editor in Chief
Joel Toner, Publisher
Stephany Skirvin, Art Director
Steven Kent, CEO
William Reed, President

News and information for the graphic design industry.
Cost: $53.00
160 Pages
Circulation: 45000
ISSN: 0032-8510
Founded in 1940
Printed in 4 colors on glossy stock

12413 **Printer's Northwest Trader**
Eagle Newspapers
650 N 1st Street
PO Box 96
Woodburn, OR 97071-450

503-981-3441
Fax: 503-981-1253
Home Page: www.eaglenewspapers.com

Rod Stollery, Publisher
Sandy Hubbard, Founder
Elmo Smith, Founder

Reviews new equipment and techniques and highlights industry leaders of note. Serves the northwestern portion of the United States.
Cost: $10.00
Frequency: Monthly
Circulation: 16000
Founded in 1933

12414 **Publication Design Annual #39**
Society of Publication Designers
17 East 47th Street
6th Floor
New York, NY 10017

212-223-3332
Fax: 212-223-5880
E-Mail: mail@spd.org
Home Page: wwww.spd.org

Bruce Ramsay, President
Amid Capeci, Treasurer
Gail Bichler, Treasurer
Nancy Stamatopoulos, Secretary

A compendium of the best designed magazine/trade and consumer newspapers. Annual reports of the year as judged by a panel. Also includes web and interactive design sites and annual reports.
Cost: $195.00
Frequency: Monthly
Circulation: 15000
ISBN: 1-564966-21-6
Founded in 1969
Printed in 4 colors on matte stock

12415 **Publish How-to Magazine**
MacWorld Communications
501 2nd St
Suite 310
San Francisco, CA 94107-1496

415-243-0505
Fax: 415-442-0766

Mike Kisseberth, CEO
Susan Gubemat, Editor

The definitive source on how to use personal computers to integrate text and graphics into printed communication.
Cost: $4.00
Circulation: 98,819

12416 **Sign & Digital Graphics**
National Business Media
PO Box 1416
Broomfield, CO 80038-1416

303-469-0424
800-669-0424
Fax: 303-465-3424
Home Page: www.sdgmag.com

Mary Tohill, Publisher
Ken Mergentime, Executive Editor
Matt Dixon, Managing Editor
James Kochevar, Associate Publisher
Sara Siauw, Production Coordinator

The most widely read industry trade publication covering the business of visual communications and offering a broad range of in-depth reporting for sign industry and wide-format digital graphics professionals. This distinguished and unique magazine provides comprehensive professional coverage on all aspects of commercial signage, commercial graphics production, electric LED-based signage and letter systems, architectural signage, electronic digital displays, vehicle wraps, and much more.
Frequency: Monthly

12417 **Southern Graphics**
PTN Publishing Company
445 Broadhollow Road
Suite 21
Melville, NY 11747-3601

FAX 631-845-7109

Rob Schweiger, Publisher
KJ Moran, Editor

Edited for those in the graphic arts industry throughout the southeastern US and the Caribbean.
Cost: $5.00
Circulation: 21,000

12418 **TAGA Journal of Graphic Technology**
Technical Association of the Graphic Arts
200 Deer Run Road
Sewickley, PA 15143

412-259-1706
Fax: 412-741-2311
Home Page: www.taga.org

Mark Bohan, Managing Director

A peer-reviewed journal designed to meet the needs of the global professional graphic applications industries and to bring together the multi-disciplinary community in further development of printing as a manufacturing process. Embraces the fundamental science and technology, application and technology transfer and the genergic problems and experience associated with the management and implementation of graphic applications.
900+ Members
Frequency: Bi-Annually
Founded in 1948

12419 **Trade Show Times**
Fichera Communications
441 S State Road
Suite 14
Margate, FL 33063

954-971-4360
800 327-8999
Fax: 954-971-4362
Home Page: www.tradeshowtimes.com

Orazio Fichera, Publisher
Rick Kelly, Contact

Hand distributed to attendees at major graphic arts trade shows. Accepts advertising.
32 Pages
Frequency: Monthly
Founded in 1974

12420 **Visual Communications Journal**
Graphic Arts Technical Foundation Association
200 Deer Run Road
Sewickley, PA 15143-2324

412-741-6860
800-910-4283
Fax: 412-741-2311
E-Mail: gain@piagatf.org
Home Page: www.gain.net

George Ryan, Executive VP/COO
Michael Makin, President/CEO
Peter Oresick, VP Publishing

Educational guide and news for scholars and students studying the graphic arts industry.

12421 **segdDESIGN**
Society for Environmental Graphic Design
1000 Vermont Ave NW
Suite 400
Washington, DC 20005-4921

202-638-5555
Fax: 202-638-0891
E-Mail: pat@segd.org
Home Page: www.segd.org

Ann Makowski, Manager

The magazine of choice for creative professionals working at the intersection of communication design and the built environment. A rich source of information on the key people, research, technologies, materials, and resources that influence communications in the built environment. International Journal of Environmental Graphic Design
Frequency: Quarterly

Trade Shows

12422 **3D Design & Animation Conference & Expo**
Miller Freeman Publications
525 Market Street
Suite 500
San Francisco, CA 94110

415-955-5533
Fax: 415-278-5341
Home Page: www.mfi.com

For animators and digital content creators, exibits include equipment supplies and services for the 3D design and animation industry. Conferences, reception and publications. Space rental available.
Frequency: Annual

12423 **Annual Automated Imaging Associates Business Conference**
Appliance Manufacturer
5900 Harper Road
Suite 105
Solon, OH 44139-1935

440-349-3060
Fax: 440-498-9121
E-Mail: jburnstein@robotics.org
Home Page: www.machinevisiononline.org

Jeff Burnstein, Executive Director

The industry's leading conference and networking event. This conference gathers over 150 top industry executives to do business with their peers and hear presentations on issues affecting the global economy in general and the machine vision industry specifically.
Frequency: Annual,February

12424 **Grafix**
Conference Management Corporation
200 Connecticut Avenue
Norwalk, CT 06854-1940

800-342-3238
Fax: 203-831-8446

Annual show of 200 exhibitors of computer hardware and software for graphic design and computer publishing, paper supplies, typesetting equipment and services, stock photography, clip art service and related equipment, supplies and services.
4000 Attendees

12425 **Graph Expo**
Graphic Arts Show Company
1189 Preston White Drive
Reston, VA 20191-5435

703-264-7200
Fax: 703-620-9187
Home Page: www.graphexpo.com

Where top executives come to learn, network and make informed intelligent purchasing decisions. Leading manufacturers and suppliers will be exhibiting at the show and many of them will be showcasing newly released products, technologies and services. The year's largest and most exciting display of live running equipment in the Americas.
40000 Attendees
Frequency: Annual/September

12426 **Graph Expo West**
Graphic Arts Show Company
1899 Preston White Drive
Reston, VA 20191

703-264-7200
Fax: 703-620-9187
E-Mail: info@gasc.org
Home Page: www.gasc.org

Lilly Kinney, Conference Manager
Chris Theil, Administrative Assistant
Erin Omwake, Administrative Assistant
Deborah Vieder, Director of Communications

Two hundred booths for the graphics industry.
13M Attendees
Frequency: November
Founded in 1982

12427 **Graphics Trade Show Expo Southwest**
910 W Mockingbird Lane
Dallas, TX 75247-5182
Jim Weinstein, Show Manager

Six hundred and fifty booths.
13M Attendees
Frequency: June

12428 **Graphics of the Americas**
Printing Association of Florida
6275 Hazeltine National Drive
Orlando, FL 32822

407-240-8009
Fax: 407-240-8333
Home Page: www.pafgraf.org

Holly Price, Booth Sales & Marketing
Michelle Torres, Attendee Info.

Largest annual international graphic commincations education and exhibit showplace. Over 450 exhibitors in 500,000 square feet.
22000 Attendees
Frequency: February

12429 **Gutenberg & Digital Outlook**
Graphic Arts Show Company
1189 Preston White Drive
Reston, VA 22091

703-264-7200
Fax: 703-620-9187
E-Mail: info@gasc.org
Home Page: www.gasc.org

Chris Thiel, VP
Kelly Kilga, Administrative Assistant
Erin Omwake, Administrative Assistant
Deborah Vieder, Director of Communications

Largest graphic design, digital prepress, printing, publishing, and converting trade show in the Westen United States. Over 100 exhibitors with the widest selection of vendors.
8000 Attendees
Frequency: Annual,June

12430 **IMPA Annual Conference**
In-Plant Printing and Mailing Association
125 S. Jefferson
Suite B-4
Kearney, MO 64060

816-903-4762
Fax: 816-902-4766
E-Mail: ipmaininfo@ipma.org
Home Page: www.ipma.org

John Sarantakos, Administrator
Larry Wright, Treasurer

Annual educational conference and vending show.

12431 **Printing Expo Conference Mid America**
Graphics Arts Show Company
1899 Preston White Drive
Reston, VA 20191

703-264-7200
Fax: 703-620-9187

E-Mail: info@gasc.org
Home Page: www.gasc.org

Paul Kaplan, Show Manager
Erin Omwake, Administrative Assistant
Deborah Vieder, Director of Communications

Exhibits by manufacturers and dealers of the latest graphics equipment and services.
3000 Attendees
Frequency: June
Founded in 1982

12432 **Sunbelt Computer and Graphics**
Printing Industry Association of Georgia
5020 Highlands Parkway
Smyrna, GA 30082

770-433-3050
800-288-1894
Fax: 770-433-3062
Home Page: www.sunbeltshow.org

Dianne McPherson, Trade Show Director
Denise Holland, VP Communications

Two hundred and fifty exhibitors of current printing technology.
18M Attendees

Directories & Databases

12433 **365: AIGA Year In Design**
American Institute of Graphic Arts
164 Fifth Avenue
New York, NY 10010-5989

212-807-1990
Home Page: www.aiga.org
Social Media: Facebook, Twitter, LinkedIn

Doug Powell, President
Zia Khan, Secretary/ Treasurer
Richard Grefe, Executive Director

About 500 works of graphic designers that have been cited for outstanding design by the American Institute of Graphic Arts.
Cost: $45.00
Frequency: Annual

12434 **Graphic Artist's Guide to Marketing and Self-Promotion**
North Light Books
1557 Dana Avenue
Cincinnati, OH 45207-1005

FAX 513-531-4082

A list of publishers of resources about marketing for the graphic artist.
Cost: $19.95

12435 **Graphic Arts Blue Book**
AF Lewis & Company
360 Lexington Ave
Suite 21
New York, NY 10017-6529

212-682-8448
Fax: 212-682-2442
Home Page: www.d-net.com/graphartsbb

Andrew Lewis, Owner
Timothy Lewis, Editor

Offers information on printing plants, bookbinders, imagesetters, platemakers, paper merchants, paper manufacturers, printing machinery manufacturers and dealers and others serving the graphic arts industry.
Cost: $85.00
Frequency: 8 Annual Editions
Circulation: 51500

12436 **Graphic Arts Monthly Sourcebook**
Reed Business Information
2000 Clearwater Dr
Oak Brook, IL 60523-8809

630-574-0825
Fax: 630-288-8781
Home Page: www.reedbusiness.com

Jeff Greisch, President
Bill Esler, Editor-in_Chief
Roger Ynostroza, Editorial Director

About 1,400 manufacturers and distributors of graphic arts equipment, supplies and services, as well as over 700 graphic arts dealers.
Cost: $50.00
Frequency: Annual March
Circulation: 85,000

12437 **Graphic Communications Association Bar Code Reporter**
International Digital Enterprise Alliance
1421 Prince St
Suite 230
Alexandria, VA 22314-2805

703-837-1060
Fax: 703-548-2867
Home Page: www.idealliance.org

David Steinhardt, CEO

The authoritative quarterly journal of bar codes, electronic data interchange, and related electronic commerce technologies in the publishing, printing, and paper industries.
Cost: $95.00
Frequency: Quarterly
Circulation: 150

12438 **Publication Design Annual**
Society of Publication Designers
27 Union Square West
Suite 207
New York, NY 10003

212-223-3332
Fax: 212-223-5880
E-Mail: mail@spd.org
Home Page: www.spd.org
Social Media: Twitter

Josh Klenert, President
Andrea Dunham, Vice President
Jennifer Pastore, Vice President
Nancy Stamatopoulos, Secretary
Gail Bichler, Treasurer

Celebrates the journalists, editorial directors, photographers, and other talented individuals who brought the year with all its triumphs and disasters to light. Featuring work published in a wide range of mediums and created by journalistic, design, and publishing talent from around the world.
Cost: $14.49
ISBN: 1-592531-81-4
Founded in 1965

12439 **RSVP: Directory of Illustration and Design**
RSVP
PO Box 050314
Brooklyn, NY 11205

718-857-9267
E-Mail: info@rsvpdirectory.com
Home Page: www.rsvpdirectory.com

Kathleen Creighton, Co-Publisher/Co-Editor
Richard Lebenson, Co-Publisher/Co-Editor

Fully illustrated resource book for the graphic arts/media industry. Showcases work of illustrators and designers, nationwide.
Circulation: 18,000

Industry Web Sites

12440 **http://gold.greyhouse.com**
G.O.L.D Grey House OnLine Databases

Grey House Publishing's online database platform, GOLD, offers Quick Search, Keyword Search and Expert Search for most business sectors including graphic design markets. The GOLD platform makes finding the information you need quick and easy - whether you're a novice searcher or an experienced database user. All of Grey House's directory products are available for subscription on the GOLD platform.

12441 **www.agcomm.org**
Association of Graphic Communications

Promtes the interest of graphic communication professionals.

12442 **www.aiga.org**
American Institute of Graphic Arts

The purpose of the AIGA is to further excellence in a communication design as a broadly defined discipline, as a strategic tool for business and as a cultural force. The AIGA is the place design professionals turn first to exchange ideas and information, participate in critical analysis and research and advance education and ethical practice.

12443 **www.gaa1900.com**
Graphic Arts Association

Promotes the interests of graphic art professionals. Members consist of suppliers and distributors of graphic arts equipment.

12444 **www.gatf.org**
Graphic Arts Technical Foundation Association

To serve the graphic comunications community as the leading source for the technical information and services through research and education.

12445 **www.graphicartistsguild.org**
Graphic Artists Guild

Promotes and protects the economic interests of member artists and is committed to improving conditions for all ceators of graphic arts and raising standards for the enitre industry.

12446 **www.greyhouse.com**
Grey House Publishing

Authoritative reference directories for most business sectors including graphic design markets. Users can search the online databases with varied search criteria allowing for custom searches by product category, geographic area, sales volume, keyword, subject and more. Full Grey House catalog and online ordering also available.

12447 **www.idealliance.org**
International Digital Enterprise Alliance

Provides the opportunity for those who create, produce, manage, and deliver content to interface with those who develop the software tools to facilitate these functions.

12448 **www.myfonts.com**
MyFonts.com

Allows a user to find fonts with simple keywords. The user can test a font. The site also offers a MyFonts forum, where users can ask the experts

12449 **www.nagasa.org**
North American Graphic Arts Suppliers Association
The association for the channel that distributes printing and imaging technologies.

12450 **www.napl.org**
National Association for Printing Leadership
NAPL publishes industry specific books and periodicals for the graphic arts community. Topics cover management in the areas of sales, marketing, human resources, finance and operations technology.

12451 **www.ppi-assoc.org**
Pacific Printing & Imaging Association
To provide programs, offer services, and promote an environment, which assists members to see and adapt to the future, while continuing to improve and profit in the present.

12452 **www.recouncil.org**
Research and Engineering Council of the National
Association for Printing Leadership
A technical trade association established to identify graphic arts industry problems, coordinate graphic arts technical activities and develop industry associated technical/education programs, conference and seminars.

12453 **www.siggraph.org**
Special Interest Group on Computer Graphics
A forum for the promotion and distribution of current computer graphics research and technology.

12454 **www.taga.org**
Technical Association of the Graphic Arts
Organized to advance the science and technology of graphic arts. Disseminates graphic arts research internationally via annual technical conference and proceedings.

Associations

12455 **American Hardware Manufacturers Association**
801 N Plaza Drive
Schaumburg, IL 60173-4977
847-605-1025
Fax: 847-605-1030
E-Mail: info@ahma.org
Home Page: www.ahma.org
Social Media: Twitter, LinkedIn

A leading industry trade association providing a wide range of programs and services for member firms as well as the entire industry, including industry conferences, events and workshops; legislative representation in Washington; domestic and international marketing support; technology initiatives; cost-saving programs; targeted publications; networking opportunities; and many other industry-directed services.
Founded in 1901

12456 **Associated Locksmiths of America**
3500 Easy St
Dallas, TX 75247
214-819-9733
800-532-2562
Fax: 214-819-9736
E-Mail: webmaster@aloa.org
Home Page: www.aloa.org
Social Media: Facebook

International professional organization of highly qualified security professionals engaged in consulting,sales,installation and maintenance of locks,keys,safes,premises security,access controls,alarms, and other secutriy relates endeavors.
10000 Members

12457 **Builders' Hardware Manufacturers Association**
355 Lexington Avenue
15th Floor
New York, NY 10017
212-297-2122
Fax: 212-370-9047
Home Page: www.buildershardware.com
Social Media: LinkedIn

Sandy Johnson, President
Scott James, 1st Vice President
Dan Picard, 2nd Vice President
Ed Pruitt, 3rd Vice President

The trade association for North American manufacturers of commercial builders hardware. Nationally recognized for its leadership role in ensuring the quality and performance of builders hardware. Any organization that manufactures and sells builders hardware in the United States is eligible for Association membership.
Founded in 1925

12458 **Door and Hardware Institute**
14150 Newbrook Drive
Chantilly, VA 20151-2232
703-222-2010
Fax: 703-222-2410
E-Mail: info@dhi.org
Home Page: www.dhi.org
Social Media: Facebook, Twitter, LinkedIn

Jerry Heppes, Sr, CAE, Chief Executive Officer
Stephen R Hildebrand, FDHI, Executive Vice President
Sharon Newport, Director of Operations
Kathleen Fite, CPA, Director of Finance
Julie Walter, Director of Events

Represents the architectural openings industry. Membership consists of individuals and consultants involved in the architectural openings industry, representing distributors, manufacturers and sales representatives/agency firms, as well as architects, specifiers and contractors who rely on such professionals. Advancing the safety and security of the built environment.
5000 Members
Founded in 1975

12459 **Hand Tools Institute**
25 North Broadway
Tarrytown, NY 10591-3221
914-332-0040
Fax: 914-332-1541
E-Mail: info@hti.org
Home Page: www.hti.org

Trade association of North American manufacturers of non-powered hand tools and tool boxes. The objectives of the Institute are to promote and further the interests of its members relative to manufacturing, safety, standardization, international trade and government relations.
Founded in 1935

12460 **International Door Association**
PO Box 246
West Milton, OH 45383-0246
937-698-8042
800-355-4432
Fax: 937-698-6153
E-Mail: info@longmgt.com
Home Page: www.doors.org
Social Media: Facebook, Twitter, LinkedIn, YouTube

Chris Long, Managing Director
Roe Long-Wagner, Meetings/Exposition Manager
Dawn Jennings, Accounting Manager
Jane Treiber, Membership Manager
Shawn Hicks, Marketing Manager

Supports all those in the door and door operator industry, especially garage doors, installation hardware, roller shades and garage door openers. Publishes bimonthly magazine.
Founded in 1996

12461 **National Lumber & Building Material Dealers Association (NLBMDA)**
2025 M Street, NW
Suite 800
Washington, DC 20036-3309
202-367-1169
Fax: 202-367-2169
E-Mail: info@dealer.org
Home Page: www.dealer.org
Social Media: Facebook, Twitter, LinkedIn

Chuck Bankston, Chair
Michael O'Brien, President
Jonathan M Paine, Chief Operations Officer
Ben Gann, Director of Legislative Affairs
Frank Moore, Regulatory Counsel

Promoting the industry and educating legislators and public policy personnel, assising legislative, regulatory, standard-setting and other government or private bodies in the development of laws, regulations and policies affecting lumber and building material dealers, its customers and suppliers.
6M Members
Founded in 1917

12462 **North American Retail Hardware Association**
6325 Digital Way
#300
Indianapolis, IN 46278-1679
317-275-9400
800-772-4424
Fax: 317-275-9403
E-Mail: nrha40@nrha.org
Home Page: www.nrha.org
Social Media: Facebook, Twitter, YouTube

Serving the needs of independent hardware retailers in the United States and Canada. Purpose is to help independent home improvement retailers become better and more profitable merchants. Providing members with a wide array of educational and training programs, financial management resources and human resource tools that are all available online with unlimited access.
Founded in 1805

12463 **Pacific Northwest Association**
PO Box 17819
Salem, OR 97305
503-375-9024
800-933-7437
Fax: 888-686-6271
Home Page: www.pnwassoc.com/

Ronald F. Moore, President
Newell Weatherly, Vice President

Serving as a bureau of information for its members, offering health and other insurance coverage. Membership is available to any person, firm or corporation regularly engaged in the retail hardware, home center, lumber, farm equipment, outdoor power and industrial equipment industry.
Founded in 1899

Newsletters

12464 **American Hardware Manufacturers Association Newsletter**
American Hardware Manufacturers Association
801 N Plaza Dr
Schaumburg, IL 60173-4977
847-605-1025
Fax: 847-605-1030
E-Mail: info@ahma.org
Home Page: www.ahma.org

Timothy Farrell, CEO

Industry association news.
36 Pages
Frequency: Monthly
Founded in 1900

12465 **MLA LINE**
Mid-America Lumbermens Association
638 W 39th St
Kansas City, MO 64111
816-561-5323
800-747-6529
Fax: 816-561-1249
E-Mail: mail@themla.com
Home Page: www.themla.com

Olivia Holcombe, Executive Vice President

Lumber Industry News Express is the e-newsletter of the MLA.
Frequency: Monthly

Magazines & Journals

12466 **Asian Sources Hardwares**
Asian Sources
PO Box 2118
Santa Fe Springs, CA 90670
562-945-4612
Fax: 562-906-2420
Home Page: www.globalsources.com

Dianna Corriero, US Circulation Manager

The leading publication providing the latest product and market information on home center/DIY, lighting, security and safety, auto parts and accessories, and machinery and industrial supplies from around the world for volume buyers worldwide.
Frequency: Monthly
Founded in 1976

12467 **Brushware**
Centaur Company
5515 Dundee Rd
Huddleston, VA 24104

540-297-1517
Fax: 540-297-1519

Carl Wurzer, Owner
Tom Goldberg, Editor

Accepts advertising.
Cost: $35.00
88 Pages
Circulation: 1200

12468 **Hardware Retailing**
National Retail Hardware Association
6325 Digital Way
#300
Indianapolis, IN 46278-1787

317-290-0338
800 772-4424
Fax: 317-328-4354
Home Page: www.nrha.org

The hardware and home improvement industry's leading trade publication. Covers hard hitting issues many retailers in the industry face. Content includes practical profitability advice and up-and-coming new products from the industry's leading manufacturers.
Cost: $50.00
Frequency: Monthly
Circulation: 36000
Founded in 1901

12469 **Hearth & Home**
Village West Publishing
PO Box 2008
Laconia, NH 03247

800-258-3772
Fax: 603-524-0643

Richard Wright, Editor

Magazine for retailers, including specialty, hardware, patio and barbecue.

12470 **Home Channel News**
Lebhar-Friedman
425 Park Ave
6th Floor
New York, NY 10022-3526

212-756-5088
Fax: 212-838-9487
E-Mail: info@lf.com
Home Page: www.lf.com

Heather Martin, Manager
Terry Evans, Editor
J.Roger Friedman, CEO

Merchandising, marketing, management, and product trends that are important to owners, managers, and buyers.
Cost: $120.00
Frequency: 50 issues per y
Circulation: 50,000
Founded in 1925

12471 **International Door & Operator Industry**
International Door Association
PO Box 246
West Milton, OH 45383-0246

800-355-4432
Fax: 937-698-6153
Home Page: www.doors.org

Art Komorowksi, Publications Manager
Shawn Hicks, Marketing Manager

The first magazine published specifically for the door and access systems industry. Informing the industry about new products, new services, and the latest industry news. In addition, the publication features articles directed to help both door and access systems dealers and those who provide them products and services.
Circulation: 14000
Founded in 1996

12472 **Keynotes**
Associated Locksmiths of America
3003 Live Oak Street
Dallas, TX 75204-6189

214-827-1701
800-532-2562
Fax: 214-827-1810
Home Page: www.aloa.org

Betty Handerson, Editor
Charles Gibson, CEO

Technical magazine for locksmiths.
Frequency: Monthly
Circulation: 8000
Founded in 1956

12473 **Modern Paint & Coatings**
2 Grand Central Tower
140 East 45th Street 40th Floor
New York, NY 10017

212-884-9528
Fax: 212-884-9514
E-Mail: jmennella@chemweek.com
Home Page: www.chemweek.com

Joe Mennella, Global Sales Director
Lyn Tattum, Vice President/ Publisher

Keep up with the latest trends in the paint/decorating industry. Read about hot topics, successful business practices, industry performance & compliance. Covers topics relating to everything from sales and marketing to business and finance to wholesale and retail trade.
Cost: $59.00
Frequency: Monthly

12474 **Outdoor Power Equipment**
Adams Business Media
111 W Jackson Blvd
7th Floor
Chicago, IL 60604-3589

312-846-4600
Fax: 312-846-4634
Home Page: www.adamsbusinessmedia.com

Joanne Juda, Circulation Manager
Steve Brackett, VP/Group Publisher
Steve Noe, Editor

Serves retailers and distributors who sell and service outdoor power equipment products, including retailers, lawn and garden supply retailers, farm supply retailers, hardware store retailers, home centers, and building supply retailers.

12475 **Power Equipment Trade**
Hatton-Brown Publishers
PO Box 2268
Montgomery, AL 36102-2268

334-834-1170
Fax: 334-834-4525
E-Mail: petnet@powerequipmenttrade.com
Home Page: www.powerequipmenttrade.com

David Knight, Co-Owner/Editor-in-Chief
Dan Shell, Managing Editor
Rich Donnell, Editor
Dianne Sullivan, General Manager
Dave Ramsey, Co-Owner Advertising Sales Manager

Service-oriented and technical articles, product evaluations, industry news, dealer surveys and business management information.
Cost: $55.00
Circulation: 21441
ISSN: 0163-0414
Founded in 1952
Printed in on glossy stock

Trade Shows

12476 **Ace Hardware Fall Convention and Exhibit**
Ace Hardware Corporation
2200 Kensington Court
Oak Brook, IL 60521

630-990-6600
Fax: 708-990-0278

Over 950 exhibitors with hardware related products for Ace Hardware dealers. Seminar and dinner are part of the event.
17000 Attendees
Frequency: Annual/October

12477 **Ace Hardware Spring Convention and Exhibit**
Ace Hardware Corporation
2200 Kensington Court
Oak Brook, IL 60521

630-990-6600
Fax: 708-990-0278

David Myer, Senior VP

Over 900 exhibitors with hardware related products for Ace Hardware dealers.
8000 Attendees
Frequency: Annual

12478 **Door & Hardware Exposition & Convention**
Door & Hardware Institute
14170 Newbrook Drive
Suite 200
Chantilly, VA 20151

703-222-2010
Fax: 703-222-2410
E-Mail: info@dhi.org
Home Page: www.dhi.org

Stephen R Hildebrand, Director Business Development
Garld Heppes Sr, Executive Assistant
Cathy Jones, Executive Assistant

Over 150 exhibitors bringing the latest in industry trends, education and developments to safely secure the built environment.
4200 Attendees
Frequency: Annual

12479 **Equipment Leasing Association Annual Meeting**
1825 K Street NW
Suite 900
Washington, DC 20006

202-238-3400
Fax: 202-238-3401
E-Mail: rscoggins@elfaonline.org
Home Page: www.elfaonline.org

Sally Maloney, Meeting Manager
Michael Fleming, President

25 booths.
1,200 Attendees
Frequency: October

12480 **Florida Building Products and Design Show**
Florida Lumber & Building Material Dealers
1303 Limit Avenue
Mount Dora, FL 32757
352-383-0366
Fax: 352-383-8756
Home Page: www.fbma.org
Bill Tucker, President
Kair Hebrank, VP Government Relations
Betty Askew, Director of Operations
A place for members of the Building Supply Industry to gather. It provides an affordable opportunity to learn about new and innovative equipment and products.
3000 Attendees
Frequency: Annual
Founded in 1920

12481 **Gemstate Industrial and Construction Show**
Trade Shows West
360 S Fort Ln
Suite 2C
Layton, UT 84041-5708
801-485-0176
800-794-3706
Fax: 801-485-0241
E-Mail: jeffwfredericks@hotmail.com
Home Page: www.facetofacemarketing.net
Exhibit focusing on the needs of the industrial, construction, and plant maintenance industries.
6049 Attendees
Frequency: Annual/November

12482 **Hardware Wholesalers: Merchandise Mart**
Hardware Wholesalers
Nelson Road
Box 868
Ft.Wayne, IN 46801
260-748-5300
Fax: 260-496-1245
11500 Attendees

12483 **International Hardware Week**
American Hardware Manufacturers Association
801 N Plaza Drive
Schaumburg, IL 60173-4977
847-605-1025
Fax: 847-605-1030
E-Mail: info@ahma.org
Home Page: www.ahma.org
William Farrell, Vice Chairman Of The Board
Timothy Farrell, President/CEO
3,000 exhibitors.
62.5M Attendees
Frequency: August
Founded in 2001

12484 **Iowa Lumber Convention**
Northwestern Lumber Association
5905 Golden Valley Road
Suite 110
Minneapolis, MN 55422-4535
763-544-6822
888-544-6822
Fax: 763-595-4060
Home Page: www.nlassn.org
Jodie Fleck, Director of Conventions
Hosts educational seminars and trade show.
Frequency: Annual/March

12485 **Lumber and Hardware Show Mid-America**
PO Box 1828
Columbus, OH 43216
614-460-6000
Fax: 614-833-6983
Joe Bailey, Show Manager
300 booths for retail lumber yard stores.
7M Attendees
Frequency: February

12486 **National Building Products Exposition & Conference**
American Hardware Manufacturers Association
801 N Plaza Drive
Schaumburg, IL 60173-4977
847-605-1025
Fax: 847-605-1030
E-Mail: info@ahma.org
Home Page: www.ahma.org
William Farrell, Vice Chairman Of The Board
Timothy Farrell, President/CEO
70000 Attendees

12487 **National Hardware Show**
Association Expositions & Services
383 Main Avenue
Norwalk, CT 06851
203-840-5622
888-425-9377
Fax: 203-840-4824
E-Mail: inquiry@hardware.reedexpo.com
Home Page: www.nationalhardwareshow.com
Timothy Farrell, Executive VP
Martin O'Rourke, Membership Manager
Held in conjunction with International Hardware Week, this is the industry's leading hardware/home improvement event, with products from over 2,000 manufacturers from around the world. Includes hardware and allied lines, plumbing, paint and home decorating, lawn and garden, building products and housewares. Also international pavilions.
70000 Attendees
Frequency: August
Founded in 1945

12488 **National Hardware Show/National Building Products Exposition & Conference**
Reed Exhibition Companies
383 Main Avenue
Norwalk, CT 06851
203-840-4800
Fax: 203-840-4801
E-Mail: inquiry@reedexpo.com
Home Page: www.reedexpo.com

12489 **Service Specialists Association Annual Convention**
Service Specialists Association
4015 Marks Road
Suite 2B
Medina, OH 44256-8316
330-725-7160
800-763-5717
Fax: 330-722-5638
E-Mail: trucksvc@aol.com
Home Page: www.truckservice.org
Cara R Giebner, Manager
Containing 70 booths and 70 exhibits.
400 Attendees

12490 **Servistar Corporation Lumber & Home Center: Fall**
Servistar Corporation
PO Box 1510
Butler, PA 16001
773-695-5000
Fax: 773-695-5172
1500 Attendees

12491 **Servistar Corporation Lumber & Home Center : Spring**
Servistar Corporation
8600 W Bryn Mawr Avenue
Chicago, IL 60631-3505
773-695-5000
Fax: 773-695-5172
1500 Attendees

12492 **Servistar Market**
Truserv Corporation
8600 W Bryn Mawr Avenue
Chicago, IL 60631-3505
773-695-5000
Fax: 773-695-5172
Johnathan Mills, Show Manager
Hardware manufacturers, suppliers and distributors.
5M Attendees
Frequency: September

Directories & Databases

12493 **Complete Directory of Hardware Items**
Sutton Family Communications & Publishing Company
920 State Route 54 East
Elmitch, KY 42343
270-276-9500
E-Mail: jlsutton@apex.net
Theresa Sutton, Editor
Lee Sutton, General Manager
Print-out from database of wholesale distributors,importers,manufacturers,close-out houses, and liquidators. Database is updated daily to guarantee the most current and up-to-date sources available.
Cost: $109.00
100+ Pages

12494 **Complete Directory of Household Items**
Sutton Family Communications & Publishing Company
920 State Route 54 East
Elmitch, KY 42343
270-276-9500
E-Mail: jlsutton@apex.net
Theresa Sutton, Editor
Lee Sutton, General Manager
Print-out from database of wholesalers, manufacturers, distributors, importers and close-out houses. Database is updated daily to guarantee the most current and up-to-date sources available.
Cost: $109.00
100+ Pages

12495 **Directory and Buyer's Guide of the Door and Hardware Institute**
Door and Hardware Institute
14150 Newbrook Dr
Suite 200
Chantilly, VA 20151-2232
703-222-2010
Fax: 703-222-2410

E-Mail: info@dhi.org
Home Page: www.dhi.org

Gerald S Heppes Sr, Executive Director
Cathy Jones, Executive Assistant

More than 700 firms which supply doors, hinges, locks, cabinets and closet hardware, door motors, smoke clothing and detection devices.
Frequency: Annual

12496 **Door and Hardware Institute: Membership Directory**
Door and Hardware Institute
14150 Newbrook Dr
Suite 200
Chantilly, VA 20151-2232

703-222-2010
Fax: 703-222-2410
E-Mail: info@dhi.org
Home Page: www.dhi.org

Gerald S Heppes Sr, Executive Director
Cathy Jones, Executive Assistant

Includes names and addresses of more than 5,000 members, including 700 manufacturing firms. Excellent resource for networking and staying in touch with your colleagues. Advertising is available.
Frequency: Annually
Founded in 1999

12497 **Home Center Operators & Hardware Chains**
Chain Store Guide
3922 Coconut Palm Dr
Suite 300
Tampa, FL 33619-1389

813-627-6700
800-927-9292
Fax: 813-627-7094
E-Mail: info@csgis.com
Home Page: www.csgis.com

Mike Jarvis, Publisher
Arthur Rosenberg, Editor
Shami Choon, Manager

The facts on more than 4,600 company headquarters and subsidiaries operating almost 23,500 units in the vast Home Improvement Building Material Industry. Also included are 19 major buying/marketing groups and coops that contribute approximately $30 billion and serve 103,243 accounts.
Cost: $30.00
Frequency: Annual, Paperback

12498 **MLA Buyer's Guide & Dealer Directory**
Mid-America Lumbermens Association
638 W 39th St
Kansas City, MO 64111

816-561-5323
800-747-6529
Fax: 816-561-1249
E-Mail: mail@themla.com
Home Page: www.themla.com

Olivia Holcombe, Executive Vice President

Industry Web Sites

12499 **http://gold.greyhouse.com**
G.O.L.D Grey House OnLine Databases

Grey House Publishing's online database platform, GOLD, offers Quick Search, Keyword Search and Expert Search for most business sectors including hardware markets. The GOLD platform makes finding the information you need quick and easy - whether you're a novice searcher or an experienced database user. All of Grey House's directory products are available for subscription on the GOLD platform.

12500 **www.ahma.org**
American Hardware Manufacturers Association

Over 280 manufacturer representatives in the hardware industry.

12501 **www.aloa.org**
Associated Locksmiths of America

Strives to educate and provide information to industry. Maintains referral service and offers insurance and bonding programs. Holds technical training.

12502 **www.americanladderinstitute.org**
American Ladder Institute

Members include manufacturers of wood, metal and fiberglass ladders. Represents US companies engaged in the research, development, manufacture and safety ladders.

12503 **www.greyhouse.com**
Grey House Publishing

Authoritative reference directories for most business sectors including hardware markets. Users can search the online databases with varied search criteria allowing for custom searches by product category, geographic area, sales volume, keyword, subject and more. Full Grey House catalog and online ordering also available.

12504 **www.hti.org**
Hand Tools Institute

Provides safety education and concerned with product standards.

12505 **www.nrha.org**
National Retail Hardware Association

An organization which features news and information for hardware retailers.

Associations

12506 **ALS Association**
1275 K Street NW
Suite 250
Washington, DC 20005
202-407-8580
Fax: 202-289-6801
Home Page: www.alsa.org/
Social Media: Facebook, Twitter, LinkedIn, YouTube
Barbara Newhouse, President, CEO
Gregory L. Mitchell, Chief Financial Officer
Carrie Martin Munk, Chief Comm. & Marketing Officer
Lucie Bruijn, PhD, Chief Scientist
Steve Gibson, Chief Public Policy Officer
National nonprofit organization fighting Lou Gehrig's Disease—leads the way in research, care services, public education, and public policy.
Founded in 1869

12507 **ARMA International**
11880 College Blvd
Suite 450
Overland Park, KS 66210
913-341-3808
800-422-2762
Fax: 913-341-3742
E-Mail: headquarters@armaintl.org
Home Page: www.arma.org
Social Media: Twitter
Komal Gulich, CRM, Chairman
Julie J. Colgan, CRM, President
Brenda Prowse, CRM, Treasurer
Nicholas De Laurentis, Chair
ARMA is a not-for-profit professional association and the authority on managing records and information. Members include records managers, archivists, corporate librarians, imaging specialists, legal professionals, IT managers, consultants, and educators, all of whom work in a wide variety of industries, including government, legal, healthcare, financial services, and petroleum.
11M Members
Founded in 1955

12508 **ASET - The Neurodiagnostic Society**
402 East Bannister Road
Suite A
Kansas City, MO 64131-3019
816-931-1120
Fax: 816-931-1145
E-Mail: info@aset.org
Home Page: www.aset.org
Social Media: Facebook, Twitter
Arlen Reimritz, Executive Director
ASET is the largest national professional association for individuals involved in the study and recording of electrical activity in the brain and nervous system. ASET's mission is to provide leadership, advocacy and professional excellence for members, creating greater awareness of the profession and establishing standards and best practices to ensure quality patient care.
4200 Members
Founded in 1959

12509 **Academy of Dental Materials**
21 Grouse Terrace
Lake Oswego, OR 97035
503-636-0861
Fax: 503-675-2738
Home Page: www.academydentalmaterials.org
Objectives of the Academy are; to provide a forum for the exchange of information on all aspects of dental materials, to enhance communication between industry, researchers and practicing dentists, to encourage dental materials research and its applications and to promote dental materials through its activities.
Founded in 1941

12510 **Academy of General Dentistry**
560 W. Lake Street
Sixth Floor
Chicago, IL 60611-6600
888-243-3368
Fax: 312-440-0559
E-Mail: abgd@agd.org
Home Page: www.agd.org
Linda J Edgar, DDS, MEd, MAGD, President
W. Mark Donald, DMD, MAGD, Vice-President
Manuel A Cordero, DDS, MAGD, Secretary
Maria A Smith, DMD, MAGD, Treasurer
W. Carter Brown, DMD, FAGD, President-Elect
Mission is to serve the needs and represent the interest of general dentists, to promote the oral health of the public, and to foster continued proficiency of general dentists through quality continuing dental education in order to better serve the public.
37M Members
Founded in 1952

12511 **Academy of Nutrition and Dietetics**
120 South Riverside Plaza
Suite 2000
Chicago, IL 60606
312-899-0040
800-877-1600
E-Mail: info@eatright.org
Home Page: www.eatright.org
Social Media: Facebook, Twitter, Google Plus, Youtube
Striving to improve the nation's health and advance the profession of dietetics through research, education, and advocacy.
70M Members
Founded in 1917

12512 **Academy of Osseointegration**
85 W Algonquin Rd
Suite 550
Arlington Hts, IL 60005-4460
847-439-1919
800-656-7736
Fax: 847-439-1569
E-Mail: academy@osseo.org
Home Page: www.osseo.org
Stephen L. Wheeler, DDS, President
Russell D. Nishimura DDS, Vice President
Kevin P. Smith, MA, MBA, Executive Director
Jean Lynch, Director of Exhibits
Gina Seegers, Director of Meeting Services
Established to provide a focus for the rapidly advancing biotechnology involving the natural bond between bone and certain alloplastic reconstructive materials.
5200 Members
Founded in 1987

12513 **Acoustic Neuroma Association**
600 Peachtree Pkwy
Suite 108
Cumming, GA 30041-6899
770-205-8211
877-200-8211
Fax: 770-205-0239
Fax: 877-202-0239
E-Mail: info@anausa.org
Home Page: www.anausa.org
Social Media: Facebook, Twitter, YouTube
Alan Goldberg, President
Karla Jacobus, Vice President
John Gigliello, Treasurer
David Puzzoў, Secretary
Jeffrey D. Barr, Immediate Past President
A patient organization that provides education and support to thosediagnosed with an acoustic neuroma.
Founded in 1981

12514 **Adult Congenital Heart Association**
6757 Greene Street,
Suite 335
Philadelphia, PA 19119-3508
215-849-1260
888-921-ACHA
Fax: 215-849-1261
E-Mail: info@achaheart.org
Home Page: www.achaheart.org
Social Media: Facebook, Twitter
John C. Fernie, Chair
Anne Gammon, Vice Chair
Heather Abbott, Treasurer
Kay Deeney, Secretary
Curt J. Daniels, MD, Medical Advisory Board Chair
Information, resources, and support for adults with congenital heart disease.
Founded in 1998

12515 **Advanced Medical Technology Association**
701 Pennsylvania Ave, NW
Suite 800
Washington, DC 20004-2654
202-783-8700
Fax: 202-783-8750
E-Mail: info@advamed.org
Home Page: www.advamed.org
Social Media: Facebook, Twitter, LinkedIn, Youtube
David C. Dvorak, Chairman of the Board
Stephen J. Ubl, President &ўChief Executive Officer
David H. Nexon, Senior Executive Vice President
JC Scott, Senior Executive Vice President
Kenneth Mendez, Senior Executive VP
Advocates for a legal, regulatory and economic environment that advances global health care by assuring worldwide patient access to the benefits of medical technology. Promoting policies that foster the highest ethical standards, rapid product approvals, appropriate reimbursement, and access to international markets.
1100 Members
Founded in 1980

12516 **Aerospace Medical Association**
320 S Henry St
Alexandria, VA 22314-3579
703-739-2240
Fax: 703-739-9652
E-Mail: rrayman@asma.org
Home Page: www.asma.org
Jeffrey C. Sventek, MS, CAsP, Executive Director
Gisselle Vargas, Operations Manager
Gloria Carter, Director, Member Services
Sheryl Kildall, Subscriptions Manager
Frederick Bonato, PhD, Editor-in-Chief
Organized exclusively for charitable, educational, and scientific purposes. It is the largest, most-representative professional membership organization in the fields of aviation, space, and environmental medicine.
3200 Members
Founded in 1929
Mailing list available for rent

12517 Alexander Graham Bell Association for the Deaf and Hard of Hearing
3417 Volta Place, NW
Washington, DC 20007

202-337-5220
Fax: 202-337-8314
E-Mail: info@agbell.org
Home Page: www.listeningandspokenlanguage.org
Social Media: Facebook, Twitter, YouTube, Pinterest

Emilio Alonso-Mendoza, Chief Executive Officer
Lisa Chutjian, Chief Development Officer
Susan Boswell, Director of Communications
Robin Bailey, Programs Specialist
Judy Harrison, Director of Programs

A resource, support network and advocate for listening, learning, talking, and living independently with hearing loss.
Founded in 2005

12518 Alzheimer's Association
225 N. Michigan Ave.
Floor 17
Chicago, IL 60601-7633
312-335-8700
Fax: 866-699-1246
E-Mail: advocate@alz.org
Home Page: www.alz.org/
Social Media: Facebook, Twitter, YouTube

Michelle Helton, Vice President, Financial Operation
Christine Foh, Vice President, Legal
Beth Kallmyer, Vice President, Constituent Service
Maria Carrillo, Chief Science Officer
Richard Hovland, Chief Operations Officer

Information on Alzheimer's disease and dementia symptoms, diagnosis, stages, treatment, care and support resources.

12519 Ambulatory Surgery Center Association
1012 Cameron Street
Alexandria, VA 22314-2427

703-836-8808
Fax: 703-549-0976
E-Mail: asc@ascassociation.org
Home Page: www.ascassociation.org
Social Media: Facebook, Twitter, LinkedIn

Nap Gary, President
Michael A. Guarino, Vice President
David S. George, MD, Secretary

Membership and advocacy organization that provides member benefits and services, combats legislative, regulatory and other challenges at the federal and state level, assists state ASC association, enhances ASC representation at the state and federal level, and has established a political action committee.

12520 America's Health Insurance Plans (AHIP)
601 Pennsylvania Avenue
NW South Building, Suite 500ÿ
Washington, DC 20004

202-778-3200
Fax: 202-331-7487
E-Mail: ahip@ahip.org
Home Page: www.ahip.org/

The national trade association representing the health insurance industry. Members provide health and supplemental benefits to more than 200 million Americans through employer-sponsored coverage, the individual insurance market, and public programs such as Medicare and Medicaid. Advocates for public policies that expand access to affordable health care coverage to all Americans through a competitive marketplace that fosters choice, quality and innovation.

12521 American Academy for Cerebral Palsy and Developmental Medicine
555 East Wells
Suite 1100
Milwaukee, WI 53202-3800

414-918-3014
Fax: 414-276-2146
E-Mail: info@aacpdm.org
Home Page: www.aacpdm.org
Social Media: Facebook, Twitter

Richard Stevenson, MD, President
Darcy Fehlings, MD MSc FRCPC, First Vice President
Eileen Fowler, PhD PT, Second Vice President
Johanna Darrah, PhD PT, Secretary
Joshua Hyman, MD, Treasurer

Mission is to provide multidisciplinary scientific education for health professionals and promote excellence in research and services for the benefit of people with cerebral palsy and childhood-onset disabilities. A global leader in the multidisciplinary scientific education of health professionals and researchers.
1100 Members
Founded in 1947

12522 American Academy of Allergy, Asthma and Immunology
555 E Wells St
Suite 1100
Milwaukee, WI 53202-3823

414-272-6071
E-Mail: info@aaaai.org
Home Page: www.aaaai.org
Social Media: Facebook

The largest professional medical specialty organization in the United States, representing allergists, asthma specialists, clinical immunologists, allied health professionals, and others with a special interest in the research and treatment of allergic disease.
6M Members
Founded in 1943

12523 American Academy of Child and Adolescent Psychiatry
3615 Wisconsin Ave NW
Washington, DC 20016-3007

202-966-7300
Fax: 202-966-2891
E-Mail: cme@aacap.org
Home Page: www.aacap.org
Social Media: Facebook, Twitter

Martin J. Drell, President
Paramjit T. Joshi, President-Elect
David R. DeMaso, Secretary
Steven P. Cuffe, Treasurer

Membership based organization, composed of child and adolescent psychiatrists and other interested physicians. Members actively research, evaluate, diagnose, and treat psychiatric disorders and pride themselves on giving direction to and responding quickly to new developments in addressing the health care needs of children and their families.
7500 Members
Founded in 1953

12524 American Academy of Dermatology
930 E. Woodfield Road
Schaumburg, IL 60173

847-240-1280
866-503-7546
Fax: 847-240-1859
E-Mail: jbarnes@aad.org
Home Page: www.aad.org
Social Media: Facebook, Twitter, Pinterest, Youtube

Dirk M Elston, MD, President
Lisa A Garner, MD, Vice President
Suzanne M Olbricht, MD, Secretary-Treasurer
Brett M Coldiron, MD, President-Elect
Elise A Olsen, MD, Vice President-Elect

The largest, most influential and most representative dermatology group in the United States. Represents virtually all practicing dermatologists in the US, as well as a growing number of international dermatologists.
13700 Members
Founded in 1938

12525 American Academy of Fixed Prosthodontics
5454 Wisconsin Avenue
Suite 1500
Chevy Chase, MD 20815
301-652-9717
Fax: 301-652-2710
E-Mail: drrasetto@comcast.net
Home Page: www.fixedprosthodontics.org

Julie A Holloway, President
Steven Morgano, Vice President
Stephen F Rosenstiel, Secretary
Richard D Jordan, Treasurer
Jack Lipkin, President-Elect

Mission is to foster excellence in the field of prosthodontics, implants and esthetic dentistry through mutual study, participation, and cooperation.
Founded in 1950

12526 American Academy of Forensic Sciences
410 N 21st St
Colorado Spring, CO 80904-2712
719-636-1100
Fax: 719-636-1993
E-Mail: awarren@aafs.org
Home Page: www.aafs.org
Social Media: Facebook

Barry K Logan, PhD, President
Stephen B Billick, MD, Vice President
John E Gerns, MFS, Secretary
Victor W Weedn, MD, JD, Treasurer
Daniel A Martell, PhD, President-Elect

Committed to the promotion of education and the elevation of accuracy, precision, and specificity in the forensic sciences. Membership consists of physicians, attorneys, dentists, toxicologists, physical anthropologists, document examiners, digital evidence experts, and others.
5M Members
Founded in 1948

12527 American Academy of Home Care Physicians
PO Box 1037
Edgewood, MD 21040-0337

410-676-7966
Fax: 410-676-7980
E-Mail: aahcp@comcast.net
Home Page: www.aahcp.org/
Social Media: Facebook, Twitter, LinkedIn, YouTube

Bruce Leff, President
Thomas Cornwell, President-Elect
Kathy A. Kemle, Secretary
Brent T. Feorene, Treasurer

Mission is to promote the art, science, and practice of medicine in the home. Members include home care physicians, physicians who make house calls, care for homebound patients, act as home health agency medical directors, or who refer patients to home care agencies.
Founded in 1988

12528 American Academy of Implant Dentistry
211 E Chicago Avenue
Suite 750
Chicago, IL 60611
312-335-1550
877-335-2243
Fax: 312-335-9090
E-Mail: info@aaid.com
Home Page: www.aaid.com
Social Media: Facebook, Twitter, LinkedIn, YouTube, Google Plus
John Minichetti, DMD, President
Richard Mercurio, DDS, Vice President
Shankar Iyer, DDS, Treasurer
David G Hochberg, DDS, Secretary
John Da Silva, DMD, MPH, President-Elect
AAID offers a rigorous implant dentistry credentialing program which requires at least 300 hours of post-docroal or continuing education instruction in implant dentistry, passing a comprehensive exam, and presenting successful cases of different types of implants to a group of examiners. It is one of the most comprehensive credentialing programs in dentistry.
4000 Members
Founded in 1951

12529 American Academy of Medical Administrators
330 N Wabash Avenue
Suite 2000
Chicago, IL 60611
312-321-6815
Fax: 312-673-6705
E-Mail: info@aameda.org
Home Page: www.aameda.org
Linda Larin, MBA, FACCA, FAC, Chairman
Dr Robert McKenney, PhD,FAAMA, Vice Chair
Kevin Baliozian, Executive Director
Christine Peck, Education Director (interim)
Genevieve Gandal, Operations Manager
To advance excellence in healthcare leadership through individual relationships, multi-disciplinary interaction, practical business tools and active engagement.
Founded in 1957

12530 American Academy of Neurology
201 Chicago Avenue
Minneapolis, MN 55415
612-928-6000
800-879-1960
Fax: 612-454-2746
E-Mail: memberservices@aan.com
Home Page: www.aan.com
Social Media: Facebook, Twitter, LinkedIn, Youtube, Pinterest, Google Plu
Bruce Sigsbee, President
Timothy A. Pedley, President Elect
Lisa M. DeAngelis, Vice President
Terrence L. Cascino, Treasurer
Lisa M. Shulman, Secretary
An international professional association of neurologists and neuroscience professionals dedicated to promoting the highest quality patient-centered neurologic care. The AAN is strongly committed to its mission and focuses its efforts on ensuring the reality of the principles and standards set forth in AAN mission statement.
18000 Members
Founded in 1948

12531 American Academy of Ophthalmology
655 Beach Street
San Francisco, CA 94109
415-561-8500
Fax: 415-561-8533
E-Mail: customer_service@aao.org
Home Page: www.aao.org
Social Media: Facebook, Twitter, LinkedIn, Youtube
Richard L. Abbott, Chair
Mission is to advance the lifelong learning and professional interests of opthalmologists to ensure that the public can obtain the best possible eye care.
80000 Members
Founded in 1979

12532 American Academy of Optometry
2909 Fairgreen Street
Orlando, FL 32803
321-710-3937
800-969-4226
Fax: 407-893-9890
E-Mail: aaoptom@aaoptom.org
Home Page: www.aaopt.org
Social Media: Facebook, Twitter, LinkedIn, Youtube
Bernard J Dolan, OD, FAAO, President
Lois Schoenbrun, CAE, FAAO, Executive Director
Joseph P Shovlin, OD, FAAO, Secretary-Treasurer
Darryl Beatty, Project Manager,ÿAdministration
Jenny Brown, Program Manager, Membership
A philanthropic organization that develops and provides financial support for optometric research and education in vision and eye health.
5000 Members
Founded in 1947

12533 American Academy of Oral and Maxillofacial Surgeons
9700 West Bryn Mawr Avenue
Rosemont, IL 60018-5701
847-678-6200
800-822-6637
Fax: 847-678-6286
Home Page: www.aaoms.org
Eric T Geist, DDS,, President
Robert C Rinaldi, PhD, CAE, Executive Director
Brett L. Ferguson, Treasurer
William J Nelson, President-Elect
Louis K Rafetto, DMD, Vice President
The professional organization representing oral and maxillofacial surgeons in the US, supporting its members' ability to practice their specialty through education, research, and advocacy. Members comply with rigorous continuing education requirements and submit to periodic office examinations, ensuring the public that all office procedures and personnel meet stringent national standards.
9M Members
Founded in 1946

12534 American Academy of Orofacial Pain
174 S. New York Ave
PO Box 478
Oceanville, NJ 08231
609-504-1311
Fax: 609-573-5064
Home Page: www.aaop.org
Social Media: Facebook, Twitter
Jeffrey A. Crandall, President
Edward F. Wright, President-Elect
Donald R. Tanenbaum, Chair
Barry Rozenberg, Treasurer
Maureen Lang, Secretary
Dedicated to alleviating pain and suffering through the promotion of excellence in education, research and patient care in the field of orofacial pain and associated disorders.
Founded in 1975

12535 American Academy of Osteopathy
3500 DePauw Boulevard
Suite 1080
Indianapolis, IN 46268
317-879-1881
800-875-6360
Fax: 317-879-0563
E-Mail: dcole@academyofosteopathy.org
Home Page: www.academyofosteopathy.org/
Social Media: Facebook
Mission is to teach, advocate, and research the science, art and philosophy of osteopathic medicine, emphasizing the integration of osteopathic principles, practices and manipulative treatment in patient care.
Founded in 1937

12536 American Academy of Otolaryngology-Head and Neck Surgery
1650 Diagonal Road
Alexandria, VA 22314-2857
703-836-4444
E-Mail: membership@entnet.org
Home Page: www.entnet.org
Social Media: Facebook, Twitter, LinkedIn, Myspace
Richard Waguespack, MD, President
J Gavin Setzen, MD, Secretary/Treasurer
David R. Nielsen, MD, Executive Vice President and CEO
Paul T Fass, MD, Director - Private Practice
Bradley F Marple, MD, Director - Academic
The world's largest organization representing specialists who treat the ear, nose, throat, and related structures of the head and neck. Represents otolaryngologist- head and neck surgeons who diagnose and treat disorders of those areas.
12M Members
Founded in 1896

12537 American Academy of Pain Medicine
8735 W. Higgins Rd.
Suite 300
Chicago, IL 60631-2738
847-375-4731
Fax: 847-375-6477
E-Mail: info@painmed.org
Home Page: www.painmed.org
Perry Fine, President
Martin Grabois, President-Elect
Lynn Webster, Treasurer
Zahid H. Bajwa, Secretary
Has evolved as the primary organization for physicians practicing the specialty of Pain Medicine in the US. Purpose is to optimize the health of patients in pain and eliminate the major public health problem of pain by advancing the practice and the specialty of pain medicine.
Founded in 1983

12538 American Academy of Pediatric Dentistry
211 East Chicago Avenue
Suite 1700
Chicago, IL 60611-6904
312-337-2169
Fax: 312-337-6329
E-Mail: info@aapd.org
Home Page: www.aapd.org
Social Media: Facebook, Twitter
Warren A Brill, D.M.D., M.S.(H., President
Robert L Delarosa, D.D.S, Vice President
Jade Miller, D.D.S., Secretary-Treasurer
Edward J. Moody, President-Elect
Mission is to advocate policies, guidelines, and programs that promote optimal oral health and oral health care for infants and children through adolescence, including those with spe-

cial health care needs. Serves and represents its membership in the areas of professional development and governmental and legislative activities. It is a liaison to other health care groups and the public.
8M Members
Founded in 1948

12539 American Academy of Periodontology
737 N Michigan Ave
Suite 800
Chicago, IL 60611-2690

312-787-5518
Fax: 312-787-3670
E-Mail: rethman@hotmail.com
Home Page: www.perio.org
Social Media: Facebook, Twitter, YouTube, Google Plus

Stuart J. Froum, President
Wayne A. Aldredge, Vice President
Terrence J. Griffin, Secretary/ Treasurer
Joan Otomo-Corgel, Secretary/ Treasurer
Kenneth S. Kornman, Editor

Purpose is to advance the periodontal and general health of the public and promote excellence in the practice of periodontics. Membership includes periodontists and general dentists from all 50 states as well as around the world.
8,400 Members
Founded in 1914

12540 American Academy of Physical Medicine and Rehabilitation (AAPMR)
9700 West Bryn Mawr Ave
Suite 200
Rosemont, IL 60018-5701

847-737-6000
Fax: 847-737-6001
E-Mail: info@aapmr.org
Home Page: www.aapmr.org
Social Media: Facebook, Twitter

Kurt M Hoppe, MD, President
Thomas E Stautzenbach, CAE, Executive Director
Gregory M Worsowicz, MD, MBA, Vice President
Darryl L Kaelin, MD, Secretary
David G. Welch, MD, Treasurer

Exclusively serving the needs of today's physical medicine and rehabilitation physician.
7M Members
Founded in 1938

12541 American Academy of Physician Assistants
2318 Mill Road
Suite 1300
Alexandria, VA 22314

703-836-2272
Fax: 703-684-1924
E-Mail: aapa@aapa.org
Home Page: www.aapa.org
Social Media: Facebook, Twitter, Youtube

Lawrence Herman, MPA, PA-C, DFA, President
James E Delaney, PA-C, Chair of the Board
L Gail Curtis, MPAS, PA-C, DF, Vice President/Speaker of the House
Jennifer L Dorn, Chief Executive Officer
Both Bush, Senior Vice President, Member Value

Advocates and educates on behalf of the profession and the patients PAs serve. AAPA works to ensure the professional growth, personal excellence and recognition of physician assistants. It also works to enhance their ability to improve the quality, accessibility and cost-effectiveness of patient-centered health care.
81M Members
Founded in 1968

12542 American Academy of Professional Coders
2480 South 3850 West
Suite B
Salt Lake City, UT 84120

801-236-2200
800-626-2633
Fax: 801-236-2258
E-Mail: info@aapc.com
Home Page: www.aapc.com
Social Media: Facebook, Twitter, LinkedIn

David B. Dunn, MD, FACS, CPC-H,, President
Maryann C Palmeter, CPC, CENTC, Secretary
Jaci Johnson, CPC, CPC-H, C, President-elect
Nancy Clark, CPC, CPB, CPMA,, Member Relations Officer

Founded to provide education and professional certification to physician-based medical coders and to elevate the standards of medical coding by providing student training, certification, ongoing education, networking, and job opportunities.
111M Members
Founded in 1988

12543 American Alliance for Health, Physical Education, Recreation and Dance
1900 Association Dr.
Reston, VA 20191-1598

703-476-3400
800-213-7193
Fax: 703-476-9527
Home Page: www.aahperd.org
Social Media: Facebook, Twitter, YouTube

Gale Wiedow, President
E. Paul Roetert, Chief Executive Officer
Dolly D Lambdin, President-Elect

Mission is to promote and support leadership, research, education, and best practices in the professions that support creative, healthy, and active lifestyles. AAHPERD envisions a society in which all individuals enjoy an optimal quality of life through appreciation of and participation in an active and creative, health-promoting lifestyle.
25M Members
Founded in 1885

12544 American Art Therapy Association
4875 Eisenhower Ave
Suite 240
Alexandria, VA 22304

888-290-0878
E-Mail: info@arttherapy.org
Home Page: www.arttherapy.org
Social Media: Facebook, Twitter, LinkedIn

Sarah Deaver, PhD, President
Donna Betts, PhD, President Elect
Joseph Jaworek, Treasurer
Cynthia Woodruff, Executive Director
Michele Basham, Director

A U.S. national professional association of over 5,000 practicing art therapy professionals, including students, educators, and related practitioners in the field art therapy.

12545 American Association for Clinical Chemistry
1850 K St NW
Suite 625
Washington, DC 20006

800-892-1400
Fax: 202-887-5093
E-Mail: custserv@aacc.org
Home Page: www.aacc.org
Social Media: Facebook, Twitter, LinkedIn, YouTube

Robert H Christenson, PhD, President
Steven H Wong, PhD, President-Elect
Elizabeth L. Frank, Phd, Secretary
Michael Bennett, PhD, Treasurer

An international scientific/ medical society of clinical laboratory professionals, physicians, research scientists and other individuals involved with clinical chemistry and related disciplines. Vision is to provide leadership in advancing the practice and profession of clinical laboratory science and its application to health care.
10M Members
Founded in 1948

12546 American Association for Continuity of Care
342 N. Main Street
West Hartford, CT 06117-2500
860-586-7525
E-Mail: info@continuityofcare.org
Home Page: www.continuityofcare.org
Social Media: Facebook, LinkedIn

A national nonprofit multidisciplinary professional organization dedicated to providing leadership and supporting excellence in practice among those involved in continuity of care within the health care system through education and patient focused advocacy.
Founded in 1982

12547 American Association for Geriatric Psychiatry
6728 Old McLean Village Drive
McLean, VA 22101
703-556-9222
Fax: 703-556-9729
E-Mail: main@aagponline.org
Home Page: www.aagponline.org
Social Media: Facebook, Twitter, LinkedIn

Susan K. Schultz, MD, President
Gary W. Small, MD, President Elect
David C. Steffens, MD, MHS, Past President
Melinda S. Lantz, MD, Secretary/Treasurer
Christopher N. Wood, Executive Director

National association that has products, activities, and publications which focus exclusively on the challenges of geriatric psychiatry.
Founded in 1978

12548 American Association for Hand Surgery
500 Cummings Center
Suite 4550
Beverly, MA 1915
978-927-8330
Fax: 978-524-8890
Home Page: www.handsurgery.org
Social Media: LinkedIn

Mark E. Baratz,, MD, President
Peter M. Murray, MD, Vice President
John D. Lubahn, M.D., Treasurer
Robert Spinner, M.D., Secretary
Michael W. Neumeister, M.D., President Elect

Resource for hand surgeons and patients.

12549 American Association for Laboratory Animal Science
9190 Crestwyn Hills Drive
Memphis, TN 38125-8538

901-754-8620
Fax: 901-753-0046
E-Mail: info@aalas.org
Home Page: www.aalas.org
Social Media: Facebook, Twitter, LinkedIn, YouTube

An association of professionals that advances responsible laboratory animal care and use to

benefit people and animals. Dedicated to the humane care and treatment of laboratory animals and the quality research that leads to scientific gains that benefit people and animals.
11M+ Members
Founded in 1950

12550 **American Association for Marriage and Family Therapy**
112 S Alfred Street
Alexandria, VA 22314-3061

703-838-9808
Fax: 703-838-9805
E-Mail: central@aamft.org
Home Page: www.aamft.org
Social Media: Facebook, Twitter, LinkedIn

The professional association for the field of marriage and family therapy. Representing the professional interests of marriage and family therapists throughout the US, Canada, and abroad. The Association facilitates research, theory development and education.
25M Members
Founded in 1942

12551 **American Association for Pediatric Ophthalmology and Strabismus**
P.O. Box 193832
San Francisco, CA 94119-3832

415-561-8505
Fax: 415-561-8531
E-Mail: aapos@aao.org
Home Page: www.aapos.org
Social Media: Facebook, Twitter, Google+

Sherwin J. Isenberg, MD, President
M. Edward Wilson, MD, Vice President
Robert E. Wiggins, Jr, MD, Vice President Elect
Sharon F. Freedman, MD, Past President
Christie L. Morse MD, Executive Vice President

An academic association of pediatric ophthalmologists and strabismus surgeons.

12552 **American Association for Respiratory Care**
9425 N MacArthur Blvd
Suite 100
Irving, TX 75063-4706

972-243-2272
Fax: 972-484-2720
E-Mail: info@aarc.org
Home Page: www.aarc.org

Tom Kallstrom, Executive Director/CEO
Doug Laher, Associate Executive Director
Sherry Milligan, Associate Executive Director
Tim Myers, Associate Executive Director
Steve Nelson, Associate Executive Director

Leading the respiratory care profession in science, education and research. Its members are committed to providing exemplary respiratory care and improving lung health worldwide.
38M Members
Founded in 1947

12553 **American Association for Thoracic Surgery**
500 Cummings Center
Suite 4550
Beverly, MA 01915

978-927-8330
Fax: 978-524-8890
E-Mail: aats@prri.com
Home Page: www.aats.org
Social Media: Facebook, Youtube

Fred A. Crawford, Jr., Chair
Thoralf M. Sundt, III, Vice-Chair
Elizabeth Dooley Crane, Secretary/ Treasurer

The promotion and fostering of education and research in the field of cardiothoracic surgery, membership consists of the world's foremost cardiothoracic surgeons representing 35 countries. Surgeons must have a proven record of distinction within the cardiothoracic surgical field and have made meritorious contributions to the extant knowledge base about cardiothoracic disease and its surgical treatment to be considered for membership.
1231 Members
Founded in 1917

12554 **American Association for the Advancement of Science**
1200 New York Ave NW
Washington, DC

202-326-6400
Home Page: www.aaas.org
Social Media: Facebook, Twitter, Google+, YouTube

Phillip A. Sharp, Chair
Gerald Fink, President
Geraldine Richmond, President-Elect
David Evans Shaw, Treasurer
Alan I. Leshner, Chief Executive Officer

A nonprofit organization that has research news, issue papers, educational programs, etc.
Founded in 1848

12555 **American Association for the Study of Liver Disease**
1001 North Fairfax Street
Suite 400
Alexandria, VA 22314

703-299-9766
Fax: 703-299-9622
E-Mail: aasld@aasld.org
Home Page: www.aasld.org
Social Media: Facebook, Twitter, LinkedIn, Instagram, YouTube

Adrian M. Di Bisceglie, MD, FACP, President
Gyongyi Szabo, MD, PhD, President Elect
J. Gregory Fitz, MD, Past President
W. Ray Kim, MD, MBA, Treasurer
Gary L. Davis, Secretary

Organization of scientists and health care professionals committed to preventing and curing liver disease.
Founded in 1950

12556 **American Association of Bioanalysts**
906 Olive Street
Suite 1200
Saint Louis, MO 63101-1448

314-241-1445
Fax: 314-241-1449
E-Mail: aab@aab.org
Home Page: www.aab.org

Mark S Birenbaum PhD, Administrator

Professional Association representing clinical laboratory directors, owners, managers and supervisors, medical technologistsm medical laboratory technicians,and physical office laboratory technicians. AAB provides a broad range of services, including representation before federal and state legislative and regulatory agencies, educational programs, and publications.
Founded in 1956

12557 **American Association of Blood Banks**
8101 Glenbrook Rd
Bethesda, MD 20814-2749

301-907-6977
Fax: 301-907-6895
E-Mail: aabb@aabb.org
Home Page: www.aabb.org

Graham Sher, MD, PhD, President
Donna M Regan, MT(ASCP)SBB, Vice President
Zbigniew Szczepiorkowski, MD, P, Secretary
Nora V Hirschler, MDÿ, Treasurer
Lynne Uhl, MDÿ, President-Elect

Advances the practice and standards of transfusion medicine and cellular therapies to optimize patient and donor care and safety. AABB vision is to be the pre-eminent knowledge-based organization focused on improving health through advancing the science and practice of transfusion medicine and cellular therapies.
Founded in 1947

12558 **American Association of Cardiovascular & Pulmonary Rehabilitation**
330 N. WabashÿAvenue
Suite 2000
Chicago, IL 60611

312-321-5146
Fax: 312-673-6924
E-Mail: aacvpr@aacvpr.org
Home Page: www.aacvpr.org
Social Media: Facebook

Barbara A Fagan, MS, RCEP, FAACV, President
Megan Cohen, Executive Director
Mike McNamara, MS, Secretary
Adam T deJong, MA, FAACVPR, Treasurer
Abigail Lynn, Operations Manager

Mission is to reduce morbidity, mortality, and disability from cardiovascular and pulmonary diseases through education, prevention, rehabilitation, research, and disease management.
Founded in 1985

12559 **American Association of Clinical Endocrinologists**
245 Riverside Ave
Suite 200
Jacksonville, FL 32202-4933

904-353-7878
Fax: 904-353-8185
E-Mail: info@aace.com
Home Page: www.aace.com
Social Media: Facebook, Twitter, LinkedIn

Jeffrey I Mechanick, MD, FACP, F, President
Donald C Jones, Chief Executive Officer
Dan Kelsey, MS,MBA,CAE, Deputy CEO
Michael Avallone, CPA, Chief Financial Officer
George Grunberger, MD, FACP,, Vice President

Professional medical organization devoted to the enhancement of the practice of clinical endocrinology. Maintains high standards in a society of qualified medical, pediatric, reproductive and surgical endocrinologists to futher the practice through advocacy and education.
6200 Members
Founded in 1991

12560 **American Association of Colleges of Nursing**
One Dupont Circle, NW
Suite 530
Washington, DC 20036

202-463-6930
Fax: 202-785-8320
E-Mail: info@aacn.nche.edu
Home Page: www.aacn.nche.edu
Social Media: Facebook, Twitter, LinkedIn

Jennifer Ahearn, COO
Jennifer Butlin, Executive Director
Lori Schroeder, Director of Accreditation Services
Crystal Pool, Associate Director
Benjamin Murray, Director of Accreditation Services

Education, research, federal advocacy, data collection, publications, and special programs for nursing education.
750 Members
Founded in 1969

12561 American Association of Critical-Care Nurses
101 Columbia
Aliso Viejo, CA 92656-4109
949-362-2000
800-899-2226
Fax: 949-362-2020
E-Mail: info@aacn.org
Home Page: www.aacn.org
Social Media: Facebook, Twitter
Mary Stahl, President
Kathryn E. Roberts, President-Elect
Maureen Seckel, Secretary
Teri Lynn Kiss, Treasurer
The largest specialty nursing organization in the world, representing the interests of nurses who are charged with the responsibility of caring for acutely and critically ill patients. The Association is dedicated to providing members with the knowledge and resources necessary to provide optimal care to critically ill patients.

12562 American Association of Diabetes Educators
200 W Madison Street
Suite 800
Chicago, IL 60606
800-338-3633
E-Mail: aade@aadenet.org
Home Page: www.diabeteseducator.org
Social Media: Facebook, Twitter, LinkedIn
Tami Ross, RD, LD, CDEÿ, President
Charles Macfarlane, FACHE, CAE, Chief Executive Officer
Laura Downes, CAEÿ, Chief Operating Officerÿ
Ruth Lipman, PhDÿ, Chief Science and Practice Officerÿ
Ken Widelka, CAE, CPAÿ, Chief Financial Officerÿ
A multidisciplinary association of healthcare professionals dedicated to integrating self-management as a key outcome in the care of people with diabetes and related chronic conditions.
10M Members
Founded in 1973

12563 American Association of Healthcare Administrative Management
11240 Waples Mill Rd
Suite 200
Fairfax, VA 22030-6078
703-281-4043
Fax: 703-359-7562
E-Mail: moayad@aaham.org
Home Page: www.aaham.org
Christine Stottlemyer, CPAM, President
Laurie A Shoaf, CPAM, Chair of the Board
Victoria DiTomaso, CPAM, National First Vice President
John D Currier, CPAM, CCT, National Second Vice President
Lori M Sickelbaugh, CPAM, National Treasurer
The premier professional organization in healthcare administrative management. Actively represents the interests of healthcare administrative management professionals through a comprehensive program of legislative and regulatory monitoring and its participation in industry goups such as ANSI, DISA, and NUBC. AAHAM is a major force in shaping the future of health care administrative management.
Founded in 1968

12564 American Association of Hip and Knee Surgeons
9400 W. Higgins Rd.
Suite 230
Rosemont, IL 60018-4976
847-698-1200
Fax: 847-698-0704
Home Page: www.aahks.org
Social Media: Facebook, Twitter, LinkedIn
Michael J. Zarski, JD, Executive Director
Eileen M. Lusk, Director of Education
Sharon M. Creed, Accounting Coordinator
Krista M. Stewart, Membership and Advocacy Coordinator
Patti Rose, Membership Assistant
Specialty society for orthopedic surgeons who specialize in hip andknee replacements.
Founded in 1991

12565 American Association of Immunologists
9650 Rockville Pike
Bethesda, MD 20814
301-634-7178
Fax: 301-634-7887
E-Mail: infoaai@aai.org
Home Page: www.aai.org
Social Media: Facebook
Marc K Jenkins, Ph.D., President
Linda A Sherman, Ph.D., Vice President
Mitchell Kronenberg, Ph.D., Secretary-Treasurer
Dan Littman, M.D., Ph.D., Councillor
Arlene H Sharpe, M.D., Ph.D., Councillor
An association of professionally trained scientists from all over the world dedicated to advancing the knowledge of immunology and its related disciplines, fostering the interchange of ideas and information among investigators, and addressing the potential integration of immunologic principles into clinical practice.
Founded in 1913

12566 American Association of Integrated Healthcare Delivery Systems
4435 Waterfront Drive
Suite 101
Glen Allen, VA 23060
804-747-5823
Fax: 804-747-5316
Home Page: www.aaihds.org
A nonprofit organization dedicated to the educational advancement of provider-based managed care professionals involved in integrated healthcare delivery. Mission is to provide managed healthcare professionals in IPAs, PHOs, health systems, hospitals and other integrated delivery systems with the tools, education, skills and resources to be successful in the marketplace.
1000 Members
Founded in 1993

12567 American Association of Managed Care Nurses
4435 Waterfront Dr
Suite 101
Glen Allen, VA 23060-3393
804-527-1905
Fax: 804-747-5316
E-Mail: keads@aamcn.org
Home Page: www.aamcn.org
Social Media: Facebook, Twitter, LinkedIn
Jacquelyn Smith, President
Nonprofit organization representing Registered Nurses, Nurse Practitioners and Licensed Practical Nurses. AAMCN seeks to offer those nurses the opportunity to become more successful, both in their workplace and their community, through interactive membership services, quality educational resources and unparalleled networking with other managed care nurses throughout the industry.
Founded in 1994

12568 American Association of Medical Assistants
20 N Wacker Dr
Suite 1575
Chicago, IL 60606-2963
312-899-1500
800-228-2262
Fax: 312-899-1259
Home Page: www.aama-ntl.org
Social Media: Facebook
Ann Naegele, President
Chris Hollander, Vice President
Charlene Couch, Secretary/ Treasurer
Mission is to provide the medical assistant professional with education, certification, credential acknowledgment, networking opportunities, scope-of-practice protection, and advocacy for quality patient-centered health care.

12569 American Association of Naturopathic Physicians
818 18th Street, NW
Suite 250
Washington, DC 20006
202-237-8150
866-538-2267
Fax: 202-237-8152
E-Mail: member.services@naturopathic.org
Home Page: www.naturopathic.org
Social Media: Facebook, LinkedIn
Michael Cronin, ND, President
Jud Richland, AANP Chief Executive Officer
Mandisa Jones, Director, Marketing and Membership
Stephanie Geller, Finance and Administration Manager
Michael Jawer, Director, Government and Public Aff
Vision is to transform the healthcare system from a disease management system to a comprehensive health program incorporating the principles of naturopathic medicine.
1800 Members
Founded in 1985

12570 American Association of Neurological Surgeons
5550 Meadowbrook Drive
Rolling Meadows, IL 60008-3852
847-378-0500
888-566-2267
Fax: 847-378-0600
E-Mail: info@aans.org
Home Page: www.aans.org
Social Media: Facebook, Twitter, LinkedIn, Youtube, iTunesU
William T Couldwell,ÿMD, PhD, FA, President
Gary M Bloomgarden,ÿMD, FAANS, Vice President
Thomas A Marshall, Executive Director
Kathleen T Craig, Deputy Executive Director
Peter B Kuhn, Chief Financial Officer
The organization that speaks for all of neurosurgery. The AANS is dedicated to advancing the specialty of neurological surgery in order to promote the highest quality of patient care.
6500+ Members
Founded in 1931

12571 **American Association of Neuromuscular and Electrodiagnostic Medicine**
2621 Superior Drive NW
Rochester, MN 55901

507-288-0100
E-Mail: aanem@aanem.org
Home Page: www.aanem.org

Vincent J. Tranchitella, MD, President
Vern C. Juel, MD, President Elect
Francis O. Walker, MD, Past President
Shirlyn A. Adkins, JDÿ, Executive Director
Patrick Aldrich, CPA, Finance Director

A nonprofit membership association dedicated to the advancement of neuromuscular, musculoskeletal medicine.
Founded in 1953

12572 **American Association of Neuromuscular and Electrodiagnostic Medicine**
2621 Superior Dr NW
Rochester, MN 55901-8350

507-288-0100
Fax: 507-288-1225
E-Mail: aanem@aanem.org
Home Page: www.aanem.org
Social Media: Facebook, Twitter, Youtube

Francis O Walker, MD, Preisdent
Shirlyn A Adkins, JD, Executive Director
Patrick Aldrich, CPA, Finance Director
Kevin R Nelson, MD, Secretary-Treasurer:
Vincent J Tranchitella, MD, President-Elect

Dedicated to the advancement of neuromuscular, musculoskeletal, and electrodiagnostic medicine. Physician members- primarily neurologists and physiatrists- now are joined by allied health professionals and PhD Researchers working to improve the quality of medical care provided to patients with muscle and nerve disorders.
5200 Members
Founded in 1953

12573 **American Association of Neuroscience Nurses**
8735 W. Higgins Road
Suite 300
Chicago, IL 60631

847-375-4733
888-557-2266
Fax: 847-375-6430
Fax: 732-460-7313ÿ
E-Mail: info@aann.org
Home Page: www.aann.org

Mary Kay Bader, MSN RN CCNS, President
Joan Kram, Executive Director
Michelle Van Demark, MSN RN CNR, Secretary/Treasurer
Susan Dollman, Education Manager
Allison Begezda, Marketing and Membership Manager

The leading authority in neuroscience nursing, inspires passion in nurses and creates the future for the specialty. AANN is committed to the advancement of neuroscience nursing as a specialty through the development and support of nurses to promote excellence in patient care.
3000 Members
Founded in 1968

12574 **American Association of Nurse Anesthetists**
222 S Prospect Avenue
Park Ridge, IL 60068-4037

847-692-7050
Fax: 847-692-6968
E-Mail: info@aana.com
Home Page: www.aana.com
Social Media: Facebook, Twitter, Youtube

Dennis C Bless, CRNA, MS, President
John F Hanlon, Jr., Vice President
Cheryl L Nimmo, Treasurer
Sharon P Pearce, President-Elect

The AANA promulgates education and practice standards and guidelines, and affords consultation to both private and governmental entities regarding nurse anesthetists and their practice.
Founded in 1931

12575 **American Association of Occupational Health Nurses**
7794 Grow Drive
Pensacola, FL 32514

850-474-6963
800-241-8014
Fax: 850-484-8762
E-Mail: AAOHN@aaohn.org
Home Page: www.aaohn.org/
Social Media: Facebook, Twitter, LinkedIn

Pam Carter, President
Grace Paranzino, Secretary
Jeannie Hanna, President-Elect
Sheila Litchfield, Director
David Allcott, Director

Dedicated to advancing and maximizing the health, safety and prductivity of domestic and global workforces by providing education, research, public policy and practice resources for occupational and environmental health nurses. Mission is to advance the profession of occupational and environmental health nursing.

12576 **American Association of Orthodontists**
401 North Lindbergh Boulevard
St. Louis, MO 63141-7816

314-993-1700
800-424-2841
Fax: 314-997-1745
E-Mail: info@aaortho.org
Home Page: www.aaoinfo.org/

Jill Nowak, Director Of Finance & Admin
Linda Gladden, Director Of Comm. & Marketing
Sarah Dvorak, Meetings Coordinator
Sherry Nappier, Member Coordinator
Mike Nappier, Shipping And Receiving Coordinator

Official organization for board qualified and board certified orthodontists.
Founded in 1900

12577 **American Association of Physician Specialists Inc.**
5550 West Executive Drive
Suite 400
Tampa, FL 33609

813-433-2277
Fax: 813-830-6599
E-Mail: wcarbone@aapsus.org
Home Page: www.aapsus.com

Douglas L. Marciniak, D.O., FA, President
Martin E Thornton, D.O., Secretary/Treasurer
Kenneth M Flowe, M.D., FAAEP, MB, President-Elect
Craig S Smith, M.D., Membership Officer

AAPS was founded to fill a professional need among physicians practicing in medical specialities. Distinct from other medical societies, the AAPS accepts qualified physicians into membership who have either an allopathic (MD) or osteopathic (DO) degree.
Founded in 1950

12578 **American Association of Poison Control Centers**
515 King St.
Suite 510
Alexandria, VA 22314

703-894-1858
800-222-1222
E-Mail: info@aapcc.org
Home Page: www.aapcc.org
Social Media: Facebook, Twitter, RSS, WordPress

Jay L. Schauben, PharmD, President
William Banner, MD, PhD, President Elect
Marsha Ford, MD, FACMT, Past President
Stuart Heard, PharmD, FCSHP, Treasurer
Julie Weber, RPh, CSPIÿ, Secretary

National voluntary health organization that supports poison centersto prevent poisonings, provide education, conduct scientific research and treat individuals exposed to poisoning.

12579 **American Association of Retired Persons**
601 E St NW
Washington, DC 20049-0003

202-434-2277
888-687-2277
Fax: 202-434-7599
E-Mail: member@aarp.org
Home Page: www.aarp.org
Social Media: Facebook, Twitter, YouTube

A Barry Rand, CEO
W. Lee Hammond, President

A nonprofit, nonpartisan membership organization for people age 50 and over. AARP is dedicated to enhancing quality of life for all.
Founded in 1958

12580 **American Association of Sexuality Educators, Counselors & Therapists**
1444 I Street NW
Suite 700
Washington, DC 20005
202-449-1099
Fax: 202-216-9646
E-Mail: info@aasect.org
Home Page: www.aasect.org

Dee Ann Walker, Executive Director
Alphonsus Baggett, Director of Education
Janet Huynh, Membership Services Coordinator

A not-for-profit, interdisciplinary professional organization that is devoted to the promotion of sexual health by the development and advancement of the fields of sexual therapy, counseling and education.
Founded in 1967

12581 **American Association of Suicidology**
5221 Wisconsin Avenue, NW
Washington, DC 20015

202-237-2280
800-273-TALK
Fax: 202-237-2282
Home Page: www.suicidology.org
Social Media: Facebook, Twitter, YouTube

Julie Cerel, PhDÿ, Board Chair
William Schmitz Jr., PsyD, President
David Miller, PhD, President Elect
Amy Boland, CPAÿ, Treasurer
Craig J. Bryan, PsyD, ABPP, Secretary

A membership organization for those involved in suicide prevention and intervention, or touched by suicide.

12582 **American Association on Intellectual and Developmental Disabilities**
501 3rd Street, NW
Suite 200
Washington, DC 20001

202-387-1968
Fax: 202-387-2193
Home Page: www.aaidd.org/
Social Media: Facebook, Twitter, LinkedIn, YouTube

Amy Hewitt, PhD, President
Susan B. Palmer, PhD, President Elect
William Gaventa, MDiv, VP
Patti N. Martin, MEd, Secretary-Treasurer
Margaret Nygren, EdD, CEO, Executive Director

An American nonprofit professional organization concerned with intellectual disability and related developmental disabilities.
Founded in 1876

12583 **American Autoimmune Related Diseases Association**
22100 Gratiot Ave.
Eastpointe, MI 48021

586-776-3900
Fax: 586-776-3903
Home Page: www.aarda.org
Social Media: Facebook, Twitter, YouTube

Betty Diamond, M.D., Chairperson
Noel R. Rose, M.D., Ph.D., Chairman Emeritus
Edward K. Christian, Advisor
Robert Meyer, CPAÿ, Advisor

Includes patient information about autoimmunity and autoimmune related diseases.

12584 **American Behcet's Disease Association**
PO Box 80576
Rochester, MN 48308

631-656-0537
800-723-4238
Fax: 480-247-5377
E-Mail: info@behcets.com
Home Page: www.behcets.com

Deb Kleber, President
Mary Burke, VP
Belinda Rivasÿ, Treasurer
Marcia Wiseÿ, Executive Secretary
Mirta Avila Santos, Executive Dir. & Comm Coordinator

Provides information and support for patients with Behcet's Diseaseand for their family members and caretakers.

12585 **American Brain Tumor Association**
8550 W. Bryn Mawr Ave.
Suite 550
Chicago, IL 60631

773-577-8750
800-886-2282
Fax: 773-577-8738
E-Mail: info@abta.org
Home Page: www.abta.org
Social Media: Facebook, Twitter, YouTube

Jeff Fougerousse, Chair
Barbara Dunn, Vice Chair
Brian Olson, Treasurer
Jim Reilly, Secretary
Jay Krames, Immediate Past Presidentÿÿÿ

National nonprofit organization dedicated to providing support services and programs to brain tumor patients and their families, as well as the funding of brain tumor research.
Founded in 1973

12586 **American Burn Association**
311 S. Wacker Drive
Suite 4150
Chicago, IL 60606

312-642-9260
Fax: 312-642-9130
Home Page: www.ameriburn.org

David H. Ahrenholz, MD, FACSÿ, President
Edward E. Tredget, MD, MSc, President Elect
Michael D. Peck, MD, ScD, FACS, First Vice President
Ernest J. Grant, RN, BSN, MSNÿ, Second Vice President
Linwood R. Haith, MD, FACS, FCCM, Treasurer

Involved in research in the methods of treating burn injuries and fostering prevention efforts.

12587 **American Chronic Pain Association**
PO Box 850
Rocklin, CA 95677

800-533-3231
Fax: 916-632-3208
E-Mail: ACPA@theacpa.org
Home Page: theacpa.org
Social Media: Facebook, YouTube, Pinterest

Penney Cowan, Founderÿ& CEO
Mary Jane Bentÿ, Board of Director
Chris Duncan, Board of Director
Daniel Galia, Board of Director
Steve Feinberg, MD, Board of Director

Information is provided concerning services, conditions, and pain management issues.
Founded in 1980

12588 **American College Health Association**
1362 Mellon Road
Suite 180
Hanover, MD 21076

410-859-1500
Fax: 410-859-1510
E-Mail: contact@acha.org
Home Page: www.acha.org
Social Media: Facebook, Twitter

Pat Ketcham, PhD, CHES, FA, President
Doyle E Randol, MS, Col. USA (, Executive Director
Keith Anderson, PhD, FACHA, Vice President
Charley Bradley, BPS, RNBC, FA, Treasurer
Sarah Van Orman, MD, MMM, FA, President-Elect

The American College Health Association (ACHA) is the principal advocate and leadership organization for college and university health. The association provides advocacy, education, communications, products, and services, as well as promoting research and culturally competent practices to enhance its members' ability to advance the health of all students and the campus community.
2600 Members
Founded in 1920

12589 **American College of Allergy, Asthma and Immunology**
85 W Algonquin Road
Suite 550
Arlington Heights, IL 60005-4460

847-427-1200
Fax: 847-427-1294
E-Mail: mail@acaai.org
Home Page: www.acaai.org
Social Media: Facebook, Twitter, LinkedIn, YouTube,Flickr

Michael B Foggs, MD, President
Bryan L Martin, MD*, Vice President
Bradley E Chipps, MD, FACAAI*, Treasurer
James L Sublett, MD, FACAAI*, President-Elect
Bob Q Lanier, MD, Executive Medical Director

Information and news service for patients, parents of patients, members, the news media, and purchasers of health care programs.
5200 Members
Founded in 1942

12590 **American College of Cardiology**
Heart House
2400 N Street NW
Washington, DC 20037-1153

202-375-6000
800-253-4636
Fax: 202-375-7000
E-Mail: resource@acc.org
Home Page: www.acc.org
Social Media: Facebook, Twitter, LinkedIn

John Gordon Harold, MD, MAC, President
Shalom Shal Jacobovitz, Chief Executive Officer
Kim Allan Williams, Sr., M, Vice President
David May, MD, PhD, FACC, Secretary
C. Michael Valentine, MD, FACC, Treasurer

The mission is to advocate for quality cardiovascular care-through education, research promotion, development and application of standards and guidelines-and to influence health care policy.
39M Members
Founded in 1949

12591 **American College of Cardiovascular Administrators (ACCA)**
American Academy of Medical Administrators
701 Lee Street
Suite 600
Des Plaines, IL 60016-4516

847-759-8601
Fax: 312-673-6705
E-Mail: info@aameda.org
Home Page: www.aameda.org/Colleges/ACCA/cardiology.html

Renee L. Mazeroll, President
Kathy A. Miller, President-Elect

Mission is to advance ACCA members and the field of cardiovascular management and promote excellence and integrity in cardiovascular leadership.

12592 **American College of Emergency Physicians**
1125 Executive Circle
Irving, TX 75038-2522

972-550-0911
800-798-1822
Fax: 972-580-2816
E-Mail: customerservice@acep.org
Home Page: www.acep.org
Social Media: Facebook

David C. Seaberg, President
Andrew E. Sama, President-Elect
Michael J. Gerardi, Secretary/ Treasurer

Promoting the highest quality emergency care, ACEP is the leading advocate for emergency physicians and their patients.
28M Members
Founded in 1968

12593 **American College of Healthcare Executives**
One North Franklin Street
Suite 1700
Chicago, IL 60606-3529

312-424-2800
Fax: 312-424-0023
E-Mail: contact@ache.org
Home Page: www.ache.org

Social Media: Facebook, Twitter, LinkedIn, Youtube

Diana L Smalley, Chairman
Deborah J Bowen, President and CEO
Christine M Candio, Chairman-Elect

An international professional society of healthcare executives who lead hospitals, healthcare systems and other healthcare organizations.
40M Members
Founded in 1933

12594 **American College of Healthcare Information Administrators (ACHIA)**
701 Lee Street
Suite 600
Des Plaines, IL 60016-4516

847-759-8601
Fax: 847-759-8602
E-Mail: info@aameda.org
Home Page: www.aameda.org/Colleges/ACHIA/healthcareinformation.html

Charles D. Chapdelaine, President

Develops innovative concepts in the field of healthcare information and promotes the advancement of its members in knowledge, professional standing, and personal achievements through continuing education and research in healthcare information administration. ACHIA focuses on providing education, support and opportunity for information technology leaders in the healthcare industry.
300 Members
Founded in 1991

12595 **American College of Medical Practice**
104 Inverness Terrace East
Englewood, CO 80112-5306

303-799-1111
877-275-6462
E-Mail: service@mgma.com
Home Page: www.mgma.com
Social Media: Facebook, Twitter, LinkedIn, YouTube, Flickr

Stephen A. Dickens, JD, FACMPE, F, Board Chair
Debra J. Wiggs, FACMPE, Vice Chair
Susan L. Turney, MD, MS, FACP,, President and CEO
Ronald W. Holder, Jr., MHA, FACM, Finance/Audit Chair

Delivering networking, professional education and resources and political advocacy for medical practice management.
3000 Members
Founded in 1926

12596 **American College of Medical Quality**
5272 River Road
Suite 630
Bethesda, MD 20816

301-718-6516
Fax: 301-656-0989
Home Page: www.acmq.org
Social Media: Facebook, Twitter, LinkedIn

James D Cross, MD, FACMQ, President
Andrew Jerdonek, Executive Director
Mark Lyles, MD, MBA, FACMQ, Vice President
Donald E Casey, Jr MD, MPH, Secretary
John Vigorita, MD, MHA, DFA, Treasurer

The mission of the American College of Medical Quality is to provide leadership and education in healthcare quality management.
Founded in 1973

12597 **American College of Oncology Administrators**
701 Lee Street
Suite 600
Des Plaines, IL 60016-4516

847-759-8601
Fax: 847-759-8602
E-Mail: info@aameda.org
Home Page: www.aameda.org/Colleges/ACOA/oncology.html

Margaret A. O'Grady, President
Bonnie J. Miller, President-Elect

Focuses on providing support and opportunity for oncology administrators and managers in all types of healthcare institutions.
300 Members
Founded in 1991

12598 **American College of Oral and Maxillofacial Surgeons**
2025 M Street NW
Suite 800
Washington, DC 20036

202-367-1182
800-522-6676
Fax: 202-367-2182
E-Mail: admin@acoms.org
Home Page: www.acoms.org
Social Media: Facebook, Twitter, LinkedIn

Bernard Dreiman, President
Leonard Spector, President-Elect
Charles Hasse, Vice President
Cyntia Battel, Treasurer
Robert A. Strauss, Secretary

The diplomates have joined together in the College for the purpose of enhancing the level of patient care. This enhancement of surgical care through the furthering of research and education in OMS surgery is achieved by the College's sponsoring of educational programs, research activities, and fellowships as a service to not only the members of the College, but to the profession at large.
2M+ Members
Founded in 1975

12599 **American College of Osteopathic Family Physicians**
330 E Algonquin Rd
Suite 1
Arlington Heights, IL 60005-4665

800-323-0794
Fax: 847-228-9755
E-Mail: membership@acofp.org
Home Page: www.acofp.org
Social Media: Facebook, Twitter, LinkedIn, Youtube

Jeffrey S. Grove, President
Peter L Schmelzer, CAE, Executive Director
Kevin de Regnier, Vice President
Larry W Anderson, Secretary/ Treasurer
Annie DeVries, Administrative Assistant

Works to promote excellence in osteopathic family medicine through quality education, visionary leadership and responsible advocacy.
20M Members
Founded in 1950

12600 **American College of Osteopathic Surgeons**
123 N Henry Street
Alexandria, VA 22314-2903

703-684-0416
800-888-1312
Fax: 703-684-3280
E-Mail: info@facos.org
Home Page: www.facos.org

Linda Ayers, Executive Director
Jennifer B Colwell, Director of Continuing Education
Sonjya Johnson, Director of Membership Recruitment
Brandon Roberts, Director of Finance
Allison Hamrick, Manager, Marketing and Promotion

Committed to assuring excellence in osteopathic surgical care through education, advocacy, leadership, development and the fostering of professional and personal relationship.
2147 Members
Founded in 1926

12601 **American College of Physician Executives**
400 North Ashley Drive
Suite 400
Tampa, FL 33602

813-287-2000
800-562-8088
Fax: 813-287-8993
E-Mail: acpe@acpe.org
Home Page: www.acpe.org
Social Media: Facebook, Twitter, LinkedIn, Youtube, Google Plus

Peter B. Angood, CEO

The nation's largest health care organization for physician executives who want to boost their leadership skills while adding weight to their CVs. The primary focus of the College is to provide superior leadership and management skills to physicians and encouraging them to assume more active roles in the leadership and management of their organizations.
10M Members
Founded in 1975

12602 **American College of Physicians**
190 North Independence Mall West
Philadelphia, PA 19106-1572

215-351-2400
800-523-1546
Fax: 215-351-2759
E-Mail: archives@acponline.org
Home Page: www.acponline.org
Social Media: Facebook, Twitter, LinkedIn

Charles Cutler, MD, FACP, Chair, Board of Regents
Molly Cooke, MD, FACP, President
Steven E. Weinberger, EVP/CEO
Robert A, Gluckman, MD, FACP
Treasurer David A., Fleming, MD, MA, FACP

Mission is to enhance the quality and effectiveness of health care by fostering excellence and professionalism in the practice of medicine.
Founded in 1956

12603 **American College of Rheumatology**
2200 Lake Boulevard NE
Atlanta, GA 30319

404-633-3777
Fax: 404-633-1870
E-Mail: acr@rheumatology.org
Home Page: www.rheumatology.org/
Social Media: Facebook, Twitter, YouTube, Flickr

Joseph Flood, MD, President
Mark Andrejeski, Executive Vice President
David Haag, MSM, CAE, ARHP, Executive Director
Steve Echard, CAE, IOM,, Foundation Executive Director

Mission is advancing rheumatology. The organization is for physicians, health professionals, and scientists that meets the mission through programs of education, research, advocacy and practice support.
Founded in 1934

12604 American College of Sports Medicine
401 West Michigan Street
Indianapolis, IN 46202-3233

317-637-9200
Fax: 317-634-7817
Home Page: www.acsm.org
Social Media: Facebook, Twitter, YouTube, Pinterest, Instagram

William Dexter, M.D., FACSM, President
Lawrence Armstrong, Ph.D., FACS, First Vice President
Stella Volpe, Ph.D., FACSM, First Vice President
Mark Hutchinson, M.D., FACS, Second Vice Presidentÿ
Carrie Jaworski, M.D., FACSM, Second Vice Presidentÿ

From academicians to students and from personal trainers to physicians, the association of sports medicine, exercise science, and health and fitness professionals is dedicated to helping people worldwide live longer, healthier lives.
45M Members
Founded in 1954

12605 American College of Surgeons
633 N Saint Clair St
Chicago, IL 60611-3211

312-202-5000
800-321-4111
Fax: 312-202-5001
E-Mail: postmaster@facs.org
Home Page: www.facs.org
Social Media: Facebook, Twitter, LinkedIn, Youtube

Gary L Timmerman, Chair, Board of Governors
Fabrizio Michelassi, MD, FACS, Vice-Chair, Board of Governors
Lorrie Langdale, MD, FACS, Secretary, Board of Governors

Dedicated to improving the care of the surgical patient and to safeguarding standards of care in an optimal and ethical practice environment.
Founded in 1913

12606 American Congress of Obstetricians and Gynecologists
409 12th Street SW
Washington, DC 20024-2188

202-638-5577
800-673-8444
E-Mail: acm@acog.org
Home Page: www.acog.org
Social Media: Facebook, Twitter, YouTube

Jeanne A Conry, MD, PhD, President
Dr. Hal C Lawrence IIIÿ, Executive Vice President
Richard C Bailey, CPA, MBA, Chief Financial Officer
Elsa P Brown, MD, Vice President, Administration
Dr Sandra Ann Carson, Vice President, Education

Serving as a strong advocate for quality health care for women, maintaining the highest standards of clinical practice and continuing education for its members, promoting patient education and stimulating patient understanding of and involvement in medical care, and increasing awareness among its members and the public of the changing issues facing women's health care.
45M Members
Founded in 1951

12607 American Congress of Rehabilitation Medicine
11654 Plaza America Drive
Suite 535
Reston, VA 20190

703-435-5335
Fax: 866-692-1619
E-Mail: info@ACRM.org
Home Page: www.acrm.org
Social Media: Facebook, Twitter, LinkedIn, Google Plus

Tamara Bushnik, PhD, FACRM, President
Jon W Lindberg, MBA, CAE, Chief Executive Officer
Douglas Katz, MD, FACRM, FAAN, Vice President
Wayne A. Gordon, PhD ABPP-CN FA, Treasurer
Cindy Harrison-Felix, PhD, Secretary

An organization of rehabilitation professionals dedicated to serving people with disabling conditions by supporting research that; promotes health, independence, productivity, and quality of life, and meets the needs of rehabilitatio clinicians and people with disabilities.
Founded in 1923

12608 American Council of Academic Plastic Surgeons
500 Cummings Center
Suite 4550
Beverly, MA 01915

978-927-8330
Fax: 978-524-8890
Home Page: www.acaplasticsurgeons.org/

Nick Vedder, President

Goal is to provide leadership and support for educational programs for plastic surgery residents.

12609 American Counseling Association (ACA)
5999 Stevenson Ave
Alexandria, VA 22304-3302

800-347-6647
Fax: 703-823-0252
E-Mail: membership@counseling.org
Home Page: www.counseling.org
Social Media: Facebook, Twitter, LinkedIn

Don W. Locke, President
Bradley T. Erford, President-Elect
Brian Canfield, Treasurer
Richard Yep, Executive Director

Dedicated to the growth and development of the counseling profession and those who are served.
45M Members
Founded in 1952

12610 American Dance Therapy Association
10632 Little Patuxent Parkway
Suite 108
Columbia, MD 21044

410-997-4040
Fax: 410-997-4048
Home Page: www.adta.org
Social Media: Facebook, LinkedIn, YouTube, Pinterest

Jody Wager, MS, BC-DMT, President
Margaret Migliorati, R-DMT, LPC, VP
Meghan Dempsey, MS, BC-DMT, L, Treasurer
Gail Wood,ÿMA, BC-DMT, NCC, Secretary
Susan D. Imus, Board of Director

Establishes and maintains standards of professional education in the field of dance/movement therapy.
Founded in 1966

12611 American Dental Association
211 East Chicago Avenue
Chicago, IL 60611-2678

312-440-2500
Fax: 312-440-2800
Home Page: www.ada.org
Social Media: Facebook, Twitter, LinkedIn, YouTube

The oldest and largest national dental society in the world. Becoming the leading source of oral health related information for dentists and their patients. The professional association of dentists that fosters the success of a diverse membership and advances the oral health of the public.
156M Members
Founded in 1859

12612 American Dental Education Association
1400 K Street
Suite 1100
Washington, DC 20005-2415

202-289-7201
Fax: 202-289-7204
E-Mail: webmaster@adea.org
Home Page: www.adea.org
Social Media: Facebook, Twitter

Stephen K Young, D.D.S., M.S., Chair of the Board
Richard W. Valachovic, D.M.D., M., Executive Director
Lily T Garcia, D.D.S., M.S.,, Chair-elect of the Board
Pamela J Hughes,ÿD.D.S.ÿ, Board Director for Hospitals
Michael A Landers, D.D.S., M.A., Board Director for Sections

The voice of dental education. Members include all US and Canadian dental schools and many allied and postdoctoral dental education programs, corporations, faculty, and students. Mission is to lead individuals and institutions of the dental education community to address contemporary issues influencing education, research, and the delivery of oral health care for the health of the public.
Founded in 1983

12613 American Dental Hygenists Association
444 North Michigan Avenue
Suite 3400
Chicago, IL 60611-3980

312-440-8900
Fax: 312-440-8929
E-Mail: member.services@adha.net
Home Page: www.adha.org
Social Media: Facebook

Ann Battrell, MSDH, Executive Director
Karen Dunn Caspers, CAE, Director, Administration
Maddie Hilpert, Director, Corporate Development
Pamela Steinbach, RN, MS, Director, Education
Isaac Carpenter, Director, Finance and MIS

Mission is to advance the art and science of dental hygiene, and to promote the highest standards of education and practice in the profession.
Founded in 1993

12614 American Dental Society of Anesthesiology
211 E Chicago Ave
Suite 780
Chicago, IL 60611-6983

312-664-8270
877-255-3742
Fax: 312-224-8624

E-Mail: adsahome@mac.com
Home Page: www.adsahome.org
Social Media: Facebook, Twitter

Ronald Kosinski, DMD, President
R. Knight Charlton, Executive Director
Michael Rollert, DDSÿ, Vice President
Morton B. Rosenberg, DMD, Treasurer
Barbara Josephson, Director of Meetings

Mission is to provide a forum for education, research, and recognition of achievement in order to promote safe and effective patient care for all dentists who have an interest in anesthesiology, sedation and the control of anxiety and pain.
Founded in 1954

12615 American Diabetes Association
1701 North Beauregard St
Alexandria, VA 22311-1742

703-549-1500
800-342-2383
Fax: 703-739-0290
E-Mail: meetings@diabetes.org
Home Page: www.diabetes.org
Social Media: Facebook, Twitter, YouTube

Karen D Talmadge, PhD, Chair
Larry Hausner, MBA, Chief Executive Officer
Lurelean B Gaines, RN, MSN, President, Health Care & Education
John E Anderson, MD, President, Medicine & Science
Patrick L Shuler, CPA, Secretary/Treasurer

Leading the fight against the deadly consequences of diabetes and fight for those affected. Funding research to prevent, cure and manage diabetes. Delivering services to hundreds of communitites. Providing objective and credible information. Giving a voice to those denied their rights because of diabetes.
Founded in 1940

12616 American Gastroenterological Association
4930 Del Ray Avenue
Bethesda, MD 20814

301-654-2055
Fax: 301-654-5920
E-Mail: member@gastro.org
Home Page: www.gastro.org
Social Media: Facebook, Twitter, LinkedIn, YouTube

Anil K Rustgi, MD, AGAF, President
Michael Camilleri, MD, AGAF, Vice President
J Sumner Bell III, MD, AGAF, Secretary/Treasurer
Lynn P Robinson, JD
Tom Serena, MBA, CPA, Co-executive vice president

Advancing the science and practice of gastroenterology.
17M Members
Founded in 1897

12617 American Head and Neck Society
11300 W Olympic Boulevard
Suite 600
Los Angeles, CA 90064

310-437-0559
Fax: 310-437-0585
E-Mail: admin@ahns.info
Home Page: www.headandneckcancer.org
Social Media: Facebook, Twitter, YouTube

Terry Day, MD, President
Dennis H Kraus, MD, Vice President
Brian B Burkey, MD, Secretary
Ehab Hanna, MD, Treasurer

The single largest organization in North American for the advancement of research and education in head and neck oncology.
Founded in 1998

12618 American Headache Society
19 Mantua Road
Mount Royal, NJ 08061

856-423-0043
Fax: 856-423-0082
E-Mail: ahshq@talley.com
Home Page: www.americanheadachesociety.org
Social Media: Facebook, Twitter

Paul Winner, Chair

Professional society of health care providers dedicated to the study and treatment of headache and face pain. Members collaborate in producing educational programs and materials, coordinating the support groups, and undertaking public awareness initiatives all aimed at improving care for headache sufferers.
Founded in 1959

12619 American Health Care Association
1201 L St NW
Washington, DC 20005-4046

202-842-4444
Fax: 202-842-3860
E-Mail: webmaster@ahca.org
Home Page: www.ahcancal.org
Social Media: Facebook, Twitter, YouTube, Flickr

Represents the long term care community to the nation at large- to government, business leaders, and the general public. Serves as a force for change, providing information, education, and administrative tools that enhance quality at every level.
12M Members
Founded in 1949

12620 American Health Information Management Association
233 N. Michigan Avenue
21st Floor
Chicago, IL 60601-5809

312-233-1100
800-335-5535
Fax: 312-233-1090
Home Page: www.ahima.org
Social Media: Facebook, Twitter, LinkedIn, RSS, YouTube

Angela Kennedy, President/Chair
Cassi Birnbaum, MS, RHIA, CP, President/Chair-elect
Jennifer McManis, RHIT, Speaker of the House
Lynne Thomas Gordon, MBA, CEO
Ann Chenoweth, MBA, RHIA, Director

Professional organization for the field of effective management of health data and medical record needed to deliver quality healthcare to the public management.
71,00 Members
Founded in 1928

12621 American Health Information Management Association
233 N Michigan Ave
21st Floor
Chicago, IL 60601-5809

312-233-1100
800-335-5535
Fax: 312-233-1090
E-Mail: info@ahima.org
Home Page: www.ahima.org
Social Media: Facebook, Twitter, LinkedIn, YouTube

Bonnie S. Cassidy, President/ Chair
Patty Thierry Sheridan, President/ Chair-Elect
Lynne Thomas Gordon, CEO

Mission is to be the professional community that improves healthcare by advocating best practices and standards for health information management and the trusted source for education, reasearch, and professional credentialing.
46M Members
Founded in 1928

12622 American Health Quality Association
1776 I Street, NW
9th Floor
Washington, DC 20006

202-331-5790
Fax: 202-331-9334
E-Mail: info@ahqa.org
Home Page: www.ahqa.org

Adrienne Mims, MD, MPH, President
Todd D Ketch, Executive Director
Bruce W Ehrle, Senior Director
Sofia Kosmetatos, Director of Communications
Christine Oelschlager, Office Assistant

Represents Quality Improvement Organizations and professionals working to improve the quality of health care in communities across America. QIOs share information about best practices with physicians, hospitals, nursing homes, home health agencies, and others. Working together with health care providers, QIOs identify opportunities and provide assistance for improvement.

12623 American Heart Association
7272 Greenville Ave
Dallas, TX 75231-4596

214-373-6300
800-242-8721
Fax: 214-570-5930
E-Mail: siebelprod@heart.org
Home Page: www.americanheart.org
Social Media: Facebook, Twitter, YouTube, Google Plus

Bernie Dennis, Chairman
Mariell Jessup, President
Nancy Brown, CEO
Sunder Joshi, Chief Administrative Officer
Suzie Upton, Chief Development Officer

A nonprofit organization funding research and providing information on the diagnosis, treatment, and prevention of heart diseases and stroke. Mission is to build healthier lives, free of cardiovascular diseases and stroke.
Founded in 1924

12624 American Horticultural Therapy Association (AHTA)
610 Freedom Business Center
Suite 110
King of Prussia, PA 19406

610-992-0020
Fax: 610-225-2364
E-Mail: martha@ahta.org
Home Page: www.ahta.org
Social Media: Facebook, Twitter, LinkedIn, Pinterest, Youtube

MaryAnne McMillan, HTR, President
Leigh Anne Starling, MS, CRC, Vice President
Rene Malone, MS, CTRS, HTR, Treasurer
Natasha Etherington, HTT, Secretary

A champion of barrier-free, therapeutic gardens that enable everyone to work, learn, and relax in the garden. Horticultural therapists are skilled at creating garden spaces that accommodate people with a wide range of abilities.
Founded in 1973

12625 American Hospital Association
155 N. Wacker Dr.
Chicago, IL 60606

312-422-3000
800-424-4301
Fax: 312-422-4500
E-Mail: ddavidson@aha.org

Home Page: www.aha.org
Social Media: Facebook, Twitter, YouTube

Benjamin K Chu, M.D., Chairman
Richard J Umbdenstock, President and CEO
James H Hinton, Chairman-Elect

Represents and serves all types of hospitals, health care networks, and their patients and communities. Provides education for health care leaders and is a source of information on health care issues and trends.
45M Members
Founded in 1898

12626 American Industrial Hygiene Association
3141 Fairview Park Drive
Suite 777
Fairfax, VA 22042

703-849-8888
Fax: 703-207-3561
E-Mail: infonet@aiha.org
Home Page: www.aiha.org
Social Media: Facebook, Twitter, LinkedIn, Youtube

Barbara J Dawso?n, CIH, CSP?, President
Daniel H Anna, PhD, CIH, CS?P?, Vice President
Steven E. Lacey, PhD, CIH, CSP?, Treasurer
Charles F Redinger, PhD, CIH, Secretary
Christine A.D. Lorenzo, CIH, President-Elect

Organization of professionals in the science of occupational and environmental health and safety. Devoted to achieving and maintaining the highest professional standards for members. Promoting certification of industrial hygienists.
Founded in 1939

12627 American Institute of Ultrasound in Medicine
14750 Sweitzer Lane
Suite 100
Laurel, MD 20707-5906

301-498-4100
800-638-5352
Fax: 301-498-4450
E-Mail: membership@aium.org
Home Page: www.aium.org
Social Media: Facebook, Twitter, LinkedIn, Youtube

Steven R Goldstein, MD, President
Carmine Valente, Chief Executive Officer
Glynis Harvey, Deputy Chief Executive Officer
Joseph R Wax, MD, First Vice President
Lisa M. Allen, BS, RDMS, RDCS,, Second Vice President

A multidisciplinary association dedicated to advancing the safe and effective use of ultrasound in medicine through professional and public education, research, development of guidelines, and accreditation.
85M Members
Founded in 1952

12628 American Institute of Ultrasound in Medici ne
14750 Sweitzer Lane
Suite 100
Laurel, MD 20707-5906

301-498-4100
800-638-5352
Fax: 301-498-4450
E-Mail: membership@aium.org
Home Page: www.aium.org

Alfred Z. Abuhamad, President
Steven R. Goldstein, President-Elect
J. Brian Fowlkes, Secretary
Beryl R. Benacerraf, President-Elect
Brian D. Colby, Treasurer

A multidisciplinary association dedicated to advancing the safe and effective use of ultrasound in medicine through professional and public education, research, development of guidelines, and accreditation.
9.8M Members
Founded in 1952

12629 American Lung Association
1301 Pennsylvania Ave. NW
Suite 800
Washington, DC 20004

202-785-3355
Fax: 202-452-1805
E-Mail: info@lungusa.org
Home Page: www.lung.org
Social Media: Facebook, Twitter, YouTube, Google Plus, RSS

Albert A. Rizzo, Chair
Ross P. Lanzafame, Esq., Chair-Elect
Christine L. Bryant, Secretary/ Treasurer

Dedicated to the prevention, cure, and control of lung diseases such as asthma, emphysema, tuberculosis, and lung cancer. The Association offers community service, public health education, advocacy, and research.
Founded in 1904

12630 American Massage Therapy Association
500 Davis Street
Suite 900
Evanston, IL 60201

877-905-0577
E-Mail: info@amtamassage.org
Home Page: www.amtamassage.org/
Social Media: Facebook, Twitter, LinkedIn, RSS, YouTube

Nancy M. Porambo, President
Jeff Smoot, President Elect
Winona Bontrager, Immediate Past President
Kathie Lea, VP
Nathan J. Nordstrom, VP

Nonprofit, professional association serving massage therapists, massage students and massage schools.

12631 American Medical Association
330 N. Wabash Avenue
Chicago, IL 60611-5885

800-621-8335
E-Mail: robin_rusell@ama-assn.org
Home Page: www.ama-assn.org
Social Media: Facebook, Twitter, LinkedIn

James L. Madara, Chief Executive Officer
Bernard L. Hengesbaugh, Chief Operating Officer
Denise M Hagerty, Senior Vice President
Robert W Davis, Senior Vice President
Craig Ethridge, Group Vice President

Mission is to promote the art and science of medicine and the betterment of public health. The American Medical Association helps doctors help patients by uniting physicians nationwide to work on the most important professional and public health issues.
Founded in 1847

12632 American Medical Directors Association
11000 Broken Land Parkway
Suite 400
Columbia, MD 21044

410-740-9743
800-876-2632
Fax: 410-740-4572
E-Mail: webmaster@amda.com
Home Page: www.amda.com
Social Media: Facebook, Twitter, LinkedIn

Jonathan M Evans, MD, CMD, President
Naushira Pandya, MD, CMD, Vice President
Milta O Little, DO, CMD, Secretary
J Kenneth Brubaker, MD, CMD, Treasurer
Leonard Gelman, MD, CMD, President-Elect

Professional association of medical directors, attending physicians, and others practicing in the long term care continuum, is dedicated to excellence in patient care and provides education, advocacy, information, and professional development to promote the delivery of quality long term care medicine.
Founded in 1978

12633 American Medical Group Association
One Prince Street
Alexandria, VA 22314-3318

703-838-0033
Fax: 703-548-1890
E-Mail: dfisher@amga.org
Home Page: www.amga.org
Social Media: Facebook, Twitter, LinkedIn, YouTube

Michael W Bukosky, MSHA, FACMPE, Chair
Donald W Fisher, Ph.D., CAE, President and CEO
Don L Wreden, M.D., Secretary
Donn E Sorensen, M.B.A., FACM, Treasurer
Howard W Graman, M.D., FACP, Chair Elect

Represents medical groups and organized systems of care, including some of the nation's largest, most prestigious integrated healthcare delivery systems. Mission is to improve health care for patients by supporting multispecialty medical groups and other organized systems of care.
113M Members
Founded in 1950

12634 American Medical Informatics Association
4720 Montgomery Lane
Suite 500
Bethesda, MD 20814

301-657-1291
Fax: 301-657-1296
E-Mail: mail@amia.org
Home Page: www.amia.org
Social Media: Facebook, Twitter, LinkedIn, YouTube, Flickr

Gilad J Kuperman, MD, PhD, FAC, Chair
Karen Greenwood, Executive Vice President & COO
Christoph Lehmann, MD, FACMI, FA, Secretary
Sarah Ingersoll, MBA, RN, Treasurer
Sara A Ward, Executive Assistant

Aims to lead the way in transforming health care through trusted science, education, and the practice of informatics. Connecting a broad community of professionals and students interested in informatics, AMIA is the bridge for knowledge and collaboration across a continuum, from basic and applied research to the consumer and public health arenas.
3200 Members
Founded in 1990

12635 American Medical Student Association
45610 Woodland Rd.
Suite 300
Sterling, VA 20166

703-620-6600
800-767-2266
Fax: 703-620-6445
E-Mail: members@amsa.org
Home Page: www.amsa.org
Social Media: Facebook, Twitter, Inex, Youtube

Nida Degesys, MD, National President
Michele Jerome, Interim Executive Director
Deb Hall, VP for Internal Affairs
Leo Lopez III, VP for Membership
Lexi Light, VP for Program Development

The oldest and largest independent association of physicians-in-training in the United States.

Committed to improving the lives of medical students.
40M Members
Founded in 1950

12636 American Medical Technologists
10700 West Higgins
Suite 150
Rosemont, IL 60018-3722

847-823-5169
800-275-1268
Fax: 847-823-0458
Home Page: www.americanmedtech.org
Social Media: Facebook, Twitter, Youtube

Mary Burden, President
Everett Bloodworth, Vice President
Jeffrey Lavender, Secretary
Janet Sesser, Treasurer
Edna Anderson, Executive Councillor

Mission is to manage, promote, expand upon and continuously improve their certification programs for allied health professionals who work in a variety of disciplines and settings, to administer certification examinations in accordance with the highest standards of accreditation, and to provide continuing education, information, advocacy services and other benefits to members.
Founded in 1939

12637 American Medical Women's Association
12100 Sunset Hills Road
Suite 130
Reston, VA 20190

703-234-4069
866-564-2483
Fax: 215-564-2175
E-Mail: info@amwa-doc.org
Home Page: www.amwa-doc.org
Social Media: Facebook, Twitter, LinkedIn, Flickr

Eleni Tousimis, MD, President
Eliza Lo Chin, MD, MPH, Executive Director
Laurel A. Waters, Treasurer
Roberta Gebhard, DO, Secretary
Farzanna Haffizulla, MD, FACP, President-Elect

An organization of women physicians, medical students and other persons dedicated to serving as the unique voice for women's health and the advancement of women in medicine.
Founded in 1915

12638 American Music Therapy Association (AMTA)
8455 Colesville Rd
Suite 1000
Silver Spring, MD 20910-3392

301-589-3300
Fax: 301-589-5175
E-Mail: info@musictherapy.org
Home Page: www.musictherapy.org
Social Media: Facebook, Twitter, YouTube

Andrea Farbman, Executive Director
Mary Ellen Wylei, AMTA President

AMTA's purpose is the progressive development of the therapeutic use of music in rehabilitation, special education, and community settings. AMTA is committed to the advancement of education, training, professional standards, credentials, and research in support of the music therapy profession.
3800 Members
Founded in 1998

12639 American Nephrology Nurses Association
East Holly Avenue
Box 56
Pitman, NJ 08071-0056

856-256-2320
Fax: 856-589-7463
E-Mail: anna@annanurse.org
Home Page: www.annanurse.org
Social Media: Facebook, Twitter, RSS

Sharon M. Longton, RNÿ, President
Cindy A. Richards, BSNÿ, President-Elect
Norma J. Gomez, MSNÿ, Immediate Past President
Charla J. Litton Scheve, MSNÿ, Treasurer
Lynda K. Ball, MSN, Secretary

Mission is to promote excellence by advancing nephrology nursing practice and positively influence outcomes for individuals with kidney disease.

12640 American Nurses Association
8515 Georgia Avenue
Suite 400
Silver Spring, MD 20910-3492

800-274-4ANA
Fax: 301-628-5001
E-Mail: anf@ana.org
Home Page: www.nursingworld.org
Social Media: Facebook, Twitter, LinkedIn, YouTube

Pamela F. Cipriano, PhD, RN, NEA, President
Cindy R. Balkstra, MS, RN, ACNS, Vice President
Gingy Harshey Meade, Treasurer
Patricia Travis, Secretary
Andrea C. Gregg, Director at Large

Advances the nursing profession by fostering high standards of nursing practice, promoting the rights of nurses in the workplace, projecting a positive and realistic view of nursing, and by lobbying the Congress and regulatory agencies on health care issues affecting nurses and the public.

12641 American Occupational Therapy Association
4720 Montgomery Lane
Ste 200
Bethesda, MD 20814-3449

301-652-6611
800-729-2682
Fax: 301-652-7711
Home Page: www.aota.org
Social Media: Facebook, Twitter, LinkedIn, RSS

Florence Clark, President
Ginny Stoffel, Vice President
Paul A. Fontana, Secretary
Saburi Imara, Treasurer

Representing the interests and concerns of occupational therapy practitioners and students of occupational therapy and to improve the quality of occupational therapy services.
42M Members
Founded in 1917

12642 American Optometric Association
243 N Lindbergh Blvd
Flr. 1
St Louis, MO 63141-7881

314-991-4100
800-365-2219
Fax: 314-991-4101
Home Page: www.aoa.org
Social Media: Facebook, Twitter, RSS, Youtube

Mitchell T. Munson, O.D, President
Steven A. Loomis, O.D., Vice President
Andrea P. Thau, O.D., Secretary/ Treasurer

National organization of optometrists, evaluates ophthalmic products and sponsors continuing education programs.
36M Members
Founded in 1898

12643 American Optometric Student Association
243 N Lindbergh Blvd
St Louis, MO 63141-7881

314-983-4231
Home Page: www.theaosa.org/

Robert Foster, Executive Director
Alan Wegener, Vice President
Vicky Wong, Secretary
Elizabeth Turnage, Treasurer

Committed to promoting the optometric profession, enhancing the education and welfare of optometry students, as well as enhancing the vision and ocular health of the public.
6M Members

12644 American Orthopaedic Foot & Ankle Society
6300 N River Rd
Suite 510
Rosemont, IL 60018-4263

847-698-4654
800-235-4855
Fax: 847-823-8125
Home Page: www.aofas.org
Social Media: Facebook, Twitter, LinkedIn

Steven L. Haddad, MD, President
Mark E. Easley, MD, Vice President
Lousanne Lofgren, CAE, Executive Director
Judi Northrup, Director of Education
Lois Bierman, Director of Membership & Marketing

Mission is to promote quality, ethical and cost effective patient care through education, research and training of orthopaedic surgeons and other health care providers, create public awareness for the prevention and treatment of foot and ankle disorders, provide leadership, and serve as a resource for government, industry and the national and international health care community.
35000 Members
Founded in 1969

12645 American Orthopaedic Foot and Ankle Society
9400 West Higgins Road
Suite 220
Rosemont, IL 60018-4975

800-235-4855
847-698-4654
Fax: 847-692-3315
E-Mail: aofasinfo@aofas.org
Home Page: www.aofas.org/
Social Media: Facebook, Twitter, LinkedIn

Bruce J. Sangeorzan, MD, President
Mark E. Easley, MD, President-Elect
Jeffrey E. Johnson, MD, Vice President
J. Chris Coetzee, MD, Treasurer
Steven L. Haddad, MD, Immediate Past President

Specialty society for orthopaedic surgeons with training and interest in the prevention and treatment of foot and ankle conditions.

12646 American Orthopaedic Society for Sports Medicine
9400 W. Higgins Road
Suite 300
Rosemont, IL 60018ÿ

847-292-4900
877-321-3500
Fax: 847-292-4905

Home Page: www.sportsmed.org
Social Media: Facebook, Twitter

Irvin E. Bomberger, Executive Director
Camille Petrick, Managing Director
Heather Hodge, Education Director
Bart Mann, Director of Research
Lisa Weisenberger, Director of Communications

Promotes sports medicine education, research, communication, and fellowship and includes national and international orthopaedic sports medicine leaders.

12647 **American Orthopsychiatric Association**
C/o Clemson University, IFNL
225 S. Pleasantburg Dr.
Suite B-11
Greenville, SC 29607

864-250-4622
Fax: 864-250-4633
E-Mail: orthocontact@aoatoday.com
Home Page: www.aoatoday.org

Andres J. Pumariega, President
Donald Wertlieb, President-Elect
Jan L. Culbertson, Secretary
William Reay, Treasurer
Robin Kimbrough-Melton, Executive Officer

Provides a common ground for collaborative study, research, and knowledge exchange among individuals from a variety of disciplines engaged in preventive, treatment, and advocacy approaches to mental health.
Founded in 1923

12648 **American Orthotic & Prosthetic Association**
330 John Carlyle Street
Suite 200
Alexandria, VA 22314

571-431-0876
Fax: 571-431-0899
E-Mail: info@aopanet.org
Home Page: www.aopanet.org
Social Media: Facebook, Twitter, LinkedIn, Youtube

Thomas F. Kirk, Ph.D., President
Charles H. Dankmeyer, Jr., CPO, Vice President
Don DeBolt, Chief Operating Officer
Lauren Anderson, Manager of Membership Services
Stephen Custer, Communications Manager

A national trade association committed to providing high quality, unprecedented business services and products to O&P professionals.
Founded in 1917

12649 **American Osteopathic Association**
142 E Ontario St
Chicago, IL 60611-2874

312-202-8000
800-621-1773
Fax: 312-202-8200
E-Mail: info@osteotech.org
Home Page: www.osteopathic.org
Social Media: Facebook, Twitter, LinkedIn, Youtube, Pinterest

Norman E. Vinn, DO, President
Craig L. Magnatta, DO, First Vice President
Geraldine O'Shea, DO, Second Vice President
Frank M. Tursi, DO, Third Vice President
Martin S. Levine, DO, Treasurer

Promotes public health, encourages scientific research, and is the accrediting agency for all osteopathic medical schools and health care facilities.
52M Members
Founded in 1897

12650 **American Osteopathic College of Dermatology**
2902 North Baltimore Street
P.O. Box 7525
Kirksville, MI 63501

660-665-2184
800-449-2623
Fax: 660-627-2623
Home Page: www.aocd.org/
Social Media: Facebook, Twitter, Tumblr

Specialty college that promotes the practice of osteopathic dermatology.
Founded in 1958

12651 **American Pain Society**
8735 W. Higgins Road
Suite 300
Glenview, IL 60631

847-375-4715
Fax: 847-375-6479
Fax: 732-460-7318
E-Mail: info@ampainsoc.org
Home Page: www.americanpainsociety.org/
Social Media: Facebook, Twitter, LinkedIn, Youtube

Roger Fillingim, PhD, President
Catherine H Underwood, MBA CAE, Executive Director
David A. Williams, PhD, Treasurer
Kathleen Sluka, PT PhD, Secretary
Gregory W Terman, MD PhD, President-Elect

The American Pain Society is a multidisciplinary community that brings together a diverse group of scientists, clinicians and other professionals to increase the knowledge of pain and transform public policy and clinical practice to reduce pain-related suffering.
Founded in 1977

12652 **American Pediatric Society/Society for Pediatric Research**
3400 Research Forest Drive
Suite B7
The Woodlands, TX 77381

281-419-0052
Fax: 281-419-0082
E-Mail: info@aps-spr.org
Home Page: www.aps-spr.org

Debbie Anagnostelis, Executive Director
Belinda Thomas, PAS Education Program Director
Stephanie Dean, Managing Editor, Pediatric Research
Antonio Moreno, Information Technology Director
Belinda Thomas, Information Services Manager

Coordinates meetings, research and further education of health professionals. Features policies, publications and details of research programs.
Founded in 1888

12653 **American Pediatric Surgical Association**
111 Deer Lake Road
Suite 100
Deerfield, IL 60015

847-480-9576
Fax: 847-480-9282
E-Mail: eapsa@eapsa.org
Home Page: www.eapsa.org/

Michael D. Klein, Presidenty
Mary Fallat, President-Elect
Thomas M. Krummel, Immediate Past Presidenty
Daniel Von Allmen, Treasurer
Mary L. Brandt, Secretary

Pediatric surgical care of patients and their families.

12654 **American Pharmacists Association (APhA)**
2215 Constitution Ave NW
Suite 400
Washington, DC 20037-2985

202-628-4410
800-237-2742
Fax: 202-783-2351
Home Page: www.pharmacist.com
Social Media: Facebook, Twitter, RSS, Youtube

Steven T. Simenson, BSPharm, FAP, President
Thomas E. Menighan, BSPharm, MBA, Executive Vice President & CEO
Anne Burns, Senior Vice President
Joseph J. Janela, Chief Financial Officer
Elizabeth K. Keyes, Chief Operating Officer

The American Pharmacists Association (APhA) is an organization whose members are recognized in society as essential in all patient care settings for optimal medication use that improves health, wellness, and quality of life. Through information, education, and advocacy, APhA empowers its members to improve medication use and advance patient care.
60000 Members
Founded in 1852

12655 **American Physical Therapy Association**
1111 N Fairfax St
Alexandria, VA 22314-1488

703-683-6748
800-999-2782
Fax: 703-684-7343
E-Mail: memberservices@apta.org
Home Page: www.apta.org
Social Media: Facebook, Twitter, LinkedIn, Youtube

Paul Rockar, Jr, PT, DPT, M, President
Sharon L. Dunn, PT, PhD, OCS, Vice President
Bonnie Polvinale, CMP, Vice President, Member Relations
Rob Batarla, Vice President, Finance & Business
Janet Bezner, PT, Vice President, Education

The principal membership organization representing and promoting the profession of physical therapy, is to furhter the profession's role in the prevention, diagnosis, and treatment of movement dysfunctions and the enhancement of the physical health and functional abilities of members of the public.
74000 Members

12656 **American Physiological Society**
9650 Rockville Pike
Bethesda, MD 20814-3991

301-634-7164
Fax: 301-634-7241
E-Mail: webmaster@the-aps.org
Home Page: www.the-aps.org
Social Media: Facebook, Twitter, Google Plus

Martin Frank, PhD, Executive Director
Robert Price, Director of Finance
Donna Krupa, Communications Director
Mike Quinn, Information Services Manager
Marsha Lakes Matyas, PhD, Director of Education Programs

A nonprofit devoted to fostering education scientific research and dissemination of information in the physiological sciences. A member of the Federation of American Societies for Experimental Biology (FASEB) a coalition of 18 independent societies that plays an active role in lobbying for the interests of biomedical scientists.
10163 Members
Founded in 1887

12657 American Podiatric Medical Association
9312 Old Georgetown Rd
Bethesda, MD 20814-1698

301-581-9200
Fax: 301-530-2752
E-Mail: mskulick@apma.org
Home Page: www.apma.org
Social Media: Facebook, Twitter, LinkedIn, Youtube, Google Plus

Matthew G. Garoufalis, DPM, President
Phillip E. Ward, DPM, Vice President
R. Daniel Davis, DPM, Treasurer
Glenn B. Gastwirth, DPM, Secretary

An association of podiatrists providing services and information on foot problems and foot health.
11000 Members
Founded in 1912

12658 American Porphyria Foundation
4900 Woodway
Suite 780
Houston, TX 77056-1837
713-266-9617
866-APF-3635
Fax: 713-840-9552
E-Mail: porphyrus@aol.com
Home Page: www.porphyriafoundation.com

James V. Young, Chairman, Board of Trustee
Desiree H. Lyon, Executive Director
Dr. William McCutchen, Board Member
Warren Hudson, Board Member
Andrew Turell, Board Member

Dedicated to improving the health and well-being of individuals andfamilies affected by Porphyria. Also advocates for public, private, and government agencies interested in funding research and educational programs.
Founded in 1982

12659 American Psychiatric Association
1000 Wilson Blvd
Suite 1825
Arlington, VA 22209-3924

703-248-0760
888-357-7924
Fax: 703-907-1085
E-Mail: apa@psych.org
Home Page: www.psych.org
Social Media: Facebook, Twitter, LinkedIn

Association for manufacturers, suppliers, distributors, publishers, state/federal agencies and psychiatric facilities.
Founded in 1844

12660 American Psychological Association
750 1st St NE
Washington, DC 20002-4242

202-336-5500
800-374-2721
Fax: 202-336-5518
Home Page: www.apa.org
Social Media: Facebook, Twitter, LinkedIn, Google Plus

Donald N. Bersoff, PhD, JD, President
Norman B. Anderson, PhD, Chief Executive Officer
L. Michael Honaker, PhD, Deputy Chief Executive Officer
Cynthia D. Belar, PhD, Executive Director, Education
Steven J. Breckler, PhD, Executive Director

The largest scientific and professional organization representing psychology in the United States and the largest association of psychologists in the world, dedicated to advancing psychology as a science and as a means of promoting health, education, and human welfare.
Founded in 1892

12661 American Public Health Association
800 I Street, NW
Washington, DC 20001

202-777-2742
Fax: 202-777-2534
Home Page: www.apha.org
Social Media: Facebook, Twitter

Deborah Dillard, Executive Assistant

Professional association dedicated to improving the public's healththrough education.

12662 American Public Human Services Association
1133 19th St NW
Suite 400
Washington, DC 20036-3623

202-682-0100
Fax: 202-289-6555
Home Page: www.aphsa.org

Reggie Bicha, President
Tracy Wareing, Executive Director
Nicole Lobban, Human Resources Director
Raymond Washington III, Director of Finance
Anita Light, Senior Deputy Executive Director

Pursues excellence in health and human services by supporting state and local agencies, informing policymakers, and working wtih our partners to drive innovative, integrated and efficient solutions in policy and practice.
Founded in 1930

12663 American Rhinologic Society
PO Box 495
Warwick, NY 10990

845-988-1631
Fax: 845-986-1527
Home Page: www.american-rhinologic.org/

Roy Casiano, MD, President
Joseph Jacobs, MD, Executive Vice President
Peter Hwang, MD, President-elect
John DelGaudio, MD, 1st Vice President
Richard Orlandi, MD, 2nd Vice President

Physician organization whose focus is upon the medical and surgicaltreatment of patients with diseases of the nose and paranasal sinuses.

12664 American School Health Association
1760 Old Meadow Road
Suite 500
McLean, VA 22102

703-506-7675
Fax: 703-503-3266
E-Mail: info@ashaweb.org
Home Page: www.ashaweb.org
Social Media: Facebook, Twitter, LinkedIn

Linda Morse, RN, MA, CHES, President
JoAnne Lyons Wooten, Interim Executive Director

Concerned with all health factors that are necessary for students to be ready to learn, including optimum nutrition, physical fitness, emotional well-being, and a safe and clean environment.
2000 Members
Founded in 1927

12665 American Sleep Apnea Association
1717 Pennsylvania Avenue, NW
Suite 1025
Washington, DC 20006

888-293-3650
Fax: 888-293-3650
Home Page: www.sleepapnea.org/
Social Media: Facebook, Twitter, Google+, YouTube, Vimeo

Will Headapohl, Chair
Adam Amdurÿ, COO
Addison Closson, Treasurer
Nancy Rothstein, Secretary
Tracy R. Nasca, Executive Director

A nonprofit organization that promotes education, awareness and research into sleep apnea.
Founded in 1990

12666 American Society for Aesthetic Plastic Surgery
36 W 44th Street
New York, NY 10036

212-921-0500
Fax: 212-921-0011
E-Mail: media@surgery.org
Home Page: www.surgery.org
Social Media: Facebook, Twitter, LinkedIn

Jack Fisher, MD, President
James C. Grotting, MD, Vice President
Daniel C. Mills, II, MD, Treasurer
Clyde H. Ishii, MD, Secretary

Organization of plastic surgeons certified by the American Board of Plastic Surgery who specialize in cosmetic surgery of the face and body.

12667 American Society for Cell Biology
8120 Woodmont Ave
Suite 750
Bethesda, MD 20814-2762

301-347-9300
Fax: 301-347-9310
E-Mail: ascbinfo@ascb.org
Home Page: www.ascb.org
Social Media: Facebook, Twitter, LinkedIn, Youtube

Don Cleveland, President
Stefano Bertuzzi, PhD, Executive Director
Thea Clarke, Director of Communications
John Fleischman, Senior Science Writer
Christina Szalinski, Science Writer/Program Coordinator

A nonprofit membership organization of biologists studying the cell, the fundamental unit of life. Membership is open to all research scientists, students, educators, and technicians who have education or research experience in cell biology or an allied field.
10M Members
Founded in 1960

12668 American Society for Dermatologic Surgery
5550 Meadowbrook Drive
Suite 120
Rolling Meadows, IL 60008
847-956-0900
Fax: 847-956-0999
E-Mail: info@asds.net
Home Page: www.asds.net
Social Media: Facebook, Twitter, LinkedIn, YouTube

Mitchel P. Goldman, MD, President
Naomi Lawrence, MD, Vice President
Katherine J. Duerdoth, CAE, Executive Director
Tara Azzano, Director of Development
Kim Santaniello, Director of Education, Meetings

To promote optimal quality care for patients as well as support and develop investigative knowledge in the field of dermatologic surgery.
Founded in 1973

12669 American Society for Histocompatability and Immunogenetics
15000 Commerce Parkway
Suite C
Mt. Laurel, NJ 08054

856-638-0428
Fax: 856-439-0525

E-Mail: info@ashi-hla.org
Home Page: www.ashi-hla.org
Social Media: Facebook, Twitter, LinkedIn

Kathy Miranda, Executive Director
Leslie Clark, Assistant Executive Director
Melissa Weeks, Accreditation Manager
Nadege Toth, Meeting Manager
Julie DiCarlo, Meeting Coordinator

Dedicated to advancing the practice and science of inherited aspects of immunity, and its impact on the quality of human life.
Founded in 1972

12670 American Society for Laser Medicine and Surgery, Inc.
2100 Stewart Ave
Suite 240
Wausau, WI 54401-1709

715 845-9283
Fax: 715-848-2493
E-Mail: information@aslms.org
Home Page: www.aslms.org
Social Media: Facebook, Twitter, LinkedIn, Google Plus, Youtube, Pinteres

Dianne Dalsky, Executive Director
Barb Brown, CAP, Program and Services Coordinator
Paula Deffner, Accounting Assistant
Diane Dodds, Member and Customer Service
Hollie Raab, Marketing & Communications Intern

Promotes excellence in patient care by advancing biomedical application of lasers and other related technologies worldwide.

12671 American Society for Microbiology
1752 N St NW
Washington, DC 20036-2904

202-737-3600
Fax: 202-942-9341
E-Mail: webmaster@asmusa.org
Home Page: www.asm.org
Social Media: Facebook, Twitter, LinkedIn, Instagram, Youtube

Jeffery Miller, President
Joseph M. Campos, Secretary

The world's largest scientific society of individuals interested in the microbiological sciences.

12672 American Society for Nutrition
9650 Rockville Pike
Bethesda, MD 20814

301-634-7050
Fax: 301-634-7892
Home Page: www.nutrition.org
Social Media: Facebook, LinkedIn, Youtube, RSS

Gordon L. Jensen, MD, PhD, President
Simin Meydani, DVM, PhD, Vice-President
John E. Courtney, Ph.D., Executive Officer
Cheryl Rock, Treasurer
Marian L. Neuhouser, Secretary

A non-profit organization dedicated to bringing together the world's top researchers, clinical nutritionists and industry to advance our knowledge and application of nutrition for the sake of humans and animals.
Founded in 1928

12673 American Society for Pharmacology and Experimental Therapeutics
9650 Rockville Pike
Bethesda, MD 20814-3995

301-634-7135
Fax: 301-634-7061
E-Mail: info@aspet.org
Home Page: www.aspet.org
Social Media: Facebook, Twitter, LinkedIn, Youtube

Judith A. Siuciak, Ph.D., Executive Director
Matthew Hilliker, Chief Financial Officer
Suzie Thompson, Director of Marketing
Richard Dodenhoff, Director of Journals
Jim Bernstein, Director of Government & Public Aff

Members research efforts help develop new medicines and therapeutic agents to fight existing and emerging diseases.
4800 Members
Founded in 1909

12674 American Society for Surgery of the Hand
822 W. Washington Boulevard
Suite 600
Chicago, IL 60607

312-880-1900
Fax: 847-384-1435
E-Mail: info@assh.org
Home Page: www.assh.org
Social Media: Facebook, Twitter, LinkedIn

The oldest medical specialty society in the United States devoted entirely to continuing medical education related to hand surgery.
2800 Members
Founded in 1946

12675 American Society for Therapeutic Radiology And Oncology
8280 Willow Oaks Corporate Dr.
Suite 500
Fairfax, VA 22031

703-502-1550
800-962-7876
Fax: 703-502-7852
E-Mail: meetings@astro.org
Home Page: www.astro.org
Social Media: Facebook, Twitter, LinkedIn, YouTube

Colleen A. F Lawton,ÿ MD, FASTRO, Chairman
Bruce G Haffty,ÿ MD, FASTRO, President
Phillip M Devlin,ÿ MD, Secretary/Treasurer
Bruce D Minsky,ÿ MD, President-elect
Jeff M Michalski,ÿ MD, MBA, F, Secretary/Treasurer-elect

Provides members with the continuing medical education, health policy analysis, patient information resources and advocacy that they need to succeed in today's ever-changing health care delivery system.
10M Members
Founded in 1958

12676 American Society of Anesthesiologists
520 N Northwest Highway
Park Ridge, IL 60068-2573

847-825-5586
Fax: 847-825-1692
E-Mail: communications@asahq.org
Home Page: www.asahq.org

Paul Pomerantz, Chief Executive Officer
Manuel Bonilla, M.S., Chief Advocacy Officer
Karen A. Buehring, M.B.A., SPHR, Chief Member
Thomas Conway, M.B.A., CPA, Chief Administrative Officer
Diane Gambill, Ph.D., Chief Learning Officer

An educational, research and scientific association of physicians organized to raise and maintain the standards of the medical practice of anesthesiology and improve the care of the patient.
39M Members
Founded in 1905
Mailing list available for rent

12677 American Society of Angiology
708 Glen Cove Ave
Glen Head, NY 11545

516-671-1975
Fax: 516-759-5524
E-Mail: anngailius@amsocang.org
Home Page: www.amsocang.org/

David K Jackson, MD, President

Striving to incorporate a variety of disciplines to encourage education and interaction in our common fields of endeavor.

12678 American Society of Bariatric Physicians
2821 S Parker Rd
Suite 625
Aurora, CO 80014-2735

303-770-2526
877-266-6834
Fax: 303-779-4834
E-Mail: info@asbp.org
Home Page: www.asbp.org
Social Media: Facebook, Twitter, LinkedIn, Youtube, RSS

David Bryman, D.O., F.A.S.B., Chairman
Eric C. Westman, M.D., M.H.S., President
Wendy Scinta, M.D., M.S., Vice President
Laurie Traetow, CAE, CPA, Executive Director
Heidi Gordon, Director of Marketing

ASBP is a nonprofit international professional medical association headquartered in Aurora, Colorado. The ASBP was awarded a seat in the House of Delegates of American Medical Association. The American Society of Bariatric Physicians has members worldwide.
Founded in 1950

12679 American Society of Cataract & Refractive Surgery
4000 Legato Rd
Suite 700
Fairfax, VA 22033-4055

703-591-2220
800-451-1339
Fax: 703-591-0614
E-Mail: ascrs@ascrs.org
Home Page: www.ascrs.org
Social Media: Facebook, Twitter, YouTube, Flickr

Eric D. Donnenfeld, MD, President
Richard A. Lewis, MD, Vice President/President Elect
David Karcher, Executive Director
Cindy Sebrell, Director of Marketing & Comm
Laura Johnson, Director of Education

The mission of the American Society of Cataract and Refractive Surgery is to advance the art and science of ophthalmic surgety and the knowledge and skills of ophthalmic surgeons. It does so by providing clinical and practice management education and by working with patients, government, and the medical community to promote the delivery of quality eye care.

12680 American Society of Clinical Oncology
2318 Mill Road
Suite 800
Alexandria, VA 22314

571-483-1591
Fax: 703-299-1044
E-Mail: confcenter@asco.org
Home Page: www.asco.org
Social Media: Facebook, Twitter, LinkedIn, Youtube

Clifford A. Hudis, MD, FACP, President
Susan Lerner Cohn, MD, Treasurer

Goal is to improve cancer care and prevention. Members include physicians and health-care

professionals in all levels of the practice of oncology.
30M Members
Founded in 1964
Mailing list available for rent

12681 American Society of Clinical Pathologists
33 West Monroe Street
Suite 1600
Chicago, IL 60603

312-541-4999
Fax: 312-541-4998
E-Mail: info@ascp.org
Home Page: www.ascp.org
Social Media: Facebook, Twitter, LinkedIn, Youtube

Steven H. Kroft, MD, FASCP, President
David N.B. Lewin, MD, FASCP, Vice President
William E. Schreiber, MD, FASCP, Secretary
Gregory N. Sossaman, MD, FASCP, Treasurer

Mission is to provide excellence in education, certification and advocacy on behalf of patients, pathologists and laboratory professionals across the globe.
100M+ Members

12682 American Society of Colon and Rectal Surgeons
85 W Algonquin Road
Suite 550
Arlington Heights, IL 60005

847-290-9184
800-791-0001
Fax: 847-290-9203
E-Mail: ascrs@fascrs.org
Home Page: www.fascrs.org
Social Media: Facebook

Rick Slawny, Executive Director
Gayle Irvin, Associate Executive Director
Mike Slawny, Consultant/Fulfillment
Linda Cullison, Director of Development
Julie Weldon, Assistant Directorÿ

The premier society for colon and rectal surgeons and other surgeons dedicated to advancing and promoting the science and practice of the treatment of patients with diseases and disorders affecting the colon, rectum and anus.
2600 Members
Founded in 1899

12683 American Society of Cytopathology
100 W. 10th Street
Suite 605
Wilmington, DE 19801-6604

302-543-6583
Fax: 302-543-6597
E-Mail: asc@cytopathology.org
Home Page: www.cytopathology.org
Social Media: Facebook, Twitter, LinkedIn

Ritu Nayar, MD, President
Elizabeth Jenkins, Executive Director
Eva M Wojcik, MD, MIAC, Vice President
Jodi Smith, Events and Education Development
JoAnn Jenkins, Finance and Online Education

A professional organization dedicated to the science and study of cells. Membership includes physicians, cytotechnologists and scientists who practice the cytologic method of diagnostic pathology. Committed to education, research, and advocacy on behalf of its membership, with the ultimate goal of improving the standards and quality of patient care.
3,000 Members
Founded in 1951

12684 American Society of ExtraCorporeal Technology
2209 Dickens Road
Richmond, VA 23230-2005
804-565-6363
Fax: 804-282-0090
E-Mail: judyr@amsect.org
Home Page: www.amsect.org

Stewart Hinckley, Executive Director
Donna Pendarvis, Association Manager
Michael Troike, Government Relations Chairman
Kimberly Robertson, CPA, Controller
Barbara Tolan, Journal ExtraCorporeal Technology

Enhancing the quality of extracorporeal (involving heart and lung machines) technology rendered to the public by engaging in the programmatic activities that will further the knowledge, skills, abilities and general proficiency of practitioners.
2000 Members
Founded in 1964

12685 American Society of Forensic Odontology
4414 82nd Street
Suite 212
Lubbock, TX 79424

Home Page: www.asfo.org
Social Media: Facebook

Dr. Roy Sonkin, President
Dr. Bruce Schrader, Executive Director
Dr. Cynthia Brzozowski, Secretary
Dr. Tom Gromling, Treasurer
Bruce Schrader, Executive Director

ASFO is one of the largest organizations representing all of those interested in forensic dentistry worldwide. Mission and goal to encourage and stimulate investigation and research in forensic odontology and related disciplines.
Founded in 1970

12686 American Society of Health-System Pharmacists
7272 Wisconsin Ave
Bethesda, MD 20814-4861

301-657-3000
866-279-0681
Fax: 301-664-8877
E-Mail: custserv@ashp.org
Home Page: connect.ashp.org
Social Media: Facebook, Twitter, LinkedIn, YouTube, RSS

Stanley S. Kent, President
Philip J. Schneider, Treasurer
Henri R. Manasse, Jr., Executive VP

ASHP is a national professional association that represents pharmacists who practice in hospitals, health maintenance organizations, long-term care facilities, home care, and other compnents of health care systems.
30K Members
Founded in 1936

12687 American Society of Hematology
2021 L Street NW
Suite 900
Washington, DC 20036-3508

202-776-0544
Fax: 202-776-0545
E-Mail: ash@hematology.org
Home Page: www.hematology.org
Social Media: Facebook, Twitter, LinkedIn, Youtube

Martha Liggett, Esq., Executive Director
Karina Fernandez, MS, Director of Information Technology
Jenifer Hamilton, CAE, Director, Communications
Patricia Frustace, Director, Development
Mark Smith, PhD, CAE, Director, Education

Mission is to further the understanding, diagnosis, treatment, and prevention of disorders affecting the blood, bone marrow, and the immunologic, hemostatic and vascular systems, by promoting research, clinical care, education, training, and advocacy in hematology.
10000 Members
Founded in 1958

12688 American Society of Human Genetics, Inc.
9650 Rockville Pike
Bethesda, MD 20814-3998

301-634-7300
Fax: 301-634-7079
E-Mail: society@ashg.org
Home Page: www.ashg.org
Social Media: Facebook, Twitter, LinkedIn, YouTube, RSS

Jeffrey C. Murray, MD, President
Joseph D. McInerney, Executive Vice President
Michael Dougherty, Director of Education
Pauline Minhinnett, Director of Meetings
Yimang Chen, Director of Information Technology

The primary professional membership organization for human genetics worldwide. Members include researchers, academicians, clinicians, laboratory practice professionals, genetic counselors, nurses and others involved in or with special interest in human genetics.
8000 Members
Founded in 1948

12689 American Society of Nephrology
1510 H Street, NW
Suite 800
Washington, DC 20005

202-640-4660
Fax: 202-637-9793
E-Mail: email@asn-online.org
Home Page: www.asn-online.org
Social Media: Facebook, Twitter, LinkedIn, Youtube, GooglePlus, Flickr, R

Ronald J. Sharon M. Moe, MD, FAS, President
Tod Ibrahim, Executive Director
Adrienne Lea, Director of Communications
Kara Page, Director of Development
Phillip Kokemueller, Chief Learning Officer

Leads the fight against kidney disease by educating health professionals, sharing new knowledge, advancing research, and advocating the highest quality care for patients.

12690 American Society of Neuroradiology
800 Enterprise Dr.
Suite 205
Oak Brook, IL 60523

630-574-0220
Fax: 630-574-0661
E-Mail: jgantenberg@asnr.org
Home Page: www.asnr.org
Social Media: RSS

Mauricio Castillo, MD, FACR, President
Laurie A. Loevner, MD, Vice President
Lorra Tannehill, Director of Scientific Meetings
Valerie Geisendorfer, Senior Manager
Tina Cheng, Director of Finance and Information

Active members must devote approximately one half or more of their professional practice to nueroradiology. Publishes a monthly journal and holds an annual meeting.
3000 Members
Founded in 1962

12691 **American Society of Ophthalmic Administrators**
4000 Legato Road
Suite 700
Fairfax, VA 22033
703-788-5777
800-451-1339
Fax: 703-547-8827
E-Mail: asoa@asoa.org
Home Page: www.asoa.org
Social Media: Facebook, Twitter

Liz Parrott, COE, President
John S. Bell MBA, COE, Vice President
Laureen Rowland CAE, Executive Director
Amy Guzewicz, Membership Manager and Project
Susan Younker, Executive Assistant to the Director

The premier organization for the business side of the ophalmic practice.
Founded in 1986

12692 **American Society of Plastic Surgeons**
444 E Algonquin Road
Arlington Heights, IL 60005
847-228-9900
888-475-2784
Fax: 847-228-9131
E-Mail: webmaster@plasticsurgery.org
Home Page: www.plasticsurgery.org
Social Media: Facebook, Twitter, Google Plus

Robert X. Murphy, Jr., MD, President
Michael D. Costelloe, JD, Executive Vice President
Keith M. Hume, Staff Vice President
Carol L. Lazier, Staff Vice President
Karen Craven, Staff Vice President

Promotes the specialty of plastic surgery and supports the highest quality patient care, professionalism and ethical standards through our role as patient and physician advocates.
Founded in 1931

12693 **American Speech-Language-Hearing Association**
2200 Research Boulevard
Rockville, MD 20850-3289
301-897-5700
800-638-8255
Fax: 301-296-8580
E-Mail: actioncenter@asha.org
Home Page: www.asha.org

Patricia A. Prelock, PhD, CCC-SLP, President
Donna Fisher Smiley, PhD, CCC-A, Vice President for Audiology
Howard Goldstein, PhD, CCC-SL, Vice President for Science
Carolyn W. Higdon, EdD, CCC-SLP, Vice President for Finance
Barbara J. Moore, EDD, CCC-SLP, Vice President for Planning

Represents the interests of medical specialists in speech, language, and hearing science and advocates for people with communication-related disorders.
Founded in 1925

12694 **American Stroke Association (ASA)**
7272 Greenville Ave
Dallas, TX 75231-5129
214-706-1556
888-478-7653
Fax: 214-570-5930
Home Page: www.strokeassociation.org
Social Media: Facebook, Twitter, Youtube

Lee Schwamm, Chairman

The American Stroke Association (ASA) is the division of the American Heart Association that's solely focused on reducing disability and death from stroke through research, education, fundraising and advocacy. The ASA offers a wide array of programs, products and services, from patient education materials to scientific statements.

12695 **American Tinnitus Association**
522 SW Fifth Avenue
Suite 825
Portland, OR 97204-2143
503-248-9985
800-634-8978
Fax: 503-248-0024
E-Mail: tinnitus@ata.org
Home Page: www.ata.org/
Social Media: Facebook, Twitter, YouTube

Thomas J Lobl, Ph.D, Chair
Cara James, Executive Director
Melanie F. West, Vice-Chair
Marsha Johnson, Treasurer
Norma Mraz, Secretary

The American Tinnitus Association (ATA) exists to cure tinnitus through the development of resources that advance tinnitus research. ATA board and staff work with researchers, tinnitus sufferers, donors, legislators and other concerned individuals to support vital tinnitus research.
Founded in 1971

12696 **American Urological Association**
1000 Corporate Blvd
Linthicum, MD 21090-2260
410-689-3700
866-746-4282
Fax: 410-689-3800
E-Mail: aua@auanet.org
Home Page: www.auanet.org
Social Media: Facebook, Twitter, LinkedIn, YouTube

Pramod C Sogani, MD, FACS, FRCS, President
Michael Sheppard, CPA, CAE, Executive Director
Gopal H. Badlani, Secretary
Steven M Schlossberg, MD, MBA, Treasurer
William W Bohnert, MD, FACS, President-Elect

The premier professional association for the advancement or urologic patient care, and works to ensure that its members are current on the latest research and practices in urology.

12697 **Arthroscopy Association of North America**
6300 North River Road
Suite 600
Rosemont, IL 60018-4228
847-292-2262
Fax: 847-292-2268
E-Mail: info@aana.org
Home Page: www.aana.org

J. W. Thomas Byrd, MD, President
Edward A Goss, Executive Director
William R. Beach, First Vice-Presidentÿ
Jeffrey S Abrams, MDÿ, Second Vice-Presidentÿ
Louis McIntyre, MDÿ, Treasurer

Goal is to promote, encourage, support and foster through continuing medical education functions, the development and dissemination of knowledge in the discipline of arthroscopic surgery.

12698 **Association for Gerontology in Higher Education**
1220 L St NW
Suite 901
Washington, DC 20005-4018
202-289-9806
Fax: 202-289-9824
E-Mail: aghe@aghe.org
Home Page: www.aghe.org

Janet C Frank, President
Leland Bert Waters, Treasurer
Kelly Niles-Yokum, Secretary
Donna L Wagner, President-Elect
M Angela Baker, Director

A membership organization devoted primarily to gerontological education, the Association for Gerontology in Higher Education (AGHE) strives to develop and sponsor education and training initiatives and to involve students, educators, researchers, and officials from across the country in providing resources for older adults and for those who serve them.

12699 **Association for Healthcare Documentation Integrity**
4230 Kiernan Avenue
Suite 130
Modesto, CA 95356
209-527-9620
800-982-2182
Fax: 209-527-9633
E-Mail: ahdi@ahdionline.org
Home Page: www.ahdionline.org
Social Media: Facebook, Twitter, LinkedIn

AHDI works tirelessly to give thousands of medical transcriptionists a voice before legislative and regulatory agencies and to ensure MTs are recognized for their contributions to patient safety and risk management.
7000 Members
Founded in 1978

12700 **Association for Medical Imaging Management**
490B Boston Post Rd
Suite 200
Sudbury, MA 01776-3367
978-443-7591
800-334-2472
Fax: 978-443-8046
E-Mail: memberservices@ahraonline.org
Home Page: www.ahraonline.org
Social Media: Facebook, Twitter, LinkedIn

Ed Yoder, CRA, FAHRA, President
Jason Newmark, CRA, Finance Director
Edward J Cronin, Jr., Chief Executive Officer
Kerri Hart-Morris, Associate Editor
Jessica Harju, Member Services Specialist

Professional association of radiology administrators from the US, Canada and several other countries. AHRA is a resource and catalyst for the development of professional leaders in imaging sciences and other health care disciplines.
4000 Members
Founded in 1972

12701 **Association for Professionals in Infection Control and Epidemiology, Inc.**
1275 K St NW
Suite 1000
Washington, DC 20005-4006
202-789-1890
Fax: 202-789-1899
E-Mail: info@apic.org
Home Page: www.apic.org
Social Media: Facebook, Twitter, LinkedIn, Youtube

Patti Grant, RN, BSN, MS, CI, President
Vickie M. Brown, RN, MPH, CIC, Treasurer
Linda R. Greene, RN, MPS, CIC, Secretary

Mission is to improve health and patient safety by reducing risks of infection. APIC advances its mission through education, research, collab-

oration, practice guidance, public policy, and credentialing.
12M Members
Founded in 1972

12702 Association for the Advancement of Medical Instrumentation
4301 N. Fairfax Drive
Suite 301
Arlington, VA 22203-1633
703-525-4890
Fax: 703-276-0793
E-Mail: customerservice@aami.org
Home Page: www.aami.org
Social Media: Facebook, Twitter, LinkedIn, Youtube

Marcy Petrini, Chair
Mary Logan, President
C. Phillip Cogdill, Treasurer/ Secretary

Mission is to increase the understanding and beneficial use of medical instrumentation through effective standards, educational programs, and publications.
Founded in 1967

12703 Association of Air Medical Services
909 N. Washington Street
Suite 410
Alexandria, VA 22314-3143
703-836-8732
Fax: 703-836-8920
E-Mail: information@aams.org
Home Page: www.aams.org/

Rick Sherlock, President & CEO
Blair Marie Beggan, Director of Communications
Natasha Ross, CMP, Director of Education & Events
Linda Beza, Controller
Kristin Discher, Project Manager

Voluntary, nonprofit organization, encourages and supports its members in maintaining a standard of performance reflecting safe operations and efficient, high quality patient care. Built on the idea that representation from a variety of medical transport services and businesses can be brought together to share information, collectively resolve problems and provide leadership in the medical transport community.
Founded in 1980

12704 Association of American Physicians and Surgeons
1601 N Tucson Boulevard
Suite 9
Tucson, AZ 85716-3450
800-635-1196
Fax: 520-325-4230
E-Mail: aaps@aapsonline.org
Home Page: www.aapsonline.org
Social Media: Facebook, Twitter

Tom Kendall, Sr., M.D., President, Executive Director
David Stumph

AAPS is a nonpartisan professional association of physicans in all types of practices and specialties across the country.
Founded in 1943

12705 Association of Applied Psychophysiology and Biofeedback
10200 W 44th Ave
Suite 304
Wheat Ridge, CO 80033-2837
303-422-8436
800-477-8892
Fax: 303-422-8894
E-Mail: info@aapb.org
Home Page: www.aapb.org

Richard Sherman, PhD, President
Stuart C. Donaldson, PhD, BCB, President-Elect
David Stumph, Executive Director
Richard Harvey, PhD, Treasurer
Michelle Cunningham, Associate Director

Goals of the association are to promote a new understanding of biofeedback and advance the methods used in this practice. Mission is to advance the development, dissemination and utilization of knowledge about applied psychophysiology and biofeedback to improve health and the quality of life through research, education and practice.
Founded in 1969

12706 Association of Family Medicine Administration
11400 Tomahawk Creek Parkway
Leawood, KS 66211-2672
800-274-2237
Fax: 913-906-6092
E-Mail: cestes@aafp.org
Home Page: www.afmaonline.org/

Becky Owens, President
Debbie Blackburn, C-TAGME, President-Elect
Rudy Martinez, LSW, Education Committee - RPS Planning
Eileen Morroni, C-TAGME, Education Committee - RAD Workshop
Gina Silvey, C-TAGME, Education Committeeÿ-ÿAudio and Web

Promotes professionalism in family practice administration. Serves as a network for sharing information and fellowship among members. Provides technical assistance to members, functions as a liaison to related professional organizations.

12707 Association of Family Medicine Residency Directors
11400 Tomahawk Creek Parkway
Suite 670
Leawood, KS 66211-2672
913-906-6000
800-274-2237
Fax: 913-906-6105
E-Mail: afprd@aafp.org
Home Page: www.afmrd.org/i4a/pages/index.cfm?pageid=1

Kevin Helm, MBA, Executive Vice President
Vickie Greenwood, Chief Administrative Officer
Katy Jaksa, Education Services
Sam Pener, Graduate Medical Education Services
Lynn Pickerel, Online Media Specialist

Inspires and empowers family medicine residency program directors to achieve excellence in family medicine residency training.
410 Members
Founded in 1990

12708 Association of Healthcare Internal Auditors
10200 W 44th Avenue
Suite 304
Wheat Ridge, CO 80033
303-327-7546
888-275-2442
Fax: 303-422-8894
E-Mail: ahia@ahia.org
Home Page: www.ahia.org
Social Media: LinkedIn, Youtube

Robert Michalski, CHC, CHPC,, Chair
Cavell Alexander, MBA, CPA, C, Secretary/Treasurer
Heidi Crosby, CPA, CIA, CHFP, Vice Chair
David Stumph, Executive Director

Promotes cost containment and increased productivity in health care institutions through internal auditing. Serves as a forum for the exchange of experience, ideas, and information among members, provides continuing professional education courses and informs members of developments in health care internal auditing. Offers employment clearinghouse services.
1000 Members
Founded in 1981

12709 Association of Otolaryngology Administrators
2400 Ardmore Boulevard
Suite 302
Pittsburgh, PA 15221
412-243-5156
Fax: 412-243-5160
E-Mail: AOA@oto-online.org
Home Page: www.oto-online.org
Social Media: Facebook, LinkedIn

Jo Ann LoForti, President
Jeff Dudley, President-Elect
James Benson, Secretary-Treasurer
Robin L. Wagner, Executive Director

Seeks to promote the concept of professional management in otolaryngology, provide a forum for interaction and exchange of information between otolaryngological managers and present educational programs. Maintains data exchange service for members researching specific topics.
1000 Members
Founded in 1983

12710 Association of Pediatric Hematology/ Oncology Nurses
8735 W. Higgins Rd
Ste 300
Chicago, IL 60631
847-375-4724
Fax: 847-375-6478
E-Mail: info@aphon.org
Home Page: www.aphon.org

Jami Gattuso, MSN RN CPON, President
Dave Bergeson, PhD CAE, Executive Director
Nicole Wallace, Senior Operations Manager
Jennifer Velazquez, Education Manager
Elizabeth Sherman, Senior Marketing Manager

Members are dedicated to promoting optimal nursing care for children, adolescents, and young adults with cancer and blood disorders, and their families. APHON provides the leadership and expertise to pediatric hematology/oncology nurses by defining and promoting the highest standards of practice and care to the pediatric, adolescent, and young adult communities.
2000 Members
Founded in 1976

12711 Association of Perioperative Registered Nurses
2170 S Parker Road
Suite 400
Denver, CO 80231-5711
303-755-6300
800-755-2676
Fax: 800-847-0045
E-Mail: custserv@aorn.org
Home Page: www.aorn.org
Social Media: Facebook, Twitter, LinkedIn, Slideshare, Pinterest, Youtube

Anne Marie Herlehy, President
Deborah Spratt, President-Elect
Jane Kusler-Jensen, Secretary
Anne Fairchild, Treasurer

A nonprofit membership association that represents the interests of perioperative nurses by

providing nursing education, standards, and clinical practice resources.
160M Members
Founded in 1954

12712 **Case Management Society of America**
6301 Ranch Drive
Little Rock, AR 72223
501-225-2229
Fax: 501-221-9068
E-Mail: cmsa@cmsa.org
Home Page: www.cmsa.org
Social Media: Facebook, Twitter, LinkedIn
Nancy Skinner, President
Mary McLaughlin-Davis, Secretary
Jose Alejandro, Treasurer
Cheri A ÿLattimer, Executive Director
Kathy Fraser, President-Elect
The leading membership association providing professional collaboration across the health care continuum to advocate for patients' wellbeing and improved health outcomes.
Founded in 1990

12713 **Catholic Health Association**
4455 Woodson Rd
St Louis, MO 63134-3797
314-427-2500
Fax: 314-427-0029
E-Mail: khewitt@chausa.org
Home Page: www.chausa.org
Carol Keehan, DC, President
Adele Gianino, Director, Meetings & Travel
Ana Hilton, Government Relations Coordinator
Betsy Taylor, Associate Editor, Catholic Health
Betty Crosby, Executive Assistant
Led by dedicated women and men, both religious and lay, who combine advanced technology and innovative treatment with caring traditdion. As provider, employer, and advocate, Catholic health care is committed to improving the health status of communities and creating quality and compassionate health care that works for everyone, especially the vulnerable.
2000+ Members
ISSN: 0882-1577
Founded in 1915

12714 **Christopher & Dana Reeve Paralysis Resource Center**
636 Morris Tpke
Suite 3A
Short Hills, NJ 07078-2608
973-467-8310
800-539-7309
Fax: 973-912-9433
E-Mail: info@crpf.org
Home Page: www.christopherreeve.org
Social Media: Facebook, Twitter, LinkedIn, Youtube, Google Plus, Pinteres
John M. Hughes, Chairman
John E. McConnell, Vice Chairman
Peter T. Wilderotter, President and CEO
Susan Howley, Executive Vice President, Research
Aimee Hunnewell, Vice President of Development
The Christopher & Dana Reeve Paralysis Resource Center (PRC) promotes the health and well-being of people living with paralysis and their families by providing comprehensive information resources and referral services.
Founded in 2001
Mailing list available for rent

12715 **Clinical Laboratory Management Association**
330 N. Wabash Avenue
Suite 2000
Chicago, IL 60611
312-321-5111
Fax: 610-995-9568
E-Mail: website@clma.org
Home Page: www.clma.org
Social Media: Facebook, Twitter
Paul L Epner, President
Meghan Carey, Chief Executive Officer
Deborah Garton, Secretary/Treasurer
Christina Kowalski, Operations Manager
Beth Jackson, Membership and Chapter Associate

12716 **Consumer Healthcare Products Association**
900 19th St Nw
Suite 700
Washington, DC 20006-2105
202-429-9260
Fax: 202-223-6835
E-Mail: cassey@chpa-info.org
Home Page: www.chpa.org
Scott Melville, President and CEO
Lisa M Early, Vice President, Finance
John F Gay, Vice President, Government Affairs
Barbara A Kochanowski, Ph.D, Vice President, Regulatory
Theodore L Peterson, Vice President, Corporate Dev
Promotes industry growth through consumer understanding, appreciation, and acceptance of responsible self-care in America's health care system by developing and sustaining a climate that provides consumers with convenient access to safe and effective nonprescription medicines and other self-care products marketed without undue restrictions.
Founded in 1881

12717 **Cremation Association of North America**
499 Northgate Parkway
Wheeling, IL 60090-2646
312-245-1077
Fax: 312-321-4098
E-Mail: info@cremationassociation.org
Home Page: www.cremationassociation.org
Social Media: Facebook, Twitter, LinkedIn, Youtube
Rick Wiseman, President
Sheri Stahlÿ, First Vice Presidentÿ(Treasurer)
Timothy R Bordenÿ, Second Vice Presidentÿ
Michael Sheedy, Third Vice President
Robert M Boetticher, Jr.ÿ, President-Elect
An International organization of over 1300 members, composed of cemeterians, cremationists, funeral directors, industry suppliers and consultants. CANA'members believe that cremation is preparation for memorialization.

12718 **Dental Group Management Association**
North Point Dental Group
2525 E Arizona Biltmore Circle
Suite 127
Phoenix, AZ 85016
602-381-8980
Fax: 602-381-1093
Home Page: www.dgma.org
Vincent Cardillo, President
Jill Nesbtt, Vice President
The DGMA is a national organization which recognizes the importance of professional management in group dental practices. The purpose of the Association is to advance dental group management and practice administration.
200 Members
Founded in 1951

12719 **Digital Phenom**
700 Princess St.
Suite 2M
Alexandria, VA 22314
202-393-0000
800-432-3247
Fax: 202-737-8406
E-Mail: info@aspirin.org
Home Page: www.digitalphenom.com
Atilla Kocsis, President
Ismaila Togola, Content Management
James Patterson, Project Management
A non-profit educational foundation with a membership of companies engaged in the manufacture, preparation, compounding or processing of aspirin and aspirin products. AFA serves as a central source of information on the health benefits of aspirin and aspirin products, when used as directed.
Founded in 1981

12720 **Emergency Nurses Association**
915 Lee St
Des Plaines, IL 60016-6569
847-460-4100
800-900-9659
Fax: 847-698-9406
Home Page: www.ena.org
Social Media: Facebook, Twitter, Google Plus
JoAnn Lazarus, MSN, RN, CEN, President
Susan M. Hohenhaus, LPD,ÿRN, CE, Executive Director
Matthew F Powers, MS, BSN, RN, M, Secretary/Treasurer
Deena Brecher,ÿMSN, RN, APRN, President-Elect
Founded in 1968

12721 **Federation of American Health Systems**
801 Pennsylvania Ave NW
Suite 245
Washington, DC 20004-2697
202-624-1500
Fax: 202-737-6462
E-Mail: info@fah.org
Home Page: www.fah.org
Charles Kahn, President
Mike Bromberg, Vice Chairman
Bruce Gilbert, Treasurer
Barry Schochet, Secretary

12722 **Gerontological Society of America**
1220 L Street NW
Suite 901
Washington, DC 20005
202-842-1275
Fax: 202-842-1150
E-Mail: geron@geron.org
Home Page: www.geron.org
James Appleby, Executive Director and CEO
Linda Krogh Harootyan, Deputy Executive Director
Paul Stearns, Senior Director, Membership
Chris Yoder, Senior Director, Finance
Carly Bushong, Meetings and Education Manager
800+ Members
Founded in 1939

12723 **Health Industry Distributors Association**
310 Montgomery St
Alexandria, VA 22314-1516
703-549-4432
Fax: 703-549-6495

E-Mail: rowan@hida.org
Home Page: www.hida.org

Matthew Rowan, President and CEO
Justin Waters, Administrative Assistant
Ian Fardy, ExecutiveÿVice President
Elizabeth Hilla, Sr. Vice President, Education
Linda Rouse O'Neill, Vice President, Government Affairs

The trade association representing medical products distributors. Provides leadership in the healthcare distribution industry.

12724 **Health Industry Manufacturers Association**
1200 G Street NW
Washington, DC 20005-3814

FAX 202-783-8750

Established as the Wholesale Surgical Trade Association. Represents manufacturers of health care technology, including medical devices, diagnostic products, and health care information systems.

12725 **Healthcare Compliance Packaging Council**
2711 Buford Road
#268
Bon Air, VA 23235-2423

804-338-5778
Fax: 888-812-4272
E-Mail: pgmayberry@aol.com
Home Page: www.hcpconline.org
Social Media: Facebook, LinkedIn

Peter G Mayberry, Executive Director
Kathleen Hemming, Staff Consultant

Nonprofit trade association promoting the benefits of unit dose blister and strip packaging — especially its ability to be designed in compliance prompting formats that help people take their medications properly.
Founded in 1990

12726 **Healthcare Convention & Exhibitors Association**
1100 Johnson Ferry Rd NE
Suite 300
Atlanta, GA 30342-1733

404-252-3663
Fax: 404-252-0774
E-Mail: hcea@kellencompany.com
Home Page: www.hcea.org
Social Media: Facebook, Twitter, LinkedIn

Sue Huff, President
Christine Farmer, Vice President
Christine DiDomenico, MBA, Treasurer
Don Schmid, MBA, CME/H, Secretary
Diane Benson, CTSM, President-Elect

Trade association of organizations involved in health care exhibiting or providing services to health care conventions, exhibitions and/or meetings.
600 Members
Founded in 1930

12727 **Healthcare Distribution Management Association**
901 North Glebe Rd
Suite 1000
Arlington, VA 22203-1853

703-787-0000
Fax: 703-812-5282
Home Page: www.healthcaredistribution.org

David Neu, Chairman
Ann W Bittman, Executive Vice President and COO
Peri L Fri, Senior Vice President
Patrick M Kelly, Senior Vice President, Government
Karen J Ribler, Executive Vice President

An organization representing all major constituents of healthcare product distribution management.

12728 **Healthcare Financial Management Association**
3 Westbrook Corporate Ctr
Suite 600
Westchester, IL 60154-5723

708-531-9600
800-252-4362
Fax: 708-531-0032
E-Mail: jfifer@hfma.org
Home Page: www.hfma.org

Joseph J Fifer, FHFMA, CPA, CEO & President
Edwin P Czopek, FHFMA, CPA, CA, Senior Vice President
Susan Brenkus, Vice President, Human Resources
Richard L Gundling, FHFMA, CMA, Vice President, Healthcare
Lee Guthrie, Vice President, Marketing

Brings perspective and clarity to the industry's complex issues for the purpose of preparing our members to succeed. Through our programs, publications and partnerships we enhance the capabilities that strengthen not only individual careers, but also the organizations from which our members come.
34000 Members
Founded in 1946

12729 **Healthcare Marketing & Communications Council**
1525 Valley Center Parkway
Bethlehem, PA 18017

610-868-8299
Fax: 610-868-8387
E-Mail: info@hmc-council.org
Home Page: www.hmc-council.org

Janis Cohen, President/CEO
Gary J Gyss, Founder

Enhancing the professional development of its members by providing continuing education and career development opportunities. The council also works toward a better understanding of the role of marketing, education, and communications in health care.

12730 **Home Medical Equipment and Services Association of New England**
515 Kempton St
New Bedford, MA 02740-3852

508-993-0700
Fax: 508-993-0797
E-Mail: info@homesne.org
Home Page: www.homesne.org

Karyn Estrella, Executive Director
Brian Simonds, President
Jim Greatorex, VP
Rebecca Godley, Secretary
Paula Finamore, Treasurer

Works together supporting the common goals and interests of the home medical equipment, respiratory, and rehab/assistive techology and home infusion therapy industry.
15 Members
Founded in 1988

12731 **Infusion Nurses Society**
315 Norwood Park South
Norwood, MA 02062-4694

781-440-9408
800-694-0298
Fax: 781-440-9409
E-Mail: ins@ins1.org
Home Page: www.ins1.org
Social Media: Facebook, Twitter, LinkedIn, Youtube

Britt Meyer, MSN, RN, CRNIr,, President
Mary Alexander, MA, RN, CRN, Chief Executive Officerÿÿ
Christopher Hunt, Executive Vice Presidentÿ
Dora Hallock, MSN, RN, CRNI, Secretary/Treasurer
Ann Earhart, MSN, RN, ACNS, President-Elect

The INS is committed to bringing innovative new resources and opportunities to a wide range of healthcare professionals who are involved with the specialty practice of infusion therapy.
6000 Members
Founded in 1973

12732 **International Anesthesia Research Society**
44 Montgomery Street
Suite 1605
San Francisco, CA 94104-4602

415-296-6900
Fax: 415-296-6901
E-Mail: iarshq@iars.org
Home Page: www.iars.org

Denise J Wedel, MD, Chair
Thomas A Cooper, Executive Director
Davy C H Cheng, MD, Treasurer
Makoto Ozaki, MD, PhD, Secretary
Laura J Kuhar, Education Director
Founded in 1922

12733 **International Association For Healthcare Security & Safety**
PO Box 5038
Glendale Heights, IL 60139

630-529-3913
888-353-0990
Fax: 630-529-4139
E-Mail: info@iahss.org
Home Page: www.iahss.org
Social Media: Facebook, Twitter, LinkedIn

Lisa Pryse, President
Dana Frentz,ÿCHPA, Vice-President/Treasurerÿ
David LaRose, CHPA, CPP, Vice-President/Secretaryÿ
Marilyn Hollier, CHPA, CPP, President-Electÿ

The International Association for Healthcare Security and Safety, (IAHSS) is an organization dedicated to professionals involved in managing and directing security and safety programs in healthcare institutions. Its members have joined together to develop educational and credentialing programs and create a body of knowledge that meets the needs of today's fast paced and ever changing environment.
2000 Members
Founded in 1968

12734 **International Association for Worksite Health Promotion**
401 West Michigan Street
Indianapolis, IN 46202

317-637-9200
E-Mail: iawhp@acsm.org
Home Page: www.acsm-iawhp.org/
Social Media: Facebook

Wolf Kirsten, MSÿ, President
Vin DeProssino, Secretary/Treasurer

Mission is to advance the global community of worksite health promotion practitioners through high-quality information, services, educational activities, personal and professional development and networking opportunities.

12735 **International Association of Healthcare Central Service Material Management**
213 W Institute Place
Suite 307
Chicago, IL 60610-3195

312-440-0078
800-962-8274
Fax: 312-440-9474
E-Mail: mailbox@iahcsmm.com
Home Page: www.iahcsmm.com

Sharon Greene-Golden, CRCST,, President
Susan Adams, Executive Director
Marilyn T Conde, CRCST, MAOM, FC, Secretary/Treasurer
Nick Baker, Certification Manager
Elizabeth Berrios, Member Services Coordinatory

Membership consists of persons serving in a technical, supervisory or management capacity in hospital central service departments responsible for the sterilization management and distribution of supplies.
9000 Members
Founded in 1958
Mailing list available for rent: 13000 names

12736 **International Bone and Mineral Society**
330 N Wabash
Suite 1900
Chicago, IL 60611
312-321-5113
Fax: 312-673-6934
E-Mail: info@ibmsonline.org
Home Page: www.ibmsonline.org

Theresa Guise, President
Kevin Baliozian, Executive Director
Jeanette Ruby, Director of Development
John Eisman, Vice Presidentў
Richard Eastell, Treasurer Secretary
3600 Members
Founded in 1977

12737 **International Oxygen Manufacturers Association**
1025 Thomas Jefferson Street, NW
Suite 500 East
Washington, DC 20007

202-521-9300
Fax: 202-833-3636
E-Mail: ioma@iomaweb.org
Home Page: www.iomaweb.org

The International Oxygen Manufacturers Association is the truly worldwide trade association of companies in the industrial and medical gas business
190 Members
Founded in 1943

12738 **International Sleep Products Association**
501 Wythe Street
Alexandria, VA 22314-1917

703-683-8371
Fax: 703-683-4503
E-Mail: info@sleepproducts.org
Home Page: www.sleepproducts.org
Social Media: Facebook, Twitter, LinkedIn, Youtube, Flickr, Google Plus,

Debi Sutton, VP, Marketing & Member Services

Maintains a strong organization to influence government actions, inform and educate the membership and act on industry issues to enhance the growth, profitability and stature of the sleep products industry. Provides members with information and services to manage their business more effectively and efficiently. Publishes a magazine devoted exclusively to the mattress industry, BEDtimes covers a broad range of issue and news important to the industry.
Cost: $65.00
650 Members
Frequency: Monthly
Circulation: 3,500
Founded in 1915

12739 **International Society for Quality-of-Life Studies**
2056 Pamplin
Virginia Tech
Blacksburg, VA 24061-0236

540-231-5110
Fax: 540-231-3076
E-Mail: sirgy@vt.edu
Home Page: www.isqols.org

M Joseph Sirgy, Executive Director/Secretary

Was founded to stimulate interdisciplincary research in quality-of-life studies and closer cooperation among scholars. Members are academic and government social/behavioral science researchers drawn from such fields as marketing, management, applied psychology, applics sociology, political science, economics, public administration, educational administration family/child development leisure/recreation studies and technology development.
Founded in 1995

12740 **Interstate Postgraduate Medical Association**
PO Box 5474
Madison, WI 53705

608-231-9045
866-446-3424
Fax: 877-292-4489
E-Mail: cmehelp@ipmameded.org
Home Page: www.ipmameded.org

George C. Mejicano, MD, MS, Board Chair

Dedicated to sponsoring clinically relevant education for primary care clinicians.
Founded in 1916

12741 **Leading Age**
2519 Connecticut Ave NW
Washington, DC 20008-1520

202-783-2242
Fax: 202-783-2255
E-Mail: info@leadingage.org
Home Page: www.leadingage.org
Social Media: Facebook, Twitter, LinkedIn

William L. Minnix, Jr., President & CEO
Katrinka Smith Sloan, COO & Sr. Vice President
Robyn I. Stone, Senior Vice President of Research
Cheryl Phillips, Senior Vice President
Majd Alwan, Senior Vice President of Technology

Focused on advocacy, leadership development, and applied research and promotion of effective services, home health, hospice, community services, senior housing, assisted living residences, continuing care communities, nursing homes, as well as technology solutions, to seniors, children, and others with special needs.
6M Members
Founded in 1961

12742 **Medical Group Management Association**
104 Inverness Terrace East
Englewood, CO 80112-5306

303-799-1111
877-275-6462
Fax: 303-643-9599
E-Mail: support@mgma.org
Home Page: www.mgma.com
Social Media: Facebook, Twitter, LinkedIn

William Jessee, CEO
Nicholas H Kupferle, Board Chair
Jyl D Bradley, Chair
Warren C White Jr, Chair
Nicholas H Kupferle III, Chair

The mission of the MGMA is to continually improve the performance of medical group practice professionals and the organizations they represent.
19000 Members
Founded in 1926

12743 **Medical Library Association**
65 E Wacker Place
Suite 1900
Chicago, IL 60601-7246

312-419-9094
Fax: 312-419-8950
E-Mail: info@mlahq.org
Home Page: www.mlanet.org / www.marketing.mlanet.org
Social Media: Facebook, LinkedIn, Youtube

Dixie A Jones, AHIP, President
Carla J Funk, Executive Director
Mary M Langman, Director, Information Issues
Linda Walton, President-Elect
Maria Lopez, Administrative Assistant

A nonprofit, educational organization that is a leading advocate for health sciences information professionals worldwide. Through it's programs and services, we provide lifelong educational opportunities, supports a knowledgebase of health information research and works with a global network of partners to promote the importance of quality information for improved health to the health care community and the public.
4500 Members
Founded in 1898
Mailing list available for rent

12744 **Medical Marketing Association**
10293 N Meridian Street
Suite 175
Indianapolis, IN 46290
317-816-1640
Fax: 317-816-1633
Home Page: www.medicalmarketingassociation.org/
Social Media: Facebook, Twitter, Google Plus

Michael L Boner, President
Steve Hamburger, Treasurer
Stewart Marsden, Secretary

Builds diagnostic industry leadership by providing market education, professional development and a forum for fellowship and the exchange of ideas.

12745 **National Association Medical Staff Services**
2025 M St NW
Suite 800
Washington, DC 20036-2422

202-367-1196
Fax: 202-367-2196
E-Mail: info@namss.org
Home Page: www.namss.org

Melissa Walters, MHA, CPMSM, C, President
Lynn Boyd, Executive Director
Tiffany Boykin, Membership and Marketing Manager
Andrew Miller, Member Services Coordinator
Chris Murphy Peck, Education & Learning Services

NAMSS' vision is to advance a healthcare environment that maximizes the patient experience through the delivery of quality services.
4000 Members
Founded in 1978

12746 **National Association for Healthcare Recruitment**
18000 W. 105th St.
Suite 103
Olathe, KS 66061-7543

913-895-4627
Fax: 913-895-4652
E-Mail: nahcr@goAMP.com
Home Page: www.nahcr.com
Social Media: Facebook, Twitter, LinkedIn, Blogger, youtube

Terry Bennett, RN, MS, CHCR, President
Julie Hill, BSN, RN, CHCR, R, Vice President
Sheila O'Neal, BA/BS, Executive Director
Jody Shelton, EdD, CAE, Education Program Director
Raven Hardin, BA, Association Manager

Individuals employed directly by hospitals and other health care organizations which are involved in the practice of professional health care recruitment. Promotes sound principles of professionals health care recruitment. Provides financial assistance to aid members in planning and implementing regional educational programs. Offers technical assistance and consultation services. Compiles statistics.
800 Members
Founded in 1975

12747 **National Association for Home Care and Hospice**
228 7th St Se
Washington, DC 20003-4306

202-547-7424
Fax: 202-547-3540
E-Mail: ads@nahc.org
Home Page: www.nahc.org
Social Media: Facebook, Twitter, Pinterest

Andrea Devoti, Chairman
Lucy Andrews, Vice Chair
Val J. Halamandaris, President
Walter W. Borginis, Treasurer
Mary Haynor, Secretary

12748 **National Association for Medical Direction of Repiratory Care (NAMDRC)**
8618 Westwood Center Drive
Suite 210
Vienna, VA 22182-2222

703-752-4359
Fax: 703-752-4360
E-Mail: execoffice@namdrc.org
Home Page: www.namdrc.org

Dennis E. Doherty, M.D., President
Phillip Porte, Executive Director
Vickie Parshall, Director Member Services
Charles W. Atwood, MD, Secretary/Treasurer
Karen Lui, RN, Associate Executive Director

The National Association for Medical Direction of Respiratory Care, our mission is to improve access to quality care for patients with respiratory disease by removing regulatory and legislative barriers to appropriate treatment. It advises on coding issues and federal reimbursement policies; provides economic and regulatory updates; and offers unique educational opportunities.
700 Members
Founded in 1977

12749 **National Association of County & City Health Officials**
1100 17th St NW
Seventh Floor
Washington, DC 20036-4619

202-783-5550
Fax: 202-783-1583
E-Mail: info@naccho.org
Home Page: www.naccho.org

Terrance Allan, RS, MPH, President
Swannie Jett, DrPHc, MSc, Vice President
Georgia F Heise, DrPH, President-Elect

Administrators of freestanding and hospital-based long-term care facilities owned and operated by county governments or city-county consolidations; elected local officials. Promotes interests of county long-term care facilities; offers guidance in relevant legislative and regulatory areas. Provides technical assistance; conducts training workshops. Compiles statistics on public policy changes, such as changes in the Medicaid program, which affect long-term care facilities.
250 Members
Founded in 1977

12750 **National Association of School Nurses**
1100 Wayne Avenue
Suite 925
Silver Spring, MD 20910

240-821-1130
866-627-6767
Fax: 207-883-2683
E-Mail: nasn@nasn.org
Home Page: www.nasn.org

Carolyn Duff, RN, MS, NCSN, President
Tia B. Campbell, RN, BSN, MSN, Vice President
Donna J. Mazyck, RN, MS, NCSN, Executive Director
Carmen Teskey, MA, BSN, RN, Secretary/Treasurer
Kenny Lull, Manager of Communications
15500 Members
Founded in 1968

12751 **National Athletic Trainers Association**
2952 N Stemmons Fwy
Suite 200
Dallas, TX 75247-6115

214-637-6282
Fax: 214-637-2206
E-Mail: webmaster@nata.org
Home Page: www.nata.org

Jim Thornton, MS, ATC, CES, President
Scott Sailor, EdD, ATC, Vice President
Dave Saddler, Executive Director
Amy Callender, Director of Government Affairs
Michael Anto Anto, Human Resources Manager
32000 Members
Founded in 1950

12752 **National Cancer Institute**
9609 Medical Center Drive
Bethesda, MD 20892-9760

800-422-6237
E-Mail: cancergovstaff@mail.nih.gov
Home Page: www.cancer.gov
Social Media: Facebook, Twitter, Youtube

Harold Varmus, Director

Conducts and supports research, training, health information dissemination and other programs with respect to the cause, diagnosis, prevention and treatment of cancer, rehabilition from cancer and the continuing care of cancer patients.

12753 **National Council for Behavioral Health**
1701 K Street NW
Suite 400
Washington, DC 20006

202-684-7457
Fax: 202-386-9391
E-Mail: communications@thenationalcouncil.org
Home Page: www.TheNationalCouncil.org
Social Media: Facebook, Twitter, LinkedIn, Youtube, Pinterest, Google Plu

Jeffrey Walter, Chair
Linda Rosenberg, President & CEO
Jeannie Campbell, Executive Vice President & COO
Charles Ingoglia, Senior Vice President
Meena Dayak, Vice President, Marketing

Advocates for public policies in mental and behavioral health that ensure that people who are ill can access comprehensive healthcare services.

12754 **National Council on the Aging**
1901 L St NW
4th Fl
Washington, DC 20036-3506

202-479-1200
Fax: 202-479-0735
E-Mail: info@ncoa.org
Home Page: www.ncoa.org
Social Media: Facebook, Twitter, Youtube, RSS

Richard Browdie, Chair
James Firman, EdD, President and CEO
Jay Greenberg, ScD, CEO, NCOA Services, LLC
Richard Birkel, PhD, MPA, Senior Vice President
Donna Whitt, Senior Vice President

12755 **National Environmental Health Association**
720 S Colorado Blvd
Suite 1000-N
Denver, CO 80246-1926

303-756-9090
866-956-2258
Fax: 303-691-9490
E-Mail: staff@neha.org
Home Page: www.neha.org
Social Media: Facebook, Twitter

Nelson Fabian, Executive Director
Ron Grimes, First VP
Rick Collins, 2nd VP

NEHA offers a variety of programs that are all in keeping with the association's mission which is as relevant today as it was when the organization was founded. The mission of NEHA is to advance the environmental health and protection professional for the purpose of providing a healthful environment for all.
5000 Members
Founded in 1937

12756 **National Managed Health Care Congress**
71 2nd Avenue
3rd Floor
Waltham, MA 02154

888-882-2500
Fax: 941-365-0157
Home Page: www.nmhcc.org

12757 **National Medical Association**
8403 Colesville Road
Suite 820
Silver Spring, MD 20910

202-347-1895
800-257-8290
Fax: 202-347-0722
E-Mail: cme@nmanet.org
Home Page: www.nmanet.org
Social Media: Facebook, Twitter

George L Saunders, III, MD, Chairman
Michael A Lenoir, MD, President
John E Arradondo, M.D., M.P.H, Secretary & Region III Trustee

C Freeman, MD, MBA, Treasurer
Lawrence Sanders, M.D., President-Elect

The mission of the NMA is to advance the art and science of medicine for people of African descent through education, advocacy, and health policy to promote health and wellness, eliminate health disparities, and sustain physician viability.
Founded in 1895

12758 National Renal Administrators Association
100 North 20th Street
Suite 400
Philadelphia, PA 19103-1462

215-320-4655
Fax: 215-564-2175
E-Mail: nraa@nraa.org
Home Page: www.nraa.org/index.php

Wayne Evancoe, President
Marc Chow, Executive Director
Anthony Messana, Secretary
Larry Emerson, Treasurer
Deb Cote, President-Elect

Administrative personnel involved with dialysis programs for patients suffering from kidney failure. Provides a vehicle for the development of educational and informational services for members. Maintains contact with health care facilities and government agencies. Operates placement serve; compiles statistics; conducts political action committee.
475 Members
Founded in 1977

12759 National Rural Health Association
4501 College Blvd
#225
Leawood, KS 66211-1921

816-756-3140
Fax: 816-756-3144
E-Mail: mail@NRHArural.org
Home Page: www.ruralhealthweb.org
Social Media: Facebook, Twitter, LinkedIn

Rebecca Olson, Manager

A national membership organization, whose mission is to improve the health care of rural Americans and to provide leadership on rural issues through advocacy, communications, education and research.

12760 National Society Of Certified Healthcare Business Consultants
12100 Sunset Hills Rd
Suite 130
Reston, VA 20190-3233

703-234-4099
Fax: 703-435-4390
E-Mail: info@nschbc.org
Home Page: www.nschbc.org
Social Media: Facebook, Twitter, LinkedIn, Pineterst, Youtube

Judith Aburmishan, MBA, CPA,, President
Carol Wynne, Executive Director
Ashlyn McKeithan, Program Manager
H. Christopher Zaenger, CHBC, NSCHBC Secretary-Treasurer

Maintains code of ethics, rules of professional conducts, and certification program; administers exams and conduct certification course. Membership by successful completion of certification examination only.
350 Members
Founded in 1975

12761 National Society for Histotechnology
8850 Stanford Boulevard
Suite 2900
Columbia, MD 21045

443-535-4060
Fax: 443-535-4055
E-Mail: histo@nsh.org
Home Page: www.nsh.org
Social Media: Facebook, Twitter, LinkedIn

Beth Sheppard, President
Carrie Diamond, Executive Director
Jerry Santiago, Vice President
Jennifer Hofecker, Secretary
Monty Hyten, Treasurer

A non-profit organization, committed to the advancement of histotechnology, its practitioners and quality standards of practice through leadership, education and advocacy.
Founded in 1974

12762 National Strength and Conditioning Association
1885 Bob Johnson Dr
Colorado Spring, CO 80906-4000

719-632-6722
800-815-6826
Fax: 719-632-6367
E-Mail: nsca@nsca.com
Home Page: www.nsca.com/Home/

Steve Fleck, PhD, CSCS, FNSC, President
Michael Embree, Executive Director
Lee Madden, Chief Financial Officer
David Szymanski, PhD, CSCS,*, Vice-President
Bill Holcomb, PhD, ATC, LAT, Secretary-Treasurer

Develops and presents the most advanced information regarding strength training and conditioning practices, injury prevention, and research findings.
30000 Members
Founded in 1978

12763 Northwest Urological Society
914 164th Street Se
Suite 145
Mill Creek, WA 98012

866-800-3118
Fax: 800-808-4749
E-Mail: support@nwurologicalsociety.org
Home Page: www.nwurologicalsociety.org/

S Larry Goldenberg, President
Martin Gleave, VP

12764 OMA: Optical Industry Association
6055A Arlington Boulevard
Falls Church, VA 22044-2721

703-237-8433
Fax: 703-237-0643

Members are makers and importers of spectacle frames, and related products.
57 Members
Founded in 1916

12765 Optical Society of America
2010 Massachusetts Ave Nw
Washington, DC 20036-1023

202-223-8130
Fax: 202-223-1096
E-Mail: info@osa.org
Home Page: www.osa.org
Social Media: Facebook, Twitter, LinkedIn, Youtube

Donna Strickland, President
Elizabeth A Rogan, Executive Director
Philip Russell, Vice President
Melissa Russell, Chief Industry Relations Officer
Sean Bagshaw, Chief Information Officer

OSA was organized to increase and diffuse the knowledge of optics, pure and applied; to promote the common interests of investigators of optical problems, of designers and of users of optical apparatus of all kinds; and to encourage cooperation among them.
Founded in 1916

12766 Orthopedic Surgical Manufacturers Association
BioMet
PO Box 38805
Germantown, TN 38183-0805

901-758-0806
Fax: 574-372-1790
E-Mail: secretary@osma.net
Home Page: www.osma.net/

Sharon Starowicz, President
Kathy Trier, Vice President
Lori Burns, Secretary
Ed Chin, Treasurer

Members are manufacturers of orthopedic surgical items. Sponsors research, information and ethics programs.
25 Members
Founded in 1954

12767 Pacific Dermatological Association
575 Market Street
Suite 2125
San Francisco, CA 94105

415-927-5729
888-388-8815
Fax: 415-764-4915
E-Mail: pda@hp-assoc.org
Home Page: www.pacificderm.org

Gordon Searles, MD, FRCPC, FA, President
Kent Lindeman, CMP, Executive Director
Janellen Smith, MD, Vice President
Anita Gilliam, MD, Ph.D., Secretary-Treasurer
Catherine Ramsay, MD, President-Elect

Provides opportunitites for exchange of information and advancement of knowledge of dermatology among physicians within the membership area. Execlusively for education, scientific and charitable purposes.

12768 Pacific Northwest Radiological Society
2033 6th Avenue
Suite 1100
Seattle, WA 98121

206-441-9762
800-552-0612
Fax: 206-441-5863
E-Mail: lmk@wsma.org
Home Page: www.pnwrs.org

Jonathan Helwig, MD, President
Crispin Chinn, MD, First Vice President
Teresa Chapman, MD, Second Vice President
Jason Clement, MD, Secretary/Treasurer
Shane Greek, MD, President Elect

12769 Professional Association of Health Care Office Management
1576 Bella Cruz Drive
Suite 360
Lady Lake, FL 32159

847-375-4717
800-451-9311
Fax: 407-386-7006
E-Mail: info@pahcom.com
Home Page: www.pahcom.com
Social Media: Facebook, Twitter, LinkedIn, Youtube

Pam Lewis, CMM, Chairperson
Daniel Labelle, Chief Technology Officer
Karen Blanchette, Association Director
Heather Schumacher, Administrative Assistant
Sherry Sullivan, Conference Manager

A national organization dedicated to promoting professionalism in physician office practice by providing professional development opportunities, continuing education in health care office management principles and practice, and certification for health care office managers.
Founded in 1988

12770 **Radiological Society of North America**
820 Jorie Blvd
Oak Brook, IL 60523-2251
630-571-2670
800-381-6660
Fax: 630-571-7837
Home Page: www.rsna.org
Social Media: Facebook, Twitter, LinkedIn, Flickr, Youtube
Ronald L Arenson, MD, Chairman
Sarah S Donaldson, MD, President
N Reed Dunnick, MD, President-elect and Secretary
Richard T Hoppe, MD, First Vice-President
James D Fraser, MD, Second Vice-President
The mission is to promote and develop the highest standards of radiology and related sciences through education and research. The society seeks to provide radiologists and allied health scientists with educational programs and materials of the highest quality and to constantly improve the content and value of these educational activities.

12771 **Radiology Business Management Association**
10300 Eaton Place
Suite 460
Fairfax, VA 22030
703-621-3355
888-224-7262
Fax: 703-621-3356
E-Mail: info@rbma.org
Home Page: www.rbma.org
Social Media: Facebook, Twitter, LinkedIn
Mike Mabry, Executive Director
The only radiology-specific business organization in existence today. Dedicated to providing managers with information, resources, educatio and networking to run a successful radiology business.
2200 Members
Founded in 1968

12772 **Sisters Network: National Headquarters**
2922 Rosedale Street
Houston, TX 77004
713-781-0255
866-781-1808
Fax: 713-780-8998
E-Mail: infonet@sistersnetworkinc.org
Home Page: www.sistersnetworkinc.org
Social Media: Facebook, Twitter, Youtube
Karen Jackson, Founder & CEO
Erie E Calloway, Executive Director
Bettie Eubanks, Vice Chair
Dr John Green, Treasurer
Kelly P Hodges, National Program Director
Committed to increasing local and national attention to the devastating impact that breast cancer has in the African American community.
3000 Members
Founded in 1994

12773 **Society for Healthcare Strategy and Market Development**
155 North Wacker Drive
Chicago, IL 60606-3421
312-422-3888
Fax: 312-278-0883
E-Mail: shsmd@aha.org
Home Page: www.shsmd.org/
Holli Salls, President
Diane Weber, RN, ExecutiveÿDirector
Emily McCracken, Senior Manager, Membership
Lisa Hinkle, MS, Education Manager
Mollie Welsh, Interactive Marketing Specialist
The society of choice for thousands of healthcare marketing, public relations, strategic planning, communications and business development professionals.
4000 Members
Founded in 1996

12774 **Society for Imaging Informatics In Medicine**
19440 Golf Vista Plaza
Suite 330
Leesburg, VA 20176-8264
703-723-0432
Fax: 703-723-0415
E-Mail: info@siimweb.org
Home Page: www.siim.org
Social Media: Facebook, Twitter, LinkedIn, Google Plus, Youtube
J Raymond Geis, MD, Chair
William W Boonn, MD, Secretary
James T Whitfill, MD, CIIP, Treasurer
David E Brown, CIIP, President-Elect
Devoted to advance informatics and information technology in medical imaging through education and research. Provides an open environment for imaging information professionals to access expert and cutting edge resources in a collegial and practical atmosphere.
2200 Members
Founded in 1980

12775 **Society of Critical Care Medicine**
500 Midway Dr
Mt Prospect, IL 60056-5811
847-827-6869
Fax: 847-827-6886
E-Mail: info@sccm.org
Home Page: www.sccm.org
Carol Thompson, President
David J Martin, Chief Executive Officer
Brian Schramm, Director Business Affairs
Professional organization devoted exclusively to the advancement of multidisciplinary, multiprofessional intensive care through excellence in patient care, education, research, and advocacy.
11000 Members
Founded in 1972

12776 **Society of Medical-Dental Management**
125 Strafford Avenue
Suite 300
Wayne, PA 19087-3318
800-826-2264
Fax: 610-687-7702
E-Mail: patricia01@aol.com
Home Page: www.smdmc.org
Joseph Cobo, President
Richard G Bock, Regional Director/Coordinator
Rex Stanley, Secretary/Treasurer
Professional medical and/or dental management consultants associated for educational and information sharing purposes. Objectives are to: advance the profession; share management techniques; improve individual skills; provide clients with competent and capable business management. Provides information on insurance and income tax. Conducts surveys; compiles statistics.
60+ Members
Founded in 1968

12777 **Society of NeuroInterventional Surgery**
3975 Fair Ridge Dr
Suite 460 South
Fairfax, VA 22033
703-691-2272
Fax: 703-537-0650
E-Mail: info@snisonline.org
Home Page: www.snisonline.org
Social Media: Facebook, Twitter
Philip M. Meyers, MD, President
Donald F. Frei, MD, Vice President
Marie Williams, CAE, Executive Director
Eddie Woods, Director of Member Services
Anthony Portillo, Administrative Coordinator
Formerly the American Society of Interventional and Therapeutic Neuroradiology, mission is to promote excellence in patient care, provide education, support research, influence health care policy, and foster the growth of the specialty.
3000 Members
Founded in 1962

12778 **Society of Nuclear Medicine & Molecular Imaging**
1850 Samuel Morse Dr
Reston, VA 20190-5316
703-708-9000
Fax: 703-708-9015
E-Mail: volunteer@snm.org
Home Page: www.snm.org
Social Media: Facebook, Twitter, LinkedIn, Youtube
Virginia Pappas, Executive Director
Nicole Kern, Program Manager
Setha Golds, Senior Educational Manager
Laura Myers, Controller
International scientific and professional organization that promotes the science, technology and practical applications of nuclear medicine.
15000 Members
Founded in 1954

12779 **Southern Medical Association**
35 W Lakeshore Dr
Birmingham, AL 35209-7254
205-945-8903
800-423-4992
Fax: 205-945-1830
E-Mail: CustomerService@sma.org
Home Page: www.sma.org
Social Media: Facebook, Twitter, Youtube
Ed Waldron, CEO
Physician's choice for education and support to enhance practice and performance and career development.
88 Members
Founded in 1906

12780 **TLPA Annual Convention & Trade Show**
Taxicab, Limousine & Paratransit Association
3200 Tower Oaks Boulevard
Suite 220
Rockville, MD 20852
301-984-5700
Fax: 301-984-5703
E-Mail: info@tlpa.com
Home Page: www.tlpa.com
Robert Werth, President
Alfred LaGasse, Chief Executive Officer
Michael Levine, Treasurer
Michael Fogarty, President-Elect
Shares information vital to owners or taxicab, limousine, airport shuttle, paratransit and nonemergency medical transportation fleets. 100 supplier exhibits of the newest products available to the industry.
1000 Attendees
Frequency: Annual

12781 The American Association of Tissue Banks
8200 Greensboro Drive
Suite 320
McLean, VA ÿ22102
703-827-9582
Fax: 703-356-2198
Home Page: www.aatb.org
Social Media: Facebook, Twitter, LinkedIn
Frank Wilton, CEO
Scott Brubaker, Chief Policy Officer
Kathy Crandall, Director of Finance & Admin
Jamien Payne, Director of Membership & Marketing
Kerry Bolton, Education Coordinator
Transplant trade organization dedicated to ensuring that human tissues intended for transplantation are safe and free of infectious disease and available in quantities sufficient to meet national needs.
Founded in 1976

12782 The American Chiropractic Association
1701 Clarendon Boulevard
Suite 200
Arlington, VA 22209
703-276-8800
Fax: 703-243-2593
E-Mail: memberinfo@acatoday.org
Home Page: www.acatoday.org
Social Media: Facebook, Twitter, LinkedIn, RSS, YouTube, Instagram
John Falardeau, SVP, Govt. Relations
Janet Ridgely, Deputy Executive Vice President
Kim Hodes, VP, Finance
Jim Potter, CEO
Dean Millard, Senior Dir., Information System
Professional organization representing chiropractors.

Newsletters

12783 AAB Bulletin
American Association of Bioanalysts
906 Olive Street
Suite 1200
Saint Louis, MO 63101-1448
314-241-1445
Fax: 314-241-1449
E-Mail: aab@aab.org
Home Page: www.aab.org
Mark S Biernbaum PhD, Administrator
Newsletter that provides the latest information on meetings, conferences, legislative and regulatoryy issues and developments.
Frequency: Quarterly
Founded in 1956

12784 AABB News
American Association of Blood Banks
8101 Glenbrook Rd
Suite 2
Bethesda, MD 20814-2747
301-907-6977
Fax: 301-907-6895
E-Mail: aabb@aabb.org
Home Page: www.aabb.org
Karen Lipton, CEO
Frequency: Monthly

12785 AAMI News
Assoc for the Advancement of Medical Instrumentat
4301 N. Fairfax Drive
Suite 301
Arlington, VA 22203-1633
703-525-4890
Fax: 703-276-0793
E-Mail: publications@aami.org
Home Page: www.aami.org
Sean Loughlin, Publications Director
Robert King, Editor
Keeps individuals up-to-date with timely and relevant infustry news, breaking information about new standards activities and AAMI benefits, and guidance from experts in the field.
Cost: $160.00
Frequency: Monthly
Circulation: 6000

12786 AAMI News Extra!
Assoc for the Advancement of Medical Instrumentat
4301 N. Fairfax Drive
Suite 301
Arlington, VA 22203-1633
703-525-4890
Fax: 703-276-0793
E-Mail: publications@aami.org
Home Page: www.aami.org
Sean Loughlin, Publications Director
Online newsletter that includes the top stories of the month; an up-to-date listing of career opportunities in the field; and updates on AAMI's standards, benefits, and services.
Frequency: Monthly

12787 ACOG Clinical Review
American College of Obstetricians/Gynecologists
409 12th Street SW
PO Box 96920
Washington, DC 20090-6920
202-638-5577
Fax: 202-484-5107
E-Mail: resources@acog.org
Home Page: www.acog.org
Kathleen Harrison, Advertising
Frequency: 6 X

12788 ACOS News
American College of Osteopathic Surgeons
123 N Henry Street
Alexandria, VA 22314-2903
703-684-0416
Fax: 703-684-3280
E-Mail: info@facos.org
Home Page: www.facos.org
Guy Beaumont, Executive Director
Judith T Mangum, Director Finance
Frequency: Monthly

12789 ACOS Review
American College of Osteopathic Surgeons
330 E Algonquin Rd
Suite 1
Arlington Hts, IL 60005-4665
847-228-6090
800-323-0794
Fax: 847-228-9755
Home Page: www.acofp.org
Peter Schmelzer, Executive Director
Frequency: Monthly

12790 AMGA's Advocacy ENewS
American Medical Group Association
One Prince Street
Alexandria, VA 22314-3318
703-838-0033
Fax: 703-548-1890
Home Page: www.amga.org
Don Fisher, CEO
Ryan O'Connor, VP, Membership/Marketing
Timely analysis on the latest issues that affect medical groups on the federal legislative and regulatory front.
375 Members

12791 AOA News
American Optometric Association
243 N Lindbergh Blvd
Suite 1
St Louis, MO 63141-7881
314-991-4100
Fax: 314-991-4101
E-Mail: info@iacconline.org
Home Page: www.aoa.org
Barry Barresi, Executive Director
Tom Cappucci, First Vice President
Michael Jones, CEO
Official newspaper of the American Optometric Association
Cost: $93.50
Circulation: 30000
ISSN: 0094-9620
Founded in 1896
Mailing list available for rent: 22,500 names at $70 per M
Printed in 4 colors on glossy stock

12792 Adult Day Services Letter
Health Resources Publishing
1913 Atlantic Ave
Suite 200
Manasquan, NJ 08736-1067
732-292-1100
Fax: 732-292-1111
E-Mail: info@healthresourcesonline.com
Home Page: www.healthresourcesonline.com
Robert K Jenkins, Publisher
Brett Powell, Regional Director
Alice Burron, Director
A monthly newsletter that contains management information, reports on trends and new developments and information about other adult day care programs across the country.
Cost: $147.00
38574 Pages
Frequency: Monthly
ISSN: 0885-4572
Founded in 1985

12793 BNA's Health Law Reporter
Bureau of National Affairs
1801 S Bell St
Arlington, VA 22202-4501
703-341-3000
800-372-1033
Fax: 800-253-0332
E-Mail: customercare@bna.com
Home Page: www.bnabooks.com
Paul N Wojcik, CEO
Of many newsletters from BNA, this contains information on health care policy, bankruptcy, antitrust, insurance and state developments, employment issues as well as a congressional and a regulatory calendar.
Cost: $1782.00
Frequency: Weekly

12794 Biomedical Market Newsletter
Biomedical Market
3237 Idaho Pl
Costa Mesa, CA 92626-2207
714-434-9500
800-875-8181

Fax: 714-434-9755
E-Mail: info@biomedical-market-news.com
Home Page: www.biomedical-market-news.com

David G Anast, President
Steve Baker, Director of Marketing/Sales
Richard Guiss, Senior Editor
George Anast, CFO

New business development, FDA, regulatory, financial, and marketing NL on medical equipment, device, diagnostic test and instrument industries worldwide.
Cost: $199.00
Frequency: Monthly
ISSN: 1064-4180
Founded in 1991
Printed in 4 colors on matte stock

12795 Bulletin on Long-Term Care Law
Health Resources Publishing
1913 Atlantic Ave
Suite 200
Manasquan, NJ 08736-1067

732-292-1100
Fax: 732-292-1111
E-Mail: info@healthresourcesonline.com
Home Page: www.healthresourcesonline.com

Robert K Jenkins, Publisher
Lisa Mansfield, Regional Director
Brett Powell, Regional Director
Alice Burron, Director

A newsletter that covers compliance problems, Medicaid and Medicare overhauls, charges of abuse, fraud, negligence, needless litigation and other concerns of those involved in long-term health care.
Cost: $227.00
Frequency: Monthly
ISSN: 1093-6939
Founded in 1978

12796 Communique
213 W Institute Place
Suite 307
Chicago, IL 60610-3195

312-440-0078
800-962-8274
Fax: 312-440-9474
E-Mail: mailbox@iahcsmm.com
Home Page: www.iahcsmm.com

Betty Hanna, Executive Director
Marilyn Corida, Secretary/Treasurer
Lisa Huber, President

Bi-monthly publication separates supervisors/directors from technicians.
Cost: $40.00
Frequency: 6/Annual
Circulation: 15M
ISBN: 1-605309-30-9
Mailing list available for rent: 13000 names

12797 Diagnostic Testing & Technology Report
Institute of Management and Administration
1 Washington Park
Suite 1300
Newark, NJ 07102

212-244-0360
Fax: 973-622-0595
Home Page: www.ioma.com

Contains up-to-the minute information and unique perspectives on where diagnostic testing is headed, covering every innovation, new product, manufacturer, market and end-user applications.
Cost: $549.00
Frequency: Monthly

12798 Directions: Looking Ahead in Healthcare
Health Resources Publishing
1913 Atlantic Ave
Suite 200
Manasquan, NJ 08736-1067

732-292-1100
888-843-6242
Fax: 732-292-1111
E-Mail: info@healthresourcesonline.com
Home Page: www.healthresourcesonline.com

Robert K Jenkins, Publisher
Lisa Mansfield, Marketing Assistant
Carolin Pense, Publisher
Brett Powell, Regional Director
Alice Burron, Director

Provides management news on such topics as alerts, trends, forecasts, profitable innovations, facts and statistics.
Cost: $127.00
Frequency: Monthly
ISSN: 1093-6920
Founded in 1978

12799 Dispatch & Division Newsletters
Taxicab, Limousine & Paratransit Association
3200 Tower Oaks Blvd
Suite 220
Rockville, MD 20852

301-984-5700
Fax: 301-984-5703
E-Mail: info@tlpa.org
Home Page: www.tlpa.org

Alfred LaGasse, CEO
Victor Dizengoff, President

Dispatch features articles on industry business issues, provides advice on running a transportation company, and comes with division specific bi-monthly newsletters.
Frequency: Bimonthly
Circulation: 6000

12800 Elderly Health Services Letter
Health Resources Publishing
1913 Atlantic Ave
Suite 200
Manasquan, NJ 08736-1067

732-292-1100
888-843-6242
Fax: 732-292-1111
E-Mail: info@themcic.com
Home Page: www.healthresourcesonline.com

Robert K Jenkins, Publisher
Lisa Mansfield, Regional Director
Brett Powell, Regional Director
Alice Burron, Director

A newsletter on projections and trends for health services provided for the elderly. Subjects include inpatient care, long-term care, outpatient, home care, primary care, ambulatory care, day care, health promotion, disease prevention, support groups, health education and residental care.
Cost: $227.00
Frequency: Monthly
ISSN: 0891-9275

12801 Emergency Department Law
Business Publishers
8737 Colesville Road
Suite 1100
Silver Spring, MD 20910-3928

301-876-6300
800-274-6737
Fax: 301-589-8493
E-Mail: custserv@bpinews.com
Home Page: www.bpinews.com

Leonard A Eiserer, Publisher
James Lawlor, Editor

Devoted entirely to legal issues pertinent to emergency medicine, and covers monthly the latest case law, legal trends, risk management, tort reform and explains how they could impact your emergency care facility.
Cost: $357.00
Frequency: Monthly

12802 Employee Assistance Program Management Letter
Health Resources Publishing
1913 Atlantic Ave
Suite 200
Manasquan, NJ 08736-1067

732-292-1100
888-843-6242
Fax: 732-292-1111
E-Mail: info@themcic.com
Home Page: www.healthresourcesonline.com

Robert K Jenkins, Publisher
Lisa Mansfield, Regional Director
Brett Powell, Regional Director
Alice Burron, Director

A briefing published monthly on the range of influences surrounding your employee assistance program.
Cost: $237.00
Frequency: Monthly
ISSN: 0896-0941
Founded in 1978

12803 Executive Report on Integrated Care & Capitation
Managed Care Information Center
1913 Atlantic Ave
Suite 200
Manasquan, NJ 08736-1067

732-292-1100
888-843-6242
Fax: 732-292-1111
E-Mail: info@themcic.com
Home Page: www.themcic.com

Robert K Jenkins, Publisher
Joseph Schmidt, Editor

A newsletter published twice a month to keep readers informed of the competitive market. Gives facts on strategic issues, mergers and acquisitions, market facts, economics, network alliances and plan affiliations.
Cost: $447.00
Frequency: Monthly
ISSN: 1085-3103

12804 Executive Report on Managed Care
Managed Care Information Center
1913 Atlantic Ave
Suite 200
Manasquan, NJ 08736-1067

732-292-1100
888-843-6242
Fax: 732-292-1111
E-Mail: info@themcic.com
Home Page: www.themcic.com

Robert K Jenkins, Publisher

A monthly report that gives news of how major employers are implementing their managed care programs. The report also aids companies in preparing to evaluate and monitor different managed care proposals to determine cost effectiveness, quality and liability to the employer.
Cost: $437.00
ISSN: 0898-9753

12805 Executive Report on Physician Organizations
Managed Care Information Center
1913 Atlantic Ave
Suite 200
Manasquan, NJ 08736-1067

732-292-1100
888-843-6242
Fax: 732-292-1111

E-Mail: info@themcic.com
Home Page: www.themcic.com

Robert K Jenkins, Publisher

The newsletter covers mergers, acquisitions, practice management agreements and strategic planes implemented in the physician marketplace. Also provides information about the ways that managed care and goverment regulations affect the physician marketplace.
Cost: $257.00
8-10 Pages
Frequency: 12 per year
ISSN: 1097-7309
Founded in 1998

12806 **Eye-Mail Monthly**
American Academy of Optometry
6110 Executive Blvd
Suite 506
Rockville, MD 20852-3929

301-984-1441
Fax: 301-984-4737
E-Mail: aaoptom@aaoptom.org
Home Page: www.aaopt.org

Lois Schoenbrun, Executive Director
Frequency: Monthly

12807 **G-2 Compliance Report**
Institute of Management and Administration
1 Washington Park
Suite 1300
Newark, NJ 07102

212-244-0360
Fax: 973-622-0595
Home Page: www.ioma.com

Designed to guide hospital, lab, and pathology professionals in developing, implementing and revising compliance programs to meet federal standards.
Cost: $469.00

12808 **HCEA Edge**
Healthcare Convention & Exhibitors Association
5775 Peachtree Dnwdy Rd
Building G, Suite 500
Atlanta, GA 30342-1556

404-252-3663
Fax: 404-252-0774
E-Mail: hcea@kellencompany.com
Home Page: www.hcea.org

Eric Allen, Executive Vice President
Nancy Hoppe, President

News and events of the trade association of over 600 organizations involved in healthcare exhibiting or providing services to healthcare conventions, exhibitions and/or meetings.
Frequency: Monthly, Members Only

12809 **HFMA's The Business of Caring**
Healthcare Financial Management Association
Two Westbrook Corporate Center
Suite 700
Westchester, IL 60154-5700

708-319-9600
800-252-4362
Fax: 708-531-0032
Home Page: www.hfma.org/boc

Robert Fromberg, Editor-in-Chief
Maggie Van Dyke, Product Manager & Editor
Chris Burke, Advertising Manager
Kurt Belisle, Sponsorhip Manager

Helps nurse managers navigate the business side of health care to become successful hospital leaders. Topics discussed include: budgeting, workforce management, cost containment, and IT implementation. Available Free Online.
Frequency: Quarterly

12810 **HMFA Healthcare Cost Containment Newsletter**
Healthcare Finance Management Association
3 Westbrook Corporate Center
Suite 600
Westchester, IL 60154

708-531-9600
Fax: 708-531-0032
Home Page: www.hfma.org/publications/healthcarecost

Issues illustrate how to implement strategic cost management that will reduce labor and supply expenses, enhance operational efficiency, satisfy your patients, and improve your competitive position.
Cost: $125.00
Frequency: Quarterly
Mailing list available for rent

12811 **HMFA Revenue Cycle Stragetist Newsletter**
Healthcare Finance Management Association
3 Westbrook Corporate Center
Suite 600
Westchester, IL 60154

708-531-9600
Fax: 708-531-0032
Home Page: www.hfma.org/publications/

Improve your organization's bottom line while maintaining regulatory compliance.
Cost: $165.00
Frequency: Quarterly
Mailing list available for rent

12812 **Health Care Reimbursement Monitor**
Health Resources Publishing
1913 Atlantic Ave
Suite 200
Manasquan, NJ 08736-1067

732-292-1100
888-843-6242
Fax: 732-292-1111
E-Mail: info@themcic.com
Home Page: www.healthresourcesonline.com

Robert K Jenkins, Publisher
Lisa Mansfield, Regional Director
Brett Powell, Regional Director
Alice Burron, Director

A monthly newsletter that covers the latest details of actions taken or proposals in Washington concerning changes to the BBA; updates on Medicaid and Medicare budget and reimbursement issues; reimbursement news for hospital operations executives as well as top financial management. Reimbursement briefings cover hospitals, home health care, long-term care, hospice, ambulatory care and physician payment.
Cost: $257.00
Frequency: Monthly

12813 **Health Product Marketing**
PRS Group
6320 Fly Rd
Suite 102
East Syracuse, NY 13057-9792

315-431-0511
Fax: 315-431-0200
E-Mail: custserv@prsgroup.com
Home Page: www.prsgroup.com

Mary Lou Walsh, President
Ben McTernan, Managing Editor
Patti Davis, Circulation Manager
Patty Redhead, Production Manager

Provides current information, analysis and ideas for strategic planning in the health industry.
ISSN: 1520-3271
Founded in 1979

12814 **Healthcare Market Reporter**
Managed Care Information Center
1913 Atlantic Ave
Suite 200
Manasquan, NJ 08736-1067

732-292-1100
888-843-6242
Fax: 732-292-1111
E-Mail: info@themcic.com
Home Page: www.themcic.com

Robert K Jenkins, Publisher

Twice-a-month newsletter to help you abreast of the fiercely competitive market. Get the facts and details you'll need on strategies issues, market facts, mergers and acquisitions, economics, network alliances and plan affiliations.
Cost: $457.00
10 Pages
ISSN: 1073-6816

12815 **Healthcare Marketers Executive Briefing**
Health Resources Publishing
1913 Atlantic Ave
Suite 200
Manasquan, NJ 08736-1067

732-292-1100
Fax: 732-292-1111
E-Mail: info@healthresourcesonline.com
Home Page: www.healthresourcesonline.com

Robert K Jenkins, Publisher
Lisa Mansfield, Regional Director
Brett Powell, Regional Director
Alice Burron, Director

Helps managers stay informed of the latest innovations and changes in the health care field. Gives contact information for other community relations, publication practioners, administrators and marketing and advertising professonals.
Cost: $237.00
Frequency: Monthly
ISSN: 0894-9980

12816 **Healthcare PR & Marketing News**
Phillips Business Information
1201 Seven Locks Road
Potomac, MD 20854-2931

301-354-1400
888-707-5814
Fax: 301-309-3847
Home Page: www.prandmarketing.com

Matthew Schwartz, Editor
Diane Schwartz, Publisher
Amy Urban, Marketing Manager

Issues faced by health care executives in PR firms and hospitals. Regular features include industry surveys, case studies and executive profiles.
Cost: $397.00
Founded in 1944

12817 **Healthcare e-Business Manager**
Managed Care Information Center
1913 Atlantic Ave
Suite 200
Manasquan, NJ 08736-1067

732-292-1100
888-843-5242
Fax: 732-292-1111
E-Mail: info@themcic.com
Home Page: www.themcic.com

Robert K Jenkins, Publisher

Monthly executive briefing on the latest developments in the proliferation of electronic commerce among healthcare and managed care organization. Focuses on the internet marketplace, reports on trends in the industry and predictions of where the market seems to be

heading.
Cost: $477.00
10 Pages
ISSN: 1526-6052

12818 Hospice Letter
Health Resources Publishing
1913 Atlantic Ave
Suite 200
Manasquan, NJ 08736-1067

732-292-1100
888-843-6242
Fax: 732-292-1111
E-Mail: info@themcic.com
Home Page: www.healthresourcesonline.com

Robert K Jenkins, Publisher
Lisa Mansfield, Regional Director
Brett Powell, Regional Director
Alice Burron, Director

Monthly newsletter reporting the latest development in the rapidly hospice concept of caring for the terminally ill. Ready by administrators and directors who follow Medicare reimbursement and hospice accreditation. How hospices are raising money and staging community events; new legislation and regulations and the latest on nursing care, volunteers and counseling programs. Delivery options: via mail or e-mail (indicate PDF or HTML format)
Cost: $227.00
10 Pages
Frequency: Monthly
ISSN: 0913-6816
Founded in 1978

12819 Integrated Healthcare News
American Association of Integrated Healthcare
4435 Waterfront Drive
Suite 101
Glen Allen, VA 23060

804-747-5823
Fax: 804-747-5316
E-Mail: bwilliams@aainds.org
Home Page: www.aaihds.org

Jerry Williams, Editorial
Mark Abernathy, Managing Director
Dalal Haldeman, PhD, MBA, Director, Marketing Operations

12820 Journal of the American Association of Forensic Dentists
1000 N Avenue
Waukegan, IL 60085

847-244-0292
E-Mail: info@andent.net
Home Page: www.andent.net

Quarterly journal that brings forensic dental knowledge not only to dentists and their staff, but also to anthropologists, attorneys and law enforcement personnel.
3000 Pages
Founded in 1978

12821 Legislative Alert
Taxicab, Limousine & Paratransit Association
3200 Tower Oaks Blvd
Suite 220
Rockville, MD 20852

301-984-5700
Fax: 301-984-5703
E-Mail: info@tlpa.org
Home Page: www.tlpa.org

Alfred LaGasse, CEO
William Rouse, President
Harold Morgan, Executive Vice President
Michelle A. Hariston, CMP, Manager of Meetings
Leah New, Manager of Communications

TLPA's members-only bulletin of early alerts to critical changes in the industry, announcing threats and opportunities on issues that are before Congress and federal agencies. Organizes operators to take action, and provides knowledge and awareness.
Circulation: 6000
Founded in 1917
Mailing list available for rent

12822 Medical Group Management Update
Medical Group Management Association
104 Inverness Ter E
Englewood, CO 80112-5313

303-799-1111
Fax: 303-643-9599
E-Mail: infocenter@mgma.com
Home Page: www.mgma.com

William Jessee, CEO
Eileen Barker, senior Vice President
Anders Gilberg, senior Vice President
Natalie Jamieson, Administrative Assistant

Monthly association newspaper offering up-to-the-minute articles on current legislation, practical management, health care trends, association activities and other timely subjects.
Frequency: Monthly

12823 National Intelligence Report
Institute of Management and Administration
1 Washington Park
Suite 1300
Newark, NJ 07102-3130

212-244-0360
Fax: 973-622-0595
E-Mail: customercare@bna.com
Home Page: www.ioma.com

Provides concise, independent coverage and analysis of fast-breaking lab, pathology, blood banking, imaging and diagnostic radiology news from the Nation's Capital.
Cost: $489.00
Frequency: Biweekly

12824 Nephrology News and Issues
Nephrology News and Issues
17797 N Perimeter Dr
Suite 109
Scottsdale, AZ 85255-5455
480-443-4635
Fax: 480-443-4528
E-Mail: info@nephnews.com
Home Page: www.nephronline.com

Melissa Laudenschlager, Publisher
Mark Neumann, Editor
Marcia Coutts, Circulation Manager
Cost: $55.00
Frequency: Monthly
Circulation: 22000
Founded in 1986

12825 News Now
American Physical Therapy Association
1111 N Fairfax St
Alexandria, VA 22314-1488

703-684-2782
Fax: 703-706-8536
E-Mail: memberservices@apta.org
Home Page: www.apta.org
Social Media: Facebook, Twitter, LinkedIn

Maryann DiGiacomo, Editor
John D. Barnes, Chief Executive Officer
Janet Bezner, VP, Education, Governance
Rob Batarla, VP, Finance & Business Development
Felicity Clancy, VP, Communications & Marketing

Reports timely legislative, health care, and Association news to APTA members and subscribers.
80000 Members
Frequency: Weekly
Mailing list available for rent

12826 Nurses' Notes
American Association of Managed Care Nurses
4435 Waterfront Dr
Suite 101
Glen Allen, VA 23060-3393

804-747-9698
Fax: 804-747-5316
E-Mail: keads@aamcn.org
Home Page: www.aamcn.org

Bill Williams, President

A quarterly newsletter published by the American Association of Managed Care Nurses. Available to members only.
Circulation: 2000

12827 Nursing News Update
American Association of Managed Care Nurses
4435 Waterfront Dr
Suite 101
Glen Allen, VA 23060-3393

804-747-9698
Fax: 804-747-5316
E-Mail: keads@aamcn.org
Home Page: www.aamcn.org

Bill Williams, President
Laura Givens, Executive Admin

A weekly electronic newsletter published by the American Association of Managed Care Nurses. Available to members only.
Circulation: 2000

12828 Physician's News Digest
Physician's New Digest
230 Windsor Ave
Suite 216
Narberth, PA 19072-2217

610-668-1040
800-220-6109
Fax: 610-668-9177
E-Mail: info@physiciansnews.com
Home Page: www.physiciansnews.com

Jeffery Barg, CEO/President
Christopher Gaudagnino, Business Manager
Ben Birenbaum, Business Manager
Cost: $35.00
Frequency: Monthly
Circulation: 40000
ISSN: 1079-6312
Founded in 1987
Printed in 4 colors on newsprint stock

12829 Public Health
State Capitals Newsletters
PO Box 7376
Alexandria, VA 22307-7376

703-768-9600
Fax: 703-768-9690
Home Page: statecapitals.com
Cost: $245.00

Frequency: Weekly

12830 Sisters Network/National Newsletter
Sisters Network
2922 Rosedale St
Suite 4206
Houston, TX 77004-6188

713-781-0255
866-781-1808
Fax: 713-780-8998

E-Mail: infonet@sistersnetworkinc.org
Home Page: www.sistersnetworkinc.org

Erie Calloway, Executive Director
Karen E. Jackson, CEO
Caleen Burtonalleen, Public Relations Manager
Cherlyn K Latham, Project Director
Kelly P. Hodges, National Program Director

Publication of the group committed to awareness of the impact that breast cancer has on the African American community, with the latest information, medical research and news about events taking place within the Sisters National Network of affiliate chapters.
Frequency: Monthly
Founded in 1994

12831 Today's School Psychologist
LRP Publications
747 Dresher Road
PO Box 980
Horsham, PA 19044-2247

215-784-0912
800-341-7874
Fax: 215-784-9639
E-Mail: webmaster@lrp.com
Home Page: www.lrp.com

Caroline Miller, Editor

In-depth guide to a school psychologists job, offering proactive strategies and tips for handling day-to-day tasks and responsibilities, encouraging change and improving professional standing and performance.
Cost: $135.00
Frequency: Monthly

12832 US Medicine Newsletter
US Medicine
39 York Street
Suite 400
Lambertville, NJ 08530

609-397-5522
Fax: 609-397-4237
E-Mail: usmedicine@usmedicine.com
Home Page: www.usmedicine.com

James F Breuning, Publisher
Brenda L. Mooney, Editorial Director
Stephen Spotswood, Correspondent
Beth Scholz, Account Manager
Anita Crandall, Production Manager

US Medicine is an organization that supports physicians and healthcare workers with medical and legal information. Publishes a newspaper. Founded in 1964.
9 Members
Founded in 1964

12833 Walking Tomorrow
Christopher Reeve Paralysis Foundation
500 Morris Ave
Springfield, NJ 07081-1027

973-467-5915
800-225-0292
Fax: 973-912-9433
Home Page: www.christopherreeve.org/

Julie Kwon, Director of Marketing
Kathy Lewis, Controller
Ed Jobst, Controller

Newsletter of the Christopher Reeve Paralysis Foundation.
Frequency: Monthly
Founded in 1982

12834 Wellness Program Management Advisor
Health Resources Publishing
1913 Atlantic Ave
Suite 200
Manasquan, NJ 08736-1067

732-292-1100
888-843-6242
Fax: 732-292-1111
E-Mail: info@themcic.com
Home Page: www.healthresourcesonline.com

Robert K Jenkins, Publisher
Lisa Mansfield, Regional Director
Brett Powell, Regional Director
Alice Burron, Director

A newsletter that is designed to help professionals manage their organization's health promotion and wellness programs. Gives information about how other wellness programs are doing in such areas as strategies adopted, expenses and return on investments. Also included are in depth profiles of wellness programs around the country that list the problems that they encountered and the steps that they took to alter them.
Cost: $247.00
Frequency: Monthly
ISSN: 1085-7125

Magazines & Journals

12835 24 X 7
HealthTech Publishing Company
6100 Center Drive
Suite 1000
Los Angeles, CA 90045

310-642-4400
Fax: 310-641-4444
E-Mail: tantikadjian@medpubs.com
Home Page: www.24x7mag.com

Tony Ramos, Publisher
Kelly Stephens, Editor
Jennifer Bezahler, Circulation Manager

News and business magazine for the healthcare service support and technology management industry.
Frequency: Monthly
Circulation: 15000
ISSN: 1091-1626
Founded in 1996
Printed in 4 colors on glossy stock

12836 AAMA Executive
American Academy of Medical Administrators
701 Lee St
Suite 600
Des Plaines, IL 60016-4516

847-759-8601
800-621-6902
Fax: 847-759-8602
E-Mail: info@aameda.org
Home Page: www.aameda.org

Renee Schleichar, CEO
Nancy L Anderson, Director of Education
Guy Snyder, Director of Education
Rhonda Guptill, Chief Financial Officer
Cost: $90.00
Frequency: Quarterly
Founded in 1957

12837 AAPS Newsmagazine
American Association of Pharmaceutical Scientists
2107 Wilson Blvd
Suite 700
Arlington, VA 22201-3042

703-243-2800
Fax: 703-243-9054
E-Mail: aaps@aaps.org
Home Page: www.aaps.org

John Lisack, Executive Director
Joy Metcalf, Managing Editor
Janelle Kihlstrom, Editorial Assistant
Ken Corch, Executive Assistant

Exclusive to AAPS members. Features expanded coverage of the industry, complete with expert information on marketplace trends, regulatory matters, and career opportunities.
Mailing list available for rent

12838 AAPS PharmSciTech Journal
American Association of Pharmaceutical Scientists
2107 Wilson Blvd
Suite 700
Arlington, VA 22201-3042

703-243-2800
Fax: 703-243-9054
E-Mail: aaps@aaps.org
Home Page: www.aaps.org

John Lisack, Executive Director
Joy Metcalf, Managing Editor
James Greif, Communications Specialist
Ken Corch, Executive Assistant

An online-only journal published and owned by the American Association of Pharmaceutical Scientists. The journal's mission is to disseminate scientific and technical information on drug product design, development, evaluation and processing to the global pharmaceutical research community, taking full advantage of web-based publishing by presenting innovative text with 3-D graphics, interactive figures and databases, video and audio files.
ISSN: 1530-9932
Mailing list available for rent

12839 AARP The Magazine
American Association of Retired Persons
601 E St NW
Washington, DC 20049-0003

202-434-2277
888-687-2277
202-434-3525
Fax: 202-434-7599
E-Mail: member@aarp.org
Home Page: www.aarp.org

Hop Backus, Executive Vice President
Steve Cone, Executive Vice President
Joann Jenkins, Foundation President
A. Barry Rand, Chief Executive Officer
Cindy Lewin, General Counsel

AARP is a nonprofit, nonpartisan organization with a membership that helps people age 50 and over have independence, choice and control in ways that are beneficial and affordable to them and society as a whole, ways that help people 50 and over improve their lives. Founded through support from staffed offices in all 50 states.
Frequency: Monthly
Founded in 1958
Mailing list available for rent

12840 ACSM's Health & Fitness Journal
Lippincott Williams & Wilkins
351 W Camden St
Baltimore, MD 21201-2436

410-949-8000
800-222-3790
Fax: 410-528-4414
Home Page: www.lww.com

J Arnold Anthony, Operations
Michael Hargrett, Publisher
Edward Howley, Editor-in-Chief

The Journal strives to help health and fitness practitioners improve their knowledge and experience through reports and recommendations from experts, CEC offerings, opportunities to question the experts, listings of job openings and more.
Cost: $40.00
Frequency: Fortnightly
Circulation: 11144
ISSN: 1091-5397
Founded in 1997
Printed in 4 colors on matte stock

12841 ADA Courier
American Dietetic Association
120 South Riverside Plaza
Suite 2000
Chicago, IL 60606-6995
312-990-0040
800-877-1600
Fax: 312-899-4757
E-Mail: affiliate@eatright.org
Home Page: www.eatright.org
Susan H Laramee, President
Ronald S Moen, CEO
Patricia M. Babjak, Executive VP
Jennifer Herendeen, Editorial Director
Jason Switt, Editor
Readers look to the Courier for current association activities, membership news, updates on continuing education opportunities, ADA policies and coverage of the Associations' lobbying efforts in Washington.
Cost: $315.00
10 Pages
Frequency: Monthly
Circulation: 80000
ISSN: 1050-7434
Founded in 1917
Printed in 4 colors on glossy stock

12842 ADA News
American Dental Association
211 E Chicago Ave
Chicago, IL 60611-2678
312-440-2897
Fax: 312-440-3538
Home Page: www.ada.org
Judy Jakush, Editor
Jill Philbein, Circulation Manager
James Bramson, CEO
Cost: $64.00
Founded in 1859

12843 AHA News
AHA
1 N Franklin St
Suite 700
Chicago, IL 60606-4425
312-895-2500
800-242-2626
Fax: 312-895-2501
E-Mail: storeservice@aha.org
Home Page: www.aha.org
Anthony Burke, CEO
Cliff Lehman, Director Membership Services
Provides extensive coverage of regulatory, judicial and legislative developments while also providing news and information from the AHA.
Cost: $45.00
Frequency: Weekly
Circulation: 40000
Founded in 1917

12844 AMA Alliance Today
AMA
515 N State St
Chicago, IL 60654-9104
312-464-4470
Fax: 312-464-5020
E-Mail: amaa@ama-assn.org
Home Page: www.ama-assn.org
Jo Posselt, Executive Director
Megan Pellegrini, General Counsel
Jon Ekdahl, General Counsel
Bernard Hengesbaugh, Chief Operating Officer
Jacqueline Drake, Secretary
Circulation: 30,000
Founded in 1922

12845 AdvaMed SmartBrief
Advanced Medical Technology Association
1200 G St NW
Suite 400
Washington, DC 20005-3832
202-408-9788
Fax: 202-408-9793
E-Mail: info@advamed.org
Home Page: www.avamed.org
Andrea Levre, President

12846 Advance for Health Information Executives
Advance Newsmagazines/Merion Publications
2900 Horizon Dr
King of Prussia, PA 19406-2651
610-265-8249
800-355-5627
Fax: 610-962-0639
Home Page: www.advanceforhie.com
Frank Irving, Editor
Maryann Kurkowski, Circulation Manager
Coverage of emerging e-health and computer-based patient record technologies.
Frequency: Monthly
Founded in 1997

12847 Aesthetic Plastic Surgery
6277 Sea Harbor Drive
Orlando Florida
Orlando, Fl 32887-7703
407-345-4000
800-364-2147
Fax: 407-363-9661
E-Mail: elspcs@elsevier.com
Home Page: www.surgery.org/
Elizabeth Sadati, Executive Editor
Paul Bernstein, Scientific Forum Editor
Stanley A Klatsky, Managing Director
Cost: $196.00
Frequency: Monthly
Founded in 1996

12848 Air Medical Journal
Mosby
11830 Westline Industrial Drive
Saint Louis, MO 63146-3318
314-453-4307
800-325-4307
Fax: 314-872-9164
E-Mail: elspcs@elsevier.com
Home Page: www.mosby.com/airmedj
David Dries, Editor
Liz Bennett-Bailey, Publisher
Eric Ferguson, Issue Manager
Cost: $85.00
Frequency: bi-monthly
Founded in 1986

12849 American Family Physician
American Academy of Family Physicians
11400 Tomahawk Creek Pkwy
Leawood, KS 66211-2680
913-906-6000
800-274-2237
Fax: 913-906-6080
E-Mail: contactcenter@aafp.org
Home Page: www.aafp.org/fpm
Michael Springer, VP
Janis Wright, Managing Editor
Dan Gowan, Director Advertising Sales
Joetta Melton, Publisher
AFP serves family physicians, general practitioners, selected office and hospital based physicians who are general internists and family practice and general practice osteopaths.
Cost: $240.00
Frequency: Monthly
Founded in 1947

12850 American Health Line
600 New Hampshire Avenue NW
Washington, DC 20037
202-295-5381
800-717-3245
Fax: 202-266-5700
E-Mail: ahl@advisory.com
Home Page: www.americanhealthline.com
Joshua Perin, Editor-in-Chief
Josh Kotzman, Editors
Frequency: Weekly
Founded in 1992

12851 American Imago: Studies In Psychoanalysis and Culture
Johns Hopkins University Press
2715 N Charles St
Baltimore, MD 21218-4319
410-516-6900
800-548-1784
Fax: 410-516-6998
E-Mail: webmaster@jhupress.jhu.edu
Home Page: www.press.jhu.edu/journals
William Brody, President
Kathleen Keane, Director
William M. Breichner, Publisher
Founded in 1878

12852 American Journal of Clinical Medicine
American Association of Physician Specialists, Inc
5550 West Executive Drive
Suite 400
Tampa, FL 33609
813-433-2277
Fax: 813-830-6599
E-Mail: wcarbone@aapsus.org
Home Page: www.aapsus.com
Nadine Simone, Executive Administrative Assistant
Debi Colmorgen, Communications Coordinator
William Carbone, Chief Executive Officer
Anthony Durante, Director of Finance & Operations
Sandy Martin, Finance & Operations Coordinator
The official peer-reviewed journal of the AAPS, an organization dedicated to promoting the highest intellectual, moral, and ethical standards of its members.
1000 Attendees

12853 American Journal of Cosmetic Surgery
737 N Michigan Ave
Suite 2100
Chicago, IL 60611-5641
312-981-6760
Fax: 312-981-6787
E-Mail: info@cosmeticsurgery.org
Home Page: www.cosmeticsurgery.org
Jeffrey Knezovich, Executive VP
Charlie Baase, Marketing Manager

12854 American Journal of Health Education (AJHE)
1900 Association Dr
Reston, VA 20191-1502
703-476-3400
800-213-7193
Fax: 703-476-9527
E-Mail: info@aahperd.org
Home Page: www.aahperd.org
Social Media: Facebook, Twitter, YouTube
Monica Mize, President
Judith C Young, VP
Paula Kun, Marketing

Covers today's health education and health promotion issues head on with timely, substantive, and thought provoking articles for professionals working in medical care facilities, professional preparation, colleges and universities, community and public health agencies, schools, and businesses.
25000 Members
Founded in 1885

12855 **American Journal of Human Genetics**
American Society of Human Genetics
9650 Rockville Pike
Bethesda, MD 20814-3998

301-634-7300
866-HUM-GENE
Fax: 301-634-7079
E-Mail: society@ashg.org
Home Page: www.ashg.org
Social Media: Facebook, Twitter, LinkedIn

Joann Boughman, PhD, Executive VP
Chuck Windle, Director of Finance/Administration
Karen Goodman, Executive Assistant
Pauline Minhinnett, Dir. of Meetings/Exhibit Management
Mary Shih, Membership Manager

ASHG is the primary professional membership organization for human genetics specialists worldwide.
8000 Members
Frequency: Monthly
Circulation: 7,199
ISSN: 0002-9297
Founded in 1948
Mailing list available for rent

12856 **American Journal of Hypertension**
148 Madison Ave
Fifth Floor
New York, NY 10016-6700

212-532-0537
Fax: 212-696-0711
E-Mail: journal@ash-us.org
Home Page: www.ash-us.org

John H Laragh, Editor In Chief
Ellen Twyne, President
Cost: $246.00
Frequency: Monthly
Founded in 1985

12857 **American Journal of Managed Care**
American Medical Publishing
241 Forsgate Drive
Jamesburg, NJ 08831

732-656-1006
Fax: 732-656-0818
E-Mail: info@ajmc.com
Home Page: www.ajmc.com

Jim King, Publisher
Lyn Beamesderfer, Editor

The American Journal of Managed Care is an independent, peer-reviewed forum for the publication of clinical research and opinion related to quality, value, and policy in health care delivery. The Journal delivers original research on patient outcomes, clinical effectiveness, cost effectiveness, quality management, and health policy to managed care decision makers.
Frequency: Monthly
Circulation: 53000
ISSN: 1088-0224
Founded in 1995

12858 **American Journal of Neuroradiology**
2210 Midwest Rd
Suite 207
Oak Brook, IL 60523-8205

630-574-1487
800-783-4903
Fax: 630-786-6251
Home Page: www.ajnr.org

Karen Halm, Managing Editor
Victor M Haughton MD, VP

Relays news and schedules of events for members.
Cost: $235.00
Circulation: 7000
Founded in 1937

12859 **American Journal of Roetgenology**
American Roentgen Ray Society
1891 Preston White Dr
Reston, VA 20191-4326
703-729-3353
800-438-2777
Fax: 703-729-4839
E-Mail: info@arrs.org
Home Page: www.arrs.org

Susan Brown, Executive Director
Connie Wolfe, Publications Assistant
Fran Schuweiler, Managing Editor
Charles Kahn, Vice President
Melissa Rosado, Secretary

A monthly journal published by the American Roentgen Ray Society.
Cost: $275.00
Frequency: Monthly
Circulation: 25,000
Founded in 1900
Mailing list available for rent: 10000 names at $160 per M

12860 **American Medical News**
American Medical Association
515 N State St
9th Floor
Chicago, IL 60654-9104

312-464-4429
800-621-8335
Fax: 312-464-4445
E-Mail: ben_mindell@ama-assn.org
Home Page: www.ama-assn.org

Ben Mindell, Vice President
John Nelson, CEO/President
Kathryn Trombatore, Manager
Jon Ekdahl, General Counsel
Bernard Hengesbaugh, Chief Operating Officer

Intended to serve as an impartial forum for information affecting physicians and their practices. The views expressed in AMNews are not necessarily endorsed by the American Medical Association.
Cost: $95.00
Frequency: Weekly
Circulation: 230,000
Founded in 1847

12861 **American Nurse Today**
American Nurses Association
600 Maryland Avenue SW
Washington, DC 20024-2571

202-651-7000
Fax: 202-651-7003
Home Page: www.NursingWorld.org

Pamela Cipriano PhD RN FAAN, Editor-in-Chief

Serves registered nurses in North America.
Frequency: 6 per year
Printed in 4 colors on glossy stock

12862 **Anesthesiology News**
545 W 45th St
8th Floor
New York, NY 10036-3409
212-957-5300
Fax: 212-957-7230
E-Mail: marsap@mcmahonmed.com
Home Page: www.anesthesiologynews.com

Adam Marcus, Managing Editor
Raymond E. McMahon, CEO/Publisher
Marsha Radebaugh, Circulation Coordinator
Cost: $65.00
Frequency: Monthly
Circulation: 39720
Founded in 1975

12863 **Annals of Allergy, Asthma & Immunology**
85 W Algonquin Road
Suite 550
Arlington Heights, IL 60005-4460

847-427-1200
Fax: 847-427-1294
E-Mail: mail@acaai.org
Home Page: www.acaai.org
Social Media: Facebook, Twitter, LinkedIn, YouTube

Dana Wallace, MD, President
Stanley Fineman, MD, MBA, President-Elect

Information and news service for patients, parents of patients, members, the news media, and purchasers of health care programs.
5200 Members
Frequency: Monthly
Circulation: 5100
ISSN: 1081-1206
Founded in 1942

12864 **Annals of Emergency Medicine**
Elsevier Publishing
1125 Executive Circle
P.O. Box 619911
Irving, TX 75038-2522
972-550-0911
800-798-1822
Fax: 972-580-2816
E-Mail: customerservice@acep.org
Home Page: www.acep.org

Nancy B Medina, CAE, Editorial Director
Tracy Napper, Managing Editor
Michael L Callaham, MD, Editor-in-Chief
Dean Wilkerson, Executive Director
Marco Coppola, Council Speaker

An international, peer-reviewed journal dedicated to improving the quality of care by publishing the highest quality science for emergency medicine and related medical specialties.
Frequency: Monthly
Circulation: 30000
ISSN: 0196-0644
Mailing list available for rent

12865 **Annals of Opthalmology**
Am. Society of Cont. Medicine, Surgery & Opth.
North Cisero Avenue
Suite 208
Chicago, IL 60712

847-677-9093
800-621-4002
Fax: 847-677-9094
E-Mail: iaos@aol.com
Home Page: www.medlit.ru/medeng/vof5.htm

Mikhail Krasnov, Editor-in-Chief
Randall Bellows MD, CEO/President

Exclusive articles written and peer-reviewed by doctors.
Frequency: bi-monthly
Founded in 1884

12866 **Annals of Periodontology**
737 N Michigan Ave
Suite 800
Chicago, IL 60611-2690

312-787-5518
Fax: 312-787-3670

E-Mail: member.services@perio.org
Home Page: www.perio.org

Alice Deforest, Executive Director
Julie Daw, Managing Editor
Vincent J. Iacono, President
Sarah Schneider, Administrative Assistant
Cost: $365.00
Frequency: Monthly

12867 Annals of Plastic Surgery
530 Walnut St
Philadelphia, PA 19106-3603

215-521-8300
Fax: 215-521-8411
Home Page: www.lww.com

Melissa Ricks, Manager
Cost: $375.00
Frequency: Monthly

12868 Applied Clinical Trials
Advanstar Communications
6200 Canoga Avenue
2nd Floor
Woodland Hills, CA 91367

818-593-5000
Fax: 818-593-5020
Home Page:
www.appliedclinicaltrialsonline.com
Social Media: Facebook, Twitter, LinkedIn

Joseph Loggia, President
Chris DeMoulin, VP
Susannah George, Marketing Director

Practical information for clinical research professionals in industry and academia who develop, execute and manage clinical trials worldwide. Regular topics include regulatory affairs, protocol development, data management and harmonization updates.
Frequency: Monthly
Circulation: 16255
ISSN: 1064-8542
Founded in 1987
Mailing list available for rent

12869 Archives of Physical Medicine and Rehabilitation
American Congress of Rehabilitation Medicine
11654 Plaza America Drive
Suite 535
Reston, VA 20190

703-435-5335
Fax: 866-692-1619
E-Mail: acrm@acrm.org
Home Page: www.acrm.org

Jon W. Lindberg, Executive Director
Dinara Suleymanova, Director of Operations
Judy Reuter, Publications & Web Development
Cindy Robinson, Marketing Coordinator
Margo Holen, Chief Meetings Officer

Available with membership to American Congress of Rehabilitation Medicine.
Frequency: Monthly
Circulation: 900
Founded in 1923

12870 Arthritis Hotline
2824 Swift Avenue
Dallas, TX 75204

972-286-6664
Fax: 214-363-2817

12871 Aviation, Space and Environmental Medicine
Aerospace Medical Association
320 S Henry St
Alexandria, VA 22314-3579

703-739-2240
Fax: 703-739-9652
E-Mail: asemjournal@att.net
Home Page: www.asma.org

Gisselle Vargas, Manager
Jeffrey C. Sventek, Executive Director
Gisselle Vargas, Operations Manager
Gloria Carter, Director, Member Services
Sheryl Kildall, Subscriptions Manager

Provides contact with physicians, life scientists, bioengineers and medical specialists working in both basic medical research and in its clinical applications.
Frequency: Monthly
Mailing list available for rent

12872 BNA's Health Care Policy Report
3 Bethesda Metro Center
Suite 250
Bethesda, MD 20814

202-452-4107
800-372-1033
Fax: 202-452-4084
E-Mail: edcontactslitigation@bna.com
Home Page: www.bna.com

Greg McCaffey, President, Bloomburg BNA
Frequency: Weekly
Founded in 1929

12873 Behavioral Health Management
MEDQUEST Communications
3800 Lakeside Ave E
Suite 201
Cleveland, OH 44114-3857

216-391-9100
Fax: 216-391-9200
Home Page: www.behavioral.net

Mark Goodman, Manager
Monica E Oss, Editor-in-Chief

Largest publication reporting on the cutting edge trends and management practices in the behavioral health field.
Cost: $94.00
52 Pages
Circulation: 21615
ISSN: 1075-6701
Printed in 4 colors on glossy stock

12874 Behavioral Neuroscience
750 1st St NE
Washington, DC 20002-4242
202-336-5500
800-374-2721
Fax: 202-336-5549
E-Mail: journals@apa.org
Home Page:
www.apa.org/pubs/journals/bne/index.aspx

Rebecca Burwell, Editor
Cost: $235.00
Circulation: 200,000
Founded in 1988

12875 Biomedical Instrumentation & Technology
Assoc for the Advancement of Medical Instrumentat
4301 N. Fairfax Drive
Suite 301
Arlington, VA 22203-1633

703-525-4890
Fax: 703-276-0793
E-Mail: publications@aami.org
Home Page: www.aami.org

Sean Loughlin, Managing Editor

Filled with practical guidance and regular features on troubleshooting, certification, career trends, management issues, sterilization, quality assurance, and more.
Cost: $182.00
Frequency: Bimonthly
Circulation: 6000
Mailing list available for rent

12876 Biomedical Safety & Standards
Aspen Publishers
280 Orchard Ridge Drive
Suite 200
Gaithersburg, MD 20878-1978
301-417-7591

Jack Bruggeman, Publisher

12877 Birth-Issues in Perinatal Care
350 Main Street
6th Floor
Malden, MA 02148-5023

781-388-8200
800-759-6102
Fax: 781-388-8210
E-Mail: books@blackwellpublishingasia.com
Home Page: www.blackwellpublishing.com

Diony Young, Editor
Gordon Tibbitts III, President
Robert Campbell, Publisher
Ginny Foley, Manager
Cost: $36.00
Frequency: Quarterly
Circulation: 1709
Founded in 1897

12878 Body Positive
19 Fulton Street
Suite 308 B
New York, NY 10038-2100

212-566-7333
800-566-6599
Fax: 212-566-4539
Home Page: www.bodypos.org/

Raymond A Smith, Editor
Eric Rodriguez, Executive Director
Cost: $40.00
Frequency: Quarterly
Circulation: 10000
Founded in 1987

12879 Bulletin
1650 Diagonal Road
Alexandria, VA 22314-3357

703-836-4444
Fax: 703-683-5100
E-Mail: membership@entnet.org
Home Page: www.entnet.org
Social Media: Facebook, Twitter

Marty Stewart, Sr Manager, Media/Public Relations
James L. Netterville, President
J. Gavin Setzen, Secretary/Treasurer
David R. Nielsen, Executive Vice President and CEO
Paul T. Fass, Director - Private Practice

Features articles written by member otolaryngologists and Academy staff, as well as regular segments on political advocacy, the grassroots member network, practice management, and the latest specialty news and information.
Frequency: Monthly
Circulation: 12,000
ISSN: 0731-8359
Mailing list available for rent

12880 Business and Health
Medical Economics Publishing
131 West First Street
Duluth, Mi 55802-2065

218-723-9200
888-346-0085
Fax: 218-723-9437
E-Mail: info@advanstar.com
Home Page: www.advanstar.com

Tracey Walker, Senior Editor
Julie Miller, Managing Editor
Daniel Corcoran, Publisher
Joseph Loggia, Chief Executive Officer
Thomas Ehardt, Chief Administrator

Provides the business and industry fields with information on manufacturing, wholesale, retail and financial, insurance companies, law/accounting firms, hospitals, HMO/PPOs, labor unions, consulting firms, and Medicare/Medicade.
Cost: $64.00
Frequency: Monthly
Circulation: 39736
Founded in 1987
Printed in 4 colors on glossy stock

12881 CA: A Cancer Journal for Clinicians
1599 Clifton Road NE
Atlanta, GA 30329-4251

404-929-6902
Fax: 404-325-9341
E-Mail: journals@cancer.org
Home Page: caonline.amcancersoc.org

Harmon J Eyre, Editor
Vickie Thaw, Publisher
John R. Seffrin, CEO
Circulation: 90,000
Founded in 1913

12882 CVS InStep with Healthy Living
Drug Store News Consumer Health Publications
425 Park Ave
New York, NY 10022-3526

212-756-5220
845-426-7612
Fax: 212-756-5250
E-Mail: jtanzola@lf.com
Home Page: www.drugstorenews.com

Lebhar Friedman, Publisher
John Tanzola, National Sales Manager
Helps educate and inform over 25 millions 45+ shoppers that visit CVS every month. Topics include health, nutrition, fitness, lifestyle, travel, coupons and CVS programs and events.
Frequency: Quarterly
Circulation: 950000
Founded in 2007

12883 Case Manager
Mosby
10801 Executive Center Drive
Suite 509
Little Rock, AR 72211

501-223-5165
Fax: 501-220-0519
Home Page: www.mosby.com

Catherine Mullahy, Editor
Tom Strickland, Editor-in-Chief
Cheri Lattimer, Executive Director
Exclusively for the case management profession.
Cost: $52.00
80 Pages
Frequency: Bi-Monthly
Circulation: 20M
Founded in 1990
Printed in 4 colors on glossy stock

12884 Circulation Research
PO Box 1620
Suite 230
Hagerstown, MD 21741
301-223-2300
800-638-3030
Fax: 301-223-2400
E-Mail: educsales@lww.com
Home Page: www.lww.com

Eduardo Marb n, Editor
Cost: $377.00
Founded in 1792

12885 CleanRooms Magazine
PennWell Publishing Company
98 Spit Brook Rd
Nashua, NH 03062-5737

603-891-0123
Fax: 603-891-9294
E-Mail: georgem@pennwell.com
Home Page: www.pennwell.com

Christine Shaw, VP
John Haystead, Editor
James Enos, Publisher
Adam Japko, President
Heidi Barnes, Circulation Manager
Serves the contamination control and ultrapure materials and process industries. Written for readers in the microelectronics, pharmaceutical, biotech, health care, food processing and other user industries. Provides technology and business news and new product listings.
Circulation: 34019
Founded in 1910

12886 Clinical Chemistry
American Association for Clinical Chemistry
1850 K St NW
Suite 625
Washington, DC 20006-2215

202-857-0717
800-892-1400
Fax: 202-887-5093
E-Mail: custserv@aacc.org
Home Page: www.aacc.org

Richard Flaherty, VP
8,000 Members
Mailing list available for rent

12887 Clinical Lab Products
MWC Allied Healthcare Group
6100 Center Drive
Suite 1000
Los Angeles, CA 90045

310-642-4400
Fax: 310-641-4444
E-Mail: tantikadjian@ascendmedia.com
Home Page: www.clpmag.com

Scott Anderson, Publisher
Carol Andrews, Editor
Sharon Marsee, Production Manager
Tony Ramos, President
Jennifer Bezahler, Circulation Director
CLP is the leading monthly product news magazine on key decision makers in the clinical diagnostic laboratory. New product annoucements and editorial features assist lab professionals in providing cost effective timely and accurate patient diagnostic information.
Cost: $125.00
Frequency: Monthly
Circulation: 45000
Founded in 1976
Printed in 4 colors on glossy stock

12888 Clinical Pulmonary Medicine
530 Walnut St
Philadelphia, PA 19106-3603

215-521-8300
800-638-6423
Fax: 215-521-8411
Home Page: www.lww.com

Barry Morrill, Publisher
Michael S Niederman MD, Editor-in-Chief
Jay Lippincott, President
Provides a forum for the discussion of important new knowledge in the field of pulmonary medicine that is of interest and relevance to the practitioner.

12889 Computers and Biomedical Research
525 B Street
Suite 1900
San Diego, CA 92101-4401

619-231-6616
800-321-5068
Fax: 619-699-6422
Home Page: www.elsevier.com

Gilbert Laporte, Editor
Bill Godfrey, Chief Information Officer
David Clark, Senior Vice President
Frequency: Monthly
Founded in 1974

12890 Computers, Informatics, Nursing
Lippincott Williams & Wilkins
10 A Beech Street
Suite 2
Portland, ME 04101

207-553-7750
Fax: 207-553-7751
E-Mail: CustomerService@NursingCenter.com
Home Page: www.nursingcenter.com

Leslie H. Nicoll, Editor
Lippin Cott, Publisher/President
Computer and informatics applications and product selection in nursing and education for nurse managers, patient care executives, nurses in direct patient care, nurse educators and researchers.
Cost: $63.00
Circulation: 4112
Founded in 1985

12891 Consultant Pharmacist
American Society of Consultant Pharmacists
1321 Duke St
Alexandria, VA 22314-3563

703-739-1300
800-355-2727
Fax: 703-739-1321
E-Mail: info@ascp.com
Home Page: www.ascp.com

John Feather, Executive Director
Patti Thompson, Production Manager
Marlene Bloom, Editor
Debbie Furman, Circulation
Official peer reviewed journal of the American Society of Consultant Pharmacists. Editorial deals with geriatric pharmacotherapy.
Cost: $210.00
76 Pages
Frequency: Monthly
Circulation: 11000
Printed in 4 colors on glossy stock

12892 Contemporary Urology
Medical Economics Publishing
5 Paragon Dr
Montvale, NJ 07645-1791

973-944-7777
888-581-8052
Fax: 973-944-7778
Home Page: www.contemporaryurology.com

Curtis Allen, President
Culley C Carson MD, Editor-in-Chief
Matthew J Holland, Publisher
Don Berman, Director Business Development
Comtemporary Urology serves medical and osteopathic physicians specializing in urology.
Cost: $120.00
Frequency: Monthly
Circulation: 4276
ISSN: 1042-2250
Founded in 1992
Printed in 4 colors on glossy stock

12893 Contingency Planning & Management
Witter Publishing Corporation

20 Commerce Street
Flemington, NJ 08822

908-788-0343
Fax: 908-788-3782
Home Page: www.witterpublishing.com

Bob Joudanin, Publisher
Paul Kirvan, Editor-in-Chief
Mike Viscel, Production Manager
Andrew Witter, President

Serves the fields of financial/banking, manufacturing industrial, transportation, utilities, telecommunications, health care, government, insurance and other allied fields.
Cost: $195.00
Frequency: Monthly
Founded in 1987

12894 **Continuing Care**
Stevens Publishing Corporation
5151 Belt Line Rd
10th Floor
Dallas, TX 75254-7507

972-687-6700
Fax: 972-687-6767
Home Page: www.stevenspublishing.com

Craig S Stevens, President/CEO
Mike Valenti, Executive Vice President
Angela Neville, Editor

To provide case management and discharge planning professions with practical and professional information to ensure quality patient services at a cost-effective price.
Cost: $119.00
Founded in 1925

12895 **Coping with Allergies and Asthma**
Media America
PO Box 682268
Franklin, TN 37068-2268

615-790-2400
Fax: 615-794-0179
E-Mail: info@copingmag.com
Home Page: www.copingmag.com

Michael D Holt, Publisher
Julie McKenna, Editor
Michael D Holt, CEO

Information, tips and news for sufferers of allergies or asthma.
Cost: $13.95
36 Pages
Circulation: 30,000
Founded in 1998

12896 **Coping with Cancer**
Media America
PO Box 682268
Franklin, TN 37068-2268

615-790-2400
Fax: 615-794-0179
E-Mail: info@copingmag.com
Home Page: www.copingmag.com

Michael D Holt, Publisher
Julie McKenna, Editor

A magazine for people whose lives have been touched by cancer. Provides knowledge, hope and inspiration to its readers including cancer patients (survivors) and their families, caregivers, healthcare teams and support group leaders.
Cost: $19.00
Circulation: 572,000
Founded in 1987

12897 **Cosmetic Surgery Times**
Advanstar Communications
7500 Old Oak Blvd
Cleveland, OH 44130-3343

440-243-8100
888-527-7008
Fax: 440-891-2740
E-Mail: info@advanstar.com
Home Page: www.advanstar.com

Claudia Shayne-Ferguson, Group Publisher
Maureen Hrehocik, Editor-in-Chief
Michelle Tackla, Senior Editor
Ray Lender, General Manager
Carol Bessick, Manager

Provides cosmetic surgeons with the most current clinical news available. Covers latest surgical techniques, medicolegal issues, updates on new technologies, and suggestions for practice management.
Cost: $95.00
Frequency: 10x/yr
Circulation: 10,003
ISSN: 1094-6810
Founded in 1987

12898 **Cost Reengineering Report**
National Health Information
PO Box 15429
Atlanta, GA 30333-0429

404-607-9500
800-597-6300
Fax: 404-607-0095
Home Page: www.nhionline.com

David Schwartz, President

Contains strategies for reengineering clinical and operational functions, and cutting costs while maintaining or improving quality.
Cost: $299.00
Frequency: Monthly

12899 **Counseling Today**
5999 Stevenson Ave
Alexandria, VA 22304-3302

703-823-9800
800-347-6647
Fax: 703-823-0252
E-Mail: membership@counseling.org
Home Page: www.counseling.org
Social Media: Facebook, Twitter

Marvin D. Kuehn, Executive Director
Tom Evenson, President

The mission of the American Counseling Association (ACA) is to enhance the quality of life in society by promoting the development of professional counselors, advancing the counseling profession, and using the profession and practice of counseling to promote respect for human dignity and diversity. ACA is a not-for-profit, professional and educational organization.
Frequency: Monthly
Circulation: 50000
Founded in 1952
Mailing list available for rent: 60M names

12900 **Critical Strategies: Psychotherapy in Managed Care**
Bill Cohen
10 Alice Street
Binghamton, NY 13904-1580

607-722-5857
800-342-9678
Fax: 607-722-6362
E-Mail: getinfo@haworthpressinc.com
Home Page: www.haworthpressinc.com

Frank DePiano, Editor
Sandra J Sickels, Marketing VP
William Cohen, Owner

Resource for innovative and effective approaches to clinical practice in relation to managed care.
Cost: $35.00
Frequency: 2 per year

12901 **Data Strategies & Benchmarks**
National Health Information
PO Box 15429
Atlanta, GA 30333-429

404-607-9500
800-597-6300
Fax: 404-607-0095
E-Mail: nhi@nhionline.net
Home Page: www.nhionline.net

David Schwartz, Publisher
Steve Larose, Editor
David Schwartz, CEO
Edgardo Rivera, Director

Provides insightful guidance and how-to advice to help them meet all the key challenges faced under managed care.
Cost: $339.00
Frequency: Monthly
Founded in 1994

12902 **Dental Economics**
PennWell Publishing Company
1421 S Sheridan Rd
Tulsa, OK 74112-6619

918-831-9421
800-331-4463
Fax: 918-831-9476
E-Mail: joeb@pennwell.com
Home Page: www.pennwell.com

Robert Biolchini, President
Lyle Hoyt, Publisher
Cost: $105.76
Frequency: Monthly
Founded in 1910

12903 **Dental Lab Products**
MEDEC Dental Communications
2 Northfield Plaza
Suite 300
Northfield, IL 60093-1219

847-441-3700
800-225-4569
Fax: 847-441-3702
Home Page: www.dentalproducts.net

Bob Kehoe, Editorial Director
Gail Weisman, Editor
Fran Martin, Managing Editor
Richard Fischer, Publisher
Tom Delaney, National Sales Manager

Serves the dental profession and the dental industry, list rentals, classifieds and other services to complete your marketing plan.$35 subscription per year
35 Pages
Circulation: 19,000
ISSN: 0146-9738
Founded in 1967
Printed in 4 colors on glossy stock

12904 **Dental Materials**
Academy of Dental Materials
21 Grouse Terrace
PO Box 980566
Lake Oswego, OR 97035

503-636-0861
Fax: 503-675-2738
E-Mail: admabstr@vcu.edu
Home Page: www.academydentalmaterials.org

David C Watts PhD FADM, Editor-in-Chief
Dr. Lorenzo Breschi, President
J. Robert Kelly, Vice President
Paulo F. Cesar, Secretary
Tom Hilton, Treasurer

12905 **Dental Practice**
MEDEC Dental Communications
2 Northfield Plaza
Suite 300
Northfield, IL 60093-1219

847-441-3700
800-225-4569

Fax: 440-826-2865
Home Page: www.dentalproducts.net

Richard Fischer, Publisher
Bob Kehoe, Editorial Director
Steven Diogo, Editor
Daniel McCann, Senior Editor
Tom Delaney, National Sales Manager

Serves the dental industry. Subscription
75 Pages
Circulation: 120,000
ISSN: 1078-1250
Printed in 4 colors on glossy stock

12906 **Dental Products Report**
MEDEC Dental Communications
2 Northfield Plaza
Suite 300
Northfield, IL 60093-1219

847-441 3700
Fax: 847-441-3702
Home Page: www.dentalproducts.net

Dolph Sharp, Publisher
Gail Weisman, Editor
Matthew LaFleur, Illustrator

Serves the dental profession and the dental industry. $120 subscription per year
141 Pages
Frequency: 12 per year
ISSN: 0011 8737
Founded in 1967
Printed in 4 colors on glossy stock

12907 **Dental Products Report Europe**
MEDEC Dental Communications
Two Northfield Plaza
Suite 300
Northfield, IL 60093-1219

847-441-3700
Fax: 847-441-3702
Home Page: www.dentalproducts.net

Richard Fisher, Publisher
Pam Johnson, Editor
Keith Easty, Circulation Director
Dennis Spaeth, Editor
Bob Kehoe, Editorial Director

Designed to inform dentists in Europe and selected Middle Eastern and North African countries and dental distributors and depot personnel worldwide of new developments and ongoing trends in the dental market.
Cost: $40.00
Circulation: 50000
Founded in 1987

12908 **Dentistry Today**
100 Passaic Ave
Fairfield, NJ 07004-3508

973-882-4700
Fax: 973-783-7112
E-Mail: admin@dentistrytoday.com
Home Page: www.dentistrytoday.com/

Paul Radcliffe, Owner
Phillip Bonner, Editor
Susan Oettinger, Treasurer, Manager
Jan Nigro, Production Manager
Janice Yawdoszyn, Director

The nation's leading clinical news magazine for dentists
Cost: $65.00
122 Pages
Frequency: Monthly
Circulation: 150,000
ISSN: 8750-2186
Founded in 1981
Printed in 4 colors on glossy stock

12909 **Devices and Diagnostics Letter**
300 N Washington Street
Suite 200
Falls Church, VA 22046-3431

703-538-7600
888-838-5578
Fax: 703-538-7676
E-Mail: customerservice@fdanews.com
Home Page: www.fdanews.com

Robert Barton, Editorial Director
Matt Salt, Publisher
Maritza Lizama, Marketing Director
Cynthia Carter, President
Cost: $987.00
Frequency: Weekly
Circulation: 3300
Mailing list available for rent

12910 **Diabetes Care**
1701 N Beauregard St
Alexandria, VA 22311-1742

703-549-1500
800-342-2383
Fax: 703-739-0290
E-Mail: askada@diabetes.org
Home Page: www.diabetes.org

Donna Lucas, Human Resources
Joseph Scheffer, Editor
Peter Banks, Publisher
Joe Herget, Marketing Manager
Cost: $314.00
Frequency: Monthly
Circulation: 13637
Founded in 1940

12911 **Diabetes Digest Family**
Drug Store News Consumer Health Publications
425 Park Ave
New York, NY 10022-3526

212-756-5220
Fax: 212-756-5250
Home Page: www.drugstorenews.com

Lebhar Friedman, Publisher

Contains health news of importance to those with diabetes.
Frequency: Annual
Circulation: 6.8mm

12912 **Diabetes Educator**
American Association of Diabetes Educators
100 W Monroe Street
Suite 400
Chicago, IL 60603

312-424-2426
800-338-3633
Fax: 312-424-2427
E-Mail: aade@aadenet.org
Home Page: www.diabeteseducator.org

James Sain, Editor
Chris Laxton, CEO
Michael Warner, Marketing Director
Tami Ross, Vice President

Published by the American Association of Diabetes Educators.
Founded in 1973
Mailing list available for rent: 10000 names at $160 per M

12913 **Diabetes Interview**
6 School St
Suite 160
Fairfax, CA 94930-1655

415-258-2828
800-234-1218
Fax: 415-258-2822
E-Mail: webmaster@diabeteshealth.com
Home Page: www.diabeteshealth.com

Nadia Al-Samarrie, Publisher
Scott King, Editorial
Daniel Trecroci, Managing Editor
Dick Young, Production
Susan Art, Director
Cost: $12.00
Frequency: Monthly
Circulation: 120,000
Founded in 1989

12914 **Diagnostic Imaging**
Miller Freeman Publications
600 Harrison Street
San Francisco, CA 94107

415-947-6478
Fax: 415-947-6099
Home Page: www.diagnosticimaging.com

John C. Hayes, Editor
Gary Marshall, President
Suzanne Johnston, Publisher
Kathy Mischak, Associate Publisher

The news magazine of imaging innovation and economics.
Cost: $113.00
90 Pages
Frequency: Monthly
Circulation: 31240
ISSN: 0194-2514
Founded in 1984
Printed in 4 colors on glossy stock

12915 **Diagnostic Imaging America Latina**
Miller Freeman Publications
600 Harrison Street
San Francisco, CA 94107

415-947-6478
Fax: 415-947-6099
Home Page: www.diagnosticimaging.com

Suzanne Johnston, Editor/Publisher
John Hayes, Editorial
Buckley Dement, Circulation
Heidi Torpey, Marketing
Cost: $113.00
Frequency: Monthly
Founded in 1996

12916 **Diagnostic Imaging Asia Pacific**
Miller Freeman Publications
600 Harrison Street
San Francisco, CA 94107

415-947-6491
Fax: 415-947-6099
Home Page: www.diagnosticimaging.com

Philip Ward, Editor
David E Lese, Publisher

A newsmagazine aimed at radiologists and allied medical professionals involved in the practice of diagnostic imaging, and provides timely articles on new diagnostic and technical developments in the field mixed with extensive coverage of important political, commercial and economic trends in the specialty.
Cost: $120.00
42 Pages
Frequency: Quarterly
Circulation: 10,000
Printed in 4 colors on glossy stock

12917 **Diagnostic Imaging Europe**
Miller Freeman Publications
600 Harrison Street
San Francisco, CA 94107

415-947-6478
Fax: 415-947-6099
Home Page: www.diagnosticimaging.com

Philip Ward, Editor
Suzanne Johnston, Publisher
Jose Joaquin, Circulation
Kim Spinoso, National Sales Manager

A newsmagazine aimed at radiologists and allied medical professionals involved in the practice of diagnostic imaging. Provides a balanced mix of timely articles on new diagnostic and

technical developments in the field mixed with extensive coverage of important political, commercial and economic trends in the specialty.
Cost: $125.00
58 Pages
Circulation: 10062
Founded in 1996
Printed in 4 colors on glossy stock

12918 Dialysis and Transplantation
Creative Age Publications
7628 Densmore Ave
Van Nuys, CA 91406-2042

818-782-7560
800-442-5667
Fax: 818-782-7450
Home Page: www.creativeage.com

Deborah Carver, Publisher/CEO
Joseph G Herman, Executive Editor
Carlos Benskin, Circulation Manager
Gail Edwards, Accounting Manager
Diane Jones, Advertising Director

Serves the renal care community. Subscription: $17.50.
Cost: $35.00
Frequency: Monthly
Founded in 1975
Printed in 4 colors on glossy stock

12919 Director
National Funeral Director Association
13625 Bishops Dr
Brookfield, WI 53005-6607

262-789-1880
800-228-6332
Fax: 262-789-6977
E-Mail: nfda@nfda.org
Home Page: www.nfda.org

Coverage concentrates on funeral service education and licensure, community service and public relations as well as public health concerns and legal, ethical and moral issues.
Cost: $45.00
84 Pages
Frequency: Monthly
Circulation: 13906
ISSN: 0199-3186
Founded in 1882
Printed in 4 colors on glossy stock

12920 Diseases of the Colon & Rectum
American Society of Colon & Rectal Surgeons
85 W Algonquin Road
Suite 550
Arlington Heights, IL 60005

847-290-9184
800-791-0001
Fax: 847-290-9203
E-Mail: ascrs@fascrs.org
Home Page: www.fascrs.org
Social Media: Facebook

Pat Oldenburg, Managing Editor
Rick Slawny, Executive Director
Stella Zedalis, Associate Executive Director
Julie Weldon, Assistant Director
John Nocera, Chief Financial Officer
2800 Members
Mailing list available for rent

12921 Drug Store News
Lebhar-Friedman
425 Park Ave
New York, NY 10022-3526

212-756-5088
800-216-7117
Fax: 212-838-9487
E-Mail: info@lf.com
Home Page: www.lf.com

Heather Martin, Manager
Tony Lisanti, Editor/Associate Publisher
Terry Nicosia, Senior Production Manager
K Dement, Circulation Manager
Wayne Bennett, Advertising Manager

Publication consists of merchandising trends and pharmacy developments. Provides extensive coverage of every major segment of chain drug retailing and combination stores.
Frequency: Monthly
Circulation: 44372
Founded in 1925

12922 Emergency Medicine
7 Century Dr
Siute 302
Parsippany, NJ 07054-4609

973-206-3434
Fax: 973-206-9378
Home Page: www.quadranthealth.com

Susan Alburtus, Manager
Michael Pepper, Publisher
Martin Dicarlantonio, Editor
Donna Sickles, Circulation Manager
Kathleen Corbett, Advertising Coordinator
Cost: $90.00
Frequency: Monthly
Circulation: 158000
Founded in 1967

12923 Emerging Trends
Trends Analysis Group
1 N Franklin
29th Floor
Chicago, IL 60606-3421

312-422-3990
Fax: 312-422-4569

Marcia Foley, Editor

Published as a community hospital trends which focuses on financial performance, personnel, utilization and facilities.
Cost: $135.00
Frequency: Quarterly
Circulation: 1,700

12924 EndoNurse
Virgo Publishing LLC
3300 N Central Ave
Suite 300
Phoenix, AZ 85012-2532

480-990-1101
Fax: 480-990-0819
E-Mail: jsiefert@vpico.com
Home Page: www.vpico.com

Jenny Bolton, President
John Siefert, CEO
Jennifer Janos, Controller
Kelly Ridley, Executive VP, CFO, Copado

EndoNurse provides the practical information and updated protocol for those practicing in hospitals and freestanding facilities.
Mailing list available for rent: 13000+ names at $var per M

12925 Endocrine
505 NW 185th Avenue
Beaverton, OR 97006-3448

503-690-5350
Fax: 503-690-5245
E-Mail: journals@ohsu.edu
Home Page: www.bioscience.org

P Michael Conn, Editor-in-Chief
Peter O Kohler, President
Cost: $365.00
Founded in 1867

12926 Endocrine Practice
American Association of Clinical Endocrinologists
245 Riverside Avenue
Suite 200
Jacksonville, FL 32202

904-353-7878
Fax: 904-353-8185
E-Mail: info@aace.com
Home Page: www.aace.com

Donald Jones, CEO
Donna Beasley, CPA, Finance Manager
Michael Avallone, CPA, Chief Financial Officer
Lynn Blanco, Executive Assistant
Lucille Killgore, Director of College Activities

To enhance the health care of patients with endocrine diseases through continuing education of practicing endocrinologists
Cost: $350.00
Frequency: Bi-Monthly
Circulation: 5000
Mailing list available for rent

12927 Endocrine Reviews
The Endocrine Society
8401 Connecticut Ave
Suite 900
Chevy Chase, MD 20815-5817

301-941-0200
888-363-6274
Fax: 301-941-0259
E-Mail: societyservices@endo-society.org
Home Page: www.endo-society.org

Scott Hunt, Executive Director
Anthony R. Means, Secretary
John Marshall, Secretary
Cost: $252.00
Circulation: 5907
Founded in 1916

12928 European Medical Device Manufacturer
Canon Communications
11444 W Olympic Blvd
Los Angeles, CA 90064-1555

310-445-4200
Fax: 310-445-4299
Home Page: www.cancom.com

Charlie Mc Curdy, President
Cost: $150.00
Circulation: 15,048
Founded in 1978

12929 Exercise and Sport Sicence Reviews
Lippincott Williams & Wilkins
530 Walnut St
Philadelphia, PA 19106-3604

215-521-8300
Fax: 215-521-8902
E-Mail: support@ovid.com
Home Page: www.lww.com

Gordon Macomber, CEO
Lori A Tish, Editorial Assistant
Michael A. Hargrett, Associate Publisher

This Journal provides premier reviews of the most contemporary scientific, medical and research-based topics emerging in the field of sports medicine and exercise science, targeted to students, professors, clinicians, scientists and professionals for practical and research applications.
192 Pages
Frequency: Quarterly
ISSN: 0091-6331
Founded in 1998
Printed in 4 colors on matte stock

12930 Extended Care Product News
HMP Communications

83 General Warren Blvd
Suite 100
Malvern, PA 19355-1252

610-560-0500
800-237-7285
Fax: 610-560-0502
E-Mail: pnorris@hmpcommunications.com
Home Page: www.hmpcommunications.com

Christine Franey, VP
Elizabeth Klumpp, Executive Editor
Peter Treaill, CEO/President
Bonnie Shannon, Manager
Michelle Koch, Circulation Manager
Serves purchasing professionals in acute, long term, and home care, offering product information, reimbursement updates, legislative news, industry trends, and a health care business focus.
24 Pages
Circulation: 100000
ISSN: 0895-2906
Founded in 1989
Printed in 4 colors on glossy stock

12931 Family Medicine
11400 Tomahawk Creek Parkway
Leawood, KS 66211

913-906-6000
800-274-2237
Fax: 913-906-6096
E-Mail: fmjournal@stfm.org
Home Page: www.stfm.org

Traci Nolte, Publisher
John Saultz, President/Editor
Stacy Brungardt, Executive Director
Circulation: 6000
Founded in 1967

12932 Family Therapy Magazine
American Assoc for Marriage and Family Therapy
112 S Alfred Street
Alexandria, VA 22314-3061

703-838-9808
Fax: 703-838-9805
E-Mail: central@aamft.org
Home Page: www.aamft.org
Social Media: Facebook, Twitter, LinkedIn

Linda S. Metcalf, PhD, President
Michael L. Chafin, President-Elect
Michael Bowers, Executive Director
Robin Stillwell, MA, Secretary
Silvia M. Kaminsky, MsED,, Treasurer
AAMFT Association has been involved with the problems, needs and changing patterns of couples and family relationships. The assocation leads the way to increasing understanding, research and education in the field of marriage and family therapy, and ensuring that the public's needs are met by trained practitioners. The AAMFT provides individuals with the tools and resources they need to succeed as marriage and family therapists.
25000 Members
Frequency: Bi-Monthly
Circulation: 25,000
Founded in 1942

12933 First Messenger
American Association of Clinical Endocrinologists
245 Riverside Avenue
Suite 200
Jacksonville, FL 32202

904-353-7878
Fax: 904-353-8185
E-Mail: info@aace.com
Home Page: www.aace.com

Donald Jones, CEO
Donna Beasley, CPA, Finance Manager
Michael Avallone, CPA, Chief Financial Officer
Lynn Blanco, Executive Assistant
Lucille Killgore, Director of College Activities
Serves as a fast track communications tool for AACE members. AACE members utilize The First Messenger to remain in touch with the latest news that may impact their practices, including legislative and socioeconomic issues, cutting edge educational programs, practice management issues and new coding changes.
Frequency: Bi-Monthly
Circulation: 5000
Mailing list available for rent

12934 General Dentistry
211 E Chicago Ave
Suite 900
Chicago, IL 60611-2637

312-440-4300
888-243 3368
Fax: 312-440-0559
E-Mail: executiveoffice@agd.org
Home Page: www.agd.org

John Maher, Manager
Mark Heiss, AGD Member
Jay Donohue, Executive Director
Circulation: 37,000
Founded in 1951

12935 General Surgery News
545 W 45th St
8th Floor
New York, NY 10036-3409

212-957-5300
Fax: 212-957-7230
E-Mail: cdahnke@mcmahonmed.com
Home Page: www.mcmahonmed.com

Raymond E Mc Mahon, CEO
Van Velle, Director
James Prudden, Director
Megan Roloff, Managing Editor
Cost: $60.00
Frequency: Monthly
Circulation: 37,268
Founded in 1974

12936 Grant Funding for Elderly Health Services
Health Resources Publishing
1913 Atlantic Ave
Suite F4
Manasquan, NJ 08736-1067

732-292-1100
888-843-6242
Fax: 732-292-1111
E-Mail: info@healthresourcesonline.com
Home Page: www.healthresourcesonline.com

Robert K Jenkins, Publisher
Lisa Mansfield, Marketing Assistant
Robert Jenkins, Editor
Brett Powell, Regional Director
Alice Burron, Director
This report will give insight into which proposals will get funds for which organization. Lists the organizations that will recieve the most funds from grantmakers during this decade and beyond. Also studies different case histories of successful grant proposals.
Cost: $147.00
Frequency: Monthly
ISBN: 1-882364-46 5
Founded in 1969

12937 Group Practice Data Management
SourceMedia
550 W Van Buren
Suite 1100
Chicago, IL 60607-6680

312-913-1334
Fax: 312-913-1959
Home Page: www.sourcemedia.com

Howard Anderson, Publisher/Editor
Melissa Sefic, Director of Sales
Analyses of trends, insights on technology and practice advice from automation pioneers for executive and physician administrators of medical groups in charge of making decisions about information technology investments. Profiles on practices, new software development updates, and ideas on plans for implementing information technology.
Frequency: Semiannual
Circulation: 15M

12938 Harvard Mental Health Letter
Harvard Health Publcations
10 Shattuck Street
Boston, MA 02115

617-432-1485
877-649-9457
Fax: 617-432-1506
E-Mail: mental_health@hms.harvard.edu
Home Page: www.health.harvard.edu/mental

Michael Craig Miller, Editor in Chief
Edward Coburn, Publishing Director
Cost: $59.00
Frequency: Monthly
Circulation: 50000
Founded in 1985

12939 Harvard Public Health Review
Harvard School of Public Health
665 Huntington Ave
Boston, MA 02115-6018

617-495-1000
Fax: 617-384-8989
E-Mail: fphelps@hsph.harvard.edu
Home Page: www.hsph.harvard.edu/review

Martha Cassin, Manager
Barry R. Bloom, Dean of the School
Martha Cassin, Manager
Flagship magazine of the Harvard School of Public Health.
60 Pages
Frequency: Bi-annually
Circulation: 10000
Founded in 1922
Printed in 4 colors on glossy stock

12940 Health Data Management
SourceMedia
550 W Van Buren
Suite 1100
Chicago, IL 60607-6680
312-913-1334
Fax: 312-913-1959
Home Page: www.healthdatamanagement.com/

Howard J Anderson, Publisher
Bill Siwicki, Editorial Director
Greg Gillespie, Managing Editor
Bill Briggs, Senior Editor
Jim Siebert, Sales/Marketing Manager
Reporting on important information technology issues in health care with emphasis on computerization trends that improve health care efficiency.
Frequency: Monthly
Circulation: 41116
Founded in 1994

12941 Health Facilities Management
American Hospital Publishing

1 N Franklin St
29th Floor
Chicago, IL 60606-3530

312-893-6800
800-821-2039
Fax: 312-422-4500
E-Mail: hfcustsvc@healthforum.com
Home Page: www.hfmmagazine.com

Mary Grayson, Publisher
Mike Hrickiewicz, Managing Editor
Gary A. Mecklenburg, Chairman
Neil J. Jesuele, Director

Reflects their highly specialized needs such as changes in codes and standards, industry news, new products and technical developments of suppliers.
Cost: $30.00
Frequency: Monthly
Circulation: 28160
Founded in 1998

12942 Health Management Technology
Nelson Publishing
2500 Tamiami Trl N
Nokomis, FL 34275-3476

941-966-9521
Fax: 941-966-2590
E-Mail: rblair@healthmgttech.com
Home Page: www.healthmgttech.com
Social Media: Facebook, Twitter

A Verner Nelson, Owner
Robin Blair, Editor

Serves the health care industry including hospitals/multi-hospital systems, managed care organizations and others allied to the field.
Cost: $60.00
66 Pages
Frequency: Monthly
Circulation: 45751
ISSN: 0745-1075
Founded in 1965
Printed in 4 colors on glossy stock

12943 Health Progress
Catholic Health Association
4455 Woodson Rd
St Louis, MO 63134-3797

314-427-2500
Fax: 314-427-0029
E-Mail: rmueller@chausa.org
Home Page: www.chausa.org

Rhonda Mueller, Senior Vice President of Operations
Monica Heaton, Editor
Martha Slover, Circulation Manager

Focuses on management concepts, ethical issues, legislative trends, and theological issues.
Cost: $50.00
Frequency: Monthly
Circulation: 12000
Founded in 1914

12944 Healthcare Executive
American College of Healthcare Executives
1 N Franklin St
Chicago, IL 60606-3529
312-424-2800
Fax: 312-424-0023
E-Mail: contact@ache.org
Home Page: www.ache.org

Thomas C Dolan, CEO
Deborah A Labb, Editor-in-Chief
Michael C Waters, Chairman
Deborah Sprindzunas, Executive Director

Serves members of the American College of Health care executives, whose primary business/industries include hospitals, managed care organizations, long-term care facilities and others allied to the field.
Cost: $65.00
Frequency: Bi-Monthly
ISSN: 0883-5381
Printed in 4 colors on glossy stock

12945 Healthcare Financial Management
2 Westbrook Corporate Ctr
Westchester, IL 60154-5723

708-531-9614
Fax: 708-531-0032
Home Page: www.hfma.org

Richard L Clarke, President

12946 Healthcare Foodservice Magazine
International Publishing Company of America
664 La Villa Dr
Miami Springs, FL 33166-6030

305-887-1700
800-525-2015
Fax: 305-885-1923
Home Page: www.healthcare-services.com

Alexander Morton, Owner
Melora Grattan, Assistant Editor

Devoted to foodservice topics for foodservice directors, foodservice managers, dieticians, foodservice supervisors, chefs, purchasing managers, purchasing agents, administrators and others.
Cost: $25.00
24 Pages
Frequency: Quarterly
Printed in 4 colors on glossy stock

12947 Healthcare Informatics
McGraw Hill
4530 W 77th St
Suite 350
Edina, MN 55435-5018

952-832-7887
Fax: 952-832-7908

Jim Dougherty, Publisher

12948 Healthcare Purchasing News
Nelson Publishing
7650 S Tamiami Trail N
Suite 10
Sarasota, FL 34275

941-927-9345
Fax: 941-927-9588
Home Page: www.hpnonline.com

Rick Dana Barlow, Senior Editor
Jeannie Akridge, New Products Editor
Kristine Russell, Publisher
Julie Williamson, Features Editor
Susan Cantrell, Infection Control Editor

Serves the field of hospital materials management, purchasing, central services and administration.
Cost: $63.00
27 Pages
Frequency: Monthly
Circulation: 33000
ISSN: 0279-4799
Founded in 1965
Printed in 4 colors on glossy stock

12949 Healthplan
American Association of Health Plans
601 Pennsylvania Ave NW
Suite 500
Washington, DC 20004-2601

202-778-3200
Fax: 202-955-4394
E-Mail: ahip@ahip.org
Home Page: www.ahip.org

Kevin New, Editor

A magazine of trends, insights and best practices.
Cost: $60.00
Circulation: 19000
Founded in 2004

12950 Home Health Products
Stevens Publishing Corporation
5151 Belt Line Rd
Dallas, TX 75254-7507

972-687-6700
Fax: 972-687-6767
Home Page: www.stevenspublishing.com

Craig S Stevens, President
Mike Valenti, Executive Vice President
Randy Dye, Publisher
Sandra Bienkowski, Editor
Cost: $119.00
Circulation: 20000
Founded in 1925

12951 Home Medical Equipment News
United Publications
106 Lafayette Street
PO Box 998
Yarmouth, ME 04096

207-846-0600
Fax: 207-846-0657
E-Mail: hmenews@hmenews.com
Home Page: www.hmenews.com

Rick Rector, Publisher
Brook Taliaferro, Editorial Director
Brenda Boothby, Circulation Director
James G. Taliaferro, President
Jim Sullivan, Editor

Serves home medical equipment providers.
Cost: $84.00
Frequency: Monthly
Circulation: 17100
Founded in 1995

12952 HomeCare
Penton Media Inc
249 W 17th St
New York, NY 10011-5390

212-204-4200
Fax: 212-206-3622
E-Mail: gwalker@homecaremag.com
Home Page: www.penton.com

Sharon Rowlands, CEO
Gail Walker, Editor
David Kieselstein, Chief Executive Officer
Kurt Nelson, Vice President, Human Resources
Andrew Schmolka, Senior Vice President

For business leaders in home medical equipment
Frequency: Monthly
Founded in 1989
Mailing list available for rent

12953 Hospital Law Manual
Publishers
111 Eighth Avenue
7th Floor
New York, NY 10011-1978

212-771-0600
800-234-1660
Fax: 212-771-0885
E-Mail: customer.service@aspenpubl.com
Home Page: www.aspenpub.com

Robert Becker, CEO
Stacey Caywood, Publisher
Richard H Kravitz, VP

Hospital law.
Cost: $1325.00
Frequency: Quarterly
Founded in 1965

12954 **Hospital Outlook**
801 Pennsylvania Ave NW
Suite 245
Washington, DC 20004-2697

202-624-1500
202-624-1500
Fax: 202-737-6462
E-Mail: info@fah.org
Home Page: www.fah.org

Charles Kahn, President
LaQuanda Washington, Editor Asst.
Richard P Coorsh, Publisher
Letitia Faison-Mahoney, Controller
Founded in 1966

12955 **Hypertension**
1516 Jefferson Highway
BH 514
New Orleans, LA 70121

504-842-3700
Fax: 504-842-3258

12956 **Immediate Care Business**
Virgo Publishing LLC
3300 N Central Ave
Suite 300
Phoenix, AZ 85012-2532

480-990-1101
Fax: 480-990-0819
E-Mail: jsiefert@vpico.com
Home Page: www.vpico.com

Jenny Bolton, President
John Siefert, CEO
Jennifer Janos, Controller
Kelly Ridley, Executive VP, CFO, Copado
Immediate Care Business provides practical business solutions to professionals who own, operate or are planning to open an urgent care/immediate care facility.
Mailing list available for rent

12957 **Infection Control Today**
Virgo Publishing LLC
3300 N Central Ave
Suite 300
Phoenix, AZ 85012-2532

480-990-1101
Fax: 480-990-0819
E-Mail: jsiefert@vpico.com
Home Page: www.vpico.com

Jenny Bolton, President
John Siefert, CEO
Jennifer Janos, Controller
Kelly Ridley, Executive VP, CFO, Copado
Infection Control Today provides science based articles for the general ward, operating room, sterile processing and environmental services departments of healthcare facilities as well as for the public health community.
Mailing list available for rent: 30000+ names at $var per M

12958 **Information Management Magazine**
ARMA International
11880 College Blvd
Suite 450
Overland Park, KS 66210

913-341-3808
800-422-2762
Fax: 913-341-3742
E-Mail: hq@arma.org
Home Page: www.arma.org

Marilyn Bier, Executive Director
Jody Becker, Associate Editor
Kerrianne Aulet, Education Program Administrator
Michael Avery, Chief Operating Officer
Paula Banes, Sales Project Manager
The leading source of information on topics and issues central to the management of records and information worldwide. Each issue features insightful articles written by experts in the management of records and information.
Cost: $115.00
10,00 Members
Frequency: Bi-monthly
Circulation: 11000
ISSN: 1535-2897
Founded in 1955
Mailing list available for rent: 9000 names
Printed in 4 colors on glossy stock

12959 **International Journal of Trauma Nursing**
Mosby/Professional Opportunities
11830 Westline Industrial Drive
St Louis, MO 63146-3318

314-453-4338
800-237-9851
Fax: 314-872-9164
E-Mail: c.kilzer@elsevier.com
Home Page: www.mosby.com/trauma

Judith Stoner Halpern, Editor
Sarah Papke Kalamazoo, EDITORIAL ASSISTANT
Carol Kilzer, Advertising Sales Service
Reaches today's trauma nurses, coordinators,and managers who direct the nursing aspects of patient care. The journal's multidisciplinary and collaborative approach to the unique needs of the trauma patient represents the vision and clinical expertise of each nursing specialty. These professionals influence the purchase of supplies and equipment for use in emergency and trauma departments.
Cost: $42.00
Frequency: Quarterly
Circulation: 1298
Founded in 1995

12960 **Internet Healthcare Strategies**
Dean Anderson
PO Box 50507
Santa Barbara, CA 93150

805-564-2177
Fax: 805-564-2146
Home Page: www.corhealth.com

12961 **JAAPA**
Medical Economics Publishing
131 W 1st Street
Duluth, MN 55802-2065

877-922-2022
Fax: 218-723-9437
E-Mail: aapa@aapa.org
Home Page: www.jaapa.com

Leslie A Kole, Editor-in-Chief
Tanya Gregory, Editor
Dominic Barone, Publisher
Miguel Van Brakle, Circulation manager
Lee Maniscalco, CEO
Official journal of the American Academy of Physican Assistants.
92 Pages
Frequency: Monthly
Circulation: 52500
ISSN: 0893-7400

12962 **Journal Of Oncology Management**
Alliance Communications Group
810 E 10th St
Lawrence, KS 66044-3018

785-843-1235
800-627-0932
Fax: 785-843-1274
Home Page: www.acgpublishing.com

Gerald Lillian, CEO
Jorgene Hallett, Chief Financial Officer
Rob Chestnut, Chief Financial Officer
Barbara Buzzi, Manager
Bi-monthly, peer-reviewed journal. Includes original research, case studies and other features pertinent to improving performance of oncology administrators.
Cost: $87.00
32 Pages
Circulation: 10000
ISSN: 1061-9364
Founded in 1935
Printed in 4 colors on glossy stock

12963 **Journal Watch**
860 Winter Street
Waltham, MA 02154

781-893-3800
800-843-6356
Fax: 781-893-3914
E-Mail: jwatch@mms.org
Home Page: www.jwatch.org

Allan S Brett, Editor In Chief
Alberta L Fitzpatrick, Publisher
Founded in 1987

12964 **Journal of Allergy and Clinical Immunology**
American Academy of Allergy, Asthma and Immunology
555 E Wells St
Suite 1100
Milwaukee, WI 53202-3800

414-272-6071
E-Mail: info@aaaai.org
Home Page: www.aaaai.org

Thomas B. Casale, MD, Executive VP
Kay A. Whalen, Executive Director
Roberta Silvensky, Associate Executive Director
Amy Flanders, Director of Grants & Development
Rachel McCormick, Executive Assistant
The official scientific journal of the American Academy of Allergy, Asthma and Immunology and the premiere journal in the field. Each issue features the very latest and best research in the allergy/immunology specialty.
6000+ Members
Frequency: Monthly
Founded in 1943

12965 **Journal of American Dietetic Association**
American Dietetic Association
120 South Riverside Plaza
Suite 2000
Chicago, IL 60606-6995

312-990-0040
800-877-1600
Fax: 312-899-4757
E-Mail: elspcs@elsevier.com
Home Page: www.adajournal.org

Linda Van Horn, Editor-in-Chief
Jason T Switt, Editors:
The Journal of American Dietetic Association serves the dietetic field.
Cost: $220.00
Frequency: Monthly
Circulation: 65000
ISSN: 0002-8223
Founded in 1925
Printed in 4 colors on glossy stock

12966 **Journal of Cardiovascular Management**
Alliance Communications Group
810 E 10th St
Lawrence, KS 66044-3018

785-843-1235
800-627-0932
Fax: 785-843-1274

E-Mail: info@aameda.org
Home Page: www.acgpublishing.com

Gerald Lillian, CEO
Jorgene Hallett, Publishing Manager
Renee S Schleicher, CEO/President
Rob Chestnut, Chief Financial Officer

Bi-monthly, peer-reviewed journal of articles pertinent to cardiovascular administration.
Cost: $87.00
32 Pages
Circulation: 12,500
ISSN: 1053-5330
Founded in 1957
Mailing list available for rent: 400 names at $350 per M
Printed in 4 colors on glossy stock

12967 Journal of Clinical Epidemiology
Elsevier Publishing
PO Box 28430
St Louis, MO 63146-0930

314-872-8370
800-545-2522
Fax: 314-432-1380
Home Page: www.elsevier.com

Erik Engstrom, CEO
Bill Godfrey, Chief Information Officer
David Clark, Senior Vice President

12968 Journal of Clinical Investigation
11830 Westline Industrial Drive
St Louis, MO 63146

314-453-7010
800-460-3110
Fax: 314-453-7095
Home Page: www.elsevier.com

A Knottnerus, Editor
P Tugwell, Editor
Laurence Zipson, Group Advertisement Manag
Karlyn Messinger, Communications Manager
Cost: $274.00
Frequency: Monthly
Founded in 1955

12969 Journal of Craniofacial Surgery
Lippencott Williams & Wilkins
16522 Hunters Green Pkwy
Hagerstown, MD 21740-2116

301-223-2300
800-638-3030
Fax: 301-223-2398
E-Mail: service@lww.com
Home Page: www.nursingdrugguide.com

Mutaz B Habal MD, Editor
Jay Lippioctt, CEO

An international journal dedicated to the art and science essential to the practice of craniofacial surgery. Online version available.
Cost: $586.00
ISSN: 1049-2275
Founded in 1998

12970 Journal of Digital Imaging
Society for Imaging Informatics in Medicine
19440 Golf Vista Plaza
Suite 330
Leesburg, VA 20176-8264

703-723-0432
Fax: 703-723-0415
E-Mail: info@siimweb.org
Home Page: www.siimweb.org

Janice Honeyman-Buck PhD, Editor-in-Chief

Goal is to enhance the exchange of knowledge encompassed by the general topic of Imaging Informatics in Medicine such as research and practice in clinical, engineering, information technologies and techniques in all medical imaging environments. JDI topics are of interest to researchers, developers, educators, physicians, and imaging informatics professionals.
Frequency: Bi-Monthly

12971 Journal of Emergency Nursing
Mosby/Professional Opportunities
PO Box 1510
Clearwater, FL 33757-1510

727-443-3047
800-237-9851
Fax: 727-445-9380
Home Page: www.mosby.com/trauma

Presents original, peer-reviewed clinical articles as well as the annual ENA Scientific Assembly program.
Circulation: 27240

12972 Journal of ExtraCorporeal Technology
American Society of ExtraCorporeal Technology
2209 Dickens Road
Richmond, VA 23230-2005

804-565-6363
Fax: 804-282-0090
E-Mail: judyr@amsect.org
Home Page: www.amsect.org

Stewart Hinckley, Executive Director
Donna Pendarvis, Associate Manager
Michael Troike, Government Relations Chairman
Kimberly Robertson, CPA, Controller
Greg Leasure, Membership Services
Cost: $225.00
2,000 Members
Frequency: Quarterly
Circulation: 2000
ISSN: 0022-1058
Founded in 1964

12973 Journal of Forensic Psychology Practice
Bill Cohen
10 Alice Street
Binghamton, NY 13904-1580

607-225-5857
607-722-5857
Fax: 607-771-0012
E-Mail: getinfo@haworthpress.com
Home Page: www.haworthpressinc.com

Bill Cohen, President/Publisher
Jim Hom, Editor

Provides the forensic psychology practicioner and professional with timely information and regional research that examines the impact of new knowledge in the field as it relates to their practice.
Cost: $60.00
Frequency: Quarterly
Circulation: 700
Founded in 1978

12974 Journal of Hand Surgery
American Society for Surgery of the Hand
822 W. Washington Boulevard
Suite 600
Chicago, IL 60607

312-880-1900
Fax: 847-384-1435
E-Mail: info@assh.org
Home Page: www.assh.org

Roy A Meals, Editor-in-Chief

Publishes original, peer-reviewed articles related to the diagnosis, treatment, and pathophysiology of diseases and conditions of the upper extremity; these include both clinical and basic science studies, along with case reports.
Frequency: Monthly
Mailing list available for rent

12975 Journal of Healthcare Quality
National Association for Healthcare Quality
4700 W Lake Ave
Glenview, IL 60025-1468

847-375-4732
800-966-9392
Fax: 888-576-4349
E-Mail: info@nahq.org
Home Page: www.nahq.org

Sheila Lee, Manager
John D Hartley, President

Professional forum that advances quality in a diverse and changing health care environment. Health care professionals worldwide depend upon the Journal for its creative solutions and scientific konwledge in the pursuit of quality.
Cost: $115.00
54 Pages
ISSN: 1062-2551
Founded in 1976
Printed in 4 colors on glossy stock

12976 Journal of Magnetic Resonance
525 B Street
Suite 1900
San Diego, CA 92101-4401

619-231-6616
800-321-5068
Fax: 619-699-6280
Home Page: www.elsevier.com/

S.J. Opella, Editor
JJH Ackerman, Associate Editor
L Frydman, Associate Editor
W.S. Brey, Founding Editor
Founded in 1880

12977 Journal of Managed Care Medicine
American Assoc of Integrated Healthcare Delivery
4435 Waterfront Drive
Suite 101
Glen Allen, VA 23060

804-747-5823
Fax: 804-747-5316
E-Mail: phulcher@aaihds.org
Home Page: www.aaihds.org

Bill Edwards, Managing Editor
Jeremy Williams, Communications Director
Mark Abernathy, Managing Director
David Tyler, Manager
Steven M. Abramson, Senior Manager

12978 Journal of Marriage & Family Therapy
American Assoc for Marriage and Family Therapy
112 S Alfred Street
Alexandria, VA 22314-3061

703-838-9808
Fax: 703-838-9805
E-Mail: central@aamft.org
Home Page: www.aamft.org
Social Media: Facebook, Twitter, LinkedIn

Linda S. Metcalf, PhD, President
Michael Chafin, President-Elect
Michael Bowers, Executive Director
Robin K. Stillwell, MA, Secretary
Silvia M. Kaminsky, MSEd, Treasurer

The AAMFT has been involved with the problems, needs and changing patterns of couples and family relationships. The association leads the way to increasing understanding, research and education in the field of marriage and family therapy, ensuring that the public's needs are met by trained practitioners.
25000 Members
Frequency: Quarterly
Circulation: 25,000
Founded in 1942

12979 Journal of Midwifery & Women's Health

American College of Nurse-Midwives
8403 Colesville Road,Suite 1550
Silver Spring, MD 20910

240-485-1815
Fax: 240-485-1817
E-Mail: jmwh@acnm.org
Home Page: www.jmwh.org/

tekoa king, Editor
Tekoa King, President, Chief Executive Officer
Kalpana Raina, Managing Partner
Cost: $130.00
Circulation: 8000

12980 Journal of Music Therapy

8455 Colesville Rd
Suite 1000
Silver Spring, MD 20910-3392

301-589-3300
Fax: 301-589-5175
E-Mail: info@musictherapy.org
Home Page: www.musictherapy.org
Social Media: Facebook, Twitter

Andrea Farbman, Executive Director
Mary Ellen Wylei, AMTA President

Founded in 1998, AMTA's purpose is the progressive development of the therapeutic use of music in rehabilitation, special education, and community settings. AMTA is committed to the advancement of education, training, professional standards, credentials, and research in support of the music therapy profession.
3800 Members
Frequency: 4 Issues Per Year
Founded in 1998

12981 Journal of Neurotherapy

Taylor & Francis Group LLC
325 Chestnut Street
Suite 800
Philadelphia, PA 19106

215-625-8900
800-354-1420
Fax: 215-625-2940
E-Mail: haworthorders@taylorandfrancis.com
Home Page: www.haworthpressinc.com

Timothy Tinius PhD, Editor
David Kaiser PhD, Editor

Provides an integrated multidisciplinary perspective on clinically relevant research, treatment and public policy for neurotherapy. The journal reviews important findings in clinical neurotherapy and electroencephalography for use in assessing baselines and outcomes of various procedures.
Frequency: Monthly

12982 Journal of Nuclear Medicine

Society of Nuclear Medicine
1850 Samuel Morse Dr
Reston, VA 20190-5316

703-708-9000
Fax: 703-708-9015
E-Mail: volunteer@snm.org
Home Page: www.snm.org

Virginia Pappas, Executive Director
Vincent Pistilli, Chief Financial Officer
Matt Dickens, Director, Information Services
Judy Brazel, Director, Meeting Services
Joanna Spahr, Director, Marketing

12983 Journal of Occupational and Environmental Hygiene

American Industrial Hygiene Association
2700 Prosperity Ave
Suite 250
Fairfax, VA 22031-4321

703-849-8267
Fax: 703-207-3561
E-Mail: infonet@aiha.org
Home Page: www.aiha.org

Peter J Oneil, Executive Director
Michael T Brandt, President

A joint publication of AIHA and ACGIH that is published to enhance the knowledge and practice of occupational and environmental hygiene and safety.

12984 Journal of Oral Implantology

American Academy of Implant Dentistry
211 E Chicago Avenue
Suie 750
Chicago, IL 60611

312-335-1550
877-335-2243
Fax: 312-335-9090
Home Page: www.aaid.org
Social Media: Facebook, Twitter, LinkedIn

James Rutkowski, Editor-in-Chief
Sheldon Winkler, Senior Editor

Dedicated to providing valuable information to general dentists, oral surgeons, prosthodontists, periodontists, scientists, clinicians, laboratory owners and technicians, manufacturers, and educators
Cost: $140.00
Frequency: Bimonthly
Circulation: 4200
ISSN: 0160-6972

12985 Journal of Prosthetics and Orthotics

351 W Camden St
Baltimore, MD 21201-7912

410-528-4000
800-638-6423
Fax: 410-528-4452
E-Mail: webmaster@lww.com
Home Page: www.lww.com

Jeffrey A Nemeth, Editor
Cost: $91.00
Frequency: Quarterly
Founded in 1792

12986 Journal of School Nursing (JOSN)

Sage Publications
2455 Teller Rd
Newbury Park, CA 91320-2234

805-499-9774
800-818-7243
Fax: 805-499-0871
E-Mail: info@sagepub.com
Home Page: www.sagepub.com

Blaise R Simqu, CEO
Janice Denehy, Executive Editor

A forum for advancing the specialty of school nursing, promoting professional growth of school nurses, and improving the health of children in school. Published bi-monthly, this is the official journal of the National Association of School Nurses.
Cost: $164.00
Frequency: bi-Monthly
Mailing list available for rent

12987 Journal of Social Behavior & Personality

Drawer 37
Corte Madera, CA 94976

415-209-9838
Fax: 415-209-6719
Home Page: www.rickcrandall.com

Rick Crandall, CEO/President
Rick Crandall, Editor
Cost: $70.00
Frequency: Quarterly
Founded in 1985

12988 Journal of Thoracic and Cardiovascular Surgery

American Association for Thoracic Surgery
500 Cummings Center
Suite 4550
Beverly, MA 01915

978-927-8330
Fax: 978-524-8890
E-Mail: aats@prri.com
Home Page: www.aats.org
Social Media: Facebook

G Alexander Patterson, President
Elizabeth Dooley Crane, Executive Director
Cost: $354.00
Frequency: Monthly
Circulation: 6000
Founded in 1917
Mailing list available for rent

12989 Journal of Trauma & Dissociation

Taylor & Francis Group LLC
325 Chestnut Street
Suite 800
Philadelphia, PA 19106

215-625-8900
800-354-1420
Fax: 215-625-2940
E-Mail: haworthorders@taylorandfrancis.com
Home Page: www.haworthpressinc.com

Jennifer J Freyd PhD, Editor

Dedicated to publishing peer reviewed scientific literature on psychological trauma, dissociation, and traumatic memory in children and adults. The journal addresses issues ranging from controlled management of traumatic memories and successful interventions to the ethical and philosophical issues entailed by trauma.
Frequency: Quarterly

12990 Journal of Ultrasound in Medicine

American Institute of Ultrasound in Medicine
14750 Sweitzer Ln
Suite 100
Laurel, MD 20707-5906

301-498-4392
800-638-5352
Fax: 301-498-4450
E-Mail: admin@aium.org
Home Page: www.aium.org

Dr Beryl R Benacenraf, Editor-in-Chief
Bruce Totaro, Director of Publications
Thomas R. Nelson, Deputy Editor

Dedicated to the rapid, accurate publication of original articles dealing with all aspects of diagnostic ultrasound, particularly its direct application to patient care, but also relevant basic science, advances in instrumentation and biologic effects. Research papers, case reports, review articles, technical notes and letters to the editor are published.
Cost: $265.00
Frequency: Monthly
Circulation: 8200
ISSN: 0278-4297
Founded in 1952
Mailing list available for rent
Printed in 4 colors on glossy stock

12991 Journal of the American Academy of Child and Adult Psychiatry

American Academy of Child and Adult Psychiatry
3615 Wisconsin Ave NW
Washington, DC 20016-3007
202-966-7300
Fax: 202-966-2891
E-Mail: communications@aacap.org

Home Page: www.aacap.org
Social Media: Facebook, Twitter

Eva Brown, Manager
Martin J. Drell, President
Virginia Anthony, Executive Director
Founded in 1953
Mailing list available for rent

12992 Journal of the American Academy of Child & Adolescent Psychiatry
Lippincott Williams & Wilkins
351 W Camden St
Baltimore, MD 21201-2436

410-949-8000
Fax: 410-528-4414
Home Page: www.lww.com
Social Media: Facebook, Twitter

J Arnold Anthony, Operations
AndrSs Martin, MD/MPH, Editor-Elect
Rebecca Jensen, Managing Editor

The official journal of the American Academy of Child & adolescent Psychiatry, the journal is recognized as the major journal exclusivley on todays psychiatric research and treatment of the child and adolescent.
Frequency: Monthly
ISSN: 0890-8567

12993 Journal of the American College of Surgeons
633 N St. Clair Street
Chicago, IL 60611

312-202-5136
800-440-5227
Fax: 312-202-5027

12994 Journal of the American Dental Association
American Dental Association
211 E Chicago Ave
Chicago, IL 60611-2678

312-440-2897
Fax: 312-440-2800
Home Page: www.ada.org

Lawrence H Meskin, Editor
Daniel M Castagna, Editorial Board

Serves the dental profession and dental industry.
Cost: $95.00
Frequency: Monthly
Circulation: 135361
ISSN: 0002-8177
Founded in 1859
Printed in 4 colors on glossy stock

12995 Journal of the American Health Information Management Association
American Health Information Management Association
633 N St. Clair Street
Chicago, IL 60611-3211

312-202-5000
800-621-4111
Fax: 312-202-5001
E-Mail: postmaster@facs.org
Home Page: www.facs.org/

Barry M. Manuel, Editor-in-chief
Paul F. Nora, Editor

Provides information in the field of health information and medical record management in all health care settings. Subscription: non-members $72,
Cost: $25.00
Frequency: Monthly
Founded in 1913
Printed in 4 colors on glossy stock

12996 Journal of the Medical Library Association
Medical Library Association
65 E Wacker Drive
Suite 1900
Chicago, IL 60601-7246

312-419-9094
Fax: 312-419-8950
E-Mail: info@mlahq.org
Home Page: www.mlanet.org

Elizabeth Lund, Director Publication
Carla J Funk, Executive Officer
Susan Talmage, Editorial Assistant
Scott Plutchak, Editor
Cost: $163.00
Frequency: Quarterly
Circulation: 5000
Founded in 1898
Mailing list available for rent

12997 Journal of the National Medical Association
4930 Del Ray Avenue
Bethesda, MD 20814

301-654-2055
Fax: 301-654-5920
E-Mail: member@gastro.org
Home Page: www.gastro.org

Robert Greenberg, Executive Vp
Michael Stolar, Senior Vp

12998 MS Connection
Lippincott Williams & Wilkins
351 W Camden St
Baltimore, MD 21201-2436

410-949-8000
800-787-8981
Fax: 410-528-4414
Home Page: www.lww.com

J Arnold Anthony, Operations
Michael Levin-Epstein, Managing Editor
Michele Swain, Marketing Manager

12999 Managed Healthcare
Advanstar Communications
7500 Old Oak Blvd
Cleveland, OH 44130-3343

440-243-8100
Fax: 440-891-2740
E-Mail: info@advanstar.com

Daniel J. Corcoran, Publisher
Michael T. McCue, Editor-In-Chief
Craig Roth, Group Publisher
Tracey L. Walker, Senior Editor
Julie Miller, Managing Editor

Valuable resource for managers charged with controlling health care costs and quality.
Cost: $64.00
Frequency: Monthly
Circulation: 40000
ISSN: 1060-1392
Founded in 1987

13000 McKnight's Long-Term Care News
McKnight Medical Communications
1 Northfield Plz
Suite 300
Northfield, IL 60093-1216

847-784-8706
800-558-1703
Fax: 847-784-9346
E-Mail: ltcn-webmaster@mltcn.com
Home Page: www.mcknightsonline.com

William Pecover, CEO
Lee Maniscalco, Executive VP
Jim Berklan, Editor
Jeff Hartford, Circulation Director

Serves the field of long term care including nursing homes, senior housing centers, assisted living facilities, hospitals with LTC units, continuing care retirement communities, nursing home chains and other allied organizations in the field.
35 Pages
Frequency: Weekly
Circulation: 46000
ISSN: 1048-3314
Printed in 4 colors on glossy stock

13001 Medical Economics
Advanstar Communications
5 Paragon Dr
Montvale, NJ 07645-1791

973-944-7777
Fax: 973-944-7778

Curtis Allen, President
Marianne Dekker Mattera, Editor-in-Chief
Mike Graziani, Publisher
Sean Keating, Managing Editor
Laura Wagner, VP Operations

Medical Economics guides physicians in the business of practicing by giving advice about malpractice, third-party reimbursement, managed care, tax strategies, legal information and counseling, fraud, abuse and anti-trust strategies. It helps them manage their practice more efficiently so they can be more effective in delivering patient care.
Cost: $109.00
Frequency: Monthly
Circulation: 154897
Founded in 1987

13002 Medical Reference Services Quarterly
Taylor & Francis Group LLC
325 Chestnut Street
Suite 800
Philadelphia, PA 19106

215-625-8900
215-625-8900
Fax: 215-625-2940
E-Mail: haworthorders@taylorandfrancis.com
Home Page: www.haworthpress.com

M Sandra Wood, Editor

Covers topics of current interest and practical value in the areas of reference in medicine and related specialties, the biomedical sciences, nursing and allied health.
Cost: $60.00
Frequency: Quarterly
ISSN: 0276-3869
Founded in 1978

13003 Medical Research Funding Bulletin
PO Box 7507
New York, NY 10150-7507

212-371-3398
Fax: 801-761-4200

John Connolly, CEO
Carroll Gordon, Circulation Manager
Cost: $75.00
Frequency: Fortnightly
Circulation: 4500
Founded in 1972

13004 Modern Healthcare
Crain Communications
360 N Michigan Ave
Chicago, IL 60601-3800

312-649-5200
Fax: 312-649-7937
E-Mail: info@crain.com
Home Page: www.crain.com

Keith Crain, CEO

Examines and reports on the issues that have a direct impact on the business decisions healthcare professionals make every day.
Frequency: Weekly
Circulation: 70180

13005 **Molecular Endocrinology**
Molecular Society Journals
8401 Connecticut Avenue
Suite 900
Chevy Chase, MD 20815-4410
301-941-0200
888-363-6274
Fax: 301-941-0259
E-Mail: societyservices@endo-society.org
Home Page: www.endo-society.org
John A Cidlowski, Editor-in-chief
Scott Hunt, Executive Director
Maggie Haworth, Managing Editor
Jessica Peterson, Marketing Manager
John Marshall, Secretary
Cost: $376.00
Frequency: Weekly
Circulation: 11000
Founded in 1916

13006 **NASN Newsletter**
National Association of School Nurses
163 US Route 1
PO Box 1300
Scarborough, ME 04074-9060
207-883-2117
877-627-6476
Fax: 207-883-2683
E-Mail: nasn@nasn.org
Home Page: www.nasn.org
Devin Dinkel, Editor
Wanda Miller, Executive Director
Donna Mazyck, President
Gloria Durgin, Administrator/Sponsorship
Kenny Lull, Communications Manager
Cost: $2.00
Founded in 1968

13007 **New England Journal of Medicine**
Massachusetts Medical Society
10 Shattuck St
Boston, MA 02115-6094
617-734-9800
Fax: 617-739-9864
E-Mail: comments@nejm.org
Home Page: www.nejm.org
Debra Weinstein, Chair
Jeffrey M Drazen, Editor-in-Chief
Gregory Curfman, Executive Editor
General medicine journal that publishes new medical research findings, review articles, and editorial opinion on a wide variety of topics of importance to biomedical science and clinical practice. Published with an emphasis on internal medicine and specialty areas including allergy/immunology, cardiology, endocrinology, gastroenterology, hematology, kidney disease, oncology, pulmonary disease, rheumatology, HIV, and infectous diseases.
Cost: $149.00
Frequency: Weekly

13008 **Nursing**
Ambler Office of Lippincott Williams and Wilkins
323 Norristown Rd
Suite 200
Ambler, PA 19002-2758
215-646-8700
800-346-7844
Fax: 215-654-1328
Home Page: www.lww.com
Mary Gill, Human Resources
Cheryl Mee, Publisher & Editor
Keith Sollweiler, Marketing
Cost: $34.00
Frequency: Monthly
Circulation: 300000
Founded in 1971

13009 **Nursing News**
48 W Street
Concord, NH 03301-3595
603-225-3783
Fax: 603-228-6672
Home Page: www.nhnurses.org
Bob Desc, CEO
Susan Fetzer, President
Cost: $26.00
Frequency: Quarterly
Circulation: 18000
Founded in 1906

13010 **Nursing Outlook**
1111 Middle Drive
Indiana, IN 46202
317-274-1486
Fax: 317-278-1842
E-Mail: mbroome@iupui.edu
Home Page: www.nursiniupui.edu
Marion Broome, Editor
Adam Herberg, President, Circulation Manager

13011 **Nutrition Business Journal**
4452 Park Boulevard
Suite 306
San Diego, CA 92116
619-295-7685
Fax: 619 295-5743
E-Mail: info@nutritionbusiness.com
Home Page: www.nutritionbusiness.com
David Nussbaum, CEO
Preston Vice, CFO
Cost: $995.00
Frequency: Monthly
Founded in 1892

13012 **O&P Almanac**
American Orthotic & Prosthetic Association
330 John Carlyle Street
Suite 200
Alexandria, VA 22314
571-431-0876
Fax: 571-431-0899
E-Mail: info@aopanet.org
Home Page: www.aopanet.org
Social Media: Facebook, Twitter, LinkedIn
Tom DiBello, President
Anita Liberman, VP
Thomas F Fise, Executive Director
Don DeBolt, Chief Operating Officer
Devon Bernard, Manager of Reimbursement
Cost: $59.00
84 Pages
Frequency: Monthly
Circulation: 13000
ISSN: 1061-4621
Founded in 1951
Mailing list available for rent
Printed in 4 colors on glossy stock

13013 **Occupational Health & Safety**
Stevens Publishing Corporation
5151 Belt Line Rd
10th Floor
Dallas, TX 75254-7507
972-687-6700
Fax: 972-687-6767
E-Mail: jlaws@stevenspublishing.com
Home Page: www.stevenspublishing.com
Craig S Stevens, President
Jerry Laws, Executive Vice President
Mike Valenti, Executive Vice President
Craig Stevens, CEO
Margaret Perry, Circulation Director
Practical advice on workplace safety and compliance with laws and regulations. Feature articles and product information.
Frequency: Monthly
Circulation: 84000
Founded in 1925

13014 **Oncology Times**
333 7th Ave
19th Floor
New York, NY 10001-5015
646-674-6544
800-933-6525
Fax: 646-674-6500
E-Mail: ot@lww.com
Home Page: www.lww.com
Serena Stockwell, Manager
Ken Senerth, Publisher
Frank Cox, Advertising Manager
Larry Klein, Director
Cost: $189.00
Circulation: 45000
Founded in 1972

13015 **Optometry: Journal of the American Optometric Association**
American Optometric Association
243 N Lindbergh Blvd
St Louis, MO 63141-7881
314-991-4100
Fax: 314-991-4101
E-Mail:
journalsonlinesupport-usa@elsevier.com
Home Page: www.optometryjaoa.com
Paul B. Freeman, OD, Editor-in-Chief
Most widely circulated scholarly optometry journal, provides a forum for research that advances the art and science of the practice of primary care optometry.
Cost: $95.00
68 Pages
Frequency: Monthly
Circulation: 34000
ISSN: 1529-1839
Founded in 1898
Printed in 4 colors on glossy stock

13016 **Ostomy Wound Management**
HMP Communications
83 General Warren Blvd
Suite 100
Malvern, PA 19355-1252
610-560-0500
800-237-7285
Fax: 610-560-0502
E-Mail:
subscriptions@hmpcommunications.com
Home Page: www.hmpcommunications.com
Social Media: Facebook, Twitter, LinkedIn
Jeff Hennessy, CEO
Barbara Zeiger, Editor
Jeremy Bowden, Publisher
Bonnie Shannon, Circulation Manager
Information on the disciplines of ostomy care, wound care, incontinence care, and related skin and nutritional issues.
Cost: $39.95
Frequency: Monthly
Circulation: 230000
ISSN: 0889-5099
Founded in 1980
Printed in 4 colors on glossy stock

13017 **PT in Motion**
American Physical Therapy Association
1111 N Fairfax St
Alexandria, VA 22314-1488
703-684-2782
Fax: 703-706-8536
E-Mail: memberservices@apta.org

Home Page: www.apta.org
Social Media: Facebook, Twitter, LinkedIn

Don Tepper, Editor
John D. Barnes, Chief Executive Officer
Janet Bezner, VP, Education, Governance
Rob Batarla, VP, Finance & Business Development
Felicity Clancy, VP, Communications & Marketing

Formerly PT Magazine, published to meet the needs and interests of APTA members and to promote physical therapy as a vital professional career, PT provides legislative, health care, human interest, and Association news and serves as a forum for discussion of professional issues and ideas in physical therapy practice.
80000 Members
Mailing list available for rent

13018 Patient Care
Medical Economics Publishing
5 Paragon Dr
Montvale, NJ 07645-1791

973-944-7777
Fax: 973-944-7778
Home Page: www.patientcareonline.com

Curtis Allen, President
Stuart Williams, Publisher
Christine Shappell, Circulation Manager
Don Berman, Director Business Development

Patient care serves selected medical and osteopathic physicians.
Cost: $51.50
Frequency: Monthly
Founded in 1967
Printed in 4 colors

13019 Physicians & Computers
Moorhead Publications
810 S Waukegan Road
#200
Lake Forest, IL 60045-2672

847-615-8333
Fax: 847-615-8345
Home Page: www.physicians-computers.com

Tom Moorhead, Publisher

Provides physicians with information on computer advances helpful in the private practice of medicine. Practice management, current medical and non-medical software, computer diagnostics, etc.
Cost: $40.00
Frequency: Monthly
Circulation: 90M

13020 Pneumogram
1961 Main Street
#246
Sacremento, CA 95076

916-441-2222
888-730-2772
Fax: 916-442-4182
E-Mail: arosenberg@csrc.org
Home Page: www.csrc.org/

Janyth Bolden, President
Abbie Rosenberg, Secretary
Sherry Blansfield, Secretary
Frequency: Quarterly
Founded in 1968

13021 Psychoanalytic Psychology
211 E 70th Street
Suite 17 H
New York, NY 10021

212-633-9162
Fax: 212-628-8453

Lori Sloan, Executive Director

13022 Psychology of Addictive Behaviors
University of South Florida
BEH 339
Department of Psychology
Tampa, FL 33620

813-974-4826
800-374-2721
Fax: 202-336-5568
Home Page: www.apa.org
Social Media: Facebook, Twitter

Stephen A. Maisto, Editor
Norman B. Anderson, Chief Executive Officer
L. Michael Honaker, Chief Operating Officer
Cynthia D. Belar, Executive Director
Tony Habash, Chief Information Officer
Mailing list available for rent

13023 Public Health Nursing
350 Main Street
6th Floor
Malden, MA 02148

781-388-8200
Fax: 781-388-8210
E-Mail: mspencer@bos.blackwellpublishing.com
Home Page: www.blackwellpublishing.com/

Sarah E Abrams, Editor
Judith C Hays, Editor
Otis Dean, Publisher
Alice Meadows, Senior Manager, Circulation
Paige Larkin, Sr. Marketing Manager
Cost: $149.00
Founded in 1922

13024 Quality Matters
385 Highland Colony Parkway
Suite 120
Ridgeland, MS 39157

601-957-1575
800-844-0500
Fax: 601-956-1713

13025 RDH
PennWell Publishing Company
1421 S Sheridan Rd
Tulsa, OK 74112-6619

918-831-9421
Fax: 918-831-9476
Home Page: www.pennwell.com

Robert Biolchini, President
Mark Hartley, Editor

National magazine for dental hygiene professionals.
Cost: $48.00
60 Pages
Frequency: Monthly
Founded in 1910

13026 RN Magazine
Medical Economics Publishing
5 Paragon Dr
Montvale, NJ 07645-1791

973-944-7777
888-581-8052
Fax: 973-944-7778
Home Page: www.rnweb.com

Curtis Allen, President
Wendy Raupers, Associate Publisher
Joy Puzzo, Marketing/Circulation Manager
Don Berman, Director Business Development

Published to serve professional nurses in hospitals, physician's offices, extended care facilities, schools of nursing, occupational and community health agencies and other professional nurses.
Cost: $35.00
Frequency: Monthly
Circulation: 2500
ISSN: 0033-7021
Founded in 1937

13027 Radiology
820 Jorie Boulevard
Oak Brook, IL 60523-2251

630-571-2670
800-381-6660
Fax: 630-571-7837
E-Mail: reginfo@rsna.org
Home Page: www.rsna.org

Anthony V. Proto, Editor
Michael Ulezlo, Senior Marketing Manager
Cost: $250.00
Frequency: Monthly
Circulation: 35000
Founded in 1915

13028 Radiology Management
American Healthcare Radiology Administrators
490B Boston Post Rd
Suite 200
Sudbury, MA 01776-3367

978-443-7591
800-334-2472
Fax: 978-443-8046
E-Mail: info@ahraonline.org
Home Page: www.ahraonline.org
Social Media: Facebook, Twitter, LinkedIn

Edward Cronin, Jr., CEO
Sarah Murray, Executive Assistant
Emily Ryan, Membership Coordinator
Debra Murphy, Publications Director

A peer reviewed journal with an editorial review board of AHRA members.
Cost: $65.00
64 Pages
Circulation: 4,000
ISSN: 0198-7097
Founded in 1978
Printed in 4 colors on glossy stock

13029 Remington Report
Remington Report
30100 Town Center Drive
Suite 421
Laguna Niguel, CA 92677

800-247-4781
800-247-4781
Fax: 949-715-1797
E-Mail: remrptedit@aol.com
Home Page: www.remingtonreport.com

Lisa Remington, Publisher
Cost: $44.50
Founded in 1993

13030 Renal Business Today
Virgo Publishing LLC
3300 N Central Ave
Suite 300
Phoenix, AZ 85012-2532

480-990-1101
Fax: 480-990-0819
E-Mail: jsiefert@vpico.com
Home Page: www.vpico.com

Jenny Bolton, President
John Siefert, CEO
Jennifer Janos, Controller
Kelly Ridley, Executive VP, CFO, Copado

Renal Business Today delivers editorials for practice management professionals. Editorials include the latest business and technology trends in renal care, expert advice, strategic business solutions written by industry leaders and human interest articles.
Mailing list available for rent

13031 Research Quarterly for Exercise and Sport
AAHPERD

1900 Association Dr
Reston, VA 20191-1598

703-476-3400
800-213-7193
Fax: 703-476-9527
Home Page: www.aahperd.org

E. Paul Roetert, CEO
Judith C Young, VP
Paula Kun, Marketing

RQES is a professional journal providing members with numerous articles and research on subjects that focus on the art and science of human movement studies.
Cost: $295.00
128 Pages
Frequency: Quarterly
Circulation: 6000
ISSN: 0270-1367
Mailing list available for rent
Printed in one color on glossy stock

13032 **Respiratory Care**
9425 N Macarthur Blvd
Suite 100
Irving, TX 75063-4725

972-243-2272
Fax: 972-484-2720
E-Mail: info@aarc.org
Home Page: www.aarc.org

Sam Giordano, CEO

Journal for the professional respiratory care therapist. Member publication of the American Association for Respiratory Care.
Cost: $89.95
Frequency: Monthly
Founded in 1947

13033 **Review of Optometry**
11 Campus Boulevard
Newton Square, PA 19073

610-492-1000
Fax: 610-492-1039
E-Mail: reviewofoptometry@jobson.com
Home Page: www.revoptom.com

Amy Hellem, Editor-in-Chief
Jeffrey S Eisenberg, Director
Paul Karpecki, Director
Frequency: Monthly

13034 **Risk Management Handbook**
NACHA: The Electronic Payments Association
13450 Sunrise Valley Drive
Suite 100
Herndon, VA 20171

703-561-1100
Fax: 703-787-0996
E-Mail: info@nacha.org
Home Page: www.nacha.org

Janet O Estep, CEO
Marcie Haitema, Chairperson

A comprehensive guide to ACH Risk Issues and Control Procedures. Explains the types of ACH payments risk, assesses the operational implications, and provides best practices for developing an effective risk management program.
Cost: $65.00
Frequency: Monthly
Founded in 1991

13035 **Rite Aid Be Healthy & Beatiful**
Drug Store News Consumer Health Publications
425 Park Ave
New York, NY 10022-3526

212-756-5220
Fax: 212-756-5250
E-Mail: jtanzola@lf.com
Home Page: www.drugstorenews.com

Lebhar Friedman, Publisher

Provides health and beauty tips to millions of women who visit Rite Aid stores.
Frequency: Quarterly
Circulation: 950,000
Founded in 2002

13036 **Scrip Magazine**
270 Madison Ave
New York, NY 10016-0601

212-262-8230
Fax: 212-262-8234
E-Mail: pharmabooks@pharmabooks.com
Home Page: www.pjbpubs.com

Ken May, Executive Director
Alice Dunmore, Circulation Manager
Jenefer Trevena, Marketing Manager
Phillip Every, Worldwide Advertising Sales

An in-depth view of the issues and challenges facing all sectors of the pharmaceutical industry worldwide. Analytical features are written by pharmaceutical experts and opinion leaders as well as specialist journalists.
Cost: $ 1190.00

13037 **Sports Medicine Digest**
351 W Camden St
Baltimore, MD 21201-7912

410-528-4000
800-787-8981
Fax: 410-528-4452
Home Page: www.lww.com

Daniel Schwartz, Publisher
Michael Levin-Epstein, Managing Editor
Cost: $125.00
12 Pages
Frequency: Monthly
ISSN: 0731-9770
Founded in 1978
Printed in one color on matte stock

13038 **SurgiStrategies**
Virgo Publishing LLC
3300 N Central Ave
Suite 300
Phoenix, AZ 85012-2532

480-990-1101
Fax: 480-990-0819
E-Mail: jsiefert@vpico.com
Home Page: www.vpico.com

Jenny Bolton, President
John Siefert, CEO
Jennifer Janos, Controller
Kelly Ridley, Executive VP, CFO, Copado

SurgiStrategies identifies and analyzes the high level trends impacting physician and corporation owned outpatient healthcare facilities with relevant, timely, ahead of the curve content.
Mailing list available for rent: 22000+ names at $var per M

13039 **Surgical Products**
Reed Business Information
100 Enterprise Drive
Suite 600
Rockaway, NJ 07866-912

973-920-7000
Fax: 630-288-8686
E-Mail: rritsma@reedbusiness.com
Home Page: www.surgprodmag.com/

Noreen Costelloe, Group VP/Publisher
Richard Ritsma, Editor-in-Chief
James Reed, Owner
Sabrina Crow, Managing Director
Steve Koppelman, Circulation Manager

Surgical products provides surgeons, OR supervisors and OR materials managers working in hospitals and surgi-centers with new product technology and equipment.
Frequency: Monthly
Circulation: 71000
Founded in 1946

13040 **The Neurodiagnostic Journal**
American Society of Electroneurodiagnostic Tech
402 East Bannister Road
Suite A
Kansas City, MO 64131-3019

816-931-1120
Fax: 816-931-1145
E-Mail: info@aset.org
Home Page: www.aset.org

Arlen Reimritz, Executive Director
Lucy Sullivan, Managing Editor

Peer-reviewed journal that contains research articles, case studies, technical articles and book reviews.
Cost: $110.00
Frequency: Quarterly
Circulation: 5000
ISSN: 1086-508X

13041 **Transplantation**
351 W Camden St
Baltimore, MD 21201-7912

410-528-4000
800-222-3790
Fax: 410-528-4452
Home Page: www.lww.com

Sherry Reed, Manager
Mark A Hardy, Editor
Jim Mulligan, Publisher
Taron Buttler, National Sales Manager
Jeff Hargrove, Manager
Cost: $657.00
Circulation: 2556

13042 **Transportation Leader**
Taxicab, Limousine & Paratransit Association
3200 Tower Oaks Blvd
Suite 220
Rockville, MD 20852

301-984-5700
Fax: 301-984-5703
E-Mail: info@tlpa.org
Home Page: www.tlpa.org

Alfred LaGasse, CEO
William Rouse, President
Harold Morgan, Executive Vice President
Michelle A. Hariston, CMP, Manager of Meetings
Leah New, Manager of Communications

Leading resource for news and information on issues, trends, and people in the private, for-hire passenger transportation industry. Provides readers with an array of features, articles, and columns that include information on managing a transportation company, industry trends, driver's tips, an industry calendar of events, coverage of TLPA events, and advertisements from the industry's leading suppliers.
Cost: $4.00
48 Pages
Frequency: Quarterly
Circulation: 6000
Founded in 1917
Mailing list available for rent. 6,000 names at $100 per M
Printed in 4 colors on glossy stock

13043 **Urologic Nursing**
Society of Urologic Nurses and Associates
East Holly Avenue
PO Box 56
Pitman, NJ 08071

856-256-2300
Fax: 856-589-7463

E-Mail: uronsg@ajj.com
Home Page: www.suna.org

Nancy Mueller, President
Robert McIlvaine, Circulation Manager
Mike Cunningham, Marketing
Jane Hokanson Hawks, Editor
Anthony Jannetti, Executive Director
Cost: $40.00
Circulation: 4500
Founded in 1981
Printed in 4 colors on glossy stock

13044 Virology
125 Park Avenue
23rd Floor
New York, NY 10017

212-309-5498
800-821-5068
Fax: 212-309-5480
E-Mail: d.weerd@elsevier.com
Home Page: www.reed-elsevier.com/

A Pinczuk, Editor-in-Chief
Karlyn Messinger, Communications Manager
Cost: $139.00
Frequency: Monthly
Circulation: 280
Founded in 1993

13045 Volunteer
119 W 24th Street
9th Floor
New York, NY 10011-1913

212-870-4940
Fax: 212-367-1236

Esperanza Jorge-Garcia, Executive Director

13046 Walgreens Diabetes & You
Drug Store News Consumer Health Publications
425 Park Ave
New York, NY 10022-3526

212-756-5220
Fax: 212-756-5250
E-Mail: jtanzola@lf.com
Home Page: www.drugstorenews.com

Lebhar Friedman, Publisher
Edward H King, Director

Contains health news of importance to those with diabetes.

13047 World Disease Weekly
2900 Paces Ferry Road
Bldg D 2nd Floor
Atlanta, GA 30339

770-507-7777
800-726-4550
Fax: 770-435-6800
E-Mail: subscribe@newsrx.com
Cost: $2329.00

Frequency: Weekly
Founded in 1984

Trade Shows

13048 AAAAI Annual Conference and Exhibition
American Academy Allergy, Asthma, and Immunology
555 E Wells Street
Suite 100
Milwaukee, WI 53202-3823

414-272-6071
800-822-2762
Fax: 414-272-6070
E-Mail: info@aaaai.org
Home Page: www.aaaai.org

Katie Ferguson, Sr. Meetings Manager

Exhibits, pharmaceuticals, medical supplies and books.
7000 Attendees
Frequency: Annual
Founded in 1943

13049 AAAAI Annual Meeting
American Academy of Allergy, Asthma and Immunology (AAAAI)
555 E. Wells Street, Suite 1100
Milwaukee, WI 53202-3823

414-272-6071
E-Mail: info@aaaai.org
Home Page: www.aaaai.org

Thomas B. Casale, MD, Executive Vice President
Kay A. Whalen, Executive Director
Roberta Slivensky, Associate Executive Director
Amy Flanders, Director of Grants & Development
Rachel McCormick, Executive Assistant

Annual gathering of immunology and allergy experts. Those attending the annual meeting include academicians, allied health professionals and clinicians.
6000+ Members
Founded in 1943

13050 AAB Annual Meeting and Educational Conference
American Association of Bioanalysts
906 Olive Street
Suite 1200
Saint Louis, MO 63101-1448

314-241-1445
Fax: 314-241-1449
E-Mail: aab@aab.org
Home Page: www.aab.org

Mark S Biernbaum PhD, Administrator

Educational programs, abstract presentations, poster presentations and exhibits.
Founded in 1956

13051 AACAP Annual Meeting
American Academy of Child & Adolescent Psychiatry
3615 Wisconsin Avenue NW
Washington, DC 20016-3007

202-966-7300
Fax: 202-966-2891
E-Mail: communications@aacap.org
Home Page: www.aacap.org
Social Media: Facebook, Twitter

Thomas F Anders, MD, President
Virginia Anthony, Executive Director
Martin J. Drell, President
Founded in 1953
Mailing list available for rent

13052 AAHP Institute & Display Forum
American Association of Health Plans
1129 20th Street NW
Washington, DC 20036

202-778-3200
Fax: 202-778-8506

13053 AAID Annual Meeting
American Academy of Implant Dentistry
211 E Chicago Avenue
Suite 750
Chicago, IL 60611

312-335-1550
877-335-2243
Fax: 312-335-9090
E-Mail: info@aaid.com
Home Page: www.aaid.com
Social Media: Facebook, Twitter, LinkedIn

Sharon Bennett, Executive Director
Max Moses, Director Communications

The 2012 meeting will be in Washington, DC.
1500 Attendees
Frequency: October 3-6, 2012

13054 AAMFT Conference
American Assoc for Marriage and Family Therapy
112 S Alfred Street
Alexandria, VA 22314-3061

703-838-9808
Fax: 703-838-9805
E-Mail: central@aamft.org
Home Page: www.aamft.org
Social Media: Facebook, Twitter, LinkedIn

Linda S. Metcalf, PhD, President
Michael L. Chafin, President-Elect
Michael Bowers, Executive Director
Robin K. Stillwell, MA, Secretary
Silvia M. Kaminsky, MSEd, Treasurer

AAMFT represents the professional interests of more than 25,000 marriage and family therapists throughout the United States, Canada and abroad.
25000 Members
1500 Attendees
Frequency: Annual
Founded in 1942

13055 AAMI Conference & Expo
Assoc for the Advancement of Medical Instrumenta
4301 N. Fairfax Drive
Suite 301
Arlington, VA 22203-1633

703-525-4890
Fax: 703-276-0793
E-Mail: customerservice@aami.org
Home Page: www.aami.org

Michael Miller, President
Ed Leonardo, Meetings/Expositions Director

Offers educational, networking, and personal-development opportunities that wil lenable you to expand your expertise, increasr your productivity, develop lasting relationships with peers, and ultimately advance your career.
Frequency: Annual

13056 AANEM Annual Meeting
American Assoc of Neuromuscular & Electro Medicine
2621 Superior Drive NW
Rochester, MN 55902-3018

507-288-0100
Fax: 507-288-1225
E-Mail: aanem@aanem.org
Home Page: www.aanem.org

Shirlyn A Adkins, Executive Director
Patrick D Aldrich, Finance Director
Emily Spaulding, Executive Assistant
Loretta Bronson, Senior Director of Operations
Catherine French, Director of Health Policy

Forty exhibits of electromyographic and electrodiagnosis equipment and accessories. Seminar, workshop and breakfast.
1000 Attendees
Mailing list available for rent

13057 AAO-HNSF Annual Meeting & OTO Expo
American Academy of Otolaryngology
1650 Diagonal Road
Alexandria, VA 22314-3357

703-836-4444
Fax: 703-683-5100

E-Mail: membership@entnet.org
Home Page: www.entnet.org

Jessica Mikulski, Sr Manager, Media/Public Relations
Matt Daigle, Media & Public Relations Manager
James L. Netterville, President
J. Gavin Setzen, Secretary/Treasurer
David R. Nielsen, Executive Vice President and CEO

The largest gathering of otolaryngologists, together with the world's largest collection of products and services for the specialty
Frequency: Septemer
Mailing list available for rent

13058 **AAOMS Scientific Meeting**
American Assn. of Oral & Maxillofacial Surgeons
9700 W Bryn Mawr Avenue
Rosemont, IL 60018-5701

847-678-6200
800-822-6637
Fax: 847-678-6286
E-Mail: inquiries@aaoms.org
Home Page: www.aaoms.org

Edwin Slade, Treasurer
Ira Cheifetz, Vice President

Educational session, reception, tours. Over 275 exhibits relating to the profession.
4000 Attendees
Frequency: Annual
Founded in 1918

13059 **AAPS Annual Scientific Meeting**
American Association of Physician Specialists, Inc
5550 West Executive Drive
Suite 400
Tampa, FL 33609-1035

813-433-2277
Fax: 813-830-6599
E-Mail: wcarbone@aapsus.org
Home Page: www.aapsus.com

Esther Berg, Director of CME/Meetings/Membership
Keely Clarke, Membership/CME Coordinator
William Carbone, Chief Executive Officer

The American Association of Physician Specialists, Inc.(AAPS) annual meeting is used to educate medical professionals on relevant medical topics that include continuing medical education(CME) credits. The association also holdsbusiness meetings at this time.
1000 Attendees

13060 **AARC International Respiratory Congress**
American Association for Respiratory Care
9425 N MacArthur Boulevard
Suite 100
Irving, TX 75063-4706

972-243-2272
Fax: 972-484-2720
E-Mail: info@aarc.org
Home Page: www.aarc.org

Sam P Giordano, Executive Director/Executive VP
Beth Binkley, Communication Coordinator
Steve Bowden, Web developer
Kathy Blackmon, Convention and Meetings Manager
Asha Desai, Customer Service Manager

Largest respiratory care meeting in the world. Offers the latest information in all aspects of respiratory care. The congress offers you an opportunity to earn all the continuing education hours required for your state license annually.
7000 Attendees
Frequency: December
Founded in 1947
Mailing list available for rent

13061 **ACA Annual Conference & Expo**
Journal of Counseling and Development
5999 Stevenson Ave
Alexandria, VA 22304-3302

703-823-9800
Fax: 703-823-0252
E-Mail: membership@counseling.org
Home Page: www.counseling.org
Social Media: Facebook, Twitter

Marvin D. Kuehn, Executive Director
Tom Evenson, President

The mission of the American Counseling Association (ACA) is to enhance the quality of life in society by promoting the development of professional counselors, advancing the counseling profession, and using the profession and practice of counseling to promote respect for human dignity and diversity. ACA is a not-for-profit, professional and educational organization. The annual expo features over 100 exhibitors.
4000 Attendees
Frequency: Annual
Founded in 1952
Mailing list available for rent

13062 **ACOFP Convention & Scientific Seminar**
American College of Osteopathic Family Physicians
330 E Algonquin Road
Arlington Heights, IL 60005

847-228-6090
Fax: 800-323-0794

2500 Attendees

13063 **AHRA Annual Meeting and Exposition**
Association for Medical Imaging Management
490B Boston Post Road
Suite 200
Sudbury, MA 01776

978-443-7591
800-334-2472
Fax: 978-443-8046
E-Mail: info@ahraonline.org
Home Page: www.ahraonline.org
Social Media: Facebook, Twitter, LinkedIn

Edward Cronin, Jr., CEO
Sarah Murray, Executive Assistant
Emily Ryan, Membership Coordinator
Debra Murphy, Publications Director

Educational event for Radiology Administration. Topics that are covered include human resources, finance, operations and communication.
3000 Attendees
Frequency: Annual

13064 **AMGA's Annual Conference**
American Medical Group Association
One Prince Street
Alexandria, VA 22314-3318

703-838-0033
Fax: 703-548-1890
Home Page: www.amga.org
Social Media: Facebook, Twitter, LinkedIn

Donald W Fisher PhD, CAE, President/CEO
Ryan O'Connor, VP Membership/Marketing
April Noland, Assistant to the President/CEO
Clyde L. Morris, C.P.A., CFO
Nanette Lewis, Administrative Asst/Office Manager

Brings together physician and nonphysician executives from the nation's leading health care organizations, medical groups and physician owned and operated IPAs. It offers both an interactive exhibit area and a relaxed environment for meeting one-on-one with management from the nation's leading health care organizations. National conference dedicated to leadership development in multispecialty medical groups.
375 Members
1100+ Attendees
Frequency: March, Arizona
Founded in 1949
Mailing list available for rent: 600 names

13065 **AORN Congress**
Association of PeriOperative Registered Nurses
2170 S Parker Road
Suite 300
Denver, CO 80231-5711

303-755-6300
800-755-2676
Fax: 303 755-4511
E-Mail: sales@aorn.org
Home Page: www.aorn.org

Garth Jordan, VP Marketing/Business
Lori Ropa, Manager

Surgical tradeshow featuring medical devices and supplies for the operating room and facilities recruiting for open OR nursing positions.
7000 Attendees
Frequency: Annual
Founded in 1954

13066 **AORN World Conference of Perioperative Nurses**
Association of PeriOperative Registered Nurses
2170 S Parker Road
Suite 300
Denver, CO 80231-5711

303-755-6300
Fax: 303-755-5411
E-Mail: sales@aorn.org
Home Page: www.aorn.org

Christine Lindmark, Exhibits Director
Lori Ropa, Manager

Seminar and 82 equipment & supplies displays used in operating room suites, and pre-surgical areas.
2500 Attendees
Frequency: Biennial
Founded in 1978

13067 **APTA Annual Conference & Exposition**
American Physical Therapy Association
1111 N Fairfax Street
Alexandria, VA 22314

703-684-2782
Fax: 703-706-3396
E-Mail: memberservices@apta.org
Home Page: www.apta.org

R Scott Ward, President
John Barnes, CEO

The national event for physical therapy.
Frequency: June

13068 **ARMA International Conference & Expo**
ARMA International
11880 College Blvd
Suite 450
Overland Park, KS 66210

913-341-3808
800-422-2762
Fax: 913-341-3742
E-Mail: hq@arma.org
Home Page: www.arma.org/conference
Social Media: Facebook, Twitter, LinkedIn

Carol Jorgenson, Meetings/Education Coordinator

Wanda Wilson, Senior Manager, Conferences
Elizabeth Zlitni, Exposition Manager

Conference, seminar, workshop, banquet, award ceremony and 175 exhibits of micrographics, optical disk, automated document storage and retrieval systems and more technology of interest to information professionals.
3500 Attendees
Frequency: Annual
Founded in 1956
Mailing list available for rent

13069 ARVO
FASEB/OSMC
9650 Rockville Pike
Bethesda, MD 20814

301-634-7100
Fax: 301-634-7014
E-Mail: info@faseb.org
Home Page: www.faseb.org/meetings

Jacquelyn Roberts, Marketing Manager
David Craven, Executive Director

13070 ASC Association Annual Conference
Ambulatory Surgery Center Association
1012 Cameron Street
Alexandria, VA 22314-2427

703-836-8808
Fax: 703-549-0976
E-Mail: asc@ascassociation.org
Home Page: www.ascassociation.org
Social Media: Facebook, Twitter, LinkedIn

Kathy Bryant, President
Sarah Silberstein, Executive Director
71000 Attendees
Frequency: April
Founded in 1970

13071 ASCRS Annual Meeting
American Society of Colon & Rectal Surgeons
85 W Algonquin Road
Suite 550
Arlington Heights, IL 60005

847-290-9184
800-791-0001
Fax: 847-290-9203
E-Mail: ascrs@fascrs.org
Home Page: www.fascrs.org
Social Media: Facebook

James W J Felshman MD, President
John H Pemberton MD, VP
Alan G Thorson MD, Treasurer
Rick Slawny, Executive Director
Stella Zedalis, Associate Executive Director
2800 Members
Mailing list available for rent

13072 ASCRS Symposium & ASOA Congress
American Society of Cataract & Refractive Surgery
American Society of Opthalmic Administrators
4000 Legato Road, # 850
Fairfax, VA 22033-4003

703-912-2220
800-451-1339
Fax: 703-591-0614
E-Mail: ascrs@ascrs.org
Home Page: www.ascrs.org

Jane Krause, Show Manager

Seminar and 700 exhibits of opthalmic related intruments of interest to opthalmologists, administrators, nurses and technicians.
7000 Attendees
Frequency: June
Founded in 1986

13073 ASHCSP Annual Conference: American Society for Heathcare Central Servi
American Hospital Association
One N Franklin
Chicago, IL 60601

312-422-2000
Fax: 312-422-4572

Conference and exhibition of health care administration supplies and services.

13074 ASHHRA'S Annual Conference & Exposition
American Society of Healthcare & Human Resources
155 North Wacker
Suite 400
Chicago, IL 60606

312-422-3720
Fax: 312-422-4577
E-Mail: ricky@corcexpo.com
Home Page: www.ashhra.org
Social Media: Facebook, Twitter, LinkedIn

Ricky Iovino, Exhibit Manager

ASHHRA's Annual Conference & Exposition is the opportunity to connect face-to-face with the top human resource executives and decision-makers in the healthcare field. The attendees come from hospital, hospital system, ambulatory care, long-term care and hospice organizations. Attendee job titles include: Chief Human Reosurce Officer; Vice President/Director of Human Resources; Director/Manager of Recruitment, Compensation, Benefits, Organizational Development or Employee Relations
500 Attendees
Frequency: September, Disneyland
Mailing list available for rent

13075 ASHP Midyear Clinical Meeting
American Society of Health-System Pharmacists
7272 Wisconsin Avenue
Bethesda, MD 20814-4836

301-657-3000
866-279-0681
Fax: 301-657-1641
E-Mail: ipa@ashp.org
Home Page: www.ashp.org
Social Media: Facebook, Twitter, LinkedIn

Kathryn R. Schultz, President
Paul W. Abramowitz, Chief Executive Officer
Philip J. Schneider, Treasurer
Gerald Meyer, Vice-Chairman

Containing 1,160 booths and 320 exhibits.
Mailing list available for rent

13076 ASNP Convention & Exhibition
American Association of Naturopathic Physicians
4435 Wisconsin Avenue NW
Suite 403
Washington, DC 20016

202-237-8150
866-538-2267
Fax: 202-237-8152
E-Mail: member.services@naturopathic.org
Home Page: www.naturopathic.org

Karen Howard, Executive Director
Michael Cronin, ND, President
Joe Pizzorno, ND, Treasurer
Shelly Nichols, Executive Administrator
Stephanie Geller, Membership Associate
900 Attendees
Frequency: Annual/August
Mailing list available for rent

13077 ASPET Annual Meeting
ASPET
9650 Rockville Pike
Bethesda, MD 20814

301-347-7060
Fax: 301-634-7061
E-Mail: info@aspet.org
Home Page: www.aspet.org

Jean Lash, Exhibit Manager
Christine Carrico, Secretary, Treasurer
Paul Czoty, Secretary, Treasurer

The American Society for Pharmacology & Experimental Therapeutics annual meeting consisting of four-hundred exhibits of pharmacology and toxicology equipment, supplies and services.
13000 Attendees
Frequency: April

13078 ASPRS/PSEF/ASMS Annual Scientific Meeting
American Society of Plastic Surgeons
444 E Algonquin Road
Arlington Heights, IL 60005

847-228-9900
888-475-2784
Fax: 847-228-9131
E-Mail: webmaster@plasticsurgery.org
Home Page: www.plasticsurgery.org

Bonnie Burkoth, Exhibit Manager

Close to four hundred exhibits of plastic surgery products, patient education and software to assist plastic surgeons, nurses and paramedical staff.
4000 Attendees
Frequency: October
Mailing list available for rentat $750 per M

13079 ASSH Annual Meeting
American Society for Surgery of the Hand
822 W. Washington Boulevard
Suite 600
Chicago, IL 60607

312-880-1900
Fax: 847-384-1435
E-Mail: info@assh.org
Home Page: www.assh.org

Mark Anderson, CEO
Daniel Nagle, President
W P Andrew Lee, Secretary/VP
3500 Members
Frequency: September
Mailing list available for rent

13080 Academy of General Dentistry Annual Meeting
Academy of General Dentistry
211 E Chicago Avenue
Suite 900
Chicago, IL 60611

312-440-4300
888-243-3368
Fax: 312-440-0559
E-Mail: executiveoffice@agd.org
Home Page: www.agd.org

Heather Nash CMP, Director Meetings
Jay Donohue, Executive Director

Educational session and over 225 dental manufacturers and supplier exhibits. Attended by dentists and the general public.
5000 Attendees
Frequency: Annual
Founded in 1954

13081 Academy of Osseointegration Convention
Smith, Bucklin and Associates
401 N Michigan Avenue
Chicago, IL 60611-4267

312-644-6610
Fax: 312-245-1082

E-Mail: info@smithbucklin.com
Home Page: www.smithbucklin.com

Henry S. Givray, President & CEO
C. Albert Koob, Executive Vice President
Carolyn Dolezal, Executive Vice President
Michael L. Payne, Executive Vice President
Cele Fogarty, Vice President - Event Services

Osseointegration medical exhibition.
Founded in 1949

13082 Adult Day Services Exposition
VNU Expositions
Dulles International Airport
PO Box 17413
Washington, DC 20041

703-318-0300
800-765-7616
Fax: 703-318-8833
Home Page: www.vnuexpo.com

Luellen Hoffman, Show Director

Adult/geriatric health care professionals gather to see exhibits of equipment, supplies, services and consulting for those who represent senior centers, adult day centers, nursing homes, hospitals and other health care markets.
300 Attendees
Frequency: Annual

13083 Air Medical Transport Conference
Association of Air Medical Services
526 King Street
Sutie 415
Alexandria, VA 22314-3143

703-836-8732
Fax: 703-836-8920
E-Mail: information@aams.org
Home Page: www.aams.org

Johanna VanArsdall, Education/Meetings Manager
Blair Marie Kelly, Commuications/Marketing Director
Andy Papovie, Member Serives Coordinator
John Fiegel, Director

Annual exhibit of air medical transport equipment, supplies and services.
1500 Attendees
Frequency: November

13084 AmSECT International Conference
American Society of ExtraCorporeal Technology
2209 Dickens Road
Richmond, VA 23230-2005

804-565-6363
Fax: 804-282-0090
E-Mail: judyr@amsect.org
Home Page: www.amsect.org

Stewart Hinckley, Executive Director
Donna Pendarvis, Associate Manager
Michael Troike, Government Relations Chairman
Kimberly Robertson, CPA, Controller
Greg Leasure, Membership Services
2000 Members
600 Attendees
Frequency: Annual
Founded in 1964
Mailing list available for rent

13085 American Academy for Cerebral Palsy and Developmental Medicine Meeting
Amer. Academy for Cerebral Palsy/Dev. Medicine
555 E Wells St
Suite 1100
Milwaukee, WI 53202-3800

414-918-3014
Fax: 414-276-2146
E-Mail: info@aacpdm.org
Home Page: www.aacpdm.org

Maureen O'Donnell, President
Scott Hoffinger, Treasurer
Richard Stevenson, First Vice President
Darcy Fehlings, Second Vice President
Annette Majnemer, Secretary

Provides dissemination of current and emerging information in the basic sciences, prevention, diagnosis, treatment and technical advances as applied to persons with cerebral palsy and developmental disabilities.
800 Attendees
Frequency: Yearly
Founded in 1940

13086 American Academy of Dermatology Annual Meeting
American Academy of Dermatology
930 N Meacham Road
PO Box 4014
Shaumburg, IL 60168-4014

708-330-1090
Fax: 708-330-1090

Seven hundred exhibits from 300 technical companies relating to skin care, professional and scientific organizations.
Frequency: Annual
Founded in 1940

13087 American Academy of Environmental Medicine Conference
American Academy of Environmental Medicine
7701 E Kellog
Suite 625
Wichita, KS 67207-1705

316-684-5500
Fax: 316-684-5709
E-Mail: centraloffice@aaem.com
Home Page: www.aaem.com

D E Rodgers, Executive Director

Environmental medicine equipment, supplies and services of interest to physicans.
175 Attendees
Frequency: October
Mailing list available for rent

13088 American Academy of Family Physicians Scientific Assembly
American Academy of Family Physicians
11400 Tomahawk Creek Parkway
Leawood, KS 66211-2680

913-906-6000
800-274-2237
Fax: 913-906-6082
E-Mail: sbiggs@aafp.org
Home Page: www.aafp.org

Sondra Biggs CMP, Meetings/Convention Director
20000 Attendees
Frequency: Annual

13089 American Academy of Fixed Prosthodontics Scientific Session
American Academy of Fixed Prosthodontics
6661 Merwin Road
Columbus, OH 43235

614-761-1927
800-860-5633
Fax: 614-292-0941
E-Mail: aafpsec@gmail.com
Home Page: www.fixedprosthodontics.org
Social Media: Facebook, Twitter

Stephen F. Rosenstiel, Secretary
Richard D. Jordan, Treasurer
Carl F. Driscoll, President
Jack Lipkin, VP

Thirty-two exhibits of prosthodontics equipment, supplies and services. Luncheon and meeting.
800 Attendees
Frequency: Annual Feb.
Founded in 1951

13090 American Academy of Forensic Sciences Annual Meeting
American Academy of Forensic Sciences
410 N 21st St
Colorado Springs, CO 80904-2712

719-636-1100
Fax: 719-636-1993
E-Mail: awarren@aafs.org
Home Page: www.aafs.org

Anne Warren, Executive Director
Nancy Jackson, Director Development

Professionals in the forensic science field attend meeting and see 120 exhibits of scientific instruments.
2300 Attendees
Frequency: Annual

13091 American Academy of Implant Dentistry Annual Meeting
American Academy of Implant Dentistry
211 E Chicago Avenue
Chicago, IL 60611

312-335-1550
877-335-2243
Fax: 312-335-9090
Home Page: www.aaid.org
Social Media: Facebook, Twitter, LinkedIn

Sharon Bennett, Executive Director
Joyce Sigmon, Director Administrative Activities
Max Moses, Director Communications
1500 Attendees
Frequency: Annual

13092 American Academy of Neurology: Annual Meeting
American Academy of Neurology
1080 Montreal Avenue
Suite 335
Saint Paul, MN 55116-2325

651-951-1940
800-879-1960
Fax: 651-695-2791
E-Mail: aan@aan.com
Home Page: www.aanos.org

Judy Larson

One hundred and seventy-four publishers, pharmaceutical companies, and related suppliers have exibits, along with the seminar, workshop, banquet and reception.
6500 Attendees
Frequency: Annual, August

13093 American Academy of Ophthalmology Annual Meeting
American Academy of Ophthalmology
655 Beach Street
P.O. Box 7424
San Francisco, CA 94109

415-618-8500
Fax: 415-561-8533
E-Mail: meetings@aao.org
Home Page: www.aao.org

Karen Cristello, Promotions Coordinator
Dunbar Hoskins, Executive VP
25000 Attendees
Frequency: November
Founded in 1896
Mailing list available for rent

13094 American Academy of Optometry Annual Meeting
American Academy of Optometry

2909 Fairgreen Street
Suite 506
Orlando, FL 32803

301-984-1441
Fax: 407-893-9890
E-Mail: aaoptom@aaoptom.org
Home Page: www.aaopt.org

Bernard J. Dolan, President
Lois Schoenbrun, Executive Director
Jenny Brown, Program Manager, Membership
Randy Consola, Office Manager
Dana Edwards, MLIS, Database Administrator

Two hundred exhibits focusing on the latest patient treatment and research. Workshop and banquet.
4000 Attendees
Frequency: Annual

13095 American Academy of Oral and Maxillofacial Radiology Annual Session
American Academy of Oral & Maxillofacial Radiology
PO Box 55722
Jackson, MS 39296
601-984-6060
Fax: 601-984-6086
Home Page: www.aaomr.org

Dr M Kevin O'Carroll, Executive Secretary
Charles Hildebolt, Treasurer
Steven Singer, Director

Over 20 exhibits relating to dental radiology, equipment, software and accessories.
120 Attendees
Frequency: November
Founded in 1949

13096 American Academy of Orofacial Pain Annual Scientific Meeting
American Academy of Orofacial Pain
19 Mantua Road
Mount Royal, NJ 00861

856-233-3629
Fax: 856-423-3420

Donna Blackmore, Manager Meetings
Bob Talley, President

Ten exhibits relating to orofacial pain and temporomandibular disorders. Medical and dental doctors attend meeting, luncheon, tours and a reception.
350 Attendees
Frequency: Annual

13097 American Academy of Orthopedic Surgeons Annual Meeting
American Academy of Orthopedic Surgeons
6300 N River Road
Rosemont, IL 60018-4262

847-823-7186
Fax: 847-323-8031
E-Mail: orthoinfo@aaos.org
Home Page: www.aaos.org

Stuart L Weinstein, President
Richard F Kyle, First VP
Karen Hackett, CEO

Three hundred and fifty-five exhibits of surgical equipment, supplies and services used by the orthopedic professional.
28000 Attendees
Frequency: Annual
Founded in 1933

13098 American Academy of Otolaryngology Mid-Winter Meeting
American Academy of Otolaryngology-Head & Neck
19 Mantua Road
Mt. Royal, NJ 08061

856-423-0041
E-Mail: headquarters@aro.org
Home Page: www.aro.org

Darla Dobson, Executive Director

Over 300 exhibits of otolaryngology, diseases of the ear, nose and throat, head and neck surgery equipment, supplies and services plus seminar.
9000+ Attendees
Frequency: February
Founded in 1896

13099 American Academy of Pain Medicine Annual Conference and Review Course
American Academy of Pain Medicine
4700 Lake Avenue
Glenview, IL 60025

847-375-4731
Fax: 847-375-4777
E-Mail: info@painmed.org
Home Page: www.painmed.org

Samuel Hassenbusch, President
Frederick Burgess, Treasurer

Meeting and exhibits relating to pain medicine, particularly related socioeconomic and governmental issues.
Frequency: Annual

13100 American Academy of Pediatric Dentistry Annual Meeting
American Academy of Pet Owners
830 Taylor Street
Suite 1700
Ft. Worth, TX 76102

312-337-2169
800-992-8044
Fax: 312-337-6329
E-Mail: info@aapd.org
Home Page: www.aapo.org
Social Media: Facebook, Twitter

Keith Morley, President
William Berlocher, Vice President
John Rutkauskas, Executive Director

Seventy-five to 100 displays of dental products and publications.
2500 Attendees
Frequency: May
Founded in 1948

13101 American Academy of Pediatrics Annual Meeting
American Academy of Pediatrics
141 NW Point Boulevard
Elk Grove Village, IL 60009

847-434-4000
Fax: 847-434-8000
E-Mail: kidsdocs@aap.org
Home Page: www.aap.org

E Stephen Edwards MD FAAP, President
Joe M Sanders Jr, MD FAAP, Executive Director
Joann Barbour, Manager

Three hundred and fifty exhibits relating to prescription and over the counter drugs, infant formulas medical equipment and publications. Reception, tours and meeting.
10000 Attendees
Frequency: Annual

13102 American Academy of Periodontology Annual Meeting & Exhibition
American Academy of Periodontology
737 N Michigan Avenue
Suite 800
Chicago, IL 60611

312-787-5518
Fax: 312-573-3225
E-Mail: member.services@perio.org
Home Page: www.perio.org

Melody Anderson, Meetings Manager
Alice Deforest, Administrative Assistant
Sarah Schneider, Administrative Assistant

Two hundred and seventy-five exhibits of products and services relating to periodontics, including dental instruments, literature, X-ray equipment, furniture, software and more.
5800 Attendees
Frequency: Annual
Founded in 1914

13103 American Academy of Physical Medicine and Rehabilitation Annual Assembly
330 N Wabash Avenue
Suite 2500
Chicago, IL 60611-7617

312-464-9700
Fax: 312-464-0227
Home Page: www.aapmr.org/assembly.htm

Steve M Gnatz MD/MHA, President
Thomas E Stautzenbach CAE, Executive Director
Joanne Constantine, Assembly Press Releases/Media
Elsa Lightfoot, Assembly Registration Coordinator
Linda Griffin, Assembly Technical Information

One hundred twenty-five exhibitors representing pharmceutical companies, diagnostics, rehabilitation equipment manufacturers and more.
2500 Attendees
Frequency: Annual/November
Founded in 1938

13104 American Academy of Professional Coders National Conferences
2480 South 3850 West
Suite B
Salt Lake City, UT 84120

801-236-2200
800-626-2633
Fax: 801-236-2258
E-Mail: info@aapc.com
Home Page: www.aapc.com

Reed Pew, CEO
Sandra Nestman, Conference Coordinator
Amy Pistorius, Conference Coordinator
Kira Golding, Conference Coordinator
Raemarie Jimenez, Conference Coordinator

Provides the opportunity to meet the National Advisory Board, members, staff and management. Mingle with local chapters from all over the country. Get education on the most popular and needed subject matter taught by industry experts.
Frequency: January and June
Founded in 1988
Mailing list available for rent

13105 American Alliance for Health, Physical Education, Recreation & Dance Expo
AAHPERD
1900 Association Drive
Reston, VA 20191

703-476-3400
800-213-7193

Fax: 703-476-9527
Home Page: www.aahperd.org

E. Paul Roetert, CEO
Judith C Young, VP
Paula Kun, Marketing

National convention and exposition that features many exhibits focusing on products, services and equipment within the fields of health, physical education, recreation and dance.
5000 Attendees
Frequency: Annual
Mailing list available for rent

13106 **American Ambulance Association Annual Conference & Trade Show**
Executive Management Services
1255 23rd Street NWrd
Suite 200
Washington, DC 20037

202-213-3999
800-523-4447
Fax: 202-452-0005
Home Page: www.the-aaa.org

David Saunders, Executive Director
Maria Bianchi, Executive Vice President
6100 Attendees
Frequency: Annual, October

13107 **American Association for Continuity of Care Annual Conference**
American Association for Continuity of Care
638 Prospect Avenue
Hartford, CT 06105-4250

860-867-7525
Fax: 203-586-7550

Seminar, reception and 35 exhibits of suppliers of health care delivery resources, products and services.
Frequency: Annual
Founded in 1982

13108 **American Association for Laboratory Animal Science National Meeting**
American Association for Laboratory Animal Science
9190 Crestwyn Hills Drive
Memphis, TN 38125

901-754-8620
Fax: 901-753-0046
E-Mail: info@aalas.org
Home Page: www.aalas.org

Ann Turner, Executive Director

Two-hundred and seventy exhibits of pharmaceuticals and laboratory animal supplies.
4,500 Attendees
Frequency: October

13109 **American Association for Medical Transcription Annual Meeting**
PO Box 576187
Modesto, CA 95357-6187

209-551-0883
800-982-2182
Fax: 209-551-9317
E-Mail: aamt@sns.com
Home Page: www.aamt.org

Daryl Ochs, Director Marketing
Terri White, Operations Manager

Exhibitors are medical transcription businesses, hardware, software, publishers and services.
750 Attendees
Frequency: Annual
Founded in 1978

13110 **American Association for Thoracic Surgery Annual Meeting**
American Association for Thoracic Surgery
500 Cummings Center
Suite 4550
Beverly, MA 01915

978-927-8330
Fax: 978-524-8890
E-Mail: aats@prri.com
Home Page: www.aats.org
Social Media: Facebook

G Alexander Patterson, President
Elizabeth Dooley Crane, Executive Director
4700 Attendees
Frequency: Annual
Founded in 1917
Mailing list available for rent

13111 **American Association for the Study of Headache Meeting**
19 Mantua Road
Mount Royal, NJ 08061

856-423-0043
Fax: 856-423-0082
E-Mail: ahshq@talley.com
Home Page:
www.americanheadachesociety.org

Paul Winner, President
David Dodick, Treasurer

Twenty-five exhibits of research equipment supplies, and services related to headache study.
650 Attendees
Frequency: Annual
Founded in 1958

13112 **American Association of Nurse Anesthetists Midyear Assembly**
222 S Prospect Avenue
Park Ridge, IL 60068-4001

847-927-7055
Fax: 847-692-6968
E-Mail: info@aana.org
Home Page: www.aana.com

Wanda Wilson, President
Daniel Vigness, Vice President

Exhibits relating to nurse anesthetists.
350 Attendees

13113 **American Association of Blood Banks Annual Meeting**
American Association of Blood Banks
8101 Glenbrook Road
Bethesda, MD 20814-2749

301-907-6977
Fax: 301-907-6895
E-Mail: aabb@aabb.org
Home Page: www.aabb.org

Daniel Connor, President
Jacquelyn Fredrick, VP

Four hundred and eighty-nine exhibits relating to blood banking and transfusion medicine, gloves, donor coaches, chairs and equipment. Seminar, workshop and banquet.
7500 Attendees
Frequency: November
Founded in 1947
Mailing list available for rent

13114 **American Association of Cardiovascular & Pulmonary Rehabilitation Conf.**
American Assoc of Cardiovascular & Pulmonary Rehab
7611 Elmwood Avenue
Suite 201
Middleton, WI 53562

608-316-6989
Fax: 608-831-5122
E-Mail: aacvpr@tmahq.com
Home Page: www.aacvpr.org

Sheil Kirshbaum, Director Meetings

Seminar and workshop, plus 70 exhibits of cardiovascular and pulmonary rehabilitation equipment, supplies and services.
1800 Attendees
Frequency: Annual
Founded in 1985

13115 **American Association of Diabetes Educators Annual Meeting & Educational Prog.**
American Association of Diabetes Educators
100 W Monroe
Chicago, IL 60603

312-424-2426
800-338-3633
Fax: 312-424-2427
Home Page: www.diabeteseducator.org

Christopher Laxton, Executive Director
Tami Ross, Vice President

Six hundred exhibits of dietary food and beverages, testing and screening tools, educational programs and publications. Banquet and reception available.
Mailing list available for rent: 10000 names at $160 per M

13116 **American Association of Homes and Services for the Aging Convention**
American Association of Homes and Services/Aging
901 E Street NW
Suite 500
Washington, DC 20004-2037

202-661-5700
Fax: 202-783-2255
E-Mail: mraynor@aahsa.org
Home Page: www.aahsa.org

Daniel Smith, VP
Mary-Louise Raynor, Secretary
Bonnie Gauthier, Secretary
Douglas Struyk, Treasurer

One thousand eight hundred exhibitors of equipment, supplies and services for housing and long term care facilities for the aged, conference and tours.
4000 Attendees
Frequency: Annual
Founded in 1980

13117 **American Association of Immunologists Annual Meeting**
American Association of Immunologists
9650 Rockville Pike
Bethesda, MD 20814

301-634-7178
Fax: 301-634-7887
E-Mail: infoaai@aai.org
Home Page: www.aai.org
Social Media: Facebook

M Michele Hogan PhD, Executive Director
Gail A. Bishop, President

Exhibits related to immunological research, equipment and supplies.
7,600 Members
10000 Attendees
Frequency: May
Founded in 1913

13118 **American Association of Managed Care Nurses Annual Conference**
American Association of Managed Care Nurses
4435 Waterfront Drive
Suite 101
Glen Allen, VA 23060

804-747-9698
Fax: 804-747-5316

E-Mail: keads@aamcn.org
Home Page: www.aamcn.org

Sloane Reed, VP Sales
Laura Givens, Executive Admin

The AAMCN Annual Conference is designed to provide registered nurses, licensed practical nurses, advanced practice, executive nurses and other healthcare professionals with current information they can use to influence their marketplace.

13119 American Association of Medical Assistants National Convention
American Association of Medical Assistants
20 N Wacker Drive
Suite 1575
Chicago, IL 60606-2963

312-899-1500
800-228-2262
Fax: 312-899-1259
E-Mail: info@aama-ntl.org
Home Page: www.aama-ntl.org

David Balasa, Executive Director
Kathy Langley, Director Of Board Services

Main exhibits, data processing equipment, pharmaceuticals, publications, insurance services, text books, coding system reference guides, health care services and more.
500 Attendees
Frequency: Annual

13120 American Association of Naturopathic Physicians Convention
American Association of Naturopathic Physicians
4435 Wisconsin Avenue NW
Suite 403
Washington, DC 20016

202-237-8150
Fax: 202-237-8152
Home Page: www.naturopathic.org

Karen Howard, Executive Director
Michael Cronin, ND, President
Joe Pizzorno, ND, Treasurer
Shelly Nichols, Executive Administrator
Stephanie Geller, Membership Associate

One hundred and twenty exhibits of Naturopathic medicine, supplies and services plus conference and banquet.
750 Attendees
Frequency: Annual
Founded in 1986
Mailing list available for rent

13121 American Association of Neurological Surgeons Annual Meeting
American Association of Neurologists
5550 Meadowbrook Drive
Rolling Meadows, IL 60008

847-378-0500
888-566-2267
Fax: 847-378-0600
E-Mail: info@aans.org
Home Page: www.aans.org

John Robertson, President
Troy Tippett, Vice President
Griffith R. Harsh, Chairperson

Two hundred manufacturers and suppliers have 500 booths of equipment, publications and supplies.
2400 Attendees
Frequency: Annual
Mailing list available for rent

13122 American Association of Neuroscience Nurses Convention
224 N Des Plaines
#601
Chicago, IL 60661

312-258-1200
800-477-2266
Fax: 312-993-0362
E-Mail: info@aann.org
Home Page: www.aann.org

Thomas O'Dowd, Manager Meetings

Sixty exhibits of nuerological and neurosurgical supplies, services and industry related recruiters.
900 Attendees
Frequency: Annual
Founded in 1968

13123 American Association of Nurse Anesthetists Annual Meeting
222 S Prospect Avenue
Park Ridge, IL 60068-4001

847-985-5400
Fax: 847-692-6968
E-Mail: meetings@aana.com
Home Page: www.aana.com

Cindy Wood, Director Programs

325 exhibits of equipment, supplies, publications and recruiters. Seminar and workshop, as well as a banquet.
3500 Attendees

13124 American Association of Nurse Anesthetists Assembly of School Faculty
222 S Prospect Avenue
Park Ridge, IL 60068-4001

847-927-7055
Fax: 847-692-6968
E-Mail: info@aana.com
Home Page: www.aana.com

Wanda Wilson, President
Daniel Vigness, Vice President

Nurse anesthetist related exhibits
250 Attendees
Frequency: Annual

13125 American Association of Office Nurses Annual Meeting & Convention
52 Park Avenue
Suite B4
Park Ridge, NJ 07656

201-391-2600
800-457-7504
Fax: 201-573-8543
Home Page: www.aanon.org

Michelle Aronowitz, Managing Director
Sherry Levy, Associate Managing Director

American Association of Office Nurses annual meeting and convention at the Eden Roc Hotel in Miami Beach, Florida.
150 Attendees
Frequency: Sept
Founded in 1988

13126 American Association of Orthodontists Trade Show and Scientific Session
401 N Lindbergh Boulevard
Saint Louis, MO 63141-7816

314-993-1700
Fax: 314-997-1745
E-Mail: info@aaortho.org
Home Page: www.aaortho.org

Chris Varanas, Manager

Five hundred and fifty exhibits of orthodontic equipment, publications, supplies and services.
9000 Attendees
Frequency: Annual

13127 American Association of Suicidology Conference
4201 Connecticut Avenue NW
Suite 408
Washington, DC 20008

202-237-2280
Fax: 202-237-2282
Home Page: www.suicidology.org

Alan Berman PhD, Executive Director

Exhibits relating to the advancement of studies to prevent suicide and life threatening behavior.
Frequency: Annual
Founded in 1969

13128 American Association of Tissue Banks Meeting
1320 Old Chain Bridge Road
Suite 450
Mc Lean, VA 22101

703-827-9582
Fax: 703-356-2198
E-Mail: aatb@aatb.org
Home Page: www.aatb.org

Robert Rigney, CEO
Scott Brubaker, Chief Policy Officer

Exhibits for the revival, preservation, storage, and distribution of tissues for transplantation.

13129 American Association on Mental Retardation Annual Meeting
444 N Capitol Street
Suite 846
Washington, DC 20001-1512

202-387-1968
800-424-3688
Fax: 202-387-2193
E-Mail: dcroser@aamr.org
Home Page: www.aamr.org

Doreen Croser, Executive Director
Paul Aitken, Director Of Finance Administration
2000 Attendees
Founded in 1876

13130 American Chiropractic Association Annual Convention and Exhibition
1701 Clarendon Boulevard
Arlington, VA 22209

703-276-8800
800-986-4636
Fax: 703-243-2593
Home Page: http://www.acatoday.org

Kevin Corcoran, VP

Fifty displays of chiropractic tables and products, mattress companies, nutritional supplements, computer software, services and supplies.
500 Attendees
Frequency: Annual
Founded in 1963

13131 American Cleft Palate Craniofacial Association Annual Meeting
104 S Estes Drive
Suite 204
Chapel Hill, NC 27514

919-933-9044
Fax: 919-933-9604
E-Mail: meetings@acpa-cpf.org
Home Page: www.acpa-cpf.org

Kathy Bogie, Manager Meetings
Nancy Smythe, Administrative Assistant
Hillary Jones, Administrative Assistant

Scientific meeting.
600 Attendees
Frequency: March
Founded in 1943

13132 American Clinical Neurophysiology Society Convention
1 Regency Drive
PO Box 30
Bloomfield, CT 06002

860-447-9408
Fax: 860-286-0787
E-Mail: info@acns.org
Home Page: www.acns.org

Mark Ross, President
Alan Legatt, First Vice President

Over 40 exhibits of electroencephalographic and neurophysiology equipment, seminar, workshop and conference.
400 Attendees
Frequency: Annual
Founded in 1946

13133 American College Health Association Annual Meeting
American College Health Association
1362 Mellon Road
Suite 180
Hanover, MD 21076

410-859-1500
Fax: 410-859-1510
E-Mail: contact@acha.org
Home Page: www.acha.org/annualmeeting13/index
Social Media: Facebook, Twitter

Jenny Haubenreiser, President
Pat Ketcham, President-Elect
Doyle Randall, Executive Director

The largest conference for college professionals. This year we honor the spirit of service and compassion that college health professionals have shown in their dedication to serving college students and their campus communities.
1800 Attendees
Frequency: Annual
Founded in 1922

13134 American College of Allergy, Asthma and Immunology Annual Meeting
85 W Algonquin Road
Suite 550
Arlington Heights, IL 60005-4460

847-427-1200
Fax: 847-427-1294
E-Mail: mail@acaai.org
Home Page: www.acaai.org

Richard G Gowes MD, President
Sami L Bahna MD, President-Elect

2006 Annual Meeting will be held November 9-15 in Philadelpia, Pennsylvania
Frequency: November
Founded in 1942
Mailing list available for rent: 4500 names at $100 per M

13135 American College of Angiology Conference
295 Northern Boulevard
Suite 104
Great Neck, NY 11021-4701

516-466-4055
Fax: 516-466-4099
Home Page: www.collegeofangiology.org

Joan Shaffer, Executive Director

CME Seminars and 50 exhibits from commercial and scientific suppliers.
300 Attendees
Frequency: October
Founded in 1954

13136 American College of Cardiology Annual Scientific Session
American College of Cardiology
2400 N Street, NW
Washington, DC 20037-1699

202-375-6000
800-253-4636
Fax: 202-375-7000
E-Mail: resource@acc.org
Home Page: www.acc.org

Christine McEntee, CEO
Julie Miller, Assistant Professor of Medicine

Seminar, workshop, dinner and 385 exhibits of products, supplies and services related to cardiovascular medicine.
30000 Attendees
Founded in 1949

13137 American College of Cardiovascular Administrator Leadership Conference
American Academy of Medical Administrators
701 Lee Street
Suite 600
Des Plaines, IL 60016

847-759-8601
Fax: 847-759-8602
E-Mail: info@aameda.org
Home Page: www.ammeda.org

Holly Estal Ed M, Director Education
Gen Hedland, Manager of Exhibits
S. Patrick Alford, Chairman
Linda R. Larin, Treasurer
Tina R. Brinton, Vice Chairman

Featuring keynote and concurrent sessions on human relations, finance and business developments, CV program development technology plus exhibitors that include the latest technological and innovative systems and products in cardiovascular health care. There are 30-40 booths.
300 Attendees
Frequency: March
Mailing list available for rent: 3,000 names at $150 per M

13138 American College of Emergency Physicians Scientific Assembly
American College of Emergency Physicians
PO Box 619911
Dallas, TX 75261-9911

972-550-0911
800-798-1822
Fax: 972-580-2816
E-Mail: publicaffairs@acep.org
Home Page: www.acep.org

Dana Bellantone, Manager Meetings

Five hundred and twenty-five exhibits of products and services related to emergency medicine.
4400 Attendees
Frequency: Annual
Founded in 1972

13139 American College of Medical Quality Annual Meeting
4334 Montgomery Avenue
2nd Floor
Bethesda, MD 20814-4402

301-913-9149
800-924-2149
Fax: 301-656-0989
E-Mail: acmq@aol.com
Home Page: www.acmq.org

Louis H. Diamond MB, ChB, President
Alan Krumholz, MD, Vice President

Seminar, reception and exhibits of computer hardware and software, publications, phamaceuticals and supplies. Medical professionals and others involved in quality assurance and utilization review and risk management attend.
150 Attendees
Founded in 1973
Mailing list available for rent

13140 American College of Nurse Practitioners
J Spargo & Associates
11208 Waples Mill Road
Suite 112
Fairfax, VA 22030

703-631-6200
800-564-4220
Fax: 703-654-6931
E-Mail: acnp@jspargo.com
Home Page: www.afcea.org
Social Media: Facebook, Twitter, LinkedIn

June LaMountain, Exhibit Sales Account Manager
Kent Schneider, President and CEO
Pat Miorin, Chief Financial Officer
Al Grasso, Chairman

The premier educational offering for nurse practitioners. It offers the opportunity to earn a full scope of continuing education contact hours at sessions led by top clinical experts in many areas.
1200 Attendees
Frequency: October
Mailing list available for rent

13141 American College of Obstetricians and Gynecologists Clinical Meeting/Expo
American College of Obstetricians
409 12th Street SW
Washington, DC 20024

202-857-3288
Fax: 202-484-3933
Home Page: http://www.acog.org

Professionally related exhibits.

13142 American College of Oral and Maxillofacial Surgeons Annual Conference
2025 M Street Nw
Washington, DC 20036

202-367-1182
800-522-6676
Fax: 202-367-2182
E-Mail: admin@acoms.org
Home Page: www.acoms.org
Social Media: Facebook, Twitter, LinkedIn

Dr Steven Guttenberg, President
Dr Leonard Spector, Secretary/Treasurer
Sunny Patel, Staff Accountant
Tina Hochberg, Sr. Director of Event Services
Steven C. Kemp, Executive Director

Fifty exhibits for oral and maxillofacial surgery.
250 Attendees
Frequency: Annual

13143 American College of Physicians Annual Convention
American College of Physicians
Independence Mall W
6th Street & Race
Philadelphia, PA 19106

215-351-2400
Home Page: http://www.acponline.org

John Tooker, CEO

Five hundred exhibits of medical supplies and services, as well as a seminar.
8000 Attendees

13144 American College of Rheumatology Scientific Meeting
Slack

4930 Del Ray Avenue
Bethesda, MD 20814

301-654-2055
Fax: 301-654-5920
E-Mail: member@gastro.org
Home Page: www.gastro.org

Robert Greenberg, Executive Vp
Michael Stolar, Senior Vp

Two hundred and ten exhibits of diagnostic testing kits, pharmaceuticals, equipment and supplies, of interest to professionals in Rheumatology.
4500 Attendees
Frequency: Annual
Founded in 1934

13145 **American College of Surgeons Annual Clinical Congress**
American College of Surgeons
633 N Saint Clair Street
Chicago, IL 60611

312-202-5000
Fax: 312-440-7143
E-Mail: postmaster@facs.org
Home Page: www.facs.org

Felix P Niespodziewanski, Conventions Manager
Thomas Russell, Chairman
Andrew Warshaw, Treasurer
Courtney Townsend, Secretary

One thousand one hundred exhibits of medical and patient care products, equipment and supplies. Conference, seminar and workshop, as well as luncheon and tours.
10000 Attendees
Frequency: Annual
Founded in 1914

13146 **American Congress of Rehabilitation Medicine Annual Meeting**
6801 Lake Plaza Drive
Suite B- 205
Indianapolis, IN 46220

317-915-2250
Fax: 317-915-2245
E-Mail: crobinson@acrm.org
Home Page: www.acrm.org

Richard D Morgan, Executive Director

Seminar, workshop and conference with 20 exhibits of rehabilitation supplies and equipment.
250 Attendees
Frequency: September/October
Founded in 1923
Mailing list available for rent: 750 names at $275 per M

13147 **American Dental Association Annual Session & Technical Exhibition**
211 E Chicago Avenue
Suite 200
Chicago, IL 60611-2678

312-440-2500
Fax: 312-440-2707
E-Mail: donovanj@ada.org
Home Page: www.ada.org

James P Donovan, Exhibit Manager
Patricia A Johnson, Manager Program Development
Vicki Guinta, Director
James Bramson, CEO

The annual session scientific program consists of over 180 programs, including science of dentistry, practice of dentistry, dental technology and general insterest programs as well as participation workshops. The leading suppliers will showcase their products and services. Dental professionals can compare products, see demonstrations, and make decisions about applying the latest technology. Attendees visiting the Technical Exhibition can also look for the ADA Seal which has long been recognizd
30000 Attendees
Frequency: October

13148 **American Dental Education Association Annual Session and Exposition**
1400 K Street NW
Suite 1100
Washington, DC 20005

202-289-7201
Fax: 202-289-7204
Home Page: www.adea.org

Rhonda Buford, Meetings Manager
Renee Latimer, Meeting Manager
Simone Smith, Meetings Manager
Novella Abrams, Senior Administrative Associate
Cassandra Allen, Program Associate

One hundred commercial and educational exhibits of supplies, video equipment, publications and more.
3000 Attendees
Frequency: Annual
Founded in 1983

13149 **American Dental Hygienists Association Conference**
444 N Michigan Avenue
Suite 3400
Chicago, IL 60611

312-440-8900
Fax: 312-440-8929
E-Mail: mail@adha.org
Home Page: www.adha.org

Ann Battrell, Executive Director
Kathy Madryk, Marketing Manager
Katie Powell, Director, Members Service
Ann Lynch, Director, Governmental Affairs
Isaac Carpenter, Director, Finance and MIS

Educational session and 120 exhibits of dental products.
1500 Attendees
Frequency: Annual
Founded in 1993
Mailing list available for rent

13150 **American Dental Society of Anesthesiology Scientific Meeting**
211 E Chicago Avenue
Suite 948
Chicago, IL 60611

312-664-8270
800-722-7788
Fax: 312-642-9713
R Knight Charlton, Executive Director

Meeting and over 15 exhibits of anesthetics and monitoring equipment.
200 Attendees
Frequency: Annual
Founded in 1954

13151 **American Diabetes Association Annual Meeting and Scientific Sessions**
1701 N Beauregard Street
PO Box 25757
Alexandria, VA 22311

703-549-1500
800-676-4065
Fax: 703-683-1351
E-Mail: meetings@diabetes.org
Home Page: www.afassano.com/ada

Anna Fassano, Director Exhibits
Lynn Nicholas, CEO

Three hundred and fifty exhibits of medical and dietary products and services, seminar and workshop.
Frequency: June
Founded in 1940

13152 **American Health Care Association Annual Convention and Exhibition**
1201 L Street NW
Washington, DC 20005

202-842-4444
Fax: 202-842-3860
E-Mail: webmaster@ahca.org
Home Page: www.ahcancal.org
Social Media: Facebook, Twitter, LinkedIn

Dave Kyllo, VP

Three hundred and fifty exhibits of supplies and information for the long term health care industry, banquet, luncheon and tours.
5000 Attendees
Frequency: Annual
Mailing list available for rent

13153 **American Health Information Management Association National Convention**
American Health Information Management Association
233 N Michigan Avenue
21st Floor
Chicago, IL 60601-5809

312-233-1100
Fax: 312-233-1090
E-Mail: info@ahima.org
Home Page: www.ahima.org
Social Media: Facebook, Twitter, LinkedIn

Erin Toth, Exhibition Manager
Linda Kloss, Executive Director
Patty Thierry Sheridan, President
Lynne Thomas Gordon, Chief Executive Officer
Beth Kost-Woodrow, Treasurer

Five hundred exhibits of interest to health information management professionals, reception.
3500 Attendees
Frequency: Annual
Founded in 1928
Mailing list available for rent

13154 **American Health Quality Association Annual Session**
1140 Connecticut Avenue NW
Washington, DC 20036

202-331-5790
E-Mail: info@ahqa.org
Home Page: www.ahqa.org

David Thomas MD, President
David Adler, Public Affairs Associate

Quality Improvement Organizations (QIOs) and professionals working to improve the quality of health care in communities across America gather for educational sessions and networking.
Frequency: March

13155 **American Heart Association Scientific Sessions**
American Heart Association
7272 Greenville Avenue
Dallas, TX 75231

214-736-6300
Fax: 214-373-3406
Home Page: www.amhrt.org

M Cass Wheeler, CEO

Conference, seminar and tours, plus 325 exhibits relating to exercise, equipment, pharmceuticals and services related to cardiovascular health care.
29000 Attendees

13156 American Hospital Association Convention
155 N. Wacker Dr.
Chicago, IL 60606
312-422-3000
800-424-4301
Fax: 312-422-4500
E-Mail: ddavidson@aha.org
Home Page: www.aha.org
Social Media: Twitter, YouTube
Richard Umbdenstock, President & CEO
Richard Pollack, VP, Advocacy
Neil Jesuelo, SVP Business Development
Exhibits of equipment, supplies and services for the medical and hopsital industry.

13157 American Industrial Hygiene Conference & Exposition (AIHce)
American Industrial Hygiene Association
2700 Prosperity Avenue
Suite 250
Fairfax, VA 22031
703-849-8888
Fax: 703-207-3561
E-Mail: infonet@aiha.org
Home Page: www.aiha.org
Carol Tobin, Education/Meetings Director
Caroline Lacey, Expositions Manager
Attracts OEHS professionals that are industrial hygienists, EHS specialists, safety professionals, risk management professionals and other who are esponsible for safety, health and the environment at their organization.
7000 Attendees
Frequency: Annual/May

13158 American Lung Association/American Thoracic Society Int Conference
1740 Broadway
New York, NY 10019-4374
212-315-8700
Fax: 212-265-5642
John Kirkwood, CEO
Two hundred and fifty exhibits of pharmaceuticals, equipment and books.
8500 Attendees
Frequency: Annual
Founded in 1904

13159 American Medical Directors Association Annual Symposium
American Medical Directors Association
11000 Broken Land Parkway, Suite 400
Suite 760
Columbia, MD 21044
410-740-9743
800-876-2632
Fax: 410-740-4572
E-Mail: info@amda.com
Home Page: www.amda.com
Megan Brey, Director Meetings
Lorraine Tarnove, Manager
Exhibits relating to geriatrics, pharmaceuticals and medical administration of long term care facilities. Long term health care physicians and professionals attend educational sessions, receptions and special events. Spouse/guest program offered.
1400 Attendees
Frequency: April
Founded in 1978

13160 American Medical Informatics Association Fall Symposium
American Medical Informatics Association
4915 Saint Elmo
Suite 401
Bethesda, MD 20814
301-657-1291
Fax: 301-657-1296
Megan Brey, Meeting Coordinator
Karen Greenwood, Manager
One hundred ten commercial and scientific medical informatics software and hardware, supplies and service dealers. Attended by medical professionals and the general public.
2500 Attendees
Frequency: Annual
Founded in 1977

13161 American Medical Student Association Convention
American Medical Student Association
1902 Association Drive
Reston, VA 20191
703-620-6600
800-767-2266
Fax: 703-620-5873
E-Mail: amsa@amsa.org
Home Page: www.amsa.org
One hundred exhibits relating to medical supplies and equipment, residency programs, physician recruitment and professional associations.
1500 Attendees

13162 American Medical Technologists Convention
American Medical Technologists
10700 West Higgins Road
Rosemont, IL 60018
847-823-5169
800-275-1268
Fax: 847-823-0458
E-Mail: dianepowell.amt@juno.com
Home Page: www.amtc.com
Diane Powell, Show Manager
Forty eight exhibits of clinical laboratory books, supplies and equipment, seminar, work shop, banquet and tours.
600 Attendees
Frequency: Annual
Founded in 1991

13163 American Medical Women's Association Annual Meeting
12100 Sunset Hills Road, Suite 130
4th Floor
Reston, VA 20190
703-234-4069
866-564-2483
Fax: 215-564-2175
E-Mail: info@amwa-doc.org
Home Page: www.amwa-doc.org
Gayatri Devi, President
Beatrice S Desper MD, President-Elect
Ana Maria Lopez, Secretary
Mary Fitzsimmons MD, Treasurer
Seminar, banquet, tours and 60 exhibits of medical equipment, supplies and services.
1000 Attendees
Frequency: Annual
Founded in 1915
Mailing list available for rent

13164 American Nephrology Nurses Association Symposium
Society of Urologic Nurses and Associates
E Holly Avenue
Box 56
Pittman, NJ 08071
856-256-2350
Fax: 856-589-7463
Mike Cunningham, Manager
One hundred fifteen companies have exhibits of equipment, supplies, pharmaceuticals and services for nephrology.
2000 Attendees
Frequency: Annual
Founded in 1970

13165 American Nurses Association Convention
600 Maryland Avenue SW
Suite 100
Washington, DC 20024-2571
202-651-7000
Fax: 301-628-5001
E-Mail: exhibits@ana.org
Home Page: www.nursingworld.org
Exhibits of nursing professional equipment, supplies and services.
Frequency: Annual

13166 American Occupational Health Conference & Exhibits
Slack
4930 Del Ray Avenue
Bethesda, MD 20814
301-654-2055
Fax: 301-654-5920
E-Mail: member@gastro.org
Home Page: www.gastro.org
Social Media: Facebook, Twitter, LinkedIn
Robert Greenberg, Executive Vp
Michael Stolar, Senior Vp
Derek Randolph, Director of Building Services
Arceli Bacsinila, Senior Director of Finance
Hillina Fetehawoke, Staff Accountant
Four hundred exhibits of pharmaceuticals, equipment, software and supplies for health professionals, offices and labs.
4500 Attendees
Mailing list available for rent

13167 American Occupational Therapy Association Annual Conference
American Occupation Therapy Association
4720 Montgomery Lane
PO Box 31220
Bethesda, MD 20824-1220
301-652-2682
Fax: 301-652-7711
Home Page: www.aota.org
M Carolyn Baum, President
Lizette Rosales, Manager
7000 Attendees
Frequency: May
Founded in 1919

13168 American Optometric Student Association Annual Meeting
243 N Lindbergh Boulevard
Saint Louis, MO 63141
314-993-8575
Fax: 314-993-8919
E-Mail: info@iacconline.org
Home Page: www.iaccnorthamerica.org
Social Media: Facebook, Twitter, LinkedIn
James Mahon, Director Marketing
Tom Cappucci, First Vice President
Optometry equipment, supplies and services.
Frequency: Annual

13169 American Organization of Nurse Executives Meeting and Exposition
American Hospital Association
1 N Franklin
Suite 27
Chicago, IL 60606
312-222-2000
312-422-4519

E-Mail: aone@aha.org
Home Page: www.aha.org

Pamela Thompson, CEO
Cliff Lehman, Director Membership Services

One hundred fifty exhibits of patient care equipment and supplies, computer hardware and software, communications systems and information for the professional in health care.
Frequency: Annual

13170 American Orthopsychiatric Association Annual Meeting
330 7th Avenue
18th Floor
New York, NY 10001

212-564-5930
Fax: 212-564-6180

Rachel L MacAulay, Program Associate

Meeting and exhibits by social service agencies, publications, computer software companies and more.
1928 Members
700 Attendees
Frequency: Annual
Founded in 1923

13171 American Orthotic & Prosthetic Association on National Assembly
American Orthotic & Prosthetic Association
330 John Carlyle Street
Suite 200
Alexandria, VA 22314

571-431-0876
Fax: 571-431-0899
E-Mail: info@aopanet.org
Home Page: www.aopanet.org

Thomas V. Di Bello, President
Bart Herman, VP
Thomas F Fise, Executive Director
Michael Chapman, Coord Membership Operations/Meeting

AOPA's goal is to advocate for policies that improve patient care.
1928 Members
2200 Attendees
Frequency: Annual
Founded in 1917

13172 American Osteopathic Association Meeting & Exhibits
American Osteopathic Hospital Association
142 E Ontario Street
Chicago, IL 60611

312-587-3709
Fax: 312-202-8212

John Crosby, Executive Director

Over 25 exhibits of products and services relating to the osteopathic health care industry, including building and finacing, marketing and operations.
500 Attendees
Founded in 1983

13173 American Pain Society Scientific Meeting
4700 W Lake Avenue
Glenview, IL 60025

847-375-4715
Fax: 877-734-8758
E-Mail: info@ampainsoc.org
Home Page: www.ampainsoc.org

Judith A Paice, President
Catherine Underwood, Executive Director
Marilyn Rutkowski, Marketing Manager
Kathryn Checea, Director of Sales
Deborah Pinkston, Managing Editor

Designed for a diverse group of pain clinicians, scientists and other professionals, the Annual Scientific Meeting features a prominent faculty presenting basic, translational, and clinical research advancements. Seminar, banquet, luncheon, breakfast and 150 exhibits of pharmceutical and medical instruments, medical equipment, products, supplies, services, and alternative delivery systems.
Frequency: Annual
Founded in 1977

13174 American Physical Therapy Association Annual Conference
American Physical Therapy Association
1111 N Fairfax Street
Alexandria, VA 22314

703-684-2782
800-999-2782
Fax: 703-706-8575
E-Mail: webmaster@apta.org
Home Page: www.apta.org

Kelly Glascoe, Director/Exposition
Frank Mallon, CEO

450 exhibits of physical therapy equipment, supplies and services.
4000 Attendees
Frequency: Annual

13175 American Physical Therapy Association: Private Practice Session
1111 N Fairfax Street
Alexandria, VA 22314

703-684-2782
800-999-2782
Fax: 703-706-8575
Home Page: http://www.apta.org

Frank Mallon, CEO

Seminar, workshop, dinner and 120 exhibits of physical therapy and rehabilitation equipment, supplies and services.
1200 Attendees
Frequency: Annual
Founded in 1983

13176 American Podiatric Medical Association Annual Meeting
9312 Old Georgetown Road
Bethesda, MD 20814

301-581-9200
Fax: 301-530-2752
Social Media: Facebook, Twitter, LinkedIn

Anne Martinez CMP, Meetings Administrator

One-hundred and fifty exhibits of medical and laser equipment, supplies and podiatric services.
1,500 Attendees
Frequency: August

13177 American Psychiatric Association Annual Meeting
1400 K Street NW
Washington, DC 20005

202-682-6100
Fax: 202-682-6132
E-Mail: gank@psych.org
Home Page: www.psych.org

Ken Robinson, Manager Meetings

Conference, seminar, workshop and 850 exhibits of computer online service and software, media products, criminal justice, dianostic tools and much more.
18000 Attendees
Frequency: Annual
Founded in 1844

13178 American Psychological Association Annual Convention
American Psychological Association
750 1st Street NE
Washington, DC 20002-4242

202-336-5500
800-374-2721
Fax: 202-336-5568
Home Page: www.apa.org

James H Bray PhD, President
Norman Anderson PhD, Executive VP/CEO
Paul L Craig PhD, Treasurer
12000 Attendees
Frequency: Annual, August

13179 American Public Health Association Annual Exhibition
American Public Health Association
800 I Street NW
Washington, DC 20001
202-777-2742
Fax: 202-777-2534
E-Mail: lynn.schoen@apha.org
Home Page: www.apha.org

Lynn Schoen, Exhibition Manager
Georges Benjamin, Executive Director

Five-hundred seventy exhibits of medical interest, pharmaceuticals, publishers, educational, governmental, software, helth promotion products and more. Scientific Sessions available.
13000 Attendees
Frequency: November

13180 American Roentgen Ray Society Meeting
American Roentgen Ray Society
44211 Slatestone Court
Leesburg, VA 20176

703-729-3353
800-438-2777
Fax: 703-729-4839
E-Mail: info@arrs.org
Home Page: www.arrs.org

Maureen Robertson, Show Manager
Noel Montesa, Vice President
Charles Kahn, Vice President
Melissa Rosado, Secretary

Forty-one and a half hours of Category ICME credits available; Categorical course on Body CT; 30 commercial exhibits; 300 scientific exhibits; scientific paper presentations.
2,500 Attendees
Frequency: April-May

13181 American School Health's Annual School Health Conference
American School Health Association
4340 East West Highway
Suite 403
Bethesda, MD 20814

301-652-8072
800-445-2742
Fax: 301-652-8077
E-Mail: info@ashaweb.org
Home Page: www.ashaweb.org
Social Media: Facebook, Twitter, LinkedIn

Mary Bamer Ramsier, Meeting Planner
Thomas Reed, Manager
Stephen Conley, Executive Director
Julie Greenfield, Marketing and Conferences Director
Lori Lawrence, Membership/Database Manager

Join school health professionals who will come together to learn, share perspectives and resources, and network during the more than 120 educational sessions and workshops. General Sessions, multiple break-outs, and exhibits.
800 Attendees
Frequency: Annual
Founded in 1927
Mailing list available for rent: 650 names

13182 American Society for Aesthetic Plastic Surgery Conference
American Society for Aesthetic Plastic Surgery
36 W 44th Street
Suite 630
New York, NY 10036
212-921-0500
Fax: 212-921-0011
E-Mail: media@surgery.org
Home Page: www.surgery.org
Educational sessions and displays of the latest prdoducts and developments.
2500 Attendees
Frequency: May

13183 American Society for Artificial Internal Organs Meeting and Exhibits
PO Box C
Boca Raton, FL 33429-8589
561-391-8589
Fax: 561-368-9153
Home Page: www.asaio.org
Workshop, and over 30 exhibits of interest to physicians, nurses, engineers, perfusionists and technicians.
1000 Attendees
Frequency: Annual
Founded in 1954

13184 American Society for Bone and Mineral Research Congress
1200 19th Street NW
Suite 300
Washington, DC 20036
202-289-5900
Fax: 202-857-1880
Home Page: www.asbmr.org
Joan Goldberg, Executive Director
Exhibits for the research of bone and mineral diseases.
Frequency: Annual
Founded in 1977

13185 American Society for Cell Biology Annual Meeting
9650 Rockville Pike
Bethesda, MD 20814
301-530-7153
Fax: 301-530-7139
E-Mail: enewman@ascb.org
Home Page: www.ascb.org/ascb
Edward Newman, Director Marketing
Joan Goldberg, Manager
Jean Schwarzbauer, Secretary
Conference and 425 exhibits of interest to biomedical researchers, scientists, and related trade professionals.
8000 Attendees
Frequency: Annual
Founded in 1961

13186 American Society for Dermatologic Surgery Annual Meeting
American Society for Dermatologic Surgery
5550 Meadowbrook Drive
Suite 120
Rolling Meadows, IL 60008
847-956-0900
Fax: 847-956-0999
E-Mail: info@asds.net
Home Page: www.asds-net.org
Alastair Carruthers, President
Kimberly Butterwick, Board of Directors
Educational session, banquet and tours plus 80 exhibits of surgical instruments, dressings, closure materials and dermatologic pharmceuticals.
800 Attendees
Founded in 1973

13187 American Society for Health Care Human Resources Administration Meeting
American Hospital Association
1 N Franklin
Chicago, IL 60606
312-222-2000
Fax: 312-422-4519
Home Page: www.aha.org
Human resources administration in health care exhibition.

13188 American Society for Healthcare Management Convention
Corcoran Expositions
100 W Monroe Street
Suite 1001
Chicago, IL 60603
312-541-0567
Fax: 312-541-0573

13189 American Society for Histocompatability and Immunogenetics
PO Box 15804
Lexana, KS 66285 5804
913-541-0009
Fax: 913-541-0156
Michael P Flanigan CAE, Executive Director
Fifty exhibits from medical suppliers relating to tissue typing.
1000 Attendees
Frequency: Annual
Founded in 1974

13190 American Society for Laser Medicine and Surgery Conference
2100 Stewart Avenue
Suite 240
Wausau, WI 54401-1709
715-845-9283
Fax: 715-848-2493
E-Mail: information@aslms.org
Home Page: www.aslms.org
Richard O Gregory MD, Board Secretary
Dianne Dalsky, Executive Director
Seventy five exhibits of laser medicine and supplies of interest to physicians, physicists, nurses, veterinarians, dentists, podiatrists and technicians.
Frequency: Annual
Founded in 1980

13191 American Society for Microbiology: General Meeting
1325 Massachusetts Avenue NW
Washington, DC 20005
202-942-9252
Fax: 202-942-9340
Professionally related exhibits.

13192 American Society for Nutrition Annual Meeting
9650 Rockville Pike
Bethesda, MD 20814-3998
301-634-7050
Fax: 301-634-7892
Home Page: www.nutrition.org
Teresa A. Davis, President
John E Courtney PhD, Executive Officer
Gordon L. Jensen, VP
Cheryl Rock, Treasurer
Catherine Field, Secretary
Exhibits relating to clinical nutrition of interest to physicians and scientists.
Frequency: Annual
Mailing list available for rent

13193 American Society for Surgery of the Hand Annual Meeting
American Society for Surgery of the Hand
6300 N River Road
Suite 600
Rosemont, IL 60018
847-384-8300
Fax: 847-384-1435
E-Mail: info@assh.org
Home Page: www.assh.org
Carissa Wehrman, Meetings/Exhibits Coordinator
Mark Anderson, Executive Director
Meeting plus exhibits of microsurgical instruments, finger splinting devices, surgical telescopes, trauma products, external fixation systems and more.
2,000 Attendees
Frequency: September

13194 American Society for Therapeutic Radiology and Oncology Annual Meeting
American Society for Therapeutic Radiology & Onc.
12500 Fairlakes Circle
Suite 375
Fairfax, VA 22033
703-502-1550
800-962-7876
Fax: 703-502-7852
E-Mail: meetings@astro.org
Home Page: www.astro.org
Laura Mulay, ASTRO Meetings Manager
Eight-hundred exhibits of products, supplies and services for the treatment of cancer.
10000 Attendees
Frequency: October

13195 American Society of Aesthetic Plastic Surgery Meeting
11081 Winners Circle
Suite 200
Los Alamitos, CA 90720-2813
562-799-2356
Fax: 310-427-2234
Robert Stanton, Manager
Meeting and 100 exhibits of plastic surgery medical instruments and equipment.
Frequency: Annual

13196 American Society of Anesthesiologists Annual Meeting
American Society of Anesthesiologists
520 N Northwest Highway
Park Ridge, IL 60068-2573
847-825-5586
Fax: 847-825-1692
E-Mail: mail@asahq.org
Home Page: www.asahq.org
Ronald Bruns, Executive Director
18000 Attendees
Frequency: Annual, October

13197 American Society of Clinical Oncology Annual Convention
J Spargo & Associates
11208 Waples Mill Road
Suite 112
Fairfax, VA 22030
703-631-6200
800-564-4220

Fax: 703-299-1044
E-Mail: info@jspargo.com
Home Page: www.jspargo.com

John Spargo, President

Three hundred exhibits of medical equipment, supplies and services used in the practice of clinical oncology.
20000 Attendees
Frequency: Annual
Founded in 1964

13198 American Society of Clinical Pathologists and College of American Pathologist
American Society of Clinical Pathologists
2100 W Harrison Street
Chicago, IL 60612

312-738-1336
Fax: 312-738-1619

John Ball, Executive VP
4500 Attendees

13199 American Society of Cytopathology Annual Scientific Meeting
100 West 10th Street
Suite 605
Wilmington, DE 19801

302-543-6583
Fax: 302-543-6597
E-Mail: asc@cytopathology.org
Home Page: www.cytopathology.org
Social Media: Facebook, Twitter, LinkedIn

Christy Myers, Meetings Manager
Elizabeth Jenkins, Manager
Andrew Renshaw, President

Premier event in the field of cytopathology. The objectives of the Annual Meeting are to update cytologists on the current practice of cytopathology, foster research in early diagnosis and effective treatment of human disease and provide a forum for advocacy on behalf of cytologists and their patients.
850 Attendees
Frequency: November
Founded in 1951

13200 American Society of Directors of Volunteer Services Leadership Training Conf
1 N Franklin
Chicago, IL 60606

312-223-3937
Fax: 312-442-4575

Audrey Harris, Executive Director

Workshop, banquet, luncheon and 55 exhibits of health care administration equipment, supplies and services.
700 Attendees
Frequency: Annual
Founded in 1964

13201 American Society of Electroneurodiagnostic Technologists Convention
American Society of Electroneurodiagnostic Tech
402 E Bannister Rd
Suite A
Kansas City, MO 64131-3019

816-931-1120
Fax: 816-931-1145
E-Mail: info@aset.org
Home Page: www.aset.org
Social Media: Facebook, Twitter

Arlen Reimnitz, Executive Director
Sarah Ecker, Marketing/Communications Manager

The premier education and exposition opportunity for the Neurodiagnostic technologists in the country. A must attend event for all neurodiagnostic professionals whether you are a technologist, laboratory manager, physician or representing a supplier. The 2012 convention will be in St. Paul, MN.
500 Attendees
Frequency: Annual

13202 American Society of Extra-Corporeal Tech. International Conference
503 Carlisle Drive
Suite 125
Herndon, VA 20170-4838

703-435-8556
Fax: 703-435-0056
E-Mail: webmaster@amsect.org
Home Page: www.amsect.org

Judy Luther, Deputy Executive Director

Seminar, workshop, conference and 75 exhibits relating to the practice of extra-corporeal technology (involving heart and lung machines).
Frequency: Annual

13203 American Society of Hand Therapists Convention
Smith, Bucklin and Associates
401 N Michigan Avenue
Chicago, IL 60611-4267

312-644-6610
Fax: 312-245-1082
E-Mail: info@smithbucklin.com
Home Page: www.smithbucklin.com

Henry S. Givray, President & CEO
C. Albert Koob, Executive Vice President
Carolyn Dolezal, Executive Vice President
Michael L. Payne, Executive Vice President
Cele Fogarty, Vice President - Event Services

Workshop and 40 - 60 exhibits of books, and hand therapy equipment.
800 Attendees
Frequency: Annual
Founded in 1949

13204 American Society of Health Care Marketing & Public Relations
1 N Franklin Street
31st Floor
Chicago, IL 60606-3421

773-327-1064
Fax: 312-422-4579

Lauren Barnett, Executive Director

Sixty booths of communications, printing, computer equipment, public relations and fund raising consultants in the health care profession.
600 Attendees
Frequency: September

13205 American Society of Hematology Annual Meeting & Exposition
1200 19th Street NW
Suite 300
Washington, DC 24226

202-857-1118
Fax: 202-847-1164

Gail Sparks

Four hundred fifty exhibits of equipment and supplies of interest to hematologists and related professionals.
15000 Attendees
Founded in 1958

13206 American Society of Human Genetics Annual Meeting
American Society of Human Genetics
9650 Rockville Pike
Bethesda, MD 20814-3998

301-634-7300
Fax: 301-634-7079
E-Mail: society@ashg.org
Home Page: www.ashg.org
Social Media: Facebook, Twitter, LinkedIn

Joann Boughman, PhD, Executive VP
Chuck Windle, Director of Finance/Administration
Karen Goodman, Executive Assistant
Pauline Minhinnett, Dir. of Meetings/Exhibit Management
Mary Shih, Membership Manager

A meeting of researchers, clinicians, trainees and others who share the most recent research findings in human genetics. Includes invited speaker sessions and about 3000 contributed abstracts; 266 to platform and the remainder to poster presentations.
8000 Members
6,000 Attendees
Founded in 1948

13207 American Society of Nephrology
American Society of Nephrology
1200 19th Street NW
Suite 300
Washington, DC 20036

202-857-1190
Fax: 202-429-5112

13000 Attendees

13208 American Society of PeriAnesthesia Nurses
American Gastroenterological Association
4930 Del Ray Avenue
Bethesda, MD 20814

301-654-2055
Fax: 301-654-5920
E-Mail: member@gastro.org
Home Page: www.gastro.org

13209 American Society of Post Anesthesia Nurses Meeting
Slack
4930 Del Ray Avenue
Bethesda, MD 20814

301-654-2055
Fax: 301-654-5920
E-Mail: member@gastro.org
Home Page: www.gastro.org

Robert Greenberg, Executive Vp
Michael Stolar, Senior Vp

One hundred seventy exhibits of pharmaceuticals and recovery room supplies.
1700 Attendees
Frequency: Annual
Founded in 1981

13210 American Society of Psychoprophylaxis in Obstetrics/Lamaze Conference
Smith, Bucklin and Associates
1200 19th Street NW
Suite 300
Washington, DC 20036-2412

202-861-6416
Fax: 202-429-5112

Leigh McMillan, Senior Convention Director

One hundred exhibitors of educational materials for Lamaze method of prepared childbirth, obstetric equipment and supplies, infant products, breast pumps and more.
500 Attendees
Frequency: Annual
Founded in 1960

13211 American Society of Transplant Physicians Scientific Meeting
Slack

4930 Del Ray Avenue
Bethesda, MD 20814

301-654-2055
Fax: 301-654-5920
E-Mail: member@gastro.org
Home Page: www.gastro.org

Robert Greenberg, Executive Vp
Michael Stolar, Senior Vp

Fifty exhibits of medical supplies and services of interest to physicans and others actively involved with transplantaion.
800 Attendees
Frequency: Annual
Founded in 1981

13212 **American Society of Transplant Surgeons Annual Meeting**
Wright Organization
716 Lee Street
Des Plaines, IL 60016 4515

847-245-5700
Fax: 708-824-0394

Sixty exhibitors of medical equipment, supplies and services relating to renal and cardiac transplants.
750 Attendees
Founded in 1974

13213 **American Society of Tropical Medicine and Hygiene Annual Scientific Meeting**
60 Revere Drive
Suite 500
Northbrook, IL 60062

847-480-9592
Fax: 847-480-9282
E-Mail: info@astmh.org
Home Page: www.astmh.org

Madhuri Carson, Conference Administrator
Judy DeAcetis, Director
Karen Goraleski, Executive Director

Reception and over 20 exhibits related to tropical medicine and hygiene, including the areas of arboviology, entomology, medicine, nursing and parasitology.
1500 Attendees
Frequency: November
Founded in 1951

13214 **American Speech-Language-Hearing Association Annual Convention**
American Speech- Language Hearing Association
10801 Rockville Pike
Rockville, MD 20852

301-897-5700
800-498-2071
Fax: 301-296-8580
E-Mail: productsales@asha.org
Home Page: www.asha.org

Mary Harding, Exhibition Manager
Arlene Pietranton, Associate Director
Amy Hasselkus, Associate Director

Four hundred exhibits of medical, educational and testing equipment, plus publications.
12000 Attendees

13215 **American Urological Association Convention**
1000 Corporate Boulevard
Linthicum, MD 21090
410-689-3700
Fax: 410-689-3800
E-Mail: convention@auanet.org
Home Page: www.auanet.org/

Jane Conway, Advertising & Exhibit Sales
Sarah Hardy, Exhibitor Customer Service
Andrew Niles, Exhibit Operations
Michael T Sheppard, Executive Director
Paul F Schellhammer, Board of Directors President

At the American Urological Association (AUA)'s Annual Meeting there are more than 10,000 urologists and health care professionals in attendance and over 300 exhibitors showcasing their urological products or services- there is no better place to learn about the latest advances in urology.
10000 Attendees
Frequency: Annual

13216 **Annual Clinical Assembly of Osteopathic Specialists**
American College of Osteopathic Surgeons
123 N Henry Street
Alexandria, VA 22314

703-684-0416
Fax: 703-684-3280
E-Mail: info@facos.org
Home Page: www.facos.org
Social Media: Facebook, Twitter, LinkedIn

Guy Beaumont, Executive Director
Judith T Mangum, Director Finance
Jennifer B. Colwell, Director of Continuing Education
Sonjya Johnson, Director of Membership Recruitment
Brandon Roberts, Director of Finance
700 Members
Frequency: Annual
Mailing list available for rent

13217 **Annual Conference on Healthcare Marketing**
Alliance for Healthcare Strategy & Marketing
11 S LaSalle Street
Suite 2300
Chicago, IL 60603

312-704-9700
Fax: 312-704-9709
Home Page: www.alliancehlth.org/hlthmktg

Workshop and social events plus 50 exhibits of marketing communications, health care information lines, strategic planning and more.
600 Attendees
Frequency: Annual
Founded in 1984

13218 **Annual Contact Lens and Primary Care Seminar, MOA**
Michigan Optometric Association
530 W Ionia Street
Suite A
Lansing, MI 48933-1062

517-482-0616
Fax: 517-482-1611
E-Mail: mioptoassn@aol.com
Home Page: www.themoa.org

William D Dansby CAE, Executive VP
Mark Margolies, Treasurer

Continuing education program and trade show for optometrists and optometric technicians/assistants.
1100 Attendees
Frequency: October, Annually
Founded in 1968

13219 **Annual Convention of American Institute of Ultrasound in Medicine**
American Institute of Ultrasound in Medicine
14750 Sweitzer Lane
Suite 100
Laurel, MD 20707

301-498-4392
800-638-5352
Fax: 301-498-4450
E-Mail: conv_edu@aium.org
Home Page: www.aium.org

Jenny Clark, Director of Development
Brenda Kinney, Meeting Coordinator
Lisa Shendan, Sales Manager
Frequency: June

13220 **Annual Convention of the American College of Osteopathic Obstetricians**
American College Of Osteopathic Obstetricians
900 Auburn Road
Pontiac, MI 48342

248-332-6360
800-875-6360
Fax: 248-332-4607
Home Page: www.acoog.com

Jaki Britton, Administrator

Workshop, reception and banquet as well as exhibits relating to women's health, medical equipment and supplies.
350 Attendees
Frequency: Annual
Founded in 1934

13221 **Annual Critical Care Update**
National Professional Education Institute
2525 Ossen Fort Road
PO Box 118
Glencoe, MO 63068-1107

636-735-5570
800-575-5575
Fax: 561-743-9596
E-Mail: JJMcDaid@aol.com
Home Page: www.npeinursing.com

Judie McDaid, Exhibitor Relations Manager
Leslie Brock, Registration Manager

The Annual Critical Care Update and Nurse Managers Conference/EXPO provides a fully integrated program dedicated to the continuing education of critical care nurses, nurse managers and other healthcare professionals. Exhibitors showcase their latest healthcare products, pharmaceuticals, services, research and facilities. Knowledge gained in the informative, entertaining EXPO Hall, will influence these nurses' purchasing decisions throughout the year.
1500 Attendees
Frequency: Annual, April
Founded in 1973

13222 **Annual Disease Management Congress: Innovative Strategies**
National Managed Health Care Congress
71 2nd Avenue
3rd Floor
Waltham, MA 02154

888-882-2500
Fax: 941-365-0157
Home Page: www.nmhcc.org

Frances Pratt, Director/Marketing

One hundred exhibits of targeted disease management and services.
1700 Attendees
Frequency: Annual
Founded in 1996

13223 **Annual Educational Conference and Exhibits**
Society for Healthcare Strategy & Market Dev.
One N Franklin
Chicago, IL 60606

312-422-3840
Fax: 312-422-4579
E-Mail: stratsoc@aha.org
Home Page: www.stratsociety.org
Frequency: September

13224 **Annual Meeting & Clinical Lab Exposition**
American Association for Clinical Chemistry
1850 K St NW
Suite 625
Washington, DC 20006-2215
202-857-0717
800-892-1400
Fax: 202-887-5093
E-Mail: custserv@aacc.org
Home Page: www.aacc.org
Jean Rhame, Director Professional Affairs
Six hundred exhibitors of clincal laboratory equipment, supplies and services for lab automation, information, robotics and OEM products. Seminar, worshop and conference.
20000 Attendees
Frequency: Annual
Mailing list available for rent: 11000 names at $150 per M

13225 **Annual Meeting & Homecare Expo**
National Association for Home Care and Hospice
228 7th Street SE
Washington, DC 20003
202-547-7424
Fax: 202-547-3540
E-Mail: webmaster@nahc.org
Home Page: www.nahc.org
Gathering of Home Care and Hospice professionals.
4000 Attendees
Frequency: October

13226 **Annual Meeting & OTO Expo**
American Academy of Otolaryngology-Head & Neck
1650 Diagonal Road
Alexandria, VA 22314-3357
703-836-4444
Fax: 703-683-5100
E-Mail: membership@entnet.org
Home Page: www.entnet.org
Marty Stewart, Sr Manager, Media/Public Relations
James L. Netterville, President
J. Gavin Setzen, Secretary/Treasurer
David R. Nielsen, Executive Vice President and CEO
Paul T. Fass, Director - Private Practice
Frequency: September
Mailing list available for rent

13227 **Annual Meeting of the American Association on Mental Retardation**
American Association on Mental Retardation
444 N Capitol Street NW
Suite 846
Washington, DC 20001-1512
202-387-1968
800-424-3688
Fax: 202-387-2193
E-Mail: dcroser@aamr.org
Home Page: www.aamr.org
Doreen Croser, Executive Director
Paul Aitken, Director Of Finance Administration
2000 Attendees
Frequency: Annual, May

13228 **Annual Meeting of the Microscopy Society of America**
Bostrom Corporation
230 E Ohio
Suite 400
Chicago, IL 60611-3265
312-644-1527
800-538-3672
Fax: 312-644-8557
E-Mail: BusinessOffices@MSA.Microscopy.com
Home Page: www.msa.microscopy.com
Judy Janes, Manager
Microscopes and related supplies of interest to medical, biological, metalurgical, and polymer research scientists, technicians and physicists interested in instrument design and improvement.
Frequency: Annual, August

13229 **Annual National Managed Health Care Congress**
71 2nd Avenue
3rd Floor
Waltham, MA 02154
888-882-2500
Fax: 941-365-0157
E-Mail: register@mnhcc.com
Home Page: www.nmhcc.org
Seminar, workshop, conference, and 600 exhibits of services and products dedicated to improving the quality of health care.
10000 Attendees
Frequency: Annual
Founded in 1989

13230 **Annual PPO Forum**
American Assn of Preferred Provider Organizations
222 South First Street
Suite 303
Louisville, KY 40202
502-403-1122
Fax: 502-403-1129
E-Mail: mcox@aappo.org
Home Page: www.aappo.org
Melissa Cox, Event Coordinator
Michael Taddeo, Chairperson
Keith Vangeison, Vice-Chairman
Kenneth Hamm, Treasurer
William Ross, Secretary
Frequency: San Diego
Founded in 1983

13231 **Annual Scientific & Clinical Congress**
American Association of Clinical Endocrinologists
245 Riverside Avenue
Suite 200
Jacksonville, FL 32202
904-353-7878
Fax: 904-353-8185
E-Mail: info@aace.com
Home Page: www.aace.com
Donald Jones, CEO
Jeffrey Garber, President
Clinical endocrinologists and endocrine surgeons gather for meeting and exhibits of equipment, supplies and services.
2000 Attendees
Frequency: April

13232 **Annual Scientific Meeting**
Aerospace Medical Association
320 S Henry Street
Alexandria, VA 22314-3579
703-739-2240
Fax: 703-739-9652
E-Mail: rrayman@asma.org
Home Page: www.asma.org
Sheryl Kildall, Subscriptions Manager
Warren Silberman DO, VP
Jeffrey C. Sventek, Executive Director
Gisselle Vargas, Operations Manager
Gloria Carter, Director, Member Services
Provides a multi-faceted forum for all aerospace medical disciplines and concurrently provides continuing education credits for those attending the meeting.
3000 Attendees
Frequency: Annual/May
Mailing list available for rent

13233 **Annual Scientific Meeting of the Gerontological Society of America**
Gerontological Society of America
1030 15th Street NW
Suite 250
Washington, DC 20005
202-842-1275
Fax: 202-842-1150
Home Page: www.geron.org
Carol Schutz, Executive Director

13234 **Applied Ergonomics Conference**
Institute of Industrial Engineers
3597 Parkway Lane
Suite 200
Norcross, GA 30097
770-449-0461
800-494-0460
Fax: 770-263-8532
E-Mail: webmaster@iienet.org
Home Page: www.iienet.org/annual
Carol LeBlanc, Conference Manager
An exclusive event for ergonomists, engineers, and safety professionals. The conference focuses on how companies have successfully implemented programs that provide excellent return on their ergonomics investment.
800 Attendees
Frequency: March
Founded in 1998

13235 **Arthroscopy Association of North America Annual Meeting**
6300 N River Road
#104
Rosemont, IL 60018
847-292-2262
Fax: 847-292-2268
E-Mail: holly@aana.org
Home Page: www.aana.org
Holly Albert, Meetings Manager
Edward Goss, Executive Director
Seminar, reception and 100 exhibits of video and arthroscopy equipment, braces, books and more.
1000 Attendees

13236 **Assisted Living Expo**
VNU Expositions
Dulles International Airport
PO Box 17413
Washington, DC 20041
703-318-0300
800-765-7616
Fax: 703-318-8833
Home Page: www.vnuexpo.com
Displays of assisted living information and equipment.

13237 **Association for Applied Psychophysiology & Biofeedback Annual Meeting**
Association for Applied Psychophysiology
10200 W 44th Avenue
Suite 304
Wheat Ridge, CO 80033
303-228-8436
800-477-8892
Fax: 303-422-8894

E-Mail: info@aapb.org
Home Page: www.aapb.org

Tina Watkins, Meetings Manager
Francine Butler, Treasurer
Fred Schaffer, Treasurer

Exhibits of biofeedback equipment, supplies, and training programs, medical supplies and software, as well as annual meeting.
500 Attendees
Frequency: March
Founded in 1969

13238 **Association for Healthcare Philanthropy Annual Int'l Educational Conference**
Association for Healthcare Philanthropy
313 Park Avenue
Suite 400
Falls Church, VA 22046

703-532-6243
Fax: 703-532-7170
E-Mail: ahp@ahp.org
Home Page: www.ahp.org

Conference and 120 exhibits with information about equipment and services for the fundraising and helatcare development community, including computer software, recognition gifts, direct mail companies, executive recriuters, special events and more.
900 Attendees
Frequency: September

13239 **Association for Professionals in Infection Control & Epidemiology**
Association for Professionals in Infection Control
1275 K Street NW
Suite 1000
Washington, DC 20005-4006

202-789-1890
800-650-9570
Fax: 202-789-1899
E-Mail: apicinfo@apic.org
Home Page: www.apic.org

Christine J Nutty, President
Carolyn E Jackson, Secretary
Katrina Crist, CEO
Jacqueline Manson, Accounting
Sara Haywood, Education

Workshop, banquet, reception and 150 exhibits of infection control products, pharmaceuticals, disinfectants, soaps, dataprocessing software, housekeeping equipment and supplies.
2700 Attendees
Frequency: Annual
Founded in 1974

13240 **Association for Worksite Health Promotion Annual International Conference**
60 Revere Drive
Suite 500
Northbrook, IL 60062-1577

847-480-9574
Fax: 847-480-9282
Home Page: www.awhp.org

Liz Freyn, Conference Manager

One hundred twenty two booths of information and supplies to promote and develop quality programs of health and fitness in business and industry. Seminar, workshop, conference, tours and luncheon.
950 Attendees
Founded in 1974

13241 **Association of Behavioral Healthcare Management Convention**
60 Revere Drive
Suite 500
Northbrook, IL 60062

847-480-9626
Fax: 847-480-9282

Exhibits related to the administation of services for the emotionally disturbed, mentally ill, mentally retarded, developmentally disabled, and those with substance abuse problems.
Frequency: Annual

13242 **Association of Healthcare Internal Auditors Conference**
PO Box 449
Onstead, MI 49265-0449

517-467-7729
Fax: 517-467-6104
E-Mail: ahia@ahia.org
Home Page: www.ahia.org

Thomas Monahan, Executive Director
Michelle Cunningham, Account Executive
Robert Michalski, Secretary, Treasurer

Exhibits concerning cost containment and increased productivity in health care institutions through internal auditing.
1000 Attendees
Founded in 1981

13243 **Association of Pediatric Oncology Nurses Annual Conference**
Association of Pediatric Nurses
4700 W Lake Avenue
Glenview, IL 60025-1485

847-375-4724
Fax: 847-375-4777
E-Mail: info@apon.org
Home Page: www.apon.org

Pamela Asfahani, Product Manager
Elizabeth Sherman, senior marketing Manager

Exhibits on caring for children who have cancer.

13244 **Association of Rehabilitation Nurses Annual Educational Conference**
4700 W Lake Avenue
Glenview, IL 60025-1485

847-375-4710
800-229-7530
Fax: 847-375-4777

Conference, educational session, workshop and 225 exhibits of rehabilitational aids and supplies, medical equipment, hospitals and rehbilitation facilities and publications of interest to rehabilitation nurses.
2300 Attendees
Founded in 1974

13245 **Benefits Health Care New York Show**
Flagg Management
353 Lexington Avenue
New York, NY 10016

212-286-0333
Fax: 212-286-0086
E-Mail: flaggmgmnt@msn.com
Home Page: www.flaggmgmt.com

Russell Flagg, President

Sponsored by Employee Benefit News, the conference will focus on the recent health care reform, as well as coping with the economic downturn. Human resources, personnel, administration and training marketplace. HRMS, systems and services 250 exhibits. $295.
Frequency: Annual
Mailing list available for rent

13246 **Building Bridges VII**
American Association of Health Plans
1129 20th Street NW
Washington, DC 20036

202-778-3200
Fax: 202-778-8506

13247 **CHPA Annual Executive Conference**
Consumer Health Care Products Association
900 19th St NW
Suite 700
Washington, DC 20006-2105

202-429-9260
Fax: 202-223-6835
E-Mail: eassey@chpa-info.org
Home Page: www.chpa-info.org

Paul L. Sturman, Chair

Join top healthcare executives from across the nation and participate in high-level education sessions focused on the industry's rapidly shifting environment.

13248 **Center for School Mental Health Assistance National Convention**
Exhibit Promotions Plus
11620 Vixens Path
Ellicott City, MD 21042

301-596-3028
Fax: 410-997-0764

Harve C Horowitz, President

Supports school health, mental health professionals by offering ongoing consutation to address administrative, clinical and systems issues relevant to school health services.
Frequency: October

13249 **Clinical Laboratory Expo**
AACC; c/o Scherago International
11 Penn Plaza
Suite 1003
New York, NY 10001

212-643-1750
Fax: 212-643-1758
E-Mail: tonym@scherago.com
Home Page: www.scherago.com/AACC

Tony Maiorino, Vice President
20000 Attendees
Frequency: July-August

13250 **Clinical Laboratory Management Association Annual Conference & Exhibition**
Clinical Laboratory Management Association
989 Old Eagle School Road
Suite 815
Wayne, PA 19087

610-995-9580
Fax: 610-995-9568
E-Mail: info@clma.org
Home Page: www.clma.org

Dana Procsal, VP
Ruth Nelson, Director of Operations

CLMA-ASCP have combined forces to offer the largest, most comprehensive laboratory conference and exhibition ever, specifically designed for laboratory professionals at all levels.
4800 Attendees
Frequency: June

13251 **Clinical and Scientific Congress of the Int'l Anesthesia Research Society**
International Anesthesia Research Society
2 Summit Park Drive
Suite 140
Cleveland, OH 44131

216-642-1124
Fax: 216-642-1127

E-Mail: info@iars.org
Home Page: www.iars.org

Donald S Prough, Chair
Hugo Van Aken, Chairman
1200 Attendees
Frequency: March

13252 **Congress on Invitro Biology**
Society for Invitro Biology
9315 Lango Drive W
Suite 255
Lango, MD 20774

301-324-5054
800-741-7476
Fax: 301-324-5057
E-Mail: sivb@sivb.org
Home Page: www.sivb.org

Marietta Ellis, Managing Director
Richard Heller, Treasurer
Focus on issues pertinent to the Vertebrate, Invertebrate, and Cellular Toxicology Sections and will give participants a unique learning experience on animal cell culture and biotechnology.
1,000 Attendees
Frequency: June

13253 **Consumer Directed Health Care Conference**
Po Box 448, East Cary Street
Suite 102
Richmond, VA 23219

804-266-7422
Fax: 804-225-7458
Home Page: www.cdhcc.com or www.consumerhealthworld.com

Carlotta Farmer, Director of Programming
Frequency: December, Washington

13254 **Digestive Disease Week Meeting & Exhibition**
American Gastroenterological Association
4930 Del Ray Avenue
Bethesda, MD 20814

301-654-2055
Fax: 301-652-3890
E-Mail: member@gastro.org
Home Page: www.gastro.org

14000 Attendees
Frequency: March

13255 **Distribution Management Conference & Expo**
Healthcare Distribution Management Association
900 N Glebe Road
Suite 1000
Arlington, VA 22203

703-787-0000
Fax: 703-935-3200
Home Page: www.healthcaredistribution.org

Lori Burke, Director Meetings/Conferences
Denise Woodson, Managing Director
Laurel Todd, Managing Director
Provides the latest information on the most important topics affecting healthcare distribution.
Frequency: June

13256 **Drug Discovery Technology**
Hynes Convention Center
900 Boylston Street
Boston, MA 02115

617-954-2000
800-845-8800
Fax: 617-954-2125
E-Mail: info@mccahome.com
Home Page: www.mccahome.com

2000 Attendees
Frequency: August

13257 **Emergency Nurses Association Scientific Assembly & Exhibits**
Emergency Nurses Association
915 Lee Street
Des Plaines, IL 60016-6569

847-460-4100
800-900-9659
Fax: 847-460-4001
E-Mail: webmaster@ena.org
Home Page: www.ena.org

David Westman, CEO
Anita Dorr, Co-Founder
Kathy Szumanski, Director
3500 Attendees
Frequency: Annual, September

13258 **Endocrine Society Annual Meeting**
Scherago International
11 Penn Plaza
Suite 1003
New York, NY 10001

212-643-1750
Fax: 212-643-1758

6500 Attendees

13259 **Experimental Biology**
FASEB/OSMC
9650 Rockville Pike
Bethesda, MD 20814

301-634-7100
Fax: 301-634-7014
E-Mail: info@faseb.org
Home Page: www.faseb.org/meetings

Pauline Minhinnett, Meeting Manager
Jean Lash, Marketing Manager
Jacquelyn Roberts, Marketing Manager
David Craven, Executive Director
12M Attendees
Frequency: April

13260 **FASEB Conference Federation for American Societies for Experimental Biology**
FASEB/OSMC
9650 Rockville Pike
Bethesda, MD 20814

301-634-7100
Fax: 301-634-7014
E-Mail: info@faseb.org
Home Page: www.faseb.org/meetings

Jean Lash, Exhibit Manager
Marcella Jackson, Marketing Manager
Jacquelyn Roberts, Marketing Manager
David Craven, Executive Director
900 Attendees
Frequency: March

13261 **Fall Symposium**
American College of Emergency Physicians
PO Box 619911
Dallas, TX 75261

972-550-0911
Fax: 972-580-2816

325 Attendees

13262 **Federation of Hospitals Public Policy Conference & Business Exposition**
Federation of American Health Systems
801 Pennsylvania Avenue NW
Suite 245
Washington, DC 20004-2604

202-624-1500
Fax: 202-737-6462
E-Mail: info@fah.org
Home Page: www.fah.org

Bonnie Moneypenny, Senior VP Administrative Services
Letitia Faison-Mahoney, Controller
The conference brings together hospital executives and leading policymakers each Spring for important discussions. It also affords an important opportunity for suppliers to meet face-to-face with hospital managers and buyers.
Frequency: Annual, March
Founded in 1966

13263 **Fire-Rescue International**
International Association of Fire Chiefs
4025 Fair Ridge Drive
Fairfax, VA 22033

703-273-0911
Fax: 703-273-9363
Home Page: www.iafc.org/conference.shtml

William Walton, CFO
Conference and exposition of the fire service industry.
16000 Attendees
Frequency: August

13264 **Food & Nutrition Conference & Expo**
American Dietetic Association
120 South Riverside Plaza
Suite 2000
Chicago, IL 60606

312-899-0040
800-877-1600
Fax: 312-899-0008
E-Mail: gandruch@eatright.org
Home Page: www.eatright.org
Social Media: Facebook, Twitter

Greg Andruch, Exhibits Manager
Allison MacMunn, Public Relations Manager
Donna Wickstrom, Manager
Karen Didriksen, Purchasing Manager
More than 8,000 professionals come to the Food & Nutrition Conference & Expo for the latest technological and nutritional advancements. This is the premier selling opportunity in the fields of nutrition and food service management. The event continues to expand-attracting a wider audience of professionals, including hotel and restaurant managers, sports, health and nutrition professionals and executive chefs.
8000 Attendees
Frequency: September, Pennsylvania
Circulation: 65000

13265 **HCEA Annual Meeting**
Healthcare Convention & Exhibitors Association
1100 Johnson Ferry Rd NE
Suite 300
Atlanta, GA 30342-1733

404-252-3663
Fax: 404-252-0774
E-Mail: hcea@kellencompany.com
Home Page: www.hcea.org

Eric Allen, Executive Vice President
Jackie Beaulieu, Associate Director
Michelle Hall, Staff Associate
Carol Wilson, Meetings Director
Frank Skinner, Executive Director
Cost varies; approximately 50 booths; 800 attendees.
200 Attendees
Frequency: Annual
Founded in 1930
Mailing list available for rent: 1400 names

13266 **HCEA Marketing Summit**
Healthcare Convention & Exhibitors Association
1100 Johnson Ferry Rd NE
Suite 300
Atlanta, GA 30342-1733

404-252-3663
Fax: 404-252-0774

E-Mail: hcea@kellencompany.com
Home Page: www.hcea.org

Eric Allen, Executive Vice President
Jackie Beaulieu, Associate Director
Michelle Hall, Staff Associate
Carol Wilson, Meetings Director
Frank Skinner, Executive Director

Cost varies; no exhibits; 200-250 attendees.
200 Attendees
Frequency: Annual
Founded in 1930
Mailing list available for rent: 1400 names

13267 **HDMA Annual Meeting**
Healthcare Distribution Management Association
900 N Glebe Road
Suite 1000
Arlington, VA 22203

703-787-0000
Fax: 703-935-3200
Home Page: www.healthcaredistribution.org

Lori Burke, Director Meetings/Conferences
Denise Woodson, Managing Director
Laurel Todd, Managing Director

Provides a unique opportunity for senior-level retailer and supplier member executives to interact and discuss strategic issues.
Frequency: October

13268 **HIDA Conference & Expo**
Health Industry Distributors Association
310 Montgomery Street
Alexandria, VA 22314-1516

703-549-4432
Fax: 703-549-4695
E-Mail: rowan@hida.org
Home Page: www.hida.org

Matt Rowan, CEO

Includes education sessions, training rotation, and the best-attended trade showin the industry.
8000 Attendees
Frequency: October

13269 **HMFA's ANI: The Healthcare Finance Conference**
Healthcare Finance Management Association
3 Westbrook Corporate Center
Suite 600
Westchester, IL 60154

708-531-9600
Fax: 708-531-0032
Home Page: www.hfma.org/events/ani

Access to education programs, speaker sessions and hundreds of vendors, as well as networking and best practices sharing opportunities.
Mailing list available for rent

13270 **HMFA's Virtual Healthcare Finance Conference & Career Fair**
Healthcare Finance Management Association
3 Westbrook Corporate Center
Suite 600
Westchester, IL 60154

708-531-9600
800-252-4362
Fax: 708-531-0032
E Mail: virtualhcfc@hfma.org
Home Page: www.hfma.org
Social Media: Facebook, Twitter, LinkedIn

Access live education programs and on-demand sessions from your office. Keynote speakers and presenters, and a virtual exhibit hall and career fair.
39000 Members
Founded in 1991
Mailing list available for rent

13271 **Healthcare Information and Management Systems Society**
HIMSS/Healthcare Information and Management
230 E Ohio
Suite 500
Chicago, IL 60611

312-664-4467
Fax: 312-664-6143

13272 **IAHCSMM Annual Conference**
213 W Institute Place
Suite 307
Chicago, IL 60610-3195

312-440-0078
800-962-8274
Fax: 312-440-9474
E-Mail: mailbox@iahcsmm.com
Home Page: www.iahcsmm.com

Betty Hanna, Executive Director
Marilyn T. Conde, Secretary/Treasurer
Bruce T. Bird, President
David Jagrosse, Executive Board Member
David Narance, Executive Board Member

International Association of Healthcare Central Service Material Management - 125 EXHIBITORSlication separates supervisors/directors from technicians.
600+ Attendees
Frequency: Annual

13273 **IAHSS Annual General Meeting**
International Association for Healthcare Security
PO Box 5038
Glendale Heights, IL 60139

888-353-0990
888-353-0990
Fax: 630-529-4139
E-Mail: info@iahss.org
Home Page: www.iahss.org

Bryan Warren, President
Evelyn Meserve, Executive Director
Jim Stankevich, President-Elect
Lisa Pryse, VP/Treasurer
Bryan Warren, VP/Secretary

Non-profit organization of healthcare security and safety executives from around the world. The association works to improve and professionalize security and safety in healthcare facilities through the exchange of information and experiences among members.
1700 Members
Founded in 1968

13274 **INTERPHEX - The World's Forum for the Pharmaceutical Industry**
Reed Exhibition Companies
383 Main Avenue
Norwalk, CT 06851

203-840-4800
Fax: 203-840-4804

Chet Burchett, President
11000 Attendees

13275 **Infusion Nurses Society**
Infusion Nurses Society
315 Norwood Park South
Norwood, MA 02062

781-440-9408
800-694-0298
Fax: 781-440-9409
E-Mail: ins@ins1.org
Home Page: www.ins1.org
Social Media: Facebook, Twitter, LinkedIn

Britt Meyer, President
Mary Alexander, CEO
Chris Hunt, Executive VP
Michaelle Frost, Accounting Manager
Chelsea McCue, Accounting Coordinator
7000 Members
1000 Attendees
Frequency: Annual
Founded in 1973
Mailing list available for rentat $200 per M

13276 **Infusion Nurses Society Annual Meeting**
Infusion Nurses Society
315 Norwood Park South
Norwood, MA 02062

781-440-9408
800-694-0298
Fax: 781-440-9409
E-Mail: ins@ins1.org
Home Page: www.ins1.org
Social Media: Facebook, Twitter, LinkedIn

Cora Vizcarra, President
Mary Alexander, CEO
Chris Hunt, Executive VP
Michaelle Frost, Accounting Manager
Chelsea McCue, Accounting Coordinator
Mailing list available for rentat $200 per M

13277 **International Conference on Head and Neck Cancer**
American Head and Neck Society
1805 Ardmore Boulevard
Pittsburgh, PA 15221

412-243-5156
Fax: 412-243-5160
E-Mail: rwagnercme@aol.com
Home Page: www.headandneckcancer.org

Robin Wagner, Show Manager

Sixty exhibits of equipment and supplies, conference, luncheon and reception.
2,500 Attendees
Frequency: August

13278 **International Congress on Ambulatory Surgery Conference**
Hynes Convention Center
900 Boylston Street
Boston, MA 02115

617-954-2000
Fax: 617-954-2125
E-Mail: info@mccahome.com
Home Page: www.mccahome.com

1500 Attendees
Frequency: May

13279 **International Society for Magnetic Resonance in Medicine**
International Society for Magnetic Resonance
2118 Milvia Street
Suite 201
Berkeley, CA 94704

510-841-1899
Fax: 510-841-2340
E-Mail: info@ismrm.org
Home Page: www.ismrm.org

Frequency: May

13280 **International Vision Exposition & Conference**
Association Expositions & Services
383 Main Avenue
Norwalk, CT 06851

203-840-4820
800-811-7151
Fax: 203-840-4824
Home Page: visionexpo.com

Eileen Baird
Ed Gallo, Sales Manager
Tracy Flacherty, Marketing Director

As the most comprehensive vision care show and conference in the US, International Vision Expo is where today's eye care professionals meet, learn and conduct business. International vision expo draws optical professionals from all career path including: Ophthalmologist, Optometrist, Opticians, Lab Personnel, Practice managers, Ophthalmic Medical Personnel, Retailers, Manufacturing Executives, Import Export buyers, Ophthalmic Assistants, Optical Interns and more.
15000 Attendees
Frequency: March/September

13281 **Managed Care Institute & Display Forum**
American Association of Health Plans
601 Pennsylvania Avenue, NW
South Building, Suite 500
Washington, DC 20004

202-778-3200
Fax: 202-331-7487
E-Mail: ahip@ahip.org
Home Page: www.aahp.org
Social Media: Twitter

Michael Abbott, President
William Cameron, Chairman

Two hundred exhibits by suppliers to the managed health care industry, conference and reception.
2000 Attendees
Frequency: Annual
Founded in 1986

13282 **Managed Care Law Conference**
American Association of Health Plans
1129 20th Street NW
Washington, DC 20036

202-778-3200
Fax: 202-778-8506

13283 **Medical Design & Manufacturing Conference & Exhibition West**
Canon Communications
11444 W Olympic Boulevard
Los Angeles, CA 90064

310-445-4200
Fax: 310-996-9499
Home Page: www.cancom.com

Diane O'Conner, Trade Show Director
Dan Cutrone, Show Marketing Manager

Devoted to the design, development, and manufacture of medical products. Visitors can preview the latest advances in medical-grade materials, assembly components, machinery, electronics, systems, software, services and more. Held at the Anaheim Convention Center in Anaheim, California.
8,500 Attendees
Frequency: January

13284 **Medical Design and Manufacturing Minneapolis Conference**
Canon Communications
11444 W Olympic Boulevard
Los Angeles, CA 90064

310-445-4200
Fax: 310-996-9499
Home Page: www.mdm-minneapolis.com

Diane O'Connor, Trade Show Director
Dan Cutrone, Show Marketing Manager

Four hundred thirty three exhibitors in 52,500 square feet of the Minneapolis Convention Center. Medical supplies and information promotional opportunities in show directory, web site advertising, conference program, sponsorships and product previews.
3374 Attendees
Frequency: October
Founded in 1994

13285 **Medical Equipment Design & Technology Exhibition & Conference**
Canon Communications
11444 W Olympic Boulevard
Los Angeles, CA 90064-1549

310-445-4200
Fax: 310-445-4299
Home Page: www.medtecshow.com

Diane O'Conner, Trade Show Director
Dan Cutrone, Show Marketing Manager

Devoted to the design, development and manufacture of medical products. Visitors can preview the latest advances in medical-grade materials, assembly components, electronics, machinery, software, systems, services and more. Held at the RAI International Exhibition and Congress Center in Amsterdam, Netherlands.
2231 Attendees
Frequency: October

13286 **Medical Group Management Association**
Medical Group Management Association
104 Inverness Terrace E
Englewood, CO 80112-5306

303-991-1111
800-275-6462
Fax: 877-329-6462
E-Mail: infocenter@mgma.com
Home Page: www.mgma.com

William Jessee, President, Chief Executive Officer
Anders Gilberg, senior Vice President
Natalie Jamieson, Administrative Assistant
3800 Attendees
Frequency: Annual, October

13287 **Medical Meetings**
Penton Media Inc
249 W. 17th St., third floor
New York, NY 10011

847-763-9504
866-505-7173
E-Mail: shatch@meetingsnet.com
Home Page: www.meetingsnet.com

Susan Hatch, Editor
Betsy Bair, Director, Content and Media
Melissa Fromento, Group Publisher
Regina McGee, Religious Conference Manager
Susan Hatch, Executive Editor

International guide for health care and meeting planners.
Cost: $57.00
106 Pages
Circulation: 12000
Founded in 1989
Printed in 4 colors on glossy stock

13288 **Medicare and Medicaid Conference**
American Association of Health Plans
1129 20th Street NW
Washington, DC 20036

202-778-3200
Fax: 202-778-8506

13289 **Medtrade West**
VNU Expositions
Dallas International Airport
PO Box 17413
Washington, DC 20041

703-318-0300
Fax: 703-318-8833

13290 **Medtrade/Comtrade**
VNU Communications
1130 Hightower Trail
Atlanta, GA 30350

770-569-1540
Fax: 703-318-8833

13291 **NCPA Rx Exposition**
NCPA
100 Daingerfield Road
Alexandria, VA 22314

703-683-8200
800-544-7447
Fax: 703-683-3619
E-Mail: info@ncpanet.com
Home Page: www.ncpanet.org

Donnie Calhoun, President
B. Douglas Hoey, Chief Executive Officer
2000 Attendees
Frequency: Annual, October
Mailing list available for rent

13292 **National Athletic Trainers Association**
National Athletic Trainers
2952 Stemmons Freeway
#200
Dallas, TX 75247

214-637-6282
Fax: 214-637-2206
E-Mail: webmaster@nata.org
Home Page: www.nata.org

Charles Kimmel, President
Charles Rozanski, VP
Mailing list available for rent

13293 **National Convention: Opticians Association of America**
Opticians Association of America
10341 Democracy Lane
Fairfax, VA 22030
703-916-8856
Fax: 703-691-8929

13294 **National Council on the Aging Annual Conference**
National Council on the Aging
1901 L Street Nw
4th Fl
Washington, DC 20036

202-479-1200
Fax: 202-479-0735
E-Mail: info@ncoa.org
Home Page: www.ncoa.org
Social Media: Facebook, Twitter

James Firman, President/CEO
Richard Browdie, Chair
Andrew Greene, Treasurer
Jay Greenberg, Senior Vice President
Donna Whitt, Senior Vice President
Mailing list available for rent

13295 **National Managed Healthcare Congress**
Po Box 3685
Boston, MA 02441-3685

888-670-8200
Fax: 941-365-2507
Home Page: www.nmhcc.com

Frequency: March Atlanta

13296 **National Medical Association Annual Convention & Scientific Assembly**
National Medical Association
8403 Colesville Road
Suite 920
Silver Spring, MD 20910

703-631-6200
800-564-4220
Fax: 703-654-6931

E-Mail: nma@jspargo.com
Home Page: www.nmanet.org
Social Media: Facebook, Twitter

June LaMountain, Exhibit Sales Account Manager
Rahn K. Bailey, President
C. Freeman, Treasurer
Darryl R. Matthews, Executive Director

Promotes the collective interests of physicians and patients of African descent. NMA carries out this mission by serving the collective voice of physicians of African descent and a leading force for purity in medicine, elimination of health disparities and optimal health.
3000 Attendees
Frequency: August
Founded in 1895

13297 **National Safety Council Congress Expo**
National Safety Council
1121 Spring Lake Drive
Itasca, IL 60143

630-775-2213
800-621-7619
Fax: 630-285-0798
E-Mail: customerservice@nsc.org
Home Page: www.congress.nsc.org

Nancy Gavin, Expo Manager
Bill Steinbach, Exhibit Sales
Janet Froetscher, CEO

Annual event for safety, health and the environment.
16000 Attendees
Frequency: September

13298 **National Society for Histotechnology Symposium/Convention**
National Society for Histotechnology
8850 Stanford Blvd
Suite 2900
Columbia, MD 21045

443-535-4060
Fax: 443-535-4055
E-Mail: histo@nsh.org
Home Page: www.nsh.org

Aubrey M J Wanner, Meeting Manager
Carrie Diamond, Executive Director
Kerry Crabb, President
Kristin Ramseur, Administrative Assistant
Beth Wise, Administrative Assistant

National gathering for all chapters, advancing professional growth through educational sessions and the exchange of ideas.
1500 Attendees
Frequency: October
Founded in 1964

13299 **Neocon South**
Designfest/NeoCon South
200 World Trade Center Chicago
Chicago, IL 60654

312-527-7999
Fax: 312-527-7782
Home Page: http://www.neocon.com

Chris Kennedy, President

13300 **Neocon West**
Designfest/Neocon South
200 World Trade Center
Chicago, IL 60654

312-527-7999
Fax: 312-527-7782
Home Page: http://www.neocon.com

Chris Kennedy, President

13301 **Neocon's World Trade Fair**
Design/Neocon South
200 World Trade Center
Chicago, IL 60654

312-527-7999
Fax: 312-527-7782

Chris Kennedy, President

13302 **New England Grows**
Hynes Convention Center
900 Boylston
Boston, MA 07115

617-954-2000
Fax: 617-954-2125
E-Mail: info@mccahome.com
Home Page: www.mccahome.com

1500 Attendees
Frequency: February

13303 **Northwest Urological Society**
Northwest Urological Society
914 164th Street Se
Suite B-12 #145
Mill Creek, WA 98012

866-800-3118
Fax: 800-808-4749
Home Page: www.nwus.org

S Larry Goldenberg, President
Martin Gleave, VP
180 Attendees

13304 **Nurse Managers Update**
National Professional Education Institute
2525 Ossen Fort Road
PO Box 118
Glencoe, MO 63068-1107

636-735-5570
800-575-5575
Fax: 561-743-9596
E-Mail: JJMcDaid@aol.com
Home Page: www.npeinursing.com

Judie McDaid, Exhibitor Relations Manager
Leslie Brock, Registration Manager

The Nurse Managers Update and Critical Care Conference/EXPO provides a fully integrated program dedicated to the continuing education of critical care nurses, nurse managers and other healthcare professionals. Exhibitors showcase their latest healthcare products, pharmaceuticals, services, research and facilities. Knowledge gained in the informative, entertaining EXPO Hall, will influence these nurses' purchasing decisions throughout the year.
1500 Attendees
Frequency: Annual, April
Founded in 1989

13305 **Obesity and Associated Conditions Symposium**
American Society of Bariatric Physicians/ASBP
5453 E Evans Place
Denver, CO 80222

303-794-4833
Fax: 303-779-4834
E-Mail: info@asbp.org
Home Page: www.asbp.org

Cathy Suski, Communications
Stacy Schmidt, Director

Learn about the latest research in obesity treatment and how to use it in your practice.
500 Attendees
Frequency: Annual

13306 **Optometry's Meeting**
American Optometric Association
243 N Lindbergh Boulevard
Saint Louis, MO 63141

314-993-8575
Fax: 314-993-8919
E-Mail: info@iacconline.org
Home Page: www.iaccnorthamerica.org

Tom Bolman, Executive VP
Jerry White, Director of Education

Main exhibits: optometric equipment, supplies and services.
8000 Attendees
Frequency: June

13307 **Osteopathic Physicians & Surgeons Annual Convention**
Osteopathic Physicians & Surgeons of California
455 Capitol Mall
Suite 230
Sacramento, CA 95814

916-561-0724

Kathleen Creason, Executive Director

13308 **Pacific Dermatological Association**
Pacific Dermatological Association
575 Market Street
Suite 2125
San Francisco, CA 94105

415-927-5729
888-388-8815
Fax: 415-764-4915
E-Mail: pda@hp-assoc.com
Home Page: www.pacificderm.org

Edgar F. Fincher, President
Catherine Ramsay, VP
Anita Gilliam, Secretary/Treasurer
Kent Lindeman, Executive Director
Ben Hsu, Executive Committee

Exclusively for education, scientific and charitable purposes. Provides opportunities for exchange of information and advancement of knowledge of dermatology among physicians within the membership area.
Frequency: August
Founded in 1948
Mailing list available for rent

13309 **Pacific Northwest Radiological Society**
Pacific Northwest Radiological Society
2033 6th Avenue
Suite 1100
Seattle, WA 98121

206-441-9762
800-552-0612
Fax: 206-441-5863
E-Mail: lmk@wsma.org
Home Page: www.pnwrs.org

Gautham Reddy, President
Eric Stern, VP
Pauline Proulx, Association Executive
Jason Clement, Secretary/Treasurer

13310 **Pediatric Academic Societies Annual Meeting**
American Pediatric Society & Society for Pediatric
3400 Research Forest Drive
Suite B7
The Woodlands, TX 77381

281-419-0052
Fax: 281-419-0082
E-Mail: info@aps-spr.org
Home Page: www.aps-spr.org

Debbie Anagnostelis, Executive Director
Kathy Cannon, Associate Executive Director
Belinda Thomas, Information Services Director
Kate Culliton, Accounting Manager
Rachael Vogler, Executive Assistant
4500 Attendees
Frequency: May

13311 **Pediatric Perfusion**
American Society of ExtraCorporeal Technology
2209 Dickens Road
Richmond, VA 23230-2005

804-565-6310
Fax: 804-282-0090
E-Mail: judyr@amsect.org
Home Page: www.amsect.org

Stewart Hinckley, Executive Director
Donna Pandarvis, Manager
Michael Troike, Government Relations Chairman
Kimberly Robertson, CPA, Controller
Greg Leasure, Membership Services
2000 Members
100 Attendees
Frequency: Bi-Annual
Founded in 1964
Mailing list available for rent

13312 **Perfusion Safety & Best Practices in Perfusion**
American Society of ExtraCorporeal Technology
2209 Dickens Road
Richmond, VA 23230-2005

804-532-2323
Fax: 804-282-0090
E-Mail: judyr@amsect.org
Home Page: www.amsect.org

Stewart Hinckley, Executive Director
Donna Pandarvis, Manager
Michael Troike, Government Relations Chairman
Kimberly Robertson, CPA, Controller
Greg Leasure, Membership Services
2000 Members
150 Attendees
Frequency: Annual/October
Founded in 1964
Mailing list available for rent

13313 **Policy Conference**
American Association of Health Plans
1129 20th Street NW
Washington, DC 20036

202-778-3200
Fax: 202-778-8506

13314 **Postgraduate Assembly in Anesthesiology**
New York State Society of Anesthesiologists
85 5th Avenue
8th Floor
New York, NY 10003

212-867-7140
Fax: 212-867-7153
Home Page: www.nyssa-pga.org

Kurt G Becker, Executive Director
David Wlody, Director

Annual conference for anesthesia professionals, held each December in New York City.
7000 Attendees
Frequency: December

13315 **Primary Care Update**
Interstate Postgraduate Medical Association
PO Box 5474
Madison, WI 53705

608-231-9045
866-446-3424
Fax: 877-292-4489
E-Mail: cmehelp@ipmameded.org
Home Page: www.ipmameded.org

Designed to enhance your practice and improve the patient's health.
Frequency: November

13316 **Radiological Society of North America's Scientific Assembly**
Radiological Society of North America
2021 Spring Road
Suite 600
Oak Brook, IL 60521

630-571-5424

62000 Attendees

13317 **SCCM Educational & Scientific Symposium**
Society of Critical Care Medicine
8101 E Kaiser Blouevard
Anaheim, CA 92808

714-282-6000

2500 Attendees

13318 **SIIM Annual Meeting & Conference**
Society for Imaging Informatics in Medicine
19440 Golf Vista Plaza
Suite 330
Leesburg, VA 20176-8264

703-723-0432
Fax: 703-723-0415
E-Mail: info@siimweb.org
Home Page: www.siimweb.org
Social Media: Facebook, Twitter, LinkedIn

Andrea Saris, Meetings Director

Provides a vibrant community and collegial forum for learning and networking with peers and thought leaders in the imaging informatics field. This is where physicians, health care IT decision-makers, PACS administrators, and vendors from around the world come together to explore the emerging field of informatics.
2000 Members
1800 Attendees
Frequency: June
Founded in 1980

13319 **Society for Disability Studies Annual Meeting**
Exhibit Promotions Plus
11630 Vixens Path
Ellicott City, MD 21042

301-596-3028
Fax: 410-997-0764
Home Page: www.epponline.com

Harve C Horowitz, President
Frequency: June

13320 **Society for Neuroscience**
Herlitz Company
1890 Palmer Avenue
Suite 202 A
Larchmont, NY 10538

914-833-1979
Fax: 914-833-0920

Bruce Herlitz, President

13321 **Society of Nuclear Medicine Annual Meeting**
Society of Nuclear Medicine
1850 Samuel Morse Drive
Reston, VA 20190

703-708-9000
Fax: 703-708-9015
E-Mail: volunteer@snm.org
Home Page: www.snm.org

Rebecca Maxey, Director
Vincent Pistilli, Chief Financial Officer
Matt Dickens, Director, Information Services
Judy Brazel, Director, Meeting Services
Joanna Spahr, Director, Marketing
7000 Attendees

13322 **Society of Thoracic Surgeons Annual Meeting**
Society of Thoracic Surgeons
633 N Saint Clair Street
Suite 2320
Chicago, IL 60611

312-202-5800
Fax: 312-202-5801
E-Mail: sts@sts.org
Home Page: www.sts.org
Social Media: Facebook, Twitter

Robert A Wynbrandt, Executive Director
Cheryl D. Wilson, Administrative Manager & Executive
Natalie Boden, Director of Marketing
Phillip A. Bongiorno, Director of Government Relations
Courtney Donovan, Director of Meetings
4200 Attendees
Mailing list available for rent

13323 **Society of Toxicology Annual Meeting**
Society of Toxicology
1821 Michael Faraday Drive
Suite 300
Reston, VA 20190

703-438-3115
Fax: 703-438-3113
E-Mail: sothq@toxicology.org
Home Page: www.toxicology.org

Shawn Lamb, Executive Director
Clarissa Russell Wilson, Contact

Professional and scholarly organization meeting of scientists from academic institutions, government and industry representing the great variety of scientists who practice toxicology in the US and abroad.
5000 Attendees
Frequency: March

13324 **Southeastern Surgical Congress Annual Assembly**
South Med. Associates
PO Box 330
Pelham, AL 35124

205-991-3552
Fax: 205-991-6771

13325 **Southern Association for Primary Care**
Southern Medical Association
35 Lake Shore Drive
Birmingham, AL 35209

205-945-1840
800-423-4992
Fax: 205-945-1830
E-Mail: ewaldron@sma.org
Home Page: www.sma.org
Social Media: Facebook, Twitter, LinkedIn

Michael C. Gosney, President
Ed Waldron, Administration
G. Richard Holt, Editor-in-Chief

13326 **Southern Medical Association Meeting**
Southern Medical Association
PO Box 190088
Birmingham, AL 35219

205-451-1840
800-423-4992
Fax: 205-945-1830

Ed Waldron, CEO
2500 Attendees

13327 **Symposium of the Protein Society**
FASEB
9650 Rockville Pike
Bethesda, MD 20814

301-634-7100
Fax: 301-530-7001

E-Mail: info@faseb.org
Home Page: www.faseb.org

David Craven, Executive Director
Jacquelyn Roberts, Marketing Manager
Richard Dunn, Director

13328 **Symposium on New Advances in Blood Management**
American Society of ExtraCorporeal Technology
2209 Dickens Road
Richmond, VA 23230-2005

804-532-2323
Fax: 804-282-0090
E-Mail: judyr@amsect.org
Home Page: www.amsect.org

Stewart Hinckley, Executive Director
Donna Pandarvis, Manager
Michael Troike, Government Relations Chairman
Kimberly Robertson, CPA, Controller
Greg Leasure, Membership Services
2000 Members
150 Attendees
Frequency: Annual/August
Founded in 1964
Mailing list available for rent

13329 **Synergist**
American Industrial Hygiene Association
2700 Prosperity Ave
Suite 250
Fairfax, VA 22031-4321

703-849-8267
Fax: 703-207-3561
E-Mail: infonet@aiha.org
Home Page: www.aiha.org

Peter J Oneil, Executive Director
Michael T Brandt, President
Frequency: Monthly

13330 **TLPA Annual Convention & Trade Show**
Taxicab, Limousine & Paratransit Association
3200 Tower Oaks Boulevard
Suite 220
Rockville, MD 20852

301-984-5700
Fax: 301-984-5703
E-Mail: info@tlpa.com
Home Page: www.tlpa.org

Alfred LaGasse, CEO
William Rouse, President
Harold Morgan, Executive Vice President
Michelle A. Hariston, CMP, Manager of Meetings
Leah New, Manager of Communications

Shares information vital to owners or taxicab, limousine, airport shuttle, paratransit and nonemergency medical transportation fleets. 100 suppliers and exhibitors of the newest products available to the industry.
1000 Attendees
Frequency: Annual
Founded in 1917
Mailing list available for rent

13331 **Today's Surgicenter Conference**
Virgo Publishing LLC
3300 N Central Avenue
Suite 300
Phoenix, AZ 85012

480-675-8177
Fax: 602-567-6841
E-Mail: mikes@vpico.com
Home Page: www.xchangemag.com
Social Media: Facebook, Twitter, LinkedIn

Mike Saxby, Group Publisher
Craig Galbraith, Senior Online Managing Editor
Buffy Naylor, Managing Editor
Khali Henderson, Contributing Editor
Melissa Budwig, Online Advertising

Offers owners and operators of ambulatory surgery centers high-caliber instructive seminars by leading industry veterans, exhibits, and networking opportunities. Decision makers attend to learn more about construction and design, technology, equipment, legal and regulatory issues, marketing and finance and development. Approximately 50 booths.
200+ Attendees
Frequency: September
Founded in 2004
Mailing list available for rent: 15000+ names

13332 **United States and Canadian Academy of Pathology**
Herlitz Company
1890 Palmer Avenue
Suite 202A
Larchmont, NY 10538

914-833-1979
Fax: 914-833-0929
E-Mail: kris@herlitz.com
Home Page: www.herlitz.com

Kris Herlitz, Show Manager
3000 Attendees
Frequency: March

13333 **Vision New England**
Hynes Convention Center
900 Boylston Street
Boston, MA 07115

617-954-2000
Fax: 617-954-2125
E-Mail: info@mccahome.com
Home Page: www.mccahome.com

24000 Attendees
Frequency: January

13334 **World Congress on Pediatric & Intensive Care**
Hynes Convention Center
900 Boylston Street
Boston, MA 02115

617-954-2000
800-845-8800
Fax: 617-954-2125
E-Mail: info@mccahome.com
Home Page: www.mccahome.com
2500 Attendees
Frequency: June

13335 **Yankee Dental Congress**
Hynes Convention Center
900 Boylston Street
Boston, MA 07115

617-954-2000
Fax: 617-954-2125
E-Mail: info@mccahome.com
Home Page: www.mccahome.com

2400 Attendees
Frequency: January

Directories & Databases

13336 **ARMA International's Buyers Guide**
ARMA International
11880 College Blvd
Suite 450
Overland Park, KS 66210

913-341-3808
800-422-2762
Fax: 913-341-3742
E-Mail: hq@arma.org
Home Page: www.arma.org/conference

Marilyn Bier, Executive Director
Jody Becker, Associate Editor
Kerrianne Aulet, Education Program Administrator
Michael Avery, Chief Operating Officer
Paula Banes, Sales Project Manager

75-100 companies listed. Free.
10,00 Members
Founded in 1955
Mailing list available for rent

13337 **American Academy of Forensic Sciences Membership Directory**
410 N 21st St
Colorado Spring, CO 80904-2712

719-636-1100
Fax: 719-636-1993
E Mail: awarren@aafs.org
Home Page: www.aafs.org

Anne Warren, Executive Director
Nancy Jackson, Director Development

Offers valuable information on over 5,000 persons qualified in forensic sciences including law, anthropology and psychiatry.
Cost: $50.00
250 Pages
Frequency: Annual

13338 **Antimicrobial Therapy in Otolaryngology Head and Neck Surgery**
American Academy of Otolaryngology
1650 Diagonal Road
Alexandria, VA 22314-3357

703-836-4444
Fax: 703-683-5100
E-Mail: membership@entnet.org
Home Page: www.entnet.org

Richard Carson, Senior Manager, Board of Govenors
Paul T. Fass, Director - Private Practice
J. Gavin Setzen, Secretary/Treasurer
David R. Nielsen, Executive Vice President and CEO
James L. Netterville, President
Frequency: Yearly
Mailing list available for rent

13339 **Catalog of Professional Testing Resources**
Psychological Assessment Resources
PO Box 998
Odessa, FL 33556

800-331-8378
Fax: 800-727-9329
Home Page: www.parinc.com

13340 **Comparative Guide to American Hospitals**
Grey House Publishing
4919 Route 22
PO Box 56
Amenia, NY 12501

518-789-8700
800-562-2139
Fax: 845-373-6390
E-Mail: books@greyhouse.com
Home Page: www.greyhouse.com
Social Media: Facebook, Twitter

Leslie Mackenzie, Publisher
Richard Gottlieb, Editor

This new edition compares all of the nation's hospitals by 24 measures of quality in the treatment of heart attack, heart failure, pneumonia, and, new to this edition, surgical procedures and pregnancy care. Plus, this edition is now available in regional volumes, to make locating

information about hospitals in your area quicker and easier than ever before.
Cost: $350.00
2000 Pages
ISBN: 1-532371-82-5
Founded in 1981

13341 **Complete Directory for Pediatric Disorders**
Grey House Publishing
4919 Route 22
PO Box 56
Amenia, NY 12501
518-789-8700
800-562-2139
Fax: 845-373-6390
E-Mail: books@greyhouse.com
Home Page: www.greyhouse.com
Social Media: Facebook, Twitter
Leslie Mackenzie, Publisher
Richard Gottlieb, Editor
Provides parents and caregivers with information about pediatric conditions, disorders, diseases and disabilities. Contains understandable descriptions of major bodily systems, descriptions of more than 200 disorders and a resource section.
Cost: $165.00
1200 Pages
ISBN: 1-592371-50-7
Founded in 1981

13342 **Complete Directory for People with Disabilities**
Grey House Publishing
4919 Route 22
PO Box 56
Amenia, NY 12501
518-789-8700
800-562-2139
Fax: 845-373-6390
E-Mail: books@greyhouse.com
Home Page: www.greyhouse.com
Social Media: Facebook, Twitter
Leslie Mackenzie, Publisher
Richard Gottlieb, Editor
Comprehensive resource for people with disabilities, detailing independent living centers, rehabilitation facilities, state and federal agencies, associations and support groups. This one-stop resource also provides immediate access to the latest products and services for people with disabilities, such as periodicals and books, assistive devices, employment and education programs and travel groups.
Cost: $165.00
1200 Pages
ISBN: 1-592373-67-4
Founded in 1981

13343 **Complete Directory for People with Chronic Illness**
Grey House Publishing
4919 Route 22
PO Box 56
Amenia, NY 12501
518-789-8700
800-562-2139
Fax: 845-373-6390
E-Mail: books@greyhouse.com
Home Page: www.greyhouse.com
Social Media: Facebook, Twitter
Leslie Mackenzie, Publisher
Richard Gottlieb, Editor
This directory provides a comprehensive overview of the support services and information resources available for people diagnosed with a chronic illness. It details the wide range of organizations, educational materials, books, newsletters, web sites, periodicals and databases that address 88 specific chronic illness.
Cost: $165.00
1200 Pages
ISBN: 1-952371-83-3
Founded in 1981

13344 **Complete Learning Disabilities Directory**
Grey House Publishing
4919 Route 22
PO Box 56
Amenia, NY 12501
518-789-8700
800-562-2139
Fax: 845-373-6390
E-Mail: books@greyhouse.com
Home Page: www.greyhouse.com
Social Media: Facebook, Twitter
Leslie Mackenzie, Publisher
Richard Gottlieb, Editor
The most comprehensive database of programs, services, curriculum materials, professional meetings and resources, camps, newsletters and support groups for teachers, students and families concerned with learning disabilities. Includes information about associations and organizations, schools, colleges and testing materials, government agencies, legal resources and more.
Cost: $145.00
800 Pages
ISBN: 1-592373-68-2
Founded in 1981

13345 **Complete Learning Disabilities Directory - Online Database**
Grey House Publishing
4919 Route 22
PO Box 56
Amenia, NY 12501-0056
518-789-8700
800-562-2139
Fax: 518-789-0556
E-Mail: gold@greyhouse.com
Home Page: www.gold.greyhouse.com
Social Media: Facebook, Twitter
Leslie Mackenzie, Publisher
Richard Gottlieb, President
The most comprehensive database of important learning disability resources, details associations and organizations, national and state programs, schools, colleges and learning centers, publishers, publications and periodicals, classroom resources, testing materials, exchange programs, and more. Locating learning disability resources has never been easier - it's only a click away.
Founded in 1981

13346 **Complete Mental Health Directory**
Grey House Publishing
4919 Route 22
PO Box 56
Amenia, NY 12501
518-789-8700
800-562-2139
Fax: 845-373-6390
E-Mail: books@greyhouse.com
Home Page: www.greyhouse.com
Social Media: Facebook, Twitter
Leslie Mackenzie, Publisher
Richard Gottlieb, Editor
Comprehensive information covering the field of behavioral health, with critical information for both the layman and mental health professional. Provides the layman with understandable descriptions of 25 mental health disorders, as well as detailed information on associations, media, support groups and mental health facilities. Offers the professional critical and comprehensive information on managed care organizations, information systems, government agencies and provider organizations.
Cost: $165.00
800 Pages
ISBN: 1-592372-85-6
Founded in 1981

13347 **Complete Mental Health Directory - Online Database**
Grey House Publishing
4919 Route 22
PO Box 56
Amenia, NY 12501-0056
518-789-8700
800-562-2139
Fax: 518-789-0556
E-Mail: gold@greyhouse.com
Home Page: www.gold.greyhouse.com
Social Media: Facebook, Twitter
Leslie Mackenzie, Publisher
Richard Gottlieb, President
This award-winning directory, now available in a quick-to-search, easy-to-use, online database provides the most comprehensive compilation of mental health resources available anywhere, with data for both layman and mental health professionals.
Founded in 1981

13348 **Detwiler's Directory of Health and Medical Resources**
Information Today
143 Old Marlton Pike
Medford, NJ 08055-8750
609-654-6266
800-300-9868
Fax: 609-654-4309
E-Mail: custserv@infotoday.com
Home Page: www.infotoday.com
Thomas H Hogan, President
Roger R Bilboul, Chairman Of The Board
Joe Menendez, Marketing Manager
John Brokenshire, Chief Financial Officer
Michael V. Zarrello, Advertising Director
A comprehensive guide to over 2,000 health and medical corporations,associations, state and federal agencies, helathcare market research firms, foundations, institutes, and more.
Cost: $195.00
ISBN: 1-573871-55-9

13349 **Directory for Pediatric Disorders - Online Database**
Grey House Publishing
4919 Route 22
PO Box 56
Amenia, NY 12501-0056
518-789-8700
800-562-2139
Fax: 518-789-0556
E-Mail: gold@greyhouse.com
Home Page: www.gold.greyhouse.com
Social Media: Facebook, Twitter
Leslie Mackenzie, Publisher
Richard Gottlieb, President
The Complete Directory for Pediatric Disorders - Online Database is an important reference tool that provides parents and caregivers with information about common pediatric and adolescent conditions, disorders, diseases, and disabilities. This comprehensive, informative database is designed to meet the growing consumer demands for current, understandable medical information on pediatric disorders.
Founded in 1981

13350 **Directory for People with Chronic Illness - Online Database**
Grey House Publishing

4919 Route 22
PO Box 56
Amenia, NY 12501-0056

518-789-8700
800-562-2139
Fax: 518-789-0556
E-Mail: gold@greyhouse.com
Home Page: www.gold.greyhouse.com
Social Media: Facebook, Twitter

Leslie Mackenzie, Publisher
Richard Gottlieb, President

This important database is structured around the 80 most prevalent chronic illnesses and provides a comprehensive overview of the support services and information resources available for people diagnosed with a chronic illness. With a subscription to the Complete Directory for People with Chronic Illness - Online Database, your organization will have immediate access to a wealth of resources available for people diagnosed with a chronic illness, their families and support systems.
Founded in 1981

13351 Directory for People with Disabilities - Online Database
Grey House Publishing
4919 Route 22
PO Box 56
Amenia, NY 12501-0056

518-789-8700
800-562-2139
Fax: 518-789-0556
E-Mail: gold@greyhouse.com
Home Page: www.gold.greyhouse.com
Social Media: Facebook, Twitter

Leslie Mackenzie, Publisher
Richard Gottlieb, President

Comprehensive resource for people with disabilities, detailing independent living centers, rehabilitation facilities, state and federal agencies, associations and support groups. This one-stop resource also provides immediate access to the latest products and services for people with disabilities, such as periodicals and books, assistive devices, and more. With a subscription to the online databse, your organization will have immediate access to a wealth of resources available.
Founded in 1981

13352 Directory of Health Care Group Purchasing Organizations
Grey House Publishing
4919 Route 22
PO Box 56
Amenia, NY 12501

518-789-8700
800-562-2139
Fax: 845-373-6390
E-Mail: books@greyhouse.com
Home Page: www.greyhouse.com
Social Media: Facebook, Twitter

Leslie Mackenzie, Publisher
Richard Gottlieb, Editor

This comprehensive directory profiles over 800 Purchasing Organizations that negotiate more than 65% of all health care products purchased by hospitals and related facilities, and the institutions they represent.
Cost: $465.00
800 Pages
ISBN: 1-592372-87-2
Founded in 1981

13353 Directory of Health Care Group Purchasing Organizations - Online Database
Grey House Publishing
4919 Route 22
PO Box 56
Amenia, NY 12501-0056

518-789-8700
800-562-2139
Fax: 518-789-0556
E-Mail: gold@greyhouse.com
Home Page: www.gold.greyhouse.com
Social Media: Facebook, Twitter

Leslie Mackenzie, Publisher
Richard Gottlieb, President

This interactive online database offers immediate access to detailed information about over 800 GPOs, over 3,000 key contacts and 16,000 member hospitals and institutions they represent. These 800+ organizations represent billions of dollars in purchasing power for the medical and device supplies industry. This data is so critical for market research, sales plans and market development.
Founded in 1981

13354 Directory of Hospital Personnel
Grey House Publishing
4919 Route 22
PO Box 56
Amenia, NY 12501

518-789-8700
800-562-2139
Fax: 845-373-6390
E-Mail: books@greyhouse.com
Home Page: www.greyhouse.com
Social Media: Facebook, Twitter

Leslie Mackenzie, Publisher
Richard Gottlieb, Editor

A Who's Who of the hospital universe, The Directory of Hospital Personnel puts you in touch with over 100,000 key decision makers. This comprehensive directory contains listings of over 6,000 hospitals within the US, arranged alphabetically by city within state.
Cost: $325.00
2300 Pages
ISBN: 1-592372-86-4
Founded in 1981

13355 Directory of Hospital Personnel - Online Database
Grey House Publishing
4919 Route 22
PO Box 56
Amenia, NY 12501-0056

518-789-8700
800-562-2139
Fax: 518-789-0556
E-Mail: gold@greyhouse.com
Home Page: www.gold.greyhouse.com
Social Media: Facebook, Twitter

Richard Gottlieb, President
Leslie Mackenzie, Publisher

The DHP Online Database is the best resource you can have at your fingertips when researching or marketing a product or service to the hospital market. A 'Who's Who' of the hospital universe, this database puts you in touch with over 140,000 key decision-makers at 5,800 hospitals nationwide.
Founded in 1981

13356 Employee Assistance Program Management Yearbook
Health Resources Publishing
1913 Atlantic Ave
Suite 200
Manasquan, NJ 08736-1067

732-292-1100
888-843-6242
Fax: 732-292-1111
E-Mail: info@themcic.com
Home Page: www.healthresourcesonline.com

Robert K Jenkins, Publisher
Lisa Mansfield, Regional Director
Brett Powell, Regional Director
Alice Burron, Director

Explore major areas of involvement for EAPS. Investigate tools for effectively managing your EAP. Learn how screening tools for mental illness can help EAPS manage care. Learn how to help families deal with workplace changes. Learn how to identify potentially violent situations in the workplace and much more.
Cost: $149.00
ISBN: 1-882364-25-2

13357 HCEA Directory of Healthcare Meetings and Conventions
Healthcare Convention & Exhibitors Association
1100 Johnson Ferry Rd NE
Suite 300
Atlanta, GA 30342-1556
404-252-3663
Fax: 404-252-0774
E-Mail: hcea@kellencompany.com
Home Page: www.hcea.org

Susan Huff, President
Carol Wilson, Meetings Director
Michelle Hall, Staff Associate
Jackie Beaulieu, Associate Director
Frank Skinner, Executive Director

Information on 6,000 health care meetings, available to members only.
500 Pages
Founded in 1930
Mailing list available for rent: 1400 names

13358 HMO/PPO Directory
Grey House Publishing
4919 Route 22
PO Box 56
Amenia, NY 12501

518-789-8700
800-562-2139
Fax: 845-373-6390
E-Mail: books@greyhouse.com
Home Page: www.greyhouse.com
Social Media: Facebook, Twitter

Leslie Mackenzie, Publisher
Richard Gottlieb, Editor

The HMO/PPO Directory is a comprehensive source that provides detailed information about Health Maintenance Organizations and Preferred Provider Organizations nationwide. Within the HMO/PPO Profiles, over 1,300 HMOs, PPOs and affiliated companies are listed, arranged alphabetically by state.
Cost: $325.00
600 Pages
ISBN: 1-592373-69-0
Founded in 1981

13359 HMO/PPO Directory - Online Database
Grey House Publishing
4919 Route 22
PO Box 56
Amenia, NY 12501-0056

518-789-8700
800 562-2139
Fax: 518-789-0556
E-Mail: gold@greyhouse.com
Home Page: www.gold.greyhouse.com
Social Media: Facebook, Twitter

Leslie Mackenzie, Publisher
Richard Gottlieb, President

The HMO/PPO Directory - Online Database is your in-depth searchable guide to health plans nationwide - their contact information, key executives, plan information and more. The on-

line database is a necessary tool when researching or marketing a product or service to this important industry.
Founded in 1981

13360 Health Funds Grants Resources Yearbook
Health Resources Publishing
1913 Atlantic Ave
Suite 200
Manasquan, NJ 08736-1067
732-292-1100
888-843-6242
Fax: 732-292-1111
E-Mail: info@themcic.com
Home Page: www.healthresourcesonline.com
Robert K Jenkins, Publisher
Judy Granholm, Regional Director
Brett Powell, Regional Director
Alice Burron, Director
A resource book that gives dollar amounts, descriptions of previous grant recipients and programs that attract funding and details of future funding trends.
Cost: $165.00
ISBN: 1-882364-30-9

13361 Managed Care Yearbook
Health Resources Publishing
1913 Atlantic Ave
Suite 200
Manasquan, NJ 08736-1067
732-292-1100
888-843-6242
Fax: 732-292-1111
E-Mail: info@themcic.com
Home Page: www.healthresourcesonline.com
Robert K Jenkins, Publisher
Judy Granholm, Regional Director
Brett Powell, Regional Director
Alice Burron, Director
Resource book that includes critical facts, statistics cost, analysis, comparisions, enrollment and trends studies on managed care. Topics also include member retention, international markets and disease management.
Cost: $29.00
608 Pages
ISBN: 1-882364-26-0

13362 Medical Abbreviations: 24,000
Niel M Davis Associates
2049 Stout Dr
B-3
Warminster, PA 18974-3861
215-442-7430
Fax: 888-333-4915
E-Mail: med@neilmdavis.com
Home Page: www.neilmdavis.com
Neil M Davis, Owner
This current edition paperback pocket book contains 16,000 medical related abbreviations and 24,000 of their possible meanings. It is current, comprehensive, and formatted so that it is easy to use. It also contains a cross-referenced listing of 3,300 generic and trade drug names.
Cost: $24.95
Frequency: Monthly
ISBN: 0-931431-09-3
Founded in 1981

13363 Medical Device Register
Grey House Publishing
4919 Route 22
PO Box 56
Amenia, NY 12501
518-789-8700
800-562-2139
Fax: 845-373-6390
E-Mail: books@greyhouse.com
Home Page: www.greyhouse.com
Social Media: Facebook, Twitter
Leslie Mackenzie, Publisher
Richard Gottlieb, Editor
The only one-stop resource of every medical supplier licensed to sell products in the US. This edition offers fast access to over 13,000 companies - and more than 65,000 products. This comprehensive resource saves you hours of time and trouble when searching for the equipment and supplies you want and the manufacturers who provide them.
Cost: $350.00
3000 Pages
ISBN: 1-592373-73-9
Founded in 1981

13364 National Directory of Integrated Healthcare Delivery Systems
Health Resources Publishing
1913 Atlantic Ave
Suite 200
Manasquan, NJ 08736-1067
732-292-1100
888-843-6242
Fax: 732-292-1111
E-Mail: info@themcic.com
Home Page: www.healthresourcesonline.com
Robert K Jenkins, Publisher
Lisa Mansfield, Regional Director
Brett Powell, Regional Director
Alice Burron, Director
Gives facts and stastics on more than 850 health care delivery systems and affiliations. Includes profiles of IHDSs by state and by alphabetical order. Also includes a directory of health care associations, a ranking of systems by revenues and an analysis of IHDSs growth projections.
Cost: $995.00
ISBN: 1-882364-31-7

13365 National Directory of Managed Care Organzatons
Health Resources Publishing
1913 Atlantic Ave
Suite 200
Manasquan, NJ 08736-1067
732-292-1100
888-843-6242
Fax: 732-292-1111
E-Mail: info@themcic.com
Home Page: www.healthresourcesonline.com
Robert K Jenkins, Publisher
Lisa Mansfield, Regional Director
Brett Powell, Regional Director
Alice Burron, Director
Published by Health Resources Publishing. Available in print ($325), database ($1695) or CD-Rom ($695).
Cost: $325.00
ISSN: 0898-9753

13366 National Directory of Physician Organizations Database On Cd-Rom
Health Resources Publishing
1913 Atlantic Ave
Suite 200
Manasquan, NJ 08736-1067
732-292-1100
888-843-6242
Fax: 732-292-1111
E-Mail: info@themcic.com
Home Page: www.healthresourcesonline.com
Robert K Jenkins, Publisher
Judy Granholm, Regional Director
Brett Powell, Regional Director
Alice Burron, Director
Detailed profiles on over 1,800 physician organizations. Listings include physician hospitals organizations (PHOs), independent practice associations, management services organizations and physician practice management companies. Key elements of the data profile include: executive officers; year founded; profits status, statue of incorporation; numbers of associates physician; market area; market analysis; affiliated/participating hospital; management service organizations used.
Cost: $995.00
ISBN: 1-882364-18-X

13367 Older Americans Information Directory
Grey House Publishing
4919 Route 22
PO Box 56
Amenia, NY 12501
518-789-8700
800-562-2139
Fax: 845-373-6390
E-Mail: books@greyhouse.com
Home Page: www.greyhouse.com
Social Media: Facebook, Twitter
Leslie Mackenzie, Publisher
Richard Gottlieb, Editor
Important resources for older americans, including national, regional, state and local organizations, government agencies, research centers, legal resources, discount travel information, continuing education programs, disability aids and assistive devices, health, print media and electronic media.
Cost: $165.00
1200 Pages
ISBN: 1-592373-57-7
Founded in 1981

13368 Older Americans Information Directory - Online Database
Grey House Publishing
4919 Route 22
PO Box 56
Amenia, NY 12501-0056
518-789-8700
800-562-2139
Fax: 518-789-0556
E-Mail: gold@greyhouse.com
Home Page: www.gold.greyhouse.com
Social Media: Facebook, Twitter
Leslie Mackenzie, Publisher
Richard Gottlieb, President
The Older Americans Information Directory is an easy to use source that offers up-to-date information on the prevalent social, health and financial issues facing older Americans in the 21st century, as well as recreational and educational opportunities to enrich their lives. With a subscription to the online database, you'll have immediate access to over 8,000 resources including national, regional, state and local organziations, government agencies, health facilities and more.
Founded in 1981

13369 Wellness Program Management Yearbook
Health Resources Publishing
1913 Atlantic Ave
Suite 200
Manasquan, NJ 08736-1067
732-292-1100
888-843-6242
Fax: 732-292-1111
E-Mail: info@themcic.com
Home Page: www.healthresourcesonline.com
Robert K Jenkins, Publisher
Lisa Mansfield, Regional Director
Brett Powell, Regional Director
Alice Burron, Director
This yearbook highlights such issues as obtaining senior management support, encouraging

employment participation in programs, finding, funding and developing different programs. Also helps in planning initiatives by providing details of the components that will be important to include about the programs that will help you to meet your goals.
Cost: $155.00
ISBN: 1-882364-39-2

Industry Web Sites

13370 **http://gold.greyhouse.com**
G.O.L.D Grey House OnLine Databases
Grey House Publishing's online database platform, GOLD, offers Quick Search, Keyword Search and Expert Search for most business sectors including healthcare markets. The GOLD platform makes finding the information you need quick and easy - whether you're a novice searcher or an experienced database user. All of Grey House's directory products are available for subscription on the GOLD platform.

13371 **www.aaaai.org**
American Academy of Allergy, Asthma And Immunology
The largest professional medical specialty organization in the United States, representing allergists, asthma specialists, clinical immunologists, allied health professionals, and others with the special interest in the research and treatment of allergic disease.

13372 **www.aaham.org**
American Association of Healthcare Administrative
Management
Business offices, credit and collection managers, and admitting officers for hospitals, clincis and other health care organizaitons. To educate members, exchange information and techniques, and keep members abreast of new regulations relating to their field. Seeks proper recognition for the financial aspect of hospital and clinic managememnt.

13373 **www.aahperd.org**
American Alliance for Hlth, Phys. Edu. Rec. Dance
Recreation & Dance

13374 **www.aaid.org**
American Academy of Implant Dentistry
Offers a rigorous implant dentistry credentialing program which requires at least 300 hours of post-docroal or continuing education instruction in implant dentistry, passing a comprehensive exam, and presenting successful cases of different types of implants to a group of examiners. It is one of the most comprehensive credentialing programs in dentistry.

13375 **www.aaihds.org**
American Association of Integrated Healthcare
Delivery Systems
Physicians, hospital executives and board members, health plan executives, and other key entities and professionals employed by all forms of IDDSs including PHOS, IPA POSOS, and MSOS. Seeks to provide advocacy for issues related to integrated health care through research, education, and communication. Conducts educational and research programs; maintains speakers' bureau and information clearinghouse.

13376 **www.aameda.org**
American Academy of Medical Administrators
Individuals involved in medical administration at the executive- or midele-management levels. Promotes educational courses for the training of persons in medical administration. Conducts research. Offers placement service.

13377 **www.aamft.org**
American Assoc for Marriage and Family Therapy
AAMFT represents the professional interests of more than 25,000 marriage and family therapists in the United States, Canada and abroad.

13378 **www.aami.org**
Assoc for the Advancement of Medical Instrumentati
The Association for the Advancement of Medical Instrumentation (AAMI), founded in 1967, is a unique alliance of over 6,000 members united by the coommon goal of increasing the understanding and use of medical instrumentation. AAMI is the primary source of consensus and timely information on medical instrumentation and technology for the industry, professionals, and the government for national and intemational standrards.

13379 **www.aaos.org**
American Academy for Cerebral Palsy and Developmental Medicine

13380 **www.aap.org**
American Academy of Pediatrics

13381 **www.academydentalmaterials.org**
Academy of Dental Materials
Formerly known as American Academy for Plastics Research in Dentistry.

13382 **www.ache.org**
American College of Healthcare Executives
International professional society of more than 30,000 healthcare executives. Credentialing and educational programs, Congress on Healthcare Management. ACHE's publishing division, Health Administration Press, is one of the largest publishers of books.

13383 **www.acpe.org**
American College of Physician Executives
Physicians whose primary professional responsibility is the management of health care organizations. Provides for continuing education and certification of the physician executive and the profession. Offers specialized career planning, counseling, recruitment and placement services, and research and information data on physican managers.

13384 **www.acrm.org**
American Congress of Rehabilitation Medicine

13385 **www.acsm.org**
American College of Sports Medicine
The ACSM promotes and integrates scientific research, education, and practical applications of sports medicine and exercise science to maintain and enhance physical performance, fitness, health, and quality of life.

13386 **www.afprd.org**
Association of Family Practice Residency Directors
Provides representation for residency directors at a national level and provides a political voice for them to appioprite arenas. Promotes cooperation and communication between residency programs and different branches of the family practice specialty. Dedicated to improving of education of family physicians. Provides a network for mutual assistance among FP, residency directors.

13387 **www.aha.org**
American Hospital Association

13388 **www.ahia.org**
Association of Healthcare Internal Auditors
Promotes cost containment and increased productivity in health care institutions through internal auditing. Serves as a forum for the exchange of experience, ideas, and information among members; provides continuing professional education courses and informs members of developments in health care internal auditing. Offers employment clearinghouse services.

13389 **www.ahqa.org**
American Health Quality Association
Central news area for the group that represents quality improvement organizations and professionals working to improve the quality of health care in communities across America.

13390 **www.ahraonline.org**
Association for Medical Imaging Management
For radiology administrators from the US, Canada, and several other countries.

13391 **www.ama-assn.org**
American Medical Association
A partnership of physicians and their professional associations dedicated to promoting the art and science of medicine and the betterment of the public health. To serve physicians and their patients by establishing and promoting ethical, educational, and clinical standards for the medical profession and by advocating for the highest principle of all - the integrity of the physician/patient relationship.

13392 **www.amga.org**
American Medical Group Association

13393 **www.apta.org**
American Physical Therapy Association
The principal membership organization representing and promoting the profession of physical therapy, is to furhter the profession's role in the prevention, diagnosis, and treatment of movement dysfunctions and the enhancement of the physical health and functional abilities of members of the public.

13394 **www.arrs.org**
American Roentgen Ray Society
102 years strong radiological association for all subspecialties.

13395 **www.ascrs.org**
American Society of Ophthalmic Administrators
A division of the American Society of Cataract and Retractive Surgery. Persons involved with the administration of an ophthalmic office or clinic. Facilitates the exchange of idease and information in order to improve management practices and working conditions. Offers placement services.

13396 **www.asma.org**
Aerospace Medical Association
Our mission is to apply and advance scientific knowledge to promote and enhance the health, safety and performance of those involved in aerospace and related activities.

13397 **www.asnr.org**
American Society of Neuroradiology

13398 **www.asrm.org**
American Society for Reproductive Medicine

Organization devoted to advancing knowledge and expertise in reproductive medicine and biology. Members of this voluntary nonprofit organization must demonstrate the high ethical principals of the medical profession, evince an interest in reproductive medicine and biotechnology, and adhere to the objectives of the Society.

13399 **www.assh.org**
American Society for Surgery of the Hand

The oldest medical specialty society in the United States devoted entirely to continuing medical education related to hand surgery.

13400 **www.awhp.org**
Association for Worksite Health Promotion

Exists to advance the profession of worksite health promotion and the career development of its practitioners and to improve the performance of the programs they administer. Represents a variety of disciplines and worksites, for decision-makers in the areas of health promotion/disease prevention and health-care cost management.

13401 **www.cdc.gov**
Centers for Disease Control and Prevention

The official website of CDC, the government's public health agency.

13402 **www.chpa-info.org**
Consumer Healthcare Products Association

Members are producers of nonprescription medicines and dietary supplements for self-care. Has an annual budget of approximately $10 million.

13403 **www.claims.org**
Alliance of Claims Assistance Professionals

Professionals dedicated to the effective management of health insurance claims. Our members are claims assistance professionals who work for patients.

13404 **www.cleftline.org**
American Cleft Palate Craniofacial Association

Organization of plastic surgeons, dentists, orthodontists, speech pathologists, geneticists, social workers and others.

13405 **www.cmsa.org**
Case Management Society of America

Exclusively for the case management profession.

13406 **www.crnusa.com**
Council for Responsible Nutrition

Government relations, scientific and regulatory affairs, publications.

13407 **www.docinfo.org**

A national data bank of disciplinary histories on US licensed physicians from the Federation of State Medical Boards; charges $9.95 per report

13408 **www.entnet.org**
American Academy of Otolaryngology-Head & Neck

13409 **www.fascrw.org**
American Society of Colon & Rectal Surgeons

13410 **www.foodallergy.org**
Food Allergy & Anaphylaxis Network

Facts, common questions, resources and news.

13411 **www.gretmar.com/webdoctor/**
General medical information.

13412 **www.greyhouse.com**
Grey House Publishing

Authoritative reference directories for most business sectors including healthcare markets. Users can search the online databases with varied search criteria allowing for custom searches by product category, geographic area, sales volume, keyword, subject and more. Full Grey House catalog and online ordering also available.

13413 **www.hcea.org**
Healthcare Convention & Exhibitors Association

Trade association of over 650 organizations involved in health care exhibiting or providing services to health care conventions, exhibitions and/or meetings.

13414 **www.healthfinder.gov**

A comprehensive guide to resources for health information from the federal government and related agencies

13415 **www.hfma.org**
Healthcare Financial Management Association

Brings perspective and clarity to the industry's complex issues for the purpose of preparing our members to succeed. Through our programs, publications and partnerships, we enhance the capabilities that strengthen not only individuals careers, but also the organizations from which our members come.

13416 **www.hida.org**
Health Industry Distributors Association

The trade association representing medical products distributors. Provides leadership in the healthcare distribution industry.

13417 **www.iahss.org**
International Association for Healthcare Security

Non-profit professional organization of healthcare security and safety executives from around the world.

13418 **www.ichbc.org**
Institute of Healthcare Business Consultants

Maintains code of ethics, rules of professional conducts, and certification program, administers examination and conducts certification course. Membership by successful completion of certification examination only.

13419 **www.jamesbeard.org**
James Beard Foundation

Not-for-profit organization dedicated to preserving the country's culinary heritage and fostering the appreciation and development of gastronomy by recognizing and promoting excellence in all aspects of the culinary arts.

13420 **www.managedcaremarketplace.com**
Managed Care Information Center

An online yellow pages for companies providing services to MCOs, hospitals and physicians groups. There are more than three dozen targeted categories, offering information on vendors from claims processing to transportation services to health care compliance.

13421 **www.medicaid.apwa.org**
National Association of Medicaid Directors

Promotes effective Medicaid policy and program administration; works with the federal government on issues through technical advisory groups. Conducts forums on policy and technical issues.

13422 **www.mgma.com**
American College of Medical Practice Executives

Professional credentialing organization. Works to encourage medical group practice administrators to improve and maintain their proficiency and to provide appropriate recognition; to establish a program with uniform standards of admission, advancement, certification and fellowship in order to achieve the highest possible standards in the profession of medical group practice administration; to participate in the development of educational and research programs.

13423 **www.mwsearch.com/**
Medical world search.

13424 **www.mywebmd.com**

The largest commercial health site, offers easy - to read information on health and wellness issues and latest medical news

13425 **www.naher.com**
National Association for Healthcare Recruitment

Individuals employed directly by hospitals and other health care organizations which are involved in the practice of professional health care recruitment. Promotes sound principles of professionals health care recruitment. Provides financial assistance to aid members in planning and implementing regional educational programs. Offers technical assistance and consultation services. Compiles statistics.

13426 **www.namdrc.org**
National Association of Medical Directors for
Respiratory Care

Works to provide educational opportunities to fit the needs of medical directors of respiratory care and represents the interests of members to regulatory agencies to ensure that the needs of respiratory patients are not overlooked. Offers educational programs; maintains speakers' bureau.

13427 **www.namss.org**
National Association Medical Staff Service

Individuals involved in the management and administration of health care provider services. Seeks to enhance the knowledge and experience of medical staff services professionals and promote the certification of those involved in the profession.

13428 **www.nerf.org**
National Eye Research Center

Improving your vision through eyecare, education and research.

13429 **www.nlm.nih.gov/databases/medline.html**

Vast bibliographic database maintained by the US National Library of Medicine. Medline contains citations and abstracts from several thousand biomedical journals, covering medicine, nursing, dentistry, vetinary medicine and other fields.

13430 **www.nraa.org/renal/**
National Renal Administrators Association

Administrative personnel involved with dialysis programs for patients suffering from kidney failure. Provides a vehicle for the development of educational and informational services for members. Maintains contact with health care facilities and government agencies. Operates placement serve; compiles statistics; conducts political action committee.

13431 www.oncolink.com
Founded by specialist at the University of Pennsylvania, provides information on wide range of childhood and adult cancers

13432 www.pahcom.com
Professional Association of Health Care Office Management

Office managers of small group and solo medical practices. Operates certification program for health care office managers.

13433 www.paralysis.org
Christopher Reeve Paralysis Foundation

Our mission is to raise money to help fing spinal cord injury research.

13434 www.quackwatch.com
A nonprofit corporation whose purpose is to combat health - related frauds, myths, fads, and fallacies and investigate phony medical news

13435 www.rbma.org
Radiology Business Management Association

Business managers for private radiology groups; corporate members include: vendors of equipment, services, or supplies. Purposes are to improve business administration of radiologists' practices to better serve patients and the medical profession; and to provide opportunities for professional development and recognition. Offers extensive educational and networking opportunities and informal placement service. Maintains information services emphasizing those aspects unique to the business.

13436 www.siim.org
Society for Imaging Informatics in Medicine

Devoted to advance informatics and information technology in medical imaging through education and research. Provides an open environment for imaging information professionals to access expert and cutting edge resources in a collegial and practical atmosphere.

13437 www.sleepproducts.org
International Sleep Products Association

Maintains a strong organization to influence government actions, inform and educate the membership and act on industry issues to enhance the growth,profitability and stature of the sleep products industry. Provides members with information and services to manage their business more effectively and efficiently. Publishes a magazine devoted exclusively to the mattress industry, BEDtimes covers a broad range of issue and news important to the industry.

13438 www.smamc.org
Society of Medical-Dental Management Consultants

Professionals medical and/or dental management consultants associated for educational and information sharing purposes. Objectives are to: advance the profession; share management techniques; improve individual skills; provide clients with competent and capable business management. Provides information on insurance and income tax. Conducts surveys; compiles statistics.

13439 www.themcic.com
Healthcare IS/IT Yearbook

The Health care IS/IT Market Yearbook is a unique and valuable sales and marketing reference tool for IT companies selling into the health and managed care industries. Great for sales and marketing research; developing reports or preparing presentations. Now, it's easy to identify what hospitals are contracting for, get information on hundreds of millions of dollars in healthcare. IT contract deals, discover what other companies are doing.

13440 www.toxicology.org
Society Of Toxicology

Members are scientists concerned with the effects of chemicals on man and the environment. Promotes the aqusition and utilization of knowledge in toxicology, aids in the protection of public health and facilitates disiplines. The society has a strong commitment to education in toxicology and to the recruitment of students and new members into the profession.

13441 www.uams.edu/afpa/
Association of Family Practice Administrators

Promotes professionalism in family practice administration. Serves as a network for sharing of information and fellowship among network for sharing of information and fellowship among members. Provides technical assistance to members; functions as a liaison to related professional organizations.

Associations

13442 ASHRAE
1791 Tullie Cir Ne
Atlanta, GA 30329-2398

404-636-8400
800-527-4723
Fax: 404-321-5478
E-Mail: ashrae@ashrae.org
Home Page: www.ashrae.org
Social Media: Facebook

William P. Bahnfleth, Ph.D., P.E, President
Jeff H Littleton, Executive VP
Douglas E. Read, Director of Government Affairs
Joslyn Ratcliff, Manager, Electronic Communications
Joyce Abrams, Director of Member Services

An international organization that fulfills its mission of advancing heating, ventilation, air conditioning and refrigeration to serve humanity and promote a sustainable world through research, standards writing, publishing and continuing education.
55000 Members
Founded in 1894
Mailing list available for rent

13443 Air Conditioning Contractors of America
2800 S Shirlington Rd
Suite 300
Arlington, VA 22206-3607

703-575-4477
E-Mail: info@acca.org
Home Page: www.acca.org
Social Media: Facebook, Twitter, LinkedIn, youtube, RSS

Paul T. Stalknecht, President/CEO
Craig Gotthardt, Vice President of Information
Kevin W. Holland, VP for Communications
Chris Hoelzel, Vice President
Kimya Bailey Cajchun, Vice President of Membership

Represents HVAC contractors and holds annual meetings and exhibits for heating, air conditioning and refrigeration equipment, supplies and services.

13444 Air Diffusion Council
1901 North Roselle Road
Suite 800
Schaumburg, IL 60195

847-706-6750
Fax: 847-706-6751
E-Mail: info@flexibleduct.org
Home Page: www.flexibleduct.org

Jack Lagershausen, President

The purpose of the Air Diffusion Council is to promote and further the interests of the manufacturers of air distribution equipment, more specifically, flexible air ducts and related products, and the interests of the general public in the areas of safety, quality, efficiency and energy conservation. Also, to develop programs approved and supported by the membership that legally promote and further these interests.
40 Members
Founded in 1961

13445 Air-Conditioning, Heating, Refrigeration Institute
2111 Wilson Boulevard
Suite 500
Arlington, VA 22201

703-524-8800
Fax: 703-562-1942
E-Mail: ahri@ahrinet.org
Home Page: www.ahrinet.org
Social Media: Facebook, Twitter

Stephen Yurek, President and CEO
Amanda M Donahue, Executive Assistant
Stephanie Murphy, CFO
Dave Calabrese, General Counsel
Henry Hwong, Senior Vice President

A trade association representing manufacturers of air conditioning, heating and commercial refrigeration equipment.
300+ Members
Founded in 1953

13446 American Boiler Manufacturers Association
8221 Old Courthouse Rd
Suite 202
Vienna, VA 22182-3839

703-356-7172
Fax: 703-356-4543
Home Page: www.abma.com
Social Media: Facebook, Twitter, LinkedIn

Kevin Hoey, Chairman of the Board
Bob Stemen, Vice Chairman
W. Randall Rawson, President/Chief Executive Officer
Geoffrey Halley, Director of Technical Affairs
Hugh K Webster, Association General Counsel Webster

Manufacturers' trade association representing companies involved in utility, industrial and commercial steam generation. Includes associate memberships for companies who sell to or work with these companies and those who own boilers. Holds technical and production conferences and publishes technical guideline publications.
Founded in 1888

13447 American Supply Association
1200 North Arlington Heights Road
Suite 150
Itasca, IL 60143

630-467-0000
Fax: 630-467-0001
E-Mail: info@asa.net
Home Page: www.asa.net

Scott Weaver, Chairman
Jeff Pope, President
Michael Adelizzi, Executive Vice President
Amy Black, Executive Director
Dan Hilton, Director of Government Affairs

The national association of full-service plumbing, heating, cooling, and piping products for wholesalers, manufacturers, and distributors.
4000 Members
Founded in 1969

13448 Association of Professional Energy
3916 W Oak Street
Suite D
Burbank, CA 91505

818-972-2159
Fax: 818-972-2863
E-Mail: buschre@earthlink.net
Home Page: www.apem.org

John Sykes, Communications
Mark Martinez, Chair/Chapter Development
Bernell Loveridge, Chair/Treasurer
Lynne Eichner Kelley, Chair/Membership

Members include individuals responsible for energy production, consumption or management decisions.
1.5M Members
Founded in 1982

13449 Cooling Technology Institute
PO Box 73383
Houston, TX 77273-3383

281-583-4087
Fax: 281-537-1721
E-Mail: vmanser@cti.org
Home Page: www.cti.org

Jack Bland, President
Frank Michell, Vice-President
Steven Chaloupka, Treasurer
Thomas Toth, Secretary
Helene Troncin, Director

Seeks to improve technology, design and performance of water conservation apparatus. Provides inspection services and conducts research.
400 Members
Founded in 1950

13450 Heating, Air Conditioning & Refrigeration Distributors International
3455 Mill Run Drive
Suite 820
Columbus, OH 43026

614-345-4328
888-253-2128
Fax: 614-345-9161
E-Mail: hardimail@hardinet.org
Home Page: www.hardinet.org
Social Media: Facebook, Twitter, LinkedIn, Flickr, Youtube, Instagram

Brian Cobble, President
William Bergamini, Vice President
Michael Meier, Secretary / Treasurer
Royce Henderson, President-Elect

Nonprofit organization dedicated to advancing the science of wholesale distribution in the HVACR industry.
1200 Members
Founded in 1947

13451 International Microwave Power Institute
PO Box 1140
Mechanicsville, VA 23111-5007

804-559-6667
Fax: 804-559-4087
E-Mail: info@impi.org
Home Page: www.impi.org
Social Media: Facebook, Twitter, LinkedIn

Bob Schifmann, President
Ben Wilson, VP
Dorin Boldor, Secretary
Amy Lawson, Treasurer
Juan Aguilar, Editor in Chief

To be the global organization that provides a forum for the exchange of information on all aspects of microwave and RF heating technologies.
Founded in 1966

13452 Masonry Heater Association of North America
2180 S Flying Q Lane
Tuscon, AZ 85731
520-883-0191
Fax: 480-371-1139
E-Mail: execdir@mha-net.org
Home Page: www.mha-net.org

Richard Smith, Executive Director
Tim Seaton, VP
Rod Zander, Treasurer
Beverly Marois, Administrator

Promotes use of masonry heaters, increases public awareness and encourages reasonable governmental regulation.
115 Members
Founded in 1989

13453 Mechanical Contractors Association of America
1385 Piccard Dr
Rockville, MD 20850-4329
301-869-5800
Fax: 301-990-9690
Home Page: www.mcaa.org
John Gentille, Executive VP
Represents heating, piping and air conditioning professionals.
1.4M Members

13454 Mobile Air Conditioning Society Worldwide
225 S Broad Street
PO Box 88
Lansdale, PA 19446
215-631-7020
Fax: 215-631-7017
E-Mail: info@macsw.org
Home Page: www.macsw.org
Social Media: Facebook, Twitter, LinkedIn
Elvis Hoffpauir, President
Marion Posen, VP Marketing/Sales
Pam Smith, Events Manager
Non-profit organization provides technical training, information and communication for the professionals in the automotive air-conditioning industry.
1700 Members
Founded in 1981

13455 National Air Duct Cleaners Association
15000 Commerce Parkway
Suite C
Mt Laurel, NJ 08054
856-380-6810
855-GON-ADCA
Fax: 856-439-0525
E-Mail: info@nadca.com
Home Page: www.nadca.com
Social Media: Facebook, Twitter, LinkedIn, Youtube
Bill Benito, President
Jodi Araujo, CEM, Executive Director
Mike Dwyer, CAE, Chief Relationship Officer
Rick MacDonald, 1st Vice President
Michael Vinick, 2nd Vice President
The trade association of the HVAC/Heating-Ventilation-Air Conditioning industry.
1000 Members
Founded in 1989

13456 National Association of Plumbing, Heating and Cooling Contractors Association
180 S Washington Street
Suite 100
Falls Church, VA 22046
703-237-8100
800-533-7694
Fax: 703-237-7442
E-Mail: naphcc@naphcc.org
Home Page: www.phccweb.org
Dawn Dalton, Administrative Coordinator
Katie Gilbert, Membership Coordinator
Merry Beth Hall, Director, Apprentice and Journeyman
Don Hawkins, Accounts Receivable Clerk
Patrice L Jackson, Coordinator, QSC Member Services
National organization designed for suppliers of equipment, supplies and services for the plumbing, heating and cooling industries.
3700 Members
Founded in 1883

13457 National Association of Power Engineers
1 Springfield St
Chicopee, MA 01013-2672
413-592-6273
Fax: 413-592-1998
Home Page: www.powerengineers.com
Social Media: Facebook, Twitter, LinkedIn
Dominick Pepe, National President
David Grinder, National Vice President
Michael (Mike)ÿ Morin, National Treasurer/Secretary
Members include power plant operators and maintenance personnel who supply the industry with process power and related building and plant services.

13458 National Environmental Balancing Bureau
8575 Grovemont Cir
Gaithersburg, MD 20877-4121
301-977-3698
866-497-4447
Fax: 301-977-9589
E-Mail: karen@nebb.org
Home Page: www.nebb.org
Robert Linder, President
Jean-Paul Le Blance, Vice President
John M. Schulte, Executive Vice President
Elana Noel, Director of Certification
Mandy Kaur, Director of Communications
NEBB is an international certification association for firms that deliver high performance building systems. Members perform testing, adjusting and balancing (TAB) of heating, ventilating and air-conditioning systems, commission and retro-commission building systems commissioning, execute sound and vibration testing, and test and certify lab fume hoods and electronic and bio clean rooms. NEBB holds the highest standards in certification.
Founded in 1971

13459 Wholesalers Association of the Northeast
200 N. Arlington Heights Rd.
Suite 150
Itasca, IL 60143
630-467-0000
Fax: 508-923-1044
E-Mail: wane5@asa.net
Home Page: www.wane5.org
Chris Murin, Executive Director
Presently comprised of the leading wholesale distributors of pluming, heating, cooling and industrial pipe supplies, located throughout the northeast states.
Founded in 1932

Newsletters

13460 HVACR News
Trade News International
4444 Riverside Drive
Suite 202
Burbank, CA 91505
818-848-6397
Fax: 818-848-1306
Home Page: www.hvacrnews.com
Gary McCarty, Editor-in -Chief
Mark Deitch, Publisher
Jordan Tolila, Associate Publisher
Barb Kerr, Executive Assistant
A monthly national trade newspaper serving contractors, technicians, mechanical engineers, manufactures, manufacturer representatives, wholesalers, distributors, trade associations, government representatives, schools, students and other in the heating, ventilating, air conditioning, refrigerating, hydronics, sheet metals, solar, and allied trades.
Frequency: Monthly
Circulation: 50000
Founded in 1981
Printed in 4 colors on n stock

13461 Heating/Combustion and Equipment News
Business Communications Company
1 Penn Plz
Suite 42
New York, NY 10119-4200
212-273-7100
800-685-4488
Fax: 212-244-3721
Home Page: www.firstalbany.com
Equipment, materials and supplies for the heating and air conditioning industry.
Cost: $12.00
Frequency: Monthly

13462 Impact Compressor/Turbines News And Patents
Impact Publishers
PO Box 3113
Ketchum, ID 83340-3113
208-726-2332
Fax: 208-726-2115
Mary Jo Helmeke, Publisher
Regular features include new product announcements, patent information and up-to-date industry news and information on current books, brochures, software, seminars and meetings.
Cost: $60.00
30 Pages
Frequency: Annual

13463 Impact Pump News and Patents
Impact Publishers
PO Box 3113
Ketchum, ID 83340-3113
208-720-4876
Fax: 208-726-2115
Mary Jo Helmeke, Publisher
Regular features include new product announcements, patent information and up-to-date industry news and information on current books, brochures software, seminars and meetings.
Cost: $100.00
25 Pages

13464 Indoor Air Quality Update
Cutter Information Corporation
37 Broadway
Suite 1
Arlington, MA 02474-5500
718-648-8700
Fax: 718-648-8707
Home Page: www.cutter.com
Social Media: Facebook, Twitter
Karen Coburn, President and CEO
Paul Bergeron, CFO and COO
Israel Gat, Director, Agile Practice
Anne Mullaney, VP, Prodct Development
Cuitlahuac Osorio, Director, Cutter Latin America
Practical control of indoor air problems.
Cost: $287.00
Frequency: Monthly

13465 MACS Action!
Mobile Air Conditioning Society Worldwide

225 S Broad Street
PO Box 88
Lansdale, PA 19446

215-631-7020
Fax: 215-631-7017
E-Mail: info@macsw.org
Home Page: www.macsw.org

Elvis Hoffpauir, President/COO
Marion Posen, VP Marketing/Sales

Industry informational newsletter of Mobile Air Conditioning Society Worldwide.
Cost: $5.00
Frequency: 8x Yearly
Circulation: 13000
ISSN: 1949-3436

13466 **MACS Service Reports**
Mobile Air Conditioning Society Worldwide
PO Box 100
East Greenville, PA 18041

215-679-2220
Fax: 215-541-4635
E-Mail: elvis@macsw.org
Home Page: www.macsw.org

Elvis Hoffpauir, Editor
Paul DeGuiseppi, Manager of Training
Amy Anderson, Production Designer
Pam Smith, Manager
Maria Whitworth, Director of Operations

Technical newsletter for mobile air conditioning industry.
Frequency: Monthly
Circulation: 1600
Founded in 1981

13467 **Residential Heat Recovery Ventilators Directory**
Cutter Information Corporation
37 Broadway
Suite 1
Arlington, MA 02474-5500

781-648-1950
Fax: 781-648-1950
Home Page: www.cutter.com

Verna Allee, Senior Consultant

A comprehensive comparative guide and product directory to heat exchangers and ventilators.
Cost: $75.00

13468 **Superinsulated House Design and Construction Workbook**
Cutter Information Corporation
37 Broadway
Suite 1
Arlington, MA 02474-5500

781-648-1950
Fax: 781-648-1950
Home Page: www.cutter.com

Verna Allee, Senior Consultant

Detailed, graphic information to design and build superior houses.
Cost: $85.00

Magazines & Journals

13469 **AHRI Trends Magazine**
Air Conditioning & Refrigeration Institute
2111 Wilson Boulevard
Suite 500
Arlington, VA 22201

703-524-8800
Fax: 703-528-3816
E-Mail: ahri@ahri.net
Home Page: www.ahrinet.org

A resource for HVAC contractors and technicians.
Frequency: Monthly

13470 **ASHRAE Journal**
1791 Tullie Circle NE
Atlanta, GA 30329

404-636-8400
800-527-4723
Fax: 404-321-5478
E-Mail: ashrae@ashrae.org
Home Page: www.ashrae.org
Social Media: Facebook

Ronald Jarnagin, President
Thomas Watson, President-Elect
William Bahnfleth, Tresurer
Constantinos A Balaras, VP
Ross D Montgomery, VP

Explores topical technical issues, such as: indoor air quality, energy management, thermal storage, alternative refrigerants, fire and life safety and more.
Printed in 4 colors on matte stock

13471 **Air Conditioning Today**
PO Box 311776
New Braunfels, TX 78131

830-627-0605
877-669-4228
Fax: 830-627-0614
E-Mail: info@ac-today.com
Home Page: ac-today.com

Joe Eaton, Editor

Updates readers on the latest products, materials and technologies available.
Frequency: Monthly
Circulation: 19000
Founded in 1986

13472 **Air Conditioning, Heating & Refrigeration News**
Business News Publishing Company
1050 IL Route 83
Suite 200
Bensenville, IL 60106-1096

630-377-5909
Home Page: www.bnpmedia.com

Katie Rotella, Manager

Timely information to contractors, wholesalers, distributors, manufacturers, owner/operators and consulting engineers. Features technical, marketing, design, engineering, installation, management, governmental and labor aspects of the heating and cooling industry. Regular columns highlight new products and literature, legal rulings, manufacturer announcements, industry events and the latest HVAC/r patents.
Cost: $49.00
Frequency: Weekly
Circulation: 32854
Founded in 1926
Mailing list available for rent: 35M names
Printed in 4 colors on glossy stock

13473 **American Supply Association News**
222 Merchandise Mart Plaza
Suite 1400
Chicago, IL 60654-1203

312-464-0090
Fax: 312-464-0091
E-Mail: info@asa.net
Home Page: www.asa.net

Joel Becker, President
Bob Christian, Vice President
Kevin Neupert, Marketing
Joel Becker, Editor

Articles on plumbing, heating, cooling, and piping products.
50 Pages
Frequency: Monthly
Circulation: 2500
Founded in 1969
Mailing list available for rent: 4,000 names
Printed in 4 colors on matte stock

13474 **Automotive Cooling Journal**
National Automotive Radiator Service Association
3000 Villiage Run Rd
Suite 103, #221
Wexford, PA 15090-6315

412-847-5747
800-551-3232
Fax: 724-934-1036
E-Mail: info@narsa.org
Home Page: www.narsa.org

Jim Holowka, National President
Chuck Braswell, National Chairman-Past President
Rick Fuller, National 1st VP
Maarten Taal, National 2nd VP
Angelo Miozza, National Treasurer

Auto cooling system service data. Free to members.
Cost: $30.00
60 Pages
Frequency: Monthly
Circulation: 10,000
Founded in 1954

13475 **Boiler Systems Engineering Magazine**
HPAC Engineering
1300 E 9th Street
Cleveland, OH 44144

216-696-7000
Fax: 216-696-3432
E-Mail: hpac@penton.com
Home Page: www.hpac.com
Social Media: Facebook, Twitter

Mike Well, Editorial Director
Scott Arnold, Executive Editor
Ron Rajecki, Senior Editor

The official publication of the American Boiler Manufacturers Association, assists consulting engineers, in-house engineers, and building managers with the design, installation, operations, maintenance and commissioning of steam and hot water systems for institutional, commercial and industrial buildings.

13476 **Contracting Business**
Penton Media
249 W 17th St
New York, NY 10011

212-204-4200
Fax: 216-696-6662
E-Mail: information@penton.com
Home Page: www.penton.com

Jane Cooper, Marketing
Michael S Weil, Editor-in-Chief
Gwen Hostnik, Marketing Manager

Directed to the residential, commercial and industrial mechanical systems contracting marketplace. HVAC mechanical systems and Design/Build/Maintain contractors, wholesalers and commercial/industrial in-house service organizations.
Cost: $75.00
120 Pages
Frequency: Monthly
Circulation: 49,001
Founded in 1944
Printed in 4 colors on glossy stock

13477 **Contractor Magazine**
Penton Media

1300 E 9th St
Cleveland, OH 44114-1503

216-696-7000
Fax: 216-696-6662
E-Mail: information@penton.com
Home Page: www.contractormag.com
Social Media: Facebook, Twitter

Jane Cooper, Marketing
Bob Mader, Managing Editor
David B. Nussbaum, CEO

For contractors who sell, install, service air conditioning, heating, piping, plumbing, air handling, heat transfer and fluid controls equipment. Accepts advertising.
70 Pages
Frequency: Monthly
Circulation: 50000
Founded in 1892

13478 **District Energy**
International District Enery Association (IDEA)
24 Lyman Streetad
Suite 230
Westborough, MA 01581

508-366-9339
Fax: 508-366-0019
E-Mail: idea@districtenergy.org
Home Page: www.districtenergy.org

Peter Myers, Editor
Rob Thornton, President

Journal of district heating and cooling industry, congeneration, physical plants and energy efficiency. Accepts advertising.
Cost: $40.00
Frequency: Quarterly

13479 **Energy Engineering**
Association of Energy Engineers
4025 Pleasantdale Rd
Suite 420
Atlanta, GA 30340-4264

770-447-5083
Fax: 770-446-3969
E-Mail: info@aeecenter.org
Home Page: www.aeecenter.org
Social Media: Facebook, Twitter, LinkedIn, YouTube

Jennifer Venola, Controller
Ruth Whitlock, Executive Admin
Albert Thumann, Executive Director
Kate Feltgen, Executive Director's Assistant

Engineering solutions to cost efficiency problems and mechanical contractors who design, specify, install, maintain, and purchase non-residential heating, ventilating, air conditioning and refrigeration equipment and components.
Cost: $40.00
Circulation: 8000

13480 **Engineered Systems**
Business News Publishing Company
1050 IL Route 83
Suite 200
Bensenville, IL 60106-1096

630-377-5909
Home Page: www.esmagazine.com

Katie Rotella, Manager
Peter F Moran, Publisher

Research conducted by us shows that end users, consulting engineers, and contractors work together closely on the specification and selection of engineered HVAC/r systems and components. We give this receptive audience solid editorial information about real-world solutions to the everyday situations faced in the industry.
72 Pages
Frequency: Monthly
Circulation: 57515
Founded in 1985
Mailing list available for rent: 57.5M names
Printed in 4 colors on glossy stock

13481 **Fuel Oil News**
Hunter Publishing Limited
3100 S King Dr
7th Floor
Chicago, IL 60616-3483

312-567-9981
Fax: 312-846-4632
Home Page: www.fueloilnews.com

Luke Hunter, Partner
Joanne Juda, Circulation Director
Kate Kenny, Publisher
Chris Traczek, Editor-in-Chief
Patricia McCartney, Associate Editor

For home heating oil retailers.
Cost: $28.00
70 Pages
Frequency: Monthly
Circulation: 15200
Founded in 1935
Printed in 4 colors on glossy stock

13482 **HVAC Insider**
Retailing Newspapers
PO Box 81489
Conveyors, GA 30013

770-787-0115
Fax: 770-787-1213
E-Mail: insider@mindsprin.com
Home Page:
www.mindspring.com/~insider/insider

Jerry M Lawson, Publisher
Robert Scott, Chief Information Officer

Up to date information on technical tips, product reviews, commercial and industrial industry new, a job bulletin, new businesses and promotions, and a calendar of events. Retailing Newspapers issues a monthly publication for the Appliance and Electronics trade. Insiders Newspapers issues a quarterly national and 14 monthly regionals for the HVAC trade and a monthly regional publication for the plumbing trade.
Frequency: Monthly
Circulation: 118740
Founded in 1969
Printed in 4 colors on newsprint stock

13483 **HVAC/R Distribution Today**
HARDI
3455 Mill Run Dr
Suite 820
Columbus, OH 43026-7578

614-345-4328
888-253-2128
Fax: 614-345-9161
E-Mail: HARDImail@Hardinet.org
Home Page: www.hardinet.org

Talbot H Gee, Executive VP & COO
Donald L Frendberg, Chairman
Susan Little, Director of Marketing
Mary Gustafson, Director of Operations
Alan Beaulieu, Chief Economist

Official publication of Heating, Air Conditioning and Refrigeration International. Uniting world class distribution.
Frequency: Quarterly
Founded in 1960

13484 **HVACR & Plumbing Distribution**
Penton Media
1300 E 9th St
Cleveland, OH 44114-1503

216-696-7000
Fax: 216-696-6662
E-Mail: information@penton.com
Home Page: www.penton.com

Jane Cooper, Marketing
Perry Clark, Publisher

Exclusively for plumbing and heating equipment distributors.
Circulation: 10,000
Founded in 1890

13485 **Hearth & Home**
Village West Publishing
PO Box 1288
Laconia, NH 03246

603-528-4285
800-258-3772
Fax: 603-524-0643
E-Mail: info@hearthnhome.com
Home Page: villagewest.com

Richard Wright, Editor
Susan Salls, Publisher

Magazine for retailers, including specialty, hardware, patio and barbecue.
Cost: $36.00
Frequency: Monthly
Circulation: 18000

13486 **Industrial Heating**
Business News Publishing Company
1910 Cochran Road
Manor Oak One, Suite 450
Pittsburgh, PA 15220

412-531-3370
Fax: 412-531-3375
E-Mail: europesales@industrialheating.com
Home Page: www.industrialheating.com
Social Media: Facebook, Twitter

Ed Kubel, Editor
Beth McClelland, Production Manager
Doug Glenn, Publisher
Kathy Pisano, Advertising Director
Patrick Connolly, Sales Representative

We have been applying the latest advances in thermal technology to practical use since 1931. With over 22,000 BPA audited circulation comprised of mostly thermal processing engineers, technical articles cover heat treatments, brazing, sintering, melting, process control, instrumentation, refractories, burners, heating elements, and other thermal processes typically in excess of 1000 degrees.
Cost: $55.00
70 Pages
Circulation: 22100
ISSN: 0019-8374
Founded in 1931
Printed in 4 colors on glossy stock

13487 **PM Engineer**
Business News Publishing Company
1050 IL Route 83
Suite 200
Bensenville, IL 60106-1096

630-377-5909
Home Page: www.pmengineer.com
Social Media: Facebook, Twitter

Bob Miodonski, Group Publisher & Editor
Mike Miazga, Senior Editor
Julius Ballanco, Editorial Director
Suzette Rubio, Online Editor
John Siegenthaler, Hydronics Editor

Provides technical sheets, manufacturer product brochures, news features and analysis of useful industry information on the engineering and design of plumbing, piping, hydronics, cooling/heating, and fire protection/sprinkler systems. Free to trade engineers.
Cost: $64.00
80 Pages
Frequency: Monthly
Circulation: 25000
Founded in 1926
Printed in 4 colors on glossy stock

13488 **RSES Journal**
Refrigeration Service Engineers Society

1666 Rand Rd
Des Plaines, IL 60016-3552

847-297-6464
800-297-5660
Fax: 847-297-5038
E-Mail: general@rses.org
Home Page: www.rses.org
Social Media: Facebook, Twitter, LinkedIn

John Iwanski, Publishing Director
Lori A Kasallis, Editor

Providing quality technical content in digital and printed forms that can be applied on the job site.
Frequency: Monthly
Circulation: 15231

13489 Reeves Journal
23421 S Pointe Drive
Suite 280
Laguna Hills, CA 92654

949-830-0881
Fax: 949-859-7845
Home Page: www.reevesjournal.com

Ellyn Fishman, Publisher
John Fultz, Editor
Tagg Henderson, CEO

An invaluable tool for Western plumbing contractors and industry professionals for more than 80 years.
Frequency: Monthly
Circulation: 13545
Founded in 1926

13490 Refrigerated Transporter
Primedia
4200 S Shepherd Drive
Suite 200
Houston, TX 77098

713-233-3826
Fax: 713-523-8384
Home Page: www.refrigeratedtrans.com/

Gary Macklin, Editor-in-Chief
Tom Rogers, Chief Executive Officer
John Wilkins, executive Vice-President
Frequency: Monthly
Circulation: 15,023

13491 Refrigeration
John W Yopp Publications
73 Sen Island Parkway Suite 21
PO Box 1147
Beaufort, SC 29901-1147

843-521-0239
800-849-9667
Fax: 843-521-1398
E-Mail: cgraffo@jwyopp.com
Home Page: www.refrigeration-magazine.com

John W Yopp, Chairman
Joe Cronley, Publisher
Mary Yopp Cronley, Associate Publsiher
Cheryl Graffo, Editor

About the plants and processes used in ice manufacture, marketing and merchandising information, news of associations, meetings and new products available.
Cost: $20.00
Frequency: Monthly
Circulation: 3200
Founded in 1919
Printed in 4 colors on glossy stock

13492 Snips
Business News Publishing Company
2401 W. Big Beaver Road
Suite 700
Troy, MI 48084

248-362-3700
Fax: 248-362-0317
E-Mail: snips@halldata.com
Home Page: www.snipsmag.com

Katie Rotella, Manager
Sally Fraser, Advertising Sales
Karen Koppins, Advertising Productions
Ann Kalb, Customer Service
Michael McConnel, Editorial Director

Magazine directed to the heating, air conditioning, sheet metal and ventilation industry. Accepts advertising.
Cost: $18.00
120 Pages
Frequency: Monthly
Circulation: 22000
Founded in 1926
Printed in 4 colors on glossy stock

13493 Tab Journal
Associated Air Balance Council
1518 K Street NW
Washington, DC 20005-1203

202-737-0202
Fax: 202-638-4833
Home Page: www.aabchq.com/

Kenneth M Sufka, Publisher
Mike Young, President

Case studies, industry updates, as well as other news of importance to engineers.
Cost: $24.00
Frequency: Quarterly
Circulation: 12000
Founded in 1965

13494 Todays A/C and Refrigeration News
Todays Trade Publications
PO Box 521247
130 W Pine Ave
Longwood, FL 32750-1247

407-332-4959
866-320-2773
Fax: 407-332-5319
Home Page: www.todays-ac.com

Thomas Fatchell, Editor

Covers industry legislation, building codes, licensing requirements and continuing educations. New product reviews and personnel changes are also included.
Frequency: Monthly
Circulation: 20000
Founded in 1988

Trade Shows

13495 ABMA Annual Meeting
American Boiler Manufacturers Association
8221 Old Courthouse Road
Suite 207
Vienna, VA 22182-3839

703-356-7172
Fax: 703-356-4543
Home Page: www.abma.com

W Randall Rawson, President/CEO
Diana McClung, Executive Assistant
Cheryl Jamall, Director of Meetings
Geoffrey Halley, Director of Technical Affairs
Hugh K Webster, Association General Counsel

The association's premier membership networking events. In casual and relaxed settings, members have the opportunity to not only learn about developments and trends, both inside and outside their industry, that are likely to influence their business, members are also afforded the opportunity, through committee and product/market group meetings to focus on issues and concerns of specific relevance to their product and market segments.
Frequency: Bi-Annual
Founded in 1888

13496 ABMA Manufacturers Conference
American Boiler Manufacturers Association
8221 Old Courthouse Road
Suite 207
Vienna, VA 22182-3839

703-356-7172
Fax: 703-356-4543
Home Page: www.abma.com

W Randall Rawson, President/CEO
Diana McClung, Executive Assistant
Cheryl Jamall, Director of Meetings
Geoffrey Halley, Director of Technical Affairs
Hugh K Webster, Association General Counsel

Designed to bring together manufacturing plant, office and others concerned with the design, fabrication, sales and distribution of ABMA'products and services to network, discuss trends and developments, and problem solve with others in the industry and with outside experts.
Frequency: Annual/October
Founded in 1888

13497 ASA Convention and ISH North America Trade Show
American Supply Association
222 Merchandise Mart Plaza
Suite 1400
Chicago, IL 60654

312-640-0090
Fax: 312-464-0091
E-Mail: info@asa.net
Home Page: www.asa.net or www.ish-na.com

Ruth Mitchell, Manager/Convention Director
Bob Jarvie, Show Manager

Annual conference for wholesalers, distributors and manufacturers of plumbing and heating pipes, valves and fittings.
1800 Attendees
Frequency: Annual/September

13498 Air Conditioning Contractors of America Annual Conference
Air Conditioning Contractors of America
1712 New Hampshire Avenue NW
Washington, DC 20009-2502

202-518-3236
Fax: 202-332-5293
Home Page: www.acca.org

Christopher Holelzel, Director Marketing
Rosemary Graeme, Executive Assistant

Annual meeting and exhibits of heating, air conditioning and refrigeration equipment, supplies and services. Over 140 exhibitors, plus seminar, workshop and banquet.
1000 Attendees

13499 Air Conditioning Heating & Refrigeration Expo Mexico - AHR
Industrial Shows of America
164 Lake Front Drive
Hunt Valley, MD 21030-2215

410-771-1445
800-638-6396
Fax: 410-771-1158
Home Page: www.isoa.com

Bryan Mayes, President
Phillip McKay, Managing Director

300 exhibitors with air conditioning, heating and refrigerating equipment, supplies and information. Attended by professionals.
5000 Attendees
Frequency: Annual

13500 Annual Campus Energy Conference
International District Energy Association

24 Lyman Street
Suite 230
Westborough, MA 01581

508-366-9339
Fax: 508-366-0019
E-Mail: idea@districtenergy.org
Home Page: www.districtenergy.org

Robert Thornton, President
Vincent Bedeli, Chair
Leonard Phillips, Director of Business Development

IDEA fosters the success of its members as leaders in providing reliable, economical, and environmentally sound district energy services.
600 Attendees
Frequency: Annual/June
Founded in 1909

13501 Hearth Products Association
1555 Wilson Boulevard
Suite 300
Arlington, VA 22209-2405

703-522-0086
Fax: 703-812-8875
Social Media: Facebook, Twitter

Joan Letch Worth, Show Manager

900 booths of products related to the residential alternative fuel heating industry.
8M Attendees
Frequency: Annual/March

13502 Heating, Air Conditioning & Refrigeration Distributors International
3455 Mill Run Drive
Suite 820
Columbus, OH 43026

614-345-4328
888-253-2128
Fax: 614-345-9161
Home Page: www.hardinet.org

Talbot H Gee, Executive VP & COO
Donald L Frendberg, Chairman
Susan Little, Director of Marketing
Mary Gustafson, Director of Operations
Alan Beaulieu, Chief Economist

Annual show of 200 exhibitors of heating and air conditioning equipment, supplies and services.
1200 Attendees
Founded in 2003

13503 International Air Conditioning, Heating, & Refrigerating Expo
ASHRAE
1791 Tullie Circle NW
Atlanta, GA 30329

404-636-8400
800-527-4723
Fax: 404-321-5478
E-Mail: ashrae@ashrae.org
Home Page: www.ashrae.org

William A Harrison, President
Jeff H Littleton, Executive VP

The largest HVAC&R event in America featuring over 1,600 exhibiting companies. Held every year in conjunction with the ASHRAE Winter Meeting.
30000 Attendees
Frequency: Annual/January
Founded in 1894

13504 International District Energy Association (IDEA) Show
1200 19th Street NW
Suite 300
Washington, DC 20036-2428

202-429-5131
Fax: 202-429-5113
Home Page: www.energy.rochester.edu/idea

John L Fiegel, Editor
Tammie Jackson, Advertising Manager

Show of the district heating and cooling industry, cogeneration, physical plants, energy efficiency. 40 booths.
450 Attendees
Frequency: Annual/June

13505 International Institute of Ammonia Refrigeration Annual Conference
1001 N Fairfax St
suite 503
Alexandria, VA 22314

703-312-4200
Fax: 202-857-1104
E-Mail: iiar_request@iiar.org

Adolfo Blasquez, Chair
Robert Port Jr, Vice Chair
Joe Mandato, Chair Elect
Marcos Braz, Treasurer
Bruce Badger, President

Show of the district heating and cooling industry, cogeneration, physical plants, energy efficiency. 40 booths.
750 Attendees
Frequency: Annual/March

13506 International Thermal Spray Conference & Exposition
ASM International
9639 Kinsman Road
Materials Park, OH 44073-0002

440-338-5151
800-336-5152
Fax: 440-338-4634
E-Mail: natalie.nemec@asminternational.org
Home Page: www.asminternational.org

Carole Chesla, Administrator, Awards
Thom Passek, Associate Managing Director
Leslie Taylor, Executive Office Manager
Stanley Theobald, Managing Director

Global annual event attracting professional interested in thermal spray technology focusing on advances in HVOF, plasma and detonation gun, flame spray and wire arc spray processes, performance of coatings, and future trends. 150 exhibitors.
1000 Attendees
Frequency: Annual/May

13507 MACS Convention & Trade Show
Mobile Air Conditioning Society Worldwide
225 S Broad Street
PO Box 88
Lansdale, PA 19446

215-631-7020
Fax: 215-631-7017
E-Mail: info@macsw.org
Home Page: www.macsw.org

Pam Smith, Events Manager
2000 Attendees
Frequency: Annual

13508 Midwest Contractors Expo
Kansas Assn of Plumbing, Heating & Cooling Contr
320 Laura Street
Wichita, KS 67211-1517

316-262-8860
Fax: 316-262-2782

Ray Katzenmeier, Owner

Annual show and exhibits of plumbing, heating and cooling equipment, supplies and services.

13509 National Plumbing, Heating, Cooling and Piping Products Exposition
Nat'l Assn of Plumbing-Heating-Cooling Contractors
180 S Washington Street
PO Box 6808
Falls Church, VA 22046

703-237-8100
800-533-7694
Fax: 703-237-7442
Home Page: www.phccweb.org
Social Media: Facebook, LinkedIn

Elicia Magruder, VP of Member Services
Cynthia A Sheridan, Foundation Chief Operating Officer
Charlotte R Perham, Senior Director of Communications

Annual show of 500 manufacturers and suppliers of equipment, supplies and services for the plumbing, heating and cooling industries.
15M Attendees
Frequency: Annual/October

13510 North American Thermal Analysis Society
Complete Conference
1540 River Park Drive
Suite 111
Sacramento, CA 95815-4608

916-922-7032
Fax: 916-922-7379

Marilyn Hauck, President

30 booths.
300 Attendees
Frequency: Annual/September

13511 Oil Heat Business and Industry Expo
20 Summer Street
#9137
Watertown, MA 02472-3468

FAX 781-924-1022

Bernard A Smith, Executive VP
Nancy Spinney, Expo Manager

This show provides a marketplace for prime purchasers of heating oil; oil heating, and air conditioning, as well as accessory equipment; fuel oil distribution equipment, trucks, transports, service and salesmen's vehicles; computers, office equipment; insurance programs and more.
8.5M Attendees
Frequency: Annual/June

13512 RSES Annual Conference and HVAC Technology Expo
Refrigeration Service Engineers Society
1666 Rand Road
Des Plaines, IL 60016-3552

847-297-6464
800-297-5660
E-Mail: general@rses.org
Home Page: www.rses.org
Social Media: Facebook, Twitter, LinkedIn

Mark Lowry, Executive Vice President
Josh Flaim, Operations Manager
Jean Birch, Conference & Seminar Manager

80 booths consisting primarily of products and services.

13513 Sheet Metal Air Conditioning Contractors National Association Show
4201 Lafayette Center Drive
Chantilly, VA 20151-1209
703-032-2980
Home Page: http://www.smacna.org
Mary Lou Taylor, Convention Director
John Sroka, Executive VP
250 booths.
2.3M Attendees
Frequency: Annual/October

13514 Southwestern Ice Association Show
823 Congress Avenue
1300
Austin, TX 78701
512-479-0425
Fax: 512-495-9031
Andrea Barnard, Executive Director
30 booths.
200 Attendees
Frequency: Annual/February
Founded in 1891

Directories & Databases

13515 AGA GasNet
American Gas Association
1515 Wilson Boulevard
Suite 100
Arlington, VA 22209-2469
703-841-8400
Fax: 703-841-8406
Offers access to news and information on and about the natural gas industry.

13516 Air Conditioning, Heating & Refrigeration News Directory Issue
The Air-Conditioning, Heating & Refrigeration New
2401 W. Big Beaver Road
Suite 700
Troy, MI 48084
248-362-3700
Home Page: www.achrnews.com
John Conrad, Publisher
Mike Murphy, Editor-in-Chief
Kyle Gargaro, Managing Editor
Greg Mazurkiewicz, Web Editor
Barbary Checket-Hanks, Service & Maintenance Editor
This issue offers a list of over 2,000 manufacturers, 5,000 wholesalers and factory outlets. Over 10,000 HVAC/R products, exporters and related trade organizations are also covered.
Cost: $35.00
618 Pages
Frequency: Annual
Circulation: 38,000
Printed in 4 colors on glossy stock

13517 Annual Member Directory
Air Conditioning & Heating Contractors of America
1712 New Hampshire Avenue NW
Washington, DC 20009-2502
202-483-9370
Fax: 202-234-4721
Rae Dorsey, Production Manager
A publication for the members of the Air Conditioning and Heating Contractors of America.
Circulation: 5,000

13518 Directory of Certified Applied Air-Conditioning Products
Air-Conditioning & Refrigeration Institute
4301 Fairfax Drive
Suite 425
Arlington, VA 22203-1634
703-248-8800
A list of 50 manufacturers of air conditioning and heating products.
Cost: $8.50
Frequency: Bi-Annual

13519 Directory of Certified Unitary Air-Conditioners & Heat Pumps
Air-Conditioning & Refrigeration Institute
4301 Fairfax Drive
Suite 425
Arlington, VA 22203-1634
703-248-8800
Air and coil heating and cooling units and air-to-air heat pumps manufacturers are profiled.
Cost: $13.00
Frequency: Bi-Annual

13520 HPAC Engineering Information
Penton Media
1300 E 9th St
Cleveland, OH 44114-1501
216-696-7000
Fax: 216-696-1752
E-Mail: information@penton.com
Home Page: www.penton.com
Jane Cooper, Marketing
Cost: $30.00
300 Pages
Frequency: Annual
Circulation: 56,000
ISSN: 1527-4055
Printed in 4 colors on glossy stock

13521 Industrial Heating Buyers Guide and Reference Handbook
Business News Publishing
1050 IL Route 83
Suite 200
Bensenville, IL 60106-1096
630-377-5909
Home Page: www.industrialheating.com
Social Media: Facebook, Twitter, LinkedIn
Katie Rotella, Manager
Companies are profiled that have over 1,200 heating products, and heat treating, and other services in the worldwide industrial heating market.
Cost: $25.00
250 Pages
Circulation: 20,000

13522 LP/Gas: Industry Buying Guide Issue
Advanstar Communications
131 W 1st St
Duluth, MN 55802-2065
218-740-7200
800-346-0085
Fax: 218-723-9122
E-Mail: info@advanstar.com
Home Page: www.advanstar.com
Kent Akervik, Manager
List of about 1,000 liquid propane gas equipment manufacturers and suppliers; list of about 700 distributors of gas appliances and equipment.
Cost: $50.00
Frequency: Annual
Circulation: 16,000
Printed in 4 colors on glossy stock

13523 PM Directory & Reference Issue
Business News Publishing
1050 IL Route 83
Suite 200
Bensenville, IL 60106-1096
630-377-5909
Home Page: www.bnpmedia.com
Katie Rotella, Manager
Manufacturers, wholesalers, exporters, associations, products, consultants and manufacturers' representatives in the industries of plumbing, piping and hydronic heating.
Cost: $30.00
Frequency: Annual/December
Circulation: 42,000

13524 Refrigeration: Ice Industry's Buyer's Guide Issue
John W Yopp Publications
PO Box 1147
Beaufort, SC 29901-1147
843-521-0239
800-849-9677
Fax: 800-849-8418
Joe Cronley
Directory of services and supplies to the industry.
Cost: $3.00
Frequency: Annual
Circulation: 3,000

Industry Web Sites

13525 http://gold.greyhouse.com
G.O.L.D Grey House OnLine Databases
Grey House Publishing's online database platform, GOLD, offers Quick Search, Keyword Search and Expert Search for most business sectors including heating and air conditioning markets. The GOLD platform makes finding the information you need quick and easy - whether you're a novice searcher or an experienced database user. All of Grey House's directory products are available for subscription on the GOLD platform.

13526 www.abma.com
American Boiler Manufacturers Association
Manufacturers trade association representing companies involved in utility, industrial and commercial steam generation. Includes associate memberships for companies who sell to or work with these companies and those who own boilers. Holds technical and production conferences, and publishes technical guideline publications.

13527 www.achrnews.com
BNP Media
News, tips and a calendar of events for the heating & cooling industry.

13528 www.aga.com
American Gas Association
Events, publications, information, etc.

13529 www.ari.org
Air Conditioning & Refrigeration Institute
Trade association representing manufacturers of more than 90% of North American produced air-conditioning and commercial refrigeration equipment.

13530 www.asa.net
American Supply Association
The National association of full-service plumbing, heating, cooling, and piping products for wholesalers, manufacturers, and distributors.

13531 **www.ashrae.org**
American Society of Heating, Refrigeration, AC

Research, activities, education and publications.

13532 **www.construction.com**
McGraw-Hill Construction (MHC), part of The McGraw-Hill Companies, connects people and projects across the design and construction industry, serving owners, architects, engineers, general contractors, subcontractors, building product manufacturers, suppliers, dealers, distributors and adjacent markets.

13533 **www.districtenergy.org**
International District Energy Association

Journal of district heating and cooling industry, congeneration, physical plants and energy efficiency. Accepts advertising.

13534 **www.gamanet.org**
Gas Appliance Manufacturers Association

Represents manufacturers of residential, commercial and industrial gas and oil fired appliances, associated controls and accessories, as well as equipment used in the production, transmission and distribution of fuel gases.

13535 **www.greyhouse.com**
Grey House Publishing

Authoritative reference directories for most business sectors including heating and air conditioning markets. Users can search the online databases with varied search criteria allowing for custom searches by product category, geographic area, sales volume, keyword, subject and more. Full Grey House catalog and online ordering also available.

13536 **www.impi.org**
International Microwave Power Institute

IMPI's members include scientists, researchers, lab technicians, product developers, marketing managers and a variety of other professionals in the microwave industry. The Institute serves the information needs of all specialists working with dielectric (microwave and RF) heating sytems, and was expanded in 1977 to meet the information needs relating to consumer microwave ovens and related products.

13537 **www.macsw.org**
Mobile Air Conditioning Society Worldwide

Information on technical training for professionals in the automotive air-conditioning industry.

13538 **www.mha-net.org**
Masonry Heater Association of North America

Promotes use of masonry heaters, increases public awareness and encourages reasonable governmental regulation.

13539 **www.sweets.construction.com**
McGraw Hill Construction

In depth product information that lets you find, compare, select, specify and make purchase decisions in the industrial product marketplace.

Associations

13540 **American Camping Association**
5000 State Road 67 N
Martinsville, IN 46151-7902
765-342-8456
800-428-2267
Fax: 765-342-2065
E-Mail: shallway@aca-camps.org
Home Page: www.acacamps.org
Social Media: Facebook, Twitter, LinkedIn, youtube, RSS, Google+
Tisha Bolger, President
Peg Smith, CEO
Brigitta Adkins, Executive Director of Indiana Field
Rhonda Begley, Chief Financial Officer
Angela Ambrosini, Director of Marketing
6600+ Members
Founded in 1910
Mailing list available for rent

13541 **American Craft Council**
1224 Marshall Street NE.
Suite 200
Minneapolis, MN 55413
612-206-3100
Fax: 612-355-2330
E-Mail: council@craftcouncil.org
Home Page: www.craftcouncil.org
Social Media: Facebook, Twitter, Flickr, Youtube
Barbara Waldman, Board Chair
Gariel Ofiesh, Board Vice Chair
Jamienne (Jamie Studley, Board Secretary
Kevin Buchi, Board Treasurer
National nonprofit, educational organization dedicated to promotion, understanding and appreciation of contemporary American craft. Sponsors annual wholesale and retail shows, a magazine, a library and seminars.
Founded in 1943
Mailing list available for rent

13542 **American Home Sewing and Craft Association**
PO Box 369
Monroeville, PA 15146
412-372-5950
Fax: 212-714-1655
E-Mail: info@sewing.org
Home Page: www.sewing.org

13543 **American Philatelic Society**
100 Match Factory Place
Bellefonte, PA 16823-1367
814-933-3803
Fax: 814-933-6128
E-Mail: wendy@stamps.org
Home Page: www.stamps.org
Social Media: Facebook, Twitter, LinkedIn, Youtube, Stamp Talk
Stephen Reinhardÿ, President
Ken Martin, Executive Director
Alex Haimann, Board of Vice Presidents
Yamil Kouri, Board of Vice Presidents
Mick Zais, Board of Vice Presidents
National organization for postage stamp collectors, monthly magazine, the American Philatelist; lending library; insurance for philatelic materials; sales division, seminars and annual conventions open to the public.
32500 Members
Founded in 1886

13544 **American Quilt Study Group**
American Quilt Study Group
1610 L St
Lincoln, NE 68508-2509
402-477-1181
Fax: 402-477-1181
E-Mail: aqsg2@americanquiltstudygroup.org
Home Page: www.americanquiltstudygroup.org
Lisa Erlandson, President
Lenna DeMarco, Vice President
Kathy Moore, Vice President
Judy J. Brott Buss, Ph.D., Executive Director
Anne E. Schuff, Member Services Coordinator
Establishes, sustains, and promotes the highest standards for quilt-related studies. We stimulate, nurture, and affirm engagement in quilt studies and provide opportunities for its dissemination.
1000 Members
Founded in 1980
Mailing list available for rent

13545 **American Specialty Toy Retailing Association**
432 N Clark Avenue
Suite 401
Chicago, IL 60654
312-222-0984
800-591-0490
Fax: 312-222-0986
E-Mail: info@astratoy.org
Home Page: www.astratoy.org
Social Media: Facebook, Twitter
Kathleen McHugh, President
Providing a unified voice for the specialty toy industry, and opportunities to exchange information and ideas with counterparts. Membership benefits include workshops and seminars, vendor representative roundtables, membership directory and annual convention.
1000 Members
Founded in 1992

13546 **American Stamp Dealers Association**
PO Box 858
Suite 205
Morris Plains, NJ 07950
973-267-1644
800-369-8207
Fax: 800-369-8207
E-Mail: asda@americanstampdealer.com
Home Page: www.asdaonline.com
Mark Reasoner, President
Stanley Piller, Vice President
Richard A. Friedberg, Secretary
James F. Bardo, Treasurer
Robert Prager, Director
800 Members
Founded in 1914

13547 **Archery Trade Association**
PO Box 70
101 N German St
New Ulm, MN 56073-0070
507-233-8130
866-266-2776
Fax: 507-233-8140
E-Mail: jaymcaninch@archerytrade.org
Home Page: www.archerytrade.org
Social Media: Facebook, Twitter
Jay McAninch, President/CEO
Jeremy Henricks, Director of Information
Patrick Durkin, Contributing Editor and Writer
Mitch King, Director of Government Relations
John Nelson, Director of Finance and Operations
Provides core funding and direction for two new foundations critical to the future of archery and bowhunting: Arrow Sport and the Bowhunting Preservation Alliance. In addition the ATA continues to direct the industry's annual archery and bowhunting trade show.
Founded in 1956
Mailing list available for rent

13548 **Association of Traditional Hooking Artists**
600 1/2 Maple Street
Endicott, NY 13760
E-Mail: jcahill29@aol.com
Home Page: www.rughookersnetwork.com
Social Media: Facebook
Joan Cahill, Membership Chairperson
Karen Balon, Guild Secretary
Mary Henck, President
Provides educational material about rug hooking, free patterns, supplies information, chapter/rug camp meetings and teacher information that is not available through any other source. Membership includes all 50 states, England, Japan and Australia.
Founded in 1996

13549 **Embroidery Trade Association**
PO Box 793967
Dallas, TX 75379-3967
972-247-0415
888-628-2545
Fax: 972-755-2561
E-Mail: info@embroiderytrade.org
Home Page: www.embroiderytrade.org
John Swinburn, Executive Director
Dolores Cheek, Director of Membership
Keith Amen, VP
An organization with the objective to continually strengthen the commercial embroidery business.
1200 Members
Founded in 1990

13550 **Game Manufacturers Association**
240 N. Fifth St.
Suite 340
Columbus, OH 43215
614-255-4500
Fax: 614-255-4499
E-Mail: president@gama.org
Home Page: www.gama.org
Social Media: Facebook
Rick Loomis, President
John Ward, Executive Director
Jamie Chambers, Vice President
Aaron Witten, Treasurer
Brian Dalrymple, Secretary
A non-profit trade association dedicated to the advancement of the hobby game business.
Founded in 1977
Mailing list available for rent

13551 **Hobby Industry Association**
319 E 54th St
Elmwood Park, NJ 07407-2712
201-835-1200
Fax: 201-797-0657
E-Mail: info@craftandhobby.org
Home Page: www.craftandhobby.org
Social Media: Facebook, Twitter, LinkedIn, Pinterest, Youtube
Maureen Ruth, Chair
Andrej Suskavcevic, CAEÿ, President & Chief Executive Officer
Natalie Cohn, Vice President, Finance
Sue Turchickÿ, Vice President, Membership
Keri Cunninghamÿ, Director of Marketing
Trade association in the craft and hobby market. The group produces an international trade show open to qualified professionals and is the industry's only market research show.
4000 Members
Founded in 1940
Mailing list available for rent

13552 **Hobby Manufacturers Association**
PO Box 315
Butler, NJ 07405-0315

973-283-9088
Fax: 973-838-7124
E-Mail: pat.koziol@hmahobby.org
Home Page: www.hmahobby.org

Fred Hill, President
Patricia S Koziol, Executive Director
Bill Jeric, Vice President
Rich Janyszek, Sec-Treasurerў
Candi Calderone, Expositions and Events Manager

The mission of the Hobby Manufacturers Association is to stimulate the growth of the model hobby industry.
292 Members
Founded in 2005

13553 **Museum Store Association**
3773 E Cherry Creek North Dr
Suite 755
Denver, CO 80209-3804

303-504-9223
Fax: 303-504-9585
E-Mail: info@museumstoreassociation.org
Home Page: www.museumdistrict.com
Social Media: Facebook, Twitter, LinkedIn

Stacey Stachow, President
Jama Rice, Executive Director/ CEO
Barbara Lenhardt, 1st Vice President
David Duddy, 2nd Vice President
Gloria Stern, Treasurer

Providing member representatives with the professional opportunities and educational resources they need to operate effectively and ethically.
2500 Members
Founded in 1955

13554 **National School Supply Equipment Association**
8380 Colesville Rd
Suite 250
Silver Spring, MD 20910-6225

301-495-0240
800-395-5550
Fax: 301-495-3330
E-Mail: memberservices@nssea.org
Home Page: www.nssea.org
Social Media: Facebook, Twitter, LinkedIn, Youtube

Jim McGarry, President/CEO
Bill Duffy, Vice President - Operations
Adrienne Dayton, Vice President - Marketing
Joe Tucker, CEM, CMP, Director of Meetings & Experiences
Michael Nercesian, Exhibits Manager

Trade Association for the educational products industry.
1400+ Members
Founded in 1916

13555 **Toy Industry Association**
1115 Broadway
Suite 400
New York, NY 10010-3466

212-675-1141
Fax. 212-633-1429
E-Mail: info@toyassociation.org
Home Page: www.toyassociation.org/
Social Media: Facebook, Twitter, LinkedIn, Youtube

Soren Torp Laursen, Chairman
Carter Keithley, President
John Gessert, Vice-Chairmanў
David Hargreaves, Secretary-Treasurer
Bob Wann, Member of Board of Directors

National organization with toy, game and holiday decoration manufacturers and their representatives, as well as toy designers, testing laboratories, licensors, sales representatives and trade magazines.
400+ Members
Founded in 1916

13556 **Western Toy & Hobby Representatives Association**
PO Box 2250
Pomona, CA 91786

909-899-3753
Fax: 909-697-2014
E-Mail: toyshow@wthra.com
Home Page: www.wthra.com

Phylis St John, Show Director

A nonprofit association organization. Produces and promotes the Western States Toy & Hobby Show.
Founded in 1961

Newsletters

13557 **American Stamp Dealers Association Newsletter**
American Stamp Dealers Association
3 School St
Suite 205
Glen Cove, NY 11542-2548

516-759-7000
Fax: 800-369-8207
Home Page: www.asdaonline.com

Joseph Savarese, Executive VP
Elizabeth Pope, Secretary
Kim Kellermann, Secretary
Thomas Jacks, Treasurer

Association news.
Frequency: Monthly
Circulation: 810
Founded in 1914
Printed in on matte stock

13558 **Bill Nelson Newsletter**
Nelson Newsletter Publishing Corporation
PO Box 90890
Tucson, AZ 85752-0890

520-297-8240
800-368-8434
Fax: 520-629-0387
Home Page: www.billnelsonnewsletter.com/

James Lee, President

Features news on the pin collecting hobby.
Cost: $20.00
8 Pages
Frequency: Monthly
Printed in one color on matte stock

13559 **Guild of Natural Science Illustration**
Guild of Natural Science Illustrators
PO Box 652
Ben Franklin Station
Washington, DC 20044-652
301-309-1514
Fax: 301-309-1514
E-Mail: gnsihome@his.com
Home Page: www.gnsi.org

Gretchen Kai Halpert, President
Erica Beade, Vice President

Non-profit organization for those interested in the field of natural science illustrations. Newsletter is published 10 times a year.
Cost: $75.00
Frequency: 10x Yearly
Circulation: 1000
Founded in 1968

13560 **This Time**
Homeworkers Organized for More Employment
PO Box 10
Orland, ME 04472

207-469-7961
Fax: 207-469-1023
E-Mail: info@homecoop.net
Home Page: www.homecoop.net/

Lucy Toulin, President
J Ralph, Editor
F Eldridge, Volunteer Coordinator

Home community newsletter, part of the world Emmaus movement, offering information on craft store items and antiques. Member of rural coalition , Washington D.C..
Cost: $5.00
16 Pages
Frequency: Quarterly
Circulation: 300
Founded in 1970

Magazines & Journals

13561 **ABCs of Retailing**
Hobby Industry Association
319 E 54th St
Suite 348
Elmwood Park, NJ 07407-2712
201-794-1133
Fax: 201-797-0657
E-Mail: afliss@rfcp.com
Home Page: www.craftandhobby.org

Steve Berger, CEO

Guide to opening and maintaining a craft/hobby retail store.
20 Pages
Founded in 1940

13562 **American Craft Magazine**
72 Spring St
New York, NY 10012-4090

212-274-0630
Fax: 212-274-0650
E-Mail: council@craftcouncil.org
Home Page: www.craftcouncil.org

Andrew Wagner, Manager
John Gourlay, Publisher
Lois Moran, Editor-in-Chief

Celebrates the excellence of contemporary craft, focusing on masterful achievements in the craft media — clay, fiber, metal, glass, wood and other materials — with the goal to create intellectual and visual interest for the reader on today's craft.
Cost: $40.00
Founded in 1943

13563 **American Philatelist**
American Philatelic Society
100 Match Factory Pl
Bellefonte, PA 16823-1367

814-237-3803
Fax: 814-933-6128
E-Mail: kpmartin@stamps.org
Home Page: www.stamps.org

Ken Martin, Executive Director

One hundred page monthly magazine for stamp collectors.
Cost: $80.00
34000 Members
100 Pages
Frequency: Monthly
Circulation: 37500
ISSN: 0003-0473
Founded in 1886

13564 Antiques and Collecting Hobbies
Lightner Publishing Corporation
1006 S Michigan Ave
Chicago, IL 60605-2216

312-939-4767
Fax: 312-939-0053

Antiques and collectible news articles.
Cost: $32.00
88 Pages
Frequency: Monthly
Circulation: 18,000
Founded in 1931

13565 Bank Note Reporter
F+W Media
38 E. 29th Street
New York, NY 10016

212-447-1400
Fax: 212-447-5231
E-Mail: contact_us@fwmedia.com
Home Page: www.fwpublications.com
Social Media: Facebook, Twitter, LinkedIn

Bill Bright, General Manager
Dave Harper, Editor
Buddy Redling, Manager
Chad Phelps, Chief Digital Officer
Stacie Berger, Communications Director

Recognized as the finest publication for paper money collectors available. Contains news on market values, 'Bank Note Clinic' (a collector Q&A), an up-to-date foreign exchange chart, 'Fun Notes' (interesting, odd & unusual notes), a price guide, a world currency section, historical features on paper money worldwide (emphasizing US issues), & hundreds of display & classified ads offering to buy, sell, & trade bank notes of all kinds. Contributors include some of the top experts in the field.
Cost: $21.98
84 Pages
Frequency: Monthly
Circulation: 8072
Founded in 1952
Mailing list available for rent

13566 Blade
F+W Media
38 E. 29th Street
New York, NY 10016

212-447-1400
Fax: 212-447-5231
E-Mail: contact_us@fwmedia.com
Home Page: www.fwpublications.com
Social Media: Facebook, Twitter, LinkedIn

David Nussbaum, CEO/Chairman
Steve Shackleford, Editor
Jim Ogle, Chief Financial Officer
Chad Phelps, Chief Digital Officer
Stacie Berger, Communications Director

Provides knifemakers, collectors, and knife enthusiasts with information concerning new knife-making techniques and processes, field tests, and the latest news and features on knives and their makers. Also includes a Q&A section, letters to the editor, features about individual knifemakers, an extensive listing of upcoming knife shows, and a reader feature entitled, 'The Knife I Carry.'
Cost: $25.98
140 Pages
Frequency: Monthly
Circulation: 38068
ISSN: 1064-5853
Founded in 1973
Mailing list available for rent

13567 Cast On Magazine
The Knitting Guild Association (TKGA)
1100-H Brandywine Blvd.
Zanesville, OH 43701-7303

740-452-4541
E-Mail: tkga@tkga.com
Home Page: www.tkga.com
Social Media: Facebook, Twitter, LinkedIn

Penny Sitler, Executive Director

Educational journal for knitters.
10000 Members
Frequency: Quarterly
Circulation: 11,000
Mailing list available for rent

13568 Coin Prices
F+W Media
38 E. 29th Street
New York, NY 10016

212-447-1400
Fax: 212-447-5231
E-Mail: contact_us@fwmedia.com
Home Page: www.fwpublications.com
Social Media: Facebook, Twitter, LinkedIn

Bill Bright, General Manager
Bob Van Ryzin, Editor
Jim Ogle, Chief Financial Officer
Chad Phelps, Chief Digital Officer
Stacie Berger, Communications Director

Coin Prices is a complete guide to retail values for collectible US coins. A market update section (value guide) by market editor Joel Edler beings each issue. Rotating special sections provide values for Canadian and Mexican coins, Colonial coins, territorial coins, errors and varieties and selected issues of US paper money. Regular departments include a guide to grading US coins.
Cost: $18.98
96 Pages
Circulation: 56611
Founded in 1952
Mailing list available for rent

13569 Coins
F+W Media
38 E. 29th Street
New York, NY 10016

212-447-1400
Fax: 212-447-5231
E-Mail: contact_us@fwmedia.com
Home Page: www.fwpublications.com
Social Media: Facebook, Twitter, LinkedIn

Bill Bright, General Manager
Bob Van Ryzin, Editor
Jim Ogle, Chief Financial Officer
Chad Phelps, Chief Digital Officer
Stacie Berger, Communications Director

Covers market trends, buying tips, and historical perspectives on all aspects of numismatics. The news section, 'Bits and Pieces,' wraps up the latest happenings in numismatics. Regular columns and departments include 'Basics& Beyond,' 'Budget Buyer,' 'Coin Clinic' (Q&A), the editor's column, coin finds, a calendar of upcoming shows nationwide, 'Coin Values Guide' and 'Market Watch.'
Cost: $20.98
120 Pages
Frequency: Monthly
Circulation: 52660
Founded in 1955
Mailing list available for rent

13570 Comics & Games Retailer
F+W Media
38 E. 29th Street
New York, NY 10016

212-447-1400
Fax: 212-447-5231
E-Mail: contact_us@fwmedia.com
Home Page: www.fwpublications.com
Social Media: Facebook, Twitter, LinkedIn

Mark Williams, Publisher
John Miller, Editor
Norma Jean Fochs, Ad Manager

Provides information to retailers about marketing, industry news, and practical how-to tips on selling comics and games at the retail level. Regular columns include 'Suggested for Mature Retailers,' 'Small Store Strategy,' 'Trade Show Calendar,' 'Retailer News,' and 'Distributor News.' Special issue focus on the comic book industry, trade shows, trading cards, gaming, display racks, and other retail store supplies. 'Market Beat' gives a national overview of the comics market.
Cost: $29.95
72 Pages
Frequency: Monthly
Circulation: 5,201
Founded in 1971
Mailing list available for rent

13571 Comics Buyer's Guide
F+W Media
38 E. 29th Street
New York, NY 10016

212-447-1400
Fax: 212-447-5231
E-Mail: contact_us@fwmedia.com
Home Page: www.fwpublications.com
Social Media: Facebook, Twitter, LinkedIn

David Nussbaum, CEO/Chairman
Maggie Thompson, Editor
Jim Ogle, Chief Financial Officer
Chad Phelps, Chief Digital Officer
Stacie Berger, Communications Director

The longest-running magazine about comic books. Each 200+ page monthly issue features new comic reviews, nostalgic retroviews, interviews and the largest monthly price guide. Aslo included is the latest convention news, opinion pieces from celebrity columnists and expanded coverage of anime, manga and other comics-related auctions.
Cost: $38.95
244 Pages
Frequency: Monthly
Circulation: 30,000
ISSN: 1064-5853
Founded in 1952
Mailing list available for rent

13572 Craftrends
Primedia Enthusiast Group Publishing
741 Corporate Circle
Suite A
Golden, CO 80401

303-278-1010
800-881-6634
Fax: 303-277-0370
Home Page: www.craftrends.com

Bill Gardner, Editorial Director
Beth Hess, Managing Editor
Dave O'Neil, VP Group Publishing
Kelly P. Conlin, President/CEO

Includes new products, coverage of industry trade shows, merchandising and promotion ideas. Also has timely information to operate a craft business and stay on top of a rapidly changing retail environment.
Cost: $26.00
Frequency: Monthly
Circulation: 22000
Founded in 1989

13573 Crafts Magazine
Primedia Enthusiast Group Publishing
PO Box 420494
Palm Coast, FL 32142-9524

800-727-2387
Fax: 386-447-2321

E-Mail: papercrafts@palmcoastd.com
Home Page: www.craftsmag.com

Valerie Pingree, Editor-in-Chief
Mike Irish, Associate Publisher
Kelly P Conlin, CEO/President

Monthly craft consumer magazine reaching the crafting enthusiast.
Cost: $15.97
112 Pages
Circulation: 300272
ISSN: 0148-9127
Founded in 1989
Printed in 4 colors on glossy stock

13574 Crafts Report
Crafts Reports Publishing
100 Rogers Road
Wilmington, DE 19801

302-656-2209
800-777-7098
Fax: 302-656-4894
E-Mail: theeditor@craftsreport.com
Home Page: www.craftsreport.com

Lammot Copeland Jr, Publisher
Heather Skelly, Editor
Stewart Abowitz, Marketing Director
Deborah Copeland, Co-Publisher

Monthly business magazine for the crafts professional, providing information on marketing, growing your craft business, time management, studio safety, retail relationships, artist/retailer profiles, show listings and more.
Cost: $29.00
Frequency: Monthly
Circulation: 30000
ISSN: 0160-7650
Founded in 1975
Printed in 4 colors on glossy stock

13575 Creative Knitting
House of White Birches
306 E Parr Rd
Berne, IN 46711-1100

260-589-8741
800-829-5865
Fax: 260-589-8093
E-Mail: customer_service@drgbooks.com
Home Page: www.whitebirches.com

David J McKee, CEO
John Boggs, Advertising Sales Director
Carl Musselman, Editor
David J McKee, Publishing Director
Greg Deily, Marketing Director

Serves the knitting industry.
Cost: $13.00
64 Pages
Frequency: Monthly
Founded in 1947

13576 Doll Artisan
Jones Publishing
N7 450 Aanstad Road
PO Box 5000
Iola, WI 54945-5000

715-445-5000
Fax: 715-445-4053
E-Mail: joejones@jonespublishing.com
Home Page: www.dollmakingartisian.com

Edited to entertain, fascinate and educate the doll maker in reproduction of antique porcelain dolls. Encourages and promotes efforts to make porcelain doll making easier, safer and more accessible to a growing number of enthusiasts.
Cost: $5.95
Frequency: Bi-Monthly

13577 Doll World
Jones Publishing
N7 450 Aanstad Road
PO Box 5000
Iola, WI 54945-5000

715-445-5000
800-331-0038
Fax: 715-445-4053
E-Mail: jonespub@jonespublishing.com
Home Page: www.jonespublishing.com

Joe Jones, President
Nayda Rondon, Editor
Trina Laube, Assistant Editor
Virginia Adams, Marketing
Brandan Hardie, Circulation Manager
Cost: $32.95
Frequency: Monthly

13578 Dollmaking
Jones Publishing
N7 450 Aanstad Road
PO Box 5000
Iola, WI 54945-5000

715-445-5000
Fax: 715-445-4053
E-Mail: jonespub@jonespublishing.com
Home Page: www.Dollmaking/Artisan.com

Resource for makers of porcelain and sculpted modern dolls, is edited for the serious costume and doll maker.
Cost: $4.95
Frequency: Bi-Monthly

13579 Essentials Magazine
National School Supply Equipment
8300 Colesville Rd
Suite 250
Silver Spring, MD 20910-6225

301-495-0240
800-395-5550
Fax: 301-495-3330
E-Mail: customerservice@nssea.org
Home Page: www.nssea.org
Social Media: Facebook, Twitter, LinkedIn

Jim McGarry, President/CEO
Rashad Cheeks, Meetings Coordinator
Tamara Davis, Bookkeeper/Office Manager
Karen Prince, Director of Membership
Bill Duffy, Vice President - Operations

13580 Family Tree
B&W Publications
1507 Dana Avenue
Cincinnati, OH 45207-1056

513-943-9464
Fax: 513-531-1843

Ideas and advice for discovering, preserving and celebrating family history.

13581 Family Tree Magazine
F+W Media
38 E. 29th Street
New York, NY 10016

212-447-1400
Fax: 212-447-5231
E-Mail: contact_us@fwmedia.com
Home Page: www.fwpublications.com
Social Media: Facebook, Twitter, LinkedIn

David Nussbaum, CEO/Chairman
Allison Stacy, Editor
Kelly Klener, Marketing
Chad Phelps, Chief Digital Officer
Stacie Berger, Communications Director

America's most popular family history magazine. It covers all areas of potential interest to family history enthusiasts, reaching beyond strict genealogy research to include ethnic heritage, family reunions, memoirs, oral history, scrapbooking, historical travel and other ways that families connect with their pasts. Each issue features the latest tools, how-to tips and expert advice to guide readers through the journey of discovering, preserving and celebrating their roots.
Cost: $27.00
84 Pages
Circulation: 80050
Founded in 1952
Mailing list available for rent

13582 Fine Woodworking
Taunton Press
63 S Main Street
PO Box 5506
Newtown, CT 06470-5506

203-270-6206
800-926-8776
Fax: 203-426-3434
E-Mail: fw@taunton.com
Home Page: www.taunton.com

David Grey, Publisher
Linda Abbett, Advertising Manager
Anatole Burkin, Editor
John Lagan, National Account Manager

Published since 1975, written by woodworkers for woodworkers regularly shows the finest work in wood being done today.
Cost: $34.95
120 Pages
Circulation: 295000
Founded in 1975
Mailing list available for rent: 185M names
Printed in 4 colors on glossy stock

13583 Gun Digest
F+W Media
38 E. 29th Street
New York, NY 10016

212-447-1400
Fax: 212-447-5231
E-Mail: contact_us@fwmedia.com
Home Page: www.fwpublications.com
Social Media: Facebook, Twitter, LinkedIn

David Nussbaum, CEO/Chairman
Steve Hudziak, Marketing
Jim Ogle, Chief Financial Officer
Chad Phelps, Chief Digital Officer
Stacie Berger, Communications Director

An all-advertising, nationwide marketplace for buyers and sellers of new, used and antique firearms. Display advertising from the nation's top dealers, manufacturers, distributors, and suppliers is found in each bi-weekly issue, along with thousands of classified word ads, organized alphabetically, from collectors all over the world. The nation's leading indexed firearms paper. Hundreds of gun show listings and knife show listings are included to help readers schedule their show attendance.
Cost: $37.98
136 Pages
Circulation: 81120
Founded in 1952
Mailing list available for rent

13584 HIA Craft/Hobby Consumer Study
Hobby Industry Association
319 E 54th St
Elmwood Park, NJ 07407-2712

201-794-1133
Fax: 201-797-0657
E-Mail: info@craftandhobby.org
Home Page: www.craftandhobby.org

Steve Berger, CEO

An extensive study of consumer behavior and buying habits relevant to the hobby/craft/creative industry. Executive summary is available on-line.
Cost: $400.00
Circulation: 5000
Founded in 2004

13585 Hobby Merchandiser
Hobby Publications

207 Commercial Court
PO Box 102
Morganville, NJ 07751-102

732-536-5160
800-969-7176
Fax: 732-536-5761
E-Mail: info@hobbymerchandiser.com
Home Page: www.hobbymerchandiser.com/

Robert Gherman, Publisher
Jeff Troy, Editor
Patrick Sarver, Associate Publisher

Trade magazine for the model hobby industry, available to professionals only.
Cost: $20.00
96 Pages
Frequency: Monthly
Circulation: 7000
ISSN: 0744-1738
Founded in 1947
Mailing list available for rent: 8,300 names at $241 per M
Printed in 4 colors on glossy stock

13586 Hobby Rocketry
California Rocketry Publishing
PO Box 1242
Claremont, CA 91711-1242

760-389-2233
Fax: 661-824-0868
E-Mail: info@v-serv.com
Home Page: www.v-serv.com/crp

Jerry Irvine, Publisher

Covers consumer rocket products which are available in hobby, toy and retail outlets. Product reviews, manufacturers notes, consumer feedback and more. Back issues available.
Cost: $16.00
16 Pages
Frequency: Quarterly
Circulation: 8M
Founded in 1992
Printed in on newsprint stock

13587 Horizons
Hobby Industry Association
319 E 54th St
Elmwood Park, NJ 07407-2712

201-794-1133
Fax: 201-797-0657
Home Page: www.craftandhobby.org

Steve Berger, CEO

Available only to members of the Hobby Association of America. This magazine offers information and updates on what is happening in the industry.
6 Pages
Frequency: Quarterly

13588 Master Embroidery Manual
Embroidery Trade Association
P.O. Box 794534
Suite 414
Dallas, TX 75379-4534

972-247-0415
888-628-2545
Fax: 972-755-2561
E-Mail: info@embroiderytrade.org
Home Page: www.embroiderytrade.org
Social Media: Twitter, LinkedIn

John Swinburn, Executive Director
Dolores Cheek, Director Of Membership
Keith Amen, VP

Developed and published by ETA, this manual is an embroiderer's encyclopedia, especially for those new to the embroidery industry. Chapters include hooping & framing, backings & toppings, common goods and fabrics, and much more.
1200 Members
Founded in 1990

13589 Model Retailer
Kalmbach Publishing Company
21027 Crossroads Circle
PO Box 1612
Waukesha, WI 53187

262-796-8776
800-533-6644
Fax: 262-796-8776
E-Mail: hmiller@modelretailer.com
Home Page: www.modelretailer.com

Kevin Keefe, Publisher
Hal Miller, Editor
Rick Albers, Advertising Sales Manager
Jim Meinhardt, Circulation Manager

The business of hobbies, from financial and shop management issues to industry news and trends, as well as the latest in product releases. Provides hobby shop entreprenuers with the information, ideas and examples they need in order to be successful retailers.
Frequency: Monthly
Circulation: 6350
Founded in 1934

13590 Needlework Retailer
Yarn Tree Designs
117 Alexander Avenue
PO Box 2438
Ames, IA 50010-2438

515-232-3121
800-247-3952
Fax: 515-232-0789
E-Mail: info@needleworkretailer.com
Home Page: www.needleworkretailer.com

Larry Johnson, VP
Megan Chriswisser, Editor

Highlights a variety of new products and designs in needlework. Includes infornation on upcoming needlework trade shows and association news.
Cost: $12.00
Circulation: 11000

13591 Numismatic News
F+W Media
38 E. 29th Street
New York, NY 10016

212-447-1400
Fax: 212-447-5231
E-Mail: contact_us@fwmedia.com
Home Page: www.fwpublications.com
Social Media: Facebook, Twitter, LinkedIn

Bill Bright, General Manager
Dave Harper, Editor
Jim Ogle, Chief Financial Officer
Chad Phelps, Chief Digital Officer
Stacie Berger, Communications Director

Provides timely reports on market happenings and news concerning collectible coins. 'Coin Clinic' is a very popular weekly Q&A column that gives readers a chance to learn all about numismatics. The 'Coin Market' section provides comprehensive pricing monthly. Each issue also includes columns with practical how-to advice and historical features by some of the top experts in the field including 'Making the Grade' and 'Facts about Fakes.' Sponsors the annual Mid-America Coin Convention.
Cost: $35.99
72 Pages
Frequency: Weekly
Circulation: 34392
Founded in 1952
Mailing list available for rent

13592 Play Meter
Skybird Publishing Company
PO Box 337
Metairie, LA 70004-0337

504-488-7003
888-473-2376
Fax: 504-488-7083
E-Mail: news@playmeter.com
Home Page: www.playmeter.com
Social Media: Facebook, Twitter, LinkedIn

Bonnie Theard, Editor
Carol P. Lally, Publisher
Carol Ann Lally, President
Bonnie Theard, Managing Editor
Courtney McDuff, Assistant Editor

Trade publication that provides members with information on the coin-operated entertainment industry, including upcoming trade shows, new products, ongoing trends and more.
Cost: $60.00
Frequency: Monthly
Circulation: 60000
Founded in 1974

13593 Playthings
Reed Business Information
360 Park Ave S
4th Floor
New York, NY 10010-1737

646-746-6400
800-309-3332
Fax: 646-756-7583
E-Mail: mlaporte@reedbusiness.com
Home Page: www.reedbusiness.com
Social Media: Twitter, LinkedIn

John Poulin, CEO
Larry Oliver, VP/Group Publisher
Micki LaPorte, Circulation Director
James Reed, Owner
Andrew Rak, Senior Vice President

Emphasizes a merchandising approach for improving sales and promotional techniques. Features include new product listings, market reports, licensing updates and general industry trends.
Cost: $33.95
80 Pages
Frequency: Monthly
Founded in 1903
Printed in 4 colors on glossy stock

13594 SCRYE
F+W Media
38 E. 29th Street
New York, NY 10016

212-447-1400
Fax: 212-447-5231
E-Mail: contact_us@fwmedia.com
Home Page: www.fwpublications.com
Social Media: Facebook, Twitter, LinkedIn

Mark Williams, Publisher
Joyce Greenholdt, Editor
Jim Ogle, Chief Financial Officer
Chad Phelps, Chief Digital Officer
Stacie Berger, Communications Director

The most respected price guide in the industry for collectible card games and collectible miniatures. SCRYE also provides collectors and players the latest news, checklists, player strategies, deck building tips and tricks for collectible card games. The latest collectible card games are reviewed in each issue in addition to related role-playing and board games.
Cost: $29.98
160 Pages
Frequency: Monthly
Circulation: 47000
Founded in 1994
Mailing list available for rent

13595 Snapshot Memories
PRIMEDIA Consumer Magazine & Internet Group

2 News Plaza
PO Box 1790
Peoria, IL 61656-1790

309-682-6626
Fax: 309-679-5057

Mike Irish, Associate Publisher
Miram Olson, Editor-in-Chief

Scrapbook page idea magazine.
Cost: $16.98
92 Pages
Frequency: Quarterly
Circulation: 90,000
Founded in 1998
Printed in 4 colors on glossy stock

13596 Sports Collectors Digest
F+W Media
38 E. 29th Street
New York, NY 10016

212-447-1400
Fax: 212-447-5231
E-Mail: contact_us@fwmedia.com
Home Page: www.fwpublications.com
Social Media: Facebook, Twitter, LinkedIn

Dean Listle, Publisher
TS O'Connell, Editor
Jim Ogle, Chief Financial Officer
Chad Phelps, Chief Digital Officer
Stacie Berger, Communications Director

The Bible of Hobby covers every aspect of modern sports collecting, including cards, memorabilia, equipment, lithographs, figurines, and autographed material. Online collecting, graded cards, memorabilia and auction news are covered each week in specially designed sections that complement columns from some of the most respected experts in the hobby and up-to-date card pricing checklisting data from expert analysts, along with display advertisements from all the major dealers in the country.
Cost: $49.95
96 Pages
Frequency: Weekly
Circulation: 23356
Founded in 1973
Mailing list available for rent

13597 Stamp Collector
F+W Media
38 E. 29th Street
New York, NY 10016

212-447-1400
Fax: 212-447-5231
E-Mail: contact_us@fwmedia.com
Home Page: www.fwpublications.com
Social Media: Facebook, Twitter, LinkedIn

Wayne Youngblood, Publisher
Jill Ruesch, Ad Manager
Jim Ogle, Chief Financial Officer
Chad Phelps, Chief Digital Officer
Stacie Berger, Communications Director

Covers a wide variety of US & foreign stamp news. Sepcial inserts cover topicals, errors, postal history, and many others. Regular columns and features include 'Decoding the Catalog,' 'Q&A,' 'Meet the Designer,' 'Postal History,' 'New Stamps of the World,' 'Stamp Values Today,' an auction guide and the most extensive stamp show calendar in the hobby. The first issue each month cotains Stamp Wholesaler - stamp dealer info that is used as a 'philatelic phone book' by the entire industry.
Cost: $32.98
60 Pages
Circulation: 13251
Founded in 1931
Mailing list available for rent

13598 Stitches
Advertising Specialty Institute
4800 E Street Rd
Langhorne, PA 19053-6698

215-953-4000
800-546-1350
Fax: 215-953-3045
E-Mail: info@asicentral.com
Home Page: www.asicentral.com
Social Media: Facebook

Timothy M Andrews, CEO

The voice and vision of the embroidery industry and the single most referenced magazine in the business.
Frequency: 13x/Year
Circulation: 40000

13599 Tole World
EGW.com
4075 Papazian Way
Suite 208
Fremont, CA 94538-4372

510-668-0268
Fax: 510-668-0280
Home Page: www.toleworld.com

Chris Slaughter, VP
Rickie Wilson, Advertisement Manager

Serving crafters in the decorative painting field; each issue features 10 to 12 projects complete with full color photographs, step-by-step instructions and line art patterns. Project designs come from the nation's leading decorative artists, many of whom are also teachers in the field.
Cost: $35.94
84 Pages
Frequency: Quarterly
Circulation: 85956
Founded in 1977

13600 Toy Book
Adventure Publishing Group
1107 Broadway
Suite 1204
New York, NY 10010

212-575-4510
Fax: 212-575-4521
Home Page: www.adventurepub.com

Owen Shorts, Owner
Nelson Lombardi, Editor
A Schwartz, Marketing
Anthony Guardiola, Production Manager

Keeps readers abreast of new products and marketing information related to the industry.
Cost: $48.00
Frequency: Monthly
Circulation: 18000
Founded in 1980

13601 Toy Shop
F+W Media
38 E. 29th Street
New York, NY 10016

212-447-1400
Fax: 212-447-5231
E-Mail: contact_us@fwmedia.com
Home Page: www.fwpublications.com
Social Media: Facebook, Twitter, LinkedIn

Mark Williams, Publisher
Tom Bartsch, Editor
David Nussbaum, CEO/Chairman
Chad Phelps, Chief Digital Officer
Stacie Berger, Communications Director

A complete marketplace for buyers and sellers of toys, action figures, Barbie, Hot Wheels, character toys, and more. Offers thousands of easy-to-read, categorized classified ads, display ads, and a complete editorial package covering baby-boomer toys, vintage collectibles, TV toys, action figures, and many helpful Q&A columns. Also contains up-to-date market trends as well as thorough auction updates and reports from toy shows nationwide.
Cost: $33.98
76 Pages
Circulation: 11577
Founded in 1988
Mailing list available for rent

13602 Trapper & Predator
F+W Media
38 E. 29th Street
New York, NY 10016

212-447-1400
Fax: 212-447-5231
E-Mail: contact_us@fwmedia.com
Home Page: www.fwpublications.com
Social Media: Facebook, Twitter, LinkedIn

Hugh McAloon, Publisher
Paul Wait, Editor
Jim Ogle, Chief Financial Officer
Chad Phelps, Chief Digital Officer
Stacie Berger, Communications Director

Contains news, in-depth features, and how-to tips on trapping, the art of predator calling, and animal damage control. Contributors include the top names in the business. Regular columns and departments include 'The Fure Shed,' 'Let's Swap Ideas,' 'Q&A,' and news from state trapping associations nationwide.
Cost: $18.95
80 Pages
Circulation: 38260
Founded in 1975
Mailing list available for rent

13603 Tuff Stuff
F+W Media
38 E. 29th Street
New York, NY 10016

212-447-1400
Fax: 212-447-5231
E-Mail: contact_us@fwmedia.com
Home Page: www.fwpublications.com
Social Media: Facebook, Twitter, LinkedIn

Dean Listle, Publisher
Rocky Landsverk, Editor
Jim Ogle, Chief Financial Officer
Chad Phelps, Chief Digital Officer
Stacie Berger, Communications Director

A guide to the sports card and collectibles hobby. Coverage of sports cards includes the latest prices on baseball, football, basketball, hockey, racing, and more. Each issue lists pricing information on Hall of Fame baseball and football memorabilia, autographed items, and commentary on the sports card industry. Columns and opinion pieces include a Q&A section, directories to professional teams, geographical and product directories, and hobby dealer listings for the US and Canada.
Cost: $29.95
Frequency: Monthly
Circulation: 175,682
Founded in 1983
Mailing list available for rent

13604 Turkey & Turkey Hunting
F+W Media
38 E. 29th Street
New York, NY 10016

212-447-1400
Fax: 212-447-5231
E-Mail: contact_us@fwmedia.com
Home Page: www.fwpublications.com
Social Media: Facebook, Twitter, LinkedIn

David Nussbaum, CEO/Chairman
James Schlender, Editor
Jim Ogle, Chief Financial Officer
Chad Phelps, Chief Digital Officer
Stacie Berger, Communications Director

Edited for serious, technical, year-round, gun and bow turkey hunters. Features emphasize success and enjoyment of the sport. Articles

focus on hunting, scouting, turkey behavior and biology, hunting ethics, new equipment, methodologies, turkey management, and current research. Columns include 'Tree Call,' 'Mail Pouch,' 'Turkey Biology,' a Q&A column, 'Hunter's Library,' 'Turkey Gear,' and 'Last Call.'
Cost: $15.95
72 Pages
Circulation: 68962
Founded in 1975
Mailing list available for rent

13605 Weekend Woodcrafts
EGW.com
1041 Shary Circle
Concord, CA 94518-2407

925-671-9852
Fax: 925-671-0692
E-Mail: info@egw.com
Home Page: www.weekendwoodcrafts.com

Chris Slaughter, Circulation Director
Rickie Wilson, Advertising

Wide selection of easy-to-finish wood projects ranging from craft fair novelties and decorative home-accents to useful housewares and wooden toys.
Cost: $35.94
68 Pages
Frequency: Monthly
Founded in 1980

13606 Wood Strokes
EGW.com
1041 Shary Circle
Concord, CA 94518-2407

925-671-9852
Fax: 925-671-0692
E-Mail: info@egw.com
Home Page: www.egw.com

Chris Slaughter, Circulation Manager

Wide selection of easy-to-finish decorative wood painting projects ranging from craft fair novelties and decorative home accents to useful housewares and wooden toys.
Cost: $5.99
76 Pages
Circulation: 110437

13607 World Coin News
F+W Media
38 E. 29th Street
New York, NY 10016
212-447-1400
Fax: 212-447-5231
E-Mail: contact_us@fwmedia.com
Home Page: www.fwpublications.com
Social Media: Facebook, Twitter, LinkedIn

Bill Bright, General Manager
Dave Harper, Editor
Jim Ogle, Chief Financial Officer
Chad Phelps, Chief Digital Officer
Stacie Berger, Communications Director

Recognized as the leading authority on world coins. It regularly reports on new issues, auctions and other coin news from around the world. Features by some of the top experts in the field provide in-depth historical information on coins and the countries that issue them. Regular features include World Coin Clinic (Q&A), World Coin Roundup (newly issued coins), Rule Britannia, Nautical Numismatics, Mexican Potpourri, and Coin Critters. Each issue provides a calendar of shows.
Cost: $30.99
84 Pages
Frequency: Monthly
Circulation: 8729
Founded in 1952
Mailing list available for rent

Trade Shows

13608 ACC Craft Show
American Craft Council
21 S Eltings Corner Road
Highland, NY 12528

845-883-6100
800-836-3670
Fax: 845-883-6130
E-Mail: shows@craftcouncil.org
Home Page: www.craftcouncil.org

Craft fair.
Frequency: Annual

13609 APS Stampshow
American Philatelic Society
100 Match Factory Place
Ballefonte, PA 16823

814-373-3803
Fax: 814-933-6128
E-Mail: stampshow@stamps.org
Home Page: www.stamps.org

Kenneth P Martin, Executive Director
Dana Guyer, Shows/Exhibits

Annual show for postage stamp collectors. Includes 150 dealers buying and selling material, more than 100 seminars, and 10,000 pages of stamps in collection.
6,000 Attendees
Frequency: Annual

13610 AQSG Conference and Annual Meeting
American Quilt Study Group
1610 L St
Lincoln, NE 68508-2509

402-477-1181
Fax: 402-477-1183
E-Mail: aqsg2@americanquiltstudygroup.org
Home Page: www.americanquiltstudygroup.org
Social Media: Twitter, LinkedIn

Lisa Erlandsonn, President
Lenna DeMarco, VP
Flavin Glover, VP
Judy J. Brott Buss, Ph.D., Executive Director
Anne E. Schuff, Member Services Coordinator

For members. Research presentations and quilt and textile study
200 Attendees
Frequency: Annual
Mailing list available for rent

13611 ASD/AMD Group
Flectcher
2950 31st Street
Suite 100
Santa Monica, CA 90405

310-255-4633
Fax: 310-396-8476

15000 Attendees

13612 AmeriStamp Expo
American Philatelic Society
100 Match Factory Place
Bellafonte, PA 16823
814-373-3803
Fax: 814-933-6128
E-Mail: stampshow@stamps.org
Home Page: www.stamps.org

Ken Martin, Director Shows/Exhibitions

Annual event for postage stamp collectors, featuring 75 dealers, 50 meetings and services, auction, 5,000 pages of exhibits and beginner actions.
2,500 Attendees
Frequency: Annual
Founded in 1998

13613 American Camping Association Conference & Exhibits
5000 State Road 67 N
Martinsville, IN 46151-7902

765-342-8456
800-428-2267
Fax: 765-342-2065
E-Mail: bwilliems@aca-camps.org
Home Page: http://www.acacamps.org

Peg Smith, CEO
Bill Willems, Director Business

One hundred fifty booths of arts and crafts, computer software, sporting goods, waterfront equipment and more plus a seminar and workshop.
1,200 Attendees
Frequency: Annual
Founded in 1943

13614 American Craft Council Fairs
ACC
21 S Elting Corners Road
Highland, NY 12528-2805

845-883-6100
800-836-3470
Fax: 612-355-2330
E-Mail: shows@craftcouncil.org
Home Page: www.craftcouncil.org

Nine fairs nationwide each year. Each show incorporates crafts from the ceramics, wood, metal, mixed media, fiber, glass, jewelry, accessories and related industries. Most fairs include retail portion (public sales); some fairs also have wholesale (trade) component.

13615 American International Toy Fair
Toy Industry Association
1115 Broadway
Suite 400
New York, NY 10010

212-675-1141
Fax: 212-675-3246
Home Page: www.toy-tia.org

Laura Green, VP Trade Shows/Meetings
Diane Cardinale, Public Information Manager

1,800-2,000 booths for producers of all types of toys and games, party and holiday items, models, hobby products, as well as collectibles, dolls, plush and miniatures. Attendees are retail buyers and trade professionals. Seminar and program.
20000 Attendees
Frequency: Annual
Founded in 1903

13616 American Needlepoint Guild Show
3410 Valley Creek Circle
Middleton, WI 53562-1990

608-831-3328
Fax: 608-831-0651
E-Mail: seminars@needlepoint.org
Home Page: www.needlepoint.org

Estelle Kelley, Seminars Director

Two hundred exhibits of needlework pieces, banquet and luncheon.
830 Attendees
Frequency: Annual
Founded in 1972

13617 American Numismatic Association Trade Show
8181 N Cascade Avenue
Colorado Springs, CO 80903
719-632-2646
E-Mail: webmaster@money.org
Home Page: www.money.org
Brenda Bishop, Show Manager
Nancy Green, Manager
Four hundred twenty five booths of coins, medals and paper money.
15M Attendees
Frequency: August

13618 American Quilt Study Group
American Quilt Study Group
1610 L St
Lincoln, NE 68508-2509
402-477-1181
Fax: 402-477-1181
E-Mail: aqsg2@americanquiltstudygroup.org
Home Page: www.americanquiltstudygroup.org
Social Media: Twitter, LinkedIn
Lisa Erlandsonn, President
Lenna DeMarco, Vice President
Kathy Moore, VP
Judy J. Brott Buss, Ph.D., Executive Director
Anne E. Schuff, Member Services Coordinator
Annual Seminar, Annual Journal member organization
Frequency: October, Kansas
Founded in 1980
Mailing list available for rent

13619 American Stamp Dealers Association Stamp Shows
3 School Street
Suite 201
Glen Cove, NY 11542-2548
516-759-7000
Fax: 800-369-8207
Joseph Savarese, Show Manager/Executive VP
Two hundred booths.
12.5M Attendees

13620 Americover
American First Day Cover Society
PO Box 1335
Maplewood, NJ 07040
973-762-2012
Fax: 973-762-7916
E-Mail: webmaster@afdcs.org
Home Page: www.afdcs.org
Steve Ripley, Show Manager
US and international first day postal covers, USPS first day ceremonies at most shows, 50 stamp dealers, cover dealers, cachetmalchers philatelic suppliers.
1500 Attendees
Frequency: Annual

13621 Annual Spring-Easter Arts & Crafts Show & Sale
Finger Lakes Craftsmen Shows
1 Freshour Road
Shortsville, NY 14548
585-289-9439
Fax: 585-289-9440
Ronald L Johnson, President
Annual show of 150 exhibitirs of arts and crafts manufacturers. Exhibits include handcrafted arts and crafts, including photos and prints.
9000 Attendees
Frequency: March
Founded in 1999

13622 Antique Arms Show
P.O. Box 2917
Cathedral City, CA 92234
760- 20- 448
Fax: 760-202-4793
Home Page: www.antiquearmsshow.com
Wallace Beinfield
Public show with 850 booths of antiques and collectibles.
4M Attendees
Frequency: January

13623 Association of Crafts and Creative Industries Show: ACCI Show
Offinger Management Company
1100-H Brandywine Boulevard
PO Box 3388
Zanesville, OH 43702
740-452-4541
888-360-2224
Fax: 740-452-2552
E-Mail: accishow@offinger.com
Home Page: www.accicrafts.org
Social Media: Facebook, Twitter, LinkedIn
Marrijane Jones, Executive Director
Erica McKenzie, ACCI Communications Manager
The ACCI Show is sponsored by the Association of Crafts and Creative Industries. Over 1,300 booths are represented, featuring general crafts, softcrafts, art materials and framing, scrapbooking materials and floral, home and garden items.
8000+ Attendees
Frequency: Annual

13624 Christmas Gift & Hobby Show
HSI Show Productions
PO Box 502797
Indianapolis, IN 46250
317-576-9933
800-215-1700
Fax: 317-576-9955
E-Mail: info@hsishows.com
Home Page: www.hsishows.com
Donell Hebererwalton, Sales Director
Todd Jameson, Show Manager
45000 Attendees

13625 Christmas Gift and Hobby Show
HSI Show Productions
PO Box 502797
Indianapolis, IN 46250-7797
317-576-9933
800-215-1700
Fax: 317-576-9955
E-Mail: info@hsishows.com
Home Page: www.hsishows.com
Donell Hebererwalton, Sales Director
Todd Jameson, Show Manager
Annual show of 360 exhibitors of arts, crafts and giftware.
70M Attendees

13626 Coin and Stamp Exposition: San Francisco
Bick International
PO Box 854
Van Nuys, CA 91408
818-997-6496
Fax: 818-988-4337
E-Mail: iibick@sbcglobal.net
Home Page: www.bick.net
Israel I Bick, Managing Director
5000 Attendees
Frequency: June/September, Annually

13627 Doll, Teddy Bear & Toy Show & Sale
Jones Publishing
9572 Forest Hills Lodge & Route 173
Rockford, IL 54945-5000
715-445-5000
JoAnn Reynolds, Contact
Great assortment of toys featuring teddy bears of all kinds.

13628 Eastern States Doll, Toy, and Teddy Bear Show and Sale
Maven Company
PO Box 937
Plandome, NY 11030
914-248-4646
Fax: 914-248-0800
Home Page: www.mavencompany.com
N Chittenden, VP
Wide variety of dolls, toys and teddy bears. Largest show of its kind in the northeast.
5000 Attendees
Frequency: November/April
Founded in 1982

13629 Ed Expo
National School Supply & Equipment Association
8380 Colesville Road
Suite 250
Silver Spring, MD 20910
301 495-0240
800-395-5550
Fax: 301-495-3330
E-Mail: nssea@nssea.org
Home Page: www.nssea.org
Bill Duffy, VP Operations
Adrienne Dayton, VP Marketing
The world's premier back-to-school purchasing event, specifically geared toward helping the educational products/parent-teacher retailer, cataloger and full-line distributor find the best teaching tools and resources for the classrooms of today, tomorrow and the future.
3000 Attendees
Frequency: Annual/April

13630 HIA: Hobby Industries of America Trade Show
Hobby Industries of America
319 E 54th Street
PO Box 348
Elmwood Park, NJ 07407
201-794-1133
Fax: 201-798-0657
E-Mail: sberger@craftandhobby.org
Home Page: www.hobby.org
Steve Berger, Executive Director
International trade show open to qualified professionals and is the industry's only market research show.
10000 Attendees

13631 Halloween Costume and Party Show
TransWorld Exhibits
1850 Oak Street
Northfield, IL 60093
847-784-6905
800-323-5462
Fax: 847-446-3523
Home Page: www.transworldexhibits.com
Don Olstinske, Manager
Stephanie Geitner, Operations Director

13632 International Coin + Stamp Collection Society
Bick International
PO Box 854
Van Nuys, CA 91408
818-997-6496
Fax: 818-988-4337

E-Mail: iibick@sbcglobal.net
Home Page: www.bick.net

Israel I Bick, Managing Director
5000 Attendees
Frequency: Annual/December/May, NV

13633 International Gift and Collectible Expo
F+W Media
38 E. 29th Street
New York, NY 10016

212-447-1400
Fax: 212-447-5231
E-Mail: contact_us@fwmedia.com
Home Page: www.fwpublications.com
Social Media: Twitter, LinkedIn

Claude Chmiel, Show Producer
John Swinburn, Executive Director
17000 Attendees
Frequency: June

13634 International JPMA Show
Juvenile Products Manufacturers Association
15000 Commerce Parkway
Suite C
Mt Laurel, NJ 08054

856-439-0500
Fax: 856-439-0525
Home Page: www.jpma.org

Linda Still, Director of Trade Show

Items of interest to retailers of children's apparel and toys.
3000 Attendees
Frequency: Annual

13635 International Miniature Collectibles Trade Show
10 Estes Street
Ipswich, MA 1938

978-356-6500
800-653-2726
Fax: 978-356-6565
Home Page: www.connection.ebscohost.com
Social Media: Facebook, Twitter, LinkedIn

Frequency: August

13636 Just Kidstuff & The Museum Source
George Little Management
10 Bank Street
Suite 1200
White Plains, NY 10606

914-486-6070
800-272-7469
Fax: 914-948-2918

George Little II, President
45000 Attendees

13637 Knitting Guild Association Conference
The Knitting Guild Association (TKGA)
1100-H Brandwine Blvd.
Zanesville, OH 43701-7303

740-452-4541
Fax: 740-452-2552
E-Mail: tkga@tkga.com
Home Page: www.tkga.com
Social Media: Facebook, Twitter, LinkedIn

Penny Sitler, Executive Director

The TKGA conference is held twice each year and offers items such as fiber, stitching tools, patterns, books, finishing accessories and more.
10000 Members
Mailing list available for rent

13638 National Dollhouse & Miniatures Trade Show & Convention
Miniatures Association of America
10 Estes Street
Ipswich, MA 1938

978-356-6500
800-653-2726
Fax: 978-356-6565
Home Page: www.connection.ebscohost.com
Social Media: Facebook, Twitter, LinkedIn

1400 Attendees

13639 National Merchandise Show
Miller Freeman Publications
One Penn Plaza
PO Box 2549
New York, NY 10119

212-714-1300
Fax: 212-714-1313

16000 Attendees

13640 National NeedleArts Association Trade Show
National Needlework Association
PO Box 3388
Zanesville, OH 43702-3388

740-452-4541
800-889-8662
Fax: 740-452-2552
E-Mail: tnna.info@offinger.com
Home Page: www.tnna.org

Joel Woodcock, VP
Frequency: January

13641 National Sewing Show: Home Sewing Association
American Home Sewing and Craft Association
1350 Broadway
Suite 1601
New York, NY 10018

212-714-1633
Fax: 212-714-1655
E-Mail: info@sewing.org
Home Page: www.sewing.org

Pat Kobishyn, Show Manager

Two hundred exhibits of fabric, notions, patterns, sewing and trimmings. Attended by professionals from major chain stores, independent retailers, wholesalers and manufacturers.
3000 Attendees
Frequency: Annual

13642 SHOPA
SHOPA
3131 Elbee Road
Dayton, OH 45439-1900

937-297-2250
800-854-7467
Fax: 937-297-2254
Home Page: www.shopa.org

Steven Jacober, President
Doris Condron, Director of Communications
7500 Attendees
Frequency: November

13643 School Equipment Show
National School Supply & Equipment Association
8380 Colesville Rd
Suite 250
Silver Spring, MD 20910-6225

301-495-0240
800-395-5550
Fax: 301-495-3330
E-Mail: customerservice@nssea.org
Home Page: www.nssea.org
Social Media: Facebook, Twitter, LinkedIn

Jim McGarry, President/CEO
Rashad Cheeks, Meetings Coordinator
Tamara Davis, Bookkeeper/Office Manager
Karen Prince, Director of Membership
Bill Duffy, Vice President - Operations

Source new products, engage in industry discussion, hear perspectives on current issues, and network with existing and potential new suppliers, distributors and purchasing influencers.
Frequency: Annual/November

13644 Souvenirs Gifts & Novelties Trade Association
Kane Communications
7000 Terminal Square
Suite 210
Upper Darby, PA 19082-2330

610-734-2420
Fax: 610-734-2423
Home Page: www.souvmag.com

Al Barry, Show Manager
Larry White, VP Marketing

Trade show serving amusements, museums, zoos, entertainment, bowling, and retailers. Seminars and networking party.
5000 Attendees
Frequency: July

13645 Variety Merchandise Show
Miller Freeman Publications
One Penn Plaza
PO Box 2549
New York, NY 10119

212-714-1300
Fax: 212-714-1313

20000 Attendees

13646 Western States Toy and Hobby Show
Western Toy and Hobby Representative Association
9397 Reserve Drive
Corona, CA 92883

951-771-1598
Fax: 909-277-1599
Home Page: www.wthra.com

Phylis St. John, Contact

If it's for kids, it's here. Show is for trade members only, not open to the public.
3000 Attendees
Frequency: March

13647 iHobby Expo
Hobby Manufacturers Association
PO Box 315
Butter, NJ 07405-0315

973-283-9088
Fax: 973-838-7124
E-Mail: pat.koziol@hmahobby.org
Home Page: www.hmahobby.org
Social Media: Twitter, LinkedIn

Patricia S. Koziol, Executive Director
Jodi Araujo, Expositions and Events Manager

Models, trains, rc, cars, boats, planes and more
Frequency: October

Directories & Databases

13648 American International Toy Fair Official Directory of Showrooms & Exhibits
Toy Industry Association
1115 Broadway
Suite 400
New York, NY 10010-3466

212-675-1142
Fax: 212-633-1429

E-Mail: info@toy-tia.org
Home Page: www.toy-tia.org

Thomas Conley, President
Diane Cardinale, Public Information Manager

Over 1,500 toy, game and hobby decoration manufacturers and their representatives are profiled.
Cost: $50.00
400 Pages
Frequency: Annual
Circulation: 12,000

13649 Complete Directory of Collectibles
Sutton Family Communications & Publishing Company
920 State Route 54 East
Elmitch, KY 42343

270-276-9500
E-Mail: jlsutton@apex.net

Theresa Sutton, Publisher
Lee Sutton, Editor

Print-out from database of wholesalers, manufacturers, distributors, importers and close-out houses. Database is updated daily to guarantee the most current and up-to-date sources available.
Cost: $67.50
100 Pages

13650 Complete Directory of Crafts and Hobbies
Sutton Family Communications & Publishing Company
920 State Route 54 East
Elmitch, KY 42343

270-276-9500
E-Mail: jlsutton@apex.net

Theresa Sutton, Editor
Lee Sutton, General Manager

Print-out from database of wholesalers, manufacturers, distributors, importers and close-out houses. Database is updated daily to guarantee the most current and up-to-date sources available.
Cost: $54.50
100+ Pages

13651 Complete Directory of Figurines
Sutton Family Communications & Publishing Company
920 State Route 54 East
Elmitch, KY 42343

270-276-9500
E-Mail: jlsutton@apex.net

Theresa Sutton, Publisher
Lee Sutton, Editor

Print-out from database of wholesalers, manufacturers, distributors, importers and close-out houses. Database is updated daily to guarantee the most current and up-to-date sources available.
Cost: $44.50
100 Pages

13652 Complete Directory of Games
Sutton Family Communications & Publishing Company
920 State Route 54 East
Elmitch, KY 42343

270-276-9500
E-Mail: jlsutton@apex.net

Theresa Sutton, Publisher
Lee Sutton, Editor

Print-out from database of wholesalers, manufacturers, distributors, importers and close-out houses. Database is updated daily to guarantee the most current and up-to-date sources available.
Cost: $39.50
100 Pages

13653 Complete Directory of Novelties
Sutton Family Communications & Publishing Company
920 State Route 54 East
Elmitch, KY 42343

270-276-9500
E-Mail: jlsutton@apex.net

Theresa Sutton, Publisher
Lee Sutton, Editor

Print-out from database of wholesalers, manufacturers, distributors, importers and close-out houses. Database is updated daily to guarantee the most current and up-to-date sources available.
Cost: $79.50
100 Pages

13654 Complete Directory of Pewter Items
Sutton Family Communications & Publishing Company
920 State Route 54 East
Elmitch, KY 42343

270-276-9500
E-Mail: jlsutton@apex.net

Theresa Sutton, Publisher
Lee Sutton, Editor

Print-out from database of wholesalers, manufacturers, distributors, importers and close-out houses. Database is updated daily to guarantee the most current and up-to-date sources available.
Cost: $39.50
100 Pages

13655 Complete Directory of Plush and Stuffed Toys and Dolls
Sutton Family Communications & Publishing Company
920 State Route 54 East
Elmitch, KY 42343

270-276-9500
E-Mail: jlsutton@apex.net

Theresa Sutton, Editor
Lee Sutton, General Manager

Print-out from database of wholesalers, manufacturers, distributors, importers and close-out houses. Database is updated daily to guarantee the most current and up-to-date sources available.
Cost: $39.50
100+ Pages

13656 Complete Directory of Posters, Buttons and Novelties
Sutton Family Communications & Publishing Company
920 State Route 54 East
Elmitch, KY 42343

270-276-9500
E-Mail: jlsutton@apex.net

Theresa Sutton, Editor
Lee Sutton, General Manager

Print-out from database of wholesalers, manufacturers, distributors, importers and close-out houses. Database is updated daily to guarantee the most current and up-to-date sources available.
Cost: $39.50
100+ Pages

13657 Complete Directory of Toys and Games
Sutton Family Communications & Publishing Company
920 State Route 54 East
Elmitch, KY 42343

270-276-9500
E-Mail: jlsutton@apex.net

Theresa Sutton, Editor
Lee Sutton, General Manager

Print-out from database of wholesalers, manufacturers, distributors, importers and close-out houses. Database is updated daily to guarantee the most current and up-to-date sources available.
Cost: $44.50
100+ Pages

13658 Directory of Manufacturer Representatives Service Suppliers
Hobby Industry Association
319 E 54th St
Elmwood Park, NJ 07407-2712

201-794-1133
Fax: 201-797-0657
E-Mail: sberger@craftandhobby.org
Home Page: www.craftandhobby.org

Steve Berger, CEO

Two hundred manufacturers representatives and 105 trade show booth demonstrators working in the hobby equipment industry.
Cost: $25.00
Frequency: Biennial

13659 Game Manufacturers Association Membership Directory
Game Manufacturers Association
240 N. Fifth St.
Suite 340
Columbus, OH 43215

614-255-4500
Fax: 614-255-4499
E-Mail: ops@gama.org
Home Page: www.gama.org
Social Media: Twitter, LinkedIn

John Ward, Executive Director
John Kaufeld, Marketing/Sales
Jonda Crutcher, Office Coordinator
Angela Ward, Financial Director
Betsy Kaplan, Sales Coordinator

Approximately 350 member manufacturers and distributors of adventure games.
Frequency: \nnual
Founded in 1977
Mailing list available for rent

13660 Games and Entertainment on CD-ROM
Mecklermedia Corporation
20 Ketchum Street
Westport, CT 06880-5908

203-341-2806
Fax: 203-454-5840

Over 1,300 multimedia encyclopedias, children's educational software and interactive 'board games'.
Cost: $29.95

13661 Hobby Industries of America Trade Show Program and Buyers Guide
Hobby Industry Association
319 E 54th St
Elmwood Park, NJ 07407-2712

201-794-1133
Fax: 201-797-0657
E-Mail: hia@ihobby.org
Home Page: www.craftandhobby.org

Steve Berger, CEO

Over 1000 manufacturers are listed that exhibit at the HIA trade show.
Cost: $25.00
170 Pages
Frequency: Annual
Founded in 1940

13662 **Hobby Merchandiser Annual Trade Directory**
Hobby Publications
207 Commercial Ct
Morganville, NJ 07751-1099

732-536-5160
Fax: 732-536-5761
Home Page: www.hobbypub.com

David Gherman, President
Jeff Troy, Editor
Ellen Gherman, Circulation Director
Tracey Decesure, Production Manager

Offers valuable information on manufacturers, wholesalers, industry suppliers and publishers of books and periodicals in the hobby trade industry.
Cost: $35.00
140 Pages
Frequency: Annual
Circulation: 7,000
Founded in 1945
Mailing list available for rent: 8M names
Printed in 4 colors on glossy stock

13663 **Hobby RoundTable**
GE Information Services
401 N Washington Street
Rockville, MD 20850-1707

301-388-8284

Cathy Ge, Owner

This database offers a forum enabling participants to share information on hobby-related topics, the hobby industry and hobby-related software.
Frequency: Bulletin Board

13664 **Radio Control Hobby Membership Directory**
Radio Control Hobby Trade Association
31632 N Ellis Avenue
Unit 111
Volo, IL 60073

847-740-1111
Fax: 847-740-1111
Home Page: www.rchta.org

Members and manufacturers of radio control products.
Founded in 1983

Industry Web Sites

13665 **http://gold.greyhouse.com**
G.O.L.D Grey House OnLine Databases

Grey House Publishing's online database platform, GOLD, offers Quick Search, Keyword Search and Expert Search for most business sectors including hobby and game markets. The GOLD platform makes finding the information you need quick and easy - whether you're a novice searcher or an experienced database user. All of Grey House's directory products are available for subscription on the GOLD platform.

13666 **www.amo-archery.org**
Archery Manufacturers & Merchants Organization

Members are producers and sellers to the archery consumer.

13667 **www.asdaonline.com**
American Stamp Dealers Association

Holds annual International Philatelic Exhibition Interpex. Sponsors the annual International Dealers course. Postage stamp mega event twice a year (spring and fall).

13668 **www.craftdesigners.org**
Society of Craft Designers

The Society of Craft Designers (SCD), founded in 1975, is a professional organization for those who believe that quality craft design is the basis of a strong and viable craft industry. It is the only membership organization exclusively serving those who design for the consumer craft industry.

13669 **www.greyhouse.com**
Grey House Publishing

Authoritative reference directories for most business sectors including hobby and game markets. Users can search the online databases with varied search criteria allowing for custom searches by product category, geographic area, sales volume, keyword, subject and more. Full Grey House catalog and online ordering also available.

13670 **www.hobby.org**
Hobby Industry Association

The world's largest trade association in the craft and hobby market. The group produces an International Trade Show open to qualified professionals and is the industrys only market research show.

13671 **www.mria.org**
Model Railroad Industry Association

Works to publicize the hobby and to keep members informed on the industry. Assists clubs and retailers in their shows.

13672 **www.nssea.org**
Naitonal School Supplu Equipment

Trade Association for the educational products industry.

13673 **www.rchta.org**
Radio Control Hobby Trade Association

For manufacturers and distributors of model hobby kits and hobby equipment, supplies and services and products associated with retail hobby stores.

13674 **www.stamps.org**
American Philatelic Society

National organization for stamp collectors; lending library; insurance for philatelic materials; sales division, seminars and annual conventions open to the public.

13675 **www.tkga.com**
The Knitting Guild Association (TKGA)

Membership organization for knitters with focus on knitting education and enhancing knitter's skills

13676 **www.tnna.org**
National Needlework Association

For maufacturers, suppliers and distributers of needlework and related equipment, supplies and services.

13677 **www.toyassociation.org**
Toy Industry Association

National organization for U.S. producers and importers of toys, games and children's entertainment products. Represents more than 500 member companies including designers, safety consultants, testing laboratories, licensors, communication professionals and inventors.

13678 **www.wccwis.gr.jp/home.html**
World Craft Council

A national organization for Handicraft

Associations

13679 American Hotel & Lodging Association
1201 New York Ave NW
Suite 600
Washington, DC 20005-3931
202-289-3100
Fax: 202-289-3199
E-Mail: webmaster@ahla.com
Home Page: www.ahla.com
Social Media: Facebook, Twitter, LinkedIn

Ronald L Vlasic, Chair of the Board
John Fitzpatrick, Vice-Chair
Joseph A McInerney, CHA, President/CEO
James Abrahamson, Secretary/ Treasurer

Supports all those involved in managing or franchising properties worldwide. Publishes annual directory.
10000 Members
Founded in 1910

13680 American Hotel & Lodging Educational Institute
800 N. Magnolia Avenue
Suite 300
Orlando, FL 32803
517-372-8800
800-344-4381
Fax: 202-289-3199
E-Mail: webmaster@ahla.com
Home Page: www.ahlei.org/
Social Media: Facebook, Twitter, LinkedIn, Google Plus, Youtube, Instagra

Robert L Steele, III, CHA, President and COO
Ed Kastli, Vice President, International Sales
George Glazer, CMHS, Senior Vice President
Chris Jack, Vice President, Certification
Joshua Sumption, Vice President, Information

Fosters education, research programming, and information regarding operating techniques in the lodging industry.
11000 Members
Founded in 1910

13681 Asian/American Hotel Owners Association
Asian American Hotel Owners Association
7000 Peachtree Dunwoody Road NE
Building 7
Atlanta, GA 30328
404-816-5759
Fax: 404-816-6260
E-Mail: info@aahoa.com
Home Page: www.aahoa.com
Social Media: Facebook, Twitter, LinkedIn, Youtube

Fred Schwartz, President
Laura Lee Blake, CHO, V.P., Fair Franchising & Government
Jonathan Albano, Vice President of Membership
Don Bollmer, Vice President of Finance
Geetika Patel, Director of Membership & HR

Supports Asian/American hotel and motel owners and operators.
8,700 Members
Founded in 1989

13682 Associated Luxury Hotels International
1000 Connecticut Ave Nw
Suite 603
Washington, DC 20036-5302
202-887-0085
Fax: 202-887-0085
E-Mail: meetings@alhi.com
Home Page: www.alhi.com
Social Media: Facebook, Twitter

Jim Schultenover, President
David Gabri, Chief Executive Officer
Don Macumber, Executive Vice President
Mike Coutu, Executive VP & CFO
Ashly Balding, Division VP - East

Provided a National Sales Network to associations and corporations in America for the distinguished hotels and resorts now in 26 states, Canada, Mexico, and the Caribbean.
Founded in 1987

13683 Bed and Breakfast League
PO Box 9490
Washington, DC 20016-9490
202-363-7767
Fax: 202-363-8396
E-Mail: bedandbreakfast/washingtondc@erols.com

Millie Groobey, Director

A reservation service for bed and breakfasts in Washington, DC, that welcome selected travelers into their homes.
Founded in 1976

13684 Educational Institute of the American Hotel & Lodging Association
2113 N High St
Lansing, MI 48906-4221
517-372-8800
800-752-4567
Fax: 517-372-5141
E-Mail: info@ei-ahla.org
Home Page: www.ei-ahla.org
Social Media: Facebook, Twitter

George Glazer, VP
Anthony Farris, Chairman
Thomas J. Corcoran Jr., Vice Chair
Brenda Moons, Senior Vice President of Sales
K.V. Simon, Regional Vice President

A nonprofit educational foundation of the American Hotel & Lodging Association and the world's largest provider of hospitality education training resources, videos, books, workbooks, seminars, management courses, complete training systems and professional certification programs.
120 Members
Founded in 1953

13685 Hospitality Financial & Technology Professionals
11709 Boulder Lane
Suite 110
Austin, TX 78726-1832
512-249-5333
800-646-4387
Fax: 512-249-1533
E-Mail: membership@hftp.org
Home Page: www.hftp.org
Social Media: Facebook, Twitter, LinkedIn

Jerry Trieber, CPA, CHAE, CF, President
Daniel N Conti, Jr., CHAE, CAM, Vice President
Ian Millar, CHTP, Treasurer
Arlene Ramirez, MBA, CHE, CHA, Secretary
Lucinda Hart, Chief Operations Officer

Professional society for those in the financial segment of the hospitality industry.
4300 Members
Founded in 1954
Mailing list available for rent

13686 Hotel Employees and Restaurant Employees
275 7th Avenue
New York, NY 10001-6708
212-265-7000
E-Mail: ccarrera@unitehere.org
Home Page: www.unitehere.org
Social Media: Facebook, Twitter, Google Plus

Bruce S Raynor, General President
John W Wihelm, President,Hospitality Industry

Hosts a diverse membership, comprised largely of immigrants and including high percentages of African-American, Latino, and Asia-American workers. The majority of members are women.
850m Members
Founded in 1891

13687 International Council on Hotel, Restaurant and Institutional Education
2810 North Parham Road
Suite 230
Richmond, VA 23294
804-346-4800
Fax: 804-346-5009
E-Mail: webmaster@chrie.org
Home Page: www.chrie.org
Social Media: Facebook, Twitter, LinkedIn

Dennis Reynolds, President
Kathy McCartyў, Chief Executive Officer
Martin O'Neill, ViceўPresident
Chris Roberts, Secretary
Stephanie Hein, Treasurer

A nonprofit professional association which provides programs and services to continually improve the quality of global education, research, service, and business operations in the hospitality and tourism industry.
Founded in 1946

13688 International Executive Housekeepers Association
1001 Eastwind Drive
Suite 301
Westerville, OH 43081-3361
614-895-7166
800-200-6342
Fax: 614-895-1248
E-Mail: excel@ieha.org
Home Page: www.ieha.org
Social Media: Facebook, Twitter, LinkedIn

Sherry Sidwell, President
Beth Risinger, CEO/Executive Director
Anna Rodriguez, Secretary/Treasurer
Janet Wiggins, President-Elect
Tina Chubb, Convention Manager

An organization for persons working in the housekeeping area of the lodging industry.
3500 Members
Founded in 1930

13689 International Facility Management Association
800 Gessner Rd
Suite 900
Houston, TX 77024-4257
713-623-4362
Fax: 713-623-6124
E-Mail: ifma@ifma.org
Home Page: www.ifma.org
Social Media: Facebook, Twitter, LinkedIn, Flickr, Youtube

Jon Seller, Chair
Tony Keane, CAE, President and CEO
James P Whittaker, P.E., CFM,, First Vice Chair
Michael D Feldman, FMP, CM, Second Vice Chair
Michael D Moss, CAE, Chief Operating Officer

Certifies facility managers, conducts research, provides educational programs, recognizes facility management degree and certificate programs and produces World Workplace, the

world's largest facility management conference and exposition.
19000 Members
Founded in 1980
Mailing list available for rent

13690 National Bed & Breakfast Association
1011 W Fifth Street
Suite 300
Austin, TX 78703

512-322-2710
Fax: 512-320-0883
E-Mail: Sales@BedandBreakfast.com
Home Page: www.bedandbreakfast.com
Social Media: Facebook, Twitter, Pinterest, Google Plus

John Banczac, Vice President
Denis Kashkin, Sr. Directory of Technology
Eric Goldreyer, Founder & President

An organization of services and supplies to the industry offering a list of the best in bed and breakfast accommodations in the USA, Canada and the Caribbean.
Founded in 1981
Mailing list available for rent

13691 Preferred Hotels and Resorts Worldwide
311 S Wacker Dr
Suite 1900
Chicago, IL 60606-6676

312-913-0400
866-990-9491
Fax: 312-913-5124
E-Mail: info@preferredhotels.com
Home Page: www.preferredhotels.com
Social Media: Facebook, Twitter, Google Plus, Youtube, Pinteres

John Ubberoth, CEO
Nora Gainer, Director Marketing

Independently owned luxury hotels and resorts. Each provides the highest standards of quality and extraordinary service.
120 Members
Founded in 1968

13692 Professional Association of Innkeepers International
295 Seven Farms Drive
Suite 236-C
Charleston, SC 29492

856-310-1102
800-468-7244
Fax: 856-310-1105
E-Mail: membership@paii.org
Home Page: www.paii.org

Jay Karen, CEO
Isabel Abreu, Membership Sales Manager
Brook Patterson, Director of Vendor Services
Ingrid Thorson, Marketing & Communications Manager
Jessie Robinson, Director of Education & Events

Serving bed and breakfast/country inn owners, aspiring innkeepers, inn sitters, vendors with educational and consultative services. International conference.
3000 Members
Founded in 1988

13693 Select Registry
501 East Michigan Avenue
PO Box 150
Marshall, MI 49068

269-789-0393
800-344-5244
Fax: 269-789-0970
E-Mail: maincontact@selectregistry.com
Home Page: www.selectregistry.com/
Social Media: Facebook, Twitter

Will Carlson, Executive Director
Carol Riggs, Membership/Quality Assurance
Lois Huver, Marketing Coordinator
Tina Amsler, Business/Administrative Coordinator

Represents the finest country inns, B&Bs, and unique small hotels from California to Nova-Scotia. The very best the travel industry has to offer.
400 Members
Founded in 1968
Mailing list available for rent

13694 Small Luxury Hotels
14673 Midway Road
Suite 201
Addison, TX 75001

972-866-8010
800-608-0273
E-Mail: lanny.grossman@slh.com
Home Page: www.slh.com

Members are independent owners and managers of deluxe hotels with fewer than 200 rooms.
233 Members
Founded in 1991

13695 Small Luxury Hotels of the World
370 Lexington Avenue
Suite 1506
New York, NY 10017

212-953-2064
800-608-0273
Fax: 212-953-0576
E-Mail: lanny.grossman@slh.com
Home Page: www.slh.com

Lanny Grossman, Marketing
Johnathan Slater, Chairman
Ed Donaldson, Manager

Collection of independently owned exclusive hotels in more than 50 countries. Selected for style and comfort, properties include spas, country houses, golf resorts, island retreats, city sanctuaries, game and wilderness lodges. Publishes directory.
300 Members
Founded in 1991

13696 Textile Rental Services Association
1800 Diagonal Rd
Suite 200
Alexandria, VA 22314-2842

703-519-0029
877-770-9274
Fax: 703-519-0026
E-Mail: trsa@trsa.org
Home Page: www.trsa.org

Roger Cocivera, President
George F. Ferencza, VP

Develops new programs and services to help textile rental operators meet today's challenges.
1400 Members
Founded in 1913

Newsletters

13697 AHA Hotline Newsletter
American Hospitality Association
603 S Pulaski
PO Box 3866
Little Rock, AR 72201

501-376-2323
800-472-5022
Fax: 501-376-6517
Home Page: www.arhospitality.org
Social Media: Facebook, Twitter, LinkedIn

Montine McNulty, Executive Director
Rita Walker, Executive Assistant
Amanda Glover, Education Coordinator
Holly Heer, Director of Membership
Kristen Smith, Director of Finance

For members, focuses on trends in the hospitality industry, upcoming events, training and education opportunities and more.
Frequency: Monthly

13698 AHF Developments
American Hotel & Lodging Association
1201 New York Ave Nw
Suite 600
Washington, DC 20005-3931

202-289-3100
Fax: 202-289-3199
E-Mail: webmaster@ahla.com
Home Page: www.ahla.com

Joseph Mc Inerney, President
Pam Inman, Executive Vice President & COO
Joori Jeon, Executive Vice President & CFO
Marlene M. Colucci, Executive Vice President
Lisa Costello, Vice President, Gov Affairs

AHF Developments is published three times a year with circulation to donors, scholarship recipients and members of the American Hotel and Motel association.
Frequency: Quarterly
Founded in 1910

13699 Cameron's Foodservice Marketing Reporter
Cameron's Publications
5423 Sheridan Drive
PO Box 676
Williamsville, NY 14231

519-586-8785
Fax: 519-586-8816
E-Mail: mail@cameronpub.com
Home Page: www.cameronpub.com

Bob McClelland, CEO
Nina Cameron, Editor

Successful promotion and advertising case histories for the restaurant and hotel industry.

13700 Epicurean Revue
PO Box 35128
Sarasota, FL 34242-5128

FAX 941-349-4370

Jean-Noel Prade, Publisher
Georgia Brown, Editor
JN Prade, Circulation Manager

The publication for the jetsetters exclusive recommendations on top class hotels and restaurants. Total analysis of the various issues of the Michelin Guide and results of the wine auctions.
Cost: $79.00
8 Pages
Frequency: Monthly
Circulation: 5,000
Printed in one color on matte stock

13701 Hospitality Law
LRP Publications
PO Box 24668
West Palm Beach, FL 33416-4668

561-622-6520
800-341-7874
Fax: 561-622-0757
E-Mail: webmaster@lrp.com
Home Page: www.lrp.com

Kenneth Kahn, President
Dave Light, Editor

Details and analyzes significant cases in the hospitality industry so you can learn from the mistakes that landed other properties in court.

You receive summaries of the latest court cases - without legalese - involving hotels, inns, resorts and restaurants.
Cost: $229.00
12 Pages
Frequency: Monthly
Circulation: 1400

13702 Hotel Technology Newsletter
Chervenak, Keane and Company
307 E 44th Street
New York, NY 10017

212-986-8230
Fax: 212-983-5275
Home Page: www.e-hospitality.com.storefronts/ckchoteltech.html

J Christmas, Publisher
L Chervenak, Editor

Covers hotel information processing, telecommunications, security, fire safety, energy and audio-visual systems.
Cost: $180.00
Frequency: Annual

13703 Hotel and Casino Law Letter
William F Harrah College of Hotel Administration
4505 Maryland Parkway
Box 456013
Las Vegas, NV 89154-6013

702-895-3161
Fax: 702-895-4109
E-Mail: hoaadvise@ccmail.nevada.edu
Home Page: hotel.unlv.edu/

Annette Kannenberg, Business Manager
Stuart H Mann, Dean
Alice Baker, Administrative Assistant
Pat Merl, Management Assistant
Sherri Theriault, Director

Legislative news for executive level management of hotels and motels.

13704 Hyatt Overseas
Hyatt International Corporation
71 S Wacker Dr
Chicago, IL 60606-4637

312-701-7063
Fax: 312-750-8578

Thomas Pritzker, CEO

A summary of news, packages and events happening at Hyatt Hotels.
2 Pages

13705 Inn Side Issues
Hotel and Motel Brokers of America
10220 N Executive Boulevard
Suite 610
Kansas City, MO 64153

816-891-8776
Fax: 816-891-7071

Robert Kralicek, Editor

News of hotel owners and investors with articles about hospitality real estate.

Magazines & Journals

13706 Bottomline
Hospitality Financial & Technology Professionals
11709 Boulder Lane
Suite 110
Austin, TX 78726-1832

512-249-5333
800-646-4387
Fax: 512-249-1533
E-Mail: Sales@hftp.org
Home Page: www.hftp.org

Jen Gonzales, Communications Manager
Theresa Pulley, Advertising Director

Official publication of the international association for individuals employed as controllers and financial officers in the hospitality industry. Articles include topics such as technology, personnel management, financial analysis, ethics and financial controls.
Cost: $200.00
Circulation: 4300
Founded in 1952
Printed in on glossy stock

13707 Cameron's Worldwide Hospitality Marketing Reporter
53256 Sheridan Drive
Williamsville, NY 14221-3503

416-636-5666
Fax: 416-636-5026

13708 Cheers
257 Park Avenue S
3rd Floor, Suite 303
New York, NY 10010

212-967-1551
Fax: 646-654-2099

John Eastman, Owner

Every issue is designed to help on-premise operators enhance the profitability of their beverage operations.

13709 Club Management Magazine
Finan Publishing Company
107 W Pacific
Saint Louis, MO 63119-3776

314-961-6644
Fax: 314-961-4809
Home Page: www.club-mgmt.com

Thomas J Finan, IV, Managing Editor
Dee Kaplan, Publisher
Dianne Dierkes, Circulation Manager

The resource for successful club operations.
Cost: $26.95
150 Pages
Founded in 1921
Mailing list available for rent: 21,000 names
Printed in 4 colors on glossy stock

13710 Consortium of Hospitality Research Information Services
Quanta Press
1313 5th St SE
Suite 223A
Minneapolis, MN 55414-4513

612-379-3618

Nancy J Hall, Owner

Consists of academic and industry groups which together have produced a comprehensive index of hospitality literature in CD-ROM format. Over 47,000 bibliographic records with abstracts from over 50 journals serving the hospitality industry.

13711 Cornell Hotel & Restaurant Administration Quarterly
Elsevier Science Publishing Company
415 Horsham Road
Horsham, PA 19044

212-633-3730
888-437-4636
Fax: 212-633-3680
E-Mail: nicole@leonardmedia.com
Home Page: www.hotelschool.cornell.edu/

Glenn Withiam, Executive Editor
Dr. Michael Sturman, Editor
Thomas Cullen, Associate Professor

A journal devoted to the development and exchange of management ideas for the hospitality industry.
Cost: $113.00
Frequency: Quarterly
Circulation: 4500
Founded in 1960

13712 Developments Magazine
American Resort Development Association
1201 15th St NW
Suite 400
Washington, DC 20005-2842

202-371-6700
Fax: 202-289-8544
E-Mail: customerservice@arda.org
Home Page: www.ardafoundation.org

Howard Nusbaum, President/CEO
Lou Ann Burney, Vice President of Marketing
Robert Craycraft, Vice President of Industry Relation
Rob Dunn, Vice President of Finance
Jason C. Gamel, Vice President of State Governments

13713 Executive Housekeeping Today (EHT)
International Executive Housekeepers Association
1001 Eastwind Dr
Suite 301
Westerville, OH 43081 3361

614-895-7166
800-200-6342
Fax: 614-895-1248
E-Mail: excel@ieha.org
Home Page: www.ieha.org
Social Media: Facebook, Twitter, LinkedIn

Beth Risinger, CEO
Laura DiGiulio, Advertising/Sales/Ed

Magazine for management personnel in the institutional housekeeping industry. Highlighting products, services, association news and industry trends.
Cost: $40.00
3500 Members
30 Pages
Frequency: Monthly
Circulation: 4130
ISSN: 0738-6583
Founded in 1930

13714 Foodservice Equipment & Supplies Specialist
Reed Business Information
2000 Clearwater Dr
Oak Brook, IL 60523-8809

630-574-0825
Fax: 630-288-8781
E-Mail: 411_webmaster@reedbusiness.com
Home Page: www.reedbusiness.com

Jeff Greisch, President
Maureen Slocum, Publisher
Paulette Cortopassi, Managing Editor
Victoria Jones, Production Manager
Andrew Rak, Senior Vice President

Magazine for professionals who specify, sell and distribute foodservice equipment, supplies and furnishings.
Frequency: Monthly
Circulation: 22719
Founded in 1948
Printed in 4 colors on glossy stock

13715 Hospitality News
PO Box 11960
Prescott, AZ 86304-1960

206-686-7378
800-685-1932

Fax: 206-463-0090
Home Page: www.hospnews.com

Linda Sanders, Publisher
Miles Small, Editor-in-Chief

Serves restaurants, lodges, health care facilities, schools, clubs, casino's, caterers, and culinary and beverage marketplaces.
Circulation: 105000
ISSN: 1084-2551
Founded in 1988

13716 **Hospitality Product News**
Advanstar Communications
2501 Colorado Avenue
Suite 280
Santa Monica, CA 90404

310-857-7500
888-527-7008
Fax: 310-857-7510
E-Mail: info@advanstar.com
Home Page: www.advanstar.com/

Doug Ferguson, Group Publisher
Helen Gardner, General Manager
Georgiann Decenzo, Director of Corporate mar
Joseph Loggia, CEO
Thomas Ehardt, Chief Administrator

Contains ADA compliance, maintenance and cleaning, fitness, leisure and entertainment, food and beverage, foodservice equipment and supplies, furnishings and fixtures, guest amenities, tabletop, technology, uniforms, and bedding and linens.
Cost: $35.00
Circulation: 30019
Founded in 1987

13717 **Hospitality Technology**
Edgell Communications
4 Middlebury Boulevard
Randolph, NJ 07869

973-252-0100
Fax: 973-252-9020
Home Page: www.htmagazine.com

Lenore O'Meara, Associate Publisher
Reid Paul, Editor
Gerald Ryerson, President
Jan Miciak, Production Manager
Leah Segarra, Account Executive

Aimed at owners/operators, franchise and chain executives, and managers in operations, finance, sales/marketing and information systems. Emphasis on applications, new products, industry news and trade show highlights.
Circulation: 16000
Founded in 1984
Printed in 4 colors on glossy stock

13718 **Hotel & Motel Management**
Advanstar Communications
757 3rd Avenue
New York, NY 10017-2013

212-951-6600
Fax: 212-951-6793
E-Mail: info@advanstar.com
Home Page: www.advanstar.com

Scott E Pierce, President
Mike Malley, Publisher
Jeff Higley, Editor-in-Chief
Mary M. Malloy, National Sales Manager

Publication reaching more than 57,000 management personnel in hotels, motels, motor inns and other related businesses.
Circulation: 53058
ISSN: 0018-6082
Founded in 1875

13719 **Hotels**
Reed Business Information
2000 Clearwater Dr
Oak Brook, IL 60523-8809

605-3 8-09
Fax: 630-288-8781
E-Mail: hotels_webmaster@reedbusiness.com
Home Page: www.reedbusiness.com

Jeff Greisch, President
Andrew Rak, Senior Vice President
Jeff Weinstein, Editor

The magazine for the worldwide hotel industry
Cost: $125.90
Frequency: Monthly
Circulation: 62000
ISSN: 1047-2975
Printed in 4 colors on glossy stock

13720 **Infoline**
Hospitality Financial & Technology Professionals
11709 Boulder Lane
Suite 110
Austin, TX 78726-1832

512-249-5333
800-646-4387
Fax: 512-249-1533
E-Mail: eliza.selig@hftp.org
Home Page: www.hftp.org

Eliza Selig, Editor
Lance Peterson, Director Marketing
Frank Wolfe, Executive ViP

Chapter and officer activities.
Frequency: Monthly
Circulation: 4000
Founded in 1952

13721 **Journal of Quality Assurance in Hospitality & Tourism**
Bill Cohen
10 Alice Street
Binghamton, NY 13904-1580

607-722-5857
800-342-9678
Fax: 607-722-6362
E-Mail: getinfo@haworthpressinc.com
Home Page: www.haworthpressinc.com

Timothy R Hinkin, Editor
Pyo Sungsoo, Editor
William Cohen, Owner

Serves as a medium to share and disseminate information coming from new research findings and superior practices in tourisim and hospitality; covers planning, development, management and marketing.
Cost: $50.00
Frequency: Quarterly
Founded in 1978

13722 **Journal of Teaching in Travel & Tourism**
Bill Cohen
10 Alice Street
Binghamton, NY 13904-1580

607-722-5857
800-342-9678
Fax: 607-722-6362
E-Mail: getinfo@haworthpress.com
Home Page: www.haworthpressinc.com

Timothy R Hinkin, Editor
Pyo Sungsoo, Editor
Cathy HC Hsu, Editor
William Cohen, Owner

Serves as an international interdisiplinary forum and reference source for travel and tourisim education at professional schools and universities.
Founded in 1978

13723 **Lodging Hospitality**
Penton Media
1300 E 9th St
Cleveland, OH 44114-1503

216-696-7000
Fax: 216-696-6662
E-Mail: ewatkins@penton.com
Home Page: www.penton.com

Jane Cooper, Marketing
Edward Watkins, Editor
David Kieselstein, CEO
Preston L. Vice, Chief Financial Officer
Andrew Schmolka, Senior Vice President

Serving the US hotel, motel and resort industry. Published 16 times per year, LH provides owners and operators with the latest trends and information on the development, operations and marketing of lodging properties
Frequency: Monthly
Circulation: 50,976
ISSN: 0148-0766
Founded in 1892
Mailing list available for rent
Printed in 4 colors on glossy stock

13724 **Market Watch**
M Shanken Communications
387 Park Ave S
Floor 8
New York, NY 10016-8872

212-684-4224
Fax: 212-684-5424
Home Page: www.cigaraficionado.com

Marvin Shanken, Publisher
Felicia Bedoya, President

Up-to-date information for individuals and businesses working in the beverage and alcohol industry.
Cost: $75.42
200 Pages
Circulation: 65000
Founded in 1981
Printed in 4 colors

13725 **Nation's Restaurant News**
Lebhar-Friedman Publications
425 Park Ave
New York, NY 10022-3526

212-756-5220
Fax: 212-756-5250
E-Mail: info@lf.com

Lebhar Friedman, Publisher
Michael Cardillo, VP Sales
Ellen Koteff, Editor

Serves commercial and onsite food service and lodging establishments including restaurants, schools, universities, hospitals, nursing homes and other health and welfare facilities, hotels and motels with food service, government installations, clubs and other related firms.
Cost: $44.95
Circulation: 85,999
Founded in 1925
Mailing list available for rent: 100,000 names at $100 per M
Printed in 4 colors on matte stock

13726 **National Culinary Review**
American Culinary Federation
180 Center Place Way
St Augustine, FL 32095-8859

904-824-4468
800-624-9458
Fax: 904-825-4758
E-Mail: acf@acfchefs.net
Home Page: www.acfchefs.org

Heidi Cramb, Executive Director
Kay Orde, Editor
Edward Leonard, Presient
Michael Feierstein, Administrative Assistant
Bryan Hunt, Graphic Designer

Accepts advertising.
Cost: $50.00
Frequency: Monthly
Circulation: 20000
Founded in 1929

13727 Restaurant Hospitality
Penton Media
1300 E 9th St
Cleveland, OH 44114-1503

216-696-7000
Fax: 216-696-6662
E-Mail: information@penton.com
Home Page: www.penton.com

Jane Cooper, Marketing
Jennifer Daugherty, Communications Manager
David Kieselstein, Chief Executive Officer
Kurt Nelson, Vice President, Human Resources
Andrew Schmolka, Senior Vice President

A national trade publication that covers the full-service restaurant industry. If offers cover story features, an extensive food section with recipes, a multi-page news section and a variety of one page profiles on rising stars, equipment, food safety, beverages, design and more.
130 Pages
Frequency: Monthly
Circulation: 117721
ISSN: 0147-9989
Founded in 1892
Mailing list available for rent
Printed in 4 colors on glossy stock

13728 Restaurants & Institutions
Reed Business Information
2000 Clearwater Dr
Oak Brook, IL 60523-8809

605-3 8-09
Fax: 630-288-8781
E-Mail: privacymanager@reedbusiness.com
Home Page: www.reedbusiness.com

Patricia B Dailey, Editor-in-Chief
Scott Hume, Managing Editor
Jim Casella, CEO
Brion Palmer, Publisher
Andrew Rak, Senior Vice President

Commercial and noncommercial foodservice establishments including restaurant, hotels, motels, fast-food chains,coffee shops, food stores with foodservice
Cost: $477.00
Frequency: Monthly
Circulation: 154,110
Founded in 1937
Printed in 4 colors on glossy stock

13729 Ski Area Management
Beardsley Publishing Corporation
PO Box 644
Woodbury, CT 06798-644

203-263-0888
Fax: 203-266-0452
Home Page: www.saminfo.com

Jennifer Rowan, Publisher
Rick Kahl, Editor
Donna Jacobs, Production Manager

Content includes technologies of skilifts, snowmaking and slope grooming, at year-round resort operations. Other features include product and supplier directories, resort architecture and design, new products, marketing, real estate and rental.
Cost: $42.00
Frequency: Monthly
Circulation: 3100
Printed in 4 colors on glossy stock

13730 Textile Rental Magazine
Textile Rental Services Association
1800 Diagonal Rd
Suite 200
Alexandria, VA 22314-2842

703-519-0029
877-770-9274
Fax: 703-519-0026
E-Mail: trsa@trsa.org
Home Page: www.trsa.org
Social Media: Facebook, Twitter, LinkedIn

Roger Cocivera, President/CEO
Jack Morgan, Editor

Packed with valuable tips and ideas.
Frequency: Monthly
Founded in 1912

Trade Shows

13731 American Hotel & Motel Association Annual Conference/Leadership Forum
1201 New York Avenue NW
Suite 600
Washington, DC 20005-3931

202-289-3100
Fax: 202-289-3158
E-Mail: webmaster@ahla.com
Home Page: www.ahlef.org

Gerald Petitt, Chairman
Joseph A. McInerney, President/Ceo
Pam Inman, Executive Vice President & COO
Joori Jeon, Executive Vice President & CFO
Marlene M. Colucci, Executive Vice President

189 exhibits of hotel supplies, equipment and information, conference and workshop.
1500 Attendees
Frequency: Annual
Founded in 1910

13732 American Hotel & Motel Association Annual Convention
1201 New York Avenue NW
Suite 600
Washington, DC 20005-3931

202-289-3100
Fax: 202-289-3199
E-Mail: webmaster@ahla.com
Home Page: www.ahlef.org
Gerald Petitt, Chairman
Joseph A. McInerney, President/Coo
Pam Inman, Executive Vice President & COO
Joori Jeon, Executive Vice President & CFO
Marlene M. Colucci, Executive Vice President

125 booths consisting of telecommunication systems, supplies and equipment for the hotel and motel industry.
1.5M Attendees
Frequency: April

13733 American Resort Development Association Convention
1201 15th Street NW
Suite 400
Washington, DC 20005-2842

202-371-6700
Fax: 202-289-8544
E-Mail: customerservice@arda.org
Home Page: www.arda.org

Howard C Nusbaum, President/CEO
Lou Ann Burney, Vice President of Marketing
Robert Craycraft, Vice President of Industry Relation
Rob Dunn, Vice President of Finance
Jason C. Gamel, Vice President of State Government

One hundred fifty booths.
3600 Attendees
Frequency: April

13734 Annual Council on Hotel, Restaurant and Institutional Education Conference
Int'l Council on Hotel & Restaurant Education
2810 North Parham Roaf
Suite 230
Richmond, VA 23294

804-346-4800
Fax: 804-346-5009
E-Mail: publications@chrie.org
Home Page: www.chrie.org

Kathy McCarty, Executive VP/CEO
Bill Shoemaker, Treasurer
Joseph Bradley, Treasurer

Terrific opportunity to gain knowledge, exchange ideas, and enjoy the camaraderie and fellowship of colleagues in the hospitality industry
6MM Attendees
Frequency: July

13735 Annual Hotel, Motel and Restaurant Supply Show of the Southeast
Leisure Time Unlimited
708 Main Street
PO Box 332
Myrtle Beach, SC 29577

843-448-9483
800-261-5991
Fax: 843-626-1513
E-Mail: hmrss@sc.rr.com
Home Page: www.hmrsss.com

Brooke P Baker, Show Director

Trade show for the hospitality industry.
23000 Attendees
Frequency: January
Founded in 1975

13736 Fall Conference for Hospitality Supply Management
Institute for Supply Management
Po Box 22160
Tempe, AZ 85285-2160

480-752-6276
800-888-6276
Fax: 480-752-7890
Home Page: www.ism.ws
Social Media: Facebook, Twitter, LinkedIn

Sidney Johnson, Chairman
Thomas W. Derry, Chief Executive Officer
Debbie Webber, Senior VP/Corporate Treasurer
Holly LaCroix Johnson, Senior VP/Corporate Secretary
Nora Neibergall, CPM, Senior VP
Frequency: Oct, Dallas, TX
Mailing list available for rent

13737 Great Southwest Lodging & Restaurant Show
Arizona Hotel and Lodging Association
1240 East Missouri Avenue
Phoenix, AZ 85014

602-604-0729
800-788-2462
Fax: 520-604-0769
E-Mail: info@azhla.com
Home Page: www.azhla.com

Britt Kimball, Show Manager

Seminars, workshops and 450+ exhibits of food service and lodging equipment, marketing, decorations, berverage services (alcoholic and non), cleaning services and pest control, furnishings, lighting, insurance, transportation and more.
5000 Attendees
Frequency: Annual
Founded in 1970

13738 IEHA's Association Convention/in Conjunction with ISSA Interclean
International Executive Housekeepers Association
1001 Eastwind Drive
Suite 301
Westerville, OH 43081-3361

614-895-7166
800-200-6342
Fax: 614-895-1248
E-Mail: excel@ieha.org
Home Page: www.ieha.org
Social Media: Facebook, Twitter, LinkedIn

Beth Risinger, CEO

Educational seminars and exhibits by firms engaged in manufacturing, marketing and distribution of cleaning and maintenance suppliers. Containing 750 exhibits.
3500 Members
15M Attendees
Frequency: Oct 23-26 Orlando Florida

13739 Innkeeping
PAII
Box 97010
Santa Barbara, CA 93190

805-965-4525

JoAnn Bell, Publisher

Offers a forum for innkeepers, hotel and motel managers, owners and operators.
500 Attendees
Frequency: March/April

13740 International Hotel/Motel & Restaurant Show
George Little Management
10 Bank Street
Suite 1200
White Plains, NY 10606-1954

914-486-6070
800-272-7469
Fax: 914-948-6180
E-Mail: ihmrs@glmshows.com
Home Page: www.ihmrs.com

Christian Falkemberg, Show Manager
George Little II, President

Products and services for lodging and food service properties organized in 12 categories: Technology; Uniforms, Linens and Bedding; Tabletop; Guest amenities and services; Food and Beverage; Cleaning and Maintenance; Food Service Equipment and Supplies; Franchise, Finance and Management; Furnishings and Fixturtes; Fitness, Leisure and Entertainment; The Environment; Advertising and Promotion
45000 Attendees
Frequency: Early November

13741 Marine Hotel Catering Duty Free Conference
PO Box 1659
Sausalito, CA 94966

415-332-1903
Fax: 415-332-9457
E-Mail: mha@mhaweb.org
Home Page: www.mhaweb.org

Caroline Prichard, Administrator

100 booths.
700 Attendees
Frequency: April

13742 National Restaurant Association: Restaurant, Hotel-Motel Show
Convention Office
150 North Michigan Avenue
Suite 2000
Chicago, IL 60601

312-853-2525
Home Page: www.restaurant.org

Mary Pat Heftman, Sr VP Conventions
Jamie Schaefer, Treasurer
Phil Hickey, Treasurer

1,800 booths.
Frequency: Annual,May

13743 Pacific Hospitality Expo Convention Center
1801 Kalakaua Avenue
Honolulu, HI 96815-2558

808-973-9790

Joanie Gribbin, Director

220 booths.
2.5M Attendees
Frequency: June

13744 Rocky Mountain Hospitality Convention and Expo
899 Logan Street
Suite 300
Denver, CO 80203-3155

303-792-9621

Bruce Whiticker, Convention Director

413 booths.
7M Attendees
Frequency: June

Directories & Databases

13745 All Suite Hotel Guide
Ten Speed Press
PO Box 7123
Berkeley, CA 94707-0123

510-559-1600
800-841-2665
Fax: 510-559-1629
Home Page: www.tenspeedpress.com

Phil Wood, President

Over 1,600 hotels are offered which have suites available consisting of two or more rooms for rent.
Cost: $14.95
336 Pages
Frequency: Annual
ISBN: 1-580080-91-

13746 America's Wonderful Little Hotels & Inns
St. Martin's Press
175 5th Ave
4th Floor
New York, NY 10010-7703

212-674-5151
Fax: 212-674-3179

John Sargent, CEO

A directory listing hotels and inns that are located throughout the United States and Canada in various volumes. Prices vary per region, per volume.
ISBN: 0-312081-30-8
Founded in 1952

13747 Bed & Breakfast Home Directory: Homes Away from Home, West Coast
Knighttime Publications
890 Calabasas Road
Watsonville, CA 95076-0418
Diane Knight, Author
Suzy Blackaby, Author
Kevin McElvain, Author

Over 250 bed and breakfast homes are listed that are located in the areas of California, Oregon, Washington and British Columbia, Canada.
Cost: $12.95
203 Pages
Frequency: Biennial
ISBN: 0-942902-03-3

13748 Bed and Breakfast Guest Houses and Inns of America
PO Box 38066
Germantown, TN 38183-0066

901-946-1902
Fax: 901-758-0816

Directory of services and supplies to the industry.
Cost: $45.00
350 Pages
Frequency: Annual
ISSN: 1056-8069

13749 Cabin Guide to Wilderness Lodging
Hammond Publishing
1500 E Tropicana Ave
Suite 110
Las Vegas, NV 89119-6515

702-878-2008
Home Page: www.prosofrealty.com

Jim Smith, Manager

Information is given on over 500 cabins in national and state forests, preserves and other wildlife areas.
Cost: $14.95
250 Pages
Frequency: Annual

13750 Complete Guide to Bed & Breakfasts, Inns and Guesthouses in US & Canada
Lanier Publishing International
963 Transport Way
Petaluma, CA 94954-8011

707-763-0271
Fax: 707-763-5762
E-Mail: lanier@travelguides.com
Home Page: www.travelguides.com

Pamela Lanier, Owner

Directory of services and supplies to the industry.
Cost: $16.95
536 Pages
Frequency: Annual

13751 Country Inns and Back Roads, North America
HarperCollins
10 E 53rd St
Cellar 1 Floor
New York, NY 10022-5299

212-207-7000
Fax: 212-207-6964
E-Mail: feedback2@harpercollins.com
Home Page: www.harpercollins.com

Brian Murray, CEO

Over 200 country inns in the United States and Canada are listed.
Cost: $13.00
450 Pages
Frequency: Annual

13752 Directory of Hotel & Lodging Companies
American Hotel & Lodging Association
1201 New York Ave NW
Suite 600
Washington, DC 20005-3931

202-289-3100
Fax: 202-289-3199

E-Mail: webmaster@ahla.com
Home Page: www.ahla.com

Joseph McInerney, President
Joori Jeon, Executive Vice President & CFO
Pam Inman, Executive Vice President & COO
Marlene M. Colucci, Executive Vice President
Lisa Costello, Vice President, Government Affairs

Lists over 1,000 companies that own, manage or franchise properties worldwide. Also lists, in 7 sections: companies by type, company/brand web site, company listings, geographical, company rankings, hotel brokers, and vendors.
Cost: $100.00
Frequency: Annual
Founded in 1931

13753 **Hotel Development Guide**
Hospitality Media
17950 Preston Rd
Suite 710
Dallas, TX 75252-5637

972-934-2040
Fax: 972-934-2070
E-Mail: Info@hospitalitymgt.com
Home Page: www.hospitalitymgt.com

Leo Spriggs, CEO
John Connor, Director of Operations
Bill Sullivan, Chief Financial Officer

Offers a list of suppliers of equipment, fixtures and services needed for new motels.
Cost: $100.00

13754 **Hotel and Travel Index**
Reed Travel Group
904 Haddonfield Rd
Subscription Department
Cherry Hill, NJ 08002-2745

856-665-4455
800-442-0900
Fax: 856-488-4867

Over 45,000 hotels worldwide are profiled in this travel directory.
Cost: $125.00
2000 Pages
Frequency: Quarterly
Circulation: 60,000

13755 **Inspected, Rated and Approved Bed and Breakfast Country Inns**
American Bed & Breakfast Association
10800 Midlothian Tpke
Suite 254
Richmond, VA 23235-4700

Home Page: www.abba.com

Beth Burgreen Stuhlman, Editor

Information on over 500 overnight accommodations in North American bed and breakfast locations are listed.
Cost: $17.95
350 Pages
ISBN: 0-934473-27-7
Founded in 1996

13756 **National Directory of Budget Motels**
Pilot Books
127 Sterling Avenue
#2102
Greenport, NY 11944-1439

631-477-0978
800-79 -ILOT
Fax: 631-477-0978

Guide to the best in economy-priced chain motel accommodations in the United States and Canada.
Cost: $12.95
346 Pages
Frequency: Annual

13757 **National Trust Guide to Historic Bed & Breakfasts, Inns & Small Hotels**
Preservation Press
1785 Massachusetts Ave NW
Washington, DC 20036-2117

202-588-6083
Fax: 202-588-6172

James Schwartz, Manager

Directory of services and supplies to the industry.
Cost: $13.95
416 Pages
Frequency: Biennial

13758 **Official Bed and Breakfast Guide**
National Bed & Breakfast Association
148 E Rocks Road
Norwalk, CT 06851

203-847-6196
Fax: 203-847-0469
Home Page: www.nbba.com

Phyllis Featherston, President

A who's who directory of services and supplies to the industry offering a list of the best in bed and breakfast accommodations in USA, Canada and the Carribbean.
Cost: $17.95
560 Pages

13759 **Official Hotel Guide**
Reed Hotel Directories Network
500 Plaza Drive
Secaucus, NJ 07094-3619

201-902-1960
Fax: 201-319-1628

Wilma Goldenberg, Editor

3 volumes of 25,000 hotels, motels and resorts worldwide.
Cost: $385.00
Frequency: Annual
Circulation: 20,000

13760 **Pelican's Select Guide to American Bed and Breakfast**
Pelican Publishing Company
1000 Burmaster St
Gretna, LA 70053-2246

504-368-1175
Fax: 504-368-1195
E-Mail: sales@pelicanpub.com
Home Page: www.pelicanpub.com

Milburn Calhoun, Publisher
Joseph Billingsley, Sales Manager

Independent guest houses, inns and bed and breakfast accommodations are profiled.
Cost: $14.95
216 Pages
ISBN: 1-589800-61-8
Printed in 2 colors on matte stock

13761 **Preferred Hotels Directory**
Preferred Hotels & Resorts Worldwide
311 S Wacker Dr
Suite 1900
Chicago, IL 60606-6676

312-913-0400
800-323-7500
Fax: 312-913-5124
Home Page: www.preferredhotels.com

John Ubberoth, CEO
Casey Ueberroth, Managing Director
80 Pages
Frequency: Annual
Circulation: 25,000

13762 **Recommended Country Inns**
Globe Pequot Press
246 Goose Lane
PO Box 480
Guilford, CT 06437

203-458-4500
888-249-7586
Fax: 800-820-2329
Home Page: www.globepequot.com

Elizabeth Squier
Elenor Berman

This series of directories offers information on country inns located in certain parts of the United States.
Cost: $18.95
416 Pages
Frequency: Biennial
ISBN: 0-762728-48-5

13763 **Where to Stay USA**
Prentice Hall Law & Business
1 Lake St
Upper Saddle Rv, NJ 07458-1828

201-236-7000
Fax: 201-236-3381

Information is given on over 1,200 places to stay and eat from $4 to $35 a night.
Cost: $16.00
350 Pages
Frequency: Biennial

Industry Web Sites

13764 **http://gold.greyhouse.com**
G.O.L.D Grey House OnLine Databases

Grey House Publishing's online database platform, GOLD, offers Quick Search, Keyword Search and Expert Search for most business sectors including hotel, motel and hospitality markets. The GOLD platform makes finding the information you need quick and easy - whether you're a novice searcher or an experienced database user. All of Grey House's directory products are available for subscription on the GOLD platform.

13765 **www.abba.com**
American Bed & Breakfast Association

National organization with information on over 500 overnight accomodations in North American bed and breakfast locations.

13766 **www.ahma.com**
American Hotel & Lodging Foundation

Trade association covering news, issues and activities of related industry groups.

13767 **www.biztravel.com**
Biztravel.com

Internet travel service offering discounts on flights, hotels, car rentals, packages and cruises.

13768 **www.chrie.org**
Int'l Council on Hotel & Restaurant Education

To enhance professionalism at all levels of the hospitality and tourism industry through education and training.

13769 **www.ei-ahla.org**
American Hotel&Lodging Educational Foundation

A non-profit educational foundation of the American Hotel & Lodging Association and the world's largest provider of hospitality education training resources, videos, books, workbooks, seminars, management courses, complete training systems and professional certification programs.

13770 **www.expedia.com**
Expedia.com
Internet travel service offers access to airlines, hotels, car rentals, vacation packages, cruises and corporate travel.

13771 **www.goworldnet.com/cgi-bin**
Worldnet USA
A database of states with hotels, theaters and museums.

13772 **www.greyhouse.com**
Grey House Publishing
Authoritative reference directories for most business sectors including hotel, motel and hospitality markets. Users can search the online databases with varied search criteria allowing for custom searches by product category, geographic area, sales volume, keyword, subject and more. Full Grey House catalog and online ordering also available.

13773 **www.hanyc.org**
Hotel Association of New York City
One of the oldest professional trade associations in the nation.

13774 **www.hotels.com**
Hotels.com
Provides discount accommodations worldwide.

13775 **www.hotwire.com**
Hotwire.com
Internet travel service offering discounts on flights, hotels, car rentals, packages and cruises.

13776 **www.ieha.org**
International Executive Housekeepers Association
An organization for persons working in the housekeeping area of the lodging industry.

13777 **www.innbook.com**
Bed and Breakfast Inns & Small Luxury Hotels
Includes the finest inns, B&Bs, and getaway retreats in Canada and the Us, carefully chosen and inspected to maintain the highest standards.

13778 **www.masslodging.com**
Massachusetts Lodging Association
A trade association representing and promoting the lodging industryin Massachusetts.

13779 **www.nmhotels.com**
New Mexico Lodging Association
New Mexico's trade association representing the lodging industry.

13780 **www.orbitz.com**
Orbitz.com
Internet travel service offering discounts on flights, hotels, car rentals, packages and cruises.

13781 **www.paii.org**
Professional Association of Innkeepers International
Serving bed and breakfast/country inn owners, aspiring innkeepers, inn sitters, vendors with educational and consultative services. International conference.

13782 **www.preferredhotels.com**
The Luxury Hotels of Preferred Hotels & Resorts Worldwide
An exclusive group of independent luxury hotels in the United States.

13783 **www.travel.lycos.com**
Lycos.com
Internet travel service offering discounts on flights, hotels, car rentals, packages and cruises.

13784 **www.travel.yahoo.com**
Yahoo.com
Internet travel service providing access to flights, hotels, car rentals, vacation packages and cruises.

13785 **www.travelocity.com**
Sabre Holdings
Travel service offering consumers access to hundreds of airlines and thousands of hotels, as well as cruises, last-minute and vacation packages and best-in-class car rental companies.

13786 **www.travelweb.com**
Travelweb.com
Internet provider of hotel accommodations.

Associations

13787 ASM International
9639 Kinsman Rd
Materials Park, OH 44073-0002

440-338-5151
800-336-5152
Fax: 440-338-4634
E-Mail: memberservices@asminternational.org
Home Page: www.asminternational.org

Stanley Theobald, Senior Director, Business
Tom Passek, Managing Director
Nichol Campana, Director of Development
Skip Wolfe, Membership Product Manager
Norina Columbaro, Senior Manager, Education

The society for materials engineers and scientists, a worldwide network dedicated to advancing industry, technology and applications of metals and materials.
35000 Members
Founded in 1913

13788 American Coatings Association
1500 Rhode Island Ave., NW
Washington, DC 20005

202-462-6272
Fax: 202-462-8549
E-Mail: members@paint.org
Home Page: www.coatingstech.org

J. Andrew Doyle, President & CEO
Thomas J. Graves, Vice President, General Counsel
Allen Irish, Counsel / Director
Alison Keane, Vice President, Government Affairs
Robin Eastman Caldwell, Senior Government Affairs

Provides technical education and professional development to its members and to the global industry through its multinational Constituent Societies and collectively as a Federation
Founded in 1922

13789 American Composites Manufacturers Association
3033 Wilson Blvd.
Suite 420
Arlington, VA 22201-4749

703-525-0511
Fax: 703-525-0743
E-Mail: info@acmanet.org
Home Page: www.acmanet.org
Social Media: Facebook, Twitter, LinkedIn, RSS

Jay Merrell, Chairman
Kevin Mcdonald, Vice Chairman
Tom Dobbins, CAE, Director
Patricia Bradford, Vice President, Finance
Heather Rhoderick, CMP, Vice President, Events & Education

A trade association serving the composites industry.
1100 Members
Founded in 1979

13790 American Electroplaters and Surface Finishers Society (AESF)
1155 15th Street NW
Suite 500
Washington, DC 20005

202-457-8401
Fax: 202-530-0659
E-Mail: info@aesf.org
Home Page: www.aesf.org
Social Media: Facebook, Twitter, LinkedIn, Google Plus

John Flatley, Executive Director
Courtney Mariette, Bookstore/Education
Holly Wills, Membership
Carrie Hoffman, Deputy Executive Director
Cheryl Clark, Director of Events

AESF is an international society that advances the science of surface finishing to benefit industry and society through education, information and social involvement, as well as those who provide services, supplies and support to the industry.
5000 Members
Founded in 1909

13791 American Society of Industrial Security
1625 Prince St
Alexandria, VA 22314-2882

703-519-6200
Fax: 703-519-6299
E-Mail: asis@asisonline.org
Home Page: www.asisonline.org

Eduard J. Emde, CPP, CISSP, Chairman
Geoffrey T. Craighead, CPP, President
Michael J. Stack, ASIS Chief Executive Officer
Dave N. Tyson, CPP, CISSP, Treasurer
David C. Davis, CPP, Secretary

The largest international organization for professionals who are responsible for security, including managers and directors of security.
38000 Members
Founded in 1955
Mailing list available for rent

13792 Asphalt Recycling and Reclaiming Associates
15 Harold Court
Suite 250
Bayshore, NY 11706

631-231-8400
Fax: 631-434-1116
E-Mail: sales@arra.com
Home Page: www.arra.com

Mike Krissoff, Executive Director

Promotes the interest of owners and manufacturers of recycling equipment, engineers, suppliers and businesses involved in the asphalt recycling industry. Newsletter published quarterly.
200 Members
Founded in 1976
Mailing list available for rent

13793 Associated Equipment Distributors
600 22nd Street
Suite 220
Oak Brook, IL 60523-8807

630-574-0650
800-388-0650
Fax: 630-574-0132
E-Mail: info@aednet.org
Home Page: www.aednet.org

Mike Quirk, Chairman
Timothy J Watters, Vice Chairman
Bob Henderson, Executive Vice President and COO
Dave Gordon, Publisher / Vice President of Sales
Kim Phelan, Executive Editor

Membership organization of independent distributors, manufacturers and other organizations involved in the distribution of construction equipment and related products and services in North America and throughout the world.
1200 Members
Founded in 1919
Mailing list available for rent

13794 Association of Equipment Manufacturers
6737 W Washington St
Suite 2400
Milwaukee, WI 53214-5647

414-272-0943
866-236-0943
Fax: 414-272-1170
E-Mail: aem@aem.org
Home Page: www.aem.org

Richard A Patek, Chair
Robert A Kolb, Vice Chair
Michael A Haberman, Treasurer
Dennis J Slater, Secretary

The trade and business development resource for companies that manufacture equipment, products and services used worldwide in the construction, agricultural, mining, forestry, and utility fields.
Founded in 2002
Mailing list available for rent

13795 Association of Machinery and Equipment Appraisers
315 South Patrick Street
Alexandria, VA 22314-3532

703-836-7900
800-537-8629
Fax: 703-836-9303
E-Mail: amea@amea.org
Home Page: www.amea.org

James Zvonar, President

Certifies and accredits the most qualified capital equipment appraisers in the appraisal industry through promotion of standards of professional practice, ethical conduct, and marketing based experience.
300 Members
Founded in 1983
Mailing list available for rent

13796 Association of Technology Management and Applied Engineering
1390 Eisenhower Place
Suite 220
Ann Arbor, MI 48108

734-677-0720
Fax: 734-677-0046
E-Mail: atmae@atmae.org
Home Page: www.atmae.org
Social Media: Facebook, Twitter, LinkedIn

Rick Coscarelli, Executive Director
Dave Monforton, Associate Director
Mary Lee, Association Manager
Keith Bretzius, Publications Coordinator

Provides support to all those involved in the industrial technology industry. Hosts trade shows and publishes various materials.
Mailing list available for rent

13797 Athletic Equipment Managers Association
460 Hunt Hill Rd
Freeville, NY 13068-9643

607-539-6300
Fax: 607-539-6340
E-Mail: aema@frontiernet.nen
Home Page: www.equipmentmanagers.org

Dan Siermine E.M., C., President
Mike Royster, Executive Director
Matthew Althoff E.M.,C., Associate Executive Director
Meli Resendiz E.M.,C, Vice Presidentý
Dorothy "Dot" Cutting, Office Manager

The purpose of the AEMA is to promote, advance, and improve the Equipment Managers Profession in all of its many phases
700 Members
Founded in 1974

13798 Casting Industry Suppliers Association
14175 W Indian School Road
Suite B4-504
Goodyear, AZ 85395
623-547-0920
Fax: 623-536-1486
E-Mail: info@cisa.org
Home Page: www.cisa.org
James Bade, President
Roger A Hayes, Executive Director
Lew Fish, 2nd Vice President
Dean Weaver, 1st Vice President
Fosters better trade practices. Serves as industry representative before the government and public. Encourages member research into new processes and methods of foundry operation. Association of suppliers to the worldwide metal casting industry.
70 Members
Founded in 1919
Mailing list available for rent

13799 Composite Can and Tube Institute
50 South Pickett Street
Suite 110
Alexandria, VA 22304-7206
703-823-7234
Fax: 703-823-7237
E-Mail: ccti@cctiwdc.org
Home Page: www.cctiwdc.org
Kristine Garland, Executive Vice President
Wayne Vance, Association Councel
Janine Marczak, Associate Manager, Events
CCTI is an international nonprofit trade association representing the interests of manufacturers of composite paperboard cans, containers, canisters, tubes, cores, edgeboard and related or similar composite products and suppliers to those manufacturers of such items as paper, machinery, adhesives, labels and other services and materials.
Founded in 1933

13800 Conveyor Equipment Manufacturers Association
5672 Strand CT
Suite 2
Naples, FL 34110
239-514-3441
Fax: 239-514-3470
E-Mail: phil@cemanet.org
Home Page: www.cemanet.org
Social Media: LinkedIn
Warren Chandler, President
Bill Pugh, VP
Robert Reinfried, Executive VP
Involved in writing industry standards, the CEMA seeks to promote among its members and the industry standardization of design manufacture and application on a voluntary basis and in such manner as will not impede development of conveying machinery and component parts or lessen competition. CEMA sponsors an annual Engineering Conference that allows Member Company Engineers to meet and develop or improve CEMA Consensus Industry Standards and National Standards that affect the conveyor industry.
96 Members
Founded in 1933

13801 Equipment Leasing and Finance Association
1825 K Street NW
Suite 900
Washington, DC 20006
202-238-3400
Fax: 202-238-3401
Home Page: www.elfaonline.org
Social Media: Facebook, Twitter, LinkedIn, Youtube
William G. Sutton, CAE, President and CEO
Amy Vogt, Vice President of Communications
Paul Stilp, Vice President of Finance
Lesley Sterling, Vice President-Business
Andy Fishburn, Vice President
Represents companies involved in the dynamic equipment leasing and finance industry to the business community, government and media.
700+ Members
Founded in 1961
Mailing list available for rent

13802 Fluid Controls Institute
1300 Sumner Avenue
Cleveland, OH 44115-2851
216-241-7333
Fax: 216-241-0105
E-Mail: fci@fluidcontrolsinstitute.org
Home Page: www.fluidcontrolsinstitute.org
Manufacturers of equipment for fluid (liquid or gas) control and conditioning. This institute is organized into product specific sections which address issues that are relevant to particular products and or/or technologies.
Founded in 1921

13803 Fluid Sealing Association
994 Old Eagle School Rd
Suite 1019
Wayne, PA 19087-1802
610-971-4850
Fax: 610-971-4859
E-Mail: info@fluidsealing.com
Home Page: www.fluidsealing.com
Robert Ecker, Executive Director
Hope Silverman, Administrative Director
Influence and support the development of related standards and to provide education in the fluid sealing area.
57 Members
Founded in 1933
Mailing list available for rent

13804 Hoist Manufacturers Institute
8720 Red Oak Boulevard
Suite 201
Charlotte, NC 28217-3996
704-676-1190
Fax: 704-676-1199
E-Mail: gbaer@mhia.org
Home Page: www.mhi.org
Social Media: Facebook, Twitter, LinkedIn
E Larry Strayhorn, Executive Chairman
Dave Young, Executive Vice Chairman
John Paxton, Vice Chairman
Arthur H Stroyd, Jr, General Counsel
An affiliate of Material Handling Industry, also a trade association of maufacturers of overhead handling hoists. The products of member companies include hand chain hoists, ratchet lever hoists, trolleys, air chain and air rope hoists, and electric chain and electric wire rope hoists.
Mailing list available for rent

13805 Independent Lubricant Manufacturers Association
400 N Columbus St
Suite 201
Alexandria, VA 22314-2264
703-684-5574
Fax: 703-836-8503
E-Mail: ilma@ilma.org
Home Page: www.ilma.org
Lon Fanning, President
Celeste Powers, CAE, Executive Director
Barbara A Bellantiÿ, Vice President
Frank H Hamilton III, Treasurer
Beth Ann Jones, Secretary
Independent blenders and compounders of lubricants.
320 Members
Founded in 2004
Mailing list available for rent: 2000 names at $750 per M

13806 Industrial & Municipal Cleaning Association
906 Olive Street
Suite 1200
Saint Louis, MO 63101-1448
314-241-1445
Fax: 314-241-1449
E-Mail: wjta-imca@wjta.org
Home Page: www.wjta.org
George A Savanick PhD, President, Jet News Editor
Kenneth C Carroll, Association Manager
International association of professionals involved in high/ultra-high waterjet technology and industrial cleaning. Members are contractors, end users, job shops, manufacturers, researchers, and academicians.
Founded in 1983

13807 Industrial Diamond Association of America
PO Box 29460
Columbus, OH 43229
614-797-2265
Fax: 614-797-2264
E-Mail: tkane-ida@insight.rr.com
Home Page: www.superabrasives.org
Mike Mustin, President
Terry M Kane, Executive Director
Troy Heuermann, Vice President
Keith Reckling, Secretary/Treasurer
Trade association for those in the superabrasives industry. Products and services provided and used in most manufacturing and constuction industries such as: stone processing, glass, construction, woodworking, electronics, medical, etc.
Founded in 1946

13808 Industrial Heating Equipment Association
5040 Old Taylor Mill Rd., PMB 13
Taylor Mill, KY 41015
859-356-1575
Fax: 859-356-0908
E-Mail: ihea@ihea.org
Home Page: www.ihea.org
Social Media: Facebook
Brian Kelly, General Manager
A voluntary national trade association representing the major segments of the industrial heat processing equipment industry. Provides services to member companies that will enhance member company capabilities to serve end users in the industrial heat processing industry and improve the member company's business performance as well.
Founded in 1929
Mailing list available for rent

13809 Industrial Supply Association
100 North 20th Street
Suite 400
Philadelphia, PA 19103
215-320-3862
866-460-2360
Fax: 215-564-2175
Fax: 877-460-2365
E-Mail: info@isapartners.org
Home Page: www.isapartners.org

Social Media: Facebook, Twitter, LinkedIn, Youtube

Michael Carr, President
Tommy Thompsonÿ, Vice President
Craig Vogel, Treasurer
John Wiborg, Secretary

ISA goal is to help members increase sales, reduce expenses and improve profitability.
600 Members
Founded in 1988

13810 Institute for Supply Management

2055 E. Centennial Circle
Tempe, AZ 85284

480-752-6276
800-888-6276
Fax: 480-752-7890
E-Mail: isminfo@ism.ws
Home Page: www.ism.ws
Social Media: Facebook, Twitter, LinkedIn, Youtube, Google Plus

Thomas Derry, CEO
Nora Neibergall, CPSM CPO
Cindy Urbaytis, Managing Director
Mary Lue Peck, Managing Director

The mission of ISM is to enhance the value and performance of procurement and supply chain management practitioners and their organizations worldwide.
45000 Members
Founded in 1915
Mailing list available for rent

13811 Institute of Industrial Engineers

3577 Parkway Lane
Suite 200
Norcross, GA 30092

770-449-0460
800-494-0460
Fax: 770-441-3295
E-Mail: cs@iienet.org
Home Page: www.iienet.org

Don Greene, P.E., C.A.E., Chief Executive Officery
Donna Calvert, Chief Operating Officer
Hope Teaque, Director of Multimedia Advertising
Heather Bradley Story, Director of Membership
Monica Elliott, Director of Communications

Supports all industrial engineers with training, education, publications, conferences, etc.
15000 Members
Founded in 1948
Mailing list available for rent

13812 International Staple, Nail and Tool

512 W Burlington Ave
Suite 203
La Grange, IL 60525-2245

708-482-8138
Fax: 708-482-8186
E-Mail: isanta@ameritech.net
Home Page: www.isanta.org

John Kurtz, Executive VP
David Rapp, Codes/Technical Services

An international organization of premier power fastening companies involved in the design, and manufacturing, and sales of power fastening tools and the fasteners they drive.
22 Members
Founded in 1966

13813 Machinery Dealers National Association

315 S Patrick St
Alexandria, VA 22314-3532

703-836-9300
800-872-7807
Fax: 703-836-9303
E-Mail: office@mdna.org
Home Page: www.mdna.org
Social Media: Facebook, Twitter, LinkedIn, Youtube

Ron Shuster, AEA, President

An international, non-profit trade association dedicated to the promotion of the used machinery industry.
400+ Members
Founded in 1941

13814 NIBA - The Belting Association

6737 W Washington St
Suite 1300
Milwaukee, WI 53214-5648

414-389-8606
800-488-4845
Fax: 414-276-7704
E-Mail: staff@niba.org
Home Page: www.niba.org
Social Media: Facebook, Twitter, LinkedIn

Randall E Rakow, Executive VP/CEO
Cie Motelet, Manager Association Services
Jennifer Rzepka, Executive Director
Sandy Kaye, Account Coordinator
Amanda Wallich, Account Coordinator

A voluntary association of individuals and organizations who have joined together to further the interests of all fabricators, distriubtors and manufacturers of belting and related products. Promtes common business interests of all distributors/fabricators and manufacturers of conveyor and flat power transmission belting and material that enhances/changes belt.
Founded in 1927
Mailing list available for rent

13815 National Corrugated Steel Pipe Association

14070 Proton Road
Suite 100, LB 9
Dallas, TX 75244

972-850-1907
Fax: 972-490-4219
E-Mail: info@ncspa.org
Home Page: www.ncspa.org
Social Media: Facebook, Twitter, Youtube, RSS

Brian C Roberts PE, Executive Director
Patrick Collings, President
Vern Cameron, 1st Vice President
Wallace Johnson, 2nd Vice President
Pat Loney, Secretary

Seeks to promote sound public policy relating to the use of corrugated steel drainage structures in private and public construction.
60 Members
Founded in 1956

13816 National Spray Equipment Manufacturers

PO Box 2147
Skokie, IL 60076

440-366-6808
Fax: 847-763-9538
E-Mail: ipp@halldata.com
Home Page: www.ippmagazine.com

Bruce Bryan, Advertising Director
Ted Klaiber, Sales Manager

Serves as a technical forum for safety and environmental matters pertaining to the spray finishing industry.
16 Members
Founded in 1922

13817 New England Equipment Dealers Association

PO Box 895
Concord, NH 03302-0895

603-225-5510
Fax: 603-225-5510

George M Becker, Managing Director

The New England Equipment Association serve equipment manufacturing companies who provide products and services to the food and beverage industry.

13818 North American Equipment Dealers Association

1195 Smizer Mill Rd
Fenton, MO 63026-3480

636-349-5000
Fax: 636-349-5443
E-Mail: naeda@naeda.com
Home Page: www.naeda.com
Social Media: Facebook, Twitter, LinkedIn

Paul Kindinger, President/CEO
Michael Williams, VP, Government Relations/Treasurer
Terry Leath, Executive Assistant
Roger Gjellstad, First Vice Chair
Lester Killebrew, Chairman

NAEDA and its affiliates provides a variety of educational, financial, legislative and legal services to equipment dealers in the United States and Canada.
5000 Members
Founded in 1900

13819 North American Sawing Association

1300 Sumner Avenue
Cleveland, OH 44115-2851

216-241-7333
Fax: 216-241-0105
E-Mail: nasa@sawing association.com
Home Page: www.sawingassociation.com

Charles M Stockinger, Secretary/Treasurer

The purpose of this association is to improve the band sawing and power tool accessoried industries.
8 Members
Founded in 1959

13820 Society of Tribologists & Lubrication Engineers

840 Busse Hwy
Park Ridge, IL 60068-2302

847-825-5536
Fax: 847-825-1456
E-Mail: information@stle.org
Home Page: www.stle.org
Social Media: Facebook, Twitter, LinkedIn, Youtube

Robert D Heverly, President
Dr. Maureen E Hunter, Vice President
Dr. Martin N.ÿ Webster, Secretary
Dr Ali Erdemir, Treasurer
Bruce Murgueitio, Digital Marketing Manager

Purpose is to advance the science of tribology and the practice of lubrication engineering in order to foster innovation, improve the performance of equipment and products, conserve resources and protect the environment.
4000 Members
Founded in 1944
Mailing list available for rent

13821 ToolBase Services

NAHB Research Center
400 Prince George's Boulevard
Upper Marlboro, MD 20774

301-494-4000
800-898-2842
E-Mail: toolbase@nahbrc.org
Home Page: www.toolbase.org

The housing industry's resource for technical information on building products, materials, new technologies, business management, and housing systems.
Mailing list available for rent

13822 **Unified Abrasive Manufacturers' Association**
30200 Detroit Rd
Cleveland, OH 44145-1967

440-899-0010
Fax: 440-892-1404
E-Mail: contact@uama.org
Home Page: www.uama.org

Jeff Wherry, Executive Director

The purpose is to undertake those activties that can be pursued more effectively by an association than individual companies in order to enable the industry to freely create and market safe, productive abrasive products throughout the world.
30 Members
Founded in 1999

13823 **WaterJet Technology Association Industrial & Municipal Cleaning Association**
906 Olive Street
Suite 1200
Saint Louis, MO 63101-1448

314-241-1445
Fax: 314-241-1449
E-Mail: wjta-imca@wjta.org
Home Page: www.wjta.org

George A Savanick PhD, President
Kenneth C Carroll, Association Manager

A professional association of high pressure waterjet and industrial vacuum equipment users, manufacturers, distributors, researchers, regulators and consultants.
Founded in 1983

13824 **Web Sling & Tiedown Association**
2105 Laurel Bush Road
Suite 200
Bel Air, MD 21015

443-640-1070
Fax: 443-640-1031
E-Mail: kristin@stringfellowgroup.net
Home Page: www.wstda.com

Tom Wynn, President
Greg Pilgrim, Vice-President
Jim Bailey, Secretary/Treasurer
Jeff Iden, President-Elect

Manufacturers of web slings which are used as hoists in various industrial lifting operations.
79 Members
Founded in 1973

Newsletters

13825 **Asphalt Recycling and Reclaiming Association**
Asphalt Recycling and Reclaiming Association
3 Church Cir
PMB Box 250
Annapolis, MD 21401-1933

410-267-0023
Fax: 410-267-7546
Home Page: www.arra.com

Mike Krissoff, Executive Director

Promotes the interest of owners and manufacturers of recycling equipment, engineers suppliers and businesses involved in the asphalt recycling industry.
Frequency: Quarterly
Circulation: 1200
Founded in 1976
Mailing list available for rent

13826 **Can Tube Bulletin**
Composite Can & Tube Institute
50 S Pickett Street
Suite 110
Alexandria, VA 22304-7206

703-823-7234
Fax: 703-823-7237
E-Mail: ccti@cctiwdc.org
Home Page: www.cctiwdc.org

Kristine Garland, Executive VP
Wayne Vance, Association Counsel
Janine Marczak, Associate Manager, Events
Frequency: Bi-monthly
Circulation: 800+

13827 **Fastener Industry News**
Business Information Services
5028 Dumont Place
Woodland Hills, CA 91364-2407

818-248-5023
800-929-5586
Fax: 818-249-1169
E-Mail: info@biscomputer.com
Home Page: www.biscomputer.com

Richard Callahan, Publisher
John Wolz, Editor
Miro Macho, CEO/President

Publication written for executives and administrators in the fastener industry. Focuses on providing readers with business and financial news from within the industry. Includes personnel notices, management ideas and related materials.
Cost: $200.00
8 Pages
Frequency: Monthly
Founded in 1971
Mailing list available for rent
Printed in 2 colors on matte stock

13828 **Instrumentation and Automation News**
Chilton Company
201 King of Prussia Rd
Radnor, PA 19087-5147

610-964-4762
800-274-2207
Fax: 610-964-1888

Matt DeJulio, Publisher

The control technology/instrumentation market's only product news tabloid.

13829 **Journal of the National Spray Equipment Manufacturers Association**
550 Randall Road
Elyria, OH 44035-2974

440-366-6808
Fax: 440-892-2018

Don R Scarbrough, Executive Secretary

Includes editorial on safety and environmental matters pertaining to the spray finishing industry. Regular monthly features.
16 Pages
Founded in 1922

13830 **Manufacturing Automation**
Vital Information Publications
754 Caravel Lane
Foster City, CA 94404-1712

650-345-7018
Home Page: www.sensauto.com

Peter Adrian, Owner
Gary Kuba, Marketing Director

Provides market research data and vital information about key products, applications, and technologies for a wide range of industrial automation segments, such as CAD/CAM, supply chain management, e-Commerce solutions, enterprise resource planning, automation software, manufacturing technology, industrial controls, and manufacturing systems.

13831 **Sensor Business Digest**
Vital Information Publications
754 Caravel Lane
Foster City, CA 94404-1712

650-345-7018
Home Page: www.sensauto.com

Peter Adrian, Owner
Gary Kuba, Marketing Director

A widely recognized as a major source of information about the sensors industry-provides unique information about vital sensor markets, products, and applications, sensor technology, as well as in-depth company profiles
Frequency: Monthly

13832 **Sensor Technology**
John Wiley & Sons
111 River St
Hoboken, NJ 07030-5774

201-748-6000
800-825-7550
Fax: 201-748-6088
E-Mail: info@wiley.com
Home Page: www.wiley.com

William J Pesce, CEO

Written for companies and enterprises involved in a broad range of industrial disciplines. Publication follows advances in sensor technologies and their applications, along with opportunities for their use in the industrial marketplace.
Cost: $565.00
10 Pages
Frequency: Daily
Founded in 1807
Mailing list available for rent: 25000 names at $180 per M
Printed in 2 colors on newsprint stock

13833 **Waterjet Technology Association-Industrial and Municipal Cleaning Association**
906 Olive Street
Suite 1200
Saint Louis, MO 63101-1448

314-241-1445
Fax: 314-241-1449
E-Mail: wjta-imca@wjta.org
Home Page: www.wjta.org

George A Savanick PhD, President, Jet News Editor
Kenneth C Carroll, Association Manager

A professional association of high pressure waterjet and industrial cleaning equipment users, manufacturers, distributors, researchers, regulators, consultants and academicians.
Founded in 1983

Magazines & Journals

13834 **Advanced Materials & Processes**
ASM International
9639 Kinsman Rd
Materials Park, OH 44073-0002

440-338-5151
800-336-5152
Fax: 440-338-4634
E-Mail: memberservices@asminternational.org
Home Page: www.asminternational.org

Joseph M Zion, Publisher
Joanne Miller, Managing Editor
Margaret Hunt, Editor-in-Chief
Gernant E. Maurer, President
Thomas S. Passek, Managing Director

AM&P, the monthly technical magazine from ASM International, is designed to keep readers aware of leading-edge developments and trends in engineering materials - metals and alloys, engineering polymers, advanced ceramics, and composites - and the methods used to select, process, fabricate, test, and characterize them.
Frequency: Monthly
Circulation: 32M
Founded in 1977

13835 American Industry
Publications for Industry
21 Russell Woods Road
Great Neck, NY 11021-4644

516-487-0990
Fax: 516-487-0809
Home Page: www.publicationsforindustry.com

Jack S Panes, Publisher

Created for those executives responsible for overall plant operations and maintenance. Editorial focus is on new products and related services.
Cost: $25.00
Circulation: 300000
Founded in 1946
Printed in 4 colors on newsprint stock

13836 American Tool, Die & Stamping News
Eagle Publications
42400 Grand River Ave
Suite 103
Novi, MI 48375-2572

248-347-3487
800-783-3491
Fax: 248-347-3492
E-Mail: info@ameritooldie.com
Home Page: www.ameritooldie.com

Applications, techniques, equipment and accessories of metal stamping, moldmaking, electric discharge machining; and new product information relating to the tool and die industry. Accepts advertising.
70 Pages
Frequency: Monthly
Circulation: 30000
ISSN: 0192-5709
Founded in 1971
Printed in 5 colors on glossy stock

13837 Asian Industrial Report
Keller International Publishing Corporation
150 Great Neck Rd
Great Neck, NY 11021-3309

516-829-9722
Fax: 516-829-9306

Gerald E Keller, President
Bryan DeLuca, Editorial Director
Terry Beirne, Publisher
Bob Herlihy, Sales manager

English language tabloid presenting new products, equipment and services.
36 Pages
Circulation: 37107
ISSN: 1076-8351
Founded in 1882
Printed in 4 colors on glossy stock

13838 Business & Industry
Business Magazines
1720 28th Street
Suite B
West Des Moines, IA 50266-1400

515-225-2545
Fax: 515-225-2318
Home Page: www.busindmag.com

James V Snyder, Publisher
RJ Balch, Editor

Industrial news publication
Cost: $24.00
56 Pages
Frequency: Monthly
Circulation: 14M
ISSN: 0021-0463
Founded in 1946
Printed in 4 colors on glossy stock

13839 Cleaner
COLE Publishing
1720 Maple Lake Dam Road
PO Box 220
Three Lakes, WI 54562-0220

715-546-3346
800-257-7222
Fax: 715-546-3786
E-Mail: info@cleaner.com
Home Page: www.cleaner.com
Social Media: Facebook, Twitter

Jeff Bruss, President
Winnie May, Advertising Sales/Subscriptions
Ted Rulseh, Editor
Bob Kendall, Co-founder

The latest tools and equipment promoting safety and efficiency, employment and enviromental concerns, as well as industry profiles.
Cost: $15.50
Frequency: Monthly
Circulation: 22780
Founded in 1979

13840 Composites Manufacturers Magazine
American Composites Manufacturers Association
1010 N Glebe Rd
Suite 450
Arlington, VA 22201-5761

703-525-0511
Fax: 703-525-0743
E-Mail: info@acmanet.org
Home Page: www.acmanet.org

Tom Dobbins, Chief Staff Executive
Patti Washburn, Deputy Chief Staff Executive
Frequency: Monthly

13841 Crane & Hoist Canada
Capamara Communications
815 1st Ave
#301
Seattle, WA 98104

250-474-3982
800-936-2266
Fax: 250-478-3979
E-Mail: jeremy@capamara.com
Home Page: www.naqua.com

Peter Chetteburgh, Editor-in-Chief
Jeremy Thain, Sales Manager
James Lewis, Production Department

Only magazine focused exclusively on Canada's crane and hoist sectors. Provides essential news and information that Canadian crane and hoist professionals need in order to operate successfully and profitably. Articles on company profiles, practical crane & rigging information, new product news, industry trends, policy & regulations, safety/training/certification, and risk management.
Cost: $27.95
Frequency: Bi-monthly
Circulation: 3,500
Founded in 1985

13842 Filtration News
Eagle Publishers
42400 Grand River Ave
Suite 103
Novi, MI 48375-2572

248-347-3487
Fax: 248-347-3492
E-Mail: info@filtnews.com

Arthur Brown, Editor
Antoinette DeWaal, Associate Publisher/VP
Ken Norberg, Editor-in-Chief

New products and events on the special aspects of filtraion ranging from new equipment applications to new trends in the filtraion industry.
Cost: $65.00
Frequency: Bi-Monthly
Founded in 1981

13843 Finer Points Magazine
Industrial Diamond Association of America
PO Box 29460
Columbus, OH 43229

614-797-2265
Fax: 614-797-2264
E-Mail: tkane-ida@insight.rr.com
Home Page: www.superabrasives.org

Terry Kane, Publisher/Editor
Joe Tabling, President

Information for people who are involved in superabrasives or superabrasive products in some way.
Cost: $35.00
Frequency: Quarterly
Circulation: 7,500
Founded in 1946

13844 Flow Control
Grand View Media Group
200 Croft Street
Suite 1
Birmingham, AL 35242

888-431-2877
Fax: 205-408-3799
E-Mail: flowcontrol@grandviewmedia.com
Home Page: www.flowcontrolnetwork.com
Social Media: Facebook, Twitter, LinkedIn

John P Harris, Publisher
Matt Migliore, Editor
Matt Migliore, Executive Director of Content
Amy W. Richardson, Managing Editor
Mary Beth Timmerman, Marketing Manager

Technology information and new products for fluid handling engineers

13845 Hauler
Hauler Magazine
166 S Main Street
PO Box 508
New Hope, PA 18938

800-220-6029
800-220-6029
Fax: 215-862-3455
E-Mail: mag@thehauler.com
Home Page: www.thehauler.com

Thomas N Smith, Publisher/Editor
Barbara Gibney, Circulation Manager
Leslie T Smith, Marketing Director

Dedicated to the refuse and solid waste industry. It is the acknowledged leader in the new and used refuse truck and equipment marketplace, and now lists hundreds of new and used trash trucks, trailers, containers, services, plus parts and accessories from the best suppliers in the industry.
Cost: $12.00
Frequency: Monthly
Circulation: 18630
Founded in 1978

13846 High Performance Composites
Ray Publishing

P.O.Box 992
Morrison, CO 80465-0992

303-467-1776
Fax: 303-467-1777
E-Mail: info@raypubs.com
Home Page: www.compositeworld.com

Approach is technical, offering cutting-edge design, engineering, prototyping, and manufacturing solutions for aerospace and other traditional and emerging structural applications for advanced composites.

13847 **I&CS-Instrumentation & Control Systems**
PennWell Publishing Company
1421 S Sheridan Rd
Tulsa, OK 74112-6619

918-831-9421
800-331-4463
Fax: 918-831-9476
E-Mail: headquarters@pennwell.com
Home Page: www.pennwell.com

Robert Biolchini, President

Regular issue features include new systems analyses, new products listings, application ideas, and tutorial technology features.
Cost: $65.00
Frequency: Monthly
Circulation: 92,618
Founded in 1910

13848 **ICS Cleaning Specialist**
BNP Media
22801 Ventura Boulevard
#115
Woodland Hills, CA 91364

818-224-8035
800-835-4398
Fax: 818-224-8042
E-Mail: kesslere@bnpmedia.com
Home Page: www.icsmag.com
Social Media: Facebook, Twitter, LinkedIn

Phil Johnson, Group Publisher
Evan Kessler, Publisher
Jeffrey Stouffer, Editor

Dedicated to providing cleaning and restoration/remediation professionals with the most current and relevant information available to the industry.
Frequency: Annual+
Circulation: 25000
Mailing list available for rent

13849 **Industrial Distribution**
199 East Badger Road
Suite 201
Madison, WI 53713

781-734-8000
Fax: 781-734-8070
Home Page: www.manufacturing.net/ind
Social Media: Facebook, Twitter

Eric Wixom, Publisher
Jeff Reinke, Editorial Director
Joel Hans, Managing Editor
Mary Ann Gajewski, Production Manager

Provides current, comprehensive, issues-oriented editorial unique to the distribution industry including news, product updates, profitable product selection, management techniques, features on distribution-manufacturer relationships, legal issues and sales improvement.
Cost: $89.90
Frequency: Monthly
Circulation: 38000+
Mailing list available for rent

13850 **Industrial Equipment News**
Thomas Publishing Company
5 Penn Plaza
Manhattan, NY 10001

212-695-0500
800-733-1127
Fax: 212-290-7206
E-Mail: dmaskin@tpmgnet.com
Home Page: www.ienonline.com

Mark Maskin, Editorial Director
Deborah Maskin, Managing Editor
Ciro Buttacavoli, Publisher
Marie Urbanowicz, Marketing Director

Serves the industrial field including manufacturing, mining, utilities, construction, transportation,governmental establishments, and educational services.
Frequency: Monthly
Circulation: 205,000+
ISSN: 0019-8258
Founded in 1898

13851 **Industrial Laser Solutions**
PennWell Publishing Company
1421 S Sheridan Rd
Tulsa, OK 74112-6619

918-831-9421
Fax: 918-831-9476
E-Mail: belforte@penwell.com
Home Page: www.pennwell.com

Robert Biolchini, President
Laureen Belleville, Associate Publisher/Senior Editor

Devoted exclusively to global coverage of industrial laser applications, technology, and the people and companies who participate in this, the largest commerical portion of the global laser market.
45 Pages
Frequency: Monthly
Circulation: 10000
ISSN: 1523-4266
Founded in 1910

13852 **Industrial Literature Review**
Thomas Publishing Company
5 Penn Plz
12th Floor
New York, NY 10001-1860

212-695-0500
Fax: 212-290-7362
E-Mail: businesslists@thomaspublishing.com
Home Page: www.thomaspublishing.com

Carl Holst-Knudsen, CEO

Created to provide the dissemination of manufacturer catalogs and literature and mailed to buyers and specifies at plants with more than twenty employees.
Founded in 1976

13853 **Industrial Maintenance & Plant Operation**
Advantage Business Media
199 E Badger Road
Suite 201
Madison, WI 53713
973-920-7787
Fax: 973-607-5599
Home Page: www.impomag.com

Tom Lynch, Group Publisher
Eric Wixom, Associate Publisher
Anna Wells, Editor
Jeff Reinke, Editorial Director

provides timely, relevant coverage of manufacturing news, technology breakthrough, and in-plant advancements for plant managers and engineers looking to increase productivity, operate more efficiently and improve competitiveness.
Frequency: Monthly
Founded in 1940

13854 **Industrial Management**
Institute of Industrial Engineers
3577 Parkway Lane
Suite 200
Norcross, GA 30092
770-449-0460
800-494-0460
Fax: 770-441-3295
E-Mail: cs@iienet.org
Home Page: www.iienet.org

Elaine Fuerst, Marketing Director
Don Greene, Chief Executive Officer
Donna Calvert, Chief Operating Officer
Heather Bradley, Director of Membership
Monica Elliott, Director of Communications

Directed to the full range of management issues including adapting and evaluating new technologies, improving productivity and quality, and motivating employees.
Cost: $35.00
Frequency: Monthly
Circulation: 8500
Founded in 1948
Mailing list available for rent

13855 **Industrial Market Place**
Wineberg Publications
7842 Lincoln Avenue
Skokie, IL 60077

847-676-1900
800-323-1818
Fax: 847-676-0063
E-Mail: info@industrialmktpl.com
Home Page: www.industrialmktpl.com

Joel Wineberg, President
Jakie Bitensky, Editor

Has advertisements on machinery, industrial and plant equipment, services and industrial auctions in each issue.
Cost: $175.00
Frequency: Bi-Weekly
Circulation: 14,000
Founded in 1951
Mailing list available for rent: 120 names at $70 per M
Printed in 4 colors on glossy stock

13856 **Industrial Purchasing Agent**
Publications for Industry
21 Russell Woods Road
Great Neck, NY 11021-4644

516-487-0990
Fax: 516-487-0809
Home Page: www.PublicationsforIndustry.com

Jack Panes, Publisher
Pearl Shaine, Editor

New products publication for industrial purchasing agent executives in largest plants in the United States. Contains new releases on products, brochures, materials handling, etc.
Cost: $25.00
Frequency: Monthly
Circulation: 27000
Founded in 1958
Printed in 4 colors on newsprint stock

13857 **International Journal of Purchasing & Materials Management**
National Association of Purchasing Management
2055 E Centennial Circle
PO Box 22160
Tempe, AZ 85285-2160

480-752-2277
Fax: 480-491-7885
Home Page: www.capsresearch.com
Social Media: Twitter

Phillip L Carter, CEO/President
Richard A. Boyle, Director of Corporate
Kristina Cahill, Research Specialist
Phillip L. Carter, Executive Director

Kim Dixon-Williams, Executive Programs Manager

Publishes articles dealing with concepts from business, economics, operations management, information systems, the behavioral sciences, and other disciplines which contribute to the advancement of knowledge in the various areas of purchasing, materials management, and related fields.
Cost: $59.00
Frequency: Quarterly
Circulation: 2800
Founded in 1986

13858 Journal of Coatings Technology
Federation of Societies for Coatings Technology
1500 Rhode Island Ave., NW
Suite 415
Washington, DC 20005

202-462-6272
Fax: 202-462-8549
E-Mail: fsct@coatingstech.com
Home Page: www.coatingstech.org

J. Andrew Doyle, President & CEO
Thomas J. Graves, VP, General Counsel
Allen Irish, Counsel / Director, Industry Affair
Alison Keane, Vice President, Government Affairs
Robin Eastman Caldwell, Senior Government Affairs

Includes practical articles, Q&A features, and roundtable discussions with coatings professionals related to industry segments, manufacturing processes, business operations, environmental concerns, and other pertinent topics.
Frequency: 11x/Year

13859 Journal of Materials Engineering and Performance
ASM International
9639 Kinsman Road
Materials Park, OH 44073-0002

440-338-5151
800-336-5152
Fax: 440-338-4634
E-Mail: memberservice@asminternational.org
Home Page: www.asminternational.org

Gernant E. Maurer, President
Thomas S. Passek, Managing Director

Peer-reviewed journal that publishes contributions on all aspects of materials selection, design, characterization, processing and performance testing. The journal for solving day-to-day engineering challenges - especially those involving components for larger systems.
Cost: $1965.00
Frequency: Bimonthly
Circulation: 305
Founded in 1992

13860 Journal of Phase Equilibria
ASM International
9639 Kinsman Rd
Materials Park, OH 44073-0002

440-338-5151
800-336-5152
Fax: 440-338-4634
E-Mail: memberservices@asminternational.org
Home Page: www.asminternational.org

Gernant E. Maurer, President
Thomas S. Passek, Managing Director

Peer-reviewed journal that contains basic and applied research results, evaluated phase diagrams, a survey of current literature, and comments or other material pertinent to the previous three areas. The aim is to provide a broad spectrum of information concerning phase equilibria for the materials community.
Cost: $1965.00
Frequency: Bimonthly
Circulation: 305

13861 Journal of Protective Coatings & Linings
Technology Publishing Company
2100 Wharton St
Suite 310
Pittsburgh, PA 15203-1951

412-431-8300
800-837-8303
Fax: 412-431-5428
E-Mail: webmaster@paintsquare.com
Home Page: www.paintsquare.com
Social Media: Facebook, Twitter

Harold Hower, Owner
Karen Kapsanis, Editor
Milissa Bogats, Production Director
Pam Simmons, Director of Marketing
Julie Birch, Marketing Manager

Focuses on good practice in the use of protective coatings for steel and concrete surfaces. Features articles on such topics as coatings selection for specific service environments, surface preparation, coating application, quality control, cost-effectiveness in maintenance programs, safety issues, and environmental regulations.
Cost: $80.00
Frequency: Monthly
Circulation: 15000
Mailing list available for rent

13862 Journal of Thermal Spray Technology
ASM International
9639 Kinsman Rd
Novelty, OH 44073-0002

440-338-5151
800-336-5152
Fax: 440-338-4634
E-Mail: Cust-Srv@asminternational.org
Home Page: www.asminternational.org

Gernant E. Maurer, President
Thomas S. Passek, Managing Director

Peer-reviewed journal which publishes contributions on all aspects, fundamental and practical, of thermal spray science, including processes, feedstock manufacture, testing and characterization. As the primary vehicle for thermal spray information transfer, its mission is to synergize the rapidly advancing thermal spray industry and related industries by presenting research and development efforts leading to advancements in implementable engineering applications of the technology.
Cost: $1577.00
Frequency: Bimonthly
Circulation: 680
Founded in 1952

13863 Lift Equipment
Group III Communications
204 W Kansas Street
Suite 103
Independence, MO 64050

816-254-8735
Fax: 816-254-2128

Terry Ford, President
Michael Scheibach, Publisher
Tracy L Bennett, Editor/Associate Publisher

The buyer's source for equipment, technology and trends. Free to qualified subscribers.
Cost: $24.00
80 Pages
Frequency: 10 per year
Circulation: 18,000
ISSN: 1056-0149
Printed in 4 colors on glossy stock

13864 Lubes-N-Greases
LNG Publishing Company
6105 Arlington Blvd
Suite G
Falls Church, VA 22044-2708

703-536-0800
Fax: 703-536-0803
E-Mail: info@LNGpublishing.com
Home Page: www.lngpublishing.com

Gloria Stienberg, Owner
Tim Sullivan, Managing Editor
Sheryl Unangst, Circulation Manager
Michele Persaud, Senior Editor
Richard Beercheck, Senior Editor

Features and informed opinions covering automotive and industrial lubricants, metalworking fluids, greases, base stocks, additives, packaging, biodegradable and synthetic products, companies, people, issues and trends affecting the industry.
Frequency: Monthly
Circulation: 16000
ISSN: 1080-9449
Founded in 1995
Printed in 4 colors

13865 Lubricating Engineering
Society of Tribologists & Lubrication Engineers
840 Busse Hwy
Park Ridge, IL 60068-2376

847-825-5536
Fax: 847-825-1456
E-Mail: information@stle.org
Home Page: www.stle.org

Ed Salek, Executive Director
Karl Phipps, Associate Managing Editor
Tracy Nicholas, National Sales Manager

Technical papers and news articles with up to date developments in the lubrication industry.
Frequency: Monthly
Circulation: 6000

13866 MRO Today
Pfingsten Publishing
730 Madison Avenue
Fort Atkinson, WI 53538-606

920-563-5225
800-932-7732
Fax: 920-563-4269
Home Page: www.mrotoday.com

Todd Rank, VP
Tom Hammel, Associate Publisher/Editorial Dir
John Mansavage, Circulation and Research
Jill Sheppard, Marketing Manager

Provides best practices for industrial maintanence, production, MRO purchasing, quality and safety personnel. MRO Today helps these pros do their jobs cheaper, better, faster and smarter.
Circulation: 120,000
ISSN: 1091-0638
Founded in 1996
Printed in on glossy stock

13867 Maintenance Technology
Applied Technology Publications
1300 S Grove Ave
Suite 105
Barrington, IL 60010-5246

847-382-8100
Fax: 847-304-8603
Home Page: www.mt-online.com

Arthur Rice, President/CEO
Bill Kiesel, Vice President/Publisher
Jane Alexander, Editor-In-Chief
Rick Carter, Executive Editor
Randy Buttstadt, Director of Creative Services

Maintenance Technology magazine serves the business and technical information needs of managers and engineers responsible for assuring availability of plant equipment and systems. It provides readers with articles on advanced technologies, strategies, tools, and services for the life-cycle management of capital assets.
Frequency: Monthly
Circulation: 50,827
Mailing list available for rent: 35,263 names at $$15 per M

13868 Measurements & Control
100 Wallace Avenue
Suite 100
Sarasota, FL 34237

941-954-8405
800-883-8894
Fax: 941-366-5743

13869 Modern Paint & Coatings
Cygnus Publishing
445 Broad Hollow Road
Melville, NY 11747-3601

631-845-2700
Fax: 631-845-2723
Home Page: www.cygnuspub.com

Esther D'Amico, Editor
Paul Bonaiuto, CFO
Kathy Scott, Director of Public Relations

The latest technology and news including chemical innovations, new production equipment,new trends and coverage of regulatory affairs.
Cost: $45.00
Frequency: Monthly
Circulation: 14,000

13870 NAEDA Equipment Dealer
North American Equipment Dealers Association
1195 Smizer Mill Rd
Fenton, MO 63026-3480

636-349-5000
Fax: 636-349-5443
E-Mail: naeda@naeda.com
Home Page: www.naeda.com
Social Media: Twitter, LinkedIn

Paul Kindinger, President/CEO
Michael Williams, VP, Government Relations/Treasurer
Terry Leath, Executive Assistant
Roger Gjellstad, First Vice Chair
Lester Killebrew, Chairman

A monthly management and merchandising magazine features articles about successful dealers, new products, new technology, industry news, insurance loss control solutions, and top management tips.
Cost: $45.00
5000 Members
32 Pages
Frequency: Monthly
ISSN: 1074-5017
Founded in 1959
Printed in 4 colors on glossy stock

13871 New Equipment Digest
Penton Media
1300 E 9th St
Cleveland, OH 44114-1503

216-696-7000
Fax: 216-696-6662
E-Mail: information@penton.com
Home Page: www.penton.com

Jane Cooper, Marketing
Diane Madzelonka, Production Manager
David Kieselstein, Chief Executive Officer
Kurt Nelson, Vice President, Human Resources
Andrew Schmolka, Senior Vice President

Serves the general industrial field which includes manufacturing, processing, engineering services, construction, transportation, mining, public utilities, wholesale distributors, educational services, libraries, and governmental establishments.
Frequency: Monthly
Circulation: 206154
Founded in 1936
Mailing list available for rent

13872 OEM Off-Highway
1233 Janesville Avenue
PO Box 803
Fort Atkinson, WI 53538-803

920-563-6388
800-547-7377
Fax: 920-328-9029
E-Mail: Leslie.Shalabi@cygnuspub.com
Home Page: www.oemoff-highway.com

Richard Reiff, Executive VP
Leslie Shalabi, Publisher/Editor
Paul Mackler, President/CEO
Barb Hesse, Circulation Manager

Offers information on off-road machinery and farm equipment.
Founded in 1965

13873 Purchasing Magazine's Buying Strategy Forecast
Reed Business Information
275 Washington St
Newton, MA 02458-1611

617-964-3030
Fax: 617-558-4327
E-Mail: kbecker@reedbusiness.com

Kathy Doyle, Publisher
Paul Teague, Chief Editor
Kathy Becker, Publisher's Assistant

Provides insight and forecasts of numerous industrial and commercial raw materials products.
Circulation: 95,095
Founded in 1960

13874 Rental Product News
Cygnus Business Media
3 Huntington Quadrangle
Suite 301N
Melville, NY 11747

631-845-2700
800-308-6397
Fax: 631-845-2741
E-Mail: info@cygnus.com
Home Page: www.cygnusb2b.com

Dave Davel, VP Publishing
Kris Flitcroft, Group Publisher
Carrier Grall, Publisher
Paul Bonaiuto, Chief Financial Officer
John French, Chief Executive Officer

Provides professional rental operators with the latest insights on equipment asset management so they can make their businesses more productive and competitive. Also provides insight on how leaders in the equipment rental field are getting the best return from their assets through better equipment selection, application, maintenance and safety techniques.
Circulation: 20000
Founded in 1966

13875 Robotics World
Douglas Publications
2807 N Parham Road
Suite 200
Richmond, VA 23294

804-762-9600
800-791-8699
570-567-1982
Fax: 570-320-2079
E-Mail: briefingsweborders@publishersserviceasso
Home Page: www.douglaspublications.com

Jack Browne, Editor
Andrew Dwyer, Publisher

Covers key developments in the field of flexible automation and intelligent machines for an audience of management level automation professionals.
Frequency: Monthly
Circulation: 87000
Founded in 1985

13876 Twin Plant News
5400 Suncrest
Suite D-5
El Paso, TX 79912

915-532-1567
Fax: 915-544-7556
E-Mail: tpn@twinplantnews.com
Home Page: www.twinplantnews.com

Michele Lee, President
Rosa Ma Nibbe, Executive Publisher
Mike Patten, Managing Editor

Focuses on the operations of major companies in the United States and the maquiladoras in Mexico. Includes articles about changes affecting the automotive, electronics, plastics and metal industries, as well as information about customs regulations on both sides of the border and other relevant topics.
Frequency: Monthly
Founded in 1985

13877 World Industrial Reporter
Keller International Publishing Corporation
150 Great Neck Rd
Great Neck, NY 11021-3309

516-829-9722
Fax: 516-829-9306
Home Page: www.supplychainbrain.com

Bryan DeLuca, Editor
Terry Beirne, Publisher
Jerry Keller, President
Mary Chavez, Director of Sales

New equipment, machinery and techniques for the industry.
34 Pages
Circulation: 37,107
Founded in 1882

Trade Shows

13878 AMSE Internation Manufacturing Science & Engineering Conference
American Society of Mechanical Engineers
Three Park Avenue
New York, NY 10016-5990

973-882-1170
800-843-2763
E-Mail: infocentral@asme.org
Home Page: www.asme.org

David Walsh, Editor
Chitra Sethi, Managing Editor
John Kosowatz, Senior Editor

The MSEC highlights cutting edge manufacturing research in technical paper, poster and panel sessions.
3200 Attendees
Frequency: Annual/Fall
Founded in 1880
Mailing list available for rentat $125 per M

13879 ASIS Annual Conference and Exhibits
American Society of Industrial Security

1625 Prince Street
Alexandria, VA 22314-2818

703-519-6200
703-519-6299
Fax: 703-519-6299
E-Mail: asis@asisonline.org
Home Page: www.asisonline.org

Eduard J. Emde, President
Michael J Stack, CEO

The most comprehensive educational and networking event in the security industry that offers high-quality and insightful educational sessions on every aspect of security; exhibits featuring the latest security technology and innovations and providing a forum for 900 companies to demonstrate the cutting-edge security products and services that are shaping the security industry.
38000 Members
14M Attendees
Frequency: September
Founded in 1955
Mailing list available for rent

13880 ASM Heat Treating Society Conference & Exposition
Materials Information Society
9639 Kinsman Road
Materials Park, OH 44073-0002

440-385-5151
800-336-5152
Fax: 440-338-4634
E-Mail:
pamela.kleinman@asminternational.org
Home Page: www.asminternational.org

Pamela Kleinma, Senior Manager, Events
Kellye Thomas, Exposition Account Manager
Gernant E. Maurer, President
Thomas S. Passek, Managing Director

Conference and exhibits of heat treating equipment and supplies plus information of interest to metallurgists, manufacturing, research and design technical professionals. 300 exhibitors.
3500 Attendees
Frequency: September, Bi-Annual
Founded in 1974

13881 ASM Materials Science & Technology (MS&T)
Materials Information Society
9639 Kinsman Road
Materials Park, OH 44073-0002

440-338-5151
800-336-5152
Fax: 440-338-4634
E-Mail:
pamela.kleinman@asminternational.org
Home Page: www.asminternational.org

Pamela Kleinman, Senior Manager, Events
Kelly Thomas, Exposition Account Manager
Gernant E. Maurer, President
Thomas S. Passek, Managing Director

Annual event focusing on testing, analysis, characterization and research of materials such as engineered materials, high performance metals, powdered metals, metal forming, surface modification, welding and joining. 350 exhibitors.
4,000 Attendees
Frequency: Annual/October
Founded in 2005

13882 ASME Annual Meeting
American Society of Mechanical Engineers
Three Park Avenue
New York, NY 10016

973-882-1170
800-843-2763
Fax: 212-591-7856
E-Mail: infocentral@asme.org
Home Page: www.asme.org

Melissa Torres, Meetings Manager
Mary Jakubowski, Meetings Manager
David Walsh, Editor
Chitra Sethi, Managing Editor
John Kosowatz, Senior Editor
Frequency: Annual/June
Founded in 1880
Mailing list available for rent

13883 ASME Gas Turbine Users Symposium (GTUS)
American Society of Mechanical Engineers/IGTI
6525 The Corners Pkwy
Ste. 115
Norcross, GA 30092

404-847-0072
Fax. 404-847-0151
E-Mail: igti@asme.org
Home Page: www.asme.org/igti

Stephanie Searsr, Coordinator, IGTI Conferences
Judy Osborn, Manager, IGTI Conferences & Expos
Michael Ireland, Managing Director
Charity Golden, Operations Director
Shirley Barton, Manager, Professional Development

A show focused on the role gas turbines will play in meeting the nation's future energy demands, provides the information related to gas turbine operations, maintenance, advances, and design.
2000 Attendees
Frequency: Annual
Mailing list available for rent

13884 AeroMat Conference and Exposition
ASM International
9639 Kinsman Road
Materials Park, OH 44073-0002

440-385-5151
800-336-5152
Fax: 440-338-4634
E-Mail: kim.schaefer@asminternational.org
Home Page: www.asminternational.org

Kim Schaefer, Event Manager
Kelly Thomas, Exposition Account Manager
Gernant E. Maurer, President
Thomas S. Passek, Managing Director

Conference for Aerospace Meterials Engineers, Structural Engineers and Designers. The annual event focuses on affordable structures and low-cost manufacturing, titanium alloy technology, advanced intermetallics and refractory metal alloys, materials and processes for space applications, aging systems, high strength steel, NDT evaluation, light alloy technology, welding and joining, and engineering technology. 150 exhibitors.
1500 Attendees
Frequency: Annual/June
Founded in 1984

13885 Association of Machinery and Equipment Appraisers Annual Conference
315 S Patrick Street
Alexandria, VA 22314-3501

703-836-7900
800-537-8629
Fax: 703-836-9303
E-Mail: amea@amea.org
Home Page: www.amea.org

Lorna Lindsey, Manager
Charles J. Winternitz, President
Pamela Reid, Director, Member Services

Exhibits of interest to machinery and equipment appraisers.
300 Members
Founded in 1983
Mailing list available for rent

13886 CCTI Annual Meeting
Composite Can & Tube Institute
50 S Pickett Street
Suite 110
Alexandria, VA 22304-7206

703-823-7234
Fax: 703-823-7237
E-Mail: ccti@cctiwdc.org
Home Page: www.cctiwdc.org

Kristine Garland, Executive VP
Wayne Vance, Association Counsel
Janine Marczak, Associate Manager, Events
Frequency: May

13887 Capital Industrial Show
Industrial Shows of America
1794 The Alameda
San Jose, CA 95126-1729

408-947-0233
Fax: 408-286-8836

Annual show and exhibits of industrial equipment, supplies and services.
4000 Attendees

13888 Dynamic Positioning Conference
Marine Technology Society
1100 H St., Nw
Suite LL-100
Washington, DC 20005

202-717-8705
Fax: 202-347-4302
E-Mail: membership@mtsociety.org
Home Page: www.mtsociety.org
Social Media: Facebook, Twitter, LinkedIn

Jerry Boatman, President
Drew Michel, President-Elect
Jerry Wilson, VP of Industry and Technology
Jill Zande, VP of Education and Research
Justin Manley, VP of Gov. & Public Affairs

Recognized as the leading symposium covering developments and technology associated with Dynamic Positioning. Industry leaders discuss DP-related vessel design, and operations, and DP manufacturers and service companies exhibit their products and services to a highly targeted and focused audience.
2M Members
Founded in 1963

13889 FABFORM
Industrial Shows of America
164 Lake Front Drive
Hunt Valley, MD 21030-2215

410-771-1445
800-638-6396
Fax: 410-771-1158

This is the most effective way to reach forming, fabricating and welding equipment buyers in the Northern California area.
3000 Attendees
Frequency: April

13890 Federation of Societies for Coatings Technology
Federation of Societies for Coatings Technology
492 Norristown Road
Blue Bell, PA 19422-2350

610-940-0777
Fax: 610-940-0292
Home Page: www.coatingstech.com

Robert Ziegler, Publisher
Patricia D Ziegler, Semior Editor
Ray Dickie, Editor

Provides a major service to the coatings industry, serves as a link between users and supplies of raw materials, production equipment, coatings, adhesives, inks, sealants, testing equipment, containers and laboratory apparatus.International Coating Expo November, Georgia World Congress Center in Atlanta, Georgia.

13891 **Great Lakes Industrial Show**
North American Expositions Company
33 Rutherford Avenue
Boston, MA 02129

617-242-6092
800-225-1577
Fax: 617-242-1817
E-Mail: dnovack@naexpo.com
Home Page: www.naexpo.com

Denise Novack, Contact

With over 300 companies exhibiting, showcases the latest technology, products, services and solutions for your manufacturing needs.
14319 Attendees
Frequency: November
Founded in 1972

13892 **ISMA/IDA Spring & Fall Conventions**
Industrial Distribution Association
100 N 20th Street
Suite 400
Philadelphia, PA 19103

215-320-3862
866-460-2360
Fax: 215-963-9785
E-Mail: info@isapartners.org
Home Page: www.isapartners.org
Social Media: Facebook, Twitter, LinkedIn

John Duffy, Director
Ed Gerber, President
Michael Carr, Vice President
Tommy Thompson, Treasurer

Semi-annual conventions for distributors and manufacturers of industrial (MROP) supplies.

13893 **Industrial Marketing Expo**
Lobos Services
16016 Perkins Road
Baton Rouge, LA 70810

225-751-5626

Debbie Balough, Show Manager

250 booths.
6M Attendees
Frequency: April

13894 **Industrial Products Expo and Conference**
Key Productions
94 Murphy Road
Hartford, CT 06114-2121

860-247-8363
880-753-9776
Fax: 860-947-6900
E-Mail: webadmin@keypro.com
Home Page: www.keypro.com

Maura Lewis, Show Manager

This show features exhibits and/or services used in manufacturing, management and warehousing.
6M Attendees
Frequency: September

13895 **Industrial Show Pacific Coast**
Industrial Shows of America
164 Lake Front Drive
Hunt Valley, MD 21030-2215

410-771-1445
800-638-6396
Fax: 410-771-1158

James K Donahue, President

Four hundred booths.
11M Attendees
Frequency: November

13896 **International Fastener and Precision Formed Parts Manufacturing Expo**
Pemco
383 Main Avenue
Norwalk, CT 06851-1543

203-840-7700
800-323-5155
Fax: 630-260-0395

Biennial show and exhibits of cold headers and header tooling, tools and dies, forming machines, parts feeding and handling equipment and test equipment for the industrial fastener and precision formed parts manufacturing industry.

13897 **International Off-Highway and Power Plant Meeting and Exposition**
Society of Automotive Engineers
400 Commonwealth Drive
Warrendale, PA 15096-0001

724-776-4841
Fax: 724-776-4026
Home Page: www.sae.org

Diane Rogne, Show Manager
Sam Barill, Treasurer
Andrew Brown, Treasurer

Annual show of 270 suppliers of parts, components, materials and systems utilized in farm and industrial machinery and off-road and recreational vehicles.
5000 Attendees
Circulation: 84,000

13898 **International Symposium for Testing & Failure Analysis**
ASM International
9639 Kinsman Road
Materials Park, OH 44073-0002

440-338-5151
800-336-5152
Fax: 440-338-4634
E-Mail: kim.schaefer@asminternational.org
Home Page: www.asminternational.org

Kim Schaefer, Event Manager
Kelly Thomas, Exposition Account Manager
Gernant E. Maurer, President
Thomas S. Passek, Managing Director

Annual event focusing on microelectronic and elcetronic device failure analysis, techniques, EOS/ESD testing and descretes aimed at failure analysis engineers and managers, technisians and new failure analysis engineers. 200 exhibitors.
1100 Attendees
Frequency: Annual/November

13899 **Mid South Industrial, Material Handling and Distribution Expo**
Industrial Shows of America
164 Lake Front Drive
Hunt Valley, MD 21030-2215

410-771-1445
800-638-6396
Fax: 410-771-1158

James K Donahue, President

300 booths of industrial and business related products and services.
8M Attendees
Frequency: June

13900 **National Association of Industrial Technology Convention**
National Association of Industrial Technology
3300 Washtenaw Avenue
Suite 220
Ann Arbor, MI 48104-4294

734-677-0720
Fax: 734-677-2407
E-Mail: nait@nait.org
Home Page: www.nait.org

Dr. Alvin Thadisill, Show Manager
Dave Monporan, Exhibit Manager
Rick Coscarelli, Executive Director

Annual convention of National Association of Industrial Technology, professional association of two and four year Industrial Technology program, faculty, standards and professionals in industry. Exhibitors desired in textbooks, training manuals, software and video; testing and training equipment, computer hardware and software, ISP's and distance learning hosts; CAD/CAM; Rapid Protyping; PC's. There are 25 booths. Next show is in Pittsburgh, Pennsylvania.
500 Attendees
Frequency: November

13901 **Pacific Coast Industrial and Machine Tool Show**
ISOA
1794 The Alameda
San Jose, CA 95126-1729

408-947-0233
800-286-2882
Fax: 408-286-8836

Annual show of 260 exhibitors of industrial equipment, machine tools, business services, hand tools and related equipment, supplies and services.
12M Attendees
Frequency: November, Santa Clara

13902 **Rocky Mountain Industrial and Machine Tool Show**
Trade Shows West
360 S Fort Ln
Suite 2C
Layton, UT 84041-5708

801-485-0176
Fax: 801-485-0241
Home Page: www.facetofacemarketing.net

A three day exhibit focusing on the needs of the industrial, manufacturing and plant maintenance industries.
8463 Attendees
Frequency: Annual/May

13903 **Salt Lake Machine Tool & Manufacturing Exposition**
Trade Shows West
2880 S Main Street
Suite 110
Salt Lake City, UT 84115

801-485-0176
Fax: 801-485-0241
E-Mail: jeffwfredericks@hotmail.com
Home Page: www.facetofacemarketing.net

13904 **Tidewater Industrial & Manufacturing Technology Show**
Industrial Shows of America
164 Lake Front Drive
Hunt Valley, MD 21030-2215

410-771-1445
800-638-6396
Fax: 410-771-1158
Home Page: www.isoa.com

Annual show of 250 suppliers and distributors of industrial and marine equipment, machine and hand tools, business services and related equipment, supplies and services.
Frequency: September, VA Beach

13905 Tri-State Industrial & Machine Tools Show
Industrial Shows of America
164 Lake Front Drive
Hunt Valley, MD 21030-2215

410-771-1445
800-638-6396
Fax: 410-771-1158

This show will bring together exhibitors and customers to preview products and discuss new technologies for the metalworking and manufacturing industries. The show will feature machine tools, metalworking equipment, services for manufacturing industrial products and supplies. Thousands of qualified decision-makers involved in management, engineering, purchasing and manufacturing will attend.
Frequency: April

13906 USA/Mexico Industrial Expo
Industrial Shows of America
164 Lake Front Drive
Hunt Valley, MD 21030-2215

410-771-1445
800-638-6396
Fax: 410-771-1158

This event draws attendees from avariety of manufacturing and assembly companies. Product categories include material handling, safety equipment, compressors, maintenance equipment, industrial water products, hydraulic/pneumatics, tools and many more. On average, attendees spend over $100,000 per year obn these products.
9000 Attendees
Frequency: June

Directories & Databases

13907 Capital Cities Regional Industrial Buying Guide
Thomas Publishing Company
5 Penn Plaza
New York, NY 10001-1810

212-950-0500

A who's who directory of supplies to the industry.
Cost: $65.00
1200 Pages
Frequency: Annual

13908 Directory of the Association of Machinery and Equipment Appraisers
Association of Machinery and Equipment Appraisers
315 S Patrick St
Alexandria, VA 22314-3532

703-836-7900
800-537-8629
Fax: 703-836-9303
E-Mail: amea@amea.org
Home Page: www.amea.org

Pamela Reid, Director, Member Services
Lorna Lindsey, Manager
Charles J. Winternitz, President

Nearly 300 member certified machinery appraisers.
300 Members
Frequency: Annual January
Founded in 1983
Mailing list available for rent

13909 IGWB Buyer's Guide
BNP Media
PO Box 1080
Skokie, IL 60076-9785

847-763-9534
Fax: 847-763-9538
E-Mail: igwb@halldata.com
Home Page: www.igwb.com

James Rutherford, Editor
Lynn Davidson, Marketing
Nikki Smith, Director

A comprehensive resource listing over 1000 gaming products and services suppliers.
Frequency: Annual

13910 Industrial Machinery Digest
Cygnus Interactive
262 Yeager Parkway
Suite C
Pelham am, AL 35124

866-833-5346
Fax: 866-826-5918
E-Mail: william.strickland@cygnusb2b.com
Home Page: www.indmacdig.com
Social Media: Facebook, Twitter, LinkedIn

William Strickland, Publisher
Adrienne Gallender, Associate Publisher
Lisa Hanschu, Sales Consultant
Amy Boelk, Art Director / Print Product
Susan Hopkins, Accounting

A leader among industrial trade publications distributed to machine shops, job shops, fabricating shops, gear manufacturers, industrial warehouses & distribution centers, large industrial facilities & manufacturing plants, material handling, retro & rebuilding machine maintenance, pipe & tube manufacturers and manchinery dealers and wholesalers.

13911 SBC Industrial Purchasing Guide
100 E Big Beaver Rd
Suite 700E
Troy, MI 48083-1248

248-524-4800
800-331-1385
Fax: 248-524-4849
Home Page: www.smartpages.com

Susan Wright, Industrial Operations Manager
Nicole Howard-Combs, Director

Providers of industrial products and services; seperate regional editions cover Illinois, Wisconsin, Indiana, Michigan, and Ohio.

13912 Sweets Directory
Grey House Publishing/McGraw Hill Construction
1221 Avenue of the Americas
New York, NY 10020-1095

212-512-2000
800-442-2258
Fax: 212-512-3840
E-Mail: webmaster@mcgraw-hill.com
Home Page: www.mcgraw-hill.com
Social Media: Facebook, Twitter

Harold W McGraw III, CEO

The leading desktop reference and preliminary research guide, featuring more than 10,000 building product manufacturers and their products.
Cost: $145.00
950 Pages
Frequency: Annual
ISBN: 1-592378-50-1
Founded in 1906

13913 ThomasNet
Thomas Publishing Company, LLC
User Services Department
5 Penn Plaza
New York, NY 10001

212-695-0500
800-699-9822
Fax: 212-290-7362
E-Mail: contact@thomaspublishing.com
Home Page: www.thomasnet.com
Social Media: Facebook, Twitter, LinkedIn

Carl Holst-Knudsen, President
Robert Anderson, VP, Planning
Mitchell Peipert, VP, Finance
Ivy Molofsky, VP, Human Resources

A way to reach qualified businesses that list their company information on ThomasNet.com. Detailed profiles promote their products, services, capabilities and brands carried. The ThomasNet.com web site is the most up-to-date compilation of 650,000 North American manufacturers, distributors, and service companies in 67,000 industrial categories.
Founded in 1898
Mailing list available for rent

13914 World Industrial Reporter: Directory of Distributors Issue
Keller International Publishing Corporation
150 Great Neck Rd
Great Neck, NY 11021-3309

516-829-9722
Fax: 516-829-9306
Home Page: www.supplychainbrain.com

Jerry Keller, President
Mary Chavez, Director of Sales

A list of over 3,000 international advertisers and their distributors with product line related to the industrial supplies and equipment industry.
Cost: $45.00
Frequency: Annual

13915 World Industrial Reporter: International Buyer's Guide Issue
Keller International Publishing Corporation
150 Great Neck Rd
Great Neck, NY 11021-3309

516-829-9722
Fax: 516-829-9306
Home Page: www.supplychainbrain.com

Jerry Keller, President
Mary Chavez, Director of Sales

Over 275 international advertisers are listed that offer industrial supplies and equipment for export.
Cost: $5.00
Frequency: Annual
Circulation: 40,000

Industry Web Sites

13916 http://gold.greyhouse.com
G.O.L.D Grey House OnLine Databases

Grey House Publishing's online database platform, GOLD, offers Quick Search, Keyword Search and Expert Search for most business sectors including industrial equipment markets. The GOLD platform makes finding the information you need quick and easy - whether you're a novice searcher or an experienced database user. All of Grey House's directory products are available for subscription on the GOLD platform.

13917 www.amea.org
Association of Machinery and Equipment Appraisers

The premier international association of appraisers who specialize in appraising machinery and equipment.

13918 www.arra.org
Asphalt Recycling and Reclaiming Association

Promotes the interest of owners and manufacturers of recycling equipment, engineers suppliers and businesses involved in the asphalt recycling industry.

13919 www.atmae.org
Assoc of Tech, Management, and Applied Engineering
Faculty, students and industry professionals dedicated to solving complex technological probelms and developing the competitive technologist and applied engineering workforce.

13920 www.greyhouse.com
Grey House Publishing
Authoritative reference directories for most business sectors including industrial equipment markets. Users can search the online databases with varied search criteria allowing for custom searches by product category, geographic area, sales volume, keyword, subject and more. Full Grey House catalog and online ordering also available.

13921 www.ida-assoc.org
Industrial Supply Association
To help members increase sales, reduce expenses and improve profiyability

13922 www.mdna.org
Machinery Dealers National Association
Represents dealers of used industrial equipment.

13923 www.mt-online.com
Applied Technology Publications
MT-online.com is the premier source of capacity assurance and best practice solutions for manufacturing, process and service operations worldwide. Online home of Maintenance Technology magazie, the dynamic MT-online.com portal serves the critical technical, business and professional-development needs of engineers, managers and technicians from across all industrial, institutional and commercial sectors.

13924 www.polysort.com
Polysort.com
A portal for the plastics and rubber industry, providing news, information about plastics and rubber industry trade shows, company links, as well as plastics and rubber classified advertising

13925 www.sweets.construction.com
McGraw Hill Construction
In depth product information that lets you find, compare, select, specify and make purchase decisions in the industrial product marketplace.

13926 www.thomasregister.com Thomas Register
Thomas Register
Comprehensive online resource for defining companies and products manufactured in North America. Use it for placing orders, downloading computer-aided design drawings, and viewing thousands of online company catalogs and websites.

Associations

13927 Alliance of Claims Assistance Professionals
9600 Escarpment
Suite 745-65
Austin, TX 78749
512-394-0008
888-394-5163
E-Mail: capinfo@claims.org
Home Page: www.claims.org
Social Media: Twitter

Rebecca Stephenson, Co-President
Katalin Goencz, Co-President

Professionals dedicated to the effective management of health insurance claims. Our members are claims assistance professionals who work for patients.
50 Members
Founded in 1998

13928 America's Health Insurance Plans
601 Pennsylvania Ave Nw
South Building, Suite 500
Washington, DC 20004-2601
202-778-3200
Fax: 202-331-7487
E-Mail: ahip@ahip.org
Home Page: www.ahip.org
Social Media: Twitter

Karen M Ignagni, President/CEO

Mission is to be an effective advocate for a workable legislative and regulatory environment at the federal and state levels in which our members can advance their vision of a health care system that meets the needs of consumers, employers and public purchasers.
1300 Members
Founded in 2003
Mailing list available for rent

13929 American Academy of Actuaries
1850 M Street NW
Suite 300
Washington, DC 20036
202-223-8196
Fax: 202-872-1948
E-Mail: cassidy@actuary.org
Home Page: www.actuary.org
Social Media: Facebook, Twitter, LinkedIn, Youtube

Mary Downs, Executive Director
Craig Hanna, Director of Public Policy
Keith Jones, General Counsel and Director
Steven Knell, Chief Financial Officer
Charity Sack, Director of Communications

AAA is a public policy organization for actuaries within the US. The Academy acts as the public information organization for the profession. Assisting public policy process through the presentation of clear actuarial analysis, the Academy regularly prepares testimony for Congress, provides information to federal elected officials, regulators and congressional staff, comments on proposed federal regulations, and works closely with state officials on issues related to insurance.
17000 Members
Founded in 1965
Mailing list available for rent

13930 American Agents Alliance
1231 I Street
Suite 201
Sacramento, CA 95814
916-283-9473
866-497-9222
Fax: 916-283-9479
E-Mail: info@agentsalliance.com
Home Page: www.agentsalliance.com
Social Media: Facebook, Twitter, LinkedIn, Google Plus

Ken May, President
Bob Kipper, Vice President
Charlie Garrison, Chief Financial Officer

Founded on the philosophy that independent producers speaking with one united voice can accomplish mch more than separate individuals. A member-driven organization dedicated to protect and serve independent insurance producers and consumers.
Founded in 1962

13931 American Association for Long Term Care Insurance
3835 E. Thousand Oaks Blvd.
Suite 336
Westlake Village, CA 91362
818-597-3227
Fax: 818-597-3206
E-Mail: info@aaltci.org
Home Page: www.aaltci.org

Jesse Slome, Media Inquiries
Joseph Howard, Board of Advisor
Don Hansen, Board of Advisor
Tom Hebrank, Board of Advisor
Larry Thomas, Board of Advisor

National trade organization for the long term care insurance industry in the United States.
Founded in 1998

13932 American Association of Crop Insurers
1 Massachusetts Ave NW
Suite 800
Washington, DC 20001-1401
202-789-4100
Fax: 202-408-7763
E-Mail: aaci@mwmlaw.com
Home Page: www.cropinsurers.com

Mike McLeod, Executive Director
David Graves, Manager/Secretary

A organization that represents companies involved with the Federal crop insurance program.
25 Members
Founded in 1980

13933 American Association of Dental Consultants
10032 Wind Hill Dr
Greenville, IN 47124
812-923-2600
800-896-0707
Fax: 812-923-2900
Home Page: www.aadc.org

Dr. Frank A Klump, President
Dr. Kay D Eckroth, President-Elect
Dr. Lawrence M Hoffman, Secretary-Treasurer

Members are dentists, insurance consultants, benefits programs administrators and other dental professionals.
350 Members
Founded in 1979

13934 American Association of Insurance Management Consultants
Eaglemark Consulting Group
PO Box 20
Lemoyne, PA 17043
717-763-7717
Fax: 717-763-7989
E-Mail: nmallouf@mrcgroup.ws
Home Page: www.aaimco.com

Lee M Hoffman, President
Mary LaPorte, Membership Director

THe premier association of consultants to the insurance industry: insurance companies, agents, brokers, and their consumers. Also dedicated to helping the insurance industry operate more efficiently and more profitably, thus enabling improved service to the buying public.
35 Members
Founded in 1979

13935 American Association of Insurance Services
701 Warrenville Roadÿ
Lisle, IL 60532
630-681-8347
800-564-AAIS
Fax: 630-681-8356
Home Page: www.aaisonline.com
Social Media: Facebook, LinkedIn

Edmund J. Kelly, President, CEO
Joan Zerkovich, SVP, Operations
Robin Westcott, VP, Govt. Affairs
John Kadous, CPCU, CPM, VP, Personal Lines
Bill Bickerton, VP, Data Analytics

A member-owned, nonprofit national insurance advisory organization that provides specialized services to property/casualty insurers.

13936 American Association of Managing General Agents
610 Freedom Business Center
Suite 110
King of Prussia, PA 19406-2832
610-992-0022
Fax: 610-992-0021
E-Mail: bernie.heinze@aamga.org
Home Page: www.aamga.org
Social Media: Facebook, Twitter, LinkedIn

Francis Mastowski, CPCU, CIW, President
Roger Ware, Senior Vice President
Michael Berry, Senior Vice President
David Thomas, Vice President
Edward Levy, CIW, Vice President

A trade association of the premier wholesale property and casualty agents and companies in the insurance industry, committed to fostering the business partnerships, networking, professionalism, trusted expertise and exchange of knowledge among its members.
Founded in 1926
Mailing list available for rent

13937 American Association of Retired Persons (AARP)
American Association of Retired Persons
601 E St Nw
Suite A1-200
Washington, DC 20049-0003
202-434-2277
888-687-2277
202-434-3525
Fax: 202-434-7599
E-Mail: member@aarp.org
Home Page: www.aarp.org
Social Media: Facebook, Twitter, Youtube

Gail E. Aldrich, Board Chair
Robert G. Romasco, President
A. Barry Rand, Chief Executive Officer, AARP
Hop Backus, Executive Vice President
Kevin Donnellan, Executive Vice President

AARP is a nonprofit membership organization of persons 50 and older dedicated to addressing their needs and interests. Services include: informing members and the public on issues important to this age group; advocating on legislative, consumer and legal issues; promoting community service, and offering a wide range of special products and services to members. There are 39+ million members within the United States.
Founded in 1958
Mailing list available for rent

13938 American Association of State Compensation Insurance Funds
P.O. Box 20073
Towson, MD 21284

877-494-3237
Fax: 800-925-9420
E-Mail: info@aascif.org
Home Page: www.aascif.org/

Tom Phelan, President
Laurence Hubbard, Past President
Ray Pickup, Vice President
Gerard Adams, Vice President
Jeff Hamilton, Treasurer/Secretary

An association of workers' compensation insurance companies from 27different states, plus 11 workers' compensation boards in Canada.

13939 American Cargo War Risk Reinsurance
30 Broad Street
7th floor
New York, NY 10004

212-405-2835
Fax: 212-344-1664
E-Mail: amich@amich.org
Home Page: www.amich.org

TD Montgomery, Chairman
RJ Decker, Vice Chairman
TA Haig Dick, Secretary/Director
Warren C Dietz, Treasurer

Reinsurance pool of member companies.
Founded in 1939

13940 American Council of Life Insurance
101 Constitution Ave NW
Suite 700
Washington, DC 20001-2133

202-624-2000
Fax: 202-624-2115
E-Mail: contact@acli.com
Home Page: www.acli.com
Social Media: Facebook, Twitter, youtube, RSS

Dirk Kempthorne, President & Chief Executive Officer
Brian Waidmann, Chief of Staff
Gary E. Hughes, Executive Vice President
J. Bruce Ferguson, Senior Vice President
Don Walker, Senior Vice President

Works to advance the interests of the life insurance industry and to provide effective government relations. Conducts investment and social research programs.
631 Members
Founded in 1976
Mailing list available for rent

13941 American Fraternal Alliance
1301 West 22nd St
Suite 700
Oak Brook, IL 60523-6022

630-522-6322
Fax: 630-522-6326
E-Mail: info@fraternalalliance.org
Home Page: www.fraternalalliance.org
Social Media: Facebook, Twitter

William B McKinneyÿ, Chair
Joseph J Annotti, President & CEO
Harald E Borrmann, Vice Chair
David C Gautsche, Secretary-Treasurer
Melanie Hinds, Director, Advocacy

The trade association of America's fraternal benefit societies.
69 Members
Founded in 1886

13942 American Institute of Marine Underwriters
14 Wall St
Suite 820
New York, NY 10005-2145

212-233-0550
Fax: 212-227-5102
E-Mail: aimu@aimu.org
Home Page: www.aimu.org

Roger F Ablett, Chairman of the Boardÿ
James M Craig, President
John A Miklus, Vice President
Frank Costa, Vice Chairman
Drew Feldman, Director of Finances

Provides information of interest to marine underwriters and promotes their interests.

13943 American Insurance Association
2101 L Street, NW
Suite 400
Washington, DC 20037-1542

202-828-7100
Fax: 202-293-1219
E-Mail: info@aiadc.org
Home Page: www.aiadc.org
Social Media: Facebook, Twitter, Youtube

Leigh Ann Pusey, President & CEO
J. Stephen Zielezienski, Senior Vice President
Joseph Digiovanni, Senior Vice President
Peter R Foley, Vice President, Claims
Eric M Goldberg, Vice President, State Government

The leading property and casualty insurance trade organization. Member companies offer all types of property and casualty insurance, as well as personal and commercial auto insurance, commercial property and liability coverage for small businesses, worker's compensation, homeowners' insurance, medical malpractice coverage, and product liability insurance.
Founded in 1964

13944 American Insurance Marketing & Sales Society
PO Box 35718
Richmond, VA 23235

804-674-6466
877-674-2742
Fax: 703-579-8896
E-Mail: info@aimssociety.org
Home Page: www.aimssociety.org/cpiaseminars.html
Social Media: Facebook, Twitter, LinkedIn

June Taylor, CPIA, CIC, CPI, President
Craig Most, CIC, Vice President
Dennis Templeton, CPIA, CIC, Vice President
Michael G Herzak CPIAL, CIC, CRM, Secretary
Martin A Lebson CPIAL, AAI, ARM, Treasurer

A sales training organization that is managed by agents for agents; makes an active effort to ensure that its sales training material is current and takes into consideration today's agency sales approaches.
Founded in 1968

13945 American Nuclear Insurers
95 Glastonbury Blvd
Glastonbury, CT 06033-4443

860-682-1301
Fax: 860-659-0002
E-Mail: info@nuclearInsurance.com
Home Page: www.amnucins.com
Social Media: Facebook

George Turner, President/CEO
John Quatrocchi, Senior VP

A joint underwriting association, and and organization created by some of the largest stock insurance companies in the United States. The purpose is to pool the financial assets pledged by these member companies to provide significant amount of property and liability insurance we make available to nuclear power plants and related facilities throughout the world.
60 Members
Founded in 1957

13946 American Risk and Insurance Association ARIA
716 Providence Road
Malvern, PA 19355-3402

610-640-1997
Fax: 610-725-1007
E-Mail: aria@theinstitutes.org
Home Page: www.aria.org

Laureen Regan, President
Andreas Richter, Vice President
Anthony Biacchi, Executive Director
Tony Biacchi, Executive Director

ARIA is the premier academic organization devoted to the study and promotion of knowledge about risk management and insurance.
500 Members
Founded in 1932

13947 American Society for Healthcare Risk Management
155 N. Wacker Drive
Suite 400
Chicago, IL 60606-4425

312-422-3980
Fax: 312-422-4580
E-Mail: ashrm@aha.org
Home Page: www.ashrm.org

Andrew Oppenberg MPH, CPHRM,, President
Kimberly Hoarle, MBA, CAE, Executive Director
Marcia Cooke, RN-BC, MSN, Director, Education & Research
Matthew B. Hornberger, MBA, CAE, Associate Executive Director
Mary LaRusso, Marketing & Communications Manager

National organization for the health care industry risk management equipment, supplies and services.
4400+ Members
Founded in 1980
Mailing list available for rent

13948 American Society of Appraisers
11107 Sunset Hills Rd
Suite 310
Reston, VA 20190
703-478-2228
800-272-8258
Fax: 703-742-8471
E-Mail: asainfo@appraisers.org
Home Page: www.appraisers.org
Social Media: Facebook, Twitter, LinkedIn, YouTube

Jim Hirt, CEO
Bonny Price, Chief Operations Officer
Joseph Noselli, MBA, CPA, Chief Financial Officer
Todd Paradis, Dir., Marketing & Comm.
Susan Fischer, Governance Operations Manager

Organization provides education and accreditation for appraisers, plus an appraiser locator service.

13949 American Society of Pension Professionals and Actuaries
4245 N. Fairfax Drive
Suite 750
Arlington, VA 22203

703-516-9300
Fax: 703-516-9308

E-Mail: customercare@asppa.org
Home Page: www.asppa.org
Social Media: Facebook, LinkedIn, RSS, YouTube

Kyla M. Keck, CPC, QPA, QKA, President
Joseph A. Nichols, MSPA, President-Elect
Kevin Barnhurst, Chief Financial Officer
Michael R. Copp, Chief Operating Officer
Brian H. Graff, Esq., APMÿ, CEO/Executive Director

(ASPPA) ia a national organization for career retirement plan professionals. The membership consists of the many disciplines supporting retirement income management and benefits policy. Its members are part of the diversified, technical, and highly regulated benefits industry. ASPPA represents those who have made a career of retirement plan and pension policy work.
16,00 Members

13950 American Society of Safety Engineers
1800 E Oakton Street
Des Plaines, IL 60018

847-699-2929
Fax: 847-768-3434
E-Mail: customerservice@asse.org
Home Page: www.asse.org

Fred Fortman, Executive Director
Kelly Fanella, Deputy Executive Director/COO
Dewey Whitmire, Director, Professional Development
Dennis Hudson, Director, Professional Affairs
Bruce Sufranski, Director, Finance/Controller

The oldest and largest professional safety organization. Its members manage, supervise and consult on safety, health, and environmental issues in industry, insurance, government and education.
30000 Members
Founded in 1911

13951 Appraisers Association of America
212 West 35th Street
#11 South
New York, NY 10001

212-889-5404
Fax: 212-889-5503
E-Mail: aaa@appraisersassoc.org
Home Page: www.appraisersassoc.org
Social Media: Facebook, Twitter, LinkedIn

Betty Krulik, AAA, President
Deborah G. Spanierman, AAA, First Vice President
Elizabeth von Habsburg, AAA, Second Vice President
Daile Kaplan, AAA, Secretary
Erica Hartman, AAA, Treasurer

The oldest non-profit professional association of personal property appraisers. The mission and primary purpose of the association is to develop and promote standards of excellence in the profession of appraising through education and the application of the highest form of professionals practice, which results in enhancing the visibility and standing of appraisers within the private and professional communities in which they serve.
900 Members
Founded in 1949
Mailing list available for rent

13952 Arbitration Forums
3350 Buschwood Park Dr
Suite 295
Tampa, FL 33618-4314

813-931-4004
866-977-3434
Fax: 813-931-4618
E-Mail: status@arbfile.org
Home Page: www.arbfile.org

Russ Smith, President & CEO
Jay Arcila, CFO/Secretary
Richard Ledbetter, Chief Information Technology Office
Geoff Engert, Director of Product Development
Ken Butler, Director, Human Resource

Arbitration Forums is a not-for-profit provider of intercompany insurance dispute resolution services. More than 2,000 insurers and self-insurers participate in AF's programs. AF resolves over 250,000 disputes with a claim value approaching one billion dollars.
Founded in 1943

13953 Associated Risk Managers International
Two Pierce Place
Itasca, IL 60143-3141

630-285-4324
Fax: 630-285-4020
E-Mail: scott_spangler@rpsins.com
Home Page: www.armiweb.com

Develops specialized insurance/risk management services for trade associations, professional groups and other industry organizations. Conducts seminars and sponsors competitions.
505 Members
Founded in 1970

13954 Association of Advanced Life Underwriters
11921 Freedom Drive
Suite 1100
Reston, VA 20190

703-641-9400
888-275-0092
Fax: 703-641-9885
Home Page: www.aalu.org

Thomas J Von Riesen, President
Mark B Murphy, Vice President & Treasurer
David J Stertzer, Chief Executive officer
Chris Foster, Secretary
Anthony J Domino, Jr, President - Elect

Offers services in complex fields of estate analysis, business, insurance, pension planning, employee benefit plans.
1.4M Members
Founded in 1957

13955 Association of Average Adjusters of the United States and Canada
126 Midwood Avenue
Farmingdale, NJ 11735

973-597-0824
E-Mail: averageadjusters@aol.com
Home Page: www.averageadjustersusca.org/

Jonathan S Spencer, Chair
Richard P Carney, Executive Chairman
Eileen M Fellin

Marine insurance and general average adjusters, ship and cargo surveyors and admiralty lawyers. Has no paid staff. Membership principally in New York area.
700+ Members
Founded in 2011

13956 Association of Finance and Insurance Professionals
4104 Felps Drive
Suite H
Colleyville, TX 76034

817-428-2434
Fax: 817-428-2534
E-Mail: info@afip.com
Home Page: www.afip.com
Social Media: Facebook, Twitter, LinkedIn

David N Robertson, Executive Director
Tarrah Lett, Sr VP
Heather M Barnett, Communications Director

A nonprofit educational foundation that serves the needs of in-dealership finance and insurance personnel for the automobile, RV, commercial truck and equipment, motorcycle, and motorized sports industries while assisting the lenders, vendors, and independent general agents who support the F&I function.
Cost: $95.00
3500 Members
Frequency: $2,500 for Company's
Founded in 1989
Mailing list available for rent

13957 Association of Financial Guaranty Insurers
139 Lancaster Street
Albany, NY 12210-1903

518-449-4698
Fax: 212-391-6920
E-Mail: tcasey@mackinco.com
Home Page: www.afgi.org

Teresa M. Casey, Executive Director
Margaret Towers, Contact Person

A trade association of the insurers and reinsurers of municipal bonds and asset-backed securities.
10 Members
Founded in 1986

13958 Association of Home Office Underwriters
1155 15th Street, Nw
Suite 500
Washington, DC 20005

202-962-0167
Fax: 202-530-0659
E-Mail: memberservices@ahou.org
Home Page: www.ahou.org
Social Media: Facebook, Twitter, LinkedIn

Lee Janecek, FALU, FLMI, President
Norm Leblond, FALUÿ, Executive Vice President
Cheryl Johns, FLMI, CLUr, AAL, Vice President, Publications
Carlo Fusco, FALU, Vice President, Treasurer
Traci Davis, AALU, FLMI, ACS, Vice President, Program Development

Founded when the Home Office Life Underwriters Association and Institute of Homes Office Underwriters joined forces to provide one unified underwriting voice. The mission is to advance the knowledge of sound underwriting of life and disability insurance risks, toward which end it holds meetings, publishes papers and discussions, and promotes educational programs.
Cost: $100.00
1400 Members
Frequency: Membership Fee
Founded in 2002
Mailing list available for rent

13959 Association of Insurance Compliance Professionals
12100 Sunset Hills Road
Suite 130
Reston, VA 20190
703-234-4074
Fax: 703-435-4390
E-Mail: aicp@aicp.net
Home Page: www.aicp.net

Doug Simino, President
Elaine Douglas, Vice President
Dawn Murphy, Secretary
Doug Geraci, Treasurer

Formerly the Society of State Filers. AICP represents individuals involved or interested in statutes, state filing methods, and/or regulatory requirements. Associate members are consultants, attorneys, association managers, education/service organizations and other interested individuals.
Cost: $175.00
1200 Members
Frequency: Membership Fee
Founded in 1998

13960 Association of Life Insurance Counsel
14350 Mundy Drive
Suite 800
Noblesville, IN 46060

317-774-7500
Fax: 317-614-7147
E-Mail: pcarey@alic.cc
Home Page: www.alic.cc/

William J. Forgione, President
Teresa J. Rasmussen, President-Elect
Sharon A. Cheever, Past President
Carl Wilkerson, Treasurer/Secretary
Paula L. Carey, Executive Director

Association for life insurance counsel.
Founded in 1913

13961 Association of Professional Insurance Women
990 Cedar Bridge Avenue
Suite B& PMB 210
Brick, NJ 08723-4157

973-941-6024
Fax: 732-920-1260
E-Mail: info@apiw.org
Home Page: www.apiw.org

Isabel Silvestri, President
Cheryl Vollweiler, Treasurer
Frances S. Mingoia, Treasurer
Angela Denny, Treasurer
Kathryn Turck-Rose, Corporate Secretary

Provides women in the insurance insudtry with opportunities for professional development and assistance in advancing their careers. Our membership consists of professional insurance women, highly regarded, decision makers with primary insurers, reinsurers, insurance brokers, risk management, professional services firms and other industry related organizations.
135 Members
Founded in 1976

13962 Association of Professional Insurance Agen ts
400 N Washington Street
Alexandria, VA 22314

703-836-9340
Fax: 703-836-1279
E-Mail: web@pianet.org
Home Page: www.pianet.com
Social Media: Facebook, Twitter, LinkedIn

John G Lee, President
Robert W Hansen, Vice President
Gareth W Blackwell, Jr., Secretary/Assistant
Richard A Clements, President-Elect
Loan Nguyen, VP Finance

Represents professional independent insurance agents in all 50 states, Puerto Rico and the District of Columbia. Our members are local Main Street Agents who serve their communities throughout America
Founded in 1931
Mailing list available for rent

13963 Automobile Insurance Plans Service Office
302 Central Ave
Johnston, RI 02919-4995

401-275-1000
Fax: 401-528-1350
Home Page: www.aipso.com

David Kohlhammer, President

AIPSO's mission is to provide high quality services for the insurance residual market at the lowest possible cost.

13964 Aviation Insurance Association
7200 W. 75th Street
Overland Park, KS 66204

913-627-9632
Fax: 913-381-2515
E-Mail: mandie@aiaweb.org
Home Page: www.aiaweb.org
Social Media: Facebook

Paul Leonard, President
Todd McCredie, Vice President
Patrick Bailey, Secretary
Mary D'Alauro, Treasurer
Mandie Bannwarth, Executive Director

A not-for-profit association dedicated to expanding the knowledge of and promoting the general welfare of the aviation insurance industry through numerous educational programs and events.
900 Members
Founded in 1976

13965 Blue Cross and Blue Shield Association
225 North Michigan Avenue
Chicago, IL 60601-6026

312-540-0460
Fax: 312-297-6609
Home Page: www.bcbs.com
Social Media: Facebook, Twitter, Youtube

Scott P Serota, Presidentÿ& Chief Executive Officer

Formerly Blue Cross Association and National Association of Blue Shield Plans. Members must be medical and/or hospital plans and operate according to established standards. Offers information, consulting, representation and operation services to members. Member plans represent over 68.1 million health care consumers.
55 Members
Founded in 1946
Mailing list available for rent

13966 Captive Insurance Companies Association
4248 Park Glen Road
Minneapolis, MN 55416

952-928-4655
Fax: 952-929-1318
E-Mail: cica@cicaworld.com
Home Page: www.cicaworld.com
Social Media: Facebook, Twitter

Tomas Wittbjer, Board Chair
Dennis P Harwick, President
Scott Beckman, Board Vice Chair
Ryan Ralston, Secretary/Treasurer
Dixie Arthur, Director

An organization dedicated to networking, educating, and promoting the captive insurance industry. Its mission is to be the first and best source of unbiased information, knowledge, and leadership for captive insurance decision makers.
Founded in 1972

13967 Casualty Actuarial Society
4350 N Fairfax Dr
Suite 250
Arlington, VA 22203-1620

703-276-3100
Fax: 703-276-3108
E-Mail: office@casact.org
Home Page: www.casact.org
Social Media: Facebook, Twitter, LinkedIn

Cynthia R Ziegler, Executive Director
Diane Tremblay, Executive Assistant
J Michael Boa, Director of Communications
Todd P Rogers, Director of Finance and Operations
Kathleen Dean, Director of Meeting Services

The purpose is to advance the body of knowledge of actuarial science applied to property, casualty and similar risk exposures, to establish and maintain standards of qualification for membership, to promote and maintain highstandards of conduct and competence for the members, and to increase the awareness of actuarial science.
3400+ Members
Founded in 1914
Mailing list available for rent

13968 Certified Claims Professional Accreditation Council
PO Box 550922
Jacksonville, FL 32255-0922

301-292-1988
Fax: 301-292-1787
E-Mail: animag@lattmag.com
Home Page: www.ccpac.com

A nonprofit organization that seeks to raise the professional standards of individuals who specialize in the administration and negotiation of freight claims. Specifically it seeks to give recognition to those who have acquired the necessary degree of experience, education, and expertise in domestic and international freight claims to warrant acknowledgment of their professional stature.
Founded in 1981

13969 Chartered Property Casualty Underwriters
720 Providence Rd
Suite 100
Malvern, PA 19355-3446

610-251-2733
800-932-2728
Fax: 610-725-5969
E-Mail: membercenter@cpcusociety.org
Home Page: www.cpcusociety.org
Social Media: Facebook, Twitter, LinkedIn

Cynthia A Baroway, CPCU, M.Ed.,, President and Chairman
Kevin H Brown, Senior Vice President
Bryan Tedford,ÿCPCU, ARM, Vice President
Brian P Savko, CPCU, CLU, ChFC, Treasurer
Jane M Wahl, CPCU, CSSBB, CMQ, President-Elect

A community of credentialed property and casualty insurance professionals who promote excellence through ethical behavior and continuing education. Mission is to meet the career development needs of a diverse membership pf professionals who have earned the CPCU designation, so that they may serve others in a competent and ethical manner
28000 Members
Founded in 1944

13970 Conference of Consulting Actuaries
3880 Salem Lake Drive
Suite H
Long Grove, IL 60047-5292

847-719-6500
Fax: 847-719-6506

E-Mail: conference@ccactuaries.org
Home Page: www.ccactuaries.org

John J Schubert, President
John H Lowell, Vice President - Communities
Robert J Reiskytl, Vice President - Member Services
Carol R Sears, Vice President - Professionalism
Donald J Segal, Vice President - Continuing Ed

The Conference advances the quality of consulting practice, supports the needs of consulting actuaries, and represents their interests.
1200+ Members
Founded in 1950

13971 Consumer Credit Industry Association
6300 Powers Ferry Road
Suite 600-286
Atlanta, GA 30339

678-858-4001
E-Mail: webmaster@ccíaonline.com
Home Page: www.cciaonline.com

Kris Nelson, Chair
Todd Schubert, President
Scott J. Cipinko, Executive Vice President
John Euwema, VP Legislative Regulatory Counsel
Stephanie Brandt, Director of Member Services

Preserves, promotes and enhances the availability, utility and integrity of insurance and related products and services delivered in connection with financial transactions.
140+ Members
Founded in 1951

13972 Council on Employee Benefits
1501 M Street, N.W
Suite 620
Washington, DC 20005

202-861-6025
Fax: 202-861-6027
E-Mail: scanfield@ceb.org
Home Page: www.ceb.org

Donna A Sexton, President
Shane Canfield, Executive Director
Karen M Welch, Vice President
John R. Collins, Treasurer
Julie R Sheehy, Secretary

Composed of major corporations having a common interest in the management of employee benefits. Stimulates the development and improves the adminstration of sound, progressive employee benefit plan among its members. Also provides an excellent medium for the exchange of ideas, thought and information on the design, operation and financing of such plans.
Founded in 1946

13973 Crop Insurance and Reinsurance Bureau
201 Massachusetts Avenue, NE
Suite C5
Washington, DC 20002

202-544-0067
Fax: 202-330-5255
E-Mail: mtorrey@cropinsurance.org
Home Page: www.cropinsurance.org

Greg Mills, Chairman
Mike Torrey, Executive Vice President
Sheri Bane, Vice-Chairwoman
Ron Rutledge, Treasurer
Tara Smith, Federal Affairs Vice President

National trade association made up of insurance providers and related organization who provide a variety of insurance products for our Nation's Farmers.
Founded in 1964

13974 Eastern Claims Conference
PO Box 863902
Ridgewood, NY 11386

732-922-7037
Fax: 212-615-7345
E-Mail: easternclaimsconference@gmail.com
Home Page: www.easternclaimsconference.com

John Healy, Executive Director

Provides education and training to examiners, managers, and officers who review medical and disability claims. Holds seminars for life, health and disability clinics.
Founded in 1977

13975 Employee Benefit Research Institute
1100 13th St NW
Suite 878
Washington, DC 20005-4051

202-659-0670
Fax: 202-775-6312
E-Mail: info@ebri.org
Home Page: www.ebri.org

Dallas L Salisburyÿ, President
Stephen Blakely, Communications Director
Martha Bobbino, Information Center Director

Mission is to contribute to, to encourage, and to enhance the development of sound employee benefit programs and sound public policy through objective research and education.
Founded in 1978
Mailing list available for rent

13976 Federal Insurance Administration
500 C Street SW
Washington, DC 20472-2110

202-646-3535
Fax: 202-646-4320

Bud Schaurte, Administrator

Administers the federal flood insurance and crime insurance programs.

13977 Federation of Defense & Corporate Counsel
11812 N 56th St
Tampa, FL 33617-1528

813-983-0022
Fax: 813-988-5837
E-Mail: mstreeper@thefederation.org
Home Page: www.thefederation.org
Social Media: Facebook, LinkedIn

Edward M Kaplan, Board Chair
Timothy A Pratt, President
Steven E. Farrar, Secretary-Treasurer
Victoria H Roberts, President-Elect

The Federation is an organization of recognized leaders in the legal community dedicated to representation of insurers and corporations.
1400+ Members
Founded in 1936

13978 Financial & Insurance Conference Planners
330 N. Wabash Avenue
Suite 2000
Chicago, IL 60611

312-245-1023
Fax: 312-321-5150
E-Mail: info@icpanet.com
Home Page: www.ficpnet.com
Social Media: Facebook, Twitter, LinkedIn, Youtube

Steve Bova, CAE, Executive Director
Mark Swets, Membership Manager
Ellie Hurley, Events Senior Manager
Lydia Kamicar, Education Manager
Kim Walsh, Marketing Senior Manager

An association of insurance and financial services industry meeting planners who exchange proven meeting management techniques and explore trends and new ideas that may enhance the value of conferences.
Founded in 1957

13979 Financial Planning Association
7535 E. Hampden Ave.
Suite 600
Denver, CO 80231

303-759-4900
800-322-4237
Fax: 303-759-0749
E-Mail: marv.tuttle@fpanet.org
Home Page: www.fpanet.org
Social Media: Facebook, Twitter, LinkedIn

Mary Tuttle, CEO
Maureen Peck, Executive Communications Manager
Lauren Schadle, Assoc Exec Dir, COO
Curt Niepoth, Assoc Exec Dir, CFO
Ian MacKenzie, Managing Dir Bus Dev, CMO

Members include accountants, financial planners, lawyers, bankers, stockbrokers, insurance professionals and others who provide financial advice and services to individuals.
15M Members
Founded in 2000
Mailing list available for rent

13980 Fraternal Field Managers' Association
Concordia Mutual Life
3020 Woodcreek Drive
Downers Grove, IL 60515

630-971-8000
Fax: 630-971-9332
Home Page: www.ffma.info

William J. Murray, President
Jay Schenk, VP

FFMA is dedicated to the promotion of higher ethical standards and the professional development of the fraternal field force, fostering harmony, unity of purpose and the exchange of ideas among the member societies.
70 Members
Founded in 1935

13981 GAMA International
2901 Telestar Ct
Suite 140
Falls Church, VA 22042-1205

703-770-8184
800-345-2687
Fax: 571-499-4302
E-Mail: gij@gamaweb.com
Home Page: www.gamaweb.com
Social Media: Facebook, Twitter, LinkedIn

Howard J Elias, President
Jeffrey R Hughes, Chief Executive Officer
Robert J Fashano, M.S.F.S., CLU, Vice President
Timothy P Schmidt, CLF FIC LUTCF, Secretary
Daralee S Barbera, CFP CLF CMFC, President-Elect

The only association dedicated to promoting the professional development needs of managers in the insurance and financial services industry. Also the only volunteer organization that focuses on the agency building tasks and skills of successful career agenices and firms.
Cost: $300.00
5500 Members
Frequency: Membership Fee
Mailing list available for rent

13982 General Agents and Managers Conference of NALU
2901 Telestar Ct
Suite 140
Falls Church, VA 22042-1205

703-770-8184
800-345-2687
Fax: 571-499-4302
E-Mail: gij@gamaweb.com
Home Page: www.gamaweb.com
Social Media: Facebook, Twitter, LinkedIn

Howard J Elias, President
Jeffrey R Hughes, Chief Executive Officer
Robert J Fashano, M.S.F.S., CLU, Vice President
Timothy P Schmidt, CLF FIC LUTCF, Secretary
Daralee S Barbera, CFP CLF CMFC, President-Elect

Seeks to improve quality of management and life insurance selling through educational programs, code of ethical practices, and research programs.
7.2M Members
Founded in 1951
Mailing list available for rent

13983 Great American Insurance Group Tower
125 Park Ave
14th Floor
New York, NY 10017-5529

212-885-1500
Fax: 212-885-1535
E-Mail: service@fcia.com
Home Page: www.greatamericaninsurancegroup.com

Lindley M Franklin, CEO

To provide credit insurance covering teh risk of non-payment on foreign and,in certain cases, domestic receivables.
Founded in 1961

13984 Group Underwriters Association of America
P.O. Box 735
Northbrook, IL 60065-0735

205-427-2638
Fax: 205-981-2901
E-Mail: info@guaa.org
Home Page: www.guaa.com/

Libby Corcillo, President
Shawn R. Dutremble, Vice President
Steve Ginsburg, Treasurer
Patty Marshall, Secretary
Jennifer Kyle, Past President

Comprised of industry professionals that promote the study, analysis, and discussion of all matters relating to the underwriting of group products.

13985 Health Insurance Association of America
601 Pennsylvania Avenue, NW South Building
Suite 500
Washington, DC 20004

202-778-3200
Fax: 202-331-7487
E-Mail: ahip@ahip.org
Home Page: www.ahip.org

A national political advocacy and trade association with about 1,300 member companies that sell health insurance coverage to Americans.

13986 Highway Loss Data Institute
1005 N Glebe Rd
Suite 700
Arlington, VA 22201-5759

703-247-1600
Fax: 703-247-1595
Home Page: www.iihs.org
Social Media: Twitter

Adrian Lund, President
Russ Rader, Senior Vice President
Shelley Shelton, Executive Assistant, Legal Affairs
Brenda O'Donnell, Vice President, Insurer Relations
Karen Koger, Communications Associate

Provides the public with insurance industry data concerning human and economic loss resulting from crashes.
12 Members
Founded in 1972
Mailing list available for rent

13987 Home Office Life Underwriters Association
Minnesota Mutual Life
400 Robert Street N
Suite A
Saint Paul, MN 55101-2098

651-665-3500
Fax: 651-665-4488

Lynn Patterson, President
Jane Hall, Executive Vice President

Offers educational programs through the Academy Life Underwriting designed for professional home office underwriters.
560 Members
Founded in 1930

13988 I-Car
5125 Trillium Blvd
Hoffman Estates, IL 60192-3600

847-590-1198
800-422-7872
Fax: 800-590-1215
E-Mail: tom.mcgee@i-car.com
Home Page: www.i-car.com

William Brower, Chair
John S. Van Alstyne, CEO & President
Rollie Benjaminÿ, Vice Chair
Dustin Wombleÿ, Secretaryÿ
Bob Keith, Treasurer

Formed by the collision industry, an international not-for-profit training organization. Develops and delivers technical training programs to professionals in all areas of the collision industry. Also provides a communication forum for anyone interested in proper collision repair.
100 Members
Founded in 1979

13989 IMCA Annual Meeting
Insurance Marketing Communications Association
4248 Park Glen Road
Minneapolis, MN 55416

206-219-9811
Fax: 866-210-2481
E-Mail: tseibert@imcanet.com
Home Page: www.imcanet.com
Social Media: Facebook, Twitter, LinkedIn

Rob Martin, President
Gloria Grove, Executive Director
Mark Friedlander, Executive Vice President
Anna Hargis, Treasurer

To promote education and development of its members.
Cost: $795.00
Frequency: Registration Fee
Mailing list available for rent

13990 Independent Automotive Damage Appraisers Association
PO Box 12291
Columbus, GA 31917-2291

800-369-IADA
Fax: 888-423-2669
E-Mail: admin@iada.org
Home Page: www.iada.org

Leo Maki, President
Mark Nathan, First Vice President
John Williams, Executive Vice President
Pete Duhamel, Secretary/Treasurer

A nationwide network of appraiser specialists with the knowledge and experience to assess vehicle damage and to make unbiased repair decisions based on the manufacturer's specifications, accepted industry procedures, and safety concerns.
731 Members
Founded in 1947

13991 Independent Insurance Agents & Brokers of America
127 S Peyton Street
Alexandria, VA 22314-2803

703-683-4422
800-221-7917
Fax: 703-683-7556
E-Mail: info@iiaa.org
Home Page: www.independentagent.com/
Social Media: Facebook, Twitter, LinkedIn, Youtube

Robert A Rusbuldt, CEO
Ronald Tubertini, Chairman

A national alliance of business owners and their employees who offer all types of insurance and financial services products. IIABA agents and brokers not only advise clients about insurance, they recommend loss-prevention ideas that can cut costs.
300M+ Members
Founded in 1896
Mailing list available for rent

13992 Information, Incorporated
6707 Democracy Blvd.
Suite 700
Bethesda, MD 20817
301-215-4688
Fax: 301-215-4600
E-Mail: acarr@mail.infoinc.com
Home Page: www.infoinc.com

Alain Carr, Manager
Organization offers evaluations of companies on their claims-paying ability. Association news services.
Founded in 1979
Mailing list available for rent

13993 Inland Marine Underwriters Association
14 Wall Street
8th Floor
New York, NY 10005

212-233-0550
Fax: 212-227-5102
E-Mail: lcolson@imua.org
Home Page: www.imua.org

Peter Opinante, Chair
Kevin O'Brien, President & CEO
Lillian Colson, Vice President & Secretary
Eileen Monreale, Education Training /Specialist
Michelle Hoehn, Deputy Chair

Serves as the collective voice of the U.S. inland marine insurance industry. Also provides its members with education, research and communications services that support the inland ma-

rine underwriting discipline.
Cost: $1750.00
400+ Members
Frequency: Membership Fee
Founded in 1930
Mailing list available for rent

13994 Institute of Home Office Underwriters
General American Life Insurance Company
1155 15th Street, Nw
Suite 500
Washington, DC 20005
202-962-0167
Fax: 202-530-0659
E-Mail: memberservices@ahou.org
Home Page: www.ahou.org
Social Media: Facebook, Twitter, LinkedIn

Lee Janecek, FALU, FLMI, President
Norm Leblond, FALUý, Executive Vice President
Cheryl Johns, FLMI, CLUr, AAL, Vice President, Publications
Carlo Fusco, FALU, Vice President, Treasurer
Traci Davis, AALU, FLMI, ACS, Vice President, Program Development

Goals are to increase underwriting knowledge of members through educational programs. Prepares program and examinations leading to Fellowship in Academy of Life Underwriting.
425 Members
Founded in 1937
Mailing list available for rent

13995 Insurance Accounting Systems Association
3511 Shannon Rd, Suite 160
PO Box 51340
Durham, NC 27707-6330
919-489-0991
Fax: 919-489-1994
E-Mail: info@iasa.org
Home Page: www.iasa.org
Social Media: Facebook, Twitter, LinkedIn, Google Plus

H Louise Ziemann, CPCU, CLU, Board Chair
Elizabeth Mercier, President
Joseph Pomilia, Executive Director
Margaret McKeon, VP-Conference
Kim Morris, Director-Exhibits

Membership includes insurance companies of all types, as well as companies that serve the insurance industry, regulators and also organizations more broadly representative of the financial services industry, including banks and investment brokerage firms.
1.7M Members
Founded in 1928
Mailing list available for rent

13996 Insurance Accounting and Systems Association
3511 Shannon Road, Suite 160
PO Box 51340
Durham, NC 27707
919-489-0991
Fax: 919-489-1994
E-Mail: info@iasa.org
Home Page: www.iasa.org/
Social Media: Facebook, Twitter, LinkedIn, YouTube

Beth Mercier, Chairman of the Board
Forrest Mills, Jr., President
Tim Morgan, President-Electý
Tom Ewbank, CFO
Joe Pomilia, Executive Director

A nonprofit education association that strives to enhance the knowledge of insurance professionals and participants from similar organizations closely allied with the insurance industry.

13997 Insurance Committee for Arson Control
3601 Vincennes Road
Indianapolis, IN 46268
317-575-5601
Fax: 317-879-8408
E-Mail: info@arsoncontrol.org
Home Page: www.arsoncontrol.org

Gregg Dykstra, Executive Director
Larry Baile, Event Director
Don Hancock, Technical Director
David Middleton, Controller
Reeda Stone, Membership Director

Serves as a national resource, education and communications organization. ICAC works to increase public awareness of the arson problem, what can be done and how the industry is responding on both the national and local levels.
Founded in 1978
Mailing list available for rent

13998 Insurance Consumer Affairs Exchange
PO Box 746
Lake Zurich, IL 60047
847-991-8454
E-Mail: nbrebner@icae.com
Home Page: www.icae.com

Nancy Brebner, Executive Director
Gail Cleary, Secretary
Carol Crosson, Treasurer
Kendra Franklin, VP & Catalyst Editor
Mitch Wilson, Web Technology

A not-for-profit organization that promotes professionalism and shapes the standards of behavior in relationships between insurance organizations, regulators and customers through proactive dialogue, research, communication and education.
110 Members
Founded in 1976

13999 Insurance Cost Containment Service
330 S Wells
Chicago, IL 60606-4701
312-427-2520
Fax: 312-368-8336

Robert Kissane, President

Assists insurance companies with property claims adjustment and arson and fraud claims investigation.

14000 Insurance Information Institute
110 William St
New York, NY 10038-3908
212-346-5500
800-942-4242
Fax: 212-732-1916
E-Mail: members@iii.org
Home Page: www.iii.org
Social Media: Facebook, Twitter, LinkedIn, Google Plus, Youtube, Flickr

Cary M Schneider, Executive Vice President
Michael Barry, Vice President, Media Relations
Jeanne M Salvatore, Senior Vice President
Andrea C Basora, Senior Vice President, Digital
Madine Singer, Vice President, Publications

A factfinding communication and media organization for all lines of insurance except life and health insurance. Affiliated with Western Insurance Information Services offering consumer information services to 10 western states. Also offers a national insurance consumer helpline.
250 Members
Founded in 1959

14001 Insurance Loss Control Association
PO Box 346
Morton, IL 61550
309-696-2551
Fax: 317-879-8408
E-Mail: administration@insurancelosscontrol.org
Home Page: www.insurancelosscontrol.org

Kevin Matthews, President
Ron Huber, CSP, ALCM, First Vice President
Larry E Peterson, CSP, Second Vice President
Dan Finn, Secretary
Stig T Ruxlow, CSP, Financial Secretary

Supports loss control professionals. Publishes quarterly newsletter.
Founded in 1931

14002 Insurance Marketing Communications Association
4248 Park Glen Road
Minneapolis, MN 55416
206-219-9811
Fax: 866-210-2481
E-Mail: tseibert@imcanet.com
Home Page: www.imcanet.com
Social Media: Facebook, Twitter, LinkedIn, Youtube

Rob Martin, President
Gloria Grove, Executive Director
Mark Friedlander, Executive Vice President
Anna Hargis, Treasurer

An international organization of insurance communications professionals who specialize in marketing, marketing communications, advertising, sales promotion, and public relations.
Cost: $500.00
180 Members
Frequency: Annual Membership Fee
Founded in 1923
Mailing list available for rent

14003 Insurance Premium Finance Association
2890 Niagara Falls Boulevard
PO Box 726
Amherst, NY 14226
716-695-8757
Fax: 716-695-8758

Eric Bouskill, Contact

Firms licensed by New York State to finance property and casualty insurance premiums.
16 Members
Founded in 1961

14004 Insurance Research Council
718 Providence Road
Malvern, PA 19355-0725
610-644-2212
Fax: 610-640-5388
E-Mail: irc@cpcuiia.org
Home Page: www.ircweb.org
Social Media: Facebook, Twitter, LinkedIn

Rhonda Aikens, Chairperson
Kevin Kelso, Treasurer
Elizabeth A Sprinkel, Secretary
Elizabeth A. Sprinkel, Senior Vice President
Victoria Kilgore, Director of Research

Non profit division of the American Institute for Chartered Property Casualty Underwriters and the Insurance Institute of America. Addresses subjects relating to all lines of property-casualty insurance, including coverages of automobiles, homes, businesses, municipalities, and professionals.
Founded in 1977

14005 Insurance Value Added Network Services
1455 E Putnam Avenue
Old Greenwich, CT 06870-1307

203-698-1900
800-548-2675
Fax: 203-698-7299
E-Mail: ivans.info@ivans.com
Home Page: www.ivans.com
Social Media: Twitter, LinkedIn

Clare DeNicola, President/CEO
Jeffery K Dobish, Sr VP/CFO
Linda Welsh, CAO

Industry-sponsored organization offering value added data communications network linking agencies, companies and healthcare providers to the insurance industry.
Founded in 1983

14006 Insured Retirement Institute
1101 New York Ave NW
Suite 825
Washington, DC 20005

202-469-3000
Fax: 202-469-3030
Home Page: www.irionline.org

Robert Moore, Chairman
Bruce Ferris, Vice Chairman
Catherine J Weatherford, President, CEO
Lee Covington, SVP, General Counsel
Danielle Holland, SVP, Communications, Marketing

An association for the retirement income industry.

14007 Intermediaries and Reinsurance Underwriters Association
971 Rte 202 North
Branchburg, NJ 08876

908-203-0211
Fax: 908-203-0213
E-Mail: info@irua.com
Home Page: www.irua.com

Amy Barra, Executive Director

A not-for-profit corporation, organized for the purposes of reinsurance education and research and the dissemination of information relevant to the reinsurance industry.
60 Members
Founded in 1967

14008 International Association for Insurance Law: United States Chapter
Chase Communications
PO Box 3028
Malvern, PA 19355-0728

FAX 914-966-3264

Stephen C Acunto, VP

Members are attorneys, professors, regulators and others who are interested in international or comparative aspects of insurance law.
700 Members
Founded in 1963

14009 International Association of Accident Reconstruction Specialists
1036 Gretchen Lane
Grand Ledge, MI 48837-1873

517-622-3135
E-Mail: brandtb@benchmarktrafficservices.com
Home Page: www.iaars.org

Fred Rice, President
Eino Butch Thompson, Vice President

Composed of members and associates from 38 states, as well as abroad. Membership comprised of law enforcement officers and civilian personnel.
152 Members
Founded in 1980

14010 International Association of Arson Investigators
2111 Baldwin Ave
Suite 203
Crofton, MD 21114

410-451-3473
800-468-4224
Fax: 410-451-9049
Home Page: www.firearson.com
Social Media: Facebook, Twitter, LinkedIn, Youtube

Deborah Neitch, Executive Director
Gloria Ryan, Dir. of Admin/Editor, F&AI
Tom Aurnhammer, Training Manager
Debra Miller, Acctg. & Finance Mgr.
Lisa Quible, Training Coordinator

Dedicated to improving the professional development of fire and explosion investigators by being the global resource for fire investigation, technology and research.
7500 Members
Founded in 1949

14011 International Association of Defense Counsel
303 West Madison
Suite 925
Chicago, IL 60606-3300

312-368-1494
Fax: 312-368-1854
E-Mail: info@iadclaw.org
Home Page: www.iadclaw.org
Social Media: Facebook, Twitter, LinkedIn

Molly H Craig, President
Mary Beth Kurzak, Executive Director
Alfred R Paliani, Vice President of Corporate
Daniel M Zureich, Vice President of Insurance
Pamela McGovern, Vice President

Formerly the International Association of Insurance Counsel. Members are defense attorneys and insurance and corporate counsels, by invitation only.
Cost: $650.00
2400 Members
Frequency: Membership Fee
Founded in 1920

14012 International Association of Industrial Accident Boards and Commissions
5610 Medical Circle
Suite 24
Madison, WI 53719

608-663-6355
Fax: 608-663-1546
E-Mail: gkrohm@iaiabc.org
Home Page: www.iaiabc.org

Jack Nolish, President
Jennifer Wolf Horejsh, Executive Director
R.D. Maynard, Vice President
Chris Godfrey, Secretary/Treasurer
Heather Lore, Manager of Membership and Marketing

A not for profit trade association representing government agencies charged with the administration of workers' compensation systems throughout most of the United States and Canada, and other nations and territories.
300+ Members
Founded in 1914

14013 International Association of Insurance Receivers
610 Freedom Business Center
Suite 110
King of Prussia, PA 19406

610-992-0015
Fax: 610-992-0021
E-Mail: bernie@accolademgt.com
Home Page: www.iair.org

Jeanne Lachapelle, Director

Founded to provide an association to individuals involved with insurance receiverships in order to receive education, promote information exchange, and enhance the standards followed those who work in this position.
Founded in 1991

14014 International Association of Insurance Pro fessionals Corporate Centre
8023 East 63rd Place
Suite 540
Tulsa, OK 74133

918-294-3700
800-766-6249
Fax: 918-294-3711
E-Mail: joinnaiw@naiw.org
Home Page: www.internationalinsuranceprofessionals.org
Social Media: Facebook

Brandi Capps, Director of Products and Education
Beth Chitnis, Executive Vice-President
John C McColloch, Director of Member Services
Michael North, Accounting
Sharon Smith, Marketing

Serves its members by providing professional education, an environment in which to build business alliances and the opportunity to make connections with people of differing career paths and levels of experience within the insurance industry.
2000 Members
Founded in 1940
Mailing list available for rent

14015 International Association of Special Investigation Units (IASIU)
11950 W. Lake Park Drive
Suite 320
Milwaukee, WI 53224

414-375-2992
Fax: 414-359-1671
E-Mail: info@iasiu.org
Home Page: www.iasiu.org

Wade Wickre, President
Sean Zavala, Vice President
Ellen Withers, Secretary
John Kloc, Treasurer

An association of more than 870 insurance company SIU professionals representing 130 of the largest property and casualty companies in the country.
4000 Members
Founded in 1984

14016 International Claim Association
1155 15th Street NW
Suite 500
Washington, DC 20005

202-452-0143
Fax: 202-530-0659
E-Mail: dchuba@claim.org
Home Page: www.claim.org
Social Media: Facebook

Marlon Nettleton, President
Christopher Murphy, Executive Director
Lisa Phillips, Secretary

Provides a forum for information exchange and a program of education tailored to the needs of its member life and health insurance companies, reinsurers, managed care companies, TPAs, and Blue Cross and Blue Shield organizations worldwide
Founded in 1909
Mailing list available for rent

14017 International Claim Association Newsletter
International Claim Association
1155 15th Street NW
Suite 500
Washington, DC 20005
202-452-0143
Fax: 202-530-0659
E-Mail: dchuba@claim.org
Home Page: www.claim.org
Social Media: Facebook
Marlon Nettleton, President
Christopher Murphy, Executive Director
Lisa Phillips, Secretary
Frequency: Quarterly
Founded in 1909
Mailing list available for rent

14018 International Cooperative and Mutual Insurance Federation
8400 Westpark Drive
Second Floor
McLean, VA 22102-5116
703-245-8077
Fax: 703-610-0211
Home Page: www.aacmis.org
Edward L Potter, CAE, Executive Director
Formerly the North American Association of the International Cooperative Insurance Federation.

14019 International Foundation of Employee Benefit Plans
18700 W. Bluemound Rd
Brookfield, WI 53045
262-786-6700
888-334-3327
Fax: 262-786-8780
E-Mail: pr@ifebp.org
Home Page: www.ifebp.org
Social Media: Facebook, Twitter, LinkedIn, Youtube
George R Laufenberg, CEBS, President and Chair of the Board
Michael Wilson, Chief Executive Officer
Thomas T Holsman, Treasurer
Regina C Reardon, Secretary
Kenneth R Boyd, President-Elect
The largest educational association serving the employees and compensation industry.
Cost: $295.00
35000 Members
Frequency: $575/Organization Fee
Founded in 1954

14020 International Insurance Society
101 Murray Street
New York, NY 10007
212-277-5171
Fax: 212-277-5172
E-Mail: cj@iisonline.org
Home Page: www.iisonline.org
Greig Woodring, Chairman
Michael Morrissey, President & Chief Executive Officer
Takeo Inokuchi, Vice Chairman
Provides a world forum for leading insurance executives, academicians and others interested in insurance to share interests and ideas on timely global issues.
1000 Members
Founded in 1965

14021 International Risk Management Institute
12222 Merit Dr
Suite 1450
Dallas, TX 75251-3297
972-996-0800
800-827-5991
Fax: 972-371-5128
Home Page: www.zeroriskhr.com
Jack P Gibson, President
Mike Poskey, Vice President
Dr. Robert Kinsel Smith, Senior Adviser/Consultant
Cathy J Roberts, Vice President
Mike Wojcik, Information Technology Director
Provides important risk and insurance information to business, legal, risk management, and insurance professionals
Founded in 1978

14022 International Society of Appraisers
225 West Wacker Drive
Suite 650
Chicago, IL 60606ÿ
312-981-6778
Fax: 312-265-2908
E-Mail: isa@isa appraisers.org
Home Page: www.isa-appraisers.org/
Social Media: Facebook, Twitter, LinkedIn, RSS
Cindy Charleston-Rosenberg, President
Christine Guernsey, Vice President
Steven R. Roach, Treasurer
Libby Holloway, Secretary
Karen S. Jackson, CAE, Director
A nonprofit, professional personal property appraisal association representing appraisers in the United States and Canada.
Founded in 1979

14023 International Tax and Investment Center
1800 K St NW
Suite 718
Washington, DC 20006-2202
202-530-9799
Fax: 202-530-7987
E-Mail: Washington@iticnet.org
Home Page: www.iticnet.org
James C Miller III, Chairman
Daniel A Witt, President
Irene Savitsky, Vice President
Elena Novak, Program Manager
Diana McKelvey, Communications Manager
A trade association that advances the use of structured settlements as a means of using periodic payments to resolve personal injury claims, workers compensation, and other types of claims.
600+ Members
Founded in 1993

14024 Intersure Ltd
3 Hotel St
Warrenton, VA 20186-3221
540-349-0969
Fax: 540-349-0971
E-Mail: info@intersurepartners.com
Home Page: www.intersurepartners.com
Millie Curtis, Executive Officer
Formerly the Association of International Insurance Agents. Founded to promote the principles of a free exchange of ideas and mutual cooperation based on the highest standards of intergrity, confidentiality and trust.
45 Members
Founded in 1965

14025 LIMRA International
Po Box 208
Hartford, CT 06141-0208
860-285-7715
800-235-4672
Fax: 860-285-7714
E-Mail: customer.service@limra.com
Home Page: www.limra.com
Social Media: Facebook, Twitter, LinkedIn, Google Plus
Robert A Kerzner, President
Howard S Drescher, Public Relations Director
James W. Kerley, President
Robert M. Baranoff, Senior Vice President
Gary Aluise, Senior Vice President
We offer our clients insight in the form of cooperative research and value added marketing and distribution expertise. Insight that helps you identify trends, evaluate options and implement solutions. All of which leads to one clear outcome; the growth of your company.
800 Members
Founded in 1916
Mailing list available for rent

14026 LOMA: Life Office Management Association
2300 Windy Ridge Pkwy SE
Suite 600
Atlanta, GA 30339
770-951-1770
800-275-5662
Fax: 770-984-0441
E-Mail: askloma@loma.org
Home Page: www.loma.org
Robert A Kerzner, CLU, ChFC, President and CEO
Jeffrey Hasty, FLMI, ACS, Senior Vice President, Assessment
Michele LaBouff, Senior Vice President
Kathy Milligan, FLMI, ACS, A, Senior Vice President, Education
Ian J Watts, Senior Vice President
Insurance worldwide association of insurance companies specializing in research and education.
1200+ Members
Founded in 1924
Mailing list available for rent

14027 Life Insurance Settlement Association
225 South Eola Drive
Orlando, FL 32801
407-894-3797
Home Page: www.lisa.org/
Alan Buerger, Chairman
Cynthia Poveda, Vice Chairman
Phil Loy, Treasurer
Vince Granieri, Secretary
Michael Freedman, Board Member
Promotes the development, integrity, and reputation of the life settlement industry and promotes a competitive market for the people it serves.
85+ Members
Founded in 1994

14028 Life Insurers Council
2300 Windy Ridge Parkway
Suite 600
Atlanta, GA 30339
770-984-3724
800-275-5662
Fax: 770-984-3780

E-Mail: askloma@loma.org
Home Page: www.loma.org/lic/

Robert A Kerzner, CLU, ChFC, President and CEO
Jeffrey Hasty, FLMI, ACS, Senior Vice President, Assessment
Michele LaBouff, Senior Vice President
Kathy Milligan, FLMI, ACS, A, Senior Vice President, Education
Ian J Watts, Senior Vice President

In 1997, the LIC merged with (LOMA) Life Office Management Association which added extensive benefits for all LIC members. Serving the basic insurance needs of the general public, including the underserved market, through various distribution methods.
62 Members
Founded in 1910
Mailing list available for rent

14029 Lightning Protection Institute
PO Box 99
Maryville, MO 64468

804-314-8955
800-488-6864
E-Mail: LPI@lightning.org
Home Page: www.lightning.org

Harold VanSickle III, Executive Director
Kim Loehr, Media/Marketing Consultant

A not-for-profit organization whose members are dedicated to insuring that today's lightning protection systems are the best possible quality in design, materials and installation, so that precious live and property can be protected from the damaging and costly effects of one of nature's most exciting phenomenons, lightning.
100 Members
Founded in 1955

14030 Loss Executives Association
Industrial Risk Insurers
Po Box 37
Tenafly, NJ 07670

201-569-3346
E-Mail: info@lossexecutives.com
Home Page: www.lossexecutives.com

Kevin L Ennis, President
Edward J Ryan, Vice President
Jean L Broderick, Treasurer
Paul Aviles, Secretary

A professional association of property loss executives providing education to the industry.

14031 Mass Marketing Insurance Institute
3007 Tilden Street, NW
Suite 7M-103
Washington, DC 20008

816-221-7575
Fax: 816-772-7765
E-Mail: gregc@robstan.com
Home Page: www.mi2.org
Social Media: Facebook, Twitter, LinkedIn, Google Plus, Youtube, Pinteres

Mark Smith, Director
Laurie Weber, Associate Director
Jim Barrett, First VP
Mary Walsh, VP Membership
Jennifer Branfort, Associate Director

The oldest not-for-profit membership organization that promotes the voluntary benefits industry by providing a forum for education, business development and fellowship.
300 Members
Frequency: Annual Meeting (Spring)
Founded in 1970

14032 Massachusetts Association of Insurance Agents
91 Cedar Street
Milford, MA 01757

508-634-2900
800-972-9312
Fax: 508-634-2929
E-Mail: info@massagent.com
Home Page: www.massagent.com

Richard A Perras, Chairman
Raymond Sirois, AAI, Vice Chairman
G.L. Lee Gaudette, III, CPCU, Secretary-Treasurer
Joseph P Leahy, Jr., National Director
Thomas F Skelly, Jr., CIC, LIA,, Chairman-Elect

Trade show for everyday use in the insurance agency office.
1800 Members
Frequency: November
Mailing list available for rent

14033 Million Dollar Round Table
325 W Touhy Ave
Park Ridge, IL 60068-4265

847-692-6378
Fax: 847-518-8921
E-Mail: info@mdrt.org
Home Page: www.mdrt.org
Social Media: Facebook, Twitter, LinkedIn, Pinterest

Guy E Baker, President
Stephen P. Stahr, Chief Executive Officer
Tammy Johnson-Peon, Organizational Communications
Wayne Schmeiser, Emerging Media Director
Laura McGrady, Accounting Manager

Provides its members with resources to improve their technical knowledge, sales and client service while maintaining a culture of high ethical standards. Mission is to be a valued, member-driven international network of leading insurance and investment financial services professionals/advisors who serve their clients by exemplary performance and the highest standards of ethics, knowledge, service and productivity.
35000 Members
Founded in 1927
Mailing list available for rent

14034 Mortgage Bankers Association of America
1919 M Street NW
5th Floor
Washington, DC 20036

202-557-2700
800-793-6222
Home Page: www.mortgagebankers.org

Bill Cosgrove, CMB, Chairman
Bill Emerson, Chairman-Elect
Rodrigo Lopez, CMB, Vice Chairman
David H. Stevens, President, CEO
Marcia Davies, COO

United States national association representing all facets of the real estate finance industry.
2200 Members

14035 Mortgage Insurance Companies of America
1425 K St Nw
Suite 210
Washington, DC 20005-3590

202-682-2683
Fax: 202-842-9252
E-Mail: info@privatemi.com
Home Page: www.privatemi.com

Suzanne Hutchinson, Executive VP

Representing the private mortgage insurance industry.
4 Members
Founded in 1973

14036 National African American Insurance Association
1718 M Street, NW
Box #1110
Washington, DC 20036

866-56 -AAIA
Fax: 513-563-9743
E-Mail: info@naaia.org
Home Page: www.naaia.org
Social Media: Facebook, Twitter, LinkedIn

Rudy Loney, Chairman
Jerald L. Tillman,ÿLUTCF, Founder
Leslie L. Skinner-Leslieÿ, Chairman of the BOD
Margaret Redd, Vice Chair of the BOD
Cherie Coffey, Treasurer

Helps create a network among minorities who are employed by insurance companies or self-employed in the insurance industry.
Founded in 1997

14037 National Alliance for Insurance Education & Research
3630 North Hills Drive
PO Box 27027
Austin, TX 78755-2027

512-457-7932
800-633-2165
Fax: 512-349-6194
E-Mail: alliance@scic.com
Home Page: www.scic.com/
Social Media: Facebook, Twitter, LinkedIn, Google Plus

William T Hold, Ph.D, CIC, CPCU,, President and CEO
Skyla Badger, Assistant Vice President
Theresa Bucek, CISR, Assistant Vice President
Paula Cook, Senior vice president
Bettie Duff, Senior Vice President

National education providers offering programs for all insurance and risk management professionals in property, liability and life insurance, with a continuing education requirement upon designation.
75000 Members
Founded in 1969

14038 National Association of Professional Agents
8430 Enterprise Circle
Suite 200
Lakewood Ranch, FL 34202

800-593-7657
Fax: 800-411-4771
Home Page: www.napa-benefits.org/
Social Media: Facebook, Twitter, LinkedIn

Offers insurance agents direct access to insurance benefits and professional services.
Founded in 1989

14039 National Association of Bar-Related Title Insurers
1430 Lee Street
Des Plaines, IL 60018

847-298-8300
Fax: 847-298-8388
E-Mail: joanne@elliottlaw.com
Home Page: www.nabrti.com

Joanne P Elliott, Executive Vice President
Kathleen Waters, Secretary/Treasurer

Members are bar-related title insurance companies registered with the US Patent Office.
10 Members
Founded in 1965

14040 National Association of Casualty and Surety Agents
316 Pennsylvania Avenue SE
Suite 400
Washington, DC 20003-1172

202-543-7500
Fax: 202-293-1219

Lawrence Zippin, Executive Director

A trade organization of insurance agentswho represent and sell for stock insurers. Its purpose is to foster the growth of its members through cooperation with the insurers its members represent.

14041 National Association of Catastrophe Adjusters
PO Box 821864
North Richland Hills, TX 76182

817-498-3466
Fax: 817-498-0480
E-Mail: naca@nacatadj.org
Home Page: www.nacatadj.org

Wanda Hogan, President
Robert Uhler, Vice President
John Postava, Secretary/Treasurer

Provides a professional organization focused on excellence in catastrophe insurance adjusting for members through education, shared resources, and technology.
347 Members
Founded in 1976

14042 National Association of Dental Plans
12700 Park Central Drive
Ste. 400
Dallas, TX 75251

972-458-6998
Fax: 972-458-2258
E-Mail: info@nadp.org
Home Page: www.nadp.org
Social Media: Twitter, LinkedIn, Youtube

Chris Swanker, FSA, MAAA, Chair
Evelyn F Ireland, CAEÿ, Executive Director
Theresa McConeghey, Vice Chair
Dr Gene Sherman, Secretary
Kirk Andrews, Treasurer

Non profit trade association representing the entire dental benefits industry; dental HMOs, dental PPOs, discount dental plans and dental indemnity products. Members include major commercial carriers, regional and single state companies, as well as companies organized as Delta and Blue Cross Blue Shield plans.
80 Members
Founded in 1989

14043 National Association of Disability Evaluating Professionals
13801 Village Mill Drive
Midlothian, VA 23113

804-378-7275
Home Page: www.nadep.com

Virgil Robert May III, Executive Director

Members are lawyers, medical doctors and other professionals involved in the evaluation and rehabilitation of persons with disabilities resulting from work or personal injuries.
Cost: $150.00
1000 Members
Frequency: Membership Fee
Founded in 1984

14044 National Association of Fire Investigators , International
857 Tallevast Road
Sarasota, FL 34243
941-359-2800
877-506-6234
Fax: 941-351-5849
E-Mail: info@nafi.org
Home Page: www.nafi.org

Heather Kennedy, Director Membership Services
Christine Kennedy, Director Training Program

Primary purpose of this association is to increase the knowledge and improve the skills of persons engaged in the investigation and analysis of fires, explosions, or in the litigation that ensues from such investigations. The Association also originated and implemented the National Certification Board.
6000 Members
Founded in 1961

14045 National Association of Fraternal Insurance Counselors
211 Canal Road
Waterloo, WI 53594

920-458-1996
866-478-3880
Fax: 920-457-4661
E-Mail: office@nafic.org
Home Page: www.nafic.org

H.E. Durbin, MBA, CFP, CLU,, President
Randall Kolarik, FIC, LUTCF, Vice President
Anna Maenner, Executive Director
Robert Cooper, FICF, Secretary and Treasurer

Promotes and educates the sales force in fraternal life insurance. Bestows quality service award and production awards annually.
3.1M Members
Founded in 1950

14046 National Association of Health Underwriters
1212 New York Avenue NW
Suite 1100
Washington, DC 20005

202-552-5060
Fax: 202-747-6820
E-Mail: info@nahu.org
Home Page: www.nahu.org
Social Media: Facebook, Twitter, LinkedIn, Youtube, RSS, B2B

Janet Trautwein, Executive Vice President & CEO
Jennifer B Murphy, Senior Vice President of Operations
Illana Maze, Senior Vice President of Technology
Brooke Willson, Vice President of Leadership
Melanie Gibson, Vice President

The mission is to improve its members' ability to meet the health, financial and retirement security needs of all Americans through education, advocacy and professional development.
18000 Members
Founded in 1930
Mailing list available for rent: 18000 names at $350 per M

14047 National Association of Independent Insurance Adjusters (NAIIA)
1880 Radcliff Ct.
Suite 117-C&B
Tracy, CA 95376

209-832-6962
Fax: 209-832-6964
E-Mail: admin@naiia.com
Home Page: www.naiia.com

T. Mark Nixon, President
Brenda Reisinger, Executive Director
Matt Ouellette, Secretary/Treasurer

Members are companies and individuals adjusting claims for insurance companies on a fee basis.
300 Members
Founded in 1937

14048 National Association of Independent Insura nce Adjusters (NAIIA)
1880 Radcliff Ct.
Suite 117-C & B
Tracy, CA 95376

209-832-6962
Fax: 209-832-6964
E-Mail: admin@naiia.com
Home Page: www.naiia.com

T. Mark Nixon, President
Brenda Reisinger, Executive Director
Matt Ouellette, Secretary/Treasurer

Membership consists of property-liability companies Supports the National Association of Independent Insurers Political Action Committee.

14049 National Association of Independent Life Brokerage Agencies
11325 Random Hills Road
Suite 110
Fairfax, VA 22030

703-383-3081
Fax: 703-383-6942
E-Mail: jnormandy@nailba.org
Home Page: www.nailba.org
Social Media: Facebook, Twitter, LinkedIn, RSS

Raymond Phillips, CLU, LTCP, Chairman
Jack Chiasson, CAE, Chief Executive Officer
Kathy Allison, Director, Membership
Sarah O'Hanley, Manager, Exhibits, Sponsorships
John Tong, Director, Administration

Influencing the independent life and health brokerage community.

14050 National Association of Insurance Commissioners
1100 Walnut Street
Suite 1500
Kansas City, MO 64106-2197

816-842-3600
Fax: 816-783-8175
E Mail: webpost@naic.org
Home Page: www.naic.org

James J. Donelon, NAIC President, Commissioner
Andrew Beal, NAIC Chief Operating Officer and Ch
Monica J. Lindeen, NAIC Vice President Commissioner
Sen. Ben Nelson, NAIC Chief Executive Officer
Michael F. Consedine, NAIC Secretary-Treasurer

Assists state insurance regulators, individually and collectively, in serving the public interest and achieving the following fundamental insurance regulatorygoals in a responsive, efficient and cost effective manner, consistent with the wishes of its members.
Founded in 1871
Mailing list available for rent

14051 National Association of Insurance and Financial Advisors
2901 Telestar Court
PO Box 12012
Falls Church, VA 22042-1205

877-866 2432
877-866-2432
Fax: 703-770-8201
E-Mail: membersupport@naifa.org
Home Page: www.naifa.org
Social Media: Facebook, Twitter, LinkedIn, Youtube

John F. Nichols, MSM, CLU, President
Susan B. Waters, EDM, CAE, Chief Executive Officer

Matthew S. Tassey, CLU, ChFC, LUT, Treasurer

Mission is to advocate for a positive legislative and regulatory environment, enhance business and professional skills, and promote the ethical conduct of our members.

Founded in 1890

14052 National Association of Mortgage Brokers

2701 W. 15th Street
Suite 536
Plano, TX 75075

972-758-1151
Fax: 530-484-2906
E-Mail: membership@namb.org
Home Page: www.namb.org
Social Media: Facebook, Twitter, LinkedIn, Youtube, RSS

Donald J. Frommeyer, CRMS, President
Rocke Andrews, CMC, CRMS, Vice President
Kay A. Cleland, CMC, CRMS, Secretary
Andy W. Harris, CRMS, Treasurer

The only national trade association representing the mortgage broker industry. Promotes the industry through programs and services such as education, professional certification and government affairs representation.

25000 Members
Founded in 1973
Mailing list available for rent

14053 National Association of Mutual Insurance Companies

3601 Vincennes Road
Indianapolis, IN 46268-0700

317-875-5250
Fax: 202-628-1601
Home Page: www.namic.org
Social Media: Facebook, Twitter

Charles M Chamness, President/CEO
Gregg Dykstra, Chief Operating Officer
Neil Alldredge, Senior Vice President
Brent N. Bahler, Vice President, Public Affairs
Pam Keeney, Vice President - Underwriting

A full service nationaltrade association with more than 1,400 member companies that underwrite 43 percent of the property/casualty insurance premium in the United States.

1400 Members
Founded in 1985
Mailing list available for rent

14054 National Association of Professional Surplus Lines Offices, Ltd.

200 NE 54th St.
Suite 200
Kansas City, MO 64118

816-741-3910
Fax: 816-741-5409
E-Mail: info@napslo.org
Home Page: www.napslo.org
Social Media: Facebook, Twitter, LinkedIn

Kevin T. Westrope, President
Hank Haldeman, Vice President
Brady Kelley, Executive Director
Mike Ardis, Director of Technology
Richard Bouhan, Counsel on Special Projects

A national trade association representing the surplus lines industry and the wholesale insurance marketing system. Acting as a source of information, spends a great deal of time identifying and explaining to regulatory, other segments of the insurance industry, the media and the public the vital role surplus lines in the insurance industry.

Founded in 1975
Mailing list available for rent

14055 National Association of Professional Insur ance Agents

400 North Washington Street
Alexandria, VA 22314

703-836-9340
Fax: 703-836-1279
E-Mail: web@pianet.org
Home Page: www.pianet.org/
Social Media: Facebook, Twitter, LinkedIn, RSS

Mike Becker, Executive Vice President & CEO
Roxanne Johnson, Executive Assistant
Patricia A. Borowski, CPIW, Senior Vice President
Jennifer Webb, Counsel & Director of Reg Affairs
Jon Gentile, Director of Federal Affairs

Voluntary, membership based, trade association representing professional independent insurance agents throughout the United States.

Founded in 1931

14056 National Association of Public Insurance Adjusters

21165 Whitfield Place
Suite 105
Potomac Falls, VA 20165

703-433-9217
Fax: 703-433-0369
E-Mail: info@napia.com
Home Page: www.napia.com

Art Jansen, Jr., SPPA, President & Chairman
David W Barrack, Executive Director
Richelle Kelly, Director, Events & Membership
Damon Faunce, Treasurer
Greg Raab, Secretary

Experts on property loss adjustment who are retained by policy holders to assist in preparing, filing and adjusting insurance claims. NAPIA members have joined together for the purpose of professional education, certification, and promotion of a code of professional conduct.

Founded in 1950
Mailing list available for rent

14057 National Association of State Comprehensive Health Insurance

580-512-1488
Home Page: www.naschip.org/

Tanya Case, Chair
Vic Kensler, Chair-Elect/Vice President
Cecil Bykerk, Treasurerÿ
Vernita McMurtrey, Secretary
Michele Eberle, Board Member

Provides educational opportunities and information for state high risk health insurance pools that have been, or are yet to be, established by state governments to serve the medically "uninsurable" population.

14058 National Association of Surety Bond Producers

1140 19th Street
Suite 800
Washington, DC 20036-5104

202-686-3700
Fax: 202-686-3656
E-Mail: info@nasbp.org
Home Page: www.nasbp.org
Social Media: Facebook, Twitter, LinkedIn

Richard Foss, Executive VP
Stephen L Cory, Second VP

International organization of professional surety bond producers and brokers.

500+ Members
Founded in 1942

14059 National Cargo Bureau

17 Battery Pl
Suite 1232
New York, NY 10004-1110

212-785-8300
Fax: 212-785-8333
E-Mail: ncbnyc@natcargo.org
Home Page: www.natcargo.org

Ian J. Lennard, President
Kristian Wiede, Corporate Secretary
Philip Anderson, Chief, Technical Department

The Bureau was created to render assistance to the United States Coast Guard in discharging its responsibilities under the 1948 International Convention for Safety of Life at Sea and for other purposes closely related thereto.

Founded in 1952

14060 National Conference of Insurance Legislators

385 Jordan Road
Troy, NY 12180

518-687-0178
Fax: 518-687-0401
E-Mail: info@ncoil.org
Home Page: www.ncoil.org

Greg Wren, AL, President
Travis Holdman, IN, Vice President
Steve Riggs, Secretary
Jason Rapert, Treasurer

NCOIL is an organization of state legislators whose main area of public policy concern is insurance legislation and regulation. Many legislators active in NCOIL either chair or are members of the committees reponsible for insurance legislation in their respective state houses across the country.

Founded in 1969

14061 National Conference of Insurance Legislato rs (NCOIL)

1100 13th Street NW
Suite 1000
Washington, DC 20005

202-955-3500
Fax: 202-955-3599
E-Mail: customersupport@ncqa.org
Home Page: www.ncqa.org
Social Media: Facebook, Twitter, LinkedIn, Youtube, Google Plus, Pinteres

Dolores L. Mitchell, Chair
Margaret E. O'Kane, President
Scott Hartranft, Chief Financial Officer
Tom Fluegel, Chief Operating Officer
Rick Moore, Chief Information Officer

Independent, non profit organization dedicated to improving healthcare quality.

Founded in 1990
Mailing list available for rent

14062 National Council of Self-Insurers

1253 Springfield Ave
PMB 345
New Providence, NJ 07974-2931

908-665-2152
Fax: 908-665-4020
E-Mail: natcouncil@aol.com
Home Page: www.natcouncil.com

Larry Holt, Executive Director
Robin R Obetz, VP

The Council believes that the workers' compensation system, properly administered by the states, is a vital part of the economic and social fabric of the United States. The Council aime to preserve it and protect it as the most effective means of resolving claims for industrial injuries and occupational diseases between employers and employees.

3500 Members
Founded in 1946

14063 National Council on Compensation Insurance
901 Pennisula Corporate Circle
Boca Raton, FL 33487-1362

561-893-1000
Fax: 561-893-1191
E-Mail: robert_pierson@ncci.com
Home Page: www.ncci.com

Robert Pierson, Affiliate Services Executive
Jennie Dennison, Account Manager

Manages the nation's largest database of workers' compensation insurance information. They analyze industry trends, prepares workers compensation insurance rate recommendations, determines the cost of propsed legislation, and provides a variety of services and tools to maintain a healthy workers compensation system.
Founded in 1922

14064 National Independent Statistical Service
3601 Vincennes Road
PO Box 68950
Indianapolis, IN 46268-0950

317-876-6200
Fax: 317-876-6210
E-Mail: questions@niss-stat.org
Home Page: www.niss-stat.org

Theresa Szwast, President

A unique resource for the property/casualty insurance industry. Collect and report timely, quality insurance data, and perform other related functions, at a reasonable cost.
Founded in 1966

14065 National Insurance Association
1133 Desert Shale Avenue
Las Vegas, NV 89120

702-269-2445
Fax: 702-269-2446

Josephine King, Executive Director

Organization of about 14 insurance companies owned or controlled by African Americans.
14 Members
Founded in 1921

14066 National Insurance Crime Bureau
1111 E Touhy Ave
Suite 400
Des Plaines, IL 60018-5804

847-544-7000
800-447-6282
Fax: 847-544-7100
E-Mail: rjones@nicb.org
Home Page: www.nicb.org
Social Media: Facebook, Twitter, LinkedIn, Youtube

Joseph H Wehrle, Jr, President
James K Schweitzer, Senior Vice President
Daniel G Abbott, Senior Vice President
Robert Jachnicki, Senior Vice President
Andrew J Sosnowski, Senior Vice President

Not for profit organization that receives support from property/casualty insurance companies. Partners with insurers and law enforcement agaencies to facilitate the identification, detection and prosecution of insurance criminals. Formed from ther merging of the National Automobile Theft Bureau and the Insurance Crime Prevention Institute.
1000 Members
Founded in 1992

14067 National Organization of Life and Health Insurance Guaranty Associations
13873 Park Center Road
Suite 329
Herndon, VA 20171

703-481-5206
Fax: 703-481-5209
E-Mail: info@nolhga.com
Home Page: www.nolhga.com/

Peter G. Gallanisy, President
William P. O'Sullivan, SVP, General Counsel
Richard W. Klipstein, EVP, COO
Paul A. Peterson, VP, Accounting & Finance
Holly L. Wilding, VP, Administrative Services

A voluntary, U.S. association made up of the life and health insurance guaranty associations of all 50 states and the District of Columbia.
Founded in 1983

14068 National Risk Retention Association
16133 Ventura Blvd.
Suite 1055
Encino, CA 91436

952-928-4656
800-928-5809
Fax: 952-929-1318
E-Mail: joe@riskretention.org
Home Page: www nrra-usa.org

Sanford Elsass, Chair
Nancy Gray, Treasurer
Robert Myers, Jr., Esq, General Counsel
Derick White, CPA, CFE, Secretary
Rod Nofziger, Chair Elect

Promotes Risk Retention Act-authorized group insurance programs as a practical, economical, efficient and financially sound option for distributing the liability risks of member insuerds.
Founded in 1987

14069 National Underwriter Company
5081 Olympic Blvd
Erlanger, KY 41018-3164

859-692-2100
800-543-0874
Fax: 859-692-2295
E-Mail: webmistress@nuco.com
Home Page: www.nationalunderwriter.com

Charlie Smith, CEO

Organization with listings which include companies, brokers and agents in each area handling all lines of insurance.

14070 National Viatical Association
1030 15th Street NW
Washington, DC 20005

202-347-7361
800-741-9465
Fax: 202-393-0336

Charles C Reely, Executive Director

NVA is dedicated to financially assisting and effectively promotingthe needs of people coping with terminal illnesses in a compassionate, professional and ethical manner. The National Viatical Association is further dedicated to educating and informing the public on the viatical settlement processs.
60 Members
Founded in 1993

14071 New England Professional Insurance Agents Association
1 Ash Street
Hopkinton, MA 01748-1822

508-497-2590

Stella Di Camilo, Manager

Supports all those in professional agents in the insurance industry in the New England region. Hosts annual trade show.

14072 Nonprofit Risk Management Center
15 N King Street
Suite 203
Leesburg, VA 20176

202-785-3891
Fax: 703-443-1990
E-Mail: info@nonprofitrisk.org
Home Page: www.nonprofitrisk.org
Social Media: Twitter

Michael A Schraer, President
Melanie Lockwood Herman, Executive Director
Lisa Prinz, Treasurer
Carolyn Hayes-Gulston, Secretary

Provides assistance and resources for community serving organizations.
Founded in 1990
Mailing list available for rent

14073 North American Pet Health Insurance Association
200 692 Osborne Street
Winnipeg, MB R3L 2B9

877-962-7442
E-Mail: info@naphia.org
Home Page: www./naphia.org
Social Media: Facebook, Twitter, LinkedIn, YouTube

Dennis Rushovich, President and Past Treasurer
Laura Bennett, Past President
Steve Popovich, Treasurer
Tim Graff, Secretary
Randy Valpy, Board Member

Represents experienced and reputable pet health insurance companiesand pet health professionals.

14074 Physician Insurers Association of America
2275 Research Blvd
Suite 250
Rockville, MD 20850-6213

301-947-9000
Fax: 301-947-9090
E-Mail: membership@piaa.us
Home Page: www.piaa.us
Social Media: Twitter

Theodore J Clarke, MD, Chair
Gloria H Everett, Vice Chair
Paul C McNabb, II, MD, Secretary
Ann G Horwich, Business Development/Mktg Director
Michael Stinson, Government Relations Director

An organization of healthcare liability insurance entities which share the common values of its founders to advocate on behalf of physicians, dentists, and other healthcare providers in the areas of legislation, education, risk management and research.
1000 Members
Founded in 1977

14075 Professional Insurance Communicators of America
3601 Vincennes Road
Po Box 60700
Indianapolis, IN 46268-0700

317-875 5250
Fax: 317-879-8408
Home Page: www.pica.pro/
Social Media: Twitter, LinkedIn

Janet EH Wright, Secretary/Treasurer

Members are editors of insurance company newsletters.
90 Members
Founded in 1955

14076 Professional Insurance Marketing Association
35 E. Wacker Dr.
Suite 850
Chicago, IL 60601-2106

817-569-7462
Fax: 312-644-8557
E-Mail: mona@pima-assn.org
Home Page: www.pima-assn.org
Social Media: Twitter, LinkedIn

Mona F. Buckley, CEO
Samuel Fleet, President
Daniel O'Brien, CLU, President-Elect
Michael Mercer, Treasurer
Mark Kelsey, Secretary

The leading national membership association of third-party administrators, insurance carriers and allied business partners involved in the direct marketing of insurance products. Also provides educational conferences, legislative updates, networking opportunities, publications and manuals to all those whose primary business is insurance marketing.
117 Members
Founded in 1974

14077 Professional Liability Underwriting Society
5353 Wayzata Blvd
Suite 600
Minneapolis, MN 55416-1335

952-746-2580
800-845-0778
Fax: 952-746-2599
E-Mail: info@plusweb.org
Home Page: www.plusweb.org
Social Media: Twitter, LinkedIn

Derek B. Hazeltine, CAE, Executive Director
David Williams, President
Paul Lavelle, Vice President
Scott A. Billey, Director of Operations
Lance Helgerson, Director of Strategic Marketing

Enhances the professionalism of its members through education and other activities and to responsibly address issues related to professional liability.
7000 Members
Founded in 1986

14078 Property Casualty Insurers Association of America
8700 West Bryn Mawr Avenue
Suite 1200S
Chicago, IL 60631-3512

847-297-7800
Fax: 847-297-5064
E-Mail: pcinet@pciaa.net
Home Page: www.pciaa.net

David A. Sampson, President
Paul Blume, Senior Vice President
Nathaniel Wienecke, Senior Vice President
Randi Cigelnik, Senior Vice President
Joanne Orfanos, Senior Vice President

Established by the Merger of the Alliance of American Insurers and the National Association Association of Independent Insurers. Provides a responsible and effective voice on public policy questions affecting insurance products and services, fosters a competitive insurance marketplace for the benefit of insurers and consumers, and provides members with the highest quality products, information and services at a reasonable cost.
1000 Members
Founded in 2004

14079 Property Insurance Loss Register
700 New Brunswick Avenue
Rahway, NJ 07065-3819

732-388-0332
Fax: 732-388-0537

Lawrence Zippin, President

A voluntary nonprofit organization administered by the American Insurance Services Group; maintains a computerized registry of property loss claims which can be used by its subscribers to fight insurance fraud, and provides data for nonactuarial/statistical research.

14080 Property Loss Research Bureau (PLRB/LIRB)
3025 Highland Pkwy
Suite 800
Downers Grove, IL 60515-1291

630-724-2200
888-711-7572
Fax: 630-724-2260
Home Page: www.plrb.org

Tom Mallin, President
Paul C Despensa, VP/General Counsel

PLRB/LIRB provides legal research, consulting and educational services in auto liablility and CGL lines, in addition to promoting education and new, beneficial developments within the property and casualty insurance industry. Members are stock and mutual insurance companies.
252 Members
Founded in 1990
Mailing list available for rent

14081 Public Agency Risk Managers Association
PO Box 6810
San Jose, CA 95150

888-907-2762
Fax: 888-412-5913
E-Mail: Info@parma.com
Home Page: www.parma.com

Jim Thyden, President
Kim Hunt, Vice President
Susan Eldridge, Secretary Treasurer
Coni Hernandez, Alliance of Schools
Jeff J Rush, Senior Claims Administrator

A forum promoting, developing and advancing education and leadership in public agency risk management. PARMA is dedicated to facilitating the exchange of ideas and innovative solutions toward risk management in government.
600+ Members
Founded in 1974

14082 Registered Mail Insurance Association
100 William Street
New York, NY 10038-4512

212-612-4000
800-969-7462
Fax: 212-425-2539

Cheryl Martinez, Assistant VP

Insurance companies providing insurance for shipments of currency, securities and other valuables. LSTD Instrument Bonds are provided to facilitate the reproduction of lost documents.
3 Members
Founded in 1921

14083 Reinsurance Association of America
1445 New York Ave
7th Floor
Washington, DC 20005

202-638-3690
Fax: 202-638-0936
E-Mail: infobox@reinsurance.org
Home Page: www.reinsurance.org
Social Media: Facebook, Twitter, LinkedIn

Franklin W Nutter, President
Dennis C Burke, Vice President, State Relations
Marsha A Cohen, Senior Vice President and Director
Tracey W Laws, Senior Vice President
Karalee C Morell, Assistant Vice President

Non profit association committed to an activist agenda that represents the interests of reinsurance professionals across the United States.
Founded in 1968

14084 Risk and Insurance Management Society
1065 6th Ave
13th Floor
New York, NY 10018-0713

212-286-9292
Fax: 212-986-9716
Home Page: www.rims.org
Social Media: Facebook, Twitter, LinkedIn

Mary Roth, Executive Director
Deborah Flam, Human Resoures Manager
Lynn Chambers, CFO
Stephanie Orange, Chief Marketing Officer
Valerie Cammiso, Membership/Chapter Services

Dedicated to advancing the practice of risk management, a professional discipline that protects physical, financial and human resources.
3900 Members
Founded in 1950
Mailing list available for rent

14085 SNL Financial
PO Box 2124
Charlottesvle, VA 22902

434-977-1600
Fax: 434-977-4466
E-Mail: customerservice@snl.com
Home Page: www.snl.com
Social Media: Facebook, Twitter, LinkedIn

Michael Chinn, President
Reid Nagle, CEO
Bjorn Turnquist, Director Product Management

This organization offers the most up-to-date information available in the insurance industry featuring the latest news releases, filings and important events. Provides current data on top-performing stocks, insider trades, ownership filings, company news and events and legislative issues.
Founded in 1987
Mailing list available for rent

14086 Securities Industry and Financial Markets Association (SIFMA)
1101 New York Ave NW
8th Floor
Washington, DC 20005-4279

202-962-7300
Fax: 202-962-7305
Home Page: www.sifma.org
Social Media: Facebook, Twitter, LinkedIn

T Timothy Ryan Jr, President/CEO
Randy Snook, Senior Managing Director/EVP
Cheryl Crispen, Executive VP, Communications
Ira D. Hammerman, Senior Managing Director
David Krasner, Chief Financial Administrator

SIFMA's mission is to champion policies and practices that benefit investors and issuers, expand and perfect global capital markets, and foster the development of new products and services. SIFMA provides an enhanced member network of access and forward-looking services, as well as premiere educational resources

for the professionals within the industry and the investors whom they serve.
Mailing list available for rent

14087 Self Insurance Institute of America
PO Box 1237
Simpsonville, SC 29681
800-851-7789
Fax: 864-962-2483
E-Mail: administration@siia.org
Home Page: www.siia.org
James A Kinder, CEO
Mike Ferguson, Executive Director
Mieka Scholten, Finance Director
Raquel Horton, Marketing Manager
James E. Burkholder, VP Finance/Chief Financial Officer
Dedicated to protecting and promoting the self insurance and alternative risk transfer industry.
1500 Members
Founded in 1981

14088 Shipowners Claims Bureau
1 Battery Park Plz
31st Floor
New York, NY 10004-1487
212-847-4500
Fax: 212-847-4599
E-Mail: info@american-club.com
Home Page: www.american-club.com
Joseph Hughes, CEO
Vincent J. Solarino, President & COO
Arpad A. Kadi, Senior Vice President - Treasurer
Donald R. Moore, Senior Vice President
Members are claim managers and adjusters for shipping lines and protection and indemnity clubs.
31 Members
Founded in 1917
Mailing list available for rent

14089 Society of Actuaries
475 N Martingale Rd
Schaumburg, IL 60173-2252
847-706-3500
Fax: 847-706-3599
E-Mail: webmaster@soa.org
Home Page: www.soa.org
Greg Heidrich, Executive Director
Stacy Lin, Deputy Executive Director/CFO
An educational, research and professional organization dedicated to serving the public and Society members. The vision is for actuaries to be recognized as the leading professionals in the modeling and management of finanacial risk and contingent events.
17000 Members
Founded in 1949

14090 Society of Certified Insurance Counselors
3630 N Hills Drive
Austin, TX 78731-3028
800-633-2165
Fax: 512-349-6194
E-Mail: alliance@scic.com
Home Page: www.scic.com
Social Media: Facebook, Twitter, LinkedIn
William Hold, President/CEO
Theresa Bucek, Senior Management Team
Glenn Cryan, Chief Operating Officer
Michelle D. Haynes, Controller
Bettie Duff, Senior VPof Customer Care
National education program in property, liability and life insurance, with a continuing education requirement upon designation.

14091 Society of Financial Examiners
174 Grace Blvd
Altamonte Spgs, FL 32714-3210
407-682-4930
800-787-7633
Fax: 888-436-8686
Home Page: www.sofe.org
Social Media: Facebook, LinkedIn
L. Brackett, Executive Director
Stephen J Szypula, Financial Administrator
Judy Estus, Administrator
Ryan Havick, President
Eric Dercher, Treasurer
The one organization where financial examiners of inusrance companies, banks, savings and loans, credit unions come together for training and to share exchange information on a formal and informal level.
1600 Members
Founded in 1973

14092 Society of Financial Service Professionals
19 Campus Blvd
Suite 100
Newtown Square, PA 19073-3230
610-526-2500
Fax: 610-527-1499
E-Mail: info@financialpro.org
Home Page: www.financialpro.org
Social Media: Facebook, Twitter, LinkedIn
Joseph E Frack, CEO
Donna Conrad, CFO
Anthony Smith, VP Marketing/Corporate Services
Jill Von Czoernig, Managing Director
Sherry Chester, Director, Professional Development
Members are dedicated to the highest standards of competence and service in insurance and financial services.
Founded in 1928
Mailing list available for rent

14093 Society of Insurance Research
631 Eastpoint Drive
Shelbyville, IN 46176-2291
317-398-3684
Fax: 317-642-0535
E-Mail: sir.mail@comcast.net
Home Page: www.sirnet.org
Ed Budd, Executive Director
Gary Hodge, President
Howard Goldstein, Secretary
F Reilly Cobb, VP Marketing
Michael Warner, Vice President - Marketing
Provides a forum for the free exchange of ideas in all areas of insurance research. The Society includes representation from many different organizations such as insurance and non-insurance companies, government agencies, institutions of higher education, and trade associations.
350 Members
Founded in 1970
Mailing list available for rent

14094 Society of Insurance Trainers and Educators
1821 University Ave W
Ste S256
St. Paul, MN 55104
651-999-5354
Fax: 651-917-1835
E-Mail: ed@insurancetrainers.org
Home Page: www.insurancetrainers.org
Social Media: Facebook, Twitter, LinkedIn
Patricia M McCarthy, President
Melissa Palank, Executive Director
Beth Gamble Riggins, VP Annual Conference
Mary Jo Burfeind, VP Membership Services
Professional organization of trainers and educators in insurance.
600 Members
Founded in 1953

14095 Society of Professional Benefit Administrators
2 Wisconsin Circle
Suite 670
Chevy Chase, MD 20815
301-718-7722
Fax: 301-718-9440
Home Page: www.spbatpa.org
Anne C Lennan, President
National Association of Third Party Administrators (TPAs) of employee benefit health and pension plans. SPBA represents TPAs who offer comprehensive services.
300 Members
Founded in 1975

14096 Society of Risk Management Consultants
330 S Executive Drive
Suite 301
Brookfield, WI 53005-4275
800-765-SRMC
Fax: 212-572-6499
E-Mail: webmaster@srmcsociety.org
Home Page: www.srmcsociety.org
Susan Kaufman, Public Relations
Mark R. Forsythe, CPCU, President
Robert Harder, ARM, Secretary
Michael Norek, Treasurer
Joy M. Gander, CPCU, ARM, President Elect
The mission is to advance these professions to benefit the consultants themselves, their clients and the public through research, education, the exchange of information, anf the promotion of professional and ethical guidlines.
150 Members
Founded in 1984

14097 Sun States Professional Insurance Agents Association
13416 N 32nd Street
Suite 106
Phoenix, AZ 85032-6000
602-482-3333
Maryls M Graser, Executive VP
Supports all those professional insurance agents who serve the southern region of the country. Hosts annual trade show.

14098 Teachers Insurance and Annuity Association
730 Third Avenue
New York, NY 10017
800-842-2252
Fax: 800-842-2252
Home Page: www.tiaa-cref.org
Social Media: Facebook, Twitter, LinkedIn, YouTube, Google+
Roger Ferguson, President, CEO
Gina Wilson, EVP, CFO
Connie Weaver, EVP, Chief Marketing Officer
Ron Pressman, EVP, Chief Operating Officer
Annabelle Bexiga, EVP, Chief Information Officer
Financial services organization that is a retirement provider for people who work in the academic, research, medical and cultural fields.

14099 The American Council of Life Insurers
101 Constitution Avenue, NW
Suite 700
Washington, DC 20001-2133

202-624-2000
E-Mail: contact@acli.com
Home Page: www.acli.com
Social Media: Facebook, Twitter, RSS, YouTube

Dirk Kempthorne, President, CEO
Brian Waidmann, Chief of Staff
Kimberly Olson Dorgan, Senior EVP, Public Policy
J. Bruce Ferguson, SVP, State Relations
Paul S. Graham, SVP, Insurance Regulation

A Washinton, D.C.-based lobbying and trade group for the life insurance industry.
300 Members

14100 The American Society of Law, Medicine & Ethics
765 Commonwealth Ave
Suite 1634
Boston, MA 02215-1401

617-262-4990
Fax: 617-437-7596
E-Mail: info@aslme.org
Home Page: www.aslme.org
Social Media: Facebook, Twitter, LinkedIn

Ted Hutchinson, Executive Director
Margo Smith, Membership Department
Katie Kenney Johnson, Conference Director
Courtney McClellan, Assistant Editor

Provides high-quality scholarship, debate, and critical thought to the community of professionals at the nexus of law, medicine, and ethics.
Founded in 1972
Mailing list available for rent

14101 The Blue Cross and Blue Shield Association
225 North Michigan Avenue
Chicago, IL 60601

E-Mail: bcbswebmaster@bcbsa.com
Home Page: www.bcbs.com/
Social Media: Facebook, Twitter, YouTube, RSS

Scott P. Serota, President, CEO
William J. Colbourne, SVP, HR and Administration
Doug Porter, SVP, Operations, CIO
Maureen E. Sullivan, SVP, Strategic Services
Robert Kolodgy, SVP, Financial Services, CFO

Trade association for the independent, locally operated Blue Cross and Blue Shield plans in the USA.

14102 The Council of Insurance Agents & Brokers
701 Pennsylvania Ave NW
Suite 750
Washington, DC 20004-2661

202-783-4400
Fax: 202-783-4410
E-Mail: ciab@ciab.com
Home Page: www.ciab.com
Social Media: Facebook, Twitter, LinkedIn

Johnny R Pitts, Chairman
Ken A Crerar, President/CEO
Steve L Brockmeyer, Vice Chairman
Bill D Henry, Treasurer
Robert Cohen, Secretary

Formerly the National Association of Casualty and Surety agents. The council represents the nation's largest commercial property and casualty insurance agencies and brokerage firms. Council members annually place some 80% of the commercial property/casualty insurance premiums in the United States. Council members who operate both nationally and internationally, specialize in a wide range of insurance products and risk management services for business, industry, government and the public.
300 Members
Founded in 1913

14103 The Griffith Insurance Education Foundation
720 Providence Rd
Suite 100
Malvern, PA 19355

855-288-7743
Fax: 610-725-5967
E-Mail: info@griffithfoundation.org
Home Page: www.griffithfoundation.org
Social Media: Facebook, Twitter

Janice Abraham, Chair
Susan Krieger, Vice Chair
Dana Rudmose, CPA, Treasurer
Michael A. Winner, Immediate Past Chairman
Kevin Brown, Esq., CAE, Executive Director

Nonprofit, nonadvocacy, educational organization that provides riskmanagement and insurance education for students and public policymakers.
Founded in 1960

14104 The Institutes
720 Providence Road
Suite 100
Malvern, PA 19355-3433

610-644-2101
800-644-2101
Fax: 610-640-9576
E-Mail: cserv@cpcuiia.org
Home Page: www.theinstitutes.org
Social Media: Facebook, Twitter, LinkedIn

Karen Burger CPCU CPIW, Director PR/Advertising
Terrie E Troxel CPCP, President/CEO
Jim Marks, Executive Director

An independent, nonprofit organization offering educational programs and professional certification to people in all segments of the property and liability insurance business. More than 150,000 insurance practitioners around the world are involved in Institute programs.
Mailing list available for rent

14105 The National Association for Fixed Annuities
1155 F Street NW
Suite 1050
Washington, DC 20004

414-332-9306
Fax: 415-946-3532
E-Mail: bailey@nafa.com
Home Page: www.nafa.com

Chip Anderson, NAFA Chair
S. Christopherÿ Johnson, NAFA Vice Chair
Brian Mann, NAFA Treasurer
Bob Phillips, NAFA Past Chair
Kim O'Brien, President, CEO

Trade association dedicated to promoting fixed annuities.

14106 The National Association of Independent Insurance Adjusters
1880 Radcliff Ct.
Tracy, CA 95376

209-832-6962
Fax: 209-832-6964
E-Mail: admin@naiia.com
Home Page: www.naiia.com/

Brenda Reisinger, Executive Director

Trade group of property and casualty claims companies.

14107 The National Association of Mutual Insurance Companies
122 C Street N.W.ÿ
Suite 540
Washington, DC 20001

202-628-1558
Fax: 202-628-1601
Home Page: www.namic.org
Social Media: Facebook, Twitter, LinkedIn, RSS, YouTube

Stuart Henderson, J.D., CPCU, Chairman
Steve Linkous, Vice Chairman
John J. Bishop, CPCU, CLU, Immediate Past Chairman
Charles Chamnessÿ, President, CEO
Paul G. Stueven, PFMMÿ, Chairman Elect

National trade association of mutual property and casualty insurance companies.

14108 The Society of Chartered Property and Casualty Underwriters (CPCU)
800-932-2728
Fax: 610-725-5969
E-Mail: MemberResources@theinstitutes.org
Home Page: www.cpcusociety.org/
Social Media: Facebook, Twitter, LinkedIn

Jane M. Wahl, CPCU, CSSBB, President, Chair
Brian P. Savko, CPCU, President-Elect
Stanley W. Plappert, JD, CPCU, Treasurer, Secretary
Cynthia A. Baroway, CPCU, Immediate Past President, Chairman
Kevin H. Brown, Esq., CAE, SVP, Executive Director

A community of credentialed property and casualty insurance professionals.
22,00 Members

14109 Think Believe Act
220 West 42nd Street
10th Floor
New York, NY 10036

646-445-7000
Fax: 646-445-7001
E-Mail: losangeles@tbaglobal.com
Home Page: www.tbaglobal.com
Social Media: Facebook, Twitter, LinkedIn

Robert Geddes, CEO

TBA is a privately-held company that is now one of the world's leading producers and marketers of brand events and experiences for Fortune 1000 companies

14110 Transportation & Logistics Council
120 Main Street
Huntington, NY 11743

631-549-8988
Fax: 631-549-8962
E-Mail: tlc@transportlaw.com
Home Page: www.tlcouncil.org

Diane Smid, Executive Secretary
Judy Selvaggio, Administrative Secretary
Nadia Martin, CCP, Secretary/ Treasurer
Bob Hochwarth, Chairman
Reed Tepper, President

Formerly the Transportation Consumer Protection Council, a not for profit trade association dedicated to the education of shippers, carriers and others involved in the transportation of goods, the prevention of transit loss and damage, the promulgation of reasonable practices, laws and regulations, and the equitable resolution of disputes invloving frieght claims, freight charges and related maters.
250 Members
Founded in 1974

14111 US Travel Insurance Association
2080 Western Avenue
Guilderland, NY 12084

800-224-6164
E-Mail: president@ustia.org
Home Page: www.ustia.org

Bruce Kirby, President
Mark Carney, Vice President
Linda Finkle, Treasurer
Mike Kelly, Past President
Henry Carpenter, Secretary

National association of insurance carriers, third-party administrators, insurance agencies and related businesses involved in the development, administration and marketing of travel insurance and travel assistance products.
Founded in 2004

14112 Underwriters Laboratories
333 Pfingsten Rd
Northbrook, IL 60062-2096

847-272-8800
877-854-3577
Fax: 847-272-8129
E-Mail: cec@us.ul.com
Home Page: www.ul.com
Social Media: Facebook, Twitter, LinkedIn, YouTube, Google+

Keith E Williams, President/CEO
Michael Saltzman, SVP & CFO
Christian Anschuetz, Senior VP and CIO
Adrian Groom, Senior Vice President
Terry Brady, SVP & Chief Legal Officer

An independent, not for profit product safety testing and certification organization. They have also tested products for public safety for more than a century.
Founded in 1894
Mailing list available for rent

14113 Women In Insurance and Financial Services
136 Everett Road
Albany, NY 12205

518-694-5506
866-264-9437
Fax: 518-935-9232
E-Mail: office@wifsnational.org
Home Page: www.w-wifs.org
Social Media: Facebook, Twitter, LinkedIn

Angelia Z. Shay, President
Susan L. Combs, President-Elect
Susan Glass, Secretary
Veronica Bell, Treasurer
Deb Duffy, Executive Director

Vision is to provide a strong network of women helping each other develop the success that lies within each of us.
1.5M Members
Founded in 1987

14114 Women in Insurance and Financial Services
136 Everett Road
Albany, NY 12205

518-694-5506
866-264-9437
Fax: 518-935-9232
E-Mail: office@wifsnational.org
Home Page: www.wifsnational.org
Social Media: Facebook, Twitter, LinkedIn

Susan Combs, PPACA, President
Susan Glass, LUTC, President-Elect
Angelia Shay, CLU, ChFC, Immediate Past President
Lisa Pilgrim, Deputy Treasurer
Evelyn Gellar, LUTCF, Secretary

National organization devoted to the success of women in the insurance and financial services fields.

14115 Workers Compensation Reinsurance Bureau
2 Hudson Place
Hoboken, NJ 07030-5515

201-798-6312
Fax: 201-792-4441

Alfred O Weller, President

An association of insurance companies which pool their workers compensation excess losses as an alternative to purchasing reinsurance.
Founded in 1912

Newsletters

14116 ARIA Newsletter
American Risk and Insurance Association
716 Providence Road
Malvern 19355-3402

610-640-1997
Fax: 610-725-1007
E-Mail: diana.lee@pciaa.net
Home Page: www.aria.org

Frequency: 2x/Year

14117 AWCP Newsletter
Association of Workers' Compensation Professionals
PO Box 760
Rancho Cordova, CA 95741-0760

916-290-8017
Fax: 916-914-1706
E-Mail: info@awcp.org
Home Page: www.awcp.org

Debra Real, President
Connie Conley, Executive Director

An educational newsletter with information about our constantly changing industry, how to contact our sponsors as well as announcing our upcoming events.
Frequency: Monthly

14118 Actuarial Studies in Non-Life Insurance
Astin Bulletin
B641 Locust Walk
Philadelphia, PA 19104-6218

215-898-2741

Jean Lemaire, Chairman

Promotes actuarial research and study and publishes the ASTIN Bulletin.
2.2M Pages
Founded in 1957

14119 Advanced Underwriting Services
Dearborn Financial Publishing
155 N Wacker Drive
Floor 1
Chicago, IL 60606-6819

312-836-4400
Fax: 312-836-1146

Georgia Mann, Publisher

Information on the law.
Cost: $395.00
Frequency: Monthly

14120 Best's Agents Guide to Life Insurance Companies
AM Best Company
Ambest Rd
Oldwick, NJ 08858

908-439-2200
800-544-2378
Fax: 908-439-3296
E-Mail: webmaster@ambest.com
Home Page: www.ambest.com

Arthur Snyder, CEO

Offers information on over 1,400 life and health insurance companies nationwide.
Cost: $150.00
Frequency: Monthly
Founded in 1899

14121 Compensation & Benefits for Law Offices
Institute of Management and Administration
1 Washington Park
Suite 1300
Newark, NY 07102-3130

212-244-0360
Fax: 973-622-0595
E-Mail: customercare@bna.com
Home Page: www.ioma.com

An indespensible reference for law firm recruitment, training, compensation, benefits, and HR managers who want and need to keep pace with what it takes to successfully, recruit, retain, train, reward, recognize, and compensatetop legal talent.
Cost: $449.00

14122 Crittenden Insurance Markets Newsletter
Crittenden Publishing
45 Leveroni Court
Suite 204
Novato, CA 94949-5721

415-475-1522
800-421-3483
Fax: 619-923-3518
E-Mail: ins@crittendenonline.com
Home Page: www.crittendenonline.com
Social Media: Twitter

Offers readers a behind-the-scenes look at everything going on in the commercial insurance market. Provides all the coverage necessary for agents to be successful in the board field of commercial insurance
Frequency: Weekly
Founded in 1972

14123 Disability Eval and Rehab Review
National Association of Disability Evaluating
13801 Village Mill Drive
Midlothian, VA 23113

804-378-7275
Home Page: www.nadep.com

This periodical is peer reviewed and addresses issues which are impacting the field of medicine and rehabilitation and which specifically address impairment rating, disability determination, functional capacity evaluation, vocational evaluation and current trends in reimbursement and how the Americans with Disabilities Act of 1990 has changed the practice of medicine and rehabilitation.
Frequency: Quarterly

14124 HELP Newsletter
Insurance Loss Control Association
PO Box 346
Morton, IL 61550

309-696-2551
Fax: 317-879-8408
E-Mail: ccarson@namic.org
Home Page: www.insurancelosscontrol.org

Brock Bell, President
Daniel Finn, VP
Stig Ruxlow, Financial Secretary

Association news and activities.
Frequency: Quarterly
Circulation: 325
Founded in 1931
Printed in 2 colors on matte stock

14125 **Highlights**
American Association of Retired Persons
601 E St Nw
Washington, DC 20049-0003
202-434-2277
Fax: 202-434-7599
E-Mail: PCMNationalOffice@aarp.org
Home Page: www.aarp.org
A Barry Rand, CEO
Ethel Andrus, Founder
Offers information and updates on the association, tax information and legal statistics.
4 Pages
Frequency: BiWeekly

14126 **IOMA's Report on Hourly Compensation**
Institute of Management and Administration
1 Washington Park
Suite 1300
Newark, NJ 07102-3130
212-244-0360
Fax: 973-622-0595
E-Mail: customercare@bna.com
Home Page: www.ioma.com
RHC is a sister publication for IOMA's Report on Salary Surveys and takes compensation and salary dates from major surveys produced by firms like Watson Wyatt Data Services, the Big Six Accounting firms and local HR groups to show benefits and compensation managers the going rate for hourly workers in a variety of positions.

14127 **Insurance Daily**
SNL Financial
One SNL Plaza
PO Box 2124
Charlottesville, VA 22902
434-977-1600
Fax: 434-293-0407
E-Mail: salesdept@snl.com
Home Page: www.snl.com
Social Media: Facebook, Twitter, LinkedIn
Akash Sinha, Editor
Tom Mason, Editor
The most comprehensive news source on the insurance sector. The news desk researches filings and investor presentations, conducts exclusive interviews with industry executives and analysts for the stories that impact the insurance market
Cost: $995.00
Frequency: Daily
Mailing list available for rent

14128 **Insurance Finance & Investment**
Institutional Investor
488 Madison Ave
New York, NY 10022-5701
212-303-3100
800-715-9195
Fax: 212-224-3491
E-Mail: iieditor@institutionalinvestor.com
Home Page: www.institutionalinvestor.com
Erik Kolk, Publisher
Chris Brown, CEO/President
Stuard Wise, Senior Editor
Nick Ferris, Marketing Director
Provides reviews of investment performance, financing strategies, overviews of ratings, and highlights of new issues.
Cost: $1495.00
Frequency: Monthly
Founded in 1905

14129 **Insurance Forum**
Insurance Forum
PO Box 245
Ellettsville, IN 47429
812-876-6502
Fax: 812-876-6572
Home Page: www.theinsuranceforum.com
Joseph M Belth, Editor
Ann I Belth, Business Manager
Jeffrey E Belth, Circulation Manager
Provides objective information and incisive analysis of important insurance topics.
Cost: $120.00
Frequency: Monthly
Founded in 1974

14130 **Insurance Performance Graph**
SNL Financial
PO Box 2124
Charlottesvle, VA 22902-2124
434-977-1600
Fax: 434-977-4466
E-Mail: isales@snl.com
Home Page: www.snl.com
Mike Deane, Editor
Matt Mueller, Chief Operating Officer
Nick Cafferillo, Chief Operating Officer
Adam Hall, Managing Director
For publicly traded insurance companies and law, accounting and consulting firms. Compares the investment performance of an insurance company to a specific SNL index or to a selected peer group and the appropriate broad multi-industry index. Covers a 5-year period or the period beginning with the IPO date.
Cost: $399.00
Frequency: Monthly
Founded in 1987

14131 **Insurance Regulation**
Wakeman Walworth Inc
PO Box 7376
Alexandria, VA 22307-7376
703-768-9600
Fax: 703-768-9690
Home Page: statecapitals.com
Keyes Walworth, Publisher
The best way to track day-to-day changes and innovations at the state level □ covers health insurance including HMOs, CHIP programs and the battle to increase health insurance benefits. It also covers life, automobile, homeowner, unemployment insurance, workers compensation and malpractice. It reports on tort reform, licensing, self-insurance, plus new approaches such as lifestyle considerations.
Cost: $245.00
Frequency: Weekly

14132 **Insurance Weekly: Life & Health**
SNL Financial
One SNL Plaza
PO Box 2124
Charlottesville, VA 22902-2124
434-977-1600
Fax: 434-977-4466
E-Mail: subscriptions@snlnet.com
Home Page: www.snl.com
Social Media: Facebook, Twitter, LinkedIn
Akash Sinha, Editor
Tom Mason, Editor
Super-focused coverage of the dynamic life and health, managed care and insurance agency sectors
Cost: $396.00
Frequency: Weekly
ISSN: 1098-8149
Mailing list available for rent

14133 **Insurance Weekly: Property & Casualty**
SNL Financial
One SNL Plaza
PO Box 2124
Charlottesville, VA 22902-2124
434-977-1600
Fax: 434-977-4466
E-Mail: subscriptions@snlnet.com
Home Page: www.snl.com
Social Media: Facebook, Twitter, LinkedIn
Akash Sinha, Editor
Tom Mason, Editor
Complete, current coverage of the property and casualty, title, financial and mortgage guaranty and insurance agency sectors
Cost: $396.00
Frequency: Weekly
ISSN: 1098-8130
Mailing list available for rent

14134 **Journal for Insurance Compliance Professionals Newsletter**
Association of Insurance Compliance Professionals
12100 Sunset Hills Road
Suite 130
Reston, VA 20190
703-234-4074
Fax: 703-435-4390
E-Mail: aicp@aicp.net
Home Page: www.aicp.net
Doug Simino, President
Darrell Turner, Editor
Elaine Douglas, Vice President
Dawn Murphy, Secretary
Doug Geraci, Treasurer
Includes topical information for members, covering regulatory and industry issues, along with the latest techniques in filings nad news from each Association Region and Chapter
Frequency: Quarterly
Founded in 1998

14135 **LIC Newsletter**
Life Insurers Council
2300 Windy Ridge Pkwy SE
Suite 600
Atlanta, GA 30339-5665
770-951-1770
800-275-5662
Fax: 770-984-0441
E-Mail: askloma@loma.org
Home Page: www.loma.org
Jeff Shaw, Executive Director
Rose Hoyt, Administrative Assistant
Includes news and analysis about issues of concern to executives and those involved in operations, plus information on upcoming events and company activities
Frequency: Monthly
Mailing list available for rent

14136 **Mealey's Catastrophic Loss**
LexisNexis Mealey's
555 W 5th Avenue
Los Angeles, CA 90013
213-627-1130
800-253-4182
E-Mail: mealeyinfo@lexisnexis.com
Home Page: www.lexisnexis.com/mealeys
Social Media: Facebook, Twitter, LinkedIn, RSS, Youtube
Tom Hagy, CEO
Maureen McGuire, Editorial Director
Gina Cappello, Editor
Mike Wash, Chief Executive Officer, Legal
Lisa Agona, Chief Marketing Officer
This report focuses on business interruption insurance claims in the aftermath of the Hurricane Katrina, September 11th, and other catastrophic loss tragedies. Additionally, the report will go beyond these claims and will offer important business interruption insurance cov-

erage news related to computer viruses, computer failures, and natural disasters.
Cost: $1075.00
100 Pages
Frequency: Monthly
Founded in 2001
Mailing list available for rent

14137 Mealey's Emerging Insurance Disputes
LexisNexis Mealey's
555 W 5th Avenue
Los Angeles, CA 90013

213-627-1130
800-253-4182
E-Mail: mealeyinfo@lexisnexis.com
Home Page: www.lexisnexis.com/mealeys
Social Media: Facebook, Twitter, LinkedIn, RSS, Youtube

Tom Hagy, CEO
Maureen McGuire, Editorial Director
Gina Cappello, Editor
Mike Wash, Chief Executive Officer, Legal
Lisa Agona, Chief Marketing Officer

The report tracks new areas of coverage liability, novel policy applications, and conflicting policy language interpretations as they arise in insurance litigation. Some areas of coverage featured are: sexual harassment and discrimination, assault and battery, professional liability, patent and trademark infringement, construction defects, directors and officers claims, emotional distress, intentional acts, technology, and insurance business practices.
Cost: $ 1229.00
100 Pages
Frequency: Semi-Monthly
Founded in 1996
Mailing list available for rent

14138 Mealey's Litigation Report: Asbestos
LexisNexis Mealey's
555 W 5th Avenue
Los Angeles, CA 90013

213-627-1130
800-253-4182
E-Mail: mealeyinfo@lexisnexis.com
Home Page: www.lexisnexis.com/mealeys
Social Media: Facebook, Twitter, LinkedIn, RSS, Youtube

Tom Hagy, CEO
Maureen McGuire, Editorial Director
Bryan Redding, Editor
Mike Wash, Chief Executive Officer, Legal
Lisa Agona, Chief Marketing Officer

The report offers unsurpassed coverage of litigation arising from asbestos-related injury and death. Key issues include: massive class action settlements involving present and future claimants, state and federal verdicts, litigation experts, medical monitoring claims, suits against the tobacco industry, discovery battles, discovery rule decisions, insurance coverage rulings, and asbestos property decisions.
Cost: $1789.00
100 Pages
Frequency: Semi-Monthly
Founded in 1984
Mailing list available for rent

14139 Mealey's Litigation Report: California Insurance
LexisNexis Mealey's
555 W 5th Avenue
Los Angeles, CA 90013

213-627-1130
800-253-4182
E-Mail: mealeyinfo@lexisnexis.com
Home Page: www.lexisnexis.com/mealeys
Social Media: Facebook, Twitter, LinkedIn, RSS, Youtube

Tom Hagy, CEO
Maureen McGuire, Editorial Director
Jennifer Hans, Editor
Mike Wash, Chief Executive Officer, Legal
Lisa Agona, Chief Marketing Officer

The Report focuses on ever-changing California and federal Ninth Circuit insurance coverage disputes and developments. Topics include California developments in bad faith litigation, earthquake damage coverage, disability insurance, products liability coverage, environmental insurance coverage, mold coverage, asbestos coverage, aviation litigation coverage, entertainment law and more.
Cost: $949.00
100 Pages
Frequency: Monthly
Founded in 2001
Mailing list available for rent

14140 Mealey's Litigation Report: Disability Insurance
LexisNexis Mealey's
555 W 5th Avenue
Los Angeles, CA 90013

213-627-1130
800-253-4182
E-Mail: mealeyinfo@lexisnexis.com
Home Page: www.lexisnexis.com/mealeys
Social Media: Facebook, Twitter, LinkedIn, RSS, Youtube

Tom Hagy, CEO
Maureen McGuire, Editorial Director
Karen Miehle, Editor
Mike Wash, Chief Executive Officer, Legal
Lisa Agona, Chief Marketing Officer

This report tracks the burgeoning number of disputes involving complex disability coverage claims. Topics covered include: claims for chronic fatigue, chronic pain, stress, psychiatric disabilities, chemical dependency and risk of relapse, plus key issues like total disability, own occupation, bad faith, ERSA, class actions and much more.
Cost: $849.00
100 Pages
Frequency: Monthly
Founded in 2000
Mailing list available for rent

14141 Mealey's Litigation Report: Insurance
LexisNexis Mealey's
555 W 5th Avenue
Los Angeles, CA 90013

213-627-1130
800-253-4182
E-Mail: mealeyinfo@lexisnexis.com
Home Page: www.lexisnexis.com/mealeys
Social Media: Facebook, Twitter, LinkedIn, RSS, Youtube

Tom Hagy, CEO
Maureen McGuire, Editorial Director
Vivi Gorman, Editor
Shawn Rice, Co-Editor
Mike Wash, Chief Executive Officer, Legal

The report tracks declaratory judgment actions regarding coverage for litigation arising from long-tail claims, including environmental contamination and latent damage and injury allegedly caused by asbestos, tox chemicals and fumes, lead, breast implants, medical devices, construction defects, and more. Key issues: allocation, occurrence, policy exclusion, choice of law, discovery, duty to defend, notice, trigger of coverage and known loss.
Cost: $2115.00
100 Pages
Frequency: Weekly
Founded in 1984
Mailing list available for rent

14142 NACA NEWS
National Association of Catastrophe Adjusters
PO Box 821864
North Richland Hills, TX 76182

817-498-3466
Fax: 817-498-0480
E-Mail: naca@nacatadj.org
Home Page: www.nacatadj.org

Lori Ringo, Executive Administrator
Robert Uhler, Vice President
John Postava, Secretary/Treasurer
Wanda Hogan, President

Contains information of interest and benefit to the members of NACA and the president of the association provides his insights for the quarter.
Frequency: Quarterly
Circulation: 2500
Founded in 1976

14143 NAPIA Newsletter
National Association of Public Insurance Adjusters
21165 Whitfield Place
Suite 105
Potomac Falls, VA 20165

703-433-9217
Fax: 703-433-0369
E-Mail: info@napia.com
Home Page: www.napia.com

David W Barrack, Executive Director
Ronald R. Reitz, President
Frequency: Quarterly
Circulation: 600
Mailing list available for rent

14144 NCOILetter
National Conference of Insurance Legislators
385 Jordan Road
Troy, NY 12180

518-687-0178
Fax: 518-687-0401
E-Mail: info@ncoil.org
Home Page: www.ncoil.org

Susan F. Nolan, Executive Director
Candace Thorson, Deputy Executive Director
Simone Smith, Director, Operations/Administration
Mike Humphreys, Director,State-Federal Relations
Jordan Estey, Dir, Legislative Affairs/Education

NCOIL is an organization of state legislators whose main area of public policy concern is insurance legislation and regulation. Many legislators active in NCOIL either chair or are members of the committees responsible for insurance legislation in their respective state houses across the country.
Frequency: Monthly
Circulation: 2500
Founded in 1969

14145 NFPA Journal Update
National Fire Protection Association
1 Batterymarch Park
Quincy, MA 02169-7471

617-770-3000
800-344-3555
Fax: 617-770-0700
E-Mail: publicaffairs@nfpa.org
Home Page: www.nfpa.org

James M. Shannon, President/CEO
Peg O'Brien, Administrator - Public Affairs
Sharon Gamache, Executive Director
Bruce Mullen, CFO
Paul Crossman, VP, Marketing

Member newsletter that contains the latest articles, features, and special online exclusives

from NFPA Journal , as well as quick access to the information and resources on NFPA's codes and standards-making process, research, training, safety information, and more.
75000 Members
Frequency: Monthly
Founded in 1896

14146 PIA Connection
Association of Professional Insurance Agents
400 N Washington Street
Alexandria, VA 22314-2312

703-836-9340
Fax: 703-836-1279
E-Mail: web@pianet.org
Home Page: www.pianet.com
Social Media: Facebook, Twitter, LinkedIn

Andrew C. Harris, President
John G. Lee, President-elect
Richard A. Clements, Vice President, Treasurer
Robert W. Hansen, Secretary/Assistant Treasurer

Contains current insurance industry news that is particularly relevant to independent insurance agents
Cost: $24.00
Frequency: 10x/Year
Mailing list available for rent

14147 Report on Property/Casualty Rates & Ratings
Institute of Management and Administration
1 Washington Park
Suite 1300
Newark, NJ 07102-3130

212-244-0360
Fax: 973-622-0595
E-Mail: customercare@bna.com
Home Page: www.ioma.com

Helps agents and brokers get competitive premium rates for their clients.
Cost: $389.00
16 Pages
Frequency: Monthly
Founded in 1755

14148 Risk Management Essentials
Nonprofit Risk Management Center
15 N King Street
Suite 203
Leesburg, VA 20176

202-785-3891
Fax: 703-443-1990
E-Mail: info@nonprofitrisk.org
Home Page: www.nonprofitrisk.org

Melanie Herman, Executive Director
Erin Gloeckner, Project Manager
Sue Weir Jones, Office Manager
Jennifer Walther, Director of Client Solutions

Each issue covers a selection of issues, showcases the Center's training and workshops, and/or highlights new publications offering risk management advice from a nonprofit perspective
16 Pages
Frequency: 3 times a year
Mailing list available for rent

14149 Riskwatch
Public Risk Management Association
700 S. Washington St.
Suite 218
Alexandria, VA 22314-1565

703-528-7701
Fax: 703-739-0200
E-Mail: info@primacentral.org
Home Page: www.primacentral.org
Social Media: Facebook, Twitter, LinkedIn

Marshall Davies, Executive Director
Jennifer Ackerman, Deputy Executive Director
Bles Dones, Manager, Member Services
Jennifer W. Morris, Manager, Meetings and Conferences
Paulette Washington, Office Administrator

E-news service that delivers handpicked, high-quality news articles relating to the public risk management industry. Provides PRIMA members with valuable association-related news. Keeps you on top of the latest news and trends in the public sector risk management field.
Frequency: Weekly
Mailing list available for rent

14150 SFFA Newsletter
Surety & Fidelity Association of America
1101 Connecticut Avenue NW
Suite 800
Washington, DC 20036

202-463-0600
Fax: 202-463-0606
E-Mail: information@surety.org
Home Page: www.surety.org
Social Media: Facebook, Twitter

Lynn Schubert, President
Mailing list available for rent

14151 Surety Association of America
Surety Association of America
1101 Connecticut Ave Nw
Suite 800
Washington, DC 20036-4347

202-463-0600
Fax: 202-463-0606
E-Mail: information@surety.org
Home Page: www.surety.org

Lynn Schubert, President

14152 UPDATE
Insurance Marketing Communications Association
PO Box 473054
Charlotte, NC 28247

704-755-5551
Fax: 704-543-6345
E-Mail: tseibert@imcanet.com
Home Page: www.imcanet.com

September J Seibert, Executive Director

Contains reviews and previews of meetings, articles on communications issues and techniques, and news of IMCA members.
Frequency: For Members Only

Magazines & Journals

14153 AHIP Solutions Directory Resource Directory of Health Plans
America's Health Insurance Plans
601 Pennsylvania Ave NW
South Building, Suite 500
Washington, DC 20004-2601

202-778-3200
877-291-2247
Fax: 202-331-7487
E-Mail: ahip@ahip.org
Home Page: www.ahip.org
Social Media: Twitter

Karen M Ignagni, President/CEO
Susan Pisano, VP Communications

More than 3,400 key executives listed, types of products offered such as HMO, PPO, POS, etc., company contact information, national enrollment by type of products, and national and state level enrollment data by company. There is also a CD-ROM availablie for $1,495.00
Cost: $492.00
Mailing list available for rent

14154 ASPPA Journal
American Society of Pension Professionals & Act
4245 Fairfax Dr
Suite 750
Arlington, VA 22203-1648

703-516-0512
Fax: 703-516-9308
E-Mail: asppa@asppa.org
Home Page: www.asppa.org

Thomas Finnegan, President

A technical publication providing critical insight into legislative and regulatory developments. Also features technical analysis of benefit plan matters as well as information regarding ASPPA's programs.
Frequency: Quarterly
Circulation: 7500

14155 Actuarial Digest
Actuarial Digest Publishing Company
PO Box 1127
Ponte Vedra, FL 32004-1127

904-273-1245
Home Page: www.theactuarialdigest.com

Gene Hubbard, Editor

Covers fields such as life, group, health, reinsurance, pension/employee benefits, government regulations and educational institutions.
Founded in 1982

14156 Actuarial Studies in Non-Life Insurance
Peeters
1600 Arch St
Philadelphia, PA 19103-2032
215-567-0097
Fax: 215-567-0107
E-Mail: webmaster@actuaries.org
Home Page: www.actuaries.org

Lucy Peters, Owner
Andrew Cairns, Editor
David G Hartman, Chairman
Carla Melvin, Executive Assistant
Katy Martin, Project Manager

Promotes actuarial research and study and publishes the ASTIN Bulletin.
Cost: $65.00
500 Pages
Frequency: Quarterly
Circulation: 3000
Founded in 1957

14157 Advisor Today
Natl Assoc of Insurance and Financial Advisors
2901 Telestar Court
Falls Church, VA 22042

703-770-8100
877-866-2432
E-Mail: membersupport@naifa.org
Home Page: www.advisortoday.com
Social Media: Facebook, Twitter, LinkedIn

Ayo Mseka, Editor-In-Chief
Julie Britt, Senior Editor
Preeti Vasishtha, Editor
Tara Heuser, Publication and Circulation

Provides practical information, sales idas resources and business strategies to hel pinsurance and financial advisors succeed.
Founded in 1906
Mailing list available for rent

14158 American Journal of Law & Medicine
American Society of Law, Medicine and Ethics

765 Commonwealth Ave
Suite 1634
Boston, MA 02215-1401

617-262-4990
Fax: 617-437-7596
E-Mail: info@aslme.org
Home Page: www.aslme.org
Social Media: Facebook, Twitter, LinkedIn

Ted Hutchinson, Executive Director
Courtney McClellan, Assistant Editor
Katie Kenney Johnson, Conference Director
Margo Buege, Membership Department
Courtney McClellan, Assistant Editor

A law review fulfilling the need to improve communication between leagal and medical professionals. Contains professional articles and case notes on themes in health law and policy, and on the legal, ethical, and economic aspects of medical practice, research, and education-and health law court decisions and book reviews.
Cost: $150.00
Frequency: Quarterly
Mailing list available for rent

14159 **Annuity Shopper**
Annuity Shopper
28 Harrison Ave.
D209
Englishtown, NJ 07726

732-521-5110
877-206-8141
Fax: 732-521-5113
Home Page: www.annuityshopper.com

Hersh Stern, Owner
Laura Stern, Editor

Helps consumers purchase the safest and most reliable lifetime income annuities for their retirement.
Frequency: Semi-annually
ISSN: 1071-4510
Founded in 1986
Mailing list available for rent

14160 **Beacon**
American Association of Dental Consultants
10032 Wind Hill Dr
Greenville, IN 47124-9673

812-923-2600
800-896-0707
Fax: 812-923-2900
Home Page: www.aadc.org

Judith Salisburty, Executive Director
Dr Larry Hoffman, Secretary/Treasurer

Informs members about the latest issues affecting dentistry and dental benefits.
Frequency: Twice/Year
Circulation: 350

14161 **Benefits Magazine**
International Foundation of Employee Benefit Plans
18700 W Bluemound Road
Brookfield, WI 53045

262-786-6700
888-334-3327
Fax: 262-786-8670
E-Mail: pr@ifebp.org
Home Page: www.ifebp.org
Social Media: Facebook, Twitter, LinkedIn

Michael Wilson, CEO
Terry Davidson, VP, Business Development
Beth Harwood, VP, Educ Program/Content Management

Covers issues such as healthcare, retirement and related trends. Authors are experienced professionals in the field.
Cost: $175.00
35000 Members
Frequency: Monthly
Circulation: 28336
ISSN: 2157-6157
Founded in 1954

14162 **Benefits Quarterly**
Int'l Society of Certified Employee Benfit Special
18700 W Bluemound Road
PO Box 209
Brookfield, WI 53008-0209

262-786-8771
Fax: 262-786-8650
E-Mail: iscebs@iscebs.org
Home Page: www.iscebs.org
Social Media: Facebook, Twitter, LinkedIn

Daniel W Graham, CEBS, Executive Director
Sandra L. Becker, Director
Jennifer Mathe, Manager Member Services
Kathy Frank, Administrative Assistant
Julie Dickow, Department Assistant

Offers comprehensive coverage of the latest trends and innovations in benefits and compensation. Features articles on health care, retirement and total compensation, each issue includes a section focused on a topic of special interest.
Cost: $125.00
Frequency: Quarterly
Circulation: 15000
Founded in 1981
Mailing list available for rent

14163 **Best's Review**
AM Best Company
Ambest Rd
Oldwick, NJ 08858

908-439-2200
800-424-2378
Fax: 908-439-3296
E-Mail: editor_br@bestreview.com
Home Page: www.ambest.com

Arthur Snyder, Chairman & President
Paul Tinnirello, CIO
Larry Mayewski, Chief Rating Officer

Best's Review, the insurance industry's premier news magazine, contains insightful, award-winning coverage of the worldwide insurance industry, giving you the information you need to make informed decisions about your business and career.
Cost: $60.00
Frequency: Monthly
ISSN: 1527-5914
Founded in 1900

14164 **BestWeek**
AM Best Company
Ambest Rd
Oldwick, NJ 08858

908-439-2200
Fax: 908-439-3296
E-Mail: bestweek@ambest.com
Home Page: www.ambest.com

Arthur Snyder, Chairman and President
Paul Tinnirello, CIO
Larry Mayewski, Chief Rating Officer

BestWeek, the cornerstone of a Best's Insurance News & Analysis subscription, now provides even more ratings information and A.M. Best-generated analytical content in three region-focused editions.
Frequency: Weekly
ISSN: 1945-4139
Founded in 1953

14165 **Broker World**
Insurance Publications
9404 Reeds Road
PO Box 11310
Overland Park, KS 66207-1010

913-383-9191
800-762-3387
Fax: 913-383-1247
E-Mail: info@brokerworldmag.com
Home Page: www.brokerworldmag.com

Rita S Reeves, Sales Manager
Sharon A Chace, Editor
Stephen P Howard, Publisher
Betsy Masters, Production Manager
Patty L Godfrey, Director of Circulation

The first and only national insurance magazine founded, focused and edited to specifically address the unique informational needs of independent like and health producers.
Frequency: Monthly
Circulation: 28600
Founded in 1980

14166 **Business Insurance**
Crain Communications
711 3rd Ave
New York, NY 10017-4014

212-210-0785
Fax: 212-210-0200
E-Mail: info@crain.com
Home Page: www.businessinsurance.com

Norm Feldman, Manager
Charmain Benton, Assistant Managing Editor
Paul Bomberger, Managing Editor
Roberto Ceniceros, Senior Editor
Matt Dunning, Associate Editor

Reports on risk management, risk financing, employee benefits management and workers compensation. Our audience also includes insurance brokers, agents, consultants, insurers, reinsurers, and others concerned with corporate insurance, risk management, alternative risk financing, employee benefits, workers compensation and reinsurance.
Frequency: Weekly
Circulation: 44639
Mailing list available for rentat $89y per M

14167 **CICA International Conference**
Captive Insurance Companies Association
4248 Park Glen Road
Minneapolis, MN 55416

952-928-4655
Fax: 952-929-1318
E-Mail: info@cicaworld.com
Home Page: www.cicaworld.com

Dennis Harwick, President

2012 International Conference is located in Scottsdale, AZ during March 11-13.
500 Attendees
Frequency: Annual

14168 **CPCU Journal**
Chartered Property Casualty Underwriters
720 Providence Rd
Malvern, PA 19355-3446

610-251-2733
Fax: 610-251-2761
Home Page: www.cpcusociety.org

Steve McElhiney, President
Cynthia Barouex, Vice President

14169 **CPCU e-Journal**
Chartered Property Casualty Underwriter Society
720 Providence Road
Suite 100
Malvern, PA 19355

610-512-2728
800-932-2728
Fax: 610-725-5969
E-Mail: membercenter@cpcusociety.org
Home Page: www.cpcusociety.org
Social Media: Facebook, Twitter, LinkedIn

James R Marks, CEO
David C Marlett, Editor
Mark A. Robinson, President and Treasurer

Provides information on practical and timely issues of interest to financial services and property and casualty insurance professionals.
Frequency: Monthly

14170 Contingencies
American Academy of Actuaries
1850 M Street NW
Suite 300
Washington, DC 20036

202-223-8196
Fax: 202-872-1948
E-Mail: webmaster@actuary.org
Home Page: www.actuary.org

Linda Mallon, Editor
Cindy Johns, Marketing/Publications Production

Magazine of the actuarial profession, available in print and digital editions; its circulation includes legislators, regulators, CEOs, and all Academy members
Cost: $24.00
Frequency: Bi-Monthly
ISSN: 1048-9851
Founded in 1965
Printed in 4 colors on glossy stock

14171 Contingency Planning & Management
Witter Publishing Corporation
20 Commerce Street
Flemington, NJ 08822

908-788-0343
Fax: 908-788-3782
Home Page: www.witterpublishing.com

Bob Joudanin, Publisher
Paul Kirvan, Editor-in-Chief
Mike Viscel, Production Manager
Courtney Witter, Circulation Manager
Andrew Witter, President

Serves the fields of financial/banking, manufacturing industrial, transportation, utilities, telecommunications, health care, government, insurance and other allied fields.
Cost: $275.00
Frequency: Monthly
Circulation: 62000
Founded in 1987

14172 Crittenden Excess & Surplus Insider
Crittenden Publishing
250 Bel Marin Keys Boulevard
PO Box 1150, #A
Novato, CA 94948-1150

415-382-2400
Fax: 415-382-2476
E-Mail: ins@crittendenonline.com
Home Page: www.crittendenonline.com

Robert Fink, Publisher

Focuses on new products, trade literature, industry news, and personnel changes.
Cost: $411.00
Frequency: Weekly
Circulation: 20,000

14173 EXAMINER Magazine
Society of Financial Examiners
174 Grace Blvd
Altamonte Spgs, FL 32714-3210

407-682-4930
800-787-7633
Fax: 407-682-3175
Home Page: www.sofe.org
Social Media: Facebook, LinkedIn

L. Brackett, Executive Director
Stephen J Szypula, Financial Administrator
Judy Estus, Administrator
Ryan Havick, President
Eric Dercher, Treasurer

A quarterly magazine offering association news and information.
Cost: $65.00
Frequency: Quarterly
Circulation: 2500
Founded in 1973
Printed in 2 colors on glossy stock

14174 GAMA International Journal
GAMA International
2901 Telestar Ct
Suite 140
Falls Church, VA 22042-1261

703-770-8184
800-345-2687
Fax: 703-770-8182
E-Mail: rwolpert@gama.naifa.org
Home Page: www.gamaweb.com
Social Media: Facebook, Twitter, LinkedIn

Mary Barnes, Director of Communications / Editor
Jeff Hughes, CEO
Miriam Hankins, Marketing Director
Stephanie Beattie, Membership and Awards Coordinator
Jen D'Alessio, Program Manager

Devoted to the professional development of leaders in the insurance and financial services industry.
Cost: $300.00
56 Pages
Circulation: 5000
ISSN: 1095-7367
Founded in 1951
Mailing list available for rent
Printed in 4 colors on glossy stock

14175 Health Insurance Underwriters
National Association of Health Underwriters
1212 New York Avenue NW
Suite 1100
Washington, DC 20005

202-552-5060
Fax: 202-747-6820
E-Mail: editor@nahu.org
Home Page: www.nahu.org
Social Media: Facebook, Twitter, LinkedIn

Martin Carr, Publisher/Editor

Covers technology, legislation and product news-everything that affects how health insurance professionals do business
Cost: $40.00
Frequency: Monthly
Circulation: 30,000
ISSN: 0017-9019
Founded in 1930
Mailing list available for rent: 19000 names at $350 per M
Printed in 4 colors on glossy stock

14176 IAIABC Journal
Int'l Assoc of Industrial Accident Boards/Commis.
5610 Medical Circle
Suite 24
Madison, WI 53719
608-663-6355
Fax: 608-663-1546
E-Mail: hlore@iaiabc.org
Home Page: www.iaiabc.org

Robert Aurbach, Editor
Jennifer Wolf Horejsh, Executive Director
Faith Howe, Manager
Christina Klein, Events and Office Administrator
Heather Lore, Manager of Membership and Marketing

Advances the understanding and management of workers' compensation system administration through the availability of data, research, policy analysis, and thoughtful opinion.
Frequency: 2x/Year
Mailing list available for rent

14177 Independent Agent Magazine
Independent Insurance Agents & Brokers of America
127 S Peyton St
Alexandria, VA 22314-2803

703-683-4422
800-221-7917
Fax: 703-683-7556
E-Mail: info@iiaba.net
Home Page: www.iiaba.net
Social Media: Facebook, Twitter

Robert A Rusbuldt, CEO
Ronald Tubertini, Chairman

Regular issue features include agency management and automation, insurance products and markets, legislative issues, and analysis of industry trends.
Cost: $24.00
Frequency: Monthly
Circulation: 57,814
Mailing list available for rent

14178 Inquiry
Excellus Health Plan
1807 Glenview Rd
Suite 100
Glenview, IL 60025-2944

847-724-9280
Fax: 847-729-2199
E-Mail: inquiry@hartleydata.com
Home Page: www.inquiryjournal.org

Howard J Berman, Publisher
Kevin P Kane, Editor-In-Chief
Alan Monheit, Editor
Ronny G. Frishman, Managing Editor

Seeks to contribute to the continued improvement of the nation's health care system by providing a thoughtful forum for the communication and discussion of relevant public policy issues, innovative concepts, and original research and demonstrations in the areas of health care organization, provision and financing
Cost: $1.00
Frequency: Quarterly
ISSN: 0046-9580

14179 Insurance & Financial Meetings Managment
Coastal Communications Corporation
2700 N Military Trail
Suite 120
Boca Raton, FL 33431

561-989-0600
Fax: 561-989-9509
E-Mail: ccceditor@att.net
Home Page: www.themeetingmagazines.com

Harvey Grotsky, Publisher/Editor-In-Chief
Susan Wyckoff Fell, Managing Editor
Susan Gregg, Managing Editor

The executive source for planning meetings and incentives for the financial and insurance sectors. With regular features and special focus on site selection, destinations, industry-related studies and activities, motivational and incentive programs, program and event planning.
Frequency: Monthly
Circulation: 40,000
Founded in 1983

14180 Insurance & Technology
TechWeb

240 West 35th Street
New York, NY 10011

212-600-3000
Fax: 212-600-3060
Home Page: www.insurancetech.com

Katherine Burger, Editorial Director
Anthony O'Donnell, Executive Editor
Nathan Golia, Associate Editor
Cara Latham, Online Managing Editor

Information on how technology can help life, health, property and casualty and multi-line insurance companies perform more productively, profitably, and competitively.
Frequency: Monthly
ISSN: 1054-0733
Mailing list available for rent

14181 Insurance Advocate

PO Box 14367
Cincinatti, OH 45250-0367

908-859-0893
E-Mail: cluke@nuco.com
Home Page: www.nationaunderwriter.com

Chris Luke, Publisher
Phil Gusman, Editor
Eric V Gilkey, Assistant Editor
Steve Acunto, Associate Publisher

Covers the people and issues affecting the insurance industry in New York, New Jersey, Connecticut and beyond. Also the source for new markets and coverages, financial trends, legislative isssues, M&A, insurance law and industry developments.
Cost: $59.00
Frequency: Weekly
Circulation: 7200
Founded in 1889
Printed in 4 colors on glossy stock

14182 Insurance Conference Planner

Penton Media Inc
249 W. 17th St., third floor
New York, NY 10011

847-763-9504
866-505-7173
E-Mail: shatch@meetingsnet.com
Home Page: www.meetingsnet.com

Susan Hatch, Editor
Betsy Bair, Director, Content and Media
Melissa Fromento, Group Publisher
Regina McGee, Religious Conference Manager
Susan Hatch, Executive Editor

Meeting and incentive strategies for the financial services industry.
Cost: $57.00
148 Pages
Circulation: 9000
Founded in 1989
Printed in 4 colors on glossy stock

14183 Insurance Insight

Professional Independent Insurance Agents of IL
4360 Wabash Ave
Springfield, IL 62711-7009

217-793-6660
800-628-6436
Fax: 217-793-6744
E-Mail: info@IIAofIllinois.org
Home Page: www.iiaofillinois.org

Sandy Cuffle, Manager
Dennis Garrett, VP Marketing/Membership
Mark Kuchar, CPA, CFO
Mike Tate, CAE, Chief Operating Officer
Peter Gulatto, Marketing Representative

Features articles that are relevant to the Illinois insurance industry, and includes topics such as industry news, technology, markets and coverages, financial planning, sales and marketing, state and federal issues, agency management, The Middleton Letter, and education.
Cost: $65.00
68 Pages
Frequency: Monthly
Circulation: 2500
Founded in 1993
Mailing list available for rent

14184 Insurance Journal West

3570 Camino Del Rio N
Suite 200
San Diego, CA 92108-1747

619-584-1100
800-897-9965
Fax: 619-584-5889
E-Mail: info@insurancejournal.com
Home Page: www.insurancejournal.com
Social Media: Facebook, Twitter, LinkedIn

Mark Wells, Publisher
Mitch Dunford, Chief Operating Officer
Katie Robley, Circulation Manager
Suzie Song, Marketing Manager
Andrea Ortega-Wells, Editor-In-Chief

Insurance Journal is written for the independent agent and broker. Insurance Journal West covers California and the western states, while Insurance Journal Texas/South Central covers Texas, Arkansas, Oklahoma & Louisiana. We cover legal issues, people, markets, regulations and legistation, the very things that affect our readers.
Cost: $58.00
Circulation: 40000
Founded in 1923
Printed in 4 colors on matte stock

14185 Insurance Networking News

SourceMedia
550 W. Van Buren St.
Suite 1110
Chicago, IL 60607

847-933-5183
Fax: 312-566-0656
Home Page: www.insurancenetworking.com
Social Media: Facebook, Twitter

Carrie Burns, Editor-In-Chief

A trusted source for information on how technology is being implemented to support insurers' strategic business objectives, providing insightful analysis of-and case studies on-how technology is being innovatively utilized to automate critical processes.
Frequency: Monthly
Founded in 1997
Mailing list available for rent

14186 Journal of Healthcare Risk Management

American Society for Healthcare Risk Management
1 N Franklin St
Chicago, IL 60606-4425

312-422-3840
Fax: 312-422-4573
Home Page: www.aha.org

Deborah Sprindzunas, Executive Director
Cliff Lehman, Director Membership Services
Cost: $80.00
Circulation: 4500
Mailing list available for rent: 4400 names

14187 Journal of Law, Medicine & Ethics

American Society of Law, Medicine and Ethics
765 Commonwealth Ave
Suite 1634
Boston, MA 02215-1401

617-262-4990
Fax: 617-437-7596
E-Mail: info@aslme.org
Home Page: www.aslme.org
Social Media: Facebook, Twitter, LinkedIn

Ted Hutchinson, Executive Director
Ted Hutchinson, Publications Director
Katie Kenney Johnson, Conference Director
Margo Buege, Membership Department
Courtney McClellan, Assistant Editor

Provides articles on such timely topics as health care quality and access, managed care, pain relief, genetics, child/maternal health, reproductive health, informed consent, assisted dying, ethics committees, HIV/AIDS, and public health. Issues review significant policy developments, health law court decisions, and books.
Cost: $140.00
Frequency: Quarterly
Circulation: 4,500+
Mailing list available for rent

14188 Journal of Reinsurance

Intermediaries and Reinsurance Underwriters Assoc
971 Rte 202 North
Branchburg, NJ 08876

908-203-0211
Fax: 908-203-0213
E-Mail: info@irua.com
Home Page: www.irua.com

Paul Walther, Editor

To encourage an exchange of ideas and to disseminiate educational information for the benefit and betterment of the Intermediarics & Reinsurance Underwriters Association membership and the reinsurance community.
Cost: $195.00
Frequency: Quarterly

14189 Journal of Risk and Insurance

Wiley-Blackwell Publishing
111 River Street
Hoboken, NJ 07030-5774

201-748-6000
Fax: 201-748-6088
E-Mail: info@wiley.com
Home Page: www.wiley.com

Georges Dionne, Editor

The flagship journal for the American Risk and Insurance Association. The JRI is the most well recognized academic risk management and insurance journal in the world and is currently indexed by the American Economic Association's Economic Literature Index, the Finance Literature Index, RePEc, the Social Sciences Citation Index, ABI/Inform, Business and Company ASAP, Lexis-Nexis, Dow Jones Interactive, and others.
Frequency: Quarterly
ISSN: 0022-4367

14190 LIMRA Marketfacts

LIMRA International
300 Day Hill Road
PO Box 208
Windsor, CT 06141-208

860-688-3358
Fax: 860-298-9555
E-Mail: bragaglia@limra.com
Home Page: www.limra.com

Brad Ragaglia, Editor
Richard Wecker, CEO

Features in-depth, timeless articles devoted to the critical issues of the day, including such topics as distribution, technology, marketing strategies, retirement, globalization, demographics, financial integration and products and services.
Cost: $500.00
Circulation: 7500

14191 LIMRA Vision
LIMRA International
PO Box 208
Hartford, CT 06141-0208
860-688-3358
800-235-4672
Fax: 860-298-9555
E-Mail: webmaster@limra.com
Home Page: www.limra.com
Robert A Kerzner, CEO
Content focuses on leadership styles and concepts, business management concerns and 21st century strategical positioning. Ideas are presented from top business leaders in a variety of industries around the globe, as well as information from today's cutting-edge sales associates. Includes full-length features, regular columns and shorter idea pieces, product reviews, and information on technology.
Cost: $59.96
Circulation: 10000
Founded in 1916

14192 Leader's Edge Magazine
Council of Insurance Agents & Brokers
701 Pennsylvania Ave NW
Suite 750
Washington, DC 20004-2661
202-783-4400
Fax: 202-783-4410
E-Mail: webmaster@ciab.com
Home Page: www.ciab.com
Ken A Crerar, President
Pat Wade, Director of Communications
Brianne Mallaghan, Director of Communications
Scott Sinder, General Counsel
Comprised of vital information and news for the industry of insurance agents and brokers.
Cost: $100.00
Frequency: Bi-Monthly

14193 Liability & Insurance Week
JR Publishing
PO Box 6654
McLean, VA 22106-6654
703-532-2235
Fax: 703-532-2236
E-Mail: jvreistrup@erols.com
John Reistrup, Publisher
Reports on political, legislative and regulatory actions affecting the insurance and legal industries.

14194 Life & Health Advisor
JonHope Communications
71 Emerson Road
PO Box 613
Walpole, MA 02081
508-668-8025
888-578-8025
Fax: 508-668-8056
E-Mail: pkelley@lifehealth.com
Home Page: www.lifehealth.com
Social Media: Facebook, Twitter, LinkedIn
Sally O'Connell, Publisher/Ad Sales Manager
Peter Kelley, Editor
Access, exposure & market visibility for financial services, investment and retirement income planningo.
Frequency: Monthly
Founded in 1995
Mailing list available for rent

14195 Life Insurance Selling
Summit Buiness Media
5081 Olympic Blvd.
Suite 550
Erlanger, KY 41018
859-692-2100
Fax: 859-692-2000
E-Mail: lis@pfpublish.com
Home Page: www.lifeinsuranceselling.com
Social Media: Facebook, Twitter, LinkedIn, RSS
Dave O'Neil, Group Publisher
John K Moore, Publisher
Brian Anderson, Editor
Tashawna Rodwell, Publisher
Bill Coffin, Group Editorial Director
The leading sales publication for life, health and financial planning professionals.

14196 Life and Health Insurance Sales Magazines
Rough Notes Company
11690 Technology Drive
Carmel, IN 46032-5600
317-582-1600
800-321-1909
Fax: 317-816-1000
E-Mail: rnc@roughnotes.com
Home Page: www.roughnotes.com
Walter Gdowski, Owner
Nancy Doucette, Senior Editor
Elisabeth Boone, CPCU, Associate Editor
Dennis Pillsbury, Associate Editor
For life and health agents, general agents, managers and brokers with prospects to culivate and clients to serve. Accepts advertising.
48 Pages
Frequency: Monthly
Founded in 1878
Mailing list available for rent

14197 Long-Term Care Insurance Sales Strategies
Sales Creators
3835 E Thousand Oaks Boulevard
Suite 336
Westlake Village, CA 91362
818-597-3205
888-599-5997
Fax: 818-597-3206
E-Mail: jslome@ltcsales.com
Home Page: www.ltcsales.com
Jesse Sloame, Publisher/President
Mindy Hartman, Ad Director
Content covers successful sales approaches, new and unexplored marekts, industry trends, and upcoming training seminars.
Cost: $24.00
Frequency: Quarterly
Circulation: 7500
Founded in 1998

14198 Momentum
Metropolitan Life Insurance Company
1 Madison Ave
New York, NY 10010-3603
212-867-2165
Fax: 212-685-8042
Home Page: www.metlife.com
Robert H Benmosche, CEO
Magazine covering the Metropolitan Life Insurance Company.
Frequency: Monthly
Founded in 1970

14199 NRRA News
National Risk Retention Association
4248 Park Glen Road
Minneapolis, MN 55416-4758
952-284-4643
800-999-4505
Fax: 952-929-1318
Home Page: www.captive.com
Judith Harrington, Editor
Cost: $195.00
Frequency: Quarterly
Circulation: 250,000

14200 National Underwriter Life & Health Financial Services Edition
33-41 Newark Street
2nd Floor
Hoboken, NJ 07030
201-526-1230
Fax: 201-526-1260
E-Mail: spiontek@nuco.com
Home Page: cms.nationalunderwriter.com
Stephen Piontek, Editor-In-Chief
Jim Connolly, Senior Editor
Uniquely positioned to provider producers, brokers, marketers and company executives with timely, insightful information. Each week, identifies, analyzes and comments on the latest trends and developments for their significance to the market-giving our readers the information they need to make critical business decisions.
Frequency: Weekly

14201 National Underwriter: Life & Health Insurance Edition
National Underwriter Company
5081 Olympic Blvd
Erlanger, KY 41018-3164
859-692-2100
800-543-0874
Fax: 859-692-2295
Home Page: www.nationalunderwriter.com
Charlie Smith, CEO
Offers features on agent activities, stocks and marketing, brokers and financial planners, trade meetings, business trends and outside developments in the industry.
Cost: $75.00
Frequency: Weekly
Circulation: 48,5070

14202 National Underwriter: Property & Casualty Risk & Benefits Management
National Underwriter Company
5081 Olympic Blvd
Erlanger, KY 41018-3164
859-692-2100
800-543-0874
Fax: 859-692-2295
Home Page: www.nationalunderwriter.com
Charlie Smith, CEO
Covers industry trends, risk management, state and federal legislation, and judicial affairs.
Cost: $149.00
Frequency: Weekly
Circulation: 485070
Founded in 1897

14203 POA Bulletin/Merritt Risk Management News and Review
POA Publishing
1625 Prince Street
Alexandria, VA 22314-2818
703-519-6200
877-663-4890
Fax: 703-519-6299
E-Mail: asis@asisonline.org
Home Page: www.asisonline.org
Michael E. Knoke, Managing Editor
Sherry Harowitz, Editor-In-Chief
Denny White, Director/Publishing
Editorial content is designed to keep security managers and risk managers abreast of legal, legislative and insurance issues, and contains

features that identify security and risk management trends and present analysis of insurance coverage and needs.
Cost: $690.00
Frequency: Quarterly
Circulation: 3400
Founded in 1955

14204 **Proceedings**
Conference of Consulting Actuaries
3880 Salem Lake Drive
Suite H
Long Grove, IL 60047-5292

847-719-6500
Fax: 847-719-6506
E-Mail: conference@ccactuaries.org
Home Page: www.ccactuaries.org

Rita K DeGraaf, Executive Director
Keith G Stewart, Director of Operations
Patricia D Johnson, Project Manager
Matthew D Noncek, Member Services Manager

The professional journal of the Conference of Consulting Actuaries. Promotes the interchange of information among actauries and the various actuarial organizations, and to keep its publics informed of the viewpoints and activities of the professional consulting actuary.
Cost: $95.00
500 Pages
Circulation: 1,200
Founded in 1950

14205 **Professional Agent**
Association of Professional Insurance Agents
400 N Washington Street
Alexandria, VA 22314-2312

703-836-9340
Fax: 703-836-1279
E-Mail: piainfo@pianet.org
Home Page: www.pianet.com

Magazine for the insurance professional.
Cost: $24.00
65 Pages
Frequency: Monthly
Circulation: 35000
Founded in 1931

14206 **Property/Casualty Insurance**
National Association of Mutual Insurance Companies
3601 Vincennes Road
PO Box 68700
Indianapolis, IN 46268

317-875-5250
Fax: 317-879-8408
E-Mail: webmaster@namic.org
Home Page: www.namic.org

Bart Anderson, Publisher
Laura Biddle-Bruckman, Managing Editor
Matt Keating, Editor
Kristen Eichhorn, Program Director

Highlights insurance industry news, personnel announcements, industry events, and new products in the field.
Cost: $20.00
Frequency: Monthly
Circulation: 2500
Founded in 1895

14207 **Public Risk**
Public Risk Management Association
700 S. Washington St.
Suite 218
Alexandria, VA 22314-1565

703-528-7701
Fax: 703-739-0200
E-Mail: info@primacentral.org
Home Page: www.primacentral.org
Social Media: Facebook, Twitter, LinkedIn

Marshall Davies, Executive Director
Jon Ruzan, Editor
Jennifer Ackerman, Deputy Executive Director
Bles Dones, Manager, Member Services
Paulette Washington, Office Administrator

Magazine exclusively targeting risk management practitioners in the public sector: state and local governments.
Cost: $130.00
Frequency: 1 Year 10 Issue
Circulation: 8250
ISSN: 0891-7183
Founded in 1978
Mailing list available for rent

14208 **Resource Magazine**
Life Office Management Association
2300 Windy Ridge Pkwy SE
Suite 600
Atlanta, GA 30339-5665

770-951-1770
800-275-5662
Fax: 770-984-0441
E-Mail: resource@loma.org
Home Page: www.loma.org

Thomas P Donaldson, President/CEO
Jerry Woo, Director
Robert Lai, Managing Director

Covers every topic of interest to management of insurance and financial services companies.
Frequency: Monthly

14209 **Risk & Insurance**
LRP Publications
PO Box 980
Horsham, PA 19044-0980

215-784-0912
800-341-7874
Fax: 215-784-9639
E-Mail: custserv@lrp.com
Home Page: www.lrp.com

Todd Lutz, CFO
Jack Roberts, Editor-in-Chief
Cyril Tuohy, Managing Editor

Provides business executives and insurance professionals with the insight, information and strategies they need to mitigate challenging business risks. Published monthly and semi-monthly in April when publish two special editions focusing on the Risk and Insurance Management Society's annual RIMS conference.
Frequency: Monthly
Circulation: 51541
Founded in 1977

14210 **Risk Management**
Risk Management Society Publishing
1065 Avenue of the Americas
13th Floor
New York, NY 10018-5637

212-286-9292
Fax: 212-986-9716
E-Mail: tdonovan@rims.org
Home Page: www.rims.org
Social Media: Facebook, Twitter, LinkedIn

Ted Donovan, Publisher
Bill Coffin, Editor-In-Chief
Morgan O'Rouke, Managing Editor
Jared Wade, Editor
Callie Nelson, Circulation Manager

The premier source of analysis, insight and news for corporate risk managers. RM strives to explore existing and emerging techniques and concepts that address the needs of those who are tasked with protecting the physical, financial, human and intellectual assets of their companies.
Cost: $64.00
Frequency: Monthly
Circulation: 17000
Founded in 1950
Mailing list available for rent

14211 **Risk Management and Insurance Review**
Wiley Publications
111 River Street
Hoboken, NJ 07030-5774

201-748-6000
Fax: 201-748-6088
E-Mail: info@wiley.com
Home Page: www.wiley.com

Mary A Weiss, Editor

Publishes respected, accessible, and high-quality applied research, and well-reasoned opinion and discussion in the field of risk and insurance. The Review's Feature Articles section includes original research involving applications and applied techniques. The Perspectives section contains articles providing new insights on the research literature, business practice, and public policy.
Frequency: Bi-Annual
ISSN: 1098-1616

14212 **Risk Report**
International Risk Management Institute
12222 Merit Dr
Suite 1450
Dallas, TX 75251-3297

972-996-0800
800-827-5991
Fax: 972-371-5128
Home Page: www.zeroriskhr.com
Social Media: Facebook, Twitter, LinkedIn

Mike Poskey, Vice President
Jack P Gibson, President
Paul D Murray, VP Marketing/Sales
Robert Kinsel Smith, Senior Adviser/Consultant
Mike Wojcik, Information Technology Director

Helps risk and insurance professionals in both of these areas with analysis and interpretation of the latest innovations in insurance
Cost: $219.00
Frequency: Monthly
Founded in 1987

14213 **Rough Notes**
Rough Notes Company
PO Box 1990
Carmel, IN 46082-1990

317-582-1600
800-428-4384
Fax: 317-816-1000
E-Mail: rnc@roughnotes.com
Home Page: www.roughnotes.com

Monthly sales and management magazine for property and casualty insurance agents.
Cost: $357.00
120 Pages
Frequency: Monthly
Founded in 1878
Printed in 4 colors on glossy stock

14214 **Round the Table Magazine**
Million Dollar Round Table
325 W Touhy Ave
Park Ridge, IL 60068-4265

847-692-6378
Fax: 847-518-8921
E-Mail: editor@mdrt.org
Home Page: www.mdrt.org

Guy E Baker, President
Kathyrn F Keuneke, Associate Editor
John Prast, Executive VP
Scott Brennan, Secretary

Productivity ideas, reaching your clients, professional knowledge, motivational stories, all this to share with clients and to help you make the sale.
Cost: $14.00
Frequency: Bi-Monthly

14215 Standard
Standard Publishing Corporation
155 Federal St
13th Floor
Boston, MA 02110-1752

617-457-0600
Fax: 617-457-0608
E-Mail: e.ayers@spcpub.com
Home Page: www.standardpub.com

John Cross, President/Publisher

Content focuses on all aspects involving legislative and regulatory developments at the state and federal levels, court decisions, trade association positions and more. Coverage includes news, feature articles and opinion pieces, with an emphasis on property/casualty insurance.
Cost: $80.00
Frequency: Weekly
Circulation: 5000
Founded in 1870

14216 The Brief (Tort & Insurance Practice Section)
American Bar Association
321 N Clark St
Chicago, IL 60654-7598

312-988-5000
800-285-2221
Fax: 312-988-6281
E-Mail: askaba@abanet.org
Home Page: www.abanet.org
Social Media: Facebook, Twitter

Jane Harper-Alport, Staff Editor
John Warren May, Editor
Janet Jackson, Director
Bill Pritchard, Assistant to the Director

The Brief explores all aspects of tort and insurance law, including the many facets of trial practice essential to the profession.
Cost: $50.00
400,0 Members
60 Pages
Frequency: Quarterly
Circulation: 30000
ISSN: 0273-0995
Founded in 1878
Printed in 4 colors

14217 Today's Insurance Woman
National Association of Insurance Women
1847 E 15th Street
PO Box 4410
Tulsa, OK 74159-0410

918-744-5195
Fax: 918-743-1968

Melissa Carlson, Editor

Focus is on business careers, legislation, leadership, management and social issues facing women in the industry.
Cost: $15.00
Frequency: Bi-Monthly
Circulation: 12,887

14218 Underwriters' Report
National Underwriters Company
5081 Olympic Boulevard
Erlanger, KY 41018

859-922-2100
800-543-0874
Fax: 800-874-1916
Home Page: www.nationalunderwriter.com

Charlie Smith, CEO

Offering complete information on fire, casualty and life insurance every week.
Cost: $45.00
40 Pages
Frequency: Weekly
Circulation: 5000

14219 Weight Loss Solutions
Field Media Publishing
200 S Main Street
Alpharetta, GA 30004

770-475-9770
Fax: 678-990-5565
Home Page: www.bcsolutionsmag.com

Doug Field, CEO/Publisher
Steve Milano, Editor

A business magazine that addresses real-world issues by delivering best-practice solutions and information to those involved in benefits and compensation decisions. Free to members.
Frequency: Monthly

14220 Worker's Compensation Monitor
LRP Publications
PO Box 24668
West Palm Beach, FL 33416-4668

561-622-6520
Fax: 561-622-0757
E-Mail: webmaster@lrp.com
Home Page: www.lrp.com

Kenneth Kahn, President
Leslie Lake, Managing Editor
Josh Clifton, Editor

Information on worker's compensation laws.
Cost: $210.00
Frequency: Monthly
Founded in 1977

Trade Shows

14221 AADC Annual Spring Workshop
American Association of Dental Consultants
10032 Wind Hill Drive
Greenville, IN 47124

812-923-2600
800-896-0707
Fax: 812-923-2900
Home Page: www.aadc.org

Dr George Koumaras, President
Dr Larry Hoffman, Secretary/Treasurer
Judith K. Salisbury, Executive Director

These meetings provide a forum to discuss topical subjects involving the Dental Benefit Industry and Clinical Dentistry as a whole. AADC presenters and lectures are recognized as leaders in the Dental Industry. 10 exhibitors.
300 Attendees
Frequency: Annual/May
Founded in 1979

14222 AHIP Annual Meeting
America's Health Insurance Plans
601 Pennsylvania Avenue NW
South Building, Suite 500
Washington, DC 20004

202-778-3200
877-291-2247
Fax: 202-331-7487
E-Mail: ahip@ahip.org
Home Page: www.ahip.org

Karen M Ignagni, President/CEO
Susan Pisano, VP Communications

This meeting continues to be the nation's leading health care conference where all segments of the health insurance industry convene to share perspectives on, and analysis of, the most recent developments in health care.
300 Attendees

14223 AHOU Annual Conference
Association of Home Office Underwriters
22300 Windy Ridge Parkway
Suite 600
Atlanta, GA 30339-8443

770-984-3715
Fax: 770-984-6418
E-Mail: ahou@loma.org
Home Page: www.ahou.org

Jennifer Richards, Convention VP
Lee Janecek, Convention Assistant VP

Providing career development, underwriting solutions, the latest medical issues and valuable insight to keep you prepared.
Frequency: Annual/October
Founded in 2001

14224 AIA Annual Conference
Aviation Insurance Association
400 Admiral Blvd
Suite 200
Kansas City, MO 64106-1508

816-221-8488
Fax: 816-472-7765
E-Mail: mandie@robstan.com
Home Page: www.aiaweb.org
Social Media: Facebook

Paul Leonard, President
Todd McCredie, Vice President
Patrick Bailey, Secretary
Mary D'Alauro, Treasurer
Mandie Bannwarth, Executive Director

Provides a forum for the biggest names and best minds in the aviaiton insurance industry. Offers top-notch speakers, continuing education classes, time with vendors and opportunities to network and develop relationships that last a lifetime.
900 Members
Frequency: April/May
Founded in 1976

14225 AICP Annual Conference
Association of Insurance Compliance Professionals
12100 Sunset Hills Road
Suite 130
Reston, VA 20190

703-234-4074
Fax: 703-435-4390
E-Mail: aicp@aicp.net
Home Page: www.aicp.net

Richard A Guggolz, Executive Director
Elaine Bailey, Conference Chair

Learning opportunities for a broad range of compliance professionals, sessions for beginners and seasoned professionals and networking opportunities with colleagues, peers and state regulators.
680 Attendees
Frequency: Annual/Sept-Oct

14226 ASPPA Annual Conference
American Society of Pension Professionals & Act
4245 N Fairfax Drive
Suite 750
Arlington, VA 22203

703-160-0512
Fax: 703-516-9308
E-Mail: asppa@asppa.org
Home Page: www.asppa.org

Tom Finnegan, President

Attendees of this conference share quality time with representatives from every aspect of the retirement plan industry. Offers 20 hours of ASPPA continuing education credits and provides Joint Board for the Enrollemnt of Actuaries credit hours for enrolled actuaries.
1600 Attendees

14227 ASSE Annual Conference & Exposition
American Society of Safety Engineers
1800 E Oakton Street
Des Plaines, IL 60018
847-699-2929
Fax: 847-768-3434
E-Mail: customerservice@asse.org
Home Page: www.asse.org
Social Media: Facebook, Twitter, LinkedIn, Blogger, Pinterest, Tumblr
Fred Fortman, Executive Director
Jim Drzewiecki, Finance/Controller Director
Diane Hurns, Manager Public Relations Department
Richard A. Pollock, President
Stephanie A. Helgerman, Vice President, Finance
Featuring more than 200 sessions, an exposition with 300 exhibitors, special pre- and post-conference seminars, conference proceedings on CD, numerous networking events and more! Learn the latest strategies to expand your knowledge base and network with other safety, health and environmental professionals
3500 Attendees
Frequency: Annual/June
Mailing list available for rent

14228 Advanced Life Underwriting Association
1922 F Street NW
Washington, DC 20006-4302
202-331-6099
Fax: 202-331-2164
Karen G Keating, Director
22 booths.
1.1M Attendees
Frequency: February

14229 Alliance of Insurance Agents and Brokers Convention & Expo
1029 J. Street
Suite 120
Sacramento, CA 95814
916-283-9473
866-497-9222
Fax: 916-283-9479
E-Mail: info@agentsalliance.com
Home Page: www.agentsalliance.com
Social Media: Facebook, Twitter
Joe Jimenez, President
David Nelson, Executive Direcetor
Mike D'Arelli, Executive Vice President
Yolanda Olquin, Sales/Marketing Manager
The largest insurance industry trade show in the western U.S. Offers the perfect blend of business networking opportunities, education seminars, and fun and laughs with old and new friends.
Frequency: Annual
Founded in 1962

14230 American Association of Managing General Agents Annual Meeting
American Association of Managing General Agents
9140 Ward Parkway
Kansas City, MO 64114-3306
816-444-3500
Fax: 816-444-0330
Jeanne Corlew-Knox, Director Meetings
Annual meeting and exhibits for managing general agents of insurance companies.
1000 Attendees
Frequency: Annual

14231 American Fraternal Alliance Annual Meeting
American Fraternal Alliance
1301 W 22nd St
Suite 700
Oak Brook, IL 60523-6022
630-522-6322
Fax: 630-522-6326
E-Mail: info@fraternalalliance.org
Home Page: www.fraternalalliance.org
Social Media: Facebook, Twitter
Joseph Annotti, President & CEO
Linda McLaughlin, Admin Services Manager
Melanie Hinds, Director, Advocacy
Allison Koppel, Executive Vice President
Andrea Litewski, Executive Administrator
Keeps members abreast of industry trends, to promote the spirit of fraternalism and to resolve mutual concerns.
Frequency: September

14232 American Society for Healthcare Risk Management Convention
American Society for Healthcare Risk Management
American Hospital Association
1 N Franklin
Chicago, IL 60606
312-422-3840
Fax: 312-422-4580
Home Page: www.aha.org
Deborah Sprindzunas, Executive Director
Cliff Lehman, Director Membership Services
Annual convention and exhibits of health care industry risk management equipment, supplies and services.
Frequency: Annual

14233 American Society of CLU and CHFC Annual Conference
American Society of CLU and CHFC
270 S Bryn Mawr Avenue
Suite 2
Bryn Mawr, PA 19010-2195
215-726-3160
Fax: 610-527-1400
Annual conference and exhibits for insurance agents and financial services professionals who hold Chartered Life Underwriter or Chartered Financial Consultant designations.
Frequency: October, San Diego

14234 Annual Conference for Public Agencies
Public Risk Management Association
1815 Fort Myer Drive
Suite 1020
Arlington, VA 22209-1805
703-527-5546
Fax: 703-528-7966
E-Mail: info@primacentral.org
Home Page: www.primacentral.org
James F Coyle, Executive Director
Tony D'Alba, Manager
Kerry Langley, Manager
Largest conference in North America for state and local government risk managers who purchase insurance, safety and training products, computer software, TPA and consultant services. 150 booths.
2000 Attendees
Frequency: June
Founded in 1979
Mailing list available for rent: 2000 names

14235 Annual National Association of Insurance Women International
1847 E 15th
PO Box 4410
Tulsa, OK 74159
918-744-5195
800-766-6249
Fax: 918-743-1968
E-Mail: naiw@ionet.net
Home Page: www.naiw.org
Mark Adams, Executive Vice-President
Equipment, information and supplies for women in the insurance industry.
900 Attendees
Frequency: Annual

14236 Appraisers Association of America National Conference
386 Park Avenue S
Suite 2000
New York, NY 10016-8804
212-889-5404
Fax: 212-889-5503
Home Page: www.appraisersassoc.org
Aleya Lehmann, Executive Director
A unique opportunity to connect with fellow appraisers as well as with allied professionals in insurance companies, law firms, government agencies, auction houses, galleries, museums, and libraries to debate and discuss the latest issues impacting the appraisal profession. We'll offer panels, specialist sessions, roundtable discussions, networking, and behind-the-scenes tours.

14237 Association for Advanced Life Underwriting
2901 Telester Court
Falls Church, VA 22042
703-641-9400
888-275-0092
Karen Keating, Communications Director
David Stertzer, Executive VP
Twenty two booths.
1M Attendees
Frequency: March

14238 CEB Spring Conference
Council on Employee Benefits
1311 King Street
Alexandria, VA 22314
703-549-6025
Fax: 703-549-6027
E-Mail: scanfiled@ceb.org
Home Page: www.ceb.org
Shane Canfield, Executive Director
Robert B. Arthur, President
John R. Collins, Treasurer
Donna A. Sexton, Vice President
Charles A. Jordan, Secretary
For members only and affords a great opportunity to exchange ideas in an interactive workshop format.
Frequency: April

14239 CIRB Annual Meeting
Crop Insurance Research Bureau
201 Massachusetts Avenue, NE
Suite C5
Washington, DC 20002
202-544-0067
Fax: 202-330-5255
E-Mail: mtorrey@cropinsurance.org
Home Page: www.cropinsurance.org
Mike Torrey, Executive VP/Federal Affairs Rep
Naomi Watson, Operations Manager
W. Kurt Henke, Legal Counsel
The annual meeting brings together crop industry leaders to learn from expert speakers and newtwork with others in their industry.
Frequency: Annual/January-February

14240 CPCU Annual Meeting & Seminar
Chartered Property Casualty Underwriter Society

720 Providence Road
PO Box 3009
Malvern, PA 19355-0709

610-251-2728
800-932-2728
Fax: 610-251-2780
E-Mail: lrizzo@cpcusociety.org
Home Page: www.cpcusociety.org

Liliana Rizzo, CMP, Meeting Services Director

Join your fellow society members, new designees and industry leaders for the best in education, networking and leadership the property and casualty insurance industry has to offer.
2600 Attendees
Frequency: Annual/October
Founded in 1944

14241 **CPCU Conferment Ceremony**
American Institute for CPCU
720 Providence Road
PO Box 3016
Malvern, PA 19355

610-251-2733
800-644-2101
Fax: 610-640-9576
E-Mail: cserv@cpcuiia.org
Home Page: www.aicpcu.org

Karen Burger CPCU CPIW, Public Relations
Roch Parayre, Senior Partner

Annual graduation ceremony for people who have earned the Chartered Property Casualty Underwriter - CPCU - designation.
Frequency: October

14242 **Captive Insurance Companies Association Conference**
Captive Insurance Companies Association
4248 Park Glen Road
Minneapolis, MN 55416

952-928-4655
Fax: 952-928-1318
Home Page: www.captiveassociation.com

Annual conference and exhibits of captive insurance equipment, supplies and services.

14243 **Chartered Property Casualty Underwriters Society Fall Seminar**
Chartered Property Casualty Underwriter Society
720 Providence Road
Malvern, PA 19355-3402

610-512-2728
Home Page: http://www.cpcusociety.org

Joseph Wisniewski, VP Finance
Jim Marks, Executive Director

Offers a forum for the exchange of ideas between insurance representatives.
3M Attendees
Frequency: October

14244 **Employee Benefits Annual Conference**
International Foundation of Employee Benefit Plans
18700 W Bluemound Road
Brookfield, WI 53045

262-786-6700
888-334-3327
Fax: 262-786-8780
E-Mail: pr@ifebp.org
Home Page: www.ifebp.org
Social Media: Facebook, Twitter, LinkedIn

Michael Wilson, CEO
Terry Davidson, VP, Business Development
Beth Harwood, VP, Educ Program/Content Management

This conference is designed to meet the specific needs of multiemployer and public sector plan trustees and administrators, attorneys, accountants, actuaries, investment managers and others who provide services or who are involved in the overall management and administration of benefit trust funds. The 2011 conference will be in New Orleans, LA.
35000 Members
4500 Attendees
Frequency: Annual/Nov 4-7

14245 **FICP Conference**
Financial & Insurance Conference Planners
330 N. Wabash Avenue
Suite 2000
Chicago, IL 60611

312-245-1023
Fax: 312-321-5150
E-Mail: jschultze@ficpnet.com
Home Page: www.ficpnet.com

James Schultze, CMP, Conference Manager
Laura Vanderbur, Conference Associate
Steve Bova, CAE, Executive Director
Mark Swets, Membership Manager
Ellie Hurley, Events Senior Manager

Exhibits, education and networking activities.
Frequency: Annual/November

14246 **Financial Service Forum**
Society of Financial Service Professionals
19 Campus Blvd
Suite 100
Newtown Square, PA 19073-3230

610-526-2500
800-392-6900
Fax: 610-526-2538
E-Mail: info@financialpro.org
Home Page: www.financialpro.org
Social Media: Facebook, Twitter, LinkedIn

Joseph E Frack, CEO
Donna Conrad, CFO
Anthony Smith, VP Marketing/Corporate Services
Jill Von Czoernig, Managing Director
Sherry Chester, Director, Professional Development

Composed of motivational speakers, break-out educational session with continuing education for insurance, CFP, PACE, CLE, CPE, ICB, and EA. Exhibithall includes demo theaters.
3000+ Attendees
Frequency: October

14247 **General Agents and Managers Life Agency Management Program**
1922 F Street NW
Washington, DC 20006-4302

202-331-6099
Fax: 202-785-5612

Jo Anne Kohler, Show Manager

80 booths including publishers, computer software and hardware manufacturers and office management services.
2.7M Attendees
Frequency: March

14248 **Health Law Professors Conference**
American Society of Law, Medicine and Ethics
765 Commonwealth Avenue
16th Floor
Boston, MA 02215

617-262-4990
Fax: 617-437-7596
E-Mail: conferences@aslme.org
Home Page: www.aslme.org
Social Media: Facebook, Twitter, LinkedIn

Ted Hutchinson, Executive Director
Katie Kenney Johnson, Conference Director
Margo Buege, Membership Department
Courtney McClellan, Assistant Editor
Frequency: June
Mailing list available for rent

14249 **I-Car International Annual Meeting**
3701 W Algonquin Road
Suite 400
Rolling Meadows, IL 60008

925-961-0393
800-422-7872
Fax: 800-590-1215
E-Mail: webmaster@i-car.com
Home Page: www.i-car.com

Pat Perren, Meetings Manager
Matt Forpanek, Customer Care Manager

A important event that brings together collision industry leaders from across the United States, Canada and New Zealand to address current trends and issues in the industry. Attendees will have the opportunity to learn about new products and technologies and share ideas with other industry leaders.
Frequency: Annual/July

14250 **IAAI Annual Conference and General Meeting**
International Association of Arson Investigators
12770 Boenker Road
Bridgeton, MO 63044

314-739-4224
Fax: 314-739-4219
E-Mail: orders@firearson.com
Home Page: www.firearson.com

Marsha Sipes, Conference/Meeting Services
Dolores Nelson, Executive Director
Dave Allen, Executive Director

Provides the means to stay abreast of the latest techniques and theories in the investigation of the crime of arson.
Frequency: Annual/April

14251 **IADC Annual Meeting**
International Association of Defense Counsel
303 West Madison
Suite 925
Chicago, IL 60606

312-368-1494
Fax: 312-368-1854
E-Mail: info@iadclaw.org
Home Page: www.iadclaw.org
Social Media: Facebook, Twitter, LinkedIn

Mary Beth Kurzak, Executive Director
Mathew Hornberger, Director Membership/Administration
Liz Anderson, Administrative Assistant
Carmela Balice, Senior Manager, Member Services
Ashley Fitzgerald, Communications Coordinator

Offering interests CLE and excellent networking opportunities in family friendly environment.
Frequency: Annual/July

14252 **IAIABC Annual Convention**
Int'l Assoc of Industrail Accident Boards/Commissi
5610 Medical Circle
Suite 24
Madison, WI 53719

608-663-6355
Fax: 608-663-1546
E-Mail: hlore@iaiabc.org
Home Page: www.iaiabc.org

Jennifer Wolf Horejsh, Executive Director
Faith Howe, EDI Manager
Christina Klein, Events/Education Coordinator
Christina Klein, Events and Office

Administrator
Heather Lore, Manager of Membership and Marketing
Brings together regulators and administrators of workers' compensation agencies and private sector professionals to discuss the industry's most common and pressing problems.
Frequency: August
Mailing list available for rent

14253 IAIR Roundtable and Meetings
International Association of Insurance Receivers
174 Grace Boulevard
Altamonte Springs, FL 32714
407-682-4513
Fax: 407-682-3175
E-Mail: info@iair.org
Home Page: www.iair.org
Daniel A Orth III, Meetings VP
Mary Cannon Veed, Vice President
Douglas Hartz, Vice President
Quarterly meetings that provides an opportunity to share information about important industry issues and topics in insurance and reinsurance as they relate specifically to insurance receiverships.
Frequency: June, Sept, December

14254 IASA Annual Conference
Insurance, Accounting & Systems Association
3511 Shannon Road
Suite 160
Durham, NC 27707
919-489-0991
Fax: 919-489-1994
E-Mail: info@iasa.org
Home Page: www.iasa.org
Thom Hoffman, Exhibit Manager
R Iovino, Account Manager
Providing the most comprehensive education program and business show targeted for financial and technology professionals in the industry.
1800 Attendees
Frequency: June

14255 ICAE's Annual Exchange
Insurance Consumer Affairs Exchange
PO Box 746
Lake Zurich, IL 60047
847-997-8454
E-Mail: nbrebner@icae.com
Home Page: www.icae.com
Mike Hammond, President
Kendra Franklin, VP
Nancy Brebner, Executive Director
Chad Batterson, Executive Committee
Gail Cleary, Secretary
A not-for-profit organization that promotes professionalism and shapes the standards of behavior in relationships between insurance organizations, regulators and customers through proactive dialogue, research, communication and education.
110 Members
Frequency: Annual/October
Founded in 1976

14256 IRU Spring Conference
Intermediaries and Reinsurance Underwriters Assoc
971 Rte 202 North
Branchburg, NJ 08876
908-203-0211
Fax: 908-203-0213
E-Mail: info@irua.com
Home Page: www.irua.com
Amy Barra, Executive Director
Frequency: Annual, March

14257 Insurance and Financial Communications Association Annual Conference
1037 N 3rd Ave
Tucson, AZ 85705
602-350-0717
E-Mail: info@ifcaonline.com
Home Page: www.ifcaonline.com
Social Media: Facebook, Twitter, LinkedIn, YouTube
Susan o'Neill, President
Ralph Chaump, VP
Kim Schultz, Secretary
Kim Schultz, Secretary
An international organization dedicated to the ongoing professional development of its members in life insurance and related financial services communications.
700 Members
Founded in 1933

14258 International Claim Association Conference
International Claim Association
1155 15th Street NW
Suite 500
Washington, DC 20005
202-452-0143
Fax: 202-530-0659
E-Mail: cmurphy@claim.org
Home Page: www.claim.org
Marlon Nettleton, President
Christopher Murphy, Executive Director
Lisa Phillips, Secretary
400 Attendees
Frequency: Annual
Founded in 1909
Mailing list available for rent

14259 LAMP Annual Meeting
GAMA International
2901 Telestar Court
Suite 140
Falls Church, VA 22042-1205
703-770-8184
Fax: 703-770-8182
E-Mail: gamamail@gamaweb.com
Home Page: www.gamaweb.com
Nicole Travers, Meetings/Products Administrator
Delaine Everett, Meetings/Convention Director
The event for field leaders in the insurance and financial services industry. Featuring top-notch main platform speaker presentations, more than 30 leading practices concurrent sessions, resource center with more than 50 exhibitors that will be offering valuable products and services and networking opportunities with your peers.
Frequency: Annual/March
ISSN: 1095-7367
Printed in 4 colors on glossy stock

14260 LIC Annual Meeting
Life Insurers Council
2300 Windy Ridge Parkway
Suite 600
Atlanta, GA 30339-8443
770-984-3724
800-275-5662
Fax: 770-984-3780
E-Mail: askloma@loma.org
Home Page: www.loma.org/IndexPage-LIC.asp
Michael H Siris, Executive Director
Rose Hoyt, Administrative Assistant
Designed to educate members about critical issues for competing in today's regulatory, legislative and business climates.
Frequency: Annual/May
Mailing list available for rent

14261 MDRT Annual Meeting
Million Dollar Round Table
325 W Touhy Avenue
Park Ridge, IL 60068-4265
847-926-6378
Fax: 847-518-8921
E-Mail: meetings@mdrt.org
Home Page: www.mdrt.org
Ray Kopcinski, Meeting Services Director
Jody Egel, Meeting Coordinator
Kathyrn H Pagura, Meeting Coordinator
John Prast, Executive Vice President
Scott Brennan, Secretary
Known throughout the industry as the premier meeting for financial professionals. Motivational stories, educational sessions, experienced colleagues, networking opportunities come together at these annual meetings.
Frequency: Annual/June

14262 NACA Convention
National Association of Catastrophe Adjusters
PO Box 821864
North Richland Hills, TX 76182-1864
817-498-3466
Fax: 817-498-0480
E-Mail: nacatadj@aol.com
Home Page: www.nacatadj.org
Lori Ringo, Executive Administrator
Annual convention and business meeting offering continuing education credits for some states; also a vendor show. Convention is held in Las Vegas, NV.
200 Attendees
Frequency: January
Founded in 1976

14263 NADP Annual Conference
National Association of Dental Plans
8111 LBJ Freeway
Suite 935
Dallas, TX 75251-1347
972-458-6998
Fax: 972-458-2258
E-Mail: info@nadp.org
Home Page: www.nadp.org
Evelyn F Ireland, CAE, Executive Director
Tim Brown, Executive Assistant
Jeremy May, Executive Assistant
Get the greater industry insight, re-energized creativity and influential contacts.
Frequency: Annual/September

14264 NAIFA Convention and Career Conference
Ntl Association of Insurance & Financial Advisors
2901 Telestar Court
PO Box 12012
Falls Church, VA 22042-1205
703-770-8100
877-866-2432
Fax: 703-770-8201
E-Mail: membersupport@naifa.org
Home Page: www.naifa.org
Robert O. Smith, President
Matthew S. Tassey, Treasurer
Juli McNeely, Secretary
Susan B. Waters, CEO
Susan B Waters, Deputy Chief Executive Officer
Features educational workshops from more than a dozen prominent speakers and the NAIFA Expo, one of the largest exhibits of financial services and products in the nation.
2000 Attendees
Frequency: Annual/September
Founded in 1890

14265 **NAIIA Annual Conference**
National Association of Independent Insurance Adj.
825 W State Street
Suite 117-C&B
Geneva, IL 60134
630-397-5012
Fax: 630-397-5013
E-Mail: assist@naiia.com
Home Page: www.naiia.com
David F Mehren, Executive Director
Brenda Reisenger, President
Mark Nixon, Secretary, Treasurer
Attendance is open to claims handling professionals.
Frequency: Annual

14266 **NAPIA Annual Meeting**
National Association of Public Insurance Adjusters
21165 Whitfield Place
Suite 105
Potomac Falls, VA 20165
703-433-9217
Fax: 703-433-0369
E-Mail: info@napia.com
Home Page: www.napia.com
David W Barrack, Executive Director
Ronald R. Reitz, President
Education sessions, networking and social events and exhibits by industry suppliers.
Frequency: Annual/June
Mailing list available for rent

14267 **National Association of Independent Life Brokerage Agencies Conference**
National Assn of Independent Life Brokerage Agents
8201 Greensboro Drive
Suite 300
Mc Lean, VA 22102-3814
703-610-9011
Fax: 703-524-2303
Annual conference and exhibits of equipment, supplies and services for licensed independent life brokerage agencies that represent at least 3 insurance companies, but are not controlled or owned by an underwriting company.
Frequency: November, San Diego

14268 **National Association of Life Underwriters Conference**
1922 F Street NW
Washington, DC 20006-4394
202-331-6099
Fax: 202-331-2179
William V Regan III, Executive VP
Teresa Bonnema, Advertising Account
Sales professionals in life and health insurance and other financial services. 110 booths.
3.5M Attendees
Frequency: September

14269 **National Association of Mutual Insurance Companies Annual Convention & Expo**
National Association of Mutual Insurance Companies
3601 Vincennes Road
#68700
Indianapolis, IN 46268-1154
317-875-5250
Fax: 317-879-8408
E-Mail: bnastally@namic.org
Home Page: www.namic.org
Charles Chamness, President
Barbara Nastally, Program Director
Kristen Eichhorn, Program Director
Gregg Dykstra, COO
Convention and exhibit show for property/casualty insurance executives. Four day event.
1700 Attendees
Frequency: Fall
Founded in 1895

14270 **New England Professional Insurance Agents Association Conference**
1 Ash Street
Hopkinton, MA 01748-1822
508-497-2590
Stella Di Camilo, Show Manager
100 booths of insurance-related products.
1.5M Attendees
Frequency: November

14271 **PIA Annual Convention and Trade Fair**
Professional Insurance Agents Association of
VA & DC
8751 Park Central Dr., Suite 140
Richmond, VA 23227
804-264-2582
Fax: 804-266-1075
E-Mail: pia@piavadc.com
Home Page: www.piavadc.com
Social Media: Facebook, Twitter
Dennis Yooom, Executive VP
Lori Lohr, Education Manager
Carol Throokmorton, Accounting Manager
Founded in 1936

14272 **PLRB/LIRB Claims Conference & Insurance Expo**
PLRB/LIRB-Property Loss Research Bureau
3025 Highland Parkway
Suite 800
Downers Grove, IL 60515-1291
630-242-2250
888-711-7572
Fax: 630-724-2260
E-Mail: pdispensa@lirb.org
Home Page: www.lirb.org
Tom Mallin, President
Paul C Despensa, VP/General Counsel
Concept sessions that feature a thorough presentation of a topic by expert panelists. A forum of experts/panels that will discuss controversial topics in response to questions and comments from participants on a range of subjects outlined in the agenda for that forum. Participants form a small discussion group to reach consensus on hypothetical problems. Each table debates and defends its conclusions with other groups.
Frequency: April
Mailing list available for rent

14273 **PRIMA Annual Conference Trade Show**
700 S. Washington St.
Suite 218
Alexandria, VA 22314
703-528-7701
Fax: 703-739-0200
E-Mail: info@primacentral.org
Home Page: www.primacentral.org
Social Media: Facebook, Twitter, LinkedIn
Marshall Davies, Executive Director
Jon Ruzan, Editor
Jennifer Ackerman, Deputy Executive Director
Bles Dones, Manager, Member Services
Paulette Washington, Office Administrator
Containing 150 exhibits concerning insuring the public.
2,200 Attendees
Frequency: June
Founded in 1976
Mailing list available for rent

14274 **Physician Insurers Association of America Annual Conference**
Physician Insurers Association of America
2275 Research Boulevard
Rockville, MD 20850-3268
301-947-9000
Fax: 301-947-9090
Annual exhibits related to physician liability insurance.

14275 **Professional Insurance Agents National Annual Conference & Exhibition**
National Association of Prof. Insurance Agents
400 N Washington Street
Alexandria, VA 22314-2312
703-836-9340
Fax: 703-836-1279
Home Page: http://www.pianet.com
Ted Besesparis, VP
Annual conference and exhibits of equipment, supplies and services for independent property and casualty agents.

14276 **Public Agency Risk Managers Association Convention**
Public Agency Risk Managers Association
PO Box 6810
San Jose, CA 95150-6810
Annual convention and exhibits of risk management equipment, supplies and services.

14277 **Risk Insurance Management Society**
1065 Avenue of Americas
13th Floor
New York, NY 10018
212-286-9292
E-Mail: chapterservices@RIMS.org
Home Page: www.rims.org
Brian Stevenson, Show Manager
Mary Roth, Manager
Fran Jordan, Manager
500 booths of premier insurance companies and associated service companies.
5M Attendees

14278 **Securities Industry and Financial Markets Association (SIFMA) Annual Meeting**
1101 New York Avenue Nw
8th Floor
Washington, DC 20005
202-962-7300
Fax: 202-962-7305
Home Page: www.sifma.org
Social Media: Facebook, Twitter, LinkedIn
T Timothy Ryan Jr, President/CEO
Randy Snook, Senior Managing Director/EVP
Cheryl Crispen, Executive VP, Communications
Ira D. Hammerman, Senior Managing Director
David Krasner, Chief Financial Officer
The Securities Industry and Financial Markets Association/SIFMA Annual Meeting and Conference program addresses a variety of topics that may include competitiveness of the U.S. capital markets, global exchange consolidation, regulatory and legal initiatives, and trends in the fixed-income and capital markets.
Mailing list available for rent

14279 **Society of Insurance Trainers and Educators Conference**
2120 Market Street
Suite 108
San Francisco, CA 94114
415-621-2830
Fax: 415-621-0889

E-Mail: ed@insurancetrainers.org
Home Page: www.insurancetrainers.org

Lois A Markovich, Executive Director

Forty booths. A major conference for those involved with training and education in the insurance industry.
200 Attendees
Frequency: June-July
Founded in 1953

14280 Sun States Professional Insurance Agents Association
13416 N 32nd Street
Suite 106
Phoenix, AZ 85032-6000

602-482-3333
Social Media: Facebook, Twitter, LinkedIn

Maryls M Graser, Executive VP

50 booths.
300 Attendees
Frequency: May

14281 VCIA Annual Meeeting
Vermont Captive Insurance Association
180 Battery Street
Suite 200
Burlington, VT 05401-5212

802-658-8242
Fax: 802-658-9365
E-Mail: vcia@vcia.com
Home Page: www.vcia.com

Richard Smith, President
Diane Leach, Education/Program Planning Director
Janice Valgoi, Membership/Development Director
Elizabeth Halpern, Communications Director
Peggy Companion, Director of Finance
Frequency: August
Founded in 1985

14282 Women Life Underwriters Confederation
1126 S 70th Street
Suite S-106
Milwaukee, WI 53214-3151

800-776-3008
Fax: 414-475-2585

Ann Wells, Managing Director

For women insurance agents, their managers and their companies. 20 booths.
100 Attendees
Frequency: September

Directories & Databases

14283 ADP Parts Exchange New
ADP Claims Services Group
2010 Crow Canyon Place
San Ramon, CA 94583

925-866-1100
Home Page: www.adpclaims.com

Provides an electronic link from your ADP estimating system to comprehensive database of new replacement parts. Data on over three and a half million parts facilitates the writing of complete, cost-effective damage reports.

14284 Adjusters Reference Guide
Bar List Publishing Company
425 Huehl Road
Building 6B
Northbrook, IL 60062-2323

847-498-6133
800-726-1007
Fax: 847-498-6695
E-Mail: info@barlist.com
Home Page: www.barlist.com

Bruce Rodgers, President
Leslie Rodgers, Production Manager

A professional service for anyone who handles insurance claims. It contains a complete set of ISO Policy and Forms and is divided into two major categories; Personal Lines and Commercial Lines.
Frequency: Annual

14285 Best's Directory of Recommended Insurance Attorneys and Adjusters
AM Best Company
Ambest Rd
Oldwick, NJ 08858

908-439-2200
Fax: 908-439-3296
E-Mail: webmaster@ambest.com
Home Page: www.ambest.com

Arthur Snyder, CEO

Includes over 5,300 insurance defense law firms and over 1,200 insurance adjusters companies recommended by the insurance industry. Includes a section on expert services providers, insurance company groups or fleets, legal and claims services, officials and a digest of insurance laws.
Cost: $1205.00
5100 Pages
Frequency: Annual
Circulation: 19,000
Founded in 1928

14286 Best's Insurance News & Analysis
AM Best Company
Ambest Rd
Oldwick, NJ 08858

908-439-2200
800-424-2378
Fax: 908-439-3296
E-Mail: editor_br@bestreview.com
Home Page: www.ambest.com

Arthur Snyder, Chairman & President
Paul Tinnirello, CIO
Larry Mayewski, Chief Rating Officer

Best's Insurance News & Analysis makes it easy to take advantage of A.M. Best's extensive insurance news and industry research. A Best's Insurance News & Analysis subscription grants you access to a full range of news products as well as unique statistical studies and special reports - all of which are accessible from one convenient online location. Allows access to receive BestDay, BestWeek, Best's Review, and Best's Special Reports.

14287 Best's Insurance Reports
AM Best Company
Ambest Rd
Oldwick, NJ 08858

908-439-2200
Fax: 908-439-3296
E-Mail: webmaster@ambest.com
Home Page: www.ambest.com

Arthur Snyder, CEO

Published in two editions - life-health insurance and property-casualty insurance, United States and Canada.
Cost: $570.00
Frequency: Annual

14288 Best's Insurance Reports: International Edition
AM Best Company
Ambest Rd
Oldwick, NJ 08858

908-439-2200
Fax: 908-439-3296
E-Mail: webmaster@ambest.com
Home Page: www.ambest.com

Arthur Snyder, CEO

Offers information on over 800 insurance companies in Canada, Europe, Asia, Africa, Australia, and South America that offer life/health and property/casulaty insurance policies.
Cost: $495.00
1200 Pages
Frequency: Annual

14289 Best's Key Rating Guide
AM Best Company
Ambest Rd
Oldwick, NJ 08858

908-439-2200
Fax: 908-439-3296
E-Mail: webmaster@ambest.com
Home Page: www.ambest.com

Arthur Snyder, CEO
Larry Mayewski, Editor

Financial and operating characteristics on over 2,600 major property/casualty insurance companies, over 1,750 major life and health insurance companies.
Cost: $95.00
Frequency: Annual August

14290 Best's Market Guide
AM Best Company
Ambest Rd
Oldwick, NJ 08858

908-439-2200
Fax: 908-439-3296
E-Mail: webmaster@ambest.com
Home Page: www.ambest.com

Arthur Snyder, CEO

In each volume, separate volumes for corporate stocks, corporate bonds, and municipal bonds, a list of insurance company investment officers are offered.
Cost: $1425.00
Frequency: 3-Volume Set

14291 Business Insurance Directory of Reinsurance Intermediaries
Crain Communications
360 N Michigan Ave
Chicago, IL 60601-3800

312-649-5200
800-678-9595
Fax: 312-649-7937
Home Page: www.crain.com

Keith Crain, CEO
Sandra L Budde, Editor

Lists nearly 100 reinsurance intermediaries in the United States and Bermuda.
Cost: $4.00
Frequency: Annual
Circulation: 53,000

14292 Captive Insurance Company Directory
Tillinghast/Towers Perrin Company
263 Tresser Boulevard
Stamford, CT 06901-3236

203-631-1900
Fax: 203-326-5498

Corinne Ramming, Editor

Lists over 3,000 captive insurance companies and their parent or sponsor companies; management companies and insurance subsidiary investment advisors.
Cost: $210.00
270 Pages
Frequency: Annual

14293 Certified Claims Professional Accreditation Council
PO Box 441110
Fort Washington, MD 20749-1110
301-292-1988
Fax: 301-292-1787
Home Page: www.lattmag.com
Dale L Anderson, Editor
Offers a variety of information on members of the CCPAC and certified claims professionals.
76 Pages
Circulation: 350

14294 Claim Service Guide
Bar List Publishing Company
425 Huehl Road
Building 6B
Northbrook, IL 60062-2323
847-498-6133
800-726-1007
Fax: 847-498-6695
E-Mail: info@barlist.com
Home Page: www.barlist.com
Bruce Rodgers, President
Edna MacMillan, Editor
National Directory of Independent Insurance Adjusters, Appraisers, Expert Consultants and Property Specialists. Distributed to every home and branch office insurance company claims manager.
Cost: $80.00
Frequency: Annual
Circulation: 13,000

14295 Corporate Yellow Book
Leadership Directories
104 5th Ave
New York, NY 10011-6901
212-627-4140
Fax: 212-645-0931
E-Mail: corporate@leadershipdirectories.com
Home Page: www.leadershipdirectories.com
Social Media: Facebook, Twitter
David Hurvitz, CEO
Contact information for over 48,000 executives at over 1,000 companies and more than 9,000 board members and their outside affiliations.
Cost: $360.00
1,400 Pages
Frequency: Quarterly
ISSN: 1058-2098
Founded in 1969

14296 Custom Publishing & News Services
Information
7707 Old Georgetown Rd
Suite 700
Bethesda, MD 20814
301-215-4688
Fax: 301-215-4600
E-Mail: acarr@mail.infoinc.com
Home Page: www.infoinc.com
Alain Carr, Owner
Offers evaluations of companies on their claims-paying ability.

14297 Directory of Corporate Buyers
Crain Communications Inc
360 N Michigan Ave
Chicago, IL 60601-3800
312-649-5200
Fax: 312-649-7937
Home Page: www.crain.com
Keith Crain, CEO
Provides complete contact information for more that 3,200 top level corporate executives from Fortune 500 companies involved in risk management and employee benefits.
Frequency: Annual

14298 Directory of Employee Assistance Program Providers
Crain Communications Inc
360 N Michigan Ave
Chicago, IL 60601-3800
312-649-5200
Fax: 312-649-7937
Home Page: www.crain.com
Keith Crain, CEO
Lists organizations that provide a variety of EAP services to employers on a direct, stand alone basis.
Frequency: Annual
Circulation: 50,000

14299 Directory of Property Loss Control Consultants
Crain Communications
360 N Michigan Ave
Chicago, IL 60601-3800
312-649-5200
Fax: 312-649-7937
Home Page: www.crain.com
Keith Crain, CEO
Lists companies that provide loss control services on a direct, unbundled basis. Consultants that provide loss control assistance only in conjunction with other services such as brokering insurance are not listed.
Frequency: Annual
Circulation: 53,000

14300 Directory of Specialty Markets Issue
Insurance Journal
9191 Towne Centre Drive
Suite 550
San Diego, CA 92122-1231
619-584-1100
Fax: 619-584-1200
Mark Wells, Editor
Lists about 200 insurance companies and surplus lines brokers offering specialty lines to insurance agents and brokers in California, Arizona, Alaska, Oregon, Hawaii and Washington.
Cost: $10.00
Frequency: SemiAnnual
Circulation: 10,400

14301 HMO/PPO Directory
Grey House Publishing
4919 Route 22
PO Box 56
Amenia, NY 12501
518-789-8700
800-562-2139
Fax: 845-373-6390
E-Mail: books@greyhouse.com
Home Page: www.greyhouse.com
Social Media: Facebook, Twitter
Leslie Mackenzie, Publisher
Richard Gottlieb, Editor
The HMO/PPO Directory is a comprehensive source that provides detailed information about Health Maintenance Organizations and Preferred Provider Organizations nationwide. Within the HMO/PPO Profiles, over 1,300 HMOs, PPOs and affiliated companies are listed, arranged alphabetically by state.
Cost: $325.00
600 Pages
ISBN: 1-592373-69-0
Founded in 1981

14302 HMO/PPO Directory - Online Database
Grey House Publishing
4919 Route 22
PO Box 56
Amenia, NY 12501-0056
518-789-8700
800-562-2139
Fax: 518-789-0556
E-Mail: gold@greyhouse.com
Home Page: www.gold.greyhouse.com
Social Media: Facebook, Twitter
Leslie Mackenzie, Publisher
Richard Gottlieb, President
The HMO/PPO Directory - Online Database is your in-depth searchable guide to health plans nationwide - their contact information, key executives, plan information and more. The online database is a necessary tool when researching or marketing a product or service to this important industry.
Founded in 1981

14303 III Data Base Search
Insurance Information Institute
110 William St
New York, NY 10038-3908
212-346-5500
Fax: 212-732-1916
Home Page: www.iii.org
Gary Johnson, Manager
Cary Schneider, Executive Vice President
Provides citations and abstracts of insurance-related literature appearing in magazines, newspapers and trade publications and books.

14304 III Insurance Daily
Insurance Information Institute
110 William St
New York, NY 10038-3908
212-346-5500
Fax: 212-732-1916
Home Page: www.iii.org
Gary Johnson, Manager
Cary Schneider, Executive Vice President
This insurance database provides summaries of news and articles relating to the property and casualty insurance industry.
Frequency: Full-text

14305 IRU Members +
Intermediaries and Reinsurance Underwriters Assoc
971 Rte 202 North
Branchburg, NJ 08876
908-203-0211
Fax: 908-203-0213
E-Mail: info@irua.com
Home Page: www.irua.com
Jim Brost, President
List of all member companies and contacts; conference and attendee list provided to attendees only.
Founded in 1967

14306 Independent Insurance
Independent Insurance Agents of America
127 S Peyton St
Alexandria, VA 22314-2803
703-683-4422
800-221-7917
Fax: 703-683-7556
E-Mail: info@iiaba.net
Home Page: www.independentagent.com
Social Media: Facebook, Twitter
Robert A Rusbuldt, CEO
Alex Soto, President
This web site contains information for consumers on property and casualty insurance includ-

ing homeowner, renter, landlord, and automobile insurance.
Frequency: Full-text
Founded in 1896
Mailing list available for rent

14307 Insurance Almanac
Underwriter Printing & Publishing Company
244 North Main St.
P.O. Box 622
New City, NY 10956

845-634-2720
Fax: 845-634-2989
E-Mail: jgcrothers@criterionpub.com
Home Page: www.criterioninsurancedirectory.com

Over 3,000 insurance companies that write fire, casualty, accident, health and life insurance policies.
650 Pages
Frequency: Annual
Circulation: 10,000

14308 Insurance Bar Directory
Bar List Publishing Company
425 Huehl Road
Building 6B
Northbrook, IL 60062-2323

847-498-6133
800-726-1007
Fax: 847-498-6695
E-Mail: info@barlist.com
Home Page: www.barlist.com

Bruce Rodgers, President
Edna MacMillin, Editor
Leslie Rodgers, Production Manager

National Directory of Insurance Defense Attorneys that is distributed to all insurance company home office and branch office company executives and claims personnel.
Cost: $80.00
Frequency: Annual
Circulation: 40,000

14309 Insurance Companies' Directory List of Mortgage Directors
Communication Network International
3918 Avenue T
Brooklyn, NY 11234-5028

718-396-6245

Listing of 210 mortgage offices of major insurance companies that make real estate mortgages and related investments.
Cost: $75.00
Founded in 1993

14310 Kelly Casualty Insurance Claims Directory
Francis B Kelley & Associates
123 Veteran Avenue
Los Angeles, CA 90024-1900

800-328-4144
Fax: 310-472-1290
Home Page: www.fbka.com

Francis B Kelley, Editor

Lists only casualty insurance claims payment offices. Workers' Compensation and Auto Insurance can pay health care providers for their services. Directory covers Casualty Insurance Companies, Independent Claims Companies, Insurance Commissioners with their Web sites.
Cost: $150.00
280 Pages
Frequency: Annual

14311 LEXIS Insurance Law Library
Mead Data Central
9443 Springboro Pike
Dayton, OH 45401

888-223-6337
Fax: 518-487-3584
Home Page: www.lexis-nexis.com

Andrew Prozes, CEO
Rebecca Schmitt, Chief Financial Officer

This full database contains the complete text of the insurance statutes for 50 states, the District of Columbia and Puerto Rico.
Frequency: Full-text

14312 LOMA's Information Center Database
Life Office Management Association
2300 Windy Ridge Pkwy SE
Suite 600
Atlanta, GA 30339-5665

770-951-1770
800-275-5662
Fax: 770-984-0441
E-Mail: infoctr@loma.org
Home Page: www.loma.org

Thomas P Donaldson, President/CEO
Jerry Woo, Director
Robert Lai, Managing Director

A team of experienced researchers provide current data utilizing our comprehensive database. More than 10,000 documents are maintained and updated. A comprehensive list of Industry Research Links can also be found in this area.
Frequency: Available to Members

14313 Life Insurance Selling: Sources Issue
Commerce Publishing Company
330 N 4th Street
Suite 200
Saint Louis, MO 63102-2041

314-421-5445
Fax: 314-421-1070

Larry Albright, Editor

Lists life insurance companies, publishers of software used in the insurance field and financial planning corporations.
Cost: $7.00
Frequency: 45000

14314 Life Office Management Association Directory
5770 Powers Ferry Road NW
Atlanta, GA 30327-4350

770-953-6872
Fax: 770-984-0441

Philippa Griffith, Editor

Offers information on life insurance and financial service companies.
190 Pages
Frequency: Annual

14315 Morningstar
Morningstar
225 W Washington Street
Chicago, IL 60602

312-384-4000
Fax: 312-696-6001
E-Mail: productinfo@morningstar.com
Home Page: www.morningstar.com

Joe Mansueto, Chairman & CEO
Chris Boruff, President, Software Division
Peng Chen, President, Global Investment Div.
Bevin Desmond, President, International Operations
Scott Cooley, Chief Financial Officer

Morningstar provides data on approximately 330,000 investment offerings, including stocks, mutual funds, and similar vehicles, along with real-time global market data on more than 5 million equities, indexes, futures, options, commodities, and precious metals, in addition to foreign exchange and Treasury markets. Morningstar also offers investment management services and has more than $167 billion in assets under advisement and management.

14316 NAIC Database
National Association of Insurance Commissioners
1100 Walnut Street
Suite 1500
Kansas City, MO 64106-2197

816-842-3600
Fax: 816-783-8175
Home Page: www.naic.org

Sandy Praeger, President
Andrew Beal, CEO
Kevin M. McCarty, President
James J. Donelon, President-Elect
Monica J. Lindeen, Secretary-Treasurer
Mailing list available for rent

14317 National Association of Catastrophe Adjusters Membership Directory
National Association of Catastrophe Adjusters
PO Box 821864
North Richland Hills, TX 76182-1864

817-498-3466
Fax: 817-498-0480
E-Mail: nacatadj@aol.com
Home Page: www.nacatadj.org

Lori Ringo, Executive Administrator
Frequency: Annual
Circulation: 2000
Founded in 1976

14318 National Insurance Law Service/Insource Insurance
NILS Publishing Company
PO Box 2507
Chatsworth, CA 91313-2507

818-998-8830
800-423-5910
Fax: 818-718-8482
Home Page: www.nils.com

Jon Fish, Circulation Director
Karen G Beaudoin, VP Marketing
Jonathon K Fish, Production Manager

This insurance database contains the complete text of insurance codes, related laws, regulations, bulletins and selected attorney general opinions for all 50 states and the federal government. Available on CD-ROm and in looseleaf print. The CD-ROM service 'Insource Insurance' is accessible for licensed users on the NILS Publishing Website.
Cost: $520.00
Frequency: Monthly Updates
Circulation: 5,000

14319 National Underwriter Kirschner's Insurance Directories (Red Book)
National Underwriter Company
5081 Olympic Blvd
Erlanger, KY 41018-3164

859-692-2100
Fax: 859-692-2295
Home Page: www.nationalunderwriter.com

Charlie Smith, CEO
Charlie Smith, Chief Exceutive Officer

This series of 24 directories are published by state or region. Listings include companies, brokers and agents and services for each state handling property and casualty.
Cost: $19.95
150+ Pages
Frequency: Semi-Annual/Annual
Printed in on matte stock

14320 Profiles: Health Insurance Edition
National Underwriter Company

5081 Olympic Blvd
Erlanger, KY 41018-3164

859-692-2100
800-543-0874
Fax: 859-692-2295
Home Page: www.nationalunderwriter.com

Charlie Smith, CEO

Your reliable resource for up-to-date news and information in the life & health insurance/financial services industry.
Cost: $39.95
300 Pages
Frequency: Annual

14321 Profiles: Property and Casualty Insurance Edition
National Underwriter Company
505 Gest Street
Cincinnati, OH 45203-1716

513-723-0012

Edward A Lyon, Editor

Offers information on more than 1,500 property and liability insurance companies.
Cost: $39.95
852 Pages
Frequency: Annual

14322 Register of North American Insurance Companies
American Preeminent Registry
PO Box 622
Old Bridge, NJ 08857-0622

732-225-5533

Brian Axelrod, Publisher

Directory of services and supplies to the industry.
Cost: $125.00
450 Pages
Frequency: Annual

14323 Risk Retention Group Directory and Guide
Insurance Communications
PO Box 50147
Pasadena, CA 91115-0147

626-796-4972
Fax: 626-796-4972
Home Page: http://www.rrr.com

Karen Cutts, Editor

Offers information on over 80 risk retention groups formed under the 1986 Risk Retention Act or the 1981 Product Liability Risk Retention Act through 1990.
Cost: $165.00
144 Pages
Frequency: Annual

14324 Shortcut 2: Insurance Markets Tracking Systems
National Underwriter Company
505 Gest Street
Cincinnati, OH 45203-1716

513-723-0012

Directory of services and supplies to the industry.
Cost: $300.00

14325 Society of Professional Benefit Administrators
Society of Professional Benefit Administrators
2 Wisconsin Circle
Suite 670
Chevy Chase, MD 20815

301-718-7722
Fax: 301-718-9440
E-Mail: info@spbatpa.org
Home Page: www.spbatpa.org

Anne Lennan, President

For members only. Discusses and analyzes government compliance requirements of administration and plan design and industry and market trends
300 Members
350 Attendees
Frequency: 2x/Year
Founded in 1975

14326 Statistics of Fraternal Benefit Societies
1240 Iroquois Avenue
Suite 300
Naperville, IL 60563-8476

630-355-6633
Fax: 630-355-0042
Home Page: www.nfcanet.org

Anthony Snyder, Communications Director

NFCA membership is currently made up of 82 fraternal benefit societies in the United States and Canada. Each of these societies pay annual membership dues to belong to the organization and it is their executives, employees and grassroots members who serve on the NFCA Board of Directors and various NFCA committees and sections.
Cost: $11.00

14327 TPA Directory
Society of Professional Benefit Administrators
2 Wisconsin Circle
Suite 670
Chevy Chase, MD 20815

301-718-7722
Fax: 301-718-9440
E-Mail: info@spbatpa.org
Home Page: www.spbatpa.org

Frederick D Hunt Jr, President
Anne C Lennan, President-Elect

Detailed description of contact information and types of plans and services and size of each firm in an easy-to-cross-reference and compare format.
Cost: $495.00
Mailing list available for rent

14328 WESTLAW Insurance Library
West Publishing Company
610 Opperman Drive
Eagan, MN 55123-1340

651-687-7327
Home Page: www.westgroup.com

This database offers information on US state laws relating to the insurance industry.
Frequency: Full-text

14329 Weiss Ratings Consumer Box Set
Grey House Publishing
4919 Route 22
PO Box 56
Amenia, NY 12501

518-789-8700
800-562-2139
Fax: 845-373-6390
E-Mail: books@greyhouse.com
Home Page: www.greyhouse.com
Social Media: Facebook, Twitter

Leslie Mackenzie, Publisher
Richard Gottlieb, Editor

Each guide in the Weiss Ratings Consumer Box Set is packed with accurate, unbiased information, including helpful, step-by-step Worksheets & Planners. The set consists of Consumer Guides to Variable Annuities, Elder Care Choices, Medicare Supplement Insurance, Medicare Prescription Drug Coverage, Homeowners Insurance, Automobile Insurance, Long-Term Care Insurance, and Term Life Insurance.
Cost: $249.00
600 Pages
Frequency: Quarterly
Founded in 1981

14330 Weiss Ratings Guide to Health Insurers
Grey House Publishing
4919 Route 22
PO Box 56
Amenia, NY 12501

518-789-8700
800-562-2139
Fax: 845-373-6390
E-Mail: books@greyhouse.com
Home Page: www.greyhouse.com
Social Media: Facebook, Twitter

Leslie Mackenzie, Publisher
Richard Gottlieb, Editor

Weiss Ratings Guide to Health Insurers is the first and only source to cover the financial stability of the nation's health care system, rating the financial safety of more than 6,000 health maintenance organizations (HMOs) and all of the Blue Cross Blue Shield plans - updated quarterly to ensure the most accurate, up-to-date informations.
Cost: $249.00
600 Pages
Frequency: Quarterly
Founded in 1981

14331 Weiss Ratings Guide to Life & Annuity Insurers
Grey House Publishing
4919 Route 22
PO Box 56
Amenia, NY 12501

518-789-8700
800-562-2139
Fax: 845-373-6390
E-Mail: books@greyhouse.com
Home Page: www.greyhouse.com
Social Media: Facebook, Twitter

Leslie Mackenzie, Publisher
Richard Gottlieb, Edtior

Each easy-to-use edition provides independent, unbiased ratings on the financial strength of 1,000 life and annuity insurers, including companies providing life insurance, annuities, guaranteed investment contracts (GICs) and other pension products.
Cost: $249.00
600 Pages
Frequency: Quarterly
Founded in 1981

14332 Weiss Ratings Guide to Property & Casualty Insurers
Grey House Publishing
4919 Route 22
PO Box 56
Amenia, NY 12501
518-789-8700
800-562-2139
Fax: 845-373-6390
E-Mail: books@greyhouse.com
Home Page: www.greyhouse.com
Social Media: Facebook, Twitter

Leslie Mackenzie, Publisher
Richard Gottlieb, Editor

Updated quarterly, this publication is the only resource that provides independent, unbiased ratings and analyses on the 2,400 insurers offering auto & homeowners, business, worker's compensation, product liability, medical malpractice and other professional liability insur-

ance in the United States.
Cost: $249.00
600 Pages
Frequency: Quarterly
Founded in 1981

14333 Yearbook of the Insurance Industry
American Association of Managing General Agents
150 S Warner Rd
Suite 156
King of Prussia, PA 19406-2832
610-225-1999
Fax: 610-225-1996
Home Page: www.aamga.org
Bernie Heinz, Executive Director
250 managing general agents of insurance companies and more than 500 branch offices; coverage includes Canada.
Frequency: Annual Spring

Industry Web Sites

14334 http://gold.greyhouse.com
G.O.L.D Grey House OnLine Databases
Grey House Publishing's online database platform, GOLD, offers Quick Search, Keyword Search and Expert Search for most business sectors including insurance markets. The GOLD platform makes finding the information you need quick and easy - whether you're a novice searcher or an experienced database user. All of Grey House's directory products are available for subscription on the GOLD platform.

14335 www.aaimco.com
American Association of Insurance Management
Consultants

Supports the insurance management industry.

14336 www.aaimedicine.org
American Academy of Insurance Medicine
This organization offers information and legislative updates for people in the medical insurance field.

14337 www.actuary.org
American Academy of Actuaries
The AAA is a public policy organization for actuaries within the US The Academy acts as the public information organization for the profession. Assisting public policy process through the presentation of clear actuarial analysis, the Academy regularly prepares testimony for Congress, provides information to federal elected officials, regulators and congressional staff, comments on proposed federal regulations, and works closely with state officials on issues related to insurance.

14338 www.aha.org
American Society for Healthcare Risk Management
National organization for the health care industry risk management equipment, supplies and services.

14339 www.aicpcu.org
Insurance Institute of America
Sponsors programs for property and casualty insurance firms, conducts exams and award certificates. Maintains a library.

14340 www.aicpeu.org
American Institute for CPCU
An independent, nonprofit educational organization that confers the Chartered Property Casualty Underwriter professional designation on those individuals who meet its education and ethics requirements.

14341 www.allianceai.org
Alliance of American Insurers
Trade association of property and casualty insurers providing educational, legislative and safety services to its members.

14342 www.apiw.org
Association of Professional Insurance Women
Promotes cooperation and understanding among members. Maintains high professional standards and provides a network of professional contacts. Encourages women in industry.

14343 www.arbifile.org
Arbitration Forums
Arbitration Forums is a not-for-profit provider of intercompany insurance dispute resolution services. More than 2,000 insurers and self-insurers participate in AF's programs. AF resolves over 250,000 disputes with a claim value approaching 1 billion dollars.

14344 www.arminet.com
Associated Risk Managers International
Develops specialized insurance/risk management services for trade associations, professional groups and other industry organizations. Conducts seminars and sponsors competitions.

14345 www.asppa.org
American Society of Pension Professionals & Act
(ASPPA) ia a national organization for career retirement paln professionals. The membership consists of the many disciplines supporting retirement income management and benefits policy. Its members are part of the diversified, technical, and highly regulated benefits industry. ASPPA represents those who have made a career of retirement plan and pension policy work.

14346 www.awpc.org
Association of Workers' Compensation Professionals
A nonprofit organization for those engaged in the field of workers' compensation, providing members with training and certification.

14347 www.ccactuaries.org
Conference of Consulting Actuaries
Full-time consulting actuaries.

14348 www.easternclaimsconference.com
Eastern Claims Conference
Provides education and training to examiners, managers, and officers who review medical and disability claims. Holds seminars for life, health and disability clinics.

14349 www.financialpro.org
Society of Financial Service Professionals
Members are dedicated to the highest standards of competence and service in insurance and financial services.

14350 www.financialratingsseries.com
Grey House Publishing
Financial Ratings Series Online combines the strength of Weiss Ratings and TheStreet Ratings to offer the library community with a single source for financial strength ratings and financial planning tools covering Banks, Insurers, Mutual Funds and Stocks. This powerful database will provide the accurate, independent information consumers need to make informed decisions about their financial planning.

14351 www.fraternalalliance.org
American Fraternal Alliance
The trade association of America's fraternal benefit societies.

14352 www.greyhouse.com
Grey House Publishing
Authoritative reference directories for most business sectors including insurance markets. Users can search the online databases with varied search criteria allowing for custom searches by product category, geographic area, sales volume, keyword, subject and more. Full Grey House catalog and online ordering also available.

14353 www.highwaysafety.org
Insurance Institute for Highway Safety
Traffic and motor vehicle safety organization supported by auto insurers.

14354 www.hwsafety.org
Highway Loss Data Institute
Provides the public with insurance industry data concerning human and economic loss resulting from crashes.

14355 www.iasa.org
Insurance Accounting Systems Association
Facilitates the exchange of ideas among insurance industry professionals and their industry-related associates.

14356 www.icae.com
Insurance Consumer Affairs Exchange
Promotes professionalism and shapes the standards of behavior in relationships between insurance organizations, regulators and customers through proactive dialogue, research, communication and education.

14357 www.insuranceallnations.com
Allnations Insurance
Provides financial and technical assistance to new and developing cooperative insurance facilities. Promotes and develops all types of cooperative insurance organizations.

14358 www.irua.org
Intermediaries & Reinsurance Underwriters Assoc
A not-for-profit corporation, organized for the purposes of reinsurance education and research and the dissemination of information relevant to the reinsurance industry.

14359 www.ivans.com
Insurance Value Added Network Services
Industry-sponsored organization offering value added data communications network linking agencies, companies and providers of data to the insurance industry.

14360 www.nacatadj.org
National Association of Catastrophe Adjusters
Association of Catstrophe Insurance Adjusters and independent adjustment companies.

14361 www.nafi.org
National Association of Fire Investigators
Primary purpose of this association is to increase the knowledge and improve the skills of persons engaged in the investigation and analysis of fires, explosions, or in the litigation that ensues from such investigations. The Association also originated and implemented the National Certification Board.

14362 **www.nafi921.org**
National Association of Fire Investigators
Primary purpose is to increase the knowledge and improve the skills of persons engaged in the investigation and analysis of fires, explosions, or in the litigation that ensues from such investigations.

14363 **www.nahu.org**
National Association of Health Underwriters
Sponsors advanced health insurance underwriting and research seminars. Testifies before federal and state committees on pending health insurance legislation. Presents numerous awards.

14364 **www.naiw.org**
National Association of Insurance Women
Professional membership association for employees in all facets of the insurance industry. The association exists to promote continuing education and networking for the professional advancement of its members, and offers education programs, meetings, publications, services and leadership opportunities for its members' benefits.

14365 **www.ncci.com**
National Council on Compensation Insurance
Develops and administers rating plans and systems for workers compensation insurance.

14366 **www.ncoil.org**
National Conference of Insurance Legislators
NCOIL is an organization of state legislators whose main area of public policy concern is insurance legislation and regulation. Many legislators active in NCOIL either chair or are members of the committees responsible for insurance legislation in their respective state houses across the country.

14367 **www.nonprofitrisk.org**
Nonprofit Risk Management Center
Publishes materials and delivers workshops and conferences on risk management, liability and insurance issues of special concern to nonprofit organizations.

14368 **www.ontherisk.org/houla/**
Home Office Life Underwriters Association
Offers educational programs through the Academy Life Underwriting designed for professional home office underwriters.

14369 **www.plrb.org**
Property Loss Research Bureau
Provides access to legal and technical databases, legal research on property and inland marine coverage issues countrywide, claims education, and daily catastrophe information for a membership of 570 property/casualty insurance companies.

14370 **www.sirnet.org**
Society of Insurance Research
Members are individuals actively engaged in some form of insurance research.

14371 **www.snl.com**
SNL Securities
News articles on banks and thrifts, insurance and other financial services. Also features vital company information.

14372 **www.snlnet.com**
SNL Securities
This organization offers the most up-to-date information available in the insurance industry featuring the latest news releases, filings and important events. Provides current data on top-performing stocks, insider trades, ownership filings, company news and events and legislative issues.

14373 **www.soa.org**
Society of Actuaries
Nonprofit professional society of 17,000 members involved in the modeling and management of financial risk and contingent events. The mission of the SOA is to advance actuarial knowledge and to enhance the ability of actuaries to provide expert advice and relevant solutions for financial, business and societal problems involving uncertain future events.

14374 **www.spbatpa.org**
Society of Professional Benefit Administrators
National Association of Third Party Administrators (TPAs) of employee benefit health and pension plans. SPBA represents TPAs who offer comprehensive services.

14375 **www.thefederation.org**
Federation of Insurance and Corporate Counsel
For members of the bar who are actively engaged in the legal aspects of the insurance business, executives of insurance companies and associations and corporate counsel engaged in the defense of claims.

14376 **www.thepiaa.org**
Physician Insurers Association
Represents domestic and international medical malpractice insurance companies which are practioner-owned or controlled.

14377 **www.transportlaw.com**
Transportation Consumer Protection Council
Dedicated to the reduction of transit losses and the improvement of freight claim and freight charge payment procedures in domestic and international commerce.

14378 **www.users.erols.com/spba**
Society of Professional Benefit Administrators
Third-party contract administration (TPA) administers employee benefit plans for client employers and unions. It is estimated that 66 percent of US workers with employee benefits are in plans administered by TPA.

Associations

14379 **American Floorcovering Alliance**
210 W Cuyler St
Dalton, GA 30720

706-278-4101
800-288-4101
Fax: 706-278-5323
E-Mail: afa@americanfloor.org
Home Page: www.americanfloor.org

Wanda J. Ellis, Executive Director

Promotes the industry's products and services to the world, and educates the members and others through seminars, press releases, and trade shows.
Founded in 1979

14380 **American Lighting Association**
2050 N Stemmons Freeway
Ste 10046
Dallas, TX 75207

214-698-9898
800-605-4448
Home Page: www.americanlightingassoc.com
Social Media: Facebook, YouTube

Wendy E. Rollins, Dir. Of Finance
Richard D Upton, President/CEO
W. Lawrence Lauck, Vice President, Communications
Eric Jacobson, Vice President, Membership
Beth Bently, Director of Confrences

A trade association uniting lighting; component manufacturers, showrooms/distributors, manufacturer representatives; industry related companies dedicated to providing quality residential illumination in the U.S., Canada and the Caribbean.
700 Members
Founded in 1945

14381 **American Society of Interior Designers**
608 Massachusetts Avenue NE
Washington, DC 20002-6006

202-546-3480
Fax: 202-546-3240
E-Mail: membership@asid.org, asid@asid.org
Home Page: www.asid.org
Social Media: Facebook, Twitter, LinkedIn, Stagram

Thom Banks, COO
Randy Fiser, EVP/ CEO
Kevin Mulavaney, Marketing/Communications
Don Davis, Government/Public Affairs
Rick Peluso, CFO

The American Society of Interior Designers (ASID) is a community of people-designers, industry representatives, educators and students committed to interior design. Through education, knowledge sharing, advocacy, community building and outreach, the Society strives to advance the interior design profession and, in the process, to demonstrate and celebrate the power of design to positively change people's lives.
34500 Members
Founded in 1975

14382 **Association of University Interior Design**
1652 Cross Center Drive
Norman, OK 73019-5050

FAX 405-325-4164
Home Page: www.auid.org

Debra Barresse, President
Sara Powell, First VP
Debi Miller, Second VP
Susan Carlyle, Secretary
Lisa Kring, Treasurer

Provides a network for individuals who work within institutions of higher education and to promote activities designed to benefit its members through education, research, and communication.
Founded in 1979

14383 **Association of the Wall and Ceiling Industry**
513 W. Broad St.
Suite 210
Falls Church, VA 22046

703-538-1600
Fax: 703-534-8307
E-Mail: info@awci.org
Home Page: www.awci.org
Social Media: Facebook, Twitter, LinkedIn, YouTube

Steven A. Etkin, EVP/ CEO
Tom Pack, Operations Director
Mike Taylor, Seretary
John E Hinson, Treasurer
Craig Daley, President

Represents acoustic systems, ceiling systems, drywall systems, exterior insulation and finishing systms, fireproofing, flooring systems, insulation, and stucco contractors, suppliers and manufacturers and those in allied trades.
2400 Members
Founded in 1918
Mailing list available for rent

14384 **Carpet Cushion Council**
23 Courtney Circle
Bryn Mawer, PA 19010

610-527-3880
Fax: 610-527-8535
Home Page: www.carpetcushion.org

Chris Bradley, President
Gary Lanser, Vice President
Bob Ambrose, Secretary
Mark Vitale, Treasurer
G. William Haines, Executive Director

Encourages distribution and use of seperate carpet cushions. Works with regulatory agencies at the national, state and local levels.
33 Members
Founded in 1976

14385 **Carpet and Rug Institute**
100 S. Hamilton St.
Dalton, GA 30720

706-278-3176
Fax: 706-278-8835
Home Page: www.carpet-rug.org
Social Media: Facebook, Twitter, LinkedIn

Jim Jolly, CEO
Georgina Sikorski, Executive Director
Werner Braun, President

CRI is a nonprofit trade association representing the manufacturers of more than 95 percent of all carpet made in the United States, as well as service providers and their suppliers.To help increase consumers' satisfaction with carpet and to show them how carpet creates a better environment, they coordinate with other segments of the industry, such as installers, distributors, and retailers.
115 Members
Founded in 1969

14386 **Council for Interior Design Accreditation**
206 Grandvill Avenue
Suite 350
Grand Rapids, MI 49503-4014

616-458-0400
Fax: 616-458-0460
E-Mail: info@accredit-id.org
Home Page: www.accredit-id.org

Robert Wright, Chair
Holly Mattson, Executive Director
Megan Scanlan, Director of Accredidation
Laura Hozeska, Office Manager
Stacy I. Peck, Site Visit and Meeting Coordinator

Leads the interior design profession to excellence by setting standards and accrediting academic programs.
135 Members
Founded in 1970

14387 **Custom Electronic Design & Installation Association**
7150 Winton Drive
Suite 300
Indianappolis, IN 46268

317-328-4336
800-669-5329
Fax: 317-735-4012
E-Mail: info@cedia.org
Home Page: www.cedia.net

Don Gilpin, Executive Director & COO
Buzz Delano, Secretary
Gordin van Zuiden, Treasurer
Fedrico Bausone, Chairman
Jamie Antcliff, Director Marketing/Public Relations

The Custom Electronic Design & Installation Association (CEDIA) is an international trade association of companies that specialize in planning and installing electronic systems for the home. CEDIA provides educational conferences, industry professional training, and certification focused on the installation and integration of residential electronic systems that consumers use to enhance their lifestyles.
Mailing list available for rent

14388 **Foundation for Design Integrity**
1950 N Main Street
Suite 139
Salinas, CA 93906

650-326-1867
Fax: 408-449-7040
Home Page: www.ffdi.org

Justin Binnix, President
Eleanor McKay, Chairman
Susan E. Farley, Esquire

Promotes original design and to fight the unethical and illegal practice of manufacturing knockoffs. Honors those who conceive, design, engineer and develop innovative new products for the Interior and Architectural Design Community and their clients.
150+ Members
Founded in 1994

14389 **Home Fashion Partners, LLC**
524 Canterbury Rd
Bay Village, OH 44140-2410

727-443-2702
Home Page: www.homefashionpartners.com

Pam Costantini, Business Manager
John James, Manager

This organization has a list of wallcovering manufacturers and distributors aimed at the interior design community.
Founded in 1977

14390 **Illuminating Engineering Society**
120 Wall St
17th Floor
New York, NY 10005-4001

212-248-5000
Fax: 212-248-5017

E-Mail: ies@ies.org
Home Page: www.iesna.org

Daniel Salinas, President
Clayton Gordon, Marketing Manager
William Hanley, Executive Vice President
Calyton Gordon, Marketing Manager
Nick Bleeker, Treasurer

To advance knowledge and disseminate information for the improvement of the lighted environment to the benefit of society. Publishes a monthly magazine.
8500 Members
Founded in 1906

14391 **Institute of Inspection Cleaning and Restoration Certification**
4317 NE Thurston Way
Ste 200
Vancouver, WA 98662

360-693-5675
800-835-4624
Fax: 360-693-4858
E-Mail: info@iicrc.org
Home Page: www.iicrc.org
Social Media: Facebook, Twitter, LinkedIn, Google+

Patrick Winters, President & CEO
Hank Unck, 1st Vice President
Pete Duncanson, 2nd Vice President
Norm Maia, Treasurer
Kevin Pearson, Secretary

Sets standards of skill and ethics in fabric restoration industry. Works with regulatory bodies to develop proficiency standards and issues certification.
1.6M Members
Founded in 1972

14392 **Interior Design Educators Council**
9100 Purdue Rd
Suite 200
Indianapolis, IN 46268

317-328-4437
Fax: 317-280-8527
E-Mail: info@idec.org
Home Page: www.idec.org
Social Media: Facebook, Twitter, LinkedIn, YouTube, Google+, Yahoo, Flick

Jeffrey Beachum, Executive Director
Christine Saricos, Event Planner
Rachel Daeger, Marketing & Membership
John Martin-Rutherford, President
Migette Kaup, Secretary/Treasurer

Dedicated to the advancement of education and research in interior design. IDEC fosters exchange of information, improvement of educational standards, and development of the body of knowledge relative to the quality of life and human performance in the interior environment.
Founded in 1963

14393 **Interior Design Society**
164 South Main
Suite 404
High Point, NC 27260

336-884-4437
Fax: 336-885-3291
E-Mail: info@interiordesignsociety.org
Home Page: www.interiordesignsociety.org
Social Media: Facebook, Twitter, YouTube, Blogspot

Snoa Garrigan, Executive Director
Anna Mavrakis, President
Bruce Knott, Vice President
Jan Cregier, Treasurer/Secretary
Melanie Hylton, Education Coordinator

The largest design organization exclusively dedicated to serving the residential interior design industry. Promote retail interior design, emphasizing education and skills improvement.
2500 Members
Founded in 1973

14394 **International Furnishings and Design Association**
610 Freedom Business Center
Suite 110
King of Prussia, PA 19406

610-992-0011
Fax: 610-992-0021
E-Mail: info@ifda.com
Home Page: www.ifda.com
Social Media: Facebook, Twitter, LinkedIn

Diane Fairburn, President
Athena Charis, Treasurer
Martha Heinze, Executive Director
Dede Radford, Director at Large
Myra Schwartz, Educational Foundation Chair

The only all-industry association whose members provide services and products to the furnishings and design industry. IFDA is the driving force, through its programs and services, to enhance the professionalism and strature of the industry worlwide.
1400 Members
Founded in 1947

14395 **National Association of Decorative Fabric Distributors**
One Windsor Cove
Suite 305
Columbia, SC 29223

800-445-8629
Fax: 803-765-0860
E-Mail: info@nadfd.com
Home Page: www.nadfd.com

Ted Sargetakis, President
Debbye Lustig, Vice President, Membership Chair
Frank Governal, 1st Vice Presiden
Dee Duncan, Director
Kathy Gowdy, Secreatry-Treasurer

Comprised of the leading fabric distributors who reach the reupholsterers, made to order drapery and home decorator markets, and more than fifty of their major suppliers, fabric mills, fabric finishers, manufacturers of upholstery and drapery supplies.
75 Members
Founded in 1968

14396 **National Council for Interior Design Qualification, Inc.**
1602 L Street, NW
Suite 200
Washington, DC 20036-5681

202-721-0220
Fax: 202-721-0221
E-Mail: info@ncidq.org
Home Page: www.ncidq.org
Social Media: Facebook, Twitter

Carol Williams-Nickelson, Executive Director
Kim Ciesynski, President
Sharon Parkinson, Dir. Of Business Development
Lola Liao, Finance Manager
Sharon Parkinson, Dir. Of Business Development

Serves to identify to the public those interior designers who have met the minimum standards for professional practice by passing the NCIDQ examination in addition to protecting the public by identifying those individuals who are competent to practice interior design.
10000 Members
Founded in 1974

14397 **National Guild of Professional Paperhangers, Inc.**
136 S Keowee Street
Dayton, OH 45402

937-222-6477
800-254-6477
Fax: 937-222-5794
E-Mail: ngpp@ngpp.org
Home Page: www.ngpp.org
Social Media: Facebook, Twitter, LinkedIn

Kimberly Fantaci, Executive Director
Bob Banker, Secretary
Cyndi Green, President
Carl Bergaman, Treasurer
Vincent LaRusso, Vice President

Promotes products, upgrades skills of paperhangers and encourages good business ethics. Holds workshops and seminars.
650 Members
Founded in 1974

14398 **National Home Furnishings Association**
3910 Tinsley Drive
Suite 101
High Point, NC 27265-3610

336-886-6100
800-888-9590
Fax: 336-801-6102
E-Mail: info@nhfa.org
Home Page: www.nhfa.org
Social Media: Facebook, Twitter, LinkedIn, YouTube

Mary Ellen Hiatt, Executive Director
Doug Kays, President
Steven Dehaan, Executive Vice President
Carolyn McManus, Director Marketing
Larry Carroll, Advertising Executive

The nation's largest organization devoted specifically to the needs and interests of home furnishings retailers. Also to provide members with the information, education, products and services they need to remain successful.
2800 Members
Founded in 1920

14399 **North American Association of Floor Covering Distributors**
330 N. Wabash Ave.
Suite 2000
Chicago, IL 60611

312-321-6836
Fax: 312-673-6962
E-Mail: info@nafcd.org
Home Page: www.nafcd.org
Social Media: LinkedIn, YouTube

David Williams, President
Joe Reddington, Vice President
Harvey Johnson, Treasurer
George Roth, Secretary
Michelle Miller, Executive Director

Organized to foster trade and commerce for those having a business, financial, or professional interest as wholesale distributors or manufacturers of floor coverings and allied products.
557 Members
Founded in 1971

14400 **Paint and Decorating Retailers Association**
1401 Triad Center Dr
St Peters, MO 63376

636-326-2636
800-737-0107
Fax: 636-229-4750
E-Mail: info@pdra.org

Home Page: www.pdra.org
Social Media: Facebook, Twitter, LinkedIn

Dan Simon, Executive VP/Publisher
Tina Sullivan, Association Coordinator
Michael Austin, Managing Editor
Jeff Baggaley, President
Phil Merlo, VP/ Treasurer

PDRA serves the independent dealer through education, membership benefits and trade shows. The Board of Director's initiative to bring top-quality, efficient education to all independent dealers has resulted in development of a new online seminar. The PDRA Coatings Specialist course eliminates the time and expense of traveling to a seminar site. This new course can be taken right in the store, during slow times or at the dealer's convenience.
1500 Members
Founded in 1947

14401 Painting and Decorating Contractors of America
2316 Millpark Drive
Maryland Heights, MO 63043

314-514-7322
800-332-7322
Fax: 314-890-2068
E-Mail: bhoran@pdca.org
Home Page: www.pdca.org
Social Media: Facebook

Beth McDaniel, CFO
David Ayala, Chairman
David Ryker, Vice Chairman
Michael Walker, Treasurer
Richard Greene, CEO

PDCA exists to lead the industry by providing quality products, programs, services, and opportunities essential to the success of our members.
5M Members
Founded in 1884
Mailing list available for rent

14402 Professional Picture Framers Association
2282 Springport Road
Suite F
Jackson, MI 49202

517-788-8100
800-762-9287
Fax: 517-788-8371
E-Mail: ppfa@ppfa.com
Home Page: www.ppfa.com
Social Media: Facebook, Twitter, LinkedIn

John Pruitt, President
Elaine Truman, Administrative
Jeff Frazine, Trade Exhibit Sales
Nick Shaver, Membership
Sheila Pursglove, FMO

An international trade association for the art and framing industry. Supporting a membership of custom picture framers, art galleries, manufacturers, and distributors.
3000+ Members
Founded in 1971

14403 Society of Glass & Ceramic Decorated Products
PO Box 2489
Zanesville, OH 43702

740-588-9882
Fax: 740-588-0245
E-Mail: sgcd@sgcd.org
Home Page: www.sgcd.org

Mark Kelly, President
Walter Lumley, VP
Nancy Klinefelter, Secretary/Treasurer

Provides decorating professionals with a competitive edge in business by providing opporotunities for networking to learn about new decorating technologies and techniques.
525 Members

14404 Window Coverings Association of America
9707 Key West Avenue
Suite 100
Rockville, MD 20850

240-404-6490
888-298-9222
Fax: 301-990-9771
E-Mail: solutions@wcaa.org
Home Page: www.wcaa.org
Social Media: Facebook, LinkedIn

Karen Groppe, Executive Director
Linda Principe, President
Michele Williams, Vice President
Carol Collord, Treasurer
Ronica VanGelder, Secretary

The only national non-profit trade association dedicated to the retail window covering industry and to the dealers, decorators, and workrooms that are our members.
1200 Members
Founded in 1987

Newsletters

14405 Architectural Lighting
1515 Broadway
34th Floor
New York, NY 10036-8901

212-360-0660
847-763-9050
Fax: 646-654-4484
E-Mail: archl@halldata.com
Home Page: www.archlighting.com

Gary Gyss, Group Publisher
Emilie Worth Sommerhoff, Editor-in-Chief
Elizabeth Donoff, Managing Editor
Carolyn Cunningham, Brand Manager
Cliff Smith, Sales Manager

Showcases the application of lighting in architectural and interior design applications.
Circulation: 25,000
Founded in 1964

14406 Installer
National Guild of Professional Paperhangers
136 S Keowee Street
Dayton, OH 45402

937-222-6477
800-254-6477
Fax: 937-222-5794
E-Mail: ngpp@ngpp.org
Home Page: www.ngpp.org

Elsie Kaptetna CP, President
Phil Curtis CP, First VP
Vincent Larusso CP, Second VP

Promotes products, upgrades skills of paperhangers and encourages good business ethics.
Frequency: Bimonthly
Circulation: 900

14407 Mirror News
Market Power
103 2nd Street N
Hopkins, MN 55343-9276

E-Mail: feedback@mirror.co.uk
Home Page: www.mirror.co.uk

Wil Tiller, Publisher
Paul Hodd, Head of Digital

Offers interior design news and developments for professionals in the industry.
Cost: $16.00
24 Pages
Frequency: Monthly

14408 National Guild of Professional Paperhangers
136 S Keowee Street
Dayton, OH 45402

937-222-6477
800-254-6477
Fax: 937-222-5794
E-Mail: ngpp@ngpp.org
Home Page: www.ngpp.org

Kim Fantaci, Executive VP
Joseph Parker, President

Accepts advertising.
16 Pages
Founded in 1974

14409 NewsFash
American Society of Interior Designers
608 Massachusetts Avenue NE
Washington, DC 20002-6006

202-546-3480
Fax: 202-546-3240
E-Mail: asid@asid.org
Home Page:
www.asid.org/designer/ASID+Member+Benefits.htm

Julie Warren, Editor
Jennifer Lipner, Associate Editor
Rick McCosh, Director of Chapter Services
Thom Banks, COO
Rick Peluso, CFO

Bi-weekly newsletter published by the American Society of Interior Designers (ASID) that provides need-to-know design and Society news delivered biweekly. Through education, knowledge sharing, advocacy, community building and outreach, the Society strives to advance the interior design profession and, in the process, to demonstrate and celebrate the power of design to positively chang
Frequency: Bi-Weekly
Founded in 1975
Mailing list available for rent

Magazines & Journals

14410 ASID ICON
American Society of Interior Designers
608 Massachusetts Avenue NE
Washington, DC 20002-6006
202-546-3480
Fax: 202-546-3240
E-Mail: asid@asid.org
Home Page:
www.asid.org/designer/ASID+Member+Benefits.htm

Julie Warren, Editor
Jennifer Lipner, Associate Editor
Rick McCosh, Director of Chapter Services
Thom Banks, COO
Rick Peluso, CFO

ASID ICON, the magazine of the American Society of Interior Designers/ASID, provides readers with success strategies bi-monthly. ASID is a community of people-designers, industry representatives, educators and students committed to interior design. Through education, knowledge sharing, advocacy, community building and outreach, the Society strives to advance the interior design profession and, in the process, to demonstrate and celebrate the

power of design to positively change people's lives.
Frequency: Monthly
Circulation: 40,000
Founded in 1975
Mailing list available for rent

14411 Better Homes and Gardens
Meredith Corporation
1716 Locust St
Des Moines, IA 50309-3023

515-284-3000
800-678-8091
Fax: 515-284-3371
E-Mail: shareholderhelp@meredith.com
Home Page: www.meredith.com

Stephen M Lacy, CEO
Daniel M. Lagani, V.P./Publisher
Karol DeWulf Nickell, Editor in Chief

Ideas and how-to information on both new and remodeled kitchen and bath.
Cost: $11.00
Frequency: Monthly
Circulation: 7.6 mill
Founded in 1902

14412 Country Home Product Guide
Meredith Corporation
1716 Locust St
Des Moines, IA 50309-3023

515-284-2015
Fax: 515-284-3684
E-Mail: shareholderhelp@meredith.com
Home Page: www.meredith.com

David Kahn, Publisher

Offers information on residential projects focusing on innovative design work for homes with a country motif.
Frequency: Monthly

14413 Decor
Pfingsten Publishing
330 N 5th Street
Saint Louis, MO 63102-2036

314-421-5445
800-867-9285
Fax: 314-421-1070
Home Page: www.decormagazine.com

Gary S Goldman, Publisher
Alice C Gibson, Editor

In the business of furnishing helpful information, education, and marketing services that will assist art and framing retailers, distributors, and wholesalers in the manufacture and sale of their products and services, and in the successful management of their business. Every article of Decor must give art and framing retailers helpful information that they can use to make their business stronger.
Cost: $20.00
Frequency: 13 per year
Circulation: 27,000

14414 Design Solutions Magazine
Architectural Woodwork Institute
46179 Westlake Drive
Suite 120
Potomac Falls, VA 20165-5874

571-323-3636
Fax: 571-323-3630
E-Mail: awiweb@vt.edu
Home Page: www.awinet.org

David Ritchey, Editor
Judith Durham, Executive VP
Matthew Lundahl, President
Randy Jensen, Vice President
Bruce Spitz, Treasurer

Covers new commercial construction, as well as renovation. Updates on doors, paneling, laminatem plywood, architectural hardware and finishes.
Cost: $25.00
Frequency: Quarterly
Circulation: 25000
Mailing list available for rent

14415 Designers West
Designers World Corporation
8914 Santa Monica Boulevard
Los Angeles, CA 90069-4902

213-748-8291
Fax: 213-748-0039

Carol Soucek King, Editor
Rafael Nadal, President

For interior designers, architects and other design professionals involved in residential, office and hospitality projects. Accepts advertising.
Cost: $30.00
120 Pages
Frequency: Monthly
Founded in 1953

14416 Designing with Tile and Stone
Tile & Stone
20 Beekman Pl
20th Floor
New York, NY 10022-8043

212-929-0500
Fax: 212-376-7723
E-Mail: ashleepub@aol.com
Home Page: www.ashlee.com

Michelle Tillou, Owner

Articles on design, selection, installation and maintenance.
Frequency: Quarterly
Circulation: 12000

14417 Donna Dewberry's One-Day Decorating
F+W Media
38 E. 29th Street
New York, NY 10016

212-447-1400
Fax: 212-447-5231
E-Mail: contact_us@fwmedia.com
Home Page: www.fwpublications.com
Social Media: Facebook, Twitter, LinkedIn

Colleen Cannon, Publisher
David Nussbaum, CEO
Jim Ogle, Chief Financial Officer
Chad Phelps, Chief Digital Officer
Stacie Berger, Communications Director

A how-to magazine for decorative painters, crafters, and do-it-yourself home decorators. Its goal is to inspire anyone interested in embellishing their home, and it features easy-to-complete, step-by-step project ideas using decorative painting, stamping, faux finishing, stenciling, and other crafting techniques.
Cost: $27.00
76 Pages
Frequency: Monthly
Circulation: 100000
Founded in 1945
Mailing list available for rent

14418 Eye on Design
American Society of Interior Designers
608 Massachusetts Avenue NE
Washington, DC 20002-6006

202-546-3480
Fax: 202-546-3240
E-Mail: asid@asid.org
Home Page: www.asid.org/designer/ASID+Member+Benefits.htm

Julie Warren, Editor
Jennifer Lipner, Associate Editor
Rick McCosh, Director of Chapter Services
Thom Banks, COO
Rick Peluso, CFO

Eye on Design, provided by the American Society of Interior Designers\ASID, focuses on industry news and developments and is delivered electronically on a weekly basis. Through education, knowledge sharing, advocacy, community building and outreach, the Society strives to advance the interior design profession and, in the process, to demonstrate and celebrate the power of design to positively change people's lives.
Founded in 1975
Mailing list available for rent

14419 Facilities Design & Management
1515 Broadway
34th Floor
New York, NY 10036-8901

212-840-0595
800-950-1314
Fax: 212-302-6273

Anne Fallucchi, Editor-in-Chief

Covers all aspects of the planning, design and management of facilities for corporate offices and related facilities, health care, government, hospitality and education.
Frequency: Monthly

14420 Floor Care Professional
Vacuum Dealers Trade Association
2724 2nd Ave
Des Moines, IA 50313-4933

515-282-9101
800-367-5651
Fax: 515-282-4483
E-Mail: mail@vdta.com
Home Page: www.vdta.com

Charles Dunham, Owner
Beth Vitiritto, Managing Editor
Rob Heater, Managing Editor
Sherry Graham, Administrative Assistant
Judy Patterson, Vice President

Offers news and information for the distributers and dealers of vacuum and sewing machines.
Cost: $100.00
Frequency: Monthly
Circulation: 18000
Founded in 1981
Printed in 4 colors on glossy stock

14421 Flora-Line
Berry Hill Press
7336 Berry Hill Drive
Palos Verdes Estates, CA 90275-4404

310-377-7040

Dody Lyness, Editor

Targeted to the home-based business person engaged in dried floral design. Its format keeps readers abreast of the floral trends in herbal growing and the most modern techniques for drying and designing with flowering herbs. Accepts advertising.
Cost: $16.95
20 Pages
Frequency: Quarterly
Circulation: 1,000
Founded in 1981

14422 Furniture Style
400 Knightsbridge Parkway
Lincolnshire, IL 60069-3613

847-634-4339
800-621-2845
Fax: 847-634-4379
E-Mail: info@vancepublishing.com
Home Page: www.vancepublishing.com

Michael R Reckling, Publisher
Judy Riggs, Director
Steve Chair, Marketing Manager

Douglas A. Riemer, Circulation Manager
William C Vance, Chairman
Cost: $49.95
Frequency: Monthly
Circulation: 25000
Founded in 1937

14423 HOW Design Ideas at Work
F&W Publications
4700 E Galbraith Rd
Cincinnati, OH 45236-2726

513-531-2690
800-333-1115
Fax: 513-531-1843
E-Mail: editorial@howdesign.com
Home Page: www.fwpublications.com

David Nussbaum, CEO
Bryn Mooth, Chief Financial Officer
Jim Ogle, Chief Financial Officer
Kate Rados, Marketing Director
Stacie Berger, Communications Director

HOW reaches visual communicators, including art directors, graphic designers, type designers, typographers, illustrators, advertising and sales promotion managers, and other design-minded executives; also manufacturers and suppliers of graphic arts products and services.
Cost: $29.96
194 Pages
Frequency: Monthly
Circulation: 39946
ISSN: 0886-0483
Founded in 1990
Printed in 4 colors on glossy stock

14424 Home Furnishings Executive
305 W High Ave
Suite 400
High Point, NC 27260-4950

336-885-6981
800-888-9590
Fax: 336-885-4424

14425 Home Lighting & Accessories
Doctorow Communications
1011 Clifton Ave
Clifton, NJ 07013-3518

973-779-1600
Fax: 973-779-3242
E-Mail: email@homelighting.com
Home Page: www.homelighting.com

Jeffrey Doctorow, President
Cost: $15.00
Frequency: Monthly
Founded in 1953

14426 Homeworld Business
45 Research Way
Suite 106
East Setauket, NY 11733

631-246-9300
Fax: 631-246-9496
Home Page: www.homeworldbusiness.com

Ian Gittlitz, Publisher/Editor-in-Chief
Peter Giannetti, Editor
Bill McLoughlin, Executive Editor
Peter Chamberlin, Circulation Manager
Hope Rosenzweig, Classified Advertising
Cost: $185.00

14427 House Beautiful
959 8th Ave
New York, NY 10019-3737

212-649-2098
Fax: 212-765-3528
Home Page: www.hearstcorp.com

Kate Kelly Smith, Publisher
Victor F Ganzi, CEO
Bruce Paisner, VP
Michael A Hurley, Marketing Director
Cost: $19.97
Frequency: Monthly
Circulation: 854627
Founded in 1887

14428 Interior Design
Reed Business Information
360 Park Avenue South
17th floor
New York, NY 10010

212-772-8300
Fax: 630-288-8686
E-Mail: custserv@espcomp.com
Home Page: www.interiordesignmag.com
Social Media: Facebook, Twitter, LinkedIn, RSS

Lawrence S Reed
Woody Goldfien, Owner
Jim Casella, CEO

Offers information on quality residential and contract design work. Recent issues include corporate offices, remodeling/restoration, kitchen and bath design, health care and hospitality.
Cost: $64.95
250 Pages
Frequency: Monthly
Circulation: 59,000
Founded in 1932
Printed in 4 colors on glossy stock

14429 Interiors and Sources
840 US Highway 1
Suite 330
North Pal Beach, FL 33408

561-627-3393
Fax: 561-694-6578
Home Page: www.isdesignet.com

Robert Nieminen, Editor
Guy De Silva, Publisher
Charlotte Vann, Circulation Manager
Adam Moore, Managing Editor

Offers national commercial and residential design work articles. Emphasizes design solu tions and focuses on challenges encountered by designers.
Cost: $27.00
Frequency: Monthly
Circulation: 28,000
Founded in 1990

14430 Kitchen & Bath Design News
Cygnus Publishing
PO Box 803
Fort Atkinson, WI 53538-0803

920-000-1111
Fax: 920-563-1699
E-Mail: ESefrin@kbdn.net
Home Page: www.cygnusb2b.com

John French, CEO
Eliot Sefrin, Director of Public Relations
Kathy Scott, Director of Public Relations
Paul Bonaiuto, CFO

Offers articles for kitchen and bath dealers, interior designers and architects.
Frequency: Monthly
Circulation: 50000
Founded in 1966

14431 Laminating Design & Technology
Cygnus Publishing
PO Box 803
Fort Atkinson, WI 53538-0803

920-000-1111
Fax: 920-563-1699
Home Page: www.cygnusb2b.com

John French, CEO
Rich Reiff, Director of Public Relations
Kathy Scott, Director of Public Relations
Paul Bonaiuto, CFO

Global design and color trends, as well as surfacing solutions for furniture architecture and interior design. Focuses on surface design, performance and application.
Cost: $30.00
44 Pages
Frequency: Monthly
Circulation: 40006
Founded in 1937

14432 Lighting Dimensions
Primedia
PO Box 12901
Shawnee Mission, KS 66282-2901

913-341-1300
Fax: 913-514-6895
E-Mail: djohnson@primediabusiness.com

Eric Jacobson, Senior VP
David Barbour, Editorial Director
Cost: $34.97
Frequency: Monthly

14433 Metropolis
Bellerophon Publications
61 W 23rd St
23rd Street
New York, NY 10010-4246

212-627-9977
800-344-3046
Fax: 212-627-9988
E-Mail: info@metropolismag.com
Home Page: www.metropolismag.com

Horace Havemeyer, Publisher
Susan S Szenasy, Editor-in-Chief
Denise Csaky, Marketing Director
Tamara Costa, Advertising Manager
Peter Sangiorgio, Circulation Controller

The only magazine that covers all facets of design: architecture, interiors, furniture, preservation, urban design, graphics and crafts.
Cost: $32.95
Circulation: 54000
Founded in 1980

14434 Michaels Create!
F+W Media
38 E. 29th Streett
New York, NY 10016
212-447-1400
Fax: 212-447-5231
E-Mail: contact_us@fwmedia.com
Home Page: www.fwpublications.com

Debbie Knauer, Publisher
Jane Beard, Editor

Features contemporary designs reflecting the latest trends with clear instructions. The home decorating, fashion, and gift ideas will inspire experienced crafters as well as seasonal crafters to explore new possibilities. Step-by-step instructions, tips, and techniques will engage crafters of all ages - including kids - with the creative skills of crafting to be enjoyed as a year-round activity.
Cost: $21.97
116 Pages
Frequency: Monthly
Circulation: 24991
Founded in 1952

14435 Midwest Retailer
8528 Columbus Ave S
Bloomington, MN 55420-2460

952-854-7610
Fax: 952-854-6460

Joan Thomasberg, Owner
Cost: $10.00
38588 Pages
Circulation: 5000
Founded in 1972
Printed in 2 colors on newsprint stock

14436 NHFA Trade Show
National Home Furnishings Association
3910 Tinsley Drive
Suite 101
Highpoint, NC 27265-3610

336-886-6100
800-888-9590
Fax: 336-801-6102
E-Mail: info@nhfa.org
Home Page: www.nhfa.org

Steve DeHaan, Executive VP
Karin Mayfield, Senior Director for Membership
Frequency: Annual

14437 National Floor Trends
Business News Publishing Company
22801 Ventura Blvd
Suite 113
Woodland Hills, CA 91364-1230

818-224-8035
Fax: 818-224-8042
E-Mail: privacy@BNPMedia.com
Home Page: www.bnpmedia.com

Phil Johnson, Publisher
Rick Arvidson, Director

For interior designers.
Frequency: Monthly
Founded in 1952

14438 Paint & Decorating Retailer Magazine
Paint and Decorating Retailers Association
1401 Triad Center Dr
St. Peters, MO 63376-7353

636-326-2636
800-737-0107
Fax: 636-229-4750
E-Mail: info@pdra.org
Home Page: www.pdra.org

Dan Simon, Executive VP/Publisher
Tina Sullivan, Dir Membership/Education/Tradeshows
Diane Capuano, Managing Editor
Renee Nolte, Director, Finance/Human Resources
Tony Sarantakis, Account Executive

Monthly trade magazine dedicated to the informational needs of paint and decorating store owners, managers and employees.
1500 Members
Frequency: Annual May
Circulation: 26,000+
Founded in 1947

14439 Panel World
Hatton-Brown Publishers
225 Hanrick Street
PO Box 2268
Montgomery, AL 36102

334-834-1170
Fax: 334-834-4525
E-Mail: rich@hattonbrown.com
Home Page: www.hattonbrown.com

Rich Donnell, Editor
David Knight, Co-Owner
Rhonda Thomas, Circulation Director
Dianne Sullivan, Chief Operating Officer
Phil Grissett, Operations Manager
Cost: $30.00
Frequency: Monthly
Circulation: 12754
ISSN: 1048-826X
Founded in 1948
Printed in on glossy stock

14440 Perspective
13-500 Merchandise Mart
Chicago, IL 60654-1104

312-467-1950
888-799-4432
Fax: 312-467-0779
E-Mail: ahq@iida.org
Home Page: www.iida.org

John Lijewski, President
Cheryl Durst, Executive Vice President
Jocelyn Pysarchuk, Managing Director, Communications
Suzanne Murphy, Director, Membership & Chapter
Robert Friedman, Editor

International magazine of IIDA.
Cost: $30.00
Frequency: Monthly
Circulation: 10000
Founded in 1994
Mailing list available for rent: 10000 names
Printed in on matte stock

14441 Picture Framing Magazine
Hobby Publications
225 Gordon's Corner Road
PO Box 420
Manalapan, NJ 07726

732-446-4900
800-969-7176
Fax: 732-446-5488
E-Mail: gcoughlin@hobbypub.com
Home Page: www.pictureframingmagazine.com

Bruce Gherman, Executive Publisher
Anne Vazquez, Editor
Deborah Salmon, Circulation Director
Alan Pegler, Production Manager of Advertising

News and trends in the picture framing trade, marketing strategies, and economic developments.
Cost: $20.00
Frequency: Monthly
Circulation: 23000
ISSN: 1052-9977
Founded in 1995

14442 Progressive Architecture
Progressive Scale
382 S Beach Avenue
Old Greenwich, CT 06870-2223

203-792-2854
Fax: 203-748-2456

Valerie Kanter Sisca, Managing Editor

This magazine has been covering the fields of architecture and interiors for more than 60 years and publishes projects that illustrate both current trends and innovative design solutions.
Cost: $48.00
Frequency: Monthly
Circulation: 65,000

14443 Upholstery Journal
Industrial Fabrics Association International
1801 County Road B W
Roseville, MN 55113-4061

651-222-2508
800-225-4324
Fax: 651-631-9334
E-Mail: generalinfo@ifai.com
Home Page: www.ifai.com

Stephen Warner, CEO
JoAnne Farris, Marketing Director

Serves as the industry resource for after-market furniture, marine and automotive upholstery. Provides education for both the craft and business of upholstery.
Frequency: Bimonthly
Circulation: 5,000

14444 Wall Paper
Waldman Publishers
570 Fashion Ave
New York, NY 10018-1603

212-730-9590
Fax: 212-391-6610

Edited for wallcovering retailers and the wallcovering industry. Accepts advertising.
Cost: $25.00
40 Pages
Frequency: Monthly
Circulation: 18,000
Founded in 1980

14445 Wallcoverings, Windows and Interior Fashion
Cygnus Publishing
445 Broad Hollow Road
Melville, NY 11747-3669

631-845-2700
Fax: 631-845-2723
Home Page: www.cygnuspub.com

Paul Bonaiuto, CFO
Kathy Scott, Director of Public Relations

14446 Walls & Ceilings
Business News Publishing Company
2401 W. Big Beaver Rd
Suite 700
Troy, MI 48084

248-362-3700
Home Page: www.bnpmedia.com
Social Media: Facebook, Twitter, LinkedIn

Katie Rotella, Manager

Information regarding management, building methods, technology, government regulations, consumer trends, and product information for the contractor involved in exterior finishes, waterproofing, insulation, metal framing, drywall, fireproofing, partitions, stucco and plaster.
Cost: $49.00
140 Pages
Frequency: Monthly
Circulation: 32800
Founded in 1939
Printed in 4 colors

Trade Shows

14447 Accent on Design
George Little Management
10 Bank Street
Suite 1200
White Plains, NY 10606-1954

914-486-6070
800-272-7469
Fax: 914-948-2867
Home Page: www.nyigf.com

George Little II, President
Elizabeth Murphy, Show Manager

370 booths of the latest and most innovative gift lines such as decorative accessories and home furnishings.
50M Attendees
Frequency: August
Founded in 1984

14448 Aidex: Asian International Interior Design Exposition
Reed Exhibition Companies
383 Main Avenue
PO Box 6059
Norwalk, CT 06851

203-840-4800
Fax: 203-840-9628

Audio visual systems, bathroom equipment, supplies and services, plus interior decorations.

More than 22 exhibitors, for trade professionals.
Frequency: Annual

14449 **American Society of Interior Designers National Conference**
American Society of Interior Designers
608 Massachusetts Avenue NE
Washington, DC 20002-6006

202-546-3480
Fax: 202-546-3240
E-Mail: asid@asid.org
Home Page: www.asid.org

Randy Fiser, Executive Vice President/CEO
Thom Banks, COO
Rick Peluso, CFO
Deanna Waldron, Government/Public Affairs
Willie Pugh, Information Technology

Workshop and annual conference with 100 manufacturers and suppliers. Exhibits include interior design merchandise, wall coverings, laminates, lighting fixtures, plumbing fixtures, carpets, furniture, office systems and fabrics.
3000 Attendees
Frequency: Annual
Founded in 1975
Mailing list available for rent

14450 **Dickens Christmas Show & Festival**
Leisure Time Unlimited
708 Main Street
Myrtle Beach, SC 29577

843-448-9483
Fax: 843-362-6153
E-Mail: dickensshow@sc.rr.com
Home Page: www.dickenschristmasshow.com

Offers a unique blend of craft and gift exhibits presented in a 19th century setting
25000 Attendees
Frequency: Annual November

14451 **Evergreen Home Show**
Westlake Promotions
8740 Golden Gardens Dr. NW
Seattle, WA 98117

206-783-5957
Fax: 206-708-7406
Home Page: www.westlakepromo.com
Social Media: Facebook, Twitter

Bill Bradley, VP
Sam Scott, Marketing Director, Operations
Michael R. Scott, President

See what's new and what you can do for your home. Fresh ideas and practical advice from our remodeling and construction specialists. See demonstrations on how to make dramatic improvements to your home.
7500 Attendees

14452 **Fall Decor**
Paint & Decorating Retailers Association
403 Axminister Drive
Fenton, MO 63026

636-326-2636
Fax: 314-991-5039
E-Mail: info@pdra.org
Home Page: www.pdra.org

Tina Sullivan, Show Coordinator
Kathy Witmeyer, Director of Trade Shows

Annual show of 350 manufacturers, suppliers and distributors of decorating and office products and related equipment, supplies and services.
4000 Attendees
Frequency: October

14453 **Galeria**
Decor Magazine
330 N 4th Street
Saint Louis, MO 63102

314-421-5445
Fax: 314-421-1070

12000 Attendees

14454 **Holiday Fair**
Textile Hall Corporation
25 Woodslake Road
Greenville, SC 29607

864-331-2277
Fax: 864-293-0619
Home Page: http://www.holidayfairgreenville.com

25000 Attendees

14455 **Home Furnishings Summer Market**
1355 Market Street
San Francisco, CA 94103-1324

415-934-1380

Donald Preiser, Show Manager

600 booths.
30M Attendees

14456 **Home World Home & Garden Show**
Show Biz Productions
16600 Harbor Blouevard
Suite F
Fountain Valley, CA 92708

714-418-2000
877-418-2001
Fax: 714-418-2009
E-Mail: marlene@sbhomeshow.com

Rachel Perry, President
Marlene Thorne, VP

Featuring vendors of window, doors, painting, heating, air conditioning, kitchens and baths, flooring, furniture, remodeling services and more.
30000 Attendees
Founded in 1991

14457 **Home and Garden Show**
Reed Exhibition Companies
255 Washington Street
Newton, MA 02458-1637

617-584-4900
Fax: 617-630-2222

Elizabeth Hitchcock, International Sales

Home products and services.
75M Attendees
Frequency: March

14458 **IDS National Conference**
Interior Design Society
164 S Main Street
Suite 404
High Point, NC 27260

336-884-4437
888-884-4469
Fax: 336-885-3291
E-Mail: info@interiordesignsociety.org
Home Page: www.interiordesignsociety.org
Social Media: Facebook, Twitter, Youtube, Blogger

Domnick Minella, President
Snoa Garrigan, Executive Director
Dennis Novosel, Treasurer
Anna Mavrakis, VP

IDS is the largest design organization exclusively dedicated to serving the residential interior design industry. Promotes retail interior design, emphasizing education and skills improvement.
3000 Members
Founded in 1973

14459 **IFAI Annual Expo**
Industrial Fabrics Association International
1801 County Road BW
Roseville, MN 55113-4061

651-222-2508
800-225-4324
Fax: 651-631-9334
E-Mail: generalinfo@ifai.com
Home Page: www.ifai.com
Social Media: Facebook, Twitter, LinkedIn, Youtube

Beth Wistrcill, Conference Manager
Mary J. Hennessy, President and CEO
Pam Egan-Blahna, Director of Human Resources
Todd V. Lindemann, Vice President
Susan R. Niemi, Publisher

Trade event in the American for the technical textiles and specialty fabrics industry.
Frequency: Annual/September

14460 **International Home Furnishings Market**
International Home Furnishings Market Authority
POBox 5243
High Point, NC 27262

336-888-3794
800-874-6492
Fax: 336-889-6999
Home Page: www.highpointmarket.org

Judy Mendenhall, President
G Bruce Miller, CEO
Tammy Covington, Director Operations
Jan Wellmon, Executive Assistant
Shannon Kennedy, Director of Marketing

Large home furnishings trade show with a variety of new opportunities to make your visit easy, cost effective and productive. Ten million square feet of exhibition space with 2,500 manufacturers represented.
80000 Attendees
Frequency: April & October
Founded in 1921

14461 **International Silk Flower Accessories Exhibition**
Dallas Market Center
2000 N Stemmons Freeway
Dallas, TX 75207

214-655-6100
800-325-6587
Fax: 214-655-6238

8000 Attendees

14462 **LightFair**
AMC
120 Wall Street
17th Floor
New York, NY 10005

212-843-8358
Fax: 212-248-5017
Home Page: www.iesna.org

Pamela R Weess, Circulation Director
Nini Schwenk, Manager

A major lighting trade show in North America featuring architectural lighting products from all spectrons of the industry. Containing 600 booths and 400 exhibits.
17M Attendees
Frequency: June
Mailing list available for rent: 10M names at $100 per M
Printed in 4 colors on glossy stock

14463 **Museum Store Association**
4100 E Mississippi Avenue
Suite 800
Denver, CO 80246-3055

303-504-9223
Fax: 303-504-9585

E-Mail: expo@msaweb.org
Home Page: www.museumdistrict.com

Beverly Barsook, Executive Director
Stacey Woldt, Assistant Director Programs
Eric Curtis, Conference & Expo Manager
2500 Attendees
Frequency: April, Annually
Founded in 1955

14464 NGPP National Convention & Trade Show
National Guild of Professional Paperhangers
136 S Keowee Street
Dayton, OH 45402

937-222-6477
800-254-6477
Fax: 937-222-5794
E-Mail: ngpp@ngpp.org
Home Page: www.ngpp.org
Elsie Kaptetna CP, President
Phil Curtis CP, First VP
Vincent Larusso CP, Second VP

Promotes products, upgrades skills of paperhangers and encourages good business ethics. Workshops and product launches with over 130 vendors.
Frequency: Annual

14465 National Decorating Product Show
Paint & Decorating Retailers Association
403 Axminister Drive
Fenton, MO 63026-2941

636-326-2636
Fax: 314-991-5039

James B Savens III, Executive Director

430 booths for home supplies, equipment and services.
10M Attendees
Frequency: November

14466 National Decorating Products Association: Western Show
1050 N Lindbergh Boulevard
Saint Louis, MO 63132-2912

314-432-6001
Fax: 314-991-5039

Ruth Williams, Convention Manager

230 booths of decorating products such as paint, furniture and more.
2.5M Attendees
Frequency: March

14467 National Decorating Products Southern Show
Paint & Decorating Retailers Association
403 Axminister Drive
Fenton, MO 63026-2941

636-326-2636
Fax: 314-991-5039

Ruth Williams, Convention Manager

850 display booths of floor coverings, paint, furniture and various interior decorating products.
4M Attendees
Frequency: February

14468 Needlework Markets
Needlework Markets
PO Box 533
Pine Mountain, GA 31822

706-663-0140
Fax: 706-663-0202
Home Page: www.stitching.com

Emily Castleberry, Owner
Frequency: February

14469 Old House New House Home Show
Kennedy Productions
1208 Lisle Place
Lisle, IL 60532-2262

630-515-1160
Fax: 630-515-1165
E-Mail: info@kennedyproductions.com
Home Page: www.kennedyproductions.com

Laura McNamara, Event Producer
Joanne Kennedy, President

Over 300 home improvement exhibitors displaying cutting-edge home enhancements for kitchens, baths, home and garden including landscape, interior remodeling, pools, spas, floors, doors and more.
8000 Attendees
Frequency: Feb/Sept
Founded in 1977

14470 PDCA Painting & Decorating Expo
Paint and Decorating Retailers Association
1401 Triad Center Dr
St. Peters, MO 63376-7353

636-326-2636
800-737-0107
Fax: 636-229-4750
E-Mail: info@pdra.org
Home Page: www.pdra.org

Dan Simon, Executive VP/Publisher
Tina Sullivan, Dir Membership/Education/Tradeshows
Diane Capuano, Managing Editor
Renee Nolte, Director, Finance/Human Resources
Tony Sarantakis, Account Executive

Over thiry education sessions, multiple special networking events and the latest in products and services to support the trade.
2000 Members
Frequency: May
Founded in 1947

14471 Paint Industries Show
492 Norristown Road
Blue Bell, PA 19422-2355

610-940-0777
Fax: 215-840-0292

Robert F Ziegler, Show Manager

Exhibits of raw materials, production equipment, instrumentation and testing apparatus for the coatings, inks and adhesives manufacturing industries. 920 booths.
3.5M Attendees
Frequency: October

14472 Painting and Decorating Contractors of America National Convention
3913 Old Lee Highway
Suite 301
Fairfax, VA 22030-2433

703-359-0826
Fax: 703-359-2976

Mary S DePersig, Director Meetings

200 booths of painting, wallcoverings, coatings and sundries.
1.2M Attendees
Frequency: March

14473 Surtex
George Little Management
10 Bank Street
Suite 1200
White Plains, NY 10606-1954

914-486-6070
800-272-7469
Fax: 914-948-6180
E-Mail: SURTEX@glmshows.com
Home Page: www.SURTEX.com

Gina DeLuca, Show Coordinator
Rita Malek, Show Manager
George Little II, President

Annual show of 350 exhibitors featuring prints and patterns for all applications-decorative fabrics, linens, and domestics, apparel and contract textiles, wall and floor coverings, greeting cards, giftwrap and other paper products, tabletop, ceramics and packaging. Available for sale and/or license.
5000 Attendees
Frequency: May

14474 TEXBO
Reed Exhibition Companies
255 Washington Street
Newton, MA 02458-1637

617-584-4900
Fax: 617-630-2222

Elizabeth Hitchcock, International Sales

International trade fair for the interior design industry.
7M Attendees
Frequency: January

14475 Tabletop Market
George Little Management
577 Airport Boulevard
Burlingame, CA 94010-2020

650-548-1200
800-272-SHOW
Fax: 650-344-5270
E-Mail: customer_relations@glmshows.com
Home Page: www.glmshows.com/table

Susan Corwin, VP

Annual show of 90 exhibitors featuring tableware, table linens, better housewares and decorative accessories.
1500 Attendees
Frequency: October

14476 West Coast Art and Frame
Art Trends/Picture Framing/Digital Fine Arts
PO Box 594
Lynbrook, NY 11563

516-596-3937
Fax: 516-596-3941

3500 Attendees

Directories & Databases

14477 Carpet & Rug Industry Buyers Guide Issue
Rodman Publishing
17 S Franklin Tpke
Ramsey, NJ 07446-2522

201-252-2552

More than 300 suppliers of machinery, equipment and colors and dyes used in the making of carpets and rugs.
Cost: $7.00
Frequency: Annual
Circulation: 5,500

14478 Carpet Cleaners Institute of the Northwest Membership Roster
Carpet Cleaners Institute of the Northwest
PMB #40 2421 South Union Avenue
Suite L-1
Tacoma, WA 98405

253-759-5762
877-692-2469
Fax: 253-761-9134
E-Mail: info@ccinw.org
Home Page: www.ccinw.org

Lyle Neville, President
Matt O'Haleck, Treasurer
Jim Thomas, Secretary
Mike Elias, Director of Education

Over 330 member companies involved in the carpet cleaning industry in Washington, Oregon, and Montana, USA and Alberta and British Columbia, Canada.
Frequency: Annual

14479 Decor-Sources Issue
Commerce Publishing Company
330 N 4th Street
Suite 200
Saint Louis, MO 63102-2041

314-421-5445

Over 1,200 wholesale suppliers of pictures, frames, interior accessories and mirrors to art galleries and home accessories retailers are profiled.
Cost: $5.00
Frequency: Annual
Circulation: 35,000

14480 Decorating Registry
Paint and Decorating Retailers Association
1401 Triad Center Dr
St. Peters, MO 63376-7353

636-326-2636
800-737-0107
Fax: 636-229-4750
E-Mail: info@pdra.org
Home Page: www.pdra.org

Dan Simon, Executive VP/Publisher
Tina Sullivan, Dir Membership/Education/Tradeshows
Diane Capuano, Managing Editor
Renee Nolte, Director, Finance/Human Resources
Tony Sarantakis, Account Executive

A searchable industry database listing paint and decorating companies, products, trademarks, distributors and manufacturer reps.
Cost: $15.00
1500 Members
200 Pages
Frequency: Annual, Magazine
Founded in 1947
Printed in on glossy stock

14481 Decorating Retailer's Decorating Registry
National Decorating Products Association
1050 N Lindbergh Boulevard
Saint Louis, MO 63132-2912

314-432-6001
800-737-0107
Fax: 314-991-5039

Ernest Stewart, Executive VP
Cindy Nusbaum, Directories Editor

Trademark and brand name directory covering paint, wallcovering, window covering, floor covering and related sundries.
Cost: $9.00
Frequency: Annual
Circulation: 30,000
Mailing list available for rent: 30,000+ names
Printed in 4 colors on glossy stock

14482 Decorating Retailer: Directory of the Wallcoverings Industry Issue
National Decorating Products Association
1050 N Lindbergh Boulevard
Saint Louis, MO 63132-2912

314-432-6001
800-737-0107
Fax: 314-991-5039

Ernest Stewart, Publisher
Cindy Nusbaum, Editor

Over 1,000 manufacturers and distributors of wallcoverings and related products are listed.
Cost: $25.00
Frequency: Annual
Circulation: 5,000
Printed in 4 colors

14483 DesignSource: Official Specifying and Buying Directory
PO Box 5059
Hoboken, NJ 07030-1501

201-963-9000

More than 10,000 companies that manufacture or supply products or services for interior designers.
Cost: $25.00
Frequency: Annual
Circulation: 40,000

14484 Directory of African American Design Firms
San Francisco Redevelopment Agency
770 Golden Gate Avenue
San Francisco, CA 94102

415-749-2400
Fax: 415-749-2526

Over 100 architectural, engineering, planning and landscape design firms.
Frequency: Annual December

14485 Draperies & Window Coverings: Directory and Buyer's Guide Issue
LC Clark Publishing Company
840 US Highway 1
Suite 330
North Palm Beac, FL 33408-3878

561-627-3393
Fax: 561-694-6578

John Clark, Owner
Sarah Christy, Associate Editor
Katie Sosnowchik, Senior Editor

Over 2,000 manufacturers and distributors of window coverings and other products used in the window coverings and interior fashions industry.
Cost: $15.00
Frequency: Annual

14486 ENR Directory of Design Firms
McGraw Hill
PO Box 182604
Columbus, OH 43272

877-833-5524
Fax: 614-759-3749
E-Mail: customer.service@mcgraw-hill.com
Home Page: www.mcgraw-hill.com
Social Media: Facebook, Twitter, LinkedIn, Blog, Youtube, Social

Paul Hermannsfeldt, Editor
Harold McGraw III, Chairman, President
Jack F. Callahan, Executive Vice President
John Berisford, Executive Vice President
Mary Jo Vittor, Executive Vice President

Profiles of 88 architects, architectural engineers, consultants and other design firms; limited to advertisers.
Cost: $95.00
Frequency: Biennial
Mailing list available for rent

14487 ENR: Top 500 Design Firms Issue
McGraw Hill
1221 Avenue of the Americas
Suite C3A
New York, NY 10020-1095

212-512-2000
Fax: 212-512-3840
E-Mail: webmaster@mcgraw-hill.com
Home Page: www.mcgraw-hill.com

Harold W McGraw III, CEO

List of 500 leading architectural, engineering and specialty design firms selected on basis of annual billings.
Cost: $35.00
Frequency: Annual April
Circulation: 71,000

14488 Flooring: Buying and Resource Guide Issue
Leo Douglas
9609 Gayton Road
Suite 100
Richmond, VA 23233-4904

Lists various manufacturers, workrooms, manufacturers' representatives and distributors of floor, and other interior surfacing products and equipment.
Cost: $38.50
Frequency: Annual
Circulation: 24,000

14489 Home Lighting & Accessories Suppliers Directory
Doctorow Communications
1011 Clifton Ave
Clifton, NJ 07013-3518

973-779-1600
Fax: 973-779-3242
E-Mail: info@homelighting.com
Home Page: www.homelighting.com

Jeffrey Doctorow, President
Linda Longo, Editor-in-Chief
Susan Grisham, Managing Editor
Dina Tamburro, Associate Publisher

A list of over 1,000 suppliers of lighting fixtures and other products for use in the retail lighting industry are provided.
Cost: $6.00
Frequency: Semi-Annual
Circulation: 9,690

14490 Interior Decorators Handbook
EW Williams Publications
370 Lexington Ave
Suite 1409
New York, NY 10017-6583

212-661-1516
Fax: 212-661-1713
Home Page: www.williamspublications.com

Philippa Hochschild, Publisher
Phillip Russo, Publishing Director
Lynne Lancaster, Advertising Sales Director

Designers resource guide with over 600 product/service categories. 3,000 suppliers are listed with their headquarters, showrooms. Addresses, phone numbers, fax numbers and e-mail.
Cost: $36.00
230 Pages
Frequency: Bi-annual
Circulation: 25,000
Founded in 1922
Printed in 4 colors on glossy stock

14491 LDB Interior Textiles Annual Buyers' Guide
EW Williams Publications
370 Lexington Ave
Room 1409
New York, NY 10017-6583

212-661-1516
Fax: 212-661-1713
Home Page: www.williamspublications.com

Philippa Hochschild, Publisher

Over 2,000 manufacturers and importers of home accessories and interior design products are listed.
Cost: $40.00
Frequency: Monthly
Circulation: 14000
Founded in 1927

14492 Market Resource Guide
International Home Furnishings Center

PO Box 828
High Point, NC 27261-0828

336-888-3700
Fax: 336-882-1873
E-Mail: marketing@ihfc.com
Home Page: www.ihfc.com

Bruce Miller, CEO

Two-volume directory offers over 1,500 manufacturers and distributors in the furniture industry with exhibits at the International Home Furnishings Market.
Cost: $25.00
624 Pages
Frequency: Semiannual
Founded in 1974
Printed in 4 colors on glossy stock

14493 **Painting and Wallcovering Contractor**
Painting and Decorating Contractors of America
2316 Millpark Drive
Suite 220
Maryland Heights, MO 63043

314-514-7322
800-332-7322
Fax: 314-514-9417
E-Mail: bhoran@pdca.org
Home Page: www.pdca.org
Social Media: Facebook

Beth Horan, VP Operations
David Ayala, Chairman
David Ryker, Vice Chairman
Darylene Dennon, Treasurer

Offers a list of over 3,300 member contractors engaged in painting, decorating and special coatings applications.
Frequency: Annual
Circulation: 3,500
Mailing list available for rent

14494 **Rauch Guide to the US Paint Industry**
Grey House Publishing
4919 Route 22
PO Box 56
Amenia, NY 12501

518-789-8700
800-562-2139
Fax: 845-373-6390
E-Mail: books@greyhouse.com
Home Page: www.greyhouse.com
Social Media: Facebook, Twitter

Leslie Mackenzie, Publisher
Richard Gottlieb, Editor

Provides industry structure and current market information about this $16.6 billion industry. The report is divided into five major chapters with 100+ tables and 20 figures in its 500 pages. Unique to the Guide is a profile over 800 industry manufacturers, with sales estimates, products, mergers and acquisitions, divestitures and other information for the 400 largest companies.
Cost: $595.00
500 Pages
ISBN: 1-592371-27-2
Founded in 1981

14495 **Specifiers' Guide and Directory of Contract Wallcoverings**
Wall Publications
570 Fashion Ave
New York, NY 10018-1603

212-730-9590

Anne Gober, Owner

A who's who directory of services and supplies to the industry.
Cost: $15.95
Frequency: Annual
Circulation: 15,000

14496 **Tile & Decorative Surfaces**
18 E 41st Street
New York, NY 10017-6222

212-376-7722
Fax: 212-376-7723
E-Mail: publisher@ashlee.com
Home Page: www.ashlee.com/tile

Jordan M Wright, President/Publisher

The Tile industry including ceramic, natural stone, terrazzo, agglomerated, cement glasstiles and others allied to the field. Architects, designers, importers, retail floor covering dealers, distributors, installers and contractors. Also, firms involved with renovation and restoration of tile. Accepts advertising.
Cost: $25.00
Frequency: Monthly
Circulation: 24,000
ISSN: 0192-9550
Founded in 1950

14497 **Wallcovering Pattern Guide and Source Directory**
Home Fashion Information Network
557 S Duncan Avenue
Clearwater, FL 33756-6255

A list of wallcovering manufacturers and distributors are offered in this comprehensive directory aimed at the interior design community.
Cost: $78.00
Frequency: Semiannual
Circulation: 10,000

14498 **Western Floors: Buyers Guide & Directory**
Specialist Publications
17835 Ventura Boulevard
Suite 312
Encino, CA 91316-3634

818-709-1437

A list of firms which manufacture, import or distribute floor coverings.
Cost: $15.00
Frequency: Annual
Circulation: 17,000

14499 **Who's Who in Floor Covering Distribution**
National Association of Floor Covering Distributor
122 S. Michigan Avenue
Suite 1040
Chicago, IL 60603

312-461-9600
Fax: 312-461-0777
E-Mail: info@nafed.org
Home Page: www.nafed.org

Jack Lidenschmidt, President
Danny Harris, Executive Director/CEO
Norbert Makowka, Vice President, Technical
Tamara Matthews, Communications Coordinator
Socorro Garcia, Office Manager

Offers information on over 400 member distributors and suppliers of floor coverings.
40 Pages
Frequency: Annual
Mailing list available for rent

Industry Web Sites

14500 **http://gold.greyhouse.com**
G.O.L.D Grey House OnLine Databases

Grey House Publishing's online database platform, GOLD, offers Quick Search, Keyword Search and Expert Search for most business sectors including interior design, decorating and lighting markets. The GOLD platform makes finding the information you need quick and easy - whether you're a novice searcher or an experienced database user. All of Grey House's directory products are available for subscription on the GOLD platform.

14501 **www.carpet-rug.com**
Carpet and Rug Institute

National association of carpet and rug manufacturers. Source for product information.

14502 **www.fider.org**
Foundation for Interior Design Education Research

Promotes excellence in interior design education through research and the accreditation of academic programs.

14503 **www.greyhouse.com**
Grey House Publishing

Authoritative reference directories for most business sectors including interior design, decorating and lighting markets. Users can search the online databases with varied search criteria allowing for custom searches by product category, geographic area, sales volume, keyword, subject and more. Full Grey House catalog and online ordering also available.

14504 **www.homeshows.net**
Home Show Management

Organizes three annual south Flordia home design and remodeling shows in Coconut Grove, Ft. Lauderdale and Miami Beach convention centers. Open to the trade and public.

14505 **www.i-d-d.com**
Interior Design Directory

Sources and links for the interior designer.

14506 **www.iesna.org**
Illuminating Engineering Society of North America

To advance knowledge and disseminate information for the improvement of the lighted environment to the benefit of society. Publishes a monthly magazine.

14507 **www.iida.org**
International Interior Design Association

Members are professionals from various facets of the interior design trade.

14508 **www.interiordesignsociety.org**
Interior Design Society

The largest design organization exclusively dedicated to serving the residential interior design industry. Promotes retail interior design, emphasizing education and skills improvement.

14509 **www.nadfd.com**
National Assn of Decorative Fabric Distributors

Promotes the textile and home furnishings manufacturers and distributors.

14510 **www.nafcd.org**
National Assn of Floor Covering Distributors

This organization offers information on over 500 member distributors and suppliers of floor coverings. Publications available to members.

14511 **www.ncidq.org**
National Council for Interior Design Qualification

Serves to identify to the public those interior designers who have met the minimum standards for professional practice by passing the NCIDQ examination.

14512 **www.ngpp.org**
National Guild of Professional Paperhangers

Promotes products, upgrades skills of paperhangers and encourages good business ethics. Holds workshops and seminars.

14513 www.nhfa.org
National Home Furnishings Association
A federation of local home furnishings representatives association.

14514 www.oikos.com
Oikos
Devoted to serving professionals whose work promotes sustainable design and construction. Oikos is a Greek word meaning house. Oikos serves as the root for two English words: ecology and economy. That may seem contradictory at first, but it makes perfect sense. Ecology is the science of interactions in natural communities. It examines the web of life where plants, animals, rocks and gases all affect one another. Healthy communities, healthy ecosystems exist ina dynamic equilibrium.

14515 www.pdra.org
Paint and Decorating Retailers Association
This organization lists 1,500 manufacturers, manufacturers' representatives, distributors, and suppliers of decorating merchandise.

14516 www.resources.com
Resources
Organized into easy point and click directories under a highly interactive database.

Associations

14517 **Academy of International Business**
The Eli Broad College of Businesss, Eppley Cent
645 N. Shaw ln Rm 7
East Lansing, MI 48824

517-432-1452
Fax: 517-432-1009
E-Mail: aib@aib.msu.edu
Home Page: aib.msu.edu
Social Media: Facebook, Twitter, LinkedIn

G Tomas M Hult, Executive Director
Tunga Kiyak, Managing Director
Irem Kiyak, Treasurer
Robert Grosse, President
Peter Liesch, VP, Administration

Leading association of scholars and specialists in the field of international business. Members include academics, consultants, researchers, and NGO representatives. AIB has chapters worldwide to facilitate networking and information exchange at a local level.
3200 Members
Founded in 1981
Mailing list available for rent: 3000 names at $250 per M

14518 **American Association of Exporters and Importers**
1050 17th St NW
Suite 810
Washington, DC 20036-5514

202-857-8009
Fax: 202-857-7843
E-Mail: hg@aaei.org
Home Page: www.aaei.org
Social Media: Facebook, Twitter

Marianne Rowden, President and CEO
Richelle Wilkins, Director Meetings & Events
Claib Cook, Secetary/ Treasurer
David A Potts, Manager Office Administration
Chris Enyart, Manager of Member & Media Affairs

Supports those involved in trade development with other countries and conducting business in the United States, as well as developments affecting trade originating from Treasury, Customs, US Courts, Commerce Department, International Trade Commission, Federal Maritime Commission and other regulatory agencies. Hosts annual trade show.
Founded in 1921

14519 **American Foreign Service Association**
2101 E Street NW
Washington, DC 20037

202-338-4045
Fax: 202-338-6820
Home Page: www.afsa.org
Social Media: Facebook, Twitter, YouTube, Flickr

Robert J. Sullivan, President
Sharon Wayne, Vice President
David Mergen, Vice President
Ian Houston, Executive Director
Patrick Bradley, Executive Assistant

Organization dedicated specifically to preserving and enhancing theintegrity of the U.S. Foreign Service.
31000 Members
Founded in 1924

14520 **American League for Exports and Security Assistance**
122 C St NW
Suite 740
Washington, DC 20001-2109

202-393-3903
Fax: 202-737-4727

David Lewis, President

Encourages and supports the sale of American defense products abroad in agreement with foreign policy, security and economic goals of the nation.
38 Members
Founded in 1976

14521 **Assist International**
90 John Street
Room 505
New York, NY 10038

212-244-2074
Fax: 831-439-9602
E-Mail: info@assist-intl.com
Home Page: www.assist-intl.com

International trade promotion and consulting firm: mailing lists, seminars, conferences, international business expo.

14522 **Association Of American Chambers of Commerce in Latin America**
1615 H St NW
Washington, DC 20062-2000

Home Page: www.aaccla.org

Nicholas Galt, Chair
Thomas H. Kenna, Vice Chair
Aldo Defilippi, VP for Executive Management
Neil Herrington, Executive Vice President
Alejandro Diaz, VP for Membership Relations

Promotes trade and investment between the United States and the countries of the region through free trade, free markets, and free enterprise.
20000 Members

14523 **CalChamber Council for International Trade**
1215 K Street
Suite 1400
Sacramento, CA 95814

916-444-6670
800-649-4921
Fax: 916-325-1272
Home Page: www.calchamber.com
Social Media: Facebook, Twitter, LinkedIn

Allan Zaremberg, President/CEO
Debi Hobson, Executive Assistant
Ann Amioka, VP, Communications
Drew Savage, VP, Corporate Relations
Karen Olson, VP, Marketing

Formed by the merging of California Council for International Trade and California Chamber of Commerce International Trade Committee. The foundation is dedicated to preserving and strengthening the California business climate and private enterprise through accurate, impartial research and education on public policy issues of interest to the California business and public policy communities.
15000 Members
Founded in 1890
Mailing list available for rent

14524 **Customs and International Trade Bar Association**

Home Page: www.citba.org

Joseph W. Dorn, President
Lawrence M. Friedman, Vice President
Melvin S. Schwechter, Chair, Export Committee
Kathleen W. Cannon, Secretary
William Sjoberg, Treasurer

Members represent importers, exporters, and domestic producers in matters involving U.S. customs laws, antidumping and countervailing duty laws, safeguards, export licensing, and other federal laws and regulations that affect imported or exported merchandise or international commerce.
Founded in 1917

14525 **FSC/DISC Tax Association**
Council for International Tax Education
PO Box 1012
White Plains, NY 10602
914-328-5656
800-207-4432
Fax: 914-328-5757
E-Mail: info@citeusa.org
Home Page: www.citeusa.org

Robert Ross, Owner

The only organization operating on a national level devoted to educational interests of companies that have set up a foreign sales corporation.
300 Members
Founded in 1984
Mailing list available for rent

14526 **Foreign Trade Association**
437 S. Cataract Avenue
Suite #4B
San Dimas, CA 91773

888-223-6459
Fax: 310-220-4474
E-Mail: info@foreigntradeassociation.com
Home Page: www.foreigntradeassociation.com
Social Media: Facebook, Twitter, LinkedIn

Keith Sanchez, Chairman
Tom Gould, President
Adonna Martin, 1st VP
Cameron Roberts, 2nd VP
Glenn Patton, Treasurer

Business association of European and International commerce that promotes the values of free trade.

14527 **Forum for International Trade Training**
116 Lisgar Street
Suite 300
Ottawa, ON K2P 0C2

613-230-3553
800-561-3488
Fax: 613-230-6808
E-Mail: info@fitt.ca
Home Page: www.fitt.ca
Social Media: Facebook, Twitter, LinkedIn, Traderead y, Flickr

Bill Walsh, Chair
Leslie Meingast, Vice Chair
Paloma Healey, Board Member
Scott Forbes, Board Member
Carl Burlock, Treasurer

Nonprofit organization that develops international business programs, sets competency standards, designs the certification and accreditation programs for the Certified International Trade Professional (CITP) designation, and generally ensures continuing professional development in the practice of international trade.
Founded in 1992

14528 **Futures Industry Association**
2001 Pennsylvia Ave. NW
Suite 600
Washington, DC 20006-1823

202-466-5460
Fax: 202-296-3184
E-Mail: info@futuresindustry.org

Home Page: www.futuresindustry.org/
Social Media: Facebook, Twitter, LinkedIn

Gerald Corcoran, Chair
Walter L. Lukken, President & CEO
Mary Ann Burns, EVP & COO
Will Acworth, SVP, Communications
Guy Sheetz, SVP & CFO

Trade association in the United States composed of futures commission merchants.
Founded in 1955

14529 **Gemini Shippers Group National Fashion Accessories Assoc**
137 West 25th St.
3rd Floor
New York, NY 10001

212-947-3424
Fax: 212-629-0361
E-Mail: info@Geminishippers.com
Home Page: www.geminishippers.com

Sara Mayes, President
Harold Sachs, Executive Director

Offers membership to importers and exporters of various products.
200 Members
Founded in 1916

14530 **Hong Kong Association of New York**
115 East 54th Street
New York, NY 10022-4563

646-770-1676
E-Mail: contact@hkany.org
Home Page: www.hkany.org

Mary Wadsworth Darby, Chair
Sylvia S. Ng, Vice Chair
Amy Shang, Vice Chair
Ying Yen, Executive Director
Raymond H. Wong, Treasurer

Nonprofit organization that promotes global cooperation, communication exchange and synergy among the Hong Kong business associations worldwide.
1100 Members
Founded in 1987

14531 **Hong Kong Trade Development Council**
38/F Office Tower
Convention Plaza, 1 Harbour Rd.
Wanchai, HK 10017-2951

852-183- 668
800-820-5188
Fax: 852-282- 024
E-Mail: hktdc@hktdc.org
Home Page: www.hktdc.com
Social Media: Facebook, Twitter, LinkedIn, Google+, YouTube, RSS Feed

Fred Lam, Executive Director
Margaret Fong, Deputy Executive Director
Raymond Yip, Asst. Executive Director
Lawrence Yipp, Asst. Executive Director

Promotes trade between the United States and Hong Kong.
Founded in 1966
Mailing list available for rent

14532 **International Chamber of Commerce (ICC)**
33-43 Ave. du President Wilson
Paris, Fr 75116

33- 0 -1 49
Fax: 3- 0- 1 4
E-Mail: icc@iccwbo.org
Home Page: www.iccwbo.org
Social Media: Facebook, Twitter, LinkedIn, Google+, YouTube

Gerard Worms, Chairman
Harold McGraw III, Vice Chairman
Founded in 1919
Mailing list available for rent

14533 **International Reciprocal Trade Association**
524 Middle Street
Portsmouth, VA 23704

FAX 757-257-4014
E-Mail: ariggs@comcast.net, ron@irta.com
Home Page: www.irta.com
Social Media: Facebook, LinkedIn, Google+, YouTube

Annette Riggs, President
Scott Whitmer, Vice President
Ron Whitney, Executive Director
Chong Kee Tan, Secretary
Mary Ellen Rosinski, Treasurer

A nonprofit organization committed to promoting just and equitable standards of practice and operation within the Modern Trade and Barter and otherAlternative Capital Systems Industry.
Founded in 1979

14534 **International Trade Administration**
U.S. Department of Commerce
1401 Constitution Ave NW
Washington, DC 20230

800-USA-TRAD
Home Page: trade.gov
Social Media: Facebook, Twitter, Blog

Tim Rosado, CFO & CAO
Kurt S. Bersani, Deputy CFO & CAO
Victor Powers, Business Operations
Michael House, Budget
Anne McDonagh, Financial Management

An agency in the United States Department of Commerce that promotesUnited States exports of nonagricultural U.S. services and goods.

14535 **International Trade and Finance Association**
PO Box 2145
Kingsville, TX 78363

E-Mail: itfaconf@ymail.com
Home Page: www.itfaconf.org

Jorge Gonzalez, President
Nathalie de Marcellis-Warin, VP of Membership
Alfred Eckes, EVP
Lucian Cernat, Board Member
Pompeo Della Posta, Board Member

A multidisciplinary association for academics and professionals interested in studying international trade and finance and in promoting a general awareness of these fields and related global economic issues.
Founded in 1988

14536 **International Trademark Association**
655 Third Avenue
10th Floor
New York, NY 10017

212-642-1700
Fax: 212-768-7796
E-Mail: memberservices@inta.org
Home Page: www.inta.org/
Social Media: Facebook, Twitter, LinkedIn

J. Scott Evans, President
Tish Berard, Vice President
Joseph Ferretti, VP- Secretary
Etienne Sanz de Acedo, CEO
Ang Eng, Dir. Of Education

A global association of trademark owners and professionals dedicated to supporting trademarks and related intellectual property in order to protectconsumers and to promote fair and effective commerce.
6400 Members
Founded in 1878

14537 **International Warehouse Logistics Association**
2800 S River Rd
Suite 260
Des Plaines, IL 60018

847-813-4699
Fax: 847-813-0115
E-Mail: email@iwla.com
Home Page: www.iwla.com
Social Media: Facebook, Twitter, LinkedIn

Joel Anderson, President/CEO
Paul Verst, Chairman
Tom Herche, Vice Chairman
Rob Doyle, Treasurer
Mark DeFabis, Secretary

The unified voice of the global logistics outsourcing industry, representing third party warehousing, transportation and logistics service providers. Our member companies provide the most timely and cost-effective global logistics solutions for their customers and are committed to protecting the free flow of products across international borders.
500 Members
Founded in 1891
Mailing list available for rent

14538 **Italian Trade Agency**
33 E 67th St
New York, NY 10065-5949

212-980-1500
Fax: 212 758-1050
E-Mail: newyork@ice.it
Home Page: www.italtrade.com

Trade promotion section of the Italian Consulate.

14539 **Latin American Studies Association**
University of Pittsburgh
416 Bellefield Hall
University of Pittsburgh
Pittsburgh, PA 15260

412-648-7929
Fax: 412-624-7145
E-Mail: lasa@pitt.edu
Home Page: lasa.international.pitt.edu/

Merilee Grindle, President
Debra Castillo, VP
Timothy J. Power, Treasurer
Philip Oxhorn, Editor of LARR
Milagros Pereyra-Rojas, Executive Director

To foster intellectual discussion, research, and teaching on Latin America, the Caribbean, and its people throughout the Americas, promote the interests of its diverse membership, and encourage civic engagement through network building and public debate.
5000+ Members
Mailing list available for rent

14540 **MIQ Logistics, LLC**
11501 Outlook Street
Suite 500
Overland Park, KS 66211

913-696-7100
877-246-4909
Fax: 913-696-7501
E-Mail: contact_us@miq.com
Home Page: www.meridianiq.com
Social Media: Facebook, Twitter, LinkedIn, Google+, RSS Feed

Brenda Stasiulis, CFO
Reid Schultz, General & Chief Adminisrator
John E. Carr, President
Dan Bentzinger, Chief Information Officer
Michael Collins, Senior Vice President

Plans and coordinates the movement of goods throughout the world.

14541 NEXCO, Inc.
Grand Central Station
PO Box 3949
New York, NY 10163

877-291-4901
Fax: 646-349-9628
E-Mail: director@nexco.org
Home Page: www.nexco.org
Social Media: Facebook, Twitter, LinkedIn, YouTube

Gerri Cristantiello, Executive Director
Valerie Oakes-Locascio, Board Treasurer
David Reiff, Board Secretary
Henry Lapidos, Director
Barney Lehrer, Board President

Members are import and export trading and import and export management companies, international trade service vendors and other international trade companies.
300 Members
Founded in 1963

14542 National Council on International Trade Development
1901 Pennsylvania Ave. NW
Suite 804
Washington, DC 20006

202-872-9280
Fax: 202-293-0495
E-Mail: cu@ncitd.org
Home Page: www.ncitd.org

Mary Fromyer, Executive Director
David Joy, Senior Counsel
Cathleen Ryan, Asst. Dir. Of Enforcement
kevin J. Wolf, Asst. Secretary of Commerce
Gerard Horner, Head of Economic Analysis Program

Non-profit membership organization dedicated to providing direct expertise on a wide range of international trade topics. Our mission is to identify impediments to all aspects of international commerce and to provide solutions to faciliting the global process.
Founded in 1967

14543 National Foreign Trade Council
1625 K Street, NW
Suite 200
Washington, DC 20006

202-887-0278
Fax: 202-452-8160
E-Mail: nftcinformation@nftc.org
Home Page: www.nftc.org
Social Media: Facebook, Twitter

William A. Reinsch, President & CEO
J. Daniel O'Flaherty, Vice President
Marshall Lane, Sr Director of Operations
Andrew Watrous, Program Manager
Catherine Schultz, VP, Tax Policy

Business organization advocating a rules-based world economy.
300 Members
Founded in 1914

14544 PromaxBDA
1522 Cloverfield Blvd.
Suite E
Santa Monica, CA 90404

310-788-7600
Fax: 310-788-7616
Home Page: www.promaxbda.org

Jim Chabin, CEO
Lee Hunt, Vice Chair/Treasurer
Michael Mischler, Secretary

International association of promotion and marketing, professionals in electronic media. Promotes the effectiveness of promotion and marketing within the industry and the academic community.
2400 Members
Founded in 1952

14545 Russian Trade Development Association
Palms & Company
6421 Lake Washington Boulevard North East
Penthouse Suite 408
Kirkland, WA 98033-6876

425-828-6774
Fax: 425-821-9101
E-Mail: Palms@PeterPalms.com
Home Page: www.peterpalms.com

Variety of industrial trade shows by SIC code occuring in the Russian Federation throughout the year. Export services from USA to purchasing agent services in Russia for buyers worldwide.
25000 Members
Founded in 1934

14546 Small Business Exporters Association

800-345-6728
E-Mail: info@sbea.org
Home Page: www.sbea.org

Jody Milanese, Government Affairs
Patrick Post, Membership
Millo Day, Media/ Press Inquires

Association for small and mid-sized exporters and serves as the international trade arm of the National Small Business Association (NSBA), the nation's first small-business advocacy organization with more than 65,000 members across the country.
65000 Members

14547 The Association of Women in International Trade
204 E. St. NE
Washington, DC 20002

202-293-2948
E-Mail: info@wiit.org
Home Page: www.wiit.org

Nancy S. Travis, President
Rowan M. Dougherty, VP of Programming
Jennifer Meek, VP of Communications
Dana Watts, VP of Professional Development
Peggy A. Clarke, Secretary

Provides educational and networking opportunities to professional women involved in international trade and business.
Founded in 1987

14548 The Federation of International Trade Associations
172 Fifth Avenue
#118
Brooklyn, NY 11217

888-491-8833
E-Mail: info@fita.org
Home Page: www.fita.org

Kimberly Park, President & CEO

Provides resources, benefits and services to the international trade community.
45000 Members
Founded in 1984

14549 The Women in International Trade Charitable Trust

Home Page: www.wiittrust.org

Nicole Bivens Collinson, Chair
Amy Breeman-Rhodes, Treasurer
Emily Ruger-Beline, Advisory Committee
Amanda DeBusk, Advisory Committee
Cami Mazard, Advisory Committee

Funds charitable, scientific, and educational activities in international trade.
Founded in 2001

14550 US China Business Council
1818 N St NW
Suite 200
Washington, DC 20036

202-429-0340
Fax: 202-775-2476
E-Mail: info@uschina.org
Home Page: www.uschina.org
Social Media: Facebook, Twitter, LinkedIn

John Frisbie, President
Erin Ennis, VP
Ryan Ong, Director/Business Advisory Services
Marc Ross, Director, Communications
Shelly Zhao, Manager, BusinessAdvisory Services

Membership association for US companies doing business with the People's Republic of China. Provides representation, practical assistance, and up-to-date information to members.
240 Members
Founded in 1973
Mailing list available for rent

14551 US Council for International Business
1212 Ave of the Americas
New York, NY 10036

212-354-4480
Fax: 212-575-0327
E-Mail: info@uscib.org
Home Page: www.uscib.org
Social Media: Facebook, Twitter, LinkedIn, YouTube

Peter M. Robinson, President
Ronnie L. Goldberg, Executive Vice President
Paul Cronin, EVP & CFO
John E Merow, Secretary
Rob Mulligan, SVP, Policy & Govt. Affairs

Addresses a broad range of policy issues with the objective of promoting an open system of world trade, finance and investment in which business can flourish and contribute to economic growth, human welfareand protection of the environment.
300 Members
Founded in 1945

14552 US International Trade Association
1401 Constitution Ave Nw
Washington, DC 20230

202-482-2867
800-USA-TRAD
Fax: 202-482-2867
Home Page: www.trade.gov
Social Media: Facebook, Twitter

David L Aaron, Manager
Adam S. Wilczewski, Chief of Staff
Kurt Bersani, CFO & Dir. Of Administration
Renee Macklin, Chief Information Officer
Mary L. Trupo, Senior Advisor

Association for those interested in export opportunities for United States businesses.

14553 US Russia Business Council
1110 Vermont Ave NW
Suite 350
Washington, DC 20005

202-739-9180
Fax: 202-659-5920
E-Mail: info@usrbc.org
Home Page: www.usrbc.org

Daniel A. Russell, President
Randi Levinas, Executive Vice President & COO
Julia Fabens, Manager of Membership
Jeff Barnett, Senior Director of Policy

Joy M. Bottalico, VP of Administration & Finance

A Washington-based trade association that provides significant business developme, dispute resolution, government relations, and market intelligence services to its American and Russian member companies.

14554 United States Council for International Business
1212 Avenue of the Americas
New York, NY 10036

212-354-4480
Fax: 212-575-0327
Home Page: www.uscib.org

Harold McGraw III, Chair
Dennis Nally, Vice Chair
Peter M. Robinson, President/ CEO
Paul Cronin, EVP & CFO
Abby Shapiro, SVP, Business Development

Promotes open markets, competitiveness and innovation, sustainable development and corporate responsibility, supported by international engagement and regulatory coherence.
300 Members
Founded in 1945

14555 WESTCONN International Trade Association

Home Page: www.westconn.org
Social Media: Facebook, Twitter, LinkedIn

Lucy Ambrosino, President
George Woods, Vice President
Mark Bishop, Treasurer
Kim Harris, Board Member
Edward Carey, Board Member

Promotes industrial and academic awareness of the importance of international trade to our national economy.
Founded in 1972

14556 Women's International Shipping & Trading Association

Home Page: www.wista.net
Social Media: Facebook, Twitter

Alexandra Anagnostis-Irons, President
Kathleen Haines, Treasurer
Parker Harrison, Membership Secretary
Laura Sherman, Board Member
Kathy Plemer, Board Member

An international organization for women in management positions involved in the maritime transportation business and related trades worldwide.
390 Members
Founded in 1997

Newsletters

14557 AAMA News
Asian American Manufacturers Association
3300 Zanker Road
Maildrop Sj2f8
San Jose, CA 95134

408-955-4505
Fax: 408-955-4516
E-Mail: aama@aamasv.com

Robert M Lee, Executive Director
Cost: $30.00
Frequency: Monthly
Circulation: 1000

14558 AIB Newsletter
Academy of International Business
Michigan State University
7 Eppley Center
East Lansing, MI 48824-1121

517-432-1452
Fax: 517-432-1009
E-Mail: aib@aib.msu.edu
Home Page: aib.msu.edu

G Tomas M Hult, Executive Director
Tunga Kiyak, Managing Director
Irem Kiyak, Treasurer

Provides feature reports and news articles. Information on upcoming events such as conference announcements, calls for papers, and publishing opportunities are also featured.
Frequency: Quarterly
ISSN: 1520-6262

14559 Asahi Shimbun Satellite Edition
Japan Access
757 3rd Avenue
Front 3
New York, NY 10017-2013

212-869-7018
Fax: 212-317-3025

Mo Matsuchita, Publisher
Cost: $3.00
Circulation: 12,000

14560 Asian Economic News
Kyodo News International
50 Rockefeller Plz
Room 803
New York, NY 10020-1605
212-603-6600
Fax: 212-397-3721
E-Mail: kni@kyodonews.com
Home Page: www.kyodonews.com

Economic business news of Asian countries and regions.

14561 Buisness IP Services in Brazil
Probe Research
3 Wing Drive
Suite 240
Cedar Knolls, NJ 07927-1000

973-285-1500
Fax: 973-285-1519
Home Page: www.proberesearch.com

Provides an overview of the business IP services market in Brazil; one of the most active IP markets in South America. Breakdown of Brazil companies. IT investment in B2B and networking applications. We discuss cable and ADSL broadband services and the e-government project. Profile of over 15 service providers.

14562 Business Russia
Economist Intelligence Unit
111 W 57th Street
New York, NY 10019-2211

212-586-1115
800-938-4685
Fax: 212-586-1181
Home Page: www.eiu.com

Hyunkyu Lee, Owner

Monthly newsletter providing financial and market information as well as current business statistics, economic forecasts and political risk analysis for Russia.
Cost: $865.00
12 Pages
Frequency: Monthly
ISSN: 1357-0293

14563 Business Africa
Economist Intelligence Unit
111 W 57th Street
New York, NY 10019-2211

212-861-1115
800-938-4685
Fax: 212-586-1181
Home Page: www.eiu.com

Daniel Franklin, Editorial Director
Richard Epstein, Director
Ingersoll Rand, Managing Director
Jane Morley, Senior Editor

Fortnightly newsletter identifying key business issues across Africa; forecasting future developments and trends and analysing their implications on Africa's business environment.
Cost: $1095.00
12 Pages
ISSN: 0968-4468
Founded in 1946

14564 Business Asia
Economist Intelligence Unit
111 W 57th Street
New York, NY 10019-2211

212-861-1115
800-938-4685
Fax: 212-586-1181
Home Page: www.eiu.com

Daniel Franklin, Editorial Director
David Butter, Editor
Euan Rellio, Executive Director

Fortnightly newsletter focusing on operating issues and analyzing current political, business and economic developments across Asia.
Cost: $1055.00
12 Pages
Frequency: Fortnightly
ISSN: 0572-7545
Founded in 1946

14565 Business China
Economist Intelligence Unit
111 W 57th Street
New York, NY 10019-2211

212-586-1115
800-938-4685
Fax: 212-586-1181
Home Page: www.eiu.com

Daniel Franklin, Editorial Director
Richard Epstein, Advertising Manager

Fortnightly newsletter alerting business executives to the political economic and legal changes that will affect corporate interests. Provides corporate case studies. Analysis financial issues in, and affecting, China. Offers practical, detailed advice.
Cost: $895.00
12 Pages
Frequency: 50 issues per y
ISSN: 1016-9766
Founded in 1946

14566 Business Eastern Europe
Economist Intelligence Unit
111 W 57th Street
New York, NY 10019-2211

212-861-1115
800-938-4685
Fax: 212-586-1181
Home Page: www.eiu.com

Daniel Franklin, Editorial Director
Richard Epstein, Advertising Manager

Fortnightly newsletter providing information for business planning on the latest political and economic developments in Eastern Europe on a country-by-country basis.
Cost: $1395.00
12 Pages
Frequency: Weekly
ISSN: 1351-8763
Founded in 1946

14567 Business Europe
Economist Intelligence Unit
111 W 57th Street
New York, NY 10019-2211

212-861-1115
800-938-4685
Fax: 212-586-1181
Home Page: www.eiu.com/

Lou Hencken, CEO/President
Paul Lewis, Editor
Nina Andrikian, Marketing

Fortnightly newsletter providing hard facts about changes in the EU's business environment; identifying opportunities for growth and analysing the impact of current issues on business in Europe.
Cost: $1435.00
12 Pages
Frequency: 44 issues per y
ISSN: 1351-8755
Founded in 1946

14568 Business India Intelligence
Economist Intelligence Unit
111 W 57th Street
New York, NY 10019-2211

212-586-1115
800-938-4685
Fax: 212-586-1181
Home Page: www.eiu.com

Helen Alexander, CEO
Lou Kelly, Marketing Manager
Louis Ceil, VP

Monthly newsletter tracking the issues and trends in India's business environment; providing information on infrastructure and industries, tariffs, taxes and economic policy and consumer markets.
Cost: $660.00
16 Pages
Frequency: Monthly
ISSN: 1352-8335
Founded in 1946

14569 Business Latin America
Economist Intelligence Unit
111 W 57th Street
New York, NY 10019-2211

212-861-1115
800-938-4685
Fax: 212-586-1181
Home Page: www.eiu.com

Daniel Franklin, Editorial Director
Richard Epstein, Director, Business Development

Weekly newsletter covering vital issues affecting business in Latin America, identifying the opportunities, and forecasting the risks to help executives make competetive corporate decisions.
Cost: $1370.00
12 Pages
Founded in 1946

14570 Caribbean Update
52 Maple Avenue
Maplewood, NJ 07040-2626

973-762-1565
Fax: 973-762-9585
E-Mail: mexcarib@cs.com
Home Page: www.caribbeanupdate.org

Kal Wagenheim, Editor/Publisher

Monthly newsletter focusing on trade and investment opportunities in the Caribbean and Central America.
Cost: $267.00
24 Pages
Frequency: Monthly
Founded in 1985
Mailing list available for rent: 2500 names
Printed in one color on newsprint stock

14571 Country Finance
Economist Intelligence Unit
111 W 57th Street
New York, NY 10019-2211

212-861-1115
800-938-4685
Fax: 212-586-1181
Home Page: www.eiu.com

Daniel Franklin, Editorial Director
Richard Epstein, Director, Business Development

Covering 47 countries, this service is a comprehensive overview of global financial issues and conditions. Provides case studies and resources to help companies find and manage finances in countries around the globe. A weekly alert service highlights changes as they happen.
Cost: $445.00
Frequency: 41 issues per y
Founded in 1946

14572 Country Forecasts
Economist Intelligence Unit
111 W 57th Street
New York, NY 10019-2211

212-861-1115
800-938-4685
Fax: 212-586-1181
Home Page: www.eiu.com

Daniel Franklin, Editorial Director

Five-year forecasts of political, economic and business trends in 60 countries. Each quarterly updated forecast focuses on the key factors affecting a country's political and economic outlook and its business environment over the next five years.
Cost: $845.00
36 Pages
Frequency: Quarterly

14573 Country Monitor
Economist Intelligence Unit
111 W 57th Street
New York, NY 10019-2211

212-861-1115
800-938-4685
Fax: 212-586-1181
Home Page: www.eiu.com

Daniel Franklin, Editorial Director
Richard Epstein, Director, Business Development

Weekly newsletter analysing the latest global economic and political events; providing risk assessment in emerging markets and facts on global trends and markets.
Cost: $895.00
12 Pages
Frequency: Weekly
Founded in 1946

14574 Country Reports
Economist Intelligence Unit
111 W 57th Street
New York, NY 10019-2211

212-861-1115
800-938-4685
Fax: 212-586-0248
Home Page: www.eiu.com

Daniel Franklin, Editorial Director
Emily Morris, Senior Editor

Quarterly updates on the situation in over 180 countries. Each report includes and analysis of a country's current political and economic climate as well as 12-18 month economic projection.
Cost: $425.00
Founded in 1946

14575 Country Risk Service
Economist Intelligence Unit
111 W 57th Street
New York, NY 10019-2211

212-861-1115
800-938-4685
Fax: 212-586-1181
Home Page: www.eiu.com

Daniel Franklin, Editorial Director

Information to assist financial risk management in emerging countries. Country Risk Service is an exclusive two-year forecasting service, assessing the solvency of 100 indebted countries. Each report includes projections of GDP, the budget deficit, trade and current account balances, financing requirements and debt-service ratio.
Cost: $760.00
60 Pages
Frequency: Quarterly
Founded in 1946

14576 East Asian Business Intelligence
International Executive Reports
717 D St Nw
Suite 300
Washington, DC 20004-2815

202-737-6366
Fax: 202-628-6618
E-Mail: execrep@aol.com

William Hearn, Publisher

Twice-a-month newsletter containing business leads and market studies on Far East business.
Cost: $345.00
8 Pages
Frequency: 22 per year
Circulation: 300
ISSN: 0888-058X
Founded in 1986
Printed in on matte stock

14577 East/West Executive Guide
WorldTrade Executive
PO Box 761
Concord, MA 01742

978-287-0301
Fax: 978-287-0302
E-Mail: info@wtexec.com
Home Page: www.wtexec.com

Alison French, Production Manager

Provides detailed information on how to do business in Russia, the CIS, and East/Central Europe. Focuses on key mechanical issues such as accounting and tax matters, local sourcing, the due diligence process, labor, finance, permits, environmental issues etc.
Cost: $656.00
Frequency: Monthly

14578 European Community
US Council for International Business
1212 Ave of the Americas
Suite 1800
New York, NY 10036-1689

212-354-4480
Fax: 212-575-0327
Home Page: www.uscib.org

Peter Robinson, President

Newssheet on developments in the European community affecting business on council activities.
Circulation: 2,800

14579 Export Update
Trade Communications
733 15th Street NW
Suite 1100
Washington, DC 20005-2112

202-737-1060
Fax: 202-783-5966

Stephen Pfeiderer, Publisher

Includes significant buying trends, specific sales leads, in-depth country market profiles, latest figures on trade activity, schedules for trade affairs and missions and insight on the affects of international news.

14580 Hong Kong Trade Development Council Newsletter
Hong Kong Development Council
219 E 46th St
Suite 1
New York, NY 10017-2951

212-838-8688
Fax: 212-838-8941
E-Mail: new.york.office@tdc.org.hk
Home Page: www.tdctrade.com

Louis Ho, Executive Director

Promotes trade between United States and Hong Kong.
Frequency: Weekly
Founded in 1966

14581 Hong Kong Trader
Hong Kong Trade Development Council
219 E 46th St
Suite 1
New York, NY 10017-2951

212-838-8688
Fax: 212-838-8941
E-Mail: new.york.office@tdc.org.hk
Home Page: www.tdctrade.com

Louis Ho, Executive Director
8 Pages
Frequency: Monthly
Printed in on glossy stock

14582 Indonesia Letter
Asia Letter Group
12508 Whitley Street
Whittier, CA 90601-2729

FAX 852-526-2950

14583 International Finance & Treasury
WorldTrade Executive
PO Box 761
Concord, MA 01742

978-287-0301
Fax: 978-287-0302
E-Mail: info@wtexec.com
Home Page: www.wtexec.com

Alison French, CEO

Focus on techniques used by leading firms to manage worldwide financial resources. Topics covered include: tax, accounting and regulatory changes, currency and interest rate risk, cash management techniques, risk management strategies, regional treasury alerts.
Cost: $1245.00
Frequency: Weekly

14584 International Observer
PO Box 5997
Washington, DC 20016-1597

202-244-7050
Fax: 202-244-5410

J Wagner, Publisher

Informs on world developments in political, diplomatic, government, security, and economic origins.
Cost: $240.00
10 Pages
Frequency: Monthly
Printed in one color

14585 International Securitization & Structured Finance
WorldTrade Executive
PO Box 761
Concord, MA 01742

978-287-0301
Fax: 978-287-0302
E-Mail: info@wtexec.com
Home Page: www.wtexec.com

Jill McKenna, Production Manager
George Veoger, Editor
Pierre Brown, Publisher
Alleesa Aughas, Marketing Manager

A twice monthly report devoted exclusively to asset-backed securities in international markets. Covers all aspects of international asset-backed securitization, including innovative product trends, issuer considerations, regulatory matters, and tax and accounting considerations. Examines what is working in emerging markets and spotlights unique US transactions.
Cost: $1296.00
Frequency: Bi-monthly
Founded in 1996

14586 International Trade Alert
American Association of Importers and Exporters
1200 G Street NW
Suite 800
Washington, DC 20005

212-944-2230
Fax: 202-661-2185
Home Page: www.aaei.org

Mathew Mermigousis, Production Manager
Stuart Iserber, Director of Events
Michelle Measel, Director of Events

Reports on current trade developments and advance notices of changes in rules for conducting business in the United States, as well as developments affecting trade originating from Treasury, Customs, US Courts, Commerce Department, International Trade Commission, Federal Maritime Commission and other regulatory agencies.
10 Pages
Frequency: Monthly
Circulation: 2,200

14587 International Trade Reporter Current Reports
Bureau of National Affairs
1801 S Bell St
Arlington, VA 22202-4501

703-341-3000
800-372-1033
Fax: 800-253-0332
E-Mail: customercare@bna.com
Home Page: www.bnabooks.com
Social Media: Facebook, Twitter, LinkedIn

Paul N Wojcik, Chairman
Gregory C. McCaffery, President and CEO
John Camp, Vice President
Lisa A. Fitzpatrick, Vice President
Audrey Hipkins, Vice President

A comprehensive source that reports and analyzes legislative and regulatory developments as well as private sector activities affecting international trade (both export and import).
Cost: $1744.00
Frequency: Weekly
Founded in 1929

14588 International Trade Reporter Decisions
Bureau of National Affairs
1801 S Bell St
Arlington, VA 22202-4501

703-341-3000
800-372-1033
Fax: 800-253-0332
E-Mail: customercare@bna.com
Home Page: www.bnabooks.com
Social Media: Facebook, Twitter, LinkedIn

Paul N Wojcik, Chairman
Gregory C. McCaffery, President and CEO
John Camp, Vice President
Lisa A. Fitzpatrick, Vice President
Audrey Hipkins, Vice President

Only available source of digested, classified and indexed judicial and administrative decisions dealing with legal issues arising from US trade law (mostly import cases).
Cost: $2265.00
ISSN: 0748-0709

14589 International Trade Reporter Import Reference Manual
Bureau of National Affairs
1801 S Bell St
Arlington, VA 22202-4501

703-341-3000
800-372-1033
Fax: 800-253-0332
E-Mail: customercare@bna.com
Home Page: www.bnabooks.com
Social Media: Facebook, Twitter, LinkedIn

Paul N Wojcik, Chairman
Gregory C. McCaffery, President and CEO
John Camp, Vice President
Lisa A. Fitzpatrick, Vice President
Audrey Hipkins, Vice President

A complete guide to the entire import process with analysis and full text of statutes, regulations, and executive orders on subjects such as customhouse brokers, dumping, countervailing duties, escape clauses, and presidential retaliation.
Cost: $1781.00

14590 Investing, Licensing & Trading
Economist Intelligence Unit
111 W 57th Street
New York, NY 10019-2211

212-586-1115
800-938-4685
Fax: 212-586-1181
Home Page: www.eiu.com

Updated twice a year, ILT outlines business requirements for operating successfully in the world's major markets. This reference service, shows how the laws work in practice, with case studies of how leading multinationals obtain government approvals, set up local companies, calculate corporate and personal taxes and overcome restrictions and other legal hurdles in 60 countries and the European Union.
Cost: $345.00

14591 Managing Imports and Exports
Institute of Management and Administration
1 Washington Park
Suite 1300
Newark, NJ 07102-3130

212-244-0360
Fax: 973-622-0595
E-Mail: customercare@bna.com
Home Page: www.ioma.com

The source of information on customs policies and procedures, BIS rules and regulations, and how to best enhance the compliance programs.
Cost: $437.00

14592 Market Europe
PRS Group
6320 Fly Rd
Suite 102
East Syracuse, NY 13057-9792

315-431-0511
Fax: 315-431-0200

E-Mail: custserv@prsgroup.com
Home Page: www.prsgroup.com

Mary Lou Walsh, President
Doris Walsh, Chairman

Demographic and lifestyle information about consumers in Europe to help businesses do a better job marketing to those consumers.
Cost: $397.00
Frequency: Monthly
Circulation: 325
Founded in 1985
Printed in one color on matte stock

14593 **Mexican Forecast**
WorldTrade Executive
2250 Main St
Suite 100
Concord, MA 01742-3838

978-287-0301
Fax: 978-287-0302
E-Mail: info@wtexec.com
Home Page: www.wtexecutive.com

Gary Brown, President
Jay Stanley, Sales Manager

Provides up-to-date information and forecasts on Mexican business. Includes coverage of foreign trade, currency, major industry sectors, market trends and investment climates.
Cost: $535.00

14594 **Middle East Business Intelligence**
International Executive Reports
717 D St Nw
Suite 300
Washington, DC 20004-2815

202-737-6366
Fax: 202-628-6618
E-Mail: execrep@aol.com

William Hearn, Publisher

Twice-a-month newsletter containing business leads and market studies on Middle East business.
Cost: $345.00
8 Pages
Circulation: 400
ISSN: 0731-5305
Printed in one color on matte stock

14595 **Middle East Trade Letter**
PO Box 472986
Charlotte, NC 28247-2986

704-536-9847
Fax: 704-543-6161

Leslie B Cohen, Publisher

Business in the Middle East.
Cost: $139.00
4 Pages
Frequency: Quarterly
Circulation: 500
Printed in one color on newsprint stock

14596 **Nielsen's International Investment Letter**
Nielsen & Nielsen
1901 South Bay Rd Ne
Olympia, WA 98506-3532

360-352-7485
Fax: 360-352-7485
Home Page: www.nelsonfurnitureworks.com

Paul Nelson, President

Tracks domestic and international stock markets and economics, precious metals and other commodities, USA and foreign bonds, interest rates, foreign currencies and real estate; offers clients specific buy and sell recommendations on domestic and international investments for both traders and investors.
Cost: $360.00
10 Pages
Frequency: Monthly
Printed in on matte stock

14597 **North American Free Trade & Investment**
WorldTrade Executive
PO Box 761
Concord, MA 01742

978-287-0301
Fax: 978-287-0302
E-Mail: info@wtexec.com
Home Page: www.wtexec.com

Alison French, Production Manager
Gary Brown, CEO/President
Gary Brown, Editor
Dana Pierce, Marketing Manager
Dana Pierce, Circulation Manager

Covers NAFTA trade and investment developments. Key topics include rules of origin, tariff phaseouts, intellectual property protection, compliance and planning options, and business opportunities.
Cost: $734.00
Frequency: Annual+
Circulation: 100
Founded in 1992

14598 **Practical Latin American Tax Strategies**
WorldTrade Executive
PO Box 761
Concord, MA 01742

978-287-0301
Fax: 978-287-0302
E-Mail: info@wtexec.com
Home Page: www.wtexec.com

Alison French, Production Manager

A monthly report on how leading companies are reacting to changes and developments in Latin American tax practice. Includes commentary from senior practitioners at major law and accounting firms and case studies from major corporations.
Cost: $645.00
Frequency: Monthly

14599 **Practical US/International Tax Strategies**
WorldTrade Executive
PO Box 761
Concord, MA 01742-761

978-287-0301
Fax: 978-287-0302
E-Mail: info@wtexec.com
Home Page: www.wtexec.com

Dana Pierce, Production Manager
Gary Brown, CEO/Publisher
David Cooper, Editor
John Nartel, Marketing Manager
Jay Stanley, Sales Manager

Analyzes how leading companies are reacting to changes in US-international tax practice. Leading experts provide practical guidance covering every area of international transactions.
Cost: $614.00
Frequency: Fortnightly
Circulation: 200
Founded in 1992

14600 **Russian Far East Update**
Russian Far East Update
PO Box 22126
Seattle, WA 98122-0126

206-447-2668
Fax: 206-628-0979
Home Page: www.russianfareast.com

Trade and economic information plus news analysis of Russia's far east.
Cost: $20.00
Circulation: 1,300

14601 **Vietnam Business Info Track**
Vietnam Access
PO Box 1210
Port Hueneme, CA 93044-1210

FAX 805-985-0839

Kahn Le, Editor

Comprehensive coverage of Vietnam market. Focuses on trade, investment and sector reports. Gives you an immediate advantage in evaluating the potential of doing business in Vietnam and operating in a timely and cost effective matter.

14602 **Vietnam Market Watch**
Vietnam Market Resources
375 Lexington Avenue
New York, NY 10017

212-499-2000
Fax: 203-256-9790
E-Mail: mail@inc.com
Home Page: www.inc.com/

Khoung Ho, Publisher
Aaron Goldstein, Chief Operating Officer
Caroline Basquez, Owner

For companies and professionals doing business in Vietnam.
Cost: $295.00
Frequency: Monthly
Circulation: 500
Founded in 2004

14603 **Weekly International Market Alert**
International Business Communications
114 E 32nd Street
#602
New York, NY 10016

212-686-1460

Johnathan Block, Publisher

International trade news.
Frequency: Monthly

14604 **World Trade**
Taipan Press
4199 Campus Drive
Suite 230
Irvine, CA 92612-4684

949-410-0980
Fax: 949-725-0306

Will Swaim, Publisher

Articles aim to help companies expand international opportunities. Accepts advertising.
Cost: $24.00
96 Pages
Frequency: Monthly

Magazines & Journals

14605 **AIB Insights**
Academy of International Business
Michigan State University
7 Eppley Center
East Lansing, MI 48824-1121

517-432-1452
Fax: 517-432-1009

E-Mail: aib@aib.msu.edu
Home Page: aib.msu.edu

Ilan Alon, Editor

Provides an outlet for short, interesting, topical, current, and thought provoking articles. Articles can discuss theoretical, empirical, practical or pedagogical issues affecting the international business community.
Frequency: Quarterly
ISSN: 1938-9590

14606 **Aaonline**
Africa-America Institute
420 Lexington Ave
Suite 1706
New York, NY 10170-0007

212-949-5666
Fax: 212-682-6174
E-Mail: aainy@aaionline.org
Home Page: www.aaionline.org

Amber Jones, Executive Assistant
Mora McLean, Vice President
Joy Phumaphi, Vice President
Frequency: Quarterly
Circulation: 3000
Founded in 1953

14607 **American Business in China**
Caravel
23545 Crenshaw Blvd
Suite 101E
Torrance, CA 90505-5201

310-325-0100
Fax: 310-325-2583
E-Mail: info@china4us.com
Home Page: www.china4us.com

Directory of US firms operating in China and Hong Kong; Hong Kong: a special administrative region; exporting to China - best US exporting prospects; China's major cities for foreign investments; marketing, advertising and exhibiting in China.
Cost: $99.00
288 Pages
Circulation: 10,000
ISBN: 0-964432-29-3
Founded in 1993
Mailing list available for rent: 2,000 names at $95 per M

14608 **Asian Finance**
Asian Finance Publications
14 Davis Drive
Armonk, NY 10504-3005

Focuses on international banking and finance.
Circulation: 13147

14609 **Asian Industrial Report**
Keller International Publishing Corporation
150 Great Neck Rd
Great Neck, NY 11021-3309

516-829-9722
Fax: 516-829-9306
E-Mail: mcamca@rad.net.id

Robert Herihly, Publisher
Brian Deluca, Editor
Jerry Keller, President

New machinery and equipment.
Cost: $85.00
36 Pages
Frequency: Monthly
Circulation: 20000
Founded in 1882
Printed in 4 colors on matte stock

14610 **Business America: the Magazine of International Trade**
US Department of Commerce
200 Constitution Ave NW
Washington, DC 20210-0001

202-693-5000
Fax: 202-219-8822
Home Page: www.dol.gov
Social Media: Facebook, Twitter, LinkedIn, Pinterest, Blogger, Tumblr

Hilda L Solis, CEO

Designed to help American exporters penetrate overseas markets by providing them with timely information on opportunities for trade and methods of doing business in foreign countries.
Cost: $2.00
Circulation: 13,000
Mailing list available for rent

14611 **Cross Border**
Economist Intelligence Unit
111 W 57th Street
New York, NY 10019-2211

212-586-1115
Fax: 212-586-1181

Debrah Langley, Publisher

Focuses on multinational management issues faced by managers of international businesses.
Circulation: 55,000

14612 **East Asian Executive Report**
International Executive Reports
717 D St NW
Suite 300
Washington, DC 20004-2815

202-737-6366
Fax: 202-628-6618
E-Mail: execrep@aol.com

William Hearn, Publisher

Monthly magazine covering the legal and practical requirements of doing business in Far Eastern countries.
Cost: $455.00
28 Pages
Frequency: Monthly
Circulation: 600
ISSN: 0272-1589
Founded in 1979
Printed in on matte stock

14613 **Economist**
PO Box 58524
Boulder, CO 80322-8524

303-945-1917
800-456-6086
Fax: 303-604-7455
E-Mail: ukpressoffice@economist.com
Home Page: www.economist.com

Helen Alexander, CEO
Kate Cooke, Group Communications Manager
David Hanger, Publisher
James Wilson, Founder

The Economist is a news and business publication written for top business decision-makers and opinion leaders who need a wide range of information and views on world events. It explores the close links between domestic and international issues, business, finance, current affairs, science and technology.
160 Pages
Frequency: Weekly
Circulation: 1009759
ISSN: 0013-0613
Founded in 1843
Printed in 4 colors on glossy stock

14614 **Export**
Adams/Hunter Publishing
2101 S Arlington Heights Road
Suite 150
Arlington Heights, IL 60005-4142

FAX 847-427-2006

David Thayer, Publisher

Covers all aspects of international trade for distributors of consumer durables in 183 countries.

14615 **Foreign Affairs**
Foreign Affairs
58 E 68th St
New York, NY 10065-5953

212-434-9522
800-829-5539
Fax: 212-861-2759
E-Mail: order@wshein.com
Home Page: www.foreignaffairs.org

David Kellogg, Publisher
Gideon Rose, Editor
Michael Pasuit, Marketing Coordinator
Eugnia Chang, Circulation Director

Reviews on events, news, people, and foreign relations.
Cost: $44.00
Founded in 1921

14616 **Global Trade**
North American Publishing Company
1500 Spring Garden St
Suite 1200
Philadelphia, PA 19130-4094

215-238-5300
Fax: 215-238-5342
Home Page: www.napco.com

Ned S Borowsky, President and CEO
Bennett Zucker, Publisher

Assists international cargo decision makers in planning, financing and documenting goods and commodities in international trade. Accepts advertising.
Cost: $45.00
Frequency: Monthly
Founded in 1958

14617 **IGT Magazine**
World Trade Winds
610 Old Campbell Rd
Suite 108
Richardson, TX 75080-3379

972-994-9816
877-861-1188
Fax: 972-699-1189
Home Page: www.asiatrademart.com

Offers information for exporters to find international buyers.
ISSN: 0259-9880
Founded in 1975

14618 **Journal of International Business Studies**
Academy of International Business
Michigan State University
7 Eppley Center
East Lansing, MI 48824-1121

517-432-1452
Fax: 517-432-1009
E-Mail: managing-editor@jibs.net
Home Page: www.aib.msu.edu

Lorraine Eden, Editor

The leading peer-reviewed, scholarly journal that publishes research across the entire range of topics encompassing the domain of international business studies.
Frequency: 9x/Year
ISSN: 0047-2506

14619 **LASA Forum**
Latin American Studies Association

946 William Pitt Union
University of Pittsburgh
Pittsburgh, PA 15260

412-648-7929
Fax: 412-624-7145
E-Mail: lasa@pitt.edu
Home Page: lasa.international.pitt.edu/

Hane Horowitz, Exhibit Management Head
Arturo Arias, Associate Editor
Sonia E Alvarez, President/Editor
Charles R Hale, VP
Milagros Pereyra-Rojas, Managing Editor

Published by the Latin American Studies Association.
Cost: $30.00
Frequency: Quarterly
Founded in 1969
Mailing list available for rent

14620 Latin Trade Magazine
Freedom Latin America
1001 Brickell Bay Drive
Suite 2700
Miami, FL 33131

305-749-0880
Fax: 786-513-2407
E-Mail: info@latintrade.com
Home Page: www.latintrade.com
Social Media: Facebook, Twitter, LinkedIn, RSS

Rosemary Winters, Chief Executive Officer
Maria Lourdes Gallo, Executive Director & Publisher
Santiago Gutierrez, Executive Editor
Elida Bustos, Managing Editor
Manny Melo, Art & Production Director

Comprehensive news coverage and analysis of business issues in Latin America and the Caribbean. Available in English or Spanish
Cost: $64.00
Frequency: Monthly
Circulation: 92,319
Founded in 1993

14621 Middle East Executive Reports
International Executive Reports
717 D St NW
Suite 300
Washington, DC 20004-2815

202-737-6366
Fax: 202-628-6618
E-Mail: execrep@aol.com

William Hearn, Publisher

Monthly magazine covering the legal and practical requirements of doing business in the Middle East.
Cost: $455.00
28 Pages
Frequency: Monthly
Circulation: 1,000
ISSN: 0271-0498
Founded in 1978
Printed in 2 colors on matte stock

14622 Showcase USA
Bobit Publishing Company
23210 Crenshaw Blvd
Torrance, CA 90505-3181

310-539-1969
Fax: 310-539-4329
Home Page: www.bobit.com

John Bebout, Owner

International marketing vehicle for American manufacturing.
Cost: $12.00
165 Pages
Founded in 1979

14623 Trade and Culture Magazine
Key Communications
PO Box 569
Garrisonville, VA 22463-0569

540-657-7174
800-544-5684
Fax: 540-720-5687
Home Page: www.key-com.com

Debra Levy, Owner
Kim White, Managing Editor
Penny Stacey, Advertising Coordinator

Published to help executives make their companies competitive worldwide, featuring 22 trade zone presentations in each issue covering every country. Trade and Culture blends cultural insight with practical how-to business information.
Cost: $39.95
96 Pages
Frequency: Quarterly
Circulation: 45000
Founded in 1993

14624 US Council for International Business
1212 Avenue of the Americas
Suite 1805
New York, NY 10036-1689

212-354-4480
Fax: 212-575-0327
E-Mail: info@uscib.org
Home Page: www.uscib.org

Peter Robinson, President
Davis Hodge, Marketing & Advertising

Monthly newsletter that supports those involved in the developments in the European community affecting business on council activities.
Frequency: Monthly
Founded in 1945

14625 US-China Business Council
US China Business Council
1818 N St NW
Suite 200
Washington, DC 20036-2470

202-429-0340
Fax: 202-775-2476
E-Mail: info@uschina.org
Home Page: www.uschina.org

John Frisbie, President
Erin Ennis, VP
Ryan Ong, Director/Business Advisory Services

Covers all aspects of doing business with China and Hong Kong.
Cost: $100.00
240+ Members
Circulation: 6000
ISSN: 0163-7169
Founded in 1973
Printed in on glossy stock

14626 Vietnam Business Journal
VIAM Communications Group
535 W 114th Street
New York, NY 10027

212-854-2271
Fax: 212-854-9099

Kenneth Felderbaum, Publisher

Research and experience based articles and graphics produces by journalists.

14627 World Trade
Freedom Magazine
2401 W. Big Beaver Rd
Suite 700
Troy, MI 48084

248-362-3700
Home Page: www.bnpmedia.com
Social Media: Facebook, Twitter, LinkedIn

Steve Beyer, Director

Articles are aimed at helping companies to expand their international opportunities.
Frequency: Monthly
Circulation: 70590
Founded in 1987

Trade Shows

14628 AIB Annual Meeting
Academy of International Business
645 N. Shaw Ln
Rm 7
East Lansing, MI 48824-1121

517-432-1452
Fax: 517-432-1009
E-Mail: aib@aib.msu.edu
Home Page: www.aib.msu.edu

G Tomas M Hult, Executive Director
Tunga Kiyak, Managing Director
Irem Kiyak, Treasurer
Robert Grosse, President
Elizabeth Rose, Vice President Administration

Features a combination of plenaries, panels, and papers.
Frequency: June-July

14629 American-Turkish Council Annual Meeting
Ideea
6233 Nelway Drive
McLean, VA 22101

703-760-0762
Fax: 703-760-0764
E-Mail: qwhiteree@ideea.com
Home Page: www.ideea.com

Quentin C Whiteeree, President

High level military and government officials and businessmen from Turkey and the United States. Seminar and over 25 exhibits of trade, defense, banking, investments and tourism.
1000 Attendees
Frequency: Annual
Founded in 1983

14630 Annual Convention and Trade Show
American Association of Exporters and Importers
1050 17th Street NW
Suite 810
Washington, DC 20036

202-857-8009
Fax: 202-857-7843
E-Mail: hq@aaei.org
Home Page: www.aaei.org
Social Media: Facebook, Twitter

Kathy Corrigan, Director Meetings/Events
Marianne Rowden, President and CEO
Terri A Lankford, Director Membership & Marketing
David A Potts, Manager Office Administration
Megan Montgomery, Director of Government Affairs

Reports on current trade developments and advance notices of changes in rules for conducting business in the United States, as well as developments affecting trade originating from Treasury, Customs, US Courts, Commerce Department, International Trade Commission, Federal Maritime Commission and other regulatory agencies. 50 exhibitors with 50 booths.
550 Attendees
Frequency: May
Founded in 1921

14631 International Business Expo
Assist International

90 John Street
Room 505
New York, NY 10038

212-442-2074
Fax: 212-725-3312
Home Page: www.assist-intl.com

Peter Robinson, Director

This expo has 170 exhibitors with 170 booths.
1800 Attendees
Frequency: April
Founded in 1999

14632 Showcase USA Trade Show
Bobit Publishing Company
3520 Challenger Street
Torrance, CA 90503

310-533-2400
Fax: 310-533-2500
E-Mail: webmaster@bobit.com
Home Page: www.bobit.com

Mike Spivak, Editor
Ty Bobit, CEO

International marketing vehicle for American manufacturing
165 Attendees
Founded in 1979

14633 USRBC Annual Meeting
US Russia Business Council
1701 Pennsylvania Avenue NW
Suite 520
Washington, DC 20006

202-739-9180
Fax: 202-659-5920
E-Mail: lawson@usrbc.org
Home Page: www.usrbc.org

Eugene K Lawson, President

Highlights the opportunities and risks that are emerging in the Russian market as it enters a new stage of development.

Directories & Databases

14634 A Basic Guide to Exporting
World Trade Press
1450 Grant Avenue
Suite 204
Novato, CA 94945

415-549-9934
800-833-8586
Fax: 415-898-1080
Home Page: www.worldtradepress.com

Alexandra Woznick

Includes significant new information on export regulations, customs benefit, and tax incentives. There are also hundreds of new sources of assistance available with updated addresses and telephone numbers.
188 Pages
ISBN: 1-885073-83-6
Founded in 1999

14635 American Business in China
Caravel
23545 Crenshaw Blvd
Sutie 101E
Torrance, CA 90505-5201

310-325-0100
Fax: 310-325-2583
E-Mail: info@china4us.com
Home Page: www.china4us.com

Davisson Chang, Owner
Sheryl Chang, Production Manager
Betty Yao, Marketing Manager

Directory of US firms operating in China and Hong Kong; Hong Kong as a special administrative region; exporting to China - best US exporting prospects; China's major cities for foreign investments; marketing, advertising and exhibiting in China. Also contains 1,000+ US contacts and 1,800+ China & Hong Kong contacts
Cost: $99.00
288 Pages
Frequency: Annual
ISBN: 0-964432-29-3
Founded in 1995
Mailing list available for rent: 2,000 names at $95 per M

14636 Arthur Andersen North American Business Sourcebook
Triumph Books
601 S La Salle St
Suite 500
Chicago, IL 60605-1725

312-939-3330
Fax: 312-663-3557
Home Page: www.triumphbooks.com

Mitch Rogatz, President/Publisher
Tom Bast, Editorial Director
Blythe Hurley, Managing Editor
Kelley Thornton, Associate Editor

Government and trade agencies and trade-related databases in the United States, Canada and Mexico are profiled.
Cost: $150.00
Founded in 1994

14637 AtoZ World Business
World Trade Press
800 Lindberg Lane
Suite 190
Petaluma, CA 94952

707-778-1124
800-833-8586
Fax: 707-778-1329
E-Mail: egh@worldtradepress.com
Home Page: www.worldtradepress.com

Edward Hinkelman, Publisher

The world's most comprehensive country-by-country resource for success in international business and trade. Consists of 100 Country Business Guides and 76 World Trade Resources. Offers entrepreneurs, business professionals and researchers access to vetted international business and trade intelligence, compiled into a single, reliable source.
Founded in 1993

14638 Brazil Tax, Law, & Business Briefing
WorldTrade Executive
2250 Main St
Suite 100
Concord, MA 01742-3838

978-287-0301
Fax: 978-287-0302
E-Mail: info@wtexec.com
Home Page: www.wtexecutive.com

Gary Brown, Owner
Jay Stanley, Sales Manager

Coverage includes economic analysis and risk assessment, new transfer pricing rules, foreign direct investment, labor regulation, environment, privatization, accessing the Mercosur market, litigation, arbitration, and debt collection in Brazil, antitrust concerns for foreign acquisition, securitizing infrastructure projects, foreign investor access to the telecommunications market, and choices in creating Brazilian subsidiaries.
Cost: $297.00
340 Pages
ISBN: 1-893323-57-9

14639 CSI Market Statistics
Commodity Systems
200 W Palmetto Park Rd
Suite 200
Boca Raton, FL 33432-3788

561-392-1556
800-274-4727
Fax: 561-392-7761
E-Mail: info@csidata.com
Home Page: www.csidata.com

Bob Pelletier, President

Offers information on daily, weekly and monthly time series of price and trading data for commodity markets worldwide, cash, futures options, index options, US stocks and mutual funds and government instruments.

14640 Chinese Business in America
Caravel
23545 Crenshaw Blvd
Suite 101E
Torrance, CA 90505-5201

310-325-0100
Fax: 310-325-2583
E-Mail: info@china4us.com
Home Page: www.china4us.com

Davisson Chang, Owner
Sheryl Chang, CEO

Directory of ethnic Chinese importers and exporters in the US; marketing, sourcing and establishing a business in the US; US business laws and immigration regulations; money saving tips and business bargains.
Cost: $88.00
288 Pages
Frequency: Annual
Circulation: 5,000
ISBN: 0-964432-26-9
Founded in 1997

14641 DACA Directory
Distributors & Consolidators of America
2240 Bernays Drive
York, PA 17404

888-519-9195
Fax: 717-764-6531
E-Mail: daca@comcast.net
Home Page: www.dacacarriers.com

Mike Wichert, Chairman
Mike Oliver, President
Steve Hubbard, VP
Andy Delaney, Secretary
Rich Eberhart, Treasurer

Firms and individuals active in the shipping, warehousing, receiving, distribution or consolidation of freight shipments.

14642 DRI Europe
DRI/McGraw-Hill
24 Hartwell Ave
Lexington, MA 02421-3103

781-860-6060
Fax: 781-860-6002
E-Mail: support@construction.com
Home Page: www.construction.com

Walt Arvin, President

Subjects covered in this database include macroeconomic, microeconomic, and financial indicators for the European countries.

14643 DRI Middle East and African Forecast
DRI/McGraw-Hill
24 Hartwell Ave
Lexington, MA 02421-3103

781-860-6060
Fax: 781-860-6002
E-Mail: support@construction.com
Home Page: www.construction.com

Walt Arvin, President

This large database offers more than 500 annual historical and forecast time series for 10 Middle Eastern and African economies.

14644 DRI/TBS World Sea Trade Forecast
DRI/McGraw-Hill
24 Hartwell Ave
Lexington, MA 02421-3103

781-860-6060
Fax: 781-860-6002
E-Mail: support@construction.com
Home Page: www.construction.com

Walt Arvin, President

This comprehensive database covers cargo movements over major water trade routes worldwide.

14645 DRI/TBS World Trade Forecast
DRI/McGraw-Hill
24 Hartwell Ave
Lexington, MA 02421-3103

781-860-6060
Fax: 781-860-6002
E-Mail: support@construction.com
Home Page: www.construction.com

Walt Arvin, President

Offers over 82,000 annual historical and forecast time series on import and export volumes, and prices in current US dollars.

14646 Dictionary of International Trade
World Trade Press
1450 Grant Avenue
Suite 190
Petaluma, CA 94952

707-778-1124
800-833-8586
Fax: 707-778-1329
E-Mail: egh@worldtradepress.com
Home Page: www.worldtradepress.com

Edward G Hinkelman

The most respected and largest-selling dictionary of trade in the world. It is in use in more than 100 countries by importers, exporters, bankers, shippers, logistics professionals, attorneys, economists, and government officials.
Cost: $55.00
688 Pages
ISBN: 1-885073-72-0
Founded in 2004

14647 Directory of US Exporters
Journal of Commerce
33 Washington Street
Floor 13
Newark, NJ 07102

973-848-7000
E-Mail: amiddlebrook@cbizmedia.com
Home Page: www.cbizmedia.com

Amy Middlebrook, Group Publisher

Provides logistics professionals with active confirmed leads for over 60,000 US companies involved in world trade.
Cost: $450.00
Frequency: Annual

14648 Directory of US Importers
Journal of Commerce
33 Washington Street
13 Floor
Newark, NJ 07102

973-848-7000
E-Mail: amiddlebrook@cbizmedia.com
Home Page: www.cbizmedia.com

Amy Middlebrook, Group Publisher

Provides logistics professionals with active confirmed leads for over 60,000 US companies involved in world trade.
Cost: $450.00

14649 Export Yellow Pages
US West Marketing Resources Group
1101 30th Street NW
Suite 200
Washington, DC 20007-3769

202-934-4584
800-228-2582
Fax: 202-944-4680

David Lee, President

Approximately 16,000 US suppliers distributed worldwide through US commerce department channels.

14650 Foreign Exchange Forecast Data Base
Global Insight
800 Baldwin Tower
Eddystone, PA 19022

610-490-4000
Fax: 610-490-2770
E-Mail: info@wefa.com
Home Page: www.wefa.com

Ben G Hackett, International Trade/Transportation

This large database covers over 130 monthly and 60 quarterly time series of historical and forecast data for foreign exchange rates.

14651 Foreign Representatives in the US Yellow Book
Leadership Directories
104 5th Ave
New York, NY 10011-6901

212-627-4140
Fax: 212-645-0931
E-Mail: info@leadershipdirectories.com
Home Page: www.leadershipdirectories.com
Social Media: Facebook, Twitter

David Hurvitz, CEO
James M Petrie, Associate Publisher

Contact information for foreign representatives of over 187 nations at embassies, consulates, and intergovernmental organizations in the US, US executives of over 1,100 foreign corporations, over 275 foreign financial institutions with offices in the US, and over 300 international media outlets with bureaus in the US.
Cost: $245.00
850+ Pages
Frequency: SemiAnnual
ISSN: 1089-5833
Founded in 1969
Mailing list available for rent: 12,000 names at $125 per M

14652 GIN International Database
Global Information Network
146 W 29th St
Suite 7E
New York, NY 10001-5303

212-244-3123
Home Page: www.globalinfo.org

Lisa Vives, Owner

This large database offers all sorts of information on developing countries, ranging from economics and finance to health and social trends.
Frequency: Full-text

14653 GLOBAL Vantage
Standard & Poor's Corporation
55 Water St
New York, NY 10041-0003

212-438-1000
800-525-8640
Fax: 212-438-0299

Deven Sharma, President

This database provides corporate financial data covering more than 2,500 US companies and over 1,500 companies in 23 other countries.

14654 Global Report
Citicorp
800 3rd Ave
New York, NY 10022-7669

212-688-1308
Home Page: www.citibank.com

One of the most comprehensive databases in the world offering information on foreign exchange, country reports, money markets, bonds, companies, industries and news.
Frequency: Full-text

14655 Importers Manual USA
World Trade Press
800 Lindberg Lane
Suite 190
Petaluma, CA 94952

707-778-1124
800-833-8586
Fax: 707-777-1329
E-Mail: egh@worldtradepress.com
Home Page: www.worldtradepress.com

Edward Hinkelman, Publisher
James Nolan, Editor
Karla Shippey, Editor

Lists of trade fairs, embassies, chambers of commerce, banks, and other sources of information on various aspects of international trade.
Cost: $145.00
960 Pages
Frequency: 2-3 per year
Circulation: 3,000
ISBN: 1-885073-93-3
Founded in 1993

14656 International Directory of Importers
1741 Kekamek NW
Poulsbo, WA 98730

360-779-1511
800-818-0140
Fax: 360-697-4696
Home Page: www.export-leads.com

Esther Camacho, Circulation

Publishes reference guides for worldwide importers, wholesalers, agents, and distributors.
Cost: $250.00
5000 Pages
Frequency: Annual
Founded in 1978

14657 Japan Economic Daily
Kyodo News International
747 3rd Ave
Suite 1803
New York, NY 10017-2803

212-935-4440
Fax: 212-508-5441
E-Mail: kni@kyodonews.com
Home Page: www.kyodonews.com

This full coverage database contains news on Japanese business, industry, economics and finance developments.
Frequency: Full-text

14658 LEXIS International Trade Library
Mead Data Central
9443 Springboro Pike
Dayton, OH 45401

888-223-6337
Fax: 518-487-3584
Home Page: www.lexis-nexis.com

Andrew Prozes, CEO
Rebecca Schmitt, Chief Financial Officer

This database contains information on international trade regulation decisions handed down from the Supreme Court and other legislative bodies.
Frequency: Full-text

14659 Local Chambers of Commerce Which Maintain Foreign Trade Services
US Chamber of Commerce-International Division
1615 H St NW
Washington, DC 20062-0002

202-659-6000
Fax: 202-463-5836
Home Page: www.uschamber.org

Thomas J Donohue, CEO
Jean Hunt, Administrative Assistant
Cost: $15.00

14660 Mexico Tax, Law,& Business Briefing
WorldTrade Executive
2250 Main St
Suite 100
Concord, MA 01742-3838

978-287-0301
Fax: 978-287-0302
E-Mail: info@wtexec.com
Home Page: www.wtexecutive.com

Gary Brown, Owner
Jay Stanley, Sales Manager
A single volume special report that provides guidance on tax and legal issues investors should consider when evaluating a possible company aquisition, starting a business or entering into a joint venture or strategic alliance in Mexico. Also featuring important guidance prepared by major accounting and law firms.
Cost: $297.00
291 Pages
ISBN: 1-893323-67-6

14661 North American Export Pages
US West Marketing Resources Group
1101 30th Street NW
Suite 200
Washington, DC 20007-3769

202-934-4584
800-288-2582
Fax: 202-944-4680

David Lee, President
Approximately 50,000 suppliers from the United States, Canada, and Mexico wishing to export products worldwide.
Cost: $39.95

14662 Official Export Guide
North American Publishing Company
1500 Spring Garden St
Suite 1200
Philadelphia, PA 19130-4094

215-238-5300
Fax: 215-238-5342
Home Page: www.napco.com

Ned S Borowsky, President and CEO
Offers information on customs officials, port authorities, embassies and consulates, chambers of commerce and other organizations involved in international trade.
Cost: $399.00
1800 Pages
Frequency: Annual
Founded in 1958

14663 Political Handbook of the World
McGraw Hill
PO Box 182604
Columbus, OH 43272

614-866-5769
Fax: 614-759-3759
E-Mail: webmaster@mcgraw-hill.com
Home Page: www.mcgraw-hill.com

Arthur S Banks, Editor
Thomas C Muller, Editor
Annual reference book containing separate sections on every country in the world and more than 100 intergovernment organizations. Each edition completely updates political developments over the past year while retaining the extensive background information necessary for researchers to place current events in a comprehensive historical perspective.
1400 Pages
Founded in 1979

14664 Practical Guide: Doing Business in Ukraine
WorldTrade Executive
PO Box 761
Concord, MA 01742-0761

978-287-0301
Fax: 978-287-0302
E-Mail: info@wtexec.com
Home Page: www.wtexec.com

Alison French, Production Manager
Topics covered include: common business structures, registration procedures, real property transactions, tax and foreign investment legislation, currency reforms and regulations, privatization programs, intellectual property.
Cost: $145.00

14665 Protecting Intellectual Property in Latin America
WorldTrade Executive
PO Box 761
Concord, MA 01742-0761

978-287-0301
Fax: 978-287-0302
E-Mail: info@wtexec.com
Home Page: www.wtexec.com

Alison French, Production Manager
A complete guide to the protection of intellectual property in Latin America, including in-depth coverage of copyright law, patents and trademarks, software, pharmaceuticals, etc. Also deals with issues of enforcement and prosecution.
Cost: $235.00

14666 Russian Far East: A Business Reference Guide
Russian Far East Advisory Group
PO Box 22126
Seattle, WA 98122-0126

206-447-2668
Fax: 206-628-0979
Home Page: www.russianfareast.com

Elisa Miller, Editor
Alexander Karp, Editor
Sourcebook for business people, travelers, and researchers focusing on trends and economic developments in the Russian Far East. Includes reviews of each of the ten administrative regions and 27 maps
Cost: $79.00
270 Pages
ISBN: 0-964128-63-2

14667 Selling Successfully in Mexico
WorldTrade Executive
PO Box 761
Concord, MA 01742-0761

978-287-0301
Fax: 978-287-0302
E-Mail: info@wtexec.com
Home Page: www.wtexec.com

Alison French, Production Manager
A detailed guide to market research, advertising, direct marketing, and trade show exhibition in Mexico, written by marketing professionals and supplemented by extensive data and key contracts.
Cost: $129.00

14668 Showcase USA: American Export-Buyers Guide and Membership
Bobit Publishing Company
3623 Artesia Boulevard
Redondo Beach, CA 90278

FAX 310-376-9043
List of member companies and organizations of Sell Overseas America.

14669 Trade Opportunity
US International Trade Association
1401 Constitution Ave NW
Washington, DC 20230-0001

202-482-2867
800-872-8723
Fax: 202-482-2867
Home Page: www.ita.doc.gov

David L Aaron, Manager
Renee Macklin, Chief Information Officer
Leads to export opportunities for United States businesses.

14670 Trade Shows Worldwide
Gale/Cengage Learning
PO Box 09187
Detroit, MI 48209-0187

248-699-4253
800-877-4253
Fax: 248-699-8049
E-Mail: gale.galeord@cengage.com
Home Page: www.gale.com
Social Media: Facebook, Twitter, Google+, Youtube

Patrick C Sommers, President
Each edition of this resource includes listings for more than 10,000 trade shows; approximately 6,000 trade show sponsoring organizations and more than 5,900 facilities, services and information sources on trade shows and exhibitions held in the United States and around the globe.
Frequency: Annual
ISBN: 1-414435-24-X

14671 US Custom House Guide
U.S. Custom House Guide

609-371-7825
888-215-6084
Fax: 609-371-7885
E-Mail: mmcarthy@ubmglobaltrade.com
Home Page: www.uscustomhouseguide.com

Monica McCarthy, Associate Editor
Amy Middlebrook, Vice President, Directories
Dennis Ferrere, Advertising Sales Rep
List of ports having customs facilities, customs officials, port authorities, chambers of commerce, embassies and consulates, foreign trade zones and other organizations; related trade services.
Cost: $399.00
Frequency: Annual January

14672 World Trade Almanac
World Trade Press
1450 Grant Avenue
Suite 204
Novato, CA 94945

415-454-9934
415-898-1124
Home Page: www.worldtradepress.com

Gayle Madison
Peter Jones

Industry Web Sites

14673 http://gold.greyhouse.com
G.O.L.D Grey House OnLine Databases
Grey House Publishing's online database platform, GOLD, offers Quick Search, Keyword Search and Expert Search for most business sectors including international trade markets. The GOLD platform makes finding the information you need quick and easy - whether you're a novice searcher or an experienced database user. All of Grey House's directory products are available for subscription on the GOLD platform.

14674 www.aib.msu.edu/
Academy of International Business
Members are executives and teachers in the international business field.

14675 www.fancyfoodshows.com
National Association for the Specialty Food Trade
Members are manufacturers, importers, distributors and retailers of specialty gourmet and fancy foods. Has an annual budget of approximately $15 million. Publications available to members.

14676 www.geminishippers.com
Gemini Shippers Group
Shippers association with global contracts for all commodities.

14677 www.greyhouse.com
Grey House Publishing
Authoritative reference directories for most business sectors including international trade markets. Users can search the online databases with varied search criteria allowing for custom searches by product category, geographic area, sales volume, keyword, subject and more. Full Grey House catalog and online ordering also available.

14678 www.iwla.com
International Warehouse Logistics Association

14679 www.ncitd.org
National Council on Int'l Trade Development
For exporters and importers and other professionals serving the international commerce industry.

14680 www.tdctrade.com
Hong Kong Trade Development Council
Promotes trade between United States and Hong Kong.

14681 www.uschina.org
US China Business Council
Membership association for US companies doing business with the People's Republic of China. Provides representation, practical assistance, and up-to-date information to members.

14682 www.vita.com
VMEbus International Trade Association (VITA)
Association for manufacturers of microcomputer boards, hardware, software, military products, controllers, bus interfaces and other accessories compatible with VMEbus architecture.

International Trade Resources

14683 Albania to the United Nations
320 E 79th Street
New York, NY 10075
212-249-2059
Fax: 212-535-2917
E-Mail: mission.newyork@mfa.gov.al
Home Page: www.albania-un.org
Social Media: Facebook, Twitter, LinkedIn, RSS Feed, Google+
Geronimo Albano, Owner
Petrik Jorgji, Minister Counselor
Olisa Cifligu, Second Secretary
Ermal Frasheri, Adviser, legal Issues
Admira Jorgji, Counselor

14684 Antigua and Barbuda Department of Tourism and Trade
25 S.E. 2nd Avenue
Suite 300
Miami, FL 33131
305-381-6762
Fax: 305-381-7908
E-Mail: cganuear@bellsouth.net
Home Page: www.antigua-barbuda.org
Byron Spencer, Manager

14685 Austrian Trade Commission
120 West 45th Street
9th Floor
New York, NY 10036
212-421-5250
Fax: 212-421-5251
E-Mail: newyork@advantageaustria.org
Home Page: www.advantageaustria.org/us
Social Media: Facebook, Twitter, RSS Feed
Peter Athanasiadis, Manager
Sabine Miller, Project Manager
Walter HAfle, Director

14686 Azerbaijan - Permanent Mission to the United Nations
866 United Nations Plaza, Ste 560
48 str. & 1 Avenue
New York, NY 10017
212-371-2559
Fax: 212-371-2784
E-Mail: azerbaijan@un.int, az.protocol@yahoo.com
Home Page: www.un.int/azerbaijan/
Eldar Kouliev, Manager

14687 Bahamas Consulate General
231 E 46th Street
New York, NY 10017
212-421-6420
Fax: 212-688-5926
E-Mail: consulate@bahamasny.com
Home Page: www.un.it/bahamas
Hon Eldred E Bethel, Contact
Forrester J. Carroll, JP, Consul General
Sandra N. McLaughlin, Vice Consul
Clemmy Eneas-varence, Sr. Information Clerk
Carolyn Young-Miller, Administrative Asst.

14688 Bulgarian General Consulate
121 E 62nd Street
New York, NY 10021
212-935-4646
Fax: 212-319-5955
E-Mail: consulate.newyork@mfa.bg
Home Page: www.consulbulgaria-ny.org

14689 Business Council for the United Nations
801 2nd Avenue
Ste 900
New York, NY 10017
212-697-3315
Fax: 212-682-9185
E-Mail: unahq@unausa.org
Home Page: www.unfoundation.org
Social Media: Facebook, Twitter, YouTube, RSS Feed
Allison B MacEachron, Executive Director
Kathy Calvin, President & CEO
Richard S. Parnell, COO
Walter Cortes, CFO
Aaron Sherinian, VP, Communications

14690 Chile Trade Commission
866 United Nations Plaza
Suite 603
New York, NY 10017
212-207-3266
Fax: 212-207-3649
Alejandro Cerda, Trade Commissioner

14691 Consulate General of Bahrain
866 2nd Avenue
14th Floor
New York, NY 10017
212-223-6200
Fax: 212-319-0687
Home Page: www.un.int/bahrain/consulate.html
Jassim Buallay, Manager

14692 Consulate General of Belgium in New York
1065 Avenue of Americas
22nd Floor
New York, NY 10018
212-586-5110
212-586-7472
Fax: 212-582-9657
E-Mail: NewYork@diplobel.fed.be
Home Page: www.diplomatie.be/newyork/
Piet Morisse, Manager
Marc Calcoen, Consul General
Leon Cortens, Deputy Consul General

14693 Consulate General of Brazil
220 E. 42nd St.
26th Floor
New York, NY 10017
917-777-7777
Fax: 212-827-0225
E-Mail: cg.novayork@itamaraty.gov.br
Home Page: http://novayork.utamaraty.gov.br/en-us/
Julio Cesar Gomes Dos Sant, Manager

14694 Consulate General of Costa Rica
14 Penn Plaza, #1202
225 West 34th Street
New York, NY 10122
212-509-3066
212-509-3066
Fax: 212-509-3068
Fax: 212-509-3068
Home Page: www.costariica-embassy.org
Otto Barcas, Manager

14695 Consulate General of Germany
871 United Nations Plaza
New York, NY 10017
212-610-9700
Fax: 212-940-0402
Bernhard Von Der Planit, Manager

14696 **Consulate General of Haiti**
815 2nd Ave.
6th Floor
New York, NY 10017

212-697-9767
Fax: 212-681-6991
E-Mail: contact@haitianconsulate-nyc.org, cg.new
Home Page: www.haitianconsulate-nyc.org

Marie Therese, Manager
Charles A. Forbin, Consul General

14697 **Consulate General of Honduras**
255 West 36th Street
First Level
New York, NY 10018

212-714-9451
Fax: 212-714-9453
Home Page: www.hondurasemb.org
Social Media: Facebook, Twitter

14698 **Consulate General of India**
3 E 64th Street
New York, NY 10065

212-774-0600
Fax: 212-861-3788
Home Page: www.indiacgny.org

Ambassador Prabhu Dayal, Consul General
Mr. P.K. Bajaj, Consul (Head of Chancery)
Shambhu Amitabh, Vice Consul (Passport & Consular)
Ajay Purswani, Consul (Visa)
Dhirendra Singh, Counsel

14699 **Consulate General of Indonesia**
5 E 68th Street
New York, NY 10021

212-879-0600

14700 **Consulate General of Israel in New York**
800 Second Avenue
New York, NY 10017
212-499-5000
E-Mail: info@newyork.mfa.gov.il
Home Page: www.israelfm.org
Social Media: Facebook, Twitter, YouTube, flickr

Ido Aharoni, Consul General
Founded in 1948

14701 **Consulate General of Kenya**
866 UN Plaza
Suite 4016
New York, NY 10017

212-421-4741
Fax: 212-486-1985
Home Page: www.kenya.embassy-online.net/kenya-consulate-general-new-york.php

Rolando Visconti, Manager

14702 **Consulate General of Lebanon in New York**
9 E 76th Street
New York, NY 10021

212-744-7905
Fax: 212-794-1510
E-Mail: lebconsny@aol.com
Home Page: www.lebconsny.org

Hassan Saad, Manager

14703 **Consulate General of Lithuania**
420 5th Avenue
3rd Floor
New York, NY 10018

212-354-7840
Fax: 212-354-7911
E-Mail: kons.niujorkas@urm.lt
Home Page: ny.mfa.lt

Rimantas Morkvenas, Manager
Valdemaras Sarapinas, Consul General

14704 **Consulate General of Malta**
249 E 35th Street
New York, NY 10016

212-725-2345
Fax: 212-779-7097

14705 **Consulate General of Morocco**
10 East 40th Street
New York, NY 10016

212-758-2625
Fax: 646-395-8077
E-Mail: info@moroccanconsulate.com
Home Page: www.moroccanconsulate.com

Ramon Xilotl, Manager
Mohammed Benabdeljalil, Consul general
Sidi Mohammed El Bakkari, Deputy Consul

14706 **Consulate General of Nigeria**
828 2nd Avenue
New York, NY 10017

212-808-0301
Fax: 212-687-1476
E-Mail: cgnny@nigeriahouse.com
Home Page: www.nigeriahouse.com

14707 **Consulate General of Paraguay**
801 2nd . Ave.
Suite 600
New York, NY 10017

212-682-9441
212-682-9442
Fax: 212-682-9443
E-Mail: info@consulparny.com
Home Page: www.consulparny.com/ingles/html/visas.html

Juan Baiardi, Manager

14708 **Consulate General of Peru**
241 East 49th St.
New York, NY 10017

646-735-3828
Fax: 646-735-3866
E-Mail: consulado@conperny.org
Home Page: www.consuladoperu.com

Fortunato Ricar Quesada Seminario, Consul General

14709 **Consulate General of Qatar**
2555 M St NW
Washington, DC 20037-1305

202-274-1600
Fax: 202-237-9880
E-Mail: info@qatarembassy.net
Home Page: www.qatarembassy.net

Mohammad Al-Madadi, Consul

14710 **Consulate General of Saudi Arabia**
866 United Nations Plaza
Suite 480
New York, NY 10017

212-752-2740

Abdulrahman Gdaia, Execellency

14711 **Consulate General of Slovenia**
120 East 56th Street
Suite 320
New York, NY 10022

212-370-3006
Fax: 212-421-1532
E-Mail: nky@gov.si

Reimo Pettai, Manager

14712 **Consulate General of South Africa**
333 E 38th Street
9th Floor
New York, NY 10016

212-213-4880
Fax: 212-213-0102
E-Mail: consulate.ny@foreign.gov.za
Home Page: www.southafrica-newyork.net

Fikile Magubane, Consul-General
Thami Sono, Consul
Leon Naidoo, Consul
George Monyemangene, Consul General

14713 **Consulate General of St. Lucia**
2005 Massachusetts Ave., NW
Washington, DC 20036-1030

202-558-2216
800-345-6541
202-364-6795
Fax: 202-318-0771
E-Mail: info@visahq.com
Home Page: saint-lucia.visahq.com

Julian Hunte, Manager

14714 **Consulate General of Switzerland**
633 3rd Avenue
30th Floor
New York, NY 10017-6706

212-599-5700
Fax: 212-599-4266
Home Page: www.eda.admin.ch

Raymond Loretan, Excellency

14715 **Consulate General of Trinidad & Tobago**
125 Maidan Lane
4th Floor
New York, NY 10038

212-682-7272
Fax: 212-232-0368
E-Mail: consulate@ttcgny.com
Home Page: www.ttcgnewyork.com
Social Media: Facebook, Twitter, YouTube, RSS Feed

Hon Harold Robertson, Contact
Rudrawatee Nan Ramgoolam, Consul General

14716 **Consulate General of Ukraine**
240 E 49th Street
New York, NY 10017

212-371-5690
Fax: 212-371-5547
E-Mail: gc_usn@mfa.gov.ua
Home Page: ny.mfa.gov.ua

Serhii Pohoreltsev, Consul General

14717 **Consulate General of Uruguay**
420 Madison Street
6th Floor
New York, NY 10017

212-753-8581
212-753-8192
Fax: 212-753-1603
E-Mail: consulado@consuladouruguaynewyork.com
Home Page: www.consuladouruguaynewyork.com

Basil Bryan, Manager
Carlos Orlando, Consul General

14718 Consulate General of Venezuela
7 E 51st Street
New York, NY 10022
212-826-1660
Fax: 212-644-7471
E-Mail: ven.newyork@gmail.com
Home Page: newyork.embavenez-us.org
Carol Delgado Arria, Consul General

14719 Consulate General of the Dominican Republic
1715 22nd Street, NW
Washington, DC 20008
202-332-6280
202-332-7670
Fax: 202-265-8057
E-Mail: embassy@us.serex.gov.do, consular@us.ser
Home Page: www.domrep.org
Social Media: Facebook, Blogspot
Jose Luis Dominguez, Minister Counselor
Felipe Herrera, Cunselor
Morela Baez, Commercial Affairs
Alejandra Hernandez, Minister Counselor
Ligia Reid Bonetti, Minister Counselor

14720 Consulate General of the Netherlands
666 Third Avenue
19th floor
New York, NY 10017
877-388-2443
Fax: 212-333-3603
E-Mail: nyc@minbuza.nl
Home Page: ny.the-netherlands.org
Social Media: Facebook, Twitter, YouTube, RSS Feed
Wanda Fleck, Manager

14721 Consulate General of the Principality of Monaco
565 5th Avenue
23rd Floor
New York, NY 10017
212-286-0500
Fax: 212-286-1574
E-Mail: info@monaco-consulate.com
Home Page: www.monaco-consulate.com
Social Media: Facebook, Twitter
Maguy Maccario-Doyle, Consul General, Minister Cousellor

14722 Consulate General of the Republic of Belarus
708 3rd Avenue
20th Floor
New York, NY 10017
212-682-5392
Fax: 212-682-5491
E-Mail: gcny@belembassy.org
Home Page: www.belarusconsul.org
Social Media: RSS Feed
Sergei Kolos, Manager

14723 Consulate General of the Russian Federation
2343 Massachusettes Ave, NW
Washington, DC 20008-2803
202-588-5899
Fax: 202-588-8937
Home Page: www.croatiaemb.org

14724 Consulate of Guyana
370 7th Avenue
New York, NY 10017
212-947-5110
Fax: 212-573-6225
Home Page: www.guyana.org
Social Media: Facebook, Twitter, Gmail, StumbleUpon,Pinterest,G
Samuel Insanally, Ambassador, Permanent Rep
Edwin Carrington, Secretary
Mohammed A. O. Ishmael, Managing Director
Amral Khan, Administrator & Editor

14725 Consulate of the Republic of Uzbekistan in New York City
801 Second Ave
20th Floor
New York, NY 10017
212-754-7403
Fax: 212-838-9812
E-Mail: info@uzbekconsulny.org
Home Page: www.uzbekconsulny.org

14726 Croatia Consulate, United States
369 Lexington Avenue
11th Floor
New York, NY 10017
212-599-3066
Fax: 212-599-3106
E-Mail: croatian.consulate@gte.net
Home Page: www.croatia.visahq.com/embassy/United-States/
Abdul Seraj, Manager

14727 Ecuadorian Consulate
2535 15th Street NW
Washington, DC 20009
202-234-7200
866-ECU-DOR
Fax: 202-667-3482
E-Mail: consuladodc@ecuador.org
Home Page: www.ecuador.us
Pablo Yanez, Consul General

14728 Egyptian Consulate Economic & Commercial Office
3521 International Ct. NW
Washingotn, DC 20008
202-895-5400
Fax: 202-244-5131
E-Mail: embassy@egyptembassy.net
Home Page: www.egyptembassy.net
Social Media: Facebook
Ayden Nour, Executive Director
Mohamed M. Tawfik, Ambassador

14729 Embassy of Australia
1601 Massachusetts Avenue NW
Washington, DC 20036
202-797-3000
Fax: 202-797-3168
Home Page: www.usa.embassy.gov.au
Social Media: Facebook, Twitter
Kim Beazley, Ambassador

14730 Embassy of Benin
2124 Kalorama Road NW
Washington, DC 20008
202-232-6656
Fax: 202-232-2611
E-Mail: info@beninembassy.us
Home Page: www.beninembassy.us
Boni T. Yayi, President
Cyrille S. Oguin, Ambassador

14731 Embassy of Bosnia and Herzegovina
2109 E Street NW
Washington, DC 20037
202-337-1500
Fax: 202-337-1502
E-Mail: info@bhembassy.org, consularaffairs@bhem
Home Page: www.bhembassy.org
Social Media: Facebook, Twitter, Google +, Pinterest
Yayi Kujundzic, Ambassador Extraordinary
Jadranka Negodic, Ambassador
Edic Sehic, Minister-Counselor Head
Haris Bazdarecic, Counselor
Adnan Hadrovic, Minister-Counselor

14732 Embassy of Cambodia
4530 16th Street NW
Washington, DC 20011
202-726-7742
202-726-7824
Fax: 202-726-8381
E-Mail: camemb.usa@mfa.gov.kh
Home Page: www.embassyofcambodia.org
Social Media: Facebook
Hem Heng, Ambassador
Mouth Keo Thida, Commercial Counselor
Koeut navuth, Defense Attache
Neang Chanthou, Finance Attache
Theam Vuth, Second Secretary

14733 Embassy of Estonia
2131 Massachusetts Avenue NW
Washington, DC 20008
202-588-0101
Fax: 202-588-0108
E-Mail: embassy.washington@mfa.ee
Home Page: www.estemb.org
Social Media: Facebook, Twitter, Flickr
Marina Kaljurand, Ambassador

14734 Embassy of Ethiopia
3506 International Drive NW
Washington, DC 20008
202-364-1200
Fax: 202-587-0195
E-Mail: ethiopia@ethiopianembassy.org
Home Page: www.ethiopianembassy.org/
Girma Birru, Ambassador
Tsegab Kebebew, Minister Counselor
Kidist Yakob, Counselor (Politcal Affairs)
Wahide Belay, Minister Counselor
Yohannes Getahun, Minster Counselor

14735 Embassy of Finland
3301 Massachusetts Avenue NW
Washington, DC 20008
202-298-5800
Fax: 202-298-6030
E-Mail: sanomat.was@formin.fi
Home Page: www.finland.org
Social Media: Facebook, Twitter
Ritva Koukku-Ronde, Ambassador

14736 Embassy of Georgia
2209 Massachusettes Avenue, NW
Washington, DC 20008
202-387-2390
Fax: 202-387-0864
E-Mail: embgeo.usa@mfa.gov.ge
Home Page: www.embassy.mfa.gov.ge
Temur Yakobashvili, Ambassador
David Rakviashvili, Envoy
Mikheil Darchiashvili, Minister
Thea Kentchadze, Sr. Counselor
Mariam Lebanidze, Counselor

14737 Embassy of Grenada
1701 New Hampshire Ave, NW
Washington, DC 20009-2501
202-265-2561
Fax: 292-265-2468
E-Mail: gdaembassydc@gmail.com
Home Page: www.grenadaembassyusa.org
Social Media: Facebook, Twitter, Google+
E. Angus Friday, Ambassador
Patricia D.M. Clarke, Counsellor

Dianne C. Perrotte, Adminstrative Asst
Lucia Amedee, Receptionist/ Clerical Asst.

14738 Embassy of Jamaica (JAMPRO)
1520 New Hampshire Ave, NW
Washington, DC 20036

202-452-0660
Fax: 202-452-0036
E-Mail: firstsec@jamaicaembassy.org
Home Page: www.embassyofjamaica.org

Audrey P. Marks, Ambassador

14739 Embassy of Jordan
3504 International Drive NW
Washington, DC 20008

202-966-2664
Fax: 202-966-3110
E-Mail: HKJEmbassyDC@jordanembassyus.org
Home Page: www.jordanembassyus.org
Social Media: Facebook, Twitter, YouTube, RSS Feed, Pinterest,

Alia Hatoung Bouran, Ambassador
Amjad Hatem Al-Mbideen, Consul
Fawaz Bilbesi, Deputy Chief of Mission
Aishabint Al hussein, Military Attache
Qais Biltaji, Fist Secretary

14740 Embassy of Mali
2130 R Street NW
Washington, DC 20008

202-332-2249
Fax: 202-332-6603
E-Mail: info@maliembassy.us
Home Page: www.maliembassy.us

Al Maamoun Baba Lamine Kehta, Ambassador
Muhamed Ouzouna Maiga, 1st Counselor
Ahmadou Barazi Maiga, 2nd Counselor
Colonel Bourama Sangare, Defence Attache
Mahama Dicko, Financial Attache

14741 Embassy of Mongolia
2833 M Street NW
Washington, DC 20007

202-333-7117
Fax: 202-298-9227
E-Mail: dc@mongolianembassy.us
Home Page: www.mongolianembassy.us

Khasbazaryn Bekhbat, Ambassador

14742 Embassy of Panama
2862 McGill Terrace NW
Washington, DC 20008

202-483-1407
202-483-1407
Fax: 202-483-8413
E-Mail: info@embassyofpanama.org
Home Page: www.embassyofpanama.org
Social Media: Facebook

Mario E. Jaramillo, Ambassador

14743 Embassy of Tanzania
1232 22nd St, NW
Washington, DC 20037

202-884-1080
202-939-6125, 202-
Fax: 202-797-7408
E-Mail: ubalozi@tanzaniaembassy-us.org
Home Page: www.tanzaniaembassy-us.org
Social Media: Facebook, Twitter

Liberata Mulamula, Ambassador
Lily Munanka, Minister/ Head of Chancery
Paul Mwafongo, Minister, Economic Affairs
B.G. Emmanuel Maganga, Defense Attache
Edward Masanja, Finacial Attache

14744 Embassy of Tunisia
1515 Massachusetts Avenue NW
Washington, DC 20005

202-862-1850
Fax: 202-862-1858
E-Mail: info@tunconusa.org
Home Page: www.tunconsusa.org/

Gordon Gray, Ambassador

14745 Embassy of Uganda
5911 16th Street NW
Washington, DC 20011

202-726-7100
Fax: 202-726-1727
E-Mail: info@ugandaembassyus.org
Home Page: www.ugandaemb.org

Oliver Wonekha, Ambassador
Alfred Nnam, Deputy Chief of Commission
Dickson Ogwang, Minister Counselor
Patrick Muganda Guma, Counselor
Sam Bhoi Omara, 1st Secretary

14746 Embassy of Vietnam
1233 20th Street NW
Suite 400
Washington, DC 20036

202-861-0737
Fax: 202-861-0917
E-Mail: info@vietnamembassy.us, vnconsular@vietn
Home Page: www.vietnamembassy-usa.org

Nguyen Quoc Cuong, Ambassador

14747 Embassy of Zimbabwe
1608 New Hampshire Avenue NW
Washington, DC 20009

202-332-7100
Fax: 202-483-9326
E-Mail: info33@zimbabwe-embassy.us
Home Page: www.zimbabwe-embassy.us

Dr. Machivenyik Mapuranga, Ambassador
Richard T. Chibuwe, Minister Counselor & Deputy Chief
Whatmore Goora, Counselor (Political)
R. Matsika, Counselor
Lt. Col. George Chinoingira, Defence Attache

14748 Embassy of the Lao People's Democratic Republic
2222 S Street NW
Washington, DC 20008

202-332-6416
202-667-0076
Fax: 202-332-4923
E-Mail: embasslao@gmail.com
Home Page: www.laoembassy.com

H.E. Seng Soukhathivong, Ambassador
Thongmoon Phongphailath, 1st Secretary
Somxai Kittanouvong, 2nd Secretary (Consular)
Kerlor Yangko, 3rd Secretary (Economy And Culture)
Sounthone Duangxaty, Attache (Economic & Culture)

14749 Embassy of the People's Republic of China
3505 International Place NW
Washington, DC 20008

202-495-2266
Fax: 202-495-2138
E-Mail: chinaembpress_us@mfa.gov.cn
Home Page: www.china-embassy.org

Cui Tiankai, Ambassador
Lu Kang, Minister

14750 Embassy of the Republic of Angola
2100-2108 16th Street, NW
Washington, DC 20009

202-785-1156
Fax: 202-822-9049
E-Mail: angola@angola.org
Home Page: www.angola.org

Alberto do Carmo Bento Ribeiro, Ambassador
Sofia Pegado da Silva, Minster Counselor
Manuel Fransisco Lourenco, 1st Secretary
Ismael Filipe, 2nd secretary- Political Affairs
Gil Cardoso, Financial Attache

14751 Embassy of the Republic of Botswana and GlobeScope, Inc.
1531-1533 New Hampshire Avenue NW
Washington, DC 20036

202-244-4990
E-Mail: smautle@botswanaembassy.org
Home Page: www.botswanaembassy.org

H.E. Dr.Tebelel Mazile Seretse, Ambassador
Ms. Sophie Heide Mautle, Deputy Head of Mission
Innocent Matengu, Counselor (Politcal Affairs)
Dineo Mpuchane, 1st Secretary (Administration)
Mighty Mohurutshe, Administrative Attache
Founded in 1965

14752 Embassy of the Republic of Fiji
2000 M Street,NW
Suite 710
Washington, DC 20036

202-466-8320
Fax: 202-466-8325
E-Mail: info@fijiembassydc.com
Home Page: www.fijiembassydc.com

Winston Thompson, Ambassador
Akuila Vuira, 1st Secretary
Teresita R. Sauler-Cooke, Executive Asst.
Lathanzuala Phillips, Chauffer

14753 Embassy of the Republic of Latvia
2306 Massachusettes Ave, NW
Washington, DC 20008

202-328-2840
Fax: 202-328-2860
E-Mail: embassy.usa@mfa.gov.lv
Home Page: www.latvia-us.org

Andrejs Pildegovics, Ambassador

14754 Embassy of the Republic of Yemen
2319 Wyoming Ave, NW
Washington, DC 20008

202-965-4760
Fax: 202-337-2017
E-Mail: ambassador@yemenembassy.org
Home Page: www.yemenembassy.org

Abdulwahab Abdulla Al-Hajjri, Ambassador
Nadia Fhashem, Asst to the Ambassador

14755 Embassy of the Republic of the Marshall Islands
2433 Massachusetts Avenue NW
Washington, DC 20008

202-234-5414
Fax: 202-232-3236
E-Mail: info@rmiembassyus.org
Home Page: www.rmiembassyus.org

Charles R. Paul, Ambassador
Dixie Lomae, 1st Secretary
Donna Dizon, Office Manager

14756 Fair Trading Commission
Good Hope, Green Hill
St. Michael, Ba BB12003

246-424-0260
Fax: 246-424-0300

E-Mail: info@ftc.gov.bb
Home Page: www.ftc.gov.bb

Peggy Griffith, CEO
Sir Neville Nicholls, Chairman
Andrew Downes, Deputy chairman
Monique Taitt, Commissioner
Kendrid Sargeant, Commissioner

14757 **French Trade Commission**
200 N Colombus Dr.
Chicago, IL 60601

312-565-8000
Fax: 312-856-1032
Home Page: www.firmafrance.com
Social Media: Facebook, Twitter, LinkedIn, RSS Feed, Google +

14758 **Gambia Mission to the United Nations**
800 2nd Avenue
Suite 400 F
New York, NY 10017
212-949-6640
Fax: 212-856-9820
E-Mail: gambia@un.int
Home Page: www.un.int/wcm/content/site/gambia

Tamsir Jallow, Ambassador

14759 **General Consulate of Luxembourg**
17 Beekman Place
New York, NY 10022

212-888-6664
Fax: 212-888-6116
E-Mail: newyork.cg@mae.etat.lu
Home Page: www.newyork-cg.mae.lu/

Jean-Claude Knebelar, Consul General
Saba Amroun-Forbes, Consular Officer

14760 **Gibraltar Information Bureau**
1156 15th Street NW
Suite 1100
Washington, DC 20005

202-452-1108
Fax: 202-452-1109

Perry Stieglitz, Executive Director

14761 **Greek Trade Commission**
150 E 58th Street
17th Floor
New York, NY 10155

212-751-2404
Fax: 212-593-2278

Yannis Papadimitriou, Manager

14762 **Hungarian Trade Commission**
425 Bloor Street, East
Suite 501
Toronto-Ontario M4W 3R4

416-923-3596
Fax: 416-923-2097
E-Mail: itdtoronto@hungariantrade.org

Gyula Cseko, Trade Commissioner

14763 **Icelandic Consulate General**
800 3rd Avenue
36th Floor
New York, NY 10022

646-282-9360
Fax: 646-282-9369
E-Mail: icecon.ny@mfa.is
Home Page: www.iceland.is/us/nyc

Hlynur Gudjonsson, Consul & Trade Commissioner

14764 **International Chamber of Commerce (ICC)**
1212 Avenue of the Americas
New York, NY 10036-1689

212-703-5065
Fax: 212-575-0327
Home Page: www.iccwbo.org
Social Media: Facebook, Twitter, LinkedIn, Google+, YouTube

Sunil Bharti Mittal, Vice-Chairman
Harold McGraw III, Chairman
Gerard Worms, Honorary Chairman
Jean-Guy Carrier, Secretary General
Founded in 1919
Mailing list available for rent

14765 **Irish Trade Board**
345 Park Avenue
17th Floor
New York, NY 10154
212-180-0800

Jean McCluskey, Marketing Executive

14766 **Japanese External Trade Organization**
1221 Avenue of the Americas
McGraw Hill Building, 42nd Floor
New York, NY 10020

212-997-0400
Fax: 212-997-0464
E-Mail: jetrony@jetro.go.jp
Home Page: www.jetro.org
Social Media: Facebook, Twitter

Hiroyuki Ishige, Chairman
Masaki Fujihara, Dir., Business Development
Daiki Nakajima, ICT/ Environment

14767 **Kazakhstan Mission to the United Nations**
305 East 47th Street
3rd Floor
New York, NY 10017

212-230-1900
Fax: 212-230-1172
E-Mail: kazakhstan@un.int
Home Page: www.kazakhstanun.org

Byrganym Aitimova, Ambassador
Akan Rakhmetulin, Deputy Permanent Rep
Israil Tilegen, Minister Counsellor
Ruslan Bultrikov, Counsellor
Col. Alexander Kabentayev, Counsellor Military Adviser

14768 **Korea Trade Promotion Center (KOTRA)**
460 Park Avenue
14th Floor
New York, NY 10022

212-826-0900
Fax: 212-888-4930
E-Mail: kotrany@hotmail.com
Home Page: www.kotrana.org

Sungpil Um, Presiden/North America
Il Hoon Ko, Deputy Director

14769 **Kyrgyzstan Mission to the United Nations**
866 United Nations Plaza
Room 477
New York, NY 10017
212-486-4214
Fax: 212-486-5259
Home Page: www.un.int/wcm/content/site/kyrgyzstan

Talaibek Kydyrov, Ambassador
Nuran Niyazaliev, Counsellor/DPR
Nurbek Kasymov, 1st secretary
Asel Davydova, Chief Administrative Specialist
Salamat Supataev, Administrative Officer

14770 **Malaysia Mission to the United Nations**
313 E 43rd Street
3rd Floor
New York, NY 10017

212-986-6310
Fax: 212-490-8576
E-Mail: malnyun@kln.gov.my
Home Page: www.kln.gov.my
Social Media: RSS Feed

Hussein Haniff, Ambassador

14771 **Mexico Trade Commission**
757 3rd Ave
Suite 2400
New York, NY 10017-2042

212-826-2978
Fax: 212-826-2979
Home Page: www.mexconnect.com
Social Media: Facebook, Twitter

14772 **Moldova Mission to the United Nations**
35 East 29th Street
New York, NY 10016

212-447-1867
Fax: 212-447-4067
E-Mail: unmoldova@aol.com
Home Page: www.un.int/wcm/content/site/moldova

Vlad Lupan, Ambassador
Larisa Miculet, Counsellor, Deputy Permanent Rep
Carolina Podoroghin, 3rd Secretary
Tatiana Dudnicenco, CFO,Head of Chancery
Litvac Sergiu, Administrator

14773 **New Zealand Trade Development Board**
222 East 41st Street
New York, NY 10017-6739

212-497-0200

14774 **Norwegian Trade Council**
2720 34th Street NW
Washington, DC 20008

202-333-6000
Fax: 202-469-3990
E-Mail: emb.washington@mfa.no
Home Page: www.norway.org
Social Media: Facebook, Twitter, Flickr, Instagram

Kare A. Aas, Ambassador
Berit Enge, Minister Counselor
Beate Anderson Varrecchia, Officer for Administrative
Harald W. Storen, Counselor
Olav Heian-Engdal, 1st Secretary

14775 **Pakistan Trade Commission**
12 E 65th Street
4th Floor
New York, NY 10021

212-879-5800

Abbas Zaidi, Manager

14776 **Permanent Mission of Armenia to the United Nations**
119 E 36th Street
New York, NY 10016

212-686-9079
Fax: 212-686-3934

Home Page: www.un.mfa.am/
Social Media: RSS

Andrezej Towpik, Manager
Garen Nazarian, Permanent Representative to the UN
Tigran Samvelian, Counsell, Deputy Permanent Rep
Nikolay Sahakov, 1st Secretary
Sahak Sargsyan, 2nd Secretary

14777 **Permanent Mission of Bangladesh to the United Nations**
820 East 2nd Avenue, Diplomat Centre
4th Floor
New York, NY 10017

212-867-3434
Fax: 212-972-4038
E-Mail: bangladesh@un.int
Home Page: www.un.int/wcm/content/site/bangladesh

Sheikh Hasina, Prime Minister

14778 **Permanent Mission of Belize to the United Nations**
675 Third Avenue
Suite 1911
New York, NY 10017

212-986-1240
Fax: 212-593-0932
E-Mail: belize@un.int
Home Page: www.belizemission.com
Social Media: Facebook, Twitter

Mohamed Latheef, Manager
Paulette Erlington, Counselor
Han Dean Barrow, Prime Minister
Lois M. Young, Ambassador
Janine felson, Deputy Permanent Representative

14779 **Permanent Mission of Ghana to the United Nations**
19 E 47th Street
New York, NY 10017

212-832-1300
Fax: 212-751-6743
E-Mail: ghanaperm@aol.com
Home Page: www.un.int/ghana

Ken Kanda, Ambassador
William A. Awinador-Kanyirige, Minister
Henry Tachie-Menson, Minister-Counsellor
N.A. Abayena, Counsellor
A. Ayebi Arthur, 1st Secretary

14780 **Permanent Mission of Myanmar (Formerly Burma)**
10 E 77th Street
New York, NY 10075

212-744-1271
Fax: 212-744-1290
E-Mail: myanmarmission@verizon.net, myanmarconsu
Home Page: www.myanmarmissionny.org

Janis Priedkalns, Manager
U Han Thu, Deputy Permanent Representative
U Aung Kyaw Zan, Minister Counsellor
U kyaw Tin, Permanent representative
U Ko Ko Shein, Minister Counselor

14781 **Permanent Mission of Saint Vincent & the Grenadines**
800 2nd Avenue
Suite 400-G
New York, NY 10017

212-599-0950
Fax: 212-599-1020
Home Page: www.suv-un.org
Social Media: Facebook, Twitter, YouTube

Camillo M. Gonsalves, Ambassador
Nedra Miguel, Minister Counsellor
Mozart Carr, Attache
Maglyn Carrington, Secretary/ Accountant
N. Pepper Alexander, Security Officer/ Aide de Camp

14782 **Permanent Mission of Slovakia to the United Nations**
801 2nd Ave.
New York, NY 10017

212-286-8880
E-Mail: un.newyork@mzv.sk
Home Page: www.mzv.sk/unnewyork

Founded in 1993

14783 **Permanent Mission of Tajikistan to the United Nations**
216 East 49th St.
4th Floor
New York, NY 10017

212-207-3315
Fax: 212-207-3855
E-Mail: tajikistan@un.int, tajikistanun@verizon.
Home Page: www.un.int/

Khamrokhon Zaripov, President
Sirodjidin Aslov, Ambassador

14784 **Permanent Mission of the Czech Republic to the United Nations**
1109-1111 Madison Avenue
New York, NY 10028

646-981-4000
Fax: 646-981-4099
E-Mail: un.newyork@embassy.mzv.cz
Home Page: www.mzv.cz/un.newyork
Social Media: RSS

Edita Hrda, Ambassador
David Cervenka, Minister Counsellor
Peter Urbanek, Counsellor
Ladislav Steinhubel, 1st Secretary
Petra Benesova, 3rd Secretary

14785 **Permanent Mission of the Kingdom of Bhutan to the United Nations**
343 East 43rd Street
New York, NY 10017

212-682-2268
Fax: 212-661-0551
E-Mail: bhutan@un.int
Home Page: www.un.int/wcm/content/site/bhutan

Lhatu Wangchuk, Ambassador

14786 **Permanent Mission of the Republic of Sudan to the United Nations**
305 East 47th Street
3 Dag Hammarskjold Plaza, 4th Floor
New York, NY 10017

212-573-6033
Fax: 212-573-6160
E-Mail: sudan@sudanmission.org
Home Page: www.un.int/wcm/content/site/sudan

Jenine Selson, Manager

14787 **Permanent Mission of the Solomon Islands to the United Nations**
800 2nd Avenue
Suite 400
New York, NY 10017-4709

212-599-6192
Fax: 212-661-8925
E-Mail: simun@foreignaffairs-solomons.org
Home Page: www.un.int/wcm/content/site/solomonislands/cache/offonce/pid/4707

B Jagne, Manager

14788 **Philippines Commercial Office**
556 5th Avenue
New York, NY 10036

212-764-1330

14789 **Poland Trade Commission**
675 3rd Avenue
19th Floor
New York, NY 10017

212-351-1713

Phyllis Poland, Owner

14790 **Portuguese Trade Commission**
590 5th Avenue
3rd Floor
New York, NY 10036

212-354-4627
Fax: 212-575-4737

Soto Moura, Manager

14791 **Romanian Consulate General**
11766 Wilshire Blvd
Suite 560
Los Angeles, CA 90025

310-444-0043
Fax: 310-445-0043
E-Mail: losangeles@mae.ro, losangeles.cons@mae.r
Home Page: http://www.romanian.com
Social Media: RSS

Corina Suteu, Manager
Eugen Chivu, Consul General

14792 **Singapore Trade Commission**
55 E 59th Street
Suite 21-B
New York, NY 10022

212-421-2200

Kc Yeoh, Executive Director

14793 **Swedish Trade Council**
150 N Michigan Avenue
Chicago, IL 60601

312-781-6222

Stefam Bergstrom, Manager

14794 **Syrian Arab Republic Embassy**
2215 Wyoming Avenue NW
Washington, DC 20008

202-232-6316
Fax: 202-265-4585
E-Mail: consular@syrembassy.net, info@syrembassy
Home Page: www.syrianembassy.us/

14795 **Taiwan Trade Center**
1 Penn Plaza
Suite 2025
New York, NY 10119

212-904-1677
Fax: 212-904-1678
E-Mail: newyork@taitra.org.tw
Home Page: http://newyork.taiwantrade.com.tw/

Kevin K. H. Wei, Director

14796 **Thailand Trade Center-Consulate General of Thailand**
401 N Michigan Avenue
Suite 544
Chicago, IL 60611

312-467-0044
Fax: 312-467-1690
E-Mail: ttcc@wwa.com

14797 Trade Commission of Denmark
3565 Piedimont Rd
NE #1-400
Atlanta, GA 30305

404-588-1588
Fax: 404-835-0799
E-Mail: atlhkt@um.dk
Home Page: /www.dtcatlanta.um.dk

Henrik Bronner, Manager

14798 Trade Commission of Spain
500 N Michigan Avenue
Suite 1500
Chicago, IL 60611

312-644-1154

14799 Turkish Trade Commission
821 United Nations Plaza
4th Floor
New York, NY 10017

212-687-1530

14800 Turkmenistan Mission to the United Nations
866 United Nations Plaza
Suite 424
New York, NY 10017

212-486-8908
Fax: 212-486-2521

Aksoltan Ataeva, Manager

14801 UK Trade & Investment
1 Victoria St.
London, UK SW1H OET

212-745-0495
E-Mail: uktiusa@ukti.gsi.gov.uk
Home Page: www.ukti.gov.uk
Social Media: Twitter, LinkedIn, Youtube, Flickr, Open to Expor

Nick Baird, CEO
Sandra Rogers, Managing Dir., Marketing
Jon Harding, COO
Charu Gorasia, Dir., Finance & IT
Michael W. Boyd, MD, Strategic Investments

14802 United Nations Mission to El Salvador
46 Park Avenue
New York, NY 10016

212-679-1616
Fax: 212-725-3467
E-Mail: elsalvador@un.int
Home Page:
www.un.int/wcm/content/site/elsalvador

Antonio Montiero, Manager
Mauricio Fiunes, President

Associations

14803 **American Gem Society Laboratories**
8917 W Sahara Ave
Las Vegas, NV 89117-5826

702-233-6120
Fax: 702-233-6125
E-Mail: support@agslab.com
Home Page: www.agslab.com
Social Media: Facebook, Twitter, RSS, Youtube, Tumblr, Blogger,

Frank Delahan, CEO
Donna Jolly, Marketing Executive

Seeks to build consumer confidence in the retail jeweler by promoting ethical business standards and professional excellence.
4.4M Members
Founded in 1934

14804 **American Gem Trade Association**
3030 LBJ Freeway
Ste 840
Dallas, TX 75342-643

214-742-4367
800-972-1162
Fax: 214-742-7334
E-Mail: info@agta.org
Home Page: www.agta.org
Social Media: Facebook, Twitter, YouTube

Kami Swinney, Operations Manager
Eric Braunwart, President
Danielle Pelletiere, Marketing Manager
Douglas K. Hucker, CEO
Joan Allen, Chief Financial Officer

Trade association for the colored gemstone industry in North America. Operates a gemological testing laboratory in New York.
750+ Members
Founded in 1981
Mailing list available for rent

14805 **American Jewelry Design Council**
P.O. Box 1149
Hermitage, PA 16148

724-979-4992
800-376-3609
E-Mail: info@ajdc.org
Home Page: www.ajdc.org
Social Media: Facebook

Todd Reed, President
Kent Raible, VP
Jane Bohan, Secretary
Geoffrey Giles, Treasurer
William Schraft, Board Member

The American Jewelry Design Council is a non-profit educational corporation that recognizes and promotes the understanding of original jewelry designs as art.
Founded in 1988

14806 **American Watch Association**
1201 Pennsylvania Avenue NW
PO Box 464
Washington, DC 20044

434-963-7773
Fax: 434-963-7776
E-Mail: egcollado@earthlink.net
Home Page: www.americanwatchassociation.com

Ronald Wolfgang, Chairman
Walter Fischer, Chairman

Trade association for communication among professionals and legislative advocacy.
45 Members
Founded in 1933

14807 **American Watchmakers-Clockmakers Institute**
701 Enterprise Drive
Harrison, OH 45030-1696

513-367-9800
866-367-2924
Fax: 513-367-1414
E-Mail: awci@awci.com
Home Page: www.awci.com
Social Media: Facebook, RSS

Jordan Ficklin, Executive Director
Paul Wadsworth, Office Manager
Jennifer Bilodeau, Assistant Editor
Elizabeth Janszen, Membership Coordinator
Cindy L. Whitehead, Education & Certification Coor

Examines and certifies master watchmakers and clockmakers. Maintains a placement service. Conducts home study courses.
2500 Members
Founded in 1892
Mailing list available for rent

14808 **Appraisers Association of America**
386 Park Ave S
Suite 2000
New York, NY 10016

212-889-5404
Fax: 212-889-5503
E-Mail: aaa@appraisersassoc.org
Home Page: www.appraisersassoc.org
Social Media: Facebook, Twitter, LinkedIn

Linda Selvin, Executive Director
Kathryn Moldenhauer, Manager, Programs
Erica Hartman, Treasurer
Daile Kaplan, Secretary
Betty Krulik, President

The oldest non-profit professional association of personal property appraisers. The mission and primary purpose of the association is to develop and promote standards of excellence in the profession of appraising through education and the application of the highest form of professional practice, which results on enhancing the visibility and standing of appraisers within the private and professional communities in which they serve.
900 Members
Founded in 1949

14809 **Brotherhood of Traveling Jewelers**
Leys, Christie & Company
342 Madison Avenue
Suite #1530
New York, NY 10013

212-869-9162

Represents traveling jewelers.
300 Members

14810 **Cultured Pearl Information Center**
331 E 53rd Street
New York, NY 10022-4923

212-688-5580
Fax: 212-688-5857
Home Page: www.pearlinfo.com

Devin MacNow, Executive Director

Conference information and buying guide for pearls.

14811 **Diamond Council of America**
3212 West End Ave
Suite 400
Nashville, TN 37203

615-385-5301
877-283-5669
Fax: 615-385-4955
Home Page: www.diamondcouncil.org
Social Media: Facebook

Peter Engel, Chairman
Terry Chandler, President/CEO

Provides courses in diamontology and gemology to retail jewelers and their employees who are DCA members. Sixty-six retailers representing 1,800 locations.
70 Members
Founded in 1944

14812 **Diamond Dealers Club**
580 5th Ave
11 West 47th St.
New York, NY 10036

212-790-3600
Fax: 212-869-5164
E-Mail: mhochbaum@nyddc.com
Home Page: www.nyddc.com
Social Media: Facebook

Reuven Kaufman, President
Dr Martin Hochbaum, Managing Director
Basant Johari, VP
Benny Simkhai, Secretary
Herman Klarsfeld, General Counsel

Seeks to foster the interest of the diamond industry, promote equitable trade principles and eliminate abuses and unfair trading practices.
Founded in 1931

14813 **Diamond Manufacturers and Importers Association of America**
580 Fifth Avenue
Suite 2000
New York, NY 10036

212-944-2066
800-223-2244
Fax: 212-202-7525
E-Mail: info@dmia.net
Home Page: www.dmia.net

Ronald VanderLinden, President
Stuart Samuels, Secretary
Parag Shah, Treasurer
Eli Haas, VP
Steve Eisen, Director, Board Member

Represents and promotes manufacturers and importers of diamonds and rare gems.
150 Members
Founded in 1931

14814 **Diamond Peacock Club Kebadjian Brothers**
Kebadjian Brothers
333 Washington Street
Ste 638
Boston, MA 02108-5111

617-523-5565
Fax: 617-523-7193
E-Mail: info@kebadjian.com
Home Page: www.kebadjian.com

Claude Kebadjian, Founder And Designer
Seta Kebadjian, Designing
Michael Kebadjian, Jewelry Design
Founded in 1957

14815 **Diamond Promotion Service**
466 Lexington Avenue
New York, NY 10017-9998

800-370-6789
Fax: 877-276-1224
E-Mail: newyorkdps@jwt.com
Home Page: www.dps.org
Social Media: Facebook, Twitter

Resource for the tools and strategies to sell more diamonds. Buy marketing materials, train your staff, find the suppliers of advertised jewelry and more.

14816 Estate Jewelry Association of America
209 Post Street
Suite 718
San Francisco, CA 94108-5209

415-834-0718
800-584-5522
Fax: 212-840-1644
E-Mail: jaa@aol.com

14817 Fashion Jewelry Association of America
3 Davol Sq
Unit 135
Providence, RI 02903-4710

401-273-1515

Nick Macris, President
150 Members
Founded in 1985

14818 Gem & Lapidary Dealers Association
120 Derwood Circle
Rockville, MD 20850

301-294-1640
Fax: 301-294-0034
E-Mail: info@glda.com
Home Page: www.glda.com

Arnold Duke, President
Brandy Swanson, Customer Service
Jennifer Guillot, Exhibit Sales/Services
Monique Anderson, PR/ Marketing & New Media
Don Wyatt, PR/ Marketing & New Media

G.L.D.A. is a firmly established, successful wholesale gem & jewelry show promotion company. For the past 30 years, our Tucson show has enjoyed a booming success growth rate. Our show has included 400 exhibit booths which is the maximum that this facility would accomodate.

14819 Gold Prospectors Association of America
43445 Business Park Drive
Suite #113
Temecula, CA 92590

951-699-4749
800-551-9707
Fax: 951-699-4062
E-Mail: info@goldprospectors.org
Home Page: www.goldprospectors.org

Thomas Massie, CEO

GPAA is the largest recreational gold prospecting club. Owner of The Outdoor Channel, a cable TV channel featuring real outdoors for real people.
35M Members
Founded in 1985
Mailing list available for rent

14820 Independent Jewelers Organization
136 Old Post Rd.
Southport, CT 06850-1302

203-846-4215
800-624-9252
Fax: 203-254-7429
E-Mail: ijo@ijo.com
Home Page: www.ijo.com
Social Media: Facebook, Twitter, LinkedIn

Penny Palmer, Member Services Director

Jewelry buying group and service organization for retail jewelers.
850 Members
Founded in 1972

14821 Indian Arts & Crafts Association
4010 Carlisle Blvd NE
Suite C
Albuquerque, NM 87107

505-265-9149
Fax: 505-265-8251
E-Mail: info@iaca.com
Home Page: www.iaca.com
Social Media: Facebook, Twitter

Gail Chehak, Manager
Joseph P. Zeller, President
Cliff Fragua, VP
Kathi Ouellet, Treasurer
Beth Hale, Secretary

Nonprofit trade association whose mission is to promote, protect and preserve Indian arts.
700 Members
Founded in 1974
Mailing list available for rent

14822 Industrial Diamond Association of America
PO Box 29460
Columbus, OH 43229

614-797-2265
Fax: 614-797-2264
E-Mail: tkane-ida@insight.rr.com
Home Page: www.superabrasives.org

Terry Kane, Executive Director
Mike Mustin, President
Keith Reckling, Secretary/Treasurer
Troy Heuermann, Vice President
Edward E. Galen, Executive Director

Association of industrial diamond, cvd diamond and polycrystalling supplies, toolmakers. Products and services provided and used in most manufacturing and constuction industries such as: stone processing, glass construction, electronics, medical, woodworking, etc.
190 Members
Founded in 1946

14823 International Colored Gemstone Association
62 W. 47th St.
Suite 905
New York, NY 10036

212-352-8814
Fax: 212-352-9054
E-Mail: claudiu@gemstone.org
Home Page: www.gemstone.org
Social Media: RSS Feed

Claudiu Margarit, Manager
Barbara Lipatapanlop, Executive Director
Pat Koziol, Manager
Benjamin Hackman, President
Jean Claude Michelou, Vice-President

Nonprofit association representing the international gemstone industry. Works to increase the understanding, appreciation and sales of colored gemstones worldwide.
Founded in 1984

14824 International Fine Jewelers Guild
257 Adams Lane
Hewlett, NY 11557

516-295-2516
Fax: 516-374-5060
E-Mail: Info@InternationalFineJewelersGuild.com
Home Page: www.internationalfinejewelersguild.com

Bertram Kalisher, Chairman
Olivia Cornell, President
Berge Abajian, Jewelry Industry Advisory Board
Kari Allen, Jewelry Industry Advisory Board
Zoltan David, Jewelry Industry Advisory Board

14825 International Precious Metals Institute
5101 N 12th Avenue
Suite C
Pensacola, FL 32504

850-476-1156
Fax: 850-476-1548
E-Mail: mail@ipmi.org
Home Page: www.ipmi.org

Uve Kupka, President
Brad Cook, Director
Robert Bullen-Smith, Secretary
Jon Potts, Treasurer
Chris Jones, VP

International association of producers, refiners, fabricators, scientists, users, financial institutions, merchants, private and public sector groups and the general precious metals community created to provide a forum for the exchange of information and technology.
Founded in 1976

14826 International Society of Appraisers
303 West Madison St.
Ste 2650
Chicago, IL 60606

312-981-6778
Fax: 312-265-2908
E-Mail: isa@isa-appraisers.org
Home Page: www.isa-appraisers.org
Social Media: Facebook, Twitter, LinkedIn

Nan B Shelton, President
Joseph M. Jackson, Executive Director
Charles Ellias, Treasurer
Sara Porter, Sr. Coordinator, Membership
Joanna Stearns, Director

Nonprofit professional association of personal property appraisers. ISA provides education and organizational support to its members, to serve the public by producing highly qualified and ethical appraisers who are recognized authorities in personal property appraising.
1400+ Members
Founded in 1979
Mailing list available for rent

14827 Jewelers Board of Trade
95 Jefferson Blvd
Warwick, RI 02888

401-467-0055
Fax: 401-467-6070
E-Mail: jbtinfo@jewelersboard.com
Home Page: www.jewelersboard.com
Social Media: Twitter

Dione Kenyen, President

Trade Association: credit and collection for the jewelry industry.
3300 Members
Founded in 1884

14828 Jewelers Vigilance Committee
25 W 45th St
Suite 1406
New York, NY 10036

212-997-2002
Fax: 212-997-9148
E-Mail: askamlexpert@aol.com
Home Page: www.jvclegal.org
Social Media: Facebook, LinkedIn

Cecilia L. Gardner, President, CEO & General Counsel
Steven P Kaiser, Treasurer
Suzan Flamm, Sr. Counsel
Jasmin Greene, Marketing & Development Associate
Jeff Mercado, Membership Services Director

The sole legal compliance association in the jewelry industry. Educates the trade to under-

stand complex rules governing the manufacture, sale and marketing of fine jewelry.
1300 Members
Founded in 1917

14829 **Jewelers of America**
120 Broadway
Suite 2820
New York, NY 10271

646-658-0246
800-223-0673
Fax: 646-658-0256
E-Mail: info@jewelers.org
Home Page: www.jewelers.org
Social Media: Facebook, Twitter, LinkedIn

Ashley Petrylak, Manager
David J. Bonaparte, President and CEO
Annie Doresca, Dir. Of Finance & Administration
Molly Fallon, Dir. Of Marketing & Communications
Carey Miller, Member Services Manager

Center of knowledge for the jeweler and an advocate for professionalism and high social, ethical and environmental standards in the jewelry trade. Our mission is to assist all members in improving their business skills and profitability. JA will provide acess to meaningful educational programs and services, leadership in public and industry affairs, and encourage members with common interests to act in the industry's best interest.
Mailing list available for rent

14830 **Jewelry Industry Distributors Association**
701 Enterprise Drive
Harrison, OH 45030

513-367-2357
Fax: 513-367-1414
E-Mail: info@jida.info
Home Page: www.jida.info

Bill Nagle, President
Harvey Cobrin, First VP
Rick Foster, Secretary/Treasurer

Sets standards of service and facilitates the exchange of information of all types among members in order to improve business, maximize opportunities, and minimize risks.
150 Members
Founded in 1946

14831 **Jewelry Information Center**
120 Broadway
Suite 2820
New York, NY 10271

646-658-0246
800-223-0673
Fax: 646-658-0256
E-Mail: info@jic.org
Home Page: www.jic.org
Social Media: Facebook, Twitter, RSS

Matthews Runzi, President and CEO
Robert Headley, Vice President & COO
Carlon Alexandr, Administrative Assistant
Carey Miller, Membership Manager

Identifies deceptive trade practices and misleading advertising. Provides advice on marketing and assists in prosecution of violations. The media side of the Jewelers Vigilance Committee.
1000 Members
Founded in 1946
Mailing list available for rent

14832 **Jewelry Manufacturers Guild**
PO Box 46099
Los Angeles, CA 90046

909-769-1820
800-359-0340
Fax: 909-769-1920

Paula Glick Hill, Operations Manager

Promotes and improves conditions in the fine jewelry manufacturing industry.
400 Members

14833 **Leading Jewelers Guild**
PO Box 64609
Los Angeles, CA 90064

310-820-3386
Fax: 310-820-3530
Home Page: www.love-story.com
Social Media: Facebook, Twitter, Google+, Pinterest

James West, President
Mailing list available for rent

14834 **Manufacturing Jewelers & Suppliers of America**
57 John L Dietsch Sq
Attleboro Falls, MA 02763

401-274-3840
800-444-6572
Fax: 401-274-0265
E-Mail: info@mjsa.org
Home Page: www.mjsa.org
Social Media: Facebook, Twitter, LinkedIn, Pinterest

James McCarthy, COO
Edward N. DeCristofaro, Chairman
David W. Cochran, President & CEO
Stuart Lee, Secretary
Michael Toback, Treasurer

National trade association for the manufacturing jewelers and silversmiths. Sponsors trade shows, expositions and social events.
1.8M Members
Founded in 1903

14835 **Manufacturing Jewelers and Silversmiths**
57 John L Dietsch Sq
Attleboro Falls, MA 02763-1027

401-274-3840
800-444-6572
Fax: 401-274-0265
E-Mail: info@mjsa.org
Home Page: www.mjsa.org

David W. Cochran, President & CEO
Corrie Silvia Berry, Director of Sales & Business
Kristin Kopaz, Operations Manager
Dawn Britland, Assistant Controller
Travis Searle, Membership Coordinator

The trade association for all segments of the American jewelry manufacturing and supply industry.
Founded in 1903

14836 **National Association of Jewelry Appraisers**
PO Box 18
Rego Park, NY 11374-0018

718-896-1536
Fax: 718-997-9057
E-Mail: office@najaappraisers.com
Home Page: www.najaappraisers.com
Social Media: Facebook

Gail Brett Levine, Executive Director

Purpose is to maintain professional standards and education in the field of jewelry appraising and provide members benefits at lower cost than can be attained individually.
720 Members
Founded in 1981

14837 **Platinum Guild International USA**
620 Newport Center Dr
Suite 800
Newport Beach, CA 92660-6420

212-404-1600
800-207-PLAT
Fax: 949-760-8780
E-Mail: info@pgiusa.com
Home Page: www.preciousplatinum.com
Social Media: Facebook, Twitter, Google+, Pinterest

Laurie A Hudson, President

Organization promoting platinum jewelry. Maintains a website where the press and the public can find helpful information.
Founded in 1975

14838 **Plumb Club**
157 Engle St
Englewood, NJ 07631

201-816-8881
Fax: 201-816-8882
E-Mail: susan@plumbclub.com
Home Page: www.plumbclub.com

Susan Lee Brandonisio, Executive Director
Michael Langhammer, Secretary
David Meleski, President
Jonathan Cohen, Vice President
Sam Sandberg, Treasurer

Exclusive social organization within the jewelry industry holding black tie events for members and their clients and exhibitor shows.

14839 **Schneider National**
3101 S Packerland Drive
Po Box 2545
Green Bay, WI 54306-2545

920-592-2000
800-558-6767
Home Page: www.schneider.com
Social Media: RSS

Don Schneider, Chairman
Christopher Lofgren PhD, President & CEO

A leading provider of transportation and logistics services with a comprehensive reach across North America and a growing presence in Europe and Asia.
Founded in 1935

14840 **Silver Institute**
1400 I St NW
Suite #550
Washington, DC 20005

202-835-0185
Fax: 202-835-0155
E-Mail: info@silverinstitute.org
Home Page: www.silverinstitute.org

Fernando Alains, President
Michael DiRienzo, Executive Director and Secretary
Mitchell Krebs, Vice President
Thomas Angelos, Treasurer
Ken Koski, Assistant Treasurer

International association of miners, refiners, fabricators and wholesalers of silver and silver products.
Founded in 1971

14841 **Silver Users Association**
3930 Walnut St.
Suite 210
Fairfax, VA 22030

703-930-7790
800-245-6999
Fax: 703-359-7562

E-Mail: pmiller@mwcapitol.com
Home Page: www.silverusersassociation.org

Bill LeRoy, President
Mike Huber, VP
Jack Gannon, Immediate Past President
Bill Hamelin, Treasurer
John King, Secretary

Represents manufacturers and distributors of products in which silver is an essential element, such as photographic materials, medical and dental supplies, batteries and electronic and electrical equipment, silverware, mirrors, commemorative art and jewelry.
27 Members
Founded in 1947

14842 Society of American Silversmiths
P.O.Box 786
West Warwick, RI 02893

401-461-6840
Fax: 401-461-6841
E-Mail: sas@silversmithing.com
Home Page: www.silversmithing.com

Jeffrey Herman, Founder/Executive Director

Organization devoted to the preservation and promotion of the silversmithing art and craft.
240 Members
Founded in 1989
Mailing list available for rent

14843 Society of North American Goldsmiths
540 Oak Street
Suite A
Eugene, OR 97401

541-345-5689
Fax: 541-345-1123
E-Mail: info@snagmetalsmith.org
Home Page: www.snagmetalsmith.org
Social Media: Facebook, Twitter, LinkedIn, Pinterest, Flickr, RSS Feed

Renee Zettle-Sterling, President
Anne Havel, Treasurer
Gwynne Rukenbrod, Executive Dir.
Tara Jecklin, Operations Manager
John Garbett, Advertising & Production Director

Promotes a favorable and enriching environment in which contemporary metalsmiths practice their art. One aspect of this process is educating the public about the quality and rich diversity within the field of metalsmithing. Exhibitions, public forums, lectures, and published documents are our primary methods of reaching out to the public. SNAG sponsors workshops, seminars, audio-visual services and an annual conference.
Founded in 1969

14844 Women's Jewelry Association
80 Washington St.
Ste 205
Poughkeepsie, NY 12601

845-473-7323
Fax: 646-355-0216
E-Mail: info@womensjewelryassociation.com
Home Page: www.womensjewelryassociation.com

Amy Rosi, Communications
Bernadette Mack, Administrative Director
Tryna Kochanek, President
Kristie Nicolosi, Treasurer
Brandee Dallow, VP of Administration

To empower women to achieve their highest goals in the international jewelry, watch and related businesses.
Founded in 1983

14845 World Gold Council
510 Madison Ave
9th Floor
New York, NY 10022

212-317-3800
Fax: 212-688-0410
E-Mail: info@gold.org
Home Page: www.gold.org
Social Media: Facebook, Twitter, LinkedIn, YouTube Flickr, RSS Feed, Goog

John Calnon, Manager
Randall Oliphant, Chairman
Brenda Bates, Director, Corporate Communications
Aram Shishmanian, Chief Executive Officer
Robin Lee, CFO

Organization formed and funded by the world's leading gold mining companies with the aim of stimulating and maximizing the demand for, and holding of gold by consumers, investors, industry and the official sector.
23 Members
Founded in 1987

Newsletters

14846 Benchmark
Manufacturing Jewelers & Suppliers of America
57 John L Dietsch Sq
Attleboro Falls, MA 02763-1027

401-274-3840
800-444-6572
Fax: 401-274-0265
E-Mail: info@mjsa.org
Home Page: www.mjsa.org

James McCarthy, COO
Bruce Coltin, Operations Manager
Kristin Kopaz, Operations Manager
Corrie Berry, Sales Manager

Offers details of association activities and industry events for members.
4 Pages
Frequency: Bi-Monthly

14847 Costume Jewelry Review
Retail Reporting Bureau
302 5th Ave
11th Floor
New York, NY 10001-3604

212-279-7000

Offers news and information on the costume jewelry industry, suppliers and manufacturers.
Cost: $108.00
Frequency: Monthly

14848 Diamond Insight
Tryon Mercantile
790 Madison Avenue
New York, NY 10021-6124

212-288-9011
Fax: 212-772-1286
Home Page: www.newsletteraccess.com

Guido Giovannini-Torelli, Editor

Penetrates the multifaceted world of diamonds, giving intelligence on the world's important stones, future price indicators, key individuals behind the trends, jewelry auctions and DeBeers/CSO Activities.
Cost: $325.00
12 Pages
Frequency: Monthly
Circulation: 250
Printed in one color on glossy stock

14849 Diamond Registry Bulletin
Diamond Registry
580 5th Avenue
New York, NY 10036-4701

212-575-0444
800-223-7955
Fax: 212-575-0722
E-Mail: info@diamondregistry.com
Home Page: www.diamondregistry.com

Joseph Schlussel, President

Monthly newsletter offering the latest trends, prices and forecasts concerning diamonds, diamond jewelry and diamond mining.
Cost: $97.00
Frequency: Monthly
ISSN: 0199-9753
Founded in 1961

14850 Jewelers' Security Alliance Newsletter
Jewelers' Security Alliance
6 E 45th St
Suite 1305
New York, NY 10017-2469

212-687-0328
800-537-0067
Fax: 212-808-9168
E-Mail: jsa2@jewelerssecurity.org
Home Page: www.jewelerssecurity.org

John J Kennedy, President
Robert W. Frank, Vice President
Helen M. Buck, Manager of Membership Services

Principal activity is providing education and information to jewelers so they can guard against loss through crimes, including burglary, robbery and theft.
Cost: $375.00
Frequency: Annual+
Founded in 1883

14851 Jewelers' Security Bulletin
Jewelers' Security Alliance
6 E 45th St
Suite 1305
New York, NY 10017-2469

212-687-0328
800-537-0067
Fax: 212-808-9168
E-Mail: jsa2@jewelerssecurity.org
Home Page: www.jewelerssecurity.org

John J Kennedy, President
Robert W. Frank, Vice President
Helen M. Buck, Manager of Membership Services

Principal activity is providing education and information to jewelers so they can guard against loss through crimes, including burglary, robbery and theft.
19500 Members
Founded in 1883
Mailing list available for rent

14852 Jewelry Newsletter International
Newsletters International
7710 T Cherry Park Drive
#421
Houston, TX 77095

888-972-4662
Home Page: www.j-i.com

Len Fox, Editor

Informs manufacturers, wholesalers, suppliers, and retailers of jewelry how to stimulate sales, increase profits, and cut costs.
Cost: $250.00
4-8 Pages
Frequency: Monthly
Founded in 1975
Printed in on matte stock

14853 Precious Metals News
International Precious Metals Institute

5101 N 12th Avenue
Suite C
Pensacola, FL 32504

850-476-1156
Fax: 850-476-1548
E-Mail: mail@ipmi.org
Home Page: www.ipmi.org

Robert Ianniello, President
Frequency: Quarterly
Circulation: 1000

14854 Spectra
American Gem Society
8917 W Sahara Ave
Las Vegas, NV 89117-5826

702-233-6120
Fax: 702-233-6125
E-Mail: support@agslab.com
Home Page: www.agslab.com

Frank Delahan, CEO

Society news covering all aspects of the jewelry world.
12 Pages
Frequency: Quarterly
Founded in 1934

Magazines & Journals

14855 AJM Magazine: The Authority on Jewelry Manufacturing
Manufacturing Jewelers & Suppliers of America
57 John L Dietsch Sq
Attleboro Falls, MA 02763-1027

401-274-3840
800-444-6572
Fax: 401-274-0265
E-Mail: info@mjsa.org
Home Page: www.mjsa.org

James McCarthy, COO
Corrie Silvia Berry, Director of Sales & Business
David W. Cochran, President & CEO
Kristin Kopaz, Operations Manager
Dawn Britland, Assistant Controller

This is the only magazine dedicated solely to jewelry manufacturers. It delivers the three T's of jewelry manufacturing: trends, technology and techniques.
Cost: $47.00
Frequency: Monthly
Founded in 1903
Printed in 4 colors on glossy stock

14856 Accent Magazine
Larkin Group
485 Fashion Ave
Suite 1400
New York, NY 10018-6804

212-594-1439
Fax: 212-594-8556

AJ Larkin, Publisher

Provides trend analysis and market forecasts for buyers and designers, for accessories, clothing, and footwear. Also covers convention and tradeshow news, and new product launches.
Cost: $24.00
Frequency: Monthly
Circulation: 13,000

14857 Adornment: Newsletter of Jewelry and Related Arts
1333A N Avenue
New Rochelle, NY 10804

914-636-3784
E-Mail: ekarlin@usa.net

Elyse Karlin, Publisher/Editor/CEO
Cost: $60.00
Frequency: Quarterly
Circulation: 800
Founded in 1999

14858 Chronos
Golden Bell Press
2403 Champa St
Denver, CO 80205-2621

303-296-1600
Fax: 303-295-2159
E-Mail: print@goldenbellpress.com
Home Page: www.goldenbellpress.com

Editorial material looks at timepieces of the past, present and future, bringing you the latest, the best and the most intriguing creation from the leading international watch and clock makers. The history of timepiece manufacturers and their significant milestones are also reported as well as armchair tours of the world's most prestigious horological museums.
Cost: $2250.00
Frequency: Quarterly
Circulation: 20000
Founded in 1933

14859 Colored Stone
PRIMEDIA
60 Chestnut Avenue
Suite 201
Devon, PA 19333-1312

610-964-6300
610-232-5700
Fax: 610-293-1717
Home Page: www.colored-stone.com

Joseph Breck, Publisher
Morgan Beard, Editor-in-Chief

Contains news and information on the gem and gemstone jewelry industry.
Cost: $29.95
64 Pages
Circulation: 10000
Founded in 1986

14860 Couture International Jeweler
Miller Freeman Publications
770 Broadway
5th Floor
New York, NY 10003-9595

212-780-0400
Fax: 847-763-9037
E-Mail: ijmag@halldata.com
Home Page: www.couturejeweler.com

Debra De Roo Ballard, Publisher
Lynda Roguso, Operations Director
Karen Stewart, Operations Director

Publication features information on hot trends in fine jewelry and fashion.
Cost: $60.00
Circulation: 20000
Founded in 1964

14861 GZ (European Jeweler)
JCK International Publishing Group
360 Park Ave S
New York, NY 10010-1710

646-746-6400
Fax: 646-746-7131
Home Page: www.jckgroup.com

Ted Smith, CEO
Donna Borrelli, Associate Publisher
Hedda Schupak, Editor-in-Chief
Tracey Peden, Marketing Manager
Nancy Walsh, Senior Vice President
Cost: $49.95
Frequency: Monthly
Founded in 1874

14862 High-Volume Jeweler
Reed Business Information
201 King of Prussia Road
Radnor, PA 19087-5114

610-889-9577
Fax: 630-288-8686
Home Page: www.reedbusiness.com

Shawn Mery, Publisher
Lisa Reed, CFO
Stuart Whayman, CFO

Provides original market research and in-depth analysis of current news and industry trends affecting this segment of the jewelry and watch market. Features operational strategies and new technological developments that can make and save money for retailers and vendors.
Cost: $60.00
Frequency: Bi-Monthly
Circulation: 5,000

14863 Horological Times
American Watchmakers-Clockmakers Institute
701 Enterprise Drive
Harrison, OH 45030-1696

513-367-9800
866-367-2924
Fax: 513-367-1414
Home Page: www.awci.com
Social Media: Facebook, RSS

James Lubic, Executive Director
Tom Pack, Operations Director
Jennifer Bilodeau, Assistant Editor
Elizabeth Janszen, Membership Coordinator

Contains articles dealing with the techniques of servicing and repairing watches and clockes; the uses of shop tool and equipment; the functional characteristics of mechanical, electronic, and antique timepieces.
Frequency: Monthly
Founded in 1892
Mailing list available for rent

14864 International Wristwatch Magazine USA
International Publishing Corporation
979 Summer Street
PO Box 110204
Stamford, CT 06905

203-259-8100
Fax: 203-295-0847
E-Mail: wristwatch@snet.net
Home Page: www.intlwristwatch.com

Gary George, Editor-in-Chief
Patricia Russo, General Manager

Editorial content provides a consumer-oriented focus on new, vintage, and collectable watches.
Cost: $7.95
150 Pages
Frequency: Bi-Monthly
Circulation: 30,000
ISBN: 0-744706-22-2
Founded in 1989
Printed in 4 colors on glossy stock

14865 JCK Magazine
JCK International Publishing Group
1018 W Ninth Avenue
King of Prussia, PA 19406-1

610-205-1100
800-305-7759
Fax: 610-205-1139
E-Mail: JCK@pub-serv.com
Home Page: www.jckgroup.com

Nancy Walsh, Senior VP
Fran Pennella, Marketing Director

Mark Smelzer, Publisher
Hedda Schupak, Editor-in-chief
Jay Jackson, Chief Operating Officer

Serves retailers, manufacturers, and vendors of fine jewelry and selected upscale gift categories, providing valuable market and design trend information and how-to information about gemology, financial management, employee relations, marketing, advertising, and visual merchandising, e-commerce, and other topics.
Cost: $49.95
Frequency: Monthly
Founded in 1869

14866 JQ Limited Edition
JQ Publishing
585 5th Street W
Sonoma, CA 95476-6831

707-938-1082
Fax: 707-935-6585
Home Page: www.retailmerchandising.net

Audrey Bromstad, Publisher
Cynthia Unninayar, Editor
Deborah Rittenberg, Marketing Manager

Issues contain articles presented with illustrations on precious colored gems and diamonds, creative jewelry designs, designers, and luxury watches.
Frequency: Monthly
Circulation: 300000
Founded in 1985

14867 Jewelers' Circular: Keystone
Reed Business Information
360 Park Ave S
New York, NY 10010-1737

646-746-6400
Fax: 646-756-7583
E-Mail: hschupak@reedbusiness.com
Home Page: www.reedbusiness.com
Social Media: Twitter, LinkedIn

John Poulin, CEO
Hedda Schupak, Editor
Victoria Jones, Production Manager
James Reed, Owner
Andrew Rak, Senior Vice President

Discusses news of interest mainly to the jewelry shop owner and manager. Covers such topics as; product notices, manufacturer news and tips on operating a successful business.
Cost: $49.95
Frequency: Monthly
Circulation: 25000
Founded in 1874
Printed in on glossy stock

14868 Jewelry Appraiser
National Association of Jewelry Appraisers
P. O. Box 18
Rego Park, NY 11374-0018

718-896-1536
Fax: 718-997-9057
E-Mail: naja.appraisers@netzero.net
Home Page: www.najaappraisers.com
Social Media: Facebook, LinkedIn

Gail Brett Levine, Executive Director

An important source for all jewelry appraisers.
Frequency: Quarterly
Founded in 1981

14869 Lapidary Journal
300 Chesterfield Parkway
Suite 100
Malvern, PA 19355-937

610-232-5700
800-676-4336
Fax: 610-232-5754
Home Page: www.lapidaryjournal.com

Merle White, Editor
Karen Nuckols, Sales Director
Joe Breck, Publisher

This publication focuses fundamentally on the all aspects of the jewelry industry.
Cost: $29.95
Frequency: Monthly
Circulation: 45000
Founded in 1947

14870 Link
National Cuff Link Society
PO Box 5970
Vernon Hills, IL 60061-5970

847-816-0035
Fax: 847-816-0035
Home Page: www.cufflink.com

Gena Klompus, President
Founded in 1990

14871 Lustre
Cygnus Publishing
19 W 44th St
Suite 1405
New York, NY 10036-6101

212-921-1091
Fax: 212-921-5539
E-Mail: lorraine.depasque@cygnuspub.com
Home Page: www.cygnusb2b.com

Tim Murphy, Publisher
Roy Kim, Sales Director
Lorraine DePasque, Editor In Chief
Barb Hesse, Circulation Manager
Paul Mackler, President/CEO
Circulation: 4000
Founded in 1966

14872 Modern Jeweler
3 Huntington Quadrangle
Suite 301N
Melville, NY 11747-3602

631-845-2700
800-255-5113
Fax: 631-845-7109
E-Mail: tim.murphy@cygnuspub.com
Home Page: www.modernjeweler.com

Matthew Kramer, Managing Editor
Timothy Murphy, Publisher
Cheryl Kremkow, Editor in Chief
Barb Hesse, Circulation Manager
Jeff Prine, Executive Editor

A trade publication serving retail jewelers, wholesalers and manufacturers of jewelry, watches and related items. Accepts advertising.
Cost: $66.00
90 Pages
Frequency: Monthly
Circulation: 30000

14873 Monroe Originals
Karen Monroe
14014 Moorpark Street
Apartment 122
Sherman Oaks, CA 91423-3492

FAX 818-783-5009

Handmade wholesale jewelry designs magazine.
Cost: $2.00
50 Pages
Frequency: Monthly

14874 Ornament
PO Box 2349
San Marcos, CA 92079-9806

760-599-0222
800-888-8950
Fax: 760-599-0228
E-Mail: ornament@sbcglobal.net
Home Page: beadwrangler.com/mag-ornament.htm

Robert Liu, Co-Editor
Carolin Denish, Co-Editor

Offers information on contemporary, ethnic, ancient jewelry and costumes.
Cost: $26.00
Frequency: Quarterly
Circulation: 38,000
Founded in 1976

14875 Professional Jeweler
Bond Communications
1500 Walnut Street
Suite 1200
Philadelphia, PA 19102-3523

215-670-0727
888-557-0727
Fax: 215-545-9629
E-Mail: askus@professionaljeweler.com
Home Page: www.professionaljeweler.com

Lee Lawrence, Publisher/President
Peggy Jo Donahue, Editor-in-Chief
Peter James, Manager
Carole Masciantonio, Marketing Coordinator
Lisa Pastore, Advertising Manager

Editorial content provides these professionals with the information they need to meet business objectives and ensure success. Regular departments offer the latest news, trends, technical and practical information on all aspects of the jewelry industry.
Cost: $49.95
105 Pages
Frequency: Monthly
Circulation: 24000
ISSN: 1097-5314
Founded in 1998
Printed in 4 colors on glossy stock

14876 Southern Jewelry News
Mullen Publications
9629 Old Nations Ford Rd
Charlotte, NC 28273-5719

704-527-5111
800-738-5111
Fax: 704-527-5114
Home Page: www.mullenpublications.com

Chip Smith, Publisher
Bill Newnam, Production Manager
Robert Cutshaw, Production Manager
Elesa Dillon, Sales Manager

Dedicated to the southern jewelry industry and contains industry news, local and regional events, personnel announcements, and pricing information.
Frequency: Monthly
Circulation: 13,431
Founded in 1945

14877 Watch and Clock Review
Golden Bell Press
2403 Champa St
Denver, CO 80205-2621

303-296-1600
Fax: 303-295-2159
E-Mail: print@goldenbellpress.com
Home Page: www.goldenbellpress.com

Offers news and information on fashion accessories and jewelry.
Cost: $19.50
48 Pages
ISSN: 1082-2453
Founded in 1935

Trade Shows

14878 ASD/AMD Las Vegas Variety Merchandise Show
ASD/AMD Merchandise Group
Las Vegas Convention Center
3150 Paradise Road
Las Vegas, NV 89109
702-892-0711
Fax: 702-892-2933
Home Page: www.lvcva.com
Features tens of thousands of unique products in hundres of popular categories.
10000 Attendees
Frequency: March

14879 Accent on Design
George Little Management
10 Bank Street
Suite 1200
White Plains, NY 10606-1954
914-486-6070
800-272-7469
Fax: 914-948-2867
Home Page: www.nyigf.com
Elizabeth Murphy, Show Manager
George Little II, President
Three hundred and seventy booths of the latest and most innovative gift lines such as decorative accessories and home furnishings.
50M Attendees
Frequency: August
Founded in 1984

14880 American Gem Society Conclave
8881 W Sahara Avenue
Las Vegas, NV 89117
702-255-6500
Fax: 702-255-7420
Home Page: www.ags.org
Glory Wade, Show Manager
One hundred and sixty booths. Conference and exhibitors.
1M Attendees
Frequency: April

14881 American Gem Trade Association Expo
3030 LBJ Freeway
Suite 840
Dallas, TX 75234
214-742-4367
800-972-1162
Fax: 214-742-7334
E-Mail: info@agta.org
Home Page: www.agta.org
Elizabeth Ross, Marketing Manager
Rick Krementz, President
Two booths featuring exhibits of loose colored gemstones and diamonds.
10.3M Attendees
Frequency: February

14882 Annual Spring New Products Show
Pacific Expositions
1600 Kapiolani Boulevard
Suite 1660
Honnolulu, HI 96814
808-945-3594
Fax: 808-946-6399
48000 Attendees
Frequency: Annual

14883 Bead and Button Show
Kalmbach Publishing Company
21027 Crossroads Circle
PO Box 1612
Waukesha, WI 53187-1612
262-796-8776
800-553-6644
262-796-8776
Fax: 262-796-1615
Home Page: www.beadandbuttonshow.com
Social Media: Facebook, Pinterest
3500 Attendees

14884 Best Bead Show
Crystal Myths
PO Box 3243
Albuquerque, NM 87190
505-883-9295
Fax: 505-889-9553

14885 Business to Business Gem Trade Show
Gem & Lapidary Wholesalers
Holiday Inn Palo Verde/Holidome
Tucson, AZ
601-879-8832
Fax: 601-879-3282
E-Mail: info@glwshows.com
Home Page: www.glwshows.com
Frequency: February

14886 Catalog in Motion
Bell Group
Tucson E Hilton
Tucson, AZ
505-839-3249
Fax: 505-839-3248
Home Page: www.riogrande.com
Frequency: February

14887 Fashion Accessories Expo
Business Journals
50 Day Street
Norwalk, CT 06854
203-853-6015
Fax: 203-852-8175
Home Page: www.busjour.com
Britton Jones, President
Lizette Chin, Show Director Market
14000 Attendees

14888 Fashion Accessories Expo Accessories to Go
Business Journals
50 Day Street
Norwalk, CT 06854
203-853-6015
Fax: 203-852-8175
Home Page: www.busjour.com
Britton Jones, President
Lorrie Frost, Accessories Publisher
14000 Attendees

14889 GJX Gem and Jewelry Show
198 S Granada Avenue
Tucson, AZ
520-824-4200
Fax: 520-882-4203
Home Page: www.gjxusa.com
Allan Norville, President
Frequency: February

14890 GLDA Gem and Jewelry Show
Gem & Lapidary Dealers Association
PO Box 2391
Tucson, AZ 85702
520-792-9431
Fax: 520-882-2836
E-Mail: info@glda.com
Home Page: www.glda.com
Paul Page, Director Marketing
Qualified buyers receive free admission. Buyers are jewerly retailers, manufacturers, wholesalers, gem dealers.
16000 Attendees
Frequency: February

14891 Gem & Jewelry Show
International Gem & Jewelry Show
120 Derwood Circle
Rockville, MD 20850-1264
301-294-1640
Fax: 301-294-0034
Herb Duke, Owner
Annual show and exhibits of jewelry and gemstones and related equipment, supplies and services.
Frequency: October, Denver

14892 Gem, Jewelry & Mineral Show
Trade Shows International
PO Box 8862
Tucson, AZ 85738
520-791-2210
Fax: 520-825-9115

14893 IJO Trade Show & Seminars
Independent Jewelers Organization
25 Seir Hill Rd
Norwalk, CT 06850-1322
203-846-4215
800-624-9252
Fax: 203-846-8571
E-Mail: ijo@ijo.com
Home Page: www.ijo.com
Penny Palmer, Member Services Director
For members only
3500 Attendees
Frequency: Semi-Annual

14894 IPMI Conference
International Precious Metals Institute
5101 N 12th Avenue
Suite C
Pensacola, FL 32504
850-476-1156
Fax: 850-476-1548
E-Mail: mail@ipmi.org
Home Page: www.ipmi.org
Robert Ianniello, President
Frequency: Annual

14895 International Gem & Jewelry Show
120 Derwood Circle
Rockville, MD 20850
301-294-1640
Fax: 301-294-0034
Home Page: www.intergem.net
Herb Duke, Owner
Jewelry, gemstones and related equipment, supplies and services.

14896 International Gift Show: The Jewelry & Accessories Expo
Business Journals
50 Day Street
Norwalk, CT 06854
203-853-6015
Fax: 203-852-8175
14000 Attendees

14897 International Jewelry Fair/General Merchandise Show-Spring
Helen Brett Enterprises

5111 Academy Drive
Lisle, IL 60532-2171

630-241-9865
800-541-8171
Fax: 630-241-9870
E-Mail: dharrington@helenbrett.com
Home Page: www.gift2jewelry.com
Social Media: Facebook

Dave Harrington, Show Manager

Containing 800 booths during the spring show and 1500 booths during the fall show. Tradeshow open to wholesale buyers only (credentials required to attend).

24000 Attendees
Frequency: May
Founded in 1946
Mailing list available for rent

14898 International Watch and Jewelry Show

Burley and Olg Bullock
5901-Z Westheimer Road
Houston, TX 77057

713-783-8188
800-554-4992
Fax: 281-589-8987
E-Mail: info@iwjg.com
Home Page: www.iwjg.com

JJ Gilbreath
Christina LeDoux

Frequency: June-Nov./January-March

14899 JA International Jewelry Show

Jewelers of America
52 Vanderbuilt Avenue
19th Floor
New York, NY 10017

646-580-0255
Fax: 212-768-8087
E-Mail: info@jewelers.org
Home Page: www.jewelers.org

Matthew Runci, President
Donald Jackson, Controller
Timothy Haake, Founder
Lauren Thompson, Communications Manager

Showcase of fine jewelry open to the trade only.

11000 Attendees
Frequency: Febuary/July

14900 JCK Orlando International Jewelry Show

Reed Exhibition Companies
383 Manin Avenue
Norwalk, CT 06850

203-404-4800
Fax: 203-840-5830
Home Page: www.jckgroup.com

Jay Jackson, Chief Operating Officer
Matthew Stuller, Founder
John Bachman, Secretary

Conference and exhibition.

2000 Attendees
Frequency: February

14901 Jewelers International Showcase (JIS)

6421 Congress Avenue
Suite 105
Boca Raton, FL 33487-2858

561-998-0205
Fax: 561-998-0209
E-Mail: jisshow@aol.com
Home Page: www.jisshow.com

Michael G Breslow CEM, President
Jordan Tuchband, Sales Director
Vito J. Miceli, Sales Manager
Cindy Corrente, Financial Coordinator
Michele Carter, Show Director

Worldwide manufacturers and wholesalers of jewelry exhibit to trade buyers from Florida, Caribbean, Central and South America, plus other USA states. Exhibits of 1000 suppliers of fine jewelry, fashion jewelry and related products and services. The leading and largest independent Jewelery Trade-Only Show in the Western Hemisphere.

12000 Attendees
Frequency: October, January, April
Founded in 1979

14902 Merchandise Mart Gift/Jewelry/ Resort Show

Denver Merchandise Mart
451 E 58th Avenue #470
Suite 4270
Denver, CO 80216

303-292-6278
800-289-6278
Fax: 303-298-8473
E-Mail: bridget@denvermart.com
Home Page: www.denvermart.com

Bridget Oakes, Gift Show Exhibit Manager

A wholesale market for retail store buyers for resorts, theme parksand national parks, specialty gift stores and interior designers. Semi - Annual Show.

7000 Attendees
Frequency: February/August

14903 Mid-South Jewelry & Accessories Fair -Spring

Helen Brett Enterprises
5111 Academy Drive
Lisle, IL 60532-2171

630-241-9865
800-541-8171
Fax: 630-241-9870
E-Mail: dharrington@helenbrett.com
Home Page: www.gift2jewelry.com
Social Media: Facebook

Dave Harrington, Show Manager

Containing over 300 booths during the spring show and 500 booths during the fall show. Tradeshow open to wholesale buyers only (credentials required to attend).

8500 Attendees
Frequency: May
Founded in 1946
Mailing list available for rent

14904 Mid-South Jewelry & Accessories Fair-Fall

Helen Brett Enterprises
5111 Academy Drive
Lisle, IL 60532-2171

630-241-9865
800-541-8171
Fax: 630-241-9870
E-Mail: dharrington@helenbrett.com
Home Page: www.gift2jewelry.com
Social Media: Facebook

Dave Harrington, Show Manager

Containing 500 booths during the fall show and over 300 booths during the spring show. Tradeshow open to wholesale buyers only (credentials required to attend).

16000 Attendees
Frequency: November
Founded in 1946
Mailing list available for rent

14905 Midwest Jewelry Expo

Wisconsin Jewelry Assocation
1 East Main Street
Suite 305
Madison, WI 53703

608-257-3541
Fax: 608-257-8755
Home Page: www.midwestjewelryexpo.com

Mary Kaja, Executive Director

The next jewelry trade show exposition is scheduled for March 24th to March 25th in 2007.

3000 Attendees
Frequency: March

14906 National Accessory Maintenance Exposition

240 Peachtree Street NW
Suite 2200
Atlanta, GA 30303-1327

404-203-3000
Fax: 404-607-8682

Jeff Portman, CEO
Charles Sydney, Manager

Offers a forum for the exchange of ideas between manufacturers and suppliers of fashion accessories.

10M Attendees
Frequency: January

14907 Pacific Jewelry Show

California Jewelers Association
911 Wilshire Boulevard
Suite 1740
Los Angeles, CA 90017-3446

213-235-5722
Fax: 213-623-5742

Richard Trujillo, Owner
Alberta E Hultman, Manager

Annual show of 250 exhibitors of jewelry and related items.

3000 Attendees
Frequency: August
Founded in 1999

14908 Stylemax

Merchandise Mart Properties Inc
222 Merchandise Mart Plaza
Suite 470
Chicago, IL 60654

312-527-4141
800-677-6278
E-Mail: sglick@mmart.com
Home Page: www.mmart.com
Social Media: Facebook

Susan Glick, VP

A women's apparel and accessory trade show with over 4,000 exhibitors.

5000 Attendees
Founded in 1920
Mailing list available for rent

14909 The Whole Bead Show

PO Box 1100
Nevade City, CA 95959

530-652-2725
800-292-2577
Fax: 530-265-2776
E-Mail: info@wholebead.com
Home Page: www.wholebead.com
Social Media: Facebook

Ava Motherwell, Owner

An international bread trade show that occurs thirteen times per year. Contemporary pieces made from glass, stone, metal, pearl, amber and porcelain. Offering antique beads, handmade, findings, buttons, charms and beaded jewelry. Access merchants, bead makers and importers

who are direct suppliers of many professional and novice jewelry makers.
N/A Attendees
Frequency: Jan/Feb/Mar/Apr
Founded in 1993
Mailing list available for rent

14910 **Trade Show for Jewelry Making**
Manufacturing Jewelers & Suppliers of America
57 John L Dietsch Sq
Attleboro Falls, MA 02763-1027
401-274-3840
800-444-6572
Fax: 401-274-0265
E-Mail: info@mjsa.org
Home Page: www.mjsa.org
James McCarthy, COO
Corrie Silvia Berry, Director of Sales & Business
David W. Cochran, President & CEO
Kristin Kopaz, Operations Manager
Dawn Britland, Assistant Controller
New regional trade show designed to service jewelry makers and manufacturers of all sizes throughout New England and surrounding areas. Providing a full range of products that industry professionals need to make their jewelry and operate their business.
1000 Attendees
Frequency: September
Founded in 1903

14911 **Transworld's Jewelry, Fashion & Accessories Show**
Transworld Exhibits
1850 Oak Street
Northfield, IL 60093
847-446-8434
800-323-5462
Fax: 847-446-3523
Home Page: www.tweshows.com/jfa
Don Olstinske, Show Manager
Yianna Manokas, Creative Director
Donna Connolly, Customer Service Rep
Ron Carlson, Logistics Manager
Hundreds of the country's finest exhibitors. Thousands of the best buyers nationwide. The perfect venue for the latest jewelry collections, the most current fashion ideas and new accessories.
25000 Attendees
Frequency: July/October/December

14912 **Tucson Gem and Mineral Show (tm)**
Tucson Gem and Mineral Society
PO Box 42588
Tucson, AZ 85733
520-322-5773
Fax: 520-322-6031
E-Mail: tgms@tgms.org
Home Page: www.tgms.org
Sponsored by the Tucson Gem and Mineral Society. Retail show open to the public at the Tucson Convention Center every February for four days. Over 200 dealers, over 100 exhibitors, children's activities.
25000 Attendees
Frequency: February
Founded in 1946

Directories & Databases

14913 **AJM Technology Sourcebook**
Manufacturing Jewelers & Suppliers of America
57 John L Dietsch Sq
Attleboro Falls, MA 02763-1027
401-274-3840
800-444-6572
Fax: 401-274-0265
E-Mail: info@mjsa.org
Home Page: www.mjsa.org
James McCarthy, COO
Corrie Silvia Berry, Director of Sales & Business
David W. Cochran, President & CEO
Kristin Kopaz, Operations Manager
Dawn Britland, Assistant Controller
This publication provides listings and specs on machinery, equipment, raw materials, and software specifically geared to jewelry manufacturing.
Cost: $4.50
Frequency: Annual
Circulation: 5,000
Founded in 1903
Printed in 4 colors on glossy stock

14914 **Accent Source Book**
Larkin Group
100 Wells Avenue
Newton, MA 02459-3210
617-326-6525
800-869-7469
Fax: 617-964-2752
Lauren Parker, Editor
Michael Corkin, Owner
Information on over 1,500 manufacturers of jewelry, watches and accessories is available in this comprehensive directory aimed at the gemology and related industries.
Cost: $25.00
200 Pages
Frequency: Annual
Circulation: 15,000
ISSN: 0192-7507

14915 **Accessories Resource Directory**
Business Journals
50 Day Street
Norwalk, CT 06854-3100
203-853-6015
Fax: 203-852-8175
Home Page: www.busjour.com
Britton Jones, President
Over 1,500 manufacturers, importers and sales representatives that produce accessories are profiled.
Frequency: Annual
Circulation: 10,000

14916 **Complete Directory of Cubic Zirconia Jewelry**
Sutton Family Communications & Publishing Company
920 State Route 54 East
Elmitch, KY 42343
270-276-9500
E-Mail: jlsutton@apex.net
Theresa Sutton, Editor
Lee Sutton, General Manager
Print-out from database of wholesalers, manufacturers, distributors, importers and close-out houses. Database is updated daily to guarantee the most current and up-to-date sources available.
Cost: $39.50
100+ Pages

14917 **Complete Directory of Earrings & Necklaces**
Sutton Family Communications & Publishing Company
920 State Route 54 East
Elmitch, KY 42343
270-276-9500
E-Mail: jlsutton@apex.net
Theresa Sutton, Editor
Lee Sutton, General Manager
Print-out from database of wholesalers, manufacturers, distributors, importers and close-out houses. Database is updated daily to guarantee the most current and up-to-date sources available.
Cost: $37.00
100+ Pages

14918 **Complete Directory of Jewelry Close-Outs**
Sutton Family Communications & Publishing Company
920 State Route 54 East
Elmitch, KY 42343
270-276-9500
E-Mail: jlsutton@apex.net
Theresa Sutton, Editor
Lee Sutton, General Manager
Print-out from database of wholesalers, manufacturers, distributors, importers and close-out houses. Database is updated daily to guarantee the most current and up-to-date sources available.
Cost: $34.50
100+ Pages

14919 **Complete Directory of Jewelry: General**
Sutton Family Communications & Publishing Company
920 State Route 54 East
Elmitch, KY 42343
270-276-9500
E-Mail: jlsutton@apex.net
Theresa Sutton, Editor
Lee Sutton, General Manager
Print-out from database of wholesalers, manufacturers, distributors, importers and close-out houses. Database is updated daily to guarantee the most current and up-to-date sources available.
Cost: $54.50
100+ Pages

14920 **Complete Directory of Low-Price Jewelry & Souvenirs**
Sutton Family Communications & Publishing Company
920 State Route 54 East
Elmitch, KY 42343
270-276-9500
E-Mail: jlsutton@apex.net
Theresa Sutton, Editor
Lee Sutton, General Manager
Print-out from database of wholesalers, manufacturers, distributors, importers and close-out houses. Database is updated daily to guarantee the most current and up-to-date sources available.
Cost: $39.50
100+ Pages

14921 **Complete Directory of Watches and Watch Bands**
Sutton Family Communications & Publishing Company
920 State Route 54 East
Elmitch, KY 42343
270-276-9500
E-Mail: jlsutton@apex.net
Theresa Sutton, Editor
Lee Sutton, General Manager

Print-out from database of wholesalers, manufacturers, distributors, importers and close-out houses. Database is updated daily to guarantee the most current and up-to-date sources available.
Cost: $39.50
100+ Pages

14922 Diamond Report
Rapaport Diamond Corporation
15 W 47th Street
Suite 600
New York, NY 10036-3305

212-540-0575
Fax: 212-840-0243
E-Mail: rap@diamonds.net
Home Page: www.diamond.net

Amber Michelle, Editor
Eillene Furrel, Advertising Manager

This large directory database offers background information and current prices for more than 100,000 stores.
Cost: $185.00
Frequency: Annual

14923 International Society of Appraisers
International Society of Appraisers
Ste 400
230 E Ohio St
Chicago, IL 60611-3646

206-241-0359
Fax: 312-265-2908
E-Mail: isa@isa-appraisers.org
Home Page: www.isa-appraisers.org

Nan B Shelton, President
Connie Davenport, Vice President
Charles Pharr, Treasurer
Philip Hawkins, Secretary

Be Certain of its Value - A Consumer's Guide To Hiring a Competent Personal Property Appraiser is available complimentary to the public. Alphabetical list of appraisers with specialty areas plus indexes: area of expertise, zip code, state and city, company, and related services.
Cost: $15.00
305 Pages
Frequency: Annual
Circulation: 1500
Founded in 1979
Printed in 2 colors

14924 Jewelers Board of Trade: Confidential Reference Book
Jewelers Board of Trade
95 Jefferson Blvd
Warwick, RI 02888-1046

401-467-0055
Fax: 401-467-1199
E-Mail: jbtinfo@jewelersboard.com
Home Page: www.jewelersboard.com

Dione Kenyen, President

Importers, distributors and retailers, close to 45,000, are profiled that are directly related to the jewelry industry.
Frequency: Semiannual
Circulation: 3,400

14925 Jewelers' Circular/Keystone: Brand Name and Trademark Guide
Chilton Company
1 Chilton Way
Wayne, PA 19089-0002

610-964-4243
800-866-0206
Fax: 610-964-4481

L Roberts, Editor

Over 5,000 manufacturers of jewelry store products.
Cost: $49.95

14926 Jewelers' Circular/Keystone: Jewelers' Directory Issue
Chilton Company
PO Box 2045
Radnor, PA 19089

610-964-4000
Fax: 610-964-4512

Kathleen Ellis, Editor

About 10,000 manufacturers, importers and wholesale jewelers providing merchandise and supplies to the jewelry retailing industry and related trade organizations.
Cost: $32.00
Frequency: Monthyly
Circulation: 30,000

14927 Lapidary Journal: Annual Buyers' Directory Issue
Lapidary Journal
60 Chestnut Avenue
Suite 201
Devon, PA 19333-1312

610-325-5700
800-676-GEMS
Fax: 610-293-1717

Michele Erazo, Marketing Executive

List of 4,000 suppliers and retailers of gem-cutting and jewelry making and mineral collecting equipment, beads, fossils, minerals and gems, gem and mineral clubs, bead societies, museums, schools and shops.
Cost: $6.50
Frequency: Annual May
Circulation: 67,000

14928 MJSA Buyers' Guide
Manufacturing Jewelers & Suppliers of America
57 John L Dietsch Sq
Attleboro Falls, MA 02763-1027

401-274-3840
800-444-6572
Fax: 401-274-0265
E-Mail: info@mjsa.org
Home Page: www.mjsa.org

James McCarthy, Coo
Bruce Coltin, Operations Manager
Kristin Kopaz, Operations Manager
Corrie Berry, Sales Manager

Contains finished jewelry as well as equipment, supplies, and components necessary for jewelry manufacturing.
Cost: $45.00
Frequency: BiAnnual
Circulation: 5,000

14929 National Jeweler: Industry Yellow Pages
Miller Freeman Publications
28 East 28th Street
12th Floor
New York, NY 10016

212-378-0400
Fax: 212-378-0470
E-Mail: sedorusa@optonline.net
Home Page: www.governmentvideo.com
Social Media: RSS

Gary Rhodes, International Sales Manager

Approximately 5,000 companies providing products and services in the jewelry and watch industries.
Cost: $10.00
Frequency: Annual December
Circulation: 36,000

Industry Web Sites

14930 http://gold.greyhouse.com
G.O.L.D Grey House OnLine Databases

Grey House Publishing's online database platform, GOLD, offers Quick Search, Keyword Search and Expert Search for most business sectors including jewelry and watch markets. The GOLD platform makes finding the information you need quick and easy - whether you're a novice searcher or an experienced database user. All of Grey House's directory products are available for subscription on the GOLD platform.

14931 www.agta.org
American Gem Trade Association

A trade association for the colored gemstone industry in North Africa. Operates gemological testing in New York.

14932 www.awi-net.org
American Watchmakers Institute

Examines and certifies master watchmakers and clockmakers. Maintains a placement service. Conducts home study courses.

14933 www.cufflink.com
National Cuff Link Society

For cuff link wearers and collectors.

14934 www.glda.com
Gem & Lapidary Dealers Association

14935 www.goldinstitue.org
Gold Institute

14936 www.greyhouse.com
Grey House Publishing

Authoritative reference directories for most business sectors including jewelry and watch markets. Users can search the online databases with varied search criteria allowing for custom searches by product category, geographic area, sales volume, keyword, subject and more. Full Grey House catalog and online ordering also available.

14937 www.iaca.com
Indian Arts & Crafts Association

Not for profit trade association. Our mission is to promote, protect and preserve Indian arts.

14938 www.independentjewlers.com
Independent Jewelers

Works to aid independent jewelers in competing in local markets through advertising, promotion, and buyers assistance.

14939 www.ipmi.org
International Precious Metals Institute

International association of producers, refiners, fabricators, scientists, users, financial institutions, merchants, private and public sector groups and the general precious metals community created to provide a forum for the exchange of information and technology.

14940 www.isa-appraisers.org
International Society of Appraisers

A not-for-profit professional association of personal property appraisers. ISA provides education and organizational support to its members, to serve the public by producing highley qualified and ethical appraisers who are recognized authorities in personal property appraising.

14941 www.jewelers.org
Jewelers of America

14942 www.jewelersboard.com
Trade association providing credit reporting, collections and marketing services to the US and overseas jewelry industries. Our members are wholesalers, manufacturers and service providers to the jewelry industry.

14943 www.jewelerssecurity.org
Jewelers' Security Alliance
Principal activity is providing education and information to jewelers so they can guard against loss through crimes, including burglary, robbery and theft.

14944 www.jewelryinfo.org
Jewelery Information Center
Identifies deceptive trade practices and misleading advertising. Provides advice on marketing and assists in prosecution of violations. The media side of the Jewelers Vigilance Committee.

14945 www.jvclegal.org
Jewelers Vigilance Committee
Identifies deceptive trade practices and misleading advertising. Provides advice on marketing and assists in prosecution of violations.

14946 www.love-story.com
Leading Jewelers Guild

14947 www.silverinstitute.org
Silver Institute

14948 www.silversmithing.com
Society of American Silversmiths

14949 www.silverusersassociation.org
Silver Users Association
Represents manufacturers and distributors of products in which silver is an essential element, such as photographic materials, medical and dental supplies, batteries and electronic and electrical equipment, silverware, mirrors, commemorative art and jewelry.

14950 www.superabrasives.org
Industrial Diamond Association of America

14951 www.womensjewelry.org
Women's Jewelry Association
For jewelry industry professionals.

14952 **National Academy of Television Journalists**
PO Box 289
Salisbury, MD 21803

410-251-2511
Fax: 410-543-0658
E-Mail: wolske@shore.intercom.net
Home Page: www.angelfire.com/md/NATJ/

Dr Catherine North, Executive Director
Dr Cathy Roche, Director

Works with newly graduated journalist school students to assist them as they enter in the world of television news. Honors those in the industtry for excellence in their field of endeaver.
Founded in 1985

Associations

14953 **Accrediting Council on Education in Journalism and Mass Communications**
1435 Jayhawk Blvd
Lawrence, KS 66045-7575

785-864-3973
Fax: 785-864-5225
Home Page: www2.ku.edu/~acejmc/

Susanne Shaw, Executive Director
Doug Anderson, VP
Peter Bhatia, President
Will Norton, Chairman
Christopher Callahan, Vice Chair

ACEJMC members are journalism and media departments, education associations and professional organizations.
113 Members
Founded in 1945

14954 **American Agricultural Editors' Association**
120 Main Street W
PO Box 156
New Prague, MN 56071

952-758-6502
Fax: 952-758-5813
E-Mail: aaea@gandgcomm.com
Home Page: www.ageditors.com
Social Media: Facebook, Twitter, LinkedIn

Den Gardner, Executive Director
Holly Spangler, President
Kenna Rathai, Associate Director
Kurt Lawton, Vice President / President Elect
Laurie Bedord, Immediate Past President

National professional development member association for agricultural communicators.
Founded in 1921

14955 **American Association of Sunday & Feature Editors**
1921 Gallows Road
Suite 600
Vienna, VA 22182-3900

703-902-1639
Fax: 703-620-4557
E-Mail: contact@aasfe.org
Home Page: www.aasfe.org

Chris Beringer, President
Gina Seay, VP
Denise Joyce, VP
Kim Marcum, Secretary-Treasurer

An organization of editors from the United States and Canada dedicated to the quality of features in newspapers and the craft of feature writing.

14956 **American Copy Editors Society**
155 E. Algonquin Road
Arlington Heights, IL 60005-4617

E-Mail: info@copydesk.org
Home Page: www.copydesk.org
Social Media: Facebook, Twitter, LinkedIn, RSS

Teresa Schmedding, President
David Sullivan, Vice President
Neil Holdway, Treasurer
Brady Jones, Secretary
Christine Steele, Director of Membership

A professional nonprofit association for copy editors at U.S. newspapers, magazines, websites, and corporations.
Founded in 1997

14957 **American Copy Editors Society (ACES)**
7 Avenida Vista Grande
Suite B7 #467
Santa Fe, NM 87508

E-Mail: info@copydesk.org
Home Page: www.copydesk.org
Social Media: Facebook, Twitter, LinkedIn, RSS

Teresa Schmedding, President
Lisa McLendon, Vice President Conferences
Neil Holdway, Treasurer
Rudy Bahr, Executive Director
David F. Sullivan, Secretary

ACES is a professional organization working toward the advancement of editors. Their aim is to provide opportunities through training, discussion and advocacy that promote the editing profession.
Founded in 1997

14958 **American Medical Writers' Association**
30 W Gude Dr
Suite 525
Rockville, MD 20850-4347

240-238-0940
Fax: 301-294-9006
E-Mail: amwa@amwa.org
Home Page: www.amwa.org
Social Media: Facebook, Twitter, LinkedIn

Susan Krug, Executive Director
Ann Silveira, Membership Manager & Database Coor
Shari Rager, Deputy Director
Samantha Nelson, Program Assistant
Melanie Canahuate, Education & Conference Asst.

Concerned with the advancement and improvement of medical communications.
3.4M Members
Founded in 1940
Mailing list available for rent

14959 **American Newspaper Representatives**
2075 W Big Beaver Rd
Suite 310
Troy, MI 48084-3439

248-643-9910
800-550-7557
Fax: 248-643-9914
E-Mail: accountsales@gotoanr.com
Home Page: www.anrinc.net

Hilary Howe, President
Robert Sontag, Executive VP/COO
John Jepsen, Controller
Melanie Cox, Regional Sales Manager

Supports those newspaper representatives and distributors in the United States. Hosts annual trade show.
Founded in 1943

14960 **American Press Institute**
4401 Wilson Boulevard
Suite 900
Arlington, VA 22203

571-366-1200
E-Mail: hello@pressinstitute.org
Home Page: www.americanpressinstitute.org/
Social Media: Facebook, Twitter, YouTube, RSS

Tom Rosenstiel, Executive Director
Jeff Sonderman, Deputy Director
Jane Elizabeth, Senior Research Project Manager
Kevin Loker, Program Coordinator
Millie Tran, Editorial Coordinator

Conducts research, training, convenes thought leaders and creates tools to help chart a path ahead for journalism in the 21st century.
Founded in 1946

14961 **American Press Institute (API)**
4401 Wilson Blvd.
Ste 900
Arlington, VA 22203

571-366-1200
Fax: 571-366-1195
E-Mail: hello@pressinstitute.org
Home Page: www.americanpressinstitute.org
Social Media: Facebook, Twitter, RSS

Thomas A. Silvestri, Chairman
Peter Bhatia, Editor
James Moroney, III, Publisher and CEO
Katharine Weymouth, Chief Executive Officer
Tom Rosenstiel, Executive Director

API is the trusted source for career leadership development for the newsmedia industry in North America and around the world. They help companies innovate and leaders realize their full potential.
Founded in 1946

14962 **American Society of Business Press Editors**
214 North Hale Street
Wheaton, IL 60187

630-510-4588
Fax: 630-510-4501
E-Mail: info@asbpe.org
Home Page: www.asbpe.org
Social Media: Facebook, Twitter, LinkedIn, RSS

Mark Schlack, President
Erin Erickson, Vice President
Tina Grady Barbaccia, Secretary/Treasurer
Janet Svazas, Executive Director
Robin Sherman, Associate Dir. & Newsletter Editor

ASBPE is the professional association for full-time and freelance editors and writers employed in the business, trade, and specialty press. It is widely known for its annual Awards of Excellence competition, which recognizes the best editorial, design, and online achievement.
Founded in 1964
Mailing list available for rent

14963 **American Society of Business Publication Editors**
214 North Hale St.
Wheaton, IL 60187

630-510-4588
Fax: 630-510-4501
E-Mail: info@asbpe.org
Home Page: www.asbpe.org

Social Media: Facebook, Twitter, LinkedIn, YouTube

Janet Svazas, Executive Director

Professional association for full-time and freelance editors and writers employed in the business, trade, and specialty press.
Founded in 1964

14964 **American Society of Journalists and Authors**
1501 Broadway
Suite 403
New York, NY 10036

212-997-0947
Fax: 212-937-2315
E-Mail: webeditor@asja.org
Home Page: www.asja.org
Social Media: Facebook, Twitter, LinkedIn, Goggle+

Alexandra Cantor Owens, Executive Director
Minda Zetlin, President
Randy Dotinga, VP
Sandra Lamb, Secretary
Neil O'Hara, Treasurer

For freelance nonfiction writers whose bylines appear in periodicals and in books.
1000+ Members
Founded in 1948

14965 **American Society of Magazine Editors**
757 Third Avenue
11th Floor
New York, NY 10017

212-872-3700
E-Mail: mpa@magazine.org
Home Page: www.magazine.org/
Social Media: Facebook, Twitter, LinkedIn, YouTube, Google+

Mary Berner, President, CEO
Meredith Wagner, EVP, Communications
William Wood, SVP and Chief Financial Officer
Eric John, SVP, Digital Strategy
Rita Cohen, SVP/ Legislative & Reg Policy

An industry trade group for editors of magazines published in the United States.
Founded in 1919

14966 **American Society of Media Photographers (ASMP)**
150 North 2nd Street
Philadelphia, PA 19106

215-451-2767
Fax: 215-451-0880
E-Mail: info@asmp.org
Home Page: asmp.org
Social Media: Facebook, Twitter, LinkedIn

Gail Mooney, Board Chair
Jenna Close, Vice Chair
Luke Copping, Treasurer
Jim Flynn, Secretary
Eugene Mopsik, Executive Director

ASMP is the premier trade association for the world's most respectd photograhers. ASMP is the leader in promoting photographers' rights, providing education in better business practices, producing business publications for photographers, and helping to connect purchasers with professional photographers.
7000 Members
Founded in 1944

14967 **American Society of News Editors (ASNE)**
209 Reynolds Journalism Institute
Mission School of Journalism
Columbia, MO 65211

573-884-2405
Fax: 703-453-1133
E-Mail: asne@asne.org
Home Page: www.asne.org
Social Media: Facebook, Twitter, Storify

Mizell Stewart III, Treasurer
Arnie Robbins, Executive Director
Pam Fine, Secretary
David Boardman, President
Christopher Peck, VP

ASNE is a membership organization for editors, producers or directors in charge of journalistic organizations or departments, deans or faculty at university journalism schools, and leaders and faculty of media-related foundations and training organizations.
Founded in 1922

14968 **Asian American Journalists Association (AAJA)**
5 Third Street
Suite 1108
San Francisco, CA 94103

415-346-2051
Fax: 415-346-6343
E-Mail: national@aaja.org
Home Page: www.aaja.org
Social Media: Facebook, Twitter, LinkedIn

Kathy Chow, Executive Director
Justin Seiter, Program Associate
Glenn E. Sugihara, Accounting Consultant
Karen A. Sugihara, Accounting Consultantÿ
Sunday Ely, Administrative Assistantÿ

AAJA provides support among Asian American and Pacific Islander journalists. It provides encouragement, information, advice and scholarship assistance to Asian American and Pacific Islander students who aspire to professional journalism careers.

14969 **Associated Press**
1825 K Street NW
Suite 800
Washington, DC 20006-1202

212-621-1500
Fax: 202-736-1107
E-Mail: info@ap.org
Home Page: www.ap.org
Social Media: Facebook, LinkedIn, Google+, Youtube

Gary Pruitt, President & CEO
Ken Dale, SVP, CFO
Mary Junck, Chairman
Roger Lockhart, Director Marketing/Communications
George Galt, Director Business Affairs

Seeks to advance journalism through radio and television, and cooperates with the AP to promote accurate and impartial news.
5.9m Members
Founded in 1846

14970 **Associated Press Media Editors**

Home Page: www.apme.com/
Social Media: Facebook, Blog

Alan D. Miller, President
Teri Hayt, Vice President
Laura Sellers-Earl, Secretary
Dennis Anderson, Treasurer
Debra Adams Simmons, Immediate Past President

Members are managing editors or executives of Associated Press News Executives.
Founded in 1930

14971 **Associated Press Media Editors (APME)**
450 West 33rd Street
New York, NY 10001

212-621-7007
E-Mail: sjacobsen@ap.org
Home Page: www.apme.com
Social Media: Facebook, Twitter, Blog

Teri Hyat, Secretary
Debra Adams Simmons, President
Alan D. Miller, VP
Dennis Anderson, Treasurer
Laura Sellers-Earl, Journalism Studies Chair

APME is an association of U.S. and Canadian editors, broadcasters and educators whose entitites are members of The Associated Press.
Founded in 1933

14972 **Associated Press Sports Editors**
9000 N. Broadway
Oklahoma City, OK 73114

405-990-0352
Fax: 405-475-3164
E-Mail: msherman@oklahoman.com
Home Page: apsportseditors.org
Social Media: Facebook, Twitter, RSS

Mike Sherman, President
Mary Byrne, First VP
Tommy Deas, Second VP
John Bednarowski, Third VP
Jack Berninger, Executive Director

A national organization that strives to improve professional standards of sports departments.

14973 **Association for Education in Journalism and Mass Communication**
234 Outlet Pointe Boulevard
Suite A
Columbia, SC 29210-5667

803-798-0271
Fax: 803-772-3509
E-Mail: aejmchq@aol.com
Home Page: www.aejmc.org/
Social Media: Facebook, Twitter, LinkedIn, Friendfeed, YouTube, RSS

Jennifer McGill, Executive Director
Felicia Greenlee Brown, Desktop Publisher
Jenni Meyer, Association Business Manager
Paula M. Poindexter, President
Lori Bergen, VP

AEJMC promotes the highest possible standards for education in journalism and mass communication, encouraging the widest possible range of communication research and the implementation of a multi-cultural society in the classroom and curriculum, defending and maintaining the freedom of expression in day-to-day living.
Founded in 1912

14974 **Association for Women in Communications**
3337 Duke Street
Alexandria, VA 22314

703-370-7436
Fax: 703-342-4311
Home Page: www.womcom.org
Social Media: Facebook, Twitter, LinkedIn, Google+, YouTube

Mitzie Zerr, Chair
Sheila Scarborough, Vice Chair
Jill Randolph, Treasurer
Judy Arent-Morency, Immediate Past Chair
Missy Kruse, Director

Supports all those professional women in the fields of journalism online media, public relations, advertising, marketing, educational communications, graphic and web design, photography and film. Hosts bi-annual conference.
Founded in 1909

14975 Association for Women in Sports Media
7742 Spalding Dr.
#377
Norcross, GA 30092

Home Page: www.awsmonline.org
Social Media: Facebook, Twitter, LinkedIn, Instagram

Kathy Kudravi, Chair of the Board
Jennifer Overman, President
Jim Jenks, VP, Convention
Jill Bouffard, VP, Convention
Stacie Shain, Treasurer

Nonprofit organization founded as a support network and advocacy group for women who work in sports writing, editing, broadcast and production, andpublic and media relations.

14976 Association of Alternative Newsmedia
116 Cass Street
Traverse City, MI 49684ÿ

703-470-2996
Fax: 866-619-9755
E-Mail: web@aan.org
Home Page: www.altweeklies.com/
Social Media: Facebook, Twitter, RSS, Google+

Sally Freeman, President
Amy Austin, Vice President
Ellen Meany, Treasurer
Tiffany Shackelford, Executive Director
Jason Zaragoza, Editor / Advertising Director

Trade association of alternative weekly newspapers in North America.
Founded in 1978

14977 Association of American Editorial Cartoonists
3899 North Front Street
Harrisburg, PA 17110

717-703-3003
Fax: 717-703-3008
Home Page: www.editorialcartoonists.com
Social Media: Twitter

14978 Association of Food Journalists
Home Page: www.afjonline.com
Social Media: Facebook

Debbie Moose, President
Bob Batz, Jr., Vice President
Patricia West-Barker, Treasurer
Nancy Stohs, Secretary
Jennifer Palcher-Silliman, Executive Director
Founded in 1974

14979 Association of Health Care Journalists
Missouri School of Journalism
10 Neff Hall
Columbia, MO 65211

573-884-5606
Fax: 573-884-5609
E-Mail: info@healthjournalism.org
Home Page: www.healthjournalism.org
Social Media: Facebook, Twitter

Karl Stark, President
Ivan Oransky, M.D., Vice President
Felice J. Freyer, Treasurer
Julie Appleby, M.P.H., Secretary
Len Bruzzeseÿ, Executive Director
1,400 Members
Founded in 1997

14980 Association of Magazine Media
810 Seventh Avenue
24th Floor
New York, NY 10019

212-872-3700
Fax: 212-906-0128
E-Mail: mpa@magazine.org
Home Page: www.magazine.org
Social Media: Facebook, Twitter, LinkedIn, Youtube, Pinterst

Mary Berner, President & CEO
Nina Fortuna, Director
Sid Holt, Chief Executive
Sarah Hansen, Events Dir.
Lucy Danziger, Secretary

ASME is the principal organization for magazine journalists in the United States. ASME works to defend the First Amendment, protect editorial independence and support the development of journalism.
700 Members
Founded in 1963

14981 Association of Opinion Journalists
2301 Vanderbilt Place
VU Station B 351669
Nashville, TN 37233-1699

E-Mail: opinionjournalists@gmail.com
Home Page: www.opinionjournalists.org/
Social Media: Facebook, Twitter

Founded in 1947

14982 Baptist Communicators Association
1519 Menlo Drive
Kennesaw, GA 30152

770-425-3728
E-Mail: office@baptistcommunicators.org, webmast
Home Page: www.baptistcommunicators.org
Social Media: Facebook, RSS

Jim Veneman, President
Shawn Elledge, Communications VP
Melissa R. Lilley, Missions VP
Barbara L. Denman, Treasurer
Stella Prather, President-Elect

PR and journalism profesionals.
300 Members
Founded in 1953

14983 Center for Investigative Reporting
925 L St.
Suite 150
Sacramento, CA 95814

916-504-4085
Fax: 916-444-7821
Home Page: cironline.org/
Social Media: Facebook, Twitter, Tumblr, Google+

Phil Bronstein, Executive Chair
Joaquin Alvarado, CEO
Judy Alexander, Chief Legal Counsel
Robert J. Rosenthal, Executive Director
Christa Scharfenberg, Managing Director
Founded in 1977

14984 Center for Media Literacy
22837 Pacific Coast Highway
#472
Malibu, CA 90265

310-804-3985
Home Page: www.medialit.org
Social Media: YouTube

Elizabeth Thoman CHM, Founder
Tessa Jolls, President, CEO
Beth Thornton, Communications

14985 Collegiate Press Association
330 21st Avenue S
Minneapolis, MN 55455-0480

612-625-3500
Fax: 612-626-0720

Tom Rolnicki, Manager

Supports all those involved in the development and betterment of collegiate press. Hosts annual trade show.

14986 Committee of Concerned Journalists
Administrative Offices
Suite 300
Columbia, MO 65211

573-884-9121
Fax: 573-884-3824
E-Mail: rji@rjionline.org
Home Page: www.rjionline.org
Social Media: Facebook, Twitter, LinkedIn, Google+, YouTube

Randy Picht, Executive Director
Roger Gafke, Director of Program Development
Edward McCain, Digital Curator of Journalism
Brian Steffens, Director, Communications
Esther Thorson, Director, Research
Founded in 2004

14987 Committee to Protect Journalists
330 7th Avenue
11th Floor
New York, NY 10001

212-465-1004
Fax: 212-465-9568
E-Mail: info@cpj.org
Home Page: www.cpj.org/
Social Media: Facebook, Twitter, YouTube, Tumblr, RSS

Joel Simon, Executive Director
Robert Mahoney, Deputy Director
John Weis, Development & Outreach Director
Sue Marcoux, Director, Finance & Admin.
Kavita Menon, Senior Program Officer
Founded in 1981

14988 Dart Center for Journalism & Trauma
Columbia University
Graduate School of Journalism, 2950
New York, NY 10027

212-854-8056
Home Page: www.dartcenter.org
Social Media: Facebook, Twitter

Bruce Shapiro, Executive Director
Kate Black, Associate Director
Kelly Boyce, Administrative Coordinator
Julian Rubinstein, Senior Producer / Web Editor

14989 Education Writers Association
3516 Connecticut Avenue NW
Washington, DC 20008

202-452-9830
Fax: 202-452-9837
Home Page: www.ewa.org
Social Media: Facebook

George Dieter, Chief Operating Officer
Caroline W. Hendrie, Executive Director
Lori Crouch, Assistant Director
Natalie Gross, Program Assistant
Emily Richmond, Public Editor

The Education Writers Association is the national professional organization of education reporters and intent of improving education reporting to the public.

14990 First Amendment Center
555 Pennsylvania Ave. N.W.
Washington, DC 20001

202-292-6288
E-Mail: kcatone@newseum.org
Home Page: www.firstamendmentcenter.org
Social Media: Facebook, Twitter, Pinterest

Peter S. Prichard, CEO
Gene Policinski, COO
Scott Williams, SVP, Marketing
Karen Catone, Director
Ashlie Hampton, Event Coordinator

14991 Football Writers Association of America

972-713-6198
E-Mail: webmaster@sportswriters.net
Home Page: www.sportswriters.net
Social Media: Twitter

Kirk Bohls, President
Steve Richardson, Executive Director
1,000 Members

14992 Garden Writers Association of America

7809 FM 179
Shallowater, TX 79363

806-832-1870
Fax: 806-832-5244
E-Mail: webtech@gardenwriters.org
Home Page: www.gardenwriters.org/
Social Media: Facebook

Larry Hodgson, President
Kirk Brown, Vice President
Becky Heath, Treasurer
Robert LaGasse, Executive Director
Debra Prinzing, Past President

14993 Gay and Lesbian Press Association

PO Box 8185
Universal City, CA 91618-8185

FAX 818-902-9576

Supports those gay and lesbian professionals in the field of journalism. Publishes quarterly newsletter.

14994 Hollywood Foreign Press Association

646 N Robertson Blvd
West Hollywood, CA 90069

310-657-1731
Fax: 310-939-9034
E-Mail: info@hfpa.org
Home Page: www.hfpa.org
Social Media: Facebook, Twitter, Youtube, RSS

Theo Kingma, President
Lorenzo Soria, VP
Lilly Lui, Executive Secretary
Yoram Kahana, Chairman
Meher Tatna, Treasurer

Foreign correspondents covering Hollywood and the entertainment industry.
Mailing list available for rent

14995 Inland Press Association

701 Lee Street
Suite 925
Des Plaines, IL 60016

847-795-0380
Fax: 847-795-0385
E-Mail: inland@inlandpress.org
Home Page: www.inlandpress.org/
Social Media: Facebook, Twitter, LinkedIn

Tom Slaughter, Executive Director
Patty Slusher, Director, Membership & Programming
Tim Mather, Financial Studies Manager
Mark Fitzgerald, Publications Editor
Maria Choronzuk, Graphic Designer
Founded in 1885

14996 Inter American Press Association

1801 Sw 3rd Ave
Miami, FL 33129

305-634-2465
Fax: 305-635-2272
E-Mail: info@sipiapa.org
Home Page: www.sipiapa.org
Social Media: Facebook, Twitter, Blogger, Youtube

Julio E. Munoz, Executive Director
Bartolome Mitre, Secretary
Diana Daniels, Second VP
Elizabeth Ballantine, President
Vivian-Anne Gittens, Treasurer

Supports all those involved in the media and journalism industry. Hosts annual trade show.
Founded in 1926

14997 International Center for Journalists

2000 M St. NW
Suite 250
Washington, DC 20036

202-737-3700
Fax: 202-737-0530
Home Page: www.icfj.org
Social Media: Facebook, Twitter, LinkedIn, YouTube, Instagram

Michael Golden, Chairman
James F. Hoge, Jr., Vice Chair
Pamela Howard, Vice Chair
Matthew Winkler, Vice Chair
Joyce Barnathan, President

14998 International Communications Association

1500 21st St Nw
Washington, DC 20036

202-955-1444
Fax: 202-955-1448
E-Mail: icahdq@icahdq.org
Home Page: www.icahdq.org
Social Media: Facebook, Twitter, LinkedIn, Google+

Michael L. Haley, Executive Director
Francois Heinderyckx, President
John Paul Gutierrez, Communication Director
Jennifer Le, Executive Assistant
Michael J. West, Publications Manager

Supports all students and professionals in the international communications industry. Publishes bi-monthly newsletter.
3400 Members
Founded in 1950
Mailing list available for rent

14999 International Food, Wine and Travel Writers Association

39252 Winchester Rd.
Ste 107 #418
Murrieta, CA 92563

877-439-8929
951-970-8326
Fax: 909-396-0014
E-Mail: admin@ifwtwa.org
Home Page: www.ifwtwa.org
Social Media: Facebook, Twitter, LinkedIn, RSS, Youtube, Instagram

Mel Greenberg, Executive Director
Michelle M. Winner, President, Board Member
Allen Cox, 2nd VP, Board Member
Linda Kissam, Secretary, 1st VP
Sherrie A. Wilkolaski, Treasurer, Board Member

Staff and/or freelance writers in the food, wine and travel field. Also includes other media professionals and industry associate members in 28 countries worldwide.
300 Members
Founded in 1956

15000 International Food, Wine and Travel Writer

39252 Winchester Rd
Ste 107 #418
Murrieta, CA 92563

877-439-8929
951-970-8326
Fax: 877-439-8929
E-Mail: admin@ifwtwa.org
Home Page: www.ifwtwa.org/
Social Media: Facebook, Twitter, LinkedIn, YouTube, RSS, Instagram

Linda Kissam, President
Allen Cox, 1st Vice President
Susan J. Montgomery, Treasurer
Michelle M. Winner, Past President
John Lamkin, Board Member

15001 International News Media Association

PO Box 740186
Dallas, TX 75374

214-373-9111
972-991-3151
Fax: 214-373-9112
E-Mail: inma@inma.org
Home Page: www.inma.org
Social Media: Facebook, Twitter, LinkedIn, RSS

Yasmin Namini, President
Matrk Challinor, VP
Scott Stines, Treasurer
Earl Wilkinson, Executive Director
Ravi Dhariwal, Past President

Individuals in marketing, circulation, research and public relations of newspapers.
1100 Members
Founded in 1930
Mailing list available for rent

15002 Investigative Reporters and Editors

141 Neff Annex
Missouri School of Journalism
Columbia, MO 65211

573-882-2042
Fax: 573-882-5431
E-Mail: info@ire.org
Home Page: www.ire.org

Sarah Cohen, Board President
Matt Goldberg, Vice President
Andrew Donohue, Treasurer
Mark Horvit, Executive Director
Jaimi Dowdell, Senior Training Directory

For individuals involved in investigative journalism.
Founded in 1975

15003 Journalism Center on Children and Families

Knight Hall, Room 1100
College Park, MD 20742

301-405-8808
E-Mail: info@journalismcenter.org
Home Page: www.journalismcenter.org
Social Media: Facebook, Twitter, LinkedIn

Julie Drizin, Director
Aysha Khan, Editorial Intern
Zoe King, Editorial Intern
Fatimah Waseem, Editorial Intern
Founded in 1993

15004 Magazine Publishers of America

757 Third Avenue
11th Floor
New York, NY 10017

212-872-3700
E-Mail: mpa@magazine.org
Home Page: www.magazine.org
Social Media: Facebook, Twitter, LinkedIn, YouTube, Google+

Mary Berner, President, CEO
Meredith Wagner, EVP, Communications
William Wood, SVP and Chief Financial Officer
Eric John, SVP, Digital Strategy
Rita Cohen, SVP / Legislative & Reg Policy
Founded in 1919

15005 Media Financial Management Association
550 W. Frontage Road
Ste. 3600
Northfield, IL 60093
847-716-7000
Fax: 847-716-7004
E-Mail: info@mediafinance.org
Home Page: www.infe.org
Mary M. Collins, President & CEO
Toimothy Mulvaney, Treasurer
Ralph Bender, Secretary/ Conference Co-Chair
Debi Borden, Administrative Manager
Chad Richardson, Chairman
Focuses on newspaper financial management, with members representing most North American newspaper companies, as well as many offshore. INFE's activities include publishing, conferences, workshops, industry surveys and studies, and offers members networking opportunities.
1000 Members
Founded in 1961

15006 National Association of Black Journalists
1100 Knight Hall
Suite 3100
College Park, MD 20742
301-405-0248
Fax: 301-314-1714
E-Mail: drmatthews@nabj.org
Home Page: www.nabj.org
Social Media: Facebook
Bob Butler, President
Dedrick Russell, Vice President/Broadcast
Errin Whack, Vice President/Print
Keith Reed, Treasurer
Lee Ivory, Secretary
An organization of journalists, students and media-related professionals that provides quality programs and services and advocates on behalf of black journalists worldwide.

15007 National Association of Broadcast Employees & Technicians
501 3rd St Nw
Washington, DC 20001
202-434-1254
Fax: 202-434-1426
E-Mail: guild@cwa-union.org
Home Page: www.nabetcwa.org
Social Media: Facebook, Youtube, RSS, Flickr
James C. Joyce, Sector President
Nikisha Lango, Technical Asst.
William Murray, Staff Representative
Charles G. Braico, Sector Vice President
Jodi Fabrizio-Clontz, Administrator of Sector Operations
Organization covering the newspaper industry, its employment practices, press freedom and labor movement.
Founded in 1934

15008 National Association of Hispanic Journalists
1050 Connecticut Avenue NW
10th Floor
Washington, DC 20036
202-662-7145
Fax: 202-662-7144
E-Mail: nahj@nahj.org
Home Page: www.nahj.org
Social Media: Facebook, Twitter, LinkedIn, YouTube
Hogo Balta, President
Mekahlo Medina, Vice President/Broadcast
Erlin Ailwoth, VP Print
Sergio Quintana, Secretary
Blanca Torres, Finanacial Officer
NAHJ is dedicated to the recognition and professional advancement of Hispanics in the news industry. NAHJ created a national voice and unified vision for all Hispanic journalists.
2300 Members
Founded in 1984

15009 National Association of Hispanic Journalis ts
1050 Connecticut Avenue NW
10th Floor
Washington, DC 20036
202-662-7145
E-Mail: NAHJ@nahj.org
Home Page: www. nahj.org/
Mekahlo Medina, President
Rebecca Aguilar, VP, Online
Barbara Rodriguez, VP, Print
Ivette Davila Richard, VP, Broadcast

15010 National Association of Science Writers
P.O. Box 7905
Berkeley, CA 94707
510-647-9500
Home Page: www.nasw.org
Social Media: Facebook, Twitter, LinkedIn, Google+
Robin Marantz Henig, President
Laura Helmuth, Vice President
Jill Adams, Treasurer
Deborah Franklin, Secretary
Tinsley Davis, Executive Director
Founded in 1934

15011 National Book Critics Circle
160 Varick Street
11th Floor
New York, NY 10013
E-Mail: info@bookcritics.org
Home Page: www.bookcritics.org
Social Media: Twitter
Laurie Muchnick, President
Jane Ciabattari, VP, Online
Rigoberto Gonzalez, VP/Awards
Michael Miller, VP/Treasurer
Karen Long, VP/Secretary
Founded in 1974

15012 National Federation of Press Women
PO Box 5556
Arlington, VA 22205
800-780-2715
Fax: 703-237-9808
E-Mail: presswomen@aol.com
Home Page: www.nfpw.org
Social Media: Facebook, Twitter, LinkedIn, RSS, Flickr, Youtube
Teri Ehresman, President
Marsha Hoffman, 1st VP
Ellen Crawford, Treasurer (Financial Advisor)
Gay Porter DeNileon, Secretary
Marianne Wolf, 2nd VP
Members are writers, editors and other communication professionals for newspapers, magazines, wire services, agencies and freelance.
2000 Members
Founded in 1937
Mailing list available for rent: 1700 names at $40 per M

15013 National Lesbian & Gay Journalists Association
2120 L St, NWÿ
Suite 850
Washington, DC 20037ÿ
202-588-9888
E-Mail: info@nlgja.org
Home Page: www.nlgja.org/
Social Media: Facebook, Twitter, LinkedIn
Jen Christensen, President
Sarah Blazucki, Vice President of Print & Online
Ken Miguel, Vice President of Broadcast
Sharif Durhams, Treasurer
Robin J. Phillips, Secretary
Founded in 1990

15014 National Lesbian and Gay Journalists Association (NLGJA)
2120 L Street NW
Suite 850
Washington, DC 20037
202-588-9888
E-Mail: info@nlgja.org
Home Page: www.nlgja.org
Social Media: Facebook, Twitter
Robin J. Phillips, Secretary
Sharif Durhams, Treasurer
Michael Tune, Executive Director
Jen Christensen, President
Jen Christensen, Vice President/Broadcast
NLGJA is an organization of journalists, media professionals, educators and students working within the news industry to foster fair and accurate coverage of LGBT issues. NLGJA opposes all forms of workplace bias and provides professional development to its members.
220 Members
Founded in 1990
Mailing list available for rent

15015 National Newspaper Association
PO Box 7540
Columbia, MO 65205-7540
573-777-4980
800-829-4662
Fax: 703-237-9808
Home Page: www.nnaweb.org
Social Media: Facebook, Twitter, RSS Feeds
Lynn Edinger, Associate Director
Robert M. Wiliams Jr., President
Chip Hutcheson, Treasurer
Merle Baranczyk, Immediate Past President
John Edgecombe Jr., VP
To protect, promote and enhance America's community newspapers.
2000 Members
Founded in 1885

15016 National Press Club
529 14th St NW
13th Floor
Washington, DC 20045
202-662-7500
Fax: 202-662-7512
Home Page: press.org/
Social Media: Facebook, Twitter, Google+
angela Greiling Keane, President
Myron Belkind, Vice President
Joel Whitaker, Secretary
John Hughes, Treasurer
Marc Wojno, Membership Secretary
A private organization composed of professional journalists who are directly related to the media. Persons must qualify to be admitted.
4.6M Members
Founded in 1921

15017 National Press Foundation
1211 Connecticut Ave NW
Suite 310
Washington, DC 20036
202-663-7280
Fax: 202-662-1232
E-Mail: maha@nationalpress.org
Home Page: www.nationalpress.org

Social Media: Facebook, Twitter, Flickr, Youtube, Google+, Scri

Bob Meyers, President/COO
John Walcott, Chairman
Linda Topping Streitfeld, Director of Programs
Jessica Jean-Francois, Operations Dir.
Kathy Gest, Secretary

Supports all those involved with national press and the media. Publishes bi-weekly newsletter.
Founded in 1976

15018 National Scholastic Press Association
2221 University Ave SE
Suite 121
Minneapolis, MN 55414

612-625-8335
Fax: 612-605-0072
E-Mail: info@studentpress.org
Home Page: www.studentpress.org
Social Media: Facebook, Twitter, Flickr, RSS

Diana mitsu Klos, Executive Director
Paul Schwarzkopf, Dir. Of Communications & Technology
Lindasy Grome, Dir. Of Community Engagement
Albert R. Tims, President
Christopher J. Ison, Treasurer

Supports all those involved in yearbook printing and photographic services, college journalism departments and video yearbook production services. Hosts annual trade show.
Founded in 1921
Mailing list available for rent

15019 Native American Journalists Association (NAJA)
OU Gaylord College
395 W. Lindsey St.
Norman, OK 73019-4201

405-325-1649
Fax: 405-325-6945
Home Page: www.naja.com/
Social Media: Facebook, Twitter, RSS

NAJA serves and empowers Native journalists through programs and actions designed to enrich journalism and promote Native cultures. NAJA educates and unifies its membership through journalism programs that promote diversity and defends challenges to free press.

15020 New England Newspaper and Press Association
370 Common Street, Barletta Hall
3rd Floor, Suite 319
Dedham, MA 02026

781-320-8050
Fax: 781-320-8055
E-Mail: info@nepa.org
Home Page: www.nenpa.org
Social Media: Facebook, Twitter

Dan Cotter, Executive Director
David Costello, VP of Technology
Peter Haggerty, Treasurer
Mark S. Mrphy, Secretary
Gary Farrugia, President/ Publisher

This organization offers a publication about the newspaper industry specifically focusing on New England newspapers and the issues that affect them, which goes to every newspaper in New England.
460 Members
Founded in 1950

15021 New Jersey Press Association
810 Bear Tavern Rd
Suite 307
West Trenton, NJ 08628-1019

609-406-0600
Fax: 609-406-0300
E-Mail: foundation@njpa.org
Home Page: www.njpa.org

Thomas M. Donovan, 2nd VP
Jennifer Cone Chciuk, Chairman
Stephen M. Parker, President
Richard Verzza, Treasurer
George H. White, Executive Director/ Secretary

Supports all those involved in the development and betterment of collegiate press. Hosts annual trade show.
49 Members
Founded in 1857

15022 Newspaper Association Managers
New England Press Association
32 Dunham Rd.
Beverly, MA 01929

978-338-2555
Fax: 978-744-0333
E-Mail: mlpiper52@comcast.net
Home Page: www.nammanagers.com

Bob New, Owner
Morley Piper, Executive Director
H. dean Ridings, President
lisa Hills, Secretary
Greg Sherrill, Director

Executives of state, regional, national and international newspaper associations.
65 Members
Founded in 1923

15023 Newspaper Association of America
4401 Wilson Blvd
Suite 900
Arlington, VA 22203

571-366-1000
Fax: 571-366-1195
E-Mail: joan.mills@naa.org
Home Page: www.naa.org
Social Media: Facebook, Twitter, LinkedIn, RSS, Youtube, Google+

Reggie Hall, Senior VP
Rebecca Albers, VP
Donna Barrett, Secretary
Joan Mills, Marketing Manager
Robert M. Nutting, Chairan

Newspaper Association of America maintains close, cooperative relations with other newspaper and journalism organizations.
2000 Members
Founded in 1992

15024 Overseas Press Club of America
40 W 45th St
New York, NY 10036

212-626-9220
Fax: 212-626-9210
E-Mail: sonya@opcofamerica.org
Home Page: www.opcofamerica.org
Social Media: Facebook, Twitter, LinkedIn, Yahoo, Stumbleupon, Google, Di

Sonya Fry, Executive Director
Michael Serrill, President
Dorinda Elliott, Treasurer
Jonathan Dahl, Secretary
Tim Ferguson, 1st VP

OPC is a private non-profit membership organization of journalists engaged in international news.
600 Members
Founded in 1939

15025 Pulic Radio News Directors Incorporated
PO Box 838
Sturgis, SD 57785

605-490-3033
Fax: 605-490-3085
E-Mail: info@prndi.org
Home Page: www.prndi.org
Social Media: Facebook, Twitter, RSS

George Bodarky, President
Bob Beck, Treasurer
Naomi Starobin, Large Station Rep
Matt Schaffer Powell, Medium Station Rep
Christine Paige Diers, Business Manager

A non-profit professional association that exists to improve local news and information programming by serving public radio journalists.
Founded in 1985

15026 Society for Features Journalism
Home Page: www.featuresjournalism.org
Social Media: Facebook, Twitter, RSS

Betsey Guzior, President
Terry Bertling, First Vice-President
Lisa Glowinski, Second Vice-President
Kathy Lu, Secretary-Treasurer
Merrilee Cox, Executive Director
Founded in 1947

15027 Society for News Design
424 E. Central Blvd.
Suite 406
Orlando, FL 32801

407-420-7748
Fax: 407-420-7697
E-Mail: snd@snd.org
Home Page: www.snd.org
Social Media: Facebook, Twitter, LinkedIn, RSS, Pinterest

Rob Schneider, President
David Kordalski, Vice President
Lee Steele, Secretary/Treasurer
Stephen Komives, Executive Director
Jonathon Berlin, Immediate Past President

An international professional organization that encourage high standards of journalism through design. An international forum and resource for all those interested in news design, SND works to recognize excellence and strengthen visual journalism as a profession.
2600 Members
Founded in 1979
Mailing list available for rent

15028 Society of American Business Editors and Writers
ASU, Walter Cronkite School of Journalism & Mas
555 North Central Ave, Suite 302
Phoenix, AZ 85004-1248

602-496-7862
Fax: 602-496-7041
E-Mail: sabew@sabew.org
Home Page: www.sabew.org
Social Media: Facebook, Twitter, RSS

Warren Watson, Executive Director
Marty Wolk, VP
David Milstead, Treasurer
Joanna Ossinger, Secretary
Lacey Clements, Marketing & Membership Director

Members are financial and economic news writers and editors for print and broadcast outlets.
3200 Members
Founded in 1964

15029 Society of American Travel Writers
11950 W. Lake Park Drive
Suite 320
Milwaukee, WI 53224-3049

414-359-1625
Fax: 414-359-1671
E-Mail: info@satw.org
Home Page: www.satw.org
Social Media: Facebook, Twitter, LinkedIn

Steven Giordano, President
Diana Lambdin Meyer, VP

Peggy Bendel, Secretary
Tom Adkinson, Treasurer
Cindy Lemek, Executive Director

Photographers and 35 associate member representatives of airlines, hotels, resorts, tourist agencies and public relations firms.
Founded in 1955

15030 Society of Environmental Journalists
PO Box 2492
Jenkintown, PA 19046

215-884-8174
Fax: 215-884-8175
E-Mail: sej@sej.org
Home Page: www.sej.org
Social Media: Facebook, Twitter, RSS

Beth Parke, Executive Director
Don Hopey, President
Linda Knouse, Records Manager
Christy George, Secretary
Carolyn Whetzel, Treasurer & Finance Chair

To advance public understanding of environmental issues by improving the quality, accuracy, and visibility of environmental reporting.
Founded in 1990
Mailing list available for rent

15031 Society of Professional Journalists
3909 N Meridian Street
Indianapolis, IN 46208

317-927-8000
Fax: 317-920-4789
E-Mail: webmaster@spj.org
Home Page: www.spj.org
Social Media: Facebook, Twitter, LinkedIn, RSS, Pinterest, Flickr, Storif

David Cuillier, President
Paul Fletcher, Secretary/Treasurer
Joe Skeel, Executive Director
Chris Vachon, Associate Executive Director
Linda Hall, Director of Membership

Broad-based journalism organization, dedicated to encouraging the free practice of journalism and stimulating high standards of ethical behavior.
9000 Members
Founded in 1909
Mailing list available for rent

15032 The American Society of Journalists and Authors
355 Lexington Avenue
15th Floor
New York, NY 10017-6603

212-997-0947
Home Page: www.asja.org/
Social Media: Facebook, Twitter, LinkedIn, Instagram, Google+

Randy Dotinga, President
Sherry Beck Paprocki, Vice President
Neil O'Hara, Treasurer
Minda Zetlin, Immediate Past President
Salley Shannon, 2nd Immediate Past President
Founded in 1948

15033 The Fund for Investigative Journalism
529 14th Street NW
13th Floor
Washington, DC 20045

202-662-7564
E-Mail: fundfij@gmail.com
Home Page: www.fij.org/
Social Media: Facebook, Twitter, RSS

Ricardo Sandoval Palos, President
Peter Eisler, Treasurer
Founded in 1969

15034 The Society of Environmental Journalists
PO Box 2492
Jenkintown, PA 19046

215-884-8174
Fax: 215-884-8175
E-Mail: sej@sej.org
Home Page: www.sej.org
Social Media: Facebook, Twitter, RSS

Beth Parke, Executive Director
Linda Knouse, Records Manager
Christy George, Secretary
Don Hopey, President
Carolyn Whetzel, Treasurer & Finance Chair

Mission is to strengthen the quality. reach and viability of journalism across all media to advance public understanding of environmental issues.
Founded in 1990
Mailing list available for rent

Newsletters

15035 AEJMC News Association for Education in Journa
234 Outlet Pointe Boulevard
Columbia, SC 29210-5667

803-798-0271
Fax: 803-772-3509
E-Mail: meirick@ou.edu
Home Page: www.aejmc.org

Jenniffer Mcgrill, CEO
Kyshra Brown, Executive Director
Jennifer McGill, Executive Director

Supports all those scholars and educators of journalism and mass communications.
Frequency: Monthly
Circulation: 3425
Founded in 1912

15036 AGENDA
National Federation of Press Women
PO Box 34798
Alexandria, VA 22334-0798

800-780-2715
Fax: 703-812-4555
E-Mail: jane@janeleecomm.com
Home Page: www.nfpw.org
Social Media: Facebook, Twitter, LinkedIn, RSS, Flickr, Youtube

Lori Potter, President

A quarterly newletter published by the National Federation of Press Women.
Cost: $51.50
4 Pages
Frequency: Quarterly
Circulation: 2000
Founded in 1937
Mailing list available for rent: 1700 names at $40 per M

15037 ASBPE News
American Society of Business Publication Editors
214 North Hale Street
Wheaton, IL 60187

630-510-4588
Fax: 630-510-4501
E-Mail: info@asbpe.org
Home Page: www.asbpe.org
Social Media: Facebook, Twitter, LinkedIn, RSS

Amy Florence Fischbach, President
Erin Erickson, Vice President
Tina Grady Barbaccia, Secretary/Treasurer
Janet Svazas, Executive Director
Robin Sherman, Associate Dir. & Newsletter Editor

ASBPE is the professional association for full-time and freelance editors and writers employed in the business, trade, and specialty press. It is widely known for its annual Awards of Excellence competition, which recognizes the best editorial, design, and online achievement.
Founded in 1964
Mailing list available for rent

15038 ASJA Newsletter
American Society of Journalists and Authors
1501 Broadway
Suite 403
New York, NY 10036-5505

212-997-0947
Fax: 212-937-2315
E-Mail: staff@asja.org
Home Page: www.asja.org
Social Media: Facebook, Twitter, LinkedIn, Goggle+

Alexandra Cantor Owens, Executive Director
Minda Zetlin, President
Barbara DeMarco- Barrett, Newsletter Editor
Dave Mosso, Art Director

Confidential news for journalists and authors, available only to members of the Society.
Frequency: Monthly
Founded in 1948
Mailing list available for rent

15039 ASMP Bulletin
American Society of Media Photographers
150 North 2nd Street
Philadelphia, PA 19106

215-451-2767
E-Mail: info@asmp.org
Home Page: www.asmp.org
Social Media: Facebook, Twitter, LinkedIn, Pinterest, Blogger, Tumblr

Peter Dyson, Director of Communications
Victor Perlman, General Counsel
Eugene Mopsik, Executive Director
Elena Goertz, General Manager
Khaisha Allford, Member Services Coordinator

ASMP is the premier trade association for the world's most respectd photograhers. The ASMP Bulletin is a newsletter benefit for members.
Founded in 1944
Mailing list available for rent

15040 Associated Press Media Editors (APME) Newsletter
450 West 33rd Street
New York, NY 10001

212-621-7007
E-Mail: sjacobsen@ap.org
Home Page: www.apme.com
Social Media: Facebook, Twitter

Brad Dennison, President
Debra Adams Simmons, Vice President
Alan D. Miller, Journalism Studies Chair
Jan Touney, Treasurer
Mark Mittelstadt, Executive Director

APME is an association of U.S. and Canadian editors, broadcasters and educators whose entitites are members of The Associated Press.
Founded in 1933

15041 Bulldog Reporter
James Sinkinson/InfoCom Group
124 Linden Street
Suite L
Oakland, CA 94607

510-596-9300
800-959-1059
Home Page: www.bulldogreporter.com

Social Media: Facebook, Twitter, RSS, Pinterest, Google+

James Sinkson, President
Jacques Guatreaux, Vice President

Journalist contact updates and intelligence on how to successfully place stories with the most influential business media and journalists in the US.
Cost: $449.00
Frequency: 24 issues per y
Founded in 1980
Mailing list available for rent

15042 Clio Among the Media
Association for Education in Journalism
234 Outlet Pointe Blvd
Suite A
Columbia, SC 29210-5667

803-798-0271
Fax: 803-772-3509
E-Mail: aejmc@aejmc.org
Home Page: www.asjmc.org

Georgia NeSmith, Assistant Editor
Jennifer McGill, Executive Director

This newsletter is aimed directly at scholars and educators of Journalism and Mass Communications.
Cost: $107.50
24 Pages
Frequency: Quarterly
Circulation: 450
Founded in 1966

15043 Communicator
American Institute of Parliamentarians
550m Ritchie Highway #271
Severna Park, MD 21146

888-664-0428
Fax: 410-544-4640
E-Mail: aip@aipparl.org
Home Page: www.aipparl.org

Rob James, Vice President
Alison Wallis, President
Mary Remson, Treasurer
Jim Jones, CPP-T, Accrediting Director
Jeanette Williams, CP-T, Education Director

Quarterly newsletter listing AIP's board of directors, committees, parliamentary activities, chapter news and activities.
Founded in 1958

15044 GP Reporter
Star Reporter Publishing Company
PO Box 60193
Staten Island, NY 10306-0193

718-981-5700
Fax: 718-981-5713

RA Lindberg, Publisher

Covers journalism for educational purposes.
Cost: $9.00
20 Pages

15045 Guild Reporter
Newspaper Guild: CWA
501 3rd St Nw
6th Floor
Washington, DC 20001-2760

202-434-1254
Fax: 202-434-1426
E-Mail: guild@cwa-union.org
Home Page: www.nabetcwa.org
Social Media: Facebook, Youtube, RSS, Flickr

John Clark, President
Carol D Rothman, Secretary/Treasurer
Andy Zipser, Guild Reporter
Charles G. Braico, Sector Vice President

Covers the newspaper industry, its employment practices, press freedom and labor movement.
Cost: $20.00
6 Pages
Frequency: Monthly
Founded in 1933

15046 ICA Newsletter
International Communications Association
1500 21st St Nw
Washington, DC 20036-1000

202-955-1444
Fax: 202-530-9851
E-Mail: icahdq@icahdq.org
Home Page: www.icahdq.org
Social Media: Facebook, Twitter, LinkedIn, Google+

Michael L. Haley, Executive Director
Sam Luna, Member Services Director
John Paul Gutierrez, Communication Director
Jennifer Le, Executive Assistant
Michael J. West, Publications Manager

Trade association publication for scholars in the field of communication.
Cost: $20.00
Frequency: 10 times a year
Founded in 1950
Mailing list available for rent
Printed in on matte stock

15047 Journalist and Financial Reporting
TJFR Publishing Company
82 Wall Street
Suite 1105
New York, NY 10005-3600

212-422-2456
Fax: 212-663-3260

Dean Rotbart, Publisher

Financial and business news.
Cost: $549.00
12 Pages
Frequency: BiWeekly

15048 Media Reporter
Gay and Lesbian Press Association
PO Box 8185
Universal City, CA 91618-8185

FAX 818-902-9576

RJ Curry, Publisher

Accepts advertising.
Cost: $40.00
16 Pages
Frequency: Quarterly

15049 N2 Newspaper Next:
American Press Institute
4401 Wilson Boulevard
Suite 900
Arlington, VA 22203

703-620-3611
Fax: 703-620-5814
E-Mail: info@americanpressinstitute.org
Home Page: www.americanpressinstitute.org
Social Media: Facebook, Twitter, LinkedIn

Thomas A. Silvestri, Chairman
Peter Bhatia, Editor
Caroline H. Little, President and CEO
Margaret G. Vassilikos, Finance & Operations
Mary Peskin, Training Programs

N2 Newspaper Next: is the forward thinking project undertaken by API - to identify and test new business models for newspaper companies. It has grown to include not just research, but two reports of the project's findings as well as cuountless seminars, worksops, tailored programs offerings and special events.
Founded in 1946
Mailing list available for rent

15050 National Press Foundation Update
National Press Foundation
1211 Connecticut Ave Nw
Suite 310
Washington, DC 20036-2709

202-663-7280
Fax: 202-662-1232
E-Mail: maha@nationalpress.org
Home Page: www.nationalpress.org
Social Media: Facebook, Twitter, RSS, Youtube, Google+, Scribd,

Bob Meyers, President/COO
Gerald Seib, Vice Chairman
Linda Topping Streitfeld, Director of Programs
Maha Masud, Programs Manager
Kerry Buker, Director of Operations

News.
4 Pages
Frequency: BiWeekly
Founded in 1993

15051 New England Press Association Bulletin
New England Press Association
360 Huntington Avenue
428CP
Boston, MA 02115-5005

617-254-4880
Fax: 617-373-5615
Home Page: www.nepa.org

Brenda Need, Publisher
Linda Conway, Marketing Director
Thomas Guenette, Circulation Manager
Brenda Need, Editor

A monthly publication about the newspaper industry specifically focusing on New England newspapers and the issues that affect them.
Cost: $15.00
Frequency: Monthly
Circulation: 1500
Founded in 1950
Printed in 4 colors on newsprint stock

15052 OCP Bulletin
Overseas Press Club of America
40 W 45th St
New York, NY 10036-4202

212-626-9220
Fax: 212-626-9210
Home Page: www.opcofamerica.org

Sonya Fry, Executive Director
David Andelman, President
Jacqueline Albert-Simon, Treasurer

Foreign correspondence news and features.
Frequency: Monthly

15053 Publisher's Auxiliary
National Newspaper Association
PO Box 7540
Columbia, MO 65205-7540

800-829-4662
E-Mail: lynnedinger@nws.org
Home Page: www.nnaweb.org
Social Media: Facebook, Twitter

Lynn Edinger, Associate Director
Merle Baranczyk, President
Robert M. Williams Jr., Vice President
John Edgecombe Jr., Treasurer

The only national publication serving America's community newspapers. First published in 1865, Publishers' Auxiliary is also the oldest newspaper serving the newspaper industry.
2000 Members
Founded in 1885

Magazines & Journals

15054 Alternative Press Review
CAL Press

PO Box 6245
Arlington, VA 22206

E-Mail: alternativepressreview@comcast.net
Home Page: www.altpr.org

Jason McQuinn, Editor

Covers alternative press including humor, opinion and art.
Cost: $16.00
Frequency: Quarterly
Circulation: 7000

15055 American Editor
American Society of Newspaper Editors
11690B Sunrise Valley Drive
Reston, VA 20191-1409

703-453-1122
Fax: 703-453-1133
Home Page: www.asne.org

Arnie Robbins, Executive Director
Kathy Bates, Development Director
Cindy L. Roe, Finance Director
Diana Mitsu Klos, Senior Project Director
Megan Schumacher, Sr. Information Specialist

A magazine published by the American Society of Newspaper Editors.
30 Pages
Frequency: Daily
Founded in 1922

15056 American Journalism Review
University of Maryland
1117 Journalism Building
College Park, MD 20742-1

301-405-8803
800-827-0771
Fax: 301-405-8323
E-Mail: editor@ajr.org
Home Page: www.ajr.org

Tom Kunkel, President
Rem Rieder, Editor
Reese Cleghorn, Publisher
Kathy Darragh, Circulation Manager
Kevin Klose, Senior Vice President

Monthly magazine for media professionals.
Cost: $24.00
Circulation: 25000
Founded in 1972

15057 American Prospect
5 Broad Street
Boston, MA 02109

617-570-8030
Fax: 617-570-8028
E-Mail: editors@prospect.org
Home Page: www.prospect.org

Robin Hutson, Publisher
Tim Lysler, Associate Publisher
Robert Kuttner, President

Progressive liberal publication
Cost: $19.95
Frequency: Monthly
Circulation: 55000
Founded in 1990
Printed in 4 colors on matte stock

15058 Brilliant Ideas for Publishers
Creative Brilliance Associates
Mathey Road
PO Box 32
Clam Lake, WI 94517

715-749-2186
800-975-5474
Fax: 715-749-2180

Naomi Shapiro, Editor

Edited and published for the newspaper industry.

15059 Catholic Journalist
3555 Veterans Memorial Highway
Unit O
Ronkonkoma, NY 11779

631-471-4730
Fax: 631-471-4804
E-Mail: cathjourn@catholicpress.org
Home Page: www.catholicpress.org

Penny Wiegert, President
Tim Walker, Executive Director
Cost: $12.00
Frequency: Quarterly

15060 Columbia Journalism Review
Columbia University
2960 Broadway
New York, NY 10027-6900

212-854-1754
888-425-7782
Fax: 212-749-0397
E-Mail: subscriptions@cjr.org
Home Page: www.columbia.edu

Robert Kasdin, Executive VP
Evan Cornog, Publisher
Michael Hoyt, Executive Editor

Evaluates all of the media as well as establishes standards for the profession.
Cost: $19.95
72 Pages

15061 ESD Technology
Kelvin Publishing
22700 Wood Street
Saint Clair Shores, MI 48080-1762

586-777-0440
Fax: 586-774-3892

John Kelvin, Editor
Kevin Campbell, VP Marketing

Technical articles highlighting new applications and research.
Founded in 1936

15062 Ideas
International Newspaper Marketing Association
10300 N Central Expressway
Suite 467
Dallas, TX 75231

214-373-9111
Fax: 214-373-9112
E-Mail: inma@inma.org
Home Page: www.inma.org
Social Media: Facebook, Twitter, LinkedIn, RSS

Earl Wilkinson, Executive Director
Marise Trevino, Editor
Earl Wilkinson, CEO/President
Dawn McMullan, Editor
Ravi Dhariwal, President

Marketing and promotion ideas for newspaper executives.
32 Pages
Frequency: Monthly
Circulation: 1200
Founded in 1930
Mailing list available for rent

15063 International Communications Association
1500 21st St NW
Washington, DC 20036-1000

202-955-1444
Fax: 202-955-1448
E-Mail: icahdq@icahdq.org
Home Page: www.icahdq.org
Social Media: Facebook, Twitter, LinkedIn, Google+

Michael L. Haley, Executive Director
Sam Luna, Member Services Director
John Paul Gutierrez, Communication Director
Jennifer Le, Executive Assistant
Michael J. West, Publications Manager

Bi-monthly newsletter that supports all students and professionals in the international communications industry.
Mailing list available for rent
Printed in on matte stock

15064 Journalism & Mass Communication Quarterly (JMC)
234 Outlet Pointe Road
Columbia, SC 29210-5667

803-798-0271
Fax: 803-772-3509
E-Mail: aejmchq@aol.com
Home Page: www.aejmc.org/
Social Media: Facebook, Twitter, LinkedIn, FriendFeed, Flickr, Youtube, R

Lillian Coleman, JMC Production Manager (AEJMC)
Dan Riffe, Editor (JMCQ Contact)
Jennifer McGill, Executive Director
Pamela Price, Membership/Subscription Coordinator
Kysh Anthony, Website Content Manager

Published by the Association for Education in Journalism and Mass Communication, the JMC Quarterly focuses on research in journalism and mass communication. Each issue features reports of original investigation, presenting the latest developments in theory and methodology of communication, international communication, journalism history, and social and legal problems. Also contains book reviews. Refereed. Four times per year. (est. 1924)
Cost: $80.00
Circulation: 4800
Mailing list available for rent

15065 Latinos in the US: A Resource Guide for Journalists
National Association of Hispanic Journalists
529 14th St Nw # 1240
Washington, DC 20045-2520

202-789-1157
Fax: 202-347-3444
E-Mail: rnutting@marketwatch.com
Home Page: www.marketwatch.com

Rex Nutting, Manager
Joseph Torres, Communications Director
Rex Nutting, Manager

Purposes are to increase educational and career opportunities in journalism for Hispanic Americans.
Cost: $8.50
Mailing list available for rentat $500 per M

15066 Magazine Media Factbook (ASME)
American Society of Magazine Editors
810 Seventh Avenue
24th Floor
New York, NY 10019

212-872-3700
Fax: 212-906-0128
E-Mail: info@magazine.org
Home Page: www.magazine.org
Social Media: Facebook, Twitter, LinkedIn, Youtube, Pinterst

Mary Berner, President & CEO
Nina Fortuna, Program Coordinator
Larry Hackett, President
Peggy Northrop, Vice President
Lucy Danziger, Secretary

A comprehensive guide of magazine media facts for advertisers, advertising agencies, media planners and consumer magazine marketers.
700 Members
Founded in 1963

15067 **Newspaper Financial Executive Journal**
Interactive & Newsmedia Financial Executives
550 W. Frontage Road
Ste. 3600
Northfield, IL 60093
847-716-7000
Fax: 703-421-4068
Home Page: www.infe.org
Mary M. Collins, President & CEO
Jamie L. Smith, Director of Operations
Arcelia Pimentel, MFM Membership Manager & Sales
Debi Borden, Administrative Manager
Cindy Laser, Sales Account Executive
Trade publication for financial management of newspapers. More than 800 members.
Frequency: Weekly
Circulation: 1000
Founded in 1947
Mailing list available for rent

15068 **Newspapers & Technology**
Conley Magazines
1623 Blake Street
Suite 250
Denver, CO 80202
303-575-9595
Fax: 303-575-9555
E-Mail: letters@newsandtech.com
Home Page: www.newsandtech.com/
Mary Van Meter, Publisher
Chuck Moozakis, Editor-in-Chief
Tara McMeekin, Editor
Hays Goodman, Associate Editor/Webmaster
Jessica Shade, Creative Services Assistant
Newspapers & Technology is a monthly trade publication for newspaper publishers and department managers involved in applying and integrating technology. Written by industry experts, News & Tech provides regular coverage of the following departments: prepress, press, postpress and new media.
Circulation: 16,874
Mailing list available for rent

15069 **Overseas Press Club of America Magazine**
Overseas Press Club of America
40 W 45th St
New York, NY 10036-4202
212-626-9220
Fax: 212-626-9210
Home Page: www.opcofamerica.org
Social Media: Facebook, Twitter, LinkedIn
Sonya Fry, Executive Director
David Andelman, President
Jacqueline Albert-Simon, Treasurer
600 Members
Frequency: Annual
Circulation: 600
Founded in 1939

15070 **Parliamentary Journal**
American Institute of Parliamentarians
550m Ritchie Highway #271
Severna Park, MD 21146
888-664-0428
Fax: 410-544-4640
E-Mail: aip@aipparl.org
Home Page: www.aipparl.org
Rob James, Vice President
Alison Wallis, President
Mary Remson, Treasurer
Jim Jones, CPP-T, Accrediting Director
Jeanette Williams, CP-T, Education Director
Wide range of subjects for AIP members
Founded in 1958

15071 **Ways With Words**
American Society of News Editors
11690B Sunrise Valley Drive
Reston, VA 20191-1409
703-453-1122
E-Mail: asne@asne.org
Home Page: www.asne.org
Social Media: Facebook, Twitter, Storify
Cindy L. Roe, Finance Director
Arnie Robbins, Executive Director
Diana Mitsu Klos, Senior Project Director
Megan Schumacher, Sr. Information Specialist
Kevin Goldberg, Legal Counsel
Ways With Words is the result of unusual, perhaps unique, collaboration among a diverse group of people who care about newspapers and reading. It may well be a model for joint research and development by journalism scholars and practitioners into the future of newspaper journalism.
Cost: $1.00
Founded in 1922

Trade Shows

15072 **AWC National Conference**
Association for Women in Communications
3337 Duke Street
Alexandria, VA 22314
703-370-7436
Fax: 703-342-4311
E-Mail: info@womcom.org
Home Page: www.womcom.org
Social Media: Facebook, Twitter, LinkedIn, Youtube
Patricia Valenzuela, National Administrator
Judy Arent-Morency, Board Chair
Pamela Valenzuela, Executive Director
Liz Booth, Membership Coordinator
Beth Veney, Communications and Programs Manager
Annual conference and exhibits of journalism, public relations, advertising, marketing, educational communications and film.
Mailing list available for rent

15073 **American Society of Journalists and Authors Conference**
1501 Broadway
Suite 403
New York, NY 10036-5501
212-997-0947
Fax: 212-937-2315
E-Mail: director@ajsa.org
Home Page: www.asja.org
Social Media: Facebook, Twitter, LinkedIn, Goggle+
Alexandra Cantor Owens, Executive Director
Minda Zetlin, President
Barbara DeMarco- Barrett, Newsletter Editor
Dave Mosso, Art Director
Bruce Miler, Web Master
A forum for the exchange of ideas between journalists.
700 Attendees
Frequency: May
Mailing list available for rent

15074 **American Society of News Editors (ASNE) Convention**
11690B Sunrise Valley Drive
2660 Woodley Road, NW
Reston, VA 20191-1409
703-453-1122
800-656-4622
E-Mail: registrar@naa.org
Home Page: www.asne.org
Social Media: Facebook, Twitter
Cindy L. Roe, Finance Director
Arnie Robbins, Executive Director
Diana Mitsu Klos, Senior Project Director
Megan Schumacher, Sr. Information Specialist
Kevin Goldberg, Legal Counsel
ASNE's annual convention is the largest annual gathering of newsroom leaders from daily newspapers and other news organizations. Editors and leaders in the field of journalism education will gather to refresh their spirits and create a roadmap to transform their newsrooms and shape the future of professional journalism.
Frequency: April
Founded in 1922

15075 **Annual Multimedia Convention & Career Expo (NAHJ)**
National Association of Hispanic Journalists
Disney's Coronado Spings Resort
1000 W Buena Vista Drive
Lake Buena Vista, FL 32830
866-257-5990
Home Page: www.nahjconvention.org
Social Media: Facebook, Twitter, LinkedIn, YouTube
Michele Salcedo, President
Manuel De La Rosa, Vice President/Broadcast
Russell Contreras, VP Print/Financial Officer
NAHJ is dedicated to the recognition and professional advancement of Hispanics in the news industry. NAHJ created a national voice and unified vision for all Hispanic journalists.
2300 Members
Frequency: August
Founded in 1984

15076 **Associated Press Media Editors (APME) Conference**
The John Seigenthaler Center, Vanderbilt Univ.
1207 18th Avenue S.
Nashville, TN 37212
615-727-1600
E-Mail: sjacobsen@ap.org
Home Page: www.apme.com
Social Media: Facebook, Twitter
Brad Dennison, President
Debra Adams Simmons, Vice President
Alan D. Miller, Journalism Studies Chair
Jan Touney, Treasurer
Mark Mittelstadt, Executive Director
APME is an association of U.S. and Canadian editors, broadcasters and educators whose entitites are members of The Associated Press.
Frequency: September
Founded in 1933

15077 **Association for Education in Journalism and Mass Communication Annual Show**
234 Outlet Pointe Boulevard
Suite A
Columbia, SC 29210-5667
803-798-0271
Fax: 803-772-3509
Home Page: www.aejmc.org/
Fred Williams, Communications & Convention Manager
Richard Burke, Business Manager/Convention Manager
Jennifer McGill, Executive Director
Annual show of publishers and educational groups. Exhibits include publications, information retrieval services and special programs.
2000 Attendees
Frequency: August
Founded in 1912

15078 Collegiate Press Association Trade Show
330 21st Avenue S
Minneapolis, MN 55455-0480
612-625-3500
Fax: 612-626-0720
Tom Rolnicki, Show Manager
20 booths including learning sessions and press conferences.
1.2M Attendees
Frequency: November

15079 International American Press Association Trade Show
2911 NW 39th Street
Miami, FL 33142-5148
305-634-2465
Julio Munoz, Executive Director
12 booths.
500 Attendees
Frequency: September
Mailing list available for rent

15080 International Newspaper Marketing Association Central
World-Herald Square
Omaha, NE 68102
402-734-7632
Fax: 402-444-1370
Terry Ausenbaugh
20 booths.
100 Attendees
Frequency: October

15081 Magazine Media Factbook (ASME)
American Society of Magazine Editors
810 Seventh Avenue
24th Floor
New York, NY 10019
212-872-3700
Fax: 212-906-0128
E-Mail: info@magazine.org
Home Page: www.magazine.org
Social Media: Facebook, Twitter, LinkedIn, Pinterest, Youtube
Sid Holt, Chief Executive
Nina Fortuna, Program Coordinator
Larry Hackett, President
Peggy Northrop, Vice President
Lucy Danziger, Secretary
A comprehensive guide of magazine media facts for advertisers, advertising agencies, media planners and consumer magazine marketers.
700 Members
Founded in 1963

15082 National Conference of the American Copy Editors Society
Sheraton New Orleans Hotel
500 Canal Street
Nw Orleans, LA 70130
504-525-2500
866-716-8106
Fax: 504-595-5552
Home Page: www.sheratonneworleans.com
Social Media: Facebook, Twitter, LinkedIn
Teresa Schmedding, President
Lisa McLendon, Vice President Conferences
Sara Hendricks, Vice President Membership
Rudy Bahr, Executive Director
Gerri Berendzen, Content Editor
ACES is a professional organization working toward the advancement of editors. Their aim is to provide opportunities through training, discussion and advocacy that promote the editing profession.
Frequency: April
Founded in 1997

15083 National Convention & Annual LGBT Media Summit
National Lesbian and Gay Journalists Association
2120 L Street NW
Suite 850
Washington, DC 20037
202-588-9888
E-Mail: info@nlgja.org
Home Page: www.nlgja.org
Social Media: Facebook, Twitter
Bach Polakowski, National Office Administrator
Matthew Rose, Membership Coordinator
Michael Tune, Executive Director
David Steinberg, President
Jen Christensen, Vice President/Broadcast
NLGJA is an organization of journalists, media professionals, educators and students working within the news industry to foster fair and accurate coverage of LGBT issues. NLGJA opposes all forms of workplace bias and provides professional development to its members.
220 Members
Founded in 1990
Mailing list available for rent

15084 National Editorial Conference
American Society of Business Publication Editors
The Gleacher Center
450 N. Cityfront Plaza Drive
Chicago, IL 60611
312-464-8787
Fax: 312-464-8683
E-Mail: info@gleachercenter.com
Home Page: www.gleachercenter.com
Social Media: Facebook, Twitter, LinkedIn
Amy Florence Fischbach, President
Erin Erickson, Vice President
Tina Grady Barbaccia, Secretary/Treasurer
Janet Svazas, Executive Director
Robin Sherman, Associate Dir. & Newsletter Editor
The National Editorial Conference focuses on the skills and ideas you need to weather the down economy and thrive in the new B2B publishing landscape.
Frequency: August

15085 National Magazine Awards
American Society of Magazine Editors
810 Seventh Avenue
24th Floor
New York, NY 10019
212-872-3700
Fax: 212-906-0128
E-Mail: info@magazine.org
Home Page: www.magazine.org
Social Media: Facebook, Twitter, LinkedIn, Pinterest, Youtube
Sid Holt, Chief Executive
Nina Fortuna, Program Coordinator
Larry Hackett, President
Peggy Northrop, Vice President
Lucy Danziger, Secretary
The National Magazine Awards honor magazines, published in print and on digital platforms, that consistently demonstrate superior execution of editirial objectives, innovative techniques, noteworthy journalistic enterprise and imaginative art direction.
Founded in 1966

15086 National Scholastic Press Association Conference
National Scholastic Press Association
330 21st Avenue S
Suite 620
Minneapolis, MN 55455-0479
612-625-8335
Fax: 612-626-0720
Tom Rolnicki, Executive Director
Annual conference and exhibits of information on yearbook printing and photographic services, college journalism departments and video yearbook production services.
1800 Attendees

15087 Newspaper Association of America/ Circulation Managers International
1921 Gallows Road
Suite 600
Vienna, VA 22182-3995
703-902-1600
Fax: 703-902-1600
James Abbott, VP
Newspaper management forum.
1M Attendees

15088 SABEW Annual Conference
Society of American Business Editors & Writers
ASU, Walter Cronkite School of Journalism
555 North Central Ave, Suite 302
Phoenix, AZ 85004-1248
602-496-7862
Fax: 602-496-7041
E-Mail: sabew@sabew.org
Home Page: www.sabew.org
Social Media: Facebook, Twitter, LinkedIn, RSS
Warren Watson, Executive Director
Lacey Clements, Marketing Director
Mark Scarp, Membership Director
Spring Eselgroth, Web/ Membership Coordinator
Defines and inspires excellence in business journalism.
Frequency: April

15089 West Coast Practicum
American Institute of Parliamentarians
550m Ritchie Highway #271
Severna Park, MD 21146
888-664-0428
Fax: 410-544-4640
E-Mail: aip@aipparl.org
Home Page: www,aipparl.org
Rob James, Vice President
Alison Wallis, President
Mary Remson, Treasurer
Jim Jones, CPP-T, Accrediting Director
Jeanette Williams, CP-T, Education Director
Topics being covered are convention committees, boards and problems related to boards, reference committees and the parliamentarian's role in consulting with boards.
Founded in 1958

Directories & Databases

15090 1,000 Worldwide Newspapers
Albertsen's
PO Box 339
Nevada City, CA 95959-0339
Over 500 English-language newspapers overseas and in the United States are listed.
Cost: $10.00
54 Pages
Frequency: Annual

15091 **American Society of Journalists and Authors Directory**
ASJA
1501 Broadway
Suite 403
New York, NY 10036-5505
212-997-0947
Fax: 212-937-2315
Home Page: www.asja.org
Social Media: Facebook, Twitter, LinkedIn, Goggle+
Alexandra Cantor Owens, Executive Director
Minda Zetlin, President
Barbara DeMarco- Barrett, Newsletter Editor
Dave Mosso, Art Director
Lists over 800 member freelance nonfiction writers.
Cost: $75.00
90 Pages
Mailing list available for rent

15092 **American Society of News Editors (ASNE) Database**
11690B Sunrise Valley Drive
Reston, VA 20191-1409
703-453-1122
E-Mail: asne@asne.org
Home Page: www.asne.org
Social Media: Facebook, Twitter, Storify
Cindy L. Roc, Finance Director
Arnie Robbins, Executive Director
Diana Mitsu Klos, Senior Project Director
Megan Schumacher, Sr. Information Specialist
Kevin Goldberg, Legal Counsel
Free access to ASNE's extensive online archive of reports and journalism studies, the gold standard in newsroom-related research.
Founded in 1922

15093 **Asian American Journalists Accountants Directory**
1182 Market St
Suite 320
San Francisco, CA 94102-4919
415-346-2051
Fax: 415-346-6343
Home Page: www.aaja.org
Ellen Endo, Executive Director
Luke Stangel, Co-Founder
Christine Choy, Director
Marcus Brauchli, Executive Editor
Student development, job referrals, fellowship and internship reports.
700 Pages
Founded in 1981

15094 **Bacon's Newspaper & Magazine Directories**
Cision U.S., Inc.
322 South Michigan Avenue
Suite 900
Chicago, IL 60604
312-263-0070
866-639-5087
E-Mail: info.us@cision.com
Home Page: us.cision.com
Joe Bernardo, President & CEO
Heidi Sullivan, VP & Publisher
Valerie Lopez, Research Director
Jessica White, Research Director
Rachel Farrell, Research Manager
Two volume set listing all daily and community newspapers, magazines and newsletters, news service and syndicates, syndicated columnists, complete editorial staff listings of each publication provided, covers U.S., Canada, Mexico, and Carribean.
Cost: $350.00
4,700 Pages
Frequency: Annual
ISSN: 1088-9639
Founded in 1951
Printed in one color on matte stock

15095 **Bacon's Radio/TV/Cable Directory**
Cision U.S., Inc.
332 South Michigan Avenue
Suite 900
Chicago, IL 60604
312-263-0070
866-639-5087
E-Mail: info.us@cision.com
Home Page: www.us.cision.com
Joe Bernardo, President & CEO
Heidi Sullivan, VP & Publisher
Valerie Lopez, Research Director
Jessica White, Research Director
Rachel Farrell, Research Manager
Includes comprehensive coverage for contact and programming information for more than 3,500 televsion networks, cable networks, television syndicators, television stations, and cable systems in the United States and Canada.
Cost: $350.00
Frequency: Annual
ISSN: 1088-9639
Printed in one color on matte stock

15096 **Burrelle's Media Directory**
BurrellesLuce
75 E Northfield Rd
Livingston, NJ 07039-4532
973-992-6600
800-631-1160
Fax: 973-992-7675
Home Page: www.burrellesluce.com
Social Media: Facebook, Twitter, LinkedIn, RSS
Robert C Waggoner, CEO
Johna Burke, Senior Vice President, Marketing
Approximately 60,000 media listings in North America. Listings cover newspapers, magazines (trades and consumer), broadcast, and internet outlets.
Cost: $795.00
Frequency: Annual

15097 **Directory of Selected News Sources Issue**
American Journalism Review
8701 Adelphi Road
Suite 310
Adelphi, MD 20783-1716
800-827-0771
Fax: 301-405-8323
Rem Reider, Editor
List of about 400 companies, organizations and associations that provide information to newspapers and freelance reporters.
Cost: $2.95
Frequency: Annual
Circulation: 28,295

15098 **FYI Directory of News Sources and Information**
JSC Group
PO Box 868
Severna Park, MD 21146-0868
410-647-1013
Fax: 410-647-9557
Home Page: www.fyinews.com
Julia Stocks Corneal, Editor
About 400 associations, corporations, individuals and sources for background story gathering for journalists.
Cost: $19.95
Frequency: Annual
Circulation: 20,000

15099 **Find A Photographer Database**
American Society of Media Photographers
150 North 2nd Street
Philadelphia, PA 19106
215-451-2767
E-Mail: info@asmp.org
Home Page: www.asmp.org
Social Media: Facebook, Twitter, LinkedIn, Pinterest, Blogger, Tumblr
Peter Dyson, Director of Communications
Victor Perlman, General Counsel
Eugene Mopsik, Executive Director
Elena Goertz, General Manager
Khaisha Allford, Member Services Coordinator
Find a Photographer is a search engine to help ASMP members connect with the most respected photographers in the industry.
Founded in 1944
Mailing list available for rent

15100 **Journalism Forum**
CompuServe Information Service
5000 Arlington Centre Blvd
Columbus, OH 43220-5439
614-326-1002
800-848-8199
This database provides information on all aspects of professional journalism.
Frequency: Full-text

15101 **National Directory of Community Newspapers**
American Newspaper Representatives
1000 Shelard Parkway
Suite 360
Minneapolis, MN 55426-4933
612-545-1116
800-752-6237
Fax: 612-545-1116
Hilary Howe, President
A directory of community and weekly newspapers in the United States offering rates, circulation, etc.
Cost: $85.00
550 Pages
Frequency: Annual
Circulation: 2,000

15102 **News Media Yellow Book**
Leadership Directories
104 5th Ave
New York, NY 10011-6901
212-627-4140
Fax: 212-645-0931
E-Mail: newsmedia@leadershipdirectories.com
Home Page: www.leadershipdirectories.com
Social Media: Facebook, Twitter
David Hurvitz, CEO
James M Petrie, Associate Publisher
Contact information for over 39,000 journalists at over 2,500 new services, networks, newspapers, television, radio stations, as well as independent journalists and syndicated columnists.
Cost: $325.00
1,200 Pages
Frequency: Quarterly
ISSN: 1071-8931
Founded in 1969
Mailing list available for rent: 32,000 names at $125 per M

15103 **Newswire ASAP**
Information Access Company
362 Lakeside Drive
Foster City, CA 94404-1171
650-378-5200
800-227-8431
Provides citations and the complete text of more than 1 million news releases and wire stories from the international news wire agencies.

Subjects covered include banking, commodities, companies, currency and economics.
Frequency: Full-text
Founded in 1983

15104 Overseas Press Club of America Directory
Overseas Press Club of America
40 W 45th St
New York, NY 10036
212-626-9220
Fax: 212-626-9210
E-Mail: sonya@opcofamerica.org
Home Page: www.opcofamerica.org
Social Media: Facebook, Twitter, LinkedIn
Sonya Fry, Executive Director
David Andelman, President
Jacqueline Albert-Simon, Treasurer
OPC is a private non-profit membership organization of journalists engaged in international news.
600 Members
Founded in 1939

Industry Web Sites

15105 http://gold.greyhouse.com
G.O.L.D Grey House OnLine Databases
Grey House Publishing's online database platform, GOLD, offers Quick Search, Keyword Search and Expert Search for most business sectors including communication, broadcast and journalism markets. The GOLD platform makes finding the information you need quick and easy - whether you're a novice searcher or an experienced database user. All of Grey House's directory products are available for subscription on the GOLD platform.

15106 www.aarwba.org
American Auto Racing Writers and Broadcasters
Association
Members are professional journalists who regularly cover auto racing and other related sports events.

15107 www.ajr.newslink.org
American Journalism Review
Provides links to sources, journalism organizations, search tools and media newsletters.

15108 www.apme.com
Associated Press Managing Editors
Members are executives of Associated Press News Executives.

15109 www.asja.org
American Society of Journalists and Authors
For freelance nonfiction writers whose bylines appear in periodicals and in books.

15110 www.asne.org
American Society of Newspaper Editors
Directing editors who determine editorial and news policy on daily newspapers and news gathering operations of daily newspapers.

15111 www.cjr.org/resources
Columbia Journalism Review
Contains resource guides and other journalism-related lists.

15112 www.drudgereport.com
Links to international news sources and columnists.

15113 www.greyhouse.com
Grey House Publishing
Authoritative reference directories for most business sectors including communication, broadcast and journalism markets. Users can search the online databases with varied search criteria allowing for custom searches by product category, geographic area, sales volume, keyword, subject and more. Full Grey House catalog and online ordering also available.

15114 www.house.gov
Association of House Democratic Press Assistants
Promotes education and professional standards of members through speakers, series, seminars and papers. Offers placement services.

15115 www.infesecure.org
International Newspaper Financial Executives
Controllers, chief accountants, auditors, business managers, treasurers, secretaries and related newspaper executives, educators and public accountants.

15116 www.inma.org
International Newspaper Marketing Association
Individuals in marketing, circulation, research and public relations of newspapers.

15117 www.ire.org
Investigative Reporters and Editors
For individuals involved in investigative journalism.

15118 www.jour.missouri.edu/home.nsf/
Resources at the University of Missouri's School of Journalism and beyond.

15119 www.jrn.columbia.edu/ressources
Columbia University School of Journalism
Access to Columbia University's Journalism School, the library's bibliographies and reference works, job listings and other associations.

15120 www.kausfiles.com
Site for journalists and media specialists.

15121 www.liberty.uc.wlu.edu
Journalism Resources
Lists of newspapers, film resources, jobs and internships and political advocacy groups.

15122 www.naa.org
Newspaper Association of America
Focuses on the major issues that affect today's newspaper industry public policy and legal matters, advertising revenue growth and audience development across the medium's broad portfolio of products and digital platforms.

15123 www.nepa.org
New England Press Association
This organizatiom offers a publication about the newspaper industry specifically focusing on New England newspapers and the issues that affect them, which goes to every newspaper in New England.

15124 www.nna.org
National Newspaper Association
Representatives of community newspapers. Founded 1885.

15125 www.nnaweb.org
National Newspaper Association
To protect, promote and enhance America's community newspapers.

15126 www.opcfamerica.org
Overseas Press Club of America
A media/journalist organization.

15127 www.poynter.org
Poynter Institute is dedicated to teaching and inspiring journalists and media leaders. Promotes excellence and integrity in the practice of craft and in the practical leadership of successful businesses.

15128 www.press.org
National Press Club
A private organization composed of professional journalists who are directly related to the media. Persons must qualify to be admitted.

15129 www.ukans.edu/~acejmc/
Accrediting Council on Education in Journalism
and Mass Communications
ACEJMC members are journalism and media departments, education associations and professional organizations.

Associations

15130 **Academy of Criminal Justice Science**
7339 Hanover Pkwy
Suite A
Greenbelt, MD 20770
301-446-6300
800-757-2257
Fax: 301-446-2819
E-Mail: manager@acjs.org
Home Page: www.acjs.org
Mittie Southerland, Executive Director
Prabha Unnithan, Association Manager
James Frank, President
Brian Payne, 1st Vice President
David F. Owens, Treasurer
An international association established to foster professional and scholarly activities in the field of criminal justice.
2500 Members
Founded in 1963

15131 **Air Force Security Forces Association**
818 Willow Creek Cir
San Marcos, TX 78666
512-396-5444
888-250-9876
Fax: 512-396-7328
Home Page: www.afspaonline.org
Jerry Bullock, Executive Director
Scott Castillo, VP
Nick Keck, Secretary
Wayne Cox, President
Jim Saulnier, Sgt-at-Arms
The mission is to bring together all those currently serving in the US Air Force as Security Forces members, past Air Police and Security Police members, as well as future Security forces members.
Founded in 1947

15132 **Airborne Law Enforcement Association**
50 Carroll Creek Way
Suite 260
Frederick, MD 21701
301-631-2406
Fax: 301-631-2466
E-Mail: webmaster@alea.org
Home Page: www.alea.org
Social Media: Facebook, LinkedIn
Steven Ingley, Executive Director
Kevin R Caffery, VP
Kurt Frisz, President
Gregg Weitzman, Secretary
Daniel B. Schwarzbach, CFO
Supports and encourages the use of aircraft in public safety and provides networking systems, educational seminars and product expositions.
3500 Members
Founded in 1968

15133 **American Academy of Forensic Sciences**
410 N 21st St
Colorado Spring, CO 80904
719-636-1100
Fax: 719-636-1993
E-Mail: awarren@aafs.org
Home Page: www.aafs.org
Social Media: Facebook
Anne Warren, Executive Director
Nancy Jackson, Director Development
Victor W. Weedn, Treasurer
Barry K. Logan, President
John E. Gerns, Secretary
The need to identify forensic scientists unequivocally qualified to provide essential professional services for the Nation's judicial and executive branches of government has long been recognized. In response to this professional mandate, The American Board of Forensic Odontology was organized under the auspices of the National Institute of Justice.
Founded in 1948
Mailing list available for rent

15134 **American Association of Motor Vehicle Administrators**
4301 Wilson Blvd
Suite 400
Arlington, VA 22203
703-522-4200
Fax: 703-522-1553
E-Mail: info@aamva.org
Home Page: www.aamva.org
Social Media: Facebook, Twitter, Youtube
Neil D Schuster, President & CEO
Sandy Bloomfield, Executive Asst.
Philip Quinlan, VP, Business Solutions
Marc Saitta, Vice President & CFO
Kathy King, Director, Program Business Services
A nonprofit association that supports both state and provincial official members throughout North America who oversee the administration and enforcement of motor vehicle laws. Services include development and research in motor vehicle administration, law enforcement and highway safety as well as being an information clearinghouse.
Founded in 1933
Mailing list available for rent

15135 **American Association of Police Polygraphists**
PO Box 657
Waynesville, OH 45068
888-743-5479
Fax: 937-488-1046
E-Mail: NOM@policepolygraph.org
Home Page: www.policepolygraph.org
Social Media: Facebook
Karen Clark, President
James Wardwell, VP
Robert C. Heard, Secretary
Bruce P. Robertson, Chaiperson
Gordon W. Moore, Treasurer
Promote and maintain the highest standards of ethics, integrity, honor and conduct in the polygraph profession; provide an opportunity and forum for the exchange of information regarding polygraph experiences, studies and research; cooperate with other national, regional and state polygraph associations and other professional organizations in matters of mutual interest and benefit to the profession.
900 Members
Founded in 1977

15136 **American Association of Police Officers**
1109 W 6th St
Suite 205
Austin, TX 78703
800-961-9773
Fax: 800-227-1042
E-Mail: contact@policeusa.com
Home Page: www.policeusa.com
Social Media: Facebook
Phil LeConte, Executive Officer
David Dierks, Financial Officer
Suzanne D'Ambrose, Law Enforement Instructor
Dennis Haley, Veteran Homicide Investigator
Curt Schwake, General Counsel & Advisor
Dedicated to bringing the wisdom of America's law enforcement veterans to the next generation of police officers and citizens. AAPO has provided a national stage for veteran law enforcement officers to share their wisdom and experience. Guided by an advisory council of law enforcement veterans and distinguished citizens, AAPO is committed to tapping into this often overlooked resource - veteran law enforcers both active duty and retired - and putting this unique knowledge to a useful purpose.

15137 **American Association of State Troopersÿ**
1949 Raymond Diehl Road
Tallahassee, FL 32308
800-765-5456
850-385-7904
Fax: 850-385-8697
E-Mail: christine@statetroopers.org
Home Page: www.statetroopers.orgÿ
Social Media: Facebook
Keith Barbier, President
Jeffrey Lane, ?First Vice President
Lee Burch, Second Vice President
Noel Houze, Secretary
Kenneth Musick, Treasurer
Founded in 1989

15138 **American Correctional Association**
206 N Washington St
Alexandria, VA 22314
703-224-0000
800-222-5646
Fax: 703-224-0179
E-Mail: jeffw@aca.org
Home Page: www.aca.org
Social Media: Twitter
Jeff Washington, Deputy Executive Director
James A Gondles Jr, Executive Director
Daron Hall, President
For individuals involved in the correctional field.
20000 Members
Founded in 1870
Mailing list available for rent

15139 **American Criminal Justice Association**
PO Box 601047
Sacramento, CA 95860-1047
916-484-6553
Fax: 916-488-2227
E-Mail: acjalae@aol.com
Home Page: www.acjalae.org
Preston Koelling, President
Karen Campbell, Executive Secretary
Janay Church-Elson, Region 1 President
Steve Atchley, VP
Objectives are to improve criminal justice through educational activities, foster professionalism in law enforcement personnel and agencies, promote professional, academic and public awareness of criminal justice issues and promote high standards of ethical conduct, professional training and higher education within the criminal justice field.
7200 Members
Founded in 1937

15140 **American Jail Association**
1135 Professional Ct
Hagerstown, MD 21740-5853
301-790-3930
Fax: 301 790 2941
E-Mail: rickn@aja.org
Home Page: www.aja.org
Social Media: Facebook, Twitter, LinkedIn, Pinterest, Google+,Tumblr, Red
Robert J. Kasabian, Executive Director
Rick Neimiller, Director of Communications
Patty Vermillion, Program Manager
Lauren McGuire, Marketing and Sales Coordinator
Nico Gentile, Dir. Of Business Development

Dedicated to supporting those who work in and operate our nations's jails. AJA is the only national association that focuses exclusively on issues specific to the operations of local correctional facilities.
5000 Members
Founded in 1981

15141 American Police Hall of Fame and Museum
6350 Horizon Drive
Titusville, FL 32780

321-264-0911
Fax: 321-264-0033
E-Mail: policeinfo@aphf.org
Home Page: www.aphf.org
Social Media: Facebook

Barry Shepherd, Executive Director
Deputy Dennis Wise, National President
Debra Chitwood, CFO
Jamie Maynard, Dir. Of Communications
Brent Shepherd, Director of Operations

Offers benefits and various types of awards to members, magazine, line of duty benefits, film and training library as well as support services, scholarships and financial assistance for police family survivors.
Founded in 1960

15142 American Police Hall of Fame and Museum
6350 Horizon Drive
Titusville, FL 32780

321-264-0911
Fax: 321-264-0033
E-Mail: policeinfo@aphf.org
Home Page: www.aphf.org
Social Media: Facebook

Donna Shepherd, CEO
Barry Shepherd, Executive Director
Debra Chitwood, Chief Financial Officer
Brent Shepherd, Director of Operations
Jamie Maynard, Director of Communications

The nation's first national police museum dedicated to law enforcement officers who have died in the line of duty.
104M Members
Founded in 1960

15143 American Polygraph Association
PO Box 8037
Chattanooga, TN 37414-0037

423-892-3992
800-APA-8037
Fax: 423-894-5435
E-Mail: manager@polygraph.org
Home Page: www.polygraph.org
Social Media: Facebook, Twitter, LinkedIn, Pinterest, Google+, Myspace

Robbie S Bennett, National Office Manager
Chuck Slupski, President
Raymond Nelson, President Elect
Barry K. Cushman, Chairman
Donnie Dutton, VP, Govt

Representing experienced polygraph examiners in private business, law enforcement and government. Professional APA polygraph examiners administer hundreds of thousands of polygraph exams each year worldwide. The APA establishes standards of ethical practices, techniques, instrumentation and research, as well as provides advanced training and continuing education programs.
3200 Members
Founded in 1966
Mailing list available for rentat $125 per M

15144 American Probation and Parole Association
PO Box 11910
Lexington, KY 40578-1910

859-244-8203
Fax: 859-244-8001
E-Mail: appa@csg.org
Home Page: www.appa-net.org
Social Media: Facebook, Twitter, LinkedIn

Carl Wicklund, Executive Director
Barbara Broderick, President
Diane Kincaid, Deputy Director
Adam Matz, Research Associate
John Higgins, Graphic Designer

An international association composed of members from the United States, Canada and other countries actively involved with probation, parole and community based corrections, inboth adult and juvenile sectors
2200 Members
Founded in 1975

15145 American Psychiatric Association
1000 Wilson Blvd
Suite 1825
Arlington, VA 22209-3901

703-907-7300
888-35 -7792
Fax: 703-907-1085
E-Mail: apa@psych.org
Home Page: www.psych.org
Social Media: Facebook, Twitter, LinkedIn

James Scully, Manager

U.S. and international member physicians work together to ensure humane care and effective treatment for all persons with mental disorder, including mental retardation and substance-related disorders. It is the voice and conscience of modern psychiatry. Its vision is a society that has available, accessible quality psychiatric diagnosis and treatment.
3500 Members
Founded in 1966

15146 American Society of Crime Laboratory Directors
139A Technology Drive
Garner, NC 27529

919-773-2044
Fax: 919-861-9930
E-Mail: ascldirector@gmail.com
Home Page: www.ascld.org

Brady Mills, President
Jean Stover, Executive Director
Ramona Robertson, Office Administrator
Jody Wolf, President Elect
Cecilia Doyle, Secretary

15147 American Society of Criminology
1314 Kinnear Rd
Suite 212
Columbus, OH 43212-1156

614-292-9207
Fax: 614-292-6767
E-Mail: asc@asc41.com, ncoldiron@asc41.com, aare
Home Page: www.asc41.com

Bonnie Fisher, Treasurer
Joanne Belknap, President-Elect
Christopher Uggen, Executive Secretary
Robert Agnew, President
Becky Block, VP

Objectives are to encourage the exchange, in a multidisciplinary setting, of those engaged in research, teaching, and practice so as to foster criminological scholarship, and to serve as a forum for the dissemination of criminological knowledge.
Founded in 1941

15148 American Speaker Association
32 East Riverhead Drive
Houstan, TX 77042-2501

713-914-9444
800-636-2722
E-Mail: info@americanspeakers.com
Home Page: www.americanspeakers.com
Social Media: Facebook, LinkedIn

Don Akers, Customer Service/Sales
Richard Alderman, Director of Consumer Law

Assists in proceedings involving legislation and arbitration.
37 Members
Founded in 1979
Mailing list available for rent

15149 American Traffic Safety Services Association
15 Riverside Parkway
Suite 100
Fredericksburg, VA 22406-1022

540-368-1701
800-272-8772
Fax: 540-368-1717
Home Page: www.atssa.com
Social Media: Facebook, Twitter, LinkedIn

Douglas Danko, Chairman
Scott Seeley, Chairman-Elect
Chad England, Traffic Director
john Tobin, Director, Manufacturers & Suppliers
Juan Arvizu, At-Large Director

Promotes uniform use of lights, signs, pavement markings and barricades. Distributes technical information and sponsors training courses for worksite traffic supervisors.
1600 Members
Founded in 1969

15150 Americans for Effective Law Enforcement
P.O. Box 75401
Chicago, IL 60675-5401

847-685-0700
Fax: 847-685-9700
E-Mail: info@aele.org
Home Page: www.aele.org
Social Media: RSS

Wayne W. Schmidt, Executive Director
Daniel B. Hales, President
Bernard J. Farber, Editor/ Research Counsel
Helen Finkel, Staff Vice President
Missy Taki, Supervisor/Manager

Incorporated as a not for profit educational organization for the purpose of establishing an organized voice for the law-abiding citizens regarding this country's crime problem, and to lend support to professional law enforcement.
Founded in 1975

15151 Association of Firearm and Tool Mark Examiners
525 Carter Hill Rd.
Montgomery, AL 36106

334-242-2938
Fax: 334-240-3284
E-Mail: kathy.richert@adfs.alabama.gov
Home Page: www.afte.org

Kathy Richert, President
Brandon Giroux, 1st Vice President
Travis Spinder, 2nd Vice President
Wendy M. Gibson, Secretary
Melissa Oberg, Treasurer

15152 Association of Paroling Authorities Inernational
Sam Houston State University
Huntsville, TX 77341-2296

877-318-2724
Fax: 936-294-1671

E-Mail: keith@apaintl.org
Home Page: www.apaintl.org

Cyndi Mausser, President
Keith Hardison, Chief Administrative Officer
Natalie Payne, Secretariat
511 Members
Founded in 1970

15153 Association of Public-Safety Communication s Officials International (APCO)
351 N Williamson Boulevard
Daytona Beach, FL 32114-1112

386-322-2500
888-272-6911
Fax: 386-322-2501
E-Mail: apco@apcointl.org
Home Page: www.apcointl.org/
Social Media: Facebook, Twitter, LinkedIn

Doreen Geary, Accounting
Gigi Smith, President
Derek Poarch, Ex-Officio
John W. Wiright, 1st VP
Ricky Marshall, Technology & Support Operations

International, nonprofit organization fostering the development and progress of the art of public safety communications by means of research, planning, training and education. Promotes cooperation between towns, cities, counties, states and federal, public safety agencies in the area of communications.
15000 Members
Founded in 1935

15154 Border Patrol Supervisors' Association
3755 Avocado
Blvd #404
La Mesa, CA 91941

Home Page: www.bpsups.org

Richard Haynes, President
Richard Marzec, Vice President
Linwood Knowles, Secretary
Logan Snider, Treasurer
Mike Diaz, Sergeant at Arms
500 Members
Founded in 1990

15155 Central Station Alarm Association
8150 Leesburg Pike
Suite 700
Vienna, VA 22182

703-242-4670
Fax: 703-242-4675
E-Mail: techadmin@csaaintl.org
Home Page: www.csaaintl.org
Social Media: Facebook, Twitter, LinkedIn, RSS

Stephen P Doyle, Executive VP/CEO
Ivan Spector, Treasurer
Robert R. Bean, President
Jay Hauhn, First Vice President
Peter Lowitt, Secretary

Represents companies offering security (alarm) monitoring systems through a central station. It also represents companies that provide services and products to the industry.
300+ Members
Founded in 1950
Mailing list available for rent

15156 Commission on Accreditation for Law Enforcement Agencies, Inc.
13575 Heathcote Boulevard
Suite 320
Gainesville, VA 20155

703-352-4225
800-368-3757
Fax: 703-890-3126
E-Mail: calea@calea.org
Home Page: www.calea.org
Social Media: RSS, Pinterest, Google+, Myspa

Sylvester Daughtry Jr, Executive Director
James D. Brown, Associate Director
Antonio T. Beatty, Administrative Services Manager
Linda Phillips, Information Technology Coordinator
Reginald Newell, Planning and Research Coordinator

Established as an independent accrediting authority by the four major law enforcement membership associations: International Association of Chiefs of Police; National Organization of Black Law Enforcement Executives; National Sheriffs' Association; and Police Executive Research Forum.
21 Members
Founded in 1979

15157 Concerns of Police Survivors
846 Old South 5
PO Box 3199
Camdenton, MO 65020

573-346-4911
Fax: 573-346-1414
E-Mail: cops@nationalcops.org
Home Page: www.nationalcops.org
Social Media: Facebook, Twitter, Youtube

Mariah Hughes, Chief Executive Officer
Erin Barnett, Programs Dir.
Sarah Slone, Public Relations Manager
Lynn Kuse, Chief Financial Officer
Suzie Sawyer, Executive Dir.

Resources are offered in the rebuilding of the lives of surviving families of law enforcement officers killed in the line of duty or determined by federal criteria. Futhermore, COPS provides training to law enforcement agencies on survivor victimizationa issues and educates the public of the need to support the law enforcement profession and its survivors.

15158 Congressional Fire Services Institute
900 2nd St NE
Suite 303
Washington, DC 20002-3557

202-371-1277
Fax: 202-682-3473
E-Mail: update@cfsi.org
Home Page: www.cfsi.org
Social Media: Facebook
William M Webb, Executive Director
Dr William Jenaway, President
James Estepp, Vice President

Designed to educate members of Congress about the needs and challenges of our nation's fire and emergency services so that the federal government provides the types of training and funding needed by our first responders.
Founded in 1989

15159 Cops Who Careÿ
PO Box 20688
Wickenburg, AZ 85358

860-500-8926
Home Page: www.copswhocare.org

Founded in 1982

15160 Criminal Justice Center
Sam Houston State University
PO Box 2296
Huntsville, TX 77341

936-294-1635
Fax: 281-294-1653
E-Mail: icc_www@shsu.edu

Vincent Webb, Director/Dean
Kristi Kreier, Business Office Director

Established to provide an educational program for students seeking careers in law enforcement, cours and corrections and for the development of a continuing education program for professionals working in the field.

15161 D.A.R.E. America
PO Box 512090
Los Angeles, CA 90051-0090

310-215-0575
800-223-DARE
Fax: 310-215-0180
E-Mail: webmaster@dare.com
Home Page: www.dare.com

Francisco X. Pergueros, Secretary
Charles Parsons, President/CEO
Louis Skip Miller, Chairman
David M. Horn, Vice Chairman
Sheriff Roy Klinger, Executive Law Enforcement Advisory

A police officer led series of classroom lessons that teaches children from kindergarten through 12th grad how to resist peer pressure and live productive drug and violence free lives.
Mailing list available for rent

15162 Dogs Against Drugs/Dogs Against Crime National Law Enforcement K9 Assn.
3320 Main St.
Suite G
Anderson, IN 46013

765-642-9447
888-323-3227
Fax: 765-642-4899
E-Mail: office@daddac.com
Home Page: www.daddac.tripod.com/
Social Media: Facebook

Darron Sparks, President/National Director

Dedicated to the betterment of law enforcement K9 operations and to educating the youth on the dangers of drug abuse. DAD/DAC provides grants to officers for purchasing highly trained special purpose dogs and related training equipment and supplies and to provide training for the officer and/or dog. Working/training seminars are offered for K9 officers on numerous topics related to police service dogs.

15163 Evidence Photographers International Council
229 Peachtree St. NE
Ste #2200
Atlanta, GA 30303

570-253-5450
866-868-EPIC
Fax: 404-614-6404
E-Mail: EPICheadquarters@verizon.net
Home Page: www.evidencephotographers.com
Social Media: Facebook

Robert F Jennings, Executive Director

Nonprofit scientific/educational organization with a primary purpose of advancement of forensic photography/videography in civil evidence and law enforcement.
Founded in 1968

15164 FBI National Academy Associates
422 Garrisonville Road
Suite 103
Stafford, VA 22554

540-628-0834
Fax: 703-632-1993
E-Mail: info@fbinna.org
Home Page: www.fbinaa.org

Laura Masterton, Executive Assistant
Greg Cappetta, Executive Director
Ashley Sutton, Communications Manager
Nell Cochran, Financial Manager
Becky Storm, Business Manager

A non-profit international organization of senior law enforcement professionals dedicated

to providing the communities and profession with the highest degree of law enforcement expertise, training, education and information.
17000 Members
Founded in 1935

15165 Federal Criminal Investigators Association
12427 Hedges Run Dr.
Suite 104
Lake Ridge, VA 22192
800-403-3374
E-Mail: info@fedcia.org
Home Page: www.fedcia.orgÿ
Founded in 1953

15166 Federal Law Enforcement Officers Association
7945 MacArthur Blvd
Suite 201
Cabin John, MD 20818
202-870-5503
866-553-5362
E-Mail: fleoa@fleoa.org
Home Page: www.fleoa.orgÿ
Social Media: Facebook, Twitter
Jon Adler, National President
Nate Catura, Executive Vice President
Chris Schoppmeyer, Vice President
Enid Febus, National Secretary
Kurtis Roinestad, Treasurer
Founded in 1977

15167 Fire Equipment Manufacturers' Association
1300 Sumner Avenue
Cleveland, OH 44115
216-241-7333
Fax: 216-241-0105
E-Mail: fema@femalifesafety.org
Home Page: www.femalifesafety.org
Social Media: YouTube, Wikipedia, Slideshare
The premier trade association representing leading brands, and spanning dozens of product categories, related to fire protection.
24 Members
Founded in 1925

15168 Fire Suppression Systems Association
5024 R Campbell Boulevard
Baltimore, MD 21236-5974
410-931-8100
Fax: 410-931-8111
E-Mail: fssa@clemonsmgmt.com
Home Page: www.fssa.net
Social Media: Facebook, Twitter, LinkedIn
Crista LeGrand, Executive Director
Cal Clemons, Managing Director
Dale Kent, President
Tim Carman, Secretary/Treasurer
Eric Burkland, VP
An organization of manufacturers, suppliers, and design-installers, dedicated to providing a higher level of fire protection. Members are specialists in protecting high value special hazardareas from fire.
Founded in 1982

15169 Fire and Emergency Manufacturers and Services Association
PO Box 147
Lynnfield, MA 01940-0147
781-334-2771
Fax: 781-334-2771
E-Mail: info@femsa.org
Home Page: www.femsa.org
Social Media: Twitter, LinkedIn
Dan Reese, President
William Lawson, VP
The leading trade association for the fire and emergency services industry whose members provide products and services to millions of fire and EMS professionals throughout the world. Works to strengthen its membership, planning for future development and directing programs that build industry opportunities.
150 Members
Founded in 1966

15170 Flight Safety Foundation
801 N. Fairfax Street
Suite 400
Alexandria, VA 22314-1774
703-739-6700
Fax: 703-739-6708
Home Page: www.flightsafety.org
Social Media: Facebook, Twitter, LinkedIn
Capt. Kevin L. Hiatt, President/CEO
David Barger, Treasurer
Robert H Vandel, Executive VP
Kenneth P. Quinn, General Counsel & Secretary
David McMillan, Chairman
Independent, nonprofit, international organization engaged in research, auditing, education, advocacy and publishing to improve aviation safety.
Founded in 1947

15171 Fraternal Order of Police
701 Marriott Dr
Nashville, TN 37214-5043
615-399-0900
Fax: 615-399-0400
E-Mail: webmaster@grandlodgefop.org
Home Page: www.fop.net
Patrick Yoes, National Secretary
Ed Brannigan, National VP
Chuck Canterbury, National President
Tom Penoza, National Treasurer
Roger Mayberry, National sergeant-at-Arms
This is the world's largest organization of sworn law enforcement officers, with more than 324,000 members in more than 2,100 lodges. It is the voice of those who dedicate their lives to protecting and serving our communities, and is committed to improving the working conditions of law enforcement officers and the safety of those served through education, legislation, information, community involvement,and employeee representation.
324M Members
Founded in 1915
Mailing list available for rent

15172 Hispanic National Law Enforcement Association
PO Box 766
Cheltenham, MD 20623
240-244-9189
E-Mail: President@hnlea.zzn.com
Home Page: www.hnlea.com
Joe Perez, President
Wendell C. Brantley, VP
Marcos Rodriguez, Secretary
Alex Zunca, Treasurer
Luis Rodriguez, Executive Director
Non-profit organization of professionals involved in the administration of justice and dedicated to the advancement of Hispanic(Latino) and minority interests within the law enforcement profession.
Founded in 1988

15173 Institute of Investigative Technology
AccuQuest
6950 Phillips Hwy, #46
Jacksonville, FL 32216-6087
904-296-0212
Fax: 904-296-7385
Home Page: www.aqonline.com/iitframeset.html
John Ramming, Director
Provides training for law enforcement and corporate clients. Programs can be designed from one-day to multiple week training courses.

15174 Institute of Police Technology and Management
University of North Florida
12000 Alumni Dr
Jacksonville, FL 32224-2678
904-620-4786
Fax: 904-620-2453
E-Mail: info@iptm.org
Home Page: www.iptm.org
Social Media: Facebook
Bob Jacob, Executive Director
Cameron Pucci, Director
Tony Becker, Administration
Kenin Al Roop, Marketing
Harry Walters, Traffic Enforcement
Mission of the Institute is to provide the law enforcement community with the highest quality of training at competitive prices. By providing this service, IPTM continues to support law enforcement's efforts in building and maintaining safer communitites.

15175 Insurance Institute for Highway Safety
1005 N Glebe Rd
Suite 800
Arlington, VA 22201
703-247-1500
Fax: 703-247-1588
E-Mail: rrader@iihs.org
Home Page: www.iihs.org
Social Media: Twitter, RSS, YouTube
Adrian Loud, President
Russ Rader, Senior Vice President
Shelley Shelton, Executive Assistant, Legal Affairs
Brenda O'Donnell, Vice President, Insurer Relations
Karen Koger, Communications Associate
Independent, nonprofit, scientific and educational organization dedicated to reducing the losses (deaths, injuries, and property damage) from crashes on the nation's highways.
Founded in 1959
Mailing list available for rent

15176 International Association for Identification
2131 Hollywood Blvd.,
Suite 403
Hollywood, FL 33020
954-589-0628
Fax: 954-589-0657
Home Page: www.theiai.org
Social Media: Facebook
Steve Johnson, President
Bridget Lewis, 1st Vice President
Harold Ruslander, 2nd Vice President
Ray Jorz, 3rd Vice President
Glen Calhoun, Chief Operations Officer
Founded in 1915

15177 International Association for Property Evidence, Inc.
903 N San Fernando Boulevard
Suite 4
Burbank, CA 91504-4327
818-846-2926
800-449-4273
Fax: 818-846-4543
E-Mail: Mail@IAPE.org

Home Page: www.iape.org
Social Media: Facebook

Joseph T. Latta, Executive Director/Lead Instructor
William Kiley, Board Member, Instructor
Steve Campbell, Secretary, Instructor
Suzanne Cox, Tresurer
Robin Lynn Trench, Founder

Established to further the education, training and professional growth of Law Enforcement Property and Evidence Personnel.
Founded in 1993

15178 International Association of Arson Investigators
2111 Baldwin Avenue
Suite 203
Crofton, MD 21114

410-451-3473
800-468-4224
Fax: 410-451-9049
Home Page: www.firearson.com
Social Media: Facebook, Twitter, LinkedIn, YouTube

Rob Rush, President
Deborah Neitch, Executive dir.
Tom Aurnhammer, Training Manager
Peter Mansi, 1st VP
Debra Miller, Accounting & Finanace Manager

Dedicated to improving the professional development of fire and explosion investigators by being the global resource for fire investigation, technology and research.
7500 Members
Founded in 1949

15179 International Association of Auto Theft Investigators
PO Box 223
Clinton, NY 13323-0223
315-853-1913
315-883-1310
Fax: 315-883-1310
E-Mail: jvabounader@iaati.org
Home Page: www.iaati.org

Peter R. Perrien, President
Robert C. Hasbrouck, Treasurer
John V Abounader, Executive Director
Heidi M. Jordan, 1st VP
Todd M. Blair, 3rd VP

Provides members who are auto theft investigators with resources to develop and maintain professional standards within the industry.
4904 Members
Founded in 1952

15180 International Association of Bloodstain Pattern Analysts

Home Page: www.iabpa.org

Pat Laturnus, President
Donald Schuessler, VP
Norman Reeves, Secretary/ Treasurer
Jeff Scozzafava, Sergeant at Arms
Stuart H James, Historian

15181 International Association of Bomb Technicians and Investigators
1120 International parkway
Fredricksburg, VA 22406

540-752-4533
Fax: 540-752-2796
E-Mail: admin@iabti.org
Home Page: www.iabti.org
Social Media: Twitter

Ralph Way, Executive Director

An independent professional association formed for countering the criminal use of explosives. This is sought through the exchange of training, expertise and information among personnel employed in the fields of law enforcement, fire and emergency services, the military, forensic science and other related fields.
4000 Members
Founded in 1973

15182 International Association of Campus Law Enforcement Administrators
342 N Main Street
West Hartford, CT 06117-2507

860-586-7517
Fax: 860-586-7550
E-Mail: info@iaclea.org
Home Page: www.iaclea.org
Social Media: Facebook

Christopher Blake, Chief Staff Officer
Lynn Sedlak, Membership/Administration Director
Kathleen Harrington, Associate Director
Lisa Phillips, Government Relations
Deborah Rondeau, Membership Services

Advances public safety for educational institutions by providing educational resources, advocacy and professional development.
Founded in 1958
Mailing list available for rent

15183 International Association of Directors of Law Enforcement Standards/Training
1330 N. Manship Pl.
Meridian, ID 83642

208-288-5491
Fax: 517-857-3826
E-Mail: mikebecar@iadlest.org, pjudge@att.net
Home Page: www.iadlest.org

Patrick Judge, Deputy Director
C. Kim Vickers, President
Michael N. Becar, Executive Director
Charles Melville, Treasurer
Mark Damitio, Secretary

An international organization of training managers and executives dedicated to the improvement of public safety personnel. The Association serves as the national forum of Peace Officer Standards and Training (POST) agencies, boards and commissions as well as statewide training academies throughout the United States.
Mailing list available for rent

15184 International Association of Law Enforcement Firearms Instructors
25 Country Club Road
Suite 707
Gilford, NH 03249

603-524-8787
Fax: 603-524-8856
E-Mail: info@ialefi.com
Home Page: www.ialefi.com

R Steven Johnson, President
Robert D Bossey, Executive Director/Treasurer
Michial Dunlap, Secretary
John T. Meyer, 1st VP
Emanuel Kapelson, 2nd VP

An independent, non-profit association whose mission is to update and modernize the instruction and teaching techniques used to train the majority of law enforcement officers.
Founded in 1981

15185 International Association of Undercover Officers
142 Banks Drive
Brunswick, GA 31523

800-876-5943
Fax: 800-876-5912
E-Mail: charlie@undercover.org
Home Page: www.undercover.org

Charlie Fuller, Executive Director
Brian Sallee, President
Steve Cook, First Vice-President
David Redemann, Second Vice-President
Frank Swirko, Treasurer

Established for the purpose of promoting safety and professionalism among undercover officers. The association continues to foster mutual cooperation, discussion and interests among its members. It provides vast international network of intelligence gathering means for today's undercover officer and sponsors high quality training programs for undercover officers.

15186 International Association of Women Police
1352 NE 47th Avenue
Portland, OR 97213

301-464-1402
Fax: 301-464-1402
E-Mail: carolpaterick@gmail.com
Home Page: www.iawp.org
Social Media: Twitter

Jane Townsley, President
Deborah Friedl, Executive Director
Karen Salisbury, Recording Secretary
Michelle Lish, Treasurer

Strengthen, unite and raise the profile of women in crimial justiceinternationally. field of law enforcement. Conferences held in South Africa, Wales and elsewhere overseas highlight the successes of the association of Women Police.
1M Attendees
Frequency: September/October
Founded in 1915

15187 International Association of Women Police
1352 NE 47th Avenue
Portland, OR 97213

301-464-1402
Fax: 301-464-1402
E-Mail: carolpaterick@gmail.com
Home Page: www.iawp.org
Social Media: Twitter

Terrie S Swann, President
Amy Ramsey, Executive Director
Glenda Baker, First VP
Michele Lish, Recording Secretary
Jo Ann Acree, Treasurer

To strengthen, unite, and raise the profile of women in criminal justice internationally.
24000 Members
Founded in 1915

15188 International Board of Certification for Safety Managers
173 Tucker Road
Suite 202
Helena, AL 35080

205-664-8412
Fax: 205-663-9541
E-Mail: info@ibfcsm.org
Home Page: www.ibfcsm.org

James Tweedy, Executive Director

A professional credentialing organization that promotes the application of managerial techniques to eliminate or control unsafe and unhealthy conditions, behavior and other factors detrimental to people and property. Offers credentials in safety, product safety, healthcare safety, patient safety, and healthcare emergency management.
2500 Members
Founded in 1976

15189 International Crime Scene Investigator's Association
15774 S. LaGrange Road
Orland Park, IL 60462
708-460-8082
Home Page: www.icsia.org
Hayden B Baldwin, Executive Director
Christopher Anderson, Caribbean Director
Paul Echols, Board of Directors
Chad Pitfield, Board of Directors
Steven W Hulsey, Board of Directors

15190 International Critical Incident Stress Foundation
3290 Pine Orchard Ln
Suite 106
Ellicott City, MD 21042
410-750-9600
Fax: 410-750-9601
E-Mail: info@icisf.org
Home Page: www.icisf.org
Donald Howell, Executive Director
Lisa Joubert, Finance Director
Richard Barton, CEO
C. Kenneth Bohn, Director of Operations
Jeannie Gow, General Information Requests
A foundation dedicated to the prevention and mitigation of disabling stress through the provision of; Education, training and support services for all Emergency Services professions, continuing education and training in Emergency Mental Health Services for Psychologists, Psychiatrists, Social Workers and Licensed Professional Counselors and Consultation in the establishment of Crisis and Disaster Response Programs for varied organizations and communities worldwide.

15191 International Footprint Association
PO Box 1652
Walnut, CA 91788
323-981-1488
877-432-3668
Fax: 323-265-4657
E-Mail: footprint@footprinter.org
Home Page: www.footprinter.org
Mike Azuela, President
Charles Zigler, First VP
A non-profit association that promotes and encourages fellowship, respect, cooperation, and helpfulness between all arms of law enforcement and all others who are sympathetic with and understanding toward law enforcement and all of its agencies.
4000 Members
Founded in 1929

15192 International Law Enforcement Educators & Trainers Association
1972 Gail Lynne Drive
Burlington, WI 53105
262-767-1406
Fax: 262-767-1813
E-Mail: info@ILEETA.org
Home Page: www.ileeta.org
Social Media: Facebook
Harvey Hedden, Executive Director
Brian Wills, Deputy Executive Dir.
Alexis Artwohl, Advisory Board Member
Massad Ayoob, Advisory Board Member
Steve Ashley, Advisory Board Member
An organization by, for and about instructors and training for the criminal justice professions. Committed to the reduction of law enforcement risk through the enhancement of training for criminal justice practitioners.
Founded in 2003

15193 International Narcotic Enforcement Officers Association
112 State Street
Suite 1200
Albany, NY 12207-2079
518-463-6232
E-Mail: ineoa@iopener.net
Home Page: www.ineoa.org
John J Bellizer Jr, Executive Director
Michael Harris, President
Basic purpose is to promote and foster mutual interest in the problems of narcotic control; provide a medium for the exchange of ideas, conduct seminars, conferences and study groups and issue publications.

15194 International Police Associationÿÿ
PO Box 516
Greystone Station
Yonkers, NY 10703-0516
Home Page: www.ipa-usa.org
Social Media: Facebook, Twitter
Kevin Gordon, President
Calvin Chow, 1st VP
Cory Freadling, 2nd VP
Joe Johnson, 3rd VP
Viola Powrie, Treasurer
Founded in 1950

15195 Law Enforcement & Emergency Services Video Association
84 Briar Creek Road
Whitesboro, TX 76273
469-285-9435
Fax: 469-533-3659
E-Mail: commngr@leva.org
Home Page: www.leva.org
Social Media: Facebook, Twitter, LinkedIn
Alan Salmon, Chairman of the Board
Scott Sullivan, Vice Chairman
Blaine Davison, President
Scott Tidwell, Executive Vice President
Scott Sullivan, Forensic Training, Program Manager
Committed to improving the quality of video training and promoting the use of state-of-the-art, effective equipment in the law enforcement and emergency services community.
Mailing list available for rent

15196 Law Enforcement Alliance of America
12427 Hedges Run Drive
Suite 113
Lake Ridge, VA 22192-1715
703-847-2677
Fax: 703-556-6485
E-Mail: membership@leaa.org
Home Page: www.leaa.org
Jim Fotis, Executive Director
Kevin Watson, Communications Director
Nation's largest nonprofit, non-partisan coalition of law enforcement professionals. Crime victims, and concerned citizens united for justice; with a major focus on public education, LEAA is dedicated to providing hard facts and real world insights into the world of law enforcement and the battle against violent crime. Fighting at every level of government for legislation that reduces violent crime while preserving the rights of honest citizens, particularly the right of self-defense.
Founded in 1992

15197 Law Enforcement Bloodhound Association
PO Box 190442
Anchorage, AL 99519-0442
907-602-3542
E-Mail: leba@gci.net
Home Page: www.leba98.com
Gerry Nichols, President
LEBA is a professional nonprofit organization dedicated to the promotion of bloodhounds in law enforcement. Also provides beginning, continuing and advanced education to law enforcement professionals and thier bloodhound partners.
Founded in 1998
Mailing list available for rent

15198 Law Enforcement Executive Development Association, Inc.
5 Great Valley Pkwy.
Suite 125
Malvern, PA 19355
877-772-7712
Fax: 610-644-3193
E-Mail: crobb@fbileeda.org
Home Page: www.fbileeda.org
Greg Hamilton, President
Sam J. Pennica, First Vice President
Chief David Boggs, Second Vice President
Charles Robb, Executive Director
Judy Pal, Director of Operations
Purpose of the association is to advance the Science and Art of Police Management and Administration; to develop and disseminate improved administrative and technical practices; promote the exchange of information and training for executives of law enforcement.

15199 Law Enforcement Legal Defense Fundÿ
1428 Duke Street
Alexandria, VA 703-807-18
E-Mail: info@leldf.org
Home Page: www.policedefense.orgÿ
Social Media: Facebook, Twitter, LinkedIn, YouTube
Alfred S Regnery, Chairman
John J Burke, Vice Chairman
Ron Hosko, President
Edwin Meese, Director
Daniel J DeSimone, Secretary-Treasurer
Founded in 1995

15200 Law Enforcement Standards Office
100 Bureau Drive
MS 8102
Gaithersburg, MD 20899-8102
301-975-2757
Fax: 301-948-0978
E-Mail: oles@nist.gov
Home Page: www.nist.gov/oles/
Patrick D. Gallagher, Director
Michael D. Herman, Executive Officer
Kevin Kimball, Chief of Staff
Henry N. Wixon, Chief Counsel
Mary Saunders, Associate Director
OLES's mission is to serve as the principal agent for standards development for the criminal justice and public safety communities. Helping criminal justice and public safety agencies acquire, on a cost-effective basis, the high quality resources they need to do their jobs.
Founded in 1901

15201 Major Cities Chiefs Police Association
E-Mail: stephens@majorcitieschiefs.com
Home Page: www.majorcitieschiefs.com

Charles H Ramsey, President
Chris Burbank, 1st Vice President
AnWilliam Blair, 2nd Vice President
J. Thomas Manger, Chief of Police
Darrel Stephens, Executive Director
Founded in 1949

15202 Metropolitan Alliance of Police
215 Remington Blvd.
Suite C
Bolingbrook, IL 60440

630-759-4925
Fax: 630-759-1902
E-Mail: mapunion@msn.com
Home Page: www.mapunion.org

Joseph Andalina, President
Keith George, Vice President
Richard Tracy, Secretary
John Ward, Board of Directors
John Holiday, Board of Directors

15203 Narcotic Enforcement Officers Association
29 N Plains Hwy
Suite 10
Wallingford, CT 06492

203-269-8940
Fax: 203-284-9103
Home Page: www.neoa.org

Michael R Rinaldi, President
Gabriel Lupo, VP
Richard Stook, Treasurer
Duane Tompkins, Secretary

A non-profit educational organization of more than a thousand law enforcement personnel and others in the criminal justicce system, includin state and local police, D.E.A., F.B.I. and customs.

15204 National Asian Peace Officers' Association
1776 I Street, NW,
Suite 900
Washington, DC 20006

646-632-5384
Fax: 202-756-1301
E-Mail: james.ng@napoaonline.com
Home Page: www.napoaonline.org

James Ng, President
Taerance Oh, 1st Vice President
Thomas Masters, Executive Director
Rolland Ogawa, Secretary
Siamone Bangphraxay, Treasurer

15205 National Association School Resource Officers
2020 Valleydale Road
Suite 207A
Hoover, AL 35244

205-739-6060
888-316-2776
Fax: 205-536-9255
E-Mail: kevin.campana@nasro.org
Home Page: www.nasro.org
Social Media: Facebook, Twitter, RSS, Youtube

Phil Bailey, President
Kevin Campana, Executive Director

A not-for-profit organization for school based law enforcement officers, school administrators, and school security/safety professionals working as partners to protect students, school faculty and staff and the schools they attend.

15206 National Association of Attorneys General
2030 M Street NW
8th Floor
Washington, DC 20036

202-326-6000
Fax: 202-331-1427
Home Page: www.naag.org

J.B. Van Hollen, President
Marty Jackley, Vice President and CWAG Chair
James McPherson, Executive Director
Scott Messing, Chief of Staff
Marjorie Tharp, Director of Communications

Founded to help Attorneys General fulfill the responsibilities of their office and to assist in the delivery of high quality legal services to the states and territorial jurisdictions.
Founded in 1907
Mailing list available for rent

15207 National Association of Chiefs of Police
6350 Horizon Drive
Titusville, FL 32780-8002

321-264-0911
Fax: 321-264-0033
E-Mail: policeinfo@aphf.org
Home Page: www.aphf.org

Jamie Maynard, Director of Communications
Barry Shepherd, Executive Director
Debra Chitwood, Chief Financial Officer
Brent Shepherd, Director of Operations

The mission is to encourage through the leadership of persons who hold a command law enforcement or security position within the United States and her territories and possessions, educational activities and services to upgrade law enforcement and security on a professional level.
Founded in 1967
Mailing list available for rent

15208 National Association of Drug Court Professionals
1029 N. Royal St
Suite 201
Alexandria, VA 22314

703-575-9400
Fax: 703-706-0577
Home Page: www.nadcp.org
Social Media: Facebook, Twitter, Youtube

West Huddleston, CEO
Meghan Wheeler, Project Director

Seeks to reduce substance abuse, crime and recidivism by promoting and advocating for the establishment and funding of Drug Courts and providing for collection and dissemination of information, technical assistance, and mutual support to association members.
Founded in 1997
Mailing list available for rent

15209 National Association of Field Training Officers
20783 N. 83rd Ave.
Ste 103 PMB 462
Peoria, AZ 85382

812-483-6588
E-Mail: director@nafto.org
Home Page: www.nafto.org
Social Media: Facebook, Twitter, RSS

Henry Loeffel, President
Sgt. David Harris, First VP
Lt. Bob Smith, Second VP
Sgt. Jeff Chapman, Executive Director

An educational and professional association concerned with apprenticeship and advance ongoing training for law enforcement, communications, and corrections personnel. Educators, administrators and other criminal justice practitioners are also encouraged to participate.

15210 National Association of Fleet Administrators
100 Wood Avenue S
Suite 310
Iselin, NJ 08830-2709

732-494-8100
Fax: 609-452-8004
E-Mail: info@nafa.org
Home Page: www.nafa.org
Social Media: Facebook, Twitter, LinkedIn, Youtube, RSS

Charles A Gibbens, President
Gayle Pratt, Senior VP

Serving the needs of those managing fleets of automobiles, light duty trucks and/or vans for US and Canadian organizations. Offers statistical research, publications, including NAFA's Fleet Executive monthly magazine, regional meetings, government representation, conferences, trade shows and seminars.
2600+ Members
Mailing list available for rent

15211 National Association of Police Organizations
317 S Patrick St
Alexandria, VA 22314-3501

703-549-0775
Fax: 703-684-0515
E-Mail: info@napo.org
Home Page: www.napo.org
Social Media: Facebook, Twitter

Thomas J. Nee, President
Mick McHale, Executive Vice President
William Johnson, Executive Director
Chris Collins, Recording Secretary
Sean Smoot, Treasurer

A coalition of police unions and associations from across the United States that serves to advance the interests of America's law enforcement officers through legislative and legal advocacy, political action and education.
241k Members
Founded in 1978
Mailing list available for rent

15212 National Black Police Association
3100 Main Street
#256
Dallas, TX 75226

855-879-6272
Fax: 202-986-0410
Home Page: www.blackpolice.org

Malik Aziz, Chairperson
Rochelle Bilal, Vice Chairperson
Carlos Bratcher, Sergeant at Arms
Sherri V. Lockett, Secretary
Donna Ross, Fiscal Officer

Law enforcement association to improve the relationship between Police Departments as institutions and the minority.
35000 Members
Founded in 1972

15213 National Burglar & Fire Alarm Association
2300 Valley View Lane
Suite 230
Irving, TX 75062-1733

214-260-5970
888-447-1689
Fax: 214-260-5979
E-Mail: MerlinG@alarm.org

Home Page: www.alarm.org
Social Media: Facebook, Twitter, Youtube

Merlin Guilbeau, Executive Director
Georgia Calaway, Communications/PR Director

Representing, promoting and enhancing the growth and professional development of the electronic life safety, security, and integrated systems industry. In cooperation with a federation of state associations, NBFAA provides government advocacy and delivers timely information, professional development tools, products and services that members use to grow and prosper their businesses.
Founded in 1948

15214 National Constables Association (NCA)
16 Stonybrook Drive
Levittown, PA 19055-2217

215-943-3110
800-292-1775
Fax: 215-943-0979
E-Mail: lefcourtapr@juno.com
Home Page: www.angelfire.com/la/nationalconstable

Hal Lefcourt APR, Executive Director
John Sindt, President
Leo Bullock, Secretary

Helping to preserve and clearly define the significant role of the constable in the delivery of justice system in the United States; to train, educate and upgrade the quality of performance of the constable; to serve as a clearing house for all positive actions to give a continued rebirth to the dignity, respect, status and duties and responsibilities of the position of constable as the heritage of the law enforcement community.
Founded in 1973

15215 National Correctional Industries Association
1202 N Charles St
Baltimore, MD 21201-5508

410-230-3972
Fax: 410-230-3981
E-Mail: info@nationalcia.org
Home Page: www.nationalcia.org
Social Media: Facebook

Gina Honeycutt, Executive Director
Wil Heslop, Director of Operations
Karl Wiley, Accounting Manager
Rebekah Zinno, Sales and Marketing Manager
Farrah Marriott, Systems Coordinator

An affiliate body of the American Correctional Association, the Jail Industries Association and The Workman Fund. The mission is to promote excellence and credibility in correctional industries through professional development and innovative business solutions.
Founded in 1941
Mailing list available for rent

15216 National Crime Prevention Council
2001 Jefferson Davis Highway
Suite 901
Arlington, VA 22202

202-466-6272
Fax: 202-296-1356
E-Mail: webmaster@ncpc.org
Home Page: www.ncpc.org

David A. Dean, Chairman
Robert F. Diegelman, Vice Chairman
Ann Harnkins, President/CEO
John P. Box, Treasurer
Jean Adnopoz, Secretary

Aids people in keeping themselves, their families, and their communities safe from crime. NCPC produces tools that communities can use to learn crime prevention strategies, engage community members, and coordinate with local agencies.
136 Members
Founded in 1982
Mailing list available for rent

15217 National Crime and Punishment Learning Center
300 S 25th Ave
Hattiesburg, MS 39401-7301

228-447-0285
Fax: 228-896-8696
E-Mail: ncplc@crimeandpunishment.net
Home Page: www.crimeandpunishment.net

William H Sanford, President/Founder

Provide free information on the most common crimes and their punishments in each state. The center is unique in its dedicated endeavor to accomplish this task by providing information to bridge the gap between the legal justice system and the American people.

15218 National Criminal Justice Association
720 7th St Nw
3rd Floor
Washington, DC 20001-3902

202-628-8550
Fax: 202-448-1723
E-Mail: info@ncja.org
Home Page: www.ncja.org
Social Media: Facebook, Twitter, LinkedIn, RSS

Jack Cutrone, President
Jeanne Smith, Vice President
Cabell Cropper, Executive Director
David Fredenburgh, Director of Program Services
Bethany Broida, Director of Communications

A national voice in shaping and implementing criminal justice policy since its founding. As the representative of state, tribal and local criminal and juvenile justice practitioners, the NCJA works to promote a balanced approach to communities' complex public safety and criminal and juvenile justice system problems.
Founded in 1971

15219 National Criminal Justice Reference Service
PO Box 6000
Rockville, MD 20849-6000

301-519-5500
800-851-3420
Fax: 301-519-5212
Home Page: www.ncjrs.gov
Social Media: Facebook, Twitter, LinkedIn, RSS, Youtube, Google+, Vimeo,

Dolores Kozloski, Executive Director

A federally funded resource offering justice and substance abuse information to support research, policy, and program development worldwide.
Founded in 1972
Mailing list available for rent

15220 National District Attorneys Association
99 Canal Center Plz
Suite 330
Alexandria, VA 22314-1548

703-549-9222
Fax: 703-836-3195
E-Mail: berryb@co.yamhill.or.us
Home Page: www.ndaa.org
Social Media: Facebook

Henry L. Garza, President
Scott Burns, Executive Director
Rick Hanes, Chief of Staff

Development resource for prosecutors at all levels of government. APRI has become a vital resource and national clearinghouse for information on the prosecutorial function. The Institute is committed to providing interdisciplinary responses to the complex problems of criminal justice. It is also committed to supporting the highest professional standards among officials entrusted with the crucial responsibility for public safety.
Founded in 1950

15221 National Drug Court Institute
1029 N. Royal St
Suite 201
Alexandria, VA 22314

703-575-9400
Fax: 703-575-9402
E-Mail: webmaster@nadcp.org
Home Page: www.ndci.org
Social Media: Facebook, Twitter, RSS, Youtube

Lars Levy, President
Milly Merrigan, President-Elect

Promote education, research and scholarship for drug court and other court-based intervention programs.

15222 National Drug Enforcement Officers Association
Drug Enforcement Administration
Office of Training/TRDS
FBI Academy, PO Box 1475
Quantico, VA 22134-1475

202-298-9653
E-Mail: paul.stevens@state.mn.us
Home Page: www.ndeoa.org

Paul Stevens, President
Steve Peterson, First VP

NDEOA's purpose and objective is to promote the cooperation, education and exchange of information among all Law Enforcement Agencies involved in the enforcement of controlled substance laws.
Founded in 1970

15223 National Emergency Number Association
1700 Diagonal Road
Suite 500
Alexandria, VA 22314

202-466-4911
Fax: 202-618-6370
Home Page: www.nena.orgÿ
Social Media: Facebook, Twitter, YouTube

Christy Williams, President
Cheri Lynn Rockwel, 1st Vice President
Renee Hardwick, 2nd Vice President
Lisa Hoffmann, Director
Bernard Buster Brown, Immediate Past President

15224 National Fire Protection Association
1 Batterymarch Park
Quincy, MA 02169-7471

617-770-3000
800-344-3555
Fax: 617-770-0700
E-Mail: custserv@nfpa.org
Home Page: www.nfpa.org
Social Media: Facebook, Twitter, LinkedIn, Youtube, RSS, Google+, Flickr

Philip C. Stittleburg, Chair
Ernest J. Grant, First Vice Chair
James M. Shannon, President and CEO
Bruce H. Mullen, Executive Vice President and CFO
Paul G. Crossman, Vice President, Marketing

Mission is to reduce the worldwide burden of fire and other hazards on the quality of life by providing and advocating scientifically based concensus codes and standards, research, training, and education. Also serves as the world's

leading advocate of fire prevention and is an authoritive source on public safety.
70000 Members
Founded in 1896

15225 National Gang Crime Research Center
Research Center
PO Box 990
Peotone, IL 60468-0090
708-258-9111
Fax: 708-258-9546
E-Mail: gangcrime@aol.com
Home Page: www.ngcrc.com
George W Knox, Director
Research on gangs and gang members, disseminate information through publications and reports, and provide training and consulting services.
Founded in 1990

15226 National Institute of Justice
US Department Of Justice
810 7th Street NW
Washington, DC 20531
202-664-4000
800-851-3420
Fax: 202-307-6394
E-Mail: askncjrs@ncjrs.org
Home Page: www.ojp.usdoj.gov
Social Media: Facebook, Twitter, RSS
Leigh Benda, Chief Financial Officer
Karol Virginia Mason, Assistant Attorney General
Karol Virginia Mason, Assistant Attorney General
Mary Lou Leary, Principal Deputy Assistant Attorney
James H. Burch, II, Deputy Assistant Attorney General
Research, development and evaluation agency of the US department of Justice. Supports all those in the justice industry with education and training, publications and trade shows.
Mailing list available for rent

15227 National Insurance Crime Bureau
1111 E Touhy Ave
Suite 400
Des Plaines, IL 60018-5804
847-544-7002
800-447-6282
Fax: 708-544-7100
Home Page: www.nicb.org
Social Media: Facebook, Twitter, LinkedIn, Youtube
Joseph H. Wehrle, President/CEO
James K. Schweitzer, Senior Vice President
Daniel G. Abbott, Senior Vice President
Robert Jachnicki, Senior Vice President
Andrew J. Sosnowski, Senior Vice President
A not for profit organization that recieves support from approximately 1,000 property/casualty insurance companies. NICB partners with insurers and law enforcement agencies to facilitate the identification, detection and prosecution of insurance criminals.
1000 Members
Founded in 1992

15228 National Latino Peace Officers Association
P O Box
23116
Santa Ana, CA 92711
Home Page: www.nlpoa.com
Social Media: Facebook
Andrew P Peralta, National President
Alfredo Dean, Vice President
Maria B. Thomas, Secretary
Cindy Rodriguez, Treasurer
Vicente Calderon, Founder
Founded in 1972

15229 National Native American Law Enforcement Association
PO Box 171
Washington, DC 20040
202-207-3065
Fax: 866-506-7631
E-Mail: info@nnalea.org
Home Page: www.nnalea.org
Joseph Wicks, President
Mark Murtha, Vice President
Gary Edwards, CEO
Dave Nichols, CFO
Daryll Davis, Senior Director
NNALEA is a nonprofit organization that promotes and fosters mutual cooperation between American Indian Law Enforcement Officers/Agents/Personnel, their agencies, tribes, private industry and public.
Founded in 1993

15230 National Organization for Victim Assistance
510 King St
Suite 424
Alexandria, VA 22314-3132
703-535-6682
800-879-6682
Fax: 703-535-5500
E-Mail: nova@trynova.org
Home Page: www.trynova.org
Social Media: Facebook, Twitter, RSS
Will Marling, Executive Director
Kristy Dyroff, Director of Communications
James Gierke, Director of Victim Services
Deborah Baroch, Director of Finance and Operations
Barbara Kendall, Director of Training
A private, non-profit organization of victim and witness assistance programs and practitioners, criminal justice agencies and professionals, mental health professionals, researchers, former victims and survivors, and others committed to the recognition and implementation of victim rights and services.

15231 National Organization of Black Law Enforcement Executives
4609 Pinecrest Office Park Dr
Alexandria, VA 22312-1442
703-658-1529
Fax: 703-658-9479
E-Mail: jakers@noblenatl.org
Home Page: www.noblenatl.org
Social Media: Facebook, Twitter, LinkedIn, Tumblr, Stumbleupon, Pinterest
Joseph Akers, National President
Wilmae Leach, Executive Assistant/Chief of Staff
Joseph Akers, Interim Executive Director
Pamela Chapman, Training Coordinator
Valerie Shuford, Director of Conferences
Ensure equity in the administration of justice in the provision of public service to all communities, and to serve as the conscience of law enforcement by being committed to justice by action.

15232 National Police Athletic/Activities League , Inc.
1662 N. US Highway 1
Suite C
Jupiter, FL 33469
561-745-5535
Fax: 561-745-3147
E-Mail: mdillhyon@nationalpal.org
Home Page: www.nationalpal.org
Social Media: Facebook, Twitter
Christopher Hill, President
Barbara Bonilla, 1st Vice President
Ronald Allen, 2nd Vice President
Donna Miller, 3rd Vice President
Frank Williams, Secretary
Exists to prevent juvenile crime and violence by providing civic, athletic, recreational, and educational opportunities and resources to PAL Chapters.
Founded in 1940

15233 National Police Bloodhound Association
E-Mail: president@npba.com
Home Page: www.npba.com
Social Media: Facebook
Doug Lowry, President
Roger G. Titus, Vice President
Angela Alexander, Secretary
Coby Webb, Treasurer
Roger G. Titus, Training
Founded in 1966

15234 National Police Institute
Central Missouri State University
200 Ming Street
Warrensburg, MO
660-543-4090
Fax: 660-543-4709
E-Mail: wiggins@cmsu.edu
Home Page: www.cmsu.edu/x4869.xml
Dr Mike Wiggins, Director
An internationally recognized police training center. Provides advanced police training in a number of areas as well as housing the Regional Police Academy.

15235 National Public Safety Information Bureau
PO Box 365
Stevens Point, WI 54481
715-345-2772
800-647-7579
Fax: 715-345-7288
E-Mail: info@safetysource.com
Home Page: www.safetyresource.com
Steve Cywinski, President/Publisher
Ronald Tippel, VP Information Services
Laura Gross, VP Data Procurement
Celia Piesik, Data Procurement Specialist
Christina Scott, Data Procurement Specialist
Working hand in hand with law enforcement, fire and emergency departments to develop the most accurate database in the public safety industry with over 70,000 contacts. The result is; the most current and comprehensive reference tools available.
Founded in 1964

15236 National Public Safety Telecommunications Council
8191 Southpark Lane
Unit 205
Littleton, CO 80120-4641
407-836-9668
866-907-4755
Fax: 303-649-1844
E-Mail: npstc@highlands-group.com
Home Page: www.npstc.org
Vincent Stile, Chair
Douglas M Aiken, Vice Chair
Marilyn Ward, Ecexutive Director
Charles Bryson, Outreach News Editor
Mark Grubb, Participant Development Coordinator
NPSTC is a federation of associations representing public safety telecommunications. They

follow up on the recommendations of the Public Safety Wireless Advisory Committee.
Founded in 1997
Mailing list available for rent

15237 National Reserve Law Officers Association
PO Box 6505
San Antonio, TX 78209
210-805-8917
Fax: 210-653-9655
E-Mail: nrloa01@earthlink.net
Home Page: www.nrlo.net
Capt. Chuck Mantkus, Director of Training
Provides members with training information and services plus the best, most extensive, and lowest cost in-line-of-duty accidental insurance coverage available.

15238 National Safety Council
1121 Spring Lake Dr
Itasca, IL 60143-3201
630-285-1121
800-621-7615
Fax: 630-285-1315
E-Mail: info@nsc.org, customerservice@nsc.org
Home Page: www.nsc.org
Social Media: RSS
Suzanne Powills, Publisher
Janet Froetscher, President & CEO
Patrick Phelan, Chief Financial Officer
Shay Gallagher, Vice President, General Manager
Paulette Moulos, Vice President, Channels
Provides information sharing opportunities, continuing education and professional fellowship to people with environmental health and safety responsibilities in higher education.
936 Members
Founded in 1912
Mailing list available for rent

15239 National Sheriffs' Association
1450 Duke St
Alexandria, VA 22314-3490
703-836-7827
800-424-7827
Fax: 703-683-5349
E-Mail: jthompson@sheriffs.org
Home Page: www.sheriffs.org
Social Media: Facebook, Twitter, LinkedIn
Aaron D. Kennard, Executive Director
John Thompson, Chief of Staff and Deputy Executive
Fred G. Wilson, Director of Operations
Ed Hutchison, Director of Traffic Safety & Triad
Greg J. MacDonald, Director of Homeland Security
Devoted to helping sheriffs and other law enforcers to execute their duties most effectively and professionally.
21M Members
Founded in 1943
Mailing list available for rent: 3M names

15240 National Tactical Officers Association
PO Box 797
Doylestown, PA 18901
215-230-7552
800-279-9127
Fax: 215-230-7552
E-Mail: membership@ntoa.org
Home Page: www.ntoa.org
Social Media: Facebook, Twitter
Deputy Chief Bo Chabali, Board Chairman
Mark Lomax, Executive Director
Rob Cartner, Director of Training
Corey Luby, Marketing Director
Marsha Martello, Membership Coordinator
Enhance the performance and professional status of law enforcement personnel by providing a credible and proven training resource, as well as a forum for the development of tactics and information exchange. The Association's ultimate goal is to improve public safety and domestic security through training, education, and tactical excellence.
32000 Members
Founded in 1983

15241 National Technical Investigators Association (NATIS)
1069 West Broad Street
Box 757
Falls Church, VA 22046
703-237-9338
800-966-2842
770-485-1820
Fax: 703-241-0353
E-Mail: admin@natia.org
Home Page: www.natia.org
Michael Woods, President
The purpose of NATIA is to further knowledge, develop skills and promote fellowship between those law enforcement and intelligence professionals who support their agencies' and departments' technical surveillance, tactical operations, and forensic activities.

15242 National United Law Enforcement Officers
256 E McLemore Avenue
Memphis, TN 38106-2833
901-774-1118
Fax: 901-774-1139
E-Mail: clydevenson@bellsouth.org
Clyde Venson, Executive Director
Samantha Macklin, Secretary
Protects the needs and interests of persons in the law enforcement industry.
5000 Members
Founded in 1969

15243 National White Collar Crime Center
10900 Nuckols Rd
Suite 325
Glen Allen, VA 23060-9288
804-967-6200
Home Page: www.nw3c.org
Social Media: Facebook, Twitter, Youtube
Don Brackman, Director
Ken Brooks, Deputy Director
Through a combination of training and critical support services, law enforcement agencies are given the skills and resources they need to tackle emerging economic and cyber crime problems.
Mailing list available for rent

15244 Naval Criminal Investigative Services
27130 Telegraph Road
Suite 2000
Quantico, VA 22134
202-433-8800
Fax: 724-794-3293
Home Page: www.ncis.navy.mil
Andrew L. Traver, Director
John Beattie, Senior Intelligence Officer
Mark D. Ridley, Deputy Director
Rod Baldwin, Executive Assistant Director
Charlton Howard, Chief Intelligence Officer
Primary law enforcement and counterintelligence arm of the United States Department of the Navy. It works closely with other local, state, federal and foreign agencies to counter and investigate the most serious crimes.

15245 Organized Crime Task Force
The Capitol
Albany, NY 12224-0341
518-474-7330
Fax: 914-422-8795
Home Page: www.ag.ny.gov
John Amodeo, Assistant Attorney General
Colleen Glavin, Public Integrity Officer
A forum that brings government, law enforcement and a range of agencies together to set priorities for tackling organized crime.
Founded in 1970

15246 Park Law Enforcement Association
E-Mail: nielsen4397@com.cast.net
Home Page: www.myparkranger.org
Tom Wakolbinger, President
William Westerfield, Vice President
Dale Steele, Secretary
Capt. Carl Nielsen, Executive Director
Steve Newsom, Treasurer
Founded in 1979

15247 Police & Firemen's Insurance Association
101 E 116th St
Carmel, IN 46032-5629
317-581-1913
800-221-7342
Fax: 317-571-5946
Home Page: www.pfia.net
Mark Kemp, President
Jeanie Williams, Operations VP
Mission of the association is to create and operate a Supreme Lodge and Subordinate Branches for the purpose of inculcating principles of friendship and brotherhood among police officers and fire fighters. Providing financial assistance to its members through disability certificates and pay final expenses for members with legal reserve life insurance policies.

15248 Police Executive Research Forum
1120 Connecticut Ave NW
Suite 930
Washington, DC 20036-3951
202-466-7820
Fax: 202-466-7826
Home Page: www.policeforum.org
Commissioner Ch Ramsey, President
Chief Tom Manger, VP
Chief Scott Thomson, Secretary
Chief Roberto Villasenor, Treasurer
Raquel Rodriguez, Accounting Manager
A national membership organization of progressive police executives from the largest city, county and state law enforcement agencies. Dedicated to improving policing and advancing professionalism through research and involvement in public policy debate.
100 Members
Founded in 1976
Mailing list available for rent

15249 Police Foundation
1201 Connecticut Ave NW
Suite 200
Washington, DC 20036-2636
202-833-1460
Fax: 202-659-9149
E-Mail: pfinfo@policefoundation.org
Home Page: www.policefoundation.org
Social Media: Facebook, Twitter, RSS, Google Plus
Weldon J. Rougeau, Chairman
Jim Bueermann, President
Karen L. Amendola, PhD, Chief Behavioral Scientist
Tari Lewis, CPA, Chief Financial Officer

Garth den Heyer, DPubPol, Senior Research Fellow

A national, nonpartisan, nonprofit organization dedicated to supporting innovation and improvement in policing through its research and evaluation, technical assistance, training, technology, professional services, and communication programs.
Founded in 1970
Mailing list available for rent

15250 **Public Safety Diving Association**

904-743-3025
E-Mail: psdahq@bellsouth.net
Home Page: www.publicsafetydivingassociation.comÿ

David Scoggins, President
Mark Reese, Director

15251 **Public Services Health and Safety Association**

4950 Yonge Street
Suite 902
Toronto, ON M2N 6K1

416-250-2131
877-250-7444
Fax: 416-250-7484
Home Page: www.pshsa.ca

Michael Papadakis, Chair
Thomas Hayes, Vice Chair
Ron Kelusky, CEO
Normand Lavallee, Treasurer
Donald MacLeod, Board of Directors

15252 **Reserve Police Officers Association**

89 Rockland Ave
Yonkers, NY 10705
800-326-9416
800-326-9416
Fax: 212-555-1234
Home Page: www.reservepolice.org

Brooke Webster, President

Dedicated to the support of law enforcement with an emphasis on the role of the reserve and auxiliary law enforcement officer.
Founded in 1996

15253 **Texas Department of Public Safety Officer's Association**

5821 Airport Boulevard
Austin, TX 78752

512-451-0571
800-933-7762
Fax: 512-451-0709
Home Page: www.dpsoa.com
Social Media: Facebook, Twitter, RSS

Sgt. Gary Chandler, President
Lt. Jimmy Jackson, VP
John M. Pike, Executive Director
Trooper Clay Taylor, Secretary/Treasurer
Patti Benson, Membership Services

Offers and executes programs that benefit Texas Troppers and the communitites around them. Also publishes DPSOA a quarterly magazine.
2650 Members
Founded in 1974

15254 **The Association of Certified Fraud Specialists**

4600 Northgate Blvd.
Suite 105
Sacramento, CA 95834

916-419-6319
Fax: 916-419-6318
E-Mail: headquarters@acfsnet.org
Home Page: www.acfsnet.org

Lance Brandon, President
Carolyn Mashburn, Secretary
Allan Wisnicky, Treasurer

Jodi Takahash, Board of Director
Patricia Fisher, Board of Director
Founded in 1993

15255 **The Commission on Accreditation forÿLaw Enforcement Agencies**

13575 Heathcote Boulevard
Suite 320
Gainesville, VI 20155

703-352-4225
Fax: 703-890-3126
Home Page: www.calea.org
Social Media: Facebook, Twitter, LinkedIn

J. Grayson Robinson, President
Craig Webre, Vice-President
W. Craig Hartley, Executive Director
Richard Myers, Secretary
Gary Margolis, Treasurer

15256 **The Federal Law Enforcement Associationÿ**

7945 MacArthur Blvd
Suite 201
Cabin John, MD 20818

202-870-5503
866-553-5362
E-Mail: fleoa@fleoa.org
Home Page: www.fleoa.org
Social Media: Facebook, Twitter

Jon Adler, National President
Nate Catura, Executive Vice President
Chris Schoppmeyer, Vice President
Enid Febus, National Secretary
Kurtis Roinestad, Treasurer
Founded in 1977

15257 **The International Association of Chiefs of Police**

44 Canal Center Plaza
Suite 200
Alexandria, VA 22314

703-836-6767
Home Page: www.theiacp.org
Social Media: Facebook, Twitter, LinkedIn, YouTube

Vincent Talucci, Co Chair
Dwight Henninger, Treasurer
Richard Beary, President
Yost Zakhary, Immediate Past President
Terry M Cunningham, First Vice President
Founded in 1893

15258 **The United Deputy Sheriffs' Association**

319 S. Hydraulic St.,
Suite B
Wichita, KS 67211

316-263-2583
E-Mail: info@usdeputy.org
Home Page: www.usdeputy.org
Social Media: Facebook

Mike Willis, Executive Director
David Hinners, Deputy Director

15259 **TheÿAssociationÿofÿPublic-Safety Communications Officials**

351 N. Williamson Blvd
Daytona Beach, FL 32114-1112

386-322-2500
Fax: 386-322-2501
E-Mail: RFAnalyst@Gmail.com
Home Page: www.apcointl.org
Social Media: Facebook, Twitter

John W Wright, President
Brent Lee, First Vice President
Cheryl J Greathouse, Second Vice President
Gigi Smith, Immediate Past President
Derek Poarch, Executive Director
Founded in 1982

15260 **Transportation Research Board National Research Council**

500 Fifth Stret NW
Washington, DC 20001

202-334-2934
Fax: 202-334-2003
Home Page: www.trb.org
Social Media: Facebook, Twitter, LinkedIn, RSS, Blogger, Pinterest, Tumbl

Robert Skinner, Executive Director
Rosa Allen, Administrative Coordinator
Stephen J. Andrle, Deputy Director
Javy Awan, Director, Publications
Terri M. Baker, Senior Program Assistant

A division of the National Research Council, which serves as an independent advisor to the federal government and others on scientific and technical questions of national importance.

15261 **Transportation Technology Center**

55500 DOT Rd.
Pueblo, CO 81001-0130

719-584-0750
Fax: 719-584-0711
E-Mail: ttci_marketing@ttci.aar.com
Home Page: www.aar.com
Social Media: Facebook, Twitter, Youtube

Roy Allen, Manager
Michele Johnson, Administrative Assistant
Mark Nordling, Assistant Director Business
Ron Lang, Manager Business Development
Michele Johnson, Executive Assistant

A wholly owned subsidiary of the Association of American Railroads. TTCI is a world-class transportation research and testing organization, providing emerging technology solutions for the railway industry throughout North America and the world.

15262 **U.S. First Responders Association**

420 Kimbrel Avenue
Panama City, FL 32404

E-Mail: Corporate@usfra.org
Home Page: www.usfra.org
Social Media: Facebook, Twitter, LinkedIn, Yahoo

15263 **United States Conference of Mayors**

1620 Eye St NW
Washington, DC 20006

202-293-7330
Fax: 202-293-2352
E-Mail: info@usmayors.org
Home Page: www.usmayors.org
Social Media: Facebook, Twitter

Mayor Scott Smith, President
Mayor Kevin Johnson, VP
Mayor Stephanie Rawlings-Blake, Second Vice President
Mayor Kevin Johnson, Second Vice President

An organization of city government officials whose primary roles are to promote the development of effective national urban/suburban policy; strengthen federal-city relationships; ensure that federal policy meets urban needs; provide mayors with leadership and management tools; and create a forum in which mayors can share ideas and information.
Founded in 1932

15264 **United States Deputy Sheriff's Association**

319 S. Hydraulic St.
Suite B
Wichita, KS 67211

316-263-2583
877-800-8854
Fax: 281-578-0669

E-Mail: info@usdeputy.org
Home Page: www.usdeputy.org

Mike Willis, Executive Director/Training
David Hinners, Deputy Director/National Trainer

Provides needed equipment, free of charge, to the mostly rural, underfunded county law enforcement agencies. All members are given an Emergency Disaster Relief of $2,000, if killed in the line of duty.
Founded in 1995

15265 United States Police Canine Association
PO Box 80
Springboro, OH 45066

937-751-6469
800-531-1614
Home Page: www.uspcak9.com
Social Media: Facebook

Russ Hess, Executive Director
Kevin Johnson, President
Melinda Roupp, Secretary
James Matarese, Treasurer

Nonprofit organization striving for the establishment of minimum standards for Police K-9 dogs through proper methods of training. Police K-9 dogs, properly trained and handled, give Law Enforcement officers one of the finest non-lethal aids in the prevention and detection of crime.
Founded in 1971

Newsletters

15266 CGAA Signals
Central Station Alarm Association
8150 Leesburg Pike
Suite 700
Vienna, VA 22182-2721

703-242-4670
Fax: 703-242-4675
E-Mail: communications@csaaul.org
Home Page: www.csaaul.org
Social Media: Facebook, Twitter, LinkedIn

Stephen P Doyle, Executive VP/CEO
Celia Besore, VP Marketing & Programs
Robert R. Bean, President
Jay Hauhn, First Vice President
Peter Lowitt, Secretary
300+ Members
Frequency: Quarterly
Circulation: 1200
Founded in 1950
Mailing list available for rent

15267 Correctional Education Bulletin
LRP Publications
747 Dresher Road Suite 500
PO Box 980
Horsham, PA 19044
215-784-0912
800-341-7874
Fax: 215-784-9639
E-Mail: webmaster@lrp.com
Home Page: www.lrp.com

Kim Yablonski, Editor

Combines and analyzes corrections education issues and management topics. You'll learn how educators are coping with shrinking budgets and the growing number of youths being sentenced as adults. Expert analysis of current legal issues and the latest regulatory updates given.
Cost: $125.00
Frequency: Monthly
Founded in 1977

15268 Corrections Professional
LRP Publications
PO Box 980
Horsham, PA 19044
215-840-0912
800-341-7874
Fax: 215-784-9639
E-Mail: webmaster@lrp.com
Home Page: www.lrp.com

Debi Pelletier, Editor
Kenneth Kahn, President

Tracks innovative strategies, proven techniques and legal developments impacting correction facilities across the country. Gives profiles of other professionals and their institutions, giving an opportunity to learn from their experiences and avoid costly mistakes. Contains Q-A section that addresses difficult situations.
Cost: $210.00
Frequency: 104 issues per
Founded in 1977

15269 Criminal Justice Newsletter
Pace Publications
443 Park Ave S
New York, NY 10016-7322

212-685-5450
Fax: 212-679-4701

Sid Goldstein, Publisher
Craig Fischer, Editor
Peter Kiers, Executive Director

Independent publication providing system-wide perspective of law enforcement.
Cost: $219.00
Frequency: BiWeekly

15270 Emergency Preparedness News
Business Publishers
2222 Sedwick Dr
Suite 101
Durham, NC 27713

800-223-8720
Fax: 800-508-2592
E-Mail: custserv@bpinews.com
Home Page: www.bpinews.com

Dedicated solely to disaster management: from securing pre-disaster mitigation and counter terrorism funds, to staying prepared for hurricanes, terrorist threats, fires, floods and other natural disasters.
Cost: $327.00

15271 FEMSA News
Fire and Emergency Manufacturers and Services Asso
PO Box 147
Lynnfield, MA 01940-0147

781-334-2771
Fax: 781-334-2771
E-Mail: info@femsa.org
Home Page: www.femsa.org
Social Media: Twitter, LinkedIn

Dan Reese, President
William Lawson, VP
Member newsletter
Frequency: 3x/Year
Circulation: 600

15272 FLEOA Newsletter
Federal Law Enforcement Officers Association
PO Box 326
Lewisberry, PA 17339-2900

717-938-2300
Fax: 717-932-2262
E-Mail: fleoa@fleoa.org
Home Page: www.fleoa.org
Social Media: Facebook, Twitter

Jon Adler, National President
Nate Catura, National Executive VP

Federal newsletter offering information, legislative updates and news for law enforcement officers nationwide.
12 Pages
Circulation: 2400
Founded in 1976

15273 Journal of the American Association of Forensic Dentists
1000 N Avenue
Waukegan, IL 60085

847-223-5077
E-Mail: info@andent.net
Home Page: www.andent.net
Social Media: RSS

Quarterly journal that brings forensic dental knowledge not only to dentists and their staff, but also to anthropologists, attorneys and law enforcement personnel.
Cost: $8.00
Frequency: Quarterly
Founded in 1978

15274 Keepers' Voice
International Association of Correctional Officers
PO Box 53
Chicago, IL 60690

312-996-5401
Fax: 312-413-0458

Jim Clark, Publisher
Jess Maghan, Editor

Of special interest to correctional officers because it focuses on current developments in the field, including practical, day-to-day training topics, current legislation, resources, conference notices and job openings.

15275 Law Enforcement Legal Publications
421 Ridgewood Avenue
Suite 100
Glen Ellyn, IL 60137-4900

630-858-6092
Fax: 630-858-6392
E-Mail: lelp@xnet.com
Home Page: www.lelp.com

James Manak, Publisher/President

Publication for law enforcement, legal professional civil liability, personnel law, labor law, criminal law and law libraries.
ISSN: 1070-9967
Founded in 1970
Printed in 3 colors on newsprint stock

15276 Law Enforcement Legal Review
Law Enforcement Legal Publications
421 Ridgewood Avenue
Suite 100
Glen Ellyn, IL 60137-4900

630-858-6392
Fax: 630-858-6392
E-Mail: lelp@xnet.com
Home Page: www.lelp.com/

James Manak, Publisher
Glen Manak, VP Marketing

Case reporter for law enforcement, legal profession and law libraries, covering criminal law, civil liability and personnel law.
Cost: $98.00
16 Pages
Frequency: Bi-monthly
Circulation: 500
ISSN: 1070-9967
Founded in 1975

15277 Legal Employment Weekly Law Bulletin Publishing Company
415 N State Street
Chicago, IL 60610-4674
312-644-7800
Fax: 312-644-1215
E-Mail: editor@lbpc.com
Home Page: www.lawbulletin.com
Bernard Judge, Publisher
Stephen Brown, Managing Editor
Lanning Macfarland, Chairman
Legal employment opportunities.
Frequency: Weekly
Founded in 1854
Printed in 2 colors on newsprint stock

15278 National Constables Association Newsletter
National Constables Association
PO Box 1172
Haverhill, MA 01831-1572
978-373-5234
800-272-1775
Fax: 978-373-1191
E-Mail: mike@constables.com
Home Page: www.constables.com
Hal Lefcourt, Executive Director
John Sindt, President
A newsletter published for the members of National Constables Association.
4 Pages
Frequency: Quarterly
Printed in one color on glossy stock

15279 Police Executive Research Forum
1120 Connecticut Avenue NW
Suite 930
Washington, DC 20036
202-466-7820
Fax: 202-466-7826
Home Page: www.policeforum.org
Chuck Wexler, Executive Director
Chief John Timoney, VP
Daniel Woods, Research Associate
Jessica Toliver, Deputy Director
Raquel Rodriguez, Accounting Manager
Members are chief executives of city, county and state police agencies. Membership dues are general $300.00, subscribing $125.00.
Cost: $35.00
Frequency: Monthly
Circulation: 1000
Founded in 1977
Mailing list available for rent

15280 Signal
American Traffic Safety Services Association
15 Riverside Parkway
Suite 100
Fredericksburg, VA 22406-1022
540-368-1701
800-272-8772
Fax: 540-368-1717
Home Page: www.atssa.com
James Baron, Communications Director
Douglas Danko, Chairman
Covers legislative updates, industry news and meeting information, as well as other items of interest to the roadway safety industry as is a full-color publication.
Frequency: Quarterly
Mailing list available for rent

15281 Women Police
International Association of Women Police
PO Box 690418
Tulsa, OK 74169
918-234-6445
E-Mail: jvanland@aol.com
Home Page: www.iawp.org/
Mona Moore, Publisher
Kim Covert, Treasurer
Accepts advertising.
Cost: $25.00
50 Pages
Frequency: Quarterly

Magazines & Journals

15282 Air Beat Magazine
Airborne Law Enforcement Association
50 Carroll Creek Way
Suite 260
Frederick, MD 21701-4786
301-631-2406
Fax: 301-631-2466
Home Page: www.alea.org
Steven Ingley, Executive Director
Kevin R. Caffery, VP
Nicole Gentile, Operations Manager
Keith Johnson, Safety Program Director
Carrie Cosens, Membership Manager
Dedicated to Airborne Law Enforcement. The subscription also includes the annual Buyer's Guide and special Convention issue with membership.
Cost: $40.00
3500 Members
Frequency: Bi-Monthly
Circulation: 6500
Founded in 1968

15283 Campus Safety Journal
Bricepac
12228 Venice Boulevard
PO Box 66515
Los Angeles, CA 90066
310-390-5277
Fax: 310-390-4777
E-Mail: tnelson@campusjournal.com
Home Page: www.campusjournal.com
John Van Horn, Publisher
Tom Nelson, Managing Editor
Wendy Rackley, Production Manager
Provides a vehicle for communicating campus safety and security issues to all interested parties at the middle, secondary, college and university levels.
40 Pages
Frequency: Monthly
Circulation: 20100
Founded in 1992
Printed in 4 colors on glossy stock

15284 Contingency Planning & Recovery Journal
Management Advisory Services & Publications
PO Box 81151
Wellesley Hills, MA 02481-0001
781-235-2895
Fax: 781-235-5446
E-Mail: info@masp.com
Home Page: www.masp.com/
An independent, subscription supported to all issues of contingency planning, disaster recovery and business continuity. Includes tutorial extensive literature review on the fields of business continuity.
Cost: $75.00
Frequency: Quarterly
Founded in 1972
Printed in on glossy stock

15285 Corrections Today
4380 Forbes Boulevard
Lanham, MD 20706
301-918-1800
800-222-5646
Fax: 301-918-1900
E-Mail: customerservice@corrections.com
Home Page: www.corrections.com/aca
Susan Clayton, Editor
Gwendolyn C Chunn, President
Harry Wilhelm, Marketing Manager
Alice Heiserman, Publications and Research Manager
Published by the American Correctional Association.
Cost: $25.00
200 Pages
Circulation: 20000
Founded in 1870
Mailing list available for rent

15286 Credit Card Crime, Law Enforcement Kit
9770 S Military Trail
Suite 380
Boynton Beach, FL 33436-4011
561-737-8700
Fax: 561-737-5800
E-Mail: sales@fraudandtheftinfo.com
Home Page: www.fraudandtheftinfo.com
Larry Schwartz, Editor
Ways to catch and punish the thieves, including corporate support of police, reverse sting operations, paying informants. Case histories, specific recommendations.
Cost: $59.95
ISBN: 0-914801-05-8
Founded in 1982

15287 Crime & Delinquency
Sage Publications
2455 Teller Rd
Newbury Park, CA 91320-2234
805-499-9774
800-818-7243
Fax: 805-499-0871
E-Mail: info@sagepub.com
Home Page: www.sagepub.com
Blaise R Simqu, CEO
Janice Denehy, Executive Editor
Offers information to probation and parole executives as well as criminologists and lawyers.
Cost: $105.00
Frequency: Quarterly
Circulation: 3250
Founded in 1965
Mailing list available for rent

15288 Law Enforcement Legal Review
Law Enforcement Legal Publications
421 Ridgewood Avenue
Suite 100
Glen Ellyn, IL 60137-4900
630-858-6392
Fax: 630-858-6392
E-Mail: lelp@xnet.com
Home Page: home.xnet.com/~lelp
James Manak, President
Glen P Manak, VP Marketing
Civil liability, criminal law and personnel law case reporter for law enforcement, legal professional and law libraries.
Cost: $98.00
Circulation: 1000
ISSN: 1070-9967
Founded in 1970
Printed in on n stock

15289 Law Enforcement Product News
100 Garfield Street
2nd Floor
Denver, CO 80206

303-322-6400
800-291-3911
Fax: 303-322-0627
Home Page: www.law-enforcement.com

Michael George, Publisher
Jeannine Heinecke, Editor
Paul Mackler, CEO
Chuck Cummings, Sales Manager
Circulation: 57000
Founded in 1966

15290 Law Enforcement Technology
Cygnus Publishing
PO Box 803
Fort Atkinson, WI 53538-0803

920-000-1111
Fax: 920-563-1699
E-Mail: Patrick.Bernardo@cygnuspub.com
Home Page: www.cygnusb2b.com

John French, CEO
Scott Cravens, Circulation Director
Gordon Gavin, VP
Ronnie Garrett, Editor
Kathy Scott, Director of Public Relations

Covers the innovative products and technology available to the law enforcement manager. Accepts advertising.
64 Pages
Frequency: Monthly
Circulation: 30,000
Founded in 1966

15291 Law and Order
Hendon
130 Waukegan Rd
Deerfield, IL 60015-4912

847-444-3300
800-843-9764
Fax: 847-444-3333
E-Mail: info@hendonpub.com
Home Page: hendonpub.com

Henry Kingwill, Owner
Bruce Cameron, Editor
Pete Kingwill, National Director
Yesenia Salcedo, Managing Editor
Tim Davis, Graphic Designer

Tailored to the law enforcement officer, the magazine updates professionals on trends, covers new methods and incorporates articles with special focuses.
Cost: $24.00
100 Pages
Frequency: Monthly
Circulation: 32304
Founded in 1953

15292 Materials Evaluation
American Society for Nondestructive Testing
PO box 28518
1711 Arlingate Lane
Columbus, OH 43228-518

614-274-6003
800-222-2768
Fax: 614-274-6899
Home Page: www.asnt.org

Paul McIntire, Publication Manager
Betsy Blazar, Marketing Manager
Wayne Holliday, Executive Director
Shelby Reeves, Owner

Research, reviews and information of nondestructive testing materials. Provides members and subscribers the latest news and technical information concerning this industry.
Frequency: Monthly
Circulation: 10200
Founded in 1941

15293 National Fire Protection Association Newsletter
1 Batterymarch Park
Quincy, MA 02169-7471

617-770-3000
800-344-3555
Fax: 617-770-0700
E-Mail: custserv@nfpa.org
Home Page: www.nfpa.org

James M. Shannon, President/CEO
Peg O'Brien, Administrator - Public Affairs
Lorraine VP - Communications, Executive Director
Bruce Mullen, CFO
Paul Crossman, VP, Marketing

Written for various fire safety professionals and covers major topics in fire protection and suppression. The Journal carries investigation reports written by NFPA specialists, special NFPA statistical studies on large-loss fires, multiple deaths, fire fighter deaths and injuries, and others annually. Articles on fire protection advances, public education and information of interest to NFPA members.
Cost: $135.00
70000 Members
Circulation: 85000
Founded in 1896

15294 Peace Officer
Dale Corporation
22150 W 9 Mile Road
Southfield, MI 48034

248-204-2244
Fax: 248-204-2240
Home Page: www.salesdoctors.com

Dale Jabolonski, President

Covers areas of interest to law enforcement personnel.
Cost: $12.00
40 Pages
Founded in 1958

15295 Perspectives Journal
American Probation and Parole Association
PO Box 11910
Lexington, KY 40578-1910

859-244-8203
Fax: 859-244-8001
E-Mail: appa@csg.org
Home Page: www.appa-net.org
Social Media: Facebook, Twitter, LinkedIn

Carl Wicklund, Executive Director
Barbara Broderick, President
Diane Kincaid, Deputy Director
Carrie Abner, Research Associate
John Higgins, Graphic Designer

Mailing list includes mailing addresses only, no email
Frequency: Quarterly
Circulation: 2200
Mailing list available for rent: 2200 names

15296 Police
Bobit Publishing Company
3520 Challenger St
Torrance, CA 90503-1640

310-533-2400
Fax: 310-533-2500
E-Mail: webmaster@bobit.com
Home Page: www.bobit.com

Edward J Bobit, CEO

The law officer's magazine. Accepts advertising.
Cost: $35.00
104 Pages
Frequency: Monthly
Circulation: 50000
Founded in 1961

15297 Police Chief
International Association of Chiefs of Police
515 N Washington St
Alexandria, VA 22314-2340

703-836-6767
800-843-4227
Fax: 703-836-4543
E-Mail: information@theiacp.org
Home Page: www.theiacp.org
Social Media: Facebook, Twitter, RSS, Youtube

Dan Rosenblatt, Executive Director
Mark L. Whitman, Chair Commissioner

A monthly magazine published by the International Association of Chiefs of Police.
Cost: $25.00
80 Pages
Frequency: Monthly
Circulation: 21300
Founded in 1893
Mailing list available for rent

15298 Police Times
American Federation of Police & Concerned Citizens
6350 Horizon Drive
Titusville, FL 32780

321-264-0911
Fax: 321-573-9819
E-Mail: policeinfo@aphf.org
Home Page: www.aphf.org
Social Media: Facebook

Barry Shepard, Executive Director
Deputy Dennis Wise, National President
Debra Chitwood, CEO
Brent Shephard, Director of Operations

Quarterly publication focusing on law enforcement, security and police survivors.
Circulation: 31,000
Founded in 1978

15299 Public Safety Communications/APCO Bulletin
Assn of Public Safety Communication Officials
351 N Williamson Boulevard
Daytona Beach, FL 32114-1112
386-322-2500
888-272-6911
Fax: 386-322-2501
E-Mail: apco@apcointl.org
Home Page: www.apcointl.org/services/publications/

Toni Edwards, Editor
George S Rice Jr, President
Susan Stowell, Member Services Director
Garry Mendez, Marketing/Communications Director
Robert Gurss Esq., Legal/Government Affairs Director

The world's oldest and largest professional organization dedicated to the enhancement of public safety communications and to serving its more than 15,000 members, the people who use public safety communications systems and services.
Cost: $12.00
Frequency: Monthly
Circulation: 13000
ISSN: 1526-1646
Founded in 1935

15300 Public Safety Product News
Cygnus Publishing
PO Box 803
Fort Atkinson, WI 53538-0803

920-000-1111
800-547-7377
Fax: 920-563-1699

E-Mail: Patrick.Bernardo@cygnusB2B.com
Home Page: www.cygnusb2b.com

John French, CEO
Sharon Haberkorn, Development Manager
Ronnie Garrett, Editor-in-Chief
Kathy Scott, Director of Public Relations
Paul Bonaiuto, CFO
Frequency: Monthly

15301 **Sheriff**
National Sherriff's Association
1450 Duke St
Alexandria, VA 22314-3490

703-836-7827
800-424-7827
Fax: 703-836-6541
E-Mail: nsamail@sheriffs.org
Home Page: www.sheriffs.org

Suzanne Kitts, Editor
Aaron Kennard, President
Thomas N Faust, Executive Director

Published for the law enforcement official.
Cost: $25.00
Circulation: 20,000
Founded in 1948

15302 **Tactical Edge**
National Tactical Officers Association
PO Box 797
Doylestown, PA 18901

215-230-7616
800-279-9127
Fax: 215-230-7552
E-Mail: membership@ntoa.org
Home Page: www.ntoa.org
Social Media: Facebook, Twitter, LinkedIn, Google+, Blogger, Bloggy, Pint

Phil Hansen, Board Chairman
Jim Torkar, Treasurer
Bob Chabali, Secretary
Mark Lomax, Executive Director
Rob Cartner, Director of Training
Cost: $40.00
Frequency: Quarterly
Circulation: 12000
Mailing list available for rent

15303 **Today's Policeman**
Towerhigh Productions
PO Box 875108
Los Angeles, CA 90087-208
Donald Mack, President

General philosophy of the police services.
Cost: $9.00
40 Pages
Founded in 1961

Trade Shows

15304 **ACFSA International Conference**
American Correctional Food Service Affiliates
210 N Glenoaks Blvd
Suite C
Burbank, CA 91502

818-843-6608
Fax: 818-843-7423
E-Mail: jonnichols@acfsa.org
Home Page: www.acfsa.org

Jon Nichols, Executive Director
150 Attendees
Frequency: Annual/August
Founded in 1969

15305 **APCO Annual Conference & Expo**
351 N Williamson Boulevard
Daytona Beach, FL 32114-1112

386-322-2500
888-272-6911
Fax: 386-322-2501
E-Mail: apco@apcointl.org
Home Page: www.apcointl.org/

Barbara Myers, Director Conference Services
Casey Epton Roush, Conference/Meeting Services Manager
Brigid Blaschak, Tradeshow Manager
Patricia Giannini, Senior Meeting Coordinator
Garry Mendez, Marketing/Communications Director

APCO's Annual Conference and Exposition brings together more than 300 vendors to provide hands-on demonstrations of new technologies you might use in your agency or call centers. The Conference also offers sessions on personal and professional development and a variety of technical skills. Banquet, breakfast and exhibitors of radio, computer, and supporting equipment companies.
6000 Attendees
Frequency: Annual
Founded in 1935

15306 **Academy of Criminal Justice Sciences Annual Meeting**
Academy of Criminal Justice Sciences
7339 Hanover Parkway
Suite A
Greenbelt, MD 20770

301-446-6300
800-757-2257
Fax: 301-446-2819
E-Mail: info@acjs.org
Home Page: www.acjs.org

Mittie Southerland, Executive Director
Cathy Barth, Association Manager
Craig Hemmens, President
James Frank, 1st Vice President
David F. Owens, Treasurer

Criminal justice educators, researchers, practicioners, students and the general public visit 45 exhibits and seminars.
2000 Attendees
Frequency: Annual
Founded in 1963

15307 **Airborne Law Enforcement Annual Conference & Expo**
Airborne Law Enforcement Association
50 Carroll Creek Way
Suite 260
Frederick, MD 21701-4786

301-631-2406
Fax: 301-631-2466
Home Page: www.alea.org

Steven Ingley, Executive Director
Kevin R. Caffery, VP
Nicole Gentile, Operations Manager
Keith Johnson, Safety Program Director
Carrie Cosens, Membership Manager

Containing 157 booths.
1100 Attendees
Frequency: July
Founded in 1968

15308 **American Academy of Forensic Sciences Annual Meeting**
American Academy of Forensic Sciences
410 N 21st St
Colorado Springs, CO 80904-2712

719-636-1100
Fax: 719-636-1993
E-Mail: awarren@aafs.org
Home Page: www.aafs.org

Nancy Jackson, Director Development
Anne Warren, Executive Director
Sondra Bynoe-Doolittle, Assistant Meetings Manager
Addie Arellano, Meetings/Exposition Assistant
Anne Warren, Executive Director

Professionals in the forensic science field attend meeting and see 120 exhibits of scientific instruments.
2300 Attendees
Frequency: Annual,February
Mailing list available for rent

15309 **American Correctional Association Congress**
206 N Washington St
Suite 200
Alexandria, VA 22314

703-224-0000
800-222-5646
Fax: 703-224-0179
E-Mail: pres@aca.org
Home Page: www.aca.org

Daron Hall, President
James Gondles Jr, Executive Director
Jeff Washington, Deputy Executive Director

Five hundred booths featuring association whose membership is concerned with correctional services.
3900 Attendees
Mailing list available for rent

15310 **American Correctional Association Winter Conference**
206 N Washington St
Suite 200
Alexandria, VA 22314

703-224-0000
800-222-5646
Fax: 703-224-0179
E-Mail: pres@aca.org
Home Page: www.aca.org

James Gondles Jr, Executive Director
Daron Hall, President
Jeff Washington, Deputy Executive Director

Three hundred and fifty booths.
3M Attendees
Frequency: January
Founded in 1935
Mailing list available for rent

15311 **American Criminal Justice Association National Conference**
American Criminal Justice Association
PO Box 601047
Sacramento, CA 95860-1047

916-484-6553
Fax: 916-488-2227
E-Mail: acjalae@aol.com
Home Page: www.acjalae.org

Joe Davenport, President
Karen Campbell, Executive Secretary
Abby Schofield, Region 1 President
Preston Koelling, Vice-President

Business meetings, awards, competitions, job fairs, physical agility competitions, safety meetings and crime scene competitions
7200 Members
Founded in 1937

15312 **American Jail Association Training Conference & Jail Expo**
1135 Professional Court
Hagerstown, MD 21740

301-790-3930
Fax: 301-790-2941
E-Mail: dorothyd@aja.org

Home Page: www.aja.org
Social Media: Facebook

Dorothy Drass, Marketing Director
Holly Nicarry, Assistant Marketing Director
Robert J. Kasabian, Executive Director
Patty Vermillion, Training Coordinator
Leslie Brozna, Marketing and Sales Coordinator

Brings together more than 2,200 participants from around the world and over 275 companies who provide products and services to jails.
2200 Attendees
Frequency: May
Founded in 1981

15313 American Society of Criminology Show
1314 Kinnear Road
Columbus, OH 43212

614-292-9207
Fax: 614-292-6767
E-Mail: webmaster@asc41.com
Home Page: www.asc41.com

Bonnie Fisher, Treasurer

Twenty-five tables.
1.5M Attendees
Frequency: October

15314 Convention & Traffic Expo
American Traffic Safety Services Association
15 Riverside Parkway
Suite 100
Fredericksburg, VA 22406-1022

540-368-1701
800-272-8772
Fax: 540-368-1717
Home Page: www.atssa.com

Douglas Danko, Chairman

The premier meeting place for roadway professionals around the world. The program and exhibits are dedicated to issues and products related to all aspects of temporary traffic control and roadway safety.
Frequency: Annual/February
Mailing list available for rent

15315 FBINAA Conference
FBI National Academy Associates
422 Garrisonville Road
Suite 103
Stafford, VA 22554

540-628-0834
Fax: 703-632-1993
E-Mail: info@fbinaa.org
Home Page: www.fbinaa.org

Timothy D Overton, National President
Steve Tidwell, Executive Director
Rhonda Stites, Administrative Assistant
Becky Storm, Business Manager
Nell Cochran, Financial Manager
Frequency: July
Mailing list available for rent

15316 FEMSA Annual Meeting
Fire and Emergency Manufacturers and Services Asso
PO Box 147
Lynnfield, MA 01940-0147

781-334-2771
Fax: 781-334-2771
E-Mail: info@femsa.org
Home Page: www.femsa.org
Social Media: Twitter, LinkedIn

Dan Reese, President
William Lawson, VP

Works to strengthen its membership, planning for future development, and directing programs that build industry opportunities
100+ Attendees
Frequency: Fall

15317 GovSec: The Govenment Security Conference & Expo
1105 Media
9201 Oakdale Avenue
Suite 101
Chatsworth, CA 91311

818-734-5200
Fax: 818-734-1522
E-Mail: info@1105media.com
Home Page: www.1105media.com

Jules Gagne, Exhibits & Sponsorships
Deborah Lovell, Conference Program
Brad Wills, Press & Media
Neal Vitale, President & Chief Executive Officer
Richard Vitale, Senior Vice President & CFO

GovSec is the premier government security conference & expo that has joined forces with the Contingency Planning & Management Network (Centric Security) and U.S. Law Enforcement Conferences, to strengthen its focus on critical infrastructure protection, cybercrime and cyberterrorism, counterterrorism and homeland security. Washington Convention Center, Washington, DC.
Frequency: Annual/April
Founded in 2001

15318 Int'l Assn of Campus Law Enforcement Administrators Annual Conference
International Assn of Campus Law Enforcement Admin
342 North Main Street
West Hartford, CT 06117-2507

860-586-7522
Fax: 860-586-7550
E-Mail: info@iaclea.org
Home Page: www.iaclea.org

Pamela Hayes, Exhibitor Contact
Peter Berry, Executive Director

Offers members an opportunity to attend informative programs to learn more about current issues and developments in campus public safety, network with peers, visit exhibitor booths, and enjoy special events.
Frequency: Annual

15319 International Association of Chiefs of Police Annual Conference
International Association of Chiefs of Police
515 N Washington Street
Alexandria, VA 22314-2357

703-836-6767
800-843-4227
Fax: 703-836-4543
E-Mail: information@theiacp.org
Home Page: www.theiacp.org
Social Media: Facebook, Twitter, RSS, Youtube

Lia Muwwakkil, Exhibits & Conferences
Colleen Phalen, Exhibits & Sponsorships
Dan Rosenblatt, Executive Director

Enables professionals to examine the state of the police industry through highly rated seminars, forums, and technical workshops. Only open to IACP members and their guests.
Frequency: Annual,September
Mailing list available for rent

15320 National Education & Training Conference
National Black Police Association
3100 Main Street
#256
Dallas, TX 75226

855-879-6272
Fax: 202-986-0410
Home Page: www.blackpolice.org

Ronald Hampton, Executive Director
Malik Aziz, Chairperson
Walter L Holloway, Vice Chairperson
Sherri Lockett, Secretary
Donna Ross, Fiscal Officer
400 Attendees
Frequency: Annual

15321 National Forensic League
125 Watson Street
PO Box 38
Ripon, WI 54971

920-748-6206
Fax: 920-748-9478
E-Mail: nflcustomerservice@nflonline.org
Home Page: www.nflonline.org

Diane Rasmussen, Associate Secretary
J Scott, Executive Director

Ten booths.
2.8M Attendees
Frequency: June

15322 National Sheriff's Association
1450 Duke Street
Alexandria, VA 22314-3490

703-836-7827
800-424-7827
E-Mail: kbright@sheriffs.org
Home Page: www.sheriffs.org

Kimberly Bright, Director, Marketing & Exhibits
Thomas Faust, Executive Director

More than 500 exhibits.
3M Attendees
Frequency: June

15323 Tactical Operations Conference
National Tactical Officers Association
PO Box 797
Doylestown, PA 18901

215-230-7616
800-279-9127
Fax: 215-230-7552
E-Mail: membership@ntoa.org
Home Page: www.ntoa.org
Social Media: Facebook, Twitter, LinkedIn, Google+, Blogger, Bloggy, Pint

Mark Lomax, Executive Director
Laura Gerhart, Conference Coordinator
Rob Cartner, Director of Training
Mary Heins, Editor
Michelle Griffin, Assistant Editor
1000 Attendees
Frequency: September
Mailing list available for rent

Directories & Databases

15324 American Academy of Forensic Sciences Membership Directory
410 N 21st St
Colorado Spring, CO 80904-2712

719-636-1100
Fax: 719-636-1993
E-Mail: awarren@aafs.org
Home Page: www.aafs.org

Anne Warren, Executive Director

Offers valuable information on over 5,000 persons qualified in forensic sciences including

law, anthropology and psychiatry.
Cost: $50.00
250 Pages
Frequency: Annual

15325 Directory of Law Enforcement and Criminal
Law Enforcement Standards Office
US National Institute of Standards
100 Bureau Drive M/S 8102
Gaithersburg, MD 20899-8102

301-975-2757
Fax: 301-948-0978

Marilyn Leach, Editor
Ruth Joel, Editor

More than 200 local, national and international organizations involved in the fields of law enforcement, corrections, forensic science and criminal justice in the US.

15326 Fire Chief: Equipment and Apparatus Directory Issue
Primedia
1300 E 9th St
Cleveland, OH 44114-1503

216-696-7000
Fax: 216-696-6662
Home Page: www.penton.com

Eric Jacobson, Senior VP
Jane Cooper, Marketing
David Kieselstein, Chief Executive Officer
Kurt Nelson, Vice President, Human Resources
Andrew Schmolka, Senior Vice President

List of approximately 1,000 suppliers of fire protection equipment, including ladder trucks, protective clothing, alarms, alternators and others.
Cost: $10.00
Frequency: Monthly
Circulation: 52901
Mailing list available for rent

15327 Grey House Homeland Security Directory
Grey House Publishing
4919 Route 22
PO Box 56
Amenia, NY 12501

518-789-8700
800-562-2139
Fax: 845-373-6390
E-Mail: books@greyhouse.com
Home Page: www.greyhouse.com
Social Media: Facebook, Twitter

Leslie Mackenzie, Publisher
Richard Gottlieb, Editor

Features the latest contact information for government and private organizations involved with Homeland Security along with the latest product information. The directory provides detailed profiles of nearly 1,500 Federal & State Organizations & Agencies and over 3,000 Officials and Key Executives involved with Homeland Security.
Cost: $195.00
800 Pages
ISBN: 1-592370-75-6
Founded in 1981

15328 Grey House Homeland Security Directory - Online Database
Grey House Publishing
4919 Route 22
PO Box 56
Amenia, NY 12501-0056

518-789-8700
800-562-2139
Fax: 518-789-0556
E-Mail: gold@greyhouse.com
Home Page: www.gold.greyhouse.com
Social Media: Facebook, Twitter

Leslie Mackenzie, Publisher
Richard Gottlieb, President

This comprehensive database presents a wide range of information that is scattered and hard to find elsewhere, providing subscribers with access to the most comprehensive, up-to-date and detailed information on the nation's homeland security contacts and services. This online database contains over 1,100 profiles of Federal and State agencies and companies along with the names of 11,000 key contacts.
Founded in 1981

15329 Grey House Safety & Security Directory
Grey House Publishing
4919 Route 22
PO Box 56
Amenia, NY 12501

518-789-8700
800-562-2139
Fax: 845-373-6390
E-Mail: books@greyhouse.com
Home Page: www.greyhouse.com
Social Media: Facebook, Twitter

Leslie Mackenzie, Publisher
Richard Gottlieb, Editor

Comprehensive resource guide to the safety and security industry, including articles, checklists, OSHA regulations and product listings. Focuses on creating and maintaining a safe and secure enviroment, and dealing specifically with hazardous materials, noise and vibration, workplace preparation and maintenance, electrical and lighting safety, fire and rescue and more.
Cost: $165.00
1600 Pages
ISBN: 1-592373-75-5
Founded in 1981

15330 Law Enforcement Technology Directory
Hendon
130 Waukegan Rd
Deerfield, IL 60015-4912

847-444-3300
800-843-9764
Fax: 847-444-3333
E-Mail: info@hendonpub.com
Home Page: www.lawandordermag.com

Henry Kingwill, Owner

Directory of manufacturers and suppliers of one type of law enforcement equipment such as computers, weapons, training, surveillance, forensics and radio and communications equipment.
Cost: $60.00
Frequency: Annual December

15331 Law and Order Magazine: Police Management Buyer's Guide Issue
Hendon
130 Waukegan Rd
2nd Floor
Deerfield, IL 60015-4912

847-444-3300
800-843-9764
Fax: 847-444-3333
E-Mail: esanow@hendonpub.com
Home Page: www.hendonpub.com

Henry Kingwill, Owner
Jennifer Gavigan, Managing Editor
Yesenia Salcedo, Managing Editor
Tim Davis, Graphic Designer
Marilou Go, Office Manager

Monthly publication for police managers, covering all aspects of law enforcement including a list of manufacturers, dealers and distributors of products and services for police departments.
Cost: $15.00
Frequency: Annual February

15332 National Directory of Law Enforcement Administrators Correctional Inst
National Public Safety Information Bureau
PO Box 365
Stevens Point, WI 54481

715-345-2772
800-647-7579
Fax: 715-345-7288
E-Mail: info@safetysource.com
Home Page: www.safetysource.com

Steve Cywinski, Publisher
John Diser, Account Manager
Christina Scott, Business Development Manager

Listing of police departments, sheriffs, criminal prosecutors, state law enforcement, criminal investigation agencies, federal law enforcement and homeland security.
Cost: $129.00
924 Pages
Frequency: Annual, paperback
Circulation: 9,000
ISBN: 1-880245-22-1
ISSN: 1066-5595
Founded in 1964

15333 National Employment Listing Service Bulletin
Criminal Justice Center
Sam Houston State University
1803 Avenue I
Huntsville, TX 77341

936-295-6371

Kay Billingsley, Editor

Job openings in police departments, sheriff's departments, courts and other law enforcement and security agencies.

15334 Police: Buyer's Guide Issue
Bobit Publishing Company
23210 Crenshaw Blvd
Torrance, CA 90505-3181

310-539-1969
Fax: 310-539-4329
E-Mail: police@bobit.com

John Bebout, Owner

List of suppliers of police products and services.
Cost: $10.00
Frequency: Annual August

15335 Transportation Security Directory & Handbook
Grey House Publishing
4919 Route 22
PO Box 56
Amenia, NY 12501

518-789-8700
800-562-2139
Fax: 845-373-6390
E-Mail: books@greyhouse.com
Home Page: www.greyhouse.com
Social Media: Facebook, Twitter

Leslie Mackenzie, Publisher
Richard Gottlieb, Editor

Provides information on everything from Regulatory Authorities to Security Enforcement, this top-flight directory brings together the relevant information necessary for creating and maintaining a security plan for a wide range of

transportation facilities.
Cost: $195.00
800 Pages
ISBN: 1-592370-75-6
Founded in 1981

15336 **Who's Who in Jail Management Jail Directory**
American Jail Association
1135 Professional Ct
Hagerstown, MD 21740-5853

301-790-3930
Fax: 301-790-2941
Home Page: www.aja.org

Gwyn Smith-Ingley, Executive Director
Kelton Chapman, Manager
Sheryl Ebersole, Business Manager
Connie Lacy, Director

Offers the most current information available on local jails in the US. Also offers an up-to-date listing of all the jails in the US that is available for rent electronically and a valuable resource for sheriffs, jail administrators and vendors.
Cost: $85.00

Industry Web Sites

15337 **http://gold.greyhouse.com**
G.O.L.D Grey House OnLine Databases
Grey House Publishing's online database platform, GOLD, offers Quick Search, Keyword Search and Expert Search for most business sectors including law enforcement and public safety markets. The GOLD platform makes finding the information you need quick and easy - whether you're a novice searcher or an experienced database user. All of Grey House's directory products are available for subscription on the GOLD platform.

15338 **www.aamva.org**
American Assn. of Motor Vehicle Administrators
Nonprofit organization represents state and provincial officials in the US and Canada who administer and enforce motor vehicle laws. Strives to develop model programs in motor vehicle administration, police traffic services and highway safety.

15339 **www.aca.org**
American Correctional Association
This organization offers information on the correctional field.

15340 **www.alea.org**
Airborne Law Enforcement Association
Members are law enforcement officers who use both fixed and rotary wing air craft, in law enforcement, and equipment suppliers.

15341 **www.apco911.org**
Association of Public-Safety Communications
Officials International

The world's oldest and largest professional organization dedicated to the enhancement of public safety communications and to serving its more than 15,000 members, the people who use public safety communications systems and services.

15342 **www.aphf.org**
American Police Hall of Fame
Offers benefits, and various types of awards to members, magazine, line of duty death benefits, film and training library as well as support services, scholarships and financial assistance for police family survivors.

15343 **www.atssa.org**
American Traffic Safety Services Association
Promotes uniform use of lights, signs, pavement markings and barricades. Distributes technical information and sponsors training courses for worksite traffic supervisors.

15344 **www.blr.com**
Business & Legal Reports
Provides essential tools for safety and environmental compliance and training needs

15345 **www.corrections.com/**
Corrections Professionals
Information about events, careers, news, legal happenings and newsletters.

15346 **www.dpsoa.com**
Texas Department of Public Safety Officer's Association

15347 **www.fema.gov**
Federal Emergency Management Agency.

15348 **www.femsa.org**
Fire and Emergency Manufacturers and Services Asso
The leading trade association for the fire and emergency services industry whose members provides products and services to millions of fire and EMS professionals throughout the world.

15349 **www.footprinter.org**
International Footprint Association

15350 **www.fssa.net**
Fire Suppression Systems Association
Designers, suppliers and installers of special hazard fire suppression equipment, gases and detectors.

15351 **www.greyhouse.com**
Grey House Publishing
Authoritative reference directories for most business sectors including law enforcement and public safety markets. Users can search the online databases with varied search criteria allowing for custom searches by product category, geographic area, sales volume, keyword, subject and more. Full Grey House catalog and online ordering also available.

15352 **www.highwaysafety.org**
Insurance Institute for Highway Safety
Traffic and motor vehicle safety organization supported by auto insurers.

15353 **www.home.xnet.com/~lelp**
Law Enforcement Legal Publications
Publication for law enforcement, legal professional and law libraries.

15354 **www.iaati.org**
International Association of Auto Theft Investigators

Provides members who are auto theft investigators with resources to develop and maintain professional standards within the industry.

15355 **www.iawp.org**
International Association of Women Police
To strengthen, unite and raise the profile of women in criminal justice internationally.

15356 **www.ncpc.org**
National Crime Prevention Council

15357 **www.neoa.org**
Narcotic Enforcement Officers Association
A non-profit educational organization of more than a thousand law enforcement personnel and others in the criminal justicce system, includin state and local police, D.E.A., F.B.I. and customs.

15358 **www.nist.gov/oles/**
Law Enforcement Standards Office

15359 **www.ntoa.org**
National Tactical Officers Association
Enhance the performance and professional status of law enforcement personnel by providing a credible and proven training resource as well as a forum for the development of tactics and information exchange.

15360 **www.policeforum.org**
Police Executive Research Forum
For chief executives of city, county and state police agencies.

15361 **www.polygraph.org**
American Polygraph Association
A merger of Academy of Scientific Interrogation, American Academy of Polygraph Examiners and National Board of Polygraph examiners.

15362 **www.psa.com**
Production Services Associates,Inc.
Dealers and dealer banks who underwrite and trade federal, state and local government securities and mortgage-backed securities.

15363 **www.sheriffs.org**
National Sherriff's Association
Devoted to helping sheriffs and other law enforcers to execute their duties most effectively and professionally.

15364 **www.theiacp.org**
International Association of Chiefs of Police
Organization that focuses on topics of interest to professional law enforcers.

15365 **www.toxicology.org**
Society of Toxicology
Members are scientists concerned with the effects of chemicals on man and the environment. Promotes the aquisition and utilization of knowledge in toxicology, aids in the protection of public health and facilitates disiplines. The society has a strong commitment to education in toxicology and to the recruitment of students and new members into the profession.

Associations

15366 American Leather Chemists Association
1314 50th Street
Suite 103
Lubbock, TX 79412
806-744-1798
Fax: 806-744-1785
E-Mail: alca@leatherchemists.org
Home Page: www.leatherchemists.org
Steve Lange, President
Sarah Drayna, Vice President
Robert F. White, JALCA Editor
Carol Adcock, Executive Secretary
Group of leather chemists who are interested in the development of methods that could be utilized to standardize both the supply and application of the tanning agents utilized by the industry.
500 Members
Founded in 1903
Mailing list available for rent

15367 American Saddle Makers Association
12155 Donovan Lane
Black Forest, CO 80908
729-494-2848
E-Mail: info@saddlemakers.org
Home Page: www.saddlemakers.org
Cheryl Rifkin, President
Bob Brenner, Executive Director
Steve Bowen, Director of Membership
Representing manufacturers of Western and English saddles in the US.

15368 International Federation Leather Guild
2264 Logan Drive
New Palestine, IN 46163
317-691-0321
E-Mail: eddjanlucas@sbcglobal.net
Home Page: www.ifolg.org
David Smith, Executive Director
Alex Madson, Assistant Director
Carol Higgins, Secretary
Monica Nibbes, Treasurer
Roger Bligan, Web Master
Supports all leather craftsmen via education, training, publications and trade shows.

15369 Leather Apparel Association
19 W 21st Street
Suite 403
New York, NY 10010
212-727-1210
Fax: 212-727-1218
E-Mail: info@leatherassociation.com
Home Page: www.leatherassociation.com
Morris Goldfarb, President
Richard Harrow, Executive Director
Represents the nation's leading leather retailers, manufacturers, cleaners and other businesses in promoting leather apparel in the US.
Founded in 1990

15370 Leather Industries of America
3050 K St NW
Suite 400
Washington, DC 20007-5100
202-342-8497
Fax: 202-342-8583
E-Mail: info@leatherusa.com
Home Page: www.leatherusa.com
John Wittenborn, President
John M. Pike, Executive Director
A trade association representing the leather industry: tanners; chemical suppliers; hide, skin and leather suppliers; and product manufacturers. Provides environmental, technical, educational, statistical, and marketing services.
Founded in 1917

15371 Leathercraft Guild
9108 Garvey Ave
Rosemead, CA 91770
Home Page: www.theleathercraftguild.com
Social Media: Facebook, Twitter, Myspace
Preserves and promotes the art of leather carving and stamping. Seeks to improve skills of members, raise standards of crafts and promote the product.
200 Members
Founded in 1949

15372 National Shoe Retailers Association
7386 N. La Cholla Blvd.
Suite G
Tucson, AZ 85741
520-209-1710
800-673-8446
Fax: 410-381-1167
E-Mail: info@nsra.org
Home Page: www.nsra.org
Social Media: Facebook, Twitter, LinkedIn, Pinterest, Google Plus
Rick Ravel, Board Chairman
Lenny Comeras, Vice Chairman
Jeff Greenberg, Vice Chairman
Membership association for independent shoe ratailers. Provides business services such as credit-card processing and shipping at special low members only prices. Also provides educational and training programs, consulting and other services.
63 Members
Founded in 1912

15373 Pedorthic Footwear Association
8400 Westpark Dr.
2nd Floor
McLean, VA 22102
703-610-9035
703-995-4456
Fax: 410-381-1167
E-Mail: info@pedorthics.org
Home Page: www.pedorthics.org
Social Media: Facebook, Twitter, LinkedIn, Google+, Blogger, Bloggy, Pint
Jay Zaffater, C. Ped., President
Robert Sobel, C. Ped., Vice President
Dean Mason, OST, C. Ped., C, Treasurer
Christopher J. Costantini, C. Ped., Secretary
Rebecca Fazzari, Meeting and Convention Manager
Membership organization for individuals and companies involved in the design, manufacture, modification and fit of therapeutic footwear. Provides educational programs, publications, legislative monitoring, marketing materials, professional liason and business operations services.
Cost: $55.00
2000 Members
Founded in 1958

15374 Proleptic, Inc.
PO Box 17817
Asheville, NC 28816
828-505-8474
Fax: 828-505-8476
E-Mail: shoptalk@proleptic.net
Home Page: www.proleptic.net
Social Media: Facebook
Daniel S Preston, PhD, Director
A Comprehensive Source for Sewing Machines, Leather working Equipment, Supplies, Tools, Horse Healthcare and Finished Products Repair Shops Retailers, Crafters, Collectors.
320 Members

15375 Sponge and Chamois Institute
10024 Office Center Ave
Suite 203
Saint Louis, MO 63128
314-842-2230
Fax: 314-842-3999
E-Mail: scwaters@swbell.net
Home Page: www.chamoisinstitute.org
Members are suppliers and dealers of natural sponges and chamois leather.

15376 Travel Goods Association
301 North Harrison Street
#412
Princeton, NJ 08540-3512
609 720-1200
Fax: 877-842-1938
E-Mail: info@travel-goods.org
Home Page: www.travel-goods.org
Michele Marini Pittenger, President/CEO
Rob Holmes, Vice President/ CFO
Kim Wong, Creative Director
Kate Ryan, Media Relations
Nate Herman, Director, Government Relations
Trade association that represents manufacturers of luggage, business and computer cases, handbags and accessories. Formerly the Luggage and Leather Goods Association.
450 Members
Founded in 1938
Mailing list available for rent

15377 Western-English Trade Association
451 East 58th Avenue
Suite 4323
Denver, CO 80216-8468
303-295-2001
Fax: 303-295-6108
E-Mail: weta@netway.net
Home Page: www.wetaonline.org
Glenda Chipps, Executive Director
Members are manufacturers and retailers of western and english style riding equipment and clothes.
158 Members
Founded in 1963

Newsletters

15378 Leather Conservation News
Minnesota Historical Society
345 Kellogg Blvd W
St Paul, MN 55102-1906
651-259-3000
Fax: 651-296-1004
E-Mail: webmaster@mnhs.org
Home Page: www.mnhs.org
Nina Archabal, Executive Director
Jackie Swanson, Secretary
Sue Leas, Executive Assistant
Research and advancements in the specialty of leather conservation and preservation; articles on materials science research and treatments; news of conferences and workshops.
Cost: $15.00
24 Pages
Frequency: 2 per year
Circulation: 250
ISSN: 0898-0128
Printed in on matte stock

15379 Leather Facts
US Hide, Skin & Leather Association

1700 N Moore Street
Suite 1600
Arlington, VA 22209

703-841-2400
Fax: 703-527-0938
E-Mail: jreddington@meatami.com
Home Page: www.meatami.com

John Reddington, President

Association news covering the leather and hide industry.

Magazines & Journals

15380 **Journal of the American Leather Chemists Association (JALCA)**
American Leather Chemists Association
1314 50th Street
Suite 103
Lubbock, TX 79412

806-744-1798
Fax: 806-744-1785
E-Mail: alca@leatherchemists.org
Home Page: www.leatherchemists.org

Carol Adcock, Executive Secretary
Robert F. White, Editor
Steven Gilberg, President
Steve Lange, Vice President
Cost: $175.00
Frequency: Monthly
Circulation: 500
Founded in 1903
Mailing list available for rent

15381 **Leather Crafters & Saddlers Journal**
222 Blackburn St
Rhinelander, WI 54501

715-362-5393
888-289-6409
Fax: 715-362-5391
E-Mail: journal@newnorth.net
Home Page: www.leathercraftersjournal.com
Social Media: Facebook

Dot Reis, Editor

Publication for leather workers. Sponsors several trade shows throughout the year which attract vendors of leather, tools, equipment and supplies.
Cost: $32.00
Frequency: Bi-Monthly
Circulation: 6000
ISSN: 1082-4480

15382 **Pedorthic Footwear Association**
7150 Columbia Gateway Drive
Suite G
Columbia, MD 21046-1151

410-381-8282
800-673-8446
Fax: 410-381-1167
E-Mail: info@pedorthics.org
Home Page: www.pedorthics.org
Social Media: Facebook, Twitter, LinkedIn, Google+, Blogger, Bloggy, Pint

Ed Habre, Board Chairman
Chuck Schuyler, President
Brian Lagana, Executive Director
Margaret Hren, Editorial, Communications
Rebecca Fazzari, Meeting and Convention Manager

Membership organization for individuals and companies involved in the design, manufacture, modification and fit of the therapeutcic footwear. Provides educational programs, publications, legislative monitoring, marketing materials, professional liason and business operations services. Dues are $225/595 (individuals/companies).
Cost: $185.00
44 Pages
Circulation: 5000
Founded in 1958
Printed in 2 colors on glossy stock

Trade Shows

15383 **ALCA Annual Meeting**
American Leather Chemists Association
1314 50th Street
Suite 103
Lubbock, TX 79412

806-744-1798
Fax: 806-744-1785
E-Mail: alca@leatherchemists.org
Home Page: www.leatherchemists.org

Carol Adcock, Executive Secretary
Robert F. White, Editor
Steven Gilberg, President
Steve Lange, Vice President
100 Attendees
Mailing list available for rent

15384 **International Federation Leather Guild Trade Show**
748 NW Wood Street
Burleson, TX 76028-2619

817-478-2335

Ernie Wayman, Executive Director

Open exhibition of leather craftsmen.
400 Attendees

15385 **Leather Allied Trade Show**
2214 S Brentwood Boulevard
Saint Louis, MO 63144-1804

314-961-2829

Virginia Breen, Secretary

Exhibition of leathers and components.
2.1M Attendees
Frequency: February

15386 **Pedorthic Footwear Association Annual Symposium**
7150 Columbia Gateway Drive
Suite G
Columbia, MD 21046-1170

410-381-8282
800-673-8446
Fax: 410-381-1167
E-Mail: info@pedorthics.org
Home Page: www.pedorthics.org
Social Media: Facebook, Twitter, LinkedIn, Google+, Blogger, Bloggy, Pint

Ed Habre, Board Chairman
Chuck Schuyler, President
Brian Lagana, Executive Director
Margaret Hren, Editorial, Communications
Rebecca Fazzari, Meeting and Convention Manager

One hundred fifty booths plus educational sessions regarding the design, manufacture or modification and fit of shoes and foot orthoses to alleviate foot problems caused by disease, congenital condition, overuse or injury.
1000 Attendees
Frequency: November

Directories & Databases

15387 **Complete Directory of Leather Goods & Luggage**
Sutton Family Communications & Publishing Company
920 State Route 54 East
Elmitch, KY 42343

270-276-9500
E-Mail: jlsutton@apex.net

Theresa Sutton, Publisher
Lee Sutton, Editor

Print-out from database of wholesalers, manufacturers, distributors, importers and close-out houses. Database is updated daily to guarantee the most current and up-to-date sources available.
Cost: $39.50
100 Pages

15388 **Leather Industries of America Membership Directory & Buyer's Guide**
3050 K St NW
Suite 400
Washington, DC 20007-5100

202-342-8497
Fax: 202-342-8583
E-Mail: info@leatherusa.com
Home Page: www.leatherusa.com

John Wittenborn, President
30 Pages
Frequency: Annual
Founded in 1917

15389 **Leather Manufacturer Directory**
Shoe Trades Publishing Company
323 Cornelia
Suite 274
Plattsburg, NY 12901

514-457-8787
800-973-7463
Fax: 514-457-5832
Home Page: www.shoetrades.com

George McLeish, Group Publisher
Inta Huns, Managing Editor

Classified directory of major leather finishers, tanneries and hide processors in the United States and Canada, and their suppliers.
Cost: $61.00
413 Pages
Frequency: Annual
Circulation: 1,200

15390 **US Leather Industry Statistics**
Leather Industries of America
3050 K St NW
Suite 400
Washington, DC 20007-5100

202-342-8497
Fax: 202-342-8583
E-Mail: info@leatherusa.com
Home Page: www.leatherusa.com

John Wittenborn, President
Cost: $18.00
10 Pages
Frequency: Annual
Founded in 1917

Industry Web Sites

15391 **http://gold.greyhouse.com**
G.O.L.D Grey House OnLine Databases

Grey House Publishing's online database platform, GOLD, offers Quick Search, Keyword Search and Expert Search for most business sectors including leather markets. The GOLD platform makes finding the information you need quick and easy - whether you're a novice searcher or an experienced database user. All of Grey House's directory products are available for subscription on the GOLD platform.

15392 www.greyhouse.com
Grey House Publishing
Authoritative reference directories for most business sectors including leather markets. Users can search the online databases with varied search criteria allowing for custom searches by product category, geographic area, sales volume, keyword, subject and more. Full Grey House catalog and online ordering also available.

15393 www.hidenet.com
Hidenet
Furnishes detailed information on the daily hide market worldwide.

15394 www.leatherusa.com
Leather Industries of America
Works to promote the leather industry through collection of statistics, chemical and technical research and public relations.

15395 www.meatami.org
US Hide, Skin & Leather Association

15396 www.ssia.info
Shoe Service Institute of America
Shop to shop chat room, links and listings of manufacturers and wholesalers plus shoe care tips.

15397 www.travel-goods.org
Travel Goods Association
Manufacturers of luggage and other leather goods.

Associations

15398 ABA Young Lawyers Division
American Bar Association
321 N Clark St
Chicago, IL 60654-7598
312-988-5000
800-285-2221
Fax: 312-988-5280
E-Mail: yld@staff.abanet.org
Home Page: www.abanet.org/yld/home.html
Social Media: Facebook, Twitter, LinkedIn, Youtube
James R. Silkenat, President
Robert M. Carlson, Chair, House of Delegates
Jack L. Rives, Executive Director
Hon. Cara Lee T Neville, Secretary
Lucian T. Pera, Treasurer
The Division is committed to assuring it is best able to represent the newest members of the profession, ensuring that it reflects the society it serves, and providing young lawyers wth the tools and opportunities for professional and personal success.
150M Members
Founded in 1878

15399 AILA's Immigration Lawyer Search
Home Page: www.ailalawyer.com
12,00 Members

15400 Academy of Family Mediators
PO Box 51090
Eugene, OR 97405
541-345-1629
E-Mail: admin@mediate.com
Home Page: www.mediate.com
Social Media: Facebook, Twitter, LinkedIn, Stumbleupon, Tumblr, RSS, Pint
Jim Melamed, CEO
Carol Knapp, CTO
Josh Remis, COO
John Blair, Business Advisor & Board Member
Byron Knapp, Systems Administrator
Produce conflict management specialists who can advance conflict resolution and engagement, as well as a functional approach to conflict within our communities and society.
2M Members
Founded in 1981
Mailing list available for rent

15401 Adjutants General Association of the United States
2001 E Capitol Street
Washington, DC 20003-1719
302-326-7008
Fax: 302-326-7196
E-Mail: president@agaus.org
Home Page: www.agaus.org
MajGen Edward Tonini, President
MG David Baldwin, VP Army
MajGen Mike Edwards, VP Air
MG Dave Sprynczynatyk, Treasurer
MajGen Scott Rice, Secretary
Composed of the commander of the National Guard in each state.
55 Members

15402 Alliance for Justice
11 Dupont Cir NW
2nd Floor
Washington, DC 20036-1206
202-822-6070
Fax: 202-822-6078
E-Mail: alliance@afj.org
Home Page: www.afj.org
Social Media: Facebook, Twitter, Youtube, Google Plus
Anne Hess, Chair
Nan Aron, President
Winsome McIntosh, Vice-Chair
Elizabeth Posner, Director of Foundation Relations
Michelle Schwartz, Director of Justice Programs
Nonprofit association of public interest advocacy organization. Offers workshops, advocacy projects, legal guides, techinical assistance and public education. Publishes a directory of public interest law centers.
Founded in 1979
Mailing list available for rent

15403 American Academy of Psychiatry and the Law
1 Regency Dr
PO Box 30
Bloomfield, CT 06002-2310
860-242-5450
800-331-1389
Fax: 860-286-0787
E-Mail: execoff@aapl.org
Home Page: www.aapl.org
Robert Weinstock, MD, President
Richard L. Frierson, MD, Vice President
Emily A. Keram, MD, Vice President
Barry W. Wall, MD, Secretary
Douglass Mossman, MD, Treasurer
Members are psychiatrists who have a professional interest in psychiatry and the law.
1500 Members
Founded in 1969

15404 American Alliance of Paralegals
4023 Kennett Pike
Suite 146
Wilmington, DE 19807-2018
E-Mail: info@aapipara.org
Home Page: www.aapipara.org
Social Media: Facebook, Twitter, LinkedIn
Carolyn M. Saenz, AACP, President
Sandra M. Herdler, Vice President
Patricia S. Carr, AACP, Treasurer
Keelie J. Fike, Secretary
Leslie L. Adams, AACP, Director of Education
Founded in 2003

15405 American Arbitration Association
1633 Broadway
Floor 10
New York, NY 10019-6707
212-716-5800
Fax: 877-304-8457
E-Mail: websitemail@adr.org
Home Page: www.adr.org
William K Slate II, CEO
Debi Miller-Moore, VP
Available to resolve a wide range of disputes through mediation, arbitration, elections and other out-of-court settlement procedures.

15406 American Association for Justice
777 6th Street, NW
Suite 200
Washington, DC 20001
202-965-3500
800-424-2725
E-Mail: membership@justice.org
Home Page: www.justice.org
Social Media: Facebook, Twitter, LinkedIn
Burton LeBlanc, President
Larry Tawwater, Vice President
Charles Jeffress, Chief Operating Officer
Kathi Berge, Chief Financial Officer
Anjali Jesseramsing, Executive Vice President
56000 Members
Founded in 1972
Mailing list available for rent

15407 American Association for Paralegal
19 Mantua Road
Suite 241
Mt. Royal, NJ 08061
856-423-2829
Fax: 856-423-3420
E-Mail: info@aafpe.org
Home Page: www.aafpe.org
Social Media: Facebook, Twitter, LinkedIn
Steve Dayton, President
Gene Terry, CAE, Executive Director
Wendy Stevens, Exhibits & Meetings Manager
Kathy Suckiel, Administrative Assistant
Robert Mongue, Secretary
National organization serving paralegal education and institutions which offer paralegal education programs.
Founded in 1981

15408 American Association for Paralegal Educati on
19 Mantua Road
Mt. Royal, NJ 8061
856-423-2829
Fax: 856-423-3420
E-Mail: info@aafpe.org
Home Page: www.aafpe.org
Social Media: Facebook, Twitter, LinkedIn
Patricia Lyons, President
Robert Mongue, President-Elect
Steve Dayton, Immediate Past President
Wm. Bruce Davis, Treasurer
Tom Pokladowski, Secretary
Founded in 1981

15409 American Association of Attorney-Certified Public Accountants
8647 Richmond Highway
Ste. 639
Alexandria, VA 22309
703-352-8064
888-288-9272
Fax: 703-352-8073
E-Mail: info@attorney-cpa.com
Home Page: www.attorney-cpa.com
Domenick R. Lioce, President
Joseph E. Cordell, President Elect/Vice President
John W. Pramberg, Treasurer
Brian Yacker, Secretary
Jo Ann M. Koontz, Assistant Treasurer/Secretary
Seeks to safeguard the professional and legal rights of CPA attorneys.
1400 Members
Founded in 1964

15410 American Association of Law Libraries
105 W Adams Street
Suite 3300
Chicago, IL 60603-6225
312-939-4764
Fax: 312-431-1097
E-Mail: aallhq@aall.org
Home Page: www.aallnet.org
Social Media: Facebook, Twitter, RSS
Steven Anderson, President
Holly Riccio, Vice President
Gail Warren, Treasurer
Julia O'Donnell, Director Membership Marketing
Ashley St. John, Director Marketing/Communications

Promotes and enhances the value of law libraries to the legal and public communities, fosters the profession of law librarianship and provides leadership in the field of legal information.
5000+ Members
Founded in 1906

15411 American Bail Coalition
3857 Lewiston Place
Fairfax, VA 22030

877-385-9009
Fax: 703-385-1809
Home Page: www.americanbailcoalition.com
Social Media: Facebook, Twitter, LinkedIn, Youtube

William B Carmichael, President
Thomas Ritchey, Treasurer

Dedicated to the long term growth and continuation of the surety bail bond industry.
Founded in 1992

15412 American Bar Association
321 N Clark St
Chicago, IL 60654-7598

312-988-5000
800-285-2221
Fax: 312-988-5280
E Mail: askaba@abanet.org
Home Page: www.abanet.org
Social Media: Facebook, Twitter, LinkedIn

James R. Silkenat, President
Jack L. Rives, Executive Director
Robert M. Carlson, Chairman
Lucian T. Pera, Treasurer
Cara Lee T. Neville, Secretary

The American Bar Association is the largest coluntary professional association in the world, with over 400,000 members. The ABA provides law school accreditation, continuing legal education, information about the law, programs to assist lawyerd and judges in their work, and initiatives to improve the legal system for the public.
400M Members
Founded in 1878
Mailing list available for rent

15413 American Bar Foundation
750 N Lake Shore Dr
Chicago, IL 60611-4403

312-988-6500
Fax: 312-988-6579
Home Page: www.americanbarfoundation.org

Hon. Bernice B. Donald, President
David A. Collins, Vice President
Ellen J. Flannery, Secretary
George S. Frazza, Treasurer
Katharine Hannaford, Senior Writer & Grants Officer

Memberships are elected and limited to one third of one percent of the lawyers in the United States.
Founded in 1955
Mailing list available for rent

15414 American Civil Liberties Union
125 Broad St
18th Floor
New York, NY 10004-2427

212-549-2500
Fax: 212-549-2646
E-Mail: membership@aclu.org
Home Page: www.aclu.org
Social Media: Facebook, Twitter, RSS, Stumbleupon, Digg

Susan N. Herman, President
Anthony D Romero, Executive Director
Steven Shapiro, Legal Director
Mark Wier, Chief Development Officer
Emily Tynes, Communications Director

Protection of civil liberties and constitutional rights through litigation, public education and legislative lobbying.
Founded in 1920
Mailing list available for rent

15415 American College of Legal Medicine
1100 E Woodfield Rd
Suite 520
Schaumburg, IL 60173

847-969-0283
Fax: 847-517-7229
E-Mail: info@aclm.org
Home Page: www.aclm.org

Vicky A. Trompler, Chairman, Counsel
Victoria L. Green, President
Wendy J. Weiser, Executive Director
Sue O'Sullivan, Associate Director
Christopher White, Secretary

Organization related to the field of health law, legal medicine or medical jurisprudence.
1400 Members
Founded in 1960

15416 American Health Lawyers Association
1620 Eye Street, NW
6th Floor
Washington, DC 20006-4010

202-833-1100
Fax: 202-833-1105
Home Page: www.healthlawyers.org
Social Media: Facebook, Twitter, LinkedIn

Kristen B. RosatiRosati, President, Chair
Peter M. Leibold, Esq., Executive Vice President
Anne H. Hoover, Vice President of Programs
Cynthia Conner, Esq., Vice President
Wayne Miller, CA, Deputy Executive Vice President

Health Lawyers offers numerous services for their members and most are freely available to nonmembers as well.
Mailing list available for rent

15417 American Immigration Lawyers Association
1331 G St NW
Suite 300
Washington, DC 20005-3142

202-507-7600
Fax: 202-783-7853
E-Mail: info@aila.org
Home Page: www.aila.org

Crystal L. Williams, Esq., Executive Director
Gregory Chen, Director, Director of Advocacy
Daniel Presser-Kroll, Marketing Coordinator
Tatia L. Gordon-Troy, Esq., Director of Publications
Grace Woods, Director of Education

Attorneys practicing in the field of immigration and naturalization law.
11200 Members
Founded in 1946
Mailing list available for rent

15418 American Inns of Court
1229 King St
2nd Floor
Alexandria, VA 22314-2993

703-684-3590
Fax: 703-684-3607
E-Mail: info@innsofcourt.org
Home Page: home.innsofcourt.org
Social Media: Facebook, Twitter, LinkedIn, Pinterest, Tumblr, Blogger, St

Donald W. Lemons, President
Carl E. Stewart, Vice President
Malinda E. Dunn, Executive Director
Cindy Dennis, Awards & Scholarships Coordinator
Andrew Young, Director of Knowledge Resources

AIC is designed to improve skills, professionalism and ethics of the bench and bar. The American Inns of Court is an amalgam of judges, lawyers, and in some cases, law professors and law students.
Mailing list available for rent

15419 American Institute of Parliamentarians
550m Ritchie Highway
#271
Severna Park, MD 21146

888-664-0428
Fax: 410-544-4640
E-Mail: aip@aipparl.org
Home Page: www.aipparl.org

Alison Wallis, JD, CP-T, PRP, President
Daniel Ivey-Soto, CP-T, PRP, Vice President
Mary Remson, CPP-T, PRP, Treasurer
Teresa Dean, CPP-T, PRP, Accrediting Director
Jeanette Williams, CP-T, Education Director

Promotes the use of effective, democratic and parliamentary practices by teaching of parliamentary procedures; training and certification of parliamentarians; promoting the use of parliamentarians; and maintaining a representative, democratic organization.
1.4M Members
Founded in 1958

15420 American Intellectual Property Law Association
241 18th Street, South
Suite 700
Arlington, VA 22202

703-415-0780
Fax: 703-415-0786
E-Mail: aipla@aipla.org
Home Page: www.aipla.org
Social Media: Facebook, Twitter, LinkedIn, Pinterest, Tumblr, Blogger, St

Wayne P. Sobon, President
Denise W. DeFranco, First Vice President
Mark L. Whitaker, Second Vice President
Q. Todd Dickinson, Executive Director
Meghan Donohoe, Chief Operating Officer

Lawyers whose specialty is trademark, patent or copyright laws.
Founded in 1897
Mailing list available for rent

15421 American Judicature Society
Center Building

2014 Broadway
Suite 100
Nashville, TN 37203

615-873-4675
800-626-4089
Fax: 615-873-4671
E-Mail: sandersen@ajs.org
Home Page: www.ajs.org
Social Media: Facebook, Twitter, Youtube

Martha Hill Jamison, President
Rebecca Lee Wiggs, Vice President
Jon Comstock, Vice President
James Alfini, Interim Executive Director
Cynthia Gray, Director, Center Judicial Ethics

Lawyers, judges and educators interested in the effective administration of justice.
5000 Members
Founded in 1913

15422 **American Law & Economics Association**
PO Box 208245
New Haven, CT 06520-8245
203-432-7801
Fax: 203-432-7225
E-Mail: alea@pantheon.yale.edu
Home Page: www.amlecon.org

Douglas G. Baird, President
Robert Scott, Vice President
Kathryn Spier, Secretary-Treasurer

Dedicated to the advancement of economic understanding of law and related areas of public policy and regulation.
Founded in 1991

15423 **American Law Institute**
4025 Chestnut St
Suite 5
Philadelphia, PA 19104-3099
215-243-1600
800-253-6397
Fax: 215-243-1636
E-Mail: ali@ali.org
Home Page: www.ali.org
Social Media: Facebook, Twitter, LinkedIn, Youtube

Roberta Cooper Ramo, President
Allen D. Black, 1st Vice President
Douglas Laycock, 2nd Vice President
Julie Scribner, Chief Financial Officer
Stephanie A. Middleton, Deputy Director

A private, nonprofit organization that seeks to promote the clarification and simplification of the law through legal research and reform activities.
Founded in 1923
Mailing list available for rent

15424 **American Law Institute Continuing Legal Education Group (ALI CLE)**
4025 Chestnut St
Suite 5
Philadelphia, PA 19104
215-243-1600
800-253-6397
Fax: 215-243-1664
E-Mail: ali@ali.org
Home Page: www.ali-cle.org

Leslie A. Belasco, Chief of Content Production
Mark T. Carroll, Chief of CLE Operations
Matthew Born, Director, Office of Marketing
Diane Schnitzer, Director of Human Resources
Frank Paul Tomasello, Director

Provides continuing legal education courses, books, and periodicals for practicing attorneys and others in the legal profession. This organization is a collaborative effort of the ALI and the ABA.
Founded in 2012

15425 **American Lawyers Auxiliary**
321 North Clark Street
Chicago, IL 60610-4714
312-988-6387
Fax: 312-988-5494
E-Mail: moisantj@staff.abanet.org
Home Page: www.americanlawyersauxiliary.org
Social Media: Facebook

Barbara Smallwood, President
Sue Bennett, President-Elect
Sue Patterson, First Vice President
Janet Bullinger, Second Vice Presidentÿ
Mary Ellen Borgelt, Secretary

Acts as a clearinghouse for state and local groups throughout the country and suggests educational programs pertaining to the law. Encourages members to volunteer their services.
75M Members
Founded in 1958

15426 **American Lawyers Newspapers Group**
1730 M Street NW
Washington, DC 20036-4513
202-457-0686

Supports all those involved in the reporting of legal issues. Publishes a weekly newsletter.
Founded in 1977

15427 **American Prepaid Legal Services Institute**
321 N Clark Street
Chicago, IL 60654
312-988-5751
Fax: 312-988-5032
E-Mail: info@aplsi.org
Home Page: www.aplsi.org
Social Media: Twitter

Alec Schwartz, Executive Director

Professional trade organization representing the legal services plan industry. The members include lawyers, sponsor representatives, administrators and marketers of legal service plans. These people have invested their time, money and organizational resources to build legal service plans into the premier mechanism for supplying affordable legal services.
Founded in 1976

15428 **American Society for Legal History**
185 West Broadway
PO Box R
New York, NY 10013
574-631-6984
Fax: 574-631-3595
E-Mail: walter.f.pratt.1@nd.edu
Home Page: www.aslh.net

Michael Grossberg, President
Sally Hadden, Secretary
Craig Evan Klafter, Treasurer
Rebecca J. Scott, President-Elect

Exhibits relating to legal history and its uses in formulating legal policy, decisions and actions; unearthing historical items; and preserving legal and legislative records.
1200 Members
Founded in 1956
Mailing list available for rent

15429 **American Society of Comparative Law**
University of Baltimore
1420 N. Charles Street
Baltimore, MD 21201
410-837-4689
Fax: 410-837-4560
E-Mail: lschnitzer@ubalt.edu
Home Page: www.comparativelaw.org

H. Patrick Glenn, President
David J. Gerber, Vice President
Franklin Gervurtz, Secretary
Richard Kay, Treasurer
Mathias W. Reimann, Editor-in-Chief

An organization of institutional and individual members devoted to study, research, and write on foreign and comparative law as well as private international law.
60 Members
Founded in 1951
Mailing list available for rent

15430 **American Society of International Law**
2223 Massachusetts Ave Nw
Washington, DC 20008-2864
202-939-6000
Fax: 202-797-7133
E-Mail: services@asil.org
Home Page: www.asil.org
Social Media: Facebook, Twitter, LinkedIn, Youtube

Dame RosalynÿHiggins, Honorary President
Donald Francis Donovan, President
Elizabeth Andersen, Executive Director/EVP
Sara Bannon, Chief Opearting Officer
Michael Farley, Director of Development

Supports all those involved with overseas litigation. Publishes monthly newsletter.
4000 Members
Founded in 1906
Mailing list available for rent

15431 **American Society of Notaries**
PO Box 5707
Tallahassee, FL 32314-5707
850-671-5164
Fax: 850-671-5165
Home Page: www.asnnotary.org

Kathleen Butler, Executive Director
Carly Heitz, Member Services Director

Helps to organize, improve and uphold high standards for notaries public.
21M Members
Founded in 1965

15432 **American Society of Trial Consultants**
1941 Greenspring Drive
Timonium, MD 21093
410-560-7949
Fax: 410-560-2563
E-Mail: ASTCOffice@astcweb.org
Home Page: www.astcweb.org

Doug Green, Ph.D., President
Ronald Matlon, Ph.D., Executive Director
Bill Grimes, Treasurer & Board Member
Carol Bauss, J.D., Secretary & Board Member

Members come from diverse professional fields: communication, psychology, theatre, marketing, linguistics, political science and law.
500+ Members
Founded in 1982
Mailing list available for rent

15433 **American Society of Trial Consultants Foun dation**
10951 West Pico Blvd.
Suite 203
Los Angeles, CA 90064
424-832-3641
E-Mail: info@astcfoundation.org
Home Page: www.astcfoundation.org

Daniel Wolfe, J.D., Ph.D., Board of Director
Karen Ohnemus Lisko, Ph.D., Board of Director
Mark Modlin, M.S., N.C.C., Board of Director
Ken Broda-Bahm, Ph.D., Board of Director
Ted Donner, Esq., Board of Director

15434 **Association of American Law Schools**
1614 20th Street, Northwest
Washington, DC 20009-1001
202-296-8851
Fax: 202-296-8869
E-Mail: aals@aals.org
Home Page: www.aals.org

Leo P Martinez, President
Judith Areen, Interim Executive Director
Jane M La Barbera, Managing Director
Regina F Burch, Associate Director
Tim Bloomquist, Staff Assistant

An association of law schools that serves as the law teachers' learned society.
Founded in 1900
Mailing list available for rent

15435 Association of Corporate Counsel
1025 Connecticut Ave NW
Suite 200
Washington, DC 20036-5425

202-293-4103
Fax: 202-293-4701
E-Mail: acc.chair@acc.com
Home Page: www.acc.com

David Allgood, Chair
Veta T. Richardson, President and CEO
Amar Sarwal, Vice President
John McAndrew, Vice President and Chief Technology
Jim Merklinger, Vice President and General Counsel

Lawyers who practice law in a corporation or other private sector entity and do not hold themselves out to the public to practice law.
15000 Members
Founded in 1982
Mailing list available for rent

15436 Association of Family and Conciliation
6525 Grand Teton Plaza
Madison, WI 53719

608-664-3750
Fax: 608-664-3751
E-Mail: afcc@afccnet.org
Home Page: www.afccnet.org
Social Media: Facebook, Twitter, LinkedIn

Nancy Ver Steegh, JD, MSW, President
Peter Salem, MA, Executive Director
Hon. Peter Boshier, Vice President
Leslye Hunter, MA, LMFT, Associate Director
Candace Walker, CMP, CMM, Program Director

AFCC is an interdisciplinary, international association of professionals dedicated to improving the lives of children and families through the resolution of family conflict.
3700 Members
Founded in 1963

15437 Association of Insolvency and Restructuring Advisors
221 Stewart Ave
Suite 207
Medford, OR 97501-3647

541-858-1665
Fax: 541-858-9187
E-Mail: aira@aira.org
Home Page: www.aira.org

Stephen Darr, CIRA, CDBVÿ, Chairman
Anthony Sasso, CIRAÿ, President
Thomas Morrow, CIRA, Vice President - CIRA, CDBV
Gina Gutzeit, CIRA, Vice President - Member Services
Grant Newton, Executive Director

Disseminates judicial and financial information relating to insolvency proceedings as well as offering methods to increase skills needed in these cases. Also administers the (CIRA) Certified Insolvency and Reorganization Account Program.
1250 Members
Founded in 1984

15438 Association of Legal Administrators
75 Tri State Intl
Suite 222
Lincolnshire, IL 60069-4435

847-267-1252
Fax: 847-267-1329
E-Mail: publications@alanet.org
Home Page: www.alanet.org
Social Media: Facebook, Twitter, LinkedIn

Paul Farnsworth, President
Oliver Yandle, JD, CAEÿ, Executive Director
Renee Tibbettsÿ, Director of Administration
Gwen Biasi, CAEÿ, Director of Marketing
Michelle Goldberg, Sr. Director Marketing

Professional support for management of private law firms and other legal organizations worldwide.
10000 Members
Founded in 1971

15439 Association of Professional Responsibility Lawyers (APRL)
20 South Clark Street
Suite 1050
Chicago, IL 60603

312-782-4396
Fax: 312-782-4725
E-Mail: admin@aprl.net
Home Page: aprl.net

Arthur J Lachman, President
Charles Lundberg, President-Elect
Lynda C Shely, Secretary
Donald Campbell, Treasurer

An organization of lawyers who concentrate on professional responsibilities issues.
300 Members
Founded in 1990

15440 Biz Law Association
PO Box 247
Springdale, UT 84767-0247

FAX 435-635-9817

Suppports all those involved in business law, especially business owners and managers. Publishes newsletter.

15441 Business & Legal Reports
100 Winners Circle
Suite 300
Brentwood, TN 37027

860-510-0100
800-727-5257
Fax: 860-510-7225
E-Mail: service@blr.com
Home Page: www.blr.com
Social Media: Facebook, Twitter, LinkedIn

Robert L Brady, JD, Founder
Dan Oswald, Chief Executive Officer
Guy Crossley, Chief Operating Officer
Lawton Miller, Chief Financial Officer
Matt Humphrey, Chief Marketing Officer

Provides essential tools for safety and environmental compliance and training needs.
32 Members
Mailing list available for rent

15442 Center for Professional Responsibility
American Bar Association
321 North Clark Street
Chicago, IL 60654

312-988-5000
800-285-2221
Fax: 312-988-5491
E-Mail: cpr@staff.abanet.org
Home Page: www.americanbar.org
Social Media: Facebook, Twitter, LinkedIn

James R. Silkenat, President
Jack L. Rives, Executive Director
Robert M. Carlson, Chair, House of Delegates
Lucian T. Pera, Treasurer
Cara Lee T. Neville, Secretary

Since 1978, the Center has provided national leadership and vision in developing and interpreting standards and scholarly resources in legal ethics, professional regulation, professionalism and client protection mechanisms.
Founded in 1878
Mailing list available for rent

15443 Center on Children and the Law
American Bar Association Young Lawyers Division
1050 Connecticut Ave. N.W.
Suite 400
Washington, DC 20036

202-662-1000
800-285-2221
Fax: 202-662-1755
E-Mail: ctrchildlaw@abanet.org
Home Page: www.americanbar.org
Social Media: Facebook, Twitter, LinkedIn

James R. Silkenat, President
Jack L. Rives, Executive Director
Robert M. Carlson, Chair, House of Delegates
Lucian T. Pera, Treasurer
Cara Lee T. Neville, Secretary

This is a program of the Young Lawyers Division that aims to improve children's lives through advances in law, justice, knowledge, practice and public policy. Areas of expertise include child abuse and neglect, child welfare and protective services system enhancement, foster care, family preservation, termination of parental rights, parental substance abuse, adolescent health, and domestic violence.
15 Members
Founded in 1878

15444 Commercial Law League of America
205 N. Michigan
Suite 2212
Chicago, IL 60601-5961

312-240-1400
800-978-2552
Fax: 312-240-1408
E-Mail: info@clla.org
Home Page: www.clla.org
Social Media: Facebook, Twitter, LinkedIn

Anthony Hilvers, Executive Vice President

Supports those involved in bankruptcy, collections, debt and insolvency legislation. Publishes quarterly magazine and weekly e-newsletter.
1500 Members
Founded in 1895
Mailing list available for rent

15445 Commission on Mental & Physical Disability Law
American Bar Association
1050 Connecticut Ave. N.W.
Suite 400
Washington, DC 20036

202-662-1000
800-285-2221
Fax: 202-442-3439
E-Mail: cdr@americanbar.org
Home Page: www.abanet.org/disability
Social Media: Facebook, Twitter, LinkedIn

Mark D. Agrast, Esq., Chair
Amy L. Allbright, Director
M. Tovah Miller, Program Specialist
Michael J. Stratton, Administrative Coordinator
Brandon M. Moore-Rhodes, Technology Associate

The Commission's mission is 'to promote the ABA's commitment to justice and the rule of law for persons with mental, physical, and sensory disabilities and to promote their full and equal participation in the legal profession.' The Commission consists of 15 members appointed by the ABA President-elect on an annual basis. It meets bi-annually at its

headquarters in Washington, D.C., to map out future plans and to direct the current activities.
15 Members
Founded in 1973
Mailing list available for rent

15446 **Copyright Society of The USA**
1 East 53rd Street
8th Floor
New York, NY 10022

Home Page: www.csusa.orgÿ
Social Media: Facebook, Twitter, LinkedIn

Eric J. Schwartz, President
Nancy E. Wolff, Vice President
Michael Donaldson, Treasurer
Judith Finell, Secretary
Kaitland Kubat, Director of Operations

15447 **Council of State Governments**
2760 Research Park Drive
PO Box 11910
Lexington, KY 40578-1910

859-244-8000
800-800-1910
Fax: 859-244-8001
E-Mail: press@csg.org
Home Page: www.csg.org
Social Media: Facebook, Twitter, Youtube

Gary Stevens, Chair
Jay Nixon, President
David Adkins, Executive Director/CEO
Carl Marcellino, Vice Chair
Mark Norris, Chair-Elect
Founded in 1933
Mailing list available for rent

15448 **Council on Legal Education Opportunity**
1101 Mercantile Lane
Suite 294
Largo, MD 20774

240-582-8600
866-886-4343
Fax: 240-582-8605
E-Mail: cleo@americanbar.org
Home Page: www.cleoscholars.org
Social Media: Facebook, Twitter

Cassandra Sneed Ogden, Executive Director
Bernetta J Hayes, Admissions Administrator
Leigh R. Allen II, Mentoring & Development Director
Lynda Cevallos, Pre-Law Coordinator
Julie D Long, Project Research Assistant

Provides law school preparation assistance for minority and disadvantaged students. Program is six-week summer institute paid for by the program. Scholarship of approximately $16,000 for the three years of law study is granted to selected and certified students, after completion of the summer program.

15449 **Council on Licensure, Enforcement and Regulation**
403 Marquis Ave
Suite 200
Lexington, KY 40502-2104

859-269-1289
Fax: 859-231-1943
E-Mail: rbrown@clearhq.org
Home Page: www.clearhq.org
Social Media: Facebook, Twitter, LinkedIn

Darrel S Crimmins, President
Adam Parfitt, Executive Director
Rosa Brown, Administrative Associate
Lisa Eads, Marketing & Communications
Jodie Markey, Program Coordinator

Supports all those involved in occupational and professional testing and credentialing. Publishes bi-annual magazine.
Mailing list available for rent

15450 **DRI-The Voice Of The Defense Bar**
55 W. Monroe Street
Suite 2000
Chicago, IL 60603

312-951-1101
Fax: 312-795-0747
E-Mail: dri@dri.org
Home Page: www.dri.org
Social Media: Facebook, Twitter, LinkedIn, Youtube

J. Michael Weston, President
Laura E Proctor, First Vice President
John e Cuttino, Second Vice President
Steven M Puiszis, Secretary-Treasurer
John Parker Sweeney, President-Elect

Service organization to improve the administration of justice and defense lawyers' skills.
Founded in 1960

15451 **Education Law Association**
2121 Euclid Avenue
LL 212
Cleveland, OH 44115-2214

216-523-7377
Fax: 216-687-5284
E-Mail: ela@educationlaw.org
Home Page: www.educationlaw.org
Social Media: Facebook, Twitter, LinkedIn

William E Thro, President
Cate K Smith, Executive Director
Patrick D Pauken, Vice President

Brings together educational and legal scholars and practitioners to inform and advance educational policy and practice through knowledge of the law. Together, our professional community anticipates trends in educational law and supports scholarly research through the highest value print and electronic publications, conferences, seminars and professional forums.
1400 Members
Founded in 1954

15452 **Equal Justice Works**
1730 M Street NW
Suite 1010
Washington, DC 20036-4511

202-466-3686
Fax: 202-429-9766
E-Mail: mail@equaljusticeworks.org
Home Page: www.equaljusticeworks.org
Social Media: Facebook, Twitter, LinkedIn, Youtube, Flickr

Laura Stein, Chair
David Stern, Executive Director
Jeanne Van Vlandren, Chief Operating Officer
David Simmons, Director of Fellowships
Sarah Snik, Program Manager, Fellowships

Founded by law students dedicated to surmounting barriers to equal justice that affect millions of low income individuals and families. Equal Justice organizes, trains and supports public service minded law students, and in creating summer and postgraduate public interest jobs.
Founded in 1986
Mailing list available for rent

15453 **Federal Bar Association**
1220 North Fillmore St.
Suite 444
Arlington, VA 22201ÿ

571-481-9100
Fax: 571-481-9090
E-Mail: fba@fedbar.org
Home Page: www.fedbar.org
Social Media: Facebook, Twitter, LinkedIn

Matthew B. Moreland, President
Mark K. Vincent, President Elect
Michael J. Newmanÿ, Treasurer
Karen Silberman, Executive Director
Heather Gaskins, Director of Development
Founded in 1920

15454 **Federal Circuit Bar Association**
1620 Eye St NW
Suite 801
Washington, DC 20006-4035

202-466-3923
Fax: 202-833-1061
Home Page: www.fedcirbar.org

James Brookshire, Executive Director
Linda Ingram, Office Coordinator
Oliver Hobbs, Administrative Coordinator
T. Andrew Hunter, Communications Coordinator
Jeremy Atkinson, Information Services Coordinator

FCBA is a national organization of attorneys who practice before the United States Court of Appeals for the Federal Circuit.
Mailing list available for rent

15455 **Federal Communications Bar Association**
1020 19th St NW
Suite 325
Washington, DC 20036-6101

202-293-4000
Fax: 202-293-4317
E-Mail: fcba@fcba.org
Home Page: www.fcba.org

Joseph M. Di Scipio, President
Stanley D. Zenor, Executive Director
Kerry Loughney, Director of Membership Services
Wendy Jo Parish, Administrative Assistant
Beth Phillips, Bookkeeper

A nonprofit organization of attorneys and other professionals involved in the development, interpretation, implementation and practice of communications law and policy.
3000 Members
Founded in 1936
Mailing list available for rent

15456 **Federal Mediation & Conciliation Service**

Home Page: www.fmcs.gov

15457 **Federation of Defense & Corporate Counsel**
11812 N 56th St
Tampa, FL 33617-1528

813-983-0022
Fax: 813-988-5837
E-Mail: mstreeper@thefederation.org
Home Page: www.thefederation.org

Edward M. Kaplan, Board Chair
Timothy A. Pratt, President
Martha J. Streeper, FDCC Executive Director
Michael W. Streeper, FDCC Financial Director
Susan J. Coone, Executive Administration

The objective and purposes of this Federation are to establish and maintain an organization consisting of members of the bar who are actively engaged in the legal aspects of the insurance business, executives of insurance companies an associations and corporate counsel engaged in the defense of claims; to assist in establishing standards for providing competent, efficient and economical legal services; to encourage and provide for legal education of the members of this Federation.
Founded in 1960

15458 First Amendment Lawyers Association
123 W. Madison St.
Suite 3100
Chicago, IL 60602
312-236-0606
Fax: 312-236-9264
E-Mail: wgiampietro@wpglawyers.com
Home Page: www.firstamendmentlawyers.org

Wayne Gianpetro, General Counsel
Lawyers concentrating on defending clients under the first amendment of the Constitution.
180 Members
Founded in 1972

15459 Hispanic National Bar Association
1900 L Street NW
Suite 700
Washington, DC 20036

202-223-4777
Fax: 202-223-2324
E-Mail: info@hnba.com
Home Page: www.hnba.com
Social Media: Facebook, Twitter, RSS

Miguel Alexander Pozo, President
Alba Cruz-Hacker, Chief Operating Officer & Executive
Jorge Barcelo, Treasurer
Rosevelie Marquez Morales, Secretary
Rafael Zahralddin, VP of External Affairs
Supports all Latino attorneys and legal professionals with publications and educational conferences.
25000 Members
Founded in 1972
Mailing list available for rent

15460 Institute of Management & Administration
3 Bethesda Metro Center
Suite 250
Bethesda, MD 20814-5377

703-341-3500
800-372-1033
Fax: 800-253-0332
E-Mail: customercare@bna.com
Home Page: www.ioma.com

An independent source of exclusive business management information for experienced senior and middle management professionals.

15461 Inter-American Bar Association
1211 Connecticut Ave NW
Suite #202
Washington, DC 20036-2712

202-466-5944
Fax: 202-466-5946
E-Mail: iaba@iaba.org
Home Page: www.iaba.org
Social Media: Facebook

Marianne Cordier, Manager
Rafael Veloz, President
The main purposes of this association are to establish and maintain relations among organizations of lawyers, national and local, in the Americas; to provide a forum for the exchange of views; to advance the science of jurisprudence particularly in the study of comparative law; to promote uniformity of the law; to disseminate knowledge of the laws; to promote the Rule of Law and the administration of justice; to preserve and defend human rights and liberties.
3M Members
Founded in 1940

15462 International Association of Defense Counsel
303 West Madison
Suite 925
Chicago, IL 60606-3401

312-368-1494
Fax: 312-368-1854
E-Mail: info@iadclaw.org
Home Page: www.iadclaw.org
Social Media: Facebook, Twitter, LinkedIn

Molly H. Craig, President
Mary Beth Kurzak, Executive Director
Amy O'Maley, Esq., Director, Professional Development
Carmela Balice, Senior Manager, Member Services
Cole Garrison, Manager, Membership
Offers continuing legal education and conducts research projects.
Cost: $650.00
2.5M Members
Founded in 1920

15463 International Bar Association
1667 K Street, NW
Suite 1230
Washington, DC 20006

202-827-3250
Fax: 202-733-5657
Home Page: www.ibanet.org
Social Media: Facebook, Twitter, LinkedIn, YouTube

David W Rivkin, President
Martin Solc, Vice President
Horacio Bernardes-Neto, Secretary-General
Mark Ellis, Executive Director
Ele Dexter, Executive Assistant
Founded in 1947

15464 International BarÿAssociation
1667 K Street, NW
Suite 1230
Washington, DC 20006

202-827-3250
Fax: 202-733-5657
Home Page: www.ibanet.org
Social Media: Facebook, Twitter, LinkedIn, YouTube

David W Rivkin, President
Martin Solc, Vice President
Horacio Bernardes-Neto, Secretary-General
Mark Ellis, Executive Director
Ele Dexter, Executive Assistant
Founded in 1947

15465 International Paralegal Management Association
980 N. Michigan Ave
Suite 1400
Chicago, IL 60611

312-214-4991
Fax: 888-662-9155
Home Page: www.paralegalmanagement.org
Social Media: Facebook, Twitter, LinkedIn

Victoria L.ÿ Snook, President
Marcia M. Bibb, President-Elect
Lynda S. McNie, Secretary-Treasurer
Brian J. Bernhard, Immediate Past President
Larry C. Smith, CAE, Executive Director
Founded in 1984

15466 International Probate Research Association
c/o Josh Butler & Company
PO Box 27
Cuyahoga Falls, OH 44222-0027

330-506-6400
E-Mail: inforequest@joshbutler.com
Home Page: www.lostheir.com/ipa.htm

Josh Butler, President
IPRA members are probate research companies.
Founded in 1989

15467 International Society of Barristers
University of Michigan Law School
802 Legal Research Building
Ann Arbor, MI 48109-1215

734-763-0165
Fax: 734-764-8309
E-Mail: reedj@umich.edu
Home Page: www.internationalsocietyofbarristers.com

John W Reed, Administrative Secretary
Members are trial lawyers interested in encouraging advocacy under the adversary system and preserving trial by jury.
750 Members
Founded in 1965

15468 Investigative Professionals, Inc.
PO Box 35
Hardyville, KY 42746
805-445-1997
Fax: 877-657-6691
Home Page: www.investigativeprofessionals.com
Social Media: Facebook, Twitter, Google+, Blogger

Larry Troxel
NALI was formed with its primary focus to conduct investigations related to litigation. Membership in NALI is open to all professional legal investigators who are actively engaged in negligence investigations for the plaintiff and/or criminal defense, and who are emplyoed by investigative firms, law firms or public defender agencies.
Mailing list available for rent

15469 Japanese American Society for Legal Studies
University of WA Law School-1100 NE Cam.
Seattle, WA 98105

206-233-9292
Fax: 206-685-4469

John Haley, Editor
Association for those interested in Japanese law and legal issues.

15470 Law and Society Association
423 Wakara Way
Suite 205
Salt Lake City, UT 84108
801-581-3219
Fax: 888-292-5515
E-Mail: lsa@lawandsociety.org
Home Page: www.lawandsociety.org
Social Media: Facebook, Twitter, LinkedIn

Carroll Seron, President
Valerie Hans, President Elect
Mario Barnes, Treasurer
Kaaryn Gustafson, Secretary
Susan Olson, Executive Director
Founded in 1964

15471 Legal Education and Admissions to the Bar Association
321 N Clark Street
21st Floor
Chicago, IL 60611-4403

312-988-5000
800-285-2221
Fax: 312-988-5681
Home Page: www.abanet.org/legaled/resources
Social Media: Facebook, Twitter

Barry Currier, Managing Director
Scott Norberg, Deputy Consultant
Camille deJorna, Associate Consultant
Carl A. Brambrink, Director of Operations
Beverly Holmes, Program Associate

Association for state bar admission administrators in the United States and its territories.
Founded in 1878
Mailing list available for rent

15472 Legal Marketing Association
330 North Wabash Ave.
Suite 2000
Chicago, IL 60611

312-321-6898
Fax: 312-673-6894
E-Mail: membersupport@legalmarketing.org
Home Page: www.legalmarketing.orgÿ
Social Media: Facebook, Twitter, LinkedIn, YouTube

Timothy B. Corcoran, President
Aleisha Gravit, Immediate Past Presidentÿ
Adam Severson, President-Elect
Mark Usellis, Treasurer
Betsi Roach, Executive Directorÿ
Founded in 1985

15473 Maritime Law Association of the United States
400 Poydras Street
27th Floor Texaco Center
New Orleans, LA 70130-324

504-680-8433
Fax: 904-421-8437
Home Page: www.mlaus.org

Robert B. Parrish, President
Robert G. Clyne, First VP
Harold K. Watson, Second VP
William Robert Connor III, Treasurer
David J. Farrell, Secretary

To advance reforms in the Maritime Law of the United States, to facilitate justice in its administration to promote uniformity in its enactment and interpretation, to furnish a forum for the discussion and consideration of problems affecting the Maritime Law and its administration to participate as a constituent member of the Comite Maritime International and as an affiliated organization of the American Bar Association.
Founded in 1899
Mailing list available for rent

15474 Mid-America Association of Law Libraries
E-Mail: jeri_hopkins@ca8.uscourts.gov
Home Page: www.aallnet.org/chapter/maall/

Jeri Kay Hopkins, President
Cynthia Bassett, Vice President/ President Elect
Rebecca Lutkenhaus, Secretary
Jenny Watson, Treasurer

Association for suppliers of law library equipment, supplies and services.
Founded in 1973

15475 NALS/The Association For Legal Professionals
8159 East 41st Street
#210
Tulsa, OK 74145

918-582-5188
Fax: 918-582-5907
E-Mail: info@nals.org
Home Page: www.nals.org
Social Media: Facebook, Twitter, LinkedIn, RSS, Youtube, Google+, Flickr

Doris T. Compton, PP, PLS, President
Tammy Hailey, CAE, Executive Director
April Collins, Meetings & Communications Manager
Saundra Bates, Membership Services Manager
Brynne Williamson, PP, PLS-SC, Secretary/Treasurer

Supports all those involved with the technology of the legal profession and the education and training of the legal administrative staff. Publishes quarterly magazine. NALS is dedicated to enhancing the competencies and contributions of members in the legal field.
Founded in 1929
Mailing list available for rent

15476 National Academy of Elder Law Attorneys
1577 Spring Hill Road
Suite 220
Vienna, VA 22182-2223

703-942-5711
Fax: 703-563-9504
E-Mail: naela@naela.org
Home Page: www.naela.org

Howard S. Krooks, CELA, CAP, President
Peter G Wacht, CAE, Executive Director
Shirley Berger Whitenack, Esq., Vice President
Ann Watkins, Operations Manager
Dannie Larkin, Meetings & Education Coordinator

Non-profit association for attorneys specializing in Elder Law and Special Needs Law.
4200 Members
Founded in 1987

15477 National American Indian Court Clerks Association
National Association of Tribal Court Personnel
920 Spring Creek Circle
Green Bay, WI 54311

E-Mail: RMJ143@compuserve.com

Robert Miller, President

Devoted to upgrading the integrity capabilities and management of tribal courts through training, testing and certification of court clerks and court administrators.
257 Members

15478 National American Indian Court Judges
3300 Arapahoe Avenue
Suite 203
Boulder, CO 80303

303-449-4112
Fax: 303-449-4038
E-Mail: info@naicja.org
Home Page: www.naicja.org
Social Media: Facebook, Youtube

Hon. Jill E. Tompkins, President
Richard Blake, First VP
Kevin Briscoe, Second VP
Winona Tanner, Treasurer
Catherine Bryan, Associate Director

National voluntary association of tribal court judges. Primarily devoted to the support of the American Indian and Alaska Native justice systems through education, information sharing and advocacy.
256 Members
Founded in 1969
Mailing list available for rent

15479 National Association for Community Mediation
611 South Palm Canyon Drive
STE 252
Palm Springs, CA 92264

602-633-4213
Fax: 202-545-8873
E-Mail: jordway@nafcm.org
Home Page: www.nafcm.org
Social Media: Facebook, Twitter, LinkedIn, Youtube, Blogger, Google+

Joanne Galindo, Senior Director
Matt Phillips, Executive Director
Malcolm D. White, Chairman
Karmit Bulman, Vice Chair
Daniel Kos, Treasurer

Supports the maintenance and growth of community-based mediation program and processes: presents a compelling voice in appropriate policy-making, legislative, professional, and other arenas; and encourages the development and sharing of resources for these efforts.
779 Members
Founded in 1994
Mailing list available for rent

15480 National Association for Court Management
300 Newport Avenue
Williamsburg, VA 23185-4147

757-259-1841
800-616-6165
Fax: 757-259-1520
E-Mail: nacm@ncsc.org
Home Page: www.nacmnet.org
Social Media: Facebook, Twitter, LinkedIn

David W. Slayton, President
Stephanie Hess, Vice President
Scott C. Griffith, Secretary/Treasurer

Members are clerks of court, court administration and others serving in a court management capacity.
2,500 Members
Founded in 1985
Mailing list available for rent

15481 National Association for Legal Career Professionals
1220 19th Street NW
Suite 401
Washington, DC 20036-2405

202-835-1001
Fax: 202-835-1112
E-Mail: info@nalp.org
Home Page: www.nalp.org
Social Media: Facebook, Twitter, LinkedIn, RSS

Stacey M. Kielbasa, President
Marilyn F. Drees, Vice-President for Member Services
Diane Downs, Vice-President for Finance
James G. Leipold, Executive Director
Frederick E. Thrasher, Deputy Director

Deals with issues such as career planning, recruiting and ethics.
Founded in 1971

15482 National Association of Attorneys General
2030 M Street Nw
8th Floor
Washington, DC 20036

202-326-6000
Fax: 202-331-1427
Home Page: www.naag.org

Attorney Genera Hollen, President
Attorney Genera Jackley, Vice President
Jim McPherson, Executive Director
Chris Toth, Deputy Executive Director
Scott Messing, Chief of Staff

Fosters interstate cooperation on legal and law enforcement issues, conducts policy research and analysis, provides advocacy.
56 Members
Founded in 1907
Mailing list available for rent: 56 names

15483 National Association of Black Criminal
1801 Fayetteville Street 106
Whiting Criminal Justice Building
Durham, NC 27707

919-683-1801
866-846-2225
Fax: 919-683-1903
E-Mail: office@nabcj.org

Home Page: www.nabcj.org
Social Media: Facebook, Twitter, RSS

Carlyle I. Holder, President
Andrea Carson, Vice President
Deborah Burwell, National Office Manager
Richard Gray, Director of Association Development
Margaret Harding, Chief Presidential Advisor

Supports all black persons who are involved in the criminal justice system. Hosts annual trade show.
Founded in 1974

15484 National Association of College and University Attorneys
One Dupont Circle
Suite 620
Washington, DC 20036-1134

202-833-8390
Fax: 202-296-8379
E-Mail: nacua@nacua.org
Home Page: www.nacua.org

Kathleen Curry, CEO
Jeanna L. Grimes, Manager of Membership and Marketing
John R. Bishop, Director of Information Services
Erica McKnight, Legal Resources Attorney
Paul L. Parsons, Deputy CEO

Educates attorneys and administrative executives about campus legal issues.
Mailing list available for rent

15485 National Association of Consumer Advocates
1215 17th Street NW
5th Floor
Washington, DC 20036

202-452-1989
Fax: 202-452-0099
E-Mail: info@consumeradvocates.org
Home Page: www.consumeradvocates.org
Social Media: Facebook, Twitter

Stuart Rossman, Co-Chair
Kirsten Keefe, Co-Chair
Daniel Blinn, Treasurer
Leslie Bailey, Secretary
Ira Rheingold, Executive Director

15486 National Association of Counsel for Children
13123 E. 16th Avenue
B390
Aurora, CO 80045

888-828-NACC
E-Mail: Advocate@NACCchildlaw.org
Home Page: www.naccchildlaw.org
Social Media: Facebook, LinkedIn, Blog

Kendall Marlowe, Executive Director
Andrew Yost, SeniorÿStaff Attorney
Brooke N. Silverthorn, Staff Attorney
Daniel Trujillo, Certification Director
Taylor Stockdell, Conference & Comm Director
Founded in 1977

15487 National Association of County Civil Attorneys
1100 17th St NW
Second Floor
Washington, DC 20036-4619

202-783-5550
Fax: 202-783-1583
E-Mail: info@naccho.org
Home Page: www.naccho.org
Social Media: Facebook, Twitter, LinkedIn, RSS, Blogger, Pinterest, Tumbl

Terrance Allan, RS, MPH, President
Swannie Jett, DrPHc, MSc, Vice President
Eli Briggs Director, Government Affairs
Paul Etkind, MPH, DrPH, Senior Director
Laura Hanen, Chief, Government & Public Affairs

An affiliate of the National Association of Counties.
240 Members
Founded in 1994
Mailing list available for rent

15488 National Association of Criminal Defense Lawyers
1660 L St NW
12th Floor
Washington, DC 20036-5632

202-872-8600
Fax: 202-872-8690
E-Mail: assist@nacdl.org
Home Page: www.nacdl.org
Social Media: Facebook, Twitter, LinkedIn, RSS, Blogger, Pinterest, Tumbl

Jerry J. Cox, President
Norman L. Reimer, Executive Director
Thomas Chambers, Deputy Executive Director
James Bergmann, Sales & Marketing Director
Ivan Dominguez, Director of Public Affairs

America's preeminent voluntary bar association supporting the Criminal Defense profession.
10000 Members
Founded in 1958

15489 National Association of Legal Assistants
1516 S. Boston
#200
Tulsa, OK 74119

918-587-6828
Fax: 918-582-6772
E-Mail: mdover@nala.org
Home Page: www.nala.orgÿ

Kelly A. LaGrave, ACP, President
Cassandra Oliver, ACP, First Vice President
Jill Francisco, ACP, Second Vice President
Debra L. Overstreet, ACP, Treasurer
Marge Dover, CAE, Executive Director

15490 National Association of Legal Investigator s
235 N. Pine Street
Lansing, MI 48933

517-702-9835
866-520-NALI
Fax: 517-372-1501
Home Page: www.nalionline.org
Social Media: Facebook, LinkedIn

David W. Luther, CLI, National Director
Don C. Johnson, CLI, CII, Assistant National Director
Neeta McClintock, National Secretary
Julian Vail, LLC, Association Management
John Hoda, CLI, Regional Director, Northeast Region
Founded in 1965

15491 National Association of Legal Vendors
Juris
5106 Maryland Way
Brentwood, TN 37027-7501

615-377-3740
Mel Goldenburg, Chairman

Trade association of organizations who sell products to the legal community.
100 Members

15492 National Association of Parliamentarians (NAP)
213 South Main Street
Independence, MO 64050-3808

816-833-3892
888-627-2929
Fax: 816-833-3893
E-Mail: hq@nap2.org
Home Page: www.parliamentarians.org
Social Media: Facebook, Twitter, RSS

Ann Guiberson, President
Mary Randolph, VP
Mike Chamberlain, MBA, CAE, Executive Director
Ann Rempel, NAP Secretary
Evan Lemoine, NAP Treasurer

An association for those interested in parliamentary law and procedure, NAP's primary objectives are teaching, promoting, and disseminating the philosophy and principles underlying the rules of deliberative assemblies.
3500 Members
Founded in 1930

15493 National Association of Women Lawyers
321 North Clark Street
Chicago, IL 60654

312-988-6186
Fax: 312-988-5100
E-Mail: nawl@nawl.org
Home Page: www.nawl.org

Doborah S. Froling, President
Marsha L. Anastasia, Vice President
Rena Calabrese, Executive Director
Lindsey Urban, Marketing and Sponsorship Director
Maureen Randolph, Membership Coordinator

Promotes the advancement and welfare of women in the legal profession. NAWL is a professional association of attorneys, judges and law students serving the educational, legal and practical interests of the organized bar and women generally. Founded in 1899, long before most local and national bar associations admitted women.
800 Members
Founded in 1899

15494 National Bar Association
1225 11th St Nw
Washington, DC 20001-4217

202-842-3900
Fax: 202-289-6170
E-Mail: headquarters@nationalbar.org
Home Page: www.nationalbar.org
Social Media: Facebook, Twitter, LinkedIn

Patricia Rosier, President
Taa Grays, Chief of Staff
Cassandra A. McClould, Deputy Chief of Staff
Robert R. Simpson, General Counsel
Catherine H. Costict, Deputy General Counsel

Represents the interests of minority attorneys, offers education and research programs.
18000 Members
Founded in 1925
Mailing list available for rent

15495 National Center for State Courts
300 Newport Ave
Williamsburg, VA 23185-4147

757-259-1819
800-616-6164
Fax: 757-220-0449
E-Mail: mmcqueen@ncsc.org
Home Page: www.ncsc.org
Social Media: Facebook, Twitter, LinkedIn, Google+, Flickr, Vimeo

Mary McQueen, President
Robert Baldwin, Executive Vice President
Jeffrey Apperson, Vice President, NCSC International
Thomas Clarke, Vice President, Research
Daniel Hall, Vice President of Court Consulting

Provides a forum for the state courts.
Founded in 1971
Mailing list available for rent

15496 National College of District Attorneys
99 Canal Center Plaza
Suite 330
Alexandria, VA 22314

703-549-9222
Fax: 703-836-3195
Home Page: www.ndaa.org
Social Media: Facebook, Yahoo

Scott Burns, Executive Director
Rick Hasey, Chief Financial Officer
Rick Hanes, Chief of Staff
Brent Berkley, Program Director
Candace Mosley, Director of Programs

Provides continuing legal education and training for prosecuting attorneys and their investigators and office administrators through programs specifically tailored to meet their needs. Programs include resident courses held each summer at the University of Houston Law Center, short courses conducted in locations throughout the country, and courses presented cooperatively with state associations and local offices.
Founded in 1950
Mailing list available for rent

15497 National Conference of Bar Examiners
302 South Bedford Street
Madison, WI 53703-3622

608-280-8550
Fax: 608-280-8552
E-Mail: contact@ncbex.org
Home Page: www.ncbex.org

Erica Moeser, President

A non-profit organization offering tests and services to state boards of bar examiners.
Founded in 1931

15498 National Conference of Bar Foundations
ABA Division For Bar Services
321 North Clark Street
Suite 2000
Chicago, IL 60654

312-988-5344
Fax: 312-988-5492
E-Mail: info@ncbf.org
Home Page: www.ncbf.org

Courtney Ward-Reichard, President
Roseanne T. Lucianek, Director, Division for Bar Services
Leonard Pataki, Treasurer
Lorrie Albert, Secretary

Serves bar foundations in the United States and Canada; conducts biannual conferences; maintains information clearinghouses.
Founded in 1977
Mailing list available for rent

15499 National Conference of Bar Presidents
321 North Clark Street
Suite 2000
Chicago, IL 60654-7598

312-988-5344
Fax: 312-988-5492
E-Mail: bware@staff.abanet.org
Home Page: www.ncbp.org
Social Media: Facebook

Carl D. Smallwood, President
Lanneau W. Lambert Jr., Treasurer
Jonathan J. Cole, Secretary

Provides a forum for the exchange of ideas and seeks to stimulate work in bar associations.
1M Members
Founded in 1950

15500 National Conference of Commissioners on US Law
211 E Ontario St
Suite 1300
Chicago, IL 60611-3242

312-283-5200
Fax: 312-915-0187
E-Mail: nccusl@nccusl.org
Home Page: www.nccusl.org

John A. Sebert, Executive Director
J. Elizabeth Cotton-Murphy, Chief Administrative Officer
Robert Stein, Secretary
Carl Lisman, Treasurer
Elizabeth Cotton, Manager

Designed to foster interstate cooperation in legal issues.
Founded in 1892
Mailing list available for rent

15501 National Conference of Women's Bar Associations
PO Box 82366
Portland, OR 97282

503-775-4396
E-Mail: info@ncwba.org
Home Page: www.ncwba.org
Social Media: Facebook, Twitter, LinkedIn

Andrea Carlise, President
Amanda Green Alexander, Vice President - Membership
Katherine L. Brown, Vice-President
Wendy E. Weigler, Vice-President-Finance
S. Diane Rynerson, Executive Director

To promote and assist the growth of local and statewide women's bar associations and ideas among women's bar associations and women's bar sections of local and statewide bar associations; to serve as a vehicle for the exchange and dissemination of information and ideas among women's bar associations and women's bar sections of local and statewide bar associations.

15502 National Conference of Womens' Bar Associations
PO Box 82366
Portland, OR 97282

503-775-4396
Fax: 503-657-3932
E-Mail: info@ncwba.org
Home Page: www.ncwba.org
Social Media: Facebook, Twitter, LinkedIn

Andrea Carlise, President
Amanda Green Alexander, Vice President - Membership
Katherine L. Brown, Vice-President
Wendy E. Weigler, Vice-President-Finance
S. Diane Rynerson, Executive Director

Supports women who are involved in the legal community and provides a forum for the exchange of ideas, thus stimulating work in bar associations.
30000 Members
Founded in 1981
Mailing list available for rent

15503 National Court Reporters Association
8224 Old Courthouse Rd
Vienna, VA 22182-3808

703-556-6272
800-272-6272
Fax: 703-556-6291
E-Mail: msic@ncra.org
Home Page: www.ncraonline.org
Social Media: Facebook, Twitter, LinkedIn, Youtube, RSS

Nancy Varallo, FAPR, RDR, CR, President
James M. Cudahy, CAE, Executive Director & CEO
Glyn Poage, FAPR, RDR, CRR, VP
Stephen A. Zinone, RPR, Secretary/Treasurer
Toni O'Neill, FAPR, RPR, Director
18000 Members
Founded in 1899

15504 National District Attorneys Association
99 Canal Center Plaza
Suite 330
Alexandria, VA 22314-1548

703-549-9222
Fax: 703-836-3195
Home Page: www.ndaa.org
Social Media: Facebook, Yahoo

Scott Burns, Executive Director
Rick Hasey, Chief Financial Officer
Rick Hanes, Chief of Staff
Brent Berkley, Program Director
Candace Mosley, Director of Programs

Supports district attorneys nationwide with education, publications, and regular conferences.
7000 Members
Founded in 1950

15505 National Federation of Paralegal Associations, Inc.
23607 Highway 99
Suite 2-C
Edmonds, WA 98026

425-967-0045
Fax: 425-771-9588
E-Mail: info@paralegals.org
Home Page: www.paralegals.org
Social Media: Facebook, LinkedIn

Robert Hrouda, President
Beth Bialis, Vice President
Lisa Vessels, CP, FRP, Vice President
Cindy Welch, RP, Vice President
Suellen Honeychuck, RP, Vice President

Nonprofit, professional organization comprising state and local paralegal associations throughout the United States and Canada. NFPA affirms the paralegal profession as an independent, self-directed profession which supports increased quality, efficiency and accessibility in the delivery of legal services. NFPA promotes the growth, development and recognition of the profession as a integral partner in the delivery of legal services.
15000 Members
Founded in 1974

15506 National Forensic Center
17 Temple Terrace
Lawrenceville, NJ 08648

609-883-0550
800-526-5177
E-Mail: jon@midi.com
Home Page: expertindex.com

Association for those interested in the application of scientific knowledge in litigation.

15507 National Institute for Trial Advocacy
1685 38th Street
Suite 200
Boulder, CO 80301-2735

800-225-6482
Fax: 720-890-7069
E-Mail: support@nita.org
Home Page: www.nita.org

Laurence Rose, President
Lonny Rose, CEO
Laurence M Rose, Executive Director
Shelly Goethals, Operations Manager
Paula Muhlherr, Owner
60 Members
Founded in 1971

15508 National Law Foundation
P. O. Box 218
Montchanin, DE 19710
302-656-4757
Fax: 302-764-8697
Home Page: www.nlfcle.com

15509 National Lawyers Association
3801 E. Florida Avenue
Suite 400
Denver, CO 80210
800-471-2994
Home Page: www.nla.org
Joshua McCaig, President
Paul Brodersen, Vice President
Lenny A. Best, CEO
Jeremiah Morgan, Board Member
Cynthia Dunbar, Board Member

15510 National Lawyers Guild
132 Nassau St
Room 922
New York, NY 10038-2486
212-679-5100
Fax: 212-679-2811
E-Mail: nlgno@nlg.org
Home Page: www.nlg.org
Social Media: Facebook, Twitter
Azadeh Shahshahani, President
Heidi Boghosian, Executive Director
Natasha Bannan, Executive Vice President

Bina Ahmad, National Vice President
Camilo Romero, National Vice President

Dedicated to seeking economic justice, social equality and the right to political dissent.
5000 Members
Founded in 1937
Mailing list available for rent

15511 National Legal Aid and Defender Associatio n
1140 Connecticut Ave NW
Suite 900
Washington, DC 20036-4019
202-452-0620
Fax: 202-872-1031
E-Mail: info@nlada.org
Home Page: www.nlada100years.org
Lillian Johnson, Chairperson
Jo-Ann Wallace, President & CEO
Edwin Burnette, Vice President
Julie Clark, Vice President, Strategic Alliances
Don Saunders, Vice President, Civil Legal Service
Private, nonprofit association that dedicates all its resources to ensuring the availability of high quality legal assistance for the poor.
3500 Members
Founded in 1911
Mailing list available for rent

15512 National Notary Association
9350 De Soto Avenue
Chatsworth, CA 91311-4926
818-739-4000
800-876-6827
Fax: 818-700-1942
E-Mail: hotline@nationalnotary.org
Home Page: www.nationalnotary.org
Social Media: Facebook, Twitter, LinkedIn
Milton G Valera, Chairman
Thomas A. Heymann, President And CEO
Deborah M Thaw, Executive VP
Ellen J. Nichols, Vice President of Human Resources
William A. Anderson, Vice President, Legislative Affairs
Supports all those involved in identity fraud and electronic notarization. Publishes newlsetter.
200M Members
Founded in 1957

15513 National Organizations of Bar Counsel
515 Fifth Street, NW
Building A, Room 127
Washington, DC 20001
202-454-1744
E-Mail: BloomL@dcobc.org
Home Page: www.nobc.org
Lawrence K. Bloom, D.C., President
Paul J. Burgoyne, Treasurer
William D. Slease, Secretary
NOBC is a non-proft of legal professionals whose members enforce ethics rules that regulate the professional conduct of lawyers who practice in the U.S., Canada and Australia. Via the website, locate your local member office for information.
Founded in 1965

15514 National Paralegal Association
23607 Highway 99
Suite 2-C
Edmonds, WA 98026
425-967-0045
Fax: 425-771-9588
E-Mail: info@paralegals.org
Home Page: www.paralegals.org
Social Media: Facebook, LinkedIn
Lisa Vessels, RP, CP, FRP, President
Beth Bialis, RP, VP, Dir. of Profession Dev.
Lynne Marie Reveliotis, VP & Director of Positions
Cindy Welch, RP, VP, Director of Membership
Nita Serrano, RP, VP, Dir. of Paralegal Certification
Founded in 1974

15515 Native American Rights Fund
1506 Broadway St
Boulder, CO 80302-6296
303-447-8760
Fax: 303-443-7776
E-Mail: webmaster@narf.org
Home Page: www.narf.org
Social Media: Facebook
Gerald L. Danforth, Chairman
John E Echohawk, Executive Director
Michael Kennedy, Chief Financial Officer
Morgan O'Brien, Director of Development
Melody McCoy, Litigation Management Committee
National legal defense fund. Provides legal services and technical assistance to Indian tribes, organizations and individuals in the areas of preservation of tribal existence, protection of tribal natural resources, promotion of human rights, accountability of governments and development of Indian law.
35000 Members
Founded in 1971
Mailing list available for rent

15516 People Against Racist Terror
Po Box 1055
Culver City, CA 90232
310-495-0299
Fax: 818-848-2680
E-Mail: la@antiracistaction.org
Home Page: www.prisonactivist.org/resources/anti-racist-action-lapart-people
Michael Novick, Publisher
Association for those interested in anti-racist activism, research and education covering neo-nazi and other racist violence, efforts at conflict resolution and social justic reforms.

15517 Practising Law Institute
1177 Avenue of the Americas
2nd Floor
New York, NY 10036
212-824-5700
800-260-4754
Fax: 212-581-4670
E-Mail: info@pli.edu
Home Page: www.pli.edu
Social Media: Facebook, Twitter, LinkedIn, RSS
Victor J Rubino, President
Sandra R. Geller, Executive Vice President
William C. Cubberley, Vice President of Publishing
Anita C. Shapiro, Vice President of Programs
Donald F. Berbary, Chief Sales & Marketing Officer
Nonprofit continuing legal education organization chartered by the Regents of the University of the State of New York. Dedicated to providing the legal community and allied professionals with the most up-to-date, revelant information and techniques which are critical to the development of a professional, competitive edge.
Founded in 1933
Mailing list available for rent

15518 RAND Institute for Civil Justice
1776 Main Street
Santa Monica, CA 90407-3208
310-393-0411
Fax: 310-393-4898
E-Mail: zakaras@rand.org
Home Page: www.rand.org/icj
Social Media: Facebook, Twitter
Michael D Rich, President
Richard Fallon, Senior Vice President
Andrew R Hoehn, Senior Vice President
Allison Elder, Vice President, Human Resources
Patrick Horrigan, Vice President, Office of Services
Nonprofit research organization within the RAND Corporation dedicated to interdisciplinary, empirical research to facilitate change in the civil justice system.

15519 Rocky Mountain Mineral Law Foundation
9191 Sheridan Blvd
Suite 203
Westminster, CO 80031-3011
303-321-8100
Fax: 303-321-7657
E-Mail: info@rmmlf.org
Home Page: www.rmmlf.org
Social Media: Facebook, Twitter, LinkedIn
David Phillips, Executive Director
Mark Holland, Associate Director
Catherine J. Boggs, President

Robert B. Keiter, Vice President
Gregory R. Danielson, Secretary
2000 Members
Founded in 1955
Mailing list available for rent

15520 The International Association for Conflict Management
Home Page: www.iacm-conflict.orgў

15521 The Sports Lawyers Association
12100 Sunset Hills Road
Suite 130
Reston, VA 20190

703-437-4377
Fax: 703-435-4390
E-Mail: sla@sportslaw.org
Home Page: www.sportslaw.org
Social Media: Facebook, Twitter, LinkedIn

Glenn M. Wong, President
Matthew J. Mitten, President Elect
Ash Narayan, Treasurer
Vered Yakovee, Secretary
Gabe Feldman, Director of Publications

15522 Trial Lawyers Marketing
1 Boston Place
Suite 1260
Boston, MA 02108-4471

617-720-5356
Fax: 617-742-5417

James Sokolve, President

Provides education and marketing information to personal injury attorneys.
300 Members
Founded in 1986

Newsletters

15523 ABA Child Law Practice
ABA Center on Children and the Law
740 15th Street, NW
Washington, DC 20005

202-662-1000
800-285-2221
Fax: 202-662-1755
E-Mail: teaguec@staff.abanet.org
Home Page: www.abanet.org
Social Media: Facebook, Twitter

Laurel Bellows, President
Jack L. Rives, Executive Director
Robert M. Carlson, Chairman
Lucian T. Pera, Treasurer
Cara Lee T. Neville, Secretary

An online periodical for lawyers who advocate for children and youth, judges handling child protection-related cases, and other professionals who want to keep abreast of cutting edge legal issues affecting children. Includes litigation strategies, analyses of new laws, policies and research, and how they apply to practice, expert interviews, advice from judges, and more.
Cost: $50.00
Frequency: Online
Founded in 1878
Mailing list available for rent

15524 ABA Washington Letter
American Bar Association Government Affairs Office
321 N Clark St
Chicago, IL 60654-7598

312-988-5000
800-285-2221
Fax: 202-662-1762
E-Mail: mcmillionr@staff.abanet.org
Home Page: www.abanet.org/poladv/home.html
Social Media: Facebook, Twitter

Thomas M. Susman, Director, GAO
Denise A. Cardman, Deputy Director
Jared D. Hess, Legislative Coordinator
Laurel Bellows, President
Jack L. Rives, Executive Director

A monthly publication produced by the GAO to report and analyze congressional and executive branch action on legislation issues of interest to the ABA and the legal profession, highlighting ABA involvment in the federal legislative process.
Cost: $30.00
Frequency: Monthly
Founded in 1957
Mailing list available for rent

15525 ACC Docket
American Corporate Counsel Association
1025 Connecticut Ave Nw
Suite 200
Washington, DC 20036-5425

202-293- 410
Fax: 202-293-4701
E-Mail: acc.chair@acc.com
Home Page: www.acc.com

Tiffani Alexander, Managing Editor
Ken Lawrence, Director Publishing
Fred Krebs, President/CEO
Moustafa W. Abdel-Kader, Marketing Manager
David Barre, Director Communications
Frequency: Monthly
Mailing list available for rent

15526 ALA News
Association of Legal Administrators
75 Tri-State International
Suite 222
Lincolnshire, IL 60069-4435

847-267-1252
Fax: 847-267-1329
E-Mail: publications@alanet.org
Home Page: www.alanet.org

Larry Smith, Executive Director
Debbie Thomas, Director, Accounting & Finance
Renee Mahovsky, Director, Administration/Operations
Bob Abramson, Director, Marketing & Communication
Jan Waugh, Director, Member Services

Member magazine focusing on association news and career improvements for administrators in the association.
Cost: $36.00
40 Pages
Circulation: 9000
Founded in 1971
Mailing list available for rent
Printed in 4 colors on glossy stock

15527 ATLA Advocate
Association of Trial Lawyers of America
1050 31st Street NW
Washington, DC 20007

202-965-3500
800-424-2725
Home Page: www.atla.org

Kathleen Flynn Peterson, President
Linda Lipsen, Chief Executive Officer
Charles Jeffress, Chief Operating Officer
Kathi Berge, Chief Financial Officer
Anjali Jesseramsing, Executive Vice President

Keeps association members abreast of association news. Not available by subscription. No advertising or announcements.
Cost: $5.00
Frequency: Monthly
Mailing list available for rent
Printed in 2 colors

15528 Administrative & Regulatory Law News
American Bar Association-Administrative/Regulatory
740 15th St NW
11th Floor
Washington, DC 20005-1022

202-662-1000
800-285-2221
Fax: 202-662-1592
E-Mail: knightk@staff.abanet.org
Home Page: www.abanet.org
Social Media: Facebook, Twitter

Laurel Bellows, President
Jack L. Rives, Executive Director
Robert M. Carlson, Chairman
Lucian T. Pera, Treasurer
Cara Lee T. Neville, Secretary

Newsletter for Section members providing information about recent developments affecting clients and practices with features such as Supreme Court News, News From the Circuits, and more.
16 Pages
Frequency: Quarterly
Circulation: 6000
Founded in 1878
Mailing list available for rent

15529 Admiralty Law Newsletter
American Bar Association - TIPS Admiralty/Maritime
321 N Clark St
Chicago, IL 60654-7598

312-988-5000
800-285-2221
Fax: 312-988-5280
E-Mail: askaba@abanet.org
Home Page: www.abanet.org
Social Media: Facebook, Twitter

Laurel Bellows, President
Jack L. Rives, Executive Director
Robert M. Carlson, Chairman
Lucian T. Pera, Treasurer
Cara Lee T. Neville, Secretary

Focuses on summaries of recent case law development, CLE programs in maritime law area, and information and articles on programs and projects.
Frequency: Quarterly
Founded in 1878
Mailing list available for rent

15530 Allen's Trademark Digest
Congressional Digest Corporation
152413 29th Street NW
Washington, DC 20007-2756

202-333-7332
800-637-9915
Fax: 202-625-6670
E-Mail: ededitor@aol.com
Home Page: www.trademarkdigest.com

Griff Thomas, President
Page Robinson, Publisher
Brooke Beyer, Editor

Monthly digest of citable and uncitable tradmark decisions issues by the US Patent and Trademark Office.
Cost: $695.00
Frequency: 12 per year
ISSN: 8990-191X
Founded in 1989

15531 American Association of Visually Impaired Attorneys
American Blind Lawyers Association
c/o American Council of the Blind
2220 Wilson Blvd, Suite 650
Arlingtonn, VA 22201

202-467-5081
800-424-8666

Fax: 703-465-5085
E-Mail: info@acb.org
Home Page: www.acb.org

Melanie Brunson, Executive Director
12000 Members
Frequency: Audio
Circulation: 150
Founded in 1961

15532 **American Corporate Counsel Association Newsletter**
Americna Corporate Counsel Association
1025 Connecticut Ave NW
Suite 200
Washington, DC 20036-5425

202-293-8439
Fax: 202-331-7454
Home Page: http://www.acc.com

Deneen Stambone, Editor

Association news.
16 Pages
Frequency: Bi-Monthly
Circulation: 9,700
Printed in 2 colors on matte stock

15533 **American Foreign Law Association Newsletter**
Forman Law School
140 W 62nd Street
New York, NY 10023

212-636-6844
Fax: 212-636-6899

James Maxelner, Publisher

Reports on programs sponsored by the Association of American Foreign Law.
Cost: $20.00
4 Pages
Frequency: Monthly

15534 **American Lawyers Newspapers Group**
American Lawyers Newspapers
1730 M St Nw
Suite 802
Washington, DC 20036-4550

202-296-1995
Fax: 202-457-0718

Ted Goldman, Manager

Supports all those involved in the reporting of legal issues.
Founded in 1977

15535 **American Notary**
American Society of Notaries
PO Box 5707
Tallahassee, FL 32314

850-671-5164
800-522-3392
Fax: 850-671-5165
Home Page: www.notaries.org

Lisa K Fisher, Publisher
Joanna Lilly, Executive Director
Kathleen Butler, Executive Director

Legislation news.
Cost: $21.00
20 Pages
Frequency: Quarterly
Circulation: 21000
Printed in 4 colors on glossy stock

15536 **American Society of International Law Newsletter**
American Society of International Law
2223 Massachusetts Ave Nw
Washington, DC 20008-2864

202-939-6000
Fax: 202-797-7133
Home Page: http://www.asil.org

Charlotte Ku, Executive Director

Association news and updates on overseas litigation.
6 Pages
Frequency: Monthly

15537 **Antitrust and Trade Regulation Report**
Bureau of National Affairs
1801 S Bell St
Arlington, VA 22202-4501

703-341-3000
800-372-1033
Fax: 800-253-0332
E-Mail: customercare@bna.com
Home Page: www.bnabooks.com
Social Media: Facebook, Twitter, LinkedIn

Paul N Wojcik, Chairman
Gregory C. McCaffery, President and CEO
John Camp, Vice President and Chief Technology
Lisa A. Fitzpatrick, Vice President
Audrey Hipkins, Vice President

Weekly comprehensive coverage of significant competition and deceptive trade practice law developments on the federal, state and international levels.
Cost: $1894.00
Frequency: Weekly

15538 **Attorneys Marketing Report**
James Publishing
3505 Cadillac Avenue
Suite H
Costa Mesa, CA 92626

714-755-5450
800-440-4780
Fax: 714-751-2709
E-Mail: customer-service@jamespublishing.com
Home Page: www.jamespublishing.com

Jim Pawell, Founder/President
Linda Standke, Editor

The latest practice development tips and news for law firms from Yellow Pages advertising to referral management.
Founded in 1981
Mailing list available for rent

15539 **BNA's Bankruptcy Law Reporter**
Bureau of National Affairs
1801 S Bell St
Arlington, VA 22202-4501

703-341-3000
800-372-1033
Fax: 800-253-0332
E-Mail: customercare@bna.com
Home Page: www.bnabooks.com
Social Media: Facebook, Twitter, LinkedIn

Paul N Wojcik, Chairman
Gregory C. McCaffery, President and CEO
John Camp, Vice President and Chief Technology
Lisa A. Fitzpatrick, Vice President
Audrey Hipkins, Vice President

Weekly notification service covering various areas of bankruptcy law.
Cost: $1331.00
Frequency: Weekly

15540 **BNA's Corporate Counsel Weekly Corporate Practice Series**
Bureau of National Affairs
1801 S Bell St
Arlington, VA 22202-4501

703-341-3000
800-372-1033
Fax: 800-253-0332
E-Mail: customercare@bna.com
Home Page: www.bnabooks.com
Social Media: Facebook, Twitter, LinkedIn

Paul N Wojcik, Chairman
Gregory C. McCaffery, President and CEO
John Camp, Vice President and Chief Technology
Lisa A. Fitzpatrick, Vice President
Audrey Hipkins, Vice President

A weekly roundup of the latest developments in law that affect business, including coverage of the courts, federal regulatory agencies, the executive branch, states and professional associations.
Cost: $722.00
8 Pages
Frequency: Weekly
Printed in one color on matte stock

15541 **BNA's Medicare Report**
Bureau of National Affairs
1801 S Bell St
Arlington, VA 22202-4501

703-341-3000
800-372-1033
Fax: 800-253-0332
E-Mail: customercare@bna.com
Home Page: www.bnabooks.com
Social Media: Facebook, Twitter, LinkedIn

Paul N Wojcik, Chairman
Gregory C. McCaffery, President and CEO
John Camp, Vice President and Chief Technology
Lisa A. Fitzpatrick, Vice President
Audrey Hipkins, Vice President

Biweekly notification service covering legislative, regulatory and legal developments affecting or pertaining to the Medicare program; also provides information about relevant developments in the Medicaid program that could have implications for Medicare.
Cost: $1108.00
Frequency: Weekly

15542 **Bankruptcy Court Decisions**
LRP Publications
PO Box 980
Horsham, PA 19044-0980

215-784-0912
800-341-7874
Fax: 215-784-9639
E-Mail: webmaster@lrp.com
Home Page: www.lrp.com

Todd Lutz, CFO
Kenneth Khan, CEO

Full-text loose leaf bankruptcy reporting service with an expanded and informative newsletter.
Cost: $900.00
Founded in 1977
Mailing list available for rent
Printed in one color on matte stock

15543 **Bankruptcy Law Letter**
Thomson West Publishing
610 Opperman Dr
Eagan, MN 55123-1340

651-687-7000
800-344-5008
Fax: 651-687-5581
Home Page: www.west.thomson.com
Social Media: Facebook, Twitter, LinkedIn, Blogger, Pinterest, Tumblr, St

Charles B Cater, Executive VP
Laurie Zenner, VP

Highly specialized coverage of case developments in the bankruptcy field. No outside submissions accepted.
Cost: $621.00
Frequency: Monthly
Circulation: 3000

15544 Biotechnology Law Report
Mary Ann Liebert
2 Madison Ave
Larchmont, NY 10538-1947

914-834-4348
800-6 5-3 23
Fax: 914-834-3688
E-Mail: info@liebertpub.com
Home Page: www.liebertpub.com/

Mary Ann Liebert, President
Gerry J Elman, Editor
Harry Matisco, Marketing

Legislative news for the world of biotechnology and science.
Cost: $1858.00
96 Pages
ISSN: 0730-031X
Founded in 1980

15545 Business Crime: Criminal Liability of the Business Community
Matthew Bender and Company
11 Penn Plz
Suite 5101
New York, NY 10001-2006

212-000-1111
Fax: 212-244-3188

Eric Blood, Data Processing

The most complete guide to the many criminal questions that can arise in modern business practice.

15546 Business Information Alert
Alert Publications
401 W Fullerton Parkway
Suite 1403E
Chicago, IL 60614-2801

773-525-7594
866-492-5266
Fax: 773-525-7015
E-Mail: info@alertpub.com
Home Page: www.alertpub.com/

Donna T Heroy, Publisher/Editor
Nina Wendt, Director Marketing

Newsletter for business and law librarians to help them make purchasing decisions for their companies. Includes product reviews and columns on industry news. Discounted price of $99 for non-profit organizations.
Cost: $167.00
12 Pages
ISSN: 1042-0746
Founded in 1981

15547 CLE Guidebook
Law Bulletin Publishing Company
415 N State St
Suite 1
Chicago, IL 60654-8116

312-644-7800
Fax: 312-644-4255
Home Page: www.lawbulletin.com

Lanning Macfarland Jr, President
Bernard M Judge, Publisher
Michael Loquercio, Sales Manager

Lists hundreds of CLE courses by date, subject and provider.
Cost: $219.00
34 Pages
Printed in 4 colors on matte stock

15548 Chapter 11 Update
Federal Managers Association
1641 Prince St
Alexandria, VA 22314-2818

703-683-8700
Fax: 703-683-8707
E-Mail: info@fedmanagers.org
Home Page: www.fedmanagers.org

Todd Wells, Executive Director
George J. Smith, National VP
Patricia J. Niehaus, National President
Richard J. Oppedisano, National Secretary
Katie L. Smith, National Treasurer

Management issues and concerns.
Frequency: Monthly
Mailing list available for rent

15549 Civil RICO Report
LRP Publications
PO Box 24668
West Palm Beach, FL 33416-4668

561-622-6520
800-341-7874
Fax: 561-622-0757
E-Mail: webmaster@lrp.com
Home Page: www.lrp.com

Kenneth Kahn, President
Robert K Latzko, Editor

Weekly report and analysis of litigation under the civil provisions of the Racketeer Influenced and Corrupt Organizations Act as well as legislative developments and state little RICO laws.
Cost: $812.00
Printed in 2 colors on matte stock

15550 Client Counseling Update
American Bar Association
321 N Clark St
Chicago, IL 60654-7598

312-988-5000
800-285-2221
Fax: 312-988-5280
E-Mail: askaba@abanet.org
Home Page: www.abanet.org
Social Media: Facebook, Twitter

Laurel Bellows, President
Jack L. Rives, Executive Director
Robert M. Carlson, Chairman
Richard J. Oppe Pera, Treasurer
Cara Lee T. Neville, Secretary

e-Newsletter contains summaries of publications and news articles concerning client counseling.
Founded in 1878
Mailing list available for rent

15551 Collective Bargaining Negotiations and Contracts
Bureau of National Affairs
1801 S Bell St
Arlington, VA 22202-4501

703-341-3000
800-372-1033
Fax: 800-253-0332
E-Mail: customercare@bna.com
Home Page: www.bnabooks.com
Social Media: Facebook, Twitter, LinkedIn

Paul N Wojcik, Chairman
Gregory C. McCaffery, President and CEO
John Camp, Vice President and Chief Technology
Lisa A. Fitzpatrick, Vice President
Audrey Hipkins, Vice President

A biweekly notificaiton and reference service containing information designed to help unions and management prepare, negotiate and administer contracts.
Cost: $1541.00
Frequency: Monthly
Founded in 1929

15552 Commercial Law Bulletin
Commercial Law League of America
205 N. Michigan
Suite 2212
Chicago, IL 60601-5961

312-240-1400
800-978-2552
Fax: 312-240-1408
E-Mail: info@clla.org
Home Page: www.clla.org

Oliver Yandle, VP
Charles R Johnson III, Treasurer

Provides news and information on bankruptcy, collections, debt and insolvency information, as well as reports from Washington DC and updates on resolutions.
Cost: $65.00
Circulation: 5000
Founded in 1895

15553 Commercial Laws of the World
Foreign Tax Law
PO Box 2189
Ormond Beach, FL 32175-2189

386-341-7405
Home Page: www.foreignlaw.com

Contains company laws, commercial codes, and related law for over 100 countries.
Cost: $100.00

15554 Communications Lawyer
American Bar Association Forum - Communication Law
321 N Clark St
Chicago, IL 60654-7598

312-988-5000
800-285-2221
Fax: 312-988-5280
E-Mail: askaba@abanet.org
Home Page: www.abanet.org
Social Media: Facebook, Twitter

Laurel Bellows, President
Jack L. Rives, Executive Director
Robert M. Carlson, Chairman
Lucian T. Pera, Treasurer
Cara Lee T. Neville, Secretary

Newsletter reviews significant activities and developments in communications law and reports on Forum activities.
Cost: $45.00
30 Pages
Frequency: Quarterly
ISSN: 0737-7622
Founded in 1878
Mailing list available for rent

15555 Computer & Internet LAWCAST
Vox Juris
PO Box 389
Pennington, NJ 08534

609-737-6543
800-LAW-CAST
Fax: 609-737-3860
E-Mail: INFO@lawcast.com
Home Page: www.lawcast.com

Jason Meyer, Publisher

Groundbreaking law arising from life and commerce in the digital age...in licensing, torts, intellectual property securities, contracts, privacy, joint ventures, antitrust, content regulation and more. If your clients use email or the internet, have their own websites, produce hardware or software or provide on-line service, listen up here. 60 minute audio and outline twice monthly
Cost: $25.00

15556 Computer Industry Litigation Reporter
Andrews Publications

175 Strafford Avenue
Building 4 Suite 140
Wayne, PA 19087
610-225-0510
800-345-1101
Fax: 610-225-0501
Home Page: www.andrewspub.com
Donna Higgins, Editor
Mary Ellen Fox, Publisher
Jodine Mayberry, Executive Editor
Covers litigation involving copyright, patent, trade secrets, employment, securities, trademark, contracts and other issues related to the computer industry.
Cost: $1226.00
Founded in 1983

15557 **Construction Claims Monthly**
Business Publishers
2222 Sedwick Dr
Suite 101
Durham, NC 27713
800-223-8720
Fax: 800-508-2592
E-Mail: custserv@bpinews.com
Home Page: www.bpinews.com
Contains summaries of important decisions from the federal and state courts, boards of contract appeals, and the Office of Comptroller General on such topics as change orders, design problems, inspection, delay, home office overhead, claims administration, termination, waivers, differing site conditions, subcontractors and insurance.
Cost: $244.00
8 Pages
Frequency: Monthly
Founded in 1962

15558 **Construction Litigation Reporter**
McGraw Hill
1221 Avenue of the Americas
New York, NY 10020-1095
212-512-2000
800-352-3566
Fax: 212-512-3840
E-Mail: webmaster@mcgraw-hill.com
Home Page: www.mcgraw-hill.com
Harold W McGraw III, CEO
Summaries of judicial and agency decisions.
Cost: $300.00
24 Pages
Frequency: Monthly

15559 **Consumer Financial Services Law Report**
LRP Publications
PO Box 980
Horsham, PA 19044-0980
215-784-0912
800-341-7874
Fax: 215-784-9639
E-Mail: webmaster@lrp.com
Home Page: www.lrp.com
Todd Lutz, CFO
Kenneth Kahn, President
Keeps you up-to-date with the latest changes and developments in the area of consumer financial services litigation. Provides timely coverage of legal developments involving fair lending, debt collection, state UDAP laws and fraud, automobile lending and leasing, damage theories and class actions, and more.
Cost: $220.00
Founded in 1977

15560 **Consumer Product Litigation Reporter**
Andrews Publications
175 Strafford Avenue
Building 4, Suite 140
Wayne, PA 19087-3331
610-225-0510
800-345-1101
Fax: 610-225-0501
Home Page: www.andrewspub.com
Robert Maroldo, Publisher
Eileen Gonyeau, Editor
Covers areas such as strict liability, assumption of risk, insurance coverage, adequacy of warning merchantability, punitive damages, component liability, forseeability and more.
Cost: $46.00

15561 **Controlling Law Firm Costs**
Institute of Management and Administration
1 Washington Park
Suite 1300
Newark, NJ 07102-3130
212-244-0360
Fax: 973-622-0595
E-Mail: customercare@bna.com
Home Page: www.ioma.com
Laurel Bellows, President
Shows law office administrators how to reduce overhead, improve the firm's profitability and efficiency, get more value for the firm's budget dollar, and improve their own professional standing. Includes strategies to control the costs of support staff, insurance, leases, taxes, computers and more.
Cost: $300.00
Frequency: Annual+

15562 **Corporate Counsel LAWCAST**
Vox Juris
PO Box 389
Pennington, NJ 08534
609-737-6543
800-LAW-CAST
Fax: 609-737-3860
E-Mail: INFO@lawcast.com
Home Page: www.lawcast.com
Jason Meyer, Publisher
Everything for the in house counsel in one lively and substantive program. In-house ethics and privileges, the law of the workplace, intellectual property, corporate governance, contracts, regulations, and more...close-ups on how top counsel meet the demands of the in-house practice. 75 minute audio and online, 15 times per year
Cost: $25.00

15563 **Corporate Legal Times**
Corporate Legal Times
656 West Randolph Street
Suite 500 East
Chicago, IL 60611
312-654-3500
Fax: 312-654-3525
Home Page: www.cltmag.com
Nat Slavin, Publisher
Larry Lannon, CEO
Written for general counsel and other in house corporate attorneys to provide information relevant to strategic planning and day-to-day operation of legal departments including in-house counsel's relationships with outside law firms.
Cost: $10.00
Frequency: Monthly
Circulation: 40000
Founded in 1991

15564 **Corporate Practice Series**
Bureau of National Affairs
1801 S Bell St
Arlington, VA 22202-4501
703-341-3000
800-372-1033
Fax: 800-253-0332
E-Mail: customercare@bna.com
Home Page: www.bnabooks.com
Social Media: Facebook, Twitter, LinkedIn
Paul N Wojcik, Chairman
Gregory C. McCaffery, President and CEO
John Camp, Vice President and Chief Technology
Lisa A. Fitzpatrick, Vice President
Audrey Hipkins, Vice President
A corporate law reference service organized into a series of portfolios written by legal experts, with a weekly newsletter. Each portfolio covers a different legal subject with detailed analyses, working papers and a bibliography.
Cost: $2426.00
ISSN: 0162-5691

15565 **Criminal Law Reporter**
Bureau of National Affairs
1801 S Bell St
Arlington, VA 22202-4501
703-341-3000
800-372-1033
Fax: 800-253-0332
E-Mail: customercare@bna.com
Home Page: www.bnabooks.com
Social Media: Facebook, Twitter, LinkedIn
Paul N Wojcik, Chairman
Gregory C. McCaffery, President and CEO
John Camp, Vice President and Chief Technology
Lisa A. Fitzpatrick, Vice President
Audrey Hipkins, VP
A weekly notification service providing coverage of court decisions, federal legislative activities and administrative developments in the field of criminal law. Fulltext of the cases highlighted in each issue are available free on CrL's web site. Subscribers can also recieve free email notification of Supreme Court decisions.
Cost: $1108.00
Frequency: Weekly
Founded in 1929

15566 **DataLaw Report**
Clark Boardman Company
155 Pflingsten Road
Deerfield, IL 60015
847-374-0400
Fax: 847-948-7099
Amelia Boss, Editor
Analyzes the changing global legal environment for electronic information.

15567 **Death Care Business Advisor**
LRP Publications
747 Dresher Road
PO Box 980
Horsham, PA 19044-980
215-784-0912
800-341-7874
Fax: 215-784-9639
E-Mail: webmaster@lrp.com
Home Page: www.lrp.com
Jay Kravetz, Editor
Dionne Ellis, Managing Editor
The only twice a month newsletter that offers you in-depth business coverage of memorialization and remembrance issues. You'll recieve news and tips on the latest trends and developments in funeral service, cemetery management and cremation and learn innovative strategies to capture the expanding preneed market and more.
Cost: $215.00
Founded in 1977

15568 Digest of Environmental Law
Strafford Publications
PO Box 13729
Atlanta, GA 30324-0729

404-881-1141
800-926-7926
Fax: 404-881-0074
E-Mail: customerservice@straffordpub.com
Home Page: www.straffordpub.com

Richard Ossoff, President
Jennifer Vaughan, Managing Editor

Monthly digest of nationally significant litigation related to the full range of environmental issues, includes annual index.
Cost: $547.00
Frequency: Monthly
ISSN: 1073-9521
Founded in 1984

15569 Disability Compliance for Higher Education
LRP Publications
747 Dresher Road
PO Box 980
Horsham, PA 19044-980

215-784-0912
800-341-7874
Fax: 561-622-2423
E-Mail: webmaster@lrp.com
Home Page: www.lrp.com

Marsha Jaquays, Editor
Nancy Grover, Managing Editor

Helps colleges determine if they are complying with the Americans with Disabilities Act (ADA) and section 504 of the Rehabilitation Act. Readers find out how to fulfill legal obligations under the law and save their college from costly litigation.
Cost: $198.00
Frequency: Monthly
Founded in 1977

15570 ELA Notes
Education Law Association
300 College Park Ave
Dayton, OH 45469-0001

937-229-3589
Fax: 937-229-3845
E-Mail: ela@educationlaw.org
Home Page: www.educationlaw.org

Mandy Schrenk, Executive Director
Jody Thornburg, Publications Editor
Cate K Smith, Executive Director
Judy Pleiman, Member Services Coordinator
Jody Thornburg, Publications Manager

ELA is a nonprofit, nonadvocacy, member-based organization found in 1954 to provide an unbiased forum for the dissemination of information about current issues in education law. Membership is open to all individuals and organizations with a special interest in education law. ELA's mission is to bring together educational and legal scholars and practioners to inform and advance educational policy and practice through knowledge of the law.
Cost: $125.00
Frequency: Quarterly
Circulation: 1300
ISSN: 0047-8997
Founded in 1954
Printed in 2 colors on matte stock

15571 Employee Benefits Cases
Bureau of National Affairs
1801 S Bell St
Arlington, VA 22202-4501

703-341-3000
800-372-1033
Fax: 800-253-0332
E-Mail: customercare@bna.com
Home Page: www.bnabooks.com
Social Media: Facebook, Twitter, LinkedIn

Paul N Wojcik, Chairman
Gregory C. McCaffery, President and CEO
John Camp, Vice President and Chief Technology
Lisa A. Fitzpatrick, Vice President
Audrey Hipkins, VP

A weekly decisional service that reports the full text of federal and state court opinions and selected decisions of arbitrators and the NLRB on employee benefits issues.
Cost: $1582.00
54 Pages
Frequency: Weekly
Circulation: 6000+
ISSN: 0273-236X
Founded in 1929
Printed in on matte stock

15572 Employment Law Report Strategist
Data Research
PO Box 490
Rosemount, MN 55068-0490

952-452-8694
800-365-4900
Fax: 952-452-8694

Covers the latest court cases and late-breaking legislation along with the most recent law review articles affecting employment.
Cost: $120.00
Frequency: Monthly
ISSN: 1058-1308

15573 Entertainment Law and Finance
345 Park Avenue S
New York, NY 10010-1707

212-779-6611
800-888-8300
Fax: 212-696-1848

Stan Soocher, Editor
Stuart M Wise, Production Manager
Kerry Kyle, Circulation Director

Laws and news in the entertainment field.
Cost: $195.00
8 Pages
Frequency: Monthly
ISSN: 0883-2455
Printed in 2 colors

15574 Entertainment and Sports Lawyer
American Bar Association
Forum-Entertainment/Sport
321 N Clark St
Chicago, IL 60654-7598

312-988-5000
800-285-2221
Fax: 312-988-5280
E-Mail: askaba@abanet.org
Home Page: www.abanet.org
Social Media: Facebook, Twitter

Laurel Bellows, President
Vered Yakovee, Editor
Jack L. Rives, Executive Director
Robert M. Carlson, Chairman
Lucian T. Pera, Treasurer

Newsletter on recent developments in the sports and entertainment industries, public policy and scholarly viewpoints.
Cost: $60.00
40 Pages
Frequency: Quarterly
ISSN: 0732-1880
Founded in 1878
Mailing list available for rent

15575 Estate Planner's Alert
Thomson Reuters
2395 Midway Rd
Suite 4
Carrollton, TX 75006

646-822-2000
800-231-1860
Fax: 646-822-2800
E-Mail: trta.lei-support@thomsonreuters.com
Home Page: www.ria.thomsonreuters.com

Laurel Bellows, President
Thomas H Glocer, CEO & Director
Robert D Daleo, Chief Financial Officer
Kelli Crane, Senior Vice President & CIO

Offers complete coverage of estate planning and law.
Cost: $195.00
Frequency: Monthly
Founded in 1935

15576 Exercise Standards and Malpractice Reporter
PRC Publishing
3976 Fulton Dr Nw
Canton, OH 44718-3043

330-492-6063
800-336-0083
Fax: 330-492-6176
Home Page: www.prcpublishingcorp.com

Molly Romig, VP
Dr. Doyice Cotton, Publisher
Mary Cotton, Publisher

Designed to cover topics of interest and concern to the exercise professionals.
Cost: $39.95
16 Pages
Circulation: 750
ISSN: 0891-0278
Founded in 1997
Printed in 2 colors on matte stock

15577 FCBA Newsletter
Federal Communications Bar Association
1020 19th St Nw
Suite 325
Washington, DC 20036-6113

202-293-4000
Fax: 202-293-4317
E-Mail: fcba@fcba.org
Home Page: www.fcba.org

Stanley Zenor, Executive Director
Kerry Loughney, Director of Membership Services
Diane J Cornell, Treasurer
Wendy Jo Parish, Administrative Assistant
Beth Phillips, Bookkeeper

A non-profit organization of attorneys and other professionals involved in the development, interpretation, implementation and practice of communications law and policy.
Frequency: Monthly
Founded in 1936
Mailing list available for rent

15578 Family Law Reporter
Bureau of National Affairs
1801 S Bell St
Arlington, VA 22202-4501
703-341-3000
800-372-1033
Fax: 800-253-0332
E-Mail: customercare@bna.com
Home Page: www.bnabooks.com
Social Media: Facebook, Twitter, LinkedIn

Paul N Wojcik, Chairman
Gregory C. McCaffery, President and CEO
John Camp, Vice President and Chief Technology
Lisa A. Fitzpatrick, Vice President
Audrey Hipkins, VP

A weekly notification and reference service dealing with all significant state and federal de-

velopments in the field of family law.
Cost: $974.00
Frequency: Weekly
Founded in 1929

15579 Federal Contract Disputes
Business Publishers
2222 Sedwick Dr
Suite 101
Durham, NC 27713
800-223-8720
Fax: 800-508-2592
E-Mail: custserv@bpinews.com
Home Page: www.bpinews.com
A monthly newsletter designed to help you avoid disputes, and successfully resolve those you can't avoid. Each issue brings you concise synopses of a dozen major decisions, from the courts, the Comptroller General, and the boards of contract appeals.
Cost: $285.00
Frequency: Monthly

15580 Federal Contracts Report
Bureau of National Affairs
1801 S Bell St
Arlington, VA 22202-4501
703-341-3000
800-372-1033
Fax: 800-253-0332
E-Mail: customercare@bna.com
Home Page: www.bnabooks.com
Social Media: Facebook, Twitter, LinkedIn
Paul N Wojcik, Chairman
Gregory C. McCaffery, President and CEO
John Camp, Vice President and Chief Technology
Lisa A. Fitzpatrick, Vice President
Audrey Hipkins, VP
A weekly reporting service providing comprehensive coverage of the latest significant developments affecting federal contracts and grants.
Cost: $1887.00
Frequency: Weekly
Founded in 1929

15581 Federal Discovery News
LRP Publications
747 Dresher Road
PO Box 980
Horsham, PA 19044-980
215-784-0912
800-341-7874
Fax: 215-784-9639
E-Mail: webmaster@lrp.com
Home Page: www.lrp.com
John Massaro, Editor
Dionne Ellis, Managing Editor
Each issue covers the whole realm of pretrial case management and discovery, especially the impact of the new civil procedure rules on discovery in federal cases. Provides a timely review of how district developments pertain to your practice.
Cost: $275.00
Frequency: Monthly
Founded in 1977

15582 Federal EEO Advisor
LRP Publications
747 Dresher Road
PO Box 980
Horsham, PA 19044-980
215-784-0912
800-341-7874
Fax: 215-784-9639
E-Mail: webmaster@lrp.com
Home Page: www.lrp.com
Allison Uehling, Editor
Clarrisa Spasyk, Staff Writer
One-of-a-kind publication provides readers with essential tips, strategies and news about the constanly changing EEO profession. Each issue includes insightful coverage on topics such as: details on major developments and trends in federal EEO; tips on how to accomplish specific objectives within the EEO program; synopses of decisions by the EEOC and related courts, etc.
Cost: $220.00
Frequency: Monthly
Founded in 1977

15583 Federal Human Resources Week
LRP Publications
747 Dresher Road, Suite 500
PO Box 980
Horsham, PA 19044
215-840-0912
800-341-7874
Fax: 215-784-9639
E-Mail: custserve@lrp.com
Home Page: www.feds.com
Daniel J Gephart, Editorial Director
Julie Davidson, Managing Editor
Kathleen Filipczyk, Staff Writer
Federal Human Resources Week helps you stay on top of changes affecting you and your workplace. This revolutionary resource enables you to experience each major development as it occurs.
Cost: $365.00
12 Pages
Frequency: Weekly
Founded in 1977
Printed in 2 colors on matte stock

15584 Financial Management Newsletter
Association of Legal Administrators
75 Tri-State International
Suite 222
Lincolnshire, IL 60069-4435
847-267-1252
Fax: 847-267-1329
E-Mail: publications@alanet.org
Home Page: www.alanet.org
Larry Smith, Executive Director
Debbie Thomas, Director, Accounting & Finance
Renee Mahovsky, Director, Administration/Operations
Bob Abramson, Director, Marketing & Communication
Jan Waugh, Director, Member Services
8 Pages
Frequency: Monthly
Founded in 1971

15585 Forum
Federal Bar Association
1220 North Fillmore St.
Ste. 444
Arlington, VA 22201
571-481-9100
Fax: 571-481-9090
E-Mail: fba@fedbar.org
Home Page: www.fedbar.org
Social Media: Facebook, Twitter, LinkedIn
Karen Silberman, Executive Director
Lori Beth Gorman, Executive Assistant
Stacy King, Deputy Executive Director
April Davis, Staff Accountant
Patty Richardson, Receptionist
A forum for the exchange of ideas, news, updates, and cases for lawyers.
Cost: $35.00
8 Pages
Frequency: Monthly
Founded in 1920
Mailing list available for rent

15586 General Aviation Accident Report
Andrews Communications
175 Stafford Street Building 4
Suite 140
Wayne, PA 19087
610-225-0510
800-345-1101
Fax: 610-225-0501
E-Mail: nick.sullivan@thomson.com
Home Page: www.andrewsonline.com/
Thomson West, Publisher
Nick Sullivan, Editor
General aviation laws.
Cost: $99.00
20 Pages
Founded in 1872

15587 HRFocus
Institute of Management and Administration
1 Wasington Park
Suite 1300
Newark, NJ 07102-3130
212-244-0360
Fax: 973-622-0595
E-Mail: customercare@bna.com
Home Page: www.ioma.com
Provides HR managers with timely information on a variety of topics, including talent management, HR legal and compliance issues, performance reviews, and workplace policies and standards.
Cost: $429.00
16 Pages
Frequency: Monthly
Printed in 4 colors

15588 Hastings Communications & Entertainment Law Journal
Hastings College of Law
200 McAllister St
2nd Floor, Room 213
San Francisco, CA 94102-4978
415-565-4600
Fax: 415-565-4854
Home Page: www.uchastings.edu
Nell Jessup Newton, Manager
Karen Gibbs, Editor
Specializing in a host of legal issues generally grouped under the rubric of communications and entertainment law. Focuses on, but is not limited to, telecommunications, broadcasting, cable and other non-broadcast video, and the print media.
Cost: $7.00
Frequency: Monthly
Circulation: 1300
Founded in 1878

15589 Health Law Week
Strafford Publications
PO Box 13729
Atlanta, GA 30324-0729
404-881-1141
800-926-7926
Fax: 404-881-0074
E-Mail: customerservice@straffordpub.com
Home Page: www.straffordpub.com
Richard Ossoff, President
Case digest of judicial decision affecting all aspects of health care operations. Topics covered include AIPS abortion antitrust, drugs, ERISA, expert testimony, informed consent, amd much more.
Cost: $1397.00
Frequency: Weekly
ISSN: 1063-4061
Founded in 1984
Mailing list available for rent: 25M names

15590 Hospital Litigation Reporter
Strafford Publications

PO Box 13729
Atlanta, GA 30324-0729

404-881-1141
800-926-7926
Fax: 404-881-0074
E-Mail: customerservice@straffordpub.com
Home Page: www.straffordpub.com

Richard Ossoff, President
Jennifer Vaughan, Editor

Monthly digest of judicial decisions that concern or affect the hospital environment. Cases are screened and selected to provide concise, comprehensive coverage of issues important to hospital attorneys and administrators.
Cost: $397.00
18 Pages
Frequency: Monthly
ISSN: 1048-5201
Founded in 1984
Mailing list available for rent: 11M names
Printed in one color

15591 Human Resources Report
Bureau of National Affairs
1801 S Bell St
Arlington, VA 22202-4501

703-341-3000
800-372-1033
Fax: 800-253-0332
E-Mail: customercare@bna.com
Home Page: www.bnabooks.com
Social Media: Facebook, Twitter, LinkedIn

Paul N Wojcik, Chairman
Gregory C. McCaffery, President and CEO
John Camp, Vice President and Chief Technology
Lisa A. Fitzpatrick, Vice President
Audrey Hipkins, VP

Covers current developments in every area of human resources; includes in-depth analysis of important events, developments or trends affecting human resource professionals.
Cost: $1140.00
28 Pages
Frequency: Weekly
ISSN: 1095-6239
Founded in 1929
Printed in one color on matte stock

15592 I-CBC Newsletter
Institute of Certified Business Counselors
18831 Willamette Dr
West Linn, OR 97068-1711

503-751-1856
877-422-2674
Fax: 503-292-8237
E-Mail: inquiry@i-cbc.org
Home Page: www.i-cbc.org

Roger Murphy, Director, Newsletter

For counselors, brokers and attorneys qualified to act as advisors for persons with business problems. Regular editorial features.
Frequency: 6/Year
Mailing list available for rent

15593 IOMA's Report on Controlling Law Firm Costs
Institute of Management and Administration
1 Washington Park
Suite 1300
Newark, NJ 07102-3130

212-244-0360
Fax: 973-622-0595
E-Mail: customercare@bna.com
Home Page: www.ioma.com

Information to control costs of law firms management.
Cost: $175.00
12 Pages
Frequency: Monthly

15594 IRR News Report
ABA Section - Individual Rights & Responsibilities
740 15th Stree, NW
10th Floor
Washington, DC 20005

202-662-1000
800-285-2221
Fax: 202-662-1031
E-Mail: askaba@abanet.org
Home Page: www.abanet.org
Social Media: Facebook, Twitter

Laurel Bellows, President
Jack L. Rives, Executive Director
Robert M. Carlson, Chairman
Lucian T. Pera, Treasurer
Cara Lee T. Neville, Secretary

A quarterly newsletter including updates on Section events, news about members, a review of recent legislative events and decision by the Supreme Court.
Circulation: 6000
Founded in 1878
Mailing list available for rent

15595 Individual Employment Rights
Bureau of National Affairs
1801 S Bell St
Arlington, VA 22202-4501

703-341-3000
800-372-1033
Fax: 800-253-0332
E-Mail: customercare@bna.com
Home Page: www.bnabooks.com
Social Media: Facebook, Twitter, LinkedIn

Paul N Wojcik, Chairman
Gregory C. McCaffery, President and CEO
John Camp, Vice President and Chief Technology
Lisa A. Fitzpatrick, Vice President
Audrey Hipkins, VP

Case reference and notification on individual employment rights issues including employment at will, privacy, polygraph testing, and other employee rights issues outside the traditional labor-management relations context.
Cost: $1227.00
Frequency: Monthly
ISSN: 0148-7981
Founded in 1929

15596 Intellectual Property LAWCAST
Vox Juris
PO Box 389
Pennington, NJ 08534-389

609-737-6543
Fax: 609-737-3860
E-Mail: INFO@lawcast.com
Home Page: www.lawcast.com

Jason Meyer, Publisher

US legal news in patents, trademarks, copyrights, trade secrets, unfair trade, etc. including comprehensive coverage of PTO policies and a regular Listening Post on legal issues in the digital age. The buzz for thousands of IP lawyers, nationwide. 60 minute audio and online, twice monthly.
Cost: $488.00

15597 Intellectual Property Law Review
Clark Boardman Company
375 Hudson St
Room 201
New York, NY 10014-3658

585-546-5530
800-323-1336

David Doughty, Publisher

Compilation of the best law review articles.
Frequency: Monthly
Founded in 1916

15598 Intellectual Property Litigation Reporter
Andrews Publications
175 Strafford Avenue
Building 4 Suite 140
Wayne, PA 19087-3331

610-225-0510
800-345-1101
Fax: 610-225-0501
Home Page: www.andrewspub.com

Robert Maroldo, Publisher
Jodine Mayberry, Editor

Covers litigation and regulation of intellectual property issues including patents, copyrights, and tradeworks.
Cost: $83.00

15599 Intellectual Property Today
Omega Communications
29 E Maryland Street
Indianapolis, IN 46204-7258

317-264-4010
Fax: 317-264-4020
E-Mail: planet@iptoday.com
Home Page: www.omegac.com

Douglas Dean, Editor
Steve Barnes, Vice President
Laura Moore, Vice President

Emphasizes developments in leading edge technology, including multimedia, genetic engineering and computer software, and how they effect disciplines of law.
Cost: $96.00
Frequency: Monthly
Circulation: 20000
Founded in 1971

15600 Inter-American Bar Association Newsletter
Inter-American Bar Association
1211 Connecticut Ave Nw
Suite 202
Washington, DC 20036-2712

202-466-5944
Fax: 202-466-5946
E-Mail: iaba@iaba.org
Home Page: www.iaba.org
Social Media: Facebook

Marianne Cordier, Secretary General
Rafael Veloz, President
Cost: $60.00
Frequency: Quarterly

15601 International Law News
American Bar Association Internat'l Law & Practice
321 N Clark St
Chicago, IL 60654-7598

312-988-5000
800-285-2221
Fax: 312-988-5280
E-Mail: askaba@abanet.org
Home Page: www.abanet.org
Social Media: Facebook, Twitter

Angela Gwizdala, Managing Editor
Laurel Bellows, President
Jack L. Rives, Executive Director
Robert M. Carlson, Chairman
Lucian T. Pera, Treasurer

Provides information concerning current, important developments pertaining to international law and practice, Section news, and other information of professional interest.
28 Pages
Frequency: Quarterly
Circulation: 15000
ISSN: 0047-0813
Founded in 1878
Mailing list available for rent

15602 Internet Lawyer
GoAhead Productions
123 7th Avenue
#137
Brooklyn, NY 11215-1301

718-399-6136
Fax: 718-499-6039
Home Page: www.internetlawyer.com

Tatia L Gordon-Troy, Editor-in-Chief
Christopher Eddings, Publisher

Gives legal advice and examines how to use the Net for research, marketing and communications purposes. Includes book reviews as well as information on current law office technology.
Cost: $149.00
Frequency: Monthly

15603 Judicial Division Record
American Bar Association Judicial Division
321 N Clark St
Chicago, IL 60654-7598

312-988-5000
800-285-2221
Fax: 312-988-6281
E-Mail: askaba@abanet.org
Home Page: www.abanet.org
Social Media: Facebook, Twitter

Laurel Bellows, President
Jack L. Rives, Executive Director
Robert M. Carlson, Chairman
Lucian T. Pera, Treasurer
Cara Lee T. Neville, Secretary

The Record is the only newsletter published by the Division, providing news about Division activites, products, publications and programs. It contains sections for each Division Conference, and an insert.
Cost: $25.00
Frequency: Free Online
Founded in 1878
Mailing list available for rent

15604 Labor Arbitration and Dispute Settlements
Bureau of National Affairs
1801 S Bell St
Arlington, VA 22202-4501

703-341-3000
800-372-1033
Fax: 800-253-0332
E-Mail: customercare@bna.com
Home Page: www.bnabooks.com
Social Media: Facebook, Twitter, LinkedIn

Paul N Wojcik, Chairman
Gregory C. McCaffery, President and CEO
John Camp, Vice President and Chief Technology
Lisa A. Fitzpatrick, Vice President
Audrey Hipkins, VP

Contains the full-text of arbitration cases, and digests of court decisions involving arbitration.
Cost: $1686.00
Frequency: Weekly
ISSN: 1043-5662
Founded in 1929

15605 Labor Arbitration in Government
LRP Publications
PO Box 980
Horsham, PA 19044-0980

215-784-0912
800-341-7874
Fax: 215-784-9639
E-Mail: webmaster@lrp.com
Home Page: www.lrp.com

Todd Lutz, CFO
Dionne Ellis, Marketing

Selected awards involving city, state, and federal employers (other than those employed by schools) are covered by this reporting service. Some of the issues arbitrated include: absenteeism, smoking policies, layoffs, and substance abuse.
Cost: $120.00
Frequency: Monthly
Founded in 1977
Printed in 2 colors on glossy stock

15606 Labor Lawyer
American Bar Association - Labor & Employment Law
321 N Clark St
Chicago, IL 60654-7598

312-988-5000
800-285-2221
Fax: 312-988-5814
E-Mail: laboremplaw@abanet.org
Home Page: www.abanet.org
Social Media: Facebook, Twitter

Laurel Bellows, President
Jack L. Rives, Executive Director
Robert M. Carlson, Chairman
Lucian T. Pera, Treasurer
Cara Lee T. Neville, Secretary

Substantive articles on developments in labor and employment law.
Frequency: Quarterly
Circulation: 2300
Founded in 1878
Mailing list available for rent

15607 Labor Relations Reporter
Bureau of National Affairs
1801 S Bell St
Arlington, VA 22202-4501

703-341-3000
800-372-1033
Fax: 800-253-0332
E-Mail: customercare@bna.com
Home Page: www.bnabooks.com
Social Media: Facebook, Twitter, LinkedIn

Paul N Wojcik, Chairman
Gregory C. McCaffery, President and CEO
John Camp, Vice President and Chief Technology
Lisa A. Fitzpatrick, Vice President
Audrey Hipkins, VP

A multi-part notification and reference service covering labor-management relations, wages and hours, labor arbitration, fair employment practices, individual employment rights and more.
Cost: $6175.00
Frequency: Weekly
ISSN: 0148-7981
Founded in 1929

15608 Labor Relations Week
Bureau of National Affairs
1801 S Bell St
Arlington, VA 22202-4501

703-341-3000
800-372-1033
Fax: 800-253-0332
E-Mail: customercare@bna.com
Home Page: www.bnabooks.com
Social Media: Facebook, Twitter, LinkedIn

Paul N Wojcik, Chairman
Gregory C. McCaffery, President and CEO
John Camp, Vice President and Chief Technology
Lisa A. Fitzpatrick, Vice President
Audrey Hipkins, VP

A weekly reporting service that provides a comprehensive overview of developments influencing labor relations in the private sector.
Cost: $1472.00
Frequency: Weekly
ISSN: 0891-4141
Founded in 1929

15609 Labor and Employment Law
American Bar Association - Labor & Employment Law
321 N Clark St
Chicago, IL 60654-7598

312-988-5000
800-285-2221
Fax: 312-988-6281
E-Mail: askaba@abanet.org
Home Page: www.abanet.org
Social Media: Facebook, Twitter

Laurel Bellows, President
Jack L. Rives, Executive Director
Robert M. Carlson, Chairman
Lucian T. Pera, Treasurer
Cara Lee T. Neville, Secretary

Offers news items of interest to members and information on the latest developments in the labor field.
Cost: $5.00
16 Pages
Frequency: Quarterly
Circulation: 22000
ISSN: 0193-5739
Founded in 1878
Mailing list available for rent

15610 Labor and Employment Law News
American Bar Association - Labor & Emplyment Law
321 N Clark St
Chicago, IL 60654-7598

312-988-5000
800-285-2221
Fax: 312-988-5280
E-Mail: service@abanet.org
Home Page: www.abanet.org
Social Media: Facebook, Twitter

Laurel Bellows, President
Jack L. Rives, Executive Director
Robert M. Carlson, Chairman
Lucian T. Pera, Treasurer
Cara Lee T. Neville, Secretary

Legal issues and trends of interest to lawyers who represent employees, unions, and management.
Cost: $5.00
16 Pages
Frequency: Monthly
Circulation: 22000
ISSN: 0193-5739
Founded in 1878
Mailing list available for rent
Printed in 4 colors

15611 Labor-Management Relations
Bureau of National Affairs
1801 S Bell St
Arlington, VA 22202-4501

703-341-3000
800-372-1033
Fax: 800-253-0332
E-Mail: customercare@bna.com
Home Page: www.bnabooks.com
Social Media: Facebook, Twitter, LinkedIn

Paul N Wojcik, Chairman
Gregory C. McCaffery, President and CEO
John Camp, Vice President and Chief Technology
Lisa A. Fitzpatrick, Vice President
Audrey Hipkins, VP

Contains a table of cases, digest-summaries of all published NLRB decisions and full-text of opinions of the US Supreme Court, US Courts of Appeals and other courts, in one bound volume, issued several times a year.
Cost: $ 1776.00
Frequency: Monthly
ISSN: 1043-5506
Founded in 1929

15612 Labor-Management Relations Analysis/News and Background Information
Bureau of National Affairs
1801 S Bell St
Arlington, VA 22202-4501

703-341-3000
800-372-1033
Fax: 800-253-0332
E-Mail: customercare@bna.com
Home Page: www.bnabooks.com
Social Media: Facebook, Twitter, LinkedIn

Paul N Wojcik, Chairman
Gregory C. McCaffery, President and CEO
John Camp, Vice President and Chief Technology
Lisa A. Fitzpatrick, Vice President
Audrey Hipkins, VP

This weekly section of the Labor Relations Reporter summarizes developments and rulings in the field of labor law, covers major non-decisional developments and recent significant arbitration awards, and provides in-depth analysis and evaluation of the week's labor news.
Cost: $507.00
Frequency: Weekly
Founded in 1929

15613 Land Use Law Report
Business Publishers
8737 Colesville Road
10th Floor
Silver Spring, MD 20910-3928

301-876-6300
800-274-6737
Fax: 301-589-8493
E-Mail: custserv@bpinews.com
Home Page: www.bpinews.com/

Leonard Eiserer, Publisher
James Esq, Editor

Zoning and land use decisions at all levels of government; impact on business community and environment.
Cost: $397.00
Founded in 1963

15614 Latin America Law and Business Report
WorldTrade Executive
2250 Main St
Suite 100
Concord, MA 01742-3838

978-287-0301
Fax: 978-287-0302
E-Mail: info@wtexec.com
Home Page: www.wtexecutive.com

Gary Brown, President
Jay Stanley, Sales Manager

Provides practical, current information on how to do business in Latin America. Covers areas such as capital markets, accounting matters, labor issues, privatization, project finance techniques, joint venture regulation, local sourcing, export/import, taxation, intellectual property, environment.
Cost: $893.00
Frequency: Monthly

15615 Law Bulletin
Andrews Publications
175 Strafford Avenue
Building 4, Suite 140
Wayne, PA 19087-3331

610-225-0510
800-345-1101
Fax: 610-225-0501
Home Page: www.andrewspub.com

Donna Higgins, Editor
Rose MacDonald, Production Manager

Newsletter covering the legal issues raided by the Millenium. Bug along with insightful commentary from attorneys and other experts.
Cost: $25.00
Frequency: Monthly
Founded in 1872

15616 Law Firm Profit Report
James Publishing
3505 Cadillac Avenue
Suite H
Costa Mesa, CA 92626

714-755-5450
800-440-4780
Fax: 714-751-2709
E-Mail: customer-service@jamespublishing.com
Home Page: www.jamespublishing.com

Jim Pawell, Founder/President
Lorraine Thinnes, Editor

How to manage a small to medium-sized law firm profitably, with tips on cost-cutting, managing automation, personnel and more.
Founded in 1981
Mailing list available for rent

15617 Law Office Management & Administration Report
Institute of Management and Administration
1 Washington Park
Suite 1300
Newark, NJ 07102-3130

212-244-0360
Fax: 973-622-0595
E-Mail: customercare@bna.com
Home Page: www.ioma.com

Covers the daily management concerns relevant for law firm administrators, office managers, and others.
Cost: $489.00
Frequency: Monthly
Founded in 1983

15618 Law Practice Today
American Bar Association
321 N Clark St
Chicago, IL 60654-7598

312-988-5000
800-285-2221
Fax: 312-988-5280
E-Mail: askaba@abanet.org
Home Page: www.abanet.org
Social Media: Facebook, Twitter

Laurel Bellows, President
Jack L. Rives, Executive Director
Robert M. Carlson, Chairman
Lucian T. Pera, Treasurer
Cara Lee T. Neville, Secretary

An e-newsletter focusing on how lawyers can improve their personal productivity in the hands-on practice of law.
Frequency: Monthly
Founded in 1878
Mailing list available for rent

15619 Law and Society Association Newsletter
Denver College of Law
1900 Olive Street
Denver, CO 80220-1857

303-871-6306
E-Mail: Exec_Office@lawandsociety.org
Home Page: www.lawandsociety.org

Joyce Sterling, Publisher

Legal updates and information on the Society.
Frequency: Monthly

15620 LawPractice.news
American Bar Association - Law Practice Management
321 N Clark St
Chicago, IL 60654-7598

312-988-5000
800-285-2221
Fax: 312-988-5280
E-Mail: askaba@abanet.org
Home Page: www.abanet.org/lpm/home.shtml
Social Media: Facebook, Twitter, Youtube

Laurel Bellows, President
Jack L. Rives, Executive Director
Robert M. Carlson, Chairman
Lucian T. Pera, Treasurer
Cara Lee T. Neville, Secretary

A monthly e-newsletter for Law Practice Management Section members, keeping them abreast of Section events, publications, promotions and member news.
Frequency: Monthly
Founded in 1974
Mailing list available for rent

15621 Lawyer's PC
West Group
1428 Dewey Ave
Rochester, NY 14613-1128

585-254-9585
800-327-2665
Fax: 585-258-3707
E-Mail: west.support@thomson.com
Home Page: www.west.thomson.com

Computer and electronics information aimed at the legal profession.
Cost: $299.00
16 Pages
Circulation: 4000
Founded in 1872
Printed in one color

15622 Lawyering Tools and Techniques
American Bar Association
321 N Clark St
Chicago, IL 60654-7598

312-988-5000
800-285-2221
Fax: 312-988-5280
E-Mail: askaba@abanet.org
Home Page: www.abanet.org
Social Media: Facebook, Twitter

Laurel Bellows, President
Jack L. Rives, Executive Director
Robert M. Carlson, Chairman
Lucian T. Pera, Treasurer
Cara Lee T. Neville, Secretary

Focuses on specific tools lawyers can use to improve the productivity of their work including electronic communications, laptops, desk publishing and resources.
Cost: $50.00
Frequency: Quarterly
Founded in 1878
Mailing list available for rent

15623 Lawyers Tax Alert
Research Institute of America
90 5th Avenue
2nd Floor
New York, NY 10011-7696
212-367-6300

Peter Grean, Manager

Tax laws and news.
Frequency: Monthly

15624 Lawyers' Letter
American Bar Association
321 N Clark St
Chicago, IL 60654-7598

312-988-5000
800-285-2221
Fax: 312-988-5280
E-Mail: askaba@abanet.org

Home Page: www.abanet.org
Social Media: Facebook, Twitter

Laurel Bellows, President
Jack L. Rives, Executive Director
Robert M. Carlson, Chairman
Lucian T. Pera, Treasurer
Cara Lee T. Neville, Secretary

Newsletter informing lawyers of new developments in court improvement and reports on Conference activities.
Founded in 1878
Mailing list available for rent

15625 Legal Advisory
WPI Communications
55 Morris Ave
Suite 300
Springfield, NJ 07081-1422

973-467-8700
800-323-4995
Fax: 973-467-0368
E-Mail: info@wpicomm.com
Home Page: www.wpicomm.com

Steve Klinghoffer, President
Marilyn Lang, Chairman

Offers updates, news and the latest legislation for lawyers.
Frequency: Monthly
Founded in 1952

15626 Legal Assistant Today Magazine
James Publishing
3505 Cadillac Avenue
Suite H
Costa Mesa, CA 92626

714-755-5450
800-440-4780
Fax: 714-751-2709
E-Mail:
customer-service@jamespublishing.com
Home Page: www.jamespublishing.com

Jim Pawell, Founder/President
Rod Hughes, Managing Editor

Written exclusively for paralegals and legal assistants. Each issue includes coverage if industry news and trends, how-to articles as well as colorful and informative pieces on unique areas and persons in the profession and sound advice for becoming more efficient in the workplace., buy wisely and use their investments to maximize productivity and profitability.
Cost: $47.98
56 Pages
Circulation: 13000
ISSN: 1055-128X
Founded in 1981

15627 Legal Review
Native American Rights Fund
1506 Broadway St
Boulder, CO 80302-6296

303-447-8760
Fax: 303-443-7776
E-Mail: webmaster@narf.org
Home Page: www.narf.org
Social Media: Facebook

John E Echohawk, Executive Director
Carly Hare, Director Development
Rose Cuny, Office Manager
Katrina Mora, Office Services Assistant
Mireille Martinez, Development Projects Manager

A bi-annual case update published by the Native American Rights Fund.
Frequency: Bi-annually
Circulation: 30000
ISSN: 0739-862x
Mailing list available for rent
Printed in 4 colors on matte stock

15628 Litigation LAWCAST
Vox Juris
PO Box 389
Pennington, NJ 08534

609-737-6543
800-529-2278
Fax: 609-737-3860
E-Mail: info@lawcast.com
Home Page: www.lawcast.com

Jason Meyer, Editor & Publisher
Linda Delp, General Manager

Analysis of legal departments and advanced strategic ideas for the most demanding litigators - whatever the subject of your litigation. Stay up to date on substance and tactics in evidence, discovery, advocacy, damages, client management and selection, settlement, ADR, and ethics, plus coverage of groudbreaking decisions affecting personal injury, commercial, and employment law. 60 min./monthly
Cost: $399.00
Frequency: Monthly
Founded in 1994

15629 Litigation News
American Bar Association Section of Litigation
321 N Clark St
Chicago, IL 60654-7598

312-988-5000
800-285-2221
Fax: 312-988-5280
E-Mail: askaba@abanet.org
Home Page: www.abanet.org
Social Media: Facebook, Twitter

Laurel Bellows, President
Jack L. Rives, Executive Director
Robert M. Carlson, Chairman
Lucian T. Pera, Treasurer
Cara Lee T. Neville, Secretary

Present articles on the latest developments in law, litigation trends, and topics of interest to litigators.
Frequency: Quarterly
Circulation: 60000
Founded in 1878
Mailing list available for rent

15630 Marketing for Lawyers
Leader Publications
345 Park Avenue S
New York, NY 10010-1707

212-799-9200
Fax: 212-696-1848

Sam Adler, Editor
Kerry Kyle, Circulation Director

Helps lawyers expand their practice through marketing.
Cost: $17.50

15631 Mealey's Asbestos Bankruptcy Report
LexisNexis Mealey's
555 W 5th Avenue
Los Angeles, CA 90013

213-627-1130
800-253-4182
E-Mail: mealeyinfo@lexisnexis.com
Home Page: www.lexisnexis.com/mealeys
Social Media: Facebook, Twitter, LinkedIn, RSS, Youtube

Tom Hagy, CEO
Maureen McGuire, Editorial Director
Lisa Schaeffer, Editor
Mike Wash, Chief Executive Officer, Legal
Lisa Agona, Chief Marketing Officer

The report provides in-depth news and analysis of asbestos bankruptcy law and the progress of bankrupt asbestos companies through the ever-evolving Chapter 11 process. Topics include: insurance issues, impacts on settlements, how asbestos bankruptcies are affecting the landscape of the litigation and which companies may be forced to file for Chapter 11 protection in the future.
Cost: $475.00
100 Pages
Frequency: Quarterly
Founded in 2000
Mailing list available for rent

15632 Mealey's California Section 17200 Report
LexisNexis Mealey's
555 5th Avenue
Los Angeles, CA 90013

213-627-1130
800-253-4182
E-Mail: mealeyinfo@lexisnexis.com
Home Page: www.lexisnexis.com/mealeys
Social Media: Facebook, Twitter, LinkedIn, RSS, Youtube

Tom Hagy, CEO
Maureen McGuire, Editorial Director
Bryan Redding, Editor
Mike Wash, Chief Executive Officer, Legal
Lisa Agona, Chief Marketing Officer

Monitors litigation and provides legislative updates on California's Unfair Competition Law. This monthly report will offer readers hard-to-find filings and briefs, new complaints, breaking news, concise case summaries, and trial updates. All major cases involving Section 17200 of the state's Business and Professions Code will be reported, including those dealings with insurance, employment, consumer law, the Internet, telecommunications, securities, fraud, product liability and many more.
Cost: $959.00
100 Pages
Frequency: Monthly
Founded in 2002
Mailing list available for rent

15633 Mealey's Catastrophic Loss
LexisNexis Mealey's
555 W 5th Avenue
Los Angeles, CA 90013
213-627-1130
800-253-4182
E-Mail: mealeyinfo@lexisnexis.com
Home Page: www.lexisnexis.com/mealeys
Social Media: Facebook, Twitter, LinkedIn, RSS, Youtube

Tom Hagy, CEO
Maureen McGuire, Editorial Director
Gina Cappello, Editor
Mike Wash, Chief Executive Officer, Legal
Lisa Agona, Chief Marketing Officer

This report focuses on business interruption insurance claims in the aftermath of the Hurricane Katrina, September 11th, and other catastrophic loss tragedies. Additionally, the report will go beyond these claims and will offer important business interruption insurance coverage news related to computer viruses, computer failures, and natural disasters.
Cost: $1075.00
100 Pages
Frequency: Monthly
Founded in 2001
Mailing list available for rent

15634 Mealey's Daubert Report
LexisNexis Mealey's
555 W 5th Avenue
Los Angeles, CA 90013
213-627-1130
800-253-4182
E-Mail: mealeyinfo@lexisnexis.com
Home Page: www.lexisnexis.com/mealeys

Social Media: Facebook, Twitter, LinkedIn, RSS, Youtube

Tom Hagy, CEO
Maureen McGuire, Editorial Director
Kristin Casler, Editor
Mike Wash, Chief Executive Officer, Legal
Lisa Agona, Chief Marketing Officer

This newsletter covers the interpretation, adoption and/or rejection of the Supreme Court's landmark expert admissibility ruling, Daubert v. Merrell Dow Pharmaceutical Inc. As the nation's jurisdictions grapple with so called junk science testimony, this monthly newsletter offers subscribers the latest key rulings in this contentious components of civil and criminal litigation.
Cost: $735.00
100 Pages
Frequency: Monthly
Founded in 1997
Mailing list available for rent

15635 **Mealey's Emerging Drugs & Devices**
LexisNexis Mealey's
555 W 5th Avenue
Los Angeles, CA 90013

213-627-1130
800-253-4182
E-Mail: mealeyinfo@lexisnexis.com
Home Page: www.lexisnexis.com/mealeys
Social Media: Facebook, Twitter, LinkedIn, RSS, Youtube

Tom Hagy, CEO
Maureen McGuire, Editorial Director
Tom Moylan, Editor
Mike Wash, Chief Executive Officer, Legal
Lisa Agona, Chief Marketing Officer

The report covers cases involving a variety of prescription drug vaccines, implants and devices. Duract, Parlodel, Accutane, fen-phen, Rezulin, Propulsid, dietary supplements and blood products are among the topics tracked. Medical devices covered include heart catheters, breast implants, heart valves, intraocular lenses, jaw implants, joint replacements, latex gloves, pacemakers, pedicle screws, penile implants, and surgical lasers.
Cost: $1249.00
100 Pages
Frequency: Semi-Monthly
Founded in 1996
Mailing list available for rent

15636 **Mealey's Emerging Insurance Disputes**
LexisNexis Mealey's
555 W 5th Avenue
Los Angeles, CA 90013

213-627-1130
800-253-4182
Fax: 610-768-0880
E-Mail: mealeyinfo@lexisnexis.com
Home Page: www.lexisnexis.com/mealeys
Social Media: Facebook, Twitter, LinkedIn, RSS, Youtube

Tom Hagy, CEO
Maureen McGuire, Editorial Director
Gina Cappello, Editor
Mike Wash, Chief Executive Officer, Legal
Lisa Agona, Chief Marketing Officer

The report tracks new areas of coverage liability, novel policy applications, and conflicting policy language interpretations as they arise in insurance litigation. Some areas of coverage featured are: sexual harassment and discrimination, assault and battery, professional liability, patent and trademark infringement, construction defects, directors and officers claims, emotional distress, intentional acts, technology, and insurance business practices.
Cost: $ 1229.00
100 Pages
Frequency: Semi-Monthly
Founded in 1996
Mailing list available for rent

15637 **Mealey's Emerging Securities Litigation**
LexisNexis Mealey's
555 W 5th Avenue
Los Angeles, CA 90013

213-627-1130
800-253-4182
Fax: 610-768-0880
E-Mail: mealeyinfo@lexisnexis.com
Home Page: www.lexisnexis.com/mealeys
Social Media: Facebook, Twitter, LinkedIn, RSS, Youtube

Tom Hagy, CEO
Maureen McGuire, Editorial Director
Mike Lello, Editor
Mike Wash, Chief Executive Officer, Legal
Lisa Agona, Chief Marketing Officer

The report covers fiduciary duties to shareholders, 401k and pension implications, class actions, damage calculations, causation questions. Daubert issues, debt bondholder implications, bankruptcy issues and accountant liability in the securities law context.
Cost: $875.00
100 Pages
Frequency: Monthly
Founded in 2002
Mailing list available for rent

15638 **Mealey's Emerging Toxic Torts**
LexisNexis Mealey's
555 W 5th Avenue
Los Angeles, CA 90013
213-627-1130
800-253-4182
Fax: 610-768-0880
E-Mail: mealeyinfo@lexisnexis.com
Home Page: www.lexisnexis.com/mealeys
Social Media: Facebook, Twitter, LinkedIn, RSS, Youtube

Tom Hagy, CEO
Maureen McGuire, Editorial Director
Bill Lowe, Editor
Mike Wash, Chief Executive Officer, Legal
Lisa Agona, Chief Marketing Officer

The report focuses on the hottest areas of toxic tort litigation including: chemical sensitivity; indoor air quality; groundwater, soil and air contamination; radiation; workplace exposure; pesticides; solvents; latex gloves; EMF's; MTBE; endocrine disruptors, and more. The report provides in-depth coverage of medical monitoring; fear of cancer/disease; stigma damages; expert admissibility; federal preemption; class actions; punitive damages and market share theory.
Cost: $1539.00
100 Pages
Frequency: Semi-Monthly
Founded in 1992
Mailing list available for rent

15639 **Mealey's International Arbitration Quarterly Law Review**
LexisNexis Mealey's
555 W 5th Avenue
Los Angeles, CA 90013

213-627-1130
800-253-4182
Fax: 610-768-0880
E-Mail: mealeyinfo@lexisnexis.com
Home Page: www.lexisnexis.com/mealeys
Social Media: Facebook, Twitter, LinkedIn, RSS, Youtube

Tom Hagy, CEO
Maureen McGuire, Editorial Director
Edie Scott, Editor
Mike Wash, Chief Executive Officer, Legal
Lisa Agona, Chief Marketing Officer

The report provides thought-provoking commentary articles authored by arbitrators, scholars and attorneys with first-hand knowledge of the complex field of commercial dispute resolution. Each issue contains analytical discussions and practical insights on current case law, new treaties and statues, arbitration principles, dispute resolution techniques, and more from our prestigious international authors.
Cost: $475.00
100 Pages
Frequency: Quarterly
Founded in 2000
Mailing list available for rent

15640 **Mealey's International Arbritation Report**
LexisNexis Mealey's
555 W 5th Avenue
Los Angeles, CA 90013

213-627-1130
800-253-4182
Fax: 610-768-0880
E-Mail: mealeyinfo@lexisnexis.com
Home Page: www.lexisnexis.com/mealeys
Social Media: Facebook, Twitter, LinkedIn, RSS, Youtube

Tom Hagy, CEO
Maureen McGuire, Editorial Director
Edie Scott, Editor
Mike Wash, Chief Executive Officer, Legal
Lisa Agona, Chief Marketing Officer

The report examines arbitration and related litigation in courts world-wide. Covers enforcement, jurisdictional disputes, forum selection, use of experts by arbitral parties, enforcement, judicial supervision, the Iran-US Claims Tribunal, the United Nations Compensation Commission, and events of interest at arbitration institutions around the globe.
Cost: $2049.00
100 Pages
Frequency: Monthly
Founded in 1986
Mailing list available for rent

15641 **Mealey's International Asbestos Liability Report**
LexisNexis Mealey's
555 W 5th Avenue
Los Angeles, CA 90013

213-627-1130
800-253-4182
Fax: 610-768-0880
E-Mail: mealeyinfo@lexisnexis.com
Home Page: www.lexisnexis.com/mealeys
Social Media: Facebook, Twitter, LinkedIn, RSS, Youtube

Tom Hagy, CEO
Maureen McGuire, Editorial Director
Lisa Schaeffer, Editor
Mike Wash, Chief Executive Officer, Legal
Lisa Agona, Chief Marketing Officer

The report covers the latest litigation, regulatory, and medical news related to worldwide asbestos exposure - including the emerging issue of subsidiary liability and the question of US jurisdiction - with in-depth case summaries and news of medical findings, full-text court documents, and exclusive expert commentary articles.
Cost: $959.00
100 Pages
Frequency: Monthly

Founded in 2003
Mailing list available for rent

15642 Mealey's Litigation Report: Insurance Fraud
LexisNexis Mealey's
555 W 5th Avenue
Los Angeles, CA 90013

213-627-1130
800-253-4182
Fax: 610-768-0880
E-Mail: mealeyinfo@lexisnexis.com
Home Page: www.lexisnexis.com/mealeys
Social Media: Facebook, Twitter, LinkedIn, RSS, Youtube

Tom Hagy, CEO
Maureen McGuire, Editorial Director
Teresa Kent Zink, Editor
Mike Wash, Chief Executive Officer, Legal
Lisa Agona, Chief Marketing Officer

The report reviews civil and criminal cases arising from efforts by policyholders and third parties to defraud insurance carriers. Topics include false and fraudulent claims, arson, reverse bad faith, restitution, RICO, incontestability clauses, material misrepresentation, rescission, qui tam actions and fraud rings. Readers receive reports on schemes involving property & casualty, health care, automobile, life, homeowners, and workers' compensation fraud.
Cost: $839.00
100 Pages
Frequency: Monthly
Founded in 1994
Mailing list available for rent

15643 Mealey's Litigation Report: Asbestos
LexisNexis Mealey's
555 W 5th Avenue
Los Angeles, CA 90013

213-627-1130
800-253-4182
Fax: 610-768-0880
E-Mail: mealeyinfo@lexisnexis.com
Home Page: www.lexisnexis.com/mealeys
Social Media: Facebook, Twitter, LinkedIn, RSS, Youtube

Tom Hagy, CEO
Maureen McGuire, Editorial Director
Bryan Redding, Editor
Mike Wash, Chief Executive Officer, Legal
Lisa Agona, Chief Marketing Officer

The report offers unsurpassed coverage of litigation arising from asbestos-related injury and death. Key issues include: massive class action settlements involving present and future claimants, state and federal verdicts, litigation experts, medical monitoring claims, suits against the tobacco industry, discovery battles, discovery rule decisions, insurance coverage rulings, and asbestos property decisions.
Cost: $1789.00
100 Pages
Frequency: Semi-Monthly
Founded in 1984
Mailing list available for rent

15644 Mealey's Litigation Report: Baycol
LexisNexis Mealey's
555 W 5th Avenue
Los Angeles, CA 90013

213-627-1130
800-253-4182
Fax: 610-768-0880
E-Mail: mealeyinfo@lexisnexis.com
Home Page: www.lexisnexis.com/mealeys
Social Media: Facebook, Twitter, LinkedIn, RSS, Youtube

Tom Hagy, CEO
Maureen McGuire, Editorial Director
Dylan McGuire, Editor
Mike Wash, Chief Executive Officer, Legal
Lisa Agona, Chief Marketing Officer

This report tracks the litigation surrounding Baycol and other statin-based anti-cholesterol drug cases. Since the voluntary withdrawl of Bayer's Baycol and Lipobay brand cerivastatin anti-cholesterol drugs, numerous complaints have been filed. The report will cover hard-to-find filings, new complaints, class actions, MDL developments, trial updates and more.
Cost: $950.00
100 Pages
Frequency: Monthly
Founded in 2002
Mailing list available for rent

15645 Mealey's Litigation Report: California Insurance
LexisNexis Mealey's
1016 W Ninth Avenue
1st Floor
King of Prussia, PA 19406-1221

215-564-1788
800-448-1515
Fax: 610-768-0880
E-Mail: mealeyinfo@lexisnexis.com
Home Page: www.lexisnexis.com/mealeys
Social Media: Facebook, Twitter, LinkedIn, Itunes, Youtube

Kumsal Bayazit, Global Senior Vice President
Haywood Talcove, Chief Executive Officer, Government
Ian McDougall, Executive Vice President
Mike Walsh, CEO
Alex Watson, Executive Vice President

The Report focuses on ever-changing California and federal Ninth Circuit insurance coverage disputes and developments. Topics include California developments in bad faith litigation, earthquake damage coverage, disability insurance, products liability coverage, environmental insurance coverage, mold coverage, asbestos coverage, aviation litigation coverage, entertainment law and more.
Cost: $949.00
100 Pages
Frequency: Monthly
Founded in 2001

15646 Mealey's Litigation Report: Class Actions
LexisNexis Mealey's
1016 W Ninth Avenue
1st Floor
King of Prussia, PA 19406-1221

215-564-1788
800-448-1515
Fax: 610-768-0880
E-Mail: mealeyinfo@lexisnexis.com
Home Page: www.lexisnexis.com/mealeys
Social Media: Facebook, Twitter, LinkedIn, Itunes, Youtube

Kumsal Bayazit, Global Senior Vice President
Haywood Talcove, Chief Executive Officer, Government
Ian McDougall, Executive Vice President
Mike Walsh, CEO
Alex Watson, Executive Vice President

This report will provide in-depth coverage of class action litigation involving mass torts and beyond - including consumer law, employment law, securities litigation and e-commerce disputes. Get the latest on: hard-to-find filings, notice plans, fairness hearings, class certification rulings, settlements, trial news and verdicts, attorney fee news, appeals, breaking news stories, new complaints, Supreme Court battles, and much more.
Cost: $1195.00
100 Pages
Frequency: Semi-Monthly
Founded in 1997

15647 Mealey's Litigation Report: Construction Defects
LexisNexis Mealey's
1016 W Ninth Avenue
1st Floor
King of Prussia, PA 19406-1221

215-564-1788
800-448-1515
Fax: 610-768-0880
E-Mail: mealeyinfo@lexisnexis.com
Home Page: www.lexisnexis.com/mealeys
Social Media: Facebook, Twitter, LinkedIn, Itunes, Youtube

Kumsal Bayazit, Global Senior Vice President
Haywood Talcove, Chief Executive Officer, Government
Ian McDougall, Executive Vice President
Mike Walsh, CEO
Alex Watson, Executive Vice President

The Report tracks the growing area of construction defect litigation, including cases involving water intrusion, building settlement, concrete corrosion, mold and other defects. Topics covered include: recovery of damages, warranty issues, contractor liability, sub-contractor liability, developer liability, architect liability and related insurance cover actions.
Cost: $979.00
100 Pages
Frequency: Monthly
Founded in 2000

15648 Mealey's Litigation Report: Copyright
LexisNexis Mealey's
1016 W Ninth Avenue
1st Floor
King of Prussia, PA 19406-1221
215-564-1788
800-448-1515
Fax: 610-768-0880
E-Mail: mealeyinfo@lexisnexis.com
Home Page: www.lexisnexis.com/mealeys
Social Media: Facebook, Twitter, LinkedIn, Itunes, Youtube
Kumsal Bayazit, Global Senior Vice President
Haywood Talcove, Chief Executive Officer, Government
Ian McDougall, Executive Vice President
Mike Walsh, CEO
Alex Watson, Executive Vice President

The report offers timely and practical analysis on the hot issues in the field. Also features in-depth reporting of copyright law, including court decisions, new suits, settlements, and trials, plus full-text court documents.
Cost: $849.00
100 Pages
Frequency: Monthly
Founded in 2002

15649 Mealey's Litigation Report: Cyber Tech & E -Commerce
LexisNexis Mealey's
1016 W Ninth Avenue
1st Floor
King of Prussia, PA 19406-1221

215-564-1788
800-448-1515
Fax: 610-768-0880
E-Mail: mealeyinfo@lexisnexis.com
Home Page: www.lexisnexis.com/mealeys
Social Media: Facebook, Twitter, LinkedIn, Itunes, Youtube

Kumsal Bayazit, Global Senior Vice President
Haywood Talcove, Chief Executive Officer,

Government
Ian McDougall, Executive Vice President
Mike Walsh, CEO
Alex Watson, Executive Vice President

The Report covers disputes arising from e-commerce. The report tracks emerging legal issues, including: Internet security, data destruction and/or alteration, defamation on the Web, software errors, hardware failure, electronic theft, e-mail trespass, online privacy, government action, shareholder lawsuits, Internet jurisdiction issues, file sharing (copyright) disputes and much more.
Cost: $999.00
100 Pages
Frequency: Monthly
Founded in 1999

15650 Mealey's Litigation Report: Disability Insurance
LexisNexis Mealey's
1016 W Ninth Avenue
1st Floor
King of Prussia, PA 19406-1221

215-564-1788
800-448-1515
Fax: 610-768-0880
E-Mail: mealeyinfo@lexisnexis.com
Home Page: www.lexisnexis.com/mealeys
Social Media: Facebook, Twitter, LinkedIn, Itunes, Youtube

Kumsal Bayazit, Global Senior Vice President
Haywood Talcove, Chief Executive Officer, Government
Ian McDougall, Executive Vice President
Mike Walsh, CEO
Alex Watson, Executive Vice President

This report tracks the burgeoning number of disputes involving complex disability coverage claims. Topics covered include: claims for chronic fatigue, chronic pain, stress, psychiatric disabilities, chemical dependency and risk of relapse, plus key issues like total disability, own occupation, bad faith, ERSA, class actions and much mbre.
Cost: $849.00
100 Pages
Frequency: Monthly
Founded in 2000

15651 Mealey's Litigation Report: Discovery
LexisNexis Mealey's
1016 W Ninth Avenue
1st Floor
King of Prussia, PA 19406-1221

215-564-1788
800-448-1515
Fax: 610-768-0880
E-Mail: mealeyinfo@lexisnexis.com
Home Page: www.lexisnexis.com/mealeys
Social Media: Facebook, Twitter, LinkedIn, Itunes, Youtube

Kumsal Bayazit, Global Senior Vice President
Haywood Talcove, Chief Executive Officer, Government
Ian McDougall, Executive Vice President
Mike Walsh, CEO
Alex Watson, Executive Vice President

This report covers all of the discovery litigation essentials, including how different districts and judges interpret federal discovery rules, procedural changes, the work product, attorney-client and common interest privileges, and discovery abuse.
Cost: $785.00
100 Pages
Frequency: Monthly
Founded in 2003

15652 Mealey's Litigation Report: ERISA
LexisNexis Mealey's
1016 W Ninth Avenue
1st Floor
King of Prussia, PA 19406-1221

215-564-1788
800-448-1515
Fax: 610-768-0880
E-Mail: mealeyinfo@lexisnexis.com
Home Page: www.lexisnexis.com/mealeys
Social Media: Facebook, Twitter, LinkedIn, Itunes, Youtube

Kumsal Bayazit, Global Senior Vice President
Haywood Talcove, Chief Executive Officer, Government
Ian McDougall, Executive Vice President
Mike Walsh, CEO
Alex Watson, Executive Vice President

The report focuses on the hottest areas of ERISA litigation, including preemption, health plan actions, exhaustion of administrative remedies, contingent worker litigation, class actions 401k plans, attorney's fees, breach of fiduciary duty, what courts consider to be equitable relief, downsizing and benefit cutbacks, blackout periods and bad faith claims against disability insurers.
Cost: $875.00
100 Pages
Frequency: Monthly
Founded in 2002

15653 Mealey's Litigation Report: Ephedra/PPA
LexisNexis Mealey's
1016 W Ninth Avenue
1st Floor
King of Prussia, PA 19406-1221
215-564-1788
800-448-1515
Fax: 610-768-0880
E-Mail: mealeyinfo@lexisnexis.com
Home Page: www.lexisnexis.com/mealeys
Social Media: Facebook, Twitter, LinkedIn, Itunes, Youtube

Kumsal Bayazit, Global Senior Vice President
Haywood Talcove, Chief Executive Officer, Government
Ian McDougall, Executive Vice President
Mike Walsh, CEO
Alex Watson, Executive Vice President
The report tracks every facet of the growing area of litigation resulting from injuries and deaths associated with over-the-counter decongestant and appetite suppressant, phenylpropanolamine (PPA), and the chemically similar weight-loss herb, ephedra. The report offers true litigation reporting of new complaints, answers, discovery motions, appeals, trials, verdicts, settlements, plus covers the latest regulatory news.
Cost: $995.00
100 Pages
Frequency: Monthly
Founded in 2001

15654 Mealey's Litigation Report: Fen-Phen/Redux
LexisNexis Mealey's
1016 W Ninth Avenue
1st Floor
King of Prussia, PA 19406-1221

215-564-1788
800-448-1515
Fax: 610-768-0880
E-Mail: mealeyinfo@lexisnexis.com
Home Page: www.lexisnexis.com/mealeys
Social Media: Facebook, Twitter, LinkedIn, Itunes, Youtube

Kumsal Bayazit, Global Senior Vice President
Haywood Talcove, Chief Executive Officer, Government
Ian McDougall, Executive Vice President
Mike Walsh, CEO
Alex Watson, Executive Vice President

The report provides detailed coverage of the litigation surrounding fen-phen, Redux and other diet drugs. The report covers new filings, class actions, MDL proceedings, trials, settlements, rulings, medical studies, FDA activity and more.
Cost: $995.00
100 Pages
Frequency: Monthly
Founded in 1997

15655 Mealey's Litigation Report: Insurance
LexisNexis Mealey's
1016 W Ninth Avenue
1st Floor
King of Prussia, PA 19406-1221

215-564-1788
800-448-1515
Fax: 610-768-0880
E-Mail: mealeyinfo@lexisnexis.com
Home Page: www.lexisnexis.com/mealeys
Social Media: Facebook, Twitter, LinkedIn, Itunes, Youtube

Kumsal Bayazit, Global Senior Vice President
Haywood Talcove, Chief Executive Officer, Government
Ian McDougall, Executive Vice President
Mike Walsh, CEO
Alex Watson, Executive Vice President

The report tracks declaratory judgment actions regarding coverage for litigation arising from long-tail claims, including environmental contamination and latent damage and injury allegedly caused by asbestos, tox chemicals and fumes, lead, breast implants, medical devices, construction defects, and more. Key issues: allocation, occurrence, policy exclusion, choice of law, discovery, duty to defend, notice, trigger of coverage and known loss.
Cost: $2115.00
100 Pages
Frequency: Weekly
Founded in 1984

15656 Mealey's Litigation Report: Insurance Bad Faith
LexisNexis Mealey's
1016 W Ninth Avenue
1st Floor
King of Prussia, PA 19406-1221
215-564-1788
800-448-1515
Fax: 610-768-0880
E-Mail: mealeyinfo@lexisnexis.com
Home Page: www.lexisnexis.com/mealeys
Social Media: Facebook, LinkedIn, Itunes, Youtube

Kumsal Bayazit, Global Senior Vice President
Haywood Talcove, Chief Executive Officer, Government
Ian McDougall, Executive Vice President
Mike Walsh, CEO
Alex Watson, Executive Vice President

The report details insurance coverage disputes arising from alleged breaches of the implied covenant of good faith and fair dealing. The topics covered involve third-party and first-party actions, statutory suits, punitive damage claims, coverage denials and delays, the definition of bad faith, relevant legislation, verdicts, and discovery disputes.
Cost: $1325.00
100 Pages
Frequency: Semi-Monthly
Founded in 1987

15657 Medical Liability Advisory Service
Business Publishers

8737 Colesville Road
10th Floor
Silver Spring, MD 20910-3928

301-876-6300
800-274-6737
Fax: 301-589-8493
E-Mail: custserv@bpinews.com
Home Page: www.bpinews.com

Eric Easton, Publisher
Bonita Becker, Editor

Gives you practical information on just what triggers a lawsuit. Information you can pass on to your staff to claim-proof your procedures.
Founded in 1963

15658 **Medical Malpractice Reports**
Matthew Bender and Company
11 Penn Plz
Suite 5101
New York, NY 10001-2006

212-000-1111
Fax: 212-244-3188

Eric Blood, Data Processing

All the facts, background information and expert analysis you need to keep on top of new legislation, new theories of liability, the impact of new medical technology and more.

15659 **Mental and Physical Disability Law Reporter: On-Line**
American Bar Association
740 15th Street NW
Washington, DC 20005-1019

202-662-1000
Fax: 202-442-3439
Social Media: Facebook, Twitter, LinkedIn

Stephen N. Zack, President
Katherine H. O'Neil, Commission Chair
John W. Parry, Commission Director
Jack L. Rives, Executive Director
Alice Richmond, Treasurer

A new online searchable database allows subscribers to research disability law cases and legislation by case name, federal or state legislation, subject area, jurisdiction, and year (beginning 2003). There are 22 subject areas that cover three main areas: civil mental disability law; criminal mental disability law; and disability discrimination law. The database, which is updated every two months, contains over 12,000 summaries of key cases and legislation.
Cost: $299.00
15 Members
Frequency: 6 X/Year
ISSN: 0883-7902
Founded in 1973

15660 **Mergers & Acquisitions Litigation Reporter**
Thomson Reuters
610 Opperman Dr
St Paul, MN 55123-1340

651-687-7000
800-344-5008
Fax: 651-687-5581
Home Page:
www.store.westlaw.com/default.aspx

Charles B Cater, Executive VP
Laurie Zenner, VP

Provides summaries and fulltext documents in key litigation concerning mergers and acquisitions. Offers general buyout and acquisition coverage as well as cases related to leveraged buyouts.
Cost: $1234.20
Frequency: Monthly
Mailing list available for rent

15661 **Money Laundering Alert**
Alert Global Media
80 SW 8th Street
Suite 2300
Miami, FL 33130-3031

305-530-0500
800-232-3652
Fax: 305-530-9434
E-Mail:
customerservice@moneylaundering.com
Home Page: www.moneylaundering.com

Charles Intriago, President

Covers legal issues, including new laws, regulations and cases related to money laundering and the bank secrecy act in the US and worldwide. Provides practical guidance and analysis and serves as a training tool. Also full text on the internet.
Cost: $945.00
15 Pages
Frequency: Monthly
ISSN: 1046-3070
Founded in 1989

15662 **Municipal Litigation Reporter**
Strafford Publications
PO Box 13729
Atlanta, GA 30324-0729

404-881-1141
800-926-7926
Fax: 404-881-0074
E-Mail: customerservice@straffordpub.com
Home Page: www.straffordpub.com

Richard Ossoff, President
Jennifer Vaughan, Managing Editor

Monthly digest of key court decisions on litigation involving local governments. Cases are screened and selected to provide concise, comprehensive coverage of issues important to municipal attorneys and others involved with the local government.
Cost: $497.00
16 Pages
ISSN: 0278-1301
Founded in 1984
Mailing list available for rent: 7.4M names
Printed in one color

15663 **NAELA News**
National Academy of Elder Law Attorneys
1577 Spring Hill Road
Suite 220
Vienna, VA 22182-2223

703-942-5711
Fax: 703-563-9504
E-Mail: naela@naela.org
Home Page: www.naela.org

Peter G Wacht, CAE, Executive Director
Nancy Sween, Director Publications
Kirsten Brown Simpson, Director, Membership & Marketing
Ann Watkins, Operations Manager
Roger Naoroji, Meetings & Education Coordinator

Communicates the activities, goals, and mission of its publisher, the National Academy of Elder Law Attorneys and seeks out and publishes information and diverse views related to Elder Law and Special Needs.
Frequency: 6x Year

15664 **NCWBA Newsletter**
National Conference of Women's Bar Associations
PO Box 82366
Portland, OR 97282

E-Mail: info@ncwba.org
Home Page: www.ncwba.org

Jeanne Cezanne Collins, President
Pamela Berman, President-Elect
Diane Rynerson, Executive Director

To promote and assist the growth of local and statewide women's bar associations and ideas among women's bar associations and women's bar sections of local and statewide bar associations; to serve as a vehicle for the exchange and dissemination of information and ideas among women's bar associations and women's bar sections of local and statewide bar associations.
Frequency: Monthly

15665 **National Bankruptcy Reporter**
Andrews Communications
175 Stafford, Building 4
Suite 140
Wayne, PA 19087

610-225-0510
800-345-1101
Fax: 610-225-0501
Home Page: www.andrewspub.com

Robert Maroldo, Publisher

Commercial bankruptcy news.
Frequency: Monthly

15666 **National Bar Bulletin**
National Bar Association
1225 11th St Nw
Washington, DC 20001-4217

202-842-3900
Fax: 202-289-6170
Home Page: www.nationalbar.org

John Crump, Executive Director
Kim M Keenan, Manager
Teka Miller, Manager

Association news and activities, legislative updates and information for lawyers.
Cost: $20.00
8 Pages
Frequency: Monthly
Founded in 1925

15667 **National Financing Law Digest**
Strafford Publications
PO Box 13729
Atlanta, GA 30324-0729

404-881-1141
800-926-7926
Fax: 404-881-0074
E-Mail: customerservice@straffordpub.com
Home Page: www.straffordpub.com

Richard Ossoff, President
Jennifer Vaughan, Managing Editor

Monthly digest of nationally significant litigation concerning secured and unsecured financing transactions, including bonds, bankruptcy collection, and lender liability.
Cost: $597.00
Frequency: Monthly
ISSN: 1073-953X
Founded in 1984

15668 **National Notary**
National Notary Association
9350 DeSoto Avenue
PO Box 2402
Chatsworth, CA 91311-2402

818-394-4000
800-876-6827
Fax: 800-833-1211
E-Mail: publications@nationalnotary.org
Home Page: www.nationalnotary.org

Deborah Thaw, Executive VP
Armando Aguirre, Editor
Milton G. Valera, Chairman
Thomas A. Heymann, President /CEO
Deborah M. Thaw, Executive Vice President

Contents range from indentity fraud and electronic notarization, to legislation and practicing tips. Also includes human interest stories involving notaries.
Circulation: 250,000
ISSN: 0894-7872

Founded in 1957
Printed in 4 colors on glossy stock

15669 National On-Campus Report
Magna Publications
2718 Dryden Drive
Madison, WI 53704-3086

608-246-3590
800-433-0499
Fax: 608-246-3597
E-Mail: support@magnapubs.com
Home Page: www.magnapubs.com

William Haight, President
Jody Glynn Patrick, VP
Therese Kattner, Editor
David Burns, Publisher
Debra Art, Director

The campus legal monthly.
Cost: $169.00
8 Pages
Founded in 1972
Printed in 2 colors on matte stock

15670 National Paralegal Reporter
National Federation of Paralegal Associations
2815 Eastlake Ave E
Suite 160
Seattle, WA 98102-3278

206-285-1851
Fax: 206-284-3481
E-Mail: info@akpreparedness.com
Home Page: www.akproductions.com
Founded in 1981

15671 National Property Law Digests
Strafford Publications
PO Box 13729
Atlanta, GA 30324-0729

404-881-1141
800-926-7926
Fax: 404-881-0074
E-Mail: customerservice@straffordpub.com
Home Page: www.straffordpub.com

Richard Ossoff, Presdient

Case digests of national significant court decisions affecting the acquisition, development, management, transfer and financing of real property.
Cost: $697.00
Frequency: Monthly
ISSN: 0363-8340
Founded in 1984
Mailing list available for rent: 25M names

15672 National Report on Substance Abuse
National Retail Federation
325 7th St Nw
Suite 1000
Washington, DC 20004-2808

202-783-7971
800-673-4692
Fax: 202-737-2849
Home Page: www.nrf.com

Tracy Mullin, President
Terry Peters, Editor
Matthew Shay, President and CEO
Vicki Cantrell, Senior Vice President, Communities
Mallory Duncan, Senior Vice President

Biweekly review of federal and state laws, regulations and court cases involving alcohol and drug abuse, with an emphasis on workplace drug testing. Also covers treatment and prevention, EAPs, ADA, local laws and policies.
Cost: $377.00
Circulation: 36000
Founded in 1981
Printed in 2 colors on matte stock

15673 National Report on Work & Family
Business Publishers
2222 Sedwick Dr
Suite 101
Durham, NC 27713

800-223-8720
Fax: 800-508-2592
E-Mail: custserv@bpinews.com
Home Page: www.bpinews.com

Independent, authoritative resource covering the latest federal and state legislative, legal and regulatory developments concerning work/family issues. Includes case studies of organizations that have implemented family-friendly policies.
Cost: $497.00
Frequency: 25 per year

15674 National Security Law Report
American Bar Association-Law & National Security
740 15th St Nw
Suite 8
Washington, DC 20005-1022

202-662-1000
Fax: 202-662-1032
E-Mail: orders@abanet.org
Home Page: www.americanbar.org/aba.html
Social Media: Facebook, Twitter

Laurel G. Bellows, President

The Report includes reports of committee conferences, pertinent law and national security updates, recent cases, book reviews, pending legislation, and other writing relevant to the field.
Frequency: Monthly
Circulation: 4000
Founded in 1991

15675 Nolo News: Legal Self-Help Newspaper
Nolo Press
950 Parker St
Berkeley, CA 94710-2576

510-704-2248
Fax: 510-859-0027
E-Mail: LibraryCS@nolo.com
Home Page: www.nolo.com

Maggie Wang, Manager
Mary Randolph, Editor

Self-help legal newspaper.
Cost: $39.99
Frequency: Weekly
Circulation: 120000
Founded in 1971

15676 On the Line: Union Labor Reports Guide
Bureau of National Affairs
1801 S Bell St
Arlington, VA 22202-4501

703-341-3000
800-372-1033
Fax: 800-253-0332
E-Mail: customercare@bna.com
Home Page: www.bnabooks.com
Social Media: Facebook, Twitter, LinkedIn

Paul N Wojcik, CEO

Reports on shopfloor issues affecting union stewards. Includes summaries of arbitration awards and court cases. $4.00 per year each subscription.
Cost: $4.00
ISSN: 1526-2863
Founded in 1929

15677 Parascope
American Bar Association
321 N Clark St
Chicago, IL 60654-7598

312-988-5000
800-285-2221
Fax: 312-988-6281
E-Mail: askaba@abanet.org
Home Page: www.americanbar.org/aba.html
Social Media: Facebook, Twitter

Tommy H Wells Jr, President
Laurel G. Bellows, President

Newsletter for nation's appellate staff attorneys. Contains book reviews and articles on matters concerning appellate courts.
Cost: $19.00
Frequency: Quarterly

15678 Partner's Report for Law Firm Owners
Institute of Management and Administration
3 Bethesda Metro Center
Suite 250
Bethesda, MD 20814-5377

703-341-3500
800-372-1033
Fax: 800-253-0332
Home Page: www.ioma.com

Keeps partners up to date on salary guidelines and benefits, aw well as provide the reader with tips on increasing profit margins and exercising leadership skills.
Frequency: Monthly
Founded in 1984

15679 Patent/Trade/Copyright Newsletter
American Bar Association
321 N Clark St
Chicago, IL 60654-7598

312-988-5000
800-285-2221
Fax: 312-988-6281
E-Mail: askaba@abenet.com
Home Page: www.americanbar.org/aba.html
Social Media: Facebook, Twitter

Tommy H Wells Jr, President
Laurel G. Bellows, President

Activities of the Section, recent developments in intellectual property law and calendar of events.
Frequency: Quarterly
Founded in 1878

15680 People and Programs
American Bar Association
321 N Clark St
Chicago, IL 60654-7598

312-988-5000
800-285-2221
Fax: 312-988-6281
E-Mail: askaba@abanet.org
Home Page: www.americanbar.org/aba.html
Social Media: Facebook, Twitter

Tommy H Wells Jr, President
Laurel G. Bellows, President

A newsletter for donors and volunteers for the ABA fund for Justice and Education, which supports over 150 public service and law-related education programs.
Founded in 1878

15681 People-to-People Newsletter
Association of Legal Administrators
75 Tri-State International
Suite 222
Lincolnshire, IL 60069-4435

847-267-1252
Fax: 847-267-1329
E-Mail: publications@alanet.org
Home Page: www.alanet.org

Larry Smith, Executive Director
Debbie Thomas, Director, Accounting &

Finance
Renee Mahovsky, Director, Administration/Operations
Bob Abramson, Director, Marketing & Communication
Jan Waugh, Director, Member Services

Offers the newest information and legislative updates for legal administrators.
Frequency: Monthly
Founded in 1971

15682 **Personal Injury Verdict Reviews**
LRP Publications
PO Box 980
Horsham, PA 19044-0980

215-784-0912
800-341-7874
Fax: 215-784-9639
E-Mail: webmaster@lrp.com
Home Page: www.lrp.com

Todd Lutz, CFO
David Light, Managing Editor
Brooke Doran, Research Associate

Each twice-monthly issue contains a statistically based feature article backed by nationwide personal injury case summaries. Each case summary includes description of the incident, names and locations of counsel and expert witnesses, verdict or settlement amount, amount of medical expense and wage loss and date and docket number.
Cost: $375.00
Founded in 1977

15683 **Personnel Legal Alert**
Alexander Hamilton Institute
70 Hilltop Rd
Suite 2200
Ramsey, NJ 07446-2816

201-825-3377
800-879-2441
Fax: 201-825-8696
E-Mail: editorial@ahipubs.com
Home Page: www.ahipubs.com

Schuyler T Jenks, President

Deals with legal aspects of personnel.
Cost: $97.00
4 Pages
Frequency: Fortnightly
Circulation: 4000
Founded in 1989
Mailing list available for rent: 7,000 names at $125 per M
Printed in 2 colors on matte stock

15684 **Personnel Manager's Legal Letter**
Institute of Management and Administration
3 Bethesda Metro Center
Suite 250
Bethesda, MD 20814-5377

703-341-3500
800-372-1033
Fax: 800-253-0332
Home Page: www.ioma.com

PMLL regularly covers title VII, the Americans with Disabilities Act, ERISA, the Family and Medical Leave Act, and human resources legal issues around hiring, teminations, compensation and much more.

15685 **Practical Law Books Reviews**
Library Managemental Services
5914 Highland Hills Drive
Austin, TX 78731-4057

512-320-0320

Judith Helburn, Publisher

Reference book separated by field specification.

15686 **Premises Liability Report**
Strafford Publications
PO Box 13729
Atlanta, GA 30324-0729

404-881-1141
800-926-7926
Fax: 404-881-0074
E-Mail: customerservice@straffordpub.com
Home Page: www.straffordpub.com

Richard Ossoff, President
Jennifer Vaughan, Managing Editor

Digest of legal developments offering liability of property owners and managers. Warning system for potential lawsuits for injuries resulting from conditions on or near premises.
Cost: $287.00
Frequency: Monthly
ISSN: 1055-730X
Founded in 1984

15687 **Preservation Law Reporter**
National Trust for Historic Preservation
1785 Massachusetts Ave Nw
Washington, DC 20036-2189

202-588-6000
800-944-6847
Fax: 202-588-6038
E-Mail: members@nthp.org
Home Page: www.nationaltrust.org

Richard Moe, CEO
Andrew Carroll, Production Manager
Bob Barron, Publisher
Doug Loescher, Director

The definitive source on preservation law. It provides informative and reliable reports on recent court decisions, tax rulings, new publications and new legislation.
Cost: $95.00
Frequency: Monthly
Circulation: 400
Founded in 1949

15688 **Preview of US Supreme Court Cases**
American Bar Association
321 N Clark St
Chicago, IL 60654-7598

312-988-5000
800-285-2221
Fax: 312-988-6281
E-Mail: askaba@abanet.org
Home Page: www.americanbar.org/aba.html
Social Media: Facebook, Twitter

Tommy H Wells Jr, President
Laurel G. Bellows, President

Previews cases coming before the US Supreme Court.
Cost: $130.00
Frequency: Annual

15689 **Private Security Case Law Reporter**
Strattford Publishers
590 Dutch Valley Road NE
Atlanta, GA 30324-729

404-881-1141
800-926-7926
Fax: 404-881-0074
E-Mail: customerservice@straffordpub.com
Home Page: www.straffordpub.com

Richard Ossoff, Publisher
Albert J Pucciarelli, VP

Monthly digest decisions on litigation involving private security operations; includes insights and trend analysis by nations leading security expert.
Cost: $347.00
Frequency: Monthly
Founded in 1984

15690 **Probate and Property**
American Bar Association
321 N Clark St
Chicago, IL 60654-7598

312-988-5000
800-285-2221
Fax: 312-988-6281
E-Mail: askaba@abanet.org
Home Page: www.americanbar.org/aba.html
Social Media: Facebook, Twitter

Tommy H Wells Jr, President
Laurel G. Bellows, President

Aimed at lawyers who devote a large part of their practice to real estate law and laws dealing with wills, trusts and estates.
Cost: $60.00
Founded in 1978

15691 **Public Contract Newsletter**
American Bar Association
321 N Clark St
Chicago, IL 60654-7598

312-988-5000
800-285-2221
Fax: 312-988-6281
E-Mail: askaba@abanet.org
Home Page: www.americanbar.org/aba.html
Social Media: Facebook, Twitter

Tommy H Wells Jr, President
Laurel G. Bellows, President

Contains informative articles on a wide range of timely topics including current developments in federal and grant law, recent developments in state and local public contract law, upcoming educational programs and legislative developments.
Cost: $60.00
Frequency: Quarterly

15692 **Purchasing Law Report**
Institute of Management and Administration
3 Bethesda Metro Center
Suite 250
Bethesda, MD 20814-5377

703-341-3500
800-372-1033
Fax: 800-253-0332
Home Page: www.ioma.com

Purchasing Law Report is the most practical, least expensive and quickest way to understand and apply new purchasing laws and regulations in your day-to-day operations without wasting time sorting through hundreds of legal documents.

15693 **Report on Disability Programs**
Business Publishers
8737 Colesville Road
Suite 1100
Silver Spring, MD 20910-3928

301-876-6300
800-274-6737
Fax: 301-589-8493
E-Mail: custserv@bpinews.com
Home Page: www.bpinews.com

Leonard A Eiserer, Publisher

Follows legislation, regulations, legal actions and funding in areas import to all persons with disabilities including health care, employment, civil rights, housing, and transportation.
Cost: $227.00
8 Pages
Frequency: Monthly
Founded in 1963
Printed in on matte stock

15694 **School Law Reporter**
Education Law Association
300 College Park Ave
Dayton, OH 45469-0001

937-229-3589
Fax: 937-229-3845

E-Mail: ela@educationlaw.org
Home Page: www.educationlaw.org
Social Media: Facebook, Twitter, LinkedIn

W Brad Colwell, President
Mandy Schrank, Executive Director
Cate K. Smith, Executive Director
Judy Pleiman, Member Services Coordinator
Jody Thornburg, Publications Manager

Member association for those with an iunterest in school law issues, such as attorneys, law professors, education professors, school administrators, and teachers.
Frequency: Monthly
ISSN: 1059-4094
Founded in 1954

15695 Search and Seizure Law Report
Clark Boardman Company
375 Hudson St
Room 201
New York, NY 10014-3658

585-546-5530
800-323-1336

Robert Bouchard, Publisher
Elizabeth Brooks, Editor

Provides detailed, current coverage of the law, procedure, trends, and developments evolving in search and seizure law.
Cost: $175.00
8 Pages
Frequency: Monthly
Circulation: 2,000
Printed in 2 colors on matte stock

15696 Section of Taxation Newsletter
American Bar Association
321 N Clark St
Chicago, IL 60654-7598

312-988-5000
800-285-2221
Fax: 312-988-6281
E-Mail: askaba@abanet.org
Home Page: www.americanbar.org/aba.html
Social Media: Facebook, Twitter

Tommy H Wells Jr, President
Laurel G. Bellows, President

Update on current tax developments, committee projects, meeting information and order forms.
Cost: $15.00
Frequency: Quarterly

15697 Security Law
Strafford Publications
PO Box 13729
Atlanta, GA 30324-0729

404-881-1141
800-926-7926
Fax: 404-881-0074
E-Mail: customerservice@straffordpub.com
Home Page: www.straffordpub.com

Richard Ossoff, President

Monthly updates on security law without all the legal jargon.
Cost: $297.00
Frequency: Monthly
ISSN: 0889-0625
Founded in 1984
Mailing list available for rent: 31.6M names
Printed in one color

15698 Sexual Harassment Litigation Reporter
Andrews Publications
175 Strafford Avenue
Building 4 Suite 140
Wayne, PA 19087-3317

610-225-0510
800-345-1101
Fax: 610-225-0501
Home Page: www.andrewspub.com

Robert Maroldo, Publisher
Linda Coady, Editor
Cost: $49.00
Frequency: Monthly

15699 Small Firm Profit Report: Attorney Edition
Professional Newsletters
Atlanta, GA 30366-1143
770-819-4151

Robert Palmer, Publisher

Practice management and marketing help for small law firms and solo practitioners.

15700 Software Law Bulletin
Andrews Publications
1735 Market Street
Suite 1600
Wayne, PA 19087

610-225-0510
800-345-1101
Fax: 610-225-0501
Home Page: www.andrewspub.com

Donna Higgins, Editor

As pantenting becomes the predominant method of protecting software, and as cases involving technological copy protection measures wind through the court system, Andrews' Software Law Bulletin provides coverage of decisions and opinions in the key cases. Detailed articles put individual developments into the big picture of the changing law landscape.
Cost: $588.00
Frequency: Monthly
Founded in 1972

15701 Special Court News
American Bar Association
321 N Clark St
Chicago, IL 60654-7598

312-988-5000
800-285-2221
Fax: 312-988-6281
E-Mail: askaba@abanet.org
Home Page: www.abanet.org

Tommy H Wells Jr, President

Newsletter apprises members of the current activities and plans of the Conference. Also provides active, continual contact with members and solicits more active participation.
Cost: $11.00
Frequency: Quarterly

15702 Special Education Law Monthly
LRP Publications
747 Dresher Road Suite 500
PO Box 980
Horsham, PA 19044-980

215-784-0912
800-341-7874
Fax: 215-784-9639
E-Mail: webmaster@lrp.com
Home Page: www.lrp.com

Jessyca Harrington, Editor
Dionne Ellis, Managing Editor

Covers court decisions and administrative rulings affecting the education of students with disabilities. Each issue begins with a brief overview of the case summaries covered allowing you to quickly focus on the decisions and hearings that affect you most.
Cost: $140.00
Frequency: Monthly
Founded in 1977

15703 Sports & Entertainment Litigation Reporter
Andrews Publications
175 Strafford Avenue
Building 4 Suite 140
Wayne, PA 19087-3317

610-225-0510
800-345-1101
Fax: 610-225-0501
Home Page: www.andrewspub.com

Robert Maroldo, Publisher
Robert Sullivan, Editor

Covers the latest news in the fast-changing world of entertainment litigation.
Cost: $775.00
Frequency: Monthly
Founded in 1960

15704 Sports Medicine Standards and Malpractice Reporter
PRC Publishing
3976 Fulton Dr Nw
Canton, OH 44718-3043

330-492-6063
800-336-0083
Fax: 330-492-6176
Home Page: www.prcpublishingcorp.com

Molly Romig, VP

Designed to keep sports medicine professionals informed about current trends in their challenging professions. Accepts advertising.
Cost: $29.95
16 Pages
Frequency: Quarterly
Circulation: 500
ISSN: 0141-696X
Founded in 1984
Printed in 2 colors on matte stock

15705 Sports, Parks and Recreation Law Reporter
PRC Publishing
3976 Fulton Dr Nw
Canton, OH 44718-3043

330-492-6063
800-336-0083
Fax: 330-492-6176
Home Page: www.prcpublishingcorp.com

Molly Romig, VP

For those professionals in the sports, parks and recreational law. Accepts advertising.
Cost: $39.95
16 Pages
Frequency: Quarterly
Circulation: 500
ISSN: 0893-8210
Founded in 1997
Printed in 2 colors on matte stock

15706 State Legislative Report
American Bar Association
1800 M Street NW
#450S
Washington, DC 20036-5802

202-662-1000
Fax: 202-331-2220

Patrick Sheehan, Publisher
Diane Gibson, Editor

A summary of key legislative developments of interest to attorneys.
Cost: $50.00
4 Pages
Circulation: 800

15707 State and Local Law News
American Bar Association
321 N Clark St
Chicago, IL 60654-7598

312-988-5000
800-285-2221
Fax: 312-988-6281
E-Mail: askaba@abanet.org

Home Page: www.americanbar.org/aba.html
Social Media: Facebook, Twitter

Tommy H Wells Jr, President
Laurel G. Bellows, President
Richard W. Bright, Staff Editor

Informs members regarding Section activities and important issues of law.
Cost: $40.00
Frequency: Quarterly
Circulation: 6000
Founded in 1878

15708 **Summary and Reports**
American Bar Association
321 N Clark St
Chicago, IL 60654-7598

312-988-5000
800-285-2221
Fax: 312 988-6281
E-Mail: askaba@abanet.org
Home Page: www.americanbar.org/aba.html
Social Media: Facebook, Twitter

Tommy H Wells Jr, President
Laurel G. Bellows, President

Contains recommendations and informational reports to the ABA House of Delegates.

15709 **Summary of Labor Arbitration Awards**
LRP Publications
PO Box 980
Horsham, PA 19044-0980

215-784-0912
800-341-7874
Fax: 215-784-9639
E-Mail: webmaster@lrp.com
Home Page: www.lrp.com

Todd Lutz, CFO
Ken Kahn, CEO
Dana Eynon, Marketing Director
Claude Werder, VP
Marcy Witt, Marketing Director

Since 1959, the summary has been providing digests of private-sector labor arbitration decisions, covering the latest topics in collective bargaining with non-governmental employers.
Cost: $120.00
16 Pages
Frequency: Monthly
Founded in 1977
Printed in 2 colors on glossy stock

15710 **Syllabus**
American Bar Association
321 N Clark St
Chicago, IL 60654-7598

312-988-5000
800-285-2221
Fax: 312-988-6281
E-Mail: askaba@abanet.org
Home Page: www.americanbar.org/aba.html
Social Media: Facebook, Twitter

Tommy H Wells Jr, President
Laurel G. Bellows, President

Newspaper describing and commenting on developments in legal education.
Cost: $15.00
Frequency: Quarterly
Founded in 1978

15711 **Tax Laws of the World**
Foreign Tax Law
PO Box 2189
Ormond Beach, FL 32175-2189

386-253-5785
Fax: 386-257-3003
Home Page: www.foreignlaw.com

Income, corporate and related tax laws for over 100 countries. Many full text translations.
Cost: $100.00

15712 **Testifying Expert**
LRP Publications
747 Dresher Road
PO Box 980
Horsham, PA 19044-2247

215-784-0912
800-341-7874
Fax: 215-784-9639
E-Mail: webmaster@lrp.com
Home Page: www.lrp.com

Patrick Byrne, Editor
Gary Bagin, Circulation Manager

A newsletter designed to help experts develop a reputation or improve their present standing as an expert. Each monthly issue contains relevant decisions affecting the expert, book reviews and seminar listings.
Cost: $140.00
Frequency: Monthly
Founded in 1977

15713 **The ALI Reporter**
American Law Institute-American Bar Association
Continuing Professional Education
4025 Chestnut Street, Suite 5
Philadelphia, PA 19104

215-243-1600
Fax: 215-243-1664
E-Mail: ali@ali.org
Home Page: www.ali-aba.org
Social Media: Facebook, Twitter, LinkedIn

Julene Franki, Executive Director
Lawrence F. Meehan, Deputy Executive Director
Judith Cole, Executive Assistant
Bennett Boskey, Treasurer

This newsletter reports on the activities of the ALI and is primarily for its members.
Frequency: Quarterly
Founded in 1947

15714 **The Air and Space Lawyer**
American Bar Association Forum on Air & Space Law
321 N Clark St
Chicago, IL 60654-7598
312-988-5000
800-285-2221
Fax: 312-988-6281
E-Mail: askaba@abanet.org
Home Page: www.americanbar.org/aba.html
Social Media: Facebook, Twitter

Kenneth P. Quinn, Editor-in-Chief
John Palmer, Staff Editor
Laurel G. Bellows, President

Newsletter of significant developments in the field of air and space law as well as reports of Forum Committee activities.
Cost: $40.00
24 Pages
Frequency: Quarterly
Circulation: 2000
ISSN: 0747-7449
Printed in 4 colors

15715 **The Construction Lawyer**
American Bar Association
321 N Clark St
Chicago, IL 60654-7598

312-988-5000
800-285-2221
Fax: 312-988-5280
E-Mail: askaba@abanet.org
Home Page: www.americanbar.org/aba.html
Social Media: Facebook, Twitter

Thomas J. Campbell, Staff Editor
John W. Ralls, Editor-in-Chief
Laurel G. Bellows, President

Newsletter containing articles on recent developments in the construction industry as well as announcements pertaining to the Forum Committee or to other organizations in the field.
Cost: $50.00
48 Pages
Frequency: Quarterly

15716 **The Health Lawyer**
American Bar Association Section on Health Law
321 N Clark St
Chicago, IL 60654-7598

312-988-5000
800-285-2221
Fax: 312-988-5280
E-Mail: askabanet@abanet.org
Home Page: www.americanbar.org/aba.html
Social Media: Facebook, Twitter

Laurel G. Bellows, President

Provides informative articles that focus on a wide range of areas in the health law field and offers incisive analysis of key issues.
Cost: $60.00
Frequency: Bi-monthly

15717 **The National Notary**
Po Box 2402
Chatsworth, CA 91313-2402

818-739-4000
800-876-6827
Fax: 818-700-1942
E-Mail: hotline@nationalnotary.org
Home Page: www.nationalnotary.org
Social Media: Facebook, Twitter, LinkedIn

Milton G Valera, President
Deborah M Thaw, Executive VP
Marc Reiser, CEO
Jane Eagle, Executive VP & CFO
Ron Johnson, VP Systems & Operations

The National Notary addresses pertinent cutting-edge notarial issues in depth, and also features helpful how-to articles on every phase of operating as a professional Notary Public in the venue of American law and commerce.
200M Members
Frequency: Bi-Monthly
Circulation: 200,000
Founded in 1957

15718 **The Procurement Lawyer**
American Bar Association - Public Contract Law
321 N Clark St
Chicago, IL 60654-7598

312-988-5000
800-285-2221
Fax: 312-988-5280
E-Mail: pubcontract@abanet.org
Home Page: www.americanbar.org/aba.html
Social Media: Facebook, Twitter

John A. Burkholder, Editor-in-Chief
Laurel G. Bellows, President

Newsletter providing news on federal, state and local government procurement professionals.
Frequency: Quarterly

15719 **The SciTech Lawyer**
American Bar Association Science & Technology Law
321 N Clark St
Chicago, IL 60654-7598
312-988-5533
800-285-2221
E-Mail: sciencetech@abanet.org
Home Page: www.americanbar.org/aba.html
Social Media: Facebook, Twitter

Shawn T Kaminski, Section Director
Julie Fleming, Co-Editor-in-Chief
Eleanor Kellett, Co-Editor-in-Chief
Laurel G. Bellows, President

Quarterly practice specific magazine featuring cutting edge news.

15720 Tobacco Products Litigation Reporter
TPLR
PO Box 1162
Back Bay Annex
Boston, MA 02117-1162

617-373-2026
Fax: 617-373-3672
Home Page: www.tplr.com

Lissy Friedman, Publisher
Richard Daynard, Editor

Tobacco industry news.
Cost: $995.00
Founded in 1975

15721 Transnational Bulletin
Lewis, D'Amato, Brisbois & Bisgaard
221 N Figueroa St
Suite 1200
Los Angeles, CA 90012-2663

213-250-1800
Fax: 213-250-7900

Legal information for the international business community written by lawyers of the firm.

15722 Trial Judges News
American Bar Association
321 N Clark St
Chicago, IL 60654-7598

312-988-5000
800-285-2221
Fax: 312-988-6281
E-Mail: askaba@abanet.org
Home Page: www.americanbar.org/aba.html
Social Media: Facebook, Twitter

Tommy H Wells Jr, President
Laurel G. Bellows, President

This newsletter informs membership of the National Conference of State Trial Judges of the activities and programs of that conference.
Frequency: Quarterly
Founded in 1978

15723 Turning the Tide
People Against Racist Terror
PO Box 1990
Burbank, CA 91507-1990
FAX 818-848-2680

Michael Novick, Publisher

Bimonthly newsletter of anti-racist activism, research and education covering neo-nazi and other racist violence, efforts at conflict resolution and social justic reforms.
Cost: $10.00
24 Pages
Frequency: BiWeekly
Circulation: 7,500
Printed in 2 colors on newsprint stock

15724 Urban Lawyer
American Bar Association
321 N Clark St
Chicago, IL 60654-7598

312-988-5000
800-285-2221
Fax: 312-988-6281
E-Mail: askaba@abanet.org
Home Page: www.americanbar.org/aba.html
Social Media: Facebook, Twitter

Tommy H Wells Jr, President
Laurel G. Bellows, President

Articles on various areas of urban, state and local government law.
Cost: $49.95
Frequency: Quarterly
Circulation: 6000
Founded in 1879

15725 Utility Section Newsletter
American Bar Association
321 N Clark St
Chicago, IL 60654-7598

312-988-5000
800-285-2221
Fax: 312-988-6281
E-Mail: askaba@aba.org
Home Page: www.americanbar.org/aba.html
Social Media: Facebook, Twitter

Tommy H Wells Jr, President
Laurel G. Bellows, President

Articles pertaining to the field of public utility law.
Frequency: Quarterly
Founded in 1878

15726 Washington Employment Law Letter
M Lee Smith Publishers
PO Box 5094
Brentwood, TN 37219-2407
615-737-7517
800-274-6774
Fax: 615-256-6601
Home Page: www.mleesmith.com

M Lee Smith, Publisher
Michael Reynvaan, Editor

Reviews of employment laws.
Cost: $157.55
8 Pages
Frequency: Monthly
Circulation: 54,000
Founded in 1975
Mailing list available for rent
Printed in 2 colors on matte stock

15727 Washington Summary
American Bar Association
740 15th St Nw
Suite 8
Washington, DC 20005-1022

202-662-1000
Fax: 202-662-1032
E-Mail: cmpdi@abanet.org
Home Page: www.americanbar.org/aba.html
Social Media: Facebook, Twitter

Stephanie A Marella, Editor
Laurel G. Bellows, President

Tracks legislation and federal regulations of interest to lawyers by abstracting the Congressional Record and Federal Register.
Cost: $55.00
Frequency: Daily
Founded in 1878

15728 White-Collar Crime Reporter
Andrews Publications
175 Strafford Avenue
Building 4, Suite 140
Wayne, PA 19087-3317

610-225-0510
800-345-1101
Fax: 610-225-0501
Home Page: www.andrewspub.com

Robert Maroldo, Publisher
Edith McFail, Editor

Major articles guest written by practitioners in the area of white collar crame and covering such topics as sentencing guidelines, corporate liability, banking and securities fraud and government contract fraud.
Cost: $66.00
Frequency: Monthly
Founded in 1872

15729 Word Progress
American Bar Association
321 N Clark St
Chicago, IL 60654-7598

312-988-5000
800-285-2221
Fax: 312-988-6281
E-Mail: askaba@abanet.org
Home Page: www.americanbar.org/aba.html
Social Media: Facebook, Twitter

Tommy H Wells Jr, President
Laurel G. Bellows, President

Newsletter of the Word Processing User Group, includes updates on more effective word processing in the law office.
Cost: $50.00
Frequency: Quarterly

15730 World Jurist
World Jurist Assn of the World Peace Through Law
1000 Connecticut Avenue NW
Suite 202
Washington, DC 20036

202-466-5428
Fax: 202-452-8540
E-Mail: wja@worldjurist.org
Home Page: http://www.worldjurist.net

Sona Pancholy, Editor
M Henneberry, Executive VP

Research for international development as a basis for future world peace.
Cost: $80.00
Frequency: Fortnightly
Circulation: 6000
Founded in 1963
Printed in on glossy stock

15731 Your School and the Law
LRP Publications
747 Dresher Road Suite 500
PO Box 980
Horsham, PA 19044-2247

215-840-0912
800-341-7874
Fax: 215-784-9639
E-Mail: webmaster@lrp.com
Home Page: www.lrp.com

Stephen Bekiiacqwa, Editor

A monthly newsletter providing practical information on current judicial decisions affecting schools.
Cost: $190.00
Founded in 1977
Mailing list available for rent
Printed in one color on matte stock

Magazines & Journals

15732 AALL Spectrum
American Association of Law Libraries
105 W Adams Street
Suite 3300
Chicago, IL 60603

312-939-4764
Fax: 312-431-1097
E-Mail: support@aall.org
Home Page: www.aallnet.org
Social Media: Facebook, Twitter

Mark Estes, Editorial Director
Hillary Baker, Marketing and Communications
Kate Hagan, Executive Director
Kim Rundle,, Executive Assistant
Emily Feltren,, Director of Government Relations

Publishes substantive, well-written articles on topics of real interest to law librarians, as well as news about the American Association of Law Libraries, including its chapters, commit-

tees and Special Interest Sections
Cost: $ 75.00

15733 ABA Journal
American Bar Association
321 N Clark St
6th Floor
Chicago, IL 60654-7598

312-988-5000
800-285-2221
Fax: 312-988-6281
E-Mail: abajournal@abanet.org
Home Page: www.abanet.org

Tommy H Wells Jr, President
Robert Brouwer, Associate Publisher
Elizabeth Sullivan, Marketing Manager

Its editorial materials include news of interest to members of the legal profession. Editorial highlights include reviews of general interest and legal books, a US Supreme Court Digest section, a section listing significant rulings of other courts and news from government agencies.
Cost: $75.00
Frequency: Monthly
Circulation: 389420
Founded in 1878

15734 APA Magazine
American Polygraph Association
PO Box 8037
Chattanooga, TN 37414-0037

423-892-3992
800-272-8037
Fax: 423-894-5435
E-Mail: office@polygraph.org
Home Page: www.polygraph.org

Robbie S Bennett, National Office Manager
Gordon L. Vaughan, General Counsel
Donald Krapohl, Editor
Robbie S. Bennett, National Office Manager
Barry Cushman, President
Cost: $125.00
Frequency: Bi-Monthly
Founded in 1966

15735 Administrative Law Review
American University Washington College of Law
4801 Massachusetts Ave Nw
Suite 622
Washington, DC 20016-8180

202-274-4433
Fax: 202-274-4130
E-Mail: alr-editor-in-chief@wcl.american.edu
Home Page:
www.wcl.american.edu/journal/alr/
Social Media: Facebook, LinkedIn

Stacey L.Z. Edwards, Editor-In-Chief
Keeley McCarty, Executive Editor
Brittany Ericksen, Managing Editor
Sharon Wolfe, Journal Coordinator

Scholarly legal journal on developments in the field of administrative law and regulatory practice.
Cost: $40.00
Frequency: Quarterly
Founded in 1949

15736 Advance Sheet
150 Lincoln Street
Boston, MA 02111

617-695-3660
Fax: 617-695-3656

15737 AmLaw Tech
American Lawyer Media
345 Park Avenue S
New York, NY 10010

212-799-9434
800-888-8300
Fax: 212-972-6258
E-Mail: customersvc@amlaw.com
Home Page: www.americanlawyermedia.com

William L Pollak, President
Aric Press, Editorial Director
Kevin Vermeulen, Senior Vice President of Legal
Frequency: Annual+
Circulation: 16,500
Founded in 1997

15738 American Bankruptcy Law Journal
American Bankruptcy Institute
235 Secret Cove
Lexington, SC 29072

803-576-6225
Fax: 703-739-1060
E-Mail: Support@abiworld.org
Home Page: www.abiworld.org

Christine Molick, Executive Director
Marilyn Shea Stonum, Editor-in-Chief
J Rich Leonard, Associate Editor

Offers information on bankruptcy, legislation and financial information.
Cost: $65.00
Frequency: Quarterly
Founded in 1982

15739 American Lawyer
American Lawyer Corporation
Lbby L5
120 Broadway
New York, NY 10271-0096

917-562-2000
800-603-6571
Fax: 212-696-1845
E-Mail: lawcatalog@amlaw.com
Home Page: www.americanlawyermedia.com

Barbara Eskin, Circulation Director

Issues affecting lawyers and the legal profession, with an emphasis on the business aspect of law firms.
Cost: $349.00
102 Pages
Frequency: Monthly

15740 American Lawyers Quarterly
American Lawyers Company
853 Westpoint Pkwy
Suite 710
Cleveland, OH 44145-1546

440-871-8700
800-843-4000
Fax: 440-871-9997
E-Mail: alq@alqlist.com
Home Page: www.alqlist.com

Thomas W Hamilton, Executive VP
Frequency: Quarterly
Founded in 1899

15741 American University Business Law Review
American University Washington College of Law
4801 Massachusetts Ave Nw
Suite 615-A
Washington, DC 20016-8180

202-274-4433
Fax: 202-274-4130
Home Page: www.wcl.american.edu/blr/

Averell Sutton, Editor-In-Chief
Cameron Chong, Executive Editor
Sara Hill, Managing Editor
Sharon Wolfe, Journal Coordinator

Scholarly legal journal publishing articles providing cutting-edge legal analysis for the business law community, scholarly articles, case law analysis, and coverage of developing trends in a variety of areas to include financial regulation, international trade, antitrust, communications, healthcare and energy.
Cost: $40.00
Frequency: Quarterly
Founded in 2011

15742 American University International Law Review
American University Washington College of Law
4801 Massachusetts Ave Nw
Suite 610
Washington, DC 20016-8180

202-274-4433
Fax: 202-274-4130
Home Page: www.auilr.org
Social Media: LinkedIn

Lauren R Dudley, Editor-In-Chief
Daniel F Martini, Executive Editor
Michelle Mora Rueda, Managing Editor
Sharon Wolfe, Journal Coordinator

Scholarly legal journal publishing articles, critical essays, comments, and casenotes on a wide variety of international law topics, including public and private international law, the law of international organizations, international trade law, international arbitration, and international human rights. AUILR also publishes pieces on topics of foreign and comparative law that are of particular interest to the international legal community.
Cost: $40.00
Frequency: Quarterly
Founded in 1986

15743 American University Journal of Gender, Social Policy & the Law
American University Washington College of Law
4801 Massachusetts Ave Nw
Suite 632
Washington, DC 20016-8180

202-274-4433
Fax: 202-274-4130
Home Page:
www.wcl.american.edu/journal/genderlaw/
Social Media: Facebook

Rafael Roberti, Editor-In-Chief
J. Peter Bodri, Executive Editor
Claire Griggs, Managing Editor
Sharon Wolfe, Journal Coordinator

Scholarly legal journal that publishes articles addressing social and political equality under the law.
Cost: $40.00
Frequency: Quarterly
Founded in 1992

15744 American University Law Review
American University Washington College of Law
4801 Massachusetts Ave Nw
Suite 616
Washington, DC 20016-8180

202-274-4433
Fax: 202-274-4130
E-Mail: alr-editor-in-chief@wcl.american.edu
Home Page:
www.wcl.american.edu/journal/alr/
Social Media: Facebook, Twitter, LinkedIn

Brian R Westley, Editor-In-Chief
Mary M Gardner, Executive Editor
Christopher J Walsh, Managing Editor
Sharon Wolfe, Journal Coordinator

Scholarly legal journal, which publishes articles from professors, judges, practicing lawyers, and renowned legal thinkers. It is the only jounal in the nation to publish an annual issue dedicated to decisions of the Court of Appeals

for the Federal Circuit regarding patent law, international trade, government contracts, and trademark law.
Cost: $40.00
Frequency: Quarterly
Founded in 1952

15745 Animal Law Report
American Bar Association
321 N Clark St
Chicago, IL 60654-7598
312-988-5000
800-285-2221
Fax: 312-988-6281
E-Mail: askaba@abanet.org
Home Page: www.americanbar.org/aba.html
Social Media: Facebook, Twitter
Tommy H Wells Jr, President
Laurel G. Bellows, President
Summarizes recent legislation, case decisions and literature.
Cost: $10.00
Frequency: SemiAnnual

15746 AntiShyster
AntiShyster
PO Box 540786
Dallas, TX 75354-786
FAX 972-386-8604
Alfred Adask, Editor
Critical examination of the American legal system.
Circulation: 10000

15747 Antitrust Law Journal
American Bar Association
321 N Clark St
Chicago, IL 60654-7598
312-988-5000
800-285-2221
Fax: 312-988-6281
E-Mail: askaba@abanet.org
Home Page: www.americanbar.org/aba.html
Social Media: Facebook, Twitter
Tommy H Wells Jr, President
Laurel G. Bellows, President
MaryAnn Dadisman, Staff Editor
Covers proceedings of Section meetings, Section reports and positions on legislation, as well as content of National Institutes on antitrust law.
Cost: $120.00
Circulation: 10,000
Founded in 1878

15748 Arbitration Journal
American Arbitration Association
1633 Broadway
Suite 2c1
New York, NY 10019-6707
212-716-5800
800-778-7879
Fax: 212-716-5905
Home Page: www.adr.org
William K Slate II, CEO
Christine Newhall, Senior Vice President
Harry Kaminsky, Vice President
Cost: $30.00
Frequency: Quarterly
Founded in 1926

15749 Association of Legal Administrators
Association of Legal Administrators
75 Tri-State International
Suite 222
Lincolnshire, IL 60069-4435
847-267-1252
Fax: 847-267-1329
E-Mail: publications@alanet.org
Home Page: www.alanet.org
Larry Smith, Executive Director
Debbie Thomas, Director, Accounting & Finance
Renee Mahovsky, Director, Administration/Operations
Bob Abramson, Director, Marketing & Communication
Jan Waugh, Director, Member Services
Professional support for management of private law firms and other legal organizations worldwide.
Cost: $10.00
9500 Members
Founded in 1971
Printed in 4 colors on glossy stock

15750 Attorney/CPA
3921 Old Lee Highway
Suite71A
Fairfax, VA 22030-3926
703-352-8064
Fax: 703-352-8073
E-Mail: cmulligan@attorney-cpa.com
Home Page: www.attorney-cpa.com
Bernard Eizen, Publisher
Clark Mulligan, Executive Director
Promotes high ethical standards of dual licensed professionals.
Cost: $44.37
Founded in 1964

15751 BNA's Patent, Trademark and Copyright Journal
Bureau of National Affairs
1801 S Bell St
Arlington, VA 22202-4501
703-341-3000
800-372-1033
Fax: 800-253-0332
E-Mail: cuatomercare@bna.com
Home Page: www.bnabooks.com
Social Media: Facebook, Twitter, LinkedIn
Paul N Wojcik, CEO
Provides an in-depth review of significant current developments in the intellectual property field. Covers congressional activity, court decisions, relevant conferences, professional associations, international developments, plus actions of the Patent and Trademark Office and the Copyright Office.
Cost: $1968.00
Frequency: Weekly

15752 Barrister
American Bar Association
321 N Clark St
Chicago, IL 60654-7598
312-988-5000
800-285-2221
Fax: 312-988-6281
E-Mail: askaba@aba.net
Home Page: www.americanbar.org/aba.html
Social Media: Facebook, Twitter
Tommy H Wells Jr, President
Laurel G Bellows, President
Magazine containing general articles about the profession, the law and society in general.
Cost: $19.95
Frequency: 5 per year

15753 Broadcasting and the Law
One SE 3rd Avenue
#1450
Miami, FL 33131-1714
305-530-1322
Fax: 305-539-0013
E-Mail: broadlaw@aol.com
Matthew L Leibowitz
Addresses legal issues within the broadcasting industry.
Frequency: Monthly
Circulation: 400

15754 Business Law Today
American Bar Association Section on Business Law
321 N Clark St
Chicago, IL 60654
312-988-5000
800-285-2221
Fax: 312-988-5280
E-Mail: askaba@abanet.org
Home Page: www.americanbar.org/aba.html
Social Media: Facebook, Twitter
John Palmer, Staff Editor
Arthur F. Ferguson, Editor
Laurel G. Bellows, President
The Business Law Section's magazine edited for busy professionals: no footnotes and lots of the latest in business law.
64 Pages
Frequency: Bimonthly
Circulation: 55000
ISSN: 1059-9436
Printed in 4 colors

15755 Business Lawyer
American Bar Association
321 N Clark St
Chicago, IL 60654-7598
312-988-5000
800-285-2221
Fax: 312-988-6281
E-Mail: askaba@abanet.org
Home Page: www.americanbar.org/aba.html
Tommy H Wells Jr, President
Journal of business and financial law, with articles on current legal topics and substantive section programs.
Cost: $20.00
Frequency: Quarterly
Circulation: 60000
Founded in 1915

15756 Business Lawyer's Computer News
American Bar Association
321 N Clark St
Chicago, IL 60654-7598
312-988-5000
800-285-2221
Fax: 312-988-6281
E-Mail: askaba@abanet.org
Home Page: www.americanbar.org/aba.html
Tommy H Wells Jr, President
Information on new developments in technology for the business lawyer and news on how business lawyers are applying technology in their practices.
Cost: $50.00
Frequency: Quarterly

15757 Champion Magazine
National Association of Criminal Defense Lawyers
1660 L St Nw
Suite 1200
Washington, DC 20036-5632
202-872-8600
Fax: 202-872-8690
E-Mail: assist@nacdl.org
Home Page: www.nacdl.org
Quintin Chatman, Editor
Offers timely, informative articles written for and by criminal defense lawyers, featuring the latest developments in search and seizure laws, DUI/DWI, grandy jury proceedings, habeas, the exclusionary rule, death penalty, RICO, federal sentencing guidelines, forfeiture,

white-collar crime, and more
Cost: $70.00
Frequency: 10x/Year
Circulation: 13000

15758 Chinese Law and Government
ME Sharpe
80 Business Park Dr
Suite 202
Armonk, NY 10504-1715

914-273-1800
800-541-6563
Fax: 914-273-2106
E-Mail: info@mesharpe.com
Home Page: www.mesharpe.com

Myron E Sharpe, President
James Tong, Executive Editor
George Lobell, Executive Editor

Translations of significant works and policy documents, primarily from the Peoples Republic of China.
Cost: $144.00
Frequency: 1 Year 6 Issues

15759 Clearinghouse Reference Guide
American Bar Association
1800 M Street NW
Washington, DC 20036-5802

202-662 1000
Fax: 202-331-2220

Patrick Sheehan, Editor
Diane Gibson, Publications Coordinator

A summary of key state legislative developments of interest to attorneys.
Frequency: Annual
Circulation: 800

15760 Columbia Law School Magazine
Columbia Law School
435 West 116 Street
Box A-2
New York, NY 10027

212-854-2640
Fax: 212-854-7801
E-Mail: webmaster@law.columbia.edu
Home Page: http://web.law.columbia.edu
Social Media: Facebook, Twitter, LinkedIn

Matthew Malady, Editor
Joy Wang, Managing Editor

Features contributions that promotes ongoing discussion of social change and related issues.
Frequency: Biennial
Founded in 1754

15761 Commercial Law Journal
Commercial Law League of America
205 N. Michigan
Suite 2212
Chicago, IL 60601

312-240-1400
800-978-2552
Fax: 312-240-1408
E-Mail: info@clla.org
Home Page: www.clla.org
Social Media: Facebook, Twitter, LinkedIn

Oliver Yandle, VP
Charles R Johnson III, Treasurer

Law review journal covering such issues as credit, debt, insolvency, banking and the Uniform Commercial Code.
Frequency: Quarterly
Circulation: 6000
Founded in 1895

15762 Communications and the Law
Fred B Rotham Company
10368 W Cenntenial Road
Littleton, CO 80127-4205

800-828-7971
Fax: 716-883-8100

Theodore Kupfeman, Publisher

Features articles and book reviews on communications law, new technologies and law.
Cost: $25.00
Circulation: 585

15763 Complete Lawyer
American Bar Association
321 N Clark St
Chicago, IL 60654-7598

312-988-5000
800-285-2221
Fax: 312-988-6281
E-Mail: askaba@abanet.org
Home Page: www.americanbar.org/aba.html

Tommy H Wells Jr, President

Magazine provides practical articles directed to general practitioners, on substantive areas of law, news of council and committee activities.
Cost: $23.00
Frequency: Quarterly
Circulation: 16743

15764 Computer Industry Litigation Reporter
Andrews Publications
175 Strafford Avenue
Building 4, Suite 140
Wayne, PA 19087-3331

610-225-0510
800-345-1101
Fax: 610-225-0501
Home Page: www.andrewspub.com

Robert Maroldo, Publisher

Legal issues as they relate to hardware, software electronic databaes and the computer industry in general.
Cost: $875.00

15765 Computer Law Strategist
Leader Publications
345 Park Avenue S
New York, NY 10010-1707

212-799-9200
Fax: 212-696-1848

Stuart Wise, Publisher

For lawyers operating in the area of computer law and intellectual property.
Frequency: Monthly

15766 Corporate Control Alert
The Deal, LLC.
14 Wall Street
New York, NY 10005

212-313-9200
888-667-3325
Fax: 212-481-8128
E-Mail: customerservice@thedeal.com
Home Page: www.thedeal.com
Social Media: Twitter

Mickey Hernandez, Advertising Sales
Elena Freed, Marketing
Frequency: Monthly
Founded in 1999

15767 Corporate Counsel
American Lawyer Media
345 Park Avenue S
New York, NY 10010

212-779-9434
800-234-4256
Fax: 212-696-1845
Home Page: www.americanlawyermedia.com

15768 Court Review
American Judges Association
300 Newport Ave
Williamsburg, VA 23185-4147

757-259-1841
Fax: 757-259-1520
E-Mail: aja@ncsc.dni.us
Home Page: aja.ncsc.dni.us

James McKay, President

Highlights court decicions and precedents through articles written by US jurists and legal scholars.
Cost: $35.00
Frequency: Quarterly
Circulation: 2000
ISSN: 0011-0647
Founded in 1959

15769 Criminal Justice
American Bar Association
321 N Clark St
Chicago, IL 60654-7598

312-988-5000
800-285-2221
Fax: 312-988-6281
E-Mail: askaba@abanet.org
Home Page: www.americanbar.org/aba.html

Tommy H Wells Jr, President

Magazine providing practical treatment of aspects of the criminal law and reporting on legislative, policy-making and educational activities of the ABA Criminal Justice Section.
Cost: $38.00
Frequency: Quarterly
Circulation: 9000
Founded in 1915

15770 Cyber Esq.
Daily Journal Corporation
PO Box 54026
Los Angeles, CA 90054-0026

213-229-5300
Fax: 213-229-5481
Home Page: www.dailyjournal.com

Gerald L Salzman, CEO

Cyber Esq. is a guide for lawyers who use technology and whose practices are affected by the impact on the latest hardware and software and analysis of cutting-edge legal issues.
52 Pages
Frequency: Quarterly
Printed in 4 colors on n stock

15771 Daily Journal
Daily Journal Corporation
PO Box 54026
Los Angeles, CA 90054-0026

213-229-5300
Fax: 213-229-5481
Home Page: www.dailyjournal.com

Gerald L Salzman, CEO
Ray Chagolla, Circulation Manager

The Daily Journal Corporation provides lawyers with concise, comprehensive and intelligent coverage of legal news throughout the city, state, and nation. Through our family of publications we are able to serve the nation's largest legal markets.
Cost: $628.00
28 Pages
Frequency: Daily
Circulation: 11000
ISSN: 1059-2636
Founded in 1888
Printed in on n stock

15772 **Decisions & Developments**
PO Box 98
Bolton, MA 01740-0098

781-890-5678
Fax: 781-890-1150

15773 **Dispute Resolution**
American Bar Association Sec. Dispute Resolution
321 N Clark St
Chicago, IL 60654-7598

312-988-5000
800-285-2221
Fax: 312-988-5280
E-Mail: askaba@abanet.org
Home Page: www.americanbar.org/aba.html

Thomas J. Campbell, Staff Editor
Chip Stewart, Editor

A clearinghouse of information on programs related to the study of existing methods for prompt and effective resolution of disputes.
Cost: $45.00
32 Pages
Frequency: Quarterly
Founded in 1978

15774 **Dispute Resolution Journal**
206 Hulston Hall
University of Missouri
Columbia, MO 65211

573-823-3645
Fax: 212-716-5906
E-Mail: umclawcdr@missouri.edu
Home Page: www.law.missouri.edu

Jonathan R Bunch, Editor-in-Chief
Cassandra A Rogers, Managing Editor
Leonard Riskin, Manager
Cost: $21.00
Founded in 1984

15775 **Docket**
150 Lincoln Street
Boston, MA 02111

617-695-3660
Fax: 617-695-3656

15776 **Duke Law Journal**
Duke University School of Law
210 Science Drive
Box 90362
Durham, NC 27708

919-613-7006
Fax: 919-681-8460
E-Mail: dlj@law.duke.edu
Home Page: www.law.duke.edu
Social Media: Facebook, Twitter, LinkedIn, Youtube

Sarah Boyce, Editor-in-Chief
Julia Wood, Managing Editor
Jennifer Brady, Executive Editor
Philip Alito, Research Editor

The journal's purpose is to publish legal writing of superior quality, to publish a collection of outstanding scholarship from established legal writers, up and coming authors, and student editors.
Frequency: 8x/year
Founded in 1951

15777 **EEOC Compliance Manual**
Bureau of National Affairs
1801 S Bell St
Arlington, VA 22202-4501

703-341-3000
800-372-1033
Fax: 800-253-0332
E-Mail: customercare@bna.com
Home Page: www.bnabooks.com
Social Media: Facebook, Twitter, LinkedIn

Paul N Wojcik, CEO

A two-binder monthly service containing the complete text of the EEOC Compliance Manual, as issued by the EEOC, with monthly notification to related developments.
Cost: $410.00

15778 **Education Law Association**
Education Law Association
300 College Park Ave
Dayton, OH 45469-0001

937-229-3589
Fax: 216-687-5284
E-Mail: ela@educationlaw.org
Home Page: www.educationlaw.org
Social Media: Facebook, Twitter, LinkedIn

Mandy Schrenk, Executive Director
Cate K. Smith, Executive Director
Judy Pleiman, Member Services Coordinator
Jody Thornburg, Publications Manager

Brings together educational and legal scholars and practitioners to inform and advance educational policy and practice through knowledge of the law. Together, our professional community anticipates trends in educational law and supports scholarly research through the highest value print and electronic publications, conferences, seminars and professional forums.
Cost: $125.00
1400 Pages
Frequency: Monthly
Circulation: 1200
Founded in 1954

15779 **Energy Law Journal**
Federal Energy Bar Association
1990 M St Nw
Suite 350
Washington, DC 20036-3429

202-223-5625
Fax: 202-833-5596
E-Mail: admin@eba-net.org
Home Page: www.eba-net.org

Lorna Wilson, Administrator
Clinton A. Vince, Secretary, Treasurer
Michelle Grant, Secretary, Treasurer
Peter Trombley, Vice President

Lawyers and consultants engaged in energy and public utility law.
Cost: $35.00
Frequency: Monthly
Circulation: 2600
ISSN: 0270-9163
Founded in 1946
Printed in 2 colors on matte stock

15780 **Environmental Forum**
Environmental Law Institute
2000 L St Nw
Suite 620
Washington, DC 20036-4919

202-939-3800
800-433-5120
Fax: 202-939-3868
E-Mail: law@eli.org
Home Page: www.eli.org

John Cruden, President
Stephen R. Dujack, Editor
Linda Ellis, Manager Customer Service
Carolyn Fischer, Editorial Associate

Uses diverse points of view to stimulate the exchange of ideas and foster solutions for pressing environmental issues.
Cost: $115.00
60 Pages
Circulation: 2100
Founded in 1985
Printed in 4 colors on matte stock

15781 **Environmental Law Journal**
State Bar of Texas
1515 S Capitol of Texas Highway
Suite 415
Austin, TX 78746-6544

512-322-5800
Fax: 512-478-7750

Jimmy Alan Hall, Editor-in-Chief
Charles Jordan, Chairman

Provides members with current legal activities, recent developments and information pertaining to environmental and natural resource law, as well as section activities and other events pertaining to this area of the law.
Cost: $ 10.00
68 Pages
Frequency: Monthly
Founded in 1969

15782 **Experience**
American Bar Association
321 N Clark St
Chicago, IL 60654-7598

312-988-5000
800-285-2221
Fax: 312-988-6281
E-Mail: askaba@abanet.org
Home Page: www.americanbar.org/aba.html

Tommy H Wells Jr, President

News magazine for one of the fastest-growing sections in the ABA. Articles cover elderlaw, Council relationships, aspects of retirement including housing and health, and other topics of interest to lawyers pre- and post retirement.
Cost: $45.00
Frequency: Quarterly
Founded in 1878

15783 **Expert and the Law**
National Forensic Center
17 Temple Terrace
Lawrenceville, NJ 08648-3254

800-562-5177
E-Mail: info@nfstc.org
Home Page: www.nfstc.org/

Betty Lipscher, Publisher
David Epstein, Chief Operations Officer
Mike Berry, Program Manager

Appilcation of scientific, medical and technical knowledge to litigation.

15784 **Fair Employment Practices/Labor Relations Reporter**
Bureau of National Affairs
1801 S Bell St
Arlington, VA 22202-4501

703-341-3000
800-372-1033
Fax: 800-253-0332
E-Mail: customercare@bna.com
Home Page: www.bnabooks.com
Social Media: Facebook, Twitter, LinkedIn

Paul N Wojcik, CEO

A guide to the regulation of fair employment practices, including federal laws, orders and regulations; policy guides and ground rules; and state and local fair employment practice laws.
Cost: $1576.00
Frequency: Weekly
Founded in 1929

15785 **Family Advocate**
American Bar Association
321 N Clark St
Chicago, IL 60654-7598

312-988-5000
800-285-2221
Fax: 312-988-6281
E-Mail: askaba@abanet.com

Home Page: www.americanbar.org/aba.html
Social Media: Facebook, Twitter

Tommy H Wells Jr, President
Laurel G. Bellows, President
Amelia Stone, Marketer
Adrienne Cook, Development Editor

A practical journal in magazine format, containing information on divorce, mental health, juveniles, custody, support and problems of the aging as well as current trends, recent court decisions and new legislation.
Cost: $39.50
Frequency: Quarterly
Circulation: 11000
Founded in 1984

15786 **Family Law Quarterly**
American Bar Association
321 N Clark St
Chicago, IL 60654-7598

312-988-5000
800-285-2221
Fax: 312-988-6281
E-Mail: askaba@abanet.org
Home Page: www.americanbar.org/aba.html
Social Media: Facebook, Twitter

Tommy H Wells Jr, President
Laurel G. Bellows, President

A scholarly journal, including regular coverage of judicial decisions, legislation, taxation, summaries of state and local bar association projects and book reviews.
Cost: $79.95
Frequency: Quarterly
Circulation: 11000
Founded in 1998

15787 **Federal Communications Law Journal**
University of California-Los Angeles
Box 951476
Los Angeles, CA 90095-1476

310-825-7768
Fax: 310-206-6489
E-Mail: webmaster@law.ucla.edu
Home Page: www.law.ucla.edu

John Alden, Editor in Chief
David Matheson, Advertising Director

Articles on legal issues relating to the communications industry.
Cost: $10.00
Circulation: 2500

15788 **Federal Lawyer**
Federal Bar Association
1220 North Fillmore St.
Ste. 444
Arlington, VA 22201

571-481-9100
Fax: 571-481-9090
E-Mail: fba@fedbar.org
Home Page: www.fedbar.org
Social Media: Facebook, Twitter, LinkedIn

Jack D. Lockridge, Executive Director
Lori Beth Gorman, Executive Assistant
Lisa Sidletsky, Director Membership
Robert J. DeSousa, President
Hon. Gustavo Gelpi, Jr., President-Elect

Chronicles the news of the association and its members as well as providing practical coverage of issues affecting federal attorneys.
Cost: $35.00
Circulation: 15200
Founded in 1931

15789 **Fidelity and Surety News**
American Bar Association
321 N Clark St
Chicago, IL 60654-7598

312-988-5000
800-285-2221
Fax: 312-988-6281
E-Mail: askaba@abanet.org
Home Page: www.americanbar.org/aba.html
Social Media: Facebook, Twitter

Tommy H Wells Jr, President
Laurel G. Bellows, President

Summarizes selected recent cases on fidelity and surety law for professionals and lawyers.
Cost: $165.00
Frequency: Quarterly
Circulation: 1000
Founded in 1878

15790 **Firestation Lawyer**
Quinlan Publishing Company
23 Drydock Avenue
Boston, MA 02215-2336

617-542-0048
Fax: 617-345-9646
Home Page: www.quinlan.com

E Michael Quinlan, Publisher
Hoss Homaier, President, Chief Executive Officer

Case summaries of recent lawsuits involving fire departments. Discusses residency requirements of firefighters, worker's compensation, pensions, discrimination, and fire department rules and regulations.
Frequency: Monthly
Founded in 1950

15791 **Franchise Law Journal**
American Bar Association
321 N Clark St
Chicago, IL 60654-7598

312-988-5000
800-285-2221
Fax: 312-988-6281
E-Mail: askaba@abanet.com
Home Page: www.americanbar.org/aba.html
Social Media: Facebook, Twitter

Tommy H Wells Jr, President
Laurel G. Bellows, President
Robert A Stein, Executive Director

Journal in newsletter format primarily on current legal trends in franchising; also reports on activities of the Forum.
Cost: $50.00
Frequency: Quarterly

15792 **Health Law Litigation Reporter**
Andrews Publications
175 Strafford Avenue
Building 4, Suite 140
Wayne, PA 19087-3331

610-225-0510
800-345-1101
Fax: 610-225-0501
Home Page: www.andrewspub.com/

John E Backe, Publisher

Focus on cases involving ERSA, experimental insurance coverage, patient dumping, Medicare and Medicaid, medical devices, and federal and state legislation.
Frequency: Monthly
Circulation: 4100

15793 **Hospital Law Manual**
Publishers
200 Orchard Ridge Drive
Gaithersburg, MD 20878-1978

301-417-7500
800-234-1660
Fax: 301-698-7931
E-Mail: customer.service@aspenpubl.com
Home Page: www.aspenpub.com

Patricia Younger, Director

Hospital law.
Cost: $1325.00
Frequency: Quarterly
Founded in 1959

15794 **Human Rights**
American Bar Association
321 N Clark St
Chicago, IL 60654-7598

312-988-5000
800-285-2221
Fax: 312-988-6281
E-Mail: askaba@abanet.org
Home Page: www.americanbar.org/aba.html
Social Media: Facebook, Twitter

Tommy H Wells Jr, President
Laurel G. Bellows, President

Magazine containing news articles, features and commentary with relevance to human rights and individual rights and responsibilities.
Cost: $17.00
Frequency: Quarterly
Circulation: 6000
Founded in 1878

15795 **IP Worldwide**
American Lawyer Media
345 Park Avenue S
New York, NY 10010

212-779-9434
Fax: 212-592-4900
Home Page: www.americanlawyermedia.com

Steve Pressman, Editor
William L Pollak, CEO/President
Kevin Vermeulen, Publisher
Frequency: Quarterly
Circulation: 8000
Founded in 1997

15796 **Institute of Management & Administration Newsletter**
Institute of Management and Administration
3 Bethesda Metro Center
Suite 250
Bethesda, MD 20814-5377

703-341-3500
800-372-1033
Fax: 800-253-0332
Home Page: www.ioma.com

Monthly newsletter that supports law office administrators by offering training on how to reduce overhead, improve the firm's profitability and efficiency, get more value for the firm's budget dollar, and improve their own professional standing.
Frequency: Monthly

15797 **International Commercial Litigation**
Euromoney Publications
173 W 81st Street
New York, NY 10024-7227

212-874-4265
Fax: 212-501-8926

International litigation and dispute resolution news and developments in commercial law.

15798 **International Lawyer**
American Bar Association
321 N Clark St
Chicago, IL 60654-7598

312-988-5000
800-285-2221
Fax: 312-988-6281
E-Mail: askaba@abanet.org
Home Page: www.americanbar.org/aba.html
Social Media: Facebook, Twitter

Tommy H Wells Jr, President
Laurel G. Bellows, President

Practical issues facing lawyers engaged in an international practice.
Cost: $7.00
Circulation: 11000

15799 Journal of Court Reporting
National Court Reporters
8224 Old Courthouse Rd
Vienna, VA 22182-3808

703-556-6272
800-272-6272
Fax: 703-556-6291
Home Page: www.ncraonline.org
Social Media: Facebook, Twitter

Melanie Humphrey-Sonntag, President
Mark Golden, Executive Director & CEO
Tami Smith, VP
Bruce Matthews, Secretary/Treasurer

Covers information and views on matters related to the court recording and captioning professions.
20000 Members
Circulation: 34000
Founded in 1905

15800 Journal of Internet Law
Apen Publishers
111 Eighth Avenue
7th Floor
New York, NY 10011

212-771-0600
800-638-8437
Fax: 212-771-0885
Home Page: www.aspenpublishers.com

Mark F Radcliffe, Editor-in-Chief
Stacey Caywood, VP/Publisher
Mark Radcliffe, Editor
Gerry Centrowitz, VP Marketing And Communication
Robert Becker, CEO

Discusses strategies utilized by top intellectual property, computer law and information technology industry experts.
Cost: $380.00
Frequency: Monthly

15801 Journal of Paralegal Education and Practice
American Association for Paralegal Education
407 Wekiva Springs Road
Suite 241
Longwood, FL 32779

407-834-6688
Fax: 407-834-4747
E-Mail: info@aafpe.org
Home Page: www.americanbar.org/aba.html

Ronald Goldfarb, President

A journal offering news and information, pertaining to paralegal education.
Frequency: Annual

15802 Judges' Journal
American Bar Association
321 N Clark St
Chicago, IL 60654-7598

312-988-5000
800-285-2221
Fax: 312-988-6281
E-Mail: askaba@abanet.org
Home Page: www.americanbar.org/aba.html
Social Media: Facebook, Twitter

Tommy H Wells Jr, President
Laurel G. Bellows, President

Created to help judges and lawyers improve the administration of justice.
Cost: $23.00
Frequency: Quarterly
Founded in 1878

15803 Judicature
American Judicature Society
The Opperman Center at Drake University
2700 University Avenue
Des Moines, LA 50311

515-271-2281
800-626-4089
Fax: 515-279-3090
E-Mail: sandersen@ajs.org
Home Page: www.ajs.org

Seth S. Andersen, Executive Director
Krista Maeder, Assistant to the Executive Director
Laury Lieurance, Accountant/Membership Coordinator
Danielle Mitchell, Program Manager
David Richert, Editor

A forum for fact and opinion relating to all aspects of the administration of justice and its improvement.
Cost: $60.00
Frequency: Bi-Monthly
ISSN: 0022-5800

15804 Jurimetrics: Journal of Law, Science and Technology
American Bar Association
321 N Clark St
Chicago, IL 60654-7598

312-988-5000
800-285-2221
Fax: 312-988-6281
E-Mail: askaba@abanet.org
Home Page: www.americanbar.org/aba.html
Social Media: Facebook, Twitter

Tommy H Wells Jr, President
Laurel G. Bellows, President

Covers a wide range of topics on legal issues in science and technology.
Cost: $29.00
Frequency: Quarterly

15805 Juvenile and Child Welfare Law Reporter
American Bar Association
321 N Clark St
Chicago, IL 60654-7598

312-988-5000
800-285-2221
Fax: 312-988-6281
E-Mail: askaba@abanet.org
Home Page: www.americanbar.org/aba.html
Social Media: Facebook, Twitter

Tommy H Wells Jr, President
Laurel G. Bellows, President

Contains abstracts of case law on juvenile delinquency, abuse and neglect, adoption, termination of parental rights and other topics on child welfare.
Cost: $145.00
Frequency: Monthly

15806 Law
National Association of Legal Professionals
314 E 3rd Street
Suite 210
Tulsa, OK 74120-2409

918-582-5188
Fax: 918-582-5907
E-Mail: moore@nals.org
Home Page: www.nals.org

Jay Moore, Editor
Tammy Hailey, Publisher
Jay Moore, Communications Manager
Tammy Hailey, Executive Director
Cindy Rosser, Executive Assistant

Published content focuses on new products, technology and items of interest to the administrative staff within the legal profession.
Cost: $40.00
Frequency: Quarterly
Circulation: 7000
Founded in 1929

15807 Law Office Computing Magazine Services Section
James Publishing
PO Box 25202
Santa Ana, CA 92799-5202

714-755-5450
800-440-4780
Fax: 714-751-2709
E-Mail:
customer-service@jamespublishing.com
Home Page: www.jamespublishing.com

Jim Pawell, Founder/President
Tina Dhamija, Assistant Editor
Adrianne Choi, Production Manager

Focuses on law office automation. Issues contain independent reviews of legal software with side-by-side comparisons of the top programs, plus how-to articles and expert columns. Targeted editorial attracts legal technology buyers and helps them plan effectively for their purchases, buy wisely and use their investments to maximize productivity and profitability.
Cost: $49.00
96 Pages
Founded in 1981

15808 Law Practice Management
American Bar Association
321 N Clark St
Chicago, IL 60654-7598

312-988-5000
800-285-2221
Fax: 312-988-6281
E-Mail: askaba@abanet.org
Home Page: www.americanbar.org/aba.html
Social Media: Facebook, Twitter

Tommy H Wells Jr, President
Laurel G. Bellows, President
Jody Thornburg, Publications Editor

The pre-eminent magazine on all phases of law office management. Includes feature articles, book reviews, reports on technical innovations and announcements of forthcoming events.
Cost: $40.00
Founded in 1878

15809 Law Reporter
The American Association for Justice
777 6th Street, NW
Washington, DC 20001

202-965-3500
800-424-2725
E-Mail: membership@justice.org
Home Page: www.justice.org/

Peter C Quinn, Editor-in-Chief
Linda Lipsen, Chief Executive Officer
Charles Jeffress, Chief Operating Officer
Kathi Berge, Chief Financial Officer
Anjali Jesseramsing, Executive Vice President

Covers civil law, including automobile ,civil rights, insurance, commercial, employment and family law, medical negligence, premises liability and products liability, and workplace safety.
Cost: $135.00
40 Pages
Circulation: 53000
ISSN: 1052-4649
Founded in 1947
Printed in 2 colors

15810 Law Technology News
American Lawyer Media

345 Park Avenue S
New York, NY 10010

212-779-9434
Fax: 212-592-4900
E-Mail: subscribe@lawtechnews.com
Home Page: www.americanlawyermedia.com

Kevin Vermuellen, Publisher
Monica Bay, Editor
William L Pollak, President/CEO

Covers the use of technology in the law profession.
Cost: $99.00
Frequency: Monthly
Circulation: 40000
Founded in 1997

15811 Law and Social Inquiry: Journal of the American Bar Foundation
American Bar Association
321 N Clark St
Chicago, IL 60654-7598

312-988-5000
800-285-2221
Fax: 312-988-6281
E-Mail: askaba@abanet.org
Home Page: www.americanbar.org/aba.html
Social Media: Facebook, Twitter

Tommy H Wells Jr, President
Laurel G. Bellows, President

An academic and legal journal containing a wide range of research reports relating to the law, the profession and legal institutions.
Frequency: Weekly
Circulation: 4,00,000
Founded in 1878

15812 Law in Japan
Japanese American Society for Legal Studies
University of WA Law School-1100 NE Cam.
Seattle, WA 98105

206-233-9292
Fax: 206-685-4469

John Haley, Editor

Academic journal with translation, original articles, comments and case notes on Japanese law and legal issues.
Cost: $13.00
Circulation: 1,400

15813 Lawyers Weekly USA
Lawyers Weekly Publications
10 Milk Street
Suite 1000
Boston, MA 02111-1203

617-451-7300
366-294-8963
Fax: 617-451-1466
E-Mail: comments@lawyersweekly.com
Home Page: www.lawyersweeklyusa.com
Social Media: Facebook, Twitter, LinkedIn

Scott Murdock, Circulation Manager
Susan Bocamazo, Editor
Reni Germer, Managing Editor

Features profiles, practice tips, technology, marketing, management and other topics related to law practice.
Cost: $249.00
Frequency: Monthly
Circulation: 2500
Founded in 1972

15814 Lawyers' Professional Liability Update
American Bar Association
321 N Clark St
Chicago, IL 60654-7598

312-988-5000
800-285-2221
Fax: 312-988-6281
E-Mail: askaba@abanet.org
Home Page: www.americanbar.org/aba.html
Social Media: Facebook, Twitter

Tommy H Wells Jr, President
Laurel G. Bellows, President

Current reports and articles on legal malpractice insurance marketplace and other aspects of legal malpractice.
Cost: $45.00
Circulation: 23,000

15815 Leadership and Management Directions
American Bar Association
321 N Clark St
Chicago, IL 60654-7598

312-988-5000
800-285-2221
Fax: 312-988-6281
E-Mail: askaba@abanet.org
Home Page: www.americanbar.org/aba.html
Social Media: Facebook, Twitter

Tommy H Wells Jr, President
Laurel G. Bellows, President

Focuses on trends, principles, and practices in law office management including financial matters, marketing, human resources, facilities and technology.
Cost: $50.00
Frequency: Quarterly

15816 Legal Management: Journal of the Association of Legal Administrators
Association of Legal Administrators
75 Tri-State International
Suite 222
Lincolnshire, IL 60069-4435

847-267-1252
Fax: 847-267-1329
E-Mail: publications@alanet.org
Home Page: www.alanet.org

Larry Smith, Executive Director
Debbie Thomas, Director, Accounting & Finance
Renee Mahovsky, Director, Administration/Operations
Bob Abramson, Director, Marketing & Communication
Jan Waugh, Director, Member Services

Covers personnel management, finance, strategic planning, the legal industry, business software, technology. leadership, interpersonal communication, time and stress management, and disaster planning.
Circulation: 25000
Founded in 1971

15817 Legal Tech
Leader Publications
345 Park Avenue S
New York, NY 10010-1707

212-799-9200
800-888-8300
Fax: 212-696-1848

Stuart Wise, Publisher
Frequency: Monthly

15818 Legal Times
American Lawyers Newspapers Group
1730 M St Nw
Suite 802
Washington, DC 20036-4550

202-296-1995
Fax: 202-457-0718
Home Page: www.legaltimes.com

Peter Scheer, Editor
Ann Pelham, Publisher
Eva Rodriguev, Editor-in-Chief
Gwen Jones, Circulation Manager
Rose Mahoney, Sales Manager

Covers law, lobbying and politics.
Cost: $349.00
36 Pages
Frequency: Weekly
Circulation: 6200
Founded in 1977

15819 Lender Liability Litigation Reporter
Andrews Communications
175 Stafford Building 4
Suite 140
Wayne, PA 19087

610-225-0510
800-328-4880
Fax: 610-225-0501

Robert Maroldo, Publisher

Journal of record, of litigation proceedings involving lender liability issues.
Cost: $650.00
Frequency: Monthly

15820 License
1 Park Avenue
2nd Floor
New York, NY 10016

212-951-6600
888-527-7008
Fax: 212-951-6714
E-Mail: info@advanstar.com
Home Page: www.licensemag.com

Joyceann Cooney, Editor-in-Chief
Lorri Freifeld, Managing Editor
Steven Ekstract, Publisher
Sharon Weisman, Sales Manager

Patents, trademarks and copyrights
Frequency: Monthly
Circulation: 25000
Founded in 1987

15821 Litigation
American Bar Association
321 N Clark St
Chicago, IL 60654-7598

312-988-5000
800-285-2221
Fax: 312-988-6281
E-Mail: askaba@abanet.org
Home Page: www.americanbar.org/aba.html
Social Media: Facebook, Twitter

Tommy H Wells Jr, President
Laurel G. Bellows, President

A journal for trial lawyers and judges, each issue of which focuses on a particular topic involving trial practice.
Cost: $39.50
Frequency: Quarterly

15822 M and A Lawyer
Glasser LegalWorks
150 Clove Road
Little Falls, NJ 07424-2138

973-890-0008
Fax: 973-890-0042
Home Page: www.legalwks.com

Steven E Bochner, Editor
Stephen W Seemer, President

News affecting all types of mergers and acquisitions transactions, including securities law, state law, international, taxation, accounting and practice areas like intellectual property, employee benefits/compensation, antitrust and environmental.
Cost: $317.00
Circulation: 500
Founded in 1995

15823 Mental & Physical Disability Law
American Bar Association

740 15th St Nw
Suite 8
Washington, DC 20005-1022

202-662-1000
Fax: 202-662-1032
E-Mail: cmpdi@abanet.org
Home Page: www.americanbar.org/aba.html
Social Media: Facebook, Twitter

William Neukom, President
Laurel G. Bellows, President
John Parry, Executive Director

A bi-monthly journal published by the Commission on Mental and Physical Disability Law, containing timely summaries of reported legal developments in 22 disability subject areas - over 1600 summaries annually.
Founded in 1878

15824 Mental & Physical Disability Law Reporter
American Bar Association
740 15th Street NW
Washington, DC 20005-1019

202-662-1570
Fax: 202-442-3439
E-Mail: cmpdl@abanet.org
Home Page: www.abanet.org/disability
Social Media: Facebook, Twitter, LinkedIn

Stephen N. Zack, President
Katherine H. O'Neil, Commission Chair
John W. Parry, Commission Director
Jack L. Rives, Executive Director
Alice Richmond, Treasurer

Published since 1976, the Reporter is the only periodical that comprehensively covers civil and criminal mental disability law and disability discrimination law. Organized by 22 subject areas, the Reporter allows you to target your research and save time. A perfect complement to your online legal research databases.
Cost: $325.00
15 Members
Frequency: 6 X/Year
Circulation: 300+
ISSN: 0883-7902
Founded in 1973

15825 Mental Health Law Reporter
Business Publishers
2222 Sedwick Drive
Durham, NC 27713

800-223-8720
Fax: 800-508-2592
E-Mail: custserv@bpinews.com
Home Page: www.bpinews.com

Sarah Terry, Managing Editor

Court decisions affecting mental health professionals.
Cost: $277.00
Frequency: Monthly
Founded in 1963

15826 Midwest Alternative Dispute Resolution Guide
Law Bulletin Publishing Company
415 N State St
Suite 1
Chicago, IL 60654-8116

312-644-7800
Fax: 312-644-4255
Home Page: www.lawbulletin.com

Lanning Macfarland Jr, President

Profiles of midwest attorneys.
Cost: $219.00
156 Pages
Frequency: Monthly
Founded in 1854

15827 Midwest Legal Staffing Guide
Law Bulletin Publishing Company
415 N State St
Suite 1
Chicago, IL 60654-8116

312-644-7800
Fax: 312-644-4255
E-Mail: editor@lbpc.com
Home Page: www.lawbulletin.com

Lanning Macfarland Jr, President
Bernard Judge, Editor
Stephen E Brown, Publisher

Monthly magazine about law, people and opportunity.
Frequency: Daily
Founded in 1854
Printed in 4 colors

15828 Midwest Legal Technology Guide
Law Bulletin Publishing Company
415 N State St
Suite 1
Chicago, IL 60654-8116

312-644-7800
Fax: 312-644-4255
Home Page: www.lawbulletin.com

Lanning Macfarland Jr, President

Supplement to the Chicago Daily Law Bulletin and Chicago Lawyer. Eliminates the confusion arising from the many new technological service and product providers.
60 Pages

15829 NAELA Journal
National Academy of Elder Law Attorneys
1577 Spring Hill Road
Suite 220
Vienna, VA 22182-2223

703-942-5711
Fax: 703-563-9504
E-Mail: naela@naela.org
Home Page: www.naela.org

Peter G Wacht, CAE, Executive Director
Nancy Sween, Director, Comm. & Publications
Kirsten Brown Simpson, Director, Membership & Marketing
Ann Watkins, Operations Manager
Roger Naoroji, Meetings & Education Coordinator

Peer-reviewed, scholarly publication of substantive articles on Elder and Special Needs Law topics.
Frequency: 2x Year

15830 National Bar Association Magazine
National Bar Association
1225 11th St Nw
Washington, DC 20001-4217

202-842-3900
Fax: 202-289-6170
E-Mail: headquarters@nationalbar.org
Home Page: www.nationalbar.org
Social Media: Facebook, Twitter, LinkedIn

John Crump, Executive Director

Founded in 1925, the National Bar Association (NBA) is the nation's oldest and largest association of African American lawyers and judges.
Cost: $32.00
Circulation: 25,000
Founded in 1925

15831 National Jurist
PO Box 939039
Sandy, CA 92193

858-503-7786
Fax: 858-503-7588
E-Mail: jurist@clark.net
Home Page: www.nationaljurist.com

Jack Crittenden, Editor-in-Chief
Keith Carter, Managing Editor
Rebecca Luczycki, Editor
Mike Wright, National Accounts Manager

Information, advice, news and entertainment for law and pre-law students to help them succeed in law school.
Cost: $30.00
Circulation: 100000
Founded in 1996

15832 National Notary
National Notary Association
9350 Desoto Avenue
Post Office Box 2402
Chatsworth, CA 91313-2402

818-739-4000
800-876-6827
Fax: 800-833-1211
E-Mail: webmaster@nationalnotary.org
Home Page: www.nationalnotary.org

Deborah M. Thaw, Executive Vice President
Milton Valera, President
Mark Valera, Managing Director
Thomas Hayden, Director of Marketing

Focuses on the importance of notaries as public servants and updates readers on related news.
Founded in 1957

15833 National Paralegal Reporter
National Federation of Paralegal Association
PO Box 2018
Edmonds, WA 98020

425-967-0045
Fax: 425-771-9588
E-Mail: info@paralegals.org
Home Page: www.paralegals.org

Features in-depth articles on timely topics such as paralegal roles and choosing vendors; how-toarticles providing readers with practical information that can be directly applied to their careers; and provides legal updated providing information that affects the paralegal profession such as case law, legislation, and technology education.
Cost: $30.00
Frequency: Bi-Monthly
Circulation: 10,000

15834 Natural Resources and Environment
American Bar Association
740 15th St Nw
Suite 8
Washington, DC 20005-1022

202-662-1000
800-285-2221
Fax: 202-662-1032
E-Mail: service@abanet.org
Home Page: www.abanet.org

Practical magazine on the latest developments in the field of natural resources law.
Cost: $60.00
Frequency: Quarterly
Circulation: 12000

15835 Negotiation Journal
Plenum Publishing Corporation
513 Pound Hall
Cambridge, MA 02138

617-495-1684
Fax: 617-495-7818
Home Page: www.pon.harvard.edu

Michael Wheeler, Editor
Nancy Waters, Managing Editor

Investigates theoretical and practical developments in the conflict resolution field.
Cost: $79.00
Frequency: Quarterly
Founded in 1998

15836 Older Americans Report
Business Publishers

8737 Colesville Road
Suite 1100
Silver Spring, MD 20910-3928

301-876-6300
800-274-6737
Fax: 301-589-8493
E-Mail: custserv@bpinews.com
Home Page: www.bpinews.com

Leonard A Eiserer, Publisher
Beth Early, Operations Director
Mark Sherman, Editor

Covers every issue and program that affects your decision-making: Older Americans Act, long term care, Social Security & SSI, nutrition, nursing home regulation, housing, retirement/pension issues, all block grants for the aged, and more.
Cost: $427.00
Frequency: Weekly
Founded in 1963

15837 **Payroll Administration Guide**
Bureau of National Affairs
1801 S Bell St
Arlington, VA 22202-4501

703-341-3000
800-372-1033
Fax: 800-253-0332
E-Mail: customercare@bna.com
Home Page: www.bnabooks.com
Social Media: Facebook, Twitter, LinkedIn

Paul N Wojcik, CEO

A notification and reference service for payroll professionals. Covers federal and state employment tax, wage-hour and wage-payment laws.
Cost: $896.00
Frequency: Bi-Weekly
Founded in 1929

15838 **Polygraph**
American Polygraph Association
PO Box 8037
Chattanooga, TN 37414-0037

423-892-3992
800-272-8037
Fax: 423-894-5435
E-Mail: office@polygraph.org
Home Page: www.polygraph.org

Robbie S Bennett, National Office Manager
Gordon L. Vaughan, General Counsel
Donald Krapohl, Editor
Robbie S. Bennett, National Office Manager
Barry Cushman, President

Features articles about the psychophysiological detection of deception, and related areas.
Cost: $125.00
Frequency: Quarterly
Founded in 1966

15839 **Preview of United States Supreme Court Cases**
American Bar Association
321 N Clark St
Chicago, IL 60654-7598

312-988-5000
800-285-2221
Fax: 312-988-6281
E-Mail: askaba@abanet.org
Home Page: www.americanbar.org/aba.html
Social Media: Facebook, Twitter

Tommy H Wells Jr, President
Laurel G. Bellows, President

Advance analysis by legal experts of the issues, facts and significance of each case being argued before the Supreme Court, plus special summer issue with all court decisions.
Cost: $340.00
Frequency: 10-12 issues

15840 **Probate Lawyer**
3415 S Sepulveda Boulevard
Suite 460
Los Angeles, CA 90034-6014

310-478-4454

Offers legislative news for probate courts.
Frequency: Annual

15841 **Professional Lawyer**
American Bar Association
321 N Clark St
Chicago, IL 60654-7598

312-988-5000
800-285-2221
Fax: 312-988-6281
E-Mail: askaba@abanet.org
Home Page: www.americanbar.org/aba.html
Social Media: Facebook, Twitter

Tommy H Wells Jr, President
Laurel G. Bellows, President

A magazine providing a forum for exchange of views and ideas on professionalism issues for bar leaders, lawyers, law school education and others interested in professionalism.
Cost: $40.00
Founded in 1878

15842 **Prosecutor**
National District Attorneys Association
44 Canal Center Plz
Suite 110
Alexandria, VA 22314-1548

703-549-4253
Fax: 703-836-3195
E-Mail: trafficemail@ndaa.org
Home Page: www.ndaa.org

Thomas Charron, Executive Director
Paul F Walsh Jr, Manager
Bill Gibbs, Manager

Covers a variety of criminal justice topics including child abuse, telemarketing fraud, violence against women, vehicular crime, DNA, juvenile justice and community prosecution.
48 Pages
Circulation: 7000
ISSN: 0027-6383
Founded in 1977
Mailing list available for rent: 6,500 names
Printed in 4 colors on glossy stock

15843 **Public Contract Law Journal**
American Bar Association
321 N Clark St
Chicago, IL 60654-7598

312-988-5000
800-285-2221
Fax: 312-988-6281
E-Mail: askaba@abanet.org
Home Page: www.americanbar.org/aba.html
Social Media: Facebook, Twitter

Tommy H Wells Jr, President
Laurel G. Bellows, President

Contains articles on all phases of federal, state and local procurement and grant law by leading authoritiies.
Cost: $60.00
Frequency: Annual+

15844 **Real Property, Property and Trust Journal**
American Bar Association
740 15th St Nw
Suite 8
Washington, DC 20005-1022

202-662-1000
Fax: 202-662-1032
E-Mail: collinsj@staff.abanet.org
Home Page: www.americanbar.org/aba.html
Social Media: Facebook, Twitter

William Neukom, President
Laurel G. Bellows, President
Jennifer Collins, Advertising Sales Coordinator

Scholarly articles in the fields of estate planning, trust law and real property law.
Cost: $60.00
Frequency: Quarterly

15845 **Review of Banking and Financial Services**
Standard & Poor's Corporation
55 Water St
New York, NY 10041-0003

212-438-1000
Fax: 212-438-0299
E-Mail: clientsupport@standardandpoors.com
Home Page: www.standardandpoors.com

Deven Sharma, President
Hendrik Kranenburg, Executive VP

Focuses on laws and regulations affecting the banking and related industries.
Founded in 1941

15846 **Review of Securities & Commodities Regulation**
Standard & Poor's Corporation
55 Water St
44th Floor
New York, NY 10041-0003

212-438-1000
Fax: 212-438-0299

Deven Sharma, President

Information on the laws and regulations affecting the securities and future industries.
Cost: $8.55
Frequency: 22 per year
Printed in on newsprint stock

15847 **Right of Way**
International Right of Way
19750 S Vermont Ave
Suite 220
Torrance, CA 90502-1144

310-538-0233
Fax: 310-538-1471
E-Mail: info@irwaonline.org
Home Page: www.irwa.net

Mark Rieck, Executive VP
Barbara Billitzer, Publisher
Cost: $425.00
Founded in 1985

15848 **Specialization Update**
American Bar Association
321 N Clark St
Chicago, IL 60654-7598

312-988-5000
800-285-2221
Fax: 312-988-6281
E-Mail: askaba@abanet.org
Home Page: www.abanet.org

Tommy H Wells Jr, President

A compilation of current news briefs and articles of interest on lawyer specialization and related topics.
Circulation: 4,00,000
Founded in 1878

15849 **Student Lawyer**
American Bar Association
321 N Clark St
Chicago, IL 60654-7598

312-988-5000
800-285-2221
Fax: 312-988-6281
E-Mail: askaba@abanet.org

Home Page: www.americanbar.org/aba.html
Social Media: Facebook, Twitter

Tommy H Wells Jr, President
Laurel G. Bellows, President

Magazine for law students featuring articles on legal, political, social issues, law school and the profession.
Cost: $20.00
Frequency: Monthly
ISSN: 0039-274X
Founded in 1972
Printed in 4 colors on glossy stock

15850 **Tax Lawyer**
American Bar Association
321 N Clark St
Chicago, IL 60654-7598

312-988-5000
800-285-2221
Fax: 312-988-6281
E-Mail: askaba@abanet.org
Home Page: www.americanbar.org/aba.html
Social Media: Facebook, Twitter

Tommy H Wells Jr, President
Laurel G. Bellows, President

Journal of scholarly articles written by highly respected attorneys in the field and a thought-provoking student notes and comments section.
Cost: $53.00
Frequency: Quarterly

15851 **Technology and Practice Guide**
ABA Publishing
321 N Clark St
Chicago, IL 60654-7598

312-988-5000
800-285-2221
Fax: 312-988-6281
E-Mail: askaba@abanet.org
Home Page: www.americanbar.org/aba.html
Social Media: Facebook, Twitter

Tommy H Wells Jr, President
Laurel G. Bellows, President

Helps law professionals of general practice in making decisions about legal information management and technology.
Cost: $18.00
Frequency: SemiAnnual
Circulation: 13,477

15852 **The Bar Examiner Magazine**
National Conference of Bar Examiners
302 South Bedford Street
Madison, WI 53703

608-280-8550
Fax: 608-280-8552
E-Mail: contact@ncbex.org
Home Page: www.ncbex.org

Erica Moeser, President

Published by the NCBE as a servuce to courts, academia, bar admissions administrators, members of bar examining boards and character committees, and others with special interest in the bar admissions process. Views and opinions in the articles are not to be taken as official expressions of the NCBE's policy unless so stated.
Frequency: 4/Year
Founded in 1931

15853 **The Rules of the Game**
Alliance for Justice
11 Dupont Cir Nw
Suite 200
Washington, DC 20036-1206

202-822-6070
Fax: 202-822-6068
E-Mail: alliance@afj.org
Home Page: www.afj.org

Nan Aron, President
Mailing list available for rent

15854 **Tort and Insurance Law Journal**
American Bar Association
740 15th St Nw
Suite 8
Washington, DC 20005-1022

202-662-1000
Fax: 202-662-1032
E-Mail: cmpdi@abanet.org
Home Page: www.americanbar.org/aba.html
Social Media: Facebook, Twitter

William Neukom, President
Laurel G. Bellows, President
Rick Paszkiet, Development Editor
Jennifer Collins, Advertising Sales Coordinator

Scholarly journal on current or emerging issues of national scope in the fields of tort and insurance law.
Cost: $23.00
Frequency: Quarterly

15855 **Trial**
The American Association for Justice
777 6th Street, NW
Washington, DC 20001

202-965-3500
800-424-2725
E-Mail: membership@justice.org
Home Page: www.justice.org/

Kathleen Flynn Peterson, President
Linda Lipsen, Chief Executive Officer
Charles Jeffress, Chief Operating Officer
Kathi Berge, Chief Financial Officer
Anjali Jesseramsing, Executive Vice President

In depth articles by experts on socio-legal issues. Evaluates legal practices, points of law, civil law and recent developments in law.
Cost: $79.00
Frequency: Monthly
Circulation: 60000
Founded in 1946

15856 **Utilities Law Review**
John Wiley & Sons
111 River St
Hoboken, NJ 07030-5790

201-748-6000
800-825-7550
Fax: 201-748-6088
E-Mail: info@wiley.com
Home Page: www.wiley.com

William J Pesce, CEO

Edited by a team of specialist UK and European lawyers, it is the leading journal in this fast-changing field. Providing detailed coverage of electricity, gas, telecommunications, transport, water and broadcasting.
Founded in 1807

15857 **Verdicts & Settlement**
Daily Journal Corporation
PO Box 54026
Los Angeles, CA 90054-0026

213-229-5300
Fax: 213-229-5481
Home Page: www.dailyjournal.com

Gerald L Salzman, CEO
Malisha Anderson, Editor
Ray Chagolla, Marketing Head
Ama Sanchev, Circulation Manager
Frequency: Weekly
Circulation: 11000
Founded in 1888

15858 **Women Lawyers Journal**
National Association of Women Lawyers
American Bar Center 15.2
321 N Clark Street
Chicago, IL 60610-4403

312-988-6186
Fax: 312-988-5491
E-Mail: nawl@nawl.org
Home Page:
www.abanet.org/nawl/journal/wlj.html

Janice Sperow, Editor
Peggy Golden, Managing Editor
Stephanie Scharf, President

Published since 1911 as a forum for the exchange of ideas and information of interest to women lawyers. Unsolicited articles and press releases about non members will not be published.
Cost: $45.00
Circulation: 1200
ISSN: 0043-7468
Founded in 1899

15859 **Young Lawyers Division Newsletter**
Young Lawyers
104 Marietta St Nw
Suite 100
Atlanta, GA 30303-2743

404-527-8700
800-334-6865
Fax: 404-527-8717
E-Mail: webmaster@gabar.org
Home Page: www.gabar.org

Cliff Brashier, Executive Director
Bryan Scott, Director
Natalie Kelly, Director
Frequency: Quarterly
Circulation: 21000
Founded in 1978

Trade Shows

15860 **ABA Annual Meeting**
American Bar Association
740 15th Street NW
9th Floor
Washington, DC 20005

202-662-1570
Fax: 202-442-3439
E-Mail: cmpdl@abanet.org
Home Page: www.americanbar.org/aba.html
Social Media: Facebook, Twitter

Carolyn B Lamm, President
Alex J Hurder, Commission Chair
Laurel G. Bellows, President

The meeting includes a CLE event on incompetency and Miranda rights, and also a reception for lawyers with disabilities.

15861 **AFCC Annual Conference**
Association of Family and Conciliation Courts
6525 Grand Teton Plaza
Madison, WI 53719

608-664-3750
Fax: 608-664-3751
E-Mail: afcc@afccnet.org
Home Page: www.afccnet.org

Peter Salem, Executive Director

Over 20 exhibits relating to family judicial issues, including child custody and marriage, family, and divorce counseling. Attended by judges, couselors, attorneys, court personnel, mediators, teachers and researchers.
Frequency: June

15862 **AIRA Annual Bankruptcy & Restructuring Conference**
Association of Insolvency & Restructuring Advisors

221 Stewart Avenue
Suite 207
Medford, OR 97501

541-858-1665
Fax: 541-858-9187
E-Mail: aira@airacira.org
Home Page: www.airacira.org

Grant Newton, Executive Director

Exhibits for professionals involved in insolvency and restructuring.
Frequency: Annual/June
Founded in 1984

15863 ALA Annual Educational Conference and Exposition
Association of Legal Administrators
75 Tri-State International
Suite 222
Lincolnshire, IL 60069-4435

847-267-1252
Fax: 847-267-1329
E-Mail: publications@alanet.org
Home Page: www.alanet.org

Larry Smith, Exhibits Manager
Debbie Thomas, Director, Accounting & Finance
Renee Mahovsky, Director, Administration/Operations
Bob Abramson, Director, Marketing & Communication
Jan Waugh, Director, Member Services

Seminar, luncheon, tours and 200 exhibitors of information about computer hardware and software, facilities management, publications, printers, suppliers, litigation support, travel consultants and more.
2000 Attendees
Frequency: May

15864 APA Annual Meeting
American Polygraph Association
PO Box 8037
Chattanooga, TN 37414-0037

423-892-3992
800-272-8037
Fax: 423-894-5435
E-Mail: office@polygraph.org
Home Page: www.polygraph.org

Robbie S Bennett, National Office Manager
Gordon L. Vaughan, General Counsel
Donald Krapohl, Editor
Robbie S. Bennett, National Office Manager
Barry Cushman, President
600 Attendees
Founded in 1966

15865 Academy of Criminal Justice Sciences
Northern Kentucky University
402 Nunn Hall
Highland Heights, KY 41099

859-572-5100
800-757-ACJS
Fax: 859-572-6665

Patricia Delancey, Executive Director

Exhibits of publications pertaining to criminal justice and related areas. 45 booths.
1.8M Attendees
Frequency: March

15866 Academy of Legal Studies in Business Annual Meeting
School of Business-Forsyth
Western Carolina University
Cullowhee, NC 28723
Daniel Hebron, Executive Secretary

15 booths.
300 Attendees
Frequency: August

15867 Adjutants General Association of the United States Annual Meeting
1 Massachusetts Avenue NW
Washington, DC 20001-1401

302-326-7008
Fax: 302-326-7196
Home Page: www.agaus.org

Government legislation.
300 Attendees
Frequency: Spring

15868 American Association for Paralegal Education Convention
American Association for Paralegal Education
2965 Flowers Road S
Suite 105
Atlanta, GA 30341-5520

770-909-9000
Fax: 913-381-9308

David Scharf, Executive Director

Annual convention of 20 exhibitors of computer hardware and software, paralegal publications and educational materials and related supplies.
200 Attendees
Founded in 1984

15869 American Association of Attorney-Certified Public Accountants Convention
American Association of Attorney-CPAs
3921 Old Lee Highway
Suite 71a
Fairfax, VA 22030

703-352-8064
888-288-9272
Fax: 703-352-8073
E-Mail: info@attorney-cpa.com
Home Page: www.attorney-cpa.com

Kenneth D Goodman, President
Susan Pollock, Membership Coordinator

Exhibits for persons licensed both as attorneys and CPAs.
Frequency: Annual

15870 American Association of Law Libraries Meeting & Conference
American Association of Law Libraries
105 W Adams Street
Suite 3300
Chicago, IL 60603

312-939-4764
Fax: 312-431-1097
E-Mail: support@aall.org
Home Page: www.aallnet.org
Social Media: Facebook, Twitter

Paul Graller, Exhibits Manager
Susan Fox, Executive Director
Kate Hagan, Executive Director
Kim Rundle,, Executive Assistant
Emily Feltren,, Director of Government Relations

Annual show of 200 booths and 175 exhibitors of library equipment, supplies and services, including computer hardware and software/publishers of legal materials/information.
2000 Attendees
Frequency: July

15871 American Bar Association Annual Meeting/ ABA Expo
American Bar Association
321 N Clark Street
Chicago, IL 60610

312-988-5000
800-285-2221
E-Mail: askaba@abanet.org
Home Page: www.americanbar.org/aba.html
Social Media: Facebook, Twitter

William Neukom, President
Laurel G. Bellows, President

Annual meeting and 200 exhibits of legal technology, law books, computers, data processing equipment and other products and services related to the legal profession.
15000 Attendees
Frequency: August
Founded in 1887

15872 American Corporate Counsel Association Conference
1025 Connecticut Avenue NW
Suite 200
Washington, DC 20036-5425

202-318-8327
Fax: 202-331-7454
Home Page: http://www.acc.com

Frederick J Krebs, Executive Director

Corporate law.
600 Attendees
Frequency: November

15873 American Immigration Lawyers Association Trade Show
American Immigration Lawyers Association
1331 G Street NW
Suite 300
Washington, DC 20005-3142

202-507-7600
Fax: 202-783-7853
E-Mail: executive@aila.org
Home Page: www.aila.org

Charles H Kuck, President
Bernard P Wolfadorf, President-Elect
David W Leopold, First VP
Gregory Chen, Director of Advocacy
Susan D. Quarles, Deputy Executive Director

628 booths.
600 Attendees
Frequency: June

15874 American Society for Legal History Annual Meeting
American Society for Legal History
Notre Dame Law School
PO Box R
Notre Dame, IN 46556-0780

574-631-6627
Fax: 574-631-3595
E-Mail: WEBMASTER@ASLH.NET
Home Page: www.aslh.net

Walter F Pratt Jr, Secretary/Treasurer

Annual meeting of scholarly presses. Exhibits relating to legal history and its uses in formulating legal policy, decisions and actions; unearthing historical items; and preserving legal and legislative records.
1200 Attendees
Frequency: Annual
Founded in 1956

15875 American Society of International Law Conference
2223 Massachusetts Avenue NW
Washington, DC 20008-2847

202-939-6005
Fax: 202-797-7133
Home Page: http://www.asil.org

Rosemarie Rauzino-Heller, Show Manager
Charlotte Ku, Executive Director

30 tables.
1M Attendees

15876 Annual Conference on Legal Medicine
American College of Legal Medicine

611 E Wells Street
Milwaukee, WI 53202-3816

414-276-1881
800-433-9137
Fax: 414-276-3349
E-Mail: info@aclm.org
Home Page: www.aclm.org

Laura Morrone, Meeting/Project Manager

Annual conference and exhibits related to the field of legal medicine or health care related issues.
225 Attendees
Mailing list available for rent: 1400 names at $150 per M

15877 **Annual Education Conference & Resource Center Exhibition**
National Association for Law Placement
1666 Connecticut Avenue NW
Suite 1110
Washington, DC 20009

202-835-1001
Fax: 202-835-1112
E-Mail: info@nalp.org
Home Page: www.nalp.org

Fred Thrasher, Deputy Director
Mark Weber, Senior Vice President
Pamela Malone, Senior Vice President

Annual conference and exhibits relating to recruitment and placement of lawyers.
800 Attendees
Frequency: Annual

15878 **Association of American Law Schools Annual Meeting**
Association of American Law Schools
1201 Connecticut Avenue NW
Suite 800
Washington, DC 20036-2605

202-296-8851
Fax: 202-296-8869
E-Mail: aals@aals.org
Home Page: www.aals.org

Mary E Cullen, Director Meetings
Carl Monk, Executive Director

Annual meeting of 51 book publishers, suppliers and distributors, computer software suppliers.
4100 Attendees
Founded in 1896

15879 **Association of Trial Lawyers Annual Summer Meeting**
The American Association for Justice
777 6th Street, NW
Washington, DC 20001

202-965-3500
800-424-2725
E-Mail: membership@justice.org
Home Page: www.justice.org/

Kathleen Flynn Peterson, President
Linda Lipsen, Chief Executive Officer
Charles Jeffress, Chief Operating Officer
Kathi Berge, Chief Financial Officer
Anjali Jesseramsing, Executive Vice President

45 booths.
3M Attendees
Frequency: July/August

15880 **Association of Trial Lawyers Mid Winter Meeting**
The American Association for Justice
777 6th Street, NW
Washington, DC 20001

202-965-3500
800-424-2725
E-Mail: membership@justice.org
Home Page: www.justice.org/

Kathleen Flynn Peterson, President
Linda Lipsen, Chief Executive Officer
Charles Jeffress, Chief Operating Officer
Kathi Berge, Chief Financial Officer
Anjali Jesseramsing, Executive Vice President

55 booths.
1.5M Attendees
Frequency: January/Febuary

15881 **Association of Trial Lawyers of America Convention/Exposition**
The American Association for Justice
777 6th Street, NW
Washington, DC 20001

202-965-3500
800-424-2725
E-Mail: membership@justice.org
Home Page: www.justice.org/

Kathleen Flynn Peterson, President
Linda Lipsen, Chief Executive Officer
Charles Jeffress, Chief Operating Officer
Kathi Berge, Chief Financial Officer
Anjali Jesseramsing, Executive Vice President

Semi-annual convention and exhibits of 130 manufacturers, suppliers and distributors of legal products/service, including computer animation videos, computer software/hardware, demonstrative evidence products, expert witness services and marketing firms, as well as high end consumer gifts.
3000 Attendees
Frequency: July
Founded in 1946

15882 **DRI- Annual Conference**
DRI-The Voice of the Defense Bar
55 W. Monroe Street
Suite 2000
Chicago, IL 60603

312-951-1101
Fax: 312-795-0749
E-Mail: dri@dri.org
Home Page: www.dri.org
Social Media: Facebook, Twitter, LinkedIn

Mary Massaron Ross, President
J. Michael Weston, President-Elect
John Parker Sweeney, First Vice President
Laura E. Proctor, Second Vice President
John E. Cuttino, Secretary/Treasurer

DRI is an international organization of attorneys defending the interests of business and individuals in civil litigation. DRI provides numerous educational and informational resources to DRI members and offers many opportunities for liaison among defense trial lawyers.

15883 **Education Law Association Annual Conference**
Education Law Association
300 College Park Avenue
Dayton, OH 45469

937-229-3589
Fax: 216-687-5284
E-Mail: ela@educationlaw.org
Home Page: www.educationlaw.org
Social Media: Facebook, Twitter, LinkedIn

Mandy Schrank, Executive Director
Cate K. Smith, Executive Director
Judy Pleiman, Member Services Coordinator
Jody Thornburg, Publications Manager

Annual conference with over 100 presenters giving presentations on current education law issues. Ten to twelve exhibitors of education law resources.
350 Attendees
Frequency: November

15884 **Federal Bar Association Convention**
Federal Bar Association
1220 North Fillmore St.
Ste. 444
Arlington, VA 22201

571-481-9100
Fax: 571-481-9090
E-Mail: fba@fedbar.org
Home Page: www.fedbar.org
Social Media: Facebook, Twitter, LinkedIn

Jack D. Lockridge, Executive Director
Lori Beth Gorman, Executive Assistant
Robert J. DeSousa, President
Hon. Gustavo Gelpi, Jr., President-Elect

Annual convention and exhibits of legal publications, computer software and insurance information.
300 Attendees

15885 **Federal Taxation Institute**
11 W 42nd Street
New York, NY 10036-8002

212-921-2300

Lorrie Ann England, Show Manager

11 booths.
1M Attendees
Frequency: November

15886 **Institute of Federal Taxation**
USC Law Center
University Park
Suite 124
Los Angeles, CA 90089-0001

FAX 213-740-9442

Karen Sprague, Director

10 booths.
1M Attendees
Frequency: January

15887 **Law and Society Association Annual Meeting**
University of Massachusetts
Hampshire House
Amherst, MA 01003

413-545-0111
Fax: 413-545-1640
E-Mail: Exec_Office@lawandsociety.org
Home Page: www.lawandsociety.org

Ronald Pipkin, Executive Officer
Lissa Ganter, Administrative Coord

The annual meeting brings together 800-1000 scholars from the US and around the world to present research in the field of socio-legal studies. This includes the place of law in relation to other social institutions, legal decision making, legal systems, and operations, and a variety of research methods and modes of analysis. 50 booths including publishers exhibit, mainly academic, in the fiels of legal studies, and social science.
Frequency: May

15888 **Legal Administrators Association**
Association of Legal Administrators
75 Tri-State International
Suite 222
Lincolnshire, IL 60069-4435

847-267-1252
Fax: 847-267-1329
E-Mail: publications@alanet.org
Home Page: www.alanet.org

Larry Smith, Executive Director
Debbie Thomas, Director, Accounting & Finance
Renee Mahovsky, Director, Administration/Operations
Bob Abramson, Director, Marketing & Communication
Jan Waugh, Director, Member Services

350 booths of products and services related to the legal industry.
2M Attendees
Frequency: April
Founded in 1971

15889 Mid-America Association of Law Libraries Convention
Mid-America Association of Law Libraries
105 W Adams Street
Suite 3300
Chicago, IL 60603

312-939-4764
Fax: 312-431-1097
Home Page: www.aallnet.org/chapter/maall/
Social Media: Facebook, Twitter

Annual show and exhibits of law library equipment, supplies and services.
Frequency: October, Omaha
Founded in 1973
Mailing list available for rent

15890 NFPA Convention
National Federation of Paralegal Associations
23607 Highway 99
Suite 2-C
Edmonds, WA 98026

425 967-0045
Fax: 425-771-9588
E-Mail: info@paralegals.org
Home Page: www.paralegals.org
Social Media: Facebook, LinkedIn

Dana Murphy-Love, Managing Director
Celeste Allen, Assistant Director
Rodney Dunham, Assistant Director

The premier annual event for legal professionals to gather for education seminars, dynamic speakers, knowledge sharing, networking, and of course product-shopping.
350 Attendees
Frequency: Annual

15891 National Association of Black Criminal Justice
1900 N Loop W
Suite 255
Houston, TX 77018-8116

713-681-3700
Fax: 713-956-8664

Keith Branch Esq, Chairman
Howard Thompson, Owner

60 booths.
700 Attendees
Frequency: July

15892 National Association of Parliamentarians (NAP) Conference
National Association of Parliamentarians
213 South Main Street
Independence, MO 64050-3850

816-833-3892
888-627-2929
Fax: 816-833-3893
E-Mail: hq@nap2.org
Home Page: www.parliamentarians.org

Ronald R Stinson, President
Naurice S Henderson, VP
Sandra K Olson, Secretary

The NAP sponsors a conference and exhibit relating to parliamentary law and procedure on a biennial basis. In addition, the Association also holds a national event once each year, providing the opportunities for members, prospective members, and guests to learn more about effective meetings, how to help others learn the fundamentals of parliamentary procedure, and how to be an effective parliamentarian.

15893 National Bar Association Annual Convention
National Bar Association
1225 11th Street NW
Washington, DC 20001-4217
202-842-3900
Fax: 202-289-6170
Home Page: www.nationalbar.org
Social Media: Facebook, Twitter, LinkedIn

Maurice Foster, Director Special Projects
Reese Marshall, Coordinator Special Projects
John Crump, Executive Director

Annual convention and exhibits of computers and legal software, office products, accounting services, financial planners, temporary employment agencies, legal publications, travel agencies, luggage and leather goods, fine arts and jewelry. Containing 50 booths.
2500 Attendees
Frequency: July-August
Founded in 1925

15894 National Court Reporters Association Annual Convention & Expo
National Court Reporters Association
8224 Old Courthouse Road
Vienna, VA 22182-3808

703-556-6272
800-272-6272
Fax: 703-556-6291
E-Mail: msic@ncra.org
Home Page: www.ncra.org
Social Media: Facebook, Twitter, LinkedIn, Youtube

James M. Cudahy, Executive Director & CEO
18000 Members
1200 Attendees
Founded in 1899

15895 National Federation Paralegal Associations
PO Box 33108
Kansas City, MO 64114

816-421-5989
Fax: 816-941-2725
E-Mail: info@paralegals.org
Home Page: www.paralegals.org

Tena Nichols, Assistant Managing Director

Thirty-five booths.
300 Attendees
Frequency: April

15896 National Forensic Center Trade Show
National Forensic Center
17 Temple Ter
Lawrenceville, NJ 08648-3254

609-883-0550
800-526-5177
Fax: 609-883-7622
E-Mail: ForenExpts@att.net
Home Page: expertindex.com

Betty Lipschner, Director

Coverage of the application of scientific, medical and technical knowledge to litigation.
200 Attendees
Printed in one color on matte stock

15897 National Judges Association
P.O. Box 325
Glendale, OR 97442

FAX 541-832-2674
E-Mail: njaoffice@yahoo.com
Home Page: www.nationaljudgesassociation.org

Whitney Sullivan, Executive Director
Charlene Hewitt, Secretary
Ralph Zeller, Vice President

10 booths.
150 Attendees
Frequency: May

15898 National Notary Association Annual National Conference
Po Box 2402
Chatsworth, CA 91313-2402

818-739-4000
800-876-6827
Fax: 818-700-1942
E-Mail: hotline@nationalnotary.org
Home Page: www.nationalnotary.org
Social Media: Facebook, Twitter, LinkedIn

Milton G Valera, President
Deborah M Thaw, Executive VP
Marc Reiser, CEO
Jane Eagle, Executive VP & CFO
Ron Johnson, VP Systems & Operations
200M Members
500+ Attendees
Frequency: Bi-Monthly
Circulation: 200,000
Founded in 1957

Directories & Databases

15899 ABA Journal Directory of Legal Software and Hardware
American Bar Association
321 N Clark St
Chicago, IL 60654-7598

312-988-5000
800-285-2221
Fax: 312-988-6281
E-Mail: askaba@abanet.org
Home Page: www.americanbar.org/aba.html
Social Media: Facebook, Twitter

Tommy H Wells Jr, President
Laurel G Bellows, President

Directory of supplies to the industry.
Cost: $7.00
Frequency: Annual
Circulation: 400,000

15900 Agricultural Law Update
American Agricultural Law Association
University of Arkansas Law Programs Building
Fayetteville, AR 72701

479-575-4671
Fax: 479-575-5830
Home Page: www.aglan-assn.org

Susan Williams, Admininstrative Assistant
Linda McGormic, Editor

Monthly update of legal issues concerning the agricultural industry(members only)
Frequency: Biennial
Circulation: 1,500

15901 American Association of Attorney-Certified Public Accountants Directory
3291 Old Lee Highway
Suite 71a
Fairfax, VA 22030
703-352-8064
888-288-9272
Fax: 703-352-8073
E-Mail: info@attorney-cpa.com
Home Page: www.attorney-cpa.com

Kenneth D Goodman, President
Susan Pollock, Membership Coordinator

Offers names, addresses and biographical data on 1,400 individuals licensed as both attorneys

and CPAs.
Cost: $175.00
100 Pages
Frequency: Annual

15902 American Bar Association Legal Education Database
American Bar Association
321 N Clark St
Chicago, IL 60654-7598

312-988-5000
800-285-2221
Fax: 312-988-6281
E-Mail: askaba@abanet.org
Home Page: www.americanbar.org/aba.html
Social Media: Facebook, Twitter

Tommy H Wells Jr, President
Laurel G. Bellows, President

Contains the complete text of the Third Tenative Draft of Law School Library Accreditation Standards.
Frequency: Full-text

15903 American College of Legal Medicine Membership Directory
611 E Wells Street
Milwaukee, WI 53202-3816

414-276-1881
800-433-9137
Fax: 414-276-3349
E-Mail: info@aclm.org
Home Page: www.aclm.org

Janet L Haynes, Director

Lists members alphabetically, specialty or area(s) of expertise, and geographic location.
Cost: $75.00
1400 Pages
Circulation: 1,425
Founded in 1960

15904 American Law Reports Library
Lawyers Co-operative Publishing Company
50 Broad Street E
Rochester, NY 14694-0001

585-719-9760

A database, updated periodically, that contains the complete text of analyses of state and federal case law.
Frequency: Full-text

15905 BNA Criminal Practice Manual
Pike & Fischer
8505 Fenton St
Suite 1400
Silver Spring, MD 20910-4499

301-562-1530
800-255-8131
Fax: 301-562-1521
E-Mail: pike@pf.com
Home Page: www.pf.com

Meg Hargreaves, President
David Heyman, Director Marketing
Karen James-Cody, Director of Communications
Kirk Swanson, Managing Editor

15906 BNA's Directory of State and Federal Courts, Judges and Clerks
BNA Books
1231 25th Street NW
Washington, DC 20037-1164

732-346-0089
800-960-1220
Fax: 732-346-1624
E-Mail: books@bna.com
Home Page: www.bnabooks.com

Margaret Hullinger, Executive Editor
Lois Smith, Marketing Manager
Janie Meidhof, Media Specialist

Complete contact information including e-mail addresses on the nation's judges and clerks, as well as comprehensive details on the structure of federal, state, and territorial courts. Includes 2,201 state courts, 214 federal courts, 14,432 judges, and 5,303 clerks, list of nominations for federal judgeships, federal appellate court jurisdiction map and list, state court structure charts, reports of judicial decisions, directory of electronic public-access services, and personal name index.
714 Pages
Frequency: Annual
Circulation: 1,300
ISBN: 1-570184-11-9
ISSN: 1078-5582
Founded in 1986

15907 Best Lawyers in America
Woodward/White
129 1st Ave Sw
Aiken, SC 29801-4862

803-648-0300
Fax: 803-641-4794
E-Mail: info@bestlawyers.com
Home Page: www.bestlawyers.com

Steven Naifeh, President

Over 11,000 attorneys who are selected as the best in their specialities by a survey of over 150,000 lawyers are profiled.
Cost: $110.00
1000 Pages
Frequency: Biennial

15908 Business Litigation Database
Trans Union Credit Information Company
20 Constance Ct
Hauppauge, NY 11788-4200

631-582-2690
Fax: 516-582-2767

Over 8 million court records on companies from New York and New Jersey are included in this database.
Frequency: Directory

15909 CEMC/ENR Directory of Law Firms
Construction Education Management Corporation
8133 Leesburg Pike
Suite 700
Vienna, VA 22182-2706

703-734-2399
Fax: 703-734-2908

Over 70 construction-oriented law firms located nationwide and overseas are listed.
Cost: $75.00
Frequency: Annual

15910 Common Market Law Review
Kluwer Law and Taxation Publishers
101 Philip Drive
Assinippi Park
Norwell, MA 02061

781-871-6600
866-269-9527
Fax: 781-681-9045

Serves as a medium for the dissemination of legal thinking on community law matters, meeting the need of both the academic and the practitioner.

15911 Comprehensive Guide to Bar Admission Requirements
Legal Education and Admissions to the Bar
321 N Clark Street
21st Floor
Chicago, IL 60610

312-988-6738
Fax: 312-988-5681
Home Page: www.americanbar.org/aba.html
Social Media: Facebook, Twitter

Laurel G. Bellows, President

Offers a list of state bar admission administrators in the United States and its territories.
Cost: $5.00
Frequency: Annual

15912 Corporate Counsel's Law Library
LexisNexis Matthew Bender
1275 Broadway
Menands, NY 12204-2694

518-487-3385
888-223-1940
Fax: 518-487-3083
E-Mail: info.in@lexisnexis.com
Home Page: www.lexisnexis.com

George Bearese, VP
Rebecca Schmitt, Chief Financial Officer

This database contains court decisions covering statutory and common law concepts related to the formation, maintenance and dissolution of corporations.
Cost: $2484.00

15913 Criminal Justice Information Exchange Directory
US National Criminal Justice Reference Service
P.O. Box 60769
Harrisburg, PA 17106-0769

717-232-7554
Fax: 717-232-2162
Home Page: www.pacounties.org

Carroll Penyak, Director
Lori Dabbondanza, Executive Secretary
Lucas Martsolf, Manager

Over 100 criminal justice-related organizations are listed.
95 Pages
Frequency: Annual

15914 Criminal Justice Periodical Index
University Microfilms International
125 Chapman Hall
1219 University of Oregon
Eugine, OR 97403-1219

541-346-5129
Fax: 541-346-2804

Mary Ann Gilbert, Editor

Offers information on more than 180,000 citations to articles in 145 magazines, journals, newsletters and law reporting periodicals on the administration of justice and law enforcement.
Cost: $315.00
Frequency: TriAnnual

15915 Current Index to Legal Periodicals
Marian Gould Gallagher Law Library-Univ. of Wash.
William H Gates Hall
Box 353025
Seattle, WA 98195-3025

206-543-4089
Fax: 206-685-2165
Home Page: lib.law.washington.edu/clip/cilp.html

Susan M Sorensen, Editor
Muriel Quick, Information Specialist

List of publishers of titles indexed in the database.
Cost: $192.00
Frequency: 52 issues
Founded in 1948
Printed in on matte stock

15916 Deskbook Encyclopedia of Employment Law
Data Research

PO Box 490
Rosemount, MN 55068-0490

952-452-8694
800-365-4900
Fax: 952-452-8694

An up-to-date compilation of summarized federal and state appellate court decisions which affect employment. The full legal citation is supplied for each case. A brief introductory note on the American judicial system is provided along with updated appendices of recent US Supreme Court cases and recently published law review articles. Also included are portions of the US Constitution which are most frequently cited in employment cases.
Cost: $85.75
500 Pages
Frequency: Annual
ISBN: 0-939675-55-2
Founded in 1996

15917 Deskbook Encyclopedia of Public Employment Law
Data Research
PO Box 490
Rosemount, MN 55068-0490

952-452-8694
800-365-4900
Fax: 952-452-8694

An up-to-datre compilation of summarized federal and state appellate court decisions which affect public employment. The full legal citation is cupplied for each case. A brief introductory note on the American judicial system is provided along with updated appendices of recent US Supreme Court cases and recently published law review articles.
Cost: $987.54
531 Pages
Frequency: Annual
ISBN: 0-939675-56-0
Founded in 1996

15918 Directory of Bar Associations
American Bar Association
321 N Clark St
Chicago, IL 60654-7598

312-988-5000
800-285-2221
Fax: 312-988-6281
E-Mail: askaba@abanet.org
Home Page: www.americanbar.org/aba.html
Social Media: Facebook, Twitter

Tommy H Wells Jr, President
Laurel G. Bellows, President

Offers information on more than 57 state bar associations, local bar associations and other local associations represented in the American Bar Association House of Delegates.
Cost: $95.00
40 Pages
Frequency: Annual

15919 Directory of Certified Business Counselors
Institute of Certified Business Counselors
18831 Willamette Dr
West Linn, OR 97068-1711

503-751-1856
877-422-2674
Fax: 503-292-8237
Home Page: www.i-cbc.org

David Finsterwald, President

120 member counselors, brokers and attorneys qualified to act as advisors for persons with business problems.

15920 Directory of Courthouses, Abstract and Title Companies of the USA
Harbors International
7020 S Yale Avenue
Suite 206
Tulsa, OK 74136-5744

918-496-3232
Fax: 918-496-8905

A who's who directory of counties, parishes and boroughs with a section on abstract and title companies.
Cost: $95.00
368 Pages
ISSN: 0896-7830

15921 Directory of Law-Related CD-ROMs
Infosource Publishing
140 Norma Road
Teaneck, NJ 07666-4234

201-836-7072

Arlene Eis, Editor

A who's who directory of supplies to the industry.
Cost: $64.00
200 Pages
Frequency: Annual

15922 Directory of Lawyer Disciplinary Agencies & Lawyers' Funds/Client Protection
Center for Professional Responsibility
321 North Clark Street
Chicago, IL 60610

312-988-5000
Fax: 312-988-6281
Home Page: www.americanbar.org/aba.html
Social Media: Facebook, Twitter

Laurel G. Bellows, President
35 Pages
Frequency: Annual

15923 Directory of Lawyer Referral Services
American Bar Association
321 N Clark St
Chicago, IL 60654-7598

312-988-5000
800-285-2221
Fax: 312-988-6281
E-Mail: askaba@abanet.org
Home Page: www.americanbar.org/aba.html
Social Media: Facebook, Twitter

Tommy H Wells Jr, President
Laurel G. Bellows, President

Names of services, sponsoring organizations, phones and names of the directors are listed for over 330 services.
Cost: $10.00
40 Pages
Frequency: Annual

15924 Directory of Legal Aid & Defender Offices in the United States & Territories
National Legal Aid and Defender Association
1140 Connecticut Ave NW
Suite 900
Washington, DC 20036-4019

202-452-0620
Fax: 202-872-1031
E-Mail: info@nlada.org
Home Page: www.nlada100years.org

Jo Ann Wallace, President & CEO
Julie Clark, Secretary
Alex Gulotta, Treasurer
Cost: $70.00

15925 Directory of Opportunities in International Law
John Bassett Moore Society of International Law
School of Law: University of VA
Charlottesville, VA 22901

Offers hundreds of possible employers in international law.
Cost: $10.00
204 Pages

15926 Directory of Private Bar Involvement Programs
American Bar Association
321 N Clark St
Chicago, IL 60654-7598

312-988-5000
800-285-2221
Fax: 312-988-6281
E-Mail: askaba@abanet.org
Home Page: www.americanbar.org/aba.html
Social Media: Facebook, Twitter

Tommy H Wells Jr, President
Laurel G. Bellows, President

A list of over 900 programs that provide free or low-cost legal services.
Cost: $7.50
210 Pages
Frequency: Annual

15927 Directory of Public Interest Law Centers
Alliance for Justice
11 Dupont Cir NW
2nd Floor
Washington, DC 20036-1206

202-822-6070
Fax: 202-822-6068
E-Mail: alliance@afj.org
Home Page: www.afj.org

Nan Aron, President

Nonprofit association of public interest advocacy organization. Offers workshops, advocacy projects, legal guides, techinical assistance and public education. Lists addresses, branch offices and directors of 200 public interest law centers around the country. Indexed by state and subject area.
Cost: $10.00
48 Pages
Founded in 1996
Mailing list available for rent

15928 Directory of State Court Clerks & County Courthouses
WANT Publishing Company
420 Lexington Ave
Room 300
New York, NY 10170-0002

212-687-3774
Fax: 212-687-3779
E-Mail: rwant@msn.com
Home Page: www.wantpublishing.com

Robert S Want, President

Allows easy access to vital information including court decisions, real estate records, UCC and tax liens, and other important documents maintained by State appellate and trial courts and county courthouses nationwide.
Cost: $ 75.00
380 Pages
Frequency: Annual
ISBN: 0-970122-91-8

15929 FCBA Directory
Federal Communications Bar Association
1020 19th St NW
Suite 325
Washington, DC 20036-6113

202-293-4000
Fax: 202-293-4317

E-Mail: fcba@fcba.org
Home Page: www.fcba.org

Stanley Zenor, Executive Director
Kerry Loughney, Director Of Membership Services
Wendy Jo Parish, Administrative Assistant

A nonprofit organization of attorneys and other professionals involved in the development, interpretation, implementation and practice of communications law and policy.
Founded in 1936

15930 **Federal Careers for Attorneys**
Federal Reports
1010 Vermont Ave NW
Suite 408
Washington, DC 20005-4945

202-393-1552
Home Page: www.attorneyjobs.com

Richard L Hermann, Owner

United States government general counsel and other legal offices throughout the federal system.
Cost: $23.95
150 Pages

15931 **Federal Law-Related Careers Directory**
Federal Reports
1010 Vermont Ave NW
Suite 408
Washington, DC 20005-4945

202-393-1552
800-296-9611
Fax: 202-393-1553
Home Page: www.attorneyjobs.com

Richard L Hermann, Owner
Richard L Hermann, Editor

Listings of over 1,000 federal government recruiting offices.
Cost: $16.95

15932 **General Bar Law Directory**
General Bar
25000 Center Ridge Rd
Suite 3
Cleveland, OH 44145-4108

440-835-2000
800-533-2500
Fax: 440-835-3636
E-Mail: service@generalbar.com
Home Page: www.generalbar.com

Charles Sonnhalter, Owner
700 Pages
Circulation: 10000
Founded in 1941

15933 **Insider's Guide to Law Firms**
Mobius Press
PO Box 3339
Boulder, CO 80307

303-188-8205
800-529-5627
Fax: 303-499-5389

Directory of services and supplies to the industry.
Cost: $28.95
740 Pages
Frequency: Annual

15934 **Judicial Yellow Book**
Leadership Directories
104 5th Ave
New York, NY 10011-6901

212-627-4140
Fax: 212-645-0931
E-Mail: judicial@leadershipdirectories.com
Home Page: www.leadershipdirectories.com

David Hurvitz, CEO
James M Petrie, Associate Publisher

Contact information for over 3,250 federal and state judges in federal and state appellate courts, including staff and law clerks, and the law schools they attended.
Cost: $245.00
1,100 Pages
Frequency: SemiAnnual
ISSN: 1082-3298
Founded in 1995
Mailing list available for rent: 13,000 names at $125 per M

15935 **Latin American Labor Law Handbook**
WorldTrade Executive
PO Box 761
Concord, MA 01742-0761

978-287-0301
Fax: 978-287-0302
E-Mail: info@wtexec.com
Home Page: www.wtexec.com

Alison French, Production Manager

Designed to give firms doing business in Latin America some basic knowledge of labor and employment law in the region. Covers countries where US and foreign investment is particularly high: Argentina, Brazil, Venezuela, Colombia, Costa Rica and Chili - providing an overview of the complex network of laws, regulations, and customs affecting social security, wages, employment security, and labor organizing.
Cost: $185.00

15936 **Law Books and Serials in Print**
R R Bowker LLC
630 Central Ave
New Providence, NJ 07974-1506

908-286-0288
888-269-5372
Fax: 908-464-3553
E-Mail: info@bowker.com
Home Page: www.bowker.com

R R Bowker
L Yuster-Freeman, Editor

Focusing on core legal and related titles, Law Books & Serials in Print includes descriptive annotations that provide expert guidance on selecting the right sources for every research need.
ISBN: 0-835249-42-3
Mailing list available for rent

15937 **Law Books in Print**
Glanville Publishers
75 Main St
Dobbs Ferry, NY 10522-1673

914-693-1320

Publishers of law books in English are listed.
Cost: $750.00
Frequency: Base Edition

15938 **Law Firms Yellow Book**
Leadership Directories
104 5th Ave
New York, NY 10011-6901

212-627-4140
Fax: 212-645-0931
E-Mail: lawfirms@leadershipdirectories.com
Home Page: www.leadershipdirectories.com

David Hurvitz, CEO
James M Petrie, Associate Publisher

Contact information for over 24,000 attorneys and administrators who make the business decisions and manage the practice areas in over 800 of the nation's leading law firms.
Cost: $245.00
1,100 Pages
Frequency: SemiAnnual
ISSN: 1054-4054
Founded in 1991
Mailing list available for rent: 19,000 names at $125 per M

15939 **Law Office Computing Directory**
James Publishing
Po Box 25202
Suite E
Santa Ana, CA 92799-5202

714-755-5450
Fax: 714-751-2709
Home Page: www.jamespublishing.com

Jim Pawell, Owner

Approximately 25 computer products and services designed for use by the legal profession.
Cost: $49.95
Frequency: Bi-Monthly
Circulation: 9,000

15940 **Law Office Economics & Management: Directory of Law Office Software**
Clark Boardman Callaghan
155 Pfingsten Road
Deerfield, IL 60015

847-374-0400
800-323-1336
Fax: 847-948-9340

Paul S Hoffman, Editor

List of about 100 suppliers of data processing equipment and software.
Cost: $15.00
Frequency: Annual June

15941 **Law and Legal Information Directory**
Gale/Cengage Learning
27500 Drake Road
Farmington Hills, MI 48331-3535

248-699-4253
800-877-4253
Fax: 877-363-4253
E-Mail: gale.galeord@cengage.com
Home Page: www.gale.cengage.com
Social Media: Facebook, Twitter, Youtube

Patrick C Sommers, President
Jacqueline O'Brien, Editor

Provides descriptions and contact information for more than 21,000 institutions, services and facilities in the law and legal information industry.
Frequency: Annual
ISBN: 1-414421-26-5

15942 **Lawyers Referral Directory**
PO Box 40335
Cleveland, OH 44140-0335

440-899-8660
800-LAW-LIST
Fax: 440-899-1005
E-Mail: Support@LawListIL.com
Home Page: www.lawlistil.com

Ted M McManamon, Editor
Richard T Ostovitz, Production Manager

Bonded reference guide to lawyers specializing in commercial law, creditors' rights and collection litigation. Free to users registering referrals sent.
700 Pages
Frequency: Annual

15943 **Lawyers' List**
Commercial Publishing Company
PO Box 2430
Easton, MD 21601-2430

410-820-4494
800-824-9911
Fax: 410-820-4474

DA Schwartz, President

A listing of law offices engaged in general, corporation and trial practice or patent, trademark and copyright practice.
1700 Pages
Frequency: Annual

15944 Legal Information Alert
Alert Publications
401 W Fullerton Parkway
Apartment 1403E
Chicago, IL 60614-2805

773-525-7594

Donna Tuke-Heroy, President

Publishers of books, databases, CD-ROM products and loose-leaf services for the legal profession are listed.
Cost: $149.00

15945 Legal Looseleafs in Print
Infosource Publishing
140 Norma Road
Teaneck, NJ 07666-4234

201-836-7072
E-Mail: aeis@carroll.com
Home Page: www.infosourcespub.com

Over 230 publishers offering 3,600 looseleaf legal information services.
Cost: $106.00
400 Pages
Frequency: Annual March
Founded in 1981

15946 Legal Newsletters in Print
Infosource Publishing
140 Norma Road
Teaneck, NJ 07666-4234

201-836-7072

Arlene Eis, Editor

Directory of services and supplies to the industry.
Cost: $90.00
400 Pages
Frequency: Annual

15947 Legal Researcher's Desk Reference
Infosource Publishing
140 Norma Road
Teaneck, NJ 07666-4234

201-836-7072

Arlene Eis, Editor

Information is provided on federal and state government officials and departments are listed, as well as publishers and law book dealers and much more.
Cost: $58.00
416 Pages
Frequency: Biennial

15948 Legal Resource Directory
McFarland & Company Publishers
PO Box 611
Jefferson, NC 28640-0611

336-246-4460
Fax: 336-246-5018
E-Mail: info@mcfarlandpub.com
Home Page: www.mcfarlandpub.com
Social Media: Facebook, Twitter, LinkedIn

Information is given on national, state and local organizations providing free or inexpensive legal advice to low-income families.
Cost: $30.95
148 Pages
Mailing list available for rent

15949 Legal Resources Index
Information Access Company
362 Lakeside Drive
Foster City, CA 94404-1171

650-378-5200
800-227-8431

This database contains more than 500,000 citations, with selected abstracts, to articles published in more than 800 key law journals, bar association publications and legal newspapers.

15950 Martindale-Hubbell Law Directory
Martindale-Hubbell/Reed Reference Publishing
121 Chanlon Rd
New Providence, NJ 07974-1544

908-464-6800
800-526-4902
Fax: 908-771-8704
E-Mail: info@martindale.com
Home Page: www.martindale.com

Ralph Colistri, President

Directory of services and supplies to the industry.
Cost: $690.00
50000 Pages
Frequency: 26 Volumes

15951 NALP Directory of Legal Employers
National Association for Law Placement
1025 Connecticut Ave NW
Suite 1110
Washington, DC 20036-5413

202-835-1001
Fax: 202-835-1112
E-Mail: info@nalp.org
Home Page: www.nalp.org

M Liepold, Executive Director
Fred Thrasher, Senior Vice President
Pamela Malone, Senior Vice President

Information on more than 1,700 employers nationwide and is an invaluable tool for job searchers, career counselors, and legal recruiters alike. Published both on-line and in print, this directory includes indexes by location and by practice area keyword.
Cost: $75.00
Frequency: Annual
Founded in 1971
Mailing list available for rent: CBC names

15952 NLADA Directory of Legal Aid and Defender Offices in the US & Territories
National Legal Aid and Defender Association
1140 Connecticut Ave NW
Suite 900
Washington, DC 20036-4019

202-452-0620
Fax: 202-872-1031
E-Mail: info@nlada.org
Home Page: www.nlada100years.org

Jo Ann Wallace, President & CEO
Julie Clark, Secretary
Alex Gulotta, Treasurer

About 3,600 civil legal aid and indigent defense organizations in the US.
Cost: $70.00
Frequency: Biennial

15953 NSA Directory
National Sheriff's Association
1450 Duke St
Alexandria, VA 22314-3490

703-836-7827

Suzanne B Litts, Editor
David Strigel, Advertising Manager

Sheriffs of the US address phone and fax.
Cost: $50.00
94 Pages
Frequency: Annual

15954 National Directory of Corrections Construction
National Institute of Justice
PO Box 6000
Rockville, MD 20849-6000

301-251-5500

Offers valuable information on over 150 correctional institutions constructed since 1985.
Cost: $32.00
354 Pages

15955 National Directory of Courts of Law
Information Resources
1110 N Glebe Road
Suite 550
Arlington, VA 22201-5762

703-525-4750

Directory of services and supplies to the industry.
Cost: $95.00
888 Pages
Frequency: Biennial

15956 National Employment Listing Service Bulletin
Criminal Justice Center
Sam Houston State University
Huntsville, TX 77341

936-295-6371
Fax: 281-294-1653

Kay Billingsley, Editor

Job openings in police departments, sheriff's departments, courts and other law enforcement and security agencies.

15957 National Hispanic American Attorney Directory
Hispanic National Bar Association
100 Seaview Drive
Secaucus, NJ 07094-1800

201-348-4900
Fax: 201-348-6609

Carlos G Ortiz

National directory listing Hispanic American Attorneys.
Cost: $65.00
Circulation: 4,000

15958 National Law Journal: Directory of Current Law & Law-Related Books
New York Law Publishing Company
345 Park Avenue S
8th Floor
New York, NY 10010-1700

212-799-9434
Fax: 212-696-1875
Home Page: www.ljextra.com

Ben Gerson, Editor
Bill Pollak, General Counsel
Michael Holston, General Counsel
David Hechler, Executive Editor
Paula Martersteck, Managing Editor

Lists over 70 publishers of law and law-related books.
Cost: $124.00
Frequency: Annual January

15959 National List
PO Box 2486
Bismark, ND 58502-2486

701-237-7202
800-227-1675
Fax: 701-223-5634

E-Mail: info@nationallist.com
Home Page: www.nationallist.com

Randy Nicola, VP
Gerry Cowgill, President
Kacey Rask, Account Executive
Leslie Herr, Director of Operations

A list of lawyers and law firms handling collections and general practice in the United States, Canada, and most foreign countries.
550 Pages
Frequency: Annual

15960 National Trial and Deposition Directory
321 W Franklin Street
Boise, ID 83702

208-344-3191
Fax: 208-345-8800
Cost: $39.95

490 Pages
Circulation: 2,000

15961 National and Federal Legal Employment Report
Federal Reports
1010 Vermont Ave NW
Suite 408
Washington, DC 20005-4945

202-393-1552
800-296-9611
Fax: 202-393-1553
Home Page: www.attorneyjobs.com

Richard L Hermann, Owner
Richard L Hermann, Editor

Listings of approximately 600 current attorney and law-related job opportunities with the US government and other public and private employers in Washington DC, nationwide and abroad.
Cost: $35.80
Frequency: Monthly

15962 Nelson's Law Office Directory
Nelson Company
53 West Jackson Blvd.
Chicago, IL 60604

877-464-6656
Home Page: www.nelson.com

Richard Nelson, Owner
Michael Andrews, Chief Financial Officer

A directory of the top rated law firms in the United States. Rated on legal ability, integrity and diligence by the leading lawyers in each state.
Cost: $23.00
210 Pages
Frequency: Annual
Founded in 1968

15963 Now Hiring: Government Jobs for Lawyers
American Bar Association
321 N Clark St
Chicago, IL 60654-7598

312-988-5000
800-285-2221
Fax: 312-988-6281
E-Mail: askaba@abanet.org
Home Page: www.americanbar.org/aba.html
Social Media: Facebook, Twitter

Tommy H Wells Jr, President
Laurel G. Bellows, President

Federal, quasi- and independent government agency jobs for lawyers.
Cost: $17.95
170 Pages

15964 Parole and Probation Compact Administrator Association Mailing List
Council of State Governments
2760 Research Park Drive
PO Box 11910
Lexington, KY 40578-1910

859-244-8000
800-800-1910
Fax: 859-244-8001
Home Page: www.csg.org

Jodi Rell, President

15965 Preview of United States Supreme Court Cases
American Bar Association
321 N Clark St
Chicago, IL 60654-7598

312-988-5000
800-285-2221
Fax: 312-988-6281
E-Mail: askaba@abanet.org
Home Page: www.americanbar.org/aba.html
Social Media: Facebook, Twitter

Tommy H Wells Jr, President
Laurel G. Bellows, President

This database contains full-text reviews of cases orally argued before the US Supreme Court.
Frequency: Full-text

15966 Representative Offices in the Russian Federation
WorldTrade Executive
PO Box 761
Concord, MA 01742-0761

978-287-0301
Fax: 978-287-0302
E-Mail: info@wtexec.com
Home Page: www.wtexec.com

Alison French, Production Manager

Combines detailed information on the legal structure within which representative offices must operate, including tax and other requirements, with a user-friendly guide to the accreditation and registration process.
Cost: $135.00

15967 Russell Law List
Commercial Publishing Company
PO Box 2430
Easton, MD 21601-2430

410-820-4494
800-824-9911
Fax: 410-820-4474

DA Schwartz, President

A listing of law offices in general practice worldwide.
147 Pages
Frequency: Annual

15968 Russia Business & Legal Briefing
WorldTrade Executive
PO Box 761
Concord, MA 01742-0761

978-287-0301
Fax: 978-287-0302
E-Mail: info@wtexec.com
Home Page: www.wtexec.com

Alison French, Production Manager

Topics include: economic analysis; hard currency regulations; investment legislation in St. Petersburg; enforcing foreign judgements in Russia; new laws on limited liability companies and bankruptcy; new commercial arbitration court in St. Petersburg; changes in tax legislation; managing the Russian tax burden.
Cost: $265.00

15969 Sourcebook of Local Court and County Records Retrievers
BRP Publications
200 E Eager Street
Baltimore, MD 21202-3704

202-312-6060
800-822-6338
Fax: - - 047

Offers information on firms that specialize in finding court and county records, including civil, criminal, probate and bankruptcy files.
Cost: $45.00
432 Pages

15970 Summer Legal Employment Guide
Federal Reports
1010 Vermont Ave NW
Suite 408
Washington, DC 20005-4945

202-393-1552
Home Page: www.attorneyjobs.com

Richard L Hermann, Owner

Directory of services and supplies to the industry.
Cost: $170.00
36 Pages
Frequency: Annual

15971 US Supreme Court Employment Cases
Data Research
PO Box 490
Rosemount, MN 55068-0490

952-452-8694
800-365-4900
Fax: 952-452-8694

A compilation of summarized US Supreme Court decisions which affect employment. The full legal citation is supplied for each case.
Cost: $64.70
288 Pages
Frequency: Annual
ISBN: 0-939675-51-0
Founded in 1995

15972 United States Probation and Pretrial Services Officers Directory
Probation Div./Admin. Office of US Courts
1 Columbus Circle NE
Suite 4-300
Washington, DC 20544-0001
FAX 202-273-1603

Federal probation offices and pretrial services offices.
Frequency: Annual

15973 WESTLAW International Law Library
West Publishing Company
610 Opperman Drive
Eagan, MN 55123-1340

651-687-7327
Home Page: www.westgroup.com

Database containing the complete information of international and US federal court decisions.
Frequency: Full-text

15974 WESTLAW Legal Services Library
West Publishing Company
610 Opperman Drive
Eagan, MN 55123-1340

651-687-7327
Home Page: www.westgroup.com

This database offers the complete text of US federal and state court decisions, statutes and regulations.

15975 WESTLAW Litigation Library
West Publishing Company

610 Opperman Drive
Eagan, MN 55123-1340

651-687-7327
Home Page: www.westgroup.com

Offers information on law reviews, bar association journals and law-related texts.
Frequency: Full-text

15976 **Want's Federal-State Court Directory**
WANT Publishing Company
420 Lexington Ave
Room 300
New York, NY 10170-0002

212-687-3774
Fax: 212-687-3779
E-Mail: rwant@msn.com
Home Page: www.wantpublishing.com

Robert S Want, President
The nation's number one court reference source, offering comprehensive information on the nation's federal, state and county courts.
Cost: $35.00
235 Pages
Frequency: Softcover

Industry Web Sites

15977 **http://gold.greyhouse.com**
G.O.L.D Grey House OnLine Databases
Grey House Publishing's online database platform, GOLD, offers Quick Search, Keyword Search and Expert Search for most business sectors including legal markets. The GOLD platform makes finding the information you need quick and easy - whether you're a novice searcher or an experienced database user. All of Grey House's directory products are available for subscription on the GOLD platform.

15978 **www.aallnet.org**
American Association of Law Libraries
Membership consists of national law library professionals.

15979 **www.abanet.org**
American Bar Association
The largest organization serving lawyers and all professionals involved in the law enforcement and legal industries. Conducts research and educational activities, encourages professional improvement and provides public service.

15980 **www.aclm.org**
American College of Legal Medicine
Organization related to the field of health law, legal medicine or medical jurisprudence.

15981 **www.aclu.org**
American Civil Liberties Union
Protection of civil liberties and constitutional rights through litigation, public education and legislative lobbying.

15982 **www.afccnet.org**
Association of Family and Conciliation
AFCC is an interdisciplinary, international association of professionals dedicated to improving the lives of children and families through the resolution of family conflict.

15983 **www.afj.org**
Alliance for Justice
Nonprofit association of public interest advocacy organization. Offers workshops, advocacy projects, legal guides, techinical assistance and public education.

15984 **www.aipparl.org**
American Institute of Parliamentarians
A not-for-profit educational organization for the advancement of the parliamentary procedure.

15985 **www.ajs.org**
American Judicature Society
Lawyers, judges and educators interested in the effective administration of justice.

15986 **www.ali-aba.org**
American Law Institute - American Bar Association
Provides continuing legal education courses, books, and periodicals for practicing attorneys and others in the legal profession.

15987 **www.ascm.vicsc.dni.us**
National Association for Court Management
Members are clerks of court, court administration and others serving in a court management capacity.

15988 **www.atlanet.org**
Association of Trial Lawyers of America

15989 **www.attorney-cpa.com**
American Association of Attorney-CPAs
Seeks to safeguard the professional and legal rights of CPA attorneys.

15990 **www.blr.com**
Business & Legal Reports
Provides essential tools for safety and environmental compliance and training needs

15991 **www.educationlaw.org**
Education Law Association
Association for manufacturers or suppliers of law education equipment, supplies and services.

15992 **www.fala.org**
First Amendment Lawyers Association
Lawyers concentrating on defending clients under the first amendment of the Constitution.

15993 **www.fcba.org**
Federal Communications Bar Association
A non-profit organization of attorneys and other professionals involved in the development, interpretation, implementation and practice of communications law and policy.

15994 **www.findlaw.com**
Online Legal Resources. Legal, Professionals, Students, Business, Legal News, etc.

15995 **www.greyhouse.com**
Grey House Publishing
Authoritative reference directories for most business sectors including legal markets. Users can search the online databases with varied search criteria allowing for custom searches by product category, geographic area, sales volume, keyword, subject and more. Full Grey House catalog and online ordering also available.

15996 **www.honet.msu.edu/~law**
American Society for Legal History
Exhibits relating to legal history and its uses in formulating legal policy, decisions and actions; unearthing historical items; and preserving legal and legislative records.

15997 **www.lexis-nexis.com**
Mead Data Central
Contains the Lexis-Nexis Source Locator, a powerful new tool for retrieving targeted information about the more 31,000 Lexi-Nexis sources.

15998 **www.nacdl.org**
National Association of Criminal Defense Lawyers
Supports all criminal defense lawyers with education, publications and trade shows.

15999 **www.naela.org**
National Academy of Elder Law Attorneys
Members are private attorneys, law professors and Title III interest in the provision of legal service to the elderly.

16000 **www.narf.org**
Native American Rights Fund
Provides legal services to Indian tribes, organizations and individuals in the areas of preservation of tribal existence.

16001 **www.ncraonline.org**
National Court Reporters Association

16002 **www.ncwba.org**
National Conference of Women's Bar Associations
To promote and assist the growth of local and statewide women's bar associations and ideas among women's bar associations.

16003 **www.paralegals.org**
National Federation of Paralegal Association
For state and local paralegal associations throughout the United States and Canada.

16004 **www.parliamentarians.org**
National Association of Parliamentarians
An association for those interested in parliamentary law and procedure, NAP's primary objectives are teaching, promoting, and disseminating the philosophy and principles underlying the rules of deliberative assemblies.

16005 **www.rand.org/icj**
Institute for Civil Justice
Nonprofit research organization within the RAND Corporation dedicated to interdisciplinary empirical research to facilitate change in the civil justice system.

16006 **www.rmmlf.org**
Rocky Mountain Mineral Law Foundation

16007 **www.romingerlegal.com**
Is a Search Engine dedicated to Legal Links, Legal Research Page, Case Law and Professional Directories for Law, etc.

16008 **www.searchcrawl.com/legal/justice.html**
Searchcrawl
List of legal resources.

16009 **www.usfca.edu/law/globaljustice**
Web site for the Center for Law and Global Justice. Focus on legal education, judicial training, free and fair elections, and the protection of human rights. The Center is an integral part of the University of San Francisco School of Law.

16010 **www.westlaw.com**
Westlaw is the premier legal and business research tool on the Internet.

16011 **www.worldjurist.org**
World Jurist Association of the World Peace Through Law
Association for those interested in future world peace.

Associations

16012 Africana Librarians Council
African Studies Association
54 Joyce Kilmer Avenue
Piscataway, NJ 08854-8045

732-932-8173
Fax: 732-445-1366
E-Mail: secretariat@africanstudies.org
Home Page: www.africanstudies.org/
Social Media: Facebook, Twitter, LinkedIn, Flickr

Abdi Samatar, President
Suzanne MoyerÿBaazet, Executive Director
James A Pritchett, Vice President
Mesfin Bezuneh, Treasurer
Kathryn Salucka, Executive Assistant

Members consist of librarians, archivists or documentalists working with materials from and about Africa or scholars interested in the preseravtionof or access to Africana.
Founded in 1957

16013 American Association of Law Libraries
105 W Adams Street
Suite 3300
Chicago, IL 60603

312-939-4764
Fax: 312-431-1097
E-Mail: aallhq@aall.org
Home Page: www.aallnet.org
Social Media: Facebook, Twitter, LinkedIn, Flickr

Kate Hagan, Executive Director
Kim Rundle, Executive Assistant
Emily Feltren, Director Government Relations
Julia O'Donnell, Director Membership Marketing
Ashley St. John, Director Marketing/Communications

Promotes and enhances the value of law libraries to the legal and public communities, fosters the profession of law librarianship and provides leadership in the field of legal information.
5000+ Members
Founded in 1906

16014 American Association of School Librarians
American Library Association
50 E Huron Street
Chicago, IL 60611

312-944-6780
800-545-2433
Fax: 312-280-5276
E-Mail: ala@ala.org
Home Page: www.ala.org/aasl/
Social Media: Facebook, Twitter, LinkedIn, Flickr, Pinterest, Google Plus

Sylvia Knight Norton, Executive Director
Jonna Ashley, Program Coordinator
Stephanie Book, Manager, Communications
Allison Cline, Deputy Executive Director
Meg Featheringham, Manager/Editor

Works to ensure that all members of the school library media field collaborate to provide leadership in the total education program, participate as active partners in the teaching and learning process, connect learners with ideas and information and prepare students for life long learning, informed decision making, a love of reading and the use of information technologies.
60000 Members

16015 American Indian Library Association
American Library Association
50 E Huron Street
Chicago, IL 60611

312-944-6780
800-545-2433
Fax: 312-664-7459
E-Mail: ala@ala.org
Home Page: www.ala.org

David Ongley, President
Kelly Webster, VP
Sara Harris, Manager

Association for Native Americans and Native Alaskans libraries and librarians.
10000 Members
Founded in 1949

16016 American Library Association
American Library Association
50 E Huron St
Chicago, IL 60611-2788

312-944-6780
800-545-2433
E-Mail: ala@ala.org
Home Page: www.ala.org

Claire Knowles, Manager
Keith Michael Fiels, Executive Director

To provide leadership for the development, promotion, and improvement of library and information services and the profession of librarianship in order to enhance learning and ensure access to information for all.
65000 Members
Founded in 1876

16017 American Society for Information Science
ASIS&T
1320 Fenwick Lane
Suite 510
Silver Spring, MD 20910

301-495-0900
Fax: 301-495-0810
E-Mail: asis@asis.org
Home Page: www.asis.org

Harry Bruce, President
Richard Hill, Executive Director
Jan Hatzakos, Director of Finance & Admin
Vanessa Foss, Director of Meetings and Membership
Sandra Holder, Receptionist, Office Assistant
4000 Members
Founded in 1937

16018 American Society of Indexing
American Society for Indexing
1628 E. Southern Avenue
Suite 9-223
Tempe, AZ 85282

480-245-6750
Fax: 303-422-8894
E-Mail: info@asindexing.org
Home Page: www.asindexing.org

Ina Gravitz, President
Charlee Trantino, Vice President and President-Elect
Gwen Henson, Executive Director
Janet Perlman, Treasurer
Connie Binder, Secretary

A national association with international membership and interests. A nonprofit charitable organization for indexers, librarians, abstractors, editors, publishers, database producers, and organizations concerned with indexing, seeking cooperation and membership of all persons, groups or institutions interested in indexing. Founded in 1968 to promote excellence in indexing and increase awareness of the value of well-written indexes.
1M Members
Founded in 1957

16019 American Theological Library Association
The American Theological Library Association
300 S Wacker Dr
Suite 2100
Chicago, IL 60606-6701

312-454-5100
888-665-2852
Fax: 312-454-5505
E-Mail: sales@atla.com
Home Page: www.atla.com
Social Media: Facebook

Brenda Bailey-Hainer, Executive Director
Marie Jacobsen, Director of Financial Services
Cameron J. Campbell, Director of Production
Miguel Figueroa, Director of Member Programs
Jim Butler, Director of Information Systems

Provides indexing services in these formats: online database, CD-ROM versions, magnetic tape for OPAC tapeload and print publications. ATLA Religion indexes in print include Religious Index One: Periodicals, Religion Index Two: Multi-Author Works, Index to Book Reviews, Research in Ministry an Index to D. Min. Project Reports and Theses.
800 Members
Founded in 1946

16020 Americans For Libraries Council
Americans For Libraries Council
P.O.Box 2046
New York, NY 10159-2046

646-336-6236
800-542-1918
Fax: 646-336-6318
E-Mail: info@lff.org
Home Page: www.lff.org

Diantha Dow Schull, President
Bruce Astrein, Executive Director
Nina Sonenberg, VP Communications
Sabrina Waldron, Program Manager
William Zeisel, Operations Director

Americans for Libraries Council (ALC) is a national non-profit organization that advocates for libraries at the national level and develops and promotes programs aimed at realizing the potential of libraries in the 21st century.

16021 Art Libraries Society of North America
Art Libraries Society of North America
232-329 March Road
Box 11
Ottawa, ON K2K-2E1

403-247-3001
800-817-0621
Fax: 414-768-8001
E-Mail: g.rodriguez@arlisna.org
Home Page: www.arlisna.org
Social Media: Facebook, Twitter, LinkedIn

Gregory P.J. Most, President
Carole Ann Fabian, Vice-President/President Elect
Eric Wolf, Secretary
Deborah Barlow Smedstad, Treasurer

Membership organization for art libraries in the US and Canada.
Founded in 1972

16022 Asian/Pacific American Librarians
Asian/Pacific American Librarians
PO Box 677593
Orlando, FL 32867

415-422-5379
E-Mail: webmaster@apalaweb.org
Home Page: www.apalaweb.org

Social Media: Facebook, Twitter, LinkedIn, Flickr

Buenaventura Ven Basco, Executive Director

Librarians and information specialists of Asian Pacific descent and those interested in APA librarianship.
310 Members
Founded in 1980

16023 Association for Library & Information Science Education
Association for Library & Information
65 East Wacker Place
Suite 1900
Chicago, IL 60601-7246

312-795-0996
Fax: 312-419-8950
E-Mail: contact@alise.org
Home Page: www.alise.org

John Budd, President
Connie Van Fleet, VP/President-Elect
Deborah York, Executive Director
Jeremy Uthank, Information Management

Provides a forum for library educators to share ideas, discuss issues and seek solutions to common problems.

16024 Association for Library Collections & Technical Services
American Library Association
50 E Huron Street
Chicago, IL 60611

312-944-6780
800-545-2433
Fax: 312-280-5033
E-Mail: ala@ala.org
Home Page: www.ala.org/alcts

Genevieve S Owens, President
Charles Wilt, Executive Director
Keri A Cascio, Director at Large
Norm Medeiros, Director at Large
Timothy T Strawn, Director at Large

Division of the American Library Association.
5M Members
Founded in 1957

16025 Association for Library Service to Children
American Library Association
50 E Huron Street
Chicago, IL 60611

312-944-6780
800-545-2433
Fax: 312-944-7671
E-Mail: ala@ala.org
Home Page: www.ala.org/alsc/

Aimee Strittmatter, Executive Director
Marsha Burgess, Program Coordinator
Joanna Ison, Program Officer - Projects
Caroline Jewell, Awards Coordinator
Kristen Sutherland, Program Officer

A network of more than 4,000 children's and youth librarians, children's literature experts, publishers, education and library school faculty members, and other adults committed to improving and ensuring the future of the nation through exemplary library service to children, their families, and others who work with children.
3500 Members

16026 Association for Population/Family Planning
Family Health International Library
PO Box 13950
Research Triangle Park, NC 27709

919-447-7040
Fax: 215-898-2124
E-Mail: info@aplici.org
Home Page: www.aplici.org
Social Media: Twitter

Allison Burns, President
Debbie Dickson, Vice President
Liz Nugent, Recording Secretary
Joann Donatiello, Acting Treasurer

Global network of communication, information and resource professionals dedicated to providing assistance and support to members and to other population and reproductive health colleagues, especially in developing nations.
Founded in 1968

16027 Association for Recorded Sound Collections
Association for Recorded Sound Collections
1299 University of Oregon
Eugene, OR 97403-1299
440-564 9340
E-Mail: execdir@arsc-audio.org
Home Page: www.arsc-audio.org
Social Media: Facebook

Sam Brylawski, President
David Seubert, VP
Louise Spear, Second VP/Program Chair
Esther Gillie, Secretary/Editor

Persons in broadcasting and recording industries, librarians, sound archivists, curators, private collectors and reviewers.
Cost: $40.00
1000 Members
Frequency: 2 Per Year
Circulation: 1000
Founded in 1966
Mailing list available for rent

16028 Association of Christian Libraries
PO Box 4
Cedarville, OH 45314

937-766-2255
Fax: 937-766-5499
E-Mail: info@acl.org
Home Page: www.acl.org
Social Media: Facebook, Twitter

Frank Quinn, President
Janelle Mazelin, Executive Director
Rodney Birch, Vice President
Sheila O Carlblom, Treasurer
Carol Reid, Secretary

Membership is composed of over 500 evangelical Christian librarians representing primarily evangelical institutions of higher education.
574 Members
Founded in 1956

16029 Association of College and Research Libraries
American Library Association
50 E Huron Street
Chicago, IL 60611

312-944-6780
800-545-2433
Fax: 312-280-2520
E-Mail: acrl@ala.org
Home Page: www.ala.org/acrl/

Mary Ellen K Davis, Executive Director
Lindsay Bosch, Program Officer
Margot Sutton Conahan, Manager of Professional Development
David Connolly, Classified Advertising Coordinator
Kathryn Deiss, Content Strategist
13M Members
ISSN: 0099-0086
Founded in 1938

16030 Association of Independent Information Professionals (AAIP)
Association of Independent Information
8550 United Plaza Boulevard
Suite 1001
Baton Rouge, LA 70809

225-408-4400
Fax: 225-922-4611
E-Mail: info@aiip.org
Home Page: www.aiip.org
Social Media: Facebook, Twitter, LinkedIn

Jocelyn Sheppard, President
Joann M Wleklinski, Secretary
Marilyn Harmacek, Treasurer
Arthur Weiss, Director - Membership
Susan Wald Berkman, Director - Marketing - Content

Provides a forum for information professionals to meet and exchange views.
700 Members
Founded in 1987

16031 Association of Jewish Libraries
Association of Jewish Libraries
PO Box 1118
Teaneck, NJ 07666

201-371-3255
E-Mail: president@jewishlibraries.org
Home Page: www.jewishlibraries.org
Social Media: Facebook, Twitter

Yossi Galron, Membership

Promotes the advancement of the interests of Jewish libraries and publications of Jewish biographical interest.
900 Members
Founded in 1966

16032 Association of Mental Health Librarians
Cedarcrest Regional Hospital, Medical Library
One Beach Street
Suite 100
San Francisco, CA 94133

860-666-4613
Fax: 845-398-5551
Home Page: www.mhlib.org/

Mary L Conlon

Provides a forum for the introduction of new audiovisual and printed materials in the field of mental health.
140 Members
Founded in 1964

16033 Association of Moving Archivists
1313 North Vine Street
Hollywood, CA 90028

323-463-1500
Fax: 323-463-1506
E-Mail: amia@amianet.org
Home Page: www.amianet.org
Social Media: Facebook, Twitter, Youtube

Caroline Frick, President and Director of the Board
Snowden Becker, Secretary and Director of the Board
Colleen Simpson, Treasurer and Director of the Board
Laura Rooney, Managing Director
Beverly Graham, Membership Manager

A non-profit professional association established to advance the field of moving image archiving by fostering cooperation among individuals and organization concerned with the acquistion, description, preservation, exhibition and use of moving image materials.
750 Members
Founded in 1991

16034 Association of Research Libraries
Association of Research Libraries

21 Dupont Circle NW
Suite 800
Washington, DC 20036

202-296-2296
Fax: 202-872-0884
E-Mail: webmgr@arl.org
Home Page: www.arl.org
Social Media: Facebook, Twitter, LinkedIn, Flickr,YouTube, Google Plus

Carol Pitts Diedrichs, President
Deborah Jakubs, Vice President/ President-Elect
Elliott Shore, Executive Director
Prudence S Adler, Associate Executive Director
Sue Baughman, Deputy Executive Director

Nonprofit organization striving to shape and influence forces affecting the future of research libraries in the process of scholarly communication.
124 Members
Founded in 1932

16035 Beta Phi Mu
University of South Florida
3141 Chestnut Street
Philadelphia, PA 19104

215-895-2492
Fax: 215-895-2494
E-Mail: betaphimu@drexel.edu
Home Page: www.beta-phi-mu.org/
Social Media: Facebook, Twitter, LinkedIn

Amanda Ros, President
Eileen G Abels, PhD, Vice-President, President-Elect
Alison M. Lewis, PhD, Executive Director
Kathleen Inman, Treasurer
Erin Gabriele, Program Director

Beta Phi Mu is an organization that recognizes and encourages scholastic achievement among library and information studies students.
Founded in 1948

16036 Black Caucus of ALA
Gladys Smiley Bell
Associate Professor and Reference Librarian
Lib. Med. Serv., Rm 161, Kent State
Kent, OH 44242-0001

330-672-3045
Fax: 330-672-3964
E-Mail: gladysb@lms.kent.edu
Home Page: www.bcala.org

Jerome Offord, Jr, President
Kelvin A Watson, Vice President
Annie M Ford, Treasurer
Diane Covington, Secretary

Association that supports black librarians. Holds annual meeting in conjunction with the American Library Association conference.

16037 Catholic Library Association
Catholic Library Association
205 W Monroe St, Ste 314
Chicago, IL 60606-5061

312-739-1776
855-739-1776
Fax: 312-739-1778
E-Mail: cla@cathla.org
Home Page: www.cathla.org
Social Media: Facebook

Sara R Baron, President
Malachy R McCarthy, Acting Executive Director
Mary Kelleher, Vice-President/Treasurer

International membership organization, providing its members professional development through educational and networking experiences, publications, scholarships and other services.
1000 Members
Founded in 1921

16038 Center for Children's Books
Center for Children's Books
501 E Daniel Street
Champaign, IL 61820

217-244-9331
Fax: 217-333-5603
E-Mail: ccb@illinois.edu
Home Page: ccb.lis.illinois.edu
Social Media: Facebook

Dr. Deborah Stevenson, Director of the Center for Children
Katelyn Boucher, Graduate Assistant
Alice Mitchell, Graduate Assistant
Thaddeus Andracki, CCB Outreach & Communications

A crossroads for critical inquiry, professional training and educational outreach related to literature for youth from birth through adolescence. In partnership with The Bulletin of the Center for Children's Books, it aims to inspire and inform adults who connect young people with resources in person, in print, and online.

16039 Center for Childrens Books
Center for Children's Books
501 E Daniel Street
Champaign, IL 61820

217-244-9331
Fax: 217-333-5603
E-Mail: ccb@illinois.edu
Home Page: ccb.lis.illinois.edu
Social Media: Facebook

Dr. Deborah Stevenson, Director of the Center for Children
Katelyn Boucher, Graduate Assistant
Alice Mitchell, Graduate Assistant
Thaddeus Andracki, CCB Outreach & Communications

16040 Chief Officers of State Library Agencies
Chief Officers of State Library Agencies
201 E Main Street
Suite 1405
Lexington, KY 40507

859-514-9151
Fax: 859-514-9166
E-Mail: lsingler@AMRms.comÿ
Home Page: www.cosla.org

Ann Joslin, President
Kendall Wiggin, Vice President/President Elect
Wayne Onkst, Secretary
Sandra Treadway, Treasurer
Laura Singler, Association Director

Association for directors of state libraries.
53 Members
Founded in 1973

16041 Chinese-American Librarians Association
UCI Libraries
PO Box 19557
Irvine, CA 92623-9557

949-824-6836
Fax: 949-857-1988
E-Mail: sctseng@uci.edu
Home Page: www.cala-web.org
Social Media: Facebook, Youtube

Sally C Tseng, Executive Director
Founded in 1973

16042 Church and Synagogue Library Association
10157 SW Barbur Boulevard
Suite 102C
Portland, OR 97219

503-244-6919
800-542-2752
Fax: 503-977-3734
E-Mail: csla@worldaccessnet.com
Home Page: www.cslainfo.org
Social Media: Facebook

Cheryl Cutchin, President
Maria Isabel Garcia, Second Vice President/Membership
Alice Campbell, Treasurer
Judith Jazen, Administrator
Monica Tenney, Media Review Editor

Provides educational guidance in the establishment and maintenance of congregational libraries
1500 Members
Founded in 1967

16043 Coalition for Networked Information
21 Dupont Circle
Suite 800
Washington, DC 20036-1109

202-296-5098
Fax: 202-872-0884
E-Mail: info@cni.org
Home Page: www.cni.org
Social Media: Facebook, Twitter, LinkedIn, Youtube, Vimeo

Clifford A Lynch, Executive Director
Joan K. Lippincott, Asociate Executive Director
Sharon Adams, Administrative Assistant
Maurice-Angelo Cruz, Systems Coordinator
Jacqueline J Eudell, Office Manager

The Coalition for Networked Information is an organization dedicated to supporting the transformative promise of networked information technology for the advancement of scholarly communication and the enrichment of intellectual productivity.
202 Members
Founded in 1990

16044 Council on Library and Information Resources
Council on Library and Information Resources
1707 L Street NW, Suite 650
Washington, DC 20036-2124

202-939-4750
Fax: 202-939-4765
E-Mail: gromero@clir.org
Home Page: www.clir.org
Social Media: Facebook, Twitter, LinkedIn, Youtube

Herman Pabbruweÿ, Chair
Charles Henry, President
David Rumsey, Vice Chair
Sharon Ivy Weiss, Chief Operations Officer
Lizzi Albert, Administrative Coordinator

The mission of the Council on Library and Information Resources is to expand access to information, however recorded and preserved, as a public good.
Founded in 1997

16045 Council on Library/Media Technicians
PO Box 256
Oxon Hill, MD 20748

202-231-3836
Fax: 202-231-3838
E-Mail: jmhite0@dia.mil
Home Page: http://colt.ucr.edu/

Jackie Hite, President
Margaret Barron, Executive Directorr
Chris Eganÿ, Vice-President/President Elect
Robin Martindill, Secretary
Stan Cieplinski, Treasurer

Supports library and media techicians by offering publications, training, networking and annual conference in conjunction with the American Library Association conference.
Founded in 1967

16046 **Ethnic Employees of the Library of Congress**
6100 Eastview Street
Bethesda, MD 20817-6004
George E Perry, President
Promotes and strengthens brotherhood among ethnic employees and ethnic members of society.
Founded in 1973

16047 **Federal Library and Information Network**
Library of Congress
101 Independence Ave SE
Washington, DC 20540-4935
202-707-4800
Fax: 202-707-4818
Home Page: www.loc.gov/flicc
Social Media: Facebook, Twitter, LinkedIn, Flickr
Roberta Shaffer, Executive Director
Robin Hatziyannis, Editor-in-Chief/Education
Joseph S Banks, Business Manager
Ruby J Thomas, Head, Member Services
Representatives of departments and agencies of the federal government.
40 Members
Founded in 1965
Mailing list available for rent

16048 **Federal and Armed Forces Libraries Roundtable**
American Library Association
50 E Huron Street
Chicago, IL 60611
312-944-6780
800-545-2433
E-Mail: ala@ala.org
Home Page: www.ala.org
Emily Sheketoff, Executive Director
Association for libraries and information services.

16049 **Friends of Libraries (FOLUSA)**
Association of Library Trustees, Advocates, Friend
50 E Huron Street
Chicago, IL 60611
312-944-6780
800-545-2433
Fax: 215-545-3821
E-Mail: ala@ala.org
Home Page: www.ala.org
Encourages the development of excellent library service to all residents of the US. Aids in forming local and state, friends branches in academic and special libraries.
1.8M Members
Founded in 1979

16050 **Herbert Hoover Presidential Library Association**
302 Park Side Drive
PO Box 696
West Branch, IA 52358
319-643-5327
800-828-0475
Fax: 319-643-2391
E-Mail: info@hooverassociation.org
Home Page: www.hooverassociation.org
Jerry Fleagle, Executive Director
Delene McConnaha, Membership and Academic Programs
Ryan Johnson, Financial Development
Brad Reiners, Communications Manager
Joan Maske, Administrative Assistant

16051 **Insurance Library Association of Boston**
Insurance Library
156 State St
Boston, MA 02109-2584
617-227-2087
Fax: 617-723-8524
E-Mail: shart@insurancelibrary.org
Home Page: www.insurancelibrary.org
Glenn Cryan, Executive Director
Meagan Stefanow, Reference Librarian
Sarah Hart, Reference Librarian
Founded in 1887, the Insurance Library Association of Boston is a resource for and provider of literature, information services, and quality professional education for the insurance industry and related interests. The Association offers a wide variety of research services and materials. The collection includes contemporary and historical versions of books, pamphlets, articles and reference materials in all areas of the insurance industry.
760+ Members
Founded in 1887
Mailing list available for rent

16052 **Interagency Council on Information**
American Nurses Association Library
8515 Georgia Avenue
Suite 400
Silver Spring, MD 20910-3492
301-628-5143
Fax: 301-628-5008
E-Mail: richard.barry@ana.org
Home Page: www.icirn.org
Susan Fowler, MLIS, President
June Levy, President
Warren Hawkes, VP
Wanda Hiestand, Treasurer
Jane Root, Secretary
To esablish an effective use of information resources available to the nursing community, and to advance the profession through the promotion and use of its literature.
26 Members
Founded in 1960

16053 **International Association of Aquatic & Mar ine Science Libraries**
The International Association of Aquatic and Marin
2030 S Marine Science Drive
Newport, OR 97365
772-460-9977
E-Mail: janet.webster@oregonstate.edu
Home Page: www.iamslic.org
Sally Taylor, President
Elizabeth Connor, Secretary
Lenora Oftedahl, Treasurer
Guillermina Cosulich, President-Elect
Kristen Anderson, President-Elect
Encourages members to exchange scientific and technical information and explore issues of mutual concern. Conducts workshops about on line databases.
200 Members
Founded in 1975

16054 **International Association of School Librarianship**
65 E. Wacker Place
Suite 1900
Chicago, IL 60601-7246
814-474-1115
Fax: 312-419-8950
Home Page: www.iasl-online.org/
Social Media: Twitter
Dr. Diljit Singh, President
Lourense Das, Vice President
Kay Hones, Vice President
Elizabeth Greef, Vice President
Katy Manck, Treasurer
IASL provides an international forum for those people interested in promoting effective school library media programs as viable instruments in the educational process.

16055 **Library Binding Institute**
4440 PGA Blvd.
Ste. 600
Palm Beach Gardens, FL 33410
561-745-6821
Fax: 561-472-8401
E-Mail: info@lbibinders.org
Home Page: www.lbibinders.org
Duncan Campbell, President
Jack Tolbert, Vice President
Debra S. Nolan, CAE, Executive Director
Alan McIntire, Treasurer
Jack McLoraine, Director
Members are firms binding books for libraries and their suppliers.

16056 **Library Leadership and Management Association**
American Library Association
50 E Huron Street
Chicago, IL 60611
312-944-6780
800-545-2433
Fax: 312-280-5033
E-Mail: lama@ala.org
Home Page: www.ala.org/llama/
Catherine Friedman, President
Kerry Ward, Executive Director
Fred Reuland, Program Officer
Works to improve and develop all aspects and levels of administration in all types of libraries.
5M Members
Founded in 1957

16057 **Library and Information Technology Association**
American Library Association
50 E Huron Street
Chicago, IL 60611
312-944-6780
800-545-2433
E-Mail: lita@ala.org
Home Page: www.ala.org/lita/
Cindi Trainor Blyberg, President
Rachel ÿVacek, Vice President
Mary C Taylor, Executive Director
Melissa Prentice, Program Planning and Marketing
Valerie A Edmonds, Program Coordinator

16058 **Major Orchestra Librarians' Association**
MOLA
1530 Locust Street
PMB 154
Philadelphia, PA 19102
E-Mail: admin@mola-inc.org
Home Page: www.mola-inc.org
Patrick McGinn, President
Mark Millidge, Vice President
Alison Mrowka, Secretary
Shannon Highland, Treasurer
International organization whose objectives include: to improve communication among orchestra librarians; present a unified voice in publisher relations; and assist librarians in providing better service to their orchestras.
630 Members
Founded in 1983

16059 Medical Library Association
65 E Wacker Place
Suite 1900
Chicago, IL 60601-7246

312-419-9094
Fax: 312-419-8950
E-Mail: info@mlahq.org
Home Page: www.mlanet.org / www.marketing.mlanet.org
Social Media: Facebook, LinkedIn, Youtube

Dixie A Jones, President
Carla J Funk, Executive Director
Michelle Kraft, Director and Secretary
Chris Shaffer, Director and Treasurer
Julia Esparza, Director

A nonprofit, educational organization that is a leading advocate for health sciences information professionals worldwide. Through it's programs and services, we provide lifelong educational opportunities, supports a knowledgebase of health information research and works with a global network of partners to promote the importance of quality information for improved health to the health care community and the public.
4500 Members
Founded in 1898

16060 Mid-America Association of Law Libraries
MidAmerican Energy Holdings Company
Po Box 657
Des Moines, IA 50306-0657

515-242-4300
800-358-6265
Fax: 515-242-4261
E-Mail: sharon.kern@lawiowa.com
Home Page: www.midamerican.com

Gregory E. Abel, Chairman, President and CEO
Patrick J. Goodman, Executive Vice President
Maureen E. Sammon, Senior Vice President
Douglas L. Anderson, Executive Vice President

Association for suppliers of law library equipment, supplies and services.
Founded in 1971

16061 Middle East Librarians' Association
Middle East Librarians Association
Main Library
Santa Barbara, CA 93106

805-637-7749
E-Mail: webmaster@mela.us
Home Page: www.mela.us
Social Media: Facebook, Twitter, LinkedIn

Sean Swanick, President
Roberta L. Dougherty, Vice President/ Program Chair
William Kopycki, Secretary/ Treasurer

Interested in aspects of librarianship that support the study or dissemination of information about the Middle East. Publishes a bulletin (semi-annually) that is distributed to members and subscriber institutions in North America, Europe, the Middle East, Asia and Africa.
150 Members
Founded in 1972

16062 Mountain Plains Library Association
14293 W. Center Drive
'
Lakewood, CO 80228

303-985-7795
Fax: 605-677-5488
E-Mail: execsecretary@mpla.us
Home Page: www.mpla.us
Social Media: Facebook, Twitter

Wendy Wendt, President
Annie Epperson, Vice-President/President Elect
Judy Zelenski, Executive Secretary
Abby Moore, Newsletter Editor
Roy Degler, Systems Administrator

Purpose is to promote the development of librarians and libraries by providing significant educational and networking opportunities. The association meets annually in joint conferences with member stats on a rotational basis, and its governed by an elected board of representatives from each member state and a number of selections and roundtables representing interests and types of libraries. In addition to its board and officers, MPLA activities are carried out by a number of committees.
1600+ Members
Founded in 1948

16063 Music Library Association
8551 Research Way
Suite 180
Middleton, WI 53562

608-836-5825
Fax: 608-831-8200
E-Mail: mla@areditions.com
Home Page: www.musiclibraryassoc.org
Social Media: Facebook

Michael Colby, President
Pamela Bristah, Recording Secretary
Paul Cary, Administrative Officer
Linda W. Blair, Assistant Administrative Officer

Promotes growth and establishment in the use of music libraries, musical instruments and musical literature.
Founded in 1931

16064 National Association of Media & Technology Centers
PO Box 9844
Cedar Rapids 52409-9844

319-654-0608
Fax: 319-654-0609
E-Mail: bettyge@mchsi.com
Home Page: www.namtc.org
Social Media: Facebook, Twitter

Sally Lindgren, President
Betty G. Ehlinge, Executive Director
Barbara Siemaszko, Secretary
Geoff Craven, Treasurer

The National Association of Media & Technology Centers is an organization committed to promoting leadership among its membership through networking, advocacy, and support activities that will enhance the equitable access to media, technology, and information services to educational committees. Current membership is over 20 million students.
Founded in 1984

16065 National Church Library Association
National Church Library Association
275 3rd St S
Suite 101A
Stillwater, MN 55082-5094

651-430-0770
E-Mail: info@churchlibraries.org
Home Page: www.churchlibraries.org
Social Media: Facebook

Non-profit support organization that endeavours to further the gospel through church libraries. New resources and support programs are always under development to serve the ever changing needs of the church librarian. Membership is open to individuals, churches or libraries of any denomination or size.
Founded in 1958

16066 National Information Standards Organization
3600 Clipper Mill Road
Suite 302
Baltimore, MD 21211

301-654-2512
Fax: 410-685-5278
E-Mail: nisohq@niso.org
Home Page: www.niso.org

Heather Reid, Chair
Todd Carpenter, Executive Director / Secretary
Nettie Lagace, Associate Director for Programs
Juliana Wood, Educational Programs Manager
Janice Fleming, Treasurer

A non-profit association accredited by the American National Standards Institute, identifies, develops, maintains, and publishes technical standards to manage information in our changing and ever-more digital environment.
70 Members
Founded in 1939

16067 National Library Service for the Blind
Library of Congress
101 Independence Avenue SE
Washington, DC 20542

202-707-4800
888-657-7323
Fax: 202-707-0712
E-Mail: nls@loc.gov
Home Page: www.loc.gov/nls
Social Media: Facebook, Twitter, LinkedIn

Frank Cylke, Manager
Martinez Majors, IT Specialist
Alice G Freeman, Program Management Assistant
Michael M Moodie, Research/Development Officer
ISSN: 0363-3805
Mailing list available for rent

16068 National Media Market
National Media Market
PO Box 87410
Tucson, AZ 85754-7410

520-743-7735
Fax: 800-952-0442
E-Mail: director@nmm.net
Home Page: www.nmm.net
Social Media: Facebook

Ursula Schwarz, Executive Director
Julie Drake, Chair

Presents an exceptional opportunity for media professionals who purchase for public libraries, universities, media/technology centers and educational broadcasting to screen the newst and best quality motion medis from fifty-five prominent producers and distributors.
55 Members
Founded in 1978

16069 New England Library Association
New England Library Association
55 North Main Street, Unit 49
Belchertown, MA 01007

413-813-5254
Fax: 978-282-1304
E-Mail: rscheier@gmail.com
Home Page: www.nelib.org
Social Media: Facebook, Twitter, Flickr, RSS

Deb Hoadley, President
Stephen Spohn, Vice President
David Bryan, Technology Contractor
Mary Ann Rupert, Conference Management Contractor
Robert Scheier, Library Association Administrator

Promotes excellence in library services to the people of New England and advances the leadership role of it's members. Holds an annual conference.

16070 Public Library Association
Public Library Association
50 E Huron Street
Chicago, IL 60611-5295

312-280-5752
800-545-2433
Fax: 312-280-5029
E-Mail: pla@ala.org
Home Page: www.ala.org/pla
Social Media: Facebook

Carolyn Anthony, President
Barb Macikas, Executive Director
Julianna Kloeppel, Program Director
Linda Bostrom, Manager, Professional Development
Mary Hirsh, Project Manager

Exists to provide a diverse program of communications and programming for its members and others interested in the advancment of public libaries.
Founded in 1944

16071 Reference and User Services Association
American Library Association
50 E Huron St
Chicago, IL 60611-2729

312-280-4395
800-545-2433
Fax: 312-944-8085
E-Mail: rusa@ala.org
Home Page: www.ala.org/RUSA

Susan Hornung, Executive Director
Andrea Hill, Manager, Web Services
Leighann Wood, Membership Assistant

Reference and User Services Association is responsible for stimulating and supporting excellence in the delivery of general library services and materials to adults, and the provision of reference and information services, collection development, and resource sharing for all ages, in every type of library.
5000 Members
Founded in 1876

16072 Society of American Archivists
17 North State Street
Suite 1425
Chicago, IL 60602

312-606-0722
866-722-7858
Fax: 312-606-0728
E-Mail: info@archivists.org
Home Page: www2.archivists.org/
Social Media: Facebook, Twitter, LinkedIn

Nancy Beaumont, Executive Director
Teresa Brinati, Director of Publishing
Solveig De Sutter, Director of Education
Tom Jurczak, Director of Finance
Matthew Black, Web and Information Systems

Association for those interested in archival theory and practice in North America.
3400 Members
Founded in 1936

16073 Southeastern Library Association
P.O. Box 950
Rex, GA 30273

678 466 4334
Fax: 678-466-4349
E-Mail: lfallon@solinet.net
Home Page: www.selaonline.org/

Gordon Baker, President
Beverly James, Treasurer
Lorene Flanders, Secretary
Diane N Baird, Treasurer

For over 60 years, the Association has been a unifying force strong enough to influence legislation and to attract foundation and federal funds for regional library projects. The accomplishments of the Association include 2 regional library surveys; the adoption of school library standards; the establishment of state library agencies and the position of state school library supervisor; the founding of library schools; the sponsoring of a variety of informative workshops.

16074 Special Libraries Association
331 S Patrick St
Alexandria, VA 22314-3501

703-647-4900
Fax: 703-647-4901
E-Mail: sla@sla.org
Home Page: www.sla.org

Deb Hunt, President
Janice R. Lachance, Chief Executive Officer
Doug Newcomb, Deputy Chief Executive Officer
Linda Broussard, Chief Financial Officer
Paula Diaz, Director, Membership

International association of information professionals who work in special libraries serving business, research, government and institutions that produce specialized information.
13M Members

16075 State University of New York Librarians Association
Office of Library & Information Services
SUNY Plaza
Albany, NY 12246

518-443-5577
Fax: 518-443-5358
E-Mail: drewwe@morrisville.edu
Home Page: www.sunyla.org
Social Media: Facebook, Twitter

April Davies, President
Alvin Dantes, 1st Vice-President/President Elect
Wendy West, 2nd Vice-President/Conference Chair
Carleen Huxley, Secretary
Greg Bobish, Treasurer

Statewide professional librarian organization.
348 Members
Founded in 1968

16076 Substance Abuse Librarians and Information
Substance Abuse Librarians & Information Specialis
PO Box 9513
Berkeley, CA 94709-0513

510-769-1831
Fax: 510-865-2467
E-Mail: salis@salis.org
Home Page: www.salis.org

Jane Shelling, Chair
Andrea Mitchell, Executive Director and Editor
Sheila Lacroix, Secretary
Karen Palmer, Treasurer

Provides professional development and exchange of information and concerns about access to and dissemination of information on substance abuse.
160 Members
Founded in 1978

16077 Theatre Library Association
40 Lincoln Center Plaza
New York, NY 10023

E-Mail: info@tla-online.org
Home Page: www.tla-online.org
Social Media: Facebook

Nancy Friedland, President
Angela Weaver, VP
Laurie Murphy, Executive Secretary
Colleen Riley, Treasurer

Supports librarians and archivists affiliated with theatre, dance, performance studies, popluar entertainment, motion picture and broadcasting collections. Promotes professional best practices in acquistion, organization, access and preservation of performing arts resources in libraries, archives, museums, private collections, and the digital environment.
300 Members
Founded in 1937

16078 U.S. National Commission on Libraries and Information Science (NCLIS)
1800 M Street NW
Suite 350 North Tower
Washington, DC 20036-5841

FAX 202-606-9203
Home Page: www.nclis.gov/

Trudi Bellardo Hahn, Executive Director
C. Beth Fitzsimmons, Chairperson

The U.S. National Commission on Libraries and Information Science is a permanent, independent agency of the federal government charged with advising the executive and legislative branches and other public and private organizations on national library and information policies and plans.
Founded in 1970

16079 Urban Libraries Council
125 S Wacker Drive
Suite 1050
Chicago, IL 60606-4477

312-676-0999
Fax: 312-676-0950
E-Mail: info@urbanlibraries.org
Home Page: www.urbanlibraries.org
Social Media: Facebook, Twitter

Melanie Huggins, Chairman
Karen Glover, Vice Chair/Chair Elect
Susan B Benton, President & CEO
Lourdes Aceves, Project Manager, Edge
Mary Colleen Bragiel, Project Manager

Works to strengthen public libraries as an essential part of urban life. Serves as a forum for research widely recognized and used by public and prrivate sector leaders.
150+ Members
Founded in 1971

Newsletters

16080 AASL Presidential Hotline
American Library Association
50 E Huron St
Chicago, IL 60611-2788

312-280-2518
800-545-2433
E-Mail: kfiels@ala.org
Home Page: www.ala.org

Keith Michael Fiels, Executive Director

School library media association news.
Frequency: Monthly
Founded in 1951

16081 Church & Synagogue Libraries Journal
Church and Synagogue Library Association
10157 SW Barbur Boulevard #102C
Portland, OR 97219

503-244-6919
800-542-2752
Fax: 503-977-3734
E-Mail: csla@worldaccessnet.com

Home Page: www.cslainfo.org
Social Media: Facebook, Twitter

Judith Jazen, Administrator/Director
Cheryl Cutchin, President
Maria Isabel Garala, Second VP/Membership Chair
Alice Campbell, Treasurer

The Church & Synagouge Library Assn. provides educational guidance in the establishment and maintenance of congreational libraries.
Cost: $35.00
Frequency: Bi-Monthly
ISSN: 0009-6342
Founded in 1967

16082 Church & Synagogue Libraries Newsletter
Church and Synagogue Library Association
10157 SW Barbur Boulevard #102C
Portland, OR 97219

503-244-6919
800-542-2752
Fax: 503-977-3734
E-Mail: csla@worldaccessnet.com
Home Page: www.cslainfo.org
Social Media: Facebook, Twitter

Judith Jazen, Religious Leader
Evelyn Pockrass, President
Cheryl Cutchin, First Vice President
David Reed, Second Vice President
Dick Burgduff, Treasurer

16083 Corporate Library Update
Reed Business Information
30 Technology Parkway South
Suite 100
Norcross, GA 30092

646-746-6400
800-424-3996
Fax: 646-756-7583
E-Mail: webmaster@reedbusiness.com
Home Page: www.reedbusiness.com

John Poulin, CEO
Lynn Blumenstein, Senior Editor
Susan DiMattia, Editor
Cost: $69.95
Frequency: Fortnightly
Circulation: 2500

16084 Libraries Alive
National Church Library Association
275 3rd St S
Suite 101A
Stillwater, MN 55082-5094

651-430-0770
E-Mail: info@churchlibraries.org
Home Page: www.churchlibraries.org
Social Media: Facebook

Sue Benish, Executive Director
Chuck Mann, President Board of Directors

Features informative articles, reviews of books and other media, a sharing of ideas, Internet resources, chapter news, news of authors and upcoming regional and national workshops.
Frequency: Quarterly

16085 Library Hotline
Library Journal/School Library Journal
360 Park Ave S
New York, NY 10010-1710

646-746-6819
800-446-6551
Fax: 646-746-6734
Home Page: www.libraryjournal.com

Ron Shank, Publisher
Justin Torres, Production Manager
Lynn Blumenstein, Senior Editor
Carol Batt, COO
Patty Braden, Director
Cost: $115.00
Frequency: Weekly
Founded in 1876

16086 MLA News
Medical Library Association
65 E Wacker Place
Suite 1900
Chicago, IL 60601-7298

312-419-9094
Fax: 312-419-8950
E-Mail: info@mlahq.org
Home Page: www.mlanet.org

Lynanne Fielen, Director Publications
Carla Funk, Editor
Lynanne Fielen, Circulation Manager
Elizabeth Rodriguez, Graphic Designer

Covers MLA programs and services as well as the medical librarian profession in general.
Cost: $58.00
Frequency: Monthly
Founded in 1898
Mailing list available for rent

16087 Marcato
MOLA/Editor
1530 Locust Street
PMB 154
Philadelphia, PA 19102

202-416-8131
Fax: 202-416-8132
E-Mail: sfriedman@kennedy-center.org
Home Page: www.mola-inc.org

Shelley Friedman, Editor
Gordon Rowley, Treasurer
Elena Lence Talley, President

Newsletter of Major Orchestra Librarians' Association.
Cost: $20.00
Frequency: Quarterly

16088 Marketing Treasures
Chris Olson & Associates
857 Twin Harbor Drive
Arnold, MD 21012-1027

410-647-6708
Fax: 410-647-0415
Home Page: www.chrisolson.com

Christine Olson, Publisher

Provinding creative ideas, helpful hints and insights on how libraries can promote thier services
6 Pages
Frequency: Monthly
Circulation: 1000
Founded in 1987
Printed in 2 colors on matte stock

16089 Report on Literacy Programs
Business Publishers
8737 Colesville Road
Suite 1100
Silver Spring, MD 20910-3928

301-876-6300
800-274-6737
Fax: 301-589-8493
E-Mail: custserv@bpinews.com
Home Page: www.bpinews.com

Dave Speights, Editor
Leonard A Eiserer, Publisher
Beth Early, Operations Director

Covers all aspects of literacy including legislation, funding, training programs, important conferences, job skills and much more.
Cost: $317.00
Founded in 1963

16090 Research Library Issues
Association of Research Libraries
21 Dupont Circle NW
Suite 800
Washington, DC 20036

202-296-2296
Fax: 202-872-0884
E-Mail: arlhq@arl.org
Home Page: www.arl.org
Social Media: Facebook, Twitter, LinkedIn, Flickr,YouTube

Charles B Lowry, Executive Director
Prudence S. Adler, Associate Executive Director
Sue Baughman, Deputy Executive Director
Julia Blixrud, Assistant Executive Director
Mary Jane Brooks, Assistant Executive Director

Member representatives
Frequency: Bi-Monthly
ISSN: 1947-4911

16091 State University of New York Librarians Association
Office of Library & Information Services
SUNY Plaza
Albany, NY 12246

518-443-5577
Fax: 518-443-5358
E-Mail: drewwe@morrisville.edu
Home Page: www.sunyla.org
Social Media: Facebook, Twitter

Wilfred Drew, President
John Schumacher, Electronic Resources Coordinator

Provides news, notes and information from SUNY campus libraries.
Frequency: 2-3/Year

16092 Technicalities
Westport Publishing
802 Broadway Street
Kansas City, MO 64105

816-842-0641

Brian Alley, Editor

A professional journal presenting discussion, opinions, and reviews on library-management topics. Typical issues include articles ranging from computer applications, on-line public access catalogs, library budgets, collection building, book reviews, automation, software, library marketplace trends, and the Library of Congress. Articles are indexed in Library Literature and LISA: Library Information Science Abstracts and are available on microfilm from UMI.
Cost: $ 47.00
16 Pages
Frequency: Monthly
Circulation: 700
Mailing list available for rent
Printed in one color on matte stock

16093 Urban Libraries Council Exchange Letter
1603 Orrington Avenue
Suite 1080
Evanston, IL 60201

847-866-9999
Fax: 847-866-9989
E-Mail: info@urbanlibraries.org
Home Page: www.urbanlibraries.org/

Eleanor Rodger, President/CEO
Linda Crismond, Editor

Newsletter for public libraries in cities with over 100,000 people. Free to members, also available without membership.
Cost: $50.00
150 Pages
Circulation: 6000
Founded in 1971

Magazines & Journals

16094 AALL Spectrum
American Association of Law Libraries
105 W Adams Street
Suite 3300
Chicago, IL 60603
312-939-4764
Fax: 312-431-1097
E-Mail: support@aall.org
Home Page: www.aallnet.org
Social Media: Facebook, Twitter
Mark Estes, Editorial Director
Hillary Baker, Marketing and Communications
Kate Hagan, Executive Director
Kim Rundle,, Executive Assistant
Emily Feltren,, Director of Government Relations
Publishes substantive, well-written articles on topics of real interest to law librarians, as well as news about the American Association of Law Libraries, including its chapters, committees and Special Interest Sections
Cost: $ 75.00

16095 Advanced Technology/Libraries
GK Hall & Company
1239 Broadway
Suite 1601
New York, NY 10001-4327
212-685-0602
Fax: 212-654-4751
E-Mail: sales@gkimport.com
Home Page: www.gkimport.com
Dina Groudan, President
Audrey Ismal, Owner
Concise, practical information on the advances in development, implementation and use of library automation. Articles cover new products, new services, legislation and grant information.
Cost: $95.00
Frequency: Monthly

16096 American Archivist
Society of American Archivists
527 S Wells Street
5th Floor
Chicago, IL 60607-3922
312-922-0140
Fax: 312-347-1452
Home Page: www.archivists.org
Susan Fox, Executive Director
Philip B Eppard, Editor
Teresa Brinati, Director of Publications
Offers information and essays on archival theory and practice in North America.
Cost: $85.00
Circulation: 4800+
Founded in 1936

16097 American Libraries
American Library Association
50 E Huron St
Chicago, IL 60611-2788
312-280-2518
800-545-2433
E-Mail: customerservice@ala.org
Home Page: www.ala.org
Claire Knowles, Manager
Carla D Hayden, President
Library development news.
Cost: $60.00
Frequency: Monthly
Founded in 1876

16098 Book Report: Magazine for Secondary School Librarians
Linworth Publishing
480 East Wilson Bridge Road
Suite L
Worthington, OH 43085
614-436-7107
800-786-5017
Fax: 614-436-9490
E-Mail: linworth@linworthpublishing.com
Home Page: www.linworth.com
Marlene Woo-Lun, Publisher
Amy Robinson, Marketing Manager
In-depth articles, helpful hints, and reviews on books, software, videos, and CD-Roms for secondary school librarians.
Cost: $49.00
105 Pages
Circulation: 15000
Founded in 1981
Printed in 4 colors on glossy stock

16099 Booklist
American Library Association
50 E Huron St
Chicago, IL 60611-2788
312-280-2518
800-545-2433
E-Mail: customerservice@ala.org
Home Page: www.ala.org
Claire Knowles, Manager
To provide a guide to current library materials in many formats appropriate for use in public libraries and school library media centers.
Cost: $89.95
Circulation: 25000
Founded in 1876

16100 Bulletin of Bibliography
Greenwood Publishing Group
88 Post Road W
P O Box 5007
Westport, CT 06881-5007
203-226-3571
800-225-5800
Fax: 203-226-6009
E-Mail: customer-service@greenwood.com
Home Page: www.greenwood.com
Bernard McTigue, Editor-in-Chief
Gerry Katz, Executive Editor
Naomi Caldwell Wood, Author
Offers bibliographies in humanities and social sciences.
Cost: $125.00
100 Pages
Frequency: Quarterly
Circulation: 1000
ISSN: 0190-745X
Printed in 2 colors on matte stock

16101 Bulletin of the Center for Children's Books
501 E Daniel Street
MC-493
Champaign, IL 61820
217-244-0324
Fax: 217-244-3302
Home Page: alexia.lis.uiuc.edu
Deborah Stevenson, Editor
Marlow Welshon, Dean
Reviews of children's books for librarians, teachers, booksellers and parents.
Cost: $50.00
34 Pages
Frequency: Monthly
Circulation: 6500
Founded in 1893

16102 CD-ROM Librarian
Mecklermedia Corporation
11 Ferry Lane W
Westport, CT 06880-5808
FAX 203-454-5840
Alan Meckler, Editor
A periodical intended for the library professional.
Cost: $80.00
Frequency: Monthly
Founded in 1986

16103 Catholic Library World
Catholic Library Association
205 W Monroe St, Ste 314
Pittsfield, MA 01201-5178
413-443-2252
Fax: 413-442-2252
E-Mail: cla@cathla.org
Home Page: www.cathla.org
Social Media: Facebook
Nancy K Schmidtmann, President
Malachy R McCarthy, VP
Jean R Bostley SSJ, Executive Director
Articles and news of interest to the library profession. Extensive section of book and media reviews
Frequency: Quarterly
ISSN: 0008-820X

16104 Choice
Association of College and Research Libraries
575 Main Street
Suite 300
Middletown, CT 06457
800-545-2433
E-Mail: acrl@ala.org
Home Page: www.ala.org/acrl/choice
Lori Goetsch, President
Irving Rockwood, Publisher
Francine Graf, Editorial Director
Lisa Gross, Information/Production Manager
Rita Balasco, Choice Reviews
Publishes reviews of books, internet sites, and microcomputer software suitable for college and university libraries.
Cost: $280.00
Frequency: Monthly
Circulation: 5000
Founded in 1938

16105 Congregational Libraries Today
Church and Synagogue Library Association
2920 SW Dolphin Court
Suite 3A
Portland, OR 97219-4055
503-244-6919
800-542-2752
Fax: 503-977-3734
Home Page: www.cslainfo.org
Jeri Zulli, Publications Editor
Contains news about CSLA and its chapters, feature stories about congregational libraries and librarians, promotion ideas, information on using computers and the internet in the library, and reviews of books, videos, CDs, and audiotapes for adults and children.
Frequency: Quarterly
Circulation: 2500

16106 Information Retrieval & Library Automation
Lomond Publications
PO Box 88
Mount Airy, MD 21771-0088
202-362-1361
Fax: 202-362-6156
Thomas Hattery, Publisher
New technology, products and equipment that improve information systems and library ser-

vices, for science, social, social science, law, medicine, academic institutions and the public.
Cost: $75.00
Frequency: Monthly

16107 Journal of the Medical Library Association
Medical Library Association
65 E Wacker Drive
Suite 1900
Chicago, IL 60601-7298
312-419-9094
800-462-6420
Fax: 312-419-8950
E-Mail: info@mlahq.org
Home Page: www.mlanet.org
Lynanne Feilen, Director Publication
Carla J Funk, Executive Director
Susan C Talmage, Editorial Assistant
Bleu caldwell, Production Assistant
Barbara Redmond, Advertising Coordinator
Cost: $163.00
Frequency: Quarterly
Mailing list available for rent

16108 Knowledge Quest
American Library Association
50 E Huron St
Chicago, IL 60611-2788
312-280-2518
800-545-2433
E-Mail: kfiels@ala.org
Home Page: www.ala.org
Keith Michael Fiels, Executive Director
Andria Parker, Marketing
Vickie William, Circulation Manager
Articles on teaching, learning process, ideas and information to prepare students for life long learning.
Cost: $40.00
Circulation: 5000
ISSN: 1094-9046
Founded in 1879
Printed in 4 colors on matte stock

16109 Library Bookseller
PO Box 9544
Berkeley, CA 94709-544
Scott Saifer, Publisher
Gail Russin, Editor
A journal focusing on suppliers to libraries.
Cost: $100.00
36 Pages

16110 Library Journal
Media Source
160 Varick Street
11th Floor
New York, NY 10013
646-380-0700
Fax: 646-380-0756
E-Mail: ljinfo@mediasourceinc.com
Home Page: www.libraryjournal.com
Ron Shank, Publisher
Francine Fialkoff, Editor-in-Chief
Brian Kenney, Editorial Director
Bette-Lee Fox, Managing Editor
Rebecca Miller, Executive Editor
Provides groundbreaking features and analytical news reports covering technology, management, policy and other professional concerns to public, academic and institutional libraries. Evaluates 8000 reviews annually of books, ebooks, audiobooks, videos/DVDs, databases, systems and websites.
Cost: $141.00
Circulation: 17936
Founded in 1876
Printed in 4 colors on glossy stock

16111 Library Resources & Technical Services
American Library Association
50 E Huron St
Chicago, IL 60611-2788
312-280-2518
800-545-2433
E-Mail: kfiels@ala.org
Home Page: www.ala.org
Keith Michael Fiels, Executive Director
Steven L Hofman, Circulation Manager
Andrea Parker Parker, Marketing Head
Offers articles to technical service librarians on acquisitions, cataloging and classification.
Cost: $30.00
Frequency: Bi-annually
Circulation: 60000
Founded in 1951

16112 Library Software Review
Sage Publications
Vanderbilt University
419 21st Avenue S
Nashville, TN 37240-0001
615-343-6094
Fax: 615-343-8834
E-Mail: info@sagepub.com
Home Page: www.sagepub.com
Marshall Breeding, Editor
Provides the library professional with information necessary to make intelligent software evaluation, procurement, integration and installation decisions. Issues review software and software books and periodicals.
Cost: $52.00
Frequency: Quarterly
Circulation: 1M

16113 Library Talk: Magazine for Elementary School Librarians
Linworth Publishing
480 E Wilson Bridge Road
Suite L
Worthington, OH 43085-2372
614-436-7107
800-786-5017
Fax: 614-436-9490
E-Mail: linworth@linworthpublishing.com
Home Page: www.linworth.com
Marlene Woo-Lun, Publisher
Amy Robinson, Marketing Manager
Carol Simpson, Consulting Editor
In-depth articles, helpful hints, and reviews on books, software, and CD-ROMS for elementary school library media and technology specialist.
Cost: $49.00
68 Pages
Circulation: 10000
Founded in 1988
Printed in 4 colors on glossy stock

16114 Library Trends
University of Illinois Press
1325 S Oak St
Champaign, IL 61820-6975
217-333-0950
866-244-0626
Fax: 217-244-8082
E-Mail: journals@uillinois.edu
Home Page: www.press.uillinois.edu
Willis Regier, Director
Ann Lowry, Journals Manager
Cheryl Jestis, Manager
Pat Hoefling, Marketing and Sales Director
A journal which offers a medium for current thought and information in the library field.
Cost: $75.00
Frequency: Quarterly
Circulation: 2600
ISBN: 0-252725-23-9
Founded in 1918

16115 Medical Reference Services Quarterly
Taylor & Francis
325 Chestnut Street
Suite 800
Philadelphia, PA 19106
800-354-1420
Fax: 215-625-2940
Home Page: www.tandf.co.uk
M Sandra Wood, Editor
An essential working tool for medical and health sciences librarians. Covers topics of current interest and practical value in the areas of reference in medicine and related specialities, the biomedical sciences, nursing and allied health.
Cost: $110.00
Frequency: Quarterly
ISSN: 0276-3869
Founded in 1975

16116 Reference and User Services Quarterly (RUSQ)
American Library Association
50 E Huron St
Chicago, IL 60611-2788
312-280-2518
800-545-2433
Fax: 312-664-7459
E-Mail: customerservice@ala.org
Home Page: www.ala.org
Keith Michael Fiels, Executive Director
Andrea Parker, Marketing Specialist
Steven L Hofmann, Manager, Communications
Connie Van Fleet, Editor in Chief
News of interest to reference and adult services librarians.
Cost: $60.00
Frequency: Quarterly
Circulation: 6,246
Founded in 1951

16117 School Library Journal
Media Source
160 Varick Street
11th Floor
New York, NY 10013
646-380-0700
Fax: 646-380-0756
E-Mail: sljinfo@mediasourceinc.com
Home Page: www.schoollibraryjournal.com
Ron Shank, Publisher
Francine Fialkoff, Editor-in-Chief
Brian Kenney, Editorial Director
Bette-Lee Fox, Managing Editor
Rebecca Miller, Executive Editor
Provides groundbreaking features and analytical news reports covering technology, management, policy and other concerns to school libraries. Evaluates 8000 reviews annually of books, ebooks, audiobooks, videos/DVDs, databases, systems and websites.
Frequency: Monthly
Circulation: 100000
Founded in 1954
Printed in 4 colors on glossy stock

16118 School Library Media Research
American Library Association
50 E Huron St
Chicago, IL 60611-2788
312-280-2518
800-545-2433
E-Mail: kfiels@ala.org
Home Page: www.ala.org
Keith Michael Fiels, Executive Director
Available online only. Current developments in the media and library field. Evaluates the most

currently available print and nonprint materials for library media centers.

16119 **Science and Technology Libraries**
Taylor & Francis
325 Chestnut Street
Suite 800
Philadelphia, PA 19106
800-354-1420
Fax: 215-625-2940
Home Page: www.tandf.co.uk
Tony Stankus, Editor-in-Chief
A peer-reviewed, scholarly journal covering all ascpects of the profession as librarians serving science, engineering, clinical investigation, and agriculture.
Cost: $110.00
Frequency: Quarterly
ISSN: 0194-262X
Founded in 1978

16120 **Today's Librarian**
Virgo Publishing LLC
3300 N Central Ave
Suite 300
Phoenix, AZ 85012-2532
480-990-1101
Fax: 480-990-0819
E-Mail: mikes@vpico.com
Home Page: www.vpico.com
Jenny Bolton, President
John Siefert, CEO
Kelly Ridley, Executive VP, CFO
Heather Wood, VP, Human Resources
Jon Benninger, VP, Health & Nutrition Network
Of interest to librarians and media professionals.

16121 **Video Librarian**
Video Librarian
3435 NE Nine Boulder Drive
Poulsbo, WA 98370
360-626-1259
Fax: 360-626-1260
E-Mail: vidlib@videolibrarian.com
Home Page: www.videolibrarian.com
Randy Pitman, Publisher
Anne Williams, Graphic Designer
Carol Kaufman, Graphic Designer
Offers video reviews and news for public, school, academic and special libraries.
Cost: $64.00
56 Pages
Circulation: 2000
ISSN: 0887-6851
Founded in 1986
Printed in 4 colors on glossy stock

Trade Shows

16122 **ACL Conference**
Association of Christian Librarians
PO Box 4
Cedarville, OH 45314
937 766-2255
Fax: 937-766-5499
E-Mail: info@acl.org
Home Page: www.acl.org
Social Media: Facebook, Twitter, Delicious
Jo Ann Rhodes, President
Alice Ruleman, VP
Janelle Mazelin, Executive Director
Sheila O. Carlblom, Treasurer
Carrie Beth Lowe, Secretary
The purpose of the conference is to provide professional information, promote Christian philosophy and ethic of librarianship, provide an opportunity for exchange of ideas and promote service to the academic community worldwide
550 Members
Founded in 1954

16123 **ALA National Conference on Asian Pacific American Librarians**
American Library Association
50 E Huron Street
Chicago, IL 60611
800-545-2433
E-Mail: customerservice@ala.org
Home Page: www.ala.org

16124 **American Association of School Librarians National Conference & Exhibition**
50 E Huron Street
Chicago, IL 60611-5295
312-280-4386
800-545-2433
Fax: 312-664-7459
E-Mail: customerservice@ala.org
Home Page: www.ala.org/aasl
Judy King, Director Program Development
Lissa Salvatierra, Meeting Planner
Biennial continuing education conference and 300-500 exhibits of equipment, supplies and services for school library media centers, including print and nonprint materials and other equipment.
3500 Attendees
Frequency: October
Founded in 1876

16125 **American Indian Library Association Conference**
American Indian Library Assn Univ. of Pittsburgh
207 Hillman Library
Pittsburgh, PA 15260
412-621-4470
Fax: 412-648-1245
Home Page: http://www.ailanet.org
Lisa A Mitten
Annual conference and exhibits relating to the development, maintenance and cultural information services on reservations and in communities of Native Americans and Native Alaskans.
Founded in 1979

16126 **American Library Association Annual Conference**
American Library Association
50 E Huron Street
Chicago, IL 60611
800-545-2433
E-Mail: customerservice@ala.org
Home Page: www.ala.org
Loriene Roy, President
Keith Michael Fiels, Executive Director
Annual meeting and exhibits of books, periodicals, reference works, audio visual equipment, films, data processing services, computer hardware and software, library equipment and supplies.

16127 **American Library Association Midwinter Meeting**
American Library Association
50 E Huron Street
Chicago, IL 60611
800-545-2433
E-Mail: customerservice@ala.org
Home Page: www.ala.org
Loriene Roy, President
Keith Michael Fiels, Executive Director
Annual meeting and 418 exhibits of books, periodicals, reference works, audio visual equipment, films, data processing services, computer hardware and software, library equipment and supplies.

16128 **Art Libraries Society of North America Annual Conference**
Art Libraries Society of North America
4101 Lake Boone Trail
Suite 201
Raleigh, NC 27607-7506
919-518-1919
800-892-7547
Fax: 919-787-4916
E-Mail: arlisna@mercury.interpath.com
Annual conference and show of publishers, book dealers, library suppliers and visual resources suppliers.
500 Attendees
Founded in 1977

16129 **Association for Library & Information Science Education Annual Conference**
11250 Roger Bacon Drive
Suite 8
Reston, VA 20190-5202
703-360-0500
Fax: 703-435-4390
Home Page: www.alise.org/index.shtml
John Budd, President
Deborah York, Executive Director
Frequency: January

16130 **Association for Population/Family Planning Libraries & Information Centers**
Assn for Population Family Planning Libraries
Surgical Contraception-79 Madison
New York, NY 10016
212-780-2687
Fax: 212-779-9439
William Record
Annual conference and exhibits for effective documentation, information systems and services in the field of population/family planning.

16131 **Association of College and Research Libraries**
American Library Association
50 E Huron Street
Chicago, IL 60611-5295
312-280-2511
800-545-2433
Fax: 312-280-2520
E-Mail: customerservice@ala.org
Home Page: www.ala.org/acrl
Mary Ellen Davis, Executive Director
Two hundred exhibitors with computers and web products, audiovisual products, furniture and library equipment.
3000 Attendees
Frequency: Biennial
ISSN: 0099-0086
Founded in 1978
Mailing list available for rent

16132 **CSLA Conference**
Church and Synagogue Library Association

2920 SW Dolphin Court
Suite 3A
Portland, OR 97219-4055

503-244-6919
800-542-2752
Fax: 503-977-3734
Home Page: www.cslainfo.org

Judith Janzen, Administrator
150 Attendees
Frequency: Annual/July

16133 Culture Keepers: Making Global Connections
Black Caucus of the American Library Association
Newark Public Library
5 Washington Street
Newark, NJ 07101

973-961-2540
Fax: 973-522-4827

Dr. Alex Boyd

Biennial show and exhibits of books, journals and library products.

16134 Federal and Armed Forces Libraries Roundtable Conference
American Library Association
50 E Huron St
Chicago, IL 60611-2729

312-944-6780
800-545-2433
Fax: 312-944-8085
E-Mail: ala@ala.org
Home Page: www.ala.org/faflrt/front

Emily Sheketoff, Executive Director

Annual conference and exhibits of equipment, supplies and services for libraries and information services.

16135 International Association of Aquatic & Marine Science Libraries Conference
Harbor Branch Oceanographic Institution
5600 US 1 N
Fort Pierce, FL 34946

800-333-4264
Fax: 772-465-2446

Annual conference and exhibits of equipment, supplies and services for marine-related libraries and information centers.
Frequency: October, Charleston

16136 Mid-Atlantic Regional Library Federation
South Maryland Regional Library
37 606 New Market Road
Charlotte Hall, MD 20622
301-884-0436

Katharine Hurrey, President

Offers exhibits by vendors who provide services and products useful to libraries and information brokers.
1M Attendees
Frequency: March

16137 Mountain Plains Library Association Annual Conference
Mountain Plains Library Association
University of SD-I D Weeks Library
Vermillion, SD 57069

FAX 605-677-5488

Annual conference and exhibits of publications and library equipment, supplies and services.
600 Attendees

16138 New England Library Association Annual Conference
New England Library Association
14 Main Street
Gloucester, MA 03031

978-820-0787
Fax: 978-282-1304
Home Page: www.nelib.org

Mary Ann Rupert, Technology Manager
Barry Blaisdell, Manager

Annual show of publishers, distributors and suppliers of books, media, supplies, furniture, equipment, hardware, software and services used by libraries. Containing 160 booths and 130 exhibits.
1,000 Attendees
Frequency: October

16139 Public Library Association National Conference
Public Library Association
50 E Huron Street
Chicago, IL 60611-5295

312-280-5752
800-545-2433
Fax: 312-280-5029
E-Mail: pla@ala.org

Barb Macikas, Show Manager

Biennial show of 200 exhibitors of books and other equipment, supplies and services for libraries.
3500 Attendees
Frequency: March

16140 Southeastern Library Association
Combined Book Exhibit
P.O. Box 950
Rex, GA 30273

678-466-4334
Fax: 678-466-4349
Home Page: http://selaonline.org/

This biennial conference, offers attendees from over 12 states. The convention offers exhibits, meetings and an open reception in the exhibit hall. The three biggest states, Georgia, North Carolina and South Carolina spend twice as much of expenditures on CD-ROM and 8% more on books than the national average, which makes this the perfect exhibition for sellers.
2.1M+ Attendees
Frequency: Fall

16141 Special Libraries Association
331 South Patrick St
Alexandria, VA 22314-3501

703-647-4900
Fax: 703-647-4901
E-Mail: janice@sla.org
Home Page: http://www.sla.org/content/SLA/contactus/index.cfm

James Mears, Conference Manager
Janice Lschance, CEO

An international professional association of people working in special libraries serving institutions and organizations that use or produce specialized information.
6M Attendees
Frequency: June

Directories & Databases

16142 Address List, Regional and Subregional Libraries for the Handicapped
Library of Congress
101 Independence Avenue SE
Washington, DC 20540

202-707-4800
888-657-7323
Fax: 202-707-0712
E-Mail: nls@loc.gov
Home Page: www.loc.gov/nls
Social Media: Facebook, Twitter, LinkedIn

Kurt Cykle, Director
25 Pages
Frequency: Semi-Annual
ISSN: 0363-3805
Mailing list available for rent

16143 American Library Association Handbook
American Library Association
50 E Huron St
Chicago, IL 60611-2788

312-280-2518
800-545-2433
E-Mail: customerservice@ala.org
Home Page: www.ala.org

Claire Knowles, Manager

Offers 56 regional groups comprised of libraries, trustees, librarians and others interested in the responsibilities of libraries in the educational and cultural needs of society.

16144 American Library Directory
Information Today
143 Old Marlton Pike
Medford, NJ 08055-8750

609-654-6266
800-300-9868
Fax: 609-654-4309
E-Mail: custserv@infotoday.com
Home Page: www.infotoday.com

Thomas H Hogan, President
Roger R Bilboul, Chariman Of The Board

Detailed profiles for more than 35,000 public, academic, special, and government libraries and library related organizations in the US and Canada. These include addresses, phone and fax numbers, e-mail addresses, network participation, expenditures, holdings and special collections, key personnel, special services and more than 40 categories of library information in all. A two volume set.
Cost: $299.00
4000 Pages
ISBN: 1-573872-04-0
Mailing list available for rent

16145 Association of Jewish Libraries Membership List
Ramaz Upper School Library
60 E 78th St
New York, NY 10075-1838

212-517-2103

Ira Miller, Principal
Cost: $100.00
100 Pages
Frequency: Annual

16146 BookQuest
ABACIS
135 Village Queen Drive
Owings Mills, MD 21117-4470

FAX 410-581-0398

This database offers descriptions of book dealers' offerings and books being sought by libraries, dealers and collectors.
Frequency: Full-text

16147 Chief Officers of State Library Agencies Directory
Chief Officers of State Library Agencies

201 E Main St
Suite 1405
Lexington, KY 40507-2004
859-514-9151
Fax: 859-514-9166
Home Page: www.cosla.org

Tracy Tucker, Executive Director

Directors, staff and consultants of state libraries.
Cost: $25.00
Frequency: Annual April

16148 Computers in Libraries: Buyer's Guide & Consultants Directory Issue
Mecklermedia Corporation
11 Ferry Lane W
Westport, CT 06880-5808

This comprehensive directory offers a list of suppliers of computer products and services for use in libraries.
Cost: $30.00
Frequency: Annual

16149 DataLinx
Faxon Company
1001 W Pines Road
Oregon, IL 61061-9507

815-732-9001
800-732-9001
Fax: 815-732-2132
Home Page: www.faxon.com

This online system was established to provide technical support to libraries for serials acquisition and control.

16150 Directory of Special Libraries and Information Centers
Gale Research
27500 Drake Road
Farmington Hills, MI 48331-3535

248-699-4253
800-877-4253
Fax: 877-363-4253
E-Mail: gale.galeord@cengage.com
Home Page: www.gale.cengage.com
Social Media: Facebook, Twitter, Youtube

Patrick C Sommers, President

Provides detailed contact and descriptive information on subject-specific resource collections maintained by various government agencies, businesses, publishers, educational and non-profit organizations, and associations around the world.
3600 Pages
Frequency: Annual
ISBN: 1-414433-49-2

16151 Directory of US Government: Depository Libraries
Joint Committee on Printing, US Congress
1309 Longworth
Washington, DC 20515

202-225-8281
Fax: 202-225-9957

Directory of federal depository libraries, regional and select throughout the United States. Includes list of GPO bookstores.
91pp Pages
Frequency: Annual

16152 EBSCONET
EBSCO Publishing
Po Box 682
Ipswich, MA 01938-0682

978-356-1372
800-653-2726
Fax: 978-356-6565
Home Page: http://www.ebsco.com

Timothy S Collins, President

This database provides technical support to libraries, information centers and purchasing departments for serials acquisitions and control.

16153 Employment Sources in the Library and Information Professions
National Center for Information Media & Technology
University of Hertfordshire, College Lane
Chicago, IL 60611

773-846-7300
E-Mail: customerservice@ala.org
Home Page: www.ala.org

Directory of services to the industry.
140 Pages
Frequency: Annual

16154 Gale Directory of Databases
Gale/Cengage Learning
27500 Drake Road
Farmington Hills, MI 48331-3535

248-699-4253
800-877-4253
Fax: 877-363-4253
E-Mail: gale.galeord@cengage.com
Home Page: www.gale.cengage.com
Social Media: Facebook, Twitter, Youtube

Patrick C Sommers, President
Bob Romanick, Editor

Profiles thousands of databases available worldwide in a variety of formats. Entries include producer name and contact information, description, cost and more.
ISBN: 1-414420-79-X

16155 Interlibrary Loan Policies Directory
Neal-Schuman Publishers
100 William St
New York, NY 10038-5017

212-925-8650
800-584-2414
Fax: 212-219-8916
E-Mail: info@neal-schuman.com
Home Page www.neal-schuman.com

Patricia Schuman, Owner

A brand new edition of the standard source of current information about the policies of over 1,425 academic, public and other libraries that offer books through interlibrary loans in the United States, Canada and Puerto Rico. Updated to include all the members of the Association of Research Libraries, Internet addresses, Ariel addresses and libraries that loan periodicals, government documents, microfilms, software, newspapers, media and foreign countries.
Cost: $119.95
800 Pages

16156 Librarian's Yellow Pages
Garance
7823 Stratford Road
Bethesda, MD 20814

240-354-1281
Home Page: www.librarianyellowpages.com

A database offering information on products and services intended for use by libraries and information centers in the United States.

16157 Library Fax/Ariel Directory
CBR Consulting Services
PO Box 22421
Kansas City, MO 64113-0421

Over 10,500 libraries with telefacsimile services in the United States and Canada and worldwide.
Cost: $49.50
475 Pages
Frequency: Annual

16158 Library Literature & Information Science
HW Wilson Company
950 Dr Martin L King Jr Blvd
Bronx, NY 10452-4297

718-588-8405
Fax: 718-590-1617
Home Page: www.hwwilson.com

Harold Regan, CEO
Kathleen McEvoy, Director of Public Relations

Comprehensive listings are offered in this database on more than 25,000 citations to articles and reviews of books, periodicals and audiovisual materials in the library and information science areas.

16159 Library Periodicals: An Annual Guide for Subscribers, Authors and Publicists
Periodical Guides Publishing
1633 Pearl Street
Alameda, CA 94501-3065

510-865-7439

Over 150 journals and newsletters in the United States and Canada of national or international scope devoted to library science.
Cost: $18.00
55 Pages
Frequency: Annual

16160 One Hundred and One Software Packages to Use in Your Library
American Library Association
50 E Huron St
Chicago, IL 60611-2788

312-280-2518
800-545-2433
E-Mail: customerservice@ala.org
Home Page: www.ala.org

Claire Knowles, Manager

Directory of services and supplies to the industry.

16161 Subject Directory of Special Libraries & Information Centers
Gale/Cengage Learning
27500 Drake Road
Farmington Hills, MI 48331-3535

248-699-4253
800-877-4253
Fax: 877-363-4253
E-Mail: gale.galeord@cengage.com
Home Page: www.gale.cengage.com
Social Media: Facebook, Twitter, Youtube

Patrick C Sommers, President

Presents entries culled from the Directory of Special Libraries and Information Centers in three volumes arranged by subject matter. This rearrangement is especially important for all users who frame their searches in a subject context. In addition to expanded international coverage, users will also find fax numbers, E-mail addresses, Web and Internet addresses and increased reporting of online services
Frequency: Annual/Set
ISBN: 1-414434-59-6

16162 Univ. of Missouri School of Journalism: Freedom of Information Center
University of Missouri
133 Neff Annex
Columbia, MO 65210-0012

573-882-7539
Fax: 573-884-6204
Home Page: www.missouri.edu/~foiwww

Charles N Davis, Executive Director
Kathleen M Edwards, Center Manager

Reference and research library serving the public and media regarding access to government information. The center has a collection of over a million articles and documents concerning access to information at state, federal and local levels and offers a wide variety of online documents through its webpage.

16163 Who's Who in Special Libraries
Special Libraries Association
1700 18th St Nw
Washington, DC 20009-2508
202-234-4700
Fax: 202-265-9317
Directory of services and supplies to the industry.
Cost: $50.00
364 Pages
Frequency: Annual

Industry Web Sites

16164 http://gold.greyhouse.com
G.O.L.D Grey House OnLine Databases
Grey House Publishing's online database platform, GOLD, offers Quick Search, Keyword Search and Expert Search for most business sectors including library markets. The GOLD platform makes finding the information you need quick and easy - whether you're a novice searcher or an experienced database user. All of Grey House's directory products are available for subscription on the GOLD platform.

16165 www.aallnet.org
American Association of Law Libraries

16166 www.acl.org
Association of Christian Librarians
Membership is composed of over 500 evangelical Christian librarians representing primarily evangelical institutions of higher education.

16167 www.aiip.org
Association Independent Information Professionals

16168 www.akla.org
Alaska Library Association

16169 www.ala.org
American Library Association
Association for librarians, libraries, trustees, students and academics, encompassing all aspects of librarianship.

16170 www.ala.org./alcts
Assn for Library Collections & Technical Services
A division of the American Library Association.

16171 www.ala.org/aasl
American Association of School Librarians
Works to ensure that all members of the school library media field collaborate to: provide leadership in the total eduction program; participate as active partners in the teaching/learning process; connect learners with ideas and information; and prepare students for life-long learning. The American Association of School Librarians is a division of the American Library Association.

16172 www.ala.org/acrl
Association of College and Research Libraries
A division of the American Library Association. Represents academic and research librarians.

16173 www.ala.org/alsc
Association for Library Service to Children
A division of the American Library Association. For persons interested in the improvement and extension of library services to children.

16174 www.ala.org/lama
Library Administrative Management Association
Works to improve and develop all aspects and levels of administration in all types of libraries. The Library Administrative Management Association is a division of the Young Adult Library Services Association, which is part of the American Library Association.

16175 www.ala.org/yalsa
The Young Adult Library Services Association
Responsible for the evaluation and selection of books and nonbook materials and the interpretation and use of materials for teenagers and young adults. The Young Adult Library Services Association is a division of the American Library Association.

16176 www.alise.org/index.shtml
Association for Library & Information Science
Education

16177 www.allanet.org
Alabama Library Association

16178 www.amianet.org
Association of Moving Image Archivists

16179 www.arl.org
Association of Research Libraries
Non profit organization striving to shape and influence forces affecting the future of research libraries in the process of scholarly communication.

16180 www.arlib.org
Arkansas Library Association
Includes constitution and bylaws, conference information, publication, membership, and links to the Arkansas State Library.

16181 www.arlisna.org
Art Libraries Society of North America
Membership organization for art libraries in the US and Canada.

16182 www.arma.org
Assoc. for Information Management Professionals

16183 www.arsc-audio.org
Association for Recorded Sound Collections
Persons in broadcasting and recording industries, librarians, sound archivists, curators, private collectors and reviewers.

16184 www.asindexing.org
American Society of Indexers
A national association with international membership and interests. A nonprofit charitable organization for indexers, librarians, abstractors, editors, publishers, database producers, and organizations concerned with indexing, seeking cooperation and membership of all persons, groups or institutions interested in indexing. Founded in 1968 to promote excellence in indexing and increase awareness of the value of well-written indexes.

16185 www.atla.com/home.html
American Theological Library Association
Provides indexing services in these formats: online database, CD-ROM versions, magnetic tape for OPAC tapeload and print publications. ATLA Religion indexes in print include Religious Index One: Periodicals, Religion Index Two: Multi-Author Works, Index to Book Reviews, Research in Ministry: an Index to D. Min. Project Reports and Theses. ETHICS Index, a new ATLA interdisciplinary index on CD-ROM, contains indexing from polygraphs, articles, journals and newspapers.

16186 www.azla.org
Arizona Library Association

16187 www.bcala.org
Black Caucus of the American Library Association
Meets annually in conjunction with the American Library Association in August.

16188 www.beta-phi-mu-org
Beta Phi Mu

16189 www.cal-webs.org/aboutus.html
Colorado Association Of Libraries

16190 www.cala-web.org
Chinese-American Librarians Association

16191 www.cla-net.org
California Library Association

16192 www.clir.org
Council on Library & Information Resources

16193 www.cni.org
Coalition for Networked Information

16194 www.csla.org
Church and Synagogue Library Association
Provides educational guidance in the establishment and maintenance of congregational libraries

16195 www.ctlibraryassociation.org
Connecticut Library Association
Professional organization of librarians, library staff, friends, and trustees working together: to improve library service to Connecticut, to advance the interests of librarians, library staff, and librarianship, and to increase public awareness of libraries and library services.

16196 www.dla.lib.de.us
Delaware Library Association

16197 www.flalib.org
Florida Library Association

16198 www.floridamedia.org
Florida Library Association

16199 www.folgers.edu
Independent Research Libraries Association
Seeks to provide consultation to members concerning mutual problems.

16200 www.folusa.com
Friends of Libraries (FOLUSA)
Encourages the development of excellent library service to all residents of the US Aids in forming local and state friends branches in academic and special libraries.

16201 www.glma-inc.org/
Georgia Media Library Association

16202 www.greyhouse.com
Grey House Publishing
Authoritative reference directories for most business sectors including library markets. Users can search the online databases with varied search criteria allowing for custom searches by product category, geographic area, sales vol-

ume, keyword, subject and more. Full Grey House catalog and online ordering also available.

16203 **www.hlaweb.org**
Hawaii Library Association

16204 **www.hooverassociation.org**
Herbert Hoover Presidential Library Association
Foster the collection, interpretation and preservation of historical resources relating to the life, ideas, values, and times of Herbert Hoover, thirty-first President of the United States; we will promote public education about and appreciation for Herbert Hoover, support the Hoover Presidential Library-Museum and the National Historic Site at West Branch, Iowa, effectively garner and prudently manage Association resources, and serve Association members.

16205 **www.idaholibaries.org**
Idaho Library Association

16206 **www.idaholibraries.org**
Idaho Library Association

16207 **www.ifla.org**
International Federation of Library Associations

16208 **www.ila.org**
Illinois Library Association

16209 **www.ilfonline.org**
Indiana Library Federation

16210 **www.iowalibraryassociation.org**
Iowa Library Association

16211 **www.kylibasn.org**
Kentucky Library Association

16212 **www.lff.org**
Americans for Libraries Council

16213 **www.library.ucr.edu/COLT**
Council on Library/Media Technicians
Meets annually in conjunction with the American Library Association in August.

16214 **www.lita.org**
Library and Information Technology Association
Concerned with information dissemination in the areas of library information technology and automation. The Library and Information Technology Association is a division of the American Library Association.

16215 **www.llaonline.org**
Louisiana Library Association

16216 **www.mainelibraries.org**
Maine Library Association

16217 **www.masslib.org**
Massachusetts Library Association

16218 **www.mdlib.org**
Maryland Library Association

16219 **www.misslib.org**
Mississippi Library Association

16220 **www.mla.lib.mi.us**
Michigan Library Association

16221 **www.mlanet.org**
Medical Library Association
MLA is dedicated to the dissemination of quality health sciences information for use in education, research, and patient care.

16222 **www.mnlibraryassociation.org**
Minnesota Library Association

16223 **www.molib.org**
Missouri Library Association

16224 **www.mtlib.org**
Montana Library Association
The mission of the Montana Library Association is to develop, promote, and improve library and information services and the profession of librarianship in order to enhance learning and ensure accesss to information to all.

16225 **www.musiclibraryassoc.org**
Music Library Association
Promotes growth and establishment in the use of music libraries, musical instruments and musical literature.

16226 **www.namtc.org**
National Association of Media & Technology Centers

16227 **www.nativeculture.com/lisamitten/aila.html**
American Indian Library Association
Association for Native Americans and Native Alaskans libraries and librarians.

16228 **www.nclaonline.org**
North Carolina Library Association

16229 **www.nclis.gov**
U.S. National Commission On Libraries & Information Science

16230 **www.ndsl.lib.state.nd.usndla**
North Dakota Library Association

16231 **www.nelib.org**
New England Library Association

16232 **www.nevadalibraries.org**
Nevada Library Association

16233 **www.niso.org**
National Information Standards Organization

16234 **www.njla.org**
New Jersey Library Association

16235 **www.nmla.org**
New Mexico Library Association

16236 **www.nmm.net**
National Media Market

16237 **www.nol.org/home/nla**
Nebraska Library Association

16238 **www.nursingworld.org/icirn/indate.htm**
Library American Journal of Nursing Compliance
Comprised of representatives from agencies and organizations concerned with library needs of nurses.

16239 **www.nyla.org**
New York Library Association

16240 **www.oelma.org**
Ohio Educational Library Media Association

16241 **www.oema.net**
Oregon Educational Media Association

16242 **www.oklibs.org**
Oklahoma Library Association

16243 **www.olaweb.org**
Oregon Library Association

16244 **www.olc.org**
Ohio Library Council

16245 **www.palibraries.org**
Pennsylvania Library Association

16246 **www.pla.org**
Public Library Association
Plans programs on current public library issues and concerns, develops publications for public librarians and disseminates statistics on public libraries. The Public Library Association is a division of the American Library Association.

16247 **www.pnla.org**
Pacific Northwest Library Association

16248 **www.rig.org**
Research Libraries Group

16249 **www.rusa.org**
Reference & User Services Association

16250 **www.salis.org**
Substance Abuse Librarians & Info. Specialists
Provides professional development and exchange of information and concerns about access to and dissemination of information on substance abuse.

16251 **www.scla.org**
South Carolina Library Association

16252 **www.seflin.org/seflin/aboutsef.cfm**
Southeast Florida Library Information Network

16253 **www.skyways.lib.ks.us/kla**
Kansas Library Association

16254 **www.sla.org**
Special Libraries Association
International association of information professionals who work in special libraries serving business, research, government and institutions that produce specialized information.

16255 **www.state.nh.us/nhla**
New Hampshire Library Association

16256 **www.taet.org**
Texas Association for Educational Technology

16257 **www.tla.library.unt.edu/default.asp**
Theatre Library Association

16258 **www.tnla.org/**
Tennessee Library Association

16259 **www.txla.org**
Texas Library Association

16260 **www.ublib.buffalo.edu/libraries/units/cts**
University of North Florida, Carpenter Library
For catalogers of audiovisual materials and electronic resources. Provides information exchange, continuing education, and works toward a common understanding of practices and standards.

16261 **www.uic.edu/depts/lib/projects/resources**
Asian/Pacific American Librarians Association
Librarians and information specialists of Asian Pacific descent working in the United States.

16262 **www.ula.org**
Utah Library Assocation

16263 **www.urbanlibraries.org**
Urban Libraries Council
Works to strengthen public libraries as an essential part of urban life. Serves as a forum for research widely recognized and used by public and private sector leaders.

16264 **www.uri.edu/library/rila/rila.html**
Rhode Island Library Association

16265 **www.usd.edu/mpla**
Mountain Plains Library Association

16266 **www.usd.edu/sdla**
South Dakota Library Association

16267 **www.vermontlibraries.org**
Vermont Library Association

16268 **www.vla.org**
Virginia Library Association

16269 **www.wla.lib.wi.us**
Wisconsin Library Association

16270 **www.wla.org**
Washington Library Association

16271 **www.worldaccessnet.com/nesla**
Church and Synagogue Library Association
Religious groups interested in promoting church or synagogue libraries comprise the membership. This association also offers a bi-monthly newsletter to all its members.

16272 **www.worldaccessnet.com/netsa**
Church and Synagogue Library Association
Religious groups interested in promoting church or synagogue libraries comprise the membership. This association also offers a bi-monthly newsletter to all its members.

16273 **www.wvla.org**
West Virginia Library Association

16274 **www.wyla.org**
Wyoming Library Association

Associations

16275 **American Agricultural Editors' Association**
American Agricultural Editors' Association
120 Main Street W
PO Box 156
New Prague, MN 56071

952-758-6502
Fax: 952-758-5813
E-Mail: aaea@gandgcomm.com
Home Page: www.ageditors.com
Social Media: Facebook, Twitter, LinkedIn

Den Gardner, Executive Director
Kenna Rathai, Associate Director
Kenna Rathai, Associate Executive Director

National professional development member association for agricultural communicators.
Founded in 1921

16276 **American Independent Writers**
1001 Connecticut Ave Nw
Suite 701
Washington, DC 20036-5547

202-775-5150
Fax: 202-775-5810
E-Mail: info@washwriter.org
Home Page: www.amerindywriters.org/

Donald Graul, Executive Director

An association that seeks to create an open and inclusive community of authors, journalists and other writers.
1800 Members
Founded in 1975

16277 **American Medical Writers' Association**
American Medical Writers' Association
30 W Gude Dr
Suite 525
Rockville, MD 20850-4347

240- 23- 094
Fax: 301-294-9006
E-Mail: amwa@amwa.org
Home Page: www.amwa.org
Social Media: Facebook, Twitter, LinkedIn

Samantha Nelson, Program Assistant
Rachel Spassiani, Membership Associate & Publications
Melanie Canahuate, Education & Conference Assistant
Becky Phillips, Conference Program Manager
Lauren Ero, Education and Certificate Program

Concerned with the advancement and improvement of medical communications.
3.4M Members
Founded in 1940

16278 **American Society of Journalists and Authors**
American Society of Journalists and Authors
1501 Broadway
Suite 403
New York, NY 10036-5505

212-997-0947
Fax: 212-937-2315
E-Mail: webeditor@asja.org
Home Page: www.asja.org
Social Media: Facebook, Twitter, LinkedIn, Google+

Minda Zetlin, President
Randy Dotinga, Vice President
Alexandra Cantor Owens, Executive Director, ASJA
Lisa Jordan, Headquarters Staff
Bruce Miller, Webmaster/IT Manager

Association for journalists and authors.
1000+ Members
Founded in 1948

16279 **American Translators Association**
American Translators Association
225 Reinekers Lane
Suite 590
Alexandria, VA 22314

703-683-6100
Fax: 703-683-6122
E-Mail: ata@atanet.org
Home Page: www.atanet.org
Social Media: Facebook, Twitter

Caitilin Walsh, President
Walter W. Bacak, Executive Director
Kirk Lawson, Accounting Manager
Jamie Padula, Division Relations
Teresa Kelly, Meetings Manager

ATA membership is open to anyone with an interest in translation and interpreting as a profession or as a scholarly pursuit.
11100 Members
Founded in 1959

16280 **Association of American Collegiate Literary Societies**
Philomathean Society
College Hall
Box G
Philadelphia, PA 19104
Andrew Smith, Governor

Works with literary societies in the United States to promote the creation of new societies, existing societies and reviving old societies.
400 Members
Founded in 1978

16281 **Association of Professional Writing**
Professional Writers Association
P.O. Box 7474
Daytona Beach, FL 32116

386-265-4279
E-Mail: pwa@prowriters.org
Home Page: www.prowriters.org
Social Media: Twitter

Lee C Johns, President

Organization founded to establish standards for writing consultants. Other goals are to draw new members into the writing consulting field. Also offers a referral system for companies looking for writing consultants.
400+ Members
Founded in 1983

16282 **Before Columbus Foundation**
The Raymond House
655 13th Street
Suite 302
Oakland, CA 94612

510-268-9775
E-Mail: info@beforecolumbusfoundation.com
Home Page: www.beforecolumbusfoundation.com

Gundars Strads, Executive Director

Participants are individuals interested in promoting contemporary American multicultural literature.
Founded in 1976

16283 **Center for the Book**
Library of Congress
101 Independence Avenue SE
Washington, DC 20540

202-707-4800
Fax: 202-707-0269
E-Mail: cfbook@loc.gov
Home Page: www.loc.gov/loc/cfbook
Social Media: Facebook, Twitter, LinkedIn

John Y Cole, Director
Anne Boni, Program Specialist

This organization strives to stimulate consumer interest in books and reading.
Founded in 1977
Mailing list available for rent

16284 **Council of Biology Editors**
1000 East Henrietta Road
Rochester, NY 14623

585-292-2000
E-Mail: webmaster@monroecc.edu
Home Page: www.monroecc.edu
Social Media: Facebook, Twitter, Youtube, Flickr

Anne M Kress, President

Represents those members in life sciences who write for journals, medical science publications, and textbooks.
1.1M Members
Founded in 1957

16285 **Council on National Literatures**
Council on National Literatures
68-02 Metropolitan Avenue
Middle Village, NY 11379

718-821-3916
E-Mail: anneandhenrypaolucci@yahoo.com
Home Page: www.cnliteratures.com

Anne Paolucci, President

Provides a forum for scholars concerned with comparative study of literature.
Founded in 1976

16286 **Dramatists Guild of America**
1501 Broadway
Suite 701
New York, NY 10036-5505
212-398-9366
Fax: 212-944-0420
E-Mail: igor@dramaguild.com
Home Page: www.dramatistsguild.com/
Social Media: Facebook, Twitter, Flickr, Tumblr, Youtube

Stephen Schwartz, President
Ralph Sevush, Executive Director, Business
Gary Garrisonÿ, Executive Director
Peter Parnell, Vice-President
Doug Wright, Secretary

Protects the rights of its international membership of playwrights, composers and lyricists. Supports fair royalty, maintenance of subsidiary rights, artistic control and ownership of copyright.
6M+ Members
Founded in 1920

16287 **Editorial Freelancers Association**
Editorial Freelancers Association
71 W 23rd St
4th Fl
New York, NY 10010-4102

212-929-5400
866-929-5425
Fax: 212-929-5439
E-Mail: office@the-efa.org
Home Page: www.the-efa.org
Social Media: Facebook, Twitter, LinkedIn

Stacie L. McClintock, Secretary
Kristine E. Hunt, Chapter Development
Jennifer Maybin, Education
Sheila Buff, Job List
Cassie Tuttle, Membership

National nonprofit, professional organization of self-employed workers in the publishing and communications industries.
Founded in 1970

16288 **Education Writers Association**
Education Writers Association

3516 Connecticut Avenue NW
Suite 201
Washington, DC 20008

202-452-9830
Fax: 202-452-9837
E-Mail: ewa@ewa.org
Home Page: www.ewa.org

Scott Elliott, President
Caroline W. Hendrie, Executive Director
George Dieter, Chief Operating Officer
Tracee Eason, Administrative Coordinator
Kenneth Terrell, Project Director

The Education Writers Association is the national professional organization of education reporters and intent of improving education reporting to the public.
800 Members
Founded in 1947

16289 Freelance Editorial Association
PO Box 380835
Cambridge, MA 02238-0835

617-643-8626
E-Mail: kramer@tiac.net
Home Page: www.freelancepubs.com

Eileen Kramer, President

Offers editorial services that include editing, writing, proofreading, graphic design, desktop publishing, and project managemant.
500 Members
Founded in 1983
Mailing list available for rent

16290 International Food, Wine and Travel Writers Association
39252 Winchester Rd
Ste 107 #418
Murrieta, CA 92563

877-439-8929
909-860-6914
951-970-8326
Fax: 877-439-8929
E-Mail: admin@ifwtwa.org
Home Page: www.ifwtwa.org
Social Media: Facebook, Twitter, LinkedIn, Youtube, RSS, Instagram

Michelle M. Winner, President, Board Member
Linda Kissam, 1st Vice President, Secretary
Allen Cox, 2nd Vice President, Board Member
Sherrie A Wilkolaski, Treasurer, Board Member

Staff and/or freelance writers in the food, wine and travel field. Also includes other media professionals and industry associate members in 28 countries worldwide.
300 Members
Founded in 1956

16291 Mystery Writers of America
1140 Broadway
Suite 1507
New York, NY 10001

212-888-8171
Fax: 212-888-8107
E-Mail: mwa@mysterywriters.org
Home Page: www.mysterywriters.org

Charlaine Harris, President
Daniel J. Hale, Executive Vice President
Cathy Pickens, Secretary
Sharon Potts, Treasurer

Professional writers of crime and mystery stories and novels. Unpublished writers are affiliate members. MWA annually gives the Edgar Awards for excellence in the mystery genre.
3000 Members
Founded in 1945

16292 National Association of Hispanic Journalists
1050 Connecticut Avenue NW
Washington, DC 20036

202-662-7145
Fax: 202-662-7144
E-Mail: nahj@nahj.org
Home Page: www.nahj.org
Social Media: Facebook, Twitter

Hugo Balta, President
Mekahlo Medina, Vice President/Broadcast
Rebecca Aguilar, Vice President, Online
Erin Ailworth, Vice President, Print
Blanca Torres, Financial Officer

NAHJ is dedicated to the recognition and professional advancement of Hispanics in the news industry. NAHJ created a national voice and unified vision for all Hispanic journalists.
2300 Members
Founded in 1984

16293 National Federation of Press Women
National Federation of Press Women
200 Little Falls Street
Suite 405
Falls Church, VA 22046

800-780-2715
Fax: 703-237-9808
E-Mail: presswomen@aol.com
Home Page: www.nfpw.org
Social Media: Facebook, Twitter, LinkedIn, Youtube, RSS, Flickr

Teri Ehresman, President
Marsha Hoffman, 1st Vice President
Marianne Wolf-Astrauskas, 2nd Vice President
Ellen Crawford, Treasurer (Financial Adviser)
Gay Porter DeNileon, Secretary

Members are writers, editors and other communication professionals for newspapers, magazines, wire services, agencies and freelance.
2000 Members
Founded in 1937
Mailing list available for rent: 1700 names at $40 per M

16294 National Writers Association
10940 S Parker Rd
Suite 508
Parker, CO 80134-7440

303-841-0246
Fax: 303-841-2607
E-Mail: natlwritersassn@hotmail.com
Home Page: www.nationalwriters.com

Sandy Whelchel, Executive Director

Exists to enhance the future of writers by fostering continuing education through award winning scholarships and providing no or low cost workshops and seminars. A non-profit organization, we provide education and an ethical resource for writers at all levels of experience.
2000 Members
Founded in 1937

16295 Newspaper Features Council
22 Byfield Lane
Greenwich, CT 06830

203-661-3386
Fax: 203-661-7337

A forum for editors, writers, columnists, cartoonists and syndicates to exchange views and improve the content of newspapers.
130 Members
Founded in 1955

16296 Outdoor Writers Association of America
615 Oak St
Suite 201
Missoula, MT 59801-1896

406-728-7434
800-692-2477
Fax: 406-728-7445
E-Mail: info@owaa.org
Home Page: www.owaa.org
Social Media: Facebook, Twitter, LinkedIn, RSS Feeds

Bill Graham, President
Mark Freeman, 1st Vice President
Lisa Densmore, 2nd Vice President
Tom Sadler, Executive Director
Ashley Schroeder, Communications Director

Nonprofit, international organization representing over 2,000 professional outdoor communicators who report on diverse interests in the outdoors.
2.4M Members
Founded in 1927

16297 Self-Employed Writers and Artists Network
PO Box 175
Towaco, NJ 07082

Home Page: www.njcreators.org

George Kamper, President
Stan Cohen, Vice President
Liz Kassler, Treasurer
Dave McCoy, Membership Director
Krista Wildermuth, Communications Director

For more then 2 decades, companies and agencies alike have relied on the NJ Creatives Network organization as a cost-efficient, reliable source for freelance talent-from writers and artists to designers and photographers, plus film and video producers, and more.

16298 Society of American Business Editors and Writers
ASU, Walter Cronkite School of Journalism
555 North Central Ave, Suite 416
Phoenix, AZ 85004-1248

602-496-7862
Fax: 602-496-7041
E-Mail: sabew@sabew.org
Home Page: www.sabew.org
Social Media: Facebook, Twitter, LinkedIn, RSS

Kevin Hall, President
Marty Wolk, VP
Warren Watson, Executive Director
Lacey Clements, Marketing and Membership Director
Spring Eselgroth, Web/ Membership Coordinator

Members are financial and economic news writers and editors for print and broadcast outlets.
3200 Members
Founded in 1964

16299 Society of American Travel Writers
11950 W. Lake Park Drive
Suite 320
Milwaukee, WI 53224

414-359-1625
Fax: 414-359-1671
E-Mail: info@satw.org
Home Page: www.satw.org
Social Media: Facebook, Twitter, LinkedIn

Steve Giordano, President
Diana Lambdin Meyer, VP
Cindy Lemek, MA, Executive Director
Kelsey Weaver, MBA, Membership Manager
Maureen Sacho, Director of Finance

Photographers and 35 associate member representatives of airlines, hotels, resorts, tourist agencies and public relations firms.
Founded in 1955

16300 Space Coast Writers Guild
PO Box 262
Melbourne, FL 32902
E-Mail: scwg-jm@cfi.rr.com
Home Page: www.scwg.org
Social Media: Facebook, Twitter, LinkedIn, Google+
Scott Tilley, President
Kit Adams, VP
Lisa De Anda, Secretary
David Polhill, Treasurer
Bill Allen, Communications & Publicity
Nonprofit, tax-exempt organization of writers of all genres.
Cost: $35.00
Frequency: Annual
Founded in 1982

16301 Writers Alliance
12 Skylark Lane
Stony Brook, NY 11790-3121
516-751-7080
Writers' organization.

16302 Writers Guild of America: West
Writers Guild of America
7000 W 3rd St
Los Angeles, CA 90048-4329
323-951-4000
800-548-4532
Fax: 323-782-4800
Home Page: www.wga.org
Social Media: Facebook, Twitter, Youtube,RSS
Chris Keyser, President
Howard A. Rodman, Vice President
Carl Gottlieb, Secretary-Treasurer
An independent labor union representing writers in motion pictures, television and radio in the west.
9500 Members
Founded in 1912

16303 Writers Research Group LLC
Po Box 891568
Oklahoma City, OK 73189-1568
405-682-2589
Fax: 405-685-3390
E-Mail: info@writersresearchgroup.com
Home Page: www.writersresearchgroup.com
Lori Packwood, Director
Writers Research Group is a professional writing and research firm. Our knowledgeable employees gather, examine, edit, and compile data to your company's specifications. Our services include research, writing, directory listing updates and new entries, indexing, copyediting, proofreading, data entry, document markup and permissions negotiations.
Founded in 2000

Newsletters

16304 AGENDA
National Federation of Press Women
PO Box 34798
Alexandria, VA 22334-0798
800-780-2715
Fax: 703-237-9808
E-Mail: jane@janeleecomm.com
Home Page: www.nfpw.org
Social Media: Facebook, Twitter, LinkedIn, Youtube
A quarterly newletter published by the National Federation of Press Women.
Cost: $51.50
4 Pages
Frequency: Quarterly
Circulation: 2000
Founded in 1937
Mailing list available for rent: 1700 names at $40 per M

16305 ASJA Newsletter
American Society of Journalists and Authors
1501 Broadway
Suite 302
New York, NY 10036-5505
212-997-0947
Fax: 212-937-2315
E-Mail: staff@asja.org
Home Page: www.asja.org
Social Media: Facebook, Twitter, LinkedIn
Alexandra Owens, Executive Director
Lisa Collier Coloradool, President
Barbara Barrett, Newsletter Editor
Confidential news for journalists and authors, available only to members of the Society.
Frequency: Monthly
Founded in 1948

16306 American Writer
American Independent Writers
1001 Connecticut Ave Nw
Suite 701
Washington, DC 20036-5547
202-775-5150
Fax: 202-775-5810
E-Mail: info@aiwriters.org
Home Page: www.amerindywriters.org/
Donald Graul, Executive Director
News and information for freelance writers.
Cost: $160.00
8 Pages
Frequency: Monthly
Founded in 1975

16307 Copy Editor
McMurry
1010 E Missouri Ave
Phoenix, AZ 85014-2602
602-395-5850
888-626-8779
Fax: 602-395-5853
Home Page: www.mcmurry.com
Chris McMurry, CEO
Barbara Wallraff, Editor
Helps editors stay up-to-date with the changing language. Articles discuss new words, changes in usage and reference books. Each issue contains interviews with copy editors.
Cost: $69.00
8 Pages
Circulation: 2000
Founded in 1990
Printed in one color

16308 EFA Newsletter
Editorial Freelancers Association
71 W 23rd St
Suite 1910
New York, NY 10010 4181
212-929-5400
866-929-5400
Fax: 212-929-5439
E-Mail: office@the-efa.org
Home Page: www.the-efa.org
Judi Greenstein, Office Manager
J P Partland, Co-Executive
Mary Ratcliffe, Editor
Martha Schuenman, Executive Director
Pat Molholt, Secretary
Book reviews, news, features and reports on matters of interest to writers, indexers and editors.
Cost: $20.00
Frequency: 6 issues/year
Founded in 1970

16309 Editorial Eye
Editorial Experts
66 Canal Center Plz
Suite 200
Alexandria, VA 22314-5507
703-683-0683
800-683-8380
Fax: 703-683-4915
E-Mail: info@eeicommunications.com
Home Page: www.eeicom.com
Jim De Graffenreid, President
Candee Wilson, Director
Robin Cormier, VP Publications
Linda B Jorgensen, Editor
Keith C. Ivey, Technical Editor
Professional standards and practices for editors, writers and publication managers.
Cost: $139.00
12 Pages
Frequency: Monthly
Circulation: 3,000
Founded in 1972

16310 Freelance Writer's Report
CNW Publishing
PO Box A
North Stratford, NH 03590
603-922-8338
800-351-9278
Fax: 603-922-8339
E-Mail: info@writers-editors.com
Home Page: www.writers-editors.com
Dana K Cassell, Executive Director
News and marketing information for freelance writers.
Cost: $39.00
Frequency: Monthly
Circulation: 1200

16311 IDEAS Unlimited for Editors
Omniprint
9700 Philadelphia Ct
Lanham, MD 20706-4405
301-731-7000
800-774-6809
Fax: 301-731-7001
E-Mail: info@omniprint.net
Home Page: www.omniprint.net
Ken Kaufman, President
Stephen Brownan, VP
Editorial ideas and graphics for editors of in-house, corporate newsletters. Provides 16 pages of fresh, ready-to-use items and ideas editors can use to fill out their publications.
Cost: $5.00
16 Pages
Frequency: Monthly
Circulation: 6310
Founded in 1973
Printed in one color on matte stock

16312 KEYSTROKES
Writers Alliance
12 Skylark Lane
Stony Brook, NY 11790-3121
516-751-7080
Kiel Stuart, Publisher
Howard Austerlitz, Editor
Charles Spataro, Circulation Manager
A writers newsletter containing marketing, how-to and computer information.
Cost: $10.00
16 Pages
Frequency: TriAnnual

Circulation: 250
Mailing list available for rent: 250 names
Printed in one color on matte stock

16313 Linington Lineup
1223 Glen Ter
Glassboro, NJ 08028-1315

856-589-1571

Rinehart S Potts, Editor

Editing, publishing, police procedural.
Cost: $12.00
16 Pages
Frequency: Bi-Monthly
Circulation: 400
Founded in 1984
Printed in one color on matte stock

16314 NWA Newsletter
National Writers Association
10940 S Parker Rd
Suite 508
Parker, CO 80134-7440

303-841-0246
Fax: 303-841-2607
E-Mail: natlwritersassn@hotmail.com
Home Page: www.nationalwriters.com

Sandy Whelchel, Executive Director

A monthly e-mail newsletter that includes information on upcoming contests and conferences, announcements and job opportunities
2000 Members
Frequency: Monthly
Founded in 1938

16315 Speechwriter's Newsletter
Ragan Communications
316 N Michigan Ave
Suite 400
Chicago, IL 60601-3773

312-960-4100
800-493-4867
Fax: 312-960-4106
E-Mail: cservice@ragan.com
Home Page: www.ragan.com

Jim Ylisela, Publisher
David Murray, Editor
Rebecca Anderson, Managing Editor

Offers speechwriting tips, examples and criticism.
Cost: $307.00
4 Pages
Frequency: Monthly
Founded in 1980

16316 Story Bag: National Storytelling Newsletter
5361 Javier St
San Diego, CA 92117-3215

858-569-9399
Fax: 858-569-0205
E-Mail: storybag@juno.com

Professional storytellers, whether freelance or working for a school or library, will find this newsletter stuffed full of tips on techniques, suggestions for handling the business, reviews of storytelling books and tapes, listings of events nationwide, bibliographies of suggested materials, and discussion of issues such as censorship. Note: Above phone is used on e-mail, if busy try again.
Cost: $15.00
8 Pages
Frequency: Bi-Monthly
Circulation: 300
Printed in one color on matte stock

16317 Strategic Employee Publications
Lawrence Ragan Communications
316 N Michigan Ave
Suite 400
Chicago, IL 60601-3773

312-960-4100
800-878-5331
Fax: 312-960-4106
E-Mail: cservice@ragan.com
Home Page: www.ragan.com

Jim Ylisela, Publisher
David Murray, Editor
Diane Tillman, Marketing Manager

Designed to help organizational editors produce their company publications.
Cost: $139.00
8 Pages
Frequency: Monthly
Circulation: 2500
Founded in 1970
Printed in 2 colors on matte stock

16318 Writers Connection
Writers Connection
1826 Crossover Roade
PMB 108
Fayetteville, AR 72703
Home Page: www.thewritersconnection.com

Provides how-to information for writers, plus listings of markets, contests and events. Accepts advertising.
Cost: $45.00
16 Pages
Frequency: Monthly

Magazines & Journals

16319 ATA Chronicle
American Translators Association
225 Reinekers Lane
Suite 590
Alexandria, VA 22314

703-683-6100
Fax: 703-683-6122
E-Mail: ata@atanet.org
Home Page: www.atanet.org
Social Media: Facebook, Twitter

Nicholas Hartmann, President
Walter Bacak, Executive Director
Kirk Lawson, Accounting Manager
Jamie Padula, Chapter & Division Relations
Teresa Kelly, Meetings Manager

Contains feature articles, announcements, reviews, and association news.
Cost: $65.00
Frequency: Monthly
Circulation: 11,100

16320 Latinos in the US: A Resource Guide for Journalists
National Association of Hispanic Journalists
529 14th St Nw # 1240
Washington, DC 20045-2520

202-789-1157
Fax: 202-347-3444
E-Mail: rnutting@marketwatch.com
Home Page: www.marketwatch.com

Rex Nutting, Manager
Joseph Torres, Communications Director
Rex Nutting, Manager

Purposes are to increase educational and career opportunities in journalism for Hispanic Americans.
Cost: $8.50
Mailing list available for rentat $500 per M

16321 Modernism/Modernity
2715 N Charles Street
Baltimore, MD 21218-4319

410-516-6900
800-548-1784
Fax: 410-516-6968
E-Mail: claity@drew.edu
Home Page: www.press.ghu.edu/journals

Jeffrey T Schnapp, Editor
Becky Brasington Clark, Marketing Director
Tom Lovett, Circulation Manager
Ken Sabol, Production Manager

Focuses systematically on the methodological, archival, and theoretical exigencies particular to modermist studies. It encourages and interdisciplinary approach linking music, architecture, the visual arts, literature, and social and intellectual history.
Cost: $40.00
Frequency: Quarterly
Founded in 1994

Trade Shows

16322 ATA Annual Conference
American Translators Association
225 Reinekers Lane
Suite 590
Alexandria, VA 22314

703-683-6100
Fax: 703-683-6122
E-Mail: ata@atanet.org
Home Page: www.atanet.org
Social Media: Facebook, Twitter

Nicholas Hartmann, President
Walter Bacak, Executive Director
Kirk Lawson, Accounting Manager
Jamie Padula, Chapter & Division Relations
eresa Kelly, Meetings Manager
2000 Attendees

16323 Agricultural Publications Summit
American Agricultural Editors' Association
120 Main Street W
PO Box 156
New Prague, MN 56071

952-758-6502
Fax: 952-758-5813
E-Mail:
aaea@gardnerandgardnercommunications.com
Home Page: www.ageditors.com

Den Gardner, Executive Director
Holly Martin, President
Kenna Rathai, Associate Executive Director
Frequency: July

16324 American Society of Journalists and Authors Conference
American Society of Journalists and Authors
1501 Broadway
Suite 302
New York, NY 10036-5501

212-997-0947
Fax: 212-937-2315
E-Mail: director@ajsa.org
Home Page: www.asja.org
Social Media: Facebook, Twitter, LinkedIn

Alexandra Owens, Executive Director
Salley Shannon, President
Barbara DeMarco- Barrett, Newsletter Editor
Stephen Morril, Web Editor
Bruce Miler, Web Master

A forum for the exchange of ideas between journalists.
700 Attendees
Frequency: May

16325 Annual Multimedia Convention & Career Expo (NAHJ)
National Association of Hispanic Journalists
Disney's Coronado Spings Resort
1000 W Buena Vista Drive
Lake Buena Vista, FL 32830

866-257-5990
Home Page: www.nahjconvention.org
Social Media: Facebook, Twitter, LinkedIn, YouTube

Michele Salcedo, President
Manuel De La Rosa, Vice President/Broadcast
Russell Contreras, VP Print/Financial Officer

NAHJ is dedicated to the recognition and professional advancement of Hispanics in the news industry. NAHJ created a national voice and unified vision for all Hispanic journalists.
2300 Members
Frequency: August
Founded in 1984

16326 SABEW Annual Conference
Society of American Business Editors & Writers
ASU, Walter Cronkite School of Journalism
555 North Central Ave, Suite 416
Phoenix, AZ 85004-1248

602-496-7862
Fax: 602-496-7041
E-Mail: sabew@sabew.org
Home Page: www.sabew.org
Social Media: Facebook, Twitter, LinkedIn

Carrie Paden, Executive Director
Rex Sciine, VP
Jon Lansner, Secretary/Treasurer
Brant Houston, Executive Director
Frequency: April

Directories & Databases

16327 AWP Official Guide to Writing Programs
Association of Writers & Writing Programs
Mail Stop 1E3
Fairfax, VA 22030

703-993-4301
Fax: 703-993-4302
E-Mail: awp@awpwriter.org

Supriya Bhatngar, Director of Publications

About 300 colleges and universities offering workshops and degree programs in creative writing; approximately 100 writers' conferences, colonies and centers; coverage includes Canada and the United Kingdom.
Cost: $24.95
400 Pages
Frequency: Biennial

16328 American Directory of Writer's Guidelines
Dustbooks
PO Box 100
Paradise, CA 95967-0100

530-877-6110
800-477-6110
Fax: 530-877-0222
E-Mail: directories@dustbooks.com
Home Page: www.dustbooks.com

Brigitte M Phillips, Editor
Susan D Klassen, Editor
Doris Hall, Editor

These guidelines help writers target their submissions to the exact needs of the individual publisher. A compilation of information for freelancers from more than 1,500 magazine editors and book publishers.
Cost: $29.95
752 Pages
ISBN: 1-884956-40-8

16329 American Library Directory
Information Today
143 Old Marlton Pike
Medford, NJ 08055-8750

609-654-6266
800-300-9868
Fax: 609-654-4309
E-Mail: custserv@infotoday.com
Home Page: www.infotoday.com

Thomas H Hogan, President
Roger R Bilboul, Chariman Of The Board

Detailed profiles for more than 35,000 public, academic, special, and government libraries and library related organizations in the US and Canada. These include addresses, phone and fax numbers, e-mail addresses, network participation, expenditures, holdings and special collections, key personnel, special services and more than 40 categories of library information in all. A two volume set.
Cost: $299.00
4000 Pages
ISBN: 1-573872-04-0
Mailing list available for rent

16330 American Society of Journalists and Authors Directory
American Society of Journalists and Authors
1501 Broadway
Suite 302
New York, NY 10036-5505

212-997-0947
Fax: 212-937-2315
Home Page: www.asja.org
Social Media: Facebook, Twitter, LinkedIn

Alexandra Owens, Executive Director

Lists over 800 member freelance nonfiction writers.
Cost: $75.00
90 Pages

16331 Applied Science & Technology Index
HW Wilson Company
950 Dr Martin L King Jr Blvd
Bronx, NY 10452-4297

718-588-8405
800-367-6770
Fax: 718-590-1617
Home Page: www.hwwilson.com

Harold Regan, CEO
Kathleen McEvoy, Director of Public Relations

Fast, convenient access to the cover-to-cover content of leading trade and industrial publications, journals issued by professional and technical societies, specialized subject periodicals, as well as buyers' guides, directories, and conference proceedings.
Frequency: Monthly on WlisonDisc

16332 Association of Professional Writing Consultants Membership Directory
Northwestern University
2315 Sheridan Rd
Evanston, IL 60201-2920

847-491 5500

Henry Bienen, President
Cost: $75.00
Frequency: Annual

16333 Authors and Artists for Young Adults
Gale/Cengage Learning
27500 Drake Road
Farmington Hills, MI 48331-3535

248-699-4253
800-877-4253
Fax: 877-363-4253
E-Mail: gale.galeord@cengage.com
Home Page: www.gale.cengage.com
Social Media: Facebook, Twitter, Youtube

Patrick C Sommers, President

A a source where teens can discover fascinating and entertaining facts about the writers, artists, film directors, graphic novelists and other creative personalities that most interest them.
ISBN: 0-787677-96-5

16334 Children's Writer's and Illustrator's Market
Writer's Market
1507 Dana Avenue
Cincinnati, OH 45207-1005

513-396-6160
800-289-0963
Fax: 513-531-4082

Offers valuable information about book and magazine publishers that publish works by authors and illustrators for young audiences.
Cost: $22.99
256 Pages
Frequency: Annual

16335 Complete Guide to Self-Publishing
Writer's Market
1507 Dana Avenue
Cincinnati, OH 45207-1005

513-396-6160
800-289-0963
Fax: 513-531-4082

Offers, in appendixes, a list of contacts and companies that help see to publication of a book at the author's expense.
Cost: $18.95

16336 Contemporary Authors
Gale/Cengage Learning
27500 Drake Road
Farmington Hills, MI 48331-3535

248-699-4253
800-877-4253
Fax: 877-363-4253
E-Mail: gale.galeord@cengage.com
Home Page: www.gale.cengage.com
Social Media: Facebook, Twitter, Youtube

Patrick C Sommers, President

Find biographical information on more than 130,000 modern novelists, poets, playwrights, nonfiction writers, journalists and scriptwriters. Sketches typically include personal information, contact information, career history, writings, biographical and critical sources, authors' comments and informative essays about their lives and work.
ISBN: 0-810319-11-X

16337 Directory of Literary Magazines
Council of Literary Magazines and Presses
154 Christopher St
Suite 3C
New York, NY 10014-2840

212-741-9110
Fax: 212-741-9112
E-Mail: info@clmp.org
Home Page: www.clmp.org

Contains names, addresses and phone numbers of nearly 600 magazines in the US and abroad that publish poetry, fiction, essays, literary reviews and more.
Cost: $17.00
Frequency: Annual

16338 Directory of Poetry Publishers
Dustbooks

PO Box 100
Paradise, CA 95967-0100

530-877-6110
800-477-6110
Fax: 530-877-0222
E-Mail: directories@dustbooks.com
Home Page: www.dustbooks.com

Len Fulton, Editor

Over 2,100 magazines, small and commercial presses and university presses that accept poetry for publication.
Cost: $25.95
300 Pages
Frequency: Annual
Circulation: 2,000
ISBN: 0-916685-47-0

16339 **Directory of Small Magazines Press Magazine Editors & Publishers**
Dustbooks
PO Box 100
Paradise, CA 95967-0100

530-877-6110
800-477-6110
Fax: 530-877-0222
E-Mail: directories@dustbooks.com
Home Page: www.dustbooks.com

Len Fulton, Editor

This directory contains more than 7,500 listings of editors and publishers in alphabetical order, along with their associated publishing companies, their addresses, phones, e-mail addresses and Web pages. Includes self publishers.
Cost: $25.95
460 Pages
Frequency: Annual
Circulation: 1,000
ISBN: 0-913218-28-6
Founded in 1967
Mailing list available for rent

16340 **Editor & Publisher International Year Book**
Editor & Publisher Company
17782 Cowan
Suite C
Irvine, CA 92614

929-660-6150
888-732-7323
Fax: 949-660-6172
E-Mail: circulation@editorandpublisher.com
Home Page: www.editorandpublisher.com

Duncan McIntosh, President/Publisher
Jeff Fleming, Editor-In-Chief
Kristina Ackermann, Managing Editor
Ralph Bayless, Sales Manager

It's the encyclopedia of the newspaper industry with listings for all dailies worldwide and all community and special interest U.S. and Canadian weeklies. Tabbed sections make it easy to find information from U.S. & Canadian dailies to foreign newspapers. Tables profile newspaper ad trends, circulation size by population groups, rankings by circulation size and more.
Cost: $125.00
600 Pages
Frequency: Annual
Founded in 1884

16341 **Editor & Publisher: Directory of Syndicated Services Issue**
Editor & Publisher Company
11 W 19th Street
10th Floor
New York, NY 10011-4209

212-929-1259

Michael Parker, President

A directory of several hundred syndicates serving newspapers in the United States and abroad with news, features and comic strips.
Cost: $7.00
Frequency: Annual

16342 **Editorial Freelancers Association: Membership Directory**
Editorial Freelancers Association
71 W 23rd St
4th Fl
New York, NY 10010-4181

212-929-5400
866-929-5425
Fax: 212-929-5439
E-Mail: office@the-efa.org
Home Page: www.the-efa.org
Social Media: Facebook, Twitter, LinkedIn

Jp Partland, Co-Executive
Judi Greenstein, Office Manager

1,100 member editorial freelancers.
Cost: $25.00
Frequency: Annual Spring

16343 **Guide to Literary Agents**
Writer's Market
1507 Dana Avenue
Cincinnati, OH 45207-1005

513-396-6160
800-289-0963
Fax: 513-531-4082
Home Page: www.writersmarket.com

Agents and representatives for professional writers.
Cost: $18.95
240 Pages
Frequency: Annual

16344 **Guide to Writers Conferences & Workshops**
Shaw Guides
PO Box 231295
New York, NY 10023

212-799-6464
Fax: 212-724-9287
E-Mail: info@shawguides.com
Home Page: www.shawguides.com

Conferences, workshops, and seminars for amateur and professional writers.
Cost: $19.95
272 Pages

16345 **Key Guide to Electronic Resources: Language and Literature**
Information Today
143 Old Marlton Pike
Medford, NJ 08055-8750

609-654-6266
800-300-9868
Fax: 609-654-4309
E-Mail: custserv@infotoday.com
Home Page: www.infotoday.com

Thomas H Hogan, President
Roger R Bilboul, Chairman Of The Board

Part of the ongoing topic related series of reference guides is an evaluative directory of electronic reference sources in the fields of language and literature.
Cost: $39.50
120 Pages
ISBN: 1-573870-20-x
Mailing list available for rent

16346 **Literary Agents of North America**
Author Aid/Research Associates International
340 E 52nd St
New York, NY 10022-6728

212-758-4213

Arthur Orrmont, Editor

More than 1,00 US and Canadian literary agencies.
Cost: $33.00

16347 **Literary Forum**
CompuServe Information Service
5000 Arlington Centre Blvd
Columbus, OH 43220-5439

614-326-1002
800-848-8199

This database covers literature, including books and poetry, writing, stage and screen, journalism and comic books.
Frequency: Bulletin Board

16348 **Market Guide for Young Writers: Where and How to Sell What You Write**
Writer's Market
1507 Dana Avenue
Cincinnati, OH 45207-1005

513-396-6160
800-289-0963
Fax: 513-531-4082
Home Page: www.writersmarket.com

A list of over 150 magazines and writers contests are profiles that all accept work from young writers for publishing purposes.
Cost: $16.95

16349 **Mystery Writer's Market Place and Sourcebook**
Writer's Market
1507 Dana Avenue
Cincinnati, OH 45207-1005

513-396-6160
800-289-0963
Fax: 513-531-4082
Home Page: www.writersmarket.com

Offers various profiles of about 50 publishers of mystery and crime books.
Cost: $17.95

16350 **Novel & Short Story Writer's Market**
Writer's Market
1507 Dana Avenue
Cincinnati, OH 45207-1005

513-396-6160
800-289-0963
Fax: 513-531-4082
Home Page: www.writersmarket.com

More than 2,000 literary magazines, publishers, agents and writer's organizations are profiled.
Cost: $19.95
Frequency: Annual

16351 **Poet's Market**
Writer's Market
1507 Dana Avenue
Cincinnati, OH 45207-1005

513-396-6160
800-289-0963
Fax: 513-531-4082
Home Page: www.writersmarket.com

Over 1,500 publishers, periodicals and other markets that accept poetry for publication are profiled.
Cost: $22.99
528 Pages
Frequency: Annual
ISSN: 0883-5470

16352 **Professional Freelance Writers Directory**
National Writers Club

314 Peoria
Suite 290
Aurora, CO 80014

303-841-0246

Over 200 professional members selected from the total membership on the basis of significant articles books or movies published.
Cost: $12.50
75 Pages
Frequency: Annual

16353 **Science Fiction and Fantasy Writers of America Membership Directory**
PO Box 877
Chestertown, MD 21620

E-Mail: exedir@sfwa.org
Home Page: www.sfwa.org

Mary Kowal, Vice-President
Robert Howe, Secretary
Amy Casil, Treasurer

Directory of services and supplies to the industry.
Cost: $60.00
40 Pages
Frequency: Annual

16354 **Self-Employed Writers and Artists Network Directory**
Po Box 175
Towacos, NJ 07653-0440

Home Page: www.swan-net.com
Social Media: Facebook, Twitter

Phil Cantor, President
Wayne Rousck, VP Marketing

Over 140 freelance writers and graphic designers, as well as illustrators, photographers and more in northern New Jersey and Metropolitan New York City are profiled.
20 Pages
Frequency: Annual

16355 **Self-Publishing Manual: How to Write, Print and Sell Your Own Book**
Para Publishing
PO Box 8206
Santa Barbara, CA 93118-8206

805-968-7277
800-727-2782
Fax: 805-968-1379
E-Mail: info@parapublishing.com
Home Page: www.parapublishing.com

Dan Poynter, Publisher

A list of wholesalers, reviewers and exporters, etc, are profiled.
Cost: $19.95
900 Pages
Frequency: Biennial
ISBN: 1-568600-73-9
Founded in 1979
Printed in one color on matte stock

16356 **Space Coast Writers Guild: Organization, Activities and Membership**
PO Box 262
Melbourne, FL 32902

E-Mail: scwg-jm@cfi.rr.com
Home Page: www.scwg.org
Social Media: Facebook, Twitter, LinkedIn

Judy Mammay, President
Bill Allen, VP
Donna Chesher, President
Andy Vazquez, Vice-President
Carol Didier, Secretary

A who's who directory of professional writing services and training to the media industry.
25 Pages
Frequency: Annual

16357 **Who's Who in Writers, Editors and Poets: US and Canada**
December Press
Apt 406
2800 N Roadrunner Pkwy
Las Cruces, NM 88011-0859

847-940-4122

Curt Johnson, President

Directory of writers and editors.
Cost: $99.00
700 Pages
Frequency: Biennial

16358 **Writer's Digest: Writers Conference Issue**
F&W Publications
1507 Dana Avenue
Cincinnati, OH 45207-1005

513-531-2222
Fax: 513-531-1843

Directory of services and supplies to the industry.
Cost: $2.95
Frequency: Annual
Circulation: 225,000

16359 **Writer's Guide to Book Editors, Publishers and Literary Agents**
Prima Publishing
3000 Lava Ridge Ct
Roseville, CA 95661-2802

916-787-7000
800-632-8676
Fax: 916-787-7004
E-Mail: sales@primapub.com
Home Page: www.primagames.com

Julie Asbury, Publisher

Offers information on more than 200 publishing houses and their editors.
Cost: $19.95
370 Pages
Frequency: Annual

16360 **Writer's Handbook**
Kalmbach Publishing Company
21027 Crossroads Circle
PO Box 1612
Waukesha, WI 53186-1612

262-796-8776
800-533-6644
Fax: 262-796-1615
Home Page: www.writermag.com

A list of more than 3,000 markets for the sale of manuscripts, ads and awards.
Cost: $29.95
Frequency: Annual

16361 **Writer's Market: Where and How to Sell What You Write**
Writer's Market
1507 Dana Avenue
Cincinnati, OH 45207-1056

513-396-6160
Fax: 513-531-4082

Directory of services and supplies to the industry.
Cost: $29.95
1000 Pages
Frequency: Annual
ISSN: 0084-2729

16362 **Writer's Northwest Handbook**
Media Weavers, Blue Heron Publishing
4140 S.E. 37
#10
Portland, OR 97202

Home Page: www.mediaweavers.net

Over 3,000 markets for writers, including newspapers, magazines and book publishers in Northwestern United States and British Columbia, Canada.
Cost: $18.95
232 Pages
Frequency: Biennial

16363 **Writers Conferences**
Poets & Writers
150 Broadway
New York, NY 10038-4381

212-566-2424
Fax: 212-587-9673
E-Mail: mpettus@pettuswilliams.com
Home Page: www.pettuswilliams.com

Marvin K Pettus
Cost: $7.50
50 Pages
Frequency: Annual

16364 **Writers Directory**
St. James Press/Gale
27500 Drake Road
Farmington Hills, MI 48331-3535

248-699-4253
800-877-4253
Fax: 877-363-4253
E-Mail: gale.galeord@cengage.com
Home Page: www.gale.cengage.com
Social Media: Facebook, Twitter, Youtube

Patrick C Sommers, President

This comprehensive resource features uptodate bibliographical, biographical and contact information for approximately 20,000 living authors worldwide who have at least one English publication.
ISBN: 1-558626-20-4

16365 **Writers Guild Directory**
Writers Guild of America, West
8455 Beverly Blvd
Los Angeles, CA 90048-3445

323-651-2600
Fax: 323-782-4802

Bob Waters, Owner

Directory of services and supplies to the industry.
Cost: $17.50
450 Pages
Frequency: Annual

Industry Web Sites

16366 **http://gold.greyhouse.com**
G.O.L.D Grey House OnLine Databases

Grey House Publishing's online database platform, GOLD, offers Quick Search, Keyword Search and Expert Search for most business sectors including literary markets. The GOLD platform makes finding the information you need quick and easy - whether you're a novice searcher or an experienced database user. All of Grey House's directory products are available for subscription on the GOLD platform.

16367 **www.asja.org**
American Society of Journalists and Authors
Association for journalists and authors.

16368 **www.dramaguild.com**
Dramatists Guild

Protects the rights of its international membership of playwrights, composers and lyricists. Supports fair royalty, maintenance of subsidiary rights, artistic control and ownership of copyright.

16369 www.freelancepubs.com
Freelance Editorial Association

Self-employed contractors, or consultants with expertise in editorial functions such as copy-editing, researching, indexing and proofreading, writing, illustrating, editing, project managing, desktop publishing, and translating.

16370 www.greyhouse.com
Grey House Publishing

Authoritative reference directories for most business sectors including literary markets. Users can search the online databases with varied search criteria allowing for custom searches by product category, geographic area, sales volume, keyword, subject and more. Full Grey House catalog and online ordering also available.

16371 www.ifwtwa.org
International Food, Wine and Travel Writers Association

Staff and/or freelance writers in the food, wine and travel field. Also includes other media professionals and industry associate members in 28 countries worldwide.

16372 www.loc.gov/loc/cfbook/
Library of Congress

This organization strives to stimulate the consumer interest in books and reading.

16373 www.mysterywriters.org
Mystery Writers of America

Professional writers of crime and mystery stories and novels. Unpublished writers are affiliate members. MWA annually gives the Edagar Awards for excellence in the mystery geare.

16374 www.nationalwriters.com
Membership organization for writers.

16375 www.nfc.council.com
Newspaper Features Council

A forum for editors, writers, columnists, cartoonists and syndicates to exchange views and improve the content of newspapers.

16376 www.nfpw.org
National Federation of Press Women

Members are writers, editors and other communication professionals for newspapers, magazines, wire services, agencies and freelance.

16377 www.owaa.org
Outdoor Writers Association of America

A nonprofit, international organization representing over 2,000 professional outdoor communicators who report on diverse interests in the outdoors.

16378 www.the-efa.org
Editorial Freelancers Association

National nonprofit, professional organization of self-employed workers in the publishing and communications industries.

16379 www.wga.org
Writers Guild of America, West

An independent labor union representing writers in motion pictures, television and radio in the west.

16380 www.writersresearchgroup.com
Writers Research Group

Associations

16381 **American Beverage Licensees**
5101 River Rd
Suite 108
Bethesda, MD 20816-1560
301-656-1494
Fax: 301-656-7539
E-Mail: info@ablusa.org
Home Page: www.ablusa.org/
Social Media: Facebook, Twitter
Harry Klock, President
John D Bodnovich, Executive Director
Susan Day Duffy, Director of Trade Relations
Steve Morris, Vice President
Warren Scheidt, Vice President
Represents over 15,000 off premise licensees in the open or license states and on-premise proprietors in markets across the nation. Offers members information on legislation and industry matters.
15000 Members
Founded in 1933

16382 **American Society for Enology and Viticulture**
PO Box 1855
Davis, CA 95617-1855
530-753-3142
Fax: 530-753-3318
E-Mail: society@asev.org
Home Page: www.asev.org
Social Media: Facebook, Twitter, Picasa
James Kennedy, President
Lyndie Boulton, Executive Director
Lise Asimont, First Vice President
Mark Greenspan, Second Vice President
James Harbertson, Secretary/Treasurer
A tax exempt professional society dedicated to the interests of enologists, viticulturists, and others in the fields of wine and grape research and production throughout the world.
2400+ Members
Founded in 1950

16383 **American Society of Brewing Chemists**
3340 Pilot Knob Rd
St Paul, MN 55121-2055
651-454-7250
800-328-7560
Fax: 651-454-0766
E-Mail: asbc@scisoc.org
Home Page: www.asbcnet.org
Social Media: Facebook, LinkedIn
Jeffery L Cornell, President
Christina Schoenberger, Vice President
Amy Hope, Executive Officer
Barbara Mock, Vice President of Finance
Kelly A Tretter, Secretary
750 Members

16384 **Association of Winery Supplies**
21 Tamal Vista Boulevard
Suite 196
Corte Madera, CA 94925-1146
415-924-2640
Social Media: 1983
Warner Executive Director
United States supplier of services and materials used in the winery industry.
John Members
Founded in 34

16385 **Beer Institute**
122 C St NW
Suite 350
Washington, DC 20001-2150
202-737-2337
800-379-2739
Fax: 202-737-7004
E-Mail: info@beerinstitute.org
Home Page: www.beerinstitute.org
Social Media: Facebook, Twitter
Joe McClain, President
Mary Jane Saunders, VP & General Counsel
The national trade association for the brewing industry. Representing both big and small brewers as well as importers and industry suppliers.
100 Members
Founded in 1986

16386 **Brewers Association**
Brewers Association
736 Pearl Street
Boulder, CO 80302
303-447-0816
888-822-6273
Fax: 303-447-2825
E-Mail: info@brewersassociation.org
Home Page: www.brewersassociation.org
Social Media: Facebook, Twitter, Youtube
Charlie Papazian, President
Bob Pease, Chief Operating Officer
Cindy Jones, Web Director
Allison Seymour, Magazine Art Director
Shane Wood, Information Technology Director
A non-profit educational and trade organization for small and craft brewers. Its mission is to make quality brewing and beer knowledge accessible to all.
1900 Members
Founded in 1978

16387 **Distilled Spirits Council of the United States**
1250 Eye St NW
Suite 400
Washington, DC 20005-3998
202-628-3544
Fax: 202-682-8844
Home Page: www.discus.org
Social Media: Facebook, Twitter
Peter H Cressy, CEO
National trade association representing producers and marketers of liquor sold in the US.
32 Members
Founded in 1973

16388 **Distillery, Wine and Allied Workers' International Union**
66 Grand Avenue
Englewood, NJ 07631-3506
201-894-8444
Fax: 201-569-9216
Home Page: www.ufew.org/
Social Media: Facebook, Twitter, YouTube, flickr, RSS
Joseph T. Hansen, International President
William T. McDonough, Executive Vice President, UFCW
Patrick J. O'Neill, Executive Vice President, UFCW
Wayne E. Hanley, International EVP
Anthony Marc, 20130116
Addresses the concerns of wine makers and fellow industry workers.
14M Members
Founded in 1979

16389 **Home Wine and Beer Trade Association**
PO Box 1373
Valrico, FL 33595
813-685-4261
Fax: 813-681-5625
E-Mail: dee@hwbta.org
Home Page: www.fermentersinternational.org/
Social Media: Facebook, Twitter, Youtube
Mark Alston, President
Steven Haynes, VP
Ray Ault, Secretary
Allison Babock, Treasurer
Dee Roberson, Executive Director
Manufacturers, wholesalers, retailers, authors and editors having a commercial interest in the beer and wine trade.
Founded in 1976

16390 **Italian Trade Commission**
33 East 67th Street
New York, NY 10065
212-980-1500
Fax: 212-758-1050
E-Mail: newyork@ice.it
Home Page: www.italtrade.com/countries/americas/usa/newyork.htm
Michelle Jones, Editor
Robert Luongo, Executive Director
Developments in the Italian wine industry and market, as well as reviews of imported wines from Italy.

16391 **Italian Wine and Food Institute**
Italian Wine and Food Institute
60 East 42nd Street, Suite 2214
Suite 2214
New York, NY 10165
212-867-4111
Fax: 212-867-4114
E-Mail: iwfi@aol.com
Home Page: www.italianwineandfoodinstitute.com
Lucio Caputo, President
Vincent Giampaoco, VP
Members are producers, distributors and marketers of Italian wines and foods.
Founded in 1983

16392 **National Alcohol Beverage Control Association**
4401 Ford Avenue
Suite 700
Alexandria, VA 22302-1433
703-578-4200
Fax: 703-820-3551
Home Page: www.nabca.org
Social Media: Facebook, Twitter, Youtube
J. Neal Insley, Chairman
James M. Sgueo, President & CEO
Jerome J. Janicki, Sr. VP of Operations, COO
Patricia Kelly, Sr. VP of Administration, CFO
Steven L. Schmidt, Sr. VP of Public Policy
Members include control jurisdictions, supplier members and industry trade associations.
175 Members
Founded in 1938

16393 **National Beer Wholesalers Association**
1101 King Street
Suite 600
Alexandria, VA 22314-2944
703-683-4300
800-300-6417
Fax: 703-683-8965
E-Mail: info@nbwa.org
Home Page: www.nbwa.org

Social Media: Facebook, Twitter, Youtube, Flickr

Greg LaMantia, Chair, NBWA Board of Directors
Craig A. Purser, NBWA President & CEO
Rebecca Spicer, VP Public Affairs/Chief
Paul Pisano, SVP Industry Affairs & Gen. Counsel

NBWA represents the interests of America's 2,850 independent, licensed beer distributors which service every congressional district and media market in the country.
Founded in 1938

16394 National Wine Distribution Association
2701 E Street
Sacramento, CA 95816-3221

916-979-3051
Fax: 916-448-9115

GM Pucilowski, Executive Director

Dedicated to promoting the interests and education of smaller wine wholesalers, importers, wineries, and others who are involved in the wine distribution business.
285 Members
Founded in 1978

16395 Wine Institute
425 Market St
Suite 1000
San Francisco, CA 94105-2487
415-512-0151
Fax: 415-356-7569
Home Page: www.wineinstitute.org

Robert P Koch, President / Chief Executive Officer
Nancy Light, Vice President, Communications
Steve Gross, Vice President, State Relations
Allison Jordan, Vice President
Steve Hayes, Vice President, Finance

Organization that represents the wine and spirit industry to state and federal lawmaking bodies.
80 Members
Founded in 1934

16396 Wine and Spirits Shippers Association
11800 Sunrise Valley Dr
Reston, VA 20191-5302

703-860-2300
800-368-3167
Fax: 703-860-2422
E-Mail: info@wssa.com
Home Page: www.wssa.com
Social Media: Facebook, Twitter, LinkedIn, RSS

V. James Andretta, Jr., Chairman of the Board
Louis Healey, President
Howard Jacobs, Vice President
Heather Randolph, Director of Operations
Alison Leavitt, Managing Director

Provides members, importers and exporters with efficient and economical ocean transportation and other logistic services.
460 Members
Founded in 1976
Mailing list available for rent

16397 Wine and Spirits Wholesalers of America
805 15th Street NW
Suite 430
Washington, DC 20005

202-371-9792
Fax: 202-789-2405
E-Mail: Info@wswa.org
Home Page: www.wswa.org

Douglas Hertz, Chairman
Alan Dreeben, Vice Chairman
Craig Wolf, President and CEO
Jim Rowland, Senior Vice President
Dawson Hobbs, Vice President, State Affairs

This association is comprised of wholesale distributors of domestic and imported wine and distilled spirits.
450 Members
Circulation: 1,000
Founded in 1943

Newsletters

16398 ASBC Newsletter
American Society of Brewing Chemists
3340 Pilot Knob Rd
Eagan, MN 55121-2055

651-454-7250
800-328-7560
Fax: 651-454-0766
E-Mail: asbc@scisoc.org
Home Page: www.asbcnet.org

Steven C Nelson, VP
Jordana Anker, Director of Publications
Karen Cummings, Director Publications
Joan A Raumschuh, Editor
Jody Grider, Director of Operations
Cost: $20.00
Frequency: Quarterly
Founded in 1934

16399 Alcoholic Beverage Control: From the State Capitals
Wakeman Walworth
PO BOX 7376
Alexandria, VA 22307-7376
703-768-9600
Fax: 703-768-9690
Home Page:
www.statecapitals.com/alcoholbev.html

Keyes Walworth, Publisher

Covers binge drinking laws, internet sales, advertising, taxes, bottle bills, Sunday sales laws, license regulation, drunk driving laws, under-age drinking, mini-bottles and other state laws affecting beer, liquor and wine distribution.
Cost: $245.00
4 Pages
Frequency: Weekly
Printed in one color on matte stock

16400 Beer Marketer's Insights Newsletter
Beer Marketer's Insights
49 E Maple Ave
Suffern, NY 10901-5507

845-624-2337
Fax: 845-624-2340
Home Page: www.beerinsights.com

Benj Steinman, President

Reports on the competitive battle among brewers for a share of the beer market. Analyzes recent legislation and factors that affect the industry.
Cost: $595.00
Frequency: 23/Year
Founded in 1975

16401 Beer Statistics News
Beer Marketer's Insights
49 E Maple Ave
Suffern, NY 10901-5507

845-624-2337
Fax: 845-624-2340
E-Mail: bmiexpress@aol.com
Home Page: www.beerinsights.com

Benj Steinman, President
Eric Shephard, Executive Editor
Andy Leinicke, Circulation Manager

Supplies data for major brewers' shipments in 39 reporting states.
Cost: $450.00
Frequency: Monthly
Founded in 1975

16402 Brewers Bulletin
PO Box 677
Thiensville, WI 53092

262-242-6105
Fax: 262-242-5133
E-Mail: bulletindigest@milwpc.com

Tom Volke, President/CEO

Brewing industry newspaper.
Cost: $53.00
Frequency: Monthly
Circulation: 500
Founded in 1907

16403 Champagne Wines Information Bureau
KCSA
800 2nd Avenue Frnt 5
New York, NY 10017-4709

212-682-6300
800-642-4267
Fax: 212-697-0910
E-Mail: info@champagnes.com
Home Page: www.champagnes.com

Jean-Louis Carbonnier, Editor

Representative of Comite Interprofessionnel duVinde Champagne, Epernay, France.
4 Pages
Frequency: TriAnnual
Circulation: 10,000
Printed in one color on matte stock

16404 Impact International
M Shanken Communications
387 Park Ave S
Suite 8
New York, NY 10016-8872
212-684-4224
800-848-7113
Fax: 212-684-5424
Home Page: www.cigaraficionado.com

Marvin Shanken, Publisher
Samantha Shanken, President

Reports on the global alcoholic beverage market.
Cost: $595.00
Frequency: Annual+
Founded in 1972

16405 Kane's Beverage Week
Whitaker Newsletters
313 S Avenue
#340
Fanwood, NJ 07023-1364

908-889-6339
800-359-6049
Fax: 415-027-0608

Whitaker Publisher, Anne
Bittner Editor, Fred
Rossi Editor

News on marketing, economic and regulatory factors affecting the alcohol beverage industry.
Cost: $131.00
Joel Members
6 Pages
Frequency: Monthly
ISSN: 0882-2573

16406 Notiziario
Italian Wine and Food Institute
60 East 42nd Street, Suite 2214
Suite 1341
New York, NY 10165

212-867-4111
Fax: 212-867-4114

E-Mail: iwfi@aol.com
Home Page: www.italianwineandfoodinstitute.com

Lucio Caputo, President
Vincent Giampaoco, VP

Provides detailed information on the Italian gastronomy and wines. It distributes information materials and give press interviews for the American radio and television. It carries out an intense public relations program, participates in the most important local promotional initiatives and events and maintains contact with the American and Italian authorities in this sector.
Cost: $250.00
Founded in 1984

16407 On Tap: Newsletter
WBR Publishing
PO Box 71
Clemson, SC 29633

864-654-2300
Fax: 864-654-5067

Steve Johnson, Publisher

North America breweries and microbreweries.
Cost: $.95
20 Pages
Frequency: Bi-Monthly
Circulation: 1000
Printed in one color on matte stock

16408 Spirited Living: Dave Steadman's Restaurant Scene
5301 Towne Woods Rd
Coram, NY 11727-2808

631-736-0436
Fax: 631-736-0436

Dave Steadman, Editor

Newsletter published Bi-Weekly except January, July, and August.
Cost: $75.00

16409 US Beer Market
Business Trend Analysts/Industry Reports
2171 Jericho Tpke
Suite 200
Commack, NY 11725-2937

631-462-5454
800-866-4648
Fax: 631-462-1842
Home Page: www.bta-ler.com

Charles J Ritchie, Executive VP
Donna Priani, Marketing Director

Profiles markets for premium, superpremium, popular and light beers.
Cost: $1495.00

16410 Uncorked
California Wine Club
2175 Goodyear Avenue
Suite 102
Ventura, CA 93006-3699

805-650-4330
800-777-4443
Fax: 800-700-1599
E-Mail: info@cawineclub.com
Home Page: www.cawineclub.com

Bruce Boring, Proprietors
Judy Reynolds, Proprietors

Uncorked is an 8 page newsletter that describes the featured winery. It provides an upclose and personal look at a small 'boutique' California Winery.
Frequency: Monthly
Circulation: 10000
Founded in 1990

16411 Vinotizie Italian Wine Newsletter
Italian Trade Commission
33 E 67th St
New York, NY 10065-5949

212-848-0300
Fax: 212-758-1050
E-Mail: newyork@newyork.ice.it
Home Page: www.italtrade.com

Aniello Musella, President
Giovanni Mafodda, Operations Manager

This newsletter discusses developments in the Italian wine industry and market, as well as reviews of imported wines from Italy.
Frequency: Monthly
Founded in 1998

16412 Wine Investor Buyers Guide
PGE Publications
1224 N Fairfax Avenue
Apartment 5
Los Angeles, CA 90046-5234
Paul Gillette, Publisher
JD Kronman, Editor

Reviews new releases of wines, recommends the best buys, predicts when wines will be at their peak and surveys markets for pricing trends. Accepts advertising.
Cost: $75.00
10 Pages
Frequency: Monthly

16413 World Beer Review
WBR Publishing
PO Box 71
Clemson, SC 29633-0071

864-654-2300

Steve Johnson, Publisher

Complete coverage of the beer and beermaking industry.

Magazines & Journals

16414 All About Beer
Chautauqua Inc
501 Washington St
Suite H
Durham, NC 27701-2169

919-530-8150
800-977-2337
Fax: 919-530-8160
E-Mail: editor@allaboutbeer.com
Home Page: www.allaboutbeer.com
Julie Bradford, Publisher
Natalie Abernethy, Circulation Manager
Quality beers, breweries and restaurants.
Cost: $19.99
64 Pages
Founded in 1981

16415 Atlantic Control States Beverage Journal
Club & Tavern
3 12th Street
Wheeling, WV 26003-3276

304-232-7620
Fax: 304-233-1236

Arnold Lazarus, Editor

A magazine for the alcoholic beverage industry. Serving bars, restaurants, clubs and industry personnel with West Virginia, Virginia, and North Carolina state editions. Includes states' liquor price lists.

16416 Bar Business Magazine
Simmons-Boardman Publishing Corporation
345 Hudson St
Suite 1201
New York, NY 10014-7123

212-620-7200
Fax: 212-633-1165
E-Mail: cytuarte@sbpub.com
Home Page: www.simmonsboardman.com

Arthur J McGinnis Jr, President

The premier How-To publication covering the best business practices and products for owners and managers of nightclubs, bars and lounges across the US.
Frequency: Monthly
Circulation: 8541

16417 Bartender Magazine
Foley Publishing Corporation
PO Box 157
Spring Lake, NJ 07762

732-449-4499
Fax: 732-974-8289
E-Mail: barmag@aol.com
Home Page: www.bartender.com
Social Media: Facebook, Twitter

Raymond Foley, Publisher
Jaclyn Wilson Foley, Editor

Serves all full service drinking establishments. Including individual restaurants, hotels, motels, bars, taverns, lounges, and all other full service on premise licenses. Subscription price is $40 for Canada, and $55 for all other foriegn countries.
Cost: $30.00
72 Pages
Frequency: Monthly
Circulation: 149044
Founded in 1979
Printed in 4 colors on glossy stock

16418 Beer Perspectives
National Beer Wholesalers Association
1101 King St
Suite 600
Alexandria, VA 22314-2965

703-683-4300
Fax: 703-683-8965
E-Mail: info@nbwa.org
Home Page: www.nbwa.org
Social Media: Facebook, Twitter

Craig A Purser, President & CEO
Michael Johnson, EVP Fed Aff/Chief Advisory Office
Rebecca Spicer, VP Public Affairs/Chief
Paul Pisano, SVP Industry Affairs & Gen. Counsel

Trade association for beer wholesalers. Provides government and public affairs outreach as well as education and training for its wholesaler members.
Founded in 1938

16419 Beverage Dynamics
The Beverage Information Group
17 High Street
2nd Floor
Norwalk, CT 06851

203-855-8499
E-Mail: lzimmerman@m2media360.com
Home Page: www.bevinfogroup.com

Liza Zimmerman, Editor-in-Chief
Jeremy Nedelka, Managing Editor

Devoted to the needs of the off-premise beverage alcohol retailer. Covers wine, beer and spirits categories as well as beset practices for retail decision makers.
Cost: $35.00
Frequency: Bi-Monthly
Founded in 1934

16420 Beverage Journal
Michigan Licensed Beverage Association

920 N Fairview Ave
Lansing, MI 48912-3238

517-374-9611
800-292-2896
Fax: 517-374-1165
E-Mail: info@mlba.org
Home Page: www.mlba.org

Lou Adado, CEO
Cathy Pavick, Executive Director
Peter Broderick, Director of Communication

Offers information on the alcoholic beverage industry/retail sales
Cost: $52.00
Frequency: Monthly
ISSN: 1050-4427
Founded in 1939
Printed in on glossy stock

16421 Beverage Network
Beverage Media Group
116 John St
Suite 2305
New York, NY 10038-3419

212-571-3232
800-723-8372
Fax: 212-571-4443
E-Mail: info@bevmedia.com
Home Page: www.bevmedia.com

Jason Glasser, CEO
S Paley, Circulation Manager
Cost: $99.00
Frequency: Monthly
Circulation: 6000
Founded in 1940

16422 Beverage Retailer Magazine
Oxford Publishing
Ste 1
1903b University Ave
Oxford, MS 38655-4150

662-236-5510
800-247-3881
Fax: 662-236-5541
Home Page: www.beverage-retailer.com

Brenda Owen, Editor
Ed Meek, Publisher
Stacy Clark, Production Manager
Jennifer Parsons, Marketing Director
Ruth Ann Wolfe, Circulation Director

A magazine covering the off premise market for retailers in the wine, beer and spirits business.
Cost: $30.00
Circulation: 25000
Founded in 1985
Printed in 4 colors on glossy stock

16423 Cheers
The Beverage Information Group
17 High St
Suite 2
Norwalk, CT 06851

203-855-8499
Fax: 203-855-9446
E-Mail: cforman@m2media360.com
Home Page: www.bevinfogroup.com

Charlie Forman, SVP/Group Publisher
Liza Zimmerman, Editor-In-Chief
Jeremy Nedelka, Managing Editor

Business magazine for on-premise hospitality professionals. Coverage includes trends and innovations in operations, merchandising, service and training, as well as new developments in beverage product segments.
Cost: $35.00
Frequency: Monthly
Founded in 1998

16424 Modern Brewery Age
Business Journals
50 Day Street
PO Box 5550
Norwalk, CT 06856-5550

203-853-6015
Fax: 203-853-8175
E-Mail: FayS@busjour.com
Home Page: www.breweryage.com

Mac Brighton, Chairman/COO
Britton Jones, President/CEO
Peter V K Reid, Editor/Publisher
Arthur Heilman, Circulation Director
Diane Apicelli, Advertising Director

A magazine for the wholesale and brewing industry.
Cost: $95.00
Founded in 1933

16425 Modern Brewery Age: Tabloid Edition
Business Journals
50 Day Street
PO Box #5550
Norwalk, CT 06856-5550

203-853-6015
Fax: 203-853-8175
Home Page: www.breweryage.com

Peter VK Reid, Editor
Peter VK Reid, Publisher
Britton Jones, President/CEO
Diane Apicelli, Advertising Director
Mac Brighton, Chairman & COO

Brewery industry tabloid.
Cost: $95.00
Frequency: Weekly
Founded in 1933

16426 Nightclub & Bar Magazine
Oxford Publishing
Ste 1
1903b University Ave
Oxford, MS 38655-4150

662-236-5510
800-247-3881
Fax: 662-281-0104
Home Page: www.nightclub.com

Ed Meek, Production Manager
Mitchell Diggs, Managing Editor
Laura McCreary, Advertising Director
Jennifer Cummins, Production Manager
Adam Alson, Founder

A monthly publication covering the nightclub and bar hospitality industry.
Frequency: Monthly
Circulation: 30,000
Printed in 4 colors on glossy stock

16427 Southern Beverage Journal
Beverage Media Group
14337 Sw 119th Ave
Miami, FL 33186-6006

305-233-7230
Fax: 305-252-2580
Home Page: www.bevnetwork.com

Sharon Mijares, President
Sharon Mijares, Circulation Manager

A magazine for the alcoholic beverage industry.
Cost: $35.00
Frequency: Monthly
Circulation: 29000
Founded in 1944

16428 StateWays
The Beverage Information Group
17 High Street
2nd Floor
Norwalk, CT 06851

203-855-8499
E-Mail: lzimmerman@m2media360.com
Home Page: www.bevinfogroup.com

Liza Zimmerman, Editor-In-Chief
Jeremy Nedelka, Managing Editor

Written for commissioners, board members, headquarters personnel, and retail store managers responsible for buying beverage alcohol in the eighteen control states. Covered editorial includes product knowledge, market trends, store operations, merchandising, warehousing, computerization, administration, training, and other topics.
Cost: $20.00
Frequency: Bi-Monthly
Circulation: 8500

16429 US Beer Market: Impact Databank Review and Forecast
M Shanken Communications
387 Park Ave S
Suite 8
New York, NY 10016-8872

212-684-4224
Fax: 212-684-5424
Home Page: www.cigaraficionado.com

Marvin Shanken, Publisher
Samantha Shanken, Marketing Manager
Cost: $9.10

16430 US Liquor Industry
Business Trend Analysts/Industry Reports
2171 Jericho Tpke
Suite 200
Commack, NY 11725-2937

631-462-5454
Fax: 631-462-1842
E-Mail: bta@li.net
Home Page: www.businesstrendanalysts.com

Charles J Ritchie, Executive VP
Donna Priani, Marketing Director
Linda Sherman, Production Manager
Jennifer Wichert, Research Director

A survey summarizing the past, current and future markets and trends in the liquor industry.
Cost: $1195.00
600 Pages
Founded in 1999

16431 US Wine Market
Business Trend Analysts/Industry Reports
2171 Jericho Tpke
Suite 200
Commack, NY 11725-2937

631-462-5454
800- 86- 464
Fax: 631-462-1842
Home Page: www.businesstrendanalysts.com

Charles J Ritchie, Executive VP
Donna Priani, Marketing Director

An analysis of the wine industry, domestic and imported.
Cost: $1995.00
470 Pages
Circulation: 2004
Founded in 1978

16432 Vineyard and Winery Management Magazine
Vineyard & Winery Management

421 E Street
Santa Rosa, CA 95404

707-577-7700
Fax: 707-577-7705
Home Page: www.vwm-online.com

Robert Merletti, CEO/Publisher
Dennis Black, General Manager
Tina Caputo, Editor-in-Chief

A leading independent award winning wine trade magazine serving all of North America.
Cost: $37.00
100 Pages
Frequency: Bi-Monthly
Circulation: 6900
ISSN: 1047-4951
Founded in 1975
Printed in 4 colors on glossy stock

16433 Wine Advocate
Robert M Parker Jr
PO Box 311
Monkton, MD 21111

410-329-6477
Fax: 410 357-4504
E-Mail: wineadvocate@erobertparker.com
Home Page: www.erobertparker.com

Robert M Parker Jr, Publisher/ Editor
Jacques Robinson, President

An independent magazine covering reviews of wine.
Cost: $60.00
64 Pages
Circulation: 40000
Founded in 1978

16434 Wine and Spirits
Winestate Publications
1748 Market Street
San Francisco, CA 94102-4997

415-255-7736
Fax: 415-255-9659
E-Mail:
mlkinney@wineandspiritsmagazine.com
Home Page:
www.wineandspiritsmagazine.com/

Joshua Greene, Editor/Publisher
Michael Kinney, Associate Publisher
Ray Isle, Managing Editor
W. Charles Squires, Circulation Director
Gilian Handelman, Marketing Manager

A consumer magazine for wine enthusiasts.
Cost: $26.00
70 Pages
Circulation: 75000
Founded in 1987
Printed in 4 colors on glossy stock

Trade Shows

16435 ASBC Annual Meeting
American Society of Brewing Chemists
3340 Pilot Knob Road
Saint Paul, MN 55121-2055

651-454-7250
800-328-7560
Fax: 651-454-0766
E-Mail: bford@scisoc.org
Home Page: www.meeting.asbcnet.org

Betty Ford, Meetings Director
Sue Casey, Meetings Coordinator
Steven Nelson, VP
300 Attendees
Frequency: June/Non-Members Fee

16436 American Beverage Licensees Annual Convention & Trade Show
American Beverage Licensees
5101 River Road
Suite 108
Bethesda, MD 20816-1560

301-656-1494
Fax: 301-656-7539
Home Page: www.nabronline.org

Harry Wiles, Executive Director
Susan Day Pirieda, Office Manager

Annual show of 75 manufacturers, suppliers and distributors of alcoholic beverages.
700 Attendees
Frequency: March

16437 American Society for Enology and Viticulture Annual Meeting
PO Box 1855
Davis, CA 95617-1855

530-753-3142
Fax: 530-753-3318
E-Mail: society@asev.org
Home Page: www.asev.org

Bill Mead, Event/Tradeshow Coordinator

With technical sessions, research forums, symposia and a supplier showcase.
Frequency: June
Founded in 1950

16438 American Wine Society
3006 Latta Road
Rochester, NY 14612-3298

585-225-7613
Fax: 585-225-7613
E-Mail: angel910@aol.com
Home Page: americanwinesociety.com

Angel E Nardone, Executive Director

12 booths.
600 Attendees
Frequency: November
Founded in 1967

16439 Beer, Wine & Spirits Industry Trade Show
Indiana Association of Beverage
200 S Meridian Street
Suite 350
Indianapolis, IN 46225-3418

317-847-7580
Fax: 317-673-4210

Teresa Koch

Annual show of 125 exhibitors of alcohol beverage distillers brewers that are recognized primary sources in the state of Indiana as supplies for retailers.
2500 Attendees

16440 Craft Brewers Conference and Brew Expo America
Brewers Association
736 Pearl Street
Boulder, CO 80302

303-447-0816
888-822-6273
Fax: 303-447-2825
E-Mail: info@brewersassociation.org
Home Page: www.brewersassociation.org
Social Media: Facebook, Twitter, Youtube

Charlie Papazian, President
Bob Pease, VP
Cindy Jones, Sales/Marketing Director
1,200 Attendees
Frequency: April

16441 Great American Beer Festival
Brewers Association
736 Pearl Street
Boulder, CO 80302

303-447-0816
888-822-6273
Fax: 303-447-2825
E-Mail: info@brewersassociation.org
Home Page: www.brewersassociation.org
Social Media: Facebook, Twitter, Youtube

Charlie Papazian, President
Bob Pease, VP
Cindy Jones, Sales/Marketing Director
Frequency: September

16442 NABR Tasting & Display Event Annual Convention
American Beverage Licensees
5101 River Road
Suite 108
Bethesda, MD 20816-1560

301-656-1494
Fax: 301-656-7539
Home Page: www.nabronline.org

Harry Wiles, Executive Director
Shawn Ross, Office Manager

Offers exhibits on spirits, beer and wine industry supplies, equipment, bar accessories and computers. The NABR Annual Convention is a gathering of alcohol beverage retailers and proprietors for networking and educational opportunities. An exclusive trade display and tasting event is held to promote brands and services of use to retailers and proprietors. There are 25-75 booths.
500+ Attendees
Frequency: March

16443 NBWA Annual Convention
National Beer Wholesalers Association
1101 King Street
Suite 600
Alexandria, VA 22314-8965

703-683-4300
Fax: 703-683-8965
E-Mail: info@nbwa.org
Home Page: www.nbwa.org
Social Media: Facebook, Twitter

Craig A Purser, President & CEO
Michael Johnson, EVP Fed Aff/Chief Advisory Office
Rebecca Spicer, VP Public Affairs/Chief
Paul Pisano, SVP Industry Affairs & Gen. Counsel

Designed to provide valuable education programs and important networking opportunities for the beer industry. Featuring speakers and seminars on a number of topics of imprtance to beer distributors .
2500 Attendees
Frequency: Fall

16444 National Beer Wholesalers Association Convention and Trade Show
Corcoran Expositions
33 N Dearborn Street
Suite 505
Chicago, IL 60602-3103

312-541-0567
800-541-0359
Fax: 312-541-0573

Al Natker, Operations Manager

Biennial show of 166 manufacturers, suppliers and distributors of brewery software and hardware, trucking, beer cleaning equipment and related equipment, supplies and services.
3000 Attendees

16445 Wineries Unlimited
Vineyard & Winery Services
3883 Airway Drive
Suite 250
Santa Rosea, CA 95403

707-577-7700
800-535-5670

Fax: 707-577-7705
Home Page: www.wineriesunlimited.com

The largest, most powerful trade show and conference for the eastern wine industry.
2000 Attendees
Frequency: March

Directories & Databases

16446 Beverage Marketing Directory
Beverage Marketing Corporation
2670 Commercial Ave
Mingo Junction, OH 43938-1613

740-598-4133
800-332-6222
Fax: 740-598-3977
Home Page: www.beveragemarketing.com

Andrew Standardi III, Director of Operations
Kathy Smurthwaite, Editor

Publication is available in Print Copy (Price-$1,465), PDF Format (Price-$1,465), CD-ROM Format (For pricing, call number listed for details or visit website), and Online.
1196 Pages

16447 Brewers Resource Directory
Brewers Association
736 Pearl Street
Boulder, CO 80302

303-447-0816
888-822-6273
Fax: 303-447-2825
E-Mail: info@brewersassociation.org
Home Page: www.brewersassociation.org
Social Media: Facebook, Twitter, Youtube

Charlie Papazian, President
Bob Pease, VP
Cindy Jones, Sales/Marketing Director

Various categories of listees are included that have a direct relation to the beer and liquor industry.
Mailing list available for rent

16448 Contacts
National Alcohol Beverage Control Association
4401 Ford Avenue, Suite 700
Alexandria, VA 22302-1507

703-578-4200
Fax: 703-820-3551
Home Page: www.nabca.org
Social Media: Facebook, Twitter

James M Sgueo, Executive Director
Dixie Jamieson, Executive Assistant

Members include control jurisdictions, supplier members and industry trade associations.

16449 Directory & Products Guide
Vineyard & Winery Services
PO Box 2358
Windsor, CA 95492

707-836-6820
800-535-5670
Fax: 707-836-6825
Home Page: vwm-online.com

Jennifer Merietti, Sales/Marketing Manager
Dennis Black, General Manager
Suzanne Webb, Marketing Director

A must have reference book that belongs on the desk of every wine professional. Whether it's tracking down a particular vendor, shopping for the best deal on oak barrels or searching for out-of-state winery contacts, the DPG is a powerhouse of information. Over 2,300 supplier listings and 2,700 winery/vineyard listings, it is a reliable resource that saves time and money.
Cost: $95.00
450+ Pages
Frequency: Annually

16450 Food & Beverage Market Place
Grey House Publishing
4919 Route 22
PO Box 56
Amenia, NY 12501

518-789-8700
800-562-2139
Fax: 845-373-6390
E-Mail: books@greyhouse.com
Home Page: www.greyhouse.com
Social Media: Facebook, Twitter

Leslie Mackenzie, Publisher
Richard Gottlieb, Editor

This information-packed 3-volume set is the most powerful buying and marketing guide for the US food and beverage industry. Includes thousands of industry freight and transportation listings.
Cost: $595.00
2000 Pages
Frequency: Annual
ISBN: 1-592373-61-5
Founded in 1981

16451 Food & Beverage Marketplace: Online Database
Grey House Publishing
4919 Route 22
PO Box 56
Amenia, NY 12501

518-789-8700
800-562-2139
Fax: 518-789-0556
E-Mail: gold@greyhouse.com
Home Page: http://gold.greyhouse.com
Social Media: Facebook, Twitter

Richard Gottlieb, President
Leslie Mackenzie, Publisher

This complete updated Food & Beverage Market Place: Online Database is the go-to source for the food and beverage industry. Anyone involved in the food and beverage industry needs this 'industry bible' and the important contacts to develop critical research data that can make for successful business growth.
Frequency: Annual
Founded in 1981

16452 Impact International Directory: Leading Spirits, Wine and Beer Companies
M Shanken Communications
387 Park Ave S
8th Floor
New York, NY 10016-8872

212-684-4224
Fax: 212-684-5424
Home Page: www.cigaraficionado.com

Marvin Shanken, Publisher

A directory offering information on the major players of the alcoholic beverage industry.
Cost: $295.00

16453 Impact Yearbook: Directory of the US Wine, Spirits & Beer Industry
M Shanken Communications
387 Park Ave S
8th Floor
New York, NY 10016-8872

212-684-4224
Fax: 212-684-5424
Home Page: www.cigaraficionado.com

Marvin Shanken, Publisher

A directory offering information on the top 40 American distributors and profiles of companies.
Cost: $170.00
Frequency: Annual

16454 US Alcohol Beverage Industry Category CD
Beverage Marketing Corporation
2670 Commercial Ave
Mingo Junction, OH 43938-1613

740-598-4133
800-332-6222
Fax: 740-598-3977
Home Page: www.beveragemarketing.com

Andrew Standardi III, Director of Operations
Kathy Smurthwaite, Editor

Contains information on approximately 3,030 companies including breweries, microbreweries, wineries, distilleries, wholesalers and importers.
Cost: $3010.00
Frequency: Annual

16455 US Beverage Manufacturers and Filling Locations Category CD
Beverage Marketing Corporation
850 Third Avenue, 18th Floor
New York, NY 10022

212-688-7640
800-332-6222
Fax: 212-826-1255
Home Page: www.beveragemarketing.com

Andrew Standardi III, Director of Operations
Kathy Smurthwaite, Editor

Contains information on approximately 2,402 companies including breweries, microbreweries, wineries, distilleries, soft drink fillers and franchise companies, bottled water fillers, juice, sports beverages and energy drinks, soy, coffee, tea, and milk manufacturers.
Cost: $2390.00
Frequency: Annual
Mailing list available for rent

16456 US Wine & Spirits Industry Category CD
Beverage Marketing Corporation
2670 Commercial Ave
Mingo Junction, OH 43938-1613

740-598-4133
800-332-6222
Fax: 740-598-3977
Home Page: www.beveragemarketing.com

Andrew Standardi III, Director of Operations
Kathy Smurthwaite, Editor

Contains information on approximately 1,484 companies including wineries, distilleries, wine & spirit wholesalers, and wine & spirit importers.
Cost: $1475.00
Frequency: Annual

16457 Vineyard & Winery Management Magazine
Vineyard & Winery Services
421 E Street
Santa Rosa, CA 95404

707-577-7700
800-535-5670
Fax: 707-577-7705
Home Page: vwm-online.com

Jennifer Merletti, Sales/Marketing Manager
Robert Merletti, Chairman/Owner
George Christie, President/CEO

A leading technical trade publication serving the North American Wine Industry and designed for today's serious wine business professional.
Founded in 1975
Mailing list available for rent

16458 Who's Who in Beer Wholesaling Directory
National Beer Wholesalers Association
1101 King Street
Suite 600
Alexandria, VA 22314-8965

703-683-4300
Fax: 703-683-8965
E-Mail: info@nbwa.org
Home Page: www.nbwa.org
Social Media: Facebook, Twitter

Craig A Purser, President & CEO
Michael Johnson, EVP Fed Aff/Chief Advisory Office
Rebecca Spicer, VP Public Affairs/Chief
Paul Pisano, SVP Industry Affairs & Gen. Counsel

A listing of more than 3,000 beer distributors and suppliers in the industry.
Cost: $50.00

16459 Wholesale Beer Association Executives of America Directory
Wholesale Beer Association Executives of America
2805 E Washington Avenue
Madison, WI 53704-5165

608-255-6464
Fax: 608-255-6466

7 Pages
Frequency: Annual

16460 Wine & Spirits Industry Marketing
Jobson Publishing Corporation
100 Avenue of the Americas
9th Floor
New York, NY 10013-1678

212-274-7000
Fax: 212-431-0500

Michael J Tansey, CEO

List of about 300 wine and liquor firms including wineries, producers, distillers and importers.
Cost: $150.00
Frequency: Annual April

16461 Wine on Line
Wine on Line International
400 E 59th St
Apartment 9F
New York, NY 10022-2342

212-755-4363
Fax: 212-755-7365

A database containing information including reviews about wines, production methods, serving advice, and more. Available on the Internet and worldwide web.
Frequency: Daily

16462 Wines and Vines Directory of the Wine Industry in North America Issue
Hiaring Company
1800 Lincoln Avenue
San Rafael, CA 94901-1221

415-453-9700
Fax: 415-453-2517
E-Mail: info@winesandvines.com
Home Page: www.winesandvines.com

Dorthy Kubota-Cordery, Editor
Phil Hiaring, Publisher
Debbie Hennessy, Editor
Renee Skiadas, Circulation Director
Chet Klingensmith, Owner

Annual guide offering listings of wineries and wine industry suppliers in the US, Canada and Mexico.
Cost: $85.00
505 Pages
Frequency: Annual
Circulation: 5000

Industry Web Sites

16463 http://gold.greyhouse.com
G.O.L.D Grey House OnLine Databases

Grey House Publishing's online database platform, GOLD, offers Quick Search, Keyword Search and Expert Search for most business sectors including alcoholic beverage markets. The GOLD platform makes finding the information you need quick and easy - whether you're a novice searcher or an experienced database user. All of Grey House's directory products are available for subscription on the GOLD platform.

16464 www.beerinstitute.org
Beer Institute

Protects the market environment from unfair burdens imposed by government bodies. Represents members interest before Congress.

16465 www.beertown.org
American Homebrewers Association

Devoted to the education of home brewed beer. Publishes the only magazine devoted exclusively to education, art and science of homebrewing. Services include: Beer Judge Certification Program, Sanctioned Competitions, World's Largest Homebrew Competition.

16466 www.cawineclub.com
California Wine Club

A wine of the month club that features only California's small boutique wineries. Each month members receive two bottles of award-winning wine.

16467 www.greyhouse.com
Grey House Publishing

Authoritative reference directories for most business sectors including alcoholic beverage markets. Users can search the online databases with varied search criteria allowing for custom searches by product category, geographic area, sales volume, keyword, subject and more. Full Grey House catalog and online ordering also available

16468 www.nbwa.org
National Beer Wholesalers Association

Research and development, quality control and ingredients.

16469 www.scisoc.org/asbc
American Society of Brewing Chemists

Annual scientific meeting for professionals in the brewing industry.

16470 www.wineinstitute.org
Wine Institute

Organization that represents the wine and spirit industry to state and federal lawmaking bodies.

16471 www.wssa.com
Wine and Spirits Shippers Association

Provides members, importers and exporters with efficient and economical ocean transportation and other logistic services.

Associations

16472 **APA - The Engineered Wood Association**
7011 S 19th Street
Tacoma, WA 98466-5333

253-565-6600
Fax: 253-565-7265
E-Mail: help@apawood.org
Home Page: www.apawood.org
Social Media: Facebook, Twitter

Mary Jo Nyblad, Chairman
Tom Temple, Vice Chairman
Dennis Hardman, President

A nonprofit trade association that represents US and Canadian manufacturers of structural engineered wood products, including plywood, oriented strand board (OSB), glued-laminated timber (glulam), wood i-joists and structural composite lumber.
160 Members
Founded in 1933
Mailing list available for rent

16473 **American Fiberboard Association**
2118 Plum Grove Rd.
#283
Rolling Meadows, IL 60008

847-934-8394
E-Mail: afa@fiberboard.org
Home Page: www.fiberboard.org
Social Media: Twitter

Rina P. McGuire, President
Jim Pieczynski, VP
Louis E. Wagner, Executive Director
William C. Ives, Legal Counsel
Blair Ruzicka, Secretary/Treasurer

The national trade organization of manufacturers of cellulose fiberboard products used for residential and commercial construction.
7 Members
Founded in 1990

16474 **American Forest & Paper Association**
AF&PA
1101 K Street, NW
Suite 700
Washington, DC 20005

202-463-2700
800-878-8878
Fax: 202-463-2785
E-Mail: info@afandpa.org
Home Page: www.afandpa.org
Social Media: Facebook, Twitter, LinkedIn, Youtube

David W. Scheible, Chairman
Donna Harman, President and CEO
Sharon Ashley, Manager of Operations
Elizabeth VanDersarl, Senior Advisor
John D. Williams, First Vice Chairman

Represents member companies and related trade associations which grow, harvest and process wood and wood fiber, manufacture pulp, paper and paperboard products from both virgin and recovered fiber and produce solid wood products.
550 Members
Founded in 1993

16475 **American Forest Foundation**
2000 M Street, NW
Suite 550
Washington, DC 20036

202-765-3660
Fax: 202-827-7924
E-Mail: info@forestfoundation.org
Home Page: www.forestfoundation.org
Social Media: Facebook, Twitter

Tom Martin, President & CEO
Jennifer Jones, Vice President, Communications
Nathan Truitt, Vice President of Development
Scott Smiley, Vice President, Finance
Kathy McGlauflin, Senior Vice President, Education

Committed to creating a future where North American forests are sustained by the public that understand and values the social, economic, and environmental benefits they provide to our communities, our nation, and the world.
120 Members
Mailing list available for rent

16476 **American Forests**
1220 L Street NW
Suite 750
Washington, DC 20005

202-737-1944
E-Mail: info@americanforests.org
Home Page: www.americanforests.org
Social Media: Facebook, Twitter

Ann Nichols, Chair
Scott Steen, Chief Executive Officer
Matthew Boyer, Vice President, Individual Giving
Peter Hutchins, Vice President, Programs
Greg Meyer, Vice President, Corporate

Restoring watersheds to help provide clean drinking water and replanting forests destroyed by human action and by natural disasters.
Founded in 1990
Mailing list available for rent

16477 **American Hardwood Export Council**
American Hardwood Export Council
1825 Michael Faraday Dr
Reston, VA 20190

703-435-2900
Fax: 703-435-2537
Home Page: www.ahec.org

Michael Snow, Executive Director
An Di H Nguyen, Manager of International Programs
Stefani Brown, International Program Coordinator

AHEC provides the global hardwood industry with promotional assistance, technical information and sources of supply for American hardwoods from its international offices.

16478 **American Institute of Timber Construction**
American Institute of Timber Construction
7012 S Revere Parkway
Suite 140
Centennial, CO 80112

503-639-0651
Fax: 503-684-8928
E-Mail: info@aitc-glulam.org
Home Page: www.aitc-glulam.org

Don DeVisser P.E., Executive VP
Skeet Rominger, Director Quality Services
Mike Schoen, Controller
Robert A Horlacher, Senior District Manager, Eastern
Tony Lewin, Western District Auditor

The national trade association of the structural glued laminiated (glulam) timber industry.
Founded in 1952

16479 **American Lumber Standard Committee**
American Lumber Standard Committee
PO Box 210
Germantown, MD 20875-0210

301-972-1700
Fax: 301-540-8004
E-Mail: alsc@alsc.org
Home Page: www.alsc.org

Thomas D Searles, President, Chief Lumber Inspector

Comprised of manufacturers, distributors, users, and consumers of lumber, serves as the standing committee for the American Softwood Lumber Standard
Founded in 1924

16480 **American Sports Builders Association**
American Sports Builders Association
8480 Baltimore National Pike
Suite 307
Ellicott City, MD 21043

410-730-9595
888-501-2722
Fax: 410-730-8833
E-Mail: info@sportsbuilders.org
Home Page: www.sportsbuilders.org
Social Media: Facebook, LinkedIn

Mark Brogan, CTCB, Chairman
Fred Stringfellow, CAE, Executive Director
Cynthia M. Sanchez, Director of Meetings/Member Service
Amy Chetelat, CAE, Financial Manager
David H. Pettit, Esq., Legal Counsel

Wood flooring manufacturers and distributors.
50 Members
Founded in 1965

16481 **American Walnut Manufacturers Association**
American Walnut Manufacturers Association
1007 North 725 West
West Lafayette, IN 47906-9431

317-873-8780
Fax: 317-873-8780
E-Mail: jackson@purdue.edu
Home Page: www.walnutassociation.org

Liz Jackson, Executive Director

A national trade group representing manufacturers of walnut lumber, veneer, gunstock and dimensions.
8 Members
Founded in 1912

16482 **American Wood Chip Export Association**
Stoel Rives
101 South Capitol Boulevard
Suite 1900
Boise, ID 83702

208-389-9000
Fax: 208-389-9040
E-Mail: mlmoody@stoel.com
Home Page: www.stoel.com
Social Media: Facebook, Twitter, LinkedIn, RSS

Kris J. Ormseth, Office Managing Partner

Researches and compiles data on the wood chip export association.
5 Members
Founded in 1907

16483 **American Wood Protection Association**
100 Chase Park S
Suite 116
Birmingham, AL 35244-1851

205-733-4077
Fax: 205-733-4075

E-Mail: email@awpa.com
Home Page: www.awpa.com

Colin McCown, Executive Vice President

A non-profit organization which is responsible for promulgating voluntary wood preservation standards.
900 Members
Founded in 1904

16484 Appalachian Hardwood Manufacturers
Appalachian Hardwood Manufacturers
816 Eastchester Drive
Suite 202
High Point, NC 27262

336-885-8315
Fax: 336-886-8865
E-Mail: tom@appalachianwood.org
Home Page: www.appalachianwood.org/

Tom Inman, President
Dinah Farrington, Administrative Assistant

Promotes the use of Appalachian hardwoods. Provides education and research programs.
154 Members
Founded in 1926

16485 Architectural Woodwork Institute
Architectural Woodwork Institute
46179 Westlake Drive
Suite 120
Potomac Falls, VA 20165-5874

571-323-3636
Fax: 571-323-3630
E-Mail: info@awinet.org
Home Page: www.awinet.org

Michael Bell, President
Kent Gilchrist, Vice President
Bruce Spitz, Treasurer

Members consist of architectural woodworkers, suppliers, design professionals and students from around the world
4000 Members
Founded in 1954

16486 Association of Equipment Manufacturers
Association of Equipment Manufacturers
6737 W Washington St
Suite 2400
Milwaukee, WI 53214-5650

414-272-0943
Fax: 414-272-1170
E-Mail: aem@aem.org
Home Page: www.aem.org
Social Media: Twitter

Richard A Patek, Chairman
Dennis Slater, President
Al Cervero, Vice President, Marketing & Global
John Nowak, Chief Financial Officer
Anne Forristall Luke, Vice President, Political & Public

Representing manufacturers of architectural, construction, forestry, materials handling and liabilty equipment.

16487 Association of Millwork Distributors
10047 Robert Trent Jones Pkwy
New Port Richey, FL 34655-4649

727-372-3665
800-786-7274
Fax: 727-372-2879
E-Mail: mail@amdweb.com
Home Page: www.amdweb.com
Social Media: Twitter, LinkedIn

Nathan Potter, President
Joe Bayer, First Vice President
Dave Ondrasek, Second Vice President
Scot Harder, Associate Vice President
Simon Sikora, Treasurer

Provides leadership, certification, education, promotion, networking and advocacy to, and for, the millwork distribution industry.
1200 Members
Founded in 1935

16488 Association of Woodworking & Furnishings Suppliers
Association of Woodworking & Furnishings
2400 E Katella Ave
Suite 340
Anaheim, CA 92806

323-838-9440
800-946-2937
Fax: 323-838-9443
E-Mail: awfsofc@aol.com
Home Page: www.awfs.org

Wade Gregory, President
Archie Thompson, VP
Angelo Gangone, Executive Vice President
Amy Bartz, Fair Sales Director
Nancy Fister, Education & Conference Director

Trade association for suppliers to the woodworking and furnishings industry. Services include three trade shows: Woodworking; Machinery and Supply Fair; Home and Commercial Furnishings.
425 Members
Founded in 1979

16489 Capital Lumber Company: Boise
Capital Lumber Company
5110 North 40th Street
Ste 242
Phoenix, AZ 85018

602-381-0709
Fax: 602-955-6191
E-Mail: info@capital-lumber.com
Home Page: www.capital-lumber.com
Social Media: Facebook, Twitter, LinkedIn, Pinterest

Dan Merrill, Division Manager
Bill Bieker, Sales Manager

Serves Idaho with a 10,000 square foot warehouse on a five acre site.
Founded in 1948

16490 Capital Lumber Company: Tacoma
Capital Lumber Company
5110 North 40th Street
Ste 242
Phoenix, AZ 85018

602-381-0709
866-479-5077
Fax: 602-955-6191
E-Mail: info@capital-lumber.com
Home Page: www.capital-lumber.com
Social Media: Facebook, Twitter, LinkedIn, Pinterest

Matt Yates, Division Manager
Jason Allen, Sales Manager
Eric Stout, Assistant Sales Manager
Sakhawat Amin, EWP Technical Supervisor
Darren Henderson, Operations Manager

Serves Western Washington, Alaska and Western Oregon through a seven acre asphalt covered yard and a 100,000 square foot fully enclosed warehouse.
Founded in 1948

16491 Cedar Shake and Shingle Bureau
Cedar Shake & Shingle Bureau
PO Box 1178
Sumas, WA 98295-1178

604-820-7700
Fax: 604-820-0266
E-Mail: info@cedarbureau.com
Home Page: www.cedarbureau.org
Social Media: Facebook, Twitter

Len Taylor Jr, Chairman
Bill Artigliere, Vice-chairman
Terry Wiens, Secretary-Treasurer
Lynne Christensen, MBA, CAE, Director of Operations
Barbara Enns, Accountant

Nonprofit trade association representing manufacturer's, distributors, approved installers and service suppliers of Certilabel™ cedar shakes and shingles.
350 Members
Founded in 1915

16492 Composite Panel Association
19465 Deerfield Avenue
Suite 306
Leesburg, VA 20176

703-724-1128
Fax: 703-724-1588
Home Page: www.compositepanel.org

Tom Julia, President
Donald Bisson, Vice President, Government
Jeannie Ervin, Vice President
Gary Heroux, Vice President, Product Acceptance
Chad Campbell, Director of Communication

Represents Northern American Particle Board and Manufacturers' sister association, Composite Wood Council. Represents manufacturers and suppliers of Composite Wood Council.
232 Members
Founded in 1960

16493 Fine Hardwood Veneer Association
American Walnut Manufacturers Association
260 S 1st Street
Suite 2
Zionsville, IN 46077

317-873-8780
Fax: 317-873-8788
E-Mail: FhvaAwmaWc@CompuServe.com
Home Page: www.h-i-solutions.com/wood/detail.htm

James Mathers, President
Larry R Frye, Executive Director

Represents the decorative veneer industry. Members are face veneer manufacturers, dealers, veneer custom cutters, rotary face and crossband manufacturers, hardwood industry suppliers, veneer salesman and veneer face plants.
15 Members
Founded in 1933

16494 Forest Industries Telecommunications
1565 Oak St
Eugene, OR 97401-4008

541-485-8441
Fax: 541-485-7556
E-Mail: license@landmobile.com
Home Page: www.landmobile.com

Kevin Mc Carthy, President

Organized to assist the forest industry in radio matters before the FCC.
600 Members
Founded in 1947

16495 Forest Landowners Association
900 Circle 75 Pkwy SE
Suite 205
Atlanta, GA 30339-3075

404-325-2954
800-325-2954
Fax: 404-325-2955
E-Mail: info@forestlandowners.com
Home Page: www.forestlandowners.com
Social Media: Facebook, Twitter

Joe Hopkins, President
Scott P. Jones, Chief Executive Officer
Susan Johnson Klco, Director of Administration

Kent Sole, Director of Development
Katelin Baker, Marketing Coordinator

Proactive, progressive, grassroots organization of timberland owners - large and small - who operate more than 47 million acres of timberland in 17 southern and eastern states.
10500 Members
Founded in 1941
Mailing list available for rent

16496 Forest Products Society
15 Technology Parkway South
Ste. 115
Peachtree Corners, GA 30092

855-475-0291
Fax: 608-231-2152
E-Mail: info@forestprod.org
Home Page: www.forestprod.org
Social Media: Facebook, Twitter, LinkedIn

Tim M. Young, PhD, President
Maureen Puettman, Vice President
Stefan A. Bergmann, Executive Vice President

An international non-profit technical association founded to provide an information network for all segments of the forest products industry.
Founded in 1947

16497 Forest Products Trucking Council
1025 Vermont Avenue NW
Suite 1020
Washington, DC 20005-3516

202-149-9250

Douglas Domenech, Secretary

An affiliate of the American Pulpwood Association.
50 Members

16498 Friends of the Trees
PO Box 165
Hot Springs, MT 59845

406-741-5809
E-Mail: michael@friendsofthetrees.net
Home Page: www.friendsofthetrees.net

Nicole D' Onofrio, President
Founded in 1978
Mailing list available for rent

16499 Great Lakes Timber Professionals Association
3243 Golf Course Road
PO Box 1278
Rhinelander, WI 54501-1278

715-282-5828
Fax: 715-282-4941
E-Mail: info@timberpa.com
Home Page: www.timberpa.com

Mark Huempfner, President
Guy Longhini, Vice President
Matt Jensen, Vice President
Henry Schienebeck, Executive Director
Aaron Nieman, Event Coordinator

A nonprofit organization that is committed to leading the Forest Products industry in sustainable forest management through advocacy, professionalism, service to members, education and training.

16500 Hall-Woolford Tank Company, Inc.
5500 N. Water Street
PO Box 2755
Philadelphia, PA 19120

215-329-9022
Fax: 215-329-1177
E-Mail: jackhillman@woodtank.com
Home Page: www.woodtank.com

Jack Hillman, Company Contact

To promote the use and to guide the proper construction methods for wooden tanks as per NWTI S-82.
Founded in 1854

16501 Hardwood Manufacturers Association
Hardwood Manufacturers Association
665 Rodi Road
Suite 305
Pittsburgh, PA 15235

412-244-0440
Fax: 412-244-9090
Home Page: www.hardwoodinfo.com
Social Media: Facebook, Twitter, Youtube, Pinterest

Susan M Regan, Executive VP

Over 100 companies with over 150 locations in the US.
55 Members

16502 Hardwood Plywood and Veneer Association
1825 Michael Faraday Dr
Reston, VA 20190-5350

703-435-2900
Fax: 703-435-2537
E-Mail: hpva@hpva.org
Home Page: www.hpva.org

Kip Howlett, HPVA President
Eva Mentel, Office Manager
Ketti Tyree, Membership and Conventions Manager
Matthew Windt, Marketing Manager

Provides public relations, advertising, marketing, and technical services to manufacturers and distributors of hardwood plywood, veneers and engineered hardwood flooring and suppliers who sell to these industries.
73 Members
Founded in 1921

16503 Hardwood Utilization Consortium
USDA Forest Service
Southern Research Station
Blacksburg, VA 24061-0503

540-231-5341
Fax: 540-231-8868
E-Mail: paraman@vt.edu
Home Page: www.consortium.forprod.vt.edu

Philip Araman, President

The role is to improve hardwood resource viability through better utilization, technology, markets, cooperative extension and education in the eastern United States.

16504 Hearth, Patio & Barbecue Association
1901 N Moore St
Suite 600
Arlington, VA 22209-1708

703-522-0086
Fax: 703-522-0548
Home Page: www.hpba.org
Social Media: Facebook, Twitter

Chet Goldman, CEO
Carter Keithley, CEO
Leslie Wheeler, Director Communications
2600 Members
Founded in 1980

16505 Intermountain Forest Association
2218 Jackson Blvd
#10
Rapid City, SD 57702

605-341-0875
Fax: 605-341-8651
E-Mail: info@intforest.org
Home Page: www.intforest.org

Tom Troxel, Executive Director
Ben Wudtke, Forest Programs Manager

Seeks to provide a unified voice for the industry. Promotes a sustained timber yield. Monitors federal legislation.
Founded in 1986

16506 International Wood Products Association
4214 King St
Alexandria, VA 22302-1555

703-820-6696
Fax: 703-820-8550
E-Mail: info@iwpawood.org
Home Page: www.iwpawood.org
Social Media: Facebook, Twitter, LinkedIn

Cindy Newman, President
Chris Connellyÿ, Vice President
Craig Forester, Treasurer
Cindy L Squires, Esq., Executive Director
Ashley A Amidon, Manager, Government

International trade association for the North American imported wood products industry, representing companies and trade organizations engaged in the import of hardwoods and softwoods from sustainably managed forests in more than 30 nations across the globe.
220 Members
Founded in 1956

16507 Laminating Materials Association
Louisiana Municipal Association
700 North 10th street
Baton Rouge, LA 70802

225-344-5001
800-234-8274
Fax: 225-344-3057
E-Mail: infor@lma.org
Home Page: www.lma.org

Tom Ed McHugh, Executive Director
Ronnie C Harris, Executive Director Elect
Brett Kriger, Deputy Director
Donald W Nijoka, Deputy Director
Penny Ambeau-Scott, General Staff

Nonprofit trade group representing all decorative overlays and edgebanding in North America. These products are applied to a composite wood substrate and used in the production of furniture, store fixtures, kitchen cabinets and more.
Founded in 1926

16508 Lumbermen's Credit Association
20 N Wacker Dr
Suite 1800
Chicago, IL 60606-2905

312-553-0943
Fax: 312-553-2149
Home Page: www.lumbermenscredit.com

Steven Smith, President/Director
Elliott Smith, VP
Richard J Arde, Secretary/Treasurer

Assist credit managers and salesmen by providing listings and credit ratings of companies which deal in lumber and wood products. Also publishes a directory.
Founded in 1876

16509 MSR Lumber Producers Council
MSR Lumber Producers Council
6300 Enterprise Lane
Madison, WI 53719

888-848-5339
Fax: 888-212-5110
E-Mail: info@msrlumber.org
Home Page: www.msrlumber.org

Dan Uskoski, President
Stacy Tiefenbach, Secretary/Treasurer
Sean Shields, Business Manager

Represents the interest of Machine Stress Rated Lumber Producers in the manufacturing, mar-

keting, promotion, utilization and technical aspects of machine stress rated lumber.
Founded in 1987

16510 **Maple Flooring Manufacturers Association**
Maple Flooring Manufacturers Association
111 Deer Lake Road
Suite 100
Deerfield, IL 60015

847-480-9138
888-480-9138
Fax: 847-480-9282
E-Mail: mfma@maplefloor.org
Home Page: www.maplefloor.org
Social Media: Facebook, Twitter

Kevin Hacke, Executive Director

International non-profit trade organization representing manufacturers of northern hard maple solid strip flooring along with flooring contractors, distributors and providers of instalation-related products and services. Maintains technical standards for product quality, grading, shipping and packaging, and quality central.
175 Members
Founded in 1897

16511 **National Association of the Remodeling Industry**
P.O. Box 4250
Des Plaines, IL 60016

847-298-9200
800-611-6274
Fax: 847-298-9225
E-Mail: info@nari.org
Home Page: www.nari.org
Social Media: Facebook, Twitter, Google+

Dean Herriges, MCR, CKBR, Chairman
Art Donnelly, MCR, CKBR, President
Mary Busey Harris, CAE Executive Vice President
Elsie Iturralde, CAE, Chief Operations Officer
Dan Taddei, Director of Education

Purpose is to establish and maintain a firm commitment to developing and sustaining programs that expand and unite the remodeling industry; to ensure the industry's growth and security; to encourage ethical conduct, sound business practices and professionalism in the remodeling industry; and to present NARI as the recognized authority in the remodeling industry.
Founded in 1983

16512 **National Food Flooring Association**
111 Chesterfield Industrial Boulevard
Suite B
Chesterfield, MO 63005

636-519-9663
800-422-4556
636-519-9663
Fax: 636-519-9664
E-Mail: info@nofma.org
Home Page: www.nofma.org
Social Media: Facebook, Twitter, LinkedIn

John Lessick, Chairman
Jeff Fairbanks, Vice Chairman
Michael Martin, President & CEO
Anita Howard, COO
Bree Urech-Boyle, CFO

It's warmer with wood. Genuine hardwoods, plus one-of-a-kind beauty. You never get tired of solid hardware floors - provides the perfect setting.
27 Members
Founded in 1908

16513 **National Frame Builders Association**
8735 W Higgins Road
Suite 300
Chicago, IL 60631

785-843-2444
800-557-6957
Fax: 847-375-6495
E-Mail: info@nfba.org
Home Page: www.nfba.org
Social Media: Facebook

Rick Hess, Chair
Greg Lehman, Secretary-Treasurer
Mike Dunipace, Director
Dan Nyberg, Director
Terry Burrow, Director

Building contractors, suppliers, design and code professionals and academic personnel specializing in the post frame construction industry.
Founded in 1969

16514 **National Hardwood Lumber Association**
National Hardwood Lumber Association
6830 Raleigh Lagrange Road
Memphis, TN 38184

901-377-1818
800-933-0318
E-Mail: membership@nhla.com
Home Page: www.nhla.com
Social Media: Facebook, Twitter, LinkedIn, RSS

Scott Heidler, President
Pem Jenkins, 1st Vice President
Mark Barford, Executive Director
Lisa Browne, Convention Director
Trisha Clariana, Office Manager

Founded to establish a uniform system of grading rules for the measurement and inspection of hardwood lumber
1600 Members
Founded in 1898

16515 **National Lumber and Building Material Dealers Association**
2025 M St NW
Suite 800
Washington, DC 20036-3309

202-367-1169
800-634-8645
Fax: 202-367-2169
E-Mail: info@dealer.org
Home Page: www.dealer.org
Social Media: Facebook, Twitter, LinkedIn

Chuck Bankston, Chair
Michael O'Brien, President/CEO
Jonathan M. Paine, Chief Operations Officer
Ben Gann, Director of Legislative Affairs
Stephen Kendrick, Communications & Operations

To advance the national agenda for America's building material suppliers.
6000 Members
Founded in 1916

16516 **National Wood Flooring Association**
111 Chesterfield Industrial
Suite B
Chesterfield, MO 63005-1219

636-519-9663
800-422-4556
Fax: 636-519-9664
E-Mail: info@nwfa.org
Home Page: www.nwfa.org
Social Media: Facebook, Twitter, LinkedIn

Michael Martin, President & CEO
Anita Howard, COO
Bree Urech-Boyle, CFO
Debbie Edgar, Human Resources Manager
Heather Wegge, Director of Conventions

A not-for-profit trade association serving the wood flooring industry
3000 Members
Founded in 1985

16517 **National Wood Window and Door Association**
330 N. Wabash Avenue
Suite 2000
Chicago, IL 60611-4267

312-321-6802
Fax: 847-299-1286
E-Mail: wdma@wdma.com
Home Page: www.wdma.com
Social Media: Facebook, Twitter, LinkedIn, RSS Feeds

Mike Salsieder, Chairman
Michael O'Brien, CAE, President & CEO
John McFee, Vice President, Certification
Jeff Lowinski, Vice President, Technical Services
Jeffrey Inks, Vice President, Code & Regulatory

Members are makers of standard building products such as doors, windows and frames.
140 Members
Founded in 1926

16518 **National Wooden Pallet & Container Association**
1421 Prince Street
Suite 340
Alexandria, VA 22314-2805

703-519-6104
Fax: 703-519-4720
E-Mail: pjsherry@nepapallet.com
Home Page: www.palletcentral.com
Social Media: Facebook, Twitter, LinkedIn, Google+

Brent J. McClendon, CAE, President/CEO
Isabel Sullivan, Vice President of Operations
Karen Wanamaker, Vice President of Industry
John A. McLeod III, Director
Annette Ferri, Communication and Education Dir

An advocacy organization communicating regularly with key lawmakers and regulators, collaborating with a broad network of business groups and wood product organizations.
700+ Members
Founded in 1947

16519 **New England Kiln Drying Association**
SUNY
200A Progress Drive Ext,
Burgaw, NC 28425

910-259-9794
Fax: 910-259-1625
E-Mail: sales@kiln-direct.com
Home Page: www.kiln-direct.com

William Smith, Executive Director

Disseminates information on the dying of wood to the wood-using industry.
650 Members
Founded in 1951

16520 **North American Wholesale Lumber Association**
3601 Algonquin Road
Suite 400
Rolling Meadows, IL 60008

847-870-7470
800-527-8258
Fax: 847-870-0201
E-Mail: info@nawla.org
Home Page: www.nawla.org
Social Media: Facebook, Twitter, LinkedIn

Mike Phillips, Chairman
Rick Ekstein, First Vice Chairman
Scott Elston, Second Vice Chairman

Gary Vitale, President/CEO
Jennifer Chan, Accountant

Supports the wholesale lumber industry. Publishes monthly NAWLA Bulletin that includes industry and association news, and produces the NAWLA Traders Market, an annual trade show bringing together over 1500 manufacturers and wholesale lumber traders at the premier event in the forest products industry. NAWLA also produces a variety of educational programs designed to enhance professionalism in the lumber industry.
600+ Members
Founded in 1893

16521 Northeastern Loggers Association
3311 State Route 28
PO Box 69
Old Forge, NY 13420-0069

315-369-3078
800-318-7561
Fax: 315-369-3736
E-Mail: nela@northernlogger.com
Home Page: www.northernlogger.com

Joseph E. Phaneuf, Executive Director
Eric A Johnson, Executive Editor
Mona Lincoln, Coordinator of Training and Safety
Debbie Haehl, Advertising Manager
Nancy E. Petrie, Circulation Manager

Works to improve the industry in the Northeast and educate the public about policies and products of the industry.
2000 Members
Founded in 1952

16522 Northern Woods Logging Association
PO Box 270
Jackman, ME 04945-0270

Provides members with a workers compensation protection program. Conducts on-site inspections and offers a first aid course and safety training program.
213 Members
Founded in 1974

16523 Northwest Forestry Association
1500 SW 1st Ave
Suite 700
Portland, OR 97201-5837

503-222-9505
Fax: 503-222-3255
Home Page: www.nwtrees.org

Tom Partin, President

Promotes forestry throughout the region to assure a permanent industry and stable economy. Works to keep informed on current changes affecting forest products.
70 Members
Founded in 1987

16524 Northwestern Lumber Association
Northwestern Lumber Association
5905 Golden Valley Road
Suite 110
Minneapolis, MN 55422-4535

763-544-6822
888-544-6822
Fax: 763-595-4060
E-Mail: info@nlassn.org
Home Page: www.nlassn.org
Social Media: Facebook

Jeff Reinhardt, Chairman of the Board
Paula Siewert, President & Secretary
Cody Nuernberg, Interim Director & Board Liaison
Jodie Fleck, Director of Conventions & Tours
Sue Jones, Accountant/ Office Manager

Retail lumber dealer in Iowa, Minnesota, North Dakota, and South Dakota.
1.5M Members
Founded in 1890
Mailing list available for rent

16525 OSBGuide
Structural Board Association
25 Valleywood Drive
Unit 27
Markham, L3R 5L9, ON

905-475-1100
Fax: 905-475-1101
E-Mail: osbguide@tecotested.com
Home Page: osbguide.tecotested.com

Members are manufacturers of structural panels.
Founded in 1978

16526 Pacific Logging Congress
Pacific Logging Congress
PO Box 1281
Maple Valley, WA 98038

425-413-2808
Fax: 425-413-1359
E-Mail: rikki@pacificloggingcongress.com
Home Page: www.pacificloggingcongress.com
Social Media: Facebook, Twitter

Rikki Wellman, Executive Director
Craig Olson, President
Ron Simon, Treasurer

Logging firms.
550 Members
Founded in 1909

16527 Pacific Lumber Exporters Association
678 SW Foresta Terrace
Portland, OR 97225

503-467-5271
Fax: 503-467-5273
E-Mail: info@lumber-exporters.org
Home Page: www.lumber-exporters.org

Provide forum to discuss trade issues and problems; promote member companies through governmental and other trade association channels.
Founded in 1923

16528 Pacific Lumber Inspection Bureau
Pacific Lumber Inspection Bureau
1010 S 336th St
Suite 300
Federal Way, WA 98003-7355

253-835-3344
Fax: 253-835-3371
E-Mail: info@plib.org
Home Page: www.plib.org

Dave Poggemoeller, President
Eric Fritch, VP
Jeff Fantozzi, Secretary-Manager/Treasurer
Ben Haynes, Technical & Special Programs
Hannah Petersen, Accounting & Benefits Administrator

Accredited for grading and grade stamping of softwood lumber. Issues certificates on domestic and export lumber shipments.
65 Members
Founded in 1903

16529 Pennsylvania Forest Products Association
301 Chestnut Street
Suite 102
Harrisburg, PA 17101

717-901-0420
800-232-4562
Fax: 717-901-0360
E-Mail: pfpa@paforestproducts.org
Home Page: www.paforestproducts.org

Alan Metzler, Chairman
Terry Stockdale, Vice-Chairman
Paul Lyskava, Executive Director
Michelle McManus, Business Manager
Bob Long, Membership Representative

Created to provide members with a unified voice on state legislative and regulatory issues.
Founded in 1980

16530 Railway Tie Association
Railway Tie Association
115 Commerce Dr
Suite C
Fayetteville, GA 30214-7335

770-460-5553
Fax: 770-460-5573
E-Mail: ties@rta.org
Home Page: www.rta.org

James Gauntt, Executive Director

Members include crosstie producers, sawmill owners, chemical manufacturers, wood preservation companies, railroad maintenance engineers, purchasing officials and others.
2500 Members
Founded in 1919

16531 Redwood Inspection Service
818 Grayson Road
Suite 201
Pleasant Hill, CA 94523

925-935-1499
888-225-7339
Fax: 925-935-1496
E-Mail: info@calredwood.org
Home Page: www.calredwood.org
Social Media: Youtube

Christopher Grover, President

Authorized by Department of Commerce to develop and supervise redwood lumber grading.
Founded in 1916

16532 Society of American Foresters
5400 Grosvenor Lane
Bethesda, MD 20814-2198

301-897-8720
866-897-8720
Fax: 301-897-3690
E-Mail: membership@safnet.org
Home Page: www.safnet.org
Social Media: Facebook, Twitter, LinkedIn

Provides access to information and networking opportunities to prepare members for the challenges and the changes that face natural resource professionals.
Founded in 1900

16533 Society of Wood Science & Technology
PO Box 6155
Monona, WI 53716-6155

608-577-1342
Fax: 608-467-8979
E-Mail: vicki@swst.org
Home Page: www.swst.org
Social Media: Facebook

Sheldon Shi, President
Eric Hansen, Vice-President
Vicki L. Herian, Executive Director
H. Michael Barnes, Editor of Wood and Fiber Science
Barb Hogan, Editorial Assistant

Promotes policies and procedures which assure the wise use of wood and wood-based products; assures high standards for professional performance of wood scientists and technologists; fosters educational programs at all levels of wood science and technology and further the

quality of such programs; represents the profession in public policy development.
450 Members
Founded in 1958

16534 Southeastern Lumber Manufacturers Association, Inc.
Southeastern Lumber Manufacturers
200 Greencastle Road
Tyrone, GA 30290

770-631-6701
Fax: 770-631-6720
Home Page: www.slma.org

Bryan Smalley, President
Alexis Sivcovich, Member Services Coordinator
Beverly Knight, Accounting Manager
Will Telligman, Government Affairs Manager

Represents membership in local, regional, and national problems that affect southeastern lumber industry. Conducts marketing and promotional activity.
350 Members
Founded in 1962

16535 Southern Cypress Manufacturers Association
Southern Cypress Manufacturers Association
400 Penn Center Boulevard
Suite 530
Pittsburgh, PA 15235

877-607-7262
Home Page: www.cypressinfo.org
Social Media: Facebook, Youtube

Administrative support provided by the Hardwood Manufacturers Association.
19 Members
Founded in 1905
Mailing list available for rent

16536 Southern Forest Products Association
2900 Indiana Ave
Kenner, LA 70065-4605

504-443-4464
Fax: 504-443-6612
E-Mail: mail@sfpa.org
Home Page: www.sfpa.org
Social Media: Twitter, Youtube

Adrian Blocker, President

The Association and its members are committed to quality, and believe that Southern Pine forest products provide a smart, environmentally friendly way to meet our world's needs for a wide range of building and industrial products.
265 Members
Founded in 1915

16537 Southern Pine Inspection Bureau
Southern Pine Inspection Bureau
Po Box 10915
Pensacola, FL 32524-0915

850-434-2611
Fax: 850-433-5594
E-Mail: spib@spib.org
Home Page: www.spib.org

Kim Merritt, Operations Manager
Tom Jones, Executive Director

Develops grading standards for Southern pine lumber and provides an inspection service and grade marking systems.
Founded in 1940
Mailing list available for rent

16538 Temperate Forest Foundation
528 Hennepin Avenue
Suite 703
Minneapolis, MN 55403

612-333-0430
Fax: 612-333-0432
E-Mail: info@forestinfo.org
Home Page: www.forestinfo.org

Robert M Owens, Chairman
Lee F Freeman, President & CEO

A tax-exempt, non-profit, public charity. Provides leadership by articulating the current realties, and a positive inspiring vision of the future. Helps people move toward the positive vision of living sustainably.
Founded in 1989

16539 Timber Products Manufacturers Association (TPM)
951 E 3rd Avenue
Spokane, WA 99202-2287

509-535-4646
Fax: 509-534-6106
E-Mail: tpm@tpmrs.com
Home Page: www.timberassociation.com

Russ Vaagen, Chairman
Tom Shaffer, Vice Chairman
Adam Molenda, President
Chris Chathams, Safety Resource Director
Jolene Skjothaug, Office Manager

Association of companies in the Timber and Wood products industry of the pacific northwest. TPM provides human resource and safety consulting, Training and employee benefits.
250 Members
Founded in 1916

16540 Tree Care Industry Association
Tree Care Industry Association
136 Harvey Road
Suite 101
Londonderry, NH 03053

603-314-5380
800-733-2622
Fax: 603-314-5386
E-Mail: tcia@tcia.org
Home Page: www.tcia.org/
Social Media: Facebook, Twitter, LinkedIn, Youtube

Benjamin G Tresselt, III, Chair
Mark Garvin, President
Bob Rouse, Chief Program Officer
Sarah Winslow, Director of Development
William P Maleyÿ, Vice Chair

Supports all those involved with trees and tree care by offering education and training, community events, and publications.
2000 Members
Founded in 1938
Mailing list available for rent

16541 Truss Plate Institute
218 North Lee Street
Suite 312
Alexandria, VA 22314-2800

703-683-1010
Fax: 866-501-4012
E-Mail: info@tpinst.org
Home Page: www.tpinst.org

Michael A Cassidy, Executive Director

The Truss Plate Institute's mission is '...to maintain the truss industry on a sound engineering basis..'. To accomplish its mission, TPI establishes methods of design and construction for trusses in accordance with the American National Standards Institute's accredited consensus procedures for coordination and development of American National Standards in addition to providing a Quality Assurance Inspection program and by contributing its expertise in other technical areas.
300 Members
Founded in 1961

16542 West Coast Lumber Inspection Bureau
PO Box 23145
Portland, OR 97281-3145

503-639-0651
Fax: 503-684-8928
E-Mail: info@wclib.org
Home Page: www.wclib.org

Ted Stock, President
Rod Lucas, Vice President
Don DeVisser, Exec. Vice Pres.
John Konecny, Sec./Treasurer

Supervises manufacturing practices, grade stamping, and inspecting.
189 Members
Founded in 1941

16543 Western Building Material Association
Western Building Material Association
909 Lakcridge Dr. SW
Olympia, WA 98502

360-943-3054
888-551-9262
Fax: 360 943-1219
E-Mail: casey@wbma.org
Home Page: www.wbma.org

Tom Simkins, President
Justin Boyer, VP
Jason Crist, Secretary-Treasurer

Regional trade association derving building material dealers throughout the states of Alaska, Idaho, Montana, Oregon and Washington and a federated association of the National Lumber and Building Material Dealers Association.
600 Members

16544 Western Forestry and Conservation Association
4033 SW Canyon Rd
Portland, OR 97221

503-226-4562
888-722-9416
Fax: 503-226-2515
E-Mail: richard@westernforestry.org
Home Page: www.westernforestry.org

Richard Zabel, Executive Director

Offers high-quality continuing education workshops and seminars for professional foresters throughout Oregon, Washington, Idaho, Montana, Northern California and British Columbia.
125 Members
Founded in 1909
Mailing list available for rent

16545 Western Red Cedar Lumber Association
Western Red Cedar Lumber Association
1501-700 West Pender Street
Pender Place 1, Business Building
Vancouver, BC V6C 1G8

604-891-1262
800-266-1910
Fax: 604-687-4930
E-Mail: wrcla@wrcla.org
Home Page: ww.realcedar.com
Social Media: Facebook, Twitter, Youtube, Pinterest

Peter Lang, General Manager
Edward Burke, Eastern Field Representative

Mission is to produce quality Western Red Cedar lumber products and support them with technical education and promotion.
Founded in 1954

16546 Western Wood Products Association
522 Sw 5th Ave
Suite 500
Portland, OR 97204-2122

503-224-3930
Fax: 503-224-3934
E-Mail: info@wwpa.org
Home Page: www2.wwpa.org

Michael O'Halloran, President
Tom Hanneman, VP/Director
Robert Bernhardt Jr, Director Information Services
Kevin CK Cheung, Director Technical Services
Kevin Binam, Director Economic Services

Represents lumber manufacturers in 12 Western states and Alaska. Provides lumber quality control, technical support, and business information to supporting mills.
135 Members
Founded in 1964

16547 Window & Door Manufacturers Association
Window & Door Manufacturers Association
330 N. Wabash Avenue
Suite 2000
Chicago, IL 60611-4267

312-321-6802
800-223-2301
Fax: 847-299-1286
E-Mail: wdma@wdma.com
Home Page: www.wdma.com
Social Media: Facebook, Twitter, LinkedIn, RSS

Michael O'Brien, CAE, President & CEO
Jeff Lowinski, Vice President, Technical Services
Jeffrey Inks, Vice President, Code & Regulatory
John McFee, Vice President
Jonathan Paine, Chief Operations Operations

A trade association representing approximately 145 U.S. and Canadian manufacturers and suppliers of windows and doors for the domestic and export markiets.

16548 Wood Component Manufacturers Association
Wood Component Manufacturers Association
5353 Wayzata Blvd
Ste 350
Minneapolis, MN 55416

952-564-3046
Fax: 952-252-8096
E-Mail: wcma@woodcomponents.org
Home Page: www.woodcomponents.org

Steven V Lawser, Executive Director

Represents manufacturers of wood component products for furniture, cabinetry, building products, and decorative wood products.
Founded in 1929

16549 Wood Machinery Maufacturers of America
Wood Machinery Maufacturers of America
2105 Laurel Bush Road
Suite 201
Bel Air, MD 21015

443-640-1052
Fax: 443-640-1031
E-Mail: info@wmma.org
Home Page: www.wmma.org
Social Media: Facebook, Twitter, LinkedIn

John Schultz, President
Jamison Scott, Vice President
Fred Stringfellow, Executive Director
Diane Schafer, Director of Meetings
Amy Chetelat, Director of Finance

WMMA has worked to increase the productivity and profitability of U.S. machinery and tooling manufacturers and the businesses that support them.
Founded in 1899

16550 Wood Moulding and Millwork Producers Association
MMPA
507 1st St
Woodland, CA 95695-4025

530-661-9591
800-550-7889
Fax: 530-661-9586
E-Mail: info@wmmpa.com
Home Page: www.wmmpa.com
Social Media: Facebook

Al Delbridge, President
Pete Delaney, VP
Jim Cadwell, 2nd Vice President
Kellie Schroeder, CMP, CAE, CEO / Exec. VP
Melissa Leal, Director Of Programs & Finance

Promote quality products produced by its members, to develop sources of supply, to promote optimum use of raw materials to standardize products, and to increase the domestic and foreign usage of moulding and millwork products.

16551 Woodworking Machinery Industry Association
27 Main St.
Suite One
New Milford, CT 06776

860-350-9642
Fax: 860-354-0677
E-Mail: info@wmia.org
Home Page: www.wmia.org
Social Media: Twitter

John Park, President
Scott Mueller, Vice President
Riccardo Azzoni, Executive Vice President
Liza Wentworth, Program Administrator
Dave Rakauskas, Secretary/Treasurer

Providing the North American wood products industry with technologically advanced woodworking systems available in the global market. A wide range of special programs provide industry awards, safety publications, scholarships and a host of other methods to support industry initiatives and address industry issues.
Founded in 1977

Newsletters

16552 American Wood Protection Association Newsletter
American Wood Protection Association
100 Chase Park South
Suite 116
Birmingham, AL 35244-1851

205-733-4077
Fax: 205-733-4075
E-Mail: info@awpa.com
Home Page: www.awpa.com

John Hall, Publisher

Reports on governmental issues and environmental news.
Cost: $7.50
12 Pages
Frequency: Monthly
Founded in 1921

16553 Association of Millwork Distributors Newsletter
Association Of Millwork Distributors
10047 Robert Trent Jones Pkwy
Trinity, FL 34655-4649

727-372-3665
800-786-7274
Fax: 727-372-2879
E-Mail: marketing@amdweb.com
Home Page: www.amdweb.com/

Rosalie Leone, CEO
Kim Cotterman, Director of Membership

Updates for wholesale millwork distribution companies.
Frequency: Monthly
Circulation: 1500
Founded in 1964
Printed in 2 colors on glossy stock

16554 Building Products CONNECTION
Northwestern Lumber Association
5905 Golden Valley Road
Suite 110
Minneapolis, MN 55422-4535

763-544-6822
888-544-6822
Fax: 763-595-4060
E-Mail: info@nlassn.org
Home Page: www.nlassn.org

Beth Stoll, Editor
Jodie Fleck, Director of Conventions & Tours
Cody Nuernberg, Manager of Membership

Dedicated to providing information on issues important to the success of the lumber and building material industry in the upper Midwest.
Cost: $300.00
Frequency: Bi-Monthly
Circulation: 2200
Mailing list available for rent

16555 Classified Exchange
Miller Publishing Corporation
PO Box 34908
Memphis, TN 38184-0908

901-372-8280
800-844-1280
Fax: 901-373-6180
E-Mail: editor@millerwoodtradepub.com
Home Page: www.millerpublishing.com

Paul J Miller, President
Sue Putnam, Editor

Pages and pages of bargains, several pages on raw material and service sources for everything from lumber to curved plywood, from dry kilns to sawmill equipment and boilers. Special liquidations and auctions offering everything from soup to nuts.
Cost: $65.00
Frequency: Monthly

16556 Connected
Association of Millwork Distributors
10047 Robert Trent Jones Pkwy
Trinity, FL 34655-4649

727-372-3665
800-786-7274
Fax: 727-372-2879
E-Mail: marketing@amdweb.com
Home Page: www.amdweb.com

Rosalie Leone, CEO

Keeps you abreast of the latest breaking news within the millwork industry regarding economics & finance; the current housing indus-

try; legislative updates; codes, standards and the AMD Certification Program information, Education special offers as well as comprehensive Millwork News.
Frequency: Weekly

16557 **Forestbytes**
American Forests
734 15th Street NW
Suite 800
Washington, DC 20005

202-737-1944
Home Page: www.americanforests.org
Social Media: Facebook, Twitter

Lynda Webster, Chair
Scott Steen, CEO

Features environmental stories and breakthroughs that impact our forests and trees and news and updates on American Forests projects and programs.
Frequency: Monthly
Founded in 1990

16558 **Forestry Source**
Society of American Foresters
5400 Grosvenor Ln
Bethesda, MD 20814-2198

301-897-8720
Fax: 301-897-3690
E-Mail: safweb@safnet.org
Home Page: www.safnet.org
Social Media: Facebook, Twitter, LinkedIn

Michael T Goergen Jr, Executive VP/CEO
Joe Smith, Editor

Offers the latest information on national forestry trends, the latest developments in forestry at the federal, state, and local levels, the newest advances in forestry-related research and technology, and up-to-date information about SAF programs and activities.
Cost: $33.00
Frequency: Monthly
Founded in 1900
Printed in 4 colors

16559 **Import/Export Wood Purchasing News**
Miller Publishing Corporation
PO Box 34908
Memphis, TN 38184-0908

901-372-8280
800-844-1280
Fax: 901-373-6180
E-Mail: editor@millerwoodtradepub.com
Home Page: www.millerpublishing.com

Paul J Miller, President
Sue Putnam, Editor

Read features about overseas buyers, U.S. factories buying imported forest products and North American exporters. Also carries forest products business trends on the domestic and international markets.
Cost: $75.00
Frequency: Bi-Monthly

16560 **MSR Council Matters**
MSR Lumber Producers Council
6300 Enterprise Lane
Madison, WI 53719
888-848-5339
Fax: 888-212-5110
E-Mail: info@msrlumber.org
Home Page: www.msrlumber.org

Steve Hardy, President

Provides updates on issues affecting members and customers
Frequency: Monthly
Founded in 1987

16561 **National Frame Builders Association Newsletter**
National Frame Builders Association
4700 W. Lake Avenue
Glenview, IL 60025

785-843-2444
800-557-6957
Fax: 847-375-6495
E-Mail: info@nfba.org
Home Page: www.nfba.org

John Fullerton, VP
Tom Knight, President

Published by the National Frame Builders Association.

16562 **National Wooden Pallet & Container Association: Newsletter**
National Wooden Pallet & Container Association
1421 Prince Street
Suite 340
Alexandria, VA 22314-3501

703-519-6104
Fax: 703-519-4720
E-Mail: palletcomm@aol.com
Home Page: www.nwpca.com

Bruce N Scholnick, President
Pamela Wilson, Publisher
Kathy Conroy, Marketing Director
Sam McAdow, Interim President
Susan Cheney, Membership Coordinator

Newsletter published by The National Wooden Pallet and Container Association.
Cost: $2995.00

16563 **SFPA E-Newsletter**
Southern Forest Products Association
2900 Indiana Ave
Kenner, LA 70065-4605

504-443-4464
Fax: 504-443-6612
E-Mail: mail@sfpa.org
Home Page: www.sfpa.org

Digges Morgan, President
Richard Wallace, VP Communications
Tami Kessler, Corporate Secretary
Stephen P. Conwell, President
Tami Kessler, Corporate Secretary & Director

The Association and its members are committed to quality, and believe that Southern Pine forest products provide a smart, environmentally friendly way to meet our world's needs for a wide range of building and industrial products.
265 Members
Frequency: Weekly/Online

16564 **Softwood Forest Products Buyer**
Miller Publishing Corporation
PO Box 34908
Memphis, TN 38184-0908

901-372-8280
800-844-1280
Fax: 901-373-6180
E-Mail: editor@millerwoodtradepub.com
Home Page: www.millerpublishing.com

Paul J Miller, President
Sue Putnam, Editor

Provides you with interesting feature articles on purchasing, inventory control, marketing, production, utilization and distribution of Softwood forest products such as lumber, plywood, moulding, etc.
Cost: $65.00
Frequency: Bi-Monthly

16565 **TPM Bulletin**
Timber Products Manufacturers Association
951 E 3rd Avenue
Spokane, WA 99202-2287

509-535-4646
Fax: 509-534-6106
E-Mail: tpm@tpmrs.com
Home Page: www.tpmrs.com

Dick Molenda, Interim President
Shelley Jeffers, Publications Coordinator

Provides insightful overviews of key employment issues that can impact every business.
Frequency: Monthly
Circulation: 250

16566 **TPM Newsletter**
Timber Products Manufacturers (TPM) Association
951 E 3rd Avenue
Spokane, WA 99202-2287

509-535-4646
Fax: 509-534-6106
E-Mail: tpm@tpmrs.com
Home Page: www.tpmrs.com

Dick MoLenda, Interim President
Jeff Bosma, Chairman

Official newsletter of Timber Products Manufacturers (TPM) Association.
Cost: $195.00
250 Members
Frequency: Monthly
Circulation: 700
Founded in 1916

16567 **Timberline**
Bear Creek Lumber
Po Box 669
Winthrop, WA 98862

800-597-7191
Fax: 509-997-2040
E-Mail: customerservice@bearcreeklumber.com
Home Page: www.bearcreeklumber.com
Social Media: Twitter, LinkedIn

Features articles about the timber industry, the construction industry, how-to information, and it also lets folks know what's new at Bear Creek Lumber.
Cost: $15.00
6000 Pages

16568 **TreeWorker**
Tree Care Industry Association
136 Harvey Road
Suite 101
Londonderry, NH 03053

603-314-5380
800-733-2622
Fax: 603-314-5386
E-Mail: tcia@tcia.org
Home Page: www.tcia.org
Social Media: Facebook, Twitter, LinkedIn, Youtube

Mark Garvin, Interim CEO/President
Peter Gerstenberger, Sr Adv Safety/Standards/Compliance
Frequency: Monthly
Founded in 1938

16569 **Two-By-Four**
Mountain States Lumber & Building Material Dealers
9034 E Easter Pl
#103
Centennial, CO 80112-2104

303-793-0859
800-365-0919
Fax: 303-290-9137
E-Mail: contact@mslbmda.org
Home Page: www.mslbmda.org

Geri Adams, Executive Director

16570 Wood Design Focus
Forest Products Society
2801 Marshall Court
Madison, WI 53705-2295

608-231-1361
Fax: 608-231-2152
E-Mail: info@forestprod.org
Home Page: www.forestprod.org
Social Media: Facebook, Twitter

Paul Merrick, President
Patrice Tardif, President-Elect
Timothy M. Young, Vice President
Stefan Bergmann, Executive Vice President

Online publication providing a communications link between design professionals, educators, reserachers, building code officials, and manufacturers of engineered wood products through the publication of technical articles related to contemporary engineered wood construction.
Cost: $125.00
Frequency: Quarterly
Founded in 1947

16571 Wood Machining News
Wood Machining Institute
PO Box 476
Berkeley, CA 94701

510-448-8363
Fax: 925-945-0947
E-Mail: szymani@woodmachining.com
Home Page: www.woodmachining.com

Ryszard Szymani, Editor
Ryszard Szymani, Director

Information on the latest technological advances in the field of wood machining, including sawing, planning and sanding operations as well as the production of veneers and chips.
Cost: $72.00
Frequency: Fortnightly
Circulation: 600
Founded in 1984

Magazines & Journals

16572 AMD Millwork Magazine
Association of Millwork Distributors
10047 Robert Trent Jones Pkwy
Trinity, FL 34655-4649

727-372-3665
800-786-7274
Fax: 727-372-2879
E-Mail: marketing@amdweb.com
Home Page: www.amdweb.com

Rosalie Leone, CEO

Digital news journal distributed to AMD members and industry professionals with an interest in the millwork industry. An inside look at the heartbeat of AMD and offers industry insights found nowhere else.
Frequency: Monthly

16573 American Forests
American Forests
734 15th Street NW
Suite 800
Washington, DC 20005

202-737-1944
Fax: 202-955-4588
Home Page: www.americanforests.org
Social Media: Facebook, Twitter

Deborah Gangloff, Executive Director
Lydia Scalettar, Art Director

Updates on forest management and environmental policy, as well as news on the programs and policies of the American Forests organization.
Cost: $25.00
Frequency: Quarterly
Circulation: 25000
Founded in 1875

16574 American Forests Magazine
American Forests
734 15th Street NW
Suite 800
Washington, DC 20005

202-737-1944
Home Page: www.americanforests.org
Social Media: Facebook, Twitter

Lynda Webster, Chair
Scott Steen, CEO

Topics covered include urban forestry methods and visiting champion trees, fighting invasive species and learning about the many incredible creatures that make their homes in forests.
Frequency: Bi-Annually
Founded in 1990

16575 Crossties
Railway Tie Association
115 Commerce Dr
Suite C
Fayetteville, GA 30214-7335

770-460-5553
Fax: 770-460-5573
E-Mail: ties@rta.org
Home Page: www.rta.org

Talty O'Connor, President/CEO

Highlights new products, industry news, and personnel changes.
Cost: $35.00
Circulation: 3000
Founded in 1983

16576 Crow's Weekly Market Report
CC Crow Publications
3635 N Farragut St
Portland, OR 97217-5954

503-241-7382
Fax: 503-646-9971
E-Mail: info@chadcrowe.com
Home Page: www.chadcrowe.com
Social Media: Facebook, Twitter, LinkedIn

Chad Crowe, President
Sam Sherrill, Editor

Tracks the wood and lumber industry, providing customers with accurate and timely pricing and analysis.
Cost: $285.00
Frequency: Weekly
Circulation: 2000
Founded in 1921
Mailing list available for rent

16577 Custom Woodworking Business
Vance Publishing
400 Knightsbridge Parkway
Lincolnshire, IL 60069

847-342-2600
800-343-2016
Fax: 847-634-4374
E-Mail: industrialinfo@vancepublishing.com
Home Page: www.iswonline.com
Social Media: Facebook, Twitter, Youtube

William C Vance, CEO
Helen Kuhl, Editor
Harry Urban, VP Publishing
Bill Esler, Associate Publisher/Editor-in-Chief
Rich Christianson, Associate Publisher/Editor-at-Large
Founded in 1937

16578 Design Solutions Magazine
Architectural Woodwork Institute
46179 Westlake Drive
Suite 120
Potomac Falls, VA 20165

571-323-3636
Fax: 571-323-3630
E-Mail: info@awinet.org
Home Page: www.awinet.org

Judy Durham, Executive VP
Philip Duvic, Marketing Director
Kirsten Ingham, President

Featuring beautiful woodwork projects manufactured by members of the Architectural Woodwork Institute (AWI). Many other related publications, including woodworking quality standards used by woodwork manufacturers and design professionals.
Cost: $25.00
Frequency: Quarterly
Circulation: 27000

16579 Evergreen Magazine
Evergreen Foundations
PO Box 1290
Bigfork, MT 59911

406-837-0966
Fax: 406-258-0815
E-Mail: editor@evergreenmagazine.com
Home Page: www.evergreenmagazine.com
Social Media: Facebook

James D Petersen, Publisher

Focuses on issues and events impacting forestry, forest communities, and the forest product industry. Includes profiles of industry leaders and advocates.
Frequency: Bi-Monthly
Circulation: 100000

16580 Fine Woodworking
Taunton Press
63 South Main Street
PO Box 5506
Newtown, CT 06470-2355

203-426-8171
800-477-8727
Fax: 203-426-3434
E-Mail: fwads@taunton.com
Home Page: www.taunton.com

James Chiavelli, Publisher
Richard West, Advertising Manager

Published since 1975, written by woodworkers for woodworkers regularly shows the finest work in wood being done today.
Cost: $34.95
120 Pages
Frequency: 7 Issues (1yr)
Circulation: 250000
Founded in 1980
Printed in 4 colors on glossy stock

16581 Forest Industries
Miller Freeman Publications
600 Harrison Street
6th Fl
San Francisco, CA 94107

415-947-6000
Fax: 415-947-6055
Home Page: www.mfi.com

Directed to foresters, loggers and manufacturers.
Cost: $55.00
90 Pages
Frequency: Monthly

16582 Forest Landowner Magazine
Forest Landowners Association
900 Circle 75 Pkwy Se
Suite 205
Atlanta, GA 30339-3075

404-325-2954
800-325-2954

Fax: 404-325-2955
E-Mail: info@forestlandowners.com
Home Page: www.forestlandowners.com

Scott P Jones, Executive VP
Joy Moore, Circulation Director

Provides members with applied, practical and current forestry information written by the most experienced and successful forestry professionals.
Cost: $50.00
Circulation: 9000
Founded in 1941

16583 Forest Products Journal
Forest Products Society
2801 Marshall Ct
Madison, WI 53705-2295

608-231-1361
Fax: 608-231-2152
E-Mail: info@forestprod.org
Home Page: www.forestprod.org
Social Media: Facebook, Twitter, LinkedIn

Carol Lewis, VP

Covers the latest research and technology from every branch of the forest products industry.
Cost: $155.00
Founded in 1945

16584 Forests and People
Louisiana Forestry Association
PO Drawer 5067
Alexandria, LA 71307

318-443-2558
Fax: 318-443-1713
E-Mail: jtompkins@laforestry.com
Home Page: www.laforestry.com
Social Media: Facebook, Twitter

Janet Tompkins, Editor
Mike Merritt, President
Buck Vandersteen, Executive Director
Karla Johnson, Admin. Assistant/Annual Meeting
Debbie Dodd, Membership/Tree Farm

Magazine
Cost: $250.00
36 Pages
Frequency: Quarterly
Circulation: 5800
ISSN: 0015-7589
Founded in 1947
Printed in 4 colors on glossy stock

16585 Frame Building News
National Frame Builders Association
4700 W. Lake Avenue
Glenview, IL 60025

785-843-2444
800-557-6957
Fax: 847-375-6495
E-Mail: info@nfba.org
Home Page: www.nfba.org
Social Media: Facebook

John Fullerton, VP
Tom Knight, President

The official publication of National Frame Builders Association.

16586 Great Lakes TPA Magazine
Great Lakes Timber Professionals Association
3243 Golf Course Road
PO Box 1278
Rhinelander, WI 54501-1278

715-282-5828
Fax: 715-282-4941
E-Mail: info@timberpa.com
Home Page: www.timberpa.com

Henry Schienebeck, Executive Director & Editor

The magazine provides education and information on the practice and promotion of sustainable forestry and seeks to instill a sense of pride and professionalism among manufacturers, operators, transporters, landowners, and foresters.
Cost: $24.00
Frequency: Monthly
Circulation: 2500

16587 Hardwood Floors
National Wood Flooring Association
111 Chesterfield Industrial
Chesterfield, MO 63005-1219

636-519-9663
800-422-4556
Fax: 636-519-9664
E-Mail: info@nwfa.org
Home Page: www.nwfa.org

Ed Korczak, Executive Director

An essential educational tool, with articles on everything from sanding and finishing techniques to industry trends and tips on running a profitable business.
Frequency: 6x/Year
Circulation: 25000

16588 International Journal of Forest Engineering
Forest Products Society
2801 Marshall Court
Madison, WI 53705-2295

608-231-1361
Fax: 608-231-2152
E-Mail: info@forestprod.org
Home Page: www.forestprod.org
Social Media: Facebook, Twitter

Paul Merrick, President
Patrice Tardif, President-Elect
Timothy M. Young, Vice President
Stefan Bergmann, Executive Vice President

Committed to serving the international forest engineering community as the voice of new ideas and developments in forest engineering. Reporting on existing practices and innovations in forest engineering by scientists and professionals from around the world which promote environmentally sound forestry practices and contribute to sustainable forest management.
Frequency: Semiannually
Founded in 1947

16589 International Wood: The Guide to Applications, Sources & Trends
International Wood Products Association
4214 King St
Alexandria, VA 22302-1555

703-820-6696
Fax: 703-820-8550
E-Mail: info@iwpawood.org
Home Page: www.iwpawood.org

Brent McClendon, Executive VP/CAE
Annette Ferri, Member Services
Brigid Shea, Government Affairs
Annette Ferri, Director, Finance & Administration
Ashley A. Amidon, Manager, Government

Formerly Imported Wood, International Wood continues to lead with innovative new designs and new product applications.
Frequency: Annual
Circulation: 25000

16590 Journal of Forestry
Society of American Foresters
5400 Grosvenor Ln
Bethesda, MD 20814-2198

301-897-8720
Fax: 301-897-3690
Home Page: www.safnet.org

Michael T Goergen Jr, Executive VP/CEO
Matthew Walls, Publications Dir/Managing Editor

To advance the profession of forestry by keeping professionals informed about significant developments and ideas in the many facets of forestry: economics, education and communication, entomology and pathology, fire, forest ecology, geospatial technologies, history, international forestry, measurments, policy, recreation, silviculture, social sciences, soils anf hydrology, urban and community forestry, utilization and engineering, and wildlife management.
Cost: $85.00
Frequency: 8 Times
ISSN: 0022-1201
Founded in 1902
Printed in 4 colors on glossy stock

16591 Loggers' World
Loggers World Publications
4206 Jackson Hwy
Chehalis, WA 98532-8425

360-262-3376
800-462-8283
Fax: 360-262-3337
E-Mail: logworld@aol.com
Home Page: www.loggersworld.com

Mike Crouse, Publisher
Kevin Core, Advertising Manager
Finley Hays, Editor
Darin Burt, Writer

Accepts advertising.
Cost: $12.00
56 Pages
Frequency: Monthly
Circulation: 16,000
Founded in 1966

16592 Logging & Sawmilling Journal
Logging & Sawmilling Journal
Po Box 86670
Vancouver, BC V7L-4L2

604-990-9970
Fax: 604-990-9971
E-Mail: stanhope@forestnet.com
Home Page: www.forestnet.com
Social Media: Facebook

Rob Stanhope, Publisher
Lil Fawcus, Production Manager
Mailing list available for rent

16593 Logging Management
Baum International Media
203-2323 Boundary Road
Vancouver, Ca V5M 4

604-298-3005
Fax: 604-298-3966
E-Mail: editor.lm@bauminternational.com
Home Page: www.bauminternational.com

Kevin Cook, Associate Publisher
Gunner Martin, Editor
Carol Lee, Circulation Manager

Logging equipment information for the United States and Canada.
Circulation: 23000

16594 Lumber Cooperator
Northeastern Retail Lumber Association
585 N Greenbush Rd
Rensselaer, NY 12144-9615

518-286-1010
800-292-6752
Fax: 518-286-1755

E-Mail: rferris@nrla.org
Home Page: www.nrla.org

Rita Ferris, President

Includes the latest industry, legislative and regulatory news, as well as issues and trends that most influence the lumber and building materials business. Readers gain insight into the newest methods, management techniques, new product ideas, family owned business concerns and key industry issues.
Cost: $40.00
100 Pages
Circulation: 5000
Founded in 1894

16595 Lumberman's Equipment Digest
Lumbermen Online
PO Box 1146
Columbia, TN 38401

931-381-1638
800-477-7606
Fax: 931-388-3564
E-Mail: publisher@lumbermenonline.com
Home Page: www.lumbermenonline.com

Brady Carr, Publisher
Tammy Coffman, Advertising Manager
Shana Hibdon, Internet Technical Support
Gina High, Graphics Department
Cost: $38.00
Frequency: Monthly
Circulation: 35,000

16596 Millwork Magazine
Association of Millwork Distributors
10047 Robert Trent Jones Pkwy
New Port Richey, FL 34655-4649

727-372-3665
800-786-7274
Fax: 727-372-2879
Home Page: www.amdweb.com
Social Media: Twitter, LinkedIn

Rosalie Leone, CEO/ Secretary
Dan Barber, President
John Crowder, 1st VP
Mark Hefley, Associate VP
George Kessel, Treasurer

Articles of interest to AMD members.
1200 Members
Frequency: Monthly
Founded in 1935

16597 Modern Woodworking
Modern Woodworking
90 West Afton Ave. #117
Yardley, PA 19067

267-519-1705
800-633-5953
Fax: 205-391-2081
E-Mail: Admin@tccmedia.com
Home Page: www.modernwoodworking.com

Brooke Wisdom, Executive Editor
W.W. Chip Wisdom, VP/Group Publisher
Mailing list available for rent

16598 National Hardwood Magazine
Miller Publishing Company
PO Box 34908
Memphis, TN 38184-0908

901-372-8280
800-844-1280
Fax: 901-373-6180
E-Mail: editor@millerwoodtradepub.com
Home Page: www.millerpublishing.com

Paul J Miller, President
Wayne Miller, VP
Sue Putnam, Editor

A monthly journal serving the hardwood industry including sawmillls, distillation, lumber yards, wholesalers and buyers and woodworkers.
Cost: $45.00
85 Pages
Frequency: Monthly
Circulation: 5000
Founded in 1927
Printed in 4 colors on glossy stock

16599 Northern Journal of Applied Forestry
Society of American Foresters
5400 Grosvenor Ln
Bethesda, MD 20814-2198

301-897-8720
866-897-8720
Fax: 301-897-3690
E-Mail: safweb@podi.com
Home Page: www.safnet.org
Social Media: Facebook, Twitter, LinkedIn

Matthew Walls, Publications Dir/Managing Editor
Kim C Steiner, Editor

Each regional journal of applies forestry focuses on research, practice, and techniques targeted to foresters and allied professionals in specific regions of the United States and Canada. This journal covers northeastern, midwestern, and boreal forests in the United States and Canada.
Cost: $75.00
Frequency: 4 Times
ISSN: 0742-6348

16600 Pallet Enterprise
Industrial Reporting
10244 Timber Ridge Dr
Ashland, VA 23005-8135

804-550-0323
800-805-0263
Fax: 804-550-2181
E-Mail: ed@ireporting.com
Home Page: www.palletenterprise.com

Edward C Brindley Jr, Publisher
Chris Edwards, Production Manager
Chaille Brindley, Assistant Publisher
Scott Brindley, Marketing Director
Laura Seal, Circulation Manager

Written for those who manufacture, repair, sell or use wooden pallets and containers. Regular features include a market column, new products section and industry events.
Cost: $60.00
104 Pages
Frequency: Monthly
Circulation: 15000
Founded in 1981
Printed in 4 colors on glossy stock

16601 PalletCentral
National Wooden Pallet & Container Association
1421 Prince Street
Suite 340
Alexandria, VA 22314-2805

703-519-6104
Fax: 703-519-4720
E-Mail: pjsherry@nepapallet.com
Home Page: www.nwpca.com

John T. Swenby, Chair
James Ruder, Chair-Elect
James Schwab, Secretary/ Treasurer
Bruce N. Scholnick, President

The technical journal for the solid wood packaging industry published by the NWPCA. First with essential news and innovations affecting wood packaging companies, going beyond reporting to provide useful analysis and strategies for coping with industry changes.
700+ Members
Frequency: Montly
Circulation: 6000
Founded in 1947

16602 Panel World
Hatton-Brown Publishers
225 Hanrick Street(36104)
PO Box 2268
Montgomery, AL 36102-3317

334-834-1170
800-669-5613
Fax: 334-834-4525
E-Mail: mail@hattonbrown.com
Home Page: www.hattonbrown.com

Rich Donnell, Editor
Rhonda Thomas, Circulation Manager
Dan Shell, Managing Editor
Jennifer McCary, Associate Editor
Tonya Cooner, Associate Editor

For people who deal with production, sales, marketing, distribution, fabrication and utilization of veneer, plywood and other panel products.
Cost: $40.00
Circulation: 12850
Founded in 1948
Printed in 4 colors on matte stock

16603 Popular Woodworking
F And W Publications
10151 Carver Road, Suite # 200
Blue Ash, OH 45242

513-531-2690
Fax: 513-531-1843
E-Mail: publicity@fwmedia.com
Home Page: www.fwpublications.com

David Nussbaum, CEO
Don Schroder, Ad Manager

Everything woodworkers need to develop their skills; in-depth tool reviews and tests, shop tips, finishing secrets, projects and more.
Cost: $28.00
104 Pages
Frequency: Monthly
Circulation: 240151
Founded in 1981

16604 Rural Builder
F And W Publications
10151 Carver Road, Suite # 200
Blue Ash, OH 45242

513-531-2690
Fax: 715-445-4087
E-Mail: publicity@fwmedia.com
Home Page: www.fwpublications.com

Steve Shanesy, Publisher
Don Schroder, Advertising Manager

16605 Southern Loggin' Times
Hatton-Brown Publishers
PO Box 2268
Montgomery, AL 36102-2268

334-834-1170
800-669-5613
Fax: 334-834-4525
E-Mail: mail@hattonbrown.com
Home Page: www.hattonbrown.com

David H Ramsey, President
Rich Donnell, Editor

Monitors the south's forest products industry.
Cost: $65.00
Frequency: Monthly
Circulation: 13,408
ISSN: 0744-2106
Founded in 1948
Printed in 4 colors on glossy stock

16606 Southern Lumberman
Hatton-Brown Publishers
PO Box 2268
Montgomery, AL 36102-2268

334-834-1170
800-669-5613
Fax: 334-834-4525

E-Mail: mail@hattonbrown.com
Home Page: www.hattonbrown.com

David H Ramsey, President
Rich Donnell, Editor

Industry news for sawmill operators and dimension manufacturers.
Cost: $21.00
60 Pages
Frequency: Monthly
Circulation: 13500

16607 Southern Pine Inspection Bureau Magazine
Southern Pine Inspection Bureau
PO Box 10915
Pensacola, FL 32524-0915

850-434-2611
Fax: 850-433-5594
E-Mail: spib@spib.org
Home Page: www.spib.org

James Loy, President
Tom Jones, Executive Director
Founded in 1940
Mailing list available for rent

16608 Timber Harvesting
Hatton-Brown Publishers
225 Hanrick Street (36104)
PO Box 2268
Montgomery, AL 36102-3317

334-834-1170
800-669-5613
Fax: 334-834-4525
E-Mail: mail@hattonbrown.com
Home Page: www.hattonbrown.com

Dave Ramsey, Co-Publisher
D K Knight, Co-Publisher
Rich Donnell, Editor

News and methods reported that are of particular interest to loggers.
Cost: $40.00
Frequency: Monthly
Circulation: 20130
ISSN: 0160-6433
Founded in 1953
Printed in 4 colors on matte stock

16609 Timber Processing
Hatton-Brown Publishers
225 Hanrick Street
PO Box 2268
Montgomery, AL 36102

334-834-1170
800-669-5613
Fax: 334-834-4525
E-Mail: rich@hattonbrown.com
Home Page: www.hattonbrown.com

David H Ramsey, Co-Publisher
Rich Donnell, Editor-in-Chief
Dan Shell, Managing Editor

Timber Processing serves sawmill/chipmill operations; consultants in mill and processing operations; machinery manufacturers, dealers and distributors, others allied to the field.
Cost: $40.00
44 Pages
Circulation: 20780
ISSN: 0885-906X
Founded in 1948
Printed in 4 colors on glossy stock

16610 Timber West Journal
Logging & Sawmilling Journal
Po Box 86670
Vancouver, BC V7L-4L2

604-990-9970
866-221-1017
Fax: 604-990-9971
E-Mail: timberwest@forestnet.com
Home Page: www.forestnet.com/timberwest
Social Media: Facebook

Sheila Ringdahl, Publisher
Diane Mettler, Managing Editor

Packed with valuable and useful stories on successful mechanized harvesting and wood processing techniques and equipment, special editorial features, plus timely information on legislation, industry news, annual events, and people and products pertinent to America's largest forestry market.
Cost: $20.00
48 Pages
Circulation: 10500
ISSN: 0192-0642
Founded in 1975
Mailing list available for rent
Printed in 4 colors

16611 Timberline
Industrial Reporting
10244 Timber Ridge Dr
Ashland, VA 23005-8135

804-550-0323
Fax: 804-550-2181
E-Mail: editor@ireporting.com
Home Page: www.palletenterprise.com

Edward C Brindley Jr, Publisher
Tim Cox, Editor
Laura Seal, Circulation

Highlights sawmill, logging, and pallet interests including environmental issues, new machinery and technologies that impact the industry.
52 Pages
Frequency: Monthly
Circulation: 30000
Founded in 1994
Mailing list available for rent: 28,000 names at $250 per M
Printed in 4 colors on newsprint stock

16612 Tree Care Industry
Tree Care Industry Association
136 Harvey Road
Suite 101
Londonderry, NH 03053
603-314-5380
800-733-2622
Fax: 603-314-5386
E-Mail: tcia@tcia.org
Home Page: www.tcia.org
Social Media: Facebook, Twitter, LinkedIn, Youtube

Mark Garvin, Interim CEO/President
Peter Gerstenberger, Sr Adv Safety/Compliance/Standards

Informative articles on tree care issues, leading advertisers, and industry almanac, and cutting edge product news combine to make TCI Magazine a must-read for tree workers, tree care company owners, and anyone who wants a fresh, insightful look at the industry
Founded in 1938

16613 Tree Farmer Magazine, the Guide to Sustaining America's Family Forests
American Forest Foundation
1111 19th St NW
Suite 780
Washington, DC 20036

202-463-2462
Fax: 202-463-2461
E-Mail: info@forestfoundation.org
Home Page: www.forestfoundation.org
Social Media: Facebook, Twitter, YouTube

Tom Martin, President & CEO
Brigitte Johnson APR, Director Communications, Editor

The official magazine of ATFS, this periodical provides practical, how-to and hands-on information and techniques, and services to help private fore landowners to become better stewards, save money and time, and add to the enjoyment of their land.

16614 Wood Digest
Cygnus Publishing
1233 Janesville Avenue
Fort Atkinson, WI 53538-0803

920-000-1111
800-547-7377
Fax: 920-563-1699
E-Mail: info@cygnus.com
Home Page: www.cygnus.com

John French, CEO
John Anfderhaar, Associate Publisher
Paul Bowers, President
Jay Schneider, Publisher

Trade magazine, Accepts advertising.
64 Pages
Frequency: Monthly
Circulation: 51000
Founded in 1965

16615 Wood Finisher
7616 Banning Way
Inver Grove Heights, MN 55077-5819
Mitchell Kohansek, Editor

Wood finishing information.
Cost: $10.00
20 Pages
Frequency: Monthly
Founded in 1981

16616 Wood and Fiber Science
Society of Wood Science & Technology
PO Box 6155
Monona, WI 53716-6155

608-577-1342
Fax: 608-467-8979
E-Mail: vicki@swst.org
Home Page: www.swst.org
Social Media: Facebook

Victoria Herian, Executive Director
James Funck, President Elect

Publishes papers with both professional and technical content. Original papers of profesional concer, or based on research dealing with the science, processing, and manufacture of wood and composite products of wood or wood fiber origin are considered for publication. All papers are peer-reviewed and must be unpublished research not offered for publication elsewhere.
Cost: $250.00
Frequency: Quarterly
Circulation: 950
ISSN: 0735-6161
Founded in 1958

16617 Wood and Wood Products
Vance Publishing
400 Knightsbridge Pkwy
Lincolnshire, IL 60069

847-634-2600
Fax: 847-634-4379
E-Mail: info@vancepublishing.com
Home Page: www.vancepublishing.com

William C Vance, Chairman
Peggy Walker, Wood & Wood Products

Leading woodworking industry publication for solid wood and panel technology.
140 Pages
Frequency: Monthly
Circulation: 48000
ISSN: 0043-7662
Founded in 1937

16618 World Wood Review
Widman Publishing

601 West Broadway
Suite 400
Vancouver, BC V5Z 4C2

604-675-6923
Fax: 604-675-6924
E-Mail: tlhaugen@widman.com
Home Page: www.widman.com

Janice Widman, Chair
Jason Roth, Director / Editor
Tamara Haugen, Director / Editor
Dick Brown, Associate Editor
Brian Haugen, Associate Editor

The premier newsletter serving the global wood products industry, with news of trends and developments in the solid wood and panel manufacturing sector.
Cost: $55.00
50 Pages
Frequency: Monthly

Trade Shows

16619 AMD Annual Convention & Tradeshow
Association of Millwork Distributors
10047 Robert Trent Jones Pkwy
Trinity, FL 34655-4649

727-372-3665
800-786-7274
Fax: 727-372-2879
E-Mail: marketing@amdweb.com
Home Page: www.amdweb.com

Rosalie Leone, CEO

16620 ATIC Annual Meeting
7012 S Revere Parkway
Suite 140
Centennial, CO 80112

303-379-2955
E-Mail: info@aitc-glulam.org
Home Page: www.aitc-glulam.org
Social Media: Facebook

R Michael Caldwell PE, Executive VP
Frequency: Annual
Founded in 1952

16621 American Forestry Association
PO Box 2000
Washington, DC 20013-2000

202-955-4500

Billl Tikkala, Show Manager
Deborah Gangloff, Executive Director

30 booths of tree planting and care equipment.
1M Attendees
Frequency: November

16622 Appalachian Hardwood Expo
Mercer County Technical Education Center
105 Old Bluefield Road
Princeton, WV 24740-8901

304-425-4583

Linda Cox

100 tables.
2M Attendees
Frequency: June

16623 Architectural Woodwork Institute Annual Convention
46179 Westlake Drive
Suite 120
Potomac Falls, VA 20165

571-323-3636
Fax: 571-323-3630
E-Mail: info@awinet.org
Home Page: www.awinet.org

Kimberly Haynes, Director Meetings & Conventions

Seminar, workshop and woodwork products such as casework, fixtures and panelings, equipment and supplies.

16624 Forest Expo
Prince George Regional Forest Exhibition Society
850 River Road
Prince George, BC V2L-5S8

250-563-8833
Fax: 250-563-3697
E-Mail: info@forestexpo.bc.ca
Home Page: www.forestexpo.bc.ca

Trudy Swaan, General Manager

Provides a showcase to display the latest in new technology, equipment, supplies and services, as well as educate the forest sector and the general public about the importance of our forests.

16625 Forest Products Machinery & Equipment Expo
Southern Forest Products Association
2900 Indiana Avenue
Kenner, LA 70065

504-443-4464
Fax: 504-443-6612
E-Mail: mail@sfpa.org
Home Page: www.sfpa.org

Digges Morgan, President
Richard Wallace, VP Communications
Tami Kessler, Corporate Secretary
Stephen P. Conwell, President
Tami Kessler, Corporate Secretary & Director

200+ exhibitors
3000 Attendees
Frequency: June, Biennial

16626 Frame Building Expo
National Frame Builders Association
4700 W. Lake Avenue
Glenview, IL 60025

785-843-2444
800-557-6957
Fax: 847-375-6495
E-Mail: info@nfba.org
Home Page: www.nfba.org
Social Media: Facebook

John Fullerton, VP
Tom Knight, President

Containing 200 booths.
2000+ Attendees
Frequency: February

16627 Greenbuild International Conference and Expo
Engineered Wood Association
7011 S 19th Street
Tacoma, WA 98466-5333

253-565-6600
Fax: 253-565-7265
E-Mail: tanya.rosendahl@apawood.org
Home Page: www.apawood.org
Social Media: Facebook, Twitter

Tanya Rosendahl, Tradeshow Coordinator

16628 HPVA Sping Conference
Hardwood Plywood & Veneer
1825 Michael Faraday Dr
Reston, VA 20190-5350

703-435-2900
Fax: 703-435-2537
E-Mail: hpva@hpva.org
Home Page: www.hpva.org

Clifford Howlett, President
Kip Howlett, HPVA President
Eva Mentel, Office Manager
Frequency: May

16629 HPVA Winter Conference
Hardwood Plywood & Veneer
1825 Michael Faraday Dr
Reston, VA 20190-5350

703-435-2900
Fax: 703-435-2537
E-Mail: hpva@hpva.org
Home Page: www.hpva.org

Clifford Howlett, President
Kip Howlett, HPVA President
Eva Mentel, Office Manager
Frequency: November

16630 Hardwood Manufacturers Association
400 Penn Center Boulevard
Suite 530
Pittsburgh, PA 15235-5605

412-244-0440
Fax: 412-244-9090

Susan Regan, Executive VP

Offers 20 booths of sawmill and logging machinery and services.
300 Attendees
Frequency: March

16631 IWPA Annual Convention
International Wood Products Association
4214 King St
Alexandria, VA 22302-1555

703-820-6696
Fax: 703-820-8550
E-Mail: info@iwpawood.org
Home Page: www.iwpawood.org

Brent McClendon, Executive VP/CAE
Annette Ferri, Member Services
Brigid Shea, Government Affairs
Annette Ferri, Director, Finance & Administration
Ashley A. Amidon, Manager, Government

The largest gethering solely dedicated to the North American imported wood products industry.
Frequency: April

16632 International Woodworking Machinery and Furniture Supply Fair: USA
Reed Exhibition Companies
1350 E Touhy Avenue
Des Plaines, IL 60018-3303

847-294-0300
Fax: 847-635-1571

Paul Pajor, National Marketing Manager

The largest woodworking machinery and furniture supply manufacturing exposition held in the Western Hemisphere. Exhibitors interface with North American furniture, cabinet, and woodworking manufacturers. One thousand booths.
37M Attendees
Frequency: August/Biennial

16633 Lake States Logging Congress & Equipment Expo
Great Lakes Timber Professionals Association
3243 Golf Course Road
PO Box 1278
Rhinelander, WI 54501-1278

715-282-5828
Fax: 715-282-4941

E-Mail: info@timberpa.com
Home Page: www.timberpa.com

Henry Schienebeck, Executive Director & Editor

Held in either Michigan or Wisconsin, the Logging Congress is a 3-day expo that takes place during the Fall season throughout the Lake States region of the United States.
3500 Attendees
Founded in 1945

16634 Live Woods Show
Pacific Logging Congress
PO Box 1281
Maple Valley, WA 98038

425-413-2808
Fax: 425-413-1359
E-Mail: rikki@pacificloggingcongress.com
Home Page: www.pacificloggingcongress.com

Rikki Wellman, Executive Director
Craig Olson, President
Ron Simon, Treasurer
3000+ Attendees
Frequency: September

16635 Logging Congress Pacific
2300 SW 6th Avenue
Suite 200
Portland, OR 97201-4915

FAX 503-612-0344

Al Wilson, Executive Director

50 booths.
800 Attendees
Frequency: September

16636 Lumbermen's Merchandising Conferences
137 W Wayne Avenue
Wayne, PA 19087-4018
610-293-7000
Fax: 215-293-7098

Jack Reznor, Show Manager
Anthony Decarlo, President

325 booths.
1.6M Attendees
Frequency: March

16637 MFMA Annual Conference
Maple Flooring Manufacturers Association
111 Deer Lake Road
Suite 100
Deerfield, IL 60015

847-480-9138
888-480-9138
Fax: 847-480-9282
E-Mail: mcarson@maplefloor.org
Home Page: www.maplefloor.org

Madhuri Carson, Conference Manager

Containing 50 booths.
300 Attendees
Frequency: Annual/March

16638 NHLA Annual Convention & Exhibit Showcase North American Hardwood Lumber Indu
National Hardwood Lumber Association
6830 Raleigh Lagrange Road
Memphis, TN 38184

901-377-1818
E-Mail: www.natlhardwood.org
Home Page: www.nhla.com

Lisa Browne, Convention Director

The premier networking opportunity for the Hardwood Industry. Provides attendees time for direct, personal contact with industry leaders and exhibitors, giving them from the opportunity to ask meaningful questions, view and compare products and services and strengthen business relationships.
Frequency: Annual

16639 NWFA Wood Flooring Convention and Expo
National Wood Flooring Association
111 Chesterfield Industrial Boulevard
Chesterfield, MO 63005
636-519-9663
800-422-4556
Fax: 636-519-9664
E-Mail: convention@nwfa.org
Home Page: www.nwfa.org

Michael Martin, CEO

The Wood Flooring Expo has become the international gathering place for wood flooring professionals: Manufacturers, Distributors, Dealer/Contractors, Inspectors, Installers, Import/Exporters, Architects & Designers of wood flooring.
2000 Attendees
Frequency: April

16640 Northeastern Forest Products Equipment Expo
Northeastern Loggers Association
3311 State Route 28 PO Box 69
Old Forge, NY 13420-0069

315-369-3078
Fax: 315-369-3736
E-Mail: nela@northernlogger.com
Home Page: http://nefpexpo.net

Joseph Phaneuf, Show Manager

Annual expo on forest products equipment, suppliers, and services. Always listed as one of the top 100 shows in the U.S. with 200+ exhibitors and indoor/outdoor demonstrations.
6000 Attendees
Frequency: Annual/May

16641 Northeastern Retail Lumber Association
Northeastern Retail Lumber Association
585 N Greenbush Road
Rensselaer, NY 12144

518-286-1010
800-292-6752
Fax: 518-286-1755
E-Mail: rferris@nrla.org
Home Page: www.nrla.org

Deborah Talar, Executive Assistant
Rita Ferris, President

500 booths or more of builiding materials and education relating to the lumber and building industry.
8M Attendees
Frequency: January

16642 Northwestern Building Products Expo
Northwestern Lumber Association
5905 Golden Valley Road
Suite 110
Minneapolis, MN 55422-4535

763-544-6822
888-544-6822
Fax: 763-595-4060
E-Mail: info@nlassn.org
Home Page: www.nlassn.org

Sally Means, Director of Conventions
Jodie Fleck, Director of Conventions & Tours
Cody Nuernberg, Manager of Membership

Building material retailers and their contractors attend this trade show and conference for continuing education and cammeraderie
1200 Attendees
Frequency: Annual
Mailing list available for rent

16643 Redwood Region Logging Conference California
Redwood Region Logging Conference
5601 South Broadway Street
Eureka, CA 95503

707-443-4091
Fax: 707-443-0926
E-Mail: rrlc@sonic.net
Home Page: www.rrlc.net/

Charles Benbow, Show Manager

100 booths of timber and forestry related products and services.
3M Attendees
Frequency: March

16644 Retail Lumbermen's Association Northeast
339 E Avenue
Rochester, NY 14604-2627
John Brill, Show Manager

681 booths of lumber and related services.
10M Attendees
Frequency: January

16645 Sawmill Logging Equipment Expo East Coast
220 E Williamsburg Road
PO Box 160
Sandston, VA 23150-0160

804-737-5625
Fax: 804-737-9437
E-Mail: info@exporichmond.com
Home Page: www.exporichmond.com

Mike Washko, Expo Manager

Logging and forestry production and distribution.
12M Attendees
Frequency: May

16646 Southeastern Lumber Manufacturers Association
Southeastern Lumber Manufacturers
200 Greencastle Road
Tyrone, GA 30290

770-631-6701
Fax: 770-631-6720
Home Page: www.slma.org/

Steve Roundtree, President
Bryan Smalley, President
Will Telligman, Government Affairs Manager
Beverly Knight, Accounting Manager

50 booths.
350 Attendees
Frequency: July

16647 Southern Forest Products Mid-Year Meeting
Southern Forest Products Association
2900 Indiana Avenue
Kenner, LA 70065

504-443-4464
Fax: 504-443-6612
E-Mail: mail@sfpa.org
Home Page: www.sfpa.org

Digges Morgan, President
Richard Wallace, VP Communications
Tami Kessler, Corporate Secretary
Stephen P. Conwell, President
Tami Kessler, Corporate Secretary & Director

200+ exhibitors
3000 Attendees
Frequency: Annual

16648 Southern Forestry Conference
Forest Landowners Association

900 Circle 75 Pkwy Se
Suite 205
Atlanta, GA 30339-3075

404-325-2954
800-325-2954
Fax: 404-325-2955
E-Mail: info@forestlandowners.com
Home Page: www.forestlandowners.com

Lisa Newsome, Manager
Stacie Lewis, Managing Editor
Frequency: May
Founded in 1941

16649 TCI Expo
Tree Care Industry Association
136 Harvey Road
Suite 101
Londonderry, NH 03053

603-314-5380
800-733-2622
Fax: 603-314-5386
E-Mail: tcia@tcia.org
Home Page: www.tcia.org
Social Media: Facebook, Twitter, LinkedIn, Youtube

Mark Garvin, Interim CEO/President
Peter Gerstenberger, Sr Adv Safety/Compliance/Standards
3500 Attendees
Frequency: Annual
Founded in 1938

16650 World of Wood Annual Convention
International Wood Products Association
4214 King Street W
Alexandria, VA 22302-1507

703-820-6696
Fax: 703-820-8550
E-Mail: info@iwpawood.org
Home Page: www.iwpawood.org

Brent J McClendon, Executive VP/CAE
Annette Ferri, Member Services
Brigid Shea, Government Affairs
Annette Ferri, Director, Finance & Administration
Ashley A. Amidon, Manager, Government

A gethering for imported wood products industry importers, distributers, manufacturers, offshore suppliers and service providers.
220 Attendees
Frequency: Annual/Spring

Directories & Databases

16651 American Papermaker Mill and Personnel
Office of Paper Recycling
785 Fulton Industrial Boulevard
Suite 3
Atlanta, GA 30336

770-395-0606

Jerome Koncel, Editor

Offers a list of pulp, paper and paperboard mills.
Cost: $40.00
Frequency: Annual
Circulation: 28,000

16652 Cedar Shake and Shingle Bureau Membership Directory/Buyer's Guide
Cedar Shake & Shingle Bureau
PO Box 1178
Sumas, WA 98295-1178

604-820-7700
Fax: 604-820-0266
E-Mail: info@cedarbureau.com
Home Page: www.cedarbureau.org

Lynne Christensen, Director of Operations
Barb Enns, Accountant
Dave Mooney, Cedar Quality Auditor
Sharron Beauregard, Accounting Assistant
Suzie Quigley, Customer Service Representative

About 102 member manufacturing mills in the Pacific Northwest and British Columbia, Canada; approximately 163 affiliated roofing applicators, builders, architects, remodelers and suppliers of related products and services.
Cost: $17.00
Frequency: SemiAnnual
Circulation: 450

16653 Dimension & Wood Components Buyer's Guide
Miller Publishing Corporation
Po Box 34908
Memphis, TN 38184-0908

901-372-8280
800-844-1280
Fax: 901-373-6180
E-Mail: editor@millerwoodtradepub.com
Home Page: www.millerpublishing.com

Paul J Miller, President
Sue Putnam, Editor

Instant access to manufacturers of furniture parts, mouldings, cabinet doors, stair parts, flooring, turnings, paneling, door parts, window parts, edge glued panels, etc. Gives the information on who to contact, firm name and address, phone number, fax number, number of employees, products manufactured, species of wood used, machining capabilities and marketing areas served.
Cost: $350.00

16654 Forest Products Export Directory
Miller Publishing Corporation
Po Box 34908
Memphis, TN 38184-0908

901-372-8280
800-844-1280
Fax: 901-373-6180
E-Mail: editor@millerwoodtradepub.com
Home Page: www.millerpublishing.com

Paul J Miller, President
Sue Putnam, Editor

The only directory published listing all the major exporters of North American forest products. Edited to help the oversease buyer find reliable suppliers for the wide variety of Softwood and Hardwood forest products available in North America.
Cost: $175.00

16655 Forest Products Research Society Membership Directory
2801 Marshall Ct
Madison, WI 53705-2295

608-231-1361
Fax: 608-231-2152
E-Mail: info@forestprod.org
Home Page: www.forestprod.org

Carol Lewis, VP
Stefan A. Bergmann, Executive Vice President
Joe Gravunder, Publications Manager
Cost: $125.00
1900 Pages
Frequency: 10 Per Year
Circulation: 3500
Founded in 1947

16656 Gebbie Press: All-In-One Media Directory
Gebbie Press
Po Box 1000
New Paltz, NY 12561

845-255-7560
Fax: 888-345-2790
Home Page: www.gebbieinc.com
Social Media: Facebook, Twitter, LinkedIn

Mark Gebbie, Associate Editor
Founded in 1955

16657 Green Book's Hardwood Marketing Directory
Miller Publishing Corporation
Po Box 34908
Memphis, TN 38184-0908

901-372-8280
800-844-1280
Fax: 901-373-6180
E-Mail: editor@millerwoodtradepub.com
Home Page: www.millerpublishing.com

Paul J Miller, President
Sue Putnam, Editor

A sales booster that lists over 7,900 woodworking plants' Hardwood lumber and other Hardwood forest products purchasing needs. Gives up-to-date, documented facts on species, grades, thicknesses and quantities purchased by each plant annually in the U.S. and Canada.
Cost: $1200.00

16658 Green Book's Softwood Marketing Directory
Miller Publishing Corporation
Po Box 34908
Memphis, TN 38184-0908

901-372-8280
800-844-1280
Fax: 901-373-6180
E-Mail: editor@millerwoodtradepub.com
Home Page: www.millerpublishing.com

Paul J Miller, President
Sue Putnam, Editor

Instant access to over 5,000 woodworking and industrial plants' Softwood lumber purchasing needs with complete, up-to-date, documented facts on species, grades, thicknesses, and quantities of Softwood lumber and other Softwood forest products bought regularly.
Cost: $900.00

16659 Hardwood Manufacturers Association: Membership Directory
Hardwood Manufacturers Association
665 Rodi Road
Suite 305
Pittsburgh, PA 15235

412-244-0440
800-373-9663
Fax: 412-244-9090
Home Page: www.hardwoodinfo.com

Susan Regan, Executive VP

Over 100 companies with over 160 locations in the US.
Frequency: Annual December

16660 Hardwood Purchasing Handbook
Miller Publishing Corporation
Po Box 34908
Memphis, TN 38184-0908

901-372-8280
800-844-1280
Fax: 907-373-6180
E-Mail: editor@millerwoodtradepub.com
Home Page: www.millerpublishing.com

Paul J Miller, President
Sue Putnam, Editor

An easy-to-use digest size directory that has all the major Hardwood suppliers in the U.S.A. and Canada of Hardwood lumber, plywood, ve-

neers, etc. Up-to-date sections describe Hardwood sawmills, wholesalers, distribution yards, etc. Complete mailing addresses, phone numbers, fax numbers, email addresses, names of sales agents, main Hardwood species handled, specialty items listed and information on production facilities and shipping methods are given.
Cost: $175.00

16661 Imported Wood Purchasing Guide
Miller Publishing Corporation
Po Box 34908
Memphis, TN 38184-0908
901-372-8280
800-844-1280
Fax: 901-373-6180
E-Mail: editor@millerwoodtradepub.com
Home Page: www.millerpublishing.com
Paul J Miller, President
Sue Putnam, Editor
A wide variety of imported suppliers of lumber, mouldings, veneers, wall paneling, furniture components, flooring, plywood, hardboard, doorskins, millwork, etc.
Cost: $175.00

16662 Imported Wood: Guide To Applications, Sources and Trends
International Wood Products Association
4214 King St
Alexandria, VA 22302-1555
703-820-6696
Fax: 703-820-8550
E-Mail: info@iwpawood.org
Home Page: www.iwpawood.org
Social Media: Facebook, Twitter, LinkedIn
Brent McClendon, Executive VP/CAE
Annette Ferri, Member Services
Brigid Shea, Government Affairs
An annual magazine featuring imported woods in applications, sustainable Forest Management issues and listing of IWPA members.
84 Pages
Frequency: Annual
Circulation: 15,000

16663 International Green Front Report
Friends of the Trees
PO Box 1064
Tonasket, WA 98855-1064
FAX 509-485-2705
E-Mail: michael@friendsofthetrees.net
Michael Pilarski, Editor
Organizations and periodicals concerned with sustainable forestry and agriculture and related fields.
Cost: $7.00
Frequency: Irregular

16664 Lumbermen's Red Book
Lumbermens Credit Association
20 N Wacker Drive
Suite 1800
Chicago, IL 60606-2905
312-553-0943
Fax: 312-533-1842
Home Page: www.lumbermanscredit.com
PD McLaughlin, Editor
Approximately 39,000 manufacturers and distributors of lumber and wood products in the US and Canada.
Cost: $1780.00
Frequency: SemiAnnual

16665 North American Forest Products Export Directory
International Wood Trade Publications
1235 Sycamore View Road
Memphis, TN 38134-7646
901-752-1246
Fax: 901-373-6180
Producers, exporters, agents, etc. of lumber, plywood, etc. in the US and Canada.
Cost: $150.00
Frequency: Annual August
Circulation: 10,000

16666 Northeastern Retail Lumber Association Buyer's Guide
Northeastern Retail Lumber Association
585 N Greenbush Rd
Rensselaer, NY 12144-9615
518-286-1010
800-292-6752
Fax: 518-286-1755
E-Mail: rferris@nrla.org
Home Page: www.nrla.org
Rita Ferris, President
Offers information on over 2,000 retail dealers in lumber and forest products located in the Northeastern states of the US.
Cost: $125.00
225 Pages
Frequency: Annual
ISSN: 0024-7294

16667 Random Lengths Big Book: Buyers' & Sellers' Directory of the Forest
Random Lengths Publications
PO Box 867
Eugene, OR 97440-0867
541-869 9925
888-686-9925
Fax: 800-874-7979
E-Mail: rlmail@rlpi.com
Home Page: www.randomlengths.com
Dave Evans, Editor
Terri Richards, Editor
About 7,500 companies, consultants and associations involved in the softwood forest product industry in the US and Canada, including sawmills, treating plants, manufacturers of panels and specialty products, wholesalers and secondary manufacturers.
Cost: $188.00
Frequency: Annual February
Circulation: 2,200

16668 Rauch Guide to the US and Canadian Pulp & Paper Industry
Grey House Publishing
4919 Route 22
PO Box 56
Amenia, NY 12501
518-789-8700
800-562-2139
Fax: 845-373-6390
E-Mail: books@greyhouse.com
Home Page: www.greyhouse.com
Social Media: Facebook, Twitter
Leslie Mackenzie, Publisher
Richard Gottlieb, Editor
Provides current market information and trends; industry economics and government regulations; company share data for each of the leading product categories; technology and raw material information; industry sources of further data; and unique profiles of 500+ pulp and paper manufacturers, a section which includes all known companies with pulp and paper sales at or over $15 million annually.
Cost: $595.00
400 Pages
ISBN: 1-592371-31-0
Founded in 1981

16669 Timber Harvesting: Logger's Resource Guide
Hatton-Brown Publishers
Po Box 2268
Montgomery, AL 36102-2268
334-834-1170
800-669-5613
Fax: 334-834-4525
E-Mail: mail@hattonbrown.com
Home Page: www.hattonbrown.com
David H Ramsey, President
Rich Donnell, Editor
Cost: $20.00
88 Pages
Frequency: Annually, January
Circulation: 20,179
ISSN: 0160-6433
Printed in on glossy stock

16670 Where to Buy Hardwood Plywood, Veneer & Engineered Hardwood Flooring
Hardwood Plywood and Veneer Association
1825 Michael Faraday Drive
Reston, VA 20190-5350
703-435-2900
Fax: 703-435-2537
E-Mail: hpva@hpva.org
Home Page: www.hpva.org
Kip Howlett, President
Eva Mentel, Office Manager
Ketti Tyree, Membership & Conventions Manager
The definitive annual guide to the species and products sold by HPVA members.
120 Pages
Frequency: Annual
Founded in 1921

16671 Wood & Wood Products: Laminating Users Guide Issue
Louisiana Municipal Association
700 North 10th street
Baton Rouge, LA 70802
225-344-5001
800-234-8274
Fax: 225-344-3057
E-Mail: infor@lma.org
Home Page: www.lma.org
George Carter, Editor
List of approximately 100 manufacturers and importers of decorative overlays, wood substrates, adhesives, laminating equipment and laminated products.
Frequency: Annual June

16672 Wood Components Buyer's Guide
Wood Component Manufacturers Association
741 Butlers Gate NE
Suite 100
Marietta, GA 30068-4207
770-565-6660
Fax: 770-565-6663
E-Mail: wcma@woodcomponents.org
Home Page: www.woodcomponents.org
Steven V Lawser, Executive Director
Over 150 member manufacturers of wood components.
Cost: $5.00
Frequency: Annual Summer

16673 Wood Technology: Buyers' Guide Issue
Miller Freeman Publications

600 Harrison Street
Suite 400
San Francisco, CA 94107-1391
800-227-4675
Fax: 415-905-2630
Home Page: www.woodtechmag.com
David A Pease, Editorial Director
Companies supplying machinery, tools and other equipment to manufacturers of wood products worldwide.
Frequency: Annual

16674 **Wood and Wood Products: Red Book Issue**
Vance Publishing
400 Knightsbridge Parkway
Lincolnshire, IL 60069
847-634-2600
Fax: 847-634-4379
Home Page: www.vancepublishing.com
William C Vance, Chairman
Peggy Walker, President
Annual directory that is the editorial and advertising leader for the woodworking industry. Listings and specifications of more than 3,000 industry suppliers.
Cost: $40.00
Frequency: Annual
Circulation: 50,000

Industry Web Sites

16675 **http://gold.greyhouse.com**
G.O.L.D Grey House OnLine Databases
Grey House Publishing's online database platform, GOLD, offers Quick Search, Keyword Search and Expert Search for most business sectors including lumber and wood markets. The GOLD platform makes finding the information you need quick and easy - whether you're a novice searcher or an experienced database user. All of Grey House's directory products are available for subscription on the GOLD platform.

16676 **www.afandpa.org**
American Forest and Paper Association
Represents member companies and related trade associations which grow, harvest and process wood and wood fiber, manufacture pulp, paper and paperboard products from both virgin and recovered fiber and produce solid wood products.

16677 **www.afma4u.org**
American Furniture Manufacturers Association
Provides a uniform voice in the furniture industry.

16678 **www.aitc-glulam.org**
American Institute of Timber Construction
The national trade association of the structural glued laminiated (glulam) timber industry.

16679 **www.alsc.org**
American Lumber Standard Committee

16680 **www.amdweb.com**
Association of Millwork Distributors
Provides leadership, certification, education, promotion, networking and advocacy to, and for, the millwork distribution industry.

16681 **www.apawood.org**
Engineered Wood Association
A nonprofit trade association that represents US and Canadian manufacturers of structural engineered wood products, including plywood, oriented strand board (OSB), glued-laminated timber (glulam), wood i-joists and structural composite lumber.

16682 **www.bearcreeklumber.com**
Bear Creek Lumber
Publishes a newsletter called the Timberline.

16683 **www.big-creek.com**
Big Creek
Produces a newspaper

16684 **www.calredwood.org**
California Redwood Association
Authorized by Department of Commerce to develop and supervise redwood lumber grading.

16685 **www.capital-lumber.com**
Capital Lumber Company
Dedicated to being the leading distributor of materials in the Western United States.

16686 **www.construction.com**
McGraw-Hill Construction
McGraw-Hill Construction (MHC), part of The McGraw-Hill Companies, connects people and projects across the design and construction industry, serving owners, architects, engineers, general contractors, subcontractors, building product manufacturers, suppliers, dealers, distributors and adjacent markets.

16687 **www.fiberboard.org**
American Fiberboard Association
The national trade organization of manufacturers of cellulosic fiberboard products used for residential and commercial construction.

16688 **www.forestinfo.org**
Temperate Forest Foundation
Source for information which is understandable, unbiased, fast, accurate, and available in a wide variety of formats.

16689 **www.forestnet.com**
Logging & Sawmilling Journal
A journal that provides information on logginf and sawmilling.

16690 **www.forestprod.org**
Forest Products Society
Focus is on the development and research of information for the wood industry.

16691 **www.fpl.fs.fed.us/swst**
Society of Wood Science & Technology
Promotes policies and procedures which assure the wise use of wood and wood-based products; assures high standards for professional performance of wood scientists and technologists; foster educational programs at all levels of wood science and technolgoy and further the quality of such programs; represents the profession in public policy development.

16692 **www.gebbieinc.com**
Gebbie Press
A directory with all information that is needed for the lumber industry.

16693 **www.greyhouse.com**
Grey House Publishing
Authoritative reference directories for most business sectors including lumber and wood markets. Users can search the online databases with varied search criteria allowing for custom searches by product category, geographic area, sales volume, keyword, subject and more. Full Grey House catalog and online ordering also available.

16694 **www.hardboard.org**
American Hardboard Association
Represents major United States producers of hardwood.

16695 **www.hlma.org**
Pennsylvania Forest Products Association
Represents the state's entire forest products industry, including foresters, loggers, sawmills, and value-added processors.

16696 **www.iwpawood.org**
International Wood Products Association
International trade association representing companies handling imported wood products of all types.

16697 **www.lma.org**
Laminating Materials Association
Nonprofit trade group representing manufacturers and importers of decorative overlays, wood substrates, adhesives, laminating equipment and laminated products.

16698 **www.loggertraining.com**
A reference site for loggers in their pursuit of training programs where they work and live. Maintained by Northeastern Loggers' Association.

16699 **www.lumber.org**
North American Wholesale Lumber Association
NAWLA Bulletin is published monthly and includes industry and association news. The Association also produces the NAWLA Traders Market, an annual trade show bringing together over 2000 manufacturer and wholesale lumber traders at the premier event in the forest products industry. NAWLA also produces a variety of educational programs designed to enhance professionalism in the lumber industry.

16700 **www.maplefloor.org**
Maple Flooring Manufacturers Association
For manufacturers of northern hard maple solid strip flooring along with flooring contractors, distributors and providers of instalation-related products and services. Maintains technical standards for product quality, grading, shipping and packaging, and quality central.

16701 **www.millerpublishing.com**
Miller Publishing Corporation
Publishes many newspapers, magazines, and directories.

16702 **www.mslbmda.org**
Mountain States Lumber & Building Materials Dealer

16703 **www.nari.org**
National Association of the Remodeling Industry
Establishes and maintains a firm commitment to developing and sustaining programs that expand and unite the remodeling industry.

16704 **www.nlassn.org**
Northwestern Lumber Association
Retail lumber dealers in Iowa, Minnesota, North Dakota, and South Dakota.

16705 **www.nofma.org**
National Oak Flooring Manufacturers Association
Formulates and administers industry standards on hardwood floorings, inspection service, and semiannual Hardwood Flooring installation school.

16706 **www.nsdja.com**
National Sash and Door Jobbers Association

For wholesale millwork distribution companies.

16707 www.nwfa.org
National Wood Flooring Association
A not-for-profit trade association serving the wood flooring industry

16708 www.nwpca.com
National Wooden Pallet & Container Association
Represents wood and pallet container organizations.

16709 www.osbguide.com
Structural Board Association
Members are manufacturers of structural panels.

16710 www.pacificloggingcongress.org
Pacific Logging Congress
Fulfills the need to provide sound technical education about the forest industry.

16711 www.pbmdf.org
Composite Panel Association
For particle board manufacturers and suppliers.

16712 www.postframe.org
National Frame Builders Association
Building contractors, suppliers, design and code professionals and academic personnel specializing in the post frame construction industry.

16713 www.sfpa.org
Southern Forest Products Association
For lumber manufacturers across the mid-Atlantic and southern states as far west as Texas.

16714 www.spib.org
Southern Pine Inspection Bureau
Develops grading standards for Southern pine lumber and provides an inspection service and grade marking systems.

16715 www.sweets.construction.com
McGraw Hill Construction
In depth product information that lets you find, compare, select, specify and make purchase decisions in the industrial product marketplace.

16716 www.swst.org
Society of Wood Science & Technology
Promotes policies and procedures which assure the wise use of wood and wood-based products; assures high standards for professional performance of wood scientists and technologists; foster educational programs at all levels of wood science and technology and further the quality of such programs; represents the profession in public policy development.

16717 www.toc.org
TOC Management Services
Serves membership in the fields of labor, industrial, and employee relations. Provides counsel in wage and contract negotiations. Provides training and safety programs.

16718 www.tpmrs.com
Timber Products Manufacturers Association
Association of companies in the Timber and Wood products industry of the pacific northwest. TPM provides human resource and safety consulting, Training and employee benefits.

16719 www.wdma.org
Window & Door Manufacturers Association
Trade association representing approximately 145 U.S. and Canadian manufacturers and suppliers of windows and doors for the domestic and export market.

16720 www.westernforestry.org
Western Forestry and Conservation Association
Offers high-quality continuing education workshops and seminars for professional foresters throughout Oregon, Washington, Idaho, Montana, Northern California and British Columbia.

16721 www.woodcomponents.org
Wood Component Manufacturers Association
Represents manufacturers of wood component products for urniture, cabinetry, building products, and decorative wood products.

16722 www.woodfloors.org
National Wood Flooring Association
For distributors, manufacturers, retailers, and contractors.

16723 www.woodtank.com
National Wood Tank Institute
To promote the use and to guide the proper construction methods for wooden tanks as per NWTI S-82.

16724 www.wrcla.org
Western Red Cedar Lumber Association
Association of 26 quality producers of Western Red Cedar lumber products in Washington, Oregon, Canada.

16725 www.wwpa.org
Western Wood Products Association
Represents lumber manufacturers in 12 Western states and Alaska. Provides lumber quality control, technical support, and business information to supporting mills.

16726 www2.dcn.org/orgs/wmmpa.wm
Wood Moulding And Millwork Producers Association
Goal is to promote quality products produced by its members, to develop sources of supply, to promote optimum use of raw materials to standardize products, and to increase the domestic and foreign usage of moulding and millwork products.

Associations

16727 ASM International
ASM International
9639 Kinsman Rd
Materials Park, OH 44073-0002

440-338-5151
800-336-5152
Fax: 440-338-4634
E-Mail: memberservices@asminternational.org
Home Page: www.asminternational.org
Social Media: Facebook, Twitter, LinkedIn

Prof. C. Ravi Ravindran, FASM, President
Dr. Sunniva R. Collins, FASM, Vice President
Thomas S Passek, Managing Director & Secretary
Jeane Deatherage, Administrator, Foundation Programs
Virginia Shirk, Foundation Executive Assistant

The society for materials engineers and scientists, a worldwide network dedicated to advancing industry, technology and applications of metals and materials.
35000 Members
Founded in 1913

16728 American Amusement Machine Association
450 E. Higgins Road
Suite 201
Elk Grove Village, IL 60007

847-290-9088
Home Page: www.coin-op.org
Social Media: Facebook, Wordpress

Pete Gustafson, President
Chris Felix, Vice President
Tina Schwartz, Business & Finance Manager
Frank Cosentino, Secretary
Rich Babich, Treasurer
Founded in 1981

16729 American Gear Manufacturers Association
American Gear Manufacturers Association
1001 N. Fairfax Street
Suite 500
Alexandria, VA 22314-1587

703-684-0211
Fax: 703-684-0242
E-Mail: webmaster@agma.org
Home Page: www.agma.org
Social Media: Facebook, Twitter

Louis Ertel, Chairman
Joe T Franklin Jr, President
Charles Fischer, Vice President, Technical Division
Dean Burrows, Treasurer
Adil Abdulmoen, Administrative Assistant

Manufacturers of gears and geared speed changers. Involved in writing industry standards.
400 Members
Founded in 1916

16730 American Mold Builders Association
American Mold Builders Association
3601 Algonquin
Suite 304
Rolling Meadows, IL 60008-3136

847-222-9402
Fax: 847-222-9437
E-Mail: info@amba.org
Home Page: www.amba.org

Todd Finley, President
Troy Nix, Executive Director
Kym Conis, Managing Director

Promotes the development, welfare and expansion of businesses engaged in the manufacture of molds and related tooling.
Cost: $50.00
400 Members
Frequency: Annual
Founded in 1973

16731 American Society of Mechanical Engineers
Three Park Ave
New York, NY 10016-5902

212-591-7000
800-843-2763
Fax: 202-429-9417
E-Mail: CustomerCare@asme.org
Home Page: www.asme.org

Madiha Kotb, President
Thomas G. Loughlin, Executive Director
Warren DeVries, Secretary/Treasurer
John Delli Venneri, Assistant Secretary
June Ling, Second Assistant Treasurer

To promote and enhance the technical competency and professional well-being of the members, and through quality programs and activities in mechanical engineering, better enable its practitioners to contribute to the well being of human kind.
12000 Members
Founded in 1880

16732 American Textile Machinery Association
American Textile Machinery Association
201 Park Washington Ct
Falls Church, VA 22046-4527

703-538-1789
Fax: 703-241-5603
E-Mail: info@atmanet.org
Home Page: www.atmanet.org

Will Motchar, Chairman
Clay D Tyeryar, President/Assistant Treasurer
Harry W. Buzzerd, Jr., ATMA Management Counsel
Susan A. Denston, ATMA Executive Vice President
Carlos F. J. Moore, ATMA International Trade & Gov

ATMA's purpose is to advance the common interests of its members, improve business conditions within the US textile machinery industry from a global perspective and market the industry and members' machinery, parts and services.
Founded in 1933

16733 Associated Equipment Distributors
600 22nd Street
Suite 220
Oak Brook, IL 60523

630-574-0650
Fax: 630-574-0132
Home Page: www.aednet.org
Social Media: Facebook, Twitter, Google+, YouTube

Timothy J. Watters, Chair
Don Shilling, Vice Chair
Brian P. McGuire, President & CEO
Bob Henderson, Executive Vice President / COO
Jason Blake, SVP/ CFO
500 Members

16734 Association for Facilities Engineering
12801 Worldgate Drive
Suite 519
Herndon, VA 20170

571-203-7171
Fax: 571-766-2142
E-Mail: info@AFE.org
Home Page: www.afe.org

Dennis M. Hydrick, CPMM, President & Chairman
Wayne P. Saya, CPE, CPMM, Executive Director
Fred King, Vice Chair of Finance
Virginia S. Gibson, Vice Chair of Membership
Stephen W. Nicholas, CPMM, VP, Professional Development
Founded in 1915

16735 Association for Machine Translation in the Americas
Home Page: www.amtaweb.org
Social Media: Twitter, LinkedIn

16736 Association for Manufacturing Technology
American Machine Tool Distributors
7901 Westpark Drive
McLean, VA 22102-4206

703-893-2900
800-524-0475
Fax: 703-893-1151
E-Mail: amt@amtonline.org
Home Page: www.amtonline.org
Social Media: Facebook, Twitter, LinkedIn, Youtube

Douglas K Woods, President
Amber L Thomas, Vice President - Advocacy
JefferyÿH Traver, Vice President - Business
PeterÿR. Eelman, Vice President - Exhibitions
LindaÿG Montfort, Vice President-Finance & HR

Since 1925, the American Machine Tool Distributors' Association has been a major voice within the machine tool industry. The AMTDA represents independent distributors and worldwide builders of machine tools and related products used in the metalworking industry. The Association's mission is to provide marketers of manufacturing technology the essential services necessary to develop and perpetuate distribution businesses that make vital contributions to North American manufacturing.
400 Members
Founded in 1925

16737 Association of Computing Machinery
2 Penn Plaza
Suite 701
New York, NY 10121-0701

212-626-0500
800-342-6626
Fax: 212-944-1318
E-Mail: acmhelp@acm.org
Home Page: www.acm.org
Social Media: Facebook, Twitter, LinkedIn, Google+, YouTube

Patrick H. Madden, Chair
Renee McCauley, Vice Chair, Operations
Alexander L. Wolf, President
Vicki Hanson, Vice President
Erik AR. Altman, Secretary/ Treasurer
Founded in 1947

16738 Association of Equipment Manufacturers
6737 West Washington Street
Suite 2400
Milwaukee, WI 53214-5647

414-272-0943
Fax: 414-272-1170
E-Mail: aem@aem.org
Home Page: www.aem.org
Social Media: Twitter

John Patterson, Chair
Leif J. Magnusson, Vice Chair
Dennis Slater, President
Wanda Sova, Executive Assistant
Judy Gaus, Sr. Di., Human Resources
850 Members

16739 Association of Machinery and Equipment Appraisers
Association of Machinery and Equipment
315 South Patrick Street
Alexandria, VA 22314-3532

703-836-7900
800-537-8629
Fax: 703-836-9303
E-Mail: amea@amea.org
Home Page: www.amea.org

James Zvonar, President

Members are appraisers of the metalworking industry.
284 Members
Founded in 1983
Mailing list available for rent

16740 Association of Vacuum Equipment Manufacturers International
201 Park Washington Court
Falls Church, VA 22046-4527

703-538-3543
Fax: 703-241-5603
E-Mail: aveminfo@avem.org
Home Page: www.avem.org

David Dedman, Chairman
Ken Harrison, Vice Chairman
Dawn M. Shiley, Executive Director
Clay Tyeryar, MAM, CAE, Assistant Treasurer
Kim Fay, Data Analyst

The only non-profit U.S. association dedicated fully to companies that manufacture vacuum equipment and supplies that serve and advance vacuum science and technology. AVEM promotes member interests and provides services to enhance the membership value and understanding of the global market.
49 Members
Founded in 1969

16741 Clinical Robotic Surgery Association
Two Prudential Plaza
180 North Stetson, Suite 3500
Chicago, IL 60601

312-268-5754
E-Mail: inquiries@clinicalrobotics.com
Home Page: www.clinicalrobotics.com

Eren Berber, President
Mark Dylewski, Vice President
Rajan Sudan, Executive Member
Chung Ngai Tang, Secretary
Joseph Colella, Treasurer

16742 Compressed Air and Gas Institutue
Compressed Air and Gas Institutue
1300 Sumner Ave
Cleveland, OH 44115-2851

216-241-7333
Fax: 216-241-0105
E-Mail: cagi@cagi.org
Home Page: www.cagi.org

John Addington, Manager

An organization representing manufacturers of compressed air system equipment, including air compressors, blowers, pneumatic tools and air and gasdryingand filtration equipment.
Founded in 1915

16743 Concrete Sawing and Drilling Association
Polycrystalline Products Association
100 2nd Ave S
Suite 402N
St. Petersburg, FL 33701

727-577-5004
Fax: 727-577-5012
E-Mail: info@csda.org
Home Page: www.csda.org
Social Media: Facebook, Youtube

Judith O'Day, President
Pat O'Brien, Executive Director
Kevin Baron, Vice President
Mike Orzechowski, Secretary/ Treasurer

An industrial trade association of tool fabricators, machine tool builders, material suppliers, educators and users of polycrystalline products.
500 Members
Founded in 1971

16744 Contractors Pump Bureau
Contractors Pump Bureau
6737 W Washington Street
Suite 2400
Milwaukee, WI 53214-5650

414-272-0943
866-AEM-0442
Fax: 414-272-1170
E-Mail: aem@aem.org
Home Page: www.aem.org/Groups/Groups/Group.asp?G=22
Social Media: Twitter

Rod Mersino, Chair
Jeff Davis, 1st Vice Chair
Juan Quiros, 2nd Vice Chair

A product group of the Association of Equipment Manufacturers, the CPB promotes matters of mutual interest to contractor pump users, manufacturers and parts and component suppliers. Membership is open to any AEM member in good standing actively engaged in the manufacture and distribution of portable contractor pumps within the USA, or supplying components to those manufacturers.
20 Members
Founded in 1938

16745 Converting Equipment Manufacturers Association
201 Springs Street
Fort Mill, SC 29715

803-948-9470
Fax: 803-948-9471
E-Mail: aimcal@aimcal.org
Home Page: www.cema-converting.org
Social Media: Facebook, Twitter, LinkedIn, YouTube, Instagram

Craig Sheppard, Executive Director
Tracey Ingram, Operations Manager
Melissa Crandall, Administrative Assistant
Ashley Wood, Event Planner
Colin Rupp, Web Designer
Founded in 1984

16746 Conveyor Equipment Manufacturers Association (CEMA)
5672 Strand CT
Suite 2
Naples, FL 34110

239-514-3441
Fax: 239-514-3470
E-Mail: kim@cemanet.org
Home Page: www.cemanet.org
Social Media: Facebook, Twitter, LinkedIn

Warren Chandler, President
Robert Reinfried, Executive Vice President
Jerry Heathman, Vice President
Jim McKnight, Secretary
Garry Abraham, Treasurer

Involved in writing industry standards, the CEMA seeks to promote among its members and the industry standardization of design manufacture and application on a voluntary basis and in such manner as will not impede development of conveying machinery and component parts or lessen competition. CEMA sponsors an annual Engineering Conference that allows Member Company Engineers to meet and develop or improve CEMA Consensus Industry Standards and National Standards that affect the conveyor industry.
96 Members
Founded in 1933

16747 Farm Equipment Manufacturers Association
Farm Equipment Manufacturers Association
1000 Executive Parkway Dr
Suite 100
St Louis, MO 63141-6369

314-878-2304
Fax: 314-732-1480
E-Mail: info@farmequip.org
Home Page: www.farmequip.org
Social Media: Twitter

Marc McConnell, President
Mike Kloster, 1st Vice President
Richard Kirby, Second VP
Vernon Schmidt, Executive Vice President
Hannah Hamontree, Communications Director

An information gathering and distributing organization for farm equipment manufacturers and suppliers.
340 Members

16748 Fire Equipment Manufacturers' Association
Fire Equipment Manufacturers' Association
1300 Sumner Avenue
Cleveland, OH 44115-2851
216-241-7333
Fax: 216-241-0105
E-Mail: fema@femalifesafety.org
Home Page: www.femalifesafety.org
Social Media: Youtube

The premier trade association representing leading brands, and spanning dozens of product categories, related to fire protection.
24 Members
Founded in 1925

16749 Fluid Power Safety Institute
2170 South 3140 West
West Valley City, UT 84119

801-908-5456
Fax: 801-908-5734
E-Mail: info@fluidpowersafety.com
Home Page: www.fluidpowersafety.com

Rory S. McLaren, Founder & Director

16750 Fluid Power Society
Fluid Power Society
1930 E Marlton Pike
PO Box 1420
Cherry Hill, NJ 08034-0054

856-489-8983
800-308-6005
Fax: 856-424-9248
E-Mail: Askus@ifps.org
Home Page: www.ifps.org

Mark Perry, CFPHS, President & Chairperson
Donna Pollander, ACA, Executive Director
Sue Tesauro, Event Planner/Certification Manager
Adele Kayser, Website/Communications Manager
Sue Dyson, Membership Coordinator

International organization for fluid power and motion control professionals.
2600 Members
Founded in 1960

16751 Food Processing Suppliers Association
Food Processing Suppliers Association

1451 Dolley Madison Blvd
Suite 101
Mc Lean, VA 22101-3850

703-761-2600
Fax: 703-761-4334
E-Mail: info@fpsa.org
Home Page: www.fpsa.org
Social Media: Facebook, Twitter, LinkedIn

Jeff Dahl, Chairman
David Seckman, President & CEO
Robyn Roche, CFO
Andy Drennan, Senior VP, International Market
Adam Finney, VP of Membership and Communications

Trade association for food and beverage processing suppliers.
350+ Members

16752 **Heat Exchange Institute**
Heat Exchange Institute
1300 Sumner Avenue
Cleveland, OH 44115-2851

216-241-7333
Fax: 216-241-0105
E-Mail: hei@heatexchange.org
Home Page: www.heatexchange.org

John H Addington, Secretary-Treasurer
Craig H Addington, Account Executive

A non-profit trade association committed to the technical advancement, promotion and understanding of a broad range of utility and industrial-scale heat exchange and vacuum apparatus.
19 Members
Founded in 1933

16753 **Industrial Distribution Association**
Industrial Distribution Association
100 N 20th Street
4th Floor
Philadelphia, PA 19103

215-320-3862
866-460-2360
Fax: 215-564-2175
E-Mail: info@isapartners.org
Home Page: www.ida-assoc.org

John Duffy, Director
Ed Gerber, Director

Promotes the industry and the use of converting equipment. Conducts research and compiles statistics for wholesalers of industrial equipment.
650 Members
Founded in 1988

16754 **International Association of Diecutting and Diemaking**
651 W Terra Cotta Ave
Suite 132
Crystal Lake, IL 60014

815-455-7519
800-828-4233
Fax: 815-455-7510
E-Mail: staff@iadd.org
Home Page: www.iadd.org
Social Media: LinkedIn

Cindy Crouse, CEO
Nikki Faul, Chapter & Meeting Assistant
Jenny Holliday, Membership & Desktop Publishing

A not-for-profit international trade association serving diecutters, diemakers, and industry suppliers worldwide. Provides conferences, educational and training programs, networking opportunities, a monthly magazine, technical articles, regional chapter meetings, publications and training manuals, recommended specifications, videos and surveys.

16755 **International Association of Machinists and Aerospace**
International Association of Machinists
9000 Machinists Pl
Upper Marlboro, MD 20772-2675

301-967-4500
Fax: 301-967-4588
E-Mail: websteward@iamaw.org
Home Page: www.goiam.org
Social Media: Facebook, Twitter, RSS, Ucubed

R Thomas Buffenbarger, CEO
Robert Martinez, Jr., General VP
Robert Roach, Jr., General Secretary-Treasurer
Diane Babineaux, Executive Assistant

Has an annual budget of approximately $101.3 million.
Founded in 1888

16756 **International Association of Professional Mechanical Engineers**
55 Public Square
Suite 612
Cleveland, OH 44113

216-453-0500
Home Page: iapme.org

Founded in 1954

16757 **Machinery Dealers National Association**
Machinery Dealers National Association
315 S Patrick St
Alexandria, VA 22314-3532

703-836-9300
800-872-7807
Fax: 703-836-9303
E-Mail: office@mdna.org
Home Page: www.mdna.org
Social Media: Facebook, Twitter, LinkedIn, Youtube

Ron Shuster, AEA, President
Richard Levy CEA, President

Represents dealers of used industrial equipment.
383 Members
Founded in 1941

16758 **Manufacturers Alliance for Productivity and Innovation**
1600 Wilson Blvd
Suite 1100
Arlington, VA 22209-2594

703-841-9000
Fax: 703-841-9514
Home Page: www.mapi.net
Social Media: Facebook, Twitter, LinkedIn, Youtube, RSS

Carlos M. Cardoso, Chairman
John M. Stropki, Vice Chairman
Stephen V. Gold, President
Cameron L. Mackey, Vice President, Sales and Marketing
Daniel J. Meckstroth, Vice President and Chief Economist

A policy research organization whose members are companies drawn from the producers and users of capital goods and allied products. Includes leading companies in heavy industry, automotive, electronics, precision instruments, telecommunications, computers, office systems. aerospace, oil/gas, chemicals and similar high technology industries.
500+ Members
Founded in 1933

16759 **Material Handling Institute**
Crane Manufacturers Association of America
8720 Red Oak Boulevard
Suite 201
Charlotte, NC 28217-3996

704-676-1190
Fax: 704-676-1199
E-Mail: jnofsinger@mhia.org
Home Page: www.mhia.org/psc
Social Media: Facebook, Twitter, LinkedIn, Youtube, Blooger, RSS

E. Larry Strayhorn, Executive Chairman
Dave Young, Executive Vice Chairman
John Paxton, Vice Chairman
Cathy Moose, Executive Assistant
Victoria Wheeler, Director Member Services

Supports crane equipment manufacturers.
22 Members
Founded in 1945

16760 **Mechanical Power Transmission Association**
Mechanical Power Transmission Association
5672 Strand Ct.
Suite 2
Naples, FL 34110

239-514-3441
Fax: 239-514-3470
E-Mail: bob@mpta.org
Home Page: www.mpta.org
Social Media: Youtube

Robert Reinfried, Executive VP

Formerly Multiple V-Belt and Mechanical Power Transmission Association.
23 Members

16761 **National Fluid Power Association**
National Fluid Power Association
3333 N Mayfair Road
Suite 211
Milwaukee, WI 53222-3219
414-778-3344
Fax: 414-778-3361
E-Mail: nfpa@nfpa.com
Home Page: www.nfpa.com
Social Media: Facebook, Twitter, LinkedIn, Google+

Roger Sherrard, Chairman of the Board
Eric Lanke, Chief Executive Officer
Denise Rockhill, Marketing and Communication Manager
Pete Alles, Director of Association Services
Sue Chase, Director of Workforce Development

Members are companies which have designed, manufactured and nationally marketed a fluid power component for a least two years in the US.
Founded in 1955

16762 **National Tooling & Machining Association**
National Tooling & Machining Association
1357 Rockside Road
Cleveland, OH 44134

301-248-6200
800-248-6862
Fax: 216-264-2840
E-Mail: info@ntma.org
Home Page: www.ntma.org
Social Media: Twitter, LinkedIn

Rob Akers, CEO
Rich Basalla, Membership Officer
Tiffany Bryson, Sales/Sponsorship Manager
John Capka, Chief Financial Officer

Members are makers of jigs, molds, tools, gages, dies and fixtures for companies doing precision machining. Supports the NTMA - Committee for A Strong Economy.
2800 Members
Founded in 1943

16763 North American Equipment Dealers Association

1195 Smizer Mill Rd
Fenton, MO 63026-3480

636-349-5000
Fax: 636-349-5443
E-Mail: naeda@naeda.com
Home Page: www.naeda.com
Social Media: Facebook, Twitter, LinkedIn

Tom Nobbe, Chairman
Michael Williams, VP, Government Relations/Treasurer
Joseph Dykes, Director of Member Services
Amy Volk, Administrative Assistant
Doug Kreienkamp, Accounting Assistant / Membership

NAEDA and its affiliates provides a variety of educational, financial, legislative and legal services to equipment dealers in the United States and Canada.
5000 Members
Founded in 1900

16764 Outdoor Power Equipment and Engine Service Association

Outdoor Power Equipment and Engine
37 Pratt Street
Essex, CT 06426-1159

860-767-1770
Fax: 860-767-7932
E-Mail: executivedirector@opeesa.com
Home Page: www.opeesa.com

Todd Winstead, President and Director
Ron Monroe, Vice President/Annual Meeting
Nancy Cueroni, Executive Director
Robert Smith, Director
Rick Bryan IV, Director

Members are distributors of outdoor power equipment to retailers with a minimum of $1 million gross sales. Associate membership is available for suppliers and finance companies associated with the industry.

16765 Packaging Machinery Manufacturers Institute

Packaging Machinery Manufacturers
11911 Freedom Drive
Suite 600
Reston, VA 20190

703-243-8555
Fax: 703-243-8556
E-Mail: pmmiwebhelp@pmmi.org
Home Page: www.pmmi.org
Social Media: Facebook, Twitter, LinkedIn, Youtube

Charles D. Yuska, President and CEO
Tom Egan, Vice President, Industry Services
Maria Ferrante, Vice President
Patti Fee, Vice President Meetings And Events
Jim Pittas, Vice President, Tradeshows

Trade association for manufacturers of packaging and packaging-related converting equipment. PMMI offers meetings, an inquiry service, statistics and surveys, and a business to business survey on its website. PMMI also offers several Pack Expos (packaging related tradeshows).

16766 Powder Actuated Tool Manufacturers' Institute

Powder Actuated Tool Manufacturers
136 South Main Street
Suite 2e
Saint Charles, MO 63301

636-578-5510
Fax: 314-725-6592
E-Mail: info@patmi.org
Home Page: patmi.org

Represents manufacturers of construction tools used to fasten to and into steel and concrete.
7 Members
Founded in 1951

16767 Power Conversion Products Council International

4 Hollis Street
PO Box 378
Sherborn, MA 01770

508-979-5935
Fax: 508-651-3920

Elizabeth Bevington-Chambers, Executive Director

Members are manufacturers and suppliers to the wall plug-in transformer/transformer charger/converter industry. Sponsor two meetings each year covering business and engineering topics.
50 Members
Founded in 1974

16768 Power Tool Institute

1300 Sumner Ave
Cleveland, OH 44115-2851

216-241-7333
Fax: 216-241-0105
E-Mail: pti@powertoolinstitute.com
Home Page: www.powertoolinstitute.com

Susan Young, Manager

The preeminent organization for building global understanding of power tools and for maintaining high standards of safety and quality control in the industry.
Founded in 1968

16769 Power-Motion Technology Representative Association

Power-Motion Technology Representative
16A Journey
Suite 200
Aliso Viejo, CA 92656

949-859-2885
888-817-PTRA
Fax: 949-855-2973
E-Mail: info@ptra.org
Home Page: www.ptra.org

Gordon Jopling, President
Doug Bower, Executive Director
Kurt Fisher, 1st Vice President
Doug Landgraf, 2nd Vice President
Bill Taylor, Treasurer

To promote the science of power transmission/motion control engineering, to promote educational programs and activities and to promote representatives placed in the industry.
Founded in 1972

16770 Precision Machined Products Association

Precision Machined Products Association
6700 West Snowville Rd
Cleveland, OH 44141-3292

440-526-0300
Fax: 440-526-5803
E-Mail: info@pmpa.org
Home Page: www.pmpa.org
Social Media: Facebook, Twitter, LinkedIn, Youtube

Darlene M. Miller, President
Tom Bernstein, Jr., First Vice President
Harry S Eighmy, Second Vice President
Charles L Kerr II, Treasurer

Produces several educational opporunities for members, emphasizing quality assurance and emerging technologies. Sponsors the PMPA Political Action Committee.

16771 Robotic Industries Association

Robotic Industries Association
900 Victors Way
Suite 140
Ann Arbor, MI 48108

734-994-6088
Fax: 734-994-3338
E-Mail: ria@robotics.org
Home Page: www.roboticsonline.com
Social Media: Facebook, Twitter, LinkedIn

Jeff Burnstein, Executive Director

Only trade group in North America specifically to serve the rototics industry.
Founded in 1974

16772 Service Dealers Association

PO Box 73796
Houston, TX 77273-3063

281-443-3063
Fax: 817-921-3741

Melinda Delgado, Executive Director

Represents dealers and distributors of power equipment.
690 Members
Founded in 1986

16773 Service Specialists Association

PO Box 936
Elgin, IL 60121

847-760-0067
800-763-5717
Fax: 330-722-5638
E-Mail: rbrothers@wade-partners.com
Home Page: www.truckservice.org

Larry Schmitz, President
Matt Thompson, Vice-President
Bill Wade, Executive Director
Toni Nastali, Treasurer
Randy Brothers, Manager

Members are persons, firms or corporations who have operated a full line heavy duty repair service shop for at least one year with sufficient inventory to service market area, having rebuilding department capable of making all necessary repairs.
140 Members
Founded in 1981

16774 Society of Manufacturing Engineers

Society of Manufacturing Engineers
1 SME Drive
PO Box 930
Dearborn, MI 48128

313-425-3000
800-733-4763
Fax: 313-425-3400
E-Mail: advertising@sme.org
Home Page: www.sme.org
Social Media: Facebook, Twitter, LinkedIn, Youtube, RSS

Dennis S. Bray, PHD, FSME, President/Interim CEO
Wayne F. Frost, CMfgE, Vice President
Dean L. Bartles, PhD, FSME, Secretary/Treasurer
Debbie Holton, Managing Director
Jeannine Kunz, Managing Director

Serves its members and others in the international manufacturing community by identifying, evaluating and explaining the adoption and integration of emerging information technologies to create business value.
7000 Members
Founded in 1932

16775 **Society of Robotic Surgery**
Two Woodfield Lake
1100 E Woodfield Road, Suite 350
Schaumburg, IL 60173

847-517-7225
Home Page: www.srobotics.org
Social Media: Facebook

16776 **The Association for Packaging and Processing Technologies**
11911 Fredom Drive
Suite 600
Reston, VA 20190

571-612-3200
Fax: 703-243-8556
Home Page: www.pmmi.org
Social Media: Facebook, Twitter

Bill L. Crist, Chair
Jeff Bigger, Vice Chair
Charles D. Yuska, President & CEO
Corrine G. Mulligan, Executive Assistant
Caroline Abromavage, Operations Director
650 Members
Founded in 1933

16777 **The FPDA Motion & Control Network**
105 Eastern Avenue
Suite 104
Annapolis, MD 21403

410-940-6347
E-Mail: info@fpda.org
Home Page: www.fpda.org

Alex Wheelock, President & Chairman
Scott Durand, VP, Finance & Treasurer
Patricia A. Lilly, Executive Director
Joseph M. Thompson, General Manager
Donald Smith, Accounting Manager
180 Members
Founded in 1974

16778 **Tooling Component Manufacturers Association**
36505 Florida Avenue
Hemet, CA 92545-3534

FAX 909-766-7443

Ray Fuhrer, Executive Secretary
Members are united primarily for the purpose of coordinating and standardizing sizes.
8 Members
Founded in 1958

16779 **Unified Abrasives Manufacturers' Association**
30200 Detroit Road
Cleveland, OH 44145-1967

440-899-0010
Fax: 440-892-1404
E-Mail: contact@uama.org
Home Page: www.uama.org

Founded in 1999

16780 **Valve Manufacturers Association of America (VMA)**
Valve Manufacturers Association of America
1050 17th St NW
Suite 280
Washington, DC 20036-5521

202-331-8105
Fax: 202-296-0378
E-Mail: wsandler@vma.org
Home Page: www.vma.org

Ivan Velan, Chairman
Greg Rogowski, Vice Chairman
William S. Sandler, President
Marc Pasternak, Vice President
Malena Malone-Blevins, Meetings Manager

VMA represents the interests of nearly 100 U.S. and Canadian valve, actuator, and control Manufacturers who account for approximately 80% of the total industrial valve shipments out of U.S. and Canadian facilities. The American valve industry supplies approximately 35% of worldwide valve demand. VMA member companies employ 20,000 men and women directly in supporting jobs. VMA is the only organization exclusively serving U.S. and Canadian manufacturers of industrial valves, controls and actuator
100 Members
Founded in 1938

16781 **Vibration Institute**
Vibration Institute
6262 Kingery Hwy
Suite 212
Willowbrook, IL 60527-2276

630-654-2254
Fax: 630-654-2271
E-Mail: information@vi-institute.org
Home Page: www.vi-institute.org
Social Media: Facebook, LinkedIn

Dave Corelli, President
Tom Spettel, Executive Vice President
Robin Ginner, Administrative Manager
Cyndy Catalano, Certification Associate
Ronald L. Eshleman, Ph.D., Technical Director

A not-for-profit organization dedicated to the exchange of practical vibration information on machines and structures.
3000 Members
Founded in 1972

16782 **Wood Machinery Maufacturers of America**
Wood Machinery Maufacturers of America
2105 Laurel Bush Road
Suite 201
Bel Air, MD 21015

443-640-1052
Fax: 443-640-1031
E-Mail: info@wmma.org
Home Page: www.wmma.org
Social Media: Facebook, Twitter, LinkedIn

John Schultz, President
Jamison Scott, Vice President
Fred Stringfellow, Executive Director
Diane Schafer, Director of Meetings
Amy Chetelat, Director of Finance
WMMA has worked to increase the productivity and profitability of U.S. machinery and tooling manufacturers and the businesses that support them.
Founded in 1899

16783 **Woodworking Machinery Industry Association**
27 Main St.
Suite 1
New Milford, CT 6776

860-350-WMIA
Fax: 860-354-0677
E-Mail: info@wmia.org
Home Page: www.wmia.org
Social Media: Facebook, Twitter

John Park, President
Scott Mueller, Vice President
Jason Howell, Chair, Education Committee
Riccardo Azzzoni, Executive Vice President
Liza Wentworth, Program Administrator
Founded in 1977

Newsletters

16784 **Association of Machinery and Equipment Appraisers - Newsletter**
Association of Machinery and Equipment Appraisers
315 S Patrick St
Alexandria, VA 22314-3532

703-836-7900
800-537-8629
Fax: 703-836-9303
E-Mail: amea@amea.org
Home Page: www.amea.org

Pamela Reid, Executive Director
Information about appraisers of the machinery equipment.
8 Pages
Circulation: 6800
Founded in 1983
Mailing list available for rent: 282 names at $100 per M
Printed in 2 colors on matte stock

16785 **CEMA Bulletin**
Conveyor Equipment Manufacturers Association
5672 Strand Ct., Suite 2
Naples, FL 34110

239-514-3441
Fax: 239-514-3470
E-Mail: cema@cemanet.org
Home Page: www.cemanet.org

Robert Reinfried, Executive Director
Association and conveyor industry news.
6 Pages
Circulation: 96
Founded in 1933

16786 **Caster and Wheel Handbook**
Youngs
55 E Cherry Ln
Souderton, PA 18964-1550

215-723-4400
800-523-5454
Fax: 800-544-3239
E-Mail: custrep@youngscatalog.com
Home Page: www.youngscatalog.com

Paul O Young Jr, President
Technical news and information.
Frequency: Monthly
Founded in 1945

16787 **Computer Aided Design Report**
CAD/CAM Publishing
711 Van Nuys Street
San Diego, CA 92109-1053

858-488-0533
Fax: 858-488-0361
E-Mail: info@cadcampub.com
Home Page: www.cadcampub.com/

Randall Newton, Editor
Uses of computers by engineers in the manufacturing trades.
Cost: $344.00
Frequency: Monthly
ISSN: 0276-749X
Founded in 1977

16788 **Computer Integrated Manufacture and Engineering**
Lionheart Publishing

2555 Cumberland Pkwy Se
Suite 299
Atlanta, GA 30339-3921

770-432-2551
Fax: 770-432-6969

Explores cutting edge developments in manufacturing systems operation management.
Circulation: 24,000

16789 High-Tech Materials Alert
John Wiley & Sons
111 River St
Hoboken, NJ 07030-5790

201-748-6000
800-825-7550
Fax: 201-748-6088
E-Mail: info@wiley.com
Home Page: www.wiley.com

William J Pesce, CEO

Details significant developments in high-performance materials ranging from alloys and metallic whiskers to ceramic and graphite fibers, their fabrication and industrial applications.
Cost: $1152.00
Frequency: Monthly
Founded in 1807

16790 Industrial Health & Hazards Update
InfoTeam
PO Box 15640
Plantation, FL 33318-5640

954-473-9560
Fax: 954-473-0544

Merton Allen, Editor

Covers occupational safety, health, hazards, and disease, mitigatioin and control of hazardous situations; waste recycling and treaqtment; environmental pollution and control; product safety and liability; fires and explosions; plant and computer security,; air pollution; surface and ground water; wastewater; soil gases; combustion and incineration; earth warming; ozone layer depletion; electromagnetic radiation; toxic materials; and many other related topics.
Frequency: Monthlyth

16791 Innovators Digest
InfoTeam
PO Box 15640
Plantation, FL 33318-5640

954-473-9560
Fax: 954-473-0544

Merton Allen, Editor

A multidisciplinary publication covering developments in science, engineering, products, markets, business development, manufacturing and other technological developments having industrial or commercial significance.
Frequency: Bi-Weekly

16792 Intelligent Manufacturing
Lionheart Publishing
506 Roswell St Se
Suite 220
Marietta, GA 30060-4101

770-422-3139
Fax: 770-432-6969
E-Mail: lpi@lionhrtpub.com
Home Page: www.lionhrtpub.com

John Llewellyn, Publisher
David Blanchard, Advertising Sales Manager
Marvin Diamond, Advertising Sales Manager

Provides expert solutions to manufacturing professionals covering production problems, developments in manufacturing systems.
Cost: $20.00
Frequency: Weekly
Circulation: 1598
Founded in 1987

16793 Machinery Outlook
Manfredi & Associates
20934 W Lakeview Pkwy
Mundelein, IL 60060-9502

847-949-9080
Fax: 847-949-9910
E-Mail: info@manfredi.com
Home Page: www.machineryoutlook.com

Frank Manfredi, President

A newsletter about and for the construction and mining machinery industry.
Cost: $550.00
14 Pages
Frequency: Monthly
Founded in 1984
Printed in one color on matte stock

16794 Machining Technology
Society of Manufacturing Engineers
1 SME Drive
PO Box 930
Dearborn, MI 48121

313-425-3000
800-733-4763
Fax: 313-425-3400
E-Mail: advertising@sme.org
Home Page: www.sme.org

Mark Tomlinson, Executive Director/General Manager
Greg Sheremet, Publisher
Bob Harris, Director Finance

Covers all aspects of machining in manufacturing, milling, grinding, honing, etc.
Cost: $60.00
8 Pages
Frequency: Quarterly
Circulation: 3770
Founded in 1932
Printed in 2 colors on matte stock

16795 Manufacturing Technology
National Technical Information Service
5285 Port Royal Rd
Springfield, VA 22161-0001

703-605-6000
Fax: 703-605-6900
E-Mail: info@ntis.gov
Home Page: www.ntis.gov

Linda Davis, VP
Patrik Ekstrom, Business Development Manager
Reuel Avila, Managing Director

Covers CAD/CAM, robotics, robots, productivity, manufacturing, planning, processing and control, plant design and computer software.

16796 NTMA Record
Tooling
9300 Livingston Road
Fort Washington, MD 20744-4905

301-248-5071
800-248-6862
Fax: 301-248-7104
E-Mail: tom@ntma.org
Home Page: www.ntma.org

Rob Akers, Operations Director/ Publisher
Richard Wills, CEO
Thomas Garcia, Manager, Marketing

Covers activities of 4,000 member companies of tool, die and precision machining industries.
Cost: $39.00
16 Pages
Frequency: Monthly
Circulation: 2000
Founded in 1943

16797 Wood Machining News
Wood Machining Institute
PO Box 476
Berkeley, CA 94701

510-448-8363
Fax: 925-945-0947
E-Mail: szymani@woodmachining.com
Home Page: www.woodmachining.com

Ryszard Szymani, Director

Information on the latest technological advances in the field of wood machining, including sawing, planning and sanding operations as well as the production of veneers and chips and equipment associated with these operations. WMN also reports on new machinery, processes and software, cutting tools and machinery and worker safety.
Cost: $72.00
38448 Pages
Circulation: 600
ISSN: 0743-5232
Founded in 1984

Magazines & Journals

16798 American Society of Mechanical Engineers
American Society of Mechanical Engineers
3 Park Ave
Suite 21
New York, NY 10016-5990

212-591-7000
800-843-2763
Fax: 202-429-9417
E-Mail: infocentral@asme.org
Home Page: www.asme.org

Thomas Loughlin, Executive Director
John G Falcioni, Editor-in-Chief
Frequency: Monthly
Founded in 1880

16799 American Tool, Die & Stamping News
Eagle Publications
42400 Grand River Ave
Suite 103
Novi, MI 48375-2572

248-347-3487
800-783-3491
Fax: 248-347-3492
E-Mail: info@ameritooldie.com
Home Page: www.ameritooldie.com

Arthur Brown, President
Joan Oakley, CEO

Applications, techniques, equipment and accessories of metal stamping, moldmaking, electric discharge machining; and new product information relating to the tool and die industry. Accepts advertising.
70 Pages
Circulation: 36000
ISSN: 0192-5709
Founded in 1971
Printed in 4 colors on glossy stock

16800 Compressed Air Magazine
Ingersoll Rand Company
200 Chestnut Ridge Road
Woodcliff, NJ 07677

201-573-0123
Fax: 201 573-3172
Home Page: www.irco.com

Michele Zayle, Circulation Director
Thomas McAloon, Editor

A magazine of applied technology and industrial management for middle and upper level managers in diversified industries.
Cost: $15.00
44 Pages
Frequency: 8 per year

Circulation: 125,000
Printed in 4 colors on matte stock

16801 Contact
Furnas Electric Company
1000 McKee Street
Batavia, IL 60510-1682

630-879-6000
Fax: 630-879-0867

Steve Wilcox, Editor

Application of electric motor controls to electrically operated machinery and equipment.
Circulation: 4,000

16802 Cutting Edge
Int'l Assoc of Diecutting and Diemaking
651 W Terra Cotta Ave
Suite 132
Crystal Lake, IL 60014

815-455-7519
800-828-4233
Fax: 815-455-7510
E-Mail: cccrouse@iadd.org
Home Page: www.iadd.org

Cindy Crouse, CEO
Jill May, Chapter Relations Coordinator

A technical journal and trade magazine written and edited specifically for diecutters, diemakers and industry suppliers who are faced with the need to stay ahead of technologies in an industry that is changing at breakneck speed.
Frequency: Monthly

16803 Diesel Progress: North American Edition
Diesel & Gas Turbine Publications
20855 Watertown Rd
Suite 220
Waukesha, WI 53186-1873

262-754-4100
Fax: 262-754-4175
E-Mail: mmcneely@dieselpub.com
Home Page: www.dieselspec.com

Michael Osenga, President
S Bollwahn, Circulation Manager

Geared towards readers interested in state-of-the-art systems technology. Features include new product listings, systems design, research and product testing as well as systems maintenance and rebuilding.
Frequency: Monthly
Circulation: 26011

16804 EE-Evaluation Engineering
Nelson Publishing Inc
2500 Tamiami Trl N
Nokomis, FL 34275-3476

941-966-9521
Fax: 941-966-2590
Home Page: www.healthmgttech.com
Social Media: Facebook

A Verner Nelson, President

Leading source of information for the electronics testing and evaluation market.
Founded in 1962

16805 Elevator World
Elevator World
PO Box 6507
Mobile, AL 36660-0507

251-479-4514
800-730-5093
Fax: 251-479-7043
E-Mail: editorial@elevator-world.com
Home Page: www.elevator-world.com

T Bruce Mackinnon, CEO
Robert S Caporale, Senior VP/Editor
Patricia Cartee, VP/Commercial Operations

International journal for those involved in short-range vertical transportation, including manufacturers, contractors, maintainers, consultants and inspectors.
Cost: $75.00
170 Pages
Frequency: Monthly
Circulation: 7,000
Founded in 1953
Printed in 4 colors on glossy stock

16806 Equip-Mart
Story Communications
116 N Camp Street
Seguin, TX 78155

830-303-3328
800-864-1155
Fax: 830-372-3011
Home Page: www.equip-mart.com

Tammy Reilly, Publisher

Largest industrial equipment magazine in North America. Received by manufacturig executives who purchase or sell industrial equipment, tools, supplies and accessories.
Frequency: Monthly
Circulation: 108,000

16807 Gear Technology
Randall Publishing Company
PO Box 1426
Elk Grove Village, IL 60009

847-437-6604
Fax: 847-437-6618
Home Page: www.geartechnology.com

Michael Goldstein, Publisher
William R Stott, Managing Editor
Dan Pels, Business Development Mana
Carol Tratar, Circulation Coordinator
Richard Goldstein, Vice President

Gear Technology offers technical articles from the top names in the industry; feature articles dealing with management and technology; top-notch tradeshow coverage; industry and products news.
Circulation: 13025
Founded in 1934
Printed in 4 colors on glossy stock

16808 High Performance Composites
Ray Publishing
P.O.Box 992
Morrison, CO 80465-0992

303-467-1776
Fax: 303-467-1777
E-Mail: info@raypubs.com
Home Page: www.compositeworld.com

Approach is technical, offering cutting-edge design, engineering, prototyping, and manufacturing solutions for aerospace and other traditional and emerging structural applications for advanced composites.

16809 Home Medical Equipment News
United Publications
106 Lafayette Street
PO Box 998
Yarmouth, ME 04096

207-846-0600
Fax: 207-846-0657
Home Page: www.hmenews.com

James G Taliaferro, CEO/President
Brenda Boothby, Circulation Director
Joline V Gilman, Production Director
Jim Sullivan, Editor
Rick Rector, Publisher

Serves home medical equipment providers.
Frequency: Monthly
Circulation: 17100
Founded in 1995

16810 Home Shop Machinist
Village Press
2779 Aero Park Drive
PO Box 968
Traverse City, MI 49685-968

231-946-3712
800-327-7377
Fax: 231-946-3289
E-Mail: info@villagepress.com
Home Page: www.villagepress.com

Robert Goff, Publisher
Neil Knopf, Editor
Joe D. Rice, Editor in Chief
Angela Sagi, Advertising Director

Articles on precision machining and metal working and how-to projects geared towards the amateur machinist and small commercial machine shops.
Cost: $25.00
Circulation: 28000

16811 IEEE Transactions on Industry Applications
IEEE Operations Center
PO Box 1331
Piscataway, NJ 08855-1331

732-981-0060
Fax: 732-981-1721
E-Mail: society-info@ieee.org
Home Page: www.ieee.org

John Vig, CEO
Johnathan Dahl, Director of Sales and Marketing

The development and applications of electrical systems, apparatus, devices and controls to the processes and equipment of industry and commerce.
Cost: $515.00
Circulation: 5100
Founded in 1980

16812 InTech
ISA Services
67 Alexander Drive
PO Box 12277
Research Triangle Park, NC 27709

919-549-8411
Fax: 919-990-9434
E-Mail: info@isa.org
Home Page: www.isa.org

Greg Hale, Editor
Richard Simpson, Publisher

Covers the most recent developments in the instrumention, measurement and control market.
Frequency: Monthly
Circulation: 75000
Founded in 1945

16813 Industrial Machine Trader
Heartland Industrial Group
1003 Central Avenue
PO Box 1415
Fort Dodge, IA 50501

515-955-1600
800-203-9960
Fax: 515-955-3753
E-Mail: ads@industrialgroup.com
Home Page: www.imtgetsresults.com/

Tony Smith, Publisher
Gele Mckinney, President
Angi Hesterman, Circulation Manager

Industrial machinery equipment, suppliers and manufacturers.
Cost: $67.85
8 Pages
Frequency: Weekly
Circulation: 234000
Founded in 1970

16814 **Industrial Market Place**
Wineberg Publications
7842 Lincoln Avenue
Skokie, IL 60077

847-676-1900
800-323-1818
Fax: 847-676-0063
E-Mail: info@industrialmktpl.com
Home Page: www.industrialmktpl.com

Joel Wineberg, President
Jackie Bitensky, Editor
Has advertisements on machinery, industrial and plant equipment, services and industrial acution in each issue.
Cost: $175.00
Frequency: Every 2 weeks
Circulation: 14,000
Founded in 1951
Mailing list available for rent: 120 names at $70 per M
Printed in 4 colors on glossy stock

16815 **Journal of Engineering for Industry**
American Society of Mechanical Engineers
3 Park Ave
Suite 21
New York, NY 10016-5990

212-591-7000
800-843-2763
Fax: 212-591-7674
E-Mail: Infocentral@asme.org
Home Page: www.asmc.org

Richard E Feigel, President
David Soukup, Managing Director
Covers interfaces of mechanical engineering.
Cost: $40.00
Founded in 1880

16816 **Journal of Materials Engineering and Performance**
ASM International
9639 Kinsman Road
Materials Park, OH 44073-0002

440-338-5151
800-336-5152
Fax: 440-338-4634
E-Mail: memberservice@asminternational.org
Home Page: www.asminternational.org
Social Media: Facebook, Twitter, LinkedIn

Jeane Deatherage, Administrator, Foundation Programs
Virginia Shirk, Foundation Executive Assistant
Peer-reviewed journal that publishes contributions on all aspects of materials selection, design, characterization, processing and performance testing. The journal for solving day-to-day engineering challenges - especially those involving components for larger systems.
Cost: $1965.00
Frequency: Bimonthly
Circulation: 305
Founded in 1992

16817 **Journal of Thermal Spray Technology**
ASM International
9639 Kinsman Rd
Novelty, OH 44072-9603

440-338-5151
Fax. 440-338 4634
E-Mail: Cust-Srv@asminternational.org
Home Page: www.asminternational.org
Social Media: Facebook, Twitter, LinkedIn
Jeane Deatherage, Administrator, Foundation Programs
Virginia Shirk, Foundation Executive Assistant
Peer-reviewed journal which publishes contributions on all aspects, fundamental and practical, of thermal spray science, including processes, feedstock manufacture, testing and characterization. As the primary vehicle for thermal spray information transfer, its mission is to synergize the rapidly advancing thermal spray industry and related industries by presenting research and development efforts leading to advancements in implementable engineering applications of the technology.
Cost: $1577.00
Frequency: Bimonthly
Circulation: 680
Founded in 1952

16818 **Locator Services**
Locator Online
315 S Patrick St
Suite 3
Alexandria, VA 22314-3532

703-836-9700
800-537-1446
Fax: 703-836-7665
E-Mail: sales@locatoronline.com
Home Page: www.locatoronline.com

Terry Pitman, Publisher
Used metalworking equipment.
Cost: $38.00
Frequency: Monthly
Circulation: 225000
Founded in 1969

16819 **Machine Shop Guide**
Worldwide Communications
401 Worthington Avenue
Harrison, NJ 07029-2039

973-977-7555
Fax: 253-872-7603
Home Page: www.machineshopguide.com

Robert L Hatschek, Executive Editor
Frederick Mason, Editor
Information on manufacturing technology, new applications for manufacturing technology and new products. Focus is metal cutting machines and tooling.
Frequency: 10 per year
Circulation: 102,893
Founded in 1996
Printed in 4 colors on glossy stock

16820 **Machinery Trader**
Sandhills Publishing
PO Box 82545
Lincoln, NE 68501-2545

402-479-2181
800-247-4898
Fax: 402-479-2195
E-Mail: feedback@sandhills.com
Home Page: www.sandhills.com

Tom Peed, CEO
Marva Wasser, Editor-in-Chief
Covering heavy equipment.
Cost: $59.00
160 Pages
Frequency: Weekly
Circulation: 20000
Founded in 1978

16821 **Managing Automation**
Thomas Publishing Company
5 Penn Plz
Suite 10
New York, NY 10001-1860
212-695-0500
Fax: 212-290-7362
E-Mail: businesslists@thomaspublishing.com
Home Page: www.thomaspublishing.com

Carl Holst-Knudsen, CEO
Robert Malone, Editor
Heather L Mikisch, Publisher
Kim Vennard, Marketing Manager
Serves the needs of those managers and engineers responsible for the planning and implementation of factory automation at both the plant and enterprise levels.
Frequency: Monthly
Circulation: 100246
Founded in 1898

16822 **Manufacturing Engineering**
Society of Manufacturing Engineers
1 SME Drive
#930
Dearborn, MI 48121

313-425-3000
800-733-4763
Fax: 313-425-3400
E-Mail: advertising@sme.org
Home Page: www.sme.org

Mark Tomlinson, Executive Director
Greg Sheremet, Publisher
Gene Nelson, President
Serves metalworking industry machining, forming, inspection, assembly and processing operations.
Frequency: Monthly
Circulation: 111966
Founded in 1932

16823 **Modern Machine Shop**
Gardner Publications
6915 Valley Ln
Cincinnati, OH 45244-3153

513-527-8800
800-950-8020
Fax: 513-527-8801
E-Mail: mmsmkt@gardnerweb.com
Home Page: www.gardnerweb.com

Rick Kline Sr, CEO
Mark D Albert, Manager
John Campos, Manager
Brian Wertheimer, Account Manager
Eddie Kania, Sales Manager
Reaches metalworking plants of all sizes - from small job shops to giant aerospace and automotive plants. It is edited for those involved in metalworking operations, particularly those performed on machine tools.
Cost: $4.00
Frequency: Monthly
Circulation: 107000
Founded in 1928
Mailing list available for rent: 106M names
Printed in 4 colors on glossy stock

16824 **Motion Control**
ISA Services
PO Box 12277
Durham, NC 27709-2277

919-549-8411
Fax: 919-990-9434
E-Mail: info@isa.org
Home Page: www.isa.org

Sam Batman, Editor
Richard Simpson, Publisher
Robert Renner, Executive Director
Information for those who design and maintain motion control systems.
Cost: $54.00
56 Pages
Circulation: 41000
ISSN: 1058-4644
Founded in 1945
Printed in 4 colors on glossy stock

16825 **Motion System Distributor**
Penton Media
1166 Avenue of the Americas/10th Fl
New York, NY 10036

212-204-4200
Fax: 216-696-6662

E-Mail: information@#penton.com
Home Page: www.penton.com

Jane Cooper, Marketing
Chris Meyer, Director, Corporate Communications

Provides selling and technical information to individuals and distributors specializing in power transmission, motion control and fluid products.

16826 **NAEDA Buyer's Guide**
North American Equipment Dealers Association
1195 Smizer Mill Road
Fenton, MO 63026-3480

636-349-5000
Fax: 636-349-5443
E-Mail: naeda@naeda.com
Home Page: www.naeda.com
Social Media: Twitter, LinkedIn

Annual directory of contact names, trade and product names of more than two thousand of the equipment industry's manufacturers and suppliers.
Cost: $35.00
5000 Members
Frequency: Annually
Founded in 1900

16827 **OEM Worldwide**
Cygnus Publishing
PO Box 803
Fort Atkinson, WI 53538-0803

920-000-1111
Fax: 920-563-1699
E-Mail: tjheinlein@cableinet.co.uk
Home Page: www.cygnusb2b.com

John French, CEO
Leslie Shalabi, Publisher
James S Rank, VP
Sue Cullen, Advertising Manager
Brett Apold, Corporate Production Director

Designed to be a resource of operational and general productivity information for original equipment manufacturers in Europe, competing in the global marketplace.
Cost: $6.00
Frequency: Monthly
Circulation: 16800
Founded in 1984

16828 **Outdoor Power Equipment**
1900 Arch Street
Philadelphia, PA 19103-1404

215-564-3484
Fax: 215-564-2175

Julie S Burns, Executive Director

Members are distributors of outdoor power equipment to retailers with a minimum of $1 million gross sales. Associate members are suppliers and finance companies.
150 Pages
Founded in 1980

16829 **Plant Engineering**
Reed Business Information
30 Technology Parkway South
Suite 100
Norcross, GA 30092

646-746-6400
800-424-3996
Fax: 646-756-7583
E-Mail: webmaster@reedbusiness.com
Home Page: www.reedbusiness.com

John Poulin, CEO
Richard L Dunn, Editor
Gerard Van de Aast, Director
Carel de Bos, Chief Information Officer

The magazine for plant engineering professionals responsible for the maintenance, repair and operations of plant facilities, equipment and systems.
Cost: $3.00
Circulation: 116700

16830 **Processing Magazine**
Grand View Media Group
200 Croft Street
Suite 1
Birmingham, AL 35242

888-431-2877
Fax: 205-408-3797
E-Mail: webmaster@grandviewmedia.com
Home Page: www.gvmg.com/

Leading source for up-to-date product and equipment solutions.

16831 **Production Machining**
Gardner Publications
6915 Valley Ln
Cincinnati, OH 45244-3153

513-527-8800
800-950-8020
Fax: 513-527-8801
E-Mail: jjordan@gardnerweb.com
Home Page: www.gardnerweb.com

Rick Kline Sr, CEO
Leo Rakowski, Senior Editor
John Jordan, Assistant Editor
Lori Beckman, Managing Editor
John Campos, Manager
Frequency: Monthly
Circulation: 200000
Founded in 1928

16832 **Pumps & Systems**
Randall Publishing Company
1900 28th Ave S
Suite 110
Homewood, AL 35209-2627

205-212-9402
Fax: 205-212-9452
Home Page: www.pump-zone.com

Walter Evans, President
George Lake, Associate Publisher
Scott Kidwell, Advertising Sales
Tom Cory, Circulation
Robert Windle, CEO
Frequency: Monthly
Founded in 2002

16833 **Sensors Magazine**
Advanstar Communications
7500 Old Oak Blvd
Cleveland, OH 44130-3343

440-243-8100
Fax: 440-891-2740
E-Mail: info@advanstar.com
Home Page: www.act-europe.org

Barbara G Goode, Editor-in-Chief
Donna Pellerin George, Associate Editor
Joseph Loggia, CEO
Georgiann Decenzo, Director of Corporate marketing
Francis Heid, Vice President of Publishing

Primary source among design and production engineers of information on sensor technologies and products, and topic integral to sensor-based systems and applications. Provides practical and in-depth yet accessible information on sensor operation, design, application, and implementation within systems. Covers the effective use of state-of-the-art resources and tools that enable readers to get the maximum benefit from their use of sensors.
Frequency: Monthly
Circulation: 75000
Founded in 1984

16834 **Valve Magazine**
Valve Manufacturers Association of America
1050 17th Street NW
Suite 280
Washington, DC 20036-5521

202-331-8105
Fax: 202-296-0378
E-Mail: wsandler@vma.org
Home Page: www.vma.org

Bill Sandler, President
Marc Pasternak, VP

Promotion of significance and application of US and Canadian manufactured industrial valves and actuators.
Frequency: Quarterly
Circulation: 26000

16835 **Vibrations Magazine**
Vibration Institute
6262 Kingery Hwy
Suite 212
Willowbrook, IL 60527-2276

630-654-2254
Fax: 630-654-2271
E-Mail: information@vi-institute.org
Home Page: www.vi-institute.org

Ronald Eshleman, Executive Director

Provides current information about activities of the Vibration Institute and news about vibration technology. Each issue contains practical, technical articles and case histories.
Frequency: Quarterly
Founded in 1975

16836 **World Industrial Reporter**
Keller International Publishing Corporation
150 Great Neck Rd
Suite 400
Great Neck, NY 11021-3309

516-829-9722
Fax: 516-829-9306
Home Page: www.supplychainbrain.com

Bryan DeLuca, Editor
Terry Beirne, Publisher
Jerry Keller, President
Mary Chavez, Director of Sales

New equipment, machinery and techniques for the industry.
34 Pages
Frequency: Monthly
Circulation: 37107
Founded in 1882

Trade Shows

16837 **ASME Annual Meeting**
American Society of Mechanical Engineers
Three Park Avenue
New York, NY 10016

973-882-1170
800-843-2763
Fax: 212-591-7856
E-Mail: CustomerCare@asme.org
Home Page: www.asme.org

Melissa Torres, Meetings Manager
Mary Jakubowski, Meetings Manager
Frequency: Annual/June

16838 **ASME Gas Turbine Users Symposium (GTUS)**
American Society of Mechanical Engineers/IGTI
Three Park Avenue
New York, NY 10016-5990

973-882-1170
800-843-2763
Fax: 404-847-0151

E-Mail: CustomerCare@asme.org
Home Page: www.asme.org/igti

Stephanie Searsr, Coordinator, IGTI Conferences
Judy Osborn, Manager, IGTI Conferences & Expos

A show focused on the role gas turbines will play in meeting the nation's future energy demands, provides the information related to gas turbine operations, maintenance, advances, and design.
2000 Attendees
Frequency: Annual

16839 **Association of Machinery and Equipment Appraisers Annual Conference**
315 S Patrick Street
Alexandria, VA 22314-3501

703-836-7900
800-537-8629
Fax: 703-836-9303
E-Mail: amea@amea.org
Home Page: www.amea.org

Lorna Lindsey, Manager
Mary Flynn, Executive Director

Exhibits of interest to machinery and equipment appraisers.
Founded in 1982
Mailing list available for rent

16840 **FloorTek Expo**
American Floorcovering Alliance
210 West Cuyler St
Dalton, GA 30720-8209

706-278-4101
800-288-4101
Fax: 706-278-5323
E-Mail: afa@americanfloor.org
Home Page: www.floor-tek.com

Wanda J Ellis, Executive Director

The only internationla flooring manufacturing tradeshow dedicated to the production and materials of the industry
3000+ Attendees
Frequency: Bi-Annual

16841 **Gear Expo**
American Gear Manufacturers Association
500 Montgomery Street
Suite 350
Alexandria, VA 22314-1581

703-684-0211
Fax: 703-684-0242
Home Page: www.gearexpo.com

Kurt Medert, VP

Biennial trade show held in October of the odd-numbered years. It is the only trade show devoted exclusively to the Gear Manufacturing process.
4.5M Attendees
Frequency: October
Founded in 1987

16842 **IADD/FSEA Odyssey**
Int'l Assoc of Diecutting and Diemaking
651 W Terra Cotta Ave
Suite 132
Crystal Lake, IL 60014

815-455-7519
800-828-4233
Fax: 815-455-7510
E-Mail: cccrouse@iadd.org
Home Page: www.iadd.org

Cindy Crouse, CEO
Jill May, Chapter Relations Coordinator

The premiere education and technology expo uniquely focused on diemaking, converting, foil stamping, embossing and bindery.
Frequency: Annual/May

16843 **International Integrated Manufacturing**
Reed Exhibition Companies
255 Washington Street
Newton, MA 02458-1637

617-584-4900
Fax: 617-630-2222

Elizabeth Hitchcock, International Sales

Expo and conference dedicated to the products and technology needed by engineering operations and management to automate and integrate manufacturing.
Frequency: March

16844 **International Manufacturing Technology Show**
7901 Westpark Drive
Mc Lean, VA 22102-4206

703-893-2900
Fax: 703-893-1151
Home Page: www.amtonline.org

John Byrd, President
Peter Eelman, VP Exhibitions

Manufacturing equipment trade show.
85M Attendees
Frequency: Biennial
Founded in 1927

16845 **International Woodworking Machinery and Furniture Supply Fair: USA**
Reed Exhibition Companies
1350 E Touhy Avenue
Des Plaines, IL 60018-3303

847-294-0300
Fax: 847-635-1571

Paul Pajor, National Marketing Manager

The largest woodworking machinery and furniture supply manufacturing exposition held in the Western Hemisphere. Exhibitors interface with North American furniture, cabinet, and woodworking manufacturers. One thousand booths.
37M Attendees
Frequency: August/Biennial

16846 **Job Shop Show: Midwest**
Edward Publishing LLC
16 Waterbury Road
Prospect, CT 06712-1215

203-758-6658
Fax: 203-758-4476
Home Page: www.jobshoptechnology.com

Jennifer Bryda, Production Manager
Christoper Davis, Manager
Gerald Schmidt, President

A source for forming, fabricating, shaping, and assemblies. The show is designed to attract the highest caliber engineers and buyers from product manufacturers. There will be 170 exhibitors and booths.
1500 Attendees

16847 **National Technical Training Symposium**
Vibration Institute
6262 S Kingery Highway
Suite 212
Willowbrook, IL 60527

630-654-2254
Fax: 630-654-2271
E-Mail: information@vi-institute.org
Home Page: www.vi-institute.org

Ronald L Eshlemann, Director

Formerly the annual meeting, provides specific training in practical vibration technology.
Frequency: Annual

16848 **Powder and Bulk Solids Conference and Exhibition**
Reed Exhibition Companies
255 Washington Street
Newton, MA 02458-1637

617-584-4900
Fax: 617-630-2222

Elizabeth Hitchcock, International Sales

Equipment and technology for processing and handling of powder and bulk solids.
8.4M Attendees
Frequency: May

16849 **South-Tec Machine Tool and Manufacturing Show**
Society of Manufacturing Engineers
1 SME Drive
#930
Dearborn, MI 48128

313-425-3000
800-733-4763
Fax: 313-425-3400
E-Mail: advertising@sme.org
Home Page: www.sme.org

Mark Tomlinson, Executive Director
Greg Sheremet, Publisher

A professional society dedicated to advancing scientific knowledge in the field of manufacturing and to applying its resources for research-ing, writing, publishing and disseminating information.
70M Attendees
Frequency: March
Founded in 1932

Directories & Databases

16850 **American Machine Tool Distributors Association Directory**
1445 Research Bowl
Suite 450
Rockville, MD 20852-1421

301-738-1200
Home Page: www.metalworld.com

Greg Safko, Editor
Ralph Nappi, President

Directory of services and supplies to the industry.
Cost: $60.00
150 Pages
Frequency: Annual
Founded in 1925

16851 **American Machinist Buyers' Guide**
Penton Media
1166 Avenue of the Americas/10th Fl
New York, NY 10036

212-204-4200
Fax: 216-696-6662
E-Mail: information@penton.com
Home Page: www.penton.com

Jane Cooper, Marketing
Pat Smith, Managing Editor
Chris Meyer, Director, Corporate Communications

Guide to over manufacturers of products and services used by metalworking industries.
Cost: $6.00
Frequency: Annual
Circulation: 80,000
Printed in 4 colors on glossy stock

16852 American Mold Builders Association
PO Box 404
Medinah, IL 60157-0404

630-980-7667
Fax: 630-980-9714
E-Mail: info@amba.org
Home Page: www.amba.org

Jeanette Bradley, Editor
Kym Conis, Managing Director
Directory of services and supplies to the industry.
Cost: $25.00
50 Pages
Frequency: Annual

16853 American Textile Machinery Association Official Directory
201 Park Washington Ct
Falls Church, VA 22046-4527

703-538-1789
Fax: 703-241-5603
E-Mail: info@atmanet.org
Home Page: www.atmanet.org

Harry W Buzzerd, Owner
Clay D Tyeryar, President/Assistant Treasurer
Susan Denston, Executive VP/Secretary
Judith O Buzzerd, Meetings Manager
The Directory of the American Textile Machinery Association/ATMA offers information on over 100 member textile machinery and accessory manufacturers. ATMA is a professional trade association devoted to the advancement of manufacturers of textile machinery, parts, and accessories in the textile industry.
100 Pages

16854 Directory of Machine Tools and Manufacturing
Association for Manufacturing Technology
7901 Westpark Drive
Mc Lean, VA 22102-4206

703-893-2900
Fax: 703-893-1151

Machine tools and related products built by members of the Association for Manufacturing Technology.
Frequency: Annual

16855 Equip-Mart
116 N Camp Street
Seguin, TX 78155

830-303-3328
800-864-1155
Fax: 830-372-3011
Home Page: www.equip-mart.com

Directory of available used metalworking equipment.
Frequency: Weekly

16856 ISA Directory
Instrumentation, Systems,and Automation Society
PO Box 12277
Durham, NC 27709-2277

919-549-8411
Fax: 919-990-9434
E-Mail: info@isa.org
Home Page: www.isa.org

Premier guide to instrumentation, systems and automation
Printed in 4 colors

16857 Industrial Machine Trader
Heartland Industrial Group
1003 Central Avenue
PO Box 1415
Fort Dodge, IA 50501

515-955-1600
800-247-2000
Fax: 515-955-3753
E-Mail: igproduction@industrialgroup.com
Home Page: www.industrialgroup.com
Social Media: Facebook, Twitter, LinkedIn

Virginia Rodriguez, Publisher
Printed directory of available used metalworking equipment.
150+ Members
Frequency: Weekly
Founded in 1966

16858 Locator Services
315 S Patrick St
Alexandria, VA 22314-3532

703-836-9700
800-537-1446
Fax: 703-836-7665
E-Mail: sales@locatoronline.com
Home Page: www.locatoronline.com

Terry Pitman, Publisher
Printed directory of available used metalworking equipment.
Frequency: Monthly
Circulation: 225,000

16859 Machine Design Product Locator
Penton Media
1166 Avenue of the Americas/10th Fl
New York, NY 10036

212-204-4200
Fax: 216-696-6662
E-Mail: information@penton.com
Home Page: www.penton.com

Jane Cooper, Marketing
Chris Meyer, Director, Corporate Communications
Directory of services and supplies to the industry.
Cost: $35.00
325 Pages
Frequency: Annual
Circulation: 180,000
Printed in 4 colors on glossy stock

16860 Metalworking Machinery Mailer
Tade Publishing Group
29501 Greenfield Road
Suite 120
Southfield, MI 48076

248-552-8583
800-966-8233
Fax: 248-552-0466
Home Page: www.tadesite.com

Tom Lynch, Editor
Printed directory of available used metalworking equipment.
Frequency: Monthly

16861 Motion Control Technical Reference and Buyers Guide
ISA Services
PO Box 12277
Durham, NC 27709-2277

919-549-8411
Fax: 919-990-9434
E-Mail: info@isa.org
Home Page: www.isa.org

The most comprehensive reference source for motion control market
Founded in 2000
Printed in 4 colors

16862 Multimedia Monograph Series
SIGDA Multimedia

E-Mail: pedram@seng.usc.edu
Home Page: atrak.usc.edu/~sigda-mm/

Massoud Pedram, Program Director
Set of electronic media publications focusing on key talks/presentations given at various ACM sponsored conferences over the last few years.

16863 Orion Blue Book: Tools
Orion Research Corporation
14555 N Scottsdale Rd
Suite 330
Scottsdale, AZ 85254-3487

480-951-1114
800-844-0759
Fax: 480-951-1117
Home Page: www.bluebook.com

Roger Rohrs, Owner
List of manufacturers of tools.
Frequency: Annual

16864 Surplus Record Machinery & Equipment Directory
Thomas Scanlan
20 N Wacker Dr
Chicago, IL 60606-3004

312-372-9077
Fax: 312-372-6537
E-Mail: surplus@surplusrecord.com
Home Page: www.surplusrecord.com

Thomas Scanlan, Publisher
Listing over 55,000 items of used/surplus machine tools, machinery, electrical apparatus, and capital equipment by more than 1200 suppliers worldwide.
Cost: $33.00
736 Pages
Frequency: Monthly Magazine
Circulation: 150000
ISSN: 0039-615X
Founded in 1924

16865 ThomasNet
Thomas Publishing Company, LLC
User Services Department
5 Penn Plaza
New York, NY 10001

212-695-0500
800-699-9822
Fax: 212-290-7362
E-Mail: contact@thomaspublishing.com
Home Page: www.thomasnet.com
Social Media: Facebook, Twitter, LinkedIn

Carl Holst-Knudsen, President
Robert Anderson, VP, Planning
Mitchell Peipert, VP, Finance
Ivy Molofsky, VP, Human Resources
A way to reach qualified businesses that list their company information on ThomasNet.com. Detailed profiles promote their products, services, capabilities and brands carried. The ThomasNet.com web site is the most up-to-date compilation of 650,000 North American manufacturers, distributors, and service companies in 67,000 industrial categories.
Founded in 1898

16866 Used Machinery Buyer's Guide
Machinery Dealers National Association
315 S Patrick St
Alexandria, VA 22314-3532

703-836-9300
800-872-7807
Fax: 703-836-9303
E-Mail: office@mdna.org
Home Page: www.mdna.org

Mark Robinson, Executive VP
Richard Levy CEA, President
Over 400 dealers in used capital equipment.
Frequency: Annual, September

Industry Web Sites

16867 **http://gold.greyhouse.com**
G.O.L.D Grey House OnLine Databases
Grey House Publishing's online database platform, GOLD, offers Quick Search, Keyword Search and Expert Search for most business sectors including machinery markets. The GOLD platform makes finding the information you need quick and easy - whether you're a novice searcher or an experienced database user. All of Grey House's directory products are available for subscription on the GOLD platform.

16868 **www.amea.org**
Association of Machinery and Equipment Appraisers
Members are appraisers of the metalworking industry.

16869 **www.americanfloor.org**
American Floorcovering Alliance
Promotes the industry's products and services to the world, and educates the members and others through seminars, press releases, and trade shows.

16870 **www.avem.org**
Association of Vacuum Equipment Manufacturers International
The only non-profit U.S. association dedicated fully to companies that manufacture vacuum equipment and supplies.

16871 **www.cemanet.org**
Conveyor Equipment Manufacturers Association
Continues to be considered the resource for conveyor safety dimensional and application standards.

16872 **www.fpmsa.org (or www.iefp.org)**
Food Processing Machinery & Supplies Association
List of exhibitors from IEFP (links included).

16873 **www.greyhouse.com**
Grey House Publishing
Authoritative reference directories for most business sectors including machinery markets. Users can search the online databases with varied search criteria allowing for custom searches by product category, geographic area, sales volume, keyword, subject and more. Full Grey House catalog and online ordering also available.

16874 **www.iadd.org**
Int'l Association of Diecutting and Diemaking
A not-for-profit international trade association serving diecutters, diemakers, and industry suppliers worldwide. IADD provides conferences, educational and training programs, networking opportunities, a monthly magazine, technical articles, regional chapter meetings, publications and training manuals, recommended specifications, videos and surveys.

16875 **www.mapi.net**
Manufacturers Alliance/MAPI
A policy research organization whose members are companies drawn from the producers and users of capital goods and allied products. Includes leading companies in heavy industry, automotive, electronics, precision instruments, telecommunications, computers, office systems. aerospace, oil/gas, chemicals and similar high technology industries.

16876 **www.mdna.org**
Machinery Dealers National Association
Represents dealers of used industrial equipment.

16877 **www.naeda.com**
North American Equipment Dealers Association
Promotes the general welfare of retail agricultural, outdoor power, construction and large property equipment dealers in the United States and Canada.

16878 **www.ntma.org**
National Tooling and Machining Association
For makers of jigs, molds, tools, gages, dies and fixtures for companies doing precision machining.

16879 **www.packexpo.com**
Packaging Machinery Manufacturers Institute (PMMI)
For manufacturers of packaging and packaging-related converting equipment.

16880 **www.pmpa.org**
Precision Machined Products Association
Member companies are producers of high precision component products. Provides educational opportunities for members, emphasizing quality assurance and emerging technologies.

16881 **www.polysort.com**
Polysort.com
Includes materials, machinery and equipment, processors and industry services.

16882 **www.taol\fema.com**
Fire Equipment Manufacturers' Association
Members are companies making devices that control or extinguish fires in residential or commercial buildings.

16883 **www.vma.org**
Valve Manufacturers Association of America

Associations

16884 AAHC American Association of Healthcare
1205 Johnson Ferry Road
Suite 136-420
Marietta, GA 30068

404-661-1710
888-350-2242
Fax: 770-874-4401
E-Mail: info@aahcmail.org
Home Page: www.aahc.net

Linda Campbell, Executive Director

To serve as the preeminent credentialing, professional and practice development organization for the healthcare consulting profession; to advance the knowledge, quality and standards of practice for consulting to management in the healthcare industry; and to enhance the understanding and image of the healthcare consulting profession and member firms among its various publics.
Founded in 1949

16885 AMR Management Services
201 East Main Street
Suite 1405
Lexington, KY 40507

859-514-9150
Fax: 859-514-9207
E-Mail: info@amrms.com
Home Page: www.amrms.com
Social Media: Facebook, LinkedIn

Rebecca Klemm, President

Seeks to enhance members skills in organizational opportunities and in planning strategies to influence external events on international objectives.
400 Members
Founded in 1982

16886 Academy of Human Resource Development
1000 Westgate Drive
Suite 252
St. Paul, MN 55114

651-290-7466
Fax: 651-290-2266
E-Mail: office@ahrd.org
Home Page: www.ahrd.orgÿ
Social Media: Facebook, Twitter, LinkedIn, RSS

Ron Jacobs, President
Darren Short, Past President
Wendy Ruona, President-Elect
Kathie Pugaczewski, Executive Director
Carissa Wolf, Meeting Planner
Founded in 1993

16887 Adizes Network International
1212 Mark Ave
Carpinteria, CA 93013

805-565-2901
Fax: 805-565-0741
E-Mail: adizes@adizes.com
Home Page: www.adizes.com

James C Morgan, Chairman and CEO
Dr Ichak Adizes, Professional Director
James Zukin, Senior Managing Director

Promotes Adizes management consulting as a profession. Facilitates discussion of ideas and conducts lectures and seminars.
115 Members
Founded in 1973

16888 American Academy of Medical Administrators
American Academy of Medical Administrators
330 N Wabash Avenue
Suite 2000
Chicago, IL 60611

312-321-6815
Fax: 312-673-6705
E-Mail: info@aameda.org
Home Page: www.aameda.org

Linda Larin, MBA, FACCA, FAC, Chairman
Kevin Baliozian, Executive Director
Eric Conde, MSA, CFAAMA, Chairman Elect
John Garrity, CFAAMA, Treasurer
Robert McKenney, PhD,FAAMA, Vice Chair

Department heads and administrators in areas of hospital and health administration.
Founded in 1957

16889 American Association of Commerce Executives
American Chambers of Congress Executives
1330 Braddock Place
Suite 300
Alexandria, VA 22314

703-998-0072
Fax: 888-577-9883
E-Mail: webmaster@acce.org
Home Page: www.acce.org
Social Media: Facebook, Twitter, LinkedIn

Betty Nokes, Chairman of the Board
Mick Fleming, President
Tamara Philbin, COO
Chris Mead, Senior VP
Jacqui Cook, Chief Financial Officer

National association uniquely serving individuals involved in the management of chambers of all sizes. Chamber executives and professionals hold positions requiring leadership, vision and strong management skills. Devoted to helping chamber executives and their staffs' play a significant leadership role ing their communities.
1300 Members
Founded in 1914

16890 American Business Women's Association
9820 Metcalf Ave
Suite 110
Overland Park, KS 66212

800-228-0007
Fax: 913-660-0101
E-Mail: webmail@abwa.org
Home Page: www.abwa.orgÿ
Social Media: Facebook, Twitter, YouTube

Nancy Griffin, National President
Meg Bell, National ViceÿPresident
Lisa Montross, National Secretary - Treasurer
Gina Berry, Vice President, District I
Frances Nicholson, Vice President, District II

16891 American Management Association
American Management Association
1601 Broadway
New York, NY 10019-7420

212-586-8100
800-262-9699
Fax: 212-903-8168
Home Page: www.amanet.org
Social Media: Facebook, Twitter, LinkedIn

Edward T Reilly, CEO

Membership-based management development organization. AMA provides valuable and practical action-oriented learning programs to people at all levels, in all industries, from companies and agencies of all sizes. More than 500,000 AMA customers and members a year learn new skills and behaviors, gain more confidence, advance their careers through a wide range of seminars, conferences and executive forums, as well as publications, research, print and online self-study courses.
20000 Members
Founded in 1923

16892 American Productivity and Quality Center
American Productivity and Quality Center
123 N Post Oak Ln
Suite 300
Houston, TX 77024-7797

713-681-4020
800-776-9676
Fax: 713-681-8578
E-Mail: cflett@apqc.org
Home Page: www.apqc.org
Social Media: Facebook, Twitter, LinkedIn, Youtube, RSS

C. Jackson Grayson, Founder and Executive Chairman
Lisa Higgins, President
Carla O'Dell, Chief Executive Officer
Cindy Hubert, Executive Director
Mike Shea, Chief Financial Officer

Seeks to improve productivity and the quality of work life in the United States. Works with businesses, unions, academics and government agencies to improve productivity and quality.
300 Members
Founded in 1977

16893 American Small Businesses Association
American Small Businesses Association
206 E College
Grapevine, TX 76034-2663

817-488-8770
800-801-2722
Fax: 817-251-8578

Bill Hill Sr, President
Wanda Johnson, Bookkeeper

Represents the interests of small businesses.
10M Members
Founded in 1975

16894 American Society for Quality
American Society for Quality
600 N Plankinton Avenue
PO Box 3005
Milwaukee, WI 53201-3005

414-272-8575
800-248-1946
Fax: 414-272-1734
E-Mail: help@asq.org
Home Page: www.asq.org
Social Media: Facebook, Twitter, LinkedIn, Youtube

John C. Timmerman, Chairman
Paul E Borawski, Executive Director
Jennifer Janzen, Director, Human Resources
Laurel Nelson-Rowe, Managing Director
Michelle Mason, Managing Director

ASQ's mission is to facilitate continuous improvement and increase customer satisfaction. Promotes quality principles, concepts and technologies. Provides information, contacts and opportunities to make things better in the workplace, in communities and in people's lives.
100M Members
Founded in 1946

16895 American Society for the Advancement of Project Management
American Society for the Advancement of
6547 North Academy
#404
Colorado Springs, CO 80918

719-488-3850
Fax: 719-487-0637
E-Mail: info@asapm.org
Home Page: www.asapm.org

Stacy Goff, President
Trevor Nelson, Vice President
Morgan Henrie, Marketing Director

Neeraj Parolia, Director of Education
Brent Hansen, Director of Member Services
Standards and guidelines to define the work of project management personnel. Requirements to standardize the norms are collection, process and then institutionalization of the applied competence with acceptable protocols in managing the work for optimization of output. This includes the knowledge, experience and attitude of the manpower involved in the handling the assigned project.

16896 American Society of Association Executives
American Society of Association Executives
1575 I St NW
Washington, DC 20005-1103
202-371-0940
888-950-2723
Fax: 202-371-8315
E-Mail: darthur@asaecenter.org
Home Page: www.asaecenter.org/
John Graham, President
Elissa Matulis Myers, VP/Publisher
24.5M Members
Founded in 1920

16897 Association For Strategic Planning
Association for Strategic Planning
191 Clarksville Road
Princeton, NJ 08550
877-816-2080
Fax: 609-799-7032
Home Page: www.strategyplus.org
Social Media: Facebook, Twitter, LinkedIn, Youtube, Picasa
Neelima Firth, President
Lee Crumbaugh, Vice President
Tom Carter, Treasurer
Kimme Carlos, Executive Director
Dedicated to advancing thought and practice in strategy development and deployment for business, non-profit and government organizations. Provides opportunities to explore cutting-edge strategic planning principles and practices that enhance organizational success and advance members' and organizations' knowledge, capability, capacity for innovations and professionalism.
Founded in 1999

16898 Association for Services Management International (AFSM)
Association for Services Management
1342 Colonial Boulevard
Suite D-25
Fort Myers, FL 33907
239-275-7887
800-333-9786
Fax: 239-275-0794
E-Mail: jschoenewald@afsmi.org
Home Page: www.afsmi.org
Tom Schlick, President
John Schoenewald, CEO
Ms Nancy Alm, VP/Americas
Henrik Moeller-Christensen, VP/Europe/Middle East/Africa
Edina Sobaleski, Director at Large
A global organization dedicated to furthering the knowledge, understanding, and career development of executives, managers and professionals in the high-technology service industry.
5000 Members
Founded in 1975

16899 Association for Systems Management
Association for Systems Management
24587 Bagley Road
Cleveland, OH 44138
216-671-1919
Fax: 440-234-2930
Paula Winrod, Public Communication
Offers seminars and conferences in all phases of business systems and management.
5M Members
Founded in 1947

16900 Association of Executive and Administrative Professionals
900 South Washington Street
Suite G-13
Falls Church, VA 22046-4009
703-237-8616
Fax: 703-533-1153
E-Mail: headquarters@theaeap.com
Home Page: www.theaeap.com
Social Media: LinkedIn
Ruth Ludeman, Director
Has helped thousands of administrative and secretarial professionals grow in their chosen careers, and supported their efforts at becoming the best that they can be. Strives to provide its members with a pathway for setting and achieving accomplishments of all types and at all levels. Publishes a newsletter 11 times per year.
3000 Members
Founded in 1975

16901 Association of Higher Education Facilities Officers (APPA)
1643 Prince St
Alexandria, VA 22314-2818
703-684-1446
Fax: 703-549-2772
E-Mail: lander@appa.org
Home Page: www.appa.org
Social Media: Facebook, Twitter, LinkedIn, Youtube
Glenn Smith, President
E. Landerÿ Medlin, Executive Vice President
John F Bernhardsÿ, Associate Vice President
Peter Strazdas, Secretary-Treasurer
Jeri Ripley Kingÿ, Vice President for Information
APPA is an association dedicated to leadership in educational facilities management and the ongoing evolution of its professionals into influential leaders in education.
5500 Members
Founded in 1914

16902 Association of Investment Management Sales Executives
Association of Investment Management
12100 Sunset Hills Road
Suite 130
Reston, VA 20190
703-234-4098
Fax: 703-435-4390
E-Mail: lyarborough@drohanmgmt.com
Home Page: www.aimse.org/
Christopherÿ Newman, President
Kathy Hoskins, Executive Director
Scott Kearney, Vice President
P. MacKenzieÿ Hurd, Treasurer
Christopher J Krein, President Emeritus
The AIMSE mission is to provide an educational forum for those employed in the investment management sales and marketing services profession worldwide. AIMSE fosters high ethical and professional standards among members regarding representation of investment products and services, with an educational emphasis on improving skills, enabling members to adapt to the changing needs of the marketplace.
1400 Members
Founded in 1977

16903 Association of Management
Association of Management
920 Battlefield Boulevard
Suite 100
Chesapeake, VA 23322
757-482-2273
Fax: 757-482-0325
E-Mail: aomgt@aom-iaom.org
Home Page: www.aom-iaom.org
Dr Karin Klenke, Co-Founder/President
Dr WM A Hamel, CEO
T J Mills, VP Comptroller
Formerly the Association of Human Resources Management and Organizational Behavior (HRMOB).
3.5M Members
Founded in 1979

16904 Association of Management Consulting Firms
Association of Management Consulting Firms
370 Lexington Avenue
Suite 2209
New York, NY 10017
212-262-3055
Fax: 212-262-3054
E-Mail: info@amcf.org
Home Page: www.amcf.org
Social Media: Facebook, Twitter, LinkedIn, Youtube
Sally Caputo, President & Chief Operating Officer
Richard Hulme, Chief Executive Officer
Dominick DiLeo, Membership & Administrative Support
Lydia Shaw, Senior Conference & Events Coor
Seeks to unite management consulting firms in order to develop and improve professional standards and practice in the field. Offers information and referral services on management consultants.
65 Members
Founded in 1929

16905 Automotive Trade Association Executives
Automotive Trade Association Executives
8400 Westpark Dr
Mc Lean, VA 22102-5116
703-821-7072
Fax: 703-556-8581
E-Mail: sjewett@nada.org
Home Page: www.asna-atae.com
Bob Israel, ATAE Chairman
Jennifer Colman, ATAE Executive Director
Promotes interest of executives of state and local auto dealers associations.
106 Members

16906 Awards and Recognition Association
Awards and Recognition Association
8735 W. Higgins Road
Suite 300
Chicago, IL 60631
847-375-4800
800-344-2148
Fax: 847-375-6480
E-Mail: info@ara.org
Home Page: www.ara.org
Social Media: Facebook, Twitter, Youtube
Mike May, President
Louise Ristau, CAE, Executive Director
Brian Fitzgerald, Senior Sales Manager
Tom Calvin, Sales Manager
Chris Schroll, Sales Manager

Membership organization of 4,000 companies dedicated to increasing the professionalism of recognition specialists and advancing the awards and engraving industry.
Founded in 1993

16907 Best Employers Association
Best Employers Association
2505 McCabe Way
Irvine, CA 92614

866-706-2225
800-237-8543
Fax: 949-553-0883
E-Mail: info@bestlife.com
Home Page: www.beassoc.org/
Social Media: Facebook, Twitter, LinkedIn

Steve Course, President
Jennifer Bolton, Sales Account Manager
Ramon Duran, Sales Account Manager
Cristina Rios, Sales Account Manager
Dorothy Sehramm, Salews Account Manager

Providing group medical, dental, long-term disability, vision and life insurance to employers.
Founded in 1970

16908 Business Management Daily
National Institute of Business Management
PO Box 9070
McLean, VA 22102-0070

703-058-8000
800-543-2055
Fax: 703-905-8040
E-Mail: Customer@BusinessManagementDaily.com
Home Page: www.businessmanagementdaily.com
Social Media: Facebook, Twitter, LinkedIn, Google+

Steve Sturm, President

Career guidance for managers and executives.
Founded in 1937

16909 Center for Breakthrough Thinking
Center for Breakthrough Thinking
PO Box 18012
Los Angeles, CA 90018

213-740-6415
Fax: 213-740-1120
E-Mail: info@breakthroughthinking.com
Home Page: www.breakthroughthinking.com
Social Media: Twitter

Dr Gerald Nadler, President
George Hathaway, Vice President

Organized to promote and institutionalize the teaching and application of Breakthrough Thinking in universities, corporations and governments for solving problems, leveraging opportunities, and achieving change.
15 Members
Founded in 1989

16910 Center for Creative Leadership
Center for Creative Leadership
One Leadership Place
PO Box 26300
Greensboro, NC 27410-6300

336-545-2810
Fax: 336-282-3284
E-Mail: info@ccl.org
Home Page: www.ccl.org/Leadership/
Social Media: Facebook, Twitter, LinkedIn, Youtube, Google Plus, Pinteres

Thomas K Hearn Jr, Chairman
John Alexander, President

An international, nonprofit educational institution devoted to behavioral science research, executive development and leadership education.
Founded in 1970
Mailing list available for rent

16911 Center for Management Effectiveness
Center for Management Effectiveness
P. O. Box 1202
Pacific Palisades, CA 90272

310-459-6052
Fax: 310-459-9307
E-Mail: info@cmeinc.org
Home Page: www.cmeinc.org
Social Media: Facebook, Twitter, LinkedIn

Jerry Feist, President
Ron Smith, General Manager
Rob Wood, Publications Director
Sam Erdman, Manager Information Systems
Christie Randolph, Management Consultants

Conducts management training programs and publishes self-scoring inventories, trainer guides and workbooks on stress management, resolution of conflict, risk taking, decision making and building managerial skills.
Founded in 1981

16912 Center for Management Systems
Center for Management Systems
PO Box 159
Akron, IA 51001-0159

FAX 712-568-3427

Provides specialized education to improve management skills.
70M Members
Founded in 1978

16913 Center for Third World Organizing
Center For Third World Organizing
900 Alice Street
Suite 300
Oakland, CA 94607

510-433-0908
Fax: 510-433-0908
Home Page: www.ctwo.org

Wendall Chin, Co-Director
Faron Mclurkin, Co-Director
Karissa Lewis, Senior Field Organizerÿ
Nancy Benavides, Operations Director

A national organization of books, periodicals and audiovisuals on transnational corporations and labor issues.
Founded in 1980

16914 Christian Management Association
Christian Management Association
1825 Hamilton Drive
San Jose, CA 95125

408-703-6568
Fax: 408-703-6568
E-Mail: info@cmanational.org
Home Page: www.christianmanagementassociation.org
Social Media: Facebook, Twitter

Frank Lofaro, CEO
Dick Bahruth, Senior Consultant
Sandy Huston, Member Services Manager
Joe Voorhies, Director Business Development
Charles S Blake, Director Finance

Designed to assist those involved in the management of Christian organizations.
3500+ Members
Founded in 1976

16915 Club Managers Association of America
1733 King St
Alexandria, VA 22314-2720

703-739-9500
Fax: 703-739-0124
E-Mail: cmaa@cmaa.org
Home Page: www.cmaa.org
Social Media: Facebook, Twitter, LinkedIn, Flickr

Richard Bayliss, Jr, President
Damon DiOrio, Vice President
James B Singerling, Chief Executive Officerÿ
Kathi Driggs, Chief Operating Officerÿ
Tony D'Errico, Secretary/Treasurer

Advances the professional of club management by fulfilling the educational and related needs of its members.
7000 Members
Founded in 1927

16916 Construction Financial Management Association
100 Village Blvd.
Suite 200
Princeton, NJ 8540

609-452-8000
888-421-9996
Fax: 609-452-0474
E-Mail: info@cfma.org
Home Page: www.cfma.orgÿ
Social Media: Facebook, Twitter, LinkedIn, YouTube

Stuart Binstock, President, CEO
Erica O'Grady, CAE, Vice President, Operations
Robert Rubin, CPA, VP, Finance & Admin.
Brian Summers, CAE, VP, Content Mgmt & Edu.
Ariel Sanchirico, Director, Online Learning
Founded in 1981

16917 Data Processing Sciences Corporation
Data Processing Sciences Corporation
11370 Reed Hartman Hwy
Cincinnati, OH 45241

513-489-4200
Fax: 513-791-2371
E-Mail: info@dpsciences.com
Home Page: www.dpsciences.com
Social Media: Facebook, Twitter, LinkedIn, Youtube, Google+

Kurt Loock, President
Scott Nesbitt, CEO
Stephen Vandegriff, EVP
Tim Shelton, CFO

DPS delivers solutions that simplify and manage technology for our clients so they can aggressively pursue their strategic business goals.

16918 Decision Sciences Institute
Decision Sciences Institute
University Plaza
Atlanta, GA 30303

404-651-4000
Fax: 404-413-7714

Lee Krajewski, Publisher

Scientific quantitative, behavioral and computational approaches to decision making.

16919 Distribution Business Management Association
2938 Columbia Ave
Suite 1102
Lancaster, PA 17603

717-295-0033
Fax: 717-299-2154
E-Mail: dbminfo@dbm-assoc.com
Home Page: www.dcenter.com

16920 Diversified Business Communications
Diversified Business Communications
Po Box 7437
Portland, ME 04112-7437

207-842-5500
Fax: 207-842-5503
E-Mail: custserv@divcom.com
Home Page: www.divbusiness.com

Theodore Wirth, President & Chief Executive Officer
Paul Clancy, Executive Vice President

Janice Rogers, Vice President, Human Resources
Vicki Hennin, Vice President, Strategic Marketing
Oakley R. Dyer, VP/Business Development

Has over 30 years of experience as trade magazine publishers and exhibition organizers. Provides exposition management services for associations and organizations seeking to expand domestically and overseas, as well as direct mail, internet, telemarketing campaigns and market research.
Founded in 1949

16921 Employer Associations of America

262-696-3473
E-Mail: Vicki.Vought@mranet.org
Home Page: www.eaahub.orgÿ

Meredith Wise, Chair
Mary Lynn Fayoumi, Chair Elect
Jennifer Graft, Secretary - Treasurer
Susan Fronk, Past Chair
Vicki Vought, Executive Director

16922 Employers Group
Employers Group
1150 S Olive St
Suite 2300
Los Angeles, CA 90015-2211

213-748-0421
800-748-8484
Fax: 213-742-0301
Home Page: www.employersgroup.com
Social Media: Facebook, Twitter, LinkedIn

Mark Wilbur, CEO

Aims to provide human resources management, management counseling and educational programs. Offers unemployment insurance services, and workers compensation programs.
3.9M Members

16923 Employers of America
Employers of America
310 Meadow Lane
Mason City, IA 50401

641-424-3187
800-728-3187
Fax: 641-424-3187
E-Mail: employer@employerhelp.org
Home Page: www.employerhelp.org

Jim Collison, President

Provides information and guidance to employers, managers, and supervisors to empower employees and make great things happen.
1600 Members
Founded in 1976

16924 Financial Management Association International
University of South Florida/College of Business
4202 E Fowler Ave
BSN 3331
Tampa, FL 33620-5500

813-974-2084
Fax: 813-974-3318
E-Mail: fma@coba.usf.edu
Home Page: www.fma.org

Kose John, President
William G Christie, VP-Program
Ronald Masulis, VP-Global Services
Javier Estradaÿ, VP-Practitioner Services
Jay R Ritter, President Elect

The mission of the FMA is to broaden the common interests between academicians and practitioners, provide opportunities for professional interaction between and among academicians, practitioners and students, promote the development and understanding of basic and applied research and of sound financial practices, and to enhance the quality of education in finance.
3000 Members
Founded in 1970

16925 Floodplain Management Association
P.O. Box 712080
Santee, CA 92072

916-231-2134
E-Mail: admin@floodplain.org
Home Page: www.floodplain.orgÿ
Social Media: Facebook, Twitter, LinkedIn, Google+

Thomas Plummer, Chair
Mark Seits, Vice Chair
Andrew Treleaseÿ, Treasurer
George Booth, Secretary
John Moynier, Director

16926 Fulfillment Management Association
Fulfillment Management Association
60 E 42nd St
Suite 2316
New York, NY 10165-1146

818-487-2090
Fax: 818-487-4501
E-Mail: info@fmanational.com
Home Page: www.fmanational.com/

Brian Knowles, President
Rochelle Boorstein, Vice President
Mike McCarthy, Treasurer
Jo Ann Binz, Executive Secretary
Greg Wolf, Recording Secretary

Educates, updates and maintains high standards of service in operations management and customer service. Sponsors four seminars per year. Members are direct mail fullfillment, marketing and circulation executives.
425 Members
Founded in 1945

16927 Independent Professional Representatives Organization (IPRO)
Independent Professional Representatives
34157 West 9 Mile Road
Farmington Hills, MI 48335

248-474-0522
800-420-4268
E-Mail: ray@avreps.org
Home Page: www.avreps.org
Social Media: Facebook, LinkedIn

Dave Humphries, President
Frank Culotta, Vice President
Mark Adams, Secretary
Mike Pecar, Treasurer

The mission of IPRO is to provide new avenues of networking; provide new and emerging resources for sound business management; enhance valuable dialogue and commmunication with business partners; and to continue to develop resources and benefits for individual members beyond the resources of individual firms.

16928 Industrial Asset Management Council
Industrial Asset Management Council
6625 The Corners Parkway
Suite 200
Peachtree Corners, GA 30092

770-325 3461
Fax: 770-263-8825
E-Mail: info@iamc.org
Home Page: www.iamc.org
Social Media: Facebook, Twitter, LinkedIn, Pinterest, Tumblr, Blogger, St

Roger Nesti, Chair
Randy Cardoza, Executive Director
Paula Korowin, Director of Meetings
Rya Hazelwood, Director of Marketing & Conference
Joel Parker, Director of Research & Education

World's leading associates of industrial asset management and corporate real estate executives, their supplies and service providers and economic developers.
135 Members
Founded in 1963

16929 Information Resources Management Association
Information Resources Management Association
701 E Chocolate Ave
Suite 200
Hershey, PA 17033-1240

717-533-8845
Fax: 717-533-8661
E-Mail: member@irma-international.org
Home Page: www.irma-international.org

Jan Travers, Executive Director
Sherif Kamel, Communications Director
Lech Janczewski PhD, IRMA World Representative Director
Gerald Grant, IRMA Doctoral Symposium Director
Paul Chalekian, IRMA United States Representative

An international professional organization dedicated to advancing the concepts and practices of information resources management in modern organizations. The primary objective of IRMA is to assist organizations and professionals in enhancing the overall knowledge and understanding of effective information resources management in the early 21st century and beyond.

16930 Institute for Supply Management Association
2055 E Centennial Circle
PO Box 22160
Tempe, AZ 85284-1898

480-752-6276
800-888-6276
Fax: 480-752-7890
E-Mail: custsvc@ism.ws
Home Page: www.ism.ws
Social Media: Facebook, Twitter, LinkedIn, Youtube, google Plus

Thomas K. Linton, Chair
Bill Michels, CPSM, C.P.M., Senior Vice President
Nora Neibergall, CPSM, C.P., Senior Vice President
Thomas W. Derry, Chief Executive Officer, ISM
Janis Kellerman, Senior Vice President/Corporate

The mission of ISM is lead supply management.
43000 Members
Founded in 1915

16931 Institute of Business Appraisers
Institute of Business Appraisers
5217 South State Street
Suite 400
Salt Lake City, UT 84107

954-482-1812
800-299-4130
Fax: 866-353-5406
E-Mail: hqiba@go-iba.org
Home Page: www.go-iba.org

Howard A. Lewis, Executive Director

The oldest professional society devoted solely to the appraisal of closely-held businesses.
3,000 Members
Founded in 1978

16932 Institute of Certified Business Counselors
Institute of Certified Business Counselors

18831 Willamette Dr
West Linn, OR 97068-1711
503-751-1856
877-422-2674
Fax: 503-292-8237
E-Mail: inquiry@i-cbc.org
Home Page: www.i-cbc.org

David Finsterwald, President
Ray Hanson, Secretary/Treasurer
Roger Murphy, Director, Newsletter

Premier association of skilled, experienced practitioners focused on the needs of businesses in ownership transition.
120 Members

16933 Institute of Management & Administration
Institute of Management & Administration
3 Bethesda Metro Center
Suite 250
Bethesda, MD 20814-5377
703-341-3500
800-372-1033
Fax: 800-253-0332
E-Mail: customercare@bna.com
Home Page: www.ioma.com

An independent source of exclusive business management information for experienced senior and middle management professionals.

16934 Institute of Management Accountant
Institute of Management Accountant
10 Paragon Dr
Suite 1
Montvale, NJ 07645-1760
201-573-9000
800-638-4427
Fax: 201-474-1600
Home Page: www.imanet.org
Social Media: Facebook, Twitter, LinkedIn, Youtube

Jeffrey C. Thomson CMA, CAE, President

A subunit of the Institute of Management Accountants, with a network of 3,000 controllers incorporating newsletters and seminars.
1.2M Members
Founded in 1919

16935 Institute of Management Consultants - USA
Institute of Management Consultants - USA
2025 M St NW
Suite 800
Washington, DC 20036-2422
202-367-1261
800-221-2557
Fax: 202-367-2134
E-Mail: norm@ecksteinconsult.com
Home Page: www.imcusa.org
Social Media: Facebook, Twitter, LinkedIn, RSS

Loraine Huchler CMC, P.E,

Chair and CEO
Cynthia E. Currence CMC, Director
Lee Czarapata CMC, Director
Don Matheson, Treasurer
Manola Robinson CMC, Director

IMC is the leading association representing management consultants in the United States, organized to establish consulting as a self-regulating profession, meriting public confidence and respect. Toward the achievement of this goal IMC awards the international appelation CMC for certified management consultants.

16936 Institute of Management and Administration
Institute of Management and Administration
3 Bethesda Metro Center
Suite 250
Bethesda, MD 20814-5377
703-341-3500
800-372-1033
Fax: 800-253-0332
E-Mail: customercare@bna.com
Home Page: www.ioma.com

An independent source of exclusive business management information for experienced senior and middle management professionals.

16937 Int'l. Association of Healthcare Central Services Material Management
Int'l. Association of Healthcare Place
213 W Institute Place
Suite 307
Chicago, IL 60610-3195
312-440-0078
800-962-8274
Fax: 312-440-9474
E-Mail: mailbox@iahcsmm.com
Home Page: www.iahcsmm.com

Sharon Greene-Golden, CRCST,, President
Susan Adams, Executive Director
Nick Baker, Certification Manager
Josephine Colacci, Government Affairs Director
Elizabeth Berrios, Member Services Coordinator

Membership consists of persons serving in a technical, supervisory or management capacity in hospital central service departments responsible for the sterilization management and distribution of supplies.
9000 Members
Founded in 1958

16938 International Association for Worksite Health Promotion
Association for Worksite Health Promotion
401 W. Michigan St.
Indianapolis, IN 46202
317-637-9200
Fax: 847-480-9282
E-Mail: iawhp@acsm.org
Home Page: ww.acsm-iawhp.org
Social Media: Facebook

Wolf Kirsten, MSÿ, President
George Pfeiffer, MSE, President-Elect
Vin DeProssino, Secretary/Treasurer

Exists to advance the profession of worksite health promotion and the career development of its practitioners and to improve the performance of the programs they administer. Represents a variety of disciplines and worksites, for decision makers in the areas of health promotion/disease prevention and health care cost management.
3000 Members

16939 International Association of Administrative Professionals
10502 N. Ambassador Dr.
Suite 100
Kansas City, MO ÿ64153
816-891-6600
Fax: 816-891-9118
Home Page: www.iaap-hq.orgÿ
Social Media: Facebook, Twitter, LinkedIn, Pinterest, RSS

Antoinette Smith, CAP-OM, President
Wendy S. Melby, CAP-OM, President Elect
Kristi Rotvold, CAP-OM, Vice President
Sharon K. McPherson, CAP-OM, Treasurer
Dortha Gray, CAP-OM, Secretary
Founded in 1942

16940 International Council for Small Business
2201 G Street NW
Suite 315
Washington, DC 20052
202-944-0704
Fax: 202-994-4930
E-Mail: info@icsb.org
Home Page: www.icsb.org
Social Media: Facebook, Twitter, LinkedIn, Stumbleupon

Jeffrey R. Alves, Ph.D., President
Semra F. Ascigil / ECSB, Senior Vice-President, Marketing
Geralyn Franklin, Senior Vice-President, Finance
Jay Krysler / CCSBE, Senior Vice-President
Ki-Chan Kim, Senior Vice-President, Research

Promotes the growth and development of small businesses by bringing together researchers, practitioners and policy makers from around the world.
2000+ Members
Founded in 1955

16941 International Council of Management Consulting Institutes
International Council of Management
858 Longview Road
Burlingame, CA 94010-6974
650-342-2250
E-Mail: icmci@icmci.org
Home Page: www.icmci.org

Camera Gaylen, Executive Director
Michael Shays, Manager
John Roethle, Advisory Council

The global association of management consultants. The members of ICMCI are national institutes from around the world that certify professional management consultants. The ICMCI maintains an international code of professional conduct, an international uniform body of knowledge, and strict standards for certification and reciprocity between nations. It promotes professional development and networking between consultants and the highest standards of performance for clients.
39 Members
Founded in 1987

16942 International Facility Management Association
International Facility Management
800 Gessner Rd.
Ste. 900
Houston, TX 77024-4257
713-623-4362
Fax: 713-623-6124
E-Mail: ifma@ifma.org
Home Page: www.ifma.org
Social Media: Facebook, Twitter, LinkedIn, Youtube, Flickr, RSS

Jon Seller, Chair
Tony Keane, CAE, President and CEO
Michael D. Moss, CAE, Chief Operating Officer
Catherine Pavick, Vice President of Education
Cheryl White, Director of Corporate Connections

Certifies facility, managers, conducts research, provides educational programs, recognizes facility management degree and certificate pro-

grams and produces World Workplace, the world's largest facility management conference and exposition.
Founded in 1980

16943 **International Leadership Association**
1110 Bonifant Street
Suite 510
Silver Spring, MD 20910
202-470-4818
Fax: 202-470-2724
E-Mail: ila@ila-net.org
Home Page: www.ila-net.org
Social Media: Facebook, Twitter, LinkedIn, Google+, YouTube, Flickr

Cynthia Cherrey, President
Shelly Wilsey, Chief Operating Officer
Bridget Chisholm, Director of Conferences
Anita Marsh, Membership Manager
Jean Portianko, I.T. and Office Manager

16944 **International Personal Management and Association for Human Resources**
Int'l Public Management Assoc for Human Resources
1617 Duke St
Alexandria, VA 22314-3406
703-549-7100
Fax: 703-684-0948
E-Mail: ipma@ipma-hr.org
Home Page: www.ipma-hr.org

Neil Reichenberg, Executive Director
Sima Hassassian, Chief Operating Officer
Irina Bowyer, Director of Membership
Jacob Jackovich, Assessment Services Coordinator
Andrey Pankov, Assessment Research Manager

Human resource professionals, representing the interests of over 6,000 individual and 1,300 agency members, at the federal, state and local levels of government. Promotes excellence in human resource management through the ongoing development of professional and ethical standards, and through its publishing and educational training programs.
6M Members
Founded in 1973

16945 **International Public Management Association**
1617 Duke Street
Alexandria, VA 22314
703-549-7100
Fax: 703-684-0948
E-Mail: nreichenberg@ipma-hr.org
Home Page: www.ipma-hr.orgÿ
Social Media: Facebook, Twitter, LinkedIn

Sima Hassassian, Chief Operating Officer
Neil Reichenberg, Executive Director
Irina Bowyer, Director of Membership
Jenny Chang, Director of Communications
Linda Sun, Director of China Programs
Founded in 1906

16946 **Life Office Management Association**
Life Office Management Association
2300 Windy Ridge Parkway
Suite 600
Atlanta, GA 30339-5665
770-951-1770
800-968-1738
Fax: 770-984-0441
E-Mail: askloma@loma.org
Home Page: www.loma.org
Social Media: Facebook, Twitter, LinkedIn, Youtube

Robert A Kerzner, CLU, ChFC, President and CEO
Jeffrey Hasty, FLMI, ACS, Senior VP, Assessment
Michele LaBouff, Senior Vice President
Kathy Milligan, FLMI, ACS, A, Senior Vice President
Ian J Watts, Senior Vice President

Insurance worldwide association of insurance companies specializing in research and education.
1250 Members
Founded in 1924

16947 **Marketing Management Association**
Home Page: www.mmaglobal.orgÿ
Social Media: Facebook, Twitter, LinkedIn, Google+, YouTube

Roscoe Hightower, President
Carrie Trimble, Immediate Past President
Brian Vander Schee, President Elect
Pam Kennett-Hensel, VP, Marketing
Michelle Kunz, Executive Director
Founded in 1977

16948 **Medical Group Management Association**
Medical Group Management Association
104 Inverness Ter E
Englewood, CO 80112-5306
303-799-1111
877-275-6462
Fax: 303-643-9599
E-Mail: service@mgma.com
Home Page: www.mgma.com
Social Media: Facebook, Twitter, LinkedIn, Youtube

Ronald S German, MBA, FACMPE, Chair of the Board
Kevin Spencer, Chief Operating Officer
Stephen A. Dickens, JD, FACMPE, F, Secretary/Treasurer

The oldest and largest professional membership association dedicated to medical practice management. Serves their members by offering timely and relevant networking and educational opportunities that keep the members up-to-date on the practice management field.
18M Members
Founded in 1926

16949 **National Association Executive Club**
1300 L Street NW
Suite 1050
Washington, DC 20005-4107
202-043-3001
Fax: 202-783-4410

Steven Fier, Secretary
Angela West, Manager

Provides networking services and facilities.
500 Members
Founded in 1953

16950 **National Association for the Self-Employed**
P.O. Box 241
Annapolis Junction, MD 20701-0241
800-649-6273
800-649-6273
E-Mail: advocacy@NASE.org.
Home Page: www.nase.org
Social Media: Facebook, Twitter, LinkedIn, Youtube

Katie Vlietstra, Director of Government Affairs
John K. Hearrell, Director of Membership
Thom Childers, Software Developer/Database Admin
Rosie Farris, Accounts Payable
Cameron T. Brown, Systems Administrator

Goal is to promote small business growth through education and discounts earned through NASE negotiating power.
225M Members
Founded in 1981
Mailing list available for rent

16951 **National Association of Corporate Directors**
2001 Pennsylvania Ave, NW
Suite 500
Washington, DC 20006
202-775-0509
Fax: 202-775-4857
E-Mail: Join@NACDonline.org
Home Page: www.nacdonline.org
Social Media: Twitter, LinkedIn, Youtube, RSS

Kenneth Daly, President/CEO
Katherine Davis, COO
Peter Gleason, Managing Director, CFO
Henry Stoever, Chief Marketing Officer
Judy Warner, Editor in Chief

A national non-profit membership organization dedicated exclusively to serving the corporate governance needs of corporate boards and individual board members.
15500 Members
Founded in 1977

16952 **National Association of Service Managers**
PO Box 250796
Milwaukee, WI 53225
414-466-6060
Fax: 414-466-0840
Home Page: www.nasm.com
Social Media: Facebook

Ken Cook, Treasurer

Service manager association for professional development
100 Members
Founded in 1955

16953 **National Business Owners Association**
480 Broadway
PO Box 3373
Saratoga Springs, NY 12866
202-839-9000
866-639-1669
Fax: 866-224-0609
Home Page: www.nboaofny.org

Ed Bolen, President

A non-profit organization representing small business owners' interests and offers several money-saving services, valuable benefits and assistance.
4.5M Members
Founded in 1986

16954 **National Businesswomens Leadership Association**
P.O. Box 419107
Kansas City, MI 64141-6107
913-432-7755
800-258-7246
Fax: 913-432-0824
E-Mail: cstserv@natsem.com
Home Page: www.nationalseminarstraining.com/AboutNBLA.cfm

Linda Truitt, President

Offers seminars and workshops on business related issues.
Founded in 1985

16955 **National Career Development Association**
305 N. Beech Circle
Broken Arrow, OK 74012
918-663-7060
866-367-6232
Fax: 918-663-7058
E-Mail: webeditor@ncda.org
Home Page: www.ncda.org

Social Media: Facebook, Twitter, LinkedIn, Pinterest

Mark Danaher, President
Lisa Severy, Past President
Cynthia Marco Scanlon, President Elect
Deneen Pennington, Executive Director
Mary Ann Powell, CDF & Conference Director
Founded in 1913

16956 National Committee for Quality Assurance
1100 13th Street NW
Suite 1000
Washington, DC 20005

202-955-3500
Fax: 202-955-3599
E-Mail: customersupport@ncqa.org
Home Page: www.ncqa.org
Social Media: Facebook, Twitter, LinkedIn, Youtube, Google+, Pinterest

Dolores L. Mitchell, Chair
Margaret E. O'Kane, President
Tom Fluegel, Chief Operating Officer
Scott Hartranft, Chief Financial Officer
Rick Moore, Chief Information Officer

Independent, non profit organization dedicated to improving healthcare quality.
Founded in 1990
Mailing list available for rent

16957 National Conference of Personal Managers
964 2nd Avenue
New York, NY 10022-6304

212-421-2670
866-91N-COPM
Fax: 212-838-5105
E-Mail: ncopmse@cox.net
Home Page: www.ncopm.com/

Clinton Ford Billups Jr, National President
Jack Rollins, National First Vice President
Stanley Evans, National Second Vice President
Peggy Becker, National Secretary
Daniel Abrahamson, Eastern Executive Director

A personal manager is engaged in the occupation of advising and counseling talent and personalities in the enternainment industry. personal managers have the expertis to find and develop new talent and create opportunities for those artists which they represent.

16958 National Contract Management Association
21740 Beaumeade Circle
Suite 125
Ashburn, VA 20147

571-382-0082
800-344-8096
Fax: 703-448-0939
E-Mail: memberservices@ncmahq.org
Home Page: www.ncmahq.org
Social Media: Facebook, Twitter, LinkedIn, Youtube

Russell J. Blaine, CPCM, Fellow, President
Michael Fischetti, J.D., CPCM,, Executive Director
John G. Horan, J.D., General Counsel
Penny L. White, J.D., Fellow, Director and Chair
Kim Rupert, CPCM, CFCM, Fe, Director and Chair, Finance

Formed in 1959 to foster the professional growth and educational advancement of its members.
19000 Members
Founded in 1959

16959 National Employee Services and Recreation Association
Employee Services Management Association
568 Spring Road
Suite D
Elmhurst, IL 60126-3896

630-559-0020
Fax: 630-559-0025
E-Mail: esmahq@esmassn.org
Home Page: www.esmassn.org

Pud Belek, President

Manufacturers and distributors offering products and services for employee discount programs and employee store merchandise to members.

16960 National Management Association
2210 Arbor Blvd
Moraine, OH 45439-1580

937-294-0421
Fax: 937-294-2374
E-Mail: nma@nma1.org
Home Page: www.nma1.org
Social Media: Facebook, LinkedIn

William T Mahaffey, Chairman
Wendell M Pichon, Vice Chairman
Doug Shaw, Manager

Seeks to develop and recognize management as a profession and to promote the free enterprise system.
22000 Members
Founded in 1925

16961 National Property Management Association
3525 Piedmont Road
Building 5, Suite 300
Atlanta, GA 30305

404-477-5811
Fax: 404-240-0998
E-Mail: hq@npma.org
Home Page: www.npma.orgÿ
Social Media: Facebook, LinkedIn

Marcia Whitson CPPM CF, National Presidentÿ
Cinda Brockman CPPM CF, Executive Vice Presidentÿ
Cheri Cross CPPM CF, Immediate Past Presidentÿ
Ivonne Bachar CPPM CF, VP, Administration
Rosanne Green CPPM CF, VP, Certification
Founded in 1970

16962 National Small Business United
1156 15th St NW
Suite 1100
Washington, DC 20005-1755

202-293-8830
800-345-6728
Fax: 202-872-8543
E-Mail: info@nsba.biz
Home Page: www.nsba.biz/
Social Media: Facebook, Twitter, LinkedIn, Google+, Stumbleupon

David Ickert, Chair
Jeffrey Van Winkle, First Vice Chair
Todd McCracken, President and CEO
C. Cookie Driscoll, Vice Chair for Advocacy
Eric Tolbert, Vice Chair for Membership

Merged with Small Business United in 1986 and sponsors and supports the NSBU Political Action Committee.

16963 National Training Systems Association
2111 Wilson Boulevard
Suite 400
Arlington, VA 22201-3061

703-247-2567
Fax: 703-243-1659
E-Mail: jrobb@ndia.org
Home Page: www.trainingsystems.org

De Voorhees, GD IT, Chairman
Pete Swan, VT MAK, Vice Chairman
James Robb, President
Debbie Dyson, Director/Exhibits
Patrick Rowe, Director of Membership Services

Represents companies in the simulation and training and training support industry. Provides forums, market surveys, and business development information and other services to members.
944 Members
Founded in 1988

16964 Newspaper Association Managers
New England Press Association
PO Box 458
Essex, MA 01929

978-338-2555
Fax: 978-744-0333
E-Mail: mlpiper52@comcast.net
Home Page: www.nammanagers.com

H. Dean Ridings, President
Michael MacLaren, Vice President
Lisa Hills, Secretary
Greg Sherrill, Director
Robin Rhodes, Director

Executives of state, regional, national and international newspaper associations.
65 Members
Founded in 1923

16965 North America Human ResourceÿManagement Association
E-Mail: casandra.merkel@shrm.org
Home Page: www.nahrma.org

Henry Jackson, President
Lic. Jorge Jauregui, HRMP, Immediate Past Presidentÿ
Cheryl Newcombeÿÿÿÿ, Secretary/Treasurer
Founded in 1979

16966 Operations Management Society
5400 Bosque Boulevard
Waco, TX 76710-4414
254-752-6315
Fax: 254-776-3767

Helen Schneider Lemay, Executive Director

Members are senior management and deans of business schools in the field of operations management.

16967 Organization Development Institute
11234 Walnut Ridge Road
Chesterland, OH 44026-1240

440-729-7419
Fax: 440-729-9319
E-Mail: donwcole@aol.com
Home Page: www.odinstitute.org

Dr. Donald W Cole RODC, President
Jim Gustafson, Editor Journal

Promotes the understanding of organization development and offers three categories of membership: professional consultant, regular and student. Offers the International Registry of O.D. Professionals and O.D. Handbook which lists names, addresses and E-mail addresses, publishes a monthly newsletter plus a quarterly journal of 100-150 pages. There are two con-

ferences held every year, one in the USA and one International.
500 Members
Founded in 1968

16968 Product Development and Management Association
330 N. Wabash Avenue
Suite 2000
Chicago, IL 60611

312-321-5145
800-232-5241
Fax: 312-673-6885
E-Mail: pdma@pdma.org
Home Page: www.pdma.org

Christina Hepner Brodie, NPDP, Chair
Charlie Noble, VP Academic Affairs
Peter Bradford, NPDP, VP of Certification
Peter Flentov, VP Chapters
Brad White, VP Conferences & Events

Provides essential information to help foster new product development, giving an overview of the total product innovation process and presenting the latest advancements in product innovation. Also assists managers in innovating and producing products more effectively and efficiently.
3200 Members
Founded in 1976

16969 Production and Operations Management Society

Home Page: www.poms.orgў

16970 Professional Convention Management Association
35 East Wacker Drive
Suite 500
Chicago, IL 60601

312-423-7262
877-827-7262
Fax: 312 423-7222
E-Mail: communications@pcma.org
Home Page: www.pcma.org
Social Media: Facebook, Twitter, LinkedIn, Youtube

Johnnie White, CMP, Chairman of Board
Deborah Sexton, President and CEO
Jason Paganessi, Vice President, Business Innovation
Sherrif Karamat, CAE, BAS, MBA, Chief Operating Officer
Michelle Russell, Editor in Chief

PCMA delivers superior and innovative education, to promote the value of professional convention management.
6100 Members
Founded in 1957

16971 Professional Managers Association
PO Box 77235
Washington, DC 20013

202-803-9597
Fax: 202-874-1739
E-Mail: info@promanager.org
Home Page: www.promanager.org

Betsy Fallacaro, National President
Jeff Eppler, National Vice President
Maria Alexander, National Secretary
Tom Burger, Executive Director

National membership association representing the interests of professional managers, management officials and non-bargaining unit employees in the federal government. Promote leadership and management excellence within the federal services.
10000 Members
Founded in 1981

16972 Project Management Institute (PMI)
14 Campus Blvd
Newtown Square, PA 19073-3299

610-356-4600
855-746-4849
Fax: 610-482-9971
E-Mail: customercare@pmi.org
Home Page: www.pmi.org
Social Media: Facebook, Twitter, LinkedIn, Youtube

Mark Langley, President & CEO
Michael Deprisco, Vice President
John J Doyle, MBA, Vice President, Finance
Craig Killough, Vice President, Organization Market
Dorothy McKelvy, MA, SPHR, Vice President, Human Resources

Fosters recognition of the need for project management professionalism. Offers professional certification and bestows awards.
105M Members
Founded in 1969
Mailing list available for rent

16973 Public Risk Management Association
700 S. Washington St.
Suite 218
Alexandria, VA 22314

703-528-7701
Fax: 703-739-0200
E-Mail: info@primacentral.org
Home Page: www.primacentral.org
Social Media: Facebook, Twitter, LinkedIn

Regan Rychetsky, ABCP, President
Betty Coulter, Past President
Dean Coughenour, ARM, President-Elect
Marshall Davies, PhD, Executive Director
Jennifer Ackerman, CAEў, Deputy Executive Director

16974 Small Business Assistance Center
119 E Locust Ln
Kennett Square, PA 19348-1717

610-444-1720
Fax: 610-444-1724
E-Mail: inquire@sbacnetwork.org
Home Page: www.sbacnetwork.org

Provides information and assistance to small businesses. To train and consult entrepreneurs through information services, seminars and professional consultations.
Founded in 1988

16975 Society for Advancement of Management
6300 Ocean Drive - OCNR 383
Unit - 5808
Corpus Christi, TX 78412-5807

361-825-3045
888-827-6077
Fax: 361-825-5609
E-Mail: moustafa@cob.tamucc.edu
Home Page: www.samnational.org

Moustafa H Abdelsamad, President/CEO
R. Clifton Poole, Secretary
Kent Byus, Treasurer

SAM members come from a variety of disciplines - productions, finance, marketing, accounting and more who all share a common bond of interest in becoming stronger managers. SAM abounds with opportunities for professional development.
3000 Members
Founded in 1912

16976 Society for Human Resource Management
SHRM/Society for Human Resource Management
1800 Duke St
Alexandria, VA 22314-3496

703-535-6000
800-283-7476
703-548-3440
Fax: 703-535-6490
E-Mail: shrmeducation@shrm.org.
Home Page: www.shrm.org
Social Media: Facebook, Twitter, LinkedIn, Youtube, RSS

Bette J. Francis, SPHR, Chair
Henry G. Jackson, CPA, President and CEO
J. Robert Carr, J.D., SPHR, SVP, Membership, Marketing
Deb Cohen, Ph.D., SPHR, SVP, Knowledge Development
Brian K. Dickson, SVP, Professional Development

World's largest association devoted to human resource management. Serves the needs of the human resource management professional by providing the most essential and comprehensive set of resources available.
18500 Members
Founded in 1948
Mailing list available for rent

16977 Stage Managers' Association
PO Box 275
Times Square Station
New York, NY 10108-0275

Home Page: www.stagemanagers.org
Social Media: Facebook, Twitter, LinkedIn

Elynmarie Kazle, Chair
Mandy L. Berry, 1st Vice Chair
Hope Rose Kelly, 2nd Vice Chair
Eileen Arnold, Treasurer
Melissa A.ў Nathan, Secretary
Founded in 1981

16978 Strategic Management Association
19102 South Blackhawk Parkway
Unit 25
Mokena, IL 60448-4066

815-806-4908
E-Mail: slfmcb@telus.net
Home Page: www.strategicleadershipforum.org

Chris Glatz, Executive Director/Administration

The international society for strategic management and planning. Presents awards, conducts seminars and foundation research.
6.5M Members
Founded in 1985

16979 Strategic Management Society
Rice Building, 815 W Van Buren Street
Suite 215
Chicago, IL 60607

312-492-6224
Fax: 312-492-6223
E-Mail: sms@strategicmanagement.net
Home Page: www.strategicmanagement.net
Social Media: Facebook, Twitter, LinkedIn, YouTube

Robert Hoskisson, President
Marjorie Lyles, President Elect
Jay Barney, Past President
Steven Floyd, Treasurer
Nikolaus Pelka, Executive Director
Founded in 1981

16980 Support Services Alliance
Po Box 130
Schoharie, NY 12157-0130

518-295-7966
800-322-3920
Fax: 518-295-8556
E-Mail:

membershipservices@ssamembers.com
Home Page: www.ssainfo.com

Steven Cole, President

Multi-state membership organization that provides cost-savings services and legislative representation for small businesses and the self-employed. Also offers services to the memberships of more than 100 affiliated state, regional and national associations.
50 Members
Founded in 1977

16981 The Association of State Floodplain Managers
575 D'Onofrio Drive
Suite 200
Madison, WI 53719

608-828-3000
Fax: 608-828-6319
Home Page: www.floods.orgÿ
Social Media: Facebook, Twitter, LinkedIn

Bill Nechamen, Chair
Ceil Strauss, Vice Chair
Karen McHugh, Treasurer
Leslie Durham, Secretary
Chad Berginnis, Executive Director
Founded in 1977

16982 The Employers Association
3020 W. Arrowood Road
Charlotte, NC 28273

704-522-8011
Fax: 704-522-8105
E-Mail: info@employersassoc.com
Home Page: www.employersassoc.com
Social Media: Facebook, Twitter, LinkedIn, RSS

Tom L. Barnhardt, Chairman
Paul DeVine, Vice Chairman
Kenny Colbert, President, CEO
Neal Alexander, Past Chairman
Cathy Graham, SPHR, Director, Benefit Services

16983 The Sales Management Association
E-Mail: support@salesmanagement.org
Home Page: www.salesmanagement.org
Social Media: Facebook, Twitter, LinkedIn, RSS

Robert J. Kelly, Chairman
Laura Hall, Managing Director

16984 TheÿAmerican SocietyÿofÿAdministrativeÿ Professionals
121 Free Street
Portland, ME 4101

888-960-ASAP
Fax: 207-842-5603
E-Mail: membership@asaporg.com
Home Page: www.asaporg.com
Social Media: Facebook, Twitter, LinkedIn, Pinterest
Founded in 2005

16985 TheÿAssociationÿfor Financial Professionals
4520 East West Highway
Suite 750
Bethesda, MD 20814ÿ

301-907-2862
Fax: 301-907-2864
Home Page: www.afponline.org
Social Media: Twitter, LinkedIn, YouTube, RSS

Anthony Scaglione, CTP, Chairman
Roberta Eiseman, CTP, Vice Chairman
Jeff Johnson, CTP, CPA, Vice Chairman
Ann Anthony, CTP, Board of Director
Terry Crawford, CTP, Board of Director

16986 Turnaround Management Association Headquarters
150 S Wacker Drive
Suite 900
Chicago, IL 60606

312-578-6900
Fax: 312-578-8336
E-Mail: info@turnaround.org
Home Page: www.turnaround.org
Social Media: Facebook, Twitter, LinkedIn

Ronald R Sussman, Chairperson
Thomas M Kim, President
Gregory J. Fine, CAE, Chief Executive Officer
Jim Gavin, Chief Financial Officer
Jennifer Bethke, Chief Learning & Certification

The only international nonprofit association dedicated to corporate renewal and turnaround management. TMA's 9,000 members in 46 regional chapters comprise a professional community of turnaround practitioners, attorneys, accountants, investors, lenders, venture capitalists, appraiser, liquidators, executive recruiters and consultants. Three international conferences each year offer networking and educational sessions on the latest trends and best practices in the restructuring field.
9000 Members
Founded in 1988

16987 U.S. Workplace Wellness Alliance
1615 H Street NW
Washington, DC 20062

Home Page: www.uswwa.org

16988 WACRA: World Association for Case Method Research & Application
23 Mackintosh Avenue
Needham, MA 02492-1218

781-444-8982
Fax: 781-444-1548
E-Mail: hans.klein@wacra.org
Home Page: www.wacra.org

Dr Hans E Klein, President/Executive Director
Denise M. Smith, Executive Assistant
Dr. Amelia J. Klein, Director Education
Dr. Lars Bengtsson, Director Public Relations
Dr. Charles H. Patti, Director of Publications

Advancing the use of the case method and other interactive methodologies in teaching, training and planning.
2000 Members
Founded in 1984

16989 Wiley
John Wiley & Sons
111 River Street
Hoboken, NJ 07030-5774

201-748-6000
800-825-7550
Fax: 201-748-6088
E-Mail: info@wiley.com
Home Page: www.wiley.com

Peter B. Wiley, Chairman of the Board
Stephen M. Smith, President and CEO
Vincent Marzano, Vice President & Treasurer
Ellis E. Cousens, Executive Vice President
John Kritzmacher, Executive Vice President

Provides information to help executives manage their companies effectively.

16990 Women in Management
Women in Management
PO Box 6690
Elgin, IL 60121-6690

877-946-6285
Fax: 847-683-3751
E-Mail: nationalwim@aol.com
Home Page: www.wimonline.org

Dana Vierck, President
Ann Louis, Secretary
Tracey Carlstedt, Treasurer
Jane Gregory, Membership
Chris Awe, Administrator

Aims to promote self-growth in management. Sponsors speakers and discussion groups.
1.7M Members
Founded in 1976

16991 Young Presidents Organization
600 East Las Colinas Boulevard
Suite 1000
Irving, TX 75039ÿ

972-587-1500
800-773-7976
Fax: 972-587-1611
E-Mail: LatinAmerica@ypo.org
Home Page: www.ypo.orgÿ
Social Media: Facebook, Twitter, LinkedIn, YouTube, Google+, Instagram

Scott Mordell, Chief Executive Officer
Sean Magennis, Chief Operating Officer
Cynthia Abbott, Chief Marketing Officer
Terry Wilson, Chief Financial Officer
Dwight Moore, Chief Information Officer
Founded in 1950

16992 Young Presidents' Organization
Young Presidents' Organization
600 East Las Colinas Boulevard
Suite 1000
Irving, TX 75039

972-587-1500
800-773-7976
Fax: 972-587-1611
E-Mail: askypo@ypo.org
Home Page: www.ypo.org
Social Media: Facebook, Twitter, LinkedIn, Youtube, Google+, Instagram

Fulton Collins, Chairman
Scott Mordell, Chief Executive Officer

Members are corporate presidents under the age of fifty whose companies employ at least fifty employees.
8000 Members
Founded in 1950

Newsletters

16993 American Academy of Medical Administration Executive Newsletter
701 Lee St
Suite 600
Des Plaines, IL 60016-4516

847-759-8601
Fax: 847-759-8602
E-Mail: renee@aameda.org
Home Page: www.aameda.org

Renee Schleichar, CEO
Guy Snyder, Director of Education
Rhonda Guptill, Chief Financial Officer

Offers information and news to upper level administration of hospitals and medical institutions.
14 Pages
Frequency: BiWeekly

16994 Best Practices Report
Management Roundtable
92 Crescent St
Waltham, MA 02453-4315

781-891-8080
800-338-2223

Fax: 781-398-1889
Home Page: www.pharmcentric.com

A monthly newsletter on the best practices in product development. How to develop and deliver great products at the lowest cost in the shortest time.

16995 Better Supervision
Economics Press
12 Daniel Road
Fairfield, NJ 07004-2565

973-227-1224
Fax: 973-227-9742

Robert Guder, Publisher

Techniques for managing people successfully.
Cost: $1.00
Circulation: 43,000

16996 Better Work Supervisor
Clement Communications
Concord Industrial Park
Concordville, PA 19331

610-459-4200
Fax: 610 459-0936

Offers important information, articles and news to upper level management.
Cost: $48.50

16997 Blue Ribbon Service
Economics Press
12 Daniel Road
Fairfield, NJ 07004-2565

973-227-1224
Fax: 973-227-9742

Robert Guder, Publisher

Shows employees the importance of giving good customer service and methods of providing that service.
Circulation: 27,760

16998 Bridging the Gap
Section for Women in Public Administration
1301 Pennsylvania Avenue NW
Suite 700
Washington, DC 20004

202-393-7878
Fax: 202-638-4952
E-Mail: info@aspanet.org
Home Page: www.aspanet.org
Social Media: Facebook, Twitter, LinkedIn

Circulation: 400
Founded in 1939
Mailing list available for rent: 400 names

16999 Bulletin to Management
Bureau of National Affairs
1801 S Bell St
Arlington, VA 22202-4501

703-341-3000
800-372-1033
Fax: 800-253-0332
E-Mail: customercare@bna.com
Home Page: www.bnabooks.com
Social Media: Facebook, Twitter, LinkedIn

Paul N Wojcik, CEO

Features summaries of current developments in human resource/personnel management and labor relations. Discusses real life job situations and provides policy guides on how companies have successfully handled employee related problems. Recurring features include statistics.
Cost: $317.00
Frequency: Weekly
Founded in 1929

17000 Business Journal
Business Journals of North Carolina
120 W Morehead St
Suite 420
Charlotte, NC 28202-1874

704-973-1200
800-948-5323
Fax: 704-973-1201
E-Mail: charlotte@bizjournals.com
Home Page: www.citybiznetwork.com

George Conley, President
Robert Morris, Editor
David Harris, Managing Editor
72 Pages
Frequency: Weekly
ISSN: 0887-5588
Printed in 4 colors on newsprint stock

17001 Business Courier
101 W 7th St
Cincinnati, OH 45202-2306

513-621-6665
800-767-3263
Fax: 513-621-2462
E-Mail: borben@bizjournals.com
Home Page: www.bizjournals.com/cincinnati/

Douglas Bolton, Publisher
Rob Daumeyer, Editor
Cost: $83.00
Frequency: Weekly
Circulation: 11000
Founded in 1947

17002 Case Strategies
Cutter Information Corporation
37 Broadway
Suite 1
Arlington, MA 02474-5500

781-648-1950
800-888-8939
Fax: 781-648-1950
E-Mail: service@cutter.com
Home Page: www.cutter.com/

Paul Harman, Editor
Kim Leonard, Customer Service Director
Karen Coburn, CEO/President
Hillel Glazer, Senior Consultant
Ron Blitstein, Director

Objective, timely information to help you successfully integrate CASE into your organization.
Cost: $387.00
16 Pages
Frequency: Monthly
Founded in 1986

17003 Cash Flow Enhancement Report
Institute of Management and Administration
3 Bethesda Metro Center
Suite 250
Bethesda, MD 20814-5377

703-341-3500
800-372-1033
Fax: 800-253-0332
Home Page: www.ioma.com

Focuses on business strategies for increasing liquidity.
Cost: $245.00
16 Pages
Frequency: Monthly

17004 Center for Creative Leadership Newsletter
Center for Creative Leadership
Attn: Client Services
PO Box 26300
Greensboro, NC 27438-6300

336-887-7210
Fax: 336-282-3284
E-Mail: info@ccl.org
Home Page: www.ccl.org

Walter Ulmer Jr, Publisher
John Alexander, President, Chief Executive Officer

A newsletter featuring issues and observations on the behavioral science research and development field.
Frequency: Monthly
Circulation: 35000
Founded in 1970

17005 Chief Executive Officers Newsletter
Center for Entreprenuel Management
47 West Street
Suite 5C
New York, NY 10014-4606

212-633-0060
Fax: 212-633-0063
E-Mail: mail@ceoclubs.org
Home Page: www.ceoclubs.org

Joseph Mancuso, President
Christopher Jones, Office Manager

Unique management insights and sources for presidents of growing businesses.
Cost: $71.00
Frequency: Monthly
Circulation: 40000
Founded in 1978

17006 Communications Insights
Comquest
112 Schubert Drive
Downingtown, PA 19335-3382

610-269-2100
Fax: 610-269-2275

Mark Schubert, Publisher

Tips and techniques for sucessful communication.

17007 Communique
213 W Institute Place
Suite 307
Chicago, IL 60610-3195

312-440-0078
800-962-8274
Fax: 312-440-9474
E-Mail: mailbox@iahcsmm.com
Home Page: www.iahcsmm.com

Betty Hanna, Executive Director
Marilyn Corida, Secretary/Treasurer
Lisa Huber, President
Bruce T. Bird, President

Bi-monthly publication separates supervisors/directors from technicians.
Cost: $40.00
Frequency: 6/Annual
Circulation: 15M
ISBN: 1-605309-30-9

17008 Contractor's Business Management Report
Institute of Management and Administration
3 Bethesda Metro Center
Suite 250
Bethesda, MD 20814-5377

703-341-3500
800-372-1033
Fax: 800-253-0332
Home Page: www.ioma.com

Delivers practical, relevant, and insightful business management guidance to contractors, subcontractors and their consultants.
Cost: $424.00

17009 Corporate EFT Report
Phillips Publishing

95 Old Shoals Road
Arden, NC 28704

301-340-2100
866-599-9491
E-Mail: feedback@healthydirections.com
Home Page: www.healthydirections.com
Social Media: Facebook, Twitter

Newsletter on business, EFT operations for corporate cash managers.

17010 Corporate Examiner
Interfaith Center on Corporate Response
475 Riverside Dr
Suite 1842
New York, NY 10115-0034

212-870-2295
Fax: 212-870-2023
E-Mail: info@interfaithcommunity.org
Home Page: www.interfaithcommunity.org

Laura Morrison, Program Coordinator
Diane Bratcher, Editor

Analyzes corporate social responsibility issues and trends, reports corporate action news, reviews publications and media and presents the ideas and opinions of leaders of the corporate social responsibility movement.
Cost: $ 35.00
8 Pages
Circulation: 1500
Founded in 1981
Printed in one color on matte stock

17011 Cost Controller
Siefer Consultants
PO Box 1384
Storm Lake, IA 50588-1384

712-732-7340
Fax: 712-732-7906

Dan Siefer, Publisher

Cost cutting techniques and ideas for business and industry.
Cost: $149.00
8 Pages
Frequency: Monthly

17012 Customer Communicator
Alexander Communications Group
1916 Park Ave
Suite 501
New York, NY 10037-3733

212-281-6099
800-232-4317
Fax: 212-283-7269
E-Mail: info@customerservicegroup.com
Home Page: www.customerservicegroup.com

Romauld Alexander, President
Adam Reif, Marketing Manager

Provides customer service representatives with the skills, techniques and motivation they need to be more productive.
Cost: $200.00
Frequency: Monthly
ISSN: 0145-8450
Founded in 1990

17013 Customer Service Manager's Letter
Bureau of Business Practice
76 Ninth Avenue
7th Floor
New York, NY 10011
212-771-0600
Fax: 212-771-0885
Home Page: www.aspenpublishers.com
Social Media: Facebook, Twitter, LinkedIn

Mark Dorman, CEO
Gustavo Dobles, VP Operations

Specially designed to show managers how to reduce their costs, their customer base, and maximize their employee capability.
Cost: $179.00
8 Pages
Frequency: 2 per year
Circulation: 5200

17014 Daily Report for Executives
Bureau of National Affairs
1801 S Bell St
Arlington, VA 22202-4501

703-341-3000
800-372-1033
Fax: 800-253-0332
E-Mail: customercare@bna.com
Home Page: www.bnabooks.com
Social Media: Facebook, Twitter, LinkedIn

Paul N Wojcik, CEO

A daily notification service covering legislative, regulatory, legal, tax and economic developments which affect both national and international businesses.
Cost: $9399.00
Frequency: Daily
ISSN: 0148-8155
Founded in 1929

17015 Deal
The Deal, LLC.
14 Wall Street
New York, NY 10005

212-313-9200
888-667-3325
E-Mail: customerservice@thedeal.com
Home Page: www.thedeal.com
Social Media: Twitter

Mickey Hernandez, Advertising Sales
Elena Freed, Marketing

Dedicated solely to reporting and analyzing all the aspects of the booming, high stakes world of the deeal economy. Areas of coverage include mergers and acquisitions, IPO's, private equity, venture capital and bankruptcies. Published in newsletter and on website.
Cost: $249.00
26 Pages
Founded in 1999

17016 Delphi Insight Series
Delphi Group
Ten Post Office Square
Suite 580
Boston, MA 02109-4603

617-247-1511
800-335-7440
Fax: 617-247-4957
Home Page: www.delphigroup.com

Thomas Koulopoulos, President
Hadley Reynolds, Director Research
Mary Ann Kozlowski, Director Public Relations

Timely and insightful analysis and review of the markets, developments, and business cases for knowledge management, corporate portals and e-business solutions. Incorporates original Delphi research findings. Written for all management titles. Includes weekly email news update on relevant issues and access to DelphiWeb, an extensive online resource of product and market information.
Cost: $20000.00
Frequency: Daily

17017 Directorship
Directorship Search Group
8 Sound Shore Drive
Suite 250
Greenwich, CT 06830-7276

203-618-7000
Fax: 203-618-7007
Home Page: www.directorship.com

Russell Reynolds Jr, CEO/President
Barrett Stephens, VP
J.P. Donlon, Editor-in-Chief

Articles and news of interest to CEOs and directors of public companies, on every aspect of corporate governance.
Cost: $395.00
12 Pages
ISSN: 0193-4279
Founded in 1975
Printed in 4 colors on glossy stock

17018 EAP Link
International Education Services and Publishing
1537 Franklin Street
#201-203
San Francisco, CA 94109-4571

415-239-4171
800-551-3005

Kendall Van Blarcom, Publisher

International news for human resource professionals.
Cost: $197.00
8 Pages
Frequency: Monthly

17019 Employee Assistance Program Management Letter
Health Resources Publishing
1913 Atlantic Ave
Suite 200
Manasquan, NJ 08736-1067

732-292-1100
888-843-6242
Fax: 732-292-1111
E-Mail: info@healthresourcesonline.com
Home Page: www.healthresourcesonline.com

Robert K Jenkins, Publisher
Lisa Mansfield, Regional Director
Brett Powell, Regional Director
Alice Burron, Director

A monthly briefing on guidelines to help companies make decisions on managing their EAP programs. Contains information on what EAP's across the country are doing; help on policy issues dealing with and monitoring costs; framing coverages and limitations; and case histories.
Cost: $227.00
Frequency: Monthly
ISSN: 0896-0941
Founded in 1978

17020 Enrollment Management Report
LRP Publications
747 Dresher Road Suite 500
PO Box 980
Horsham, PA 19044-980

215-840-0912
800-341-7874
Fax: 215-784-9639
E-Mail: webmaster@lrp.com
Home Page: www.lrp.com

Jay Margolis, Editor

Provides solutions and strategies for recruitment, admissions, retention and financial aid for higher-education institutions. Shows readers how to face the challenge of working across departmental lines to improve retention rates and how to respond to the upcoming surge in

non-traditional students who apply.
Cost: $198.00
Frequency: Monthly
Founded in 1977

17021 Executive Administrator
Seifer Consultants
P.O.Box 1384
Storm Lake, IA 50588-1384
712-732-7340
Fax: 712-732-7906
John Siefer, Publisher
Management, job opportunities and news.
Cost: $70.00
Frequency: Monthly

17022 Executive Advantage
Briefings Publishing Group
1101 King St
Suite 110
Alexandria, VA 22314-2944
703-548-3800
800-888-2084
Fax: 703 684-2136
Home Page: www.briefings.com
Tina Ragland, Editorial Assistant
Lois Willingham, Marketing Manager
Deirdre Hackett, Executive Editor
William Dugan, Group Publisher
Michelle Cox, Publisher
A publication designed to help you learn the key interpersonal secrets to business success through proper etiquette and protocol.
Cost: $147.00
8 Pages
Frequency: Monthly
Founded in 1981
Mailing list available for rent: 6000 names at $125 per M
Printed in 2 colors on matte stock

17023 Executive Edge
28 W 23rd Street
10th Floor
New York, NY 10010
212-367-4100
Fax: 212-367-4137
Rich Karlgaard, Publisher
David Hallerman, Editor
Covers quality customer service and marketing techniques.

17024 Executive Issues
Wharton School
255 S 38th St
Philadelphia, PA 19104-3706
215-386-8300
Fax: 215-573-6138
E-Mail: editor@wharton.upenn.edu
Home Page: www.wharton.upenn.edu
Jason Fisher, President
Discusses current business issues, business continuing information.
Circulation: 40000

17025 Executive Recruiter News
Kennedy Information
1 Phoenix Mill Lane
Floor 3
Peterborough, NH 03458
603-924-1006
800-531-0007
E-Mail: customerservice@kennedyinfo.com
Home Page: www.kennedyinfo.com
Joseph McCool, Editor
William Allen, Managing Director
The authoritative voice of the recruiting industry, covering news, analysis, practice, advice, proprietary data and opinion.
Cost: $229.00
8 Pages
Frequency: Monthly
ISSN: 0271-0781
Founded in 1980
Printed in 2 colors on matte stock

17026 Executive Report on Managed Care
Health Resources Publishing
1913 Atlantic Ave
Suite 200
Manasquan, NJ 08736-1067
732-292-1100
888-843-6242
Fax: 732-292-1111
E-Mail: info@themcic.com
Home Page: www.healthresourcesonline.com
Robert K Jenkins, Publisher
Lisa Mansfield, Regional Director
Brett Powell, Regional Director
Alice Burron, Director
Bi-monthly report giving news of how major employers are implementing managed care programs. Helps companies prepare to evaluate and monitor various managed care proposals in terms of their cost effectiveness, quality and ability to the employer.
Cost: $497.00
Frequency: Weekly
ISSN: 0898-9753
Founded in 1978

17027 Executive Report on Physician Organizations
Health Resources Publishing
1913 Atlantic Ave
Suite 200
Manasquan, NJ 08736-1067
732-292-1100
800-516-4343
Fax: 732-292-1111
E-Mail: info@themcic.com
Home Page: www.healthresourcesonline.com
Robert K Jenkins, Publisher
Lisa Mansfield, Marketing Assistant
Caroline Pense, Editor
Brett Powell, Regional Director
Alice Burron, Director
A bi-monthly newsletter published by Health Resources Publishing.
Cost: $197.00
Frequency: Monthly
Circulation: 5000
ISSN: 0898-9753
Founded in 1978

17028 Executive Solutions
Dartnell Corporation
4660 N Ravenswood Avenue
Chicago, IL 60640-4510
773-907-9500
800-727-1227
Fax: 561-622-2423
E-Mail: customerservice@dartnellcorp.com
Home Page: www.dartnellcorp.com
Clark Fertridge, Publisher
John Aspley, Founder
Modern management techniques for executive training.

17029 Executive Wealth Advisory
National Institute of Business Management
Po Box 906
Williamsport, PA 17703-9933
703-058-8000
800-433-0622
Fax: 570-567-0166
E-Mail: customer@nibm.net
Home Page: www.nibm.net
10 Pages
Frequency: Monthly
ISSN: 1049-4855

17030 Federal Personnel Guide
LRP Publications
360 Hiatt Drive
Palm Beach Gardens, FL 33418
561-622-6520
800-341-7874
Fax: 561-622-0757
E-Mail: webmaster@lrp.com
Home Page: www.lrp.com
Kenneth Kahn, President
Annual almanac for US civilian federal personnel and training officers and individual federal and postal employees. An up-to-the-minute summary of rules and regulations affecting federal employees, including employment, pay and benefits.
Cost: $12.95
Circulation: 55000
ISBN: 1-881097-12-9
ISSN: 0163-7665
Founded in 1978

17031 Financial Management Association International (FMA)
University of South Florida
4202 E Fowler Ave
Tampa, FL 33620-9951
813-974-2011
Fax: 813-974-5530
E-Mail: fma@coba.usf.edu OR info@fma.org
Home Page: www.usf.edu
Judy L Genshaft, President
William Christie, Financial Management Editor
Keith M Howe, Journal of Applied Finance Editor
James Schallheim, FMA Survey Synthesis Series Editor
John Finnerty, Editor FMA Online
Financial books, textbooks, databases, newspapers, research services, software and related products and services.
Frequency: Quarterly
Founded in 1970
Mailing list available for rent

17032 Global Environmental Change Report
Cutter Information Corporation
111 Eighth Avenue 7th Floor
New York, NY 10011-5552
212-771-0600
Fax: 212-771-0885
E-Mail: jrohaly@aspenpublishers.com
Home Page: www.aspenpublishers.com
Wolters Kluwer, CEO
Richard Richard, Executive VP
An exclusive international service reporting on policy trends, industry actions and global environmental change.
Cost: $565.00
8 Pages
Frequency: Monthly

17033 HIPAA Bulletin for Management
Health Resources Publishing
1913 Atlantic Ave
Suite 200
Manasquan, NJ 08736-1067
732-292-1100
888-843-6242
Fax: 732-292-1111
E-Mail: info@healthresourcesonline.com
Home Page: www.healthresourcesonline.com
Robert K Jenkins, Publisher
Lisa Mansfield, Regional Director

Brett Powell, Regional Director
Alice Burron, Director

A monthly newsletter published by Health Resources Publishing.
Cost: $147.00
Frequency: Monthly
ISSN: 0898-9753
Founded in 1978

17034 HMFA Healthcare Cost Containment Newsletter
Healthcare Finance Management Association
3 Westbrook Corporate Center
Suite 600
Westchester, IL 60154

708-531-9600
Fax: 708-531-0032
Home Page: www.hfma.org/publications/healthcarecost

Issues illustrate how to implement strategic cost management that will reduce labor and supply expenses, enhance operational efficiency, satisfy your patients, and improve your competitive position.
Cost: $125.00
Frequency: Quarterly

17035 HMFA Revenue Cycle Stragetist Newsletter
Healthcare Finance Management Association
3 Westbrook Corporate Center
Suite 600
Westchester, IL 60154

708-531-9600
Fax: 708-531-0032
Home Page: www.hfma.org/publications/

Improve your organization's bottom line while maintaining regulatory compliance.
Cost: $165.00
Frequency: Quarterly

17036 HR Briefings
Bureau of Business Practice
111 8th Avenue
New York, NY 10011

212-771-0733
800-243-1660
Fax: 800-901-9075
Home Page: www.aspenpublishers.com/

Alicia Pierce, President

Designed to help HR professionals become more effective on the job. It offers hands-on advice from other personnel managers who have experienced the kinds of problems facing readers.
Cost: $259.00
8 Pages
Frequency: Monthly
Founded in 1925

17037 HR News
Int'l Public Management Assoc for Human Resources
1617 Duke St
Alexandria, VA 22314-3406

703-549-7100
Fax: 703-684-0948
E-Mail: ipma@pma-hr.org
Home Page: www.ipma-hr.org

Neil Reichenberg, Executive Director
Sima Hassassian, COO
Tina Chiappetta, Sr Director Gov't Affairs/Comm
Frequency: Monthly
Circulation: 8000

17038 HR Weekly
SHRM/Society for Human Resource Management
1800 Duke St
Alexandria, VA 22314-3494

703-535-6000
866-898-4724
Fax: 703-535-6474
E-Mail: shrmeducation@shrm.org.
Home Page: www.shrm.org
Social Media: Facebook, Twitter, LinkedIn, Youtube

Susan R Meisinger, CEO

Weekly e-newsletter highlighting critical HR/Human Resourace issues.

17039 HR on Campus
LRP Publications
747 Dresher Road
PO Box 980
Horsham, PA 19044-980

215-784-0912
800-341-7874
Fax: 215-784-9639
E-Mail: webmaster@lrp.com
Home Page: www.lrp.com

Jay Margolis, Editor/publisher

Gives you the tools you need to solve your institution's human resource challenges. Provides pratical tips for handling real-life, day-to-day problems, along with the latest news and significant developments in higher education.
Cost: $165.00
Frequency: Monthly
Founded in 1977

17040 HRmadeEasy
Employers of America
310 Meadow Lane
Mason City, IA 50401

641-424-3187
800-728-3187
Fax: 641-424-3187
E-Mail: employer@employerhelp.org
Home Page: www.employerhelp.org

Jim Collison, President

A weekly e-newsletter published by Employers of America.
Cost: $149.00
Frequency: Weekly
Circulation: 600
Founded in 1976

17041 Hiring the Best
Briefings Publishing Group
1101 King St
Suite 110
Alexandria, VA 22314-2944

703-548-3800
800-888-2084
Fax: 703-684-2136
Home Page: www.briefings.com

Deirdre Hackett, Editor
William G Dugan, Publisher
Tina Ragland, Editorial Assistant
Lois Willingham, Marketing Manager

A publication designed to help executives recruit, screen, and retain the best employees.
Cost: $697.00
8 Pages
Frequency: Monthly
Circulation: 1300
Founded in 1981
Mailing list available for rent: 6000 names at $125 per M
Printed in 2 colors on matte stock

17042 Human Resource Department Management Report
Institute of Management and Administration
3 Bethesda Metro Center
Suite 250
Bethesda, MD 20814-5377

703-341-3500
800-372-1033
Fax: 800-253-0332
Home Page: www.ioma.com

Shows HR department heads how to boost staff motivation and productivity, improve department automation, and cut costs while improving service.
Cost: $299.00
Frequency: Monthly

17043 Human Resources Management Reporter
Thomson Reuters
2395 Midway Rd
Carrollton, TX 75006

646-822-2000
800-431-9025
Fax: 888-216-1929
E-Mail: trta.lei-support@thomsonreuters.com
Home Page: www.ria.thomsonreuters.com

Elaine Yadlon, Plant Manager
Thomas H Glocer, CEO & Director
Robert D Daleo, Chief Financial Officer
Kelli Crane, Senior Vice President & CIO

For personnel practitioners.
Founded in 1935

17044 IOMA's Pay for Performance Report
Institute of Management and Administration
3 Bethesda Metro Center
Suite 250
Bethesda, MD 20814-5377

703-341-3500
800-372-1033
Fax: 800-253-0332
Home Page: www.ioma.com

Helps human resource and compensation executives improve their company's productivity through the use of variable pay and bonus programs for all types of employees.

17045 IOMA's Report on Managing Flexible Benefit Plans
Institute of Management and Administration
3 Bethesda Metro Center
Suite 250
Bethesda, MD 20814-5377

703-341-3500
800-372-1033
Fax: 800-253-0332
Home Page: www.ioma.com

Information to manage a firm's flex plan.
Cost: $245.00
16 Pages
Frequency: Monthly

17046 IT Services Business Report
Staffing Industry Analysts
881 Fremont Ave
Suite A3
Los Altos, CA 94024-5637

650-948-9303
800-950-9496
Fax: 650-232-2360
Home Page: www.sireport.com

Ron Mester, President/CEO
Peter Yessne, Chairman/Publisher

Business news and industry trends analysis for professionals.
Cost: $297.00
Frequency: Monthly
Founded in 1989

17047 Information Advisor
Information Advisory Services

143 Old Marlton Pike
Medford, NJ 08055-8750

609-654-6266
Fax: 609-654-4309
E-Mail: dpanara@infotoday.com
Home Page: www.informationadvisor.com

Robert Berkman, Editor

Compares and evaluates business information services - print, online and CD-ROM. Covers international data, information quality, and new noteworthy products.
Frequency: Monthly
Circulation: 700

17048 International Council for Small Business
2201 G Street NW
Suite 315
Washington, DC 20052

202-944-0704
Fax: 202-994-4930
E-Mail: icsb@gwu.edu
Home Page: www.icsb.org

David Smallbone, President
Don B. Bradley, III, President-Elect
Rita Grant, VP/Finance/Control
Ayman El Tarabishy, Executive Director
Michael Bataglia, Operations Manager

Promotes the growth and development of small businesses by bringing together researchers, educators, practitioners, and policy makers from around the world.
2000+ Members
Founded in 1956
Printed in 2 colors on glossy stock

17049 International Management Council
608 S 114th Street
Omaha, NE 68154-3153

402-330-6310
800-688-9622
Fax: 402-330-7424
E-Mail: imcoffice@msn.com
Home Page: www.imc-ymca.org/join.html

Jodeen Sterba, National Administrator

Information on developing leadership and management skills through a network of shared experiences and education.
Printed in 2 colors on matte stock

17050 International Quality
Underwriters Laboratories
2600 N.W. Lake Rd.
Camas, WA 98607-8542

847-412-0136
877-854-3577
Fax: 360-817-6278
E-Mail: cec.us@us.ul.com
Home Page: www.ul.com

Keith E Williams, CEO
John Drengenberg, Manager Consumer Affairs

Free standards and other quality management topics.
Frequency: Monthly
Circulation: 18000
Founded in 1894

17051 Inventory Reduction Report
Institute of Management and Administration
3 Bethesda Metro Center
Suite 250
Bethesda, MD 20814-5377

703-341-3500
800-372-1033
Fax: 800-253-0332
Home Page: www.ioma.com

Focuses on reducing inventory costs, JIT methods and improving profitability.
Cost: $245.00
16 Pages
Frequency: Monthly

17052 Issues and Observations
Center for Creative Leadership & Jossay-Bass
350 Sansome Street
San Francisco, CA 94104-1304

415-334-4700
888-378-2537
Fax: 800-605-2665
E-Mail: info@ccl.org
Home Page: www.ccl.org

John Alexander, President
Patricia Ohlott, President, Chief Executive Officer

Contains articles about leadership and management.
Cost: $99.00
Frequency: Quarterly
Circulation: 3000
ISSN: 1093-6092
Founded in 1970

17053 Job Safety and Health
Bureau of National Affairs
1801 S Bell St
Arlington, VA 22202-4501

703-341-3000
800-372-1033
Fax: 800-253-0332
E-Mail: customercare@bna.net
Home Page: www.bnabooks.com
Social Media: Facebook, Twitter, LinkedIn

Paul N Wojcik, CEO

A biweekly review of workplace health and safety regulations, policies, practices and trends.
Cost: $898.00
ISSN: 0149-7510
Founded in 1929

17054 Jots and Jolts
Economics Press
12 Daniel Road
Fairfield, NJ 07004-2565

973-227-1224
Fax: 973-227-9742

John Beckley, Publisher

Monthly planner for supervisors; includes information management theory.
Cost: $1.00
Circulation: 32000

17055 Kennedy's Career Strategist
Career Strategies
1150 Wilmette Avenue
Wilmette, IL 60091-2603

847-251-1661
800-728-1709
Fax: 847-251-5191
E-Mail: mmkcareer@aol.com
Home Page: www.moatskennedy.com/newsletter.html

Marilyn Moat Kennedy, Editor
Linda Mitchell, Production Manager
Cost: $65.00
Frequency: Monthly
ISSN: 0891-2572
Founded in 1986

17056 Laboratory Industry Report
Institute of Management and Administration
3 Bethesda Metro Center
Suite 250
Bethesda, MD 20814-5377

703-341-3500
800-372-1033
Fax: 800-253-0332
Home Page: www.ioma.com

An insider's view of the lab industry's most important business and financial trends.
Cost: $449.00

17057 Law Office Management & Administration Report
Institute of Management and Administration
3 Bethesda Metro Center
Suite 250
Bethesda, MD 20814-5377

703-341-3500
800-372-1033
Fax: 800-253-0332
Home Page: www.ioma.com

Covers the daily management concerns relevant for law firm administrators, office managers, and others.
Cost: $489.00
Frequency: Monthly
Founded in 1983

17058 Leadership Strategies
Briefings Publishing Group
1101 King St
Suite 110
Alexandria, VA 22314-2944

703-548-3800
800-888-2084
Fax: 703-684-2136
Home Page: www.briefings.com

Deirdre Hackett, Editor
Jacqueline Stonis, Production Manager
William G. Duggan, Group Publisher
Lois Willingham, Marketing Manager

A publication designed to sharpen your management and leadership abilities, improve your productivity, and accelerate your professional success.
Cost: $199.00
8 Pages
Frequency: Monthly
Circulation: 8500
Founded in 1981
Mailing list available for rent: 7000 names at $125 per M
Printed in 2 colors on matte stock

17059 Management Policies and Personnel Law
Business Research Publications
1533 H Street NW
Suite 200W
Washington, DC 20005-1005

202-364-6473
800-822-6338
Fax: 202-466-3509

Susan Sonnesyn-Brooks, Editor

Leading newsletter designed to give managers an inside view into the best run companies.
Frequency: BiWeekly

17060 Manager's Legal Bulletin
Alexander Hamilton Institute
70 Hilltop Rd
Suite 220
Ramsey, NJ 07446-2816

201-825-3377
800-879-2441
Fax: 201-825-8696
E-Mail: custsvc@ahipubs.com
Home Page: www.ahipubs.com

Schuyler T Jenks, President

Shows managers how to handle problems in the workplace without provoking lawsuits for illegal discrimination in hiring, firing, promotions, sexual harassment or discipline decisions.
Cost: $66.00
4 Pages
Frequency: Fortnightly
Circulation: 20000
Founded in 1909
Mailing list available for rent: 8M names at $125 per M
Printed in 2 colors on matte stock

17061 **Managing Benefits Plans**
Institute of Management and Administration
3 Bethesda Metro Center
Suite 250
Bethesda, MD 20814-5377

703-341-3500
800-372-1033
Fax: 800-253-0332
Home Page: www.ioma.com

The result of combining two newsletters into one, stronger report. Managers who oversee the enrollment, communications, and administration of employee benefits are the best subscribers to MBP.
Cost: $399.00
Founded in 1982

17062 **Managing Customer Service**
Institute of Management and Administration
3 Bethesda Metro Center
Suite 250
Bethesda, MD 20814-5377

703-341-3500
800-372-1033
Fax: 800-253-0332
Home Page: www.ioma.com

Boost the productivity, efficiency and visibility of your department, and keep it on the cutting edge.

17063 **Managing Logistics**
Institute of Management and Administration
3 Bethesda Metro Center
Suite 250
Bethesda, MD 20814-5377

703-341-3500
800-372-1033
Fax: 800-253-0332
Home Page: www.ioma.com

Covers new technologies and strategies, how to negotiate with outsourced service providers.

17064 **Managing Training & Development**
Institute of Management and Administration
3 Bethesda Metro Center
Suite 250
Bethesda, MD 20814-5377

703-341-3500
800-372-1033
Fax: 800-253-0332
Home Page: www.ioma.com

Covers all aspects of measuring, learning, development, getting employees trained for their jobs, and justifying the cost of training to upper management.

17065 **Medical Group Management Update**
Medical Group Management Association
104 Inverness Ter E
Englewood, CO 80112-5313

303-799-1111
Fax: 303-643-9599
E-Mail: infocenter@mgma.com
Home Page: www.mgma.com

William Jessee, CEO
Eileen Barker, senior Vice President
Anders Gilberg, senior Vice President
Natalie Jamieson, Administrative Assistant

Monthly association newspaper offering up-to-the-minute articles on current legislation, practical management, health care trends, association activities and other timely subjects.
Frequency: Monthly

17066 **Object-Oriented Strategies**
Cutter Information Corporation
37 Broadway
Suite 1
Arlington, MA 02474-5500

781-648-1950
800-888-8939
Fax: 781-648-1950
E-Mail: service@cutter.com
Home Page: www.cutter.com

Paul Harman, Editor
Kim Leonard, Customer Service Director
Karen Coburn, CEO
Hillel Glazer, Senior Consultant
Ron Blitstein, Director

Designed for managers and developers of object-oriented systems.
Cost: $495.00
16 Pages
Frequency: Monthly
Founded in 1986

17067 **Orlando Business Journal**
Business Journals
Ste 700
255 S Orange Ave
Orlando, FL 32801-5007

407-649-8470
888-649-6254
Fax: 407-420-1625
E-Mail: orlando@bizjournals.com
Home Page: www.bizjournals.com/orlando

Ann Sonntag, Publisher
Ken Cogburn, Editor
Cindy Barth, Managing Editor
Sue Ross, Ad Director
Alan Byrd, Director of Marketing/Circulation
Cost: $79.00
64 Pages
Frequency: Weekly
ISSN: 8750-8686
Founded in 1995
Printed in 4 colors on newsprint stock

17068 **PMI Today**
Project Management Institute
14 Campus Blvd
Newtown Square, PA 19073-3299

610-356-4600
Fax: 610-356-4647
Home Page: www.pmi.org

Gregory Balestrero, CEO
Mark Langley, Managing Director
Louis Mercken, Chairman
Van Goldfisher, Editor
Jane Farley, Secretary

A monthly newsletter published by the Project Management Institute.
6 Pages
Frequency: Monthly
Circulation: 150000
Founded in 1969
Mailing list available for rent

17069 **PSMJ Principal Strategies**
PSMJ Resources
10 Midland Avenue
Newton, MA 02458-1000

617-965-0055
800-537-7765
Fax: 617-965-5152
E-Mail: info@psmj.com
Home Page: www.psmj.com

Frank Stasiowski, Production Manager

Offers management tactics and techniques for the design industry.
Cost: $195.00
8 Pages
Frequency: Monthly
Founded in 1974
Mailing list available for rentat $125 per M
Printed in 2 colors on matte stock

17070 **PSMJ Project Delivery**
PSMJ Resources
10 Midland Avenue
Newton, MA 02458-1000

617-965-0055
800-537-7765
Fax: 617-965-5152
E-Mail: info@psmj.com
Home Page: www.psmj.com

Frank Stasiowski, Production Manager

Offers project management tactics and techniques to the design industry.
Cost: $196.00
8 Pages
Frequency: Monthly
Mailing list available for rentat $125 per M
Printed in 2 colors on matte stock

17071 **Payroll Manager's Letter**
Bureau of Business Practice
111 8th Avenue
7th Floor
New York, NY 10011

212-771-0600
800-638-8437
E-Mail: rfecustomer@aspenpubl.com
Home Page: www.aspenpublishers.com

Marc Jennings, VP
Gerry Centrowitz, VP, Marketing and Commu

Contains concise, plain-English explanations of the latest federal payroll developments which helps companies comply with rapidly changing employment tax and minimum wage/overtime laws.
Cost: $235.00
8 Pages
Circulation: 7000
Founded in 1920
Printed in one color on glossy stock

17072 **Personal Report for the Administrative Professional**
National Institute of Business Management
1750 Old Meadow Rd
Suite 302
Mc Lean, VA 22102-4304

703-905-8000
800-543-2049
Fax: 703-905-8042
E-Mail: customer@nibm.net
Home Page: www.nibm.net

Steve Sturm, President
Phil Ash, Marketing Director
Cost: $54.00
10 Pages
Frequency: Monthly
ISSN: 1049-4855
Founded in 1937

17073 **Preventing Business Fraud**
Institute of Management and Administration
3 Bethesda Metro Center
Suite 250
Bethesda, MD 20814-5377

703-341-3500
800-372-1033
Fax: 800-253-0332
Home Page: www.ioma.com

Stop corporate fraud before it happens. Get guidance on how to avoid supplier collusion and kickbacks, false invoicing, health insurance and workers' compensation fraud, payroll, petty cash and T and E overstatements, theft of equipment and materials and more.

17074 **Professional Advisor**
Int'l Society of Speakers, Authors & Consultants
PO Box 6432
Kingwood, TX 77325-6432

281-441-3558
Fax: 281-441-3538

Bernard Zick, Publisher

Includes information of the consulting industry.
Cost: $120.00
10 Pages
Frequency: Monthly

17075 **Profit Line**
Ernst and Young
9920 Pacific Heights Blvd
Suite 200
San Diego, CA 92121

858-452-6800
800-200-7763
Fax: 858-452-6998
E-Mail: media@profitline.com
Home Page: www.profitline.com

Gary Martino, Chief Financial Officer

Business information newsletter for entrepreneurs.

17076 **Quality Assurance Bulletin**
Bureau of Business Practice
76 Ninth Avenue
7th Floor
New York, NY 10011

212-771-0600
Fax: 212-771-0885
Home Page: www.aspenpublishers.com
Social Media: Facebook, Twitter, LinkedIn

Mark Dorman, CEO
Gustavo Dobles, VP Operations

Helps quality professionals improve the company's question-answer function.
Cost: $118.80
8 Pages
Frequency: 2 per year

17077 **Real Estate & Leasing Report**
Business Journals
120 W Morehead St
Suite 420
Charlotte, NC 28202-1874

704-973-1200
Fax: 704-973-1201
Home Page: www.citybiznetwork.com

George Conley, President
Joanne Skoog, Editor
Cost: $70.00
70 Pages
Frequency: Weekly
ISSN: 0887-5588
Printed in 4 colors on newsprint stock

17078 **Report on Salary Surveys**
Institute of Management and Administration
3 Bethesda Metro Center
Suite 250
Bethesda, MD 20814-5377

703-341-3500
800-372-1033
Fax: 800-253-0332
Home Page: www.ioma.com

Analyzes data from major salary surveys released during the year by the biggest compensation survey companies, WorldatWork, SHRM, state HR societies, and the Big Four accounting firms, to give readers an overview of those expensive, hard-to-manage services.
Cost: $429.00
Founded in 1993

17079 **Rodenhauser Report**
Consulting Information Services
191 Washington Street
Keene, NH 03431

603-355-1560
Home Page: www.consultinginfo.com

Tom Rodenhauser, President

Rodenhauser Report is a monthly electronic briefing that forecasts consulting trends for senior management advisors and business executives.
Frequency: Monthly
Founded in 1998

17080 **Servicing Management**
LDJ Corporation
70 Edwin Avenue
PO Box 2180
Waterbury, CT 06708-2180

203-755-0158
800-325-6745
Fax: 203-755-3480
Home Page: www.sm-online.com/

Paul Zackin, Publisher
Michael Bates, Editor
June Han, Circulation Manager
Jeanette Laliberte, Subscriptions

Delivers news and how-to advice to executives and personnel in the servicing of mortgage loans nationwide.
Cost: $48.00
Frequency: Monthly
Circulation: 18000
Founded in 1969

17081 **Small-Biz Growth**
Support Services Alliance
PO Box 130
Schoharie, NY 12157-0130

518-295-7966
800-322-3920
Fax: 518-295-8556
E-Mail: info@ssamembers.com
Home Page: www.smallbizgrowth.com

Steven Cole, President

Keeps SSA members and their employees up-to-date on developments affecting small-business communties.
Cost: $25.00
Frequency: Monthly
Circulation: 17,000
Founded in 1977

17082 **Small-Business Strategies**
Page Group
PO Box 116
Dundee, IL 60118-0116

847-695-7887

Phillip Grisolia, Publisher

Contains practical ideas for use in successfully starting and profitably managing small businesses. Accepts advertising.
Cost: $95.00
4 Pages
Frequency: BiWeekly

17083 **Sound Thinking**
Jay Mitchell Associates
PO Box 1285
Fairfield, IA 52556-0022

641-472-4087
Fax: 641-472-2071

Jay Mitchell, Publisher

Notes and comments on the radio industry and related fields, specializing in an outside-in view.
Cost: $65.00
2 Pages
Frequency: Monthly

17084 **Source**
Rachel PR Services
1650 S Pacific Coast Highway
Suite 200C
Redondo Beach, CA 90277-5625
Janis Brett-Elspas, Editor
Jamie Steiner, Advertising/Sales

Annual reference guide for job hunters in advertising, public relations, marketing and journalism offering more than 2,000 resources for finding jobs at all levels in all 50 states. Listings includes job banks, job hotlines, executive recruiters, books/directories, trade publications, industry associations and more.
Cost: $39.00
40 Pages
Frequency: Annual
Circulation: 30,000
Printed in on matte stock

17085 **Southeastern Association Executive**
Special Edition Publishing
999 Douglas Ave
Suite 3317
Altamonte Spgs, FL 32714-2063

407-862-7737
Fax: 407-862-8102
E-Mail: specedpub@earthlink.net
Home Page: www.specedpub.com

A Sciuto, Publisher
Nichole Wunduke, Editor
Betty Harper, Director of Sales & Marke

Monthly news magazine serving associations meetings and hospitality executives in the southeast .
25 Pages
Frequency: Monthly
Circulation: 5200
Founded in 1973
Printed in 4 colors on glossy stock

17086 **Staffing Industry Report**
Staffing Industry Analysts
881 Fremont Ave
Suite A3
Los Altos, CA 94024 5637

650-948-9303
800-950-9496
Fax: 650-232-2360
E-Mail: memberservices@staffingindustry.com
Home Page: www.staffingindustry.com

Ron Mester, Managing Director
Tim Murphy, Editor
Joyce Routson, Managing Editor
Greg Palmer, CEO
Jason Ezratty, Managing Partner

A twice monthly newsletter for temporary help, staff leasing and employment service companies. Industry information, company news, training and automation resource reviews, financial coverage, labor demand and supply analysis, key interviews. Association news, public company stock tables. SI Report sponsors an annual Staffing Industry Executive Forum in April. Emphasis is on business news. Includes advertising supplement.
Cost: $385.00
Circulation: 3000
Founded in 1989
Mailing list available for rent: 3500 names
Printed in 2 colors on matte stock

17087 **Success in Recruiting and Retaining**
National Institute of Business Management
1750 Old Meadow Rd
Suite 302
Mc Lean, VA 22102-4304

703-905-8000
800-543-2049

Fax: 703-905-8042
E-Mail: customer@nibm.net

Steve Sturm, President
10 Pages
Frequency: Monthly
ISSN: 1049-4855

17088 Successful Self-Management
Stahlka Associates
60 Westchester Road
Williamsville, NY 14221-5021

716-347-7070
Fax: 716-626-4188
E-Mail: wendystahlka@verizon.net
Home Page: www.stahlkamarketing.com

Clayton A Stahlka, Production Manager
Wendy Stahlka, President

Mastering changes in yourself and your environment to be the best you can be with what you have.
Cost: $24.00
5 Pages
Frequency: Quarterly
Circulation: 1800
Founded in 1975
Printed in one color on matte stock

17089 Supplier Selection and Management Report
Institute of Management and Administration
3 Bethesda Metro Center
Suite 250
Bethesda, MD 20814-5377

703-341-3500
800-372-1033
Fax: 800-253-0332
Home Page: www.ioma.com

Focuses on supplier selection, partnering and management issues.
Cost: $289.00
16 Pages
Frequency: Monthly
Circulation: 180,000
Founded in 1980

17090 Travel Manager's Executive Briefing
Health Resources Publishing
1913 Atlantic Ave
Suite 200
Manasquan, NJ 08736-1067

732-292-1100
888-843-6242
Fax: 732-292-1111
E-Mail: info@themcic.com
Home Page: www.healthresourcesonline.com

Robert K Jenkins, Publisher
Judith Granholm, Regional Director
Brett Powell, Regional Director
Alice Burron, Director

A digest published twice a month that covers developments in the field of travel and expense cost control. Topics include discounts in air fare, car rentals, hotel bills, travel alternatives, phone savings, planning for meetings trends in government legislation affecting business travel costs, and case histories of companies that have successfully cut costs. Ideal for travel managers of corporations, small businesses and nonprofit organizations.
Cost: $447.00
ISSN: 0272-569X
Founded in 1978

17091 WACRA News
World Assoc for Case Method Research & Application
23 Mackintosh Avenue
Needham, MA 02492-1218

781-444-8982
800-523-6468
Fax: 781-444-1548
E-Mail: wacra@rcn.com
Home Page: www.wacra.org

Dr Hans E Klein, President/Executive Director
Dr Charles H Patti, Publications Director

17092 WACRA Newsletter
World Assoc for Case Method Research & Application
23 Mackintosh Avenue
Needham, MA 02492-1218

781-444-8982
800-523-6468
Fax: 781-444-1548
E-Mail: hans.klein@wacra.org
Home Page: www.wacra.org

Dr Hans E Klein, President/Executive Director
Dr Charles H Patti, Publications Director
Frequency: Biannual

17093 Wage-Hour Compliance Report
Institute of Management and Administration
3 Bethesda Metro Center
Suite 250
Bethesda, MD 20814-5377

703-341-3500
800-372-1033
Fax: 800-253-0332
Home Page: www.ioma.com

Covers white-collar exemptions, how to pay employees for rest and overtime periods, legal holidays, how to handle vacation, severance and negotiated termination pay rules, and give managers a concise rundown of new federal and state withholding and minimum wage changes, new rules, rates and requirements.

17094 What's Ahead in Personnel
Remy Publishing Company
1439 W Summerdale Ave
Suite 440
Chicago, IL 60640-2115

773-769-6760
800-542-6670
Fax: 773-464-0166
E-Mail: webmaster@passportnewsletter.com
Home Page: www.passportnewsletter.com

Contains information on current HR trends, legal issues and company practices.
Frequency: SemiMonthly

17095 What's Working In Consulting
Kennedy Information
1 Pheonix Mill Lane
Floor 3
Fitzwilliam, NH 03447

603-924-1006
800-531-0007
E-Mail: customerservice@kennedyinfo.com
Home Page: www.kennedyinfo.com

Alan Weiss, Editor
Provides practical guidance on improving consulting skills and managing a consulting practice.
Cost: $197.00
Frequency: Monthly
ISSN: 1535-3036

17096 Women in Business
Business Journal of Portland
851 Sw 6th Ave
Suite 500
Portland, OR 97204-1342

503-274-8733
800-486-3289
Fax: 503-219-3450
E-Mail: borben@bizjournals.com
Home Page: www.bizjournals.com/portland

Craig Wessel, Publisher
Dan McMillan, Managing Editor
Rob Smith, Editor
George Vaughan, Advertising Director

Special supplement of The Business Journal that celebrates the achievements of women making a difference in the business world and community
Cost: $89.00
36 Pages
ISSN: 0742-6550
Printed in 4 colors on newsprint stock

17097 Work and Family Life
230 W 55th Street
Apartment 6B
New York, NY 10019-5212

212-557-3555
Fax: 212-557-6555
E-Mail: susan@workandfamilylife.com
Home Page: www.workandfamily.com

Ellen Galinsky, Executive Editor
Susan Ginsberg, Editor/Publisher
Anne Perryman, Editor
Susan Seitel, President

Provides information and practical solutions to a wide range of family, job and health issues. Purpose is to help readers find pleasure and satisfaction in their many roles at work, at home, and in their communities.
Cost: $ 295.00
Frequency: Monthly
Circulation: 50000
Founded in 1984
Printed in 4 colors on matte stock

17098 Working Smart
National Institute of Business Management
1750 Old Meadow Rd
Suite 302
Mc Lean, VA 22102-4304

703-905-8000
800-543-2055
Fax: 703-905-8042
E-Mail: customer@nibm.net
Home Page: www.nibm.net

Steve Sturm, President
Morey Stettner, Editor
Phil Ash, Marketing Director

Ready, relevant and reliable advice for managers on workplace issues.
Cost: $48.00
10 Pages
Frequency: Monthly
ISSN: 1049-4855
Founded in 1937
Printed in 2 colors on matte stock

Magazines & Journals

17099 AFSM: Professional Journal
Assoication for Services Management International
11031 Via Frontera
Suite A
San Diego, CA 92127

239-275-7887
800-333-9786
Fax: 239-275-0794
E-Mail: info@afsmi.org
Home Page: www.afsmi.org

Jb Wood, President/CEO
John Schoenewald, Executive Director

A journal aimed at management issues.
64 Pages
Frequency: Monthly
Founded in 1975

17100 APICS: The Performance Advantage
APICS Association for Operations Management

8430 West Bryn Mawr Avenue
Suite 1000
Chicago, IL 60631

773-867-1777
800-444-2742
Fax: 773-639-3000
E-Mail: webmaster@apics.org.
Home Page: www.apics.org
Social Media: Facebook, Twitter, LinkedIn, Youtube

Doug Kelly, Editor
Jennifer Procter, Managing Editor
Beth Rennie, Senior Editor

Provides comprehensive articles on enterprise resources planning, supply chain management, e-business, materials management and production and inventory management.
Cost: $65.00
64 Pages
Frequency: 10/Year
Circulation: 66,000
ISSN: 1056-0017
Mailing list available for rent: 40,000 names at $100 per M
Printed in 4 colors on glossy stock

17101 **American Academy of Medical Administrators**
American Academy of Medical Administrators
701 Lee St
Suite 600
Des Plaines, IL 60016-4516

847-759-8601
Fax: 847-759-8602
E-Mail: info@aameda.org
Home Page: www.aameda.org

Renee Schleichar, CEO
Holly Estal, Director of Education
Guy Snyder, Director of Education
Rhonda Guptill, Chief Financial Officer
24 Pages
Frequency: Quarterly
Founded in 1957
Mailing list available for rent
Printed in 2 colors on glossy stock

17102 **American Cemetery**
Kates-Boylston Publications
11300 Rockville Pike
Suite 1100
Rockville, MD 20852

800-500-4585
800-500-4585
Fax: 301-287-2150
E-Mail: AmericanFD@aol.com
Home Page: www.kates-boylston.com

Adrian F Boylston, Publisher
Thomas Lorge, Executive Director
Thomas Parmalee, Executive Director
Amy Fidalgo, Production Manager

Features articles on cemetery administration, maintenance, sales and public relations. Also includes coverage of conventions, new cemeteries and new building ideas.
Cost: $39.95
Frequency: Monthly
Circulation: 5800

17103 **American Small Businesses Association**
206 E College St
Suite 201
Grapevine, TX 76051-5381

817-488-8770
800-801-2722
Fax: 817-251-8578

Bill Will Sr, President
Wanda Johnson, Bookkeeper

Represents the interests of small businesses.
Printed in on glossy stock

17104 **Association Management Magazine**
American Society of Association Executives
1575 I St Nw
Suite 11
Washington, DC 20005-1103

202-626-2700
888-950-2723
Fax: 202-371-8315
E-Mail: publicpolicy@asaenet.org
Home Page: www.asaenet.org/

Karl Ely, Publisher
Keith C Skillman, Editor

Serves the field of trade business professional and philanthropic associations.
Cost: $30.00
Frequency: Monthly
Circulation: 22507
Founded in 1920

17105 **Benchmarking: A Practitioner's Guide for Becoming & Staying the Best**
Quality & Productivity Management Association
300 N Martingale Road
Suite 230
Schaumburg, IL 60173-2407

FAX 847-619-3383

William Ginnodo, Publisher
Lesley Williams, Publications Manager

Promotes benchmarking as a technique for comparing processes, products or services with the world's best encouraging ways to do things faster, better, and less cost.

17106 **Bits and Pieces**
Economics Press
12 Daniel Road
Fairfield, NJ 07004-2565

973-227-1224
Fax: 973-227-9742

Arthur Lenehan, Publisher

Management and common sense plus anecdotes and quotes.
Cost: $1.00
Circulation: 266,000

17107 **Bloomberg Businessweek**
Bloomberg
731 Lexington Avenue
New York, NY 10022

212-318-2000
800-955-4003
Fax: 212-617-5999
Home Page: www.bloomberg.com

Daniel L. Doctoroff, President/CEO
Peter T. Grauer, Chairman
Beth Mazzeo, Head of Global Data Products Div.
Thomas F. Secunda, Head of Global Financial Products
Matthew Winkler, Editor-in-Chief

Offers a global perspective to help senior executives profit from faster, smarter, and more informed decisions. Bloomberg Businessweek reaches more C-level executives than any other business magazine.
Cost: $4.95
Frequency: Weekly
Founded in 1981

17108 **Building Operating Management**
Trade Press Publishing Corporation
2100 W Florist Avenue
Milwaukee, WI 53209-3799

414-228-7701
Fax: 414-228-1134
E-Mail: info@tradepress.com
Home Page: www.tradepress.com

Edward Sullivan, Editor
Bobbie Reid, Production Director
Scott Cunningham, Associate Publisher
Eric Muench, Director of Circulation
Robert J Wisniewski, President/CEO

Serves the field of facilities management, encompassing commercial building: office buildings, real estate/property management firms, developers, financial institutions, insurance companies, apartment complexes, civic/convention centers, including members of the Building Owners and Managers Association
Frequency: Monthly
Circulation: 70000
Founded in 1943

17109 **Business Facilities**
Group C Communications
PO Box 2060
Red Bank, NJ 07701-0901

732-842-7433
800-524-0337
Fax: 732-758-6634
E-Mail: webmaster@groupc.com
Home Page: www.groupc.com

Edgar T Coene, President
Ted Coene, Publisher
Karim Khan, Editor
Beth Sicignano, Marketing Manager
Connie Donatantonio, Circulation Manager

Magazine covering the fields of corporation expansion, economic development and real estate.
Cost: $30.00
Frequency: Monthly
Circulation: 30309
Founded in 1969

17110 **Business First**
Business News
455 S 4th St
Suite 278
Louisville, KY 40202-2551

502-583-1731
Fax: 502-587-1703
E-Mail: borben@bizjournals.com
Home Page: www.bizjournals.com

Tom Monahan, President
Carol Brando Timmons, Editor
Judith Berzof, Associate Editor
Rebecca Ray, Assistant Editor
Cost: $83.00
Frequency: Monthly

17111 **C2M Consulting to Management**
Journal of Management Consulting
858 Longview Road
Burlingame, CA 94010-6974

650-342-1954
Fax: 650-344-5005
Home Page: www.c2m.com

E Michael Shays, Publisher
Marsha Lewin, Chairman Editorial

The journal, which is read in over 60 countries, presents methods and processes for management consultants helping them to enlarge and perfect their skills and service to clients.
Cost: $80.00
Frequency: Quarterly
Circulation: 5000
ISSN: 0158-7778
Founded in 1981

17112 **CFO: the Magazine for Chief Financial Officers**
CFO Publishing Corporation

253 Summer St
Suite 3
Boston, MA 02210-1114

617-345-9700
Fax: 617-951-4090
Home Page: www.cfo.com

Frank Quigley, President

Features insurance, cash management, taxes, benefits, accounting, buyers guide.
Circulation: 365,409

17113 COM-SAC, Computer Security, Audit & Control
Management Advisory Services & Publications
PO Box 81151
Wellesley Hills, MA 02481-0001

781-235-2895
Fax: 781-235-5446
E-Mail: Info@masp.com
Home Page: www.masp.com

Presents tutorials and articles of current interest in computer security and audit, presents a comprehensive digest of all key articles and books published on the fields of computer security and control.
Cost: $98.00
Frequency: Quarterly
Founded in 1973

17114 Central Penn Business Journal
Journal Publications
101 N 2nd Street
2nd Floor
Harrisburg, PA 17101-1600

717-236-4300
Fax: 717-909-6803
E-Mail: webmaster@journalpub.com
Home Page: www.centralpennbusiness.com

David A Schankweiler, Publisher
Gary Nalbandian, CEO/President
Jason Klinger, Editor

Provides comprehensive news for the business community.
Cost: $64.95
56 Pages
Frequency: Weekly
Circulation: 10,500
ISSN: 1058-3599
Founded in 1985

17115 Chain Leader
Raymond Herrmann
2000 Clearwater Drive
Oak Brook, IL 60523
630-288-8242
Fax: 630-288-8215
Home Page: www.chainleader.com

Mary Boltz Chapman, Editor-in-Chief
Maya Norris, Managing Editor
Ray Herrmann, Publisher

Targets senior management of chain restaurant companies.
Frequency: Monthly
Circulation: 17323
Founded in 1960

17116 Chief Executive
Chief Executive Group
110 Summit Avenue
Montvale, NJ 07645

201-930-5959
Fax: 201-930-5956
E-Mail: contact@chiefexecutive.net
Home Page: www.chiefexecutive.net

Carol Evans, Publisher
Robin Uhl, Circulation Manager
William J. Holstein, Editor-in-Chief
Edward M. Kopko, CEO/Chairman
Chris Chalk, Vice President of Sales

A journal of strategy and analysis by and for chief executives.
75 Pages
Frequency: Monthly
Circulation: 42000
Founded in 1976

17117 Club Management Magazine
Finan Publishing Company
107 W Pacific
Saint Louis, MO 63119

314-961-6644
Fax: 314-961-4809
Home Page: www.club-mgmt.com

Thomas J Finan, Publisher/Editor
Dee Kaplan, Publisher
Dianne Dierkes, Circulation Manager

The resource for successful club operations.
Cost: $26.95
Frequency: 3 Issues a year
Founded in 1927
Mailing list available for rent: 21,000 names
Printed in 4 colors on glossy stock

17118 Commitment Plus
Quality & Productivity Management Association
300 N Martingale Road
Suite 230
Schaumburg, IL 60173-2407

FAX 847-619-3383

William Ginnodo, Editor/Author

This monthly newsletter is for managers who want to improve quality, productivity and service through people. It contains brief case studies, written primarily by QPMA staff, showing how operating managers, or their people, went about implementing improvements in their organizations' operating managers, and regularly reinforce the improvement message. This newsletter is free to members.
Cost: $95.00
4 Pages
Frequency: Monthly

17119 Competitive Intelligence Review
John Wiley & Sons
111 River St
Hoboken, NJ 07030-5790

201-748-6000
800-825-7550
Fax: 201-748-6088
E-Mail: info@wiley.com
Home Page: www.wiley.com

William J Pesce, CEO

Collection and analysis of business information.
Cost: $68.95
Frequency: Quarterly
Circulation: 3250
Founded in 1807

17120 Consulting Magazine
Kennedy Information
One Phoenix Mill Lane
Floor 3
Peterborough, NH 03458

603-924-1006
800-531-0007
E-Mail: bookstore@kennedyinfo.com
Home Page: www.kennedyinfo.com

Jack Sweeney, Editor-in-Chief
Mina Landrisina, Managing Director

The only magazine written exclusively for management consultants, consulting is dedicated to fostering performance excellence and career success. Consulting serves the information needs of those responsible for shaping the business strategies of their clients.
Cost: $99.00
Frequency: Monthly
ISSN: 1525-4321
Founded in 1970

17121 Contingency Planning & Management
Witter Publishing Corporation
20 Commerce Street
Flemington, NJ 08822

908-788-0343
Fax: 908-788-3782
Home Page: www.witterpublishing.com

Bob Joudanin, Publisher
Paul Kirvan, Editor
Courtney Witter, Print Circulation/Subscriptions
Andrew Witter, President

Serves the fields of financial/banking, manufacturing industrial, transportation, utilities, telecommunications, health care, government, insurance and other allied fields.
Cost: $195.00
Frequency: Monthly
Founded in 1987

17122 Contingency Planning & Recovery Journal
Management Advisory Services & Publications
PO Box 81151
Wellesley Hills, MA 02481-0001

781-235-2895
Fax: 781-235-5446
E-Mail: Info@masp.com
Home Page: www.masp.com

The only independent quarterly that is membership and subscriber supported. It presents current state of affairs in emergency preparedness, contingency planning and business resumption planning and business continuity.
Cost: $ 75.00
16 Pages
Frequency: Quarterly
Founded in 1972
Printed in 2 colors

17123 Corporate Meetings & Incentives
Penton Media Inc
10 Fawcett Street
Suite 500
Cambridge, MA 02138

847-763-9504
866-505-7173
E-Mail: shatch@meetingsnet.com
Home Page: www.meetingsnet.com
Social Media: Facebook, Twitter, LinkedIn

Susan Hatch, Editor

Serves those involved in organizing business meetings, conventions, corporate travel agencies, and related fields.
Cost: $87.00
Frequency: Monthly
Circulation: 32200
Founded in 1980
Printed in 4 colors

17124 Corporate Security
Strafford Publications
PO Box 13729
Atlanta, GA 30324-0729

404-881-1141
800-926-7926
Fax: 404-881-0074
E-Mail: customerservice@straffordpub.com
Home Page: www.straffordpub.com

Richard Ossoff, Publisher
Joan McKenna, Editor
Marianne Mueller, Marketing

Intelligence briefing on the latest security developments, best practices, the most important trends and new technolgies.
Cost: $330.00
23 Pages
ISSN: 0889-0625
Founded in 1984

17125 Cost Engineering Journal
AACE International
1265 Suncrest Towne Centre Drive
Morgantown, WV 26505-1876

304-296-8444
800-858-2678
Fax: 304-291-5728
E-Mail: info@aacei.org
Home Page: www.aacei.org

Marvin Gelhausen, Managing Editor
Noah Kinderknecht, Editor
International hournal of cost estimation, cost/schedule control, and project management read by cost professionals around the world to get the most up-to-date information about the profession.
Frequency: Monthly
Founded in 1956

17126 Crain's New York Business
Crain Communications
711 3rd Ave
New York, NY 10017-4014

212-210-0100
Fax: 212-210-0200
E-Mail: customerservice@crainsnewyork.com.
Home Page: www.crainsnewyork.com
Social Media: Facebook, Twitter, LinkedIn

Norm Feldman, President
Dedicated to exclusive coverage of business in New York City, Crain's keeps tabs on the people, the companies, the products, the politics and much more.
Frequency: Weekly
Circulation: 61000
Mailing list available for rent

17127 Customer Interaction Solutions
Technology Marketing Corporation
800 Connecticut Ave
1st Floor East
Norwalk, CT 06854-1936

203-852-6800
800-243-6002
Fax: 203-866-3326
E-Mail: tmc@tmcnet.com
Home Page: www.tmcnet.com
Social Media: Twitter

Rich Tehrani, CEO
Dedicated to teleservices and e-services outsourcing, marketing and customer relationship management issues.
Frequency: Monthly
Founded in 1972

17128 Decision Sciences Journal
Decision Sciences Institute
35 Broad Street
Atlanta, GA 30303

404-651-4000
Fax: 404-413-7714
E-Mail: dsi@gsu.edu
Home Page: www.decisionsciences.org

Gary L Ragatz, President
Julie Kendall, Treasurer
Carol J. Latta, Executive Director
Terrell G. Williams, Marketing Director
Vicki Smith-Daniels, Editor
Scientific quantitative, behavioral and computational approaches to decision making.
Cost: $100.00
Frequency: Quarterly
Circulation: 5000
Founded in 1968

17129 Destination KC
Show-Me Publishing
306 E 12th Street
Suite 1014
Kansas City, MO 64106

816-358-8700
Fax: 814-474-1111
E-Mail: ingrams@unicom.net

Joe Sweeney, Editor-in-Chief
Kansas City's business relocation and information guide.
Cost: $36.00
984 Pages
Frequency: Monthly
ISSN: 1046-9958
Printed in 4 colors on glossy stock

17130 Direct
Primedia
1166 Avenue of the Americas/10th Fl
New York, NY 10036

212-204-4200
Fax: 913-514-6895
E-Mail: sales@rmsreprints.com
Home Page: www.penton.com

Eric Jacobson, Senior VP
Charles Vietri, Managing Editor
Cheryll Richter, Marketing Manager
Andria Gennlauderslager, Circulation Manager
Chris Meyer, Director, Corporate Communications
Serves the marketing and media industries.
Circulation: 46500
ISSN: 1046-4174
Printed in 4 colors

17131 Director
NFDA Publications
13625 Bishops Dr
Brookfield, WI 53005-6607

262-789-1880
800-228-6332
Fax: 262-789-6977
E-Mail: nfda@nfda.org
Home Page: www.nfda.org

Christine Pepper, CEO
Chris Raymond, Editor
Benjamin Lund, Assistant Editor
Fay Spano, Director of Public Relations
The Director is specifically designed to inform and educate the funeral service professional in today's world.
Cost: $45.00
114 Pages
Frequency: Monthly
Circulation: 14,761
ISSN: 0199-3186
Founded in 1882
Printed in 4 colors on glossy stock

17132 Discovery
Cooper Group
381 Park Ave S
Suite 801
New York, NY 10016-8822

212-696-2512
Fax: 212-696-2517
Home Page: www.cooperdirect.com

Harold Cooper, CEO
Focusing on critical management issues that drive growth, profitability and shareholder value.
Cost: $10.00
Circulation: 1500
Founded in 1984

17133 Economist
PO Box 58524
Boulder, CO 80322-8524

303-945-1917
800-456-6086
Fax: 303-604-7455
E-Mail: ukpressoffice@economist.com
Home Page: www.economist.com

Helen Alexander, CEO
Kate Cooke, Group Communications Manager
David Hanger, Publisher
James Wilson, Founder
The Economist is a news and business publication written for top business decision-makers and opinion leaders who need a wide range of information and views on world events. It explores the close links between domestic and international issues, business, finance, current affairs, science and technology.
160 Pages
Frequency: Weekly
Circulation: 1009759
ISSN: 0013-0613
Founded in 1843
Printed in 4 colors on glossy stock

17134 Executive Update
Greater Washington Society of Assn Executives
1300 Pennsylvania Avenue NW
Washington, DC 20004

202-048-8014
Fax: 202-326-0995
Home Page: www.gwsae.org

Liz Whittenmore, Publisher
Scott Briscoe, Editor
Theresa Magner, Director Advertising
Jam Armstrong, Circulation Manager
Susane Sarsati, CEO/President
Association news aimed at the executive level.
120 Pages
Frequency: Monthly
Circulation: 13300
Founded in 1980

17135 Expansion Management
Penton Media
1166 Avenue of the Americas/10th Fl
New York, NY 10036

212-204-4200
Fax: 216-696-6662
E-Mail: information@penton.com
Home Page: www.penton.com

Jane Cooper, Marketing
Bill King, Chief Editor
Jodi Svenson, Production Manager
Chris Meyer, Director, Corporate Communications
Mary Abood, Vice President
Employs charts, graphs and art to lead readers through well organized sections, such as regional reviews, state reports, industry news, case studies and international reports. Addresses the key issues that attract executives in companies that need facts on resource management.
Frequency: Monthly
Circulation: 45015
Founded in 1986

17136 Facilities Manager
APPA
1643 Prince St
Alexandria, VA 22314-2818

703-684-1446
Fax: 703-549-2772

E-Mail: lander@appa.org
Home Page: www.appa.org

Steve Glazner, Editor
Anita Dosik, Managing Editor
Cost: $120.00
Frequency: Bimonthly
Circulation: 5,500
ISSN: 0882-7249

17137 Financial Management Journal
Financial Management Association International
4202 E Fowler Ave
Suite 3331
Tampa, FL 33620-9951

813-974-2084
Fax: 813-974-3318
E-Mail: fma@coba.usf.edu
Home Page: www.fma.org

Jack S Rader, Executive Director
Jeffrey Coles, Advisory Editor

Financial Management serves both academicians and practitioners who are concerned with the financial management of non-financial businesses, financial institutions, and public and private not-for-profit organizations. The journal serves the profession by publishing significant new scholarly research in finance that is of the highest quality.
Frequency: Quarterly

17138 Financial Manager
Broadcast Cable Financial Management Association
550 W Frontage Rd
Suite 3600
Northfield, IL 60093-1243

847-716-7000
Fax: 847-716-7004
E-Mail: info@mediafinance.org
Home Page: www.bcfm.com

Mary Collins, President
Jamie Smith, Director of Operations
Rachelle Brooks, BCCA Sales

A bi-monthly magazine published by the Broadcast Cable Financial Management Association.
Cost: $69.00
36 Pages
Circulation: 300
Founded in 1961
Mailing list available for rent: 1100 names at $495 per M

17139 Forbes Magazine
Forbes Media LLC.
60 5th Ave
New York, NY 10011-8868
212-620-2200
Fax: 212-620-1857
E-Mail: readers@forbes.com
Home Page: www.forbes.com

Malcolm S Forbes Jr, CEO
Bruce Rogers, VP Marketing
Paul Maidment, Executive Editor
Michael Smith Maidment, VP, GM Operations

A magazine giving detailed information about business and finance.
Frequency: Monthly

17140 Fortune Magazine
Time Inc./Time Warner
1271 Avenue of the Americas
16th Floor
New York, NY 10020-1393

212-522-1212
800-274-6800
Fax: 212-522-0602
Home Page: www.timeinc.com
Social Media: Facebook, Twitter

Laura Lang, CEO
Howard M. Averill, CFO
Leslie Picard, President
Stephanie George, Chief Marketing Officer
John Huey, Editor-in-Chief

FORTUNE is a global leader in business journalism. The magazine has a great history of providing analysis and news critical to business people.
Cost: $5.00
Frequency: Annual/18
Circulation: 1M
Founded in 1930

17141 Global IT Consulting Report
Kennedy Information
1 Kennedy Place
Route 12 S
Fitzwilliam, NH 03447

212-973-3855

Martin Zook, Editor

The business of information technology consulting, featuring news, analysis, benchmasking data and our exclusive Intelligence Briefing.
Cost: $895.00
16 Pages
Frequency: Monthly

17142 Golf Course Management
Golf Course Superintendents Association of America
1421 Research Park Dr
Lawrence, KS 66049-3859
785-841-2240
800-472-7878
Fax: 785-832-4488
E-Mail: hrmail@gcsaa.org
Home Page: www.gcsaa.org

Mark Woodward, CEO
Lacy Stattelman, Marketing Specialist
Carla Sturgeon, Sales Coordinator
Shelly Howard, Publications Coordinator

Golf Course Superintendent, economical, research and commercial interests concerned with golf course management and improvement. Provides information, education and representation for golf course managment profession.
Cost: $ 48.00
Frequency: Monthly
Circulation: 40000
ISSN: 0192-3048
Founded in 1926

17143 HR Magazine
SHRM/Society for Human Resource Management
1800 Duke St
Alexandria, VA 22314-3494

703-535-6000
866-898-4724
Fax: 703-535-6474
E-Mail: shrmeducation@shrm.org.
Home Page: www.shrm.org
Social Media: Facebook, Twitter, LinkedIn, Youtube

Susan R Meisinger, CEO
Leon Rubis, Editor

The world's leading HR resource, offering perspective and in-depth information to leading HR professionals for over 50 years.
Cost: $70.00
Frequency: Monthly
Circulation: 197000
ISSN: 1047-3149
Founded in 1956

17144 IJCRA
World Assoc for Case Method Research & Application
23 Mackintosh Avenue
Needham, MA 02492-1218

781-444-8982
800-523-6468
Fax: 781-444-1548
E-Mail: wacra@rcn.com
Home Page: www.wacra.org

Dr Hans E Klein, President/Executive Director
Dr Charles H Patti, Publications Director

Provides members and case writers and case teachers from around the world the opportunity to share their work with colleagues, to learn from colleagues and to create an international network for ccase writing, case teaching and interactive teaching applications.
Frequency: Quarterly
ISSN: 1554-7752

17145 Information Resources Management Journal
Information Resources Management Association
701 E Chocolate Ave
Suite 200
Hershey, PA 17033-1240

717-533-8845
Fax: 717-533-8861
E-Mail: members@irma-international.org
Home Page: www.irma-international.org

Jan Travers, Executive Director

An applied research, refereed, international journal providing coverage of challenges, opportunities, problems, trends, and solutions encountered by both scholars and practitioners in the field of information technology management.
Cost: $95.00
Frequency: Quarterly
ISSN: 1040-1628

17146 Institute of Management & Administration Newsletter
Institute of Management and Administration
3 Bethesda Metro Center
Suite 250
Bethesda, MD 20814-5377

703-341-3500
800-372-1033
Fax: 800-253-0332
Home Page: www.ioma.com

Monthly newsletter that offers information for all those involved in international sales, looking for new distribution channels and how to reduce exports costs and risks.
Circulation: 180,000

17147 International Cemetery & Funeral Management
International Cemetery & Funeral Association
1895 Preston White Drive
Suite 220
Reston, VA 20191-5434

703-391-8400
800-645-7700
Fax: 703-391-8416
Home Page: www.icfa.org

Susan Loving, Managing Editor
Larry Stuart Jr, General Manager

Serves as the primary communication vehicle for ICFA news, membership activities, legislation, marketing and management, including the financial aspects of cemetery and funeral home operation.
Cost: $25.00
64 Pages
Circulation: 6200
ISSN: 0270-5281
Founded in 1887
Printed in 4 colors on glossy stock

17148 Journal of Corporate Renewal
Turnaround Management Association
150 S Wacker Drive
Suite 900
Chicago, IL 60606

312-578-6900
Fax: 312-578-8336
E-Mail: info@turnaround.org
Home Page: www.turnaround.org
Social Media: Facebook, Twitter, LinkedIn

Lisa Poulin, President
Patrick Lagrange, Chairman
Linda Delgadillo, Executive Director

The only international nonprofit association dedicated to corporate renewal and turnaround management. TMA's 9,000 members in 46 regional chapters comprise a professional community of turnaround practitioners, attorneys, accountants, investors, lenders, venture capitalists, appraiser, liquidators, executive recruiters and consultants. Three international conferences each year offer networking and educational sessions on the latest trends and best practices in the restructuring field.
Frequency: 9/Year
Circulation: 9000+

17149 Journal of Information Technology Management
Association of Management
920 Battlefield Boulevard
Suite 100
Chesapeake, VA 23322

757-482-2273
Fax: 757-482-0325
E-Mail: aomgt@aom-iaom.org
Home Page: www.aom-iaom.org

Dr Al Bento, Editor-in-Chief

A forum for the communication of solutions found by practitioners and academicians to the mulitfaceted problems associated with managing information and information technology as a corporate resource.
Frequency: Quarterly

17150 Journal of Management Systems
Association of Management
920 Battlefield Boulevard
Suite 100
Chesapeake, VA 23322

757-482-2273
Fax: 757-482-0325
E-Mail: aomgt@aom-iaom.org
Home Page: www.aom-iaom.org

Dr John Saee, Editor-in-Chief

Promotes the integreation and cross-fertilization of the behavioral/organizational and information sciences and to encourage, sharpen and expand the dialogue between academicians and practitioners from an interdisiplinary perspective

17151 Journal of Quality Technology
American Society for Quality
600 N Plankinton Avenue
PO Box 3005
Milwaukee, WI 53201-3005

414-272-8575
800-248-1946
Fax: 414-272-1734
E-Mail: help@asq.org
Home Page: www.asq.org
Social Media: Facebook, Twitter, LinkedIn

Roberto M Saco, President
Paul E Borawski, Executive Director
Erica Gumieny, Sales
Fay Spano, Communications/Media Relations

Published by the American Society for Quality, the JQT is a quarterly, peer-reviewed journal that focuses on the subject of quality control and the related areas of reliability and similar disciplines.
Cost: $30.00
100M Members
Frequency: Quarterly
Founded in 1946

17152 MSI
Reed Business Information
30 Technology Parkway South
Suite 100
Norcross, GA 30092

630-574-0825
800-424-3996
Fax: 630-288-8781
E-Mail: webmaster@reedbusiness.com
Home Page: www.reedbusiness.com

Jeff Greisch, President
Kevin Parker, Editorial Director
Jim Casella, CEO
Nancy Bartels, Senior Editor
Eric Roth, Circulation Manager
Frequency: Monthly
Founded in 1977

17153 MWorld: Journal of the American Mangement Association
American Management Association
1601 Broadway
Suite 7
New York, NY 10019-7420

212-586-8100
Fax: 212-903-8168
E-Mail: customerservice@amanet.org
Home Page: www.amanet.org

Edward T Reilly, CEO
Florence M Stone, Senior Vice President
Arthur Levy, Senior Vice President
Roger Kelleher, Manager
Jorge Rubio, Managing Director

Free quarterly mangement journal for American Management Association's executive and individual members.
48 Pages
Frequency: Quarterly
Circulation: 25,000
Founded in 2002
Printed in 2 colors on glossy stock

17154 Maintenance Technology
Applied Technology Publications
1300 S Grove Ave
Suite 105
Barrington, IL 60010-5246

847-382-8100
Fax: 847-304-8603
Home Page: www.mt-online.com

Arthur Rice, President/CEO
Bill Kiesel, Vice President/Publisher
Jane Alexander, Editor-In-Chief
Rick Carter, Executive Editor
Randy Buttstadt, Director of Creative Services

Maintenance Technology magazine serves the business and technical information needs of managers and engineers responsible for assuring availability of plant equipment and systems. It provides readers with articles on advanced technologies, strategies, tools, and services for the life-cycle management of capital assets.
Frequency: Monthly
Circulation: 50,827
Mailing list available for rent: 35,263 names at $$15 per M

17155 Manage
National Management Association
2210 Arbor Blvd
Suite A
Moraine, OH 45439-1580

937-294-0421
Fax: 937-294-2374
E-Mail: nma@nma1.org
Home Page: www.nma1.org

Douglas Shaw, Publisher
Richard Hergert, Owner
Steve Bailey, CEO
Mike McCulley, Chief Operations Officer

Association news for executives.
32 Pages
Frequency: Quarterly
Founded in 1925

17156 Management Consultants International
Kennedy Information
37 Beach Rd
Singapore 199597

65 -100-0688
Fax: 656-234-0688
E-Mail: corporate@cacmci.com
Home Page: www.cacmci.com

News and business intelligence on management consulting worldwide. Monthly issues feature country by country surveys of local consulting firms.
Cost: $1122.00
16 Pages
Frequency: Monthly
ISSN: 0956-3253

17157 Medical Group Management Journal
Medical Group Management Association
104 Inverness Ter E
Englewood, CO 80112-5313

303-799-1111
Fax: 303-643-9599
E-Mail: infocenter@mgma.com
Home Page: www.mgma.com

William Jessee, CEO
Eileen Barker, senior Vice President
Anders Gilberg, senior Vice President
Natalie Jamieson, Administrative Assistant

Encompasses pertinent problems, questions and issues relating to group practice management.
Frequency: Bi-Monthly

17158 New Mobility
PO Box 220
415 Horsham Road
Horsham, PA 19044

215-675-9133
888-850-0344
Fax: 215-675-9376
E-Mail: info@newmobility.com
Home Page: www.newmobility.com
Social Media: Facebook, Twitter, MySpace

Tim Gilmer, Editor
Jean Dobbs, Editorial Director, VP
Kim Brennan, Circulation/List Manager
Amy Blackmore, VP of Sales
Jeff Leonard, SVP of Marketing + Communication

New Mobility encourages the integration of active-lifestyle wheelchair users into mainstream society, while simultaneously reflecting the vibrant world of disability-related arts, media, advocacy and philosophy. Our stories foster a sense of community.
Cost: $27.95
Frequency: Monthly

17159 Operations & Fulfillment
Primedia

11 River Bend Drive South
PO Box 4242
Stamford, CT 06907-242

203-589-9900
800-775-3777
Fax: 203-358-5823
Home Page: www.multichannelmerchant.com

Sherry Chiger, Editorial Director
Melisa Dowling, Executive Editor
Len Roberto, Circulation Manager
Kate Dimarco, Creative Director of Production
Barry Litwin, VP Sales/Marketing

Provides executives information they can't get anywhere else and reach executives and managers with purchasing authority in all areas of operations management. Information on direct to customer fulfillment..
Cost: $85.00
Circulation: 40000
Founded in 1984

17160 Organization Development Journal
Organization Development Institute
11234 Walnut Ridge Road
Chesterland, OH 44026-1240

440-729-7419
Fax: 440-729-9319
E-Mail: dian@odinstitute.com
Home Page: www.odinstitute.org/

Dr. Donald W Cole, Publisher
Dr. Donald W Cole, CEO/President
Jenny Maes, Editor

A journal published quarterly for human resource people, managers and organization development people. The most frequently cited OD/OB publication in the world.
Cost: $80.00
100 Pages
Frequency: Quarterly
Circulation: 700
ISSN: 0889-6402
Founded in 1968
Mailing list available for rent: 9M names
Printed in one color on newsprint stock

17161 PM Network
Project Management Institute
14 Campus Blvd
Newtown Square, PA 19073-3299

610-356-4600
Fax: 610-356-4647
Home Page: www.pmi.org

Gregory Balestrero, CEO
Louis J Mercken, Chair
Iain Fraser, Vice Chair
James McGeehan, Public Relations
Jane Farley, Secretary

A monthly magazine published by the Project Management Institute.
75 Pages
Frequency: Monthly
Mailing list available for rent

17162 Print Solutions Magazine
Document Management Industries Association
433 E Monroe Avenue
Alexandria, VA 22301-1693

703-836-6232
800-336-4641
Fax: 703-549-4966
Home Page: www.printsolutionsmag.com/

Peter L Colaianni, Editor-in-Chief
Darin Painter, Managing Editor
Preeti Vasishtha, Assistant Editor
Andrew Brown, Assistant Editor

Source for marketing, management and product information.
Frequency: Monthly
Circulation: 42000
ISSN: 0532-1700
Founded in 1962
Printed in 4 colors on glossy stock

17163 Professional Journal
AFSM International
11031 Via Frontera
Suite A
San Diego, CA 92127-1709

858-673-3055
800-333-9786
Fax: 239-275-0794
E-Mail: info@asfmi.org
Home Page: www.afsmi.org

John Schoenewald, Executive Director
Jb Wood, President/Ceo

A magazine for executives, managers and professionals in the high-technology services industry.
Cost: $90.00
114 Pages
Circulation: 7000
ISSN: 1049-2135
Founded in 1975
Printed in 4 colors on glossy stock

17164 Project Management Journal
Project Management Institute
14 Campus Blvd
Newtown Square, PA 19073-3299

610-356-4600
Fax: 610-356-4647
Home Page: www.pmi.org

Gregory Balestrero, CEO
Mark Langley, Managing Director
Gary Boyler, Publisher
Dan Goldfischer, Editor in Chief
Beverly Cook, Production Manager

A quarterly journal published by the Project Management Institute.
65 Pages
Frequency: Quarterly
Mailing list available for rent

17165 Purchasing
Reed Business Information
6 Alfred Circle
Bedford, MA 00173

972-980-8810
Fax: 630-288-8686
Home Page: www.designnews.com
Social Media: Facebook, Twitter, LinkedIn

Kathy Doyle, Publisher
Lockie Montgomery, Production Manager
Anne Millen Porter, Business Manager
Paul Teague, Chief Editor.

About the purchasing professional in American industry.
Founded in 1920

17166 Quality Engineering
American Society for Quality
600 N Plankinton Avenue
PO Box 3005
Milwaukee, WI 53201-3005

414-272-8575
800-248-1946
Fax: 414-272-1734
E-Mail: help@asq.org
Home Page: www.asq.org
Social Media: Facebook, Twitter, LinkedIn

Roberto M Saco, President
Paul E Borawski, Executive Director
Erica Gumieny, Sales
Fay Spano, Communications/Media Relations

Co-published with Taylor and Francis, this journal is for professional practitioners and researchers whose goal is quality engineering improvements and solutions.
Cost: $34.75
100M Members
Frequency: Quarterly/Members Price
Founded in 1946

17167 Quality Management Journal
American Society for Quality
600 N Plankinton Avenue
PO Box 3005
Milwaukee, WI 53201-3005

414-272-8575
800-248-1946
Fax: 414-272-1734
E-Mail: help@asq.org
Home Page: www.asq.org
Social Media: Facebook, Twitter, LinkedIn

Roberto M Saco, President
Paul E Borawski, Executive Director
Erica Gumieny, Sales
Fay Spano, Communications/Media Relations

Published by the American Society for Quality, the QMT is a quarterly, peer-reviewed journal that focuses on the subject of quality management practice and provides a discussion forum for both practitioners and academics in the area of research.
Cost: $50.00
100M Members
Frequency: Quarterly
Founded in 1946

17168 Quality Progress
American Society for Quality
600 N Plankinton Avenue
PO Box 3005
Milwaukee, WI 53201-3005

414-272-8575
800-248-1946
Fax: 414-272-1734
E-Mail: help@asq.org
Home Page: www.asq.org
Social Media: Facebook, Twitter, LinkedIn

Roberto M Saco, President
Paul E Borawski, Executive Director
Erica Gumieny, Sales
Fay Spano, Communications/Media Relations

Published by the American Society for Quality, QP is a peer-reviewed journal that focuses on the subject of quality control, discussing the usage and implementation of quality principles including the subject areas of organizational behavior, knowledge management and process improvement.
Cost: $55.00
100M Members
Founded in 1946

17169 Recruiting Trends
Kennedy Information
One Phoenix Mill Lane
Floor 3
Peterborough, NH 03458

603-924-1006
800-531-0007
E-Mail: customerservice@kennedyinfo.com
Home Page: www.kennedyinfo.com

Joseph McCool, Editor
Mina Landrisina, Managing Director

Provides strategies and tactics for creating and maintaining a competitive workforce.
Cost: $99.00
8 Pages
Frequency: Monthly
ISSN: 0034-1827
Founded in 1970

17170 Retail Merchandiser
MacFadden Publishing

233 Park Ave S
6th Floor
New York, NY 10003-1606

212-979-4800
Fax: 212-979-7342
Home Page: www.retail-merchandiser.com

Jeff Friedman, Publisher
Greg Masters, Managing Editor
Toni Riggio, Sales Coordinator
Anita M Wise, Production Manager

Serves those in management positions of mass retail and discount companies.
Cost: $99.00
Frequency: Monthly
Circulation: 34,188
Founded in 1961

17171 Risk Management
Risk & Insurance Management Society
655 3rd Avenue
2nd Floor
New York, NY 10017

212-286-9292
Fax: 212-286-9716
E-Mail: chapterservices@RIMS.org
Home Page: www.rims.org

Ted Donovan, Publisher
Bill Coffin, Editor-in-Chief
Jared Wade, Associate Editor
Callie Nelson, Circulation Manager
Todd Lockwood, Advertising Sales Manager
Cost: $64.00
Frequency: Monthly
Circulation: 15000
Founded in 1950

17172 SAM Advanced Management Journal
Society for Advancement of Management
Corpus Christi - College of Business
6300 Ocean Drive - Unit 5807
Corpus Christi, TX 78412-5807

361-825-6045
Fax: 361-825-2725
E-Mail: moustafa@cob.tamucc.edu
Home Page: www.samnational.org

Moustafa H. Abdelsamad, President/CEO
R. Clifton Poole, Secretary
S.G. Fletcher, Treasurer
Everette Anderson, VP, Sales & Marketing
Anthony Buono, Director

A quarterly, refereed publication especially designed for general managers.
Cost: $64.00
3000 Members
Frequency: Quarterly
Founded in 1912

17173 SAM Management In Practice
Society for Advancement of Management
Corpus Christi - College of Business
6300 Ocean Drive, Unit 5807
Corpus Christi, TX 78412-5807

361-825-6045
Fax: 361-825-2725
E-Mail: moustafa@cob.tamucc.edu
Home Page: www.samnational.org

Moustafa H. Abdelsamad, President/CEO
R. Clifton Poole, Secretary
S.G. Fletcher, Treasurer
Everette Anderson, VP, Sales & Marketing
Anthony Buono, Director

A quarterly, refereed publication especially designed for general managers.
3000 Members
Frequency: Quarterly
Founded in 1912

17174 Shelby Report
Shelby Publishing Company
517 Green St Nw
Gainesville, GA 30501-3300

770-534-8380
Fax: 770-535-0110
E-Mail: shelbpub@bellsouth.net
Home Page: www.shelbypublishing.com

Ron Johnston, President
Chuck Gilmer, Editor

Serving the grocery industry in Arizona, Arkansas, Colorado, Kansas, Louisana, Missouri, New Mexico, Oklahoma, and Texas,
Cost: $36.00
Frequency: Monthly
Circulation: 25201
Founded in 1966

17175 Si Review
Staffing Industry Analysts
881 Fremont Ave
Suite A3
Los Altos, CA 94024-5637

650-948-9303
800-950-9496
Fax: 650-232-2360
Home Page: www.sireport.com

Ron Mester, President
Theresa Daly, Production Manager

Tools and techniques for staffing industry professionals. How-to's and survey articles for branch management, upper management, owners, and sales/service personnel in employment service companies. Display advertising included.
Cost: $99.00
Frequency: 22 issues per y
Founded in 1989
Printed in 4 colors on glossy stock

17176 Software Quality Professional
American Society for Quality
600 N Plankinton Avenue
PO Box 3005
Milwaukee, WI 53201-3005

414-272-8575
800-248-1946
Fax: 414-272-1734
E-Mail: help@asq.org
Home Page: www.asq.org
Social Media: Facebook, Twitter, LinkedIn

Roberto M Saco, President
Paul E Borawski, Executive Director
Erica Gumieny, Sales
Fay Spano, Communications/Media Relations

Published by the American Society for Quality, the SQP is a quarterly, peer-reviewed journal for software development professionals that focuses on the subject of quality practice principles in the implementation of software and the development of software systems.
Cost: $45.00
100M Members
Frequency: Quarterly
Founded in 1946

17177 South Florida Business Journal
American City Business Journals
120 W Morehead St
Suite 400
Charlotte, NC 28202-1874

704-973-1000
800-486-3289
Fax: 704-973-1001
E-Mail: borben@bizjournals.com
Home Page: www.bizjournals.com

Whitney R Shaw, CEO
Megan Foley, Marketing Director
David Harris, Managing Editor

Covers all aspects of business in South Florida.
Cost: $99.00
Frequency: Weekly
ISSN: 1528-0527

17178 Staffing Management
SHRM/Society for Human Resource Management
1800 Duke St
Alexandria, VA 22314-3494

703-535-6000
866-898-4724
Fax: 703-535-6474
E-Mail: shrmeducation@shrm.org.
Home Page: www.shrm.org
Social Media: Facebook, Twitter, LinkedIn, Youtube

Susan R Meisinger, CEO
Leon Rubis, Editor

Formerly known as Employment Management Today, this magazine provides information on the latest techniques and trends in recruiting and retaining your most important commodity: your employees.
Cost: $35.00
56 Pages
Frequency: Quarterly
Circulation: 10000
Founded in 1995

17179 Supermarket News - Retail/Financial
Fairchild Publications
7 W 34th St
New York, NY 10001-8100

212-630-3880
800-204-4515
Fax: 212-630-3868
E-Mail: custserv@espcomp.com
Home Page: www.supermarketnews.com

Dan Bagan, Publishing Director
David Orgel, Editor-in-Chief
Christina Veiders, Managing Editor
Joy Kulick, Marketing
Cost: $45.00
Frequency: Weekly
ISSN: 0039-5803
Founded in 1892

17180 Supervision Magazine
National Research Bureau
320 Valley St
Burlington, IA 52601-5513

319-752-5415
Fax: 319-752-3421
E-Mail: mail@national-research-bureau.com
Home Page: www.national-research-bureau.com

Diane M Darnall, President
Teresa Levinson, Editor

Dedicated to providing the most timely and relevant information to today's supervisors and managers.
Frequency: Monthly
Circulation: 1200
Founded in 1930

17181 Supply Chain Management Review
Reed Business Information
225 Wyman St
Suite 3
Waltham, MA 02451-1216

781-734-8000
Fax: 781-734-8076
Home Page: www.reedbusiness.com

Mark Finklestein, President
Frank Quinn, Chief Editor
Susan Lacefield, Associate Editor
Mary Ann Gajewski, Production Manager
Stuart Whayman, CFO

Contains in-depth feature articles on various aspects of Supply Chain Management. SCM is the science of integrating the flow of goods and information from initial souring and purchasing, order processing and fulfillment, production planning and scheduling, inventory management, transportation, distribution and

customer service. Each issue delivers in-depth feature articles from the thought leaders in the supply chain community.
Cost: $199.00
Circulation: 12000

17182 Supply Chain Technology News
Penton Media
1166 Avenue of the Americas/10th Fl
New York, NY 10036

212-204-4200
Fax: 216-696-6662
E-Mail: information@penton.com
Home Page: www.penton.com

Jane Cooper, Marketing
Chris Meyer, Director, Corporate Communications

Focuses on the practical application of technology accross a broad range of supply chain functions.

17183 Tapping the Network Journal
Quality & Productivity Management Association
300 N Martingale Road
Suite 230
Schaumburg, IL 60173-2407

708-619-2909
Fax: 847-619-3383

William Ginnodo, Editor/Author

This quarterly publication is, By and For Organizational Change Agents. Most articles are written by QPMA members. Its purpose is to share - in a straightforward, factual and practical manner - what has been learned within the authors' organization during the course of a particular change effort. It is provided free to members, and made available to non-member subscribers.

17184 Training
50 S 9th Street
Minneapolis, MN 55402

612-333-0471
Fax: 612-333-6526
Home Page: www.vnu.com

Rob van den Bergh, CEO
Rob Ruijter, CFO
AC Nielsen, Marketing
Founded in 1960

17185 WACRA: World Association for Case Method Research & Application
23 Mackintosh Avenue
Needham, MA 02492-1218

781-444-8982
Fax: 781-444-1548
E-Mail: wacra@rcn.com
Home Page: www.wacra.org

Dr Hans E Klein, President/Executive Director
Denise Smith, Conference Office

Advancing the use of the case method and other interactive methodologies in teaching, training and planning.
Cost: $75.00
2000 Members
Circulation: digital
ISSN: 1931-7549
Founded in 1984

17186 Warehousing Management
Reed Business Information
30 Technology Parkway South
Suite 100
Norcross, GA 30092

646-746-6400
800-424-3996
Fax: 646-756-7583
E-Mail: webmaster@reedbusiness.com
Home Page: www.reedbusiness.com

John Poulin, CEO
John R Johnson, Editor-in-Chief
James Reed, Owner
Jane Burgess, Marketing Director

Warehousing Management targets warehousing and distribution center operations managers with analysis, news, trends, equipment and events.
Circulation: 47185
Founded in 1977

17187 Workgroup Computing Report
Patricia Seybold Group
Po Box 783
Needham Heights, MA 02492

617-742-5200
800-826-2424
Fax: 617-742-1028
E-Mail: feedback@customers.com
Home Page: www.psgroup.com
Social Media: Twitter

Patricia Seybold, Founder/CEO

Provides information on implementing workflow, document management, groupware, and business process reengineering.
Cost: $440.00
Frequency: Monthly
Mailing list available for rent

17188 World
Economist
111 W 57th Street
The Economist Building
New York, NY 10019

212-541-5730
Fax: 212-541-9378
E-Mail: usrights@economist.com

Dudley Fishburn, Editor
David Hanger, Publisher
124 Pages
ISBN: 0-862181-66-6
Printed in 4 colors on glossy stock

17189 Young Presidents' Organization - Magazine
Young Presidents' Organization
451 Decker Drive
Suite 200
Irving, TX 75062-3954

972-504-4600
Fax: 972-650-4777
Home Page: www.ypo.org

Thomas Stauffer, Executive Director
Les Ward, Manager
Frequency: BiAnnual
Circulation: 8000
Printed in on glossy stock

Trade Shows

17190 AACE Annual Meeting
AACE International
1265 Suncrest Towne Centre Drive
Morgantown, WV 26505-1876

304-296-8444
800-858-2678
Fax: 304-291-5728
E-Mail: info@aacei.org
Home Page: www.aacei.org
Social Media: Facebook, LinkedIn

Andrew S Dowd Jr, Executive Director
Jennie Amos, Marketing/Meetings Manager
Frequency: June

17191 AHRA Annual Meeting & Exposition
Association for Medical Imaging Management
490B Boston Post Road
Suite 200
Sudbury, MA 01776

978-443-7591
800-334-2472
Fax: 978-443-8046
E-Mail: info@ahraonline.org
Home Page: www.ahraonline.org
Social Media: Facebook, Twitter, LinkedIn

Edward Cronin, Jr., CEO
Sarah Murray, Executive Assistant
Emily Ryan, Membership Coordinator
Debra Murphy, Publications Director

A resource and catalyst for the development of professional leadership in imaging sciences. A driving force toward improving the healthcare environment. Containing 171 booths and 171 exhibits.
5000 Members
Mailing list available for rent: 4000 names at $250 per M

17192 Administrative Assistants Executive Secretaries Seminar
PA Douglas & Associates
644 Strander Boulevard
#411
Seattle, WA 98188

206-244-6441
Fax: 780-444-8002
Home Page: www.padouglas.com

Dr. Paul A Douglas MBA, PhD, CMC, Leader

To provide seminars, workshops and educational materials to individuals from the United States, Canada, and Europe. Includes an intensive three-day workshop for exploring and developing intellectual, organizational and interpersonal abilities.
Founded in 1975

17193 American Society of Association Executives Annual Meeting & Expo
American Society of Association Executives
The ASAE Building
1575 I Street NW
Washington, DC 20005

202-262-2723
Fax: 202-371-8315
E-Mail: publicpolicy@asaenet.org
Home Page: www.asaenet.org

John Graham, Executive Director

Professional service companies that specialize in providing management services for association on a fee-for-service basis. Exhibits related to managing associations.
Frequency: Annual

17194 Annual Lean Six Sigma Conference
American Society for Quality
600 N Plankinton Avenue
PO Box 3005
Milwaukee, WI 53201-3005

414-272-8575
800-248-1946
Fax: 414-272-1734
E-Mail: help@asq.org
Home Page: www.asq.org
Social Media: Facebook, Twitter, LinkedIn

Roberto M Saco, President
Paul E Borawski, Executive Director
Erica Gumieny, Sales
Fay Spano, Communications/Media Relations

An exclusive two-day briefing and networking event designed by and for the top practitioners in the Six Sigma community.
100M Members
Frequency: Annual/February
Founded in 1946

17195 Annual Quality Audit Conference
American Society for Quality
600 N Plankinton Avenue
PO Box 3005
Milwaukee, WI 53201-3005

414-272-8575
800-248-1946
Fax: 414-272-1734
E-Mail: help@asq.org
Home Page: www.asq.org
Social Media: Facebook, Twitter, LinkedIn

Roberto M Saco, President
Paul E Borawski, Executive Director
Erica Gumieny, Sales
Fay Spano, Communications/Media Relations

Topics of interest include: new innovating audit/process approaches, value added involvement, corporate expectations, corporate/social responsibility, auditing in the overall corporate scheme.
100M Members
Frequency: October
Founded in 1946

17196 Annual Service Quality Conference
American Society for Quality
600 N Plankinton Avenue
PO Box 3005
Milwaukee, WI 53201-3005

414-272-8575
800-248-1946
Fax: 414-272-1734
E-Mail: help@asq.org
Home Page: www.asq.org
Social Media: Facebook, Twitter, LinkedIn

Roberto M Saco, President
Paul E Borawski, Executive Director
Erica Gumieny, Sales
Fay Spano, Communications/Media Relations

The sessions we plan will help you to navigate through unpredictable consumer behavior and increasing competition to build a strong foundation for reaching superior levels of quality service.
100M Members
Frequency: September
Founded in 1946

17197 Annual World Conference on Quality and Improvement
American Society for Quality
600 N Plankinton Avenue
PO Box 3005
Milwaukee, WI 53201-3005

414-272-8575
800-248-1946
Fax: 414-272-1734
E-Mail: help@asq.org
Home Page: www.asq.org
Social Media: Facebook, Twitter, LinkedIn

Roberto M Saco, President
Paul E Borawski, Executive Director
Erica Gumieny, Sales
Fay Spano, Communications/Media Relations

Conference focuses on quality and improvement with more than 2,000 exhibits and attendees. Keynote speakers and sessions discuss quality tools, techniques and methodologies. Provides the opportunity for members to meet and network with colleagues in the industry.
100M Members
Frequency: May
Founded in 1946

17198 Association for Services Management
11031 Via Frontera
Suite A
San Diego, CA 92127

239-275-7887
800-333-9786
Fax: 239-275-0794
E-Mail: info@afsmi.org
Home Page: www.afsmi.org

John Schoenwald, Executive Director
Jb Wood, President/Ceo

Management convention and exposition.
Frequency: Fall

17199 Association for Strategic Planning Annual Conference
Association for Strategic Planning
12021 Wilshire Boulevard
Suite 286
Los Angeles, CA 90025-1200

877-816-2080
Fax: 323-954-0507
Home Page: www.strategyplus.org
Social Media: Facebook, Twitter, LinkedIn

Dr Stanley G Rosen, President
Janice Laureen, Executive Director

Nation's premier forum for professional discussion and exchange of information and experiences among strategic planning practitioners.
Frequency: February

17200 Association for Worksite Health Promotion Annual International Conference
60 Revere Drive
Suite 500
Northbrook, IL 60062-1577

847-480-9574
Fax: 847-480-9282
Home Page: www.awhp.org

Liz Freyn, Conference Manager

122 booths of information and supplies to promote and develop quality programs of health and fitness in business and industry. Seminar, workshop, conference, tours and luncheon.
950 Attendees
Founded in 1974

17201 Association of Management Meeting
Association of Management
920 Battlefield Boulevard
Suite 100
Chesapeake, VA 23322

757-482-2273
Fax: 757-482-0325
E-Mail: aomgt@aom-iaom.org
Home Page: www.aom-iaom.org

Dr Karin Klenke, Co-Founder/President
Dr WM A Hamel, CEO
T J Mills, VP Comptroller
800 Attendees
Frequency: Annual

17202 Circulation Managers Association International
11600 Sunrise Valley Drive
Reston, VA 20191-1412

703 506-1661

Joseph Forsee, Show Manager

100 booths exhibiting products such as news racks, rubber products and software.
225 Attendees
Frequency: June

17203 Coaching and Teambuilding Skills for Managers and Supervisors
SkillPath Seminars
6900 Squibb Road
PO Box 2768
Mission, KS 66201-2768

913-623-3900
800-873-7545
Fax: 913-362-4241
E-Mail: webmaster@skillpath.com
Home Page: www.skillpath.com

One-day workshop to sharpen your leadership skills and boost your team's productivity. Various locations and dates.

17204 Construction Specifications Institute Annual Show & Convention
110 South Union Street
Suite 100
Alexandria, VA 22314

703-684-0300
800-689-2900
Fax: 703-684-8436
E-Mail: csi@csinet.org
Home Page: www.csinet.org
Social Media: Facebook, Twitter, LinkedIn, Youtube,Slideshare,Flickr

Eugene A Valentine, President
W Richard Cooper, VP

Education sessions that focus on industry topics such as; Business and Professional Development, Design & Pre-Construction Activities, Facility Management, Formats & Documents, Legal, Public Facilities & Communities, Safety & Security, Specialty Construction, and Specifications.
6,000 Attendees
Frequency: Annual
Founded in 1954

17205 EMA Annual Conference & Exposition
SHRM/Society for Human Resource Management
1800 Duke Street
Alexandria, VA 22314

703-535-6000
866-898-4724
Fax: 703-535-6474
E-Mail: shrmeducation@shrm.org.
Home Page: www.shrm.org/
Social Media: Facebook, Twitter, LinkedIn, Youtube

Johnny C Taylor Jr, Chairman
Susan Meisinger, President/CEO
Robert O Gonzales, Secretary
Robb E Van Cleave, Treasurer

Conference devoted to employment management issues.
700 Attendees
Frequency: March/April

17206 Financial Management Association International Annual Meeting
University of South Florida
College of Business Administration/BSN 3331
4202 E Fowler Avenue
Tampa, FL 33620-5500

813-974-2084
Fax: 813-974-3318
E-Mail: fma@coba.usf.edu
Home Page: www.fma.org/

Jonathan Karpoff, President Director
Jacqueline Garner, Vice President Financial Education
Rawley Thomas, VP Practitioner Services
Kenneth Eades, Vice President Global Services
Anthony Saunders, Vice President Annual Meeting

Annual meeting and exhibits of financial management related equipment, supplies and services.
Frequency: October

17207 Fundamentals of Personnel Law for Managers and Supervisors
Human Resources Council
6900 Squibb Road
PO Box 804441
Kansas City -4441

800-601-4636

Rose Miller, Trainer

One-day seminar covering the legal issues affecting everyday management of employees. Various locations and dates.

17208 Hartford Conference on Leadership Development & Teambuilding
SkillPath Seminars
6900 Squibb Road
PO Box 2768
Mission, KS 66201-2768

913-623-3900
800-873-7545
Fax: 913-362-4241
E-Mail: enroll@skillpath.net

Conference teaches practical leadership skills thorough real-life examples, pratical methods and techniques. Suitable for managers, supervisors, team leaders and team members.

17209 IRMA Annual Conference
Information Resources Management Association
701 E Chocolate Avenue
Suite 200
Hershey, PA 17033

717-533-8845
Fax: 717-533-8661
E-Mail: member@irma-international.org
Home Page: www.irma-international.org

Mehdi Khosrow-Pour PhD, President
Sherif Kamel PhD, Communications Director
Gerald Grant PhD, IRMA Doctoral Symposium Director
Lech Janczewski PhD, IRMA World Representative Director
Paul Chalekian, IRMA United States Representative

Provides forums for researchers and practitioners to share leading-edge knowledge in the global resource information management area. Various seminars, conventions and conferences, and other training programs are offered by IRMA throughout the year.
Frequency: May

17210 Int'l. Association of Healthcare Central Svc. Material Management
IAHCSMM Annual Conference
213 W Institute Place
Suite 307
Chicago, IL 60610-3195

312-440-0078
800-962-8274
Fax: 312-440-9474
E-Mail: mailbox@iahcsmm.com
Home Page: www.iahcsmm.com

Betty Hanna, Executive Director
Marilyn Corida, Secretary/Treasurer
Lisa Huber, President
Bruce T. Bird, President

125 EXHIBITORSlication separates supervisors/directors from technicians.
600+ Attendees
Frequency: Annual

17211 International Public Management Associatio n for Human Resources Trade Show
Int'l Public Management Assoc for Human Resources
1617 Duke St
Alexandria, VA 22314-3406

703-549-7100
Fax: 703-684-0948
E-Mail: ipma@pma-hr.org
Home Page: www.ipma-hr.org

Neil Reichenberg, Executive Director
Sima Hassassian, COO
Tina Chiappetta, Sr Director Gov't Affairs/Comm
500 Attendees

17212 Labor-Management Initiative (LMI)
International Association of Fire Chiefs
4025 Fair Ridge Dr
Fairfax, VA 22033-2868

703-273-0911
Fax: 703-273-9363
Home Page: www.iafc.org
Social Media: Facebook, LinkedIn

Al H. Gillespie, President & Chairman of the Board
Hank Clemmensen, First Vice President
William R. Metcalf, Second Vice President
Richard Carrizzo, Treasurer
Luther L. Fincher, Jr., Director-At-Large

Provides exceptional networking opportunities and dynamic education to foster and enhance cooperative and collaborative labor-management relationships.
12000 Members
Founded in 1873

17213 National Quality Education Conference
American Society for Quality
600 N Plankinton Avenue
PO Box 3005
Milwaukee, WI 53201-3005

414-272-8575
800-248-1946
Fax: 414-272-1734
E-Mail: help@asq.org
Home Page: www.asq.org
Social Media: Facebook, Twitter, LinkedIn

Roberto M Saco, President
Paul E Borawski, Executive Director
Erica Gumieny, Sales
Fay Spano, Communications/Media Relations

Provides teachers, administrators, and support personnel opportunities to examine continuous improvement principles used in education. It provides resources and best practices to help you address requirements of No Child Left Behind, while helping you increase student achievement and improve overall performance.
100M Members
Frequency: November
Founded in 1946

17214 New York Social Media Marketing Conference
SkillPath Seminars
6900 Sqibb Road
PO Box 2768
Mission, KS 66201-2768

913-623-3900
800-873-7545
Fax: 913-362-4241
E-Mail: webmaster@skillpath.com
Home Page: www.skillpath.com

Steve Nichols, Customer Care Representative
Robb Garr, President

This state-of-the-art conference walks through everything needed to start using social media to drive real business results, even for someone who doesn't know the difference between a tweet and a like button. There's no reason to miss out any longer on the proven, bottom-line benefits of marketing with social media.
Frequency: Semi-Annual, April

17215 Project Management for IT Professionals
CompuMaster
6900 Squibb Road
PO Box 2973
Mission, KS 66201-1373

913-362-3900
800-867-4340
Fax: 913-432-4930
E-Mail: compumaster@mcimail.com
Home Page: www.compumaster.net

Casey Smith, Customer Service

A two-day workshop that will help you meet complex project deadlines and budgets. Held in various locations in November and December. Customization at your location available for groups of twenty or more.

17216 Society for Advancement of Management, Inc. (SAM)
Society for Advancement of Management
Corpus Christi - College of Business
6300 Ocean Drive, Unit 5808
Corpus Christi, TX 78412-5808

361-825-3045
888-827-6077
Fax: 361-825-5609
E-Mail: sam@samnational.org
Home Page: www.samnational.org

Moustafa H. Abdelsamad, President/CEO
Ken E. Byus, Treasurer
Everette Anderson, VP, Sales & Marketing

Featuring speakers, sponsors, presentations, workshops and discussions.
2500 Members
Founded in 1912

17217 Turnaround Management Association Annual Fall Conference
Turnaround Management Association
150 S Wacker Drive
Suite 900
Chicago, IL 60606

312-578-6900
Fax: 312-578-8336
E-Mail: info@turnaround.org
Home Page: www.turnaround.org
Social Media: Facebook, Twitter, LinkedIn

Lisa Poulin, President
Patrick Lagrange, Chairman
Linda Delgadillo, Executive Director

The only international nonprofit association dedicated to corporate renewal and turnaround management. TMA's 9,000 members in 46 regional chapters comprise a professional community of turnaround practitioners, attorneys, accountants, investors, lenders, venture capitalists, appraiser, liquidators, executive recruiters and consultants. Three international conferences each year offer networking and educational sessions on the latest trends and best practices in the restructuring field.
600 Attendees
Frequency: Annual/Fall

17218 Turnaround Management Association Spring Conference
Turnaround Management Association
150 S Wacker Drive
Suite 900
Chicago, IL 60606

312-578-6900
Fax: 312-578-8336
E-Mail: info@turnaround.org
Home Page: www.turnaround.org
Social Media: Facebook, Twitter, LinkedIn

Lisa Poulin, President
Patrick Lagrange, Chairman
Linda Delgadillo, Executive Director

The only international nonprofit association dedicated to corporate renewal and turnaround management. TMA's 9,000 members in 46 regional chapters comprise a professional community of turnaround practitioners, attorneys, accountants, investors, lenders, venture capitalists, appraiser, liquidators, executive recruiters and consultants. Three international conferences each year offer networking and educational sessions on the latest trends and best practices in the restructuring field.
600 Attendees
Frequency: Annual/Spring

17219 **Volunteer & Combination Officers Section Symposium in the Sun**
International Association of Fire Chiefs
4025 Fair Ridge Dr
Fairfax, VA 22033-2868
703-273-0911
Fax: 703-273-9363
Home Page: www.iafc.org
Social Media: Facebook, LinkedIn

Al H. Gillespie, President & Chairman of the Board
Hank Clemmensen, First Vice President
William R. Metcalf, Second Vice President
Richard Carrizzo, Treasurer
Luther L. Fincher, Jr., Director-At-Large

Addresses the unique needs of volunteer and combination departments including transitioning from a volunteer to a combination department, recruitment and retention, leadership and management, staffing and more.
12000 Members
Founded in 1873

17220 **WACRA Annual Conference Research & Application**
World Assoc for Case Method Research & Application
23 Mackintosh Avenue
Needham, MA 02492-1218
781-444-8982
Fax: 781-444-1548
E-Mail: hans.klein@wacra.org
Home Page: www.wacra.org

Dr Hans E Klein, President/Executive Director
Dr Joelle Piffault, Director/Development/Membership
Dr Pavel Zufan, Director/Business/Economics

Directories & Databases

17221 **ABI/INFORM**
UMI/Data Courier
620 S 3rd Street
Suite 400
Louisville, KY 40202-2475
800-626-2823
Fax: 502-589-5572

This database contains more than 675,000 citations, appearing in over 900 international periodicals covering business and management related areas.

17222 **ARMA International's Buyers Guide**
ARMA International
11880 College Blvd
Suite 450
Overland Park, KS 66215
913-341-3808
800-422-2762
Fax: 913-341-3742
E-Mail: hq@arma.org
Home Page: www.arma.org/conference
Social Media: Facebook, Twitter, LinkedIn

Formerly the Association of Record Managers and Administrators, this guide has 75-100 companies listed.

17223 **Analysis of Workers' Compensation Laws**
Chamber of Commerce of the United States
1615 H St Nw
Washington, DC 20062-0002
202-659-6000
Fax: 202-463-5836
Home Page: www.uschamber.org

Thomas J Donohue, CEO
Jean Hunt, Administrative Assistant

Offers a list of workers' compensation administrators.
Cost: $25.00
Frequency: Annual

17224 **Association of Management Consulting Firms**
AMCF
380 Lexington Avenue
Suite 1700
New York, NY 10168
212-551-7887
Fax: 212-551-7934
E-Mail: info@amcf.org
Home Page: www.amcf.org

Elizabeth A Kovacs, President/CEO
Kathleen Fish, Director Programs
Samantha Colon, Executive Administrator

About 50 management consulting firms that are members of ACME.
Cost: $50.00
Frequency: Biennial
Founded in 1929

17225 **Business Information Desk Reference: Where to Find Answers to Questions**
Palgrave Macmillan
175 5th Ave
New York, NY 10010-7728
212-982-3900
Fax: 212-307-5035
Home Page: www.ibtauris.com

Bruce McKenzie, President
Stuart Weir, Production Director
Paul Davighi, Marketing Director
Liz Stuckey, Secretary

Over 1,000 print material, online databases and federal agencies covering over 24 business areas are listed.

17226 **Business Information Resources - Online Database**
Grey House Publishing
4919 Route 22
PO Box 56
Amenia, NY 12501
518-789-8700
800-562-2139
Fax: 518-789-0556
E-Mail: gold@greyhouse.com
Home Page: http://gold.greyhouse.com
Social Media: Facebook, Twitter

Leslie Mackenzie, Publisher
Richard Gottlieb, Editor

This one-stop, business building database provides immediate access to the resources you need for success in the industry of your choice. This is the kind of must have information that, before now, could take hours to find. With a subscription to the Directory of Business Information Resources - Online Database, you'll have immediate access to over 17,000 associations, magazines, journals, newsletters, trade shows, directories, databases, and web sites for 100 industry groups.
Founded in 1981

17227 **Business Library**
Dow Jones & Company
4300 North Route 1
South Brunswick, NJ 08852
609-520-4000

Covers all types of topics and subjects that are of interest to US business markets.
Frequency: Full-text

17228 **Business Opportunities Handbook**
Enterprise Magazines
1020 N Broadway
Suite 111
Milwaukee, WI 53202-3157
414-272-9977
Fax: 414-272-9973
E-Mail: info@busop1.com
Home Page: www.franchisehandbook.com

Betsy Green, Owner

Over 2,500 listings of franchises, dealers and distributors that offer business opportunities to individuals.
Cost: $5.99
150 Pages
Frequency: Quarterly

17229 **Career Guide: Dun's Employment Opportunities Directory**
Dun & Bradstreet Information Service
3 Sylvan Way
Parsippany, NJ 07054-3822
973-605-6000
Fax: 973-605-9630

Offers information on more than 5,000 companies, leading employers of the United States, that provide career opportunities in sales, marketing and management.
Cost: $385.00
2700 Pages
Frequency: Annual

17230 **Company Intelligence**
Information Access Company
362 Lakeside Drive
Foster City, CA 94404-1171
650-378-5200
800-227-8431

Offers company news and financial information with an emphasis placed on hard-to-find privately held companies in the United States and worldwide.

17231 **Corporate Technology Database**
One Source Information Services
300 Baker Ave
Concord, MA 01742-2131
978-318-4300
800-554-5501
Fax: 978-318-4690
E-Mail: sales@onesource.com
Home Page: www.onesource.com

Philip J Garlick, President
John Brewer, Vice Chairman
Brad Haigis, VP/Products
Beth Jacaruso, VP/Content

Offers profiles of over 45,000 public and private US corporations and operating units of large corporations that develop or manufacture some 100,000 high-technology products.
Frequency: Directory

17232 **Corporate Yellow Book**
Leadership Directories

104 5th Ave
New York, NY 10011-6901

212-627-4140
Fax: 212-645-0931
E-Mail: corporate@leadershipdirectories.com
Home Page: www.leadershipdirectories.com

David Hurvitz, CEO

Contact information for over 48,000 executives at over 1,000 companies and more than 9,000 board members and their outside affiliations.
Cost: $360.00
1,400 Pages
Frequency: Quarterly
ISSN: 1058-2098
Founded in 1986

17233 Directory of Business Information Resources
Grey House Publishing
4919 Route 22
PO Box 56
Amenia, NY 12501

518-789-8700
800-562-2139
Fax: 845-373-6390
E-Mail: books@greyhouse.com
Home Page: www.greyhouse.com
Social Media: Facebook, Twitter

Leslie Mackenzie, Publisher
Richard Gottlieb, Editor

The source for contacts in over 98 business areas, from advertising and agriculture to utilities and wholesalers. This carefully researched volume details, for each business industry, the associations representing each industry, the newsletters that keep members current, the magazines and journals that are important to the trade, the top conventions and industry web sites that provide important marketing information. Includes contact names with phone, fax, website and e-mail information.
Cost: $195.00
2300 Pages
Frequency: Annual
ISBN: 1-592371-93-0
Founded in 1981

17234 Directory of Executive Recruiters
Kennedy Information
One Phoenix Mill Lane
Floor 3
Peterboro, NH 03458

603-924-1006
800-531-0007
E-Mail: customerservice@kennedyinfo.com
Home Page: www.kennedyinfo.com

Lists over 8,900 offices of 5,678 executive search firms in the US, Canada and Mexico. Includes key data and contact info on each firm. Directory is indexed by recruiter specialities, function, industry, key principals, and geography. Corporate edition is specially designed for corporate buyers of search services and search providers.
Cost: $179.95
1180 Pages
Frequency: Annual
ISBN: 1-885922-81-7
ISSN: 0090-6484

17235 Directory of Management Consultants
Kennedy Information
1 Phoenix Mill Lane
Floor 3
Peterborough, NH 03458

603-924-1006
800-531-0007
E-Mail: bookstore@kennedyinfo.com
Home Page: www.kennedyinfo.com

The premier directory of management consulting firms, published since 1979. The 10th edition profiles more than 2,400 firms in North America. Indexed by services, industries, geography, and key contacts.
Cost: $295.00
850 Pages
Frequency: Biennial
ISBN: 1-885922-69-8
ISSN: 0743-6890
Founded in 1919
Mailing list available for rent: 7600 names at $200 per M

17236 Directory of Management Information Systems Faculty
Management Information Systems Research Center
355 Humphrey-271 9th Avenue S
Minneapolis, MN 55455

763-783-7496
Fax: 612-626-1316
E-Mail: jdegross@csom.umn.edu
Home Page: www.webfoot.csom.umn.edu

Gordon B Davis, Editor
Janice I DeGross, Manager
Kate Terry, Manager
Abby Pinto, Managing Director

College-level teachers of subjects related to management information systems and technology.
Cost: $25.00

17237 Directory of Outplacement & Career Management Firms
Kennedy Information
One Phoenix Mill Lane
Floor 3
Peterborough, NH 03458

603-924-1006
800-531-0007
E-Mail: customerservice@kennedyinfo.com
Home Page: www.kennedyinfo.com

Profiles 365 firms in 1,351 offices worldwide and identifies 1,875 key principals. Includes key data on revenues, staff sizes, fees & expense policies, and contact information. Indexed by industry specialty, geography and individual outplacement professional.
Cost: $129.00
606 Pages
ISBN: 1-885922-65-5

17238 Directory of US Labor Organizations
BNA Books
3 Bethesda Metro Center
Suite 250
Bethesda, MA 02814-5377

703-341-3500
800-372-1033
Fax: 800-253-0332
E-Mail: customercare@bna.com
Home Page: www.bna.com

Gregory C McCaffery, President

Over 200 national unions and professional and state employees associations engaged in labor representation are profiled.
Cost: $55.00
110 Pages
Frequency: Annual

17239 Diversity in Corporate America
Hunt-Scanlon Corporation
700 Fairfield Avenue
Stamford, CT 06902

203-352-2920
Fax: 203-352-2930

James A Mueller, Founder
Scott Scanlon, CEO
Smooch S Reynolds, President
A David Brown, Managing Director
John D Delpino, Director - Executive Staffing

2,200 listings of executives responsible for managing corporate diversity in the US.
Cost: $179.00
Frequency: Biennial

17240 Employee Service Management: NESRA Buyers Directory
National Employee Services & Recreation Assn
568 Spring Road
Suite D
Elmhurst, IL 60126

630-559-0020
Fax: 630-559-0025
E-Mail: esmahq@esmassn.org
Home Page: www.esmassn.org

Renee Mula, Editor

Includes a list of over 200 member manufacturers and distributors offering products and services for employee discount programs and employee store merchandise to members.
Frequency: Annual

17241 Employment, Hours and Earnings
US Department Of Commerce
200 Constitution Ave Nw
Washington, DC 20210-0001

202-693-5000
Fax: 202-219-8822
E-Mail: webmaster@dol.gov
Home Page: www.dol.gov

Hilda L Solis, CEO
Sonya Carrion, Director

This database aimed at employees and management cover US employment, hours and earnings.

17242 Fortune Magazine
Time Inc./Time Warner
1271 Avenue of the Americas
16th Floor
New York, NY 10020-1393

212-522-1212
800-274-6800
Fax: 212-522-0602
Home Page: www.timeinc.com
Social Media: Facebook, Twitter

Laura Lang, CEO
Howard M. Averill, CFO
Leslie Picard, President
Stephanie George, Chief Marketing Officer
John Huey, Editor-in-Chief

FORTUNE is a global leader in business journalism. The magazine has a great history of providing analysis and news critical to business people.
Founded in 1922

17243 Fortune: Deals of the Year Issue
Time Inc./Time Warner
1271 Avenue of the Americas
16th Floor
New York, NY 10020-1393

212-522-1212
800-274-6800
Fax: 212-522-0602
Home Page: www.timeinc.com

Laura Lang, CEO
Howard M. Averill, CFO
Leslie Picard, President
Stephanie George, Chief Marketing Officer
John Huey, Editor-in-Chief

Offers information on 50 of the largest United States corporate financial transactions, including mergers, acquisitions and leveraged buyouts.
Cost: $5.00
Frequency: Annual
Founded in 1922

17244 Gale Group Management Contents®
Gale/Cengage Learning
2250 Perimeter Park Drive
Suite 300
Morrisville, NC 27560

919-804-6400
800-334-2564
Fax: 919-804-6410
E-Mail: gale.content@A@cengage.com
Home Page: www.library.dialog.com
Social Media: Facebook, Twitter, LinkedIn, Youtube

Patrick C Sommers, President
A specialized database that provides current information on business practices and management techniques from key management journals. The database provides theoretical background and practical how to approaches to key management disciplines.
Frequency: Weekly

17245 International Directory of Executive Recruiters
Kennedy Information
One Phoenix Mill Lane
Floor 3
Peterborough, NH 03458

603-924-1006
800-531-0007
E-Mail: customerservice@kennedyinfo.com
Home Page: www.kennedyinfo.com

A comprehensive source of worldwide executive recruiting firms and consultancies. List full contact information for search firms in 60 countries. Indexed by management function, industry, firm, and search firm principals.
Cost: $149.00
800 Pages
ISBN: 1-885922-53-1

17246 International Registry of OD Professional
Organization Development Institute
11234 Walnut Ridge Road
Chesterland, OH 44026-1240

440-729-7419
E-Mail: donwcole@aol.com

Dr. Donald W Cole RODC, President
A who's who directory of services and supplies to the industry. Includes: The OD Code of Ethics; a Statement on the Knowledge and Skill Necessary for Competence in O.D.; a listing of not just names and addresses, but the credential of all those registered with us; a list of all the OD organizations in the world and all the OD/OB academic programs in the world.
Cost: $25.00
300 Pages
Frequency: Annual

17247 Labor Arbitration Information System
LRP Publications
747 Dresher Road, Suite 500
PO Box 980
Horsham, PA 19044-0980

215-840-0912
Fax: 215-784-9639
E-Mail: webmaster@lrp.com
Home Page: www.lrp.com

Sandy Johnson, Director/Manager
Comprehensive indexing system for arbitration awards available. The easy-to-use, one-stop indexing system covers all the major arbitration reporting services including AAA, BNA, and CCH.
Cost: $515.00
Frequency: Monthly
Founded in 1977

17248 Meeting the Needs of Employees with Disabilities
Resources for Rehabilitation
22 Bonad Road
Winchester, MA 01890

781-368-9094
Fax: 781-368-9096
Home Page: www.rfr.org

Offers various descriptions of organizations and products that assist those involved in the employment of people with disabilities.
Cost: $42.95
Frequency: Biennial

17249 SHRM Membership Directory Online
SHRM/Society for Human Resource Management
1800 Duke St
Alexandria, VA 22314-3494

703-535-6000
866-898-4724
Fax: 703-535-6474
E-Mail: shrmeducation@shrm.org.
Home Page: www.shrm.org
Social Media: Facebook, Twitter, LinkedIn, Youtube

Susan R Meisinger, CEO
Robert O Gonzales, Secretary
Robb E Van Cleave, Treasurer
An exclusive benefit for SHRM members, the SHRM Membership Directory Online is a searchable database catagorized by by name, title, company, company size, job function or location.

17250 Small Business Sourcebook
Gale/Cengage Learning
27500 Drake Road
Farmington Hills, MI 48331-3535

248-699-4253
800-877-4253
Fax: 877-363-4253
E-Mail: gale.galeord@cengage.com
Home Page: www.gale.cengage.com
Social Media: Facebook, Twitter, Youtube

Patrick C Sommers, President
In this two volume annotated guide you'll discover more than 340 specific small business profiles and 99 general small business topics, small business programs and assistance programs in the US, its territories and Canadian provinces and US federal government agencies and offices specializing is small business issues, programs and assistance.
Frequency: Annual/2 Volumes
ISBN: 1-414421-75-3

17251 Small Business or Entrepreneurial Related Newsletter
Prosperity & Profits Unlimited
PO Box 416
Denver, CO 80201-0416

303-573-5564

A Doyle, Editor
A mini directory of listings for small businesses.
Cost: $19.95
8 Pages
Frequency: Every 2 Years
Circulation: 2,500
Founded in 1990
Printed in one color on matte stock

17252 Staffing Industry Sourcebook
Staffing Industry Analysts
881 Fremont Ave
Suite A3
Los Altos, CA 94024-5637

650-948-9303
800-950-9496
Fax: 650-232-2360
Home Page: www.sireport.com

Ron Mester, Manager
Jeff Reeder, Mgr Editor/SI Review
Sona Sharma, Mgr Editor/IT Serv Business Report
Linda Hubbard, Director of Marketing
Leslie Austin, Customer/Membership
Source Book, Facts and Figures for Market Research on the staffing industry.
Cost: $285.00
451 Pages
Frequency: BiAnnual
ISBN: 1-883814-10-3

17253 Transnational Corporations and Labor: A Directory of Resources
Third World Resources
1218 E 21st Street
Oakland, CA 94606

510-533-7583
Fax: 510-533-0923

Danielle Mahones, Executive Director
This directory is a source for books, periodicals and audiovisuals on transnational corporations and labor issues.
Cost: $14.95
160 Pages

Industry Web Sites

17254 http://gold.greyhouse.com
G.O.L.D Grey House OnLine Databases
Grey House Publishing's online database platform, GOLD, offers Quick Search, Keyword Search and Expert Search for most business sectors including management markets. The GOLD platform makes finding the information you need quick and easy - whether you're a novice searcher or an experienced database user. All of Grey House's directory products are available for subscription on the GOLD platform.

17255 www.aahc.net
AAHC American Association of Healthcare Consultant

17256 www.aaimnhta.com
American Association of Industrial Management
Dedicated to better management and the over-all objective which is the formulation of broad management principles and strategies that will insure sucessful management and promote the principles of free, private and competitive enterprise with individual opportunity and freedom under a constitutional government.

17257 www.aameda.org
American Academy of Medical Administrators
Department heads and administrators in areas of hospital and health administration.

17258 www.afsmi.org
AFSM International
A global organization dedicated to furthering the knowledge, understanding, and career development of executives, managers and professionals in the high-technology service industry.

17259 www.amanet.org
American Management Association
Offers a full range of business education and management development programs for indivdual and organizations in Europe, the Americas and Asia. Learn superior business skills and best management practices through a

variety of seminars, conferences and special events.

17260 **www.amcf.org**
AMCF
Seeks to unite management consulting firms in order to develop and improve professional standards and practice in the field. Offers information and referral services on management consultants.

17261 **www.americanassocofindmgmt.com**
American Association of Industrial Management
Dedicated to better management and the formulation of broad management principles and strategies that will ensure sucessful management and promote the principles of free, private and competive enterprise with individual opportunity and freedom under a constitutional government.

17262 **www.aom-iaom.org**
Association of Management
Formerly the Association of Human Resources Management and Organizational Behavior.

17263 **www.apics.org**
APICS Association for Operations Management
The primary purpose of this specific industry group is to educate food and beverage manufacturers on effective marketing strategies, market trends and material management.

17264 **www.aspanet.org**
American Society for Public Administration
The nation's most respected society representing all forums in the public service arena. Advocate for greater effectiveness in government agents of goodwill and professionalism addressing key public service issues by promoting change at both the local and international levels, we can enhance the quality of lives worldwide.

17265 **www.awhp.org**
Association for Worksite Health Promotion
Exists to advance the profession of worksite health promotion and the career development of its practitioners and to improve the performance of the programs they administer. Represents a variety of disciplines and worksites, for decision-makers in the areas of health promotion/disease prevention and health-care cost management.

17266 **www.besthealthplans.com**
Best Employers Association
Market and administer medical and dental insurance for large and small groups. Specializes in group insurance and employee benefits.

17267 **www.bizintell.com**
Business Intelligence Association
Business to business research on a wide variety of industries. Specialize in primary and hard-to-find secondary information.

17268 **www.cmaa.org**
Club Managers Association of America
Professional association for managers of membership clubs. Members manage country, city, athletic, faculty, yacht, town and military clubs. Objectives to promote and advance friendly relations among persons connected with the management of clubs and other associations of similar character.

17269 **www.cmaonline.org**
The Christian Management Association
Designed to assist those involved in the management of Christian organizations.

17270 **www.cmeinc.org**
Center for Management Effectiveness
Conducts management training programs and publishes self-scoring inventories, trainer guides and workbooks on stress management, resolution of conflict, risk taking, decision making and building managerial skills.

17271 **www.corptech.com**
CORPTECH Information Services
Corporations and operating units of large corporations that develop or manufacture some 100,000 high-technology products.

17272 **www.emsnetwork.com/cbt**
Center for Breakthrough Thinking
Organized to promote and institutionalize the teaching and application of Breakthrough Thinking in universities, corporations and governments in solving problems, leveraging opportunities, and achieving change.

17273 **www.expedia.com**
Expedia.com
Internet travel service offers access to airlines, hotels, car rentals, vacation packages, cruises and corporate travel.

17274 **www.greyhouse.com**
Grey House Publishing
Authoritative reference directories for most business sectors including management markets. Users can search the online databases with varied search criteria allowing for custom searches by product category, geographic area, sales volume, keyword, subject and more. Full Grey House catalog and online ordering also available.

17275 **www.iamc.org**
Industrial Asset Management Council
Members are companies engaged in the management of two or more organizations on a professional client basis.

17276 **www.icmci.org**
ICMCI Intn'l Council of Mgnt Consulting Institutes
For national institutes from around the world that certify professional management consultants; promotes professional development and networking between consultants and the highest standards of performance for clients.

17277 **www.icsa.com**
International Customer Service Association
Dedicated to promoting the development and awareness of the customer service profession through networking, education and research.

17278 **www.icsb.org**
International Council for Small Business
Management development.

17279 **www.imc-ymca.org/join.html**
International Management Council
IMC provides individuals with opportunities for continually developing their leadership and management skills through a network of shared experiences and education.

17280 **www.imcusa.org/**
IMC-USA Institute of Management Consultants-USA
For management consultants in the United States, organized to establish consulting as a self-regulating profession, meriting public confidence and respect. Toward the achievement of this goal IMC awards the international appelation CMC for certified management consultants.

17281 **www.ioma.com**
Institute of Management & Administration
Organization helps to provides information and guidance to management teams for various businesses.

17282 **www.ipma-hr.org**
International/Public Management Assn For Human Res
Human resource professionals, representing the interests of over 6,000 individual and 1,300 agency members, at the federal, state and local levels of government. Promotes excellence in human resource management through the ongoing development of professional and ethical standards, and through its publishing and educational training programs.

17283 **www.members.aol.com/odinst**
Organization Development Institute
Promotes the understanding of organization development and offers three categories of membership: professional consultant, regular and student.

17284 **www.mgma.com**
Medical Group Management Association
The oldest and largest professional membership association dedicated to medical practice management. Serves their members by offering timely and relevant networking and educational opportunities that keep the members up-to-date on the practice management field.

17285 **www.mt-online.com**
Applied Technology Publications
MT-online.com is the premier source of capacity assurance and best practice solutions for manufacturing, process and service operations worldwide. Online home of Maintenance Technology magazie, the dynamic MT-online.com portal serves the critical technical, business and professional-development needs of engineers, managers and technicians from across all industrial, institutional and commercial sectors.

17286 **www.nacdonline.org**
National Association of Corporate Directors
Fosters research, surveys, seminars and director for corporate. Maintains placement service.

17287 **www.naesaa.com**
National Association of Executive Secretaries and Administrative Assistants
Publishes a newsletter 11 times per year.

17288 **www.nsha.biz**
National Small Business United
Volunteer-led association. Primary mission is to advocate state and federal policies that are beneficial to small business, the state and the nation and to promote the growth of free enterprise.

17289 **www.pmi.org**
Project Management Institute
Fosters recognition of the need for project management professionalism. Offers professional certification and bestows awards.

17290 **www.promanager.org**
Professional Managers Association
A national membership association representing the interests of professional managers, management officials and non-bargaining unit employees in the federal government.

17291 **www.rbma.org**
Radiology Business Management Association

Promotes management education and study of practice economics, legislative issues and consumer trends.

17292 www.samnational.org
Society for Advancement of Management
SAM members come from a variety of disciplines - productions, finance, marketing, accounting and more who share a common bond of interest in becoming stronger managers.

17293 www.shrm.org
Society for Human Resource Management

17294 www.shrm.org/ema
Society for Human Resources/Employment Mgt Assn
A national association comprised primarily of corporate human resource professionals responsible for hiring and staffing.

17295 www.ssainfo.com
Support Services Alliance
Multi-state membership organization that provides cost-savings services and legislative representation for small businesses and the self-employed. Also offers services to the memberships of more than 100 affiliated state, regional and national associations.

17296 www.wacra.org
World Assn for Case Method Research & Application
Members are professional and academicians with an interest in the use of the case method in teaching, training and planning. Interactive, innovative teaching and learning methods.

17297 www.ypo.org
Young Presidents' Organization
Members are corporate presidents under the age of fifty whose companies employ at least fifty employees.

Associations

17298 **APICS: Association for Operations Management**
8430 West Bryn Mawr Avenue
Suite 1000
Chicago, IL 60631

773-867-1777
800-444-2742
Fax: 773-639-3000
E-Mail: webmaster@apics.org.
Home Page: www.apics.org
Social Media: Facebook, Twitter, LinkedIn, Youtube

Robert D Boyle, Chair of the Board
Abe Eshkenazi, CSCP, CPA,, Chief Executive Officer
Sharon Rice, Executive Director
Dean Martinez, Executive Vice President
Jennifer K Daniels, Vice President, Marketing

Provides lifelong learning for lifetime success. APICS certification programs, training tools and networking opportunities increase workplace performance. The society supports 20,000 manufacturing and service industry companies worldwide.
Cost: $110.00
60000 Members
Frequency: Membership/Professional
Founded in 1957

17299 **ASM International**
9639 Kinsman Rd
Materials Park, OH 44073-0002

440-338-5151
800-336-5152
Fax: 440-338-4634
E-Mail: memberservices@asminternational.org
Home Page: www.asminternational.org
Social Media: Facebook, Twitter, LinkedIn

Prof. C. Ravi Ravindran, FASM, President
Dr. Sunniva R. Collins, FASM, Vice President
Thomas S Passek, Managing Director & Secretary
Jeane Deatherage, Administrator, Foundation Programs
Virginia Shirk, Foundation Executive Assistant

The society for materials engineers and scientists, a worldwide network dedicated to advancing industry, technology and applications of metals and materials.
35000 Members
Founded in 1913

17300 **Adhesive & Sealant Council**
7101 Wisconsin Ave
Suite 990
Bethesda, MD 20814-4805

301-986-9700
Fax: 301-986-9795
E-Mail: info@ascouncil.org
Home Page: www.ascouncil.org
Social Media: Twitter, LinkedIn

C. Russell Thompson, Jr., Chairman
Matt Croson, President
Steve Duren, Senior Director, Member Services
Kate Zando, Director, Finance
Mark Collatz, Director, Government Relations

A North American trade association dedicated to representing the adhesive and sealant industry. ASC is bound by the collective efforts of its members, and strives to improve the industry operating government and strengthen its member companies.
Founded in 1958

17301 **American Bearings Manufacturers Association**
2025 M St NW
Suite 800
Washington, DC 20036-3309

202-367-1155
Fax: 202-367-2155
E-Mail: info@americanbearings.org
Home Page: www.americanbearings.org
Social Media: Facebook, Twitter

Pete Eich, Chair
Brian Lindsay, Vice Chair
Scott Lynch, President & Secretary
Kelly Sherrard, AssociationÿCoordinatorÿ
Peter Shapiro, Senior Associate

Promotes bearing standardization. Sponsors Bearing Technical Committee.
36 Members
Founded in 1917

17302 **American Brush Manufacturers Association**
736 Main Ave, Suite 7
Durango, CO 81301

720-392-2262
Fax: 866-837-8450
E-Mail: info@abma.org
Home Page: www.abma.org
Social Media: Facebook, Twitter, LinkedIn

David Park, Executive Director

Trade association representing North American manufacturers of brooms, brushes, mops and rollers.
175 Members
Founded in 1917

17303 **American Machine Tool Distributors Association**
AMTDA
7901 Westpark Drive
McLean, VA 22102-4206

703-893-2900
800-524-0475
Fax: 703-893-1151
E-Mail: amt@amtonline.org
Home Page: www.amtonline.org

Pete Borden, President

AMTDA will lead distributors of manufacturing technology by providing essential programs and services that help its members gain global recognition from customers and supplies as the preferred method of distribution.
Cost: $50.00
8-12 Pages
Frequency: Monthly
Circulation: 3400
Founded in 1924

17304 **American Society for Quality**
American Society for Quality
600 N Plankinton Avenue
PO Box 3005
Milwaukee, WI 53201-3005

414-272-8575
800-248-1946
Fax: 414-272-1734
E-Mail: help@asq.org
Home Page: www.asq.org
Social Media: Facebook, Twitter, LinkedIn, Youtube

John C. Timmerman, Chairman
Paul E Borawski, Executive Director
Jennifer Janzen, Director, Human Resources
Laurel Nelson-Rowe, Managing Director
Michelle Mason, Managing Director

ASQ's mission is to facilitate continuous improvement and increase customer satisfaction. Promotes quality principles, concepts and technologies. Provides information, contacts and opportunities to make things better in the workplace, in communities and in people's lives.
100M Members
Founded in 1946

17305 **American Textile Machinery Association**
201 Park Washington Ct
Falls Church, VA 22046-4527

703-538-1789
Fax: 703-241-5603
E-Mail: info@atmanet.org
Home Page: www.atmanet.org

Will Motchar, Chairman
Clay D Tyeryar, President/Assistant Treasurer
Harry W. Buzzerd, Jr., ATMA Management Counsel
Susan A. Denston, ATMA Executive Vice President
Carlos F. J. Moore, ATMA International Trade

The American Textile Machinery Association/ATMA's purpose is to advance the common interests of its members, improve business conditions within the US textile machinery industry from a global perspective and market the industry and members' machinery, parts and services.
Founded in 1933

17306 **Association for Manufacturing Technology**
7901 Westpark Drive
McLean, VA 22102-4206

703-893-2900
800-524-0475
Fax: 703-893-1151
E-Mail: amt@amtonline.org
Home Page: www.amtonline.org
Social Media: Facebook, Twitter, LinkedIn, Youtube

Douglas K Woods, President
Amber L Thomas, Vice President - Advocacy
JefferyÿH Traver, Vice President - Business
PeterÿR. Eelman, Vice President - Exhibitions
LindaÿG Montfort, Vice President-Finance & HR

Represents American providers of manufacturing machinery and equipment. Its goal is to promote technological advancements and improvements in the design, manufacture and sale of member's products in those markets and act as an industry advocate on trade organizations thoroughout the world.
Founded in 1902

17307 **Association of Equipment Manufacturers**
6737 W Washington St
Suite 2400
Milwaukee, WI 53214-5650

414-272-0943
866-236-0442
Fax: 414-272-1170
E-Mail: aem@aem.org
Home Page: www.aem.org
Social Media: Twitter

Richard A Patek, Chairman
Dennis Slater, President
Al Cervero, Vice President, Marketing
John Nowak, Chief Financial Officer
Anne Forristall Luke, Vice President, Political & Public

Composed of manufacturers of screens and feeders used in aggregates, mining and industrial processing. Promotes and furthers the interests of members in safety, production, engineering, government relations and other industry matters.
8 Members
Founded in 1959

17308 **Contract Packaging Association**
1833 Centre Point Circle
Suite 123
Naperville, IL 60563-4848

630-544-5053
Fax: 630-544-5055
E-Mail: info@contractpackaging.org
Home Page: www.contractpackaging.org
Social Media: Twitter, LinkedIn

Chris Nutley, President
Vicky Smitley, Vice President
Tim Koers, Treasurer

Formed for contract packaging firms and those businesses related to them. Promotes the growth and welfare of member firms.
155 Members
Founded in 1992

17309 **Conveyor Equipment Manufacturers Association (CEMA)**
5672 Strand CT
Suite 2
Naples, FL 34110

239-514-3441
Fax: 239-514-3470
E-Mail: kim@cemanet.org
Home Page: www.cemanet.org
Social Media: Facebook, Twitter, LinkedIn

Warren Chandler, President
Robert Reinfried, Executive Vice President
Jerry Heathman, Vice President
Jim McKnight, Secretary
Garry Abraham, Treasurer

Involved in writing industry standards, the CEMA seeks to promote among its members and the industry standardization of design manufacture and application on a voluntary basis and in such manner as will not impede development of conveying machinery and component parts or lessen competition. CEMA sponsors an annual Engineering Conference that allows Member Company Engineers to meet and develop or improve CEMA Consensus Industry Standards and National Standards that affect the conveyor industry.
96 Members
Founded in 1933

17310 **Flexible Packaging Association**
971 Corporate Blvd
Suite 403
Linthicum, MD 21090-2253

410-694-0800
Fax: 410-694-0900
E-Mail: fpa@flexpack.org
Home Page: www.flexpack.org

Marla Donahue, President

One of the leading trade associations for converters of flexible packaging and suppliers to the industry. Also provides a wealth of information to its members through focused services and benefits of membership.

17311 **Food & Beverage Marketplace Directory**
Grey House Publishing
4919 Route 22
PO Box 56
Amenia, NY 12501

518-789-8700
800-562-2139
Fax: 518-789-0556
E-Mail: books@greyhouse.com
Home Page: www.greyhouse.com
Social Media: Facebook, Twitter

Richard Gottlieb, President
Leslie Mackenzie, Publisher

A three-volume set that is the most comprehensive resource in the food and beverage industry. Available in print, a subscription-based online database, as well as a mailing list and database formats.
Cost: $595.00
2000 Pages
Frequency: Annual

17312 **Grocery Manufacturers Association**
1350 Eye St NW
Suite 300
Washington, DC 20005-3377

202-639-5900
Fax: 202-639-5932
E-Mail: info@gmaonline.org
Home Page: www.gmabrands.com
Social Media: Facebook, Twitter, RSS

Pamela G Bailey, President
Jim Flannery, Senior Executive Vice President
Dr. Leon Bruner, DVM, Ph.D., Senior Vice President
Louis Finkel, Executive Vice President
Sean Darragh, Executive Vice President, Global

Manufacturers of food and nonfood products sold through the grocery trade. US sales are more than $500 billion, GMA members employ more than 2.5 million workers in the nation.
135 Members
Founded in 1908

17313 **International Packaged Ice Association**
238 East Davis Blvd
Suite 213
Tampa, FL 33606

813-258-1690
E-Mail: jane@packagedice.com
Home Page: www.packagedice.com

Bob Morse, Chairman
Bo Russell, Vice Chairman/Treasurer
John Smibert, Secretary/Assistant Treasurer
Mike Ringstaff, Associate Member

Manufacturers and distributors of ice and their suppliers.
150 Members
Founded in 1917

17314 **Manufacturers' Agents National Association**
16-A Journey
Suite 200
Aliso Viejo, CA 92656-3317

949-859-4040
877-626-2776
Fax: 949-855-2973
E-Mail: MANA@MANAonline.org
Home Page: www.manaonline.org

Tom Hayward, CPMR, Chairman
Charles Cohon, CPMR, President and CEO
Jerry Leth, Vice President and General Manager
Lisa Ball, Member Services Coordinator
Doug Bower, Director of Strategic Alliances

Association for independent agents and firms representing manufacturers and other businesses in specified territories on a commission basis, including consultants and associate member firms interested in the manufacturer/agency method of marketing.
Founded in 1947

17315 **Material Handling Institute**
8720 Red Oak Blvd # 201
Suite 201
Charlotte, NC 28217-3996

704-676-1190
Fax: 704-676-1199
E-Mail: gbaer@mhia.org
Home Page: www.mhia.org
Social Media: Facebook, Twitter, LinkedIn, Youtube, Blooger, RSS

E. Larry Strayhorn, Executive Chairman
Dave Young, Executive Vice Chairman
John Paxton, Vice Chairman

Industrial steel shelving is loaded by hand and generally stores materials that are small in size, with multiple parts stores on a given shelf separated by dividers, boxes and drawers.
400 Members
Founded in 1945

17316 **National Association of Display Industries**
4651 Sheridan Street
Suite 470
Hollywood, FL 33021

954-893-7300
Fax: 954-893-7500
E-Mail: nadi@nadi-global.com
Home Page: www.nadi-global.com

Klein Merriman, Executive Director
Tracy Dillon, Director Communications

A leading association for the visual merchandising profession. As visual merchandising has evolved over the years into playing an integral role in retail, NADI has always taken the lead in information and educating members. The association's already significant support for the visual design profession has grown with NADI's exclusive sponsorship of GlobalShop's Visual Merchandising Show and StoreXpo.
350 Members
Founded in 1942

17317 **National Association of Manufacturers**
733 10th Street NW
Suite 700
Washington, DC 20001

202-637-3000
800-814-8468
Fax: 202-637-3182
E-Mail: manufacturing@nam.org
Home Page: www.nam.org
Social Media: Facebook, Twitter, LinkedIn, Youtube, RSS, Flickr

Douglas R. Oberhelman, Chairman
Jay Timmons, President
Ann E. Heins, Senior Vice President, Members
Linda E. Kelly, Senior Vice President, Legal
Richard I. Klein, Senior Vice President

Enhances the competitiveness of manufacturers and improves American living standards by shaping a legislative and regulatory environment conductive to US economic growth and to increase understanding among policy makers, the media and the general public about the importance of manufacturing to America's economic strength.
14000 Members
Founded in 1895

17318 **National Automatic Merchandising Association**
20 N Wacker Dr # 3500
Suite 3500
Chicago, IL 60606-3102

312-346-0370
Fax: 312-704-4140
E-Mail: dmathews@vending.org
Home Page: www.vending.org
Social Media: Facebook, Twitter, YouTube

Peter A. Tullio, NCE, CCS, Chairman
Howard Chapman, NCE, CCS, Vice Chairman
Carla Balakgie, FASAE, CAE, President & CEO
Dan Mathews, NCE5, CCS, Executive Vice President & COO
Eric Dell, Senior Vice President, Government

Serves food and refreshment, vending, contract foodservice management and office coffee service industries.
2500 Members
Founded in 1936

17319 National Cotton Batting Institute
4322 Bloombury St
Southaven, MS 38672

901-218-2393
Fax: 662-449-0046
E-Mail: info@natbat.com
Home Page: www.natbat.com

Weston Arnall, President
Greg Windsperger, VP
Fred Middleton, Executive Secretary-Treasurer

NCBI respresents U.S. companies that manufacture and sell batting for use in mattresses, futons, home furnishing, and upholstered products. It provides a range of services to assist its members in expanding markets, monitoring and contributing to legislative and regulatory decisions that affect the industry, and conducting consumer education and information programs.
27 Members
Founded in 1954

17320 North American Punch Manufacturers Association
21 Turquoise Avenue
Naples, FL 34114

239-775-7245
Fax: 239-775-7245
E-Mail: bobjanmay@napma.org
Home Page: www.napmaa.org/aboutus.asp

Robert E May, Executive Secretary

Principal program of NAPMA is the standardization of all punches, dies and retainers manufactured by the various member companies.
23 Members
Founded in 1963

17321 Pressure Vessel Manufacturers Association
800 Roosevelt Rd.
Building C,Suite 312
Glen Ellyn, IL 60137

630-942-6590
Fax: 630-790-3095
E-Mail: info@pvma.org
Home Page: www.pvma.org/

Jeff Church, Executive Director
Briana Gunn, Association Coordinatorÿÿÿ

Members are manufacturers of ASME code pressure vessels and suppliers, components and services to pressure vessel manufacturers.
31 Members
Founded in 1975

17322 Production and Operations Management Society
Dept. of Management-Univ. of Baltimore
1420 N Charles Street
Baltimore, MD 21201-5720

410-837-4727
Fax: 410-837-5675
E-Mail: poms@eng,fiu.edu
Home Page: www.poms.org/

Sushil Gupta, PhD, Executive Director
Chelliah Sriskandarajah, Ph.D., Associate Executive Director
Metin Єakanyildirim, Associate Professor of Operations

Members are professionals and academics with an interest in production and operations management.
1200 Members
Founded in 1989

17323 Refractories Institute
PO Box 8439
Pittsburgh, PA 15218

412-244-1880
Fax: 412-244-1881
E-Mail: info@refractoriesinstitute.org
Home Page: www.refractoriesinstitute.org

Robert Crolius, President

National trade association for refractory manufacturers, suppliers of equipment and raw materials and installers of refractory products.
80 Members
Founded in 1951

17324 Remanufacturing Industries Council
RICI
4401 Fair Lakes Ct
Suite 210
Fairfax, VA 22033-3848

FAX 703-968-2878
Home Page: www.rici.org

Larry Rice, CEO

A coalition of associations and companies in the remanufacturing industry.
Founded in 1997

17325 Remanufacturing Institute
Po Box 48
Lewisburg, PA 17837

570-523-0992
Fax: 705-555-5555
E-Mail: rgiuntini@reman.org
Home Page: www.reman.org

Ron Giuntini, Executive Director

A coalition of associations and companies in the entire manufacturing industry. There are over 73,000 companies in this industry. Our goal is to unite them into a powerful organization.
11 Members
Founded in 1997

17326 The Benchmarking Network
4606 Fm 1960 Rd W
Suite #250
Houston, TX 77069-4617

281-440-5044
Fax: 281-440-6677
Home Page: www.benchmarkingnetwork.com
Social Media: Facebook, Twitter

AMBC is a focused group of manufacturing process improvement professionals that looks to identify the best practices surrounding manufacturing issues for the overall operations of the members.

17327 Ultrasonic Industry Association
PO Box 2307
Dayton, OH 45401-2301

937-586-3725
Fax: 937-586-3699
E-Mail: uia@ultrasonics.org
Home Page: www.ultrasonics.org

Mark Hodnett, President
Mark Schafer, VP
Ron Stault, Treasurer
Janet Devine, Secretary

Improving processes, techniques and materials through the application of ultasonic technology.
70 Members
Founded in 1956

17328 United Association of Manufacturers Representatives
PO Box 784
Branson, MO 65615

417-779-1575
Fax: 417-779-1576
E-Mail: info@uamr.com
Home Page: www.uamr.com/

Karen Mazzola, Executive Director

Benefits manufacturers and independent sales representatives and is a national marketing association.
3,000 Members
Founded in 1965

17329 Waste Equipment Technology Association
4301 Connecticut Ave Nw
Suite 300
Washington, DC 20008-2304

202-244-4700
800-424-2869
Fax: 202-966-4824
E-Mail: wastecinfo@WASTEC.org
Home Page: www.environmentalistseveryday.org
Social Media: Facebook, Twitter, Youtube

Mike Savage, Chairman
Sharon H. Kneiss, President and CEO
Philip Hagan, Director, Safety
Sheila R. Alkire, Director, Education
Catherine Maimon, Manager, Meetings

Manufacturers of waste handling, collection and processing equipment.
Founded in 1972

Newsletters

17330 Infocus Newsletter
319 SW Washington Street
Suite 710
Portland, OR 97204-2618

503-227-3393
Fax: 503-274-7667
Home Page: www.bfma.org

Lea Anne A Fuchs, President
Andy Palatka, Executive Director
Tonya Macalino, Adversiting and Sales

Infocus is a newsletter focused on industry topics and products.
Cost: $75.00
Circulation: 1,100
Founded in 1960
Mailing list available for rent: 1M names at $200 per M

17331 Innovators Digest
InfoTeam
PO Box 15640
Plantation, FL 33318-5640

954-473-9560
Fax: 954-473-0544

Merton Allen, Editor

A multidisciplinary publication covering developments in science, engineering, products, markets, business development, manufacturing and other technological developments having industrial or commercial significance.
Frequency: Bi-Annual

17332 Intelligent Manufacturing
Lionheart Publishing
2555 Cumberland Pkwy Se
Suite 299
Atlanta, GA 30339-3921

770-432-2551
Fax: 770-432-6969
E-Mail: llewellyn@lionhrtpub.com

John Llewellyn, Publisher
David Blanchard, Editor

Provides expert solutions to manufacturing professionals covering production problems,

developments in manufacturing systems.
Cost: $20.00
Circulation: 1,598

17333 Manufacturing Technology
National Technical Information Service
5285 Port Royal Rd
Springfield, VA 22161-0001
703-605-6000
Fax: 703-605-6900
E-Mail: info@ntis.gov
Home Page: www.ntis.gov
Linda Davis, VP
Patrik Ekstr"m, Business Development Manager
Reuel Avila, Managing Director
Covers CAD/CAM, robotics, robots, productivity, manufacturing, planning, processing and control, plant design and computer software.

17334 News & Views
American Mold Builders Association
3601 Algonquin Rd
Suite 304
Rolling Meadows, IL 60008-3136
847-222-9402
Fax: 630-980-9714
E-Mail: info@amba.org
Home Page: www.amba.org
Melissa Millhuff, Executive Director
Peter Manship, Managing Director
Kym Conis, Managing Director
Frequency: Quarterly
Circulation: 2000
Founded in 1973

17335 Noise Regulation Report
Business Publishers
2222 Sedwick Drive
Durham, NC 27713
800-223-8720
Fax: 800-508-2592
E-Mail: custserv@bpinews.com
Home Page: www.bpinews.com
Exclusive coverage of airport, highway, occupational and open space noise, noise control and mitigation issues.
Cost: $511.00
10 Pages
Frequency: 12 per year
Printed in on matte stock

17336 RPA Newsletter
Retail Packaging Association
2205 Warwick Way, Suite 110
Marriottsville, MD 21104
410-925-9809
Fax: 513-527-4999
E-Mail: info@retailpackaging.org
Home Page: www.retailpackaging.org
Joel Zaas, President
Frequency: Weekly
Founded in 1989

17337 Service Management
National Association of Service Management
PO Box 250796
Milwaukee, WI 53225
414-466-6060
Fax: 414-466-0840
Home Page: www.nasm.com
Don Buelow, Publisher
Caryn Anderson, Editor
Ken Cook, Treasurer
Offers information on manufacturing and service companies.
40 Pages
Frequency: Quarterly
Circulation: 300

17338 Vision
Society of Manufacturing Engineers
1 SME Drive
PO Box 930
Dearborn, MI 48128
313-425-3000
800-733-4763
Fax: 313-425-3400
E-Mail: service@sme.org
Home Page: www.sme.org
Mark Tomlinson, Executive Director
Greg Sheremet, Publisher
The newsletter highlights the latest developments in the machine vision industry including applications, techniques and methods.
Cost: $75.00
Frequency: Quarterly
Circulation: 1,100
ISSN: 1544-3531
Founded in 1984

Magazines & Journals

17339 APICS: The Performance Advantage
APICS Association for Operations Management
5301 Shawnee Road
Alexandria, VA 22312-2317
703-548-8851
Fax: 703-354-8106
E-Mail: webmaster@apics.org
Home Page: www.apics.org
Doug Kelly, Editor
Jennifer Procter, Managing Editor
Jeffery Raynes, CEO
Provides comprehensive articles on enterprise resources planning, supply chain management, e-business, materials management and production and inventory management.
Cost: $65.00
64 Pages
Circulation: 66000
ISSN: 1056-0017
Mailing list available for rent: 40,000 names at $100 per M
Printed in 4 colors on glossy stock

17340 Adhesives & Sealants
Business News Publishing Company
PO Box 400
Flossmoor, IL 60422
708-922-0761
Fax: 708-922-0762
E-Mail: mcphersont@bnpmedia.com
Home Page: www.adhesivesmag.com
Susan Love, Publisher
Teresa Mc Pherson, Editor
Kari Rowe, Circulation Manager
Violeta Ivezaj, Senior Marketing Manager
Cost: $33.00
Frequency: Monthly
Circulation: 15000
Founded in 1926

17341 Adhesives Age
2 Grand Central Tower
140 East 45th Street,40th Floor
New York, NY 10017
212-884-9528
Fax: 212-884-9514
E-Mail: ltattum@chemweek.com
Home Page: www.chemweek.com
Lyn Tattum, Group Vice President/Publisher
Joe Minnella, Global Sales Director
Adhesives Age provides readers with vital information: global industry coverage of the development, manufacture, and application of adhesives, sealants, and related products.
Cost: $75.00
62 Pages
Frequency: Weekly
Circulation: 22994
ISSN: 0001-821X
Founded in 1958
Mailing list available for rent
Printed in 4 colors on glossy stock

17342 Advanced Materials & Processes
ASM International
9639 Kinsman Rd
Materials Park, OH 44073
440-338-5151
800-336-5152
Fax: 440-338-4634
E-Mail: memberservices@asminternational.org
Home Page: www.asminternational.org
Social Media: Facebook, Twitter, LinkedIn
Joseph M Zion, Publisher
Joanne Miller, Managing Editor
Margaret Hunt, Editor-in-Chief
Jeane Deatherage, Administrator, Foundation Programs
Virginia Shirk, Foundation Executive Assistant
AM&P, the monthly technical magazine from ASM International, is designed to keep readers aware of leading-edge developments and trends in engineering materials - metals and alloys, engineering polymers, advanced ceramics, and composites - and the methods used to select, process, fabricate, test, and characterize them.
Frequency: Monthly
Circulation: 32M
Founded in 1977

17343 American Fastener Journal
Carol McGuire
11305 E. Monument Drive
Scottsdale, AZ 85262-4746
480-488-3500
Fax: 480-488-3247
E-Mail: mmcguire@fastenerjournal.com
Home Page: www.fastenerjournal.com
Mike McGuire, Publisher/Editor
Jackie McGuire, Executive Editor
Micki Leopard, Circulation Manager
This journal for the fastener industry covers technical articles, inspections, quality assurance, materials applications, specifications and standards, as well as manufacturer, distributors and supplier profiles. Publishes annual buyers guide - The American Fastener Source Guide
Cost: $45.00
Circulation: 13000
Founded in 1981
Printed in 4 colors on glossy stock

17344 American Funeral Director
Kates-Boylston Publications
11300 Rockville Pike
Suite 1100
Rockville, MD 20852
800-500-4585
800-500-4585
Fax: 732-730-2515
Home Page: www.kates-boylston.com
Adrian F Boylston, Publisher
Thomas Parmalee, Executive Director
Amy Fidalgo, Production Manager
Articles on funeral home construction, finance, mortuary law, shipment of human remains by air transportation, sales and display methods, advertising and public relations, new equipment and other association activiies. Also includes personnel news about funeral directors and related supply firms.
Cost: $49.95
Frequency: Monthly
Circulation: 12168
Founded in 1918

17345 **Automatic Machining Magazine**
Screw Machine Publishing Company
1066 Gravel Rd
Suite 201
Webster, NY 14580-1769

585-787-0820
800-610-6950
Fax: 585-787-0868
Home Page: www.automachmag.com

Wayne Wood, President
Linda Iobiondo, Circulation Manager

General industry news for professionals in the metal turning and cold forming fields.
Cost: $55.00
142 Pages
Frequency: Monthly
Circulation: 13000
Founded in 1939
Printed in 4 colors on glossy stock

17346 **CNC West**
Arnold Publications
14340 Bolsa Chica Avenue E
PO Box 100
Westminster, CA 92684-100

714-899-0733
Fax: 714-899-0738
E-Mail: larnold@cnc-west.com
Home Page: www.cnc-west.com

Shawn Arnold, Publisher
Chuck Bush, Editor
Shawn Arnold, CEO/President
Shawn Arnold, Circulation Manager
Shawn Arnold, Marketing Manager

News and trends on western jobshops and manufacturers
Cost: $32.50
Circulation: 22000
Founded in 1981
Printed in 4 colors on glossy stock

17347 **Card Manufacturing**
International Card Manufacturing Association
PO Box 727
Princeton Junction, NJ 08550-727

609-799-4900
Fax: 609-799-7032
E-Mail: info@icma.com
Home Page: www.icma.com

Lynn McCullough, Association Manager
Jeffrey E Barnhart, Communications Manager
Kaitlin Friedmann, Communications Manager
Al Vrancart, Founder

Advertiser supported trade magazine featuring industry news and features on all aspects of the plastic card production worldwide, and the news of the ICMA.
Cost: $75.00
Circulation: 3000

17348 **Coatings World**
Rodman Publishing
70 Hilltop Rd
Suite 3000
Ramsey, NJ 07446-1150

201-825-2552
Fax: 201-825-0553
E-Mail: info@rodpub.com
Home Page: www.nutraceuticalsworld.com
Social Media: Facebook, Twitter, LinkedIn

Rodman Zilenziger Jr, President
Matt Montgomery, VP

Coatings World is directed at industry personnel concerned with developing and manufacturing paints, coatings, adhesives and sealants. Feature articles and industry news are directed at chemists, formulators and all levels of management that must keep abreast of technical products and market developments.
Cost: $50.00
136 Pages
Frequency: Monthly
Circulation: 17315
ISSN: 1527-1129
Mailing list available for rent
Printed in 4 colors on glossy stock

17349 **Composites Fabrication**
Composites Fabricators Association
1010 N Glebe Rd
Suite 450
Arlington, VA 22201-4749

703-525-0714
Fax: 703-525-0743
E-Mail: info@acmanet.org
Home Page: www.acmanet.org/

Elly Shariat, Marketing Manager
Andy Rusnak, Editor
Roxanne Fraver, Marketing & Circulation
Sabeena Hickman, Deputy Director
Jessica Howard, Production Manager

Presents information on new technology, trends and techniques for manufacturers in the fiberglass and composites industry.
Cost: $41.00
114 Pages
Circulation: 8000
ISSN: 1084-841X
Printed in 4 colors on glossy stock

17350 **Consumer Goods Technology**
Edgell Communications
4 Middlebury Boulevard
Randolph, NJ 07869

973-252-0100
Fax: 973-252-9020
Home Page: www.consumergoods.com

Andrew Gaffney, Group Publisher
Steve Rosenstock, Publisher
Tim Clark, Editor-in-Chief
Alliston Ackerman, Assistant Editor
Pat Wisser, Production Manager

Provides case histories, technology overviews, new products and industry news to assist corporations and management in the consumer goods industry.
Frequency: Monthly
Circulation: 25000
Founded in 1984

17351 **Contingency Planning & Management**
Witter Publishing Corporation
20 Commerce Street
Flemington, NJ 08822

908-788-0343
Fax: 908-788-3782
Home Page: www.witterpublishing.com

Bob Joudanin, Publisher
Paul Kirvan, Editor In Chief
Courtney Writter, Circulation Manager
Andrew Witter, President

Serves the fields of financial/banking, manufacturing industrial, transportation, utilities, telecommunications, health care, government, insurance and other allied fields.
Frequency: Monthly
Founded in 1987

17352 **Contract Management**
National Contract Management Association
1912 Woodford Road
Vienna, VA 22182-3728

703-489-9231
800-344-8096
Fax: 703-448-0939
E-Mail: memberservices@ncmahq.org
Home Page: www.ncmahq.org

Amy Miedema, Editor-in-Chief
Neal Couture, Executive Director

It covers the myriad aspects of government and commercial contract management. News and features provide information on such topics as procurement policy, on-the-job techniques, regulations, case law, ethics, contract administration, electronic commerce, international and small business matters, education and career development.
Cost: $75.00
80 Pages
Frequency: Monthly
Circulation: 22000
Founded in 1959
Printed in 4 colors on glossy stock

17353 **Control Design**
Putman Media
555 W Pierce Rd
Suite 301
Itasca, IL 60143-2626

630-467-1300
Fax: 630-467-0197
E-Mail: lgoldberg@putman.net
Home Page: www.putman.net

John Cappelletti, President
Mike Bacidore, Editor-in-Chief/Publisher
Anetta Gauthier, Production Manager
Lori Goldberg, Operations Manager

Markets to the manufacturing facilities under the government's standard industry classification (SIC) code 35, which manufacture a broad range of products from turbines, conveyors and machine tools to food processing, printing presses and computers.
Cost: $96.00
Circulation: 50,046
ISSN: 1094-3366
Founded in 1938
Printed in 4 colors

17354 **Design News**
Reed Business Information
30 Technology Parkway South
Suite 100
Norcross, GA 30092

646-746-6400
800-424-3996
Fax: 646-756-7583
E-Mail: webmaster@reedbusiness.com
Home Page: www.reedbusiness.com

John Poulin, CEO
Karen Auguston Field, Editor-in-Chief
James Reed, Owner

Informs professionals in the technology industry of all the latest in new product introductions in fields such as bearings, fastening/joining and new technology.
Circulation: 170000

17355 **Distributor's Link**
4297 Corporate Sq
Naples, FL 34104-4754

239-643-2713
800-356-1639
Fax: 239-643-5220
E-Mail: leojcoar@linkmagazine.com
Home Page: www.linkmagazine.com/

Maryann Marzocchi, President
Tracey Lumia, Director of Sales and Marketing

Information aimed at the fastener distributors nationwide.
Cost: $45.00
Frequency: Quarterly
Circulation: 50000
Founded in 1975

17356 Edplay
Fahy-Williams Publishing
PO Box 1080
Geneva, NY 14456-8080
315-789-0458
800-344-0559
Fax: 315-789-4263
Home Page: www.edplay.com
Kevin Fahy, Publisher
Tina Manzer, Editorial Director
Mark Stash, Art Director
Alyssa Lafaro, Associate Editor
Serves toy manufacturers and dealers. Offers product reviews, industry profiles, and reader surveys.
Circulation: 13000
Founded in 1984

17357 Fastener Technology International
Initial Publications
PO Box 5451
Akron, OH 44334-0451
330-864-2122
Fax: 330-864-5298
E-Mail: mcnulty@fastenertech.com
Home Page: www.fastenertech.com
Job Lippincott, Publisher
Michael J. McNulty, Vice President and Editor
Contains articles on company profiles, new equipment, literature, products, fastener topics and patents.
Cost: $40.00
Circulation: 13,000
Founded in 1981
Printed in 4 colors on glossy stock

17358 Fastening
Mike McGuire
293 Hopewell Drive
Powell, OH 43065-9350
614-848-3232
800-848-0304
Fax: 614-848-5045
Home Page: www.fastening.com
Mike McGuire, Publisher
In-depth and up-to-date information about fastening products, design/applications, people, companies, fastening industry events and specifications.
Cost: $30.00
Frequency: Quarterly
Circulation: 28,000
Founded in 1995
Printed in 4 colors on glossy stock

17359 Forming & Fabricating
Society of Manufacturing Engineers
1 SME Drive
Box 930
Dearborn, MI 48128
313-425-3000
800-733-4763
Fax: 313-425-3400
E-Mail: advertising@sme.org
Home Page: www.sme.org
Mark Tomlinson, Executive Director
Greg Sheremet, Publisher
News and features regarding the forming and fabricating industry with the intention of improving process productivity and project quality. Special focus on technology and its applications in manufacturing.
Frequency: Monthly
Circulation: 66616

17360 ITE Solutions
Institute of Industrial Engineers
25 Technology Pkwy S
Suite 150
Norcross, GA 30092-2946
770-449-0461
Fax: 770-263-8532
E-Mail: webmaster@iienet.org
Home Page: www.iienet.org

17361 InTech
Instrumentation, Systems,and Automation Society
67 Alexander Drive
Research Triangle Park, NC 27709
919-549-8411
Fax: 919-990-9434
E-Mail: info@isa.org
Home Page: www.isa.org
Richard Simpson, Publisher
Greg Hale, Editor
Rob Renner, Executive Officer
Chip Lee, Publication Director
Regular issue features include new product developments, new processes, research updates and general industry news.
Cost: $75.00
Frequency: Monthly
Circulation: 67000
Founded in 1945

17362 Industrial Equipment News
Thomas Publishing Company
5 Penn Plz
Suite 10
New York, NY 10001-1860
212-695-0500
800-733-1127
Fax: 212-290-7362
E-Mail: businesslists@thomaspublishing.com
Home Page: www.thomaspublishing.com
Carl Holst-Knudsen, CEO
Joseph Rosta, Editor-in-Chief
Marie Urbanowicz, Marketing Manager
Serves the industrial field including manufacturing, mining, utilities, construction, transportation,governmental establishments, and educational services.
Frequency: Monthly
ISSN: 0019-8258
Founded in 1898

17363 Industrial Maintenance & Plant Operation
Reed Business Information
199 East Badger Road
Suite 201
Madison, WI 53713
973-920-7787
Fax: 973-920-7531
E-Mail: hpendrak@reedbusiness.com
Home Page: www.impomag.com
Scott Sward, Publisher
Rick Carter, Editor-in-Chief
R Reed, Owner
Kyle Orr, Circulation Manager
Hank Pendrak, Marketing Director
Circulation: 100000
Founded in 1975

17364 Industrial Market Place
Wineberg Publications
7842 Lincoln Avenue
Skokie, IL 60077
847-676-1900
800-323-1818
Fax: 847-676-0063
E-Mail: info@industrialmktpl.com
Home Page: www.industrialmktpl.com
Joel Wineberg, President
Jackie Bitensky, Editor
Has advertisements on machinery, industrial and plant equipment and services and industrial auctions in each issue.
Cost: $175.00
Circulation: 14000
Founded in 1951
Mailing list available for rent: 120 names at $70 per M
Printed in 4 colors on glossy stock

17365 Job Shop Technology
Edward Publishing
16 Waterbury Road
Prospect, CT 06712-1215
203-758-4474
800-317-0474
Fax: 203-758-3427
Home Page: www.jobshoptechnology.com
Mark W Shortt, Editor
Cindy Wilkinson, Circulation Director
Published to aid product manufacturers who outsource parts and manufacturing services. Specializes in manufacturing processes for the metals, plastics, rubber, and electronics industries, including virtually any outsourced manufacturing service.
Frequency: Quarterly
Circulation: 100,000
Founded in 1986
Mailing list available for rent: 90875 names at $125 per M
Printed in 4 colors on glossy stock

17366 Journal of Coatings Technology
Federation of Societies for Coatings Technology
527 Plymouth Rd
Suite 415
Plymouth Meetin, PA 19462-1641
610-940-0777
Fax: 610-940-0292
Home Page: www.coatingstech.org
Robert F Ziegler, Publisher
Patricia D Ziegler, Administrative Assistant
Shelby Ferguson, Administrative Assistant
Chris Hobson, Communications Manager
Lance Edwards, Director
For the industrial and service organizations in paint and manufacturing plants, raw materials suppliers for coatings, printing inks and sealants.
Cost: $120.00
Frequency: Monthly

17367 Journal of Materials Engineering and Performance
ASM International
9639 Kinsman Road
Materials Park, OH 44073-0002
440-338-5151
800-336-5152
Fax: 440-338-4634
E-Mail: memberservice@asminternational.org
Home Page: www.asminternational.org
Social Media: Facebook, Twitter, LinkedIn
Jeane Deatherage, Administrator, Foundation Programs
Virginia Shirk, Foundation Executive Assistant
Peer-reviewed journal that publishes contributions on all aspects of materials selection, design, characterization, processing and performance testing. The journal for solving day-to-day engineering challenges - especially those involving components for larger systems.
Cost: $1965.00
Frequency: Bimonthly
Circulation: 305
Founded in 1992

17368 Journal of Phase Equilibria
ASM International

9639 Kinsman Rd
Materials Park, OH 44072

440-338-5151
800-336-5152
Fax: 440-338-4634
E-Mail: memberservices@asminternational.org
Home Page: www.asminternational.org
Social Media: Facebook, Twitter, LinkedIn

Jeane Deatherage, Administrator, Foundation Programs
Virginia Shirk, Foundation Executive Assistant

Peer-reviewed journal that contains basic and applied research results, evaluated phase diagrams, a survey of current literature, and comments or other material pertinent to the previous three areas. The aim is to provide a broad spectrum of information concerning phase equilibria for the materials community.
Cost: $1965.00
Frequency: Bimonthly
Circulation: 305

17369 Journal of Process Control
Butterworth Heinemann
313 Washington Street
Newton, MA 02458-1626

617-928-5460
Fax: 781-933-6333

JD Perkins, Editor
T McAvoy, Regional Editor

Covers the application of control theory, operations research, computer science and engineering principles to the solution of process control problems.

17370 Journal of Quality Technology
American Society for Quality
600 N Plankinton Avenue
PO Box 3005
Milwaukee, WI 53201-3005

414-272-8575
800-248-1946
Fax: 414-272-1734
E-Mail: help@asq.org
Home Page: www.asq.org
Social Media: Facebook, Twitter, LinkedIn

Roberto M Saco, President
Paul E Borawski, Executive Director
Erica Gumieny, Sales
Fay Spano, Communications/Media Relations

Published by the American Society for Quality, the JQT is a quarterly, peer-reviewed journal that focuses on the subject of quality control and the related areas of reliability and similar disciplines.
Cost: $30.00
100M Members
Frequency: Quarterly
Founded in 1946

17371 Maintenance Technology
Applied Technology Publications
1300 S Grove Ave
Suite 105
Barrington, IL 60010-5246
847-382-8100
Fax: 847-304-8603
Home Page: www.mt-online.com

Arthur Rice, President/CEO
Bill Kiesel, Vice President/Publisher
Jane Alexander, Editor-In-Chief
Rick Carter, Executive Editor
Randy Buttstadt, Director of Creative Services

Maintenance Technology magazine serves the business and technical information needs of managers and engineers responsible for assuring availability of plant equipment and systems. It provides readers with articles on advanced technologies, strategies, tools, and services for the life-cycle management of capital assets.
Frequency: Monthly
Circulation: 50,827
Mailing list available for rent: 35,263 names at $$15 per M

17372 Managing Automation
Thomas Publishing Company
5 Penn Plz
Suite 10
New York, NY 10001-1860

212-695-0500
800-733-1127
Fax: 212-290-7362
E-Mail: contact@thomaspublishing.com
Home Page: www.thomaspublishing.com

Carl Holst-Knudsen, CEO
Greg MacSweeney, Managing Editor
Kim Vennard, Senior Marketing Manager
Shawn Jacobs, Director of Sales

Serves the needs of those managers and engineers responsible for the planning and implementation of factory automation at both the plant and enterprise levels.
Cost: $60.00
Frequency: Monthly
Circulation: 100246
Founded in 1898

17373 Manufacturers Mart
Philip G Cannon Jr
PO Box 310
Georgetown, MA 01833-0410

978-352-3320
800-835-0017
Fax: 401-348-0797
E-Mail: info@manufacturersmart.com
Home Page: www.manufacturersmart.com

Phillip Cannon, Publisher
Linda Smith, Editor

Information and news on manufacturing companies with a regional focus in New England. New product articles, coverage of advances in technology, compliance issues, case studies, announcements and calendar events. Online version includes searchable index of products and services.
32 Pages
Frequency: Monthly
Circulation: 30000
Founded in 1978
Printed in 4 colors on newsprint stock

17374 Manufacturing Engineering
Society of Manufacturing Engineers
1 SME Drive
PO Box 930
Dearborn, MI 48128

313-425-3000
800-733-4763
Fax: 313-425-3400
E-Mail: advertising@sme.org
Home Page: www.sme.org

Mark Tomlinson, Executive Director
Greg Sheremet, Publisher
Karen Manardo, Director of Communication
Tom Drozda, Publisher/Advertising

Serves metalworking industry machining, forming, inspection, assembly and processing operations.
Frequency: Monthly
Circulation: 1,11,966
Founded in 1932

17375 Manufacturing News
Publishers & Producers
PO Box 36
Annandale, VA 22003

703-750-2664
Fax: 703-750-0064
E-Mail: editor@manufacturingnews.com
Home Page: www.manufacturingnews.com

Richard McCormack, Publisher/Editor

Gives in-depth analysis of critical manufacturing trends, insightful interviews with top players in industry and government and up-to-the-minute business news about issues that directly affect your ability to compete and prosper and takes a look at software and hardware, sucessful manufacturers, and profound technological changes.
Cost: $495.00
12 Pages
Frequency: Fortnightly
Circulation: 30,000
ISSN: 1078-2397
Founded in 1994
Printed in on matte stock

17376 Manufacturing Systems
2000 Clearwater Drive
Oak Brook, IL 60523-8809

630-288-8000
Fax: 630-320-7373
Home Page: www.manufacturing.net

Michelle Palmer, Publisher
Mary Ann Brockway, Circulation Manager
David Greenfield, Editor

Information management for increased manufacturing productivity.
Cost: $6.00
Frequency: Monthly
Circulation: 114682

17377 Marketeer
1602 E Glen Avenue
Peoria, IL 61614-5451
VB Cook, Editor

New products for manufacturing.
Cost: $15.00
16 Pages
Frequency: Monthly
Founded in 1952

17378 Marking Industry Magazine
Marking Devices Publishing Company
136 W Vallette St
Suite 6
Elmhurst, IL 60126-4377

630-832-5200
Fax: 630-832-5206
Home Page: www.markingdevices.com

David Hachmeister, President

New products, processes and services, MDAI and other association news, shows and seminars, sales and management methods.
Cost: $54.00
Frequency: Monthly
Circulation: 1300
Founded in 1907

17379 Material Handling Equipment Distributors Association
Data Key Communications
201 US Highway 45
Vernon Hills, IL 60061-2398

847-680-3500
Fax: 847-362-6989
E-Mail: connect@mheda.org
Home Page: www.mheda.org

Loren Swakow, President
Elizabeth Richard, Editor/Executive VP
Kathy Carter, Marketing Manager

Updates on technology, association news and announcements, industrial perspectives and outlook and new product information.
Cost: $24.00
Frequency: Quarterly
Circulation: 4000
Founded in 1954

17380 Material Handling Network
Network Publishing
252 E Washington Street
East Peoria, IL 61611-338

309-699-4431
800-447-6901
Fax: 309-698-0801
Home Page: www.mhnetwork.com

Andra Stephens, Editor
Bob Behrens, General Manager
Andra Stephens, Advertising/Sales
Mindi Mitzelfelt, Graphic Designer

Monthly journal written for material handling distributors/dealers and people who sell racks, bins, conveyors, dock equipment, lift trucks, batteries, and pallet jacks - both power and non-power.
Cost: $65.00
156 Pages
Frequency: Monthly
Circulation: 12058
Founded in 1981
Printed in 4 colors on n stock

17381 Material Handling Product News
Reed Business Information
225 Wyman St
Suite 3
Waltham, MA 02451-1216

781-734-8000
Fax: 781-734-8076
Home Page: www.reedbusiness.com

Mark Finklestein, President
Joseph Pagnotta, Editor-in-Chief
Joanna Schumann, Marketing Manager
Michael Holowchuck, Circulation Manager
Steve McCoy, Associate Publisher

Literature reviews, new product listings and new systems and services are featured regularly.
Frequency: Monthly
Founded in 1977

17382 Materials at High Temperatures
Butterworth Heinemann
313 Washington Street
Newton, MA 02458-1626

617-928-5460
Fax: 781-933-6333

T Suzuki, Co-Editor
TB Gibbons, Co-Editor

Serves the needs of those developing and using materials for high temperature applications in the power, chemical, engine, processing and furnace industries.

17383 Mid-America Commerce & Industry
Mid-America Commerce & Industry
2432 Sw Pepperwood Rd
Topeka, KS 66614-5293

785-272-5280
Fax: 785-272-3729
E-Mail: maci@maci-mag.com
Home Page: www.maci-mag.com/

David Lippe, President

Regional industrial magazine covering manufacturing in Missouri, Kansas, Nebraska, Oklahoma, Arizona and Iowa
Cost: $18.00
Frequency: Monthly

17384 Midrange ERP
MFG Publishing
9 W Street
Beverly, MA 01915-2225

978-927-1419
Fax: 978-921-1255
E-Mail: editor@mfg-erp.com
Home Page: www.mfg-erp.com

Deborah A Turbide, Publisher

Planning and scheduling issues, polices and procedures, as well as system improvements.
Circulation: 40000
Founded in 1996

17385 Modern Applications News
Nelson Publishing
2500 Tamiami Trl N
Nokomis, FL 34275-3476

941-966-9521
Fax: 941-966-2590
E-Mail: nelpub@ix.netcom.com
Home Page: www.healthmgttech.com
Social Media: Facebook

A Verner Nelson, President
John Mullaly, Editor
Bob Olree, Publisher
Joan Southerland, Marketing
Wyanne Harwell, Circulation Manager

Information includes coverage of abrasives and grinding, automated handling and robotics, CAD/CAM, coatings and finishings, coolants, lubricants and filters, cutting tools, heat treating, ID marking, lasers, machining centers, and shop control software.
Cost: $127.00
Frequency: Monthly
Circulation: 80340
Founded in 1962

17386 NC Shop Owner
Penton Media
1166 Avenue of the Americas/10th Fl
New York, NY 10036

212-204-4200
Fax: 216-696-6662
E-Mail: information@penton.com
Home Page: www.penton.com

Jane Cooper, Marketing
Chris Meyer, Director, Corporate Communications

News of industry events, new product information, updates on manufacturing technology and a special technology focus section.
Frequency. Semiannual
Circulation: 120,000

17387 National Association of Relay Manufacturers
2500 Wilson Boulevard
Arlington, VA 22201

703-907-8025
Fax: 703-875-8908
E-Mail: narm@ecaus.org
Home Page: www.ecaus.org/narm

Electronical relay and associated switching devices. Engrs. Relay HB - 5th Edition - $60.00 plus $7.00 postage and handling; IRC Proceeding 2002 - $60.00 plus $7.00 postage and handling
Cost: $60.00
Circulation: 1000
Founded in 1947

17388 New Equipment Digest
Penton Media
1166 Avenue of the Americas/10th Fl
New York, NY 10036

212-204-4200
Fax: 216-696-6662
E-Mail: information@penton.com
Home Page: www.penton.com

Chris Meyer, Director, Corporate Communications
Robert F King, Editor
Sarah Hughes, Production Manager
Bobbie Macy, Circulation Manager
David B. Nussbaum, CEO

Serves the general industrial field which include manufacturing, processing, engineering services, construction, transportation, mining, public utilities, wholesale distributors, educational services, libraries, and governmental establishments.
Frequency: Monthly
Circulation: 206154
Founded in 1892

17389 Off-Highway Engineering
SAE
400 Commonwealth Dr
Warrendale, PA 15086-7511

724-776-4841
877-606-7323
Fax: 724-776-5760
E-Mail: sohe@sae.org
Home Page: www.saesections.org

Richard O Schaum, President

Off-Highway Engineering serves the international off highway design and manufacturing field which consists of producers of construction, lawn and garden, agricultural equipment, and industrial vehicles. Also served are makers of engines and parts and components and others allied to the field.
Cost: $70.00
66 Pages
Circulation: 16308
ISSN: 1074-6919
Founded in 1905
Printed in 4 colors on glossy stock

17390 Planning Guidebook
Reed Business Information
6 Alfred Circle
Bedford, MA 00173

972-980-8810
Fax: 617-558-4700
E-Mail: corporatecommunications@reedbusiness.com
Home Page: www.designnews.com

William Shordon, Editor
Jim Casella, CEO

Offers information and news on manufacturing companies.
Frequency: Monthly
Founded in 1946

17391 Plant
Rogers Media Publishing
777 Bay Street
Toronto, Ontario M5W1A

416-596-5729
Fax: 416-596-5552
Home Page: www.plant.ca

Joe Terrett, Editor
Kathy Smith, Production Manager
Jessica Jubb, Manager

PLANT serves manufacturing and processing industries in Canada.
Cost: $125.00
Frequency: 18 per year
ISSN: 0845-4213
Founded in 1941

17392 Plant Services
Putman Media
555 W Pierce Rd
Suite 301
Itasca, IL 60143-2626

630-467-1300
Fax: 630-467-0197
E-Mail: mbrenner@putman.net
Home Page: www.putman.net

John Cappelletti, CEO
Mike Bacidore, Editor-in-Chief
Mike Brenner, Group Publisher
Keith Larson, VP Content

For maintenance and engineering managers responsible for keeping manufacturing plants

running efficiently.
Cost: $96.00
Circulation: 80100
Founded in 1938
Mailing list available for rent: 10,000 names
Printed in 4 colors on glossy stock

17393 Plating and Surface Finishing
1155 Fifteenth Street, NW
Suite 500
Washington, DC 20005

202-457-8401
Fax: 407-281-6446
E-Mail: aesf@aesf.org
Home Page: www.aesf.org

Jon Bednerik CAE, Publisher
Tom Urban, Advertising Manager
Donn Berry, Editor
Dan Denston, Executive Director
John Flatley, Senior Advisor and NASF Liaison

AESF is an international society that advances the science of surface finishing to benefit industry and society through education information and social involvement, as well as those who provide services, supplies and support to the industry.
Cost: $125.00
Frequency: Monthly
Circulation: 4000
Founded in 1909

17394 Powder Coating
OSC Publishing
1300 E 66th Street
Minneapolis, MN 55423-2642

612-866-2242
Fax: 612-866-1939

Richard R Cress, Publisher
Richard Link, Manager

Our information focuses on the application, pre-treatment, materials, materials handling, and curing processes. Also features case histories.
Frequency: 9 per year
Circulation: 23587

17395 Precision Manufacturing
Minnesota Precision Manufacturing Association
3131 Fernbrook Ln N
Suite 111
Minneapolis, MN 55447-5336

763-473-4090
Fax: 763-473-2804
Home Page: www.mpma.com

Dennis A Olson, President
Garry Bultnick, Sales Manager
LuAnn Bartley, Executive Director

Publication for job shop owners, managers and engineers and industrial suppliers, distributors, OEM buyers and purchasing agents, manufacturing representatives and technical colleges.
Circulation: 7900
Founded in 1958
Printed in on glossy stock

17396 Process Cooling & Equipment
Business News Publishing Company
1050 IL Route 83
Suite 200
Bensenville, IL 60106-1096

630-377-5909
Fax: 630-694-4002
E-Mail: meaneys@bnpmedia.com
Home Page: www.process-cooling.com

Katie Rotella, President
Linda Becker, Editor
Sean Meaney, Sales Manager

Focuses on temperatures down through cryogenic levels in industrial processes and in equipment cooling.

17397 Process Heating
Business News Publishing Company
155 Pfingsten Road
Suite 205
Deerfield, IL 60015

847-405-4000
Fax: 248-502-1001
E-Mail: PHeditors@bnpmedia.com
Home Page: www.process-heating.com
Social Media: Facebook, Twitter

Anne Armel, Publisher
Linda Becker, Associate Publisher/Editor
Beth McClelland, Production Manager
Sean Meaney, Sales Manager
Caroline Eychenne, European Sales Representative

Magazine covers heat processing at temperatures up to 1000 degrees F at end user and OEM plants in 9 industries. Follow us at twitter.com/ProcessHeating, www.facebook.com/ProcessHeating
Circulation: 25000
Founded in 1994

17398 Products Finishing
Gardner Publications
6915 Valley Ln
Cincinnati, OH 45244-3153

513-527-8800
800-950-8020
Fax: 513-527-8801
E-Mail: narnold@gardnerweb.com
Home Page: www.gardnerweb.com

Rick Kline Sr, CEO
Matthew J Little, Editor
Nancy Eigel-Miller, Marketing Director
Nancy Arnold, Circulation Manager
John Campos, Manager

Covers production, management, engineering, design, etc. in plants where metal and plastic products are eletroplated, anodized, painted, buffed, cleaned or otherwise finished.
Cost: $89.00
Frequency: Monthly
Circulation: 42000
Founded in 1928
Printed in 4 colors on glossy stock

17399 Progressive Distributor
Pfingsten Publishing
730 Madison Avenue
Fort Atkinson, WI 53538

920-563-5225
800-932-7732
Fax: 920-563-4269
Home Page: www.progressivedistributor.com

Rich Vurva, Editor
Pat OBrien, Executive Director
Mitch Bouchard, Secretary, Treasurer

Sales and marketing magazines for top manager, salespeople and marketing executives in industrial and construction distribution firms.
Circulation: 24337
Founded in 1996
Printed in 4 colors on glossy stock

17400 Quality
Business News Publishing
1050 IL Route 83
Suite 200
Bensenville, IL 60106-1096

630-377-5909
Fax: 630-227-0204
E-Mail: williamst@bnpmedia.com
Home Page: www.qualitymag.com

Katie Rotella, President
Thomas A Williams, Publisher
Christopher Sheehy, Manager

Quality is a monthly business publication serving the quality assurance and process improvement needs of more than 80,000 North American manufacturing professionals.
Cost: $75.00
74 Pages
Frequency: Monthly
Circulation: 64000
ISSN: 0360-9936
Founded in 1962
Printed in 4 colors on glossy stock

17401 Quality Engineering
American Society for Quality
600 N Plankinton Avenue
PO Box 3005
Milwaukee, WI 53201-3005

414-272-8575
800-248-1946
Fax: 414-272-1734
E-Mail: help@asq.org
Home Page: www.asq.org
Social Media: Facebook, Twitter, LinkedIn

Roberto M Saco, President
Paul E Borawski, Executive Director
Erica Gumieny, Sales
Fay Spano, Communications/Media Relations

Co-published with Taylor and Francis, this journal is for professional practitioners and researchers whose goal is quality engineering improvements and solutions.
Cost: $34.75
100M Members
Frequency: Quarterly/Members Price
Founded in 1946

17402 Quality Management Journal
American Society for Quality
600 N Plankinton Avenue
PO Box 3005
Milwaukee, WI 53201-3005

414-272-8575
800-248-1946
Fax: 414-272-1734
E-Mail: help@asq.org
Home Page: www.asq.org
Social Media: Facebook, Twitter, LinkedIn

Roberto M Saco, President
Paul E Borawski, Executive Director
Erica Gumieny, Sales
Fay Spano, Communications/Media Relations

Published by the American Society for Quality, the QMT is a quarterly, peer-reviewed journal that focuses on the subject of quality management practice and provides a discussion forum for both practitioners and academics in the area of research.
Cost: $50.00
100M Members
Frequency: Quarterly
Founded in 1946

17403 Quality Observer: ICSS Journal
Quality University Press
3970 Chain Bridge Road
PO Box 1111
Fairfax, VA 22030-3316

703-691-9496
Home Page: www.thequalityobserver.com

Johnson A Edosomwan, Editor

Case studies, interviews, international and national news and regular colums covering service in manufacturing, high-tech, government

agencies and non-profit organizations.
Cost: $139.00
50 Pages
Frequency: 4 per year
Circulation: 15,000
ISSN: 1057-9583
Printed in 4 colors on glossy stock

17404 **Quality Progress**
American Society for Quality
600 N Plankinton Avenue
PO Box 3005
Milwaukee, WI 53201-3005
414-272-8575
800-248-1946
Fax: 414-272-1734
E-Mail: help@asq.org
Home Page: www.asq.org
Social Media: Facebook, Twitter, LinkedIn
Roberto M Saco, President
Paul E Borawski, Executive Director
Erica Gumieny, Sales
Fay Spano, Communications/Media Relations
Published by the American Society for Quality, the QP is a peer-reviewed journal that focuses on the subject of quality control, discussing the usage and implementation of quality principles including the subject areas of organizational behavior, knowledge management and process improvement.
Cost: $55.00
100M Members
Founded in 1946

17405 **Scan Tech News**
Reed Business Information
30 Technology Parkway South
Suite 100
Norcross, GA 30092
630-574-0825
800-424-3996
Fax: 630-288-8781
E-Mail: webmaster@reedbusiness.com
Home Page: www.reedbusiness.com
Jeff Greisch, President
Updates in trends in ADC technology and standards, the latest news from leading industry events, and product developments that streamline the flow of essential information in industrial settings.
Frequency: Monthly
Circulation: 82M

17406 **Software Quality Professional**
American Society for Quality
600 N Plankinton Avenue
PO Box 3005
Milwaukee, WI 53201-3005
414-272-8575
800-248-1946
Fax: 414-272-1734
E-Mail: help@asq.org
Home Page: www.asq.org
Social Media: Facebook, Twitter, LinkedIn
Roberto M Saco, President
Paul E Borawski, Executive Director
Erica Gumieny, Sales
Fay Spano, Communications/Media Relations
Published by the American Society for Quality, the SQP is a quarterly, peer-reviewed journal for software development professionals that focuses on the subject of quality practice principles in the implementation of software and the development of software systems.
Cost: $45.00
100M Members
Frequency: Quarterly
Founded in 1946

17407 **Solid State Technology**
PennWell Publishing Company
1421 S. Sheridan Road
Tulsa, OK 74112
918-835-3161
800-331-4463
Fax: 603-891-9294
Home Page: www.pennwell.com
Christine Shaw, VP
David Barach, Publisher
Serves firms involved in the manufacturing and testing of semi-conductor materials, equipment, device/circuits manufacturing and OEM manufacturing with in-house IC manufacturing facilities.
Cost: $213.00
Frequency: Monthly
ISSN: 0038-111X
Founded in 1958
Mailing list available for rent

17408 **Solid Surface**
Cygnus Publishing
PO Box 803
Fort Atkinson, WI 53538-0803
920-000-1111
800-547-7377
Fax: 920-563-1699
E-Mail: paul.bowers@cygnuspub.com
Home Page: www.cygnusb2b.com
John French, CEO
Russ Lee, Editor
Paul Bowers, Group VP
Charlie Lillis, Content Licensing
Kathy Scott, Director of Public Relations
Solid surfaces link between fabricator, distributor, supplier, and manufacturer. It is dedicated to providing reliable and timely information, including updates on the latest fabrication trends and techniques, with a fresh perspective and a sense of humor.
Cost: $25.00
Circulation: 4,500
Founded in 1966

17409 **Springs Manufacturer Institute**
Spring Manufacturers Institute
2001 Midwest Rd
Suite 106
Oak Brook, IL 60523-1378
630-495-8588
Fax: 630-495-8595
E-Mail: info@smihq.org
Home Page: www.smihq.org
Lynne Carr, President
Rita Schauer, Editor
Kim Kostecki, Member Services Coordinator
Pashun McNulty, Financial Admin Coordinator
Russ Bryer, Secretary, Treasurer
Provides how-to and technical articles on inspection methods, design, finishes, manufacturing proccesses, materials and equipment, also contains financial and management articles on the interests of precision mechanical spring manufacturers.
130 Pages
Frequency: Quarterly
Circulation: 12,000
Printed in 4 colors on glossy stock

17410 **Supply Chain e-Business**
Keller International Publishing Corporation
150 Great Neck Rd
Suite 400
Great Neck, NY 11021-3309
516-829-9722
Fax: 516-829-9306
Home Page: www.supplychainbrain.com
Thomas A Foster, Editor-in-Chief
Russell W Goodman, Managing Editor
Jerry Keller, President
Mary Chavez, Director of Sales
Offers a thorough analysis of on-line solutions designed to help corporations achieve greater supply-chain visiblity and real-time connections with suppliers and customers
Frequency: Bi-Monthly
Circulation: 45M
ISSN: 1525-4887
Printed in 4 colors on glossy stock

17411 **Target**
Association for Manufacturing Excellence
380 W Palatine Road
Wheeling, IL 60090-5831
847-520-3282
Fax: 847-520-0163
E-Mail: info@ame.org
Home Page: www.ame.org
Robert W Hall, Editor-in-Chief
Dick Barton, Director of Advertising
Contains coverage on educational events, opinion columns, a networking section and more, reflecting manufacturing competitiveness, and improvement concepts and activities for the members of the Association for Manufacturing Excellence and interested academia.
Cost: $125.00
Frequency: Quarterly
Circulation: 5000
Founded in 1985

17412 **US Industries Today**
Postitive Publications
225 Madison Avenue
Morristown, NJ 07960
973-292-2600
Fax: 973-292-2696
Home Page: www.usitoday.com
Peter Mercer, Editor
Sabastian Fraser, CEO/President
Provides information on the latest developments across the whole range of the US manufacturing industry, covering stock market analysis, US business leaders, business profiles and industry sector reports, as well as new products and services.
Cost: $15.00
Circulation: 65000
Founded in 1998

Trade Shows

17413 **AES/EPA Conference/Exhibit: Environmental Control for Surface Finishing**
American Electroplaters and Surface Finishers Soc.
1155 Fifteenth Street, NW
Suite 500
Washington, DC 20005
202-457-8401
Fax: 407-281-6446
E-Mail: exhibit@aesf.org
Home Page: www.aesf.org
Kathy Shumacher, Show Manager
Dan Denston, Executive Director
John Flatley, Senior Advisor and NASF Liaison
One-hundred exhibitors of waste treatment, pollution control, surface finishing equipment and surfaces.
600 Attendees
Frequency: June

17414 **AESF SUR/FIN Annual Technical Conference and Exhibit of Surface Finishers**
American Electroplaters and Surface Finishers Soc.

1155 Fifteenth Street, NW
Suite 500
Washington, DC 20005

202-457-8401
Fax: 407-281-6446
E-Mail: exhibit@aesf.org
Home Page: www.aesf.org

Dan Denston, Executive Director
John Flatley, Senior Advisor and NASF Liaison

More than 300 suppliers to the industry will attend.
Frequency: June

17415 AESF Week - Society's Annual Winter Meeting
American Electroplaters and Surface Finishers Soc.
1155 Fifteenth Street, NW
Suite 500
Washington, DC 20005

202-457-8401
Fax: 407-281-6446
E-Mail: exhibit@aesf.org
Home Page: www.aesf.org

Dan Denston, Executive Director
John Flatley, Senior Advisor and NASF Liaison
Frequency: June

17416 AME Annual Conference
Association for Manufacturing Excellence
380 W Palatine Road
Suite 7
Wheeling, IL 60090-5863

847-520-3282
Fax: 847-520-0163
E-Mail: info@ame.org
Home Page: www.ame.org

Vivian Bartt, Manager
Dick Barton, Director of Advertising
Frequency: November
Founded in 1985

17417 AMSE International Manufacturing Science & Engineering Conference
American Society of Mechanical Engineers
Three Park Avenue
New York, NY 10016-5990

973-882-1170
800-843-2763
E-Mail: CustomerCare@asme.org
Home Page: www.asme.org

The MSEC highlights cutting edge manufacturing research in technical paper, poster and panel sessions.
3200 Attendees
Frequency: Annual/Fall

17418 ASM Heat Treating Society Conference & Exposition
ASM International
9639 Kinsman Road
Materials Park, OH 44073

440-385-5151
800-336-5152
Fax: 440-338-4634
E-Mail: pamela.kleinman@asminternational.org
Home Page: www.asminternational.org
Social Media: Facebook, Twitter, LinkedIn

Pamela Kleinma, Senior Manager, Events
Kellye Thomas, Exposition Account Manager
Jeane Deatherage, Administrator, Foundation Programs
Virginia Shirk, Foundation Executive Assistant
Conference and exhibits of heat treating equipment and supplies plus information of interest to metallurgists, manufacturing, research and design technical professionals. 300 exhibitors.
3500 Attendees
Frequency: September, Bi-Annual
Founded in 1974

17419 ASM Materials Science & Technology (MS&T)
ASM International
9639 Kinsman Road
Materials Park, OH 44073-0002

440-338-5151
800-336-5152
Fax: 440-338-4634
E-Mail: pamela.kleinman@asminternational.org
Home Page: www.asminternational.org
Social Media: Facebook, Twitter, LinkedIn

Pamela Kleinman, Senior Manager, Events
Kelly Thomas, Exposition Account Manager
Jeane Deatherage, Administrator, Foundation Programs
Virginia Shirk, Foundation Executive Assistant

Annual event focusing on testing, analysis, characterization and research of materials such as engineered materials, high performance metals, powdered metals, metal forming, surface modification, welding and joining. 350 exhibitors.
4,000 Attendees
Frequency: Annual/October
Founded in 2005

17420 Adhesive and Sealant Council Fall Convention
Adhesive & Sealant Council
7101 Wisconsin Avenue
Suite 990
Bethesda, MD 20814

301-986-9700
Fax: 301-986-9795
E-Mail: bob.willis@ascouncil.org
Home Page: www.ascouncil.org

Bob Willis, Senior Manager Conventions/Meetings
Frequency: October

17421 AeroMat Conference and Exposition
ASM International
9639 Kinsman Road
Materials Park, OH 44073-0002

440-385-5151
800-336-5152
Fax: 440-338-4634
E-Mail: kim.schaefer@asminternational.org
Home Page: www.asminternational.org
Social Media: Facebook, Twitter, LinkedIn

Kim Schaefer, Event Manager
Kelly Thomas, Exposition Account Manager
Jeane Deatherage, Administrator, Foundation Programs
Virginia Shirk, Foundation Executive Assistant

Conference for Aerospace Meterials Engineers, Structural Engineers and Designers. The annual event focuses on affordable structures and low-cost manufacturing, titanium alloy technology, advanced intermetallics and refractory metal alloys, materials and processes for space applications, aging systems, high strength steel, NDT evaluation, light alloy technology, welding and joining, and engineering technology. 150 exhibitors.
1500 Attendees
Frequency: Annual/June
Founded in 1984

17422 Annual Elevator Convention and Exposition
356 Morgan Avenue
PO Box 6507
Mobile, AL 36660

251-479-4514
800-730-5093
Fax: 251-479-7043
E-Mail: naec@mindspring.com
Home Page: www.elevator-world.com

Ricia S Hendrick, President/Publisher
Robert Caporale, Senior VP and Editor
Frequency: Annual

17423 Annual Lean Six Sigma Conference
American Society for Quality
600 N Plankinton Avenue
PO Box 3005
Milwaukee, WI 53201-3005

414-272-8575
800-248-1946
Fax: 414-272-1734
E-Mail: help@asq.org
Home Page: www.asq.org
Social Media: Facebook, Twitter, LinkedIn

Roberto M Saco, President
Paul E Borawski, Executive Director
Erica Gumieny, Sales
Fay Spano, Communications/Media Relations

An exclusive two-day briefing and networking event designed by and for the top practitioners in the Six Sigma community.
100M Members
Frequency: Annual/February
Founded in 1946

17424 Annual Meeting & Leadership Conference
Private Label Manufacturers Association (PLMA)
630 Third Avenue
New York, NY 10017

212-972-3131
Fax: 212-983-1382
E-Mail: info@plma.com
Home Page: www.plma.com

Brian Sharoff, President
Myra Rosen, VP
Tom Prendergast, Director, Research Services

Members look at key issues for the years ahead.
3200+ Members
Frequency: Annual
Founded in 1979

17425 Annual Quality Audit Conference
American Society for Quality
600 N Plankinton Avenue
PO Box 3005
Milwaukee, WI 53201-3005

414-272-8575
800-248-1946
Fax: 414-272-1734
E-Mail: help@asq.org
Home Page: www.asq.org
Social Media: Facebook, Twitter, LinkedIn

Roberto M Saco, President
Paul E Borawski, Executive Director
Erica Gumieny, Sales
Fay Spano, Communications/Media Relations

Topics of interest include: new innovating audit/process approaches, value added involvement, corporate expectations, corporate/social responsibility, auditing in the overall corporate scheme.
100M Members
Frequency: October
Founded in 1946

17426 Annual Service Quality Conference
American Society for Quality
600 N Plankinton Avenue
PO Box 3005
Milwaukee, WI 53201-3005

414-272-8575
800-248-1946
Fax: 414-272-1734
E-Mail: help@asq.org
Home Page: www.asq.org
Social Media: Facebook, Twitter, LinkedIn

Roberto M Saco, President
Paul E Borawski, Executive Director
Erica Gumieny, Sales
Fay Spano, Communications/Media Relations

The sessions we plan will help you to navigate through unpredictable consumer behavior and increasing competition to build a strong foundation for reaching superior levels of quality service.
100M Members
Frequency: September
Founded in 1946

17427 Annual World Conference on Quality and Improvement
American Society for Quality
600 N Plankinton Avenue
PO Box 3005
Milwaukee, WI 53201-3005

414-272-8575
800-248-1946
Fax: 414-272-1734
E-Mail: help@asq.org
Home Page: www.asq.org
Social Media: Facebook, Twitter, LinkedIn

Roberto M Saco, President
Paul E Borawski, Executive Director
Erica Gumieny, Sales
Fay Spano, Communications/Media Relations

Conference focuses on quality and improvement with more than 2,000 exhibits and attendees. Keynote speakers and sessions discuss quality tools, techniques and methodologies. Provides the opportunity for members to meet and network with colleagues in the industry.
100M Members
Frequency: May
Founded in 1946

17428 Association of Loudspeaker Mfg. & Acoustics (ALMA) Symposium
ALMA International
55 Littleton Road
13B
Ayer, MA 01432

978-772-6977
E-Mail: management@almainternational.org
Home Page: www.almainternational.org

Spiro Iraclianos, President, VP

Unlike other audio-related events, ALMA Symposia focuses exclusively on products, services and technical and business topics relevant to the loudspeaker industry. Invited speakers present technical papers to keep attendees abreast of the latest developments and expert panelists discuss the latest topics. Training programs are also offered. Exhibit hall features more than 30 industry professionals.
100 Members
Frequency: Annual
Founded in 1962

17429 Atlantic Design Engineering
Canon Communications
11444 W Olympic Boulevard
Suite 900
Los Angeles, CA 90064-1549

310-445-4200
Fax: 310-445-4299
Home Page: www.cancom.com/

Shannon Cleghorn, Customer & Media Coordinator
Erwin Laner, Promotional Manager

The Atlantic Design Engineering show serves the East Coast's design, process and manufacturing marketplace. Product classifications include Coatings & Finishes, composites, Computer Aided Design/Computer Aided Manufacturing, Electrical/Electronic, Electro Optical Components & Equipment, Engineered Safety Products, Engineering Management & Tools, Fasteners, Fluid Media, Fluid Power & Control and more. Held at the Jacob K. Javits Convention Center in New York, New York.
1319 Attendees
Frequency: June

17430 CleanRooms East
PennWell Conferences and Exhibitions
1421 S. Sheridan Road
Tulsa, OK 74112

918-835-3161
800-331-4463
Fax: 603-891-9200
E-Mail: andrear@pennwell.com
Home Page: www.pennwell.com

Andrea Rollins, Show Manager
Lisa Gowern, Registration Manager
Meg Villeure, Conference Manager

CleanRooms shows, the international forums exclusively serving the contamination control industry, couples exhibits with 100% technology-driver conference programs.
3000 Attendees
Frequency: March
Mailing list available for rent

17431 Close the Loop Technical Symposium
2001 Midwest Road
Suite 106
Oak Brook, IL 60523-1335

630-495-8588
Fax: 630-495-8595
E-Mail: info@smihq.org
Home Page: www.smihq.org

Russ Bryer, Secretary, Treasurer
Jim Kobrinetz, Technical Director
Christy Johnson, Manager

Symposium will highlight the latest technolgy and best practice solutions to difficult technical problems that are regularly experienced by the spring designer, spring user and manufacturing personel.

17432 Contract Packaging Association Annual Meeting
Contract Manufacturing & Packaging
1601 Bond Street
Suite 101
Naperville, IL 60563

630-544-5053
Fax: 630-544-5055
Home Page: www.contractpackaging.com

John Mazelin, President
John Riley, VP
Frequency: April

17433 Dollar Store Expo
Retail Dollar Store Association
11540 S Eastern Avenue
Suite 100
Henderson, NV 89052

702-893-9090
800-859-9247
Fax: 702-893-9227
E-Mail: info@bentleyintl.net
Home Page: www.dollarstoreexpo.com

Kristina Mullen, Show Manager
Wendy Witherspoon, Manager

Four-hundred and fifty booths for products that retail for a dollar or less. Wholesalers, distributors, manufacturers, importers and representatives for surplus, jewelry, hair and beauty, automotive, food items, household goods, gifts, toys, party supplies, seasonal and closeouts.
2,500 Attendees
Frequency: June
Founded in 2002

17434 Int'l Conference on Powder Injection Molding of Metals & Ceramics
Innovative Material Solutions
605 Severn Drive
State College, PA 16803

814-867-1140
Fax: 814-867-2813
E-Mail: info@imspowder.com
Frequency: March

17435 International Integrated Manufacturing Technology Trade Exhibition
Reed Exhibition Companies
383 Main Avenue
Norwalk, CT 06851

203-840-4800
Fax: 203-840-4801
E-Mail: inquiry@reedexpo.com
Home Page: www.reedexpo.com/app/homepage

Elizabeth Hitchcock, International Sales

Expo and conference dedicated to the products and technology needed by engineering operations and management to automate and integrate manufacturing.
Frequency: June

17436 International Manufacturing Technology Show
7901 Westpark Drive
Mc Lean, VA 22102-4206

703-893-2900
800-828-7469
Fax: 703-827-5250
E-Mail: peelman@AMTonline.org
Home Page: www.amtonline.org

Peter Eelman, VP Exhibitions
Michelle Edmonson, Exhibitions Operations Manager

Manufacturing equipment trade show.
85M Attendees
Frequency: Biennial
Founded in 1927

17437 International Symposium for Testing & Failure Analysis
ASM International
9639 Kinsman Road
Materials Park, OH 44073

440-338-5151
800-336-5152
Fax: 440-338-4634
E-Mail: kim.schaefer@asminternational.org
Home Page: www.asminternational.org
Social Media: Facebook, Twitter, LinkedIn

Kim Schaefer, Event Manager
Kelly Thomas, Exposition Account Manager
Jeane Deatherage, Administrator, Foundation Programs
Virginia Shirk, Foundation Executive Assistant

Annual event focusing on microelectronic and elcetronic device failure analysis, techniques, EOS/ESD testing and descretes aimed at failure analysis engineers and managers, technisians

and new failure analysis engineers. 200 exhibitors.
1100 Attendees
Frequency: Annual/November

17438 International Thermal Spray Conference & Exposition
ASM International
9639 Kinsman Road
Materials Park, OH 44073
440-338-5151
800-336-5152
Fax: 440-338-4634
E-Mail: natalie.nemec@asminternational.org
Home Page: www.asminternational.org
Social Media: Facebook, Twitter, LinkedIn
Natalie Neme, Event Manager
Kelly Thomas, Exposition Account Manager
Jeane Deatherage, Administrator, Foundation Programs
Virginia Shirk, Foundation Executive Assistant
Global annual event attracting professional interested in thermal spray technology focusing on advances in HVOF, plasma and detonation gun, flame spray and wire arc spray processes, performance of coatings, and future trends. 150 exhibitors.
1000 Attendees
Frequency: Annual/May

17439 Lean Management and Solutions Conference
Institute of Industrial Engineers
3577 Parkway Lane
Suite 200
Norcross, GA 30092
770-449-0460
800-494-0460
Fax: 770-441-3295
E-Mail: cs@iienet.org
Home Page: www.iienet.org
Elaine Fuerst, Marketing Director
The place to find the leaders in lean management and all the tools that you need for success.
300 Attendees
Frequency: September

17440 METALfab
532 Forest Parkway
Suite A
Forest Park, GA 30297-6137
404-363-4009
Fax: 404-366-1852
E-Mail: nommainfo@nomma.org
Home Page: www.nomma.org
Martha Pennington, Show Manager
Todd Daniel, Editor
Barbara Cook, Executive Director
Martha Pennington, Meetings Manager
Trade show sponsored by National Ornamental and Miscellaneous Metals Association.
1000 Attendees
Frequency: March

17441 Medical Design & Manufacturing Exhibition East/West
Canon Communications
11444 W Olympic Boulevard
Los Angeles, CA 15494
310-445-4200
Fax: 310-996-9499
Home Page: www.cancom.com
Shannon Cleghorn, Customer & Media Coordinator
Erwin Laner, Promotional Manager
Design, development, and manufacture of medical products, from high-volume, single-use disposables to next-generation diagnostic instruments and advanced imaging systems. Preview the latest advances in medical-grade materials, assembly components, electronics, machinery, software, systems, services, and more.
Frequency: May

17442 Medical Equipment Design & Technology Conference
Canon Communications
11444 W Olympic Boulevard
Los Angeles, CA 90064-1549
310-445-4200
Fax: 310-996-9499
Home Page: www.cancom.com
Shannon Cleghorn, Customer & Media Coordinator
Erwin Laner, Promotional Manager
Design, development, and manufacture of medical products, from high-volume, single-use disposables to next-generation diagnostic instruments and advanced imaging systems. Preview the latest advances in medical-grade materials, assembly components, electronics, machinery, software, systems, services and more.
Frequency: September

17443 Midwest Job Shop Show
Edward Publishing
16 Waterbury Road
Prospect, CT 06712-1215
203-758-4474
Fax: 203-758-4476
Home Page: www.jobshoptechnology.com
Jennifer Bryda, Production Manager
Christoper Davis, Manager
Gerald Schmidt, President
A source for forming, fabricating, shaping, and assemblies. The show is designed to attract the highest caliber engineers and buyers from product manufacturers. There will be 170 exhibitors and booths.
1500 Attendees

17444 National Manufacturing Week
Reed Exhibition Companies
383 Main Street
Norwalk, CT 06851
203-840-4800
Fax: 203-840-4801
E-Mail: inquiry@reedexpo.com
Home Page: www.reedexpo.com/app/homepage
Elizabeth Hitchcock, International Sales
The pre-eminent American forum for the display of industrial technology.
1.5M Attendees
Frequency: March

17445 National Plant Engineering and Facilities Management Show and Conference
Reed Exhibition Companies
383 Main Avenue
Norwalk, CT 06851
203-840-4800
Fax: 203-840-4801
E-Mail: inquiry@reedexpo.com
Home Page: www.reedexpo.com/app/homepage
Frequency: June

17446 National Quality Education Conference
American Society for Quality
600 N Plankinton Avenue
PO Box 3005
Milwaukee, WI 53201-3005
414-272-8575
800-248-1946
Fax: 414-272-1734
E-Mail: help@asq.org
Home Page: www.asq.org
Social Media: Facebook, Twitter, LinkedIn
Roberto M Saco, President
Paul E Borawski, Executive Director
Erica Gumieny, Sales
Fay Spano, Communications/Media Relations
Provides teachers, administrators, and support personnel opportunities to examine continuous improvement principles used in education. It provides resources and best practices to help you address requirements of No Child Left Behind, while helping you increase student achievement and improve overall performance.
100M Members
Frequency: November
Founded in 1946

17447 Pacific Design Engineering
Canon Communications
11444 W Olympic Boulevard
Los Angeles, CA 90064
310-445-4200
Fax: 310-996-9499
Home Page: www.cancom.com
Shannon Cleghorn, Customer & Media Coordinator
Erwin Laner, Promotional Manager
Serves the West Coast's dynamic design, process, and manufacturing marketplace. Product classifications include: Coatings and Finishes, Composites, Computer Aided Design/Computer Aided Manufacturing, Electrical/Electronic, Electrc Optical Compnents and Equipment, Engineered Safety Products, Engineering Management and Tools, Fasteners, Fluid Media, Fluid Power and Control.
Frequency: January

17448 Packaging & All That Jazz Trade Show
Retail Packaging Association
PO Box 43517
Cincinnati, OH 45243
513-527-4333
Fax: 513-527-4999
E-Mail: info@retailpackaging.org
Home Page: www.retailpackaging.org
Joel Zaas, President
Provides exhibitors and attendees opportunities to enjoy the great city of New Orleans and network and conduct business, all without losing valuable days in the office.
600 Attendees
Frequency: Annual

17449 Simulation Solutions Conference
Institute of Industrial Engineers
3577 Parkway Lane
Suite 200
Norcross, GA 30092
770-449-0460
800-494-0460
Fax: 770-441-3295
E-Mail: cs@iienet.org
Home Page: www.iienet.org
Elaine Fuerst, Marketing Director
Simulation techniques. Tools and software used in a wide range of industries and applications.
250 Attendees

17450 South-Tec Machine Tool and Manufacturing Show
Society of Manufacturing Engineers
1 SME Drive
#930
Dearborn, MI 48121
313-425-3000
800-733-4763
Fax: 313-425-3400

E-Mail: service@sme.org
Home Page: www.sme.org

Mark Tomlinson, Executive Director
Greg Sheremet, Publisher
70M Attendees
Founded in 1932

17451 **Southern Job Shop Show**
Edward Publishing
16 Waterbury Road
Prospect, CT 06712-1215

203-758-4474
Fax: 860-768-4475
Home Page: www.jobshoptechnology.com

Mark W Shortt, Editor
Gerald Schmidt, President
Christopher Davis, Manager

The show is designed to attract the highest caliber engineers and buyers from your major DEM product manufacturers.
1500 Attendees
Frequency: March

17452 **Spring World Expo**
PO Box 1144
Highland Park, IL 60035

847-433-1335
Fax: 847-433-3769
E-Mail: info@casmi-springworld.org
Home Page: www.springworld.org

Gerald H Reese, Executive Director
Tracy Hodge, Director
4500 Attendees
Frequency: October

Directories & Databases

17453 **Agricultural & Industrial Manufacturers Membership Directory**
Agricultural & Industrial Manufacturers Rep Assn
7500 Flying Cloud Drive
Suite 900
Eden Prairie, MN 55344

952-253-6230
866-759-2467
Fax: 952-835-4774
Home Page: www.aimrareps.org

Michael J Kowalczyk, President
Ronald R Reed, VP
Cost: $25.00
Frequency: Annual October

17454 **Directory of Manufacturing Research Centers**
Manufacturing Technology Information
10 W 35th Street
Chicago, IL 60616-3717

312-431-1442
800-421-0586
Fax: 312-567-4736
E-Mail: info@iitri.org
Home Page: www.iitri.org

Paula Marggraf, Editor
Cost: $75.00
Frequency: Irregular

17455 **Directory of Waste Equipment Manufacturers and Distributors**
WASTEC Equipment Technology Association
4301 Connecticut Ave NW
Suite 300
Washington, DC 20008-2304

202-966-4701
Fax: 202-966-4818
Home Page: www.wastec.org

Christine Hutcherson, Director Member Services
Bruce Parker, President
Gary T Satterfield, Executive VP
Sandra Price, Director Member Services

About 250 member manufacturers of waste handling, collection and processing equipment.
Cost: $5.00
Frequency: Annual

17456 **Encyclopedia of American Industries**
Grey House Publishing
4919 Route 22
PO Box 56
Amenia, NY 12501

518-789-8700
800-562-2139
Fax: 845-373-6390
E-Mail: books@greyhouse.com
Home Page: www.greyhouse.com
Social Media: Facebook, Twitter

Leslie Mackenzie, Publisher
Richard Gottlieb, Editor

A two volume set, Volume I provides separate coverage of nearly 500 manufacturing industries, while Volume II presents nearly 600 essays covering the vast array of services and other non-manufacturing industries in the United States. Combined, these two volumes provide individual essays on every industry recognized by the U.S. Standard Industrial Classification (SIC) system.
Cost: $650.00
3000 Pages
ISBN: 1-592372-44-9
Founded in 1981

17457 **Manufacturers Representatives of America: Yearbook and Directory of Members**
Manufacturers Representatives of America
PO Box 150229
Arlington, TX 76015-6229

817-465-5511
Fax: 817-561-7275

WR Bess, Executive Director

Several hundred independent manufacturers' representatives in paper, plastic, packaging and sanitary supplies.
Cost: $250.00
Frequency: Annual Fall
Circulation: 1,200

17458 **Manufacturing & Distribution USA**
Gale/Cengage Learning
27500 Drake Road
Farmington Hills, MI 48331-3535

248-699-4253
800-877-4253
Fax: 877-363-4253
E-Mail: gale.galeord@cengage.com
Home Page: www.gale.cengage.com
Social Media: Facebook, Twitter, Youtube

Patrick C Sommers, President

This new edition also features enhanced coverage of input-output data by industrial sector when available as well as classifications of leading public and private corporations in each industry.
ISBN: 1-414408-67-6

17459 **Rauch Guide to the US Rubber Industry**
Grey House Publishing
4919 Route 22
PO Box 56
Amenia, NY 12501

518-789-8700
800-562-2139
Fax: 845-373-6390
E-Mail: books@greyhouse.com
Home Page: www.greyhouse.com
Social Media: Facebook, Twitter

Leslie Mackenzie, Publisher
Richard Gottlieb, Editor

Provides current market information and trends; industry economics and government regulations; company share data for each of the leading product categories; technology and raw material information; industry sources of further data; and unique profiles of 847 rubber manufacturers, a section which includes all known companies with rubber sales at or over $1 million annually.
Cost: $595.00
500 Pages
ISBN: 1-592371-30-2
Founded in 1981

17460 **Small Business Inovation Research**
1000 Independence Avenue SW
Washington, DC 20585-1207

202-571-1300
Home Page: www.er.doe.gov/

Lawrence Small, CEO
Frequency: Annual

17461 **Sound and Vibration: Buyer's Guide Issue**
Acoustical Publications
PO Box 40416
27101 E. Oviatt Road
Bay Village, OH 44140-0416

440-835-0101
Fax: 440-835-9303
E-Mail: sv@mindspring.com
Home Page: www.sandv.com.home/htm

Jack Mowry, Editor and Publisher
Scott J Lothes, Assistant Editor/Webmaster

This directory offers a list of manufacturers of products for noise and vibration control.
Frequency: Monthly
Circulation: 19,000
ISBN: 0-038181-09-9
Mailing list available for rent: 21M names
Printed in 4 colors on glossy stock

17462 **ThomasNet**
Thomas Publishing Company, LLC
User Services Department
5 Penn Plaza
New York, NY 10001

212-695-0500
800-699-9822
Fax: 212-290-7362
E-Mail: contact@thomaspublishing.com
Home Page: www.thomasnet.com
Social Media: Facebook, Twitter, LinkedIn

Carl Holst-Knudsen, President
Robert Anderson, VP, Planning
Mitchell Peipert, VP, Finance
Ivy Molofsky, VP, Human Resources

A way to reach qualified businesses that list their company information on ThomasNet.com. Detailed profiles promote their products, services, capabilities and brands carried. The ThomasNet.com web site is the most up-to-date compilation of 650,000 North American manufacturers, distributors, and service companies in 67,000 industrial categories.
Founded in 1898

17463 **Who Audits America**
Data Financial Press

PO Box 668
Menlo Park, CA 94026-0668

650-321-4553
Fax: 650-321-4427

A who's who directory of services and supplies.
Cost: $133.00
600 Pages
Frequency: SemiAnnual

Industry Web Sites

17464 **http://gold.greyhouse.com**
G.O.L.D Grey House OnLine Databases
Grey House Publishing's online database platform, GOLD, offers Quick Search, Keyword Search and Expert Search for most business sectors including a wide variety of manufacturing markets. The GOLD platform makes finding the information you need quick and easy - whether you're a novice searcher or an experienced database user. All of Grey House's directory products are available for subscription on the GOLD platform.

17465 **www.abrasiveengineering.com**
Abrasive Grain Association
Members manufacture natural and artificial grains used in grinding wheels, coated abrasives etc.

17466 **www.aesf.org**
American Electroplaters and Surface Finishers Soc.
AESF is an international society that advances the science of surface finishing to benefit industry and society through education information and social involvement, as well as those who provide services, supplies and support to the industry.

17467 **www.agma.org**
American Gear Manufacturers Association
Manufacturers of gears and geared speed changers.

17468 **www.ahma.org**
American Hardware Manufacturers Association
Over 280 manufacturer representatives in the hardware industry.

17469 **www.amba.org**
American Mold Builders Association
Promotes the development, welfare, and expansion of businesses engaged in the manufacture of molds and related tooling.

17470 **www.amtda.org**
American Machine Tool Distributors Association
For distributors of manufacturing technology.

17471 **www.ararental.org**
American Rental Association
For rental business owners and equipment suppliers.

17472 **www.arcat.com**
National Association of Relay Manufacturers
NARM is a trade association for the electro-mechanical relay and associated switching devices industry. An affiliate of Electronic Industries Alliance.

17473 **www.asphaltinstitute.org**
Asphalt Institute
Conducts education, research, and engineering services related to asphalt products; conducts seminars and sells publications and videos on asphalt technology.

17474 **www.awci.com/**
American Watchmakers-Clockmakers Institute
Examines and certifies master watchmakers and clockmakers. Maintains a placement service. Conducts home study courses.

17475 **www.awci.org**
Association of the Wall and Ceiling Industries
Offers information on contractors, manufacturers, suppliers and organizations affiliated with the interior design, building and contracting community. Strives to provide services and undertake activities that enhance the members ability to operate a successful business.

17476 **www.bia.org**
Brick Industry Association
Supports the industry by rendering technical assistance to architects and designers, by providing marketing assistance to the industry, by monitoring and positively influencing governmental actions, by working to assure the long term availability of bricklayers and by providing other member services as appropriate.

17477 **www.cancentral.com**
Can Manufacturers Institute
Industry, environmental and consumer information.

17478 **www.carpet ushion.org**
Carpet Cushion Council
Encourages distribution and use of seperate carpet cushions. Works with regulatory agencies at the national, state and local levels.

17479 **www.cl2.com**
Chlorine Institute
Promotes safe handling of chlorine and caustic materials and sponsors awards.

17480 **www.cmit.edi.gatech.edu/**
Center for Manufacturing Information
Provides a non-instrusive environment in which manufacturers can objectively evaluate and compare the latest computer-based technologies.

17481 **www.cottonseed.com**
National Cottonseed Products Association
Services include the administration of trading rules and standards, a research program, information service center and product promotion of cotton seed food and feed products.

17482 **www.cti.org**
Cooling Technology
Seeks to improve technology, design and performance of water conservation apparatus. Provides inspection services and conducts research.

17483 **www.divbusiness.com**
Diversified Business Communications
Provides management services for associations and organizations seeking to expand domestically and overseas, as well as direct mail, internet, telemarketing campaigns and market research.

17484 **www.fluidcontrolsinstitute.org**
Fluid Controls Institute
Manufacturers of devices for fluid control, such as temperature and pressure regulators, strainers, gauges, control valves, solenoid valves, steam traps, etc.

17485 **www.fluidsealing.com**
Fluid Sealing Association
An international association of manufacturers of mechanical packings, sealing devices, gaskets, rubber expansion joints and allied products.

17486 **www.graphicsPor.org**
Graphics Products Association
Independent manufacturers and suppliers of paperboard packaging. Purposes are to futher development, use and sale of members product. Compiles statistics and bestows awards.

17487 **www.greyhouse.com**
Grey House Publishing
Authoritative reference directories for most business sectors including a wide variedy of manufacturing markets. Users can search the online databases with varied search criteria allowing for custom searches by product category, geographic area, sales volume, keyword, subject and more. Full Grey House catalog and online ordering also available.

17488 **www.housewares.org**
National Housewares Manufacturers Association
Links to other associations.

17489 **www.iccsafe.org/**
International Code Council
Nonprofit membership association with more than 16,000 members who span the building community, from code enforcement officials to materials manufacturers. Dedicated to preserving the public health, safety and welfare in the built environment through the effective use and enforcement of model codes.

17490 **www.icea.net**
Insulated Cable Engineers Association
Professional organization dedicated to developing cable standards for the electric power, control and telecommunications industries. Ensures safe, economical and efficient cable systems utilizing proven state-of-the-art materials and concepts. ICEA documents are of interest to cable manufacturers, architects and engineers, utility and manufacturing plant personnel, telecommunication engineers, consultants and OEMs.

17491 **www.ifai.com**
Industrial Fabrics Association International
Provides many products, services and programs to industry members.

17492 **www.ilma.org**
Independent Lubricant Manufacturers Association
Independent blenders and compounders of lubricants.

17493 **www.iopp.org**
Institute of Packaging Professionals
Association for packing professionals.

17494 **www.ipc.org**
IPC-Association Connecting Electronics Industries
Works to develop standards in circuit board assembly equipment. Brings together all players in the electronic interconnection industry, including designers, board manufacturers, assembly companies, suppliers and original equipment manufacturers. Offers workshops, conferences, meetings and online communications.

17495 **www.isri.org**
Institute of Scrap Recycling Industries

Members include processors, brokers and consumers of scrap metal, rubber, paper, textiles, plastics and glass.

17496 www.marinecanvas.com
Marine Fabricators Association
Firms and individuals engaged in the design, construction, and installation of marine fabric products. Provides certification and product standards.

17497 www.mechanical.com
Mechanical.Com
Manufacturing industry database.

17498 www.mep.nist.gov
Manufacturing Extension Partnership
A nationwide network of more thatn 70 not-for-profit centers whose sole purpose is to provide small and medium-sized manufacturers with the help they need to succeed.

17499 www.mfgworld.com/index.html
Manufacturing World Online
Manufacturing news, software, industry reports and links.

17500 www.mhia.org/psc/PSC_Products_Racks.cfm
Rack Manufacturers Institute
Makers of steel industrial storage racks.

17501 www.mt-online.com
Applied Technology Publications
MT-online.com is the premier source of capacity assurance and best practice solutions for manufacturing, process and service operations worldwide. Online home of Maintenance Technology magazie, the dynamic MT-online.com portal serves the critical technical, business and professional-development needs of engineers, managers and technicians from across all industrial, institutional and commercial sectors.

17502 www.naima.org
North American Insulation Manufacturers Assn

17503 www.nam.org
National Association of Manufacturers
Represents industry's views on national and international problems to government.

17504 www.naumd.com
North American Assoc. of Uniform Manufacturers
Promotes interests of manufacturers and distributors of uniforms and career wear.

17505 www.ncspa.org
National Corrugated Steel Pipe Association
NCSPA seeks to promote sound public policy relating to the use of corrugated steel drainage structures in private and public construction.

17506 www.nei.org
Nuclear Energy Institute
Members are of utilities, manufacturers of electrical generating equipment, researchers, architects, engineers, labor unions, and others interested in the generation of electricity by nuclear power.

17507 www.nomma.org
National Ornamental and Miscellaneous Metals
Association

Publishes the Ornamental and Miscellaneous Metals Fabricator magazine. Holds annual convention and trade show (METALfab). Membership dues: $275 fabricators, $250 local supplier, $325 regional supplier, $425 nationwide supplier.

17508 www.nwpca.org
National Wooden Pallet & Container Association
Represents manufacturers, recyclers and distributors of pallets, containers and reels.

17509 www.p3-ny.org/
Women in Production
Promotes the interests of women in the production profession.

17510 www.patmi.org
Powder Actuated Tool Manufacturers Institute
Represents manufacturers of construction tools used to fasten to and into steel and concrete.

17511 www.powertoolinstitute.com
Power Tool Institute
Trade association representing manufacturers of power tools.

17512 www.reman.org
Remanufacturing Institute International
A coalition of associations and companies in the entire manufacturing industry. There are over 73,000 companies in this industry. Our goal is to unite them into a powerful organization.

17513 www.sawingassociation.com/
North American Sawing Association

17514 www.smma.org
SMMA: Small Motors & Motion Association
Manufacturing trade association. Members include electric motor and motion control companies, as well as suppliers, users, and associated businesses such as consultants, universities and distributors.

17515 www.steeltubeinstitute.org
Steel Tube Institute of North America
Members produce steel tubes and pipes from carbon, stainless or alloy steel for applications ranging from large structural tubing to small redrawn tubing.

17516 www.sunglassassociation.com
Sunglass Association of America
A nonprofit trade association of manufacturers and import-wholesale sunglasses, sunglass parts, components, materials, and reading glasses.

17517 www.thomasnet.com/index.html
Thomas Register of American Manufacturers
Industrial buying guide of US and Canadian manufacturers.

17518 www.tileusa.com
Tile Council of America
Manufacturers and suppliers of ceramic wall and floor tiles.

17519 www.tpatube.org
Tube & Pipe Association International
TPA is an educational technology association serving the metal tube and pipe producing and fabricating industries.

17520 www.ttmanet.org
Truck Trailer Manufacturers Association
News of interest to trailer manufacturers and suppliers.

17521 www.vending.org
National Automatic Merchandising Association
For makers and operators of automatic vending equipment.

17522 www.westernroofing.net/
Roof Tile Institute
Manufacturers of clay and concrete roof tiles. Emphasis is on technical issues and codes that involve tile. Has annual budget of approximately $300,000 a year. Publications available to members.

Associations

17523 Academy of Marketing Science
PO Box 248012
Coral Gables, FL 33124-8012
305-284-6673
Fax: 305-284-3762
Home Page: www.ams-web.org
Dr. Harold W Berkman, Director
Sally Sultan, Coordinator
Fosters education professional standards in marketing science. Sponsers the AMS Foundation which provides grants for the advancement of teaching and research.
1500 Members
Founded in 1971

17524 American Association of Family & Consumer Sciences
400 N Columbus Street
Suite 202
Alexandria, VA 22314-2264
703-706-4600
800-424-8080
Fax: 703-706-4663
E-Mail: store@aafcs.org
Home Page: www.aafcs.org
Social Media: Facebook, Twitter, LinkedIn, Flickr, Pintrest
Peggy Wild, CFCS, President
Carolyn Jackson, CFCS, Executive Director
Gwynn Mason, Director of Communications
Beverly Card, CFCS, President-Elect
Victoria Marie Gribschaw, S.C.,, Treasurer
An association dedicated to Family & Consumer Sciences professionals. AAFCS strives to improve the quality and standards of individual and family life by providing educational programs, influencing public policy, and through communication.
10000 Members

17525 American Chamber of Commerce Executives
1330 Braddock Place
Suite 300
Alexandria, VA 22314
703-998-0072
Fax: 888-577-9883
E-Mail: webmaster@acce.org
Home Page: www.acce.org
Social Media: Facebook, Twitter, LinkedIn
Betty Nokes, Chairman of the Board
Mick Fleming, President
Tamara Philbin, COO
Chris Mead, Senior VP, Members
Jacqui Cook, Chief Financial Officer
1300+ Members
Founded in 1914

17526 American Marketing Association
American Marketing Association
311 S Wacker Dr # 5800
Suite 5800
Chicago, IL 60606-6629
312-542-9000
800-262-1150
Fax: 312-542-9001
Home Page: www.themarketingfoundation.org
Social Media: Facebook, Twitter, LinkedIn, Youtube, amaconnect
Jerome D. Williams, Chairperson
Dennis L. Dunlap, Chief Executive Officer
Roger A. Kerin, Vice Chairperson
Donald R. Lehmann, Vice Chairperson
William Cron, Treasurer
A professional association for individuals and organizations involved in the practice, teaching and study of marketing worldwide.
40000 Members
Founded in 1992
Mailing list available for rent

17527 Association for Innovative Marketing
34 Summit Avenue
Sharon, MA 02067-2149
508-668-2575
Facilitates sharing of innovative ideas; bestows awards, maintains library and speaker bureau.
Founded in 1989

17528 Association for Postal Commerce
1800 Diagonal Road
Suite 320
Alexandria, VA 22314-2862
703-524-0096
Fax: 703-997-2414
Home Page: www.postcom.org
Gene Del Polito, President
National organization representing those who use, or who support, the use of mail as a medium for communication and commerce. Publishes a weekly newsletter covering postal policy and operational issues.
231 Members
Founded in 1947

17529 Association of Marketing Service Providers
Mailing & Fulfillment Service Association
1800 Diagonal Road
Suite 320
Alexandria, VA 22314-2806
703-836-9200
Fax: 703-548-8204
E-Mail: mfsa-mail@mfsanet.org
Home Page: www.amsp.org
Social Media: Facebook, Twitter, LinkedIn, Youtube, RSS, Vimeo
Ken Garner, President/CEO
Leo Raymond, Vice President
Michelle Raymond, Director of Marketing/Communication
Patty Dumas, Director of Accounting
Tyler T. Keeney, Director of Member Satisfaction
The national trade association for the mailing and fulfillment services industry.
Founded in 1920
Mailing list available for rent

17530 Association of Marketing and Communication Professionals
127 Pittsburgh St.
Dallas, TX 75207
214-377-3524
Fax: 214-377-3548
E-Mail: info@amcpros.com
Home Page: amcpros.com
Social Media: Facebook, LinkedIn, YouTube, Google+, RSS
Founded in 1995

17531 Association of Sale Marketing Companies
1010 Wisconsin Avenue NW
Suite 900
Washington, DC 20007
202-337-9351
Fax: 202-337-4508
E-Mail: info@asmc.org
Home Page: www.asmc.org
Mark Baum, President/CEO
Karen Connell, Contact
Provides referral service and other methods of assistance in locating sales and marketing companies.
250 Members
Founded in 1995

17532 Biomedical Marketing Association
10293 N Meridian Street
Suite 175
Indianapolis, IN 46290
317-816-1640
800-278-7886
Fax: 317-816-1633
E-Mail: info@bmaonline.org
Home Page: www.bmaonline.org
Michael L Boner, President
Builds diagnostic industry leadership by providing market education, professional development and a forum for fellowship and the exchange of ideas.

17533 Brand Activation Association
650 First Avenue
Suite 2-SW
New York, NY 10016-3207
212-420-1100
Fax: 212-533-7622
E-Mail: pma@pmalink.org
Home Page: www.baalink.org/
Bonnie J Carlson, President
Noelle Boddewyn, Executive Assistant
Mike Kaufman, VP of Marketing
Marybeth Petescia, Marketing Manager
Christine Goonan, Director of Membership
Mission is to encourage the highest standards of excellence in promotion marketing. Represents member interests and promotes better understanding promotion in the marketing mix.
700 Members
Founded in 1911

17534 Business Marketing Association
1833 Centre Point Cir
Suite 123
Naperville, IL 60563-4848
630-544-5054
Fax: 630-544-5055
E-Mail: info@marketing.org
Home Page: www.marketing.org
Social Media: Facebook, Twitter, LinkedIn
Katherine Button Bell, Chairman
Stephen Liguori, Vice Chair
George Stenitzer, VP, Thought Leadership
Chris Schermer, VP, Marketing
Bob Felsenthal, VP, Membership
The Business Marketing Association/BMA, a preeminent service organization for professionals, provides expertise in business-to-business marketing and communications. The BMA offers an information-packed Website, online skills-building, marketing certification programs, and industry surveys and papers. In addition, members have the opportunity to interact with peers at seminars, chapter training programs and the BMA Annual Conference.
Founded in 1922

17535 Business Marketing Association: Atlanta
2801 Buford Highway
Druid Chase Suite 375
Atlanta, GA 30329
404-641-9417
800-664-4262
Fax: 312-822-0054
E-Mail: info@bmaatlanta.com
Home Page: www.bmaatlanta.com
Social Media: Facebook, Twitter, LinkedIn, Youtube
Martine Hunter, President
Rory Carlton, Treasurer

Eduardo Esparza, Co-Chair of Marketing
Mark Potter, Membership Chairperson
Nancy Bistritz, Public Relations

The Atlanta chapter of the BMA includes marketing executives from a variety of industries and backgrounds including research, advertising, promotions, events, Web development, printing and more. The BMA offers an information-packed Website, online skills-building, marketing certification programs, and industry surveys and papers. In addition, members have the opportunity to interact with peers at seminars, participate in chapter training programs and the BMA Annual Conference.
Founded in 1922

17536 Business Marketing Association: Boston
246 Hampshire Street
Cambridge, MA 02130

617-418-4000
800-664-4262
Fax: 312-822-0054
E-Mail: info@thebmaboston.com
Home Page: www.thebmaboston.com/

Michael Lewis, President
Will Robinson, VP Public Relations
Matthew Mamet, VP Internet Marketing
Larry Perreault, VP Finance
Chris Perkett, VP Programming

BMA Boston helps members improve their ability to manage business-to-business marketing and communications for greater productivity and profitability by providing unique access to information, ideas, and the experience of peers. The BMA offers an information-packed Website, online skills-building, marketing certification programs, and industry surveys and papers. In addition, members have the opportunity to interact with peers at seminars, chapter training programs and the BMA Annual Conference.

17537 Business Marketing Association: Houston
PO Box 710350
Houston, TX 77271-0350

713-723-1325
Fax: 713-723-1326
E-Mail: info@bmahouston.com
Home Page: www.bmahouston.org
Social Media: Facebook, Twitter, LinkedIn, Youtube

Diana Salerno, President
Linda Ivon, Executive Director
Megan Coffing, Vice President
Bob Wallace, Treasurer

Dedicated to serving the needs of business to business Associations worldwide.
Founded in 1922

17538 Business Marketing Association: Hudson Valley
304 Wall Street
Kingston, NY 12401

845-340-4708
800-664-4262
E-Mail: alviankamaly@gmail.com
Home Page: www.bma-hv.org

Bud Clarke, President
Joan Giewat, First Vice President
June Bisel, Second Vice President
Rebecca D Jones, Treasurer
John Bassler, Secretary

Offers ways for its members to expand their business expertise and grow professionally.

17539 Business Marketing Association: Indy
8650 Commerce Park Place
Indianapolis, IN 46268

800-664-4262
Fax: 317-285-2068
E-Mail: information@bmaindy.org
Home Page: www.bmaindy.org

John Faust, President
Christine Johnston, Secretary
Judy Knafel, Treasurer

To promote the quality and effectiveness of Indiana-developed business-to-business marketing communications through the continuous learning of its members.

17540 Cable & Telecommunications Association for Marketing
120 Waterfront Street, Suite 200
National Harbor, MD 20745

301-485-8900
Fax: 301-560-4964
E-Mail: info@ctam.com
Home Page: www.ctam.com
Social Media: Facebook, Twitter, LinkedIn, Youtube

David Juliano, Chair
Char Beales, President and CEO
Angie Britt, Vice President of Advanced Products
Jonathan Hargis, Vice Chair
David Preschlack, Secretary / Treasurer

CTAM is dedicated to the discipline and development of consumer marketing excellence in cable television, new media and telecommunications services.
5500 Members
Founded in 1976

17541 Communications Marketing Association
PO Box 5680
Lago Vista, TX 78645

512-656-7747
Home Page: www.cma-cmc.org

Rex Reed, President
Larry Weber, Vice President
Karen Hollingsworth, Executive Director
Tony Fulton, Treasurer
Larry Seige, Secretary

17542 Communications Roundtable
1250 24th Street NW
Suite 250
Washington, DC 20037

202-755-5180
Fax: 202-466-0544
Home Page: www.roundtable.org

Michael Reichgut, Chairman
Shawn Dolley, CEO

Association of more than 20 public relations, marketing, graphics, advertising, training and other communications organizations with more than 12,000 professional members. The goals include furthering professionalism, cooperation between member organizations, career and employment support, and employer assistance.

17543 Construction Marketing Association
1220 Iroquois Ave.
Ste. #210
Naperville, IL 60563

630-868-5061
Home Page: www.constructionmarketingassociation.org
Social Media: Facebook, Twitter, LinkedIn, YouTube, Pinterest, Google+

Neil M. Brown, Chair/ Founder
Kevin Enke, Board Member, Rick
Kean O'Brien, Board Member
Deborah Hodges, Board Member
Founded in 2009

17544 Construction Marketing Research Council C/O CMPA
4625 South Wendler Drive
Suite 111
Tempe, AZ 85282

602-431-1441
Fax: 602-431-0637
E-Mail: info@c-m-r-c.com
Home Page: www.c-m-r-c.com/

Craig Schulz, President
Don Johnson, Director at Large
Jim McMahon, Treasurer

Members are professionals in the construction products industry with responsiblities for their firms' corporate strategic planning and the conduct of marketing research activities. Membership is restricted to the highest level marketing research or planning professional within a company.
25 Members
Founded in 1992

17545 Council for Marketing and Opinion
110 National Drive
2nd Floor
Glastonbury, CT 06033

860-657-1881
Fax: 330-645-6750
E-Mail: information@cmor.org
Home Page: www.cmor.org

Donna Gillin, Director of Operations

A non-profit organization which works on behalf of the survery research industry to improve respondent cooperation in research, and to promote positive legislation and prevent restrictive legislation which could impact the survey research industry.
150+ Members
Founded in 1992

17546 Data-Driven Marketing
Direct Marketing Association
1120 Avenue of the Americas
New York, NY 10036-6700

203-358-3702
E-Mail: ed_berkowitz@primediabusiness.com
Home Page: thedma.org

Ed Berkowitz, Sales Director

Offers strategies and tactics for getting your message to the right consumers.

17547 Destination Marketing Association International
2025 M Street NW
Suite 500
Washington, DC 20036

202-296-7888
Fax: 202-296-7889
E-Mail: info@destinationmarketing.org
Home Page: www.destinationmarketing.org
Social Media: Facebook, Twitter, Google+

Cleo Battle,CDME, Chair
Gary Sherwin, CDME, Secretary/ Treasurer
Bob Lander, Chair Elect
Jerard Bachar, CDME, Board Member
Kevin Kane, Board Member

17548 Direct Marketing Association
1120 Avenue of the Americas
New York, NY 10036-6700

212-768-7277
Fax: 212-302-6714
E-Mail: customerservice@the-dma.org

Home Page: www.the-dma.org
Social Media: Facebook, Twitter, LinkedIn

Monfradi Dunn, Chairman
Arjan Dijk, Vice Chairman
Linda A. Woolley, J.D., CEO & President, Direct Marketing
Thomas J. Benton, Chief Operating Officer
Jerry Cerasale, J.D., Senior Vice President

The leading global trade association of businesses and nonprofit organizations using and supporting multichannel direct marketing tools and techniques. DMA advocates standards for responsible marketing, promotes relevance as the key to reaching consumers with desirable offers, and provides cutting edge research, education and networking opportunities to improve results throughout the end to end direct marketing process.
3100 Members
Founded in 1917

17549 Distributive Education Clubs of America
1908 Association Dr # A
Reston, VA 20191-1594

703-860-5000
Fax: 703-860-4013
E-Mail: info@deca.org
Home Page: www.deca.org
Social Media: Facebook, Twitter, LinkedIn, Youtube, RSS

Jim Brock, President
Edward Davis, Executive Director
Lynore Levenhagen, Secretary
Mary Peres, Treasurer

To enhance the co-curricular education of students with interest in marketing, management, and entrprenuership. Helps students to develop skills and competence for marketing careers, to build self-esteem, to experience leadership and to practice community service.

17550 Diving Equipment & Marketing Association

800-862-DIVE
Home Page: www.dema.org
Social Media: Facebook, Twitter

Stephen Ashmore, President & Director
William Cline, Director
Jenny Collister, Director
Scott Daley, Director
Stuart Cove, Director
1300 Members

17551 EMarketing Association
4259 Old Post Road
Charlestown, RI 02813

401-315-2194
800-496-2950
Fax: 408-884-2461
E-Mail: service@emarketingassociation.com
Home Page: www.emarketingassociation.com
Social Media: Facebook, Twitter, LinkedIn

An international association of emarketing professionals. Members include governments, professionals and students involved with the emarketing arena. The eMA provides marketing resources, services, research, certifications, educational programs and events to its members and the marketing community.
2500 Members
Founded in 1997

17552 Electronic Retailing Association
607 14th Street, NW
Suite 530
Washington, DC 20005

703-841-1751
800-987-6462
Fax: 425-977-1036
E-Mail: webadmin@retailing.org
Home Page: www.retailing.org
Social Media: Facebook, Twitter, LinkedIn, Youtube.Flickr

Elliott Segal, Chairman of the Board
Julie Coons, President & CEO
Kevin Kelly, Chief Financial Officer
Bill McClellan, Vice President, Government Affairs
Dave Martin, Vice President, Marketing

The trade association that represents the leaders of direct response: members who maximize revenues through electronic retailing on television, online and on radio. ERA strives to protect the regulatory and legislative climate of direct response while ensuring a favorable landscape that enhances e-retailers' ability to bring quality products and services to the consumer.

17553 Entertainment Resource & Marketing Association
2315 28th Street
Suite 204
Santa Monica, CA 90405

310-985-9029
E-Mail: Tami@erma.org
Home Page: http://erma.org/

Michael Schrager, President
Amy Ferguson, Vice President
Eric Dahlquist, Treasurer
Nikki David, Secretary
Tami Cooper, Ethics Committee

17554 Foodservice Sales & Marketing Association
1810-J York Road #384
Lutherville, MD 21093

410-715-4084
800-617-1170
Fax: 888-668-7496
E-Mail: info@fsmaonline.com
Home Page: www.fsmaonline.com
Social Media: Facebook, Twitter, LinkedIn, Youtube

Stuart Wolff, Chairman of the Board
Rick Abraham, President & CEO
Sharon Boyle, Vice President
Jessica Muffoletto, Manager, Membership & Meetings
Barry Maloney, General Counsel

Specializes in selling food and related products to foodservice companies.
150 Members
Founded in 2003
Mailing list available for rent

17555 Global Retail Marketing Association

Home Page: www.thegrma.com
Social Media: Twitter, LinkedIn

Bill Brand, Advisory Board Member
Brian Beitler, Advisory Board Member
Ron Bonacci, Advisory Board Member
Lily Chang, Advisory Board Member
Shane Coker, Advisory Board Member

17556 Healthcare Public Relations & Marketing Association
5406 Hazeltine Ave.
Sherman Oaks, CA 91401

714-647-2430
E-Mail: info@hprma.org
Home Page: www.vnetitclients.com/hprma2
Social Media: Facebook, Twitter, LinkedIn

Pamela Westcott, President
Ava Alexander, Sponsorships
Jennifer Heinley, Secretary
Kathleen Curan, Communications
Lisa Killen, Membership

17557 Hospitality Sales and Marketing Association
7918 Jones Branch Drive
Suite 300
McLean, VA 22102

703-506-3280
Fax: 703-506-3266
E-Mail: info@hsmai.org
Home Page: www.hsmai.org
Social Media: Facebook, Twitter, LinkedIn

Rob Torres, Chair
Marina MacDonald, Vice Chair
Robert A. Gilbert, CHME, CHA, President & CEO
Juli Jones, Vice President
Fran Brasseux, CHSE, Executive Vice President
7000 Members

17558 Incentive Marketing Association
1601 North Bond Street
Suite 303
Naperville, IL 60563

603-369-7780
Fax: 630-369-3773
E-Mail: karen@incentivemarketing.org
Home Page: www.ima.site-ym.com
Social Media: Facebook, Twitter, LinkedIn, Stumbleupon, Tumblr, Blogger,

Mike Arvelo, CPIM, President
Louise Anderson, CPIM, Executive Vice President
Richard Low, Vice President
Carla R. DeFlorio, CAE, Executive Director/CAE
Steve Maselko, CPIM, CITE, Treasurer

Members are professional premium/incentive marketing executives.
650 Members
Founded in 1998

17559 Incentive Performance Center
5008 Castle Rock Way
Naples, FL 34112

914-591-7600
Fax: 239-775-7537
E-Mail: info@incentivecentral.org
Home Page: www.incentivecentral.org

Howard C Henry, Executive Director/CAE

Your portal to new ways of achieving business goals by capturing the power of your best customers and employees.
150 Members
Founded in 1984

17560 Insurance Marketing & Communications Association
4248 Park Glen Road
Minneapolis, MN 55416
952-928-4644
Fax: 952-929-1318
E-Mail: info@imcanet.com
Home Page: imcanet.com
Social Media: Facebook, Twitter, LinkedIn, YouTube

Mark Friedlander, President
Gloria Grove, Executive Director
Anna Hargis, Executive Vice President
John Abbott, Member
Emily Hathcoat, Treasurer
Founded in 1923

17561 Internet Marketing Association
10 Mar Del Rey
San Clemente, CA 92673

949-443-9300
Fax: 949-443-2215
E-Mail: info@imanetwork.org
Home Page: imanetwork.org

Social Media: Facebook, Twitter, LinkedIn, RSS, Google+, YouTube

Sinan Kanatsiz, CIM, Chairman & Founder
Matthew Langie, CIM, Vice Chair of Education
Rachel Reenders, CIM, Executive Director
Vince Walden, Finance Director
David Steinberg, CIM, VP of Business Alliances
90000 Members
Founded in 2001

17562 **Legal Marketing Association**
330 North Wabash Avenue
Suite 2000
Chicago, IL 60611-4267

312-321-6898
Fax: 312-673-6894
E-Mail: membersupport@legalmarketing.org
Home Page: www.legalmarketing.org
Social Media: Facebook, Twitter, LinkedIn, Youtube

Betsi Roach, Executive Director
Susan Lane, Director of Operations
Adrianne Watson, Membership Services
Lizzie Duvall, Membership Services
Justine Gershak, Membership Services
LMA is a nonprofit organization dedicated to serving the needs and maintaining the professional standards of the men and women involved in marketing within the legal profession.
2700 Members
Founded in 1986

17563 **Life Insurance Direct Marketing Association**
3227 S. Cherokee Lane
Suite 1320
Woodstock, GA 30188
770-516-0207
866-890-LEAD
E-Mail: info@lidma.org
Home Page: lidma.org
Social Media: Facebook, Twitter, LinkedIn

Pat Wedeking, Chair
Andy Meehan, President
Jeff McCauley, Vice President
Staci Birk, Director
Cindy Farrow, Secretary/ Treasurer

17564 **Manufacturers Agents National Association**
16-A Journey
Suite 200
Aliso Viejo, CA 92656-3317
949-859-4040
877-626-2776
Fax: 949-855-2973
E-Mail: mana@manaonline.org
Home Page: www.manaonline.org

Tom Hayward, CPMR, Chairman
Charles Cohon, CPMR, President and CEO
Jerry Leth, Vice President and General Manager
Lisa Ball, Member Services Coordinator
Doug Bower, Director of Strategic Alliances
6600 Members
Founded in 1947

17565 **Marketing Agencies Association Worldwide**
60 Peachcroft Drive
Bernardsville, NJ 07924

908-428-4300
Fax: 908-766-1277
E-Mail: vincentsottosanti@maaw.org
Home Page: www.maaw.org

Simon Mahoney, President
Aldo Cundari, 1st Vice President
Dan Mortimer, VP On-line Services
John Williams, Executive Director
Rick Shaver, Treasurer
The Marketing Agencies Assocation Worldwide (MAA) is the only global organization dedicated solely to the CEOs, Presidents,Managing Directors and Principals of top marketing services agencies.
75 Members
Founded in 1963

17566 **Marketing Education Association**
PO Box 27473
Tempe, AZ 85285-7473

602-750-6735
E-Mail: mea@nationalmea.org
Home Page: www.nationalmea.org

Fosters the development and expansion of education for and about marketing as a descrete, clearly defined profession. Members are high school and postsecondary marketing educations as well as university-level teacher educations and collegiate marketing teacher education students.
Founded in 1982

17567 **Marketing Research Association**
1156 15th Street NW
Suite 302
Washington, DC 20005

202-800-2545
Fax: 888-512-1050
E-Mail: membership@marketingresearch.org
Home Page: www.marketingresearch.org
Social Media: Facebook, Twitter, LinkedIn

David Almy, CEO
The Marketing Research Association's Blue Book Research Services Directory is the research industry number one reference source.
Founded in 1957

17568 **Marketing Science Institute**
Marketing Science Institute
1000 Massachusetts Avenue
Cambridge, MA 02138-5396

617-491-2060
Fax: 617-491-2065
E-Mail: msi@msi.org
Home Page: www.msi.org
Social Media: Facebook, Twitter, LinkedIn

Kevin Lane Keller, Executive Director
Marni Zea Clippinger, Chief Operating Officer
Earl Taylor, Chief Marketing Officer
Liza Hostetler-Ingalls, Administrative Assistant
Susan Keane, Editorial Director
MSI publishes research done on a variety of marketing topics, including: E - Commerce, Metrics, Branding, New Products and Innovations, Communications and more. Individual papers and subscriptions are available. We accept proposals and papers for grant consideration.
65 Members
Founded in 1961

17569 **Mass Marketing Insurance Institute**
3007 Tilden Street, NW
Suite 7M-103
Washington, DC 20008

816-221-7575
Fax: 816-772-7765
E-Mail: Jeffrey.M.Collins@MedStar.net
Home Page: www.mi2.org
Social Media: Twitter, Youtube, Pinterest, RSS, Googl

Greg Carlile, Executive Director
Laurie Weber, Associate Director
Provides a forum for professionals engaged in marketing, sales and administration of employee benefits such as worksite marketing, payroll deduction and other mass marketed services.

17570 **Materials Marketing Associates**
136 South Keowee Street
Dayton, OH 45402

937-222-1024
Fax: 937-222-5794
E-Mail: email@mma4u.com
Home Page: www.mma4u.com

Kimberley Fantaci, President
Members are chemical distributors representing manufacturers marketing chemical raw material specialties to makers of coatings, inks, pharmaceuticals, adhesives, cosmetics, plastics, soaps, detergents, etc.
19 Members
Founded in 1963

17571 **Midwest Direct Marketing Association**
P.O. Box 75
Andover, MN 55304

763-607-2943
Fax: 763-753-2240
E-Mail: office@mdma.org
Home Page: www.mdma.org

Ben DuBois, Communications Director
Jolee Molitor, Programs Director
Vicki Erickson, Secretary/Treasurer
Dedicated to the advancement of professional and ethical practice of direct response marketing by members throughout the Upper Midwest.
600 Members
Founded in 1960

17572 **Mobile Marketing Association**
770 Broadway
2nd Floor
New York, NY 10003

646-257-4515
E-Mail: northamerica@mmaglobal.com
Home Page: www.mmaglobal.com
Social Media: Facebook, Twitter, LinkedIn, Google+

Greg Stuart, Chief Executive Officer
Sheryl Daija, CSO & GM, Global Events
Chris Babayode, Managing Director, EMEA
Fabiano Destri Lobo, Managing Director, Latam
Michael Wis, SVP, Global Finance Administration
800 Members

17573 **Multi-Level Marketing International Association**
119 Stanford Court
Irvine, CA 92612-1671

949-854-0484
Fax: 949-854-7687
E-Mail: doriswood@mlmia.com
Home Page: www.mlmia.com
Social Media: Facebook, Twitter, LinkedIn

Doris Wood, Chairman/President Emeritus
Linda Bruno, Secretary
Seeks to strengthen and improve the Direct Sales/Network Marketing/Multi-Level Marketing industry in the United States and abroad.
Founded in 1985

17574 **Multicultural Marketing Resources**
150 West 28th Street
Suite 1501
New York, NY 10001

212-242-3351
Fax: 212-691-5969
E-Mail: lisa@multicultural.com

Home Page: www.multicultural.com
Social Media: Facebook, Twitter, LinkedIn

Lisa Skriloff, President
Cassandra Richardson-Coughlin, Marketing/Sales Assistant
Kelleh Jian, Marketing/Sales Assistant
Mukti Ajmeri, Marketing/Sales Assistant
Nadia M, Marketing/Sales Assistant

A place where corporate executives can find diverse resources, experts and information on how to market to multicultural (ethnic and niche) consumer markets.
Founded in 1994

17575 National Association of Display Industries
4651 Sheridan Street
Suite 470
Hollywood, FL 33021

954-893-7300
Fax: 954-893-7500
E-Mail: nadi@nadi-global.com
Home Page: www.nadi-global.com

Klein Merriman, Executive Director
Tracy Dillon, Director Communications

A leading association for the visual merchandising profession. As visual merchandising has evolved over the years into playing an integral role in retail, NADI has always taken the lead in informing and educating members. The association's already significant support of the visual design profession has grown with NADI's exclusive sponsorship of GlobalShop's Visual Merchandising Show and StoreXpo.
Founded in 1942

17576 National Energy Marketers Association
3333 K Street, NW
Suite 110
Washington, DC 20007

202-333-3288
Fax: 202-333-3266
Home Page: www.energymarketers.com

Dan Verbanac, Chair, Executive Committee
Chris Hendrix, 1st Vice Chair, Executive Committee
Pierre Koshakji, 2nd Vice Chair, Executive Committee
Craig Goodman, President
Harry Warren, Chair Emeriti

17577 North American Farmers' Direct Marketing Association
62 White Loaf Road
Southampton, MA 1073

FAX 413-233-4285
E-Mail: Charlie @ Whiteloafridge.com
Home Page: www.farmersinspired.com
Social Media: Facebook, Twitter, Pinterest, YouTube

Cynthia Chiles, President/ Chair
Charlie Touchette, Executive Director
Becky Walters, VP of Membership
Ben Beaver, VP of Education
Mike Dunn, Treasurer/ Finance Team Chair

17578 Performance Marketing Association
364 East Main St.
Suite 444
Middletown, DE 19709

805-233-7987
Home Page: thepma.org
Social Media: Facebook, Twitter, LinkedIn, RSS, Google+

Brian Littleton, President
Tony Pantano, Treasurer
Tricia Meyer, Secretary
Todd Crawford, Board Member
Rachel Honoway, Board Member
20000 Members
Founded in 2008

17579 Petroleum Marketers Association of America
1901 North Fort Myer Drive
Suite 500
Arlington, VA 22209

703-351-8000
Fax: 703-351-9160
E-Mail: info@pmaa.org
Home Page: www.pmaa.org

Grady Gaubert, Chairman
Mike Bailey, Vice Chair
Mark Whitehead, 2nd Vice Chair
Benny Hodges, Brands Division Director
Greg Benson, West Region Chair
Founded in 1909

17580 Photo Marketing Association International
2282 Springport Road, Suite F
Jackson, MI 49202

517-788-8100
800-762-9287
Fax: 517-788-8371
E-Mail: pma_information_central@pmai.org
Home Page: www.pmai.org
Social Media: Facebook, Twitter, LinkedIn

Allen Showalter, President
Robert L. Hanson, Vice President
Jim Esp, Executive Director/Secretary
Bill Eklund, Treasurer
18000 Members
Founded in 1924

17581 Power Marketing Association
Home Page: www.powermarketers.com

Ralph E. Beaty III, Membership/Communications Manager
Carol Ofiesh, Member Services Manager
Phil Ofiesh, Data Services Manager
Scott Spiewak, Publisher

17582 Private Label Manufacturers Association
630 Third Avenue
New York, NY 10017-6770

212-972-3131
Fax: 212-983-1382
E-Mail: info@plma.com
Home Page: www.plma.com

Myra Rosen, Vice President
Brian Sharoff, President

Trade Association promoting the Private Label Industry.
3200+ Members
Founded in 1979

17583 Produce Marketing Association
1500 Casho Mill Road
Newark, DE 19711

302-738-7100
Fax: 302-731-2409
Home Page: www.pma.com
Social Media: Facebook, Twitter, Pinterest, Flickr

Cathy Burns, President
Bryan Silbermann, Chief Executive Officer
Tony Parassio, Chief Operating Officer
Yvonne Bull, Chief Financial Officer
Margi Prueitt, Executive Director

17584 Producers Livestock Marketing Association
PO Box 819
Greeley, CO 80632

970-353-4121
800-791-BEEF
Home Page: www.producerslivestock.com

Rick O'Brien, General Manager
Brad Jones, Branch Manager
Bob Elliot, Assistant Branch Manager
Vivian Reed, Office Manager
Founded in 1935

17585 Professional Insurance Marketing Association
35 E. Wacker Dr
Suite 850
Chicago, IL 60601-2106

817-569-PIMA
Fax: 312-644-8557
E-Mail: mona@pima-assn.org
Home Page: www.pima-assn.org
Social Media: Twitter, LinkedIn

Daniel O'Brien, CLU, President
Mona F. Buckley, MPA, Chief Executive Officer
William Suneson, Secretary
Mark Kelsey, Treasurer
Dave Armstrong, Director
120 Members

17586 Promotion Industry Council
1805 N Mill Street
Naperville, IL 60563-1275

630-369-7781
Fax: 630-369-3773

Manufacturers, distributors and users of promotion premiums. Increases understanding of incentives and the premium promotion process.
100 Members
Founded in 1940

17587 Re:Gender
11 Hanover Square
24th Floor
New York, NY 10005-2819

212-785-7335
Fax: 212-785-7350
E-Mail: info@regender.org
Home Page: www.regender.org
Social Media: Facebook, Twitter, RSS

Lucie Lapovsky, Chair
Aine Duggan, President
Andrea Greenblatt, Vice President of Operations
Debbie Kellogg, Vice President for External Rel
Gail Cooper, Vice President for Programs

A network of 120 leading research, policy and advocacy centers committed to improving the lives of women and girls. Provides the latest news, information and strategies needed to ensure fully informed debates, effective policies and inclusive practices.
3,000 Members
Founded in 1981

17588 Restaurant Marketing & Delivery Association
3636 Menaul Blvd.
Ste. 323
Albuquerque, NM 87110

E-Mail: membership@rmda.info
Home Page: www.rmda.info

Paul Birrell, President
David Farmer, Vice President
Wes Garrison, Treasurer
Anu Mehra, Convention
Luke Katuin, Technology
Founded in 1990

17589 **Sales and Marketing Executives International**
PO Box 1390
Sumas, WA 98295-1390
312-893-0751
Fax: 312-893-0751
E-Mail: admin@smei.org
Home Page: www.smei.org
Social Media: Facebook, Twitter, LinkedIn, Youtube, RSS
Clinton J. Schroeder MBA, CME, CS, Chairman
Willis Turner CAE CME CSE, President & Chief Executive Officer
Hans-Benno Mastboom, Senior Vice Chair
Antonio Rios-Ramirez, Senior Vice Chair
Nathalie Roemer CME, Secretary Treasurer
Members are most commonly professionals in the fields of sales and marketing management, market research management, sales training, distribution management and other senior executives in small and medium businesses.
10000 Members
Frequency: Annual Meeting (Fall)
Founded in 1935

17590 **Search Engine Marketing Professional Organization**
401 Edgewater Pl.
Suite 600
Wakefield, MA 1880
718-876-8866
E-Mail: info@sempo.org
Home Page: www.sempo.org
Social Media: Facebook, Twitter, LinkedIn, Blogpot, YouTube, Google+
Mike Grehan, Chair
Mike Gullaksen, President
Simon Heseltine, VP of Education
Marc Engelsman, VP of Research
Krista LaRiviere, VP of Local Group
Founded in 2002

17591 **Society for Marketing Professional Services**
123 North Pitt Street
Suite 400
Alexandria, VA 22314
703-549-6117
800-292-7677
Fax: 703-549-2498
E-Mail: info@smps.org
Home Page: www.smps.org
Social Media: Facebook, Twitter, LinkedIn, Youtube,Pinterest
Ronald D. Worth, CAE, FSMPS, CPS, CEO
Lisa Bowman, Senior Vice President
Mark DellaPietra, Vice President of Education
Tina Myers, CAE, Senior Vice President
Michele Santiago, Director of Marketing
Serving marketing and business development professionals employed by architectural, engineering and construction firms, SMPS provides education and networking opportunities tailored to build your bottom line.
5600 Members
Founded in 1973
Mailing list available for rent: 6000 names at $200 per M

17592 **Society of Independent Gasoline Marketers**
3930 Pender Drive
Suite 340
Fairfax, VA 22030
703-709-7000
Fax: 703-709-7007
E-Mail: sigma@sigma.org
Home Page: www.sigma.org
Tom Schmidt, President
Kenneth A. Doyle, CAE, Executive Vice President
Mary Alice Kutyn, Director Meetings
Dennis Cuevas, Director of Education
Mary Alice Kutyn, Director of Meetings
Members are independent gasoline marketers.
270 Members
Founded in 1958

17593 **Specialty Equipment Market Association**
1575 S. Valley Vista Drive
Diamond Bar, CA 91765-0910
909-610-2030
Fax: 909-860-0184
E-Mail: sema@sema.org
Home Page: www.sema.org
Social Media: Facebook, Twitter, Google+
Nate Shelton, Chairman
Christopher J. Kersting, President and CEO
George Afremow, Vice President
Steve McDonald, Vice President of Government Affair
John Kilroy, Vice President/General Manager, PRI
Represents the automotive aftermarket industry with government agencies and trade and consumer groups.
5200 Members
Founded in 1963

17594 **Sport Marketing Association**
1972 Clark Ave.
Alliance, OH 44601
330-829-8207
E-Mail: smaoffice@mountunion.edu
Home Page: www.sportmarketingassociation.com
Social Media: Facebook, Twitter, LinkedIn
Nancy Lough, President
Khalid Ballouli, VP of Academic Affairs
Elizabeth Gregg, VP of Student Affairs
Steven McKelvey, VP of Industry Relations
Beth Grupsmith, Social Media Consultant

17595 **Strategic Account Management Association**
10 N. Dearborn St.
2nd Floor
Chicago, IL 60602
312-251-3131
Fax: 312-251-3132
E-Mail: napolitano@strategicaccounts.org
Home Page: www.strategicaccounts.org
Social Media: Facebook, Twitter, LinkedIn, Pinterest, Google+
Bernard Quancard, President/CEO
Katherine Gotsick, Chief Operations Officer
Frankie Cusimano, Senior Manager, Membership
Matt Fegley, Chief Business Development Officer
Richard Rottsolk, Senior Manager, Corporate Resource
The Strategic Account Management Association is a non-profit organization devoted to developing and promoting the concept of customer-supplier partnering. SAMA is dedicated to the professional and personal development of the executives charged with managing national, global, and strategic account relationships, and to elevating the status of the profession as a whole. SAMA provides literature, training and research into best practices in large, complex, global customer account management.
2000 Members
Founded in 1964

17596 **Thomson Reuters**
Thomson Reuters
2395 Midway Rd
Carrollton, TX 75006
646-223-4000
888-885-0206
Fax: 888-216-1929
E-Mail: trta.lei-support@thomsonreuters.com
Home Page: www.tax.thomsonreuters.com
David K R Thomson, Chairman
Thomas H Glocer, CEO & Director
Robert D Daleo, Chief Financial Officer
Kelli Crane, Senior Vice President & CIO
A national organization that focuses on marketing and sales intelligence for top level marketing executives.

17597 **Trade Show Exhibitors Association**
2214 NW 5th St.
Suite 1005
Bend, OR 97701
541-317-8768
Fax: 541-317-8749
E-Mail: tsea@tsea.org
Home Page: www.tsea.org
Social Media: Facebook
Amanda Helgemoe, President
Michael Mulry, Vice President
Glenda Brundgardt, Treasurer
Chris Griffin, Secretary
Members are companies using exhibits for marketing, advertising or public relations.
1800 Members
Founded in 1966

17598 **Transportation Marketing & Sales Association**
9382 Oak Avenue
Waconia, MN 55387
952-466-6270
Home Page: www.tmsatoday.org/
Social Media: Facebook, Twitter, LinkedIn
David Hoppens, Chairman
Dino Moler, President
Beth Carroll, VP-Administration & Finance
Candi Cybator, VP- Content & Strategy
Andy Williams, VP- Membership & Outreach
Founded in 1924

17599 **Word of Mouth Marketing Association**
65 E. Wacker Place
Suite #500
Chicago, IL 60601
312-853-4400
Fax: 312-275-7687
E-Mail: membership@womma.org
Home Page: www.womma.org
Social Media: Facebook, Twitter, LinkedIn, YouTube, Google+
Suzanne Fanning, President
Chris Spallino, Director of Marketing
Jennifer Connelly, Events Manager
Chelsea Hickey, Marketing Manager & Editor
The Word of Mouth Association is dedicated to word of mouth and social media marketing. It is the leader in ethical word of mouth marketing practices through eduation including the WOMMA summit, professional marketing opportunities and knowledge sharing.
Founded in 2004

Newsletters

17600 **Advanced Selling Power**
Thompson Group

6850 Austin Center Blvd
Suite 100
Austin, TX 78731-3201

512-418-8869
Fax: 512-418-1209
E-Mail: carol@thompson-group.com
Home Page: www.thompson-group.com

Terry E Thompson, Publisher
Valerie A Canaday, Editor
Carol Thompson, President

Provides sales tactics, strategies and ideas to sales professinals and entrepreneurs. Each issue helps salespeople learn how to put together presentations, develop openings that keep customers interested, use testimonials correctly and more.
Cost: $10.00
Circulation: 1000
Founded in 1993

17601 Airline Financial News
Phillips Business Information
1201 Seven Locks Road
Suite 300
Potomac, MD 20854-2931

301-541-1400
Fax: 301-309-3847

Grier Graham, Editor

Newsletter that provides the most timely financial reports and market analysis for the entire airline industry.
Cost: $695.00
Frequency: Weekly

17602 Antin Marketing Letter
Alan Antin/Antin Marketing Group
19888 Sw Monte Vista Dr
Suite 205
Beaverton, OR 97007-5412

503-356-0504
Fax: 913-663-5552
E-Mail: AMG@commonsensemarketing.com
Home Page:
www.commonsensemarketing.com

Brad Antin, President
Alan Antin, Director of Marketing
William Hammond, Director of Marketing

How-to info on marketing for professionals and entrepreneurs (service businessess, retailers, wholesalers, professional practice).
Cost: $197.00
Frequency: Monthly

17603 Application Servers and Media Servers
Probe Research
3 Wing Drive
Suite 240
Cedar Knolls, NJ 07927-1000

973-285-1500
Fax: 973-285-1519
Home Page: www.proberesearch.com

This bulletin describes the market for both applications and media servers; examines key issues and provides a profile of selected players in various product categories.

17604 Art of Self Promotion
Ilise Benun/Creative Marketing and Management
PO Box 23
Hoboken, NJ 07030

201-653-0783
800-737-0783
Fax: 201-222-2494
E-Mail: ilise@marketing-mentor.com
Home Page: www.artofselfpromotion.com

Lisa Cyr, Author
Ilise Benun, Marketing Manager

Nuts'n bolts for manageable marketing for small business owners and self employed professionals.
Cost: $100.80
8 Pages
Frequency: Quarterly
Founded in 1995

17605 Association of Incentive Marketing News
Association of Incentive Marketing
1601 North Bond Street, Suite 303
Naperville, IL 60563

603-369-7780
Fax: 603-369-3773
E-Mail: karen@incentivemarketing.org
Home Page: www.incentivemarketing.org

George Meredith, Editor
Susan Peterson, Director of Membership
Nicole Sweigart, Administrative Director
Paul Cernohous, Director
Karen Renk, Executive Director

Articles cover promotion industry news and Association information and events.
Frequency: Quarterly
Circulation: 300

17606 Auctioneer
National Auctioneers Association
8880 Ballentine
Overland Park, KS 66214

913-541-8084
Fax: 913-894-5281
E-Mail: hcombest@auctioneers.org
Home Page: auctions.auctioneers.org

Robert Shively, CEO
Wendy Dellinger, Advertising Manager
Steve Baska, Publications Editor
Ryan Putnam, Assistant Editor

Keeps members of the National Auctioneers Association informed of trends and legal issues related to auctioneering. Chronicles activities of the Association and its membership.
Frequency: Monthly
Circulation: 7000
Founded in 1948

17607 Automated and Self-Provisioning Servers
Probe Research
3 Wing Drive
Suite 240
Cedar Knolls, NJ 07927-1000

973-285-1500
Fax: 973-285-1519
Home Page: www.proberesearch.com

A look at service provider implementation of automated and self - provisioning software systems. An explanation of the causes of delay and QoS degradation in IP networks.

17608 BDA
BDA News
900 W Sunset Boulevard
Suite 900
Los Angeles, CA 90069

310-712-0040
Fax: 310-712-0039
Home Page: www.bda.tv

Jill Masters, VP Member Services
Jim Chabin, President

Newsletter, awards annual, magazine and directory published by BDA for designers in the motion graphics industry.
Cost: $5.00
Frequency: Monthly
Circulation: 2000
Printed in 4 colors on glossy stock

17609 Bandwidth Management: Driving Profitablity to the Botton Line
Probe Research
3 Wing Drive
Suite 240
Cedar Knolls, NJ 07927-1000

973-285-1500
Fax: 973-285-1519
Home Page: www.proberesearch.com

Provides an analysis of the type of issues that require Bandwidth Management solutions. Makes a comparison of the types of technical solutions implemented in different parts of the network and the major benefits of each solution. Also analyzes the trends seen in IP traffic and inter - relationship with bandwidth management.

17610 Bulletproof Marketing for Small Businesses
Kay Borden/Franklin-Sarrett Publishers
3761 Vinyard Trce Ne
Marietta, GA 30062-5227

770-578-9410
Fax: 770-977-5495

Kay Borden, President

Publicity for small businesses, particularly producing news releases that get printed.
Cost: $15.00
Frequency: SemiAnnual
Founded in 1994

17611 Business Owner
Mailing & Fulfillment Service Association
1421 Prince Street
Suite 410
Alexandria, VA 22314-2806

703-836-9200
Fax: 703-548-8204
E-Mail: mfsa-mail@mfsanet.org
Home Page: www.mfsanet.org
Social Media: Facebook, Twitter, LinkedIn

David L Perkins Jr, Editor
Leo Raymond, Vice President

Developed specifically to communicate with owners and CEOs on issues unique to them. You'll receive a wealth of knowledge on growing your business, tax issues, insurance, estate planning, management, finance and much more.
Frequency: Bi-Monthly

17612 Business-2-Business Marketer
Business Marketing Association
Ste 123
1833 Centre Point Cir
Naperville, IL 60563-4848

630-544-5054
Fax: 630-544-5055
E-Mail: info@marketing.org
Home Page: www.marketing.org
Social Media: Facebook, Twitter, LinkedIn

Jeffrey Hayzlett, Chairman
Gary Slack, Vice Chairman
Bob Goranson CBC, Treasurer

Editorial covers all apsects of integrated marketing disciplines, including: sales management, trade show marketing, datbase and direct mail marketing, presentations, telemarketing, public relations, advertising and electronic marketing.
Cost: $150.00
16 Pages
Circulation: 4300
ISSN: 1073-4538
Founded in 1922
Printed in 4 colors on glossy stock

17613 Cable & Wireless
Probe Research

3 Wing Drive
Suite 240
Cedar Knolls, NJ 07927-1000

973-285-1500
Fax: 973-285-1519
Home Page: www.proberesearch.com

A look at cable & wireless IP infrastructure, how the company is operating it, and how it is managing services on its network.

17614 Cable Headed Equipment Markets Upstarts
Probe Research
3 Wing Drive
Suite 240
Cedar Knolls, NJ 07927-1000

973-285-1500
Fax: 973-285-1519
Home Page: www.proberesearch.com

This bulletin analyses the CMTS market and the role the equipment plays in the plans of the major cable operators to move towards the goal of full service operators. A market forecast is included and the major players profiled.

17615 Cambridge Reports Trends and Forecasts
Cambridge Reports
955 Massachusetts Ave
Suite 8
Cambridge, MA 02139-3178

617-661-0110
Fax: 617-661-3575

Gene Pokorny, Publisher

Key changes in consumer and public opinions.

17616 Career News Update
American Marketing Association
311 S Wacker Dr
Suite 5800
Chicago, IL 60606-6629

312-542-9000
800-262-1150
Fax: 312-542-9001
Home Page: www.marketingpower.com
Social Media: Facebook, Twitter, LinkedIn, Youtube

Dennis Dunlap, CEO

You'll receive the latest career and hiring advice as well as useful job resources and employment listings.
Frequency: Monthly
Mailing list available for rent

17617 Collegiate Trends
Strategic Marketing
550 N Maple Ave
Suite 102
Ridgewood, NJ 07450-1611

201-612-8100
Fax: 201-612-1444
E-Mail: weil@studentmonitor.com
Home Page: www.studentmonitor.com

Marketing and media trends for marketers targeting college students.
Cost: $95.00
Frequency: Quarterly
Founded in 1987

17618 Colloquy
Frequency Marketing
PO Box 610
Milford, OH 45150-0610

513-248-2882
Fax: 513-248-2672
E-Mail: info_de@epsilon.com
Home Page: www.epsilon.com

Bryan Kennedy, President/CEO
Jill Z. McBride, Chief Operating Officer
Catherine Lang, Chief Operating Officer
Paul Dundon, Chief Financial Officer
Jeanette Fitzgerald, General Counsel

Frequency Marketing, is the publisher of the COLLOQUY newsletter and COLLOQUY.com Web site, which are dedicated tot he discrimination of information about analysis of frequency marketing strategies and programs worldwide. COLLOQUY also provides educational and research services on a global basis to the loyalty marketing industry, and offers substantial news, research libraries and program archives to qualified subscribers at COLLOQUY.com.
Frequency: Quarterly
Circulation: 16,000+
Founded in 1990

17619 Competitive Advantage
Competitive Advantage
PO Box 10828
Portland, OR 97296-0828

503-274-2953
Fax: 503-274-4349

Jim Moran, Publisher
Tonya Shrives, Promotional Director

Provides sales, marketing and management tools to make careers and companies more prosperous.
Circulation: 10,000

17620 Conference Board Management Briefing - Marketing
Conference Board
845 3rd Ave
Suite 2
New York, NY 10022-6600

212-759-0900
Fax: 212-980-7014
E-Mail: june.shelp@conference-board.org
Home Page: www.conference-board.org

Jonathan Spector, CEO

Trends and practices in marketing.
Frequency: Monthly

17621 Creative Marketing Newsletter
Association of Retail Marketing Services
10 Drs James Parker Boulevard
Suite 103
Red Bank, NJ 07701-1500

732-842-5070
Fax: 732-219-1938
E-Mail: info@goarms.com
Home Page: www.goarms.com

Gerri Hopkins, Executive Director
Lisa McCauley, Administrative Director

Retail promotion marketing newsletter for supermarkets, convenience stores, drug chains and suppliers of retail promotions.
Frequency: Quarterly
Printed in 3 colors on matte stock

17622 Creative Selling
Bentley-Hall
120 E Washington St
Suite 913
Syracuse, NY 13202-4003

315-701-0308
Fax: 315-471-2138

Contains training material for sales managers and sales training managers.
Cost: $7.00
Circulation: 6,500

17623 Current Global Carrier Market Environment, Global Carrier
Probe Research
3 Wing Drive
Suite 240
Cedar Knolls, NJ 07927-1000

973-285-1500
Fax: 973-285-1519
Home Page: www.proberesearch.com

Addresses a sweeping review of current strategic, business, economic, financial, network technology, network operations and service portfolio topics now at work in global and international carriage. Also includes a discussion of the potential risk assessment value of existing and future bandwidth trading and arbitrage exchanges.

17624 Current Thinking on Network Evolution and Its Laws
Probe Research
3 Wing Drive
Suite 240
Cedar Knolls, NJ 07927-1000

973-285-1500
Fax: 973-285-1519
Home Page: www.proberesearch.com

This issue focuses on three laws of network evolution used by new entrants and by vendors. These three laws seem to be justified when the stock market rewarded new entrants with enormous valuations simply based on technology and expensive business plans. Now that the stock market no longer rewards such ventures, an analysis of these three laws is warranted and what impact thay have had on the carrier business.

17625 Customers First
Dartnell Corporation
4660 N Ravenswood Avenue
Chicago, IL 60640-4510

773-907-9500
Fax: 773-561-3801

Clark Fetridge, Publisher
Jim Nawrocki, Editor

A practical periodical that provides employees with an organized plan of action for building and improving customer relations.
Cost: $62.00

17626 Daily News E-Mail (3D)
Direct Marketing Association
1120 Avenue of the Americas
New York, NY 10036-6700

212-768-7277
Fax: 212-302-6714
E-Mail: customerservice@the-dma.org
Home Page: www.the-dma.org

Lawrence M Kimmel, CEO

Delivers the essential news, research, hot trends, and technological developments from the nations leading newspapers, trade publications, and the government all in an easy-to-read, time-saving format.

17627 Dartnell Sales and Marketing Executive Report
Dartnell Corporation
4660 N Ravenswood Avenue
Chicago, IL 60640-4510

773-907-9500
800-341-7874
Fax: 773-907-0645
E-Mail: infochicago@insightpd.com
Home Page: www.insightpd.com

Craig Scherer, Senior Partner
Anthony Annibale, General Manager
Cost: $168.00
Frequency: Monthly
Founded in 1917

17628 Data Service: ISDN, Private Lines, Frame Relay and ATM
Probe Research
3 Wing Drive
Suite 240
Cedar Knolls, NJ 07927-1000

973-285-1500
Fax: 973-285-1519
Home Page: www.proberesearch.com

We survey and highlight four major data transport technologies detailing the technology's strengths, weakness, specific applications, and basic carrier strategies.

17629 Defining the M-Commerce Value Chain
Probe Research
3 Wing Drive
Suite 240
Cedar Knolls, NJ 07927-1000

973-285-1500
Fax: 973-285-1519
Home Page: www.proberesearch.com

Defines and unifies all participants in a mobile commerce transaction using the sentence Selecting, ordering and paying for items using a mobile device in a secure fashion. Examines the m-commerce business models selected carriers, ASPs and other vendors.

17630 Delaney Report
PRIMEDIA Intertec-Marketing & Professional Service
149 5th Avenue
#725
New York, NY 10010-6801

212-979-7881
Fax: 212-979-0691
E-Mail: tdrinfo@aol.com
Home Page: http://www.delaneyreport.com

Thomas Delaney, Editor

Provides information on personnel changes, trade literature and indsutry events for advertising, media, media, and public relations executives. Reports on global news and developments.
Cost: $74.00

17631 Digital Subscriber Line Access Multiplexer Upstarts
Probe Research
3 Wing Drive
Suite 240
Cedar Knolls, NJ 07927-1000

973-285-1500
Fax: 973-285-1519
Home Page: www.proberesearch.com

This bulletin examines the major DSALM vendors and forecast the market for DSLAM ports and equipment revenue until 2006.

17632 Downtown Promotion Reporter
Alexander Communications Group
1916 Park Ave
Suite 501
New York, NY 10037-3733

212-281-6099
800-232-4317
Fax: 212-283-7269
E-Mail: info@downtowndevelopment.com
Home Page: www.downtowndevelopment.com

Romauld Alexander, President
Nadine Harris, Marketing Manager

Tested ideas for promotion, public relations, marketing, increasing business, participation, downtown image building, sales, and events.
Cost: $189.00
Frequency: Monthly
Founded in 1954

17633 Drop Shippng News
Consolidated Marketing Services
PO Box 7838
New York, NY 10150

212-688-8797
Fax: 212-688-8797
Home Page: www.drop-shipping-news.com

Nicholas T Scheel, Editor/Publisher

Covers all facets of Drop Shipping; source directory for 300,000 consumer products. Book 'Drop Shipping' marketing methods.
Cost: $25.00
Frequency: Monthly
Founded in 1977

17634 Dynamic Selling
Economics Press
12 Daniel Road
Fairfield, NJ 07004-2565

973-227-1224
Fax: 973-227-9742

Covers sales issues and ways to improve sales.

17635 Effective Telephone Techniques
Dartnell Corporation
4660 N Ravenswood Avenue
Chicago, IL 60640-4510

773-907-9500
Fax: 773-561-3801

Clark Fetridge, Publisher
Kim Anderson, Editor

Training bulletin helps your team build profitable customer relations with every call.
Cost: $62.00

17636 Empoyment Points
Mailing & Fulfillment Service Association
1421 Prince Street
Suite 410
Alexandria, VA 22314-2806

703-836-9200
Fax: 703-548-8204
E-Mail: mfsa-mail@mfsanet.org
Home Page: www.mfsanet.org
Social Media: Facebook, Twitter, LinkedIn

Leo Raymond, Vice President

The content is written for business owners and operators who want to stay informed about current employment issues. The editorial is targeted on human resource issues and employment practices in the mailing and fulfillment services industry.
Frequency: 4x/Year
Circulation: 2000

17637 Fiberoptics Market Intelligence
KMI Corporation
98 Spit Brook Rd
Suite 400
Nashua, NH 03062-5737

603-243-8100
Fax: 603-891-9172
Home Page: www.kmiresearch.com

Richard Mack, VP/General Manager
David Janoff, President
Kurt A Ruderman, Analyst/Editor

Markets, technologies, strategic planning, issues, standards and competition in the fiber optics industry.
Cost: $595.00
Frequency: Fortnightly
Founded in 1974

17638 Frohlinger's Marketing Report
Marketing Strategist Communications
7 Coppel Drive
Tenafly, NJ 07670-2903

201-569-6088
Fax: 201-568-8538

Joseph Frohlinger, Editor/Publisher

Global marketing, advertising and media NL with emphasis on strategic and trend articles.
Cost: $200.00
Frequency: Bi-Monthly
Founded in 1988

17639 Growth Strategies
Growth Strategies
2118 Wilshire Blvd
#826
Santa Monica, CA 90403-5704

310-721-6322
Fax: 310-828-0427

Roger Selbert, President

A newsletter published twice a monthly since 1981 has been presciently reporting on economic, social, political, technological, demographic, lifestyle, consumer, business, management, workforce and marketing trends.
Cost: $146.00
Frequency: Monthly
Founded in 1981
Printed in 2 colors on glossy stock

17640 Guerrilla Marketing International
Cascade Seaview Corporation
PO Box 1336
Mill Valley, CA 94942-1336

415-383-5426
Fax: 415-381-8361

William Shear, Publisher

Marketing insights, trends and tips for small business.
Cost: $59.00
8 Pages
Frequency: Bi-Monthly
Founded in 1989
Printed in one color on glossy stock

17641 Home Business Idea Possibility Newsletter
Prosperity & Profits Unlimited
PO Box 416
Denver, CO 80201-0416

303-573-5564

A Doyle, Editor

Possibilities for home businesses.
Cost: $7.50
4 Pages
Frequency: Annual
Circulation: 1,000
Founded in 1996
Printed in one color on matte stock

17642 How Long Can Traffic Grow?
Probe Research
3 Wing Drive
Suite 240
Cedar Knolls, NJ 07927-1000

973-285-1500
Fax: 973-285-1519
Home Page: www.proberesearch.com

Carrier lack of agreement on standard metrics for traffic measurement allows for any interpretation of data, misleads investors and vendors. Optical networking's future depends on a more rational approach to traffic statistics. An assessment of the three drivers for optical networking are discussed.

17643 INFO Marketing Report
Towers Club Press

9170 NW 11th Avenue
Vancouver, WA 98665

360-574-3084

Jerry Buchanan, Editor

Focuses on marketing of HOW TO information in all its many forms: print, audio, video, public speaking, etc.
Cost: $69.95
Frequency: Monthly
Founded in 1974

17644 **Imaging Market Forum**
Technology Marketing Corporation
800 Connecticut Ave
1st Floor East
Norwalk, CT 06854-1936

203-852-6800
800-243-6002
Fax: 203-866-3326
E-Mail: tmc@tmcnet.com
Home Page: www.tmcnet.com
Social Media: Twitter

Rich Tehrani, CEO

Case studies and opinions.

17645 **Infomercial Marketing Report**
Steven Dworman and Associates
11533 Thurston Circle
Los Angeles, CA 90049-2426

310-472-6360

Steve Dworman, Editor/Publisher

Insider information on the infomercial industry.
Cost: $395.00
Frequency: Monthly

17646 **Information Advisor**
Information Today
143 Old Marlton Pike
Medford, NJ 08055-8750

609-654-6266
800-300-9868
Fax: 609-654-4309
E-Mail: custserv@infotoday.com
Home Page: www.infotoday.com

Thomas H Hogan, President
Roger R Bilboul, Chairman Of The Board

Provides comprehensive evlauation of research tools, timely and specific information you will use, new sources valuable to researchers and head to head analysis of the most popular information services.
Cost: $165.00
Frequency: Monthly
Mailing list available for rent

17647 **International Marketing Service Newsletter**
IDG Communications
375 Cochituate Road
#9171
Framingham, MA 01701-4653
Frank Cutitta, Publisher

This newsletter concentrates on the overseas advertising and marketing industry.

17648 **International Product Alert**
Marketing Intelligence Service
482 N Main St
Canandaigua, NY 14424-1049

585-374-6326
800-836-5710
Fax: 585-374-5217
Home Page: www.productscan.com

Tom Vierhile, Editor

Reports product introductions from Europe, Asia and throughout the world.
Cost: $795.00
Frequency: Fortnightly
Founded in 1983

17649 **JonesReport**
PO Box 50038
Indianapolis, IN 46250-7830

317-576-9889
800-878-9024
Fax: 317-576-0441
E-Mail: ctrmktg@jonesreport.com
Home Page: www.jonesreport.com

William Willburn, Publisher/President
William Willburn, Editor
Lue Dyar, Circulation Manager

Monthly newsletter for shopping center marketing professionals. Free Resource Guide in September. Salary Survey results in December. Christmas planner issues in April. STEALable marketing ideas in every issue. Sample copies are available.
Cost: $145.00
16 Pages
Frequency: Monthly
Circulation: 1000
Founded in 1980
Mailing list available for rent: 6M names at $110 per M
Printed in 2 colors on matte stock

17650 **Levin's Public Relations Report**
Levin Public Relations & Marketing
2 East Ave
Suite 201
Larchmont, NY 10538-2419

914-834-2570
Fax: 914-834-5919
Home Page: www.saralevin.com

Sara B Levin, President
Sylvia Moss, Editor

Strategies, tactics for the CEO, VP Sales and Marketing seeking new marketing/public relations effectiveness.
Cost: $29.00
Frequency: Quarterly
Founded in 1978

17651 **Licensing Journal**
PO Box 1169
Stamford, CT 06904-1169

203-358-0848

Charles Grimes, Publisher

A publication directed to leaders in the Intellectual Property, Technology and Entertainment Communities. Accepts advertising.
Cost: $150.00
23 Pages
Frequency: Annual
Circulation: 1,000

17652 **Licensing Letter**
EPM Communications
19 W. 21st St., #303
New York, NY 10010

212-941-0099
888-852-9467
Fax: 212-941-1622
E-Mail: info@epmcom.com
Home Page: www.epmcom.com

Ira Mayer, President
Michele Khan, Marketing

Contains features on licensed properties, market trends and survey analysis.
Cost: $467.00
Frequency: 22x Year
Founded in 1977

17653 **Long Haul Market**
Probe Research
3 Wing Drive
Suite 240
Cedar Knolls, NJ 07927-1000

973-285-1500
Fax: 973-285-1519
Home Page: www.proberesearch.com

In this report, we take a look into the long haul market space and discuss some of the reasons - supply, demand and the resulting prices - that have reversed these service providers fortunes so dramatically over the past year or so. We also discuss long haul product lines, new networking technology and provide a table comparing market participants for convenient reference.

17654 **M-Commerce Security**
Probe Research
3 Wing Drive
Suite 240
Cedar Knolls, NJ 07927-1000

973-285-1500
Fax: 973-285-1519
Home Page: www.proberesearch.com

In this bulletin, we examine the issue of security in the m-commerce transaction and the technologies that are appering to address it. We also create international m-commerce forecasts by region.

17655 **Mainly Marketing**
Schoonmaker Associates
30150 Telegraph Road
Suite 155
Bringham Farms, MI 48025

248-594-7800
Fax: 866-211-5711
E-Mail: info@mainlymkt.com
Home Page: www.mainlymkt.com

WK Schoonmaker, Publisher

Marketing high technology products.

17656 **Make It Happen**
Action Marketing
3747 NE Sandy Boulevard
Portland, OR 97232-1840

503-287-8321
Fax: 503-282-2980

CE Colwell, Publisher

Marketing news for starting a business and marketing products.

17657 **Market: Africa/Mid-East**
PRS Group
6320 Fly Rd
Suite 102
East Syracuse, NY 13057-9792

315-431-0511
Fax: 315-431-0200
E-Mail: custserv@prsgroup.com
Home Page: www.prsgroup.com

Mary Lou Walsh, President
Patti Davis, Chairman
Ben McTernan, Managing Editor
Patty Redhead, Production Manager

Demographic and lifestyle information about consumers in Africa and the Middle East.
Cost: $397.00
Frequency: Monthly
Founded in 1979

17658 **Market: Asia Pacific**
PRS Group
6320 Fly Rd
Suite 102
East Syracuse, NY 13057-9792

315-431-0511
Fax: 315-431-0200

E-Mail: custserv@prsgroup.com
Home Page: www.prsgroup.com

Mary Lou Walsh, President
Patti Davis, Chairman
Ben McTernan, Managing Editor
Patty Redhead, Production Manager

Population and lifestyle trend information about consumers in the Asia-Pacific region.
Cost: $397.00
Frequency: Monthly
Circulation: 225
Founded in 1979
Printed in 2 colors on matte stock

17659 Market: Latin America

PRS Group
6320 Fly Rd
Suite 102
East Syracuse, NY 13057-9792

315-431-0511
Fax: 315-431-0200
E-Mail: custserv@prsgroup.com
Home Page: www.prsgroup.com

Mary Lou Walsh, President
Patti Davis, Chairman
Ben McTernan, Managing Editor
Patty Redhead, Production Manager

Population and lifestyle trend information about consumers in the Latin America region.
Frequency: Monthly
Founded in 1979

17660 Marketing Academics Newsletter

American Marketing Association
311 S Wacker Dr
Suite 5800
Chicago, IL 60606-6629

312-542-9000
800-262-1150
Fax: 312-542-9001
Home Page: www.marketingpower.com
Social Media: Facebook, Twitter, LinkedIn, Youtube

Dennis Dunlap, CEO

This newsletter provides news and information that affect and inform this important constituency. It reviews Academic Council activities, profiles Academic SIGS and highlights upcoming events.
Mailing list available for rent

17661 Marketing Communications Report

14629 SW 104 Street
#272
Miami, FL 33186-4929

305-595-0063
Fax: 305-595-0380

Pete Silver, Editor

Highlights prevalent thoughts on successful marketing strategies and reviews new products.
Frequency: Monthly

17662 Marketing Dynamics

Recognition Technologies Users Association
10 High Street
Suite 630
Boston, MA 02110-1605

FAX 617-426-8911

Franklin Cooper, Publisher

Focuses on strategic marketing and planning in technology and industrial areas including technology commercialization. Also features articles on government programs and how to participate in them. International market and business development also are featured.
Cost: $120.00
Frequency: Bi-Monthly
Circulation: 5,000
Printed in 2 colors on glossy stock

17663 Marketing Insights

WPI Communications
55 Morris Ave
Suite 300
Springfield, NJ 07081-1422

973-467-8700
800-323-4995
Fax: 973-467-0368
E-Mail: info@wpicomm.com
Home Page: www.wpicomm.com

Steve Klinghoffer, President
Marilyn Lang, Chairman
Founded in 1952

17664 Marketing Library Services

Information Today
143 Old Marlton Pike
Medford, NJ 08055-8750

609-654-6266
800-300-9868
Fax: 609-654-4309
E-Mail: custserv@infotoday.com
Home Page: www.infotoday.com

Thomas H Hogan, President
Roger R Bilboul, Chairman Of The Board

Provides information professional in all types of libraries with specfic ideas for marketing their services.
Cost: $79.95
Frequency: Bi Monthly
ISSN: 0896-3908
Mailing list available for rent

17665 Marketing Matters Newsletter

American Marketing Association
311 S Wacker Dr
Suite 5800
Chicago, IL 60606-6629

312-542-9000
800-262-1150
Fax: 312-542-9001
Home Page: www.marketingpower.com
Social Media: Facebook, Twitter, LinkedIn, Youtube

Dennis Dunlap, CEO

This e-newsletter updates readers on the latest happenings in the marketing profession through news briefs, indepth features and interviews
Frequency: 2x/Monthly
Mailing list available for rent

17666 Marketing Power Newsletter

American Marketing Association
311 S Wacker Dr
Suite 5800
Chicago, IL 60606-6629

312-542-9000
800-262-1150
Fax: 312-542-9001
Home Page: www.marketingpower.com
Social Media: Facebook, Twitter, LinkedIn, Youtube

Dennis Dunlap, CEO

This update of the latest news, research and trends in the marketing industry and allied fields.
Frequency: Weekly
Mailing list available for rent

17667 Marketing Pulse

Unlimited Positive Communications
11 N Chestnut Street
New Paltz, NY 12561-1706

845-565-0615
Fax: 845-255-2231

Bill Harvey, Editor/Publisher

Focus on all aspects of new electronic media, advertising, entertainment, and marketing.
Cost: $300.00
Frequency: Monthly
Founded in 1979

17668 Marketing Report

Progressive Business Publications
PO Box 3019
Malvern, PA 19355-0719

610-695-0201
800-220-5000
Fax: 610-647-8098
E-Mail: customer_service@pbp.com
Home Page: www.pbp.com

Ed Satell, CEO
Christine Wheeler, Marketing Manager
Cost: $264.00
8 Pages
Founded in 1989

17669 Marketing Researchers Newsletter

American Marketing Association
311 S Wacker Dr
Suite 5800
Chicago, IL 60606-6629

312-542-9000
800-262-1150
Fax: 312-542-9001
Home Page: www.marketingpower.com
Social Media: Facebook, Twitter, LinkedIn, Youtube

Dennis Dunlap, CEO

This e-newsletter provides members with content designed to educate and inform researchers or any member interested in marketing research topics.
Mailing list available for rent

17670 Marketing Science Institute Newsletter

Marketing Science Institute
1000 Massachusetts Ave
Suite 1
Cambridge, MA 02138-5379

617-491-2060
Fax: 617-491-2065
E-Mail: msi@msi.org
Home Page: www.msi.org

Russ Winer, Executive Director
Leana McAlister, CEO

Focuses on people and events of MSI.
Circulation: 8000
Founded in 1968

17671 Marketing Technology

Zhivago Marketing Partners
381 Seaside Dr
Jamestown, RI 02835-2376

401-423-2400
Fax: 401-423-2700
E-Mail: kristin@zhivago.com
Home Page: www.zhivago.com

Kristin Zhivago, President
Philip Zhivago, CEO
Thomas Baker, Owner

Solutions to internal political problems encountered by high-tech marketers, critiques marketing campaigns, and discuss what's working.
Cost: $269.00
Frequency: Monthly
Founded in 1970

17672 Marketing Thought Leaders Newsletter

American Marketing Association

311 S Wacker Dr
Suite 5800
Chicago, IL 60606-6629

312-542-9000
800-262-1150
Fax: 312-542-9001
Home Page: www.marketingpower.com
Social Media: Facebook, Twitter, LinkedIn, Youtube

Dennis Dunlap, CEO

These articles focus on the issues and concepts that shape marketing today and tomorrow.
Frequency: Monthly
Mailing list available for rent

17673 Marketing to Emerging Minorities
EPM Communications
19 W. 21st St., #303
New York, NY 10010

212-941-0099
888-852-9467
Fax: 212-941-1622
E-Mail: info@epmcom.com
Home Page: www.epmcom.com

Ira Mayer, President
Michele Khan, Marketing
Melanie Shreffler, Editor

Research, trends and lifestyle coverage of minority markets.
Cost: $377.00
Frequency: Monthly

17674 Marketscan International
Miller Freeman Publications
2655 Seely Avenue
San Jose, CA 95134

408-943-1234
Fax: 408-943-0513

Paul W Kelash, Editor/Publisher

PC and Networking news in Europe, Asia, and Latin America.
Cost: $395.00
Frequency: Monthly
Founded in 1987

17675 Master Salesmanship
Clement Communications
10 LaCrue Avenue
PO Box 36
Concordville, PA 19331

610-459-4200
888-358-5858
Fax: 610-459-4582
E-Mail: customerservice@clement.com
Home Page: www.clement.com

Andrew B Clancy, Managing Editor
George Clement, President

Newsletter for professional salespeople.
Cost: $156.00
Founded in 1919

17676 Meditation Software Market
Probe Research
3 Wing Drive
Suite 240
Cedar Knolls, NJ 07927-1000

973-285-1500
Fax: 973-285-1519
Home Page: www.proberesearch.com

Examines the mediation market, the major and niche players, functionality of the solutions, and service provider deployments.

17677 Multimedia Strategist
Leader Publications
345 Park Avenue S
New York, NY 10010-1707

212-779-9200
800-888-8300
Fax: 212-696-1848
E-Mail: reprintscustomerservice@alm.com
Home Page: www.alm.com

Stuart M Wise, Editor
Kerry Kyle, Circulation Director
William L Pollak, CEO/President
Aric Press, Editorial Director
Kevin Vermeulen, Vice President, Group Publisher
Cost: $175.00
Frequency: Monthly
ISSN: 1080-3904
Founded in 1997

17678 New Account Selling
Dartnell Corporation
4660 N Ravenswood Avenue
Chicago, IL 60640-4510

773-907-9500
Fax: 773-561-3801

Clark Fetridge, Publisher
Terry Breen, Editor

Timely and effective techniques for building sales and improving profits. Instructive series ideal for training new sales people and for increasing the productivity of your sales veterans.
Cost: $62.00

17679 New Age Marketing Opportunities Newsletter
New Editions International
PO Box 2578
Sedona, AZ 86339-2578

928-282-9574
800-777-4751
Fax: 928-282-9730
Home Page: www.newagemarket.com

Sophia Tarila PhD, Production Manager

Focuses on issues dealing with good marketing buys, resources and pertinent marketing programs dealing in the historic, visionary marketplace.
Cost: $24.00
4 Pages
Frequency: Bi-Monthly
Circulation: 450
Mailing list available for rent
Printed in one color on matte stock

17680 Next Genaration IAD for SOHO Markets
Probe Research
3 Wing Drive
Suite 240
Cedar Knolls, NJ 07927-1000

973-285-1500
Fax: 973-285-1519
Home Page: www.proberesearch.com

Examines the market for VoDSL - comapatible Integrated Access Devices (IAD) targeted toward SOHO customers. Identifies key issues associated with development, analyzes competitive dynamics and market requirements and reviews selected vendor products.

17681 On The Move
Transportation Marketing Communications Assoc
9382 Oak Avenue
Waconia, MN 55387

952-442-5638
Fax: 952-442-3941
E-Mail: briano7@tmcatoday.org
Home Page: www.tmcatoday.org

John Ferguson, President
Tom Nightingale, VP
Tracy Robinson, Treasurer
Edward Moritz, Secretary
Brian Everett, Executive Director

Provides regular feature articles on ways to effectively create more impact in transportation marketing, sales and communications strategies.

17682 Online Marketing Letter
Cyberware Media
1005 Terminal Way
Suite 110
Reno, NV 89502

808-874-0089
Home Page: www.cyberware.com

Jonathan Mizel, Editor/Publisher

Reviews the marketing of products and services over commercial online services of the internet.
Cost: $195.00
Frequency: Quarterly
Founded in 1993

17683 Online Marketplace
Jupiter Communications Company
627 Broadway
2nd Floor
New York, NY 10012-2612

212-533-8885
Fax: 212-780-6075

Adam Schoenfeld, Editor
Gene DeRose, Publisher

Interactive transaction.
Cost: $545.00
Frequency: Monthly

17684 Organized Executive
Briefings Publishing Group
1101 King St
Suite 110
Alexandria, VA 22314-2944

703-548-3800
800-722-9221
Fax: 703-684-2136
Home Page: www.briefings.com

Stephanie Winston, Editor-in-Chief
Lois Willingham, Production Manager

A publication designed to help busy people more effectively master their activities and time by applying advanced organizational strategies developed by Stephanie Winston.
Cost: $97.00
8 Pages
Frequency: Monthly
Circulation: 30000
Founded in 1981
Mailing list available for rent: 6000 names at $125 per M
Printed in 2 colors on matte stock

17685 Overcoming Objections
Dartnell Corporation
4660 N Ravenswood Avenue
Chicago, IL 60640-4510

773-907-9500
Fax: 773-561-3801

Clark Fetridge, Publisher
Christen Heide, Editor

Designed to give sales team practical responses to every objection they're likely to face and imparts proven techniques for turning every type of sales objection into a sales opportunity
Cost: $62.00

17686 Perspectives
1375 King Avenue
PO 12279
Columbus, OH 43212-2220

614-486-6708
800-448-0398
Fax: 614-486-1819

E-Mail: service@mark-ed.com
Home Page: www.mark-ed.org

J Gleason, President
Mary Carlisi, Production Manager

Information on education and marketing. Provides professional support and materials. Primary clients are schools, colleges and educational institutions.
Cost: $25.00
Circulation: 7500
Founded in 1971
Printed in 4 colors on matte stock

17687 Photo Marketing
Photo Marketing Association International
3000 Picture Pl
Jackson, MI 49201-8853

517-788-8100
Fax: 517-788-8371
Home Page: www.pmai.org

Ted Fox, CEO
Terri Cameron, Publisher
Cost: $30.00
Frequency: Monthly
Founded in 1980

17688 PostScripts
Mailing & Fulfillment Service Association
1421 Prince Street
Suite 410
Alexandria, VA 22314-2806

703-836-9200
Fax: 703-548-8204
E-Mail: mfsa-mail@mfsanet.org
Home Page: www.mfsanet.org
Social Media: Facebook, Twitter, LinkedIn

Leo Raymond, Editor
Leo Raymond, Vice President

Each issue of PostScripts highlights a theme relevant to mailing or fulfillment operations, such as production management or information technology.
Frequency: 18x/Year
Circulation: 2800

17689 Postal Points
Mailing & Fulfillment Service Association
1421 Prince Street
Suite 410
Alexandria, VA 22314-2806

703-836-9200
Fax: 703-548-8204
E-Mail: mfsa-mail@mfsanet.org
Home Page: www.mfsanet.org
Social Media: Facebook, Twitter, LinkedIn

Leo Raymond, Editor
Leo Raymond, Vice President

Deals exclusively with current and pending postal and delivery issues. Here you will find the facts and analysis of developing postal issues.
Frequency: 18x/Year

17690 Premium Marketing Club of New York
Association of Retail Marketing Services
10 Drs James Parker Boulevard
Suite 103
Red Bank, NJ 07701-1500

732-842-5070
Fax: 732-219-1938
Home Page: www.goarms.com

Gerri Hopkins, Executive Director
Lisa McCauley, Administrative Director

Provides education and networking information.
Frequency: 10 per year
Founded in 1930
Printed in one color

17691 Pricing Advisor
Pricing Advisor
3535 Roswell Rd
Suite 59
Marietta, GA 30062-8828

770-509-9933
Fax: 770-509-1963
E-Mail: info@pricingsociety.com
Home Page: www.pricingsociety.com

Eric Mitchell, President
Michelle Darko, Editor
Sobem Nwoko, COO

Pricing strategy and tactics for marketing and corporate executives.
Cost: $400.00
8 Pages
Frequency: Monthly

17692 Product Alert
Marketing Intelligence Service
482 N Main St
Canandaigua, NY 14424-1049

585-374-6326
800-836-5710
Fax: 585-374-5217
Home Page: www.productscan.com

Christine Dengler, Marketing Manager
Tom Vierhile, CEO
Diane Beach, Editor

A twice-monthly briefing on new packaged goods introduced in North America. Featuring product pictures and descriptions with indexing provided in two convenient formats. Also available in a twice monthly, international version.
Cost: $795.00

17693 Promos & Premiums
New World Media
PO Box 95
Newton Centre, MA 02156

781-483-8967
Fax: 617-367-9151

Jennifer Sawyer English, Editor/Publisher
Barbara Kalunian, Publisher

Informs consumers, collectors, dealers, and marketing executives about the best special offers available nationwide.
Cost: $19.95
Frequency: Monthly
Founded in 1994

17694 Research Alert
EPM Communications
19 W. 21st St., #303
New York, NY 10010

212-941-0099
888-852-9467
Fax: 212-941-1622
E-Mail: info@epmcom.com
Home Page: www.epmcom.com

Ira Mayer, President
Michele Khan, Marketing
Melanie Shreffler, Editor

Analyzes research on consumer behavior and attitudes.
Cost: $389.00
Frequency: 24x Year

17695 Revisiting R&D
Probe Research
3 Wing Drive
Suite 240
Cedar Knolls, NJ 07927-1000

973-285-1500
Fax: 973-285-1519
Home Page: www.proberesearch.com

With the collapse of the bull market and the apparent collapse of viable wireline competition, the ILECs must focus on the role of wireless as a major competitor. The new Bush administration appears to be pro-ILEC and this will translate into a series of regulatory initiatives that may in total favor the ILECs R&D agendas have to shift to support innovative solutions in the access domain and in mobile.

17696 Roper's Public Pulse
Roper Starch Worldwide
29 W 35th Street
5th Floor
New York, NY 10001-2299

212-240-5300
Fax: 212-564-0465
E-Mail: dcrispell@roper.com
Home Page: www.roper.com

Diane Crispell, Editor

Content includes the latest research on demographic trends, new insights from opinion research experts as to what Americans think, concise, brand-focused data, current consumer attitudes toward dozens of American themes, as well as news updates on special markets and brands.
Cost: $299.00
Frequency: Monthly
Circulation: 2000

17697 SBC
Probe Research
3 Wing Drive
Suite 240
Cedar Knolls, NJ 07927-1000

973-285-1500
Fax: 973-285-1519
Home Page: www.proberesearch.com

Discussion and analysis of ILEC/vendor market dynamics; case study of SBC's metro optical architecture; technology evolution; new services offered; incorporation of passive optical networking and metro DWDM rollouts; strategy going forward.

17698 Sales Bullet
Economics Press
12 Daniel Road
Fairfield, NJ 07004-2565

973-227-1224
Fax: 973-227-9742

Robert Guder, Editor
Diane Cody, Promotional Director

Covers the fundamental and subtleties of professional selling with methods, principles and ideas all salespoeple will find useful.
Circulation: 9,000

17699 Sales Manager's Bulletin
Bureau of Business Practice
76 Ninth Avenue
7th Floor
New York, NY 10011

212-771-0600
Fax: 212-771-0885
Home Page: www.aspenpublishers.com

Robert Becker, CEO
Gustavo Dobles, VP Operations

For front-line sales management. Focus on sales hiring, training, managing, motivation, results. Reports what people in sales management field are doing to produce measurable sales profits.
Cost: $9.00
Circulation: 4,290

17700 Sales Productivity Review
Penoyer Communications
PO Box 2509
Santa Clara, CA 95055-2509

408-248-5458
800-248-5458

Fax: 408-296-6917
E-Mail: info@penoyer.com
Home Page: www.penoyer.com

Flyn Penoyer, President

Edited for sales management with an editorial focus that will assist in improving sales productivity and effectiveness.
Cost: $5.00
Frequency: 6 issues per ye

17701 Sales Promotion Monitor
Commerce Communications
418 N 3rd Street
Suite 303
Milwaukee, WI 55410-2444

414-225-9085
Fax: 414-225-9095
E-Mail: tom@com-broker.com
Home Page: www.com-broker.com

K Sederberg, Publisher
Tom Millitzer, Contact

News and information concerning all aspects of sales promotion.

17702 Sales Rep's Advisor
Alexander Communications Group
1916 Park Ave
Suite 501
New York, NY 10037-3733

212-281-6099
800-232-4317
Fax: 212-283-7269
E-Mail: info@repsadvisor.com
Home Page: www.repsadvisor.com

Romauld Alexander, President
Bill Keenan, Editor
Adam Reis, Marketing

For independent manufacturers sales representatives. Filled with concise advice and ideas for reducing costs and increasing profits.
Cost: $199.00
Frequency: Monthly
ISSN: 0278-5048
Founded in 1954

17703 Sarah Stambler's E-Tactics Letter
E-Tactics
370 Central Park W
#210
New York, NY 10025-6517

212-222-1713
Fax: 212-678-6357
E-Mail: info@e-tactics.com
Home Page: www.e-tactics.com

Sarah Stambler, President
Shlomo Bar-Ayal, Circulation Manager

Publication devoted to the creative use of electronic alternative media in the design and implementation of customer driven marketing, research and publication strategies.
Circulation: 5000
ISSN: 1070-809X
Founded in 1984

17704 School Marketing Newsletter
School Market Research Institute
1721 Saybrook Road
PO Box 10
Haddam, CT 06438

860-345-8183
800-838-3444
Fax: 860-345-3985
E-Mail: school.market@snet.net
Home Page: www.school-market.com

Bob Stimolo, Publisher
Lynn Stimolo, Account Executive
Sally Chittenden, Account Executive

How to articles, trends, original research, interviews with experts on school marketing Pre-K - 12th.
Cost: $119.00
12 Pages
Frequency: Monthly
Circulation: 500
ISSN: 0882-701X
Founded in 1980
Printed in one color on matte stock

17705 Selling Advantage
Progressive Business Publications
PO Box 3019
Malvern, PA 19355-0719

610-695-0201
800-220-5000
Fax: 610-647-8098
E-Mail: webmaster@pbp.com
Home Page: www.pbp.com

Ed Satell, CEO
Phillip Ahr, Editor

Business-to-business sales advice to assist sales staff and sales managers.
Cost: $94.56
Circulation: 60,000
Founded in 1989

17706 Selling To Kids
Phillips Publishing
PO Box 611130
Potomac, MD 20859-2931

301-208-6787
Fax: 301-340-1451
Home Page: www.phillips.com/cgi/catalog/info?m2k

Angela Duff, Associate Publisher

Editorial offers news and practical advice on strategies in successful marketing. Includes information on market research, buying trends, and media opportunities and features news on conferences as well as a look at new products and services.
Cost: $495.00
Frequency: BiWeekly

17707 Selling to Seniors
CD Publications
8204 Fenton St
Silver Spring, MD 20910-4571

301-588-6380
800-666-6380
Fax: 301-588-6385
E-Mail: info@cdpublications.com
Home Page: www.cdpublications.com

Michael Gerecht, President
Jean Van Ryzin, Editor

Published as a subscriber driven newsletter targeting marketers and advertisers of products and services for the mature market.
Cost: $294.00
Frequency: Monthly
Founded in 1961
Mailing list available for rent: 2,000 names at $160 per M

17708 Service Level Agreements
Probe Research
3 Wing Drive
Suite 240
Cedar Knolls, NJ 07927-1000

973-285-1500
Fax: 973-285-1519
Home Page: www.proberesearch.com

Details service level agreements that are being offered by several major service providers, and examines many of the popular software solutions taht are being used in their networks. Also a briefly discusses XML, and its potential uses.

17709 Siedlecki on Marketing
Richard Siedlecki Business & Marketing
4767 Lake Forrest Drive NE
Atlanta, GA 30342-2539

770-436-8271
Fax: 403-303-9939

Richard Siedlecki, Editor

Tips, techniques, and insights on marketing.
Cost: $49.00
6 Pages
Frequency: BiWeekly
Circulation: 500
Printed in one color on matte stock

17710 Strategic Health Care Marketing
Health Care Communications
11 Heritage Lane
PO Box 594
Rye, NY 10580-594

914-967-6741
Fax: 914-967-3054
E-Mail: healthcomm@aol.com
Home Page: www.strategichealthcare.com

Michele von Dambrowski, Editor/Publisher
Michele von Dambrowski, CEO

Business development and marketing startegies for health care executives.
Cost: $279.00
12 Pages
Frequency: Monthly
Circulation: 1200
Founded in 1984
Printed in 2 colors on matte stock

17711 Subscribe
PO Box 194
Bryn Mawr, PA 19010-0194
Lynn Kerrigan, Editor
Gail Jennings, Administration

A newsletter offering marketing ideas to help gain new subscribers and retain old ones.
Cost: $49.00
Frequency: Quarterly

17712 Successful Closing Techniques
Dartnell Corporation
4660 N Ravenswood Avenue
Chicago, IL 60640-4510

773-907-9500
Fax: 773-561-3801

Clark Fetridge, Publisher
Terry Breen, Editor

Fail-safe techniques for acquiring bigger sales and more frequent closings.
Cost: $62.00

17713 Target Market News
Target Market News
228 S Wabash Ave
Suite 210
Chicago, IL 60604-2383

312-408-1881
Fax: 312-408-1867
E-Mail: TargetMarketNews@aol.com
Home Page: www.targetmarketnews.com
Social Media: Facebook, Twitter

Ken Smikle, President
Hallie Mummert, Editor

News and developments in the areas of black consumer marketing and black-oriented media.
Cost: $40.00
12 Pages
Frequency: Monthly
Founded in 1988

17714 Trends Journal
Trends Research Institute

P.O.Box 3476
Kingston, NY 12402-3476

845-876-6700
Fax: 845-758-5252
Home Page: www.trendsresearch.com

Gerald Celente, Editor
Emily Arter, Manager

Offers the inside track on trends affecting your business, your profession, your life. Forecasts on over 300 trend categories - consumer, social, economic, political, media, health, family, education, and other domestic and international trends.
Cost: $185.00
Frequency: Quarterly
Founded in 1980
Printed in 2 colors on glossy stock

17715 Upline
MLM Publishing
106 W South Street
Charlottesvle, VA 22902-5039

FAX 434-979-1602

John Milton Fogg, Editor
Randolph Byrd, Publisher

Distribution training for network (multilevel) marketers.
Founded in 1990

17716 Video Marketing Newsletter
Outback Group Productions
PO Box 872
Harrison, AR 72602-0872

FAX 870-741-4727

Dan Reynolds, Editor/Publisher

Information, business opportunities, marketing tips, product reviews. For people interested in producing and marketing their own videos.
Cost: $185.00
Frequency: Monhtly
Founded in 1989

17717 What's Working in Sales Management
Progressive Business Publications
PO Box 3019
Malvern, PA 19355-0719

610-695-0201
800-220-5000
Fax: 610-647-8098
E-Mail: webmaster@pbp.com
Home Page: www.pbp.com

Ed Satell, CEO
Richard Kern, Editor

Sales management news and issues.
Cost: $264.00
Founded in 1989

17718 Youth Markets Alert
EPM Communications
19 W. 21st St., #303
New York, NY 10010
212-941-0099
888-852-9467
Fax: 212-941-1622
E-Mail: info@epmcom.com
Home Page: www.epmcom.com

Ira Mayer, President
Michele Khan, Marketing
Larissa Faw, Editor

Research reports on trends in youth response to marketing techniques and buying.
Cost: $447.00
Frequency: 24x Year

Magazines & Journals

17719 ADCLIP
National Research Bureau
320 Valley St
Burlington, IA 52601-5513

319-752-5415
Fax: 319-752-3421
E-Mail: mail@national-research-bureau.com
Home Page: www.national-research-bureau.com

Diane M Darnall, President
Nancy Heinzel, Circulation Manager

Individualized adclipping service providing market intelligence information on various retail operations. Includes full size, pages, market strategies, advertising promotion ideas, new store openings and more.

17720 Adage Global
Crain Communications
711 3rd Ave
New York, NY 10017-4014

212-210-0785
Fax: 212-210-0200
E-Mail: info@crain.com
Home Page: www.crain.com

Norm Feldman, President
Scott Donaton, Editor
David Klein, Publisher
Philip Scarano, Circulation Director
Vanessa Reed, Marketing Director

Dedicated to being the world's essential advertising, marketing and media publication, with editors around the world, Adage covers topics of significance form Times Square to Taiwan.
Cost: $69.95
Frequency: Weekly
Circulation: 57,800
Founded in 1943
Printed in 4 colors

17721 Advertising Age
Ad Age Group/Division of Crain Communications
711 3rd Ave
New York, NY 10017-4014

212-210-0785
Fax: 212-210-0465
E-Mail: jbloom@adage.com
Home Page: www.adage.com

Norm Feldman, President

Editorial insights, exclusive analysis and proprietary data take readers beyond the day's news giving it context helping our audience understand ongoing and emerging trends.
Frequency: Weekly
Circulation: 56650

17722 Adweek
Prometheus Global Media
770 Broadway
New York, NY 10003-9595

212-493-4100
Fax: 646-654-5368
Home Page: www.prometheusgm.com
Social Media: Facebook, Twitter, RSS

Richard D. Beckman, CEO
James A. Finkelstein, Chairman
Madeline Krakowsky, Vice President Circulation
Tracy Brator, Executive Director Creative Service

Adweek is the source for advertising and agency news, information and opinion. Covering the industry from an agency perspective Adweek focuses on the image makersand those who create the strategy and the ads as well as those who buy the media and handle client relations.
Cost: $149.00
Frequency: Weekly
Circulation: 36032
Founded in 1978

17723 Agency Sales Magazine
Manufacturers Agents National Association
16-A Journey
Suite 200
Aliso Viejo, CA 92656

949-859-4040
877-626-2776
Fax: 949-855-2973
E-Mail: mana@manaonline.org
Home Page: www.manaonline.org

Jack Foster, Editor

Chronicling the changes which continue to take place nationwide that affect you and your business. Explores the latest tax developments, sales tips, market data, management aids, legal bulletins and more.
96 Pages
Frequency: Monthly
Circulation: 50000
Printed in on glossy stock

17724 Agri Marketing Magazine
Henderson Communications LLC
1422 Elbridge Payne Rd
Suite 250
Chesterfield, MO 63017-8544

636-728-1428
Fax: 636-777-4178
E-Mail: info@agrimarketing.com
Home Page: www.agrimarketing.com

Lynn Henderson, President

Covers the unique interests of corporate agribusiness executives, their marketing communications agencies, the agricultural media, ag trade associations and other ag related professionals.
Circulation: 8000
Founded in 1962

17725 AgriSelling Principles and Practices
Henderson Communications LLC
1422 Elbridge Payne Rd
Suite 250
Chesterfield, MO 63017-8544

636-728-1428
Fax: 636-777-4178
E-Mail: info@agrimarketing.com
Home Page: www.agrimarketing.com

Lynn Henderson, President
Marilyn Holschuh, Editor

This 448-page book is utilized by many major agribusiness corporations and academic institutions for training its sales and marketing staff and or students.

17726 American Demographics
Primedia
Customer Service
PO Box 2042
Marion, OH 43306-8142

800-529-7502
Fax: 740-389-5574
Home Page: www.demographics.com

Kerry J Smith, Publisher
Seema Nayyar, Editor

Coverage includes regional and national consumer trends, lifestyles, media preferences and purchasing behaviors. Regular features present case histories and in-depth demographic profiles.
Cost: $69.00
Frequency: Monthly
Circulation: 34,304

17727 **Brand Marketing**
Fairchild Publications
7 W 34th St
New York, NY 10001-8100
212-988-2882
Fax: 212-630-3868
E-Mail: info@brandmarketingltd.com
Home Page: www.brandmarketingltd.com

Richard Faul, Publisher
Mary Berner, President

Covers how manufactureres launch and build brands, and how they leverage brand equity in new ways using new techniques. These ways include partnerships with retailers via trade marketing and information technology and a variety of cost-reduction strategies such as everyday low pricing and efficient consumer response.
Cost: $90.00
Frequency: Monthly
Circulation: 18,543

17728 **Brandweek**
Prometheus Global Media
770 Broadway
New York, NY 10003-9595
212-493-4100
Fax: 646-654-5368
Home Page: www.prometheusgm.com

Richard D. Beckman, CEO
James A. Finkelstein, Chairman
Madeline Krakowsky, Vice President Circulation
Tracy Brater, Executive Director Creative Service

Focuses on marketing strategy and services, brand identity, sponsorships, licensing, media usage and distribution and promotions.
Frequency: Weekly
Circulation: 25784
Founded in 1991

17729 **Broker News**
Broker Publishing
PO Box 20287
Fountain Hills, AZ 85269-0287
480-816-1400
800-475-3565
Fax: 480-836-7767
Home Page: www.brokernews-online.com

Joanne Genualdi, Account Executive

Serving insurance producers and financial planners across the country.
Cost: $12.00
32+ Pages
Frequency: Bi-Monthly
Founded in 1990

17730 **BtoB Magazine**
Ad Age Group/ Division of Crain Communications
711 3rd Ave
New York, NY 10017-4014
212-210-0785
Fax: 212-210-0200
E-Mail: info@crain.com
Home Page: www.crain.com

Norm Feldman, President

Dedicated to integrated business to business marketing. Every page is packed with substance news, reports, technologies, benchmarks, best practices served up by the most knowledgeable journalists.
Frequency: Monthly
Circulation: 45000

17731 **Business Journal**
120 W Morehead Street
Suite 200
Charlotte, NC 28202
704-472-2340
800-948-5323
Fax: 704-973-1102
E-Mail: borben@bizjournals.com
Home Page: www.bizjournals.com/charlotte

Robert Morris, Editor
Megan Foley, Marketing Manager
Jeannie Falknor, Publisher

Provides marketing solutions and caring service.
Cost: $82.00
Frequency: Monthly

17732 **CRM Magazine**
Information Today
143 Old Marlton Pike
Medford, NJ 08055-8750
609-654-6266
800-300-9868
Fax: 609-654-4309
E-Mail: custserv@infotoday.com
Home Page: www.infotoday.com

Thomas H Hogan, President
Roger R Bilboul, Chairman Of The Board

Offers vital information that will help you benefit from the experience of others in the industry.
Cost: $23.95
Mailing list available for rent: 4M names
Printed in 4 colors on glossy stock

17733 **Catalog Success**
North American Publishing Company
1500 Spring Garden St
Suite 1200
Philadelphia, PA 19130-4094
215-238-5300
Fax: 215-238-5342
E-Mail: phatch@napco.com
Home Page: www.catalogsuccess.com

Ned S Borowsky, CEO
Matt Griffin, Associate Editor
Peggy Hatch, VP Group Publishing

Putting marketing management to the test.
Frequency: Monthly
Circulation: 20000
ISSN: 1524-2307
Founded in 1999
Printed in 4 colors

17734 **Chamber Executive Magazine**
American Chamber of Commerce Executives
4875 Eisenhower Ave
Suite 250
Alexandria, VA 22304-4850
703-998-0072
Fax: 703-212-9512
E-Mail: webmaster@acce.org
Home Page: www.acce.org
Social Media: Facebook, Twitter, LinkedIn

Mick Flemming, President
Frequency: 5X a year

17735 **Circulation Management**
Primedia
1166 Avenue of the Americas/10th Fl
New York, NY 10036
212-204-4200
Fax: 913-514-6895
Home Page: www.penton.com

Eric Jacobson, Senior VP
Ron Wall, Chief Officer
Chris Meyer, Director, Corporate Communications

Serves consumer/special interest and business/trade/association publications.
Frequency: Monthly
ISSN: 0888-8191
Founded in 1986
Printed in 4 colors

17736 **Connect**
Media-Mark
114 Sansome St
Suite 1224
San Francisco, CA 94104-3803
415-743-6220
Fax: 415-421-6225
E-Mail: connect@media-mark.com
Home Page: www.media-mark.com

Art Garcia, Publisher

Features report on news-making agencies and corporate departments making news, as well as the people managing them, and rate/review PR services and products. Regular sections also report on international PR/marketing andmedia, women in marketing, investor relations, internet marketing, senior-level moves and promotions, account changes, trends, case studies and industry chatter.

17737 **Consumer Goods Technology**
Edgell Communications
4 Middlebury Boulevard
Randolph, NJ 07869
973-252-0100
Fax: 973-252-9020
E-Mail: cs@e-circ.net
Home Page: www.edgellcommunications.com

Gabriele A. Edgell, Chairman & CEO
Joe Skorupa, Editor-in-Chief
Andrew Gaffney, Group Publisher
Gerald Ryerson, President

Consumer Goods Technology serves manufacturers of accessories, shoes, apparel, appliances, consumer electronics, office products, automotive aftermarket products, seasonal merchandise, transporters of consumer products, consultants and others allied to the field.
Frequency: Monthly
Circulation: 25035
Founded in 1984
Printed in 4 colors on glossy stock

17738 **Currents**
Council for Advancement & Support of Education
1307 New York Ave Nw
Suite 1000
Washington, DC 20005-4726
202-393-1301
Fax: 202-387-4973
E-Mail: memberservicecenter@case.org
Home Page: www.case.org

John Lippincott, President
Deborah Bongiorno, Editor in chief
Tracy Baird, Marketing
Anne Eigeman, Editor

Offers articles on integrated marketing, technology and other industry related information.
Cost: $115.00
Frequency: Monthly
ISSN: 0748-478X
Founded in 1975

17739 **Customer Interaction Solutions**
Technology Marketing Corporation
800 Connecticut Ave
1st Floor East
Norwalk, CT 06854-1936
203-852-6800
800-243-6002
Fax: 203-866-3326
E-Mail: tmc@tmcnet.com

Home Page: www.tmcnet.com
Social Media: Twitter

Rich Tehrani, CEO
Tracey Schelmetic, Editorial Director

Dedicated to teleservices ans e-services outsoucing, marketing and customer relationship management issues.
Frequency: Monthly
Circulation: 13400

17740 CyberDealer
Meister Publishing Company
37733 Euclid Ave
Willoughby, OH 44094-5992

440-942-2000
800-572-7740
Fax: 440-975-3447
Home Page: www.meisternet.com

Gary Fitzgerald, President

Helps agricultural dealerships better manage their operations.
Frequency: 6 per year

17741 DECA Dimensions
Distributive Education Clubs of America
1908 Association Dr
Suite A
Reston, VA 20191-1594

703-860-5000
Fax: 703-860-4013
E-Mail: info@deca.org
Home Page: www.deca.org

Edward Davis, Executive Director
Cindy Allen, Assistant Director
Christopher Young, Assistant Director

For student members interested in marketing, management, and entrepreneurial careers. Delivered to members in the classroom and integrated into the curriculum. Exhibitors welcome to our national and regional conferences.
Cost: $ 5.00
Circulation: 185,000
ISSN: 1060-6106
Founded in 1948
Printed in 4 colors

17742 Daily Record
11 E Saratoga St
Baltimore, MD 21202-2199

410-752-3849
Fax: 410-752-2894
E-Mail: editor@mddailyrecord.com
Home Page: www.mddailyrecord.com

Chris Eddings, Publisher
Mark Chashir, Editor
Susan Hoettner, Marketing
Kris Charddo, Circulation Manager
Cost: $190.00
Frequency: Daily
Circulation: 9000
Founded in 1888

17743 Dealerscope Merchandising
North American Publishing Company
1500 Spring Garden St
Suite 1200
Philadelphia, PA 19130-4094

215-238-5300
800-818-8174
Fax: 215-238-5342
E-Mail: gclauser@napco.com
Home Page: www.napco.com

Ned S Borowsky, CEO
Eric Schwartz, President
Grant Clauser, Editorial Director
David Dritsas, Editor-in-Chief
Sean Downey, Managing Editor

Offers news on the marketing of appliances and consumer electronics on a national and regional basis.
Frequency: Monthly
Circulation: 20000
Founded in 1958

17744 Direct
Primedia
3585 Engineering Drive
Suite 100
Norcross, GA 30092

678-421-3000
800-216-1423
Fax: 212-206-3622
E-Mail: dkarbowski@primedia.com
Home Page: www.primedia.com

Jack Condon, Chief Operating Officer
Ray Schultz, Editorial Director
Charles Vietri, Managing Editor
Elizabeth O'Connor, Publisher

Magazine of direct marketing management.
Cost: $85.00
Circulation: 46,527
Founded in 1989

17745 Do-It-Yourself Retailing
5822 W 74th St
Indianapolis, IN 46278-1756

317-297-1190
Fax: 317-328-4354
Home Page: www.nrha.org

John Hammond, Executive Director

17746 Exhibitor Magazine
206 S Broadway
Suite 745
Rochester, MN 55903-0368

507-289-6556
888-235-6155
Fax: 507-289-5253
Home Page: www.exhibitoronline.com
Social Media: Facebook, Twitter, LinkedIn

Lee Knight, President
John Pavek, VP of Publishing

Mission is to provide trade show marketing professionals with the tools and education to produce high-performance programs with measurable results.
Cost: $78.00
Frequency: Monthly
ISSN: 0739-6821

17747 Greenville Magazine
303 Haywood Rd
Greenville, SC 29607-3426

864-271-1105
Fax: 864-271-1165
Home Page: www.greenvillemagazine.com

Paul Gesimondo, President

Features content summary, web-only extras, advertiser links, and access to reader service forms and various contests and programs.
Frequency: Monthly
Circulation: 10,002

17748 Journal of International Marketing
American Marketing Association
311 S Wacker Dr
Suite 5800
Chicago, IL 60606-6629

312-542-9000
800-262-1150
Fax: 312-542-9001
Home Page: www.marketingpower.com
Social Media: Facebook, Twitter, LinkedIn, Youtube

Dennis Dunlap, CEO

Presents scholarly and managerially relevant articles on international marketing.
Mailing list available for rent

17749 Journal of Marketing Research
American Marketing Association
311 S Wacker Dr
Suite 5800
Chicago, IL 60606-6629

312-542-9000
800-262-1150
Fax: 312-542-9001
Home Page: www.marketingpower.com
Social Media: Facebook, Twitter, LinkedIn, Youtube

Dennis Dunlap, CEO

Covers a wide range of marketing research concepts, methods and applications. You'll read about new techniques, contributions to knowledge based on experimental methods and developments in related fields that have a bearing on marketing research.
Mailing list available for rent

17750 Journal of Nonprofit & Public Sector Marketing
Taylor & Francis
325 Chestnut Street
Suite 800
Philadelphia, PA 19106

800-354-1420
Fax: 215-625-2940
Home Page: www.tandf.co.uk

Gillian Sullivan Mort, Editor

A peer reviewed journal devoted to the study of the adaption of traditional marketing principles for use by nonprofit organizations and government agencies.
Cost: $186.00
Frequency: Quarterly
Circulation: 500
ISSN: 1049-5142
Founded in 1976

17751 Journal of Public Policy & Marketing
American Marketing Association
311 S Wacker Dr
Suite 5800
Chicago, IL 60606-6629

312-542-9000
800-262-1150
Fax: 312-542-9001
Home Page: www.marketingpower.com
Social Media: Facebook, Twitter, LinkedIn, Youtube

Dennis Dunlap, CEO

Each issue features a wide ranging forum for the research, findings and discussion of marketing subjects related to business and government.
Mailing list available for rent

17752 Journal of the Academy of Marketing Science
Sage Publications
2455 Teller Rd
Newbury Park, CA 91320-2234

805-499-9774
800-818-7243
Fax: 800-583-2665
E-Mail: info@sagepub.com
Home Page: www.sagepub.com

Blaise R Simqu, CEO

Promotes research and the dissemination of research results through the study and improvement of marketing as an economic, ethical and social force.
Cost: $112.00
112 Pages
Frequency: Bi-annually

Circulation: 1100
Founded in 1965

17753 License Magazine
Advanstar Communications
641 Lexington Ave
Suite 8
New York, NY 10022-4503
212-951-6600
Fax: 212-951-6793
E-Mail: sekstract@advanstar.com
Home Page: www.licensemag.com
Joseph Loggia, CEO
Tony Lisanti, Editor
Detailed coverage and research on the $177+ billion licensed consumer product business including: retail and merchandising trends; promotional partnerships; available and recently granted property licenses; research reports; and case studies on licensed consumer product categories based on publishing and art, entertainment, brands, sports, fashion, home decor, and interactive media properties
Cost: $59.00
Frequency: Monthly
Circulation: 25000
Founded in 1998
Printed in 4 colors

17754 Magnet Marketing & Sales
Graham Communications
40 Oval Rd
Suite 2
Quincy, MA 02170-3813
617-328-0069
800-659-0069
Fax: 617-471-1504
Home Page: www.grahamcomm.com
John R Graham, President
Cynthia Cantrell, Editor
John Graham, CEO
Jonathan Bloom, Marketing manager
A marketing and sales newsletter.
Cost: $18.95
9 Pages
Frequency: Quarterly
Printed in 2 colors on matte stock

17755 Marketing
Mane/Marketing
13901 NE 175th Street
#M
Woodinville, WA 98072-8548
425-487-9111
Fax: 425-487-3158
E-Mail: coff@marketings.com
Larry Coffman, Publisher
Features important area events, industry projects, awards and executives of note. Highlights the latest information on marketing trends and pattern analysis. Free subscription.
Frequency: Monthly
Circulation: 11M

17756 Marketing Health Services
American Marketing Association
311 S Wacker Dr
Suite 5800
Chicago, IL 60606-6629
312-542-9000
800-262-1150
Fax: 312-542-9001
Home Page: www.marketingpower.com
Social Media: Facebook, Twitter, LinkedIn, Youtube
Dennis Dunlap, CEO
Specifically aimed at senior level healthcare marketers and managers, offers targeted information, practical strategies and thought provoking commentary to help achieve your goals and shape your vision
Frequency: Quarterly
Mailing list available for rent

17757 Marketing Management
American Marketing Association
311 S Wacker Dr
Suite 5800
Chicago, IL 60606-6629
312-542-9000
800-262-1150
Fax: 312-542-9001
Home Page: www.marketingpower.com
Social Media: Facebook, Twitter, LinkedIn, Youtube
Dennis Dunlap, CEO
Focuses on strategic marketing issues that marketing managers face every day.
Frequency: 6x/Year
Mailing list available for rent

17758 Marketing Recreation Classes
Learning Resources Network
1554 Hayes Drive
Manhattan, KS 66502-5068
785-539-5376
Fax: 888-234-8633
E-Mail: draves@lern.org
Home Page: www.lern.org/
William Draves, Editor
This magazine offers information on marketing and advertising trends.
8 Pages
Frequency: Monthly
Founded in 1980

17759 Marketing Research
American Marketing Association
311 S Wacker Dr
Suite 5800
Chicago, IL 60606-6629
312-542-9000
800-262-1150
Fax: 312-542-9001
Home Page: www.marketingpower.com
Social Media: Facebook, Twitter, LinkedIn, Youtube
Dennis Dunlap, CEO
Researchers and managers count on this resource to help stay on top of current methodologies and issues, management concerns and the latest books and software.
Frequency: Quarterly
Mailing list available for rent

17760 Marketing Science: INFORMS
INFORMS
7240 Parkway Dr
Suite 310
Hanover, MD 21076-1344
410-850-0300
800-446-3676
Fax: 410-757-3515
E-Mail: informs@informs.org
Home Page: www.informs.org
Mark Doherty, Executive Director
Barry List, Director Marketing
Patricia Shaffer, Director Publications
Richard C Larson, President
Marketing journal offering marketing and advertising articles. Provides help for marketing decision makers and deeper understanding of marketing phenomena.
Cost: $172.00
Frequency: Quarterly
Circulation: 1800
ISSN: 0732-2399
Founded in 1982

17761 Marketing to Women
EPM Communications
19 W. 21st St., #303
New York, NY 10010
212-941-0099
888-852-9467
Fax: 212-941-1622
E-Mail: info@epmcom.com
Home Page: www.epmcom.com
Ira Mayer, President
Larissa Faw, Editor
Topics covers attitudes and buying behaviors of the female consumer, market segment demographics, gender gap and health issues, media preferences and the role of technology.
Cost: $35.00
Frequency: Monthly

17762 Marketrac
Marketrac San Diego
4 First American Way
Santa Ana, CA 92707
714-250-6400
800-345-7334
Home Page: www.facorelogic.com
Gerald Schultz, Editor
Jim Lucich, Promotional Manager
Marketing communications: people, places, events, trends, new products, technology, public relations, advertising, broadcast, TV, radio, video production, promotions, market research, direct mail, trademark, copyright law, accounting, employee management printing, graphics, color separations, novelty promotions.
Cost: $15.00
32 Pages
Frequency: Monthly

17763 NAPRA ReView
109 N Beach Road
PO Box 9
Eastsound, WA 98245-9
360-376-2001
800-367-1907
Fax: 360-376-2704
E-Mail: marilyn@marilynmcguire.com
Home Page: www.napra.com
Erin Johnson, Advertising Sales
Marilyn McGuire, Editor
Marilyn McGuire, CEO/President
Frequency: 10 issues ayear
Circulation: 180000
Founded in 1986

17764 POINT
Direct Marketing Association
1120 Avenue of the Americas
New York, NY 10036-6713
212-768-7277
Fax: 212-302-6714
Home Page: www.the-dma.org
Social Media: Facebook, Twitter, LinkedIn
John A. Greco Jr, President & CEO
DMA's digital magazine.

17765 POP Design
In-Store Marketing Institute
8550 W. Bryn Mawr
#200
Chicago, IL 60631
773-992-4450
Fax: 773-992-4455
E-Mail: info@instoremarketer.org
Home Page: www.p2pi.org/
Peter Hoyt, President
Serves the news and product information needs of producers and designers of instore displays, signs and fixtures. Each issue features the latest

trends and technologies vital to building and designing successful instore merchandising.
Frequency: Monthly
Circulation: 18000
Printed in 4 colors on glossy stock

17766 PSMJ Marketing Tactics
PSMJ Resources
10 Midland Avenue
Newton, MA 02458-1000

617-965-0055
800-537-7765
Fax: 617-965-5152
E-Mail: info@psmj.com
Home Page: www.psmj.com

Frank Stasiowski, Production Manager

Provides marketing tactics and techniques for the design industry.
Cost: $267.00
8 Pages
Frequency: Monthly
Founded in 1975
Mailing list available for rentat $125 per M
Printed in 2 colors on matte stock

17767 Personal Selling Power
1140 International Parkway
PO Box 5467
Fredericksburg, VA 22406-467

540-752-7000
800-752-7355
Fax: 540-752-7001
E-Mail: feedback@sellingpower.com
Home Page: www.sellingpower.com

John Nuzzi, VP / Associate Publisher
Laura Gschwandtner, CEO

Sales education/motivation magazine designed to train, educate, motivate salespeople.
Cost: $33.00
140 Pages
Frequency: 10 times a year
ISSN: 1093-2216
Printed in 4 colors on glossy stock

17768 Point of Purchase Magazine
1115 Northmeadow Parkway
Roswell, GA 30076

847-647-7987
800-241-9034
Fax: 847-647-9566
E-Mail: popmag@halldata.com
Home Page: www.popmag.com

Murray Kasmenn, Publisher
Julie Andrews, Sales Manager
Larry Shore, Sales Manager
Ted Eshleman, Account Executive
Alison Medina, Executive Editor

Addresses the industry perspective of the brand marketer and the retailer and focuses on retail trends, case studies, statistics and profitability.
Cost: $60.00
Frequency: 9 per year
Circulation: 18,506

17769 Politically Direct
Direct Marketing Association
1120 Avenue of the Americas
New York, NY 10036-6700

212-768-7277
Fax: 212-302-6714
E-Mail: customerservice@the-dma.org
Home Page: www.the-dma.org

Lawrence M Kimmel, CEO

Published both in print and digital versions, this newsletter on DMA advocacy efforts keeps DMA members informed and involved in the politics and policies that impact them today and ahead of the curve on developments that will affect them tomorrow.

17770 PromaxBDA
PROMAX
1522 Cloverfield Blvd.
Suite E
Santa Monica, CA 90404

310-788-7600
Fax: 310-788-7616
Home Page: www.promaxbda.org

Jonathan Black-Verk, President & CEO
Jill Lindeman, General Manager

Magazine, newsletter and directory published by PROMAX for members only, promotion and marketing professionals in electronic media.
Frequency: Annual
Circulation: 2500
Founded in 1952
Printed in 4 colors on glossy stock

17771 Quirk's Marketing Research Review
Quirk Enterprises
4662 Slater Rd
Eagan, MN 55122-2362

651-379-6200
Fax: 651-379-6205
E-Mail: info@quirks.com
Home Page: www.quirks.com
Social Media: Facebook, Twitter, LinkedIn

Steve Quirk, President
Joe Rydholm, Editor
Evan Tweed, Vice President Sales
Alice Davies, Manager

Emphasizes marketing research case histories and techniques used by researchers in a variety of industries, from consumer products to advertising, includes directories of research services and new products and features personnel announcements.
Cost: $70.00
30000 Members
Circulation: 16013
Founded in 1986
Mailing list available for rent: 17000 names
Printed in 4 colors on glossy stock

17772 Recharger Magazine
Recharger Magazine
1050 E Flamingo Rd
Suite N237
Las Vegas, NV 89119-7427

702-438-5557
877-902-9759
Fax: 702-873-9671
E-Mail: info@rechargermag.com
Home Page: www.rechargermag.com

Tom Enerson, Publisher
Amy Turner, Manager
Becky Fenton, Manager
Amy Weiss, Director
Nancy Calabrese, Sales Manager

Information including articles that cover business and marketing, technical updates, association and industry news, and company profiles. Related features focus on the importance of recycling, government legislation, and product comparisons.
Cost: $45.00
Frequency: Monthly
Circulation: 8000
Founded in 1997

17773 Response TV
Advanstar Communications
Ste 300
17770 Cartwright Rd
Irvine, CA 92614-5815

714-513-8400
800-527-7008
Fax: 714-513-8412
E-Mail: george@directresponsetv.com
Home Page: www.directresponsetv.com

John Yarring, Publisher
Thomas Haire, Editor
Joe Logia, CEO/President
Jodi Dressig, Circulation manager
Gina Cohen, Manager

Addresses industry concerns regarding regulatory issues, production, fulfillment and aftermarketing. Designed for direct marketers, product owners and related agencies.
Cost: $39.00
Frequency: Monthly
Circulation: 21345
Founded in 1993

17774 Sales Executive
Sales Marketing Executives of Greater New York
13 E 37th Street
#8
New York, NY 10016-2821

212-685-3613
Fax: 212-725-3752

Edward Glanegan, Publisher
Patricia Israel, Editor

For sales executives in New York.
Circulation: 2,500

17775 Sales Upbeat
Economics Press
12 Daniel Road
Fairfield, NJ 07004-2565

973-227-1224
Fax: 973-227-9742

John Beckley, Publisher
Robert Guder, Editor

Sales methods and techniques, quotes and anecdotes about selling.
Cost: $2.00
Circulation: 52,000

17776 Salesmanship
LRP Publications/Dartnell Corporation
PO Box 980
Horsham, PA 19044-0980

215-784-0912
800-341-7874
Fax: 215-784-9639
E-Mail: webmaster@lrp.com
Home Page: www.lrp.com

Todd Lutz, CFO

Enhances training program with engaging and instructive reminders and shape-up tips that pay off in greater gains from sales force.
Cost: $62.00

17777 Say Yes Marketing Script Presentations
Frieda Carrol Communications
PO Box 416
Denver, CO 80201-0416

303-575-5676

This reference contains marketing presentations for various kinds of businesses.
Cost: $52.95

17778 Security Distributing & Marketing
Reed Business Information
1050 IL Route 83
Suite 200
Bensonville, IL 60106

630-616-0200
Fax: 630-227-0214
Home Page: www.sdmmag.com

Bill Zalud, Editorial Director
Susan Whitehurst, Production Manager
Lyn Sopala, Production Manager

Security Distributing and Marketing serves security installing dealers, security installing dealers with central station equipment, central station services, access control system specialists and systems integrators.
Cost: $82.00
104 Pages
Frequency: 19 per year
Circulation: 28,298
ISSN: 0049-0016
Founded in 1971
Printed in 4 colors on glossy stock

17779 Selling Magazine
Selling Magazine
477 Madison Avenue
New York, NY 10022-5802

212-751-0485
Fax: 212-224-3592

Marjorie Weiss, Publisher

Selling is targeted to business-to-business salespeople.
Cost: $5.00
Circulation: 155162

17780 Senior Marketwatch
Campbell Associates
185 Martling Ave
Tarrytown, NY 10591-4703

914-332-1177
Fax: 914-332-1177

Arnold Thiesfeldt, Publisher

Features research based on tastes, trends, and resources of the senior market, as a means for advertisers and marketers to target and focus their products.
Cost: $242.00
12 Pages
Frequency: Monthly
Founded in 1997

17781 Southern California Marketing Media
Southern California Marketing Media
5 Via Caseta
Rancho Santa Margarita, CA 92688-4947

949-713-3188
Fax: 714-713-3188
E-Mail: gklayman@pacbell.net

Gary Klayman, Publisher

Written to report on marketing strategies, techniques and new products for the Southern California area, includes various company, client and media updates, new trends, and guides to developing individualized marketing programs.

17782 Subscription Marketing
Blue Dolphin Communications
526 Boston Post Road
Wayland, MA 01778-1833

978-358-5795
Fax: 508-358-5795
E-Mail: subs@bluedolphin.com
Home Page: www.bluedolphin.com

Donald L Nicholas, Publisher

Offers trade strategies for maximizing product profitability. Provides perspective on success and failure stories.
Cost: $195.00
Frequency: Monthly

17783 Supermarket News
Fairchild Publications
750 3rd Ave
New York, NY 10017-2703

212-630-4000
800-204-4515
Fax: 212-630-3563
E-Mail: customerservice@fairchildpub.com
Home Page: www.supermarketnews.com

Mary G Berner, CEO
David Merrefield, Editorial Director
Cost: $44.50
40 Pages
Frequency: Weekly
Circulation: 36346
ISSN: 0039-5803
Founded in 1892

17784 TODAY - The Journal of Work Process Improvement
Recognition Technologies Users Association
185 Devonshire Street
Suite 770
Boston, MA 02110-1407

617-426-1167
Fax: 617-521-8675
E-Mail: info@tawpi.org
Home Page: www.tawpi.org

Dan Bolita, Editor
Frank Moran, CEO/President
Jason Glass, VP Sales
Cost: $27.69
Circulation: 5000
ISSN: 1073-2233
Founded in 1997
Printed in 2 colors on glossy stock

17785 Target Marketing
North American Publishing Company
1500 Spring Garden St
Suite 1200
Philadelphia, PA 19130-4094

215-238-5300
Fax: 215-238-5342
E-Mail: editor.tm@napco.com
Home Page: www.targetmarketingmag.com
Social Media: Facebook, Twitter, LinkedIn

Ned S Borowsky, CEO
Lisa Yorgey, Managing Editor
Drew James, Sales Manager

Covers telemarketing, list rental, testing and management, circulation, catalogue and online/web marketing, and direct response advertising.
Cost: $65.00
Frequency: Monthly
Circulation: 42,000
Mailing list available for rent

17786 Telemarketing & Call Center Solutions
Technology Marketing Corporation
800 Connecticut Ave
1st Floor East
Norwalk, CT 06854-1924

203-852-6800
800-243-6002
Fax: 203-866-3326
E-Mail: tmc@tmcnet.com
Home Page: www.tmcnet.com
Social Media: Twitter

Nadji Tehrani, President
Linda Driscoll, Editor

First and only authoritative guide to effective and profitable marketing through business telecommunications. Provides information on technology and services releases, new techniques and management strategies.
Cost: $7.00
Frequency: 24 times
Circulation: 31419
Founded in 1972

17787 Velocity
Strategic Account Management Association
33 N La Salle Street
Suite 3700
Chicago, IL 60602

312-251-3131
Fax: 312-251-3132
Home Page: www.strategicaccounts.org

Greg Bartlett, Editor

Contains exclusive, in-depth articles on topics such as negotiation, customer management, internal alignment and effective team communications.
Cost: $65.00
52 Pages
Frequency: Quarterly
Circulation: 2000
Founded in 1964
Printed in 4 colors

17788 Wireless for the Corporate User
Probe Research
3 Wing Drive
Suite 240
Cedar Knolls, NJ 07927-1000

973-285-1500
Fax: 973-285-1519

Jack Killion, Publisher

Edited for the corporate user/decision maker to keep abreast of the growth product and service offerings, the expanding uses and the technological, political and standardization issues of the wireless arena.
Circulation: 43000

17789 World Trade
BNP Media
2401 W. Big Beaver Rd, Suite 700
Troy, MI 48084

248-362-3700
Home Page: www.bnpmedia.com
Social Media: Facebook, Twitter, LinkedIn

Katie Rotella, President
Cost: $37.00
58 Pages
Frequency: Monthly

Trade Shows

17790 Annual Conference and Mailing Fulfillment Expo
Mailing & Fulfillment Service Association
1421 Prince Street
Suite 410
Alexandria, VA 22314-2806

703-836-9200
Fax: 703-548-8204
E-Mail: mfsa-mail@mfsanet.org
Home Page: www.mfsanet.org
Social Media: Facebook, Twitter, LinkedIn

Ken Garner, President
Jennifer Root, Director
Bill Stevenson, Director Marketing
Leo Raymond, Vice President

Quality educational sessions, industry specific exhibit hall, networking and more.
Frequency: Annual

17791 Annual Conference for Catalog & Multichannel Merchants (ACCM)
Direct Marketing Association
1120 Avenue of Americas
New York, NY 10036

212-768-7277
Fax: 212-302-6714
Home Page: www.the-dma.org
Social Media: Facebook, Twitter, LinkedIn

Julie Hogan, SVP Conference & Events
10M Attendees

17792 Annual Conference on Healthcare Marketing
Alliance for Healthcare Strategy & Marketing
11 S LaSalle Street
Suite 2300
Chicago, IL 60603
312-704-9700
Fax: 312-704-9709
Home Page: www.alliancehlth.org/hlthmktg
Workshop and social events plus 50 exhibits of marketing communications, health care information lines, stategic planning and more.
600 Attendees
Frequency: Annual
Founded in 1984

17793 Business Intelligence Conference
The Conference Board
845 Third Avenue
New York, NY 10022
212-339-0345
Fax: 212-836-9740
Home Page: www.conference-board.org/intelligence.htm
Shows how you can utilize business intelligence in your own organization to enhance performace and drive results.
Frequency: June, Chicago

17794 DMA Annual Conference & Exhibition
Direct Marketing Association
1120 Avenue of Americas
New York, NY 10036-6700
212-768-7277
Fax: 212-302-6714
E-Mail: dmaconferences@the-dma.org
Home Page: www.the-dma.org
Lawrence M Kimmel, CEO
Julie A Hogan, SVP Conferences/Events
Brings together thousands of practitioners and experts from the entire marketing continuum to discuss solutions and best practices to achieve optimal channel mix and integration that lead to measurable results and increase real-time customer engagement.
12000 Attendees
Frequency: October

17795 DMB: Direct Marketing to Business Conference
Target Conference Corporation
11 Riverbend Drive S
Stamford, CT 06907-0949
203-358-9900
Fax: 203-358-5815
Ed Berkowitz
National conference for business to business direct marketers. 75 table tops
1000+ Attendees
Frequency: March
Mailing list available for rent

17796 Direct Marketing Conference National Conference
DMB Miami
Fontainebleau Hilton Resort and Towers
Miami, FL 33152
203-358-3751
800-927-5007
Home Page: www.intertecevents.com
Information on improving R.O.I. and stay ahead of the competition, create customer centric business, synthesize traditional marketing strategies with the internet.

17797 Electronic Retailing Association Annual Convention
Electronic Retailing Association
607 14th Street, NW, Suite 530
Washington, DC 20005
703-841-1751
800-987-6462
Fax: 425-977-1036
E-Mail: contact@retailing.org
Home Page: www.retailing.org
Social Media: Facebook, Twitter, LinkedIn, Youtube.Flickr
Karla Kelly, VP Meetings/Conventions
Christy Brzonkala Hopkins, Meetings Coordinator

17798 Email Evolution Conference
Direct Marketing Association
1120 Avenue of Americas
New York, NY 10036-6700
212-768-7277
Fax: 212-302-6714
E-Mail: dmaconferences@the-dma.org
Home Page: www.the-dma.org
Julie A Hogan, SVP Conference/Events
Lawrence M Kimmel, CEO
Focuses on the ever-changing and evolving world of email marketing, providing you with the best ways to capitalize on the high ROI this low-cost communication tool can provide both on its own, and integrated with social, search, mobile, video and other email enhancers.
10M Attendees
Frequency: Annual/February

17799 Exhibitor Conference
Exhibitor Magazine Group
206 S Broadway
Suite 745
Rochester, MN 55904-6565
507-289-6556
888-235-6155
Fax: 507-289-5253
E-Mail: exhibitorshow@heiexpo.com
Home Page: www.exhibitoronline.com
Social Media: Facebook, Twitter, LinkedIn
Carol Fojtik, Managing Director/Sr Vice President
Conference program combined with exhibit hall featuring latest products and resources shaping the future of exhibiting and corporate event programs. Anyone responsible for planning, managing or implementing trade show or corporate event marketing functions should attend. Conference is held annually in Las Vegas, NV.
5M Attendees
Frequency: March, Las Vegas
Founded in 1989

17800 FSMA Top 2 Top Conference
1810-J York Road #384
Lutherville, MD 21093
410-715-4084
800-617-1170
Fax: 888-668-7496
E-Mail: info@fsmaonline.com
Home Page: www.fsmaonline.com
Bob Watson, Chair
Rick Abraham, President
Frequency: Annual/February
Mailing list available for rent

17801 High Performance Linux on Wall Street
Flagg Management
353 Lexington Avenue
New York, NY 10016
212-286-0333
Fax: 212-286-0086
E-Mail: flaggmgmnt@msn.com
Home Page: www.flaggmgmt.com
Russell Flagg, President
Featuring Linux and HPC futures discussions, virtualization, cloud computing and service-driven datacenters, open source meets low latency, VLDB architectures, cost reduction with Linux, and more.
1000 Attendees
Frequency: Annual
Founded in 2001

17802 MBA Research Conclave
MBAResearch and Curriculum Center
1375 King Avenue
PO Box 12279
Columbus, OH 43212
614-486-6708
800-448-0398
Fax: 614-486-1819
E-Mail: servic@mbaresearch.org
Home Page: www.mbaresearch.org
Marsha Dyer, Customer Service Manager
Kimberly Holstlaw, Executive Adminstrator
James Gleason, President/CEO
Containing 20 booths and 15 exhibits.
500 Attendees
Frequency: June
Founded in 1971

17803 MDMA's Annual Direct Marketing Conference & Expo
Midwest Direct Marketing Association
P.O. Box 75
Andover, MN 55304
763-607-2943
Fax: 763-753-2240
E-Mail: office@mdma.org
Home Page: www.mdma.org
Joan Forde, President
Cindy McCleary, Director
Containing 55 booths and 50 companies exhibiting.
Frequency: April
Mailing list available for rent: 1.1M+ names

17804 MFSA Midwinter Executive Conference
Mailing & Fulfillment Service Association
1421 Prince Street
Suite 410
Alexandria, VA 22314-2806
703-836-9200
Fax: 703-548-8204
E-Mail: mfsa-mail@mfsanet.org
Home Page: www.mfsanet.org
Social Media: Facebook, Twitter, LinkedIn
Ken Garner, President
Jennifer Root, Director
Bill Stevenson, Director Marketing
Leo Raymond, Vice President
Will address financial operations and business valuation, marketing your own company, the changing world of postal regulations, technology in fulfillment, building a sales team, being strong in digital printing and the landscape of employment law.

17805 MLMIA Annual Corporate Convention and Expo
Multi-Level Marketing International Association
119 Stanford Court
Irvine, CA 92612-1671
949-854-0484
Fax: 949-281-2114
E-Mail: info@mlmia.com

Home Page: www.mlmia.com
Social Media: Facebook, Twitter

Doris Wood, Chair/President Emeritus
Del Hickman, Executive Director
Eugene Argent, VP Support
Kate Jackson, Treasurer
Linda Bruno, Secretary

Seeks to strengthen and improve the Direct Sales/Network Marketing/Multi-Level Marketing industry in the United States and abroad. Members are companies which market their products and services directly to consumers through independent distributors, suppliers to the industry and distributors who interface with consumers.
Founded in 1985

17806 **Mailer Strategies Conference**
Mailing & Fulfillment Service Association
1421 Prince Street
Suite 410
Alexandria, VA 22314-2806

703-836-9200
Fax: 703-548-8204
E-Mail: mfsa-mail@mfsanet.org
Home Page: www.mfsanet.org
Social Media: Facebook, Twitter, LinkedIn

Ken Garner, President
Jennifer Root, Director
Bill Stevenson, Director Marketing
Leo Raymond, Vice President

This conference will focus solely on postal issues that are important to your operations.

17807 **Marketing Federation's Annual Conference on Strategic Marketing**
Marketing Federation
109 58th Avenue
Saint Petersburg, FL 33706-2203

727-363-7805
Fax: 727-367-6545

Greg Stemm

Offers attendees information on how to boost attendance at their seminars, conferences and expositions.

17808 **NCDM Conference**
Direct Marketing Association
1120 Avenue of Americas
New York, NY 10036-6700

212-768-7277
Fax: 212-302-6714
E-Mail: dmaconferences@the-dma.org
Home Page: www.the dma.org

Julie A Hogan, SVP Conference/Events
Lawrence M Kimmel, CEO

Presents industry experts and hard-hitting case studies from a variety of verticals, such as financial services, retail, automotive, publishing, non-profit and many more, who will share the latest strategies and methodologies in gathering, analyzing, leveraging and protecting your most valuable business asset - customer data.
10M Attendees
Frequency: Annual/December

17809 **NCDM Conferences National Center for Database Marketing**
Primedia Business Exhibitions
11 River Bend S
PO Box 4254
Stamford, CT 06907

203-358-9900
Fax: 203-358-5815
Home Page: www.ncdmsummer.com or www.ncdmwinter.com

Ed Berkowitz, Director Sales

A conference offering a highly qualified audience of database marketing decision-makers from all over the country, including a high concentration of marketers from the Midwest and West coast. Containing 210 booths and 100 exhibits.
2500 Attendees
Frequency: July/December

17810 **National Conference on Operations & Fulfillment (NCOF)**
Direct Marketing Association
1120 Avenue of Americas
New York, NY 1003-6700

212-768-7277
Fax: 312-302-6714
E-Mail: dmaconferences@the-dma.org
Home Page: www.the-dma.org

Julie A Hogan, SVP Conference/Events
Lawrence M Kimmel, CEO

Focus on innovative solutions for warehouse, distribution, operations, and ecommerce needs in the ever-changing world of operations and fulfillment.
10M Attendees
Frequency: Annual/April

17811 **National Hispanic Market Trade Show and Media Expo (Se Habla Espanol)**
Hispanic Business
5385 Hollister Avenue, Ste. 204
Santa Barbara, CA 93111

805-964-4554
800-806-4268
Fax: 805-964-5539
E-Mail: info@hispanstar.com
Home Page: www.hispanicbusiness.com
Social Media: Facebook, Twitter, LinkedIn

John Pasini, Cfo/Coo

Annual show of 100 exhibitors of market/research, media, advertising, public relations, information services and recruitment.
1500 Attendees
Mailing list available for rent

17812 **National Mail Order Merchandise Show**
Expo Accessories
47 Main Avenue
Clifton, NJ 07014-1917

973-661-9681

Martin Deeks, Show Manager

300 booths.
5M Attendees
Frequency: January

17813 **New York Nonprofit Conference**
Direct Marketing Association
1120 Avenue of Americas
New York, NY 10036-6700

212-768-7277
Fax: 212-302-6714
E-Mail: dmaconferences@the-dma.org
Home Page: www.the-dma.org

Julie A Hogan, SVP Conference/Events
Lawrence M Kimmel, CEO

Discover which acknowledgement programs work best-and why, increase the revenue with membership options-as well as traditional fund-raising appeals, learn how the Internet and e-mail campaigns can improve fundraising, lower costs and increase advocacy.
10M Attendees

17814 **PROMO Live**
Prism Business Media
PROMO Live
11 River Bend South
Stamford, CT 06907

508-743-0105
800-927-5007
Fax: 508-759-4552
E-Mail: registration@prism2b.com
Home Page: www.thepromoevent.com

Kim Stolfi, Conference/Show Coordinator
Florence Torres, Conference Program Manager
Frequency: Oct. Chicago

17815 **Photo Marketing Association International**
3000 Picture Place
Jackson, MI 49201

517-788-8100
Fax: 517-788-8371
E-Mail: pma_education@pmai.org
Home Page: www.pmai.org

Ted Fox, Executive Director
Mary Anne LaMarre, Operations Officer

Containing 3,230 booths and 645 exhibits. Promoting the growth of the photography industry through cooperation.
24M Attendees
Frequency: February

17816 **Promo Expo**
Promo Expo Sales
The Navy Pier
Chicago, IL 60606

800-927-5007
Fax: 203-358-3751
Home Page: www.promoexpo.com

The largest conference and exhibition dedicated to the promotion marketing industry, and the one event where you can meet with over four thousand promotion marketing decision makers.
Frequency: October

17817 **Publishers Multinational Direct Conference**
1501 3rd Avenue
New York, NY 10028-2101

212-734-7040
Fax: 212-986-3757

Alfred Goodloe, President

Offers publishers information and seminars on how to build sales and profits in foreign markets.
Frequency: March

17818 **Securities Industry and Financial Markets Association (SIFMA) Annual Meeting**
1101 New York Avenue NW
8th Floor
Washington, DC 20005

202-962-7300
Fax: 202-962-7305
Home Page: www.sifma.org
Social Media: Facebook, Twitter, LinkedIn

T Timothy Ryan Je, President/CEO
Randy Snook, Senior Managing Director/EVP
Donald D Kittell, CFO

The Securities Industry and Financial Markets Association/SIFMA Annual Meeting and Conference program addresses a variety of topics that may include competitiveness of the U.S. capital markets, global exchange consolidation, regulatory and legal initiatives, and trends in the fixed-income and capital markets.
Mailing list available for rent

17819 **SourceMedia Conferences & Events**
SourceMedia
One State Street Plaza
27th floor
New York, NY 10004

212-803-6093
800-803-3424
Fax: 212-803-8515
E-Mail: abconferences@sourcemedia.com

Home Page: www.sourcemedia.com/
Social Media: Facebook, Twitter, LinkedIn

James M Malkin, Chairman & CEO
William Johnson, CFO
Steve Andreazza, VP, Sales & Customer Service
Celie Baussan, SVP, Operations
Anne O'Brien, EVP Marketing & Strategic Planning

SourceMedia Conferences & Events attract over 20,000 attendees worldwide. The content embraces a variety of formats, including: conferences, executive roundtables, expositions, Web seminars, custom events and pod casts. With over 70 events annually, participants are provided with premier content as well as access to the industry's top solution providers. Markets served include: accounting; banking; capital markets; financial services; information technology; insurance; and real estate.
Mailing list available for rent

17820 TMCA Annual Conference & Marketing Expo
Transportation Marketing Communications Assoc
9382 Oak Avenue
Waconia, MN 55387

952-442-5638
Fax: 952-442-3941
E-Mail: brian07@tmcatoday.org
Home Page: www.tmcatoday.org

John Ferguson, President
Tom Nightingale, VP
Tracy Robinson, Treasurer
Edward Moritz, Secretary
Brian Everett, Executive Director
200 Attendees
Frequency: Annual

Directories & Databases

17821 Adweek Directory
Prometheus Global Media
770 Broadway
New York, NY 10003-9595

212-493-4100
Fax: 646-654-5368
Home Page: www.prometheusgm.com

Richard D. Beckmand, CEO
James A. Finkelstein, Chairman
Madeline Krakowsky, Vice President Circulation
Tracy Brater, Executive Director Creative Service

Adweek Directories Online is where you will find searchable databases with comprehensive information on ad Agencies, brand marketers and multicultural media.
Frequency: Annual
Circulation: 800
Founded in 1981

17822 Affluent Markets Alert
EPM Communications
488 E 18th Street
Brooklyn, NY 11226-6702

FAX 718-469-7124

Offers complete coverage on affluent market trends containing complete contact and price information on books, monographs, journals and newspapers.
Frequency: Full-text

17823 AmericanProfile
Donnelley Marketing Information Services
25 Tremont Ave
#10250
Stamford, CT 06906-2330

203-325-9801
800-866-2255
Fax: 203-553-7276
Home Page: www.donnellyestates.com

Richard Donnelly, Owner

A database retrieval and reporting system that contains 1980 and 1990 census data, current year updates and 5-year projections of selected demographic characteristics and proprietary statistics.

17824 Annual Directory of Marketing Information Companies
American Demographics
PO Box 4949
Stamford, CT 06907-0949

203-358-9900

Offers a list of firms offering demographic and research services, data retrieval and analysis, market evaluation and forecasting.
Frequency: Annual
Circulation: 5,000

17825 Annual Mail Order Sales Directory & Mail Order 750 Report
Marketing Logistics
1460 Cloverdale Avenue
Highland Park, IL 60035-2817

847-831-1575

Arnold L Fishman, President

This comprehensive directory offers a list of mail order businesses reporting at least 5 million dollars in annual sales. The 750 report gives mail order companies, businesses and mail order catalogs, 250 listings of each.
Cost: $1095.00
Frequency: Annual

17826 Boomer Report
FIND/SVP
625 Avenue of the Americas
New York, NY 10011-2020

212-807-2656
800-346-3787
Fax: 212-645-7681

Andrew P Garvin, President

With over 77 million baby boomers, this report carefully tracks news stories, market surveys, and interviews the experts to help you spot opportunities and position your products.
Cost: $195.00
8 Pages
Frequency: Monthly

17827 Bradford's Directory of Marketing Research Agencies & Consultants
Bradford's Directory of Marketing Research Agency
9991 Caitlin Center
Manassas, VA 20110-4282
703-614-4000

Thomas Bradford, Owner

Over 2,500 companies that are involved in management or market research are listed.
Cost: $90.00
400 Pages
Frequency: Biennial
Circulation: 5,000

17828 Business Marketing Association Membership Directory & Yellow Pages
Business Marketing Association
Ste 123
1833 Centre Point Cir
Naperville, IL 60563-4848

630-544-5054
Fax: 630-544-5055
E-Mail: info@marketing.org
Home Page: www.marketing.org
Social Media: Facebook, Twitter, LinkedIn

Jeffrey Hayzlett, Chairman
Gary Slack, Vice Chairman
Bob Goranson, Treasurer

Offers information on over 4,500 member business communications professionals in the field of advertising, marketing communications and marketing. Additional benefits of membership include opportunites for networking, professional development seminars, and access to marketing research and studies.
Frequency: Annual

17829 Catalog Connection
Holy B Pasiuk
210 E 5th Street
Greenville, NC 06437-0527

252-758-8612
Home Page: www.catalogconnection.net

Over 400 companies that supply catalogs of their merchandise to consumers and businesses are profiled in this directory.
55 Pages
Frequency: Biennial

17830 Catalog Handbook
Enterprise Magazines
1020 N Broadway
Suite 111
Milwaukee, WI 53202-3157

414-272-9977
Fax: 414-272-9973
Home Page: www.franchisehandbook.com

Offers information on companies that offer product catalogs.
Cost: $6.99
106 Pages
Frequency: Quarterly
Circulation: 30,000
Founded in 1989

17831 Complete Directory of Mail Order Catalog Products
Sutton Family Communications & Publishing Company
920 State Route 54 East
Elmitch, KY 42343

270-276-9500
E-Mail: jlsutton@apex.net

Theresa Sutton, Editor
Lee Sutton, General Manager

Print-out from database of wholesalers, manufacturers, distributors, importers and close-out houses. Database is updated daily to guarantee the most current and up-to-date sources available.
Cost: $157.50
100+ Pages

17832 Directory Marketplace
Todd Publications
PO Box 635
Nyack, NY 10960-0635

845-358-6213
Fax: 845-358-1059
E-Mail: toddpub@aol.com

Barry Klein, Editor

Directories and Reference Books for business, education, and libraries; news of new directories.
Cost: $25.00
Frequency: Bi-Monthly
Founded in 1987

17833 Directory of Franchising Organizations
Pilot Books
127 Sterling Avenue
PO Box 2102
Greenport, NY 11944
631-477-0978
800-797-4568
Fax: 631-477-0978
Over 1,300 current franchise opportunities in 45 categories.
Cost: $12.95
Frequency: Annual
Circulation: 0
ISBN: 0-875762-15-8

17834 Directory of Mail Order Catalogs
Grey House Publishing
4919 Route 22
PO Box 56
Amenia, NY 12501
518-789-8700
800-562-2139
Fax: 845-373-6390
E-Mail: books@greyhouse.com
Home Page: www.greyhouse.com
Social Media: Facebook, Twitter
Leslie Mackenzie, Publisher
Richard Gottlieb, Editor
The premier source of information on the mail order catalog industry. Covers over 13,000 consumer and business catalog companies with 44 different product chapters from Animals to Toys and Games.
Cost: $395.00
1600 Pages
Frequency: Annual
ISBN: 1-592373-96-8
Founded in 1981

17835 Directory of Mail Order Catalogs - Online Database
Grey House Publishing
4919 Route 22
PO Box 56
Amenia, NY 12501
518-789-8700
800-562-2139
Fax: 845-373-6390
E-Mail: gold@greyhouse.com
Home Page: http://gold.greyhouse.com
Social Media: Facebook, Twitter
Leslie Mackenzie, Publisher
Richard Gottlieb, Editor
Reach over 10,000 consumer catalog companies in one easy-to-use source with The Directory of Mail Order Catalogs - Online Database. Filled with business-building detail, each company profile gives you the information you need to access that organization quickly and easily. Listings provide key contacts, sales volume, employee size, printing information, circulation, list data, product descriptions and much more.
Frequency: Annual
Founded in 1981

17836 Entertainment Marketing Letter
EPM Communications
19 W. 21st St., #303
New York, NY 10010
212-941-0099
888-852-9467
Fax: 212-941-1622
E-Mail: info@epmcom.com
Home Page: www.epmcom.com
Ira Mayer, Owner
Terence Keegan, Editor
Database covering marketing techniques used in the entertainment industry.
Cost: $449.00
Frequency: 24 Issues/Year

17837 Food & Beverage Market Place
Grey House Publishing
4919 Route 22
PO Box 56
Amenia, NY 12501
518-789-8700
800-562-2139
Fax: 845-373-6390
E-Mail: books@greyhouse.com
Home Page: www.greyhouse.com
Social Media: Facebook, Twitter
Leslie Mackenzie, Publisher
Richard Gottlieb, Editor
This information packed three volume set is the most powerful buying and marketing guide for the US food and beverage industry. Includes thousands of industry freight and transportation listings.
Cost: $595.00
2000 Pages
Frequency: Annual
ISBN: 1-592373-61-5
Founded in 1981

17838 Food & Beverage Marketplace: Online Database
Grey House Publishing
4919 Route 22
PO Box 56
Amenia, NY 12501
518-789-8700
800-562-2139
Fax: 518-789-0556
E-Mail: gold@greyhouse.com
Home Page: http://gold.greyhouse.com
Social Media: Facebook, Twitter
Richard Gottlieb, President
Leslie Mackenzie, Publisher
This complete updated Food & Beverage Market Place: Online Database is the go-to source for the food and beverage industry. Anyone involved in the food and beverage industry needs this 'industry bible' and the important contacts to develop critical research data that can make for successful business growth.
Frequency: Annual
Founded in 1981

17839 GreenBook: Worldwide of Market Research Companies and Services
NY American Marketing Association
116 East 27th Street
6th Floor
New York, NY 10016-1799
212-687-3280
Fax: 212-202-7920
E-Mail: info@greenbook.org
Home Page: www.greenbook.org
Social Media: Twitter, LinkedIn
Lucas Pospichal, Managing Director
Comprehensive listings of over 1,500 market research firms in the US and Canada. Listings in over 300 service categories and market industries. The most reliable reference resource for buyers of marketing research services.
Cost: $350.00
880 Pages
Frequency: Yearly
Circulation: 4,500
Founded in 1962

17840 Infomercial Marketing Sourcebook
Prometheus Global Media
770 Broadway
New York, NY 10003-9595
212-493-4100
Fax: 646-654-5368
Home Page: www.prometheusgm.com
Richard D. Beckman, CEO
James A. Finkelstein, Chairman
Madeline Krakowsky, Vice President Circulation
Tracy Brater, Executive Director Creative Service
A complete resource guide for everyone involved in the infomercial industry.

17841 International Directory of Marketing Research Companies & Services
New York Chapter/American Marketing Association
310 Madison Avenue
New York, NY 10017-6009
212-986-1418
Offers more than 1,500 marketing research consultants and suppliers of marketing research data.
Cost: $105.00
600 Pages
Frequency: Annual
Circulation: 6,000

17842 International Network Marketing Reference Book & Resource Directory
MLM Group Publications
12 Rose Center
Norwood, MA 02062-2603
Offers valuable information on over 800 companies in the multi-level marketing industry.
Cost: $15.75
85 Pages

17843 Leadership Library on Internet and CD-ROM
Leadership Directories
104 5th Ave
New York, NY 10011-6901
212-627-4140
Fax: 212-645-0931
E-Mail: info@leadershipdirectories.com
Home Page: www.leadershipdirectories.com
David Hurvitz, CEO
Makes all 14 leadership directories available over the Internet and on CD-ROM in one integrated directory. They provide subscribers with complete contact information in one database. Subscription includes Internet access and four CD-ROM editions quarterly.
Cost: $3065.00
Frequency: Updated Daily
ISSN: 1075-3869
Founded in 1999
Mailing list available for rent
Printed in A colors on B stock

17844 MDMA Membership and Resource Directory
Midwest Direct Marketing Association
P.O. Box 75
Andover, MN 55304
763-607-2943
Fax: 763-753-2240
E-Mail: office@mdma.org
Home Page: www.mdma.org
Ed Harrington, Manager
Cindy McCleary, Director
400 Pages
Frequency: April
Mailing list available for rent: 1.1M+ names

17845 Mail Order Business Directory
B Klein Publishers

PO Box 8503
Coral Springs, FL 33075-8503
Bernard Klein, Editor

A listing of over 12,000 corporations in the US and 500 international firms doing business by mail order and catalogs.
Cost: $95.00
400 Pages
Frequency: Annual

17846 Mail Order Product Guide
Todd Publications
PO Box 635
Nyack, NY 10960-0635

845-358-6213
800-747-1086

A listing of over 1,500 manufacturers and importers to the mail order industry worldwide.
Cost: $50.00
250 Pages
Frequency: Triennial
Circulation: 5,000

17847 Market Scope
Trade Dimensions
45 Danbury Rd
Wilton, CT 06897-4445

203-563-3000
Fax: 203-563-3131
Home Page: www.tradedimensions.com

Lynda Gutierrez, Managing Editor

The definitive source of market share and category sales data for supermarkets. The book configures the information in Trade Dimensions' database to determine market share by Nielsen, DMA, MSA and IRI definitions - over 300 markets in all. Market Scope also provides extensive category sales data as reported by Nielsen and IRI.
Cost: $325.00
Frequency: Annual

17848 Marketing Guidebook
Trade Dimensions
45 Danbury Rd
Wilton, CT 06897-4445

203-563-3000
Fax: 860-563-3131
Home Page: www.tradedimensions.com

Lynda Gutierrez, Managing Editor
Jane Sheulin, Editor

The 'blue book' sales and marketing professionals have depended on for 30 years. The directory details the supermarket industry from distribution standpoint, comprising over 800 profiles, organized into 52 market areas. Includes all grocery chains and wholesalers that do a minimum of $30 million in sales. Also includes food brokers, non-food distributors, and small wholesalers in each market.
Cost: $340.00
Frequency: Annual

17849 Marketing Made Easier: Directory of Mailing List Companies
Todd Publications
PO Box 635
Nyack, NY 10960-0635

845-358-6213
800-747-1056
Fax: 845-358-3203
E-Mail: toddpubQ@aol.com
Home Page: toddpublications.com

Barry Klein, Editor

Over 1,100 companies that sell mailing lists and the type of lits they handle.
Cost: $55.00
100 Pages
Frequency: Biennial
Circulation: 5,000
ISBN: 0-915344-83-1

Founded in 1972
Mailing list available for rent: 1,000 names at $100 per M
Printed in 2 colors

17850 Marketing Tools Directory
American Demographics
PO Box 4949
Stamford, CT 06907-0949

203-358-9900
800-832-1486
Fax: 607-273-3196

List of firms offering demographic and research services, data retrieval, and analysis, market evaluation and forecasting media services.
Frequency: Annual

17851 Marketing on a Shoestring: Low-Cost Tips for Marketing Products & Services
John Wiley & Sons
111 River St
Hoboken, NJ 07030-5790

201-748-6000
800-825-7550
Fax: 201-748-6088
E-Mail: info@wiley.com
Home Page: www.wiley.com

William J Pesce, CEO

Business and professional associations that can assist individuals or companies in improving their marketing are profiled.
Cost: $14.95
236 Pages

17852 National Agri-Marketing Association
11020 King St
Suite 205
Overland Park, KS 66210-1201

913-491-6500
Fax: 913-491-6502
E-Mail: agrimktg@nama.org
Home Page: www.nama.org
Social Media: Facebook, Twitter, LinkedIn, Youtube,Flickr

Jennifer Pickett, CEO
Vicki Henrickson, Vice President
2500 Pages
Frequency: Annual Spring
Founded in 1956

17853 National Directory of Addresses and Telephone Numbers
Omnigraphics
2500 Penobscot Building
Detroit, MI 48226

313-961-1340

This new edition provides the most current names and addresses for businesses and services throughout the United States, arranged alphabetically and by business type.
Cost: $60.00
1,500 Pages
Frequency: Hardcover
ISBN: 0-780800-20-6

17854 National Trade and Professional Associations of the United States
Columbia Books
1212 New York Avenue NW
Suite 330
Washington, DC 20005-3987

202-641-1662
888-265-0600
Fax: 202-898-0775
E-Mail: info@columbiabooks.com
Home Page: www.columbiabooks.com

Buck Downs, Senior Editor

Lists 7,600 national trade associations, professional societies and labor unions. Five convenient indexes enable you to look up associations by subject, budget, geographic area, acronym and executive director. Other features include: contract information, serial publications, upcoming convention schedule, membership/staff size, budget figures, and background information.
Cost: $99.00
Frequency: Annual Feburary

17855 New Marketing Opportunities
New Editions International
PO Box 2578
Sedona, AZ 86339-2578

928-282-9574
800-777-4751
Fax: 928-282-9730
Home Page: www.newagemarket.com

Sophia Tarila, Author
Pat Bush, CEO

7,000 New Age and Metaphysical publishers, events, retailers, distributors, services, publications, reviewers, catalogers, media connections, internet connections, associations and other resources.
Cost: $139.95
Frequency: Annual
ISBN: 0-944773-18-4
Mailing list available for rent

17856 Procter & Gamble Marketing Alumni Directory
Ward Howell International
300 S Wacker Drive
Suite 2940
Chicago, IL 60606-6703

Membership directory listings.
120 Pages
Frequency: Annual

17857 Quirk's Marketing Research Review
Quirk Enterprises
PO Box 23536
Minneapolis, MN 55423-0536

952-854-5101
Fax: 612-854-8191
E-Mail: evan@quirks.com
Home Page: www.quirks.com

Thomas Quirk, Publisher
Evan Tweed, Associate Publisher
Joseph Rydholm, Editor
Alice Davies, Manager

Publishing case histories and discussions of techniques which can be used by purchasers of research products and services. Also directories of research services. Accepts advertising.
Cost: $60.00
64 Pages
Frequency: 11 per year
Circulation: 15,500
Mailing list available for rent: 15.5M names
Printed in 4 colors on glossy stock

17858 Shop-at-Home Directory
Belcaro Group
7100 E Belvue
Suite 305
Greenwood Village, CO 80111
Marc Braunstein, President

This valuable informational source offers information on over 400 companies that offer direct mail order sales.
Cost: $3.00
60 Pages
Frequency: SemiAnnual

17859 Source Book Of Multicultural Experts
Multicultural Marketing Resources

101 5th Ave
Suite 10B
New York, NY 10003-1008

212-242-3351
Fax: 212-691-5969
E-Mail: lisa@multicultural.com
Home Page: www.multicultural.com
Social Media: Facebook, Twitter, LinkedIn

Lisa Skriloff, President
Agata Porter, Account Executive & Editor
Yartish Bullock-Okeke, Public Relations/Sales Manager
Melanie Eisenberg, Director, Client Services
Annette Chow, Director Sales/Business Development

An annual directory that includes companies with expertise in marketing to different cultural and lifestyle markets. Resources include how to reach ethnic consumers, and contacts and leads for possible business alliances.
Cost: $19.99
Frequency: Annually
Circulation: 4000
Founded in 1994

17860 **Sports Market Place Directory**
Grey House Publishing
4919 Route 22
PO Box 56
Amenia, NY 12501

518-789-8700
800-562-2139
Fax: 518-789-0556
E-Mail: books@greyhouse.com
Home Page: www.greyhouse.ocm
Social Media: Facebook, Twitter

Leslie Mackenzie, Publisher
Richard Gottlieb, Editor

For over 20 years, this comprehensive, up-to-date directory has offered direct access to the Who, What, When & Where of the Sports Industry. With this directory on your desk, you have a comprehensive tool providing current key information about the people, organizations and events involving the explosive sports industry at your fingertips.
Cost: $225.00
1800 Pages
Frequency: Annual
ISBN: 1-592373-48-8
Founded in 1981

17861 **State and Regional Associations of the United States**
Columbia Books
1212 New York Avenue NW
Suite 330
Washington, DC 20005-3987

202-641-1662
888-265-0600
Fax: 202-898-0775
E-Mail: info@columbiabooks.com
Home Page: www.columbiabooks.com

Buck Downs, Senior Editor

Lists 7,200 of the largest and most significant state and regional trade and professional organizations in the US Look up associations by subject, budget, state, acronym, or chief executive. Also lists contract information, serial publications, upcoming convention schedule, membership/staff size, budget figures, and background information.
Cost: $79.00
Frequency: Annual March

17862 **Who's Who: MASA Buyer's Guide to Blue Ribbon Mailing Services**
Mailing & Fulfillment Service Association
1421 Prince Street
Suite 410
Alexandria, VA 22314-2806

703-836-9200
Fax: 703-548-8204
E-Mail: mfsa-mail@mfsanet.org
Home Page: www.mfsanet.org
Social Media: Facebook, Twitter, LinkedIn

Ken Garner, President
Bill Stevenson, Director Marketing
Leo Raymond, Vice President

Offers a detailed listing of suppliers of equipment, products and services to the direct mail industry, most containing a description of the specific products they provide.
Frequency: Annual

Industry Web Sites

17863 **http://gold.greyhouse.com**
G.O.L.D Grey House OnLine Databases
Grey House Publishing's online database platform, GOLD, offers Quick Search, Keyword Search and Expert Search for most business sectors including advertising and marketing markets. The GOLD platform makes finding the information you need quick and easy - whether you're a novice searcher or an experienced database user. All of Grey House's directory products are available for subscription on the GOLD platform.

17864 **www.adweek.com**
Adweek
Leading decision makers in the advertising and marketing field go to Adweek.Com everyday for breaking news, insight, buzz, opinion, analysis, research and classifieds. The resources of all six regional editions of Adweek, as well as the national edition of Brandweek are combined with the knowledge of our online editors and the multimedia/interactive capabilities of the web to deliver vital information quickly and effectively to our target audience.

17865 **www.ama.org**
American Marketing Association
Represents marketers and keeps members informed of trends in advertising. Fosters research, sponsors seminars and provides educational placement service.

17866 **www.apmaw.org**
Assn of Promotion Marketing Agencies Worldwide
A trade association of sales promotion agencies with at least two years experience.

17867 **www.assist-intl.com**
Assist International
International trade promotion and consulting firm: mailing lists, seminars, conferences, international business expo.

17868 **www.awmanet.org**
American Wholesale Marketers Association
Government affairs, trade shows, publications, and products.

17869 **www.bmahouston.org**
Business Marketing Association: Houston
Dedicated to serving the needs of business to business Associations worldwide.

17870 **www.choosecherries.org**
Cherry Marketing Institute
An organization providing cherry information and promoting material to food manufacturers, food service operators and others.

17871 **www.fmi.org**
Food Marketing Institute
Events, publications, industry and consumer information and media.

17872 **www.greyhouse.com**
Grey House Publishing
Authoritative reference directories for most business sectors including advertising and marketing markets. Users can search the online databases with varied search criteria allowing for custom searches by product category, geographic area, sales volume, keyword, subject and more. Full Grey House catalog and online ordering also available.

17873 **www.inma.org**
International Newspaper Marketing Association
Individuals in marketing, circulation, research and public relations of newspapers.

17874 **www.manaonline.org**
Manufacturers Agents National Association
A national organization for manufacturer's agents and manufacturers who contract for the services of these representatives.

17875 **www.mark-ed.org**
Marketing Education Center
Committed to education for and about marketing. Provides professional support and training materials. Primary clients are schools, colleges, and educational institutions.

17876 **www.marketing.org**
Business Marketing Association
Pre-eminent service organization for professional's in this vital industry.

17877 **www.marketingpower.com**
American Marketing Association
A professional association for individuals and organizations involved in the practice, teaching and study of marketing worldwide.

17878 **www.mfsanet.org**
Mailing & Fulfillment Service Association
The national trade association for the mailing and fulfillment services industry.

17879 **www.mlmia.com**
Multi-Level Marketing International Association
Seeks to strengthen and improve the multi level marketing industry in the United States and abroad.

17880 **www.msi.org**
Marketing Science Institute
Seeks to improve marketing practice and education, conducts research.

17881 **www.nacda.com**
National Assn of Collegiate Marketing Admin.
Members are public relations and marketing professionals in college and university athletic departments. Promotes standards and provides professional support.

17882 **www.pdma.org**
Product Development and Management Association
International association serving those with a professional interest in improving the management of product innovation.

17883 **www.pma.com**
Produce Marketing Association
Products and services, issues and information, conventions and expos.

17884 **www.pmc-ny.com**
Premium Marketing Club of New York
Provides education and networking opportunities for members from all areas of the marketing field

17885 **www.printing.org**
Graphic Arts Marketing Information Service
A section of Printing Industries of American that provides market research and statistics to its members. Research is member selected and directed.

17886 **www.promax.tv**
PROMAX
International association of promotion and marketing, professionals in electronic media. Promotes the effectiveness of promotion and marketing within the industry and the academic community.

17887 **www.retailing.com**
Electronic Retailing Association
Members include infomercial producers, marketers, product developers, broadcasters and other industries serving the infomercial market.

17888 **www.riahome**
Research Institute of America
A national organization that focuses on marketing and sales intelligence for top level marketing executives.

17889 **www.sigma.org**
Society of Independent Gasoline Marketers
Members are independent gasoline marketers.

17890 **www.smps.org**
Society for Marketing Professional Services
Promotes new business development of architectural, engineering, planning, design and construction management firms.

17891 **www.strategicaccounts.org**
Strategic Account Management Association
Dedicated to the professional and personal development of the executives charged with managing national, global, and strategic account relationships, and to elevating the status of the profession as a whole.

17892 **www.teleport.com**
International Trade Resources
An overview of the steps required to market abroad. Updated guide to the web's best global business sites and more.

17893 **www.the-dma.org**
Direct Marketing Association
Leading global trade association of business and nonprofit organizations using and supporting direct marketing tools and techniques.

17894 **www.tpnregister.com**
TPN Register
Business to business marketplace.

International Trade Resources

17895 **Albania Mission to the United Nations**
320 E 79th Street
New York, NY 10075
212-249-2059
Fax: 212-535-2917
E-Mail: mission.newyork@mfa.gov.al
Home Page: www.albania-un.org
Geronimo Albano, Owner

17896 **Antigua and Barbuda Department of Tourism and Trade**
25 S.E. 2nd Avenue
Suite 300
Miami, FL 33131
305-381-6762
Fax: 305-381-7908
E-Mail: cganuear@bellsouth.net
Home Page: www.antigua-barbuda.org
Byron Spencer, Manager

17897 **Austrian Trade Commission**
120 West 45th Street
9th Floor
New York, NY 10036
212-421-5250
Fax: 212-421-5251
E-Mail: newyork@advantageaustria.org
Home Page: www.advantageaustria.org/us
Peter Athanasiadis, Manager
Sabine Miller, Project Manager
Walter HAfle, Director

17898 **Belize Mission to the United Nations**
675 Third Avenue
Suite 1911
New York, NY 10017
212-986-1240
Fax: 212-593-0932
E-Mail: belize@un.int
Home Page: www.un.int/belize/staff.htm
Janine Coye-Felson, Minister-Counsellor
Dina S. Shoman, Counsellor/Director of Trade
Alfonso Gahona, First Secretary

17899 **Botswana Embassy**
1531-1533 New Hampshire Avenue NW
Washington, DC 20036
202-244-4990
E-Mail: smautle@botswanaembassy.org
Home Page: www.botswanaembassy.org
H.E. Ms. Tebelelo Seretse, Ambassador
Ms. Sophie Heide Mautle, Deputy Head of Mission

17900 **British Trade and Investment Office**
845 3rd Avenue
9th Floor
New York, NY 10022
212-745-0495
E-Mail: uktiusa@ukti.gsi.gov.uk
Home Page: www.ukti.gov.uk
Social Media: Twitter, LinkedIn, YouTube, flickr
Nick Baird, Chief Executive Officer
Jon Harding, Chief Operating Officer
Crispin Simon, Managing Director, Trade
Michael Boyd, Managing Director
Sandra Rogers, Managing Director, Marketing

17901 **Bulgarian General Consulate**
121 E 62nd Street
New York, NY 10021
212-935-4646
Fax: 212-319-5955
E-Mail: consulate.newyork@mfa.bg
Home Page: www.consulbulgaria-ny.org

17902 **Business Council for the United Nations**
801 2nd Avenue
2nd Floor
New York, NY 10017
212-907-1300
Fax: 212-682-9185
E-Mail: unahq@unausa.org
Home Page: www.unausa.org/bcun
Social Media: Facebook, Twitter, YouTube, flickr
Allison B MacEachron, Executive Director

17903 **Chile Trade Commission**
866 United Nations Plaza
Suite 603
New York, NY 10017
212-207-3266
Fax: 212-207-3649
Alejandro Cerda, Trade Commissioner

17904 **Colombia Government Trade Bureau**
1701 Pennsylvania Avenue, N W
Suite 560
Washington, DC 20006
202-887-9000
Fax: 202-223-0526
E-Mail: Fadul@coltrade.org

17905 **Consulate General of Bahrain**
866 2nd Avenue
14th Floor
New York, NY 10017
212-223-6200
Fax: 212-319-0687
Home Page: www.un.int/bahrain/consulate.html
Jassim Buallay, Manager

17906 **Consulate General of Belgium**
1065 Avenue of Americas
22nd Floor
New York, NY 10018
212-586-5110
212-586-7472
Fax: 212-582-9657
E-Mail: NewYork@diplobel.fed.be
Home Page: www.diplomatie.be/newyork/
Piet Morisse, Manager

17907 **Consulate General of Bolivia**
211 E 43rd Street
Suite 702
New York, NY 10017
212-599-6767
Fax: 212-687-0532
Jorge Heredia Cavero, Manager

17908 **Consulate General of Brazil**
1185 Avenue of the Americas
21st Floor
New York, NY 10036-2601
917-777-7777
Fax: 212-827-0225
E-Mail: cg.novayork@itamaraty.gov.br
Home Page: http://novayork.itamaraty.gov.br/en-us/
Julio Cesar Gomes Dos Sant, Manager

17909 **Consulate General of Costa Rica**
14 Penn Plaza, #1202
225 West 34th Street
New York, NY 10122
212-509-3066
212-509-3066
Fax: 212-509-3068
Fax: 212-509-3068
Home Page: www.costariica-embassy.org
Otto Barcas, Manager

17910 **Consulate General of Germany**
871 United Nations Plaza
New York, NY 10017
212-610-9700
Fax: 212-940-0402
Bernhard Von Der Planit, Manager

17911 Consulate General of Haiti
815 2nd Avenue
6th Floor
New York, NY 10017

212-697-9767
Fax: 212-681-6991
Home Page: www.haitianconsulate-nyc.org
Social Media: Facebook, Twitter

Marie Therese, Manager

17912 Consulate General of Honduras
255 West 36th Street
First Level
New York, NY 10018

212-714-9451
Fax: 212-714-9453
Home Page: www.hondurasemb.org
Social Media: Facebook, Twitter

17913 Consulate General of India
3 E 64th Street
New York, NY 10065

212-774-0600
Fax: 212-861-3788
E-Mail: info@bls-india-usa.com
Home Page: www.indiacgny.org
Social Media: Facebook, Twitter, Youtube

Dnyaneshwar M Mulay, Consul General
Mr. P.K. Bajaj, Consul (Head of Chancery)

17914 Consulate General of Indonesia
5 E 68th Street
New York, NY 10021

212-879-0600

17915 Consulate General of Israel
800 Second Avenue
New York, NY 10017

212-499-5000
E-Mail: info@newyork.mfa.gov.il
Home Page: www.israelfm.org
Social Media: Facebook, Twitter, YouTube, flickr

Ido Aharoni, Consul General

17916 Consulate General of Kenya
866 UN Plaza
Suite 4016
New York, NY 10017

212-421-4741
Fax: 212-486-1985
Home Page:
www.kenya.embassy-online.net/kenya-consulate-general-new-york.php

Rolando Visconti, Manager

17917 Consulate General of Lebanon
9 E 76th Street
New York, NY 10021

212-744-7905
Fax: 212-794-1510
E-Mail: lebconsny@aol.com
Home Page: www.lebconsny.org/

Hassan Saad, Manager

17918 Consulate General of Lithuania
420 5th Avenue
3rd Floor
New York, NY 10018

212-354-7840
Rimantas Morkvenas, Manager

17919 Consulate General of Malta
249 E 35th Street
New York, NY 10016

212-425-2345

17920 Consulate General of Morocco
10 East 40th Street
New York, NY 10016

212-758-2625
Fax: 646-395-8077
Home Page: www.moroccanconsulate.com/

Ramon Xilotl, Manager

17921 Consulate General of Nicaragua
820, 2nd Avenue, 8th floor.,
Suite 802
New York, NY 10017

212-983-1981
Fax: 212-989-5528
E-Mail: info@ConsuladoDeNicaragua.com
Home Page: consuladodenicaragua.com

Jose Flores, Manager
Nohelia Urcuyo, Consul

17922 Consulate General of Nigeria
828 2nd Avenue
New York, NY 10017

212-808-0301
Fax: 212-687-1476
E-Mail: cgnny@nigeriahouse.com
Home Page: www.nigeriahouse.com/
Social Media: Facebook

17923 Consulate General of Paraguay
801 2nd Avenue
Suite 600
New York, NY 10017

212-682-9441
Fax: 212-682-9443
E-Mail: info@consulparny.com
Home Page: www.consulparny.com/ingles/

Juan Baiardi, Manager

17924 Consulate General of Peru
215 Lexington Avenue
21st Floor
New York, NY 10016

212-481-7410
Home Page: www.consuladoperu.com/

17925 Consulate General of Qatar
809 United Nations Plaza
4th Floor
New York, NY 10017

212-486-9335

17926 Consulate General of Russia
2790 Green St
San Francisco, CA 94123

415-928- 687
Fax: 415-929-0306
E-Mail: russianlegal@sbcglobal.net
Home Page: www.consulrussia.org/eng

17927 Consulate General of Saudi Arabia
866 Second Avenue
5th Floor
New York, NY 10017

212-752-2740
Home Page:
www.saudiembassy.net/embassy/us_offices.aspx
Abdulrahman Gdaia, Excellency

17928 Consulate General of Slovenia
600 3rd Avenue
24th Floor
New York, NY 10016

212-370-3007
Fax: 212-370-3581
Home Page: www.culturalprofiles.net/slovenia

Reimo Pettai, Manager
Sayed Jahangit, Director of Publications

17929 Consulate General of South Africa
333 E 38th Street
9th Floor
New York, NY 10016

212-213-4880
Fax: 212-213-0102
E-Mail: consulate.ny@foreign.gov.za
Home Page:
www.southafrica-newyork.net/consulate/
Social Media: Facebook

George Monyemangene, Consul General

17930 Consulate General of St. Lucia
800 2nd Avenue
9th Floor
New York, NY 10017

212-499-5000

Julian Hunte, Manager

17931 Consulate General of Switzerland
633 3rd Avenue
30th Floor
New York, NY 10017

212-599-5700

Raymond Loretan, Excellency

17932 Consulate General of Trinidad & Tobago
125 Maiden Lane
Unit 4A, 4th Floor
New York, NY 10038

212-682-7272
Fax: 212-232-0368
E-Mail: consulate@ttcgny.com
Home Page: www.ttcgnewyork.com/
Social Media: Facebook, Twitter, You Tube

Hon Harold Robertson, Contact

17933 Consulate General of Ukraine
240 E 49th Street
New York, NY 10017

212-371-6965
Fax: 212-371-5547
E-Mail: gc_usn@mfa.gov.ua
Home Page: www.ny.mfa.gov.ua/en

17934 Consulate General of Uruguay
420 Madison Avenue
6th Floor
New York, NY 10017

212-753-8191
Fax: 212-753-1603
E-Mail:
consulado@consuladouruguaynewyork.com
Home Page:
www.consuladouruguaynewyork.com/english-1/

Basil Bryan, Manager

17935 Consulate General of Venezuela
7 E 51st Street
New York, NY 10022

212-826-1660

17936 **Consulate General of the Commonwealth of the Bahamas**
231 E 46th Street
2nd Floor
New York, NY 10017

212-717-5643

Hon Eldred E Bethel, Contact

17937 **Consulate General of the Dominican Republic**
1715 22nd Street NW
Washington, DC 20008

202-332-6280
Fax: 202-265-8057

17938 **Consulate General of the Netherlands**
666 Third Avenue
19th Floor
New York, NY 10017

877-388-2443
Fax: 212-246-9769
E-Mail: nyc@minbuza.nl
Home Page: http://ny.the-netherlands.org/
Social Media: Facebook, Twitter

Wanda Fleck, Manager

17939 **Consulate General of the Principality of Monaco**
565 5th Avenue
New York, NY 10017

212-286-0500

Magguy Maccario-Doyle, Manager

17940 **Consulate General of the Republic of Croatia**
369 Lexington Avenue
11th Floor
New York, NY 10017

212-972-2277

Abdul Seraj, Manager

17941 **Consulate General of the Republic of Belarus**
708 3rd Avenue
21st Floor
New York, NY 10017

212-682-5392

Sergei Kolos, Manager

17942 **Consulate of Guyana**
866 United Nations Plaza
New York, NY 10017

212-527-3215

Brentnold Evans, Manager

17943 **Consulate of the Republic of Uzbekistan**
866 United Nations Plaza
Suite 327-A
New York, NY 10017-7671

212-754-6178

17944 **Cyprus Embassy Trade Center**
13 E 40th Street
New York, NY 10016

212-213-9100
Fax: 212-213-2918
E-Mail: ctcny@cyprustradeny.org
Home Page: www.cyprustradeny.org/

Aristos Constantine, Trade Commissioner

The commission's primary role is to further and expand the economic interests of the Republic of Cyprus through promoting, facilitating and attracting foreign investment and fostering the expansion of exports of Cyprus' goods and services, in addition to monitoring related market and policy issues.

17945 **Department of Trade- Government of Antigua & Barbuda**
610 5th Avenue
Suite 311
New York, NY 10020

212-541-4117

17946 **Ecuadorian Consulate**
2535 15th Street NW
Washington, DC 20009

202-234-7200
Fax: 202-667-3482
E-Mail: consuladodc@ecuador.org
Home Page: www.ecuador.us

Pablo Yanez, Consulate

17947 **Egyptian Consulate Economic & Commercial Office**
3521 International Ct. NW
Washingotn, DC 20008

202-895-5400
Fax: 202-244-4319
E-Mail: embassy@egyptembassy.net
Home Page: www.egyptembassy.net
Social Media: Facebook

Ayden Nour, Executive Director

17948 **Embassy of Australia**
1601 Massachusetts Avenue NW
Washington, DC 20036

202-797-3000
Fax: 202-797-3168
Home Page: www.usa.embassy.gov.au
Social Media: Facebook, Twitter

Kim Beazley, Ambassador

17949 **Embassy of Benin**
2124 Kalorama Road NW
Washington, DC 20008

202-232-6656
Fax: 202-265-1996
E-Mail: info@beninembassy.us
Home Page: www.beninembassy.us

Cyrille Segbe Oguin, President

17950 **Embassy of Bosnia and Herzegovina**
2109 E Street NW
Washington, DC 20037

202-337-1500
Fax: 202-337-1502
E-Mail: info@bhembassy.org
Home Page: www.bhembassy.org

Mitar Kujundzic, Ambassador Extraordinary

17951 **Embassy of Cambodia**
4530 16th Street NW
Washington, DC 20011

202-726-7742
202-726-7824
Fax: 202-726-8381
E-Mail: camemb.usa@mfa.org.kh
Home Page: www.embassyofcambodia.org
Social Media: Facebook

Hem Heng, Ambassador

17952 **Embassy of Ethiopia Trade Affairs**
3506 International Drive NW
Washington, DC 20008

202-364-1200
Fax: 202-587-0195
E-Mail: ethiopia@ethiopianembassy.org
Home Page: www.ethiopianembassy.org

Girma Birru, Ambassador

17953 **Embassy of Finland**
3301 Massachusetts Avenue NW
Washington, DC 20008

202-298-5800
Fax: 202-298-6030
E-Mail: sanomat.was@formin.fi
Home Page: www.finland.org
Social Media: Facebook, Twitter

Ritva Koukku-Ronde, Ambassador
Kristiina Vuorenp,,,,, Assistant to the Ambassador
Tarja Thatcher, Social Secretary

17954 **Embassy of Georgia**
2209 Massachusettes Avenue, NW
Washington, DC 20008

202-387-2390
Fax: 202-387-0864
E-Mail: georgianconsulate1@verizon.net
Home Page: www.embassy.mfa.gov.ge

Temur Yakobashvili, Ambassador

17955 **Embassy of Grenada**
1701 New Hampshire Ave, NW
Washington, DC 20009-2501

202-265-2561
Fax: 292-265-2468
E-Mail: embassy@grenadaembassyusa.org
Home Page: www.grenadaembassyusa.org
Social Media: Facebook, Twitter, Google Plus

E. Angus Friday, Ambassador
Patricia D Clarke, Counsellor
Dianne C Perrotteÿ, Administrative Assistant
Lucia Amedee, Receptionist/Office Assistant

17956 **Embassy of Jamaica (JAMPRO)**
1520 New Hampshire Ave, NW
Washington, DC 20036

202-452-0660
Fax: 202-452-0036
E-Mail: firstsec@jamaicaembassy.org
Home Page: www.embassyofjamaica.org

Dr Stephen Vasciannie, Ambassador

17957 **Embassy of Mali**
2130 R Street NW
Washington, DC 20008

202-332-2249
Fax: 202-332-6603
E-Mail: info@maliembassy.us
Home Page: www.maliembassy.us

Al Maamoun Baba Lamine Keita, Ambassador
Muhamed Ouzouna Maiga, The First Counselor
Ahmadou Barazi Maiga, The Second Counselor
Salif Sanogo, The Third Counselor-Communication
Colonel Bourama Sangare, Defence Attache

17958 **Embassy of Mongolia**
2833 M Street NW
Washington, DC 20007

202-333-7117
Fax: 202-298-9227
E-Mail: dc@mongolianembassy.us
Home Page: www.mongolianembassy.us
Social Media: Facebook, Twitter, Youtube

H.E. Altangerel Bulgaa, Ambassador
Gansukh Damdin, Minister Counsellor, Deputy Chief
Munkhjargal Byamba, Counsellor
Colonel Boldbat Khasbazar, Defense Attache
Gantulga Chadraabal, Political Affairs/ Counsellor

17959 **Embassy of Panama**
2862 McGill Terrace NW
Washington, DC 20008
202-483-1407
202-483-8416
Fax: 202-483-8413
E-Mail: info@embassyofpanama.org
Home Page: www.embassyofpanama.org
Social Media: Facebook
Mario E. Jaramillo, Ambassador

17960 **Embassy of Tanzania**
1232 22nd St, NW
Washington, DC 20037
202-884-1080
202-939-6125
Fax: 202-797-7408
E-Mail: ubalozi@tanzaniaembassy-us.org
Home Page: www.tanzaniaembassy-us.org
H.E. Liberataÿ Mulamula, Ambassador
Lily Munankaÿ, Minister
Paul Mwafongoÿ, Minister Plenipotentiary, Economics
B. GÿEmmanuel Maganga, Defense Attach,
Edward Masanja, Financial Attache

17961 **Embassy of Tunisia**
1515 Massachusetts Avenue NW
Washington, DC 20005
202-862-1850
Fax: 202-862-1858
Home Page: www.tunconsusa.org/
Gordon Gray, Ambassador

17962 **Embassy of Uganda**
5911 16th Street NW
Washington, DC 20011
202-726-7100
Fax: 202-726-1727
E-Mail: owonekha@ugandaembassyus.org
Home Page: www.ugandaemb.org
Social Media: Facebook, Twitter
Oliver Wonekha, Ambassador
Alfred Nnam, Deputy Chief of Mission (DCM)
Dickson Ogwang, Minister Counselor
Patrick Muganda Guma, Counselor
Sam Bhoi Omara, First Secretary

17963 **Embassy of Vietnam**
1233 20th Street NW
Suite 400
Washington, DC 20036
202-861-0737
Fax: 202-861-0917
E-Mail: info@vietnamembassy.us
Home Page: www.vietnamembassy-usa.org
Nguyen Quoc Cuong, Ambassador

17964 **Embassy of Zimbabwe**
1608 New Hampshire Avenue
Washington, DC 20009
202-332-7100
Fax: 202-483-9326
E-Mail: info33@zimbabwe-embassy.us
Home Page: www.zimbabwe-embassy.us
Machivenyika Mapuranga, Ambassador
Richard T Chibuwe, Minister Counselor and Deputy Chief
R Matsika, Counselor
Whatmore Goora, Counselor (Political)
Col. George Chinoingira, Defence Attache

17965 **Embassy of the Hashemite Kingdom of Jordan**
3504 International Drive NW
Washington, DC 20008
202-966-2664
Fax: 202-966-3110
E-Mail: HKJEmbassyDC@jordanembassyus.org
Home Page: www.jordanembassyus.org
Social Media: Facebook, Twitter, Youtube, Pintrest
Alia Hatoug Bouran, Ambassador

17966 **Embassy of the Lao People's Democratic Republic**
2222 S Street NW
Washington, DC 20008
202-332-6416
202-667-0076
Fax: 202-332-4923
E-Mail: embasslao@gmail.com
Home Page: www.laoembassy.com
Seng Soukhathivong, Ambassador

17967 **Embassy of the People's Republic of China**
3505 International Place NW
Washington, DC 20008
202-495-2266
Fax: 202-495-2138
E-Mail: chinaembpress_us@mfa.gov.cn
Home Page: www.china-embassy.org
Zhang Yesui, Ambassador

17968 **Embassy of the Republic of Angola**
2100-2108 16th Street, NW
Washington, DC 20009
202-785-1156
Fax: 202-822-9049
E-Mail: angola@angola.org
Home Page: www.angola.org
Alberto do Carmo Bento Ribeiro, Ambassador
Sofia Pegado da Silva, Minister Counselor
Manuel Francisco Louren‡o, First Secretary - Head of Consular
Ineclito Lima, First Secretary - Consular Section
ÿMercedes Quintino, First Secretary - Consular Section

17969 **Embassy of the Republic of Fiji**
2000 M Street,NW
Suite 710
Washington, DC 20036
202-466-8320
Fax: 202-466-8325
E-Mail: info@fijiembassydc.com
Home Page: www.fijiembassydc.com
Winston Thompson, Ambassador

17970 **Embassy of the Republic of Latvia**
2306 Massachusettes Ave, NW
Washington, DC 20008
202-328-2840
Fax: 202-328-2860
E-Mail: embassy.usa@mfa.gov.lv
Home Page: www.mfa.gov.lv/en/usa/
Social Media: Facebook, Twitter, Flickr
Andris Razans, Ambassador
Jurijs Pogrebnaks, Deputy Chief of Mission and Counsel
Vineta Mekoneÿ, Counselloÿ
Gita Leitlandeÿ, Defense Counselloÿ
Valts Vitums, First Secretary

17971 **Embassy of the Republic of Liberia**
5201 16th Street N. W.
Washington, DC 20011
202-723-0437
Fax: 202-723-0436
Home Page: www.liberianembassyus.org/
Charles Minor, President

17972 **Embassy of the Republic of Yemen**
2319 Wyoming Ave, NW
Washington, DC 20008
202-965-4760
Fax: 202-337-2017
E-Mail: ambassador@yemenembassy.org
Home Page: www.yemenembassy.org
Abdulwahab Abdulla Al-Hajjri, Ambassador
Nadia Hashem, Assistant to the Ambassador

17973 **Embassy of the Republic of the Marshall Islands**
2433 Massachusetts Avenue NW
Washington, DC 20008
202-234-5414
Fax: 202-232-3236
E-Mail: info@rmiembassyus.org
Home Page: www.rmiembassyus.org
Charles R. Paul, Ambassador

17974 **Estonian Embassy in Washington**
2131 Massachusetts Avenue NW
Washington, DC 20008
202-588-0101
Fax: 202-588-0108
E-Mail: Embassy.Washington@mfa.ee
Home Page: www.estemb.org
Marina Kaljurand, Ambassador
Tanel Sepp, Deputy Chief of Mission
Indrek Kannik, Counselor (Security Policy)
Oleg Dmitrijev, First Secretary (Political Affairs)
Marju Korts, Third Secretary (Economic Affairs)

17975 **Fair Trading Commission**
800 2nd Avenue
2nd Floor
New York, NY 10017
246-424-260
Fax: 246-424-0300
E-Mail: info@ftc.gov.bb
Home Page: www.ftc.gov.bb
Peggy Griffith, CEO
Founded in 1955

17976 **French Trade Commission**
1 E Wacker Drive
Suite 3730
Chicago, IL 60601
312-661-1880
Fax: 310-843-1700
Home Page: www.ubifrance.com
Social Media: Facebook, Twitter, LinkedIn

17977 **Gambia Mission to the United Nations**
800 2nd Avenue
Suite 400 F
New York, NY 10017
212-949-6640
Fax: 212-856-9820
Home Page: www.gambiamissionun.org
Tamsir Jallow, Ambassador

17978 **General Consulate of Luxembourg**
17 Beekman Place
New York, NY 10022
212 888 6664
Fax: 212-888-6116
E-Mail: newyork.cg@mae.etat.lu
Home Page: http://newyork-cg.mae.lu/en/The-Consulate-General
Jean-Claude Knebeler, Consul General
Saba Amroun-Febres, Consular Officer

17979 Gibraltar Information Bureau
1156 15th Street NW
Suite 1100
Washington, DC 20005

202-452-1108
Fax: 202-452-1109

Perry Stieglitz, Executive Director

17980 Greek Trade Commission
150 E 58th Street
17th Floor
New York, NY 10155

212-751-2404
Fax: 212-593-2278

Yannis Papadimitriou, Manager

17981 Guatemala Trade Office
57 Park Avenue
New York, NY 10017

212-689-1014
Fax: 212-689-6414
E-Mail: guatrade@aol.com

Roberto Rosenberg, Manager

17982 Hong Kong Trade Development Council
219 E 46th Street
New York, NY 10017-2951

212-838-8688
Fax: 212-838-8941
E-Mail: hktdc@hktdc.org
Home Page: www.tdctrade.com

Jack So Chak Kwong, Chairman

Promotes trade between the United States and Hong Kong.
Founded in 1966

17983 Hungarian Trade Commission
425 Bloor Street, East
Suite 501
Toronto-Ontario M4W 3R4

416-923-3596
Fax: 416-923-2097
E-Mail: itdtoronto@hungariantrade.org

Gyula Cseko, Trade Commissioner

17984 Icelandic Consulate General
800 3rd Avenue
36th Floor
New York, NY 10022

212-593-2700
646-282-9360
Fax: 646-282-9369
E-Mail: icecon.ny@mfa.is
Home Page: www.iceland.is/us/nyc
Social Media: Facebook

Hlynur Gudjonsson, Consul & Trade Commissioner
Berg_¢ra Laxdal, Cultural Representative
Founded in 1939

17985 International Chamber of Commerce (ICC)
1212 Avenue of the Americas
New York, NY 10036-1689

212-703-5065
Fax: 212-575-0327
Home Page: www.iccwbo.org
Social Media: Facebook, Twitter, LinkedIn, Youtube

Gerard Worms, Chairman
Harold McGraw III, Vice-Chairman
Founded in 1919

17986 Irish Trade Board
345 Park Avenue
17th Floor
New York, NY 10154

212-180-0800

Jean McCluskey, Marketing Executive

17987 Italian Trade Commission
33 East 67th Street
New York, NY 10065-5949

212-980-1500
Fax: 212-758-1050
E-Mail: newyork@ice.it
Home Page: www.italtrade.com/countries/americas/usa/newyork.htm

Michelle Jones, Editor
Robert Luongo, Executive Director

Developments in the Italian wine industry and market, as well as reviews of imported wines from Italy.

17988 Japanese External Trade Organization
1221 Avenue of the Americas
42nd Floor
New York, NY 10020
212-997-0400
Fax: 212-997-0464
E-Mail: jetrony@jetro.go.jp
Home Page: www.jetro.org
Social Media: Facebook, Twitter

Masaki Fujiharaÿ, Director, Business Developmentÿ
Daiki Nakajimaÿ, ICT/Environmentÿ

17989 Kazakhstan Mission to the United Nations
305 East 47th Street
3rd Floor
New York, NY 10017

212-230-1900
Fax: 212-230-1172
E-Mail: kazakhstan@un.int
Home Page: www.kazakhstanun.org

Byrganym Aitimova, Ambassador
Akan Rakhmetulin, DeputyPermanent Representative
Israil Tilegen, Minister Counsellor
Ruslan Bultrikov, Counsellor
Tluezan Seksenbay, Counsellor

Historic contributions in the field of nuclearÿdisarmamentand non-proliferation by voluntarily eliminating its nuclear arsenal, acceding to the NPT as a non-nuclear state and shutting down the former Semipalatinsk nuclear testing ground, thus ensuring global and regional stability
Founded in 1992

17990 Korea Trade Promotion Center (KOTRA)
460 Park Avenue
14th Floor
New York, NY 10022

212-826-0900
Fax: 212-888-4930
E-Mail: kotrany@hotmail.com
Home Page: www.kotrana.org

Sungpil Umo, President
Il Hoon Ko, Deputy Director

17991 Kyrgyzstan Mission to the United Nations
866 United Nations Plaza
Suite 477
New York, NY 10017

212-486-4214
Fax: 212-486-5259
Home Page: www.un.int/wcm/content/site/kyrgyzstan

Talaibek Kydyrov, Ambassador
Nuran Niyazaliev, Counsellor
Nurbek Kasymov, First Secretary
Diana Sarygulova, Third Secretary
Asel Davydova, Chief Administrative Specialist

Landlocked republic in the eastern part of Central Asia which is bordered in the north by Kazakhstan, in the east by China, in the south by China and Tajikistan, and in the west by Uzbekistan. Bishkek is the capital and largest city.
Founded in 1993

17992 Malaysia Trade Commission
313 E 43rd Street
3rd Floor
New York, NY 10017
212-986-6310
Fax: 212-490-8576
E-Mail: malnyun@kln.gov.my
Home Page: www.kln.gov.my

Hussein Haniff, Ambassador

17993 Mexico Trade Commission
757 3rd Avenue
Suite 2400
New York, NY 10017-2042

212-826-2978

17994 Moldova Mission to the United Nations
35 East 29th Street
New York, NY 10016

212-447-1867
Fax: 212-447-4067
E-Mail: unmoldova@aol.com
Home Page: www.un.int/wcm/content/site/moldova

Vlad Lupan, Ambassador
Larisa Miculet, Counsellor
Carolina Podoroghin, Third Secretary
Tatianana Dudnicenco, Chief Financial Officer
Litvac Sergiu, Administrator
Founded in 1992

17995 New Zealand Trade Development Board
222 East 41st Street
New York, NY 10017-6739

212-497-0200

17996 Norwegian Trade Council
2720 34th Street NW
Washington, DC 20008

202-333-6000
Fax: 202-469-3990
E-Mail: emb.washington@mfa.no
Home Page: www.norway.org
Social Media: Twitter, LinkedIn, Flickr, Instagram, Tumblr

Kare R.Aas, Ambassador
Lajla Jakhelin, Minister
Elin Kylvag, Personal Assistant
Berit Enge, Minister Counsellor

Innovation Norway promotes nationwide industrial development profitable to both the business economy and Norways national economy, and helps release the potential of different districts and regions by contributing towards innovation, internationalisation and promotion. Innovation Norway also promotes tourism to Norway

17997 **Pakistan Trade Commission**
12 E 65th Street
4th Floor
New York, NY 10021

212-879-5800

Abbas Zaidi, Manager

17998 **Permanent Mission of Bangladesh to the United Nations**
820 East Diplomat Center, 2nd Avenue
4th Floor
New York, NY 10017

212-867-3434
Fax: 212-972-4038
E-Mail: bangladesh@un.int
Home Page:
www.un.int/wcm/content/site/bangladesh

A.K.Abdul Momen, Ambassador
Mustafizur Rahman, Permanent Representative
Andalib Elias, Counsellor
Samia Anjum, Counsellor

Peaceful settlement of disputes, promotion of human rights, protection of environment, sustainable development and so on.
Founded in 1990

17999 **Permanent Mission of Ghana to the United Nations**
19 E 47th Street
New York, NY 10017

212-832-1300
Fax: 212-751-6743
E-Mail: ghanaperm@aol.com
Home Page: www.un.int/ghana

Ken Kanda, Ambassador
William Kanyirige, Minister
Henry T.Menson, Minister-Counsellor
J.R Adogla, Minister-Counsellor
N.A Abayena, Counsellor
Founded in 1957

18000 **Permanent Mission of Myanmar (Formerly Burma)**
10 E 77th Street
New York, NY 10075

212-744-1271
Fax: 212-744-1290
E-Mail: mynmarmnission@verizon.net
Home Page: www.myanmarmissionny.org

H.E.U. Kyaw Tin, Ambassador
A.Kyaw Zan, Minister counsellor
Ko Ko Shien, Minister Counsellor

18001 **Permanent Mission of Saint Vincent & the Grenadines to the United Nations**
800 2nd Avenue
Suite 400-G
New York, NY 10017

212-599-0950
Fax: 212-599-1020
E-Mail: mission@svg-un.org
Home Page: www.svg-un.org
Social Media: Facebook, Twitter, YouTube

Camillo M. Gonsalves, Ambassador
Nedra Miguel, Minister Counsellor
Mozart Carr, Attache
Maglyn Carrington, Secretary/Accountant

Primary channel for communications between the Vincentian Government and the United Nations in New York City.
Founded in 1998

18002 **Permanent Mission of the Czech Republic to the United Nations**
1109-1111 Madison Avenue
New York, NY 10028

646-981-4001
Fax: 646-981-4099
E-Mail: un.newyork@embassy.mzv.cz
Home Page: www.mzv.cz/un.newyork
Social Media: Facebook, Twitter, LinkedIn

Edita Hrda, Amabassador
David Cervanka, Deputy Permanent Representative
Founded in 1945

18003 **Permanent Mission of the Kingdom of Bhutan to the United Nations**
343 East 43rd Street
New York, NY 10017

212-682-2268
Fax: 212-661-0551
E-Mail: bhutan@un.int
Home Page:
www.un.int/wcm/content/site/bhutan

Lhtu Wangchuk, Ambassador

18004 **Permanent Mission of the Republic of Sudan to the United Nations**
655 3rd Avenue
Suite 500-10
New York, NY 10017

212-593-0999

Jenine Selson, Manager

18005 **Permanent Mission of the Republic of Armenia to the United Nations**
119 E 36th Street
New York, NY 10016

212-752-3370

Andrezej Towpik, Manager

18006 **Permanent Mission of the Solomon Islands to the United Nations**
800 2nd Avenue
Suite 400
New York, NY 10017

212-599-6192
Fax: 212-661-8925
E-Mail: simun@foreignaffairs-solomons.org
Home Page:
www.un.int/wcm/content/site/solomonislands

Collin Beck, Ambassador
Hellen Beck, Counsellor
Vanessa M.Kenilorea, Third Secretary
B Jagne, Manager

18007 **Philippines Commercial Office**
556 5th Avenue
New York, NY 10036

212-764-1330

18008 **Poland Trade Commission**
675 3rd Avenue
19th Floor
New York, NY 10017

212-351-1713

Phyllis Poland, Owner

18009 **Portuguese Trade Commission**
590 5th Avenue
3rd Floor
New York, NY 10036

212-354-4403
Fax: 212-575-4737
E-Mail: chamber@portugal-us.com
Home Page: www.portugal-un.org

18010 **Romanian Consulate General**
11766 Wilshire Blvd
Suite 560
Los Angeles, CA 90025

310-444-0043
Fax: 310-445-0043
Home Page: http://www.romanian.com

Corina Suteu, Manager

The Romanian projects are on hold, as inhouse resources were diverted to more lucrative projects hosted at NetSide. If you have an interst to develop something in Romanian, please let me know and perhaps we can work something out.

18011 **Singapore Trade Commission**
55 E 59th Street
Suite 21-B
New York, NY 10022

212-421-2869
Fax: 212-421-2206
E-Mail: newyork@contactsingapore.org

Kc Yeoh, Executive Director

18012 **Slovak Republic Mission to the United Nations**
866 United Nations Plaza
Suite 493
New York, NY 10017

212-980-1558

18013 **Swedish Trade Council**
150 N Michigan Avenue
Chicago, IL 60601

312-781-6222
Social Media: Facebook, Twitter

Stefam Bergstrom, Manager

18014 **Syrian Arab Republic Embassy**
2215 Wyoming Avenue NW
Washington, DC 20008

202-232-6313
Fax: 202-265-4585
E-Mail: consular@syrembassay.net

18015 **Taiwan Trade Center**
5201 Great America Parkway
Suite 306
Santa Clara, CA 95054-112

408-988-5018
Fax: 408- 98-5029
E-Mail: office@taiwantradesf.org
Home Page: http://sf.taiwantrade.com.tw/

Founded in 1970

18016 **Tajikistan Mission to the United Nations**
136 E 67th Street
New York, NY 10021

212-744-2196
Fax: 212-472-7645

Khamrokhon Zaripov, President
Abduvokhid Karimov, Minister

18017 **Thailand Trade Center- Consulate General of Thailand**
401 N Michigan Avenue
Suite 544
Chicago, IL 60611

312-467-0044
Fax: 312-467-1690
E-Mail: ttcc@wwa.com

18018 **Trade Commission of Denmark**
285 Peachtree Road NE
Suite 920
Atlanta, GA 30303

404-588-1588
Fax: 678-904-9714
E-Mail: atlhkt@um.dk

Taksoe Jensen, Ambassador
Henrik Bronner, Manager

18019 **Trade Commission of Spain**
500 N Michigan Avenue
Suite 1500
Chicago, IL 60611

312-644-1154
Home Page: www.spaintechnology.com

18020 **Turkish Trade Commission**
821 United Nations Plaza
4th Floor
New York, NY 10017

212-687-1530

18021 **Turkmenistan Mission to the United Nations**
866 United Nations Plaza
Suite 424
New York, NY 10017

212-486-8908
Fax: 212-486-2521
E-Mail: turkmenistan@un.int

Aksoltan Ataeva, Manager

18022 **United Nations Mission to El Salvador**
46 Park Avenue
New York, NY 10016

212-679-1616
Fax: 212-725-3467
E-Mail: elsalvador@un.int
Home Page:
www.un.int/wcm/content/site/elsalvador

Antonio Montiero, Manager

Associations

18023 AMT: Association for Manufacturing Technology
7901 Westpark Dr
Mc Lean, VA 22102-4206

703-893-2900
800-524-0475
Fax: 703-893-1151
E-Mail: AMT@amtonline.org
Home Page: www.amtonline.org
Social Media: Facebook, Twitter, Youtube

Bob Simpson, President
Douglas K. Woods, First Vice Chairman
John Byrd, President

ÿThe Association For Manufacturing Technology represents and promotes U.S.-based manufacturing technology and its members-those who design, build, sell, and service the continuously evolving technology that lies at the heart of manufacturing
370 Members
Founded in 1902

18024 APMI International Advancement of Powder Metallurgy
105 College Road E
Princeton, NJ 08540-6992

609-452-7700
Fax: 609-987-8523
E-Mail: apmi@mpif.org
Home Page: www.apmiinternational.org

Dean Howard, President
Michael E Lutheran, Director
C James Trombino CAE, Director

A non-profit professional society which promotes the advancement of powder metallurgy (PM) and particulate materials as a science. Its purpose is to disseminate and exchange information about PM and particulate materials through publications, conferences, and other activities of the society.
Founded in 1959

18025 ASM International
9639 Kinsman Rd
Materials Park, OH 44072

440-338-5151
800-336-5152
Fax: 440-338-4634
E-Mail: memberservices@asminternational.org
Home Page: www.asminternational.org
Social Media: Facebook, Twitter, LinkedIn

Stanley Theobald, Managing Director
Thomas S Passek, Association Managing Director
Joseph M Zion, Director, Sales & Marketing
Jeane Deatherage, Administrator, Foundation Programs
Virginia Shirk, Foundation Executive Assistant

The society for materials engineers and scientists, a worldwide network dedicated to advancing industry, technology and applications of metals and materials.
35000 Members
Founded in 1913

18026 ASM International Materials Information Society
9639 Kinsman Road
Materials Park, OH 44073-0002

440-338-5151
800-336-5152
E-Mail:
memberservicecenter@asminternational.org
Home Page: www.asminternational.org
Social Media: Facebook, Twitter, LinkedIn

Founded in 1913

18027 Aluminum Anodizers Council (AAC)
1000 North Rand Road
Suite 214
Wauconda, IL 60084

847-526-2010
Fax: 847-526-3993
E-Mail: mail@anodizing.org
Home Page: www.anodizing.org
Social Media: LinkedIn

Todd Hamilton, Chairman
Gregory T Rajsky CAE, President

Represents the interests of aluminum anodizers worldwide and is the principal trade organization for the andozing industry in North America. It promotes the interests of its members through technical exchange, ongoing education, statistical data, market promotion and industry representation.
85 Members
Founded in 1988

18028 Aluminum Association
Aluminum Association
1525 Wilson Blvd
Suite 600
Arlington, VA 22209-2444

703-358-2960
Fax: 703-358-2961
Home Page: www.aluminum.org

J Stephen Larkin, President
A.Robin King, VP, Public Affairs
Heidi Biggs Brock, President
Nicholas Adams, Vice President, Business Informatio

Members are manufacturers of aluminum mill products and producers of aluminum.
70 Members

18029 Aluminum Extruders Council
1000 North Rand Road
Suite 214
Wauconda, IL 60084

847-526-2010
Fax: 847-526-3993
E-Mail: mail@aec.org
Home Page: www.aec.org
Social Media: LinkedIn

James Bine, Chairman
Duncan Crowdis, Vice Chairman
Rand A Baldwin CAE, President

An international association dedicated to helping manufacturers, engineers, architects and others to discover why aluminum extrusoin is the preferred material process for better products
135 Members
Founded in 1950

18030 American Association of Professional Farriers
1313 Washington Street
Unit 5
Shelbyville, KY 40065

Home Page: www.professionalfarriers.comÿ

Dave Farley APF CF, President
Steve Prescott APF CJF, Vice President
Roy Bloom APF CJF, Treasurer
Jeff Ridley APF CJF TE, Immediate Past President
Bryan Quinsey, Executive Director
Founded in 2011

18031 American Ceramic Society
600 N. Cleveland Ave.
Suite 210
Westerville, OH 43082

240-646-7054
866-721-3322
Fax: 240-396-5637
E-Mail: customerservice@ceramics.org
Home Page: www.ceramics.orgÿ
Social Media: Facebook, Twitter, LinkedIn, RSS, Google+, YouTube

18032 American Electroplaters and Surface Finishers Society (AESF)
1155 15th Street NW
Suite 500
Washington, DC 20005

202-457-8401
Fax: 202-530-0659
E-Mail: info@aesf.org
Home Page: www.aesf.org
Social Media: Facebook, Twitter

John Flatley, Executive Director
Courtney Mariette, Bookstore/Education
Holly Wills, Membership
Dan Denston, Executive Director
John Flatley, Senior Advisor and NASF Liaison

AESF is an international society that advances the science of surface finishing to benefit industry and society through education, information and social involvement, as well as those who provide services, supplies and support to the industry.
5000 Members
Founded in 1911

18033 American Farriers Association
4059 Iron Works Pkwy
Suite 1
Lexington, KY 40511-8488

859-233-7411
Fax: 859-231-7862
E-Mail: info@americanfarriers.org
Home Page: www.americanfarriers.org

Craig Trnka, President
Bob S.Earle, VP
Bryan Quinsey, Executive Director
Rachel Heighton, Office Manager
Founded in 1971

18034 American Foundry Society
1695 N Penny Ln
Schaumburg, IL 60173-4555

847-824-0181
800-537-4237
Fax: 847-824-7848
E-Mail: library@afsinc.org
Home Page: www.afsinc.org

Jerry Call, Executive VP
Ian Kay, VP
David Peterson, Membership Director

Trade association representing the interests of foundry workers across the nation. Offers publications, seminars and networking to promote business in the trade.
10000 Members
Founded in 1896

18035 American Galvinizers Association
6881 South Holly Circle,
Suite 108
Centennial, CO 80112

720-554-0900
Fax: 720-554-0909
E-Mail: aga@galvanizeit.org
Home Page: www.galvanizeit.orgÿ
Social Media: Facebook, Twitter, LinkedIn, Google+, YouTube

Tommy Rose, President
John Gregor, First Vice President
Tim Pendley, Second Vice President
Philip G. Rahrig, Executive Director
Dr. Tom Langill, Technical Director
Founded in 1933

18036 American Institute of Mining, Metallurgical & Petroleum Engineers
8307 Shaffer Parkway
Po Box 270728
Littleton, CO 80127-0013

303-948-4255
Fax: 303-948-4260
E-Mail: aime@aimehq.org
Home Page: www.aimeny.org

Rick Rolater, Executive Director
James R Jorden, President

Organized and operated exclusively to advance, record and disseminate significant knowledge of engineering and the arts and sciences involved in the production and use of minerals, metals, energy sources and materials for the benefits of humankind, both directly as AIME and through memeber societies.

18037 American Institute of Steel Construction
One East Wacker Drive
Suite 700
Chicago, IL 60601-1802

312-670-2400
Fax: 312-670-5403
E-Mail: solutions@aisc.org
Home Page: www.aisc.org
Social Media: RSS

Roger E. Ferch, President

18038 American Iron & Steel Institute
25 Massachusetts Ave., NW, Suite 800
Washington, DC 20001

202-452-7100
Fax: 202-496-9702
E-Mail: webmaster@steel.org
Home Page: www.recycle-steel.org
Social Media: Facebook, Twitter, Youtube

Chip Foley, VP
David Bell, VP/CEO

Works with market development communications programs in automotive, construction and container markets.

18039 American Society for Metals
9639 Kinsman Road
Materials Park, OH 44073-0002

440-338-5151
800-336-5152
E-Mail: memberservicecenter@asminternational.org
Home Page: www.asminternational.org
Social Media: Facebook, Twitter, LinkedIn
Founded in 1913

18040 American Welding Society
8669 Doral Boulevard, Suite 130
Doral, FL 33166

305-443-9353
800-443-9353
Fax: 305-443-7559
Home Page: www.aws.org

Ray Shook, Manager
Andy Cullison, Publisher
Amy Nathan, Public Relations Manager

Involved in writing industry standards.
48000 Members
Founded in 1919

18041 American Wire Cloth Institute
25 North Broadway
Tarrytown, NY 10591

914-332-0040
Fax: 914-332-1541
E-Mail: info@hti.org
Home Page: www.hti.org

Richard C Byrne, Executive Director

Formerly the Industrial Wire Cloth Institute (1978)
Founded in 1933

18042 American Wire Producers Association
PO Box 151387
Alexandria, VA 22315

703-299-4434
Fax: 703-299-4434
E-Mail: info@awpa.org
Home Page: www.awpa.org
Founded in 1981

18043 American Zinc Association
American Bearing Manufacturers Association
2025 M St NW
Suite 800
Washington, DC 20036-2422

202-367-1155
Fax: 202-367-2232
E-Mail: zincinfo@zinc.org
Home Page: www.americanbearings.org

Scott Lynch, President
Joseph Spiciarich, Chairman
K.Kelly Sherrard, Senior Associate
Laura Somerville, Senior Associate

Washington D.C. based trade organization comprised of primary and secondary producers of zinc metal, zinc oxide and zinc dust marketed in the United States, as well as consumers.
18 Members
Founded in 1990

18044 Artist-Blacksmiths Association of North
PO Box 816
Farmington, GA 30638-816

706-310-1030
Fax: 423-913-1023
E-Mail: abana@abana.org
Home Page: www.abana.org

Don Kemper, President
Clare Yellin, First VP
Dorothy Stiegler, Treasurer
Jerry Kagele, Secretary

For the professional and amateur blacksmith.
4500 Members
Founded in 1973
Mailing list available for rent

18045 Association for Iron & Steel Technology (AIST)
186 Thorn Hill Rd
Warrendale, PA 15086-7528

724-814-3000
Fax: 724-814-3001
E-Mail: memberservices@aist.org
Home Page: www.aist.org

Ronald E Ashburn, Executive Director
Lori Wharrey, Board Administrator
Chris McKelvey, Assistant Board Administrator
Stacy Vermecky, Membership Services Manager
Penny English, Member Administrator

The Association for Iron & Steel Technology (AIST) is an international technical association representing iron and steel producers, their allied suppliers and related academia. The association is dedicated to advancing the technical development, production, processing and application of iron and steel.
12300 Members
Founded in 2004

18046 Association for Manufacturing Technology
7901 Westpark Drive
McLean, VA 22102

703-893-2900
877-578-4000
Fax: 703-893-1151
E-Mail: amt@mfgtech.org
Home Page: www.amtonline.org

Bob Simpson, President
Douglas K. Woods, First Vice Chairman
John Byrd, President

ÿThe Association For Manufacturing Technology represents and promotes U.S.-based manufacturing technology and its members-those who design, build, sell, and service the continuously evolving technology that lies at the heart of manufacturing

18047 Association of Battery Recyclers
PO Box 290286
Tampa, FL 33687

813-626-6151
Fax: 813-622-8387
E-Mail: joycemorales@aol.com
Home Page: batteryrecyclers.com

Joyce Morales, Secretary/Treasurer

Investigates means and methods to achieve compliance with OSHA and EPA regulations impacting the secondary lead smelting industry.
Founded in 1976

18048 Association of Industrial Metallizers, Coaters and Laminators (AIMCAL)
201 Springs Street
Fort Mill, SC 29715

803-948-9470
Fax: 803-948-9471
E-Mail: aimcal@aimcal.org
Home Page: www.aimcal.org
Social Media: Facebook

Bob Connelly, President
Dan Bemi, VP
Craig Sheppard, Executive Director
Tracey Ingram, Senior Administrator
Danis Roy, Treasurer

Nonprofit trade organization for makes of coated, laminated and metalized papers.
Founded in 1970
Mailing list available for rent

18049 Association of Steel Distributors
401 N Michigan Avenue
Chicago, IL 60611

312-673-5793
Fax: 312-527-6705
E-Mail: headquarters@steeldistributors.org
Home Page: www.steeldistributors.org

Ron Pietrzak, Executive Director

ASD is a nonprofit organization, providing the steel distribution industry a forum for ideas exchange and market information.

18050 Association of Women in the Metal Industries
19 Mantua Road
Mt Royal, NJ 08061

856-423-3201
Fax: 856-423-3420
E-Mail: awmi@talley.com
Home Page: www.awmi.org
Social Media: Facebook, LinkedIn

Haley Brust, Executive Director

An international, professional organization dedicated to promoting and supporting the advancement of women in the metal industries.

18051 Cast Iron Soil Pipe Institute
3008 Preston Station Drive
Hixson, TN 37343

423-842-2122
Home Page: www.cispi.org

Founded in 1949

18052 Cast Metals Institute
1695 N Penny Ln
Schaumburg, IL 60173-4555

847-824-0181
800-537-4237
Fax: 847-824-7848
Home Page: www.castmetals.com
Social Media: Facebook, Twitter, LinkedIn

Mark Nagel, Executive VP
Sandy Salisbury-Linton, Vice Chairman

Supports all those involved in the cast metal industry. Hosts annual trade show.
Founded in 1956

18053 Closure & Container Manufacturers Association
421 N NW Highway
Suite 201
Barrington, IL 60010

847-438-2700
E-Mail: candyr@@closureandcontainer.org
Home Page: www.closureandcontainer.org
Social Media: Facebook, Twitter, LinkedIn

Candace M Renwall, President

Conducts public relations for member companies and establishes industry standards.
38 Members
Founded in 1984

18054 Copper Development Association
260 Madison Ave
New York, NY 10016-2403

212-251-7200
800-232-3282
Fax: 212-251-7234
E-Mail: questions@cda.copper.org
Home Page: www.copper.org
Social Media: Facebook, Twitter

Andrew G Kireta, President & CEO
Victoria Prather, Manager Communications
Michels Harold, VP Technaloy Services
Luis Lozano, Technical Consultant
Lorraine Herzing Mills, VP/Finance/Administration

Seeks to expand the uses and applications of copper and copper products. Responsible for industry-wide market statistics and research.
75 Members
Founded in 1963

18055 Copper and Brass Servicenter Association
994 Old Eagle School Road
Suite 1019
Wayne, PA 19087-1866

610-971-4850
Fax: 913-345-1006
Home Page: www.copper-brass.org

Daniel Erck, President
Robert A Lewis, VP

Distriburors (servicenters) of fabricated copper and copper alloy products (sheet, plate, coil, rod bar, tube, etc) and their brass mill suppliers.
75 Members
Founded in 1951

18056 Ductile Iron Pipe Research Association
245 Riverchase Pkwy E
Suite O
Birmingham, AL 35244-1856

205-402-8700
Fax: 205-402-8730
Home Page: www.dipra.org

Troy F Stroud, President
Richard W Bonds, Technical Director

Established as the Cast Iron Pipe Publicity Bureau.
7 Members
Founded in 1915

18057 Ductile Iron Society
15400 Pearl Rd
Suite 234
Strongsville, OH 44136-6017

440-665-3686
Fax: 440-878-0070
E-Mail: jwood@ductile.org
Home Page: www.ductile.org

Patricio Gill, President
Robert O.Rourke, VP
Pete Guidi, Treasurer
James N.Wood, Executive and Technical Director

A technical society servicing the ductile iron industry. To advance the technology, art, science of ductile iron production and to disseminate all such information to the members.
102 Members
Founded in 1958

18058 Edison Welding Institute
1250 Arthur E Adams Dr
Columbus, OH 43221-3585

614-688-5000
Fax: 614-688-5001
E-Mail: info@ewi.org
Home Page: www.ewi.org
Social Media: Facebook, Twitter

Henry Cialone, President
Dr Karl Graff, Executive Director

Companies and organizations with an interest in new developments in welding equipment and technology.

18059 Electrical Manufacturing & Coil Winding Association
PO Box 278
Imperial Beach, CA 91933-0278

619-435-3629
Fax: 619-435-3639
E-Mail: cthurman@earthlink.net
Home Page: www.emcwa.org

Richard Duke, President
Charles Thurman, Executive Director
Don Stankiewicz, Vice President

A non-profit voluntary organization dedicated to the furtherance of the conception, research, design, manufacturing, marketing and use of electrical products. The Association provides an array of educational opportunities that enhance the development, knowledge, and use of electrical technology and products. Providing an annual forum to display products, ideas and innovations is a key element in this educational process.
400 Members
Founded in 1973
Mailing list available for rent

18060 Fabricators and Manufacturers Association
Fabricators and Manufacturers Association
833 Featherstone Road
Rockford, IL 61107-6302

815-399-8700
Fax: 815-484-7700
E-Mail: info@fmanet.org
Home Page: www.fmanet.org
Social Media: Facebook, Twitter, LinkedIn

Gerald M Shankel, President/CEO
Jim Warren, Director/Membership + Education
Vicki Webb, Director/Information Technology
Mark Hoper, Director/Expositions
Michael Long, Director/Education

FMA is an educational association serving the metal forming and fabricating industry. Technology areas include sheet metal fabricating, stamping, roll forming, coil processing, punching and plate structural fabricating.
1500 Members
Founded in 1971

18061 Forging Industry Association
1111 Superior Ave.
Suite 615
Cleveland, OH 44114

216-781-6260
Fax: 216-781-0102
E-Mail: info@forging.org
Home Page: www.forging.org
Social Media: Facebook, Twitter, LinkedIn

Roy W. Hardy, President
Joe Boni, CFO
Don Farley, Director of Marketing
Theresa Ferry, Executive Assistant
Pat Kasik, Executive Assistant

18062 Global Platinum & Gold
5380 S 154th St
Gilbert, AZ 85298-6138

480-946-1242
Fax: 480-946-1242
Home Page: www.globalplatinumonline.com

A natural resources mining company engaged in the processing and commercial extraction of precious metals from complex ores.

18063 Gold Prospectors Association of America
Po Box 891509
Temecula, CA 92589-1509

951-699-4749
800-551-9707
Fax: 951-699-4062
E-Mail: info@goldprospectors.org
Home Page: www.goldprospectors.org

Thomas Massie, CEO

GPAA is the largest recreational gold prospecting club. Owner of The Outdoor Channel, a cable TV channel featuring real outdoors for real people.
35M Members
Founded in 1985

18064 Industrial Diamond Association of America
P.O. Box 29460ÿ
Columbus, OH 43229

614-797-2265
614-425-0712
Fax: 614-797-2264
E-Mail: tkane-ida@insight.rr.com
Home Page: www.superabrasives.org

Terry M. Kane, Executive Director

18065 Industrial Metal Containers Section of the Material Handling Institute
8720 Red Oak Boulevard
Suite 201
Charlotte, NC 28217-3996

704-676-1190
Fax: 704-676-1199
E-Mail: gbaer@mhia.org
Home Page: www.mhia.org
Social Media: Facebook, Twitter, LinkedIn, Yahoo

Greg Baer, Senior Sales Associate
Jennifer Breadling, Manager Of Communications

Promotes the market and develops a code of ethics. Serves as liaison among members and other groups.
9 Members
Founded in 1972

18066 Industrial Perforators Association
6737 W. Washington St
Milwaukee, WI 53214

414-389-8618
Fax: 414-276-7704
E-Mail: infof@iperf.org
Home Page: www.iperf.org

Delores Morris, Executive Secretary

Members are companies making perforated metal products.

18067 Innovative Material Solutions
225 Canterbury Drive
State College, PA 16803

814-867-1140
Fax: 814-867-2813
E-Mail: info@imspowder.com

Supports all those involved in research in the materials industry. Hosts annual trade show.

18068 Institute of Scrap Recycling Industries
1615 L St NW
Suite 600
Washington, DC 20036-5664

202-662-8500
Fax: 202-626-0900
E-Mail: dennywhite@scrap.org
Home Page: www.isri.org

Robin K.Wiener, President
Sandy Bishop, VP Finance/Administration
Rachel Bookman, Admin Assistant
Thomas Crane, Director of Membership

ISRI provides education, advocacy, and compliance training while promoting public awareness of the role recycling plays in the U.S. economy, global trade, the environment and sustainable development.

18069 International Chromium Development Association

Home Page: www.icdacr.com

18070 International Copper Association
260 Madison Ave
16th Floor
New York, NY 10016-2403

212-251-7240
Fax: 212-251-7245
Home Page: www.copperalliance.org

Francis J Kane, President

Promoting the use of copper by communicating the unique attributes that make this sustainable element an essential contributor to the formation of life, to advances in science and technology, and to a higher standard of living worldwide.
Founded in 1989

18071 International Council on Mining and Metals

Home Page: www.icmm.com

18072 International Hard Anondizing
PO Box 579
Moorestown, NJ 08057-0579

856-234-0330
Fax: 856-727-9504
E-Mail: Denise.Downing@comcast.net
Home Page: www.ihanodizing.com

Denise Downing, Executive Director

Formed by companies in the hard anodizing business to provide a forum for the exchange of technical information and to act as a clearing house for information about the industry.
Founded in 1989

18073 International Lead Management Center
2525 Meridian Parkway
Suite 100
Durham, NC 27713

919-287-1872
Fax: 919-361-1957
E-Mail: info@ilmc.org
Home Page: www.ilmc.orgÿ

18074 International Lead Zinc Research Organization
1822 NC Highway 54 East
Suite 120
Durham, NC 27713-5243

919-361-4647
Fax: 919-361-1957
E-Mail: jhendric@ilzro.org
Home Page: www.ilzro.org

Stephen Wilkinson, President
Judith Hendrickson, Corporate Secretary

Members are miners, smelters and refiners of lead and zinc. Supports research and development of new uses for the metals and refinement existing uses. Has an annual budget of approximately $5.3 million.
77 Members
Founded in 1958

18075 International Magnesium Association
1000 N Rand Rd
Suite 214
Wauconda, IL 60084-1180

847-526-2010
Fax: 847-526-3993
E-Mail: info@intlmag.org
Home Page: www.intlmag.org

Greg Patzer, Executive VP
Eileen Hoblit, Administrative Coordinator

IMA is to promote the use of the metal magnesium in material selection and encourage innovative applications of the versatile metal.
125 Members
Founded in 1943

18076 International Platinum GroupÿMetals Association

Home Page: www.ipa-news.com

18077 International Precious Metals Institute
5101 N 12th Avenue
Suite C
Pensacola, FL 32504

850-476-1156
Fax: 850-476-1548
E-Mail: mail@ipmi.org
Home Page: www.ipmi.org

Robert Ianniello, President

International association of producers, refiners, fabricators, scientists, users, financial institutions, merchants, private and public sector groups and the general precious metals community created to provide a forum for the exchange of information and technology.
Founded in 1976

18078 International Thermal Spray Association
208 Third Street
Fairport Harbor, OH 44077

440-357-5400
Fax: 440-357-5430
E-Mail: itsa@thermalspray.org
Home Page: www.thermalspray.org
Social Media: Facebook, LinkedIn

Kathy M Dusa, Administrative Assistant

Strengthens the level of awareness in general industry and government on the increasing capabilities and advantages of thermal spray technology for surface engineering through business opportunities, technical support and a social network. Contributes to growth and education in the thermal spray industry.
70 Members
Founded in 1948

18079 International Titanium Association
11674 Huron Street
Suite 100
Northglenn, CO 80234

303-404-2221
Fax: 303-404-9111
E-Mail: ita@titanium.org
Home Page: www.titanium.org
Social Media: titanium2011.pathable.com

Brett S.Paddock, President & CEO
Donn S.Hickton, VP
Hunter R.Dalton, Treasurer
Susan M.Abkowitz, Director
Jennifer Simpson, Executive Director

International Titanium Association is an international membership based trade association dedicated to the titanium metal industry. Established in 1984, ITA strives to connect the public interested in using titanium with specialists from across the globe who offer sales and technical assistance.
120 Members
Founded in 1984

18080 Lead Industries Association
13 Main Street
Sparta, NJ 07871

973-726-5323
Fax: 973-726-4484
E-Mail: miller@leadinfo.com
Home Page: www.leadinfo.com

Jeffrey T Miller, Executive Director

Nonprofit trade association representing the lead industries in the US and abroad. It collects and distributes information about the users of lead products in industry, vehicles, radioactive waste disposal and noise barriers. Its services are availble, generally free of charge, to anyone interested in the uses of lead and lead products.

18081 **Machinery Dealers National Association**
Machinery Dealers National Association
315 S Patrick St
Alexandria, VA 22314-3532

703-836-9300
800-872-7807
Fax: 703-836-9303
E-Mail: office@mdna.org
Home Page: www.mdna.org

Ron Shuster, President
Mark Robinson, Executive VP

Supports manufacturers involved in metal working machine tools. Publishes annual directory.

18082 **Magnet Distributors and Fabricators Association**
8 S Michigan Avenue
Suite 1000
Chicago, IL 60603

312-541-2667
Fax: 312-580-0165

August L Sisco, Executive Secretary

Distributors and magnetic materials and fabricators of magnetic components, plus suppliers to the distributor/fabricators.
31 Members
Founded in 1991

18083 **Metal Building Contractors and Erectors Association**
PO Box 499
Shawnee Mission, KS 66201

913-432-3800
800-866-6722
Fax: 913-432-3803
Home Page: www.mbcea.org

Angela M Cruse, Executive Director
Tim Seyler, President

To support the professional advancement of metal building contractors, erectors, and the industry.
235 Members
Founded in 1968

18084 **Metal Building Manufacturers Association**
1300 Sumner Avenue
Cleveland, OH 44115-2851

216-241-7333
Fax: 216-241-0105
E-Mail: mbma@mbma.com
Home Page: www.mbma.com

Charles M Stockinger, General Manager
Charles E Praeger, Assistant General Manager
W Lee Shoemaker, Ph.D., P.E., Director of Research & Engineering
Dan J.Walker, Senior Technical Enginner
Jay D.Johnson, Director of Architectural Services

Promotes the design and construction of metal building systems in the low-rise, non-residential building marketplace.
Founded in 1956

18085 **Metal Construction Association**
4700 W Lake Ave
Glenview, IL 60025-1468

847-375-4718
Fax: 847-375-6488
E-Mail: mca@metalconstruction.org
Home Page: www.metalconstruction.org

Dedicated to promoting the use of metal in construction. Initiative include market development, educational programs, issue and product awareness compaigns and publication of technical guidelines and specifications manuals. Also monitors and confronts challenges affecting the industry such as code restructions.
100 Members
Founded in 1983

18086 **Metal Findings Manufacturers**
30-R Houghton Street
Providence, RI 02904

401-861-4667
Fax: 401-861-0429
E-Mail: info@mfma.net
Home Page: www.mfma.net

John Augustyn, Executive Officer

Makers of metal parts and fittings used in the assembly of jewelry.
Founded in 1930

18087 **Metal Injection Molding Associationÿ**
105 College Road East
Princeton, NJ 8540

609-452-7700
609-987-8523
E-Mail: info@mpif.org
Home Page: www.mimaweb.org

18088 **Metal Powder Industries Federation**
105 College Rd E
Princeton, NJ 08540-6692

609-452-7700
Fax: 609-987-8523
E-Mail: info@mpif.org
Home Page: www.mpif.org

Michael Latheran, President, CEO
Jilliane Regan, VP
Jim Adams, Manager
James R.Dale, VP

As its name states, it is aÿfederation of trade associations-six in all-that are concerned with some aspect of powder metallurgy, metal powders, or particulate materials.
210 Members
Founded in 1944

18089 **Metal Service Center Institute**
4201 Euclid Ave
Suite 550
Rolling Meadows, IL 60008-2025

847-485-3000
Fax: 847-485-3001
E-Mail: info@msci.org
Home Page: www.msci.org
Social Media: Facebook, Twitter, LinkedIn

Bob Weidner, President
Jonathan Kalkwarf, VP Finance/Administration
Rose Manfredini, VP Member Information Services
Chris Marti, VP Technology
375 Members
Founded in 1907

18090 **Metals Service Center Institute**
4201 Euclid Ave
Rolling Meadows, IL 60008

847-485-3000
Fax: 847-485-3001
E-Mail: info@msci.org
Home Page: www.msci.org
Social Media: Facebook, Twitter, LinkedIn

Bob Weidner, President/ Chief Executive Officer
Ann D'Orazio, Vice President, Marketing-Growth
Ashley DeVecht, Director of Communications
Rose Manfredini, Vice President, Membership
Chris Marti, Vice President, Research
400+ Members

18091 **Mineral Information Institute**
12999 E. Adam Aircraft Circle
Englewood, CO 80112-4167

303-948-4200
Fax: 800-763-3132
E-Mail: MEC@smenet.org
Home Page: www.MineralsEducationCoalition.org

Sharon Schonhaut, Director
Rebecca Smith, Curriculum Coordinator
Rachel Grimes, Outreach Coordinator
Carol Kiser, Purchases dept

Nonprofit organization dedicated to educating youth about the science of minerals and other natural resources and about their importance in our everyday lives.

18092 **Minerals, Metals & Materials Society**
184 Thorn Hill Road
Warrendale, PA 15086-7514

724-769-9000
800-759-4867
Fax: 724-776-3770
E-Mail: webmaster@tms.org
Home Page: www.tms.org

Alexander Scott, Executive Director
Nellie Luther, Professional Affairs Coordinator
Gail Miller, Executive Assistant

Supports all those devoted to exploring the many aspects of materials science and engineering. Publishes monthly magazine.
Founded in 1993

18093 **Mining and Metallurgical Society**
PO Box 810
Boulder, CO 80306-0810

303-444-6032
Fax: 415-897-1380
E-Mail: contactmmsa@mmsa.net
Home Page: www.mmsa.net
Social Media: Facebook, Twitter, LinkedIn

Betty L. Gibbs, Executive Director
Matt Bender, President
Barney Guarnera, VP
Paul C. Jones, Treasurer
Michael Blois, Secretary

Concerned with the conservation of the nation's mineral resources and the best interest of the mining and metallurgical industries.
350 Members
Founded in 1908

18094 **National Association for Surface Finishing**
1155 15th Street NW
Suite 500
Washington, DC 20005

202-457-8404
Fax: 202-530-0659
Home Page: www.nasf.org
Social Media: Facebook, Twitter

Rick Delawder, President
Erik Welys, VP
Paul Brancato, Secretary/Treasurer
Jery Wahlin, Executive

The National Association for Surface Finishing is a trade association whose mission is to promote the advancement of the surface finishing industry worldwide.

18095 **National Association of Aluminum Developers**
4201 Euclid Ave
Suite 550
Rolling Meadows, IL 60008-2025

847-485-3000
Fax: 773-867-8750

E-Mail: info@msci.org
Home Page: www.msci.org

Bob Weidner, President
Jonathan Kalkwarf, VP Finance/Administration
Rose Manfredini, VP Member Information Services
Chris Marti, VP Technology
Ann Zastrow, VP

NAAD is the trade association of North American service centers and principal suppliers engaged in marketing aluminum products.
400 Members
Founded in 1914

18096 National Blacksmiths and Welders
PO Box 123
Arnold, NE 69120

308-848-2913
Home Page: www.arcat.com

Dave Christen, President
Jim Lindquist, First Director
Gerry Westhoff, Second VP
James Holman, Executive Director

Blacksmiths, welders and manufacturing machine shops. Organize and offer assistance to state organizations for the advancement of their members with education and guiding measures for the present and future prospects of the trade.
175 Members
Founded in 1895

18097 National Coil Coating Association
1300 Sumner Ave
Cleveland, OH 44115-2851

216-241-3333
Fax: 216-781-0621
E-Mail: ncca@coilcoilcoating.org
Home Page: www.coilcoating.org

NCCA is an established trade organization dedicated to the growth of coil coated products. A unified organization that provides resources and leadership in order to ensure that coil coated materials are the product of choice.
Founded in 1962

18098 National Institute for Metal Working Skills
10565 Fairfax Boulevard
Suite 203
Fairfax, VA 22030

703-352-4971
Fax: 703-352-4991
E-Mail: kdoyle@nims-skills.com
Home Page: www.nims-skills.org

James Wall, Executive Director
David Morgan, Director of Business Development
Catherine Ross, Accrediation Incharge

A nonprofit organization formed by metalworking trade associations, national labor organizations, a council of state governors, companies and educators to support the development of a skilled workforce for the metalworking industry.
Founded in 1995
Mailing list available for rent

18099 National Ornamental & Miscellaneous Metals Association
805 South Glynn St.,
Ste. 127 #311
Fayetteville, GA 30214

404-363-4009
Fax: 888-279-7994
E-Mail: nommainfo@nomma.org
Home Page: www.nomma.org

Curt Witter, President
Chris Connelly, VP/Treasurer

Supports all those involved in the ornamental and miscellaneous metal industry. Publishes bi-monthly magazine.
1000 Members
Founded in 1959

18100 National Ornamental and Miscellaneous Metals
805 South Glynn St.
Ste. 127 #311
Fayetteville, GA 30214

888-516-8585
Fax: 888-279-7994
E-Mail: nommainfo@nomma.org
Home Page: www.nomma.org

Todd Daniel, Executive Director
Liz Harris, Member Care & Operations Manager
Martha Pennington, Meetings & Exposition Manager
Founded in 1958

18101 National Tooling & Machining Association
National Tooling & Machining Association
1357 Rockside Road
Cleveland, OH 44134

800-248-6862
800-248-6862
Fax: 216-264-2840
E-Mail: info@ntma.org
Home Page: www.ntma.org

Rob Akers, CEO
Rich Basalla, Membership Officer
Tiffany Bryson, Sales/Sponsorship Manager
John Capka, Chief Financial Officer

Trade organization representing the precision custom manufacturing industry throughout the US. Has an active safety & education program.
Founded in 1972

18102 National Welding Supply Association
Fernley & Fernley
1900 Arch St
Philadelphia, PA 19103-1404

215-564-3484
Fax: 215-564-2175
Home Page: www.nwsa.com

GA Fernley, Director
1200 Members
Founded in 1945

18103 Non-Ferrous Founders' Society
1480 Renaissance Drive
Suite 310
Park Ridge, IL 60068

847-299-0950
Fax: 847-299-3598
E-Mail: nffstaff@nffs.org
Home Page: www.nffs.org

James L Mallory, Executive Director
Jerrod A Weaver, Director Of Education and Training
Ryan J Moore, Member Services Manager

Manufacturers of bronze, brass and aluminum castings.
185 Members
Founded in 1943

18104 North American Die Casting Association
3250 Arlington Heights Rd
Suite 101
Arlington Heights, IL 60004

847-279-0001
Fax: 847-279-0002
E-Mail: nadca@diecasting.org
Home Page: www.diecasting.org
Social Media: Facebook

Neal Shapiro, Affairs Committee Chairman

Supports all those involved in the die casting industry. Publishes bi-monthly magazine.
Founded in 1957

18105 Precision Metalforming Association
6363 Oak Tree Blvd
Cleveland, OH 44131-2500

216-901-9667
Fax: 216-901-9190
E-Mail: pma@pma.org
Home Page: www.pma.org

Nels Leutwiler, Chairman
Dennis J Keat, First Vice Chairman
Bernie Rosselli Jr, Second Vice Chairman/Treasurer
William Gaskin, President

Members include producers of metal stampings, spinnings, washers and precision sheet metal fabrications as well as suppliers of equipment, materials and services.
1300 Members
Founded in 1913

18106 Resistance Welder Manufacturers
1900 Arch St
Philadelphia, PA 19103-1404

215-564-3484
Fax: 305-442-7451
E-Mail: rwma@aws.com
Home Page: www.aws.org/rwma/
Social Media: Facebook, LinkedIn

Mark Gramelspacher, Chairman
Ed Langhenry, Vice Chairman
Tom Snow, Vice Chairman

Strives to create widespread awareness and use of the various resistance welding processes and equipment, improve relations between individual manufacturers, foster higher ethical standards throughout the industry, develop industry standards to assist users of resistance welding equipment.
82 Members
Founded in 1935

18107 Sheet Metal Workers International Association
1750 New York Avenue, NW
6th Floor
Washington, DC 20006

Home Page: www.smwia.org

18108 Sheet Metal and Air Conditioning Contractors' National Association
4201 Lafayette Center Dr
Chantilly, VA 20151-1219

703-803-2980
Fax: 703-803-3732
Home Page: www.smacna.org

Vincent Sandusky, CEO

An international trade association representing 4,500 contibuting contractor firms in the sheet metal and air conditioning industry. Develops technical standards and manuals addressing all facets of the sheet metal and air conditioning industry.
1944 Members
Founded in 1943

18109 Silver Institute
1400 I Street, NW
Suite 550
Washington, DC 20005

202-835-0185
Fax: 202-835-0155
E-Mail: info@silverinstitute.org
Home Page: www.silverinstitute.org

Fernando Alanis, President
Mitchell Krebs, VP
Thomas Angelos, Treasurer

Michael Dirienzo, Executive Director and Secretary

International association of miners, refiners, fabricators and wholesalers of silver and silver products.
Founded in 1971

18110 Silver Users Association
3930 walnut Street
Suite 210
Fairfax, VA 22030

703-934-0219
800-245-6999
Fax: 703-359-7562
E-Mail: silverusers@capitolonellc.com
Home Page: www.silverusersassociation.org

Mike Merolla, President
John Gannon, VP

Represents the interests of corporations that make, sell and distribute products and services in which silver is an essential part. SUA membership includes representatives from the photographic, electronic, silverware and jewelry industries; producers of semi-fabricated and industrial products; and, mirror manufacturers.
30 Members
Founded in 1947

18111 Society of American Silversmiths
PO Box 786
West Warwick, RI 02893

401-461-6840
Fax: 401-461-6841
E-Mail: sas@silversmithing.com
Home Page: www.silversmithing.com

Jeffrey Herman, Founder/Executive Director

Founded to preserve the art and history of handcrafted holloware and flatware plus provide support, networking and greater access to the market for its artisan members. Artisans are silversmiths both practicing and retired who now or used to smith as a livelihood. Educates the public as to the aesthetic and investment value of this art form and demystifies silversmithing techniques through its literature and national exhibits.
240 Members
Founded in 1989

18112 Society of Manufacturing Engineers
Society of Manufacturing Engineers
One SME Drive
PO Box 930
Dearborn, MI 48121

313-425-3000
800-733-4763
Fax: 313-425-3400
E-Mail: advertising@sme.org
Home Page: www.sme.org

Dennis S.Bray, President
Debbie Holton, Managing Director
Mark Tomlinson, Executive Director
Greg Sheremet, Publisher
Jeannine Kunz, Managing Director

Supports all those involved in the metalworking industry, specifically machining, forming, inspection, assembly and processing operations. Publishes magazine.
70M Members
Founded in 1932

18113 Society of North American Goldsmiths
540 Oak Street, Suite A
Eugene, OR 97401

541-345-5689
Fax: 541-345-1123
Home Page: www.snagmetalsmith.org
Social Media: Facebook, Twitter, LinkedIn

Micki Lippe, President
Peggy Eng, Conferences

Promotes a favorable and enriching environment in which contemporary metalsmiths practice their art. One aspect of this process is educating the public about the quality and rich diversity within the field of metalsmithing. Exhibitions, public forums, lectures, and published documents are our primary methods of reaching out to the public. SNAG sponsors workshops, seminars, audio-visual services and an annual conference.
Founded in 1969

18114 Specialty Steel Industry of North America
3050 K Street, N.W.
Washington, DC 20007

202-342-8630
800-982-0355
Fax: 202-342-8451
Home Page: www.ssina.comÿ

18115 Steel Deck Institute
PO Box 25
Fox River Grove, IL 60021-0025

847-458-4647
Fax: 412-487-3326
E-Mail: steve@sdi.org
Home Page: www.sdi.org

Steven A Roehrig, Managing Director

Trade association providing uniform industry standards for the engineering, design, manufacture and field usage of steel decks.
29 Members
Founded in 1939

18116 Steel Door Institute
30200 Detroit Rd
Cleveland, OH 44145-1967

440-899-0010
Fax: 440-892-1404
Home Page: www.steeldoor.org

Jeff Wherry, Executive Director

Producers of all metal frames and doors for commercial, industrial and residential construction.

18117 Steel Founders Society of America
780 McArdle Dr
Unit G
Crystal Lake, IL 60014-8155

815-455-8240
Fax: 815-455-8241
E Mail: monroe@sfsa.org
Home Page: www.sfsa.org
Social Media: Facebook

Raymond Monroe, Executive VP
Rick Boyd, Vice President of Technology
Kelly DiGiacomo, CPA, Director of Finance
Rob Blair, Manager of Information Services
David Poweleit, Director of Engineering

A technically oriented trade association serving the steel casting industry.
Founded in 1902

18118 Steel Manufacturers Association
1150 Connecticut Ave NW
Suite 715
Washington, DC 20036-4131

202-296-1515
Fax: 202-296-2506
E-Mail: cipicchio@steelnet.org
Home Page: www.steelnet.org

Thomas A Danjczek, President

The majority of SMA members are minimills companies engaged in electric air furnace/continuous caster steel productions as well as hot and cold rolling of steel mill products. A growing number of integrated steel producers are also members.

18119 Steel Plate Fabricators Association
944 Donata Ct
Lake Zurich, IL 60047-5025

847-438-8265
Fax: 847-438-8766
E-Mail: info@steeltank.com
Home Page: www.steeltank.com
Social Media: Facebook, Youtube

Anne Kiefer, Director Of Administration
Wayne B. Geyer, President
J Michael Braden, VP
Jerry Stetzler, Treasurer

Protection of the environment and preservation of air and water quality are key concerns for the owners and operators of tanks, pressure vessels, specialty fabrications and piping systems.
Founded in 1916

18120 Steel Service Center Institute
4889 Neo Parkway
Cleveland, OH 44128

216-827-7816
Fax: 847-485-3001
E-Mail: info@ssci.org
Home Page: www.ssci.org

Thomas Conley, President
S Harbke, Director
570 Members
Founded in 1909

18121 Steel Shipping Container Institute
1101 Vermont Ave NW
Suite 2020
Washington, DC 20005-3521

202-408-1900
Fax: 503-581-2221

Jeffrey Steele, President

18122 Steel Tank Institute
944 Donata Ct
Lake Zurich, IL 60047-5025

847-438-8265
Fax: 847-438-8766
E-Mail: info@steeltank.com
Home Page: www.steeltank.com
Social Media: Facebook, Youtube

Anne Kiefer, Director Of Administration
Wayne B. Geyer, President
J Michael Braden, VP
Jerry Stetzler, Treasurer

Protection of the environment and preservation of air and water quality are key concerns for the owners and operators of tanks, pressure vessels, specialty fabrications and piping systems.
Founded in 1916

18123 Steel Tube Institute of North America
2516 Waukegan Road, Suite 172
Glenview, IL 60025

847-461-1701
Fax: 847-660-7981
E-Mail: sti@apk.net
Home Page: www.steeltubeinstitute.org
Social Media: Facebook, LinkedIn

Timothy F Andrassy, Executive Director
Peggy Sams, Executive Assistant
Mary Gregel, Administrative Assistant

Members produce steel tubes and pipes from carbon, stainless or alloy steel, for applications ranging from large structural tubing to small redrawn tubing.
87 Members
Founded in 1930

18124 The Aluminum Association
1525 Wilson Boulevard
Suite 600
Arlington, VA 22209

703-358-2960
E-Mail: mmeenan@aluminum.org
Home Page: www.aluminum.org
Social Media: Facebook, Twitter, LinkedIn

Layle Smith, Chairman
Garney B. Scott, III, Vice Chairman
Michelle O'Neill, Second Vice Chair
Heidi Brock, President
Karen Bowden, Vice President, Administration

18125 The American Institute of Mining, Metallur gical and Petroleum Engineers
12999 East Adam Aircraft Circle
Englewood, CO 80112

303-325-5185
Fax: 888-702-0049
E-Mail: aime@aimehq.org
Home Page: www.aimehq.org
Social Media: Facebook, LinkedIn, YouTube, RSS

Behrooz Fattahi, President
Garry W. Warren, President Elect
Nikhil C. Trivedi, President-Elect Designate
Dale E. Heinz, Past President
Drew Meyer, Trustee
Founded in 1871

18126 The Fabricators & Manufacturers Association
833 Featherstone Road
Rockford, IL 61107

815-399-8700
888-394-4362
Home Page: www.fmanet.org
Social Media: Facebook, Twitter, LinkedIn, YouTube

Edwin Stanley, Chair
Al Zelt, First Vice Chairman
Vivek Kumar Gupta, Second Vice Chairman
Lyle Menke, Secretary/ Treasurer
Carlos Borjas, Immediate Past Chair
Founded in 1970

18127 The Minerals, Metals, and Materials Society
184 Thorn Hill Road
Warrendale, PA 15086-7514

800-759-4867
Fax: 724-776-3770
E-Mail: webmaster@tms.org
Home Page: www.tms.org
Social Media: Facebook, LinkedIn, YouTube

Hani Heneinÿ, President
Elizabeth A. Holm, Past President
Patrice E. A. Turchi, Vice President
James Robinson, Secretary/ Executive Director
Robert W. Hyers, Financial Planning Officer

18128 The Silver Users Association
3930 walnut Street
Suite 210
Fairfax, VA 22030

703-930-7790
Fax: 703-359-7562
E-Mail: pmiller@mwcapitol.com
Home Page: www.silverusersassociation.orgÿ

Bill LeRoy, President
Mike Huber, Vice President
Jack Gannon, Immediate Past President
Bill Hamelin, Treasurer
John King, Secretary
Founded in 1947

18129 Tube and Pipe Association International
833 Featherstone Road
Rockford, IL 61107

815-399-8700
Fax: 815-484-7700
E-Mail: info@tpatube.org
Home Page: www.tpatube.org
Social Media: Facebook, Twitter, LinkedIn, Youtube

Gerald Shankel, President
Mike Hedges, VP Finance/CFO

TPA is an educational technology association serving the metal tube and pipe producing and fabricating industries. It is an affiliate association of the Fabricators and Manufacturers Association International.
Founded in 1970

18130 US Magnetic Materials Association
717-898-2294
Home Page: www.usmagneticmaterials.com

Ed Richardson, Chairman/ President/ Treasurer
Peter Dent, Vice President
Daniel McGroarty, Vice President
Rob Strahs, Secretary/ Vice President
Kerry LaPierre, Board Member

18131 US Pipe and Foundry Company
PO Box 10406
Birmingham, AL 35202-0406

205-547-7254
Fax: 205-254-7494

David Mize, Plant Manager

Supports all those involved with the foundry industry. Publishes semi-monthly newsletter.
Founded in 1928

18132 Unified Abrasives Manufacturers Association
30200 Detroit Road
Cleveland, OH 44145-1967

440-899-0010
Fax: 440-892-1404
E-Mail: contact@uama.org
Home Page: www.uama.org
Founded in 1999

18133 United States Cutting Tool Institute
1300 Sumner Ave
Cleveland, OH 44115-2851

216-241-7333
Fax: 216-241-0105
E-Mail: uscti@uscti.com
Home Page: www.uscti.com

Charles M Stockinger, Secretary-Treasurer

The premier trade association for all manufacturers of any type of cutting tools designed and sold to the metalworking, woodworking, and other industrial and consumer markets.
60 Members
Founded in 1988

18134 Welding Research Council
PO Box 1942
New York, NY 10156

216-658-3847
Fax: 216-658-3854
E-Mail: mprager@forengineers.org
Home Page: www.forengineers.org/wrc

Coordinates welding research.
Founded in 1935

18135 Welding Research Council, Inc.
PO Box 201547
Shaker Heights, OH 44122

216-658-3847
Fax: 216-658-3854
E-Mail: mpc@forengineers.org
Home Page: www.forengineers.org

Martin Prager, PhD, Executive Director

An outgrowth of the ASTM-ASME Joint Committee on the effect of temperature on the properties of metals which was founded in 1925 to meet the apparent need for information on the subject in the construction of central power stations.
600 Members
Founded in 1966

18136 Wire Association International
1570 Boston Post Road
PO Box 578
Guilford, CT 06437-0578

203-453-2777
Fax: 203-453-8384
Home Page: www.wirenet.org

Steven J Fetteroll, Executive Director
Phyilis Conon, Technical Information Director

Technical association serving the global wire and cable industry by providing educational materials, sponsoring trade shows and international technical conferences.
Founded in 1930

18137 Wiring Harness Manufacturers Association
3335 N Arlington Heights Road
Suite E
Arlington Heights, IL 60004

847-577-7200
Fax: 847-577-7276
E-Mail: whma@whma.org
Home Page: www.whma.org

Andrew Larsen, Executive Director

To provide the cooperative forum through which members companies can solve both their specific problems and also help resolve industry problems.
4 Pages
Frequency: Quarterly
Circulation: 5,000

Newsletters

18138 Abrasive Users News Fax
Meadowlark Technical Services
144 Moore Rd
Butler, PA 16001-1312

724-282-6210
Fax: 724-234-2376
E-Mail: aes@abrasiveengineering.com
Home Page: www.abrasivesmall.com

Ted Giese, Executive Director

Newsletter from the Abrasive Engineering Society.
Cost: $50.00
Circulation: 500
Founded in 1957

18139 American Iron and Steel Institute News
American Iron and Steel Institute
25 Massachusetts Ave., NW, Suite 800
Suite 705
Washington, DC 20001

202-452-7100
Fax: 202-496-9702
E-Mail: steelnews@steel.org
Home Page: www.recycle-steel.org
Social Media: Facebook, Twitter, Youtube

Chip Foley, VP
Dave James, Marketing

Publication of the nonprofit trade organization representing approximately 65 percent of steel companies in the US, Canada and Mexico.
Circulation: 6000
Founded in 1855

18140 American Metal Market
Michael G Botta
825 7th Avenue
New York, NY 10019-6014

212-887-8510
Fax: 212-887-8522
E-Mail: custserv@amm.com
Home Page: www.amm.com

Gloria T LaRue, Editor
Catalino Abrei, Owner

A daily newspaper of the metals industry covering news and pricing information for corporate, purchasing and manufacturing management.
Frequency: Daily
Circulation: 10,500

18141 Anodizing Newsline
Aluminum Anodizers Council (AAC)
1000 North Rand Road
Suite 214
Wauconda, IL 60084

847-526-2010
Fax: 847-526-3993
E-Mail: mail@anodizing.org
Home Page: www.andoizing.org

Todd Hamilton, Chairman
Gregory T Rajsky CAE, President
Frequency: Quarterly
Circulation: 250

18142 Building & Architecture News
Copper Development Association
260 Madison Ave
New York, NY 10016-2403

212-251-7200
800-232-3282
Fax: 212-251-7234
E-Mail: questions@cda.copper.org
Home Page: www.copper.org

Andrew G Kireta, President & CEO
Victoria Prather, Manager Communications
Michels Harold, VP Technaloy Services
Arnold W Ray, VP Environmental Division
Lorraine Herzing Mills, VP/Finance/Administration

A special-edition newsletter that focuses onthe use of copper and copper alloys in commercial and residential design and construction.
Frequency: Monthly

18143 CBSA Capsules
Copper and Brass Servicenter Association
994 Old Eagle School Road
Suite 1019
Wayne, PA 19087

610-971-4850
Fax: 610-971-4859
Home Page: www.cbsa.copper-brass.org

Daniel Erck, President
Robert A Lewis, VP

Content includes information about conventions and seminars, programs and activities sponsored by the CBSA, general business/industry news, legislation information and government regulations.
Cost: $35.00
6 Pages
Frequency: Monthly
Circulation: 200
Founded in 1951

18144 Cables Industry Analyst
CRU International
6305 Ivy Ln
Suite 422
Greenbelt, MD 20770-6339

301-441-8997
Fax: 301-441-4726
E-Mail: sales@crugroup.com
Home Page: www.crugroup.com

Florence Kauffman, VP

Written for managers and executives in the wire industry around the globe. Spotlights effective management techniques and superior administrative skills in the industry, profiles industry leaders, notes personnel movements and features general industry news.
Cost: $965.00
12 Pages
Frequency: Monthly
ISSN: 1368-4191

18145 Futuretech
John Wiley & Sons
111 River St
Hoboken, NJ 07030-5790

201-748-6000
800-825-7550
Fax: 201-748-6088
E-Mail: info@wiley.com
Home Page: www.wiley.com

William J Pesce, CEO

Edited for product development and technology transfer engineers. Intelligence service that deals with new technologies with demonstrated commercial appeal still in the early stages of development in leading corporate, academic and university labs. Contains analysis and exploitation information.
Cost: $1500.00
24 Pages
Frequency: Monthly

18146 IMA Weekly Updates
1000 N Rand Rd
Suite 214
Wauconda, IL 60084-1180

847-526-2010
Fax: 847-526-3993
E-Mail: info@intlmag.org
Home Page: www.intlmag.org

Greg Patzer, Executive Vice-President
Heidi Diederich, Administrative Coordinator

Develops international use and acceptance of magnesium metal and its alloys in all product forms. Members are organizations or individuals engaged in the production, manufacture or marketing of metallic magnesium or those supplying materials, equipment or consulting.
Cost: $90.00
Frequency: Weekly
Circulation: 5000
Founded in 1943
Printed in 2 colors on glossy stock

18147 IMPI Conference
International Precious Metals Institute
5101 N 12th Avenue
Suite C
Pensacola, FL 32504

850-476-1156
Fax: 850-476-1548
E-Mail: mail@ipmi.org
Home Page: www.ipmi.org

Robert Ianniello, President

annual conference holds technical sessions, evening social receptions and a golf tournament. Also some product demonstrations.
400 Attendees
Frequency: Annual

18148 MBCEA Newsletter
Metal Building Contractors & Erectors Association
PO Box 499
Shawnee Mission, KS 66201

913-432-3800
Fax: 913-432-3803
E-Mail: MBCEA@kc.rr.com
Home Page: www.mbcea.org

Angela M Cruse, Executive Director
Tim Seyler, President

Official newsletter of the Metal Building Contractors and Erectors Association (MBCEA), a trade association, formed in 1968 to provide programs and services, as well as to support the interests of metal building contractors and erectors.

18149 Metal Construction Association
MCA Newsletter
4799 West Lake Street
Glenview, IL 60025

847-375-4718
Fax: 877-665-2234
E-Mail: mengle@amctec.com
Home Page: www.metalconstruction.org

Mark Engle, Executive VP
Julie Weldon, Chairman

Dedicated to promoting the use of metal in construction. Initative include market development, educational programs, issue and product awareness campaigns, and publication of technical guidelines and specifications manuals.
100 Pages
Frequency: Quartly
Founded in 1983

18150 Precious Metals News
International Precious Metals Institute
5101 N 12th Avenue
Suite C
Pensacola, FL 32504

850-476-1156
Fax: 850-476-1548
E-Mail: mail@ipmi.org
Home Page: www.ipmi.org

Robert Ianniello, President
Cost: $30.00
Frequency: Quarterly
Circulation: 1000
Founded in 1976

18151 R&D Focus
International Lead Zinc Research Organization
2525 Meridian Parkway
PO Box 12036
Research Triangle Park, NC 27709-2036

919-361-4647
Fax: 919-361-1957
E-Mail: rputnam@ilzro.org
Home Page: www.ilzro.org

Rob Putnam, Publisher
Doug Zabor, President

Reports on current research and development products in the metal industry.
Frequency: Quarterly
Circulation: 100
Founded in 1958

18152 Steel Industry Weekly Review
2 Uxbridge Road
Scarsdale, NY 10583-2725
Karl Keffer, Publisher

Offers industry news for steel workers.
Cost: $75.00
Frequency: Monthly

18153 Titanium
International Titanium Association

2655 W Midway Blvd
Suite 300
Broomfield, CO 80020-7187

303-404-2221
299-942-5371
Fax: 303-404-9111
E-Mail: jsimpson@titanium.org
Home Page: www.titanium.org

Frequency: Quarterly
Circulation: 5000
Founded in 1960

18154 US Piper
US Pipe and Foundry Company
PO Box 10406
James Canada
Birmingham, AL 35202-406

205-547-7254
Fax: 205-254-7494
Home Page: www.uspipe.com

George Bogs, Publisher
Ray Torok, President
Walter Knollenberg, VP

Articles deal with advantages of using new products.
16 Pages
Circulation: 9000
Founded in 1899

18155 WRC Bulletin
Welding Research Council
3 Park Avenue
27th Floor
New York, NY 10016-5902

212-591-7956
Fax: 212-591-7183
E-Mail: bulletinsales@forengineers.org
Home Page: www.forengineers.org/wrc

CR Felmley Jr, Publisher

Offers information and updates for the welding community.
Cost: $300.00
Frequency: Monthly
Circulation: 900

Magazines & Journals

18156 AISE Steel Technology
Association of Iron & Steel Engineers
186 Thorn Hill Road
Warrendale, PA 15086

724-776-6040
Fax: 724-776-1880
E-Mail: info@aist.org
Home Page: www.aise.org

Ronald Ashburn, Managing Director
Marge Baker, Editor
Gerry Kane, Sales Manager
Karen Hadley, Managing Editor
Janet McConnell, Production Editor

Information relating to the design and construction of equipment, machinery and plants for the production and processing of iron and steel.
Cost: $115.00
Frequency: Monthly
Circulation: 8000
Founded in 2004

18157 APMI International
105 College Road E
Princeton, NJ 08540-6622

609-452-7700
Fax: 609-987-8523
E-Mail: apmi@mpif.org
Home Page: www.mpif.org

Christopher Adam, President
David L Schaefer, Director
Jim Adams, Manager

Monthly newsletter for all those involved the metal powder producing and consuming industries. Regular editorial features.
Founded in 1965

18158 Abrasives
PO Box 11
Byron Center, MI 49315

616-530-3220
Fax: 616-530-6466
Home Page: www.abrasivesmagazine.com

Rose Trevino, Publisher/Editor

Covers research and development in the abrasives field including information about grinding and finishing applications.
Cost: $27.00
Frequency: Annual+
Circulation: 35000

18159 Advanced Materials & Processes
ASM International
9639 Kinsman Rd
Materials Park, OH 44073

440-338-5151
800-336-5152
Fax: 440-338-4634
E-Mail: memberservices@asminternational.org
Home Page: www.asminternational.org
Social Media: Facebook, Twitter, LinkedIn

Joseph M Zion, Publisher
Joanne Miller, Managing Editor
Margaret Hunt, Editor-in-Chief
Jeane Deatherage, Administrator, Foundation Programs
Virginia Shirk, Foundation Executive Assistant

AM&P, the monthly technical magazine from ASM International, is designed to keep readers aware of leading-edge developments and trends in engineering materials - metals and alloys, engineering polymers, advanced ceramics, and composites - and the methods used to select, process, fabricate, test, and characterize them.
Frequency: Monthly
Circulation: 32M
Founded in 1977

18160 Aluminum Recycling & Processing for Energy Conservation and Sustainability
Aluminum Association
1525 Wilson Blvd
Suite 600
Arlington, VA 22209-2444

703-358-2960
Fax: 703-358-2961
Home Page: www.aluminum.org

John Green, Editor
Heidi Biggs Brock, President
Nicholas Adams, Vice President, Business
Frequency: Yearly

18161 American Machinist
Penton Media
1166 Avenue of the Americas/10th Fl
New York, NY 10036

212-204-4200
Fax: 216-696-6662
E-Mail: ameditor@penton.com
Home Page: www.penton.com

Jane Cooper, Marketing
Patricia L Smith, Executive Editor
Charles Bates, Senior Editor
Jim Benes, Associate Editor
Chris Meyer, Director, Corporate Communications

Magazine of the manufacturing business. Plays an integral role in educating and informing our readers of the significant developments of manufacturing technology. The intent of every issue is to describe new metalworking technologies that help the readership speed production, cut costs, and stay competitive in the global market.
Frequency: Monthly
Circulation: 80000
Founded in 1892
Printed in 4 colors

18162 American Metal Market
Reed Business Information
225 Park Avenue South
New York, NY 10003

646-274-6257
Fax: 630-288-8686
Home Page: www.amm.com
Social Media: Twitter, LinkedIn

Lawrence S Reed, President
Gloria LaRue, Editor-in-Chief
Catalino Abrei, Owner

Thoroughly covers the metals industry, from production to distribution to recycling. American Metal Market is comprehensive, timely, reliable and invaluable daily newspaper for today's metal industry professionals.
Cost: $725.00
16 Pages
Frequency: Daily
Circulation: 10000
Printed in on glossy stock

18163 American Tool, Die & Stamping News
Eagle Publications
42400 Grand River Ave
Suite 103
Novi, MI 48375-2572

248-347-3487
800-783-3491
Fax: 248-347-3492
E-Mail: info@ameritooldie.com
Home Page: www.ameritooldie.com

Arthur Brown, President
Joan Oakley, CEO

Applications, techniques, equipment and accessories of metal stamping, moldmaking, electric discharge machining; and new product information relating to the tool and die industry. Accepts advertising.
70 Pages
Circulation: 36000
ISSN: 0192-5709
Founded in 1971
Printed in 5 colors on glossy stock

18164 Anvil Magazine
PO Box 1810
Georgetown, CA 95634-1810

530-333-2142
800-942-6845
Fax: 530-333-2906
Home Page: www.anvilmag.com

Rob Edwards, Publisher
Timothy Sebastian, Editor-in-Chief
Jody Edwards, Advertising Manager

World-wide coverage of the blacksmithing and farrier trades.
Cost: $29.50
Frequency: Monthly
Circulation: 5000
Founded in 1980

18165 Anvil's Ring
Artist-Blacksmiths' Association of North America

5821 Helias Drive
Jefferson, MO 65101-9316

573-395-3304
Fax: 573-395-3201

Jim McCarty, Editor

Covers such topics as architectural iron, decorative design, primitive artifacts, advice, and Association news. Also discusses supply sources, formal blacksmithing instruction and employment opportunities.
Frequency: Monthly
Circulation: 4000

18166 Association of Iron and Steel Engineers Steel Technology
Three Gateway Center
Suite 1900
Pittsburgh, PA 15222-1004

412-281-6323
Fax: 412-281-6216
E-Mail: rashburn@aist.org
Home Page: www.aise.org

Ronald E Ashburn, Executive Director
Frank E Farmer, Graphic Designer
Chris Brown, Graphic Designer
Stacy Varmecky, General Manager

AISE Steel Technology is the monthly technical journal of AISE. Highly authorative, it contains exclusive technical information relating to all phaes of iron and steelmaking and finishing.
50+ Pages
Frequency: Monthly
Printed in 4 colors

18167 Automatic Machining Magazine
Screw Machine Publishing Company
1066 Gravel Rd
Suite 201
Webster, NY 14580-1769

585-787-0820
800-610-6950
Fax: 585 787 0868
Home Page: www.automachmag.com

Wayne Wood, President

General industry news for professionals in the metal turning and cold forming fields.
Cost: $45.00
142 Pages
Frequency: Monthly
Circulation: 13000
Founded in 1941
Printed in 4 colors on glossy stock

18168 Casting World
Continental Communications
104 Florence Ln
Fairfield, CT 06824-2215

203-255-7752
Fax: 203-377-7230

Wilburt W Troland, President

In-depth news on all aspects of ferrous and non-ferrous casting.
Cost: $99.00
Frequency: Quarterly
Circulation: 35000

18169 Coil World
CJL Publishing
8 High Point
Cedar Grove, NJ 07009

973-571-7155
Fax: 973-571-7102
E-Mail: philcola@optonline.net
Home Page: www.coilworld.com

Philip E Colaiacovo, Editor-in-Chief/Publisher
Carl Hoffman, Circulation Manager
Shawn A Savage, Creative Director
A L Colaiacovo, Production/Advertising Svcs Manager

Offers articles on coil coating operations, fabricatiors, service centers, OEMs which use prepainted metals, new products, upcoming events, industry news, personnel announcements and committee updates.
Frequency: Quarterly
Circulation: 10000

18170 Cutting Technology
Penton Media
1166 Avenue of the Americas/10th Fl
New York, NY 10036

212-204-4200
Fax: 216-696-6662
E-Mail: information@penton.com
Home Page: www.penton.com

Jane Cooper, Marketing
Patricia Smith, Executive Editor
Gil Apelis, Manager
Chris Meyer, Director, Corporate Communications

Covers the full gamut of information essential to the success and productivity of those involved in metalcutting manufacturing.
Cost: $35.00
Circulation: 40000
Founded in 1892
Printed in 4 colors

18171 Cutting Tool Engineering
CTE Publications
40 Skokie Blvd
Suite 450
Northbrook, IL 60062-1698

847-498-9100
866-207-1450
Fax: 847-559-4444
E-Mail: alanr@jwr.com
Home Page: www.ctemag.com

John Wm Roberts, CEO
Alan Richter, CEO
Alan Rooks, Director

Cutting Tool Engineering serves manufacturing plants in the metal working industries.
Cost: $65.00
72 Pages
Frequency: Monthly
Circulation: 34871
ISSN: 0011-4189
Founded in 1955
Printed in 4 colors on glossy stock

18172 Die Casting Engineer Magazine
North American Die Casting Association
241 Holbrook Drive
Wheeling, IL 60090

847-279-0001
Fax: 847-279-0002
E-Mail: nadca@diecasting.org
Home Page: www.diecasting.org
Social Media: Facebook, Twitter, LinkedIn, youtube, Flickr

Donna Peterson, Editor
Norwin A Merens, Managing Director

Provides members with the latest industry information, technology innovation and state-of-the-art developments. Each issue presents readers with up to date die casting news topics, opinion features of interest, and an editorial theme.
Cost: $150.00
1000 Pages
Frequency: Bi-Monthly
Founded in 1989

18173 Die Casting Management
C-K Publishing
PO Box 247
Wonder Lake, IL 60097-0247

815-728-0912
Fax: 815-728-0912
Home Page: www.diecastmgmt.com

Rob Crofts, Publisher

The main content focuses on profitable management, and includes articles on finance, marketing, technology, engineering, industry developments, and government legislation.
Frequency: Bi-Monthly
Circulation: 4500

18174 Ductile Iron News
Ductile Iron Society
15400 Pearl Rd
Suite 234
Strongsville, OH 44136-6017

440-665-3686
Fax: 440-878-0070
E-Mail: jwood@ductile.org
Home Page: www.ductile.org

Scott Gledhill, President
Patricio Gill, VP
Pete Guidi, Treasurer

The main material focuses on the technical data and applications, production statistics, and profiles of foundries.
Frequency: 3-4x/Yeur

18175 Engineering and Mining Journal
Mining Media
8751 E Hampden Ave
Suite C1
Denver, CO 80231-4930

303-751-5370
Fax: 303-283-0641
E-Mail: info@mining-media.com
Home Page: www.e-mj.com

Peter Johnson, President
Steve Fiscor, Editor-in-Chief
Russ Carter, Managing Editor
Gina Tverdak, Assistant Editor

Serves the field of mining including exploration, development, milling, smelting, refining of metals and nonmetallics.
Cost: $79.00
Frequency: Monthly
Circulation: 10523
Founded in 1866
Printed in 4 colors on glossy stock

18176 Equip-Mart
116 N Camp Street
Seguin, TX 70155

830-303-3328
800-864-1155
Fax: 830-372-3011
E-Mail: story@storycomm.com
Home Page: www.equip-mart.com

James Story, President
Tammy Reilly, Publisher
Kim Wiemann, Circulation Manager

Used metalworking equipment.
Cost: $50.00
Frequency: Monthly
Circulation: 36000
Founded in 1994

18177 Fabricator
Fabricators and Manufacturers Association
833 Featherstone Road
Rockford, IL 61107

815-227-8281
866-879-9144
Fax: 815-484-7700
E-Mail: dand@thefabricator.com
Home Page: www.thefabricator.com

Dan Davis, Executive Editor

North America's leading magazine for the metal forming and fabricating industry that delivers the news, technical articles, and case histories that enable fabricators to do their jobs more efficiently.
Cost: $75.00
Frequency: Monthly
Circulation: 55000
Founded in 1970
Printed in 4 colors on glossy stock

18178 Finishers' Management
Publication Management
4350 Di Paolo Center
Glenview, IL 60025-5212

847-699-1700
Fax: 847-699-1703
Home Page: www.finishers-management.com

David Friedman, Publisher
Kristy Judycki, Editor

Our publishing highlights include new product developments, equipment innovations, new production methods and reviews of current industry financial trends in the finishing industry.
Cost: $35.00
50 Pages
Frequency: 10 per year
Circulation: 12000
ISSN: 0015-2358
Founded in 1957
Printed in 4 colors on glossy stock

18179 Forging
Penton Media
1166 Avenue of the Americas/10th Fl
New York, NY 10036

212-204-4200
Fax: 216-696-6662
E-Mail: forgeditor@penton.com
Home Page: www.penton.com

Jane Cooper, Marketing
Robert Brooks, Editor
Melody Berendt, Circulation
Chris Meyer, Director, Corporate Communications

Dedicated to providing industrial part forgers with current market, product, process and equipment news and trend analysis.
Cost: $31.50
62 Pages
Circulation: 5000
ISSN: 1054-1756
Founded in 1990
Printed in 4 colors on glossy stock

18180 Foundry Management & Technology
Penton Media
1166 Avenue of the Americas/10th Fl
New York, NY 10036

212-204-4200
Fax: 216-696-6662
E-Mail: jwright@penton.com
Home Page: www.penton.com

Jane Cooper, Marketing
Dave Shanks, Publisher
Melody Berendt, Circulation Manager
Chris Meyer, Director, Corporate Communications

Received by management, production, engineering, research and technical professionals in the foundry industry.
Cost: $54.00
70 Pages
Frequency: Monthly
ISSN: 0360-8999
Printed in 4 colors on glossy stock

18181 Gases & Welding Distributor
Penton Media
1166 Avenue of the Americas/10th Fl
New York, NY 10036

212-204-4200
Fax: 216-696-6662
E-Mail: infomation@penton.com
Home Page: www.penton.com

Jane Cooper, Marketing
Patricia L Smith, Executive Editor
Charles Bates, Senior Editor
Jim Benes, Associate Editor
Melody Berendt, Circulation Manager

Marketing, management and technology magazine that aids distributors of welding supplies, industrial/medical/specialty gases, and safety products to sell more effectively to diverse markets.
Cost: $55.00
74 Pages
Frequency: six issues ayea
ISSN: 1079-3909
Printed in 4 colors

18182 Heat Treating Progress
ASM International
9639 Kinsman Rd
Novelty, OH 44072-9603

440-338-5151
800-336-5152
Fax: 440-338-4634
E-Mail: MemberServiceCenter@asminternational.org
Home Page: www.asminternational.org

Stanley Theobald, Executive Director
Dean Peters, Editor-in-Chief
Lana Shapowal, Manager
Tina Long, Circulation Manager
Vin LeGendre, Publisher
Frequency: Monthly
Founded in 1913

18183 Industrial Paint & Powder Magazine
Reed Business Information
30 Technology Parkway South
Suite 100
Norcross, GA 30092

630-574-0825
800-424-3996
Fax: 630-288-8781
E-Mail: webmaster@reedbusiness.com
Home Page: www.reedbusiness.com

Jeff Greisch, President
Coatings on manufacturing.
Cost: $55.00
Frequency: Monthly
Circulation: 38000
Founded in 1924

18184 Industrial Product Bulletin
Gordon Publications
301 Gibraltar Drive
#650
Morris Plains, NJ 07950-3400
973-292-5100
Fax: 973-539-3476

Todd Baker, Publisher
Anita LaFond, Editor

Publication for executives and professionals in the process and metalworking industries.
Cost: $7.00
Circulation: 200,050

18185 Inspection Trends
American Welding Society
550 Nw 42nd Ave
Miami, FL 33126-5699

305-443-9353
800-443-9353
Fax: 305-443-7559
E-Mail: info@aws.org
Home Page: www.aws.org

Ray Shook, President
Jeff Hufsey, Deputy Executive Director
Ray Shook, Executive Director
Kristin Campbell, Assistant Editor
Robert Pali, Treasurer

Our information assists inspection personnel through information and reports on new technology and equipment, tips on inspection techniques and interpretation, as well as by giving examples of practical methodology.
Cost: $50.00
Frequency: Quarterly
Circulation: 18000
Founded in 1989

18186 International Journal of Powder Metallurgy
APMI International
105 College Road E
Princeton, NJ 08540-6992

609-452-7700
Fax: 609-987-8523
E-Mail: apmi@mpif.org
Home Page: www.apmiinternational.org

Dr Alan Lawley, Editor-in-Chief
Peter K Johnson, Contributing Editor

Embraces a wide range of materials and processes including classical press and sinter PM and advanced particulate materials.
Cost: $230.00
Frequency: Bi-Monthly
ISSN: 0888-7462

18187 Iron & Steel Technology
Association for Iron & Steel Technolgy (AIST)
186 Thorn Hill Rd
Warrendale, PA 15086-7528

724-814-3000
Fax: 724-814-3001
E-Mail: memberservices@aist.org
Home Page: www.aist.org
Social Media: Facebook, Twitter, LinkedIn

Karen D Hickey, Managing Editor
Amanda Blyth, Technical Editor
Janet McConnell, Production Editor

The official monthly publication of AIST, this is the premier technical journal for metallurgical, engineering, operating and maintenance personnel in the global iron and steel industry.
Cost: $20.00
Frequency: Monthly
Circulation: 9600

18188 Journal of Materials Engineering and Performance
9639 Kinsman Road
Materials Park, OH 44073-2

440-338-5151
Fax: 440-338-4634
E-Mail: cust-srv@asminternational.org
Home Page: www.asm-intl.org

Ash Khare, President
Stanley Theobald, Managing Director

Peer-reviewed journal which publishes contributions on all aspects of materials selection, design, characterization, processing and performance testing. The scope includes all materials used in engineering applications: those that typically result in components for larger systems.
Cost: $1184.00
Circulation: 645
Founded in 1913

18189 Journal of Minerals, Metals & Materials Society
Minerals, Metals & Minerals Society

184 Thorn Hill Road
Warrendale, PA 15086-7511

724-776-9000
Fax: 724-776-3770
E-Mail: webmaster@tms.org
Home Page: www.tms.org

Alexander R Scott, Executive Director
Robert Makowski, Communications Director

To promote the global science and engineering profession's concerned with minerals, metals and materials. Founded in 1871. Publishes a monthly magazine.
Cost: $20.00
Frequency: Monthly
Circulation: 10000
Founded in 1880

18190 Journal of Phase Equilibria
ASM International
9639 Kinsman Rd
Materials Park, OH 44072

440-338-5151
800-336 5152
Fax: 440-338-4634
E-Mail: memberservices@asminternational.org
Home Page: www.asminternational.org
Social Media: Facebook, Twitter, LinkedIn

Jeane Deatherage, Administrator, Foundation Programs
Virginia Shirk, Foundation Executive Assistant

Peer-reviewed journal that contains basic and applied research results, evaluated phase diagrams, a survey of current literature, and comments or other material pertinent to the previous three areas. The aim is to provide a broad spectrum of information concerning phase equilibria for the materials community.
Cost: $1965.00
Frequency: Bimonthly
Circulation: 305

18191 Light Metal Age
Fellom Publishing Company
170 S Spruce Ave
Suite 120
S San Francisco, CA 94080-4557

650-588-8832
Fax: 650-588-0901
E-Mail: lma@lightmetalage.com
Home Page: www.buffalowildwings.com

Ann Marie Fellom, Publisher
Cost: $45.00
Frequency: Monthly
Circulation: 5000
ISSN: 0024-3345
Founded in 1944
Printed in 4 colors on glossy stock

18192 Locator Services
Locator Online
315 S Patrick St
Suite 3
Alexandria, VA 22314-3532

703-836-9700
800-537-1446
Fax: 703-836-7665
E-Mail: webmaster@locatoronline.com
Home Page: www.locatoronline.com

Terry Pitman, Publisher

Used metalworking equipment.
Frequency: Monthly
Circulation: 225000
Founded in 1969

18193 Machine Shop Guide
Worldwide Communications
401 Worthington Avenue
Harrison, NJ 07029-2039

973-497-7555
Fax: 973-497-7556

Robert L Hatschek, Executive Editor

Information on manufacturing technology, new applications for manufacturing technology and new products.
Circulation: 102893

18194 Manufacturers Showcase
Heartland Communications Group
1003 Central Avenue
Po Box 1052
Fort Dodge, IA 50501

515-955-1600
800-203-9960
Fax: 515-955-3753
E-Mail: ads@imtproduction.com
Home Page: www.imtgetsresults.com

Natalie Fevold, Operations Manager
Sandy Simonson, Sales Manager

A magazine for new metalworking machinery, tooling and supplies.
Frequency: Monthly

18195 Manufacturing Engineering
Society of Manufacturing Engineers
1 Sme Drive
PO Box 930
Dearborn, MI 48121

313-425-3000
800-733-4763
Fax: 313-425-3400
E-Mail: advertising@sme.org
Home Page: www.sme.org

Mark Tomlinson, Executive Director
Greg Sheremet, Publisher
Gene Nelson, President

Serves metalworking industry machining, forming, inspection, assembly and processing operations.
Frequency: Monthly
Circulation: 111966
Founded in 1932

18196 Metal Architecture
Modern Trade Communications
7450 Skokie Blvd
Suite 200
Skokie, IL 60077-3374

847-674-2200
Fax: 847-674-3676
Home Page: www.moderntrade.com

John Lawrence, President
Mark Wiebusch, Marketing & Operations
Shawn Zuver, Editorial & Production

Low-rise construction involving architects, engineers and specifiers.
Frequency: Monthly
Circulation: 29513

18197 Metal Center News
Reed Business Information
30 Technology Parkway South
Suite 100
Norcross, GA 30092

630-574-0825
800-424-3996
Fax: 630-288-8781
E-Mail: webmaster@reedbusiness.com
Home Page: www.reedbusiness.com

Jeff Greisch, President

Reports on verious phases of metal center operations.

18198 Metal Finishing
Elsevier Science
655 Avenue of the Americas
New York, NY 10010-5107

212-633-3800
Fax: 212-633-3850
E-Mail: PressOffice@elsevier.com
Home Page: www.elsevier.com

Young Suk Chi, President
Patti Ann Frost, Managing Editor
Susan Canalizo, Director, Manager
Greg Valero, Manager

Finishes and finishing of metal products.
Cost: $87.00
Frequency: Monthly
Circulation: 19824
Founded in 1903

18199 Metal Mecanica
Gardner Publications
901 poncedeleon blvd
sute 601
Coral Gables, FL 33134-3029

513-527-8977
800-950-8020
Fax: 305-448-9942
E-Mail: trivas@metalmecanica.com
Home Page: www.metalmecanica.com

David Ash, President
Eduardo Tovar, Editor
Holgar Hilkinger, Circulation Manager
Alfredo Domador, Publisher
Circulation: 12157
Founded in 1905

18200 MetalForming
Precision Metalforming Association
6363 Oak Tree Blvd
Cleveland, OH 44131-2500

216-901-9667
Fax: 216-901-9190
E-Mail: pma@pma.org
Home Page: www.metalformingmagazine.com

Brad Kuvin, Editor
Kathy DeLollis, Publisher
William Gaskin, President
Daniel Ellashek, VP
Lou Kren, Senior Editor

Edited for decision makers in the precision metal forming industry.
Cost: $59.95
100 Pages
Frequency: Monthly
Circulation: 60000
Founded in 1967
Printed in 4 colors on matte stock

18201 Metallurgical and Materials Transactions
Minerals, Metals & Materials Society
184 Thorn Hill Road
Warrendale, PA 15086-7528

724-776-9000
Fax: 724-776-3770
E-Mail: webmaster@tms.org
Home Page: www.tms.org

Robert Makowski, Publishing Director
Cost: $1467.00
Frequency: 13 issues
ISSN: 1073-5615

18202 Metalsmith
Society of North American Goldsmiths
5009 Londonderry Drive
Tampa, FL 33647-1336

813-977-5326
Fax: 813-977-8462
E-Mail: editor@snagmetalsmith.org
Home Page: www.snagmetalsmith.org

Suzanne Ramljak, Editor
Dana Singer, Executive Director
Ken Bova, President

Jean Savarese, Advertising Director
Ellen Laing, Program Manager

Information which explores new work in the jewelry, holloware, blacksmithing, and sculpture fields. Profiles of master metalsmiths are included.
Cost: $65.00
Circulation: 13,500
Founded in 1969

18203 Metalworking Digest
Reed Business Information
30 Technology Parkway South
Suite 100
Norcross, GA 30092

973-920-7000
800-424-3996
Fax: 973-920-7531
E-Mail: webmaster@reedbusiness.com
Home Page: www.reedbusiness.com

Rich Stevancsecz, Editor
Joe May, Publisher
Cloin Ungaro, CEO/President
Steve Koppelman, Circulation Manager
R Reed, Owner
Frequency: Monthly
Circulation: 115000
Founded in 1969

18204 Metalworking Distributor
Penton Media
1166 Avenue of the Americas/10th Fl
New York, NY 10036

212-204-4200
Fax: 216-696-6662
E-Mail: information@penton.com
Home Page: www.penton.com

Jane Cooper, Marketing
Thomas Grasson, Editor
Susan Cubranich, Production Manager
Chris Meyer, Director, Corporate Communications

Publication exclusively devoted to distributors and wholesales in the metalworking industry to help improve marketing, management, and technology knowledge as well as provide information on new markets.
Frequency: Quarterly
Circulation: 5,000
Printed in 4 colors

18205 Modern Applications News
Nelson Publishing
2500 Tamiami Trl N
Nokomis, FL 34275-3476

941-966-9521
Fax: 941-966-2590
E-Mail: subscriptions@nelsonpub.com
Home Page: www.healthmgttech.com
Social Media: Facebook

A Verner Nelson, President

Information includes coverage of abrasives and grinding, automated handling and robotics, CAD/CAM, coatings and finishings, coolants, lubricants and filters, cutting tools, heat treating, ID marking, lasers, machining centers, and shop control software.
Frequency: Monthly
Circulation: 84000
Founded in 1967

18206 Modern Casting
American Foundrymen's Society
1695 N Penny Ln
Schaumburg, IL 60173-4555

847-824-0181
800-537-4237
Fax: 847-824-7848
E-Mail: circ@afsinc.org
Home Page: www.afsinc.org

Jerry Call, Executive VP
Sandy Salisbury-Linton, Vice Chairman
Kyle Bauer, Editor
Barbara Jackowski, Circulation Manager
Alfred Spada, Editor-In-Chief

Designed to promote the technological advances in the industry.
Cost: $50.00
Frequency: Monthly
Circulation: 19000
Founded in 1896

18207 Modern Machine Shop
Gardner Publications
6915 Valley Ln
Cincinnati, OH 45244-3153

513-527-8800
800-950-8020
Fax: 513-527-8801
E-Mail: mmsmkt@gardnerweb.com
Home Page: www.gardnerweb.com

Rick Kline Sr, CEO
Mark D Albert, Editor-in-Chief
Dianne Hight, Circulation Manager
John Campos, Manager
Brian Wertheimer, Account Manager

Reaches metalworking plants of all sizes - from small job shops to giant aerospace and automotive plants. It is edited for those involved in metalworking operations, particularly those performed on machine tools.
Cost: $89.00
Frequency: Monthly
Circulation: 107000
Founded in 1928
Mailing list available for rent: 106M names
Printed in 4 colors on glossy stock

18208 Occupational Hazards
Penton Media
1166 Avenue of the Americas/10th Fl
New York, NY 10036

212-204-4200
Fax: 216-696-6662
E-Mail: information@penton.com
Home Page: www.penton.com

Jane Cooper, Marketing
Bob Marinez, Publisher
David B Nussbaum, CEO
Jennifer Daugherty, Communications Manager
Chris Meyer, Director, Corporate Communications

Analysis of qualified recipients who have indicated that they recommend, select and/or buy the safety equipment, fire protection and other occupational health products.
65 Pages
Frequency: Monthly
Circulation: 65777
ISSN: 0029-7909
Founded in 1892
Printed in 4 colors on glossy stock

18209 Ornamental and Miscellaneous Metals Fabricator
National Ornamental & Miscellaneous Metals Assn
532 Forest Parkway
Suite A
Forest Park, GA 30297-6137

404-363-4009
Fax: 404-366-1852
E-Mail: nommainfo@nomma.org
Home Page: www.nomma.org

Curt Witter, CEO/President
Todd Daniel, Editor

Magazine published by National Ornamental and Miscellaneous Metals Association.
Cost: $30.00
Circulation: 10000
Founded in 1958

18210 Platt's Metals Week
McGraw Hill
3333 Walnut Street
Boulder, CO 80301

720-548-5000
800-752-8878
Fax: 720-548-5701
E-Mail: metals@platts.com
Home Page: www.mcgraw-hill.com

Jackie Roche, Editor-in-Chief
Terry McGraw, CEO
Harry Sachinsis, President
Jackie Roche, Publisher

Extensive price listings in four currencies.
Frequency: Weekly

18211 Powder Coating
OSC Publishing
1300 E 66th Street
Minneapolis, MN 55423-2642

612-866-2242
Fax: 612-866-1939

Richard R Cress, Publisher
Richard Link, Manager

Our information focuses on the application, pre-treatment, materials, materials handling, and curing processes. Also features case histories.
Cost: $95.00
Frequency: Monthly
Circulation: 23587

18212 Practical Welding Today
Fabricators and Manufacturers Association
833 Featherstone Road
Rockford, IL 61107-6302

815-399-8700
Fax: 815-484-7700
E-Mail: info@fmanet.org
Home Page: www.fmanet.org

Gerald M Shankel, President/CEO
Michael Hedges, VP Finance/CFO
Scott Stevens, Publisher
Kim Clothier, Director of Circulation
Jim Gorzek, Marketing

Practical Welding Today is the only hands on, down-to-earth magazine with information that welders can use in the shop or out in the field. Published six times per year with more than 40,000 subcribers, it covers topics such as systems and equipment, safety, consumables, cutting and welding prep, welding inspection and more. In addition, Practical Welding Today has a regular lineup of application articles, welder profiles, product highlights and valuable buyers' guides.
Circulation: 40000
Printed in 4 colors on glossy stock

18213 Products Finishing
Gardner Publications
6915 Valley Ln
Cincinnati, OH 45244-3153

513-527-8800
Fax: 513-527-8801
E-Mail: narnold@gardnerweb.com
Home Page: www.gardnerweb.com

Rick Kline Sr, CEO
Beverly Graves, Manager
John Campos, Manager
Brian Wertheimer, Account Manager
Eddie Kania, Sales Manager

Covers production, management, engineering, design, etc. in plants where metal and plastic products are eletroplated, anodized, painted,

buffed, cleaned or otherwise finished.
Cost: $89.00
Frequency: Monthly
Circulation: 45552
Founded in 1928
Printed in 4 colors on glossy stock

18214 Projects in Metal
Village Press
2779 Aero Park Drive
PO Box 629
Traverse City, MI 49686-9101

231-463-3712
Fax: 231-946-3289
E-Mail: villagepre@aol.com
Home Page:
www.members.aol.com/vpshop/pim/htm

Robert Goff, Publisher

In each issue you will find plans for valuable tools and accessories, and challenging hobby projects. Every project is complete in one issue.
Frequency: Bi-Monthly
Circulation: 15000

18215 Recycling Today
GIE Media
4012 Bridge Avenue
Cleveland, OH 44113-3320

216-961-4130
800-456-0707
Fax: 216-961-0364
E-Mail: btaylor@gie.net
Home Page: www.recyclingtoday.com

Jim Keefe, Group Publisher
Brian Taylor, Editor
Richard Foster, CEO
Helen Duerr, Director of Production
Megan Ries, Advertising Coordinatior

Published for the secondary commodity processing/recycling market.
Cost: $30.00
Frequency: Monthly
Founded in 1980

18216 SCRAP
Institute of Scrap Recycling Industries
1615 L Street NW
Suite 600
Washington, DC 20036-5664

202-662-8500
Fax: 202-626-0900
E-Mail: kentkiser@scrap.org
Home Page: www.scrap.org

Kent Kiser, Publisher
Marian Weiss, Production Manager
Rachel H Pollack, Editor-In-Chief
Valerie Hillyer, Circulation/Advertising Associate

A bi-monthly magazine that covers all aspects of the international scrap recycling industry, including market trends, business management, personnel issues, equipment and technology, regulations and legislation, and more.
Cost: $36.00
16 Pages
Frequency: 6 per year
Circulation: 7400
ISSN: 1092-8618
Founded in 1928

18217 Secondary Marketing Executive
LDJ Corporation
P.O.Box 2180
Waterbury, CT 06722-2180

203-755-0158
800-325-6745
Fax: 203-755-3480

John Florian, Editorial Director
Linda Herrmann, Account Executive

Delivers news, analysis and how-to advice to people involved in the buying and selling of mortgage loans and servicing rights nationwide.
Cost: $48.00
44 Pages
Frequency: Monthly
Circulation: 21,000
Founded in 1986

18218 Shop Owner
Penton Media
1166 Avenue of the Americas/10th Fl
New York, NY 10036

212-204-4200
Fax: 216-696-6662
E-Mail: information@penton.com
Home Page: www.penton.com

Jane Cooper, Marketing
Thomas J Grasson, Editorial Director
Charles Bates, Senior Editor
Melody Berendt, Circulation Manager
Janet Marioneaux, Administrative Assistant

Digest-sized publication covering information essential to the success of the small to medium manufacturing shop.
Frequency: Quarterly
Circulation: 120000
Founded in 1998
Printed in 4 colors

18219 Stamping Journal
Fabricators and Manufacturers Association
833 Featherstone Road
Rockford, IL 61107-6302

815-399-8700
Fax: 815-484-7700
E-Mail: info@fmanet.org
Home Page: www.fmanet.org

Gerald Shankel, President/CEO
Michael Hedges, CFO
Scot Stevens, Publisher
Jim Gorzek, Sales Manager
Kim Clothier, Circulation Manager

Stamping Journal, the only North American magazine devoted exclusively to metal stamping, has been delivering the industry's latest techniques, news and ideas to subscribers worldwide for 13 years. Published six times per year, with more than 35,000 subscribers, Stamping Journal focuses on metal stamping technology including, tool and die, material handling, coil processing, stamping presses, press feeding, quick die change and more.
Cost: $65.00
Frequency: Monthly
Circulation: 35000
Founded in 1970
Printed in 4 colors on glossy stock

18220 Tooling & Production
NP Communications, LLC
2500 Tamiami Trail N
Nokomis, FL 34275

941-966-9521
Fax: 941-966-2590
E-Mail: vnelson@nelsonpub.com
Home Page: www.toolingandproduction.com

Vern Nelson, Publisher/Editorial Director
Bob West, Managing Editor/Associate Publisher

Provides information to metalworking professionals working in large, high-throughput plants. Original editorial delivers technology, products, and processes applying to aerospace, automotive, medical equipment, mold, tool & die manufacturing, and much more.
100 Pages
Frequency: Monthly
Circulation: 70000
ISSN: 0040-9243
Founded in 1934
Printed in 4 colors on glossy stock

18221 Tube & Pipe Journal
Fabricators and Manufacturers Association
833 Featherstone Road
Rockford, IL 61107-6302

815-998-8700
Fax: 815-484-7701
E-Mail: info@fmanet.org
Home Page: www.fmanet.org

Gerald Shankel, President/CEO
Michael Hedges, CFO

The Tube and Pipe Journal is North America's only magazine devoted exclusively to metal tube and pipe manufacturing. Published 8 times per year and with more than 30,000 subscribers, TPJ covers topics such as tube producing, bending and forming, cutting and sawing, welding, tooling, coil and material handling, and more. TPJ also provides expanded coverage of hydroforming technology in the Hydroforming Journal, a separate supplement published four time per year alongside TPJ.
Cost: $200.00
Circulation: 30000
Founded in 1970
Printed in 4 colors on glossy stock

18222 US Glass, Metal & Glazing
Key Communications
PO Box 569
Garrisonville, VA 22463

540-577-7174
Fax: 540-720-5687
E-Mail: info@glass.com
Home Page: www.glass.com

Debra Levy, Publisher
Ellen Giard Chilcoat, Editor
Penny Stacey, Advertising Coordinator

Serves manufactures/fabricators, contract glaziers, distributors and wholesalers, retailors/dealers of glass/metal and or glass/metal products and other allied to the field.
Frequency: Monthly
Circulation: 15000
ISSN: 0041-7661
Founded in 1995
Printed in 4 colors on glossy stock

18223 Welding Design & Fabrication
Penton Media
1166 Avenue of the Americas/10th Fl
New York, NY 10036
212-204-4200
Fax: 216-696-6662
E-Mail: information@penton.com
Home Page: www.penton.com

Jane Cooper, Marketing
Dean Peters, Editor
David Nussbaum, CEO
Chris Meyer, Director, Corporate Communications

Reaches designers, engineers, managers, superviisors, and buyers in plants and field sites in the US and Canada who conduct welding and fabricating operations. Reports on processes and equipment, materials, safety, testing and inspection in the manufacturing of fabricated metal products, structural projects and equipment maintenance.
Frequency: Monthly
Circulation: 40000
Founded in 1892
Printed in 4 colors

18224 Welding Innovation
James F Lincoln Arc Welding Foundation

22801 Saint Clair Ave
Cleveland, OH 44117-2524

216-481-4300
Fax: 216-383-8220
Home Page: www.jflf.org/

Roy Morrow, President
Richard D Seif, Chairman
Vicki Wilson, Administrative Assistant
Dave Manning, Executive Director

Informative articles related to welding steel structures such as bridges and buildings, as well as notices of related conferences.
Circulation: 40000
Founded in 1936

18225 Welding Journal
American Welding Society
550 Nw 42nd Ave
Miami, FL 33126-5699

305-443-9353
800-443-9353
Fax: 305-443-7559
E-Mail: info@aws.org
Home Page: www.aws.org

Ray Shook, President
Jefferey Weber, Publisher
Cecilia Barbier, Senior Coordinator Market
Robert Pali, Treasurer

Our feature articles include new product listings, book reviews and the application of new operating procedures.
Frequency: Monthly
Circulation: 46000
Founded in 1919

18226 Wire Rope News & Sling Technology
Wire Rope News
PO Box 871
Clark, NJ 07066-871

908-486-3221
Fax: 732-396-4215
E-Mail: vsent@aol.com
Home Page: www.wireropenews.com

Edward J Bluvias, Publisher
Conrad Miller, Editor

Wire Rope News & Sling Technology is edited for manufacturers and distributors of wire rope, chain, cordage, related hardware, and sling fabricators. Content includes technical articles, news, and reports describing the manufacture and use of wire rope in marine, construction, mining, aircraft and offshore drilling operations. Cordage, slings, chain and fittings are also covered. Editorial content contains articles about fabricating companies, new products and people in the news.
Cost: $20.00
Circulation: 4400
ISSN: 0740-1809
Founded in 1979
Printed in 4 colors on glossy stock

Trade Shows

18227 AFS/CMI Advanced Foundry Operations Conference
American Foundrymen's Society
1695 N Penny Ln
Schaumburg, IL 60173-4555

847-824-0181
800-537-4237
Fax: 847-824-7848
Home Page: www.afsinc.org

Frequency: March

18228 AISTech Conference & Exposition
Association for Iron & Steel Technology
186 Thorn Hill Rd
Warrendale, PA 15086-7528

724-814-3000
Fax: 724-814-3001
E-Mail: memberservices@aist.org
Home Page: www.aist.org
Social Media: Facebook, Twitter, LinkedIn

Ronald E Ashburn, Executive Director
William A Albaugh, Technology Programs Manager
Joann Cantrell, Publications Manager/Editor
Mark Didiano, Finance & Administration Manager
Stacy Varmecky, Membership Communications Manager

Featuring technologies from across the globe, allowing steel producers to compete in today's global market. Submit technical papers for presentation at the event. 300 exhibitors. Registration starts at $425.
4500 Attendees
Frequency: Annual/Spring

18229 ASM Heat Treating Society Conference & Exposition
ASM International
9639 Kinsman Road
Materials Park, OH 44073

440-385-5151
800-336-5152
Fax: 440-338-4634
E-Mail:
pamela.kleinman@asminternational.org
Home Page: www.asminternational.org
Social Media: Facebook, Twitter, LinkedIn

Pamela Kleinma, Senior Manager, Events
Kellye Thomas, Exposition Account Manager
Jeane Deatherage, Administrator, Foundation Programs
Virginia Shirk, Foundation Executive Assistant

Conference and exhibits of heat treating equipment and supplies plus information of interest to metallurgists, manufacturing, research and design technical professionals. 300 exhibitors.
3500 Attendees
Frequency: September, Bi-Annual
Founded in 1974

18230 ASM Materials Science & Technology (MS&T)
ASM International
9639 Kinsman Road
Materials Park, OH 44073-0002

440-338-5151
800-336-5152
Fax: 440-338-4634
E-Mail:
pamela.kleinman@asminternational.org
Home Page: www.asminternational.org
Social Media: Facebook, Twitter, LinkedIn

Pamela Kleinman, Senior Manager, Events
Kelly Thomas, Exposition Account Manager
Jeane Deatherage, Administrator, Foundation Programs
Virginia Shirk, Foundation Executive Assistant

Annual event focusing on testing, analysis, characterization and research of materials such as engineered materials, high performance metals, powdered metals, metal forming, surface modification, welding and joining. 350 exhibitors.
4,000 Attendees
Frequency: Annual/October
Founded in 2005

18231 Advanced Productivity Conference and Expo- Cleveland
Society of Manufacturing Engineers
1 SME Drive
PO Box 930
Dearborn, MI 48121

313-425-3000
800-733-4763
Fax: 313-425-3400
E-Mail: advertising@sme.org
Home Page: www.sme.org

Mark Tomlinson, Executive Director
Greg Sheremet, Publisher

200 Exhibits of equipment, supplies and services for the tool and manufacturing engineering fields.
13800 Attendees
Frequency: Biennial
Founded in 1984

18232 AeroMat Conference and Exposition
ASM International
9639 Kinsman Road
Materials Park, OH 44073-0002

440-385-5151
800-336-5152
Fax: 440-338-4634
E-Mail: kim.schaefer@asminternational.org
Home Page: www.asminternational.org
Social Media: Facebook, Twitter, LinkedIn

Kim Schaefer, Event Manager
Kelly Thomas, Exposition Account Manager
Jeane Deatherage, Administrator, Foundation Programs
Virginia Shirk, Foundation Executive Assistant

Conference for Aerospace Meterials Engineers, Structural Engineers and Designers. The annual event focuses on affordable structures and low-cost manufacturing, titanium alloy technology, advanced intermetallics and refractory metal alloys, materials and processes for space applications, aging systems, high strength steel, NDT evaluation, light alloy technology, welding and joining, and engineering technology. 150 exhibitors.
1500 Attendees
Frequency: Annual/June
Founded in 1984

18233 American Foundrymen's Society Castings Congress and Cast Expo
505 State St
Des Plaines, IL 60016-2267

847-824-0181
Fax: 847-824-7845

Kristy Glass, Show Manager

300 booths including technical papers and panel sessions for the metal casting industry.
12000 Attendees
Frequency: Annual

18234 American Society Engineers: Design International
Systems and Design Group
3 Park Avenue
Floor 27
New York, NY 10016-5902

212-903-4160

Fred Goldfarb, Program Manager
Virgil Carter, CEO

150 booths.
2.5M Attendees
Frequency: August

18235 American Welding Show
American Welding Society
8669 Doral Boulevard, Suite 130
Doral, FL 33166

305-443-9353
800-443-9353

Fax: 305-443-7559
Home Page: www.aws.org

Ray Shook, Executive Director
Jefferey Weber, Publisher
Amy Nathan, Public Relations Manager

350 booths of welding and allied industries held in conjunction with metal form.
Frequency: Annual

18236 **American Zinc Association**
1112 16th Street NW
Suite 240
Washington, DC 20036-4818

202-478-8200
Fax: 202-835-0155
E-Mail: info@zinc.org
Home Page: www.zinc.org

George Vary, Executive Director
David Adkins, Secretary
Frequency: February

18237 **Annual International Titanium Conference**
International Titanium Association
1871 Folsom Street
Suite 200
Boulder, CO 80302-5714

303-443-7515
Fax: 303-443-4406
Home Page: www.titanium.org

Amy Fitzgerald, Manager
800 Attendees
Frequency: October
Founded in 1984

18238 **Artist-Blacksmiths Association of North America**
PO Box 206
Washington, MO 63090

636-390-2133
Fax: 423-913-1023
Home Page: www.abasna.otg

Marcus Vickery, Conference Coordinator

Meeting and exhibitions, workshops, demonstrations and artistic metalwork for the professional and amateur blacksmith.

18239 **Association of Industrial Metallizers, Coaters and Laminators Conference**
201 Springs Street
Fort Mill, SC 29708

803-802-7820
Fax. 803-802-7821
E-Mail: aimcal@aimcal.org
Home Page: www.aimcal.org

Craig Sheppard, Executive Director
Erin Davis, Communications Manager

Displays relating to coaters and laminators, metallizers and producers of metallized film and or paper on continuous rolls, suppliers of plastic films, papers and adhesives.
Frequency: Annual
Founded in 1970

18240 **Cast Expo**
Cast Metals Institute
1695 N Penny Ln
Schaumburg, IL 60173-4555

847-824-0181
800-537-4237
Fax: 847-824-7848
Home Page: www.castmetals.com
Social Media: Facebook, Twitter, LinkedIn

CastExpo attracts thousands of decision-making metalcasters from around the world, all of whom are looking for the latest advancements in equipment, technology and services to use in their own facilities.
Frequency: May

18241 **Electrical Manufacturing & Coil Winding Expo**
PO Box 278
Imperial Beach, CA 91933-0278

619-435-3629
Fax: 619-435-3639
E-Mail: cthurman@earthlink.net
Home Page: www.emcwa.org

Richard Duke, President
Charles Thurman, Executive Director
Don Stankiewicz, Vice President

An annual technical conference and exhibition related to the manufacture of electrical products. Exhibitors include suppliers of materials and process equipment used in manufacturing electric motors, trnasformers, and other electrical devices. 150 exhibitors, free admission.
2000 Attendees

18242 **FABTECH International**
Fabricators and Manufacturers Association
833 Featherstone Road
Rockford, IL 61107-6302

815-399-8700
Fax: 815-399-7279
E-Mail: info@fmametalfab.org
Home Page: www.fmametalfab.org

Mark Hoper, Director

Metal forming, fabricating, finishing and welding event that gives all the tools neded to improve productivity, increase profits and find new ways to survive in today's competitive business environment.
25000 Attendees
Frequency: Annual/November

18243 **Furnaces North America**
Metal Treating Institute
504 Osceola Ave
Jacksonville Beach, FL 32250

904-249-0448
Fax: 904-249-0459
Home Page: www.heattreat.net

Tom Morrison, Show Manager

North America's Premier Heat Treat Only Event, Furnaces North America 2012, will be held October 1-3, 2012 in Nashville, TN.
340 Members
1200 Attendees
Frequency: September
Founded in 1933

18244 **International Anodizing Conference & Exposition**
Aluminum Anodizers Council (AAC)
1000 North Rand Road
Suite 214
Wauconda, IL 60084

847-526-2010
Fax: 847-526-3993
E-Mail: mail@anodizing.org
Home Page: www.andoizing.org

Terry D Snell, Chairman
Todd Hamilton, Vice Chairman
Gregory T Rajsky CAE, President
120 Attendees
Frequency: Annual

18245 **International Symposium for Testing and Failure Analysis**
ASM International
9639 Kinsman Road
Materials Park, OH 44073-0002

440-385-5151
Fax: 440-338-4634

Jan DiRosa, Expositions Sales

Annual event focusing on microelectronic and electronic device failure analysis, techniques, EOS/ESD testing and discretes aimed at failure analysis engineers and managers, technicians and new failure analysis engineers. Santa Clara Convention Center, Santa Clara, California.
1,100 Attendees
Frequency: November

18246 **International Thermal Spray Conference & Exposition**
ASM International
9639 Kinsman Road
Materials Park, OH 44073

440-338-5151
800-336-5152
Fax: 440-338-4634
E-Mail: natalie.nemec@asminternational.org
Home Page: www.asminternational.org
Social Media: Facebook, Twitter, LinkedIn

Natalie Neme, Event Manager
Kelly Thomas, Exposition Account Manager
Jeane Deatherage, Administrator, Foundation Programs
Virginia Shirk, Foundation Executive Assistant

Global annual event attracting professional interested in thermal spray technology focusing on advances in HVOF, plasma and detonation gun, flame spray and wire arc spray processes, performance of coatings, and future trends. 150 exhibitors.
1000 Attendees
Frequency: Annual/May

18247 **Iron & Steel Exposition**
Association of Iron & Steel Engineers
3 Gateway Center
Suite 1900
Pittsburgh, PA 15222-1000

412-281-6323
Fax: 412-281-4657
Home Page: www.aise.org

Ronald E Ashiurn, Managing Director
Chris Brown, Graphic Designer
Stacy Varmecky, General Manager

Includes technical sessions and exhibits of equipment, supplies and services for the metals producing industry.
25M Attendees

18248 **MBCEA Annual Conference**
Metal Building Contractors & Erectors Association
PO Box 499
Shawnee Mission, KS 66201

913-432-3800
Fax: 913-432-3803
E-Mail: MBCEA@kc.rr.com
Home Page: www.mbcea.org

Angela M Cruse, Executive Director
Tim Seyler, President

Annual conference with the mission to support the professional advancement of metal building contractors, erectors and our industry.
Frequency: February

18249 **METALFORM**
Precision Metalforming Association
6363 Oak Tree Boulevard
Independence, OH 44131

216-901-8800
Fax: 216-901-9190
E-Mail: rjudson@pma.org
Home Page: www.metalform.com

Amy Primiano, Director Expositions
William Gaskin, President

A regional networking and educational event that brings buyers and sellers from metal stamping and fabricating markets together in a dynamic and interactive environment.
5,000 Attendees
Frequency: March

18250 Metalworking Machine Tool Expo
Marketing International Corporation
200 N Glebe Road
Suite 900
Arlington, VA 22203-3728

703-527-8000
Fax: 703-527-8006

Annual show of 100 machine tools suppliers.
8000 Attendees

18251 NFFS Summit Conference
Non-Ferrous Founders' Society
1480 Renaissance Drive
Suite 310
Park Ridge, IL 60068

847-299-0950
Fax: 847-299-3598
E-Mail: staff@nffs.org
Home Page: www.nffs.org

Frequency: February

18252 National Ornamental and Miscellaneous Metals Association
532 Forest Parkway
Suite A
Forest Park, GA 30297-6137

404-363-4009
Fax: 888-279-7994
E-Mail: nommainfo@nomma.org
Home Page: www.nomma.org

Barbara Cook, Executive Director
Todd Daniel, Editor
Cyndi Smith, Office Manager
Martha Pennington, Meetings/Exposition Manager

This annual convention and trade show — METALfab — is for all those involved in the ornamental and metallury industries.
900 Attendees
Founded in 1958

18253 PowderMet
APMI International
105 College Road E
Princeton, NJ 08540-6992

609-452-7700
Fax: 609-987-8523
E-Mail: info@mpif.org
Home Page: www.mpif.org

Nicholas T Mares, President
Michael E Lutheran, Director
C James Trombino CAE, Director

An annual international conference serving the powder metallurgy industry with a standalone exhibit featuring industry service providers and equipment suppliers.
1000 Attendees
Frequency: Annual

18254 SMACNA Annual Convention
Sheet Metal and Air Conditioning Contractor's Natl
4201 Lafayette Center Drive
Chantilly, VA 20151-1219

703-803-2980
Fax: 703-803-3732
E-Mail: info@smacna.org
Home Page: www.smacna.org

Vincent R Sandusky, CEO

Sheet metal and air conditioning contractors explore the newest ideas, technologies, and trends in the construction industry.
Frequency: October

18255 TMS Annual Meeting Exhibition
Minerals, Metals & Materials Society
184 Thorn Hill Road
Warrendale, PA 15086

724-776-9000
Fax: 724-776-3770
E-Mail: webmaster@tms.org
Home Page: www.tms.org

Cindy Wilson, Show Manager
Alexander Scott, Executive Director

International metals and materials exhibition. Production, processing, engineering and research. Held in Charlotte, North Carolina.
3,500 Attendees
Frequency: March

18256 WESTEC-Advanced Productivity Expo
Society of Manufacturing Engineers
1 SME Drive
PO Box 930
Dearborn, MI 48121

313-425-3000
800-733-4763
Fax: 313-425-3400
E-Mail: advertising@sme.org
Home Page: www.sme.org

Mark Tomlinson, Executive Director
Greg Sheremet, Publisher

600 booths displaying machine tools and metalworking products and services.
40M Attendees
Frequency: Annual

Directories & Databases

18257 Aluminum Association Aluminum Standards & Data
Aluminum Association
900 19th Street NW
Washington, DC 20006-2105

202-862-5100

Contains the nominal composition and composition limits, typical mechanical and physical properties and tensile properties limits for US wrought aluminum alloys. Updated periodically.

18258 Aluminum Extruders Council Buyer's Guide
1000 North Rand Road
Suite 214
Wauconda, IL 60084

847-526-2010
Fax: 847-526-3993
E-Mail: mail@aec.org
Home Page: www.aec.org
Social Media: LinkedIn

Thomas J Schabel, Chairman
Duncan Crowdis, Vice Chairman
Rand A Baldwin CAE, President
135 Members
Frequency: Annual
Founded in 1950

18259 DRI Steel Forecast
DRI/McGraw-Hill
24 Hartwell Ave
Lexington, MA 02421-3103

781-860-6060
Fax: 781-860-6002
E-Mail: support@construction.com
Home Page: www.construction.com

Walt Arvin, President

This comprehensive database offers over 500 quarterly and annual forecasts on production, shipment, and consumption of raw steel and steel products in the United States.

18260 Directory Iron and Steel Plants
Association for Iron & Steel Technology
186 Thorn Hill Rd
Warrendale, PA 15086-7528

724-814-3000
Fax: 724-814-3001
E-Mail: memberservices@aist.org
Home Page: www.aist.org
Social Media: Facebook, Twitter, LinkedIn

Ronald E Ashburn, Executive Director
William A Albaugh, Technology Programs Manager
Joann Cantrell, Publications Manager/Editor
Mark Didiano, Finance & Administration Manager
Stacy Varmecky, Membership Communications Manager

The Directory lists more than 2,000 companies and 17,500 individuals. Featuring data on essentially ever steel producer in the USA, Canada and Mexico, including names and titles of executive, enginnering, maintenance and operating personnel. Also includes an alpha listing of all major equipment, product and service providers to the international iron and steel industry, and a listing of associations affiliated with the industry, with complete geo-indexing. Softbound book with CD.
Cost: $95.00
Frequency: M-$95/NM-$135
ISBN: 1-935117-00-1

18261 Dun's Industrial Guide: Metalworking Directory
Dun & Bradstreet Information Service
3 Sylvan Way
Parsippany, NJ 07054-3822

973-605-6000
800-526-0651
Fax: 973-605-9630

Over 78,000 original equipment manufacturers, metal distributors, and machine tools/metalworking machinery distributors.
Cost: $775.00
Frequency: Annual

18262 EDM Today Yearbook
EDM Publications
230 W Parkway
Suite 3-1
Pompton Plains, NJ 07444-1065

973-831-1334
Fax: 973-831-1195

Jack Sebzda, Editor
Frequency: Annual

18263 Economic Handbook of the Machine Tool Industry
AMT - The Association for Manufacturing Technology
7901 Westpark Dr
Mc Lean, VA 22102-4206

703-893-2900
Fax: 703-893-1151
E-Mail: amt@amtonline.org
Home Page: www.amtonline.org

Bob Simpson, President

Complete statistics for the US machine tool industry, including exports and imports.
Cost: $295.00
Frequency: Annual
Printed in one color on matte stock

18264 Equip-Mart
116 N Camp Street
Seguin, TX 78155

830-303-3328
800-864-1155

Fax: 830-372-3011
Home Page: www.equip-mart.com

Directory of available used metalworking equipment.
Frequency: Weekly

18265 Foundry Management & Technology: Where to Buy Directory Issue
Penton Publishing Company
1166 Avenue of the Americas/10th Fl
New York, NY 10036

212-204-4200
Fax: 216-696-1752
E-Mail: information@penton.com
Home Page: www.penton.com

Dean Peters, Editor
Chris Meyer, Director, Corporate Communications

Listing of about 1,700 manufacturers of foundry products.
Cost: $15.00
Frequency: Annual, September
Circulation: 22,000

18266 Fundamentals of Steel Product Physical Metallurgy
Association for Iron & Steel Technology (AIST)
186 Thorn Hill Road
Warrendale, PA 15086-7528

724-814-3000
Fax: 724-814-3001
E-Mail: memberservices@aist.org
Home Page: www.steellibrary.com

Bruno C De Cooman, Author
John G Speer, Author

This directory is an introduction to steel products for industry professionals. With its readily accessible style, the book allows the reader to easily grasp important scientific topics that play an essential role in current steel research, product development and applications. ISBN: 978-1-935117-16-2
Cost: $110.00
Frequency: Annual

18267 Industrial Laser Review: Buyers' Guide of Companies & Products
PennWell Publishing Company
10 Tara Boulevard
5th Floor
Nashua, NH 03062-2800

603-891-0123
Fax: 603 891 0574
Home Page: www.industrial-lasers.com/index.html

David Belforte, Editor
Frequency: Annual July

18268 Industrial Machine Trader
Heartland Industrial Group
1003 Central Avenue
PO Box 1415
Fort Dodge, IA 50501

515-955-1600
800-247-2000
Fax: 515-955-3753
E-Mail: igproduction@industrialgroup.com
Home Page: www.industrialgroup.com
Social Media: Facebook, Twitter, LinkedIn

Virginia Rodriguez, Publisher

Printed directory of available used metalworking equipment.
150+ Members
Frequency: Weekly
Founded in 1966

18269 International Lead and Zinc
WEFA Group
800 Baldwin Tower Boulevard
Eddystone, PA 19022-1368

610-490-4000
Fax: 610-490-2770
E-Mail: info@wefa.com
Home Page: www.wefa.com

This database contains quarterly and annual time series on lead and zinc.

18270 International Powder Metallurgy Directory
Metal Powder Industries Federation
105 College Rd East
Princeton, NJ 08540-6692

609-452-7700
Fax: 609-987-8523
E-Mail: info@mpif.org
Home Page: www.mpif.org

Michael Lutheran, President
Jim Adams, Director, Technical Services
C. James Trombino, Executive Director, CEO
Jillaine K. Regan, VP, Finance & Administration
Jessica Tamasi, Advertising & Exhibit Manager

Leading reference source for powder metallurgy parts producers and industry suppliers worldwide.
Cost: $30.00
210 Members
504 Pages
Frequency: Annual, Paperback
Founded in 1944

18271 Iron and Manganese Ore Databook
Metal Bulletin
220 5th Avenue
New York, NY 10001-7708
212-136-6202
800-MET-L 25
Fax: 212-213-6273

John Bailey, Editor

Iron and manganese ore producers and traders worldwide.
Cost: $179.00
Frequency: Quadrennial

18272 Iron and Steel Works of the World
Metal Bulletin
220 5th Avenue
19th Floor
New York, NY 10001-7781

212-213-6202
Fax: 202-213-1870
Home Page: www.metalbulleton.com

Henry Cooke, Editor

Lists over 1,500 major iron and steel plants worldwide.
Cost: $439.00
730 Pages

18273 Locator Services
315 S Patrick St
Alexandria, VA 22314-3532

703-836-9700
800-537-1446
Fax: 703-836-7665
E-Mail: sales@locatoronline.com
Home Page: www.locatoronline.com

Terry Pitman, Publisher

Printed directory of available used metalworking equipment.
Frequency: Monthly
Circulation: 225,000

18274 Metal Bulletin's Prices and Data Book
Metal Bulletin
220 5th Avenue
19th Floor
New York, NY 10001-7781

212-213-6202
Fax: 212-213-1870
E-Mail: help@metalbulletin.com
Home Page: www.metalbulletin.com

Richard ODonoghue, Manager
Ania Tumm, Marketing Manager
Julius Pike, Account Manager

A list of national and international associations and trading organizations concerned with iron, steel and nonferrous ores and metals.
Cost: $165.00
Frequency: Annual

18275 Metal Casting Industry Directory
Penton Media
1166 Avenue of the Americas/10th Fl
New York, NY 10036

212-204-4200
Fax: 216-696-6662
E-Mail: information@penton.com
Home Page: www.penton.com

Jane Cooper, Marketing
Chris Meyer, Director, Corporate Communications

Directory of services and supplies to the industry.
Cost: $425.00
300 Pages

18276 Metal Center News: Metal Distribution Issue
Hitchcock Publishing Company
191 S Gary Avenue
Carol Stream, IL 60188-2095

630-690-5600

Joseph Marino, Editor

Offers a list of producers and industrial metals and metal products, manufacturers of metal processing and handling equipment.
Cost: $25.00
Frequency: Annual
Circulation: 14,000

18277 Metal Finishing Guidebook Directory
Metal Finishing/Elsevier Science
360 Park Ave S
New York, NY 10010-1736

212-633-3980
Fax: 212-633-3913
E-Mail: metalfinishing@elsevier.com
Home Page: www.elsevier.com

Ys Chi, President
Patti Ann Frost, Managing Editor
Matthew Smaldon, Circulation Manager
Bill Godfrey, Chief Information Officer
Cost: $87.00
Founded in 1962

18278 Metal Finishing: Guidebook Directory
Metal Finishing/Elsevier Science
650 Avenue of Americas
New York, NY 10011

212-633-5100
Fax: 212-633-5140
Home Page: www.metalfinishing.com

Eugene Nadel, Publisher
Don Walsh, Director of operations
Enthone Taps, Communications Manager
Jonathan Timms, Director of Marketing
Frequency: Annual January

18279 Metal Statistics
American Metal Market

350 Hudson Street
4th Floor
New York, NY 10014-4504

212-666-2420
800-662-4445
Fax: 212-519-7522
E-Mail: custserv@amm.com
Home Page: www.amm.com

Gloria Larme, Editor-in-Chief

The statistical guide to North American metals. Hardcover $265.00, Softcover $185.00.
404 Pages
Frequency: Annual
ISBN: 0-910094-01-2
Founded in 1908

18280 **Metal Statistics: Ferrous Edition**
American Metal Market
350 Hudson Street
4th Floor
New York, NY 10014-4504

212-662-2420
800-662-4445
Fax: 818-487-4550
E-Mail: custserv@amm.com
Home Page: www.amm.com

Machael Botta, Publisher
Gloria LaRue, Editor-in-Chief

Statistics for North American metals, also Canadian and Mexican statistucs, International tables and graphs, International trade labor contractsand recycling and scrap alternatives.
Cost: $265.00
Frequency: Annual
ISBN: 0-910094-00-4

18281 **Metals Datafile**
Materials Information
ASM International
Materials Park, OH 44073

440-930-4888
Fax: 440-338-4634

This database contains designation and specification numbers for ferrous and non-ferrous metals and alloys.
Frequency: Full-text

18282 **Metalworking Machinery Mailer**
Tade Publishing Group
29501 Greenfield Road
Suite 120
Southfield, MI 48076

248-552-8583
800-966-8233
Fax: 248-552-0466
Home Page: www.tadesite.com

Tom Lynch, Editor

Printed directory of available used metalworking equipment.
Frequency: Monthly

18283 **Mineral and Energy Information**
Mineral Information Institute
505 Violet St
Golden, CO 80401-6714

303-277-9190
Fax: 303-277-9198
E-Mail: mii@mii.org
Home Page: www.mii.org

Profiles of associations, government agencies and special interest groups in North America that are sources of publications and products on mineral related subjects.
Cost: $15.00

18284 **Modern Machine Shop: CNC & Software Guide Software Issue**
Gardner Publications
6915 Valley Ln
Cincinnati, OH 45244-3153

513-527-8800
Fax: 513-527-8801
Home Page: www.gardnerweb.com

Rick Kline Sr, CEO
Richard Kline, Manager
John Campos, Manager
Brian Wertheimer, Account Manager
Eddie Kania, Sales Manager
Frequency: Annual April

18285 **Parts Cleaning: Master Source Buyer's Guide**
Witter Publishing Corporation
84 Park Avenue
Suite 32
Flemington, NJ 08822-1172

908-788-0343
Fax: 908-788-3782
Home Page: www.partscleaningweb.com

Andrew Witter, Owner
Frequency: Annual July

18286 **Pipe and Tube Mills of the World with Global Technical Data**
Preston Publishing Company
715 S Sheridan Rd
Tulsa, OK 74112-3139

918-834-2356
Fax: 918-299-4795
E-Mail: preston@webzone.net
Home Page: www.prestonpipe.com

Richard Preston, Owner
LaSondra L O'Farrell, President

We also have a monthly trade journal The Preston Pipe and Tube Report.
Cost: $245.00
842 Pages
Frequency: BiAnnual
Founded in 1995
Printed in one color on matte stock

18287 **Powder Metallurgy Suppliers Directory**
Metal Powder Industries Federation
105 College Rd East
Princeton, NJ 08540-6692

609-452-7700
Fax: 609-987-8523
E-Mail: info@mpif.org
Home Page: www.mpif.org

Michael Lutheran, President
Jim Adams, Director, Technical Services
C. James Trombino, Executive Director, CEO
Jillaine K. Regan, VP, Finance & Administration
Jessica Tamasi, Advertising & Exhibit Manager

Over 50 producers and suppliers of metal powder who belong to the Metal Powder Producers Association or Refractory Metals Association.
210 Members
Frequency: Paperback
Founded in 1944

18288 **Precision Cleaning: Master Source Buyer's Guide**
Witter Publishing Corporation
84 Park Avenue
Suite 32
Flemington, NJ 08822-1172

908-788-0343
Fax: 908-788-3782
Home Page: www.precisioncleaningweb.com

Andrew Witter, Owner
Frequency: Annual

18289 **Purchasing Magazine**
Reed Business Information
275 Washington St
Newton, MA 02458-1611

617-964-3030
Fax: 617-558-4327
E-Mail: support@designnews.com
Home Page: www.designnews.com

About 1,800 metal producers, distributors, die casters, foundries, forgers, coil coaters and powder metals.
Cost: $15.00
Frequency: Annual

18290 **Reference Book for Metal Working Machinery**
Machinery Dealers National Association
1110 Spring St
Silver Spring, MD 20910-4019

301-585-9496
800-872-7807
Fax: 301-588-7830

Nearly 1,000 metal working machine tool manufacturers; international coverage.
Cost: $75.00

18291 **Serial Number Reference Book**
Machinery Dealers National Association
315 S Patrick St
Alexandria, VA 22314-3532

703-836-9300
800-872-7807
Fax: 703-836-9303
E-Mail: office@mdna.org
Home Page: www.mdna.org

Mark Robinson, Executive VP
Richard Levy CEA, President

Sourcebook for metalworking machinery has been designed to lead the reader as quickly as possible to the specific serial number/age information he is seeking.
Cost: $29.95
778 Pages

18292 **Silver Refiners of the World and their Identifying Ingot Marks**
Silver Institute
1112 16th St Nw
Suite 240
Washington, DC 20036-4818

202-347-8200
Home Page: www.silverinstitute.org

Over 80 refiners in over 18 countries are profiled.
Cost: $33.00
85 Pages

18293 **Welding Design & Fabrication**
Penton Media
1166 Avenue of the Americas/10th Fl
New York, NY 10036

212-204-4200
Fax: 216-696-6662
E-Mail: information@penton.com
Home Page: www.penton.com

Jane Cooper, Marketing
Chris Meyer, Director, Corporate Communications

For owner operators and managers of professional welding shops.
Frequency: Annual, December

18294 **Who's Who in Powder Metallurgy Membership Directory**
Metal Powder Industries Federation
105 College Rd East
Princeton, NJ 08540-6692

609-452-7700
Fax: 609-987-8523

E-Mail: info@mpif.org
Home Page: www.mpif.org

Michael Lutheran, President
Jim Adams, Director, Technical Services
C. James Trombino, Executive Director, CEO
Jillaine K. Regan, VP, Finance & Administration
Jessica Tamasi, Advertising & Exhibit Manager

An annual listing of the members of the APMI International and the Metal Powder Industries Federation.
Cost: $105.00
210 Members
88 Pages
Frequency: Annual
ISSN: 0361-6304
Founded in 1944

Industry Web Sites

18295 **http://gold.greyhouse.com**
G.O.L.D Grey House OnLine Databases
Grey House Publishing's online database platform, GOLD, offers Quick Search, Keyword Search and Expert Search for most business sectors including metals and metalworking markets. The GOLD platform makes finding the information you need quick and easy - whether you're a novice searcher or an experienced database user. All of Grey House's directory products are available for subscription on the GOLD platform.

18296 **www.ace.org**
Aluminum Extruders Council
An international trade association representing aluminum extruders.

18297 **www.aimcal.org**
Association of Industrial Metallizers, Coaters
and Laminators

Packaging equipment.

18298 **www.aisc.org**
American Institute of Steel Construction
Nonprofit trade association and technical institute established to serve the structural steel industry in the US. Our purpose is to promote the use of structural steel through research activities, market development, education, codes and specifacations, technical assistance, quality certifacation and standardization.

18299 **www.aise.org**
Association of Iron & Steel Engineers
Production and processing of iron and steel.

18300 **www.amea.org**
Association of Machinery and Equipment Appraisers
Members are appraisers of the metalworking industry.

18301 **www.asminternational.org**
ASM International provides information and networking for metals and materials professionals through its website.

18302 **www.aws.org**
American Welding Society

18303 **www.cbsa.copper-brass.org**
Copper and Brass Servicenter Association
Distributors of fabricated copper and copperalloy products, Sheets,plate, coil, rod, bar, pipe, tubing, etc.

18304 **www.cmadc.org**
Closure Manufacturers Association
Conducts public relations for member companies and establishes idustry standards.

18305 **www.coilcoaters.org**
National Coil Coaters Association

18306 **www.construction.com**
McGraw-Hill Construction
McGraw-Hill Construction (MHC), part of The McGraw-Hill Companies, connects people and projects across the design and construction industry, serving owners, architects, engineers, general contractors, subcontractors, building product manufacturers, suppliers, dealers, distributors and adjacent markets.

18307 **www.copper.org**
Copper Development Association
Seeks to expand the uses and applications of copper and copper products. Responsible for industry-wide market statistics and research.

18308 **www.ductile.org**
Ductile Iron Society
A technical society servicing the ductile iron industry. To advance the technology, art, science of ductile iron production and to disseminate all such information to the members.

18309 **www.emcw.org**
Electrical Manufacturing & Coil Winding Assn
Promotes welfare of the motor and coil industry. Offers courses and workshops.

18310 **www.fmanet.org**
Fabricators and Manufacturers Association
FMA is an educational association serving the metal forming and fabricating industry. Technology areas include sheet metal fabrucating, stamping, roll forming, coil processing, punching, and plate structural fabricating.

18311 **www.forengineers.org/wrc**
Welding Research Council
Coordinates welding research.

18312 **www.greyhouse.com**
Grey House Publishing
Authoritative reference directories for most business sectors, incluidng metal and metalworking markets. Users can search the online databases with varied search criteria allowing for custom searches by product category, geographic area, sales volume, keyword, subject and more. Full Grey House catalog and online ordering also available.

18313 **www.ilzro.org**
International Lead Zinc Research Organization
For miners, smelters and refiners of lead and zinc. Supports research and developement of new uses for the metals and refinement existing uses.

18314 **www.intlmag.org**
International Magnesium Association
Develops international use and acceptance of magnesium metal and its alloys in all product forms. Members are organizations or individuals engaged in the production, manufacture or marketing of metallic magnesium or those supplying materials, equipment or consulting.

18315 **www.ipmi.org**
International Precious Metals Institute
Miners, refiners, producers and users of precious metals, as well as research scientists and mercantilists.

18316 **www.iss.org**
Iron & Steel Society
Seeks to be the premier professional and technical society serving its members and advancing knowledge exchange in the global iron and steel industry. Publishes a monthly magazine.

18317 **www.mbcea.org**
Metal Building Contractors & Erectors Association
To support the professional advancement of metal building contractors, erectors, and the industry.

18318 **www.mdna.org**
Machinery Dealers National Association

18319 **www.metalforming.com**
Precision Metalforming Association
For producers of metal stampings, spinnings, washers and precision sheet metal fabrications as well as suppliers of equipment, materials and services.

18320 **www.mfgtech.org**
Association for Manufacturing Technology

18321 **www.mhia.org**
Material Handling Institute
Promotes the market and develops a code of ethics. Serves as liaison among members and other groups.

18322 **www.mmsa.net**
Mining and Metallurgical Society of America
A professional organization dedicated to increasing public awareness and understanding about mining and why mined materials are essential to modern society and human well being.

18323 **www.mpif.org**
Metal Powder Industries Federation
Promotes the science and industry of powder metallurgy through technical meetings, seminars, conferences, and publications.

18324 **www.naad.org**
National Association of Aluminum Distributors
NAAD is the trade association of North American service centers and principal suppliers engaged in marketing aluminum products.

18325 **www.nffs.org**
Non-Ferrous Founder's Society
Manufacturers of bronze, brass and aluminum castings.

18326 **www.nwsa.com**
Fernley & Fernley

18327 **www.powdercoating.org**
Powder Coating Institute

18328 **www.scra.org/amc/tfa**
Ferroalloys Association
Promotes the ferroalloy industry in the areas of technology, international trade, environment and health, safety and government relations.

18329 **www.sdi.org**
Steel Deck Institute
Trade association providing uniform industry standards for the engineering, design, manufacture and field usage of steel decks.

18330 **www.silversmithing.com**
Society of American Silversmiths
Founded to preserve the art and history of handcrafted holloware and flatware plus provide support, networking and greater access to

the market forsilversmiths. Educates the public as to the aesthetic and investment value of this art form.

18331 www.smacna.org
Sheet Metal and Air Conditioning Contactor's Natl

An international trade association representing 4,500 contibuting contractor firms in the sheet metal and air conditioning industry. Develops technical standards and manuals addressing all facets of the sheet metal and air conditioning industry.

18332 www.spfa.org
Steel Plate Fabricators Association

18333 www.ssci.org
Steel Service Center Institute

18334 www.steel.org
American Iron and Steel Institute

Works to protect interests of manufacturers in the steel industry.

18335 www.steeldistributors.org/asd
Association of Steel Distributors

Bestows Steel Distributor of The Year Award and the Presidents Award of Merit.

18336 www.steelnews.com
Association for Iron and Steel Technology (AIST)

SteelNews.com is a publication created by the Association for Iron and Steel Technology (AIST) for the steel community. The site features daily updates of the latest global headlines.

18337 www.steeltubeinstitute.org
Steel Tube Institute of North America

Members produce steel tubes and pipes from carbon, stainless or alloy steel, for applications ranging from large structural tubing to small redrawn tubing.

18338 www.sweets.construction.com
McGraw Hill Construction

In depth product information that lets you find, compare, select, specify and make purchase decisions in the industrial product marketplace.

18339 www.taol.com/uscti
United States Cutting Tool Institute

For those in the domestic cutting tool market.

18340 www.thermalspray.org
International Thermal Spray Association

Strengthens the level of awareness in general industry and government on the increasing capabilities and advantages of thermal spray technology for surface engineering through business opportunities, technical support and a social network. Contributes to growth and education in the thermal spray industry.

18341 www.titanium.org
International Titanium Association

Contact ITA for mailing list price.

18342 www.uschamber.org/chamber/mall
Silver Users Association

Represents the interests of corporations that make, sell and distribute products and services in which silver is an essential part. SUA membership includes representatives from the photographic, electronic, silverware and jewelry industries; producers of semi-fabricated and industrial products; and, mirror manufacturers.

18343 www.wirenet.org
Wire Association International

Technical association serving the global wire and cable industry by providing educational materials, sponsoring trade shows and international technical conferences.

18344 www.zinc.org
American Zinc Association

Provides information on the zine industry and hosts international conference on zinc.

Associations

18345 Alabama Surface Mining Commission
PO Box 2390
Jasper, AL 35502

205-221-4130
Fax: 205-221-5077
E-Mail: asmc@asmc.alabama.gov
Home Page: www.surface-mining.state.al.us

Dr. Randall C. Johnson, Director
Ann Miles, Executive Secretary
Carla D.Lightsey, Chief Divison of SMCR
Milton McCarthy, Legal Division

Doing its part to balance civilization's demands for natural resources and environmental conservation in the state of Alabama.
Founded in 1972

18346 Alaska Miners Association
3305 Arctic Blvd
Suite 105
Anchorage, AK 99303-4375

907-563-9229
Fax: 907-563-9225
E-Mail: ama@alaskaminers.org
Home Page: www.alaskaminers.org

Steven Borell, Executive Director

Works to promote the mining industry in Alaska. It advocates the development and use of Alaska's mineral resources to provide an economic base for the State. AMA monitors the activities of State and Federal Government, Congress and the Legislature that affect mineral development.

18347 American Association for Crystal Growth
6986 S. Wadsworth Court
Litteton, CO 80128

303-539-6907
Fax: 303-482-2775
E-Mail: AACG@comcast.net
Home Page: www.crystalgrowth.org

Anthony L Gentile, Executive Administrator
David Bliss, Chairman
Russ Dupuis, Chair

AACG is a nonprofit technical membership organization where the primary function is a organic conference in the fall of crystal growth and characterization. A newsletter is published 3 times per year and distributed to members.
600 Members
Founded in 1966

18348 American Coal Ash Association
15200 E Girard Ave
Suite 3050
Aurora, CO 80014-3955

720-870-7897
Fax: 720-870-7889
E-Mail: info@acaa-usa.org
Home Page: www.acaa-usa.org

Thomas H Adams, Executive Director

To advance the management and use of coal combustion products in ways that are environmentally responsible, technically sound, commercially competitive, and supportive of a sustainable global community
126 Members
Founded in 1968

18349 American Exploration and Mining Association
10 N Post St
Suite 305
Spokane, WA 99201-0722

509-624-1158
Fax: 509-623-1241
E-Mail: info@miningamerica.org
Home Page: www.miningamerica.org

Joe Baird, President
Rich DeLong, 1st Vice President
Richard Brown, 2nd Vice President
Peter G. Scott, Secretary
Laura Skaer, Executive Director

Provides liaison between mining, industry and government. Offers short course on current technology.
2000 Members
Founded in 1890

18350 American Geosciences Institute
4220 King St
Alexandria, VA 22302-1502

703-379-2480
Fax: 703-379-7563
E-Mail: keane@agiweb.org
Home Page: www.agiweb.org
Social Media: Facebook, Twitter

P.Patrick Leahy, Executive Director
Dr. Wayne D. Pennington, President
Dr. Sharon Mosher, President Elect
Ann Benow, Outreach and Development Director
Walter R.Sisson, Finance and administrator Director

A nonprofit federation of 45 geoscientific and professional associations that represents more than 120,000 geologists, geophysicists, and other earth scientists.
45 Members
Founded in 1948

18351 American Institute of Mining, Metallurgical & Petroleum Engineers
12999 East Adam Aircraft Circle
Eglewood, CO 80112-5991

303-325-5185
Fax: 888-702-0049
Home Page: www.aimehq.org
Social Media: Facebook, LinkedIn, YouTube

Brajendra Mishra, President
George Luxbacher, President-Elect
Randy Skagen, Treasurer
L. Michele Lawrie-Munro, Executive Director

Supporting member societies by exercising fiscal responsibility, distributing funds, facilitating interaction with the larger scientific and engineering community, enhancing collaboration among the member societies, and honoring the legacy and traditions of AIME.
130M Members
Founded in 1871

18352 American Institute of Professional Geologists
1200 Washington St.
Thornton, CO 80241-3134

303-412-6205
Fax: 303-253-9220
E-Mail: aipg@aipg.org
Home Page: www.aipg.org
Social Media: Facebook, LinkedIn

William J Siok, Executive Director
Wendy J.Davidson, Assistant Director
Cathy L.Duran, Professional Services
Cristie J.Valero, Office Assistant
Vickie Hill, Membership Services

Founded to certify the credentials of practicing geologists and to advocate on behalf of the profession.
5000 Members
Founded in 1963

18353 Arizona Mining Association
5150 N 16th Street
Suite B-134
Phoenix, AZ 85016-3900

602-266-4416
Fax: 602-230-8413
Home Page: www.azcu.org

Sydney Hay, President
June Castelhano, Administrative Assistant

Recognizes the importance of educating Arizona's citizens about the critical role the mining industry plays not only in our state and nation, but also in the world.
Founded in 1965

18354 Arizona State Mine Inspectors
1700 West Washington
4th Floor
Phoenix, AZ 85007-4655

602-542-5971
Fax: 602-542-5335
E-Mail: admin@mi.state.az.us
Home Page: www.asmi.az.gov

John Stanford, Sr.Deputy Mine Inspector
Tim Evans, Assistant State Mine Inspector
Jack Speer, Deputy Mine Inspector Reclamation
Wiiliam Schifferns, Deputy Mine Inspector

Priority mission is to enforce state mining laws which protect mine employees, residents, and the Arizona environment. Focused on providing the best customer service to Arizona residents and mining enterprises.
330 Members
Founded in 1912

18355 Association for Mineral Exploration British Columbia
889 W Pender Street
Suite 800
Vancouver, BC V6C-3B2

604-689-5271
Fax: 604-681-2363
E-Mail: info@amebc.ca
Home Page: www.amebc.ca
Social Media: Facebook, Twitter

Gavin C Dirom, President/CEO
Rick Conte, Vice President
Michael Mcphie, Chair
Andrew Davies, Vice Chair
Sam Adkins, Director

AME BC is the predominant voice of mineral exploration and development in British Columbia.
5400 Members
Founded in 1912

18356 Association of Bituminous Contractors
1250 Eye St NW
Suite 620
Washington, DC 20005-5976

202-296-5745
Fax: 202-331-8049

William H Howe, President

Members are general and independent contractors constructing coal mines and coal mine facilities and also bargains with the United Mine Workers.
150 Members
Frequency: Annual/March

18357 Association of Equipment Manufacturers
10 S Riverside Plaza
Suite 1220
Chicago, IL 60606-3710

312-321-1470
Fax: 312-321-1480
E-Mail: aem@aem.org

James Ebbinghaus, VP

Representing manufacturers of architectural, construction, forestry, materials handling and liabilty equipment.

18358 Bureau of Land Management
1849 C Street NW
Room 5665
Washington, DC 20240

202-208-3801
Fax: 202-208-5242
Home Page: www.blm.gov

Ted Bingham, President
Robert C Bruce, VP

18359 California Mining Association
1029 J Street
Suite 420
Sacramento, CA 95814

916-554-1000
E-Mail: spridmore@calcima.org
Home Page: www.calmining.org

Adam Harper, Association Manager
Stephanie Pridmore, Association Administrator

Represents the breadth and depth of California's mining industry including producers of precious metals (such as gold and silver), industrial minerals (including borates, limestone, rare earth elements, clays, gypsum and tungsten) and rock, sand and gravel.

18360 Canadian Institute of Mining, Metallurgy and Petroleum
3400 de Maisonneuve Boulevard W
Suite 1250
Westmount, QC H3Z-3C1

514-939-2710
Fax: 514-939-2714
E-Mail: cim@cim.org
Home Page: www.cim.org

Russell E Hallbauer, CIM President
Jean Vavrek, CIM Executive Director

The leading technical society of professionals in the Canadian minerals, metals, materials and energy industries.
12000 Members
Founded in 1898

18361 China Clay Producers Association CCPA
113 Arkwright Landing
Macon, GA 31210

478-757-1211
Fax: 478-757-1949
E-Mail: info@georgiamining.org
Home Page: www.kaolin.com/

Lee Lemke, Executive VP

The mission of the China Clay Producers Association is to promote the common business interest of producers of china clay and the development of coordinated policies, which assure the industry will continue to provide jobs and contribute to the Georgia economy. In addition, objectives also include informing members of proposed legislation, regulatory actions and other matters affecting the kaolin industry, and to maintain the industry's strong community commitment.
Founded in 1978

18362 Colorado Mining Association
216 16th St
Suite 1250
Denver, CO 80202-5161

303-575-9199
Fax: 303-575-9194
E-Mail: colomine@coloradomining.org
Home Page: www.coloradomining.org

Stuart Sanderson, President
Fred J. Menzer, Chairman
William Zisch, Chairman-Elect
Stephen A. Onorofskie, Treasurer

Composed of both small and large enterprises engaged in the exploration for, production and refining of, metals, coal, oil shale, and industrial minerals; firms that manufacture and distribute mining and mineral processing equipment and supplies; and other institutions providing services and supplies to the mineral industry.
Founded in 1876

18363 Copper Development Association
260 Madison Ave
New York, NY 10016-2403

212-251-7200
Fax: 212-251-7234
E-Mail: questions@cda.copper.org
Home Page: www.copper.org
Social Media: Facebook, Twitter

Andrew G Kireta, President & CEO
Victoria Prather, Manager Communications
Michels Harold, VP Technaloy Services
Luis Lozano, Technical Consultant
Lorraine Herzing Mills, VP/Finance/Administration

Promoting the use of copper by communicating the unique attributes that make this sustainable element an essential contributor to the formation of life, to advances in science and technology, and to a higher standard of living worldwide.
75 Members
Founded in 1963

18364 Desert Research Institute
2215 Raggio Pkwy
Reno, NV 89512-1095

775-673-7300
Fax: 775-673-7421
Home Page: www.dri.edu
Social Media: Facebook, Twitter

Stephen G Wells, President

A nonprofit statewide division of the university and community college system of Nevada, DRI pursues a full-time program of basic and applied environmental research on a local, national, and international scale. DRI employees nearly 400 full and part-time staff scientists, technicians, and support personnel.
Founded in 1959

18365 Environmental Information Association
6935 Wisconsin Avenue
Suite 306
Chevy Chase, MD 20815-6112

301-961-4999
888-343-4342
Fax: 301-961-3094
E-Mail: info@eia-usa.org
Home Page: www.eia-usa.org

Brent Kynoch, Managing Director
Kim Goodman, Membership and marketing Manager
Kelly Rut, Development Manager
Nehmesah Israel, Admin Assistant
Chris Gates, Treasurer

Providing the environmental industry with the information needed to remain knowledgeable, responsible, and competitive in the environmental health and safety industry.

18366 Excavation Engineering Associates
1352 SW 175th Street
Seattle, WA 98166

206-248-7388
Fax: 206-244-7994
Home Page: www.expeditionsonline.org
Social Media: Facebook, Twitter, LinkedIn

Estelle Friant, Secretary
James E.Friant, President

Underground excavation.

18367 Federal Mine Safety and Health Review Commission
1331 Pennsylvania Avenue, NW, Suite 520N
Washington, DC 20004-1710

202-434-9900
Fax: 202-434-9906
E-Mail: info@fmshrc.gov
Home Page: www.fmshrc.gov

Richard Baker, Executive Director

Independent adjudicative agency that provides administrative trial and apellate review of legal disputes arising under the Federal Mine Safety and Health Amendments Act of 1977 (mine act).

18368 Geological Society of America
PO Box 9140
Boulder, CO 80301-9140

303-357-1000
800-472-1988
Fax: 303-357-1070
E-Mail: web@geosociety.org
Home Page: www.geosociety.org
Social Media: Facebook, Twitter, LinkedIn, YouTube

John W. Geissman, President
George H. Davis, Vice President
Jonathan G. Price, Treasurer
John W. Hess, Executive Director/ Secretary

Provides access to elements that are essential to the professional growth of earth scientists at all levels of expertise and from all sectors, academic, government, business, and industry. Membership unites thousands of earth scientists from every corner of the globe in a common purpose to study the mysteries of our planet and share scientific findings.
16000 Members
Founded in 1888

18369 Gold Prospectors Association of America
Po Box 891509
Temecula, CA 92589-1509

951-699-4749
800-551-9707
Fax: 951-699-4062
E-Mail: info@goldprospectors.org
Home Page: www.goldprospectors.org

Thomas Massie, CEO

GPAA is the largest recreational gold prospecting club. Owner of The Outdoor Channel, a cable TV channel featuring real outdoors for real people.
35M Members
Founded in 1968

18370 Idaho Mining Association
802 W Bannock St
Suite 301
Boise, ID 83702-5840

208-342-0031
Fax: 208-345-4210
E-Mail: ima@mineidaho.com

Home Page: www.mineidaho.com/
Social Media: Twitter

Kent Watson, President
Randy Vranes, 1st Vice President
Dennis Facer, 2nd Vice President
Jack Lyman, Executive Vice President

Founded to further the interests of Idaho's mining industry and minerals production. Mission is to act as the unified voice for its members to ensure the long-term health and well being of Idaho's mining industry.
Founded in 1903

18371 International Lead Association
17a Welbeck Way
London
+44(0)20 7499 8422
Fax: 44(0)207493 1555
E-Mail: enq@ila-lead.org
Home Page: http://www.ila-lead.org

Nonprofit trade association representing the lead industries in the US and abroad. It collects and distributes information about the users of lead products in industry, vehicles, radioactive waste disposal and noise barriers. Its services are availble, generally free of charge, to anyone interested in the uses of lead and lead products.

18372 Lignite Energy Council
1016 E. Owens Avenue
PO Box 2277
Bismarck, ND 58502-2277

701-258-7117
800-932-7117
Fax: 701-258-2755
E-Mail: lec@lignite.com
Home Page: www.lignite.com
Social Media: Facebook, Twitter, LinkedIn, YouTube

John Dwyer, President/CEO
Alan Hodnik, Chairman
Robert McLennan, Chairman-Elect

Regional Trade Association - promotes policies and activities that maintain a viable lignite industry and enhance development of our regions' lignite resources.
355 Members
Founded in 1974

18373 Mine Safety Institue of America
319 Paintersville Road
Hunker, PA 15139
724-925-5150
E-Mail: sikora.lisa@dol.gov
Home Page: www.miningorganizations.org/msia.htm

Frank Linkous, President
Ronnie Biggerstaff, 1st VP
Joseph Sbaffoni, 2nd VP
William Gerringer, 3rd VP
Gerald E. Davis, Secretary/Treasurer

The objectives of the Mine Safety Institute of America is to provide successful educational programs, safer and healthier working conditions, more productivity in the mining industry, and support of good legislature pertaining to mining.
Founded in 1908

18374 Mine Safety and Health Administration
1100 Wilson Blvd
21st Floor
Arlington, VA 22209-3939

202-693-9400
800-746-1553
Fax: 202-693-9401
Home Page: www.msha.gov

David G Dye, Executive Director

Administers the Federal Mine Safety and Health Act of 1977 (Mine Act) and enforces compliance with mandatory safety and health standards as a means to eliminate fatal accidents; to reduce the frequency and severity of nonfatal accidents, to minimize health hazards and to promote mineral processing operations in the US, regardless of size, employees, commodity mined or method of extraction.

18375 Mineral Economics and Management Society
Colorado School Of Mines
Golden, CO 49931

303-273-3150
Fax: 906-487-2944
Home Page: www.outreach.mines.edu

Patricia Dillon, President

A society for mineral, energy, and natural resource professionals who apply economics, finance and policy analysis to the issues facing the minerals and materials industries. These issues include supply and demand of mineral commodities, international trade in mineral and energy raw materials, environmental issues, natural resource, mineral and energy conservation, and related government policies.
200 Members
Founded in 1991

18376 Mineral Information Institute
12999 E. Adam Aircraft Circle
Englewood, CO 80112

303-948-4236
Fax: 303-948-4265
E-Mail: mii@mii.org
Home Page: www.mii.org

Jaqueline S. Dorr, Manager

Nonprofit organization dedicated to educating youth about the science of minerals and other natural resources and about their importance in our everyday lives.

18377 Minerals, Metals & Materials Society
184 Thorn Hill Road
Warrendale, PA 15086-7514

800-759-4867
800-759-4867
Fax: 724-776-3770
E-Mail: webmaster@tms.org
Home Page: www.tms.org
Social Media: Facebook, LinkedIn

James Robinson, Executive Director
Adrianne Carolla, Deputy Executive Director
Peter DeLuca, Accountant

Dedicated to the development and dissemination of the scientific and engineering knowledge bases for materials-centered technologies.

18378 Mining Foundation of the Southwest
PO Box 42317
Tucson, AZ 85733

520-577-7519
Fax: 520-577-7073
E-Mail: admin@miningfoundationsw.org
Home Page: www.miningfoundationsw.org

Advances the science of mining and related industries by educating members and the public. Annual American Mining Hall of Fame First Saturday in December. A newsletter is published.
92 Members
Founded in 1993

18379 Mining and Metallurgical Society of America
PO Box 810
Boulder, CO 80306-0810

303-444-6032
Fax: 415-897-1380
E-Mail: contactmmsa@mmsa.net
Home Page: www.mmsa.net
Social Media: Facebook, Twitter, LinkedIn

Alan K Burton, Business Manager
Mark leVier, President
Robert Schafer, VP
Kenneth Brunk, Treasurer

Concerned with the conservation of the nation's mineral resources and the best interest of the mining and metallurgical industries.
350 Members
Founded in 1908

18380 National Association of State Land Reclamationists
Coal Research Center/Southern Illinois University
Carbondale, IL 62901-4623

618-536-5521
Fax: 618-453-7346
E-Mail: aharrington@crc.siu.edu
Home Page: www.crc.siu.edu/nasir.htm

Ed Haigler, President
Tom Gragg, Vice President
Anna Harringon Caswell, Secretary/Treasurer

The National Association of State and Land Reclamationists advocates the use of research, innovative technology and professional discourse to foster the restoration of lands and waters affected by mining related activities.
140 Members
Founded in 1972

18381 National Lime Association
200 N Glebe Rd
Suite 800
Arlington, VA 22203-3728

703-243-5463
Fax: 703-243-5489
Home Page: www.lime.org

William C.Herz, Executive Director
Arline Seeger, General Counsel
Hunter Prillaman, Director Of Government Affairs
Robert Hirsch, Director of Environment
Lori D.Oney, Admin Director

Trade association for US and Canadian manufacturers of high calcium quicklime, dolomitic quicklime and hydrated lime, collectively referred to as lime. NLA represents the interests of its members in Washington, provides input on standards and specifications for lime, and funds and manages research on current and new uses for lime.
63 Members
Founded in 1902

18382 National Mining Association
101 Constitution Ave Nw
Suite 500 East
Washington, DC 20001-2133

202-463-2600
Fax: 202-463-2666
E-Mail: webmaster@nma.org
Home Page: www.nma.org

Craig Naaz, President
Carol L Raulston, Senior VP
Connie Holmes, Executive Director

Membership within the National Mining Association includes corporations involved in all aspects of the mining industry including coal, metal and industrial mineral producers, mineral processors, equipment manufacturers, state associations, bulk transporters, engineering firms, consultants, financial institutions and other companies that supply goods and services to the mining industry.
325 Members
Founded in 1995

18383 National Ocean Industries Association
1120 G St NW
Suite 900
Washington, DC 20005-3801

202-347-6900
Fax: 202-347-8650
Home Page: www.noia.org
Social Media: Facebook, Twitter, LinkedIn, YouTube

Randall Luthi, President
Franki Stuntz, Sr.VP

National organization engaged in offshore construction, drilling and petroleum production, geophysical exploration, ship building and repair, deep-sea mining and related activities in the development and use of marine resources.
300 Members
Founded in 1972

18384 National Ready Mixed Concrete Association
900 Spring St
Silver Spring, MD 20910-4015

240-485-1139
Fax: 301-585-4219
E-Mail: info@nrmca.org
Home Page: www.nrmca.org
Social Media: Facebook, LinkedIn, YouTube

Robert Garbini, President
Deana Angelastro, Executive Administrator

The mission of the National Ready Mixed Concrete Association is to provide exceptional value for our members by responsibly representing and serving the entire ready mixed concrete industry through leadership, promotion, education, and partnering to ensure ready mixed concrete is the building material of choice.
1200 Members
Founded in 1930

18385 National Stone, Sand & Gravel Association
1605 King St
Alexandria, VA 22314-2726

703-525-8788
800-342-1415
Fax: 703-525-7782
E-Mail: jwilson@nssga.org
Home Page: www.nssga.org

Jennifer Joy Wilson, President & CEO
Gus Edwards, Executive Vice President
Janice B. Springs, Executive Assistant

Represents the stone, sand and gravel — or aggregate — industries. Our members account for 90 percent of the crushed stone and 70 percent of the sand and gravel produced annually in the US.
25 Members
Founded in 1916

18386 Nevada Mining Association
201 W. Liberty Street
Suite 300
Reno, NV 89501

775-829-2121
Fax: 775-852-2631
Home Page: www.nevadamining.org
Social Media: Facebook, Twitter, YouTube

Tim Crowley, President
Dylan Shaver, Public Affairs
Lauren Arends, Office Manager
Joseph Riney, Information System Administrator

Represents all aspects of the mining industry. Provides representation for the broad mining industry in public outreach activities such as public relations, media relations, and community relations.

18387 North American Insulation Manufacturers Association
44 Canal Center Plaza
Suite 310
Alexandria, VA 22314

703-684-0084
Fax: 703-684-0427
Home Page: www.naima.org

Jeff Templeton, Chairman
Jeffrey Brisley, Vice Chairman
Kate Offringa, President & CEO/ Treasurer
Angus Crane, Executive Vice President

An authoritative resource on energy-efficiency, sustainable performance, and the application and safety of fiber glass, rock wool, and slag wool insulation products. The voice of the insulation industry for architects and builders, design, process and maintenance engineers, contractors, code groups and standards organizations, government agencies, public interest, energy and environmental groups, and homeowners.

18388 Perlite Institute
4305 North 6th Street
Suite A
Harrisburg, PA 17110

717-238-9723
Fax: 717-238-9985
E-Mail: info@perlite.org
Home Page: www.perlite.org

Kathryn Liu, President
Linda Chirico, Vice President
Paul Dunlavey, Secretary/Treasurer
Denise Calabrese, Executive Director

An international association which establishes product standards and specifications, and which encourages the development of new product uses through research.
183 Members
Founded in 1949

18389 Rocky Mountain Association of Geologists
Ste 1125
910 16th St
Denver, CO 80202-2997

303-573-8621
Fax: 303-628-0546
E-Mail: rmagdenver@aol.com
Home Page: www.rmag.org

Donna Anderson, President
Mark Sonnenfeld, First VP
Jewel Wellborn, Second VP
Sandi Pillissier, Executive Director
2200 Members
Founded in 1922

18390 Silver Institute
1400 I Street, NW
Suite 550
Washington, DC 20005

202-835-0185
Fax: 202-835-0155
E-Mail: info@silverinstitute.org
Home Page: www.silverinstitute.org

Robert Quartermain, President
Michael Dirienzo, Executive Director

International association of miners, refiners, fabricators and wholesalers of silver and silver products.

18391 Silver Users Association
3930 walnut Street
Suite 210
Fairfax, VA 22030

703-930-7790
Fax: 703-359-7562
E-Mail: pmiller@mwcapitol.com
Home Page: www.silverusersassociation.org

Bill Le Roy, President
Mike Huber, VP
John King, Secretary
Bill Hamelin, Treasurer
29 Members
Founded in 1947

18392 Silver Valley Mining Association
604 Bank St.
Wallace, ID 83873

208-556-1621
Home Page: www.silverminers.org

Dedicated to promoting the Silver Valley of northern Idaho and its mining industry. Informs the public of the history and merits of the region, serving various beneficiary needs of the mining industry, and serving those who work in the industry and the investing public.

18393 Society for Mining, Metallurgy & Exploration
12999 E. Adam Aircraft Circle
Englewood, CO 80112

303-948-4200
800-763-3132
Fax: 303-973-3845
E-Mail: sme@smenet.org
Home Page: www.smenet.org
Social Media: Facebook, Twitter, LinkedIn

John N. Murphy, President
Drew A. Meyer, President-Elect

Advances the worldwide mining and minerals community through information exchange and professional development.
13000 Members
Founded in 1957

18394 Society of Economic Geologists
7811 Shaffer Pkwy
Littleton, CO 80127-3732

720-981-7874
Fax: 720-981-7874
E-Mail: seg@segweb.org
Home Page: www.segweb.org
Social Media: Facebook, Twitter, LinkedIn

Brian G Hoal, Executive Director
Virginia S Gillerman, VP

International organization of individual members with interests in the field of economic geology. Membership includes representatives from the industry, academia and government institutions. Annual meetings, publications, field conferences and short courses ensure active communication of economic geology related concepts with the membership and the economic geology profession at large.
3400 Members
Founded in 1920

18395 Society of Exploration Geophysicists
8801 South Yale
Suite 500
Tulsa, OK 74137-3575

918-497-5500
Fax: 918-497-5557
E-Mail: web@seg.org
Home Page: www.seg.org/index.shtml
Social Media: Facebook, Twitter, LinkedIn

Dr. Bob A. Hardage, President
Dr. David James Monk, President-Elect
Dr. Wafik Bulind Beydoun, Vice-President
Nancy Jo House, Secretary/ Treasurer
Dr. Tamas Nemeth, Editor

The Society of Exploration Geophysicists/SEG is a not-for-profit organization that promotes the science of geophysics and the education of applied geophysicists. SEG fosters the expert and ethical practice of geophysics in the explo-

ration and development of natural resources, in characterizing the near surface, and in mitigating earth hazards.
Founded in 1930

18396 Society of Mineral Analysts
PO Box 50085
Sparks, NV 89435-0085
562-467-8980
Home Page: www.sma-online.org
Patrick Brown, Director
The Society of Mineral Analysts is a non-profit organization, whose members are assayers, chemists, laboratory managers, geologists, suppliers and vendors both in and serving the mineral analysis industry.
250 Members
Founded in 1986

18397 Solution Mining Research Institute
105 Apple Valley Circle
Clarks Summit, PA 18411
570 585 8092
Fax: 570-585-8091
E-Mail: smri@solutionmining.org
Home Page: www.solutionmining.org
John O Voight, Executive Director
Carolyn L Diamond, Assistant Executive Director
Members are companies interested in the production of salt brine and solution mining of potash and soda ash, as well as production of slt covers, used for storage of oil, gas, chemicals, compressed air and waste.
100 Members
Founded in 1958

18398 Sorptive Minerals Institute
1155 15th St NW
Suite 500
Washington, DC 20005-2725
202-289-2760
Fax: 202-530-0659
E-Mail: lcoogan@navista.net
Home Page: www.sorptive.org
Lee Coogan, Executive Director
The Sorptive Minerals Institute represents the absorbent clay industry and is a not-for-profit industry trade association that would serve as the marketing, promotion and research arm of the absorbent clay indsutry with the goal of enhancing long-range growth and profitability.
Founded in 1970

18399 Sulphur Institute
1020 19th Street NW, Suite 520
Washington, DC 20036
202-331-9660
Fax: 202-293-2940
E-Mail: sulphur@sulphurinstitute.org
Home Page: www.sulphurinstitute.org
Robert J Morris, President
Thomas W.Dunn, Director
Joshua C.Maak, Communications Manager
Donald S.Messik, V.P,Communications
The Sulphur Institute (TSI) is an international, non-profit organization established in 1960. The Institute is the global advocate for sulphur, representing all stakeholders engaged in producing, consuming, trading, handling or adding value to sulphur. We seek to provide a common voice for all stakeholders to promote the uninterrupted, efficient and safe handling and transportation of all sulphur products while protecting the best interests of the environment
Founded in 1960

18400 US Geological Survey
950 National Ctr
Reston, VA 20192-0001
703-648-4302
Fax: 703-648-6373
E-Mail: dc_va@usgs.gov
Home Page: www.usgs.gov
Founded in 1879

18401 United Mine Workers of America International Union
18354 Quantico Gateway Drive
Suite 200
Triangle, VA 22172
703-291-2400
Fax: 703-208-7227
Home Page: www.umwa.org
Cecil E Roberts, President
Daniel J Kane, Secretary/Treasurer
The United Mine Workers of America International Union is an organization with a diverse membership that includes coal miners, clean coal technicians, health care workers, truck drivers, manufacturing workers and public employees throughout the United States and Canada. The Union works to fight for safe workplaces, good wages and benefits, and fair representation.
120M Members
Founded in 1890

18402 Utah Mining Association
136 S Main St
Suite 709
Salt Lake City, UT 84101-1683
801-364-1874
Fax: 801-364-2640
E-Mail: mining@utahmining.org
Home Page: www.utahmining.org
Mark Compton, President
Robert Frayser, Chairman
Marilyn Tuttle, Office Manager
Provides its members with full-time professional industry representation before the State Legislature; various government regulatory agencies on the federal, state and local levels; other associations, and business and industry groups. Helps to promote and protect the mining industry.
Founded in 1915

18403 Vibrating Screen Manufacturers Association
6737 W Washington Street
Suite 2400
Milwaukee, WI 53214-5650
414-272-0943
866-236-0442
Fax: 414-272-1170
E-Mail: aem@aem.org
Home Page: www.aem.org
Social Media: Twitter
Dennis Slater, President
Al Cervero, Senior VP
AEM is teh international trade and business development resource for companies that manufacture equipment, products andservices used worldwide in the construction, agricultural, minimg, forestry, and utility industries.
8 Members
Founded in 1959

18404 Women in Mining National Organization
PO Box 260246
Lakewood, CO 80226-0246
303-298-1535
866-537-9697
E-Mail: wim@womeninmining.org
Home Page: www.womeninmining.org/aboutwim.htm
Betty Mahaffey, President
Christine Ballard, Vice President
Stephen Tibbals, Treasurer
Hannah McNally, Secretary
Women in Mining/WIM was founded in 1972 in Denver, Colorado, by several women whose intent was to facilitate education about the mining industry for themselves and for those not acquainted with the role the industry plays in their lives. In addition to providing valuable educations benefits, the WIM organization offers members an opportunity to become acquainted and work with others involved in the mining industry and thereby acquire new personal and professional contacts.
600 Members

18405 World Gold Council
510 Madison Ave
9th Floor
New York, NY 10022
212-317-3800
Fax: 212-688-0410
Home Page: www.gold.org
Organization formed and funded by the world's leading gold mining companies with the aim of stimulating and maximizing the demand for, and holding of gold by consumers, investors, industry and the official sector.
Founded in 1987

Newsletters

18406 AME BC News
Assoc for Mineral Exploration British Columbia
889 W Pender Street
Suite 800
Vancouver, BC V6C-3B2
604-689-5271
Fax: 604-681-2363
E-Mail: info@amebc.ca
Home Page: www.amebc.ca
Gavin C Dirom, President/CEO
A member e-newsletter that captures essential mineral exploration and mining news, announces important upcoming events, gives an inside look at what is happening within AME BC, announces new and renewed members and more.
5400 Members
Frequency: Bi-Weekly
Founded in 1912

18407 Alaska Geology Survey News
Alaska Division of Geological Survey
3354 College Rd
Fairbanks, AK 99709-3707
907-451-5000
Fax: 907-451-5050
E-Mail: dggsnews@dnr.state.ak.us
Home Page: www.dggs.dnr.state.ak.us
Robert Swenson, Executive Director
Trudy Wassel, Business Manager
John Parrott, Manager
Alaska miners and earth scientists.
4 Pages
Frequency: Monthly
Printed in on glossy stock

18408 Ash at Work
American Coal Ash Association

15200 E Girard Ave
Suite 3050
Aurora, CO 80014-3955

720-870-7897
Fax: 720-870-7889
E-Mail: info@acaa-usa.org
Home Page: www.acaa-usa.org

Thomas Adams, Executive Director

Association news. non-profit trade association.
160 Members
Frequency: 2x/Year
Founded in 1968
Printed in 4 colors on glossy stock

18409 Bulletin
Northwest Mining Association
10 N Post St
Suite 220
Spokane, WA 99201-0722

509-624-1158
Fax: 509-623-1241
E-Mail: nwma_info@nwma.org
Home Page: www.nwma.org

Laura Skaer, Executive Director
Mike Heywood, Marketing Director

Published every six weeks. 12-16 page newsletter covering issues relevant to the hardrock mining industry.
Circulation: 1500
Founded in 1895

18410 Coal Week International
McGraw Hill
PO Box 182604
Columbus, CO 43272

877-833-5524
800-752-8878
Fax: 614-759-3749
E-Mail: customer.service@mcgraw-hill.com
Home Page: www.mcgraw-hill.com

John Slater, Publisher

Offers information and news to and of the mining industry in North America.
Cost: $467.00
Frequency: Monthly
Founded in 1884

18411 Coaldat Productivity Report
Pasha Publications
1600 Wilson Boulevard
Suite 600
Arlington, VA 22209-2510

703-528-1244
800-424-2908
Fax: 703-528-1253

Harry Baisden, Group Publisher
Michael Hopps, Editor
Kathy Thorne, Circulatin Manager

Shows quarterly and year-to-date total coal production in tons, productivity in tons per miner per day, average number of employees for each mine, mining methods used, controlling company, mine location, district number, union affiliation and whether the mine is surface or underground. Both a controlling company and a state/country format are available.
Cost: $545.00
60 Pages
Frequency: Quarterly

18412 Control
Putman Media Company
555 W Pierce Rd
Suite 301,Pierce Road
Itasca, IL 60143-2626

630-467-1300
Fax: 630-467-0197
E-Mail: jcappelletti@putman.net
Home Page: www.putman.net

John Cappelletti, President
Walter Boies, Circulation Manager

Designed for instrumentation and control systems professionals.
Frequency: Fortnightly
Circulation: 35000
Founded in 1945

18413 Legal Quarterly Digest of Mine Safety and Health Decisions
Legal Publication Services
888 Pittsford Mendon Center Road
Pittsford, NY 14534

585-582-3211
Fax: 585-582-2879
E-Mail: MineSafety@aol.com
Home Page: www.minesafety.com

Ellen Smith, Owner/publisher
Melanie Aclander, Editor

Covers legal decisions on health and safety law in the mining industry.
Cost: $525.00
100 Pages
Frequency: Annual+
Founded in 1991

18414 Machinery Outlook
Manfredi & Associates
20934 W Lakeview Pkwy
Mundelein, IL 60060-9502

847-949-9080
Fax: 847-949-9910
E-Mail: frank@manfredi.com
Home Page: www.machineryoutlook.com

Frank Manfredi, President

A newsletter about and for the construction and mining machinery industry.
Cost: $365.00
14 Pages
Frequency: Monthly
Founded in 1984
Printed in one color on matte stock

18415 Mine Regulation Reporter
Pasha Publications
1600 Wilson Boulevard
Suite 600
Arlington, VA 22209-2509

703-528-1244
800-424-2908
Fax: 703-528-1253

Harry Baisden, Group Publisher
Michael Hopps, Editor
Kathy Thorne, Circulation Manager

The only biweekly newsletter and document service in the US for mine safety and environmental managers and attorneys. It covers mine safety, health and environmental regulations, legislation and court decisions that affect mine operations.
Cost: $785.00
Frequency: BiWeekly

18416 Mining Foundation of the Southwest
PO Box 42317
Tucson, AZ 85733

520-577-7519
Fax: 520-577-7073
E-Mail: admin@miningfoundationsw.org
Home Page: www.miningfoundationsw.org

William Dresher, President
Jean Austin, Office Manager

Advances the science of mining and related industries by educating members and the public. Annual American Mining Hall of Fame First Saturday in December.
90 Pages
Founded in 1973

18417 Mining and Metallurgical Society of America Newsletter
476 Wilson Avenue
Novato, CA 94947-4236

415-897-1380
Fax: 415-899-0262
E-Mail: contactmmsa@mmsa.net
Home Page: www.mmsa.net

Alan K Burton, Executive Director

Society news and information for professionals in the mining industry.
6 Pages
Founded in 1908

18418 Reclamation Matters
American Society of Mining and Reclamation
3134 Montevesta Road
Lexington, KY 40502-3548

859-351-9032
Fax: 859-335-6529
E-Mail: asmr@insightbb.com
Home Page: www.asmr.us
Social Media: Facebook

Dennis Neuman, President
Richard Bamhisel, Executive Secretary

Newsletter of the ASMA. Free to members or $10/year.
500 Members
Founded in 1983

18419 Utah Mining Association Newsletter
Utah Mining Association
136 South Main Street
Suite 709
Salt Lake City, UT 84101-1683

801-364-1874
Fax: 801-364-2640
E-Mail: mining@utahmining.org
Home Page: www.utahmining.org

Todd Bingham, President
Bryan Nielson, Chairman
Marilyn Tuttle, Office Manager

Provides updates on the mining industry.

18420 e-DIGEST & Washington Watch Newsletter
National Stone, Sand & Gravel Association
1605 King St
Alexandria, VA 22314-2726

703-525-8788
800-342-1415
Fax: 703-525-7782
E-Mail: jwilson@nssga.org
Home Page: www.nssga.org

Jennifer Joy Wilson, President & CEO
Gus Edwards, Executive Vice President
Janice B. Springs, Executive Assistant

Member benefit of the NSSGA. Available online only.
25 Members
Frequency: Weekly
Founded in 1916

Magazines & Journals

18421 ASH at Work
American Coal Ash Association
15200 E Girard Ave
Suite 3050
Aurora, CO 80014-3955

720-870-7897
Fax: 720-870-7889
E-Mail: info@acaa-usa.org
Home Page: www.acaa-usa.org

Thomas H Adams, Executive Director

The only magazine covering all facets of the coal combustion products industry. Read by ACAA members and others interested in the use and management of coal combustion products.
126 Members
Frequency: Bi-Annually
Circulation: 10000
Founded in 1968

18422 Alaska Miner
Alaska Miners Association
3305 Arctic Blvd
Suite 105
Anchorage, AK 99503-4575

907-563-9229
Fax: 907-563-9225
E-Mail: ama@alaskaminers.org
Home Page: www.alaskaminers.org

Steven Borell, Executive Director

News and developments regarding Alaskan mining efforts.

18423 Alaska Miners Association Journal
Alaska Miners Association
3305 Arctic Boulevard
Suite 105
Anchorage, AK 99503-4575

907-563-9229
Fax: 907-563-9225
E-Mail: ama@alaskaminers.org
Home Page: www.alaskaminers.org

Steven Borell, Executive Director

18424 CIM Magazine
Canadian Inst of Mining, Metallurgy & Petroleum
3400 de Maisonneuve Boulevard W
Suite 855
Montreal, QC H3Z-3B8

514-939-2710
Fax: 514-939-2714
Home Page: www.cim.org

Dawn Nelley, Publications

Provides important information on mine developments, new technologies, safety, HR, products and services, and business issues.
Frequency: 8x's a Year
Circulation: 11,289

18425 Coal
MacLean Hunter
29 N Wacker Drive
Floor 9
Chicago, IL 60606-3298

312-726-2802
Fax: 312-726-4103

Art Sanda, Editor
Elisabeth O'Grady, Executive Director

Articles cover maintenance and production of coal mines.
Cost: $62.50
Frequency: Monthly
Circulation: 22,000
Founded in 1964

18426 Coal Age
Primedia
29 N Wacker Avenue
10th Floor
Chicago, IL 60606

312-726-2802
Fax: 312-726-2574
Home Page: www.coalage.com

Peter Johnson, Publisher
Stever P Fiscor, Editor-in-Chief
Ben Fromenthal, Production Manager

Geared primarily toward professionals in the coal mining and processing industries. Coal Age focuses on news, with in-depth features on coal mining operations and changing technologies.
Cost: $49.00
54 Pages
Frequency: Monthly
Circulation: 17900
ISSN: 1040-7820
Founded in 1911
Printed in 4 colors on glossy stock

18427 Coal Journal
PO Box 3068
Pikeville, KY 41502-3068

606-432-0206
Fax: 606-432-2162

Terry L May, Publisher

Information concentrating on government regulations, emerging technologies and trade literature, and analyzes governmental actions and their impact on the coal industry.
Frequency: Quarterly
Circulation: 10000

18428 Coal People
Al Skinner Enterprises
PO Box 6247
Charleston, WV 25362-247

304-342-4129
800 235-5188
Fax: 304-343-3124
E-Mail: cpm@newwave.net
Home Page: www.coalpeople.com

Al Skinner, Editor
Christina Karaum, Managing Editor
Beth Terranova, Sales Manager
Angela McNealy, Circulation Manager

Features special news and product sections for the coal industry. Home interest, historical pices, coal industry personalities.
Cost: $25.00
60 Pages
Frequency: 10 times ayear
Circulation: 11500
Founded in 1976
Printed in 4 colors on glossy stock

18429 EARTH Magazine
American Geosciences Institute
4220 King St
Alexandria, VA 22302-1502

703-379-2480
Fax: 703-379-7563
E-Mail: agi@agiweb.org
Home Page: www.earthmagazine.org
Social Media: Facebook, Twitter

Patrick Leahy, Executive Director
Dr. Wayne D. Pennington, President
Dr. Sharon Mosher, President Elect
Michael D. Lawless, Treasurer
Dr. Berry H. Tew, Jr., Secretary

The science behind the headlines.
Frequency: Monthly
Founded in 1948

18430 Engineering & Mining Journal
Primedia Publishing
330 N Wabash Avenue
Suite 2300
Chicago, IL 60611

312-595-1080
Fax: 312-595-0295
E-Mail: info@mining-media.com
Home Page: www.e-mj.com

Peter Johnson, Publisher
Steve Fiscor, Editor

Serves the field of mining including exploration, development, milling, smelting, refining of metals and nonmetallics
108 Pages
Frequency: Monthly
Circulation: 20589
ISSN: 0095-8948
Founded in 1866
Printed in 4 colors on glossy stock

18431 Environmental & Engineering Geoscience
Geological Society of America
PO Box 9140
Boulder, CO 80301-9140

303-357-1019
800-472-1988
Fax: 303-357-1070
E-Mail: gsa@geosociety.org
Home Page: www.geosociety.org
Social Media: Facebook, Twitter, LinkedIn, YouTube

John W. Geissman, President
George H. Davis, Vice President
Jonathan G. Price, Treasurer
John W. Hess, Executive Director/ Secretary

Contains new theory, applications, and case histories illustrating the dynamics of the fast-growing environmental and applied disciplines.
16000 Members
Frequency: Quarterly
Founded in 1888

18432 GSA Today
Geological Society of America
PO Box 9140
Boulder, CO 80301-9140

303-357-1019
800-472-1988
Fax: 303-357-1070
E-Mail: gsa@geosociety.org
Home Page: www.geosociety.org
Social Media: Facebook, Twitter, LinkedIn, YouTube

John W. Geissman, President
George H. Davis, Vice President
Jonathan G. Price, Treasurer
John W. Hess, Executive Director/ Secretary

Lead science articles are refereed and should present the results of exciting new research or summarize and synthesize important problems or issues.
16000 Members
Frequency: Monthly
Founded in 1888

18433 Geology
Geological Society of America
PO Box 9140
Boulder, CO 80301-9140

303-357-1019
800-472-1988
Fax: 303-357-1070
E-Mail: gsa@geosociety.org
Home Page: www.geosociety.org
Social Media: Facebook, Twitter, LinkedIn, YouTube

John W. Geissman, President
George H. Davis, Vice President
Jonathan G. Price, Treasurer
John W. Hess, Executive Director/ Secretary

Articles cover all earth-science disciplines and include new investigations and provocative topics. Professional geologists and university-level students in the earth sciences use this widely read journal to keep up with scientific research trends.
16000 Members
Frequency: Monthly
Founded in 1888

18434 Geophysics
Society of Exploration Geophysicists

8801 South Yale
Suite 500
Tulsa, OK 74137-3575

918-497-5500
Fax: 918-497-5557
E-Mail: web@seg.org
Home Page: www.seg.org/index.shtml
Social Media: Facebook, Twitter, LinkedIn

Dr. Bob A. Hardage, President
Dr. David James Monk, President-Elect
Dr. Wafik Bulind Beydoun, Vice-President
Nancy Jo House, Secretary/ Treasurer
Dr. Tamas Nemeth, Editor

Encompasses all aspects of research, exploration, and education in applied geophysics.
Founded in 1930

18435 Geosphere
Geological Society of America
PO Box 9140
Boulder, CO 80301-9140

303-357-1019
800-472-1988
Fax: 303-357-1070
E-Mail: gsa@geosociety.org
Home Page: www.geosociety.org
Social Media: Facebook, Twitter, LinkedIn, YouTube

John W. Geissman, President
George H. Davis, Vice President
Jonathan G. Price, Treasurer
John W. Hess, Executive Director/ Secretary

Electronic journal, peer-reviewed covering all geoscience disciplines in a medium that accommodates animations, sound, and movie files.
16000 Members
Frequency: Bimonthly
Founded in 1888

18436 Geotimes
American Geological Institute
4220 King St
Alexandria, VA 22302-1502

703-379-2480
Fax: 703-379-7563
Home Page: www.agiweb.org/
Social Media: Facebook, Twitter

Dr. Wayne D. Pennington, President
Dr. Sharon Mosher, President Elect
Michael D. Lawless, Treasurer
Dr. Berry H. Tew, Jr., Secretary

Nonprofit federation of 40 geoscientific and professional associations that represents more than 100,000 geologists, geophysicsts, and other earth scientists. AGI provides information services to geoscientists, serves as a voice of shared interests in our profession, plays a major role in strengthening geoscience education, and strives to increase public awareness of the vital role the geosciences play in society's use of resources and interaction with the environment.
Cost: $42.95
250M Members
40 Pages
Frequency: Monthly
Circulation: 100000
Founded in 1948

18437 Hydrogeology Journal
Geological Society of America
PO Box 9140
Boulder, CO 80301-9140

303-357-1019
800-472-1988
Fax: 303-357-1070
E-Mail: gsa@geosociety.org
Home Page: www.geosociety.org
Social Media: Facebook, Twitter, LinkedIn, YouTube

John W. Geissman, President
George H. Davis, Vice President
Jonathan G. Price, Treasurer
John W. Hess, Executive Director/ Secretary

Features peer-reviewed papers on theoretical and applied hydrogeology. Describes worldwide progress in the science integrating subsurface hydrology and geology with supporting disciplines.
16000 Members
Frequency: Bi-Monthly
Founded in 1888

18438 JOM: The Member Journal of TMS
Minerals, Metals & Minerals Society
184 Thorn Hill Road
Warrendale, PA 15086-7514

724-776-9000
800-759-4867
724-776-9000
Fax: 724-776-3770
E-Mail: tmsgeneral@tms.org
Home Page: www.tms.org
Social Media: Facebook, LinkedIn

Garry W. Warren, President
Wolfgang A. Schneider, Vice President
Warren Hunt, Jr., Secretary/ Executive Director
Adrian C. Deneys, Director/ Chair

A technical journal devoted to exploring the many aspects of materials science and engineering. Reports scholarly work that explores the state-of-the-art processing, fabrication, design, and application of metals, ceramics, plastics, composites, and other materials.
Cost: $131.00
Frequency: Monthly
Circulation: 10000
Founded in 1948

18439 Journal of Electronic Materials
Minerals, Metals & Materials Society
184 Thorn Hill Road
Warrendale, PA 15086-7514

800-759-4867
Fax: 724-776-3770
E-Mail: webmaster@tms.org
Home Page: www.tms.org
Social Media: Facebook, LinkedIn

Reports on the science and technology of electronic materials while examining new applications for semiconductors, magnetic alloys, insulators, and optical and display materials.
Frequency: Monthly

18440 Lithosphere
Geological Society of America
PO Box 9140
Boulder, CO 80301-9140

303-357-1019
800-472-1988
Fax: 303-357-1070
E-Mail: gsa@geosociety.org
Home Page: www.geosociety.org
Social Media: Facebook, Twitter, LinkedIn, YouTube

John W. Geissman, President
George H. Davis, Vice President
Jonathan G. Price, Treasurer
John W. Hess, Executive Director/ Secretary

Peer-reviewed journal focusing on processes that affect the crust, upper mantle, landscapes, and/or sedimentary systems at all spatial and temporal scales.
16000 Members
Frequency: Bimonthly
Founded in 1888

18441 Metallurgical and Materials Transactions
Minerals, Metals & Materials Society
184 Thorn Hill Road
Warrendale, PA 15086-7514

800-759-4867
Fax: 724-776-3770
E-Mail: webmaster@tms.org
Home Page: www.tms.org
Social Media: Facebook, LinkedIn

Highly respected, peer-reviewed journals for metallurgy and materials science.
Frequency: Monthly

18442 Mine Safety and Health News
Legal Publication Services
888 Pittsford Mendon Center Road
Pittsford, NY 14534

585-582-3211
Fax: 585-582-2879
E-Mail: MineSafety@aol.com
Home Page: www.minesafety.com

Ellen Smith, Owner
Melanie Aclander, Editor
Cost: $525.00
Founded in 1991

18443 Mine and Quarry Trader
Primedia
7355 N Woodland Drive
PO Box 603
Indianapolis, IN 46206

317-991-1350
800-827-7468
Fax: 317-299-1356
Home Page: www.mineandquarry.com

John Owen, Production Manager
Colleen Leath, Circulation Director
Kyle Agert, Publisher
Laura Larahaag, Marketing
Ellen Rolett, Manager

Equipment and services geared to the mining, aggregate and heavy construction industries.
Cost: $21.00
76 Pages
Frequency: Monthly
Circulation: 34406
Founded in 1976
Printed in 4 colors on matte stock

18444 Miners News
Miners News
9792 W Glen Ellyn Street
PO Box 4965
Boise, ID 83711

800-624-7212
Fax: 208-658-4901
E-Mail: minersnews@msn.com
Home Page: www.minersnews.com

Gary White, Publisher
Shirley White, Public Relations

Information on mining history and provides insight into new technology and products used in mining.
Cost: $25.00
Circulation: 6512
ISSN: 0890-6157
Founded in 1985

18445 Mines Magazine
Colorado School of Mines Alumni Association
1600 Arapahoe Street
PO Box 1410
Golden, CO 80402

303-733-3143
Fax: 303-273-3583
E-Mail: magazine@mines.edu

Home Page: www.minesmagazine.com
Social Media: Facebook, Twitter, LinkedIn

Nick Sutcliffe, Editor
Anita Pariseau, CEO/President
Amie Chitwood, Manager
Heidi Boersma, Administrative Assistant

Mines magazine is a critical communication serving the Colorado School of Mines community. Its mission is to keep readers informed about the school, to further the goals of the school and the alumni association, and to foster connectedness.
Cost: $35.00
Frequency: Quarterly
Circulation: 20000
Founded in 1910
Printed in 4 colors on glossy stock

18446 Mining Record
Mining Record Company
PO Box 1630
Castle Rock, CO 80104-6130

303-888-8871
800-441-4708
Fax: 303-663-7823
E-Mail: customerservice@miningrecord.com
Home Page: www.miningrecord.com

Don E Howell, Editor
Dale Howell, Marketing

Has been in continuous publication for 115 years and is recognized as the industry's leading newspaper. Focuses on timely and credible news reporting on exploration, discovery, development, production, joint ventures, acquisitions, operating results, legislation, government reports and metals prices. Its readership is concentrated in the mining industry proper; mining companies and all individuals engaged in large or small mine production.
Cost: $45.00
16 Pages
Frequency: Monthly
Circulation: 5100
ISSN: 0026-5241
Founded in 1889
Printed in on newsprint stock

18447 New Equipment Digest
Penton Media
1300 E 9th St
Suite 316
Cleveland, OH 44114-1503

216-696-7000
Fax: 216-696-6662
E-Mail: information@penton.com
Home Page: www.pentonmsc.com

Jane Cooper, Marketing
Jennifer Daugherty, Communications Manager
John DiPaola, Group Publisher
Robert F King, Editor
Bobbie Macy, Circulation Manager

Serves the general industrial field which includes manufacturing, processing, engineering services, construction, transportation, mining, public utilities, wholesale distributors, educational services, libraries, and governmental establishments.
Cost: $65.00
Frequency: Monthly
Circulation: 206000
Founded in 1892

18448 North American Mining
Mining Media
1005 Terminal Way
#140
Reno, NV 89502-2179

775-323-1553
Fax: 775-323-1553

Dorothy Y Kosich, Editor

Information broken into departments which include environment, finance, government, management, new product news, profiles, safety issues and development technology updates.
Frequency: Bi-Monthly
Circulation: 7000

18449 Northern Miner
Southam Magazine Group
950 Wadsworth Boulevard
Suite 308
Lakewood, CO 80215

303-607-0853
800-459-8314
Fax: 303-607-0862
E-Mail: northernminer2@northernminer.com
Home Page: www.northernminer.com

John Cumming, Editor
Brian Warriner, Sales Representatives

News and information for the mining industry.
Cost: $89.00
Frequency: Weekly
Founded in 1915
Printed in 4 colors on glossy stock

18450 Pay Dirt
Copper Queen Publishing Company
Copper Queen Plaza
PO Drawer 48
Bisbee, AZ 85603-48

520-432-2244
Fax: 520-432-2247

Gary Dillard, Editor
Caryl Larkins, CEO
Frank Barco, Publisher
Gruce Rubin, Marketing

Keeps readers informed on current mining developments, changes in policies and decisions by state and federal agencies affecting mining. Accepts advertising.
Cost: $30.00
34 Pages
Frequency: Monthly
Circulation: 2200
ISSN: 0886-0920
Founded in 1938

18451 Pit & Quarry Magazine
The Aggregates Authority
1360 E. Ninth St.
Suite 1070
Cleveland, OH 44114

216-706-3700
800-669-1668
Fax: 216-706-3711
E-Mail: scarr@questex.com
Home Page: www.pitandquarry.com

Sean Carr, Publisher

Exclusively for nonmetallic minerals producers.

18452 Professional Geologist
American Institute of Professional Geologists
1200 N Washington St
Suite 285
Thornton, CO 80241-3134

303-412-6205
Fax: 303-253-9220
E-Mail: aipg@aipg.org
Home Page: www.aipg.org

William J Siok, Executive Director
Wendy Davidson, Assistant Director
Frequency: Bi-Monthly

18453 Reclamation Matters
American Society of Mining and Reclamation
3134 Montevesta Road
Lexington, KY 40502-3548

859-351-9032
Fax: 859-335-6529
E-Mail: asmr@insightbb.com
Home Page: www.asmr.us

Dennis Neuman, President
Richard Bamhisel, Executive Secretary

Dissemination of technical information relating to the reclamation of lands disturbed by mineral extraction. Members yearly issue is paid out of proceeding.
500 Members
Founded in 1973

18454 Silver Valley Mining Journal
414 Sixth Street
Wallace, ID 83873

208-556-1621
E-Mail: silverminers@usamedia.tv
Home Page: www.silverminers.com

Provides information about silver mining.

18455 Skillings Mining Review
WestmorelandFlint
11 E Superior St
Suite 514
Duluth, MN 55802-3015

218-727-1552
Fax: 218-733-0463
Home Page: www.westmorelandflint.com

John Hyduke, President
Ivan Hohnstadt, General Manager
Holly Olson, Circulation Manager

Skillings Mining Review covers breaking news about mining companies and their suppliers, dynamics of the global marketplace, technical aspects of mining and processing, people in the industry and their contributions to it. Also production and shipping reports, and the latest news from coal and power industries.
Cost: $69.00
28 Pages
Frequency: Monthly
Circulation: 1500
ISSN: 0037-6329
Founded in 1912
Printed in 4 colors on glossy stock

18456 The Leading Edge
Society of Exploration Geophysicists
8801 South Yale
Suite 500
Tulsa, OK 74137-3575

918-497-5500
Fax: 918-497-5557
E-Mail: web@seg.org
Home Page: www.seg.org/index.shtml
Social Media: Facebook, Twitter, LinkedIn

Dr. Bob A. Hardage, President
Dr. David James Monk, President-Elect
Dr. Wafik Bulind Beydoun, Vice-President
Nancy Jo House, Secretary/ Treasurer
Dr. Tamas Nemeth, Editor

Gateway publication introducing new geophysical theory, instrumentation, and established practices to scientists in a wide range of geoscience disciplines. Most material is presented in a semitechnical manner that minimizes mathematical theory and emphasizes practical applications.
Frequency: Monthly
Founded in 1930

18457 United Mine Workers Journal
United Mine Workers of America
900 15th Street NW
Washington, DC 20005-2585

202-842-7200
Fax: 202-842-7227

E-Mail: sales@wmwa.net
Home Page: www.wmwa.net

Doug Gibson, Editor

Information sent to members of the United Mine Workers of America, retirees, other labor unions, politicians and opinion makers in the United States and abroad. Reports on issues inside and outside the UMWA that are of interest to its members. Also contains features on politics, the arts, media and the culture of US workers.
Frequency: Monthly
Circulation: 200000

18458 Valley Gazette
Hometown Publications
1000 Bridgeport Ave
Suite 3-2
Shelton, CT 06484-4676

203-926-2080
Fax: 203-926-2091
Home Page: www.zwire.com

Gina Burkhart, CEO
Susane Hunter, Editor
Sharon Sakal, Circulation Manager
John Schneider, Marketing Manager
Frequency: Weekly
Circulation: 12322

18459 World Dredging, Mining & Construction
Placer Corporation
PO Box 17479
Irvine, CA 92623-7479

949-474-1120
Fax: 949-863-9261
E-Mail: info@worlddredging.com
Home Page: www.worlddredging.com

MJ Richardson, Publisher
Steve Richardson, Editor
Robert Lindaur, Circulation Manager

International and national news for the dredging.
Cost: $40.00
100 Pages
Frequency: Monthly
Circulation: 3400
ISSN: 1045-0343
Founded in 1965
Printed in 4 colors on glossy stock

18460 World Mining Equipment
13544 Eads Road
Prairieville, LA 70769

225-673-9400
Fax: 225-677-8277
E-Mail: info@mining-media.com
Home Page: www.mining-media.com

Steve Fiscor, Editor in chief
Richard Johnson, Managing Editor
Russ Carter, Managing Editor
Victor Matteucci, National Sales Manager
Cost: $29.95
Frequency: Monthly
Circulation: 10,523
Founded in 1866

Trade Shows

18461 ACAA Annual Meeting
American Coal Ash Association
38800 Country Club Drive
Farmington Hills, MI 48331-3439

720-870-7897
Fax: 720-870-7889
E-Mail: info@acaa-usa.org
Home Page: www.acaa-usa.org

Thomas Adams, Executive Director
150 Attendees

18462 ASMA Annual Meeting
American Society of Mining and Reclamation
3134 Montevesta Road
Lexington, KY 40502-3548

859-351-9032
Fax: 859-335-6529
E-Mail: asmr@insightbb.com
Home Page: www.asmr.us
Social Media: Facebook

Dennis Neuman, President
Richard Bamhisel, Executive Secretary

Approximately 30 exhibitors.
300 Attendees
Frequency: Annual

18463 Alaska Miners Association Convention
Alaska Miners Association
3305 Arctic Boulevard
Suite 105
Anchorage, AK 99503-4575

907-563-9229
Fax: 907-563-9225
E-Mail: ama@alaskaminers.org
Home Page: www.alaskaminers.org

Steven Borell, Executive Director

Forty booths supporting businesses of the mining industry and state and federal agencies involved with regulating the industry.
500 Attendees
Frequency: Annual/March

18464 American Federation Mineralogical Society Rocky Mountain
816 Whipporwhill Sourt
Bartlesville, OK 74006

918-827-6405

T Alf, President

One hundred tables of gems, minerals and fossils for wholesale and retail dealers.
4M Attendees
Frequency: September

18465 American Gem & Mineral Suppliers Association
PO Box 741
Patton, CA 92369-0741

760-241-3191

Renata Williams, Executive Chairman

Ten booths.
100 Attendees
Frequency: February

18466 Arminera
Marketing International
200 N Glebe Road
Suite 900
Arlington, VA 22203

703-527-8000
Fax: 703-527-8006

Seminar, banquet and 400 exhibits of supplies, equipment and services for the mining industry.
8500 Attendees
Frequency: Biennial

18467 Ash at Work Transportation Research Board
American Coal Ash Association
15200 E Girard Ave
Suite 3050
Aurora, CO 80014-3955

720-870-7897
Fax: 720-870-7889
E-Mail: info@acaa-usa.org
Home Page: www.acaa-usa.org

Thomas Adams, Executive Director

Non-profit trade association.
160 Members
Frequency: 2x/Year
Founded in 1968
Printed in 4 colors on glossy stock

18468 EIA National Conference & Exposition
Environmental Information Association
6935 Wisconsin Avenue
Suite 306
Chevy Chase, MD 20815-6112

301-961-4999
888-343-4342
Fax: 301-961-3094
E-Mail: info@eia-usa.org
Home Page: www.eia-usa.org

Dana Hudson, President
Mike Schrum, President Elect
Kevin Cannan, Vice President
Joy Finch, Secretary
Chris Gates, Treasurer

Providing the environmental industry with the information needed to remain knowledgeable, responsible, and competitive in the environmental health and safety industry.
Frequency: Annual/March

18469 MIACON Construction, Mining & Waste Management Show
Finocchiaro Enterprises
2921 Coral Way
Miami, FL 33145-3053

305-441-2865
Fax: 305-529-9217
Home Page: www.miacon.com

Michael Finocchiaro, President
Jose Garcia, VP
Justine Finocchiaro, Chief Operations

Annual show of 650 manufacturers, suppliers, distributors and exporters of equipment, machinery, supplies and services for the construction, mining and waste managment industries. There will be 600 booths.
10M Attendees
Frequency: December
Founded in 1994

18470 MINExpo International
National Mining Association
101 Constitution Avenue NW
Suite 500 East
Washington, DC 20001-2133

202-463-2600
Fax: 202-463-2666
Home Page: www.minexpo.com

Harold P. Quinn, Jr., President & CEO

MINExpo is the mining industry's premier showcase for companies specializing in every facet of mining: open pit, underground, processing and preparation, mine site development, exploration and surveying, smelting and refining, and reclamation.
30000 Attendees
Frequency: Annual/September

18471 Mineral Exploration Roundup
Assoc for Mineral Exploration British Columbia

889 W Pender Street
Suite 800
Vancouver, BC V6C 3B2
604-689-5271
Fax: 604-681-2363
E-Mail: info@amebc.ca
Home Page: www.amebc.ca
Social Media: Facebook, Twitter

Simone Hill, Acting Dir., Member Relations
Morgen Andoff, Acting Manager, Special Events
Roxanne Finnie, Manager, Member Relations

AME BC is the predominant voice of mineral exploration and development in British Columbia. AME BC represents members including geoscientists, prospectors, engineers, students, exploration and mining companies and suppliers who are engaged in mineral exploration and develoment in BC and throughout the world. AME BC annually hosts international guests from around the world during the annual Mineral Exploration Roundup conference that takes place every January.
5000 Members
Frequency: Annual/January
Founded in 1912

18472 National Western Mining Conference & Exhibition
Colorado Mining Association
216 16th Street
Suite 1250
Denver, CO 80202-5161

303-575-9199
Fax: 303-575-9194
E-Mail: colomine@coloradomining.org
Home Page: www.coloradomining.org

Stuart Sanderson, President

Annual show of 90 exhibitors of equipment and support services for the mining industry.
1000 Attendees

18473 Northwest Mining Association Annual Meeting and Exposition
Northwest Mining Association
10 N Post Street
Suite 220
Spokane, WA 99201

509-624-1158
Fax: 509-623-1241
Home Page: www.nwma.com

Pat Nelsen, Operations Director

Annual mining convention in the US. Containing 335 booths, 280 exhibits and more than 20 technical sessions. The second largest annual mining convention in the USA. Founded in 1895.
2.5M Attendees
Frequency: December

18474 Randol Gold Forum
Randol International Limited
18301 W Colfax Avenue
#T1B
Golden, CO 80401-4834

303-526-7618
Fax: 303-271-0334
Home Page: http://www.randol.com

Hans Von Michaelis, President
Patti Hamilton, Sales Coordinator

Mining companies exposition.
350 Attendees
Frequency: September

18475 Rapid Excavation Tunneling Conference Expo
PO Box 625002
Littleton, CO 80162-5002

303-973-9550

DD Daley, Meeting Manager

75 booths.
1M Attendees
Frequency: June

18476 SME Annual Meeting
Society of Mining, Metallurgy, and Exploration
12999 E. Adam Aircraft Circle
Englewood, CO 80112

303-948-4200
800-763-3132
Fax: 303-973-3845
E-Mail: sme@smenet.org
Home Page: www.smenet.org
Social Media: Facebook, Twitter, LinkedIn

John N. Murphy, President
Drew A. Meyer, President-Elect
David L. Kanagy, Executive Director

Mine to Market: Now It's Global.
4M Attendees
Frequency: Annual/February

18477 UMA Annual Convention
Utah Mining Association
136 S Main St
Suite 709
Salt Lake City, UT 84101-1683

801-364-1874
Fax: 801-364-2640
E-Mail: mining@utahmining.org
Home Page: www.utahmining.org

Todd Bingham, President
Terry Maio, Chairman
Marilyn Tuttle, Admininistrator
Frequency: August

Directories & Databases

18478 Coal Data
National Coal Association
100 Independence Ave, SW
Washington, DC 20585

202-586-8800

Offers important data on the 50 largest coal mines in the country.
Cost: $50.00

18479 Coal Mine Directory
Primedia
29 N Wacker Drive
10th Floor
Chicago, IL 60606-3203

312-726-2802
800-621-9907
Fax: 312-726-2574
Home Page: www.primediabusiness.com

Art Sanda, Editor
Patricia L Yos, Editor

Over 2,000 coal mines are profiled that are based in the United States and Canada.
Cost: $149.00
Frequency: Annual January
Circulation: 700

18480 DRI Coal Forecast
DRI/McGraw-Hill
24 Hartwell Ave
Lexington, MA 02421-3103

781-860-6060
Fax: 781-860-6002
E-Mail: support@construction.com
Home Page: www.construction.com

Walt Arvin, President

Offers valuable information on the mining of coal by supply region and producing state; total coal by demand region; cost and demand by the consumer sector.

18481 Engineering and Mining Journal: Buying Directory Issue
Primedia
29 N Wacker Drive
10th Floor
Chicago, IL 60606

312-726-2802
800-621-9907
Fax: 312-726-2574
Home Page: www.primediabusiness.com

Robert Wyllie, Editor

List of manufacturers and suppliers of mining equipment.
Cost: $35.00
Frequency: Annual November
Circulation: 23,000

18482 Expanded Shale, Clay and Slate Institute Roster of Members
Expanded Shale, Clay and Slate Institute
35 East Wacker Dr.
Suite 850
Chicago, IL 60601

801-272-7070
Fax: 312-644-8557
E-Mail: info@escsi.org
Home Page: www.escsi.org

John Riese, President

About 15 producers by the rotary kiln method of lightweight aggregates of expanded shales, clays, and slates; international coverage.

18483 Geophysical Directory
Geophysical Directory
PO Box 130508
Houston, TX 77219-0508

713-291-1922
800-929-2462
Fax: 713-529-3646
Home Page: www.geophysicaldirectory.com

Claudia LaCalli, Editor
Stewart Schafer, Owner

About 4,500 companies that provide geophysical equipment, supplies or services and mining and petroleum companies that use geophysical techniques.
Cost: $135.00
400 Pages
Frequency: Annual March
Circulation: 2,000
Founded in 1946
Mailing list available for rent: 2500 names
Printed in 4 colors on glossy stock

18484 Iron and Manganese Ore Databook
Metal Bulletin
220 5th Avenue
#Enus-19T
New York, NY 10001-7708

212-136-6202
800 MET-L 25
Fax: 212-213-6273

John Bailey, Editor

Iron and manganese ore producers and traders worldwide.
Cost: $179.00
Frequency: Quadrennial

18485 Keystone Coal Industry Manual
Primedia

29 N Wacker Drive
10th Floor
Chicago, IL 60611

312-726-2802
800-621-9907
Fax: 312-726-2574
Home Page: www.primediabusiness.com

Art Sanda, Editor
Patricia L Yos, Editor

Coal companies and mines, coke plants, coal preparation plants, domestic and export coal sales companies.
Cost: $260.00
Frequency: Annual January
Circulation: 1,400

18486 Landmen's Directory and Guidebook
American Association of Professional Landmen
4100 Fossil Creek Boulevard
Fort Worth, TX 76137-2723

817-847-7700
Fax: 817-847-7704
E-Mail: aapl@landman.org
Home Page: www.landman.org

Le'ann Callihan, Editor/Publications Department

About 7,500 member specialists in assembling or disposing of land or rights required for oil, gas, coal andmineral exploration and exploitation in the US and Canada.
Cost: $100.00
Frequency: Annual November
Circulation: 7,500
ISSN: 0272-8370

18487 Minerals Yearbook
US Geological Survey
1730 E Parham Rd
Richmond, VA 23228-2202

804-261-2600
Fax: 804-261-2659
E-Mail: dc_va@usgs.gov
Home Page: www.usgs.gov

Charles G Groats, Director

The Minerals Yearbook discusses the performance of the worldwide minerals and materials industry and provides background information to assist in interpreting that performance. Contents of the individual Minerals Yearbook volumes are, Volume I, Metals and Minerals, Volume II, Area Reports:Domestic, and Volume III, Area Reports: International.
200+ Pages
Frequency: Annual
Founded in 1935

18488 Mining Directory
Metal Bulletin
220 5th Avenue
10th Floor
New York, NY 10001-7708

212-213-6202
800-MET-L 25
Fax: 212-213-6273
E-Mail: 72610.3721@compuserve.com
Home Page: www.metbul.com/metbul/mbhome

Don Nelson, Editor

Offers valuable information on mines, mining equipment manufacturers, suppliers of equipment and services to the industry and industry consultants.
Cost: $158.00

18489 Mining Engineering: SME Membership Directory
Society of Mining, Metallurgy & Exploration
12999 E. Adam Aircraft Circle
Englewood, CO 80112

303-948-4200
800-763-3132
Fax: 303-973-3845
E-Mail: sme@smenet.org
Home Page: www.smenet.org
Social Media: Facebook, Twitter, LinkedIn

John N. Murphy, President
Drew A. Meyer, President-Elect

A list of over 18,000 persons engaged in the location, exploration,treatment and marketing of all classes of minerals except petroleum.
Cost: $150.00
Frequency: Annual
Circulation: 20,000
ISSN: 0026-5187

18490 National Ocean Industries Association: Directory of Membership
National Ocean Industries Association
1120 G St NW
Suite 900
Washington, DC 20005-3801

202-347-6900
Fax: 202-347-8650
Home Page: www.noia.org

Tom Fry, President

Over 300 firms engaged in offshore construction, drilling and petroleum production, geophysical exploration, ship building and repair, deep-sea mining and related activities in the development and use of marine resources.
Frequency: Annual

18491 Pit & Quarry: Reference Manual & Buyers' Guide Issue
Advanstar Communications
2501 Colorado Avenue
Suite 280
Santa Monica, CA 90404-4503

310-857-7500
Fax: 310-857-7510
E-Mail: info@advanstar.com
Home Page: www.advanstar.com

List of approximately 1,000 manufacturers and other suppliers of equipment, products and services to the nonmetallic mining and quarrying industry.
Cost: $25.00
Frequency: Annual
Circulation: 25,000

18492 Randol Buyer's Guide
Randol International Limited
18301 W Colfax Avenue
#T-2
Golden, CO 80401-4834

303-526-7618
800-726-3652
Fax: 303-278-9229
Home Page: http://www.randol.com

Hans Von Michaelis, Editor

Approximately 10,000 companies that offer equipment and services used in the mining industry.
Cost: $35.00
Frequency: Annual
Circulation: 10,000

18493 Randol Mining Directory
Randol International Limited
18301 W Colfax Avenue
#T1B
Golden, CO 80401-4834

303-526-7618
Fax: 303-271-0334
Home Page: http://www.randol.com

Hans Von Michaelis, President
Patti Hamilton, Sales Coordinator

The most comprehensive source of information on all mines in the USA. Used for systematic marketing to mines and exploration companies, statistical research and more, offering 10,000 industry contacts.

18494 Rock Products: Buyer's Guide Issue
Primedia
29 N Wacker Drive
10th Floor
Chicago, IL 60606

312-726-2802
Fax: 312-726-2574
Home Page: www.primediabusiness.com

Rick Marley, Editor
Scot Bieda, Publisher
David Pistello, Classified

List of about 1,500 providers worldwide of equipment and services for the nonmetallic mineral mining and processing industry.
Cost: $100.00
Frequency: Annual November
Circulation: 23,000

18495 Silver Refiners of the World and their Identifying Ingot Marks
Silver Institute
1112 16th St NW
Suite 240
Washington, DC 20036-4818

202-347-8200
Home Page: www.silverinstitute.org

Over 80 refiners in over 18 countries are profiled.
Cost: $33.00
85 Pages

18496 Western Mining Directory
Howell Publishing Company
1758 Blake St
Denver, CO 80202-1226

303-296-8000
800-441-4748
Fax: 303-296-1123
E-Mail: howell@rmi.net

Dave Howell, Owner

Directory of mining companies and mines nationwide.
Cost: $49.00
Circulation: 5,000
Founded in 1968

18497 World Aluminum: A Metal Bulletin Databook
Metal Bulletin
220 5th Avenue
19th Floor
New York, NY 10001-7781

212-213-6202
Fax: 212-213-1870
E-Mail: help@metalbulletin.com
Home Page: www.metalbulletin.com

Richard ODonoghue, Manager
Ania Tumm, Marketing Manager
Julius Pike, Account Manager

Offers information on producers and traders of aluminum and aluminum alloys.
Cost: $247.00
540 Pages
ISSN: 0951-2233

18498 World Mining Equipment
Metal Bulletin
220 5th Avenue
New York, NY 10001

212-213-6202
Fax: 212-213-6619
Home Page: www.wme.com

Mike Woof, Editor

Manufacturers of mining equipment.
Cost: $246.00
66 Pages
Circulation: 13M
ISSN: 0746-729X
Printed in 4 colors on glossy stock

Industry Web Sites

18499 **ca.uky.edu/assmr**
American Society of Mining and Reclamation

18500 **http://gold.greyhouse.com**
G.O.L.D Grey House OnLine Databases
Grey House Publishing's online database platform, GOLD, offers Quick Search, Keyword Search and Expert Search for most business sectors including mining markets. The GOLD platform makes finding the information you need quick and easy - whether you're a novice searcher or an experienced database user. All of Grey House's directory products are available for subscription on the GOLD platform.

18501 **www.acaa-usa.org**
American Coal Ash Association
Promotes the beneficial use of coal cumbustion products.

18502 **www.aem.org**
Vibrating Screen Manufacturers Association

18503 **www.agiweb.org**
American Geological Institute
Provides information services to geoscientists, serves as a voice of shared interests in our profession.

18504 **www.aimeny.org**
American Institute of Mining & Petroleum Engineers
Organization was founded to further the arts and sciences employed to recover the earth's minerals and convert them to useful products.

18505 **www.aipg.org**
American Institute of Professional Geologists
Founded to certify the credentials of practicing geologists and to advocate on behalf of the profession.

18506 **www.alaskaminers.org**
Alaska Miners Association
Encourage and support responsible mineral production in Alaska.

18507 **www.amebc.ca**
Assn for Mineral Exploration British Columbia
Supports and promotes the mineral exploration community and related services by disseminating information to the public and governments, thereby assisting in the creation of wealth and jobs through sustainable mineral developement.

18508 **www.asmi.state.az.us**
State Mine Inspector

18509 **www.azcu.org**
Arizona Mining Association
Provides information about mining, specifically copper mining and the impact it has on our lives.

18510 **www.blm.org**
Bureau of Land Management

18511 **www.calmining.org**
California Mining Association
Represents the breadth and depth of California's mining industry.

18512 **www.ces.ca.uky.edu/assmr**
American Society for Surface Mining & Reclamation
Dissemination of Technical information relating to the reclamation of lands disturbed by mineral extraction. Members yearly issue is paid out of proceedings. Membership dues - $50/regular; $10/students.

18513 **www.chamberofmines.bc.ca**
BC & Yukon Chamber of Mines
A list of mines in the Unites States.

18514 **www.cim.org**
Canadian Inst of Mining, Metallurgy & Petroleum
Strives to be the association of choice for professionals in the minerals industries.

18515 **www.coloradomining.org**
Colorado Mining Association
Serves as a spokesman for the mining industry in Colorado.

18516 **www.copper.org**
Copper Development Association

18517 **www.crc.siu.edu/nasir.htm**
National Association of State Land Reclamationists

18518 **www.crystalgrowth.org**
American Association for Crystal Growth
For those interested in organic crystal growth.

18519 **www.dri.edu**
Desert Research Institute
Information on basic and applied environmental research on a local, national, and international scale. For scientists, technicians, and support personnel.

18520 **www.fmshre.gov**
Federal Mine Safety and Health Review Commission

18521 **www.geosociety.org**
Geological Society of America

18522 **www.gold.org**
World Gold Council

18523 **www.goldprospecters.org**
Gold Prospectors Association

18524 **www.greyhouse.com**
Grey House Publishing
Authoritative reference directories for most business sectors, including mining markets. Users can search the online databases with varied search criteria allowing for custom searches by product category, geographic area, sales volume, keyword, subject and more. Full Grey House catalog and online ordering also available.

18525 **www.idahomining.org**
Idaho Mining Association
Founded to further the interests of Idaho's mining industry and minerals production.

18526 **www.kaolin.com**
China Clay Producers Association

18527 **www.leadinfo.com**
Lead Industries Association

18528 **www.lignite.com**
Lignite Energy Council
Promotes policies and directs activities that maintain a viable lignite industry and enhance the development of our regions lignite resources.

18529 **www.lime.org**
National Lime Association
Trade association for US and Canadian manufacturers of high calcium quicklime, dolomitic quicklime and hydrated lime, collectively referred to as lime.

18530 **www.minecon.com/index.html**
Mineral Economics and Management Society

18531 **www.miningfoundationsw.org**
Mining Foundation of the Southwest

18532 **www.miningorganizations.org/msia.htm**
Mine Safety Institute of America

18533 **www.miningusa.com**
Mining Associations-National
A list of associations throughout the United States.

18534 **www.mmsa.net**
Mining and Metallurgical Society of America
A professional organization dedicated to increasing public awareness and understanding about mining and why mined materials are essential to modern society and human well being.

18535 **www.msha.gov**
Mine Safety and Health Administration

18536 **www.naima.org**
Mineral Insulation Manufacturers Association
Trade association of North American manufacturwers of fiberglass, rock wool, and slag wool insulation products.

18537 **www.nevadamining.org**
Nevada Mining Association
Represents all aspects of the mining industry in the state of Nevada.

18538 **www.nma.org**
National Mining Association
The only national trade organization represents the interests of mining before Congress, the Administration, federal agencies, the judiciary and the media.

18539 **www.noia.org**
National Ocean Industries Association
National organization engaged in offshore construction, drilling and petroleum production, geophysical exploration, ship building and repair.

18540 **www.nssga.org**
National Stone, Sand & Gravel Association

18541 **www.nwma.org**
Northwest Mining Association
Provides liaison between mining industry and government. Offers short course on current technology.

18542 **www.perlite.org**
Perlite Institute

18543 **www.pitandquarry.com**
The Aggregates Authority-Pit and Quarry
A magazine exclusively for nonmetallic minerals producers.

18544 **www.rheology.org**
Society of Rheology

18545 **www.rmag.org**
Rocky Mountain Association of Geologists

18546 **www.seg.org**
Society of Exploration Geophysicists

18547 **www.segweb.org**
Society of Economic Geologists
The society of economic geologists is an international organization of individual members with interest in the field of economic geology.

18548 **www.silverinstitute.org**
Silver Institute

18549 **www.silverminers.org**
Silver Valley Mining Association
dedicated to promoting the Silver Valley of northern Idaho and its mining industry.

18550 **www.smenet.org**
Society for Mining, Metallurgy & Exploration
Advances the worldwide mining and minerals community through information exchange and professional development.

18551 **www.solutionmining.org**
Solution Mining Research Institute

18552 **www.sorptive.org**
Sorptive Minerals Institute

18553 **www.sulphurinstitute.org**
Sulphur Institute

18554 **www.surface-mining.state.al.us**
Alabama Surface Mining Commission
Balance civilization's demands for natural resources and environmental conservation in the state of Alabama.

18555 **www.tmra.com**
Texas Mining & Reclamation Association

18556 **www.tms.org**
Minerals, Metals & Materials Society
Dedicated to the development and dissemination of the scientific and engineering knowledge bases for materials-centered technologies.

18557 **www.umwa.org**
United Mine Workers of America

18558 **www.usgs.gov**
US Geological Survey

18559 **www.utahmining.org**
Utah Mining Association
Helps to promote and protect the mining industry. Provides its members with full-time professional industry representation before the State Legislature; various government regularoty agencies on the federal, state and local levels, other associations, and business and industry groups.

18560 **www.womeninmining.org**
Women in Mining

Associations

18561 Academy of Motion Picture Arts and Sciences
8949 Wilshire Blvd
Beverly Hills, CA 90211-1972
310-247-3000
Fax: 310-271-3395
Home Page: www.oscars.org
Social Media: Facebook, Twitter, LinkedIn, Youtube
The Academy was founded to advance the arts and sciences of motion pictures; foster cooperation among creative leaders for cultural, educational and technological progress; recognize outstanding achievments; cooperate on technical research and improvement of methods and equipment; provide a common forum and meeting ground for various branches and crafts; represent the viewpoint of actual creators of the motion picture. Hosts annual Academy Awards.
6000 Members
Founded in 1927

18562 Academy of Science Fiction Fantasy and Horror Films
334 W 54th St
Los Angeles, CA 90037-3806
323-752-5811
Fax: 323-752-5811
E-Mail: scifiacademy@ca.rr.com
Home Page: www.saturnawards.org
Robert Holguin, President
Roger Fenton, VP
Michael Laster, Director
Culminated from the Count Dracula Society, the Academy hosts the annual Science Fiction Film Awards, called the Saturn Awards.
Founded in 1972

18563 American Cinema Editors
100 Universal City Plaza
Verna Fields Building 2282 Room 190
Universal City, CA 91608
818-777-2900
Fax: 818-733-5023
E-Mail: americancinema@earthlink.net
Home Page: www.ace-filmeditors.org
Social Media: Facebook, Twitter
Alan Heim, President
Stephen Rivkin, VP
Lillian Bennson, Secretary
Ed Abroms, Treasurer
Jan Ambler, A.C.E
A non-profit corporation committed to the encouragement of mutually-beneficial dialogue with other members of the motion picture industry and to educating the general public. Holds the annual ACE Eddie Awards honoring the nominees for the Film Editing Award given by the Academy of Motion Pictures Arts and Sciences.
Founded in 1950

18564 American Society of Cinematographers
1782 N Orange Drive
PO Box 2230
Hollywood, CA 90028
323-969-4333
800-448-0145
Fax: 323-882-6391
E-Mail: office@theasc.com
Home Page: www.theasc.com
Social Media: Facebook
Daryn Okadaan, President
Michael Negrin, Secretary
Victor J Kemper, Treasurer
The ASC is not a labor union or guild, but is an educational, cultural and professional organization. Membership is possible by invitation and is extended only to directors of photography with distinguished credits in the industry. Publishes 'American Cinematographer' magazine.
Founded in 1919

18565 Art Directors Guild
11969 Ventura Blvd
Suite 200
Studio City, CA 91604-2619
818-762-9995
Fax: 818-762-9997
E-Mail: lydia@artdirectors.org
Home Page: www.adg.org
Social Media: Facebook, Twitter
Scott Roth, Executive Director
Lisa Frazza, Secretary
Michael Baugh, Treasurer
Alexandra Schaaf, Manager Membership Department
The creative talents that concieve and manage the background and settings for most films and television projects are members of the Art Directors Guild, Local 800. They and most other crafts of the entertainment industry are members of the International Alliance of Theatrical Stage Employees, Moving Picture Technicians, Artists and Allied Crafts of the United States, its Territories and Canada.
935 Members
Founded in 1937

18566 Assistant Directors Training Program
15301 Ventura Blvd.
Bldg E #1075
Sherman Oaks, CA 91403
818-386-2545
Fax: 818-386-2876
E-Mail: mail@dgptp.org
Home Page: www.trainingplan.org
Tom Joyner, Chair
Provides motion picture and television industry training as directed by the Alliance of Motion Picture and Television Producers and the Directors Guild of America.
Founded in 1965

18567 Association of Cinema and Video Laboratories
Bev Wood C/O Deluxe Laboratories
1377 North Serrano Avenue
Hollywood, CA 90027
323-462-6171
Fax: 206-682-6649
E-Mail: beverly.wood@bydeluxe.com
Home Page: www.acvl.org
Bev Wood, President
Chip Wilkenson, First VP
John Carlson, Second VP
Kevin Dillon, Treasurer
Bob Olson, Secretary
Provides opportunities for discussion and exchange of ideas in connection with administrative, technical and managerial problems in the motion picture and video industry. The Association is concerned with improvements in technical practices and procedures, public and industry relations, product specifications to vendors, the impact of current and impending governmental regulations, and any and all other areas of interest to the laboratory industry.
80 Members
Founded in 1953

18568 Association of Talent Agents
9255 Sunset Blvd
Suite 930
Los Angeles, CA 90069-3317
310-274-0628
Fax: 310-274-5063
E-Mail: shellie@agentassociation.com
Home Page: www.agentassociation.com
Sandy Bresler, President
Sheldon Sroloff, VP
Jim Gosnell, Secretary/Treasurer
Karen Stuart, Executive Director
Shellie Jetton, Administrative Director
A non-profit trade association representing talent agencies in the industry. ATA is the voice of unified talent and literary agencies. ATA agencies represent the vast majority of working artists, including actors, directors, writers, and other artists in film, stage, television, radio, commercial, literary work, and other entertainment enterprises.
Founded in 1937

18569 Casting Society of America
606 N Larchmont Blvd
Los Angeles, CA 90004-1309
323-463-1925
Fax: 323-463-4753
E-Mail: info@castingsociety.com
Home Page: www.castingsociety.com
Larry Raab, Manager
CSA is the largest professional association of Casting Directors in the world. They work in all areas of entertainment in film, television and theatre. CSA continually seeks to expand their standing in the industry by providing information and opportunities that support is members.
500+ Members
Founded in 1982

18570 Children in Film
11271 Ventura Blvd.
Studio City, CA 91604
818-432-7400
800-902-9001
E-Mail: contact@childreninfilm.com
Home Page: www.childreninfilm.com
Toni Casala, Founder & President
Trisha Noble, Director, Permit Services
Heather Broeker, Director, Marketing
To provide tools and information needed to successfully employ a child in the entertainment industry while also lending a healthy, positive view into the world of child actors.
Founded in 2000

18571 Directors Guild of America
7920 W Sunset Blvd
Los Angeles, CA 90046-3347
310-289-2000
800-421-4173
Fax: 310-289-2029
E-Mail: LDavis@dga.org
Home Page: www.dga.org
Jay Roth, President
Steven Soderbergh, National VP
Gilbert Cates, Secretary/Treasurer
The DGA represents Film and Television Directors, Unit Production Managers, First Assistant Directors, Second Assistant Directors, Technical Coordinators and Tape Associate Directors, Stage Managers and Production Assistants.

18572 Film Society of Lincoln Center
70 Lincoln Center Plz
New York, NY 10023-6595
212-875-5601
Fax: 212-875-5636

E-Mail: webmaster@filmlinc.com
Home Page: www.filmlinc.com
Social Media: Facebook, Twitter

Serge Joseph, Manager
Daniel H Stern, President
Wendy Keys, Secreatry
James Bouras, Treasurer
Claudia Bonn, Executive Director

Celebrates American and international cinema, recognizes and supports new filmmakers, and enhances awareness, accessibility and understanding of the art among a broad and diverse film going audience. The Film Society is best known for two international festivals - the New York Film Festival and the New Directors/New Films festival.
Founded in 1969

18573 Greek Americans in the Arts and Entertainment
3916 Sepulveda Blvd
Suite 107
Culver City, CA 90230

323-651-3507
Fax: 310-933-0250
E-Mail: info@americanhellenic.org
Home Page: www.americanhellenic.org
Social Media: Facebook, Twitter

Michael Galanakis, President
Alexander Mizan, Executive Director
Michael Sarris, VP, finance

Follows the legacy of Greek-Americans in the arts and entertainment field.

18574 Historians Film Committee
Rural Route 3
Box 80
Cleveland, OK 74020-9515

918-243-7637
Fax: 202-544-8307
E-Mail: rollinspc@aol.com
Home Page: www.filmandhistory.org

Peter C Rollins, Editor-in-Chief

The Committee exists to further the use of film sources in teaching and research, to disseminate information about film and film use to historians and other social scientists, to work for an effective system of film preservation so that scholars may have ready access to film archives, and to organize periodic conferences dealing with film.
Founded in 1970

18575 Hollywood Arts Council
PO Box 931056
Hollywood, CA 90093

323-462-2355
Fax: 323-465-9240
E-Mail: admin@hollywoodartscouncil.org
Home Page: www.hollywoodartscouncil.org
Social Media: Facebook

Nyla Arslanian, President
Nancy J Brown, VP
Steve Tronson, Treasurer
Shauna McClure, Executive Director

Promotes, nurtures and supports the arts in Hollywood. Has served the community through advocacy, coalition building, free public arts events and after school programs.
400 Members
Founded in 1978

18576 Independent Film & Television Alliance
10850 Wilshire Blvd
9th Floor
Los Angeles, CA 90024-4628

310-446-1000
Fax: 310-446-1600
E-Mail: info@ ifta-online.org
Home Page: www.ifta-online.org

Jean Prewitt, CEO
Jonathan Wolfe, Executive VP/Managing Director
Michael Ryan, Chairman
Lew Horwitz, Vice Chairman Finance

A non-profit association whose mission is to provide the independent film and television industry with high-quality marketplace-oriented services and worldwide representation. The Alliance actively lobbies the United States and Eurpoean governments and the international organizations on measures that impact production and distribution.
Founded in 1980

18577 International Animated Film Society
2114 W Burbank Blvd
Burbank, CA 91506-1232

818-842-8330
Fax: 613-232-6315
E-Mail: info@asifa-hollywood.org
Home Page: www.animationarchive.org

Amtran Manoogian, President

A California nonprofit organization established to promote and encourage the art and craft of animation. They support and encourage animation education, supports the preservation and critical evaluation of animation history, recognize achievement of excellence in the art and field of animation, strive to increase the public awareness of animation, act as a liaison to encourage the free exchange of ideas within the animation community, as well as a variety of other goals.
350 Members
Founded in 1974

18578 International Cinematographers Guild
7755 W Sunset Boulevard
Hollywood, CA 90046
323-876-0160
Fax: 323-876-6383
E-Mail: admin@camerguild.com
Home Page: www.cameraguild.com

Steven Poster, President
Tom Weston, National VP
Paul V Ferrazzi, Secretary/Treasurer
Bruce C Doering, Executive Director

The International Cinematographers Guild welcomes camera professionals from across the United States and around the world.

18579 International Documentary Association
3470 Wilshire Blvd
Suite 980
Los Angeles, CA 90010

213-232-1660
Fax: 213-232-1669
E-Mail: michael@documentary.org
Home Page: www.documentary.org
Social Media: Facebook, Twitter, LinkedIn, Youtube

Michael Lumpkin, Executive Director
Cindy Chyr, Development Director
Andrew Kaiser, Development Associate
Jina Chung, Associate
Amy Halpin, Manager

A nonprofit membership organization dedicated to supporting the efforts of nonfiction film and video makers throughout the United States and the world; promoting the documentary form; and expanding opportunities for the production, distribution, and exhibition of documentary.
2800+ Members
Founded in 1982

18580 International Stunt Association
11331 Ventura Boulevard
Suite 100
Studio City, CA 91604
818-760-2072
Fax: 818-501-5656
E-Mail: info@isastunts.com
Home Page: www.isastunts.com
Social Media: Facebook, Twitter

Leading the industry in exciting action while holding safety above all else, ISA is a fraternal organization whose membership is by invitation only. It is comprised of the top stuntment, stunt coordinators and second unit directors that Hollywood has to offer and a safety record that is second to none.
Founded in 1980

18581 Motion Picture Association of America
15301 Ventura Boulevard
Building E
Sherman Oaks, CA 91403

818-995-6600
Fax: 818-285-4403
Home Page: www.mpaa.org

Christopher J Dodd, President/CEO

Serves as the voice and advocate of the American motion picture, home video and television industries. The association advocates for strong protection of the creative works produced and distributed by the industry, fights copyright theft around the world, and provides leadership in meeting new and emerging industry challenges.
7 Members
Founded in 1922

18582 Motion Picture Editors Guild
7715 Sunset Boulevard
Suite 200
Hollywood, CA 90046

323-876-4770
800-705-8700
Fax: 323-876-0861
E-Mail: webmester@editorsguild.com
Home Page: www.editorsguild.com
Social Media: Facebook

Lisa Zeno Churgin, President
Carol Littleton, VP
Martin Levenstein, Second Vice Presdient
Diane Adler, Secretary
Rachel B Igel, Treasurer

A national labor organization representing freelance and staff post-production professionals. MPED negotiates new collective bargaining agreements and enforces existing agreements with employers involved in post-production. They provide assistance for securing better conditions, including but not limted to financial, medical, safety and artistic concerns.
6000 Members
Founded in 1937

18583 Motion Picture Pilots Association
7435 Valjean Avenue
Van Nuys, CA 91406

818-947-5454
E-Mail: moviepilots@cox.net
Home Page: www.moviepilots.com

Cliff Fleming, Board Director
Dirk Vahle, Board Director
Rick Shuster, Board Director
Neil Looy, Board Director
Kevin LaRosa, Board Director

The MPPA promotes aviation safety and the interest of aviators working in the motion picture, television and entertainment industries; establishes, conducts and maintains such activities which promote higher aviation standards and better business methods as may assist in

the advancement of aviation in the Entertainment Aviation Profession; cooperates with those government agencies, industry organizations, entities or association whose objective is the betterment or advancement of the industry.
Founded in 1997

18584 Producers Guild of America
8530 Wilshire Blvd
Suite 450
Beverly Hills, CA 90211-3115

310-358-9020
Fax: 310-358-9520
E-Mail: info@producersguild.org
Home Page: www.producersguild.org

Marshall Herskovitz, President
Vance Van Paten, Executive Director
Grant Stoner, Director Membership
Courtney Cowan, Treasurer
Gale Ann Hurd, Secretary

The PGA represents, protects and promotes the interests of all members of the producing team by providing employment opportunities and health and welfare benefits for all members of the producing team; combating deceptive or unearned credits within the producing team; and representing the interests of the entire producing team. The producing team consists of all those whose interdependency and support of each other are necessary for the creation of motion pictures and television programs.
500 Members
Founded in 1950

18585 Society for Cinema & Media Studies
640 Parrington Oval
Wallace Old Science Hall Room 300
Norman, OK 73019

405-325-8075
Fax: 405-325-7135
E-Mail: office@cmstudies.org
Home Page: www.cmstudies.org
Social Media: Facebook, Twitter

Stephen Prince, President
Eric Schaefer, Secretary
Amy Villarejo, Treasurer
Jane Dye, Administrative Coordinator

A professional organization of college and university educators, filmmakers, historians, critics, scholars, and others devoted to the study of the moving image. The gaols of SCMS are to promote all areas of media studies within universities and two- and four-year colleges; to encourage and reward excellence in scholarship and writing; to facilitate and improve the teaching of media studies as disciplines and to advance multi-cultural awareness and interaction.
1M Members
Founded in 1959

18586 Society of Camera Operators
PO Box 2006
Toluca Lake, CA 91610

818-382-7070
Fax: 323-856-9155
E-Mail: info@soc.org
Home Page: www.soc.org

Dan Dodd, Director

Non-profit organization which advances the art and creative contribution of the operating cameraman in the Motion Picture and Television Industries.
Founded in 1979
Mailing list available for rent

18587 Society of Motion Picture & Television Engineers
3 Barker Ave
5th Floor
White Plains, NY 10601-1509

914-761-1100
Fax: 914-761-3115
Home Page: www.smpte.org
Social Media: Facebook, Twitter, LinkedIn, Youtube

Barbara Lange, Executive Director
Sally-Ann D'Amato, Director Operations
Roberta Gorman, Manager
Peter Symes, Director Engineering
Amiee Ricca, Marketing and Communications

The SMPTE is the leading technical society for the motion imaging industry. It was founded to advance theory and development in the motion imaging field. Today, it publishes ANSI-approved Standards, Recommended Practices, and Engineering Guidelines. SMPTE holds conferences and local Section meetings to bring people and ides together, allowing for useful interaction and information exchange.
100 Members
Founded in 1916

18588 Stuntmen's Association of Motion Pictures
5200 Lankershim Blvd.
Suite 190
North Hollywood, CA 91601

818-766-4334
Fax: 818-766-5943
E-Mail: hq@stuntmen.com
Home Page: www.stuntmen.com

Chris Doyle, Manager
Jeff Wolfe, First VP
Alex Daniels, Second VP
Toby Holguin, Secretary
Hugh Aodh O'Brien, Treasurer

Seeks to improve working conditions for stuntmen. Encourages members to uphold high professional standards.
135 Members
Founded in 1961

18589 Stuntwomen's Association of Motion Pictures
3760 Cahuenga Blvd
Suite 104
Studio City, CA 91604-2411

818-588-8888
888-817-9267
Fax: 818-762-0907
E-Mail: INFO@STUNTWOMEN.COM
Home Page: www.stuntwomen.com
Social Media: Facebook

Jane Austin, President

A professional association for stuntwomen and stunt coordinators which seeks to uphold professional standards and improve working conditions.
Founded in 1967

18590 Sundance Institute
1825 Three Kings Drive
PO Box 684429
Park City, UT 84060

435-658-3456
Fax: 435-658-3457
E-Mail: Institute@sundance.org
Home Page: www.sundance.org

Robert Redford, President
Keri Putnam, Executive Director
Geoffrey Gilmore, Director Sundance Film Festival
Brooke McAffee, Director Finance
Ellen Oh, Associate Director Marketing

Non-profit organization dedicated to the discovery and development of independent artists and audiences. The Institute seeks to discover, support, and inspire independent film and theatre artists from the United States and around the world, and to introduce audiences to their new work. The Institutes programs include the annual Sundance Film Festival, held in Park City, Utah each January.
Founded in 1981

18591 University Film and Video Association
UFVA Membership Office C/O Cheryl Jestis
University of Illinois Press
1325 South Oak Street
Champaign, IL 61820-6903

217-244-0626
866-244-0626
Fax: 217-244-9910
E-Mail: ufvahome@gmail.com
Home Page: www.ufva.org
Social Media: Facebook, Twitter

Karla Berry, President
Thomas Tomasulo, Executive VP
Beverly Seckinger, Secretary
Peter Bukalski, Treasurer
Cheryl Jestis, Membership Coordinator

Supports those interested in the fields of film and video production, history, criticism, and aesthetics. Provides training, education, and a quarterly magazine.
Cost: $75.00
Founded in 1947

18592 Women in Film
6100 Wilshire Blvd
Suite 710
Los Angeles, CA 90048-5107

323-935-2211
Fax: 323-935-2212
E-Mail: info@wif.org
Home Page: www.wif.org

Tichi Wilkerson-Kassel, Founder
CiCi Holloway, President
Glen Alpert, VP Membership
Nicole Katz, CFO
Gayle Nachlis, Executive Director

WIFs purpose is to empower, promote, nurture, and mentor women in the industry through a network of valuable contacts, events, and programs.
10000 Members
Founded in 1974

Newsletters

18593 American Academy of Arts & Sciences Bulletin
American Academy of Arts & Sciences
136 Irving Street
Cambridge, MA 02138

617-576-5000
Fax: 617-576-5050
E-Mail: vsp@amacad.org
Home Page: www.amacad.org

Leslie Berkowitz, President
Mark Robinson, Director, Operations
Paul Karoff, Director, Communications

Features the following departments: Academy News; Around the Country; Noteworthy; and Remembrance.
Frequency: 2x/year

18594 Festival Rag
541 Main Street
Union, WV 24983
FAX 888-813-5457
E-Mail: markus@kemek.com
Home Page: www.kemek.com/independent-film/the-festival-rag

Markus Varjo, Publisher
Cil Ripley, Editor-In-Chief
Dave Roberts, Managing Editor
Carl Merrick, Content & Development

Dedicated to true independent filmmaking and filmmakers, and broadcast to thousands of media-industry subscribers. Provides information on film festivals worldwide, including interviews with filmmakers and programmers.

18595 Film Advisory Board Monthly
Film Advisory Board
263 W Olive Avenue
#377
Burbank, CA 91502

323-461-6541
Fax: 323-469-8541
Home Page: www.filmadvisoryboard.org
Social Media: Facebook, Twitter, LinkedIn

Janet Stokes, President

Information and news on the entertainment industry.
Frequency: Monthly
Founded in 1975
Printed in one color on glossy stock

18596 Hollywood Arts Council
PO Box 931056
Hollywood, CA 90093

323-462-2355
Fax: 323-465-9240
E-Mail: bianca@hollywoodartcouncil.org
Home Page: www.hollywoodartscouncil.org

Promotes, nurtures and supports the arts field in Hollywood. Newsletter is included with membership.
Founded in 1978
Printed in 4 colors on glossy stock

18597 Preview Family Movie & TV Review
Movie Morality Ministries
6302 Riverside Dr
Irving, TX 75039

972-409-9960
800-807-8071
Fax: 785-255-4316
E-Mail: preview@fni.com
Home Page: www.merchantcircle.com

Dave Haverty, President
Greg Shull, Editor
Susan Haverty, Desktop Publisher/Office Manager

Reviews current films and TV series from a Christian and family values perspective.
Cost: $34.00
Frequency: Monthly
ISSN: 0892-6468
Printed in 2 colors on matte stock

Magazines & Journals

18598 Advanstar
Advanstar Communications
641 Lexington Ave
Suite 8
New York, NY 10022-4503

212-951-6600
Fax: 212-951-6793
E-Mail: info@advanstar.com
Home Page: www.advanstar.com

Joseph Loggia, CEO

News and features emphasize innovation in equipment technology and creative technique for editing, graphics, and special effects. Covers all budget levels from desktop post to feature films.
130 Pages
Frequency: Monthly
Circulation: 31464
Founded in 1986

18599 American Cinematographer
American Society of Cinematographers
1782 North Orange Drive
PO Box 2230
Hollywood, CA 90078-2230

323-969-4333
800-448-0145
Fax: 323-876-4973
E-Mail: office@theasc.com
Home Page: www.theasc.com

Covers feature films, television, commercials, music videos, digital video, new equipment, DVD and book releases and much more. An exploration and a reflection of today's cinematography. A publication of the American Society of Cinematographers.
Cost: $29.95
Frequency: Monthly
Circulation: 42000
Founded in 1919
Mailing list available for rent

18600 Animation Magazine
Animation Magazine
26500 W.Agoura Rd
Suite 102
Calabasas, CA 91302

818-883-2884
Fax: 818-883-3773
E-Mail: info@animationmagazine.net
Home Page: www.animationmagazine.net

Jean Thoren, President

Promotes the art and business of animation and gives recognition to those animators and technicians who make the world of animation what it is today.
Cost: $50.00
Frequency: Monthly
Circulation: 30000
ISSN: 1041-617X
Founded in 1986
Printed in 4 colors on glossy stock

18601 Celebrity Service
8833 W Sunset Boulevard
Suite 401
Los Angeles, CA 90069-2171

213-883-3671
Fax: 310-652-9244

Robert Dean, Manager/Director

A listing of celebrities names and addresses. Publisher of the Celebrity Bulletin informing the entertainment and news industry of which celebrities are traveling to Hollywood and New York
Frequency: Bi-Monthly

18602 Cineaste
Cineaste Magazine
243 5th Ave
Suite 706
New York, NY 10016

212-366-5720
Fax: 212-366-5724
E-Mail: cineaste@cineaste.com
Home Page: www.cineaste.com

Gary Crowdus, Editor-in-Chief
Cynthia Lucia, Editor
Richard Porton, Editor
Dan Georgakas, Consulting Editor
Vicki Robinson, Production Assistant

An internationally recognized independent film magazine. Features contributions from many of America's most articulate and outspoken writers, critics and scholars. Focussing on both the art and politics of the cinema.
Cost: $ 20.00
Frequency: Quarterly
Circulation: 11000
ISSN: 0009-7004
Founded in 1967
Mailing list available for rent

18603 Cinefantastique
CFQ Media
PO Box 34425
Los Angeles, CA 90034-0425

310-204-0825
Fax: 310-204-5882
E-Mail: info@cfq.com
Home Page: www.cfq.com

Frederick Clarke, Editor

Provides coverage of genre entertainment. Each issue features in-depth coverage of sci-fi, fantasy and horror films, TV, DVDs, games, toys, books, comics and more.
Cost: $34.95
Frequency: Monthly
Circulation: 40,000

18604 Cinefex
79 Daily Drive
#309
Camarillo, CA 93010

805-383-0800
Fax: 805-383-0803
E-Mail: advertising@cinefex.com
Home Page: www.cinefex.com

A quarterly magazine devoted to motion picture special effects.
Cost: $32.00
180 Pages
Frequency: Quarterly
Circulation: 30000
ISSN: 0198-1056
Founded in 1980
Printed in 4 colors

18605 Cinema Journal
University of Texas Press
2100 Comal
PO Box 7819
Austin, TX 78713-7819

512-471-7233
800-252-3206
Fax: 512-232-7178
E-Mail: utpress@uts.cc.utexas.edu
Home Page: www.utexas.edu/utpress

Sponsored by the Society for Cinema and Media Studies. The journal presents recent scholarship by SCMS members. It publishes essays on a wide variety of subjects from diverse methodological perspectives. A 'Professional Notes' section informs Society of Cinema and Media Studies readers about upcoming events, research opportunities, and the latest published research. Cinema Journal is a member of the CELJ, the Conference of Editors of Learned Journals.
Cost: $42.00
144 Pages
Frequency: Quarterly
Circulation: 2800
ISSN: 0009-7101
Founded in 1950
Printed in on matte stock

18606 Daily Variety/Gotham
360 Park Avenue South
New York, NY 10010-3659
646-746-7001
Fax: 646-746-6977
E-Mail: vtccustserv@cdsfulfillment.com
Home Page: www.variety.com
Peter Bart, Editor-in-Chief
Timothy M Gray, Editor
Ted Johnson, Managing Editor
Kathy Lyford, Managing Editor
Phil Gallo, Associate Editor
Focus is on Broadway theater, network television headquarters, regional music business, and local film production. Explores the role of New York City in relation to the national and global entertainment industries.
Cost: $259.00
Frequency: Daily
Founded in 1905

18607 Daily Variety/LA
5900 Wilshire Boulevard
Suite 3100
Los Angeles, CA 90036-3659
323-617-9100
Fax: 323-857-0494
E-Mail: vtccustserv@cdsfulfillment.com
Home Page: www.variety.com
Peter Bart, Editor-in-Chief
Timothy M Gray, Editor
Ted Johnson, Managing Editor
Kathy Lyford, Managing Editor
Phil Gallo, Associate Editor
Focus is on Hollywood, network television headquarters, regional music business, and local film production. Explores the role of Hollywood in relation to the national and global entertainment industries.
Cost: $259.00
Frequency: Daily
Founded in 1905

18608 Film & History
Historians Film Committee
Lawrence University,Memorial Hall B5
711 E Boldt Way
Appleton, WI 54911
920-832-6649
E-Mail: centre@filmandhistory.org
Home Page: www.h-net.org/~filmhis
Peter C Rollins, Director
Deborah Carmichael, Editor-in-Chief
Cynthia Miller, Associate Editor-in-Chief
An Interdisciplinary Journal of Film and Television Studies concerned with the impact of motion pictures on our society. Film and History focuses on how feature films and documentary films both represent and interpret history. Types of articles include: Analysis of individual films and/or television programs from a historical perspective, survey of documents related to the production of films, or analysis of history as explored through film.
Cost: $50.00
Frequency: Bi-annually
Circulation: 1000
ISSN: 0360-3695
Founded in 1970

18609 Film & Video Magazine
110 William Street
11th Floor
New York, NY 10038
212-621-4900
Fax: 212-621-4635
Home Page:
www.studiodaily.com/filmandvideo
Bryant Frazer, Editor-in-Chief
Pete Putman, Senior Editor
Alison Johns, Editor-in-Chief
Scott Gentry, Group Publisher
Jarrett Cory, Classified Sales
Covers new ideas in creating entertainment by focusing on technique in the production and finishing of features, TV programming, music videos and commercials. No longer publishes print copies, magazine is 100% digital
Frequency: Monthly
Founded in 1983
Printed in 4 colors

18610 Film Journal International
VNU Business Media
770 Broadway,7th Floor
New York, NY 10003-9595
212-493-4097
Fax: 646-654-7694
E-Mail: subscriptions@filmjournal.com
Home Page: www.filmjournal.com
Penny Vane, President
Sid Holt, Editorial Director
Robert Sunshine, Publisher/Editor
Robin Klamfoth, Advertising Director
Kevin Lally, Executive Editor
A trade publication covering the motion picture industry, including theatrical exhibition, production, distribution, and allied activities. Articles report on US and international news, with features on current production, industry trends, theatre design, equipment, concessions, sound, digital cinema, screen advertising, and other industry-related news. Each issue also includes the Buying and Booking Guide, with comprehensive feature film reviews.
Cost: $65.00
Frequency: Monthly
Founded in 1934
Mailing list available for rent

18611 Film Threat
Film Threat International Headquarters
5042 Wilshire Boulevard
PMB 1500
Los Angeles, CA 90036
FAX 310-274-7985
E-Mail: advertise@filmthreat.com
Home Page: www.filmthreat.com
Social Media: Facebook, Twitter
Mark Bell, Editor-in-Chief
Eric Campos, Senior Contributing Editor
Chris Gore, Founder/Publishjer
The print edition of Film Threat retired in 1997, but the legend has lived on as an internet journalism mainstay. FilmThreat.com delivers film reviews, film festival coverage, exclusive filmmaker interviews and original video content.
Cost: $10.50
Frequency: Bi-Monthly
Circulation: 100,000
Founded in 1985

18612 Hollywood Life
Movieline Magazine
10537 Santa Monica Blvd
Suite 250
Los Angeles, CA 90025-4952
310-234-9501
Fax: 310-234-0332
E-Mail: hollywoodlife@pcspublink.com
Home Page: www.hollywoodlive.net
Anne Volokh, President
Formerly called Movieline, an entertainment lifestyle featuring interviews with stars, directors and producers; as well as information on celebrity shopping, up and coming talent, soundtracks, electronics and fashion associated with hollywood style and trends.
Cost: $13.75
Frequency: Monthly
Founded in 1989
Printed in 4 colors on glossy stock

18613 Hollywood Reporter
Prometheus Global Media
770 Broadway
New York, NY 10003-9595
212-493-4100
Fax: 646-654-5368
Home Page: www.prometheusgm.com
Social Media: Facebook, Twitter, YouTube
Richard D. Beckman, CEO
James A. Finkelstein, Chairman
Madeline Krakowsky, Vice President Circulation
Tracy Brater, Executive Director Crative Service
Gives fresh ideas for film and TV. Covers the full spectrum of craft and commerce in the entertainment industry.
Cost: $199.00
Frequency: Weekly
Circulation: 34770

18614 International Cinematographers Guild Magazine
7755 W Sunset Blvd
Suite 300
Los Angeles, CA 90046-3911
323-876-0160
Fax: 323-876-6383
E-Mail: info@icgmagazine.com
Home Page: www.cameraguild.com
Steven Poster, President
John McCarthy, Marketing
Serves as the journal of 'how to' for film and digital techniques. It incorporates a wide range of editorial for specific job categories in relation to cinematography for Film/Hi-Def/Digital production and defines the tools and technology necessary for advancement in this field. The magazine is written for members of the International Cinematographers Guild, including cinematographers, camera operators, camera assistants, still photographers, publicists, film loaders, and others in the field.
Cost: $48.00
Frequency: Monthly
Founded in 1929

18615 International Documentary Magazine
International Documentary Association
Ste M270
1201 W 5th St
Los Angeles, CA 90017-1476
213-534-3600
Fax: 213-534-3610
E-Mail: tom@documentary.org
Home Page: www.documentary.org
Thomas White, Editor
Tamara Krinsky, Associate Editor
Jodi Pais Montgomery, Manager Advertising Sales
Michael Lumpkin, Executive Director
Devoted exclusively to nonfiction media.
Frequency: Monthly
Founded in 1982
Printed in 4 colors on glossy stock

18616 Journal of Film and Video
University Film and Video Association
University of Illinois Press
1325 S Oak Street
Champaign, IL 61820
217-244-0626
866-244-0626
Fax: 217-244-9910
E-Mail: journals@uiuc.edu
Home Page: www.ufva.org
Stephen Tropiano, Editor
Cheryl Jestis, Membership
Focuses on scholarship in the fields of film and video production, history, criticism, and aes-

thetics. Topics include film and related media, education in these fields, and the function of film and video in society.
Cost: $40.00
Frequency: Quarterly
Circulation: 1200

18617 Journal of Popular Film and Television
Heldref Publications
1319 18th St Nw
Suite 2
Washington, DC 20036-1802

202-296-6267
800-365-9753
Fax: 202-296-5149
E-Mail: subscribe@heldref.org
Home Page: www.heldref.org

James Denton, Executive Director
Gary Edgerton, Co-Executive Editor

Articles discuss networks, genres, series and audiences, as well as celebrity stars, directors and studios. Regular features include essays on the social and cultural background of films and television programs, filmographies, bibliographies, and commisioned book and video reviews.
Cost: $51.00
Frequency: Quarterly
ISSN: 0195-6051
Founded in 1956

18618 Keyframe Magazine
DMG Publishing
2756 N Green Valley Pkwy
Suite 261
Henderson, NV 89014-2120
702-990-8656
Fax: 702-992-0471
E-Mail: info@dmgpublishing.com
Home Page: www.dmgpublishing.com

Dariush Derakhshani, Editor-in-Chief
Cheri Madison, Managing Editor
Charles Edgin, Editorial Director
Alice Edgin, Executive Editor

In response to reader requests, Keyframe is adding to its LightWave and Photoshop tutorials and content additional bonus pages covering other tools used by digital artists. As Keyframe evolves into this larger, better magazine, its new title with be HDRI 3D.
Cost: $54.00
Circulation: 9000
Founded in 1997

18619 Millimeter Magazine
PO Box 2100
Skokie, IL 60076-7800

847-763-9504
866-505-7173
Fax: 847-763-9682
E-Mail: millimeter@pbinews.com
Home Page: www.millimeter.com

Cynthia Wisehart, Editor

In a fast-changing and challenging industry, Millimeter anticipates the future. Its early coverage of important technology-driven trends such as 24p production, desktop post, and digital cinema has helped readers remain competitive and plan their business investments. Millimeter is an authoritative resource for professionals in production, postproduction, animation, streaming, and visual effects for motion pictures, television and commercials.
Cost: $70.00
Frequency: Monthly

18620 Movie Collectors World
Arena Publishing
PO BOX 309
Fraser, MI 48026

586-774-4311
Fax: 703-940-4566
E-Mail: mail@mcwonline.com
Home Page: www.mcwonline.com

Brian Bukantis, Editor

Leading collector's publication for collectors of movie memorabilia, with an emphasis on collectible movie posters. Each issue is filled with ads from dealers and collectors all over the world. In any monthly issue, you will find movie posters common and rare - everything from the 'Golden Age' to today's blockbusters.
Cost: $36.00
36-44 Pages
Frequency: Monthly
Circulation: 6000

18621 MovieMaker
MovieMaker Magazine
8328 De Soto Ave.
Canoga Park, CA 91304
310-742-7214
888-881-5861
Fax: 818-349-9922
Home Page: www.moviemaker.com

Timothy Rhys, Publisher/Editor-in-Chief
Jennifer M Wood, Editor
Phillip Williams, Editor at Large
Ian Bage, New Marketing Services
Liza Kelley, Production Manager

MovieMaker is the world's most widely - read independent movie magazine that focuses on the art and business of making movies. Its editorial mix is a progressive mix of in depth interviews and criticism combined by practical techniques and advice on financing, distribution and production strategies.
Cost: $18.00
Frequency: Quarterly
Circulation: 54000
Founded in 1993
Mailing list available for rentat $175 per M

18622 Premiere Magazine
Hachette Filipacchi Media US Inc
1633 Broadway
Suite 41
New York, NY 10019-6708

212-767-6000
Fax: 212-481-6428
Home Page: www.premiere.com

Jessica Letkemann, Editor
Jennifer Cooper, Producer

A magazine for young adults, which focuses on the art and commerce of the film industry. Premiere's feature articles, profiles and monthly columns include original photgraphy, interviews with Hollywood's A-list and up-and-coming talent, studio heads and producers.

18623 Produced By
The Producers Guild of America
8530 Wilshire Blvd
Suite 450
Beverly Hills, CA 90211-3115
310-358-9020
Fax: 310-358-9520
E-Mail: info@producersguild.org
Home Page: www.producersguild.com

Vance Van Petter, Executive Director
Audra Whaley, Director Operations
Kyle Katz, Director Member Benefits
Chris Greenr, Director Communications
Dan Dodd, Advertising

Provided as a benefit with membership to the Producers Guild of America.
Frequency: Quarterly
Circulation: 325
Founded in 1962

18624 Producer
Testa Communications
25 Willowdale Avenue
Port Washington, NY 11050-3779
516-767-2500
Fax: 516-767-9335
Home Page: avvproducersguide.com

Randi Altman, Editor
Sande Seidman, Advertising Manager

Magazine aimed at producers, directors and creative people in the image and sound realms, with production stories on feature films, television, commercials, documentary, and corporate video projects. Accent is on the creative application of technology, following producers into the field and onto the studio set.
Cost: $15.00
Frequency: Bi-Monthly
Circulation: 18,300

18625 SMPTE Journal
Society of Motion Picture & Television Engineers
3 Barker Ave
Sute 5
White Plains, NY 10601-1509

914-761-1100
Fax: 914-761-3115
E-Mail: smpte@smpte.org
Home Page: www.smpte.org
Social Media: Facebook, Twitter

Kimberly Maki, Executive Director
Charlie Barone, Administrative Assistant

Featuring industry-leading papers and standards, each month the Journal keeps its members on the cutting edge of the industry. Each issue provides the latest research and papers, ranging in style from technical, scientific, and tutorial, to applications/practices. Readers are kept up-to-date on events and meetings, the latest publications and brochures, and new products and developments.
Cost: $140.00
Frequency: Monthly
Circulation: 10000
Founded in 1916
Printed in on glossy stock

18626 San Francisco Cinematheque
San Francisco Cinematheque
145 Ninth Street
Suite 240
San Francisco, CA 94103
415-552-1990
Fax: 415-552-2067
E-Mail: sfc@sfcinematheque.org
Home Page: www.sfcinematheque.org

Stephen Anker, Executive Director
Alfonso Alvarez, Board Director
Gina Basso, Board Director
Aimee Friberg, Board Director
Jeff Lambert, Board Director

Supports risk-taking art, cutting edge artists and the boundless potential of creative expression.
Cost: $15.00
Frequency: Monthly
Founded in 1961

18627 Script
Forum
5638 Sweet Air Road
Baldwin, MD 21013-9009

410-592-3466
888-245-2228

Fax: 410-592-8062
E-Mail: scriptmag@fwmedia.com
Home Page: www.scriptmag.com
Social Media: Facebook, YouTube, RSS

Mark Madnick, Publisher
David Geatty, Founding Publisher
Shelly Mellot, Editor-in-Chief
Andrew Schneider, Managing Editor
Maureen Green, Editor

A leading source of information on the crage and business of writing for film and television. Each issues delivers informative articles on writing, developing and marketing screenplays and television scripts. Most articles are written by working writers. Additionally, development executives, agents, managers and entertainment attorneys contribute regularly.
Cost: $24.95
Frequency: Bi-Monthly
Circulation: 12000

18628 Starlog
1372 Broadway
2nd Floor
New York, NY 10018

212-689-2830
800-934-6788
E-Mail: rita@starloggroup.com
Home Page: www.starlog.com

David McDonnel, Editor
Norman Jacobs, Founder

Information on science fiction happenings in the movies and television industries.
Cost: $56.97
Frequency: Monthly
Circulation: 350000

18629 Variety
Reed Business Information
5700 Wilshire Boulevard
Suite 120
Los Angeles, CA 90036-3659

323-857-6600
866-698-2743
Fax: 323-857-0494
E-Mail: VTCCustserv@cdsfulfillment.com
Home Page: www.variety.com

Charles C Koones, Publisher
Peter Bart, Editor-in-Chief
Timothy Gray, Editor
Kathy Lyford, Managing Editor
Christopher Wessel, Circulation Director

Variety covers all aspects of film, television and cable, homevideo, music, new media and technolgy, theater and finance. Topics run from people, companies, products and performances, to development, financing, distribution, regulation and marketing.
Cost: $259.00
Frequency: Weekly
Circulation: 35168
Founded in 1905

Trade Shows

18630 American Film Institute Festival: AFI Fest
American Film Institute
2021 N Western Avenue
Los Angeles, CA 90027-1657

323-856-7896
866-234-3378
Fax: 323-856-9118
E-Mail: AFIFEST@AFI.com
Home Page: www.afifest.com

Jennifer Morgerman, Publicity Director
Stacey Leinson, Publicity Manager
Lagan Sebert, Publicity Coordinator
John Wildman, Filmmaker Press Liaison
Alison Deknatel, Director Communications

A 10-day event held each November, the festival features a rich slate of films from emerging filmmakers, nightly red-carpet gala premieres and global showcases of the latest work from the great film masters. AFI runs concurrently with the American Film Market. Together, AFT Fest and AFM provide the film industry with the only concurrent festival/market event in North America.
60000 Attendees
Frequency: November
Founded in 1986

18631 International Cinema Equipment (ICECO) Showest
Magna-Tech Electronic Company
5600 NW 32nd Avenue
Miami, FL 33142

305-573-7339
Fax: 305-573-8101
E-Mail: www.iceco@iceco.com
Home Page: www.showest.com

Steven H Krams, President
Dara Reusch, VP
Julio Urbay, VP International Sales/Marketing
Fancisco Blanco, VP Technical Services
Arturo Quintero, Architectural Design/Development

Annual convention for the Motion Picture industry. It is an international gathering devoted exclusively to the movie business. It is also the single largest international gathering of motion picture professionals and theatre owners in the world, with delegates from more than 50 countries in attendance each year.
Frequency: March
Founded in 1975

18632 International Cinema Equipment Company ICECO Show East
Magna-Tech Electronic Company,Inc.
1998 NE 150th Street
North Miami, FL 33181

305-573-7339
Fax: 305-573-8101
E-Mail: iceco@aol.com
Home Page: www.iceco.com

Steven H Krams, President
Dara Reusch, VP
Julio Urbay, VP International Sales/Marketing
Francisco Blanco, VP/Technical Services
Arturo Quintero, Architectural Design & Development

This annual convention brings together over 1300 colleagues from the motion picture industry in the United States, Latin America and the Caribbean. The convention provides information on industry trends, screen films and product reels, state-of-the-art theatre equipment along with services and technologies vital to the industry.
1300 Attendees
Founded in 1975

18633 Moondance Film Festival
970 9th Street
Boulder, CO 80302

303-545-0202
E-Mail: director@moondancefilmfestival.com
Home Page: www.moondancefilmfestival.com

Elizabeth English, Festival Founder/Executive Director
Kyle/Erica Saylors, Festival Director/Event Coordinator
Karina Pyudik, Registration Coordinator
Douglis C Garvin, Special Events Coordinator
Roy Bodner, Publicist/Media Relations

The Festival's primary goal is to present films and scripts which have the power to raise awareness about vital social issues, educating writers and filmmakers, as well as festival audiences, and inspiring them to take positive action. The Festival's objective is to promote and encourage independent filmmakers, screenwriters and playwrights, and the best works in films, screenplays, stageplays, TV scripts, radioplays, film scores, lyrics, librettos, music videos, and short stories.
Frequency: Annual

18634 New York Film Festival
Film Society of Lincoln Center
70 Lincoln Center Plaza
New York, NY 10023

212-875-5610
888-313-6085
E-Mail: filminfo@filmlinc.com
Home Page: www.filmlinc.com
Social Media: Facebook, Twitter

Rose Kuo, Executive Director
Richard Pena, Program Director
Lesli Klainberg, Managing Director

Celebrates American and international cinema and recognizes and supports new filmmakers.
Frequency: Annual

18635 Sundance Film Festival
Sundance Institute
1825 Three Kings Drive
PO Box 684426
Park City, UT 84060

435-658-3456
Fax: 435-658-3457
E-Mail: Institute@sundance.org
Home Page: www.sundance.org

Robert Redford, Founder
Keri Putnam, Executive Director
Jill Miller, Managing Director

Annual festival held in Park City, Utah as a US showcase for American and International independent film. The Institute is dedicated to the development of artists of independent vision and the exhibition of their new work. Since its inception, the Institute has grown into an internationally recognized resource for thousands of independent artists.
Frequency: January
Founded in 1981

18636 Telluride Film Festival
National Film Preserve
800 Jones Street
Berkeley, CA 94710

510-665-9494
Fax: 510-665-9589
E-Mail: mail@telluridefilmfestival.org
Home Page: www.telluridefilmfestival.org

Bill Pence, Founder
Stella Pence, Founder

Well situated on the international film festival calendar, Terruride takes place in Telluride, Colorado, and is defined by sense of purity and commitment.
Founded in 1974

18637 Toronto International Film Festival
TIFF Bell Lightbox
350 King Street West
Toronto

888-599-8433
Home Page: www.tiff.net

William Marshall, Founder
Piers Handling, Director & CEO
Noah Cowan, Artistic Director, Bell Lightbox
Cameron Bailey, Co-Director

Publicly attended film festival that takes place each September in Toronto, Ontario, Canada, showing upwards of 400 films from more than 60 countries. The festival is currently head-

quartered at TIFF Bell Lightbox, which opened in 2010.
Founded in 1976
Mailing list available for rent

Directories & Databases

18638 **Annual Index to Motion Picture Credits**
Academy of Motion Picture Arts and Sciences
8949 Wilshire Blvd
Beverly Hills, CA 90211-1972
310-247-3000
Fax: 310-271-3395
Home Page: www.oscars.org
The Index is closely tied to the annual Academy Awards presentation. As part of the Academy Awards process, the Academy of Motion Picture Arts and Sciences gathers credits for each film hoping to qualify for awards. These credits, compiled and verified by the film's producer or distributor, are the core of the Annual Index and IMPC database. In addition to personal credits, IMPC also records index production and releasing dates, MPAA ratings, running times, color, language, and more.
Frequency: Annual
ISBN: 0-942102-37-1
ISSN: 0163-5123
Founded in 1934

18639 **Blu-Book Production Directory**
Hollywood Creative Directory
5055 Wilshire Blvd
Los Angeles, CA 90036-6103
323-525-2369
800-815-0503
Fax: 323-525-2398
E-Mail: hcdcustomerservice@hcdonline.com
Home Page: www.hcdonline.com
Valencia McKinley, Manager
A comprehensive directory for professionals in the production and post-production industries. Provides current contact information needed to produce a film, TV program, commercial, or music video. The directory contains a special tabbed section on premier below-the-line craft professionals, along with selective credits, and has been expanded to include New York production facilities and services, making it one of the only bi-coastal resources of its kind.
Cost: $39.95
450 Pages
Frequency: Annual
ISBN: 1-928936-44-X

18640 **Boxoffice: Circuit Giants**
Boxoffice
PO Box 1634
Des Plains, IL 60019
212-627-7000
Home Page: www.boxoffice.com
Peter Cane, Publisher
Joe Policy, CEO
Annlee Ellingson, Editor
Francesca Dinglasan, Senior Editor
Bob Vale, VP Advertising and Sales
Directory of the largest exhibition chains. Available to subscribers of Boxoffice magazine
Cost: $59.95
Frequency: Annual
Founded in 1990

18641 **Boxoffice: Distributor Directory**
Boxoffice
PO Box 1634
Des Plains, IL 60019
212-627-7000
Home Page: www.boxoffice.com
Peter Cane, Publisher
Joe Policy, CEO
Annlee Ellingson, Editor
Francesca Dinglasan, Senior Editor
Bob Vale, VP Advertising and Sales
Listings of studio and independent film suppliers. Available to subscribers of Boxoffice magazine
Cost: $59.95
Frequency: Annual
Founded in 1990

18642 **Directors Guild of America Directory of Members**
Directors Guild of America
7920 W Sunset Blvd
Los Angeles, CA 90046-3347
310-289-2000
800-421-4173
Fax: 310-289-2029
Home Page: www.dga.org
Jay Roth, President
Morgan Rumpf, Director Communications
Paul Zepp, Membership Administrator
Darrell L Hop, Editor DGA Monthly/Website
Michael Apted, Secretary
The DGA represents Film and Television Directors, Unit Production Managers, First Assistant Directors, Second Assistant Directors, Technical Coordinators and Tape Associate Directors, Stage Managers and Production Associates. The Directory is available in print and on-line
Cost: $25.00
Frequency: Annual

18643 **Editors Guild Directory**
Motion Picture Editors Guild
7715 Sunset Boulevard
Suite 200
Hollywood, CA 90046
323-876-4770
800-705-8700
Fax: 323-876-0861
E-Mail: info@editorsguild.com
Home Page: www.editorsguild.com
Ron Kutak, Executive Director
Tomm Carroll, Publications Director
Serena Kungr, Director Membership Services
Adriana Iglesias-Dietl, Membership Administrator
Tris Carpenter, Manager
An invaluable resource for producers, directors and post production professionals alike. It lists contact, credit, award and classification information for all of the Guild's active members at the time of publication, as well as a list of Oscar and Emmy winners for every year since the awards began. It also includes a retirees section.
Cost: $25.00
Frequency: Bi-Annual
Founded in 1994

18644 **Fame Index**
Hollywood Madison Group
11684 Ventura Boulevard
#258
Studio City, CA 91604-2499
818-762-8008
Fax: 818-762-8089
Home Page: holllywood-madison.com
Jonathan Holiff, Founder/President/CEO
Search over 10,000 celebrities from actors to athletes to find every performer who meets your needs. The Index has more than 250 searchable criteria including: age, sex, children, birthplace, genre, fees, ethnicity/heritage, biography, statistics, interests, hobbies, sports, personality attributes, charity affiliations, medical conditions, and endorsement histories. Contact information includes agent, manager, publicist, business manager, attorney, and personal assistant.
Founded in 1996

18645 **Film Journal: Distribution Guide Issue**
Film Journal International
770 Broadway
5th Floor
New York, NY 10003-9595
646-654-7680
Fax: 646-654-7694
Home Page: www.filmjournal.com
Robert Sunshine, Publisher/Editor
Kevin Lally, Executive Editor
Rex Roberts, Associate Editor
Andrew Sunshine, Advertising Director
Katey Rich, Editorial Assistant
The International Distribution and subdistribution Guide supplements the regular monthly Buying and Booking Guide. It is designed to furnish ready reference information on the who, what, where and how of theatrical sales. It lists the names, addresses, personnel, telephone numbers and product of domestic and international distributors, both major and independent, along with similar information on regional exchanges together with national companies they handle.
Frequency: Annual

18646 **Film Journal: Equipment Guide**
Film Journal International
770 Broadway
5th Floor
New York, NY 10003-9595
646-654-7680
Fax: 646-654-7694
Home Page: www.filmjournal.com
Robert Sunshine, Publisher/Editor
Kevin Lally, Executive Editor
Robin Klamfoth, Advertising Director
Rex Roberts, Associate Editor
Katey Rich, Editorial Assistant
The Equipment, Concessions and Services Guide is designed to provide ready reference information on the theatrical equipment and concessions industry. It lists in detail the company names, addresses, telephone numbers, personnel, affiliations and products of equipment and concession manufacturers and service companies, along with similar information on US and foreign service dealers and suppliers, arranged in alphabetical order according to state or country.
Frequency: Annual

18647 **Film Journal: Exhibition Guide**
Film Journal International
770 Broadway
5th Floor
New York, NY 10003-9595
212-493-4097
Fax: 646-654-7694
E-Mail: subscriptions@filmjournal.com
Home Page: www.filmjournal.com
Robert Sunshine, Publisher/Editor
Kevin Lally, Executive Editor
Robin Klamfoth, Advertising Director
Rex Roberts, Associate Editor
Sarah Sluis, Editorial Assistant
The exhibition Guide is an alphabetical listing designed to provide ready reference information on the leading theatrical motion picture circuits. It lists in comprehensive detail such data as company names, addresses and phone numbers, total screens and new screens pro-

jected, division office locations, top personnel, recent circuit acquisitions, and a state-by-state breakdown of screens.
Frequency: Annual
Founded in 1934
Mailing list available for rent

18648 Film Superlist: Motion Pictures in the Public Domain
Hollywood Film Archive
8391 Beverly Blvd
Ste. 321
Los Angeles, CA 90048-2633
323-655-4968
Richard Baer, Executive Director
Created by Walter E. Hurst and updated by Richard Baer. 1992-1994. Three volumes to date, covering 50,000 films from the years 1894-1939, 1940-1949 and 1950-1959.

18649 Grey House Performing Arts Directory
Grey House Publishing
4919 Route 22
PO Box 56
Amenia, NY 12501
518-789-8700
800-562-2139
Fax: 845-373-6390
E-Mail: books@greyhouse.com
Home Page: www.greyhouse.com
Social Media: Facebook, Twitter
Leslie Mackenzie, Publisher
Richard Gottlieb, Editor
The most comprehensive resource covering the Performing Arts. This directory provides current information on over 8,500 Dance Companies, Instrumental Music Programs, Opera Companies, Choral Groups, Theater Companies, Performing Arts Series, Performing Arts Facilities and Artist Management Groups.
Cost: $185.00
1200 Pages
Frequency: Annual
ISBN: 1-592373-76-3
Founded in 1981

18650 Grey House Performing Arts Directory - Online Database
Grey House Publishing
4919 Route 22
PO Box 56
Amenia, NY 12501
518-789-8700
800-562-2139
Fax: 518-789-0556
E-Mail: gold@greyhouse.com
Home Page: www.gold.greyhouse.com
Social Media: Facebook, Twitter
Leslie Mackenzie, Publisher
Richard Gottlieb, Editor
The Grey House Performing Arts Directory - Online Database provides immediate access to dance companies, orchestras, opera companies, choral groups, theater companies, series, festivals and perfoming arts facilities across the country, or in their region, state, or in your own backyard. It offers unequaled coverage of the Performing Arts - over 8,500 listings - of the major performance organization, facilities, and information resources.
Frequency: Annual
Founded in 1981

18651 International Motion Picture Alamanc
Quigley Publishing Company
64 Wintergreen Lane
Groton, MA 01450
860-228-0247
800-231-8239
Fax: 860-228-0157
E-Mail: quigleypub@aol.com
Home Page: www.quigleypublishing.com
William J Quigley, President/Publisher
Eileen Quigley, Editor
Contains over 400 pages of biographies and 500 pages of reference material. From 1928 to the present day, the complete set contains the biography of everyone who has ever been of importance to the Industry. Each edition includes thousands of company listings, credits for current films and films released in the prior ten years, statistics and awards and complete coverage of all aspects of the industry, including production, distribution and exhibition.
Cost: $175.00
Frequency: Annual

18652 International Television and Video Almanac
Quigley Publishing Company
64 Wintergreen Lane
Groton, MA 01450
860-228-0247
800-231-8239
Fax: 860-228-0157
E-Mail: quigleypub@aol.com
Home Page: www.quigleypublishing.com
William J Quigley, President/Publisher
Eileen Quigley, Editor
Each edition contains over 400 pages of biographies and an additional 500 pages of reference material on television programs, broadcast, cable and satellie, production services, the video industry, statistics and awards. Included are detailed listings for thousands of companies, as well as coverage outside the United States.
Cost: $175.00
Frequency: Annual
Founded in 1955

18653 Mini Reviews
Cineman Syndicate
31 Purchase St
Suite 203
Rye, NY 10580-3013
914-967-5353
Home Page: www.minireviews.com
John P McCarthy, Editor
An easy to read, easy to use guide for movie watchers updated weekly.
Frequency: Weekly
Founded in 2000

18654 Motion Picture TV and Theatre Directory
Motion Picture Enterprises
PO Box 276
Tarrytown, NY 10591-0276
212-245-0969
Fax: 212-245-0974
Home Page: www.mpe.net
Neal R Pilzer, Publisher
The Guide is mailed to members of 59 trade associations, unions and professional societies; decision-makers at advertising agencies, production companies, TV stations, and government agencies; faculty and students of nearly 200 film schools; and other prime purchasers of film and TV equipment and services nationwide. Companies are listed both by category and company name. Listings include company name, address and telephone number as well as fax numbers, e-mail addresses, and web site URLs.
Cost: $18.80
335 Pages
Frequency: Annual
Circulation: 82500
Founded in 1963

18655 Movie World Almanac
Hollywood Film Archive
8391 Beverly Blvd
PMB 321
Los Angeles, CA 90048-2633
323-655-4968
Richard Baer, Executive Director
Lists over 200 major American and foreign film distributors who handle old and contemporary films.

18656 Reel Directory
Lynetta Freeman
PO Box 1910
Boyes Hot Springs, CA 95416
415-531-9760
Fax: 707-581-1725
E-Mail: info@reeldirectory.com
Home Page: www.reeldirectory.com
Lynetta Freeman, Manager
Keith Marsalis, Director
Katie Carney, Director of Marketing
Source for Film, Video and Multimedia in Northern California.
Cost: $25.00
700 Pages
Frequency: Annual
Circulation: 5,000
Founded in 1979

18657 Studio Report: Film Development
Hollywood Creative Directory
5055 Wilshire Blvd
Los Angeles, CA 90036-6103
323-525-2369
800-815-0503
Fax: 323-525-2398
E-Mail: hcdcustomerservice@hcdonline.com
Home Page: www.hcdonline.com
Valencia McKinley, Manager
The only directory of its kind, in print for the first time. A complete breakdown of film development project tracking. A-Z listings by title, spec screenplays sold, hot studio projects, cross-referenced by studio, production company and genre. The directory's main body consists of an alphabetical listing of all in-development projects that have achieved a forward-moving milestone some time in the last five months. Subsequent sections sort and cross-reference the information to highlight aspects
Cost: $19.95
190 Pages
ISBN: 1-928936-49-0

Industry Web Sites

18658 http://gold.greyhouse.com
G.O.L.D Grey House OnLine Databases
Grey House Publishing's online database platform, GOLD, offers Quick Search, Keyword Search and Expert Search for most business sectors including motion picture and entertainment markets. The GOLD platform makes finding the information you need quick and easy - whether you're a novice searcher or an experienced database user. All of Grey House's directory products are available for subscription on the GOLD platform.

18659 www.actioncutprint.com
Action-Cut-Print
Website for filmmakers. filmmaking resources, free ezine for directors, film and TV bookstore. The Director's Chair magazine by director Peter D. Marshall.

18660 www.artdirectors.org
Art Directors Guild
Conceive and manage the background and settings for most films and television projects.

18661 www.asatalent.com
ASA/Affordable Services
Entertainment services are brought to you as you need them and when you need them at the best price available. Security services, studio teachers, and medical services.

18662 www.castingsociety.com
Casting Society of America
An organization representing casting directors.

18663 www.discoverhollywood.com
Hollywood Arts Council
Promotes, nurtures and supports the arts field in Hollywood. Discover Hollywood on line.

18664 www.documentary.org
International Documentary Association
A nonprofit association founded to promote non-fiction film and video, to support the efforts of documentary film and video makers around the world, and to increase public appreciation and demand for the documentary.

18665 www.greyhouse.com
Grey House Publishing
Authoritative reference directories for most business sectors including motion picure and entertainment markets. Users can search the online databases with varied search criteria allowing for custom searches by product category, geographic area, sales volume, keyword, subject and more. Full Grey House catalog and online ordering also available.

18666 www.iqfilm.org
International Quorum of Film and Video Producers
Fosters the exchange of information and ideas. Seeks to raise professional standards. Disseminates information on new concepts and technology.

18667 www.millimeter.com
Millimeter Magazine
Authoritative resource for more than 33,000 qualified professionals in production, postproduction, animation, streaming and visual effects for motion pictures, television and commercials.

18668 www.mpaa.org
Motion Picture Association of America
Promotes high moral and artistic standards in motion picture production. Maintains Motion Picture Association Political Action Committee.

18669 www.nyfa.com
New York Film Academy
Educational institution devoted to providing focused filmmaking and acting instructions. Geared to offer an intensive, hands-on experience which gives students the opportunity to develop their creative skills to the fullest extent possible.

18670 www.oscars.org
Academy of Motion Picture Arts and Sciences
Current information on motion pictures, the arts and sciences, events and screenings.

18671 www.producersguild.com
Producers Guild of America
Members are producers of motion pictures and television shows mainly in the Los Angeles area.

18672 www.resumegenie.com
Motion Pictures job listings, salary information and job search tips.

18673 www.smpte.org
Society of Motion Picture & Television Engineers
Advances the practice and theory of engineering in television and film industry.

18674 www.stuntnet.com
International Stunt Association
Represents those involved in stunt work for the entertainment industry.

18675 www.stuntwomen.com
Stuntwomen's Association of Motion Pictures
A professional association for stuntwomen and stunt coordinators which seeks to uphold professional standards and improve working conditions.

18676 www.sundance.org
Sundance Institute
Nonprofit corporation dedicated to the support and development of emerging screenwriters and directors of vision. Hosts the Sundance Film Festival.

18677 www.wif.org
Women in Film
For global entertainment,communication and media industries. Focuses on contemporary issues facing women and provides an extensive network of valuable contacts, educational programs, scholars, film finishing funds, grants, community outreach, advocacy and practical services that promote, nurture and mentor women to achieve their highest potential.

Associations

18678 American Historic Racing Motorcycle Association
309 Buffalo Run
Goodlettsville, TN 37072
615-420-6435
Fax: 615-420-6438
E-Mail: dlamberth@comcast.net
Home Page: www.ahrma.org
Social Media: Facebook
Dave Janiec, Chairman
Matthew Benson, Communications Director
Mark Hatten, Treasurer
Carl Anderson, Secretary
Mark Hatten, Treasurer
For individuals interested in vintage racing mo torcycles.
5M Members
Founded in 1989

18679 American Motorcyclist Association
13515 Yarmouth Dr
Pickerington, OH 43147-8273
614-856-1900
800-AMA-JOIN
Fax: 614-856-1920
E-Mail: tlindsay@ama-cycle.org
Home Page: www.amadirectlink.com
Rob Dingman, President
Maggie McNally, Chair
Russel Brenan, Vice Chairman
Scott Papenfus, Marketing Director
Ken Ford, Assistant Treasurer
The association's purpose is to pursue, protect and promote the interests of motorcyclists, while serving the needs of its members.
270M Members
Founded in 1924

18680 Breakdown & Legal Assistance for Motorcyclists
13047 Ventura Blvd
Suite 100
Studio City, CA 91604-2250
818-377-6280
800-424-5377
Fax: 818-377-6290
E-Mail: russbrown@russbrown.com
Home Page: www.russbrown.com
J Russell Brown II, President
A support group for motorcyclists. Offers roadside assistance for emergencies and breakdowns. Attorney referral service specializing in motorcycle accident cases. Brochures and guest speakers available upon request, also offers a twenty-four hour toll-free hotline.
100M Members
Founded in 1983

18681 Harley Owners Group
National H.O.G. Office
PO Box 453
Milwaukee, WI 53201
800-258-2464
Fax: 414-343-4515
Home Page: www.harleydavidson.com
James L Ziemer, President/CEO
Harley Davidson established the Harley Owners Group in response to a growing desire by Harley riders for an organized way to share their passion and show their pride.
60000 Members
Founded in 1983

18682 Motorcycle & Moped Industry Council
716 Gordon Baker Road
Suite 100
North York, M2H 3B4, ON
416-491-4449
877-470-6642
Fax: 416-493-1985
E-Mail: info@mmic.ca
Home Page: www.mmic.ca
Robert Ramsay, President
National nonprofit trade association which represents the responsible interest of the major motorcycle distributors, as well as the manufacturers, distributors and the retail outlets of motorcycle-related products and services, and individual owners and riders of motorcycles in Canada.
140 Members
Founded in 1971

18683 Motorcycle Industry Council
2 Jenner Street
Suite 150
Irvine, CA 92618-3806
949-727-4211
Fax: 949-727-3313
E-Mail: dkopf@mic.org
Home Page: www.mic.org
Robert Moffit, Chairman
Tim Buche, President
David Kopf, Manager
A nonprofit national trade association created to represent the motorcycle industry.
Cost: $25.00
300 Members
Frequency: Annual
ISSN: 0149-3027
Founded in 1940

18684 Motorcycle Riders Foundation
236 Massachusetts Ave NE
Suite 204
Washington, DC 20002-4980
202-546-0983
Fax: 202-546-0986
E-Mail: jeff@mrf.org
Home Page: www.mrf.org
Kirk Willard, President
Mike Kerr, Vice President
Paulette Pinkham, Secretary
Chuc Coulter, Treasurer
Tiffany Latimer, Office Manager
To continue developing an aggressive, independent national advocate for the advancement of motorcycling and its associated lifestyle which is financially stable and exceeds the needs of motorcycling enthusiasts.
Founded in 1987

18685 Motorcycle Safety Foundation
2 Jenner
Suite 150
Irvine, CA 92618-3812
949-727-3227
Fax: 949-727-4217
Home Page: www.msf-usa.org
Tim Buche, President
Founded by the five leading manufacturers and distributors of motorcycles for the purpose of public safety education.
7 Members
Founded in 1972

18686 Women in the Wind
PO Box 8392
Toledo, OH 43605-0392
E-Mail: becky@womeninthewind.org
Home Page: www.womeninthewind.org
Becky Brown, Founder/Treasurer
Gale Collins, President
Lauranne Bailey, VP
Peggy Zeeb, Secretary
Seeks to promote a positive image for women motorcyclists. Educates members on maintenance and safety.
1000 Members
Founded in 1979

Newsletters

18687 AHRMA Newsletter
American Historic Racing Motorcycle Association
PO Box 882
Wausau, WI 54402-0882
715-842-9699
Fax: 715-842-9545
Home Page: www.ahrma.org
Jeff Smith, Director
Matt Benson, Executive Director
David Lamberth, Executive Director
For individuals interested in vintage motorcycles.
Cost: $2.00
Circulation: 5,000

18688 MRF Reports
Motorcycle Riders Foundation
236 Massachusetts Ave Ne
Suite 204
Washington, DC 20002-4980
202-546-0983
Fax: 202-546-0986
E-Mail: jeff@mrf.org
Home Page: www.mrf.org
Eric Hampton, Editor/Publisher
Frequency: Bi-Monthly

Magazines & Journals

18689 American Motorcyclist
American Motorcyclist Association
13515 Yarmouth Dr
Pickerington, OH 43147-8273
614-856-1900
800-262-5646
Fax: 614-856-1920
E-Mail: membership@ama-cycle.org
Home Page:
http://www.americanmotorcyclist.com
Rob Dingman, President
Bill Wood, Editor-in-Chief
Grant Parsons, Managing Editor
John Holliday, Circulation
Magazine covers every facet of motorcycling. Each monthly issue details the people, places and events - from road rallies to road races - that make up the American motorcycling experience.
Cost: $39.00
Frequency: Monthly
Circulation: 260000
Founded in 1924
Printed in 4 colors on glossy stock

18690 Biker
Paisano Publishers

PO Box 3075
Agoura Hills, CA 91376-3075

818-898-8740
800-962-985
Fax: 818-889-1252
Home Page: easyridersevents.com

Joe Teresi, Publisher
Dean Shawier, Editor

Events and charity events for the motorcycle enthusiast.
Cost: $15.00
96 Pages
Founded in 1971

18691 Cycle World
Hachette Filipacchi Media US
1499 Monrovia Ave
Newport Beach, CA 92663-2752

949-720-5300
Fax: 949-631-2374
Home Page: www.hfmus.com

Nancy Laporte, Executive Director
David Edwards, Editor-in-Chief

Publication for motorcycle enthusiasts.
Cost: $16.00
136 Pages
Frequency: Monthly
Circulation: 325000

18692 Cycling USA
United States Cycling Federation
1 Olympic Plz
Colorado Spring, CO 80909-5775

719-866-4581
Fax: 719-866-4628
E-Mail: web@usacycling.org
Home Page: www.usacycling.org

Gerard Bisceglia, CEO
Sean Petty, Chief of Staff

Bike racing magazine.
Cost: $10.00
24 Pages
Circulation: 3000
Founded in 1920

18693 Dealernews Magazine
Advanstar Communications
New York
New York, NY 10016-5778

212-951-6600
800-854-3112
Fax: 212-951-6793
E-Mail: info@advanstar.com
Home Page: www.dealernews.com

Mike Vaughan, Publisher
Mary Slepicka, Associate Publisher
Arlo Redwine, Managing Editor

Written for and read by a qualified power sports dealer network and related industry associates. It features articles on merchandising, sales techniques and profiles of successful retailers. Industry trends and business conditions are monitored through exclusive industry research.
Frequency: Monthly
Circulation: 17535
Founded in 1965
Printed in 4 colors on glossy stock

18694 Easyriders
Paisano Publishers
3547 Old Conejo Rd
Suite 106
Newbury Park, CA 91320

800-962-9857
800-825-7294
Fax: 805-375-4591
E-Mail: info@easyridersevents.com
Home Page: easyridersevents.com

Joe Teresi, Publisher
Keith Ball, Editor
John Green, President

Motorcycle magazine.
Cost: $39.95
136 Pages
Frequency: Monthly
Founded in 1971

18695 Motorcycle Dealer News
Edgell Communications
4500 Campus Drive
Suite 100
Santa Ana, CA 92705

FAX 949-252-0499

Don Emde, Publisher

For dealers of power sports equipment and supplies.
Cost: $25.00

18696 Motorcycle Industry Magazine
Industry Shopper Publishing
PO Box 160
Gardnerville, NV 89410-160

775-782-0222
800-576-4624
Fax: 775-782-0266
Home Page: www.mimag.com

Rick Campbell, Publisher
Rick Campbell, Editor
Caroline Carr, Sales Manager

Provides information to the motorcycle and accessory dealer and or retailer on products, services, events and people aiming to maximize profitablity and growth, also includes personal watercraft vehicles, ATV's and snowmobiles.
Frequency: Monthly
Circulation: 14000
ISSN: 0884-626X
Founded in 1976
Printed in 4 colors on glossy stock

18697 Shootin the Breeze
Women in the Wind
PO Box 8392
Toledo, OH 43605-0392

Home Page: www.womeninthewind.org

Becky Brown, Founder
Gale Collins, President
Lauranne Bailey, VP
Peggy Zeeb, Secretary

Available to all Women in the Wind members.
Frequency: 6x/year

18698 Upshift Magazine
Motorcycle & Moped Industry Council
3000 Steeles Avenue East
Suite 201
Markham, Ontario L3R 4T9

416-491-4449
877-470-6642
Fax: 416-493-1985
E-Mail: info@mmic.ca
Home Page: www.mmic.ca

Steve Thornton, Producer

Features articles and information on motorcycles.
Frequency: Quarterly

Trade Shows

18699 AMA Members Tour
American Motorcyclist Association
13515 Yarmouth Drive
Pickerington, OH 43147

614-856-1900
Fax: 614-856-1920
E-Mail: tlindsay@ama-cycle.org
Home Page:
http://www.americanmotorcyclist.com

Will Stoner, Director Special Events

The goal is to spread awareness of the benefits of membership and the importance of the work of the AMA does in protecting all motorcyclists' right to ride.
Frequency: Semi-Annual, June

18700 AMA Vintage Motorcycle Days
American Motorcyclist Association
13515 Yarmouth Drive
Pickerington, OH 43147

614-856-1900
Fax: 614-856-1920
E-Mail: tlindsay@ama-cycle.org
Home Page: www.amadirectlink.com

Will Stoner, Director Special Events

Will benefit the Motorcycle Hall of Fame Museum and will feature an exhibit of classic motorcycles and memorabilia.
Frequency: July

18701 Annual Meeting of the Minds
Motorcycle Riders Foundation
236 Massachusetts Avenue NE
Suite 510
Washington, DC 20002-4980

202-546-0983
Fax: 202-546-0986
E-Mail: downs@mrf.org
Home Page: www.mrf.org

Carol Downs, Conference Director

Designed to educate and motivate those in the motorcyclists' rights community. The premier leadership conference that boasts an audience from across the nation and around the world.
Frequency: September

18702 Beast of the East
Motorcycle Riders Foundation
236 Massachusetts Avenue NE
Suite 510
Washington, DC 20002-4980

202-546-0983
Fax: 202-546-0986
E-Mail: downs@mrf.org
Home Page: www.mrf.org

Carol Downs, Conference Director

Designed to educate and motivate those in the motorcyclists' rights community. These events are a great chance to meet other people who are as passionate about motorcyclists' rights as you are.
Frequency: April

18703 Best of the West
Motorcycle Riders Foundation
236 Massachusetts Avenue NE
Suite 510
Washington, DC 20002-4980

202-546-0983
Fax: 202-546-0986
E-Mail: downs@mrf.org
Home Page: www.mrf.org

Carol Downs, Conference Director

Designed to educate and motivate those in the motorcyclists' rights community. These events are a great chance to meet other people who are as passionate about motorcyclists' rights as you are.
Frequency: June

18704 International Motorcycle Show
Advanstar Communications

201 E Sandpointe
Suite 600
Santa Ana, CA 92707

714-138-8400
Fax: 714-513-8481
Home Page: www.motorcycleshows.com

Jeff D'Entremont, Show Director
Leah Stevens, Account Manager
Chris Alonzo, Account Manager

Exposition for motorcyclists and enthusiasts.

18705 Los Angeles Calendar Motorcycle Show
Breakdown & Legal Assistance for Motorcyclists
13047 Ventura Boulevard
Suite 100
Studio City, CA 91604

323-321-1483
800-424-5377
Fax: 818-377-6290
E-Mail: russbrown@russbrown.com
Home Page: www.russbrown.com

Russ Brown, President

Biggest custom and performance streetbike event.
Frequency: July
Founded in 1983

18706 Motocross American Reunion and Exhibit Grand Opening
American Motorcyclist Association
13515 Yarmouth Drive
Pickerington, OH 43147

614-856-1900
800-262-5646
Fax: 614-856-1920
Home Page: americanmotorcyclist.com

Since 1924, the AMA has protected the future of motorcycling and promoted the cotorcycle lifestyle. As the world's largest motorcycling rights organization, the AMA advocates for motorcyclists' interests in the halls of local, state and federal government, the committees of international governing organizations, and the court of pulic opinion.
Frequency: July
Founded in 1924

18707 Motorcycle and Parts
Glahe International
PO Box 2460
Germantown, MD 20875-2460

301-515-0012
Fax: 301-515-0016
Home Page: www.glahe.com

Exhibits of motorcycle equipment, supplies and services.

18708 Summer Nationals
Women in the Wind
PO Box 8392
Toledo, OH 43605-0392

Home Page: www.womeninthewind.org

Becky Brown, Founder/Treasurer
Gale Collins, President
Lauranne Bailey, VP
Peggy Zeeb, Secretary
Frequency: July

Directories & Databases

18709 MSF Guide to Motorcycling Excellence
Motorcycle Safety Foundation
2 Jenner
Irvine, CA 92618-3812

949-727-3227
Fax: 949-727-4217
Home Page: www.msf-usa.org

Tim Buche, President

Covering the skills, knowledge and strategies for riding right. Subjects include: preparing yourself and your bike, developing street strategies, and advanced theory for experienced riders.
Cost: $24.95
176 Pages

18710 Motorcycle Statistical Annual
Motorcycle Industry Council
2 Jenner Street
Suite 150
Irvine, CA 92618-3806

949-727-4211
Fax: 949-727-3313

This industry-related directory offers statistical information on US motorcycle manufacturers and distributors, as well as national and state motorcycle associations.
Cost: $25.00
Frequency: Annual
ISSN: 0149-3027

Industry Web Sites

18711 http://gold.greyhouse.com
G.O.L.D Grey House OnLine Databases
Grey House Publishing's online database platform, GOLD, offers Quick Search, Keyword Search and Expert Search for most business sectors including motorcycle and biking markets. The GOLD platform makes finding the information you need quick and easy - whether you're a novice searcher or an experienced database user. All of Grey House's directory products are available for subscription on the GOLD platform.

18712 www.ahrma.org
American Historic Racing Motorcycle Association
For individuals interested in vintage racing motorcycles.

18713 www.amadirectlink.com
American Motorcyclist Association
Covers every facet of motorcycling: the people, places and events that make up the American motorcycling experience. In addition, this award winning website offers profiles of issues affecting everyone who rides, and provides tools that help motorcyclists communicate directly with legislators, business leaders and the news media.

18714 www.greyhouse.com
Grey House Publishing
Authoritative reference directories for most business sectors including motocycle and biking markets. Users can search the online databases with varied search criteria allowing for custom searches by product category, geographic area, sales volume, keyword, subject and more. Full Grey House catalog and online ordering also available.

18715 www.mic.org
Motorcycle Industry Council
Nonprofit national trade association created to represent the motorcycle industry.

18716 www.mmic.ca
Motorcycle & Moped Industry Council
National nonprofit trade association which represents the responsible interest of the major motorcycle distributors, as well as the manufacturers, distributors and the retail outlets of motorcycle related products and services, and individual owners and riders of motorcycles in Canada.

18717 www.msf-usa.org
Motorcycle Safety Foundation
Founded by the five leading manufacturers and distributors of motorcycles for the purpose of public safety education.

18718 www.russbrown.com
Breakdown & Legal Assistance for Motorcyclists
A support group for motorcyclists. Offers roadside assistance for emergencies and breakdowns. Attorney referral service specializing in motorcycle accident cases. Brochures and guest speakers available upon request, also offers a twenty-four hour toll-free hotline.

Associations

18719 Academy of Country Music
5500 Balboa Blvd
Suite 200
Encino, CA 91316-1505

818-788-8000
Fax: 818-788-0999
E-Mail: info@acmcountry.com
Home Page: www.acmcountry.com

Gayle Holcomb, Chairman
David Young, Director Operations
Tiffany Moon, Secretary
Brandi Brammer, Project Manager
Tree Paine, Director Marketing

Involved in numerous events and activities promoting country music. Presents annual awards.
4M Members
Founded in 1964

18720 Accordian Federation of North America
14126 E Rosencrans Boulevard
Santa Fe Springs, CA 90670

562-921-5058
E-Mail: afna@musician.org
Home Page: www.afnafestival.org
Social Media: Facebook, Twitter

Madeleine D'Ablaing, President
Debbie Gray, VP
Oakley Yale, Secretary
Prisscilla Martinez, Treasurer
Larry Demian, Parliamentarian

Members are primarily teachers and music school owners with the primary purpose to encourage young people to pursue their music study. Holds festivals and competitions
75 Members
Founded in 1972

18721 Accordion Teachers Guild
10349 Century,Lane
Overland Park, KS 66215

913-722-5625
E-Mail: Betty@BettyJoSimon.com
Home Page: www.accordions.com/atg

Betty Jo Simon, President
Liz Finch, First VP
Amy Jo Sawyer, Second VP
Joan C. Sommers, Executive Secretary
John Neu, Treasurer

ATG members are accordion teachers and professionals committed to furthering the progress of the accordion by improving teaching standards, music and all phases of music education.
Founded in 1940

18722 Acoustical Society of America
2 Huntington Quadrangle
Suite 1NO1
Melville, NY 11747-4502

516-576-2360
Fax: 516-576-2377
E-Mail: asa@aip.org
Home Page: www.acousticalsociety.org

David Bradley, President
Michael Stinson, Vice President
David Feit, Treasurer
Paul Shomer, Standards Director
Charles Schmid, Executive Director

Premier international scientific society in acoustics, dedicated to increasing and diffusing the knowledge of acoustics and its practical applications.

18723 American Choral Directors Association
545 Couch Drive
Oklahoma City, OK 73102

405-232-8161
Fax: 405-232-8162
Home Page: www.acdaonline.org

Timothy Sharp, Executive Director
Jerry Mccoy, President
Haiary Aphelstadt, VP
Jo-Ann Miller, Treasurer

Nonprofit music-education organization whose central purpose is to promote excellence in choral music through performance, composition, publication, research and teaching. In addition, ACDA strives to elevate choral music's position in American society through arts advocacy. Holds annual convention.
Cost: $90.00
19500 Members
Founded in 1959

18724 American College of Musicians
PO Box 1807
Austin, TX 78767

512-478-5775
Fax: 512-478-5843
E-Mail: ngpt@pianoguild.com
Home Page: www.pianoguild.com

Richard Allison, President
Julia Kruger, VP

Provides student awards and teachers benefits.
Founded in 1931

18725 American Federation of Musicians of the United States and Canada
1501 Broadway
Suite 600
New York, NY 10036-5501

212-869-1330
Fax: 212-764-6134
E-Mail: info@afm.org
Home Page: www.afm.org

Thomas Lee, President
Linda Patterson, Executive Secreatry to President

AFM is an association of professional musicians united through their locals so that they can live and work in dignity; produce work that will be fulfilling and compensated fairly; have a meaningful voice in decisions that affect them; have the opportunity to develop their talents and skills; whose collective voice and power will be realized in a democratic and progressive union; and who oppose the forces of exploitation through their union solidarity.
10K Members
Founded in 1896

18726 American Federation of Violin and Bow Makers
1121 East Avenue
Red Wing, MN 55066

507-396-3411
E-Mail: info@afvbm.org
Home Page: www.afvbm.com

Peter Seman, President
Yung Chin, Vice President
William Scott, Treasurer
Lisbeth N.Butler, Secretary

Members are those with recognized professional abilities and experience in either making or repairing violins and bows. They are elected to the Federation and are entitled to all privileges and duties of membership. The Federation has designed programs to held develop the technical skills and knowledge of the membership through seminars and regular meeting events. The Federation sponsors exhibitions as a forum for makers,musicians and the general public.
Cost: $300.00
Founded in 1980

18727 American Gamelan Institute
603-448-6060
Fax: 603-448-6060
E-Mail: agi@gamelan.org
Home Page: www.gamelan.org

Founded in 1983

18728 American Guild of Music
PO Box 599
Warren, MI 48090

248-686-1975
E-Mail: agm@americanguild.org
Home Page: www.americanguild.org

Barry Carr, President
Joanne Darby, Treasurer
Lorelei Eccleston Dart, First VP
Steve Petrunak, Second VP

The worls's oldest international music organization. Its membership is oipen to independent music teachers, music store owners and their teaching staffs, music publishers and instrument manufacturers and music students.
6000 Members

18729 American Guild of Musical Artists
1430 Broadway
14th Floor
New York, NY 10018-3308

212-265-3687
Fax: 212-262-9088
E-Mail: agma@musicalartists.org
Home Page: www.musicalartists.org
Social Media: Facebook

Alan S.Gordon, Executive Director
Gerry Angel, Director of Operations
Deborah A.Maher, Associate Executive Director
Gerry Angel, Director of Operations

AGMA is a labor union. It negotiates collective bargaining agreements for its members that provide them with these vital benefits: guaranteed salaries; rehearsal and overtime pay; regulated work hours; vacation and sick pay; access to low-cost health benefits; good-faith resolution of disputes; and protection of their legal and contractual rights.
5700 Members
Founded in 1936

18730 American Guild of Organists
475 Riverside Drive
Suite 1260
New York, NY 10115-0055

212-870-2310
Fax: 212-870-2163
E-Mail: info@agohq.org
Home Page: www.agohq.org

James Thomashower, Executive Director
Marcia Van Oyen, Director

Membership in the American Guild of Organists is primarily through local chapters, which hold regular meetings featuring performances, lectures, seminars, and discussions on a wide variety of topics. Many chapters also offer monthly newsletters, scholarship programs, musician placement services, and substitute referrals to employing institutions. Membership can also be without chapter affiliation.
20000 Members
Founded in 1896

18731 **American Harp Society**
PO Box 278
Greenfield Center, NY 12833

518-893-7495
E-Mail: elizabetharp@juno.com
Home Page: www.harpsociety.org

Delaine Fedson, President
Randall Pratt, 1st VP
Lillian Lau, 2nd VP
Jaymee Haefner, Secretary
Ashanti Pretlow, Executive Secretary

Promotes and fosters the appreciation of the harp as a musical instrument, to encourage the composition of music for the harp and to improve the quality of performance of harpists.
Cost: $50.00
3000 Members
Founded in 1962

18732 **American Music Therapy Association**
8455 Colesville Rd
Suite 1000
Silver Spring, MD 20910-3392

301-589-3300
Fax: 301-589-5175
E-Mail: info@musictherapy.org
Home Page: www.musictherapy.org

Andrea Farbman, Executive Director
Brian Abrams, Mid Atlantic Region President

The mission of the American Music Therapy Association is to advance public awareness of the benefits of music therapy and increase access to quality music therapy services in a rapidly changing world.
3800 Members
Founded in 1998

18733 **American Musical Instrument Society**
1106 Garden Street
Hoboken, NJ 07030

201-656-0107
E-Mail: amis@guildassoc.com
Home Page: www.amis.org
Social Media: Facebook

Albert R Rice, President
Carolyn Bryant, Vice-President
Deborah Check Reeves, Secretary
Joanne Kopp, Treasurer

Promotes better understanding of all aspects of history, design, construction, restoration, and usage of musical instruments in all cultures and from all periods. The membership of AMIS includes collectors, historians, curators, performers, instrument makers, restorers, dealers, conservators, teachers, students, and many institutional members.
Founded in 1971

18734 **American Musicological Society**
6010 College Station
Brunswick, ME 04011-8451

207-798-4243
877-679-7648
Fax: 877-679-7648
E-Mail: ams@ams-net.org
Home Page: www.ams-net.org

Robert Judd, Executive Director

Advances research in the various fields of music as a branch of learning and scholarship.
3600 Members
Founded in 1934

18735 **American Orff-Schulwerk Association**
PO Box 391089
Cleveland, OH 44139-8089

440-543-5366
Fax: 440-600-7332
E-Mail: info@aosa.org
Home Page: www.aosa2.org

Katharine P. Johnson, Executive Director
Jo Ella Hug, President
Julie Scott, VP
Jennifer Hartman, Treasurer

Professional organization of music and movement educators dedicated to the creative teaching approach developed by Carl Orff and Gunild Keetman.
Cost: $70.00

18736 **American School Band Directors Association**
227 N 1st Street
PO Box 696
Guttenberg, IA 52052-0696

563-252-2500
Fax: 563-252-2500
E-Mail: asbda@alpinecom.net
Home Page: www.asbda.com
Social Media: Facebook

Kebin Beaber, President
Valerie Gaffney, Secretary
Blair Callaway, Treasurer
Dennis Hanna, Manager
Russ Hilton, Treasurer

Nationwide organization dedicated to the support of professional and college band conductors. Membership by invitation only.
1200 Members
Founded in 1953

18737 **American Society of Composers, Authors and Publishers (ASCAP)**
1 Lincoln Plaza
New York, NY 10023-7097

212-621-6000
Fax: 212-621-8453
E-Mail: info@ascap.com
Home Page: www.ascap.com

Paul Williams, President/Chairman
James M Kendrick, Treasurer
Kathyr Spanberger, Secretary
John Lofrumento, CEO

Performing rights organization created and controlled by composers, songwriters and music publishers. Protects the rights of its members by licensing and distributing royalties for the non-dramatic public performances of their copyrighted works. An online newsletter is also available filled with the most up-to-date information about professional opportunities, legislative issues, member benefits and more.
26000 Members
Founded in 1914

18738 **American Society of Music Arrangers and Composers**
5903 Noble Ave
Van Nuys, CA 91411-3026

818-994-4661
Fax: 818-994-6181
E-Mail: asmac@theproperimageevents.com
Home Page: www.asmac.org
Social Media: Facebook, Twitter, LinkedIn, Youtube

Scherr Lillico, Executive Director
Duane L Tatro, Vice President
Ray Charles, Vice President

Professional society for arrangers, composers, orchestrators, and musicians. Monthly meetings with great speakers from the music industry.
500 Members
Founded in 1938

18739 **American Song Writers Association**

205-815-8180
E-Mail:
info@americansongwritersassociation.com
Home Page:
www.americansongwritersassociation.com

18740 **American String Teachers Association**
4155 Chain Bridge Rd
Fairfax, VA 22030-4102

703-279-2113
Fax: 703-279-2114
E-Mail: asta@astaweb.com
Home Page: www.astaweb.com

Donna Hale, Executive Director
Beth Danner-Knight, Deputy Director
Mary Jane Dye, Deputy Director

A membership organization for string and orchestra teachers and players, helping them to develop and refine their careers. Members range from budding student teachers to artist-status performers, businesses who supply goods and services to the string and orchestra world plus colleges, universities, music programs and conservatories.
11300 Members
Founded in 1946

18741 **American Union of Swedish Singers**

E-Mail: president@auss.org
Home Page: www.auss.org

500+ Members

18742 **American Viola Society**
14070 Proton Rd
Suite 100
Dallas, TX 75244-3601

972-233-9107
Fax: 972-490-4219
E-Mail: info@avsnationaloffice.org
Home Page: www.americanviolasociety.org
Social Media: Facebook, Twitter

Nokunthula Ngwenyama, President
Madeline Crouch, General Manager
Karin Brown, Secretary
Michelle Sayles, Treasurer

An association for the promotion of viola performance and research. AVS membership is accompanied by two print issues of the Journal of the American Viola Society (JAVS) each year.
1000 Members

18743 **Americana Music Association**
The Factory at Franklin
PO Box 628
Franklin, TN 37065

615-386-6936
Fax: 615-386-6937
E-Mail: press@americanamusic.org
Home Page: www.americanamusic.org
Social Media: Facebook, Twitter, Pinterest, YouTube

Jed Hilly, Executive Director
Danna Strong, Director of Operations
Michelle Aquilato, Director of Marketing
Sarah Comardelle, Manager of Marketingÿ
Whitney Holmes, Manager of Member Relations

18744 **Association for Electronic Music**

Home Page:
www.associationforelectronicmusic.orgÿ
Social Media: Twitter

Mark Lawrence, CEO

18745 Association of Concert Bands
6613 Cheryl Ann Drive
Independence, OH 44131-3718

800-726-8720
Fax: 216-524-1897
Home Page: www.acbands.org

Allen Beck, President
Nada Vencl, Secretary
Mike Montgomery, CIO
Howard Habenicht, Treasurer

The purpose of ACB is to encourage and foster adult concert community, municipal, and civic bands and to promote the performance of the highest quality traditional and contemporary literature for band.
750 Members
Founded in 1977

18746 Blues Foundation
421 S.Main St
Memphis, TN 38103-4464

901-527-2583
Fax: 901-529-4030
E-Mail: jay@blues.org
Home Page: www.blues.org
Social Media: Facebook, Twitter, LinkedIn, YouTube, RSS

Jay Sieleman, President
Joey Whitmer, DeputuDirector
Cindy James, Membership
Chadd Webb, Treasurer

A nonprofit corporation which serves as the hub for the worldwide passion for Blues Music.
Founded in 1980

18747 Carnatic Music Association of North America
P O Box 234
Fords, NJ 8863

908-521-0500
800-362-6137
E-Mail: webmaster@cmana.org
Home Page: www.cmana.orgÿ

Aravind Narasimhan, President
Chithra Krishnan, Vice President
Rajesh Nathan, Secretary
Rhama Narayanan, Treasurer

18748 Chamber Music America
99 Madison Avenue
5th Floor
New York, NY 10016

212-242-2022
Fax: 646-430-5667
Home Page: www.chamber-music.org

Susan Dadian, Program Director
Margaret M Lioi, CEO
Louise Smith, Chair

Promotes artistic excellence and economic stability within the profession and to ensure that chamber music is a vital part of American life. Their vision is that chamber music serves as a model of cooperation and collaboration, that audiences become more committed to supporting chamber music and the professionals who devote their lives to this art form, and that opportunities for the performance of chamber music increase in traditional concert venues and beyond.
Founded in 1977

18749 Chinese Arts and Music Association
P.O. Box 50531
Seattle, WA 98015-0531

206-817-6888
E-Mail: chinamusic@comcast.net
Home Page: www.uschinamusic.org

Warren Chang, President
Angel Yan, Board Member
Janelle Yeung, Board Member
Minghwa Chiem, Board Member
Buyun Zhao, Director

18750 Chorus America
1156 15th St NW
Suite 310
Washington, DC 20005-1747

202-331-7577
Fax: 202-331-7599
E-Mail: service@chorusamerica.org
Home Page: www.chorusamerica.org
Social Media: Facebook, Twitter, Youtube

Ann Meier Baker, President & Chief Executive Officer
Rollo Dilworth, Chairman
Michael McCarthy, Treasurer

Chorus America's mission is to build a dynamic and inclusive choral community so that more people are enriched by the beauty and power of choral singing.
2100 Members
Founded in 1977

18751 Church Music Association of America
12421 New Point Drive
Richmond, VA 23233

505-263-6298
E-Mail: contact@musicasacra.com
Home Page: www.musicasacra.comÿ
Social Media: Facebook, Twitter, Google+

Founded in 1964

18752 College Music Society
312 E Pine St
Missoula, MT 59802-4624

406-721-9616
Fax: 406-721-9419
E-Mail: cms@music.org
Home Page: www.music.org
Social Media: Facebook, Twitter

Robby D Gunstream, Executive Director
David B. Williams, President

A consortium of college, conservatory, university and independent musicians and scholars interested in all disciplines of music. Its mission is to promote music teaching and learning, musical creativity and expression, research and dialogue, and diversity and interdisciplinary interaction.
9500 Attendees
Founded in 1958

18753 Conductors Guild
719 Twinridge Ln
Richmond, VA 23235

804-553-1378
Fax: 804-553-1876
E-Mail: guild@conductorsguild.org
Home Page: www.conductorsguild.org

Amanda Burton Winger, Executive Director
Scott Winger, Assistant Director
David Leibowitz, Editor
Rufus Jones Jr, Editor

The Conductors Guild is the only music service organization devoted exclusively to the advancement of the art of conducting and to serving the artistic and professional needs of conductors.
1850+ Members
Founded in 1975

18754 Contemporary Record Society
724 Winchester Road
Broomall, PA 19008

610-544-5920
Fax: 610-544-5920
E-Mail: crsnews@verizon.net
Home Page:
www.mysite.verizon.net/vzeeewvp/contemporaryrecordsociety/

Caroline Hunt, Contact

Promotes both a fellowship in the musical arts between artists, composers and presenters and commercial recordingsa of participants in this endeavor. The intent of the Society is to advance the cause of music in the United States and throughout the world, promoting an association among its constituents. The scope of the Society's repertoire includes the musical masterworks of both well-known and relatively unknown composers of all periods.
Cost: $45.00
Founded in 1981

18755 Country Music Association
One Music Circle S
Nashville, TN 37203

615-244-2840
Fax: 615-242-4783
Home Page: www.cmaworld.com

Gary Overton, Chairman
Troy Tomlison, President
Jessie Schmidt, Secretary/Treasurer
Steve Moore, CEO

CMA is dedicated to bringing the poetry and emotion of Country Music to the World. They will continue a tradition of leadership and professionalism, promoting the music and recognizing excellence in all its forms. They foster a spirit of community and sharing, and respect and encourage creativity and the unique contributions of everyone. It is a place to have fun and celebrate success.
5000+ Members
Founded in 1958

18756 Country Radio Broadcasters
819 18th Ave S
Nashville, TN 37203-3218

615-327-4487
Fax: 615-329-4492
E-Mail: news@crb.org
Home Page: www.crb.org

Ed Salamon, Executive Director
Chasity Crouch, Business Manager
Bill Mayne, VP
Carole Bowen, Secretary
Jeff Walker, Treasurer

A nonprofit eductional organization. It is the principal entity that brings Country radio together with the Country music industry for learning opportunities that promote growth.
Founded in 1969

18757 Creative Musicians Coalition
PO Box 6205
Peoria, IL 61601-6205

309-685-4843
800-882-4262
Fax: 309-685-4879
E-Mail: aimcmc@aol.com
Home Page:
www.creativemusicianscoalition.com

Ronald Wallace, Founder/President

An international organization dedicated to the advancement of new music and the success of independent musicians.
1000 Members
Founded in 1984

18758 East-2-West Marketing & Promotion
559 Wanamaker Road
Jenkintown, PA 19046-2219

215-884-3308
Fax: 215-884-1083

Jackie Paul, President/CEO

Marketing and promotion.
Mailing list available for rent

18759 Folk Alliance International
510 S Main St
First Floor
Memphis, TN 38103-6417
901-522-1170
Fax: 816-221-3658
E-Mail: fa@folk.org
Home Page: www.folkalliance.org
Lewis Meyers, Executive Director
Van Denn, VP
Alan Korolenko, Secretary
Mark Moss, Treasurer
The service association for the field, working on behalf of the folk music and dance industry year round. They offer a business directory of contacts for members, and a non-profit group exemption program for US-based organizations.
Cost: $70.00
Founded in 1989

18760 Folklife Center Of International House
3701 Chestnut Street
Philadelphia, PA 19104
215-387-5125
Fax: 215-895-6550
Osagie Imasogie, President
Tanya Steinberg, Executive Director
William Parker, Director Of Communications Events
To present the highest caliber of traditional arts.

18761 Freelance Musicians' Association
E-Mail: info@freelancemusicians.org
Home Page: www.freelancemusicians.org

18762 Gospel Music Association
741 cool Springs Blvd.
Franklin, TN 37067
615-242-0303
Fax: 615-254-9755
E-Mail: service@gospelmusic.org
Home Page: www.gospelmusic.org
Social Media: Facebook, Twitter, LinkedIn, Youtube
John Styll, President
Scott Brickell, Director
Charles Dorris, Founder/Chairman
Ed Harper, Director
Ed Leonard, Director
Our mission is to expose, promote and celebrate the gospel through music. GMA serves as a voice for the Christian music community. It provides an atmosphere in which artists, industry leaders, retail stores, radio stations, concert promoters and local churches can coordinate their efforts for the purpose of benefitting the industry as a whole, while remaining true to the purpose of communicating the gospel message.
Cost: $85.00
5000 Members
Founded in 1964

18763 Guitar Accessory and Marketing Association (GAMA)
Po Box 757
New York, NY 10033
212-795-3630
Fax: 212-795-3630
E-Mail: assnhdqs@earthlink.net
Home Page: www.discoverguitar.com
Membership is comprised of guitar and guitar accessory manufacturers and various consumer magazines.
Founded in 1933

18764 Guitar Foundation of America
P.O.Box 171269
Austin, TX 78717
877-570-1651
Fax: 877-570-3409
E-Mail: info@guitarfoundation.org
Home Page: www.guitarfoundation.org
Social Media: Facebook, Twitter
Brian Head, President
Jill Winchell, Operations Manager
Martha Masters, Executive VP
Jeff Cogan, VP
Robert Lane, Vice President/Secretary
Provides its members the combined advantages of a guitar society, a library, a publisher, a continuing education resource, and an artis council. The GFA is a non-profit educational and literacy organization devoted to furthering the knowledge of and interest in the guitar and its music.
Cost: $40.00
Founded in 1973

18765 International Association for the Study of Popular Music
Home Page: www.iaspm.net
Founded in 1981

18766 International Association of Electronic Keyboard Manufacturers
305 Maple Avenue
Wyncote, PA 19095-3228
617-747-2816
Home Page: www.iaekm.org
An association that comprises the global manufacturers of electronic keyboards and affiliated software and publications.

18767 International Association of Jazz Education
PO Box 724
Manhattan, KS 66505
785-776-8744
Fax: 785-776-6190
E-Mail: bill@iage.org
Home Page: www.iaje.org
Bill McFarlin, Executive Director
Chuck Owen, President
Ronald Carter, VP
Laura Johnson, Treasurer
Brian Coyle, Secretary
To ensure the continued development and growth of jazz through education and outreach.
Cost: $70.00
8000 Members
Founded in 1989

18768 International Bluegrass Music Association
608 West, Irish Drive
Nashville, TN 37204
615-256-3222
888-438-4262
Fax: 615-256-0450
E-Mail: info@ibma.org
Home Page: www.ibma.org
Social Media: Facebook, Twitter, LinkedIn, Youtube
Dan Hayes, Executive Director
Stan Zdonik, Vice Chair/Associations
Peter D'Addario, Treasurer
Lee Michael Demsey, Secretary
IBMA works together for high standards of professionalism, a greater appreciation for our music, and the success of the worldwide bluegrass community.

18769 International Clarinet Association
14070 Proton Rd
Suite 100 LB9
Dallas, TX 75244
972-233-9107
Fax: 972-490-4219
E-Mail: membership@clarinet.org
Home Page: www.clarinet.org
John Cipolla, President
Tod Kerstetter, Treasurer
Caroline Hartig, Secretary
So Rhee, Executive Director
A community of clarinetists and clarinet enthusiasts that supports projects that will benefit clarinet performance; provides opportunities for the exchange of ideas, materials and information among its members; fosters the composition, publication, recording, and distribution of music for the clarinet; encourages the research and manufacture of a more definitive clarinet; and encourages and promotes the perfomance and teaching of a wide variety of repertoire for the clarinet.
4000 Members
Founded in 1990

18770 International Computer Music Association
1819 Polk St.
Suite 330
San Francisco, CA 94109
FAX 734-878-3031
E-Mail: icma@umich.edu
Home Page: www.computermusic.org
Tom Erbe, President
Michael Gurevitchý, VP, Membership
Margaret Schedel, VP, Conferences
Chryssie Nanou, Treasurer, Secretary
Christopher Haworth, Array Editor
Founded in 1974

18771 International Horn Society
E-Mail: exec-secretary@hornsociety.org
Home Page: www.hornsociety.org
Frank Lloyd, President
Joseph Ognibene, VP
Marian Hesse, Secretary/Treasurer
Heidi Vogal, Executive Secretary
Cost: $35.00
3500 Members
Founded in 1970

18772 International Music Products Association NAMM
5790 Armada Drive
Carlsbad, CA 92008-4608
760-438-8001
800-767-6266
Fax: 760-438-7327
E-Mail: info@namm.org
Home Page: www.namm.org
Larry Morton, President
Mark Goff, President/Owner
Robin Walents, President/CEO
Chris Martin, Chairman/CEO
Joe Lamond, President/CEO
An association whose mission is to unify, lead and strengthen the international music products industry and increase active participation in music making.
9000 Members
Founded in 1901

18773 International Piano Guild
PO Box 1807
Austin, TX 78767
512-478-5775
E-Mail: ngpt@pianoguild.com
Home Page: www.pianoguild.com
Richard Allison, President

A division of the American College of Musicians Professional society of piano teachers and music faculty members. Its primary function is to establish definite goals and awards for students of all levels, from the earliest beginner to the gifted prodigy. Its purpose is to encourage growth and enjoyment through the study of piano.
118m Members
Founded in 1929

18774 International Polka Association
4608 S Archer Ave
Chicago, IL 60632-2932

773-254-7771
800-867-6552
E-Mail: ipa@internationalpolka.com
Home Page: www.internationalpolka.com

Dave Ulczycki, President
Rick Rzeszutko, First VP
Fred Kenzierski, Second VP
Marlene Gill, Secretary
Linda Niewierowski, Treasurer

An educational and charitable organization for the preservation, promulgation and advancement of polka music and to promote, maintain and advance public interest in polka entertainment; to advance mutual interests and encourage greater cooperation among its members who are engaged in polka entertainment; and to encourage and pursue the study of polka music, dancing and traditional folklore. Responsible for the continued operation and growth of the Polka Music Hall of Fame and Museum.
Cost: $15.00
8M Members
Founded in 1968

18775 International Society of Folk Harpers and Craftsmen
1614 Pittman Drive
Missoula, Mt 59803

406-542-1976
E-Mail: harps@thorharp.com
Home Page: www.folkharpsociety.org

Dave Kolacny, President
Timothy Habinski, First VP
Verlene Schermer, Second VP
Alice Williams, Secretary
Barbra Bailey Bradley, Treasurer

The mission of the ISFHC is: to promote the playing and enjoyment of the folk harp by all; to promote education, creation and development in the building of the folk harp; to increase awareness of professional folk harpers; and to increase public awareness of the music and joys of the folk harp.
Cost: $30.00
Founded in 1985

18776 Keyboard Teachers Association International
361 Pin Oak Lane
Westbury, NY 11590-1941

516-333-3236
Fax: 516-997-9531
Home Page: www.musiciansnetwork.com

Dr. Albert DeVito, President

18777 League of American Ochestras
33 W 60th Street
New York, NY 10023-7905

212-262-5161
Fax: 212-262-5198
E-Mail: league@symphony.org
Home Page: www.symphony.org

Henry Fogel, CEO
Jesse Rosen, President/CEO
Aja Stephens, Assistant to President
Peter D Cummings, Vice Chair
Heather Noonan, Vice Chair

Provides leadership and service to American orchestras while communicating to the public the value and importance of orchestras and the music they perform. The League links a national network of thousands of musicians, conductors, managers, board members, volunteers, staff members and business partners, providing a wealth of services, information, and educational opportunities to its members.
1200 Members
Founded in 1942
Mailing list available for rent

18778 Metropolitan Opera Guild
70 Lincoln Center Plz
New York, NY 10023-6593
212-769-7000
Fax: 212-769-7007
E-Mail: info@metguild.org
Home Page: www.metoperafamily.org/guild/

David Dik, Manager

Seeks to encourage the appreciation of opera and to support the Metropolitan Opera. The guild provides programs and services in many areas designed to further these goals. Publishes monthly magazine and organizes special events throughout the year to raise funds.
100M Members
Founded in 1935

18779 Midland Center For The Arts Midland Music And Concert Series
1801 W. St Andrews Road
Midland, MI 48640

989-631-8250
Fax: 989-631-7890
E-Mail: hohmeyer@mcfta.org
Home Page: www.mcfta.org
Social Media: Facebook, Twitter, LinkedIn, Youtube

Michael Tiknis, President
James Hohmeyer, Artistic Director
Robb Wouose, Managing Director
Mark Bachman, Director
David Blakemore, Director

encourage concert audiences; Providing students with opportunities to experience professional performances.

18780 Music Business Association
1 Eves Drive
Suite 138
Marlton, NJ 8053

856-596-2221
Fax: 856-596-7299
Home Page: www.musicbiz.org
Social Media: Facebook, Twitter, RSS

Fred Beteille, Chairman
Steve Harkins, Vice Chairman
John Trickett, Treasurer
Ryan Redington, Secretary
James Donio, President

18781 Music Distributors Association
14070 Proton Rd
Suite 100 LB9
Dallas, TX 75244-3601

972-233-9107
Fax: 972-490-4219
E-Mail: office@musicdistributors.org
Home Page: www.musicdistributors.org

International, nonprofit trade association representing and serving manufacturers, wholesalers, importers and exporters of musical instruments and accessories, sound reinforcement products and published music.
Cost: $675.00
Founded in 1939

18782 Music Library Association
8551 Research Way
Suite 180
Middleton, WI 53562

608-836-5825
Fax: 608-831-8200
E-Mail: mla@areditions.com
Home Page: www.musiclibraryassoc.org
Social Media: Facebook

Michael Colby, President
Pamela Bristah, Secretary
Paul Cary, Admin Officer
Linda W.Blair, Admin Officer

Provides a forum for issues surrounding music, music in libraries, and music librarianship.
Cost: $90.00
Founded in 1931

18783 Music Performance Fund
1501 Broadway
Suite 600
New York, NY 10036

212-391-3950
Fax: 212-221-2604
E-Mail: lwilliamson@musicpf.org
Home Page: www.musicpf.org
Social Media: Facebook

Den Beck, Trustee
Al Elvin, Director of Finance
Linda Williamson, Manager

A nonprofit public service organization headquartered in New York City. MPF is the world's largest sponsor of live, admission-free musical programs.
Founded in 1948

18784 Music Performance Trust Funds
1501 Broadway
Suite 600
New York, NY 10036

212-391-3950
Fax: 212-221-2604
E-Mail: sramos@musicpf.org
Home Page: www.musicpf.org
Social Media: Facebook

Dan Beck, Trustee
Vidrey Blackburn, Grant Review Process
Al Elvin, Director of Finance
Samantha Ramos, Team Member
Founded in 1948

18785 Music Publishers Association
243 5th Ave
Suite 236
New York, NY 10016-8728
212-675-7354
Fax: 212-675-7381
E-Mail: mpa-admin@mpa.org
Home Page: www.mpa.org

Kathleen Marsh, President
Bryndon Bay, Treasurer
Todd Vunderink, Secretary
Lauren Keiser, Second VP

The MPA fosters communication among publishers, dealers, music educators, and all ultimate users of music. It is a nonprofit association which addresses itself to issues pertaining to every area of music publishing with an emphasis on the issues relevant to the publishers of print music for concert and educational purposes.
75 Members
Founded in 1895

18786 Music Teachers National Association
441 Vine St
Suite 3100
Cincinnati, OH 45202-3004

513-421-1420
888-512-5278

Fax: 513-421-2503
E-Mail: mtnanet@mtna.org
Home Page: www.mtna.org
Social Media: Facebook, Twitter

Gary L Ingle, Executive Director
Gail Berenson, President
Janice Wenger, VP

The mission of the MTNA is to advance the value of music study and music making to society and to support the professionalism of music teachers.
24000 Members
Founded in 1876
Mailing list available for rent: 23,000 names at $85 per M

18787 Music Video Production Associationÿ

E-Mail: infomvpa@gmail.com
Home Page: www.mvpa.com

Coleen Haynes, President
Missy Galanadia, Vice President
Kim Dellara, Vice President
Grant Cihlar, Treasurer
Amanda Fox, Board of Director

18788 Music for All Foundation

39 W Jackson Place
Suite 150
Indianapolis, IN 46225

317-636-2263
Fax: 317-524-6200
E-Mail: info@music-for-all.org
Home Page: www.musicforall.org

Eric Martin, President/CEO
Nancy H.Carlson, Executive VP/CFO
Carolyn Ealy, Education and Office Manager
Tonya Bullock, Accounting manager

Committed to expanding the role of music and the arts in education, to heightening the public's appreciation of the value of music and arts education, and to creating a positive environment for the arts through societal changes.
Founded in 1975
Mailing list available for rent

18789 Musical Box Society International

MBSI Member Registration
PO Box 10196
Springfield, MO 65808-0196

FAX 417-886-8839
Home Page: www.mbsi.org
Social Media: Facebook, Twitter, Digg, Yahoo, Reddit, StumbleUp

A nonprofit organization dedicated to the enjoyment, sstudy and preservation of all automatic musical instruments. Members receive the bimonthly scholarly journal, Mechanical Music, covering educational articles, relevant events, activities, news, information, and advertisements and the biennial, Directory of Members, Museums and Dealers. Hosts annual convention.
Cost: $55.00
2.8M Members
Founded in 1949

18790 Musicians Foundation

875 Sixth Avenue
Suite 2303
New York, NY 10001-3507

212-239-9137
Fax: 212-239-9138
E-Mail: info@musiciansfoundation.org
Home Page: www.musiciansfoundation.org

BC Vermeersch, Executive Director
Hans E Tausig, President
Joseph Hertzberg, Treasurer

Representing interests on the condition and social welfare of professional musicians and their families. Provides emergency financial assistance to meet current living, medical and allied expenses.
Founded in 1914

18791 National Academy of Recording Arts and Sciences

3030 Olympic Blvd.ÿ
Santa Monica, CA 90404

310-392-3777
Fax: 310-392-2188
Home Page: www.grammy.org
Social Media: Facebook, Twitter, YouTube, Instagram

Ryan Seacrest, Honorary Chair
Tim Bucher, Chair
Geoff Cottrillÿ, Vice Chair
Rachna Bhasin, Secretary/Treasurer
Rusty Rueff, Chair Emeritus
Founded in 1988

18792 National Association for Music Education MENC

1806 Robert Fulton Drive
Reston, VA 20191

703-860-4000
800-336-3768
Fax: 703-860-1531
Home Page: www.menc.org

John J Mahlmann, Executive Director
Lynn Brinckmeyer, President

Mission is to advance music education by encouraging the study and making of music by all.
Founded in 1907

18793 National Association of Band Instrument Manufacturers

2026 Eagle Road
PO Box 51
Normal, IL 61761

309-452-4257
Fax: 309-452-4825
E-Mail: napbirt@napbirt.org
Home Page: www.napbirt.org
Social Media: Facebook

Jerome Hershman, Contact

A trade association of band instrument manufacturers, importers and distributors including accessories selling to the trade only.
34 Members
Founded in 1976

18794 National Association of College Wind and Percussion Instructor

Division of Fine Arts
Truman State University
Kirksville, MO 63501

660-785-4442
Fax: 660-785-7463
E-Mail: cmoore@fsu.edu
Home Page: www.nacwpi.org

Chris Moore, President
Michael Dean, VP
Richard K Weerts, Executive Secretary/Treasurer

A forum for communication within the profession of applied music on the college campus. The Association is composed of university, college, and conservatory teachers.
Cost: $35.00
600 Members
Founded in 1951

18795 National Association of Composers

P.O. Box 49256
Barrington Station
Los Angeles, CA 90049

Home Page: www.music-usa.org/nacusa

Greg A. Steinke, Ph.D., President/ Chair
Wieslaw V Rentowski ÿ, Vice President
Sylvia ÿ Constantinidis, M.M., Secretary
Joe L. Alexander, Treasurer
Daniel Kessner, Past President
Founded in 1933

18796 National Association of Negro Musicians Inc

931 Monroe Drive NE
Suite A102-159
Atlanta, GA 30308

404-647-7217
Fax: 404-745-0128
E-Mail: info@nanm.org
Home Page: www.nanm.org

David E Morrow, President
Byron J. Smith, First VP
Glenn L Jones, Second VP
Ona B Campbell, Executive Secretary
Daniel.J Long, Treasurer

Dedicated to the preservation, encouragement and advocacy of all genres of the music of African Americans. Holds a national convention in a different city eac year, offering a chance to participate in workshops, seminars, lectures and performances. NANM invites the professional artists, the educator, the student, the amateur, the lover of music to become a part of this organization's 'Pride in a Cultural Heritage.'
2.5M Members
Founded in 1919

18797 National Association of Pastoral Musicians

962 Wayne Ave
Suite 210
Silver Spring, MD 20910-4461

240-247-3000
Fax: 240-247-3001
E-Mail: npmsing@npm.org
Home Page: www.npm.org

J Michael Mc Mahon, President
Kathleen Haley, Director Membership Services
Lowell Hickman, Office Manager/Executive Assistant
Joseph Lively, Comptroller

Fosters the art of musical liturgy. The members of NPM serve the Catholic Church in the United States as musicians, clergy, liturgists, and other leaders of prayer.
9000 Members
Founded in 1976

18798 National Association of Professional Band Instrument Repair Technicians

2026 Eagle Road
PO Box 51
Normal, IL 61761

309-452-4257
Fax: 309-452-4825
E-Mail: napbirt@napbirt.org
Home Page: www.napbirt.org
Social Media: Facebook

Bill Mathews, President

A nonprofit international educational association dedicated to the advancement of the craft of band instrument repair. Their mission is to promote the highest possible standards of band instrument repair, restoration and maintenance by providing members with multi-level professional development by offering technical training, continuing education and the publication

of their bi-monthky trade journal.
Cost: $95.00
1300 Members
Founded in 1976

18799 National Association of Recording Merchandisers
9 Eves Drive
Suite 120
Marlton, NJ 08053-3130

856-596-2221
Fax: 856-596-3268
E-Mail: donio@narm.com
Home Page: www.narm.com

Sue Peterson, Chair
Scott Wilson, Vice Chairman
Bob Schneider, Treasurer
Rachelle Friedman, Secretary
Jim Donio, President

A not-for-profit trade association that serves the music retailing community in the areas of networking, advocacy, information, education and promotion. Membership includes music and other entertainment retailers, wholesalers, distributorsm record labels, multimedia suppliers, and suppliers of related products and services, as well as individual professionals and educators in the music business field.
Founded in 1958

18800 National Association of Schools of Music
11250 Roger Bacon Drive
Suite 21
Reston, VA 20190-5248

703-437-0700
Fax: 703-437-6312
E-Mail: info@arts-accredit.org
Home Page: www.arts-accredit.org

Don Gibson, President
Mark Wait, VP
Mellasenah Y Morris, Treasurer

An organization of schools, conservatories, colleges and universities. NASM provides information to potential students and parents, consultations, stastistical information, professional development and policy analysis. It is the national accrediting agency for music and music-related disciplines.
635 Members
Founded in 1924

18801 National Association of Teachers of Singing
9957 Moorings Drive
Suite 401
Jacksonville, FL 32257-2416

904-992-9101
Fax: 904-262-2587
E-Mail: info@nats.org
Home Page: www.nats.org
Social Media: Facebook, Twitter, LinkedIn

Allen Henderson, Executive Director
Deborah Guess, Director of Operations

To encourage the highest standards of the vocal art and of ethical principles in the teaching of singing; and to promote vocal education and research at all levels, both for the enrichment of the general public and for the professional advancement of the talented.
7000 Members
Founded in 1944

18802 National Ballroom and Entertainment Association
PO Box 274
Decorah, IA 52101-7600

563-382-3871
E-Mail: nbea@q.com
Home Page: www.nbea.com

John Matter, Executive Director

National nonprofit association which advocates that social dancing is a life-long activity that contributes to the physical, mantal, and social well-being of an individual. They believe that social dancing should be preserved for current and future generations and introduced to today's youth as an alternate form of social interaction.
450 Members
Founded in 1947

18803 National Band Association
Membership Office
745 Chastain Road-Ste 1140
PO Box 102
Kennesaw, GA 30144

601-297-8168
Fax: 601-266-6185
E-Mail: info@nationalbandassociation.org
Home Page: www.nationalbandassociation.org

Roy Holder, President
Richard Good, First VP
Scott Casagrande, Second VP
Linda Moorehouse, Secretary/Treasurer
David Gregory, Advisor to the President

The purpose of the NBA to promote the musical and educational significance of bands and is dedicated to the attainment of a high level of excellence for bands and band music. It is open to anyone and everyone interested in bands, regardless of the length if his/her experience, type of position held, or the specific area at which he/she works. The membership roster includes men and women from every facet of the band world.
3M Members
Founded in 1960

18804 National Endowment for the Arts
400 7th Street, SW
Washington, DC 20506-0001

202-682-5400
E-Mail: webmgr@arts.gov
Home Page: www.arts.govÿ

Jane Chu, Chairman
Laura Callanan, Senior Deputy Chairman
Beth Bienvenu, Accessibility Director
Wendy Clark, Director of Museums
Ayanna N. Hudson, Arts Education Director

18805 National Federation of Music Clubs
1646 W Smith Valley Rd
Greenwood, IN 46142-1550

317-882-4003
Fax: 317-882-4019
E-Mail: info@nfmc-music.org
Home Page: www.nfmc-music.org
Social Media: Facebook, Twitter, LinkedIn, Youtube

Carolyn Nelson, President
Michael Edwards, First VP
Kay Hawthorne, Secretary
Barbara Hildebrand, Treasurer
Jennifer Keller, Administrative Manager

NFMC provides opportunities for musical study, performance and appreciation to more than 200,000 senior, student and junior members in 6,500 music-related clubs and organizations nationwide. Members are professional and amateur musicians, vocalists, composers, dancers, performing artists, arts and music educators, music students, generous music patrons and benefactors, and music lovers of all ages.
170M Members
Founded in 1898

18806 National Music Council of the United States
425 Park Street
Montclair, NJ 07043ÿ

Home Page: www.musiccouncil.org

Michael Butera, President
Carolyn Nelson, First Vice President
Paul Williams, Second Vice President
Del R. Bryant, Third VP
Linda Lorence, Treasurer
Founded in 1940

18807 National Opera Association
PO Box 60869
Canyon, TX 79016-0869

806-651-2857
Fax: 806-651-2958
Home Page: www.noa.org

Robert Hansen, Executive Director
JoElyn Wakefield-Wright, President
Carole Notestine, Secretary
Robert Thieme, Editor Opera Journal
Philip Hagemann, Treasurer

The NOA seeks to promote a greater appreciation of opera and music theatre, to enhance pedagogy and performing activities, and to increase performance opportunities by supporting projects that improve the scope and quality of opera. Members in the United States, Canada, Europe, Asia and Australia participate in a wide array of activities in support of this mission.
775 Members
Founded in 1955
Mailing list available for rent

18808 NationalÿAssociationÿofÿMusicÿMerchants
5790 Armada Drive
Carlsbad, CA 92008ÿ

760-438-8001
800-767-6266
Fax: 760-438-7327
E-Mail: info@namm.org
Home Page: www.namm.org
Social Media: Facebook, Twitter, Pinterest, YouTube

Larry Morton, Chairman
Mark Goff, Vice Chairman
Robin Walenta, Treasurer
Chris Martin, Secretary
Joe Lamond, President/ CEO

18809 North American Basque Organizations
E-Mail: info@naBASQUE.org
Home Page: www.nabasque.org

Valerie Arrechea, President
Mary Gaztambide, Vice President
Grace Mainvil, Treasurer
Marisa Espinalÿ, Secretary
Kate Camino, Administrator
Founded in 1973

18810 Opera America
330 7th Ave
16th Floor
New York, NY 10001-5248

212-796-8620
Fax: 212-796-8631
E-Mail: frontdesk@operaamerica.org
Home Page: www.operaamerica.org

Marc A Scorca, President
Frayda B. Lindemann, Chairman
Timothy O'Leary, Treasurer

James W Wright, Secretary
Rebecca Ackerman, Membership Manager

Opera America serves and strengthens the field of opera by providing a variety of informational, technical, and administrative resources to the greater opera community. Its fundamental mission is to promote opera as exciting and accessible to individuals from all walks of life.

18811 Organization of American Kodaly Educators
10951 Pico Blvd
Suite 405
Los Angeles, CA 90064

310-441-3555
Fax: 310-441-3577
E-Mail: info@oake.org
Home Page: www.oake.org

Joan Dahlin, Manager
Penny Whalen, VP
Paul Baumann, Secretary
Greg Williams, Treasurer
Joan Dahlin, Administrative Director

The purpose of this organization is to promote Zoltan Kodaly's concept of Music for Everyone, through the improvment of music education in schools.
Founded in 1973

18812 Pedal Steel Guitar Association
PO Box 20248
Floral Park, NY 11002-0248

516-616-9214
Fax: 516-616-9214
E-Mail: bobpsga@optonline.net
Home Page: www.psga.org

Kelly Foster Griffin, President
Jane Smith, VP
Kathy Hickey, Treasurer
David Gadberry, Secretary
Doug Mack, Newsletter Editor

A nonprofit organization whose primary purpose is to share information on playing the steel guitar and in particular the pedal steel guitar. Publishes the Pedal Steel Newsletter ten times per year
1540 Members
Founded in 1973

18813 Percussive Arts Society
110 W Washington Street
Suite A
Indianapolis, IN 46204

317-974-4488
Fax: 317-974-4499
E-Mail: percarts@pas.org
Home Page: www.pas.org

Lisa Rogers, President
Steve Houghton, VP
Julie Hill, Secretary
Michael Balter, Treasurer
Larry Jacobson, Executive Director

A music service organization promoting percussion education, research, performance and appreciation throughout the world. Offers two print publications, the Percussive Arts Society International Headquarters/Museum and the annual Percussive Arts Society International Convention.
Cost: $85.00
7000 Members
Founded in 1961

18814 Piano Technicians Guild
4444 Forest Ave
Kansas City, KS 66106

913-432-9975
Fax: 913-432-9986
E-Mail: ptg@ptg.org
Home Page: www.ptg.org

Barbara Cassaday, Executive Director
Allan Gilreath RPT, President
Jim Coleman Jr RPT, VP

A nonprofit organization serving piano tuners, technicians, and craftsmen throughout the world, organized to promote the highest possible service and technical standards among piano tuners and technicians.
4100 Members
Founded in 1957

18815 Positive Music Association

Home Page:
www.positivemusicassociation.comÿ

Sambodhiÿ Prem, Composer/ Guitarist
400 Members
Founded in 2003

18816 Production Music Association
9220 Sunset Blvd.
Suite 220
Los Angeles, CA 90069

E-Mail: hunter@pmamusic.com
Home Page: www.pmamusic.com
Social Media: Facebook, Twitter, YouTube

Randy Thornton, Chairman
Adam Taylor, Vice Chairman
Ivy Tombak, Treasurer
Ron Mendelsohn, Secretary
Joel Goodman, Board Member
Founded in 1997

18817 Recording Industry Association of America
1025 F ST N.W.
10th Floor
Washington, DC 20004

202-775-0101
Home Page: www.riaa.com

Mitch Glazier, Sr. Executive Vice President
Steven M. Marks, Chief, Digital Business

18818 Retail Print Music Dealers Association
2650 Midway Rd
Suite 230
Carrolton, TX 75006

972-818-1333
Fax: 214-483-7004
E-Mail: cwilbur@penders.com
Home Page: www.printmusic.org

Madeleine Crouch, Owner
Myrna Sislen, VP/Secretary
Christie Smith, VP/Treasurer

A professional trade organization founded to address the special needs and interests of the print music industry. RPMDA provides a common meeting ground for the congenial interchange of ideas among print music dealers; promotes ethical standards and policies in dealing with music publishers; promotes better dealer/publisher relations; serves the public and encourages music education; provides association-sponsored activities and publications that help its members prepare for future trends.
275 Members
Founded in 1976

18819 Rhythm and Blues Foundation
P.O.Box 22438
Philadelphia, PA 19101

215-985-4822
Fax: 215-985-1195
E-Mail: info@rhythmblues.org
Home Page: www.rhythm-n-blues.org

Patricia Wilson Aden, Executive Director
Jim Fifield, Vice Chairman
Jeff Harleston, Treasurer
Kenneth Gamble, Secretary

Nonprofit service organization dedicated to the historical and cultural preservation of Rhythm and Blues music. The Foundation provides financial support, medical assistance and educational outreach through various grants and programs to support R&B amd Motown artists of the 40s, 50s, 60s and 70s.
Founded in 1988

18820 Society of Professional Audio Recording Services
9 Music Square S
Suite 222
Nashville, TN 37203

800-771-7727
Fax: 214-722-1422
E-Mail: spars@spars.com
Home Page: www.spars.com

Karen Brinton, President
Eric W Johnson, Secretary
Andrew Kautz, Treasurer

SPARS is dedicated to excellence through innovation, education and communication.
200 Members
Founded in 1979
Mailing list available for rent

18821 Songwriters Guild of America
5120 Virginia Way
Suite C22
Brentwood, TN 37027

615-742-9945
800-524-6742
Fax: 615-630-7501
E-Mail: corporate@songwritersguild.com
Home Page: www.songwritersguild.com

Joe Whitt, Manager

Provides agreements between songwriters, composers and publishers. The SGA will take such lawful actions as will advance, promote and benefit the profession.
4000 Members
Founded in 1931

18822 Sweet Adelines International
PO Box 470168
Tulsa, OK 74147-0168

918-622-1444
800-992-7464
Fax: 918-665-0894
E-Mail: admin@sweetadelineintl.org
Home Page: www.sweetadelineintl.org

Donna Kerley, Dicector Finance/Administration
Kelly Kirchoff, Director Communications
Jane Hanson, Marketing/Membership Coordinator

A worldwide organization of women singers committed to advancing the musical art form of barbershop harmony through education and performances. Their motto is to 'Harmonize the World.'
27000 Members
Founded in 1945

18823 The Society for American Music
Stephen Foster Memorial
University of Pittsburgh
Pittsburgh, PA 15260

412-624-3031
E-Mail: sam@american-music.org
Home Page: www.american-music.org
Social Media: Facebook

Judy Tsouÿ, Board of Trustee/ President
Kay Norton, Board of Trustee, VP
Sabine Feisst, Treasurer
Mariana Whitmer, Executive Director
Neil Lerner, Secretary
Founded in 1975

18824 **United States Germanic Music Association**
E-Mail: mikesurrattmusic@gmail.com
Home Page: www.usgma.us

18825 **World Piano Competition/AMSA**
441 Vine St
Suite 1030
Cincinnati, OH 45202-2832
513-421-5342
Fax: 513-421-2672
E-Mail: info@amsa-wpc.orgm
Home Page: www.amsa-wpc.org
Gloria Ackerman, Founder, CEO
William Selnick, Treasurer
Stanley Aronoff, Event Chair
Leon Fleisher, President
Provides an continuum of services and role models to assist youth in need. Their task is to provide a venue of excitement and compassion to teach them to do their best to prepare for the enormous challenges they will face as they approach adulthood.
2.5M Members
Founded in 1956

Newsletters

18826 **American Guild Associate News Newsletter**
American Guild of Music
PO Box 599
Warren, MI 48090-4905
248-686-1975
Fax: 630-968-0197
E-Mail: agm@americanguild.org
Home Page: www.americanguild.org
Richard Chizmadia, Editor-in-Chief
Offers information and news for professionals in the music profession.
Cost: $25.00
5000 Members
Frequency: Quarterly
Founded in 1901

18827 **American Music Center Opportunity Update**
American Music Center
322 8th Ave
Suite 1001
New York, NY 10001-6774
212-366-5263
Fax: 212-366-5265
E-Mail: center@amc.net
Home Page: www.amc.net
Joanne Cossa, Executive Director
A listing of composition competitions, calls for scores, workshops, and other opportunities delivered every month via e-mail to members of the American Music Center.
Frequency: Monthly
Founded in 1939

18828 **American Musical Instrument Society Newsletter**
AMIS
1106 Garden Street
Hoboken, NJ 07030
201-656-0107
E-Mail: amis@guildassoc.com
Home Page: www.amis.org
Albert R Rice, President
Carolyn Bryant, Vice-President
Deborah Check Reeves, Secretary
Joanne Kopp, Treasurer
Official notices and news of the Society's activites; short articles and communications; recent acquisition lists from member institutions; news of members; and classified ads.
Frequency: 2x/Year

18829 **American Musicological Society Inc**
University of Iowa
6010 College Station
Brunswick, ME 04011-8451
207-798-4243
877-679-7648
Fax: 207-798-4254
E-Mail: ams@ams-net.org
Home Page: www.ams-net.org
Peter Alexander, Editor
Robert Judd, Executive Director
Al Hipkins, Office Manager
Melissa Kapocius, Secretary
The AMS Newsletter is published simiannually in February and August. The February Newsletter is mailed with the new Directory and Ballot each year. The August Newsletter is mailed with the Annual Meeting information and registration form each year.
Frequency: Semi-Annually
Founded in 1934

18830 **American School Band Directors Association Newsletter**
American School Band Directors Association
227 N 1st Street
PO Box 696
Guttenberg, IA 52052-0696
563-252-2500
Fax: 563-252-2500
E-Mail: asbda@alpinecom.net
Home Page: www.asbda.com
Monte Dunnum, President
Valerie Gaffney, Secretary
Blair Callaway, Treasurer
Reports and information for members of the ASBDA
Frequency: Quarterly
Founded in 1953
Printed in 2 colors on matte stock

18831 **American Viola Society Newsletter**
American Viola Society
14070 Proton Rd
Suite 100
Dallas, TX 75244-3601
972-233-9107
Fax: 972-490-4219
E-Mail: stemple@comcast.net
Home Page: www.madcrouch.com
Madeleine Crouch, President
A monthly e-newsletter. It contains announcements from the AVS, upcoming local chapter events, and other important items.
Frequency: Monthly

18832 **Banjo Newsletter**
PO Box 3418
Annapolis, MD 21403-0418
800-759-7425
Fax: 410-263-6503
E-Mail: bnl@infionline.net
Home Page: www.banjonews.com
Newletter focusing on Bluegrass banjo music.
Mailing list available for rent

18833 **Bluegrass Music Profiles**
Bluegrass Publications
PO Box 850
Nicholasville, KY 40340-0850
859-333-6456
E-Mail: info@bluegrassmusicprofiles.com
Home Page: www.bluegrassmusicprofiles.com
Social Media: Facebook, Twitter
Information on Bluegrass music.

18834 **Bluegrass Now**
PO Box 2020
Rolla, MO 65402
573-341-7335
E-Mail: Bgn@fidnet.com
Home Page: www.bluegrassnow.com
Information on Bluegrass music.

18835 **Bluegrass Unlimited**
PO Box 771
Warrenton, VA 20188-0771
540-349-8181
800-258-4727
E-Mail: info@bluegrassmusic.com
Home Page: www.bluegrassmusic.com
Information on Bluegrass music.
Mailing list available for rent

18836 **Brooklyn Institute for Studies in American Music**
Brooklyn College
2900 Bedford Ave
Brooklyn, NY 11210-2889
718-951-5000
Home Page: www.brooklyn.cuny.edu/bb/fac/american.htm
Karen L Gould, President
Music news and Academy activities.
Frequency: Semi-Annual
Founded in 1861

18837 **CMS Newsletter**
College Music Society
312 E Pine Street
Missoula, MT 59802
406-721-9616
Fax: 406-721-9419
E-Mail: cms@music.org
Home Page: www.music.org
Robby D Gunstream, Executive Director

18838 **Dirty Linen**
PO Box 6660
Baltimore, MD 21239-6600
410-583-7973
E-Mail: office@dirtylinen.com
Home Page: www.dirtylinen.com
Information on Bluegrass music.

18839 **Early Music Newsletter**
New York Recorder Guild
145 W 93 Street
New York, NY 10025-7559
212-662-2946
E-Mail: mzumoff@nyc.rr.com
Home Page: www.priceclan.com/nyrecorderguild/
Michael Zumoff, Executive Director
A publication of the New York Recorder Guild
10 Pages
Frequency: Monthly

18840 **Flatpicking Guitar**
High View Publications
PO Box 2160
Pulaski, VA 24301
540-980-0338
800-413-8296
Fax: 540-980-0557
E-Mail: info@flatpickinqmercantile.com
Home Page: www.flatpick.com
Information on Bluegrass music and the Flatpick guitar.
Mailing list available for rent

18841 GMA Update
Gospel Music Association
PO Box 22697
Nashville, TN 37202

615-242-0303
Fax: 615-254-9755
E-Mail: info@gospelmusic.org
Home Page: www.gospelmusic.org

John Styll, President
Jackie Patillo, Executive Director

GMA's industry e-newsletter available to any non-GMA member who wishes to receive it. Sent out once a month, GMA Update contains the latest news about the Christian music industry and valuable information about the GMA.
Frequency: Monthly
Mailing list available for rent

18842 GMAil
Gospel Music Association
PO Box 22697
Nashville, TN 37202

615 242-0303
Fax: 615-254-9755
Home Page: www.gospelmusic.org

John Styll, President

E-newsletter sent weekly to GMA members. Includes weekly music sales, charts, news, links to valuable resources, and information about upcoming GMA and industry events.
Frequency: Weekly
Founded in 1964

18843 Girl Groups Gazette
PO Box 69A04
Department HSND
West Hollywood, CA 90069-0066
Louis Wendruck, Editor/Publisher

For fans of girl groups and female singers of the 1960's and 70's including photos, discographies, records, t-shirts, postcards, and videos.
Cost: $20.00
Frequency: Quarterly
Founded in 1988

18844 In the Groove
Michigan Antique Phonograph Society
60 Central St
Battle Creek, MI 49017-3704

269-968-1299
E-Mail:
ITG@michiganantiquephonographsociety.org
Home Page:
www.michiganantiquephonographsociety.org

Phil Stewart, Editor
Eileen Stewart, Editor

The Newsletter of the Michigan Antique Phonograph Society. Includes show, sales and auction announcements, MAPS chapter news, President's message, monthly feature articles, letters to the editor, and swap shop.
Cost: $25.00
24 Pages
Frequency: Monthly
Founded in 1976

18845 International Bluegrass Music Association
IBMA
2 Music Cir S
Suite 100
Nashville, TN 37203-4381

615-256-3222
888-438-4262
Fax: 615-256-0450
E-Mail: info@ibma.org
Home Page: www.ibma.org

Dan Hays, Executive Director

Information on Bluegrass music from the IBMA

18846 Music for the Love of It
67 Parkside Drive
Berkeley, CA 94705-2409

510-654-9134
Fax: 510-654-4656
E-Mail: tedrust@musicfortheloveofit.com
Home Page: www.musicfortheloveofit.com

Edgar Rust, Publisher/Editor
Janet Telford, Co-Editor

A newsletter for people everywhere who love making music. Every issues brings new enthusiasm, new ideas and new opportunities for making music.
Frequency: Bi-Monthly
ISSN: 0898-8757
Founded in 1988
Printed in on matte stock

18847 National Music Museum Newsletter
National Music Museum
414 E Clark St
Vermillion, SD 57069-2307

605-677-5306
Fax: 605-677-6995
E-Mail: smm@usd.edu
Home Page: www.usd.edu/smm/

Andre Larson, Director

Quarterly Newletter which includes feature articles written by the curatorial staff and lists recent acquisitions. Published in February, May, August and November. It is available with basic museum membership.
Cost: $35.00
Printed in 4 colors

18848 No Depression
908 Halcyon Avenue
Nashville, TN 37204

615-292-7084
Home Page: www.nodepression.net

Information on Bluegrass music
Founded in 1995

18849 Notes a Tempo
West Virginia University
Fairmount State University
1201 Locust Avenue
Fairmont, WV 26554

304-293-4841
Home Page:
www.wvmea.tripod.com/Notes_a_Tempo_Winter_10.pdf

David Bess, Co-Editor
Becky Terry, Co-Editor

The official publication of the West Virginia Music Educators. Published Fall, Winter and Spring
20-32 Pages
Frequency: 3 per year
Circulation: 1115

18850 Old Time Herald
P.O.Box 61679
Durham, NC 27715-1679

919-286-2041
E-Mail: info@oldtimeherald.org
Home Page: www.oldtimeherald.org

Sarah Bryan, Editor-in-chief
Peter Honig, Business Director

Information on Bluegrass music
Mailing list available for rent

18851 Pedal Steel Newsletter
Pedal Steel Guitar Association
PO Box 20248
Floral Park, NY 11002-0248

516-616-9214
Fax: 516-616-9214
E-Mail: bobpsga@optonline.net
Home Page: www.psga.org

Doug Mack, Editor
Bob Maickel, President

Dedicated to the art of playing pedal steel guitar. Every issue contains tablature arrangements of songs for the steel guitar as well as coming events, record reviews, product reports and news concerning the instrument.
Frequency: 10 x Per Year
ISSN: 1088-7954
Founded in 1973
Mailing list available for rent

18852 Percussion News
Percussive Arts Society
110 W Washington Street
Suite A
Indianapolis, IN 46204

317-974-4488
Fax: 317-974-4499
E-Mail: percarts@pas.org
Home Page: www.pas.org

Rick Mattingly, Editor
Hillary Henry, Art Director
Lisa Rogers, President

Newsletter devoted to membership activities. This colorful newsletter also features a Classified Advertising section. Percussion News is published in January, March, May, July, September and November.
Frequency: 6 Editions Per Year
Founded in 1961
Mailing list available for rent

18853 Rolling Stone
Rolling Stone Magazine
1290 Ave of the Americas
2nd Floor
New York, NY 10104-0298

212-484-1616
800-283-1549
Fax: 212-484-1771
E-Mail: rollingstone@real.com
Home Page: www.rssoundingboard.com
Social Media: Facebook, Twitter, YouTube, RSS, Foursqare

Jann Wenner, President

A monthly newsletter geared for marketing, advertising and music exexecutives. It includes information on such matters as rock tours and musician endorsements, ad campaigns and rock contests.
Cost: $50.00
Frequency: Monthly
Founded in 1967
Mailing list available for rent

18854 Roots and Rhythm Newsletter
Roots and Rhythm
PO Box 837
El Cerrito, CA 94530

510-526-8373
888-766-8766
Fax: 510-526-9001
E-Mail: roots@toast.net
Home Page: www.rootsandrhythm.com

Frank Scott, Owner
Nancy Scott-Noennig, Co-Owner

Lists, reviews and makes available for sale, recordings of blues, rhythm and blues, rockabilly, country, folk, ethnic, nostalgia and jazz music. Each newsletter reviews about 400 items and lists another 500 without reviews.
Frequency: Bi-Monthly
Circulation: 10000

Founded in 1974
Printed in 2 colors on newsprint stock

18855 Sing Out!
PO Box 5460
Bethlehem, PA 18015-0460

610-865-5366
Fax: 215-895-3052
E-Mail: info@singout.org
Home Page: www.singout.org

Information on Bluegrass music
Mailing list available for rent

18856 Tempo
Academy of Country Music
5500 Balboa Blvd
Suite 200
Encino, CA 91316-1505

818-788-8000
Fax: 818-788-0999
E-Mail: info@acmcountry.com
Home Page: www.acmcountry.com

Butch Waugh, Chairman

Devoted exclusively to the country music industry.
12 Pages
Frequency: Quarterly
Circulation: 4500
Founded in 1964

18857 The Voice
1156 15th St NW
Suite 310
Washington, DC 20005-1747

202-331-7577
Fax: 202-331-7599
E-Mail: service@chorusamerica.org
Home Page: www.chorusamerica.org

Ann Meier Baker, President & Chief Executive Officer
1600 Members
Frequency: Quarterly
Circulation: 5000
ISSN: 1074-0805
Founded in 1977

18858 Westfield Center
Westfield Center for Early Keyboard Studies
726 University Ave,Room 102
Cornell University
Ithaca, NY 14850-3914

607-255-3065
E-Mail: info@westfield.org
Home Page: www.westfield.org

Annette Richards, Executive Director
Maja Anderson, Program Coordinator
Evan Cortens, Administrative Assistant

E-newsletter providing information to professional keyboard musicians.
12 Pages
Frequency: Monthly
Founded in 1979

18859 Women in Bluegrass Newsletter
PO Box 2498
Winchester, VA 22604
800-227-2357
E-Mail: Nmhentry@visuallink.com
Home Page:
www.murphymethod/com/womeninbluegrass.cfm

Information on women in bluegass music

Magazines & Journals

18860 AfterTouch: New Music Discoveries
Music Discovery Network
PO Box 6205
Peoria, IL 61601-6205

309-685-4843
800-882-4262
Fax: 309-685-4878
E-Mail: aimcmc@aol.com
Home Page: www.musicdiscoveries.com

Ronald Wallace, Editor

A magazine for music lovers who would like to experience new sights and sounds and would like to keep their fingers on the pulse of the music industry.
Frequency: Annual
Circulation: 10,000
Founded in 1984
Printed in on glossy stock

18861 American Music
University of Illinois Press
1325 South Oak Street
MC-566
Champaign, IL 61820-6903

217-244-0626
866-244-0626
Fax: 217-244-8082
E-Mail: journals@uillinois.edu
Home Page: www.press.uillinois.edu

Michael Pisani, Editor
Jeff McArdle, Journals Marketing/Advertising Mgr.

Publishes articles on American composers, performers, publishers, institutions, events, and the music industry as well as book and recording reviews, bibliographies, and discographies.
Cost: $45.00
Frequency: Quarterly
Circulation: 1650
ISSN: 0734-4392
Founded in 1981
Mailing list available for rent: 1,650 names at $100 per M
Printed in 2 colors on glossy stock

18862 American Music Teacher
Music Teachers National Association
441 Vine St
Suite 505
Cincinnati, OH 45202-2813

513-421-1420
888-512-5278
Fax: 513-421-2503
E-Mail: mtnanet@mtna.org
Home Page: www.mtna.org

Gary L Ingle, Executive Director
Gail Berenson, President
Janice Wenger, VP

Provides articles, reviews and regular columns that inform, educate and challenge music teachers and foster excellence in the music teaching profession.
Cost: $30.00
Circulation: 35000
Founded in 1876
Mailing list available for rent: 24000 names at $85 per M
Printed in 4 colors on glossy stock

18863 American Organist
American Guild of Organists
475 Riverside Dr
Suite 1260
New York, NY 10115-0055

212-870-2310
800-246-5115
Fax: 212-870-2163
E-Mail: info@agohq.org
Home Page: www.agohq.org
Social Media: Facebook

James Thomashower, Executive Director

Most widely read journal devoted to organ and choral music in the world. Officialjournal of the American Guild of Organists, the Royal Canadian College of Organists, and the Associated Pipe Organ Builders of America.
Cost: $ 52.00
Frequency: Monthly
Circulation: 24000
ISSN: 0164-3150
Founded in 1967

18864 American String Teachers Journal
American String Teachers Association
4155 Chain Bridge Rd
Fairfax, VA 22030-4102

703-279-2113
Fax: 703-279-2114
E-Mail: asta@astaweb.com
Home Page: www.astaweb.com

Donna Hale, Executive Director
Beth Danner-Knight, Deputy Director

Available to members. Provides an overview of current articles featured in the journal. Also answers questions about content, advertising, and contact information.
Cost: $90.00
Frequency: Quarterly
Circulation: 11,300
Mailing list available for rent: 10M+ names

18865 American Viola Society Journal
American Viola Society
14070 Proton Rd
Suite 100LB
Dallas, TX 75244-3601

972-233-9107
Fax: 972-490-4219
E-Mail: info@avsnationaloffice.org
Home Page: www.americanviolasociety.org

Nokuthula Ngwenyama, President
Karin Brown, Secretary
Michelle Sayles, Treasurer
Kathryn Steely, Webmaster

Peer reviewed journal which promotes interest in the viola.
Cost: $42.00
Frequency: Annually
Circulation: 1500
Founded in 1984

18866 BMI Musicworld
Broadcast Music
7 World Trade Center
250 Greenwich Street
New York, NY 10007-0030

212-220-3000
Fax: 212-246-2163
Home Page: www.bmi.com

Del Bryant, CEO
John E Cody, COO/EVP

Performing rights organization. Articles of interest to the songwriting community.
Founded in 1985

18867 Billboard Magazine
Prometheus Global Media
770 Broadwaye Blvd.
New York, NY 10003-9595

212-493-4100
Fax: 646-654-5368

Home Page: www.prometheusgm.com
Social Media: Facebook, Twitter

Richard D. Beckman, CEO
James A. Finkelstein, Chairman
Madeline Krakowsky, Vice President Circualtion
Tracy Brater, Executive Director Creative Service

Packed with in-depth music and entertainment features including the latest in new media and digital music, global coverage, music and money, touring, new artists, radio news and retail reports.
Cost: $149.00
Frequency: Weekly
Founded in 1894

18868 CCM Magazine
Salem Publishing
402 BNA Drive
Suite 400
Nashville, TN 37217

615-386-3011
Fax: 615-386-3380
E-Mail: info@ccmcom.com
Home Page: www.ccmmagazine.com
Social Media: Facebook, Twitter, RSS

Jim Cumbee, President

The voice of Contemporary Christian Music. Each monthly issue features music news, exclusive interviews, and an in-depth look at the spiritual lives of today's leading Christian music artists.
Cost: $19.95
Frequency: Monthly
Founded in 1978
Printed in 4 colors on glossy stock

18869 Callboard
Theatre Bay Area
1663 Mission St
Suite 525
San Francisco, CA 94103-2487

415-430-1140
Fax: 415-430-1145
E-Mail: tba@theatrebayarea.org
Home Page: www.theatrebayarea.org
Social Media: Facebook, Twitter, YouTube

Karen Mc Kevitt, Manager

Provides trade information for professionals in the Bay Area. The magazine contains the following departments: Letterbox, Inside the Industry, Community News, How Did They Do That, Keep An Eye On, Editors' Picks and Encore.
Cost: $65.00
Frequency: Monthly
ISSN: 1064-0703
Founded in 1976
Printed in 2 colors on matte stock

18870 Chamber Music Magazine
Chamber Music America
UPS Box 458
243 Fifth Avenue
New York, NY 10016

212-242-2022
Fax: 212-242-7955
Home Page: www.chamber-music.org

Susan Dadian, Program Director
Margaret M Lioi, CEO
Louise Smith, Chair
Cost: $5.95
Frequency: Bi-Monthly
Circulation: 6000
Founded in 1977

18871 Choral Journal
American Choral Directors Association
545 Couch Drive
Oklahoma City, OK 73102

405-232-8161
Fax: 405-232-8162
Home Page: www.acdaonline.org

Carroll Gonzo, Editor
Ron Granger, Managing Editor

Contains articles and columns of a scholarly and practical nature in addition to reviews of newly released CD recordings, books, and printed music.
Frequency: Monthly

18872 Clarinet Journal
International Clarinet Society
PO Box 5039
Wheaton, IL 60189-5039

630-665-3602
Fax: 630-665-3848
E-Mail: info@clarinet.org
Home Page: www.clarinet.org

James Gillespie, Editor
So Rhee, Executive Director
Maxine Ramey, President
Caroline Hartig, Secretary
Tod Kerstetter, Treasurer

Contains articles in wide variety of areas written by performers and scholars.
Cost: $25.00
Frequency: Quarterly
Circulation: 3000

18873 Clavier
Instrumentalist Publishing Company
200 Northfield Road
Northfield, IL 60093-3390

847-446-5000
888-446-6888
Fax: 847-446-6263
E-Mail: editor@theinstrumentalist.com
Home Page: www.instrumentalistmagazine.com
Social Media: Facebook

James Rohner, Publisher
Judy Nelson, Editor

Provides new ideas and advice for piano teachers from leading educators. The focus of each issue is to offer practical advice for teachers. Articles include interviews with prominent performers, teachers and composers, the latest teaching methods, tributes to great artists of the past, and reviews of newly publshed music, educational software and videos.
Cost: $17.00
Frequency: 10X Per Year
Circulation: 16000
Founded in 1965
Mailing list available for rent

18874 Close Up Magazine
Country Music Association
One Music Circle S
Nashville, TN 37203

615-244-2840
Fax: 615-242-4783
E-Mail: international@cmaworld.com
Home Page: www.cmaworld.com

Profiles of country music artists, various songwriters and industry news. Members of the Association receive the magazine as a benefit of their membership.
Circulation: 8000
Founded in 1958

18875 Country Weekly Magazine
American Media Inc
1000 American Media Way
T-Rex Technology Center
Boca Raton, FL 33464-1000

561-997-7733
Fax: 561-989-1298
Home Page: www.nationalenquirer.com

David J Pecker, CEO

Devoted to country music and entertainment. Packed with feature articles and photos of country music personalities, music and video reviews, tour dates and late breaking news from the world of country music.
Cost: $34.95
Frequency: Bi-Weekly

18876 DJ Times
Testa Communications
25 Willowdale Avenue
Port Washington, NY 11050-3779

516-767-2500
800-937-7678
Fax: 516-767-9335
E-Mail: djtimes@testa.com
Home Page: www.djtimes.com

Jim Tremayne, Editor-in-Chief
Steve Thorakos, Production Manager

Colorful tabloid magazine dedicated to professional mobile and club DJs. Specialized music sections, new product departments for sound and lighting, record reviews, business columns, informative entertainer profiles and more.
Cost: $19.40
Frequency: Monthly
Circulation: 30000
Founded in 1988

18877 Diapason
Scranton Gillette Communications
3030 W Salt Creek Lane
Suite 201
Arlington Heights, IL 60005-5025

847-391-1000
Fax: 847-390-0408
E-Mail: jbutera@sgcmail.com
Home Page: www.thediapason.com

Jerome Butera, Editor/Publisher
Joyce Robinson, Associate Editor

Devoted to the organ, the harpischord, the carillon, and church music. Includes feature articles, reviews, reports, news, organ specifications, and a calendar, as well as classified advertisements.
Cost: $35.00
Frequency: Monthly
ISSN: 0012-2378
Founded in 1909

18878 Discoveries
700 East State Street
Ioal, WI 54990-0001

715-445-2214
800-258-0929
Fax: 715-445-4087
E-Mail: wayne.youngblood@fwpubs.com
Home Page: www.discoveriesmag.com

Mark Willliams, Publisher
Wayne Youngblood, Editorial Director
Cathy Bernardy, Associate Editor
Todd Whitesel, Associate Editor
Trevor Lauber, Advertising Sales Manager

Keeps close watch on market trends for collectible records, CDs and memorabilia. The Market Watch pages serve to interpret the mass of information available online and break it down to the most useful data collectors need. Each monthly issue is full of personality and opinion, with many reviews to help you determine where to spend your money. Coverage includes rock 'n' roll, rhythm &'blues, pop, doo-wop, classic jazz and country western re-

cordings.
Cost: $28.00
Frequency: Monthly
Circulation: 10,859
Founded in 1988

18879 Downbeat
102 N Haven Road
PO Box 906
Elmhurst, IL 60126
630-941-2030
800-554-7470
Fax: 630-941-3210
E-Mail: service@downbeat.com
Home Page: www.downbeat.com

Kevin Maher, CEO

Monthly magazine includes such features as Readers Poll results, festival reviews, CD reviews, feature articles and more.
Cost: $29.95
Frequency: Monthly
Mailing list available for rent

18880 Electronic Musician
PRIMEDIA
6400 Hollis Street
Suite 12
Emeryville, CA 94608-1086
510-653-3307
E-Mail: emeditorial@prismb2b.com
Home Page: www.emusician.com
Social Media: Facebook, Twitter

Steve Oppenheimer, Editor-in-Chief
Joe Perry, Associate Publisher
Marie Briganti, List Manager

Magazine for musicians recording and producing music in a home or personal studio environment. They are a source of user-friendly technical information for musicans. Features include: Tech Page, ProFile, Working Musician, Sound Design Workshop, Making Tracks, Square One, Reviews, What's New, Master Class, Final Mix, and Editors Choice Awards.
Cost: $23.97
Frequency: Monthly
Circulation: 61102
Founded in 1986
Mailing list available for rent

18881 Flute Talk
Instrumentalist Company
200 Northfield Road
Northfield, IL 60093-3390
847-446-5000
888-446-6888
Fax: 847-446-6263
E-Mail: fteditor@instrumentalistmagazine.com
Home Page: www.instrumentalistmagazine.com
Social Media: Facebook

Flute Talk is written for professional flute players, teachers, and advanced students. Frequent topics include performance analyses of flute repertoire, current teaching techniques, piccolo articles, interviews with prominent performers and teachers, and reviews of new music, recordings, and books for flutists.
Cost: $13.00
Frequency: 10 x Per Year
Circulation: 12000
Founded in 1981

18882 Goldmine
700 E State Street
Iola, WI 54990-0001
715-445-2214
800-258-0929
Fax: 715-445-4087
E-Mail: susan.sliwicki@fwmedia.com
Home Page: www.goldminemag.com
Social Media: Facebook, YouTube, RSS, Pinterest

Jeff Pozorski, Publisher
Brian Earnest, Editorial Director
Peter Lindblad, Associate Editor
Tim Neely, Research Director
Trevor Lauber, Advertising Sales Manager

The world's largest marketplace for collectible records, CDs, and music memorabilia covering Rock N' Roll, Blues, Country, Folk, and Jazz. Large volumes of For Sale and Wanted ads are placed by collectors and dealers. Includes articles on recording stars of the past and present with discographies listing all known releases, a listing of upcoming record-and-CD-collector conventions, album reviews, hobby and music news, a collecting column, a letters section, and Collector Mania (Q&A).
Cost: $39.95
Frequency: Bi-Weekly
Circulation: 17026
Founded in 1974
Mailing list available for rent

18883 Guitar One
Cherry Lane Magazines
6 E 32nd St
Suite 11
New York, NY 10016-5422
212-561-3000
800-825-4942
Fax: 212-447-6885
E-Mail: guitarshop@worldnet.att.net
Home Page: www.guitarmag.com

Peter W Primont, CEO
Jonathan Simpson-Bint, President
Holly Klingel, VP Circulation
Steve Aaron, Publishing Director
Greg Di Benedetto, Publisher

Information on everything from the guitar equipment evaluations to news on the latest trends and technological developments to special insider pieces covering the sound secrets of today's top players.
Cost: $24.95
Frequency: Monthly
Circulation: 105,000
Founded in 1985

18884 Guitar Review
Albert Augustine Limited
151 W 26th St
Suite 4
New York, NY 10001-6810
917-661-0220
Fax: 917-661-0223
E-Mail: mail@guitarreview.com
Home Page: www.albertaugustine.com

Steven Griesgraber, President
Eliot Fisk, Associate Editor
David Starobin, Associate Editor
Ian Gallagher, Music Editor
Matthew Hough, Circulation

Scholarly articles related to the classical guitar.
Cost: $28.00
48 Pages
Frequency: Quarterly
Circulation: 4000
Founded in 1946

18885 HipHop Weekly
Z & M Media
401 Broadway
New York, NY
212-696-0831
Home Page: www.hiphopweekly.com
Social Media: Facebook, Twitter

Covers the entire hip hop culture.

18886 Instrumentalist
Instrumentalist Company
200 Northfield Road
Northfield, IL 60093-3390
847-446-5000
888-446-6888
Fax: 847-446-6263
E-Mail: insteditor@instrumentalistmagazine.com
Home Page: www.instrumentalistmagazine.com
Social Media: Facebook

A magazine school band and orchestra directors can depend on for practical information to use for then ensembles. The articles written by veteran directors and performers cover a wide range of topics, including rehearsal techniques, conducting tips, programming ideas, instrument clinics, repertoire analyses, and much more. Monthly new music reviews guide directors to selecting the best music for their students.
Cost: $21.00
Frequency: Monthly
Circulation: 16,000
Founded in 1945
Printed in 4 colors

18887 International Musician
American Federation of Musicians
1501 Broadway
Suite 600
New York, NY 10036-5501
212-869-1330
Fax: 212-764-6134
E-Mail: info@afm.org
Home Page: www.afm.org

Thomas Lee, President

Delivers the latest happenings in music. Focuses on the overall well-being of all musicians. Provides news pertaining to symphonic, rock, freelance, recording and touring musicians. IM features aricles on pressing issues sich as piracy, legislation, on-the-job struggles, and the effects of technology.
Cost: $25.00
Frequency: Monthly
Circulation: 110000
Founded in 1896
Printed in on n stock

18888 JAMIA
American Musical Instrument Society
389 Main Street
Suite 202
Malden, MA 02148
781-397-8870
Fax: 781-397-8887
E-Mail: amis@guildassoc.com
Home Page: www.amis.org

Stewart Carter, President
Joanne Kopp, Treasurer

Presents peer-reviewed articles that assist in both professionals and students to develop and apply biomedical and health informatics to patient care, teaching, research, and health care administration.
Frequency: Bi-Monthly
Founded in 1971

18889 Jazz Education Journal
JazzTimes Magazine,Madavor Media
85 Quincy Ave
Suite 2
Quincy, MA 02169
617-706-9110
Fax: 617-536-0102
E-Mail: karen@iage.org
Home Page: www.jazztimes.com

Leslie M Sabina, Editor
Karen Mayse, Advertising

Provides news and information in the field of jazz education. Contains information of to-

day's top jazz artists, reviews, transcriptions, industry news, and articles on improvisation, teaching techniques, history, performance, composition, arranging and music business.
Cost: $23.95
100 Pages
Circulation: 10,000
Founded in 1968
Mailing list available for rent
Printed in on glossy stock

18890 Journal of American Organbuilding
American Institute of Organ Builders
PO Box 35306
Canton, OH 44735

330-806-9011
E-Mail: robertsullivan@pipeorgan.org
Home Page: www.pipeorgan.org

Jeffrey L Weiler, Editor

Features technical articles, product and book reviews, and a forum for the exchange of building and service information and techniqes. Subscriptions are provided free to AIO members, and are available to non-members for $24.00 per year.
Cost: $24.00
Frequency: Quarterly
Founded in 1974
Mailing list available for rent: 350 names at $250 per M
Printed in on glossy stock

18891 Journal of Music Theory
Yale University
Department of Music
PO Box 208310
New Haven, CT 06520-8310

203-432-2985
Fax: 203-432-2983
E-Mail: jmt.editor@yale.edu
Home Page: www.yale.edu/jmt/

Ian Quinn, Editor
David Clampitt, Associate Editor
Richard Cohn, Associate Editor
Daniel Harrison, Associate Editor
Patrick McCreless, Associate Editor

Publishes peer-reviewed reseach in Music Theory.
Cost: $30.00
Frequency: Annual
Founded in 1957

18892 Journal of Music Therapy
American Music Therapy Association
8455 Colesville Rd
Suite 1000
Silver Spring, MD 20910-3392

301-589-3300
Fax: 301-589-5175
E-Mail: info@musictherapy.org
Home Page: www.musictherapy.org

Andrea Farbman, Executive Director

Research in the area of music therapy and rehabilitation, a forum for authoratative articles of current music therapy research and theory, use of music in the behavioral sciences, book reviews, and guest editorials.
Cost: $120.00
Frequency: Quarterly
Circulation: 6000
ISSN: 0022-2917
Founded in 1998

18893 Journal of Research in Music Education
MENC Subscription Office
PO Box 1584
Birmingham, AL 35201

800-633-4931
E-Mail: menc@ebsco.com
Home Page: www.menc.org
Social Media: Facebook, Twitter

Keeps members informed of the latest music education research. Offers a collection of reports that includes thorough analyses of theories and projects by respected music researchers. Issued four times yearly.
Frequency: Quarterly
Founded in 1907
Printed in on matte stock

18894 Journal of Singing
National Association of Teachers of Singing
9957 Moorings Dr
Suite 401
Jacksonville, FL 32257-2416

904-992-9101
Fax: 904-262-2587
E-Mail: info@nats.org
Home Page: www.nats.org

Richard Dale Sjoerdsma, Editor-in-Chief

Provides current information regarding the teaching of singing as well as results of recent research in the field. The Journal serves as a historical record and a venue for teachers of singing and other scholars to share the resilts of their work in areas such as history, diction, voice science, medicine, and voice pedagogy.
Frequency: 5x times/year

18895 Journal of the American Musicological Society
University of California Press, Journals Division
2000 Center Street Way
Suite 203
Berkeley, CA 94704-1223

510-643-7154
Fax: 510-642-9917
E-Mail: journals@ucpress.edu
Home Page: www.ucpressjournals.com

Bruce Alan Brown, Editor
Louise Goldberg, Assistant Editor
Julie Cumming, Book Review Editor

The JAMS publishes scholarship from all fields of musical inquiry: from historical musicology, critical theory, music analysis, iconography and organology, to performance practice, aesthetics and hermeneutics, ethnomusicology, gender and sexuality, popular music and cultural studies. Each issue includes articles, book reviews, and communications.
Cost: $42.00
Frequency: Tri-Annual
Circulation: 5000
ISSN: 0003-0139
Founded in 1893

18896 Jukebox Collector Magazine
2545 SE 60th Court
Pleasant Hill, IA 50327-5099

515-265-8324
Fax: 515-265-1980
E-Mail: JukeboxCollector@att.net
Home Page: www.jukeboxmagazine.com

Rick Botts, Editor

Focuses on collectors of jukeboxes from the 40's, 50's, and 60's. There are approximately 150 jukeboxes for sale each month, along with show events information. Accepts advertising.
Cost: $33.00
36 Pages
Frequency: Monthly
Circulation: 1800
Founded in 1977

18897 Live Sound International
111 Speen Street
Framingham, MA 01701

415-387-4009
800-375-8015
Fax: 866-449-3761
E-Mail: amclean@livesoundint.com
Home Page: www.livesoundint.com

Mark Herman, Publisher
Jeff MacKay, Editor
Mitch Gallagher, Associate Editor
Sara Elliott, Advertising

The editorial focus is performance audio and event sound. Contains audio production techniques, new products, equipment applications and associated commercial concerns.
Cost: $60.00
Frequency: Monthly
Circulation: 20,000
Mailing list available for rent
Printed in on glossy stock

18898 Mix
Prism Business Media
6400 Hollis St
Suite 9
Emeryville, CA 94608-1052

510-658-3793
866-860-7087
Fax: 510-653-5142
E-Mail: mixeditorial@prismb2b.com
Home Page: www.mixonline.com

Melinda Paras, Owner
Erika Lopez, Associate Publisher
Tom Kenny, Editor
John Pledger, Publisher
Christen Pocock, Marketing Director

Mix covers a wide range of topics including: recording, live sound and production, broadcast production, audio for film and video, and music technology. In addition, Mix includes coverage of facility design and construction, location recording, tape/disc manufacturing, education, and other topics of importanct to audio professionals. Distributed in 94 countries.
Cost: $35.97
Frequency: Monthly
Circulation: 45244
Founded in 1977

18899 Modern Drummer
Modern Drummer Publications
12 Old Bridge Rd
Cedar Grove, NJ 07009-1288

973-239-4140
Fax: 973-239-7139
E-Mail: mdinfo@moderndrummer.com
Home Page: www.moderndrummer.com

Isabel Spagnardi, Owner
Tracy A Kearns, Associate Publisher
Bill Miller, Editor-in-Chief
Rick Van Horn, Senior Editor
Adam Budofsky, Managing Editor

Every issue of Modern Drummer includes interviews with the world's leading drummers, a full roster of columns on all facets of drumming, complete drum charts, solos and patterns performed by your favorite players, insightful reviews on the hottest new geat, the best in CDs, books, and DVDs for drummers, and giveaways worth thousands of dollars.
Cost: $29.97
Frequency: Monthly
Circulation: 6000
ISSN: 1078-1757
Founded in 1993
Mailing list available for rent
Printed in 4 colors on glossy stock

18900 Music
102 N Haven Road
PO Box 906
Elmhurst, IL 60126-2932

630-941-2030
Fax: 630-941-3210

E-Mail: subscriptions@musicincmag.com
Home Page: www.musicincmag.com

Zach Phillip, Editor
Kevin Maher, CEO
John Cahill, Eastern Advertising
Tom Burns, Western Advertising
Chris Maher, Classified Ads

Offered free to those involved in music products retailing. Delivers news you can use for the musical products industry. Geared toward store owners and managers in musical product retail and repair shops in the United States and Canada.
Frequency: 11 Per Year
Circulation: 8,949
Founded in 1934

18901 Music & Sound Retailer
Testa Communications
25 Willowdale Avenue
Port Washington, NY 11050

516-767-2500
800-937-7678
Fax: 516-767-9335
E-Mail: testa@testa.com
Home Page: www.testa.com

Brian Berk, Editor

News magazine serving owners, managers and sales personnel in retail musical-instument and sound-product dealershops. The magazine's emphasis is on full-line and combo dealerships offering guitars, drums, electronic keyboards and digital pianos, recording and sound-reinforcement products, lighting, DJ equipment, software, print and accessories. Recurring features include 'MI Spy,' 'Top Ten,' 'Veddatorial,' 'Selling Points,' and editor's letter
Cost: $18.00
Frequency: Monthly
Circulation: 11000
Founded in 1985

18902 Music Row
1231 17th Avenue S
PO Box 158542
Nashville, TN 37215-8542

615-321-3617
Fax: 615-329-0852
E-Mail: sales@musicrow.com
Home Page: www.musicrow.com

David M Ross, CEO/President

Written for people who work in the music business. Contents include record reviews, current news items, timely interviews or discovering hot talent first. Music Row subscriptions include six print issues per year, daily Afternoon News updates via e-mail and @Musicrow reports every Tuesday, Thursday and Friday via e-mail.
Cost: $159.00
Frequency: Six Per Year
Circulation: 14000
Founded in 1981
Printed in 4 colors on glossy stock

18903 Music Trades Magazine
Music Trades
80 West Street
Englewood, NJ 07631-0432

201-871-1965
800-423-6530
Fax: 201-871-0455
E-Mail: music@musictrades.com
Home Page: www.musictrades.com

Brian Majeski, Publisher
Richard T Watson, Managing Editor
Juanita Hampton, Circulation Manager

A blend of industry news, hard sales and marketing data, trend analysis and management tips in every issue. Target audience is retailers, distributors, and manufacturers of musical instruments, professional audio equipment and related products, worldwide.
Cost: $16.00
Frequency: Monthly
Circulation: 7500
Founded in 1890
Mailing list available for rent

18904 Music and Sound Journal
912 Carlton Road
Tarpon Spring, FL 34689

727-938-0571
E-Mail: sound@masj.com
Home Page: www.masj.com

Don Kulak, Founder/Owner

Brings readers the future of sound today, with new music, experimental sound, cutting edge audio and acoustics and alternative media. MSJ is written for people who are discriminating about music, audio, and sound - people who want to improve their sonic environments on all levels, without having to study pages of data - people who want to more fully understand the profound impact sound has on every aspect of their daily lives.
ISSN: 1541-8545
Founded in 1988

18905 Musical Merchandise Review
21 Highland Circle
Suite One
Needham, MA 02494

781-453-9310
800-964-5150
Fax: 781-453-9389
E-Mail: mprescott@symphonypublishing.com
Home Page: www.mmrmagazine.com

Lee Zapis, President
Sidney L Davis, Group Publisher
Richard E Kessel, Publisher/Advertising Sales
Maureen Johan, Classified Sales

Serves retailers of musical instruments, accessories, and related services as well as wholesalers, importers/exporters and manufacturers of related products. Its purpose is to communicate facts and ideas that will benefit musical merchandisers and their daily business operations as well as help them enhance their growth. Its editorial approach includes features on industry trends and innovations, new product promotion, in-store display techniques, financing, planning and dealer surveys.
Cost: $32.00
Frequency: Monthly
Founded in 1879
Mailing list available for rentat $100 per M
Printed in 4 colors

18906 New on the Charts
Music Business Reference
70 Laurel Place
New Rochelle, NY 10801-7105

914-632-3349
Fax: 914-633-7690
E-Mail: lenny@notc.com
Home Page: www.notc.com

Leonard Kalikow, Publisher/Editor

Circulation limited to professionals only, provides major signings, contracts and directories.
Cost: $365.00
Frequency: Monthly
Circulation: 5,000
ISSN: 0276-7031
Founded in 1976

18907 Notes
Music Library Association
8551 Research Way
Suite 180
Middleton, WI 53562

608-836-5825
Fax: 608-831-8200
E-Mail: mla@areditions.com
Home Page: www.musiclibraryassoc.org

Michael Colby, President
Jane Gottlieb, Editor

18908 Opera America Newsline
Opera America
330 7th Ave
Suite 1600
New York, NY 10001-5248

212-796-8620
Fax: 212-796-8631
E-Mail: info@operaamerica.org
Home Page: www.operaamerica.org

Marc Scorca, President

Provides company news from around the world, articles on issues affecting the field, professional opportunities, and updates on OPERA America programs and activities. Complimentary subscription with all membership levels, excluding stand-alone professional subscriptions.
Frequency: 10X Per Year
Founded in 1970

18909 Opera News
Metropolitan Opera Guild
70 Lincoln Center Plz
New York, NY 10023-6577

212-769-7000
Fax: 212-769-7007
E-Mail: info@metguild.org
Home Page: www.metoperafamily.org

David Dik, Manager

Monthly magazine that reports on opera around the world. Issues include reviews of commercial recordings and live performances, profiles of artists and articles by eminent writers on the music scene.
Cost: $29.95
Frequency: Monthly
Circulation: 60000
Founded in 1883

18910 Percussive Notes
Percussive Arts Society
110 W Washington Street
Suite A
Indianapolis, IN 46204

317-974-4488
Fax: 317-974-4499
E-Mail: percarts@pas.org
Home Page: www.pas.org

Rick Mattingly, Editor
Hillary Henry, Managing Editor

The official journal of the Percussive Arts Society. Published in February, April, June, August, October and December, this magazine features a variety of articles and advertising aimed at professional and student percussionists. Regular sections are devoted to drumset, marching percussion, world percussion, symphonic percussion, technology, keyboard, health and wellness, research and reviews.
Cost: $85.00
Frequency: 6 Times Per Year
Circulation: 8000
Founded in 1961
Mailing list available for rent

18911 Piano Guild Notes
Piano Guild Publications

PO Box 1807
Austin, TX 78767-1807

512-478-5775
Fax: 512-478-5843
E-Mail: ngpt@pianoguild.com
Home Page: www.pianoguild.com

Richard Allison, President
Music industry publication focusing on Piano Guild members and activities.
Cost: $16.00
Frequency: Quarterly
Circulation: 11000
Founded in 1929
Printed in 2 colors

18912 Piano Technicians Journal
Piano Technicians Guild
4444 Forest Avenue
Kansas City, KS 66106

913-432-9975
Fax: 913-432-9986
E-Mail: ptg@ptg.org
Home Page: www.ptg.org

Barbara Cassaday, Executive Director
Jim Coleman Jr RPT, President
Norman R Cantrell RPT, VP
Monthly technical magazine covering all phases of working on pianos. Articles explore new tools, industry news and organizational issues. Feature articles range from setting up a repair shop to rebuilding techniques.
Cost: $ 150.00
Frequency: Monthly
Circulation: 4300
ISSN: 0031-9562

18913 Pitch Pipe
Sweet Adelines International
9110 S Toledo
PO Box 470168
Tulsa, OK 74137-0168

918-622-1444
800-992-7464
Fax: 918-665-0894
E-Mail: Joey@sweetadelineintl.org
Home Page: www.sweetadelineintl.org

Pat LeVezu, President
Joey Mechell Stenner, Editor
Kelly Kirchhoff, Director Communications
Official publication of Sweet Adelines International, the world's largest singing performance and music education organization for women. The Pitch Pipe informs, educates and recognizes the members who have made the organization a success. The subscription price for members is included in the annual per capita fee.
Cost: $12.00
Frequency: Quarterly
Circulation: 30,000
Founded in 1947
Mailing list available for rent: 30M names
Printed in 4 colors on glossy stock

18914 Playback
American Society of Composers, Authors & Publisher
1 Lincoln Plz
New York, NY 10023-7097

212-621-6027
800-952-7227
Fax: 212-362-7328
E-Mail: Playback@ascap.com
Home Page: www.ascap.com

Marilyn Bergman, President
Phil Crossland, Executive Editor
Jin Moon, Deputy Editor
Mike Barsky, Advertising
David Pollard, Design
The Society's magazine is loaded with full-color photos, features the latest news on ASCAP events, new member listings, legislative updates, feature articles on members, distribution info, upcoming workshops and showcases and much more.
Cost: $12.00
Frequency: Annual
Circulation: 100,000
ISSN: 1080-1391

18915 Pro Audio Review
IMAS Publishing
28 East 28th Street
12th Floor
New York, NY 22041

212-378-0400
Fax: 212-378-0470
E-Mail: letters@proaudioreview.com
Home Page: www.proaudioreview.com

John Gatski, Publisher/Executive Editor
Brett Moss, Managing Editor
Claudia Van Veen, Advertising
Reviews of the latest new equipment written by audio professionals in the field, from bench tests checking the specs, to new product announcements.
Cost: $24.95
Frequency: Monthly
Circulation: 26000
ISSN: 1083-6241
Founded in 1995
Mailing list available for rent: 30,000 names at $145 per M
Printed in 4 colors on glossy stock

18916 Pro Sound News
United Business Media
28 East 28th Street
12th Floor
New York, NY 10019

212-378-0400
Fax: 212-378-2160
E-Mail: sedorusa@optonline.net
Home Page: www.governmentvideo.com

Gary Rhodes, International Sales Manager
Provides timely and accurate news, industy analysis, features and technology updates to the expanded professional audio community.
Cost: $30.00
Frequency: Monthly
Circulation: 250003
Printed in 4 colors

18917 RePlay Magazine
PO Box 572829
Tarzana, CA 91357-7004

818-776-2880
Fax: 818-776-2888
E-Mail: editor@replaymag.com
Home Page: www.replaymag.com

Edward Adlum, President
Barry Zweben, Marketing
A trade publication for those within the coin-operated amusement machine industry, primarily distributors, manufacturers and operators of jukeboxes and games.
Cost: $65.00
Frequency: Monthly
Circulation: 36000
ISSN: 1534-2328
Founded in 1975
Mailing list available for rent
Printed in 4 colors on glossy stock

18918 Rolling Stone Magazine
1290 Ave of the Americas
Floor 2
New York, NY 10104-0295

212-484-1616
Fax: 212-484-1771
Home Page: www.rssoundingboard.com
Social Media: Facebook, Twitter

Jann Wenner, President
Covers pop culture, politics etc in a massive amount of music articles, interviews, news, reviews, photos, and sound clips.

18919 Sheet Music Magazine
PO Box 58629
Boulder, CO 80323

914-244-8500
800-759-3036
Fax: 914-244-8560
Home Page: www.sheetmusicmagazine.com

Ed Shanaphy, Publisher
Features actual reproduction of popular songs, both words and music, articles on various aspects of musical performance and interest for many types of musicians, and self improvement features for keyboard and fretter instrument players. A single year's subscription brings you at least 66 great songs best-loved standards and today's most lyrical hits.
Cost: $22.97
Frequency: Bi-Monthly
Circulation: 50,000

18920 Society News
Contemporary Record Society
724 Winchester Road
Broomall, PA 19008

610-544-5920
Fax: 915-808-4232
E-Mail: crsnews@verizon.net
Home Page:
www.mysite.verizon.net/vzeeewvp/contemporaryrecordsociety/id3.

Jack M Shusterman, Advertising
Offers opportunities to CRS consitituents, progress notes on its associates, various awards and performance possibilities. The Society News offers feature articles of renowned composers/performers and reviews of music, recordings and music books.
Founded in 1983

18921 Southwestern Musician
Texas Music Educators Association
7900 Centre Park
PO Box 140465
Austin, TX 78714-0465

512-452-0710
888-318-8632
Fax: 512-451-9213
E Mail: rfloyd@tmea.org
Home Page: www.tmea.org

Robert Floyd, Executive Director
Karen Kneten, Communications Manager
Tesa Harding, Advertising/Exhibit Manager
Laura Kocian, Financial Manager
Rita Ellinger, Membership Assistant
The official magazine of the TMEA. Publsihed monthly August through May. Included with membership. A President's newsletter is published each June when necessary to provide an update on TMEA activities. The purposed of this publication is to serve the music educators of Texas as a means of communication or professional philosophy and action and to promote the field of music education within the state.
Circulation: 14000
Founded in 1938
Mailing list available for rent: 10,000 names
Printed in 4 colors on glossy stock

18922 Symphony Magazine
American Symphony Orchestra League

33 W 60th St
Suite 5
New York, NY 10023-7905

212-262-0638
Fax: 212-262-5198
E-Mail: editor@symphony.org
Home Page: www.symphony.org

Henry Fogel, CEO
Stephen Alter, Advertising Manager
Michael Rush, Production Manager

Bimonthly magazine of the American Symphony Orchestra League. Discusses issues critical to the orchestra community and communicates the value and importance of orchestras and the music they perform. Publishes articles on compelling issues and trends relevant to the entire orchestra field. Its readers include professional staff, musicians, and board members in the orchestra industry and related fields; orchestra patrons and volunteers; and music critics and arts and media professionals.
Cost: $22.00
Frequency: Bi-Monthly
Circulation: 18000
Founded in 1942
Mailing list available for rent
Printed in 4 colors

18923 **Symposium**
312 E Pine Street
Missoula, MT 59802

406-721-9616
800-729-0235
Fax: 406-721-9419
E-Mail: cms@music.org
Home Page: www.music.org

Robby D Gunstream, Executive Director
Cynthia Taggart, President
Glenn Stanley, Editor

Serves as a vehicle for the dissemination of information and ideas on music in higher education. The content of the publication highlights concerns of general interest and reflects the work of the Society in the areas of music represented on its Board of Directors.
Frequency: One Per Year
Circulation: 8000
Founded in 1968
Printed in one color on matte stock

18924 **Vibe**

E-Mail: vbecustserv@cdsfulfillment.com
Home Page: www.vibe.com

Mimi Valdez, Editor-In-Chief

Covers the trends, the events, and culture of the urban scene. Film, fashion and art to politics and music-pop, jazz, R&B, dance, hip hop, rap, house and more.
Cost: $11.95
Frequency: Monthly

Trade Shows

18925 **ASTA National Conference**
American String Teachers Association
4155 Chain Bridge Road
Fairfax, VA 22030

703-279-2113
Fax: 703-279-2114
E-Mail: asta@astaweb.com
Home Page: www.astaweb.com

Donna Sizemore Hale, Executive Director
Beth Danner-Knight, Deputy Director
Jody McNamara, Deputy Director

Recognizing the wealth of our rich traditions as well as offer members new horizons in teaching and performing strings. Cost of attendance begins at $255. 150 exhibitors.
2000 Attendees
Frequency: Annual/March

18926 **American Choral Directors Association National Conference**
American Choral Directors Association
545 Couch Drive
Oklahoma City, OK 73102

405-232-8161
Fax: 405-232-8162
Home Page: www.acdaonline.org

Dr Tim Sharp, Executive Director

4 full days of concerts, interest sessions, exhibits, and networking.
Frequency: Annual/March

18927 **American Guild of Organists, National Conference**
475 Riverside Drive
Suite 1260
New York, NY 10115

212-870-2310
Fax: 212-870-2163
E-Mail: info@agohq.org
Home Page: www.agohq.org

James Thomashower, Executive Director
Jennifer Madden, Manager Membership
Harold Calhoun, Mgr Competitions

Over 20 exhibits and a workshop for professional, amatuer and student organists.
Frequency: Biennial

18928 **American Harp Society National Conference**
3416 Primm Lane
Birmingham, AL 35216

205-795-7130
Fax: 205-823-2760
E-Mail: execsecretary@harpsociety.org
Home Page: www.harpsociety.org

Christa Grix, National Conference Chair
Lynne Aspnes, Conference Program Advisory Chair
Delaine Fedson, President

Conference will explore the mind-body-music connection, the creative process, and the connection between creativity and learning. The conference will include multiple disciplines including educators, composers, performers, therapists and practioners.
300 Attendees
Frequency: Annual
Founded in 1962

18929 **American Institute of Organbuilders Annual Convention**
American Institute of Organ Builders
PO Box 130982
Houston, TX 77219

713-529-2212
Fax: 713-529-2212
E-Mail: pipes@pipeorgan.org
Home Page: www.convention.pipeorgan.org

Rene Marceau, Convention Committee Chairman

Annual convention includes supplier exhibits, technical lectures, sight-seeing tours, professional examinations, lectures and organ demonstrations.
Frequency: October
Founded in 1974
Mailing list available for rent: 350 names at $250 per M

18930 **American Music Therapy Conference**
National Music Therapy Association
8445 Colesville Road
Suite 1000
Silver Spring, MD 20910

301-589-3300
Fax: 301-589-5175
Home Page: www.musictherapy.org

Seminar and exhibits of publications, musical instruments, books, learning aids and recordings.
Frequency: November

18931 **American Musical Instrument Society**
1106 Garden Street
Hoboken, NJ 07030

202-656-0107
E-Mail: amis@guildassoc.com
Home Page: www.amis.org

Susan Thompson, Program Co-Chair
Kathryn Libin, Program Co-Chair

A broad range of topics include the history, design, use, care and acoustics of musical instruments in all cultures and from all periods.
Frequency: Annual

18932 **American Musicological Society Annual Meeting**
American Musicological Society
6010 College Station
Brunswick, ME 04011-8451

207-798-4243
877-679-7648
Fax: 877-679-7648
E-Mail: ams@ams-net.org
Home Page: www.ams-net.org

Robert Judd, Executive Director

A society of professional musicologists and university educators. The annual meetings are held in the fall each year; 2007- Quebec; 2008- Nashville; 2009- Philadelphia.
2000 Attendees
Frequency: Annual
Founded in 1948
Mailing list available for rent: 3515 names at $100 per M

18933 **American Orff-Schulwerk Association National Conference**
American Orff-Schulwerk Association
PO Box 391089
Cleveland, OH 44139-8089

440-543-5366
Fax: 440-600-7332
E-Mail: info@aosa.org
Home Page: www.aosa2.org

Karen Medley, Conference Chair

One hundred exhibits of music, music books, software, insturments, and gifts in addition to National Conference of 2000+ music educators.
2400 Attendees
Frequency: November
Founded in 1969

18934 **American Symphony Orchestra League National Conference**
33 W 60th Street
5th Floor
New York, NY 10023

212-262-5161
Fax: 212-262-5198
E-Mail: league@symphony.org
Home Page: www.symphony.org

Stephen Alter, Advertising and Meetings Manager
Meghan Whitbeck, Advertising/Meetings Coordinator
Henry Fogel, President/CEO

Ninety booths incorporating all facets of classical music industries including industry suppliers, music publishers and computer technology.
1200 Attendees
Frequency: June

18935 CMS National Conference
College Music Society
312 E Pine Street
Missoula, MT 59802

406-721-9616
Fax: 406-721-9419
E-Mail: cms@music.org
Home Page: www.music.org

Robby D Gunstream, Executive Director

Presents higher education's broadest array of topics dealing with music. Attendees are faculty, administrators, graduate students, independent scholars, composers, publishers, and music business personnel who share a common interest and dedication to the improvement of music and its relationship to the other academic disciplines of higher education.
450 Attendees
Frequency: Annual/October

18936 Chamber Music America National Conference
Chamber Music America
305 7th Avenue
5th Floor
New York, NY 10001

212-242-2022
Fax: 212-242-7955
Home Page: www.chamber-music.org

Susan Dadian, Program Director
Margaret M Lioi, CEO
Louise Smith, Chair
700 Attendees
Frequency: Annual

18937 Chorus America Annual Conference
910 17th Street NW
Washington, DC 20006

202-776-0215
Fax: 202-776-0224
E-Mail: service@chorusamerica.org
Home Page: www.chorusamerica.org

Ann Meier Baker, President/CEO
Melanie Garrett, Membership Services Manager

This four day conference offers seminars, workshops, concerts, expert consultations and peer-group meetings in a friendly, dynamic environment.
500 Attendees
Frequency: June
Printed in 2 colors on matte stock

18938 Country Radio Seminar
Country Radio Broadcasters
819 18th Avenue S
Nashville, TN 37203

615-327-4487
Fax: 615-329-4492
E-Mail: info@crb.org
Home Page: www.crb.org

Ed Salamon, Executive Director
Chasity Crouch, Business Manager
Carole Bowen, Secretary

Conference attendess include major radio groups and record labels as well as independents, Features include exhibits, seminars and shows.
2300 Attendees
Frequency: Annual
Founded in 1969

18939 Folk Alliance Annual Meeting
Folk Alliance
510 South Main
1st Floor
Memphis, TN 38103

901-522-1170
Fax: 816-221-3658
E-Mail: fa@folk.org
Home Page: www.folkalliance.org

200+ artists, 4 nights of show cases, four days of feature concerts, exhibit hall parties, panels, workshops, clinics and much more all under one roof.
3000 Attendees

18940 Gospel Music Week
Gospel Music Association
PO Box 22697
Nashville, TN 37202

615-242-0303
Fax: 615-254-9755
E-Mail: info@gospelmusic.org
Home Page: www.gospelmusic.org

Jackie Patillo, Executive Director

Listen to new music as you experience over 100 eclectic performances throughout the week from today's top artists and tomorrow's hit-makers, invent new waysof enhancing your ministry through educational opportunities found in over 100 seminars and panels and through the sharing of your ideas with colleagues. Connect with your industry peers and friends at various networking opportunities including receptions, roundtables and more.
3,000 Attendees
Frequency: April
Founded in 1964

18941 Gospel Music Workshop America
PO Box 34635
Detroit, MI 48208

313-898-6900
Fax: 313-898-4520
E-Mail: manager@gmwanational.org
Home Page: www.gmwanational.org

Rev Albert L Jamison, Sr, Chair, Board of Directors
Sheila Smith, Director Operations
Mark Smith, Convention Manager

Conferences open with a highly spirited service including Sacraments, music from choirs within the GMWA, Psalmists and the preached Word. This is followed by lectures, speakers, preachers and over 100 courses offered during the week. Nightly musicals include chapter choirs and national recording artists. Midnight services are held which include music, preaching and various recordings by the Women's Division, Men's Division, Youth/Young Adult division and a service by Bishop Richard White.
16M Attendees
Frequency: August
Founded in 1967

18942 Horns Over the Sea
Central Washington University Music Department
400 E University Way
Ellensburg, WA 98926-7458

509-963-1226
Fax: 509-963-1239
E-Mail: gross@music.ucsb.edu
Home Page: www.hornsociety.org

Jeffrey Snedeker, President
Steven Gross, Conference Coordinator
Heidi Vogel, Membership Coordinator

Features renowned hornists, guest ensembles, recitals and master classes
450 Attendees
Frequency: August

18943 International Association of Jazz Educators Conference
International Association of Jazz Education
PO Box 724
Manhattan, KS 66505

785-776-8744
Fax: 785-776-6190
E-Mail: info@iage.org
Home Page: www.iaje.org

Bill McFarlin, Executive Director

This four-day conference fatures a 75,000 square-food music industry exposition, commission premieres, technology presentations, research papers, award ceremonies, and performances by over 500 of the world's most respected professional jazz groups and musicians.
8000 Attendees
Frequency: Annual

18944 International Computer Music Conference
International Computer Music Association
1819 Polk Street
Suite 330
San Francisco, CA 94109

FAX 734-878-3031
E-Mail: icma@umich.edu
Home Page: www.computermusic.org
Social Media: Facebook

Tae Hong Park, President
Margaret Schedel, VP of Conference
Chryssie Nanou, Treasurer/Secretary
Tom Erbe, VP, Membership
Sandra Neal, Administrative Assistant

The International Computer Music Association is an international affiliation of individuals and institutions involved in the technical, creative, and performance aspects of computer music. It serves composers, engineers, researchers and musicians who are interested in the integration of music and technology.
Founded in 1974

18945 International Horn Competition of America
BGSU Continuing and Extended Education
14 College Park
Bowling Green, OH 43403-0200

509-963-1226
Fax: 509-963-1239
Home Page: www.ihcamerica.org

Jeffrey Snedeker, President
Andrew Pelletier, Host

International competition specifically for the horn as a solo instrument.
450 Attendees
Frequency: July

18946 International Steel Guitar Convention
College Music Society
312 East Pine Street
Missoula, MT 59802

406-721-9616
Fax: 406-721-9419
E-Mail: cms@music.org
Home Page: www.music.org
Social Media: Facebook, Twitter, YouTube, RSS

Dewitt Scott Sr, President
Mary Scott, Secretary

Sixty-five booths that provide entertainment from steel guitarists and various instruments including the bass guitar.
3M Attendees
Frequency: August

18947 Mid-South Horn Conference
Central Washington University Music Department

400 E University Way
Ellensburg, WA 98926-7458

509-963-1226
Fax: 509-963-1239
E-Mail: campbellel@umkc.edu
Home Page: www.hornsociety.org

Jeffrey Snedeker, President
Ellen Campbell, Event Host
Heidi Vogel, Membership Coordinator

Features renowned hornists, guest ensembles, recitals and master classes
450 Attendees
Frequency: March

18948 Midwest International Band & Orchestra Clinic
Midwest International Band & Orchestra Clinic
111 E Touhy Ave
Suite 250
Des Plaines, IL 60018

847-424-4163
Fax: 773-321-1509
E-Mail: info@midwestclinic.org
Home Page: www.midwestclinic.org

The purpose to the clinic is to raise the standards of music education, to develop new teaching techniqes, to examine, analyze, analyze and appraise literature dealing with music, demonstrations for the betterment of music education. 350 exhibitors, 565 booths, 30 concerts, and 50 instructional clinics.
12000 Attendees
Frequency: December

18949 Music Teachers National Association Convention
441 Vine Street
Suite 3100
Cincinnati, OH 45202

513-421-1420
888-512-5278
Fax: 513-421-2503
E-Mail: mtnanet@mtna.org
Home Page: www.mtna.org

Gary L Ingle, Executive Director
Gail Berenson, President
Janice Wenger, VP

Atendees include independent music teachers, college faculty, students and parents from all over North America.
2500 Attendees
Frequency: Annual
Founded in 1876
Mailing list available for rent: 23000 names at $85 per M

18950 NAMM: International Music Products Association
5790 Armada Drive
Carlsbad, CA 92008-4608

760-438-8001
800-767-6266
Fax: 760-438-7327
E-Mail: tradeshow@namm.com
Home Page: www.thenammshow.com

Joe Lamond, President

NAMM's trade shows are all about the experience. The experience of checking out the latest gear, of networking with other music product professionals, of attending free business-boosting classes. From the cook exhibits to the sizzling hot nightlife, music and music making always take center stage.
80000 Attendees
Frequency: January

18951 NATS National Conference
National Association of Teachers of Singing
9957 Moorings Dr
Suite 401
Jacksonville, FL 32257-2416

904-992-9101
Fax: 904-262-2587
E-Mail: info@nats.org
Home Page: www.nats.org

Allen Henderson, Executive Director
Deborah L Guess, Director of Operations
Frequency: June/July

18952 National Association for Music Education Conference
1806 Robert Fulton Drive
Reston, VA 20191-4348

703-860-4000
800-336-3768
Fax: 703-860-1531
Home Page: www.menc.org
Social Media: Facebook, Twitter, LinkedIn

John J Mahlmann, Executive Director
Margaret Jamborsky, Director Meetings/Conventions
Elizabeth Lasko, Director Public Relations/Marketing
Amanda Kidwell, Membership Director

To advance music education by encouraging the study and making of music by all.
5M Attendees
Frequency: April

18953 National Association of Pastoral Musicians Convention
National Association of Pastoral Musicians
962 Wayne Avenue
Suite 210
Silver Spring, MD 20910-4461

240-247-3000
Fax: 240-247-3001
E-Mail: npmsing@npm.org
Home Page: www.npm.org

J Michael McMahon, President
Kathleen Haley, Membership Services Director
Paul H Colloton, Continuing Education Director
Lowell Hickman, Executive Assistant/Office Manager

200 workshop sessions, 5 major addresses, music education classes, clinics, new music showcases and exhibits, musical performances, prayer and songs, adult and children's choirs, handbells, youth gatherings, Liturgical Space Tour.
4000 Attendees
Frequency: July

18954 National Association of Recording Merchandising Trade Show
9 Eves Drive
Suite 120
Marlton, NJ 08053-3130

856-596-2221
Fax: 859-596-3268
E-Mail: still@narm.com
Home Page: www.narm.com
Social Media: Facebook, Twitter, RSS

Jim Donio, President
Pat Daly, Meeting Planner
Evelyn Dichter, Membership Coordinator
Susan L'Ecuyer, VP Communications/Marketing

One-on-One meeting opportunities, welcome reception, keynote speakers, marketplace exhibits, live performances, forums, receptions and awards dinner
3M Attendees
Frequency: April/May

18955 National Association of Schools of Music Annual Meeting
National Association of Schools of Music
11250 Roger Bacon Drive
Suite 21
Reston, VA 20190-5248

703-437-0700
Fax: 703-437-6312
E-Mail: info@arts-accredit.org
Home Page: www.arts-accredit.org

Don Gibson, President
Mark Wait, VP
Mellasenah Y Morris, Treasurer
Frequency: November

18956 National Opera Association Conference
National Opera Association
PO Box 60869
Canyon, TX 79016
806-651-2857
Fax: 806-651-2958
E-Mail: rhansen@mail.wtamu.edu
Home Page: www.noa.org
Social Media: Facebook, RSS

Robert Hansen, Executive Director
Robert Thieme, Editor

Annual conference and exhibits of opera related equipment, supplies and services.
775 Attendees
Frequency: Annual
Founded in 1954

18957 Northeast Horn Workshop
Central Washington University Music Department
400 E University Way
Ellensburg, WA 98926-7458

509-963-1226
Fax: 509-963-1239
E-Mail: rdodsonw@mansfield.edu
Home Page: www.hornsociety.org

Jeffrey Snedeker, President
Rebecca Dodson, Workshop Host
Heidi Vogel, Membership Coordinator

Features renowned hornists, guest ensembles, recitals and master classes
450 Attendees
Frequency: February

18958 Opera America Conference
Opera America
330 7th Avenue
16th Floor
New York, NY 10001-5248

212-796-8620
Fax: 212-796-8631
Home Page: www.operaamerica.org
Social Media: RSS

Session topics include identifying ways to harness the power of the best new technologies, how to reach current and prospective audiences, how to gain support from donors, and how to enrich the lives of children and adults who are now downloading podcasts, reading blogs, and designing their own multimedia communications.
275 Attendees
Frequency: April

18959 Piano Technicians Guild Annual Convention
Piano Technicians Guild
4444 Forest Avenue
Kansas City, KS 66106

913-432-9975
Fax: 913-432-9986

E-Mail: ptg@ptg.org
Home Page: www.ptg.org

Barbara J Cassaday, Executive Director
Jim Coleman Jr RPT, President
Norman R Cantrell RPT, VP

Come for the learning: find a hands-on class for your skill level; pick from sessions covering every type of piano service; squeeze in a mini-tech; prepare for the RPT exams; see the latest and greatest piano products.
650 Attendees
Frequency: June

18960 Sweet Adelines International Convention
Sweet Adelines International
PO Box 470168
Tulsa, OK 74147-0168

918-622-1444
800-992-7464
Fax: 918-665-0894
Home Page: www.sweetadelineintl.org

Kathy Hayes, Director Meetings/Corporate Service
Ruth Cameron, Meetings/Exhibits Coordinator
Jane Hanson, Marketing Coordinator
Connie Heyer, Membership Registrar
Kellye Kirchhoff, Director Communications

Heart-pounding chorus competitions, the rush and excitement of the quartet competition, education classes, shopping in the Harmony Bazaars and good times with old friends and new are all included in the International Convention.
8M Attendees
Frequency: October

18961 Winter Music Conference
3450 NE
12th Terrace
Fort Lauderdale, FL 33334

954-563-4444
Fax: 954-563-1599
E-Mail: info@wintermusicconference.com
Home Page: www.wintermusicconference.com

Regarded as the singular networking event in the dance music industry, attracting professionals from over 60 different countries.

18962 World of Bluegrass
International Bluegrass Music Association
2 Music Circle South
Suite 100
Nashville, TN 37203

615-256-3222
888-438-4262
Fax: 615-256-0450
E-Mail: info@ibma.org
Home Page: www.ibma.org

Dan Hays, Executive Director
Nancy Cardwell, Special Projects Coordinator
Jill Snider, Member/Convention Services

Build relationships with event producers, record label reps, agents and managers, broadcasters, association leaders, educators, the media, instrument builders, artists and composers. Educational and networking events like seminars, facilitated discussions and workshops are the primary focus of the conference. Browse through 100+ booths in the Exhibit Hall. You will hear bluegrass music around the clock for seven days. The Highpoint of the Conference is the International Bluegrass Music Awards.
1,800 Attendees
Frequency: October

Directories & Databases

18963 American Music Center Directory
American Music Center
90 John Street
Suite 312
New York, NY 10038

212-645-6949
Fax: 212-366-5265
E-Mail: library@newmusicusa.org
Home Page: www.amc.net

Joanne Cossa, Executive Director
Lyn Liston, Director New Music Information
Peter Shavitz, Director Development
Lisa Taliano, Director Information Technology
Carlos Camposeco, Director Finance and Administration

Mailing lists include all United States members; all International and United States members; Composer Members in the United States; Members in the New York City Metropolitan area; and Members in the United States and Canada.

18964 American Society of Composers, Authors and Publishers
American Soc. of Composers, Authors & Publishers
1 Lincoln Plz
New York, NY 10023-7097

212-621-6027
Fax: 212-621-8453
E-Mail: ACE@ascap.com
Home Page: www.ascap.com

Marilyn Bergman, President
Johnny Mandel, Writer Vice Chairman
Jay Morgenstern, Publisher Vice Chairman
Arnold Broido, Treasurer
Kathy Spanberger, Secretary

ASCAP created the dial-up ACE system as a useful tool for music professionals. An enhanced World Wide Web version of this database is now available. The database contains information on all compositions in the ASCAP repertory which have appeared in any of ASCAP's domestic surveys, including foreign compositions licensed by the ASCAP in the United States.
Frequency: Annual
Founded in 1993

18965 AudArena International Guide
Billboard Directories
PO Box 15158
North Hollywood, CA 91615

818-487-4582
800-562-2706
E-Mail: info@billboard.com
Home Page: www.orderbillboard.com

Arkady Fridman, Inside Sales Manager

Complete data on over 4,400 venues worldwide, including Amphitheaters, Arenas, Stadiums, Sports Facilities, Concert Halls and New Constructions. Also includes complete listings of companies offering services to the touring industry in the Facilty Buyer's Guide. The guide features contact names, phone and fax numbers, e-mail and web site addresses, market population, facility capacities and staging configurations, and rental fees and ticketing rights.
Cost: $99.00
325 Pages
Frequency: Annual

18966 Billboard Subscriber File
Edith Roman Associates
PO Box 1556
Pearl River, NY 10965

845-620-9000
800-223-2194
Fax: 845-620-9035
E-Mail: john.logiudice@edithroman.com
Home Page: www.edithroman.com

Steve Roberts, President
Wayne Nagrowski, E-Mail List Info Contact

Directory listees include booking agencies and agents, clubs, music publishers, promoters, radio stations, record labels, sound and lighting services, retailers, video, venues, wholesalers, equipment and manufacturing and general services.
Frequency: Annual

18967 Bluegrass Resource Directory
International Bluegrass Music Association
2 Music Cir S
Suite 100
Nashville, TN 37203-4381

615-256-3222
888-438-4262
Fax: 615-256-0450
E-Mail: info@ibma.org
Home Page: www.ibma.org

Member Directory can only be accessed by IBMA members.
Cost: $25.00
88 Pages
Frequency: Annual

18968 Gospel Music Industry Directory
Gospel Music Association
P.O Box 22697
Nashville, TN 37202

615-242-0303
Fax: 615-254-9755
E-Mail: info@gospelmusic.org
Home Page: www.gospelmusic.org
Social Media: Facebook, YouTube

John Styll, President
Scott Brickell, Director
Ed Harper, Director

Formerly called the Networking Guide, the GMA Music Industry Directory is a comprehensive listing of Christian and Gospel music artists, managers, booking agents, record companies, publishing companies and more. Active GMA Professional members get a copy of the directory free. Associate and Student GMA members can purchase one for a discounted rate.

18969 Grey House Performing Arts Directory
Grey House Publishing
4919 Route 22
PO Box 56
Amenia, NY 12501

518-789-8700
800-562-2139
Fax: 845-373-6390
E-Mail: books@greyhouse.com
Home Page: www.greyhouse.com
Social Media: Facebook, Twitter

Leslie Mackenzie, Publisher
Richard Gottlieb, Editor

The most comprehensive resource covering the Performing Arts. This directory provides current information on over 8,500 Dance Companies, Instrumental Music Programs, Opera Companies, Choral Groups, Theater Companies, Performing Arts Series, Performing Arts Facilities and Artist Management Groups.
Cost: $185.00
1200 Pages
Frequency: Annual
ISBN: 1-592373-76-3
Founded in 1981

18970 Grey House Performing Arts Directory - Online Database
Grey House Publishing
4919 Route 22
PO Box 56
Amenia, NY 12501-0556
518-789-8700
800-562-2139
Fax: 518-789-0556
E-Mail: gold@greyhouse.com
Home Page: www.gold.greyhouse.com
Social Media: Facebook, Twitter
Leslie Mackenzie, Publisher
Richard Gottlieb, Editor
The Grey House Performing Arts Directory - Online Database provides immediate access to dance companies, orchestras, opera companies, choral groups, theater companies, series, festivals and perfoming arts facilities across the country, or in their region, state, or in your own backyard. It offers unequaled coverage of the Performing Arts - over 8,500 listings - of the major performance organization, facilities, and information resources.
Frequency: Annual
Founded in 1981

18971 International Buyers Guide
Billboard Directories
PO Box 15158
North Hollywood, CA 91615
818-487-4582
800-562-2706
E-Mail: info@billboard.com
Home Page: www.billboard.com/directories
Arkady Fridman, Inside Sales Manager
A must-have resource for doing business in the music industry, covers every aspect of the recording business worldwide. The latest edition includes contact information on: record labels, video and digital music companies, distributors and importers/exporters; music publishers and rights organizations - blank media manufacturers, pressing plants and services; manufacturers of jewel boxes and other packaging and equipment services; and suppliers of store fixtures, security and accessories.
Cost: $179.00
340 Pages
Frequency: Annual

18972 International Talent and Touring Guide
Billboard Directories
PO Box 15158
North Hollywood, CA 91615
818-487-4582
800-562-2706
E-Mail: info@billboard.com
Home Page: www.billboard.com/directories
Arkady Fridman, Inside Sales Manager
A reference guide for anyone who books, promotes or manages talent. Features over 30,000 listings, including 12,900 artists, managers and agents worldwide, including the USA and Canada. The guide includes contact names, phone and fax numbers, e-mail and website addresses, artists and their record labels, managers and agents, tour services and merchandise, sound and lighting vendors, equipment and instrument rentals, limo rentals, security services, plus national promoters and their key personnel
Cost: $139.00
242 Pages
Frequency: Annual

18973 Keyboard Teachers Association International
Dr. Albert DeVito
361 Pin Oak Lane
Westbury, NY 11590-1941
516-333-3236
Fax: 516-997-9531
Albert DeVito, President
Music teachers and those related to keeping members updated as to activity going on in music world.
Frequency: Quarterly
Founded in 1963

18974 MLA Membership Handbook
Music Library Association
8551 Research Way
Suite 180
Middleton, WI 53562
608-836-5825
Fax: 608-831-8200
E-Mail: mla.areditions.com
Home Page: www.musiclibraryassoc.org
Philip Vandermeer, President
A mailing list that is available for rental in a variety of formats.
Cost: $25.00
Founded in 1931

18975 Music Library Association Membership Directory
Music Library Association
8551 Research Way
Suite 180
Middleton, WI 53562
608-836-5825
Fax: 608-831-8200
E-Mail: mla@areditions.com
Home Page: www.musiclibraryassoc.org
Jerry L. McBride, President
The MLA mailing list is available for rental in a variety of formats. Members include music librarians, librarians who work with music as part of their responsibilities, composers and music scholars, and others interested in the program of the association.

18976 Musical America Directory
Musical America
PO Box 1330
Highstown, NJ 08520
609-448- 334
800-221-5488
Fax: 609-371-7879
E-Mail: info@musicalamerica.com
Home Page: www.musicalamerica.com
Social Media: Facebook, Twitter, YouTube
Joyce Wasserman, Subscription Information
Bob Hudoba, Contact
Provides thousands of names, phone numbers, addresses, and Email and Web site addresses for manangers, orchestras, opera companies, festivals, presenters, venues and more around the world.
Cost: $125.00
Mailing list available for rent

18977 Musician's Guide
Billboard Directories
PO Box 15158
North Hollywood, CA 91615
818-487-4582
800-562-2706
E-Mail: info@billboard.com
Home Page: www.billboard.com/directories
Arkady Fridman, Inside Sales Manager
Everything the working musician needs to book gigs, contact record labels, find a manager, and locate tour services. The latest edition includes A & R Directory, Music Business Services, and City by City listings.
Cost: $15.95
170 Pages
Frequency: Annual

18978 National Opera Association Membership Directory
PO Box 60869
Canyon, TX 79016-0869
806-651-2857
Fax: 806-651-2958
E-Mail: rhansen@mail.wtamu.edu
Home Page: www.noa.org
Social Media: Facebook, RSS
Robert Hansen, Executive Director
JoElyn Wakefield Wright, President
Edith Kirkpatrick Vrenios, VP Resources
Philip Hageman, Treasurer
Carol Notestine, Recording Secretary
Members of the National Opera Association are entitled to receive the NOA Freelance Artists and Production Resources databases, the NOA membership directory, and access to the NOA e-mail listserve.
Frequency: Annual
Mailing list available for rent

18979 Orion Blue Book: Guitars and Musical Instruments
Orion Research Corporation
14555 N Scottsdale Rd
Suite 330
Scottsdale, AZ 85254-3487
480-951-1114
Fax: 480-951-1117
E-Mail: sales@UsedPrice.com
Home Page: www.orionbluebook.com
Roger Rohrs, Owner
77,834 products listed; products listed from 1970s to present; over 450 manufacturers listed; 2 volumes - hardbound or on CD-ROM. Lists musical instruments from Accordians to Xylophones
Cost: $195.00
Frequency: Annual
Founded in 1981

18980 Orion Blue Book: Professional Sound
Orion Research Corporation
14555 N Scottsdale Rd
Suite 330
Scottsdale, AZ 85254-3487
480-951-1114
800-844-0759
Fax: 480-951-1117
E-Mail: sales@UsedPrice.com
Home Page: www.orionbluebook.com
Roger Rohrs, Owner
Features over 48,964 products from the 1950's to present. Over 350 manufacturers listed. Comes in hardbound or on CD-ROM. Lists products from Cartridge Players to Wireless Microphone Systems.
Cost: $150.00
970 Pages
Frequency: Annual
Founded in 1973

18981 Orion Blue Book: Vintage Guitar
Orion Research Corporation
14555 N Scottsdale Rd
Suite 330
Scottsdale, AZ 85254-3487
480-951-1114
800-844-0759
Fax: 480-951-1117
E-Mail: sales@UsedPrice.com
Home Page: www.orionbluebook.com
Roger Rohrs, Owner

Features more than 11,413 products from the 1800's to present. Over 30 manufacturers listed. Comes in hardbound or CD-ROM, Lists products from Banjos to Ukuleles.
Cost: $50.00
Frequency: Quarterly
Founded in 1990

18982 **Record Retailing Directory**
Billboard Directories
PO Box 15158
North Hollywood, CA 91615

818-487-4582
800-562-2706
E-Mail: info@billboard.com
Home Page: www.billboard.com/directories

Arkady Fridman, Inside Sales Manager

Over 5,500 listings covering the entire retailing community. Provides access to major chain headquarters and local outlets; complete coverage of independent retailers; hard-to-find audiobook retailers; and the booming world of online record retailing, plus store genre or specialization; executives, owners, buyers and planners; address, phone, fax, email and web.
Cost: $215.00
Frequency: Annual

18983 **Source Directory of Books, Records and Tapes**
Sutton's Super Marketplace
153 Sutton Lane
Fordsville, KY 42343

270-276-9880
E-Mail: mtsutton32@earthlink.net
Home Page: www.pubdisco.com

Jerry Sutton, Owner/Founder

Publishers, recording studios, wholesalers, distributors, manifacturers and importers. Approximatley 450 records. Changes daily as updated.
Cost: $55.20

18984 **Source Directory of Musical Instruments**
Sutton's Super Marketplace
153 Sutton Lane
Fordsville, KY 42343

270-276-9880
E-Mail: mtsutton32@earthlink.net
Home Page: www.pubdisco.com

Jerry Sutton, Owner/Founder

Listings in directory include names, addresses, phone and fax numbers, and product descriptions from wholesale distributors, Importers, Manufacturers, Close-out houses and Liquidators. Updated daily.
Cost: $55.20

Industry Web Sites

18985 **http://gold.greyhouse.com**
G.O.L.D Grey House OnLine Databases

Grey House Publishing's online database platform, GOLD, offers Quick Search, Keyword Search and Expert Search for most business sectors including music and performance markets. The GOLD platform makes finding the information you need quick and easy - whether you're a novice searcher or an experienced database user. All of Grey House's directory products are available for subscription on the GOLD platform.

18986 **www.acdaonline.org**
American Choral Directors Association

Nonprofit music-education organization whose central purpose is to promote excellence in choral music through performance, composition, publication, research and teaching.

18987 **www.acmcountry.com**
Academy of Country Music

Involved in numerous events and activities promoting country music. Presents annual awards.

18988 **www.afm.org**
American Federation of Musicians of the United
States and Canada

Union representing over 100,000 professional musicians, performing in all genres of music.

18989 **www.afvbm.com**
American Federation of Violin and Bow Makers

Strives to elevate professional standards of craftmanship and ethical conduct among members. Helps members develop technical skills and knowledge.Research and study organization.

18990 **www.agohq.org**
American Guild of Organists

Promotes the organ in its historic and evolving roles and provides a forum for mutual support, inspiration, education and certification.

18991 **www.ascap.com**
American Society of Composers Authors & Publishers

Membership association of more than 260,000 US composers, song writers, lyricists and music publishers.

18992 **www.asmac.org**
American Society of Music Arrangers and Composers

Professional society for arrangers, composers, orchestrators, and musicians. Monthly meetings with great speakers from the music industry.

18993 **www.billboard.com**

The ultimate music industry research tool and information source. The Member Service database is state-of-the-art electronic information service, enabling users to efficiently access information from a variety of music industry databases via the World Wide Web.

18994 **www.chorusamerica.org**
Chorus America

National service for orchestral choruses, independent choruses and professional choruses.

18995 **www.clarinet.org**
International Clarinet Association

Seeks to focus attention on the importance of the clarinet and to foster communication of the fellowship between clarinetists.

18996 **www.cmaworld.com**
Country Music Association

Promotes and publicizes country music.

18997 **www.creativemusicalcoalition.com**
Creative Musician Coalition

A national organization that brings the world of new music to its readers. Includes in depth music reviews, informative artist interviews, interesting articles and feature columns, and valuable resource material.

18998 **www.flmusiced.org**
Florida Music Educators Association

Florida Music Educators Association and Florida School Music Association.

18999 **www.folkharpsociety.org**
International Society of Folk Harpers and Craftsmen

Conducts technical and artistic programs and promotes craft exchange.

19000 **www.gospelmusic.org**
Gospel Music Association

Dedicated to providing leadership, direction and unity for all facets of the gospel music industry. Through education, communication, information, promotion and recognition, the GMA is striving to help those involved in gospel music.

19001 **www.greyhouse.com**
Grey House Publishing

Authoritative reference directories for most business sectors including music and performance markets. Users can search the online databases with varied search criteria allowing for custom searches by product category, geographic area, sales volume, keyword, subject and more. Full Grey House catalog and online ordering also available.

19002 **www.guitarfoundation.org**
Guitar Foundation of America

Supports the serious studies of the guitar.

19003 **www.harpsociety.org**
American Harp Society

Improves the quality of the instrument and performance.

19004 **www.horndoggie.com/horn**
International Horn Society

A national organization that focuses on music industry news and information.

19005 **www.iaekm.org**
International Association of Electronic Keyboard
Manufacturers

Global manufacturers of electronic kayboards and affiliated software and publications.

19006 **www.ibma.org**
World of Bluegrass

IBMA: working together for high standards of professionalism, a greater appreciation for our music, and the success of the world-wide bluegrass community.

19007 **www.imeamusic.org**
Indiana Music Educators Association

Supports and advances music education in Indiana.

19008 **www.internationalpolka.com**
International Polka Association

Educational organization concerned with the preservation and advancement of polka music. Operates the Polka Music Hall of Fame and Museum, and presents the International Polka Fesitval every year during the complete first weekend of August.

19009 **www.metguild.org**
Metropolitan Opera Guild

Seeks to promote greater understanding and interest in opera.

19010 **www.mpa.org**
Music Publishers Association of the United States

Encourages understanding of the copyright laws and works to protect musical works against infringements and piracy.

19011 **www.mtna.org**
Music Teachers National Association
This is a nonprofit organization of independent and collegiate music teachers committed to furthering the art of music through teaching, performance, composition and scholarly research.

19012 **www.music.org**
College Music Society
The Society is a national service organization for college conservatory and university music teachers.

19013 **www.musicalartists.org**
American Guild of Musical Artists
Exclusive bargaining agent for all concert musical artists.

19014 **www.musicdistributors.org**
Music Distributor Association
A trade association of 160 manufactures, importers, wholesalers of musical instruments and accessories, domestic and international selling to the trade only

19015 **www.musiclibraryassoc.org**
Music Library Association
Promotes growth and establishment in the use of music libraries, musical instruments and musical literature.

19016 **www.nacwpi.org**
National Association of College Wind and Percussion Instructors

Teachers of wind and percussion instruments in American colleges and universities.

19017 **www.napbirt.org**
National Association of Professional Band Instrument Repair Technicians

Promotes technical integrity in the craft. Surveys tools and procedures to improve work quality. Makes available emergency repair of band instruments. Provides placement services.

19018 **www.narm.com**
National Association of Recording Merchandisers
Not-for-profit trade association that represents the retailers, wholesalers, and distributors of prerecorded music in the United States.

19019 **www.nats.org**
National Association of Teachers of Singing
To encourage the highest standards of the vocal art and of ethical principals in the teaching of singing; and to promote vocal education and research at all levels, both for the enrichment of the general public and for the professional advancement of the talented.

19020 **www.nbea.com**
National Ballroom and Entertainment Association
Provides exchange for owners and operators of ballrooms.

19021 **www.noa.org**
National Opera Association
To advance the appreciation, composition and production of opera.

19022 **www.npm.org**
National Association of Pastoral Musicians
Membership organization primarily composed of musicians, musician-liturgist, clergy, and other leaders of prayer devoted to serving the life and mission of the Church through fosterering the art of musical liturgy in Roman Catholic worshiping communities in the United States.

19023 **www.nyssma.org**
New York State School Music Association
Advocates and improves the education in music of all people in New York State.

19024 **www.pas.org**
Percussive Arts Society
Promotes drums and percussion through a viable network of performers, teachers, students, enthusiasts and sustaining members. Offers publications, a worldwide network of the World Percussion Network, the Percussive Arts Society International Headquarters/Museum and the annual Percussive Arts Society International Convention.

19025 **www.pianoguild.com**
International Piano Guild
A division of the American College of Musicians Professional society of piano teachers and music faculty members. Sponsers national examinations.

19026 **www.printmusic.org**
Retail Print Music Dealers Association
The voice of the print music industry.

19027 **www.ptg.org**
Piano Technicians Guild
Conducts technical institutes at conventions and seminars. Promotes public education in piano care. Bestows awards. Publishes monthly technical journal by subscriptions.

19028 **www.spars.com**
Society of Professional Audio Recording Services
Members are individuals, companies and studios connected with the professional recording industry.

19029 **www.symphony.org**
American Symphony Orchestra League
The national nonprofit service and educational organization dedicated to strengthening symphony and chamber orchestras. It provides artistic, organizational and financial leadership and service to orchestral conductors, managers, volunteers and staff.

19030 **www.tmea.org**
Texas Music Educators Association
Promoting excellence in music education.

Associations

19031 **ARMA International**
11880 College Blvd
Suite 450
Overland Park, KS 66210

913-341-3808
800-422-2762
Fax: 913-341-3742
E-Mail: hq@arma.org
Home Page: www.arma.org

Marilyn Bier, Executive Director
Komal Gulich, President
Brenda Prowse, Treasurer

A not-for-profit professional association and the authority on managing records and information.
11000 Members
Founded in 1955

19032 **Business and Institutional Furniture Manufacturers Association**
678 Front Ave NW
Suite 150
Grand Rapids, MI 49504-5368

616-285-3963
Fax: 616-285-3765
E-Mail: email@bifma.org
Home Page: www.bifma.org
Social Media: Twitter, LinkedIn

Chuck Saylor, President
Thomas Reardon, Executive Director
Franco Bianchi, Treasurer

BIFMA is a not-for-profit trade association of furniture manufacturers and suppliers, addressing issues of common concern.
245+ Members
Founded in 1973

19033 **Graphic Arts Information Network**
200 Deer Run Road
Sewickley, PA 15143

412-741-6860
800-910-4283
Fax: 412-741-2311
E-Mail: printing@printing.org
Home Page: www.gain.net

Michael F Makin, President

Members are companies printing labels for food or consumer products.
40 Members

19034 **Independent Office Products & Furniture Dealers Association**
3601 E. Joppa Road
Baltimore, MD 21234

410-931-8100
Fax: 410-931-8111
E-Mail: info@iopfda.org
Home Page: www.iopfda.org
Social Media: Twitter, LinkedIn

Mike Tucker, President
Paul Miller, Director Government Affairs
Paula Kreuzburg, M.D
Alicia Ellis, Director, Marketing

Association for independent office product and office furniture dealers. IOPFDA is comprised of the National Office Products Alliance (NOPA) and the Office Furniture Dealers Alliance (OFDA).
1500 Members
Founded in 1904

19035 **Office Furniture Distribution Association**
282 N.Ridge Rd
Brooklyn, MI 49230

517-467-9355
Fax: 517-467-9056
E-Mail: kmassoc@splusnet.com
Home Page: www.theofda.org

75 Members
Founded in 1923

19036 **Office Products Representatives**
3131 Elbee Road
Dayton, OH 45439

937-297-2250
800-447-1684
Fax: 937-297-2254
E-Mail: info@oprareps.org
Home Page: www.oprareps.org

Carol Hinton, Owner
100 Members
Founded in 1974

19037 **Office Products Wholesalers Association**
5024 Campbell Boulevard
Baltimore, MD 21236

410-931-8100
Fax: 410-931-8111
E-Mail: info@BusinessSolutionsAssociation.com
Home Page: www.opwa.org

Cal Clemons, Executive Vice President
Paula Kreuzberg, Associate Director

Members are chief executives of office product wholesalers and manufacturers.
165 Members
Founded in 1995

19038 **Society for Service Professionals in Printing**
433 E Monroe Ave
Alexandria, VA 22301-1645

703-684-0044
866-600-8820
Fax: 703-548-9137
E-Mail: ssppsupport@sspp.org
Home Page: www.sspp.org

Peter Colaianni, Executive Director
Marj Green, Director

Individual membership society dedicated to the needs of customer service professionals in the printing industry.
8 Members
Founded in 1993

Newsletters

19039 **BTA Hotline Online**
Business Technology Association
12411 Wornall Rd
Suite 200
Kansas City, MO 64145-1212

816-941-3100
800-325-7219
Fax: 816-941-2829
E-Mail: info@bta.org
Home Page: www.bta.org

Brent Hoskins, Executive Director
Terry Chapman, President

Current copier/printer and network systems industry news.
Founded in 1926

19040 **Digital Image Review**
Buyers Laboratory
20 Railroad Avenue
Hackensack, NJ 07601-3309

201-896-6439
Fax: 201-488-0461
E-Mail: info@buyerslab.com
Home Page: www.buyerslab.com

Daria Hoffman, Managing Editor
Michael Danziger, CEO

Devoted to digital topics, all types of digital office products, industry news and trends, trade show, pricing changes and much more.
Cost: $305.00
16 Pages
Frequency: Monthly
Founded in 1961

19041 **Executary**
National Association of Executive Secretaries
900 S Washington Street
Suite G13
Falls Church, VA 22046-4009

703-237-8616
Fax: 703-533-1153
E-Mail: headquarters@theaeap.com
Home Page: www.theaeap.com
Social Media: LinkedIn

Ruth Ludeman, Director

Packed with practical advice on various issues of interest to administrative professionals. Seeks to support AEAP's mission to assist members in achieving their career goals by keeping you informed of advances and changes in the administrative profession.
Frequency: 10x/Year
Mailing list available for rent: 5000 names

19042 **Form & Document Industry Newsletter**
319 SW Washington Street
Suite 710
Portland, OR 97204-2618

503-227-3393
Fax: 503-274-7667
E-Mail: bfma@bfma.org
Home Page: www.bfma.org

Andy Palatka, Executive Director
Tonya Macalino, Editor
Tonya Macalino, Marketing

Industry newsletter containing educational articles and rules on the latest processes, techniques, and products in the form and document industry. Library rate is $35.00 per year.
Cost: $50.00
38574 Pages
Circulation: 700
Founded in 1958
Mailing list available for rent: 1000 names at $400 per M

19043 **Jot and Jolts**
Economics Press
12 Daniel Road
Fairfield, NJ 07004-2565

973-227-1224
800-526-2554
Fax: 973-227-8360
Home Page: www.epinc.com

Monthly planner for supervisors to the office products industry.
Cost: $16.20
26 Pages
Frequency: Monthly
Printed in on glossy stock

19044 **MFP Report**
Bissett Communications

Apt 44
20919 Bloomfield Ave
Lakewood, CA 90715-1840

562-809-8917
Fax: 562-809-1627
Home Page: http://www.mfpreport.com

Brian R Bissett, Publisher

A newsletter providing information on manufacturers, suppliers, sellers, and managers of multifunction peripherals and connected office equipment of the latest MFP business, market and technology issues and their impact.
Frequency: Monthly

19045 Scanner
Private Label Manufacturers Association (PLMA)
630 Third Avenue
New York, NY 10017-6506

212-972-3131
Fax: 212-983-1382
E-Mail: info@plma.com
Home Page: www.plma.com

Brian Sharoff, President
Myra Rosen, VP
Tom Prendergast, Director, Research Services

News and information for the private label industry.
3200+ Members
6 Pages
Frequency: Quarterly
Circulation: 12000
Founded in 1979

Magazines & Journals

19046 Better Buys for Business
Progressive Business Publications
PO Box 3019
Malvern, PA 19355-0719

610-695-0201
800-247-2185
Fax: 610-647-8098
E-Mail: webmaster@pbp.com
Home Page: www.pbp.com

Ed Satell, CEO
Steve Hannaford, Editor

Publishes 10 non-advertising buyer's guides for office equipment (copiers, printers, fax machines and scanners), with objective, unbiased information and evaluations. Each issue includes in-depth write-ups on all manufacturers and their models, easy to read specifications and price charts to compare models and Editor's Choice selections - awarded to the best machines in each product category
Cost: $149.00
Circulation: 4,000
ISSN: 1084-2055
Founded in 1980
Printed in 4 colors on matte stock

19047 Business Documents
North American Publishing Company
1500 Spring Garden St
Suite 1200
Philadelphia, PA 19130-4094

215-238-5300
800-627-2689
Fax: 215-238-5342
E-Mail: tbay@napco.com
Home Page: www.napco.com

Ned S Borowsky, CEO
Brian C Ludwick, Publisher

For professional buyers of forms, labels and electronic systems. Emphasizes internal and external design, production and management of business documents either as traditionally printed forms or electronically generated documents.
Cost: $24.00
42 Pages
Frequency: Monthly
Founded in 1958
Mailing list available for rent
Printed in 2 colors on matte stock

19048 Business Forms, Labels & Systems
North American Publishing Company
1500 Spring Garden St
Suite 1200
Philadelphia, PA 19130-4094

215-238-5300
800-627-2689
Fax: 215-238-5342
E-Mail: webmaster@napco.com
Home Page: www.napco.com/

Ned S Borowsky, CEO
Judith Cavaliere, Publisher
Maggie DeWitt, Senior Editor
Cynthia Graham, Associate Editor
Jennifer Hans, Associate Editor

For independent manufacturers and distributors in the forms and systems industry. Emphasizes product applications, marketing and sales ideas and new technology.
Cost: $49.00
Frequency: Monthly
Circulation: 12000
Founded in 1958
Mailing list available for rent
Printed in 4 colors on glossy stock

19049 Business Solutions
Corry Publishing
5539 Peach Street
Erie, PA 16506

814-380-0025
800-290-5460
Fax: 814-864-2037
E-Mail: editor@corrypub.com
Home Page: www.corrypub.com

John Clifton, Group Publisher
Melinda Reed-Fadden, Circulation Manager
Dan Schell, Editor
Carrie Brocious, Marketing Director
Jim Roddy, President

Informative magazine including analysis of technological and marketing developments.
Frequency: Monthly
Circulation: 43000
Founded in 1980

19050 Business Technology Association
Buiness Technology Association
12411 Wornall Rd
Suite 200
Kansas City, MO 64145-1212

816-941-3100
800-325-7219
Fax: 816-941-2829
E-Mail: info@bta.org
Home Page: www.bta.org
Social Media: Facebook, Twitter, LinkedIn

Brent Hoskins, Executive Director
Ron Hulett, Vice President

An international trade organization serving dealers, value added resellers, systems integrators, manufacturers and distributors in the network computing and office automation industries. The association provides educational programs, professional forums, discount services and other benefits designed to help members be more profitable and competitive. BTA members provide business solutions in local area networks, wide area networks, document management and a wide variety of office technologies.
Cost: $30.00
Frequency: Monthly
Circulation: 3500
ISBN: 1-092916-9
Founded in 1927
Mailing list available for rent: 1200 names

19051 Digital Information Network
Buyers Laboratory
20 Railroad Avenue
Hackensack, NJ 07601-3309

201-587-0828
Fax: 201-488-0461
E-Mail: info@buyerslab.com
Home Page: www.buyerslab.com

Daria Hoffman, Managing Editor

A comprehensive test report service which provides test reports on all the office products BLI evaluates. Subscribers will also get a sixteen page monthly newsletter called Digital Imaging Review, and will recieve a copy of BLI's Multifunctional Specification Guide, Facsimile-Based Products, Copier-Based Products and the Printer Specification Guide, as well as updated specifications throughout the term of their subscription.
Cost: $755.00

19052 Hard Copy Supplies Journal
Lyra Research
PO Box 9143
Newtonville, MA 02640-9143

617-454-2600
Fax: 617-454-2601
Home Page: www.lyra.com

Charles LeCompte, Publisher
Frank Stefansson, CEO/President
Jim Forrest, Managing Editor
Jennifer Sprague, Vice President of Sales
Andre Rebelo, Marketing Manager

In-depth coverage of current innovations in marketing materials and media, including ink jet cartridges, toner, paper and film, and monitors the fast-moving corporate developments, such as lawsuits, mergers, distribution, tactics, and marketing campaigns.
Cost: $550.00
Frequency: Monthly
Circulation: 2,000
Founded in 1991

19053 Information Management Magazine
ARMA International
11880 College Blvd
Suite 450
Overland Park, KS 66210

913-341-3808
800-422-2762
Fax: 913-341-3742
E-Mail: hq@arma.org
Home Page: www.arma.org

Marilyn Bier, Executive Director
Jody Becker, Associate Editor
Brenda Prowse, Treasurer

The leading source of information on topics and issues central to the management of records and information worldwide. Each issue features insightful articles written by experts in the management of records and information.
Cost: $115.00
Frequency: Bi-monthly
Circulation: 11000
ISSN: 1535-2897
Mailing list available for rent: 9000 names
Printed in 4 colors on glossy stock

19054 Mail: Journal of Communication Distribution
Excelsior Publications

One Millstone Road
Gold Key Box 2425
Milford, PA 18337

570-861-1969
Fax: 570-686-3495

Francis P Ruggiero, Publsher
Circulation: 43000

19055 Office Dealer
Quality Publishing
252 N Main Street
Suite 200
Mount Airy, NC 27030-3810

336-783-0000
Fax: 336-783-0045
E-Mail: bcomer@os-od.com
Home Page: www.os-od.com/

Richard Kunkel, Publisher
Simon DeGroot, Editorial Director
Bessie Comer, Sales/Advertising Coor
Scott Cullen, Managing Editor
Debbie Hooker, Director of Publishing Services

Information including the latest industry news pertaining to resellers, plus office dealer conventions and other newsworthy events.
Circulation: 17020

19056 Office Solutions
Quality Publishing
252 N Main Street #200
PO Box 1028
Mount Airy, NC 27030-3810

336-783-0000
Fax: 336-783-0045
E-Mail: osod@os-od.com
Home Page: www.os-od.com

Richard Kunkel, Publisher
Simon Degroot, Editorial Director
Debbey Hooker, Circulation Manager
Bill Middleton, Marketing Manager
Scott Cullen, Managing Editor

Information on state of the art, survey and overview of articles and product offerings. Emphasis on personal computing, software, telecommunications, personnel and financial management.
Cost: $36.00
Circulation: 81250
Founded in 2003

19057 Office Systems Research Journal
SW Missouri Council of Governments
901 S National Avenue
Springfield, MO 65804

417-836-5000
Fax: 417-836-4146
Home Page: www.smsu.edu

Diane May, Executive Director

A journal offering research and news of the office supplies and products industry.
Cost: $35.00
Circulation: 400

19058 Print Solutions Magazine
Document Management Industries Association
433 E Monroe Avenue
Alexandria, VA 22301-1693

703-836-6232
Fax: 703-549-4966
Home Page: www.printsolutionsmag.com

Peter L Colaianni CAE, Editor-in-Chief

Source for marketing, management and product information.
Cost: $49.00
276 Pages
Frequency: Monthly
ISSN: 0532-1700
Printed in 4 colors on glossy stock

19059 Recharger Magazine
Recharger Magazine
1050 E Flamingo Rd
Suite N237
Las Vegas, NV 89119-7427

702-438-5557
877-902-9759
Fax: 702-873-9671
E-Mail: info@rechargermag.com
Home Page: www.rechargermag.com

Phyllis Gurgevich, Publisher
Amy Turner, Managing Editor
Michael MacDonald, Graphics Director
Sara Feest, Sales Assistant
Monica Miceli, Associate Editor

Information including articles that cover business and marketing, technical updates, association and industry news, and company profiles. Related features focus on the importance of recycling, government legislation, and product comparisons.
Cost: $45.00
Frequency: Monthly
Circulation: 8000

Trade Shows

19060 ARMA International Conference & Expo
ARMA International
11880 College Blvd
Suite 450
Overland Park, KS 66215

913-341-3808
800-422-2762
Fax: 913-341-3742
E-Mail: hq@arma.org
Home Page: www.arma.org/conference
Social Media: Facebook, Twitter, iConference

Carol Jorgenson, Meetings/Education Coordinator
Wanda Wilson, Senior Manager, Conferences
Elizabeth Zlitni, Exposition Manager

Conference, seminar, workshop, banquet, award ceremony and 175 exhibits of micrographics, optical disk, automated document storage and retrieval systems and more technology of interest to information professionals.
3500 Attendees
Frequency: Annual
Founded in 1956

19061 American Business Women's Association Convention
9100 Ward Parkway
PO Box 8728
Kansas City, MO 64114

816-361-6621
800-228-0007
Fax: 816-361-4991
E-Mail: abwa@abwa.org
Home Page: www.abwa.org

Wendy Mabrey, Corporate Sponsorship Coordinator
Carolyn Elman, Executive Director

One-hundred exhibits of equipment, supplies and services for women in business, seminar and banquet.
2000 Attendees
Frequency: November

19062 American Society for Training & Development Conference & Exposition
American Society for Training & Development
1640 King Street
PO Box 1443
Alexandria, VA 22313-2043

703-683-8100
Fax: 703-683-8103
E-Mail: customercare@astd.org
Home Page: www.astd.org

Michael Neff, Executive Director
2000 Attendees

19063 Business Show
INPEX
217 9th Street
Pittsburgh, PA 15222-3506

412-881-1300
800-544-6739
Fax: 412-288-4546
E-Mail: info@inventionshow.com
Home Page: www.inventionshow.com/

Nevin Arora, Product Manager

Annual show of 150 exhibits of office furniture, supplies and machines; computers; media; specialty items; financial services; printing services; security systems; entertainment; cellular phones and pagers; sinage; travel agencies; audio-visual equipment and car rental agencies.
5000 Attendees

19064 Business Technology Association
Business Technology Association
12411 Wornall Road
Suite 200
Kansas City, MO 64145-1212

816-941-3100
800-325-7219
Fax: 816-941-4838
E-Mail: info@bta.org
Home Page: www.bta.org
Social Media: Facebook, Twitter, LinkedIn

Brent Hoskins, Executive Director
Ron Hulett, Vice President
Founded in 1926
Mailing list available for rent: 1200 names

19065 Document World/American Business Equipment and Computer Show
Key Productions
116 Murphy Road
Hartford, CT 06114-2121

860-247-8363

Eldred Codling, Show Manager

Features exhibits of computer software, hardware, supplies and services.
6M Attendees
Frequency: April

19066 National Stationery Show
George Little Management
10 Bank Street
White Plains, NY 10606-1954

914-486-6070
800-272-7469
Fax: 914-948-6180
Home Page: www.

Lori Robinson, VP
Kelly Bristol, Assistant Show Manager
George Little II, President

A show for greeting cards and social stationery, writing instruments and home office products, party ware and giftwrap, scrapbooking and craft supplies, albums, frames and much more.
14000 Attendees
Frequency: May

Directories & Databases

19067 ARMA International's Buyers Guide
ARMA International
11880 College Blvd
Suite 450
Overland Park, KS 66215

913-341-3808
800-422-2762
Fax: 913-341-3742
E-Mail: hq@arma.org
Home Page: www.arma.org/conference

75-100 companies listed. Free.

19068 Directory of Mail Order Catalogs
Grey House Publishing
4919 Route 22
PO Box 56
Amenia, NY 12501

518-789-8700
800-562-2139
Fax: 845-373-6390
E-Mail: books@greyhouse.com
Home Page: www.greyhouse.com
Social Media: Facebook, Twitter

Leslie Mackenzie, Publisher
Richard Gottlieb, Editor

The premier source of information on the mail order catalog industry. Covers over 13,000 consumer and business catalog companies with 44 different product chapters including office supplies, stationery and more.
Cost: $395.00
1900 Pages
Frequency: Annual
ISBN: 1-592373-96-8
Founded in 1981

19069 Directory of Mail Order Catalogs - Online Database
Grey House Publishing
4919 Route 22
PO Box 56
Amenia, NY 12501

518-789-8700
800-562-2139
Fax: 845-373-6390
E-Mail: gold@greyhouse.com
Home Page: http://gold.greyhouse.com
Social Media: Facebook, Twitter

Leslie Mackenzie, Publisher
Richard Gottlieb, Editor

Reach over 10,000 consumer catalog companies in one easy-to-use source with The Directory of Mail Order Catalogs - Online Database. Filled with business-building detail, each company profile gives you the information you need to access that organization quickly and easily. Listings provide key contacts, sales volume, employee size, printing information, circulation, list data, product descriptions and much more.
Frequency: Annual
Founded in 1981

19070 Orion Blue Book: Copier
Orion Research Corporation
14555 N Scottsdale Rd
Suite 330
Scottsdale, AZ 85254-3487

480-951-1114
800-844-0759
Fax: 480-951-1117
E-Mail: support@orionbluebook.com
Home Page: www.orionbluebook.com/

Roger Rohrs, Owner

List of manufacturers of copiers and other office equipment.
Cost: $39.00
Frequency: Annual

Industry Web Sites

19071 http://gold.greyhouse.com
G.O.L.D Grey House OnLine Databases

Grey House Publishing's online database platform, GOLD, offers Quick Search, Keyword Search and Expert Search for most business sectors, including office supplies and services makrets. The GOLD platform makes finding the information you need quick and easy - whether you're a novice searcher or an experienced database user. All of Grey House's directory products are available for subscription on the GOLD platform.

19072 www.americanpayroll.org
American Payroll Association

Association of payroll and human resource professionals. Website furthers information exchange and meeting announcements.

19073 www.bfma.org
Business Forms Management Association

For form systems professionals interested in the effective capture distribution and management of information in electronic and paper forms.

19074 www.bifma.org
Business and Institutional Furniture Manufacturers
Association

The voice of the office furniture industry, BIFMA members are manufacturers and suppliers of goods and services to the industry.

19075 www.dmia.org
Document Management Industries Association

19076 www.greyhouse.com
Grey House Publishing

Authoritative reference directories for most business sectors including office products and services markets. Users can search the online databases with varied search criteria allowing for custom searches by product category, geographic area, sales volume, keyword, subject and more. Full Grey House catalog and online ordering also available.

19077 www.iopfda.org
Independent Office Products & Furniture Dealers
Association

Association for independent office product and office furniture dealers. IOPFDA is comprised of the National Office Products Alliance (NOPA) and the Office Furniture Dealers Alliance (OFDA).

19078 www.oprareps.org
Office Products Representatives Association

Provides programs and services that promote the role of the independant manufactures' representative in the various distribution channels within the entire office products industry.

19079 www.sspp.org
Society for Service Professionals in Printing

Individual membership society dedicated to the needs of customer service professionals in the printing industry.

19080 www.theofda.org
Office Furniture Distribution Association

Associations

19081 American Forest & Paper Association
1111 19th St NW
Suite 800
Washington, DC 20036-3652

202-463-2700
800-878-8878
Fax: 202-463-2785
E-Mail: info@afandpa.org
Home Page: www.afandpa.org

James B. Hannan, Chairman
Doyle R. Simons, 1st Vice Chairman
Alexander Toeldte, 2nd Vice Chairman
Donna A. Harman, President & CEO
Jan A. Poling, Vice President & Secretary

To provide significant value to member companies through outstanding performance in those areas that are key to members' success and where an association can be more effective than individual companies.
Founded in 1993

19082 American Paper Machinery Association
201 Park Washington Ct
Falls Church, VA 22046-4527

703-538-1787
Fax: 703-241-5603
E-Mail: apmahq@aol.com
Home Page: www.papermachinery.org

Clay D Tyeryar, Chief Administrative Executive
Judith O Buzzerd, Manager Meetings
Sharon Kelly, Coordinator Member Services

To promote the global common interests, image and business relations of the membership.
35 Members
Founded in 1971

19083 Association of Independent Corrugated Converters
PO Box 25708
Alexandria, VA 22313

703-836-2422
877-836-2422
Fax: 703-836-2795
E-Mail: info@aiccbox.org
Home Page: www.aiccbox.org
Social Media: Facebook, Twitter, LinkedIn, YouTube

A Steven Young, President
Maria Frustaci, Administrative Director
David Core, CAE, Director Education
Taryn Pyle, Director Meetings
Chris Richards, Webmaster/Systems Manager

Represents and protects, the business interests of the independent sector of the corrugated packaging industry. Dedicated to strengthening the independent's position in the marketplace through programs and publications that empower our members to compete successfully in a rapidly changing industry and an increasingly competitive and global business environment.
750 Members
Founded in 1974

19084 Fibre Box Association
25 NW Point Boulevard
Suite 510
Elk Grove VLG, IL 60007-1033

847-364-9600
Fax: 847-364-9639
E-Mail: fba@fibrebox.org
Home Page: www.fibrebox.org
Social Media: LinkedIn

Robert McIlvaine, Chairman
Daniel Pyne, First Vice Chairman
Dennis J. Colley, President

A non-profit association that represents and serves the corrugated industry. It also brings together the North American manufacturers to improve the overall well being of the industry and to provide an array of services that enable member companies to conduct their business more effectively , responsibly and efficiently.
170 Members
Founded in 1940

19085 Foodservice/Packaging Institute
201 Park Washington Ct
Suite 204
Falls Church, VA 22046-4527

703-538-3550
Fax: 703-241-5603
E-Mail: fpi@fpi.org
Home Page: www.fpi.org

Lynn Dyer, President
Natha Freiburg, VP
Caron Mason, Communications Manager

A national association comprised of manufacturers and suppliers of single-use foodservice packaging products.
25 Members
Founded in 1933

19086 International Corrugated Packaging Foundation
113 S West Street
Alexandria, VA 22314-2858

703-549-8580
Fax: 703-549-8670
E-Mail: info@icpfbox.org
Home Page: www.icpfbox.org

Richard M Flaherty, President
Thomas W.H. Walton, Vice Chairman
A Steven Young, Treasurer
Paul Vishny, Secretary

An industry led philantropic organization dedicated to building a knowledgeable workforce for the corrugated packaging industry.
Founded in 1985

19087 International Molded Fiber Association
1425 W Mequon Rd
Suite C
Mequon, WI 53092-3262

262-241-0522
Fax: 262-241-3766
E-Mail: info@imfa.org
Home Page: www.imfa.org
Social Media: Facebook, Twitter, LinkedIn

Cassandra Niesing, Asst. Director
Joseph Grygny, Chairman

Acts as an information center for the molded fiber industry with worldwide membership of users and manufacturers of molded fiber producs. Promotes use of natural and recycled fibers.
Founded in 1996

19088 National Council for Air and Stream Improvement
PO Box 133138
Research Triangle Park, NC 27709-3318

919-941-6400
Fax: 919-941-6401
E-Mail: ryeske@ncasi.org
Home Page: www.ncasi.org

NCASI's mission is to serve the forest products industry as a center of excellence for providing technical information and scientific research needed to achieve the industry's environmental goals and principles.
Founded in 1943

19089 National Paper Trade Association
330 North Wabash Avenue
Suite 2000
Chicago, IL 60611

312-321-4092
800-355-6782
Fax: 312-673-6736
E-Mail: NPTA@goNPTA.com
Home Page: www.gonpta.com

Greg Savage, Chairman
Donald C Clampitt, First Vice Chairman
Travis M. Mlakar, Second Vice Chairman
William Frohlich, President
Hilton Maze, Treasurer

Supports all those professionals in the paper, packaging and allied products distribution industries. Publishes monthly magazine.
2000 Members
Founded in 1903

19090 National Paperbox Association
1350 Main Street
Suite 1508
Springfield, MA 01103-1670

413-686-9191
Fax: 413-747-7777
E-Mail: npahq@paperbox.org
Home Page: www.paperbox.org

Ben Markens, President
Lou Kornet, Vice President
Kim Guarnaccia, Director of Marketing
Brian Chaisson, Director of Industry Benchmarking
Jennie Markens, Director of General Leaders

Serves as the voice of the paperbox and packaging industry. Also represents the concerns of boxmaker nationally, internationally and at the local level through its Regional Divisions. Publishes bi-monthly magazine and holds an annual convention.
100 Members
Founded in 1839

19091 Paper Distribution Council
National Paper Trade Association
330 North Wabash Avenue
Suite 2000
Chicago, IL 60611

312-321-4092
Fax: 312-673-4092
E-Mail: NPTA@goNPTA.com
Home Page: www.gonpta.com

Greg Savage, Chairman
Donald C Clampitt, First Vice Chairman
Travis M. Mlakar, Second Vice Chairman
William Frohlich, President
Hilton Maze, Treasurer

Association for paper, packaging and applied products distribution channels.
35 Members
ISBN: 1-092807-3 -
Founded in 1958

19092 Paper Industry Management Association
15 Technology Parkway South
Norcross, GA 30092

770-209-7230
Fax: 770-209-7359
E-Mail: mcornell@pimaweb.org
Home Page: www.pimaweb.com
Social Media: Facebook, Twitter, Youtube

Ralph W Feck, President
Terry M Gallagher, Regional VP
Jim Weir, Executive VP/COO
Julie Weldon, Senior Manager
Patrick Andrus, Marketing Coordinator

Contributes to the strength of the international pulp and paper community by providing the means for our members to address relevant in-

dustry issues and to develop their management and leadership skills.
4500 Members
Founded in 1919

19093 Paper Shipping Sack Manufacturers Association
5050 Blue Church Road
Coopersburg, PA 18036

610-282-6845
Fax: 610-282-1577
E-Mail: admin@pssma.org
Home Page: www.pssma.com

Richard E. Storat, President
Ross Barett, Chairman
Donald P Belmont, Vice Chairman

Provides its member companies with programs and services which further the industry's objectives and in doing so promote and enhance the welfare of the industry.
45 Members
Founded in 1933

19094 Paperboard Packaging Council
1350 Main Street
Suite 1508
Springfield, MA 01103-1670

413-686-9191
Fax: 413-747-7777
E-Mail: paperboardpackaging@ppcnet.org
Home Page: www.ppcnet.org
Social Media: Facebook, Twitter

Ben Markens, President
Lou Kornet, Vice President

Members are companies making folding cartons. Provides publications and instructional materials on the paper industry and recycling.
92 Members
Founded in 1929

19095 Technical Association of the Pulp & Paper Industry
15 Technology Parkway South
Norcross, GA 30092

770-446-1400
800-322-8686
Fax: 770-446-6947
E-Mail: webmaster@tappi.org
Home Page: www.tappi.org

Larry N Montague, CEO
Thomas J Garland, Vice Chairman

To engage the people and resources of our association in providing technically sound solutions to the workplace problems and opportunities that challenge our current and future members.
12000 Members
ISSN: 0734-1415
Founded in 1915

19096 United Paperworkers International Union
100 Decatur Street SE
PO Box 3967
Atlanta, GA 30303-3202

404-413-2820
Fax: 404-651-4314
E-Mail: libdgg@langate.gsu.edu
Home Page: www.library.gsu.edu

Mike Dees, President

Bestows awards and conducts training seminars.
Founded in 1972

Newsletters

19097 American Forest & Paper Association Report
American Forest & Paper Association
1111 19th St NW
Suite 800
Washington, DC 20036-3652

202-463-2700
Fax: 202-463-2785
E-Mail: info@afandpa.org
Home Page: www.afandpa.org

Covers events of the paper, wood and forest industry. Distribution is limited to association members only.
Cost: $1200.00
4 Pages
Frequency: Weekly
Founded in 1993

19098 Conservatree Greenline
Greenline Publications
PO Box 590780
San Francisco, CA 94159-780

415-386-8646
Fax: 415-391-7890
Home Page: www.conservatree.com

Alan Davis, Founder/Publisher
Susan Kinsella, Editor

Reports on efforts and achievements by businesses on the environmental front.
Cost: $59.00
Circulation: 25000
Founded in 1976

19099 Essential Resources, LLC
45 S Park Pl
Suite 330
Morristown, NJ 07960-3924

908-832-6979
Fax: 908-832-6970

Newsletters for plastic, chemical, pharmaceutical, and packaging industries.
5-15 Pages

19100 Official Board Markets
Advanstar Communications
2835 N Sheffield Avenue
Suite 226
Chicago, IL 60657-9213

312-553-8922
Fax: 312-553-8929
Home Page: www.packaging-online.com

Mark Arzoumanian, Editor-in-Chief
Esther Durkalski, Managing Editor

Covers the corrugated container and folding carton converting industries.
Cost: $180.00
24 Pages
Frequency: Weekly
Circulation: 5900
Founded in 1915
Printed in on glossy stock

19101 Seaboard Bulletin
International Paper
PO Box 1200
Bucksport, ME 04416-1200

207-469-1700
Fax: 207-469-1705

David Bailey, President

Paper industry news.

Magazines & Journals

19102 Asia Pacific PaperMaker
Paper Industry Management Association
4700 West Lake Avenue
Glenview, IL 60025-1485

847-375-6860
Fax: 877-527-5973
E-Mail: info@pimaweb.org
Home Page: www.pima-online.org

Jim Weir, Executive VP/CEO
Patrick Andrus, Marketing Coordinator
Patrick Filippelli, Sales Manager
Sarah Walsh, Administrative Assistant
Mary Cornell, Account Manager
Founded in 1919

19103 Board Converting News
NV Business Publishers Corporation
43 Main St
Avon By the Sea, NJ 07717-1051

732-502-0500
Fax: 732-502-9606
E-Mail: tvilardi@NVPublications.com
Home Page: www.nvpublications.com

Ted Vilardi, Owner
Jim Curley, Editor-in-Chief
Robyn Smith, Executive Publisher
Gail Kalina, Production Manager
Dan Brunton, Managing Director

News for the corrugated box and folding carton industry along with box and carton transacted prices.
Cost: $180.00
140 Pages
Frequency: Weekly

19104 Converting Magazine
Reed Business Information
2000 Clearwater Dr
Oak Brook, IL 60523-8809

630-574-0825
Fax: 630-288-8781
E-Mail: psaran@reedbusiness.com
Home Page: www.reedbusiness.com

Jeff Greisch, President
Mark Spaulding, Editor-in-Chief
Steve Reiss, VP
Frequency: Monthly
Circulation: 4000

19105 Distribution Sales & Management
National Paper Trade Association
500 B1 - County Boulevard
Suite 200E
Farmingdale, NY 11735-5402

631-777-2223
Fax: 631-777-2224
Home Page: www.goNPTA.com

Debra Ray, Editor
Bill Fronlinch, Publisher

The business magazine for the paper, packaging and allied products distribution channel.
Cost: $49.00
48 Pages
Frequency: Monthly
Circulation: 17000
ISSN: 1092-8073
Founded in 1959
Printed in on matte stock

19106 European PaperMaker
Paper Industry Management Association

1699 Wall Street
Suite 212
Mount Prospect, IL 60056

847-699-1706
Fax: 847-956-0520
Home Page: www.pima-online.org

Mary Cornell, Account Manager

19107 **International Paper Board Industry**
Brunton Publications & NV Public
43 Main Street
Avon By The Sea, NJ 07717-1051

732-502-0500
Fax: 732-502-9606
E-Mail: jcurley@NVPublications.com
Home Page: www.nvpublications.com

Mike Brunton, Publisher
Jim Curley, Editor-in-Chief
Gail Kalina, Production Manager
Tom Vilardi, President
Dan Brunton, Managing Director

Information on corrugated paper and converting industry, encompassing news and production worldwide.
Cost: $60.00
Frequency: Monthly
Circulation: 10021

19108 **Latin American PaperMaker**
Paper Industry Management Association
1699 Wall Street
Suite 212
Mount Prospect, IL 60056

847-956-0250
Fax: 847-956-0520
E-Mail: info@pima-online.org
Home Page: www.pima-online.org

Ralph W. Feck, President
Jim Weir, COO/Executive VP
Patrick Andrus, Marketing Coordinator
Patrick Filippelli, Sales Manager
Sarah Walsh, Administrative Assistant
Founded in 1919

19109 **Mill Trade Journal's Recycling Markets**
NV Business Publishers Corporation
43 Main St
Avon By the Sea, NJ 07717-1051

732-502-0500
800-962-3001
Fax: 732-502-9606
E-Mail: advertising@NVPublications.com
Home Page: www.nvpublications.com

Ted Vilardi, Owner
Roy Bradbrook, Editor
Jim Curley, Editor-in-Chief
Gail Kalina, Production Manager
Robyn Smith, Executive Publisher

Information on recycling mills paper stock, scrap metal and plastics brokers and dealers used by the municipal governments and private organizations as a basis for letting contracts.
Cost: $130.00
Frequency: Fortnightly
Circulation: 3625
Founded in 1984
Printed in 2 colors on matte stock

19110 **NPTA Distribution Sales & Management**
111 Great Neck Road
Suite 418
Great Neck, NY 11021-5402

516-829-3070
Fax: 516-829-3074

19111 **North American PaperMaker**
Paper Industry Management Association
4700 West Lake Avenue
Glenview, IL 60025-1485

847-375-6860
Fax: 877-527-5973
E-Mail: info@pimaweb.org
Home Page: www.pima-online.org

Jim Weir, Executive VP/COO
Pam Oddi, Administrative Assistant
Patrick Filippelli, Sales Manager
Patrick Andrus, Marketing Coordinator
Julie Weldon, Senior Manager
Founded in 1919

19112 **Paper Age Magazine**
O'Brien Publications
20 Schofield Rd
Suite 200B
Cohasset, MA 02025-1922

781-749-5255
Fax: 781-749-5896
E-Mail: info@paperage.com
Home Page: www.paperage.com

John O'Brien, Owner
John O'Brien, Managing Editor
Michael O'Brien, Publisher

For management and supervisory personnel of pulp, paper and paperboard mills. Tabloid-sized magazine covering the pulp, paper and converting industry, with a unique mix of timely and insightful coverage of corporate strategies, mill operations, technological innovations, industry issues, as well as analysis of the latest production and marketing trends.
Cost: $90.00
Circulation: 36156
Founded in 1884

19113 **Paper Industry Equipment Magazine**
PO Box 5675
Montgomery, AL 36103

604-264-1158
888-224-6611
Fax: 604-264-1367
E-Mail: info@paperindustrymag.com
Home Page: www.paperindustrymag.com

Tim Shaddick, Publisher
Peter N Williamson, Editor

Services and equipment for the pulp/paper industry.
Cost: $12.00
32 Pages
Circulation: 1900
Founded in 1984
Printed in 4 colors on glossy stock

19114 **Paper Stock Report: News and Trends of the Paper Recycling Markets**
McEntee Media Corporation
13727 Holland Road
Brook Park, OH 44142

216-362-7979
Fax: 216-362-6553
Home Page: www.recyle.cc

Ken McEntee, President

Covers news and trends of the scrap paper markets.
Cost: $115.00
Frequency: BiWeekly
Founded in 1990

19115 **Paper, Paperboard and Wood Pulp Monthly Statistical Summary**
American Forest & Paper Association
1111 19th St NW
Suite 800
Washington, DC 20036-3652

202-463-2700
800-878-8878
Fax: 202-463-2700
E-Mail: info@afandpa.org
Home Page: www.afandpa.org

Donna Harman, CEO
Henson Moore, President

For the pulp and paper industry.
Cost: $435.00
Frequency: Monthly
Founded in 1878

19116 **Recycled Paper News**
McEntee Media Corporation
9815 Hazelwood Ave
Strongsville, OH 44149-2305

440-238-6603
Fax: 440-238-6712
E-Mail: info@recycle.cc
Home Page: www.recycle.cc

Ken Mc Entee, Owner

Coverage of markets and environmental issues related to recycled paper and environmentally friendly paper making process.
Cost: $235.00
Frequency: Monthly
Founded in 1990

19117 **Solutions! for People, Processes and Paper**
TAPPI and PIMA
15 Technology Parkway S
Norcross, GA 30092

770-446-1400
800-322-8686
Fax: 770-446-6947
E-Mail: webmaster@tappi.org
Home Page: www.tappi.org

Larry N Montague, CEO
Thomas J Garland, Vice Chairman

19118 **TAPPI Journal**
Technical Association of the Pulp & Paper Industry
15 Technology Parkway S
Norcross, GA 30092

770-446-1400
800-322-8686
Fax: 770-446-6947
E-Mail: webmaster@tappi.org
Home Page: www.tappi.org

Larry N Montague, CEO
Thomas J Garland, Vice Chairman

Serves domestic and international pulp, paper, paperboard, packaging and converting industries; manufacturers and suppliers of machinery, equipment, chemicals and other material.
Cost: $350.00
130 Pages
Frequency: Monthly
Circulation: 40637
ISSN: 0734-1415
Founded in 1915
Printed in 4 colors on glossy stock

19119 **Walden's Paper Report**
Walden-Mott Corporation
225 N Franklin Tpke
Ramsey, NJ 07446-1600

201-818-8630
888-292-5336
Fax: 201-818-8720
E-Mail: editorial@walden-mott.com
Home Page: www.waldenmott.com

Alfred F Walden, President
Linda Colhen, Director of Operations
Kirk Hardy, Director of Operations

Reports on company expansions and general financial notes on the manufacturers, as well as personnel changes and appointments. Concise review of news on the North American paper

industry.
Cost: $240.00
8 Pages
Circulation: 500
Founded in 1884

Trade Shows

19120 Annual Information Technology Conference
PIMA-Paper Industry Management Association
4700 West Lake Avenue
Glenview, IL 60025-1485
847-375-6860
Fax: 877-527-5973
E-Mail: info@pimaweb.org
Home Page: www.pimaweb.org
Carol Waugh, Meetings Manager
Three-day conference to bring together IT and process control professionals from around the world to share their knowledge of information technology in the pulp and paper industry and to promote systems applications. The only IT conference planned for and by IT professionals.
500 Attendees
Frequency: Annual, April

19121 International Bioenergy and Bioproducts Conference (IBBC)
Technical Association of the Pulp & Paper Industry
15 Technology Parkway S
Norcross, GA 30092
770-446-1400
800-322-8686
Fax: 770-446-6947
E-Mail: webmaster@tappi.org
Home Page: www.tappi.org
Norman F. Marsolan, Chair
Thomas J. Garland, Vice Chair
Larry N. Montague, President & CEO
Focusing on technical advancements and commercialization of bioconversion technologies that leverage the forest products manufacturing infrastructure and will include technical presentations, expert panels, case studies, and reports from projects that address feedstock and harvesting improvements to increase yield and quality of biomass, and much more.
500 Attendees
Frequency: Annual/October

19122 National Paper Trade Association Convention Expo
National Paper Trade Association
111 Great Neck Road
Suite 418
Great Neck, NY 11021-5497
516-829-3070
Fax: 312-673-6736
E-Mail: bill@goNPTA.com
Home Page: www.gonpta.com
William Frohlich, President
Annual convention of 135 manufacturers, suppliers and distributors of paper products, including packaging materials, health care disposables, industrial and retail packaging supplies, sanitary supplies and computer equipment.
3000 Attendees
Frequency: Annual September
Founded in 1903

19123 National Stationery Show
George Little Management
10 Bank Street
White Plains, NY 10606-1954
914-486-6070
800-272-7469
Fax: 914-948-6180
Home Page: www.
Lori Robinson, VP
Kelly Bristol, Assistant Show Manager
George Little II, President
A show for greeting cards and social stationery, writing instruments and home office products, party ware and giftwrap, scrapbooking and craft supplies, albums, frames and much more.
14000 Attendees
Frequency: May

19124 National Trade Association Paper Plastics Allied Products Exposition
National Paper Trade Association
111 Great Neck Road
Suite 418
Great Neck, NY 11021-5402
516-829-3070
E-Mail: bill@goNPTA.com
Home Page: www.gonpta.com
William Frohlich, President
Industrial and retail packaging, computer products and supplies and equipment. 30 booths.
7M Attendees
Frequency: October

19125 Paper, Plastics and Allied Products Exposition
National Paper Trade Association
111 Great Neck Road
Suite 418
Great Neck, NY 11021-5497
516-829-3070
Fax: 516-829-3074
Home Page: www.gonpta.com
William Frohlich, President
Annual show and exhibits of industrial papers, plastics and plastic products allied to the paper industry.
7000 Attendees

19126 Pulp and Paper
Glahe International
PO Box 2460
Germantown, MD 20875-2460
301-515-0012
Fax: 301-515-0016
Exhibits of equipment, supplies and services for the pulp and paper industries.

Directories & Databases

19127 Directory of Corrugated Plants
Fibre Box Association
2850 Golf Road
Suite 412
Rolling Meadows, IL 60008
847-364-9600
Fax: 847-364-9639
E-Mail: shuske@fibrebox.org
Home Page: www.fibrebox.org
Sharlene Huske
Lists companies and their related plant facilities that manufacture corrugated and solid fiber paperboard products in North America.
Cost: $200.00

19128 Grade Finder's Competitive Grade Finder
Grade Finders
622 Exton Commons
Exton, PA 19341
610-524-7070
Fax: 610-524-8912
E-Mail: info@gradefinders.com
Home Page: www.gradefinders.com
Mark A Subers, President
Phyllis Subers, Office Manager
List of about 5500 manufacturers and distributors of paper. Also lists 6,000 grades of paper competitive classification.
Cost: $60.00
700 Pages
Frequency: Annual April
Circulation: 13,000
ISBN: 0-929502-14-0
Founded in 1967
Printed in one color on matte stock

19129 Grade Finder's Paper Buyers Encyclopedia
Grade Finders
622 Exton Commons
Exton, PA 19341
610-524-7070
Fax: 610-524-8912
E-Mail: info@gradefinders.com
Home Page: www.gradefinders.com
Mark Subers, President
A list of about 6,700 manufacturers, converters and suppliers to the paper industry. In addition, it lists over 4,000 grades of paper categorized into competitive classifications showing each grades rating, opacity, color availability, etc. Also contains an extensive how-to buy paper section.
Cost: $150.00
530 Pages
Frequency: Annual
Circulation: 7000

19130 National Institute of Packaging and Handling Logistics Engineers
5903 Ridgeway Drive
Grand Prairie, TX 75052
817-466-7490
866-464-7453
Fax: 570-523-0606
E-Mail: admin@niphle.com
Home Page: www.niphle.com
Social Media: Facebook, Twitter, LinkedIn
Richard D Owen, Executive Director
An assemblage of professionals whose interest in the complex and diverse practice of distribution and logistics is a common bond.

19131 PIMA Buyers Guide
Paper Industry Management Association
4700 W Lake Avenue
Glenview, IL 60025-1485
847-375-6860
Fax: 877-527-5973
E-Mail: info@pimaweb.org
Home Page: www.pimaweb.org
Jospeph Agnew, Editor
Pam Oddi, Editorial Support
Directory aimed at the paper and pulp industry offering various information on manufacturers of chemicals and supplies used in the manufacturing of paper.
Cost: $120.00
60 Pages
Frequency: Annual
Circulation: 2,000
Printed in on matte stock

19132 Rauch Guide to the US and Canadian Pulp & Paper Industry
Grey House Publishing

4919 Route 22
PO Box 56
Amenia, NY 12501

518-789-8700
800-562-2139
Fax: 845-373-6390
E-Mail: books@greyhouse.com
Home Page: www.greyhouse.com
Social Media: Facebook, Twitter

Leslie Mackenzie, Publisher
Richard Gottlieb, Editor

Provides current market information and trends; industry economics and government regulations; company share data for each of the leading product categories; technology and raw material information; industry sources of further data; and unique profiles of 500+ pulp and paper manufacturers, a section which includes all known companies with pulp and paper sales at or over $15 million annually.
Cost: $595.00
400 Pages
ISBN: 1-592371-31-0
Founded in 1981

19133 TAPPI Membership Directory and Company Guide
Technical Association of the Pulp & Paper Industry
15 Technology Parkway S
Norcross, GA 30092

770-446-1400
800-322-8686
Fax: 770-446-6947
E-Mail: webmaster@tappi.org
Home Page: www.tappi.org

Larry N Montague, CEO
Thomas J Garland, Vice Chairman

About 35,000 member executives, managers, engineers, technologists and superintendents in the pulp, paper, packaging, converting, non-wovens and allied industries.
Cost: $140.00
Frequency: October

19134 Walden's ABC Guide and Paper Production Yearbook
Walden-Mott Corporation
225 N Franklin Tpke
Ramsey, NJ 07446-1600

201-818-8630
Fax: 201-818-8720
Home Page: www.waldenmott.com

Alfred F Walden, President
Kirk Hardy, Director of Operations

Offers a large list of manufacturers and suppliers of printing papers.
Cost: $117.50
300 Pages
Frequency: Annual January

Industry Web Sites

19135 http://gold.greyhouse.com
G.O.L.D Grey House OnLine Databases

Grey House Publishing's online database platform, GOLD, offers Quick Search, Keyword Search and Expert Search for most business sectors including paper and allied products markets. The GOLD platform makes finding the information you need quick and easy - whether you're a novice searcher or an experienced database user. All of Grey House's directory products are available for subscription on the GOLD platform,

19136 www.afandpa.org
American Forest and Paper Association

Serves forest, paper, paperboard and wood products packaging industry

19137 www.fibrebox.org
Fibre Box Association

For national corrigated manufacturers.

19138 www.fpi.org
Foodservice & Packaging Institute

Manufacturers, suppliers and distributors of one-time use products used for food service, as well as packaging products made from paper, plastic, aluminum and other materials. Membership dues based on sales.

19139 www.gonpta.com
National Paper Trade Association

Association for paper, packaging and applied products distribution channel.

19140 www.greyhouse.com
Grey House Publishing

Authoritative reference directories for most business sectors including paper and allied products markets. Users can search the online databases with varied search criteria allowing for custom searches by product category, geographic area, sales volume, keyword, subject and more. Full Grey House catalog and online ordering also available.

19141 www.tappi.org
Technical Association of the Pulp & Paper Industry

Associations

19142 Actors Equity Association
165 W 46th St
New York, NY 10036-2500

212-869-8530
Fax: 212-719-9815
Home Page: www.actorsequity.org

Alan Eisenberg, CEO
Mark Zimmerman, President
David Lotz, National Director of Communications
Mary Lou Westerfield, Natioanl Director Policy
Flora Stamatiades, National Director Organizing

A labor union that represents Actors and Stage Managers in the United States. Seeks to advance, promote and foster the art of live theatre as an essential component of our society. Negotiates wages and working conditions and provides a wide range of benefits, including health and pension plans.
45000 Members
Founded in 1913

19143 African Performing Arts Association
PO Box 660573
Atlanta, GA 30366

E-Mail: info@africanperformingarts.org
Home Page: www.africanperformingarts.org

Founded in 2001

19144 Alternate ROOTS
1083 Austin Avenue
Room 7
Atlanta, GA 30307

404-577-1079
Fax: 404-577-7991
E-Mail: ennis@alternateroots.org
Home Page: www.alternateroots.org
Social Media: Facebook, Twitter, Flickr

19145 American Alliance for Theatre and Education
4908 Auburn Avenue
Bethesda, MD 20814-3474

301-200-1944
Fax: 301-280-1682
E-Mail: info@aate.com
Home Page: www.aate.com
Social Media: Facebook

Jo B.Gonzalez, President
Rachel Prouty, Treasurer
Amy P.Jenson, Advocacy Director
Jeremy Kisling, Communications Director
Mitch Mattson, Planning Director

The national voice for theatre and education, representing artists and educators serving young people in theatre and education. Its members play a vital role in advocating for the interests of children who benefit from theatre in their communities and classrooms. AATE embraces diversity and encourages inclusion of all races, social classes, ages, genders, religions, sexual orientations, national organizations and abilities.
700 Members
Founded in 1986

19146 American Association of Community Theatre
1300 Gendy St Forth Worth
Lago Vista, TX 76107

817-732-3177
866-687-2228
Fax: 817-732-3178
E-Mail: info@aact.org
Home Page: www.aact.org

Julie Crawford, Executive Director
Linda Lee, President
Gary Walker, Executive VP
Frank Peot, Secretary
Tim Jebsen, Treasurer

The national voice of community theatre, representing the interests of its members and over 7,000 theatres across the US and with the armed services overseas. Its mission is to foster the encouragement and development of, and commitment to, the highest standards by community theatres, including standards of excellence for production, management, governance, community relations and service.
1800 Members
Founded in 1986

19147 American Composers Forum
522 Landmark Cente
75 West 5th Street
Saint Paul, MN 55102-1439

651-228-1407
Fax: 651-291-7978
E-Mail: lhoeschler@gmail.com
Home Page: www.composersforum.org
Social Media: Facebook, Twitter

Mary Ellen Childs, Chair
Patrick Castillo, Vice Chair
Dan Thomas, Vice Chair
David Ranheim, Secretary
Sam Hsu, Treasurer

2000 Members
Founded in 1973

19148 American Dance Therapy Association
10632 Little Patuxent Pkwy
Suite 108
Columbia, MD 21044-3263

410-997-4040
Fax: 410-997-4048
E-Mail: info@adta.org
Home Page: www.adta.org

Gloria Farrow, Manager
Jody Wager, VP
Gloria J Farrow, Operations Director
Meghan Dempsey, Treasurer
Ty Tedmon Jones, Secretary

Professional organization of dance movement therapists, with members both nationally and internationally; offers training, research findings, and a newsletter. Holds annual conference.

1.1M Members
Founded in 1966

19149 American Disc Jockey Association
20118 N 67th Avenue
Suite 300-605
Glendale, AZ 85308

888-723-5776
888-723-5776
Fax: 866-310-4676
E-Mail: office@adja.org
Home Page: www.adja.org
Social Media: Facebook, Twitter, YouTube

Rob Snyder, Director

An association of professional mobile entertainers. Encourages success for its members through continuous education, camaraderie, and networking. The primary goal is to educate Disc Jockeys so that each member acts ethically and responsibly.

19150 American Federation of Musicians of the United States and Canada
1501 Broadway
Suite 600
New York, NY 10036-5501

212-869-1330
Fax: 212-764-6134
E-Mail: info@afm.org
Home Page: www.afm.org

Thomas Lee, President
Linda Patterson, Executive Secreatry to President

AFM is an association of professional musicians united through their locals so that they can live and work in dignity; produce work that will be fulfilling and compensated fairly; have a meaningful voice in decisions that affect them; have the opportunity to develop their talents and skills; whose collective voice and power will be realized in a democratic and progressive union; and who oppose the forces of exploitation through their union solidarity.
10K Members
Founded in 1896

19151 American Indian Registry for the Performing Arts
1717 N Highland
Suite 614
Los Angeles, CA 90028

213-962-6574
Home Page: www.afn.org/~native/orgnztns.htm

Organization of American Indian performers and technical personnel in the entertainment field.

19152 American Institute of Organ Builders
PO Box 35306
Canton, OH 44735

330-806-9011
E-Mail: robert_sullivan@pipeorgan.org
Home Page: www.pipeorgan.org
Social Media: Twitter

Matthew M Bellocchio, President
Patrick J. Murphy, Vice President
Louis E Patterson, Secretary
Charles R Eames, Treasurer

Sponsors training seminars, quarterly journal and annual convention for pipe organ builders and service technicians.
385 Members
Founded in 1974
Mailing list available for rent: 350 names at $250 per M

19153 American Institute of Organbuilders
PO Box 35306
Canton, OH 44735

330-806-9011
E-Mail: robert_sullivan@pipeorgan.org
Home Page: www.pipeorgan.org
Social Media: Facebook

Matthew M. Bellocchio, President
Patrick J. Murphy, Vice President
Robert Sullivan, Executive Secretary
Joseph O'Donnell, Secretary
Charles R. Eames, Treasurer
Founded in 1974

19154 Americans for the Arts
1000 Vermont Avenue, NW
6th Floor
Washington, DC 20005

202-371-2830
Fax: 202-371-0424
Home Page: www.americansforthearts.org

Social Media: Facebook, Twitter, LinkedIn, YouTube, Instagram

Abel Lopez, Chair
Ramona Baker, Vice Chair
C. Kendric Fergeson, Immediate Past Chair
Michael Spring, Secretary
Julie Muraco, Treasurer
Founded in 1960

19155 Associated Pipe Organ Builders of America
PO Box 155
Chicago Ridge, IL 60415

800-473-5270
800-473-5270
Home Page: www.apoba.com

Bob Rusczyk, Executive Director
Richard Parsons, President
Paul Lytle, Vice President
Randall Dyer, Secretary
Seth Marshall, Treasurer

A professional association of North American firms engaged in building traditional pipe organs. Members are a select group of organbuilders who have passed stringent membership requirements which include commitment to principles regarding the use of electronic technology in organ building.
27 Members

19156 Association for Theatre in Higher Education
PO Box 1290
Boulder, CO 80306-1290

303-530-2167
888-284-3737
Fax: 303-530-2168
E-Mail: info@athe.org
Home Page: www.athe.org

Bill Doane, President
Terry Brino Dean, Secretary
Nina Lenoir, Treasurer

ATHE serves the interests of its diverse individual and organization members. Its vision is to advocate for the field of theatre and performance in higher education. It serves as an intellectual and artistic center for producing new knowledge about theatre and performance-related disciplines. cultivating vital alliances with other scholarly and creative disciplines, linking with professional and community-based theatres, and promoting access and equity.
1700 Members
Founded in 1986

19157 Association of Arts Administration Educators
Bolz Center for Arts Administration
N4460 Allan Rd
Portage, WI 53901

608-561-2040
Fax: 608-265-2735
E-Mail: info@artsadministration.org
Home Page: www.artsadministration.org

Andrew Taylor, President/Director
John McCann, VP
Phyllis Johnson, Treasurer
Stephen Boyle, Secretary

The Association of Administration Educators (AAAE) is an international organization incorporated as a nonprofit institution within the United States. Its mission is to represent college and university graduate and undergraduate programs in the arts administration, encompassing training in the management of visual, performing, literary, media, cultural and arts service organizations.
Founded in 1975

19158 Association of Hispanic Arts
P.O.Box 1169
El Barrio, NY 10029

212-876-1242
888-876-1240
Fax: 212-876-1285
E-Mail: informacion@latinoarts.org
Home Page: www.latinoarts.org

Nicholas L Arture, Executive Director
Julia L Gutierrez-Rivera, Program Officer/Arts Service Coord.
Crystal Chaparro, Office Assistant
Gregory Castro, Comptroller
Brenda L Jiminez, Board Chair

A nonprofit arts service organization serving the Latino arts and cultural community. AHA was established out of the need to create funding and presenting opportunities for individual Latino artists and cultural organizations whose contributions were unrecognized and whose efforts were underserved by mainstream public and private institutions.
Founded in 1975

19159 Association of Performing Arts Presenters
1211 Connecticut Ave NW
Suite 200
Washington, DC 20036-2716

202-833-2787
888-820-2787
Fax: 202-833-1543
E-Mail: info@artspresenters.org
Home Page: www.artspresenters.org
Social Media: Facebook, Twitter

Sandra Gibson, President
Josh Labelle, Chair
Terri Trotter, Vice Chairman
Johann Zietsman, Vice Chair

A national membership and advocacy organization dedicated to bringing performing artists and audiences together.
1900 Members
Founded in 1957

19160 Broadcast Music Incorporated BMI
7 World Trade Center
250 Greenwich Street
New York, NY 10007-0030

212-220-3000
Fax: 212-246-2163
E-Mail: newyork@bmi.com
Home Page: www.bmi.com
Social Media: Facebook, Twitter

Del Bryant, CEO
John E Cody, COO/Executive VP

American performing rights organization that represents approximately 300,000 songwriters, composers and music publishers in all genres of music. The nonprofit company collects license fees on behalf of those American creators it represents, as well as thousands of creators from around the world who chose BMI for representation in the US. These fees are then distributed as royalties to the writers, composers and copyright holders it represents.
300m Members
Founded in 1939

19161 Chinese Music Society of North America
PO Box 5275
Woodridge, IL 60517-0275

630-910-1551
Fax: 630-910-1561
Home Page: www.chinesemusic.net

Sin-Yan Shen, President
Kok-Koon Ng, VP
Yuan-Yuan Lee, Executive Director
Billie Jefferson, Artistic Administrator
Der-Tung Yuan, Membership

A national nonprofit organization founded to increase and diffuse the knowledge of Chinese music and performing arts. Today it has grown to become the national association of Chinese musicians and scholars and National and International organization specializing in Research and Educational Material in English concerning Music/Theater/Dance and Musical Instruments from China and Non-Western Cultures.
Founded in 1969

19162 Chorus America
1156 15th Street, NW
Suite 310
Washington, DC 20005

202-331-7577
Fax: 202-331-7599
E-Mail: webmaster@chorusamerica.org
Home Page: www.chorusamerica.org
Social Media: Facebook, Twitter

Rollo Dilworth, Chairman
Gayle. M Ober, Immediate Past Chairman
Mitch Menchaca, Interim CEO
Michael McCarthy, Treasurer
Mary Lyons, Secretary
2000 Members
Founded in 1977

19163 Classical Action
165 W 46th St
Suite 1300
New York, NY 10036-2514

212-997-7717
Fax: 212-840-0551
E-Mail: classicalaction@broadwaycares.org
Home Page: www.classicalaction.org
Social Media: Facebook, Twitter

Charles Hamlen, Founding Director
Chris Kenney, Associate Director

Since 1993, Classical Action has provided a unified voice for all those within the performing arts community to help combat HIV/AIDS and the devastating effects of this epidemic.
Founded in 1993

19164 Conductors Guild
719 Twinridge Ln
Richmond, VA 23235

804-553-1378
Fax: 804-553-1876
E-Mail: guild@conductorsguild.org
Home Page: www.conductorsguild.org
Social Media: Facebook, Twitter, LinkedIn

Gordon Johnson, President
Amanda Burton Winger, Executive Director
Erin Freeman, VP
Christopher Blair, Treasurer
David Leibowitz, Secretary

The Conductors Guild is the only music service organization devoted exclusively to the advancement of the art of conducting and to serving the artistic and professional needs of conductors.
1850+ Members
Founded in 1975

19165 Congress on Research in Dance
SUNY College of Brockport
3416 Primm Lane
Birmingham, AL 35216

205-823-5517
Fax: 205-823-2760
E-Mail: ashanti@cordance.org
Home Page: www.cordance.org

Marta Savigliano, President
Helen Thomas, Chair, Editorial Board

A not-for-profit, interdisciplinary organization with an open, international membership. Its purposes are: to encourage research in all as-

pects of dance, including related fields; to foster the exchange of ideas, resources, and methodology, through publication, international and regional conferences and workshops; to promote the accessibility of research materials.
Cost: $35.00
750 Members
Founded in 1965
Mailing list available for rent

19166 Costume Society of America

Home Page: www.costumesocietyamerica.com
Social Media: Facebook, Twitter, LinkedIn, YouTube

19167 Country Dance & Song Society
116 Pleasant St
Suite 345
Easthampton, MA 01027-2759

413-203-5467
Fax: 413-203-5471
E-Mail: office@cdss.org
Home Page: www.cdss.org

Rima Dael, Executive/Artistic Director
Carol Compton, Financial Manager
Christine Dadmun, Membership Admin
Bob Blondin, Business Manager
Robin Hayden, Development Director

A national organization dedicated to the preservation and promotion of English and Anglo-American traditional and historical folk dance, music and song. Composed of individual members and affiliate groups, it functions both as an international service bureau and as a facilitator in building and maintaining local and regional dance, music and song communities. It exists to meed needs for community-based activity, for active participation, and for sharing and keeping historical and folk
3400 Members
Founded in 1915

19168 Dance Critics Association
Old Chelsea Station
PO Box 1882
New York, NY 10011

732-643-4008
E-Mail: dancecritics@hotmail.com
Home Page: www.dancecritics.org

Kena Herod, Co-Chair
Linda Traiger, Co-Chair

Encourages excellence in dance criticism through education, research and the exchange of ideas. Produces quarterly newsletter.
Cost: $50.00
300 Members
Founded in 1974

19169 Dance Educators of America
3340 S.E Federal Highway
Suite262
Stuart, FL 34997

914-636-3200
800-329-3868
Fax: 914-636-5895
E-Mail: info@dancedea.com
Home Page: http://usadance.dancedea.com/
Social Media: Facebook, Twitter, Youtube

Vickie Sheer, Executive Director
Fran Peters, President
Charles Kelley, Treasurer
Robyn Bourdeau, Chief Financial Officer
Stephen Ball, Events and DEA Coordinator

Dedicated to improving the quality and teaching abilities of its member teachers and enhancing their education of students, as well as furthering the professional and ethical standards in the performing arts and of dance in all its form. Membership is limited to qualified teachers.
Cost: $150.00
1800 Members
Founded in 1932

19170 Dance Films Association
48 W 21st St
Suite 907
New York, NY 10010-6989

212-727-0764
Fax: 212-727-0765
E-Mail: info@dancefilms.org
Home Page: www.dancefilms.org

Deidra Towers, Executive Director
Latika Young, Education Director
Anna Brady Nuse, Festival Coordinator
Julian Barnett, Research/Development

Supports all those professionals in both the dance and the film community. Publishes bi-monthly magazine.
Cost: $50.00
Founded in 1956

19171 Dance Masters of America
PO Box 610533
Bayside, NY 11361

718-255-4013
Fax: 718-225-4293
E-Mail: dmamann@aol.com
Home Page: www.dma-national.org

Shely Pack Manning, National President
Robert Mann, National Executive Secretary
Charleen Locascio, National Treasurer

An international organization of dance educators who have been certified by test to teach whose main focus is advancing the art of dance and improving the practice of its teaching.
2.5M Members
Founded in 1884

19172 Dance USA
1111 16th St NW
Suite 300
Washington, DC 20036-4830

202-833-1717
Fax: 202-833-2686
E-Mail: danceusa@danceusa.org
Home Page: www.danceusa.org
Social Media: Facebook, Twitter

Amy Fitterer, Executive Director
Tom Thielen, Director Finance/Operations
Katherine Fabian, Membership Manager

Provides a forum for the discussion of issues of concern to members and a support network for exchange of information.
400 Members
Founded in 1982

19173 Dance/USA
1111 16th Street NW Ste. 300
Washington, DC 20036

202-833-1717
Home Page: www.danceusa.org
Social Media: Facebook, Twitter, YouTube, Vimeo

Houston Ballet, Chair
Charlotte Ballet, Chair Elect
Andrea Clark-Smith, Vice Chair
Sarah Thompson, Secretary
Pam Robinson, Treasurer

19174 Dramatists Guild of America
1501 Broadway
Suite 701
New York, NY 10036-5505

212-398-9366
Fax: 212-944-0420
E-Mail: igor@dramaguild.com
Home Page: www.dramatistsguild.com

Ralph Sevush, Executive Director Business Affairs
Gary Garrison, Executive Director Creative Affairs
Abby Marcus, Managing Director
Roland Tec, Director of Membership

The Dramatists Guild of America was established over eighty years ago, and is the only professional association that advances the interests of playwrights, composers, lyricists and librettists writing for the living stage.
6000+ Members
Founded in 1964

19175 Educational Theatre Association
2343 Auburn Ave
Cincinnati, OH 45219-2819

513-421-3900
Fax: 513-421-7077
Home Page: www.schooltheatre.org
Social Media: Facebook, Twitter

Jay Seller, President
Frank Pruet, VP
Julie Woffington, Executive Director
Jim Flanagan, Director of Operations
Ginny Butsch, Community Manager

EdTA is a professional organization for theatre educators. In addition to providing professional development, advocacy, and networking support to its members, Edta oprtates the International Society, an honorary organization for high school and middle school theatre students.
4600+ Members
Founded in 1929

19176 Esperanza Performing Arts Association
Po Box 502591
San Diego, CA 92150

858-391-1311
E-Mail: info@esperanzaarts.org
Home Page: www.esperanzaarts.org

Alan Cox, Executive Director
Adam Stout, Assistant Director

19177 Fractured Atlas
248 W. 35th Street, 10th Fl.
New York, NY 10001
888-692-7878
Fax: 212-277-8025
Home Page: www.fracturedatlas.orgÿ

Holly Sidford, Chair
Russell Wills Taylor, Vice Chair
Adam Forest Huttler, Executive Director
Adam Huttler, Secretary
Alanna Weifenbach, Treasurer
Founded in 1998

19178 Fritz and Lavinia Jensen Foundation
Foundation for the Carolinas
220 N Tryon Street
Charlotte, NC 28202

704-973-4500
Fax: 704-973-4599
E-Mail: info@jensenfoundation.org
Home Page: www.jensenfoundation.org

Ann Todd, Competition Coordinator

Sponsors voice competitions supporting opera and other classical singers.

19179 Gina Bachauer International Piano Foundation
138 W Broadway
Suite 220
Salt Lake City, UT 84101-1913

801-297-4250
Fax: 801-521-9202
E-Mail: info@bachauer.com

Home Page: www.bachauer.com
Social Media: Facebook, Twitter, Flickr

Thomas Holst, Manager
Kimi Kawashima, Manager
Arlo McGinn, Secretary
Nathan Morgan, Treasurer

The mission of the Foundation is to further the pianistic art, foster excellence in performance and teaching, develop opportunities for pianists beyond the scope of the organization and offer leadership in developing a musically-educated community.
Founded in 1976

19180 **Guild of American Luthiers**
8222 S Park Ave
Tacoma, WA 98408-5226

253-472-7853
Fax: 253-472-7853
E-Mail: orders@luth.org
Home Page: www.luth.org
Social Media: Facebook

Debra G Olsen, Executive Director
Tim Olsen, Editor
Kurt Kendall, Membership

Manufacturers and repairs stringed instruments; offers quarterly journal and triennial meeting.
Cost: $45.00
3000 Members
Founded in 1972

19181 **Institute of Outdoor Drama**
201 Erwin Building
Mail Stop 528
Greenville, NC 27858-4353

252-328-5363
Fax: 252-328-0968
Home Page: www.outdoor-theatre.org

Michael C. Hardy, Director
Susan D. Phillips, Business Manager
Founded in 1963

19182 **International Association of Round Dance Teachers**
176 S Cole Road
Boise, ID 83709-0932

208-377-1232
800-346-7522
Fax: 208-377-1236
E-Mail: roundalab@roundalab.org
Home Page: www.roundalab.org

Gil & Judy Martin, General Chairman
Jeanne & Warren Shane, Vice Chairman
Chuck & Becky Jaworski, Marketing Membership

Supports all those involved in the field of square dancing. Publishes quarterly magazine.
Founded in 1976
Mailing list available for rent

19183 **International Computer Music Association**
1819 Polk Street
Suite 330
San Francisco, CA 94109

FAX 734-878-3031
E-Mail: icma@umich.edu
Home Page: www.computermusic.org
Social Media: Facebook

Tae Hong Park, President
Margaret Schedel, VP Of Conference

The International Computer Music Association is an international affiliaton of individuals and institutions involved in the technical, creative, and performance aspects of computer music. It serves composers, engineers, researchers and musicians who are interested in the integration of music and technology.
Cost: $63.52
450 Members

19184 **International Festivals and Events Association**
2603 W Eastover Ter
Boise, ID 83706-2800

208-433-0950
Fax: 208-433-9812
E-Mail: nia@ifea.com
Home Page: www.ifea.com

Steven Schmader, President
Nia Hovde, VP/Marketing

A voluntary association of events, event producers, event suppliers, and related professionals and organizations whose common purpose is the production and presentation of festivals, events, and civic and private celebrations.
2000 Members
Founded in 1956

19185 **International Performing Arts for Youth**
1417 North 2nd Street
Studio 23A
Philadelphia, PA 19122

267-690-1325
Fax: 267-519-3343
Home Page: www.ipayweb.org

Ms. Peg Schuler-Armstrong, President
Ms. Pamela K. Lieberman, Vice President
Ms. Mary Kate Barley-Jenkins, Immediate Past President
Jeremy Boomer Stacey, Executive Director
Ms. Nadine Carew, Treasurer
Founded in 2001

19186 **International Planned Music Association**
5900 S Salina Street
Syracuse, NY 13205

315-469-7711
Fax: 315-469-8842
Home Page: www.ipmanet.com

Roy Salgado, President
Steve Seiden, VP
Larry Zaiser, Secretary
Jon Baker, Treasurer

IPMA is a trade organization made up of providers of planned and programmed music services and key vendors. The Associatin exists to provide members with a common ground on which to share informatio about running exciting, profitable franchises and to provide associate members with opportunities to expand their sales in markets all over the world.
200 Members

19187 **International Society for the Performing Arts**
630 9th Avenue
Suite 213
New York, NY 10036-4752

212-206-8490
Fax: 212-206-8603
E-Mail: info@ispa.org
Home Page: www.ispa.org
Social Media: Facebook

Martha H Jones, Chair
Willem Brans, Treasurer
Horacio Lecona, Secretary
Johann Zietsman, CEO
Lynne Caruso, Membership Manager

A nonprofit organization of executives and directors of concert and performance halls, festivals, performing companies, and artists competitions; government cultural officials; artists' managers; and other interested parties with a professional involvement in the performing arts around the world, and in every arts disciple. The purpose of ISPA is to develop, nurture, energize and educate an international network of arts leaders and professionals who are dedicated to advancing its field.
600 Members
Founded in 1949

19188 **International Theatre Equipment Association**
770 Broadway
5th Floor
New York, NY 10003-9595

646-654-7680
Fax: 212-257-6428
E-Mail: info@itea.com
Home Page: www.itea.com

Robert Sunshine, Executive Director
Barry Ferrell, President
Jack Panzeca, VP
Joe DeMeo, Treasurer
Sarah Fuller, Secretary

Fosters and maintains professional, business and social relationships among its members within all segments of the motion picture industry. Bestows annual Teddy Award to manufacturer of the year and the annual Rodney Award to dealer of the year.
Cost: $375.00
180 Members
Founded in 1971

19189 **International Ticketing Association**
10401 N Meridian St
Suite 300
Indianapolis, IN 46290

212-629-4036
Fax: 212-629-8532
E-Mail: info@intix.org
Home Page: www.intix.org

Jennifer Aprea, Board Chair
Gary Lustig, Chair-Elect
Mardi S Dilger, Past Chair
Jena L Hoffman, President
Amber E Kinney, Treasurer

Non-profit association committed to the improvement, progress and advancement of ticket management. Provides educational programs, trade shows, conducts surveys, conference proceedings, and its valuable membership directory.
Founded in 1982

19190 **Jazz Education**
3303 South Rice, Suite 107
PO Box 8031
Houston, TX 77056

713-839-7000
Fax: 715-839-8266
E-Mail: jazzed@jazzedcation.org
Home Page: www.jazzeducation.org
Social Media: Facebook, LinkedIn

Tracy Scott, Executive Director

Nonprofit music organization providing worthwhile educational activities for school-aged youth in the field of music. Includes many subjects not covered by school systems. Promotes appreciation and understanding of Jazz.
Founded in 1970

19191 **League of American Orchestras**
33 West 60th Street
New York, NY 10023

212-262-5161
Fax: 212-262-5198
E-Mail: member@americanorchestras.org
Home Page: www.americanorchestras.org
Social Media: Facebook, Twitter, YouTube

Patricia A Richards, Chair
Steven C. Parrish, Vice Chair
Jesse Rosen, President/ CEO

Barry A Sanders, Secretary
Robert A Peiser, Treasurer
800 Members
Founded in 1942

19192 League of American Theatres and Producers
729 Seventh Avenue
5th Floor
New York, NY 10019
212-764-1122
Fax: 212-944-2136
E-Mail: league@broadway.org
Home Page: www.livebroadway.com
Social Media: Facebook, Twitter, LinkedIn, Pinterest
Charolette St Martin, Executive Director
Colin Gibson, Director Finance
Jane Svendsen, Director Marketing
Ed Sandler, Director Membership Services
National trade association for the commercial theatre industry whose principal activity is negotiation of labor contracts and government relations.
400 Members
Founded in 1930

19193 League of Historic American Theatres
2105 Laurel Bush Rd
Suite 201
Bel Air, MD 21015
443-640-1058
877-627-0833
Fax: 443-640-1031
E-Mail: info@lhat.org
Home Page: www.lhat.org
Frances Holden, Executive Director
Thomas Johnson, VP
Lance Olson, Treasurer
The League of Historic American Theatres, a nonprofit membership association, promotes the rescue, rehabilitation and sustainable operation of historic theatres throughout North America. Founded in 1976, the League serves its members through educational programs, publications, specialized services and an annual conference and theatre tour.
500+ Members
Founded in 1976

19194 Literary Managers and Dramaturgs of the Americas
PO Box 36
New York, NY 10129
212-561-0315
800-680-2148
E-Mail: lmdanyc@hotmail.com
Home Page: www.lmda.org
Cynthia M SoRelle, Chair
Vicki Stroich, President
Danielle Carroll, Administrative Director
Beth Blickers, Treasurer
The mission of the LMDA is to affirm the role of dramaturgy, to expand the possibilities of the field to other media and institutions and to cultivate, develop and promote the function of dramaturgy and literary management.
500 Members

19195 Mid-Atlantic Arts Foundation
201 N Charles Street
Suite 401
Baltimore, MD 21201-4102
410-539-6656
Fax: 410-837-5517
E-Mail: info@midatlanticarts.org
Home Page: www.midatlanticarts.org
Alan Cooper, Executive Director
E Scott Johnson, Secretary
MAAF celebrates, promotes and supports the richness and diversity of the region's art resources and works to increase access to the arts and other cultures of the region and the world.
40000 Members
Founded in 1979
Mailing list available for rent: 30,000 names

19196 Music Distributors Association
14070 Proton Road
Suite 100 LB 9
Dallas, TX 75244-3601
972-233-9107
Fax: 972-490-4219
E-Mail: office@musicdistributors.org
Home Page: www.musicdistributors.org
An international nonprofit trade association representing and serving manufacturers, wholesalers, importers and exporters of musical instruments and accessories, sound reinforcement products and published music.
Cost: $675.00
Founded in 1939

19197 National Alliance for Musical Theatre
520 Eighth Avenue
Suite 301
New York, NY 10018
212-714-6668
Fax: 212-714-0469
E-Mail: info@namt.org
Home Page: www.namt.orgÿ
Donna Lynn Hilton, President
Kevin Moriarty, Vice President
Betsy King Militelo, Executive Director
Peter Rothstein, Secretary
Jeff Loeb, Treasurer
30000 Members
Founded in 1985

19198 National Association for Drama Therapy
44365 Premier Plaza
Suite 220
Ashburn, VA 20147
585-381-5618
Fax: 571-223-6440
E-Mail: nadt.office@nadt.org
Home Page: www.nadt.org
Nisha Sajnani, President
Lisa Merrell, VP
Gary Raucher, Secretary
Mary Caligiure, Treasurer
Nancy Sondag, Membership
A nonprofit association which establishes and upholds high standards of professional competence and ethics among drama therapists; to develop criteria for training and registration; to sponsor publications and conferences; and to promote the profession of drama therapy through information and advocacy.
Founded in 1979

19199 National Association for Music Education
1806 Robert Fulton Drive
Reston, VA 20191
703-860-4000
800-336-3768
Fax: 703-860-1531
Home Page: www.menc.org
Social Media: Facebook, Twitter, LinkedIn
Lynn M Brinckmeyer, President
The mission of MENC is to advance music education by encouraging the study and making of music by all. MENC offers more than 100 books, videos and compact discs, as well as two general-interest magazines on music education and four more closely targeted journals.
Founded in 1907
Mailing list available for rent: 60,000 names

19200 National Association of Performing Arts Managers and Agents
459 Columbus Avenue
#133
New York, NY 10024
E-Mail: tuluck@fairpoint.net
Home Page: www.napama.org
Jerry Ross, President
David Wannen, Vice President
Jeff Laramie, Vice President
Laurelle Favreau, Secretary
Robin Pomerance, Treasurer
Founded in 1979

19201 National Corporate Theatre Fundÿ
505 Eighth Avenue
Suite 2303
New York, NY 10018
212-750-6895
Fax: 212-750-6977
Home Page: www.nctf.org
Social Media: Facebook, YouTube
Richard Thomas, Honorary Chair
James S Turley, Chairman
Gretchen Shugart, President
Bruce R Ewing, Secretary
Frank Orlowski, Treasurer

19202 National Costumers Association
121 N Bosart Avenue
Indianapolis, IN 46201-3729
317-351-1940
800-622-1321
Fax: 317-351-1941
E-Mail: office@costumers.org
Home Page: www.costumers.org
Janie Westendorf, President
Deborah Meredith, First Vive President
Linda Adams Foat, Second VP
Jennifer Skarstedt, Secretary/Treasurer
The objectives on the NCA are to establish and maintain professional and ethical standards of business in the costume industry. They encourage and promote a greater and more diversified use of costumes in all fields of human activity. They provide trade information, cooperation and friendship among its members together with a sound public relations policy.
400 Members
Founded in 1923

19203 National Dance Association
1900 Association Dr
Reston, VA 20191-1502
703-476-3400
800-213-7193
Fax: 703-476-9527
E-Mail: nda@aahperd.org
Home Page: www.aahperd.org/nda
Social Media: Facebook, Twitter
Colleen Dean, Manager
Marcey E Siegel, VP Dance Education
Mary Ann Laverty, VP Dance Performance
A nonprofit service organization dedicated to increasing knowledge, improving skills and encouraging sound professional practices in dance education while promoting and supporting creative and healthy lifestyles through high quality dance programs.
2000 Members
Founded in 1932

19204 National Dance Education Organization
8609 2nd Avenue
Suite 203 B
Silver Spring, MD 20910
301-585-2880
Fax: 301-585-2888

E-Mail: info@ndeo.org
Home Page: www.ndeo.org

Susan McGreevy-Nichols, Executive Director
Patricia Cohen, Treasurer

A nonprofit organization dedicated to promoting standards of excellence in dance education.
2000 Members
Founded in 1998

19205 National Endowment for the Arts
1100 Pennsylvania Ave NW
Washington, DC 20506

202-682-5400
Fax: 202-682-5611
E-Mail: webmgr@arts.gov
Home Page: www.arts.endow.gov
Social Media: Facebook, Twitter

Dana Gioia, CEO
Guilomar Barbi, Scheduler
Sarah Cook, Executive Assistant
Jon P Peede, Counselor to the Chairman
Sydney Smith, Administrative Specialist

The National Endowment for the Arts, an investment in America's living heritage, serves the public good by nurturing the expression of human creativity, supporting the cultivation of community spirit, and fostering the recognition and appreciation of the excellence and diversity of our nation's artistic accomplishments.

19206 National Music Publishers Association
101 Constitution Avenue NW
Suite 705 East
Washington, DC 20001

202-742-4375
Fax: 202-393-6673
E-Mail: pr@nmpa.org
Home Page: www.nmpa.org

Martin Bandier, President/CEO
John Eastman, Director

The NMPA is committed to promoting and advancing the interests of music publishers and their songwriting partners. Their goal is to foster a business climate that allows its members to thrive creatively and financially.
800 Members
Founded in 1917

19207 National Performance Network
1024 Elysian Fields Avenue
New Orleans, LA 70117

504-595-8008
Fax: 504-595-8006
E-Mail: info@npnweb.org
Home Page: www.npnweb.org
Social Media: Facebook, Twitter

Abe Rybeck, Chair
Yolanda Cesta Cursach, Vice Chair
MK Wegmann, President/ CEO
Meena Natarajan, Secretary
Shannon Daut, Treasurer
Founded in 1985

19208 National Piano Travelers Association
401 Sawkill Road
PO Box 2264
Kingston, NY 12401-2264

845-338-1464
Fax: 845-338-5751
Home Page: www.pianotravelers.com

Roy Chandler, President
Bob dove, VP
Dawn Demars, Secretary/Treasurer

Buys and sells pianos.
110 Members

19209 Network of Ensemble Theaters
1709 N. Avenue 56
Los Angeles, CA 90042

E-Mail: info@ensembletheaters.net
Home Page: www.ensembletheaters.net

Laurie McCants, President
August Schulenburg, Vice President
Mark Valdez, Executive Director
Cynthia Ling Lee, Secretary
Bruce Allardice, Treasurer
Founded in 1995

19210 New England Theatre Conference
215 Knob Hill Drive
Hamden, CT 06518

617-851-8535
Fax: 203-288-5938
E-Mail: mail@netconline.org
Home Page: www.netconline.org

Sabine Klein, President
Jeffrey Watts, Executive VP
Charles Emmons, VP Administration/Finance

Non-profit corporation, composed of individuals and organizations in the six-State region of New England, who are active and interested in the performing arts. The NETC promotes excellence in theatre for their region, and supports quality theatre and performance in all of its diversity.
500 Members
Founded in 1952

19211 North American Drama Therapy Association
1450 Western Avenue
Suite 101
Albany, NY 12203

888-416-7167
Fax: 518-463-8656
E-Mail: office@nadt.org
Home Page: www.nadta.org

Nadya Trytan, President
Jason Butler, President-Elect
Jeremy Segall, Vice President
Whitney Sullivan, Secretary
Dani York, Treasurer

19212 North American Performing Arts Managers and Agents
459 Columbus Ave
Suite 133
New York, NY 10024-5129

212-362-8304
800-867-3281
E-Mail: info@napama.org
Home Page: www.napama.org

Richard Baird, Owner
David Wannen, VP
Jerry Ross, VP
Susan Endrizzi Moris, Secretary
Robin Pomerance, Treasurer

National nonprofit trade association dedicated to promoting the professionalism of its members and the vitality of the performing arts. NAPAMA promotes the mutual advancement and the best interests of performing arts managers and agents; promotes open discourse among members and within the larger field; gives active consideration and expression of opinion on questions affecting the industry and develops and encourages ethical and sound business practices.
Cost: $150.00
Founded in 1979

19213 OPERA America
330 Seventh Avenue
New York, NY 10001

212-796-8620
Fax: 212-796-8621
E-Mail: Info@operaamerica.org
Home Page: www.operaamerica.orgÿ

Dr. Frayda B. Lindemann, Chairman
Susan F. Morris, Vice Chairman
Marc A. Scorca, President/ CEO
William Florescu, Secretary
Timothy O'Leary, Treasurer
Founded in 1973

19214 Oratorio Society of New York
1440 Broadway
23rd Floor
New York, NY 10018-9759

212-400-7255
E-Mail: president@oratoriosocietyofny.org
Home Page: www.oratoriosocietyofny.org
Social Media: Facebook, Twitter, Youtube

Richard A Pace, President/Chairman
Mary J.Knight, Vice President
Marie Gangemi, Treasurer
Jay Jacobson, Secretary
Kent Tritle, Music Director

New York City's second oldest cultural organization. On December 25, 1874 the society began what has become an unbroken tradition of annual performances of Handel's Messiah (at Carnegie Hall since its opening in 1891).
Founded in 1873

19215 Performing Arts Association
719 Edmond St
St Joseph, MO 64501-2268

816-279-1225
E-Mail: info@paastjo.org
Home Page: www.paastjo.org

David Cripe, President
Elaine Smith, VP
Debbie Demuth, Secretary
Kim Lueger, Treasurer

Mission is to provide a diverse selection of performing arts in the St. Joseph area by presenting programs that foster, increase and promote public knowledge and appreciation of music, theatre and dance and lectures on subjects of cultural interests.
Founded in 1979

19216 Performing Arts Medicine Association
PO Box 117
Englewood, CO 80151

303-808-5643
Fax: 866-408-7069
E-Mail: webmaster@artsmed.org
Home Page: www.artsmed.org

Julie Massaro, Executive Director
Mary Fletcher, Consultant
John Chong, President
Dorry Allen, Manager of Member Services

Organization for physicians and other professionsl persons who are involved in treatment and/or research in the field of Performing Arts Medicine.
Founded in 1989

19217 Piano Manufacturers Association
14070 Proton Road
Suite 100
Dallas, TX 75244

972-233-9107
Fax: 972-490-4219
Home Page: www.pianonet.com

Donald W Dillon, Executive Director

Piano industry trade association.
Founded in 1991

19218 Piano Technicians Guild
4444 Forest Avenue
Kansas City, KS 66106

913-432-9975
Fax: 913-432-9986
E-Mail: ptg@ptg.org
Home Page: www.ptg.org

Barbara Cassaday, Executive Director
Jim Coleman, President
Norman R. Cantrell, VP
Phil A Bondi, Secretary/Treasurer

A nonprofit organization serving piano tuners, technicians, and craftsman throughout the world, organized to promote the highest possible service and technical standards among piano tuners and technicians.
4100 Members
Founded in 1957

19219 Production Music Library Association
8551 Research Way
Suite 180
Middleton, WI 53562

608-836-5825
Fax: 608-831-8200
E-Mail: mla@areditions.com
Home Page: www.musiclibraryassoc.org

Jerry L McBride, President
Michael Colby, VP
Pamela Bristah, Secretary

Provides a forum for issues surrounding music, music in libraries, and music librarianship. Members include music librarians, librarians who work with music as part of their responsibilities, composers and music scholars, and others interested in the program of the association.
20 Members
Founded in 1931

19220 Professional Women Singers Association
PO Box 231162
New York, NY 10023

212-969-0590
Fax: 928-395-2560
E-Mail: info@womensingers.org
Home Page: www.womensingers.org
Social Media: Facebook

Elissa Weiss, President
Allison Atteberry, First VP
Sarah Downs, Second VP
Ruth Ann Cunningham, Secretary
Mary Lou Zobel, Treasurer

Non-profit networking organization for professional women singers. The group sponsors concerts, master classes and seminars for both singers and the community at large.
40 Members
Founded in 1982

19221 Screen Actors Guild
5757 Wilshire Blvd
7th Floor
Los Angeles, CA 90036-3600

323-954-1600
855-724-2387
Fax: 323-549-6792
Home Page: www.sag.org

Allen Rosenburg, President
Kent McCord, First VP
Paul Christie, Second VP
Steve Fried, Third Vice President
Connie Stevens, Secretary/Treasurer

Labor union affiliated with AFL-CIO which represents actors in film, television and commercials. The Guild exists to enhance actors' working conditions, compensation and benefits and to be a powerful, unifed voice on behalf of artists' rights.
120M Members
Founded in 1933

19222 Society of American Magicians
PO Box 510260
Saint Louis, MO 63151-0260

314-846-5659
Fax: 314-846-5659
E-Mail: rmblowers@aol.com
Home Page: www.magicsam.com

J.Christopher Bontjes, President
Bruce Kalver, First VP
Mike Miller, Second VP
Chuck Lehr, Secretary
Mary Ann Blowers, Treasurer

Founded to promote and maintain harmonious fellowship among those interested in magic as an art, to improve ethics of the magical profession, and to foster, promote and improve the advancement of magical arts in the field of amusement and entertainment. Membership includes professional and amateur magicians, manufacturers of magical apparatus and collectors.
5.5M Members
Founded in 1902

19223 Society of Stage Directors & Choreograhers
1501 Broadway
Suite 1701
New York, NY 10036

212-391-1070
Fax: 212-302-6195
E-Mail: Info@SDCweb.org
Home Page: www.sdcweb.org
Social Media: Facebook, Twitter, LinkedIn, Google+

Susan H Schulman, President
John Rando, Executive Vice President
Leigh Silverman, Vice President
Oz Scott, Secretary
Ethan McSweeny, Treasurer

19224 Society of Stage Directors and Choreographers
1501 Broadway
Suite 1701
New York, NY 10036-5653

212-391-1070
800-541-5204
Fax: 212-302-6195
E-Mail: info@ssdc.org
Home Page: www.ssdc.org
Social Media: Facebook

Laura Penn, Executive Director
Sue Lawless, Secretary
Doug Hughes, Treasurer
Barbara Hauptman, Executive Director
Gretchen M Michelfeld, Membership Coordinator

An independent labor union representing directors and choreographers in American theatre.
1700 Members
Founded in 1959
Mailing list available for rent

19225 Southern Arts Federation
1800 Peachtree St NW
Suite 808
Atlanta, GA 30309-2512

404-874-7244
Fax: 404-873-2148
Home Page: www.southarts.org

Susie Surkamer, Executive Director
Stephanie Conner, Secretary
Ken May, Treasurer
David Batley, Marketing/Communications Director

In partnership with nine state arts agencies: promotes and supports arts regionally, nationally and internationally; enhances the artistic excellence and professionalism of Southern Arts Organizations and artists; serves the diverse population of the south.
Founded in 1975

19226 Stage Directors and Choreographers Foundation
1501 Broadway
Suite 1701
New York, NY 10036

212-391-1070
Fax: 646-524-2226
E-Mail: Foundation@SDCweb.org
Home Page: www.sdcfoundation.org

Susan H Schulman, President
John Rando, Executive Vice President
Leigh Silverman, Vice President
Oz Scott, Secretary
Ethan McSweeny, Treasurer
Founded in 1965

19227 The Actors' Fund
729 Seventh Avenue, 10th floor
New York, NY 10019

212-221-7300
Home Page: www.actorsfund.org
Social Media: Facebook, Twitter, LinkedIn, YouTube

Brian Stokes Mitchell, Chairmen
Philip S. Birsh, Vice Chair
Marc Grodman, Secretary
Abby Schroeder, Assistant Secretary
Steve Kalafer, Treasurer
Founded in 1882

19228 The United States Disc Jockey Association
Post Office Box 43252
Nottingham, ML 21236

443-903-2013
E-Mail: support@usdja.com
Home Page: www.usdja.com
Social Media: Facebook, Twitter, Vimeo

Jason Walsh, President

19229 Theatre Authority
165 West 46th Street
New York, NY 10036

212-869-8530
Fax: 212-719-9815
Home Page:
www.actorsequity.org/benefits/theatreauthority.asp

Presides over theatrical agencies and performing arts organizations.

19230 Theatre Bay Area
1663 Mission Street
Suite 525
San Francisco, CA 94103

415-430-1140
Fax: 415-430-1145
E-Mail: tba@theatrebayarea.org
Home Page: www.theatrebayarea.org
Social Media: Facebook, Twitter, YouTube

Karen Mc Kevitt, Executive Director
Dale Albright, Director, Member Services
Clayton Lord, Director, Audience Development

Theatre Bay Area's mission is to unite, strengthen and promote the theatre community in the San Francisco Bay Area, working on behalf of their conviction that the performing arts are an essential public good, critical to a healthy and truly democratic society, and in-

valuable as a source of personal enrichment and growth.
3,000 Members
Founded in 1976

19231 Theatre Communications Group
520 8th Ave
24th Floor
New York, NY 10018-8666

212-609-5900
Fax: 212-609-5901
E-Mail: tcg@tcg.org
Home Page: www.tcg.org
Social Media: Facebook, Twitter

Theresa Eyring, Executive Director
Jennifer Cleary, Director of Membership

The mission of the TCG is to strengthen, nurture and promote the professional not-for-profit American theatre. TCG believes that their diversity as a field is their greatest strength. They celebrate differences in aesthetic, culture, organizational structure, and geography. They believe that every theatre makes a contribution to the greater field as a whole, that every performance expands the artistic vocabulary for us all, and that we all benefit from one another's presence.
Cost: $39.95
14000 Members
Frequency: Monthly
Founded in 1961

19232 Theatre Development Fund
520 Eight Avenue
Suite 801
New York, NY 10018-6507

212-912-9770
E-Mail: info@tdf.org
Home Page: www.tdf.org
Social Media: Facebook, RSS

Earl D. Weiner, Chairman
Sandra Kresch, Vice Chairman
Robert T. Goldm Treasurer, Deborah Hartnett Secretary

Not-for-profit service organization for the performing arts. TDF administers a wide range of audience development and financial assistance programs that encourage production of new plays and musicals and enable more New Yorkers and visitors to enjoy the riches and variety of the city's theatre, dance and music.
Cost: $25.00
Founded in 1968

19233 US Institute for Theatre Technology
315 S Crouse Ave
Suite 200
Syracuse, NY 13210-1835

315-463-6463
800-938-7488
Fax: 315-463-6525
E-Mail: info@.usitt.org
Home Page: www.usitt.org
Social Media: Facebook, LinkedIn

Carol Carrigan, Manager
Patricia Dennis, Secretary
Travis DeCastro, Treasurer

Association of design, production and technology professionals in the performing arts and entertainment industry whose mission is to promote the knowledge and skills of its members. International in scope, USITT draws its board of directors from across the US and Canada. Sponsors projects, programs, research, symposia, exhibits and annual conference. Disseminates information on aesthetic and technical developments.
3700 Members
Founded in 1960

19234 USA Dance Inc
PO Box 152988
Cape Coral, FL 33915-2988

800-447-9047
Fax: 239-573-0946
E-Mail: central-office@usadance.org
Home Page: usadance.org
Social Media: Facebook, Twitter, LinkedIn

Lydia Scardina, National President
Bill Rose, Sr.Vice President
Greg Warner, National Secretary
Esther Freeman, National Treasurer
Ken Richards, VP, Dance Sports

Nonprofit organization working to promote ballroom dancing, both as a recreational activity and as a competitive sport, and to educate the public about the mental, physical and social benefits of dance.
23000 Members
Founded in 1965

19235 United Square Dancers of America
E-Mail: usda@usda.org
Home Page: www.usda.org
Social Media: Facebook

Mike Matsko, President
L Paul Schmidt, Vice President
Jim Maczko, Past President
Milene McCall, Secretary
Jim Taylor, Treasurer
Founded in 1981

19236 United States Institute for Theatre Technology
315 South Crouse Avenue
Suite 200
Syracuse, NY 13210

315-463-6463
Fax: 800-938-7488
E-Mail: info@usitt.org
Home Page: www.usitt.org
Social Media: Facebook, Twitter, LinkedIn

Lea Asbell Swanger, President
Carolyn Satter, Vice President
David Grindle, Executive Director
Jimmie Byrd, Secretary
Dan Culhane, Treasurer
Founded in 1960

19237 Voice and Speech Trainers Association
773-888-2782
E-Mail: president@vasta.org
Home Page: www.vasta.org

Lynn Watson, President
Betty Moulton, President Elect
Mandy Rees, Past President
Melanie Julian, Secretary
Artemis Preeshl, Treasurer
Founded in 2005

19238 Women in the Arts Foundation
C/O E Butler
PO Box 1258
New York, NY 10276

212-941-0130
E-Mail: reginas@anny.org
Home Page:
www.anny.org/2/orgs/womeninarts/

Regina Stewart, Executive Director
Eric Butler, Executive Coordinator
Linda Butti, Executive Coordinator
Sari Menna, Financial Coordinator

WIA works to overcome discrimination against women artists. They provide information to help women function effectively as professional artists. WIA is open to all women interested in the arts.
150 Members
Founded in 1971

19239 Writers Guild of America
7000 West Third Street
Los Angeles, CA 90048

323-951-4000
Fax: 323-782-4800
Home Page: www.wga.org
Social Media: Facebook, Twitter, YouTube

Chris Keyser, President
Howard A. Rodman, Vice President
Carl Gottlieb, Secretary/ Treasurer
Billy Ray, Board of Directors
Shawn Ryan, Board of Directors
Founded in 1921

Newsletters

19240 American Dance
240 West 14th Street
New York, NY 10011

212-932-2789
E-Mail: info@americandanceguild.org
Home Page: www.americandanceguild.org
Social Media: Facebook

Gloria McLean, President
Tina Croll, VP

Contains articles on member news, dance, and education.
Frequency: 4 per year
Founded in 1956

19241 Artsearch
Theatre Communications Group
520 8th Ave
Suite 305
New York, NY 10018-4156

212-609-5900
Fax: 212-609-5901
E-Mail: tcg@tcg.org
Home Page: www.tcg.org

Theresa Eyring, Executive Director

Artsearch is divided into five main categories: Administration, Artistic, Production/Design, Career Development, and Education.
Cost: $75.00
Frequency: Bi-Monthly
ISSN: 0730-9023
Founded in 1961
Printed in on newsprint stock

19242 Broadside
Theatre Library Association
New York Public Library for Performing Arts
40 Lincoln Center Plaza
New York, NY 10023
E-Mail: info@tla-online.org
Home Page:
www.tla-online.org/publications/broadside.htm
l

Nancy Friedland, President
Angela Weaver, VP
Rebecca Lord, Executive Secretary
Collen Reilly, Treasurer

Features articles and news items related to exhibitions and collections, information about TLA-sponsored events, book reviews, and other items of interest in the fields of theatre, film, and dance.
ISSN: 0068-2748
Founded in 1937

19243 Country Dance and Song Society News
Country Dance and Song Society

116 Pleasant St
Suite 345
Easthampton, MA 01027-2759

413-203-5467
Fax: 413-203-5471
E-Mail: news@cdss.org
Home Page: www.cdss.org

Caroline Batson, Editor
Rima Dael, Executive Director
Bob Blondin, Business Manager

A selection of articles, letters and poems. CDSS News is available as a benefit of membership in the Country Dance and Song Society.
ISSN: 1070-8251
Founded in 1915

19244 **DNBulletin**
151 W 30th Street
Suite 202
New York, NY 10001

212-564-0985
Fax: 212-216-9027
E-Mail: dnbinfo@dancenotation.org
Home Page: www.dancenotation.org

Senta Driver, Editor

Dance news for consumers and professionals.
Founded in 1940
Printed in 2 colors on matte stock

19245 **Dancedrill**
3101 Poplarwood Court
Suite 310
Raleigh, NC 27604-1010

919-872-7888
Fax: 919-872-6888

Susan Wershing, Publisher
Kay Crawford, Editor

Publication informs members of dance drill teams and their directors.
Frequency: 4 per year

19246 **Dramatists Guild Newsletter**
Dramatists Guild of America
1501 Broadway
Suite 701
New York, NY 10036-5505

212-398-9366
Fax: 212-944-0420
Home Page: www.dramaguild.com

Ralph Sevush, Executive Director

Supplement to 'The Dramatist,' available only to Guild members, includes bi-monthly reports from New York and Los Angeles, advice from the Business Affairs Department, the latest information on submission and career development opportunities, and reminders of approaching deadlines.

19247 **INTIX Bulletin**
International Ticketing Association
One College Park, 8910 Purdue Road
Suite 480
Indianapolis, IN 46268

212-629-4036
Fax: 212-628-8532
E-Mail: info@intix.org
Home Page: www.intix.org

Jena L Hoffman, President
Kathleen O'Donnell, Director

E-bulletin provides news from the International Ticketing Association including information about upcoming events, conferences and exhibitions, industry news.
1200 Members
Frequency: Monthly
ISSN: 1071-6254
Founded in 1979
Printed in 4 colors on glossy stock

19248 **In Focus**
National Association of Theatre Owners
13190 SW 68th Parkway
Suite 200
Portland, OR 97223-8368

503-207-4700
877-388-8385
Fax: 503-207-1937
Home Page: http://www.infocus.com

19249 **In Theater**
Parker Publishing & Communications
214 Sullivan St
Suite 2C
New York, NY 10012-1354

212-228-1225
Fax: 212-719-4477
E-Mail: intheater@aol.com
Home Page: www.parkerhodges.com

Emily Parker, President

Offers the reader a behind-the-scenes perspective of how a show is technically conceived, rehearsed and staged. Regular departments center on drama and musical reviews, listings of shows in major cities and columnist options.
Cost: $78.00
Frequency: Weekly
Circulation: 71,068

19250 **InLEAGUE**
League of Historic American Theatres
2105 Laurel Bush Rd
Suite 201
Bel Air, MD 21015

443-640-1058
877-627-0833
Fax: 443-640-1031
E-Mail: info@lhat.org
Home Page: www.lhat.org

Frances Holden, Executive Director
John Bell, VP
Darlene Smolik, Treasurer
Edward Kelsey, Secretary

Quarterly newsletter which reports news from historic theatre progects around the country and features articles on all facets of historic theatre restoration and operation. The newsletter solicits articles and information from the membership.
Frequency: Quarterly
Founded in 1976

19251 **Job Contact Bulletin**
Southeastern Theatre Conference
1175 Revolution Mill Dr.
Studio 14
Greensboro, NC 27405

336-272-3645
Fax: 336-272-8810
E-Mail: arpil@setc.org
Home Page: www.setc.org

April J'C Marshall, Contact
Jack Benjamin, President
H. Duke Guthrie, Treasurer

On-line employment listing of Classified Ads for theatrical positions, auditions, and more.
Founded in 1949

19252 **Performing Arts Insider**
PAI C/O Total Theater
PO Box 31
Greeley, CO 80632

970-405-3077
E-Mail: totalpost@totaltheater.com
Home Page: performingartsinsider.com

A leading source of information about the perfoming arts in New York City and around the country. Each issue includes day-by-day calendar listings of shows on broadway, off and off-off broadway, plus dance, opera, cabaret and special events. Also includes comprehensive theatre guides, listing the author, director, cast, designers, synopsis, theater and box office details, as well as contact information for producers, press agents, general managers and casting directors.
Cost: $275.00
Frequency: Monthly+9 Mid-Month Updat
Founded in 1944
Printed in on matte stock

19253 **SETC News**
Southeastern Theatre Conference
1175 Revolution Mill Dr.
Studio 14
Greensboro, NC 27405

336-272-3645
Fax: 336-272-8810
E-Mail: deanna@setc.org.net
Home Page: www.setc.org

Deanna Thompson, Editor
Jack Benjamin, President
H. Duke Guthrie, Treasurer

Provides news and important information to members of the Southeaster Theatre Conference on upcoming SETC events, advocacy efforts, awards and competitions as well as items of special interest to the various divisions and interest areas. In addition, SETC News publishes news about people and organizations based in the Southeast.
Circulation: 4000
Founded in 1949

19254 **Spotlight**
American Association of Community Theatre
1300 Gendy St Forth Worth
Forth Worth, TX 76107

817-732-3177
866-687-2228
Fax: 817-732-3178
E-Mail: info@aact.org
Home Page: www.aact.org
Social Media: Facebook, Twitter

Julie Angelo, Executive Director
John Sullivan, President

News and updates on issues pertinent to community theatre.
Cost: $2.00
24 Pages
Circulation: 2000
Founded in 1958
Mailing list available for rent: 9,500 names at $180 per M
Printed in on matte stock

19255 **Technical Brief**
Yale School of Drama
222 York Street
PO Box 208244
New Haven, CT 06520

203-432-8188
Fax: 203-432-8129
E-Mail: bronislaw.sammler@yale.edu
Home Page: www.technicalbrief.org

Ben Sammler, Editor
Dan Harvey, Editor

Produced for technical managers in theater. Written by professionals for professionals, its purpose is simple: communication. Technical Brief provides a dailogue between technical practitioners from the several performing arts who all share similar problems.
Cost: $15.00
Frequency: 3 X Year
Founded in 1924

19256 **Women in the Arts Bulletin**
Women in the Arts Foundation

32-35 30th Street
D24
Long Island City, NY 11106

212-941-0130
E-Mail: reginas@anny.org
Home Page:
www.womenintheartsfoundation.org

Erin Butler, Editor
Regina Stewart, Executir Director
Sandra Cockerham, President

Gallery information and reviews. Women in the Arts Foundation works to overcome discrimination against women artists.
Frequency: Monthly
Founded in 1971

Magazines & Journals

19257 American Dancer
USA Dance
PO Box 152988
Cape Coral, FL 33915-2988

800-447-9047
Fax: 239-573-0946
Home Page: www.usadance.org

Shawn Fisher, Editor

News of interests to dance enthusiasts.
Cost: $25.00
Frequency: Bi-Monthly
Circulation: 23000

19258 American Theatre Magazine
Theatre Communications Group
520 8th Ave
Suite 305
New York, NY 10018-8666

212-609-5900
Fax: 212-609-5901
E-Mail: custserve@tcg.org
Home Page: www.tcg.org

Jim O'Quinn, Editor in Chief
Nicole Estvanik Taylor, Managing Editor
Cost: $35.00

19259 Applause Magazine
Denver Center for Performing Arts
1101 13th St
Denver, CO 80204-5319

303-893-3272
800-641-1222
Fax: 303-893-3206
Home Page: www.denvercenter.org

Randy Weeks, President
Daniel L. Ritchie, Chairman &CEO

A publication of the Denver Center Theatre Company and Dever Center Attractions
Frequency: 8-10 per year
Founded in 1988
Printed in 4 colors on glossy stock

19260 Asian Pacific American Journal
Asian American Writers Workshop
16 W 32nd St
Suite 10A
New York, NY 10001-1093

212-494-0061
Fax: 212-494-0062
E-Mail: desk@aaww.org
Home Page: www.aaww.org

Ken Chen, Executive Director
Jeannie L Wong, Administrative Director
Anjali Goyal, Programs Assistant
Jeffrey Lin, Designer
Hanya Yanagihara, Journal Editor

Features include short fiction, poems, essays, stage scripts, translations and artwork.
Frequency: Semi-Annual
ISSN: 1067-778X
Founded in 1992

19261 Back Stage
770 Broadway 7th Floor
New York, NY 10003

212-493-4420
800-658-8372
E-Mail: advertising@backstage.com
Home Page: www.backstage.com

Charles Weiss, Manager
Jamie Painter Young, Editor-in-Chief
Jenelle Riley, Film/TV Editor
Leonard Jacobs, Theatre Editor
Sherry Eaker, Editor-at-Large

Four print, four interactive and two face-to-face publications. Provides casting, news, articles and other resources for working actors, cingers, dancers and behind-the-scenes staff and crew.
Cost: $84.00
Circulation: 30,000
Founded in 1960
Mailing list available for rent

19262 Bomb Magazine
New Art Publications
80 Hanson Pl
Suite 703
Brooklyn, NY 11217-1506

718-636-9100
866-354-0334
Fax: 718-636-9200
E-Mail: info@bombsite.com
Home Page: www.bombsite.com
Social Media: Facebook, Twitter, YouTube

Betsy Sussler, Publisher/Editor
Mary-Ann Monforton, Associate Publisher
Nell McClister, Senior Editor
Lucy Raven, Managing Editor
Paul W Morris, Director Marketing/Special Projects

Focuses on contemporary art, literature, theater, film, music.
Cost: $495.00
Frequency: Quarterly
Circulation: 60,000
Founded in 1981
Mailing list available for rent
Printed in 4 colors on matte stock

19263 BoxOffice Magazine
BoxOffice Media
9107 Wilshire Blvd.
Suite 450
Beverly Hills, CA 90210-4241

310-876-9090
Home Page: www.boxoffice.com

Peter Crane, Publisher
Kenneth James Bacon, Creative Director
Phil Contrino, Editor
Amy Nicholson, Editor

The premier trade magazine covering the latest developments in the movie industry, from films in production to digital cinema and everything in between.
Founded in 1948

19264 Callaloo
Johns Hopkins University Press
2715 N Charles St
Baltimore, MD 21218-4363

410-516-6900
800-537-5487
Fax: 410-516-6998
Home Page:
www.press.jhu.edu/journals/callaloo

William Brody, President
Kyle G Dargan, Managing Editor

Journal of African and African-American issues. Content includes original works by, and critical studies of, black writers worldwide. Offers a rich mixture of fiction, poetry, plays, critical essays, cultural studies, interviews, and visual art, as well as special thematic issues.
Frequency: Quarterly
Circulation: 2,500
ISSN: 0161-2492
Founded in 1976

19265 Canadian Theatre Review
University of Toronto Press
5201 Dufferin Street
Toronto, ON M3H-5T8

416-667-7810
800-221-9985
Fax: 416-667-7881
E-Mail: journals@utpress.utoronto.ca
Home Page: www.utpjournals.com
Social Media: Facebook, Twitter, Blog

Anne Marie Corrigan, VP
Audrey Greenwood, Advertising/Marketing Coordinator

Provides critical analysis and innovative coverage of current developments in Canadian theatre. Advocates new issues and artists. Publishes at least one significant new playscript per issue. Each issue includes at least one complete playscript related to the issue theme, insightful articles, and informative reviews.
Cost: $40.00
Frequency: Quarterly
ISSN: 0315-0836
Founded in 1974
Mailing list available for rentat $250 per M

19266 Confrontation
CW Post Campus English Department
720 Northern Blvd
Greenvale, NY 11548-1300

516-626-0099
Fax: 516-299-3566
E-Mail: confrontation@liu.edu
Home Page: www.liunet.bkstore.com

Jayne Mo, Manager

Brings new talent to light in the shadows cast by well-known authors. Each issue contains orignal work by famous and by lesser known writers.
Cost: $10.00
Frequency: Twice Yearly
Founded in 1968

19267 Contact Quarterly Journal of Dance and Improvisation
Contact Collaborations
PO Box 603
Northampton, MA 01061

413-586-1181
Fax: 413-586-9055
E-Mail: info@contactquarterly.com
Home Page: www.contactquarterly.com

Lisa Nelson, Co-Editor
Nancy Stark Smith, Co-Editor
Melinda Buckwalter, Associate Editor
Kristin Horrigan, Operations Manager/Advertising
Bill McCully, Development/Marketing

A journal of dance, improvisation, performance and contemporary movement arts. Presents materials that spring from the experience of doing. Encourages articulation and dialogue and stimulates activity and exploration within the

field of movement and its performance.
Cost: $22.00
Frequency: BiAnnual
Founded in 1978

19268 Cue Magazine
PO Box 2027
Burlingame, CA 94011-2027
415-348-8004
Fax: 650-348-7781
Home Page: www.cuemagazines.com
Devoted to the Northern California, Seattle and Portland commercial film, video and multimedia industries and locations that support production.
Frequency: Monthly

19269 Dance Chronicle
Taylor & Francis Group
270 Madison Ave
Floor 4
New York, NY 10016-0601
212-679-3853
Fax: 212-564-7854
Home Page: www.summitcom.com
George Dorris, Co-Editor
Jack Anderson, Co-Editor
Edwin Bayrn, Associate Editor
Covers a wide variety of topics, including dance and music, theater, film, literature, painting and aesthetics.
Cost: $465.00
Frequency: TriAnnual
ISSN: 0147-2526

19270 Dance Magazine
Macfadden Performing Arts Media
333 7th Avenue
11th Floor
New York, NY 10001
212-979-4800
Home Page: www.dancemagazine.com
Amy Cogan, VP/Group Publisher
Karen Hildebrand, VP Editorial
Jessi Petrov, Publishing/Marketing Director
Wendy Perron, Editor-in-Chief
The must read magazine for professional and aspiring dancers. From Broadway to ballet and tap to hip hop, not other magazine keeps you in touch with what is going on in all disciplines of dance.
Cost: $34.95
Frequency: Monthly
Circulation: 300,000
ISSN: 0011-6009
Founded in 1927
Printed in 4 colors on glossy stock

19271 Dance Research Journal
Congress on Research in dance
3416 Primm Lane
Birmingham, AL 24702-6170
205-823-5517
Fax: 205-823-2760
E-Mail: ashanti@cordance.org
Home Page: www.cordance.org
Ann Dils, Co-Editor
Jill Green, Co-Editor
Published twice a year by the Congress on Research in Dance, this journal carries scholarly articles, book reviews, lists of books and journals received, and reports of scholarly conferences, archives and other projects of interest to the field.
Cost: $65.00
Frequency: Bi-annually
ISSN: 0149-7677
Founded in 1965
Mailing list available for rent: 750+ names at $75 per M

19272 Dance Spirit
Macfadden Performing Arts Media, LLC
333 7th Avenue
11th Floor
New York, NY 10001
212-979-4800
Home Page: www.dancespirit.com
Amy Cogan, VP/Group Publisher
Karen Hildebrand, VP Editorial
Jessi Petrov, Publishing/Marekting Director
Kayte Lydon, Editor-in-Chief
Dedicated to inspiring the next generation of dancers. Packed with expert advice on dance techniques and performing, health and nutrition tips and the latest styles to keep you looking your best from studio to stage to school.
Cost: $16.95
Frequency: 10 Per Year
Founded in 1980

19273 Dance Teacher Magazine
Macfadden Performing Arts Media
333 7th Avenue
11th Floor
New York, NY 10001
212-979-4800
Fax: 646-459-4900
Home Page: www.dance-teacher.com
Amy Cogan, VP/Group Publisher
Karen Hildebrand, VP Editorial/Editor-in-Chief
Jessie Petrov, Publishing/Marketing Director
The only magazine written just for dance professionals. Packed with useful ideas that will help you and your students become better dancers.
Cost: $24.95
Frequency: Monthly
Circulation: 60000
Founded in 1979
Printed in 4 colors

19274 Dance on Camera Journal
Dance Films Association
48 W 21st St
Suite 907
New York, NY 10010-6989
212-727-0764
Fax: 212-727-0764
E-Mail: info@dancefilms.org
Home Page: www.dancefilms.org
Social Media: Facebook, Twitter
Deidra Towers, Executive Director
Marta Renzi, President
Harry Streep, VP
Amy Meharg, Treasurer
Nolini Barretto, Secretary
Subjects range from reviews and essays, news items regarding dance films, festivals, opportunites, and issues facing artists
Frequency: Bi-Monthly
Founded in 1956

19275 Dance/USA Journal
Dance/USA
1111 16th St Nw
Suite 300
Washington, DC 20036-4830
202-833-1717
Fax: 202-833-2686
E-Mail: danceusa@danceusa.org
Home Page: www.danceusa.org
Andrea Snyder, Executive Director
Tom Thielen, Director Finance/Operations
Katherine Fabian, Membership Manager
The journal features articles on issues of importance to the dance community; news stories relating to arts and dance; essays from leaders in the dance field; notes on changes, transitions and opportunties in the field; calendar of up coming events; and highlights of Dance/USA sponsored events. Subscription is free to members of Dance/USA.
Cost: $40.00
28-36 Pages
Frequency: Quarterly
Founded in 1982
Printed in 2 colors on glossy stock

19276 Descant
50 Baldwin Street
PO Box 314 Station P
Toronto, ON M5S-2S8
416-593-2557
Fax: 416-593-9362
E-Mail: info@descant.ca
Home Page: www.descant.on.ca
Social Media: Facebook
Karen Mulhallen, Editor-in-Chief
Vera DeWaard, Managing Editor
Mary Newberry, Project Manager
Stacey May Fowles, Circulation Manager
Pasha Malla, Director of Outreach
A quarterly journal publishing new and established contemporary writers and visual artists from Canada and around the world. Devoted to the discovery and development of new writers, and places their work in the company of celebrated writers.
Cost: $28.00
Frequency: Quarterly
Circulation: 1200
ISSN: 0382-909X
Founded in 1970
Mailing list available for rent

19277 Drama Review
MIT Press
55 Hayward Street
Cambridge, MA 02142-1493
617-253-5646
800-207-8354
Fax: 617-258-6779
E-Mail: journals-info@mit.edu
Home Page: www.mitpress.mit.edu
Social Media: Facebook, Twitter, RSS
Rebbecca Mc Leod, Owner
TDR focuses on performances in their social, economic, and political contexts. It emphasizes experimental, avant-garde, intercultural and interdisciplinary performance. TDR covers dance, theatre, performance art, visual art, popular entertainment, media, sports, rituals, and performance in politics and everyday life.
Frequency: Quarterly
Founded in 1955

19278 Dramatics Magazine
Educational Theatre Association
2343 Auburn Ave
Cincinnati, OH 45219-2819
513-421-3900
Fax: 513-421-7077
E-Mail: jpalmarini@schooltheatre.org
Home Page: schooltheatre.org
Social Media: Facebook, Twitter
Donald A Corathers, Publications Director
James Palmarini, Editor
Dramatics is the only magazine that is edited exclusively for students and teachers of theatre. Contents include practical articles about acting, directing, playwriting, design, and technical theatre; interviews with working professionals that illuminate the process of becoming a theatre artist; options for higher education and training in theatre; playscripts; reports on new shows and other important events in the theatre world; book, video, and CD-ROM reviews, and more.
Cost: $27.00
4000 Members
Frequency: 9x/ A Year
Circulation: 34100

ISSN: 0012-5989
Founded in 1929

19279 Encore Performance Publishing
PO Box 95567
South Jordan, UT 84095-0567

801-282-8159
E-Mail: encoreplay@aol.com
Home Page: www.encoreplay.com

Michael C Perry, President

Publishes a variety of publications for those professionals in the performing arts industry.

19280 Gospel Today
Gospel Today
PO Box 800
Fairburn, GA 30213

770-719-4825
Fax: 770-716-2660
E-Mail: admin@gospeltoday.com
Home Page: www.gospeltoday.com

Dr Teresa Hairston, Publisher

To provide a quality publication to inspire, educate, inform, and empower readers towards standards of Godly excellence.
Cost: $17.97
Frequency: 8 Per Year
Circulation: 250000
Founded in 1989
Printed in 4 colors on glossy stock

19281 Hispanic Arts News
Association of Hispanic Arts
1025 Connecticut Ave
Suite 1000
Washington, DC 20036

202-657-5158
888-876-1240
Fax: 202-478-2767
E-Mail: informacion@latinoarts.org
Home Page: www.hispanics.einnews.com
Social Media: Facebook, Twitter

Features in depth articles on the local and national arts community, including artist profiles and a calendar of events.
Frequency: 9 Per Year
Mailing list available for rent: 5000 names at $80 per M

19282 JazzTimes
JazzTimes Magazine
Madavor Media,85 Quincy Ave
Suite 2
Quincy, MA 02169

617-706-9110
800-437-5828
Fax: 617-536-0102
Home Page: www.jazztimes.com

Glen Sabin, CEO
Eric Wynne, Consumer Advertising Director

JazzTimes contains extensive news coverage, award winning jazz journalism, hundreds of CD, Book and Video reviews, World class photography and award winning graphics, informative features and columns, special theme issues, special directories, readers poll and critic pics, and sound$weeps giveaways and prizes.
Cost: $23.95
Frequency: 10 Issues per y
Circulation: 86000
Founded in 1980

19283 Journal of Arts Management, Law, Society
Heldref Publishers
325 Chestnut Street
Suite 800
Philadelphia, PA 19106

215-625-8900
800-354-1420
Fax: 202-296-5149
E-Mail:
customer.service@taylorandfrancis.com
Home Page: www.heldref.org

James Denton, Executive Director

A resource for arts policymakers and analysts, sociologists, arts and cultural administrators, educators, trusteed, artists, lawyers, and citizens concerned with the performing, visual, and media arts as well as cultural affairs. Articles, commentaries, and reviews of publications address marketing, intellectual property, arts policy, arts law, governance, and cultural production and dissemination, from a variety of philosophical, disciplinary, and national and international perspectives.
Cost: $79.00
Frequency: Monthly
ISSN: 1063-2921
Founded in 1956

19284 Journal of Dance Education
National Dance Education Organization
8609 2nd Avenue
Suite 203 B
Silver Spring, MD 20910

301-585-2880
Fax: 301 585 2888
E-Mail: info@ndeo.org
Home Page: www.ndeo.org
Social Media: Facebook, Twitter

Susan McGreevy-Nichols, Executive Director
Jane Bonbright EdD, Executive Director
Patricia Cohen, Treasurer
Cost: $90.00
Frequency: Quarterly
Circulation: 2000
ISSN: 1529-0824

19285 Lighting Dimensions
Primedia Business
249 W 17th St
New York, NY 10011-5382

212-206-1894
800-827-3322
Fax: 212-514-3719
Home Page: lightingdimensions.com

Doug MacDonald, Group Publisher
David Johnson, Associate Publisher/Editorial
Marian Sandberg-Dierson, Editor
Mark Newman, Managing Editor
Jennifer Hirst, Director

Trade publication for lighting professionals in film, theatre, television, concerts, clubs, themed environments, architecctural, commercial, and industrial lighting. Sponsors of the LDI Trade Show and the Broadway Lighting Master Classes.
Cost: $34.97
Frequency: 12/year
Circulation: 14,177
Founded in 1989

19286 Mid-Atlantic Events Magazine
1800 Byberry Road
Suite 901
Huntingdon Valley, PA 19006

215-947-8600
800-521-8588
Fax: 215-947-8650
E-Mail: editor@eventsmagazine.com
Home Page: www.eventsmagazine.com
Social Media: Facebook, Twitter, YouTube

Jim Cohn, Publisher
Rich Kupka, Editor
Fred Cohn, VP Sales
Katie O'Connell, Director Sales/Marketing
Dana Kurtbek, Production

Focused on Hospitality in the Mid-Atlantic area. It assists the Associations, Corporations, Government, Group and Independent Meeting, Event and Travel Planners who are responsible for arranging Conventions, Trade Shows, Hotel Accommodations, Corporate/Group Travel, Meetings, Seminars, Conferences, Symposiums, Site Selections, Special Events, Banquets, Entertainment, Corporate Golf Outings and Golf Tournaments, Company Picnics, Team Building, Retreats, Board Meetings, Training & Development.
Circulation: 26000
ISSN: 0896-3967
Founded in 1987
Mailing list available for rent
Printed in 8 colors on glossy stock

19287 National Squares
National Square Dance Convention
C/O Gene and Connie Triplett
2760 Polo Club Boulevard
Matthews, NC 28105

704-847-1265
E-Mail: Richp27890@aol.com
Home Page:
www.nationalsquaredanceconvention.com

Dick/Linda Peterson, Editors
Gene/Connie Triplett, Circulation Managers
Dick/Linda Peterson, Public Relations

A national square dance magazine published by the National Executive Committee of the National Square Dance Convention.
Cost: $7.00
Frequency: Quarterly

19288 New England Theatre Journal
New England Theatre Conference
215 Knob Hill Drive
Hamden, CT 06518

617-851-8535
Fax: 203-288-5938
E-Mail: mail@netconline.org
Home Page: www.netconline.org

Sabine Klein, President
Jeffrey Watts, Executive VP
Charles Emmons, VP Administration/Finance

Scholarly publication produced once per year. Includes book and theatre reviews, historical analyses, and other well-written articles by noted authors. Free to NETC members. Specifically designed to provide members, and others interested in live theatre arts, with the information and resources they need to enhance their careers, promote their groups, and sharpen their theatre skills.
Cost: $10.00
Frequency: Annual
Founded in 1952

19289 Nouveau Magazine
Barbara Tompkins
5933 Stoney Hill Rd
New Hope, PA 18938-9602

215-794-5996
Fax: 215-794-8305
E-Mail: info@nouveaumagazine.com
Home Page: www.nouveaumagazine.com

Barbara Tompkins, Publisher

Features theater reviews.
Frequency: Monthly
Founded in 1981
Printed in 4 colors on glossy stock

19290 OffBeat
OffBeat
421 Frenchmen St
Suite 200
New Orleans, LA 70116-2039

504-944-4300
877-944-4300
Fax: 504-944-4306
E-Mail: offbeat@offbeat.com

Home Page: www.offbeat.com
Social Media: Facebook, Twitter, Flickr

Jan Ramsy, Publisher
Joseph L Irrera, Managing Editor
Bunny Matthews, Senior Editor
Michael Jastroch, Magazine Design/Production
Doug Jackson, Distribution Manager

Consumer-oriented music magazine focusing on New Orleans and Louisiana music. Regular columns on Cajun music, zydeco, traditional and contemporary jazz, brass band (Mardi Gras second-line music), New Orleans R & B, Louisiana and delta blues, Gospel, modern and roots rock and our internationally-appreciated culture and cusine. Information on music fairs and festivals in the region is given.
Cost: $29.00
Frequency: Monthly
Circulation: 50000
ISBN: 1-090081-0 -
Founded in 1985
Mailing list available for rent: 15000 names
Printed in 4 colors on newsprint stock

19291 Performing Arts Insider Magazine
PAI C/O Total Theater
PO Box 31
Greeley, CO 80632

970-405-3077
E-Mail: paipress@aol.com
Home Page: www.performingartsinsider.com

David Lefkowitz, Publisher/Editor
Richmond Shepard, Publisher
J. Weil, Advertising Sales

Includes day-by-day calendar listings of shows on Broadway, Off and Off-Off Broadway, plus dance, opera, cabaret and special events. Also included are comprehensive theater guides, listing the author, director, cast, designers, synopsis, theater and box office details, as well as contact information for producers, press agents, general managers and casting directors.
Cost: $275.00
Frequency: Monthly+9 Updates
Circulation: 2000
Founded in 1944

19292 Performing Arts Resources
Theatre Library Association
New York Public Library for Performing Arts
40 Lincoln Center Plaza
New York, NY 10023

E-Mail: info@tla-online.org
Home Page:
www.tla-online.org/publications/par.html

Nancy Friedland, President
Angela Weaver, VP
Rebecca Lord, Executive Secretary
Colleen Reilly, Treasurer

Features articles on resource materials in the fields of theatre, popular entertainment, film, television and radio, information on public and private collections, and essays on conservation and collection management of theatre arts materials.
Cost: $30.00
Frequency: Irregular
Circulation: 500
ISSN: 0360-3814
Founded in 1974

19293 Playbill
34-15 61st Street
Woodside, NY 11377

212-557-5757
Fax: 212-682-2932
E-Mail: agans@playbill.com
Home Page: www.playbill.com

Andrew Gans, Editor

The exclusive magazine for Broadway and Off-Broadway theatregoers, providing the information necessary for the understanding and enjoyment of each show, including features articles and columns by and about theatre personalities, entertainment, travel, fashion, dining and other editorial pieces geared to the lifestyle of the upscale, active theatre attendee. Playbill also serves New York's three most prominent performing arts venues - the Metropolitan Opera House, Lincoln Center and Carnegie Hall
Cost: $24.00
Frequency: Monthly
Founded in 1884

19294 Plays: Drama Magazine for Young People
Plays Magazine
PO Box 600160
Newton, MA 02460

617-630-9100
800-630-5755
Fax: 617-630-9101
E-Mail: lpreston@playsmag.com
Home Page: www.playsmag.com

Elizabeth Preston, Editor

Includes eight to ten royalty-free one-act plays, arranged by age level. Modern and traditional plays for the celebration of all important holidays and occasions. Adaptable to all cast sizes with easy to follow instructions for settings and costumes. A complete source of original plays and programs for school-age actors and audiences.
Cost: $39.00
Frequency: 7 X Per Year
Circulation: 6000
Founded in 1940
Printed in on matte stock

19295 Pointe Magazine
Macfadden Performing Arts Media LLC
333 7th Avenue
11th Floor
New York, NY 10001

212-979-4800
Home Page: www.pointemagazine.com

Amy Cogan, VP/Group Publisher
Karen Hildebrand, VP Editorial
Jessie Petrov, Publishing/Marketing Director

Dedicated exclusively to the world of ballet.
Frequency: Bi-Monthly
Circulation: 120000

19296 Pollstar: Concert Hotwire
Pollstar
4697 W Jacquelyn Ave
Fresno, CA 93722-6443

559-271-7900
Fax: 559-271-7979
E-Mail: info@pollstar.com
Home Page: www.pollstar.com

Gary Smith, COO
Shari Rice, VP
Gary Bongiovanni, CEO

Trade publication for the concert industry offering global coverage and information including concert tour schedules, ticket sales information and more.
Cost: $449.00
Frequency: Weekly
Circulation: 20000
Printed in 4 colors

19297 Shakespeare Bulletin
University of North Carolina
Department of English
9201 University City Boulevard
Charlotte, NC 28223

E-Mail: sbeditor@email.uncc.edu
Home Page: www.shakespeare-bulletin.org

Seymour Isenberg, Founding Editor
Andrew James Hartley, Editor
Jeremy Lopez, Theatre Review Editor
Genevieve Love, Book Review Editor
Kirk Melnikoff, Shakespeare on Film Editor

A peer-reviewed journal of performance and criticism and scholarship which provides commentary on Shakespeare and Renaissance drama through feature articles, thatre and film reviews, and book reviews. The journal is a member of the Conference of Editors of Learned Journals.
Cost: $35.00
Frequency: Quarterly
ISSN: 0748-2558
Founded in 1982
Mailing list available for rent
Printed in on matte stock

19298 Show Music
Po Box A
East Haddam, CT 06423-0466

860-873-8664
Fax: 860-873-2329
E-Mail: rklink@goodspeed.org
Home Page: www.showmusic.org

Ryan Klink, Managing Editor
Maz O Preeo, Editor-In-Chief

Internationally acclaimed by professionals and fans as the premier magazine covering musical theatre around the world. Show music combines insightful interviews and reviews of productions, recordings, videos and books.

19299 Sondheim Review
PO Box 11213
Chicago, IL 60611-0213

773-275-4254
800-584-1020
Fax: 773-275-4254
E-Mail: info@sondheimreview.com
Home Page: www.sondheimreview.com

Dedicated to the work of the musical theater and Broadway's foremost composer and lyricist, Stephen Sondheim. Each issue containes news, interviews, upcoming productions in the area, puzzles and more.
Cost: $19.95
Frequency: Quarterly
Circulation: 40000
ISSN: 1076-450X
Founded in 1994
Mailing list available for rent: 6,000 names at $105 per M
Printed in on glossy stock

19300 Southern Theatre
Southeastern Theatre Conference
1175 Revolution Mill Dr.
Studio 14
Greensboro, NC 27405

336-272-3645
Fax: 336-272-8810
E-Mail: setc@setc.org
Home Page: www.setc.org

Elizabeth Baun, Executive Director
April J'Callahan Marshall, Professional Theatre Services Mgr
Hardy Koenig, Educational Services Manager

Spotlights people, places and organizations within the region that are paving new paths in theatre. Includes low-cost strategies for design success, tips on hot markets for playwrights, new books of special interest, innovative ideas for marketing theatre, inside track on new trends and some of the region's up-and-coming theatre stars. Subscription is free with SETC membership.
Cost: $18.75
Frequency: Quarterly
Circulation: 4000+
Founded in 1949

19301 Spectrum
110 S Jefferson Street
Dayton, OH 45402-3412

937-220-1600
800-247-1614
Fax: 937-220-1642
E-Mail: comments@thinktv.org
Home Page: www.thinktv.org
Social Media: Facebook, Twitter, YouTube

Jerry Kathman, President&CEO
Brad Mays, Treasurer
Alisa Poe, Secretary

ThinkTV's monthly member magazine. Contains program listings for both ThinkTV 16 and ThinkTV14 as well as interesting feature stories, station news and more.
Frequency: Weekly
Circulation: 18000
Founded in 1959

19302 Stage of the Art
American Alliance for Theatre and Education
4908 Auburn Avenue
Bethesda, MD 20814-3474

301-200-1944
Fax: 301-280-1682
E-Mail: info@aate.com.edu
Home Page: www.aate.com
Social Media: Facebook, Twitter, RSS

David Young, Editor
JoBeth Gonzalez, Director Publications/Research

Published by the American Alliance for Theatre and Education.
Mailing list available for rent: 700 names at $150 per M

19303 Stagebill
Stagebill
144 E 44th Street
New York, NY 10017

212-476-0640
Fax: 212-983-5976
E-Mail: bmattison@stagebill.com
Home Page: www.avant-rus.com/stagebill

Fred B Tarter, Chairman/President/CEO
Gerry Byrne, Chairman/President/CEO
Ben Mattison, Editorial Contact

Publisher of the program magazines for the leading, theaters, symphonies, dance companies and performing arts centers in the United States. A national performing arts magazine.
Frequency: Monthly
Founded in 1924

19304 Stages
Curtains
301 W 45th Street
Apartment 5A
New York, NY 10036-3825

FAX 201-836-4107

Frank Scheck, Editor
Cost: $20.00
Frequency: Monthly
Circulation: 35,000

19305 TD & T: Theatre Design & Technology
US Institute for Theatre Technology
315 South Crouse Avenue
Suite 200
Syracuse, NY 13210

315-463-6525
Fax: 315-463-6525
E-Mail: info@.usitt.org
Home Page: www.usitt.org
Social Media: Facebook, Twitter

David Roger, Editor
Arnold Wengrow, Book Review Editor
Michelle Smith, Membership/Advertising Manager
N Deborah Hazlett, Art Director

Published by United States Institute for Theatre Technology. Focuses on USITT's ten interest areas: architecture, costume design and technology, education, engineering, health and safety, lighting, management, scene design, sound design, and technical production.
3700 Members
Frequency: Quarterly

19306 Teaching Theatre Journal
Educational Theatre Association
2343 Auburn Ave
Cincinnati, OH 45219-2819

513-421-3900
Fax: 513-421-7077
E-Mail: jpalmarini@schooltheatre.org
Home Page: schooltheatre.org
Social Media: Facebook, Twitter

Donald A Corathers, Publications Director
James Palmarini, Editor

For professional theatre educators. A typical issue includes an article on acting, directing, playwriting, or technical theatre; a profile of an outstanding educationl theatre program; a piece on curriculum design, assessment, or teaching methodology; and reports on current trends or issues in the field, such as funding, standards, or certification.
4000 Members
Frequency: Quarterly
Circulation: 4000
ISSN: 1077-2561
Founded in 1929

19307 Technical Brief
Yale School of Drama
222 York Street
PO Box 208244
New Haven, CT 06520

203-432-8188
Fax: 203-432-8129
E-Mail: bronislaw.sammler@yale.edu
Home Page: www.technicalbrief.org

Ben Sammler, Co-Editor
Don Harvey, Co-Editor

Written by professionals for professionals, providing a dialogue between technical practitioners from the several performing arts. The succinct articles, complete with mechanical drawings, represent the best solutions to recurring technical problems. Published October, January and April.
Cost: $15.00
Frequency: 3X Per Year
Founded in 1924

19308 Theater Magazine
Yale School of Drama
1120 Chapel Street
P.O Box 1257
New Haven, CT 06505

203-432-1234
Fax: 203-432-6423
E-Mail: yalerep@yale.edu
Home Page: www.yale.edu/drama

Tom Sellar, Editor
Laraine Sammler, Business Manager
Alex Grennan, Director of Business/Comm

Periodicals, essays and articles of the Yale School of Drama.
Cost: $22.00
Frequency: Annual+
Circulation: 2500
Founded in 1924
Mailing list available for rent: 1.5M names
Printed in one color on matte stock

19309 Theatre Bay Area Magazine
1663 Mission Street
Suite 525
San Francisco, CA 94103

415-430-1140
Fax: 415-430-1145
E-Mail: tba@theatrebayarea.org
Home Page: www.theatrebayarea.org
Social Media: Facebook, Twitter, YouTube

Karen Mc Kevitt, Executive Director
Dale Albright, Director, Member Services
Clayton Lord, Director, Audience Development
Cost: $5.95
Frequency: Monthly
Circulation: 4500

19310 Theatre Bill
Jerome Press
332 Congress St
Suite 2
Boston, MA 02210-1217

617-423-3400
Fax: 617-423-7108
Home Page: www.showofthemonthtravel.com

Jerome Rosenfeld, Owner

19311 Theatre Journal
Johns Hopkins University Press
2715 N Charles St
Baltimore, MD 21218-4363

410-516-6900
800-537-5487
Fax: 410-516-6968
E-Mail: webmaster@jhupress.jhu.edu
Home Page: www.press.jhu.edu

William Brody, President
David Z Saltz, Co-Editor
Sonja Arsham Kuftinec, Performance Review Editor
James Peck, Book Review Editor
Bob Kowkabany, Managing Editor

One of the most authoritative and useful publications of theatre studies available today. Theatre Journal features social and historical studies, production reviews, and theoretical inquiries that analize dramatic texts and production. Official journal of the Association for Theatre in Higher Education.
Cost: $40.00
Frequency: Quarterly
Circulation: 2492
ISSN: 0192-2882
Founded in 1878
Mailing list available for rent

19312 Theatre Symposium
Auburn University
1175 Revolution Mill Dr.
Studio 14
Greensboro, NC 27405

336-272-3645
Fax: 336-272-8810
E-Mail: setc@setc.org
Home Page: www.setc.org

M Scott Phillips, Editor

An annual publication of works of scholarship resulting from a single topic meeting held on a southeastern university campus each year. Available to adult members only. A copublication of the Southeaster Theatre Conference and the University of Alabama Press.

19313 Theatre Topics
Johns Hopkins University Press
2715 N Charles St
Baltimore, MD 21218-4363

410-516-6900
800-537-5487
Fax: 410-516-6998

E-Mail: webmaster@jhupress.jhu.edu
Home Page: www.press.jhu.edu

William Brody, President
Sandra G Shannon, Co-Editor
DeAnna Toten Beard, Book Review Editor
Elanore Lampners, Managing Editor
Beverley Pevitts, Founding Editor

Focuses on performance studies, dramaturgy, and theatre pedagogy. Concise and timely articles on a broad array of practical, performance-oriented subjects, with special attention to topics of current interest to the profession. Keeps readers informed of the latest developments on the stage and in the classroom. The official journal of the Association for Theatre in Higher Education. Published in March and September.
Cost: $32.00
Frequency: Semi-Annually
Circulation: 1528
ISSN: 1054-8378
Founded in 1878
Mailing list available for rent

19314 Youth Theatre Journal
American Alliance for Theatre and Education
4908 Auburn Ave
Bethesda, MD 20814

301-200-1944
Fax: 301-235-7108
E-Mail: info@aate.com
Home Page: www.aate.com

A scholarly journal dedicated to advancing the study and practice of theatre and drama with, for, and by the people of all ages. It is concerned with all forms of scholarship of the highest quality that inform the fields of theatre for young audiences and drama/theatre education.
Cost: $25.00
Frequency: 2x/Year
Circulation: 1000
ISSN: 0892-9092
Mailing list available for rent: 700 names at $150 per M

Trade Shows

19315 CinemaCon
National Association of Theatre Owners
750 1st St NE
Suite 1130
Washington, DC 20002-4241

202-962-0054
Fax: 202-962-0370
E-Mail: nato@natodc.com
Home Page: www.natoonline.org

John Fithian, President
Gary Klein, VP
Kathy Conroy, Executive Director

A gathering of cinema owners and operators.
4000 Members
Frequency: Annual/March

19316 EXPO
Theatre Bay Area
870 Market Street
Suite 375
San Francisco, CA 94102-3002

415-430-1140
Fax: 415-430-1145
E-Mail: dale@theatrebayarea.org
Home Page: www.theatrebayarea.org

Dale Albright, Director of Individual Services

Theatre Bay Area's EXPO is where attendees can meet those kinds of businesses that might offer services to the theatre community: theatre companies, actors, etc. There are also break-out sessions discussing issues of interest to the theatre community.
500+ Attendees
Frequency: May

19317 EdTA Thespian Festival
Educational Theatre Association
2343 Auburn Ave
Cincinnati, OH 45219-2819

513-421-3900
Fax: 513-421-7077
Home Page: www.schooltheatre.org
Social Media: Facebook, Twitter

Michael Peitz, Executive Director
Gloria McIntyre, President
Jay Seller VP

The premiere showcase for high school theatre, drawing students and teachers from throughout the United States and abroad.
3000 Attendees

19318 Educational Theatre Association Conference
Educational Theatre Association
2343 Auburn Ave
Cincinnati, OH 45219-2819

513-421-3900
Fax: 513-421-7077
Home Page: www.schooltheatre.org
Social Media: Facebook, Twitter

Michael Peitz, Executive Director
Gloria McIntyre, President
Jay Seller VP
400 Attendees
Frequency: Annual

19319 International Association of Venue Managers
International Association of Assembly Managers
635 Fritz Drive
Suite 100
Coppell, TX 75019-4442

972-906-7441
800-935-4226
Fax: 972-906-7418
E-Mail: mike.meyers@iaam.org
Home Page: www.iaam.org

Steven Peters, President
Robyn Williams, First Vice President
Frequency: Annual

19320 NDEO National Conference
National Dance Education Organization
8609 2nd Avenue
Suite 203 B
Silver Spring, MD 20910

301-585-2880
Fax: 301-585-2888
E-Mail: info@ndeo.org
Home Page: www.ndeo.org

Susan McGreevy-Nichols, Executive Director
Jane Bonbright EdD, Executive Director
Patricia Cohen, Treasurer

Provides 200+ professional development sessions for artists, educators and administrators teaching or supporting dance education programs in PreK-12, colleges/universities, private studio/schools of dance, community centers and performing arts organizations.
800 Attendees
Frequency: Annual

19321 National Black Theatre Festival
610 Coliseum Drive
Suite 1
Winston-Salem, NC 27106

336-723-2266
E-Mail: nbtf@bellsouth.net
Home Page: www.nbtf.org

Patrice Toney, President
Frequency: Annual, Winston-Salem

19322 National Square Dance Convention
PO Box 5790
Topeka, KS 66605-5790

317-635-4455
Home Page: www.57nsdc.com

Ernie Stone, Executive Committee
Barbara Stone, Executive Committee

250 booths and 250 exhibitors.
20M+ Attendees
Frequency: June

19323 New England Theatre Conference
215 Knob Hill Drive
Hamden, CT 06518

617-851-8535
Fax: 203-288-5938
E-Mail: mail@netconline.org
Home Page: www.netconline.org

Sabine Klein, President
Jeffrey Watts, Executive VP
Charles Emmons, VP Administration/Finance

Promoting excellence in theatre, a conference of New England's oldest, largest regional theatre association.
800+ Attendees
Frequency: November
Founded in 1952

19324 North Carolina Southeastern Theatre Conference
1175 Revolution Mill Drive
Suite 14
Greensboro, NC 27405-0868

336-272-3645
Fax: 336-272-8810
E-Mail: info@setc.org
Home Page: www.setc.org

Betsey Baun, Executive Director
April Marshall, Contact/Pro. Theatre Services

Join over 4,000 Theatre Artists for education, exchanges, ideas, products, networking and great theatre. Convention activities include keynote speakers, auditions, guest speakers, festivals, design competition, commercial and educational expo exhibits, scholarship awards, social events and workshops.
4000+ Attendees

19325 Prescott Park Arts Festival
105 Marcy Street
PO Box 4370
Portsmouth, NH 03802-4370

603-436-2848
Fax: 603-436-1034
E-Mail: info@prescottpark.org
Home Page: www.prescottpark.org
Social Media: Facebook

Ben Anderson, Executive Director
John Moynihan, General Manager
Catherine Wejchert, Development Coordinator

Provide a financially accessible, quality multi-arts festival to a diverse audience.

19326 TCG National Conference
Theatre Communications Group

520 8th Ave
24th Floor
New York, NY 10018-4156

212-609-5900
Fax: 212-609-5901
E-Mail: tcg@tcg.org
Home Page: www.tcg.org

Theresa Eyring, Executive Director
Jennifer Cleary, Membership Director

19327 US Institute for Theatre Technology Annual Conference & Stage Expo
USITT
315 S Crouse Avenue
Suite 200
Syracuse, NY 13210

315-463-6463
800-938-7488
Fax: 315-463-6525
E-Mail: info@usitt.org
Home Page: www.usitt.org
Social Media: Facebook, Twitter, LinkedIn

Carl Lefko, President
Patricia Dennis, Secretary
Travis DeCastro, Treasurer

The Conference offers over 175 sessions featuring design, technology, costume, sound, architecture, management, engineering, and production. The Stage Expo showcases businesses, products, services, and eductional opportunities in the performing arts and entertainment industry. With over 150 exhibitors, Stage Expo provides conference attendees with the opportunity to see the newest and best products and services on the market today.
3700 Members
3800 Attendees
Frequency: March
Founded in 1960

Directories & Databases

19328 Academy Players Directory
2210 W Olive Avenue
Suite 320
Burbank, CA 91506

310-247-3058
Fax: 310-550-5034
E-Mail: info@playersdirectory.com
Home Page: www.playersdirectory.com

The Players Directory appeared in 1937 as the first reliable casting directory that listed both featured stars and extras. Today, more than 16,000 actors are included.
Cost: $75.00
Founded in 1937

19329 American Association of Community Theatre Membership Directory
1300 Gendy St Forth Worth
St Forth Worth, TX 76107

817-732-3177
866-687-2228
Fax: 817-732-3178
E-Mail: info@aact.org
Home Page: www.aact.org

Julie Angelo, Executive Director
Linda Lee, President
Carole Ries, VP Public Relations
Frank Peot, Secretary
Tim Jebsen, Treasurer

The database includes addresses for over 7,000 community theatre organizations in the USA. Only available to members.
Mailing list available for rent: 10000 names at $180 per M

19330 Americans for the Arts Field Directory
Americans for the Arts
1 E 53rd St
2nd Floor
New York, NY 10022-4242

212-223-2787
Fax: 212-980-4857
Home Page: www.artsactionfund.org
Social Media: Facebook, Twitter, RSS, You Tube

Suzanne Niemeyer, Editor
Robert L Lynch, President/CEO
Liz Bartolomeo, Public Relations/Marketing Coord
Chad Bauman, Director Print/Multimedia
Graham Dunstan, Assoc Director Publication Sales

A must-have resource for anyone working in the arts and community development. The directory provides contact information for local, state, regional, and national arts service organizations-more than 4,000 entries broken down by state and region. Also includes contact information for professional consultants working in the nonprofit arts field. A great networking tool.
Cost: $35.00
262 Pages

19331 Association of Performing Arts Presenters Membership Directory
APAP
1211 Connecticut Ave NW
Suite 200
Washington, DC 20036-2716

202-833-2787
888-820-2787
Fax: 202-833-1543
E-Mail: info@artspresenters.org
Home Page: www.artspresenters.org

Sandra Gibson, President
Sean Handerhan, Marketing

An invaluable resource for keeping in touch with colleagues. Puts more than 1,450 presenters, service organizations, artists, management companies, consultants, and vendors at your fingertips. An excellent networking tool for everyone on your staff.
1900 Members
Frequency: Annual
Founded in 1957

19332 Complete Catalogue of Plays
Dramatists Play Service
440 Park Ave S
New York, NY 10016-8012
212-683-8960
Fax: 212-213-1539
E-Mail: webmasters@dramatists.com
Home Page: www.dramatists.com
Social Media: Facebook

Stephen Fultan, President
Rafael J Rivera, VP Finance/Administration
Michael Q Fellmeth, VP Publications/IT
Tamra Feifer, Director Operations

The Complete Catalogue is published in odd years and the Supplement of New Plays in even years. Both books are distributed, without charge, to current customers in the Fall of each year.
412 Pages
Founded in 1936

19333 Costume Designers Guild Directory
Costumer Designers Guild
4730 Woodman Avenue
Suite 430
Sherman Oaks, CA 91423-2400

818-905-1557
Fax: 818-905-1560
E-Mail: cdgia@earthlink.net
Home Page: www.costumedesignersguild.com

Cheryl Downey, Executive Director
Deborah N Landis, President

Directory includes members' names, classification, and other statistical information.
Frequency: Annual

19334 Dance Annual Directory
Dance Magazine
333 7th Ave
11th Floor
New York, NY 10001-5109

212-979-4800
Fax: 212-979-4817
E-Mail: emacel@dancemagazine.com
Home Page: www.dancemagazine.com

Karla Johnson, Publisher
Emily Macel, Editor
Karen Hildebrand, Editorial Director
Wendy Perron, Editor-in-Chief
Hanna Rubin, Managing Editor

Reach 300,000+ dancers, dance teachers, and dance professionals in the dance world.
Cost: $100.00
Frequency: Annual

19335 Dance Magazine College Guide
Dance Magazine
333 7th Ave
11th Floor
New York, NY 10038-3900

212-979-4800
Fax: 212-979-4817
E-Mail: subscriptions@dancemagazine.com
Home Page: www.dancemagazine.com

Karla Johnson, President
Karen Hildebrand, Editorial Director
Wendy Perron, Editor-in-Chief
Hanna Rubin, Managing Editor
Kate Lydon, Education Editor

With over 500+ listings, Dance Magazine College Guide is a comprehensive source for dance degree programs in higher education. Find application deadlines and audition dates. Get student perspectives and career advice. Online database offers the ability to identify programs that match an individual's personal criteria for degree, type of dance, location, department size, tuition and more.
Cost: $29.95
Frequency: Annual

19336 Dance Magazine: Summer Dance Calendar Issue
Dance Magazine
33 W 60th Street
Floor 10
New York, NY 10023-7905

212-245-9050
800-331-1750
Home Page: www.dancemagazine.com

A list of dance workshops and special programs for students are listed.
Cost: $3.95
Frequency: Annual
Circulation: 100,000

19337 Dance/USA Annual Directory and List-Serv
Dance/USA
1111 16th St NW
Suite 300
Washington, DC 20036-4830

202-833-1717
Fax: 202-833-2686

E-Mail: danceusa@danceusa.org
Home Page: www.danceusa.org

Andrea Snyder, Executive Director
Tom Thielen, Director Finance/Operations
Katherine Fabian, Membership Manager

On-going list-servs keep many peer councils in touch throughout the year, by providing a quick and easy connection to peer counseling when members have an immediate question or problem. Information about dance companies, schools, presenters, service organizations and commercial suppliers is included in the annual copy of Dance Annual Directory.
Frequency: Annual
Circulation: 400+

19338 Directory of Theatre Training Programs

Theatre Directories
P.O.Box 2409
Manchester Center, VT 05255-2409

802-867-9333
Fax: 802-867-2297
E-Mail: info@theatredirectories.com
Home Page: www.theatredirectories.com

Peg Lyons, Editor
PJ Tumielewicz, Editor

Profiles admissions, tuition, faculty, curriculum, facilities, productions and philosophy of training at 475 programs in the US, Canada and abroad: Colleges, Universities, Conservatories, Undergraduate and Graduate degrees. Includes Combined Auditions information. Indexed by degrees offered in each program.
Cost: $39.50
ISBN: 0-933919-61-1

19339 Dramatics College Theatre Directory

Educational Theatre Association
2343 Auburn Ave
Cincinnati, OH 45219-2815

513-421-3900
Fax: 513-421-7077
Home Page: www.edta.org
Social Media: Facebook, Twitter

Michael Peitz, Executive Director
Gloria McIntyre, President
Jay Seller, VP

Lists more than 250 college, university, and conservatory theatre programs, offering a sketch of each based on information provided by the schools. The listings can be used to measure each school against one's own criteria for location, setting, courses of study, admission requirements, and cost. Find out which programs offer merit scholarships and grants and how those funds are awarded. Use the contact information to get in touch with the programs that seem to offer the best fit for your needs
Cost: $9.00
Frequency: Annual

19340 Dramatics Magazine: Summer Theatre Directory

Educational Theatre Association
2343 Auburn Ave
Cincinnati, OH 45219-2815

513-421-3900
Fax: 513-421-7077
Home Page: www.edta.org
Social Media: Facebook, Twitter

Michael Peitz, Executive Director
Gloria McIntyre, President
Jay Seller, VP

Lists nearly 200 summer theatre programs and stock companies, offering a sketch of each based on factual information provided by the schools, camps, and theatre companies. The listings can be used to measure each program against one's own criteria for location, setting, housing, courses of study, admission requirements and fees.
Cost: $9.00
Frequency: Annual

19341 Dramatist's Sourcebook

Theatre Communications Group
520 8th Ave
24th Floor
New York, NY 10018-4156

212-609-5900
Fax: 212-609-5901
E-Mail: tcg@tcg.org
Home Page: www.tcg.org

Theresa Eyring, Executive Director
Kelly Haydon, Database Manager
Jennifer Cleary, Director Membership
Terence Nemeth, Publisher
Kathy Sova, Editorial Director

Completely revised, with more than 900 opportunities for playwrights, translators, composers, lyricists, and librettists, as well as opportunities for screen, radio, and television writers. Thoroughly indexed, with a calendar of deadlines. The Sourcebook contains scrip-submission procedures for more than 350 theatres seeking new plays; guidelines for more than 150 prizes; and sections on agents, fellowships and residencies.
Cost: $22.95
Frequency: Annual
ISBN: 1-559362-94-4
Founded in 1980

19342 Dramatists Guild Annual Resource Directory

Dramatists Guild of America
1501 Broadway
Suite 701
New York, NY 10036-5505

212-398-9366
Fax: 212-944-0420
Home Page: www.dramaguild.com

Ralph Sevush, Executive Director

The Resource Directory is an annual sourcebook available only to Guild members, sent automatically as one of the privileges of Guild members. It includes lists of conferences and festivals, contests, producers, publishers, agents and attorneys, fellowships and grants, and workshops throughout the US and the world.
Frequency: Annual

19343 Encyclopedia of Exhibition

National Association of Theatre Owners
750 1st St Ne
Suite 1130
Washington, DC 20002-4241

202-962-0054
Fax: 202-962-0370
E-Mail: nato@natodc.com
Home Page: www.natoonline.org

John Fithian, President
Gary Klein, VP
Kathy Conroy, Executive Director

Packed with information on film grosses, upcoming releases, and filmgoer demographics. Also features a directory of international and domestic exhibitors and distributors, cinema companies ranked by screen count, trade publications and more
Cost: $500.00
Frequency: Annual

19344 Feedback Theatrebooks and Prospero Press

Feedback Theatrebooks & Prospero Press
PO Box 174
Brooklin, ME 04616

207-359-2781
Fax: 207-359-5532

Publishes theatre histories, cookbooks, directories, anthologies of plays, plays published before WWII, and format guidelines for playwrights.

19345 Grey House Performing Arts Directory

Grey House Publishing
4919 Route 22
PO Box 56
Amenia, NY 12501

518-789-8700
800-562-2139
Fax: 845-373-6390
E-Mail: books@greyhouse.com
Home Page: www.greyhouse.com
Social Media: Facebook, Twitter

Leslie Mackenzie, Publisher
Richard Gottlieb, Editor

The most comprehensive resource covering the Performing Arts. This directory provides current information on over 8,500 Dance Companies, Instrumental Music Programs, Opera Companies, Choral Groups, Theater Companies, Performing Arts Series, Performing Arts Facilities and Artist Management Groups.
Cost: $185.00
1200 Pages
Frequency: Annual
ISBN: 1-592373-76-3
Founded in 1981

19346 Grey House Performing Arts Directory - Online Database

Grey House Publishing
4919 Route 22
PO Box 56
Amenia, NY 12501-0056

518-789-8700
800-562-2139
Fax: 518-789-0556
E-Mail: gold@greyhouse.com
Home Page: www.gold.greyhouse.com
Social Media: Facebook, Twitter

Leslie Mackenzie, Publisher
Richard Gottlieb, Editor

The Grey House Performing Arts Directory - Online Database provides immediate access to dance companies, orchestras, opera companies, choral groups, theater companies, series, festivals and perfoming arts facilities across the country, or in their region, state, or in your own backyard. It offers unequaled coverage of the Performing Arts - over 8,500 listings - of the major performance organization, facilities, and information resources.
Frequency: Annual
Founded in 1981

19347 Money for Film and Video Artists

Americans for the Arts
1 E 53rd St
2nd Floor
New York, NY 10022-4242

212-223-2787
Fax: 212-980-4857
Home Page: www.artsactionfund.org
Social Media: Facebook, Twitter, RSS, You Tube

Suzanne Niemeyer, Editor
Robert L Lynch, President/CEO
Liz Bartolomeo, Public Relations/Marketing Coord
Chad Bauman, Director Print/Multimedia
Graham Dunstan, Assoc Director Publication Sales

A comprehensive resource guide to fellowships, grants, awards, low-cost facilities, emergency assistance programs, technical assistance, and support services. Entries include contact information; type of award and/or scope of service; eligibilty requirements; application procedures; deadlines and more.
Cost: $14.95
317 Pages
ISBN: 1-879903-09-1

19348 Money for International Exchange in the Arts
Americans for the Arts
1 E 53rd St
2nd Floor
New York, NY 10022-4242

212-223-2787
Fax: 212-980-4857
Home Page: www.artsactionfund.org
Social Media: Facebook, Twitter, RSS, You Tube

Suzanne Niemeyer, Editor
Robert L Lynch, President/CEO
Liz Bartolomeo, Public Relations/Marketing Coord
Chad Bauman, Director Print/Multimedia
Graham Dunstan, Assoc Director Publication Sales

This resource includes grants, fellowships and awards for travel and work abroad; support and technical assistance for international touring and exchange; international artists' residencies; programs that support artists' professional development, and more. Indexed by region, discipline and type of support.
Cost: $14.95
122 Pages
ISBN: 1-879903-01-6

19349 Money for Performing Artists
Americans for the Arts
1 E 53rd St
2nd Floor
New York, NY 10022-4242

212-223-2787
Fax: 212-980-4857
Home Page: www.artsactionfund.org
Social Media: Facebook, Twitter, RSS, You Tube

Suzanne Niemeyer, Editor
Robert L Lynch, President/CEO
Liz Bartolomeo, Public Relations/Marketing Coord
Chad Bauman, Director Print/Multimedia
Graham Dunstan, Assoc Director Publication Sales

Lists awards, grants, fellowships, competitions, auditions, workshops, and artists' colonies, as well as emergency and technical assistance programs.
Cost: $12.00
240 Pages
ISBN: 0-915400-96-0
Founded in 1991

19350 Money for Visual Arts
Americans for the Arts
1 E 53rd St
2nd Floor
New York, NY 10022-4242

212-223-2787
Fax: 212-980-4857
Home Page: www.artsactionfund.org
Social Media: Facebook, Twitter, RSS, You Tube

Suzanne Niemeyer, Editor
Robert L Lynch, President/CEO
Liz Bartolomeo, Public Relations/Marketing Coord
Chad Bauman, Director Print/Multimedia
Graham Dunstan, Assoc Director Publication Sales

A guide to grants, fellowships, awards, artist colonies, emergency and technical assistance, and support services. Entries include contact information; type of award and/or scope of service; eligibility requirements; application procedures; deadlines and more.
Cost: $14.95
340 Pages

19351 Musical America International Directory of the Performing Arts
Commonwealth Business Media
50 Millstone Rd
Suite 200
East Windsor, NJ 08520-1418

609-371-7700
800-221-5488
Fax: 609-371-7879
E-Mail: info@musicalamerica.com
Home Page: www.cbizmedia.com

Stephanie Challener, Publisher
Sedgwick Clark, Editor
Susan Elliot, News Editor
Bob Hudoba, Data Editor

Features over 14,000 detailed listings of worldwide arts organizations, including key contact information such as name, address, phone, fax, Web site and E-mail addresses, budget category, type of event and seating capacity. In addition, through advertising, over 10,000 artists are indexed in the alphabetical and categorical indexes. Categories include artist managers, orchestras, opera companies, concert series, festivals, competitions, music schools and departments, record companies, and more.
Founded in 1898

19352 NYC/On Stage
Theatre Development Fund
520 Eight Avenue
Suite 801
New York, NY 10018-6507

212-912-9770
E-Mail: info@tdf.org
Home Page: www.tdf.org
Social Media: Facebook

Earl D. Weiner, Chair
Sandra Kresch, Vice Chairman
Robert T. Goldman, Treasurer
Deborah Hartnett, Secretary

Theater, dance, and music companies and performing arts centers in New York City.
Founded in 1995

19353 National Network For Artist Placement
National Network for Artist Placement
935 W Avenue 37
Los Angeles, CA 90065

323-222-4035
800-354-5348
E-Mail: NNAPnow@aol.com
Home Page: www.artistplacement.com

Warren Christensen, Consultant

Internship opportunities in dance, music, theatre, art and film.
Cost: $85.00
375 Pages
Frequency: Bi-Annual
ISBN: 0-945941-13-7

19354 Opera America Membership Directory
Opera America
330 7th Ave
16th Floor
New York, NY 10001-5248

212-796-8620
Fax: 212-796-8631
E-Mail: info@operaamerica.org
Home Page: www.operaamerica.org
Social Media: YouTube

Marc Scorca, President

Directory of Opera America's Company, Business, Library, and Affilliate Members, indexed alphabetically and geographically. Includes the Annual Report to Members, a description of Opera America's programs and services, and a list of individual members.
Cost: $25.00
Frequency: Annual

19355 Plays and Playwrights
International Society of Dramatists
1638 Euclid Avenue
Miami Beach, FL 33139-7744

305-882-1864
Home Page: http://blog.nytesmallpress.com/

Offers valuable information on over 1,000 dramatists producing works in English.
Cost: $29.95
200 Pages
Frequency: Annual
Circulation: 10,000

19356 Regional Theatre Directory
Theatre Directories
P.O.Box 2409
Manchester Center, VT 05255-2409

802-867-9333
Fax: 802-867-2297
Home Page: www.theatredirectories.com

Peg Lyons, Editor
PJ Tumielewicz, Editor

Profiles over 400 theatres including dinner theatres, equity and non-equity. Find out when/where auditions are held, when resumes shoul be sent, housing and transportation policy, and general description of company. If you want to find a job or an internship as an actor, designer, technician or staff in a professional regional or dinner theatre anywhere in the country, this directory can help you.
Cost: $29.50
Frequency: Annual
ISBN: 0-933919-63-8
Founded in 1984

19357 ShowBiz Bookkeeper
Theatre Directories
P.O.Box 2409
Manchester Center, VT 05255-2409

802-867-9333
Fax: 802-867-2297
E-Mail: info@theatredirectories.com
Home Page: www.theatredirectories.com

The tax record-keeping system for professionals working in the arts.
Cost: $22.95

19358 Stars in Your Eyes...Feet on the Ground
Theatre Directories
P.O.Box 2409
Manchester Center, VT 05255-2409

802-867-9333
Fax: 802-867-2297
E-Mail: info@theatredirectories.com
Home Page: www.theatredirectories.com

PJ Tumielewicz, Editor
Peg Lyons, Editor

For teens who want to act...Practical advice for young actors: learning how show business works; agents and managers; local cable shows and television commercials; auditioning for stage, student films and TV; choosing a school; dealing with rejection; parental support and more. Written by a 19-year old professional

actress.
Cost: $16.95
ISBN: 0-933919-42-5

19359 Student's Guide to Playwriting Opportunities
Theatre Directories
P.O.Box 2409
Manchester Center, VT 05255-2409
802-867-9333
Fax: 802-867-2297
E-Mail: info@theatredirectories.com
Home Page: www.theatredirectories.com
Michael Write, Directory Editor
Christi Pyland, Directory Editor
PJ Tumielewicz, Theatre Directories, Inc Editor
Peg Lyons, Theatre Directories, Inc Editor
An essential tool for every high shool or college student with an interest in playwriting. Comprehensive listings of 79 academic programs and another 80 professional development programs geared for the young writer. New essays on the art, process and business of playwriting.
Cost: $23.95
128 Pages
ISBN: 0-933919-53-0

19360 Summer Theatre Directory
Theatre Directories
P.O.Box 2409
Manchester Center, VT 05255-2409
802-867-9333
Fax: 802-867-2297
E-Mail: info@theatredirectories.com
Home Page: www.theatredirectories.com
Opportunities at over 350 summer theatres, theme parks, and summer training programs.
Cost: $29.50

19361 Theatre Profiles Database
Theatre Communications Group
520 8th Ave
24th Floor
New York, NY 10018-4156
212-609-5900
Fax: 212-609-5901
E-Mail: tcg@tcg.org
Home Page: www.tcg.org
Theresa Eyring, Executive Director
Kelly Haydon, Database Manager
Jennifer Cleary, Director Membership
Terence Nemeth, Publisher
Kathy Sova, Editorial Director
Online database of more than 400 theatre members in 47 states, 17,000 individual members, 100 Trustee Leadership Network members and a growing number of University, Funder and Business Affiliates.
Frequency: Annual

19362 Whole Arts Directory
Midmarch Arts Press
300 Riverside Dr
Apartment 8A
New York, NY 10025-5279
212-666-6990
Fax: 212-865-5510
E-Mail: info@midmarchpress.org
Home Page: www.midmarchartspress.org
Cynthia Navaregga, Manager
Directory to arts resources, organiztions, museums, galleries, colonies, retreats, art therapy, information services, and much more. Highly useful material for all artists, students, organizations and institutions.
Cost: $12.95
175 Pages
ISBN: 0-960247-67-x
Founded in 1987
Printed in on matte stock

Industry Web Sites

19363 http://gold.greyhouse.com
G.O.L.D Grey House OnLine Databases
Grey House Publishing's online database platform, GOLD, offers Quick Search, Keyword Search and Expert Search for most business sectors including performing arts markets. The GOLD platform makes finding the information you need quick and easy - whether you're a novice searcher or an experienced database user. All of Grey House's directory products are available for subscription on the GOLD platform.

19364 www.aact.org
American Association of Community Theatre
Non-profit corporation fostering excellence in community theatre productions and governance through community theatre festivals, educational opportunity publications, network, resources, and website.

19365 www.aahperd.org/nda
National Dance Association
A nonprofit service organization dedicated to increasing knowledge, improving skills and encouraging sound professional practices in dance education while promoting and supporting creative and healthy lifestyles through high quality dance programs.

19366 www.aate.com
American Alliance for Theatre and Education
Members are artists, teachers and professionals who serve youth theatres and theatre educational programs.

19367 www.absolutewrite.com
Absolute Write
Advice for writers, including playwrights.

19368 www.actorsequity.org
Actors Equity Association
Labor union affiliated with AFL-CIO which represents actors in film, television and commercials.

19369 www.actorsite.com
Actor Site
Audition and other information.

19370 www.actorsource.com
Actorsource
Extensive information and resources for actors.

19371 www.actorstheatre.org
Actors Theatre of Louisville
Supports new playwrights. For information on entering a play, click Humana Festival.

19372 www.adta.org
American Dance Therapy Association
Founded in 1966; professional organization of dance movement therapists, with members both nationally and internationally; offers training, research findings, and a newsletter.

19373 www.aislesay.com
Aislesay
Internet magazine of stage reviews and opinions.

19374 www.americandanceguild.org
American Dance Guild
Non-profit membership organization; sponsors professional seminars, workshops, a student scholarship and other projects and institutes programs of national significance in the field of dance.

19375 www.americantheaterweb.com
American Theater Web
Find theaters, Broadway shows and musicals.

19376 www.answers4dancers.com
Answers for Dancers
Dance Magazine sponsors this site.

19377 www.artsmed.org
Performing Arts Medicine Association
Organization for physicians and professionals interested in the research of Performing Arts Medicine.

19378 www.artspresenters.org
Association of Performing Arts Presenters
Celebrates rich and diverse performing arts to the public.

19379 www.artstabilization.org
National Arts Strategies
Offers training and technical assistance to arts organizations.

19380 www.bachauer.com
Gina Bachauer International Piano Foundation
Produce a yearly piano international competition

19381 www.backstage.com
Backstage.com
Information for actors, casting calls, film reviews, auditions and acting jobs.

19382 www.backstagejobs.com
Theatre Design and Technical Jobs Page
Employment opportunities.

19383 www.backstageworld.com
Backstage World
Post your resume and search for design and technical job opportunities worldwide.

19384 www.bmi.com
BMI
Secures the rights of songwriters/composers. Collects license fees for the public performance of music and pays royalties to its copyright owners.

19385 www.catf.org
Contemporary American Theater Festival
Dedicated to providing and developing new American Theater.

19386 www.cincinnatiarts.org
Cincinnati Arts Association
Dedicated to supporting performing and visual arts.

19387 www.classicalaction.org
Classical Action
Provides a unified voice for all those within the performing arts community to help combat HIV/AIDS.

19388 www.computermusic.org
International Computer Music Association
Supports the performance aspects of computer music; publishes newsletter and holds annual conferance.

19389 www.conductorsguild.org
Conductors Guild
Dedicated to encouraging the highest standards in the art and profession of conducting.
Founded in 1975.

19390 **www.contactimprov.net**
Contact Improv
Improvisation for dancers.

19391 **www.costume-con.org**
Costume Connections
Costume conferences.

19392 **www.costume.org**
International Costumers' Guild
An affiliation of amateur hobbyist and professional costumers.

19393 **www.costumegallery.com**
Costume Gallery
A central location on the web for fashion and costume since 1996.

19394 **www.costumers.org**
National Costumers Association
Seeks to establish and maintain professional and ethical standards of business in the costume industry.

19395 **www.costumes.org**
Costumer's Manifesto
Online book, information and links.

19396 **www.costumesocietyamerica.com**
Costume Society of America
Education, research, presentation and design.

19397 **www.creativedir.com**
Creative Directory Services
Diectory of suppliers for costumes, sets, special effects and stunts.

19398 **www.criticaldance.com**
Dance Critics Association
Critical dance forum and ballet dance magazine

19399 **www.csulb.edu/~jvancamp/copyrigh.html**
Csulb.edu
Copyrighting choreographic works.

19400 **www.csusa.org/face/index.htm**
Friends of Active Copyright Education
Playwrights should click on Words, then Copyright Basics.

19401 **www.cyberdance.org**
Cyber Dance
Collection of links to modern dance and classical ballet resources.

19402 **www.danceart.com/edancing**
Danceart.com
Ballet and dance art, features, chat and more.

19403 **www.dancenotation.org**
Dance Notation Bureau
Notation basics, Notated Theatrical Dances Catalogue and links.

19404 **www.dancepages.com**
Dance Pages.com
Offers resources to dance teachers.

19405 **www.dancer.com/dance-links**
Dance Links
Links to many dance sites.

19406 **www.danceusa.org**
Dance/USA
Provides a forum for the discussion of issues of concern to membersand a support network for exchange of information; also bestows awards.

19407 **www.deadance.com**
Dance Educators of America
Promotes the education of teachers in the performing arts.

19408 **www.dma-national.org**
Dance Masters of America
An organization of dance teachers.

19409 **www.dramaguild.com**
Dramatists Guild
Comprehensive organization that deals solely with Broadway and off-Broadway producers, off-off-Broadway groups, agents, theatres and sources of grants.

19410 **www.dramaleague.org**
Drama League
Seeks to strengthen American theatre through the nurturing of stage directors.

19411 **www.dtw.org**
Dance Theater Workshop
Identifies, presents and supports independent contemporary artists and dance companies to advance dance and live performances in New York and worldwide.

19412 **www.edta.org**
Educational Theater Association
Theater educators working to increase support for theater programs in the educational system.

19413 **www.esperanzaarts.org**
Esperanza Performing Arts Association

19414 **www.etecnyc.net**
Entertainment Technology Online
For employment in design and technical theatre, click on Classifieds. Also offers resources and buyers guides for theatrical lighting.

19415 **www.gmn.com**
Global Music Network
Go backstage, watch rehearsals, listen to performances of classical and jazz artists.

19416 **www.goldmime.com**
Goldston Mime Foundation: School for Mime
Holds summer seminars and workshops.

19417 **www.greyhouse.com**
Grey House Publishing
Authoritative reference directories for most business sectors including performing arts markets. Users can search the online databases with varied search criteria allowing for custom searches by product category, geographic area, sales volume, keyword, subject and more. Full Grey House catalog and online ordering also available.

19418 **www.harada-sound.com/sound/handbook**
Kai's Sound Handbook
Information for sound designers.

19419 **www.hawaii.edu**
Association for Theatre in Higher Education
Promotes quality in theatre education.

19420 **www.heniford.net/1234**
Small Cast One-Act Guide Online
List of short plays.

19421 **www.ifea.com**
International Festivals and Events Association
Network for planning events and exchange programs; publishes quarterly magazine.

19422 **www.intix.org**
International Ticketing Association
Not-for-profit association representing 22 countries worldwide and more than 1,200 members. Committed to the improvement, progress and advancement of ticket management, and to reach this goal provides educational programs, trade shows, conducts surveys and conference proceedings and produces a membership directory.

19423 **www.ispa.org**
International Society for the Performing Arts
Foundation

Supports international cooperation, facilitates networking and enhances professional dialogue.

19424 **www.jensenfoundation.org**
Fritz and Lavinia Jensen Foundation
Sponsors competitions.

19425 **www.latinoarts.org**
Association of Hispanic Arts
A multidisciplary organization which supports Hispanic arts organizations and individual artists with technical assistance. The organization facilitates projects and programs designed to foster the appreciation, growth, and well being of the Latino cultural community. It's quarter publication, AHA; Hispanic Arts News, features in depth articles on the local and national arts community, including artist profiles and a calendar of events.

19426 **www.lib.colum.edu/costwais.html**
Costume Image Database
Access costume images.

19427 **www.light-link.com**
Lightsearch.com
Lists of lighting equipment suppliers.

19428 **www.livebroadway.com**
League of American Theatres and Producers
National trade association for the commercial theatre industry whose principal activity is negotiation of labor contracts and government relations.

19429 **www.lmda.org**
Literary Managers and Dramaturgs of the Americas
Voluntary membership organization.

19430 **www.luth.org**
Guild of American Luthiers
Manufacturers and repairs stringed instruments; offers quarterly journal and triennial meeting.

19431 **www.lycos.com**
Lycos
Click Arts and Entertainment, then Dance, Theatre or Performing Arts.

19432 **www.magicsam.com**
Society of American Magicians
Founded to promote and maintain harmonious fellowship among those interested in magic as an art, to improve ethics of the magical profession, and to foster, promote and improve the advancement of magical arts in the field of amusement and entertainment. Membership includes professional and amateur magicians, manufacturers of magical apparatus and collectors.

19433 **www.makeupmag.com**
Make-Up Artist Magazine
Make-up artist magazine online.

19434 **www.members.aol.com/thegoop/gaff.html**
Gaff Tape Webring
Tech theatre.

19435 **www.midatlanticarts.org**
Mid Atlantic Arts Foundation
Provides leadership and support for artists and arts organizations in the Mid-Atlantic region and beyond.

19436 **www.milieux.com/costume**
Costume Source
Provides online sources for materials, costumes, accessories and books.

19437 **www.mtishows.com**
Music Theatre International
Scripts, cast recordings, study guides, production slides and other resources.

19438 **www.musicalamerica.com**
Musicalamerica.com
Late-breaking industry news, full search capabilities, immediate interaction between Presenter and Artist Manager/Artist.

19439 **www.musicianshealth.com**
Chiropractic Performing Arts Association
To educate amateur and professional entertainers, musicians and dancers about reaching optimum health potential through natural, drug-free, conservative chiropractic care.

19440 **www.nadt.org**
National Association for Drama Therapy
Promotes the profession of Drama Therapy.

19441 **www.namm.org**
NAMM-International Music Products Association
Offers professional development seminars; sells musical instruments and allied products.

19442 **www.napama.org**
North American Performing Arts Managers and Agents
A cooperative voice in a competitive business.

19443 **www.natoonline.org**
National Association of Theatre Owners
Exhibition trade organization, representing more than 30,000 movie screens in all 50 states, and additional cinemas in 50 countries worldwide.

19444 **www.nbtf.org**
National Black Theatre Festival

19445 **www.netconline.org**
New England Theatre Conference
Non-profit educational corporation founded to develop, expand and assist theatre activity in community, educational and professional levels in New England. Holds annual auditions.

19446 **www.netsword.com/stagecombat.html**
Netsword
Lessons on stage combat.

19447 **www.newplaysforchildren.com**
New Plays Online
Plays for children and young adults.

19448 **www.nmpa.org**
National Music Publishers' Association
Publishes a quarterly newsletter and holds an annual meeting.

19449 **www.ntcp.org**
Non-Traditional Casting Project
Promotes inclusive practices in television, theatre and film.

19450 **www.nyfa.org**
New York Foundation for the Arts
Employment openings in the arts.

19451 **www.nypl.org/reseach/lpa/lpa.html**
New York Public Library for the Performing Arts
Primary research collection.

19452 **www.nytimes.com**
New York Times on the Web
Arts and Theatre contains play reviews.

19453 **www.oobr.com**
Off-Off-Broadway Review
Lists information on off-off broadway shows such as: title of show, author, director, producing company, theatre, address, box-office phone number, dates and times, admission price and contact info.

19454 **www.opencasting.com**
Open Casting
Bulletin board containing auditions, crew calls, casting notices and links.

19455 **www.paastjo.org**
Performing Arts Association
Provides a diverse selection of performing arts.

19456 **www.pen.org**
PEN: American Center
Site of the international literary community organization.

19457 **www.performingarts.net**
Performing Arts Online
Dedicated to the perpetuation of quality performing arts.

19458 **www.pianonet.com**
Piano Manufacturers Association International
Manufacturers and suppliers of pianos and parts; holds annual trade show.

19459 **www.pipeorgan.org**
American Institute of Organ Builders
Sponsers training seminars, quarterly journal and annual convention for pipe organ builders and service technicians.

19460 **www.plasa.org**
Professional Lighting and Sound Association
Web site for PLASA, a leading trade body for Lighting and Sound Professionals.

19461 **www.playbill.com**
Playbill Online
Listings for Broadway and off Broadway theatre productions. Also guides for sites, including summer stock, national touring shows and regional theatres worldwide.

19462 **www.playwrights.org**
Playwrights Center of San Francisco
Playwrites directory.

19463 **www.playwrightshorizons.org**
Playwrights Horizon
At home page click arrow. On next page click working with PH. You will see Writing Submissions.

19464 **www.playwrightsproject.com**
Playwrights Project
Promotes literacy, creativity and communication skills in young people through drama-based activities.

19465 **www.press.jhu.edu/press/journals/paj**
Johns Hopkins University Press
A journal of performance and art.

19466 **www.press.jhu.edu/press/journals/tj**
Johns Hopkins University Press
Theatre Journal

19467 **www.press.jhu.edu/press/journals/tt**
Johns Hopkins University Press
Theatre Topics

19468 **www.proppeople.com**
Proppeople.com
Online home for props professionals.

19469 **www.renfaire.com/Language/index.html**
Renfaire.com
Lessons on proper Elizabethan accents.

19470 **www.rigging.net**
Rigger's Page
Technical information on stage rigging equipment.

19471 **www.roundalab.org**
Roundalab
A professional international society of individuals who teach round dancing at any phase.

19472 **www.safd.org**
Society of American Fight Directors
Promotes safety in directing staged combat and theatrical violence.

19473 **www.sag.org**
Screen Actors Guild
Labor union affiliated with AFL-CIO which represents actors in film, television and commercials.

19474 **www.sapphireswan.com/dance**
Dance Directory
Dance resources.

19475 **www.setc.org**
Southeastern Theatre Conference
Annual conventions include auditions.

19476 **www.sfballet.org**
San Francisco Ballet Association
Provides a repertoire of classical and contemporary ballet; to provide educational opportunities for professional dancers and choreographers; to excel in ballet, artistic direction and administration.

19477 **www.southarts.org**
Southern Arts Federation
Serves as the leadership voice to increase the regional, national and international awareness and prominence of Southern arts. Creates mechanisms and partnerships to expand local, regional, national and international markets for Southern arts.

19478 **www.spolin.com**
Spolin Center
Information on improvisational theatre.

19479 **www.ssdc.org**
Society of Stage Directors and Choreographers
An independent labor union representing directors and choreographers in American theatre.

19480 **www.stage-directions.com**
Stage Directions Magazine
The practical and technical side of theatrical operations.

19481 **www.stageplays.com/markets.htm**
Playwrights Noticeboard
Information on contests, publishing and production opportunities.

19482 **www.stetson.edu/csata/thr_guid.html**
McCoy's Guide to Theatre and Performance Studies
A brief guide to internet resources in theatre and performance studies put out by Stetson University.

19483 **www.summertheater.com**
Directory of Summer Theater in the United States
Search for summer theater opportunities by alphabetized listings or geographic region.

19484 **www.talkinbroadway.com**
Talkin' Broadway
Theatrical events and information on and off Broadway and other selected geographical locations.

19485 **www.tcg.org**
Theatre Communications Group
Supports alliances among playwrights, theatres and communities. Promotes not-for-profit theatre and offers resources to jobseekers. Offers financial support to designers and directors through its Career Development Program.

19486 **www.tdf.org**
Theatre Development Fund
Not-for-profit service organization. Provides support for every area of the dance, music and professional theatre field. Founded 1968.

19487 **www.teleport.com/~bjscript/index.htm**
Essays on the Craft of Dramatic Writing
Essays on writing a screenplay, play or novel.

19488 **www.theatre-resource.com**
Theatre Resource
Career and employment information.

19489 **www.theatrebayarea.org**
Theatre Bay Area
Serving more than 400 member theatre companies and 3,000 individual members in the San Francisco Bay Area and Northern California, Theatre Bay Area provides monthly classes, workshops, events, information and publications.

19490 **www.theatrecrafts.com**
Theatrecrafts.com
Practical information about technical theatre techniques for theatre folk at any level.

19491 **www.theatrejobs.com**
Theatrejobs.com
Online job placement. Festival listings, summer stock, assistantships, apprenticeships, fellowships and internships.

19492 **www.theatrelibrary.org/links**
Performing Arts Links
General resources including applied and interactive theatre, performing arts data service and art sites. Digital librarian includes glossary of technical theatre terms.

19493 **www.theatrelibrary.org/links/index.html**
Theatrelibrary.org
Master categories are Theatre, Dance, Cinema and Reviews.

19494 **www.thecastingnetwork.com/webring.html**
Casting Network.com
By and for actors.

19495 **www.theplays.org**
Electronic Literature Foundation
William Shakespeare's plays online.

19496 **www.top20performingarts.com**
Top 20 Performing Arts
Online directory for Perfoming Arts education.

19497 **www.towson.edu/worldmusiccongresses**
World Music Congresses
1997-2010 World Cello Congress' II-V, 2004 The First World Guitar Congress and 2008 World Guitar Congress II. Celebrations of music with international gatherings of the world's greatest musicians, composers, conductors, instrument manufacturers students, and music lovers from around the globe.

19498 **www.unc.edu/depts/outdoor**
Institute of Outdoor Drama
Summer jobs for all theatrical personnel.

19499 **www.ups.edu/professionalorgs/dramaturgy**
Dramaturgy Northwest
Relevant information for all dramaturgs.

19500 **www.urta.com**
University/Resident Theatre Association
Coalition of theatre training programs. Sponsors unified auditions.

19501 **www.usabda.org**
USA Dance
Non-profit organization working to promote ballroom dancing, both as a recreational activity and as a competetive sport.

19502 **www.usitt.org**
United States Institute for Theatre Technology
The association of design, production and technology professionals in the performing arts and entertainment industry whose mission is to promote the knowledge and skills of its members. International in scope, USITT draws its board of directors from across the US and Canada. Sponsors projects, programs, research, symposia, exhibits, and annual conference. Disseminates information on aesthetic and technical developments.

19503 **www.variety.org**
Variety
e-version of the show business newspaper.

19504 **www.vcu.edu/artweb/playwriting**
Playwriting Seminars
An opinionated web companion on the art and craft of playwriting for theatre and dance.

19505 **www.vl-theatre.com**
WWW Virtual Library
Links to theatre and drama resources. Updated daily.

19506 **www.writersguild.com**
Writers Guild of America
List of Agents and information on Mentor program.

19507 **www.wwar.com**
World Wide Arts Resources
Links to Theatre and Dance.

19508 **www2.sundance.org**
Sundance Institute
Information on the Sundance Theatre Laboratory summer workshop for directors, playwrights, choreographers, solo performers and composers. For information on submitting a play, click Theatre Program on home page.

Associations

19509 ADSC International Association of Foundation Drilling
8445 Freeport Parkway Suite 325
Irving, TX
469-359-6000
Fax: 469-359-6007
E-Mail: adsc@adsc-iafd.com
Home Page: www.adsc-iafd.com
Social Media: Facebook, Twitter, LinkedIn

Al Rasband, President
Martin McDermott, Vice President
Lance Kitchens, Treasurer
Rick Marshall, Director
Greg Sullivan, Director

19510 American Association of Drilling Engineers
P.O. Box 107
Houston, TX 77001
281-293-9800
E-Mail: info@aade.org
Home Page: www.aade.org
Social Media: Facebook

Founded in 1978

19511 American Association of Petroleum Geologists
1444 S. Boulder
PO Box 979
Tulsa, OK 74119
918-584-2555
800-364-2274
Fax: 918-560-2632
E-Mail: bulletin@aapg.org
Home Page: www.aapg.org
Social Media: Facebook, Twitter, LinkedIn, YouTube

Paul Weimer, President
Denise M. Cox, Secretary
Edward Beaumont, President-Elect
James S. McGhay, Treasurer
Stephen E. Laubach, Editor

Supports those professionals involved in the field of geology as it relates to petroleum, natural gas, and other energy products. Publishes monthly journal of peer-reviewed articles.
30000 Members
Founded in 1917

19512 American Association of Petroleum Geologis ts Foundation
P.O. Box 979
Tulsa, OK 74101-0979
918-560-2644
855-302-2743
Fax: 918-560-2642
Home Page: foundation.aapg.org
Social Media: Facebook, Twitter, Stumbleupon

David Curtiss, Executive Director
David E. Lange, Deputy Executive Director
April Stuart, Program Coordinator
Tamra Campbell, Administrative Assistant
Karen Piqune, Librarian
Founded in 1967

19513 American Association of Professional Landmen
4100 Fossil Creek Boulevard
Fort Worth, TX 76137
817-847-7700
Fax: 817-847-7704
E-Mail: aapl@landman.org
Home Page: www.landman.org
Social Media: Facebook, Twitter, LinkedIn, YouTube

Jack C. Richards, President
Jim R. Dewbre, 1st Vice President
Martin Schardt, Executive VP
Bernard J. Ulicy, 2nd Vice President
C.Craig Young, Sr.Director

AAPL's mission is to promote the highest standards of performance for all land professionals, to advance their stature and to encourage sound stewardship of energy and mineral resources.
7000 Members
Founded in 1955

19514 American Fuel & Petrochemical Manufacturer s
1667 K Street NW
Ste. 700
Washington, DC 20006
202-457-0480
Fax: 202-457-0486
Home Page: www.afpm.org
Social Media: Facebook, Twitter, RSS

David Lamp, Chairman
Gregory J. Goff, Vice Chair
Charles T. Drevna, Executive Assistant
Rich Moskowitz, General Counsel
Diana Cronan, Communications Director
450 Members
Founded in 1902

19515 American Gas Association
400 N Capitol Street NW
Washington, DC 20001
202-824-7000
Fax: 202-824-7092
E-Mail: ykorolevich@aga.org
Home Page: www.aga.org
Social Media: Facebook, Twitter, LinkedIn, Myspace, Flickr

John W. Somerhalder, II, Chairman
Dave McCurdy, President & CEO
Lawrence T. Borgard, 1st Vice Chair
Ronald W. Jibson, 2nd Vice Chair

The American Gas Association advocates the interests of its members and their customers, and provides information and services promoting efficient demand and supply growth and operational excellence in the safe, reliable and efficient delivery of natural gas.
Founded in 1918

19516 American Institute of Mining Metallurgical & Petroleum Engineers
12999 East Adam Aircraft Circle
Englewood, CO 80112
303-325-5185
Fax: 888-702-0049
E-Mail: aime@aimehq.org
Home Page: www.aimehq.org
Social Media: Facebook, LinkedIn, YouTube

Brajendra Mishra, President
George Luxbacher, President-Elect
Randy Skagen, Treasurer
L. Michele Lawrie-Munro, Executive Director

AIME is and shall be a New York State Nonprofit Corporation organized and operated to advance and disseminate, through the programs of the Member Societies, knowledge of engineering and the arts and sciences involved in the production and use of minerals, metals, energy sources and materials for the benefit of humankind, and to represent AIME and the Member Societies within the larger engineering community.
90000 Members
Founded in 1871

19517 American Oil & Gas Historical Society
1201 15th Street
Ste 300
Washington, DC 20005
Home Page: aoghs.org

Bruce A. Wells, Executive Director
Founded in 2003

19518 American Petroleum Institute
1220 L St NW
Washington, DC 20005-4070
202-682-8000
Fax: 202-682-8232
Home Page: www.api.org
Social Media: Facebook, Twitter, YouTube, Flickr

Jack N.Gerard, President & CEO

The only national trade association that represents all aspects of America's oil and natural gas industry. Members are producers, refiners, suppliers, pipeline operators and marine transporters, as well as service and supply companies that support all segments of the industry.
400+ Members
Founded in 1919

19519 Association of Desk and Derrick Clubs
5321 South Sheridan Road
Suite 24
Tulsa, OK 74145
918-622-1749
Fax: 918-622-1675
E-Mail: ado@addc.org
Home Page: www.addc.org

Linda Rodgers, President
Connie Harrison, Vice President
Maggi Franks, Treasurer
Babara Ann Pappas, Secretary
Sheryl Minear, RP, Parliamentarian
Founded in 1949

19520 Association of Drilled Shaft Contractors
8445 Freeport Parkway
Suite 325
Irving, TX 75063
469-359-6000
Fax: 469-359-6007
E-Mail: adsc@adsc-iafd.com
Home Page: www.adsc-iafd.com
Social Media: Facebook, LinkedIn

Tom Witherspoon, President
Tom Tuozzolo, Vice President
Luke Schuler, Treasurer
Tom Bird, Chairman

A professional, internationa, nonprofit trade association representing the anchored earth retention, drilled shaft, micropile, and other heavy civil construction/design industries. Members include specialty subcontractors, manufacturers and suppliers, academicians and design engineers in the private and public sectors.
Founded in 1972

19521 Association of Energy Service Companies
14531 FM 529
Suite 250
Houston, TX 77095-3528
713-781-0758
800-672-0771
Fax: 713-781-7542
E-Mail: pjordan@aesc.net
Home Page: www.aesc.net

Kenny Jordan, Executive Director
Patty Jordan, Publisher/Sales Manager
Angla Fails, Administrative Manager

Professional trade association for well-site service contractors and businesses providing goods and services to well-site contractors. Develops and sells training and safety materials.
600 Members
Founded in 1956

19522 Association of International Petroleum Negotiators
11767 Katy Freeway
Suite 412
Houston, TX 77079

281-558-7715
Fax: 281-558-7073
E-Mail: president@aipn.org
Home Page: www.aipn.org

John Bowman, President
Judith Kim, VP - Communication
Steven Otillar, VP - Education
Kimberly Reeder, VP - Membership
Joseph Wesley, VP - Planning
Founded in 1982

19523 Association of Oil Pipe Lines
1808 Eye St NW
Suite 300
Washington, DC 20006-5423

202-408-7970
Fax: 202 280-1949
E-Mail: aopl@aopl.org
Home Page: www.aopl.org
Social Media: Facebook, Twitter

Andrew J.Black, President
Steven M.Kramer, General Counsel
John Stoody, Director
Heather Keith, Director
Rekha Chandrasekher, Industry Analyst

Acts as an information clearinghouse for the public, the media and the pipeline industry; provides coordination and leaderships for the industry's ongoing joint Environmental Safety Initiative; and represents common carrier crude and product petroleum pipleines in Congress, before regulatory agencies, and in the federal courts.
47 Members
Founded in 1947

19524 Association of Petroleum Industry Cooperative Managers
Home Page: www.apicom.org
Founded in 1972

19525 Association of Petroleum Surveying & Geomatics
Home Page: www.apsg.info
Social Media: Facebook, Twitter, LinkedIn

Jackie Portsmouth, Chairman
Ashok Wadwani, Vice Chair
Kevin Crozier, Nominations Chair
Alma Alling, Communications Chair
Robert Edwards, Secretary/ Treasurer

19526 Concrete Sawing & Drilling Association
100 2nd Ave South
Ste 240N
St. Petersburg, FL 33701

727-577-5004
E-Mail: info@CSDA.org
Home Page: www.csda.org

Judith O'Day, President
Kevin Baron, Vice President
Patrick O'Brien, Executive Director
Jim Dvoratchek, Past President
Mike Orzechowski, Secretary/ Treasurer

19527 Coordinating Research Council
3650 Mansell Rd
Suite 140
Alpharetta, GA 30022-3067

678-795-0506
Fax: 678-795-0509
E-Mail: jantucker@crcao.com
Home Page: www.crcao.org

Brent Bailey, Executive Director
Christopher Tennant, Deputy Director
Debra Carter, Controller

A nonprofit organization that directs, through committee action, engineering and environmental studies on the interaction between automotive/other mobility equipment and petroleum products.
1M Members
Founded in 1942

19528 Council of Petroleum Accountants Societies
445 Union Blvd.
Suite 207
Lakewood, CO 80228

303-300-1311
877-992-6727
Fax: 303-300-3733
Home Page: www.copas.org
Social Media: Facebook, LinkedIn

Tom Wierman, Executive Director
Cheri McCallister, Administrator
Anita Hartz, Creative Specialist

Members are accountants involved in, or closely related to, the oil and gas industry. Also provides ethical standards for energy accountants and is the certification organization for the Accredited Petroleum Accountant program.
3200 Members
Founded in 1961

19529 Domestic Petroleum Council
101 Constitution Avenue NW
Suite 800
Washington, DC 20001-2133

202-742-4300
Home Page: www.dpcusa.org/

William F Whitsitt, President

To work constructively for sound energy, environmental and related public policies that encourage responsible exploration, development, and production of natural gas and crude oil to meet consumer needs and fuel our economy.
24 Members
Founded in 1975

19530 Drilling Engineering Association
10370 Richmond Ave, Suite 760
Houston, TX 77042

713-292-1945
Fax: 713-292-1946
E-Mail: scott.maddox@iadc.org
Home Page: dea-global.org

Ben Bloys, Chairman
David Dowell, Advisory Board Member
Glenda Wylie, Advisory Board Member
Robert Estes, Advisory Board Member
Scott Maddox, Secretary/ Treasurer

19531 Energy Security Council
2611 FM 1960 West
Suite F-121
Houston, TX 77068

281-587-2700
Fax: 281-587-2715
E-Mail: info@energysecuritycouncil.org
Home Page: www.energysecuritycouncil.org

Alex de Alvarez, Chairman
Rick Williams, Vice-Chairman

Founded as Petroleum Industry Security Council and assumed its current name in 1999. Provides support to security professionals and business developers in the energy industry.
450 Members
Founded in 1976

19532 Energy Telecommunications and Electrical Association
5005 Royal Lane
Suite 116
Irving, TX 75063

888-503-8700
Fax: 972-915-6040
Home Page: www.entelec.org
Social Media: LinkedIn

Dan Mueller, President
Michael Burt, 1st Vice President
James Coulter, 2nd Vice President
Becky Holland, 3rd Vice President
Richard Nation, Secretary/ Treasurer

A user association that focuses on communications and control technologies used by petroleum, natural gas, pipeline and electric utility companies. Primary goal is to provide education for its members.
Founded in 1928

19533 Energy Traffic Association
3303 Main Street Corridor
Houston, TX 77002

713-528-2868
Fax: 713-464-0702
E-Mail: russell@energytraffic.org
Home Page: www.energytraffic.org

Ralph Lopez, President
Renee Ahmed, Vice President/ Secretary
Ernest M. Powell, Executive Director

A nonprofit educational association of logistics professionals in the energy industry. Membership consists of managers of energy industry logistics departments and those logistics providers serving the energy industry.
100 Members
Founded in 1941

19534 Fiberglass Tank and Pipe Institute
11150 S Wilcrest Drive
Suite 101
Houston, TX 77099-4343

713-690-7777
Fax: 713-690-2842
E-Mail: info@fiberglasstankandpipe.com
Home Page: www.fiberglasstankandpipe.com

Bobby Jin, President

The fiberglass-reinforced, thermosetting, plastic tank and pipe manufacturing industry. Members are domestic manufacturers.
5 Members
Founded in 1987

19535 Foundation Drilling Magazine
Association of Drilled Shaft Contractors
8445 Freeport Parkway
Suite 325
Irving, TX 75063

469-359-6000
Fax: 469-359-6007
E-Mail: adsc@adsc-iafd.com
Home Page: www.adsc-iafd.com
Social Media: Facebook, LinkedIn

Tom Witherspoon, President
Tom Tuozzolo, Vice President
Luke Schuler, Treasurer
Tom Bird, Chairman

The best news source within our industry. Filled with information about design, projects and updates on what's going on where, Foundation Drilling Magazine is devoted to report-

ing on the drilled shaft, anchored retention, and other related industries.
Frequency: 8x Yearly
Founded in 1972

19536 Gas Research Machinery Council
3030 LBJ Freeway
Suite 1300
Dallas, TX 75234
972-620-4026
Fax: 972-620-1613
E-Mail: memberservices@southerngas.org
Home Page: www.gmrc.org
Bob Bahnick, Chairman
Roland Trevino, Vice Chairman
Members are companies in the natural gas, oil and petrochemical industries in mechanical and fluid systems design.
75 Members
Founded in 1952

19537 Independent Liquid Terminals Association
1005 North Glebe Road
Suite 600
Arlington, VA 22201
703-875-2011
Fax: 703-875-2018
E-Mail: info@ilta.org
Home Page: www.ilta.org
E David Doane, President
Melinda Whitney, Director/Government Affairs
Michael J. Burgett, Chairman
Burton S Russell, Treasurer
Supports all those bulk, liquid terminal owners/operators and establishments supplying equipment, goods and services to the bulk liquid terminaling industry. Publishes monthly newsletter.
Founded in 1974

19538 Independent Lubricant Manufacturers
400 N Columbus St
Suite 201
Alexandria, VA 22314-2264
703-684-5574
Fax: 703-836-8503
E-Mail: ilma@ilma.org
Home Page: www.ilma.org
Celeste Powers, Executive Director
Martha Jolkovski, Director Publications/Advertising
Glenn Boyle, Second Vice President
Dixon W Benz II, Executive Sales Manager
Independent blenders and compounders of lubricants.
Founded in 1976

19539 Independent Terminal Operators Association
1150 Connecticut Avenue NW
9th Floor
Washington, DC 20036-4129
202-828-4100
Fax: 202-828-4130
E-Mail: wbode@bode.com
William H Bode, Secretary & General Counsel
Represents indepedent petroleum distributors.
15 Members
Founded in 1970

19540 Institute of Gas Technology
1700 S Mount Prospect Rd
Des Plaines, IL 60018-1804
847-768-0664
Fax: 847-768-0669
Home Page: www.gastechnology.org
Social Media: Facebook, Twitter, LinkedIn, YouTube
David Carroll, President & CEO
Chris Herman, Treasurer & CFO
Paul Chromek, General Counsel & Secretary
An independent, not-for-profit center for energy and environmental research, development, education and information. Main function is to perform sponsored and in-house research, development and demonstration, provide educational programs and services, and disseminate scientific and technical information.
Founded in 1941

19541 International Association for Energy Economics
28790 Chagrin Blvd.,
Ste 350
Clevelend, OH 44122
216-464-5365
E-Mail: iaee@iaee.org
Home Page: www.iaee.org
Peter R. Hartley, President
Anne Neumann, VP - Publication
Jurgis Vilemas, VP -Finance
Lori Smith Dschell, VP -Communications
Ponald D. Ripple, VP -Conferences

19542 International Association of Directional Drilling
281-288-6484
Home Page: www.iadd-intl.org
Jim Oberkircher, Founder/ CEO
Arstrong Lee Agbaji, Assistant Director
Bill Bailey, Board Member
Ed Dew, Board Member
Chris McCartney, Board Member

19543 International Association of Drilling Contractors
10370 Richmond Ave
Suite 760
Houston, TX 77042-9687
713-292-1945
Fax: 713-292-1946
E-Mail: info@iadc.org
Home Page: www.iadc.org
Social Media: Facebook, Twitter, LinkedIn
Stephen Colville, President and CEO
Steve Kropla, Executive VP
Mike Killalea, Group VP
Jason McFarland, Corporate Development
Bob Warren, VP-Interantional Dept
Dedicated to enhancing the interests of the oil-and-gas and geothermal drilling and completion industry worldwide
1239 Members
Founded in 1940

19544 International Coiled Tubing Association
PO Box 1082
Montgomery, TX 77356
936-520-1549
Fax: 832-201-9977
E-Mail: ababin@icota.com
Home Page: www.icota.com
Jason Skufca, Senior Chair
Alan Turner, Junior Co-Chair
Brian Schwanitz, Treasurer
Allison Babin, Secretary
Federico Botero, Board Member

19545 International Energy Credit Association
15000 Commerce Parkway
Suite C
Mt. Laurel, NJ 08054
856-380-6854
Fax: 856-439-0525
E-Mail: mbiordi@ahint.com
Home Page: www.ieca.net
Social Media: Facebook, Twitter, LinkedIn
Michele Biordi, Executive Director
Greg Cortez, President
Paul Krebs, 1st VP
Alyson Beiker, Treasurer
Members are credit and financial executives with companies whose product is a petroleum derivative.
800 Members
Founded in 1923

19546 International Geophysical Association
1225 North Loop West
Suite 220
Houston, TX 77008
866-558-1756
Fax: 713-957-0008
E-Mail: iagc@iagc.org
Home Page: www.iagc.org
Social Media: Youtube
Chip Gill, President
Walt Rosenbusch, VP
Karen St.John, Group VP
Gail Adams, Director Of Communications
Nikki Martin, Director-Environment Regulations
Represents the industry that provides geophysical services to the oil and gas industry.
203 Members
Founded in 1971

19547 International Oil Scouts Association
PO Box 940310
Houston, TX 77094-7310
512-472-8138
Home Page: www.oilscouts.com
James Yorek, President
Compiles statistics on exploration and development wells in the United States. Offers professional development and scholarship programs.
175 Members
Founded in 1924

19548 International Slurry Surfacing Association
3 Church Cir
PMB 250
Annapolis, MD 21401-1933
410-267-0023
Fax: 410-267-7546
E-Mail: krissoff@slurry.org
Home Page: www.slurry.org
Social Media: Facebook
Mike Krissoff, Executive Director
W. Pierre Peltier, President
Doug Ford, Vice President
Christine Deneuvillers, Secretary
Eric Reimschiissel, Treasurer
A non profit association dedicated to the interests, education, and success of slurry surfacing professionals and corporations around the world.
200 Members
Founded in 1963

19549 International Union of Petroleum and Industrial Workers
8131 E Rosecrans Avenue
Paramount, CA 90723
562-630-6232
800-624-5842
Fax: 562-408-1073
E-Mail: petroleumworkers@aol.com
George R Beltz, International President
Pamela Parlow, Internat'l Secretary/Tresurer
5000 Members
Founded in 1951

19550 Interstate Natural Gas Association of America
20 F Street, NW
Suite 450
Washington, DC 20001
202-216-5900
Fax: 202-216-0870
Home Page: www.ingaa.org
Richard Hoffmann, Executive Director
Donald F. Santa, Jr., President & CEO
Trade association of natural gas pipelines in the United States, Canada, Mexico and Europe.
30 Members
Founded in 1944

19551 Interstate Oil and Gas Compact Commission
900 NE 23rd Street
Oklahoma City, OK 73105
405-525-3556
Fax: 405-525-3592
E-Mail: iogcc@iogcc.state.ok.us
Home Page: www.iogcc.state.ok.us
Mike Smith, Executive Director
Mary Fallin, Chairman
Berry Tew, Jr., Vice Chairman
William S. Daugherty, 2nd Vice Chairman
Gerry Baker, AssociatcExecutive Director
The members are states that produce oil or gas; associate states support the conservation of America's energy resources. Also establishes rules andguidelines for the proper maintenance of wells.
700 Members
Founded in 1935

19552 Liaison Committee of Cooperating Oil and Gas Association
1718 Columbus Road SW
PO Box 535
Granville, OH 13023-0535
740-587-0444
Fax: 202-857-4799
E-Mail: stewart@ooga.org
Home Page: www.energyconnect.com/liason
Thomas E Stewart, Secretary/Treasurer
Established to facilitate communication among state and regional oil and gas associations.
25 Members
Founded in 1957

19553 Mid-Continent Oil and Gas Association
730 North Blvd.
Baton Rouge, LA 70802-5727
225-387-3205
Fax: 225-344-5502
Home Page: www.lmoga.com
Social Media: Facebook, Twitter, Flickr
Chris John, President
Mike Lyons, General Counsel
Brent Golleher, Manager of Govt Relations
Richard Metcalf, Director of Environmental Affairs
Debra Boehringer, Financial Services
At the forefront of the continually changing legal, legislative and regulatory issues facing a growing and diverse membership.
7.5M Members
Founded in 1917

19554 NLGI
4635 Wyandotte St
Suite 202
Kansas City, MO 64112-1537
816-931-9480
Fax: 816-753-5026
E-Mail: nlgi@nlgi.org
Home Page: www.nlgi.org
Social Media: LinkedIn
Kim Bott, Executive Director
Barbara A. Bellanti, President
Chuck Coe, Vice President
Bruce M. Urban, Secretary
David J. Como, Treasurer
Members are companies that manufacture and market all types of lubricating greases, additive or equipment suppliers, and research and educational groups whose interests are primarily technical.
280 Members
Founded in 1933

19555 NORA Association of Responsible Recyclers
5965 Amber Ridge Rd
Haymarket, VA 20169-2623
703-753-4277
Fax: 703-753-2445
E-Mail: sparker@noranews.org
Home Page: www.noranews.org
Chris Ricci, President
Brandon Velek, Executive Vice President
Bill Hinton, Vice President
Members are companies that reprocess used antifreeze, wastewater, oil filters, chemicals and companies that provide products or services to the industry.
211 Members
Founded in 1984

19556 National Association of Convenience Stores
1600 Duke Street
Alexandria, VA
703-518-4221
E-Mail: panderson@nacsonline.com
Home Page: www.nacsonline.com
Social Media: Facebook, Twitter, LinkedIn, YouTube, Instagram
Henry Armour, President and CEO
Paige Anderson, Director, Government Relations
Chris Blasinsky, Editorial Projects Director
Laura Beck, Marketing Specialist
Reed Armstrong, Products & Services Manager
Founded in 1961

19557 National Association of Division Order Analysts
PO Box 746327
Arvada, CO 80006
972-715-4489
E-Mail: administrator@nadoa.org
Home Page: www.nadoa.org
Social Media: Facebook, Twitter, LinkedIn
Jason Lucas, President
Deborah Walker, Consultant
Lynn S McCord, Administrator
900 Members
Founded in 1974

19558 National Association of Oil and Energy Services Professionals
PO Box 67
East Petersburg, PA 17520-0067
717 625-3076
888-552-0900
Fax: 717-625-3077
E-Mail: info@naohsm.org
Home Page: www.naohsm.org
Social Media: Facebook, Twitter, YouTube
David Bessette, President
Judy Garber, Executive Administrator
Members are oil heat service managers and small business owners. Also provides members with technical tapes, books and speakers to train thei employee technicians.
1400 Members
Founded in 1952

19559 National Association of Petroleum Investment Analysts
415 Hayward Mill Road
Concord, MA 01742-4604
978-369-0084
Fax: 978-369-0086
E-Mail: dbm@napia.org
Home Page: www.napia.org
Gregory B. Barnett, Membership Chairman
Michael D. Smolinski, President
D. Barry McKennitt, Executive Director
Tyler Dann II, Board Member
Nancy J. F. Prue, Board Member
Founded in 1974

19560 National Association of Royalty Owners
15 W 6th St
Suite 2626
Tulsa, OK 74119
918-794-1660
800-558-0557
Fax: 918-794-1662
E-Mail: NARO@NARO-us.org
Home Page: www.naro-us.org
Social Media: Facebook, Twitter
David Sikes, President
Linn Willers, Vice President
Robyn Guest, Corporate Secretary
JIm Leonard, Treasurer
Assists mineral and royalty owners in the effective management of their mineral properties. Provides information on tax, regulatory, and legislative matters. Conducts seminars and bestows awards.
5M Members
Founded in 1980

19561 National Drilling Association
1545 W 130th Street
Suite A2
Hinckley, OH 44233
877-632-4748
Fax: 216-803-9900
E-Mail: info@nda4u.com
Home Page: www.nda4u.com
Peggy McGee, President
Dan Dunn, Vice President
Jim Howe, Secretary/ Treasurer
A non-profit trade association of contractors, manufacturers and affiliated members from the drilling industry representing the geotechnical, environmental and mineral exploration sectors of this industry.
250+ Members
Founded in 1972

19562 National Ocean Industries Association
1120 G St NW
Suite 900
Washington, DC 20005-3801
202-347-6900
Fax: 202-347-8650
E-Mail: rmyers@noia.org
Home Page: www.noia.org
Social Media: Facebook, Twitter, LinkedIn, YouTube
Randall Luthi, President
Franki Stunz, Sr.Vice President
Ann Chapman, VP Conferences and Events
Michael Kerns, VP Government Relations
Nicoltte Nye, VP Communications
Represents all facets of the domestic offshore and related industries. Member companies are dedicated to the development of offshore oil

and natural gas for the continued growth and security of the US.
300 Members
Founded in 1972

19563 **National Petrochemical & Refiners Association**
1667 K Street, NW
Suite 700
Washington, DC 20006-1654

202-457-0480
Fax: 202-457-0486
E-Mail: info@npra.org
Home Page: www.npra.org

Charles Drevna, President
Gerald R. Van De Velde, CFO
Rebbie J. Riley, Executive Assistant

Association that represents the petrochemical and refining industries, sponsors periodic conferences, and seeks to inform policymakers and the public. Issues include the recycling of used oils and other liquid wastes.
450 Members

19564 **National Petroleum Council**
1625 K St NW
Suite 600
Washington, DC 20006-1656

202-393-6100
Fax: 202-331-8539
E-Mail: info@npc.org
Home Page: www.npc.org

David J. O'Reilly, Chair
Douglas L. Foshee, Vice Chair
Marshall W. Nichols, Executive Director

Self-supporting, federal advisory body to the Secretary of Energy established in 1946 at the request of President Truman.
175 Members
Founded in 1946

19565 **National Petroleum Energy Credit Association**
1302 Clayton Nolen Drive
Horseshoe Bay, TX 78657

830-220-3797
Fax: 817-796-1080
E-Mail: ContactUs@npeca.org
Home Page: www.npeca.org

Mike Swillo, President
Mark L. Macha, 1st Vice President
Della White, 2nd Vice President
Laura Roussel, 3rd Vice President
Terry Faber, Secretary
Founded in 1937

19566 **National Propane Gas Association**
1899 L St NW
Suite 350
Washington, DC 20036-3804

202-466-7200
Fax: 202-466-7205
E-Mail: info@npga.org
Home Page: www.npga.org

Carl Hughes, Chairman
David Lugar, Treasurer
Richard Roldan, President & CEO
Ray Murray, Chairman-Elect

Members are producers and distributors of liquified petroleum gas and equipment manufacturers.
3500 Members
Founded in 1931

19567 **National Stripper Well Association**
1201 15th St NW
Suite 300
Washington, DC 20005-2842

202-857-4722
Fax: 202-857-4799

E-Mail: webmaster@ipaa.org
Home Page: www.ipaa.org
Social Media: Twitter, Youtube

Michael Watford, Chairman
Mak K.Miller, Vice Chair
Diemer True, Treasurer
Barry Russell, President & CEO

This operates under the Independent Petroleum Association, which is an informed voice for the exloration and production segment of the industry. It provides economic and statistical information, and develops investment symposia and other opportunities for its members.
300 Members
Founded in 1934

19568 **Natural Gas Supply Association**
1620 Eye St., NW
Suite 700
Washington, DC 20006

202-326-9300
Fax: 202-326-9330
Home Page: www.ngsa.org

R. Skip Horvath, President
Patricia W. Jagtiani, Senior Vice President

Represents U.S.-based producers and marketers of natural gas on issues that affect the natural gas industry, including the residential and industrial consumers who rely on the fuel for a myriad of purposes.

19569 **Newport Associates**
7400 E Orchard Road
Suite 320
Englewood, CO 80111-2528

FAX 303-779-0908

Association for over 450 oil companies in over 20 world regions.

19570 **Nuclear Energy Institute**
1776 I Street NW
Suite 400
Washington, DC 20006-3708
202-739-8000
Fax: 202-785-4019
E-Mail: membership@nei.org
Home Page: www.nei.org

William D. Johnson, Chairman
John F. Young, Vice Chairman
Marvin S. Fertel, President & CEO
Phyllis M. Rich, CFO

Members are of utilities, manufacturers of electrical generating equipment, researchers, architects, engineers, labor unions, and others interested in the generation of electricity by nuclear power.
370 Members
Founded in 1981

19571 **Paper, Allied-Industrial, Chemical and Energy Workers International Union**
3340 Perimeter Hill Drive
Nashville, TN 37211

615-834-8590
Fax: 615-731-6362
E-Mail: jhill@isdn.net
Home Page: www.paceunion.org

Jim Pannell, VP
Lynne Baker, Associate Director Communications
Joan Hill, Director Research & Education
Elaine Piper, Owner

Work to make life better for the workers and their families.
320M Members
Founded in 1884

19572 **Petroleum Equipment & Services Association**

713-932-0168
E-Mail: info@pesa.org
Home Page: pesa.org
Social Media: Facebook, Twitter, LinkedIn, Google+, YouTube

Paul Coppinger, Chairman
Gary Halverson, Vice Chairman
Leslie Shockley Beyer, President
Michael Perini, Executive Vice President
Molly Smart, Communications Director

19573 **Petroleum Equipment Institute**
PO Box 2380
Tulsa, OK 74101-2380

918-494-9696
Fax: 918-491-9895
E-Mail: dooley@pei.org
Home Page: www.pei.org
Social Media: Facebook, Twitter, LinkedIn

Robert Renkes, Executive Director
Joeky Cheek, President
Terry Cooper, VP

Members are makers and distributors of equipment used in service stations, bulk plants and other petroleum marketing facilities.
1580 Members
Founded in 1951
Mailing list available for rent: 1600 names at $275 per M

19574 **Petroleum Investor Relations Association**
c/o Rowan Companies Inc
2800 Post Oak Road
Houston, TX 77056-6196

713-960-7575
Fax: 978-369-0086
Home Page: www.rowancompanies.com

William Provine, President
Robert E Wright, Secretary/Treasurer

Represents investor communications professional in the peroleum and natural gas industry
100 Members
Founded in 2000

19575 **Petroleum Marketers Association**
1901 Fort Myer Dr
Suite 1200
Arlington, VA 22209-1609

703-351-8000
Fax: 703-351-9160
Home Page: www.pmaa.org

Daniel F Gilligan, President
Nancy Kniher, Director Member Service
Cost: $50.00
700 Members

19576 **Petroleum Marketers Association of America**
1901 North Fort Myer Drive
Suite 500
Arlington, VA 22209

703-351-8000
Fax: 703-351-9160
E-Mail: info@pmaa.org
Home Page: www.pmaa.org

Grady Gaubert, Chairman
Mike Bailey, Vice Chair
Mark Whitehead, 2nd Vice Chair
Benny Hodges, Brands Division Director
Greg Benson, West Region Chair
Founded in 1909

19577 **Petroleum Retailers & Auto Repair Association**
Brinton Executive Center
1051 Brinton Road Suite 304
Pittsburgh, PA 15221

412-241-2380
Fax: 412-241-2815
Home Page: www.prara.com

Jeff Decker, President
Dennis Budzynski, 1st Vice President
Gauttam Patel, 2nd Vice President
Nancy Maricondi, Executive Director
Ray Moore, Treasurer
Founded in 1937

19578 **Petroleum Technology Transfer Council**
PO Box 710942
Oak Hill, VA 20171

703-620-4797
Fax: 571-485-8255
E-Mail: kchapman@pttc.org
Home Page: www.pttc.org
Social Media: Facebook

J.C. Hall, Chairman
Barry Tew, Vice Chairman
Mary Carr, Executive Director
Jeremy Viscomi, Executive Director
Kathy Chapman, Director of Operations

Fosters the effective transfer of exploration and production technology to US petroleum producers through regional resource centers, workshops, websites, publications, etc.
Founded in 1993

19579 **Pipeline Research Council International**
3141 Fairview Park Drive
Suite 525
Falls Church, VA 22042

703-205-1600
Fax: 703-205-1607
E-Mail: gtenely@prci.com
Home Page: www.prci.org

George W Tenley Jr, Manager

Sponsors research on technical issues facing the natural gas transmission industry. Members are companies operating pipeline systems.
24 Members
Founded in 1952
Mailing list available for rent

19580 **Rocky Mountain Oil and Gas Association**
1900 Grant Street
Denver, CO 80203

303-860-0099
Fax: 303-861-0373

Jess D Cooper, General Manager
Linda Swain, Manager

A trade association, representing oil and gas industries.
600 Members
Founded in 1920

19581 **Service Station Dealers of America**
1532 Pointer Ridge Place
Bowie, MD 20716

301-390-4405
Fax: 301-390-3161
E-Mail: mgates@wmda.net
Home Page: www.ssda-at.org

Peter S Kischak, President
Paul Fiore, Executive Vice President

Service Station Dealers of America/National Coalition of Petroleum Retailers and Allied Trades is a national association composed of individual and state affiliate associations representing service station dealers, repair facilities, car washes and convenience stores.
Founded in 1947

19582 **Society of Independent Gasoline Marketers**
3930 Pender Drive
Suite 340
Fairfax, VA 22030

703-709-7000
E-Mail: sigma@sigma.org
Home Page: www.sigma.org

Tom Gresham, President
David Baker, 1st Vice President
William Bradford, 2nd Vice President
Dennis Cuevas, Education Director
Nancy Muskett, Marketing Director
260 Members
Founded in 1958

19583 **Society of Petroleum Engineers**
222 Palisades Creek Drive
Richardson, TX 75080

972-329-9393
800-456-6863
Fax: 972-952-9435
E-Mail: spedal@spe.org
Home Page: www.spe.org
Social Media: Facebook, Twitter, LinkedIn, You Tube

Jeff Spath, President
Peter Goode, VP Finance
Alex Neyin, Director Africa Region
Ali R Al-Jarwan, Director Middle East Region
Mark Rubin, Executive Director

Supports those professionals involved in the field of exploration, drilling, production, and reservoir management, as well as related manufacturing and service organizations. Publishes monthly magazine.
55000 Members
Founded in 1957

19584 **Society of Petroleum Evaluation Engineers**
5535 Memorial Drive
Houston, TX 77007

713-651-1639
Fax: 713-951-9659
E-Mail: bkspee@aol.com
Home Page: www.spee.org

B K Buongiorno, Executive Secretary
E Bernard Brauer, President
S Tim Smith, VP

Members are engineers specializing in the fields of petroleum and natural gas properties.
495 Members
Founded in 1962

19585 **Society of Petrophysicists and Well Log Analysts**
8866 Gulf Freeway
Suite 320
Houston, TX 77017-6531

713-947-8727
Fax: 713-947-7181
E-Mail: info@spwla.org
Home Page: www.spwla.org
Social Media: Facebook

Elton Frost Jr, President
Thaimar Ramirez, VP Technology
Brett L.Wendt, VP Education
Oliver Mullin, VP Publications

Provides information services to scientists in the petroleum and mineral industries, serves as a voice of shared interests in our profession, plays a major role in strengthening petrophysical education, and strives to increase the awareness of the role petrophysics has in the Oil and Gas Industry and the scientific community.
3300 Members
Founded in 1961

19586 **Society of Professional Well Log Analysts**
8866 Gulf Freeway
Suite 320
Houston, TX 77017

713-947-8727
Fax: 713-947-7181
E-Mail: info@spwla.org
Home Page: www.spwla.org
Social Media: Facebook

Vicki J King, Executive Director
Sharon Johnson, Admin Asst

Promotes the evaluation of formations, through well logging techniques, in order to locate gas, oil and other minerals.
2800 Members
Founded in 1959

19587 **Solution Mining Research Institute**
105 Apple Valley Circle
Clarks Summit, PA 18411

570-585-8092
Fax: 570-585-8091
E-Mail: info@solutionmining.org
Home Page: www.solutionmining.org
Social Media: LinkedIn

John O Voigt, Executive Director
Carolyn L Diamond, Assistant Executive Director

Members are companies interested in the production of salt brine and solution mining of potash and soda ash, as well as production of salt covers, used for storage of oil, gas, chemicals, compressed air and waste.
100 Members
Founded in 1958

19588 **Southern Gas Association**
3030 LBJ Freeway
Ste 1500
Dallas, TX 75234

972-620-8505
Fax: 972-620-1613
E-Mail: memberservices@southerngas.org
Home Page: www.southerngas.org
Social Media: Facebook, Twitter, YouTube, RSS

Henry P. Linginfelter, Chairman
Frank Yoho, 1st Vice Chair
Jerry L. Morris, 2nd Vice Chair
Mike Grubb, President & CEO
Kimberly Watson, Secretary - Treasurer
Founded in 1908

19589 **Spill Control Association of America**
103 Oronoco Street
Suite 200
Alexandria, VA 22314

571-451-0433
Fax: 443-640-1086
E-Mail: info@scaa-spill.org
Home Page: www.scaa-spill.org

Andrew Altendorf, President
Scott Metzger, VP
Robert Chambers, Treasurer
Rick Lewis, Secretary
Michael Sapala, Manager

Members are companies concerned with cleaning up spills of oil and hazardous products and manufacturers of specialized products for spill control.
Founded in 1973

19590 The Independent Petroleum Association of America
1201 15th St NW
Suite 300
Washington, DC 20005-2842

202-857-4722
Fax: 202-857-4799
Home Page: www.ipaa.org

Barry Russell, President
Teresa McCafferty, VP Administration/Chief of Staff
Lee Fuller, VP Government Relations
Tina Hamlin, VP Meetings
Fred Lawrence, VP Economics & International Affair

Members are small producers of oil and natural gas and their suppliers.
5500 Members
Founded in 1929

19591 The National Petroleum Management Association
10908 Courthouse Rd
Ste 102-301
Fredericksburg, VA 22408

540-507-4371
Fax: 540-507-4372
Home Page: www.npma-fuelnet.org

Jack Lavin, President
Alan Reynolds, VP - Communication
Ruth Lavin, Marketing Officer
Erin Creese, San Antonio Office Manager
Al Pond, Board Member

19592 The Society of Exploration Geophysicists
8801 South Yale Suite 500
Tulsa, OK 74137-3575

918-497-5500
Fax: 918-497-5557
Home Page: www.seg.org/seg
Social Media: Facebook, Twitter, LinkedIn

Christopher Lee Linr, President
Robert R. Stewart, 1st Vice President
Eve S. Sprunt, 2nd Vice President
Evert Slob, Editor
Alison Small, Treasurer

19593 Tubular Exchanger Manufacturers Association, Inc.
25 North Broadway
Tarrytown, NY 10591
914-332-0040
Fax: 914-332-1541
E-Mail: tema@tema.org
Home Page: www.tema.org

Richard C Byrne, Secretary

Sets standards for the industry, known as TEMA Standards, which are sold to the chemical processing and petroleum refining industries
18 Members
Founded in 1939

19594 US Oil & Gas Association
1101 K Street NW, Suite 425
Washington, DC 20005

202-638-4400
Home Page: www.usoga.org
Social Media: Facebook, Twitter

Walter G. Mayfield, Chairman
Albert L. Modiano, President
Tim Stewart, Vice President
Founded in 1917

19595 Western Petroleum Marketers Association
PO Box 571500
Murray, UT 84157-1500

801-263-9762
888-252-5550
Fax: 801-262-9413
E-Mail: info@wpma.com
Home Page: www.wpma.com
Social Media: Facebook, Twitter

Gene Inglesby, Executive Director
Robert Fung, President
Larry Poulton, VP

Trade magazine for petroleum marketers, c-store owners, and businesses associated with petroleum marketing.
700 Members
Founded in 1953

19596 Western States Petroleum Association
1415 L St
Suite 600
Sacramento, CA 95814-3964

916-444-9981
Fax: 916-444-5745
Home Page: www.wspa.org

Joe Sparano, President
Catherine Reheis-Boyd, COO
Steven Arita, Senior Environmental Coordinator
Barbara Chichester, Bookkeeper

Trade association that represents the full spectrum of those companies that refine, produce, transport, and market petroleum and petroleum products in six western states: Arizona, California, Oregon, Nevada, Hawaii and Washington.
35 Members
Founded in 1907

Newsletters

19597 Butane-Propane News
PO Box 660698
Arcadia, CA 91066-698

626-357-2168
800-214-4386
Fax: 626-303-2854
Home Page: www.bpnews.com

Natalie Peal, Publisher
Ann Rey, Editorial Director

Petroleum and propane industry news.
Cost: $32.00
Frequency: Monthly
Founded in 1939

19598 Clean-Coal/Synfuels Letter
McGraw Hill
PO Box 182604
Columbus, OH 43272

614-304-4000
877-833-5524
Fax: 614-759-3749
E-Mail: customer.service@mcgraw-hill.com
Home Page: www.mcgraw-hill.com
Social Media: Facebook, Twitter, You Tube

John Higgins, Publisher

Provides worldwide coverage of the development of clean-coal technologies.
Cost: $840.00
6 Pages
Frequency: Monthly
Founded in 1899

19599 Cold Water Oil Spills
Cutter Information Corporation
37 Broadway
Suite 1
Arlington, MA 02474-5500

781-648-1950
800-888-8939
Fax: 781-648-1950
E-Mail: service@cutter.com
Home Page: www.cutter.com

Kim Leonard, Editor
Karen Coburn, Senior Consultant
Hillel Glazer, Senior Consultant
Ron Blitstein, Director

Clean up and control of oil spills in cold and icy waters.
Cost: $175.00
Founded in 1986

19600 Fuel Line
National Petrochemical & Refiners Association
1667 K Street, NW
Suite 700
Washington, DC 20006-1654

202-457-0480
Fax: 202-457-0486
E-Mail: info@npra.org
Home Page: www.npra.org

Charles Drevna, President
Gerald R. Van De Velde, CFO
Rebbie J. Riley, Executive Assistant

Addresses motor fuels regulations, policy and related issues. Available online only for NPRA members.
450 Members
Frequency: Weekly

19601 Gas Daily
1200 G Street NW
#1000
Washington, DC 20005

202-383-2100
800-752-8878
Fax: 202-383-2125
E-Mail: support@platts.com
Home Page: www.gasdaily.com

Mark Davidson, Publisher
Bill Loveless, Director
Larry Foster, Director
Dixie Barrett, Vice President

Information on spot prices cash markets and regulatory developments for the natural gas industry.
Cost: $2255.00
Frequency: Daily

19602 Gas Storage Report
Pasha Publications
1600 Wilson Boulevard
#600
Arlington, VA 22209-2510

703-528-1244
Fax: 703-528-7821
Home Page: www.pasha.com

Jeff Pruzan, Editor

Detailed charts that list monthly storage activity of all interstate pipelines and covers all phases of the underground storage of natural gas.
Cost: $495.00
Frequency: Monthly

19603 Golob's Oil Pollution Bulletin
World Information Systems
PO Box 535
Cambridge, MA 02238-0535
FAX 617-492-3312

Richard S Golob, Publisher
Roger B Wilson Jr, Editor

Provides news analysis on oil pollution prevention, control and cleanup. Covers oil spills worldwide, regulations, legislation and court decisions, technical reports, new equipment and products, contract opportunities and awards, and conference notices.
Cost: $335.00
Frequency: BiWeekly
Circulation: 20,000

19604 Green Room Report
National Petrochemical & Refiners Association
1667 K Street, NW
Suite 700
Washington, DC 20006-1654

202-457-0480
Fax: 202-457-0486
E-Mail: info@npra.org
Home Page: www.npra.org

Charles Drevna, President
Gerald R. Van De Velde, CFO
Rebbie J. Riley, Executive Assistant

Addresses current environmental and safety events, including regulation and policy issues of EPA and OSHA. Available only online to NPRA members.
450 Members
Frequency: Weekly ,

19605 Gulf of Mexico Newsletter
Offshore Data Services
3200 Wilcrest Dr
Suite 170
Houston, TX 77042-3366

832-463-3000
Fax: 832-463-3100
Home Page: www.ods-petrodata.com

Thomas E Marsh, President
Hannah Hartland, Chairman

Aimed at the supply and service people of the off-shore oil and gas industry in the Gulf of Mexico, covers all significant industry news and events, and summarizes construction and field development activities.
Cost: $259.00
Frequency: Weekly
Circulation: 2150
Founded in 2002

19606 Hart's Renewable Fuel News
Hart Evepy Publishing LP
1201 Seven Locks Road
#300
Potomac, MD 20854

301-354-2100
Fax: 301 424-7260
Home Page: www.worldfuels.com

Rachel Gantz, Editor
Robert Gaph, Executive Editor
Jack Peckham, Executive Editor
Theresa Ward, Managing Editor

Refinery updates, oxygenation schemes, capital spending, strategic alliances and essential business intelligence on corporate moves.
Cost: $1495.00
Frequency: Weekly
Founded in 1973

19607 ILMA Compoundings
Independent Lubricant Manufacturers Association
400 N Columbus St
Suite 201
Alexandria, VA 22314-2264

703-684-5574
Fax: 703-836-8503
E-Mail: ilma@ilma.org
Home Page: www.ilma.org

Celeste Powers, Executive Director
Martha Jolkovski, Director Publications/Advertising

Focuses on legislative, regulatory, marketing and industry news of concern to independent blenders and compounders of high-quality lubricants. Accepts advertising.
Cost: $150.00
20 Pages
Frequency: Monthly
Circulation: 1800
Founded in 1948

19608 Independent Liquid Terminals Association Newsletter
Independent Liquid Terminals Association
1444 I St Nw
Suite 400
Washington, DC 20005-6538
202-842-9200
Fax: 703-875-2018
E-Mail: info@ilta.org
Home Page: www.ilta.org

E David Doane, President
Gwen Butler, Office Manager

Monthly publication detailing federal, state and local legislative and regulatory action, ILTA response and ILTA events. Geared specifically to bulk liquid terminal owners/operators and establishments supplying equipment, goods and services to the bulk liquid terminaling industry.
8 Pages
Frequency: Monthly
Printed in 2 colors

19609 Institute of Gas Technology
Institute of Gas Technology
1700 S Mount Prospect Rd
Des Plaines, IL 60018-1804

847-768-0500
Fax: 847-768-0501
E-Mail: publicrelations@gastechnology.org
Home Page: www.gastechnology.org

David Carroll, President/CEO
Edward Johnston, Managing Director
Carol Worster, Manager

Newsletter
Cost: $495.00
Founded in 1945

19610 International Directory of Oil Spills and Control Products and Services
Cutter Information Corporation
37 Broadway
Suite 1
Arlington, MA 02474-5500

781-648-8700
Fax: 781-648-8707
E-Mail: consortium@cutter.com
Home Page: www.cutter.com
Social Media: Facebook, Twitter, LinkedIn, RSS

Verna Allee, Senior Consultant

Products and services listed by category.
Cost: $75.00

19611 International Gas Technology Highlights
Institute of Gas Technology
1700 S Mount Prospect Rd
Des Plaines, IL 60018-1804

847-768-0664
Fax: 847-768-0669
E-Mail: gtiadmin@gastechnology.org
Home Page: www.gastechnology.org

David Carroll, President/CEO
Edward Johnston, Managing Director

A biweekly newsletter covering international developments in energy with a focus on natural gas.
Cost: $100.00
4 Pages
Circulation: 1600
Founded in 1946
Printed in 2 colors on matte stock

19612 International Oil News
William F Bland
709 Turmeric Ln
Durham, NC 27713-3103

919-544-1717
Fax: 919-544-1999
E-Mail: mbs@PetroChemical-News.com
Home Page: www.petrochemical-news.com/pcn.htm

Susan Kensil, President
Mollie B Sandor, Circulation Director

A weekly report of current news about all areas of the international petroleum industry, exploration, production, processing, transportation and marketing.
Cost: $857.00
Frequency: Weekly
Founded in 1963

19613 International Summary and Review of Oil Spills
Cutter Information Corporation
37 Broadway
Suite 1
Arlington, MA 02474-5500

781-648-8700
Fax: 781-648-8707
Home Page: www.cutter.com

Verna Allee, Senior Consultant

International coverage of the gas and oil industry.
Cost: $100.00
Frequency: Monthly
Founded in 1986

19614 LNG Observer
Institute of Gas Technology
1700 S Mount Prospect Rd
Des Plaines, IL 60018-1804

847-768-0664
Fax: 847-768-0669
Home Page: www.gastechnology.org

David Carroll, President/CEO

A bimonthly publication covering the worldwide liquefied natural gas industry, including political developments, technology, economics, statistics and interviews with industry leaders.
Cost: $395.00
24 Pages
Frequency: Bi-Monthly
Circulation: 2,000
ISBN: 1-053694-9 -

19615 Leading Edge
Society of Exploration Geophysicists
PO Box 702740
Tulsa, OK 74170-2740

918-497-5500
Fax: 918-497-5557
E-Mail: web@seg.org
Home Page: www.seg.org
Social Media: Facebook, Twitter, LinkedIn

Mary Fleming, Executive Director
Vladimir Grechka, Editor
David J Monk, President
Richard D Miller, First V.P
Dennis A Cooke, Second V.P.

19616 Lundberg Letter
Lundberg Survey

911 Via Alondra
Camarillo, CA 93012-8048

805-383-2400
800-660-4574
Fax: 805-383-2424
E-Mail: lsi@lundbergsurvey.com
Home Page: www.lundbergsurvey.com

Trilby Lundberg, President

News on the US gasoline and diesel market. Retail and wholesale prices, market shares, consumption, taxes, station populations and consumer trends.
Cost: $399.00
Founded in 1950

19617 **NGI's Daily Gas Price Index**
Intelligence Press
PO Box 70587
Washington, DC 20024

202-583-2596
800-427-5747
Fax: 202-318-0597
E-Mail: subscriptions@intelligencepress.com
Home Page: intelligencepress.com

Ellen Beswick, Publisher
Mike Nazzaro, Managing Editor
Alexander Steis, Managing Editor

Gas industry news, reports and statistics.
Cost: $1045.00
Frequency: Daily

19618 **National Association of Royalty Owners**
12316 Andrews Drive
Suite B
Oklahoma City, OK 73120-5779

405-573-2972
800-558-0557
Fax: 405-286-9402
E-Mail: naro@naro-us.org
Home Page: www.naro-us.org

Paul Covert, VP
Wana Box, President
David Guest, Manager

Newsletter for members. Also a book is available Look Before You Lease.
Cost: $6.50
Frequency: Monthly
Founded in 1980

19619 **Natural Gas Intelligence/Gas Price Index**
Intelligence Press
PO Box 70587
Washington, DC 20024

202-583-2596
800-427-5747
Fax: 202-318-0597
E-Mail: ellen@intelligencepress.com
Home Page: www.intelligencepress.com

Ellen Beswick, Publisher
Alexander Steis, Managing Editor

Statistics and research for the gas and petroleum industry.
Cost: $1195.00
Frequency: Weekly
Founded in 1981

19620 **Natural Gas Week**
Energy Intelligence Group
1401 New York Ave Nw
Suite 500
Washington, DC 20005-2102

202-393-5113
Fax: 202-393-5115
E-Mail: info@accion.org
Home Page: www.accion.org

Maria Otero, President
Mike Sultan, Managing Director
John Lwande, Managing Director
Melissa Baez, Project Manager

Economics news covering the gas industry.
Cost: $1860.00
20 Pages
Frequency: Weekly
Founded in 1985
Printed in 2 colors on matte stock

19621 **News Fuel & Vehicles Report**
Inside Washington Publishers
1919 S Eads St
Suite 201
Arlington, VA 22202-3028

703-418-3981
800-424-9068
Fax: 703-416-8543
E-Mail: support@iwpnews.com
Home Page: www.iwpnews.com

Latest news, research and reports on alternative fuels and vehicles development aimed toward the program managers, lobbyists, policy makers, and auto, oil and corn chemical industries.
Cost: $985.00
Founded in 1980

19622 **Ocean News & Technology**
Technology Systems Corporation
PO Box 1096
Palm City, FL 34991-7174

772-221-7720
Fax: 772-221-7715
E-Mail: techsystems@sprintmail.com
Home Page: www.ocean-news.com

Dan White, Editor
Sharon White, Circulation Manager

Magazine focusing on the major business areas of the ocean industry. News articles and technology developments are covered in areas including defense, offshore oil, diving, science, environment and marine.
Cost: $45.00
Founded in 1981

19623 **Offshore Rig Newsletter**
Offshore Data Services
3200 Wilcrest Dr
Suite 170
Houston, TX 77042-3366

832-463-3000
Fax: 832-463-3100
Home Page: www.ods-petrodata.com

Thomas E Marsh, President
Barry Young, Chairman

Emerging markets, accidents, new technology, financing schemes, insurance trends, rig construction, moves, sales, and rates, labor problems, attrition, marketing strategies, and the corporate activities of drilling contractors.
Cost: $220.00
Frequency: Monthly
Circulation: 900
Founded in 1973

19624 **Oil Daily**
Energy Intelligence Group
1401 New York Ave Nw
Suite 500
Washington, DC 20005-2102

202-393-5113
Fax: 202-393-5115
E-Mail: info@accion.org
Home Page: www.accion.org

Maria Otero, President
John Lwande, Managing Director
Melissa Baez, Project Manager

Magazine on the petroleum and oil industry, available on line.
Cost: $1880.00
Frequency: Daily
Circulation: 60000
Founded in 1951

19625 **Oil Express**
United Communications Group
11300 Rockville Pike
Street 1100
Rockville, MD 20852-3030

301-287-2700
Fax: 301-816-8945
E-Mail: webmaster@ucg.com
Home Page: www.ucg.com

Benny Dicecca, President

Information for gasoline marketers.
Cost: $447.00
8 Pages
Frequency: Monthly
Founded in 1977

19626 **Oil Spill Intelligence Report**
Aspen Publishers
111 8th Ave
Suite 700
New York, NY 10011-5207

212-771-0600
800-234-1660
Fax: 212-771-0885
Home Page: www.aspenpublishers.com

Richard Kravits, Executive VP
Gerry Centrowitz, Marketing/Communications Manager

Provides timely coverage of oil spills worldwide.
Cost: $695.00
6 Pages
Frequency: Weekly
Founded in 1978

19627 **Oil Spill United States Law Report**
Aspen Publishers
76 Ninth Avenue
7th Floor
New York, NY 10011

212-771-0600
800-638-8437
Home Page: www.aspenpublishers.com

Mark Dorman, CEO
Gustavo Dobles, VP Operations

Professionals who need to stay abreast of US federal and state regulations.
Cost: $7.67
12 Pages
Frequency: Monthly

19628 **Oil, Gas and Petrochem Equipment**
PennWell Publishing Company
1421 S Sheridan Rd
Tulsa, OK 74112-6619
918-835-3161
800-331-4463
Fax: 918-831-9476
E-Mail: headquarters@penwell.com
Home Page: www.pennwell.com

Robert Biolchini, President
Tim L Tobeck, Group Publisher
J B Avants, Publisher & Editor

The petroleum industry's only all new products and services magazine. Each month it announces the newest developments in equipment, products, systems and services for drilling, production, refining, petrochemical manufacturing, pipeline/storage and gas processing.
Cost: $35.00
Frequency: Monthly
Circulation: 32000
Founded in 1955

Mailing list available for rent: 32,000 names
Printed in 4 colors on glossy stock

19629 PIW's Oil Market Intelligence
286 Madison Ave
Suite 14
New York, NY 10017-6368

212-557-3000
Fax: 212-557-5051
Home Page: www.piw.pubs.com

Offers information on oil and gas stocks and bonds.
Frequency: Monthly

19630 PTTC Network News
Petroleum Technology Transfer Council
16010 Barkers Point Lane
Suite 220
Houston, TX 77079

281-921-1720
Fax: 281-921-1723
E-Mail: hq@pttc.org
Home Page: www.pttc.org

Kristi Lovendahl, Webmaster/Newsletter Editor
Norma Gutierrez, Circulation Director
Donald Duttlinger, Executive Director
Russell Lindsay, Advertising Sales Director

16 page newsletter with east to read summaries of new oil and natural gas technologies.
Frequency: Quarterly
Circulation: 17000
Founded in 1994

19631 PetroChemical News
William F Bland
PO Box 16666
Chapel Hill, NC 27516-6666

919-490-0700
Fax: 919-490-3002

Susan D Kensil, Editor

A fast, accurate report of significant world petrochemical developments.
Cost: $739.00
4 Pages
Frequency: Weekly

19632 Petroleum Intelligence Weekly
5 E 37th St
Suite 5
New York, NY 10016-2807

212-532-1112
Fax: 212-532-4479
E-Mail: info@energyintel.com
Home Page: www.energyintel.com

Tom Wallin, President
Peter Kemp, Editor
Raja W. Sidawi, Chairman
Sarah Miller, Editor-at-Large

News of the oil and gas industries worldwide.
Cost: $3340.00
Frequency: Weekly
Founded in 1961

19633 Platt's Oilgram News
McGraw Hill
3333 Walnut Street
Boulder, CO 80301-2525

720-485-5000
800-752-8878
Fax: 720-548-5701
E-Mail: support@platts.com
Home Page: www.platts.com
Social Media: Facebook, Twitter, LinkedIn, YouTube,LinkedIn,RSS,Blog

O Marashian, Publisher
James Keener, Marketing
Harry Sachinsis, President

News of the oil and gas industries worldwide.
Frequency: Daily
Founded in 1888
Mailing list available for rent

19634 Public Gas News
American Public Gas Association
201 Massachusetts Ave Ne
Suite C-4
Washington, DC 20002-4957

202-464-0240
Fax: 202-464-0246
E-Mail: website@apga.org
Home Page: www.apga.org

Bert Kalisch, President
Bob Beauregard, Marketing
Chuck Warrington, Managing Director

Written for public gas managers to keep them apprised of industry news.
Cost: $50.00
Circulation: 1000
Founded in 1961
Printed in on matte stock

19635 Security Watch
National Petrochemical & Refiners Association
1667 K Street, NW
Suite 700
Washington, DC 20006-1654

202-457-0480
Fax: 202-457-0486
E-Mail: info@npra.org
Home Page: www.npra.org

Charles Drevna, President
Gerald R. Van De Velde, CFO
Rebbie J. Riley, Executive Assistant

Important security-related events, announcements, and background stories from government and industry. Written for members of the refining and petrochemical industries who have facility security responsibilities.
450 Members
Frequency: Weekly

19636 Tech Update
National Petrochemical & Refiners Association
1667 K Street, NW
Suite 700
Washington, DC 20006-1654

202-457-0480
Fax: 202-457-0486
E-Mail: info@npra.org
Home Page: www.npra.org

Charles Drevna, President
Gerald R. Van De Velde, CFO
Rebbie J. Riley, Executive Assistant

Highlights developments in safety, plant security, technology, government regulations, and NPRA technical meetings for the petroleum refining and petrochemical industries.
450 Members
Frequency: Bi-Weekly

19637 WPMA Weekly Update
Western Petroleum Marketers Association
PO Box 571500
Murray, UT 84157

801-263-9762
888-252-5550
Fax: 801-262-9413
E-Mail: info@wpma.com
Home Page: www.wpma.com

Gene Inglesby, Executive Director
Rob Franklin, President
Bob Ogan, VP

E-newsletter.
Frequency: Weekly
Founded in 1953

19638 Washington Report
Interstate Natural Gas Association of America
555 13th St Nw
Suite 300W
Washington, DC 20004-1109

202-637-8600
Fax: 202-637-8615
Home Page: www.stonebridge-international.com

Anthony S Harrington, CEO
Samuel Berger, Manager

Natural gas newsletter places a special emphasis on developments that affect the interstate pipeline industry. It covers Congress, the Federal Energy Regulatory Commission and other federal agencies, state and Canadian regulatory boards and company news.

19639 Weekly Propane Newsletter
Butane-Propane News
PO Box 660698
Arcadia, CA 91066-0698

626-357-2168
Fax: 626-303-2854
Home Page: www.bpnews.com

Natalie Peal, Publisher
Kurt Ruhl, National Sales Manager

Weekly updates and rates on the propane and gas industry.
Cost: $205.00
8 Pages
Frequency: Weekly
Circulation: 2000
Founded in 1939
Printed in one color on matte stock

19640 Western Petroleum Marketers Association
PO Box 571500
Salt Lake, UT 84157-1500

801-263-9762
Fax: 801-262-9413
E-Mail: info@wpma.com
Home Page: www.wpma.com
Social Media: Facebook, Twitter

Gene Inglesby, Executive Director
Sandra Peterson, Editor
Brett Adams, President
Robert Fung, First V.P
Lary Poulton, Second V.P.

Accepts advertising.
Founded in 1953

19641 World Gas Intelligence
575 Broadway
New York, NY 10012-3230

212-941-5500
Fax: 212-941-5509
Home Page: www.piw.pubs.com

Edward L Morse, Publisher
Jocelyn Strauber, Circulation Director

International coverage of the oil and gas industry.
Cost: $985.00
Frequency: SemiMonthly
Mailing list available for rent

Magazines & Journals

19642 AAPG Bulletin
American Association of Petroleum Geologists
PO Box 979
Tulsa, OK 74101-979

918-584-2555
Fax: 918-560-2632

E-Mail: bulletin@aapg.org
Home Page: www.aapg.org

Beverly Molyneux, Managing Editor
David Curtiss, CEO/President
Larry Nations, Marketing

Peer reviewed articles that cover major extent and detailed geologic data. Information on petroleum, natural gas, and other energy products.
Cost: $305.00
Frequency: Monthly
Circulation: 30000
ISSN: 0149-1423
Founded in 1917

19643 AAPG Explorer
American Association of Petroleum Geologists
1444 S Boulder Avenue
PO Box 979
Tulsa, OK 74101-979

918-584-2555
800-288-7636
Fax: 918-560-2665
E-Mail: postmaster@aapg.org
Home Page: www.aapg.org

Patrick J F Gratton, President
Ernest A Mancini, Editor
Brenda Merideth, Advertising Sales Manager

News for explorationists of oil, gas and minerals as well as for geologists with environmental and water well concerns.
Cost: $50.00
Frequency: Monthly
Circulation: 30000
ISBN: 0-195298-6 -
Founded in 1917
Printed in 4 colors on matte stock

19644 American Gas Magazine
American Gas Association
400 N Capitol Street NW
Suite 450
Washington, DC 20001

202-824-7000
Fax: 202-824-7092
Home Page: www.aga.org
Social Media: Facebook, Twitter, YouTube,RSS,Flickr

Dave McCurdy, CEO
Kevin Hardardt, CFO/CAO
Ysabel Korolevich, Membership Services
Frequency: 10x/Year
Founded in 1918

19645 American Oil and Gas Reporter
National Publishers Group
PO Box 343
Derby, KS 67037

316-788-6271
800-847-8301
Fax: 316-788-7568
E-Mail: reporter@feist.com
Home Page: www.fiest.com

Charlie Cookson, Publisher
Bill Campbell, Managing Editor

The American Oil & Gas Reporter serves the exploration, drilling and production segments of the oil and gas industry.
Cost: $65.07
Frequency: Monthly
Circulation: 7384
Founded in 1958

19646 BIC - Business & Industry Connection
BIC Alliance
Po Box 3502
Covington, LA 70434

985-893-8692
Fax: 985-893-8693
E-Mail: bic@bicalliance.com
Home Page: www.bicalliance.com

Jamie Craig, Editor
Earl Heard, CEO/President
Kathy Dugas, Administrator
Joe Storer, Manager

Information on oil and gas, refining, petrochemical, environmental, construction, engineering, pulp and paper, state agencies and municipalities business.
Cost: $45.00
Circulation: 75000

19647 Bloomberg Natural Gas Report
Bloomberg Financial Markets
100 Business Park Drive
Princeton, NJ 08542-840

609-279-3000
800-395-9403
Fax: 917-369-7000
E-Mail: munis@bloomberg.com
Home Page: www.bloomberg.com/energy

Michael Bloomberg, Publisher
Ronald Henkoff, Editor

News, interviews, and analysis of topics of importance to all levels of the natural gas market.
12 Pages
Frequency: Weekly
Circulation: 1700
Founded in 1980

19648 Butane-Propane News
Butane-Propane News
PO Box 660698
Arcadia, CA 91006

626-357-2168
800-214-4386
Fax: 626-303-2854
Home Page: www.bpnews.com

Natalie Peal, Publisher
Ann Rey, Editorial Director
Kurt Ruhl, Sales Manager

Petroleum and propane industry news.
Cost: $32.00
56 Pages
Frequency: Monthly
Circulation: 16500
Founded in 1939
Printed in 4 colors on glossy stock

19649 Coal People
Al Skinner Enterprises
PO Box 6247
Charleston, WV 25362-0247

304-342-4129
800-235-5188
Fax: 304-343-3124
E-Mail: cpm@newwave.net
Home Page: www.coalpeople.com

A Skinner, Owner
Christina Karawan, Managing Editor
Beth Terranova, Sales Manager
Angela McNealy, Circulation Manager
C K Lane, Senior Vice President

Features special news and product sections for the coal industry.
Cost: $25.00
60 Pages
Circulation: 11500
Founded in 1976
Printed in 4 colors on glossy stock

19650 Compressor Tech Two
Diesel & Gas Turbine Publications
20855 Watertown Rd
Suite 220
Waukesha, WI 53186-1873

262-754-4100
Fax: 262-754-4175
E-Mail: slizdas@dieselpub.com
Home Page: www.dieselspec.com

Michael Osenga, President
Brent Haight, Managing Editor
Kara Kane, Advertising Manager
Christa Johnson, Production Manager
Sheila Lizdas, Circulation Manager

Covers oil and gas exploration, drilling, oilfield contracting, gas and petrochemical pipeline and storage, as well as petrochemical, hydrocarbon and gas processing industries.
Circulation: 12000

19651 Diesel Progress: North American Edition
Diesel & Gas Turbine Publications
20855 Watertown
Suite 220
Waukesha, WI 53186-1873

262-754-4100
800-558-4322
Fax: 262-832-5075
E-Mail: mosenga@dieselpub.com
Home Page: www.dieselspec.com

Michael Osenga, President
Sheila Lizdas, Circulation Manager
Lynne Diefenbach, Advertising Manager
Christa Johnson, Production Manager

Geared towards readers interested in state-of-the-art systems technology. Features include new product listings, systems design, research amd product testing as well as systems maintenance and rebuilding.
Frequency: Monthly
Circulation: 26011
Founded in 1969

19652 Drill Bits
National Drilling Association
1545 W 130th St
Suite A2
Hinckley, OH 44233-9121

330-273-5756
877-632-4748
Fax: 216-803-9900
E-Mail: info@nda4u.com
Home Page: www.nda4u.com

Peggy McGee, President
Dan Dunn, VP
Jim Howe, Secretary/Treasurer
Tim Cleary, Board of Directors
R. Alan Garrard, Board of Directors

A non-profit trade association of contractors, manufacturers and affiliated members from the drilling industry representing the geotechnical, environmental and mineral exploration sectors of this industry.
250+ Members
Frequency: 2 X/Year
Founded in 1972

19653 Drilling Contractor
International Association of Drilling Contractors
10370 Richmond Ave
Suite 760
Houston, TX 77042-9687

713-292-1945
Fax: 713-292-1946
E-Mail: info@iadc.org
Home Page: www.iadc.org

Lee Hunt, President
Tom Terrell, Senior VP Business Development

All drilling, all completing, all the time.
Cost: $50.00
40 Pages
Frequency: 6x/Year
Circulation: 34500
Printed in 4 colors

19654 Energy Markets
Hart Publications
4545 Post Oak Place
#210
Houston, TX 77027

713-993-9320
Fax: 713-840-8585

Linda K Rader, Editor
Robert C Jarvis, Publisher

Energy Markets serves the following energy industry business classifications: utilities, municipalities, consultants and financial services, regulators, and other companies allied to or supportive of the energy industry.
Frequency: Monthly
Circulation: 25,751
Founded in 1993

19655 Energy Network
Gulf Publishing Company
PO Box 2608
Houston, TX 77252

713-529-4301
800-231-6275
Fax: 713-520-4433
E-Mail: store@gulfpub.com
Home Page: www.gulfpub.com
Social Media: Twitter, LinkedIn, RSS,YouTube

John D Royall, President/CEO
Ron Higgins, VP Sales/Publisher

Edited for companies that sell products to the oil and gas industry.
Founded in 1916
Mailing list available for rent

19656 Fuel Oil News
Hunter Publishing Limited
3100 S King Dr
Suite 1004
Chicago, IL 60616-3483

312-567-9981
Fax: 312-846-4632
Home Page: www.fueloilnews.com

Luke Hunter, Partner
Joanne Juda, Circulation Director
Kate Kenny, Publisher
Keith Reid, Senior Editor
Patricia McCartney, Associate Editor

For home heating oil retailers.
Cost: $28.00
70 Pages
Frequency: Monthly
Circulation: 18000
Founded in 1935
Printed in 4 colors on glossy stock

19657 Gas Turbine World
Pequot Publishing
PO Box 447
Southport, CT 36490

203-259-1812
Fax: 203-254-3431
Home Page: http://www.gtwbooks.com

Robert Farmer, Editor
Victor Debiasi, Publisher
Janes Janson, Marketing
Peg Walker, Circulation Manager

Serves the electric, utility and non-untility power generation, oil/gas production and pro cessing industries.
Cost: $135.00
Frequency: Weekly
Circulation: 11000
Founded in 1979

19658 Gas Utility Manager
James Informational Media
6301 Gaston Avenue
#541
Dallas, TX 75214-6204

214-827-4630
Fax: 847-391-9058
E-Mail: ruth@BetterRoads.com
Home Page: www.betterroads.com

Mike Porcaro, Publisher
Mike Porcaro, CEO/President
Carole Spohr, Marketing Manager
Stacy Stiglic, Circulation Manager
Ruth Stidger, Editor

Federal and international regulations, new supply projects, research and development projects and gas industry news.
Cost: $95.00
40 Pages
Frequency: Annual+
Circulation: 40000
Founded in 1931

19659 Georgia Petroleum Marketer
Georgia Oilmen Association
1775 Spectrum Drive
Suite 100
Lawrenceville, GA 30043

770-995-7570
Fax: 770-995-9757
E-Mail: rlane@gaoilassoc.com
Home Page: www.georgiaoilmenassoc.com

Roger T Lane, President/Editor
Mary R Franklin, Associate Editor
100 Pages
Frequency: Annual
Circulation: 800

19660 Hart's E & P
Hart Publications
1616 S Voss Rd
Suite 1000
Houston, TX 77057-2641

713-993-9320
Fax: 713-840-8585
E-Mail: directoryeditor@hartenergy.com
Home Page: www.hartenergy.com

Rich Eichler, CEO
Joe Fisher, Senior Vice President
Kristine Klavers, Senior Vice President
Frederick Potter, Executive Vice President

Technical approaches and improvements related to both offshore and land drilling and extraction of petroleum products, also new product information and personality profiles.
Cost: $59.00
Frequency: Monthly
Circulation. 25000

19661 Hart's Gas/LPG Markets
Hart Publications
6011 Executive Drive
#200
Rockville, MD 20852-3804

301-468-1039
Fax: 301-468-1039
Home Page: www.hartpub.com

Robert Gough, Editor

Financial reports on individual natural gas and liquid gasoline companies, their stock analysis, value and future mergers or acquisitions that may affect the pricing of gasoline or companies involved in the industry.
Cost: $ 1497.00
Frequency: Monthly

19662 Hart's Oil & Gas Interests
Hart Publications
6011 Executive Boulevard
#200
Rockville, MD 20852-3804

301-468-1039
Fax: 301-468-1039
Home Page: www.hartpub.com

Brian Crotty, Group Publisher

Designed to keep readers abreast of developments and investment ideas in the petroleum and natural gas industry.
Frequency: Monthly

19663 Hart's Oil & Gas Investor
Hart Publications
1616 S Voss Rd
Suite 1000
Houston, TX 77057-2641

713-993-9320
800-874-2544
Fax: 713-840-8585
E-Mail: directoryeditor@hartenergy.com
Home Page: www.hartenergy.com

Rich Eichler, CEO
Leslie Haines, Editor-in-Chief
Nissa Darbonne, Executive Editor
Kristine Klavers, Senior Vice President
Frederick Potter, Executive Vice President

Company performance, investment forecasts, economic outlooks, management strategy reports, focusing on the financial aspects of the petroleum and natural gas industry.
Cost: $297.00
Frequency: Monthly
Circulation: 5100
Printed in 4 colors

19664 Hart's World Refining
Hart Publications
4545 Post Oak Place
Suite 210
Houston, TX 77027-3105

713-993-9320
800-874-2544
Fax: 713-840-8585
Home Page: www.hartpub.com

David Coates, Publisher
Jeremy Grunt, Executive Editor
Terry Higgins, Executive Publisher
Robert Gough, Editorial Director
Rich Eichler, President

Covers projects, financing and market developments, along with feedstock and product supply, demand, pricing information, technical and regulatory events associated with the manufacture, supply, and use of transportation fuels refining technologies, business strategies and fuel policy legislation.
Cost: $149.00
Circulation: 15,693
Founded in 1980

19665 Hydrocarbon Processing
Gulf Publishing Company
PO Box 2608
Houston, TX 77252-2608

713-529-4301
800-231-6275
Fax: 713-520-4433
E-Mail: store@gulfpub.com
Home Page: www.gulfpub.com
Social Media: Twitter, LinkedIn, RSS,YouTube

John D Royall, President/CEO
Ron Higgins, VP Sales/Publisher

Concentrates on the problems facing management and technical personnel in the worldwide hydrocarbon processing industry. Accepts advertising.
Cost: $120.00
Frequency: Monthly
Circulation: 30000

Founded in 1916
Mailing list available for rent
Printed in on glossy stock

19666 **Journal of Geophysical Research**
American Geophysical Union
2000 Florida Ave Nw
Washington, DC 20009-1277

202-462-6900
800-966-2481
Fax: 202-328-0566
E-Mail: usaha@usaha.org
Home Page: www.agu.org
Social Media: Facebook, Twitter, LinkedIn, YouTube,RSS,Flickr,Blog

Christine McEntee, Executive Director
John Orcutt, Publisher

There are five sections covering soid earth, oceans, atmosphere, planets, and space physics.
Cost: $20.00
Frequency: Monthly
Circulation: 10,000
Founded in 1919

19667 **Journal of Petroleum Technology**
Society of Petroleum Engineers
PO Box 833836
Richardson, TX 75083-3836

972-952-9300
800-456-6863
Fax: 972-952-9435
E-Mail: service@spe.org
Home Page: www.spe.org

Mark Rubin, Executive Director
Giovanni Paccaloni, President
Paul Thone, Senior Manager of Sales
Niki Bradbury, Managing Director

Journal of Petroleum Technology serves the field of exploration, drilling, production, and reservoir management as well as related manufacturing and service organizations.
98 Pages
Frequency: Monthly
Circulation: 51205
Founded in 1949
Printed in 4 colors on glossy stock

19668 **LP/Gas**
Advanstar Communications
131 W 1st St
Duluth, MN 55802-2065

218-740-7200
800-346-0085
Fax: 218-740-7079
E-Mail: info@advanstar.com
Home Page: www.advanstar.com

Kent Akervik, Manager
Sean Carr, Publisher
Joseph Loggia, CEO
Kris Meyer, Circulation Manager
Brian Kanaba, National Sales Manager

The propane industry's premier information source.
Cost: $30.00
36 Pages
Frequency: Monthly
Circulation: 15320
ISSN: 0024-7103
Printed in 4 colors on glossy stock

19669 **Landman**
American Association of Professional Landmen
4100 Fossil Creek Boulevard
Fort Worth, TX 76137-2723

817-847-7700
Fax: 817-847-7704
E-Mail: aapl@landman.org
Home Page: www.landman.org

Le'ann Callihan, Editor
Robin Forte, President

Accepts advertising.
Cost: $50.00
76 Pages
Founded in 1955

19670 **Lubricants World**
4545 Post Oak Place
Suite 230
Houston, TX 77027

713-840-0378
Fax: 713-840-0379

Kathryn B Carnes, Editor

19671 **NLGI Spokesman**
National Lubricating Grease Institute
4635 Wyandotte St
Suite 202
Kansas City, MO 64112-1537

816-931-9480
Fax: 816-753-5026
E-Mail: nlgi@nlgi.org
Home Page: www.nlgi.org

Kim Bott, Executive Director
Kim Bott, Administrative Assistant

About 50% of technical or scientific information amied at the manufacturers, users and suppliers of lubricating grease.
Cost: $53.00
Frequency: Monthly
Circulation: 2500
Founded in 1933

19672 **National Petroleum News**
Bel-Av Communications
359 Galahad Rd
Bolingbrook, IL 60440-2108

E-Mail: kreid@m2media360.com
Home Page: www.npnweb.com

Keith Reid, Editor-in-Chief
Debra Reschke, Managing/Research Editor

The independent voice of the petroleum industry, content is aimed at the owner, operator or senior manager-the people who make the big decisions that require capital, time and resources.
Cost: $64.00
90 Pages
Frequency: Monthly
Circulation: 38000
Founded in 1909

19673 **Natural Gas Fuels**
RP Publishing
2696 S Colorado Blvd
Suite 595
Denver, CO 80222-5944

303-863-0521
Fax: 303-863-1722
E-Mail: info@rppublishing.com
Home Page: www.rppublishing.com

Frank Rowe, President

Technological advances, marketing strategies, legislative activities, successful applications, and corporate and government initiatives to promote natural gas-powered vehicles
Circulation: 7000
Founded in 1992

19674 **O&A Marketing News**
KAL Publications
559 S Harbor Blvd
Suite A
Anaheim, CA 92805-4547

714-563-9300
Fax: 714-563-9310
Home Page: www.kalpub.com

Kathy Laderman, President
Doreen Philbin, Advertising Sales Manager
Jim Penn, Circulation Manager
Linda Squeo, Marketing Manager

Coverage of industry events and related shows for wholesale and retail marketers of gasoline, oil and automotive service replacement products in the thirteen Pacific-Western states.
Cost: $20.00
Circulation: 7000
Founded in 1966

19675 **Offshore**
PennWell Publishing Company
1421 S Sheridan Rd
Tulsa, OK 74112-6619

918-835-3161
800-331-4463
Fax: 918-831-9476
E-Mail: Headquarters@PennWell.com
Home Page: www.pennwell.com

Robert Biolchini, President
Biol Chini, CEO
Tommie Grigg, Circulation Manager
Elbon Ball, Editor
Jayne Gilfinger, Marketing Manager

Offshore serves the international oil and gas industry in its marine/offshore operations.
Cost: $75.00
186 Pages
Frequency: Monthly
Circulation: 40000
ISSN: 0030-0608
Founded in 1910
Mailing list available for rent
Printed in 4 colors on glossy stock

19676 **Oil & Gas Journal**
PennWell Publishing Company
1700 West Loop S
#1000
Houston, TX 77027-3005

713-621-9720
Fax: 713-963-6285
E-Mail: sales@pennwell.com
Home Page: www.ogjonline.com

Tom T Terrell, Publisher
Tim Sullivant, Regional Sales Manager
Mike Moss, Regional Sales Manager

Detailed interpreation and information of the world developments in the oil and gas industry
Cost: $79.00
Frequency: Weekly
Circulation: 36090
Founded in 1990
Printed in 4 colors on glossy stock

19677 **Oil Spill Contingency Planning: A Global Perspective**
Aspen Publishers
76 Ninth Avenue
7th Floor
New York, NY 10011

212-771-0600
800-638-8437
Home Page: www.aspenpublishers.com

Mark Dorman, CEO
Gustavo Dobles, VP Operations

Hands-on guidebook to contingency planning for oil spills.
Cost: $195.00

19678 **Oilheating**
Industry Publications
3621 Hill Rd
Parsippany, NJ 07054-1001

973-331-9545
Fax: 973-331-9547
E-Mail: info@oilheating.com
Home Page: www.spraytechnology.com
Social Media: Facebook

Cynthia Hundley, Publisher

Addresses issues on dispatching and delivery efficiency, residential and commercial fuel oil use, as well as sales and services of oilfired

equipment.
Cost: $42.00
Frequency: Monthly
Circulation: 13280
ISSN: 1092-6003
Founded in 1922
Mailing list available for rent

19679 Petroleo International
Keller International Publishing Corporation
150 Great Neck Rd,
Suite 400
Great Neck, NY 11021-3309

516-829-9722
Fax: 516-829-9306
Home Page: www.supplychainbrain.com

Victor Prieto, Editor
Sean Noble, Publisher
Steve Kann, Circulation Manager
Jerry Keller, President
Mary Chavez, Director of Sales

Spanish language petroleum/petrochemical magazine.
100 Pages
Circulation: 10,314
Founded in 1943

19680 SPE Drilling & Completion
Society of Petroleum Engineers
PO Box 833836
Richardson, TX 75083-3836

972-529-9300
800-456-6863
Fax: 972-952-9435
E-Mail: service@spe.org
Home Page: www.spe.org

Giovanni Paccaloni, President
Shashana Pearson, Editor
Mary Jane, Advertising Manager
Georgeann Bilich, Publisher
Niki Bradbury, Managing Director

Technical papers selected for the drilling profession reviewed by peers on topics such as casing, instrumentation, bit technology, fluids, measurment, deviation control, telemetry, completion and well control.
Cost: $60.00
Frequency: Quarterly
Circulation: 3588
Founded in 1984

19681 Sea Technology Magazine
Compass Publications, Inc.
1501 Wilson Blvd
Suite 1001
Arlington, VA 22209-2403

703-524-3136
Fax: 703-841-0852
E-Mail: oceanbiz@sea-technology.com
Home Page: www.sea-technology.com
Social Media: Twitter

Amos Bussmann, President/Publisher
Joy Carter, Circulation Manager
Meghan Ventura, Managing Editor

Worldwide information leader for marine/offshore business, science and engineering. Read in more than 110 countries by management, engineers, scientists and technical personnel working in industry, government and education.
Cost: $40.00
Frequency: Monthly
Circulation: 16304
ISSN: 0093-3651
Founded in 1960
Mailing list available for rentat $80 per M
Printed in 4 colors

19682 Society of Professional Well Log Analysts
8866 Gulf Freeway
Suite 320
Houston, TX 77017

713-947-8727
Fax: 713-947-7181
Home Page: www.spwla.org

Vicki J King, Executive Director
Sharon Johnson, Admin Asst
Julian Singer, VP Publications
Cost: $105.00
Frequency: Annual+
Circulation: 2900
Founded in 1959

19683 Today's Refinery
Chemical Week Associates
2 Grand Central Tower,140 East 45th Street
40th floor
New York, NY 10017

212-884-9528
Fax: 212-884-9514
E-Mail: ltattum@chemweek.com
Home Page: www.chemweek.com
Social Media: Twitter, RSS,Blog

John Rockwell, VP
Joe Minnella, Global Sales Director
LYN TATTUM, Publisher
Robert Westervelt, Editor-in-Chief

Editorials from industry leaders focusing on current problems facing the industry. Highlights on legistation, activity, government regulations,and reports on major industry meetings.
Frequency: Monthly
Circulation: 10,000
Mailing list available for rent

19684 Utility & Pipeline Industries
WMO DannHausen Corporation
330 North Wabash
Suite 3201
Chicago, IL 60611

312-628-5870
Fax: 312-628-5878
E-Mail: wod@dannhausen.com
Home Page: www.gasindustries.com

Bob Higgins, Publisher
Heidi Liddle, Production Manager
Karen Ebbesmeyer, Circulation Manager
Ruth W. Stidger, Editor-in-Chief
Cory Sekine Pettite, Managing Editor

Market to federal agencies, bureaus, government departments and toll authorities. Accepts advertising.
Cost: $20.00
62 Pages
Frequency: Monthly
Circulation: 10680

19685 Washington Report
National Ocean Industries Association
1120 G St Nw
Suite 900
Washington, DC 20005-3801

202-347-6900
Fax: 202-347-8650
Home Page: www.noia.org
Social Media: Facebook, Twitter, YouTube

Tom Fry, President
Franki K Stuntz, Director Administration
Nolty J Thuriot, Director Congressional Affairs
Frequency: Bi-Weekly

19686 Well Servicing
Workover Well Servicing Publications
10200 Richmond Avenue
Suite 275
Houston, TX 77042

713-781-0758
800-692-0771
Fax: 713-781-7542
E-Mail: kjordan@aesc.net
Home Page: www.aesc.net

Kenny Jordan, Executive DIrector
Polly Fisk, Editor
Patty Jordan, Circulation

New products listing and reviews, field reports, and information on companies in the industry. Written and edited for energy service company professionals, and oil & gas operations.
40 Pages
Circulation: 11000
ISSN: 0043-2393
Founded in 1956

19687 Western Petroleum Marketers News Magazine
Western Petroleum Marketers Association
PO Box 571500
Murray, UT 84157

801-263-9762
888-252-5550
Fax: 801-262-9413
E-Mail: info@wpma.com
Home Page: www.wpma.com

Gene Inglesby, Executive Director
Rob Franklin, President
Bob Ogan, VP
Frequency: Quarterly

19688 World Oil
Gulf Publishing Company
PO Box 2608
Houston, TX 77252

713-529-4301
800-231-6275
Fax: 713-520-4433
E-Mail: store@gulfpub.com
Home Page: www.gulfpub.com
Social Media: Twitter, LinkedIn, RSS,YouTube

John D Royall, President/CEO
Ron Higgins, VP Sales/Publisher

Reaches the exploration, drilling, producing, and well servicing segments of the oil and gas industry.
Cost: $34.00
100 Pages
Frequency: Monthly
Circulation: 36000
ISSN: 0043-8790
Founded in 1916
Mailing list available for rent
Printed in 4 colors on glossy stock

Trade Shows

19689 American Association of Petroleum Geologists Annual Convention/Expo
American Association of Petroleum Geologists
PO Box 979
Tulsa, OK 74119

918-584-2555
800-364-2274
Fax: 918-560-2665
E-Mail: convene@aapg.org
Home Page: www.aapg.org
Social Media: Facebook, Twitter, LinkedIn, YouTube

Randa Reeder-Briggs, Annual Meeting Manager
Melissa Howerton, Annual Meeting Assistant

Steph Benton, Exhibit Manager
Rick Fritz, Executive Director
Edward 'Ted' Beaumont, President

Exhibits of instrumentation, equipment, supplies, services and publications for petroleum geologists, geophysicists and engineers.
7000 Attendees
Frequency: Annual/April

19690 American School of Gas Measurement Technology Meeting
PO Box 3991
Houston, TX 77253-3991

903-486-7875
Fax: 512-267-9243
Home Page: www.asgmt.com

Seminar, workshop, and tours, plus 95 exhibits of gas measurement, equipment, supplies and services.
600 Attendees
Frequency: Annual
Founded in 1927

19691 Asia Pacific Improved Oil Recovery Conference
Society of Petroleum Engineers-Texas
222 Palisades Creek Drive
PO Box 833836
Richardson, TX 75083-3868

972-952-9300
Fax: 972-952-9435
Home Page: www.spe.org

Oil recovery exhibition.
Mailing list available for rent

19692 Beaumont Industrial Petrochemical Trade Show
Lobos Services
16016 Perkins Road
Baton Rouge, LA 70810-3631

225-751-5626

Debbie Balough, Show Manager

Informs local industry of the full array of industrial equipment for the chemical industries.
5M Attendees
Frequency: January

19693 Circum-Pacific Council Energy Mineral Resources
5100 Westheimer Road
Houston, TX 77056-5596

713-709-9071
Fax: 713-622-5360

Mary Stewart, Show Manager
Napoleon Carcamo, Owner

50 booths.
1.2M Attendees
Frequency: November

19694 Eastern Oil and Gas Equipment Show
Pennsylvania Oil and Gas Association
412 N 2nd Street
Harrisburg, PA 17101-1342

717-939-9551

Stephen Rhoads, Show Manager

175 booths displaying new technologies, products and services relating to the oil and gas industries.
1M Attendees
Frequency: June

19695 Entelec Conference & Expo
Energy Telecommunications and Electrical Assoc
5005 W Royal Lane
Suite 116
Irving, TX 75063

972-929-3169
888-503-8700
Fax: 972-915-6040
E-Mail: blaine@entelec.org
Home Page: www.entelec.org

Blaine Siske, Executive Manager
Susan Joiner, Exhibits Manager
Michael Blurt, President
James C Coulter, First V.P
Kenneth Clouse, Second V.P.

To bring together communications and control technology professionals from the petroleum, natural gas, pipeline, and electric utility companies for three days of quality training, seminars, exhibits and networking.
Frequency: Annual/May
Founded in 1928

19696 Europe International Offshore Exchange
222 Palisades Creek Drive
Richardson, TX 75080-2040
Donna Anderson, Show Manager

1,100 booths.
21M Attendees
Frequency: September

19697 International Thermal Spray Conference & Exposition
ASM International
9639 Kinsman Road
Materials Park, OH 44073

440-338-5151
800-336-5152
Fax: 440-338-4634
E-Mail: natalie.nemec@asminternational.org
Home Page: www.asminternational.org
Social Media: Facebook, Twitter, LinkedIn

Natalie Neme, Event Manager
Kelly Thomas, Exposition Account Manager

Global annual event attracting professional interested in thermal spray technology focusing on advances in HVOF, plasma and detonation gun, flame spray and wire arc spray processes, performance of coatings, and future trends. 150 exhibitors.
1000 Attendees
Frequency: Annual/May

19698 Landman
American Association of Petroleum Landmen
4100 Fossil Creek Boulevard
Fort Worth, TX 76137-2723

817-847-7700
Fax: 817-847-7704
Home Page: http://www.landman.org

Carolyn Stephens, Editor
Le Ann Pembroke, Advertising Manager

50 booths.
1.5M Attendees
Frequency: June

19699 Liquified Gas Association Southwest
PO Box 9925
Austin, TX 78766-0925

FAX 512-834-0758

Cheryl Tomanetz, Show Manager

125 booths.
1.8M Attendees
Frequency: September

19700 Liquified Natural Gas
Reed Exhibition Companies
255 Washington Street
Newton, MA 02458-1637

617-584-4900
Fax: 617-630-2222

Elizabeth Hitchcock, International Sales

Presentation for the liquefied natural gas industry.
2.5M Attendees
Frequency: May

19701 Liquified Petroleum Gas Exposition Midwest
4100 Country Club Drive
Jefferson City, MO 65109-0302

573-634-5345
Fax: 573-893-2623

Emma Krommel, Show Manager

100 booths of large transport and bobtail delivery trucks.
1M Attendees
Frequency: June

19702 Midwest Petroleum & Convenience Tradeshow
Illinois Petroleum Marketers Association
PO Box 12020
Springfield, IL 62791-2020

217-544-4609
Fax: 217-789-0222

Bill Fleischli, Executive VP, Managing Editor

Suppliers and manufacturers to petroleum marketing and convenience store trades, including pumps, computers, trucks, safety devices, canopies, car washes and tank testing. 300 booths.
4M Attendees
Frequency: June

19703 National Petro Refiners Association Refinery Petrochemical Plant
1899 L Street NW
Suite 1000
Washington, DC 20036-3810

202-457-0480
Home Page: http://www.npra.org

Robert Dzuiban, Show Manager
Robert Slaughter, President

A forum for the exchange of technical information and services to the petroleum industry.
1.3M Attendees
Frequency: May

19704 Offshore Technology Conference
222 Palisades Creek Drive, Richardson
Richardson, TX 75080-2040

972-952-9494
866-229-2386
Fax: 972-952-9435
E-Mail: service@spe.org
Home Page: www.spe.org

Alan Wegener, Show Manager
Niki Bradbury, Managing Director

Consisting of a forum to disseminate technical information for the advancement of engineering.
30M Attendees
Frequency: May

19705 Petroleum Computer Conference
Society of Petroleum Engineers
222 Palisades Creek Drive
Richardson, TX 75080-2040
972-952-9300
Fax: 972-952-9435
E-Mail: service@spe.org
Home Page: www.spe.org

Niki Bradbury, Managing Director

Annual show of 50 microcomputer manufacturers and suppliers who provide hardware and software to the petroleum industry.
650 Attendees

19706 Petroleum Equipment Institute (CONVEX) and Exhibits
Petroleum Equipment Institute

PO Box 2380
Tulsa, OK 74101-2380

918-494-9696
Fax: 918-491-9895
E-Mail: cdooley@pei.org
Home Page: www.pei.org

Connie Dooley, Administrative Director
Robert Renkes, Marketing Director
Sarah West, Marketing Director
Rick Long, General Manager

Annual show of manufacturers of petroleum marketing equipment. There are 215 exhibiting companies with 675 booths.
4500 Attendees
Frequency: October
Founded in 1951

19707 **Society Petro Engineers Annual Meeting**
PO Box 833836
Richardson, TX 75083-3836

972-952-9300
Fax: 972-952-9435

Lois Woods, Show Manager
Mark Rubin, Executive Director

Conference with exhibits of drilling and production equipment and materials.
10M Attendees
Frequency: September

19708 **Society Petro Engineers Permian Basin Oil Gas Recovery Conference and Expo**
PO Box 833836
Richardson, TX 75083-3836

972-952-9300

Susan Bell, Event Manager

70 booths.
400 Attendees
Frequency: March

19709 **Society Petro Engineers Petroleum Computer Conference and Expo**
PO Box 833836
Richardson, TX 75083-3836

972-952-9300

Georgie Cumiskey, Event Manager

30 booths of microcomputer hardware and software for the petroleum industry.
300 Attendees
Frequency: July

19710 **Society Petro Engineers Production Operations Symposium**
PO Box 833836
Richardson, TX 75083-3836

972-952-9300

Karen Rodgers, Event Manager
Mark Rubin, Executive Director

70 booths of oil and gas industry related products and services.
1M Attendees
Frequency: March

19711 **Society Petro Engineers Rocky Mountain**
PO Box 833836
Richardson, TX 75083-3836

972-952-9300

Georgie Cumiskey, Event Manager

60 booths.
300 Attendees
Frequency: April

19712 **Society Petro Engineers Western Regional Meeting**
PO Box 833836
Richardson, TX 75083-3836

972-952-9300

Lois Woods, Exchange Manager
Mark Rubin, Executive Director

65 booths.
700 Attendees
Frequency: May

19713 **Society of Petro Engineers Eastern Regional Meeting**
PO Box 833836
Richardson, TX 75083-3836

972-952-9300

Susan Bell, Event Manager
Mark Rubin, Executive Director

Offers a forum for the exchange of ideas between petroleum and gas engineers.
500 Attendees
Frequency: October

19714 **Society of Petro Engineers Enhanced Oil Recovery Symposium and Exchange**
PO Box 833836
Richardson, TX 75083 3836

972-952-9300

Georgie Cumiskey, Event Manager
Mark Rubin, Executive Director

100 booths.
1.6M Attendees
Frequency: April

19715 **Southeast Petro Food Marketing Expo**
7300 Glenwood Avenue
Raleigh, NC 27612

919-782-4411
Fax: 919-782-4414
E-Mail: svinson@ncpma.org
Home Page: www.sepetro.org

Sharon Vinson, Show Manager

550 booths and 400+ exhibitors serving the petroleum and convenience store industries in the southeast.
2,000 Attendees
Frequency: March

19716 **WPMA Convention & Convenience Store Expo**
Western Petroleum Marketers Association
Po Box 571500
Salt Lake, UT 84157-1500

801-263-9762
Fax: 801-262-9413
E-Mail: info@wpma.com
Home Page: www.wpma.com
Social Media: Facebook, Twitter

Gene Inglesby, Executive Director
Jan Roothoff, Administration Director

In addition to Las Vegas entertainment and special events, the convention offers keynote speakers around current issues and topics, as well as workshops. Over 400 exhibits. Registration costs vary.
3750 Attendees
Frequency: Annual/Winter

19717 **Western Petroleum Marketers Convention & Convenience Store Expo**
Western Petroleum Marketers Association
PO Box 571500
Salt Lake, UT 84157-1500

801-263-9762
888-252-5550
Fax: 801-262-9413
E-Mail: info@wpma.com
Home Page: www.wpma.com
Social Media: Facebook, Twitter

Gene Inglesby, Executive Director
Jan Roothoff, Administration Director
Bob Ogan, VP

430 booths.
3500 Attendees
Frequency: February

19718 **World Gas Conference**
American Gas Association
400 N Capitol Street NW
Washington, DC 20001

202-824-7000
Fax: 202-824-7092
E-Mail: ykorolevich@aga.org
Home Page: www.aga.org
Social Media: Facebook, Twitter, LinkedIn, Myspace, Flickr

John W. Somerhalder, II, Chairman
Dave McCurdy, President & CEO
Lawrence T. Borgard, 1st Vice Chair
Ronald W. Jibson, 2nd Vice Chair

Information towards building a sustainable future for the gas industry.
Frequency: Quadrennial
Founded in 1918

Directories & Databases

19719 **APILIT**
American Petroleum Institute
275 7th Avenue
9th Floor
New York, NY 10001-6708

212-989-9001
Fax: 212-366-4298

Over 500,000 citations are offered from 1978, to the literature related to the oil refining and petrochemical industries.

19720 **Africa-Middle East Petroleum Directory**
PennWell Directories
1700 West Loop S
Suite 1000
Houston, TX 77027-3005

713-621-9720
800-752-9764
Fax: 281-499-6310
E-Mail: susana@penwell.com
Home Page: www.petroleumdirectories.com

Jonelle Moore, Editor
Tim Sullivant, Manager

A directory for: associations, government agencies, drilling, exploration and production of natural gas, petrochemicals, pipeline operators etc.
Cost: $125.00
156 Pages

19721 **American Oil and Gas Reporter Directory**
Domestic Petroleum Publishers
PO Box 343
Derby, KS 67037-0343

316-788-6271
Fax: 316-788-7568

Bill Campbell, Editor
Charlie Cookson, Publisher

State oil and natural gas regulatory agencies.
Cost: $25.00
Frequency: Annual March
Circulation: 13,540

19722 American Oil and Gas Reporter: American Drilling Rig Directory Issues
National Publishers Group
PO Box 343
Derby, KS 67037-0343

316-788-6271
Fax: 316-788-7568

Bill Campbell, Editor
Charlie Cookson, Publisher

List of contractors engaged in onshore drilling for petroleum and gas.
Cost: $25.00
Frequency: SemiAnnual
Circulation: 13,540

19723 American Oil and Gas Reporter: Directory of Crude Oil Purchasers Issue
Domestic Petroleum Publishers
PO Box 343
Derby, KS 67037-0343

316-788-6271
Fax: 316-788-7568
Bill Campbell, Editor
Charlie Cookson, Publisher

List of companies buying crude oil in the US.
Cost: $25.00
Frequency: Annual July
Circulation: 13,540

19724 Armstrong Oil Directories
Armstrong Oil
Po Box 52106
Amarillo, TX 79159-2106

806-457-9300
Fax: 806-457-9301
E-Mail: support@armstrongoil.com
Home Page: www.armstrongoil.com

Alan Armstrong, Owner

Directory of services and supplies to the industry.
Cost: $53.50
300 Pages
Frequency: Annual

19725 Brown's Directory of North American and International Gas Companies
Advanstar Communications
131 W 1st St
Duluth, MN 55802-2065

218-740-7200
800-346-0085
Fax: 218-740-7079
E-Mail: info@advanstar.com
Home Page: www.advanstar.com

Kent Akervik, Manager
Joseph Loggia, CEO

Operating gas companies, brokers and refineries are listed in this comprehensive directory with worldwide coverage.
Cost: $265.00
350 Pages
Frequency: Annual
Circulation: 1,000

19726 Canadian Oil Industry Directory
PennWell Directories
1700 West Loop S
Suite 1000
Houston, TX 77027-3005

713-621-9720
800-752-9764
Fax: 281-499-6310
E-Mail: susana@penwell.com
Home Page: www.petroleumdirectories.com

Susan Anderson, Editor
Tim Sullivant, Manager

A directory for: associations, government agencies, drilling contractors, engineering, construction, exploration, production, petrochemicals, pipeline operators, etc.
Cost: $135.00

19727 Congress Legislative Directory
American Gas Association
1515 Wilson Boulevard
Suite 100
Arlington, VA 22209-2469

703-841-8400

Offers information on members of both houses of the United States Congress, federal government agencies relevant to the natural gas industry.
Cost: $10.00
220 Pages
Frequency: Annual

19728 Contracts for Field Projects & Supporting Research on Enhanced Oil Recovery
US Department of Energy
PO Box 1398
Bartlesville, OK 74005

918-336-0307
Fax: 918-337-4418

Herbert A Tiedemann, Editor

Energy Department technical project officers and contractors.
97 Pages
Frequency: Quarterly
Founded in 1997

19729 Crude Oil Analysis Data Bank
PO Box 2565
Bartlesville, OK 74005-2565

918-336-2400

Contains over 9,000 analyses, obtained from the Bureau of Mines, of worldwide crude oil deposits.
Frequency: Full-text

19730 DRI/Platt's Oil Prices
DRI/McGraw-Hill
24 Hartwell Ave
Lexington, MA 02421-3103

781-860-6060
Fax: 781-860-6002
E-Mail: support@construction.com
Home Page: www.construction.com

Walt Arvin, President

Database provides weekly, monthly and daily time series of worldwide petroleum product prices.

19731 Drilling & Well Servicing Contractors
Midwest Publishing Company
2230 E 49th Ste E
Tulsa, OK 74105-8771

918-582-2000
800-829-2002
Fax: 918-587-9349
E-Mail: info@midwestpub.com
Home Page: www.midwestpub.com

Will L Hammack, Owner

Approximately 4,000 drilling and well servicing contractors, equipment suppliers, manufacturers and service companies.
Cost: $150.00
Frequency: Annual, September
Founded in 1943

19732 Dwight's Offshore and Bid Data
Dwight's Energydata
1633 Firman Drive
Suite 100
Richardson, TX 75081-6790

972-783-8002
800-468-3381
Fax: 972-783-0058

This large database offers the most current information on bids, lease ownership data, and competitive intelligence data on the petroleum industry.

19733 Fuel Oil News-Source Book Issue
Fuel Oil News
3496 E Lake Lansing Road
Suite 150
East Lansing, MI 48823-6223

517-337-4040
Home Page: http://fueloilnews.com/Media/MediaManager/2010%20FON%20Media%20Ki

Offers a list of over 600 manufacturers and suppliers of oil handling, heating and delivering companies.
Cost: $10.00
Frequency: Annual
Circulation: 17,000

19734 GOA Membership Directory
Georgia Oilmen Association
1775 Spectrum Drive
Suite 100
Lawrenceville, GA 30043-5745

770-995-7570
Fax: 770-995-9757
E-Mail: kcarter@gaoilassoc.com
Home Page: www.georgiaoilmensassoc.com

Roger T Lane, President/Editor
Mary R Franklin, Associate Editor
Karen Carter, Executive Assitant

Directory of active and associate members and other valuable information.
Cost: $250.00
42 Pages
Frequency: Monthly
Circulation: 1,300
Printed in on glossy stock

19735 Gas and Oil Equipment Directory
Underwriters Laboratories
2600 N.W.Lake Rd
Camas, WA 98607-8542

847-412-0136
877-854-3577
Fax: 847-272-8129
E-Mail: cec.@us.ul.com
Home Page: www.ul.com
Social Media: Facebook, Twitter, YouTube

Keith E Williams, CEO
John Drengenberg, Manager Consumer Affairs

Companies that have qualified to use the UL listing mark or classification marking on or in connection with products that have been found to be in compliance with UL's requirements.
Cost: $9.00
Frequency: Annual October

19736 Hart Energy Publishing
4545 Post Oak Place Drive
Suite 210
Houston, TX 77027-3105

713-993-9320
800-874-2544
Fax: 713-840-8585
E-Mail: jeff@grainnet.com
Home Page: www.hartenergy.com

Jeff Miller, Director Marketing
Matt Beltz, Marketing Associate
Rich Eichler, President

Kristine Klavers, Senior Vice President
Frederick Potter, Executive Vice President

Hart Energy Publishing is the worldwide leader in energy industry publishing. With fiver energy magazines, E & P, Oil and Gas investors, Pipeline gas technology, energy markets and world refining. Hart Energy Publishing also has a range of newsletters and centers devoted to the downstream Energy industry.
15 Pages
Frequency: Monthly

19737 Hart Publications
4545 Post Oak Place Drive
Houston, TX 77027-3105

713-993-9320
800-874-2544
Fax: 713-840-8585
Home Page: www.hartpub.com

Gina Acosta, Fulfillment
Rich Eichler, President

Directories, magazines and newsletters of the oil and gas industry
15 Pages
Frequency: Annually

19738 International Oil Spill Control Directory
Cutter Information Corporation
37 Broadway
Suite 1
Arlington, MA 02474-5500

781-648-8700
Fax: 781-648-8707
E-Mail: consortium@cutter.com
Home Page: www.cutter.com
Social Media: Facebook, Twitter, LinkedIn, RSS

Verna Allee, Senior Consultant
Karen Coburn, President & CEO
Paul Bergeron, CFO & COO
Anne Mullaney, Vice-President

Offers valuable information on more than 1,000 suppliers of more than 3,500 oil spill cleanup, prevention and control products and services.
Cost: $95.00
225 Pages
Frequency: Annual

19739 Marketers, Purchasers & Trading Companies
Midwest Publishing Company
2230 E 49th Ste E
Tulsa, OK 74105 8771

918-582-2000
800-829-2002
Fax: 918-587-9349
E-Mail: info@midwestdirectories.com
Home Page: www.midwestdirectories.com

Will Hammack, Editor

Over 5,300 purchasers, marketers and traders of refined products, crude oil and natural gas.
Cost: $145.00
Frequency: Annual October

19740 McGraw-Hill GasWire
DRI/McGraw-Hill
24 Hartwell Ave
Lexington, MA 02421-3103

781-860-6060
Fax: 781-860-6002
E-Mail: support@construction.com
Home Page: www.construction.com

Walt Arvin, President

Contains news and analyses of the US natural gas market.
Frequency: Full-text

19741 Member Directory and Oil & Gas Agencies
Interstate Oil and Gas Compact Commission
PO Box 53127
Oklahoma City, OK 73152-3127

405-525-3556
800-822-4015
Fax: 405-525-3592
E-Mail: iogcc@iogcc.state.ok.us
Home Page: www.iogcc.state.ok.us

Christine Hansen, Executive Director
Alesha Leemaster, Communications Manager

About 600 state representatives to the commission from 29 oil and gas producing states and seven associate states and committee members from related industries and government agencies.
Cost: $11.00
Frequency: Annual

19742 NOIA Leaders
National Ocean Industries Association
1120 G St NW
Suite 900
Washington, DC 20005-3801

202-347-6900
Fax: 202-347-8650
Home Page: www.noia.org
Social Media: Facebook, Twitter, YouTube

Tom Fry, President
Franki K Stuntz, Director Administration
Nolty J Thuriot, Director Congressional Affairs
Frequency: Annual
Founded in 1972

19743 National Petroleum News: Buyer's Guide Issue
2101 S Arlington Heights Road
Arlington Heights, IL 60005-4185

847-427-9512
Fax: 847-427-2041

Jim Bursch, Publisher
Don Smith, Editor

A comprehensive listing of products and services for the petroleum industry.
Cost: $30.00
Frequency: Annual
Circulation: 18,000

19744 National Petroleum News: Market Facts Issue
2101 S Arlington Heights Road
Arlington Heights, IL 60005-4185
847-427-9512
Fax: 847-427-2041

Jim Bursch, Publisher
Don Smith, Editor

Offers the industry's most up-to-date compilation of petroleum/convenience store facts, figures and trends.
Cost: $75.00
Frequency: Annual
Circulation: 18,000

19745 Natural Gas Industry Directory
PennWell Directories
1700 West Loop S
Suite 1000
Houston, TX 77027-3005

713-621-9720
800-752-9764
Fax: 281-499-6310
E-Mail: susana@penwell.com
Home Page: www.petroleumdirectories.com

Susan Anderson, Editor
Tim Sullivant, Manager

Major divisions of the natural gas industry worldwide.
Cost: $165.00

19746 Offshore Services and Equipment Directory
Greene Dot
11686 Jocatal Center
San Diego, CA 92127-1147

858-485-0189
Fax: 858-485-5139

Renee Garza, Editor

About 5,000 suppliers of equipment and services to the offshore petroleum exploration and production industry worldwide.
Cost: $235.00
Frequency: Annual May
Circulation: 4,000

19747 Oil and Gas Directory
Geophysical Directory
Po Box 130508
Houston, TX 77219-0508

713-529-1922
800-929-2462
Fax: 713-529-3646
Home Page: www.geophysicaldirectory.com

Stewart Schafer, Owner

Valuable information is listed on over 5,000 companies worldwide that are involved in petroleum exploration and drilling.
Cost: $130.00
700 Pages
Frequency: Annual, October
Circulation: 2,000
Founded in 1970

19748 Oil and Gas Field Code Master List
US Energy Information Administration
1000 Independence Av SW
#E1-231
Washington, DC 20585-0001

202-586-8800
Fax: 202-586-0727
Home Page: www.eia.doe.gov

John H Weiner, Executive Director

All identified oil and gas fields in the US.
Cost: $27.00
Frequency: Annual December

19749 Permit Data On-Line
Petroleum Information Corporation
PO Box 2612
Denver, CO 80201-2612

303-595-7500
800-645-3282

Oil well drilling permits granted by regional governmental agencies.
Frequency: Weekly

19750 PetroProcess HSE Directory
Atlantic Communications LLC
1635 W Alabama St
Houston, TX 77006-4101

713-831-1768
Fax: 713-523-7804
E-Mail: info@oilonline.com
Home Page: www.oilonline.com

Shaun Wymes, President
Rob Garza, General Manager
Graham Thomson, General Manager
Ray Vanegas, Manager
Doug Duguid, Managing Director
Cost: $79.00
650 Pages
Frequency: Annual
Founded in 1990

19751 Petroleum Equipment Directory
Petroleum Equipment Institute

6514 E 69th St
Tulsa, OK 74133-1729

918-494-9696
Fax: 918-491-9895
E-Mail: rrenkes@pei.org
Home Page: www.pei.org

Robert N Renkes, Executive VP
Sarah West, Marketing Director
Rick Long, General Manager

Member manufacturers, distributors and installers of petroleum marketing equipment worldwide are offered.
Cost: $50.00
395 Pages
Frequency: Annual
Circulation: 3,000

19752 Petroleum Marketers Association of America Directory
Petroleum Marketers Association of America
1901 Fort Myer Dr
Suite 500
Arlington, VA 22209-1609

703-351-8000
800-300-7622
Fax: 703-351-9160
Home Page: http://www.pmaa.org

Daniel F Gilligan, President
Sarah Dodge, Director/Legislative Affairs
Patricia Murrey, Director/Administration
Holly Tuminello, VP
Izua Yang, Manager/Communications/Conferences

About 45 state and regional member associations. A national organization representing the nation's independent petroleum marketers.
Cost: $50.00
Frequency: Annual February
Circulation: 2,000

19753 Petroleum Marketing Management Buyers Guide
Graphic Concepts
1801 Rockville Pike
Suite 330
Rockville, MD 20852-1633

A list of suppliers of products, equipment and services to combination gas station owners and convenience stores.
Frequency: Annual
Circulation: 20,000

19754 Petroleum Software Directory
PennWell Publishing Company
3050 Post Oak Boulevard
Suite 200
Houston, TX 77056-6570

713-219-9720
800-752-9764
Fax: 713-963-6228
E-Mail: susana@pennwell.com

More than 800 companies that produce over 1,800 micro-, mini- and mainframe computer software packages designed for petroleum industry applications.
Cost: $195.00
Frequency: Annual June
Circulation: 1,000

19755 Petroleum Supply Annual
Superintendent of Documents
1000 Independence Ave SW
Washington, DC 20585

202-586-8800
Home Page: http://www.eia.doe.gov/oil_gas/petroleum/data_publications/petrol

Contains information on the supply and disposition of crude oil and petroleum products. Reflects data collected by the petroleum industry during 1998 through annual and monthly surveys, it is divided in to two volumes. The first volume contains three sections, Summary Statistics, Detailed Statistics, and Refinery Capacity, each with final annual data. Volume 1 cost is $17.00, volume 2 $51.00
175 Pages
Frequency: Annual
Founded in 1999

19756 Pipeline & Gas Journal: Buyer's Guide Issue
Oildom Publishing Company of Texas
PO Box 941669
Houston, TX 77094-8669

281-558-6930
Fax: 281-558-7029
Home Page: www.oildompublishing.com

Jeff Share, Editor

List of over 700 companies supplying products and services used in construction and operation of cross country pipeline and gas distribution systems.
Cost: $75.00
Frequency: May

19757 Pipeline & Gas Journal: Directory of Pipeline Operating Companies
Oildom Publishing Company of Texas
PO Box 941669
Houston, TX 77218-9368

281-558-6930
Fax: 281-558-7029
Home Page: www.oildompublishing.com

Jeff Share, Editor
Oliver Klinger, Editor

List of companies operating oil and gas transmission pipelines worldwide.
Cost: $80.00
Frequency: September
Circulation: 27,000

19758 Platts Insight
The McGraw-Hill Companies
1221 Avenue of the Americas
New York, NY 10020

212-904-2000
E-Mail: power@platts.com
Home Page: www.platts.com

Glenn Goldberg, President, Information & Media

A comprehensive look at the energy industry, with year end outlook editions on global energy, sustainability, electric power, nuclear and more.

19759 SPE: Annual Membership Directory
Society of Petroleum Engineers
PO Box 833836
Richardson, TX 75083-3836

972-952-9300
800-456-6863
Fax: 972-952-9435

Georgeann Bilich, Editor

List of 52,000 member petroleum engineers.
Cost: $150.00
Frequency: Annual May
Circulation: 5,000

19760 Supply, Distribution, Manufacturing and Service
Midwest Publishing Company
2230 E 49th Ste E
Tulsa, OK 74105-8771

918-582-2000
800-829-2002
Fax: 918-587-9349
E-Mail: info@midwestdirectories.com
Home Page: www.midwestdirectories.com

Will Hammack, Editor

8,000 oil well supply stores, service companies and equipment manufacturers.
Cost: $165.00
Frequency: Annual, September
Founded in 1943

19761 TULSA Database
Petroleum Abstracts
101 Harwell
Tulsa, OK 74104-3189

918-631-2297
800-247-8678
Fax: 918-599-9361
Home Page: www.pa.utulsa.edu

Pam Weaver, Assistant Director
David Brown, Assistant Director of Marketing
Pam Jenni, Managing Editor

Contains more than 700,000 citations, with abstracts, to the worldwide literature and patents on the exploration, development and production of petroleum resources.
Frequency: Weekly Updates

19762 US Non-Utility Power Directory on CD-ROM
PennWell Publishing Company
PO Box 1260
Tulsa, OK 74101-1260

918-835-3161
800-752-9764
Fax: 918-831-9555

Gockel Delma, Sales

Offers a unique source of information to industry professionals including a listing of over 1,423 plant locations including project names, site addresses, plant types, fuels, installed capacity, power contract information, operating control systems, ownership and more.
Cost: $695.00
Frequency: Annual

19763 US Offshore Oil Company Contact List
Offshore Data Services
PO Box 19909
Houston, TX 77224-1909

713-781-7094
Fax: 713-781-9594

Marie Sheffer, Editor
Linda Parino, Circulation Director

Approximately 265 oil companies with US offshore leases.
Cost: $135.00
Frequency: Annual
Circulation: 800
ISBN: 1-058587-7-
Mailing list available for rent

19764 USA Oil Industry Directory
PennWell Publishing Company
3050 Post Oak Boulevard
Suite 200
Houston, TX 77056-6570

713-219-9720
800-752-9764
Fax: 713-963-6228
E-Mail: susana@pennwell.com

Laura Bell, Editor
Susan Anderson, Publisher

Over 3,600 independent oil producers, fund companies, petroleum marketing companies, crude oil brokers and integrated oil firms.
Cost: $165.00
Frequency: Annual October
Circulation: 5,000

19765 USA Oilfield Service, Supply and Manufacturers Directory
PennWell Publishing Company
3050 Post Oak Boulevard
Suite 200
Houston, TX 77056-6570

713-219-9720
800-752-9764
Fax: 713-963-6228
E-Mail: susana@pennwell.com

Guntis Moritis, Editor

About 3,600 companies that provide oilfield equipment, supplies and services to the oil industry.
Cost: $145.00
Frequency: Annual October
Circulation: 2,500

19766 West Coast Petroleum Industry Directory
Economic Insight
3004 Sw 1st Ave
Portland, OR 97201-4708

503-222-2425
Fax: 503-242-2968
E-Mail: info@econ.com
Home Page: www.econ.com

Sam Van Vactor, President

Individuals and companies that refine, buy and sell oil and petroleum products are listed.
Cost: $85.00
204 Pages
Frequency: Quarterly

19767 World Oil-Marine Drilling Rigs
Gulf Publishing Company
3301 Allen Parkway
Houston, TX 77019-1896

713-294-4301

Offers information on over 600 mobile and self-contained drilling rigs including submersibles, drillships and barges.
Cost: $11.00
Frequency: Annual
Circulation: 30,000

Industry Web Sites

19768 http://gold.greyhouse.com
G.O.L.D Grey House OnLine Databases

Grey House Publishing's online database platform, GOLD, offers Quick Search, Keyword Search and Expert Search for most business sectors including petroleum and allied services markets. The GOLD platform makes finding the information you need quick and easy - whether you're a novice searcher or an experienced database user. All of Grey House's directory products are available for subscription on the GOLD platform.

19769 www.aesc.net
Association of Energy Service Companies

Professional trade association for well-site service contractors and businesses providing goods and services to well site contractors. Develops and sells training and safety materials.

19770 www.aopl.org
Association of Oil Pipe Lines

Assembles statistics and other data relating to the pipeline industry for presentation to Congress, government departments, trade associations, and the public.

19771 www.api.org
American Petroleum Institute

Seeks to maintain cooperation between government and industry, fosters foreign and domestic trade in American petroleum products, conducts research.

19772 www.bpnews.com
Butane-Propane News

Petroleum and propane industry news.

19773 www.entelec.org
Energy Telecommunications and Electrical Assoc

A user association focusing on communications and control technologies used by petroleum, natural gas, pipeline and electric utility companies.

19774 www.greyhouse.com
Grey House Publishing

Authoritative reference directories for most business sectors including petroleum and allied products marktes. Users can search the online databases with varied search criteria allowing for custom searches by product category, geographic area, sales volume, keyword, subject and more. Full Grey House catalog and online ordering also available.

19775 www.iadc.org
International Association of Drilling Contractors

Conducts educational and training programs. Sponsors safety contest and bestows awards.

19776 www.igt.org
Institute of Gas Technology

An independent not-for-profit center for energy and environmental research, development, education and information. Main function is to perform sponsored and in-house research, development and demonstration, provide educational programs and services, and disseminate scientific and technical information.

19777 www.iosc.org
Oil Spill Conference

Strives to create a global colloquim for public, government and business ideas addressing all aspects of oil spills impacting the environment. International exchange of information and ideas dealing with spill prevention, planning, response and restoration processes, protocols and technology.

19778 www.liquidrecyclers.org
NORA, An Association of Responsible Recyclers

Members are companies that reprocess used antifreeze, wastewater, oil filters, chemicals and companies that provide products or services to the industry.

19779 www.naro-us.org
National Association of Royalty Owners

Assists mineral and royalty owners in the effective management of their mineral properties. Provides information on tax, regulatory, and legislative matters. Conducts seminars and bestows awards.

19780 www.noraoil.com
National Oil Recyclers Association

Members are companies that reprocess used oil into fuel oil or recycle antifreeze, wastewater, oil filters and companies that provide products or services to the industry.

19781 www.npc.org
National Petroleum Council

Self-supporting federal advisory body to the Secretary of Energy established in 1946 at the request of President Truman.

19782 www.npga.org
National Propane Gas Association

Members are producers and distributors of liquefied petroleum gas and equipment manufacturers.

19783 www.npradc.org
National PetroChemical & Refiners Association

Members are petroleum, petrochemical and refining companies.

19784 www.oilscouts.org
International Oil Scouts Association

Compiles statistics on exploration and development wells in the US. Offers professional development and scholarship programs.

19785 www.pei.org
Petroleum Equipment Institute

Members are makers and distributors of equipment used in service stations, bulk plants and other petroleum marketing facilities.

19786 www.pttc.org
Petroleum Technology Transfer Council

Fosters the effective transfer of exploration and production technology to US petroleum producers through regional resource centers, workshops, websites, publications, etc.

19787 www.spwla.org
Society of Professional Well Log Analysts

Promotes the evaluation of formations, through well logging techniques, in order to locate gas, oil and other minerals.

19788 www.wspa.org
Western States Petroleum Association

For companies that refine, produce, transport, and market petroleum and petroleum products in six western states: Arizona, California, Oregon, Nevada, Hawaii and Washington.

Associations

19789 ASPCA
424 E 92nd St
New York, NY 10128-6804

212-876-7566
Fax: 212-876-0014
E-Mail: information@aspca.org
Home Page: www.aspca.org
Social Media: Facebook, Twitter, Pinterest,YouTube

Ed Sayres, President

Society for the humane treatment of animals, established in 1866.
300+ Members
Founded in 1866

19790 American Animal Hospital Association
12575 W Bayaud Ave
Lakewood, CO 80228-2021

303-986-2800
Fax: 303-986-1700
E-Mail: info@aahanet.org
Home Page: www.aahanet.org
Social Media: Facebook, Twitter, LinkedIn, Youtube

John Albers, Executive Director
Ellin Davis, Secretary

A group of hospitals and animal practitioners serving the industry.
33000 Members
Founded in 1933

19791 American Boarding Kennels Association
1702 E Pikes Peak Avenue
Colorado Springs, CO 80909

719-667-1600
Fax: 719-667-0116
E-Mail: info@abka.com
Home Page: www.abka.com

James Krack, Executive Manager

Information about the pet industry products, including pet foods, supplements, retail supplies, construction materials, cages, computers and software.
Founded in 1977

19792 American Cat Fanciers Association
PO Box 1949
Nixa, MO 65714-1949

417-725-1530
Fax: 417-725-1533
E-Mail: ACFA@aol.com
Home Page: www.acfacat.com

James Mendenhall, President
Doug Blackmore, First VP
Don Finger, Second VP

Central registry for cats. Sanctions shows, publishes a bimonthly newsletter, offers a yearbook and maintains pedigree records.
800 Members
Founded in 1955

19793 American Farriers Association
4059 Iron Works Pkwy
Suite 1
Lexington, KY 40511-8488

859-233-7411
Fax: 859-231-7862
E-Mail: info@americanfarriers.org
Home Page: www.americanfarriers.org
Social Media: Facebook

John Blombach, President
Thomas Dubois, VP
Bryan Quinsey, Executive Director
Bruce worman, Treasurer
Jon Johnson, Secretary

To further the professional development of farriers, to provide leadership and resource for the benefit of the farrier industry, and to improve the welfare of the horse through continuing farrier education.
2.4M Members
Founded in 1971

19794 American Federation of Aviculture
STAT Marketing
11240 Waples Mill Road
Suite 200
Fairfax, VA 22030

703-281-4043
Fax: 703-359-7562
E-Mail: moayad@aaham.org
Home Page: www.aaham.org
Social Media: Facebook, Twitter, LinkedIn, YouTube

Christine Stottlemyer, National President
Laurie A Shoaf, Chair
Victoria DiTomaso, First VP
John D Currier, Second VP
Lori M. Sickelbaugh, Treasurer

Information for manufacturers, suppliers, distributors and retailers of exotic birds and related products, including feed, seeds, cages, toys, vitamins and minerals.
Founded in 1974

19795 American Humane Association
1400 16th Street NW
Suite 360
Washington, DC 20036

800-227-4645
800-227-4645
Fax: 818-762-0908
E-Mail: info@americanhumane.org
Home Page: www.americanhumane.org
Social Media: Facebook, Twitter, LinkedIn, YouTube,RSS

Marie Wheatley, President
Dale Austin, Chief Operating Officer

Protects children and animals from cruelty, neglect, abuse, and exploitation.
Founded in 1877

19796 American Kennel Club
8051 Arco Corporate Drive
Suite 100
Raleigh, NC 27617-3390

212-696-8295
Fax: 212-696-8239
E-Mail: info@akc.org
Home Page: www.akc.org
Social Media: Facebook, Twitter, YouTube

Barbara Kolk, Manager
James P Crowley, Executive Secretary
John Lyons, Chief Operations Officer
James T Steven, Chief Financial Officer
Charley Kneifel, Chief Information Officer

The prinicipal registry of pure-bred dogs in the United States. More ways to enjoy your dog.

19797 American Morgan Horse Association
4066 Shelburne Rd
Suite 5
Shelburne, VT 05482

802-985-4944
Fax: 802-985-8897
E-Mail: info@morganhorse.com
Home Page: morganhorse.com
Social Media: Facebook, Twitter, LinkedIn, Youtube

Julie Broadway, Executive Director
Harry Sebring, President
Linnea Sidi, VP

Information for Morgan horse breeders and owners.

19798 American Paint Horse Association
PO Box 961023
Fort Worth, TX 76161-0023

817-834-2742
Fax: 817-834-3152
Home Page: http://www.apha.com

Carl Parker, President
Richard Cox, VP
Alice Singleton, Senior Committee Member
Ed Robert, Executive Secretary

Information for owners and riders of American Paint Horses.

19799 American Pet Products Manufacturers Association
255 Glenville Road
Greenwich, CT 06831

203-532-0000
800-452-1225
Fax: 203-532-0551
E-Mail: andy@appma.org
Home Page: www.appma.org

Bob Vetere, COO/Managing Director
Jennifer Bilbao, Marketing/PR Administrator
Andrew Darmohraj, VP/Deputy Managing Director
Jamie Cavanaugh, Trade Show Coordinator
Edith Martingnetti, General Mgr/Exhibitor Registration

Information for manufacturers of pet products and service providers in the pet industry.
Frequency: Annual
Founded in 1959

19800 American Rabbit Breeders Association
PO Box 5667
Bloomington, IL 61702

309-664-7500
Fax: 309-664-0941
E-Mail: info@arba.net
Home Page: arba.net

Mike Avesing, President
Randy Shumaker, VP
Eric Stewart, Executive Director
David Freeman, Treasurer
Cliff Dick, Director

Information for rabbit breeders and owners.
Founded in 1910

19801 American Veterinary Medical Association
1931 N Meacham Rd
Suite 100
Schaumburg, IL 60173-4340

847-303-6142
800-248-2862
Fax: 847-925-1329
E-Mail: sgranskog@avma.org
Home Page: www.avma.org
Social Media: Facebook, Twitter, LinkedIn, YouTube,Flickr

Tim Frey, Manager
Michael Walters, Director Communications Division
Dr. Gail Golab, Assistant Director

Publishes various journals and information for members. Acts as a clearinghouse for veterinarians.
67M Members
Founded in 1863

19802 Animal Health Institute
1325 G St NW
Suite 700
Washington, DC 20005-3127

202-637-2440
Fax: 202-393-1667
E-Mail: rphillips@ahi.org
Home Page: www.ahi.org
Social Media: Facebook, Twitter, Flickr, Utube

Alexander S.Mathews, President & CEO
Ron Phillips, VP Legislative/Public Affairs
Dr Richard A A.Carnevale, VP, Regulator
Dr Kent McClure, General Counsel
Carolyn S Ayers, VP, Admin. & Finance

Represents manufacturers of animal health care products.
24 Members
Founded in 1941

19803 Animal Legal Defense Fund
170 E Cotati Ave
Cotati, CA 94931-4474

707-795-2533
Fax: 707-795 7280
E-Mail: info@aldf.org
Home Page: www.aldf.org
Social Media: Facebook, Twitter

Joyce Tischler, Executive Director
Steve Ann Chambers, President
Stephen Wells, Director/Animal Law Program
Pamela Frasch, Director/Anti-Cruelty Division
Roger Brigham, Director/Communications

Information on animal protection, wildlife conservation and animal rights.
18 Members
Founded in 1979

19804 Association of Pet Dog Trainers
The Association of Pet Dog Trainers
104 South Calhoun Street
Greenville, SC 29601

864-331-0767
800-738 3647
E-Mail: information@apdt.com
Home Page: www.apdt.com
Social Media: Facebook, Twitter, LinkedIn

Richard Spencer, Executive Director
Mychelle Blake, President
Teoti Anderson, VP
Jackie Powell, Manager Operations
Alicia Reynolds, Chief Operationg Officer

Enhancing the human/dog relationship by educating trainers, other animal professionals and the public and advocating dog friendly training.

19805 Delta Society
875 124th Ave NW
Suite 101
Bellevue, WA 98005-2531

425-226-7357
800-869-6898
Fax: 425-679-5539
E-Mail: info@deltasociety.org
Home Page: www.deltasociety.org

R.Stephen Browning, President & CEO
Michelle Matheson, Director of Finance
Jill F. Bentler, Executive Assistant

Information on human-animal interactions. Service Dog Center provides information and advocacy for dogs trained to assist people with disabilities. Pet Partners Program trains volunteers, health professionals, animals for animal-assisted therapy and activities.
4.6M Members
Founded in 1977

19806 International Association of Pet Cemeteries & Crematories
4991 Peachtree Road
Atlanta, GA 30341

518-594-3000
800-952-5541
Fax: 770-457-8160
E-Mail: info@iaopc.com
Home Page: www.iaopc.com

Stephen Drown, Executive Director

Educates the public on pet burials and the disposal of sick and diseased animals to eliminate contamination of ground and water. Conducts workshops and research projects.
175 Members
Founded in 1971

19807 International Professional Groomers
6475 Wallace Rd NW
Salem, OR 97304-9743

847-758-1938
Fax: 503-581-1220
E Mail: jkurpiel@aol.com
Home Page: www.ipgcmb.com

Judy Kurpiel, President

Represents the professional pet grooming industry, providing continuing education to members and public information on the proper care treatment. also publishes a quarterly newsletter.
500 Members
Founded in 1988

19808 National Association of Professional Pet Care
15000 Commerce Parkway
Suite C
Mt. Laurel, NJ 08054
856-439-0324
Fax: 856-439-0525
E-Mail: napps@petsitters.org
Home Page: www.petsitters.org

Sherry L Suhosky, President
Marcia Breithaupt, Secretary/Treasurer
Jessica Dwyer, Director
Michele Gonzalez, Director
Kara Jenkins, Director

Nonprofit organization dedicated to serving the needs of professional pet care providers. Promotes ethical standards and fosters cooperation among members in the pet care industry.
24 Members
Founded in 1989

19809 National Congress of Animal Trainers
23675 W Chardon Rd
Grayslake, IL 60030-9584

847-546-0717
Fax: 847-546-3454

John F Cuneo, President

For trainers and breeders of rare animals.
300 Members

19810 National Dog Groomers Association of American
PO Box 101
Clark, PA 16113-0101
724-962-2711
Fax: 724-962-1919
E-Mail: ndga@nationaldoggroomers.com
Home Page: www.nationaldoggroomers.com

Jeffrey Reynolds, Executive Director

To unite groomers through membership and offer optional certification testing throughout the United States.
2.4M Members
Founded in 1969

19811 National Humane Education Society
PO Box 340
Charles Town, WV 25414-340

304-725-0506
Fax: 304-725-1523
E-Mail: information@nhes.org
Home Page: www.nhes.org

Anna C Briggs, Founder
James D Taylor, President
Cynthia L Taylor, President
Virginia Dungan, Treasurer
Christina B Fernandez, Secretary

Mission to foster a sentiment of kindness to animals.
400M+ Members
Founded in 1948

19812 National Pigeon Association
PO Box 950088
Oklahoma City, OK 73195-0088

405-604-8792
E-Mail: store@npausa.com
Home Page: www.npausa.com

John Heppner, President
Lennie Mefferd, Secretary/Treasurer
Amy Klopman, Eastern Vise President
Keith Casteel, Western Vice President

Special information for members.
Founded in 1920

19813 National Taxidermists Association
PO Box 549
Green Forest, AR 72638

440-786-8100
Fax: 440-786-8176
E-Mail: info@NationalTaxidermists.com
Home Page: www.nationaltaxidermists.com

Mitch Webb, President
Jim Ellis, Vice President

Preserving animals to their natural form.
2500 Members
Founded in 1972

19814 PETCO Foundation
9125 Rehco Rd
San Diego, CA 92121-2270

858-453-7845
888-824-7257
Fax: 858-784-3489
Home Page: www.petco.com
Social Media: Facebook, Twitter, YouTube,Blog

James M Myers, CEO
Drian Devine, Chairman

We put animals first. The Petco Foundation supports community organization and efforts that enhance the lives of companion animals.

19815 People for the Ethical Treatment of Animals (PETA)
501 Front Street
Norfolk, VA 23510

757-622-7382
Fax: 757-622-0457
E-Mail: info@peta.org
Home Page: www.peta.org
Ingrid Newkirk, President

Opposes all forms of animal exploitation. Seeks to educate the public on what the group sees as the three major institutionalized cruelty issues: the exploitation and abuse of animals in experimentation, the manufacturing of fur apparel, and slaughtering for human consumption.
80000 Members
Founded in 1980

19816 Pet Care Services Association
2760 N Academy Boulevard
Suite 120
Colorado Springs, CO 80917
719-667-1600
877-570-7788
Fax: 719-667-0116
E-Mail: info@petcareservices.org
Home Page: www.petcareservices.org
Joan Saunders, CEO
Seeks to upgrade the industry through educational programs and conventions. Promotes code of ethics and accreditation programs for kennel operators.
2400 Members
Founded in 1977

19817 Pet Food Institute
2025 M St NW
Suite 800
Washington, DC 20036-2422
202-367-1120
Fax: 202-367-2120
E-Mail: info@petfoodinstitute.org
Home Page: www.petfoodinstitute.org
Duane H Ekedahl, Executive Director
Represents dog and cat food manufacturers. Supporting initiative to advance the quality of dog and cat food. Supporting research in pet nutrition and the important role of pets in our society. Promoting the overall care and well-being of pets.
100 Members
Founded in 1958

19818 Pet Industry Distributors Association
3465 Box Hill Corporate Center Dr.
Suite H
Abingdon, MD 21009
443-640-1060
Fax: 443-640-1086
E-Mail: pida@kingmgmt.org
Home Page: www.pida.org
Amy Chetalat, Manager
Perry Parks, Chairman
Randy Reber, Vice Chairman
Scott Rath, Secretary/Treasurer
Ced Damby, Director
Represents wholesaler-distributors of pet products, providing training and education to members.
190 Members
Founded in 1968

19819 Pet Industry Joint Advisory Council
1146 19th St NW
Suite 350
Washington, DC 20036-2438
202-452-1525
800-553-7387
Fax: 202-452-1516
E-Mail: info@pijac.org
Home Page: www.pijac.org
Social Media: Facebook
Michael Addox, VP & General Counsel
Michael Canning, President
Monitors federal and state regulations and legislation affecting industry. Sponsors research and educational projects including certification programs in veterinary care and husbandry for companion animals, in-store training videos, etc.
1500 Members
Founded in 1971

19820 Pet Lovers Association
PO Box 145
Joppa, MD 21085
410-679-0978
Elden Harrison, President
Advises pet owners of their responsibilities.
Founded in 1983

19821 Pet Pride
P.O. Box 1055
Pacific Palisades, CA 90272
310-836-5427
Home Page: www.petpride.org
Ruth Argust, President
Public education programs for proper cat care.
50000 Members
Founded in 1965

19822 Pet Sitters International
201 East King Street
King, NC 27021-9163
336-983-9222
Fax: 336-983-5266
E-Mail: info@petsit.com
Home Page: www.petsit.com
Social Media: Facebook, Twitter, LinkedIn, YouTube
Terry Chance, Marketing Director
Beth Stultz, Marketing Manager
Chris Sutphin, Member Services Manager
Patti Moran, President
Mike Moran, Vice President
Society of professional pet sitters. Membership provides valuable benefits - educational resources for those engaged in the pet-sitting industry. Also provides a forum to network with peers who share a common vision of excellence in at-home pet care.
2.5M Members
Founded in 1994

19823 PetCenter.Com: Internet Animal Hospital PetFoodDirect.com
189 Main Street
Harleysville, PA 19438
215-513-1999
Fax: 215-513-7286
Home Page: www.the petcenter.com
T J Dunn, Jr DVM, Director
Award winning virtual animal hospital for dog and cat love. Mission of providing dog and cat caretakers with a better understanding of the medical and surgical treatment of pets. Created by veterinarians under the direction of Dr T.J. Dunn, all articles are presented in non-medical terms, just as if the veterinarian was speaking to you personally in a real exam room. Associated with PetFoodDirect.com

19824 PetFoodDirect.com
189 Main St
Harleysville, PA 19438
215-513-1999
877-738-3663
Fax: 215-513-7286
Home Page: www.petfooddirect.com
Social Media: Facebook, Twitter
Brock Weatherup, CEO
Jon Roska, Jr, Founder & VP of Merchandising
Rose Hamilton, Chief Marketing Officer
Matthew Murray, VP, Finance
Joe Falkenstein, CFO & VP of Operations
Largest pure play entailer for premium pet food, supplies and accessories on the internet. Our customers can order from a huge selection of pet products, have access to value-added services, including information on pet healthcare and nutrition.
Founded in 1997

19825 US Animal Health Association
4221 Mitchell Ave
Saint Joseph, MO 64507
816-671-1144
Fax: 816-671-1201
E-Mail: usaha@usaha.org
Home Page: www.usaha.org
Dr. Stephen Crawford, President
Linda B. Ragland, Meeting Coordinator
Kelly Janicek, Executive Asst.
Benjamin Richey, Executive Director
Dr. Annette Whiteford, Treasurer
Science-based, non-profit, voluntary organization. Concerning disease eradication, animal health, emerging diseases, food safety, public health, animal welfare, and international trade.
1400 Members
Founded in 1897

19826 United Kennel Club
100 E Kilgore Rd
Kalamazoo, MI 49002-5584
269-343-9020
Fax: 269-343-7037
E-Mail: webmaster@ukcdogs.com
Home Page: www.ukcdogs.com
Wayne Cavanaugh, President
Tanya Raab, VP of Corporate Operations
Sarah Chinsell, Legal Counsel
Andrea Hunderman, Customer Service Manager
Allen Gingerich, Senior Director of Hunting Events
Responsible for dog pedigrees and transfer of ownership of pedigree dogs. Best registry of pure-bred dogs.
50 Members
Founded in 1898

19827 Western and English Sales Association
451 E 58th Avenue
Suite 4128
Denver, CO 80216
303-295-1040
800-295-1041
Fax: 303-295-0941
E-Mail: info@denver-wesa.com
Home Page: www.denver-wesa.com
Social Media: Facebook
Scott Piper, VP
Gene House, Chairman
Mark Broughton, President
Gerald Adame, Treasurer
Jay Phillips, Secretary
Trade association
1200 Members
Founded in 1921

19828 World Pet Association
135 West Lemon Ave.
Monrovia, CA 91016
626-447-2222
Fax: 626-447-8350
E-Mail: info@wpamail.org
Home Page: worldpetassociation.org
Doug Poindexter, President
Jim Boschee, CFO
Lewis M. Sutton, Chairman of the Board
Michael Twain, 1st Vice chair
Barry Berman, Secretary
A non-profit, membership-controlled trade association organized to represent its members and the interests of the companion animal and product industry. America's oldest pet industry trade association. Our mission is to promote responsible pet care worldwide.

19829 World Society for the Protection of Animals
89 South Street
2nd Floor
Boston, MA 02111
508-879-8350
800-833-9772

Fax: 212-564-4250
E-Mail: wspa@wspausa.com
Home Page: www.wspa.usa.org
Social Media: Facebook, Twitter, YouTube

Laura Simpson, USA Director
Peter Davies, Director General
Robert S Cummings, President
John Bowen, Secretary
Carter Luke, Treasurer

International animal protection news reports. Lobbies for effective animal welfare laws and provides educational material.
12 Members

Newsletters

19830 **ASPCA Report**
424 E 92nd St
New York, NY 10128-6804

212-876-7566
Home Page: www.aspca.com

Janice Borzendowski, Publisher
Ed Sayres, Director
Kathryn Investigations, Director
Bonnie Shelter, Operations Manager

Pet care news, issues, features and reviews.
Frequency: Weekly
Founded in 1866

19831 **Animals International**
World Society for the Protection of Animals
34 Deloss Street
Framingham, MA 01702

508-879-8350
Fax: 508-620-0786
E-Mail: wspa@wspausa.com
Home Page: www.wspa-international.org/

Laura Salter, USA Director
Susan Sherwin, Press Contact

International animal protection news reports.
Cost: $10.00
12 Pages
Frequency: Quarterly
Founded in 1981

19832 **Animals' Advocate**
Animal Legal Defense Fund
170 E Cotati Avenue
Cotati, CA 94931-4474

707-795-2533
Fax: 707-795-7280
E-Mail: info@aldf.org
Home Page: www.aldf.org/action.htm

Stephen Wells, Executive Director

A newsletter offering information on animal protection, wildlife conservation and animal rights.
4 Pages
Frequency: Monthly

19833 **Anthrozoos**
Delta Society
875 124th Ave Ne
Suite 101
Bellevue, WA 98005-2531

425-226-7357
Fax: 425-235-1076
E-Mail: info@deltasociety.org
Home Page: www.deltasociety.org

Lawrence Norvell, CEO
Robert T Franklin, Secretary
Stephanie LaFarge, Secretary
David BellRetired, Treasurer

Scientific journal on the interactions of people, animals and nature.
Cost: $40.00
72 Pages
Frequency: Quarterly
Circulation: 800
Founded in 1977

19834 **Association of Pet Dog Trainers Newsletter**
750 Executive Center Dr
Box 35
Greenville, SC 29615

864-331-0764
800-738-3647
Fax: 856-439-0525
E-Mail: information@apdt.com
Home Page: www.apdt.com

Richard Spencer, Executive Director
Pat Miller, Treasurer
Sue Pearson, Treasurer
Kellyann Conway-Payne, Vice President
Pia Silvani, Secretary

Building better trainers through education.
Founded in 1993

19835 **Cat Industry Newsletter**
Good Communications
PO Box 10069
Austin, TX 78766-1069

512-454-9062
800-968-1738
Fax: 512-454-3420
Home Page: www.petfoodnews.com

Ross Becker, Editor

Business newsletter for catfood, cat products and cat litter industries. Covers business news, marketing, new products in the pipeline, industry data.
Cost: $295.00
6 Pages
Frequency: Monthly
ISSN: 1074-7788
Founded in 1992
Printed in on matte stock

19836 **Dog Industry Newsletter**
Good Communications
PO Box 10069
Austin, TX 78766-1069

512-454-9062
800-968-1738
Fax: 512-454-3420
Home Page: www.petfoodnews.com

Ross Becker, Editor

Business newsletter for petfood,and pet products industries.Covers business news, marketing, new products in the pipeline, industry data.
Cost: $295.00
10 Pages
Frequency: Monthly
ISSN: 1074-777X
Founded in 1990
Printed in on matte stock

19837 **Humane News**
Associated Humane Societies
124 Evergreen Ave
Newark, NJ 07114-2133

973-824-7080
Fax: 973-824-5937
E-Mail: associatedhumane@aol.com
Home Page: www.associatedhumanesocieties.org

Roseann Trezza, Executive Director

News concerning animal welfare.
24 Pages
Frequency: Monthly
Circulation: 75000
Founded in 1906

19838 **IPG Newsletter**
International Professional Groomers
6475 Wallace Rd NW
Salem, OR 97304-9743

847-758-1938
800-258-4765
Fax: 847-758-8031
E-Mail: jkurpiel@aol.com
Home Page: www.ipgcmb.com

Judy Kurpiel, President

A quarterly newsletter published by the International Professional Groomers.
6 Pages
Frequency: Quarterly
Circulation: 500
Founded in 1988

19839 **International Pet Industry News**
Good Communications
PO Box 10069
Austin, TX 78766-1069

512-454-9062
800-968-1738
Fax: 512-454-3420
Home Page: www.petfoods.com

Ross Becker, Editor

Business newsletter for internatioal petfood, pet products industries. Covers business news, marketing, new products in the pipeline, industry data.
Cost: $295.00
8 Pages
Frequency: Monthly
ISSN: 1074-780X
Founded in 1993
Printed in on matte stock

19840 **K-9 Courier**
PO Box 49
Jerico Springs, MO 64756

Monthly newsletter for breeders.
Frequency: Monthly

19841 **Pet Gazette**
Gazette Publishing
1309 N Halifax Avenue
Daytona Beach, FL 32118-3658
E-Mail: editor@petgazette.net
Home Page: www.petgazette.net

Robin Nudd, Advertising Coordinator
Amy McWilliams, Circulation

Pictures, anecdotes, cartoons and more for the pet industry.
Cost: $12.50
24 Pages
Frequency: Quarterly
Circulation: 300

19842 **Pet Partners Newsletter**
Delta Society
875 124th Ave Ne
Suite 101
Bellevue, WA 98005-2531

425-226-7357
Fax: 425-235-1076
E-Mail: info@deltasociety.org
Home Page: www.deltasociety.org

Lawrence Norvell, CEO
Stephanie LaFarge, Secretary
David BellRetired, Treasurer

How-to newsletter for pet owners who volunteer in animal-assisted therapy and activity programs.
Cost: $6.00
2 Pages
Frequency: Monthly
Circulation: 2500
Founded in 1977

19843 Pet Planet Newsletter
PO Box 150899
Denver, CO 80215-0899

303-986-2800
Fax: 303-986-1700
Home Page: www.healthypet.com

John W Albers, Executive Director
Gregg Takashima, Vice President

A group of hospitals and animal practitioners serving the industry.
Cost: $60.00
64 Pages
Frequency: Bi-Monthly
Circulation: 14,000
Founded in 1985
Printed in on glossy stock

19844 Pet Stuff
Pet Stuff
608 Tumbleweed Lane
Fall Brook, CA 92028-9446

760-728-9306
Fax: 760-728-9735

Robert Tanner, Publisher

A direct co-op mailing service to the pet industry. Accepts advertising.
Frequency: BiWeekly

19845 PetLetter
Pet Industry Joint Advisory Council
1146 19th St NW
Suite 350
Washington, DC 20036-2438

202-452-1525
800-553-7387
Fax: 202-452-1516
E-Mail: info@pijac.org
Home Page: www.pijac.org

Michael Addox, VP & General Counsel
Michael Canning, President

Contains a breadth of information on the current status of pending state and federal legislation, science and educational program news, the release of PIJAC publications, other PIJAC news, and a list of the newest Certified Anical Specialists

19846 Veterinary Industry Newsletter
Good Communications
PO Box 10069
Austin, TX 78766-1069

512-454-9062
800-968-1738
Fax: 512-454-3420
Home Page: www.petfoodsnews.com

Ross Becker, Editor

Business newsletter for petfood, animal health and veterinary industries.Covers business news, marketing, new products in the pipeline, industry data.
Cost: $295.00
10 Pages
Frequency: Monthly
ISSN: 1074-7796
Founded in 1993
Printed in one color on matte stock

19847 Watchbird
PO Box 56218
Phoenix, AZ 85079

602-484-0931
Fax: 602-484-0109
E-Mail: webmaster@afabirds.org
Home Page: www.afabirds.org/

Jerry Crowley, Executive VP
S Rosenbeltt, Circulation Director
Benny Gallaway, President

Journal on conservation, education, bird keeping and breeding.
Circulation: 6000
Founded in 1974

Magazines & Journals

19848 Animal Fair
7 Penn Plaza
11th Floor
New York, NY 10001

212-629-0392
Fax: 212-988-7486
E-Mail: editor@animalfair.com
Home Page: www.animalfair.com

Wendy Diamond, Editorial Director
Wendy Diamond, CEO/President
Cost: $19.95
Frequency: Bi-annually
Founded in 1999

19849 Aquarium Fish Magazine
Fancy Publications
PO Box 6050
Mission Viejo, CA 92690

949-855-8822
Fax: 949-855-3045
E-Mail: aquariumfish@fancypubs.com
Home Page: www.animalnetwork.com

Devoted to pet stores and readers who keep freshwater and saltwater species of tropical fish.
Cost: $15.97
Frequency: Monthly
Circulation: 49,700
Founded in 1905

19850 Bird Talk
Fancy Publications
3 Burroughs
Irvine, CA 92618

949-855-8822
Fax: 949-855-3045
E-Mail: ibt@bowtieinc.com
Home Page: www.birdtalkmagazine.com

Edward Bauman, Editor

Pet news.
Cost: $13.99
64 Pages
Frequency: Monthly
Founded in 1983

19851 BirdTimes
Pet Publishing
7-L Dundas Circle
Greensboro, NC 27407

336-292-4047
Fax: 336-292-4272
Home Page: www.petpublishing.com

Mike Hammond, Publisher
Cost: $17.97
Circulation: 50000
ISSN: 1096-7923
Founded in 1992
Printed in 4 colors on glossy stock

19852 Bloodlines
United Kennel Club
100 E Kilgore Rd
Portage, MI 49002-5584

269-343-9020
Fax: 269-343-7037
E-Mail: webmaster@ukcdogs.com
Home Page: www.ukcdogs.com

Wayne Cavanaugh, President
Rosie Reeds, Advertising

A comprehensive publication covering breeding, showing and registering of animals.
Cost: $24.00
Frequency: Monthly
Founded in 1898

19853 Cat Fancy Magazine
Fancy Publications
3 Burroughs
Irvine, CA 92618

949-855-8822
Fax: 949-855-3045
Home Page: www.animalnetwork.com

Susan Logan, Editor
Sandy Meyer, Managing Editor

Offers information to cat owners and pet shop owners regarding cats.
Cost: $14.99
Frequency: Monthly
Founded in 1965

19854 Cats & Kittens
Pet Publishing
7-L Dundas Circle
Greensboro, NC 27407

336-292-4047
Fax: 336-292-4272
Home Page: www.petpublishing.com

Mike Hammond, Publisher
Rita Davis, Editor

Cat enthusiast magazine.
Cost: $19.97
52 Pages
Circulation: 50000
ISSN: 1079-8285
Founded in 1998
Printed in 4 colors on glossy stock

19855 Cats Magazine
PRIMEDIA Enthusiast Group
3585 Engineering Drive
Suite 100
Norcross, GA 30092

678-421-3000
800-216-1423
Fax: 212-745-0121
E-Mail: information@primedia.com
Home Page: www.primedia.com

Mike Carney, Publisher
Doug Stange, Editor
Kelly P Conlin, CEO

For cat owners.
Founded in 1989

19856 Dog & Kennel
Pet Publishing
7-L Dundas Circle
Greensboro, NC 27407

336-292-4047
Fax: 336-292-4272
Home Page: www.petpublishing.com

Mike Hammond, Publisher
Rita Davis, Editor

Dog enthusiast magazine.
Cost: $4.99
64 Pages
Circulation: 50000
ISSN: 1079-8277
Founded in 1996
Printed in 4 colors on glossy stock

19857 Dog Fancy Magazine
Fancy Publications
3 Burroughs
Irvine, CA 92618

949-855-8822
800-546-7730
Fax: 949-855-3045

E-Mail: bowtiepress@bowtieinc.com
Home Page: www.animalnetwork.com

Susane Chney, Editor
Scott Montey, Publisher
Dock Style, CEO/President
Christy Chism, Circulation Manager
Steven Sapoher, Marketing Manager

A magazine covering the world of dogs.
Cost: $96.00
Frequency: Monthly

19858 Dog World Magazine
Charels A Tupta
3 Burroughs
Irvine, CA 92618

949-855-8822
800-361-8056
Fax: 949-855-3045
E-Mail: letters@dogworld.com
Home Page: www.dogworldmag.com/

Charels A Tupta, Publisher
Donna Marcel, Chairman

Written for the serious dog enthusiast, Dog World is the authority on dog care. Special editorial on behavior, nutrition, health care and training, plus thousands of classified and display listings in every issue.
Cost: $14.99
132 Pages
Frequency: Monthly
Circulation: 64876
Founded in 1916

19859 Dogs USA
Fancy Publications
3 Burroughs
Irvine, CA 92618

949-855-8822
Fax: 949-855-3045
Home Page: www.animalnetwork.com

Edward Bauman, Editor

Registration, breeding, pedigree news, bloodlines, etc. for dogs.
Cost: $5.95
Frequency: Annual

19860 Equestrian Retailer
Morris Communications
PO Box 7980
Colorado Springs, CO 80907-5339

719-633-5524
Fax: 719-633-1392
Home Page: www.equestrianretailer.com

Rick Swan, Associate Publisher
Kathy Swan, Executive Editor
William S Morris, President
Karen Ficklin, Circulation Manager
Rob Fulkerson, General Manager

Serves to promote profitablity in the equine industry.
60 Pages
Circulation: 11000
Founded in 1998
Printed in 4 colors on matte stock

19861 Freshwater and Marine Aquarium Magazine
RC Modeler Corporation
PO Box 487
Sierra Madre, CA 91025-0487

626-355-1476
800-523-1736
Fax: 626-355-6415
Home Page: www.mag-web.com

Patricia Crews, President

A magazine aimed at aquarium pertaining to fish and marine life, hobbyists.
Cost: $22.00
200 Pages
Frequency: Monthly
Circulation: 65000
Founded in 1978
Printed in 4 colors on glossy stock

19862 Good Dog!
PO Box 10069
Austin, TX 78766-1069

512-454-9062
800-968-1738
Fax: 512-454-3420
E-Mail: help@gooddogmagazine.com
Home Page: www.gooddogmagazine.com

Judith Becker, Editor
Ross Becker, Publisher

Consumer magazine for dog owners. Nationally known for its test reports on dog food and products for dogs. Also publishes books on dog food, puppy selection and genetics.
Cost: $12.00
36 Pages
Circulation: 40000
ISSN: 0899-6024
Founded in 1988
Printed in 4 colors

19863 NAPPS Network
Association of Professional Pet Sitters
15000 Commerce Parkway
Suite C
Mt Laurel, NJ 08054

856-439-0324
Fax: 856-439-0525
E-Mail: napps@ahint.com
Home Page: www.petsitters.org

Sally Liddick, Co-Director
Charlotte Reed, Editor/Publisher
Jerry Wentz, President
Caitlin Dougherty, Manager
Kimberly Libucki, Administrative Assistant

Official publication of the Association of Professional Pet Sitters.
Frequency: Quarterly
Circulation: 1500
Founded in 1989

19864 Pet Age Magazine
HH Backer Associates
18 S Michigan Ave
Suite 1100
Chicago, IL 60603-3233

312-578-1818
Fax: 312-578-1819
E-Mail: hhbacker@hhbacker.com
Home Page: www.hhbacker.com

Patty Backer, President
Karen MacLeod, Editor in Chief
Mark Mitera, VP
Beth Morrissey, Production Coordinator
Cathy Foster, Senior Editor

Pet AGE helps pet/pet suppliers fatailers suceed in today competive marketplace. Editorial features emphasize progressive management and trends and issues. Accepts advertising.
Cost: $70.00
80 Pages
Frequency: Monthly
Circulation: 23076
ISSN: 0098-5406
Founded in 1965
Printed in on glossy stock

19865 Pet Business Magazine
Pet Business
333 7th Ave
11th Floor
New York, NY 10001-5004

212-979-4861
Fax: 646-674-0102
E-Mail: emckiernan@petbusiness.com
Home Page: www.petbusiness.com

Craig Rexford, VP
Mike Burnette, Founder
Jerry Thom, Founder
David Litwak, Editor In Chief
Nisa Cirulnick, Sales & Marketing Coordinator

Trade magazine for the pet industry. News, new products, animal care and legislative topics. Accepts advertising.
Cost: $49.97
Circulation: 24,000
Founded in 1973
Mailing list available for rent: 19.5M names
Printed in 4 colors on glossy stock

19866 Pet Product News Magazine
Fancy Publications
3 Burroughs
PO Box 6040
Irvine, CA 92618

949-855-8822
Fax: 949-855-3045
Home Page: www.animalnetwork.com

Edward Bauman, Editor

Journal focusing on new products and other industry news.

19867 Pet Sitter's World
Pet Sitters International
201 E King St
King, NC 27021-9161

336-983-9222
Fax: 336-983-5266
E-Mail: info@petsit.com
Home Page: www.petsit.com

Patti Moran, President

Designed to educate pet sitters and affiliated firms on pet-sitting industry buiness practices, ideas, products, field-tested consumer tips and trends
Cost: $36.00
56 Pages
Frequency: Bimonthly
Circulation: 8500
Founded in 1985
Printed in on glossy stock

19868 Petfood Industry
WATT Publishing Company
303 N Main Street
Suite 500
Rockford, IL 61101

815-966-5400
Fax: 815-966-6416
Home Page: www.wattnet.com

James Watt, Chairman/CEO
Greg Watt, President/COO
Jeff Swanson, Publishing Director

The leading global information source for the petfood manufacturing industry, connecting manufacturing organizations with their supplier counterparts.
Cost: $48.00
46 Pages
Frequency: Monthly
Circulation: 9795
ISSN: 0031-6245
Founded in 1959
Printed in 4 colors on glossy stock

Trade Shows

19869 AVMA Annual Convention
American Veterinary Medical Association

1931 N Meacham Road
Suite 100
Schaumburg, IL 60173-4360

847-036-6142
800-248-2862
Fax: 847-925-1329
E-Mail: avmaininfo@avma.org
Home Page: www.avma.org
Social Media: Facebook, Twitter, LinkedIn, YouTube

Larry Corry DVM, 2009-10 President
Larry Kornegay DVM, 2009-10 President-Elect

Seminar and more than 300 exhibits of products, materials, equipment, data, and services for veterinary medicine. Education and hands-on labs, exhibit hall, charitable events and networking
10000 Attendees
Frequency: Annual/July

19870 America's Family Pet Expo
World Wide Pet Supply Association
406 S 1st Avenue
Arcadia, CA 91006-3829

626-447-2222
800-999-7295
Fax: 626-447-8350
Home Page: www.wwpsa.com

Rick Newman, President
Lewis M Sutton, CFO
Steve Segner, First VP
Russ Feller, Second Vice President
Dr. Robert Bray, Equine Outreach

Brings together all elements of the companion animal world and promotes responsible pet ownsership. Demonstrations, speakers, product exhibits, hobbyist shows, rides for the children, contests and more. 500 booths. April, Orange County, CA
80M Attendees
Frequency: April/September
Founded in 1990

19871 American Animal Hospital Association Annual Meeting
American Animal Hospital Association
12575 W Bayaud Avenue
Lakewood, CO 80228

303-986-2800
Fax: 303-986-1700
E-Mail: donna.johnson@aahanet.org
Home Page: www.aahanet.org

Donna Johnson, Exhibit Coordinator
Chuck Potter, Annual Meeting Manager
John Albers, Executive Director

250 scientific displays related to small animal veterinary care, computer software, marketing consulting services and pet care products.
3000 Attendees
Frequency: Annual
Founded in 1933

19872 American Boarding Kennels Association Annual Convention & Trade Show
1702 E Pikes Peak Avenue
Colorado Springs, CO 80909

719-667-1600
Fax: 719-667-0116
E-Mail: info@abka.com
Home Page: www.abka.com

James Krack, Executive Manager
Kathryn Eddy, Show Manager

Annual show and exhibit of pet industry products, including pet foods, supplements, retail supplies, construction materials, cages, computers and software.
300 Attendees
Frequency: October
Founded in 1977

19873 American College of Veterinary Opthalmologists Conference
2316 West Northern Avenue
Phoenix, AZ 85021

602-995-2871
Fax: 602-995-1770

Lisa Schultz, Practice Manager

Meeting and 30 exhibits of opthamology equipment and information.
400 Attendees
Frequency: Annual

19874 American College of Veterinary Surgeons - Veterinary Symposium
American College of Veterinary Surgeons
19785 Crystal Rock Dr,
Suite 305
Germantown, MD 20874

301-916-0200
Fax: 301-916-2287
E-Mail: acvs@acvs.org
Home Page: www.acvs.org

Ann T Loew, Executive Director
William B Henry, VP
Mark Markel, Chair
Marvin L Olmstead, ACVS President
Ann Loew, Executive Director

Over 150 exhibits featuring veterinary equipment, supplies and services.
1500 Attendees
Frequency: October 5-7
Founded in 1965

19875 American Federation of Aviculture Inc
STAT Marketing
PO Box 91717
Austin, TX 78709

512-585-9800
Fax: 512-858-7029
E-Mail: afaoffice@afabirds.org
Home Page: www.afabirds.org
Social Media: Facebook, Twitter

Nancy Speed, National President
Linda Sheaffer, Chair
Jamie Whittaker, First VP
Brent Gattis, Second VP
Brent Andrus, CFO

Annual convention for manufacturers, suppliers, distributors and retailers of exotic birds and related products, including feed, seeds, cages, toys, vitamins and minerals. 65 booths.
750 Attendees
Founded in 1974

19876 American Humane Association Annual Meeting and Training Conference
American Humane Association
1400 16th Street NW
Suite 360
Washington, DC 20036

303-792-9900
800-227-4645
Fax: 818-762-0908
E-Mail: info@americanhumane.org
Home Page: www.americanhumane.org
Social Media: Facebook, Twitter, RSS,YouTube,Pinterest

Robert R Ganzert, President/CEO
Clifford Rose, CFO

Over 50 exhibits of animal welfare equipment, including pet food, cages, trucks, id programs and veterinary services. Breakfast, luncheon, reception.
700 Attendees
Frequency: Annual
Founded in 1982

19877 American Morgan Horse Association Grand National Show
3 Bostwick Road
PO Box 960
Shelburne, VT 05482-0960

802-985-4944
Fax: 802-985-8897
E-Mail: info@morganhorse.com
Home Page: morganhorse.com

Raymond Gifford, Show Manager
Fred Braden, Executive Director

Offers you a way to enjoy your Morgan in a competitive setting, while enjoying the company of other Morgan exhibitors. 30 booths.
8M Attendees
Frequency: October

19878 American Paint Horse Association World Championship Horse Shows
PO Box 961023
Fort Worth, TX 76161-0023

817-834-2742
Fax: 817-834-3152
Home Page: http://www.apha.com

Carl Parker, President
Richard Cox, VP
Alice Singleton, Senior Committee Member
Ed Robert, Executive Secretary

A 14 day annual event that has become the proving ground for competitors striving to show that they ride or own the best American Paint Horses in the world. 100 booths.
5M Attendees
Frequency: July

19879 American Pet Products Manufacturers Association National Tradeshow
255 Glenville Road
Greenwich, CT 06831

203-532-0000
800-452-1225
Fax: 203-532-0551
E-Mail: andy@appma.org
Home Page: www.appma.org

Bob Vetere, COO/Managing Director
Jennifer Bilbao, Marketing/PR Administrator
Andrew Darmohraj, VP/Deputy Managing Director
Jamie Cavanaugh, Trade Show Coordinator
Edith Martingnetti, General Mgr/Exhibitor Registration

Breakfast, reception, and 1400 pet products manufacturers exhibits.
Frequency: Annual
Founded in 1959

19880 American Rabbit Breeders Association National Convention
8 Westport Court
Bloomington, IL 61704

309-664-7500
Fax: 309-664-0941
Home Page: arba.net

Glen Carr, Executive Director

Seminar, banquet, luncheon and 1500 rabbit breeders exhibits.
3000 Attendees
Frequency: Annual
Founded in 1910

19881 American Veterinary Medical Association Annual Convention
American Veterinary Medical Association
1931 N Meacham Road
Suite 100
Schaumburg, IL 60173

847-036-6142
Fax: 847-925-1329

E-Mail: convention@avma.org
Home Page: www.avma.org

Dr Bonnie Beaver, President
David Little, Director

Seminar and 310 exhibits of products, materials, equipment, data, and services for veterinary medicine.
10000 Attendees
Frequency: Annual

19882 Annual Pet Industry Trade Show
World Wide Pet Supply Association
406 S 1st Avenue
Arcadia, CA 91006-3829

626-447-2222
Fax: 626-447-8350
Home Page: www.wwpsa.com

Doug Poindexter, Executive VP

A comprehensive collection of exhibits and educational events unparalleled in the industry.

19883 HH Backer Pet Industry Christmas Trade Show
HH Backer Associates
200 S Michigan Avenue
Suite 840
Chicago, IL 60604

312-663-4040
Fax: 312-663-5676
E-Mail: hhbacker@hhbacker.com
Home Page: www.hhbacker.com

Patty Backer, President/Publisher
Karen Long MacLeod, Assoc Publisher/Editor in Chief
M Christopher Mitera, VP
Colette Fairchild, CMP, Trade Show Director
Julie Wichert, Sales Manager

Containing 1000 plus booths and 550 plus exhibits consisting of pet supplies, products and services.
9M Attendees
Frequency: October
Founded in 1967

19884 HH Backer Pet Industry Spring Trade Show
HH Backer Associates
200 S Michigan Avenue
Suite 840
Chicago, IL 60604

312-663-4040
Fax: 312-663-5676
E-Mail: hhbacker@hhbacker.com
Home Page: www.hhbacker.com

Patty Backer, President/Publisher
Karen Long MacLeod, Assoc Publisher/Editor in Chief
M Christopher Mitera, VP
Collette Fairchild, CMP, Trade Show Director
Julie Wichert, Sales Manager

Containing 1000 plus booths and 550 plus exhibits consisting of pet supplies, products and services.
10M Attendees
Frequency: April
Founded in 1967

19885 NAPPS Annual Convention: National Assoc. of Professional Pet Sitters
17000 Commerce Parkway
Suite C
Mt. Laurel, NJ 08054

856-439-0324
Fax: 856-439-0525
E-Mail: napps@ahint.com
Home Page: www.petsitters.org

Felicia Lembesis, Administrative Director
Rebecca Haines, Registration Coordinator
Kelly Calzaretta, Meeting/Exhibit Manager
Cathe Delaney, Membership Coordinator
Caitlin Dougherty, Manager

Exhibits, business sessions and networking opportunities. Provide tools and support to foster the success of members' businesses. To promote the value of pet sitting to the public and the advocate the welfare of animals.
Frequency: September

19886 National Pet Products Controlled Marketing Conference
Controlled Marketing Conferences
PO Box 1771
Monument, CO 80132

719-488-0226
888-316-0226
Fax: 719-488-8168
E-Mail: nlginfo@nlgshow.com
Home Page: www.nlgshow.com

Robert Mikulas, President
Chris Wolf, VP

This event is run in conjunction with the National Lawn and Garden Show.
3000 Attendees
Frequency: June

19887 National Pigeon Association
1717 SE 43rd Terrace
Topeka, KS 66609-1728

785-267-5732
Fax: 785-783-2846
E-Mail: secretary@npausa.com
Home Page: www.npausa.com

Frank Barrachina, President
Pat Avery, Secretary, Treasurer
James Avery, Secretary/Treasurer
Jerry McCalmon, Show Manager

Special information and exhibits about our members and the hobby of pigeon raising.
500 Attendees
Frequency: January
Founded in 1920

19888 Pet Exposition Trade Show
Pet Industry Distributors Association
2105 Laurel Bush Road
Suite 200
Bel Air, MD 21015

443-640-1060
Fax: 443-640-1086
E-Mail: pida@kingmgmt.org
Home Page: www.pida.org

Steven T King CAE, President
Fred Schober, Chairman
Perry Parks, 2nd Vice Chairman
Randy Reber, Secretary/Treasurer
Steven T King, President

Containing 500 booths and 300 exhibits.
3000 Attendees
Frequency: March
Founded in 1968

19889 Pet Food Institute Meeting and Trade Show
Pet Food Institute
2025 M Street NW
Washington, DC 20036

202-367-1120
Fax: 202-367-2120
E-Mail: info@petfoodinstitute.org
Home Page: www.petfoodinstitute.org

Stephen Payne, Public Relations Manager
Duane Ekedahl, Executive Director

Annual exhibits of equipment, supplies and services for manufacturers of commercially prepared dry, semi-moist and canned pet foods.
250 Attendees
Frequency: October

19890 Petfood Forum
WATT Publishing Company
303 N Main Street
Suite 500
Rockford, IL 61101

815-966-5400
Fax: 815-966-6416
E-Mail: blentine@wattmm.com
Home Page: www.wattnet.com

Tim Phillips, Editor
Clay Schreiber, Publisher
James Watt, Owner

A technical trade show and symposium for the pet food industry including manufacturers, suppliers to the industry as well as other pet food professsionals. Containing 143 booths.
850 Attendees
Frequency: April
Founded in 1993
Mailing list available for rent

19891 Quest for Excellence
Pet Sitters International
201 East King Street
King, NC 27021-9163

336-983-9222
Fax: 336 983-3755
E-Mail: info@petsit.com
Home Page: www.petsit.com

Kay Calzemari, Operating Manager
Beth Stoltz, Member Service Coordinator
Amy Woodleaf, Manager/Membership
John Long, Public Relations Coordinator
Dotty Shantz, Member Service

Containing 20+ exhibits.
250 Attendees
Frequency: September
Founded in 1994

19892 Super Zoo Annual WWPSA Pet Industry Trade Show
World Wide Pet Supply Association
406 S 1st Avenue
Arcadia, CA 91006-3829

626-447-2222
Fax: 626-447-8350
Home Page: www.wwpsa.com

Caryn Cohan-Bates, Manager

America's oldest pet industry trade show offering over 450 exhibitors with 850 booths. Seminars, workshops, grooming events and more are held for retailers and wholesalers.
9000 Attendees
Frequency: July
Founded in 1951

19893 Tufts Animal Expo
Hynes Convention Center
900 Boylston Street
Boston, MA 02115

617-954-2000
800-845-8800
Fax: 617-954-2125
E-Mail: info@mccahome.com
Home Page: www.mccahome.com

Animal care professionals addressed the social and medical impact pets have on human lives.
7000 Attendees
Frequency: October

19894 World of Private Label International Trade Show
Private Label Manufacturers Association (PLMA)
630 Third Avenue
New York, NY 10017

212-972-3131
Fax: 212-983-1382

E-Mail: info@plma.com
Home Page: www.plma.com

Brian Sharoff, President
Myra Rosen, VP
Tom Prendergast, Director, Research Services

This show has brought retailers together with manufacturers to help them find new products, make new contacts, and discover new ideas that will help their private label programmers succeed and grow.

Directories & Databases

19895 **American Humane Association Directory**
American Humane Association
1400 16th Street NW
Suite 360
Washington, DC 20036

303-792-9900
800-227-4645
Fax: 818-762-0908
E-Mail: info@americanhumane.org
Home Page: www.americanhumane.org
Social Media: Facebook, Twitter, RSS,YouTube,Pinterest

Robert R Ganzert, President
Clifford Rose, CFO

Animal protection agencies; Canadian and some other foreign agencies are available; national and individual state editions are available.

19896 **Directory of Animal Care and Control Agencies**
American Humane Association
63 Inverness Dr E
Englewood, CO 80112-5117

303-792-9900
800-227-4645
Fax: 303-792-5333
E-Mail: info@americanhumane.org
Home Page: www.americanhumane.org

Marie Wheatley, President

Over 6,000 animal protection agencies; Canadian and some other foreign agencies are available; national and individual state editions are available.
Cost: $75.00

19897 **Market Research Report**
Animal Health Institute
1325 G St NW
Suite 700
Washington, DC 20005-3127

202-637-2440
Fax: 202-393-1667
E-Mail: amathews@ahi.org
Home Page: www.ahi.org

Alexander Mathews, President
Dr Richard A Carnevale, VP Regulatory, Scientific, Int'l
Ron Phillips, VP/Legislative/Public Affairs
Sandra L Phelan, Director Regulatory Affairs
Carolyn S Ayers, VP Administration/Finance

An annual directory published by the Animal Health Institute.
Cost: $150.00
50 Pages
Frequency: Annual
Founded in 1941

19898 **Pets/Animals Forum**
CompuServe Information Service
5000 Arlington Centre Blvd
Columbus, OH 43220-5439

614-326-1002
800-848-8199

This database provides a forum for the discussion of typical house and exotic pets.
Frequency: Bulletin Board

19899 **Veterinary Economics**
Veterinary Healthcare Communications
8033 Flint
Lenexa, KS 66214

913-492-4300
800-255-6864
Fax: 913-492-4157
Home Page: www.vetmedpub.com

Daniel R. Verdon Chapman, Executive Director
Ray Click, VP/General Manager

Publishes two monthly magazines, a full drug list resource, and business books; conducts the Central Veterinary Conference trade show; rents its mail lists and does custom communication projects.
Frequency: Monthly
Circulation: 52,000
Mailing list available for rent: 48M+ names
Printed in 4 colors on matte stock

Industry Web Sites

19900 **http://gold.greyhouse.com**
G.O.L.D Grey House OnLine Databases
Grey House Publishing's online database platform, GOLD, offers Quick Search, Keyword Search and Expert Search for most business sectors including pet and pet supply markets. The GOLD platform makes finding the information you need quick and easy - whether you're a novice searcher or an experienced database user. All of Grey House's directory products are available for subscription on the GOLD platform.

19901 **www.aahanet.org**
American Animal Hospital Association
A group of hospitals and animal practitioners serving the industry.

19902 **www.abka.com**
American Boarding Kennels Association
Seeks to upgrade the industry through educational programs and conventions. Promotes code of ethics and accreditation programs for kennel operators.

19903 **www.ahi.org**
Animal Health Institute
Resource for you to learn more about how animals health products work, how they are used and their many benefits.

19904 **www.akc.org**
American Kennel Club
The principal registry of pure-bred dogs in the US.

19905 **www.allpets.com**
Dog.com
Best selection of dog supplies and prices, news and forum about dogs, health issues, grooming and the well-being for our four-legged friends.

19906 **www.apdt.com**
Association of Pet Dog Trainers
Official web site of the association. Includes members in the news, training events, industry news, trainer search engine, conference news and merchandise.

19907 **www.aspca.org**
ASPCA
Society for the humane treatment of animals, established in 1866.

19908 **www.avma.org**
American Veterinary Medical Association
Publishes various journals and information for members. Acts as a clearinghouse for veterinarians.

19909 **www.deltasociety.org**
Delta Society
Information on human-animal interactions. Service Dog Center provides information and advocacy for dogs trained to assist people with disabilities. Pet Partners Program trains volunteers, health professionals, animals for animal-assisted therapy and activities.

19910 **www.greyhouse.com**
Grey House Publishing
Authoritative reference directories for most business sectors including pet and pet supply markets. Users can search the online databases with varied search criteria allowing for custom searches by product category, geographic area, sales volume, keyword, subject and more. Full Grey House catalog and online ordering also available.

19911 **www.nhes.org**
National Humane Education Society
Fights for the prevention of cruelty to animals in any form. Fostering a sentiment of kindness since 1948.

19912 **www.npausa.com**
National Pigeon Association
Special information for members and for the hobby of pigeon raising.

19913 **www.peta.org**
People for the Ethical Treatment of Animals (PETA)
Opposes all forms of animal exploitation. Seeks to educate the public on what the group sees as the three major institutionalized cruelty issues: the exploitation and abuse of animals in experimentation, the manufacturing of fur apparel, and slaughtering for human consumption.

19914 **www.petfoodinstitute.org**
Pet Food Institute
Represents the manufacturer of 97% of all dog and cat food produced in the US. Dedicated to promoting the overall care and well-being of pets. Research in pet nutrition, proper feedings and pet care.

19915 **www.petpride.org**
Pet Pride
Operates a no kill free shelter for the lifetime of homeless cats.

19916 **www.petsit.com**
Pet Sitters International
Society of professional pet sitters. Membership provides valuable benefits - educational resources for those engaged in the pet-sitting industry. Also provides a forum to network with peers who share a common vision of excellence in at-home pet care.

19917 **www.petsitters.org**
National Association of Professional Pet Sitters
The only non-profit organization dedicated to serving the needs of professional pet care providers. Promotes ethical standards and fosters cooperation among members in the pet care industry.

19918 www.pida.org
Pet Industry Distributors Association
Represents wholesaler-distributors of pet products, providing training and education to members.

19919 www.pijac.org
Pet Industry Joint Advisory Council
Monitors federal and state regulations and legislation affecting the industry. Sponsors research and educational projects including certification programs in veterinary care and husbandry for companion animals, in-store training videos, etc.

19920 www.usaha.org
United States Animal Health Association
Science-based, non-profit, voluntary organization. Members are state and federal animal health officials, universities, veterinarians, livestock producers, research scientists, and extension services all to control livestock diseases in the US.

19921 www.wspa.americas.org
The Resource Center of the Americas
International animal protection news reports. Informs, educates and organizes economic justice and cross-cultural understanding in the Americas.

19922 www.wwpsa.com
World Wide Pet Supply Association
Seeks to advance the economic interests of members. Promotes responsible pet ownership. Sponsors consumer and trade shows for the pet industry.

Associations

19923 **Advertising Photographers of America**
419 Lafayette St,2nd Floor
New York, NY 10003

212-807-0399
Fax: 212-727-8120
E-Mail: jocelyn@apany.com
Home Page: www.apanational.com

Martin Trailer, President
Matthew Klein, VP
Julia Graham, Director

Our goal is to establish, endorse and promote professional practices, standards and ethics in the photographic and advertising community.
650 Members
Founded in 1981

19924 **American Photographic Artists Guild**
568 Main Street
Wilbraham, MA 01095

E-Mail: katfalls@tdi.net
Home Page: www.useassociations.com

D John McCarthy, President
Joanie Ford, Historian/Merits/Degrees
Miles Andonov, Education
Lori Smith, Membership/Public Relations
Joanie Ford, Chairman

Encourages a better understanding between the photographer, the color artist and the retoucher. Conducts educational programs, sponsors competitions and bestows awards.
Founded in 1966

19925 **American Photography Association**

877-627-2360
Home Page:
www.americanphotographyassociation.org
Social Media: Facebook, Twitter

To promote the interest, appreciation and participation in photography by all levels of photographers.

19926 **American Photograpic Artists**
369 Montezuma Ave
#567
Santa Fe, NM 87501

Home Page: apanational.org
Social Media: Facebook, Twitter

Theresa Raffetto, National Board President
Michael Grecco, National Board EVP
Ric Kasnoff, National Board SVP
John Durant, National Board Vice President
Andrew Strauss, National Board Treasurer

A not-for-profit organization for professional photographers.
Founded in 1981

19927 **American Society for Photobiology**
PO Box 7065
Lawrence, KS 66044

785-865-9405
800-627-0326
Fax: 785-843-6153
E-Mail: phot@allenpress.com
Home Page: www.photobiology.org
Social Media: Facebook, LinkedIn

Linda Hardwick, Executive Secretariat
Tayyaba Hasan, Past-President
Beth Gaillard, President
Don Forbes, Secretary
John Streicher, Treasurer

Founded to further the scientific study of the effects of light on all living organisms.
1600 Members
Founded in 1972

19928 **American Society for Photogrammetry and Remote Sensing**
5410 Grosvenor Lane
Suite 210
Bethesda, MD 20814-2160

301-493-0290
Fax: 301-493-0208
Home Page: www.asprs.org
Social Media: Facebook, Twitter

Dr. A. Stewart Walker, CP, President
Dr. E. Lynn Usery, President Elect
Dr. Charles K. Toth, CP, Vice President
Dr. Stephen D. DeGloria, Past President
Dr. Donald T.ÿ Lauer, Treasurer

A professional scientific association to advance the knowledge of and improve mapping sciences.

19929 **American Society of Media Photographers**
150 North 2nd Street
Philadelphia, PA 19106

215-451-2767
E-Mail: info@asmp.org
Home Page: asmp.org
Social Media: Facebook, Twitter, LinkedIn

Tom Kennedy, Executive Director
Victor Perlman, General Counsel
Elena Goertz, General Manager
Chris Chandler, Bookkeeper
Peter Dyson, Director of Communications

A trade association which protects and promotes the interests of photographers whose work is for publication.

19930 **American Society of Photographers**
3120 N. Argonne Dr.
Milwaukee, WI 53222

979-272-0900
Fax: 978-272-5201
E-Mail: jonallyn@aol.com
Home Page: www.asofp.com
Social Media: RSS

Doug Box, Executive Director
John Maxwell, President

Membership requirements include membership in Professional Photographers of America and either a Master of Photography, a Photographic Craftsmen, or a photographic specialist. Publishes a quarterly newsletter.
800 Members
Founded in 1937

19931 **American Society of Picture Professionals**
217 Palos Verdes Blvd
Suite 700
Redondo Beach, CA 90277

424-247-9944
Fax: 424-247-9844
E-Mail: cathy@aspp.com
Home Page: www.aspp.com
Social Media: Facebook, Twitter, LinkedIn, RSS

Jain Lemos, Executive Director
Michael Masterson, President
Sam Merrell, VP
Mary F Loftus, Treasurer
Ellen Herbert, Secretary

Members are image producers, stock photo agencies, and image users.Provides networking and educational opportunities in the image transaction industry.
800 Members
Founded in 1969

19932 **Antique and Amusement Photographers International**
3395 S.Jones Blvd
Suite 4
Las Vegas, NV 89146

860-578-2274
Fax: 877-865-1052
E-Mail: gail@oldtimephotos.org
Home Page: www.oldtimephotos.org
Social Media: Facebook, LinkedIn

Susan K. Crutchfield, Executive Director
Mike Glasser, President
Michele Powers, Secretary
Scott Henry, Treasurer
Trent Edwards, Vice President

Members are photography studies and photographers, primarliy in the US and Canada, specializing in costume photography and suppliers to the industry.
200 Members
Founded in 1993

19933 **Association of International Photography Art Dealers**
1609 Connecticut Ave NW
Suite 200
Washington, DC 20009-1034

202-232-5740
Fax: 202-318-4003
E-Mail: AIPAD@aol.com
Home Page: www.photoshow.com

Kathleen Ewing, Executive Director

Galleries and private dealers in fine photography who have been in business for at least three years.
125 Members
Founded in 1979

19934 **BioCommunications Association**
220 Southwind Lane
Hillsborough, NC 27278

919-245-0906
Fax: 919-245-0906
E-Mail: office@bca.org
Home Page: www.bca.org
Social Media: Facebook, Twitter, LinkedIn

Nancy Hurtgen, Manager Central Office
Joseph Kane, President
James Koepfler, Secretary/ Treasurer
Connie Johansen, VP
Laurie Lizotte, Dir. Of Communications

Made up of professionals who create and use the highest quality images and presentations in visual communications media for teaching and documentation in the life sciences and medicine.
140 Members
Founded in 1931

19935 **Center for Photography at Woodstock**
59 Tinker St
Woodstock, NY 12498

845-679-9957
Fax: 845-679-6337
E-Mail: info@cpw.org
Home Page: www.cpw.org
Social Media: Facebook, Twitter, Flickr, Vimeo, Pinterest

Ariel Shanberg, Executive Director
Akemi Hiatt, Program Associate
Lewrence Lewis, Operations Manager
Akemi Hiatt, Program Associate
Phil Mansfield, Digital Lab Manager

The Center for Photography at Woodstock is a not-for-profit, artist-centered organization dedicated to supporting artists working in photography and related media and engaging audiences through opportunities in which creation, discovery, and education are made possible.
Founded in 1977

19936 Council on Fine Art Photography
5613 Johnson Ave
Bethesda, MD 20817-3503

301-897-0083

Lowell Anson Kenyon, Executive Director

Members are fine art photographers employing silver processes.
50 Members
Founded in 1982

19937 Digital Media Licensing Association
3165 S. Alma School Road
#29-261
Chandler, AZ 85248-3760

714-815-8427
E-Mail: execdirector@pacaoffice.org
Home Page: www.pacaoffice.org/index.shtml
Social Media: Facebook, Twitter, LinkedIn, RSS, Skype

Sarah Fix, President
Elena Flanagan-Eister, Vice President
Chris Carey, Treasurer
Julie Zentmaier, Secretary
Geoff Cannon, Member at Large

A community of visual media licensing professionals.

19938 Evidence Photographers International Council
600 Main Street
Honesdale, PA 18431

570-253-5450
800-356-3742
Fax: 570-253-5011
E-Mail: epicheadquarters@verizon.net
Home Page: www.epic-photo.org

Robert Jennings, Executive Director

A non profit educational and scientific organization with the primary purpose is the advancement of forensic photography/videography in civil evidence and law enforcement.
2000 Members
Founded in 1968

19939 IEEE Standards Association
445 Hoes Lane
Piscataway, NJ 08854-4141

732-981-0060
Fax: 732-562-1571
E-Mail: i3amembership@i3a.org
Home Page: www.i3a.org
Social Media: Facebook, Twitter, LinkedIn

Karen Bartleson, President
John Kulick, Chairman
Don Wright, Treasurer
Konstantinos Karachalios, Secretary
Dennis Brophy, Corporate Advisory Group

Formerly (1997) National Association of Photographic Manufacturers and (2001) Photographic and Imaging Maufacturers Association. The Silver Council is a program sponsored by I3A that monitors environmental regulation of commercial silver use. Membership fee varies,based on annual sales.
81 Members
Founded in 1946

19940 Independent Photo Imagers
2518 Anthem Village
Suite 104
Henderson, NV 89052

702-617-1141
Fax: 702-617-1181
E-Mail: ipimemberinfo@ipiphoto.com
Home Page: www.ipiphoto.com
Social Media: Facebook, Twitter, YouTube, Pinterest

Brent Bowyer, Executive Director
Erin von Holdt, Marketing Director
Tom Skaggs, Treasurer
Koby Marowelli, Secretary
Larry Steiner, Chairman

An association of independent photographers, who use various means of developing their pictures.
45 Members
Founded in 1982

19941 International Color Consortium
1899 Preston White Drivey
Reston, VA 20191y

703-264-7200
Home Page: www.color.org

Thomas Lianza, Co-Chair
William Li, Co-Chair
Max Derhak, Vice Chair
Deborah Orf, Secretary
Phil Green, Technical Secretary

An association to promote the use and adoption of open, vendor-neutral, cross-platform color management.
Founded in 1993

19942 International Fire Photographers Association
143 40th Street
New Orleans, LA 70124

504-482-9616
Fax: 504-486-4946
E-Mail: president@ifpaonline.com
Home Page: ifpafirephotos.org/
Social Media: Facebook, Twitter, Google+, Yahoo

Chris E Mickal, President
Michael Heller, VP

Promote professionalism in all aspects of fire photography, specifically in the fields of fire, educational, and investigative photography and the recognition of all fire photography organizations as an important tool in the fire service and law enforcement
200 Members
Founded in 1964

19943 International Graphic Arts Education Association
1899 Preston White Drive
Reston, VA 20191

703-758-0595
Home Page: www.igaea.org

Monika Zarzycka, President
Kelly Glentz Brush, Secretary
Dr. Jerry Waite, Treasurer
Tony Cimaglia, First Vice-President (Publications)
Michael Williams, President-Elect

An association of educators in partnership with industry, dedicated to sharing theories, principles, techniques, and processes relating to graphic communications and imaging theory.
800 Members
Founded in 1923

19944 Naples Art Association
The von Liebig Art Center
585 Park St.
Naples, FL 34102

239-262-6517
Home Page: www.naplesart.org
Social Media: Facebook, Twitter, LinkedIn, Pinterest, YouTube

Stacey Bulloch, Board President
Aimee Schlehr, Executive Director
Shea Lindner, Programs Manager
Peter Franklin, Operations Manager
Callie Spilane, Education Director

A nonprofit organization to promote and advance education, interest and participation in the visual arts.
Founded in 1954

19945 National Association of Photo Equipment Technicians
300 Picture Place
Jackson, MI 49201
517-788-8100
Fax: 517-788-8371
E-Mail: bcovey@pmai.org
Home Page: wwww.pmai.org

William Covey, Executive Liaison

Provides information on the photogrpahic industry to those engaged in the photographic repair.
250 Members
Founded in 1973

19946 National Association of Quick Printers (NAQP)
One Meadowlands Plaza
Suite 1511
East Rutherford, NJ 07073

201-634-9600
800-642-6275
Fax: 201-634-0324
E-Mail: webmaster@napl.org
Home Page: www.naqp.com
Social Media: Facebook, Twitter, LinkedIn, YouTube,RSS, Pinterest, Google

Joseph Truncale, President & CEO
Nigel Worme, Chairman
Willam Gavigan, Treasurer/ Secretary
Niels Winther, Vice Chairman
Mike Philie, Senior Vice President

Furthers the business of quick printers, copy shops, and small format commercial printers. Also welcomes manufacturers and suppliers of equipment and consumables, trade publications, and consultants to the quick print industry.
900 Members
Founded in 1975

19947 National Photograpic Society
847-803-9450
Home Page: www.thenps.com

David Simm, Chairman
Rod Pascoe, Chairman
Damian McGillicuddy, Head of Training, Mentoring
Paul Spiers, Head of marketing
Vicki Boulter, Mentor & Magazine Producer

A society for both professional as well as enthusiast photographers.

19948 National Press Photographers Association
3200 Croasdaile Drÿ
Suite 306
Durham, NC 27705

919-383-7246
Fax: 919-383-7261
Home Page: nppa.org
Social Media: Facebook, Twitter, LinkedIn, Vimeo

Mark Dolan, President
Scott Mc Kiernan, Vice President
Jim Michalowski, Treasurer
Michael King, Secretary
Michael Borland, Immediate Past President

Sponsors numerous, annual television and print media workshops. Conducts annual competition for news photos and television news film. Monthly magazine job information bank given to all members.
Founded in 1946

19949 National Stereoscopic Association
E-Mail: strwld@teleport.com
Home Page: stereoworld.org
Social Media: Facebook

Lawrence Kaufman, Chairman
Lee Pratt, President
John Bueche, Vice President
John Dennis, Stereo World Editor
Ronald Gold, Vice President, Marketing

A nonprofit organization to promote research, practice, collection and use of vintage and contempory stereoviews, stereo cameras and equipment.
Founded in 1974

19950 North American Nature Photography Association
6382 Charleston Road
Alma, IL 62807

618-547-7616
Fax: 618-547-7438
E-Mail: info@nanpa.org
Home Page: www.nanpa.org
Social Media: RSS

David Stumph, Owner
Francine Butler, Executive Director
Gabby Salazar, Preisdent-Elect
Bruce Haley, President
Ron Rosenstock, Treasurer

Committed solely to serving the field of nature photography. Provides education, information develops standards and promotes nature photography as an art form and teaching medium.
Founded in 1993

19951 North American Nature Photography Associat ion
6382 Charleston Road
Alma, IL 62807

618-547-7616
Fax: 618-547-7438
E-Mail: info@nanpa.org
Home Page: www.nanpa.org
Social Media: Facebook, Twitter, LinkedIn, RSS, Google+

Gabby Salazar, President
Sean Fitzgerald, President Elect
Bruce Haley, Past-President, Treasurer
Clay Bolt, Board Member
Gary Farber, Board Member

An organization dedicated to photography of nature.

19952 PERA
Pera Innovation Park, Nottingham Rd.
Melton Broadway
Leicestershire, UK LE13 0PB

166-450-1501
800-776-8616
Fax: 408-512-5254
E-Mail: enquiries@peraconsulting.com
Home Page: www.pera.com
Social Media: Facebook, Twitter

Tanya Allen, Marketing Dircetor
Glyn Goddard, Chief Financial Officer
Amanda Lee-Bennett, Finanace Director
John Hill, Executive Chairman
John Collier, Chief Executive Officer

An association for production equipment rental personnel and organizations.
75 Members
Founded in 1973

19953 Photo Chemical Machining Institute
11 Robert Toner Blvd
234
North Attleboro, MA 02763

508-385-0085
Fax: 508-232-6005
E-Mail: cflaherty@pcmi.org
Home Page: www.pcmi.org

Catherine Flaherty, Executive Director
Joseph Beck, President
William Fox, Vice-President
Eric Kemperman, Treasurer
Philip Greiner, Secretary

Members are companies producing metal products through photo chemical machining. In addition the Institute includes companies that service the PCM industry and supply its needs.
210 Members
Founded in 1967

19954 Photo Marketing Association International
2282 Springport Road
Suite F
Jackson, MI 49202

517-788-8100
800-762-9287
Fax: 517-788-8371
E-Mail: pma_advertising@pmai.org
Home Page: www.pmai.org
Social Media: Facebook, Twitter, LinkedIn

Gabrielle Mullinax, President-Elect
Allen Showalter, President
Robert L. Hanson, Vice-President
Bill Eklund, Treasurer
Jim Esp, Secretary/Executive Director

A national organization of associations and manufacturers and suppliers of photographic equipment; also members of the National Association of Photo Equipment Technicians and of the Professional School Photographers of America.
18000 Members
Founded in 1924

19955 Photographic Society of America
8241 S Walker Avenue
Suite 104
Oklahoma City, OK 73139

405-843-1437
855-772-4636
Home Page: www.psa-photo.org

John Davis, FPSA, PPSA, President
Charlie Burke, FPSA, EPSA, Executive Vice President
Jan Lee, APSA, EPSA, Treasurer
Elena McTighe, FPSA, EPSA, Secretary
Stan Bormann, APSA, EPSA, Conference Vice President

Worldwide interactive organization for anyone interested in photography, professional or serious amateur. Offers a wide variety of activities, monthly magazine, photo and digital competitions, study groups via mail and Internet, how-to programs, an annal conference, and many other activites and services.
Founded in 1934

19956 Photoimaging Manufacturers and Distributor s Association
7600 Jericho Turnpike
Suite 301
Woodbury, NY 11797

516-802-0895
Fax: 516-364-0140
E-Mail: jackie@pmda.com
Home Page: www.pmda.com
Social Media: Facebook, Twitter, LinkedIn

Dan Unger, President
Michelle Fernandez, VP
Jay Kelbley, VP
Christine Moossmann, VP
Jerry Grossman, Executive Director

Contributes to the progress and welfare of the photoimaging industry.
Founded in 1939

19957 Picture Agency Council of America
23046 Avenida De La Carlota
Suite 600
Laguna Hills, CA 92653

714-815-8427
Fax: 949-679-8224
E-Mail: execdirector@pacaoffice.org
Home Page: www.stockindustry.org

Cathy Aron, Executive Director
Maria Kessler, President

Trade association for stock picture companies in North America. Serves member agencies, their clients and their contributing photographers by promoting communication among photo agencies and other professional groups.
150 Members
Founded in 1951

19958 Professional Aerial Photographers' Association
12069 Cessna Place
Brookshire, TX 77423

703-887-8703
Fax: 703-281-6700
Home Page: professionalaerialphotographers.com

Chuck Boyleÿ, President
Laura Boyko, VP, Programs
Kent Larson, VP, Membership
John Mooney, Treasurer, Secretary
Julie Belanger, ExecutiveÿDirector

A professional trade organization for aerial photographers.
Founded in 1974

19959 Professional Photographer Magazine
229 Peachtree St NE
Suite 2200
Atlanta, GA 30303

404-522-8600
800-742-7468
Fax: 404-614-6406
E-Mail: ppmag@omeda.com
Home Page: www.ppmag.com
Social Media: Facebook, Twitter, Pinterest

David Trust, CEO
Bob Lloyd, President
Dana Groves, Marketing Executive

Portrait, commercial, wedding, industrial and specialized photographers and photographic artists.
14000 Members
Founded in 1869

19960 Professional Photographers Association
Professional Photographers Assoc. of New England
PO Box 316
Willimantic, CT 06226

860-423-1402
Fax: 860-423-9402
E-Mail: ppanerl@aol.com
Home Page: www.ppane.com

Roland L Laramie, Show Manager/Executive Director
1000 Attendees
Frequency: September
Founded in 1860

19961 Professional Photographers of America
229 Peachtree St. NE
Suite 2200
Atlanta, GA 30303

404-522-8600
Fax: 404-614-6400
Home Page: www.ppa.com

Social Media: Facebook, Twitter, LinkedIn, Google+, Instagram, YouTube

Ralph Romaguera, Chairman
Susan Michal, President
Michael Timmons, Vice President
Lori Craft, Treasurer
Rob Behm, Director

A nonprofit trade association for photographers.
Founded in 1869

19962 **Professional Picture Framers Association**
2282 Springport Road
Suite F
Jackson, MI 49202

517-788-8100
800-762-9287
Fax: 517-788-8371
E-Mail: ppfa@ppfa.com
Home Page: www.ppfa.com
Social Media: Facebook, Twitter, LinkedIn

John Pruitt CPF, President
Fran Gray MCPF, VP

A trade association of manufacturers, wholesalers, print publishers, importers and retailers selling art, framing and related supplies.
3000 Members
Founded in 1971

19963 **Professional Travelogue Sponsors**
El Camino College Foundation
16007 Crenshaw Boulevard
Torrance, CA 90506

310-323-3670
Fax: 310-715-7875
E-Mail: artstickets@elcamino.edu
Home Page: www.centerforthearts.org

Thomas Fallow, President
Bruce Spain, Executive Director

Currently the largest documentary Travel Film Program Sponsor and Presenter.
55 Members
Founded in 1967

19964 **Professional Women Photographers**
Metropolitan Opera Guild
119 W. 72nd St.
#223
New York, NY 10023

212-867-7745
E-Mail: info@pwponline.org
Home Page: www.pwponline.org
Social Media: Facebook, Twitter, LinkedIn, Amazon, RSS

Fran Dickson, President
Gloria Waslyn, VP
Lenore Janis, President

To support and promote the work of women photographers through the sharing of ideas, resources and experience, to provide educational forums to engourage artistic growth and photographic development, and to stimulate public interst in and support for the art of photography
170 Members
Founded in 1975
Mailing list available for rent

19965 **SPIE, the international society for optics and photonics**
1000 20th Street
Bellingham, WA 98225-6705

360-676-3290
888-504-8171
Fax: 360-647-1445
E-Mail: help@spie.org
Home Page: www.SPIE.org
Social Media: Facebook, Twitter, LinkedIn, RSS, YouTube, Blogspot

Eugene G Arthurs, CEO
William H. Arnold, President
Prof. Toyohiko Yatagai, VP
Brian Lula, Secretary/ Treasurer
H. Philip Stahl, President-Elect

Members are scientists, engineers, researchers and companies interested in technology and applications of optical, electro-optical, fiber-optic, laser, and photonic systems.
14000 Members
Founded in 1955

19966 **Silver Users Association**
3930 Walnut St.
Suite 210
Fairfax, VA 22030

703 930 7790
Fax: 703-359-7562
E-Mail: pmiller@mwcapitol.com
Home Page: www.silverusersassociation.org

Paul A Miller, Executive Director
Bill LeRoy, President
Mike Huber, VP
John King, Secretary
Bill Hammerle, Treasury

Represents manufacturers and distributors of products in which silver is an essential element. Works for the recognition of silver as a commodity and the removal of governmental regulations which retard its free exchange in commerce both foreign and domestic. Also helps provide a stable trading climate in the metal, it monitors the silver market to insure that silver information available to the industry and public is accurate.
28 Members
Founded in 1947

19967 **Society for Photographic Education**
2530 Superior Avenue
Suite 403
Cleveland, OH 44114

216-622-2733
Fax: 216-622-2712
E-Mail: membership@spenational.org
Home Page: www.spenational.org

Virginia Morrison, Executive Director
Jeff Curto, Vice-Chair
Michael Marshall, Chair
Nancy Stuart, Treasurer
Nate Larson, Secretary

The Society for Photographic Education is a non-profit membership organization that provides a forum for the discussion of photogrphy and related media as a means of creative expression and cultural insight. Through its interdisciplinary porgrams, services and publications, the society seeks to promote a broader understanding of the medium in all its forms, and to foster the development of its practice, teaching, scholarship and criticism.
1800 Members
Founded in 1963

19968 **Society of American Travel Writers**
11950 W Lake Park Drive
Suite 320
Milwaukee, WI 53224-3049

414-359-1625
Fax: 414-359-1671
E-Mail: info@satw.org
Home Page: www.satw.org
Social Media: Facebook, Twitter, LinkedIn

Steve Giordano, President
Diana Lambdin Meyer, VP
Peggy Bendel, Secretary
Tom Adkinson, Treasurer
Annette Thompson, President-Elect

Photographers and 35 associate member representatives of airlines, hotels, resorts, tourist agencies and public relations firms.
Founded in 1955

19969 **Student Photographic Society**
229 Peachtree St. NE
Suite 2200
Atlanta, GA 30303

888-722-1334
E-Mail: info@studentphoto.com
Home Page: studentphoto.com
Social Media: Facebook, Twitter, Google+

Ralph Romaguera, Chairman
Susan Michal, President
Michael Timmons, Vice President
Lori Craft, Treasurer
Rob Behm, Director

Provides career building resources, networking opportunities and information for photography students.
Founded in 1999

19970 **Take Great Pictures**
109 White Oak Lane
Suite 72F
Old Bridge, NJ 08857

732-679-3460
Fax: 516-364-0140
E-Mail: bclarkpmda@aol.com
Home Page: www.takegreatpictures.com
Social Media: RSS

Willard Clark, Executive Director

Founded as Photographic Merchandising and Distributing Association and became Photographic Manufacturers and Distributors Association before assuming its present name in 1999. Membership is $500/year for associate members and $1,000/year for voting members.
20000 Members
Founded in 1939

19971 **The Association of Independent Architectural Photographers**
4531 Cambridge Court
Bountiful, UT 84010

801-738-8786
E-Mail: aiap@photographer.org
Home Page: www.aiap.net

A professional organization for architectural photographers.

19972 **The Society for Photographic Education**
Home Page: www.spenational.org
Social Media: Facebook

A nonprofit ogranization for the advancement of education in photography.

19973 **University Photographers Association of America**
SUNY Brockport
350 New Campus Drive
Brockport, NY 14420-2931

716-395-2133
Fax: 662-915-1298
E-Mail: jdusen@brockport.edu
Home Page: www.upaa.org

Glenn Carpenter, President
Robert Jordan, VP
Nick Romanenko, Treasurer
Mark Carriveau, Secretary
Bill Bitzinger, Board Member

Members are college and university photographers who are concerned with the application and practice of photography.
250 Members
Founded in 1961

19974 Wedding & Portrait Photographers International
85 Broad St.
20th Floor
New York, NY 10004

646-654-4500
Fax: 310-846-4770
Home Page: www.wppionline.com
Social Media: Facebook, Twitter, YouTube, Instagram

Stephen Sheanin, CEO/President
John McGeary, Managing Director
Lauren Wendle, VP, Publisher
Cathy Griffith, Operations Director
Jason Groupp, Director

Promotes high artistic and technical standards. Serves as a forum for an exchange of technical knowledge. Members are offered the opportunity to purchase special products and services.
2.8M Members
Founded in 1970

19975 Wedding Photojournalist Association

Home Page: www.wpja.com

A resource of photojournalists and candid wedding photographers.
Founded in 2002

19976 White House News Photographers Association
7119 Ben Franklin Station
Washington, DC 20044-7119

202-785-5230
E-Mail: info@whnpa.org
Home Page: www.whnpa.org
Social Media: Facebook, Twitter

Ron Sachs, President
Doug Wilkes, VP
Jon Elswick, Treasurer
Joshua Roberts, Secretary
Dennis Brack, Ex Officio

Volunteer association of professional photographers covering the Washington political venue. Activities include educational seminars, work with high school students and an annual awards contest. Our work is seen in newspapers, magazines, television and on the Internet.
500 Members
Founded in 1941

19977 Worldwide Community of Imaging Association
2282 Springport Road
Suite F
Jackson, MI 49202ÿ

517-788-8100
800-762-9287
Fax: 517-788-8371
Home Page: www.pmai.org
Social Media: Facebook, Twitter, LinkedIn

Bill Eklund, President
Gabrielleÿ Mullinax, Senior Vice President
Jerry Sullivan, Vice President
Mark Klostermeyer, MCPF, Treasurer
Jim Esp, Secretary, Executive Director

United diverse professionals in the imaging industry worldwide.
Founded in 1924

Newsletters

19978 American Society of Media Photgraphers Bulletin
Photo District News
150 North Second Street
Philadelphia, PA 19106

215-451-2767
Fax: 215-451-0880
E-Mail: info@asmp.org
Home Page: www.asmp.org
Social Media: Facebook, Twitter, LinkedIn

Holly Hughes, Editor
Jeffery Roberts, President

Member publication that addresses the news and preoccupations of the photography industry.
Frequency: Quarterly
Circulation: 5500
Founded in 1944

19979 BCA News
BioCommunications Association
220 Southwind Lane
Hillsborough, NC 27278-7907

919-245-0906
Fax: 919-245-0906
E-Mail: khensley@mdanderson.org
Home Page: www.bca.org
Social Media: Facebook, Twitter, LinkedIn, Blog,Tumblr

Karen Hensley, Editor
Susanne Loomis, President
Joseph Kane, Vice-President
James Koepfler, Secretary-Treasurer

Keeps members informed about such things as annual meetings, chapter activities, awards and member updates.
Frequency: 2-3x/Year

19980 Dance on Camera Journal
Dance Films Association
48 W 21st St
Suite 907
New York, NY 10010-6989

212-727-0764
Fax: 212-727-0764
E-Mail: info@dancefilmsassn.org
Home Page: www.dancefilms.org

Deidra Towers, Executive Director
Louise Spain, CEO

The only service organization in the world dedicated to both the dance and the film community.
Cost: $45.00
Circulation: 350
Founded in 1956

19981 Future Image Report
Future Image
520 South El Camino Real
Suite 206A
San Mateo, CA 94402
650-579-0493
800-749-3572
Fax: 650-579-0566
E-Mail: hbravo@futureimage.com
Home Page: www.futureimage.com

Alexis J Gerard, Editor/Publisher
Paul Worthington, Managing Editor
Heidy Bravo, Circulaion Manager

News and analysis of technology and market developments in photo-digital imaging, for management-level industry professionals.
Cost: $500.00
Founded in 1991

19982 Light Impressions Review
PO Box 940
Rochester, NY 14603-0940

716-271-8960

William Edwards, Publisher
Lance Speer, Director

Photography notes and news.
Cost: $15.00
16 Pages
Frequency: Monthly

19983 NTIS Alert- Photography & Recording Devices
National Technical Information Service
5285 Port Royal Rd
US Department of Commerce
Alexandria, VA 22312

703-605-6000
800-553-6847
Fax: 703-605-6900
E-Mail: info@ntis.gov
Home Page: www.ntis.gov

Linda Davis, VP
Cost: $140.00
Founded in 1955

19984 Photo Marketing
Photo Marketing Association International
2282 Springport Road
Suite F
Jackson, MI 49202

517-788-8100
800-762-9287
Fax: 517-788-8371
E-Mail: gpageau@pmai.org
Home Page: www.pmai.org
Social Media: Facebook, Twitter, LinkedIn

Ted Fox, CEO
Allen Showalter, President
Mark Klostermeyer, Vice-President
Robert L Hanson, Treasurer

News of interest to the photo business on both a national and international basis.
Cost: $5.00
4 Pages
Frequency: Monthly
Circulation: 12,141
Founded in 1925

19985 PhotoDaily
PhotoSource International
1910 35th Ave
Pine Lake Farm
Osceola, WI 54020-5602

715-248-3800
800-624-0266
Fax: 715-248-7394
E-Mail: info@photosource.com
Home Page: www.photosource.com

Rohn Engh, President
Bruce Swenson, Production Manager
Jonna Zehma, Editor

Pairs photographers with the picture needs of magazine and book editors.
Cost: $330.00
Frequency: Daily
Founded in 1976

19986 Photobulletin
PhotoSource International
1910 35th Ave
Osceola, WI 54020-5602

715-248-3800
800-624-0266
Fax: 715-248-7394
E-Mail: info@photosource.com
Home Page: www.photosource.com

Rohn Engh, President

Lists photographic needs of photobuyers buying in the top-notch markets.
Frequency: Daily
Founded in 1980
Printed in one color

19987 Photofinishing News
Photofinishing News

219 Lafeyette Avenue
Westwood, NJ 07675-904

201-819-2533
E-Mail: hans@photo-news.com
Home Page: www.photo-news.com

Hans Kuhlman, Editor

Technical / marketing coverage of worldwide photography / photo-imaging industry, reviews of new products, tradeshows and market statistics.
Cost: $150.00
12 Pages
ISBN: 0-889239-3 -
ISSN: 1536-6553
Founded in 1970
Printed in one color on matte stock

19988 Photograph Collector
140 East Richardson Avenue
Suite 301
Langhorne, PA 19047-2824

215-891-0214
E-Mail: info@photoreview.org
Home Page: www.photoreview.org

Stephen Perloff, Editor

News and analysis for collectors, curators and dealers. Current coverage of the auction market, trends, discoveries, museums and trade shows. Accepts advertising.
Cost: $149.95
8 Pages
Frequency: Monthly
ISBN: 0-271083-8 -
Founded in 1980
Printed in one color on matte stock

19989 Professional Photographers Association of New England
98 Windham Street
PO Box 316
Willimantic, CT 06226-316

203-488-2334
860-423-1402
Fax: 860-423-9402
E-Mail: info@ppane.com
Home Page: www.ppane.com

Harvey Goldstein, Editor
Ruth Clegg, CEO/President
Circulation: 1000
Founded in 1961
Printed in on glossy stock

19990 WPPI Newsletter
Wedding & Portrait Photographers International
770 Broadway
New York, NY 10003

646-654-4500
Fax: 310-846-4770
Home Page: www.wppionline.com

Stephen Sheanin, CEO/President
Lauren Wendle, Vice-President
Michael Zorich, Marketing Director
Frequency: Monthly

Magazines & Journals

19991 Advanced Imaging
Cygnus Publishing
102 Wilmont Road
Suite 470
Deerfield, IL 60015-3601

847-405-0257
E-Mail: larry.adams@cygnusb2b.com
Home Page: www.cygnusb2b.com

Dave Brambert, Group Publisher
Larry Adams, Editor-in-Chief
Richard Reiff, President
Hank Russell, Managing Editor

Contains information on professional photographic techniques and new approaches in all forms of media.
Cost: $60.00
Frequency: Monthly
Circulation: 44009
Founded in 1966

19992 Afterimage
Visual Studies Workshop
31 Prince Street
Rochester, NY 14607-1405
585-442-8676
Fax: 585-442-1992
E-Mail: info@vsw.org
Home Page: www.vsw.org/afterimage/index.html

Karen VanMeenen, Editor
Joanna Heatwole, Managing Editor

Geared toward media arts and photography artists, curators, academics, administrators and students. Features photography, independent film and video coverage, artist's books, alternative publishing and cultural studies issues. Also highlights conference and festival reports and scholarly feature articles.
Cost: $33.00
Circulation: 10000
Founded in 1980

19993 American Photo
1633 Broadway
43rd Floor
New York, NY 10019

212-676-6000
800-274-4514
Fax: 212-489-4217
E-Mail: jiannello@hfmus.com
Home Page: www.hfmus.com/

David Schonauer, Editor-in-Chief
Krissa Cavouras, Associate Editor
Richard Rabinowitz, Publisher

Profiles of professional photographers and other photographic topics.
Cost: $4.99
Frequency: 6 Issues per year
Circulation: 27,733
Founded in 1888

19994 Aperture
Aperture Foundation
547 W 27th St
Suite 4
New York, NY 10001-5511

212-505-5555
800-825-0061
Fax: 212-979-7759
E-Mail: info@aperture.org
Home Page: www.aperture.org

Michael Culloso, President
Cathy Kaplan, Vice-Chairman
Frederick Smith, Treasurer

Dedicates itself to celebrating the finest in creative photography. Through the periodicals exquisitely reproduced images, rivaling the quality of the photographers' original prints, subscribers experience a wealth of challenging, beautiful pictures on a series of significant topics. Accepts advertising.
Cost: $40.00
80 Pages
Frequency: Quarterly
Founded in 1952
Mailing list available for rent

19995 Exposure
Society for Photographic Education
2530 Superior Avenue
Suite 403
Cleveland, OH 44114

216-622-2733
Fax: 216-622-2712
E-Mail: membership@spenational.org
Home Page: www.spenational.org

Virginia Morrison, Executive Director
Nina Barcellona, Advertising & Publications
Meghan Borato, Registrar
Carla Pasquale, Office/Accounts Manager
Cost: $15.00
Frequency: Biannual
Mailing list available for rent: 700 names

19996 History of Photography
Routledge Publishing
7625 Empire Drive
Florence, KS 41042-2919

800-354-1420
E-Mail: orders@taylorandfrancis.com
Home Page: www.taylorandfrancis.com

Graham Smith, Editor
Ann Haddrell, Advertising Manager

An international publication devoted to the history and criticism of the basic sematic unit of all modern media.
Cost: $396.00
92 Pages
Frequency: Annual+
ISSN: 0308-7298
Founded in 1977

19997 Imaging Business
Cygnus Business Media
3 Huntington Quadrangle
Suite 301N
Melville, NY 11747-4618

631-845-2700
800-308-6397
Fax: 631-845-7109
E-Mail: bill.schiffner@cygnuspub.com
Home Page: www.labsonline.com

Bill Schiffner, Associate Publisher

Formerly called Photographic Processing. Covers photographic equipment, processing, suppliers and dealers. No longer in publication, but last six years of issues available in online archive.
Cost: $66.00
Frequency: Monthly
Circulation: 21000
ISSN: 0031-8744
Founded in 1936
Printed in 4 colors

19998 News Photographer
National Press Photographers Association
3200 Croasdaile Dr
Suite 306
Durham, NC 27705-2588

919-383-7246
Fax: 919-383-7261
E-Mail: info@nppa.org
Home Page: www.nppa.org
Social Media: Facebook, Twitter, LinkedIn, Vimeo

Mindy Hutchison, Executive Director
Robert Gould, President

Features articles, news and profiles about still and television news photography.
Cost: $38.00
Frequency: Monthly
Circulation: 10500
ISSN: 0199-2422
Founded in 1946
Printed in 4 colors

19999 Outdoor Photographer
Werner Publshing Corporation

12121 Wilshire Blvd
Suite 1200
Los Angeles, CA 90025-1168

310-820-1500
Fax: 310-826-5008
E-Mail: editors@outdoorphotographer.com
Home Page: www.outdoorphotographer.com
Social Media: Facebook, Twitter

Steve Warner, Owner
Ibarionex Perello, Associate Editor
Cost: $14.97
Founded in 1965
Mailing list available for rent

20000 PC Photo
Werner Publishing
12121 Wilshire Blvd # 1200
12th Floor
Los Angeles, CA 90025-1168

310-820-1500
Fax: 310-826-5008
E-Mail: editors@pcphotomag.com
Home Page: www.wernerpublishing.com

Steve Werner, Owner
Rob Shepherd, Editor

Covers the new desktop darkroom or home photo lab technologies, trends and methods. Designed to stimulate desktop photographers through the listing of new products and technologies.
Cost: $11.97
Founded in 1965

20001 PCPhoto Magazine
Werner Publishing Corporation
12121 Wilshire Blvd
Suite 1200
Los Angeles, CA 90025-1176

310-820-1500
Fax: 310-826-5008
E-Mail: rjones@wernerpublishing.com
Home Page: www.wernerpublishing.com

Steve Werner, Owner

Shows you how to enjy the exciting and affordable new world of computers and photography. Features step-by-step instructions, evaluations of the latest equipment, tips from the pros, and more!
Cost: $11.97
Frequency: 9 Issues
Mailing list available for rent

20002 PHOTO Techniques
Preston Publications
6600 W Touhy Ave
Niles, IL 60714-4516

847-647-2900
Fax: 847-647-1155
E-Mail: jwhite@phototechmag.com
Home Page: www.prestonpub.com

Tinsley Preston, Owner
Joe White, Editor
Connie Turgon, Marketplace Advertising

PHOTO Techniques offers practical articles that help solve shooting, processing, lighting and printing problems. This is the one magazine that walks you step by step through new techniques. Every other issue contains a digital section. Departments you can rely on include; Master Printing Class, David Vestal's commentary, Photochemistry and more. There are valuable guides to cameras, papers, films, useful accessories and darkroom suppliers.
Cost: $27.99
Founded in 1979
Mailing list available for rent: 30,000 names at $145 per M

20003 Photo District News
Prometheus Global Media
770 Broadway
New York, NY 10003-9595

212-493-4100
Fax: 646-654-5368
Home Page: www.prometheusgm.com

Richard D. Beckman, CEO
James A. Finkelstein, Chairman
Madeline Krakowsky, Vice President Circulation
Tracy Brator, Executive Director Creative Service

Delivers the information photographers need to survive in a competitive business from marketing and business advice to legal issues, photographic techniques, new technologies and more.
Frequency: Monthly
Founded in 1980

20004 Photo Insider
123 US Hwy 46 (West)
Fairfield, NJ 07004

973-377-2007
800-631-0300
E-Mail: editor@photoinsider.com
Home Page: www.photoinsider.com
Social Media: Facebook, Twitter, LinkedIn, YouTube,Foursquare,Flickr,Pint

Founded in 1947

20005 Photo Lab Management
PLM Publishing
1312 Lincoln Boulevard
Santa Monica, CA 90401-1706

310-451-1344
Fax: 310-395-9058
E-Mail: info@plmpublishing.co.uk
Home Page: www.plmpublishing.co.uk/home.htm

Claire F Irwin, Editor
Paula L McCulloch, Publishing Director
John DH Colley, Marketing Manager

Specifically for those who work in the photo lab business. Contains articles on personnel and technical information.
Cost: $15.00
52 Pages
Frequency: Monthly
Founded in 1979

20006 Photo Marketing
Photo Marketing Association International
2282 Springport Road
Suite F
Jackson, MI 49202

517-788-8100
800-762-9287
Fax: 517-788-8371
E-Mail: PMA_Publications@pmai.org
Home Page: www.pmai.org
Social Media: Facebook, Twitter, LinkedIn

Ted Fox, CEO
Allen Showalter, President
Mark Klostermeyer, Vice-President
Robert L Hanson, Treasurer

Directed to the marketing and advertising professionals, offers information on marketing photography nationally and internationally.
Cost: $50.00
80 Pages
Frequency: Monthly
Circulation: 12141
Founded in 1924

20007 Photo Metro
1590 Golden Gate Avenue
San Francisco, CA 94115

415-243-9917
Fax: 415-243-9919
Home Page: www.photometro.com

Henry Brimmer, Publisher

Image-oriented magazine dedicated to photography, features portfolios, interviews and book reviews. Accepts advertising.
Cost: $20.00
32 Pages
Frequency: Monthly
Founded in 1982

20008 Photo Stock News
1910 35th Road
Pine Lake Farm
Osceola, WI 54020

715-248-3800
Fax: 715-248-7394
E-Mail: info@photosource.com
Home Page: www.photosource.com
Social Media: Facebook, Twitter

Ron Engh, Editor
Angela Dober, Managing Editor

Contains information of interest to freelance stock photographers, includes the latest industry trends and strategies. Regular issue features include Electronic Highway.
Frequency: 12 per year

20009 PhotoStockNotes
PhotoSource International
1910 35th Ave
Osceola, WI 54020-5602

715-248-3800
800-624-0266
Fax: 715-248-7394
E-Mail: info@photosource.com
Home Page: www.photosource.com

Rohn Engh, Owner
Angela Dober, Managing Editor

Trends in the editorial stock photo industry.
Cost: $36.00
3 Pages
Frequency: Monthly
Founded in 1976

20010 Photography Quarterly
Center for Photography at Woodstock
59 Tinker St
Woodstock, NY 12498-1236

845-679-9957
Fax: 845-679-6337
E-Mail: info@cpw.org
Home Page: www.cpw.org
Social Media: Facebook, Twitter

Ariel Shanberg, Executive Director
Akemi Hiatt, Program Associate
Lawrence Lewis, Operations Manager
Lindsay Stern, Education Coordinator

Founded in 1977, tthe Center for Photography at Woodstock is a not-for-profit 501 (c)3 artist-centered organization dedicated to supporting artists working in photography and related media and engaging audiences through opportunities in which creation, discovery and education are made possible.
Cost: $25.00
Frequency: Quarterly
Circulation: 2500
ISSN: 0890-4639
Founded in 1977
Printed in one color on glossy stock

20011 Photoletter
PhotoSource International

1910 35th Ave
Osceola, WI 54020-5602

715-248-3800
800-624-0266
Fax: 715-248-7394
E-Mail: info@photosource.com
Home Page: www.photosource.com

Rohn Engh, Owner

A publication covering the world of photography.
Cost: $264.00
4 Pages
Frequency: Weekly

20012 Photopro Magazine
Patch Communications
5211 S Washington Avenue
Titusville, FL 32780-7315

321-268-5010
Fax: 321-267-1894

Christi Ashby, Publisher
Suzanne Odistro, Advertising Manager

A professional trade publication covering photography nationally and internationally.
Cost: $16.95
80 Pages
Frequency: Monthly
Founded in 1990

20013 Picture Magazine
319 Lafayette Street
No 135
New York, NY 10012

212-352-2700
Fax: 212-352-2155
E-Mail: picmag@aol.com
Home Page: www.picturemagazine.com

Brock Wylan, Pulisher
Katherine Nguyen, Associate Editor

Phot industry trade publication.

20014 Popular Photography
Hachette Filipacchi Magazines
1633 Broadway
43rd Floor
New York, NY 10019-6708

212-767-6000
800-876-6636
Fax: 212-767-5600
E-Mail: popphoto@neodata.com
Home Page: www.popularphotography.com

Alain Lemarchand, CEO
Tami Kelly, Founder
Nate Silver, Founder

A publication offering information and updates to the photography world.
Cost: $12.00
80 Pages
Frequency: Monthly
ISSN: 0032-4582

20015 Popular Photography & Imaging American PHOTO Magazine
Bonnier Corp
1633 Broadway
Suite 4200
New York, NY 10019-6708

212-767-6000
Fax: 212-767-5600
E-Mail: popphoto@hfnm.com
Home Page: www.popphoto.com
Social Media: Facebook, Twitter, RSS

Jeffrey Roberts, Publisher
Russell Brock, Associate Editor

Comprehensive coverage of the latest equipment, inspiring images by leading photographers, in-depth how-to articles and wuthoritative reports. Draws upon top professionals in the field to inform committed readers who are passionate about pictures.
Mailing list available for rent

20016 Professional Photographer
PPA Publications
229 Peachtree Street NE
International Tower, Suite 2200
Atlanta, GA 30303-1608

404-522-8600
800-786-6277
Fax: 404-614-6405
E-Mail: ppa@bframe.com
Home Page: www.ppmag.com

Cameron Bishopp, Senior Manager Publications
Jeff Kent, Senior Editor
Dana Groves, Marketing Executive

Business magazine for professional photographers. Delivers valuable articles packed with money making ideas to improve photography techniques and business skills. Accepts advertising.
Cost: $27.00
80 Pages
Frequency: Monthly
Circulation: 30000
Founded in 1910

20017 Rangefinder Magazine
Rangefinder Publishing
6255 W Sunset Blvd
Los Angeles, CA 90028

323-817-3500
Fax: 323-817-1994
Home Page: www.rangefindermag.com

Steve Sheanin, CEO
Bill Hurter, Editor

Includes product and new equipment reviews, lighting and technical pieces, how-to's, promotion and marketing stories, portraiture tips, accessories and system round-ups, computer technology, black-and-white shooting, lens reviews, processing techniques
Frequency: Monthly

20018 Select Magazine
Select Worldwide
18-20 Farringdon Lane
1st Floor Clerks Court
London UK EC1R 3AU

4.40207E+12
Fax: 4.40207E+12
E-Mail: info@select-magazine.com
Home Page: www.select-magazine.com
Social Media: Twitter, Blog

Joe Carbonara, Managing Editor

Select is used worldwide by creative decision makers in the advertising, graphic design, fashion and retail world.
Frequency: 2x/Year
Circulation: 7500

20019 Shutterbug
1415 Chaffee Drive
Suite #10
Titusville, FL 32780

321-269-3212
Fax: 321-225-3146
E-Mail: editorial@shutterbug.com
Home Page: www.shutterbug.net

Ron Leach, Publisher
Eileen Meister, Advertising Sales Manager
Josh Heitsenrether, Marketing Coordinator
George Schaub, Editor
Cost: $17.95
Frequency: Monthly
Founded in 1989

20020 Studio Photography
Cygnus Business Media
1233 Janesville Avenue
Fort Atkinson, WI 53538

631-963-6200
800-547-7377
E-Mail: circulation@spdonline.com
Home Page: www.imaginginfo.com/spd/
Social Media: RSS

Liz Vickers, Group Publisher
Alice B Miller, Editor
Jackie Dandoy, Circulation Manager
Ashley Birkholz, Classified Sales
Barry Ancona, List Rental Manager

Formerly Studio Photography & Design. Showcases the hottest portrait, wedding, commercial, digital, and travel photographers every month. It is also supported by a selection of supplementary guides, tech tips, tutorials, and product round-ups.
Frequency: Monthly
Circulation: 50000
Founded in 1936

Trade Shows

20021 ASPRS Annual Conference
American Society for Photogammetry/Remote Sensing
5410 Grosvenor Lane
Suite 210
Bethesda, MD 20814-2160

301-493-0290
Fax: 301-493-0208
E-Mail: asprs@asprs.org
Home Page: www.asprs.org
Social Media: Facebook, Twitter

James Plasker, Executive Director
Kimberly A Tiley, Assistant Executive Director
Jesse Winch, Program Manager

Educational sessions and exhibits committed to advancing knowledge in the mapping sciences and promoting the responsible application of photogrammetry, remote sensing and related technologies.

20022 BIOCOMM
BioCommunications Association
220 Southwind Lane
Hillsborough, NC 27278-7907

919-245-0906
Fax: 919-245-0906
E-Mail: office@bca.org
Home Page: www.bca.org
Social Media: Facebook, Twitter, LinkedIn

Nancy Hurtgen, Manager Central Office
Susanne Loomis, President
Joseph Kane, Vice-President
James Koepfler, Secretary-Treasurer

Includes a packed program of seminars, workshops, a juried media salon, and commercial exhibits to provide attendees with inspiration and the latest information on visual media in the life sciences.
Frequency: Annual

20023 PMA Annual Convention and Trade Show
3000 Picture Place
Jackson, MI 49201

517-885-5980
Fax: 517-788-8371
E-Mail: pma_trade_exhibits@pmai.org
Home Page: www.pmai.org

Rod Folland, Trade Exhibit Sevices Executive
Mary Anne LaMarre, Operations Officer
Ted Fox, Executive Director

Formerly the Photo Marketing Association, PMA is a global forum for photo imaging in-

dustry education, networking and introductions of new products and technologies. Includes conferences and meetings of the Association of Professional Color Imagers, the Digital Imaging Marketing Association, the Photo Imaging Education Association, the Professional Picture Framers Association, the Professional Scrapbook Retailers Organization and the Professional School Photographers Association.
24M Attendees
Frequency: February/March

20024 Photohistory
Photographic Historical Society
PO Box 39563
Rochester, NY 14604-9563
585-461-4545
Triennial show and exhibits of cameras and photographic images.
Frequency: October, Rochester

20025 Photovision
Glahe International
PO Box 2460
Germantown, MD 20875-2460
301-515-0012
Fax: 301-515-0016
Exhibits of photography equipment, supplies and services.

20026 Professional Photographer American Expo
Professional Photographers of America
229 Peachtree Street NE
International Tower, Suite 2200
Atlanta, GA 30303-1608
404-522-8600
Fax: 404-614-6401
Home Page: http://www.ppa.com
Dana Groves, Advertising Director
Devoted to new technologies in the photography field. 300 booths.
5M Attendees
Frequency: July

20027 SPE Regional & National Conference
Society for Photographic Education
2530 Superior Avenue
Suite 403
Cleveland, OH 44114
216-622-2733
Fax: 216-622-2712
E-Mail: membership@spenational.org
Home Page: www.spenational.org
Virginia Morrison, Executive Director
Nina Barcellona, Advertising & Publications
Meghan Borato, Registrar
Carla Pasquale, Office/Accounts Manager
1000 Attendees
Frequency: Annual

20028 SPIE Photonics West
1000 20th Street
PO Box 10
Bellingham, WA 38227-0010
360-676-3290
888-504-8171
Fax: 360-647-1445
E-Mail: help@spie.org
Home Page: www.SPIE.org
Social Media: Facebook, Twitter, LinkedIn
Eugene G Arthurs, Executive Director
Conference proceedings, and SPIE digital library.
14000 Members
Founded in 1955

Directories & Databases

20029 Complete Directory of Film & Photo Products
Sutton Family Communications & Publishing Company
920 State Route 54 East
Elmitch, KY 42343
270-276-9500
E-Mail: jlsutton@apex.net
Theresa Sutton, Publisher
Lee Sutton, Editor
Print-out from database of wholesalers, manufacturers, distributors, importers and close-out houses. Database is updated daily to guarantee the most current and up-to-date sources available.
Cost: $34.50
100 Pages

20030 Directory of Free Stock Photography
Infosource Publishing
10 E 39th Street
6th Floor
New York, NY 10016-0111
212-683-8905
Offers valuable information on federal, state and local governments which will provide photographs free of charge for commercial use.
Cost: $14.50
150 Pages
Frequency: Biennial

20031 Green Book: Directory of Natural History and General Stock Photography
AG Editions
41 Union Sq W
Suite 525
New York, NY 10003-3230
212-929-0959
Fax: 212-924-4796
E-Mail: info@agpix.com
Home Page: www.ag-editions.com
Ann Guifoyle, Editor
Sharon Powers, Manager
Over 400 photographers and photo agencies that provide stock photography.
Cost: $28.00
368 Pages
Frequency: Biennial
Circulation: 6500
Founded in 1986

20032 Guide to Photography Workshops
Shaw Guides
P.O. Box 231295
New York, NY 10023
212-799-6464
Fax: 212-724-9287
E-Mail: info@shawguides.com
Home Page: http://photoworkshops.shawguides.com
Workshops are profiled that are aimed at amateurs and professionals, including photo tours, studio intensives and specialized instruction.
Cost: $19.95
300 Pages
Frequency: Biennial

20033 Hemingway's Glamour Photographer's Resource Directory
Looking Glass Photography
5975 Keller Road
Saint Louis, MO 63128-3359
314-849-8952
Buyers of glamour photography, including film and video producers are profiled.
Cost: $40.00
200 Pages
Frequency: Biennial
Circulation: 1,000

20034 Industrial Photography: Gold Book Issue
PTN Publishing Company
445 Broadhollow Road
Melville, NY 11747-3669
516-465-7684
Steve Shaw, Editor
A list of manufacturers of photographic equipment and supplies, motion picture laboratories, videotape production facilities, equipment rental services, custom developing services and photographic repair services.
Cost: $5.75
Frequency: Annual December
Circulation: 40,000

20035 Orion Blue Book: Camera
Orion Research Corporation
14555 N Scottsdale Rd
Suite 330
Scottsdale, AZ 85254-3487
480-951-1114
800-844-0759
Fax: 480-951-1117
Home Page: www.bluebook.com
Roger Rohrs, Owner
List of manufacturers of cameras.
Frequency: Annual

20036 Photographer's Complete Guide to Exhibition & Sales Spaces
Consultant Press
13 Laight St
#201
New York, NY 10013-2119
212-431-3130
Bob Speirs, Owner
Directory of services and supplies to the industry.
Cost: $24.95
280 Pages

20037 Photographic Trade News: Master Buying Guide
Cygnus Business Media
445 Broad Hollow Road
Melville, NY 11747-3669
631-845-2700
Fax: 631-845-2723
Home Page: www.cynuspub.com
Offers a list of manufacturers and distributors of photographic equipment and photography associations.
Frequency: Annual

20038 Photography Forum
CompuServe Information Service
5000 Arlington Centre Blvd
Columbus, OH 43220-5439
614-326-1002
800-848-8199
Offers a forum for the discussion of photography on both the amateur and professional levels.
Frequency: Bulletin Board

20039 Photography RoundTable
GE Information Services

401 N Washington Street
Rockville, MD 20850-1707

301-388-8284

Cathy Ge, Owner

Provides a forum for the exchange of photography tips and information.
Frequency: Bulletin Board

20040 Who's Who in Photographic Management
Photo Marketing Association International
2282 Springport Road
Suite F
Jackson, MI 49202

517-788-8100
800-762-9287
Fax: 517-788-8371
Home Page: www.pmai.org
Social Media: Facebook, Twitter, LinkedIn

Ted Fox, CEO
Allen Showalter, President
Mark Klostermeyer, Vice-President
Robert L Hanson, Treasurer

Over 15,500 members of the association and manufacturers and suppliers of photographic equipment; also members of the National Association of Photo Equipment Technicians and of the Professional School Photographers of America.
Cost: $75.00
Frequency: Annual

Industry Web Sites

20041 http://gold.greyhouse.com
G.O.L.D Grey House OnLine Databases

Grey House Publishing's online database platform, GOLD, offers Quick Search, Keyword Search and Expert Search for most business sectors including photography markets. The GOLD platform makes finding the information you need quick and easy - whether you're a novice searcher or an experienced database user. All of Grey House's directory products are available for subscription on the GOLD platform.

20042 www.aspp.com
American Society of Picture Professionals

Members are image producers, stock photo agencies, and image users.Provides networking and educational opportunities in the image transaction industry.

20043 www.bca.org
BioCommunications Association

Made up of professionals who create and use the highest quality images and presentations in visual communications media for teaching and documentation in the life sciences and medicine.

20044 www.cpw.org
Center for Photography at Woodstock

Founded in 1977, the Center for Photography at Woodstock is a not-for-profit 501(c)3 artist centered organization dedicated to supporting artists working in photography and related media and engaging audiences through opportunities in which creation, discovery and education are made possible.

20045 www.editorialphoto.com
Editorial Photographers

Internet discussion forum on business issues with more than 3000 subscribers participating from over 30 countries around the globe. Via the forum photographers exchange information on business practices, copyright and contract concerns. Useful resources such as sample business forms, publisher contract reviews and more can be found here.

20046 www.greyhouse.com
Grey House Publishing

Authoritative reference directories for most business sectors including photography markets. Users can search the online databases with varied search criteria allowing for custom searches by product category, geographic area, sales volume, keyword, subject and more. Full Grey House catalog and online ordering also available.

20047 www.nppa.org
National Press Photographers Association

Sponsors numerous annual television and print media workshops. Conducts annual competition for newsphotos and television newsfilm. Monthly magazine job information bank given to all members.

20048 www.ppa.com
Professional Photographers of America

Portrait, commercial, wedding, industrial and specialized photo- graphers and photographic artists.

20049 www.stockindustry.org
Picture Agency Council of America

The trade association for stock picture agencies in North America.

Associations

20050 **ASM International**
9639 Kinsman Rd
Materials Park, OH 44073-0002

440-338-5151
800-336-5152
Fax: 440-338-4634
E-Mail: memberservices@asminternational.org
Home Page: www.asminternational.org
Social Media: Facebook, Twitter, LinkedIn

Terry Mosier, Finance Director
Janice Farmwald, Senior Manager, Human Resources
Skip Wolfe, Director, Sales & Marketing
Prof. C. Ravi Ravindran, President
Stanley Theobald, Sr. Director, Business Development

The society for materials engineers and scientists, a worldwide network dedicated to advancing industry, technology and applications of metals and materials.
35000 Members
Founded in 1913

20051 **American Chemistry Council**
American Chemistry Council
700 Second St.,NE
Washington, DC 20002

202-249-7000
Fax: 202-249-6100
E-Mail: api@plastics.org
Home Page: www.polyurethane.org
Social Media: Facebook, Twitter, LinkedIn, RSS

Anne Womack Koltan, VP of Communications
Nacole B. Hinton, Managing Dir. Of Human Resources
Calvin M. Dooley, President and CEO
Dell Perelman, Chief of staff and General Counsel
Raymond O'Bryan, CFO & Chief Administration Officer

API is composed of companies that supply polyurethane resins or chemicals used in polyurethane resins, manufacture polyurethanes, produce machinery used in the manufacture or processing polyurethane, or engage in the business of applying polyurethane products in end use applications. API consists of several groups that focus on critical industry issues such as product stewardship, recycling, communications.
80 Members
Founded in 1977

20052 **American Composites Manufacturers Association**
3033 Wilson Blvd
Suite 420
Arlington, VA 22201

703-525-0511
Fax: 703-525-0743
E-Mail: info@acmanet.org
Home Page: www.acmanet.org

Patricia Bradford, VP, Finance & Administration
Jay Merrell, Chairman
Jeff Craney, Chairman-Elect/ Treasurer
Jake Axel, Secretary
Kevin McDonald, Vice Chairman

Presents information on new technology, trends and techniques for manufacturers in the fiberglass and composites industry.
Founded in 1940

20053 **American Electroplaters and Surface Finishers Society (AESF)**
1155 15th Street NW
Suite 500
Washington, DC 20005

202-457-8404
Fax: 202-530-0659
E-Mail: info@aesf.org
Home Page: www.aesf.org
Social Media: Facebook, Twitter, LinkedIn, RSS, Google+

John Flatley, Executive Director
Courtney Mariette, Bookstore/Education
Melissa Walker, Membership
Carrie Hoffman, Deputy Executive Director

AESF is an international society that advances the science of surface finishing to benefit industry and society through education, information and social involvement, as well as those who provide services, supplies and support to the industry.
5000 Members
Founded in 1909

20054 **American Plastics Council**
American Chemistry Council
700 Second St.,NE
Washington, DC 20002

202-249-7000
800-243-5790
Fax: 202-249-6100
Home Page: www.plastics.org
Social Media: Facebook, Twitter, LinkedIn, RSS

Calvin M Dooley, President
Anne Womack Koltan, VP of Communications
Nacole B. Hinton, Managing Dir. Of Human Resources
Dell Perelman, Chief of staff and General Counsel
Raymond O'Bryan, CFO & Chief Administration Officer

Major trade association for the US plastics industry. We demonstrate that plastics are a responsible choice and promote the countless ways that plastics make lives better, healthier and safer.
24 Members

20055 **American Society for Plasticulture**
526 Brittany Drive
State College, PA 16803

814-238-7045
Fax: 814-238-7051
E-Mail: contact@plasticulture.org
Home Page: www.plasticulture.org

Henry Taber, President
William Tietjen, Chairman
Patricia Heuser, Executive Director
Jodi Fleck-Arnold, VP

Promotes research, education and technology application for plastics used in agricultural and horticultural production systems. Hosts a congress every year or so; published proceedings of research presentations.
100 Members
Founded in 1962

20056 **Association of Industrial Metallizers, Coaters and Laminators**
201 Springs Street
Fort Mill, SC 29715

803-948-9470
Fax: 803-948-9471
E-Mail: aimcal@aimcal.org
Home Page: www.aimcal.org

Craig Sheppard, Executive Director
Tracey Ingram, Operations Manager
Dana Bemi, VP
Danis Roy, Treasurer
Bob Connelly, President

Nonprofit trade organization for makers of coated, laminated and metalized papers. AIMCAL serves as the global forum for the flexible metallizing, coating and laminating industry by providing resources, services and information. AIMCAL collects and distributes information to increase industry knowledge, while fostering an environment that builds relationships and a spirit of cooperation between member companies worldwide.
Founded in 1970

20057 **Association of Postconsumer Plastic Recyclers**
1001 G Street, NW
Suite 500 West
Washington, DC 20001

202-316-3046
Home Page: www.plasticsrecycling.org

Steve Alexander, Executive Director
Josh Standish, Technical Director
Dave Cornell, Technical Consultant
Kara Pochiro, Communications Director
Liz Bedard, Rigids Program Director

Represents companies that acquire, reprocess and sell the output of more than 90 percent of the post-consumer plastic processing capacity in North America.
Founded in 1992

20058 **Association of Rotational Molders International**
800 Roosevelt Rd
Suite C-312
Glen Ellyn, IL 60137
630-942-6589
Fax: 630-790-3095
E-Mail: info@rotomolding.org
Home Page: www.rotomolding.org
Social Media: Facebook, LinkedIn

Adam Webb, Managing Director
Rick Carlsen, President
Conchita Miranda, Treasurer/Secretary
Corey Claussen, VP
Rick Church, Executive Dircetor
Seeks to increase awareness of roto-molding, exchange technical information, provide education, and standardize production guidelines.
425 Members
Founded in 1976

20059 **Berkshire Plastics Network**
Downtown Pittsfield Office
66 Allen Street
Pittsfield, MA 01201

413-499-4000
800-438-9572
Fax: 413-447-9641
E-Mail: info@berkshirechamber.com
Home Page: www.berkshirechamber.com
Social Media: Facebook, Twitter, LinkedIn, YouTube

Robert D Fanelli, Vice Chairman
Michael Supranowicz, President & CEO
June Roy-Martin, VP Member Services
Darci Hess, Dir. Of Marketing & Communications
Diana L. Murphy, Dir. Of Finance & Administration

A consortium of more than 40 independent companies, representing virtually every discipline in the design and production of molds, components and plastic products.

20060 International Association of Plastics Distribution
6734 W 121st St
Overland, KS 66209
913-345-1005
Fax: 913-345-1006
E-Mail: iapd@iapd.org
Home Page: www.iapd.org
Social Media: Facebook, Twitter, LinkedIn, YouTube, Flickr
Susan E. Avery, Chief Executive Officer
Jane Saale, President
Kevin Short, Vice-President
Mitchell Opalich, Treasurer
Wayne Gono, Secretary
The International Association of Plastics Distribution, founded in 1956, is an international trade association comprised of companies engaged in the distribution and manufacture of plastics materials. Represented are materials in semi-finished stock shapes, such as sheet, rod, tube, pipe, valves, fittings, film and related products. Members' materials are produced and distributed for a wide variety of engineering and high performance applications.
Founded in 1956

20061 International Molded Fiber Association
1425 W Mequon Rd
Suite C-D
Mequon, WI 53092
262-241-0522
Fax: 262-241-3766
E-Mail: info@imfa.org
Home Page: www.imfa.org
Social Media: Facebook, Twitter, LinkedIn
Cassandra Niesing, Asst. Director
Joseph Grygny, Chairman/ Founder
Hubert Ranger, Founder
Acts as an information center for the molded fiber industry with worldwide membership of users and manufacturers of molded fiber producs. Promotes use of natural and recycled fibers.
Founded in 1997

20062 National Association for PET Container Resources
PO Box 1327
Sonoma, CA 95476
707-996-4207
Fax: 707-935-1998
E-Mail: information@napcor.com
Home Page: www.napcor.com
Social Media: Facebook
Dennis Sabourin, Executive Director
Mike Schedler, Technical Director
Kate Eagles, Communications Director
National association for the PET plastic industry. Promotes the use of PET plastic packaging and facilitates the recycling of PET containers.
13 Members
Frequency: Bi-Monthly
Founded in 1987

20063 National Certification In Plastics (NCP)
Society of the Plastics Industry
1667 K St NW
Suite 1000
Washington, DC 20006-1620
202-496-4400
888-627-3660
Fax: 202-496-4444
E-Mail: ncp@socplas.org
Home Page: www.certifyme.org/?source=IDES.com
Barbara Darby, Manager Plastics Learning Network
Barry Eisenberg, Director Communications/Marketing
The National Certification in Plastics (NCP) program is a national, voluntary certification examination that tests plastics operations employees' skills and knowledge. The National Certification in Plastics exam tests the knowledge and skill level of plastics operations employees in one of the four major plastics processes - injection molding, extrusion, thermoforming or blow molding.The NCP program is sponsored by the Society of the Plastics Industry.

20064 Plastic Pipe and Fittings Association
800 Roosevelt Rd
Building C, Suite 312
Glen Ellyn, IL 60137
630-858-6540
Fax: 630-790-3095
Home Page: www.ppfahome.org/
Social Media: Facebook, RSS
Richard W Church, Executive Director
The Plastic Pipe and Fittings Association (PPFA) is a national trade association comprised of member companies that manufacture plastic piping, fittings and solvent cements for plumbing and related applications, or supply raw materials, ingredients or machinery for the manufacturing process.
Founded in 1978

20065 Plastic Shipping Container Institute
1701 Pennsylvania Ave NW
Suite 300
Washington, DC 20006
202-253-4347
Fax: 202-330-5092
E-Mail: info@pscionline.org, mebership@pscionlin
Home Page: www.pscionline.org/
David H Baker, General Counsel
The Plastic Shipping Container Institute (PSCI) is an international organization of producers of plastic pails (rigid, plastic shipping containers). The Institute's mission is to promote the common interests of, and the general well being of, the plastic shipping container industry, including consideration of local, state and federal regulatory and legislative issues and international trade issues impacting customers, suppliers and consumers.
Founded in 1976

20066 Plastics Institute of America
University of Massachusetts Lowell, Plastics Engin
Ball Hall Room 204
One University Avenue
Lowell, MA 01854
978-934-2575
Fax: 978-934-3089
E-Mail: contactus@plasticsinstitute.org
Home Page: www.plasticsinstitute.org/
Aldo Crugnola, Executive Director
Angelo Sabatalo, Chair Elect
Dana Mielcarek, Chair
Nick R. Schott, Secretary/ Director of Training
Marlene Gosling, Treasurer
The Plastics Institute of America is a not-for-profit educational and research organization dedicated to providing service to the plastics industries. We support, foster and guide plastics education and research at all levels to ensure the continued growth of the industry. Since our founding the Institute has held to this mission with ongoing educational programs and resources for skilled workers, professionals and industry executives.
Founded in 1961

20067 Plastics Learning Network
Society of the Plastics Industry
7 North Laurens Street
Greenville, SC 29601
864-239-2939
Fax: 864-239-0549
E-Mail: bdarby@socplas.org
Home Page: www.plasticslearning.org/
Barbara Darby, Manager Plastics Learning Network
Barry Eisenberg, Director Communications/Marketing
Training opportunities are available for plastics employers and employees through the Plastics Learning Network (PLN) which is sponsored by the Society of the Plastics Industry's (SPI). Courses from qualified instructors are presented as on-site courses tailored to individual work schedules. Courses currently available are Operator Training in Injection Molding and Extrusion. Financial aid is available.
Founded in 2001

20068 Plastics Pipe Institute
105 Decker Court
Suite 825
Irving, TX 75062
469-499-1044
Fax: 469-499-1063
E-Mail: info@plasticpipe.org
Home Page: www.plasticpipe.org
Social Media: Facebook, LinkedIn
Tony Radoszewski, Executive Director
Camille Rubeiz, Director Engineering
Sarah Patterson, Technical Director
Dana gecker, Marketing Communications Manager
Vicki Hackett, Office Manager/Executive Assistant
The major trade association representing all segments of the plastics piping industry. As an association, PPI focuses collaborative efforts to accumulate data, concentrate facts and target resources toward advancements in applications and increases in widespread usage.
131 Members
Founded in 1950

20069 Plastics USA
1667 K St.NW.
Suite 1000
Washington, DC 20006
202-974-5200
Fax: 202-296-7005
E-Mail: tradeshows@socplas.org
Home Page: www.socplas.org/about/services/shows.htm
Social Media: Facebook, Twitter, LinkedIn
Adam Krumhans, Trade Show Coordinator
Donald Duncan, President
Plastics USA, sponsored by The Society of the Plastics Industry/SPI, is held once every three years. The three-day trade show and educational program, which is sponsored by the Society of Plastics Engineers, has proven to be an ideal business forum for the North American plastics industry. Last held in Chicago in 2001, Plastics USA attracted over 15,000 attendees and the show featured 435 exhibiting companies occupying 95,000 square feet of exhibit space.
12M Members

20070 Polymer Processing Institute
New Jersey Institute Of Technology
University Heig
Guttenberg Information Technologies Center
Suite 3901
Newark, NJ 07102-1982
973-596-5256
Fax: 973-642-4594

E-Mail: info@polymers-ppi.org
Home Page: www.polymers-ppi.org/

Ming-Wan Young, Ph.D, President
Costas G. Gogos, Ph.D, Senior Advisor/President Emeritus
Mariann Pappagallo, Administrative Consultant
Niloufar Faridi, Ph.D, Research Consulting Engineer
Linjie Zhu, Ph.D., Technical Director

The Polymer Processing Institute is an independent research corporation headquartered at New Jersey Institute of Technology, Newark, New Jersey. Its mission is to assist industry by implementing the advanced knowledge in the field of polymer technology and related areas through sponsored research, development and education, and to disseminate information via technology transfer.
Founded in 1999

20071 Polystyrene Packaging Council (PSPC)
American Chemistry Council
700 Second St.,NE
Washington, DC 20002

202-249-7000
Fax: 202-249-6100
Home Page: www.polystyrenepackaging.co.za/
Social Media: Facebook, Twitter, RSS

Michael H. Levy, Senior Director
Annie F. Walton, Administrative Assistant
Calvin M. Dooley, President and CEO
Dell Perelman, Chief of staff and General Counsel

PSPC, a business unit of the American Plastics Council, is a nonprofit trade association dedicated to providing accurate information on the environmental impact of polystyrene packaging, including polystyrene recycling programs. PSPC's membership includes manufacturers of polystyrene resin, polystyrene foam and rigid food service packaging.

20072 Polyurethane Manufacturers Association
6737 W Washington Avenue
Suite 1300
Milwaukee, WI 53214

414-431-3094
Fax: 414-276-7704
E-Mail: info@pmahome.org
Home Page: www.pmahome.org
Social Media: Facebook, Twitter, LinkedIn

Mike Kocak, President
Terry Hudson, Director
Robert Adkins, Director
Phil Green, Vice President/ Treasurer
Payam Towfigh, Past President

The Polyurethane Manufacturers Association is the trade association of the cast polyurethane elastomer industry, serving processors of polyurethane products, materials and equipment suppliers and independent agents. PMA exchanges and disseminates information on standards, materials, processes and technical matters, in addition to monitoring regulatory and legislative activity affecting the urethane industry.
90 Members
Founded in 1971

20073 SPI
1667 K St NW
Suite 1000
Washington, DC 20006

202-974-5200
888-627-3660
Fax: 202-296-7005
Home Page: www.plasticbag.com
Social Media: Facebook, Twitter, LinkedIn

Donna Dempsey, Executive Director
Betsy Coleman, Assistant Director
Yvonne Wade, Assistant Manager
Jack Riopelle, Chairman
John Wilhite, Vice Chairman

Members are US and Canadian manufacturers of plastic retail bags. A business unit of the Society of the Plastics Industry, Inc. that actively promotes the growth of the plastic film and bag industry. FBF membership includes companies that are in the plastic bag segment of the industry as well as those in the film sector.
50 Members
Founded in 1937

20074 Society of Plastics Engineers
13 Church Hill Road
Newtown, CT 06470

203-775-0471
Fax: 203-775-8490
E-Mail: info@4spe.org
Home Page: www.4spe.org
Social Media: Facebook, Twitter, LinkedIn, RSS

Susan Oderwald, Executive Director
Jon Ratzlaff, President
Dick Cameron, Vice President/Treasurer
Dr. Jeffery H. Helms, Vice President/Secretary
William De Vos, Chief Executive Officer

The premier source of peer-reviewed technical information for plastics professionals. SPE takes action every day to help individuals and companies in the plastics industry succeed by spreading knowledge, strengthening skills, and promoting plastics.
15000 Members
Founded in 1942

20075 Society of the Plastics Industry
1667 K St NW
Suite 1000
Washington, DC 20006

202-974-5200
Fax: 202-296-7005
E-Mail: feedback@plasticindustry.org
Home Page: www.plasticsindustry.org
Social Media: Facebook, Twitter, LinkedIn

William Cartuaex, President
Gene Janders, VP Trade Shows
Jon Kurrie, VP Government Affairs/Public Policy
Al Damico, Executive VP

Trade association representing one of the largest manufacturing industries in the US. Members represent the entire plastics industry supply chain, including processors, machinery and equipment manufacturers and raw material suppliers. The US plastics industry employs 1.5 million workers and provides $304 billon in annual shipment.
1100 Members
Founded in 1937

20076 Thermoforming Institute
1667 K St NW
Suite 240
Washington, DC 20006-1620

202-974-5200
Fax: 202-296-7005
E-Mail: feedback@plasticindustry.org
Home Page: www.thermoforminginstitute.org
Social Media: Facebook, Twitter, LinkedIn

William Cartuaex, President
Gene Janders, VP Trade Shows

A business unit of the Society of the Plastics Industry, Incorporated,the Thermoforming Institute is comprised of principal officers of companies or divisions significantly engaged in the manufacture of custom thermoformed products.
1200 Members
Founded in 1937

Newsletters

20077 ACM Monthly
Composite Market Reports
PO Box 137
Gilbert, AZ 85299-0137

480-507-6882
Fax: 480-507-6986
E-Mail: info@compositemarketreports.com
Home Page: www.compositemarketreports.com/

John R. White, Executive Director/CEO
Patricia Ryan, Operations/COO
Russell Harris, Director Financial Services
Wayne Graves, Director Information Systems
Brian Hebert, Marketing/Communications Manager

Reports on market and technology intelligence for materials suppliers.

20078 Additives for Polymers
Reed Elsevier Science Direct
9555 Springboro Pike
Miamisburg, OH 45342

937-865-6800
Fax: 937-865-1349
E-Mail: s.barrett@elsevier.com
Home Page: www.elsevier.com

Guy Kitteringhem, Publisher
A Weawer, Editor
S. Barrett, Program Editor
Marike Westra, Director Corporate Relations
Ylann Schemm, Communications Executive

Each issue identifies and details relevant materials and products, new applications, new research and technical developments, newly issued US and British patents.
Frequency: Monthly
Founded in 1887
Printed in on matte stock

20079 Advanced Materials & Composites News
Composites Worldwide
991 C Lomas Santa Fe Drive
PMB469
Solana Beach, CA 92075-2141

858-755-1372
Fax: 858-755-5271
E-Mail: compositesnews@adelphia.net
Home Page: www.compositesnews.com

Steve Loud, Editor
Susan Loud, Managing Editor

Focuses on the processes, applications markets, design, international activities and more related to composites and other advanced materials, particularly for civil engineering and construction, but for all markets and structural applications, including aerospace, transportation, and industrial.
Cost: $598.00
Circulation: 1000

20080 Composite Industry Monthly
Composite Market Reports
PO Box 137
Gilbert, AZ 85299

480-507-6882
Fax: 480-507-6986
E-Mail: info@compositemarketreports.com

Home Page:
www.compositemarketreports.com

William Benjamin, Publisher
John R. White, Executive Director/CEO
Patricia Ryan, Operations/COO
Wayne Graves, Director Information Systems
Russell Harris, Director Financial Services

Market and technology intelligence for users, prime and sub-contractors, universities, government and others.
Cost: $1495.00
Frequency: Monthly
Circulation: 8177
Founded in 1971

20081 Modern Plastics Worldwide
Canon Communications
11444 W Olympic Blvd
Suite 900
Los Angeles, CA 90064-1555

310-445-4200
Fax: 310-445-4299
E-Mail: info@modplas.com
Home Page: www.modplas.com/

Charlie Mc Curdy, President
Kevin O'Grady, Publisher

Industry trends and developments. Accepts advertising.
Cost: $150.00
125 Pages
Frequency: Monthly

20082 POF Newsletter
Information Gatekeepers
PO Box 35880
Brighton, MA 02135-1000

617-782-5033
800-323-1088
Fax: 617-782-5735
E-Mail: info@igigroup.com
Home Page: www.igigroup.com

Paul Polishuk, CEO
Bev Wilson, Managing Editor
Will Ashley, IT Director/Media Manager

Covers recent developments in the plastic optical fiber industry. Also provides updates on components, systems, applications, standards and a calendar of related events.
Cost: $395.00
Founded in 1977

20083 Plastic Focus
Plastics Connection
PO Box 814
Amherst, MA 01004-0814

413-549-5020
Fax: 413-549-9955
Home Page: www.trplastics.com

Michael L Berins, Publisher
Armando Honegger, CEO

Newsletter for buyers, sellers, and users of plastic.
Cost: $275.00
Frequency: Bi-Weekly

20084 Plastics Brief Newsletter
Plastic Marketing News Brief Market Search
2727 North Holland Sylvania Road
Suite A
Toledo, OH 43615-1800

419-535-7899
Fax: 419-535-1243
Home Page: www.sagepub.com

James Best, Publisher

For plastic sales and marketing executives. Covers new materials, new applications, market trends, price changes.
Cost: $249.00
Frequency: Monthly

20085 Plastics Machinery & Auxiliaries
Canon Communications
Ste 370
3300 E 1st Ave
Denver, CO 80206-5806

303-321-2322
Fax: 303-321-3552
E-Mail: msnyder@pma-magazine.com
Home Page: www.pma-magazine.com/

Merle R. Snyder, Editor
Jamie Quanbeck, Online Editor
Heidi Hill, Managing Editor
Kate Hunley, Associate Editor

Plastics Machinery & Auxiliaries provides readers with a forum for learning about new products and services used in a wide range of plastics processes. Plastics Machinery & Auxiliaries is distributed free of charge to qualified professionals in the plastics processing industry, in the USA and Canada.

20086 Plastics News
Crain Communications
1725 Merriman Rd
Suite 300
Akron, OH 44313-5283

330-836-9180
Fax: 330-836-2831
E-Mail: info@crain.com
Home Page: www.crain.com

Robert S Simmons, VP
Linda Whelan, Marketing Manager

Delivers breaking news, features, detailed rankings, economic data and materials pricing to readers around the world.
Frequency: Weekly
Circulation: 60054
Founded in 1989

20087 Plastics Recycling Update
PO Box 42270
Portland, OR 97242-0270

503-233-1305
Fax: 503-233-1356
E-Mail: info@resource-recycling.com
Home Page:
www.resource-recycling.com/rr.html
Social Media: Facebook, Twitter, RSS

Jerry Powell, Editor/Publisher
Rick Downing, Advertising Director
Dylan de Thomas, Managing Editor
Mary Lynch, Assistant Publisher
Chad Powell, Director of Research

Resource Recycling is the journal of recycling and composting professionals. Each month, the latest information is provided about post-consumer waste recovery efforts including: collection system assessments; processing developments; markets analyses, and legislative and regulatory reviews. Additional features includes special commodity and regular departments on equipment, recycling and composting programs, association and state activities.
Cost: $58.00
Frequency: Monthly
ISSN: 0147-2429
Founded in 1981
Printed in 2 colors

20088 Plastics Week
Market Search
Laguna Beach, CA

949-212-7400
Home Page: www.plasticsweek.com

James R Best, Publisher
Linda Best, Production Manager
Jim Best, Editor
Jim Best, CEO

Weekly newletters on plastics. Focusing on strategies, markets, technology, recycling and environmental issues.
Cost: $480.00
6 Pages
Founded in 1961

20089 Polymer Blends, Alloys, and Interpenetrating Polymer Networks
Sage Publications
2455 Teller Rd
Newbury Park, CA 91320-2234

805-499-9774
800-818-7243
Fax: 805-499-0871
E-Mail: info@sagepub.com
Home Page: www.sagepub.com

Blaise R Simqu, CEO
David P McCune, Director

Survey and summary of the growing literature and patents in the promising area of plastics technology. Each issue provides new information on chemistry, properties and performance, testing, processing, and application.
Cost: $ 455.00
40 Pages
Frequency: Monthly
ISSN: 0893-6684
Printed in 2 colors on matte stock

20090 Polyurethane Newsletter
Polyurethane Manufacturers Association
1155 Gratiot Ave
Detroit, MI 48207-2732

313-446-6000
E-Mail: info@pmahome.org
Home Page: www.pmahome.org

Mike Katz, President
Jane Sviniski, Executive Director
Jennifer Rzepka, Assoc. Executive Director
Frequency: Quarterly

20091 Rubber and Plastics News
Crain Communications
1725 Merriman Rd
Suite 300
Akron, OH 44313-5283

330-836-9180
Fax: 330-836-2831
E-Mail: info@crain.com
Home Page: www.crain.com

Robert S Simmons, VP

It provides news, features, technical and marketing information in print and daily on the Internet to rubber manufacturers, suppliers, consultants and laboratories worldwide.
Frequency: Bi-Weekly
Circulation: 16387

Magazines & Journals

20092 Advanced Composites Monthly
Composite Market Reports
PO Box 137
Gilbert, AZ 85299-0137

480-507-6882
Fax: 480-507-6986
E-Mail: info@compositemarketreports.com
Home Page:
www.compositemarketreports.com

William Benjamin, President/Editor
Chris Red, Market Research
Cher Benjamin, VP
Joe Benjamin, Office Manager

Provides information to personnel at all levels in the advanced composite manufacturing industry.
10 Pages
Frequency: Monthly
Founded in 1975

20093 **Advanced Materials & Processes**
ASM International
9639 Kinsman Rd
Materials Park, OH 44073
440-338-5151
800-336-5152
Fax: 440-338-4634
E-Mail: memberservices@asminternational.org
Home Page: www.asminternational.org
Joseph M Zion, Publisher
Thomas S. Passek, Managing Editor
Margaret Hunt, Editor-in-Chief
AM&P, the monthly technical magazine from ASM International, is designed to keep readers aware of leading-edge developments and trends in engineering materials - metals and alloys, engineering polymers, advanced ceramics, and composites - and the methods used to select, process, fabricate, test, and characterize them.
Frequency: Monthly
Circulation: 32M
Founded in 1977

20094 **Digest of Polymer Developments**
STR-Specialized Technology Resources
10 Springborn Ctr
Enfield, CT 06082-4814
860-749-8371
Fax: 860-749-8234
E-Mail: strnet@strus.com
Home Page: www.strlab.com
Dennis Jilot, CEO
Covers domestic and international information on new plastics applications, potential growth and market performance, as well as current events in the plastics and allied chemicals industries. Contains a cumulative index by market and another by plastics materials for quick reference.
Cost: $625.00

20095 **GraFiber News**
Composite Market Reports
PO Box 137
Gilbert, AZ 85299-0137
480-507-6882
Fax: 602-507-6986
E-Mail: info@compositemarketreports.com
Home Page:
www.compositemarketreports.com
William Benjamin,
President/Publisher/Editor/CEO
Cher Benjamin, VP
Chris Red, Market Research
Joe Benjamin, Office Manager
Provides global coverage of the aerospace industry for advanced material suppliers.
Cost: $2556.25
10 Pages
Frequency: Monthly
ISSN: 1058-9023
Founded in 1973
Printed in 4 colors on matte stock

20096 **IAPD Magazine**
International Association of Plastics Distribution
6734 W 121st St
Leawood, KS 66209-2002
913-345-1007
Fax: 913-345-1006
E-Mail: iapd@iapd.org
Home Page: www.iapd.org
Deborah Hamlin, Manager
Patrick M Foose, Board President
Howard J Natal, VP Board of Directors
Published by the International Association of Plastics Distributors/IAPD, the magazine provides information on the plastics industry with special emphasis on profitability and advances in technology. IAPD fosters the development of the plastics industry through the collection, production and dissemination of quality information and education, and by being a catalyst in assuring proactive representation in the governmental and public arenas.
Cost: $90.00
68 Pages
Frequency: Monthly
Circulation: 10000
Founded in 1956
Printed in 4 colors on glossy stock

20097 **Injection Molding Magazine**
Canon Communications
11444 W Olympic Blvd
Ste.900
Los Angeles, CA 90064
310-445-4200
E-Mail: cburke@immnet.com
Home Page: www.immnet.com
Social Media: Facebook, Twitter, LinkedIn
Paul Miller, President/CEO
Stephen Corrick, Publisher/VP/Sales & Marketing
Jeff Tade, Publications Production Manager
Willy Bruijns-Miller, VP Circulation
Custom and captive molding operations, product design, moldmaking, processing information, new materials and equipment, and management issues are the editorial focus.
Cost: $168.57
Frequency: Monthly
Circulation: 37500
Founded in 1999

20098 **Journal of Cellular Plastics**
Sage Publications
2455 Teller Rd
Newbury Park, CA 91320-2234
805-499-9774
800-818-7243
Fax: 805-499-0871
E-Mail: journals@sagepub.com
Home Page: www.sagepub.com
Blaise R Simqu, CEO
A permanent record for international achievements in the science, technology, and economics of cellular plastics. It has been a major source of information on this topic for 35 years. Each issue presents outstanding technical advances in chemistry, formulation, processing, testing, properties, performance, and applications.
Cost: $901.00
96 Pages
Frequency: Bi-Monthly
ISSN: 0021-955X
Printed in 2 colors on matte stock

20099 **Journal of Composite Materials**
Sage Publications
2455 Teller Rd
Newbury Park, CA 91320-2234
805-499-9774
800-818-7243
Fax: 805-499-0871
E-Mail: journals@sagepub.com
Home Page: www.sagepub.com
Blaise R Simqu, CEO
Thomas Hahn, Editor
The leading medium for composite materials technology transfer. Featuring original studies from international material scientists, the journal seeks to emphasize practical applications with no compromise in technical integrity.
Cost: $4576.00
96 Pages
Frequency: Bi-Monthly
ISSN: 0021-9983
Founded in 1965
Printed in 2 colors on matte stock

20100 **Journal of Elastomers and Plastics**
Sage Publications
2455 Teller Rd
Newbury Park, CA 91320-2234
805-499-9774
800-818-7243
Fax: 805-499-0871
E-Mail: journals@sagepub.com
Home Page: www.sagepub.com
Blaise R Simqu, CEO
S. Qutubuddin, Editorial Board
The latest contributions to the technology and properties of elastomers and related polymeric products. Major emphasis is placed on specialty and high performance elastomers. The journal regularly presents current information on the chemistry, processing, properties, and applications of recently developed and improved elastomeric materials.
Cost: $867.00
96 Pages
Frequency: Quarterly
ISSN: 0095-2443
Printed in 2 colors on matte stock

20101 **Journal of Materials Engineering and Performance**
American Society for Metals
9639 Kinsman Road
Materials Park, OH 44073-0002
440-338-5151
800-336-5152
Fax: 440-338-4634
E-Mail: memberservices@asminternational.org
Home Page: www.asminternational.org
Gernant E. Maurer, President
Thomas S. Passek, Managing Director
Peer-reviewed journal that publishes contributions on all aspects of materials selection, design, characterization, processing and performance testing. The scope includes all materials used in engineering applications, those that typically result in components for larger systems.
Cost: $1397.00
Frequency: Bimonthly
Circulation: 645

20102 **Journal of Materials Processing**
Elsevier ScienceDirect
360 Park Ave S
New York, NY 10010-1736
212-989-5800
888-437-4636
Fax: 212-633-3990
E-Mail: journals@sagepub.com
Home Page: www.elsevier.com
Erik Engstrom, CEO
J. Gunasekera, Regional Editor North America
Original papers developments in traditional and innovative processing technologies for metals, polymers, composites, ceramics, and specialty materials. The scope is international and interdisciplinary.
Cost: $5208.00
96 Pages
Frequency: 42 Issues Per Year
ISSN: 0924-0136
Printed in 2 colors on matte stock

20103 **Journal of Phase Equilibria**
ASM International
9639 Kinsman Rd
Materials Park, OH 44073-0002
440-338-5151
800-336-5152
Fax: 440-338-4634
E-Mail: memberservices@asminternational.org
Home Page: www.asminternational.org
Gernant E. Maurer, President
Thomas S. Passek, Managing Director

Peer-reviewed journal that contains basic and applied research results, evaluated phase diagrams, a survey of current literature, and comments or other material pertinent to the previous three areas. The aim is to provide a broad spectrum of information concerning phase equilibria for the materials community.
Cost: $1965.00
Frequency: Bimonthly
Circulation: 305
Mailing list available for rent

20104 Journal of Plastic Film & Sheeting
Sage Publications
2455 Teller Rd
Newbury Park, CA 91320-2234

805-499-9774
800-818-7243
Fax: 805-499-0871
E-Mail: journals@sagepub.com
Home Page: www.sagepub.com

Blaise R Simqu, CEO

The Journal of Plastic Film and Sheeting improves communication concerning plastic film and sheeting with major emphasis on the propagation of knowledge which will serve to advance the science and technology of these products and thus better serve industry and the ultimate consumer. The journal reports on the wide variety of advances that are rapidly taking place in the technology of plastic film and sheeting.
Cost: $795.00
88 Pages
Frequency: Quarterly
ISSN: 8756-0879
Printed in 2 colors on matte stock

20105 Journal of Polymer Science
John Wiley & Sons
111 River St
Hoboken, NJ 07030-5790

201-748-6000
Fax: 201-748-6088
E-Mail: info@wiley.com
Home Page: www.wiley.com

William J Pesce, CEO

The Journal of Polymer Science provides a continuous forum for the dissemination of thoroughly peer-reviewed, fundamental, international research into the preparation and properties of macromolecules. Part A: Polymer Chemistry is devoted to studies in fundamental organic polymer chemistry and physical organic chemistry. Polymer Physics (Part B) details contemporary research on all aspects of polymer physics.
200 Pages
Frequency: 48 Issues Per Year
ISSN: 0887-624X

20106 Journal of Reinforced Plastics and Composites
Sage Publications
2455 Teller Rd
Newbury Park, CA 91320-2234

805-499-9774
800-818-7243
Fax: 805-499-0871
E-Mail: journals@sagepub.com
Home Page: www.sagepub.com

Blaise R Simqu, CEO
Christos C. Chamis, Editorial Board

The Journal of Reinforced Plastics and Composites presents research studies on a broad range of today's reinforced plastics and composites. The journal provides a permanent record of achievements in the science, technology, and economics of reinforced plastics and composites. Reports on special topics are regularly included such as recycling, environmental effects, novel materials, computer-aided design, predictive modelling, and composite materials.
Cost: $4509.00
Frequency: 18 Times Per Year
ISSN: 0731-6844
Founded in 1962

20107 Journal of Thermoplastic Composite Materials
Sage Publications
2455 Teller Rd
Newbury Park, CA 91320-2234

805-499-9774
800-818-7243
Fax: 805-499-0871
E-Mail: journals@sagepub.com
Home Page: www.sagepub.com

Blaise R Simqu, CEO
M.N. Ghasemi Jejhad, Associate Editor

An international forum for the presentation of new advances in the technology of this class of materials. Emphasis is given to the fundamental areas of new material development and characterization, design, rheological behavior in short, discontinuous, and continuous fiber systems; process development, manufacturing science, matrix-fiber interphase charaterization; short and long-term performance prediction; and engineering data base assistance for thermoplastic composites.
Cost: $1186.00
96 Pages
Frequency: Bi-Monthly
ISSN: 0892-7057
Printed in 2 colors on matte stock

20108 Journal of Vinyl and Additive Technology
John Wiley & Sons
111 River St
Hoboken, NJ 07030-5790

201-748-6000
Fax: 201-748-6088
E-Mail: subinfo@wiley.com
Home Page: www.wiley.com

William J Pesce, CEO
Elliot L. Weinberg, Associate Editor

Journal of Vinyl and Additive Technology is a peer-reviewed technical publication for new work in the fields of polymer modifiers and additives, vinyl polymers and selected review papers. Over half of all papers in JVAT are based on technology of additives and modifiers for all classes of polymers: thermoset polymers and both condensation and addition thermoplastics. Papers on vinyl technology include PVC additives.
Cost: $336.00
Frequency: Quarterly
Circulation: 625
ISSN: 1083-5601
Founded in 1942

20109 Journal of Wide Bandgap Materials
Sage Publications
2455 Teller Rd
Newbury Park, CA 91320-2234

805-499-9774
800-818-7243
Fax: 805-499-0871
E-Mail: journals@sagepub.com
Home Page: www.sagepub.com

Blaise R Simqu, CEO
Shojiro Komatsu, Editorial Advisory Board

The Journal of Wide Bandgap Materials is an international journal publishing original peer-reviewed papers on fundamental, experimental and theoretical developments in the science and engineering of wide bandgap materials. The Journal provides a broad-based forum for the publication and sharing of ongoing research and development efforts in the field of wide bandgap materials.
Cost: $245.00
96 Pages
Frequency: Quarterly
ISSN: 1524-511X
Printed in 2 colors on matte stock

20110 Medical Plastics & Biomaterials
Canon Communications
11444 W Olympic Blvd
Suite 900
Los Angeles, CA 90064-1555

310-445-4200
800-243-9696
Fax: 310-445-4299
E-Mail: feedback@cancom.com
Home Page: www.cancom.com

Charlie Mc Curdy, President
Tonna Anuligo, Technical Editor
Kevin O'Grady, Group Publisher

Technical information on the full range of plastics and biomaterials used in manufacturing and packaging medical products.
Cost: $59.00
Frequency: Monthly
Circulation: 61200
Founded in 1978

20111 Modern Plastics
Canon Communications
11444 W Olympic Blvd
Suite 900
Los Angeles, CA 90064-1555

310-445-4200
Fax: 310-445-4299
E-Mail: info@modplas.com
Home Page: www.modplas.com/
Social Media: Facebook, Twitter, LinkedIn

Charlie Mc Curdy, President
Kevin O'Grady, Publisher

Serves companies utilizing plastics. Developments in resin technology, machinery/processing techniques and additive innovation.
Cost: $59.00
Frequency: Monthly
Circulation: 50300
Founded in 1978

20112 PM/USA Green Sheet
Marketing Handbook
PO Box 243687
Boynton Beach, FL 33424-3687

561-732-5858
Fax: 561-732-2607
E-Mail: results@greensheetads.com
Home Page: www.greensheetads.com

Lee Noe, Publisher/Editor
Bob Miller, Technical Director

For those responsible for manufacturing operations.
Cost: $45.00
Frequency: Monthly
Founded in 1972

20113 PMA Polytopics
Polyurethane Manufacturers Association
6737 W Washington Avenue
Suite 1300
Milwaukee, WI 53214

414-431-3094
Fax: 414-276-7704
E-Mail: info@pmahome.org
Home Page: www.pmahome.org

Mike Katz, President

The Polyurethane Manufacturers Association is the trade association of the cast polyurethane elastomer industry, serving processors of polyurethane products, materials and equipment suppliers and independent agents. PMA exchanges and disseminates information on standards, materials, processes and technical

matters, in addition to monitoring regulatory and legislative activity affecting the urethane industry.
90 Members
Frequency: Quarterly
Circulation: 250
Founded in 1971

20114 Plastics Business News
Plastics Universe
2727 Holland Sylvania Road
Suite A
Toledo, OH 43615

419-535-7899
Fax: 419-535-1243
E-Mail: mberins@javanet.com
Home Page: www.plasticx.com/pub/plast_11.html

Michael L. Berins, Publisher

A weekly newsletter published for the professionals in the plastic industry. Covers advances in materials and processes, pricing, new applications and markets, international competition, etc.
Cost: $327.00
Frequency: Weekly
Founded in 1972

20115 Plastics Distributor and Fabricator Magazine
KLW Enterprises
PO Box 669
LaGrange, IL 60525-0669

708-588-1845
Fax: 708-588-1846
E-Mail: pdfm@plasticsmag.com
Home Page: www.plasticsmag.com

David Whelan, Editor/Publisher
Riia O'Donnell, Associate Editor
Lynette Zeitler, Art Director

Contains industry and products news relevant to the manufacture, distribution and fabrication of plastic rod, sheet and tube.
Founded in 1983
Printed in 4 colors on glossy stock

20116 Plastics Engineering
Society of Plastics Engineers
13 Church Hill Rd
Newtown, CT 06470

203-775-0471
Fax: 203-775-8490
E-Mail: info@4spe.org
Home Page: www.4spe.org

Susan Oderwald, Executive Director

Communication to SPE's global audience of plastics professionals about current developments in the industry, technology, and activities of the Society.
Frequency: Monthly
Circulation: 35000

20117 Plastics Focus
Plastics Universe
2727 Holland Sylvania Road
Suite A
Toledo, OH 43615

419-535-7899
Fax: 419-535-1243

James Best, CEO

Bi-Monthly updates on new applicationsand markets for plastics, new polymers, alloys and blends as well as machinery, processing developments, and international competitions and opportunities.
Cost: $295.00

20118 Plastics Hotline
Industry Marketing Solutions
809 Central Avenue
PO Box 893, 2nd Floor
Fort Dodge, IA 50501-1052

888-247-2006
Fax: 515-574-2237
E-Mail: steve@plasticshotline.com
Home Page: www.plasticshotline.com
Social Media: Facebook, Twitter, LinkedIn, YouTube

Steve Scanlan, Publisher
Jim Rykhus, List Marketing Specialist
Cara Jondle, Tradeshow & Marketing Manager
Jody Kirchoff, Operations

Plastics Hotline has been published since 1983. This weekly periodical continues to be the National Marketplace for Plastic Processors to buy and sell equipment, parts and services.
Cost: $69.00
Frequency: Weekly
Founded in 1990

20119 Plastics Machining & Fabricating
Onsrud Cutter
800 Liberty Dr
Libertyville, IL 60048-2374

847-362-1560
Fax: 847-362-5028
E-Mail: info@plasticsmachining.com
Home Page: www.plasticsmachining.com

Harry Urban, Publisher

Plastics Molding & Fabricating is an online technical and management magazine dedicated to the secondary plastics processing industry. It is edited for qualified professionals whose operations include: machining, milling, fabricating, forming, bending, bonding, molding, printing and finishing of plastics. Editorial subjects include case studies, technology updates, trends & news and opinion pieces.
Frequency: Bi-Monthly
Circulation: 15,015

20120 Plastics Technology
Gardner Publications
6915 Valley Ln
Cincinnati, OH 45244-3153

513-527-8800
800-950-8020
Fax: 513-527-8801
E-Mail: cnorman@gardnerweb.com
Home Page: www.gardnerweb.com

Rick Kline Sr, CEO
Sherry Fuchs, Managing Editor
Theresa Basso, Production Editor
Joe Grande, Senior Editor

A premier source of technical and business information for plastics processors, each issue reports on technological innovations and developments in the plastics processing market and reaches more than 47,000 processors who depend on authoritative coverage on applying new technology, evaluating products and practical manufacturing.
Frequency: Monthly
Circulation: 47559
Founded in 1928

20121 Polymer Engineering & Science
John Wiley & Sons
111 River St
Hoboken, NJ 07030-5790

201-748-6000
Fax: 201-748-6088
E-Mail: subinfo@wiley.com
Home Page: www.wiley.com

William J Pesce, CEO
Alan J Lesser, Associate Editor
Laura Espinet, Journal Production
Kim Thompkins, Advertising/Media

Presents papers of fundamental significance to engineers and scientists interested in polmeric materials.
Cost: $545.00
Frequency: Monthly
Circulation: 86000
Founded in 1945

Trade Shows

20122 ANTEC
Society of Plastics Engineering
13 Church Hill Road
Newtown, CT 06470

203-775-0471
Fax: 203-775-8490
E-Mail: info@4spe.org
Home Page: www.4spe.org

Susan Oderwald, Executive Director

The largest technical conference for the plastics industry

20123 ASM Heat Treating Society Conference & Exposition
ASM International
9639 Kinsman Road
Materials Park, OH 44073

440-385-5151
800-336-5152
Fax: 440-338-4634
E-Mail: pamela.kleinman@asminternational.org
Home Page: www.asminternational.org

Pamela Kleinma, Senior Manager, Events
Kellye Thomas, Exposition Account Manager

Conference and exhibits of heat treating equipment and supplies plus information of interest to metallurgists, manufacturing, research and design technical professionals. 300 exhibitors.
3500 Attendees
Frequency: September, Bi-Annual
Founded in 1974

20124 ASM Materials Science & Technology (MS&T)
ASM International
9639 Kinsman Road
Materials Park, OH 44073-0002

440-338-5151
800-336-5152
Fax: 440-338-4634
E-Mail: pamela.kleinman@asminternational.org
Home Page: www.asminternational.org

Pamela Kleinman, Senior Manager, Events
Kelly Thomas, Exposition Account Manager

Annual event focusing on testing, analysis, characterization and research of materials such as engineered materials, high performance metals, powdered metals, metal forming, surface modification, welding and joining. 350 exhibitors.
4,000 Attendees
Frequency: Annual/October
Founded in 2005

20125 AeroMat Conference and Exposition
ASM International
9639 Kinsman Road
Materials Park, OH 44073-0002

440-385-5151
800-336-5152
Fax: 440-338-4634
E-Mail: kim.schaefer@asminternational.org
Home Page: www.asminternational.org

Kim Schaefer, Event Manager
Kelly Thomas, Exposition Account Manager

Conference for Aerospace Meterials Engineers, Structural Engineers and Designers. The annual

event focuses on affordable structures and low-cost manufacturing, titanium alloy technology, advanced intermetallics and refractory metal alloys, materials and processes for space applications, aging systems, high strength steel, NDT evaluation, light alloy technology, welding and joining, and engineering technology. 150 exhibitors.
1500 Attendees
Frequency: Annual/June
Founded in 1984

20126 Association of Industrial Metallizers, Coaters and Laminators
201 Springs Street
Fort Mill, SC 29715

803-948-9470
Fax: 803-948-9471
E-Mail: aimcal@aimcal.org
Home Page: www.aimcal.org

Craig Sheppard, Executive Director
Caleb Howe, Communications Manager
Ed Cohen, Technical Consultant
Norma Bryant, Office Manager

Displays relating to coaters and laminators, metallizers and producers of metallized film and or paper on continuous rolls, suppliers of plastic films, papers and adhesives.
Frequency: Annual
Founded in 1970

20127 Health Pack Innovative Technology Conference
1833 Centre Point Circle
Suite 123
Naperville, IL 60563

630-544-5051
Fax: 630-544-5055
E-Mail: info@healthpack.net
Home Page: www.healthpack.net

Heather Jayson, Show Coordinator
Steve Bunell, Operations Manager
Curtis Larson, Program Coordinator
John Spitzley, Program Co-Chairman
Angela Holty, Owner

Unique annual conference focuses exclusively on medical device packaging, bringing together medical device manufacturers, packaging materials suppliers and converters, contract packagers, test labs, and other service providers. Food and beverage functions served in the exhibition area provide repeated opportunities for networking between exhibitors, attendees, and conference speakers. Conference location in St. Petersburg, Florida, 20 booths.
100 Attendees
Frequency: March

20128 International Association of Plastics Distributors Convention
6734 W 121st Street
Overland Park, KS 66209

913-345-1005
Fax: 913-345-1006
E-Mail: iapd@iapd.org
Home Page: www.iapd.org

Susan E Avery, Executive Director
Patrick M Foose, Board President
Howard J Natal, VP Board of Directors

IAPD is an international trade association comprised of companies engaged in the distribution and manufacture of plastics materials. The annual convention features numerous exhibits that represent a variety of materials in the plastics industry including semi-finished stock shapes, such as sheet, rod, tube, pipe, valves, fittings, film and related products. 76 booths.
450 Attendees
Frequency: September
Founded in 1956

20129 International Plastics Show
1801 K Street NW
Suite 1000
Washington, DC 20006

202-974-5200
Fax: 202-296-7005
E-Mail: tradeshows@socplas.org
Home Page: www.socplas.org or www.npe.org

Ken Rietz, President
Brigid Hughes, Director Trade Show Promotions
Adam Krumhansl, Trade Show Coordinator

Containing 2,000 exhibits.
85M+ Attendees
Frequency: June

20130 National Agricultural Plastics Congress
American Society for Plasticulture
526 Brittany Drive
State College, PA 16803

814-238-7045
Fax: 814-238-7051
E-Mail: info@plasticulture.org
Home Page: www.plasticulture.org

William Tietjen, Chairman Plastics Congress
Henry Taber, President
Jodi Fleck-Arnold, VP
Edward Carey, Secretary/Treasurer
Patricia Heuser, Executive Director

Plastic products used in agriculture. 15-25 booths.
150 Attendees
Frequency: March/November

20131 National Plastics Exposition
Society of the Plastics Industry
1667 K Street NW
Suite 1000
Washington, DC 20006

202-974-5200
Fax: 202-296-7005
E-Mail: feedback@plasticsindustry.org
Home Page: www.plasticsindustry.org
Social Media: Facebook, Twitter, LinkedIn

William R Carteaux, President/CEO
Jon Kurrie, VP Government Affairs/Public Policy
Al Damico, Executive VP

This expo features exhibits of molded, extruded, fabricated, laminated and calendered plastics, raw materials, machinery and laboratory equipment for the industry.
75M Attendees
Frequency: June

20132 PLASTEC East Trade Show
Canon Communications
11444 West Olympic Boulevard
Los Angeles, CA 90064-1549

310-445-4200
Fax: 310-996-9499
E-Mail: register@cancom.com
Home Page: www.plasteceast.com

Diane O'Connor, Trade Show Director
Shannon Cleghorn, Customer & Media Coordinator

Five co-located shows, 1,750 plastic exhibitors. The Trade Show takes place every 2 years, in odd years.
32000 Attendees

20133 PLASTEC West Trade Show
Canon Communications
2901 28th Street
Suite 100
Santa Monica, CA 90405

310-445-4200
Fax: 310-996-9499
E-Mail: Tssalesadmin@ubm.com
Home Page: www.plastecwest.com
Social Media: Twitter

Diane O'Connor, Trade Show Director
Jane Sullivan, Exhibit Contact

Five co-located shows, 3,000 exhibitors, trade show features plastics, packaging and manufacturing industries.
45000 Attendees
Frequency: January/February

20134 PMA Annual Meeting
Polyurethane Manufacturers Association
6737 W Washington Avenue
Suite 1300
Milwaukee, WI 53214

414-431-3094
Fax: 414-276-7704
E-Mail: info@pmahome.org
Home Page: www.pmahome.org

Mike Katz, President

The Polyurethane Manufacturers Association is the trade association of the cast polyurethane elastomer industry, serving processors of polyurethane products, materials and equipment suppliers and independent agents. PMA exchanges and disseminates information on standards, materials, processes and technical matters, in addition to monitoring regulatory and legislative activity affecting the urethane industry.

20135 POLYCON
International Cast Polymer Association
3033 Wilson Blvd
Suite 4200
Arlington, VA 22201

703-525-0511
Fax: 703-525-0743
E-Mail: icpa@icpa-hq-org
Home Page: www.icpa-hq.org

Jeanne McCormack, Director Conferences & Meetings
Elizabeth Cookson, Mgr Conferences & Program Dvlpmt
Debbie Cannon, President

The program includes three days of in-depth educational programming, exhibits, a product showcase, and more. Sponsored annually by the International Cast Polymer Association/ICPA, POLYCON is the largest convention and trade show for the cast polymer industry. Over 800 industry professionals attend the convention to network, attend educational sessions, and visit with over 70 exhibitors.
Frequency: Annual

20136 PPI Annual Meeting
Plastics Pipe Institute
105 Decker Court
Suite 2
Irving, TX 75062

469-499-1044
Fax: 469-499-1063
E-Mail: info@plasticpipe.org
Home Page: www.plasticpipe.org

Tony Radoszewski, Executive Director
Camille Rubeiz, Director Engineering
Stephen Boros, Technical Director
Frequency: May

20137 Polyurethane Manufacturers Association Meeting
Polyurethane Manufacturers Association
6737 W Washington Avenue
Suite 1300
Milwaukee, WI 53214
414-431-3094
Fax: 414-276-7704

E-Mail: info@pmahome.org
Home Page: www.pmahome.org

Payam Towfigh, President
Jane Sviniski, Executive Director
Jennifer Rzepka, Assoc. Executive Director
150 Attendees
Frequency: Annual/April

20138 Polyurethanes Technical Conference
Alliance for the Polyurethanes Industry
700 Second St.,NE
Arlington, VA 22209

703-741-5103
Fax: 703-741-5655
E-Mail: api@plastics.org
Home Page: www.polyurethane.org

Richard E Mericle, Executive Director
Kaye Robinson, Conference Planning Committee

Semi-annual trade show for the polyurethanes industry in North America. International technical conference and exposition will feature technical and industry issues sessions, poster session and exhibits.
Frequency: September/October
Founded in 1977

20139 World Adhesive Conference & Expo
Adhesive & Sealant Council
7101 Wisconsin Avenue
Suite 990
Bethesda, MD 20814

301-986-9700
Fax: 301-986-9795
E-Mail: bob.willis@ascouncil.org
Home Page: www.ascouncil.org
Social Media: Twitter, LinkedIn, RSS

Bob Willis, Senior Manager Conventions/Meetings
Glenn E Frommer, President
C.Russell Thompson Jr, President and CEO
Christine A Byrant, Director
Frequency: April

Directories & Databases

20140 American Mold Builders Association/AMBA Membership Directory
American Mold Builders Association
3601 Algonquin Rd
Suite 207
Rolling Meadows, IL 60008-3136

847-222-9402
Fax: 630-980-9714
E-Mail: info@amba.org
Home Page: www.amba.org or amba.org/adOppGrid.php

Melissa Millhuff, Executive Director

AMBA represents nearly 325 member companies comprised of approximately 9,000 employees and representing just over $2 billion in annual tooling sales. Members span 35 states with 12 chapter affiliations. AMBA member companies serve original equipment manufacturers in every industry including automotive, medical, electronics/electrical, toys, recreation and sporting goods, building and construction, lawn and garden, consumer, and industrial. Free to members and available to others for $50.00.
Cost: $50.00
Frequency: Annual
Circulation: 2,200
Founded in 1973

20141 Handbook of Plastic Compounds, Elastomers and Resins
John Wiley & Sons
10475 Crosspoint Blvd
Indianapolis, IN 46256-3386

317-572-3000
Fax: 317-572-4000
Home Page: www.wiley.com

Lou Peragallo, Manager
Michael Ash, Editor

Directory of services and supplies to the industry. A complete, accurate, and current data source on primary material tradename products for the rubber and plastic industries. This handbook gives short, easy-to-find information on over 15,000 chemical trademark products currently sold throughout the world.
Cost: $385.00
ISBN: 0-471188-30-1

20142 IAPD Membership Directory
International Association of Plastics Distribution
6734 W 121st St
Overland Park, KS 66209-2002

913-345-1005
Fax: 913-345-1006
E-Mail: iapd@iapd.org
Home Page: www.iapd.org

Susan Avery, Executive Director

The IAPD Membership Directory lists almost 400 companies by membership category with their locations, phone and fax numbers, key personnel and plastics products. There is also a listing of companies by geographical location, as well as an alphabetical listing of individuals from the various companies.
Cost: $150.00
Frequency: Annual May

20143 Plastics Business News
Plastics Universe
2727 Holland Sylvania Road
Suite A
Toledo, OH 43615

419-535-7899
Fax: 419-535-1243
E-Mail: mberins@javanet.com
Home Page: www.plasticx.com/pub/plast_11.html

Michael L. Berins, Publisher

Offers information on the plastics industry, forecasts, mergers, and new product developments.
Cost: $327.00
Frequency: Weekly
Founded in 1972

20144 Plastics Compounding Redbook
Advanstar Communications
2501 Colorado Avenue
Suite 280
Santa Monica, CA 90404

310-857-7500
Fax: 310-857-7510
E-Mail: info@advanstar.com
Home Page: www.advanstar.com

Joseph Loggia, CEO
Chris DeMoulin, VP
Susannah George, Marketing Director

List of suppliers — over 1,000 — of resin, additives, fillers and other materials compounding equipment and services to the plastic industry.
Cost: $150.00
280 Pages
Frequency: Annual
Circulation: 12,000

20145 Plastics Digest/PA Index
IHS/Information Handling Services
15 Inverness Way E
Englewood, CO 80112-5710

303-736-3000
800-525-7052
Fax: 303-736-3150
Home Page: www.ihsenergy.com
Social Media: Facebook, Twitter, LinkedIn

Jerre Stead, CEO
Michael Armstrong, Director

A list of over 200 manufacturers and suppliers of plastics materials are listed in this comprehensive directory. CD format only.
Cost: $768.00

20146 Plastics Engineering Handbook of the Society of the Plastics Industry
Society of the Plastics Industry
1667 K St NW
Suite 1000
Washington, DC 20006-1620

202-974-5200
800-541-0736
Fax: 202-296-7005
E-Mail: feedback@plasticsindustry.org
Home Page: www.plasticsindustry.org
Social Media: Facebook, Twitter, LinkedIn

William Cartuaex, President
Jon Kurrie, VP Government Affairs/Public Policy
Al Damico, Executive VP

Educational groups, associations, consultants and providers of technical data, literature and materials to the reinforced plastics industry.
Cost: $175.00

20147 Plastics News Datebook Online
Crain Communications
1725 Merriman Rd
Suite 300
Akron, OH 44313-5283

330-836-9180
Fax: 330-836-2831
E-Mail: info@crain.com
Home Page: www.crain.com

Robert S Simmons, VP
Linda Whelan, Marketing Manager

This business to business buyers guide highlights products and services such as extruders, sheet manufacturers, film, rod and sheet suppliers, processors, roto-molding equipment, injection molding, polyurethane machinery, resin producers and compounders. The Plastics News Online Directory helps you, as a BtoB buyer, research products and make smart buying decisions.

20148 Plastics News Web Watch Directory
Crain Communications
1725 Merriman Rd
Suite 300
Akron, OH 44313-9006

330-836-9180
800-678-9595
Fax: 330-836-2831
E-Mail: editorial@plasticsnews.com
Home Page: www.crain.com

Robert S Simmons, VP
Anthony Eagan, Publisher

Contains processors, primary equipment, auxiliary equipment, resin suppliers, compounders, recyclers, tooling and molds, design and prototyping, trade associations, industry services and more.
154 Pages
ISSN: 1042-802X
Printed in 4 colors on glossy stock

20149 Rauch Guide to the US Adhesives & Sealants Industry
Grey House Publishing
4919 Route 22
PO Box 56
Amenia, NY 12501
518-789-8700
800-562-2139
Fax: 845-373-6390
E-Mail: books@greyhouse.com
Home Page: www.greyhouse.com
Social Media: Facebook, Twitter
Leslie Mackenzie, Publisher
Richard Gottlieb, Editor
Contains information providing data on industry economics, government regulations, technology, raw materials, products and markets in addition to industry activities, organizations and sources of information on trade shows, exhibits, professional associations and societies. Provides unique profiles of more than 700 suppliers.
Cost: $595.00
361 Pages
ISBN: 1-592371-29-9
Founded in 1981

20150 Rauch Guide to the US Plastics Industry
Grey House Publishing
4919 Route 22
PO Box 56
Amenia, NY 12501-0056
518-789-8700
800-562-2139
Fax: 518-789-0556
E-Mail: books@greyhouse.com
Home Page: www.greyhouse.com
Social Media: Facebook, Twitter
Leslie Mackenzie, Publisher
Richard Gottlieb, Editor
Offers comprehensive data on the $182 billion industry, the Guide is a highly valued industry resource covering the economics, processes, materials, sales and activities of leading U.S. plastics producers. Additional features include a personnel index with key industry executives and an enhanced company listing containing detailed information indicating subsidiary, division or parent information, Internet site addresses, E-mail addresses, and key contacts.
Cost: $595.00
646 Pages
ISBN: 1-592371-28-0
Founded in 1981

20151 Who's Who in World Petrochemicals and Plastics
Reed Business Information
3355 West Alabama
Suite 700
Houston, TX 77098
713-523-2613
888-525-3255
Fax: 713-525-2659
E-Mail: csc@icis.com
Home Page: www.icis.com/
Jamie Reed, Owner
Andy Soloman, Global Editorial Director
Chrissy Salisbury, Manager
More than 9,600 individuals from 3,700 petrochemical and plastic companies worldwide.
Cost: $276.00
Frequency: Annual November
Circulation: 1,500

20152 Worldwide Petrochemical Directory
PennWell Directories
1455 West Loop South
Suite 400
Houston, TX 77027-3005
713-621-9720
800-736-6935
Fax: 713-963-6285
E-Mail: billw@pennwell.com
Home Page: www.pennwell.com
Bob Tippee, Editor
David Nakamura, Refining/Petrochemical Editor
Guntis Moritis, Production Editor
Tim Sullivant, Manager
2,980 operative petrochemical plants with 8,675 personnel in 4,320 locations are listed with their parent companies, plant locations, products produced, capacities, and current production volumes if available. Approximately 9,340 locations having 13,145 Email and 4,330 Website addresses are listed for engineering, construction, manufacturing, supply and service companies with a description of products and services provided. Included are 350 cross-references reflecting mergers and acquisitions.
Cost: $150.00
Frequency: Annual November
Circulation: 3,500
Mailing list available for rent

Industry Web Sites

20153 http://gold.greyhouse.com
G.O.L.D Grey House OnLine Databases
Grey House Publishing's online database platform, GOLD, offers Quick Search, Keyword Search and Expert Search for most business sectors including plastics markets. The GOLD platform makes finding the information you need quick and easy - whether you're a novice searcher or an experienced database user. All of Grey House's directory products are available for subscription on the GOLD platform.

20154 www.aimcal.org
Association of Industrial Metallizers, Coaters
and Laminators
Packaging equipment.

20155 www.americanmanufacturers.com
AmericanManufacturers.com
Product exchanges and electronic requests for quotes.

20156 www.apexq.com
American Plastics Exchange
Molders and extruders can review data sheets and bid for prime virgin resin.

20157 www.ariba.com
Ariba
Allows buyers and sellers to find trading partners and negotiate prices.

20158 www.assettrade.com
AssetTrade.com
Used equipment and machinery.

20159 www.berkshireplastics.org
Berkshire Plastics Network
Consortium of more than 40 independent companies, representing virtually every discipline in the design and production of molds, components and plastics products.

20160 www.chematch.com
CheMatch.com
Buyers and sellers exchange for plastic materials.

20161 www.chemconnect.com
ChemConnect
Buyers and sellers can find partners and negotiate price.

20162 www.chemcross.com
ChemCross
Online trading offered by Asian producers of plastics and chemicals.

20163 www.commerxplasticsnet.com
Commerx
Online training.

20164 www.dovebid.com
DoveBid
Bidding on used equipment, as well as capital assets.

20165 www.e-resin.com
e-Resin.com
Direct negotiation with suppliers for additives, materials and finished products.

20166 www.efodia.com
eFodia
Online purchasing of chemical processing, compounding and additives, other materials.

20167 www.elastomersolutions.com
ElastomerSolutions
Online trading for the elastomers industry.

20168 www.ewinwin.com
eWinWin
Associations, cooperatives, buyers and suppliers can employ an aggregation system for lower priced purchases.

20169 www.freemarkets.com
FreeMarkets
Reverse auction in which suppliers submit online bids for commodities, services, parts and materials.

20170 www.getplastic.com
GetPlastic.com
Materials designed for those who purchase resins.

20171 www.greyhouse.com
Grey House Publishing
Authoritative reference directories for most business sectors including plastics markets. Users can search the online databases with varied search criteria allowing for custom searches by product category, geographic area, sales volume, keyword, subject and more. Full Grey House catalog and online ordering also available.

20172 www.i2i.com
Industry to Industry
Buying and selling of plastics.

20173 www.justforplastics.com
Justforplastics.com
Marketplace for plastic services, tooling, equipment and products.

20174 www.mfgconnect.com
Mfgconnect.com
Exchange product development information and CAD files prior to bidding on contracts.

20175 www.napcor.com
National Association for Pet Container Resources

National trade association which promotes the recycling of pet con-tainers and the usage of pet plastic.

20176 www.omnexus.com
Omnexus Corporation
Trading in equipment, services, materials and tooling for central injection and blow molders.

20177 www.onechem.com
OneChem
Software applications and transactional storefront for global commercial transactions in plastics and chemicals.

20178 www.packagingexchange.com
PackagingExchange.Com
Storefront transactions and online auction for packaging products, equipment and materials.

20179 www.packexpo.com
Packexpo.com
Source for packaging materials, machinery, parts and services.

20180 www.packtion.com
Packtion Corporation
Informational tools and exchange opportunites for packaging services.

20181 www.plasticlink.com
PlasticLink.Com
Materials, equipment and products for thermoformers, extruders and semifinished shape processors.

20182 www.plasticpipe.org
Plastics Pipe Institute
The major trade association representing all segments of the plastics piping industry. As an association, PPI focuses collaborative efforts to accumulate data, concentrate facts and target resources toward advancements in applications and increases in widespread usage.

20183 www.plastics.org
American Plastics Council
Gateway to plastics on the internet.

20184 www.plasticsandchemicals.com
Plasticsandchemicals.com
Bid-based marketplace.

20185 www.plasticsbin.com
NetVendor
Trading in scrap resin and surplus plastic inventory.

20186 www.plasticsindustry.org
Society of the Plastics Industry
The Society of the Plastics Industry is the trade association representing one of the largest manufacturing industries in the US. SPI's 1,500 members represent the entire plastics industry supply chain, including processors, machinery and equipment manufacturers and raw material suppliers. The US plastics industry employs 1.5 million workers and provides $304 billon in annual shipment.

20187 www.plasticsrecycling.org
AssociationOd Postconsumer Plastic Recyclers
Represents companies that acquire, reprocess and sell the output of more than 90 percent of the post-consumer plastic processing capacity in North America.

20188 www.plasticulture.com
American Society for Plasticulture
Promotes research, education, and technology application for plastics used in agricultural and horticultural production systems. Hosts a congress every year or so; published proceedings of research presentations.

20189 www.pmahome.org
Polyurethane Manufacturers Association
The Polyurethane Manufacturers Association is the trade association of the cast polyurethane elastomer industry, serving processors of polyurethane products, materials and equipment suppliers and independent agents. PMA exchanges and disseminates information on standards, materials, processes and technical matters, in addition to monitoring regulatory and legislative activity affecting the urethane industry.

20190 www.polymeradditives.com
PolymerAdditives.com
Purchase brand-name polymer additives online.

20191 www.polymersite.com
PolymerSite.com/PolySort
Exchange site for resins and compounds. Flexible negotiations in a sealed bid environment.

20192 www.polyurethane.org
Alliance for the Polyurethanes Industry
For companies that supply polyurethane resins or chemicals used in polyurethane resins, manufacture polyurethanes, produce machinery used in the manufacture or processing polyurethane, or engage in the business of applying polyurethane products in end use applications.

20193 www.primeadvantage.com
Prime Advantage Corporation
Buying consortium offers volume discounts on resins and components.

20194 www.sorcity.com
Sorcity.com
Reverse auction in which buyer files request for quote and supplier bids.

20195 www.supplierone.com
SupplierOne.com
Supply chain management and e-marketplace for manufactured components.

20196 www.thedock.com
The Dock Exchange
Buying and selling of equipment online.

20197 www.theplasticsexchange.com
ThePlasticsExchange.com
Trading in commodity prime resins.

20198 www.worldwideplastics.com
TheBuyersNet.com
Catalog of semifinished materials.

Associations

20199 **American Society of Plumbing Engineers**
6400 Shafer Ct.
Suite 350
Rosemont, IL 60018-4914

847-296-0002
Fax: 847-296-2963
E-Mail: info@aspe.org
Home Page: www.aspe.org

Jim Kendzel, Executive Director/CEO, Secretary
William F. Hughes Jr., President
Jeffery L. Ingertson, Vice President, Education
Gary Mahoney, Treasurer
Mitch Clemente, Vice President, Technical

The American Society of Plumbing Engineers (ASPE) is a professional organization dedicated to the advancement of the science of plumbing engineering, to the professional growth and advancement of its members and the health, welfare and safety of the public. The Society disseminates technical data and information, sponsors activities that facilitate interaction with fellow professionals, and, through research and education, expands the base of knowledge of the plumbing engineering industry.
7500 Members
Founded in 1964

20200 **American Society of Sanitary Engineering**
18927 Hickory Creek Dr.
Suite 220
Mokena, IL 60448

708-995-3019
Fax: 708-479-6139
Home Page: www.asse-plumbing.org

John F. Flader, Treasurer
Steve Silber, International President
Scott Hamilton, Executive Director
Michele Kilpatrick, Administrative asst.
Stanley Nickell, Technical Services Coordinator

Members are from all segments of the plumbing industry, including contractors, engineers, inspectors, journeymen, apprentices and others who are involved in various segments of the industry. Provides information, an opportunity to exchange ideas, solve problems and offers a forum where all sides can express their views.
300 Members
Founded in 1906

20201 **American Supply Association**
1200 N. Arlington Heights Rd.
Suite 150
Itasca, IL 60143

630-467-0000
Fax: 630-467-0001
E-Mail: info@asa.net
Home Page: www.asa.net

Michael Adelizzi, Executive VP, Secretary
John Strong, President-Elect
Scott Weaver, Chairman
Rick Fantham, Treasurer
Jeff Pope, President

ASA is a not-for-profit national organization serving wholesale distributors and their suppliers in the plumbing, heating, cooling and industrial pipe, valves, and fittings industries. ASA provides a forum for trading partners from around the country to discuss critical issues facing them, and offers a menu of products and services uniquely geared to their needs.
800 Members
Founded in 1969

20202 **International Association of Plumbing and Mechanical Officials (IAPMO)**
4755 E Philadelphia Street
Ontario, CA 91761

909-472-4100
800-854-2676
Fax: 909-472-4150
E-Mail: info@iapmo.org
Home Page: www.iapmo.org
Social Media: Facebook, Twitter, LinkedIn

Gary Hile, President
Bruce Pfeiffer, VP
Russ Chaney, CEO
Robert Bud Riestenberg, Treasurer/ Secretary
Neil Bogatz, General counsel

IAPMO has been protecting the public's health and safety for more than eighty years by working in concert with government and industry to implement comprehensive plumbing and mechanical systems around the world.
5000 Members
Founded in 1926

20203 **Manufacturers Standardization Society**
127 Park St NE
Vienna, VA 22180-4602

703-281-6613
Fax: 703-281-6671
E-Mail: info@mss-hq.org
Home Page: www.mss-hq.org

Robert O'Neill, Executive Director

The Manufacturers Standardization Society (MSS) of the Valve and Fittings Industry is a non-profit technical association organized for development and improvement of industry, national and international codes and standards for valves, valve actuators, valve modifications, pipe fittings, pipe hangers, flanges, and associated seals.
Cost: $1800.00
Founded in 1924

20204 **Midwest Distributors Association (MWDA)**
1200 N. Arlington Heights Rd.
Suite 150
Itasca, IL 60143

630-467-0000
Fax: 312-464-0091
E-Mail: info@mwda.net
Home Page: www.mwda.net

Tim Milford, President
Steve Walsh, Treasurer
Dave Poteete, President-Elect
Chris Murin, Executive Director
Ryan Curry, Director

The mission of the MWDA is to professionally promote the improvement of the industry by providing quality programs, educational and training opportunities to improve operational efficiency and marketing effectiveness, and by facilitating the exchange of ideas and information throughout the distribution channel. The MWDA serves the states of Illinois, Iowa, Kansas, Minnesota, Missouri, Nebraska, North Dakota, South Dakota, Upper Michigan and Wisconsin.
110 Members
Founded in 1942

20205 **National Kitchen and Bath Association**
687 Willow Grove St
Hackettstown, NJ 07840

908-850-1206
800-843-6522
Fax: 908-852-1695
E-Mail: feedback@nkba.org
Home Page: www.nkba.org
Social Media: Facebook, Twitter, LinkedIn, Pinterest

John K. Morgan, President
John A. Petrie, President-Elect
Carolyn F. Cheetham,CMKBD, VP
debnise M. Dick, Secretary
Debra H. Robinson, Treasurer

The NKBA enhances the success of its members in the kitchen and bath industry through networking, education, certification, marketing and business tools, leadership opportunities, and the annual Kitchen/Bath Industry Show.
40000 Members
Founded in 1963

20206 **North Central Wholesalers Association/NCWA**
7107 Crossroads Blvd
Suite 106
Brentwood, TN 37027

615-371-5004
Fax: 615-371-5444
E-Mail: dan310@earthlink.net
Home Page: www.northcentralwholesalers.org

terry Shafer, Executive VP
Linda Wilbourn, Administrative Assistant
Deborah Schnelle, Bookeeper

The NCWA serves wholesale distributors of plumbing, heating, cooling and piping products in Indiana, Michigan, Ohio, Western Pennsylvania and West Virginia, sponsoring educational conferences and offering networking opportunities. During the year NCWA offers its members seminars, workshops, newsletters, industry statistics, an annual regional convention and other traditional trade association programs.
75 Members
Founded in 2003

20207 **Pacific Southwest Distributors Association**
7345 E Evans Rd
No. 7
Scottsdale, AZ 85260

480-991-5703
Fax: 480-991-5704
E-Mail: rbluth@qwestoffice.net
Home Page: www.thepsda.info

Bob Bluth, Owner

Made up of distributors of heating, cooling and plumbing supplies.
Founded in 1946

20208 **Plastic Pipe and Fittings Association**
800 Roosevelt Rd
Building C, Suite 312
Glen Ellyn, IL 60137

630-858-6540
Fax: 630-790-3095
Home Page: www.ppfahome.org
Social Media: Facebook, RSS

Richard W Church, Executive Director

The Plastic Pipe and Fittings Association (PPFA) is a national trade association of member companies that manufacture plastic piping, fittings and solvent cements for plumbing and related applications, and supply raw materials, ingredients or machinery for the manufacturing process. The PPFA provides relevant information needed to properly design, specify and install plastic piping systems, promoting an understanding of the environmental impact and benefits of thermoplastic piping products.
78 Members
Founded in 1978

20209 Plumbing Heating Cooling Contractors Association
180 South Washington Street
Suite 100
Falls Church, VA 22046

703-237-8100
800-533-7694
Fax: 703-237-7442
E-Mail: naphcc@naphcc.org
Home Page: www.phccweb.org
Social Media: Facebook, LinkedIn, RSS

Kevin Tindall, President-Elect
Charles Chip E. Greene, Vice President
Gerry Kennedy, Executive Vice President
Steven A. Rivers, President
Laurie Crigler, Secretary

National organization designed for suppliers of equipment, supplies and services for the plumbing, heating and cooling industries.
3700 Members
Founded in 1883

20210 Plumbing Manufacturers International
1921 Rohlwing Rd
Unit G
Rolling Meadows, IL 60008

847-481-5500
Fax: 847-481-5501
E-Mail: bhiggens@pmihome.org
Home Page: www.pmihome.org/

Jeff Baldwin, President
Tim Kilbane, First VP
Fernando Fernandez, Second VP
Pul Patton, Treasurer
Stewart Yang, Immediate Past President

The Plumbing Manufacturers Institute (PMI) is the trade association of plumbing products manufacturers. The Institute functions as a sounding board for its members, a source for industry and market information, and as a coordinating and decision-making body for dealing with industry issues. It is active in many arenas as it helps develop and maintain standards and codes, and works closely with government agencies at all levels - federal, state and local.
44 Members
Founded in 1975

20211 Plumbing and Drainage Institute
800 Turnpike Street
Suite 300
North Andover, MA 01845

978-557-0720
800-589-8956
Fax: 978-557-0721
E-Mail: pdi@pdionline.org
Home Page: www.pdionline.org

William Whitehead, Executive Director

An association of manufacturers of engineered plumbing products. Our members and licensees make products such as; flood drains, roof drains, sanitary floor drains, cleanouts, water hammer arresters, swimming pool drains, backwater valves, grease interceptors, fixture supports and other drainage specialties.
14 Members

20212 Plumbing and Mechanical Contractors Association of Oregon
14695 SW Millikan Way
Beaverton, OR 97006

503-626-6666
Fax: 503-626-6630
E-Mail: fwall@pmcaoregon.com
Home Page: www.pmcaoregon.com/

Frank Wall, Executive Director
Founded in 1975

20213 Southern Wholesalers Association
201 Seaboard Lane
7107 Crossroads Blvd
Suite 106
Brentwood, TN 37027-7972

615-371-5004
Fax: 615-371-5444
E-Mail: terry@southernwholesalers.org
Home Page: www.southernwholesalers.org/
Social Media: Facebook

Harry Hays, President
Coley Herrin, First VP/ Treasurer
Travis Elrod, Second VP
Reggie Hickman, Chairman Ex-Officio
Randy Wool, Chairman of the Board

The Southern Wholesalers Association is a regional association composed of leading Wholesalers of plumbing, heating, and cooling equipment and supplies; pipe, valves and fittings; and water systems throughout the southeast, as well as, Associate Member suppliers and reps to the phcp, pvf and water systems industry.
850 Members
Founded in 1928

20214 Valve Manufacturers Association of America
1050 17th Street NW
Suite 280
Washington, DC 20036-5521

202-331-8105
Fax: 202-296-0378
E-Mail: wsandler@vma.org
Home Page: www.vma.org

William S. Sandler, President
Marc Pasternak, Vice President
Malena Malone-Blevins, Meetings Manager
Dianne Ekblad, Bookkeeper/Administrative Assistant
Judy Tibbs, Director of Education

VMA represents the interests of nearly 100 U.S. and Canadian valve actuator, and control manufacturers who account for approximately 80% of the total industrial valve shipments out of U.S. and Canadian facilities. The American valve industry supplies approximately 35% of worldwide valve demand. VMA member companies employ 20,000 men and women directly in supporting jobs. VMA is the only organization exclusively serving U.S. and Canadian manufacturers of industrial valves, controls and actuator
100 Members
Founded in 1938

20215 Western Suppliers Association
3423 Investment Blvd
Suite 204
Hayward, CA 94545

510-670-0962
800-752-8833
Fax: 510-670-9081
E-Mail: wsadon@sbcglobal.net
Home Page:
www.westernsuppliersassociation.com

Don Robertson, President
Paul Davis, Executive Director
Debbie Wagner, Administrative Manager

A regional office that represents various wholesalers in the heating, plumbing and piping fields.
Founded in 1952

Newsletters

20216 Plumbing Systems & Design
2980 River Rd
Des Plaines, IL 60018

847-296-0002
Fax: 773-695-9007
E-Mail: info@aspe.org
Home Page: www.psdmagazine.com

Gretchen Pienta, Managing Editor
David Jern, Executive Publisher
Rachel Boger, Graphic Designer
Richard Albrecht, Website

Industry leading technical publication with ASPE news and features. Free to ASPE members and subscribers.
Frequency: Monthly
Circulation: 27000
Founded in 1965
Printed in on glossy stock

Magazines & Journals

20217 Directory of Listed Plumbing Products Official Magazine
Int'l Assn of Plumbing & Mechanical Officials
4755 E Philadelphia St
Ontario, CA 91761-2816

909-472-4100
Fax: 909-472-4150
Home Page: www.iapmo.org
Social Media: Facebook, Twitter, LinkedIn, YouTube

Gary Hice, VP
Dan Daniels, President
Russ Chancy, CEO
Dwight Perkins, Senior Director
Cost: $75.00
7000 Members
1300 Pages
Frequency: 6x Yearly
Circulation: 26,000
Founded in 1926

20218 OFFICIAL Magazine
Int'l Assn of Plumbing & Mechanical Officials
4755 E Philadelphia St
Ontario, CA 91761-2816

909-472-4100
800-854-2676
Fax: 909-472-4150
E-Mail: info@iapmo.org
Home Page: www.iapmo.org

Gary Hile, President
Bruce Pfeiffer, VP
Russ Chancy, CEO

The nation's leading source for information about plumbing and mechanical safety codes. This publication is geared toward plumbers, mechanical contractors, manufacturers and government safety officials who need to know safety code information
Cost: $75.00
9000 Members
Frequency: Bi-Monthly
Circulation: 26000
Founded in 1958

20219 PM Engineer
Business News Publishing Company

155 N Pfingsten Rd
#205
Deerfield, IL 60015

630-377-5909
Fax: 248-502-1023
E-Mail: privacy@BNPMedia.com
Home Page: www.pmengineer.com

Bob Miondonski, Group Publisher & Editor
Mike Miazga, Ednior Editor
Julius Ballanco, Editorial Director
Suzette Rubio, Online Editor
John Siegenthaler, Hydronics Editor

Provides technical sheets, manufacturer product brochures, news features and analysis of useful industry information on the engineering and design of plumbing, piping, hydronics, cooling/heating, and fire protection/sprinkler systems. Free to trade engineers.
80 Pages
Circulation: 25000
Printed in 4 colors on glossy stock

20220 PM Plumbing & Mechanical
Business News Publishing Company
155 N Pfingsten Rd
#205
Deerfield, IL 60015

630-377-5909
Fax: 248-502-1023
E-Mail: privacy@BNPMedia.com
Home Page: www.pmmag.com/

Bob Miondonski, Group Publisher & Editor
Mike Miazga, Ednior Editor
Julius Ballanco, Editorial Director
Suzette Rubio, Online Editor
John Siegenthaler, Hydronics Editor

Serves plumbing, hydronic heating and mechanical contractors.
Frequency: Monthly
Circulation: 45091

20221 Plumbing Engineer
TMB Publishing
2165 Shermer Rd
Suite A
Northbrook, IL 60062-5474

847-564-1127
Fax: 847-564-1264
E-Mail: editor@plumbingengineer.com
Home Page: www.plumbingengineer.com

John Mesenbrink, Chief Editor
Marilyn Cunningham, Assistant Editor
Cate Brown, Production Manager
Sadie Bechtold, Production Assistant
Mark Bruno, Art Director

Offers news and updates to plumbing engineers and manufacturers.
Cost: $35.00
Frequency: Monthly
Founded in 1973

20222 Plumbing Standards
American Society of Sanitary Engineering
901 Canterbury Rd
Suite A
Cleveland, OH 44145-1480

440-835-3040
Fax: 440-835-3488
Home Page: www.asse-plumbing.org

James Bickford, President
Donald R Jr. Summers, First VP
Steve Silber, Second VP
Scott Hamilton, Third VP
Ron Murray, Immiate Past President

Topics include standards information, updates, water, wastewater, plumbing design guidelines, and technical information pertaining to the water industry.
Cost: $12.00
Frequency: Quarterly
Circulation: 15000
Founded in 1906

20223 Reeves Journal
23421 South Pointe Drive
Suite 280
Laguna Hills, CA 92653

949-830-0881
Fax: 949-859-7845
E-Mail: hendersont@bnpmedia.com
Home Page: www.reevesjournal.com

Ellyn Fishman, Publisher
Kati Larson, Advertising Sales
Jack Sweet, Editor
Souzan Azar, Production

Reeves Journal, one of the oldest publications in the plumbing industry, addresses the regional opportunities and challenges facing plumbing/heating/cooling-phc contractors, wholesalers and engineers in the 14 western United States, focusing on the products, issues, codes and regulations relevant to the phc industry.
Frequency: Monthly
Founded in 1926

20224 Supply House Times
American Supply Association
155 N Pfingsten Rd
#205
Deerfield, IL 60015

312-464-0090
Fax: 312-464-0091
E-Mail: info@asa.net
Home Page: www.supplyht.com

Bob Miondonski, Group Publisher & Editor
Mike Miazga, Ednior Editor
Julius Ballanco, Editorial Director
Suzette Rubio, Online Editor
John Siegenthaler, Hydronics Editor

Articles on plumbing, heating, cooling, and piping products.
50 Pages
Frequency: 6x Yearly
Circulation: 2,500
Mailing list available for rent: 4,000 names
Printed in 4 colors on matte stock

20225 United Association Journal
United Associations of Journeymen
3 Park Place
Annapolis, MD 21401

410-269-2000
Fax: 202-628-5024
Home Page: www.ua.org/

Martin Maddaloni, President
Patrick Perno, General Secretary/Treasurer
Stephen F. Kelly, Assistant General President

On union issues, politics, economics, legislation, energy, environment and consumer affairs.
Frequency: Monthly
Circulation: 315000
Founded in 1889

20226 Valve Magazine
Valve Manufacturers Association of America
1050 17th Street NW
Suite 280
Washington, DC 20036-5521

202-331-8105
Fax: 202-296-0378
E-Mail: wsandler@vma.org
Home Page: www.valvemagazine.com

William S Sandler, President
Judy Tibbs, Associate Publisher/Editor-in-Chief
Sue Partyke, Advertising Director
Chris Guy, New Products, Media & Industry News
Michelle Wandres, Art Director/Production Manager

Promotion of significance and application of US and Canadian manufactured industrial valves and actuators.
Frequency: Quarterly
Circulation: 2600

Trade Shows

20227 ASPE Engineered Plumbing Exposition
National Trade Show Productions
313 South Patrick Street
Alexandria, VA 22314-1117

703-683-8500
800-687-7469
Fax: 703-836-4486
Home Page: www.ntpshow.com/ or www.aspe.org

Robert E Harar, Chairman and CEO
Karin Frendrich, Chief Operating Officer
Jennifer Hoff, Executive Director

A biennial exhibits trade show for the plumbing and engineering industry, the Engineered Plumbing Exposition, sponsored by the American Society of Plumbing Engineers/ASPE, is a gathering of plumbing, engineering and design products, equipment and services. Everything from pipes to pumps to fixtures, from compressors to computers and consulting services, is on display to allow engineers and specifiers to view the newest and most innovative design materials available to them.
7000 Attendees
Founded in 1964

20228 Business and Education Conference
Int'l Assoc of Plumbing and Mechanical Officials
4755 E Philadelphia Street
Ontario, CA 91761

909-472-4100
800-854-2676
Fax: 909-472-4150
E-Mail: info@iapmo.org
Home Page: www.iapmo.org

GP Russ Chaney, Chief Executive Officer
Gaby Davis, Director of Worldwide Operations
Neil Bogatz, General Counsel
Monte Bogatz, Associate General Counsel
Tricia Schwenke, Executive Assistant

IAPMO's annual conference brings together the public health and safety officials dedicated to plumbing and mechanical systems. for more than eighty years this venue allows for the free flow of information about changes in these necessary systems and provides technical education allowing these professionals hig competency in the associated cides and standards.
9000 Members
600 Attendees
Frequency: Annual/September
Founded in 1923

20229 Directory of Listed Plumbing Products Annual Conference
Int'l Assn of Plumbing & Mechanical Officials
4755 E Philadelphia St
Ontario, CA 91761-2816

909-472-4100
Fax: 909-472-4150
Home Page: www.iapmo.org

Social Media: Facebook, Twitter, LinkedIn, YouTube

Gary Hice, VP
Dan Daniels, President
Russ Chancy, CEO
Dwight Perkins, Senior Director
7000 Members
450 Attendees
Founded in 1926

20230 MSS Annual Meeting
Manufacturers Standardization Society
127 Park St NE
Vienna, VA 22180-4602

703-281-6613
Fax: 703-281-6671
E-Mail: orders@mss-hq.org
Home Page: www.mss-hq.org

Robert O'Neill, Executive Director
Frequency: Annual/May
Founded in 1924

20231 Mid-Atlantic Plumbing Heating Cooling Expo
Reber-Friel Company
221 King Manor Drive
Suite A
King Of Prussia, PA 19406-2500

610-272-4020
Fax: 610-272-5190

Richard Retzback, Show Manager

350 booths featuring products and services used by the plumbing, heating and cooling industries.
4.3M Attendees
Frequency: Annual/November

20232 National Plumbing, Heating, Cooling and Piping Products Exposition
American Supply Association
222 Merchandise Mart Plaza
Suite 1400
Chicago, IL 60654

312-464-0090
Fax: 312-464-0091
E-Mail: info@asa.net
Home Page: www.asa.net/

Karen Weeks, Show Manager
Bob Higgason, Owner
George Conyngham Jr., President
Colin Perry, Treasurer
Inge Calderon, Secretary

Offers information and a forum for the exchange of ideas among plumbing, heating and cooling engineers.
11M Attendees

20233 NetworkASA
American Supply Association
222 Merchandise Mart
Suite 1400
Chicago, IL 60654

312-464-0090
Fax: 312-464-0091
E-Mail: info@asa.net
Home Page: www.asa.net

Ruth Mitchell, Meetings/Conventions Director

For distributors and manufacturers in the PHCP/PVF industry. Provides information and opportunities that cannot be found with other organizations or events.
Frequency: Annual

20234 Spring Septic System Conference
Granite State Designers & Installers Association
53 Regional Drive
Concord, NH 03301-3520

603-228-1231
Fax: 603-228-2118
E-Mail: info@gsdia.org
Home Page: www.gsdia.org

Carl Hagstrom, Director
Randy Orvis, Director

Conference and trade show with 30 exhibitors and booths for septic system professionals and other allied industries.
400 Attendees
Frequency: Annual/March

Directories & Databases

20235 Complete Directory of Plumbing Products
Sutton Family Communications & Publishing Company
National Fleamarketeer
155 Sutton Lane
Fordsville, KY 42343

270-740-0870
E-Mail: jlsutton@apex.net
Home Page: www.fleamarketeer.net

Theresa Sutton, Editor
Lee Sutton, General Manager

Print-out from database of wholesalers, manufacturers, distributors, importers and close-out houses. Database is updated daily to guarantee the most current and up-to-date sources available.
Cost: $55.20
100+ Pages

20236 Directory of Custom Compounders
Delphi Marketing Services
400 E 89th Street
Apartment 2J
New York, NY 10128-6728
Dr. Newman Giragosian, Editor

Offers information on manufacturers of custom mixtures of plastics and resins.
Cost: $295.00
115 Pages
Frequency: Annual

20237 Directory of Listed Plumbing Products
Int'l Assn of Plumbing & Mechanical Officials
4755 E Philadelphia St
Ontario, CA 91761-2816

909-472-4100
Fax: 909-472-4150
Home Page: www.iapmo.org

Leticia Wilson, Manager
Dan Daniels, VP
Russ Chancy, Executive Director

Directory of products and supplies to the plumbing industry.
Cost: $93.00
1300 Pages
Frequency: Monthly

20238 Plumbing Engineer: Product Directory Issue
TMB Publishing
2165 Shermer Rd
Suite A
Northbrook, IL 60062-5474

847-564-1127
Fax: 847-564-1264
E-Mail: editor@plumbingengineer.com
Home Page: www.tmbpublishing.com

John Mesenbrink, Chief Editor
Marilyn Cunningham, Assistant Editor
Cate Brown, Production Manager
Sadie Bechtold, Production Assistant
Mark Bruno, Art Director

Over 400 plumbing products from approximately 250 manufacturers.
Frequency: Annual/January
Circulation: 2,6104

20239 Who's Who in the Plumbing-Heating-Cooling Contracting Business
Nat'l Assn of Plumbing-Heating-Cooling Contractors
180 South Washington Street
PO Box 6808
Falls Church, VA 22046-2900

703-237-8100
800-533-7694
Fax: 703-237-7442
E-Mail: naphcc@naphcc.org
Home Page: www.phccweb.org

Frank Maddalon, President
Keith Bienvenu, President-Elect
David Dugger, VP
Kevin Tindall, Secretary
Gerry Kennedy, Executive VP

About 6,000 professional plumbing/heating/cooling contractors and member firms.
Cost: $75.00
Frequency: Annual
Circulation: 15,000
Founded in 1883

Industry Web Sites

20240 http://gold.greyhouse.com
G.O.L.D Grey House OnLine Databases

Grey House Publishing's online database platform, GOLD, offers Quick Search, Keyword Search and Expert Search for most business sectors including plumbing and heating markets. The GOLD platform makes finding the information you need quick and easy - whether you're a novice searcher or an experienced database user. All of Grey House's directory products are available for subscription on the GOLD platform.

20241 www.asa.net
American Supply Association

For industry wholesale distributors and manufacturers.

20242 www.aspe.org
American Society of Plumbing Engineers

Seeks to resolve professional problems in plumbing engineering. Operates a certification program.

20243 www.asse-plumbing.org
American Society of Sanitary Engineering

Members are from all segments of the plumbing industry, including contractors, engineers, inspectors, journeymen, apprentices and others involved in the industry. Provides information, the opportunity to exchange ideas, solve problems and offers forum where all sides can express their views.

20244 www.construction.com
McGraw-Hill Construction

McGraw-Hill Construction (MHC), part of The McGraw-Hill Companies, connects people and projects across the design and construction industry, serving owners, architects, engineers, general contractors, subcontractors, building product manufacturers, suppliers, dealers, distributors and adjacent markets.

20245 www.greyhouse.com
Grey House Publishing

Authoritative reference directories for most business sectors including plumbing and heating markets. Users can search the online databases with varied search criteria allowing for custom searches by product category, geographic area, sales volume, keyword, subject and more. Full Grey House catalog and online ordering also available.

20246 www.iapmo.org
Int'l Assoc of Plumbing and Mechanical Officers
IAPMO has been protecting the public's health and safety for more than eighty years by working in concert with government and industry to implement comprehensive plumbing and mechanical systems around the world.

20247 www.pdionline.org
Plumbing and Drainage Institute
For manufacturers of engineered plumbing products, flood drains, roof drains, sanitary floor drains, cleanouts, water hammer arresters, swimming pool drains, backwater valves, grease interceptors, fixture supports, and other drainage specialties.

20248 www.sweets.construction.com
McGraw Hill Construction
In depth product information that lets you find, compare, select, specify and make purchase decisions in the industrial product marketplace.

20249 www.uboiler.com
Uniform Boiler and Pressure Vessel Laws Society
Established to promote uniformity in rules, laws and regulations for boiler and pressure vessel safety based on the requirements of the American Society of Mechanical Engineers Boiler and Pressure Vessel Code and other related national standards.

20250 www.vma.org
Valve Manufacturers Association of America

Associations

20251 Amalgamated Printers Association
304 Mountain View Lane
Laurel, MT 59044-2047

406-928-4757
E-Mail: TWOEMPRESS@aol.com
Home Page: www.apa-letterpress.org/
Social Media: Facebook, Twitter, LinkedIn, Google+, Pinterest

Ernie Blitzer, President
Dick Neihaus, VP
Howard Gelbert, Secretary/Treasurer
Rich Hopkins, Director
David Kent, Archivist

The Amalgamated Printers' Association was organized in 1958 as a hobby printers group so that members could improve their skills, expand their knowledge, and exchange samples of their letterpress work in addition to encouraging excellence of printing content, design, and techniques.
150 Members
Founded in 1958

20252 Assoc. Suppliers of Printing, Publishing & Converting Technologies
1899 Preston White Drive
Reston, VA 20191-4367

703-264-7200
Fax: 703-620-0994
E-Mail: npes@npes.org
Home Page: www.npes.org/news/whatsnew.html

Ralph J. Nappi, President
William K. Smythe, VP
Douglas Sprei, Director Communications/Marketing
Mercedes Florio, International Exhibitions Manager
Steve Prejsner, Manager of Technology

The Association for Suppliers of Printing , Publishing and Converting Technologies is a trade association that represents manufacturers, importers and distributors of equipment, supplies, systems and software used in every printing, publishing and converting process from design to distribution. Virtually all industry products and processes are represented by the member companies, which range in size from under $1 million in annual sales revenue to more than $1 billion.
460 Members
Founded in 1933

20253 Binding Industries of America
Printing Industry of Illinois
200 Deer Run Road
Sewickley, PA 15143

412-741-6860
800-910-4283
Fax: 412-741-2311
E-Mail: printing@printing.org
Home Page: www.bindingindustries.org
Social Media: Facebook, Twitter, LinkedIn, Google+, Pinterest

Frederick A. Hartwig, Manager, Environment ane Health
Gary A. Jones, Assistant Vice President
Chris Eckhart, Chairman
Chris Webbert, Vice-Chairman

A trade association representing bindery and looseleaf manufacturers, graphic finishers, and supplies to those industries
350 Members
Founded in 1955

20254 Book Manufacturers' Institute (BMI)
2 Armand Beach Drive
Suite 1B
Palm Coast, FL 32137-2612

386-986-4552
Fax: 386-986-4553
E-Mail: info@bmibook.com
Home Page: www.bmibook.org

Daniel N Bach, Executive VP & Secretary
Jac B. Garner, President
Kent H. Larson, President-Elect/ Vice President
Paul Genovesse, Treasurer
Robert J. Boyd, General counsel

Since 1933, the Book Manufacturers' Institute, Inc. (BMI) has been the leading nationally recognized trade association of the book manufacturing industry. BMI member companies annually produce the great majority of books ordered by the U. S. book publishing industry. Today, BMI is a vital part of the industry, playing a leading role by providing an intra-industry communications link among book manufacturers, publishers, suppliers and governmental bodies.
90 Members
Founded in 1933

20255 Center for Book Arts
28 W 27th St
3rd Floor
New York, NY 10001

212-481-0295
Fax: 212-481-9853
E-Mail: info@centerforbookarts.org
Home Page: www.centerforbookarts.org
Social Media: Facebook, Twitter, YouTube,Flickr, Blog

Alexander Campos, Executive Director & Curator
Brian Hannon, Vice Chair
Robert J. Ruben, Chairman, MD
Aaron Salik, Treasurer
David W. Lowden, Secretary

The Center for Book Arts is dedicated to preserving the traditional crafts of book-making, as well as exploring and encouraging contemporary interpretations of the book as an art object. Each year the Center offers three terms of courses, workshops and seminars taught by experienced book artists, and providing hands-on training in all aspects of traditional and contemporary bookmaking, including bookbinding, letterpress printing, papermaking, and other associated arts.
Founded in 1974

20256 Flexographic Technical Association Inc.
3920 Veterans Memorial Highway
Suite 9
Bohemia, NY 11716

631-737-6020
Fax: 631-737-6813
E-Mail: memberinfo@flexography.org
Home Page: www.flexography.org

Mark Cisternino, President
Joe Tuccitto, Director of Education
Doreen Monteleone, Sustainability Specialist
Sharon Cox, Director of Marketing
Milena Flores, Accounting & Human Resource Manager

Technical society devoted exclusively to the flexographic printing industry.
1500 Members
Founded in 1958

20257 In-Plant Printing and Mailing Association
455 S. Sam Barr Drive
Suite 203
Keaney, MO 64060
816-903-4762
Fax: 816-902-4766
E-Mail: ipmainfo@ipma.org
Home Page: www.ipma.org
Social Media: Facebook, LinkedIn

Carma Goin, Executive Director
Rob Lingard, President
Larry Wright, Secretary/Treasurer
Alvin Griffin, President-Elect
Debbie Pavletich, Vendor Representative

The professional association for all segments of the in-house corporate printing and mailing professionals who work for educational institutions, the government, and private industry.
600 Members
Founded in 1964

20258 International Waterless Printing Association
International Waterless Printing Association
5 Southside Dr Unit 11-328
Clifton Park, NY 12065

518-557-2981
800-850-0660
Fax: 518-310-2383
E-Mail: info@waterless.org
Home Page: www.waterless.org

John O'Rourke, Vice president
Brian Amos, Secretary
Julie Leonhard, Treasurer
Joel Friedman, Executive Director
Ruud Kempers, Director European Operations

Dedicated to the informational and educational needs of its printer and sponsor members. Seeks to inform designers and print buyers about the many benefits the process offers.
Founded in 1992

20259 Printing Brokerage Buyers Association
1530 Locust Street
Mezanine 124
Philadelphia, PA 19102

215-821-6581
866-586-9391
Fax: 561-845-7130
E-Mail: info@ pbbai.net
Home Page: www.pbba.org
Social Media: RSS

Vincent Mallardi, Chairman

Promotes business relationships among brokers, buying groups, manufacturers and related companies. Sets standards, codes and supplies information and referrals.

20260 Printing Impressions
North American Publishing Company (NAPCO)
1500 Spring Garden St
12th Floor
Philadelphia, PA 19130

215-238-5300
Fax: 212-431-5786
E-Mail: webmaster@napco.com
Home Page: www.piworld.com
Social Media: Facebook, Twitter, LinkedIn, Yahoo,Windows Live

Rosemary Sirico, President
Diane Pesce, VP
Mark T. Michelson, Editor-in-Chief
Erik Cagle, Senior Editor, PI Weekly Editor
Alex Schwartz, Senior Editor, PI Weekly Editor

Promotes the interests of women in the production profession.
Founded in 1966

20261 Printing Industries of America
200 Deer Run Rd
Sewickley, PA 15143

412-741-6860
800-910-4283
Fax: 412-741-2311
E-Mail: info@printing.org
Home Page: www.printing.org
Social Media: Facebook, Twitter, LinkedIn, Pinterest

Michael F. Makin, President/CEO
Mr Michael S Wurst, Treasurer
Paul L Cousineau, Chairman, Research Committee
Jeff Ekstein, Chairman of the Board of Directors
David A. Olberding, 1st Vice Chairman

A graphic arts trade association representing our members in this industry. Printing Industries of America, along with its affiliates, delivers products and services that enhance the growth, efficiency and profitability of its members and the industry through advocacy, education, research and technical information
10000 Members
Founded in 1887

20262 Printing Industries of New England
5 Crystal Pond Road
Southborough, MA 01772

508-804-4100
800-365-7463
Fax: 508-804-4119
E-Mail: webmaster@pine.org
Home Page: www.pine.org
Social Media: Facebook, Twitter, LinkedIn

Tad Parker, President
Joe La Valla, Chairman
Bob Clement, Secretary/Treasurer
Justin Pallis, Member-at-Large
Kurt Peterson, Vice Chairman

Serves more than 450 commercial printing and graphic communications companies throughout five New England states. Provides products and services on an ongoing basis to help member companies operate more profitably.
450 Members
Founded in 1887

20263 Printing Industries of Northern California
665 3rd St
Suite 500
San Francisco, CA 94107-1956

415-495-8242
800-659-3363
Fax: 415-543-7790
E-Mail: info@pinc.org
Home Page: www.pinc.org

Dan Nelson, Executive Director
David Katz, VP
Gerry Bonetto, Government Affairs
Jim Frey, Executive VP
Laura Vargas, Member Programs Director

The Printing Industries of Northern California (PINC) is a non-profit trade association serving several industry segments in Northern California, primarily the print production and print buying segments.

20264 Printing Industry Association of the South
305 Plus Park Blvd
Nashville, TN 37217

615-366-1094
Fax: 615-366-4192
E-Mail: info@pias.org
Home Page: www.pias.org

Ed Chalifoux, President

The Printing Industry Association of the South (PIAS), a non-profit trade association, is dedicated to assisting the entire industry to continue to expand in the region and help the industry prosper across the seven-state region of Alabama, Arkansas, Kentucky, Louisiana, Mississippi, Tennessee and West Virginia.
520 Members

20265 Printing and Graphic Communications Association
6411 Ivy Lane
Suite 700
Greenbelt, MD 20770

Home Page: www.pgca.org

Serves the graphic communications community in the Washington, D.C. metropolitan area.
Founded in 1914

20266 Society for Service Professionals in Printing (SSPP)
Document Management Industries Association
433 E Monroe Ave
Alexandria, VA 22301-1645

703-684-0044
877-777 7398
Fax: 703-548-9137
E-Mail: ssppinfo@sspp.org
Home Page: www.sspp.org

Peter Colainni, Executive Director
Marj Green, Director
Kevin Cooper, Billing Coordinator
Pam Decker, Webmaster

A national organization that focuses on rates, service and trends in the printing industry for consumers. SSPP provides information about both printing and customer service to its members through three monthly newsletters and special interest bulletins. SSPP sponsors the national Certification Examination for Printing Service Specialists (CPSS), which recognizes those printing service specialists who have attained a proscribed body of knowledge about both printing and customer service.
Cost: $150.00

20267 Specialty Graphic Imaging Association
10015 Main St
Fairfax, VA 22031-3489

703-385-1335
888-385-3588
Fax: 703-273-0456
E-Mail: sgia@sgia.org, webmaster@sgia.org
Home Page: www.sgia.org
Social Media: Facebook, Twitter, LinkedIn, Wordpress

Michael Robertson, President
James Gill, Associate Vice Chairman
Pete Gallo, Chairman
Michael Mockridge, Treasurer
Edward Cook Jr, Secretary

Participants include corporations, institutions and individuals interested in screen printing and digital imaging. Conducts technical research and training workshops.
Founded in 1986

Newsletters

20268 Binding Edge
Printing Industry of Illinois
200 Deer Run Road
Sewickley, PA 15143

412-741-6860
800-910-4283
Fax: 412-741-2311
E-Mail: gain@piagatf.org
Home Page: www.bindingindustries.org
Social Media: Facebook, Twitter, LinkedIn

Michael Makin, President/CEO
Justin Goldstein, Manager

Includes articles designed to help bindery and loose leaf facilities improve their processes and keep up on the latest technologies.
Frequency: Quarterly
Circulation: 12000

20269 Business Printing Technologies Report
DMIA
433 East Monroe Avenue
Alexandria, VA 22301-1645

703-836-6232
Fax: 703-836-2241
E-Mail: dmia@dmia.org
Home Page: www.dmia.org

Timothy J Mehl, President
Peter L Colaianni, Executive VP
Brad Holt, VP Media/Publications
Robert O'Connell, Treasurer
Marj Green, VP Operations

Offers a complete overview of the printing industry.
Frequency: Annual
Circulation: 5600
Founded in 1955

20270 Economic Edge
National Association for Printing Leadership
One Meadowlands Plaza
Suite 1511
East Rutherford, NJ 07073

201-634-9600
800-642-6275
Fax: 201-634-0324
E-Mail: webmaster@napl.org
Home Page: www.napl.org
Social Media: Facebook, Twitter, LinkedIn, YouTube,RSS

Joseph Truncale, President
Timothy Fischer, Executive VP/COO

Economic analysis of the graphic arts industry.
Cost: $150.00
12 Pages
Frequency: Quarterly
Founded in 1933

20271 Footprints
Footprint Communications
1339 Massachusetts Street
Lawrence, KS 66044
800-488-8316
Fax: 785-832-0087
E-Mail: mike@footcom.com
Home Page: www.footprints.com

Dick Vinocur, Publisher

A newsletter for the printing industry reporting news, management, marketing and financial data (including industry stock indexes), product introductions, personnel changes, association affairs and recent acquisitions and mergers. Footprints also reports on exhibits, shows, meetings and conferences in the graphic arts industry.
Cost: $327.00
Frequency: Fortnightly

20272 Graphic Arts Monthly Online
Reed Business Information
4709 Golf Road
Skokie, IL 60076

800-217-7874
Fax: 630-288-8781

E-Mail: psaran@reedbusiness.com
Home Page: www.reedbusiness.com

Jeff Greisch, President
Bill Esler, Editor-in-Chief
Lisa Cross, Web Site Editor
Stephanie Kauffman, Reprint Management Services
Mark Kelsey, CEO

Graphic Arts Monthly Online is a subscriber-based Web portal for printing professionals and print buyers featuring current and archived news, research and business tools, online classifieds, used equipment marketplace and online training and education.
Cost: $159.00
Frequency: Monthly

20273 **Graphic Communicator**
Graphic Communications International Union
25 Louisiana Avenue N.W
Washington, DC 20001

202-624-6800
Fax: 202-721-0600
E-Mail: webmessenger@gciu.org
Home Page: www.gciu.org
Social Media: Facebook, Twitter

James P Hoffa, President
Ken Hall, Secretary-Treasurer

Tabloid size newspaper for and about members of the GCIU. The international union represents workers in the printing/publishing industry. Members range from desktop operators to paper handler.
Cost: $12.00
Circulation: 100000
Founded in 1983

20274 **NAQP Network**
National Association for Printing Leadership
One Meadowlands Plaza
Suite 1511
East Rutherford, NJ 07073

201-634-9600
800-642-6275
Fax: 201-634-0324
E-Mail: webmaster@napl.org
Home Page: www.naqp.com
Social Media: Facebook, Twitter, LinkedIn, YouTube,RSS

Joseph P Truncale, President & CEO
Dean D' Ambrosi, Vice President
Carol Rocke, Marketing Coordinator

Editorial content covers technologic advances, product news, profiles on industry leaders, and club events.
Frequency: Monthly
Circulation: 900

20275 **Printing News**
Cygnus Publishing
3 Huntington Quadrangle
Suite 301N
Melville, NY 11747-3601
631-845-2700
800-308-6397
Fax: 631-249-5774
E-Mail: editor@printingnews.com
Home Page: www.printingnews.com
Social Media: Facebook, Twitter, LinkedIn

David Kastriner, Publisher
Michael Zerner, Associate Publisher
David Lindsay, Editor-in-Chief
Rachel Frank, Editor

Includes timely news and information on a variety of subjects including technological breakthroughs, industry trends, marketing, finance, as well as industry leader and corporate profiles.
Cost: $39.95
Frequency: Weekly
Circulation: 9000
Founded in 1928
Mailing list available for rent

20276 **SGIA Journal**
Specialty Graphic Imaging Association
10015 Main St
Fairfax, VA 22031-3489

703-385-1335
888-385-3588
Fax: 703-273-0456
E-Mail: sgia@sgia.org
Home Page: www.sgia.org
Social Media: Facebook, Twitter, LinkedIn

Michael Robertson, President
Sondra Fry Benoudiz, VP Membership
Lynn Krinsky, Chairman
Pete Gallo, First Vice Chairman
Tim Markley, Second Vice Chairman

Provides members with access to information relative to industry trends and the latest news such as emerging markets, government regulations, and technological developments.
Cost: $149.00
Frequency: Bi-Monthly
Circulation: 3800
Founded in 1948
Printed in 2 colors on glossy stock

20277 **Signature Service**
Signature Service Real Estate Rainier
302 Binghampton Street W
PO Box 8
Rainier, WA 98576

360-446-4646
877-446-4647
Fax: 360-446-2400
E-Mail: ssppinfo@sspp.org
Home Page: www.signatureservice.com

Peter Colaianni, Executive Director
Marj Green, Director
Kevin Cooper, Billing Coordinator
Pam Decker, Webmaster

Newsletter covering rates, service and trends in the printing industry for consumers.
Cost: $115.00
8 Pages
Frequency: Monthly
Circulation: 2000

Magazines & Journals

20278 **American InkMaker**
Cygnus Publishing
PO Box 803
Fort Atkinson, WI 53538-0803

920-000-1111
800-547-7377
Fax: 920-563-1699
E-Mail: Rich.Reiff@CygnusPub.com
Home Page: www.cygnusb2b.com

John French, CEO
Robert Stange, Senior VP Marketing

Offers information to the professional ink manufacturer. The editorial content consists of contributed technical papers and nontechnical features about trends, technology and global happenings to help our readers to improve their profitability in addition to featuring a monthly interview with printers.
Cost: $46.00
Circulation: 3800
Founded in 1923

20279 **American Printer**
American Printer
2100 West Loop South
Suite 900
Houston, TX 77027-3515

713-300-0674
E-Mail: info@AmericanPrinter.com
Home Page: www.americanprinter.com
Social Media: Facebook, Twitter, RSS

Katherine O'Brien, Editor
Michael P Koch, Senior Art Director
Denise Kapel, Managing Editor
Carrie Cleaveland, Assistant Editor
Jill Roth, Director Brand Development

Regular issue features include new products listings, new equipment technology and reports on system developments.
Frequency: Monthly
Circulation: 86037
Founded in 1883
Mailing list available for rent

20280 **Awards & Engraving Magazine**
National Business Media
PO Box 1416
Broomfield, CO 80038-1416

303-469-0424
800-669-0424
Fax: 303-469-5730
E-Mail: steve@nbm.com
Home Page: www.nbm.com
Social Media: Facebook, Twitter, LinkedIn

Bob Wieber, President
Dave Pomeroy, Publisher

Content includes a special focus, and regular articles on signage, the glass market, business management, people profiles, and advances in technology.
Cost: $38.00
Frequency: Monthly
Founded in 1985

20281 **Big Picture**
325 Public Street
Providence, RI 02905

401-752-3442
800-421-1321
Fax: 401-752-3528
E-Mail: webmaster@bigpicturelearning.org
Home Page: www.bigpicture.org

Tedd Swormstedt, CEO
Ronald A. Wolk, Chairman

This publication reports on digital printing of visual communications with coverage of digital printing from image capture and processing to finishing and display.
Frequency: Monthly
Circulation: 48000
Founded in 1996

20282 **Dealer Communicator**
Fichera Communications
441 South State Road 7
Suite 14
Margate, FL 33068-2823
954-971-4360
800-327-8999
Fax: 954-971-4362
E-Mail: omike@dealercommunicator.com
Home Page: www.dealercommunicator.com

Orazio Fichera, Publisher/President
Particia Leavitt, VP

Provides national and international coverage for the graphic arts and printing industries.
Cost: $30.00
32 Pages
Frequency: Monthly
Circulation: 13619
Founded in 1982
Printed in 4 colors on glossy stock

20283 **Digital Graphics**
National Business Media

PO Box 1416
Broomfield, CO 80038-1416

303-469-0424
800-669-0424
Fax: 303-465-3424
E-Mail: kmergent@nbm.com
Home Page: www.nbm.com
Social Media: Facebook, Twitter, LinkedIn

Bob Wieber, President
Ken Mergentime, Editor

Regular departments track public stock comapnies of interest to the industry, report on international graphics news and highlight recent technological advances.
64 Pages
Frequency: Monthly
Circulation: 18583
Founded in 1985
Printed in 4 colors

20284 Digital Output
Rockport Custom Publishing
100 Cummings Ctr
Suite 321E
Beverly, MA 01915-6101

978-921-7850
Fax: 978-921-7870
E-Mail: edit@rockportpubs.com
Home Page: www.rockportpubs.com

Thomas Tetreault, CEO
Lynn Weese, Account Executive

Provides case studies and trend updates, as well as discussing how and why companies integrate and coordinate their marketing strategies.
Frequency: 12 + 2 Buyers Guides

20285 Document Processing Technology
RB Publishing Company
2424 American Lane
PO Box 259906
Madison, WI 53725-9906

608-277-8785
800-536-1992
Fax: 608-241-8666
E-Mail: rbpub@rbpub.com
Home Page: www.rbpub.com

Ron Brent, Publisher/President
Allison Lloyd, Managing Editor
Marll Thiede, Executive Editor/VP
Rachel Spahr, Circulation Manager
Tonjia Weber, Production Manager

Covers digital printing, publishing and distribution. Feature and special topic articles focus on industry trends, technology and strategies for high-volume document processors.
Frequency: Monthly
Circulation: 10000
Founded in 1988

20286 Electronic Publishing
PennWell Publishing Company
1421 S Sheridan Rd
Tulsa, OK 74112-6619

918-835-3161
800-331-4463
Fax: 918-831-9476
E-Mail: Headquarters@PennWell.com
Home Page: www.pennwell.com

Robert Biolchini, President
Courtney E Howard, Managing Editor
Frank J Romano, Sr Contributing & Founding Editor
Nancy A Hitchcock, Senior Associate Editor

For those who communicate in print, including service bureaus, printers, prepress houses and desktop publishers, it provides latest products, news and related developments.
Cost: $59.00
Frequency: Monthly
Circulation: 68441
Founded in 1910
Mailing list available for rent

20287 Flash Magazine
BlackLighting
252 Riddle Pond Road
West Topsham, VT 05086

800-252-2599
800-252-2599
Fax: 802-439-6462
E-Mail: salesBL@BlackLightning.com
Home Page: www.flashweb.com

Walter Vose Jeffries, Publisher

Flash Magazine was started in 1989 and is all about desktop publishing, book-on-demand binding, inkjet & laser printinting, heat transfers and other topics of interest to the small time publisher and graphic artist. The Flash is filled with great how-to articles that will help you take care of your printer, do maintenance & repairs yourself, teach you about graphics, digital photography, scanning and laser etching glass and book-on-demand publishing, binding and so much more.
Cost: $20.00
Frequency: Monthly
Circulation: 112000

20288 Flexo Magazine
Flexographic Technical Association
3920 Veterans Memorial Highway
Suite 9
Bohemia, NY 11716

631-737-6020
Fax: 631-737-6813
E-Mail: membership@flexography.org
Home Page: www.flexography.org
Social Media: Facebook, LinkedIn

Robert Moran, Publisher
Christian Bonawandt, Editor

Trade publication for the flexographic printing industry.
1300 Members
Frequency: Monthly

20289 Forms & Direct Mail Manufacturer's Marketplace
Bulls-Eye Communications
211 Champion Avenue
Webster, NY 14580

585-265-3045
E-Mail: waterford@waterfordweb.com

Marsha A Thompson, Editor

The resource magazine of business forms and direct mail printers. Spotlights news and products in the industry.
Cost: $49.00
Frequency: Bi-Monthly
Circulation: 4,870

20290 Graphic Communications World
Hayzlett & Associates
3313 South Western Avenue
Sioux Falls, SD 57106

605-355-5531
Fax: 605-275-2087
Home Page: www.hayzlett.com/index.htm

Jeanette Clinkunbroomer, Editor
Jeff Hayzlett, Owner

Offers a comprehensive overview of the graphic arts and communications industry.
Cost: $347.00
Frequency: Monthly
Founded in 1968

20291 Gravure
Gravure Association of America
1200A Scottsville Road
Rochester, NY 14624-5703

585-436-2150
Fax: 585-436-7689
E-Mail: lwshatch@gaa.org
Home Page: www.gaa.org

Laura Wayland-Smith Hatch, Editor
William Martin, President/CEO

Editorial coverage focuses on the technical developments in gravure printing, the financial performance of the industry and association member activities.
Cost: $67.00
Circulation: 3500
ISSN: 0894-4946
Founded in 1987
Printed in 4 colors on matte stock

20292 High Volume Printing (HVP)
Innes Publishing Company
28100 North Ashley Circle
PO Box 7280
Libertyville, IL 60048

847-816-7900
800-247-3306
Fax: 847-247-8855
E-Mail: meinnes@innespub.com
Home Page: www.innespub.com

Mary Ellen Innes, Publisher
Ray Roth, Editor
Barb Pettersen, Circulation Manager
Mary Ellin Innes, President
Judy Abbott, Administrative Assistant

HVP offers a strategic mix of management and production-oriented editorial content, and has consistently led in coverage of new technologies and regulatory issues. It focuses on the bottom-line realities involved in merging tomorrow's technologies with today's operating environment. Subjects include prepress, press, and postpress equipment and technology, sales and marketing management, training, regulatory issues and more.
Circulation: 39057
Founded in 1982

20293 IPA Bulletin
IPA: Association of Graphic Solutions Providers
7200 France Ave S
Suite 223
Edina, MN 55435-4309

952-896-1908
800-255-8141
Fax: 708-596-5112
E-Mail: bessie@ipa.org
Home Page: www.ipa.org

Steven Bonnoff, Executive Director
Becky Walroth, Editorial Assistant
Steven Bonoff, President

Association news offering information on prepress and graphic arts.
Cost: $20.00
6 Pages
Circulation: 2,100
ISSN: 1539-137X
Founded in 1911
Printed in 4 colors on glossy stock

20294 In Plant Graphics
North American Publishing Company
1500 Spring Garden St
Suite 1200
Philadelphia, PA 19130-4094

215-238-5300
Fax: 215-238-5342
E-Mail: editor.ipg@napco.com
Home Page: www.ipgonline.com

Ned S Borowsky, CEO
Glen Reynolds, Publisher
Dorlissa Goodrich, Production Manager

Maggie Tajack, Advertising Promotion Manager
Brian Ludwig, Group Publisher

Articles include management advice, technical information, industry news and reader profiles.
Cost: $65.00
60 Pages
Frequency: Monthly
Circulation: 20,000
ISSN: 1087-2817
Founded in 1996
Printed in 4 colors on glossy stock

20295 In Plant Printer
Innes Publishing Company
28100 North Ashley Circle
Suite 101
Libertyville, IL 60048

847-816-7900
800-247-3306
Fax: 847-247-8855
E-Mail: meinnes@innespub.com
Home Page: www.innespub.com

Mary Ellin Innes, President
Jack Klasnic, Editor
Barbara Pettersen, Circulation Manager
Teri Saeed, Production Manager
Judy Abbott, Administrative Assistant

Serves printing, graphics and typesetting facilities located in business, industry, education, government, hospitals, associations, and non-profit organizations.
Cost: $110.00
70 Pages
Frequency: Monthly
Circulation: 247637
ISSN: 0891-8996
Founded in 1977
Printed in 4 colors on glossy stock

20296 Ink World
Ink World Direct Limited
108 Queens Road
Nuneaton, WI 07446-1150

800-011-2011
E-Mail: info@rodpub.com
Home Page: www.ink-world.com

Rodman Zilenziger Jr, President
Matt Montgomery, VP

Covers the printing inks, coatings and allied industries.
64 Pages
Frequency: Monthly
Circulation: 6187
Founded in 1994
Printed in 4 colors on glossy stock

20297 Inside Finishing Magazine
Foil & Speciality Effects Association
2150 Southwest Wesport Drive
Suite 101
Topeka, KS 66614

785-271-5816
Fax: 785-271-6404
E-Mail: fseamail@fsea.com
Home Page: www.fsea.com

Jeff Peterson, Executive Director
Gayla Peterson, Sales Director
Kym Conis, Assistant Director
Eric.J Carter, Art Director & Webmaster

A quarterly magazine published by the Foil Stamping and Embossing Association, Inside Finishing has a targeted circulation of 6,000 graphic finishing decision makers. These include trade finishers, folding carton companies, greeting card manufacturers, and commercial printers with finishing/bindery operations. It also includes a small percentage of graphic designers involved in the foil stamping and embossing industry, and, of course, industry suppliers to the graphic finishing industry.
56 Pages
Frequency: 4 issues
Founded in 1994

20298 Instant and Small Commercial Printer ISCP
Innes Publishing Company
28100 North Ashley Circle
PO Box 7280
Libertyville, IL 60048-7280

847-816-7900
800-247-3306
Fax: 847-247-8855
E-Mail: daninnes@innespub.com
Home Page: www.innespub.com

Dan Innes, Publisher
Linda Casey, Editor
Barb Pettersen, Circualtion MAnager
Mary Ellin Innes, President

ISCP magazine publishes how-to articles and case histories on printing and photocopy reproduction. Emphasis on desktop publishing and short-run digital technologies reflects the growth of this service in instant printing operations. Management stories are aimed at helping the publication's largely entrepreneurial audience grapple successfully with everyday problems and spot new opportunities for growth.
Frequency: Monthly
Circulation: 413671
Founded in 1982

20299 Label & Narrow Web Industry
Rodman Publishing
70 Hilltop Rd
Suite 3000
Ramsey, NJ 07446-1150

201-825-2552
Fax: 201-825-0553
E-Mail: label@rodpub.com
Home Page: www.labelandnarrowweb.com
Social Media: Facebook, Twitter, LinkedIn, RSS

Rodman J. Zilenziger Jr, President
Matthew Montgomery, VP
Kathleen Scully, Publisher
Steve Katz, Editor
Catherine Diamond, Associate Editor

Label and Narrow Web serves manufacturers of label and narrow web including labels, tags, tape, materials, substrates, machinery, and equipment and others allied to the field.
80 Pages
Circulation: 11000
ISSN: 1095-3248
Founded in 1996
Mailing list available for rent
Printed in 4 colors on glossy stock

20300 New England Printer and Publisher
Printing Industries of New England
5 Crystal Pond Rd
Southborough, MA 01772-1758

508-804-4100
800-365-7463
Fax: 508-804-4119
E-Mail: jtepper04@pine.org
Home Page: www.pine.org

John Scibelli, Manager
Joe La Valla, Chairman
Brie Drummond, Production Manager
Kurt Peterson, Vice-Chairman
Bob Clement, Secretary-Treasurer

Trade magazine for printers and publishers.
Cost: $2.40
48 Pages
Frequency: Monthly
Circulation: 4000
Founded in 1938
Printed in 4 colors on matte stock

20301 New Pages: Alternatives in Print and Media
New Pages Press
PO Box 1580
Bay City, MI 48706

989-671-0081
Fax: 313-743-2730
E-Mail: newpagesonline@hotmail.com
Home Page: www.newpages.com

Casey Hill, Publisher
Denise Hill, Editor

News and information for bookstores and libraries.
Cost: $12.00
64 Pages
Frequency: Quarterly

20302 Newspapers & Technology
Conley Magazines
1623 Blake Street
Suite 250
Denver, CO 80202

303-575-9595
Fax: 303-575-9555
Home Page: www.newsandtech.com/

Mary Van Meter, Publisher
Chuck Moozakis, Editor-in-Chief
Tara McKeekin, Editor
Hays Goodman, Associate Editor/Webmaster

Newspapers & Technology is a monthly trade publication for newspaper publishers and department managers involved in applying and integrating technology. Written by industry experts, News & Tech provides regular coverage of the following departments: prepress, press, postpress and new media.
Circulation: 16,874

20303 PC Presentations Productions
Pisces Publishing Group
1400 South Nova Road
Suite 303
Daytona Beach, FL 32114-5851

203-877-1927
Fax: 203-877-1927
Home Page: www.piscespub.com

Don Johnson, Editor/Publisher
Douglas Finlay, Managing Editor

PC Presentations Productions is a free online magazine intended for both the high-end professional and the student. Graphic and video tutorials for intermediate and advanced content producers are regular features as are HTML and Javascript tutorials and Website design tutorials intended for students and others wishing to add these skills.
Frequency: Weekly
ISSN: 1065-9699

20304 Package Printing
North American Publishing Company
1500 Spring Garden St
Suite 1200
Philadelphia, PA 19130-4094

215-238-5300
800-627-2689
Fax: 215-238-5342
E-Mail: customerservice@napco.com
Home Page: www.packageprinting.com
Social Media: Facebook, Twitter, LinkedIn, Yahoo,Windows Live

Ned S Borowsky, CEO
Brian Ludwick, Publisher
Robert Margulies, Sales Manager
Megan Wolf, Assistant Editor
Sean Sams, Advertising Account Manager

Trade publication serving the business and technology needs of presidents and CEOs of flexible packaging, tag and label, folding rigid

boxes and directing operations.
Cost: $99.50
75 Pages
Frequency: Monthly
Circulation: 24000
Founded in 1958
Mailing list available for rent

20305 Paper Magazine
365 Broadway
6th Floor
New York, NY 10013

212-226-4405
800-829-9160
Fax: 212-226-0062
E-Mail: edit@papermag.com
Home Page: www.papermag.com

Sharon Phair, Advertising & Marketing
Kim Hastreiter, Publisher
Alexis Swerdloff, Executive Editor
Nobu Massiah, Editor
Carol Lee, Creative Director

PAPER Magazine focuses on the latest trends in pop culture, style, music and film, including information on New York art exhibits, club listings, literary events, movie reviews and shows. Includes night-life guide.
Cost: $9.97
Frequency: 10 Issues Per Year
Circulation: 90,000
Founded in 1984

20306 Print Business Register
Cygnus Business Media
3 Huntington Quadrangle
Suite 301 North
Melville, NY 11747

631-845-2700
800-308-6397
Fax: 631-845-2741
Home Page: www.cygnusb2b.com
Social Media: Facebook

Michael Zerner, Publisher
Rachel Frank, Editor

Editorial material reports on mergers, acquisitions, reorganizations and major issues affecting the marketplace of the commercial printing industry.
Frequency: Weekly
Circulation: 650
Mailing list available for rent

20307 Print Magazine
RC Publications
38 east 29th street, 4th floor
New York, NY 10016
212-447-1400
Fax: 212-447-5231
E-Mail: info@printmag.com
Home Page: www.printmag.com
Social Media: Facebook, Twitter, Flickr

Joel Toner, Publisher

Regular highlights include advertising and promotion design, corporate identity, design education and film/TV production. Also covered are creative trends and technological advances in photography, printing, web design, illustration, motion graphics and packaging. Includes profiles of visual artists, ad agencies and graphic design firms.
Cost: $37.00
Frequency: Monthly
Circulation: 54149
Mailing list available for rent

20308 Print Solutions Magazine
Document Management Industries Association
330 N Wabash Ave
Suite 2000
Chicago, IL 60611

800-230-0175
Fax: 312-673-6880
Home Page: www.psda.org

Peter L Colaianni CAE, Editor-in-Chief
Preeti Vasishtha, Assistant Editor
Lashell Stratton, Assistant Editor
Rebecca Trela, Assistant Editor

The independent's source for marketing, management and product information.
Cost: $49.00
276 Pages
Frequency: Monthly
Circulation: 42000
ISSN: 0532-1700
Founded in 1962
Printed in 4 colors on glossy stock

20309 Print on Demand Business
Cygnus Business Media
1233 Janesville Avenue
Fort Atkinson, WI 53538

631-845-2700
800-547-7377
Fax: 631-845-2741
E-Mail: info@cygnus.com
Home Page: www.cygnusb2b.com/

Bob Hall, Executive Editor
Denise Gustavson, Managing Editor
Paul Bonaiuto, CFO
John French, CEO

Editorial includes a look at new products, industry news, updated technology, tips on the best equipment and a look ahead with an upcoming calendar of events.
Frequency: Bi-Monthly

20310 Printing Impressions
North American Publishing Company
1500 Spring Garden St
Suite 1200
Philadelphia, PA 19130-4094

215-238-5300
800-627-2689
Fax: 215-238-5342
E-Mail: mmichelson@napco.com
Home Page: www.napco.com

Ned S Borowsky, CEO
Chris Bauer, Managing Editor
Tunisia Bey, Circulation Manager

Offers news, articles, updates, statistics, research reports and more for the printing industry including printers involved in commercial and newspaper printing and trades.
Frequency: Weekly
Circulation: 83035
Founded in 1958
Mailing list available for rent

20311 Printing Industry Association of the South - Magazine
Printing Industry Association of the South
PO Box 290249
Nashville, TN 37229-0249

615-366-1094
Fax: 615-366-4192
E-Mail: info@pias.org
Home Page: www.pias.org

Ed Chalifoux, President
James Tepper, Board Member

Print industry information. Free with membership.
Frequency: Monthly
Circulation: 5000
Printed in 4 colors on glossy stock

20312 Printing Manager
National Association of Printing Leadership
One Meadowlands Plaza
Suite 1511
East Rutherford, NJ 07073

201-634-9600
800-642-6275
Fax: 201-634-0324
E-Mail: webmaster@napl.org
Home Page: www.napl.org

Joseph P Truncale, President/CEO
Timothy Fischer, Executive Vp/COO

Provides current news for printing executives including the latest industry, marketing and management news.
40 Pages
Frequency: Quarterly
Circulation: 6000
Founded in 1933
Mailing list available for rent
Printed in 4 colors

20313 Printing News Magazine
Cygnus Business Media
3 Huntington Quadrangle
Suite 301N
Melville, NY 11747

631-845-2700
Fax: 631-845-2741
E-Mail: editor@printingnews.com
Home Page: www.printingnews.com
Social Media: Facebook, Twitter, LinkedIn, RSS

David Nathenson, Publisher
Michael Zerner, Associate Publisher
David Lindsay, Editor-in-Chief
Rachel Frank, Editor

News and information on the graphic arts industry in New York, Connecticut, New Jersey and Pennsylvania.
Cost: $39.95
44 Pages
Circulation: 7000
Founded in 1937

20314 Printing News Online
Cygnus Business Media
3 Huntingon Quadrangle
Suite 301N
Melville, NY 11747

631-845-2700
800-308-6397
Fax: 631-845-2741
E-Mail: editor@printingnews.com
Home Page: www.printingnews.com
Social Media: Facebook, Twitter, LinkedIn, RSS

David Nathenson, Publisher
Michael Zerner, Associate Publisher
David Lindsay, Editor-in-Chief
Rachel Frank, Editor

Includes timely news and information on a variety of subjects including technological breakthroughs, industry trends, marketing, finance, as well as industry leader and corporate profiles.

20315 Publishing Executive
North American Publishing Company
1500 Spring Garden St
Suite 1200
Philadelphia, PA 19130-4094

215-238-5300
Fax: 215-238-5342
E-Mail: nskodzinski@napco.com
Home Page: www.printmediamag.com/

Ned S Borowsky, CEO
Noelle Skodzinski, Editor-in-Chief
Matt Steinmetz, Associate Editor
Rhoda Dixon, Circulation Manager
Candas Carmen, Associate Publisher

Publishing Executive (formerly PrintMedia) delivers information to magazine publishers,

associations, corporate publishers, advertising and marketing agencies.
Circulation: 17500

20316 Quick Printing
Cygnus Business Media
3 Huntington Quadrangle
Suite 301 North
Melville, NY 11747-803

631-845-2700
800-308-6397
Fax: 631-845-2741
E-Mail: Bob@quickprinting.com
Home Page: www.quickprinting.com
Social Media: Facebook

Jann Levesque, Group Publisher
Kelley Holmes, Publisher
Bob Hall, Editor
Denise Gustavson, Managing Editor

Business journal for those in the printing business.
Cost: $66.00
Frequency: Monthly
Circulation: 48000
Founded in 1937
Mailing list available for rent

20317 SGIA Journal
Specialty Graphic Imaging Association
10015 Main St
Fairfax, VA 22031-3489

703-385-1335
888-385-3588
Fax: 703-273-0456
E-Mail: sgia@sgia.org
Home Page: www.sgia.org
Social Media: Facebook, Twitter, LinkedIn

Michael Robertson, President
Sondra Fry Benoudiz, VP Membership

Published quarterly in January, April, July and October.
Circulation: 14000
Founded in 1948

20318 Screen Printing
ST Media Group International
11262 Cornell Park Dr
Cincinnati, OH 45242-1812

513-421-2050
800-421-1321
Fax: 513-421-5144
E-Mail: customer@stmediagroup.com
Home Page: www.stmediagroup.com

Tedd Swormstedt, CEO
Brian Foos, CFO
Mark Kissling, Director

Screen printing professionals have relied on Screen Printing for landmark coverage of the latest techniques and technologies that save time, energy and money.
Frequency: Monthly
Circulation: 17000
Founded in 1953
Mailing list available for rent: 17,000 names at $200 per M

20319 Signs of the Times & Screen Printing en Espanol
ST Media Group International
11262 Cornell Park Dr
Cincinnati, OH 45242-1812

513-421-2050
800-421-1321
Fax: 513-421-5144
E-Mail: customer@stmediagroup.com
Home Page: www.stmediagroup.com

Tedd Swormstedt, CEO
Brian Foos, CFO
Mark Kissling, Director

Covering the industries of signmaking, screen printing and digital imaging for Spanish speaking visual communications markets.
Frequency: Monthly
Circulation: 17000
Founded in 1906
Mailing list available for rent

20320 Wide Format Imaging Magazine
Cygnus Publishing
3 Huntington Quadrangle
Suite 301 North
Melville, NY 11747

631-845-2700
800-308-6397
Fax: 631-845-2741
E-Mail: davis@wide-formatimaging.com
Home Page: www.wide-formatimaging.com
Social Media: Facebook, Twitter, LinkedIn, RSS

David Nathenson, Publisher
Karen Lowry-Hall, Editor
Denise M Gustavson, Managing Editor/Web Editor
Charlie Lillis, Director Content Licensing
Katie Brennan, Vice President

Wide Format Imagingimg Magazine provides information on new technologies, analysis of new products, business management tips, and profiles of significant people in the industry. The magazine is a monthly business publication serving 18,000 wide-format professionals. These mostly small business owners are responsible for wide- and large-format drawings, blueprints, soft signage, outdoor signage, posters, POP displays, digital fine art printmaking, and large trade show graphics.
Cost: $25.00
Frequency: Monthly
Mailing list available for rent

Trade Shows

20321 BIA Mid Management Conference
Printing Industry of Illinois
200 Deer Run Road
Sewickley, PA 15143

412-741-6860
800-910-4283
Fax: 412-741-2311
E-Mail: printing@printing.org
Home Page: www.bindingindustries.org
Social Media: Facebook, Twitter, LinkedIn

Michael Makin, President/CEO
Justin Goldstein, Manager

Brings together mid-managers from trade binderies, graphic finishing, information packaging, custom loose leaf manufacturing, and the suppliers to those industries.
600 Attendees
Frequency: Annual/May

20322 CMM International
Romeland house
Romeland Hill
St Albans
Herdfordshire

212-268-4160
Fax: 212-268-4178
E-Mail: info@mackbrooks.co.uk
Home Page: www.cmmshow.com

The premier converting and package printing event for thousands of professionals.
Frequency: June4-7 Chicago
Founded in 1978

20323 Graphic Arts
Graphic Arts Show Company
1899 Preston White Drive
Reston, VA 20191-5468

703-264-7200
Fax: 703-620-9187
E-Mail: info@gasc.org
Home Page: www.gasc.org

Chris Price, VP
Kelly Kilga, Director Operations
Ralph Nappi, President

One of America's foremost regional prepress, printing, publishing, and converting trade shows. 300 booths, 70,000 square feet.
18000 Attendees
Frequency: March
Founded in 1982

20324 Graphics of the Americas
Printing Association of Florida
6275 Hazeltine National Drive
Orlando, FL 32822

407-240-8009
800-331-0461
Fax: 407-240-8333
E-Mail: gain@piagatf.org
Home Page: www.goa.2013.com

Bill Maguire, Chairman
Larry Kudeviz, Treasurer
Rob Hasson, First Vice Chairman
Art Abbott, Second Vice Chairman
George Ryan, CEO

We are the second largest Graphic Arts and Converting show in America. We give you two vital markets, Southeast US and Latin America: Mexico, South America, Central America and the Caribbean. Our 28 year track record reflects our success with both exhibitors and show visitors.
20000 Attendees

20325 Gutenberg Festival
American Printer
2100 West Loop South
Suite 900
Houston, TX 77027-3515

713-300-0674
E-Mail: info@AmericanPrinter.com
Home Page: www.americanprinter.com
Social Media: Facebook, Twitter, RSS

Kelly Kilga, Conference/Show Operations Director
Lilly Kinney, Conference Manager
Tina Scott, Exhibit Sales Director
Chrissie Hahn, Exhibit Sales Manager

The top printing event on the west coast and the only place to see live running equipment both traditional and digital.
15000 Attendees
Frequency: April
Mailing list available for rent

20326 Interquest
Interquest Ltd.
513-D Stewart Street
Charlottesville, VA 22902

434-979-9945
*Fax:*434-979-9959
E-Mail: iquest@inter-quest.com
Home Page: www.inter-quest.com

David Davis, Director

Interquest analysts will present key results from the company's latest research in the field.
Frequency: March

20327 Labelexpo America
Tarsus Group Plc

E-Mail: sales@labelexpo.com
Home Page: www.labelexpo-americas.com

Label, printing, decoration, web printing and converting industry's largest expo.
Frequency: Sept, Chicago

20328 **National Association of Professional Print Buyers**
15050 Northeast 20th Avenue
Suite A
North Miami, FL 33181-1123

305-956-9563

Vincent Mallardi, Executive Director
400 booths.
2.5M Attendees
Frequency: April
Founded in 1969

20329 **Non-Impact Printing Conference and Exhibit**
IS&T-The Society for Imaging Science & Technology
7003 Kilworth Lane
Springfield, VA 22151-4008

703-642-9090
Fax: 703-642-9094
E-Mail: info@imaging.org
Home Page: www.imaging.org

Robert R Buckley, President
Ingeborg Tastl, Secretary
Scott Silence, Treasurer

Annual conference and exhibits of non-impact printing equipment, supplies and services, including printer components, printer consumables, paper and document handling devices and display units.
620 Attendees

20330 **Print**
Graphic Arts Show Company
1899 Preston White Drive
Reston, VA 20191-5435

703-264-7200
Fax: 703-620-9187
E-Mail: info@gasc.org
Home Page: www.gasc.org

Ralph Nappi, President
Chris Price, Vice President
Kelly Kilga, Director Communications
Lilly Kinney, Conference Manager

This is the largest, most comprehensive event for the commercial, package printing and converting industry in the world in 2013. This huge international event held every four years offers you more running machinery under one roof than any other event anywhere.
40000 Attendees
Frequency: September/Annual
Founded in 1968
Mailing list available for rent

20331 **Print Media Conference & Expo**
c/o North American Publishing Company
1500 Spring Garden St, Suite 1200
Philadelphia, PA 19130-4094

888-627-2630
Fax: 215-409-0100
E-Mail: printmediaexpo@napco.com
Home Page: www.pubxpo.com

20332 **SGIA Technology Show**
Specialty Graphic Imaging Association
10015 Main Street
Fairfax, VA 22031-3489

703-385-1335
888-385-3588
Fax: 703-273-0456
E-Mail: sgia@sgia.org
Home Page: www.sgia.org
Social Media: Facebook, Twitter, LinkedIn

Michael Robertson, President/CEO
Sondra Fry Benoudiz, VP Membership

Technologies showcased include: embossing, printing, graphics, digital imaging, screen printing and embroidering.
14000 Attendees
Frequency: September
Founded in 1948

20333 **Tools of Change for Publishing Conference**
O'Reilly Media, Inc.
1005 Gravenstein Highway North
Sebastopol, CA 95472

707-827-7019
800-889-8969
Fax: 707-824-8268
E-Mail: orders@oreilly.com
Home Page: www.oreilly.com
Social Media: Facebook, Twitter, YouTube,RSS

Gina Blaber, Vice President, Conferences
Suzanne Axtell, Communications Manager
Shirley Bailes, Speaker Manager

Expect coverage with a range of practical, in-depth sessions that cover the innovations rocking every aspect of the art, craft, and business of publishing in the 21st century.
Frequency: February

20334 **Vue/Point Conference**
Graphic Arts Show Company
1189 Preston White Drive
Reston, VA 22091-4367

703-264-7200
Fax: 703-620-9187
E-Mail: info@gasc.org
Home Page: www.gasc.org

David Poulos, Conference Coordinator

Presents topics via panel discussions composed of printing professionals who are willing to share their experiences.

Directories & Databases

20335 **Coldset Web Offset Directory**
Printing Industries of America/Graphic Arts
200 Deer Run Rd
Sewickley, PA 15143-2600

412-741-6860
800-910-4283
Fax: 412-741-2311
E-Mail: printing@printing.org
Home Page: www.printing.org
Social Media: Facebook, Twitter, LinkedIn

Michael F Makin, President
Eric Delzer, Chairman

Over 600 printing firms with more than 1,000 presses in the US, Puerto Rico and Canada are profiled.
Cost: $120.00
Frequency: BiAnnual

20336 **Corporate and Incentive Travel**
Coastal Communications Corporation
2700 N Military Trail
Suite 120
Boca Raton, FL 33431-6394

561-989-0600
Fax: 561-989-9509
E-Mail: ccceditor@att.net
Home Page: www.themeetingmagazines.com

Harvey Grotsky, Publisher/Editor-In-Chief
Susan Wycoff Fell, Managing Editor
Susan S Gregg, Managing Editor
Mitch D Miller, Creative Director

Read by over 40,000 ABC audited meeting and incentive travel planners and key executives responsible for meeting decisions. Articles range monthly from in-depth how-to's, to issue oriented features, examinations of professional concerns, thoroughly researched destination reports, and columns by industry experts
Cost: $50.00
Frequency: Annual
Circulation: 60,000
Founded in 1983
Mailing list available for rent

20337 **Directory International Suppliers/Printing Publishing/Converting Technologies**
Association for Suppliers of Printing, Publishing
& Converting Technologies
1899 Preston White Drive
Reston, VA 20191-4367

703-264-7200
Fax: 703-620-0994
E-Mail: npes@npes.org
Home Page: www.npes.org

Ralph J Nappi, President
Douglas Sprei, Director Marketing/Communications
Jesus A Romero, Database Manager
Steve Prejsner, Manager of Technology

An online, freely accessible, association database of NPES member companies and more than 500 products, searchable by product category, keyword or company name.
220 Pages
Frequency: Biennial

20338 **Heatset Web Offset Directory**
Printing Industries of America/Graphic Arts
200 Deer Run Rd
Sewickley, PA 15143-2600

412-741-6860
800-910-4283
Fax: 412-741-2311
E-Mail: gain@piagatf.org
Home Page: www.printing.org
Social Media: Facebook, Twitter, LinkedIn

Michael Makin, President
Eric Delzer, Chairman

Offers information on nearly 500 heatset web printing firms in the United States, Puerto Rico and Canada including products produced.
Cost: $50.00
110 Pages
Frequency: BiAnnually

20339 **In Plant Reproductions: Buyer's Guide Issue**
North American Publishing Company
1500 Spring Garden St
Suite 1200
Philadelphia, PA 19130-4094

215-238-5300
800-627-2689
Fax: 215-238-5342

Ned S Borowsky, CEO

Firms that manufacture or supply equipment, materials and services to printing facilities of firms or organizations, including art, paste-up and copy preparation, mailing systems, darkroom equipment, presses, paper, word processing, computerized composition and electronic publishing.
Cost: $35.00
Frequency: Annual December
Circulation: 41,000

20340 **International Directory of Private Presses**
Educators Research Service

2443 Fair Oaks Boulevard
Suite 316
Sacramento, CA 95825-7684

Home Page: www.briarpress.org

Offers valuable information on over 1,200 private presses and hobbyist printers worldwide.
Cost: $50.00
300 Pages
Frequency: Annual

20341 Print Image International
401 N Michigan Avenue
Suite 2100
Chicago, IL 60611-4245

312-268-8015
800-234-0640
Fax: 312-321-6869
Home Page: www.printimage.org

John Giles, Editor
Steve Johnson, President
300 Pages

20342 Rauch Guide to the US Ink Industry
Grey House Publishing
4919 Route 22
PO Box 56
Amenia, NY 12501-0056

518-789-8700
800-562-2139
Fax: 518-789-0556
E-Mail: books@greyhouse.com
Home Page: www.greyhouse.com
Social Media: Facebook, Twitter

Leslie Mackenzie, Publisher
Richard Gottlieb, Editor

The Guide to this complex and diffuse $4.2 billion ink industry provides market facts and figures in a highly organized format, ideal for today's busy personnel. The report serves as a ready-reference for top executives as well as the industry newcomer.
Cost: $595.00
700 Pages
ISBN: 1-592371-26-4
Founded in 1981

20343 Rauch Guide to the US and Canadian Pulp & Paper Industry
Grey House Publishing
4919 Route 22
PO Box 56
Amenia, NY 12501-0056

518-789-8700
800-562-2139
Fax: 518-789-0556
E-Mail: books@greyhouse.com
Home Page: www.greyhouse.com
Social Media: Facebook, Twitter

Leslie Mackenzie, Publisher
Richard Gottlieb, Editor

Provides current market information and trends to; industry economics and government regulations; company share data for each of the leading product categories; technology and raw material information; industry sources of further data; and unique profiles of 500+ pulp and paper manufacturers, a section which includes all known companies with pulp and paper sales at or over $15 million annually.
Cost: $595.00
400 Pages
ISBN: 1-592371-31-0
Founded in 1981

20344 Who's Who SGIA
Specialty Graphic Imaging Association
10015 Main St
Fairfax, VA 22031-3489

703-385-1335
888-385-3588
Fax: 703-273-0456
E-Mail: sgia@sgia.org
Home Page: www.sgia.org
Social Media: Facebook, Twitter, LinkedIn

Michael Robertson, President
Sondra Fry Benoudiz, VP Membership
Circulation: 3,800
Founded in 1948

Industry Web Sites

20345 http://gold.greyhouse.com
G.O.L.D Grey House OnLine Databases

Grey House Publishing's online database platform, GOLD, offers Quick Search, Keyword Search and Expert Search for most business sectors including printing and allied markets. The GOLD platform makes finding the information you need quick and easy - whether you're a novice searcher or an experienced database user. All of Grey House's directory products are available for subscription on the GOLD platform.

20346 www.fsea.com
Foil Stamping and Embossing Association

For companies engaged in the process of hot stamping or embossing in the graphics industry and companies that manufacture, distribute or provide services to the hot stamping/embossing industry.

20347 www.gaa.org
Gravure Association of America

Members are gravure printers, converters, suppliers and users.

20348 www.greyhouse.com
Grey House Publishing

Authoritative reference directories for most business sectors including printing and allied markets. Users can search the online databases with varied search criteria allowing for custom searches by product category, geographic area, sales volume, keyword, subject and more. Full Grey House catalog and online ordering also available.

20349 www.iaphc.org
International Assn of Printing House Craftsmen

A voluntary graphic arts organization in which many people share their knowledge and their skill with one another. Open to anyone in any part of the graphic arts community who wish technical information.

20350 www.ipa.org
International Prepress Association

Members produce pre-press material for the graphics industry.

20351 www.magazine.org
Magazine Publishers of America

Promotes magazines as an advertising medium. Provides information services and assistance to members in areas of circulation marketing.

20352 www.napim.org
National Association of Printing Ink Manufacturers

Purpose is to represent the printing ink industry in the U.S.A.

20353 www.napl.org
National Association for Printing Leadership

Promotes the interests in leadership for priniting professionals.

20354 www.npes.org
NPES-Association for Suppliers of Printing &
Publishing Technology

Members are manufacturers and distributors of graphic arts equipment, systems, software and supplies. Promotes marketing, safety and industry standards, international trade and government relations.

20355 www.pbbai.net
Printing Brokerage Buyers Assoc International

Promotes business relationships among brokers, buying groups, manufacturers and related companies. Sets standards and codes and supplies information and referrals.

20356 www.pgca.org
Printing and Graphic Communications Association

Serving the graphic communications community in the Washington, D.C. metropolitan area.

20357 www.pias.org
Printing Industry Association of the South

Represents the print industry.

20358 www.pinc.org
Print Buyers Association

For professionals in print buying.

20359 www.pine.org
Printing Institute of New England

20360 www.polymers.com
Polymers DotCom

20361 www.printing.org
Printing Industries of America (PIA)

The largest graphic arts organization founded over 100 years ago.

20362 www.teched.Vt.edu/gcc
Graphic Comm Central

Web portal for education in the graphic communications industry.

20363 www.waterless.org
Waterless Printing Association

Dedicated to the informational and educational needs of its printer and sponsor members.

Associations

20364 American Society of Health Care Marketing
1 N Franklin Street
Chicago, IL 60606-3421

773-327-1064
Fax: 312-422-4579

20365 Arthur W Page Society
317 Madison Ave
Suite 1607
New York, NY 10017

212-400-7959
Fax: 347-474-7399
Home Page: www.awpagesociety.com
Social Media: Twitter, LinkedIn, YouTube, RSS

Julia Hood, President
Jon Iwata, Chairman
Valerie Di Maria, Secretary
Robert De Fillippo, Treasurer
Nicholas Ashooh, Vice Chair

Professional public relations organization with a single mission, to strengthen the management policy role of the chief public relations officer. Conducts seminars and conferences.
397 Members
Founded in 1983

20366 Association of Women in Communications
3337 Duke Street
Alexandria, VA 22314

703-370-7436
Fax: 703-342-4311
E-Mail: info@womcom.org
Home Page: www.womcom.org
Social Media: Facebook, Twitter, LinkedIn, YouTube, Wordpress

Maria Henneberry, Chair
Sheryl Liddle, Special Projects Coordinator
Billie L. Rodely, Secretary
Aliah Davis-McHenry, Vice Chair
Mitzie Zerr, Treasurer

Professional organization that champions the advancement of women across all communications disciplines by recognizing excellence, promoting leadership and positioning its members at the forefront of the evolving communications era. Hosts a bi-annual conference.
3500 Members
Founded in 1909

20367 Baptist Communicators Association
1519 Menlo Drive
Kennesaw, GA 30152

770-425-3728
E-Mail: office@baptistcommunicators.org
Home Page: www.baptistcommunicators.org
Social Media: Facebook, RSS

Jim Veneman, President
Barbara L Denman, Treasurer
Stella Prather, President-Elect
Terry Barone, Program Chair-Elect
Polly House, Program Chairs

PR and Journalism professionals.
300 Members
Founded in 1953

20368 Business Marketing Association: Atlanta
2801 Buford Highway, Druid Chase
Suite 375
Atlanta, GA 30329

404-641-9417
800-664-4262
Fax: 312-822-0054
E-Mail: info@bmaatlanta.com
Home Page: www.bmaatlanta.com
Social Media: Twitter, LinkedIn, YouTube,RSS

Martine Hunter, President
Rory Carlton, Treasurer
Eduardo Esparza, Marketing
Mark Potter, Membership
Nancy Bistritz, Public Relations

The Atlanta chapter of the BMA includes marketing executives from a variety of industries and backgrounds including research, advertising, promotions, events, Web development, printing and more. The BMA offers an information-packed Website, online skills-building, marketing certification programs, and industry surveys and papers. In addition, members have the opportunity to interact with peers at seminars, participate in chapter training programs and the BMA Annual Conference.
Founded in 1922

20369 Business Marketing Association: Boston
246 Hampshire Street
Cambridge, MA 02130

617-418-4000
800-664-4262
Fax: 312-822-0054
E-Mail: info@thebmaboston.com
Home Page: www.thebmaboston.com/

Michael Lewis, President
Will Robinson, VP Public Relations
Matthew Mamet, VP Internet Marketing
Larry Perreault, VP Finance
Chris Perkett, VP Programming

BMA Boston helps members improve their ability to manage business-to-business marketing and communications for greater productivity and profitability by providing unique access to information, ideas, and the experience of peers. The BMA offers an information-packed Website, online skills-building, marketing certification programs, and industry surveys and papers. In addition, members have the opportunity to interact with peers at seminars, chapter training programs and the BMA Annual Conference.

20370 Communications Roundtable
1250 24th Street NW
Suite 250
Washington, DC 20037

202-755-5180
Fax: 202-466-0544
Home Page: www.roundtable.org

Michael Reichgut, Chairman
Shawn Dolley, CEO

Association of more than 20 public relations, marketing, graphics, advertising, training and other communications organizations with more than 12,000 professional members. The goals include furthering professionalism, cooperation between member organizations, career and employment support, and employer assistance.

20371 Consultants in Public Relations SA
4200 Massachusetts Avenue NW
Washington, DC 20016

202-244-2580
Fax: 202-224-2581
E-Mail: jreed94680@ad.com

John M Reed, Chairman
Founded in 1970

20372 Council of Communications Management
65 Enterprise
Aliso Viejo, CA 92656

866-463-6226
Fax: 303-850-6819
E-Mail: info@thecommunicationexchange.org
Home Page: www.ccmconnection.com

Barry Mike, President
Sherry Scott, Past President
John Jensen, Secretary
Steve Forsyth, Vice President
Leila Bryner, Director-at-Large

Established more than 40 years ago as a forum for seasoned professionals to share best practices in organizational communications.
Founded in 1955

20373 Council of Public Relations Firms
317 Madison Ave
Suite 2320
New York, NY 10017

646-588-0139
Fax: 646-651-4770
E-Mail: info@prfirms.org
Home Page: www.prfirms.org
Social Media: Twitter, YouTube,RSS, Pinterest, Flickr

Kathy Cripps, President
Matt Shaw, Senior Vice President
Matthew Soriano, Manager, Online & Member Services
Kathy Tunheim, Secretary
Dave Senay, Chairman

20374 Institute for Public Relations
University of Florida
PO Box 118400
2096 Weimer Hall
Gainesville, FL 32611-8400

352-392-0280
Fax: 352-846-1122
E-Mail: ace@ifas.ufl.edu
Home Page: www.instituteforpr.org
Social Media: Facebook, Twitter, LinkedIn, YouTube,RSS

Frank Ovaitt, President & CEO
Mike Fernandez, Co-Chairs
David M Albritton, Member
Gary Sheffer, Treasurer
Amy Bimder, Member

Improving the effectiveness of organizations by advancing the professional knowledge and practice of public relations through research and education.
Founded in 1956
Mailing list available for rent

20375 International Association of Business Communicators
601 Montgomery Street
Suite 1900
San Francisco, CA 94111

415-544-4700
800-776-4222
Fax: 415-544-4747
E-Mail: service centre@iabc.com
Home Page: www.iabc.com

Robin R. McCasland, Chair
Russell L. Grossman, Vice Chair
Terry Cerisoles, Finance Director
Tom D. Roux, Trustee
Mari Pavia, Director, HR Aministration

International knowledge network for professionals engaged in strategic business communication management.
13500 Members
Founded in 1970

20376 Original Equipment Suppliers Association
Original Equipment Suppliers Association
1301 W Long Lake Road
Suite 225
Troy, MI 48098

248-952-6401
Fax: 248-952-6404
E-Mail: info@oesa.org
Home Page: www.autopr.org
Social Media: RSS

Margaret Beck, Director
Neil De Koker, President Emeritus
Julie A Fream, President & CEO
Margaret Baxter Baxter, Senior Vice President, Operations
Dave Andrea, Senior Vice President

Provides a forum for information exchange among communication professionals with the automotive industry. Two conferences are held every year, topics are integrated marketing, communications and the automotive industry.
Founded in 1998

Newsletters

20377 Bulldog Reporter
InfoCom Group
5900 Hollis Street
Suite L
Emeryville, CA 94608-2008

510-653-3035
800-959-1059
Fax: 510-596-9331
Home Page: www.infocomgroup.com

James Sinkinson, Publisher
Tim Gray, President

Emphasis on placement opportunities and media profiles, as well as personnel changes at media outlets throughout the US.
Cost: $599.00
Frequency: Fortnightly
Circulation: 5000
Founded in 1980

20378 Contacts: Media Pipeline for PR People
Larimi Communications Association
500 Executive Boulevard
Ossining on Hudson, NY 10562-1114

914-923-9400
Fax: 914-923-9484
E-Mail: info@mercommawards.com
Home Page: www.mercommawards.com/

Michael M Smith, Publisher
Madeleine Gillis, Editor

Provides pipeline of communications between what an editor needs and a public relations person can supply.
Cost: $287.00
1 Pages
Frequency: Weekly
Founded in 1975
Printed in one color

20379 Downtown Promotion Reporter
Alexander Communications Group
1916 Park Ave
Suite 501
New York, NY 10037-3733

212-281-6099
800-232-4317
Fax: 212-283-7269
E-Mail: info@downtowndevelopment.com
Home Page: www.downtowndevelopment.com/

Romauld Alexander, President

Tested ideas for promotion, public relations, marketing, increasing business, participation, downtown image building, sales, and events.
Cost: $189.00
Frequency: Monthly
ISSN: 0363-2830

20380 Healthcare PR & Marketing News
Phillips Business Information
1201 Seven Locks Road
Suite 300
Potomac, MD 20854-2931

301-354-1400
Fax: 301-340-1451

Sharmi Banik, Editor
Kismet Toksu Gould, Publisher

Issues faced by health care executives in PR firms and hospitals. Regular features include industry surveys, case studies and executive profiles.
Cost: $397.00
Frequency: Bi-Monthly
Founded in 1992

20381 High-Tech Hot Sheet
Hot Sheet Publishing
114 Sansome Street
Suite 1224
San Francisco, CA 94104

415-421-6225
Fax: 415-421-6225

Art Gracia, Editor/Publisher

Reporting updates and changes in staff, beat assignments, new publications, suspension of publishing in high-tech media.
Cost: $395.00
Frequency: Monthly
Founded in 1987

20382 Holmes Report
Holmes Group
271 W 47th St
Suite 23A
New York, NY 10036-1447

212-333-2300
Fax: 212-333-2624
E-Mail: gdrury@holmesreport.com
Home Page: www.holmesreport.com

Paul Holmes, President
Greg Drury, Managing Editor
Arun Sudhaman, Managing Editor

Source of information for public relations and corporate communications professionals.
Cost: $290.00
Frequency: Weekly
Circulation: 15,000
ISBN: 0-972364-50-1
Founded in 2001
Printed in 4 colors on glossy stock

20383 Interactive PR & Marketing News
Phillips Publishing
1201 Seven Locks Road
#300
Potomac, MD 20854-2931

301-354-1400
Fax: 301-424-8602
E-Mail: editor@interactivepr.com
Home Page: www.phillips.com

Angela Duff, Publisher

Covers the latest trends and news on the World Wide Web and Internet markets and looks at their users.
Cost: $347.00
Frequency: 23 per year
Circulation: 5M

20384 Interactive Public Relations
Ragan Communications
316 N Michigan Ave
Suite 400
Chicago, IL 60601-3773

312-960-4100
800-493-4867
Fax: 312-960-4106
E-Mail: cservice@ragan.com
Home Page: www.ragan.com

Jim Ylisela, Publisher
Mark ragan, CEO
Kasia Chalko, Marketing Director

Includes targeted newsletters in the areas of employment communication, Web PR, organizational writing and editing, sales and marketing, media relations, motivational management, and investor relations.
Cost: $279.00
Founded in 1970

20385 Jack O'Dwyer's Newsletter
JR O'Dwyer Company
271 Madison Ave
Suite 600
New York, NY 10016-1013

212-683-2750
Fax: 212-683-2750
E-Mail: jack@odwyerpr.com
Home Page: www.odwyerpr.com

Jack O'Dwyer, President
Fay Shapiro, Publisher
Eileen Kelly, Sales Manager
John ODwyer, Advertising Sales Manager

Covers current happenings in both electronic and print media, including new PR products and accounts, PR campaigns, and books about public relations.
Cost: $295.00
Frequency: Weekly
Founded in 1970

20386 Levin's Public Relations Report
Levin Public Relations & Marketing
2 East Ave
Suite 201
Larchmont, NY 10538-2419

914-834-2570
Fax: 914-834-5919
Home Page: www.saralevin.com

Sara B Levin, President
Sylvia Moss, Editor

Strategies, tactics for the CEO, VP Sales and Marketing seeking new marketing/public relations effectiveness.
Cost: $29.00
Frequency: Monthly
Founded in 1984

20387 Media Relations Insider
InfoCom Group
124 Linden Street
Oakland, CA 94607

510-596-9300
800-959-1059
Home Page: www.infocomgroup.com
Social Media: Facebook, Twitter, LinkedIn, RSS

Eastern and Western editions give you media news and exclusive interviews with top business journalists in your region.
Cost: $399.00
Frequency: Monthly
Mailing list available for rent

20388 Media Relations Report
Ragan Communications
316 N Michigan Ave
Suite 400
Chicago, IL 60601-3773

312-960-4100
800-493-4867

Fax: 312-960-4106
E-Mail: cservice@ragan.com
Home Page: www.ragan.com

Jim Ylisela, Publisher
Mark Ragan, CEO
Cost: $28.92
Frequency: Monthly
Circulation: 1000
Founded in 1975
Mailing list available for rent
Printed in 2 colors on matte stock

20389 MediaQuest
MediaQuest Publishing
PO Box 9222
Boston, MA 02114-0996

617-536-5353
Fax: 617-367-9151

Barbara Kalunian, Editor/Publisher

Media placement becomes easier for PR professionals through behind the scenes interviews with leading journalists at top broadcast and print outlets.
Cost: $295.00
Frequency: Bi-Monthly
Founded in 1990

20390 Memo to the President
American Association State Colleges & Universities
1307 New York Ave Nw
Suite 5
Washington, DC 20005-4723

202-293-7070
800-542-2062
Fax: 202-296-5819
E-Mail: chilcotts@aascu.org
Home Page: www.aascu.org

Edward Elnendorf, President
Susan M Chilcott, Editor
Cost: $100.00
6 Pages
Frequency: Monthly
Circulation: 1200
ISSN: 0047-6692
Founded in 1961
Printed in 2 colors on matte stock

20391 O'Dwyers Washington Report
JR O'Dwyer Company
271 Madison Ave
#600
New York, NY 10016-1013

212-683-2750
Fax: 212-683-2750
E-Mail: jack@odwyerpr.com
Home Page: www.odwyerpr.com

Jack O'Dwyer, President
Kevin McCowley, Advertising Sales Manager
John ODwyer, Advertising Sales Manager

Covers Washington public relations and public affairs lobbying news.
Cost: $95.00
8 Pages

20392 Opportunity
Career Skills Press/Brody Communications
815 Greenwood Ave
Suite 8
Jenkintown, PA 19046-2800

215-886-1688
800-726-7936
Fax: 215-886-1699
E-Mail: info@brodypro.com
Home Page: www.brodypro.com

Marjorie Brody, President
Miryam S Raddy, Marketing Manager

Feature products published by Career Skills Press unit.
4 Pages
Frequency: Quarterly
Circulation: 10000
Founded in 1983
Printed in 4 colors on glossy stock

20393 PR Intelligence Report
Lawrence Ragan Communications
316 N Michigan Ave
Suite 400
Chicago, IL 60601-3773

312-960-4100
Fax: 312-960-4106
E-Mail: cservice@ragan.com
Home Page: www.ragan.com

Jim Ylisela, Publisher
Mark Regan, CEO

Digs below the surface to provide the details, insights and information you need to improve your career, make your next campaign a success, or avoid costly mistakes.
Cost: $279.00
8 Pages
Circulation: 1000
Founded in 1970
Printed in 2 colors on matte stock

20394 PR News
Phillips Business Information
4 Choke Cherry Rd
Fl 2
Rockville, MD 20850-4024

301-450-0035
Fax: 301-340-3169
Home Page: www.prandmarketing.com

Matthew Schwartz, Editor
Diane Schwartz, Publisher

Briefing on the latest PR trends, what's working and what's not. We feature case studies of successful PR campaigns.
Cost: $697.00
10 Pages
Frequency: Weekly
Founded in 1944

20395 PR Reporter
Lawrence Ragan Communications
316 N Michigan Ave
Suite 400
Chicago, IL 60601-3773

312-960-4100
800-493-4867
Fax: 312-960-4106
E-Mail: cservice@ragan.com
Home Page: www.ragan.com

Jim Ylisela, Publisher
Mark Ragan, President
Rebecca Anderson, Managing Editor

Weekly publication dedicated to the behavioral aspects of public relations, public affairs and communication strategies. Its quick read format keeps you up to date on the latest theories, research, public opinions, case studies and successful public relations techniques.
Frequency: Weekly
Founded in 1970

20396 PR Tactics
Public Relations Society of America
33 Maiden Ln
Suite 11
New York, NY 10038-5150

212-460-1400
Fax: 212-995-0757
E-Mail: helpdesk@prsa.org
Home Page: www.prsa.org

Catherine Bolton, President
Philip Bonaventura, Chief Financial Officer
Cost: $75.00
32 Pages
Frequency: Monthly
Circulation: 25000
Founded in 1947
Printed in 4 colors on newsprint stock

20397 PR Watch
Center for Media and Democracy
520 University Ave
Suite 227
Madison, WI 53703-4929

608-260-9713
Fax: 608-260-9714
E-Mail: editor@prwatch.org
Home Page: www.prwatch.org

Lisa Graves, Executive Director
Dave Ross, Secretary
Sheldon Rampton, Research Director
Kristian Knutsen, Administrative Assistant

Investigates and exposes how the public relations industry and other professional propagandists manipulate public information, perceptions and opinion on behalf of governments and special interests.
Frequency: Quarterly
Founded in 1993

20398 PR Week
114 W 26th Street
3rd Floor
New York, NY 10001

646-638-6000
Fax: 646-638-6115
E-Mail: letters@prweek.com
Home Page: www.prweek.com

Lisa Kirk, Publishing Director
Julia Hood, Editor-in-Chief

Cutting-edge newsletter of public relations.
Frequency: Weekly

20399 Partyline Publishing
PartyLine Publishing Company
35 Sutton Place
New York, NY 10022-2464

212-755-3487
Fax: 212-755-4859
E-Mail: byermon@ix.netcom.com
Home Page: www.partylinepublishing.com

Morton Yarmon, Editor
Betty Yarmon, Publisher/Editor-in-chief

Weekly media newsletter, delivered by E-mail, that informs their readers of the latest happenings in the media world...new editors, new publications, new networks, new shows on existing networks, new producers, any and all media news.
Cost: $139.50
Frequency: Weekly
Circulation: 1,400
Founded in 1960

20400 Pro Motion
Beyond the Byte
PO Box 388
Fallston, MD 21047

410-877-3524
800-861-1235
Fax: 410-877-7064
Home Page: www.pro-motionsnetwork.com

Emily Laisy, President

News of interest to Media Escort and publicists.
Cost: $12.00
4 Pages
Frequency: Quarterly
Circulation: 325
ISSN: 0886-6104
Founded in 1985
Printed in one color on matte stock

20401 Public Relations Career Opportunities
CEO Update

1575 I Street NW
#1190
Washington, DC 20005-1105

202-408-7900
Fax: 202-408-7907

James Zaniello, Editor

Public relations and publis affairs job opportunities compensating $35,000 plus nationwide.
Cost: $217.00
Frequency: Bi-Monthly
Founded in 1986

20402 Ragan's Interactive Public Relations
Lawrence Ragan Communications
316 N Michigan Ave
Suite 400
Chicago, IL 60601-3773

312-960-4100
800-878-5331
Fax: 312-960-4106
E-Mail: cservice@ragan.com
Home Page: www.ragan.com

Jim Ylisela, Publisher

Dedicated to helping PR people navigate cyberspace.
Cost: $269.00
8 Pages
Frequency: Monthly
Circulation: 800
Founded in 1970
Printed in 2 colors on matte stock

20403 Ragan's Media Relations Report
Lawrence Ragan Communications
316 N Michigan Ave
Chicago, IL 60601-3773

312-960-4100
800-493-4867
Fax: 312-960-4106
E-Mail: cservice@ragan.com
Home Page: www.ragan.com

Jim Ylisela, Publisher
David Murray, Editor
Diane Tillman, Marketing Manager

Content focuses on personal changes, moves and additions in various media, including television, radio and print. Offers tips on angles to take, interviews top journalists on what type of information they prefer, and continuously updates contact numbers and addresses.
Cost: $317.00
Frequency: Monthly
Founded in 1970
Printed in 2 colors on matte stock

20404 West Coast PR Newsletter
West Coast MediaNet
5928 Lindley Avenue
Encino, CA 91316-1047

818-893-3449
Fax: 818-776-1930
Home Page: www.westcoastprjobs.com

Darren Shuster, Publisher
Ken West, Manager

Delivers in-depth inteviews and features, new media contacts and personnel updates, tips from experts in various fields, and listings of new PR markets. Regular coverage includes media web site and book reviews, as well as how-to articles, all with a West Coast angle.
Cost: $75.00
16 Pages
Frequency: 12 issues
Circulation: 1M

Magazines & Journals

20405 ACH Product & Marketing Handbook for Financial Institutions & Companies
NACHA: The Electronic Payments Association
13450 Sunrise Valley Drive
Suite 100
Herndon, VA 20171

703-561-1100
Fax: 703-787-0996
E-Mail: info@nacha.org
Home Page: www.nacha.org

Janet O Estep, CEO
Marcie Haitema, Chairperson

Designed for full financial institutions and companies to assist them in understanding ACH products and services-their benefits, risk management considerations, marketing techniques and FAQs from both corporate and consumer perspectives.
Cost: $70.00
Frequency: Annual+

20406 Communication World
Int'l Association of Business Communicators
601 Montgomery Street
Suite 1900
San Francisco, CA 94111

415-544-4700
Fax: 415-544-4747
E-Mail: cwmagazine@iabc.com
Home Page: www.iabc.com

Natasha Nicholson, Executive Editor
Sue Khodarahmi, Managing Editor
Sue Cavallaro, Production Editor

Covers the latest in communication research, technology and trends through in-depth reports and insightful interviews.
Cost: $150.00
Frequency: Bi-Monthly
Founded in 1970

20407 Currents
Council for Advancement & Support of Education
1307 New York Ave Nw
Suite 1000
Washington, DC 20005-4726
202-393-1301
Fax: 202-387-4973
E-Mail: memberservicecenter@case.org
Home Page: www.case.org

Deborah Bangiorno, Editor
Donald Falkenstein, Vice President of Finance
Will Hayden, Production Coordinator
John Lippincott, President
Marla Misek, Senior Editor

Offers information on campus fund raising, public relations,and alumni administration.
Cost: $115.00
Circulation: 15000
Founded in 1974

20408 International Public Relations Review
18 W Church Street
Saint Frederick, MD 31701
229-567-8074
Fax: 912-845-2991

John Reed, Publisher

Public relations international communications issues for senior level PR professionals.

20409 Jack O'Dwyer's Services Report
JR O'Dwyer Company
271 Madison Ave
Suite 600
New York, NY 10016-1013

212-683-2750
Fax: 212-683-2750
E-Mail: jack@odwyerpr.com
Home Page: www.odwyerpr.com

Jack O'Dwyer, Owner
John ODwyer, Advertising Sales Manager
Eileen Kelly, Sales Manager

Information on film, videotape, database and release distribution industries which serve public relations professionals.
Cost: $45.00
Frequency: Monthly
Circulation: 4500
Founded in 1980

20410 Jack O'Dwyers Washington Report
JR O'Dwyer Company
271 Madison Ave
Suite 600
New York, NY 10016-1013

212-683-2750
Fax: 212-683-2750
E-Mail: jack@odwyerpr.com
Home Page: www.odwyerpr.com

Jack O'Dwyer, Owner
John ODwyer, Advertising Sales Manager
Cost: $60.00
Frequency: Weekly
Founded in 1970

20411 Managing Media Relations in a Crisis
NACHA: The Electronic Payments Association
13450 Sunrise Valley Drive
Suite 100
Herndon, VA 20171

703-561-1100
Fax: 703-787-0996
E-Mail: info@nacha.org
Home Page: www.nacha.org

Janet O Estep, CEO
Marcie B Haitema, Chairperson

This guide is designed to assist your organization to develop, test and execute a crisis communication plan. Understand how to address the issues, know whom to call and in what order to alert them, which vendors you can count on to help, and how to develop a means to track the crisis as it grows or abates.
Cost: $30.00

20412 Public Relations Quarterly
Howard Penn Hudson
44 W Market Street
PO Box 311
Rhinebeck, NY 12572-311

845-876-2081
800-572-3451
Fax: 845-876-2561
Home Page: www.hudsonsdirectory.com

Howard Penn Hudson, Editor/Publisher
Elaine F Newman, Executive Editor
Berecah Sullivan, Circulation Manager
Nichole Latierre, Marketing Manager

Independent public relations magazine, now 48 years old, presenting articles and columns on the theory and process of public relations and communications.
Cost: $65.00
Frequency: Quarterly
ISSN: 0033-3700
Founded in 1955
Printed in on matte stock

20413 Public Relations Review
Elsevier

6277 Seaharbor Drive
Orlando, FL 32887

877-839-7126
Home Page: www.elsevier.com

Jan D Achenbach, Editor-In-Chief
Bill Godfrey, Chief Information Officer
David Clark, Senior Vice President

Covers public relations, education, government, survey research, public policy, history and bibliographies.
Cost: $110.00
Frequency: 12 issues
Circulation: 1M
ISSN: 0363-0111

20414 Public Relations Strategist
Public Relations Society of America
33 Maiden Ln
Suite 11
New York, NY 10038-5150

212-460-1400
Fax: 212-995-0757
E-Mail: william.murray@prsa.org
Home Page: www.prsa.org

Gary McCormick, Chairman/CEO
William Murray, President & COO
Philip Bonaventura, CFO
Jeneen Garcia, Vice President

With emphasis on the issues and trends affecting public relations management, it examines the changing concepts and challenges current practices with relevant, original and thought-provoking articles.
Cost: $100.00
Frequency: 4 issues per ye
Circulation: 20538
Founded in 1947

20415 Public Relations Tactics
Public Relations Society of America
33 Maiden Ln
Suite 11
New York, NY 10038-5150

212-460-1400
Fax: 212-995-0757
E-Mail: helpdesk@prsa.org
Home Page: www.prsa.org

Gary McCormick, Chairman/CEO
Gale Spreter, Marketing Manager
Alison Stateman, Managing Editor
Catherine A Bolton, Executive Director
Philip Bonaventura, Chief Financial Officer

News, trends and how-to information for public relations people.
Cost: $75.00
Frequency: Monthly
Circulation: 20538
Founded in 1947

20416 Reputation Management
Editorial Media & Marketing International
708 3rd Avenue
Frnt 2
New York, NY 10017-4201

212-687-5260
E-Mail: kingraham@prcentral.com
Home Page: www.prcentral.com

Kara T Ingraham, Publisher/COO

Editorial focuses on finance, marketing, human resources, government and society. Highlights domestic and international corporate news presenting observations and perspectives vital to the industry.
Cost: $52.00
Frequency: Bi-Monthly
Circulation: 12M
Founded in 1995

Trade Shows

20417 American Society of Health Care Marketing and Public Relations Trade Show
1 N Franklin Street
31st Floor
Chicago, IL 60606-3421

773-327-1064
Fax: 312-422-4579

Lauren Barnett, Executive Director

Sixty booths of communications, printing, computer equipment, public relations and fund raising consultants in the health care profession.
600 Attendees
Frequency: September

20418 Arthur W Page Society
Arthur W Page Society
317 Madison Ave
Suite 1607
New York, NY 10017-5201
212-400-7959
Fax: 347-474-7399
Home Page: www.awpagesociety.com
Social Media: Facebook, Twitter, YouTube,RSS

Roger Bolton, President
Gary Shepper, Chairman
Valerie Di Maria, Secretary
Frequency: Annual/September
Founded in 1986

20419 National Hispanic Market Trade Show and Media Expo (Se Habla Espanol)
Hispanic Business Inc
5385 Hollister Avenue
Suite 204
Santa Barbara, CA 93111

800-806-4268
Fax: 805-964-5539
E-Mail: info@hispanstar.com
Home Page: www.hispanstar.com
Social Media: Facebook, Twitter, LinkedIn

John Pasini, Cfo/Coo

Annual show of 100 exhibitors of market/research, media, advertising, public relations, information services and recruitment.
1500 Attendees

20420 National School for Public Relations
15948 Derwood Rd
Rockville, MD 20855

301-519-0496
Fax: 301-519-0494
E-Mail: info@nspra.org
Home Page: www.nspra.org

Mildred Wainger, Administration Services

Offers information and news for professionals in the field of public relations.
600 Attendees
Frequency: July

20421 Strategic Media Relations Conference
Ragan Communications
316 N Michigan Avenue
Chicago, IL 60601

312-960-4100
800-878-5331
Fax: 312-960-4106
E-Mail: cservice@ragan.com
Home Page: www.raganinstitute.com

Showcase of best practices for winning top media coverage in a new era. Learn how peers have garnered more ink, managed crises, built their brands and gone global. Attend pre- and post-conference sessions that provide career-boosting skills in crisis survival, media training, online media relations, PR writing, persuasive communications, PR management, digital PR and pitching stories.
Frequency: March

Directories & Databases

20422 Adweek Directory
Prometheus Global Media
770 Broadway
New York, NY 10003-9595

212-493-4100
Fax: 646-654-5368
Home Page: www.prometheusgm.com

Richard D. Beckman, CEO
James A. Finkelstein, Chairman
Madeline Krakowsky, Vice President Circulation
Tracy Brater, Executive Director Creative Service

Adweek Directories Online is where you will find searchable databases with comprehensive information on ad agencies, brand marketers and multicultural media.
Frequency: Annual
Circulation: 800
Founded in 1981

20423 Bacon's Newspaper & Magazine Directories
Cision U.S., Inc.
322 South Michigan Avenue
Suite 900
Chicago, IL 60604

312-263-0070
866-639-5087
E-Mail: info.us@cision.com
Home Page: us.cision.com

Joe Bernardo, President & CEO
Heidi Sullivan, VP & Publisher
Valerie Lopez, Research Director
Jessica White, Research Director
Rachel Farrell, Research Manager

Two volume set listing all daily and community newspapers, magazines and newsletters, news service and syndicates, syndicated columnists, complete editorial staff listings of each publication provided, covers U.S., Canada, Mexico, and Carribean.
Cost: $350.00
4,700 Pages
Frequency: Annual
ISSN: 1088-9639
Founded in 1951
Printed in one color on matte stock

20424 Bacon's Radio/TV/Cable Directory
Cision U.S., Inc.
332 South Michigan Avenue
Suite 900
Chicago, IL 60604

312-263-0070
866-639-5087
E-Mail: info.us@cision.com
Home Page: www.us.cision.com

Joe Bernardo, President & CEO
Heidi Sullivan, VP & Publisher
Valerie Lopez, Research Director
Jessica White, Research Director
Rachel Farrell, Research Manager

Includes comprehensive coverage for contact and programming information for more than 3,500 televsion networks, cable networks, television syndicators, television stations, and cable systems in the United States and Canada.
Cost: $350.00
Frequency: Annual
ISSN: 1088-9639
Printed in one color on matte stock

20425 **Burrelle's Media Directory**
BurrellesLuce
75 E Northfield Rd
Livingston, NJ 07039-4532
973-992-6600
800-631-1160
Fax: 973-992-7675
E-Mail: inquiry@burrellesluce.com
Home Page: www.burrellesluce.com
Social Media: Facebook, Twitter, LinkedIn, RSS
Robert C Waggoner, CEO
Approximately 60,000 media listings in North America. Listings cover newspapers, magazines (trades and consumer), broadcast, and internet outlets.
Cost: $795.00
Frequency: Annual

20426 **Corporate Yellow Book**
Leadership Directories
104 5th Ave
New York, NY 10011-6901
212-627-4140
Fax: 212-645-0931
E-Mail: corporate@leadershipdirectories.com
Home Page: www.leadershipdirectories.com
David Hurvitz, CEO
Contact information for over 48,000 executives at over 1,000 companies and more than 9,000 board members and their outside affiliations.
Cost: $360.00
1,400 Pages
Frequency: Quarterly
ISSN: 1058-2098
Founded in 1986

20427 **Leadership Library in Print**
Leadership Directories
104 5th Ave
New York, NY 10011-6901
212-627-4140
Fax: 212-645-0931
E-Mail: info@leadershipdirectories.com
Home Page: www.leadershipdirectories.com
David Hurvitz, CEO
Complete set of all 14 leadership directories. Provides subscribers with complete contact information for the 400,000 individuals who constitute the institutional leadership of the US.
Cost: $2300.00
Frequency: Semiannually
Founded in 1996

20428 **O'Dwyer's Directory of Corporate Communications**
JR O'Dwyer Company
271 Madison Ave
Suite 600
New York, NY 10016-1013
212-683-2750
Fax: 212-683-2750
E-Mail: jack@odwyerpr.com
Home Page: www.odwyerpr.com
Jack O'Dwyer, Owner
John ODwyer, Advertising Sales Manager
Public relations departments are profiled that represent the United States companies that are listed on the New York Stock Exchange.
Cost: $110.00
400 Pages
Frequency: Annual

20429 **PR News**
Phillips Business Information
7811 Montrose Road
Potomac, MD 20854
301-340-2100
E-Mail: feedback@healthydirections.com
Home Page: www.healthydirections.com
This database offers information on public relations issues.
Cost: $597.00
Frequency: 48 issues

20430 **PR Newswire**
150 E 58th Street
31st Floor
New York, NY 10155-0002
212-355-0090
Fax: 212-832-9406
This comprehensive database offers current news, financial news, earnings statements, mergers, acquisitions, proxy contests and general features pertaining to the public relations industry.
Frequency: Directory

20431 **Public Relations Tactics**
Public Relations Society of America
33 Maiden Ln
New York, NY 10038-5150
212-460-1400
Fax: 212-995-0757
E-Mail: william.murray@prsa.org
Home Page: www.prsa.org
Catherine Bolton, Manager
List of products and services used by public relations professionals worldwide.
Frequency: Annual June

20432 **Public Relations Tactics: Register Issue/The Blue Book**
Public Relations Society of America
33 Maiden Ln
New York, NY 10038-5150
212-460-1400
Fax: 212-995-0757
E-Mail: william.murray@prsa.org
Home Page: www.prsa.org
Catherine Bolton, Manager
About 17,000 public relations practitioners in business government education etc., who are members.
Cost: $100.00
Frequency: Annual July

20433 **Publicity at Your Finger Tips**
Federal Systems
PO Box 298-L
Oliver Springs, TN 37840-0298
865-483-3579
Offers a comprehensive list of magazines, newspapers and other publications in the United States that provide publicity for businesses, churches and charitable organizations.
Cost: $24.95

20434 **Staffing Industry Supplier Directory and Buyers Guide**
Staffing Industry Analysts
881 Fremont Ave
Suite A3
Los Altos, CA 94024-5637
650-948-9303
800-950-9496
Fax: 650-232-2360
Home Page: www.sireport.com
Ron Mester, Manager
Complete listing of suppliers and products for temporary help, placement and recruiting firms in the staffing industry.
Cost: $89.50
295 Pages
Frequency: Annual
ISBN: 1-883814-11-1

Industry Web Sites

20435 **http://gold.greyhouse.com**
G.O.L.D Grey House OnLine Databases
Grey House Pubishing's online database platform, GOLD, offers Quick Search, Keyword Search and Expert Search for most business sectors including public relations and media markets. The GOLD platform makes finding the information you need quick and easy - whether you're a novice searcher or an experienced database user. All of Grey House's directory products are available for subscription on the GOLD platform.

20436 **www.absolutelypr.com**
Absolutely Public Relations
Results-driven media relations - local, trade, national.

20437 **www.achieva.info**
ACHIEVA

20438 **www.aem.org**
Construction Equipment Advertisers and Public
Relations Council
A council of AEM that works to promote marketing, sales and advertising of construction equipment.

20439 **www.afgcan.org**
AFHCAN Project

20440 **www.aprc-online.org**
Automotive Public Relations Council
Provides a forum for information exchange among communication professionals with the automotive industry.

20441 **www.bloomgross.com**
Bloom Gross & Associates
Executive recruitment firm with corporate communications, public relations, marketing/branding/market research, and direct marketing/sales promotion practice areas.

20442 **www.case.org**
Council for the Advancement and Support of Ed.
Offers information on campus fund raising, public relations and alumni administration.

20443 **www.cof.org**
Council on Foundations
Non profit trade association for foundations

20444 **www.greyhouse.com**
Grey House Publishing
Authoritative reference directories for most business sectors including public relations and media markets. Users can search the online databases with varied search criteria allowing for custom searches by product category, geographic area, sales volume, keyword, subject and more. Full Grey House catalog and online ordering also available.

20445 www.iabc.com
International Association of Business Communicators

An international association for members who are professionals in organizational communications and public relations. Accepts advertising.

20446 www.instituteforpr.com
Institute for Public Relations
To improve the effectiveness of organizations by advancing the professional knowledge and practice of public relations through research and education.

20447 www.kscpublivrelations.com
KSC Public Relations
Full-service advertising, public relations and marketing firm serving real estate developers, health care automotive, and manufacturers.

20448 www.magnetcom.com
Magnet - Communications
Public relations firm.

20449 www.mediaaccessgroup.com
Media Access Group

20450 www.multicultural.com
Multicultural Marketing Resources Asian American
Advertising Federation

A public relations/marketing firm where corporate executives will find diverse resources, experts and information on how to market to multicultural (ethnic and niche) consumer markets.

20451 www.niri.org
National Investor Relations Institute
Professional association of corporate officers and investors relations consultants.

20452 www.petersgrouppr.com
PetersGroup Public Relations
Provides a full range of marketing and public relations programs to national and international businesses. The agency works closely with technology clients ranging from Funded start-ups to Fortune 500 companies, to integrate the right mix of research, strategy, positioning and media to help customers meet their ongoing business and communication goals.

20453 www.pinnacleww.com
Pinnacle Worldwide
For independent public relations firms in major markets around the globe.

20454 www.progressivepr.com
PPR Communications

20455 www.prpublishing.com
Public Relations Publishing Company
Case studies, research and trends in public relations and information on issues of importance to PR professionals.

20456 www.prsa.org
Public Relations Society of America
A major professional association of public relations practitioners.

20457 www.prweek.com
PR Week

20458 www.silveranvil.org
Silver Anvil Resource Center
Online database of public relations campaigns.

20459 www.washingtonpost.com
Washington Post

20460 www.wepr.org
Women Executives in Public Relations
Provides a support network for women in public relations. Offers grants and scholarships for courses in public relations and for college students studying communications.

Associations

20461 Alliance for Audited Media
48 W Seegers Road
Arlington Heights, IL 60005-3913

224-366-6939
Fax: 224-366-6949
E-Mail: service@accessabc.com
Home Page: www.accessabc.com
Social Media: Facebook, Twitter, LinkedIn, YouTube

Sunni Boot, Chairman
Scott Kruse, Vice Chair
Michael Lavery, President/Managing Director
Rob Fisher, Secretary
Scott H Heekin, Treasurer

The world's largest circulation-auditing organization, ABC provides circulation data on 1,400+ newspapers and more than 1,100 periodicals to ABC-member publications, advertisers and advertising agencies.
4.1M+ Members
Founded in 1914

20462 Alliance of Area Business Publications
Ste 330
1970 E Grand Ave
El Segundo, CA 90245

310-364-0193
Fax: 310-364-0196
E-Mail: info@bizpubs.org
Home Page: www.bizpubs.org

C James Dowden, Executive Director
Shelly Elmore, President
David Snyder, Vice President
Jeff Nuttall, Secretary-Treasurer
Ben Kinney, Director

Represents metropolitan area and state wide business to business publications with conventions, newsletters, and other services.
80 Members
Founded in 1979

20463 American Black Book Writers' Association
269 S Beverly Drive Street 2600
Beverly Hills, CA 90212

310-306-4042

Will Gibson, President

Members include all African Americans who are involved with any aspects of the publishing industry.
4M Members

20464 American Book Producers Association
151 W 19th Street
3rd Floor
New York, NY 10011

917-741-1919
800-209-4575
Fax: 212-675-1364
E-Mail: office@abpaonline.org
Home Page: www.abpaonline.org
Social Media: Facebook

Richard Rothschild, President
David Katz, Manager
Nancy Hall, Vice President
Valerie Tomaselli, Treasurer
Kristen Hall, ABPA Administrator

Increases the book industry's awareness of members capabilities and exchanges information on improving business. Develops concepts for books and other publications.
Founded in 1980

20465 American Booksellers Association
333 Westchester Avenue
Suite S202
White Plains, NY 10604
914-406-7500
800-637-0037
Fax: 914-417-4013
E-Mail: info@bookweb.org
Home Page: www.bookweb.org
Social Media: Facebook, Twitter, YouTube

Oren Teicher, CEO
Dan Cullen, Content Officer
Eleanor Chang, CFO
Greg Galloway, Marketing Manager & designer
Matt Supko, Technology Director

Trade organization pledge to protecting the well-being of book retailers and promoting the availability of books.
2000 Members
Founded in 1900

20466 American Library Association
50 E Huron St
Chicago, IL 60611

312-944-6780
800-545-2433
Fax: 312-440-9374
E-Mail: ala@ala.org
Home Page: www.ala.org
Social Media: Facebook, Twitter, LinkedIn, Stumbleupon,friendfeed,reddit

Claire Knowles, Manager
Keith Michael Fiels, Executive Director
Barbara Stripling, President
Mario Gonzalez, Treasurer
Robert E. Banks, COO

To provide leadership for the development, promotion, and improvement of library and information services and the profession of librarianship in order to enhance learning and ensure access to information for all.
65000 Members
Founded in 1876

20467 American Society of Journalists & Authors
1501 Broadway
Suite 403
New York, NY 10036

212-997-0947
Fax: 212-937-2315
E-Mail: staff@asja.org
Home Page: www.asja.org
Social Media: Facebook, Twitter, LinkedIn, Google+

Alexandra Canto Owens, Executive Director
Neil O'Hara, Treasurer
Minda Zetlin, President
Randy Dotinga, Vice-President
Sandra Lamb, Secretary
Founded in 1948

20468 Antiquarian Booksellers Association of America
20 W 44th St
Suite 507
New York, NY 10036

212-944-8291
Fax: 212-944-8293
E-Mail: hq@abaa.org
Home Page: www.abaa.org
Social Media: Facebook, Twitter, RSS

Susan Benne, Executive Director
John Thomson, President
Thomas Goldwasser, Vice-President/ Secretary
Sam Hessel, Treasurer

A trade association of rare book dealers.
480 Members
Founded in 1949

20469 Arizona Book Publishing Association
6340 South Rural Road
#118-152
Tempe, AZ 85283

602-274-6264
E-Mail: info@azbookpub.com
Home Page: www.azbookpub.com

Sam Henrie, President
Mike Wentz, Managing Editor

20470 Associated Church Press
924 Woodcrest Way
Oviedo, FL 32762

407-341-6615
Fax: 407-386-3236
E-Mail: acpoffice@earthlink.net
Home Page: www.associatedchurchpress.org
Social Media: Facebook, Twitter, RSS

Mary Lynn Hendrickson, Executive Director

Aims to share ideas and concerns in religious publishing and to stimulate higher standards of religious journalism to exert a more positive influence.
240 Members
Founded in 1916

20471 Association for Information and Image Management
1100 Wayne Avenue
Suite 1100
Silver Spring, MD 20910

301-587-8202
800-477-2446
Fax: 301-587-2711
E-Mail: aiim@aiim.org
Home Page: www.aiim.org
Social Media: Facebook, Twitter, LinkedIn, RSS,YouTube

John Newton, Chairman
Timothy Elmore, Vice Chair
John Chickering, Immediate Past Chair
Martyn Christian, Executive Committee Member at Large
Paul Engel, Treasurer

Members are users and manufacturers of equipment and supplies of the information and image industry.
10M Members
Founded in 1943

20472 Association of American Publishers (AAP)
455 Massachusetts Avenue NW
Suite 700
Washington, DC 20001-2777

202-347-3375
Fax: 202-347-3690
E-Mail: info@publishers.org
Home Page: www.publishers.org
Social Media: Twitter, RSS

Tom Allen, President & CEO
Tina Jordan, Vice President
Allan R Adler, General Counsel
Jay Diskey, Executive Director, PreK-12
Gail Kump, Director, Membership Marketing

AAP is the trade association for the US book publishers, providing advocacy and communications on behalf of the industry. AAP represents the industry's priorities on policy, legislative and regulatory issues regionally, nationally and worldwide. These include protection of intellectual property rights and worldwide copyright enforcement, digital and new technology issues, funding for education and libraries, tax and trade, censorship and literacy.
300 Members

20473 Association of American University Presses
28 West 36th Street
Suite 602
New York, NY 10018
212-989-1010
Fax: 212-989-0975
E-Mail: info@aaupnet.org
Home Page: www.aaupnet.org
Social Media: Facebook, Twitter, RSS
Peter Givler, Executive Director
Anna Weidman, Assistant Director
Philip Cercone, President
Erik Smist, Treasurer
Mike Bieker, Treasurer Elect
Members are university presses and a limited number of presses of non-degree-granting scholarly institutions.
125 Members
Founded in 1937
Mailing list available for rent: 2.2M names

20474 Association of Directory Publishers
116 Cass Street
PO Box 1929
Traverse City, MI 49684
800-267-9002
Fax: 231-486-2182
E-Mail: hq@adp.org
Home Page: www.adp.org
Social Media: Facebook, Twitter, LinkedIn, YouTube
Laura Hill, Chairman
Todd McKnight, First Vice Chairman
Jim Hail, Treasurer
Danny Bills, Secretary
Cindi A. Aldrich, President/CEO
The association is the communication link to the Telephone Directory industry. It provides a forum for the exchange of ideas and information among publishers of telephone, city and special interest directories and provides continuous training to assist in the enhancement of the publisher's operation.
240 Members
Founded in 1898

20475 Association of Free Community Papers
7445 Morgan Rd
Suite 203
Liverpool, NY 13090
877-203-2327
Fax: 781-459-7770
E-Mail: afcp@afcp.org
Home Page: www.afcp.org
Social Media: Facebook, Twitter, LinkedIn, YouTube
Loren Colburn, Executive Director
Carol Toomey, President
Karen Sawicz, Secretary / Treasurer
Greg Birkett, 1st Vice President
Cassey Recore, Administrative Assistant
Offers national classified advertising placement services; conducts charitable programs, sponsors competition, compiles statistics.
250 Members
Founded in 1951

20476 Author's Coalition of America
280 Moross Road
Grosse Pointe Farms, MI 48236
313-884-6026
Fax: 313-882-3047
E-Mail: asst.admin@authorscoalition.org
Home Page: www.authorscoalition.org
Dorien Kelly, Assistant Administrator
An organization of U.S. based authors and creators united to receive and distribute non-title specific reprographic royalties to member organizations, assist in further development of collective licensing programs and act for the general benefit of authors. The ACA is an association of twenty independent authors' organizations representing text writers, songwriters, visual artists, illustrators and photographers.
20 Members
Founded in 1994

20477 Book Industry Study Group (BISG)
145 W. 45th Street
Suite 601
New York, NY 10036
646-336-7141
Fax: 646-336-6214
E-Mail: info@bisg.org
Home Page: www.bisg.org
Social Media: Twitter, RSS
Len Vlahos, Executive Director
Julie Morris, Project Manager, Standards
Thomson Guster, Coordinator, Education & Events
Nadine Vassallo, Project Manager, Research
Jeanette Zwart, Marketing Strategist
BISG is the leading US book trade association for standardized best practices, research and education.
170 Members
Founded in 1976

20478 Book Manufacturers' Institute
2 Armand Beach Drive
Suite 1B
Palm Coast, FL 32137-2612
386-986-4552
Fax: 386-986-4553
E-Mail: info@bmibook.com
Home Page: www.bmibook.org
Daniel N Bach, Executive VP
Kent H Larson, Vice President/ President- Elect
Jac B Garner, President
Paul Genovese, Treasurer
Daniel N Bach, Executive Vice President
Since 1933, the Book Manufacturers' Institute, Inc (BMI) has been the leading nationally recognized trade association of the book manufacturing industry. BMI member companies annually produce the great majority of books ordered by the U.S. book publishing industry. Today, BMI is a vital part of the industry, playing a leading role by providing an intra-industry communications link among book manufacturers, publishers, suppliers and governmental bodies.
94 Members
Founded in 1933

20479 Guild of Book Workers
521 5th Avenue
New York, NY 10175-0038
212-285-5581
E-Mail: secretary@guildofbookworkers.org
Home Page: www.guildofbookworkers.org
Chela Metzger, Membership
Mark Andersson, President
Bexx Caswell, Vice President
Catherine Burkhard, Secretary
Alicia Bailey, Treasurer
To broaden public awareness of the hand book arts, to stimulate commissions of fine bindings, and to stress the need for sound book conservation and restoration.
900+ Members
Founded in 1906

20480 Impact Publishers, Inc.
Impact Publishers
PO Box 6016
Atascadero, CA 93423-6016
805-466-5917
80-2-6 72
Home Page: www.impactpublishers.com
Social Media: Facebook, Twitter, Pinterest
Offers the finest in practical, reader-friendly help on a wide variety of personal interpersonal matters: relationships, divorce recovery, parenting, stress, personal growth, and mental health.
Founded in 1970

20481 Independent Book Publishers Association
1020 Manhattan Beach Blvd
Suite 204
Manhattan Beach, CA 90266
310-546-1818
Fax: 310-546-3939
E-Mail: info@ibpa-online.org
Home Page: www.ibpa-online.org
Social Media: Facebook, Twitter, LinkedIn, Flickr, RSS
Angela Bole, Executive Director
Rana DiOrio, Secretary
Florrie Binford-Kichler, President
Roy M Carlisle, Treasurer
Deltina Hay, Chair
Provides cooperative marketing programs, education and advocacy within the publishing industry.
4000+ Members
Founded in 1983

20482 Independent Free Papers of America
107 Hemlock Drive
Rio Grande, NJ 08242
937-473-2028
800-441-4372
Home Page: www.ifpa.com
Deborah Phillips, President
Barbara Perry, VP
Katie Thomas, Sergeant-at-arms
Gary Rudy, Executive Director
Bob Cole, Treasurer
Bestows awards and compiles statistics.
300 Members
Founded in 1980

20483 International Digital Enterprise Alliance
1600 Duke Street
Suite 420
Alexandria, VA 22314
703-837-1070
Fax: 703-837-1072
E-Mail: info@idealliance.org
Home Page: www.idealliance.org
David Steinhardt, CEO
Frank Balser, Managing Director
Chip Harding, Chairman
Laura C Reid, Vice-Chairman
Aaron Holm, Treasurer
Founded as The Graphic Communications Association , was formed to help member companies apply the latest computer-related technologies to all forms of print and electronic publishing
Founded in 1966

20484 Jenkins Independent Publishers
Jenkins Group
1129 Woodmere Ave.
Suite B
Traverse City, MI 49686
231-330-0445
800-706-4636

Fax: 231-933-0448
Home Page: www.bookpublishing.com

Jerrold R. Jenkins, Chairman And CEO

Provides comprehensive marketing and custom book publishing services for independent and small press book publishers.
160 Members
Founded in 1996

20485 Magazine Publishers of America
810 7th Ave
24th Floor
New York, NY 10019

212-872-3700
Fax: 212-888-4217
E-Mail: mpa@magazine.org
Home Page: www.magazine.org
Social Media: Facebook, Twitter, LinkedIn, YouTube,Pinterest

Mary Berner, President and CEO
Shoshana Shapiro, Executive Assistant
Michael A. Clinton, Chairman
Thomas Harty, Treasurer
Declan Moore, Secretary

Promotes magazines as an advertising medium. Provides information services and assistance to members in areas of circulation marketing.
240 Members
Founded in 1919

20486 National Association of Desktop Publishers
462 Old Boston Road
Topsfield, MA 01983-1232

978-876-6855
800-874-4113
E-Mail: nadtp@aol.com

Barry Harrigan, Owner

Trade organization which serves the desk top publishing industry and offers information resources.
5M Members
Founded in 1987

20487 National Association of Hispanic Publications
National Press Building
529 14th Street NW
Suite 1126
Washington, DC 20045

202-662-7250
Fax: 703-610-9005
E-Mail: directory@nahp.org
Home Page: www.nahp.org

Clara Escobedo, President
Martha Montoya, Vice President, Membership
Christina Monte Scott, Treasurer
Norma Condreay, Secretary
Jesus Cobian, Membership Chair

Promotes the Hispanic print media as a valuable means of communication. Works to ensure that member publications are listed in National Media Directories.
200 Members
Founded in 1982

20488 National Association of Independent
PO Box 430
Highland City, FL 33846-0430

863-648-4420
E-Mail: naip@aol.com
Home Page: www.publishersreport.com

Betty A Lampe, Executive Director

Assists and educates small publishing companies. Conducts seminars on marketing strategies, target audience, and techniques of book distribution. Especially helpful for the beginning or self-publisher.
500 Members
Founded in 1979

20489 National Association of Publishers' Representatives
25224 Brucefield Road
Cleveland, OH 44122

866-288-0354
Fax: 847-885-8393
E-Mail: bsgrep@aol.com
Home Page: www.naprassoc.com/

Raymond Coppola, President
Everett Knapp III, Executive Director

Provides information for publishers' representatives selling advertising space.
250 Members
Founded in 1950

20490 National Music Publishers Association
975 F Street, NW
Suite 375
Washington, DC 20004

202-393-NMPA
Fax: 202-393-6673
E-Mail: admin@mpa.org
Home Page: www.nmpa.org

David Israelite, President/CEO
Bryan Bradley, Vice President
Todd Vunderink, Secretary
Bryndon Bay, Treasurer
Williard Ahdritz, Board Member

An advocate for the protection of music copyrights.
800 Members
Founded in 1919

20491 National Newspaper Association
PO Box 7540
Columbia, MO 65205-7540

573-777-4980
800-829-4662
Fax: 703-237-9808
E-Mail: briansteffens@nna.org
Home Page: www.nna.org
Social Media: Facebook, Twitter, RSS Feeds

Brian Steffens, Executive Director
Lynn Edinger, Associate Director
Robert M. Williams Jr, President
Chip Hutcheson, Treasurer
John Edgecombe Jr, Vice President

Industry trade newspaper. Accepts advertising.
2000 Members
Founded in 1885

20492 National Paper Trade Association
330 North Wabash Avenue
Suite 2000
Chicago, IL 60611

312-321-4092
800-355-6782
Fax: 312-673-6736
E-Mail: gerri@goNPTA.com
Home Page: www.gonpta.com
Social Media: LinkedIn, YouTube

William Frohlich, President
Jack Vaccaro, VP
Donald C. Clampitt, Chairman
Hilton Maze, Treasurer, 2nd VP
Kevin Gammonley, CEO

An Association for the paper, packaging, and supplies distribution industry.
2000 Members
Founded in 1903

20493 Newspaper Association of America
4401 Wilson Blvd
Suite 900
Arlington, VA 22203

571-366-1000
Fax: 571-366-1195
E-Mail: joan.mills@naa.org
Home Page: www.naa.org
Social Media: Facebook, Twitter, LinkedIn, YouTube,RSS, Google+

James M. Moroney III, Past Chairman
Robert J. Dickey, Vice Chairman
Donna Barrett, Secretary
Robert M Nutting, Chairman
Stephen P. Hills, Treasurer

Founded by the merger of seven associations serving the newspaper industry. Focuses on the major issues that affect today's newspaper industry public policy and legal matters, advertising revenue growth and audience development across the medium's broad portfolio of products and digital platforms.
2000 Members
Founded in 1992

20494 Online Publishers Association (OPA)
1350 Broadway
Suite 606
New York, NY 10018

646-473-1000
Fax: 646-473-0200
E-Mail: info@online-publishers.org
Home Page: www.online-publishers.org
Social Media: Twitter

John Kosner, Chairman
Fran Hauser, Vice Chairman
Drew Schutte, Treasurer
Jim Spanfeller, OPA Secretary
Pam Horan, President

The Online Publishers Association (OPA) is a not-for-profit trade organization dedicated to representing high-quality online content providers before the advertising community, the press, the government and the public.
Founded in 2001

20495 PSP American Medical Publishers Committee
Association of America Publishers, Inc
71 Fifth Avenue
2nd Floor
New York, NY 10003-3004

212-255-0200
Fax: 212-255-7007
E-Mail: jtagler@publishers.org
Home Page: www.PSPcentral.org

Maureen DeRosa, Co-Chair
Thane Kerner, Co-Chair
Sara Pinto, Director
John Tagler, VP & Executive director
Kate Kolendo, Project Manager

The primary goals of the PSP/AMPC are to educate, advocate, engage in outreach and philanthropy and frame issues of relevance to medical publishers, including promoting a positive image of scientific and medical publishing.
300 Members
Founded in 1960

20496 Society for Collegiate Journalists
1584 Wesleyan Drive
Virginia Inesleyan College
Norfolk, VA 23502-5599

757-455-3419
Fax: 757-461-5025
E-Mail: wjruehlmann@vwc.edu
Home Page: www.scj.us
Social Media: Facebook

Mary Beth Earnheardt, Executive Director
Frank Barnas, President
Vivian Wagner, Second VP
Martha Collins, Third V.P
Rick Stewart, First Vice President

A collegiate journalism organization.
1200 Members
Founded in 1975

20497 Society for Scholarly Publishing
10200 W 44th Ave
Suite 304
Wheat Ridge, CO 80033

303-422-3914
Fax: 303-422-8894
E-Mail: info@sspnet.org
Home Page: www.sspnet.org
Social Media: Facebook, Twitter, LinkedIn, RSS

Carol Anne Meyer, Past President
Jerry Bowman, Executive Director
Kent Anderson, President
Todd A Carpenter, Secretary/Treasurer
Howard Ratner, President-Elect

A group that represents scholarly publications, such as journals, university publications and magazines.
800 Members
Founded in 1978

20498 Society of National Association Publications
12100 Sunset Hills Road
Suite 130
Reston, VA 20190

703-234-4063
Fax: 703-435-4390
E-Mail: info@associationmediaandpublishing.com
Home Page: www.snaponline.org
Social Media: Facebook, Twitter, LinkedIn, Flickr

Sarah Patterson, Executive Director
Larry Price, Vice President, Treasurer
Carla Kalogeridis, Editorial Director
Liz Jones, Coordinator, Marketing
Kathryn Kovacs, Membership Coordinator

Develops standards for editorial and advertising content of association and professional society magazines.
1045 Members
Founded in 1963

20499 Software & Information Industry Association
1090 Vermont Ave NW
6th Floor
Washington, DC 20005-4905
202-289-7442
Fax: 202-289-7097
E-Mail: privacy@siia.net
Home Page: www.siia.net
Social Media: Facebook, Twitter, LinkedIn

Ken Wasch, President
Robert Merry, Chairman

Members are microcomputer software firms. Services include data collection program, software protection, contracts reference disk, conferences and lobbying.
1200 Members
Founded in 1984

20500 Special Libraries Association
331 S Patrick St
Alexandria, VA 22314-3501

703-647-4900
Fax: 703-647-4901
E-Mail. sla@sla.org
Home Page: www.sla.org
Social Media: Facebook, Twitter, LinkedIn, Youtube, RSS

Kate Arnold, President-Elect
Deb Hunt, President
John DiGilio, Treasurer
Linda Broussard, Chief Financial Officer
Janice R. Lachance, Chief Executive Officer

International association of information professionals who work in special libraries serving business, research, government and institutions that produce specialized information.
13M Members
Founded in 1856

20501 Specialized Information Publishers Association
1090 Vermont Ave NW
Sixth Floor
Washington, DC 20005-4095

202-289-7442
800-356-9302
Fax: 202-289-7097
Home Page: www.sipaonline.com
Social Media: Facebook, Twitter, LinkedIn, Digg, Google+

Henry Greene, Executive Director
Ken Wasch, President
Keith Kupferschmid, General Counsel and SVP
Tom Davin, Senior Vice President
Tom Meldrum, Vice President, Finance

International trade association serving the interests of publishers of newsletters and specialized information services.
450 Members
Founded in 1977
Mailing list available for rental $65 per M

20502 The Association of Publishers for Special Sales
PO Box 9725
Colorado Springs, CO 80932-0725

719-924-5534
Fax: 719-213-2602
E-Mail: kaye@bookpass.org
Home Page: www.spannet.org
Social Media: Facebook, Twitter, Google+, Yahoo

Scott Flora, President
Brian Jud, Executive Director
Guy Achtzehn, Board of Directors
Bob Erdmann, Board of Directors
Cevin Bryerman, Board of Directors

A nonprofit trade association for independent presses and self-publishers who want to produce better books and market them successfully. SPAN offers a monthly newsletter with information-rich articles and great benefits.
1300 Members
Founded in 1996

20503 University of Denver
University of Denver
2199 S. University Blvd
Denver, CO 80208

303-871-2570
Fax: 303-871-2501
E-Mail: pi-info@du.edu
Home Page: www.du.edu/publishinginstitute
Social Media: Facebook, Twitter, YouTube, Flickr

Joyce Meskis, Director
Jill Smith, Co-Director

A certificate program that combines workshops in editing and marketing with lecture/teaching sessions conducted by leading experts from all areas of publishing.
Founded in 1864

20504 Western Publications Association
823 Rim Crest Dr
Westlake Village, CA 91361

805-495-1863
888-735-1545
Fax: 866-735-1545
E-Mail: wpa@wpa-online.org
Home Page: www.wpa-online.org
Social Media: Facebook, Twitter, LinkedIn

Jane Silbering, Executive Director
Rieva Lesonsky, VP
John Brooks, Treasurer/Secretary
Jeff Berend, Director

Represents magazine publishing companies and companies related to publishing industry, in the western United States.
200 Members
Founded in 1951

20505 Women in Production
276 Bowery
New York, NY 10012

212-334-2106
Fax: 212-431-5786
E-Mail: admin@p3-ny.org
Home Page: www.p3-ny.org

Rosemary Sirico, President
Diane Pesce, VP

Nonprofit profesional and educational association whose mission is to facilitate career growth and education through peer support and the exchange of information.
500 Members
Founded in 2003

20506 Women's National Book Association
FDR Station
PO Box 237
New York, NY 10150

212-208-4629
Fax: 212-208-4629
E-Mail: info@wnba-books.org
Home Page: www.wnba-books.org
Social Media: Facebook, Twitter, LinkedIn, RSS

Jill A Tardiff, President
Laurie Beckelman, VP
Susannah Greenburg, Public Relations

An organization of women and men in all occupations allied to the book industry.
800 Members
Founded in 1917

20507 Yellow Pages Publishers Association
Connell Corporate Park
400 Connell Drive
Suite 1100
Berkeley Heights, NJ 07922-2747

908-286-2380
Fax: 908-286-0620
E-Mail: KimberlyEnik@ypassociation.org
Home Page: www.yellowpageblues.com
Social Media: Facebook, Twitter, LinkedIn, YouTube,Blog

George Burnett, Chairman
Dennis Payne, Vice Chairman
Neg Norton, President

Trade association which represents the Yellow Pages industry. YPPA's publisher members collectively produce over 96 percent of all directories published in the United States and account for 99 percent of the revenues generated by Yellow Pages advertising.
340 Members
Founded in 1988

Newsletters

20508 AAP Monthly Report
Association of American Publishers
71 5th Ave
Suite 2
New York, NY 10003-3004

212-255-1407
Fax: 212-255-7007

E-Mail: jtagler@publishers.org
Home Page: www.pspcentral.org

John Tagler, VP/Executive Director
Sara Pinto, Director
Kate Kolendo, Project Manager

A report offering information and news to the publishing community.
Cost: $800.00

20509 American Book Producers Association Newsletter
American Book Producers Association
151 W 19th Street
3rd Floor
New York, NY 10011

917-741-1919
800-209-4575
Fax: 212-675-1364
E-Mail: office@abpaonline.org
Home Page: www.abpaonline.org

David Rubel, Publisher
Dan Tucker, Co-President
David Katz, Manager
Richard Rothschild, President
Kirsten Hall, Administrator

Trade association of independent book producers in the United States and Canada.
6 Pages
Frequency: Monthly
Circulation: 2500
Founded in 1980
Printed in 2 colors on matte stock

20510 Augsburg Fortress Newsletter for Church Leaders
Augsburg Fortress
PO Box 1209
Minneapolis, MN 55440-1209

612-330-3300
800-328-4648
Fax: 800-722-7766
Home Page: www.augsburgfortress.org

Roderick Olson, Publisher

Monthly newsletter designed to equip pastors, church leaders, Christian leaders, Christian Educators and volunteers with valuable and timely resources, promotions, and ministry ideas.
Frequency: Monthly eNewsletter

20511 BISG Bulletin
BISG Book Industry Study Group
145 W 45th Street
Suite 601
New York, NY 10017-6588

646-336-7141
Fax: 646-336-6214
E-Mail: info@bisg.org
Home Page: www.bisg.org
Social Media: Twitter, RSS

Len Vlahos, Executive Director
Dominique Raccah, Co-Chair
Kelley Maier, Vice-Chair
Judith Appelbaum, Secretary
George Tattersfield, Treasurer

News and information from the Book Industry Study Group regarding book industry technologies, conferences, opinions, policy development, supply chain and more.
Founded in 1976

20512 Book Arts
Center for Book Arts
28 W 27th St
Suite 3
New York, NY 10001-6906

212-481-0295
Fax: 212-481-9853
E-Mail: info@centerforbookarts.org
Home Page: www.centerforbookarts.org
Social Media: Facebook, Twitter, YouTube,Flickr

Alexander Campos, Executive Director

Center news and activities.
Founded in 1974

20513 Book News
American Book Producers Association
151 W 19th Street
3rd Floor
New York, NY 10011

917-741-1919
800-209-4575
Fax: 212-675-1364
E-Mail: office@abpaonline.org
Home Page: www.abpaonline.org

Richard Rothschild, President
Bok Hee, Manager
Bill Raggio, Contact

Monthly newsletter is part of the membership benefits; provides a transcript of the monthly member luncheon's speaker, as well as association and member news.
Frequency: Benefit of Membership
Founded in 1980

20514 Bookselling This Week
American Booksellers Association
200 White Plains Rd
Suite 600
Tarrytown, NY 10591

800-637-0037
Fax: 914-591-2720
E-Mail: info@bookweb.org
Home Page: www.bookweb.org

Oren Teicher, CEO
Len Viahos, COO
Ellie Chang, CFO
Frequency: Weekly
Circulation: 10000

20515 Educational Marketer
Simba Information
60 Long Ridge Rd
Suite 300
Stamford, CT 06902-1841

203-325-8193
888-297-4622
Fax: 203-325-8975
E-Mail: customerservice@simbainformation.com
Home Page: www.simbanet.com/

Linda Kopp, Publisher

Reports on the entire educational publishing spectrum from el-hi to College. It covers the complete range of print and electronic tools including software, and multimedia materials. It details mergers, acquisitions, financial reports, distribution, adoption and enrollment trends, legislative issues
Cost: $650.00
8 Pages
Founded in 1989
Printed in 4 colors

20516 Exchange
Association of American University Presses
Rm 602
30 W 36th St
New York, NY 10018-8063

212-989-1010
Fax: 212-989-0275
E-Mail: aaupny@netcom.com
Home Page: aaupnet.org/

Hollis Holmes, Publisher
Peter J Givler, Executive Director
Rachel Weiss, Marketing Manager
Latasha Watters, Marketing Coordinator

Reports on issues relevant to scholarly publishing.
Cost: $10.00
16 Pages
Frequency: Quarterly

20517 Footprints Newsletter
Evangelical Christian Publishers Association
4816 S Ash Ave
Suite 101
Tempe, AZ 85282-7735

480-966-3998
Fax: 480-966-1944
E-Mail: info@ecpa.org
Home Page: www.ecpa.org

Mark Kuyper, President
Kelly Gallagher, VP
Dave Bird, Marketing

An international, not-for-profit, trade organization serving its industry by promoting excellence and professionalism, sharing relevant data, stimulating Christian fellowship, raising the effectiveness of member houses, and equipping them to meet the needs of the changing marketplace.
Frequency: Monthly
Circulation: 280

20518 Fusion Magazine
Newspaper Association of America
4401 Wilson Blvd
Suite 900
Arlington, VA 22203-4195

571-366-1000
Fax: 571-366-1195
E-Mail: joan.mills@naa.org
Home Page: www.naa.org
Social Media: Facebook, Twitter, LinkedIn, YouTube,RSS

Reggie Hall, Senior VP
James M Moroney, Chairman
Robert Dickey, Secretary
Donna Barrett, Treasurer
Robert M Nutting, Vice Chairman

This newsletter focuses on the business of diversity within the newspaper industry. In it you will find new strategies for making diversity work in advertising, news and editorial, circulation, marketing, production, human resources and the business office.
Frequency: Quarterly
Mailing list available for rent

20519 Guild of Book Workers-Newsletter
Guild of Book Workers
521 5th Avenue
17th Floor
New York, NY 10175-1799

212-285-5581
Home Page: palimpsest.stanford.edu/byorg/gbw

Margaret Johnson, Publisher
Bernadette Callery, Membership Secretary

Information for the book arts field.
Circulation: 800

20520 Hotline
1825 Ponce de Leon
Suite 429
Coral Gables, FL 33133

703-992-9339
800-356-9302
Fax: 703-992-7512
E-Mail: sipa@online.com
Home Page: www.hotline.com

Henry Greene, Executive Director

Furthers the professional and economic interests of members. Future plans include semi-

nars, research and representing members before federal agencies. Available only to members.
Founded in 1977
Printed in one color on matte stock

20521 Independent Book Publishers Association Newsletter
Independent Book Publishers Association
1020 Manhattan Beach Blvd
Suite 204
Manhattan Beach, CA 90266
310-546-1818
Fax: 310-546-3939
E-Mail: info@ibpa-online.org
Home Page: www.ibpa-online.org
Social Media: Facebook, Twitter, LinkedIn, Flickr,RSS
Terry Nathan, Executive Director
Lisa Krebs, Assistant Director
Steve Mettee, Board Chair
Roy M Carlisle, Treasurer
Florrie Kichler, President
Publicity, sales, legal, and marketing opportunities and news articles for independent book publishers.
Frequency: Monthly
Circulation: 6000

20522 Independent Publishers Trade Report
PO Box 176
Southport, CT 06490-176
860-669-5848
Fax: 203-332-7629
Henry Berry, Publisher
News and information for independent publishers, monthly column in the COSMEP Newsletter.

20523 Independent Small Press Review
WHW Publishing
930 Via Fruteria
Santa Barbara, CA 93110-2322
609-408-8000
Home Page: www.ifpa.com
Gary Rudy, Executive Director
Offers a comprehensive look at the concerns and issues of the small business publisher.

20524 John Kremer's Book Marketing Tip of the Week
Open Horizons Publishing
PO Box 2887
Taos, NM 87571
575-751-3398
800-796-6130
Fax: 575-751-3100
E-Mail: info@bookmarket.com
Home Page: www.bookmarket.com
John Kremer, Editor
Robert Sanny, Advertising/Sales Manager
Email newletter offering new PR and sales leads and tips every week.
Frequency: Weekly
Founded in 1982
Mailing list available for rent

20525 Lifelong Learning Market Report
Simba Information
60 Long Ridge Rd
Suite 300
Stamford, CT 06902-1841
203-325-8193
888-297-4622
Fax: 203-325-8975
E-Mail: customerservice@simbainformation.com
Home Page: www.simbanet.com
Linda Kopp, Publisher
News and analysis for content and service providers of corporate training and professional development materials. Includes news on merger and aczuisitions, industry financial performance and trends, product development and distribution.
Cost: $625.00
Founded in 1989

20526 MBR Bookwatch
Midwest Book Review
278 Orchard Drive
Oregon, WI 53575-1129
608-835-7937
E-Mail: mbr@execpc.com
Home Page: www.midwestbookreview.com
James A Cox, Editor-in-Chief
A monthly online book review publication that will showcase the reviews and commentaries of those MBR editors and specialized reviewers who've demonstrated expertise in their field. Bookwatch will also feature author interviews and editorial observations of various aspects of the publishing world, offered by knowledgeable and articulate participants.
140 Pages
Frequency: Monthly
Circulation: 30,000
Founded in 1976

20527 National Association of Professional Print Buyers
15050 NE 20th Avenue
Suite A
North Miami, FL 33181-1123
305-956-9563
Vincent Millardi, Publisher
Accepts advertising.
Cost: $315.00
296 Pages
Frequency: Monthly

20528 NewsInc.
Cole Group
PO Box 719
Pacifica, CA 94044-719
650-557-9595
Fax: 650-475-8479
E-Mail: admin@colegroup.com
Home Page: www.colegroup.com
David M Cole, Publisher/Editor
Marge Wetmore, Circulation Manager
The weekly newsletter about the business of the newspaper business, written for media executives and the investments community. subscriptions available in digital or print formats, as well as for archive access.
Cost: $99.00
Frequency: 48/Yr, for Digital Access
Founded in 1989

20529 Newsletter on Newsletters
Newsletter on Newsletters
PO Box 348
Rhinebeck, NY 12572-0348
845-876-5222
Fax: 845-876-4943
E-Mail: newsonnews@newsletterbiz.com
Home Page: www.newsletterbiz.com
Paul Swift, Editor
Graphics, editorial, promotions, management and reports on the entire newsletter industry.
Cost: $275.00
Founded in 1970

20530 Online Publishing Update E-Newsletter
Newspaper Association of America
4401 Wilson Blvd
Suite 900
Arlington, VA 22203-4195
571-366-1000
Fax: 571-366-1195
E-Mail: joan.mills@naa.org
Home Page: www.naa.org
Social Media: Facebook, Twitter, LinkedIn, YouTube,RSS
Reggie Hall, Senior VP
James M Moroney, Chairman
Robert Dickey, Secretary
Donna Barrett, Treasurer
A round-up of news, research, industry trends, best practices and more, focusing on items of interest to newspaper and digital media executives. Online Publishing Update e-newsletter is published every Monday, Wednesday and Friday.
Frequency: 3x/Weekly

20531 PMA Newsletter
Publishers Marketing Association
627 Aviation Way
Manhattan Beach, CA 90266-7107
310-372-2732
Fax: 310-374-3342
E-Mail: info@ibpa-online.org
Home Page: www.pma-online.org
Terry Nathan, Executive Director
Publishing law, copyrighting, marketing, business management all directed toward the independent book publishing community.
Frequency: Monthly
Circulation: 10000
Founded in 1983

20532 Personal Composition Report
Graphic Dimensions
134 Caversham Woods
Pittsford, NY 14534-2834
585-381-3428
Michael Kleper, Publisher
Covers all aspects of electronic publishing and imaging including news, reviews and in-depth analysis. Begun in 1979 by Professor Michael Kleper of RIT, the newsletter has provided consistent, valuable information for its readers.
Cost: $100.00
16 Pages
Frequency: Annual
Printed in one color on matte stock

20533 Pleasures of Publishing
Columbia University
2960 Broadway
New York, NY 10027-6900
212-854-1754
Fax: 212-749-0397
Home Page: www.columbia.edu
Robert Kasdin, Executive VP
Mathew Martg, Marketing
Industry news.

20534 Professional Publishing Report
Simba Information
60 Long Ridge Rd
Suite 300
Stamford, CT 06902-1841
203-325-8193
Fax: 203-325-8915
E-Mail: customerservice@simbainformation.com
Home Page: www.simbanet.com
Linda Kopp, Publisher
Charlie Friscia, Marketing
John Fuller, Executive Editor
Newletter focuses on the $10 billion professional publishing industry. Features in-depth analysis of each of the four major professional

publishing categories: scientific/technical, medical, legal and business. Provides revenue breakdowns by media and market, merger and acquisition news, and analysis of market trends.
Cost: $715.00
Founded in 1989

20535 Publishers Monthly Domestic Sales
Association of American Publishers
50 F St Nw
Suite 400
Washington, DC 20001-1565

202-347-3375
Fax: 202-347-3690
E-Mail: info@publishers.org
Home Page: www.publishers.org

Tom Allen, CEO
Katie Blough, Editor
Patricia Schroeder, President
Tina Jordan, Vice President
Kate Kolendo, Project Manager

Sales charts, index and rates for the publishing community.
Frequency: Monthly
Founded in 1970

20536 Publishers Multinational Direct
Direct International
1501 Third Avenue
New York, NY 10028-2101

212-861-4188
Fax: 212-628-5070
E-Mail: directin@ix.netcom.com
Home Page: www.publishersmultinational.com

Alfred Goodloe, Editor

National and international coverage of the publishing community including printing, prepress and direct marketing.
Cost: $195.00
Frequency: Monthly

20537 Publishers Report
National Association of Independent Publishers
PO Box 430
Highland City, FL 33846-430

863-648-4420
Fax: 836-648-4420
E-Mail: naip@aol.com
Home Page: www.publishersreport.com

Betsy A Lampe, Publisher

Provides a clearinghouse of information on small/independent publishing for its members. Accepts advertising. Departments include: 'New Books, Audios & Videos,' It's a Date,' 'NAIP Book Review,' 'New Media Sources,' 'Wanted,' 'In the Know,' 'F41,' and various others helpful for new publishers and self-publishers.

20538 Publishers' Auxiliary
National Newspaper Association
1010 N Glebe Road
Suite 450
Arlington, VA 22201

703-658-8808
Fax: 703-907-7901
E-Mail: info@nna.org
Home Page: www.nna.org

Stan Schwartz, Managing Editor
Lynn Edinger, Marketing Manager

Providing personnel announcements, new technology, economic trends, and new publicaiton and distribution methods for executives in the newpaper industry.
Cost: $85.00
Frequency: Monthly
Circulation: 8102
Founded in 1885

20539 Publishing Markets
Reed Business Information
275 Washington St
Newton, MA 02458-1611

617-964-3030
Fax: 617-558-4327
Home Page: www.designnews.com

Deborah Selsky, Publisher
San Buchan, Editor

Economic and demographic trends that affect the book publishing market.
Cost: $129.00

20540 Publishing Poynters
Para Publishing
PO Box 8206-240
Santa Barbara, CA 93118-8206

805-968-7277
800-727-2782
Fax: 805-968-1379
E-Mail: danpoynter@parapublishing.com
Home Page: www.parapublishing.com
Social Media: Facebook, Twitter

Dan Poynter, Editor
Becky Carbone, Production Manager

Book publishing news and ideas: marketing, promotion and distribution.
Cost: $9.95
20 Pages
Frequency: Monthly
Circulation: 16000
ISSN: 1530-5694
Founded in 1969
Printed in one color

20541 Report on Preschool Programs
Business Publishers,Inc
2222 Sedwick Drive
Durham, NC 27713

800-223-8720
Fax: 800-508-2592
E-Mail: custserv@bpinews.com
Home Page: www.bpinews.com

The one source to turn to for timely, accurate coverage of important developments in Head Start, child care, health care, special education and much more.
Cost: $357.00
8 Pages
Founded in 1963

20542 SPAN
Small Publishers Association of North America
1618 W Colorado Avenue
Colorado Springs, CO 80904-4029

719-475-1726
Fax: 719-471-2182
E-Mail: span@spannet.org
Home Page: www.spannet.org

Marilyn Ross, Editor
Cathy Bowman, Production Manager

Includes money-making articles and book industry information.
24 Pages
Frequency: Monthly
Circulation: 4000
Founded in 1996

20543 SPAN Internet Newsletter
Small Publishers Association of North America
PO Box 9725
Colorado Springs, CO 80932-0725

719-924-5534
Fax: 719-213-2602
E-Mail: brad@spannet.org
Home Page: www.spannet.org
Social Media: Facebook, Twitter

Marilyn Ross, Executive Director/Editor
Tom Ross, VP

The SPAN Internet Newsletter features timely and useful information on many aspects of writing and the publishing industry, including articles on book marketing and publicity in addition to providing links to industry related Websites.
Frequency: Monthly
Circulation: 4000
Founded in 1996

20544 Small Publisher Co-Op
Nigel Maxey
1521 SE Palm Court
PO Box 1620
Stuart, FL 34994-1620

772-287-8117
E-Mail: spcoop@hotmail.com
Home Page: www.spco-op.com

Niyel Maxey, President/Editor
Kevin Hawken, Member Service Manager

This monthly newsletter offers a guide to publishing and marketing books, reports, periodicals, etc.
Cost: $15.00
Circulation: 5900

20545 Span Connection
Small Publishers Association of North America
PO Box 1306
Buena Vista, CO 81211-1306

719-395-4790
Fax: 719-395-8374
E-Mail: span@spannet.org
Home Page: www.spannet.org

Scoot Flora, Editor
Scoot Flora, CEO

Wide variety of news and information about small-scale and individual publishing.
Cost: $105.00
Frequency: Monthly
Circulation: 4000
Founded in 1996

20546 Specialty Directory Publishing Market Forecast
Simba Information
60 Long Ridge Rd
Suite 300
Stamford, CT 06902-1841

203-325-8193
888-297-4622
Fax: 203-325-8975
E-Mail: info@simbanet.com
Home Page: www.simbanet.com

Kathy Mickey, Managing Editor/Analyst
David Goddard, Senior Editor/Analyst
Michael Norris, Senior Editor/Analyst

Complete market size, revenue and growth figures and forecasts including revenues driven by electronic products and exclusive reanking of leading publishers by revenue.
Cost: $495.00
Frequency: Anually
Founded in 1989

20547 The Bookwoman
Women's National Book Association
PO Box 237
FDR Station
New York, NY 10150

212-208-4629
Fax: 212-208-4629
Home Page: www.wnba-books.org

Social Media: Facebook, Twitter, LinkedIn, RSS

Joan Gelfand, President
Mary Grey James, Vice President/President-Elect
Ruth Light, Secretary
Margaret E Auer, Treasurer
Shannon Janeczek, The Bookwoman, Managing Editor

Bi-annual journal for members of the Women's National Book Association. Stories of interest for people in the world of books. Book review are includes, how-to information and chapter news from across the United States. Ad space available.
2 Pages
Frequency: Biennial
Circulation: 1000
Founded in 1917

Magazines & Journals

20548 AP Special Edition
Associated Press
450 W 33rd St
New York, NY 10001-2647

212-621-1849
Fax: 212-833-7574
E-Mail: info@ap.org
Home Page: www.apme.com

Collins Munro, Manager
Kathelene Carroll, Editor
Laure Morris, Marketing Manager
Alan Miller, Managing Editor
Debra Simmons, Secretary
Frequency: Monthly
Circulation: 7000
Founded in 1848

20549 American Libraries Magazine
50 East Huron Street
Chicago, IL 60611

800-545-2433
Fax: 312-944-7841
E-Mail: membership@ala.org
Home Page: www.ala.org

Keith Fields, Publisher, ALA Executive Director
Mary Mackay, Marketing & Sales Director
Camila Alire, ALA President

News and information on legislation concerning libraries, new publications and technology issues
Cost: $70.00
Frequency: 10x/Yr $ incl in ALA dues
Circulation: 60,000
ISSN: 0002-9769
Founded in 1876

20550 Book Dealers World
North American Bookdealers Exchange
PO Box 606
Cottage Grove, OR 97424

541-942-7455
Fax: 541-942-7455
Home Page: www.bookmarketingprofits.com

Al Galasso, Editorial Director
Steve Sherman, Publisher

The book marketing magazine for independent publishers and mail order entrepreneurs. A publication of the North American Book Dealers Exchange, an international book marketing organization, specializing in cooperative opportunities at trade shows, in mail order, press releases and more.
Cost: $45.00
32 Pages
Frequency: Quarterly
Circulation: 10000
ISSN: 1098-8521
Founded in 1980
Printed in on newsprint stock

20551 Book Promotion Hotline
Ad-Lib Publications
51 1/2 W Adam
PO Box 1102
Fairfield, IA 52556-3226

515-472-6617
800-669-0773
Fax: 641-472-3186

Marie Kiefer, Editor/Publisher

Provides media contacts and other marketing sources of interest to the publisher/marketing trade.
Cost: $150.00
4 Pages
Frequency: Weekly
Circulation: 1,000

20552 Booklist
American Library Association
50 E Huron St
Chicago, IL 60611-2788

312-280-2518
800-545-2433
E-Mail: kfiels@ala.org
Home Page: www.ala.org

Keith Michael Fiels, Executive Director
Mary Ellen Quinn, Editor

The purpose of this guide is to provide information on materials worthy of consideration for purchase by small and medium sized public libraries.
Cost: $79.95
Founded in 1876

20553 CBA Marketplace
Association for Christian Retail
9240 Explorer Drive
Suite 200
Colorado Spring, CO 80920

719-265-9895
800-252-1950
Fax: 719-272-3510
E-Mail: info@cbaonline.org
Home Page: www.cbaonline.org

Bill Anderson, President/CEO
Cliff Goins, Treasurer
Greg Thornton, Director of Publications
George Thomsen, Chairman
Robin Hogan, Secretary

Resource for Christian retailers & suppliers.
Cost: $59.95
Frequency: Monthly
Circulation: 8000
Mailing list available for rent

20554 Christian Retailing
Strang Communications Company
600 Rinehart Rd
Lake Mary, FL 32746-4868

407-333-0600
Fax: 407-333-7100
Home Page: www.strang.com

Stephen Strang, CEO
Tircia Stafford, Circulation Director

A trade journal designed to inform Christian bookstore owners about books, music and gifts, videos, etc. Also it features topics to help retailers run a successful business.
Cost: $75.00
72 Pages
Frequency: Monthly
Circulation: 10000
Founded in 1975

20555 Circulation Management
PRIMEDIA Intertec-Marketing & Professional Service
PO Box 4235
Stamford, CT 06907-0235

212-475-2212
Fax: 203-358-5823
Home Page: www.circman.com

Roberta Thomas, Publisher

Subscriptions, renewals, direct mail, list selection, circulation planning, data management, fulfillment and list management.
Cost: $39.00
Frequency: Monthly
Circulation: 10,000

20556 Collegiate Journalist
Society for Collegiate Journalists
1584 Wesleyan Drive
Virginia Wesleyan College
Virginia Beach, VA 23502-5599

757-455-3419
Fax: 757-461-5025
E-Mail: wjruehlmann@vwc.edu
Home Page: www.scj.us

J D Tarpley, Publisher
William Ruehlmann, CEO/President
Adam Earnheardt, Editor

For editors of yearbooks, magazines and newspapers.
Cost: $5.00
28 Pages
Frequency: Monthly

20557 Complete Guide to Self-Publishing
Communication Creativity
425 Cedar
Buena Vista, CO 81211-0909

719-395-8659
800-331-8355
Fax: 719-395-8374

Marilyn Ross, Publisher
Matthew Sullivan, Editor

The most comprehensive resource available about the business of publishing. Offers everything you need to know to write, publish, promote and sell books.
Cost: $19.99
521 Pages
ISBN: 1-582970-91-2

20558 Desktop Publishers Journal
462 Boston Street
Topsfield, MA 01983

FAX 800-492-1014
Home Page: www.dtpjournal.com

Barry Harrigan, Contact

Offers a comprehensive array of news, analysis, features and reviews on the latest products and services on the market today.
Cost: $15.00
Frequency: 12 issues

20559 Editor & Publisher
Editor & Publisher International Yearbook
11 W 19th Street
10th Floor
New York, NY 10011-4234

212-291-1259
Fax: 212-691-7287
Home Page: www.mediainfo.com

Michael Parker, President

Covers all facets of the newspaper business today and is regarded as the bible of the newspaper industry.
Cost: $184.00
Frequency: 46 issues
Founded in 1884

20560 Editorial Eye
EEI Communications
66 Canal Center Plz
Suite 200
Alexandria, VA 22314-5507

703-683-0683
Fax: 703-683-4915
E-Mail: info@eeicommunications.com
Home Page: www.eeicom.com

James T Degrafferei, CEO
Robin Cormier, VP
Candee Wilson, Director
Linda B. Jorgensen, Editor

Offering information on written excellence, editorial information and communication skills for readers.
Cost: $125.00
Frequency: Monthly
Founded in 1972

20561 Electronic Publishing
PennWell Publishing Company
10 Tara Boulevard
5th Floor
Nashua, NH 03062-2880

603-891-0123
Fax: 603-891-0539
E-Mail: genepri@pennwell.com
Home Page: www.electronic-publishing.com

Gene Pritchard, Publisher

For those who communicate in print, including service bureaus, printers, prepress houses and desktop publishers, it provides latest products, news and related developments.
Cost: $45.00
Frequency: Monthly
Circulation: 68,441

20562 F&W Publications
1507 Dana Avenue
Cincinnati, OH 45207

513-396-6160
Fax: 513-531-1025
Home Page: www.writersdigest.com

Jeff Lapin, President

Articles that reflect the current state of American freelance writing.
72 Pages
Frequency: 8 per year
Circulation: 85,000
ISBN: 7-148602-50-8
Founded in 1930

20563 FLEXO Magazine
Flexographic Technical Association Inc
900 Marconi Avenue
Ronkonkoma, NY 11779-7212

631-737-6020
Fax: 631-737-6813
Home Page: www.flexography.org

Robert Moran, President
Christian Bonawandt, Editor

Up-to-date on the changes and advances in the rapidly-expanding flexographic industry.
Cost: $55.00
Frequency: Monthly

20564 Folio: Magazine for Magazine Management
Red 7 Media, LLC
10 Norden Place
Norwalk, CT 06855

203-854-6730
Fax: 203-854-6735
E-Mail: tsilber@red7media.com
Home Page: www.foliomag.com

Stefanie Botelho, Associate Editor
Kerry Smith, President /CEO
Dan Trombetto, Group Creative Director
Tony Silber, General Manager
John Ellertson, Director Advertising Sales Manager

Written for the people who run the nation's magazines. Offers authoritative intelligence on the magazine market to enable industry professionals to navigate the widening range of strategic options. Every issue delivers features on the people and technologies that are transforming the magazine business, along with useful columns and departments, thought-provoking analysis and tactical advice for building successful magazines.
Cost: $96.00
Frequency: Monthly
Circulation: 11550
Founded in 1971

20565 ForeWord Reviews
ForeWord Magazine
425 Boardman Avenue
Traverse City, MI 49684

231-933-3699
Fax: 231-933-3899
Home Page: www.forewordreviews.com

Victoria Sutherland, Owner
Stacy Price, Director Advertising Sales

Review books and other servies for authors and small publishers.
Cost: $40.00
Frequency: Monthly
Circulation: 20000
Founded in 1998
Printed in 4 colors on 6 stock

20566 INFO FLEX
Flexographic Technical Association Inc
3920 Veterans Memorial Highway
Suite 9
Bohemia, NY 11716

631-737-6020
Fax: 631-737-6813
E-Mail: memberinfo@flexography.org
Home Page: www.flexography.org

Mark Cisternino, President
Greg Platt, Chairman
Dan Doherty, Treasurer
Jason Barrier, Director

The show floor boasts 200+ booths manned by flexography's leading suppliers, as well as a presentation theater, and educational pavilion, a social event and more
Frequency: Annual/May

20567 Independent Publisher Magazine
Jenkins Group
1129 Woodmere Avenue
Suite B
Traverse City, MI 49686-4275

231-933-0445
800-706-4636
Fax: 231-933-0448
Home Page: www.bookpublishing.com

Jerrold R Jenkins, President
Jim Barmes, Editor
Andrew Pargel, Marketing Manager

Trade journal for the independent publishing, community, university presses, librarians, bookstores and professionals.
Cost: $40.00
Frequency: Monthly
Circulation: 8000
Founded in 1988
Mailing list available for rent: 42M names
Printed in 4 colors on glossy stock

20568 Information Publishing: Business/ Professional Markets & Media
Simba Information
60 Long Ridge Rd
Suite 300
Stamford, CT 06902-1841

203-325-8193
Fax: 203-325-8915
E-Mail: simbainfo@simbanet.com
Home Page: www.simbanet.com

Linda Kopp, Publisher
Donna Devall, Marketing Director
Charlie Friscia, Director of Advertising

Demonstrates how publishers are profiting from media. Discover the opportunities in newsletters, directories, books, magazines, journals and electronic information services. More than 300 pages of information and analysis, 100 tables and charts, financial and operating information on more than 50 key publishing companies, 16 principal information markets reviewed in-depth, with five year forecasts by market and by media.
Cost: $1995.00
Founded in 1989

20569 Inside Edge
International Publishing Management Association
1205 W College Street
Liberty, MO 64068

816-781-1111
Fax: 660-781-2790
E-Mail: ipmainfo@ipma.org
Home Page: www.ipma.org

Larry Aaron, Executive Director
Susan Murphy, Editor
Jack Welch, CEO
Lea Holt, Director

Offers information on the association's activities, industry trends, and corporate publishing facility profiles.
Cost: $50.00
24 Pages
Frequency: Monthly
Circulation: 1500
Mailing list available for rent: 2M names

20570 MultiMedia & Internet @Schools
Information Today
143 Old Marlton Pike
Medford, NJ 08055-8750

609-654-6266
800-300-9868
Fax: 609-654-4309
E-Mail: custserv@infotoday.com
Home Page: www.infotoday.com

Thomas H Hogan, President
Roger R Bilboul, Chairman Of The Board
John C Yersak, Vice President
Sue Hogan, Director
John Brokenshire, CFO

A practical guide for K-12 library media specialists, technology coordinators and other educators with information on how to get high-performance learning from technology-based school products, services and resources.
Cost: $ 39.95
Frequency: 6 issues/yr
Mailing list available for rent: 4M names
Printed in 4 colors on glossy stock

20571 New Age Publishing and Retailing Alliance Trade Journal
PO Box 9
Eastsound, WA 98245-0009

360-376-2702
Fax: 360-376-2704

Marilyn McGuire, Executive Director
Carole Scarfuto, Administrative Director

Covers the publishing and retailing trades.
Frequency: Bi-Monthly
Circulation: 10,000

20572 NewsInc
PO Box 719
Pacifica, CA 94044-719
650-557-9595
Fax: 650-557-9696
E-Mail: news@newsinc.net
Home Page: www.newsinc.net

David Cole, Publisher/Editor
Cost: $147.00
Frequency: Weekly
Founded in 1989

20573 Newspapers & Technology
Conley Magazines
1623 Blake Street
Suite 250
Denver, CO 80202
303-575-9595
Fax: 303-575-9555
E-Mail: letters@newsandtech.com
Home Page: www.newsandtech.com/

Mary Van Meter, Publisher
Chuck Moozakis, Editor-in-Chief
Tara McMeekin, Editor
Hays Goodman, Associate Editor/Webmaster

Newspapers & Technology is a monthly trade publication for newspaper publishers and department managers involved in applying and integrating technology. Written by industry experts, News & Tech provides regular coverage of the following departments: prepress, press, postpress and new media.
Circulation: 16,874
Mailing list available for rent

20574 Poets & Writer's Magazine
Poets & Writers
150 Broadway
New York, NY 10038-4381
212-566-2424
Fax: 212-587-9673
E-Mail: editor@pw.org
Home Page: www.pettuswilliams.com

Marvin K Pettus, President
Christine Cassidy, Marketing Director
William Hayes, Finance Executive

Interviews, essays, grants and awards, practical information for poets and writers.
Cost: $19.95
Circulation: 60000

20575 Progressive Review
1312 18th Street NW
5th Floor
Washington, DC 20036
202-835-0770
Fax: 202-835-0779
E-Mail: news@prorev.com
Home Page: www.prorev.com

Sam Smith, Editor
Frequency: Monthly
Founded in 1964

20576 Publish
462 Boston Street
Suite 310
Topsfield, MA 01983
978-887-6855
Fax: 978-887-9245

Barry Harrigan, Owner

20577 Publishers Weekly
PO Box 51593
Harlan, IA 51593
800-278-2991
Fax: 712-733-8019
E-Mail: pwycustserv@cdsfulfillment.com
Home Page: www.publishersweekly.com
Social Media: Facebook, Twitter, LinkedIn, RSS

Jim Milliot, Co-Editorial Director
Michael Coffey, Co-Editorial Director
Diane Roback, Children's Book Editor
Louisa Ermelino, Reviews Director
Calvin Reid, News Editor

PW is the international journal of book publishing and bookselling including business news, reviews and bestseller lists targeted at publishers, booksellers, librarians and literary agents.
Frequency: Weekly
Founded in 1872

20578 Publishing & Production Executive
Mark Hertzog
1500 Spring Garden Street
Suite 1200
Philadelphia, PA 19130
215-238-5300
Fax: 215-238-5457
Home Page: www.ppe-online.com

Allison Schill Eckel, Managing Editor
Gretchen Kirby, Editor

Addresses technological trends and issues relevant to print production managers specializing in books, magazines, catalogs, agency or corporate communications
Frequency: 12 per year
Circulation: 30,000

20579 Quill
PO Box 94080
Palatine, IL 60094-v
765-653-3333
800-789-1331
Fax: 800-789-8955
Home Page: www.quill.com

20580 Searcher: Magazine for the Database Professional
Information Today
143 Old Marlton Pike
Medford, NJ 08055-8750
609-654-6266
800-300-9868
Fax: 609-654-4309
E-Mail: custserv@infotoday.com
Home Page: www.infotoday.com
Social Media: Facebook, Twitter

Thomas H Hogan, President
Roger R Bilboul, Chairman Of The Board

Explores and deliberates on a comprehensive range of issues important to the professional database researcher. Combines evaluations of data content with discussions of delivery media.
Cost: $86.95
Frequency: 10 issues/yr
Mailing list available for rent: 4M names
Printed in 4 colors on glossy stock

20581 Student Press Review
Columbia University
2960 Broadway
New York, NY 10027-6900
212-854-1754
Fax: 212-749-0397
E-Mail: cspa@columbia.edu
Home Page: www.columbia.edu

Robert Kasdin, Executive VP
Helen F Smith, Editor
Edmund J Sullivan, Publisher

Reports and advises on high school and college student media. Offers how-to articles and features to improve student newspapers, magazines and yearbooks in schools, colleges, and universities.
Frequency: Quarterly
Circulation: 2200
Founded in 1925

20582 Volt Report on Directory Publishing
Volt Directory Marketing
1800 Byberry Road
Suite 800
Huntingdon Valley, PA 19006-3520
800-677-3839
Fax: 215-938-5549

Kathy Wolden, Editor

As the monitor of the directory publishing industry, the Morgan report provides news on the people, companies, products and opportunities shaping the industry today. Includes practical how-to guidance on key facets of the directory publishing process as well as strategic overviews.
Cost: $95.00
12 Pages
Frequency: Monthly

20583 Writer Magazine
21027 Crossroads Circle
PO Box 1612
Waukesha, WI 53187-1612
262-796-8776
800-533-6644
Fax: 262-796-1615
Home Page: corporate.kalmbach.com

Sylvia Burack, Publisher
Elfrieda Abbe, Executive Vice President
Chuck Croft, Executive Vice President

Practical guide to instruct, inform, and inspire writers as they work toward the goal of publication. Writers of short stories, novels, poetry, plays or science fiction, readers will find straightforward advice, up-to-date market lists and tips on manuscript submission.
Cost: $29.00
Frequency: Monthly
Circulation: 43000
Founded in 1987

20584 Writer's Digest
F&W Publications
4700 E Galbraith Rd
Cincinnati, OH 45236-2726
513-531-2690
800-258-0929
Fax: 513-531-1843
E-Mail: WritersDig@fwpubs.com
Home Page: www.fwpublications.com

David Nussbaum, CEO
Jim Ogle, Chief Financial Officer
Kate Rados, Marketing Director
Stacie Berger, Communications Director

Information and how to tips for freelance writers.
Cost: $19.96
Frequency: Monthly
Founded in 1920

Trade Shows

20585 AAP General Annual Meeting
Association of American Publishers (AAP)
455 Massachusetts Avenue NW
Suite 700
Washington, DC 20001-2777
202-347-3375
Fax: 202-347-3690
E-Mail: info@publishers.org

Home Page: www.publishers.org
Social Media: Twitter

Karen Abramson, President & CEO
Tina Jordan, Vice President
Allan R Adler, VP for Legal & Government Affairs
Jay Diskey, Executive Director, School Division
Gail Kump, Director, Membership Marketing

Discussion topics include the state of digital content, distribution channels and copyright protection as seen through the prism of publishers and their historic partners.
200 Members
Frequency: Annual

20586 American Library Association Annual Conference
American Library Association
50 E Huron Street
Chicago, IL 60611

800-545-2433
E-Mail: customerservice@ala.org
Home Page: www.ala.org

Loriene Roy, President
Keith Michael Fiels, Executive Director

Annual meeting and exhibits of books, periodicals, reference works, audio visual equipment, films, data processing services, computer hardware and software, library equipment and supplies.

20587 American Medical Publishers' Association Annual Meeting
71 Fifth Avenue
2nd Floor
New York, NY 10003

212-255-0200
Fax: 212-255-7007
E-Mail: jtagler@publishers.org
Home Page: www.pspcentral.org
Social Media: LinkedIn

John Tagler, VP/Executive Director
Sara Pinto, Director
Kate Kolendo, Project Manager

Information provided to medical publishing field.
Frequency: Annual
Founded in 1960

20588 Association of American University Presses Conference
Association of American University Presses
71 W 23rd Street
Suite 901
New York, NY 10010-3264

212-989-1010
Fax: 212-989-0275
E-Mail: annualmeeting@aaupnet.org
Home Page:
www.aaup.uchicago.edu/aaup_home.html

Peter Givler, Executive Director
Timothy Muench, Assistant Director

Annual conference and exhibits of equipment, supplies and services for scholarly publishing divisions of colleges and universities.
125 Attendees
Frequency: Annual

20589 Association of College and Research Libraries
American Library Association
50 E Huron Street
Chicago, IL 60611-5295

312-280-2511
800-545-2433
Fax: 312-280-2520
E-Mail: customerservice@ala.org
Home Page: www.ala.org/acrl

Mary Ellen Davis, Executive Director

Two hundred exhibitors with computers and web products, audiovisual products, furniture and library equipment.
3000 Attendees
Frequency: Biennial
ISSN: 0099-0086
Founded in 1978
Mailing list available for rent

20590 Association of Free Community Papers
1630 Miner Street
Suite 204, Box 1989
Idaho Springs, CO 80452

877-203-2327
Fax: 781-459-7770
Home Page: www.afcp.org

Craig Mullin, Executive Director
Brianne Janes, Graphic Designer

Exhibits for publishers of free circulation papers and shopping/advertising guides.
Frequency: Annual
Founded in 1951

20591 Book Expo America
Reed Exhibitions
383 Main Avenue
Norwalk, CT 06851

203-404-4800
800-840-5614
E-Mail: cmuller@reedexpo.com
Home Page: www.bookexpoamerica.com
Social Media: Facebook, Twitter, LinkedIn, YouTube,Pinterest

Courtney Muller, Event Manager
Cathy Glickstein, Registration
Lisa Montanaro, Sales Executive

Sponsored by American Booksellers Association and Association of American Publishers. More than 2,000 exhibits, 500 authors, over 60 conference sessions as well as a special area for rights business, all the latest titles across genres, uncover hidden gems, network, and meet the industry contacts to put you instantly on top of what you need to know for your business and job.
Frequency: May/June
Founded in 2000

20592 Christian Booksellers Association
9240 Explorer Drive
Colorado Springs, CO 80920

800-252-1950
Fax: 719-272-3510
E-Mail: info@cbaonline.org
Home Page: www.cbaonline.org

Bill Anderson, President
Mike Regennitter, Executive Director
Scott Graham, Director

Exhibition and sales of Christian oriented products to include categories of books and Bibles, music, framed art, jewelry, videos, clothing gifts, cards, stationary, children products, computer software, church supplies, curriculum and store supplies.
12M Attendees
Frequency: July

20593 Digital Book Printing Forum
Interquest Ltd.
513-D Stewart Street
Charlottesville, VA 22902

434-979-9945
Fax: 434-979-9959
E-Mail: iquest@inter-quest.com
Home Page: www.inter-quest.com

David Davis, Director

Interquest analysts will present key results from the company's latest research in the field.
Frequency: March

20594 Digital Book World
FAX new

Jeremy Greenfield, Editorial Director
Raymond Kyle, Business Development Manager
Gary Lynch, Group Publisher
Amanda Malek, Online Product Development

A year-round platform offering educational and networking resoruces for consumer publishing professionals and their partners - including agents ,booksellers and technology vendors - online and in person

20595 FFTA Annual Forum & INFO FLEX Exhibition
Flexographic Technical Association Inc
3920 Veterans Memorial Highway
Suite 9
Bohemia, NY 11716

631-737-6020
Fax: 631-737-6813
E-Mail: memberinfo@flexography.org
Home Page: www.flexography.org

Mark Cisternino, President
Joe Tuccitto, Director of Education
Doreen Monteleone, Director Environmental Affairs
Sharon Cox, Director of Marketing
Katie Dubois, Creative Services Manager

Presents the most promising technological advances and emerging market opportunities to keep you and your company up to date.
1600+ Attendees

20596 FOLIO Show
Red 7 Media, LLC
10 Norden Place
Norwalk, CT 06855

203-854-6730
Fax: 203-854-6735
Home Page: www.folioshow.com/
Social Media: Facebook, Twitter, LinkedIn

Tony Silberg, Publisher/General Manager
John Ellertson, Group Sales Director
Magan Sprenger, Account Executive
Tania Babiuk, Account Executive
Kerry Smith, President

Biennial show and exhibits of publishing supplies, paper, printing equipment, color separators, fulfillment houses, lists and related equipment, supplies and services to the magazine and book publishing trades.
7,000 Attendees

20597 InfoCommerce
InfoCommerce Group Inc
2 Bala Plaza
Suite 300
Bala Cynwyd, PA 19004

610-649-1200
Fax: 610-471-0515
E-Mail:
rchristensen@infocommercegroup.com
Home Page: www.infocommercegroup.com

Roxanne Christensen, Dir Awards Conferences & Consulting

Convenes all kinds of publishers who are bound only by their ability and willingness to take risks.
Frequency: Oct, Philadelphia

20598 NCRW Annual Conference
National Council for Research on Women
11 Hanover Square
24th Floor
New York, NY 10005-2819

212-785-7335
Fax: 212-785-7350

E-Mail: ncrw@ncrw.org
Home Page: www.ncrw.org

Mariam K Chamberlain, Founding President
Linda G Basch, President
Frequency: June

20599 New England Booksellers Association Annual Trade Show
1770 Massachusetts Avenue
#332
Cambridge, MA 02140

617-576-3070
800-466-8711
Fax: 617-576-3091
Home Page: www.newenglandbooks.org/

Allan Schmid, President
Dale Szczeblowski, VP

Offers the opportunity for publishers to get their products in the hands of the booksellers in an area with one of the highest concentrations of readers in the country. This traditional multi-media exhibition is the largest of the regional conference in bookseller attendance.
2M+ Attendees
Frequency: September/October

20600 Publishing Institute
Publishing Institute
University of Denver
2000 E. Asbury Ave
Denver, CO 80208

303-832-5280
Fax: 303-871-2501
E-Mail: pi-info@du.edu
Home Page: www.du.edu/publishinginstitute

Elizabeth Geiser, Director
Joyce Meskis, Director

A certificate program that combines workshops in editing and marketing with lecture/teaching sessions conducted by leading experts from all areas of publishing.
90 Attendees
Frequency: July-August

20601 Publishing University
Independent Book Publishers Association
1020 Manhattan Beach Blvd
Suite 204
Manhattan Beach, CA 90266

310-546-1818
Fax: 310-546-3939
E-Mail: info@ibpa-online.org
Home Page: www.ibpa-online.org

Terry Nathan, Executive Director
Lisa Krebs, Assistant Director
Steve Mettee, Board Chair
Roy M Carlisle, Treasurer
Florrie B Kichler, President

A 2-day publishing conference focusing on education and networking. 40 exhibitors.
300 Attendees
Frequency: Annual

20602 Small Press Book Fair
Small Press Center
20 W 44th Street
New York, NY 10036-6604

212-764-7021
Fax: 212-354-5365
E-Mail: smallpress@aol.com
Home Page: www.smallpress.org

Mary Bertschmann, Chair
Lloyd Jassin, Vice Chair
Mashala Solammi, Owner

One of the major book fairs for small press. Containing 100 booths and 100 exhibits.
2,500 Attendees
Frequency: March

20603 Tools of Change for Publishing Conference
O'Reilly Media, Inc.
1005 Gravenstein Highway North
Sebastopol, CA 95472

707-827-7000
800-998-9938
Fax: 707-829-0104
E-Mail: conf-webmaster@oreilly.com
Home Page: www.oreilly.com
Social Media: Facebook, Twitter, LinkedIn, RSS

Gina Blaber, Vice President, Conferences
Suzanne Axtell, Communications Manager
Shirley Bailes, Speaker Manager

Expect coverage with a range of practical, in-depth sessions that cover the innovations rocking every aspect of the art, craft, and business of publishing in the 21st century.
Frequency: February
Mailing list available for rent

20604 Writing Academy Seminar
Writing Academy
4010 Singleton Road
Rockford, IL 61114

815-877-9675
Home Page: www.wams.org/indexhtm

Annual seminar and exhibits by Christian writers.

20605 Yellow Pages Publishers Association Convention
Yellow Pages Publishers Association
116 Cass Street
Traverse City, MI 49684

800-267-9002
Fax: 231-486-2182
E-Mail: hq@adp.org
Home Page: www.adp.org/

R. Lawrence Angove, President
Bonnie Pintozzi, COO
Vernon Smith, Treasurer

Annual convention and exhibits of equipment, supplies and services for the publication of Yellow Pages telephone directories.

Directories & Databases

20606 2,224 Public Libraries Data Files
Open Horizons Publishing
PO Box 2887
Taos, NM 87571

575-751-3398
800-796-6130
Fax: 575-751-3100
E-Mail: info@bookmarket.com
Home Page: www.bookmarket.com

John Kremer, Editor
Robert Sanny, Advertising/Sales Manager

Database features 2,224 general public libraries, with name and address; no phone, fax, or email. Download in your choice of formats along with an information sheet.
Cost: $40.00
Frequency: Database
Founded in 1982

20607 Advertising and Publicity Resources for Scholarly Books
Association of American University Presses
Rm 602
30 W 36th St
New York, NY 10018-8063

212-989-1010
Fax: 212-989-0275
E-Mail: info@aaupnet.org
Home Page: www.aaupnet.org

Peter Givler, Executive Director
Timothy Muench, Marketing Coordinator
Latasha Watters, Marketing Coordinator

This comprehensive directory lists periodicals which accept advertising or review copies of scholarly publications.
Cost: $189.00
425 Pages

20608 Alternative Publications: A Guide to Directories and Other Sources
Mcfarland & Company
Po Box 611
Jefferson, NC 28640-0611

336-246-4460
Fax: 336-246-5018
E-Mail: info@mcfarlandpub.com
Home Page: www.mcfarlandpub.com
Social Media: Facebook, Twitter, LinkedIn

Robert Franklin, President

Offers indexes and abstracts, review sources and bibliographies dealing with alternative publications.
Cost: $18.95
96 Pages

20609 American Book Producers Directory
American Book Producers Association
160 5th Avenue
New York, NY 10010-7003

212-645-2368
800-209-4575
Fax: 212-242-6799
E-Mail: office@ABPAonline.org
Home Page: www.abpaonline.org

David Rubel, President
David Katz, Treasurer
Valerie Tomaselli, Treasurer
Nancy Hall, Vice President
40 Pages
Circulation: 2,000
Founded in 1980
Printed in 2 colors on matte stock

20610 American Book Trade Directory
Information Today
143 Old Marlton Pike
Medford, NJ 08055-8750

609-654-6266
800-300-9868
Fax: 609-654-4309
E-Mail: custserv@infotoday.com
Home Page: www.infotoday.com
Social Media: Facebook, Twitter

Thomas H Hogan, President
Roger R Bilboul, Chairman Of The Board

A US book trade community. Profiles 25,500 retail and antiquarian book dealers, plus 1,200 book and magazine wholesalers, distributors, and jobbers in all 50 states and US territories.
Cost: $299.00
1800 Pages
ISBN: 1-573872-12-1

20611 American Directory of Writer's Guidelines
Dustbooks
PO Box 100
Paradise, CA 95967-0100

530-877-6110
800-477-6110
Fax: 530-877-0222
E-Mail: directories@dustbooks.com
Home Page: www.dustbooks.com

Brigitte M Phillips, Editor
Susan D Klassen, Editor
Doris Hall, Editor

These guidelines help writers target their submissions to the exact needs of the individual publisher. A compilation of information for freelancers from more than 1,500 magazine editors and book publishers.
Cost: $29.95
752 Pages
ISBN: 1-884956-40-8

20612 **Association of American University Presses Directory**
Association of American University Presses
Rm 602
30 W 36th St
New York, NY 10018-8063
212-989-1010
Fax: 212-989-0275
E-Mail: info@aaupnet.org
Home Page: www.aaup.uchicago.edu/aaup_home.html
Peter Givler, Executive Director
Timothy Muench, Assistant Director
114 presses and affiliates worldwide.
Cost: $14.95
Frequency: Annual November

20613 **Bacon's Newspaper & Magazine Directories**
Cision U.S., Inc.
322 South Michigan Avenue
Suite 900
Chicago, IL 60604
312-263-0070
866-639-5087
E-Mail: info.us@cision.com
Home Page: us.cision.com
Joe Bernardo, President & CEO
Heidi Sullivan, VP & Publisher
Valerie Lopez, Research Director
Jessica White, Research Director
Rachel Farrell, Research Manager
Two volume set listing all daily and community newspapers, magazines and newsletters, news service and syndicates, syndicated columnists, complete editorial staff listings of each publication provided, covers U.S., Canada, Mexico, and Carribean.
Cost: $350.00
4,700 Pages
Frequency: Annual
ISSN: 1088-9639
Founded in 1951
Printed in one color on matte stock

20614 **Bacon's Radio/TV/Cable Directory**
Cision U.S., Inc.
332 South Michigan Avenue
Suite 900
Chicago, IL 60604
312-263-0070
866-639-5087
E-Mail: info.us@cision.com
Home Page: www.us.cision.com
Joe Bernardo, President & CEO
Heidi Sullivan, VP & Publisher
Valerie Lopez, Research Director
Jessica White, Research Director
Rachel Farrell, Research Manager
Includes comprehensive coverage for contact and programming information for more than 3,500 televsion networks, cable networks, television syndicators, television stations, and cable systems in the United States and Canada.
Cost: $350.00
Frequency: Annual
ISSN: 1088-9639
Printed in one color on matte stock

20615 **Book Marketing 105: Choosing a Book Distribution System**
Open Horizons Publishing
PO Box 2887
Taos, NM 87571
575-751-3398
800-796-6130
Fax: 575-751-3100
E-Mail: info@bookmarket.com
Home Page: www.bookmarket.com
John Kremer, Editor
Robert Sanny, Advertising/Sales Manager
A mini-guide including criteria for deciding how to distribute books. Also includes complete information on 30 distributors, 4 library distributors, 89 book publishers who also distribute for other publishers, 3 sales reps to the chains, 27 bookstore wholesalers, 34 library wholesalers, and 23 Spanish-launguage wholesalers. Plus a sample distribution contract.
Cost: $30.00
Frequency: Ebook Download
Founded in 1982

20616 **BookStats**
Association of American Publishers (AAP)
455 Massachusetts Avenue NW
Suite 700
Washington, DC 20001-2777
202-347-3375
Fax: 202-347-3690
E-Mail: info@publishers.org
Home Page: www.publishers.org
Social Media: Twitter
Karen Abramson, President & CEO
Tina Jordan, Vice President
Allan R Adler, VP for Legal & Government Affairs
Jay Diskey, Executive Director, School Division
Gail Kump, Director, Membership Marketing
Provides a comprehensive view of the size and shape of the US book publishing industry measured by publisher net unit and dollar sales.
Frequency: Annual

20617 **Books and Periodicals Online**
Literary Technology Alliance
264 Lexington Avenue
Room 4C
New York, NY 10016-4182
212-686-8816
Fax: 212-686-8776
E-Mail: info@booksandperiodicals.com
Home Page: www.booksandperiodicals.com/
Nuchine Nobari MLS, MBA, Editor
BPO is an international directory of periodicals included in onlinedatabases. Arranged alphabetically, entries include Publication title, dates covered in each database, whether coverage is in Full text, Abstract, or Index, ISSN, and title changes. Online hosts and addresses for producers and vendors are given in separate list. Lists over 97,000 sources and includes an appendix of newspapers and their URL, in alphabetical and geographic order.
Cost: $399.00
3400 Pages
Frequency: 4 issues
Circulation: 1400
ISBN: 0-963027-78-X
Founded in 1987
Printed in 2 colors

20618 **Business Info USA**
InfoUSA
5711 S 86th Cir
Omaha, NE 68127-4146
402-593-4500
888-260-7943
Fax: 402-331-6287
E-Mail: karen.peters@infousa.com
Home Page: www.infousa.com
Vinod Gupta, CEO
Karen Peters, Account Executive
Cost: $2750.00
Frequency: Monthly
Circulation: 4000000
Founded in 1972

20619 **Business Periodicals Index**
HW Wilson Company
950 Dr Martin L King Jr Blvd
Bronx, NY 10452-4297
718-588-8405
800-367-6770
Fax: 718-590-1617
Home Page: www.hwwilson.com
Harold Regan, CEO
Kathleen McEvoy, Director of Public Relations
Designed for businesses, business schools and libraries, business periodicals index covers English-language business periodicals and trade journals. Users enjoy quick access to feature articles, product reviews, interviews, biographical sketches, corporate profiles, obituaries, surveys, book reviews, reports from associations, societies, trade shows and conferences, and more. The database also provides SIC codes for industries and names of corporations used as subject headings.

20620 **Catalog Sales Data Files**
Open Horizons Publishing
PO Box 2887
Taos, NM 87571
575-751-3398
800-796-6130
Fax: 575-751-3100
E-Mail: info@bookmarket.com
Home Page: www.bookmarket.com
John Kremer, Editor
Robert Sanny, Advertising/Sales Manager
Database features the top 1,350 catalogs, internet bookstore sites, chain store outlets, wholesalers, distributors, and other special sales outlets. Includes catalog names, buyers, addresses, phone and fax numbers, emails, website, types of books carried, and other important details.
Cost: $30.00
Frequency: Database
Founded in 1982

20621 **Celebrate Today**
Open Horizons Publishing
PO Box 2887
Taos, NM 87571
575-751-3398
800-796-6130
Fax: 575-751-3100
E-Mail: info@bookmarket.com
Home Page: www.bookmarket.com
John Kremer, Editor
Robert Sanny, Advertising/Sales Manager
Database with 18,290 holidays, special days, weeks, months and historical anniversaries. Searchable by subject interest. Includes contact info and websites in most cases. Useful for setting pub dates and doing PR tie-ins.
Cost: $30.00
Frequency: Database
Founded in 1982

20622 **Complete Directory of Large Print Books and Serials**
4919 Route 22
PO Box 56
Amenia, NY 12546
518-789-8700
800-562-2139
Fax: 518-789-0556

E-Mail: customerservice@greyhouse.com
Home Page: www.greyhouse.com

R R Bowker

Provides nine easy to use indexes including Title, Author, General Reading Subject, Textbook Subject, Children's Subject, Serials Subject, and Serials Title. For easy acquisition, full contact information on publishers, wholesalers and distributors is provided in a separate index.
Frequency: Annual
ISBN: 0-835249-41-6

20623 Corporate Yellow Book
Leadership Directories
398 RXR Plaza
Uniondale, NY 11556

516-730-1900
E-Mail: corporate@leadershipdirectories.com
Home Page: www.corporate.yellowbook.com

David Hurvitz, CEO
Bryan Turner, CFO
Jim McCusker, President

Contact information for over 48,000 executives at over 1,000 companies and more than 9,000 board members and their outside affiliations.
Cost: $400.00
1,400 Pages
Frequency: Quarterly
ISSN: 1058-2098
Founded in 1986

20624 Directories in Print
Gale/Cengage Learning
10650 Toebben Drive
Independence, KY 41051

800-824-5179
800-354-9706
Fax: 800-487-8488
E-Mail: higheredcs@cengage.com
Home Page: www.gale.com

Patrick C Sommers, President

Describes more than 16,000 active rosters, guides and other print and nonprint address lists published in the United States and worldwide.
Frequency: Annual
ISBN: 1-414421-75-3

20625 Directory of Poetry Publishers
Dustbooks
PO Box 100
Paradise, CA 95967-0100

530-877-6110
800-477-6110
Fax: 530-877-0222
E-Mail: directories@dustbooks.com
Home Page: www.dustbooks.com

Len Fulton, Editor

Over 2,100 magazines, small and commercial presses and university presses that accept poetry for publication.
Cost: $25.95
300 Pages
Frequency: Annual
Circulation: 2,000
ISBN: 0-916685-47-0

20626 Directory of Small Magazines Press Magazine Editors & Publishers
Dustbooks
PO Box 100
Paradise, CA 95967-0100

530-877-6110
800-477-6110
Fax: 530-877-0222
E-Mail: directories@dustbooks.com
Home Page: www.dustbooks.com

Len Fulton, Editor

This directory contains more than 7,500 listings of editors and publishers in alphabetical order, along with their associated publishing companies, their addresses, phones, e-mail addresses and Web pages. Includes self publishers.
Cost: $25.95
460 Pages
Frequency: Annual
Circulation: 1,000
ISBN: 0-913218-28-6
Founded in 1967
Mailing list available for rent

20627 Editor & Publisher International Yearbook
Editor & Publisher Company
770 Broadway
New York, NY 10003-9595

212-291-1259
800-336-4380
Fax: 646-654-5370
Home Page: www.editorandpublisher.com

Sid Holt, Editor-in-Chief
Greg Mitchell, Editor
Michael Parker, President

Daily and Sunday newspapers in the US and Canada; weekly newspapers; foreign daily newspapers; special service newspapers; newspaper syndicates; news servides; journalism schools; foreign language and Black newspapers in the US; news, picture and press services; feature and news syndicates; comic and magazine services; advertising clubs; trade associations; clipping bureaus; house organs; journalism awards; manufacturers of equipment and supplies.
Cost: $230.00
Frequency: Annual March

20628 Editor & Publisher Market Guide
Editor & Publisher Company
770 Broadway
New York, NY 10003-9595

212-291-1259
800-336-4380
Fax: 646-654-5370
Home Page: www.editorandpublisher.com

Sid Holt, Editor-in-Chief
Greg Mitchell, Editor
Michael Parker, President

More than 1,700 newspaper markets in the US and Canada.
Cost: $100.00
Frequency: Annual November
Circulation: 4,500

20629 Editor & Publisher: Journalism Awards and Fellowships Directory Issue
Editor & Publisher Company
770 Broadway
New York, NY 10003-9595

212-291-1259
800-336-4380
Fax: 646-654-5370
Home Page: www.editorandpublisher.com

Sid Holt, Editor-in-Chief
Greg Mitchell, Editor
Michael Parker, President

Over 500 cash prizes, scholarships, fellowships and grants available to journalists and students for work on special subjects or in specific fields.
Cost: $4.00
Frequency: Annual December
Circulation: 28,500

20630 Grey House Publishing
4919 Route 22
PO Box 56
Amenia, NY 12546

518-789-8700
800-562-2139
Fax: 518-789-0556
E-Mail: customerservice@greyhouse.com
Home Page: www.greyhouse.com

Leslie Mackenzie, Publisher
Richard Gottlieb, Editor

Publishes over 100 titles including reference directories in the areas of business, education, health, statistics and demographics, as well as educational encyclopedias and business handbooks. All titles offer detailed information in well-organized formats. Many titles available online.
Founded in 1981

20631 IBPA Directory
Independent Book Publishers Association
627 Aviation Way
Manhattan Beach, CA 90266

310-318-2270
Fax: 310-374-3342
E-Mail: info@ibpa-online.org
Home Page: www.ibpa-online.org

Terry Nathan, Executive Director
Lisa Krebs, Assistant Director

A directory of members and one of regional affiliates is available online with multi-level search options.

20632 International Directory of Little Magazines & Small Presses
Dustbooks
PO Box 100
Paradise, CA 95967-0100

530-877-6110
Fax: 530-877-0222
E-Mail: directories@dustbooks.com
Home Page: www.dustbooks.com

Len Fulton, Editor

Lists more than 4,000 book and magazine publishers of literary, avant garde, cutting-edge contemporary, left wing, right wing and radical chic fiction to non-fiction essays, reviews, artwork, music, satire, criticism, commentary, letters, parts of novels, longpoems, concrete art, collages, plays, news items and more.
Cost: $55.00
Frequency: Annual/Cloth
Circulation: 1,000
ISBN: 0-916685-49 7

20633 International Literary Market Place
Information Today
143 Old Marlton Pike
Medford, NJ 08055-8750

609-654-6266
800-300-9868
Fax: 609-654-4309
E-Mail: custserv@infotoday.com
Home Page: www.infotoday.com
Social Media: Facebook, Twitter

Thomas H Hogan, President
Roger R Bilboul, Chairman of the Board
John C Yersak, Vice President
John Brokenshire, CFO

The directory of the international book publishing industry with 16,500 up to date profiles with book related concerns, including trade organizations, distributors, dealers, literary associations, trade publications, book trade events, and other resources conveniently organzied in a country by counrty format
Cost: $240.00
1800 Pages
ISBN: 1-573871-75-3

20634 Livestock Publications Council Membership Directory
Livestock Publications
910 Currie Street
Fort Worth, TX 76107
817-336-1130
Fax: 817-232-4820
E-Mail: dianej@flash.net
Home Page: www.livestockpublications.com
Offers information on over 100 US and Canadian LPC-member livestock magazines, newspapers and newsletters.
40 Pages

20635 Magazines for Libraries
R R Bowker LLC
630 Central Ave
New Providence, NJ 07974-1506
908-286-0288
888-269-5372
Fax: 908-219-0098
E-Mail: info@bowker.com
Home Page: www.bowker.com
R R Bowker
Magazines for Libraries provides the serials information you need to build and maintain a quality collection that best meets the needs of your library's users.
Frequency: Triennial
ISBN: 1-600301-16-2

20636 National Journal
National Journal
600 New Hampshire Ave NW
Washington, DC 20037-2403
202-739-8400
800-207-8001
Fax: 202-833-8069
E-Mail: service@nationaljournal.com
Home Page: www.nationaljournal.com
John Fox Sullivan, President
Steve Hull, Senior VP
Timothy B Clark, VP
Publishes directories in the area of government.

20637 Progressive Periodicals Directory
Progressive Education
PO Box 120574
Nashville, TN 37212-0574
615-367-1874
Craig T Canan, Editor
About 600 social-concerns periodicals.
Cost: $16.00

20638 Publishers, Distributors and Wholesalers of the United States
R R Bowker LLC
630 Central Ave
New Providence, NJ 07974-1506
908-286-0288
888-269-5372
Fax: 908-219-0098
E-Mail: info@bowker.com
Home Page: www.bowker.com
R R Bowker
In this 2 volume set locate publishers, museum and association imprint and trade organizations that publish, software firms, audio-cassette producers and even publishers that have gone out of business.
Frequency: 2 Volumes
ISBN: 0-835249-66-9

20639 Publishing & Production Executive: Who's Who of Suppliers and Services
North American Publishing Company
1500 Spring Garden St
Suite 1200
Philadelphia, PA 19130-4094
215-238-5300
800-777-8074
Fax: 215-238-5342
E-Mail: customerservice@napco.com
Home Page: www.napco.com
Ned S Borowsky, CEO
Directory of services and supplies to the industry.
Circulation: 30,000
Mailing list available for rent

20640 Single Unit Supermarkets Operators
Chain Store Guide
3922 Coconut Palm Dr
Tampa, FL 33619-1389
813-627-6700
800-778-9794
Fax: 813-627-7094
E-Mail: info@csgis.com
Home Page: www.csgis.com
Mike Jarvis, Publisher
Shami Choon, Manager
Discover more than 7,100 single-unit supermarkets with annual sales topping $500,000 dollars. This comprehensive desktop reference makes it easy to reach our compiled list of 21,000 key executives and buyers, plus their primary wholesalers.
Cost: $335.00
725 Pages
Frequency: Annual

20641 Small Publishers Association of North America (SPAN)
PO Box 1306
Buena Vista, CO 81211-1306
719-395-4790
Fax: 719-395-8374
Home Page: www.spannet.org
Marilyn Ross, Executive Director/Editor
Tom Ross, VP
Cathy Bowman, Production Manager
Online resource for book publishing know-how. Works to advance the image and profits of self publishers and independent publishers through education and marketing opportunities.

20642 Something About the Author
Gale/Cengage Learning
Po Box 09187
Detroit, MI 48209-0187
248-699-4253
800-877-4253
Fax: 248-699-8049
E-Mail: gale.galeord@cengage.com
Home Page: www.gale.com
Patrick C Sommers, President
An easy to use source for librarians, students and other researchers each volume in this series provides illustrated biographical profiles of approximately 75 children's authors and artists. This critically acclaimed series covers more than 12,000 individuals, ranging from established award winners to authors and illustrators who are just beginning their careers.
ISBN: 1-414442-17-3

20643 Standard Periodical Directory
Oxbridge Communications
39 W. 29 St.
301
New York, NY 10001
212-741-0231
800-955-0231
Fax: 212-633-2938
E-Mail: custserv@mediafinder.com
Home Page: www.mediafinder.com
Patricia Hagood, President
Circulation, advertising and list rental info for more than 75,000 North American periodicals.
Cost: $1495.00
2,326 Pages
Frequency: Annual
Circulation: 3,500
ISBN: 1-891783-23-8
ISSN: 0085-6630
Founded in 1964
Printed in 4 colors

20644 Top 700 Independent Bookstores
Open Horizons Publishing
PO Box 2887
Taos, NM 87571
641-472-6130
800-796-6130
Fax: 641-472-1560
E-Mail: info@bookmarket.com
Home Page: www.bookmarket.com
John Kremer, Editor
Robert Sanny, Advertising/Sales Manager
Database of 790 stores with address, book buyer, owner, event coordinator, phone, fax, email, website and more. Lists the largest bookstores that work with authors and that buy from indy book publishers. Compiled from industry news, author and publisher recommendations, and research.The report comes as a data file download in your choice of Access, Excel, comma- or tab-delimited ASCII, d-Base or rich text format.
Cost: $40.00
Frequency: Database
Founded in 1982

20645 Ulrich's Periodicals Directory
R R Bowker LLC
630 Central Ave
New Providence, NJ 07974-1506
908-286-1090
888-269-5372
Fax: 908-219-0098
E-Mail: info@bowker.com
Home Page: www.bowker.com
Michael Cairns, CEO
Annie Callanan, COO
An essential reference tool for any serials librarian the Ulrich's Periodicals Directory™ is overflowing with the latest international bibliographic information on journals, magazines and newspapers.

Industry Web Sites

20646 http://gold.greyhouse.com
G.O.L.D Grey House OnLine Databases
Grey House Publishing's online database platform, GOLD, offers Quick Search, Keyword Search and Expert Search for most business sectors including publishing and allied markets. The GOLD platform makes finding the information you need quick and easy - whether you're a novice searcher or an experienced database user. All of Grey House's directory products are available for subscription on the GOLD platform.

20647 www.aaup.princetou.edu
Exchange
Reports on issues relevant to scholarly publishing.

20648 www.aaupnet.org/membership/directory
Association of American University Presses

Members are university presses and a limited number of presses of non-degree-granting scholarly institutions.

20649 www.abaa.org
Antiquarian Booksellers Association of America
A trade association of rare book dealers.

20650 www.abpaonline.org
American Book Producers Association
Increases the book industry's awareness of members capabilities and exchanges information on improving business. Develops concepts for books and other publications.

20651 www.accessabc.com
Audit Bureau of Circulations
The world's largest circulation-auditing organization, ABC provides circulation data on 1,400+ newspapers and more than 1,100 periodicals to ABC-member publications, advertisers and advertising agencies.

20652 www.ampaonline.org
American Medical Publishers' Association
Information provided to the medical publishing field.

20653 www.bisg.org
Book Industry Study Group
Promotes and supports research, enabling various sectors of the industry to develop and expand their professional and business plans. Book Industry Study Group has various paperback publications.

20654 www.bizpubs.org
Alliance of Area Business Publications
Represents metropolitan area and state-wide business to business publications with conventions, newsletters, and other services.

20655 www.bookbuilders.org
Bookbuilders West
A nonprofit organization that provides a forum for publishers and suppliers to share experiences via dinners, social events and educational seminars.

20656 www.bookmarketingprofits.com
North American Bookdealers Exchange
Independent publishers and mail order entrepreneurs. An international book marketing organization specializing in cooperative opportunities at trade shows, in mail order, press releases, and more.

20657 www.bookpublishing.com
Jenkins Independent Publishers

20658 www.catholicpress.org
Catholic Press Association of the US and Canada

20659 www.clmp.org
Council of Literary Magazines and Presses
Membership is open to any noncommercial literary magazine or press that publishes at least one or more books per year.

20660 www.columbia.edu/eu/cspa
Columbia Scholastic Press Association
International student press association composed of writing students, journalists and faculty advisers in schools and colleges through educational conferences, idea exchanges and recognition programs.

20661 www.du.edu/pi
Publishing Institute
A national organization that combines workshops in editing and marketing with lecture/teaching sessions conducted by leading experts from all areas of publishing.

20662 www.ecpa.org
Evangelical Christian Publishers Association
Promotes excellence and professionalism, shares relevant data, and equips Christian publishers to meet the needs of the changing marketplace.

20663 www.flexography.org
Flexographic Technical Association

20664 www.flexography.org/flexsys/index.cfm
Flexographic Technical Assn Education & Training
Magazine publishing.

20665 www.greyhouse.com
Grey House Publishing
Authoritative reference directories for most business sectors including publishing and allied markets. Users can search the online databases with varied search criteria allowing for custom searches by product category, geographic area, sales volume, keyword, subject and more. Full Grey House catalog and online ordering also available.

20666 www.interquest.Com
FAX new
A market and technology research and consulting firm in the field of digital printing and publishing that produces studies on topics such as digital printing, transactional printing, variable imaging, etc.

20667 www.ipma.org
International Publishing Management Association
The professional association for in-house corporate publishing professionals who work for educational institutions, governments and private industry.

20668 www.naa.org
Newspaper Association of America
Founded by the merger of seven associations serving the newspaper industry. Focuses on the major issues that affect today's newspaper industry public policy and legal matters, advertising revenue growth and audience development across the medium's broad portfolio of products and digital platforms.

20669 www.ncrw.org
National Council for Research on Women
A network of 120 leading research, policy and advocacy centers dedicated to improving the lives of women and girls. Provides the latest news, analysis and strategies needed to ensure fully informed debates, effective policies and inclusive practices.

20670 www.newsletters.org
Newsletter & Electronic Publishers Association
International trade association serving the interests of publishers of newsletters and specialized information services.

20671 www.nmpa.org
National Music Publishers' Association

20672 www.p3-ny.org/
Partnership in Print Production
Promotes the interests of women.

20673 www.pacificpress.com
Pacific Press Publishing Association
Promotes the interests of publishing, press, and media professionals.

20674 www.papertrade.com
National Paper Trade Association

20675 www.publishers.org
Association of American Publishers
Principal trade association for the US book publishing industry members comprise most of the major commerical book publishers in the US, as well as smaller and medium-sized houses, not-for-profit publishers, university presses, and scholarly societies.

20676 www.publishersreport.com
National Association of Independent Publishers
Assists and educates small publishing companies. Conducts seminars on marketing strategies, target audience, and techniques of book distribution. Especially helpful for the beginning or self-publisher.

20677 www.snaponline.org
Society of National Association Publications
Develops standards for editorial and advertising content of association and professional society magazines.

20678 www.spannet.org
Small Publishers Association of North America
For independent presses and self-publishers who want to produce better books and market them more successfully.

20679 www.sspnet.org
Society for Scholarly Publishing
A group that represents scholarly publications, such as journals, university publications and magazines.

20680 www.theacp.org
Associated Church Press
Aims to share ideas and concerns in religious publishing and to stimulate higher standards of religious journalism to exert a more positive influence.

20681 www.thomson.com
Thomson.Com
A shared Web service that provides critical tools for more than 35 publishers.

20682 www.wpa-online.org
Western Publications Association
Represents magazine publishing companies and companies related to publishing industry, in the western United States.

Associations

20683 Accredited Review Appraisers Council
ARAC
303 W Cypress Street
San Antonio, TX 78212
800-486-3676
Home Page: www.arac.lincoln-grad.org

Provides education and designation in appraisal and real estate review.

20684 American Association of Certified Wedding Planners
14902 Preston Road
Suite 404.324
Dallas, TX 75254
214-342-2378
E-Mail: info@aacwp.org
Home Page: www.aacwp.org
Social Media: Facebook, Twitter

Trudy Baade, President
Wendy Kidd, Vice-President
Karen Radford, Treasurer/Secretary
Micki Novak, Executive Director
Sarabeth Quattlebaum, Education

A national organization that offers designations to qualified appraisers, teaches courses on latest appraisal information and offers courses on home inspection.

20685 American College of Real Estate Lawyers
11300 Rockville Pike
Suite 903
Rockville, MD 20852
301-816-9811
Fax: 301-816-9786
E-Mail: webmaster@acrel.org
Home Page: www.acrel.org

Jill Pace, Executive Director
Kenneth M.Ken Jacobson, VP
Kathryn C.Kathy Murphy, Treasurer
Roger D. Winston, Secretary
Thomas F. tom Kaufman, Presiednt-Elect

Members are CPAs working in the real estate field.

20686 American Homeowners Foundation
6776 Little Falls Rd
Arlington, VA 22213-1213
703-536-7776
800-489-7776
Fax: 703-536-7079
E-Mail: ahga@amricanhomeowners.org
Home Page: www.americanhomeowners.org

Bruce Itahn, President

A national consumer organization representing the nation's 75 million homeowners.
Founded in 1984

20687 American Industrial Real Estate
Pacific Financial Center
800 West 6 Th Street
Suite 800
Los Angeles, CA 90017
213-687-8777
Fax: 213-687-8616
E-Mail: jcruz@airea.com
Home Page: www.airea.com

Joy D'La Cruz, Chief Operations Officer
Tim Hayes, Executive Director
David M Harding, President
Jason K Jamison, Vice-President
Joseph Lin, Secretary/Treasurer

Encourages high professional standards. Has developed industrial multiple listing system and standard lease form. Publishes a quarterly newsletter.
1300+ Members
Founded in 1960

20688 American Land Title Association
1828 L St NW
Suite 705
Washington, DC 20036
202-296-3671
800-787-ALTA
Fax: 202-223-5843
E-Mail: service@alta.org
Home Page: www.alta.org
Social Media: Facebook, Twitter, LinkedIn, YouTube, Google+

Kurt Pfotenhauer, CEO
William Burding Jr., Chair, Finance Committee
Rob Chapman, President
Peter J. Birnbaum, Treasurer
Diane Evans, President-Elect

Trade organization for title insurers, abstractors and agents.
1800 Members
Founded in 1907
Mailing list available for rent: 3000 names at $500 per M

20689 American Planning Association
122 S Michigan Ave
Suite 1600
Chicago, IL 60603-6111
312-431-9100
Fax: 312-431-9985
E-Mail: CustomerService@planning.org
Home Page: www.planning.org
Social Media: Facebook, Twitter, LinkedIn, YouTube, Flickr, RSS

Paul Farmer, Executive Director/CEO
Kenneth East, Marketing Director
Charlotte McCaskill, COO

A public interest and research organization representing practicing planners, officials, and citizens involved with urban and rural planning issues. APA's objective is to encourage planning that will meet the needs of people and society more effectively.

20690 American Rental Association
1900 19th St
Moline, IL 61265-4198
309-764-2475
800-334-2177
Fax: 309-764-1533
E-Mail: ara@ararental.org
Home Page: www.ararental.org

Chris Wehrman, CEO/ Executive Vice-President
Mike Blaisdell, President
Mike Flesher, Chairman
Paul Phelon, President-Elect
Terry Turner, Party & Event Services SIG Chairman

Benefits members (rental business owners and equipment suppliers) by promoting, representing and enhancing the rental industry, resulting in improved rental services to the public.
8600 Members
Founded in 1955

20691 American Resort Development Association
1201 15th St Nw
Suite 400
Washington, DC 20005-2842
202-371-6700
Fax: 202-289-8544
E-Mail: customerservice@arda.org, webmaster@arda
Home Page: www.ardafoundation.org

Howard C. Nusbaum, President & CEO
Rob Dunn, Vice President of Finance
Peter Roth, Vice President of Marketing
May Crowley, Executive Assistant
Sarah Oshel, HR Manager

International trade association composed of resort developers and resort industry suppliers.
1000 Members
Founded in 1969

20692 American Society of Appraisers
11107 Sunset Hills Rd
Suite 310
Reston, VA 20190
703-478-2228
800-272-8258
Fax: 703-742-8471
E-Mail: asainfo@appraisers.org
Home Page: www.appraisers.org
Social Media: Facebook, Twitter, LinkedIn, YouTube

Jane Grimm, Executive VP
Susan Fischer, Governance Manager
J. Mark Penny, International President
Linda B. Trugman, International Secretary/Treasurer
Gary L. Smith, International Vice President

Professional association of appraisers of all disciplines.
5000 Members
Founded in 1936

20693 American Society of Farm Managers and Rural Appraisers
950 S Cherry St
Suite 508
Denver, CO 80246-2664
303-758-3513
Fax: 303-758-0190
Home Page: www.asfmra.org
Social Media: Facebook, Twitter

Douglas W Slothower, Executive VP
LeeAnn E. Moss, Academic Vice President
Merrill E. Swanson, First Vice President
Jim Rickert, President
Fred L. Hepler, President-Elect

Premier professional organization for professionals who provide management, consultation and valuation services on rural and agricultural assets. Provides members with the resources, information and leadership that enables them to provide valuable services to the agricultural community.
Founded in 1929

20694 Building Owners and Managers Association International
1201 New York Ave Nw
Suite 300
Washington, DC 20005-3917
202-408-2662
Fax: 202-371-0181
E-Mail: info@boma.org
Home Page: www.boma.org/splash

Henry Chamberlain, President
Richard W. Greninger, Chair & Chief Elected Officer
Henry Chamberlain, Presdent & COO
Patricia M. Areno, Senior Vice President
Ann Coslett, Director of Executive

Owners and managers of commercial office buildings.
7.5M Members
Founded in 1907

20695 Commercial Real Estate Women
655 15th Street NW
Washington, DC 20005
202-737-3262
Home Page: www.crewdc.org
Social Media: LinkedIn
Kim Dize, Director of Special Events
Elizabeth A Karmin, President
Marci Basham, Treasurer
Susan Denner, Director of Communications
Jeniffer Bognet, President-Elect
Provides a forum for women who are involved in commercial real estate and wish to network as well as reap the benefits of their courses.
125 Members
Founded in 1979

20696 Commercial-Investment Real Estate Institute
430 N Michigan Avenue
Chicago, IL 60611-4002
312-270-0273
Steven F Pope, Executive VP
Functions as a professional association of real estate practitioners who have successfully completed its certification program or are striving toward it.
4M Members

20697 Community Associations Institute
6402 Arlington Blvd
Suite 500
Falls Church, VA 22042
703-970-9220
888-224-4321
Fax: 703-970-9558
E-Mail: caidirect@caionline.org
Home Page: www.caionline.org
Social Media: Facebook, Twitter, LinkedIn
Composed of community and condominium associations managers, management companies and other business partners.
15000 Members
Founded in 1973

20698 CoreNet Global
CoreNet Global Inc
133 Peachtree ST NE
Suite 3000
Atlanta, GA 30303
404-589-3200
800-726-8111
Fax: 404-589-3201
E-Mail: david.harris@sun.com
Home Page: www.corenetglobal.org
Social Media: Facebook, Twitter, LinkedIn, YouTube,Flickr
Angela Cain, CEO
Jim Scannell, Chairman
John Davis, Controller
Larry Bazrod, COO
Walter Showers, IT Specialist
Formerly NACORE International.

20699 Council of Real Estate Brokerage Managers
Country Radio Broadcaster's Inc
430 N. Michigan Ave.
Chicago, IL 60611
615-327-4487
Fax: 31- 3-9 88
E-Mail: info@crb.com
Home Page: www.crb.com
Social Media: Facebook, Twitter, LinkedIn
Darren Kittleson, President
Ginny Shipe, CEO
Tara Maric, Manager, Member Services
Bette McTamney, Finance Vice President
Jean Crosby, President-Elect
Members are real estate firm owners and managers.
7000 Members
Founded in 1968

20700 Council of Residential Specialists
430 N Michigan Ave
3rd Floor
Chicago, IL 60611
312-321-4400
800-462-8841
Fax: 312-329-8551
E-Mail: crshelp@crs.com
Home Page: www.crs.com
Social Media: Facebook, Twitter, LinkedIn, YouTube, Google+, RSS
Lana Vukovljak, CEO
Dale Carlton, Vice Chair
Mark T. Minchew, Chair of Nominating
Ron Canning, Chair
Janelle Pfleiger, 1st VP
Seeks to establish cooperation among brokers engaged in buying, selling, trading and leasing of real estate.
40000 Members
Founded in 1976

20701 Council of Residential Specialties
430 N Michigan Avenue
3rd Floor
Chicago, IL 60611
312-321-4400
800-462-8841
Fax: 312-329-8882
E-Mail: info@crs.com
Home Page: www.crs.com
Social Media: Facebook, Twitter, LinkedIn, RSS, Google+, Youtube
Sara Patterson, Director Communications
Ron Canning, Chair
Dale Carlton, Vice Chair
Lana Vukoljak, CEO
Janelle Pfleiger, 1st VP
A council of the Realtors National Marketing Institute.
40000 Members
Founded in 1976

20702 Counselors of Real Estate
430 N Michigan Ave
Chicago, IL 60611
312-329-8427
Fax: 312-329-8881
E-Mail: info@cre.org
Home Page: www.cre.org
Mary Walker Fleischmann, President & CEO
Alice Muncaster, Director Marketing/Communications
Shea Shumpert, CAO
Christiane Rodes, Executive Assistant
Carol Scherf, Communications Manager
Association members provide the public with expert, objective advice on property and land related matters. Individuals invited to join are awarded the CRE designation.
1200 Members
Founded in 1953

20703 Institute for Responsible Housing Preservation
401 9th St NW
Suite 900
Washington, DC 20004
20- 5-5
Fax: 202-585-8080
E-Mail: info@housingpreservation.org
Home Page: www.nixonpeabody.com
Margaret Wagner, Vice president
Greg Gossard, Treasurer
Alex Viorst, President
Brian Poulin, Chairman
Steve Whyte, Secretary
IRHP members are owners and managers of Low Income Housing Preservation and Resident Housing Act housing and ELIHPA housing and concerned professionals.
Founded in 1989

20704 Institute of Real Estate Management
430 N Michigan Ave
Chicago, IL 60611
800-837-0706
Fax: 800-338-4736
E-Mail: custserv@irem.org
Home Page: www.irem.org
Social Media: Facebook, Twitter, LinkedIn, YouTube
Michael T. Lanning, Senior Vice President
Christopher Mellen, Secretary/ Treasurer
Randy Eagar, First VP
Joseph Greenblatt, President
Lori Burger, President-Elect
Awards property manager certificate to qualifying individuals and accreditates management organizations and management firms. Offers management courses.
40000 Members
Founded in 1976

20705 International Council of Shopping Centers
1221 Ave of the Americas
41st Floor
New York, NY 10020-1099
646-728-3800
Fax: 732-694-1690
E-Mail: membership@icsc.org
Home Page: www.icsc.org
Social Media: Facebook, Twitter, LinkedIn, YouTube, Google+, Pinterest, I
Michael P Kercheval, CEO
Jennifer Collin, Manager, Membership Development
Peter E Baccile, Managing Director
Sheri Pupello, Member Communications
Cecilia Perrino, Customer Service/ Info Center
Fosters professional standards of performance in the development, construction, financing, leasing, management and operation of shopping centers throughout the world.
44000 Members
Founded in 1957

20706 International Exchangers Association
PO Box L
Rancho Santa Fe, CA 92067-0560
973-496-5784
Fax: 973-496-5784
Works to standardize procedures and establish professional ethics.
3.2M Members
Founded in 1978

20707 International Real Estate Federation
1050 Connecticut Ave NW
Suite 1000
Washington, DC 20036
202-772-3308
E-Mail: bill@fiabci-usa.com
Home Page: www.fiabci-usa.com
Bonnie Carris, President
Bill Endsley, Secretary General
Ruth Kruger, Treasurer
maire Rosol, Vice President
Edward Alford, President-Elect
Encourages private ownership of real property and understanding of property rights and obligations.

20708 International Real Estate Institute
810 N Farrell Drive
Palm Springs, CA 92262
760-327-5284
877-743-6799
Fax: 760-327-5631
E-Mail: support@assoc-hdqts.org
Home Page: www.irei-assoc.org
Bale Ekdaho, Production Manager
Robert Johnson, Executive Director
An organization comprised of thousands of real estate professionals from over 98 countries around the world. Acts as a voting member of, and property advisor to, the United Nations. Members specialize in real estate and property management. Arranges and promotes international educational real estate seminars.
2000 Members
Founded in 1975

20709 Maine Apartment Owners and Managers Association, Inc.
P.O. Box 282
Bath, MN 04530
207-623-3480
800-204-4311
E-Mail: maoma@maoma.org
Home Page: www.maineapartmentowners.com
A national organization that presents the facts and information builder/developer/owners/manager members need to keep abreast of in the world of multi-family housing. Monthly issue will bring the reader timely insight on real estate, tax news, financing techniques, and effective management procedures, and keeps readers aware of the new developments in the condominium market.

20710 Mortgage Bankers Association of America
Mortgage Bankers Association
1919 M Street NW
5th Floor
Washington, DC 20036
202-557-2700
E-Mail: membership@mortgagebankers.org
Home Page: www.mortgagebankers.org
Social Media: Facebook, Twitter, LinkedIn, YouTube
Kieran Quinn, Chairman
Margaret A. Colon, President/CEO
Debra Still, Chairman
Marcia Davies, Chief of Staff & SVP
Teresa F. Betz, Executive Dircetor & Treasurer
Seeks to improve methods of originating, servicing and marketing loans.
2.8M Members
Founded in 1914

20711 National Affordable Housing Management
400 N Columbus Street
Suite 203
Alexandria, VA 22314
703-683-8630
Fax: 703-683-8634
Home Page: www.nahma.org
Kris C Cook, Executive Director
Daria Jakubowski, Deputy Director
Michelle L. Kitchen, Director, Govt. Affairs
Rajni Agarwal, Director, Finance & Administration
Scott McMillen, Coordinator, Govt. Affairs
Trade association representing individuals involved in the management of affordable multifamily housing.
Founded in 1990

20712 National Apartment Association
4300 Wilson Blvd
Suite 400
Alexandria, VA 22203
703-518-6141
Fax: 703-248-9440
E-Mail: webmaster@naahq.org
Home Page: www.naahq.org
Social Media: Facebook, Twitter, LinkedIn, YouTube, Google+, Pinterest, F
Doug Culkin, President &CEO
Chanal Thomas, Office Manager
Karen Goggin, VP Governance
Bob Pinnegar, EVP & COO
Lynn Miller, Adminstartor
The largest organization dedicated solely to rental housing-serves 26,000 rental housing professionals representing 3.4 million apartments nationwide. NAA lobbies for the industry, provides education programs, publishes Units Magazine, and conducts an annual Education Conference and Trade Show.
25M Members
Founded in 1939

20713 National Association of Home Builders
1201 15th St Nw
Washington, DC 20005
202-266-8200
800-368-5242
Fax: 202-266-8400
E-Mail: info@nahb.org
Home Page: www.nahb.org
Social Media: Facebook, Twitter, LinkedIn, Pinterest
Gerald M Howard, CEO
Rick Judson, Chairman
Kevin Kelly, 1st Vice Chairman of the Board
Tom Woods, 2nd Vice Chairman of the Board
Ed Brady, 3rdVice Chairman
Represents the building industry by serving its members and affiliated state and local builders associations.
22000 Members
Founded in 1942

20714 National Association of Housing Cooperatives
1444 I Street NW
Suite 700
Washington, DC 20005-6542
202-737-0797
Fax: 202-216-9646
E-Mail: info@nahc.coop
Home Page: www.coophousing.org
Linda Brockway, Treasurer
Ralph Marcus, Chairman
Gregory Carlson, President
Fred Gibbs, Vice President
Anne Hills, Secretary
A nonprofit national federation of housing cooperatives, professionals, organizations and individuals promoting the interests of cooperative housing communities. Housing cooperatives are a form of multi family home ownership.
1000 Members
Founded in 1960

20715 National Association of Master Appraisers
303 W Cypress St
San Antonio, TX 78212-5512
210-271-0781
800-229-6262
Fax: 210-225-8450
E-Mail: djd@masterappraisers.org
Home Page: www.masterappraisers.org
Del Martinez, Manager
Christopher Deane, Marketing And Production Manager
Provides basic and advanced courses in techniques, management practices and marketing strategies. Offers designations in real estate appraisal MRA (Master Residential Appraisers), MFLA (Master Farm & Land Appraiser) and MSA (Master Senior Appraiser).

20716 National Association of Real Estate Investment Trusts
1875 I St NW
Suite 600
Washington, DC 20006
202-739-9400
800-3 N-REIT
Fax: 202-739-9401
E-Mail: info@nareit.org
Home Page: www.nareit.com
Social Media: Facebook, Twitter, Google+, YouTube, RSS
Steven A. Wechsler, President &CEO
David J. Neithercut, 1st Vice Chair
David B. Henry, 2nd Vice Chair
Edward Fritsch, Treasurer
Ronald L. Havner, Jr., Chairman
NAREIT is the representative voice for U.S. REITs and publicly traded real estate companies worldwide. Members are real estate investment trusts and other businesses that own, operate and finance income-producing real estate, as well as those firms and individuals who advise, study and service these businesses.

20717 National Association of Realtors
430 N Michigan Ave
Chicago, IL 60611-4087
312-645-7730
800-874-6500
Fax: 312-329-8576
Home Page: www.realtor.org
Social Media: Facebook, Twitter, LinkedIn, YouTube, Skype, Google+
Dale Stinton, CEO
Chris Polychron, President-Elect
Steve Brown, President
Mike McGrew, Treasurer
Beth L. Peerce, Vice President
Promotes education, high professional standards and modern techniques of real estate work.
40000 Members
Founded in 1908

20718 National Association of Residential Property Managers
638 Independence Parkway
Suite 100
Chesapeake, VA 23320
757-466-3336
800-782-3452
Fax: 866-466-2776
E-Mail: info@narpm.org
Home Page: www.narpm.org
Social Media: Facebook, Twitter, LinkedIn, RSS
James E. Tungsvik, President
Gail S. Phillips, Executive Director
Stephen Foster, President-Elect
Andrew Propst, Treasurer
Jayci Grana, Past President
Provides education and publications for the single-family residential property manager.
Founded in 1987

20719 National Association of Review Appraisers and Mortgage Underwriters
P.O Box 879
Palm Springs, CA 92263
760-327-5284
877-743-6805
Fax: 760-327-5631
E-Mail: support@assoc-hdqts.org
Home Page: www.naramu.org
Robert G Johnson, Executive Director
Fred Simon, Production Manager
Conducts educational seminars. Maintains library, speakers bureau and operates a placement service.
6.5M Members
Founded in 1976

20720 National Council of Exchangors
8255 Las Vegas Blvd South
Suite #1202
Las Vegas, NV 89123
85- 2-2 16
Fax: 928-771-2323
E-Mail: nce@ncexchangors.com
Home Page: www.NCExchangors.com
William Jones, President
Kenneth L Kisner, Ex. President
John Stavely, Secretary
Lance Warner, Treasurer
William Jones, Chairman
A non-profit association and is a nationwide network of real estate professionals who specilize in marketing real estate equities primarily through the medium of the real estate exchange. This network is comprised of local groups organized into regional chapters.
400+ Members

20721 National Low Income Housing Coalition
727 15th St NW
6th Floor
Washington, DC 20005
202-662-1530
Fax: 202-393-1973
E-Mail: info@nlihc.org
Home Page: www.nlihc.org
Social Media: Facebook, Twitter, pinterest, Blog
Sheila Crowley, President &CEO
Bill Shields, Vice President for Operations
Khara Norris, Director of Administration
Sarah Brundage, Communications Director
Christina Reyes, Executive Assistant
A national nonprofit organization representing housing advocates, organizers, tenants and professionals in the housing field. The Coalition advocates, represents and educates for decent housing and neighborhoods for all low-income people. It works with Congress and the executive branch to obtain adequate Federal support for low-income housing and related programs.
Founded in 1974

20722 National Property Management Association
4025 Tampa Road
Suite 1203
Oldsmar, FL 34677
813-475-6998
Fax: 813-749-0812
E-Mail: hq@nmpa.org
Home Page: www.npma.org
Wesley Carter, Executive Vice President
Marcia Whitson, National President
Sara Legault, Office Manager
Lesley Martin, Education Coordinator
Maria Maggio, Events and Education Manager
Nonprofit professional association dedicated to the cost effective management of personal property and fixed assets.
3700 Members
Founded in 1970

20723 National Real Estate Investors Association
7265 Kenwood Rd.
Ste 110
Cincinnati, OH 45236
859-261-3335
888-422-4916
Fax: 859-422-4916
E-Mail: info@nationalreia.com
Home Page: www.nationalreia.com
Social Media: Twitter
Rebecca Mc Lean, Executive Director
Scott Whaley, VP
Anna Mills, Treasurer
Lisa Kay Hansen, Secretary
Lori Hudson, Office Manager
Coalition of trade associations serving real estate investors, landlords and owners. Provides education and product services for officers and members.
115 Members
Founded in 1985

20724 National Residential Appraisers Institute
Registered Financial Planners Institute
2001 Cooper Foster Park Rd
Amherst, OH 44001
44- 9-5 16
Fax: 440-282-8027
E-Mail: info@repi.com
Home Page: www.nraiappraisers.com
Brian Schreiber, President
Jack Braman, Vice President/Education Director
Adrian Fredrick, Secretary
Rich Farina, Director
Promotes professionalism in the evaluation of residential real estate and requires demonstration appraisals and testing for professional certification.
451 Members
Founded in 1977

20725 National Society of Environmental Consultants
Po Box 12528
San Antonio, TX 78212-0528
210-225-2897
800-486-3676
Fax: 210-225-8450
Home Page: www.nsec.lincoln-grad.org
Deborah Deane, President
Provides standards, education and a forum for real estate environmental site consultants. Provides a designation program for individuals doing environmental assessments and promotes education and further information about real estate environmental problems.

20726 National Society of Professional Surveyors
National Society of Professional Surveyors
5119 Pegasus Court
Suite Q
Frederick, MD 21704
240-439-4615
Fax: 240-439-4952
E-Mail: curtis.sumner@nsps.us.com
Home Page: www.acsm.net
Curt Sumner, Executive Director
Lamar Evers, President
Rick Howard, Chairman
Jon Warren, Vice President
John Fenn, Secretary/Treasurer
Organization of professionals for networking and education in the topographical field.
5500 Members
Frequency: Annual
Founded in 1942

20727 National Trust for Historic Preservation
1785 Massachusetts Ave Nw
Washington, DC 20036-2117
202-588-6000
800-944-6847
Fax: 202-588-6038
Home Page: www.preservationnation.org
Social Media: Facebook, Twitter, Pinterest, RSS
Stephanie K. Meeks, President &CEO
Tabitha Almquist, Chief of Staff
Rosemarie Rae, CFO
Paul Edmondson, chief Legal Officer
Terry Richey, Chief Marketing officer
A private, nonprofit membership organization dedicated to saving historic places and revitlizing America's communities. Also provides leadership, education, advocacy, and resources to save America's diverse historic places and revitalize the communities.
270k Members
Founded in 1949
Mailing list available for rent

20728 Neighborhood Reinvestment Corporation
92 Argonaut
Suite 255
Aliso Viejo, CA 92656-3100
949-770-2000
800-808-3372
Fax: 949-770-2157
E-Mail: sales@federalregister.com
Home Page: www.federalregister.com
Supplies training, grants, developmental assistance, and a range of other technical services designed to help the local partnerships achieve substantially self-reliant neighborhoods. The goal is to improve a neighborhood's housing and physical conditions, build a positive community image, and establish a healthy real estate market and a core of neighbors capable of managing the continued health of their neighborhood.
Founded in 1978

20729 Professional Certification Board
Po Box 12528
San Antonio, TX 78212-0528
210-225-2897
800-486-3676
Fax: 210-225-8450
Home Page: www.nsec.lincoln-grad.org
Deborah Deane, President
Provides education and board certificates for the real estate appraisal specialties of manufactured housing valuation, business valuation and litigation management.

20730 Professional Housing Management Association
154 Fort Evans Road NE
Leesburg, VA 20176
703-771-1888
Fax: 703-771-0299
E-Mail: mkcooper@earthlink.net
Home Page: www.phma.com
Social Media: Facebook, Twitter
Barry Scribner, Treasurer
Del Eulberg, President
Elijah A. Wilki Wilkerson, Executive Vice President

Jon R. Moore, Exective Director
Chris Cole, Secretary

Members are federal government employees, civilian or military, who are directly involved in housing management or provides direct support to the field.
3,120 Members
Founded in 1973

20731 Property Owners Association
1072 Madison Ave
Lakewood, NJ 08701

732-780-1966
Fax: 732-780-1611
E-Mail: info@poanj.org
Home Page: www.poanj.org
Social Media: Facebook

Jeffery Feld, Sergeant-At-Arms
Marc Tunis, Treasurer
Tom Pahos, President
Larry Rosen, Vice President
Jerry Cheslow, Secretary

The Property Owners Association of New Jersey, Inc. brings together owners and operators of residential real estate, interested persons, and related industry personnel for educational and information sharing purposes.
550 Members
Founded in 1949

20732 Real Estate Buyers Agent Council
430 N Michigan Avenue
Chicago, IL 60611

800-648-6224
800-648-6224
Fax: 312-329-8632
E-Mail: rebac@realtors.org
Home Page: www.rebac.net
Social Media: Facebook, YouTube

Walter T McDonald, President
Larry Von Feldt, VP/Liaison to Gov Affairs
Pat Kaplan, VP Liaison to Committees
Amy Gunaka, Marketing Manager

Represents professional real estate agents who act as buyers' agents.
40000 Members
Founded in 1988
Mailing list available for rent

20733 Real Estate Capital Resources Association
1350 I Street NW
Washington, DC 20005-3305

202-663-3740
Fax: 202-371-0069

G David Fensterheim, Executive Director

Represents firms that provide third party workout and capital recovery services in connection with distressed real estate and real estate related assets.
100 Members
Founded in 1989

20734 Real Estate Educators Association
7739 E Broadway
Suite 337
Tuscon, AZ 85710

520-609-2380
Fax: 856-423-3420
E-Mail: info@reea.org
Home Page: www.reea.org

Karel Murray, President
Michael McAllister, Secretary
Chad Kumpe, Treasurer
Beverly McCormick, President-Elect
Kris Inman, Executive Director

Individuals involved in training and education.
1,400 Members
Founded in 1979

20735 Real Estate Information Providers Association
1420 16th Street NW
Washington, DC 20036-2218

202-298-8169
Fax: 202-332-2301
E-Mail: reipa@aol.com
Home Page: www.reipa.com

Randy Dyer, Executive Director

Supports professional information providers in the real estate industry.
Founded in 1995

20736 Real Estate Roundtable
801 Pennsylvania Ave NW
Suite 720
Washington, DC 20004

202-639-8400
Fax: 202-639-8442
E-Mail: info@rer.org
Home Page: www.rer.org

Robert S. Taubamn, Chairman
Jeffrey D DeBoer, President/CEO
Jeanne Kane, Chairman-Elect
William C. Rudin, Secretary
Thomas M. Flexner, Treasurer

Actively involves public and private real estate owners, advisors, builders, investors, lenders and managers on key tax, capital and credit, energy, environmental and homeland security policy issues in Washington. Its members are senior principals from every spectrum of the commercial real estate industry and leaders of major national real estate trade associations.
230 Members
Founded in 1999

20737 Realtors Land Institute
430 N Michigan Ave
Floor 11
Chicago, IL 60611

312-329-8440
800-441-5263
Fax: 312-329-8633
E-Mail: rli@realtors.org
Home Page: www.rliland.com
Social Media: Facebook, Twitter, LinkedIn, Google+

Gloria Bowman, Executive VP
George Clift, President
Terri Jensen, President-Elect
Bob Turner, Vice President
Charles Chuck Wingert, Immediate Past President

Promotes competence and accredits members. Maintains educational programs for real estate brokers.
1.9M Members
Founded in 1944

20738 Society of Industrial and Office Realtors
1201 New York Ave NW
Suite 350
Washington, DC 20005-6126

202-449-8200
Fax: 202-216-9325
E-Mail: admin@sior.com
Home Page: www.sior.com
Social Media: Facebook, Twitter, LinkedIn, Pinterest Google+, Youtube

Richard Hollander, Executive VP
Mike Hills, President
Angela L. West, President-Elect
Allen Gump, Vice-President
Del Markward, Treasurer

Active members are brokers, consultants and appraisers.
1,800 Members
Founded in 1939

20739 SourceMedia
One State Street Plaza
27th floor
New York, NY 10004

212-803-8200
800-803-3424
Fax: 212-843-9608
E-Mail: custserv@sourcemedia.com
Home Page: www.sourcemedia.com

Douglas J. Manoni, CEO
Rebecca Knoop, CFO
David Longobardi, EVP & Chief Content Officer
Minna Rhee, Chief Digital Officer
Karl Elken, EVP & Managing Director

SourceMedia provides market information, including news, analysis, and insight to the financial services and related industries such as accounting and technology, through its publications, industry-standard data applications, seminars and conferences. The informational services that SourceMedia delivers are available in print or online, including newspapers and magazines, reference directories, database products, software, web seminars and live events.

20740 The American Real Estate & Urban Economics Association
PO Box 3061110
Tallahassee, FL 32306-1110

850-644-7898
Fax: 850-644-4077
E-Mail: elaffitte@fsu.edu
Home Page: www.areuea.org

Gary D. Painter, President
Yongheng Deng, First VP
Marsha J. Courchane, Executive Vice President
Liz Laffitte, Executive Director
David H. Downs, Treasurer

Addresses academic and commercial concerns in real estate and commercial economics.
1200 Members
ISSN: 1080-8620
Founded in 1964

20741 Women's Council of Realtors
430 N Michigan Ave
Chicago, IL 60611

312-329-8483
800-245-8512
Fax: 312-329-3290
E-Mail: wcr@wcr.org
Home Page: www.wcr.org
Social Media: Facebook, Twitter, LinkedIn, Pinterest,Instagram

Gary Krysler, Executive Vice President
Carol Raabe, VP Operations
Jo Kenney, President
Sherri Souza, Financial Secretary
Sindy Ready, President-elect

Provides opportunities for women in real estate at the local, state and national level. Offers courses in leadership training and referral and relocation buisness.
40000 Members
Founded in 1930

20742 Worldwide ERC
4401 Wilson Blvd
Suite 510
Arlington, VA 22203

703-842-3400
Fax: 703-527-1552
E-Mail: customercare@worldwideerc.org
Home Page: www.erc.org
Social Media: Facebook, Twitter, LinkedIn, Pinterest

H Cris Collie, President
Cindy Salter, Vice Chair- Finance
Pandra Richie, Chair-Elect

C. Matthew Spinolo, Chairman
Anita Blanchett, Vice Chair-Membership

A national organization that examines key issues affecting the relocation industry for the benefit of corporations, government agencies, and firms or individuals providing specific services to relocated employees and their families. Accepts advertising.
160 Members
Founded in 1964

Newsletters

20743 ACREL News
American College of Real Estate Lawyers
11300 Rockville Pike
Suite 903
Rockville, MD 20852-3034

301-816-9811
Fax: 301-816-9786
E-Mail: webmaster@acrel.org
Home Page: www.acrel.org

Jill Pace, Executive Director
Frequency: Monthly

20744 AOMA Newsletter
Apartment Owners & Managers Assn of America
65 Cherry Avenue
Cherry Plaza
Watertown, CT 06795

FAX 860-274-2580

Robert J McGough, Editor
Pietro

Each month the AOMA newsletter presents the facts and information builder/developer/owners/manager members need to keep abreast of in the world of Multi-Family housing. Every monthly issue will bring the reader timely insight on Real Estate, tax news, financing techniques, and effective management procedures, and keeps readers aware of the new developments in the condominium market.
Cost: $125.00
Frequency: 12 issues
Circulation: 6,200
Mailing list available for rent
Printed in one color

20745 ASFMRA News
Amer. Society of Farm Managers & Rural Appraisers
950 S Cherry St
Suite 508
Denver, CO 80246-2664

303-758-3513
Fax: 303-758-0190
E-Mail: asfmra@agri-associations.org
Home Page: www.asfmra.org

Cheryl L Cooley, Manager Communications
Thomas V. Boyer, President

Informs ASFMRA members of education, member, event, meeting and government issues.
Cost: $24.00
Founded in 1929
Mailing list available for rent: 2500 names at $1M per M

20746 Accredited Review Appraiser
Accredited Review Appraisers Council
303 W Cypress Street
San Antonio, TX 78212-5512

800-486-3676
Fax: 210-225-8450
E-Mail: rlp@lincoln-grad.org
Home Page: arac.lincoln-grad.org

Deborah J Deane, Publisher
Rachel L Phelps, Marketing Manager

Offers information on appraisals and real estate reviews.
8 Pages
Frequency: Quarterly
Founded in 1987
Printed in one color on matte stock

20747 Advise and Counsel
National Association of Counselors
303 W Cypress St
San Antonio, TX 78212-5512

210-271-0781
800-229-6262
Fax: 210-225-8450
E-Mail: djd@masterappraisers.org
Home Page: www.masterappraisers.org

Offers information on real estate and appriasal counseling services.
Cost: $45.00
8 Pages
Frequency: Quarterly
Circulation: 4000

20748 American Chapter News
American Chapter International Real Estate Assn
30700 Russell Ranch Road
Westlake Village, CA 91362

805-557-2300
Fax: 805-557-2680
Home Page: www.realtors.com

Teresa Salmon, Publisher

International real estate news and information.
Cost: $110.00
8 Pages
Frequency: Monthly

20749 American Industrial Real Estate Association Newsletter
American Industrial Real Estate Association
700 S Flowers Street
Suite 600
Los Angeles, CA 90017

213-687-8777
Fax: 213-687-8616
E-Mail: support@airea.com
Home Page: www.airea.com

Ron Surace, COO
6 Pages
Frequency: Quarterly
Founded in 1964
Printed in 3 colors on glossy stock

20750 American Society of Farm Managers and Rural Appraisers Newsletter
Amer. Society of Farm Managers & Rural Appraisers
950 S Cherry St
Suite 508
Denver, CO 80246-2664

303-758-3513
Fax: 303-758-0190
E-Mail: asfmra@agri-associations.org
Home Page: www.asfmra.org

Cheryl L Cooley, Manager Communications/IT/PR
Hope S. Evans, Membership Coordinator

Provides professionals involved in rural property issues such as management and appraisal, with information on the industry as well as educational opportunities. Includes membership and information from the American Society of Farm Manager and Rural Appraisers.
Cost: $30.00
Frequency: Annual+
ISSN: 1076-3856
Founded in 1929
Mailing list available for rent: 2500 names at $1M per M
Printed in 2 colors on glossy stock

20751 Andrews Report
Report Publications
9595 Whitney Drive
#100
Indianapolis, IN 46280
William Woburn, Publisher

For owners and operators of small shopping centers.
Cost: $147.00
12 Pages
Frequency: Monthly

20752 Apartment Management Newsletter
AMN Publishing
PO BOX 352
Massapequa, NY 11758

516-551-5343
E-Mail: amnpub@aol.com
Home Page: amnpub.tripod.com/id4.html

Helene Mandelbaum, Editor
Vera West, Circulation Manager

News and information for apartment owners and managers, including tips and techniques for marketing, maintenance, personnel and compliance with national laws and requirements.
Cost: $6.00
Founded in 2001

20753 Apartment Management Report
Apartment Owners & Managers Assn of America
65 Cherry Avenue
Cherry Plaza
Watertown, CT 06795-238

FAX 860-274-2580

Robert J McGough, Editor
Janet Pietro, Circulation Manager

Researched and written for the owner/manager, overall property manager, and for the on site managers. Typical in depth subjects cover the nuts and bolts of every day management. Research reports on tenant renting strategies, model apartments, security, outside maintenance, how to avoid and handle tenant complaints, and more.
Cost: $72.85
6 Pages
Frequency: Monthly
Circulation: 6200
Mailing list available for rent: 6000 names
Printed in one color

20754 Asset Watch
LDI Publishing
1401 16th Street NW
Washington, DC 20036-2201

202-232-2144
Fax: 202-232-4757

Steve Sullivan, Publisher

News and analysis of federal asset sales RDIC, LRTC, HUD, etc., contracting and resolutions.
Cost: $475.00
6 Pages
Frequency: 5 per year

20755 Asset-Backed Alert
Harrison Scott Publications
5 Marine View Plz
Suite 301
Hoboken, NJ 07030-5722

201-386-1491
800-283-9363
Fax: 201-659-4141

E-Mail: info@hspnews.com
Home Page: www.hspnews.com

Andy Albert, Chairman/Publisher
Thomas J Ferris, Director
Michelle Lebowitz, Director

A weekly update on global securitization
Cost: $2297.00
20 Pages
Frequency: Weekly
Circulation: 500
Founded in 1990
Mailing list available for rent: 900 names at $400 per M
Printed in one color on matte stock

20756 Bulletin
Property Management Association
7508 Wisconsin Ave
Suite 4
Bethesda, MD 20814-3561

301-657-9200
Fax: 301-907-9326
E-Mail: info@pma-dc.org
Home Page: www.pma-dc.org

Tom Cohn, Executive Director

News and events surrounding the real estate industry.
Cost: $100.00
24 Pages
Frequency: Monthly

20757 Commercial Lease Law Insider
Brownstone Publishers
149 5th Ave
Suite 10
New York, NY 10010-6832

212-473-8200
Fax: 212-473-8786
E-Mail: vendomecs@qualitycustomercare.com
Home Page: www.brownstone.com

John M Striker Esq, Publisher
Nicole Lefton Esq, Editor

Commercial leasing strategies, techniques and insights with practical aids such as model lease clauses, checklists, do's and dont's, as well as coverage of new court decisions affecting commercial leases. Readership consists of commercial property owners, managers and real estate attorneys.
Cost: $337.00
Frequency: Monthly
Mailing list available for rentat $110 per M
Printed in 2 colors on matte stock

20758 Commercial Property News
Miller Freeman Publications
600 Harrison Street
Suite 400
San Francisco, CA 94107-1391

FAX 415-905-2239

David Nussbaum, Publisher
Maxine Jaffe, Editor

Tabloid newspaper edited for commercial property professionals.
Cost: $4.00
Circulation: 34,000

20759 Commercial Real Estate Digest
Vestal Communications
334 Humphrey Drive
Evergreen, CO 80439-9655
Robert Vestal, Publisher

Master copy newsletter allowing unlimited copy additions before subscriber prints and distributes to clients.
Cost: $495.00
2 Pages
Frequency: Quarterly

20760 Community Association Law Reporter
Community Associations Institute
6402 Arlington Blvd
Suite 500
Falls Church, VA Falls Chur

Fal-s C-urch
888-224-4321
Fax: 703-970-9558
E-Mail: caidirect@caionline.org
Home Page: www.caionline.org

Daniel Brannigan, Editor

Information on legal cases and court decisions concerning condominium, cooperative and homeowner associations.
Cost: $208.00
8 Pages
Frequency: Monthly
Founded in 1973

20761 Community Associations Institute News
Community Associations Institute
6402 Arlington Blvd
Suite 500
Falls Church, VA Falls Chur

Fal-s C-urch
888-224-4321
Fax: 703-970-9558
E-Mail: caidirect@caionline.org
Home Page: www.caionline.org

Daniel Brannigan, Editor

Real estate news and reports.
Frequency: Monthly
Founded in 1973

20762 Community Management
Community Associations Institute
6402 Arlington Blvd
Suite 500
Falls Church, VA Falls Chur

Fal-s C-urch
888-224-4321
Fax: 703-970-9558
E-Mail: caidirect@caionline.org
Home Page: www.ciaonline.org

Daniel Brannigan, Editor

Bimonthly newsletter of news, strategies and trends written especially for managers of condominium and homeowner associations. This easy to read, award-winning newsletter comes packed with how-to information on such subjects as cutting expenses, complying with federal laws, working effectively with boards of directors, ensuring community safety and resolving disputes. It often features case studies of succcessful new approaches in community association management and operations.
Cost: $59.00
8 Pages
Founded in 1973

20763 Daily Commerce
Daily Journal Corporation
PO Box 54026
Los Angeles, CA 90054-0026

213-229-5300
Fax: 213-229-5481
Home Page: www.dailyjournal.com

Gerald L Salzman, CEO
Ray Chagolla, Circulation Manager
Lisa Churchill, Editor

personnel announcements, datebook information, consumer news, and the internet, information on government foreclosers, default notices, lending reports and probate estate sales.
Cost: $237.00
Frequency: Monthly
Circulation: 10000

20764 Environmental Consultant
National Society of Environmental Consultants
PO Box 12528
San Antonio, TX 78212-0528

210-225-2897
800-486-3676
Fax: 210-225-8450
Home Page: nsec.lincoln-grad.org/

Deborah Deane, President

Offers information, articles and news of interest to real estate environmental site consultants.
Cost: $50.00
16 Pages
Frequency: Quarterly
Circulation: 4000
Founded in 1992

20765 Housing Affairs Letter
CD Publications
8204 Fenton St
Silver Spring, MD 20910-4571

301-588-6380
800-666-6380
Fax: 301-588-6385
E-Mail: info@cdpublications.com
Home Page: www.cdpublications.com

Michael Gerecht, President
Tom Edwards, Editor

The latest news on housing activity nationwide, including private, public and subsidized housing, legislation and regulations.
Cost: $559.00
Frequency: Weekly
Founded in 1961
Mailing list available for rent: 2,000 names at $160 per M

20766 Housing the Elderly Report
CD Publications
8204 Fenton St
Silver Spring, MD 20910-4571

301-588-6380
800-666-6380
Fax: 301-588-6385
E-Mail: info@cdpublications.com
Home Page: www.cdpublications.com

Michael Gerecht, President
Jeff Pines, Editor

News and advice for owners and managers of long-term care facilities on marketing and managing all types of elderly housing, with profiles of new senior housing projects, business reports and an exclusive annual salary survey.
Cost: $294.00
Frequency: Monthly
Founded in 1961
Mailing list available for rent: 2,000 names at $160 per M

20767 Inside IREM
Institute of Real Estate Management
430 N Michigan Ave
Suite 7
Chicago, IL 60611-4011

312-329-6000
Fax: 312-661-0217
E-Mail: info@crs.com
Home Page: www.irem.org

Russell Salzman, CEO

Membership newsletter for members of the Institute of Real Estate Management. It includes news on IREM policies, programs and new products. Federal, state and local legislative developments affecting real estate and asset management are also reported.
40000 Pages
Founded in 1976

20768 Inspector
American Society of Home Inspectors

932 Lee Street
Suite 101
Des Plaines, IL 60016-3520

847-759-2820
800-248-2744
Fax: 847-759-1620
E-Mail: webmaster@ashi.org
Home Page: www.ashi.org

Richard Clough, Executive Director
Paul Christensen, President

Newsletter for members of New England chapter of American Society of Home Inspectors.
Cost: $250.00
Frequency: Monthly
Circulation: 6000
Founded in 1976

20769 International Real Estate Newsletter
1224 N Nokomis NE
Alexandria, MN 56308-5072

320-763-4648
Fax: 320-763-9290
E-Mail: iami@iami.org
Home Page: www.iami.org/

David Held, Production Manager
Robert Johnson, CEO

A compilation of international real estate information which is disseminated to the International Real Estate Institute's membership and to other subscribers. This publication also reviews the latest accomplishments of the Institute and those of its high quality professional members.
Cost: $29.50
4 Pages
Frequency: Monthly
Founded in 1975
Printed in one color on newsprint stock

20770 Ledger Quarterly
Community Associations Institute
6402 Arlington Blvd
Suite 500
Falls Church, VA Falls Chur

Fal-s C-urch
888-224-4321
Fax: 703-970-9558
E-Mail: caidirect@caionline.org
Home Page: www.caionline.org

Quarterly newsletter of financial news for condominium, cooperative and homeowner associations. If you participate in any way in the financial management of an association, this eight-page newsletter is a resource you should have. It's absolutely vital for keeping up-to-date on trends in asssociation accounting practices, calculating the best strategies to minimize association taxes, and advising the board on investments.
Cost: $67.00
Frequency: Quarterly
Circulation: 12000+
Founded in 1973

20771 Mac News
Mid-Atlantic Council of Shopping Centers
8811 Colesville Road
Silver Spring, MD 20910-4343

301-890-1467

Tom Cohn, Publisher

News of the council.
Cost: $100.00
20 Pages
Frequency: Monthly

20772 Managing Housing Letter
CD Publications
8204 Fenton St
Silver Spring, MD 20910-4571

301-588-6380
800-666-6380
Fax: 301-588-6385
E-Mail: info@cdpublications.com
Home Page: www.cdpublications.com

Michael Gerecht, President
Charles Wisniowski, Editor

News and advice for owners, managers and professionals dealing with apartments and the real estate industry.
Cost: $269.00
Frequency: Monthly
Founded in 1978
Mailing list available for rent: 2,000 names at $160 per M

20773 Mobilehome Parks Report
Thomas P Kerr
3807 Pasadena Ave
Suite 100
Sacramento, CA 95821-2880

916-971-0489
800-392-5180
Fax: 916-971-1849
E-Mail: tkerr@aol.com
Home Page: www.aol.com

Reports on trends, issues, court decisions, legislation, financing and other matters of concern to owners and developers of manufactured housing communities. Valuable to attorneys and others who specialize in this segment of the Housing Industry.
Cost: $125.00
8 Pages
Frequency: Monthly
Circulation: 350
Founded in 1998
Printed in one color on matte stock

20774 National Association of Neighborhoods Newsletter
1300 Pennsylvania Avenue
NW Suite 700
Washington, DC 20004

202-332-7766
Fax: 202-332-2314
E-Mail: staff@nanworld.org
Home Page: www.nanworld.org

C Y Doyd, Editor
Ricardo C Byrd, President

Offers news and information to the community real estate industry.
Frequency: Quarterly
Circulation: 10,000
Founded in 1975

20775 New England Real Estate Journal
East Coast Publications
PO Box 55
Accord, MA 02018

781-878-4540
800-654-4993
Fax: 781-871-1853
E-Mail: nerej@rejournal.com
Home Page: www.rejournal.com

Tom Murray, Publisher
David Denelle, Editor

Business publication for the commercial-industrial-investment real estate industries.
Cost: $2.00
Frequency: Weekly
Circulation: 13000
Founded in 1961
Printed in on newsprint stock

20776 Professional Apartment Management
Brownstone Publishers
149 5th Ave
Suite 10
New York, NY 10010-6832

212-473-8200
800-643-8095
Fax: 212-473-8786
E-Mail: custserv@brownstone.com
Home Page: www.brownstone.com

Mary Lopez, Production Manager
Michael Koplin, Circulation Director

Strategies, techniques and suggestions for attracting and retaining paying tenants, and avoiding legal disputes. Includes model language for leases, sample ads, plus coverage of legal issues, recent court decisions and the like.
Cost: $217.00
Frequency: Monthly
Founded in 1972
Printed in 2 colors on matte stock

20777 Real Estate Alert
Harrison Scott Publications
5 Marine View Plz
Suite 301
Hoboken, NJ 07030-5722

201-386-1491
Fax: 201-659-4141
E-Mail: info@hspnews.com
Home Page: www.hspnews.com

Andy Albert, Chairman/President
Michelle Lebowitz, Director

Contains information for real estate and financial professionals looking for opportunities to buy or manage assets.
Cost: $1397.00
8 Pages
Frequency: Weekly
Circulation: 300+
Founded in 1989
Printed in 4 colors

20778 Real Estate Asset Manager
Lincoln Graduate Center - Executive Offices
PO Box 12528
San Antonio, TX 78212-0528

210-225-2897
800-531-5333
Fax: 210-225-8450
E-Mail: ms@lincoln-grad.org
Home Page: www.lincoln-grad.org

Debroah Deane, President
Rachel Phelps, Marketing Manager

Offers news and information on environmental concerns, real estate and appraisals.
8 Pages

20779 Real Estate Brokers Insider
Alexander Communications Group
1916 Park Ave
Suite 501
New York, NY 10037-3733

212-281-6099
800-232-4317
Fax: 212-283-7269
E-Mail: info@brokersinsider.com
Home Page: www.brokersinsider.com/

Romauld Alexander, President
Nadine Harris, Marketing Manager

Provides agency broker/owners with in depth information on how to run their businesses better.
Cost: $247.00
8 Pages
Frequency: Fortnightly
ISSN: 1086-2935
Founded in 1978

20780 Real Estate Economics
AREUEA

PO Box 9958
Richmond, VA 23228-1148

866-273-8321
Fax: 877-273-8323
E-Mail: areuea@areuea.org
Home Page: www.areuea.org

Susan Watcher, Publisher
David C. Ling, Editor

Discussions on topics such as housing prices, office markets, real estate valuation and appraisal.
Cost: $100.00
Frequency: Quarterly
Founded in 1964

20781 Real Estate Investor's Monthly
John T Reed Publishing
342 Bryan Dr
Alamo, CA 94507-2858

925-820-6292
Fax: 925-820-1259
E-Mail: johnreed@johntreed.com
Home Page: www.johntreed.com

John T Reed, President

Information for owners who manage and own their own property, suggestions for increasing their investment returns.
Cost: $125.00
8 Pages
Frequency: Monthly
Circulation: 500
Founded in 1980

20782 Tax Credit Advisor
1400 16th St Nw
Suite 420A
Washington, DC 20036-2216

202-939-1790
Fax: 202-265-4435
E-Mail: info@housingonline.com
Home Page: www.housingonline.com

Peter Bell, President
Glenn Petherick, Executive Director
Thom Amdur, Executive Director
David Abromowitz, Secretary

Monthly newsletter providing comprehensive coverage of all aspects of the federal low-income housing tax credit program, the primary incentive for low-income apartment development. Covers legislation, IRS rules, equity and debt programs, and market trends.
Cost: $269.00
12 Pages
Frequency: Monthly
Circulation: 750

20783 Upward Directions
Community Associations Institute
6402 Arlington Blvd.
Suite 500
Falls Church, VA 22042

703-970-9220
888-224-4321
Fax: 703-970-6558
Home Page: www.caionline.org

Tom Skiba, CEO

NBBC-CAM's quarterly newsletter for the further education and professional development of CMCA Certificants. Program news, updates on state credentialing activities, legislation and regulation and continuing education opportunities make this newsletter required reading for Certified Managers of Community Associations (CMCA's. Everything you need to know to earn, maintain and optimize the benefits from manager certification from the National Board of Certification.
Frequency: Quarterly

Magazines & Journals

20784 ALQ Real Estate Intelligence Report
Common Communications
PO Box 5702
Portsmouth, NH 03802-5702

800-299-9961
800-299-9961
Fax: 603-436-5202
E-Mail: IRexec@REintel.com
Home Page: www.reintel.com

Pat Remick, Editor
Frank Cook, Publisher

A close examination of buyer agency movement, services rendered by brokerages, the impact of technology on real estate and success stories.
Cost: $200.00
Frequency: Quarterly
Founded in 1989

20785 Affordable Housing Finance
Alexander & Edwards Publishing
33 New Montgomery St
Suite 290
San Francisco, CA 94105-4520

415-315-1241
800-989-7255
Fax: 415-315-1248
Home Page: www.hanleywood.com

Rob Britt, Manager
Andre Shashaty, President
Susan Piel, Conference Director
Michael Premsrirat, Circulation Manager
Carol Yee, Office Manager

Offers practical information on obtaining debt and equality financing from federal, state, and local governments as well as private resources. In-depth coverage on the federal low-income housing tax credit program, tax-exempt bond financing, corporate tax credit investigation.
Cost: $119.00
Frequency: Monthly
Circulation: 9000

20786 Alliance
John W Yopp Publications
6540 Julian Road
Gainesville, GA 30506-5550

800-849-9677
Fax: 800-849-8418
E-Mail: info@jwyopp.com
Home Page: www.jwyopp.com

Mary Y Cronley, Associate Pubisher/Editor
Natalie Gilmer, Accounts Manager

Articles provide news and information on topics of interest, including marketing and sales, pre-need campaigns and other operational topics.
Frequency: Monthly
Circulation: 8000
Founded in 1919

20787 American Cemetery
Kates-Boylston Publications
11300 Rockville Pike
Suite 1100
Rockville, MD 20852

800-500-4585
800-500-4585
Fax: 301-287-2150
E-Mail: AmericanFD@aol.com
Home Page: www.kates-boylston.com

Adrian F Boylston, Publisher
Thomas Lorge, Executive Director
Thomas Parmalee, Executive Director
Amy Fidalgo, Production Manager

Features articles on cemetery administration, maintenance, sales and public relations. Also includes coverage of conventions, new cemeteries and new building ideas.
Cost: $39.95
Frequency: Monthly
Circulation: 5800

20788 Apartment Age Magazine
Apartment Association of Greater Los Angeles
621 S Westmoreland Ave
Los Angeles, CA 90005-3962

310-536-0281
Fax: 213-382-3970
E-Mail: webmaster@aagla.org
Home Page: www.aagla.org

Charles Isham, VP
Kevin Postema, Editor/Advertising Director
Larry Cannizzaro, President

Serving the interests of residential rental property owners.
Cost: $48.00
80 Pages
Frequency: Monthly
Circulation: 40000
ISSN: 0192-0030

20789 Apartment Finance Today Magazine
Hanley Wood LLC
One Thomas Circle, NW
Suite 600
Washington, DC 20005

202-452-0800
Fax: 202-785-1974
Home Page: www.hanleywood.com

John McManus, Editorial Director
Shabnam Mogharabi, Editor-In-Chief

Provides in-depth and inbiased reporting and insightful alaysis for owners, developers and asset managers.
Cost: $29.00
80 Pages
Circulation: 11784
ISSN: 1097-4059
Founded in 1995
Printed in 4 colors on glossy stock

20790 Apartment News
Arizona Multi-Housing Consulting Corporation
5110 N 44th Street
Suite L160
Phoenix, AZ 85018-2107
602-224-0135
800-316-6403
Fax: 602-224-0657
E-Mail: info@azama.org
Home Page: www.azama.org

Terry Feinberg, President
Mitchell McBay, Marketing Manager
Erick Richard, Editor
Wayne Kaplan, Director of Community Relations
Marilyn Everroad, Events Manager

Articles on state and national government affairs, education, marketing, crime prevention, maintenance and legal issues relating to the Arizona multihousing industry.
Cost: $50.00
Frequency: Monthly
Circulation: 2500
Founded in 1964
Printed in on glossy stock

20791 Area Development
Halcyon Business Publications

400 Post Avenue
Westbury, NY 11590-2267

516-338-0900
Fax: 516-338-0100
Home Page: www.areadevelopment.com

Dennis Shea, Publisher/CEO
Geraldie Gambale, Editor
Gertrude Staudt, Circulation Manager

Focuses on the factors necessary for a successful corporate expansion or relocation, labor, taxes, incentives, quality of life, market access, and transportation.
Cost: $75.00
Circulation: 45000
Founded in 1970

20792 Brownfield Renewal
Brownfield Renewal
2200 E Devon Ave
Suite 354
Des Plains, IL 60018

312-488-4830
Fax: 312-488-4220
E-Mail: editorial@brownfieldrenewal.com
Home Page: www.brownfieldrenewal.com

Steve Dwyer, Editorial Director
Monica Acuna, Circulation Director

Dedicated to the remediation, redevelopment and reuse of brownfields.
Cost: $79.95
Frequency: Bimonthly
ISSN: 1554-8791
Founded in 1999

20793 Building Operating Management
Trade Press Publishing Corporation
2100 West Florist Avenue
Milwaukee, WI 53209-3799

414-228-7701
Fax: 414-228-1134
E-Mail: info@tradepress.com
Home Page: www.tradepress.com

Scott G Holverson, Regional Sales Manager
Edward Sullivan, Editor
Eric Muench, Director of Circulation
Bobbie Reid, Production Director
Robert Wisniewski, President/CEO

Serves the field of facilities management, encompassing commercial building: office buildings, real estate/property management firms, developers, financial institutions, insurance companies, apartment complexes, civic/convention centers, including members of the Building Owners and Managers Association
Frequency: Monthly
Circulation: 70000
Founded in 1915

20794 Business Facilities
Group C Communications
PO Box 2060
Red Bank, NJ 07701-0901

732-842-7433
800-524-0337
Fax: 732-758-6634
E-Mail: jsemple@groupc.com
Home Page: www.groupc.com

Edgar T Coene, President
Jim Semple, Production Manager
Mary McCandless, Production Manager
Bill MacRae, Marketing Director

Magazine covering the fields of corporation expansion, economic development and real estate.
Cost: $30.00
Frequency: Monthly
Circulation: 43500
Founded in 1968

20795 Business Journal
120 W Morehead Street
Suite 200
Charlotte, NC 28202

704-347-2340
800-948-5323
Fax: 704-973-1102
E-Mail: borben@bizjournals.com
Home Page: www.bizjournals.com/charlotte

Robert Morris, Editor
David Harris, Managing Editor
Kim Moser, Advertising Assistant
Megan Foley, Marketing Director
Jeannie Falknor, Publisher

Provides marketing solutions and caring service.
Cost: $82.00
Frequency: Daily

20796 CF Apartment Reporter
PO Box 480894
Denver, CO 80248-894

303-663-0606
Fax: 303-663-1616
Home Page: www.clayfil.com

Peggy Berg, President
Cost: $199.00
Frequency: Quarterly
Founded in 1984

20797 CF Industrial Reporter
Clayton-Fillmore
PO Box 480894
Denver, CO 80248-894

303-663-0606
Fax: 303-663-1616
Home Page: www.clayfil.com

Howard Treibitz, Editor

Briefs of the markets broken down into specific cities, includes briefs of the economy and average manufacturing.
Cost: $189.00
Frequency: Monthly

20798 Commercial
Oakland Press
28 W Huron St
Pontiac, MI 48342-2100

248-745-4794
248-332-1988
Fax: 248-332-3003

Edward Moss, Owner

A showcase of available commercial properties in the region.
Cost: $18.00
Frequency: Monthly
Circulation: 30,000

20799 Common Ground
Community Associations Institute
6402 Arlington Blvd
Suite 500
Falls Church, VA Falls Chur

Fal-s C-urch
888-224-4321
Fax: 703-970-9558
E-Mail: caidirect@caionline.org
Home Page: www.caionline.org

Dori Meinert, Editor

CAL's award-winning bimonthly magazine for condominium and homeowner associations, managers and other industry professionals. Would you like to learn how a Web site can help your community association? Or peruse tips on cutting your budget? Or find out about the New Urbanism and other community development trends? Stay informed and involved via features and departments on the legal, political mechanical, personal, and day-to-day realities of community association life.
Cost: $69.00
Frequency: Monthly
Founded in 1978

20800 Comparative Statistics of Industrial and Office Real Estate Markets
Society of Industrial & Office Realtors
1201 New York Ave NW
Suite 350
Washington, DC 20005-6126

202-449-8200
Fax: 202-216-9325
E-Mail: admin@sior.com
Home Page: www.sior.com

Richard Hollander, Executive VP
Craig S Meyer, President

A comprehensive publication that summarizes the results of a nationwide survey of industrial and office real estate market activity.
Cost: $135.00
300 Pages
Frequency: Annual+
Circulation: 3000

20801 Condo Management
Papers
342 Hathaway Boulevard
Suite 26
New Bedford, MA 02740

978-524-1758
888-412-6636
Fax: 508-993-2329
E-Mail: editor@condomgmt.com
Home Page: www.condomgmt.com

Melanie L Lange, Publisher
Lisa Zimmerer, Marketing Manager
Ken Sheldon, Editorial Support

News and features on condominium management issues throughout these regions, regular features on financial services, product services and other related topics.
Cost: $50.00
Circulation: 10000

20802 Connections
Women's Council of Realtors
430 N Michigan Ave
Chicago, IL 60611-4011

312-329-8483
800-462-8841
Fax: 312-329-3290
E-Mail: info@crs.com
Home Page: www.wcr.org

Gary Krysler, Executive Director
Carol Raabe, VP Operations

Top producers in the real estate industry share their strategies for success.
32 Pages
Circulation: 14000
Founded in 1966
Printed in 4 colors on matte stock

20803 Cooperative Housing Journal
National Association of Housing Cooperatives
630 Eye St NW
Washington, DC 20001-3736
202-289-3500
Fax: 202-289-8181
E-Mail: nahro@nahro.org
Home Page: www.nahro.org

Saul Ramirez, Executive Director
Deniz Tunder, Editor

Articles of lasting value to leaders in cooperative housing.
Cost: $25.00
Circulation: 3000
Founded in 1933

20804 Cooperator
Yale Robbins Publications
102 Madison Ave
5th Floor
New York, NY 10016-7417

212-683-5700
Fax: 212-545-0764
E-Mail: mrosales@mrofficespace.com
Home Page: www.mrofficespace.com

Yale Robbins, Owner
Pam Liebman, CEO/President
Judith C Grover, Managing Editor
George Rubin, Circulation Manager
Ellen Levy, Advertising Manager

Articles covering management, maintenance business, finance, law, interior design and related topics.
Cost: $30.00
Frequency: Monthly
Circulation: 75000
Founded in 1985
Printed in 4 colors

20805 Daily Record
11 E Saratoga St
Baltimore, MD 21202-2199

410-752-3849
Fax: 410-752-2894
E-Mail: editor@mddailyrecord.com
Home Page: www.mddailyrecord.com

Chris Eddings, Publisher
Suzanne Fischer-Huettner, VP Sales
Christopher J Chardo, Circulation Director
Mark R Cheshire, Editor-in-Chief
Jeffrey Raymond, Editor
Cost: $190.00
Frequency: Daily
Founded in 1888

20806 Development
National Assn of Industrial & Office Properties
2201 Cooperative Way
3rd floor
Herndon, VA 20171-4583

703-904-7100
800-666-6780
Fax: 703-904-7942
E-Mail: feedback@naiop.org
Home Page: www.naiop.org

Thomas Bisacquino, President
Shirley A Maloney, Publisher

Articles pertaining to industrial and office real estate - development, ownership, management, investment, financing, leasing, etc.
Cost: $65.00
72 Pages
Frequency: Quarterly
Circulation: 14000
ISSN: 0888-6067
Founded in 2000
Printed in 4 colors on glossy stock

20807 Developments
American Resort Development Association
1201 15th St NW
Suite 400
Washington, DC 20005-2842

202-371-6700
Fax: 202-289-8544
E-Mail: hnusbaum@arda.org
Home Page: www.ardafoundation.org

Howard Nusbaum, President

Serves the timeshare industry.
Frequency: Monthly
Circulation: 1,000
Founded in 1978

20808 Financial Freedom Report
2450 Fort Union Boulevard
Salt Lake City, UT 84121-3337

FAX 801-944-4334

Carolyn Tice, Editor

An investor's information services company which specializes in home business start-up, analysis, acquisition and maintenance of real property.
Cost: $119.00
72 Pages
Frequency: 4 issues
Founded in 1976

20809 First Tuesday
Realty Publications
PO Box 20069
Riverside, CA 92516-69

909-781-7300
Fax: 909-781-4721

Fred Crane, Publisher

Provides practical assistance to real estate professional. Includes legal and economic updates affecting the commercial and residential developments.
Frequency: Monthly
Circulation: 5000

20810 Global Property Investor
Alexander & Edwards Publishing
220 Sansome Street
11th Floor
San Francisco, CA 94104-2326

415-151-1241
800-989-7255
Fax: 415-249-1595
Home Page: www.housingfinance.com

Shabnam Mogharabi, Director
Christine Serlin, Executive Editor

Objective, independent journal covering commercial property investment and development trends with readership in Europe, Asia and North America.

20811 Hotel Journal
Stacey Horowitz
45 Research Way
Suite 106
East Setauket, NY 11733

631-246-9300
Fax: 631-246-9496
E-Mail: Info@hoteljournal.com
Home Page: www.hoteljournal.com

Stacey Silver, Group Publisher
Stefani C O'Connor, Executive News Editor
Cathy Urell, Senior Desk Editor
Barbara Jordan, Production Manager
Hope Rosenzweig, Advertising Manager
Cost: $85.00
Frequency: Monthly

20812 In Business
Business Information
2718 Dryden Drive
Madison, WI 53704

608-246-3599
Fax: 608-246-3597

Jody Glynn Patrick, Publisher
Joseph Vanden Plas, Editor

The business magazine for the Greater Madison Market.
48 Pages
Frequency: Monthly
Circulation: 15,000
ISSN: 0192-7450

20813 Ingram's
Show-Me Publishing, Inc
PO Box 411356
Kansas City, MO 64141-1356

816-842-9994
Fax: 816-474-1111
E-Mail: editorial@ingramsonline.com
Home Page: www.ingramsonline.com

Joe Sweeney, Editor-in-Chief/Publisher
Jack Cashill, Executive Editor

Kansas City's business magazine.
Cost: $36.00
114 Pages
Frequency: Monthly
ISSN: 1046-9958
Printed in 4 colors on glossy stock

20814 Institutional Real Estate Letter
Institutional Real Estate
2274 Camino Ramon
San Ramon, CA 94583

925-244-0500
Fax: 925-244-0520
Home Page: www.irei.com

H Lawrence Hull Jr, Chairman
Geoffrey Dohrmann CRE, Founder/President/CEO
Larry Gray, Editorial Director

Offers analysis of market trends related to pension fund investment in real estate.
Cost: $2495.00
Frequency: Monthly
Founded in 1987

20815 International Real Estate Journal
International Real Estate Institute
810 N Farrell Drive
Palm Springs, CA 92262

760-327-5284
877-743-6799
Fax: 760-327-5631
E-Mail: info@irei-assoc.org
Home Page: www.irei-assoc.org

Roger Wood, Production Manager
James Held, Production Manager
Robert Johnson, CEO

A full color magazine dedicated to discussing and promoting real estate opportunities all over the world. The articles cover a wide array of international Real Estate topics and are written by top international professionals.
Frequency: Monthly
Circulation: 10,000
Founded in 1977

20816 Journal of Property Management
Institute of Real Estate Management
430 N Michigan Ave
Suite 7
Chicago, IL 60611-4011

312-329-6000
Fax: 312-661-0217
E-Mail: custserv@irem.org
Home Page: www.irem.org

Russell Salzman, CEO
Anthony Smith, President

Features articles on management, leasing and development of all property types.
Cost: $69.95
Circulation: 18000
Founded in 1976

20817 Journal of Real Estate Taxation
Thomson Reuters
195 Broadway
New York, NY 10007

817-332-3709
800-431-9025
Fax: 888-216-1929
Home Page: ria.thomsonreuters.com

Paul D Carman, Editor-in-Chief
Robert J Murdich JD, Managing Editor

Complete, ongoing coverage of all aspects of real estate tax planning. In-depth articles by leading attorneys, accountants, and real estate authorities keep you abreast of the latest developments and how they affect real estate tax planning.
Cost: $315.00
Frequency: Quarterly

20818 MB News
Monument Builders of North America
401 N Michigan Avenue
Suite 2200
Chicago, IL 60611-4267
800-233-4472
Fax: 312-673-6732
Home Page: www.monumentbuilders.org
Greg Patzer, Executive VP
Marty Kraslen, Manager
The Monument Builders of North America represent the leading retail, wholesale and manufacturing and supply firms of the monument industry. Articles promote public interest, knowledge and appreciation of memorialization.
Cost: $70.00
Frequency: 12 issues
Circulation: 1400

20819 Midwest Real Estate News
The Law Bulletin Publishing Company
415 N State St
Suite 1
Chicago, IL 60654-8116
312-644-7800
Fax: 312-644-4255
E-Mail: dwalsh@lbpc.com
Home Page: www.lawbulletin.com
Lanning Macfarland Jr, President
Tricia Haddon, Associate Publisher
Bob Craig, Editor
Robert Carr, Associate editor
The Midwest's only commercial real estate source.
Cost: $60.00
Frequency: Monthly
Circulation: 16914
Founded in 1854
Printed in 4 colors on glossy stock

20820 Mobility Magazine
Worldwide ERC
4401 Wilson Boulevard
Suite 510
Arlington, VA 22203
703-842-3400
Fax: 703-527-1552
E-Mail: webmaster@worldwideerc.org
Home Page: www.worldwideerc.org
Anita Brienza GMS, SVP Communications/Marketing
Frank Mauck, Managing Editor
Relocation leaders share experiences, offer new solutions to age-old challenges, set industry trends, describe best practices and policies, as well as comment on key issues affecting the relocation profession.
Cost: $48.00
68 Pages
Frequency: Monthly
Circulation: 12500
Founded in 1960

20821 Mortgage and Real Estate Executives Report
PO Box 64833
Saint Paul, MN 55164-0833
212-929-7500
800-950-1205
Fax: 212-367-6718

20822 Multifamily Executive
MGI Publications
1 Thomas Cir NW
Suite 600
Washington, DC 20005-5803
202-452-0800
Fax: 202-785-1974
E-Mail: arice@hanleywood.com
Home Page: www.hanleywood.com
Ed McNeill, President
Stephanie Davis, Production Manager
Alison Rice, Editor
Nicola Pellegrini, Marketing
J Michael Boyle, Publisher
Software and technology innovations, legislation, property development, management and renovation topics. Subscription free to qualified individuals.
Frequency: Monthly
Circulation: 25000
ISSN: 1089-4721
Founded in 1976
Printed in 4 colors on glossy stock

20823 National Real Estate Investor
Penton Media
249 W 17th Street
New York, NY 10011
212-204-4200
E-Mail: david.bodamer@penton.com
Home Page: www.nreionline.com
Marianne Rivera, Publisher
David Bodamer, Editorial Director
Susan Piperato, Managing Editor
The leading authority on commercial real estate trends. Readers represent a cross-section of disciplines-brokerage, construction, owner/development, finance/investment, property managment, corporate real estate, and real estate services.
Circulation: 33000
Founded in 1939

20824 National Relocation & Real Estate Magazine
RISMedia, Inc
69 E Avenue
Norwalk, CT 06851
203-855-1234
800-724-6000
E-Mail: realestatemagazinefeedback@rismedia.com
Home Page: rismedia.com
John Featherston, Publisher
Steve Empey, CEO
Information on emerging trends and important issues affecting the various industries that are involved in relocating people and the home buying process.
Cost: $42.84
Frequency: Monthly
Circulation: 34,500
Founded in 1985

20825 New Homes Guide
4902 Eisenhower Boulevard
Suite 216
Tampa, FL 33634
813-823-3535
Fax: 813-290-7380
Emily Boyd, Manager
Sharon Kirkbride, Contact

20826 Office & Industrial Properties
MGI Publications
301 Oxford Valley Road
#1301
Yardley, PA 19067-7706
215-321-5112
Fax: 215-321-5122
Edward McNeill Jr, President/Editor-in-Chief
Contains business, technology, design and financial aspects concerning large private properties.
Cost: $36.00
Frequency: Bi-Monthly
Circulation: 15,000

20827 Office Buildings Magazine
Yale Robbins Publications
102 Madison Ave
5 Floor
New York, NY 10016-7417
212-683-5700
800-411-2229
Fax: 212-545-0764
E-Mail: mrosales@mrofficespace.com
Home Page: www.mrofficespace.com
Yale Robbins, Owner
Henry Robbins, Marketing
Debbie Estock, Editor
Danc Pedupo, Circulation
Offers information on appraising and betterment of the real estate community in major markets in the Northeast.
Cost: $675.00
Frequency: Annual+
Founded in 1982
Printed in 4 colors

20828 Pest Control
Questex Media
600 Superior Ave E
Suite 1100
Cleveland, OH 44114-2614
216-706-3620
800-669-1668
Fax: 216-706-3711
E-Mail: pestcon@questex.com
Home Page: www.questex.com
Tony Davino, Executive VP
Matt Waddell, Publisher
Matt Simoni, Sales Manager
Frank Andorka, Editorial Director
Serves the structural pest control industry.
Frequency: Monthly
Circulation: 21600
ISSN: 0031-6121
Founded in 1933
Printed in 4 colors on glossy stock

20829 Plants, Sites & Parks
12350 NW 39th Street
Suite 101
Coral Springs, FL 33065
954-753-2660
800-753-2660
Fax: 954-755-7048
Kevin Castellani, Group Publisher
Steve Chaffin, Publisher/Editor-in-Chief
Lisa M Bouchey, Managing Editor
Industrial office and economic development, facility planning and site selection for manufacturing and service industries.
Circulation: 44,500

20830 Professional Report
Society of Industrial & Office Realtors
1201 New York Ave NW
Suite 350
Washington, DC 20005-6126
202-449-8200
Fax: 202-216-9325

E-Mail: admin@sior.com
Home Page: www.sior.com

Richard Hollander, Executive VP
Craig S Meyer, President

Articles by industry experts focusing on new paradigm in the practice of commercial real estate.
Cost: $295.00
Frequency: Quarterly
Circulation: 2,200
Founded in 1991

20831 **RCI Timeshare Business**
RCI
PO Box 80229
Indianapolis, IN 46280-0229

317-805-9000
Fax: 317-805-9618
E-Mail: alyssa.chase@rci.com
Home Page: www.rci.com

Alyssa Chase, Editor
Katherine Jones, Publisher
David Tontius, CEO/President

Serves timeshare resorts/developers, hoteliers, operations and others allied to the field.
42 Pages
Frequency: Monthly
Circulation: 9000
Founded in 1974
Printed in 4 colors on glossy stock

20832 **RCI Ventures Magazine**
RCI
9998 N Michigan Road
Carmel, IN 46032

317-059-9584
Fax: 317-805-9507
E-Mail: alyssa.chase@rci.com
Home Page: www.rciventures.com

Alyssa Chase, Editor
Nicole Keller, Senior Editor

Gathering of more than 4,000 of timesharing's best and brightest executives.
Frequency: April
Circulation: 35000
ISSN: 1099-6753
Printed in 4 colors on 6 stock

20833 **Real Estate Business**
Realtors National Marketing Institute
430 N Michigan Avenue
#300
Chicago, IL 60611-4002

312-321-4400
Fax: 312-329-8882
E-Mail: spatterson@crs.com
Home Page: www.crs.com

Sara Patterson, Editor-in-Chief
Eric Berkland, Marketing
Nina Cottrell, CEO
Ron Canning, Vice President

Information for real estate agents and brokers engaged in US residential sales activities.
Cost: $24.00
64 Pages
Circulation: 48000
Founded in 1976

20834 **Real Estate Executive**
Sunshine Media
735 Broad Street
Suite 708
Chattanooga, TN 37402

423-266-3234
800-624-7496
Fax: 423-266-7960
E-Mail: info@sunshinemedia.com
Home Page: www.sunshinemedia.com

Tony Young, President
Jim Martin, President/CEO
David McDonald, Publisher

About real estate professionals from real estate professionals. Reaches 100 percent of the professional real estate audience in each market it serves. Each issue profiles a leading realty executive or agency within your local real estate market, as well as an assortment of new products, services and innovations.
Cost: $36.00
Frequency: Monthly
Circulation: 3000
Founded in 1996

20835 **Real Estate Finance Journal**
Thomson Reuters
610 Opperman Drive
Eagan, MN 55123

652-168-7700
Home Page: www.west.thomson.com

Examines the opportunities and pitfalls facing real estate owners, developers, investors and lenders. Focuses on financing, liability, investments, taxes and asset management.
Cost: $558.00
Frequency: Quarterly

20836 **Real Estate Finance Today**
Mortgage Bankers Association of America
1919 Pennsylvania Avenue NW
Washington, DC 20006-3404

202-557-2700
E-Mail: membership@mortgagebankers.org
Home Page: www.mortgagebankers.org

Features inside news reports on events and trends affecting the residential and commercial mortgage markets.

20837 **Real Estate Forum**
Real Estate Media
120 Broadway
Suite 5
New York, NY 10271

212-929-6976
Home Page: www.reforum.com

Michael G Desiato, VP/Group Publisher
Sule Aygoren Carranza, Editor
Paul Bubny, Managing Editor
Alexa Faulkner, Circulation

The one source for market intelligence and business generation.
Frequency: Monthly
Circulation: 53821
Founded in 1940

20838 **Real Estate Review**
Thomson Reuters
195 Broadway
Suite 4
New York, NY 10007-3124

646-822-2000
800-231-1860
Fax: 646-822-2800
E-Mail: trta.lei-support@thomsonreuters.com
Home Page: www.ria.thomsonreuters.com

Elaine Yadlon, Plant Manager
Thomas H Glocer, CEO & Director
Robert D Daleo, Chief Financial Officer
Kelli Crane, Senior Vice President & CIO

Information on financing, mortgage banking, investments, and related legal and tax issues, also covers US commercial, indiustrial and residential development.
Frequency: Quarterly
Circulation: 5,500

20839 **Real Property, Property and Trust Journal**
American Bar Association
321 N Clark St
Chicago, IL 60654-7598

312-988-5000
800-285-2221
Fax: 312-988-6281
E-Mail: askaba@abanet.org
Home Page: www.abanet.org

Tommy H Wells Jr, President
Jennifer Collins, Advertising Sales Coordinator

Scholarly articles in the fields of estate planning, trust law and real property law.
Cost: $60.00
Frequency: Quarterly
Founded in 1878

20840 **Realtor Magazine**
New York State Association of Realtors
430 N Michigan Avenue
Suite 430
Chicago, IL 60611-4087

800-874-6500
Fax: 312-329-5978
E-Mail: narpubs@realtors.org
Home Page: http://realtormag.realtor.org

Stacey Mancrieff, Editor
Frank Sibley, Senior VP/Publisher
Christina H Spira, Managing Editor
Wanda Clark, Publications Assistant
Pamela G Kabati, Vice President / Editorial Director

The business tool for real estate professionals. The New York Report is given after page 8.
Cost: $56.00
70 Pages
Frequency: Monthly
ISSN: 1522-0842
Founded in 1908
Printed in 4 colors on glossy stock

20841 **Rental Management**
1900 19th Street
Moline, IL 61265-4179

309-764-2475
800-334-2177
Fax: 309-764-1533
Home Page: www.ararental.org

Chris Wehrman, Executive VP
Joe Lynch, Deputy Executive VP

A monthly magazine published by the American Rental Association
Frequency: Monthly
Circulation: 18000

20842 **Residential Specialist**
430 N Michigan Ave
Suite 3
Chicago, IL 60611-4011

312-828-9129
Fax: 312-329-8882
E-Mail: info@crs.com
Home Page: www.crs.com

Nina Cottrell, CEO
Eric Berkland, Director Marketing
Carol Raabe, Vice President of Operations
Carlee Londo, Marketing Manager
Richard Lawson, Director of Products

Published by the Council of Residential Specialists.
Cost: $29.95
64 Pages
Circulation: 40000
Founded in 1976

20843 **Site Selection Magazine**
Conway Data

6625 the Corners Pkwy
Suite 200
Peachtree Corners, GA 30092-3334

770-446-6996
Fax: 770-263-8825
Home Page: www.conway.com

Adam Jones-Kelley, Managing Director
Loura Lyne, President
Julie Clark, Circulation Manager

Focus is on political, international and quality of life issues, also provides development groups, business parks, labor factors, relevant technology, real estate and finance information.
Cost: $90.00
Frequency: Monthly
Circulation: 45000
Founded in 1954

20844 Timeshare Business
RCI
PO Box 80229
Indianapolis, IN 46280-0229

317-805-9000
Fax: 317-805-9618
E-Mail: alyssa.chase@rci.com
Home Page: www.rci.com

Alyssa Chase, Editor
Nicole keller, Senior Associate Editor
Rita Corea, Circulation Manager

Magazine for resort developers, property managers, sales and marketing professionals, homeowners association boards, and other key personnel in the timeshare industry.
42 Pages
Frequency: Monthly
Circulation: 35000
ISSN: 1099-6753
Founded in 1974
Printed in 4 colors on 6 stock

20845 US Sites & Development
Vulcan Publications
PO Box 12846
Birmingham, AL 35202-2846

205-328-6198
Home Page: www.vulcanpub.com

Val Carrier, Publisher

Includes tax laws, real estate trends, as well as labor and work force issues.

20846 Unique Homes
327 Wall St
Princeton, NJ 08540-1518

609-688-1110
877-688-1110
Fax: 609-688-0201
E-Mail: krussell@uniquehomes.com
Home Page: www.uniquehomes.com

Kathleen Carlin-Russell, Manager
Lauren Baier Kim, Managing Editor
Cheryl Jock, Production Manager
Robert Burke, Custom Publishing Manager
Cost: $24.97
Circulation: 54,856
Founded in 1978

20847 Units Magazine
National Apartment Association
4300 Wilson Boulevard
Siote 400
Arlington, VA 22203

703-518-6141
Fax: 703-248-9440
E-Mail: webmaster@naahq.org
Home Page: www.naahq.org

Doug Culkin, President
Paul Bergeron, Communications Director

Contains news and information essential to all facets of the apartment industry-with a focus eacho month on managemetn, marketing, maintenance and politics.
Cost: $99.00
80 Pages
Frequency: Monthly
Circulation: 80,000
Printed in on glossy stock

20848 Vacation Industry Review
Interval International
PO Box 431920
Miami, FL 33243-1920

305-666-1861
Fax: 305-663-2227
Home Page: www.resortdeveloper.com

Craig M Nash, CEO
Alina Betancourt, Account Executive
Ximena Villegas, Account Executive

Vacation Industry Review is a quarterly trade publication covering the global timeshare, fractional, vacation ownership resort industry. It discusses industry issues and trends and showcases new resort developments and key markets. It also covers products and services of interest to the industry, and the activities of prominent individuals and companies.
48/64 Pages
Frequency: Quarterly
Circulation: 28,000
Founded in 1984
Printed in 4 colors on glossy stock

20849 Vacation Ownership World
CHB Company
8701 Collins Ave Ph
Miami, Fl 33154

305-864-6083
Fax: 305-864-6085
E-Mail: resort@nas.com
Home Page: www.vomagazine.com

Jon Paulisin, Publisher/President
Lou Skidmore, Editor
Howard White, Circulation Manager

News and feature stories, in depth analysis of the issues and trends affecting the industry of global timesharing.
Founded in 1984

20850 Valuation Insights & Perspectives
Appraisal Institute
550 W Van Buren St
Suite 1000
Chicago, IL 60607-3850

312-335-4100
Fax: 312-335-4400
E-Mail: puborders@appraisalinstitute.org
Home Page: www.appraisalinstitute.org

Fred Grubbe, CEO
Larisa Phillips, President

Offers a collection of high interest articles, and features industry and institute news section and columns on legal matters, technology, marketing and timely appraisal issues.
Cost: $48.00
18 Pages
Frequency: Quarterly
Circulation: 82000
Founded in 1996
Printed in 4 colors on glossy stock

Trade Shows

20851 American Congress on Surveying & Mapping Annual Conference
6 Montgomery Village Avenue
Suite 403
Gaithersburg, MD 20879

240-680-0765
Fax: 240-632-1321
E-Mail: curtis.sumner@acsm.net
Home Page: www.acsm.net

Curt Sumner, Executive Director
Ilse Genovese, Communications Director
Bob Jupin, Accounting Manager

One hundred and thirty exhibits of industry related equipment, supplies and services plus workshop and conference.
2000 Attendees
Frequency: Annual
Founded in 1954

20852 American Land Tree Association Annual Convention
1828 L Street NW
Suite 705
Washington, DC 20036-5104

202-296-3671
Home Page: http://www.alta.org

James Maher, VP
1M Attendees
Frequency: October

20853 American Real Estate Society Annual Meeting
American Real Estate Society
Cleveland State University-BU327
Dept. Finance, Business College
Cleveland, OH 44114

216-687-4732
Fax: 216-687-9331
Home Page: www.aresnet.org

Annual meeting and 10 exhibitors that are publishers, data providers, technical foundtions. Exhibits relate to decision-making within real estate finance, real estate market analysis, investment, valuation, development and other areas related to real estate.
300 Attendees
Frequency: April

20854 American Society of Appraisers International Appraisal Conference
11107 Sunset Hills Rd
Suite 310
Reston, VA 20190

703-478-2228
800-272-8258
Fax: 703-742-8471
E-Mail: asainfo@appraisers.org
Home Page: www.appraisers.org
Social Media: Facebook, Twitter, LinkedIn, YouTube

Jane Grimm, Executive VP
Susan Fischer, Governance Manager
Jack Washbourn, President

Exhibits for professional appraisers.
5000 Members
Frequency: Annual
Founded in 1936

20855 Apartment Association of Greater Dallas Annual Trade Show
4230 LBJ Freeway
Suite 140
Dallas, TX 75244

972-385-9091
Fax: 972-385-9412
E-Mail: pkelley@aagdallas.com
Home Page: www.aagdallas.com

Paula Kelley CMP, Director of Events
Gerry Henigsman, Executive Assistant
Marsha Stephenson, Executive Assistant
Bradley Elliott, Director of Communications
Donna Derden, Vice President

Tours and 240 displays of industry related supplies and services.
3000 Attendees
Frequency: April
Founded in 1963

20856 Apartment Association of Metro Denver Educational Expo and Trade Show
650 S Cherry Street
Suite 635
Denver, CO 80246

303-290-0403
Fax: 303-329-0403

Mark Williams, Executive Director

Seminar, reception and 142 exhibits of property management equipment, supplies, services and information.
1500 Attendees
Frequency: Annual

20857 BOMA Winter Business Meeting & Leadership Conference
Building Owners & Managers Association Int'l
1201 New York Avenue NW
Suite 300
Washington, DC 20005

202-408-2662
Fax: 202-371-0181
E-Mail: info@boma.org
Home Page: www.boma.org

Henry Chamberlain, President/CEO
Laura Best, Conference Director

Opportunity for business professionals to discuss problems, security, exchange ideas and share experience and knowledge.
Frequency: January

20858 BUILDINGS-New York
Reed Exhibition Companies
383 Main Avenue
Norwalk, CT 06851-1543

203-840-4800
Fax: 203-840-9570

Annual show of 425 exhibitors of products and services for the building owner, developer, manager, co-ops and superintendents in the commercial and residential real estate market, including asbestos abatement, waterproofing, restoration, financial services, utilities, laundry equipment, cleaning services, computer software, elevators, heating and air conditioning, light safety/security, renovation and restoration.
9,000 Attendees

20859 Coldwell Bankers Annual National Show
27271 Las Ramblas
Mission Viejo, CA 92691-6386

949-673-3650
Fax: 973-496-5784

Sandra Deering, Manager

Seventy-five booths.
4.5M Attendees

20860 MIPIM
Reed Exhibition Companies
255 Washington Street
Newton, MA 02458-1637

617-584-4900
Fax: 617-630-2222

Elizabeth Hitchcock, International Sales

International property market conference.
4M Attendees
Frequency: March

20861 National Association of Realtors Meetings and Trade Show
430 N Michigan Avenue
Chicago, IL 60611-4087

312-645-7730
800-874-6500
E-Mail: infocentral@realtors.org
Home Page: www.realtor.org

Karen Crafton, Convention Executive Secretary
Sue Gourley, Conventions VP
Terrence McDermott, CEO
Bill Armstrong, Treasurer

Seminars and networking, plus updates in the industry. More than 200 exhibiting companies.
6500 Attendees
Frequency: May

20862 National Association of Realtors Trade Exposition
National Association of Realtors
430 N Michigan Avenue
Chicago, IL 60611-4002

312-645-7730
Fax: 312-329-8882
E-Mail: info@crs.com
Home Page: www.crs.com

Sara Patterson, Director Communications
Terrence McDermott, Vice President
Ron Canning, Vice President

Spring show of 250 exhibitors of real estate industry equipment, supplies and services, including hardware and software, marketing programs, office products, mortgage and financial services and insurance.
40000 Attendees
Founded in 1976

20863 Old House New House Home Show
4051 E Main Street
St Charles, IL

630-515-1160
E-Mail: kp@corecomm.net
Home Page: www.kennedyproductions.com
Social Media: Facebook

Beth Wall, Contact

Discover the latest innovations, seeing creative solutions and gathering the motivation to tackle home improvement projects.
Frequency: Sept/Oct Illinois

20864 Real Show
Journal of Property Management
430 N Michigan Avenue
Chicago, IL 60611-4002

312-329-6064
Fax: 312-329-8882
E-Mail: info@crs.com
Home Page: www.crs.com

Sara Patterson, Director Communications
Ron Canning, Vice President

A trade show with 275 exhibitors and 450 booths, for professional owners and managers of investment residential and commercial property.
40000 Attendees
Founded in 1976

20865 Realmart
National Association of Industrial & Office Prop.
Woodlyn Park-2201 Coop. Way
Herndon, VA 22071

703-267-6665
Fax: 703-904-7974
E-Mail: garvin@naiop.org

Annual show of 100 suppliers of companies catering to the commercial real estate industry.
1,000 Attendees

20866 Realtors Conference & Expo
National Association of Realtors
430 N Michigan Avenue
Chicago, IL 60611

312-457-7730
800-628-6338
Fax: 312-329-8873
Home Page: www.REALTOR.org/conference

Lisa Nicola, Director of Sales
Bill Armstrong, Treasurer
Steve Brown, Vice President
20 K+ Attendees
Frequency: November

20867 SourceMedia Conferences & Events
SourceMedia
One State Street Plaza
27th floor
New York, NY 10004

212-803-6093
800-803-3424
Fax: 212-803-8515
E-Mail: abconferences@sourcemedia.com
Home Page: www.sourcemedia.com/

James M Malkin, Chairman & CEO
William Johnson, CFO
Steve Andreazza, VP, Sales & Customer Service
Celie Baussan, SVP, Operations
Anne O'Brien, EVP Marketing & Strategic Planning

SourceMedia Conferences & Events attract over 20,000 attendees worldwide. The content embraces a variety of formats, including: conferences, executive roundtables, expositions, Web seminars, custom events and pod casts. With over 70 events annually, participants are provided with premier content as well as access to the industry's top solution providers. Markets served include: accounting; banking; capital markets; financial services; information technology; insurance; and real estate.
Mailing list available for rent

20868 Trade Expo
Professional Housing Management
PO Box 4251
Leesburg, VA 20177

703-327-6873
800-543-7188
Fax: 703-327-4005
E-Mail: phmainfo@earthlink.net
Home Page: www.phma.com

Jon Moore, Director
Mona Pearson, Trade Expo Coordinator

At the expo there will be 230 booths with 150 exhibitors.
1,200 Attendees
Frequency: January

Directories & Databases

20869 America's Top-Rated Cities
Grey House Publishing
4919 Route 22
PO Box 56
Amenia, NY 12501

518-789-8700
800-562-2139
Fax: 518-789-0556
E-Mail: books@greyhouse.com
Home Page: www.greyhouse.com
Social Media: Facebook, Twitter

Leslie Mackenzie, Publisher
Richard Gottlieb, Editor

Provides current, comprehensive statistical information in one easy-to-use source on the 100 top cities that have been cited as the best for business and living in the US. Available as a four volume set or individual volumes (South-

ern, Western, Central and Eastern)
Cost: $225.00
2000 Pages
ISBN: 1-592373-49-6
Founded in 1981

20870 America's Top-Rated Smaller Cities
Grey House Publishing
4919 Route 22
PO Box 56
Amenia, NY 12501

518-789-8700
800-562-2139
Fax: 845-373-6390
E-Mail: books@greyhouse.com
Home Page: www.greyhouse.com
Social Media: Facebook, Twitter

Leslie Mackenzie, Publisher
Richard Gottlieb, Editor

America's Top-Rated Smaller Cities provides current, comprehensive data on 110 US cities, all top-ranked by population growth, median income, unemployment rate and crime rate. This informative handbook allows readers to see, at a glance, a concise social, business, economic, demographic and environmental profile of each city, including brief evaluative comments.
Cost: $195.00
1800 Pages
ISBN: 1-592372-84-8
Founded in 1981

20871 American Resort Development Association: Membership Directory
American Resort Development Association
1201 15th St Nw
Suite 400
Washington, DC 20005-2842

202-371-6700
Fax: 202-289-8544
E-Mail: hnusbaum@arda.org
Home Page: www.ardafoundation.org

Howard Nusbaum, President
Lou Ann Burney, VP
Rob Dumm, Finance
Alexa Antonuk, Communications Manager

Over 800 member firms in the resort development industry, including developers, finance companies, architectural firms, audiovisual companies, direct mail companies, rental and vacation exchange companies and law firms.
Frequency: Annual Winter

20872 American Society of Appraisers Directory
American Society of Appraisers
11107 Sunset Hills Rd
Suite 310
Reston, VA 20190

703-478-2228
800-272-8258
Fax: 703-742-8471
E-Mail: asainfo@appraisers.org
Home Page: www.appraisers.org
Social Media: Facebook, Twitter, LinkedIn, YouTube

Jane Grimm, Executive VP
Susan Fischer, Governance Manager
Jack Washbourn, President

Directory of association members who are accredited appraisers.
Cost: $12.50
5000 Members
Circulation: 8,000
Founded in 1936

20873 Buyers Broker Registry
Who's Who in Creative Real Estate
PO Box 23275
Ventura, CA 93002-3275

Offers valuable information on over 650 real estate agents in the United States who have met performance requirements set by the publisher.
Cost: $25.00
136 Pages
Frequency: Annual

20874 CRB/CRS Referral Directory
Realtors National Marketing Institute
430 N Michigan Avenue
Suite 300
Chicago, IL 60611-4002

FAX 312-329-8882
Home Page: http://www.crs.com

Gwen Voelker, Editor

Aimed at the real estate industry, this directory lists over 32,000 real estate brokerage managers and residential sales specialists.
Cost: $45.00
776 Pages
Frequency: Annual
Circulation: 32,000

20875 CRE Member Directory
Counselors of Real Estate
430 N Michigan Ave
Chicago, IL 60611-4019

312-329-8427
Fax: 312-329-8881
Home Page: www.cre.org

Mary Fleischmann, President
Frequency: Annual March

20876 Commercial Investment Real Estate
CCIM Institute
430 N Michigan Ave
Chicago, IL 60611-4011

312-321-4460
Fax: 312-321-4530
E-Mail: magazine@ccim.com
Home Page: www.ccim.com

Jonathan Falk, Manager
Ken Setlak, Chief Financial Officer
Sara Drummond, Executive Editor

Directory of services and supplies to the industry.
40000 Pages
Founded in 1976

20877 Comparative Guide to American Suburbs
Grey House Publishing
4919 Route 22
PO Box 56
Amenia, NY 12501

518-789-8700
800-562-2139
Fax: 845-373-6390
E-Mail: books@greyhouse.com
Home Page: www.greyhouse.com
Social Media: Facebook, Twitter

Leslie Mackenzie, Publisher
Richard Gottlieb, Editor

Covers statistics on the 2,000+ suburban communities surrounding the 60 largest metropolitan areas - their population characteristics, income levels, economy, school systems and important data on how they compare to one another.
Cost: $150.00
1000 Pages
ISBN: 1-592371-80-9
Founded in 1981

20878 Crime in America's Top-Rated Cities
Grey House Publishing
4919 Route 22
PO Box 56
Amenia, NY 12501

518-789-8700
800-562-2139
Fax: 845-373-6390
E-Mail: books@greyhouse.com
Home Page: www.greyhouse.com
Social Media: Facebook, Twitter

Leslie Mackenzie, Publisher
Richard Gottlieb, Editor

Details over twenty years of crime statistics in all major crime categories: violent crimes, property crimes and total crime. Conveniently arranged by city, it offers details that compare the number of crimes and crime rates for the city, suburbs and metro area with national crime trends for violent, property and total crimes. Statistics on anti-crime programs, crime risk, hate crimes, illegal drugs, law enforcement, correctional facilities, death penalty, laws and much more.
Cost: $155.00
839 Pages
ISBN: 1-891482-84-X
Founded in 1981

20879 Crittenden's Real Estate Buyers Directory
Crittendon Research
250 Bel Marin Keys Boulevard
Novato, CA 94949-5727

415-382-2400
800-421-3483
Fax: 415-382-2476
Home Page: www.crittendenonline.com

John Goodwin, Editor/Publisher
Vitlario Laeson, Marketing Director
Pati Bess, Customer Service Director

A list of over 500 real estate buyers, including private institutional investors, banks, pension funds and real estate investment trusts.

20880 Crittendon Directory of Real Estate Financing
Crittendon Research
250 Bel Marin Keys Boulevard
Novato, CA 94949-5727

415-382-7790
Fax: 415-382-2476

Listing of over 400 major lenders, investors and joint ventures enagged in commercial and residential real estate financing and investing.
Cost: $387.00
500 Pages
Frequency: Semiannual

20881 DAMAR Real Estate Information Service Online Database
3550 W Temple Street
Los Angeles, CA 90004-3620

800-873-2627

This comprehensive database offers real estate information, with an emphasis on California.
Frequency: Full-text

20882 Directory of 2,500 Active Real Estate Lenders
International Wealth Success
PO Box 186
Merrick, NY 11566-0186

516-766-5850
800-323-0548
Fax: 516-766-5919
E-Mail: admin@iwsmoney.com
Home Page: www.iwsmoney.com

Tyler G Hicks, President

Lists 2,500 names and addresses of direct lenders or sources of information on possible lend-

ers for real estate.
Cost: $25.00
197 Pages
Frequency: Annually
ISBN: 1-561503-37-1
Founded in 1985

20883 Directory of Accredited Real Property Appraisers
American Society of Appraisers
PO Box 17265
Washington, DC 20041-7265
202-337-0037
800-272-8258
Fax: 202-742-8471
Rebecca Ewing, Publication Manager
Approximately 1,700 urban, residential, rural, ad valorem and timberland appraisers; limited international coverage.
Frequency: Annual January

20884 Directory of Professional Appraisal Services
American Society of Appraisers
PO Box 17265
Washington, DC 20041-7265
202-337-0037
800-272-8258
Fax: 202-742-8471
E-Mail: asainfo@appraisers.org
Home Page: www.appraisers.org
Rebecca Ewing, Publisher/Editor
Over 3,000 tested and accredited members appraisers of real and personal property, businesses, machinery and equipment are listed.
Cost: $10.00
275 Pages
Frequency: Annual
Circulation: 8,000

20885 Directory of Real Estate Development and Related Education Programs
Urban Land Institute
625 Indiana Avenue NW
Suite 400
Washington, DC 20004-2923
202-247-7116
Over 60 programs are profiled that are currently being offered at colleges and universities in the area of real estate.
Cost: $19.00
132 Pages
Frequency: Biennial

20886 ERC Directory of Real Estate Appraisers and Brokers
Employee Relocation Council
1720 N Street NW
Washington, DC 20036-2900
202-857-0857
Tina Lung, Editor
Cost: $35.00
1,100 Pages
Frequency: Annual

20887 European Investment in United States Real Estate
Mead Ventures
PO Box 44952
Phoenix, AZ 85064-4952
Investors, developers and brokers located in Europe are the focus of this valuable directory.
Cost: $195.00
406 Pages
Frequency: Annual

20888 Executive Guide to Specialists in Industrial and Office Real Estate
Society of Industrial & Office Realtors
1201 New York Ave NW
Suite 350
Washington, DC 20005-6126
202-449-8200
Fax: 202-216-9325
E-Mail: admin@sior.com
Home Page: www.sior.com
Richard Hollander, Executive VP
Craig S Meyer, President
Thousands of specialists are listed that are integrated with industrial real estate and related industries.
Cost: $60.00
210 Pages
Frequency: Annual

20889 FDIC: Investment Properties Publication
Federal Deposit Insurance Corporation
550 17th St Nw
Washington, DC 20429-0002
202-000-1111
Fax: 202-898-8595
Mitchell L Glassman, Plant Manager
Offers information on properties owned by the Federal Deposit Insurance Corporation, including land, commercial real estate, multifamily dwellings and hotels and motels.
200 Pages
Frequency: Quarterly

20890 Guide to Real Estate and Mortgage Banking Software
Real Estate Solutions
2609 Klingle Road NW
Washington, DC 20008-1202
202-362-9854
Lists approximately 500 real estate and mortgage banking computer software, hardware and products.
Cost: $49.95
640 Pages
Frequency: Biennial

20891 Income & Cost for Organization & Servicing of 1-4 Unit Residential Loans
Mortgage Bankers Association of America
1919 Pennsylvania Avenue NW
Washington, DC 20006-3404
202-557-2700
E-Mail: membership@mortgagebankers.org
Home Page: www.mortgagebankers.org
Annual report provides data and analysis on the income and expenses associated with the organization, warehousing, marketing and servicing or one-to-four-unit residential marketing loans.
80 Pages
Frequency: $150 Member/$300 Non

20892 Japanese Investment in US Real Estate Review
Mead Ventures
PO Box 44952
Phoenix, AZ 85064-4952
FAX 602-234-0076
This is a complete database listing documenting Japanese purchases of US golf courses, houses, office buildings and industrial properties.
Frequency: Full-text

20893 Journal of the American Society of Farm Managers and Rural Appraisers
ASFMRA
950 S Cherry St
Suite 508
Denver, CO 80246-2664
303-758-3513
Fax: 303-758-0190
E-Mail: asfmra@agri-associations.org
Home Page: www.asfmra.org
Cheryl L Cooley, Manager Communications/PR
Mailing list available for rent: 2500 names at $1M per M

20894 Major Cities Canada
Grey House Publishing
4919 Route 22
PO Box 56
Amenia, NY 12501
800-562-2139
Fax: 845-373-6390
Fax: new
Home Page: www.greyhouse.ca
Richard Gottlieb, President
Provides an in-depth comparison and analysis of the 50 most populated cities in Canada. Split into 4 major categories; background, study rankings, development offices, and statistical tables
Cost: $180.00
793 Pages

20895 Million Dollar Guide to Business and Real Estate Loan Sources
International Wealth Success
PO Box 186
Merrick, NY 11566-0186
516-766-5850
800-323-0548
Fax: 516-766-5919
E-Mail: admin@iwsmoney.com
Home Page: www.iwsmoney.com
Tyler G Hicks, President
Lists hundreds of business and real estate lenders, giving their lending data in very brief form.
Cost: $25.00
201 Pages
Frequency: Annually
Founded in 1990

20896 Monthly Resort Real Estate Property Index
MDR Telecom
4742 La Villa Marina
Unit A
Marina Del Rey, CA 90292-7086
Mario Collura, Editor
Offers information on resort timeshares and resort condominiums for rent or sale.
Cost: $10.00
80 Pages
Frequency: Monthly

20897 Mortgage Banking Performance Report
Mortgage Bankers Association of America
1919 Pennsylvania Avenue NW
Washington, DC 20006-3404
202-557-2700
E-Mail: membership@mortgagebankers.org
Home Page: www.mortgagebankers.org
The report includes an annual summary, is a financial statement analysis of mortgage banking company performance.
80 Pages
Frequency: $125 Member/$175 Non
Founded in 1992

20898 Mortgage Banking Sourcebook
Mortgage Bankers Association of America

1919 Pennsylvania Avenue NW
Washington, DC 20006-3404

202-557-2700
E-Mail: membership@mortgagebankers.org
Home Page: www.mortgagebankers.org

Comprehensive directory to federal and state government agencies, industry trade associations colleges and universities, and other organizations and sources of information on mortgage lending, Includes an entire network of industry contact complete with addresses, telephone and fax numbers and internet website addresses.
Cost: $40.00
144 Pages
Founded in 1997

20899 Mortgage Finance Database
Mortgage Bankers Association of America
1919 Pennsylvania Avenue NW
Washington, DC 20006-3404

202-557-2700
Home Page: www.mortgagebankers.com

This database contains the most comprehensive and up-to-date collection of mortgage-related variables currently available.

20900 National Association of Independent Fee Appraisers: Membership Directory
National Association of Independent Fee Appraisers
7501 Murdoch Avenue
Saint Louis, MO 63119-2810

314-645-7583
Fax: 314-781-2872

Donna Walters, Publications

Five thousand and five hundred independent real estate appraisers.
Frequency: Annual January

20901 National Association of Master Appraisers Membership Directory
National Association of Master Appraisers
303 W Cypress St
San Antonio, TX 78212-5512

210-271-0781
800-229-6262
Fax: 210-225-8450
E-Mail: djd@masterappraisers.org
Home Page: www.masterappraisers.org

Del Martinez, Manager
Christopher Deane, Marketing And Production Manager

Approximately 3,500 real estate appraisers.
Frequency: Annual January
Circulation: 3,500

20902 National Association of Real Estate Appraisers
P.O. Box 879
Palm Springs, CA 92263

76- 32- 528
877-815-4172
Fax: 760-327-5631
E-Mail: info@narea-assoc.org
Home Page: www.narea-assoc.org

Dallas Martin, President

A complete guide to the REIT industry with approximately 240 real estate investment trusts, and over 1,000 associate members listed.
Cost: $695.00
600 Pages
Frequency: Annual

20903 National Association of Real Estate Companies: Membership Directory
National Association of Real Estate Companies
216 W Jackson Blvd
Suite 625
Chicago, IL 60606-6945

312-263-1755
Fax: 312-750-1203
E-Mail: info@narec.org
Home Page: www.narec.org

Kim Klein, Administrator

About 200 real estate development companies.
Frequency: Quarterly

20904 National Directory of Exchange Groups
Creative Real Estate Magazine
PO Box L
Rancho Santa Fe, CA 92067-0560

858-756-1441
Fax: 818-156-1111

Lists over 125 professional real estate marketing groups practicing tax-deferred real estate exchanges.
Cost: $72.00
48 Pages
Frequency: Monthly
Circulation: 51,000
ISBN: 0-194722-2 -

20905 National Real Estate Directory
Real Estate Publishing Company
P.O. Box 180635
Coronado, CA 92118

866-431-5223
Fax: 619-615-2350
Home Page:
www.national-real-estate-directory.com

Over 22,000 federal and state agencies, offices and departments related to the regulation of real estate, real estate associations and publications are listed.
Cost: $29.95
110 Pages
Frequency: Biennial

20906 National Real Estate Investor Sourcebook
Primedia
5680 Greenwood Plaza Boulevard
Suite 300
Greenwood Village, CO 80111

303-741-2901
Fax: 720-489-3101
Home Page: www.primediabusiness.com

Barbara Katinsky, Editor

List of about 7,000 companies and individuals in 18 real estate fields.
Cost: $78.95
Frequency: Annual, September
Circulation: 33,000

20907 National Referral Roster
Candy Holub
615 5th Street SE
Cedar Rapids, IA 52401-2158

319-364-6167
800-553-8878
Fax: 319-369-0029
Home Page: www.roster.com

Candy Holub, Publisher
Mary Richeson, Business Developer
Joey Grim, Business Developer

Approximately 90,000 Real Estate offices nationwide. Provides an effective, comprehensive and easy-to-use tool for realtors to make successful referrals to other relators nationwide.
Cost: $95.00
936 Pages
Frequency: Annual
Circulation: 18,000
ISSN: 1075-1084
Founded in 1923
Printed in 2 colors on newsprint stock

20908 National Toll-Free 800 Guide to Real Estate Publications and Publishers
Real Estate Publishing Company
4580 Brookside Rd
Cameron Park, CA 95682-9619

530-677-3864

Joe Wgle, President

Directory of publications to the industry.
Cost: $15.95
82 Pages
Frequency: Biennial

20909 Nelson's Directory of Institutional Real Estate
Nelson Publications
2500 Tamiami Trl N
Nokomis, FL 34275-3476

941-966-9521
Fax: 941-966-2590
E-Mail: webmaster@nelsonpub.com
Home Page: www.healthmgttech.com

A Verner Nelson, Owner
Marcia Boysen, Editor

Institutional investors who invest in real estate: investment managers, real estate service firms, insurance companies, plan sponsors, corporations and REIT's.
Cost: $335.00
Frequency: Annual August

20910 One List Directory
MRH Associates
365 Willard Avenue
Suite 2K
Newington, CT 06111-2373

800-727-5478

Over 700 companies and 6,000 company divisions are involved as listees in this comprehensive directory. Included is a section of over 12,000 contact personnel in the real estate and construction industry.
Cost: $545.00
750 Pages
Frequency: Annual

20911 Professional Relocation and Real Estate Services Directory
Relocation Information Service
113 Post Road E
2nd Floor
Westport, CT 06880-3410

203-256-1079
Fax: 203-227-3800

Offers over 6,000 real estate brokerage companies, appraisal firms, home inspectors and services companies.
Cost: $95.00
800 Pages
Frequency: Annual
Circulation: 35,000

20912 Profiles of America
Grey House Publishing
4919 Route 22
PO Box 56
Amenia, NY 12501

518-789-8700
800-562-2139
Fax: 845-373-6390
E-Mail: books@greyhouse.com
Home Page: www.greyhouse.com
Social Media: Facebook, Twitter

Leslie Mackenzie, Publisher
Richard Gottlieb, Editor

This four volume set details over 40,000 places, from the biggest metropolis to the smallest unicorporated hamlet and provides sta-

tistical details and information on over 50 different topics including: geography, climate, population, economy, income, taxes, education, housing, health and environment, public safety, transportation, presidential election results and more.
Cost: $795.00
10000 Pages
ISBN: 1-891482-80-7

20913 Profiles of...Series - State Handbooks
Grey House Publishing
4919 Route 22
PO Box 56
Amenia, NY 12501

518-789-8700
800-562-2139
Fax: 845-373-6390
E-Mail: books@greyhouse.com
Home Page: www.greyhouse.com
Social Media: Facebook, Twitter

Leslie Mackenzie, Publisher
Richard Gottlieb, Editor
Each state-by-state volume in this new series provides at-a-glance detailed demographic and statistical data on every populated place in the state, along with easy-to-use comparative rankings. Series includes 20 states. Additional states added each year.
Founded in 1981

20914 Real Estate & Land Use Regulation in Eastern and Central Europe
WorldTrade Executive
PO Box 761
Concord, MA 01742-0761

978-287-0301
Fax: 978-287-0302
E-Mail: info@wtexec.com
Home Page: www.wtexec.com

Alison French, Production Manager
Topics covered include: leasing in Russia: helpful hints for tenants; a guide to government agencies regulating development in Moscow and St. Petersburg; current law and practice for the Russian real estate market; the real estate lease in the Czech Republic; environmental considerations for acquisition of property in Hungary.
Cost: $135.00

20915 Real Estate Applications Software Directory
Real Estate Center
Texas A and M University
College Station, TX 77843-0001

979-845-2031
800-244-2144
Fax: 713-845-0460
E-Mail: info@recenter.tamu.edu
Home Page: www.recenter.tamu.edu

David S Jones, Senior Editor
Ted C Jones, Director
Gary Maler, Director
About 300 suppliers of several hundred software packages with applications related to the real estate industry.
Cost: $30.00
Frequency: Annual October

20916 Real Estate Books and Periodicals in Print
Real Estate Publishing Company
PO Box 41177
Sacramento, CA 95841-0177

530-677-3864

John Johnsich, Publisher
Over 400 publishers of real estate books and periodicals and their product lines are profiled in this directory.
Cost: $29.95
256 Pages
Frequency: Annual
ISBN: 0-914256-33-5
Founded in 1975

20917 Real Estate Data
DataQuick Information Systems
9620 Towne Centre Dr
San Diego, CA 92121-1963

858-455-6900
800-863-INFO
Fax: 858-455-7848
E-Mail: customercare@dataquick.com
Home Page: www.dataquick.com

Sara Stephenson, Marketing
More than 12 million developed and undeveloped real properties in California, Arizona, Nevada, Oregon and Washington.
Frequency: Daily

20918 Real Estate RoundTable
GE Information Services
801 Pennsylvania Ave
NW Suite 720
Washing, DC 20004

202-639-8400
Fax: 202-639-8442
E-Mail: info@rer.org
Home Page: www.rer.org

Cathy Ge, Owner
Clifton Rodgers, Senior Vice President
This database provides a forum for discussions between professional realtors and individuals interested in the buying and selling of residential and commercial property.
Frequency: Bulletin Board

20919 Real Estate Software Directory and Catalog
Z-Law Software
PO Box 40602
Providence, RI 02940-0602

401-273-5588
800-526-5588
Fax: 401-421-5334
Home Page: www.z-law.com
Social Media: Facebook

Gary L Sherman, President
A comprehensive guide to real estate and mortgage banking software. Includes IBM and MAC applications for realtors, landlords, property managers, investors, developers, attorneys, contractors, appraisers, loan agents, and anyone in real estate.
Frequency: SemiAnnual

20920 Timeshare Multiple Listing Service
MDR Telecom
11965 Venice Boulevard
Suite 204
Los Angeles, CA 90066-3954

323-539-9701
800-423-6377
Fax: 310-915-7212
E-Mail: triwest@att.net
Home Page: www.triwest-timeshare.com
Mario A Collura, Production Manager
Mario A Collura, Author
Approximately 6,000 pieces of timeshare real estate in the US, Mexico, and Carribean.
Cost: $10.00
60 Pages
Frequency: Monthly
ISBN: 1-888176-11-3
Founded in 1984

20921 Timeshare Vacation Owners HIP Resort Directory
TRI Publishing
11965 Venice Boulevard
Suite 204
Los Angeles, CA 90066-3954

800-423-6377
Fax: 310-915-7212
Home Page: www.triwest-timeshare.com
Mario A Collura, President
Viccie Mac, Managing Editor
This is the only combined resort directory for buyers, owners and industry professionals. Over 3,000 resorts.
Cost: $18.95
111 Pages
Frequency: Every 2 Years
ISBN: 1-888176-12-1
Founded in 1995

20922 US Real Estate Register
Barry
312 Main St
Wilmington, MA 01887-2791

978-658-7174

Joe Barry, Owner
Offers information on real estate departments of large national companies, industrial organizations and chambers of commerce involved in real estate development.
Cost: $58.00
575 Pages
Frequency: Annual

20923 United National Real Estate Catalog
United National Real Estate
4700 Belleview Avenue
Kansas City, MO 64112-1315

816-561-1115
800-999-1020
Fax: 816-231-5599

James Marinovich
Offers information on several thousand farms, ranches and country estates.
Cost: $4.95
200 Pages
Frequency: Semiannual

20924 Who's Who in Luxury Real Estate
JBL
2110 Western Avenue
Seattle, WA 98121-2110

206-441-7900
800-488-4066
Fax: 206-441-5297

Approximately 500 international luxury real estate brokers.
Cost: $19.95
Frequency: Annual

Industry Web Sites

20925 http://gold.greyhouse.com
G.O.L.D Grey House OnLine Databases
Grey House Publishing's online database platform, GOLD, offers Quick Search, Keyword Search and Expert Search for most business sectors including real estate and allied markets. The GOLD platform makes finding the information you need quick and easy - whether you're a novice searcher or an experienced database user. All of Grey House's directory products are available for subscription on the GOLD platform.

20926 www.aagdallas.com
Apartment Association of Greater Dallas

20927 www.airea.com
American Industrial Real Estate Association
Encourages high professional standards. Has developed industrial multiple listing system and standard lease form. Publishes a quarterly newsletter

20928 www.americanhomeowners.org
American Homeowners Foundation
Serves as an educational and research consumer group offering books, model contracts, special studies, home buying, selling,investing, building, financing and remodeling.

20929 www.appraisalinstitute.org
Appraisal Institute
Promotes a code of ethics and uniform standards of the real estate appraisal practice. Publishes periodicals, books and appraisal-related materials, and sponsors courses and seminars.

20930 www.appraisers.org
American Society of Appraisers
Professional association of appraisers of all kinds.

20931 www.arcuea.org
American Real Estate and Urban Economics Assoc
Addresses academic and commercial concerns in real estate and commercial economics.

20932 www.asfmra.org
American Soc of Farm Managers and Rural Appraisers
Provides professionals involved in rural property issues such as management and appraisal, with information on the industry as well as educational opportunities. Includes membership and information from the American Society of Farm Manager and Rural Appraisers.

20933 www.commercialsources.com
The official commercial real state site of the National Association Of Realtors.

20934 www.crb.com
Council of Real Estate Brokerage Managers
Members are real estate firm owners and managers.

20935 www.cre.org
Couselors of Real Estate
Association members provide the public with expert, objective advice on property and land related matters. Individuals invited to join are awarded the CRE designation.

20936 www.erc.org
Employee Relocation Council
A national organization that examines key issues affecting the relocation industry for the benefit of corporations, government agencies, and firms or individuals providing specific services to relocated employees and their families. Accepts advertising.

20937 www.fiabci-usa.com
FIABCI-USA
Encourages private ownership of real property and understanding of property rights and obligations.

20938 www.greyhouse.com
Grey House Publishing
Authoritative reference directories for most business sectors including real estate and allied markets. Users can search the online databases with varied search criteria allowing for custom searches by product category, geographic area, sales volume, keyword, subject and more. Full Grey House catalog and online ordering also available.

20939 www.homestore.com
Homestore.com's family of sites is the leading destination for the home and the real estate- related information on the Internet. Provides informatin on Finance and Insurance, Home Improvement, Decorating, Lawn and garden, Home Electronics amd more.

20940 www.iaia.org
International Association for Impact Assessment
IAIA provides a forum for the exchange of the ideas and experiences to stimulate innovation in assessing, managing and mitigating the consequences of development.

20941 www.icsc.org
International Council of Shopping Centers
Fosters professional standards of performance in the development, construction, financing, leasing, management and operation of shopping centers throughout the world.

20942 www.nahma.org
National Affordable Housing Management Association
Trade association representing companies and individuals involved in the management of affordable multifamily housing.

20943 www.npma.org
National Property Management Association
Represents asset management professionals and keeps members a breast of trends in asset accountability technologies. Sponsors seminars, training courses: certification program.

20944 www.realtor.com
National Association of Realtors
Seeks to establish cooperation among brokers engaged in buying, selling, trading and leasing for realestate.

20945 www.realtylocator.com
Realty Locator
Over 100,000 real estate links nationwide in 10,000 cities and towns in all 50 states.

20946 www.reea.org
Real Estate Educators Association
Individuals involved in training and education.

20947 www.reipa.com
Real Estate Information Providers Association
Supports professional information providers in the real estate industry.

20948 www.relibrary.com/index.html
Real Estate Library
Contains essential resources for buyers, sellers, home owners and real estate professionals.

20949 www.rfpi.com/wrai.htm
National Residential Appraisers Institute
Promotes professionalism in the evaluation of residential real estate and requires demonstration appraisals and testing for professional certification.

Associations

20950 **American Bakers Association**
1300 I Street NW
Suite 700 West
Washington, DC 20005

202-789-0300
Fax: 202-898-1164
E-Mail: info@americanbakers.org
Home Page: americanbakers.org
Social Media: Twitter, LinkedIn, YouTube, RSS

Rich Scalise, Chairman
Fred Penny, First Vice Chairman
Allen L. Shiver, Second Vice Chairman
Robb MacKie, President/ CEO
Erin Sharp, Treasurer

Represents the interests of bakers.
Founded in 1897

20951 **American Bakers Institute**
1300 I St Nw
Suite 700W
Washington, DC 20005

202-789-0300
Fax: 202-898-1164
E-Mail: info@americanbakers.org
Home Page: www.americanbakers.org
Social Media: Twitter, LinkedIn, YouTube, RSS

Robb Mac Kie, President & CEO
James Hamilton, Counsel
Howard R. Alton, Chairman
Lee Sanders, Secretary
Albert Lepage, Treasurer

Association comprised of wholesale bakers.
300 Members
Founded in 1897

20952 **American Culinary Federation**
180 Center Place Way
St. Augustine, FL 32095

800-624-9458
Fax: 904-940-0741
E-Mail: acf@acfchefs.net
Home Page: www.acfchefs.org
Social Media: Facebook, Twitter, LinkedIn, RSS, Flickr

Thomas Macrina, CEC, CCA, AAC, President
Michael Ty, Immediate Past President
William Tillinghast, Treasurer
James Taylor, Secretary
Kyle Richardson, Vice President, Central Region

Professional chefs' organization.
Founded in 1929

20953 **American Culinary Federation: Chef & Child Foundation**
180 Center Place Way
St Augustine, FL 32095

904-824-4468
800-624-9458
Fax: 904-825-4758
E-Mail: acf@acfchefs.net
Home Page: www.acfchefs.org
Social Media: Facebook, Twitter, Flickr, RSS

Heidi Cramb, Executive Director
Thomas J. Macrina, Presiednt
James Taylor, Secretary
William Tillinghast, Treasurer
Michael Ty, Immediate Past President

Seeks to teach children proper nutrition and feed hungry children in the US.
20000 Members
Founded in 1929

20954 **American Edged Products Manufacturers Association**
30200 DetroitRd.
Westlake, OH 44145

440-899-0010
Fax: 440-892-1404
E-Mail: info@aepma.org
Home Page: www.aepma.org
Social Media: Facebook, Twitter, LinkedIn, You Tube

J. Jeffery Wherry, Executive Director
Rick Joswick, VP
Alan Peppel, Treasurer
Bob Clemence, President
Gregory Borrosch, Associate Member Representative

Serves the marketing and manufacturing of the cutlery industry.
23 Members
Founded in 1951

20955 **American Hotel and Lodging Association**
1201 New York Avenue, N.W.
Suite 600
Washington, DC 20005-3931

202-289-3100
Fax: 202-289-3199
E-Mail: eiinfo@ahla.com
Home Page: www.ahla.com
Social Media: Facebook, Twitter, LinkedIn

John Fitzpatrick, Chair
Jim Abrahamson, Vice Chair
Mark Carrier, Secretary/ Treasurer
Katherine Lugar, President/ CEO

Organization focused on the needs of every aspect of the lodging industry.

20956 **American Institute of Baking**
PO Box 3999
Manhattan, KS 66505-3999

785-537-4750
800-633-5137
Fax: 785-537-1493
E-Mail: sales@aibonline.org
Home Page: www.aibonline.org
Social Media: Facebook, Twitter, LinkedIn

Committed to protecting the safety of the food supply chain worldwide and providing high value technical programs.

20957 **American Institute of Wine and Food**
P.O. Box 4961
Louisville, KY 40204

800-274-2493
Fax: 502-456-1821
E-Mail: info@aiwf.org
Home Page: www.aiwf.org
Social Media: Facebook

Brian Calvert, CMP, Executive Director

A nonprofit organization dedicated to advancing the understanding, appreciation and quality of wine and food.
Founded in 1981

20958 **American Personal & Private Chef Associati on**
4572 Delaware Streetÿ
San Diego, CA 92116

619-294-2436
800-644-8389
E-Mail: webmaster@personalchef.com
Home Page: www.personalchef.com
Social Media: Facebook, Twitter, LinkedIn, Pinterest

Candy Wallace, Founder, Executive Director

Organization for professional chefs.

20959 **American Restaurant Association**
PO Box 51482
Sarasota, FL 34232

941-379-2228
E-Mail: info@americanrestaurantassociation.com
Home Page: www.americanrestaurantassociation.com

An organization for the entire restaurant business.
Founded in 1996

20960 **American Society of Baking**
7809 N Chestnut Avenue
Kansas City, MO 64119

800-713-0462
Fax: 888-315-2612
E-Mail: info@asbe.org
Home Page: www.asbe.org
Social Media: Facebook, Twitter

Anthony Turano, Chairman
Ramon Rivera, 1st Vice Chairman
Steve Berne, 2nd Vice Chairman
Mario Somoza, 3rd Vice Chairman
Dr. Lin Carson, Secretary/ Treasurer

Promoting the advancement of baking science and technology through the exchange of information and interaction among baking industry professionals.
Founded in 1924

20961 **Association of Correctional Food Service Affiliates**
210 N. Glenoaks Blvd.
Suite C
Burbank, CA 91502

818-843-6608
Fax: 818-843-7423
Home Page: www.acfsa.org
Social Media: Facebook, Twitter

Robin Sherman, CCFP, CFSM, President
Phil Atkinson, Past President
Laurie Maurino, RD, Vice President
Timothy Thielman, CFSM, CCFP, VP Elect / Treasurer
Karen Candito, CCFP, CFSM, Secretary

An organization dedicated to advancing all aspects of food service in correctional facilities.
Founded in 1969

20962 **Commercial Food Equipment Service Association**
3605 Centre Circle
Fort Mill, SC 29715

336-346-4700
336-346-4745
Home Page: www.cfesa.com
Social Media: Facebook, LinkedIn, YouTube

Paul Toukatly, President
John Schwindt, Vice President
Gary Potvin, Vice President
Wayne Stoutner, Treasurer
David Hahn, Secretary

An organization for certified technicians servicing food equipment.
Founded in 1963

20963 **Cookie and Snack Bakers Association**
7517 Winton Drive
Indianapolis, IN 46268

888-789-3090
Home Page: casba.us

Kevin M. Boyle, President
Crockett Cobble, Immediate Past President
Tom Lugar, Treasurer
Stu Kriegermeierÿ, Secretary
Craig S. Parrish, Executive Director

An organization for cookie and snack bakers.
Founded in 1970

20964 **Cookware Manufacturers Association**
PO Box 531335
Birmingham, AL 35253-1335

205-592-0389
Fax: 205-599-5598
E-Mail: hrushing@usit.net
Home Page: www.cookware.org
Social Media: Facebook, Twitter, LinkedIn

Jay Zalinskas, President
Gene Karlson, VP
Hugh J Rushing, Executive VP

Represents manufactures of cookware and bakeware in the US and Canada. Publishes consumer guides to cookware and engineering standards for industry.
21 Members
Founded in 1920

20965 **Foodservice Consultants Society International**
P.O. Box 4961
Louisville, KY 40204

502-379-4122
E-Mail: Info@fcsi.org
Home Page: www.fcsi.org
Social Media: Facebook, Twitter

Jonathan Doughty, FCSI, President
James Petersen, FCSI, Treasurer/ Secretary
Toni Clarke, FCSI, Board of Director
William Taunton, FCSI, Board of Director
Martin Rahmann, FCSI, Board of Director

A foodservice association with members in over 30 countries.

20966 **Green Restaurant Association**
89 South Streetÿ
Suite 802
Boston, MA 2111

617-737-3344
E-Mail: info@dinegreen.com
Home Page: www.dinegreen.com
Social Media: Facebook, Twitter

Nonprofit organization that provides information and resources for making aspects of restaurants more eco-friendly.
Founded in 1990

20967 **Home Baking Association**
785-478-3283
Fax: 785-478-3024
Home Page: www.homebaking.org
Social Media: Facebook, Twitter, Flickr

Kent Symns, President
Sam Garlow, 1st Vice President
Eric Wall, 2nd Vice President

National organization promoting scratch baking education and practice.

20968 **International Association of Culinary Professionals**
1221 Avenue of the Americas
42nd floor
Louisville, NY 10020

64- 3-8 49
86- 3-8 49
Fax: 86- 3-8 25
E-Mail: iacp@hqtrs.com
Home Page: www.iacp.com
Social Media: Facebook, Twitter, LinkedIn, Vimeo

Kerry Edwards, Sr Member Services Representative
Doug Duda, Immediate Past President
Julia M. Uhser, President
Raghavan Iyer, Vice President
Margaret Bradley-Foley, Secretary-Treasurer

A not for profit organization whose members represent virtually every profession in the culinary universe: teachers, cooking school owners, caterers, writers, chefs, media cooking personalities, editors, publishers, food stylists, food photographers, restauranteurs, leaders of major food corporations and vintners. Literally a who's who of the food world. Founded in 1978.

20969 **International Caterers Association**
3601 East Joppa Road
Baltimore, MD 21234

410-931-8100
Fax: 410-931-8111
E-Mail: paulak@clemonsmgmt.com
Home Page: internationalcaterers.org

Jennifer Perna, President
Pat Christofolo, Immediate Past President
Jen Delaye, President's Council Chairÿ
Roxann Torelli, Treasurer
Linda Sample, Secretary
Organization for catering professionals.

20970 **International Food Service Executives Association Headquarters**
4955 Miller Street
Suite 107
Wheat Ridge, CO 80033

702-838-8821
800-893-5499
Fax: 702-838-8853
E-Mail: ifseahqoffice@gmail.com
Home Page: www.ifsea.com
Social Media: Facebook, Twitter, LinkedIn

Grant Thompson, Chairman of the Board
Edward Manley, President/COO
David Orosz, International Chairman of the Board
Gina Vance, International Chairman of the Board

Provides education and community service to the foodservice industry.
3,000 Members
Founded in 1901

20971 **James Beard Foundation**
167 W 12th St
New York, NY 10011

212-675-4984
800-362-3273
Fax: 212-645-1438
E-Mail: info@jamesbeard.org
Home Page: www.jamesbeard.org
Social Media: Facebook, Twitter

Susan Ungaro, President
Mitchell Davis, Executive Vice President
Marilyn Platzer, Chief Financial & Operating Officer
Nancy Kull, Executive Asst. to the President
Michelle Santoro, Project Manager

Nonprofit organization dedicated to preserving the country's culinary heritage and fostering the appreciation and development of gastronomy by recognizing and promoting excellence in all aspects of the culinary arts.
Founded in 1986

20972 **Mobile Industrial Caterers' Association**
7300 Artesia Boulevard
Buena Park, CA 90621-1804

714-632-6800
Fax: 714-632-5405
Home Page: www.mobilecaterers.com

Kelly Ramirez, Executive Director

Aids with problems common within the industry through exchange of ideas, advice on legal problems, safety standards and licensing regulations.
185 Members
Founded in 1964

20973 **National Association for Catering and Events**
9891 Broken Land Parkway
Suite 301
Columbia, MD 21046

410-290-5410
Fax: 410-290-5460
E-Mail: INFO@NACE.NET
Home Page: www.nace.net
Social Media: Facebook, Twitter, LinkedIn, Pinterest, YouTube

Linwood Campbell, CPCE, President
Joe Mahoney, CPCE, First Vice President
Donnell Bayot, Second Vice President
Kate Patay, CPCE, Secretary/ Treasurer
Lisa Hopkins Barry, Immediate Past President

Serves catering professionals and the vendors and suppliers that support them.

20974 **National Bar & Restaurant Management Association**
307 Jackson Avenue W
Oxford, MS 38655

662-236-5510
800-247-3881
Fax: 662-236-5541
E-Mail: jrobinson@oxpub.com
Home Page: www.nightclub.com
Social Media: Facebook, Twitter, RSS

Jon Taffer, President
Leo J. Squatrito, VP, Sale & Marketing
Erica Mercke, Marketing Manager
Greg Goulski, Director of Sales, Digital Media
Kristen Santoro, Content & Conference Dircetor

20975 **National Council of Chain Restaurants**
325 7th St NW
Suite 1100
Washington, DC 20004

202-783-7971
800-673-4692
Fax: 202-737-2849
E-Mail: purviss@nrf.com
Home Page: www.nccr.net

Jack Whipple, President
Chip Kunde, Chairman
Cicely Simpson, Treasurer
Lynn Liddle, Secretary
Mary Schell, Vice Chairman

A division of the National Retail Federation, NCCR was formed by a group of foodservice and restaurant executives who felt that they were not receiving adequate government relations representation from existing organizations. The NCCR helps shape federal legislative and regulatory issues that are of uniform significance to our member companies. Comprised of nearly 40 of the largest chain restaurant companies in the country.
Frequency: Inquire For Membership
Founded in 1965

20976 **National Restaurant Association**
2055 L Street NW
Suite 700
Washington, DC 20036

202-331-5900
800-424-5156
Fax: 202-331-2429
Home Page: www.restaurant.org
Social Media: Facebook, Twitter, YouTube

Ken Conrad, Chair
Jack Crawford, Vice Chair
Joe Kadow, Treasurer
Dawn Sweeney, President/ Chief Executive Officer
Ed Beck, SVP, Technology

Supports food service industry with programs in education, promotion and government relations.

20977 North American Association of Food Equipment Manufacturers
161 North Clark Street
Suite 2020
Chicago, IL 60601

312-821-0201
Fax: 312-821-0202
E-Mail: info@nafem.org
Home Page: www.nafem.org
Social Media: Facebook, Twitter, LinkedIn

Deirdre Flynn, Executive Vice President
Thomas R. Campion, President
Kevin Flink, Secretary/ Treasurer
Michael L. Whiteley, President-Elect
Marianne Byrne, Marketing Manager

Dealers and distributors of foodservice equipment and supplies.
700 Members
Founded in 1979

20978 North American Association of Foodservice Equipment Manufacturers
161 North Clark Street
Suite 2020
Chicago, IL 60601

312-821-0201
Fax: 312-821-0202
E-Mail: info@nafem.org
Home Page: www.nafem.org
Social Media: Facebook

Michael L. Whiteley, CFSP, President
Kevin Fink, CFSP, President-Elect
Joseph Carlson, CFSP, Secretary/Treasurer
Deirdre Flynn, CFSP, Executive Vice President
Charlie Souhrada, CFSP, Director, Member Services

Trade association for foodservice and food equipment manufacturers.

20979 Professional Chef's Association
P.O. Box 453
Frederick, CO 80530

720-379-8759
E-Mail: info@ProfessionalChef.com
Home Page: professionalchef.com
Social Media: Facebook, Twitter, LinkedIn

Organization for professional chefs.
Founded in 1997

20980 Restaurant Facility Management Association
5600 Tennyson Parkway
Suite 265
Plano, TX 75024

972-805-0905
Fax: 972-805-0906
Home Page: www.rfmaonline.com

Roger Goldstein, Chair
Kevin Carringer, First Vice Chair
Maria Johnson, Immediate Past Chair
Vance Arndt, Treasurer
Richard Ross, Secretary

Association for restaurant facility management professionals.

20981 United States Personal Chef Association
7680 Universal Blvd.
Suite 550
Orlando, FL 32819

800-995-2138
E-Mail: info@uspca.com
Home Page: www.uspca.com
Social Media: Facebook, Twitter, LinkedIn, RSS, Google+

Larry Lynch, President
Robert Lynch, Vice President
Vince Likar, Director of Member Service
Annise Jackson, Manager of Membership
Dan Chancellor, Marketing Manager

Organization offering all the necessary resources for those interested in starting their own personal chef business.
Founded in 1991

Newsletters

20982 AEPMA News & Views
American Edged Products Manufacturers Association
21165 Whitfield Pl
Suite 105
Sterling, VA 20165

703-433-9281
Fax: 703-433-0369
E-Mail: info@aepma.org
Home Page: www.aepma.org

David Barrack, Executive Director
Robert Clemence, VP
Tom Arrowsmith, Treasurer

Serves the marketing and manufacturing of the cutlery industry.
Frequency: Twice/Year

20983 American Culinary Federation Newsletter
American Culinary Federation
180 Center Place Way
St Augustine, FL 32095-8859

904-824-4468
800-624-9458
Fax: 904-825-4758
Home Page: www.acfchefs.org

Heidi Cramb, Executive Director
Edward G Leonard, President
Brent T. Frei, Director of Marketing
Kay Orde, Editor
Michael Feierstein, Administrative Assistant

The official membership newsletter of the American Culinary Federation.
Frequency: Monthly
Circulation: 21000
Founded in 1929
Printed in 2 colors on matte stock

20984 Baker's Math
American Bakers Institute
1300 I St Nw
Suite 700W
Washington, DC 20005-7203

202-789-0300
Fax: 202-898-1164
Home Page: www.americanbakers.org

Robb Mac Kie, President

20985 CHRIE Communique
Int'l Council on Hotel, Restaurant Institute Edu.
2810 North Parham Road
suite 230
Richmond, VA 23294-3006

804-747-4971
Fax: 804-346-5009
E-Mail: publications@chrie.org
Home Page: www.chrie.org

Dale Gaddy, Publisher
Mike Zema, President
Kathy McCarty, CEO
Joseph Bradley, Treasurer

Monthly newsletter offering information on industry, significant hospitality and tourism education job listings.
Cost: $65.00
Frequency: Monthly
Circulation: 1800
Founded in 1946

20986 Cameron's Foodservice Marketing Reporter
Cameron's Publications
5423 Sheridan Drive
PO Box 676
Williamsville, NY 14231

519-586-8785
Fax: 519-586-8816
E-Mail: products@cameronpub.com
Home Page: www.cameronpub.com

Nina T Cameron, Editor
Bob McClelland, Publisher
Peggy Kelly, Circulation Manager

Successful promotion and advertising case histories for the restaurant and hotel industry.
Cost: $197.00
Frequency: Fortnightly
Founded in 1970

20987 Center of the Plate
American Culinary Federation
180 Center Place Way
St Augustine, FL 32095-8859

904-824-4468
800-624-9458
Fax: 904-825-4758
E-Mail: acf@acfchefs.net
Home Page: www.acfchefs.org

Heidi Cramb, Executive Director
Edward Leonard, Administrative Assistant
Michael Feierstein, Administrative Assistant
Bryan Hunt, Graphic Designer
Patricia Carroll, Director of Communications

Official membership newsletter of the American Culinary Federation.
Cost: $50.00
Frequency: Monthly
Circulation: 25000+
Founded in 1929

20988 Wine on Line Food and Wine Review
Enterprise Publishing
PO Box 328
Blair, NE 68008-0328

402-426-2121
Fax: 402-426-2227
E-Mail: news@enterprisepub.com
Home Page: www.enterprisepub.com

Mark Rhoades, President
Dough Barber, Editor
Lynette Hansen, Sales Manager
Bill Smutko, Circulation Manager
Dave Smith, Production Manager

Reviews, feature articles and information on all areas of food and wine, including restaurants, hotels, trains and airlines. Accepts advertising.
Cost: $36.00
10 Pages
Circulation: 13150
Founded in 1800

Magazines & Journals

20989 Chain Store Information Guide
3922 Coconut Palm Dr
Tampa, FL 33619

800-778-9794
Fax: 813-627-6888
Home Page: www.chainstoreguide.com

A national organization that serves the commercial and institutional food and lodging industry.
Founded in 1967

20990 Cheers
257 Park Avenue S
3rd Floor, Suite 303
New York, NY 10010

212-967-1551
Fax: 646-654-2099

John Eastman, Owner

Every issue is designed to help on-premise operators enhance the profitability of their beverage operations.

20991 Chef
Talcott Communications Corporation
20 N Wacker Dr
Suite 3900
Chicago, IL 60606-3188

312-726-2410
Fax: 312-726-2554
Home Page: www.ucco.com/tc.htm

Laura Herold, President
Rob Benes, Senior Editor
Morgan Holzman, Contributing Editor
David Pizzimenti, Circulation Manager

Information on food production and presentation, includes chef profiles, trend studies, marketing information and restaurant profiles.
Cost: $32.00
Frequency: Monthly
Circulation: 38769
ISSN: 1087-061X
Founded in 1956
Printed in 4 colors on glossy stock

20992 Coffee & Cuisine
Coffee Talk
1218 3rd Avenue
#1315
Seattle, WA 98101-3021

206-521-7247
Fax: 206-623-0446
Home Page: www.coffeecuisine.com

Kerri Goodman, Publisher

Covers new products, personnel moves, industry news, how to articles, education, and techniques to increase sales growth for the coffee, cold beverage and foodservice industry.
Cost: $36.00
Frequency: Monthly
Circulation: 30000

20993 Cooking for Profit
CP Publishing
PO Box 267
Fond du Lac, WI 54936-267

920-923-3700
Fax: 920-923-6805
E-Mail: comments@cookingforprofit.com
Home Page: www.cookingforprofit.com

Colleen Phalen, Editor-in-Chief

Paid subscription trade magazine targeted to foodservice owners, managers and chefs. Each month features current trends in food preparation with step-by-step recipes and photographs; effective management techniques; and the latest in foodservice equipment — all written by industry experts. Also features in-depth profiles of a successful foodservice operation.
Cost: $26.00
28 Pages
Frequency: Monthly
Founded in 1932
Printed in 4 colors on glossy stock

20994 Cornell Hotel & Restaurant Administration Quarterly
Elsevier Science Publishing Company
537 Statler Hall
Ithaca, NY 14853-6902

607-255-9780
Fax: 607-254-2922
E-Mail: hosp_research@cornell.edu
Home Page: www.hotelschool.cornell.edu

Dr. Michael Sturman, Editor
Glenn Withiam, Executive Editor
Nicole Roach, Marketing

A journal devoted to the development and exchange of management ideas for the hospitality industry.
Cost: $113.00
Frequency: Quarterly
Circulation: 4500
Founded in 1963

20995 Culinary Trends
Culinary Trends Publications
6285 E Spring Street
#107
Long Beach, CA 90808-4000

310-496-2558
Fax: 310-421-8993
Home Page: www.culinarytrends.com

Fred Mensigna, Publisher
Linda Mensinga, Editor

Information for food and beverage managers along with managers of hotels and restaurants.
Cost: $21.60
Frequency: Quarterly
Circulation: 10000

20996 El Restaurante Mexicano
Maiden Name Press
1010 Lake St
Suite 604
Oak Park, IL 60301-1136

708-848-3200
800-407-5845
Fax: 708-445-9477
E-Mail: kfurore@restmex.com
Home Page: www.restmex.com

Joe Madden, President
Kathleen Furore, Managing Director
Jessica Pantanini, Managing Director

A bilingual magazine featuring industry specific food news, features restaurant profiles and new product information for personnel of restaurants serving mexican/southwestern menu items nationwide.
Cost: $18.00
Circulation: 27000
Founded in 1997

20997 FEDA News & Views
Foodservice Equipment Distributors Association
223 W Jackson Boulevard
#620
Chicago, IL 60606-6911

312-427-9605
Fax: 312-427-9607
E-Mail: feda@feda.com
Home Page: www.feda.com

Stacy Ward, Managing Editor
Ray Herrick, Executive VP
Adela Ramos, Administration Director, Manager
Bruce Gulbas, President

Focus is on sales, technology, new products and other areas of benefit to dealers, as well as industry trends and news.
Cost: $150.00
Circulation: 1200
Founded in 1933

20998 Food & Beverage News
Food & Beverage News
1886 W Bay Drive
#E6
Largo, FL 33770-3017

727-585-7745
Fax: 727-585-7245
Home Page: www.fbnews.com

Dennis J Regan, Publisher

News on the latest liquor law, new products, and government legislation.
Cost: $28.00
Frequency: Monthly
Circulation: 16,880

20999 Food Arts Magazine
M Shanken Communications
387 Park Ave S
Suite 8
New York, NY 10016-8872

212-684-4224
Fax: 212-684-5424
Home Page: www.cigaraficionado.com

Marvin Shanken, Publisher

A magazine devoted to the restaurant industry.
Cost: $40.00
Frequency: Monthly
Founded in 1988

21000 Foodservice Equipment & Supplies Specialist
Reed Business Information
1350 E Touhy Avenue
Des Plaines, IL 60018-3358

630-320-7000
Fax: 630-288-8686
Home Page: www.reedbusiness.com

Mitchell Schechter, Editor-in-Chief
Niles Crum, Publisher

Magazine for professionals who specify, sell and distribute foodservice equipment, supplies and furnishings.
Cost: $69.95
64+ Pages
Frequency: Monthly
Circulation: 27M
Founded in 1947
Printed in 4 colors on glossy stock

21001 Foodservice Equipment Reports
Robin Ashton
2000 Clearwater Drive
Oak Brook, IL 60523-3358

630-288-8000
800-446-6551
Fax: 630-288-8265
E-Mail: webmaster@reedbusiness.com
Home Page: www.reedbusiness.com

Josph Carbonara, Editor-in-Chief
Maureen Slocum, Publisher
Keithy Mcnamara, Marketing
katy Tucker, Circulation Manager
Jeff Greisph, CEO

Geared toward manufacturers of foodservice equipment and their agencies.
Cost: $106.90
Frequency: Monthly
Circulation: 22719
Founded in 1947

21002 Fresh Cup Magazine
Fresh Cup Publishing Company
537 SE Ash Street Suite 300
PO Box 14827
Portland, OR 97293-827

503-236-2587
800-868-5866
Fax: 503-236-3165
E-Mail: jan@freshcup.com
Home Page: www.freshcup.com

Julie Beals, Editor
Nicole Maas, Sales/Marketing Associate
Bill Berninger, Circulation Director
Ward Barbee, Publisher
Jan Gibson, Owner
Cost: $57.00
68 Pages
Frequency: Monthly
Circulation: 14000
Founded in 1992
Printed in 4 colors on glossy stock

21003 Gourmet News
Oser Communications Group
1877 N Kolb Road
Tucson, AZ 85715

520-721-1300
Home Page: www.gourmetnews.com

Rocelle Aragon, Editor
Kate Seymour, Senior Associate Publisher

The business newspaper for the gourmet industry.
40 Pages
Frequency: Monthly
Circulation: 23381
ISSN: 1052-4630
Founded in 1991
Printed in 4 colors on glossy stock

21004 Journal of Foodservice Business Research
Taylor & Francis
325 Chestnut Street
Suite 800
Philadelphia, PA 19106

800-354-1420
Fax: 215-625-2940
Home Page: www.tandf.co.uk

David A Cranage, Editor

Features articles from international experts in various disciplines, including management, marketing, finance, law, food technology, nutrition, psychology, information systems, anthropology, human resources, and more.
Cost: $ 92.00
Frequency: Quarterly
ISSN: 1537-8020
Founded in 1978

21005 Midsouthwest Restaurant
3800 North Portland Avenue
Oklahoma City, OK 73112-2982

405-942-8181
800-375-8181
Fax: 405-942-0541
Home Page: www.okrestaurants.com

Jim Hopper, President/CEO
Shannon Moad, Editor
Debra Bailey, Deputy Director
Frequency: Quarterly
Circulation: 2500
Founded in 1933

21006 Nation's Restaurant News
Lebhar-Friedman Publications
425 Park Ave
Suite 6
New York, NY 10022-3526

212-756-5220
Fax: 212-756-5250
E-Mail: info@lf.com

Lebhar Friedman, Publisher
Michael Cardillo, VP Sales
Leslie Wolowitz, Advertising

Serves commercial and onsite food service and lodging establishments including restaurants, schools, universities, hospitals, nursing homes and other health and welfare facilities, hotels and motels with food service, government installations, clubs and other related firms.
Cost: $44.95
Frequency: Weekly
Circulation: 85999
Founded in 1925
Mailing list available for rent: 100,000 names at $100 per M
Printed in 4 colors on matte stock

21007 National Culinary Review
American Culinary Federation
180 Center Place Way
St Augustine, FL 32095-8859

904-824-4468
800-624-9458
Fax: 904-825-4758
Home Page: www.acfchefs.org

Heidi Cramb, Executive Director
Edward G Leonard, Administrative Assistant
Michael Feierstein, Administrative Assistant
Bryan Hunt, Graphic Designer
Patricia Carroll, Director of Communications

Accepts advertising.
Cost: $50.00
Frequency: Monthly
Founded in 1929

21008 National Dipper
US Exposition Corporation
1028 W. Devon Avenue
Elk Grove Village, IL 60007

847-301-8400
Fax: 847-301-8402
E-Mail: lynda@nationaldipper.com
Home Page: www.nationaldipper.com

Lynda Utterback, Publisher

Information for retail ice cream and frozen yogurt owners and operators, includes changes and developments in the business.
Cost: $55.00
Circulation: 17000
Founded in 1985
Printed in 4 colors on glossy stock

21009 Restaurant Digest
Panagos Publishing
3930 Knowles Avenue
#305
Kensington, MD 20895-2428

301-929-6200
Fax: 301-929-6550
Home Page: www.foodservicedepot.com

Bruce Panagos, Publisher

Developments and news of interest to owners, managers, and operators of dining and entertainment establishments in the region.

21010 Restaurant Hospitality
Donohue/Meehan Publishing
1801 E 9th St
Suite 920
Cleveland, OH 44114-3103

216-931-7258
Fax: 216-696-1752
E-Mail: rheditor@penton.com
Home Page: www.restaurant-hospitality.com

Jeff Donohoe, President
Jess Grossberg, Publisher
Gail Bellamy, Managing Editor
Sue Apple, Production Manager
Frequency: Monthly
Circulation: 117,721
Founded in 1892

21011 Restaurant Marketing
Oxford Publishing
Ste 1
1903b University Ave
Oxford, MS 38655-4150

662-236-5510
800-247-3881
Fax: 662-281-0104
Home Page: www.restaurant-marketing.net

Frequency: Bi-Monthly

21012 Restaurant Wine
Wine Profits
PO Box 222
Napa, CA 94559-222
707-224-4777
Fax: 707-224-6740
Home Page: www.restaurantwine.com

Ronn Wiegand, Publisher
Paul Grieco, Co-Owner

Information on the marketing of wine in restaurants, hotels and clubs, wine and food pairing ideas and review of wines.
Cost: $99.00
Frequency: Monthly
Circulation: 3000
ISSN: 1040-7030
Printed in 2 colors on matte stock

21013 Restaurants & Institutions
Reed Business Information
2000 Clearwater Dr
Oak Brook, IL 60523-8809

630-574-0825
Fax: 630-288-8781
E-Mail: jamie.popp@reedbusiness.com
Home Page: www.reedbusiness.com

Jeff Greisch, President
Scott Hume, Managing Editor

Commercial and noncommercial foodservice establishments including restaurant, hotels, motels, fast-food chains,coffee shops, food stores with foodservice
Frequency: Monthly
Circulation: 155512
Founded in 1937
Printed in 4 colors on glossy stock

21014 Restaurants USA
National Restaurant Association
1200 17th St NW
Washington, DC 20036-3006

202-331-5900
800-424-5156
Fax: 202-331-2429
Home Page: www.restaurant.org

Dawn M Sweeney, CEO
Sarah Hamaker, Treasurer
Phil Hickey, Treasurer

A trade magazine offering information for restaurant owners and managers, including industry trends, operational pointers, management principles and association activities.
Cost: $125.00
48 Pages
Frequency: Monthly
Circulation: 44000
Founded in 1980
Printed in 4 colors

21015 Restaurants, Resorts & Hotels
Publishing Group
PO Box 318
Trumbull, CT 06611-0318

860-279-0149
Fax: 203-254-7104

James Martone, Publisher

Information on new products, supplies, food and equipment for those executives and managers who have responsibility for the food.
Cost: $24.00
Frequency: Monthly
Circulation: 97,000

21016 Southeast Food Service News
8805 Tamiami Trail N #301
Naples, FL 34108

239-514-1258
E-Mail: efischer@sfsn.com
Home Page: www.sfsn.com
Social Media: Y
Elliott R Fischer, Marketing Director
John P Hayward, Account Executive
Elsie Olson, Production Manager
Frequency: Monthly
Founded in 1977

21017 Southwest Food Service News
4011 W Plano Pkwy
Suite 121
Plano, TX 75093-5620

972-943-1254
Fax: 972-943-1258
Home Page: www.southwestfoodservice.com

Sam Ballard, Publisher

21018 Total Food Service
PO Box 2507
Greenwich, CT 06836-2507

203-661-9090
Fax: 203-661-9325
Home Page: www.totalfood.com

Fred Klashman, President

21019 Yankee Food Service
Griffin Publishing Company
201 Oak St
Suite A
Pembroke, MA 02359

781-294-4700
866-677-4700
Fax: 781-829-0134
E-Mail: info@griffinpublishing.net
Home Page: www.griffinpublishing.net

Kevin Griffin, President
Lynda Bassett, Editor
Henry Zacchini, Associate Publisher
Karen Harty, Vice President
Julie Mignosa, Office Manager

Reports news and happenings of the food service industry in New England.
Cost: $47.00
48 Pages
Frequency: Monthly
Circulation: 26110
Founded in 1979

Trade Shows

21020 AEPMA Annual Meeting
American Edged Products Manufacturers Association
21165 Whitfield Pl
Suite 105
Sterling, VA 20165

703-433-9281
Fax: 703-433-0369
E-Mail: info@aepma.org
Home Page: www.aepma.org

David Barrack, Executive Director
Robert Clemence, VP
Tom Arrowsmith, Treasurer

Offering training and certificate programs, and management courses.
Frequency: Annual

21021 American Culinary Federation Central Regional Conference
American Culinary Federation
10 San Bartola Drive
Saint Augustine, FL 32085

904-824-4468
800-624-9458
Fax: 904-825-4758
E-Mail: acf@acfchefs.net
Home Page: www.acfchefs.org

Brent Frei, Director Marketing
Michael Baskette, Administrative Assistant
Michael Feierstein, Administrative Assistant
Bryan Hunt, Graphic Designer
Patricia Carroll, Director of Communications

Culinary equipment, supplies and services. Seminars, workshops, cooking demos, more.

21022 American Culinary Federation National Convention
10 San Bartola Drive
Saint Augustine, FL 32086

904-824-4468
800-624-9458
Fax: 904-825-4758
E-Mail: acf@acfchefs.net
Home Page: www.acfchefs.org
Brent Frei, Director Marketing
Michael Baskette, Administrative Assistant
Michael Feierstein, Administrative Assistant
Bryan Hunt, Graphic Designer
Patricia Carroll, Director of Communications

200 booths of products and foodstuffs for the food service industry. Seminars, workshops, cooking demos, more.

21023 American Culinary Federation Northeast Regional Conference
American Culinary Federation
10 San Bartola Drive
Saint Augustine, FL 32086

904-824-4468
800-624-9458
Fax: 904-825-4758
E-Mail: acf@acfchefs.net
Home Page: www.acfchefs.org
Brent Frei, Director Marketing
Michael Baskette, Administrative Assistant
Michael Feierstein, Administrative Assistant
Bryan Hunt, Graphic Designer
Patricia Carroll, Director of Communications

Culinary equipment, supplies and services. Seminars, workshops, cooking demos, more.

21024 American Culinary Federation Southeast Regional Conference
American Culinary Federation
10 San Bartola Drive
Saint Augustine, FL 32086

904-824-4468
800-624-9458
Fax: 904-825-4758
E-Mail: acf@acfchefs.net
Home Page: www.acfchefs.org

Brent Frei, Director Marketing
Michael Baskette, Administrative Assistant
Michael Feierstein, Administrative Assistant
Bryan Hunt, Graphic Designer
Patricia Carroll, Director of Communications

Culinary equipment, supplies and services. Seminars, workshops, cooking demos, more.

21025 American Culinary Federation Western Regional Conference
American Culinary Federation
10 San Bartola Drive
Saint Augustine, FL 32086

904-824-4468
800-624-9458
Fax: 904-825-4758
E-Mail: acf@acfchefs.net
Home Page: www.acfchefs.org

Brent Frei, Director Marketing
Michael Baskette, Administrative Assistant
Michael Feierstein, Administrative Assistant
Bryan Hunt, Graphic Designer
Patricia Carroll, Director of Communications

Culinary equipment, supplies and services. Seminars, workshops, cooking demos, more.

21026 Annual Hotel, Motel and Restaurant Supply Show of the Southeast
Leisure Time Unlimited
708 Main Street
PO Box 332
Myrtle Beach, SC 29577

843-448-9483
800-261-5991
Fax: 843-626-1513
E-Mail: hmrss@sc.rr.com
Home Page: www.hmrsss.com

Brooke P Baker, Show Director

Trade show for the hospitality industry.
23000 Attendees
Frequency: January
Founded in 1975

21027 Fancy Food Show
Specialty Food Association, Inc.
136 Madison Avenue
12th Floor
New York, NY 10016

212-482-6440
Fax: new
Home Page: www.specialtyfood.com

Mike Silver, Chair
Becky Renfro Borbolla, Treasurer
Dennis Deschaine, Past Chairperson
Shawn McBride, Vice Chair
Matt Nielsen, Secretary

Over 80,000 on-trend and best-in-class products, including confections, cheese, coffee, snacks, spices, ethnic, natural, organic and more. 1,300 exhibitors representing specialty foods and beverages from across the United States and 35 countries and regions.

21028 Hospitality Food Service Expo Southeast and Atlanta International Wine
Reed Business Information
275 Washington Street
Boston, MA 02458

617-261-1166
Fax: 617-558-4327
Home Page: www.cahners.com

Patrick Paleno, Show Manager
Barry Reed Jr, CFO
Stuart Whayman, CFO

400 booths featuring educational seminars, culinary salon, and exhibits of products and services.
12M Attendees
Frequency: October

21029 National Restaurant Association: Restaurant, Hotel-Motel Show
1200 17th Street NW
Washington, DC 20036-3006
202-331-5900
Home Page: http://www.nraef.org
Reed Hayes, President, Chief Operating Officer
Steven Anderson, President
1,800 booths for the food service industry exhibiting food and beverages.
105M Attendees
Frequency: May

21030 Year of Enchantment
Int'l Council on Hotel, Restaurant Institute Edu.
1200 17th Street NW
Washington, DC 20036-3006
202-467-6300
E-Mail: publications@chrie.org
Home Page: www.chrie.org
Susan Gould, Manager
Joseph Bradley, Treasurer
Containing 70+ booths and 50+ exhibits.
750 Attendees
Frequency: August
Founded in 1946

Directories & Databases

21031 Chain Restaurant Operators Directory
Chain Store Guide
3922 Coconut Palm Dr
Tampa, FL 33619-1389
813-627-6700
800-972-9202
Fax: 813-627-7094
E-Mail: info@csgis.com
Home Page: www.csgis.com
Mike Jarvis, Publisher
Arthur Sciarrotta, Senior VP
Discover more than 5,600 listings and more than 26,000 unique personnel within the Restaurant Chain, Foodservice Management, and Hotel/Motel Operator markets in the U.S. and Canada. Each company must have at least $1 million in annual sales either system wide or industry and have two or more units/accounts.
Cost: $335.00
Frequency: Annual

21032 Culinary Collection Directory
International Association/Culinary Professionals
304 W Liberty Street
Suite 201
Louisville, KY 40202
502-587-7953
800-928-4227
Fax: 502-589-3602
E-Mail: info@iacp.com
Home Page: www.iacp.com
Kerry Edwards, Sr Member Services Representative
Trina Gribbins, Manager
Teachers, cooking school owners, caterers, writers, chefs, media cooking personalities, editors, publishers, food stylists, food photographers, restauranteurs, leaders of major food corporations and vintners. Literally a who's who of the food world.

21033 Food & Beverage Market Place
Grey House Publishing
4919 Route 22
PO Box 56
Amenia, NY 12501
518-789-8700
800-562-2139
Fax: 845-373-6390
E-Mail: books@greyhouse.com
Home Page: www.greyhouse.com
Social Media: Facebook, Twitter
Leslie Mackenzie, Publisher
Richard Gottlieb, Editor
This information packed three-volume set is the most powerful buying and marketing guide for the US food and beverage industry. Includes thousands of industry freight and transportation listings.
Cost: $595.00
2000 Pages
Frequency: Annual
ISBN: 1-592373-61-5
Founded in 1981

21034 Food & Beverage Marketplace: Online Database
Grey House Publishing
4919 Route 22
PO Box 56
Amenia, NY 12501
518-789-8700
800-562-2139
Fax: 845-373-6390
E-Mail: gold@greyhouse.com
Home Page: http://gold.greyhouse.com
Social Media: Facebook, Twitter
Richard Gottlieb, President
Leslie Mackenzie, Publisher
This complete updated Food & Beverage Market Place: Online Database is the go-to source for the food and beverage industry. Anyone involved in the food and beverage industry needs this 'industry bible' and the important contacts to develop critical research data that can make for successful business growth.
Frequency: Annual
Founded in 1981

21035 Getaways for Gourmets in the Northeast
Wood Pond Press
365 Ridgewood Rd
West Hartford, CT 06107-3517
860-521-0389
Fax: 860-313-0185
Home Page: www.green-cuisine.com
Richard M Woodworth, Owner
Directory of services and supplies to the industry.
Cost: $14.95
514 Pages

21036 High Volume Independent Restaurants Database
Chain Store Guide
3922 Coconut Palm Dr
Tampa, FL 33619-1389
813-627-6700
800-778-9794
Fax: 813-627-7094
E-Mail: info@csgis.com
Home Page: www.csgis.com
Mike Jarvis, Publisher
Shami Choon, Manager
Covers this growing niche through its nearly 5,900 listings featuring casual dining, family restaurants and fine dining establishments. Plus, access to over 15,000 key personnel names puts you in contact with key decision makers.
Cost: $335.00
1,000 Pages
Frequency: Annual

21037 International Association of Culinary Professionals
304 W Liberty Street
Suite 201
Louisville, KY 40202
502-587-7953
800-928-4227
Fax: 502-589-3602
E-Mail: info@iacp.com
Home Page: www.iacp.com
Kerry Edwards, Sr Member Services Representative
Trina Gribbins, Manager
A not for profit organization whose members represent virtually every profession in the culinary universe: teachers, cooking school owners, caterers, writers, chefs, media cooking personalities, editors, publishers, food stylists, food photographers, restauranteurs, leaders of major food corporations and vintners. Literally a who's who of the food world. Founded in 1978.

21038 Restaurant Hospitality: Hospitality 500 Issue
Penton Media
1166 Avenue of the Americas
New York, NY 10036
212-204-4200
Fax: 216-696-6662
E-Mail: information@penton.com
Home Page: www.penton.com
Social Media: Facebook, Twitter, LinkedIn
Jane Cooper, Marketing
Chris Meyer, Director
Bev Walter, Service Manager
500 independent restaurants selected on basis of sales.
Cost: $25.00
Frequency: Annual, June
Circulation: 123,000

21039 Restaurants and Institutions: Annual 400 Issues
Reed Business Information
1350 E Touhy Avenue
Suite 200E
Des Plaines, IL 60018-3358
847-962-2200
Fax: 630-288-8686
Home Page: www.reedbusiness.com
Roland Dietz, CEO
Stuart Whayman, CFO
Cost: $25.00
Frequency: Annual
Circulation: 16,000

21040 Zagat.com Restaurant Guides
Zagat Survey
4 Columbus Cir
New York, NY 10019-1180
212-977-6000
Fax: 212-977-9760
E-Mail: customerservice@zagat.com
Home Page: www.zagat.com
Tim Zagat, CEO
Zagat.com was launched in May of 1999 and contains the most trusted and authoritive dining information online for over 20,000 restaurants in twenty eight cities worldwide, with 17 more cities to be added shortly. Based in New York City, the Zagat survey was founded in 1979 by Tim and Nina Zagat.

Industry Web Sites

21041 http://gold.greyhouse.com
G.O.L.D Grey House OnLine Databases

Grey House Publishing's online database platform, GOLD, offers Quick Search, Keyword Search and Expert Search for most business sectors including restaurant markets. The GOLD platform makes finding the information you need quick and easy - whether you're a novice searcher or an experienced database user. All of Grey House's directory products are available for subscription on the GOLD platform.

21042 www.acfchefs.org
American Culinary Federation

Member organization of professional chefs and cooks. Certifies chefs, accredits culinary programs and promotes culinary arts.

21043 www.chefcertification.com
American Culinary Federation

Offers the required courses for ACF certification online.

21044 www.chowbaby.com

This web site is search engine for restaurants.It makes finding the perfect eatery close to your home or travel destination. Online reservations, maps, menus and more. You can search by Internatinal Location, US Location, US Map, or Cuisine type.

21045 www.chrie.org
Int'l Council on Hotel, Restaurant Institute Edu.

To enhance professionalism at all levels of the hospitality and tourism industry through education and training.

21046 www.greyhouse.com
Grey House Publishing

Authoritative reference directories for most business sectors including restaurant markets. Users can search the online databases with varied search criteria allowing for custom searches by product category, geographic area, sales volume, keyword, subject and more. Full Grey House catalog and online ordering also available.

21047 www.iacp.com
International Association of Culinary Professionals

A not for profit organization whose members represent virtually every profession in the culinary universe: teachers, cooking school owners, caterers, writers, chefs, media cooking personalities, editors, publishers, food stylists, food photographers, restauranteurs, leaders of major food corporations and vintners. Literally a who's who of the food world. Founded in 1978.

21048 www.ifsea.org
International Food Service Executives

Provides education and community service to the foodservice industry.

21049 www.restaurant.org
National Restaurant Association

Trends, government affairs, training, research, dining guides and links.

21050 www.therestaurantfinder.com

This search engine help to find restaurants by type or location.

Associations

21051 American Beverage Licensees
5101 River Rd
Suite 108
Bethesda, MD 20816-1560

301-656-1494
Fax: 301-656-7539
E-Mail: info@ablusa.org
Home Page: www.ablusa.org
Social Media: Facebook, Twitter, RSS

Harry Wiles, Executive Director
Harry Klock, President
Ray Cox, Treasurer
Steve Morris, Vice President
John D. Bodnovich, Executive Director

Supports all those involved with the retailing of beverages.

21052 American Booksellers Association
333 Westchester Avenue
Suite S202
White Plains, NY 10604

914-406-7500
800-637-0037
Fax: 914-417-4013
E-Mail: info@bookweb.org
Home Page: www.bookweb.org
Social Media: Facebook, Twitter, YouTube

Oren Teicher, CEO
Dan Cullen, Content Officer
Eleanor Chang, CFO
Steve Bercu, President
Betsy Burton, Vice President/Secretary

Trade organization pledge to protecting the well-being of book retailers and promoting the availability of books.
2000 Members
Founded in 1900

21053 American Collegiate Retailing Association
Loyola University/Department of Marketing
6363 Saint Charles Avenue
New Orleans, LA 70118-6195

504-865-2011
Fax: 504-865-3496
Home Page: www.acraretail.org

Barry Berman, President
Rodney Runyan, Vice President
Jane Swinney, Secretary
Susan S. Fiorito, Treasurer
Leigh Sparks, Member-at-Large

Organization of faculty from colleges with a background in retailing.
400 Members
Founded in 1950

21054 Associated Surplus Dealers/Associated Merchandise Dealers
ASD/AMD Merchandise Group
2950 31st Street
Suite 100
Santa Monica, CA 90405-3037

310-396-6006
800-421-4511
Fax: 310-399-2662
Home Page: www.merchandisegroup.com

Leading producer of trade shows and publications in the variety and general merchandise industry.
15000 Members
Founded in 1961

21055 Association for Retail Technology
325 7th Street NW
Suite 1100
Washington, DC 20004

202-783-7971
800-673-4692
Fax: 202-737-2849
E-Mail: arts@nrf.com
Home Page: www.nrf.com

Matthew Shay, President and CEO
Carleen Kohut, COO
Mallory Duncan, SVP& General Counsel
David French, SVP, Govt. Relations
Mike Gatti, SVP, Member Relations

Subsidiary of the National Retail Federation, this is a retailer-driven membership organization dedicated to creating an international, barrier-free technology environment for retailers. ARTS was established to ensure that technology works to enhance a retailer's ability to develop store level business solutions and avoid situations that limit a retailer's ability to implement change while providing industry standards designed to provide greater value at lower costs.
175 Members
Founded in 1993

21056 Association of Retail Marketing Services
10 Drs James Parker Boulevard
Suite 103
Red Bank, NJ 07701-1500

732-842-5070
866-231-6310
Fax: 732-219-1938
E-Mail: info@goarms.com
Home Page: www.goarms.com

Gerri Hopkins, Executive Director
Lisa McCauley, Administrative Director

Supports all those involved with the marketing of all aspects of the retail industry, manufacturing, distribution, representation.
100 Members
Founded in 1957

21057 Black Retail Action Group
1 Penn Plz
Suite 5315
New York, NY 10119-5315

212-736-5300
Fax: 212-234-3053

Jeffrey Block, President
500 Members
Founded in 1976

21058 Christian Booksellers Association (CBA)
9240 Explorer Drive
Suite 200
Colorado Spring, CO 80920

719-265-9895
800-252-1950
Fax: 719-272-3508
E-Mail: info@cbaonline.org
Home Page: www.cbaonline.org
Social Media: Facebook, Twitter

Curtis Riskey, President
Sue Smith, Chairman
Robin Hogan, Secretary
Bill Couey, Treasurer
Andrew Criswell, Sr., Vice Chairman

Provides products and services to assist and support Christian retail stores.
3.4M Members
Founded in 1950

21059 Electronic Retailing Association
607 14th Street, NW
Suite 530
Washington, DC 20005

703-841-1751
800-987-6462
Fax: 425-977-1036
E-Mail: webadmin@retailing.org
Home Page: www.retailing.org
Social Media: Facebook, Twitter, LinkedIn, YouTube, Flickr

Julie Coons, President and CEO
Elliott Segal, Chairman
Rich Yoegel, Secretary
Brian S. Archibald, Treasurer
Chris Reinmuth, Chairman-Elect

To foster growth, development and acceptance of the rapidly growing direct response industry worldwide for the companies who use the power of electronic media to sell goods and services to the public.
Founded in 1991
Mailing list available for rent

21060 Franchise Consultants International Association
5147 S Angela Road
Memphis, TN 38117-3454

901-368-3881
Fax: 202-628-0812
E-Mail: franmark@msn.com
Social Media: Facebook, Twitter, LinkedIn

William Richey, Executive Director

Seeks to coordinate effective and professional franchise consulting, serves as a clearinghouse and operates a library.
800 Members
Founded in 1980

21061 Institute of Store Planners
25 N Broadway
Tarrytown, NY 10591-3221

914-332-1806
Fax: 914-332-1541
E-Mail: adminisp@ispo.org
Home Page: www.ispo.org

Richard C Byrne, Manager
Kenneth Nisch, VP
Ronald Kline, Chairman
Richard Byrne, Manager

Provides a forum for debate and discussion by store design experts and retailers. Sponsors student design programs.
1300 Members
Founded in 1961

21062 International Center for Companies of Food
3800 Moore Place
Alexandria, VA 22305-1219

703-549-4525
Home Page: www.international-center.com
Social Media: Facebook, Twitter, LinkedIn

Shaker Al-Samman, MD

Provides management research on problems related to food distribution and serves as an international forum where food chain store executives can meet to exchange ideas and information.
500 Members
Founded in 1960

21063 International Council of Shopping Centers
1221 Ave of the Americas
41 St. Fl.
New York, NY 10020-1099

646-728-3800
Fax: 732-694-1690

E-Mail: membership@icsc.org
Home Page: www.icsc.org
Social Media: Facebook, Twitter, LinkedIn, YouTube, Blog, Pinterest, Goog

Sheri Pupello, Member Commincations Representative
Cecilia Perrino, Customer Service/ InfoCenter
Glen Hale, CFO
Jesse Tron, Manager, Communications
Jennifer Collin, Manager, Membership Development

Supports all those involved with any aspect of shopping centers.

21064 **International Franchise Association**
1501 K St Nw
Suite 350
Washington, DC 20005-1412

202-628-8000
Fax: 202-628-0812
Home Page: www.franchise.org

Matthew Shay, President
Debra Moss, VP Operations

Membership consists of companies franchising the distribution of goods or services.

21065 **International Map Trade Association**
2629 Manhattan Avenue
PMB 281
Hermosa Beach, CA 90254

310-376-7731
Fax: 949-458-0300
E-Mail: imta@maptrade.org
Home Page: www.maptrade.org

Chris Knoebel, President
Sanford J Hill, Executive Director

Membership comprised of retail stores featuring maps, travel books, globes, and travel products, plus publishers and manufacturers producing these products. Publishes a monthly newsletter.
800 Members
Founded in 1981

21066 **International Premium Cigar & Pipe Retailers Association**
4 Bradley Park Ct
Suite 2H
Columbus, GA 31904-3637

706-494-1143
Fax: 706-494-1893
E-Mail: info@rtda.org
Home Page: www.rtda.org
Social Media: Facebook, Twitter, LinkedIn, YouTube

Matt Dogali, State Legislative Affairs
Dawn Conger, Associate Member Services
Mandy Cross, Legislative Affairs/IT
Amy Mitchell, Finance
Kyle Whalen, Public Relations

Trade association of high quality tobacconists.
2,350 Members
Founded in 1933

21067 **Marine Retailers Association of America**
8401 73rd Ave. N.
Suite 71
Minneapolis, MN 55428

763-315-8043
Fax: 708-763-9236
E-Mail: matt@mraa.com
Home Page: www.mraa.com
Social Media: Facebook, Twitter, LinkedIn, RSS

Matt Gruhn, President
Michael Geatz, Marketing Coordinator
Steve Baum, Chairman
Randy Wattenbarger, Vice Chairman
Joe Lewis, Secretary/ Treasurer

Raising the standards of retailing within the industry. Promotes activities for the recreational boating industry and holds seminars to improve management.
2.5M Members
Founded in 1972

21068 **Museum Store Association**
3773 E Cherry Creek North Dr
755
Denver, CO 80209-3804

303-504-9223
Fax: 303-504-9585
E-Mail: info@museumstoreassociation.org
Home Page: www.museumdistrict.com

Adriana Herald, Systems Administrator
Stacey Stachow, President
Gloria Stern, Treasurer
Jama Rice, Executive Director/ CEO
Kathy Cisar, Communications Manager
2500 Members
Frequency: April, Annually
Founded in 1955

21069 **National Advisory Group**
2063 Oak Street
Jacksonville, FL 32204

904-845-5989
E-Mail: info@nagconvinience.com
Home Page: www.nag-net.com
Social Media: Facebook

Joseph Howton, Executive VP
Mary Banmiller, President
Publisher Bill, Donahe
Ben Jatlow, Chairman

This association represents senior level management of retail companies organized to enhance buying power, merchandising programs and an exchange of ideas. Membership dues: Retail Average $300, Associations $350.
500 Members
Founded in 1983

21070 **National Association General Merchandise Representatives**
1037 Us Highway 46
Suite C102
Clifton, NJ 07013-2461

973-614-9211
Fax: 973-916-1986
E-Mail: frankp@performancesales.com
Home Page: www.nagmr.org
Social Media: Facebook, Twitter, Pinterest, RSS

David Perrone, President
Jordan Stone, VP
Ronald Ross, Treasurer
Rich Siporin, Secretary
Bruce Funk, Director

A professional association of consumer product brokers representing leading manufacturers to the drug, mass merchandise and food trade.

21071 **National Association of Catalog Showrooms**
PO Box 736
Northport, NY 11768-0736

631-754-4364
Fax: 631-754-4364
Home Page: www.businessfinance.com
Social Media: Facebook, Twitter, LinkedIn

Members are catalog showroom operators and catalog publishers & associate members are suppliers.
350 Members
Founded in 1972

21072 **National Association of Chain Drug Stores**
1776 Wilson Blvd
Suite 200
Arlington, VA 22209

703-549-3001
Fax: 703-836-4869
E-Mail: contactus@nacds.org
Home Page: www.nacds.org
Social Media: Facebook, Twitter, LinkedIn, You Tube, Flickr

Steven C Anderson, President/CEO
Bob Narveson, Chairman
Juna Ortiz, Treasurer
John Standley, Vice Chairman
Jose Barra, Director

The chief purpose of NACDS is to represent the views and policy positions of member chain drug companies.
105 Members
Founded in 1933

21073 **National Association of College Stores**
528 E Lorain St
Oberlin, OH 44074-1298

440-775-7777
800-622-7498
Fax: 440-774-5315
E-Mail: service@nacscorp.com
Home Page: www.nacscorp.com

Kurt K. Schoen, President & COO
Marc Fleischaker, Secretary/ Legal Counsel
Brian E Cartier, CEO
Frank Sulen, CFO & Treasurer
Estella McCollum, Chairperson

Provides educational and support services and products to college stores. Promotes business methods and ethics. Conducts manager certification, educational services and research.
3.9M Members
Founded in 1963

21074 **National Association of Convenience Stores**
1600 Duke Street
Alexandria, VA 22314-3436

703-684-3600
800-966-2329
Fax: 703-836-4564
Home Page: www.nacsonline.com
Social Media: Facebook, Twitter, LinkedIn, You Tube

Henry Armour, Staff Liason
R. Timothy Columbus, Legal Counsel
Kathy LeBeouf, Executive Director
Brian E Cartier, CEO
Brad Call, Chairman

Association supporting key industry trends and innovative practices of convenience store companies.
2.3M Members
Founded in 1961
Mailing list available for rent

21075 **National Association of Music Merchants**
5790 Armada Dr
Carlsbad, CA 92008

760-438-8001
800-767-6266
Fax: 760-438-7327
Home Page: www.namm.org

Joe Lamond, President
Robin Walenta, Treasurer
Chris Martin, Secretary
Larry Morton, Chairman
Mark Goff, Vice Chairman

Retailers of musical instruments.
3.6M Members

21076 National Association of Resale Professionals
PO Box 80707
St Clair Shores, MI 48080

586-294-6700
800-544-0751
Fax: 586-294-6776
E-Mail: info@narts.org
Home Page: www.narts.org

Adele R. Meyer, Executive Director
Gail A. Seigel, Director of Membership Services

A national trade association for owners and managers of resale thrift shops. Purpose is to provide educational networking to promote the industry.
950 Members
Founded in 1984

21077 National Automatic Merchandising Association
20 N Wacker Dr
Suite 3500
Chicago, IL 60606

312-346-0370
800-331-8816
Fax: 312-704-4140
E-Mail: dmathews@vending.org
Home Page: www.vending.org
Social Media: Facebook, Twitter, YouTube

Peter A. Tullio, Chairman
Mark Dieffenbach, Past Chair
Howard Chapman, Vice Chairman
Patrick Hagerty, Secretary/ Treasurer
Carla Balakgie, President & CEO

Collectively advancing and promoting the automatic merchandising and coffee service industries, members include service companies, equipment manufacturers and suppliers of products and services to operating service companies.
2500 Members
Founded in 1982

21078 National Council of Chain Restaurants
325 7th St NW
Suite 1100
Washington, DC 20004

202-783-7971
800-673-4692
Fax: 202-737-2849
E-Mail: info@nrf.com
Home Page: www.nccr.net

Chip Kunde, Chairman
Rob Green, Executive Director
Scott Vinson, Vice President
Cicely Simpson, Treasurer
Lynn Liddle, Secretary

The leading trade association exclusively representing chain restaurant companies. Working to advance sound public policy that best serves the interests of restaurant businesses and the millions of people they employ.
Founded in 1965

21079 National Grocers Association
1005 N Glebe Rd
Suite 250
Arlington, VA 22201-5758

703-516-0700
Fax: 703-516-0115
E-Mail: amamone@nationalgrocers.org
Home Page: www.ngacampus.com
Social Media: Facebook, Twitter, LinkedIn

Peter J. Larkin, President & CEO
Richard Niemann, Senior Vice President
Joseph Seridan, Chairman
Kevin Doris, Treasurer
Neal Berube, Secretary

Works to advance understanding, trade, and cooperation in the food industry. Represents members interests before the government. Offers store planning, and engineering, training and advertising.
1.5M Members
Founded in 1982

21080 National Ice Cream Retailers Association
1028 West Devon Ave.
Elk Grove Village, IL 60007

847-301-7500
866-303-7500
Fax: 847-301-8402
E-Mail: info@nicra.org
Home Page: www.nicyra.org

Lynda Utterback, Executive Director
Nanette Frey, President
Jim Oden, VP
Carl Chaney, President-Elect
David Zimmerman, Past President

Members are in retail frozen dessert businesses. Some offer food services either full of limited and some operate convenience stores. The common denominator is that all members offer frozen desserts for take home or on site consumption.
350 Members
Founded in 1933

21081 National Restaurant Association
2055 L St. NW
Suite 400
Washington, DC 20036

202-331-5900
800-424-5156
Fax: 202-331-2429
Home Page: www.restaurant.org
Social Media: Facebook, Twitter, YouTube

Phil Hickey, Chair
Ken Conrad, Vice Chair
Jack Crawford, Treasurer
Dawn Sweeney, President & CEO
Ed Beck, Chief Information Officer & SVP

Striving to help members build customer loyalty, find financial success and provide rewarding careers in foodservice.
60000 Members
Founded in 1919

21082 National Restaurant Association Education Foundation
2055 L St. NW
Washington, DC 60604-2814

312-715-1010
800-424-5156
Fax: 312-583-9767
Home Page: www.nraef.org
Social Media: Facebook, Twitter, YouTube

Denise Marie Fugo, Chair
Michel Hickey, Treasurer
Mike Gibbons, Vice-Chairman
Dawn Sweeney, President & CEO

NRAEF is the philanthropic foundation of the National Restaurant Association. Committed to enhancing the restaurant industry's service to the public through education, community engagement and promotion of career opportunities.
Founded in 1987

21083 National Retail Federation
325 7th St Nw
Suite 1100
Washington, DC 20004

202-783-7971
800-673-4692
Fax: 202-737-2849
Home Page: www.nrf.com
Social Media: Facebook, Twitter, LinkedIn

Matthew R. Shay, President/CEO
Mindy 2nd vice Chair, Secret, Executive Director
Autor Erik, Vice President
Stephen I. Sadove, Chairman
Kip Tindell, Treasurer & Chairman of Finance

Retail trade association with membership that comprises all retail formats and channels of distribution including department, specialty, discount, catalog, Internet and independent stores. NRF members represent an industry that encompasses more than 1.4 million US retail establishments which employ more than 23 million people — about one in five American workers — and registered 2002 sales of $3.6 trillion. NRF's international members operate stores in more than 50 nations.
55M Members
Founded in 1990

21084 National Shoe Retailers Association
7386 N. La Cholla Blvd
Tucson, AZ 85741

520-209-1710
800-673-8446
Fax: 410-381-1167
E-Mail: info@nsra.org
Home Page: www.nsra.org
Social Media: Facebook, Twitter, LinkedIn, Google+, Pinterest

Rick Ravel, Board Chairman
Chuck Schuyler, President
Lenny Comeras, Vice Chairman
Mark Denkler, Past Chairman
Jeff Greenberg, Vice Chairman

Membership association for independent shoe ratailers. Provides busisness services such as credit-card processing and shipping at special low members only prices. Also provides educational and training programs, consulting and other services.
1400 Members
Founded in 1912

21085 National Ski & Snowboard Retailers Association
1601 Feehanville Drive
Suite 300
Mount Prospect, IL 60056

847-391-9825
888-527-1168
Fax: 847-391-9827
E-Mail: info@nssra.com
Home Page: www.nssra.com

Larry Weindruch, President
Paul Prutzman, Chairman

The retail voice for the ski and snowboard industries and provides information and services you need to operate more successfully.
250 Members
Founded in 1987

21086 National Sporting Goods Association
1601 Feehanville Drive
Suite 300
Mount Prospect, IL 60056

847-296-6742
800-815-5422
Fax: 847-391-9827
E-Mail: info@nsga.org
Home Page: www.nsga.org

Ken Meehan, Chairman of the Board
Matt Carlson, President/CEO
Dan Wiersma, CFO
Randy Nill, Treasurer/ Chairman-Elect
Jeff Rosenthal, Past chairman

Association of retailers, manufacturers and suppliers of sports equipment, footwear and apparel.
2000+ Members
Founded in 1929

21087 North American Equipment Dealers Association
1195 Smizer Mill Rd
Fenton, MO 63026-3480
636-349-5000
Fax: 636-349-5443
E-Mail: naeda@naeda.com
Home Page: www.naeda.com
Social Media: Facebook, Twitter
Gary Manke, President
Joe Nash, Immediate Past President
Brian Carpenter, 2nd Vice Chair & Secretary
Blaine Bingham, First Vice Chair & Treasurer
Tom Nobbe, Chairman
NAEDA and its affiliates provides a variety of educational, financial, legislative and legal services to equipment dealers in the United States and Canada.
5000 Members
Founded in 1900

21088 North American Retail Dealers Association
222 South Riverside Plaza
Suite 2100
Chicago, IL 60606
312-648-0649
800-621-0298
Fax: 312-648-1212
E-Mail: nardasvc@narda.com
Home Page: www.narda.com
Leon Barbachano, Chairman
Timothy W. Seavey, First Vice Chairman
Leon Barbachano, Second Vice Chairman
Michael Fischer, Past Chairman & Treasurer
Otto Papasadero, Executive Director
A national organization of association members, independent retailers selling and servicing major appliances, consumer electronics products, furniture and computers. Emphasis is placed on ideas that help readers become better, more profitable businesses. Articles are featured regularly on displays, salesmanship, financial analysis and service management.
1000 Members
Founded in 1943

21089 Oriental Rug Importers Association
100 Park Plaza Dr
Suite 200N
Secaucus, NJ 07094-3637
201-866-5054
Fax: 201-866-6169
E-Mail: oria@oria.org
Home Page: www.oria.org
Lucille Laufer, Executive Director
Andrew Peykar, VP
Membership is concentrated in the New York area.
Founded in 1958

21090 Point-of-Purchase Advertising International
440 N. Wells Street
Suite 740
Chicago, IL 60654
312-863-2900
Fax: 312-229-1152
E-Mail: bcotter@popai.com
Home Page: www.popai.com
Social Media: LinkedIn
Berk Cotter, Director of Member Services
Michael Heneghan, VP
Richard Carrigan, Treasurer
Michelle Adams, Secretary
John Anderson, Chairman
Supports all those involved with in-store promotional programs — and research on marketing and retail trends.
Founded in 1936

21091 Professional Audio-Video Retailers Association
10 E 22nd Street
Suite 310
Lombard, IL 60148-6191
630-268-1500
800-621-0298
Fax: 630-953-8957
Debra Smith, Executive Director
Supports owners and operators of independently owned, audio/video stores. Members includes manufacturers of high-end audio/video equipment.
204 Members
Founded in 1979

21092 Professional Sales Association
5045 Park Ave West
Suite 1B
Seville, CO 44273
330-299-7343
Fax: 300-408-0075
Home Page: www.profsales.com
James Mcgonical, President
An organization of manufacturers' representative firms which sell hardware, housewares, lawn and garden products and traffic appliances to the retail trade.
25 Members
Founded in 1969

21093 Retail Advertising & Marketing Association
325 7th St Nw
Suite 1100
Washington, DC 20004
202-783-7971
800-673-4692
Fax: 202-737-2849
Home Page: www.rama-nrf.org
Social Media: Facebook, Twitter, LinkedIn, Google+
Libby Landen, VP, Strategic Marketing
Mike Gatti, Executive Director
Kelly Gilmore, Senior Vice president
Kathy Grannis, Manager, Media Relations
Marcia Tabler, RAMA Consultant
Provides visionary leadership that promotes creativity, innovation and excellence within all marketing disciplines that strategically elevates our members and our industry.
1600 Members
Founded in 1952

21094 Retail Industry Leaders Association
1700 N Moore St
Suite 2250
Arlington, VA 22209
703-841-2300
Fax: 703-841-1184
Home Page: www.rila.org
Social Media: Facebook, Twitter, LinkedIn
Gregory Wasson, 2nd Vive chairman
Gregg Steinhafel, Chairman
Erica Wiseman, Treasurer
Richard Dreiling, Vice Chairman
Robert Niblock, Secretary
Retail Industry Leaders Association is a trade association of the lasgest and fastest growing companies in the retail industry, its members include over 400 retailers, product manufacturers, and service suppliers.
400+ Members
Founded in 1969

21095 Retail Packaging Association
2205 Warwick Way
Suite 110
Marriottsville, MD 21104
410-925-9809
Fax: 410-741-3004
E-Mail: info@retailpackaging.org
Home Page: www.retailpackaging.org
Deborah Gage, President
Bob Gant, VP
Joel Zaas, Treasurer~
Ed Kastenbaum, Secretary
Serves its members and the entire retail packaging industry. Also organizes the largest trade show and conference of its kind in the US. A self-governed not-for-profit organization comprised of professionals involved in all facets of production and distribution of retail packaging products.
Founded in 1990

21096 Retail Systems Alert Group
377 Elliot Street Po Box 332
Newton Upper Falls, MA 02464
617-527-4626
Fax: 617-527-8102
E-Mail: info@retailsystems.com
Home Page: www.retailsystems.com
Brian Kilcourse, President
Tom Friedman, Chairman
Karen Moss, Editor
Lisa Gayle, Advertising Manager
Retail Systems Alert Group has helped companies reach a highly qualified audience of Extened Retail Industry professionals through advertising, sponsorship, research, and exhibiting opportunities.
Founded in 1870

21097 Scuba Retailers Association
4 Florence Street
Somerville, MA 02145
617-623-7722
Social Media: Facebook, Twitter, LinkedIn
James Estabrook, Executive Director
Members are stores selling scuba and association underwater equipment.
500 Members
Founded in 1989

21098 Small Business Technology Council
National Small Business Association
1156 15th St Nw
Suite 1100
Washington, DC 20005
202-662-9700
800-835-6728
Home Page: www.sbtc.org
Social Media: Facebook, Twitter, RSS
James Morrison, President
Robert Schmidt, Co-Chair
Heidi Jacobus, Co-Chair
Jere Glover, Executive Director
Larry Nannis, Treasurer
Working with and providing web sites for the very small business.
120 Members
Founded in 2000

21099 Vacuum and Sewing Dealers Trade Association
2724 2nd Ave
Des Moines, IA 50313-4933
515-282-9101
800-367-5651

Fax: 515-282-4483
E-Mail: mail@vdta.com, ads@vdta.com
Home Page: www.vdta.com

Craig Dorman, Sales
Charley Dunham, Chairman
Judy Patterson, President
Marlin Graham, Vice-President
Beth Vitiritto, Managing Editor

Seeks to increase the independent vacuum cleaner and sewing machine dealer market share.
20,00 Members
Founded in 1981

21100 Wine and Spirits Guild of America
3530 Vinings Ridge Court
Atlanta, GA 30339

770-956-8808
Fax: 770-988-8634
E-Mail: info@wineandspiritsguild.com
Home Page: www.wineandspiritsguild.com

Barbara Owen, Conference Manager
Cedric Martin, President
Steve Herman, Ex-Officio President & Director
Gary Fisch, 2nd Vice President and Treasurer
Brad Feuerbacher, 1st Vice President

Promotes the exchange of information on merchandising, marketing and buying of wines and spirits.
40 Members
Founded in 1948

Newsletters

21101 American Collegiate Retailing Association Newsletter
Loyola University/Department of Marketing
PO Box 121
New Orleans, LA 70118

504-865-2011
Fax: 504-865-3851
E-Mail: admit@loyno.edu
Home Page: www.loyno.edu

Kevin Wildes, President
Alice Glenn, Secretary
Cynthia Tucker, Editor
Mary Degnan, Marketing Manager
Janice Long, Circulation Manager

Educational retailing news and information.
Frequency: Quarterly
Founded in 1923

21102 Bookselling This Week
American Booksellers Association
200 White Plains Rd
Suite 600
Tarrytown, NY 10591

800-637-0037
Fax: 914-591-2720
E-Mail: info@bookweb.org
Home Page: www.bookweb.org

Oren Teicher, CEO
Len Viahos, COO
Ellie Chang, CFO
Frequency: Weekly
Circulation: 10000

21103 Campus Marketplace
National Association of College Stores
500 E Lorain St
Oberlin, OH 44074-1238

440-775-0120
800-622-7498
Fax: 440-775-4769
E-Mail: webteam@nacs.org
Home Page: www.nacs.org

Brian Cartier, CEO
Carrie Tompkins, Editor

Weekly newsletter covering college store industry: sales, trends, news, personnel and address changes for stores as well as vendors.
Frequency: Monthly
Circulation: 4000
Founded in 1982

21104 For the President's Eyes Only
Bureau of Business Practice
76 Ninth Avenue
7th Floor
New York, NY 10011

212-771-0600
Fax: 212-771-0885
Home Page: www.aspenpublishers.com

Robert Becker, CEO
Gustavo Dobles, VP Operations

Provides the latest information on areas of vital interest to the head of the company.
12 Pages
Frequency: 2 per year

21105 Insider
Trade Dimensions
45 Danbury Rd
Wilton, CT 06897-4445

203-563-3000
Fax: 203-563-3131
Home Page: www.tradedimensions.com

Brain Thomas, Editor
Kristina Castle, Circulation Coordina

Shopping center weekly newsletter that profiles the latest retailer expansion plans, giving - in addition to the numbers of stores operated and planned, the areas targeted, and the type of locations sought - a thumbnail sketch of what makes the concept unique, and what the company specifically looks for in a site.
Cost: $299.00
Frequency: Weekly
Founded in 1970

21106 International Map Trade Association
2629 Manhattan Avenue
PMB 281
Hermosa Beach, CA 90254-2447

310-376-7731
Fax: 949-458-0300
Home Page: www.maptrade.org

Sandy Hill, Executive Director
Linda Hill, Editor

Membership comprised of retail stores featuring maps, travel books, globes, and travel products, plus publishers and manufacturers producing these products. Publishes a monthly newsletter
Cost: $60.00
20 Pages
Frequency: Monthly
ISSN: 1065-6324
Founded in 1981
Printed in on matte stock

21107 Mouser Report
CAMCO
124 E Carolina Avenue
Crewe, VA 23930-1802

434-645-1993
800-448-8595
Fax: 434-645-8232

Charles Mouser, Publisher
Brend DeLuca, Circulation Director

Newsletter covers the latest trends in retail and advertising.
Cost: $96.00
16 Pages
Frequency: Monthly

21108 NRF-BTM Retail Executive Opinion Survey
National Retail Federation
325 7th St
Suite 1101
Washington, DC 20004-2808

202-783-7971
800-673-4692
Fax: 202-737-2849
Home Page: www.nrf.com
Social Media: Facebook, Twitter, LinkedIn

Matthew Shay, President
Scott Krugman, Publisher
Mader Richard, Executive Director
Michael Gatti, VP/Marketing
David French, VP

Gathers the opinions of the industry's top executives on trends in merchandising, hiring, sales expectations, customer traffic and special seasonal related developments.
Frequency: Monthly

21109 NRF/BIGresearch Consumer Intentions and Actions Survey
National Retail Federation
325 7th St Nw
Suite 1101
Washington, DC 20004-2808

202-783-7971
800-673-4693
Fax: 202-737-2849
Home Page: www.nrf.com

Matthew Shay, President
Scott Krugman, Publisher
Mader Richard, Executive Director
Michael Gatti, VP/Marketing
David French, VP

Index on consumer shopping behavior. The survey also gauges consumer spending during holidays.
Frequency: Weekly

21110 NSSRA Newsletter
National Ski and Snowboard Retailers Association
1604 Feehanville Drive
Suite 300
Mount Prospect, IL 60056-6213

847-228-8277
Fax: 847-439-0111
E-Mail: info@nssra.com
Home Page: www.nssra.com

Larry Weindruch, President
Paul Prutzman, Chairman

Keeps members informed on critical industry issues, such as guidelines, litigation exposure and marketing
Frequency: Quarterly
Circulation: 1000

21111 National Research Bureau Newsletter
National Research Bureau
320 Valley St
Burlington, IA 52601-5513

319-752-5415
Fax: 319-752-3421
E-Mail: contactus@supervisionmagazine.com
Home Page: www.national-research-bureau.com

Diane M Darnall, President
William H. Wood, Founder

A newsletter is created for a company by combining a customized masthead with a four page,

monthly issue of helpful information on a business field selected by the company.
4 Pages
Frequency: Daily
Founded in 1933
Printed in 3 colors

21112 **Retail CEO Insider**
National Retail Federation
325 7th St Nw
Suite 1100
Washington, DC 20004-2808

202-783-7971
800-673-4693
Fax: 202-737-2849
Home Page: www.nrf.com
Social Media: Facebook, Twitter, LinkedIn, You Tube

Matthew Shay, President
Scott Krugman, Publisher
Mader Richard, Executive Director
Michael Gatti, VP/Marketing
David French, VP

Two-page private news briefing for CEOs, chairpersons and presidents of National Retail Federation member companies. Provides concise, bullet-point coverage of issues facing the industry in the style of the Kiplinger Washington Letter, with a heavy emphasis on government affairs and public policy. Distributed to approximately 650 C-level executives.
Frequency: Monthly

21113 **Retail Sales Outlook**
National Retail Federation
325 7th St Nw
Suite 1101
Washington, DC 20004-2808

202-783-7971
800-673-4693
Fax: 202-737-2849
Home Page: www.nrf.com
Social Media: Facebook, Twitter, LinkedIn

Matthew Shay, President
Scott Krugman, Publisher
Mader Richard, Executive Director
Michael Gatti, VP/Marketing
David French, VP

Economic analysis of the retail industry.
Frequency: Quarterly

21114 **Shopping Center Management Insider**
6 East 32nd St
8th Floor
New York, NY 10016

212-812-8420
800-519-3692
E-Mail: info@vendomegrp.com
Home Page: www.vendomegrp.com

Steven Gordon Esq, Editor

Tested management techniques, legal insights and how-to guidelines for running a shopping center or mall. Includes model notices to tenants, letters, agreements, rules, etc.
Cost: $297.00
Frequency: Monthly
Founded in 1985
Printed in 2 colors on matte stock

21115 **T-Shirt Business Info Mapping Newsletter**
Prosperity & Profits Unlimited
PO Box 416
Denver, CO 80201-0416

303-575-5676

A Doyle, Editor

How-to T-shirt business and information.
Cost: $8.00
8 Pages
Frequency: Annual
Circulation: 1,450
Founded in 1989
Printed in one color on matte stock

Magazines & Journals

21116 **Accessory Merchandising**
Vance Publishing
400 Knightsbridge Pkwy
Lincolnshire, IL 60069-3628

847-634-2600
Fax: 847-634-4379
E-Mail: mreckling@vancepublishing.com
Home Page: www.vancepublishing.com

Peggy Walker, President
Chandra Palermo, Editor
Michael R. Reckling, Group Publisher
Steven J. Kulikowski, Marketing Manager
Douglas Riemer, Circulation Director

21117 **Army/Navy Store & Outdoor Merchandiser**
445 Broad Hollow Road
Suite 21
Melville, NY 11747

631-845-2700
Fax: 631-845-2797

Military surplus, workwear, casual apparel, camping, hunting and sporting goods, and outdoor clothing industries.
Cost: $25.00
Frequency: Monthly
Circulation: 12M

21118 **Barnard's Retail Trend Report**
Barnard Enterprises
17 Kenneth Road
Upper Montclair, NJ 07043-2541

973-655-8888
Home Page: www.retailtrends.com

Kurt Barnard, Publisher/Editor
Jim Adamson, CEO

Forecasts market trends in the retailing industry and on consumer spending.
Cost: $179.00
10 Pages
Circulation: 1200
Founded in 1984
Printed in 2 colors on newsprint stock

21119 **Casual Living**
Reed Business Information
2000 Clearwater Dr
Oak Brook, IL 60523-8809

630-574-0825
Fax: 630-288-8781
Home Page: www.reedbusiness.com

Jeff Greisch, President
Mark Kelsey, MD
Jeremy Knibbs, Chief Executive

21120 **Chain Merchandiser**
Merchandising Publications Company
PO Box 95C
Baker City, OR 97814-0095

FAX 541-523-2063

Ruth Sanders, Business Manager
Henry Von Morpurgo, Editor/Publisher

A national service and promotion program incorporating Specialty Foods and Beverages and Deli-Dairy World. Devoted to improved merchandising methods at every level of the marketing and distributing processes - from the field and factory and warehouse to retail sales persons - to provide better customer values, lower costs and greater profits.

21121 **Chain Store Age**
Lebhar-Friedman
425 Park Ave
Suite 6
New York, NY 10022-3526

212-756-5088
800-216-7117
Fax: 212-838-9487
E-Mail: info@lf.com
Home Page: www.lf.com

Heather Martin, Manager
John Rapuzzi, Group Publisher
Antonia Peterson, Desk Editor
J Roger Friedman, President

Offers a full overview of chain stores, including management, operation, construction and modernization, store equipment, real estate and advertising.
Frequency: Monthly
Circulation: 35551
Founded in 1925

21122 **College Store**
Executive Business Media
PO Box 1500
Westbury, NY 11590-0812

516-334-3030
Fax: 516-334-3059
E-Mail: webteam@nacs.org
Home Page: www.nacs.org

Cynthia D'Angelo, President
Ron Stevens, Editor

Covers the college bookstore market retail industry.
Cost: $40.00
40 Pages
Frequency: Bi-Monthly
Circulation: 6,800

21123 **College Store Executive**
Executive Business Media
825 Old Country Road
PO Box 1500
Westbury, NY 11590-812

516-334-3030
Fax: 516-334-3059
E-Mail: ebm-mail@ebmpubs.com
Home Page: www.ebmpubs.com

Ken Baglino, Editor
Nancy Wilderwith, Advertising Manager

A merchandising and news magazine edited for those responsible for buying and merchandising products for college retail stores.
Cost: $35.00
36 Pages
Circulation: 8547
ISSN: 0010-1141
Founded in 1970
Printed in 4 colors on glossy stock

21124 **College Store Magazine**
National Association of College Stores
500 E Lorain St
Oberlin, OH 44074-1238

440-775-0120
800-622-7498
Fax: 440-775-4769
E-Mail: webteam@nacs.org
Home Page: www.nacs.org

Brian Cartier, CEO
Keith Galestock, Editor
Tara Ellis, Associate Editor

Covers the college store industry's long term issues and trends, focusing on retailing, technology and serving campus communities.
Cost: $66.00
Mailing list available for rent

21125 **DSN Retailing Today**
Lebhar-Friedman

425 Park Ave
Suite 6
New York, NY 10022-3526

212-756-5088
800-216-7117
Fax: 212-838-9487
E-Mail: info@lf.com
Home Page: www.dsnretailingtoday.com

Heather Martin, Manager
Tim Craig, Editor-in-Chief
Tony Lisanti, Editorial Director
Roger Friedman, CEO

Leading international newspaper serving the growing mass market.
Frequency: Monthly
Circulation: 34000
Founded in 1925

21126 **Dealerscope**
North American Publishing Company
1500 Spring Garden St
Suite 1200
Philadelphia, PA 19130-4094

215-238-5300
800-818-8174
Fax: 215-238-5342
E-Mail: sdowney@napco.com
Home Page: www.dealerscope.com
Social Media: Facebook, Twitter, LinkedIn

Ned S Borowsky, CEO
David Dritsas, Editor-in-Chief
Eric Schwartz, President/Publishing
Rhoda Dixon, Circulation Manager
Suzanne DeFruscio, Advertising Promotion Manager

Dedicated to delivering peer-based knowledge and experience, Dealerscope is the ultimate vehicle for presenting product and service solutions to the consumer.
Founded in 1958

21127 **Display & Design Ideas**
Shore Varrone
6255 Barfield Road
#200
Atlanta, GA 30328-4332

404-848-0077
Fax: 404-252-4436
Home Page: www.svi-atl.com

Doug Hope, Publisher
Steve Kaufman, Editor
Lee Pritcher, Owner

Product news and design solutions for those in the retail chain indusrty.
Cost: $60.00
Frequency: Monthly
Circulation: 18,039

21128 **Do-It-Yourself Retailing**
5822 W 74th St
Indianapolis, IN 46278-1756

317-297-1190
Fax: 317-328-4354
E-Mail: vecchie@sbcglobal.net
Home Page: www.nrha.org

John Hammond, Executive Director
Kevin Hohman, Publisher
Frequency: Monthly
Circulation: 44333

21129 **Drug Store News**
Lebhar-Friedman
425 Park Ave
Suite 6
New York, NY 10022-3526

212-756-5088
Fax: 212-838-9487
E-Mail: tlisanti@lf.com
Home Page: www.drugstorenews.com

Heather Martin, Manager
Tony Lisanti, Editor

Publication consists of merchandising trends and pharmacy developments. Provides extensive coverage of every major segment of chain drug retailing and combination stores.
Cost: $189.00
Frequency: Weekly
Circulation: 40000
Founded in 1925

21130 **Edplay**
Fahy-Williams Publishing
PO Box 1080
Geneva, NY 14456-2137

315-789-0458
800-344-0559
Fax: 315-789-4263
Home Page: www.fwpi.com

J Kevin Fahy, Publisher
Tina Manzer, Editorial Director
Jason Hagerman, Advertising Account Rep
Bradley G Gordner, Senior Editor
Tricia King, Office Manager

Serves toy manufacturers and dealers. Offers product reviews, industry profiles, and reader surveys.
Cost: $22.00
Frequency: Quarterly
Circulation: 7684

21131 **Flea Markets Magazine**
FleaMarkets.com
1156 15th St NW
Suite 1100
Washington, DC 20005-1755

202-293-8830
800-835-6728
Home Page: www.fleamarkets.com

Todd McCracken, President

A quarterly magazine published by FleaMarkets.com.
Cost: $15.00
Frequency: Quarterly
Circulation: 3000
Founded in 1989

21132 **Gacs Today**
Naylor Publications
PO Box 855
Snellville, GA 30078-855

770-736-9723
Fax: 770-736-9725
Home Page: www.gacs.com

Jim Tudor, CEO
Frequency: Quarterly
Circulation: 2500
Founded in 1973

21133 **Garden Center Merchandising & Management**
Branch-Smith Publishing
PO Box 1868
Fort Worth, TX 76101-1868

817-882-4110
800-433-5612
Fax: 817-882-4121
E-Mail: webmaster@branchsmith.com
Home Page: www.branchsmith.com

David Branch, President
Terri Smith, Director Circulation
Carol Miller, Editor
Frequency: Monthly
Circulation: 15143
Founded in 1915

21134 **Garden Center Products & Supplies**
Branch-Smith Publishing
PO Box 1868
Fort Worth, TX 76101-1868

817-882-4110
800-433-5612
Fax: 817-882-4121
E-Mail: dbranch@branchsmith.com
Home Page: www.branchsmith.com

David Branch, President
Patrice Kuhl, Publisher/Sales Director
Frequency: Monthly
Founded in 1910

21135 **Hearth & Home**
Village West Publishing
PO Box 1288
Laconia, NH 03247-2008

603-528-4285
800-258-3772
Fax: 603-524-0643
Home Page: www.homehearth.com

Richard Wright, Editor
Jackie Avignone, Sales Manager

Information for retailers and others selling hearth products, patio furnishing, barbecues, spas, garden accessories, and other outdoor products.
Cost: $11.95
Circulation: 18000
ISSN: 0273-5695
Founded in 1980

21136 **International Gaming and Wagering Business**
BNP Media
PO Box 1080
Skokie, IL 60076-9785

847-763-9534
Fax: 847-763-9538
E-Mail: igwb@halldata.com
Home Page: www.igwb.com
Social Media: Facebook, Twitter, LinkedIn

James Rutherford, Editor
Lynn Davidson, Marketing
Tammie Gizicki, Director

Focuses on business strategy, legislative information, food service and promotional concerns.
Frequency: Monthly
Circulation: 25000

21137 **Kitchenware News**
United Publications
PO Box 1056
Yarmouth, ME 04096-2056

207-846-0600
Fax: 207-846-0657
Home Page: www.kitchenwares.com

Brooke Taliaferro, President
Jim McNeil, Publisher

News and information on the latest products and equipment for the retail kitchenware industry.
Cost: $45.00
Frequency: Monthly
Circulation: 12,117

21138 **MMR/Mass Market Retailers**
Racher Press
220 5th Avenue
New York, NY 10001-7798

212-213-6000
Fax: 212-725-4594
E-Mail: info@racherpress.com
Home Page: www.massmarketretailers.com

Susan Schinitsky, Publisher
David Pinto, Editor
John Dioguardi, Director Sales/Marketing
Kevin Burke, Group Advertising Director
Pam Vandernoth, Circulation Director

News, analysis, trends, and events for drug, discount, and supermarket chain executives.
Cost: $185.00
Circulation: 21645
Founded in 1984

21139 Magazine Retailer
MetaMedia
124 W 24th Street
#3-D
New York, NY 1011-1920
212-989-6978
Fax: 212-255-7143
David Orlow, Publisher
Djalal Mohammadi, President
Merchandising tips, new tiles, publication changes, consumer purchasing trends, industry news and media impact on sales.
Cost: $19.00
Frequency: Quarterly
Circulation: 10,326

21140 Mass Market Retailer
Racher Press
220 5th Avenue
New York, NY 10001-7708
212-213-6000
Fax: 212-725-3961
E-Mail: info@racherpress.com
Home Page: www.massmarketretailers.com
Susan Schinitsky, Publisher
David Pinto, Editor
Susan Schinitsky, CEO/President
John Dioguardi, Marketing
Pam Vandernoth, Circulation Manager
News and information on the drug store chain industry.
Cost: $35.00
30 Pages
Founded in 1984

21141 Military Market
Gannet Company
6883 Commercial Dr
Springfield, VA 22151-4202
703-750-8643
Fax: 703-750-8717
E-Mail: rhynema@atpco.com
Home Page: www.gannettoffset.com
Dennis V Washburn, CEO
David Craig, Managing Editor
Provides trade information, trends, and news for military commisionary and post/base exchange managers.
Cost: $84.00
Frequency: Monthly
Circulation: 12000
Founded in 1940

21142 Museum Store Magazine
Museum Store Association
4100 E Mississippi Ave
Suite 800
Denver, CO 80246-3055
303-504-9223
Fax: 303-504-9585
E-Mail: membership@museumdistrict.com
Home Page: www.museumdistrict.com
Beverly J Barsook, Executive Director
Amy Nicholas, Editor
Cost: $34.00
Frequency: Quarterly
Circulation: 3000
Founded in 1955
Printed in 4 colors on glossy stock

21143 Museums & More Specialty Shops Product News
Museums & More Specialty Product News
PO Box 128
Sparta, Mi 49345-2122
616-887-9008
Fax: 616-887-2666
Home Page: www.museumsandmore.com
Julie McCallum, Editor
Jon Kaufman, Publisher
Product highlights and marketing strategies for the owners and oporators of gift shops in museums and other public attractions.
Cost: $35.00
Frequency: Quarterly
Circulation: 28014

21144 NACS SCAN
National Association of Convenience Stores
1600 Duke St
Suite 700
Alexandria, VA 22314-3436
703-684-3600
Fax: 703-836-4564
E-Mail: webmaster@nacsonline.com
Home Page: www.nacsonline.com
Hank Armour, President
A bi-monthly magazine offering information on key industry trends and innovative practices of convenience store companies.
Cost: $840.00
Frequency: Monthly
Circulation: 3000
Founded in 1961

21145 NAEDA Equipment Dealer
North American Equipment Dealers Association
1195 Smizer Mill Rd
Fenton, MO 63026-3480
636-349-5000
Fax: 636-349-5443
E-Mail: naeda@naeda.com
Home Page: www.naeda.com
Social Media: Twitter, LinkedIn
Paul Kindinger, President/CEO
Michael Williams, VP, Government Relations/Treasurer
Terry Leath, Executive Assistant
Roger Gjellstad, First Vice Chair
Lester Killebrew, Chairman
Monthly management and merchandising magazine featuring articles about successful dealers, new products, new technology, industry news and much more.
Cost: $40.00
5000 Members
Frequency: Monthly
Circulation: 9,500
ISSN: 1074-5017
Founded in 1900
Printed in 4 colors on glossy stock

21146 NARDA Independent Retailer
North American Retail Dealers Association
10 E 22nd Street
Suite 310
Lombard, IL 60148-6191
630-953-8950
800-621-0298
Fax: 630-953-8957
Home Page: www.narda.com
Tom Drake, CEO/President
Gennifer Michalek, Chairman
Emphasis is placed on ideas that help readers become better, more profitable businesses. Articles are featured regularly on displays, salesmanship, financial analysis and service management.
Cost: $78.00
36 Pages
Frequency: Monthly
Circulation: 2000
ISSN: 1098-9714
Founded in 1943
Mailing list available for rent: 2,000 names
Printed in 4 colors on glossy stock

21147 New Age Retailer
Continuity Publishing
2183 Alpine Way
Bellingham, WA 98226-8045
360-676-0789
800-463-9243
Fax: 360-676-0932
E-Mail: info@newageretailer.com
Home Page: www.newageretailer.com
Molly Trimble, CEO
Ray Hemachandra, Editor-in-Chief
Laurel Leigh, Editor
Stephanie R Hager, Circulation Manager
Ellen Koolen, Production Manager
Provides information on new products and business to business trade magazine that supports store owners by providing independent product reviews, retail advice and coverage of the new age and spirtual lviing industry.
Cost: $ 85.00
192 Pages
Circulation: 10000
Founded in 1987
Mailing list available for rent: 6,000 names at $150 per M

21148 POP Design
In-Store Marketing Institute
7400 Skokie Blvd
Skokie, IL 60077-3339
847-675-7400
Fax: 847-675-7494
E-Mail: info@instoremarketer.org
Home Page: www.instoremarketer.org
Social Media: Facebook, Twitter, LinkedIn
Peter Hoyt, President
Serves the news and product information needs of producers and designers of instore displays, signs and fixtures. Each issue features the latest trends and technologies vital to building and designing successful instore merchandising.
Frequency: Monthly
Circulation: 18000
Printed in 4 colors on glossy stock

21149 POPAI News
Point-of-Purchase Advertising Institute
1600 Duke Street
Suite 400
Alexandria, VA 22314
703-373-8815
Fax: 703-373-8801
E-Mail: bcotter@popai.com
Home Page: www.popai.com
Social Media: Facebook, Twitter, LinkedIn
Berk Cotter, Director Member Services
Richard Blatt, CEO/President
Stephen Morant, Manager Production Services
Sean Simmons, General Manager
Provides the point-of-purchase industry with coverage of marketing and retail trends, with an emphasis on in-store promotional programs. Editorial offers coverage of marketing programs, display case histories, preview of new promotional campaigns, sales volume and trends. Accepts advertising.
Cost: $40.00
Frequency: Monthly
Founded in 1940

21150 Pollution Engineering
Reed Business Information
2000 Clearwater Dr
Oak Brook, IL 60523-8809
630-574-0825
Fax: 630-288-8781
E-Mail: greenr@bnpmedia.com

Home Page: www.reedbusiness.com
Social Media: Facebook, Twitter, LinkedIn

Jeff Greisch, President
Erin Purananda, Marketing Manager
Seth Fisher, Products Editor
Mark Kelsey, Chief Executive Officer

Serves the field of pollution control in manufacturing industries, utilities, consulting engineers and constructors. Also serves government agencies including administration of federal, state and local environmental programs.
Frequency: Monthly
ISSN: 0032-3640
Founded in 1977

21151 Publishers Weekly
PO Box 51593
Harlan, IA 51593

800-278-2991
Fax: 712-733-8019
E-Mail: pwycustserv@cdsfulfillment.com
Home Page: www.publishersweekly.com
Social Media: Facebook, Twitter, LinkedIn

George Slovik, President
Michael Coffey, Co-Editorial Director
Diane Roback, Children's Book Editor
Louisa Ermelino, Reviews Director
Calvin Reid, News Editor

PW is the international journal of book publishing and bookselling including business news, reviews and bestseller lists targeted at publishers, booksellers, librarians and literary agents.
Frequency: Weekly
Founded in 1872

21152 Retail Cost of Doing Business
American Floorcovering Association
2211 E Howell Avenue
Anaheim, CA 92806-6009

714-572-8370

Offers an overview of the retail trade.
Frequency: Annual

21153 Retail Focus
National Sporting Goods Association
1601 Feehanville Drive
Suite 300
Mount Prospect, IL 60056

847-296-6742
800-815-5422
Fax: 847-391-9827
E-Mail: info@nsga.org
Home Page: www.nsga.org

Bob Dickman, Chairman of the Board
Matt Carlson, President/CEO
Dan Kasen, Director of Information Services

Magazine for members only
Frequency: Bi-Monthly
Mailing list available for rent

21154 Retail Observer
Retail Observer
1442 Sierra Creek Way
San Jose, CA 95132-3618

408-272-8974
800-393-0509
Fax: 408-272-3344
E-Mail: info@retailobserver.com
Home Page: www.retailobserver.com/

Chuck Edmonds, Publisher
Lee Boucher, Editor

Edited for owners, managers and retail sales personnel of appliance stores, home entertainment stores and kitchen and bath dealers.
Frequency: Monthly
Circulation: 11750

21155 Retail Systems Alert
Retail Systems Alert Group
PO Box 332
Newton Upper Falls, MA 02464-02

617-527-4626
Fax: 617-527-8102
Home Page: www.retailsystems.com

Thomas H Friedman, Publisher

Provides updated information on automation news and trends, including decision systems, information systems implementation, in-store merchandise management, and case studies of retailers.
Cost: $295.00
8 Pages
Frequency: Monthly
Founded in 1988

21156 Retail Systems Reseller
Edgell Communications
4 Middlebury Boulevard
Suite 107
Randolph, NJ 07869-1111

973-252-0100
Fax: 973-252-9020
Home Page: www.edgellcommunications.com

Michael Kachmar, Publisher
Joseph S King, Editor-in-Chief
Gabriele A Edgell, CEO
Dan Ligorner, Director of Marketing

Offers information to retailers, dealers, systems integraters, VARs, VADs, etc., on retail technology for small to mid-size retailers.

21157 RetailTech
770 Broadway
New York, NY 10003-9522

646-654-7480
Fax: 646-654-7568
Home Page: www.retail-merchandiser.com

21158 STORES Magazine
National Retail Federation
325 7th St NW
Suite 1101
Washington, DC 20004-2808

202-783-7971
800-673-4693
Fax: 202-737-2849
E-Mail: pennw@nrf.com
Home Page: www.nrf.com
Social Media: Facebook, Twitter, LinkedIn

Matthew Shay, President
Scott Krugman, Publisher
Mader Richard, Executive Director
Michael Gatti, VP/Marketing
David French, VP

Magazine of the National Retail Federation. Provides timely information of importance to senior retail headquarters executives. Every issue reports on trends in retail technology, credit and payment systems, logistics and supply chain and other vital store operations.
Cost: $120.00
Frequency: Monthly
Circulation: 35000

21159 Succe$$ful $ource$
Sutton Family Communications & Publishing Company
155 Sutton Lane
Fordsville, KY 42343

270-740-0870
E-Mail: jlsutton@apex.net
Home Page: www.fleamarketeer.net

Theresa Sutton, Publisher

The #1 trade magazine for multi-billion dollar flea market industry.
Cost: $5.00
Circulation: 100000
Founded in 1977

21160 Supermarket News
Fairchild Publications
750 3rd Ave
New York, NY 10017-2703

212-630-4000
800-204-4515
Fax: 212-630-3563
E-Mail: customerservice@fairchildpub.com
Home Page: www.supermarketnews.com

Mary G Berner, CEO
David Merrefield, Editorial Director
Dan Bagan, Publishing Director
David Orgel, Editor-in-Chief
Cost: $44.50
40 Pages
Frequency: Weekly
Circulation: 36346
ISSN: 0039-5803
Founded in 1892

21161 Today's Grocers
Florida Grocer Publications
PO Box 430760
S Miami, FL 33246

305-661-0792
800-440-3067
Fax: 305-661-6720

Jack Nobles, Publisher
Dennis Kane, Editor

Provides the latest food industry news and trends to Florida, Georgia, Alabama, Louisiana, Mississippi and the Carolinas.
Cost: $29.00
24 Pages
Frequency: Monthly
Circulation: 19,000
ISSN: 1529-4420
Founded in 1956
Printed in on newsprint stock

Trade Shows

21162 ASD/AMD Houston Variety Merchandise Show
ASD/AMD Merchandise Group
2950 31st Street
Suite 100
Santa Monica, CA 90405

310-396-6006
800-421-4511
Fax: 310-399-2662
Home Page: www.merchandisegroup.com

Julie Ichiba, Show Director

Our newest variety and general merchandise trade show offers buyers in the southwestern US and Mexico terrific product sourcing opportunities for all types of popular consumer goods.
12000 Attendees

21163 ASD/AMD Las Vegas Trade Show
ASD/AMD Merchandise Group
2950 31st Street
Suite 100
Santa Monica, CA 90405

310-396-6006
800-421-4511
Fax: 310-399-2662
Home Page: www.merchandisegroup.com

Julie Ichiba, Show Director

The summer edition of the largest variety merchandise event in the US attracts over 50,000 buyers to Las Vegas. Tens of thousands of unique products in hundreds of popular con-

sumer product categories are on display at this even
50000 Attendees
Frequency: August

21164 **ASD/AMD's Atlantic City Variety Merchandise Show**
ASD/AMD Merchandise Group
2950 31st Street
Suite 100
Santa Monica, CA 90405

310-396-6006
800-421-4511
Fax: 310-399-2662
Home Page: www.merchandisegroup.com

Julie Ichiba, Show Director

Held in Atlantic City, New Jersey, this event is a popular destination for east coast retailers to make deals and place orders for variety and general merchandise in hundreds of popular consumer categories before the summer selling season begins.
10000 Attendees
Frequency: May

21165 **ASD/AMD's Fall Variety Merchandise Show**
ASD/AMD Merchandise Group
2950 31st Street
Suite 100
Santa Monica, CA 90405

310-396-6006
800-421-4511
Fax: 310-399-2662
Home Page: www.merchandisegroup.com

Julie Ichiba, Show Director

The fall edition of the general merchandise event on the east coast takes place in New York City. It's the last opportunity of the year for retailers to place orders for goods before the busy holiday buying season.
12000 Attendees
Frequency: September

21166 **ASD/AMD's Las Vegas Merchandise Expo**
ASD/AMD Merchandise Group
2950 31st Street
Suite 100
Santa Monica, CA 90405

310-396-6006
800-421-4511
Fax: 310-399-2662
Home Page: www.merchandisegroup.com

Julie Ichiba, Show Director

Held in Las Vegas, Nevada, this event is strategically timed for western US retailers to stock their shelves with quality, value-priced variety and general merchandise in between our larger Las Vegas Trade Shows in March and Agust.
5,000 Attendees
Frequency: June

21167 **ASD/AMD's New York Variety Merchandise Show**
ASD/AMD Merchandise Group
2950 31st Street
Suite 100
Santa Monica, CA 90405

310-396-6006
800-421-4511
Fax: 310-399-2662
Home Page: www.merchandisegroup.com

Julie Ichiba, Show Director

Held in New York City, this event is the first opportunity of the New Year for variety and general merchandise retailers to stock their shelves after the holidays with popular, value-priced consumer goods in hundreds of product categories.
12500 Attendees
Frequency: January

21168 **ASD/AMD's Orlando Variety Merchandise Show**
ASD/AMD Merchandise Group
2950 31st Street
Suite 100
Santa Monica, CA 90405

310-396-6006
800-421-4511
Fax: 310-399-2662
Home Page: www.merchandisegroup.com

Julie Ichiba, Show Director

Held in Orlando, Florida, this event is a popular destination for southeastern US retailers to make deals and place orders for variety and general merchandise in hundreds of popular consumer categories.
5,500 Attendees
Frequency: April

21169 **Accent on Design**
George Little Management
10 Bank Street
Suite 1200
White Plains, NY 10606-1954

914-486-6070
800-272-7469
Fax: 914-948-2867
Home Page: www.nyigf.com

Elizabeth Murphy, Manager
George Little II, President

370 booths of the latest and most innovative gift lines such as decorative accessories and home furnishings.
50M Attendees
Frequency: August
Founded in 1984

21170 **American Beverage Licensees Annual Convention & Trade Show**
National Association of Beverage Retailers
5101 River Road
Suite 108
Bethesda, MD 20816-1560

301-656-1494
Fax: 301-656-7539
Home Page: www.nabronline.org

Harry Wiles, Executive Director
Shawn Ross, Office Manager

Annual show of 75 manufacturers, suppliers and distributors of alcoholic beverages.
1,000 Attendees

21171 **Associated Surplus Dealers/Associated Merchandise Dealers Trade Show**
ASD/AMD Merchandise Group
2950 31st Street
Suite 100
Santa Monica, CA 90405

310-255-4633
800-421-4511
Fax: 310-399-3662
Home Page: www.merchandisegroup.com

Sam Bundy, Group President

Gifts, souvenirs and assorted merchandise for professional buyers.
15000 Attendees
Frequency: Annual/March

21172 **Book Expo America**
Reed Exhibitions
383 Main Avenue
Norwalk, CT 06851

203-404-4800
800-840-5614
E-Mail: cmuller@reedexpo.com
Home Page: www.bookexpoamerica.com
Social Media: Facebook, Twitter, LinkedIn

Courtney Muller, Event Manager
Cathy Glickstein, Registration

Sponsored by American Booksellers Association and Association of American Publishers. More than 2,000 exhibits, 500 authors, over 60 conference sessions as well as a special area for rights business, all the latest titles across genres, uncover hidden gems, network, and meet the industry contacts to put you instantly on top of what you need to know for your business and job.
Frequency: May/June
Founded in 2000

21173 **CMM International: FLEX Expo**
Bruno Blenheim
Fort Lee Executive Park
Fort Lee, FL 07024

800-829-3976
Fax: 201-346-1602

Nick Helyer, President

Exhibits by franchisers and sellers to the franchise industry. 125 booths.
5M Attendees
Frequency: June

21174 **Customer Relationship Management Course: C RMretail**
National Retail Federation
325 7th Street NW
Suite 1101
Washington, DC 20004

202-783-7971
Fax: 202-737-2849
E-Mail: exhibit@nrf.com
Home Page: www.nrf.com
Social Media: Facebook, Twitter, LinkedIn

Michaal Tuttle, Director Exhibits
Cindy Shin, Director Sales

CRMretail is a cross-industry conference, bringing together retail business leaders and the leading technology companies, solutions providers, consultants and academicians in the field of customer relationship management. Annual CRMretail research conducted by Gartner Dataquest is also released at this conference.
200 Attendees
Frequency: Late Spring
Founded in 1993

21175 **Green Profit's Retail Experience**
Green Profit Magazine
335 N River Street
Batavia, IL 60510

630-208-9080
888-888-0013
Fax: 630-208-9350
E-Mail: info@ballpublishing.com
Home Page: www.ballpublishing.com/conferences

Michelle Mazza, Show Manager

Educational event and tradeshow dedicated exclusively to garden center retailing. Covers topics from store layout and design to merchandising strategies and business management. 20 booths
300 Attendees
Frequency: September
Founded in 2006

21176 International Council of Shopping Centers Fall Convention Trade & Exposition
International Council of Shopping Centers
1221 Ave Of The Americas
41st Fl
New York, NY 10020-1099

646-728-3800
Fax: 732-694-1755
E-Mail: icsc@icsc.org
Home Page: www.icsc.org

Michael Kercheval, President/CEO
Denise Adrian, Director Of Marketing

21177 International Franchise Association Expo
1501 K St NW
Suite 350
Washington, DC 20005-1412

202-628-8000
Fax: 202-628-0812

Matthew Shay, President
Patricia Langfeld, VP

75 booths.
1M Attendees
Frequency: February

21178 Internet Retailer Conference & Exhibition
Internet Retailer
300 S Wacker Drive
Suite 602
Chicago, IL 60606

FAX 312-362-9532
Home Page: www.internetretailer.com
Social Media: Facebook, Twitter, LinkedIn

Learn the strategies, practices and tools to lift your site into e-retailing's second decade of growth. Network with your peers in the only show serving e-retailers from all merchant channels.
Frequency: Annual

21179 Logistics
Retail Industry Leaders Association
1700 N Moore Street
Suite 2250
Arlington, VA 22209
703-841-2300
Fax: 703-841-1184
Home Page: www.imra.org

Britt Wood, VP
Sean Nodland, Manager

This event brings together retailers, consumer product companies, and suppliers of goods and service logistics side of business
400 Attendees
Frequency: February

21180 Loss Prevention Conference & Exhibition
National Retail Federation
325 7th Street NW
Suite 1100
Washington, DC 20004

202-783-7971
Fax: 202-737-2849
E-Mail: exhibit@nrf.com
Home Page: www.nrf.com
Social Media: Facebook, Twitter, LinkedIn

Michaal Tuttle, Director Exhibits
Scott Krugman, Publisher
Mader Richard, Executive Director
Michael Gatti, VP/Marketing
David French, VP

Major conference for Loss Prevention, Internal Audit and Risk Management professionals in the retail industry.
1500 Attendees
Frequency: June
Founded in 1993

21181 Loss Prevention, Auditing & Safety Conference
Retail Industry Leaders Association
1700 N Moore Street
Suite 2250
Arlington, VA 22209

703-841-2300
Fax: 703-841-1184
E-Mail: rhett.asher@retail-leaders.org
Home Page: www.retail-leaders.org
Social Media: Facebook, Twitter, LinkedIn

Rhett Asher
Annual information exchange.
325 Attendees
Frequency: April

21182 Marketing Conference
International Mass Retail Association
1700 N Moore Street
Suite 2250
Arlington, VA 22209

703-841-2300
Fax: 703-841-1184
Home Page: www.imra.org

Peter Kim, Owner

21183 NACS Show Annual Meeting and Exposition
National Association of Convenience Stores
1600 Duke Street
Alexandria, VA 22314

703-684-3600
Fax: 703-836-4564
E-Mail: nacs@nacs.com
Home Page: www.nacsshow.com

Jane Berzan, VP Events/Mktg/Supplier Relations
Sherry Romello, Director Meetings and Conventions
24000 Attendees
Frequency: October

21184 National Lawn & Garden Controlled Marketing Conference
Controlled Marketing Conferences
PO Box 1771
Monument, CO 80132

719-488-0226
888-316-0226
Fax: 719-488-8168
Home Page: www.nlgshow.com / www.marketingconferences.com

Robert Mikulas, President
Chris Wolf, VP

This year CMC events will be linked to the National Lawn ans Garden Show - The Expo Division. Don't miss out on the industries most important lawn and garden headlines event.
3000 Attendees
Frequency: June

21185 National Retail Federation Annual Conference and Expo
National Retail Federation
325 7th Street NW
Suite 1100
Washington, DC 20004-2808

202-783-7971
Fax: 202-783-0581
E-Mail: webmaster@nrf.com
Home Page: www.nrf.com

Michaal Tuttle, Director Exhibits
Cindy Shin, Director Sales
Tracy Mullin, President

600 booths exhibiting the latest in retail technology, new developments in credit validation, security and materials handling.
12M Attendees
Frequency: January

21186 Retail Advertising Conference: RAC
Retail Advertising & Marketing International
325 7th Street NW
Suite 1100
Washington, DC 20004

202-626-8183
Fax: 202-737-2849
Home Page: www.rama-nrf.org

Mike Gatti, VP Marketing

Definitive event for retail advertising and marketing professionals each year featuring the RAC Awards gala dinner and Retail Hall of Fame induction annually.
1000 Attendees
Frequency: February

21187 Retail Promotion Show
Association of Retail Marketing Services
10 Drs James Parker Boulevard
Suite 103
Red Bank, NJ 07701-1500

732-842-5070
866-331-6310
Fax: 732-219-1938
E-Mail: info@goarms.com
Home Page: www.goarms.com

Gerri Hopkins, Executive Director

Annual show of 65 manufacturers, suppliers, distributors and representatives of dinnerware, glassware, housewares, books, videos, games, sweepstakes, dolls and plush toys suppliers used as retail promotions.
1200 Attendees
Frequency: March, Annual

21188 Shop.org Annual Summit
Shop.org
325 7th Street NW
Suite 1100
Washington, DC 20004

202-626-8183
Fax: 202-626-8191
Home Page: www.shop.org

Diane Furstenberg, COO
Lane Bryant, VP Marketing

Provides a unique opportunity for Internet and multi-channel retail industry leaders to exchange ideas, perspectives, opportunities and challenges in an intimate and comfortable setting. The Summit features dialogues with distinguished keynote speakers, provocative panels and debates on timely issues, and important original research.
600 Attendees
Frequency: September

21189 Shop.org Members' Forum
Shop.org
325 7th Street NW
Suite 1100
Washington, DC 20004

202-626-8183
Fax: 202-626-8191
Home Page: www.shop.org

Diane Furstenberg, COO
Lane Bryant, VP Marketing

Attendees see presentations for an online holiday recap and new multichannel retail research

sessions as well as roundtable discussions and other networking events.
350 Attendees
Frequency: January

21190 Southern Convenience Store & Petroleum Show
PO Box 855
Snellville, GA 30078
770-736-9723
Fax: 770-736-9725
E-Mail: jtudor@aol.com
Home Page: www.gacs.com
Jim Tudor, President
Contains 250 exhibits.
3,000 Attendees
Founded in 2003

21191 Store Fixturing Show
Shore Varrone
6255 Barfield Road NE
Suite 200
Atlanta, GA 30328-4332
404-848-0077
800-241-9034
Fax: 770-252-4436
Russ Eisenhardt, VP Trade Shows
Lee Pritcher, Owner
The largest annual store design event in the world. The event also includes The Visual Merchandising Show, the Retail Operations & Construction Expo, the POPAI Expo and the Exhibit Ideas Show. 800 exhibitors in total.
15M Attendees
Frequency: April

21192 Store Operations & Human Resources Conference
International Mass Retail Association
1700 N Moore Street
Suite 2250
Arlington, VA 22209
703-841-2300
Fax: 703-841-1184
Home Page: www.imra.org
This educational event provides attendees with an opportunity to learn from experts in their fields on the most pressing topics of the day

Directories & Databases

21193 Annual Trade Show Directory
Forum Publishing Company
383 E Main St
Centerport, NY 11721-1538
631-754-5000
Fax: 631-754-0630
Home Page: www.forum123.com
Martin Stevens, Owner
Over 1,800 merchandise trade shows throughout the United States and Canada.
Cost: $39.95
312 Pages
Frequency: Annual

21194 Association of Retail Marketing Services Membership Directory
Association of Retail Marketing Services
10 Drs James Parker Boulevard
Suite 103
Red Bank, NJ 07701-1500
732-842-5070
Fax: 732-219-1938
Home Page: www.goarms.com
Gerri Hopkins, Executive Director
Lisa McCauley, Administrative Director
Membership directory.
Cost: $25.00
Frequency: Annual

21195 Directory of Convenience Stores
Trade Dimensions
45 Danbury Rd
Wilton, CT 06897-4445
203-563-3000
Fax: 860-563-3131
Home Page: www.tradedimensions.com
Jennifer Gillbert, Editor
Lynda Guticulez, Managing Editor
The directory comprises nearly 1,500 detailed profiles on the companies you need to do business with - extensive dependable information on the grocery industry's most volatile segment.
Cost: $245.00
Frequency: Annual

21196 Directory of High Discount Merchandise Sources
B Klein Publishers
Po Box 6578
Delray Beach, FL 33482-6578
561-496-3316
Fax: 561-496-5546
Bernard Klein, Owner
Approximately 1,200 sources of products offered at high discounts.
Cost: $35.00
Frequency: Annual

21197 Directory of Mail Order Catalogs
Grey House Publishing
4919 Route 22
PO Box 56
Amenia, NY 12501
518-789-8700
800-562-2139
Fax: 845-373-6390
E-Mail: books@greyhouse.com
Home Page: www.greyhouse.com
Social Media: Facebook, Twitter
Leslie Mackenzie, Publisher
Richard Gottlieb, Editor
The premier source of information on the mail order catalog industry. Covers over 13,000 consumer and business catalog companies with 44 different product chapters from Animals to Toys and Games.
Cost: $395.00
1900 Pages
Frequency: Annual
ISBN: 1-592373-96-8
Founded in 1981

21198 Directory of Mail Order Catalogs - Online Database
Grey House Publishing
4919 Route 22
PO Box 56
Amenia, NY 12501
518-789-8700
800-562-2139
Fax: 845-373-6390
E-Mail: gold@greyhouse.com
Home Page: http://gold.greyhouse.com
Social Media: Facebook, Twitter
Leslie Mackenzie, Publisher
Richard Gottlieb, Editor
Reach over 10,000 consumer catalog companies in one easy-to-use source with The Directory of Mail Order Catalogs - Online Database. Filled with business-building detail, each company profile gives you the information you need to access that organization quickly and easily. Listings provide key contacts, sales volume, employee size, printing information, circulation, list data, product descriptions and much more.
Frequency: Annual
Founded in 1981

21199 Directory of Major Malls
PO Box 837
Nyack, NY 10960-0837
845-348-7000
Fax: 845-426-0802
Tama J Shor, Editor/Publisher
Murray Shor, Consulting Publisher
Contains 2865 listings with over 1800 leasing/site plans of major malls, with many showing the anchors, design layout, intersecting streets, peripheral land, and major highways.
ISBN: 0-932599-13-3

21200 Directory of Mass Merchandisers
Trade Dimensions
45 Danbury Rd
Wilton, CT 06897-4445
203-563-3000
Fax: 860-563-3131
Home Page: www.tradedimensions.com
Lynda Gutierrez, Managing Editor
Jennifer Gilbert, Editor
This directory defines this complex class of retail trade. Includes profiles of the chains and leading mass merchandisers by market area. Also includes HBC suppliers and store type breakdowns by state/region.
Cost: $245.00
Frequency: Annual

21201 Discount & General Merchandising Stores
Chain Store Guide
3922 Coconut Palm Dr
Tampa, FL 33619-1389
813-627-6700
800-972-9292
Fax: 813-627-7094
E-Mail: info@csgis.com
Home Page: www.csgis.com
Mike Jarvis, Publisher
Shami Choon, Manager
This database is an in-depth look at the mass-merchandising segment, bringing you access to more than 7,000 listings along with over 23,000 key personnel. This report includes targeted research from sectors such as Discount Department Stores, General Merchandise Stores, Dollar Stores, Automotive Aftermarket Retailers and Computer & Consumer Electronics Chains.
Cost: $335.00
720 Pages
Frequency: Annual

21202 Discount Merchandiser
McFadden Publishing Company
233 Park Ave S
6th Floor
New York, NY 10003-1606
212-979-4800
Fax: 212-979-7342
Steven Jacober, Editor
Profiles of the top 55 chains and list of top 85 discount merchandising companies.
Cost: $40.00
Frequency: Annual June

21203 International Franchise Association - Franchise Opportunities Guide
1501 K St NW
Suite 350
Washington, DC 20005-1412

202-628-8000
Fax: 202-628-0812
Home Page: www.franchise.org

Matthew Shay, President

This directory lists over 3,000 companies offering franchises.
Cost: $21.00
300 Pages
Frequency: SemiAnnual

21204 Leading Chain Tenants Database
Chain Store Guide
3922 Coconut Palm Dr
Tampa, FL 33619-1389

813-627-6700
800-778-9794
Fax: 813-627-7094
E-Mail: info@csgis.com
Home Page: www.csgis.com

Mike Jarvis, Publisher
Arthur Sciarrotta, Senior VP

Information on more than 8,600 retailers in the U.S. and Canada with over 32,000 personnel contacts. This database will lead you to new real estate prospects across a vast range of industries. Whether you are in real estate development, leasing or sales, the opportunities are endless.
Cost: $365.00

21205 NRB Shopping Center Directory
Trade Dimensions
45 Danbury Rd
Wilton, CT 06897-4445

203-563-3000
Fax: 860-563-3131
Home Page: www.nrbonline.com

Patricia Kelly, Managing Editor
Stephanie Strano, Circulation Director

The most comprehensive book on shopping centers available. Encompassing over 37,000 centers from neighborhood to super regional, the Directory is organized into four volumes: East, Midwest, South, West. A fifth volume is dedicated exclusively to the industry's top contacts, comprising the names and contact information for anyone who owns, leases, or manages three or more centers.
Cost: $325.00
Frequency: Annual

21206 Outlet Project Directory
Value Retail News
29399 Us Highway 19 N
Suite 370
Clearwater, FL 33761-2138

727-781-7557
800-669-1020
Fax: 727-536-4389
Home Page: www.valueretailnews.com

Cher Russell-Street, Editor

Factory outlet projects.
Cost: $179.00
Frequency: SemiAnnual

21207 Outlet Retail Directory
Off-Price Specialists, Value Retail News
14250 49th St N
Clearwater, FL 33762-2800

727-464-6460
Fax: 727-453-7419

James Pierce, Manager

Over 500 outlet retail chains are profiled.
280 Pages
Frequency: Semiannual

21208 Products & Services Directory
Value Retail News
29399 Us Highway 19 N
Suite 370
Clearwater, FL 33761-2138

727-781-7557
800-669-1020
Fax: 727-536-4389
Home Page: www.valueretailnews.com

Cher Russell-Street, Editor

More than 2,000 service companies specializing in outlet or off-price retailing and development industries.
Cost: $49.00
Frequency: Annual

21209 Productscan Online
Marketing Intelligence Service
6473 State Route 64
Naples, NY 14512-9726

585-374-6326
Fax: 585-374-5217
Home Page: www.productscan.com

Tom Vierhile, Manager
Julie Fox, Finance Executive

This database is dedicated solely to new launches of consumer packaged goods. Includes label copy, in-depth reports on innovations, and product pictures capable of statistical analysis and manufacturer history reports.
Cost: $ 3995.00

21210 Retail Industry Buying Guide: STORES Magazine
National Retail Federation
325 7th St NW
Suite 1100
Washington, DC 20004-2808

202-783-7971
800-673-4693
Fax: 202-737-2849
E-Mail: pennw@nrf.com
Home Page: www.nrf.com
Social Media: Facebook, Twitter, LinkedIn

Matthew Shay, President
Scott Krugman, Publisher
Mader Richard, Executive Director
Michael Gatti, VP/Marketing
David French, VP

Capital spending in the products and services that are imperitive to running a smooth and efficient retail operation were particularly hard hit in the past year. In the face of continued uncertainty, it's essential that retailers make informed decisions on how to best invest their limited capital to ensure a positive return on their investment. This directory is that source of information.
Frequency: Monthly
Circulation: 35000

21211 Retail Tenant Directory
Trade Dimensions
45 Danbury Rd
Wilton, CT 06897-4445
203-563-3000
Fax: 860-563-3131
Home Page: www.tradedimensions.com

Garrett Van Siclen, Publisher
Thomas Donato, Editor

Complete and accurate details for 5,000+ growing retailers that are looking for space. Holding company section lists corporate profiles for major parent companies which own two or more major retail chains in the US. Individual company profiles include retail classifications, total number of stores, operating names, sales volume, who to contact, extensive site selection criteria including demographic preferences, expansion plans, acquisitions, format changes and more.
Cost: $ 345.00
1500 Pages
Frequency: Annual
ISBN: 0-911790-29-2

21212 Shippers Guide to Department & Chain Stores Nationwide
Shippers Guides
PO Box 112
Duarte, CA 91009-0112

626-357-6430
Fax: 626-357-6366

Profiles over 1,000 department stores and chain stores and information about routing and freight movement.
Cost: $349.00
350 Pages
Frequency: Annual
Mailing list available for rent: 1,000 names at $299 per M

21213 Shopping Center Directory
National Research Bureau
333 W Wacker Drive
Suite 900
Chicago, IL 60606-1284
312-346-3900

This large directory offers information on over 30,000 shopping centers in four regional volumes.
Cost: $225.00
3,200 Pages
Frequency: Annual

21214 Single Unit Supermarkets Operators
Chain Store Guide
3922 Coconut Palm Dr
Tampa, FL 33619-1389

813-627-6700
800-778-9794
Fax: 813-627-7094
E-Mail: info@csgis.com
Home Page: www.csgis.com

Mike Jarvis, Publisher
Shami Choon, Manager

Discover more than 7,100 single-unit supermarkets with annual sales topping $500,000 dollars. This comprehensive desktop reference makes it easy to reach our compiled list of 21,000 key executives and buyers, plus their primary wholesalers.
Cost: $335.00
725 Pages
Frequency: Annual

21215 Stores: Top 100 Retailers Issue
National Retail Federation
325 7th St NW
Suite 1100
Washington, DC 20004-2808

202-783-7971
800-673-4694
Fax: 202-737-2849
E-Mail: pennw@nrf.com
Home Page: www.nrf.com
Social Media: Facebook, Twitter, LinkedIn

Matthew Shay, President
Scott Krugman, Publisher
Mader Richard, Executive Director
Michael Gatti, VP/Marketing
David French, VP

100 US retail companies having largest estimated sales during preceding year.
Cost: $75.00
Frequency: Annual July
Circulation: 35,000

21216 **Supermarket, Grocery & Convenience Stores**
Chain Store Guide
3922 Coconut Palm Dr
Tampa, FL 33619-1389

813-627-6700
800-778-9794
Fax: 813-627-7094
E-Mail: info@csgis.com
Home Page: www.csgis.com

Mike Jarvis, Publisher
Shami Choon, Manager

Contains information on close to 3,400 U.S. and Canadian supermarket chains, each with at least $2 million in annual sales - one of the most profitable segments in this sector of the economy. The companies in this database operate over 41,000 individual supermarket, superstore, club store, gourmet supermarkets and combo-store units. A special convenience store section profiles 1,700 convenience store chains operating over 85,000 stores.
Cost: $335.00
Frequency: Annual

21217 **Top Shopping Centers: Major Markets 1-50**
National Research Bureau
333 W Wacker Drive
Suite 900
Chicago, IL 60606-1284

312-346-3900
Cost: $895.00

21218 **US Trade Pages**
Global Source
1511 K Street NW
Washington, DC 20005-1403
Kara Kent, Editor

These directories including a volume on Brazil, Chile, Canada, Mexico, Venezuela, and Argentina list trade associations and professional services that provide information on imports and exports between the US and the above listed companies.
Cost: $59.95
Frequency: 6 Volumes

21219 **World Federation of Direct Selling Associations Directory**
WFDSA
1776 K St Nw
Washington, DC 20006-2304

202-546-5330
Fax: 202-453-9010
Home Page: www.wfdsa.org
Social Media: Facebook, Twitter, LinkedIn

A Harold, President
Founded in 1789

Industry Web Sites

21220 **http://gold.greyhouse.com**
G.O.L.D Grey House OnLine Databases

Grey House Publising's online database platform, GOLD, offers Quick Search, Keyword Search and Expert Search for most business sectors including retailing markets. The GOLD platform makes finding the information you need quick and easy - whether you're a novice searcher or an experienced database user. All of Grey House's directory products are available for subscription on the GOLD platform.

21221 **www.aamp.com**
American Association of Meat Processors

The membership consists of small to medium sized meat, poultry and food businesses including: packers, processors, wholesalers, home food service businesses, retailers, deli and catering operators. AAMP is also affiliated with 34 state, regional and provincial organizations which represent meat and poultry businesses.

21222 **www.bookweb.org**
American Booksellers Association

Trade association for retail booksellers. Not for profit.

21223 **www.fdi.org**
International Center for Companies of Food Trade
and Industry/North America

Provides management research on problems related to food distribution and serves as an international forum where food chain store executives can meet to exchange ideas and information.

21224 **www.fleamarkets.org**
National Flea Market Association

Represents Flea Market and Swap Meet owners and managers and disseminates information to the general public and media regarding the flea market industry worldwide.

21225 **www.goarms.com**
Association of Retail Marketing Services

Approximately 60 retailers involved in the ARMS retail promotion show, held annually.

21226 **www.greyhouse.com**
Grey House Publishing

Authoritative reference directories for most business sectors including retail markets. Users can search the online databases with varied search criteria allowing for custom searches by product category, geographic area, sales volume, keyword, subject and more. Full Grey House catalog and online ordering also available.

21227 **www.ispo.org**
Institute of Store Planners

Provides a forum for debate and discussion by store design experts and retailers. Sponsors student design programs.

21228 **www.maptrade.org**
International Map Trade Association

Membership comprised of retail stores featuring maps, travel books, globes, and travel products, plus publishers and manufacturers producing these products. Publishes a monthly newsletter

21229 **www.mraa.com**
Marine Retailers Association of America

Promotes activities for the recreational boating industry and holds seminars to improve management.

21230 **www.nacs.org**
National Association of College Stores

Provides educational and support services and products to college stores. Promotes business methods and ethics. Conducts manager certification, educational services and research.

21231 **www.nag-net.com**
Convenience Stores/Petroleum Marketers Association

This association represents senior level management of retail companies organized to enhance buying power, merchandising programs and an exchange of ideas. C-Stores/Petroleum Marketers membership dues: Retail Av. $300, Assoc. $500

21232 **www.nagmr.org**
National Association General Merchandise Repr

A professional association of consumer product brokers representing leading manufacturers to the retail trade.

21233 **www.narda.com**
North American Retail Dealers Association

A national organization of association members, independent retailers selling and servicing major appliances, consumer electronics products, furniture and computers. Emphasis is placed on ideas that help readers become better, more profitable businesses. Articles are featured regularly on displays, salesmanship, financial analysis and service management.

21234 **www.nationalPawnbrokers.org**
National Pawnbrokers Association

Nonprofits organization that supports all those involved with the retail pawnbrokers.

21235 **www.nationalgrocers.org**
National Grocers Association

Works to advance understanding, trade, and cooperation in the food industry. Represents members interests before the government. Offers store planning, and engineering, training and advertising.

21236 **www.nicyra.org**
National Ice Cream & Yogurt Retailers Association

Members are in retail frozen dessert businesses. Some offer food services either full of limited and some operate convenience stores. The common denominator is that all members offer frozen desserts for take-home or on-site consumption.

21237 **www.nrf.com**
National Retail Federation

Retail trade association with membership that comprises all retail formats and channels of distribution including department, specialty, discount, catalog, Internet and independent stores. NRF members represent an industry that encompasses more than 1.4 million US retail establishments which employ more than 23 million people — about one in five American workers — and registered 2002 sales of $3.6 trillion. NRF's international members operate stores in more than 50 nations.

21238 **www.nsgachicagoshow.com**
National Sporting Goods Association

Members consist of retailers, wholesalers, suppliers, sales agents and media. Sponsor of NSGA World Sports EXPO, held annually in Chicago, and the NSGA Management Conference. Has an annual budget of approximately $8 million.

21239 **www.nssra.com**
National Ski & Snowboard Retailers Association

The retail voice for the ski and snowboard industries and provides information and services you need to operate more successfully.

21240 **www.retailsystems.com**
Retail Systems Alert Group

For retail and supply chain professionals. Access to community centers, newsletter information, and online ordering information is also available.

21241 **www.rtda.org**
Retail Tobacco Dealers of America

Trade association of high quality tobacconists.

21242 **www.shop.org**
Shop.org
Association for retailers online. It's where professional retailerscome together to garner the insight, knowledge and intellegence to make better decisions in the evolving world of the Internet and multi-channel retailing.

21243 **www.smallbusinesslocator.com**
Small Business Association
Providing information to mom and pop businesses.

Associations

21244 Acrylonitrile Group
1250 Connecticut Ave Nw
Suite 700
Washington, DC 20036

202-419-1500
Fax: 202-659-8037
E-Mail: angroup@regnet.com
Home Page: www.angroup.org

Robert J Fensterheim, Executive Director

Represents producers and users of the industrial chemical used to make plastics, fibers and synthetic rubber products.
Founded in 1981

21245 American Chemical Society: Rubber Division
411 Wolf Ledges
Akron, OH 44311

330-972-7814
Fax: 330-972-5269
Home Page: www.rubber.org

John Long, Councilor
Doug Ruch, Chair-Elect
Leonard Thomas, Chair
Terry DeLapa, Treasurer
William Stahl, Secretary

The Rubber Division of the American Chemical Society is a professional organization dedicated to providing educational programs, technical resources and other vital services for the people associated with rubber and affiliated industries.
Founded in 1909

21246 Engineering with Rubber: How to Design Rubber Components
American Chemical Society: Rubber Division
411 Wolf Ledges
Akron, OH 44311

330-972-7814
Fax: 330-972-5269
Home Page: www.rubber.org

John Long, Councilor
Doug Ruch, Chair-Elect
Leonard Thomas, Chair
Terry DeLapa, Treasurer
William Stahl, Secretary

Teaches the beginning engineer the principles of rubber science and technology what rubber is, how it behaves, and how to design simple engineering components.
Founded in 1909

21247 International Institute of Synthetic Rubber Producers, Inc.
2077 S Gessner Road
Suite 133
Houston, TX 77063

713-783-7511
Fax: 713-783-7253
E-Mail: info@iisrp.com
Home Page: www.iisrp.com

James L McGraw, Managing Director/CEO
Roxanna Bauza-Petrovic, General Director of Programs
Sue Flynn, Executive Assistant/ Event Coor
Robin Boyd, Manager of Accounts
Mary O'Connor, European Section Secretariat

International trade association for synthetic rubber producers to receive and benefit from statistical, environmental, and technical information in order to keep abreast of the world's market growth and events.
40 Members
Founded in 1960

21248 North American Recycled Rubber Association
1621 Mcewen Drive
Unit 24
Whitby Ontario, CA L1N-9A5

905-433-7669
Fax: 905-433-0905
E-Mail: narra@oix.com
Home Page: www.recycle.net

Diane Sarracini, Contact

Created to bring together the various stakeholders affiliated with the recycled rubber industry.
Founded in 1994

21249 Polyurethane Foam Association
9724 Kingston Pike
334 Lakeside Plaza
Loudon, TN 37774

865-657-9840
Fax: 865-381-1292
E-Mail: rluedeka@pfa.org
Home Page: www.pfa.org

Robert Luedeka, Executive Director

The mission of the Polyurethane Foam Association (PFA) is to educate customers and other groups about flexible polyurethane foam (FPF) and to promote its use in manufactured and industrial products.
Founded in 1980

21250 Polyurethane Manufacturers Association
6737 W Washington Avenue
Suite 1300
Milwaukee, WI 53214

414-431-3094
Fax: 414-276-7704
E-Mail: info@pmahome.org
Home Page: www.pmahome.org
Social Media: Facebook, Twitter, LinkedIn

Mike Kocak, President
Robert Adkins, Director
Terry Hudson, Director
Phil Green, VP/Treasurer/Secretary
Payam Towfigh, Past President

The Polyurethane Manufacturers Association is the trade association of the cast polyurethane elastomer industry, serving processors of polyurethane products, materials and equipment suppliers and independent agents. PMA exchanges and disseminates information on standards, materials, processes and technical matters, in addition to monitoring regulatory and legislative activity affecting the urethane industry.
90 Members
Founded in 1971

21251 Rubber Division, American Chemical Society
411 Wolf Ledges
Akron, OH 44311

330-972-7814
Fax: 330-972-5269
E-Mail: crubber.org
Home Page: www.rubber.org

John Long, Councilor
Doug Ruch, Chair-Elect
Leonard Thomas, Chair
Terry DeLapa, Treasurer
William Stahl, Secretary

Rubber division of the American Chemical Society is a professional association dedicated to providing educational programs, technical resources and other vital services for the people associated with rubber and affiliated industries.

Serves as a global resource for networking and partnerships with academics and industry.
3200 Members
Founded in 1909

21252 Rubber Manufacturers Association
1400 K St Nw
Suite 900
Washington, DC 20005

202-682-4800
Fax: 202-682-4854
E-Mail: info@rma.org
Home Page: www.rma.org
Social Media: Facebook, Twitter, YouTube

Charlie Cannon, President & CEO
Tracey Norberg, Senior Vice President
Daniel Zielinski, Senior Vice President

National trade association for makers of tires and other rubber products.
100 Members
Founded in 1915

21253 Rubber Pavements Association
1801 S Jentilly Ln
Suite A-2
Tempe, AZ 85281-5738

480-517-9944
877-517-9944
Fax: 480-517-9959
E-Mail: dougc@rubberpavements.org
Home Page: www.rubberpavements.org

Mark Belshe, Executive Director
Guadalupe Dickerson, Office Manager
Cliff Ashcroft, President

Dedicated to encouraging greater usage of high quality, cost effective asphalt pavements containing recycled tire rubber.
Founded in 1985

21254 Single Ply Roofing Institute
411 Waverley Oaks Road
Suite 331B
Waltham, MA 02452

781-647-7026
Fax: 781-647-7222
E-Mail: info@spri.org
Home Page: www.spri.org

SPRI represents sheet membrane and related component suppliers in the commercial roofing industry.

21255 Society of the Plastics Industry
1667 K St Nw
Suite 1000
Washington, DC 20006

202-974-5200
202-296-7005
Fax: 202-296-7005
Home Page: www.plasticsindustry.org
Social Media: Facebook, Twitter, LinkedIn

William Cartuaex, President

Represents the entire plastics industry in a manner that promotes development of the industry and enhances public understanding of its contributions while meeting the needs of society and providing value to members.
Founded in 1937

21256 Tire Industry Association
1532 Pointer Ridge Place
Suite G
Bowie, MD 20716-1883

301-430-7280
800-876-8372
Fax: 301-430-7283
E-Mail: info@tireindustry.org
Home Page: www.tireindustry.org
Social Media: Facebook, Twitter, LinkedIn

Roy Littlefield, Executive VP
Tom Formanek, Treasurer

Freda Pratt-Boyer, Secretary
Randy Groh, President
Larry Brandt, Past President

TIA is an international association representing all segments of the tire industry, including those that manufacture, repair, recycle, sell, service or use new or retreaded tires, and also those suppliers or individuals who furnish equipment, material or services to the industry. TIA was formed by the July 2002 merger of the International Tire & Rubber Association (ITRA) and the Tire Association of North America (TANA).
4500 Members
Founded in 2002

21257 Tire Retread and Repair Information Bureau
1013 Birch St.
Falls Church, VA 22046

703-533-7677
877-394-6811
Fax: 703-533-7678
E-Mail: info@retread.org
Home Page: www.retread.org
Social Media: Facebook, Twitter

David Stevens, Managing Director
Brian Hayes, President
Phil Boarts, Secretary/ Treasurer
Eddie Burleson, Vice President
Mike Berra, Director

Our goal is to provide the motoring public (both in the private and public sectors) with the most up-to-date information about the economic and environmental benefits of tire retreading and tire repairing.

21258 Tread Rubber Manufacturers Group
Piper and Marbury
1200 19th Street NW
Washington, DC 20036-2430

202-614-4171

Works to improve tire retreading techniques and to safeguard the public interest in retreading.

Newsletters

21259 Rubber Chemistry and Technology
Rubber Division, American Chemical Society
PO Box 499
Akron, OH 44325-3801

330-972-7883
Fax: 330-972-5269

Lu Ann Blazeff, Publisher

Information on materials and equipment pertaining to the rubber industry. Accepts advertising.
Cost: $487.50
Frequency: 5 Times per Year

21260 Rubber and Plastics News
Crain Communications
1725 Merriman Rd
Suite 300
Akron, OH 44313-5283

330-836-9180
800-678-9595
Fax: 330-836-2831
E-Mail: editorials@rubbernews.com
Home Page: www.crain.com

Robert S Simmons, VP
Edward Noga, Editor

Discusses production, research and development, management, sales and marketing.
Cost: $79.00
24 Pages
Frequency: Monthly
Circulation: 16258
Founded in 1971
Printed in 4 colors on glossy stock

21261 Worldwide Rubber Statistics
Int'l Institute of Synthetic Rubber Producers
2077 S Gessner Rd
Suite 133
Houston, TX 77063-1150

713-783-7511
Fax: 713-783-7253
E-Mail: orderfs@iisrp.com
Home Page: www.iisrp.com
Social Media: Facebook, Twitter, LinkedIn

Jim Mc Graw, CEO
Dr K Leon Loh Sr, Senior Director of Programs
Sue Flynn, Executive Assistant
Robin Boyd, Manager of Accounts

Guide to the synthetic and natural rubber industry, including Centrally Planned Economy Countries.
Cost: $1050.00
40 Members
Founded in 1960

Magazines & Journals

21262 Global Tire News.com
Rubber & Plastic News
1725 Merriman Rd
Suite 300
Akron, OH 44313-5283

330-836-9180
330-836-9180
Fax: 330-836-1005
E-Mail: dsector@crain.com
Home Page: www.rubbernews.com
Social Media: Facebook, Twitter, LinkedIn

Dave Cielasko, Publisher
Don Sector, Advertising Coordinator
Mike McNulty, Rubber & Plastics News Staff Writer
Brent Weaver, Classified Coordinator

Provides rubber industry information relative to tire manufacturers; top tire company managers; plant listings and other data. Subscription to annual publication includes access to Global Tire News.com.
Cost: $79.00
Frequency: Annual

21263 PMA Polytopics
Polyurethane Manufacturers Association
6737 W Washington Avenue
Suite 1300
Milwaukee, WI 53214

414-431-3094
Fax: 414-276-7704
E-Mail: info@pmahome.org
Home Page: www.pmahome.org

Mike Katz, President
Mike Cocak, VP
Mike Cocak, Secretary
Paul Blasco, Director Public Relations

The Polyurethane Manufacturers Association is the trade association of the cast polyurethane elastomer industry, serving processors of polyurethane products, materials and equipment suppliers and independent agents. PMA exchanges and disseminates information on standards, materials, processes and technical matters, in addition to monitoring regulatory and legislative activity affecting the urethane industry.
90 Members
Frequency: Quarterly
Circulation: 250
Founded in 1971

21264 Rubber World
Lippincott & Peto
PO Box 5451
Akron, OH 44334-0451

330-864-2122
Fax: 330-864-5298
E-Mail: jhl@rubberworld.com
Home Page: www.rubberworld.com

Job Lippincott, President
Dennis Kennelly, VP Sales
Don R Smith, Editor
Darlene Ballard, Director of Marketing Services
Jill Rohrer, Managing Editor

Provides complete technical coverage to the rubber industry.
Cost: $34.00

Trade Shows

21265 International Latex Conference
Crain Communications
1725 Merriman Road
Suite 300
Akron, OH 44313-5283

330-836-9180
Fax: 330-836-1005
E-Mail: cstevens@crain.com
Home Page: www.rubbernews.com

Twelve exhibitors with 12 booths.
Frequency: July

21266 International Tire Exhibition and Conference
Crain Communications
1725 Merriman Road
Suite 300
Akron, OH 44313-5283

330-836-9180
Fax: 330-836-1005
E-Mail: cstevens@crain.com
Home Page: www.rubbernews.com

One-hundred and thirty exhibitors with 110 booths.
Frequency: September

21267 PMA Annual Meeting
Polyurethane Manufacturers Association
6737 W Washington Avenue
Suite 1300
Milwaukee, WI 53214

414-431-3094
Fax: 414-276-7704
E-Mail: info@pmahome.org
Home Page: www.pmahome.org

Mike Katz, President
Mike Cocak, VP
Mike Cocak, Secretary
Paul Blasco, Director Public Relations

The Polyurethane Manufacturers Association is the trade association of the cast polyurethane elastomer industry, serving processors of polyurethane products, materials and equipment suppliers and independent agents. PMA exchanges and disseminates information on standards, materials, processes and technical matters, in addition to monitoring regulatory and legislative activity affecting the urethane industry.

21268 Rubber Expo
American Chemical Society-Rubber Division
PO Box 499
Akron, OH 44309-0499

330-972-7814
800-227-5558
Fax: 330-972-5269
E-Mail: help@acs.org
Home Page: www.chemistry.org

Sherri L Poorman, Exhibition Manager

Biennial show of 300 manufacturers and suppliers of equipment, supplies and services for the rubber industry, including machinery, chemicals, raw rubber, finished rubber products, quality control equipment and related equipment.
8,000 Attendees
Frequency: October, Cleveland

21269 Rubber Mini Expo
American Chemical Society-Rubber Division
PO Box 499
Akron, OH 44309-0499
330-972-7814
Fax: 330-972-5269
E-Mail: shbarr@rubber.org
Home Page: www.rubber.org

Sue Barr, Exposition & Future Sites Manager

Biennial show of 150 manufacturers, suppliers and custom services for the rubber industry, including machinery, chemicals, raw rubber, finished rubber products, quality control equipment and related equipment.
3000 Attendees
Frequency: October

21270 Rubber and Plastics Industry Conference of the United Steelworkers of America
5 Gateway Center
Pittsburgh, PA 15220

412-562-6971
Fax: 412-562-6963

John Sellers, Executive VP
90M Attendees
Founded in 1935

Directories & Databases

21271 Rauch Guide to the US Rubber Industry
Grey House Publishing
4919 Route 22
PO Box 56
Amenia, NY 12501

518-789-8700
800-562-2139
Fax: 845-373-6390
E-Mail: books@greyhouse.com
Home Page: www.greyhouse.com
Social Media: Facebook, Twitter

Leslie Mackenzie, Publisher
Richard Gottlieb, Editor

Provides industry structure and current market information about the $39 billion US rubber industry which faces intense inter-material competition and severe government regulation. The report contains a wealth of marketing and related technical information about the busines.
Cost: $595.00
500 Pages
ISBN: 1-592371-30-2
Founded in 1981

21272 Rubber World Blue Book: Materials, Compounding and Machinery
Lippincott & Peto
Po Box 5451
Akron, OH 44334-0451

330-864-2122
Fax: 330-864-5298
Home Page: www.rubberworld.com

Job Lippincott, Owner

Over 850 suppliers of over 8,000 chemicals, materials and compounding ingredients for rubber manufacturers.
Cost: $103.00
Frequency: Annual
Circulation: 4,000

21273 Rubber World: Custom Mixers Directory
Lippincott & Peto
Po Box 5451
Akron, OH 44334-0451

330-864-2122
Fax: 330-864-5298
Home Page: www.rubberworld.com

Job Lippincott, Owner

A list of rubber manufacturers providing custom mixes.
Cost: $3.00
Frequency: Annual

21274 Rubber World: Machinery Suppliers Issue
Lippincott & Peto
Po Box 5451
Akron, OH 44334-0451
330-864-2122
Fax: 330-864-5298
Home Page: www.rubberworld.com

Job Lippincott, Owner

Lists suppliers of used and rebuilt machinery and instrumentation and test equipment to the rubber industry.
Cost: $3.00
Frequency: Annual
ISBN: 0-035957-2 -

21275 Rubber and Plastics News: Rubicana Issue
Crain Communications
1725 Merriman Rd
Suite 300
Akron, OH 44313-5283

330-836-9180
800-678-9595
Fax: 330-836-2831
Home Page: www.crain.com

Robert S Simmons, VP

A list of over 1,000 rubber product manufacturers and suppliers of equipment, services and materials.
Cost: $85.00
Frequency: Annual
Circulation: 15,000

Industry Web Sites

21276 http://gold.greyhouse.com
G.O.L.D Grey House OnLine Databases

Grey House Publishing's online database platform, GOLD, offers Quick Search, Keyword Search and Expert Search for most business sectors including rubber markets. The GOLD platform makes finding the information you need quick and easy - whether you're a novice searcher or an experienced database user. All of Grey House's directory products are available for subscription on the GOLD platform.

21277 www.greyhouse.com
Grey House Publishing

Authoritative reference directories for most business sectors including rubber markets. Users can search the online databases with varied search criteria allowing for custom searches by product category, geographic area, sales volume, keyword, subject and more. Full Grey House catalog and online ordering also available.

21278 www.iisrp.com
Int'l Institute of Synthetic Rubber Producers

For manufacturers of synthetic rubber.

21279 www.itra.com
International Tire and Rubber Association

Information on tire retreading and repairing, new tires, scrap tire reduction and removal equipment, rubber recycling technologies, recycled rubber products and allied services including brake equipment, wheel alignment, tire balancers, tire changers, service trucks, marketing/sales and management programs and computer systems.

21280 www.rma.org
Scrap Tire Management Council

For tire manufacturers marketers of scrap tires.

Associations

21281 **AAA Foundation for Traffic Safety**
607 14th Street NW
Suite 201
Washington, DC 20005

202-638-5944
Fax: 202-638-5943
E-Mail: info@aaafoundation.org
Home Page: www.aaafoundation.org
Social Media: Facebook, Twitter, RSS

Peter Kissinger, President/CEO
Kenneth Johnson, Treasurer
Bruce Hamilton, Manager of Research & Communication
Paul C. Petrillo, Chairman
John Tomlin, Secretary

AAA Foundation for Traffic Safety is dedicated to saving lives and reducing injuries on the roads. It is a not-for-profit, publicly-supported charitable educational and research organization.
Founded in 1947

21282 **ASIS International**
1625 Prince St
Alexandria, VA 22314-2818

703-519-6200
888-968-1968
Fax: 703-519-6299
E-Mail: asis@asisonline.org
Home Page: www.asisonline.org
Social Media: Facebook, Twitter, LinkedIn, You Tube

Richard E. Widup, President-Elect
Geoffrey T. Craighead, President
Dave N. Tyson, Treasurer
David C. Davis, Secretary
Eduard J. Emde, ?Chairman

The largest organization for security professionals. ASIS is dedicated to increasing the effectiveness and productivity of security professionals by developing educational programs and materials that cover broad security interests, such as the ASIS Annual Seminar and Exhibits, as well as specific topics. ASIS also advocates the role and value of the security management profession to the media, governmental entities, and the public.
Founded in 1955

21283 **Academy of Security Educators & Trainers**
PO Box 802
Berryville, VA 22611

540-554-2540
Fax: 540-554-2558
Home Page: www.asetcse.org

Dr Richard W Kobetz, Executive Director
Dr HHA Cooper, President
Mary E Kobetz, Secretary-Treasurer

Non-profit organization of security professionals dedicated to exploring the large spectrum of issues confronting the security field. Meetings are held to discuss, design, develop, and exchange thoughts and ideas in an open forum. Awards the CST (certified security trainer) designation.
300 Members
Founded in 1980

21284 **Advanced Medical Technology Association: AdvaMed**
701 Pennsylvania Ave Nw
Suite 800
Washington, DC 20004-2654

202-783-8700
Fax: 202-783-8750
E-Mail: info@advamed.org
Home Page: www.advamed.org
Social Media: Facebook, Twitter, LinkedIn, You Tube

Stephen J Ubl, President/CEO
David Nexon, Senior Executive VP
Kenneth Mendez, Sr. Executive Vice President
David C. David C., Chairman
Jason Rupp, Vice President

Dedicated to providing members with the advocacy, information, education and tangible solutions necessary for success in a world of increasingly complex medical regulations.
1300 Members

21285 **Advocates for Highway and Auto Safety**
750 1st St NE
Suite 901
Washington, DC 20002

202-408-1711
Fax: 202-408-1699
E-Mail: advocates@saferoads.org
Home Page: www.saferoads.org
Social Media: Facebook, Twitter

Judith Lee Stone, President
Jacqueline Gillan, VP
Judie Pasquini, Director
Peter Kurdock, Advocates' State Coordinator

An organization whose members advocate the support and advancement of highway and auto safety through the implementation of state and federal laws, programs and policies.
Founded in 1989

21286 **American Association for Aerosol Research (AAAR)**
15000 Commerce Parkway
Suite C
Mount Laurel, NJ 08054

877-777-6753
Fax: 856-439-0525
E-Mail: info@aaar.org
Home Page: www.aaar.org

Barbara Wyslouzil, President
Sheryl Ehrman, Vice President Elect
Jay Turner, Vice President
Lynn Russell, Treasurer
Suresh Dhaniyala, Secretary

AAAR is a nonprofit professional organization for scientists and engineers who wish to promote and communicate technical advances in the field of aerosol research. The Association fosters the exchange of information among members and with other disciplines through conferences, symposia and publication of a professional journal. Committed to the development of aerosol and its application to important social issues, AAAR offers an international forum for education, communication and networking.
1000 Members
Founded in 1982

21287 **American Association of Occupational Health Nurses**
2920 Brandywine Rd # 100
Suite 100
Chamblee, GA 30341-5539

770-455-7271
Fax: 850-484-8762
Home Page: www.gonursing.org
Social Media: Facebook, Twitter, LinkedIn

Ann Cox, Executive Director

AAOHN is a principal force in developing and promoting the profession of occupational and environmental health nursing by providing education, resources, and advocacy.
Founded in 1942

21288 **American Association of Poison Control Centers**
3201 New Mexico Ave Nw # 310
Suite 330
Washington, DC 20016-2739

202-895-4259
800-222-1222
Fax: 202-362-8377
E-Mail: info@aapcc.org
Home Page: www.poison.org
Social Media: Facebook

M Litovitz, Executive Director
Toby Litovitz, Executive Director

Nonprofit nationwide organization of poison centers and others interested in the prevention and treatment of poisoning. Promotes the reduction of injury, illness and death from poisonings through public and professional education and scientific research. Promotes universal access to certified regional poison centers.
Founded in 1958

21289 **American Bio-Recovery Association**
39 St.Mary Street
Norwalk, OH 44857

419-663-2819
888-979-2272
Fax: 440-499-9959
Home Page: www.americanbiorecovery.org

James Monath, President

A nationwide non-profit association of crime and trauma scene recovery professionals who are dedicated to upholding the highest technical, ethical and educational guidelines of the biohazard remediation industry.

21290 **American Biological Safety Association**
1200 Allanson Rd
Mundelein, IL 60060-3808

847-949-1517
866-425-1385
Fax: 847-566-4580
E-Mail: info@absa.org
Home Page: www.absa.org

Edward Stygar Iii, Executive Director
Paul J Meechan, President
Marian Downing, President-Elect
Carol McGhan, Treasurer
Julie Johnson, Councilor

ABSA's goals are to provide a professional association that represents the interest and needs of practitioners of biological safety, and to providea forum for the continued and timely exchange of biosafety information.
Founded in 1984

21291 **American Chemical Society**
1155 16th St Nw
Washington, DC 20036-4892

202-872-4600
800-227-5558
Fax: 202-872-4615
E-Mail: service@acs.org
Home Page: www.acs.org

Madeleine Jacobs, CEO
Madeleine Jacobs, Executive Director
Bassam Z. Shakhashiri, President
William F. Carroll, Chair
George M. Bodner, Director Publications

Supports chemists and companies who work with chemicals and their by-products.
158 M Members
Founded in 1876

21292 American College of Occupational and Environmental Medicine
25 Northwest Point Blvd
Suite 700
Elk Grove Village, IL 60007-1030

847-818-1800
Fax: 847-818-9266
E-Mail: acoeminfo@acoem.org
Home Page: www.acoem.org
Social Media: Twitter, YouTube

Kaul Auerbach, Past President
Mark A. Roberts, Vice President
Ronald R. Loeppke, President
Kathryn L. Mueller, Prseident-Elect
James A. Tacci, Secretary-Treasurer

Occupational and environmental medicine is devoted to the prevention and management of occupational and injury, illness and disability, and promotion of health and productivity of workers, thier families and communities.
5000 Members
Founded in 1916

21293 American Conference of Governmental Industrial Hygienists
1330 Kemper Meadow Drive
Cincinnati, OH 45240

513-742-2020
Fax: 513-742-3355
E-Mail: mail@acgih.org
Home Page: www.acgih.org

Robert F. Herrick, Chair
J. Torey Nalbone, Vice Chair
Heather D. Borman, Secretary/ Treasurer
A. Anthony Rizzuto, Executive Director
Susan Arnold, Director

A member-based organization and community of professionals that advances worker health and safety through education and the development and dissemination of scientific and technical knowledge.
Founded in 1938

21294 American Correctional Association
206 N. Washington Street
Alexandria, VA 22314

703-224-0000
Fax: 703-224-0179
E-Mail: IndiaV@aca.org@aca.org
Home Page: www.aca.org
Social Media: Facebook, Twitter, LinkedIn, YouTube

Michael Wade, President
Mary L Livers, President-Elect
Daron Hall, Past President
James A Gondles, Secretary
Lannette C. Linthicum, Treasurer

Formerly known as the National Prison Association.
Founded in 1870

21295 American Fire Safety Council
1909 K St Nw
Suite 400
Washington, DC 20006-1168

202-338-0022
Fax: 202-955-6215
E-Mail: info@fire-safety.net
Home Page: www.fire-safety.net
Social Media: Facebook, Twitter, LinkedIn

Mike Heimowitz, President

Improving fire safety through enhancement of fire codes and standards and promoting responsible use of flame retardants and flame retardant products. AFSC was created to provide a stronger and broader voice on advocacy and safety issues.
Founded in 2003

21296 American Fire Sprinkler Association
12750 Merit Drive
Suite 350
Dallas, TX 75251

214-349-5965
Fax: 214-343-8898
E-Mail: afsainfo@firesprinkler.org
Home Page: www.firesprinkler.org

Steve Muncy, President
Janet Knowles, VP/Marketing & Communications

Nonprofit international association representing open shop fire sprinkler contractors, dedicated to the educational advancement of its members and promotion of the use of automatic sprinkler systems. Offers a convention and exhibition, correspondence course, monthly magazine and a monthly newsletter.
900 Members
Founded in 1981

21297 American Gas Association
400 N Capitol Street NW
Washington, DC 20001

202-824-7000
Fax: 202-824-7092
E-Mail: ykorolevich@aga.org
Home Page: www.aga.org
Social Media: Facebook, Twitter, LinkedIn, YouTube, Flickr, Wordpress

Dave McCurdy, President/CEO
Lawrence T. Borgard, Immediate Past Chairman
Terry D. McCallister, 2nd Vice Chairman
Ronald W. Jibson, Chairman
Gregg S. Kantor, 1st Vice Chairman

The American Gas Association advocates the interests of its members and their customers, and provides information and services promoting efficient demand and supply growth and operational excellence in the safe, reliable and efficient delivery of natural gas.
Founded in 1918

21298 American Industrial Hygiene Association
3141 Fairview Park Drive
Suite 777
Falls Church, VA 22042

703-207-3561
Fax: 703-207-3561
E-Mail: infonet@aiha.org
Home Page: www.aiha.org
Social Media: Facebook, Twitter, LinkedIn, YouTube, RSS

Daniel H. Anna, Vice President
Barbara J. Dawso?n, President
C?hristine A.D. Lorenzo, President-Elect
Steven E. Lacey, Treasurer
Charles F. Redinger, Secretary

AIHA promotes healthy and safe environments by advancing the science, principles, practice, and value of industrial hygiene and occupational and environmental health and safety.
10400 Members
Founded in 1939

21299 American Insurance Association
Ste 400
2101 L St NW
Washington, DC 20037-1542

202-828-7100
Fax: 202-293-1219
E-Mail: info@aiadc.org
Home Page: www.aiadc.org
Social Media: Facebook, Twitter, LinkedIn, YouTube, RSS

Leigh Ann Pusey, President/CEO
J. Stephen Zielezienski, SVP & General Counsel
Joseph Dogiovanni, SVP, State Affairs
David S. Lauer, VP/ Treasurer
Peter R. Foley, VP, Claims Administration

A property, casualty insurance trade organization representing more than 40,000 insurers that write more than $120 billion in premiums each year. AIA member companies offer all types of property-casualty insurance, including personal and commercial auto insurance, commercial property and liability coverage for small businesses, worker's compensation, medical malpractice coverage, and product liability insurance.
40000 Members
Founded in 1866

21300 American National Standards Institute ANSI
1819 L St Nw
11th Floor
Washington, DC 20036

202-293-8020
Fax: 202-293-9287
E-Mail: info@ansi.org
Home Page: www.ansi.org
Social Media: Facebook, Twitter, LinkedIn, YouTube, Google+

Joe Bhatia, President/CEO
Susan Bosc, Manager Membership Services
Tricia Power, Manager, Corporate Governance
James T. Pauley, Chairman
Patricia A. Griffin, Vice President and General Counsel

To enhance the global competition of business and quality of life by promoting and facilitating voluntary consensus standards and conformity assessment systems, and safeguarding their integrity.
1000 Members
Founded in 1916

21301 American Polygraph Association
PO Box 8037
Chattanooga, TN 37414-0037

423-892-3992
800-APA-8037
Fax: 423-894-5435
E-Mail: manager@polygraph.org
Home Page: www.polygraph.org

Robbie Bennett, National Office Manager
Chuck Slupski, President
Barry Cushman, Chairman
Gordon L. Vaughan, General Counsel
Donnie Dutton, VP, government

Representing experienced polygraph examiners in private business; law enforcement and government. Professional APA polygraph examiners administer hundreds of thousands of polygraph exams each year worldwide. The APA establishes standards of ethical practices, techniques, instrumentation and research, as well as provides advanced training and continuing education programs.
3200 Members
Founded in 1966

21302 American Public Health Association
800 I Street NW
Washington, DC 20001

202-777-2742
Fax: 202-777-2534
E-Mail: comments@apha.org
Home Page: www.apha.org

Dr Georges C Benjamin, Executive Director
Joyce R. Gaufin, President
Richard J. Cohen, Treasurer
Pamela Aaltonen, Vice Chair
Shiriki Kumanyika, President Elect

Influencing policies and setting priorities for over 125 years. Thoughout its history it has been in the forefront of numerous efforts to prevent disease and promote health.

21303 American Red Cross
2025 E. St.,NW
Washington, DC 20006

202-303-5214
800-733-2767
Fax: 202-639-3021
E-Mail: info@usa.redcross.org
Home Page: www.redcross.org

Gail J McGovern, President/CEO
Bonnie McElveen-Hunter, Chairman
Brian J. Rhoa, CFO
David Meltzer, General Counsel
Jennifer L. Hawkins, Corporate Secretary

The American Red Cross is where people moblilze to help their neighbors across the street, across the country and across the world, in emergencies. Each year, in communities large and small, victims of some 70,000 disasters turn to the nearly one million volunteers and 35,000 employees of the Red Cross.
31000 Members
Founded in 1881

21304 American Safety & Health Institute
4148 Louis Avenue
Holiday, FL 34691

727-437-7560
800-682-5067
E-Mail: info@ashinstitute.org
Home Page: www.ashinstitute.org
Social Media: Facebook, Twitter, LinkedIn

Frank Swiger, Manager

Nonprofit association of professional safety & health educators providing nationally recognized training programs through more than 5000 approved training centers across the US and in several foreign countries.
30000 Members
Founded in 1996

21305 American Society for Industrial Security
1625 Prince Street
Alexandria, VA 22314-2818

703-519-6200
Fax: 703-519-6299
E-Mail: asis@asisonline.org
Home Page: www.asisonline.org

Geoffrey T. Craighead, President
Michael J Stack, CEO
Dave N. Tyson, Treasurer
David C. Davis, Secretary
Eduard J. Emde, Chairman

ASIS International (ASIS) is the largest organization for security professionals, with more than 33,000 members worldwide. ASIS is dedicated to increasing the effectiveness and productivity of security professionals by developing educational programs and materials that address broad security interests, such as the ASIS Annual Seminar and Exhibits, as well as specific security topics.
33000 Members
Founded in 1955

21306 American Society for Nondestructive Testing
1711 Arlingate Lane
PO Box 28518
Columbus, OH 43228-0518

614-274-6003
800-222-2768
Fax: 614-274-6899
Home Page: www.asnt.org
Social Media: Twitter, LinkedIn, YouTube

Michelle Thomas, Executive Director's Admin
Roger Engelbart, Vice- President
L. Terry Clausing, Secreatry/ Treasurer
Robert J. Potter, Chair
Raymond G. Morasse, President

ASNT is the world's largest technical society for nondestructive tests (NDT) professionals.
12000 Members
Founded in 1941

21307 American Society of Crime Laboratory Directors (ASCLD)
139A Technology Drive
Garner, NC 27529

919-773-2044
Fax: 919-861-9930
E-Mail: president@ascld.org
Home Page: www.ascld.org

Jay Henry, President
Jodi Wolf, Secretary
Brady Mills, President-Elect
Jean Stover, Executive Director
Ramona Robertson, Office Administrator

The American Society of Crime Laboratory Directors (ASCLD) is a nonprofit professional society of crime laboratory directors and forensic science managers dedicated to providing excellence in forensic science through leadership and innovation.
Founded in 1973

21308 American Society of Criminology
1314 Kinnear Rd
Suite 212
Columbus, OH 43212-1156

614-292-9207
Fax: 614-292-6767
E-Mail: asc@asc41.com
Home Page: www.asc41.com

Candace Kruttschnitt, President-Elect
Chris Eskridge, Executive Director
Joanne Belknap, President
Karen Heimer, Vice President
Bonnie Fisher, Treasurer

The American Society of Criminology is an international organization concerned with criminology, embracing scholary, scientific and profesional knowledge concerning the etiology, prevention, control, and treatment of crime and delinquency.

21309 American Society of Industrial Security
1625 Prince St
Alexandria, VA 22314-2818

703-519-6200
Fax: 703-519-6299
E-Mail: asis@asisonline.org
Home Page: www.asisonline.org
Social Media: Facebook, Twitter, LinkedIn, YouTube

Eduard J. Emde, Chairman
Geoffrey T. Craighead, President
Michael J. Stack, CEO
Dave N. Tyson, Treasurer
David C. Davis, Secretary

The largest international organization for professionals who are responsible for security, including managers and directors of security.
33000 Members
Founded in 1955

21310 American Society of Mechanical Engineers
Two Park Ave
New York, NY 10016-5990

800-843-2763
800-843-2763
973-882-1170
Fax: 202-429-9417
E-Mail: customercare@asme.org
Home Page: www.asme.org

J. Robert Sims, Jr., President- Nominee
Madiha Kotb, President
Marc Goldsmith, Immediate Past President
Warren DeVries, Secretary/ Treasurer
Thomas G. Loughlin, Executive Director

Through its initiatives in education, advocacy and public policy, the ASME. Foundation impacts all aspects of the mechanical engineering community.
120 M Members
Founded in 1880

21311 American Society of Safety Engineers
1800 E Oakton Street
Des Plaines, IL 60018

847-699-2929
Fax: 847-768-3434
E-Mail: customerservice@asse.org
Home Page: www.asse.org
Social Media: Facebook, Twitter

Kathy A. Seabrook, President
Fred J. Fortman, Secretary & Executive Treasurer
Patricia M. Ennis, President-Elect
Michael Belcher, SVP
Stephanie A. Helgerman, VP, Finance

The oldest and largest professional safety organization. Its members manage, supervise and consult on safety, health, and environmental issues in industry, insurance, government and education.
30000 Members
Founded in 1911

21312 American Traffic Safety Services Association
15 Riverside Parkway
Suite 100
Fredericksburg, VA 22406-1022

540-368-1701
800-272-8772
Fax: 540-368-1717
Home Page: www.atssa.com
Social Media: Facebook, Twitter, Google+

Douglas Danko, Chairman
Scott Seeley, Chairman Elect
Brook Jerzyk, At-large-Director
Sue Riss, Foundation President (Non-Voting)
Debra Lee Ricker, Pavement Marking Division- Director

The American Traffic Safety Services Association, is an international trade association founded in 1969. It has has represented companies and individuals in the traffic control and roadway safety industry.
1600 Members
Founded in 1969

21313 American Welding Society
8669 NW 36 St.
Suite 130
Miami, FL 33126-6672

305-443-9353
800-443-9353
Fax: 305-443-7559
E-Mail: info@aws.org
Home Page: www.aws.org

Dennis Harwig, VP of Technology & Business Dev
Gesana Villegas, CFO
Coleen Mitchell, Meetings Manager
Cassie Burrell, Senior Associate Executive Director
Jim Lankford, Managing Director

The mission of the American Welding Society is to advance the science, technology and application of welding and allied joining and cutting processes, including brazing, soldering and thermal spraying.
50000 Members
Founded in 1919

21314 Associated Locksmiths of America
3500 Easy St
Dallas, TX 75247

214-819-9733
800-532-2562
Fax: 214-819-9736
E-Mail: aloa@aloa.org
Home Page: www.aloa.org
Social Media: Facebook, Twitter, LinkedIn

David Lowell, Executive Director
Charles Gibson, Secretary

ALOA is an international professional organization of highly qualified security professionals engaged in consulting, sales, installation and maintenance of locks, keys safes, premises security, access controls, alarms, and other security related endeavors.
10M Members
Founded in 1956

21315 Association of Air Medical Services
909 N. Washington St.
Suite 410
Alexandria, VA 22314

703-836-8732
Fax: 703-836-8920
E-Mail: information@aams.org
Home Page: www.aams.org

Dawn Mancuso, Executive Director
Melissa Porter, Membership Manager
David P. Thompson, Vice Chair
Rick Sherlock, CEO & President
Dave Evans, tresaurer

AAMS is built on the idea that representation from a variety of medical transport services and businesses can be brought together to share information, collectively resolve problems and provide leadership in the medical transport community.
581 Members
Founded in 1980

21316 Association of Certified Fraud Examiners
716 West Ave
Austin, TX 78701-2727

512-478-9000
800-245-3321
Fax: 512-478-9297
E-Mail: memberservices@acfe.com
Home Page: www.acfe.com
Social Media: Facebook, Twitter, LinkedIn

John D. Gill, VP- Education
James D. Ratley, President/CEO
Joseph T. Wells, Chairman
Bruce Dorris, Program Director & Vice President
Jaenette LeVie, VP- Administration

The mission of the Association of Certified Fraud Examiners is to reduce the incidence of fraud and white-collar crime and to assist its members in its dectection and prevention.
35000 Members
Founded in 1988

21317 Association of Christian Investigators
2553 Jackson Keller
Suite 200
San Antonio, TX 78230

210-342-0509
Fax: 210-342-0731
E-Mail: kelmar@kelmarpi.com
Home Page: www.a-c-i.org

Kelly E Riddle, President
Hugo Briseno, Director, Georgia
Timothy Friend, Director, California (Northern)
Andrew Smart, Director
Paul Jacob, Director, Alaska

Provides a spirit-filled organization that promoste the investigative profession in a non-competitive atmosphere. Provides an environment in which investigators can create meaningful and long-term relationships with other investigators outside the professional bonds.
500 Members
Founded in 1996

21318 Association of Contingency Planners
7044 S 13th St
Oak Creek, WI 53154

414-908-4945
800-445-4227
Fax: 414-768-8001
E-Mail: j.tucker@naspa.com
Home Page: www.naspa.com
Social Media: LinkedIn

Leo A Wrobel, President
Scott Sherer, Chairman
Dan Newton, Director Education
Jim Coleman, Director Public Relations
Sharon Wrobel, Treasurer/Director/ Secretary

Nonprofit trade association dedicated to fostering continued professional growth and development in effective contingency and business resumption planning.
1700 Members
Founded in 1986

21319 Association of Professional Industrial Hygienists
2288 Gunbarrel Rd
Ste 154/364
Chattanooga, TN 37421

888-481-3006
E-Mail: APIH@epbfi.com
Home Page: www.apih.usў

Offers credentialing to industrial hygienists.
Founded in 1994

21320 Association of Public Safety Communication Officials-International
351 N Williamson Boulevard
Daytona Beach, FL 32114-1112

386-322-2500
888-272-6911
Fax: 386-322-2501
E-Mail: apco@apcointl.org
Home Page: www.apcointl.org
Social Media: Facebook, Twitter, LinkedIn, psconnect

Terry Hall, Immediate Past President
Gigi Smith, President
John W. Wright, 1st VP
Brent Lee, 2nd VP
Derek Poarch, Ex-Officio

The Association of Public-Safety Communications Officials International (APCO) is a member driven association of communications professionals that provides leadership; influences public safety communications decisions of government and industry; promotes professional development; and, fosters the development and use of technology for the benefit of the public.
16000 Members
Founded in 1935

21321 Association of State Dam Safety Officials
239 S. Limestone
Lexington, KY 40508

859-550-2788
E-Mail: info@damsafety.org
Home Page: www.damsafety.orgў

Michael Johnson, President
Jim Pawloski, President Elect
Tom Woosley, Past President
Jon Garton, Secretary
Dusty Myers, Treasurer

Organization for safety officials overseeing state dams.
Founded in 1983

21322 Association of State Floodplain Managers
575 D'Onoforio Dr.
Suite 200
Madison, WI 53719
608-828-3000
Fax: 608-828-6319
E-Mail: asfpm@floods.org
Home Page: www.floods.org
Social Media: Facebook, Twitter, LinkedIn

Larry A Larson, DirectorEmeritus, Sr. Policy Adviso
Ceil Strauss, Vice Chair
Joe Ruggeri, Treasurer
Joy Duperault, Secretary
Bill Nechamen, Chair

It is the mission of the Association to mitigate the losses, costs and human suffering caused by flooding and to promote wise use of the natural and beneficial functions of floodplains.
6500 Members
Founded in 1976

21323 Automatic Fire Alarm Association
PO Box 1569
14 Sammy McGhee Blvd., Suite 103
Jasper, GA 30143

678-454-3473
Fax: 678-454-3474
E-Mail: fire-alarm@afaa.org
Home Page: www.afaa.org
Social Media: Facebook, Twitter, LinkedIn, Yahoo

Thomas P Hammerberg, President/Executive Director
Rodger Reiswig, Secretary
Jeanne Hammerberg, Office Manager
Art Black, Chairman
William Koffel, Treasurer

Striving to be the foremost industry advocate organization dedicated to improving the quality, reliability and value of fire and life safety systems.
Founded in 1953

21324 Aviation Safety Institute
PO Box 2480
Carlingford, AS NSW 2118

128-819-2455
Fax: 128-572-5248
E-Mail: sales@asi.net.au
Home Page: www.asi.net.au
Social Media: Twitter, LinkedIn

Edward H Wachs, President/Chair
Thomas Clevinger, VP/Treasurer

An aviation safety research center established in 1973. Studying the most overlooked, most important area of aviation safety.
Founded in 1973

21325 Board of Certified Safety Professionals
2301 W. Bradley Avenue
Champaign, IL 61821

217-359-9263
Fax: 217-359-0055
E-Mail: bcsp@bcsp.org
Home Page: www.bcsp.org
Social Media: Facebook, Twitter, LinkedIn, Google+

Angie Kluth, Chief accounting Officer
Andrea Kamradt, Examination Manager
Treasa Turnbeaugh, CEO

Robert Schneller, COO
Teresa Hasken, CFO

Operating solely as a peer certification board with the purpose of certifying practitioners in the safety profession.
Founded in 1969
Mailing list available for rent: 20,000 names

21326 Business Disaster Preparedness Council
Lee County Emergency Management
PO Box 398
Ft. Meyers, FL 33902-398

239-399-9779
Fax: 941-477-3636
E-Mail: board@leegov.com

Bob Lee, Owner

Public and private partnership whose goal it is to assist business in planning for and recovering from natural disasters and emergencies.
Founded in 1998

21327 CPWR: Center for Construction Research and Training
8484 Georgia Ave
Suite 1000
Silver Spring, MD 20910

301-578-8500
Fax: 301-578-8572
E-Mail: cpwrwebsite@cpwr.com
Home Page: www.cpwr.com
Social Media: Facebook, Twitter, RSS

Sean McGarvey~, President
Mary Watters, Director Communications Department
Chris Trahan, Deputy Director
Pete Stafford, Executive Director
Brent Booker, Secretary/ Treasurer

CPWR is committed to preventing illness, injury, and death in the construction industry through its safety and health research, broad network of trainers, and on-going outreach to workers and employers.
Founded in 1990

21328 Canada Safety Council
1020 Thomas Spratt Place
Ottawa, ON K1G 5L5

613-739-1535
Fax: 613-739-1566
E-Mail: cs@safety-council.org
Home Page: www.safety-council.org
Social Media: Facebook, Twitter

Jack Smith, President
Raynald Marchand, General Manager, Programs
Judy Lavergne, Secretary
Peter Slivar, Manager, Finance & Administration
Lewis Smith, Traffic Coordinator

The Canada Safety Counil is a national, non-government, charitable organization dedicated to safety. Mission is to lead in the national effort to reduce preventable deaths, injuries and economic loss in public and private places throughout Canada.
Founded in 1968

21329 Canadian Alarm & Security Association
50 Acadia Avenue
Suite 201
Markham, ON L3R 0B3

905-513-0622
800-538-9919
Fax: 905-513-0624
E-Mail: staff@canasa.org
Home Page: www.canasa.org
Social Media: Facebook, Twitter, LinkedIn

JF Champagne, Ex-Officio
Carl Jorgensen, Vice president
Carol Cairns, Treasurer
Kevin Hincks, Secretary
Philippe Bouchard, President

A national non-profit organization dedicated to promoting the interests of its members and the safety and security of all Canadians.
Founded in 1977

21330 Central Station Alarm Association
8150 Leesburg Pike
Suite 700
Vienna, VA 22182

703-242-4670
Fax: 703-242-4675
E-Mail: techadmin@csaaintl.org
Home Page: www.csaaul.org
Social Media: Facebook, Twitter, LinkedIn, RSS

Steve Doyle, Executive VP/CEO
Joe Nuccio, 2nd VP
Jay Hauhn, President
Graham Westphal, Secretary
Ivan Spector, Secretary

Represents companies offering security (alarm) monitoring systems through a central station. It also represents companies that provide services and products to the industry.
300+ Members
Founded in 1950

21331 Clery Center
110 Gallagher Road
Wayne, PA 19087

484-580-8754
888-251-7959
Fax: 484-580-8759
Home Page: www.securityoncampus.org
Social Media: Facebook, Twitter, LinkedIn, YouTube

Constance B. Clery, Co-Founder
Howard K. Clery, Co-Founder
Benjamin F. Clery, Treasurer
Mary Swanson, Chairwoman
Christopher F. McConnell, Vice Chairman

A non-profit organization whose mission is to prevent violence, substance abuse and other crimes in college and university campus commumities across the United States, and to compassionately assist the vicitims of these crimes.
Founded in 1986

21332 Commercial Vehicle Safety Alliance
6303 Ivy Lane
Suite 310
Greenbelt, MD 20770-6319

301-830-6143
Fax: 301-830-6144
E-Mail: cvsahq@cvsa.org
Home Page: www.cvsa.org
Social Media: Facebook, Twitter, LinkedIn

Stephen Campbell, Executive Director
Paul M Bomgardner, Administration Director

The Commercial Vehicle Safety Alliance (CVSA) is a nonprofit organization, established to promote an environment free of commercial vehicle accidents and incidents. Our mission is to promote commercial motor vehicle safty and security by providing leadership to enforcement, industry and policy makers.
540 Members
Founded in 1980

21333 Computer Security Institute
350 Hudson St.
Suite 300
New York, NY 10014

415-947-6320
Fax: 415-947-6023
E-Mail: csi@ubm.com
Home Page: www.gocsi.com
Social Media: Facebook, Twitter, LinkedIn

Jody Nurre, Sales Director
Mary Griffin, Membership Director
Robert Richardson, Director
Terri Curran, Director
Cheryl Jackson, Information Systems

Computer Security Institute serves the needs of information security professionals through membership, educational events, security surveys and awareness tools.
Founded in 1974

21334 Consumer Data Industry Association
1090 Vermont Ave Nw
Suite 200
Washington, DC 20005-4964

202-371-0910
Fax: 202-371-0134
E-Mail: cdia@cdiaonline.org
Home Page: www.cdiaonline.org

Norm Magnuson, VP
Betty Byrnes, Member Services

The Consumer Data Industry Association is an international trade association, founded in 1906, that represents consumer information companies that provide fraud prevention and risk management products, credit and mortgage reports, tenant and employment screening services, check fraud and verification services, and collection services.
395 Members
Founded in 1906

21335 Conveyor Equipment Manufacturers Association (CEMA)
5672 Strand CT
Suite 2
Naples, FL 34110

239-514-3441
Fax: 239-514-3470
E-Mail: phil@cemanet.org
Home Page: www.cemanet.org
Social Media: Facebook, Twitter, LinkedIn

Warren Chandler, President
Jerry Heathman, VP
Robert Reinfried, Executive VP
Jim McKnight, Secretary
Garry Abraham, Tresaurer

Involved in writing industry standards, the CEMA seeks to promote among its members and the industry standardization of design manufacture and application on a voluntary basis and in such manner as will not impede development of conveying machinery and component parts or lessen competition. CEMA sponsors an annual Engineering Conference that allows Member Company Engineers to meet and develop or improve CEMA Consensus Industry Standards and National Standards that affect the conveyor industry.
96 Members
Founded in 1933

21336 Council of International Investigators
783 N York Rd.
Elmhurst, IL 60126-1313

630-941-1700
888-759-8884
Fax: 206-367-8777
E-Mail: office@cii2.org
Home Page: www.cii2.org

Alan Marr, Executive Regional Director
John Sexton, President

Eduard Sigrist, Past president/ Treasurer
Debbra Macdonald, Secretary
Galen Clements, VP/ Executive Regional Director

The Council of International Investigators was formed to encourage a greater association among owners and operators of investigation agencies while developing mutual trust and respect.
Founded in 1955

21337 Council on Certification of Health, Environmental & Technologists
2301 W. Bradley Avenue
Champaign, IL 61821

217-359-9263
Fax: 217-359-0055
E-Mail: cchest@cchest.org
Home Page: www.cchest.org
Social Media: Facebook, Twitter, LinkedIn, Google+

Angie Kluth, Chief accounting Officer
Andrea Kamradt, Examination Manager
Treasa Turnbeaugh, CEO
Robert Schneller, COO
Teresa Hasken, CFO

CCHEST is recognized as the leader in high-quality, third-party accredited health, safety, and environmental credentialing for technologists, technicians, supervisors, and workers.
3000 Members
Founded in 1969

21338 Dangerous Goods Advisory Council
1100 H St Nw
Suite 740
Washington, DC 20005

202-289-4550
Fax: 202-289-4074
E-Mail: info@dgac.org
Home Page: www.dgac.org
Social Media: Facebook, Twitter

Frits Wybenga, Technical dircetor
Vaughn Arthur, Secreatry & President
Greg Allen, Treasurer
Deborah Hooper, Chair
Ben Barrett, Vice Chair

DGAC fulfills its mission by providing education, technical assistance and information to the private and public sectors. Members incude shippers in the chemical, petroleum, and pharmaceutical industries, manufacturers, carriers, container manufacturers and reconditioners, emergency/waste clean-up companies, trade associations, and others involved in the transport of dangerous goods.
Founded in 1978

21339 Electrical Safety Foundation International
1300 N 17th Street
Suite 100
Rosslyn, VA 22209

703-841-3229
Fax: 703-841-3329
E-Mail: info@esfi.org
Home Page: www.esfi.org
Social Media: Facebook, Twitter, YouTube

David Tallman, Chairman
John Engel, Vice Chairman
Brett Brenner, President
Even Gaddis, Treasurer
Barbara Guthrie, Secretary

The mission of the Electrical Safety Foundation International (ESFI) is to advocate electrical safety in the home and in the workplace in order to reduce electrically-related fatalities, injuries and property loss. ESFI is committed to: Being the unbiased authority in electrical safety issues for consumers, the workforce, and the media; Identifying and addressing evolving electrical safety needs; Advocating safety technology, compliance with codes and standards, and risk-reducing behaviors.
Founded in 1994

21340 Electronic Security Association
6333 North State Highway 161
Suite 350
Irving, TX 75038

972-807-6800
888-447-1689
Fax: 972-807-6883
Home Page: www.esaweb.org
Social Media: Facebook, Twitter, LinkedIn

Marshall Marinace, President
Roy Pollack, Vice President
Merlin Guilbeau, Executive Director
Jon Sargent, Secretary
Tom Eggebrecht, Treasurer

Trade association representing the electronic security industry.
Founded in 1948

21341 Environmental Information Association
6935 Wisconsin Ave
Suite 306
Chevy Chase, MD 20815-6112

301-961-4999
888-343-4342
Fax: 301-961-3094
E-Mail: info@eia-usa.org
Home Page: www.cia-usa.org

Kevin Cannan, Prseident- Elect
Chris Gates, Vice Prseident
Mike Schrum, President
joy Finch, Secretary
Stve Fulford, Treasurer

Nonprofit organization dedicated to providing environmental information to individuals, members and industry. Disseminates information on the abatement of asbestos and lead-based paint, indoor air quality, safety and health issues, analytical issues and environmental site assessments.

21342 Executive Protein Institute
Executive Protection Institute
16 Penn Plaza
Suite 1130
New York, NY 10001

212-268-4555
Fax: 212-563-4783
E-Mail: info@personalprotection.com
Home Page: www.personalprotection.com

John Negus, Asst. Executive Director
Jerry Heying, Executive Director
Eugene Ferrara, Chief Instructor
John Musser, Chief to Staff
Ana Paula Alfonso, Operations Director

A non-profit professional society whose members include academics, trainers, students, law enforcement and government officials, self-employed professionals, security officers, directors from major intenational corporations, security service organizations, and communications, energy, retail, chemicals, insurance, petroleum and utility companies.
2800 Members
Founded in 1978

21343 False Alarm Reduction Association
10024 Vanderbilt Circle
Unit 4
Rockville, MD 20850

301-519-9237
Fax: 301-519-9508
Home Page: www.faraonline.org

Brad Shipp, Executive Director

Primarily made up of persons employed by government and public safety agencies in charge of, or working in, False Alarm Reduction Units. The goal is to assist these individuals in reducing false alarms for their jurisdiction.
Founded in 1997

21344 Federal Law Enforcement Officers Association
7945 MacArthur Blvd.
Ste 201
Cabin John, MD 20818

202-870-5503
866-553-5362
Fax: 717-932-2262
E-Mail: fleoa@fleoa.org
Home Page: www.fleoa.org
Social Media: Facebook, Twitter

Jon Adler, National President
Nate Catura, National Executive VP
Chris Schoppmeyer, Vp- Agency affairs
lazaro Cosme, VP-Operations
Frank Terri, VP-Legislative affairs

Founded by a group of concerned federal agents from Customs, the IRS, FBI and INS, its goal is to assure that legal assistance and representation are a phone call away.
24000 Members
Founded in 1977

21345 Financial & Security Products Association (FSPA)
1024 Mebane Oaks Rd.
Suite 273
Mebane, NC 27302
919-648-0664
800-843-6082
Fax: 919-648-0670
E-Mail: info@fspa1.com
Home Page: www.fspa1.com

J. James Cozzi, Chairman
Randy Hall, President
Gene Polito, Director
Linda Abell, Vice President
L.A. Amith, Secretary/ Treasurer

Independent dealers, manufacturers and associates whose outstanding products and services give financial institutions a crucial edge in performance, efficiency and economy.
Founded in 1973

21346 Fire Apparatus Manufacturers' Association (FAMA)
PO Box 397
Lynnfield, MA 01940

781-334-2911
Fax: 781-334-2911
E-Mail: info@fama.org
Home Page: www.fama.org

Harold Boer, President
Bruce Whitehouse, VP

Membership association for manufacturers of emergency vehicles and components affixed to or carried upon the vehicle.
125 Members
Founded in 1946

21347 Fire Equipment Manufacturers' Association
1300 Sumner Avenue
Cleveland, OH 44115

216-241-7333
Fax: 216-241-0105
E-Mail: fema@femalifesafety.org
Home Page: www.femalifesafety.org

Social Media: YouTube, Wordpress, Slideshare

The premier trade association representing leading brands, and spanning dozens of product categories, related to fire protection.
27 Members
Founded in 1925

21348 Fire Suppression Systems Association
5024 R Campbell Boulevard
Baltimore, MD 21236

410-931-8100
Fax: 410-931-8111
E-Mail: fssa@clemonsmgmt.com
Home Page: www.fssa.net
Social Media: Facebook, Twitter, LinkedIn

Matt Euson, Director
Carla Pizzarello, Immediate Past President
Eric Burkland, Vice President
Tim Carman, Secretary/ Treasurer
Dale Kent, President

An organization of manufacturers, suppliers, and design-installers, dedicated to providing a higher level of fire protection. Members are specialists in protecting high value special hazardareas from fire.
Founded in 1982

21349 Flight Safety Foundation
801 N. Fairfax Street
Suite 400
Alexandria, VA 22314-1774

703-739-6700
Fax: 703-739-6708
Home Page: www.flightsafety.org
Social Media: Facebook, Twitter, LinkedIn

Capt. Kevin L. Hiatt, President/CEO
Stephanie Mackin, Support Services Manager
David Barger, Tresurer
David McMillan, Chair
Kenneth P. Quinn, General Counsel & Secretary

Flight Safety Foundation is an independent, nonprofit, international organization engaged in research, auditing, education, advocacy and publishing to improve aviation safety. The Foundation's mission is to pursue the continuous improvement of global aviation safety and the prevention of accidents.
Founded in 1947

21350 Homeland Security Industries Association
666 11th Street NW
Suite 315
Washington, DC 20001

202-386-6471
Fax: 202-331-8191
E-Mail: info@hsianet.org
Home Page: www.hsianet.org

Brenda Boone, Owner

Nonprofit group providing a mechanism for government and the private sector to coordinate on a wide range of homeland security issues. Monitors legislation, regulations and hearings, provides training, and develops position papers reflecting industry concerns.
200+ Members
Founded in 2002

21351 Institute for Health & Productivity Management
17470 N. Pacesetter Way
Scottsdale, AZ 85255

480-305-2100
Fax: 480-305-2189
E-Mail: sean@ihpm.org
Home Page: www.ihpm.org

Sean Sullivan, President/CEO
W C Williams III, Senior VP & CFO
Pamella Thomas, Chief Medical Officer
Steve Priddy, Executive Director
Deborah Love, EVP & COO

Nonprofit organization making employee health an investment in corporate success through enhanced workplace performance.
Founded in 1997

21352 Institute for Intergovernmental Research
PO Box 12729
Tallahassee, FL 32317-2729

850-385-0600
Fax: 850-422-3529
E-Mail: nygc@iir.com
Home Page: www.iir.com

Keith G Burt, Advisory Board
Emory B. Williams, Chairman
D. Douglas Bodrero, President
Bob Cummings, Executive Vice President
Gina Hartsfield, Senior Vice President

21353 Insurance Institute for Highway Safety
1005 N Glebe Rd
Suite 800
Arlington, VA 22201

703-247-1500
Fax: 703-247-1678
E-Mail: rrader@iihs.org
Home Page: www.iihs.org
Social Media: Twitter, YouTube, RSS

Adrian Loud, President
Russ Rader, SVP, Communications
Eric Williams, Attorney
Shelly Shelton, Senior Legal Administrator
brenda O'Donnell, VP, InsurerRelations

The Insurance Institute for Highway Safety is a nonprofit research and communications organization funded by auto insurers.

21354 Int'l Association for Counterterrorism & Security Professionals
PO Box 10265
Arlington, VA 22210

201-461-5422
E-Mail: acsp@aol.com
Home Page: www.iacsp.com

Steven Fustero, Executive Director

Our goals include creating a center of information and educational services for those concerned about the challenges now facing all free societies, and promoting professional ethics in the counter terrorism field.
Founded in 1992

21355 International Association For Healthcare Security and Safety
PO Box 5038, Glendale Heights
Illinois, US 60139

630-529-3913
888-353-0990
Fax: 630-529-4139
E-Mail: info@iahss.org
Home Page: www.iahss.org
Social Media: Facebook

David LaRose, President
Jeff A. Young, President Elect
Ben Scaglione, Vice President
Colleen Kucera, Executive Director
Nancy Felesena, Executive Assistant

An association dedicated to professionals involved in managing and directing security and safety in healthcare establishments.
Founded in 1968

21356 International Association for Identification
2131 Hollywood Blvd.
Suite 403
Hollywood, FL 33020

954-589-0628
Fax: 954-589-0657
Home Page: www.theiai.org
Social Media: Facebook

Bridget Lewis, 2nd VP
Lesley Hammer, President
Steve Johnson, 1st VP
Phyllis Karasov, legal Counsel
Glen Calhoun, COO

This is a forum where forensic specialists worldwide can interact as a whole. The main focus of any forensic organization is training and research to ensure all specialists maintain the highest levels of integrity and professionalism in order to meet the constant challenges to our individual disciplines.
Founded in 1915

21357 International Association for Computer Systems
6 Swarthmore Lane
Dix Hills, NY 11746

631-499-1616
Fax: 631-462-9178
E-Mail: iacssjalex@aol.com
Home Page: www.iacss.com

Robert J Wilk, President

Promotes the security of computer information systems. Certifies individuals as Computer Systems Security Professionals.
Founded in 1981

21358 International Association for Healthcare Security and Safety
PO Box 5038
Glendale Heights, IL 60139

630-529-3913
888-353-0990
Fax: 630-529-4139
E-Mail: info@iahss.org
Home Page: www.iahss.org

Lisa Pryse, President
Martin Green, Member-at-Large
Marilyn Hollier, President-Elect
Dana Frentz, VP/Treasurer
David LaRose, VP/Secretary

Nonprofit professional organization of healthcare security and safety executives around the world. Works to improve and professionalize security and safety in healthcare facilities through the exchange of information and experiences among members. A magazine, newsletter and an annual meeting are benefits of membership.
1700 Members
Founded in 1968

21359 International Association of Arson Investigators
2111 Baldwin Ave
Suite 203
Crofton, MD 21114

410-451-3473
800-468-4224
Fax: 410-451-9049
Home Page: www.firearson.com
Social Media: Facebook, Twitter, LinkedIn, YouTube

Rob Rush, President
Peter Mansi, 1st VP
Dan Heenan, 2nd VP
Roger Krupp, Past President
Rick Jones, Director

Dedicated to improving the professional development of fire and explosion investigators by

being the global resource for fire investigation, technology and research
7500 Members
Founded in 1949

21360 International Association of Black Professional Firefighters
1200 G St. nW
Suite 800
Washington, DC 20005

202-434-4526
Fax: 202-434-8707
E-Mail: iabpff@email.msn.com
Home Page: www.iabpff.org

James Hill, President
Sam Aubrey, Treasurer
Kenyatta Smith, EVP
Melanie Anderson, Financial Secreatry
Freddie Jackson, Sergeant at Arms

Promotes interracial progress throughout the fire service and encourages African American firefighters to seek elevated ranks. Offers an annual convention, education courses an an online resource page.
Founded in 1970

21361 International Association of Bomb Technicians and Investigators
1120 International Parkway
Suite 129
Fredericksburg, VA 22406

540-752-4533
Fax: 540-752-2796
E-Mail: admin@iabti.org
Home Page: www.iabti.org
Social Media: Facebook, Twitter, LinkedIn

Ralph Way, Executive Director

The IABTI is an independent, non-profit, professional association formed for countering the criminal use of explosives. This is accomplished through the exchange of training, expertise and information among personnel employed in the fields of law enforcement, emergency services, the military, forensic science and other related fields.
Founded in 1973

21362 International Association of Campus Law Enforcement Administrators
342 N Main Street
West Hartford, CT 06117-2507

860-586-7517
Fax: 860-586-7550
E-Mail: info@iaclea.org
Home Page: www.iaclea.org
Social Media: Facebook, LinkedIn

Peter J Berry, Chief Staff Officer
Anne P. Glavin, Immediate Past President
Vickie L. Weaver, President
David L. Perry, President- Elect
Jasper Cooke, Treasurer

Advances public safety for educational institutions by providing educational resources, advocacy and professional development.
Founded in 1958

21363 International Association of Chiefs of Police
44 Canal Center Plaza
Suite 200
Alexandria, VA 22314

703-836-6767
800-THE-IACP
Fax: 703-836-4543
E-Mail: information@theiacp.org
Home Page: www.theiacp.org
Social Media: Facebook, Twitter, RSS, YouTube

Mary Ann Viverette, President
Daniel N Rosenblatt, Executive Director

The association's goals are to advance the science and art of police services; to develop and disseminate improved administrative. technical and operation practices and promote their use in police work; to foster police cooperation and the exchange of information and experience among police administrators throughout the world; to bring about recruitment and training in the police profession of qualified person.
15000 Members
Founded in 1893

21364 International Association of Crime Analysts
9218 Metcalf Ave.
Suite 364
Overland Park, KS 66212

919-940-3883
800-609-3419
E-Mail: iaca@iaca.net
Home Page: www.iaca.net
Social Media: Facebook, Twitter, LinkedIn, RSS

Ericka Jackson, VP, Membership
Susan C. Smith, President
Carolyn Cassidy, VP, Administration
Tamara Otley, Treasurer
Dawn Clausius, Secretary

The International Association of Crime Analysts was formed in 1990 to help crime analysts around the world improve their skills and make valuable contacts, to help law enforcement agencies make the best use of crime analysis, and to advocate for standards of performance and technique within the profession itself. This is accomplished through training, networking, and publications.
Founded in 1990

21365 International Association of Dive Rescue Specialists
Box 171
8103 East US Highway
Avon, IN 46123

317-464-9787
800-423-7911
Fax: 317-641-0730
E-Mail: info@iadrs.org
Home Page: www.iadrs.org

Blades Robinson, Executive Director
Susan Watson, Operations Director
David Owens, Dir. Of communications
Fred Jackson, Advisory Board
Steven Orusa, Board of Directors

IADRS is dedicated to helping water rescue professionals stay informed about advances in training, equipment, and life saving techniques.
Founded in 1977

21366 International Association of Fire Chiefs
4025 Fair Ridge Dr
Fairfax, VA 22033

703-273-0911
Fax: 703-273-9363
E-Mail: jashley@iafc.org
Home Page: www.iafc.org
Social Media: Facebook, LinkedIn, RSS

Mark Light, Executive Director
Chief Stephen Dean, 2nd VP
Chief William R Metcalf, President and Chairman of the Board
Chief G. Keith Bryant, 1st VP
Chief Richard R Carrizzo, Treasurer

Provides leadership to career and volunteer chief, chief fire officers and managers of emergency service organization throughout the international community through vision, information, education, services and representation to enhance their professionalsim and capabilities.
12000 Members
Founded in 1873

21367 International Association of Firefighters
1750 New York Ave Nw
Suite 300
Washington, DC 20006-5395

202-737-8484
Fax: 202-737-8418
E-Mail: pr@iaff.org
Home Page: www.iaff.org
Social Media: Facebook, Twitter

Harold Schaitberger, President
Jim Lee, Chief of Operations
Peter L. Gorman, Chief of Staff
Thomas H. Miller, Secretary/ Treasurer
William Romaka, 1st VP

Represents city and county firefighters and state and federal workers such as forestry firefighters and emergency medical workers at certain industrial facilities. Addressed are health and safety, labor relations, training, hazardous materials and burn injuries and education.
240k Members
Founded in 1903

21368 International Association of Personal Protection Agents
PO Box 266
Arlington Heights, IL 60006-0266

847-870-8007
Fax: 847-870-8990
E-Mail: proproserv@aol.com
Home Page: www.iappa.net
Social Media: Facebook

Stephen R. Barnhart, Executive Director
Charles Mallice, Operations & Training Director
Nikolai Ehlers, CCPA, Senior Security Consultant
James A. King, Chief Advisor
Arnaldo B. Merli, CCPA, International Security Consultant

Professional, nonprofit membership body open to military and civilian law enforcement personnel and people from the public and private sector who are engaged in the protection of royalty, presidential, state and diplomatic officials, government, military and corporate executives, personalities from the entertainment world and those involved in witness and prisoner protection.
Founded in 1989

21369 International Association of Professional Security Consultants
575 Market St.
Suite 2125
San Francisco, CA 94105

415-536-0288
Fax: 415-764-4915
E-Mail: iapsc@iapsc.org
Home Page: www.iapsc.org
Social Media: LinkedIn

Frank Pisciotta, President
Harold Gillens, Vice President
Kerry Parker, Executive Director
Alan Brockbank, Secretary
James Kelton, Treasurer

The International Association of Professional Security Consultants (IAPSC) is a widely recognized consulting association in the security industry. Its rigid membership requirements ensure that potential clients may select from the most elite group of professional, ethical and

competent security consultants available to them.
Founded in 1984

21370 **International Biometrics & Identification Association**
1666 K Street, NW
Washington, DC 20006

202-587-4855
Fax: 202-587-4888
E-Mail: ibia@ibia.org
Home Page: www.ibia.org
Social Media: Facebook, Twitter, RSS

Rebecca Dornbush, Information Officer
Christer Bergman, Secretary
Robert Harbour, President and Chairman of the Board
Walter Hamilton, Vice Chairman
Mike DePasquale, Treasurer

IBIA provides strong and growing value to its members, expanding business opportunities for the industry, advocating government support for the useof biometrics in leading commercial and public-sector applications, and reporting on key issues of strategic importance to the membership.
Founded in 1998

21371 **International Biometrics Industry Association**
919 18th Street, NW
Suite 901
Washington, DC 20006

202-587-4855
Fax: 202-587-4888
Home Page: www.ibia.org
Social Media: Facebook, Twitter

Robert Harbour, Chairman/ President
Walter Hamilton, Vice Chairman
Raffie Beroukhim, Director
Christer Bergman, Secretary
Mike DePasquale, Treasurer

Trade association representing developers, manufacturers and integrators of biometric hardware and software.

21372 **International Centre for the Prevention of Crime**
465 St-Jean Street
Bureau 803
Montreal, QU H2Y-2R6

514-288-6731
Fax: 514-288-8763
E-Mail: cipc@crime-prevention-intl.org
Home Page:
www.crime-prevention-intl.org/english

Vincenzo Castelli, Administrator
Erich Marks, VP
Chantal Bernier, President
Elizabeth Johnston, Secretary
Paul Girard, Treasurer

The ICPC is an international forum for national government local authorities, public agencies, specialized institutions, and non-government organisations of exchange experience, consider emerging knowledge, and improve policies and programs in crime prevention and community safety. ICPC staff monitors developments, provides direct assistance to members, and contributes to public knowledge and understanding in the field.
Founded in 1994

21373 **International Consumer Product Health & Safety Organization**
7044 S. 13th Street
Oak Creek, WI 53154

414-908-4949
Fax: 301-601-3543
E-Mail: customercare@icphso.org
Home Page: www.icphso.org
Social Media: Twitter, LinkedIn

Alan Kaufman, Vice President
Carol Pollack-Nelson, President
Ann M. Weeks, President-Elect
Ross Koeser, Executive Director
Joan Mattson, Padt prseident

ICPHSO holds a unique position in its ability to attract the interest of a broad range of health and safety professionals and interested consumers, world-wide.
Founded in 1993

21374 **International Fire Service Training Association**
930 N Willis
Stillwater, OK 74078

405-744-5723
Fax: 405-744-8204
E-Mail: customer.service@osufpp.org
Home Page: www.ifsta.org
Social Media: Facebook, Twitter, LinkedIn

Michael Moore, Marketing
Steve Ashbrock, Fire Dept.
Steve Austin, Fire Service Affiliate
Mike Wieder, Fire Organisation

Nonprofit organization associated with Fire Protection Publications, a department of the College of Engineering, Architecture and Technology at Oklahoma State University.
Founded in 1934

21375 **International Foundation for Protection Officers**
PO Box 771329
Naples, FL 34107-1329

239-430-0534
Fax: 239-430-0533
E-Mail: sandi@ifpo.com
Home Page: www.ifpo.org
Social Media: Facebook, Twitter, LinkedIn

Sandi J Davies, Executive Director
Michael Stroberger, Secretary/Treasurer
Rck Daniels, Chairman
Karl Poulin, Director
Tom M. Conley, Past Chairman

Nonprofit organization for the purpose of facilitating the training and certification needs of protection officers and security supervisors from both the commercial and proprietary sectors.
Founded in 1988

21376 **International High Technology Crime Investigation Association**
3288 Goldstone Drive
Roseville, CA 95747

916-408-1751
Fax: 916-408-7543
Home Page: www.htcia.org
Social Media: Facebook, Twitter, LinkedIn

Carol Hutchings, Executive Director
Tom Quilty, International President
Jimmy Garcia, International Training Conference
Carol Hutchings, Executive Director
Anna Valdavia, Finance

Designed to encourage, promote, aid and effect the voluntary interchange of data, information, experience, ideas and knowledge about methods, processes, and techniques relating to investigations and security in advanced technologies among its membership.
3500 Members
Founded in 1986

21377 **International Hologram Association**
2149 Cascade Ave
Suite 106
Hood River, OR 97031-1087

541-386-9449
Fax: 541-386-1564
E-Mail: info@ihma.org
Home Page: www.hairmasterssalon.com

More than 60 of the worlds leading hologram manufacturers are members. Dedicated to promoting the interests of those quality hologram manufacturers worldwide and to helping our customers to achieve their security, packaging graphic and other objectives through the effective use of holography.
Founded in 1993

21378 **International Hologram Manufacturers Association**
4 Windmill Business Village
Brooklands Close, SU TW167DY

193-278-5680
Fax: 193-278-0790
Home Page: www.ihma.orgÿ

Mike Messmer, Chairman
Nuray Yilmaz, Board Member
Manoj Kochar, ASPA Representative
Diana Newcomb, Board Member
Rajan Thomas, Asian Representative

A not for profit organization serving the hologram manufacturing industry.
Founded in 1993

21379 **International Locksmiths Association**
PO Box 9560
Naperville, IL 60567-0560

866-745-5625
E-Mail: keys150@juno.com
Home Page: www.ilanational.org

Bob Gress, Chairman
Don O'Shall, Vice President
Kurt Kloeckner, Treasurer
Kevin T. Piiper, National President
John Rendle, Secretary

Members are locksmiths, carpenters and building engineers who are employed by colleges, universities, hospitals, companies and government facilities. Dedicated to the education of members and the benefit of our institutions.

21380 **International Municipal Signal Association**
165 E Union Street
PO Box 539
Newark, NY 14513-0539

315-331-2182
800-723-4672
Fax: 315-331-8205
E-Mail: info@imsasafety.org
Home Page: www.imsasafety.org
Social Media: Facebook, Twitter, LinkedIn

Marilyn Lawrence, Executive Director/Publisher
Sharon Earl, Executive Assistant
Jeff Knight, President
Mike Flanigan, President-Elect
Perry Hill, Director-at-Large

Basic purpose of the organization is to keep its members and others in the profession, up-to-date on proper procedures of construction and maintenance of signal systems and informed on new products and equipment developments.
10000 Members
Founded in 1896

21381 International Photoluminescent Safety
5050 Industrial Road
Farmingdale, NJ 07727
732-751-0100
Fax: 732-751-0508
E-Mail: usmsa@usmsa.org
Home Page: www.ipspc.org
Tom Thompson, Executive Director
A leader in the marine safety and implementation of the highest possible performance, manufacturing maintenance, service and training standards, for all lifesaving, survival and emergency rescue equipment.
131 Members
Founded in 1986

21382 International Process Servers Association
2854 Larimer St
Denver, CO 80205
585-232-8590
800-611-2774
Fax: 877-824-2482
E-Mail: richard@processservers.com
Home Page: www.iprocessservers.com
Unifies process servers in the United States and throughout the world, as the single greatest resource for all process servers and private investigators.

21383 International Safety Equipment Association
1901 N Moore Street
Arlington, VA 22209-1762
703-525-1695
Fax: 703-528-2148
E-Mail: isea@safetyequipment.org
Home Page: www.safetyequipment.org
Social Media: Facebook, LinkedIn
Daniel K Shipp, President
Daniel I Glucksman, Public Affairs Director
Ann M. Feder, Office Services Manager
Brian Lyons, Chairman
Mitch Lewellen, Past Chairman
Trade association in the US for companies that manufacture safety equipment. Member companies are world leaders in the design and manufacture of clothing and equipment used in factories, construction sites, hospitals and clinics, farms, schools, laboratories, and in the home — anywhere people are doing work. Our common goal is to protect the health and safety of people exposed to hazardous and potentially harmful environments.
Founded in 1933

21384 International Security Management Association
PO Box 623
Buffalo, IA 52728-0623
563-381-4008
800-368-1894
Fax: 563-381-4283
E-Mail: susan.pohlmann@isma.com
Home Page: isma.com/
Ken Wheatley, President
Susan W Pohlmann, Executive Director
David Saenz, Second VP
Liz Chamberlin, Deputy Executive Director
ISMA's mission is to provide and support an international forum of selected security executives whose combined expertise wil be utilized in a synergistic manner in developing, assimilating, sharing knowledge within security disciplines for the ultimate purpose of enhancing professional and business standards.
400 Members
Founded in 1983

21385 International System Safety Society
PO Box 70
Unionville, VA 22567-0070
540-854-8630
Fax: 540-854-4561
E-Mail: syssafe@ns.gemlink.com
Home Page: www.system-safety.org
Bob Schmedake, President
Gary Braman, Immediate Past President
Matt Johnson, Executive Secretary
Rod Simmons, Executive Vice President
Pam Kniess, Treasurer
The System Safety Society is a non-profit organization dedicated to supporting the safety professional in the application of system engineering and systems management to risk analysis. The Society is international in scope and draws members throughout the world.
4500 Members
Founded in 1962

21386 International of Personal Protection Agents
PO Box 266
Arlington Heights, IL 60006-0266
847-870-8007
Fax: 847-870-8990
E-Mail: proproserv@aol.com
Home Page: www.iappa.net
Social Media: Facebook
Patrick Spoerry, Executive Director
Charles Mallice, Operations &Training Director
Professional, nonprofit membership body open to military and civilian law enforcement personnel and people from the public and private sector who are engaged in the protection of royalty, presidential, state and diplomatic officials, government, military and corporate executives, personalities from the entertainment world and those involved in witness and prisoner protection.
Founded in 1989

21387 Investigators of America
PO Box 4243
Downey, CA 90241
562-869-2535
877-393-7792
Fax: 562-869-5268
E-Mail: dkalepi@earthlink.net
Home Page: www.investigatorsofamerica.com
John R. Spencer, Director
Dave Blair, Director
Roberto A. Rivera, Director
Edwin C. Hodges, Director
Steven Rambam, Director
Investigators of America is a rapidly growing association comprised of elite private investigators, insurance adjusters, and expert witnesses across the United States with affiliates in other countries.

21388 Laser Institute of America
13501 Ingenuity Dr
Suite 128
Orlando, FL 32826
407-380-1553
800-345-2737
Fax: 407-380-5588
E-Mail: lia@lia.org
Home Page: www.lia.org
Social Media: Facebook, Twitter, LinkedIn, Google+
Reinhart Poprawe, Past President
Yongfeng Lu, President Elect
Klaus Loeffler, President
Stephen Capp, Treasurer
Robert Thomas, Secretary
The Laser Institute of America is the professional membership society dedicated to fostering lasers, laser applications and safety worldwide. Its mission is to foster lasers, laser applications, and laser safety worldwide. Serving the industrial, medical, research and government communities, LIA offers technical information and networking opportunities to laser users from around the globe.
1200 Members
Founded in 1968

21389 Mine Safety and Health Administration
1100 Wilson Blvd
21st Floor
Arlington, VA 22209-3939
202-693-9400
800-746-1553
Fax: 202-693-9401
Home Page: www.msha.gov
David G Dye, Executive Director
Mission is to enforce compliance with mandatory safety and health standards as a means to eliminate fatal accidents, reduce the frequency and severity of nonfatal accidents, minimnize health hazards, and to promote improved safety and health conditions in national mines.
Founded in 1978

21390 Motorcycle Safety Foundation
2 Jenner
Suite 150
Irvine, CA 92618
800-446-9227
E-Mail: msf@msf-usa.org
Home Page: www.msf-usa.orgÿ
Social Media: Facebook, Twitter, YouTube
Russ Brenan, Chair
Joseph Dagley, Vice Chair
Tim Buche, President & CEO
Robert Gladden, Vice President
Steve Piehl, Secretary/ Treasurer
Provides information on rider training, licensing, and goverment relations.

21391 National Alarm Association of America
PO Box 3409
Dayton, OH 45401
937-461-2208
800-283-6285
Fax: 937-461-4759
E-Mail: info@naaa.org
Home Page: www.naaa.org
Gene Riddlebaugh, President
Grant Angell, Senior VP Associate Affairs
Ricardo Gonzales, Vice President
Mission is to advance the welfare of members through the free exchange, among members of ideas and the dissemination of information concerning trade practices, business conditions, technical developments, within the industry, and any related subject of concern to the security industry.
Founded in 1984

21392 National Association of Elevator Safety Authorities
6957 Littlerock Road SW
Suite A
Tumwater, WA 98512
360-292-4968
800-746-2372
Fax: 360-292-4973
E-Mail: dotty@naesai.org
Home Page: www.naesai.org
Dotty Stanlaske, Executive Director
Bill Snyder, President
Doug Warne, VP

Jonathan Brooks, Treasurer
Michael Stewart, Secretary

Elevator inspector certification and continuing education.
2500 Members
Founded in 1969

21393 National Association of Fire Equipment Distributors
122 S Michigan Avenue
Suite 1040
Chicago, IL 60603

312-461-9200
Fax: 312-461-0777
E-Mail: dharris@nafed.org
Home Page: www.nafed.org
Social Media: Facebook

Ken May, President
Danny Harris, Ex Officio
George Seymour, Treasurer
Ed Hugill, President Elect
Michael Kint, Director

Mission is to improve the economic environment, business performance, and technical competence in the fire protection industry.
Founded in 1963

21394 National Association of Fraud Investigators
2519 NW 23rd St.
Suite 204
Oklahoma City, Ok 73107

E-Mail: RBrown2150@aol.com
Home Page: www.nafraud.com

Established to improve communications and expand the network of professional fraud investigators.

21395 National Association of Legal Investigators
235N Pine Street
Lansing, MI 48933

517-702-9835
866-520-NALI
Fax: 517-372-1501
E-Mail: val@julianvail.com, larry@julianvail.co
Home Page: www.nalionline.org
Social Media: Facebook

David W. Luther, National Director
Don C. Johnson, Assistant National Director
Neeta McClintock, National Secretary
Julian Vail, Association Management
John Hoda, Regional Director- Northeast Region

Membership in NAL is open to all professional legal investigators who are actively engaged in negligence investigations for plaintiff and/or criminal defense, and who are employed by investigative firms, law firms or public defender agencies.
Founded in 1967

21396 National Association of Safety Professionals
2015 East Marion Street
Shelby, NC 28152

800-922-2219
Fax: 704-487-1579
Home Page: www.naspweb.com
Social Media: Facebook, Twitter

Eric Gislason, Executive Director
Jon Beard, IT Analyst

A nonprofit membership organization providing training, consultative services as well as certifications.
10000 Members

21397 National Association of Security Companies
444 North Capitol Street, NW
Suite 345
Washington, DC 20001

202-347-3257
Fax: 202-393-7006
E-Mail: information@nasco.org
Home Page: www.nasco.org

Jim McNulty, Chair
Stephen Kasloff, 1st Vice Chair
Julie Payne, 2nd Vice Chair
Lynn Oliver, Secretary
David Buckman, Treasurer

To promote standards and professionalism for private security officers and within contract security.

21398 National Burglar & Fire Alarm Association
2300 Valley View Lane
Suite 230
Irving, TX 75062

214-260-5970
888-447-1689
Fax: 214-260-5979
E-Mail: MerlinG@alarm.org
Home Page: www.alarm.org
Social Media: Facebook, Twitter, YouTubee

Merlin Guilbeau, Executive Director
Georgia Calaway, Communications/PR Director

A professional trade association with the purpose of representing, promoting and enhancing the growth and professional development of the electronic life safety, security, and integrated systems industry.
Founded in 1948

21399 National Classification Management Society
994 Old Eagle School Rd
Suite 1019
Wayne, PA 19087-1866

610-971-4856
Fax: 610-971-4859
E-Mail: info@classmgmt.com
Home Page: www.classmgmt.com
Social Media: Facebook

Sharon K. Tannahill, Executive Director
Leonard Moss, President
Debbie Young, Vice President
Dean Young, Treasurer
Dennis Arriaga, Secretary

Advancing the practice of classification management in the disiplines of industrial security, information security, government designated unclassified information, and intellectual property, and to foster the highest qualities of security professionalism among its members.
1,300 Members
Founded in 1964

21400 National Council of Investigation & Security Services
7501 Sparrows Point Boulevard
Baltimore, MD 21219-1927

800-445-8408
Fax: 410-388-9746
E-Mail: nciss@comcast.net
Home Page: www.nciss.org

Carolyn Ward, Executive Director
Francie Koehler, President
Bruce Hulme, Legislative Director
Don C. Johnson, Editor

A cooperative of those companies and associations responsible for providing private security and investigation services to the legal profession, business community, government and the public.
1300 Members
Founded in 1975

21401 National Counterterrorism Center
National Counterterrorism Center
Washington, DC 20511

E-Mail: nctcpao@nctc.gov
Home Page: www.nctc.govÿ
Nicholas J. Rasmussen, Director

The primary organization in the United States Government for integrating and analyzing all intelligence pertaining to counterterrorism.

21402 National Crime Justice Association
720 7th Street NW
Third Floor
Washington, DC 20001

202-628-8550
Fax: 202-448-1723
E-Mail: info@ncja.org
Home Page: www.ncja.org
Social Media: Facebook, Twitter, LinkedIn, Pinterest, RSS

Cabell C. Cropper, Executive Director
Kay Chopard-Cohen, Deputy Executive Director
Jack Cutrone, President
Jeanne Smith, Vice President
Kristen Mahoney, Immediate Past President

Exists to promote the developemtn of justice systems in states, tribal nations, and units of local government that enhance public saftety ; prevent and reduce the harmful effects of criminal and delinquent behavior on victims, individuals and communities; adjudicate defendants and sanction offenders fairly and justly; and that are effective and efficient.
Founded in 1971

21403 National Crime Prevention Council
2001 Jefferson Davis Highway
Suite 901
Arlington, VA 22202-4801

202-466-6272
Fax: 202-296-1356
E-Mail: webmaster@ncpc.org
Home Page: www.ncpc.org

David Dean, Chairman
Ann Harnkins, President & CEO
Jean Adnopoz, Secretary
John p. Box, Treasurer
Robert F. Diegelman, Vice Chair

Aids people in keeping themselves, their families, and their communities safe from crime. NCPC produces tools that communities can use to learn crime prevention strategies, engage community members, and coordinate with local agencies.
136 Members
Founded in 1979

21404 National Defense Industrial Association
2111 Wilson Blvd
Suite 400
Arlington, VA 22201-3061

703-522-1820
Fax: 703-522-1885
E-Mail: info@ndia.org
Home Page: www.ndia.org

Lawrence P. Farrell, President & CEO
Bron P. Prokuski, Secreatry/ Treasurer
Barry D. Bates, VP, Operations
Peter Steffes, VP, Government Policy
Dino Pignotti, VP, Advertising

A leading defense idustry association whose mission is to promote national security through

a variety of means, including education, training and advocacy.
28100 Members
Founded in 1919

21405 National Electrical Manufacturers
1300 17th St N
Suite 900
Arlington, VA 22209

703-841-3200
Fax: 703-841-5900
E-Mail: webmaster@nema.org
Home Page: www.nema.org
Social Media: Facebook, Twitter, LinkedIn, RSS, YouTube, Google+

Evan R Gaddis, President
Christopher B. Curtis, Chairman
Thomas S. Gross, Vice Chair
Donald J. Hendler, Treasurer
John W. Estey, Board Committee Chairman

NEMA's mission is to promote the competitiveness of its member companies by providing quality services that will impact positively on standrds, government regulation and market economics.
400 Members
Founded in 1926

21406 National Emergency Equipment Dealers Association
8521 Frost Way
Annandale, VA 22003

703-280-4622
Fax: 703-280-0942
E-Mail: KentonPl@aol.com
Home Page: www.needa.org
Social Media: Facebook, Twitter, LinkedIn

Kenton Pattie, Executive Director

Serves dealers who sell and service fire, rescue, and emergency rescue systems equipment and apparatus. Preserves and strengthens the free market system for dealers through advocacy, information and training. Assists dealers profitably deliver high quality products and support to the nation's emergency services.
Founded in 1915

21407 National Fire Protection Association
1 Batterymarch Park
Quincy, MA 02169-7471

617-770-3000
800-344-3555
Fax: 617-770-0700
E-Mail: publicaffairs@nfpa.org
Home Page: www.nfpa.org

James M. Shannon, President/CEO
Philip C. Stittleburg, 1st VP
Philip C. Stittleburg, Chairman
Randolph W. Tucker, Secretary
H. Wayne Boyd, Treasurer

The mission of the NFPA is to reduce the worldwide burden of fire and other hazards on the quality of life by providing and advocating consensus codes and standards, research, training and education.
75000 Members
Founded in 1896

21408 National Fire Sprinkler Association
40 Jon Barrett Rd.
Patterson, NY 12563

845-878-4200
Fax: 845-878-4215
E-Mail: info@nfsa.org
Home Page: www.nfsa.org
Social Media: Facebook, Twitter, LinkedIn, YouTube, Google+

Russell P. Fleming, President
Alan Wiginton, Director
Dennis Coleman, Chairman
James Boulanger, Treasurer
Larry Thau, Vice Chair

The goal is to create a market for the widespread acceptance of competently installed automatic fire sprinkler systems in new and existing construction. Members are makers and installers of automatic fire sprinklers and related equipment.
Founded in 1905

21409 National Floor Safety Institute (NFSI)
PO Box 92607
Southlake, TX 76092

817-749-1700
Fax: 817-749-1702
E-Mail: info@nfsi.org
Home Page: www.nfsi.org
Social Media: Facebook, Twitter, LinkedIn

Laura Cooper, Manager, Membership Relations
Russell Kendzior, President & Chairman
Howard W. Harris, Treasurer
Steven C. Spencer, Treasurer

Mission is to aid in the prevention of slip-and-fall accidents through education, training and recearch. The NFSI is led by a fifteen-member Board of Directors representing product manufacturers, insurance underwriters, trade associations, and independent consultants.
Founded in 1997

21410 National Institute for Occupational Safety & Health
1600 Clifton Rd
Atlanta, GA 30333

404-639-3385
800-232-4636
Fax: 513-533-8573
E-Mail: eidtechinfo@cdc.gov
Home Page: www.cdc.gov/niosh/homepage.html
Social Media: Facebook, Twitter, RSS, MySpace, YouTube, Flickr

John Howard MD, Director
Hubert H Humphrey, Chief of Staff
Max Lum EdD, Assoc Director Health

To promote health and quality of life by preventing and controlling disease, injury, and disability.

21411 National Institute of Standards and Technology (NIST)
100 Bureau Dr
Suite 1070
Gaithersburg, MD 20899-1070

301-975-6478
800-877-8339
Fax: 301-948-6107
E-Mail: inquiries@nist.gov
Home Page: www.nist.gov
Social Media: Facebook, Twitter, LinkedIn, RSS, YouTube, Flickr

William Jeffrey, CEO
Patrick D. Gallagher, Director
Kevin Kimball, Chief of Staff
Thomas Klausing, Chief Financial Officer
Mike Herman, Executive Officer

Promotes US innovation and industrial competitiveness by advancing measurement science, standards, and technology in ways that enhance economic security and improve quality of life. It's four cooperative programs are NIST Laboratories, Baldrige National Quality Program, Manufacturing Extension Partnership, and Advanced Technology Program.
Founded in 1901

21412 National Nuclear Security Administration
1000 Independence Ave., S.W.
Washington, DC 20585

202-586-5000
800-342-5363
Fax: 202-586-7371
Home Page: www.nnsa.energy.gov
Social Media: Facebook, Twitter, LinkedIn, YouTube, Flickr

Frank G. Klotz, Administrator
Madelyn Creedon, Principal Deputy Administrator
Dr. Donald L. Cook, Deputy Administrator
Bruce Diamond, General Counsel
Don Nichols, Associate Administrator

Organization for advancing nuclear sciences, technologies and engineering.
Founded in 2000

21413 National Safety Council
1121 SpringLake Dr.
Itasca, IL 60143-3201

630-775-1121
800-621-7615
Fax: 630-285-1315
E-Mail: customerservice@nsc.org
Home Page: www.nsc.org
Social Media: RSS

Alan C McMillan, CEO
Edward D Bullard, Chairman

Nonprofit, nongovernmental, international public service organization dedicated to protecting life and promoting health.
48000 Members
Founded in 1913

21414 National Safety Management Society
PO Box 4460
Walnut Creek, CA 94596-0460

800-321-2910
E-Mail: nsmsinc@yahoo.com
Home Page: www.nsms.us
Social Media: Facebook, Twitter, LinkedIn, RSS

Roosevelt Smith, President
John H Bridges III, Director
Jeffery Chung, Board Member
Marilyn Clark Alston, Board Member
Charles W. McGlothlin, Board Member

Mission is to support managers and their employees in their responsibility to assure the safety of all employees.
Founded in 1966

21415 National Sheriffs' Association
1450 Duke Street
Alexandria, VA 22314

800-424-7827
Fax: 703-838-5349
E-Mail: mkendall@sheriffs.org
Home Page: www.sheriffs.org
Social Media: Facebook, Twitter, LinkedIn, Google+

John E. Aubrey, President
John Thompson, Interim Executive Director
Linda Foldvik, Director of Finance
Miriam Kendall, Executive Secretary
Fred G. Wilson, Director of Operations

An organization to promote criminal justice, homeland security and public safety.
Founded in 1940

21416 National Society of Professional Insurance Investigators
PO Box 88
Delaware, OH 43015

888-677-4498
Fax: 740-369-7155
E-Mail: nspii@nspii.com

Home Page: www.nspii.com
Social Media: LinkedIn, RSS

Jack Morgan, President
Matthew J Smith, First VP
John R Yust, Secretary/Membership Chairman

A professional society for research and education.
590 Members
Founded in 1983

21417 National Tooling & Machining Association
1357 Rockside Road
Cleveland, OH 44134

301-248-6200
800-248-6862
Fax: 216-264-2840
E-Mail: info@ntma.org
Home Page: www.ntma.org
Social Media: Twitter, LinkedIn

Rob Akers, CEO

Supports its members through education, training and resources.
2700 Members
Founded in 1943

21418 NationalÿAssociationÿof SchoolÿSafetyÿand Law Enforcement Officials
Home Page: www.nassleo.org
Social Media: Twitter

Augustine Pescatore, Chairman
Larry D. Johnson, President
Chief Ian Moffett, President Elect
Hector Garcia, Secretary
Rudy Perez, Treasurer

Provides levels of resources for school law enforcement and safety officials.

21419 Professional Investigators & Security Association
PO Box 521
Manassas, VA 20108

703-818-0552
Fax: 703-818-0551
E-Mail: kbreenpi@yahoo.com
Home Page: www.vapisa.com

Al Donker, 1st, Vice President
Angela Collins, 2nd Vice President
Bob Blansfield, President
Kristopher Wilgus, Secretary
Charmaine Zilliox, Treasurer

PISA is recognized as the preeminent professional organization representing members of the Private Security Services.
Founded in 1984

21420 Professional Records & Information Service s Management
8735 W Higgins Rd
Suite 300
Chicago, IL 60631

847-375-6344
800-336-9793
Fax: 847-375-6343
E-Mail: info@prismintl.org
Home Page: www.prismintl.org
Social Media: Facebook, LinkedIn

Jim Booth, Executive Director
Nathan Campbell, President
Chris Kelly, Vice President
Michael Fruchter, Secretary/ Treasurer
Chris Pearson, Asst. Secretary

A nonprofit trade association for the commercial information management industry whose vision is to be the primary global resource for commercial information management outsourcing providers.
Founded in 1930

21421 SAFE Association
PO Box 130
Creswell, OR 97426-0130

541-895-3012
Fax: 541-895-3014
E-Mail: safe@peak.org
Home Page: www.safeassociation.com
Social Media: Facebook

Joel Albinowski, President
W. Barry Shope, President-Elect
Randy J. Epperly, Vice President
Steve Goldner, Treasurer
Margaret Kearney, Secretary

Dedicated to the preservation of human life. Provides a common meeting ground for the sharing of problems, ideas and information.
Founded in 1956

21422 Safe & Vault Technicians Association
3500 Easy St
Dallas, TX 75247

214-819-9733
800-532-2562
Fax: 214-819-9736
Home Page: www.savta.org

Charles Gibson, President

Provides a host of benefits to help its members stay informed, solving day to day problems, and out-performing the competition. Has helped thousands of safe and vault techicians achiveve personal and professional success.
Founded in 1986

21423 Safety Equipment Distributors Association
1901 North Moore Street
Arlington, VA 22209-1762

703-525-1695
Fax: 703-528-2148
E-Mail: jackie@ksgroup.org
Home Page: www.safetycentral.org
Social Media: Facebook, LinkedIn

Eric Beck, Board of Trustee
Mitch Lewellen, Past Chairman
Daniel K. Shipp, President
Bob Weber, Vice Chairman
Brian Lyons, Chairman

The Saftey Equipment Distributor's Association is the trade association comprised of companies that distribute safety equipmant and related products and services. Its member companies are leaders in the distribution of personal protective equipment to a broad spectrum of users, including general industry, construction, municipalities, utilities, schools and laboratories.
175 Members
Founded in 1933

21424 Safety Glazing Certification Council
P.O. Box 730
100 W. Main St.
Sackets Harbor, NY 13685

315-646-2234
Fax: 315-646-2297
E-Mail: staff@amscert.com
Home Page: www.sgcc.org

John Kent, Administrative Staff
Erin Ackley, Administrative Staff

Nonprofit corporation that provides for the certifacation of safety glazing materials, comprised of safety glazing manufacturers and other parties concerned with public safety. SGCC is managed by a board of directors comprised of representatives from the safety glazing industry and the public interest sector.
105 Members
Founded in 1971

21425 Scaffold & Access Industry Association
400 Admiral Blvd
Kansas City, MO 64106

816-595-4860
866-687-7115
Fax: 602-257-1166
E-Mail: rjm@scaffold.org
Home Page: www.scaffold.org
Social Media: Facebook, Twitter, LinkedIn, RSS

Paula Manning, Secretary
Marty Coughlin, President
Mike Russell, President Elect
Jeff Stachowiak, Vice President
Colby Hubler, Treasurer

Nonprofit organization which promotes scaffold safety and education through its publications, conventions, tradeshows and training programs.
Founded in 1972

21426 Scaffold and Access Industry Association
400 Admiral Blvd
Kansas City, MO 64106

816-595-4860
Fax: 816-472-7765
E-Mail: info@saiaonline.org
Home Page: www.saiaonline.org
Social Media: Facebook, Twitter, LinkedIn

Mike Russell, President
Paula Manning, President Elect
Ted Beville, Vice President
Colby Hubler, Secretary
Frank Frietsch, Treasurer

To promote, represent and enhance the access, scaffolding and forming industry for the benefit of its members.

21427 Security Hardware Distributors Association
105 Eastern Avenue
Suite 104
Annapolis, MD 21403

410-940-6346
Fax: 410-263-1659
E-Mail: info@shda.org
Home Page: www.shda.org

Karen Hoffman-Kahl, President
Jeff Floeck, Director
Steve Dyson, Immediate Past President
Stan Maziuk, Vice President
Jennie Berg Pagano, Treasurer

Offers education and services to its members.
150 Members
Founded in 1940

21428 Security Industry Association
8405 Colesville Road
Suite 500
Silver Spring, MD 20910

301-804-4700
866-817-8888
Fax: 301-804-4701
E-Mail: info@siaonline.org
Home Page: www.siaonline.org
Social Media: Facebook, Twitter, LinkedIn

Donald Erickson, CEO
Rand Price, COO
Dennis Hebert, Treasurer
V. John Storia, Chairman
Scott Schaffer, Secretary

SIA is dedicated to promoting growth, advancement, and professionalism within the security industry. Its activities fall into four core concentrations: government relations, research

& technology, education & training, and standards.
510 Members
Founded in 1969

21429 Semiconductor Environmental Safety & Health Association
1313 Dolly Madison Boulevard
Suite 402
McLean, VA 22101

703-790-1745
Fax: 703-790-2672
E-Mail: sesha@burkinc.com
Home Page: www.seshaonline.org

Steven Trammell, President
Brett J Burk, Executive Director
Steven Roberge, Treasurer
Hilary Matthews, Secretary
Paul M Connor, President-Elect

SESHA is the premier association serving the global semiconductor and associated technology industries by providing education and professional development.
1500 Members
Founded in 1978

21430 Society for Occupational & Environmental Health
1010 Vermont Ave., NW
Suite 513
Washington, DC 20005

202-347-4976
Fax: 202-347-4950
E-Mail: kkirklamd@aoec.org
Home Page: www.soeh.org

Ronald Denny Dobbin CIH, President
Katherine H. Kirrkland, Executive Director
Sarah Shiffert, Association Director
Mark Catlin, Governing Board

The Society plays a unique, integrating role by bringing together professionals in government, and academia. It reduces occupational and environmental hazards through the presentation of scientific data and the dynamic exchange of information across institutions and disciplines.
Founded in 1972

21431 Society of Fire Protection Engineers
7315 Wisconsin Ave
Suite 620E
Bethesda, MD 20814

301-718-2910
Fax: 301-718-2242
E Mail: sfpehqtrs@sfpe.org
Home Page: www.sfpe.org
Social Media: Facebook, Twitter, LinkedIn

Kathleen Almand, Director
Joshua W. Elvove, President
Carl F. Baldassarra, President-Elect
Michael Madden, Secretary
David Barber, Vice President

The purpose of the Society is to advance the science and practice of fire protection engineering and its allied fields, to maintain a high ethical standard among its members and to foster fire protection engineering education. The Society provides a program of educational offerings and provides technical publications.
4500 Members
Founded in 1950

21432 The American Association of Safety Council s
Home Page: www.safetycouncils.orgÿ

Jim Meade, President
Darby Vorce, Vice President
Dianna Braud, Past President
Lynndee Riley, Secretary
Toni Burrows, Treasurer

An international association of safety professionals

21433 The Association of State Floodplain Managers
575 D'Onofrio Drive
Suite 200
Madison, WI 53719

608-828-3000
Fax: 608-828-6319
E-Mail: memberhelp@floods.org
Home Page: www.floods.orgÿ
Social Media: Facebook, Twitter, LinkedIn

Bill Nechamen, Chair
Ceil Strauss, Vice Chair
Chad Berginnis, Executive Director
Leslie Durham, Secretary
Karen McHugh, Treasurer

To promote education, policies and activities that mitigate current and future losses, costs and human suffering caused by flooding.

21434 The International Biometric Society
1444 I Street, NW
Suite 700
Washington, DC 20005

202-712-9049
Fax: 202-216-9646
E-Mail: ibs@biometricsociety.org
Home Page: www.biometricsociety.org
Social Media: Facebook, Twitter, LinkedIn

John Hinde, President
Clarice Dem,trio, Outgoing President
Dee Ann Walker, Executive Director
Wesley Johnson, Director
James Carpenter, Secretary/ Treasurer

21435 The National Burglar & Fire Alarm Association
440 North Broad Street
Suite 130
Philadelphia, PA 19130

215-400-6428
Fax: 215-400-4717
E-Mail: secretary@nassleo.org
Home Page: www.alarm.org
Social Media: Facebook, Twitter, YouTube

21436 The World Institute for Security Enhancement
702-722-7779
E-Mail: training@worldinstitute.org
Home Page: www.worldinstitute.org

G.F. Bryant, Executive Director
Henry D Infante, Director of Operations
Rubern Bala, Director of International Marketing
Kunal Bhogal, Director of Operations
Lisa A Kane, Director of Health

21437 Transportation Security Administration
866-289-9673
E-Mail: TSA-ContactCenter@tsa.dhs.gov
Home Page: www.tsa.govÿ
Social Media: Facebook, Twitter, LinkedIn, YouTube

Melvin Carraway, Administrator
Kenneth Fletcher, Chief Risk Officer
Thomas McDaniels, Chief of Staffs
Francine Kerner, Chief Counsel
Pat Rose, Finance
Founded in 2001

21438 U.S. Fire Administration
16825 S. Seton Ave.
Emmitsburg, MD 21727

301-447-1000
888-382-3827
Fax: 301-447-1441
E-Mail: netcadmissions@fema.dhs.gov
Home Page: www.usfa.fema.gov
Social Media: Facebook, Twitter, YouTube

Ernest Mitchell, US Fire Administrator
Kyle Blackman, Executive Officer
Vanetta Crouch, Secretary
Angela Cunningham, Staff Assistant
Elizabeth Miller, Budget Analysis

21439 U.S. Security Associatesÿ
200 Mansell Court Fifth Floor
Roswell, GA 30076

770-625-1500
800-730-9599
Home Page: www.ussecurityassociates.com
Social Media: Facebook, Twitter, LinkedIn, YouTube, Google+
Founded in 1993

21440 Underwriters Laboratories
333 Pfingsten Rd
Northbrook, IL 60062-2096

847-412-0136
Fax: 847-272-8129
E-Mail: northbrook@us.ul.com
Home Page: www.ul.com
Social Media: Facebook, Twitter, LinkedIn, YouTube, Google+

Christian Anschuetz, SVP & Chief Information Officer
Terry Brady, SVP & Chief Legal Officer
Weifang Zhou Weifang Zhou, SVP & Chief Commercial Officer
Michael Saltzman, SVP & CFO
August Schaefer, SVP & Public Safety Officer

Underwriters Labdoratories Inc. is an independent, not-for-profit product-safty testing and certification organization, that has been testing products for safety for more than a century.
Founded in 1894

21441 United States Association of Professional Investigators
175 Hutton Ranch Rd
Ste 103-165
Kalispell, MO 59901

877-894-0615
Fax: 877-851-0794
E-Mail: info@usapi.org
Home Page: www.usapi.orgÿ
Social Media: Twitter

21442 United States Marine Safety Association
5050 Industrial Road
Suite 2
Wall Township, NJ 7727

732-751-0102
Fax: 732-751-0508
E-Mail: fhornig@vanebrothers.com
Home Page: www.usmsa.orgÿ

Frank Hornig, President
Karen Hansen, Vice President
Tom Thompson, Executive Director
Maureen Fackenthal, Administrative Director
Nancy Draper, Event Planner

21443 United States Society on Damsÿ
1616 Seventeenth Street
Suite 483
Denver, CO 80202

303-628-5430
Fax: 303-628-5431
E-Mail: stephens@ussdams.org
Home Page: www.ussdams.org

Keith A. Ferguson, President
John S. Wolfhope, Vice President
Daniel L. Wade, Secretary/Treasurer

Larry D. Stephens, Executive Director
Ross Boulanger, Board of Director

21444 Veterans of Safety
201 Humphreys Bldg
Suite 323 C
Warrensburg, MO 64093

660-543-4281
Home Page: www.vetsofsafety.org

Our mission is the promotion of safety, health, and environmental awareness by using and making available the lifetime experience of professionals throughout the world.
Founded in 1941

21445 Western States Auto Theft Investigators Association Southern Chapter
6 Hutton Centre Drive
Suite 1040
Santa Ana, CA 92707

714-434-9600
E-Mail: webmaster@wsati.org
Home Page: www.wsati.org
Social Media: Facebook, Twitter

Rob Manning, President
Tim Jackson, VP
Aristeed Powell, Secretary
Treasurer Yori, Treasurer
Richard O. Knapp, Legal Counsel

A non-profit organization that is comprised of professionals representing law enforcement, rental car and insurance companies, and other individuals whose goal is to reduce vehicle theft.

21446 Women Investigators Association
PO Box 18305
Encino, CA 91416

800-603-3524
E-Mail: womeninvas@aol.com
Home Page: www.w-i-a.org

Debra J Burdette, Executive Director
Robinette Desrochers, VP/Membership Director

Offering education and training, certification, networking, group discounts and represents women in our industry to the media.

Newsletters

21447 ACP Sentinel
Association of Contingency Planners
7044 S 13th St
Oak Creek, WI 53154-1429

414-768-8000
800-445-4227
Fax: 414-768-8001
E-Mail: Membership@techenterprises.net
Home Page: www.naspa.com

Scott Sherer, Executive Director
Shirley Runnels, Membership

News and event information for national and local chapters dedicated to fostering continued professional growth and development in effective contingency and business planning.
Cost: $75.00
Frequency: Quarterly
Founded in 1983

21448 American Society of Crime Laboratory Directors
139K Technology Drive
Garner, NC 27529

919-773-2044
Fax: 919-773-2602
E-Mail: info@nfstc.org
Home Page: www.ascld.org

William E Marbaker, President
Susan C Scholl, Membership

Contains useful information and news to maintain and improve communications among crime laboratory directors and their staff.
Cost: $100.00
Frequency: Quarterly
Founded in 1973

21449 CGAA Signals
Central Station Alarm Association
8150 Leesburg Pike
Suite 700
Vienna, VA 22182-2721

703-242-4670
Fax: 703-242-4675
E-Mail: communications@csaaul.org
Home Page: www.csaaul.org

Stephen P Doyle, Executive VP/CEO
Celia Besore, VP Marketing & Programs
300+ Members
Frequency: Quarterly
Circulation: 1200
Founded in 1950

21450 Councilor
Safety & Health Council of Northern New England
57 Regional Dr
Suite 6
Concord, NH 03301-8518

603-228-1401
800-834-6472
Fax: 603-224-0998
E-Mail: safety@shcnne.org
Home Page: www.shcnne.org

Lyman Cousens, Executive Director

Covers current regulatory issues as well as health and safety information. Free to members.
16 Pages
Frequency: Monthly
Founded in 2004
Printed in 2 colors on matte stock

21451 Emergency Preparedness News
Business Publishers
2601 University Boulevard W
#200
Silver Spring, MD 20902

301-929-5700
800-274-6737
Fax: 301-949-8844
E-Mail: custserv@bpinews.com
Home Page: www.bpinews.com

Adam P Goldstein, Publisher
Deborah Eby, Editor
David Henderson, Director
Melissa Worcester, Service

Dedicated solely to disaster management: from securing pre-disaster mitigation and counter terrorism funds, to staying prepared for hurricanes, terrorist threats, fires, floods and other natural disasters. Only available online now.
Cost: $357.00
Frequency: Monthly
ISSN: 0275-3782

21452 FAMA Flyer
Fire Apparatus Manufacturers' Association
PO Box 397
Lynnfield, MA 01940-0397

781-334-2911
Fax: 781-334-2911
E-Mail: info@fama.org
Home Page: www.fama.org

Grady North, President
Greg Kozey, VP

A newsletter that is written specifically for Fire Apparatus Manufactures and Fire Associations across the United States.
Frequency: 3x/Yr
Circulation: 500

21453 HTCIA Newsletter
3288 Goldstone Drive
Roseville, CA 95747

916-408-1751
Fax: 916-408-7543
Home Page: www.htcia.org

Carol Hutchings, Executive Director

For members only
Frequency: Quarterly

21454 Homeland Security & Defense
McGraw Hill
1200 G St Nw
Suite 900
Washington, DC 20005-3821

202-383-2377
Fax: 202-383-2438
Home Page: www.aviationnow.com

Jennifer Michels, President
Paul Hoversten, Managing Editor
Mark Lipowicz, Publisher
Iain Blackhall, Managing Director

News items for defense and homeland security professionals. Available in print or electronically.
Cost: $595.00
Frequency: Weekly
Founded in 1920

21455 Nine Lives Associates: Newsletter
Executive Protection Institute
PO Box 802
Berryville, VA 22611

540-554-2540
Fax: 540-554-2558
E-Mail: info@personalprotection.com
Home Page: www.personalprotection.com

Ronald J. Wilczynski, President
Tom Quilty, VP
Peter Morin, Tresurer
Jose Soltero, Secretary

Personal protection news and announcements for member graduates of Executive Protection Institute.
Founded in 1980

21456 Progress
National Association of Elevator Safety
6957 Littlerock Road SW
Suite A
Tumwater, WA 98512

360-292-4968
800-746-2372
Fax: 360-292-4973
E-Mail: dotty@naesai.org
Home Page: www.naesai.org
Social Media: Facebook, Twitter, LinkedIn

Dotty Stanlaske, Executive Director
Dean McLellan, President
Bill Snyder, VP

Informs members of the newest developments in the elevator industry; listings of all currently-scheduled seminars, updated classes and workshops; a message from the Executive Director with news from the main office; articles addressing code questions and issues; news from around the globe and advertising opportunities.
Frequency: Monthly

21457 Progress Report: The Foundation Newsletter
AAA Foundation for Traffic Safety

14th Street NW
Suite 201
Washington, DC 20005

202-638-5944
Fax: 202-638-5943
Home Page: www.aaafoundation.org

Fairley Mahlum, Communications Director
Frequency: Monthly

21458 Protection News
International Foundation for Protection Officers
PO Box 771329
Naples, FL 34107-1329

239-430-0534
Fax: 239-430-0533
E-Mail: sandi@ifpo.com
Home Page: www.ifpo.org

Sandi J Davies, Executive Director
Michael Stroberger, Secretary/Treasurer

Circulation to all IFPO members and candidates in associated programs. Publication is designed to keep professionals current on trends within the security industry and is full of valuable information and commentary pertinent to the enhancement of life, safety and property protection.
Cost: $18.00
Frequency: Quarterly
Founded in 1988

21459 SAFE Symposium News
SAFE Association
PO Box 130
Creswell, OR 97426

541-895-3012
Fax: 541-895-3014
E-Mail: safe@peak.org
Home Page: www.safeassociation.com
Social Media: Facebook

Al Loving, President
John Fair, President-Elect

The SAFE Association is dedicated to the preservation of human life. It provides a common meeting ground for the sharing of problems, ideas and information. SAFE is a non-profit international association headquartered in Oregon, with chapters located throughout the world. SAFE publishes a quarterly Newsletter and Proceedings of the Annual SAFE Symposium. These publications are valuable reference sources for the professional involved in all forms of safety and survival.
1100+ Attendees
Frequency: Quarterly
Founded in 1954

21460 SIA News
Security Industry Association
8405 Colesville Road
Suite 500
Alexandria, MD 20109

301-804-4700
866-817-8888
Fax: 301-804-4701
E-Mail: info@siaonline.org
Home Page: www.siaonline.org

Richard Chace, CEO
Rand Price CAE, COO
Donald Erickson, Government Relations Director

Informs and educates members and prospective members of SIA activities, news, and information. Available online only.
Frequency: 2 X'S Monthly
ISSN: 1071-6713
Founded in 1969

21461 Safety Compliance Letter
Bureau of Business Practice
111 Eight Avenue
New York, NY 10011

800-638-8437
Home Page: www.aspenpublishers.com

Alicia Pierce, Publisher
Michele Rubin, Editor

Monitors and reports on the regulatory environment and provides subscribers with up-to-date information in a concise and easy-to-read format, with references and resources (including internet addresses) to get additional help on particular topics.
Cost: $289.00
Frequency: Monthly
ISBN: 9-900003-20-0
Founded in 1920

21462 Salt & Highway Deicing
Salt Institute
700 N Fairfax St
Suite 600
Alexandria, VA 22314-2085

703-549-4648
Fax: 703-548-2194
E-Mail: info@saltinstitute.org
Home Page: www.saltinstitute.org

Richard L Hanneman, President
Tammy Goodwin, Administrative Director

A quarterly e-newsletter published by the Salt Institute.
Frequency: Quarterly
Circulation: 8000
Founded in 1914
Printed in on glossy stock

21463 Security Director's Report
Institute of Management and Administration
1 Washington Park
Suite 1300
Newark, NJ 07102

212-244-0360
Fax: 973-622-0595
Home Page: www.ioma.com

Designed to help security directors keep pace with the rapidly evolving world of corporate security. Alerts to critical news, import new security products, and up-to-date advice that you need to know to effectively manager your security department.
Cost: $419.00
Frequency: Monthly

21464 Signal
American Traffic Safety Services Association
15 Riverside Parkway
Suite 100
Fredericksburg, VA 22406-1022

540-368-1701
800-272-8772
Fax: 540-368-1717
Home Page: www.atssa.com
Social Media: Facebook, Twitter

James Baron, Communications Director

Covers legislative updates, industry news and meeting information, as well as other items of interest to the roadway safety industry as is a full-color publication.
Frequency: Quarterly

21465 Society Update
American Society of Safety Engineers
1800 E Oakton Street
Des Plaines, IL 60018

847-699-2929
Fax: 847-768-3434
E-Mail: customerservice@asse.org
Home Page: www.asse.org
Social Media: Facebook

Fred J Fortman, Executive Director
Jim Drzewiecki, Finance/Controller Director
Diane Hurns, Manager Public Relations Department

Membership benefit via e-mail with news, information on training, plus happenings in the 150 chapters throughout the US.
Cost: $60.00
Founded in 1911

21466 Workplace Substance Abuse Advisor
LRP Publications
PO Box 24668
West Palm Beach, FL 33416-4668

561-622-6520
800-341-7874
Fax: 561-622-0757
E-Mail: custserve@lrp.com
Home Page: www.lrp.com

Kenneth Kahn, President

Current developments affecting how your workplace deals with alcohol and drug abusing employees. Comprehensive overview of all the areas you need to know to create and maintain an effective substance abuse program in your company.
Cost: $377.00
Frequency: 2 X'S Month
Founded in 1977

Magazines & Journals

21467 Access Control & Security Systems
PRIMEDIA Business Magazines & Media
1166 Avenue of the Americas
Shawnee Mission, NY 10036

212-204-4200
Fax: 913-514-6895
E-Mail: prothman@primediabusiness.com
Home Page: www.penton.com

Eric Jacobson, Senior VP
Gregg Herring, Publisher
Paul Rothman, Associate Editor
Brenda Wiley, Advertising Production Manager
Marty McCallen, National Sales Manager

Product overview articles and columns cover topics on door entry, CCTV, operators and gates, sensors and perimeter security.
Frequency: Monthly
Circulation: 38000+
Founded in 1905

21468 American Industrial Hygiene Association Journal
American Industrial Hygiene Association
2700 Prosperity Ave
Suite 250
Fairfax, VA 22031-4321

703-849-8888
Fax: 703-207-3561
E-Mail: infonet@aiha.org
Home Page: www.aiha.org
Social Media: Facebook, Twitter, LinkedIn

Lisa Junker, Senior Editor
Michael Brandt, President
Dave Bentley, Marketing Manager
Sheila Brown,, Associate Editor
Peter Oneil, Executive Director

Essential source of information on occupational health and evironmental health and safety issues. Available in print and online.
780 Pages
Frequency: Monthly
Founded in 1982

21469 Business & Legal Reports
Business & Legal Reports
PO Box 6001
Old Saybrook, CT 06475-6001
860-510-0100
800-727-5257
Fax: 860-510-7225
E-Mail: service@blr.com
Home Page: www.blr.com
Robert L Brady, CEO
Peggy Carter-Ward, Editor-in-Chief
Provides essential tools for safety and environmental compliance and training needs.
32 Pages

21470 Campus Safety Journal
Bricepac
12228 Venice Boulevard Suite 541
PO Box 66515
Los Angeles, CA 90066
310-390-5277
Fax: 310-390-4777
E-Mail: tnelson@campusjournal.com
Home Page: www.campusjournal.com
Pat Restivo, Circualtion
John Horn, President
Provides a vehicle for communicating campus safety and security issues to all interested parties at the middle, secondary, college and university levels.
40 Pages
Frequency: Monthly
Circulation: 20000
Founded in 1992
Printed in 4 colors on glossy stock

21471 Compliance Magazine
Briefings Media Group
PO Box 787
Williamsport, PA 17703
800-791-8699
Fax: 570-320-2079
Home Page: www.compliancemag.com
Betty Hintch, Editor
Laura Daugherity, Production Coordinator
Compliance Magazine offers the latest in government regulations, including the materials and information needed to stay in compliance, safety trends, and a complete Safety Buyers' Guide.
Frequency: Annual
Founded in 1985

21472 Computer Fraud & Security
Elsevier Science
360 Park Ave S
New York, NY 10010-1736
212-633-3980
Fax: 212-633-3913
Home Page: www.elsevier.com
Provides practical, usable information to effectively manage and control computer and information security within commercial organizations.
Frequency: Monthly
ISSN: 1361-3723
Founded in 1979

21473 Computer Security Journal
Computer Security Institute
600 Harrison Street
San Francisco, CA 94107
415-947-6320
Fax: 415-947-6023
E-Mail: csi@cmp.com
Home Page: www.gocsi.com
Social Media: Facebook, Twitter, LinkedIn
Russell Kay, Publisher
Keeps you informed with comprehensive, practical articles, case studies, reviews and commentaries written by knowledgeable computer security professionals.
Cost: $224.00
Frequency: Quarterly
Circulation: 3000
Founded in 1974

21474 Computers & Security
Elsevier Science
360 Park Ave S
New York, NY 10010-1736
212-633-3980
Fax: 212-633-3913
Home Page: www.elsevier.com
Social Media: Facebook, Twitter, LinkedIn
Provides a blend of leading edge research and sound practical management advice.
Frequency: Monthly
ISSN: 0167-4048
Founded in 1997

21475 Corporate Security
Strafford Publications
PO Box 13729
Atlanta, GA 30324-0729
404-881-1141
800-926-7926
Fax: 404-881-0074
E-Mail: custserv@straffordpub.com
Home Page: www.straffordpub.com
Richard Ossoff, President
George Coleman, Manager
Intelligence briefing on the latest security developments, best practices, the most important trends and new technolgies.
Cost: $330.00
Frequency: Bi-Monthly
ISSN: 0889-0625
Founded in 1984

21476 EMS Product News
Cygnus Publishing
PO Box 803
Fort Atkinson, WI 53538-0803
920-000-1111
800-547-7377
Fax: 920-563-1699
E-Mail: Ronnie.Garret@cygnuspub.com
Home Page: www.cygnusb2b.com
Social Media: Facebook, Twitter, LinkedIn
John French, CEO
Nancy Perry, Editor
Product information written with the emergency medical service professional in mind.
Cost: $53.00
Frequency: 6 Issues
Circulation: 20000

21477 Emergency Medical Product News
Cygnus Business Media
PO Box 803
Fort Atkinson, WI 53538-0803
920-000-1111
800-547-7377
Fax: 920-563-1699
Home Page: www.cygnusb2b.com
John French, CEO
Ronnie Garrett, Director of Public Relations
Kathy Scott, Director of Public Relations
Paul Bonaiuto, CFO
A bi-monthly tabloid-sized magazine showcasing new products in the Emergency Medical Technician's scope of use.

21478 Emergency Medical Services
Cygnus Business Media
PO Box 803
Fort Atkinson, WI 53538-0803
920-000-1111
Fax: 920-563-1699
E-Mail: scott.cravens@cygnusb2b.com
Home Page: www.cygnusb2b.com
Social Media: Facebook, Twitter, LinkedIn
John French, CEO
Nancy Perry, Associate Publisher
A magazine designed for both career and volunteer EMS professionals. This magazine has been rated number one for editorial quality, reader interest and advertising pages.
Frequency: Monthly

21479 Fire & Arson Investigator Magazine
International Association of Arson Investigators
2111 Baldwin Ave
Suite 203
Crofton, MD 21114
410-451-3473
Fax: 410-451-9049
Home Page: www.firearson.com
David Nichols, President
Cost: $75.00
Frequency: Quarterly

21480 Fire EMS
PennWell
PO Box 1260
Tulsa, OK 74101-1260
918-835-3161
800-331-4463
Fax: 918-831-9497
E-Mail: headquarters@pennwell.com
Home Page: www.pennwell.com
Social Media: Facebook, Twitter
Robert F Biolchini, CEO
Junior Isles, Publisher/Editor
News, product information and feature articles of interest to paramedics.
Cost: $30.00
Frequency: Monthly
Printed in 4 colors on glossy stock

21481 Fire Engineering
PennWell
PO Box 1260
Tulsa, OK 74101-1260
918-835-3161
800-962-6484
Fax: 918-831-9497
E-Mail: dianef@pennwell.com
Home Page: www.pennwell.com
Social Media: Facebook, Twitter
Robert F Biolchini, CEO
Diane Feldman, Executive Editor
Bobby Halton, Editor-in-Chief
Provides education and training to the fire service through a hands-on, technically oriented editorial package.
Cost: $29.95
106 Pages
Frequency: Monthly
Circulation: 44824
ISSN: 0015-2587
Printed in 4 colors on glossy stock

21482 Fire Protection Engineering
Society of Fire Protection Engineers
7315 Wisconsin Ave
Suite 620E
Bethesda, MD 20814-3234
301-718-2910
Fax: 301-718-2242
E-Mail: sfpehqtrs@sfpe.org
Home Page: www.sfpe.org
David D Evans, Executive Director
Rebecca Salzman, Membership Coordinator
Samuel Dannaway, Publisher
James D Mike, President

Technical magazine advancing the science and practice of fire protection and its allied fields.
Cost: $145.00
Frequency: Quarterly
Circulation: 4500
Founded in 1950

21483 IMSA Journal
International Municipal Signal Association
165 E Union Street
PO Box 539
Newark, NY 14513-0539

315-331-2182
800-723-4672
Fax: 315-331-8205
E-Mail: info@imsasafety.org
Home Page: www.imsasafety.org

Marilyn Lawrence, Publisher & Executive Director
Sharon Earl, Editor

Each issue focuses on different topics, including Dispatch/Public Safety Telecommunications, Fire Alarm Interior, Fire Alarm Municipal, FCC Licensing, Flagging, Roadway Lighting, Signs & Markings, Traffic Signal Systems, Two-Way Radios, Wireless Data, Wireless Traffic Control, and Work Zone Safety.
Cost: $700.00
Frequency: Bimonthly
Circulation: 12,000
ISSN: 1064-2560

21484 Industrial Hygiene News
Rimbach Publishing
8650 Babcock Blvd
Suite 1
Pittsburgh, PA 15237-5010

412-364-5366
800-245-3182
Fax: 412-369-9720
E-Mail: info@rimbach.com
Home Page: www.rimbach.com

Norberta Rimbach, President
Karen Galante, Circulation Manager

Articles, news and product information for professionals in Occupational Health and Industrial Hygiene.
Circulation: 60,111
Founded in 1978

21485 Industrial Safety & Hygiene News
Business News Publishing
2401 W Big Beaver RD
Suite 700
Troy, MI 48084

248-244-6498
800-837-7370
Fax: 248-244-6439
E-Mail: bradfordd@bnpmedia.com
Home Page: www.ishn.com
Social Media: Facebook, Twitter, LinkedIn

Katie Rotella, President
Dave Johnson, Editor
Randy Green, Advertising Manager

Feature articles and product information for safety, health and environmental professionals. Free subscription to qualified professionals.
Cost: $58.00
Frequency: Monthly
Founded in 1926

21486 Infection Control Today
Virgo Publishing LLC
3300 N Central Ave
Suite 300
Phoenix, AZ 85012-2532

480-675-9925
Fax: 480-990-0819
E-Mail: peggyj@vpico.com
Home Page: www.vpico.com

Jenny Bolton, President
Kelly Ridley, VP
Jennifer Janos, Controller

Infection Control Today provides science based articles for the general ward, operating room, sterile processing and environmental services departments of healthcare facilities as well as for the public health community.
Mailing list available for rent: 30000+ names

21487 Journal of Fire Sciences
Sage Publications
2455 Teller Rd
Newbury Park, CA 91320-2234

805-499-9774
800-818-7243
Fax: 805-499 0871
E-Mail: info@sagepub.com
Home Page: www.sagepub.com
Social Media: LinkedIn

Blaise R Simqu, CEO

Reporting new developments in related technology. Peer-reviewed articles by recognized specialists from around the world. In-depth articles provide new science based information useful in materials research and product development.
Cost: $1281.00
88 Pages
Frequency: Bi-Monthly
ISSN: 0734-9041
Founded in 1965
Printed in 2 colors on matte stock

21488 Journal of Occupational and Environmental Medicine (JOEM)
American College of Occupational/Environmental Med
25 Northwest Point Blvd
Suite 700
Elk Grove Village, IL 60007

847-818-1800
Fax: 847-818-9266
E-Mail: acoeminfo@acoem.org
Home Page: www.acoem.org

Barry Eisenberg, Executive Director
Marianne Dreger, Communications Director

The official publication of the ACOEM, the Journal provides the latest data on reseach, as well as practical information for use in everyday practice. Readers find articles, case reviews, news and calendar of events, book reviews, and information about new product offerings.
Cost: $338.00
Frequency: Monthly/Free for Members
ISSN: 1076-2752
Founded in 1916

21489 Journal of Security Education
Academy of Security Educators & Trainers
PO Box 802
Berryville, VA 22611

540-554-2540
Fax: 540-554-2558
Home Page: www.asetcse.org

Dr Richard W Kobetz, Executive Director
Dr HHA Cooper, President
Mary E Kobetz, Secretary-Treasurer

21490 Law and Order Magazine
Hendon Publications
130 Waukegan Rd
Suite 202, 2nd Floor
Deerfield, IL 60015-4912

847-444-3300
800-843-9764
Fax: 847-444-3333
E-Mail: info@hendonpub.com
Home Page: www.hendonpub.com

Henry Kingwill, President
Henry Kingwill, Publisher
Kathryn Murnik, Director

Latest news of interest to police and law enforcement professionals. New product and service information, available in print and online.
Cost: $24.95
Frequency: Monthly
Circulation: 32304
Founded in 1953

21491 Materials Evaluation
American Society for Nondestructive Testing
1711 Arlingate Lane
PO Box 28518
Columbus, OH 43228-518

614-274-6003
800-222-2768
Fax: 614-274-6899
E-Mail: kwie@asnt.org
Home Page: www.asnt.org

Paul McIntire, Publication Manager
Betsy Blazar, Marketing Manager
Shelby Reeves, Owner
Wayne Hollile, Executive Director

Research, reviews and information of nondestructive testing materials. Provides members and subscribers the latest news and technical information concerning this industry.
Cost: $10.00
Frequency: Monthly

21492 National Defense Magazine
National Defense Industrial Association
2111 Wilson Blvd
Suite 400
Arlington, VA 22201-3061

703-522-1820
703-247-9469
Fax: 703-522-1885
E-Mail: info@ndia.org
Home Page: www.ndia.org

Lawrence Farrell, President
Sandra I Erwin, Editor
Sharon Foster, Circulation Manager

Places main focus on issues concerning the U.S. defense industry. Provides the trends in national security, including technology advancement, acquisition policy, critical industry sectors, and marketing are editorial staples.
Cost: $40.00
Frequency: Monthly
Circulation: 30000
ISSN: 0092-1491
Founded in 1946

21493 National Fire Protection Association Newsletter
National Fire Protection Association
1 Batterymarch Park
Quincy, MA 02169-7471

617-770-3000
800-344-3555
Fax: 617-770-0700
E-Mail: publicaffairs@nfpa.org
Home Page: www.nfpa.org

James M. Shannon, President/CEO
Peg O'Brien, Administrator - Public Affairs
Sharon Gamache, Executive Director
Bruce Mullen, CFO
Paul Crossman, VP, Marketing

Written for various fire safety professionals and covers major topics in fire protection and suppression. The Journal carries investigation reports written by NFPA specialists, special NFPA statistical studies on large-loss fires, multiple deaths, fire fighter deaths and injuries and others annually and articles on fire protec-

tion advances, public education and information of interest to NFPA members.
75000 Members
Frequency: Monthly
Founded in 1896

21494 National Locksmith
National Publishing Company
1533 Burgundy Pkwy
Streamwood, IL 60107-1811

630-837-1250
Fax: 630-837-1210
E-Mail: natllock@aol.com
Home Page: www.locksmithledger.net

Marc Goldberg, Publisher
Greg Mango, Editor

New products, marketing, sales, merchandising, and the array of factors involved in successful locksmith enterprises and services. Informs professionals about the latest news and techniques in security.
Cost: $46.00
Frequency: Monthly
Circulation: 17000
Founded in 1983

21495 Occupational Hazards
Penton Media
1166 Avenue of the Americas
Suite 316
Cleveland, NY 10036
212-204-4200
Fax: 216-696-6662
E-Mail: information@penton.com
Home Page: www.penton.com

Jane Cooper, Marketing
Bob Marinez, Publisher
Rob Howlette, Advertising Manager
Chris Meyer, Director
Bev Walter, Customer Service

Analysis of qualified recipients who have indicated that they recommend, select and/or buy the safety equipment, fire protection and other occupational health products.
Cost: $50.00
65 Pages
Frequency: Monthly
Circulation: 71,000
ISSN: 0029-7909
Founded in 1892
Printed in 4 colors on glossy stock

21496 Oregon Investigator
PO Box 2705
Portland, OR 97208

866-584-8645
E-Mail: webmaster@oali.org
Home Page: www.oali.org

Ted J Tolliver, Executive Director
Patricia Vollbrect, President

Official journal of the organization setting a standard of excellence among investigators. Legislative issues and news of upcoming seminars.
Founded in 1983

21497 Pest Control Technology
GIE Media
4012 Bridge Avenue
Cleveland, OH 44113

216-961-4130
800-456-0707
Fax: 216-961-0364
Home Page: www.pctonline.com

Dan Moreland, Publisher
Jodi Dorsch, CEO

Directed towards technological and educational advancement in the pest control industry.
Cost: $35.00
76 Pages
Frequency: Monthly
ISSN: 0730-7608
Founded in 1972
Printed in 4 colors on glossy stock

21498 Pollution Equipment News
Rimbach Publishing
8650 Babcock Blvd
Suite 1
Pittsburgh, PA 15237-5010
412-364-5366
800-245-3182
Fax: 412-369-9720
E-Mail: info@rimbach.com
Home Page: www.rimbach.com

Norberta Rimbach, President
Karen Galante, Circulation Manager
Paul Henderson, VP of Sales and Marketing
Richard Rimbach, Owner

Provides information to those responsible for selecting products and services for air, water, wastewater and hazardous waste pollution abatement.
Frequency: Bi-Annually
Circulation: 91000
Founded in 1968

21499 Process Safety Progress
John Wiley & Sons
1475 Crosspoint Boulevard
Indianapolis, IN 46256

877-762-2974
Fax: 800-597-3299
Home Page: www.wiley.com
Social Media: LinkedIn

D A Crowl, Editor
Joseph F Louvar, Editor

Practical information for engineering professionals. Focuses on chemical and hydrocarbon safety, loss prevention and health.
Cost: $345.00
Frequency: Quarterly
ISSN: 1066-8527
Founded in 1908

21500 Professional Safety
American Society of Safety Engineers
1800 E Oakton Street
Des Plaines, IL 60018

847-699-2929
Fax: 847-768-3434
E-Mail: customerservice@asse.org
Home Page: www.asse.org
Social Media: Facebook, Twitter

Fred Fortman, Executive Director
Jim Drzewiecki, Finance/Controller Director
Diane Hurns, Manager Public Relations Department

Journal of the well known professional safety, health and environmental organization. Articles provide in-depth examination of health and safety concerns.
Cost: $60.00
Frequency: Monthly
Founded in 1990

21501 Public Safety Communications/APCO Bulletin
Association of Public-Safety Comm Officials Int'l
351 N Williamson Boulevard
Daytona Beach, FL 32114-1112

386-322-2500
888-272-6911
Fax: 386-322-2501
E-Mail: apco@apcointl.org
Home Page: www.apcointl.org/
Social Media: Facebook, Twitter, LinkedIn, You Tube

Toni Edwards, Managing Editor
George S Rice Jr, Executive Director
Susan Stowell, Member Services Director
Garry Mendez, Marketing/Communications Director
Robert Gurss Esq., Legal/Government Affairs Director

Newsletter dedicated to the enhancement of public safety communications and to serving its more than 15,000 members, the people who use public safety communications systems and services. Subscription is a member benefit.
Frequency: Monthly
Circulation: 13000
ISSN: 1526-1646
Founded in 1935

21502 Quality Digest
Quality Control International
555 East Avenue
P.O. Box 1769
Chico, CA 95926

530-893-4095
Fax: 530-893-0395
E-Mail: qualitydigest@qualitydigest.com
Home Page: www.qualitydigest.com
Social Media: Facebook

Michael Richman, Managing Editor
Dirk Dusharme, Technical Editor
Scott Papon, Publisher
April Johnson, Circulation Manager

Serves the field of quality-related activites in manufacturing, financial services, communications, utilities, transportation, government, military, retail, educational institutions, health care, consulting, aerospace, software, agricultural, forestry, fishing, mining, construction and other industries. Available in print and free online.
Cost: $59.00
Frequency: Monthly
ISSN: 1049-8699
Founded in 1981

21503 SAFE Newsletter
SAFE Association
PO Box 130
Creswell, OR 97426

541-895-3012
Fax: 541-895-3014
E-Mail: safe@peak.org
Home Page: www.safeassociation.com

Marcia Baldwin, President
Bryan Billings, President-Elect
Frequency: 4-6x/Year
Circulation: 1000
Founded in 1957

21504 SC Magazine
Haymarket Media
161 Worcester Road
Suite 201
Framingham, MA 01701

508-879-9792
Fax: 508-879-2755
E-Mail: iarmstrong@westcoast.com
Home Page: www.scmagazine.com
Social Media: Facebook, Twitter, LinkedIn

Illena Armstrong, Editor-in-Chief
Gil Torren, Sales Director
Sherry Oommen, Circulation Director

Covers all industries that use information security systems. Provides data on information security products, services, market trends and industry developments.
Cost: $60.00
133 Pages
Frequency: Monthly
Circulation: 40,000
ISSN: 1096-7974
Founded in 1999
Printed in 4 colors

21505 Safe & Vault Technology
Safe & Vault Technicians Association

3500 Easy St
Dallas, TX 75247-6416

214-819-9771
Fax: 214-819-9736
Home Page: www.savta.org

Charles Gibson, President
Mike Oelert, Editor

Industry news, reviews, announcements and new products of paticular interest to readers.
Cost: $45.00
Frequency: Monthly
Circulation: 3000
Founded in 1986

21506 Safety & Health
National Safety Council
PO Box 558
Itasca, IL 60143-0558

630-775-2213
800-621-7615
Fax: 630-285-1315
E-Mail: info@nsc.org
Home Page: www.nsc.org

Alan C McMillan, CEO
Melissa J Ruminski, Managing Editor
Suzanne Powills, Publisher

Coverage of safety news and changes, trade shows and training courses.
Cost: $58.50
Frequency: Monthly
Founded in 1954
Mailing list available for rent

21507 Security Dealer
Cygnus Publishing
PO Box 803
Fort Atkinson, WI 53538-0803

920-000-1111
800-547-7377
Fax: 920-563-1699
Home Page: www.cygnusb2b.com

John French, CEO
Susan Brady, Editor-in-Chief
Susan Whitehurst, Group Publisher

Trade publication for those in the electronic burglary and fire alarm system business.
Cost: $112.00
Frequency: Monthly
Circulation: 25500
Founded in 1966

21508 Security Distributing and Marketing
Business News Publishing
1050 IL Route 83
Suite 200
Bensenville, IL 60106-1096

630-377-5909
Fax: 630-227-0214
E-Mail: zaludb@bnpmedia.com
Home Page: www.sdmmag.com

Katie Rotella, President
Laura Stepanek, Editor
Russ Gager, Senior Editor

Information source for the electronic security, life safety and home systems industries. Subscription free to professionals.
Frequency: Monthly
Circulation: 28000

21509 Security Industry Buyers Guide
ASIS International

21510 Security Magazine
Business News Publishing
2401 W Big Beaver Rd
Suite 700
Troy, MI 48084-3333

248-362-3700
Fax: 248-362-0317
E-Mail: zalud@bnpmedia.com
Home Page: www.bnpmedia.com

Mitchell Henderson, CEO
Mark McCourt, Publisher
Russ Gager, Senior Editor
Laura Stepanek, Editor
Mark McCourt, Pulisher

Covers all types of businesses, including industrial manufacturing, service companies, institutions and government, as well as consulting, design, and integrator firms that specify security. News, columns and security product information. No charge to professionals.
Frequency: Monthly
Circulation: 40590
Founded in 1964
Printed in 4 colors on glossy stock

21511 Security Management
American Society for Industrial Security
1625 Prince Street
Alexandria, VA 22314-2818

703-519-6200
800-368-5685
Fax: 703 519-6299
E-Mail: sharowitz@asisonline.org
Home Page: www.securitymanagement.com

Denny White, Publisher
Sherry Harowitz, Editor-in-Chief
Carlton Purvis, Associate Editor

Features, news and trends in the security world. In print and online.
Cost: $48.00
Frequency: Monthly
Founded in 1955

21512 Security Products
Stevens Publishing Corporation
5151 Belt Line Rd
10th Floor
Dallas, TX 75254-7507

972-687-6700
Fax: 972-687-6767
Home Page: www.stevenspublishing.com

Craig S Stevens, President
Margaret Perry, Circulation Director
Russell Lindsay, Publisher
Ralph Jensen, Editor
Karina Sanchez, Managing Editor

Offers examples of security solutions set by such facilities as casinos and hospitals, and explores such issues as false alarm reduction and personnel training, it also highlights new technologies.
Cost: $75.00
Frequency: Monthly
Circulation: 65000
Founded in 1925

21513 Security Sales & Integration
Bobit Publishing Company
3520 Challenger St
Torrance, CA 90503-1640

310-533-2400
Fax: 310-533-2500
E-Mail: info@securitysales.com
Home Page: www.bobit.com

Edward J Bobit, CEO
Scott Goldfine, Editor-in-chief
Michael Zawinski, Publisher

News, feature articles, columnists and new products in the field ofelectronic security.
Cost: $15.00
Frequency: Monthly
Founded in 1981

21514 Security and Privacy
IEEE Computer Society
10662 Los Vaqueros Drive
PO Box 3014
Los Alamitos, CA 90720-1314

714-821-8380
800-272-6657
Fax: 714-821-4010
E-Mail: help@computer.org
Home Page: www.computer.org/security

Angela Burgess, Publisher
Kathy Clark-Fisher, Lead Editor
Georgann Carter, Circulation Manager
George Cybenko, Editor-in-Chief

Trans-border data flow issues, protocols, database management and security. Available online to members and in print to others.
Cost: $29.00
Frequency: 6 Issues/Year
Circulation: 1600
Founded in 1979

21515 Sound & Video Contractor
Primedia
PO Box 12914
Overland Park, KS 66282

913-341-1300
Fax: 913-967-1903
E-Mail: mjohnson@primediabusiness.com
Home Page: www.svconline.com

Michael Goldman, Editor
Cynthia Wisehart, Editorial Director
Charissa Young, Associate Editor

Contains information on sound systems, video display, security, CCTV, home theater, and automation. Delivers in depth instruction and examples of successful installations, fundamental acoustical and video theory and news on new technologies affecting the systems contracting business.
Cost: $35.00
Frequency: Monthly
Circulation: 21000
Founded in 1983
Mailing list available for rent: 20,500 names at $110 per M

21516 The Poison Line
American Association of Poison Control Centers
3201 New Mexico Ave NW
Suite 310
Washington, DC 20016-2739

202-895-4259
800-222-1222
Fax: 202-362-8377
E-Mail: info@aapcc.org
Home Page: www.poison.org

M Litovitz, Executive Director
Frequency: Biannual
Founded in 1958

21517 Underground Focus
Planet Underground
411 South Evergreen
Manteno, IL 60950

815-468-7814
Fax: 815-468-7644
E-Mail: ufmagazine@underspace.com
Home Page: www.underspace.com
Social Media: Facebook, Twitter, LinkedIn

Ron Rosencrans, Founder
Amy Chmura, Editor

Documents the importance of careful excavation and helps them get the budgets to do the job. Powerfully dramatizes the need for underground damage prevention, excavation safety, and the hazards of not protecting the subsurface infrastructure.
Cost: $25.00
46 Pages
Circulation: 21800
ISSN: 1090-400X

Founded in 1986
Printed in 4 colors on glossy stock

Trade Shows

21518 **AAAR Annual Meeting**
American Association for Aerosol Research
15000 Commerce Parkway
Suite C
Mount Laurel, NJ 08054

856-439-9080
Fax: 856-439-0525
E-Mail: dbright@ahint.com
Home Page: www.aaar.org

Lynn Russell, Program Chair
Melissa Baldwin, Executive Director

Exibits related to aerosol research in areas including industrial process, air pollution, and industrial hygiene. Over 600 professionals attend.
600 Attendees
Frequency: Annual, October

21519 **ASFPM Annual Conference**
Association of State Floodplain Managers
2809 Fish Hatchery Road
Suite 204
Madison, WI 53713

608-274-0123
Fax: 608-274-0696
E-Mail: asfpm@floods.org
Home Page: www.floods.org

Larry Larson, Executive Director
Becky Head, Member Services Coordinator

Focus on floodproofing techniques, materials, floodproofing and elevation contractors, current issues and programs, new federal tax impications and the various means of funding floodproofing projects. implications. Held June in Norfolk, VA.
Frequency: Annual
Founded in 1951

21520 **ASIS International**
1625 Prince Street
Alexandria, VA 22314-2818

703-519-6200
Fax: 703-519-6299
E-Mail: asis@asisonline.org
Home Page: www.asisonline.org

Shannon Burch, Exhibits Manager
Michael Stack, Executive Director

Exhibits related to loss prevention and security for public and private organizations. Held September 24-26, 2007 at the Las Vegas Convention Center in Las Vegas, Nevada.
Frequency: September
Founded in 1955

21521 **America's Fire & Security Expo**
ROC Exhibitions
1963 University Lane
Lisle, IL 60532

630-271-8210
Fax: 630-271-8234
E-Mail: info@rocexhibitions.com
Home Page: www.americassecurity.com

Jerry Carter, Marketing Director

Annual 3 day marketplace featuring state-of-the-art security products, systems and services. Over 50 free educational sessions. Emphasis on the markets of Latin America, the Caribbean and the Southeastern US.
Frequency: July

21522 **American Biological Safety Association Conference**
1200 Allanson Road
Mundelein, IL 60060-3808

847-949-1517
847-566-4580
Fax: 847-566-4580
E-Mail: absa@covad.net
Home Page: www.absa.org

LouAnn Burnett, Chair

Exhibits of biological safety equipment, supplies and services. Held October at the Opryland Hotel in Nashville, Tennessee.
300 Attendees
Frequency: October
Founded in 1984

21523 **American Fire Sprinkler Association Annual Convention & Exhibition**
American Fire Sprinkler Association
12750 Merit Drive
Suite 350
Dallas, TX 75251

214-349-5965
847-949-1517
Fax: 214-343-8898
E-Mail: afsainfo@firesprinkler.org
Home Page: www.firesprinkler.org

Steve Muncy, President
Janet Knowles, VP/Makreting & Communications

120 exhibits of sprinkler heads, pipe, hangers, tools and other equipment. Seminar, workshop and tours. Held September in Phoenix, Arizona.
1000 Attendees
Frequency: September
Founded in 1981

21524 **American Industrial Hygiene Association Conference and Exposition**
American Industrial Hygiene Association
2700 Prosperity Avenue
Suite 250
Fairfax, VA 22031

703-849-8888
Fax: 703-207-3561
E-Mail: infonet@aiha.org
Home Page: www.aiha.org
Social Media: Facebook, Twitter, LinkedIn

Caroline Lacey, Expo Manager
Carol Tobin, Director
Peter Oneil, Executive Director
Michael Brandt, President

Conference for occupational and environmental health and safety professionals around the globe. Held June in Philadelphia, Pennsylvania.
10400 Members
4,000 Attendees
Frequency: Annual

21525 **American Society for Nondestructive Testing Conference**
1711 Arlingate Lane
PO Box 28518
Columbus, OH 43228-0518

614-274-6003
800-222-2768
Fax: 614-274-6899
E-Mail: kwie@asnt.org
Home Page: www.asnt.org

Michael O'Toole, Senior Manager Conferences
Jacquie Giunta, Meeting Coordinator
Ruth Staat, Exhibit/Event Supervisor

Seminar, conference and 150 exhibits of nondestructive testing equipment, services, supplies and laboratory representatives. Holds a smaller conference in the spring. Held November in Las Vegas, Nevada.
3000 Attendees
Frequency: Fall

21526 **American Society of Crime Laboratory Directors Annual Symposium**
139 Technology Drive
Suite K
Garner, NC 27529-7970

919-773-2044
Fax: 919-773-2602
E-Mail: rkahn@ag.state.oh.us
Home Page: www.ascld.org

Bill Marbaker, President

Devoted to providing training in leadership and management techniques in the field of forensic science. Also offers membership the opportunity to network with other laboratory directors.
Frequency: October

21527 **American Society of Safety Engineers Professional Development Conference**
American Society of Safety Engineers
1800 E Oakton Street
Des Plaines, IL 60018

847-699-2929
Fax: 847-768-3434
E-Mail: customerservice@asse.org
Home Page: www.asse.org

Fred Fortman, Executive Director
Jim Drzewiecki, Finance/Controller Director
Diane Hurns, Manager Public Relations Department

Annual conference and expo of 250 manufacturers and suppliers of safety equipment and health products. Held June
3500 Attendees
Frequency: June

21528 **Annual American Occupational Health Conference**
American College of Occupational/Environmental Med
25 Northwest Point Blvd
Suite 700
Elk Grove Village, IL 60007

847-818-1800
Fax: 847-818-9266
E-Mail: acoeminfo@acoem.org
Home Page: www.acoem.org
Social Media: Facebook, Twitter, LinkedIn, You Tube

Barry Eisenberg, Executive Director
Marianne Dreger, Communications Director

AOHC
Frequency: Annual/Spring

21529 **Applied Ergonomics Conference**
Institute of Industrial Engineers
3577 Parkway Lane
Suite 200
Norcross, GA 30092

770-449-0461
800-494-0460
Fax: 770-263-8532
E-Mail: cs@iienet.org
Home Page: www.iienet.org/annual

Carol LeBlanc, Conference Manager

An exclusive event for ergonomists, engineers, and safety professionals. The conference focuses on how companies have successfully implemented programs that provide excellent return on their ergonomics investment. Held May Nashville, Tennessee.
800 Attendees
Frequency: March
Founded in 1998

21530 Associated Locksmiths of America & Safe and Vault Tech Security Expo
Associated Locksmiths of America
3500 Easy Street
Dallas, TX 75247-6416
214-819-9733
800-532-2562
E-Mail: convention@aloa.org
Home Page: www.aloa.org
Social Media: Facebook
Karen Lyons, Conventions/Meetings
Kim Hammond, Exhibits/Sales
Features industry innovation, training, networking and education in the security world. Over 350 exhibitors with cash and carry merchandise. Held July, in Charlotte, North Carolina.
4000 Attendees
Frequency: July
Founded in 1956

21531 BOMA Annual Convention
Building Owners & Managers Association Int'l
1201 New York Avenue NW
Suite 300
Washington, DC 20005
202-408-2662
Fax: 202-326-6377
E-Mail: info@boma.org
Home Page: www.boma.org
Social Media: Facebook, Twitter, LinkedIn
Henry Chamberlain, President/COO
Kurt R Padavano, Chairman & CEO
Richard Gringer, Chair
Ray Mackry, Circulation Manager
Opportunity for business professionals to discuss problems, security, exchange ideas and share experience and knowledge. Held July 21-24, 2007 at the Jacob K Javits Convention Center in New York City.
Frequency: July

21532 Bomb Technicians & Investigators Annual Conference
PO Box 160
Goldvein, VA 22720-0160
540-752-4533
Fax: 540-752-2796
E-Mail: admin@iabti.org
Home Page: www.iabti.org
Ralph Way PhD, Executive Director
Speakers on the latest information on bomb and bio threats.Attendes are in the fields of law enforcement, fire and emergency services, the military, forensic science and other related fields.
Founded in 1973

21533 CSAA Electronic Security Forum & Exposition
Central Station Alarm Association
440 Maple Avenue E
Suite 201
Vienna, VA 22180
703-242-4670
Fax: 703-242-4675
E Mail: meetings@csaaul.org
Home Page: www.csaaul.org
John McDonald, Meetings/Conferences
Exhibitors, speakers and workshops for the alarm and security professional. Held May
Frequency: May

21534 California Alarm Association Winter Convention
3401 Pacific Avenue
Suite 1C
Marina del Rey, CA 90292
310-305-1277
800-437-7658
Fax: 310-305-2077
E-Mail: info@caaonline.org
Home Page: www.caaonline.org
Jon Sargent, President
Jerry Lenander, Executive Director
George DeMarco, Southern VP
Ron Galippo, Secretary
Annual meeting of state trade association comprised of licensed alarm company operators and suppliers of products and services. Nearly 200 alarm companies and 50 suppliers are members. Alarm companies represent 70% of the electronic security industry in California. Held December in San Francisco, California.
Frequency: December

21535 Campus Law Enforcement Administrators Annual Conference
342 N Main Street
Hartford, CT 06117-2507
860-586-7517
Fax: 860-586-7550
E-Mail: info@iaclea.org
Home Page: www.iaclea.org
Delores Stafford, President
Carol Ewing, Professional Development
Presentations on sucessful or new programs and current trends.
Frequency: June

21536 Campus Safety Conference
Bricepac
12228 Venice Boulevard
PO Box 66515
Los Angeles, CA 90066
310-390-5277
Fax: 800-758-0935
Home Page: www.campusjournal.com
Sandra Watson, Conferences/Training
Training conference designed especially for campus safety professionals at both the secondary school and higher education levels. Features more than 13 seminars of critical importance to campus safety decision makers and staff.
Frequency: 2 Days/November

21537 Card Tech/Secur Tech: CTST Conference & Exhibition
SourceMedia
One State Street Plaza
27th Floor
New York, NY 10004
212-258-6093
800-803-3424
Fax: 212-803-8515
E-Mail: abconference@sourcemedia.com
Home Page: www.ctst.com
Social Media: Facebook, Twitter, LinkedIn
Nicoal Crawford, Director of Operations
Nikole Tenbrink, Custom Events
250 booth exhibit hall, seminars, luncheons and keynote speakers in the advanced card and biometric technology field. Explores real world applications in several industries including financial services, goverment and security. Held May in San Francisco, California.
50000 Attendees
Frequency: April

21538 Computer Security Conference & Expo
Computer Security Institute
600 Harrison Street
San Francisco, CA 94107
415-947-6320
Fax: 415-947-6023
E-Mail: csi@cmp.com
Home Page: www.gocsi.com
Social Media: Facebook, Twitter
Jennifer Stevens, Conference Director
Annual event with over 150 educational sessions and exhibitor hall. Held October in Orlando, Florida.
Frequency: November

21539 Contingency Planning & Management
WPC Expositions
84 Park Avenue
Flemington, NJ 08822
908-788 0343
Fax: 908-788-0316
Home Page: www.contingencyplanningexpo.com
Greg Sgroi, Events Director
Brad Lewis, Sales/Exhibits
Courtney Witter, Expo Manager
Serves the fields of financial/banking, manufacturing industrial, transportation, utilities, telecommunications, health care, government, security, assurance, insurance and other allied fields. Shows held in both the east and west coasts.
Frequency: May/November
Founded in 1996

21540 Convention & Traffic Expo
American Traffic Safety Services Association
15 Riverside Parkway
Suite 100
Fredericksburg, VA 22406-1022
540-368-1701
800-272-8772
Fax: 540-368-1717
Home Page: www.atssa.com
Joe Jeffrey, Chairman
The premier meeting place for roadway professionals around the world. The program and exhibits are dedicated to issues and products related to all aspects of temporary traffic control and roadway safety.
Frequency: Annual/February

21541 Counterterrorism & Security Professionals Annual Conference
PO Box 10265
Arlington, VA 22210
201-461-5422
Home Page: www.iacsp.com
Steven Fustero, Executive Director
We believe that all elements of the world's societies must become better educated about the threats of terrorism as a first step toward developing innovative and effective countermeasures to combat these ongoing threats. A better informed society will result in a freer one.
Frequency: May
Founded in 1992

21542 Crime Analysts Annual Conference
9218 Metcalf
PMB 364
Overland Park, KS 66212
919-940-3883
E-Mail: nfritz@du.edu
Home Page: www.iaca.net
Noah Fritz, Director
Christopher Bruce, VP Administration
Annual themed conference helping crime analysts around the world improve their skills and

make valuable contacts. Aids law enforcement agencies in making the best use of crime analysis and advocates for standards of performance and technique within the profession itself.
Frequency: October
Founded in 1990

21543 Disaster Response & Recovery Exposition NDMS Conference
J Spargo & Associates
11208 Waples Mill Road
Suite 112
Fairfax, VA 22030

703-631-6200
800-564-4220
Fax: 703-654-6931
E-Mail: drre@jspargo.com
Home Page: www.drrexpo.com
Social Media: Facebook, Twitter, LinkedIn

Nathan Wills, Account Manager

Held in conjunction with the NDMS Conference; it is an opportunity for local, State and Federal public health practitioners and policy makers to discover the latest equipment, technologies and services available.
2700 Attendees
Frequency: August

21544 Eastern Ergonomics Conference & Exposition
Continental Exhibitions
370 Lexington Avenue
New York, NY 10017

212-370-5005
800-222-2596
Fax: 212-370-5699
E-Mail: information@ergoexpo.com
Home Page: www.ergoexpo.com

Lenore Kolb, Vice President of Sales
Walter Chamizon, President

Learn how to use ergonomics to increase productivity and safety at over 80 educational sessions. Try new products from over 100 companies, in over 2,000 square feet of floor space.
Frequency: June

21545 Emergency Preparedness & Response Conference & Exposition: READY
National Trade Productions
313 S Patrick Street
Alexandria, VA 22314
703-683-8500
800-687-7469
Fax: 703-706-8234
E-Mail: ready@ntpshow.com
Home Page: www.readyinfousa.com

Janie Bridgeman, Sales Director
Maria Chaloux, Industry Relations

Annual symposium and trade show for personnel from federal, state and local agencies to learn about the latest emergency response equipment, technology, strategies and applications.
Frequency: July

21546 Emergency Response Conference & Expo
PBI Media
1201 Seven Locks Road
Suite 300
Potomac, MD 20854

301-541-1400
Fax: 301-309-3847
Home Page: www.pbimedia.com

Robert Lewis, Conference Coordinator

Annual event for first responders and the companies who support them, working together on land, air and sea to save lives and property. Conference and exhibitors.
Frequency: November

21547 Energy Security Expo
EJ Krause & Associates
6550 Rock Spring Drive
Suite 500
Bethesda, MD 20817-1126

301-493-5500
Fax: 301-493-5705
Home Page: www.pipelinesecurity.com

Michael Rosenburg, Show Manager
Edward Krause, President

Intensive conference with workshops led by leading international experts from government and industry. Exhibit area featuring technologies, products and services for pipeline and energy infrastructure including oil, gas, electric grids, power plants and dams.
Frequency: May

21548 Fire-Rescue International
International Association of Fire Chiefs
4025 Fair Ridge Dr
Fairfax, VA 22033-2868

703-273-0911
Fax: 703-273-9363
Home Page: www.iafc.org
Social Media: Facebook, LinkedIn

Al H. Gillespie, President & Chairman of the Board
Hank Clemmensen, First Vice President
William R. Metcalf, Second Vice President
Richard Carrizzo, Treasurer
Luther L. Fincher, Jr., Director-At-Large

FRI education covers all areas of the emergency service: navigating the political environment, managing change, ethical leadership, EMS issues, career development and moor. Exhibitors showcase the newest fire service innovations in apparatus, technology, equipment, gear and more.
12000 Members
Founded in 1873

21549 Fire-Rescue Med (FRM)
International Association of Fire Chiefs
4025 Fair Ridge Dr
Fairfax, VA 22033-2868

703-273-0911
Fax: 703-273-9363
Home Page: www.iafc.org
Social Media: Facebook, LinkedIn

Al H. Gillespie, President & Chairman of the Board
Hank Clemmensen, First Vice President
William R. Metcalf, Second Vice President
Richard Carrizzo, Treasurer
Luther L. Fincher, Jr., Director-At-Large

Each spring, Fire-Rescue Med is the conference for fire-based EMS leaders, providing education and training on hiring and retaining EMTs, public and private integration challenges, embracing technology, billing for services, illness prevention programs and more.
12000 Members
Founded in 1873

21550 Global Fire Service Leadership Summit
International Association of Fire Chiefs
4025 Fair Ridge Dr
Fairfax, VA 22033-2868

703-273-0911
Fax: 703-273-9363
Home Page: www.iafc.org
Social Media: Facebook, LinkedIn

Al H. Gillespie, President & Chairman of the Board
Hank Clemmensen, First Vice President
William R. Metcalf, Second Vice President
Richard Carrizzo, Treasurer
Luther L. Fincher, Jr., Director-At-Large

Discuss important issues, share experiences and learn from one another. In turn, summit participants will generate new ideas to strengthen and advance the cause of the fire service worldwide.
12000 Members
Founded in 1873

21551 Gov't Convention on Emerging Technologies Partnerships for Homeland Security
National Conference Services
6440-C Dobbin Road
Columbia, MD 21045

301-596-8899
888-603-8899
Fax: 301-596-6274
Home Page: www.federalevents.com

Fredrick Martin, Director
Anne Slobodien, Chief Executive Officer

Forum for representatives from federal, state and local governments, along with the private sector to collaborate on and experiment with information technology that addresses mission needs critical to homeland security. Exhibits, workshops and simulation exercises.
Frequency: January

21552 GovSec
National Trade Productions
313 S Patrick Street
Alexandria, VA 22314

703-838-8500
Fax: 703-836-4486
Home Page: www.govsecinfo.com

Denise Medved, General Manager

Provides a full spectrum of security solutions for federal, state, and local governments tasked with developing comprehensive strategies that address physical security, information security and cyber security needs. Educational programs held in conjunction with displays of a wide variety of security products and services designed specifically for government users.
Frequency: Annual/May

21553 HTCIA International Training Conference & Expo
Int'l High Technnology Crime Investigation Assoc
3288 Goldstone Drive
Roseville, CA 95747
916-408-1751
Fax: 916-408-7543
Home Page: www.htcia.org

Carol Hutchings, Executive Director
Ronald J Wilczynski, First VP/Conference Chair

Intended to attract participants from all over the world to take advantage of the training and networking opportunities that is offered.
Frequency: Annual

21554 Homeland Security Expo & Conference
E-Gov Conferences
3141 Fairview Park Drive
Suite 777
Falls Church, VA 22042-4507
703-876-5060
800-746-0099
Fax: 703-876-5059
E-Mail: info@e-gov.com
Home Page: www.e-gov.com

Mike Smoyer, General Manager

Keynote presentations, conference sessions, plenary session and exhibition of solutions and

technologies to enhance homeland security efforts.
Frequency: November/December

21555 IMSA Conference
International Municipal Signal Association
165 E Union Street
PO Box 539
Newark, NY 14513-0539

315-331-2182
800-723-4672
Fax: 315-331-8205
E-Mail: info@imsasafety.org
Home Page: www.imsasafety.org
Social Media: Facebook, Twitter, LinkedIn

Marilyn Lawrence, Executive Director/Publisher
Sharon Earl, Executive Assistant/Assistant Editor

Schools, technical sessions, exhibit floor and product demos.
1300 Attendees

21556 ISC Expo International Security Conference and Expo-Las Vegas
Reed Exhibition Companies
383 Main Avenue
Norwalk, CT 06851

203-840-4800
Fax: 203-840-9322
E-Mail: inquiry@isc.reedexpo.com
Home Page: www.iscwest.com
Social Media: Facebook, Twitter, LinkedIn

Amie Cangelosi, Marketing Coordinator
Kara Buonanno, Marketing/Conference Manager

From around the globe, every relevant manufacturer, product, service and industry expert will be on hand for three days under one roof.
Frequency: March/April

21557 ISC: International Security Conference & Expo
Reed Exhibitions
383 Main Avenue
Norwalk, CT 06851

203-840-4800
Fax: 203-840-9322
E-Mail: inquiry@isc.reedexpo.com
Home Page: www.isceast.com
Social Media: Facebook, Twitter, LinkedIn

Amie Cangelosi, Marketing Coordinator
Kara Buonanno, Marketing/Conference Manager

From around the globe, relevant manufacturers, products, services and industry experts will be on hand under one roof.
Frequency: November

21558 Inside ID: Identification Solutions Mega Show
Inside ID
8900 Saunders Lane
Bethesda, MD 20817

301-365-0186
Fax: 301-365-2519
Home Page: www.insideid.com

Ben Miller, President
Liz Wenchel, CEO

Helps define and center the evolution of the emerging disipline of Identity Management. Education and displays of new products and technologies in identification. Facilitates the marketplace of buyers and sellers, provides a broad-based forum, and gathering place for standards groups and associations around the world.

21559 International Cargo Security Council
1400 I Street NW
Suite 1050
Washington, DC 20005-2209

202-821-1787
Fax: 410-956-0679
E-Mail: icsc@cargosecurity.com
Home Page: www.cargosecurity.com

Joe Baker Jr, Executive Director
Ellen Parkereman, Meeting Director

Workshops and 60 booth exposition for cargo transportation and security professionals from the entire spectrum of cargo security: air, truck, rail maritime and intermodal.
450 Attendees
Frequency: Annual
Founded in 1973

21560 International Consumer Product Health & Safety Organization Annual Meeting
PO Box 1785
Germantown, MD 20875-1785

301-601-3240
Fax: 301-601-3543
E-Mail: icphso@aol.com
Home Page: www.icphso.org

Dedicated to the health and safety issues related to consumer products manufactured and marketed in the global marketplace. Serving both health and safety professionals and consumers by sponsoring national and regional workshops. Annual meeting and training syposium.
Frequency: March
Founded in 1993

21561 NAESA Annual Workshop
National Association of Elevator Safety
6957 Littlerock Road SW
Suite A
Tumwater, WA 98512

360-292-4968
800-746-2372
Fax: 360-292-4973
E-Mail: dotty@naesai.org
Home Page: www.naesai.org
Social Media: Facebook, Twitter, LinkedIn

Dotty Stanlaske, Executive Director
Dean McLellan, President
Bill Snyder, VP
Frequency: August

21562 National Council of Investigation & Security Annual Conference
7501 Sparrows Point Boulevard
Baltimore, MD 21219-1927

800-445-8408
Fax: 410-388-9746
E-Mail: nciss@comcast.net
Home Page: www.nciss.org

Carolyn Ward, Executive Director
Francie Koehler, President
Bruce Hulme, Legislative Director

State associations and firms providing contract security services and investigative services. Our cooperative effort includes a legislative watch and providing accurate information reguarding our profession.
Frequency: March

21563 National Ergonomics Conference & Exposition
Continental Exhibitions
370 Lexington Avenue
New York, NY 10017

212-370-5005
800-222-2596
Fax: 212-370-5699
E-Mail: lkolb@ergoexpo.com
Home Page: www.ergoexpo.com

Lenore Kolb, Vice President of Sales
Walter Chamizon, President

Learn how to use ergonomics to increase productivity and safety at over 80 educational sessions. Try new products from over 100 companies, in over 2,000 square feet of floor space.
Frequency: December

21564 National Fire Protection World Safety Conference & Exposition
National Fire Protection Association
1 Batterymarch Park
Quincy, MA 02169-7471
617-770-3000
800-344-3555
Fax: 617-770-0700
E-Mail: publicaffairs@nfpa.org
Home Page: www.nfpa.org

James M. Shannon, President/CEO
Peg O'Brien, Administrator - Public Affairs
Sharon Gamache, Executive Director
Bruce Mullen, CFO
Paul Crossman, VP, Marketing

Professional development, networking and hundreds of booths from key industry suppliers.
75000 Members
Frequency: May
Founded in 1896

21565 National Safety Council Congress Expo
National Safety Council
1121 Spring Lake Drive
Itasca, IL 60143

630-775-2213
800-621-7619
Fax: 630-285-0798
E-Mail: customerservice@nsc.org
Home Page: http://congress.nsc.org
Nancy Gavin, Expo Manager
Christine Paplaczyk, Exhibit Sales
Alan McMillan, CEO

Annual event for safety, health and the environment.
16000 Attendees
Frequency: September

21566 Police and Security Expo
PO Box 20068
Sarasota, FL 34276-0368

609-466-2111
800-323-1927
Fax: 609-466-2675
E-Mail: webmaster@police-security.com
Home Page: www.police-security.com

Displaying goods, products and services for law enforcement and security professionals.
Frequency: June

21567 Professional Security Consultants Annual Conference
525 SW 5th Street
Suite A
Des Moines, IA 50309-4501

515-282-8192
Fax: 515-282-9117
E-Mail: iapsc@iapsc.org
Home Page: www.iapsc.org

David G Aggleton, President
Robert A Schultheiss, VP
Dick Goodson, Executive Director
Harold Gillens, Secretary
Frank Pisciotta, Treasurer

Seeks to enhance members knowledge through seminars, training programs, and educational

materials. Works to foster public awareness of the security consulting industry.
Frequency: April
Founded in 1984

21568 Professional Security Alliance Conference & Exhibits
PSA Security Network
12011 N Tejon Street
Denver, CO 80234

303-520-0137
Fax: 303-252-1741
E-Mail: lisa@psasecurity.com
Home Page: www.psasecurity.com

Lisa Speyer, Conference/Marketing
Shelley Binder, Customer/Vendor Service
Michelle Medina, Membership

For corporate management, salespeople, project managers and other technicians for PSA member companies. Educational sessions and pavillion featuring video surveillance, access control and biometrics.

21569 Prove It! Measuring Safety Performance Symposium
American Society of Safety Engineers
1800 E Oakton Street
Des Plaines, IL 60018

847-699-2929
Fax: 847-768-3434
E-Mail: customerservice@asse.org
Home Page: www.asse.org
Social Media: Facebook

Terrie S. Norris, President
Richard A. Pollock, President Elect
Kathy Seabrook, Senior Vice President
Fred J. Fortman, Jr., Secretary & Executive Director
James D. Smith, Vice President, Finance

Demonstrate the performance of your safety program and the value of safety. This symposium will show you how and the rewards are great. Develop leading indicators specific to safety, learn what and how to measure, and learn to use metrics to improve safety performance.
30000 Members
Founded in 1911

21570 Rocky Mountain Health & Safety Conference
Colorado Safety Association
4730 Oakland Street
Suite 500
Denver, CO 80239

303-373-1937
Fax: 303-373-1955
E-Mail: info@coloradosafety.org
Home Page: www.coloradosafety.org

Melodye Turek, President
Jan Harris, Finance Manager
Judy Sapp, Manager

Over 100 exhibitors of safety products, regulatory compliance updates and networking. Educational sessions are offered on various safety topics.
Frequency: April
Founded in 1968

21571 SAFE Association Annual Symposium
SAFE Association
PO Box 130
Creswell, OR 97426

541-895-3012
Fax: 541-895-3014
E-Mail: safe@peak.org
Home Page: www.safeassociation.com
Social Media: Facebook

Marcia Baldwin, President
Bryan Bailey, President-Elect

Presentation topics range from desert survival to the latest aircraft passenger egress aids, cockpit design, restraint systems, and school bus design to international symbols related to transportation and safety, and crew training. Attended by an international group of professionals who are there to share problems and solutions in the field of safety and survival.
1200+ Attendees

21572 SAFE Symposium
SAFE Association
PO Box 130
Creswell, OR 97426

541-895-3012
Fax: 541-895-3014
E-Mail: safe@peak.org
Home Page: www.safeassociation.com
Social Media: Facebook

Al Loving, President
John Fair, President-Elect

The SAFE Association is dedicated to the preservation of human life. It provides a common meeting ground for the sharing of problems, ideas and information. SAFE is a non-profit international association headquartered in Oregon, with chapters located throughout the world. SAFE publishes a quarterly Newsletter and Proceedings of the Annual SAFE Symposium. These publications are valuable reference sources for the professional involved in all forms of safety and survival.
1100+ Attendees
Frequency: Quarterly
Founded in 1954

21573 Safetech
Safe & Vault Technicians Association
3003 Live Oak Street
Dallas, TX 75204-6128

214-199-9771
Fax: 214-827-1810
Home Page: www.savta.org

Joanne Mims, Conventions/Meetings Manager

Annual symposium and trade show for professionals in the valuables protection industry.
Frequency: March

21574 Securing New Ground
Securing New Ground
10100 Sherman Road
Chardon, OH 44024

440-286-4900
Fax: 440-286-9169
E-Mail: info@securingnewground.com
Home Page: www.securingnewground.com

Dini Jones, Conference Coordinator
Rebecca Reed, Manager

Annual 2 day conference with influential people impacting the security industry. Learn about financing, new trends and opportunities for the security industry. Breakfast, lunch and reception included.
Frequency: October

21575 Security Canada Trade Shows
Canadian Alarm & Security Association
610 Alden Road
Suite 100
Markam, ON L3R-9Z1

905-513-0622
Fax: 905-513-0624
E-Mail: hewitson@canasa.org
Home Page: www.canasa.org

Tracy Cannata, Executive Director
Joyce Everton, Administrative Manager
Lynne Hewiston, Trade Show Manager

Offering four shows annually. Security Canada East is in April, Security Canada Atlantic is in September, Security Canada West is in June and Security Canada Central is in October. These gaterings offer professional development, information, networking and new products to dealers, distributors, manufacturers and monitoring companies across Canada.
Founded in 1977

21576 Sensors Expo & Conference
Advanstar Communications
1 Phoenix Mill Lane
Peterborough, NH 03458

603-924-5400
Fax: 603-924-5401
Home Page: www.sensorsexpo.com

Cathy Walters, Show Director
Jeanne DuVal, Sales Manager

Informative, sensor related sessions, exhibits and special events for thousands of professionals who will help shape the future of sensing technology.
Frequency: June

21577 Texas Association of Fire Educators Annual Instructors Conference
13492 Research Boulevard
Suite 120, PMB 262
Austin, TX 78750-2254

Home Page: www.tx-tafe.org

Alan Storck, President
Tim Sendelbach, VP
Jim Lee, Secretary
Patricia Clinton, Treasurer

Annual gathering for state fire safety instructors to network and learn the latest in the industry.
Frequency: January

21578 Texas Burglar & Fire Alarm Assn. Annual Meeting, Trade Show & Golf Classic
PO Box 59982
Dallas, TX 75229-1982

877-908-2322
Fax: 877-908-2522
E-Mail: president@tbfaa.org
Home Page: www.tbfaa.org

Rex Adams, President
JD Benfer, VP
Jan Wilson, Secretary
Malcolm Reed, Treasurer

Annual gathering of a large number of professional security and fire alarm companies that operate in the state of Texas.
Frequency: October

21579 US Maritime Security Expo
EJ Krause & Associates
6550 Rock Spring Drive
Suite 500
Bethesda, MD 20817-1126

301-493-5500
Fax: 301-493-5705
Home Page: www.maritimesecurityexpo.com

Lindsey Field, Show Manager
Edward Krause, President

Annual conference and exhibitor hall attended by those who protect ports, harbors, bridges, cargo containers, power plants, off shore oil rigs, railroads, cargo and passenger ships.
Frequency: September

21580 Wildland Urban Interface Conference
International Association of Fire Chiefs
4025 Fair Ridge Dr
Fairfax, VA 22033-2868

703-273-0911
Fax: 703-273-9363

Home Page: www.iafc.org
Social Media: Facebook, LinkedIn

Al H. Gillespie, President & Chairman of the Board
Hank Clemmensen, First Vice President
William R. Metcalf, Second Vice President
Richard Carrizzo, Treasurer
Luther L. Fincher, Jr., Director-At-Large

Brings together leaders from the local, state and federal levels to collaborate against the fastest growing fire threat in the world. From education and mitigation, suppression strategies, high-hazard operations to policy, WUI addresses the toughest challenges facing the wildland firefighting community.
12000 Members
Founded in 1873

Directories & Databases

21581 American Society for Industrial Security: Annual Membership Directory
American Society for Industrial Security
1625 Prince Street
Alexandria, VA 22314-2818

703-519-6200
800-368-5685
Fax: 703-519-6299
E-Mail: asis@asisonline.org
Home Page: www.asisonline.org

Keith Goins, Membership Manager
Michael Stack, Executive Director

25,000 member management specialists in the private and public sectors who formulate security policy and direct security programs to prevent terrorism, dcoument piracy. Available as a membership benefit only.

21582 BCSP Directory and International Registry of Certified Safety Professionals
Board of Certified Safety Professionals
2301 W. Bradley Avenue
Champaign, IL 61874-9571

217-359-9263
Fax: 217-359-0055
E-Mail: bcsp@bcsp.org
Home Page: www.bcsp.org

Thomas L Adams, Executive Director

Directory includes over 10,000 safety professionals holding the Certified Safety Professional (CSP) or Associate Safety Professional (ASP) designation.
Circulation: 20000
Founded in 1969
Mailing list available for rent: 20,000 names
Printed in on matte stock

21583 Business Insurance Directory of Safety Consultants & Rehabilitation Mgt.
Crain Communications
360 N Michigan Ave
Chicago, IL 60601-3800

312-649-5200
Fax: 312-649-7937
E-Mail: KCrain@crain.com
Home Page: www.crain.com

Keith Crain, CEO
Ronnie Drachman, Director Communications

List of more than 150 employee safety consultants and over 70 employee rehabilitation management providers.
Cost: $4.00
Frequency: Annual
Circulation: 53,000

21584 Central Station Alarm Association Directory
8150 Leesburg Pike
Suite 201
Vienna, VA 22182-2721

703-242-4670
Fax: 703-242-4675
Home Page: www.csaaul.org

Steve Doyle, Executive Director
Celia Besore, Director Marketing/Communications
Cost: $195.00
94 Pages
Frequency: Annual
Circulation: 1,000

21585 Computer Security Buyers Guide
Computer Security Institute
600 Harrison Street
San Francisco, CA 94107-1387

415-947-6320
800-227-4675
Fax: 415-905-2218
E-Mail: wwilson@infi.com
Home Page: www.gocsi.com/csi

Patrice Rapalus, Editor

About 650 suppliers and consultants of computer security products, including communications and network security, disaster recovery, media security, personnel security and security training.
Cost: $197.00
Frequency: Annual
Circulation: 4,500

21586 Directory of Mail Drop Addresses and Zip Codes
Fraud & Theft Information Bureau
8400 96th Ct S
Boynton Beach, FL 33472-4400

561-732-3653
Fax: 561-732-4928
E-Mail: sales@fraudandtheftinfo.com
Home Page: www.fraudandtheftinfo.com

Pat Ford, Owner
Pearl Say, Editor/VP

Identifies every one of the 35,000 mail drops used by credit card thieves to steel your merchandise. Thousands of credt card thieves use thse address, which sound like residential addresses, to hide their identity and true address while stealing from you with stolen credit card numbers.
Cost: $605.50
Frequency: Annual
ISBN: 0-914801-07-4
Founded in 1982

21587 Disaster Resource Guide
Disaster Resource Guide
PO Box 15243
Santa Ana, CA 92735

FAX 714-558-8901
Home Page: www.disaster-resource.com

Articles, business resources and product information for public and private emergency preparedness. Free of charge if subscriber is registered annually.
Frequency: Annual

21588 Fire Protection Equipment Directory
Underwriters Laboratories
333 Pfingsten Rd
Northbrook, IL 60062-2096

847-412-0136
877-854-3577
Fax: 847-272-8129
E-Mail: cec@us.ul.com
Home Page: www.ul.com
Social Media: Facebook, Twitter, LinkedIn, You Tube

Keith E Williams, CEO
John Drengenberg, Manager Consumer Affairs

Companies that have qualified to use the UL listing mark or classification marking on or in connection with products that have been found to be in compliance with UL's requirements.
Cost: $35.00
Frequency: February

21589 Fire Resistance Directory
Underwriters Laboratories
333 Pfingsten Rd
Northbrook, IL 60062-2096

847-412-0136
877-854-3577
Fax: 847-272-8129
E-Mail: cec@us.ul.com
Home Page: www.ul.com
Social Media: Facebook, Twitter, LinkedIn, You Tube

Keith E Williams, CEO
John Drengenberg, Manager Consumer Affairs

Companies that have qualified to use the UL listing mark or classification marking on or in connection with products that have been found to be in compliance with UL's requirements. 4 book set.
Cost: $110.00
Frequency: February

21590 Fire Retardant Chemicals Association: Membership Directory
Fire Retardant Chemicals Association
851 New Holland Avenue
Lancaster, PA 17601-5644

202-530-4590
Fax: 717-295-4538
E-Mail: frca@fireretardants.org
Home Page: www.fireretardants.org

Approximately 35 member manufacturers and distributors of chemical fire retardants and related supplies.

21591 Fire Suppression Systems Association: Membership Directory
Fire Suppression Systems Association
5024 Campbell Boulevard
Suite R
Baltimore, MD 21236

410-931-2374
Fax: 410-931-8111

Approximately 120 member companies that design, manufacture, distribute, install or repair and maintain fire suppression systems.
Frequency: Annual

21592 Grey House Homeland Security Directory
Grey House Publishing
4919 Route 22
PO Box 56
Amenia, NY 12501

518-789-8700
800-562-2139
Fax: 845-373-6390
E-Mail: books@greyhouse.com
Home Page: www.greyhouse.com
Social Media: Facebook, Twitter

Leslie Mackenzie, Publisher
Richard Gottlieb, Editor

Features the latest contact information for government and private organizations involved with Homeland Security along with the latest product information. The directory provides detailed profiles of nearly 1,500 Federal & State Organizations & Agencies and over 3,000 Officials and Key Executives involved with

Homeland Security.
Cost: $195.00
800 Pages
ISBN: 1-592371-96-5
Founded in 1981

21593 Grey House Homeland Security Directory - Online Database
Grey House Publishing
4919 Route 22
PO Box 56
Amenia, NY 12501
518-789-8700
800-562-2139
Fax: 845-373-6390
E-Mail: gold@greyhouse.com
Home Page: www.gold.greyhouse.com
Social Media: Facebook, Twitter

Leslie Mackenzie, Publisher
Richard Gottlieb, Editor

This comprehensive database presents a wide range of information that is scattered and hard to find elsewhere, providing subscribers with access to the most comprehensive, up-to-date and detailed information on the nation's homeland security contacts and services. This online database contains over 1,100 profiles of Federal and State agencies and companies along with the names of 11,000 key contacts.
Founded in 1981

21594 Grey House Safety & Security Directory
Grey House Publishing
4919 Route 22
PO Box 56
Amenia, NY 12501
518-789-8700
800-562-2139
Fax: 845-373-6390
E-Mail: books@greyhouse.com
Home Page: www.greyhouse.com
Social Media: Facebook, Twitter

Leslie Mackenzie, Publisher
Richard Gottlieb, Editor

Comprehensive guide to the safety and security industry, including articles, checklists, OSHA regulations and product listings. Focuses on creating and maintaing a safe and secure enviroment, and dealing specifically with hazardous materials, noise and vibration, workplace preparation and maintenance, electrical and lighting safety, fire and rescue and more.
Cost: $165.00
1600 Pages
ISBN: 1-592373-75-5
Founded in 1981

21595 Grey House Transportation Security Directory
Grey House Publishing
4919 Route 22
PO Box 56
Amenia, NY 12501
518-789-8700
800-562-2139
Fax: 845-373-6390
E-Mail: books@greyhouse.com
Home Page: www.greyhouse.com
Social Media: Facebook, Twitter

Leslie Mackenzie, Publisher
Richard Gottlieb, Editor

Information on everything from Regulatory Authorities to Security Equipment, this top-flight database brings together the relevant information necessary for creating and maintaining a security plan for a wide range of transportation facilities.
Cost: $195.00
800 Pages
ISBN: 1-592370-75-6
Founded in 1981

21596 Kodex Security Equipment/Systems Database
Security Defense Systems
139 Chestnut Street
#626
Nutley, NJ 07110-2311
973-235-0606
800-325-6339
Fax: 973-235-0132
Home Page: www.securitydefense.com

More than 32,000 manufacturers and distributors worldwide of home and office security equipment and systems.
Cost: $295.00
Frequency: Biennial

21597 Material Safety Data Sheet Reference
C&P Press
565 5th Ave
5th Floor
New York, NY 10017-2413
212-587-8620
Fax: 646-733-6010
Home Page: www.cppress.com

Regulatory and product safety requirements. Contains full text MSDS's for products listed in the Crop Protection Reference plus additional safety information such as DOT shipping information, SARA Title III regulations, Hazardous Chemical inventory reporting information plus much more. Available in print, database, continually updated electronic version or CD-ROM.

21598 NFPA Journal: Buyers' Guide
National Fire Protection Association
1 Batterymarch Park
Quincy, MA 02169-7471
617-770-3000
800-344-3555
Fax: 617-770-0700
E-Mail: publicaffairs@nfpa.org
Home Page: www.nfpa.org

James M. Shannon, President/CEO
Peg O'Brien, Administrator - Public Affairs
Sharon Gamache, Executive Director
Bruce Mullen, CFO
Paul Crossman, VP, Marketing

List of manufacturers and consultants of fire protection, fire safety and fire service products.
Cost: $30.00
75000 Members
Frequency: February
Circulation: 95,000
Founded in 1896

21599 National Directory of Fire Chiefs & EMS Administrators
National Public Safety Information Bureau
2173 Church Street, Suite 201
PO Box 365
Stevens Point, WI 54481-0365
715-345-2772
800-647-7579
Fax: 715-345-7288
E-Mail: info@safetysource.com
Home Page: www.safetysource.com

Laura Gross, Vice President of Procurement
Steve Cywinski, Account Manager
John Diser, Account Manager
Christina Scott, Business Development Manager

Vital contact resource for busy professionals. Contact nearly every fire and emergency department in the US, nearly 35,000 departments.
Cost: $129.00
Frequency: June
Circulation: 10000
Founded in 1964

21600 National Directory of Law Enforcement Administrators
National Public Safety Information Bureau
2173 Church Street, Suite 201
PO Box 365
Stevens Point, WI 54481-0365
715-345-2772
800-647-7579
Fax: 715-345-7288
E-Mail: info@safetysource.com
Home Page: www.safetysource.com

Laura Gross, Vice President of Procurement
Steve Cywinski, Account Manager
John Diser, Account Manager
Christina Scott, Business Development Manager

Listing of police departments, sheriffs, criminal prosecutors, state law enforcement, criminal investigation and homeland security agencies.
Cost: $129.00
Frequency: June
Circulation: 10000
ISBN: 1-880245-22-1
Founded in 1964

21601 National Work Zone Safety Information Clearinghouse
Texas Transportation Institute
3135 Tamu
College Station, TX 77843-0001
979-845-1715
888-447-5556
E-Mail: workzone@tamu.edu
Home Page: www.wzsafety.tamu.edu

Cooperative partnership between the American Road and Transportation Builders Association and the Texas Transportation Institute. Offers information traffic accidents and crashes, equipment and technology, legislation, research projects and training.

21602 Occupational Safety & Health Database
American Industrial Hygiene Association
2700 Prosperity Ave
Suite 250
Fairfax, VA 22031-4321
703-849-8267
Fax: 703-207-3561
E-Mail: infonet@aiha.org
Home Page: www.aiha.org

Steven Davis, Executive Director
Wanda Barbour, Chairman
Paul DeBiase, Secretary

Web accessible database with over 22,000 original abstracts covering virtually all aspects of the occupational safety and health field. Records contain original abstracts as well as complete bibliographic information. Documents represented are from sources dating back to the early 1970s as well as important articles from earlier literature.
Cost: $240.00
Frequency: Individual Subscription

21603 Security Industry Sourcebook
PRIMEDIA Business Magazines & Media
1166 Avenue of the Americas
Shawnee Mission, NY 66282-2901
212-204-4200
Fax: 913-514-6895
E-Mail: landerson@primediabusiness.com
Home Page: www.penton.com

Eric Jacobson, Senior VP

Listings of over 600 manufacturers and distributors of security and safety products.
Frequency: Annual
Circulation: 28,400

21604 Society of Fire Protection Engineers: Membership Roster
Society of Fire Protection Engineers
7315 Wisconsin Ave
Suite 1225W
Bethesda, MD 20814-3234
301-718-2910
Fax: 301-718-2242
E-Mail: info@aiia-sfpe.org
Home Page: www.sfpe.org
Pamela A Powell, Editor
Kathleen Almond, Executive Director
Allan Freedman, Executive Director
Frequency: Annual February

Industry Web Sites

21605 http://gold.greyhouse.com
G.O.L.D Grey House OnLine Databases
Grey House Publishing's online database platform, GOLD, offers Quick Search, Keyword Search and Expert Search for most business sectors including safety and security markets. The GOLD platform makes finding the information you need quick and easy - whether you're a novice searcher or an experienced database user. All of Grey House's directory products are be available for subscription on the GOLD platform.

21606 www.abih.org
American Board of Industrial Hygiene
Information on credientials for Certified Industrial Hygienist status.

21607 www.afaa.org
Automatic Fire Alarm Association
Members are made up of manufacturers, installers and others interested in fire alarm and detection equipment. Seminars are conducted on a national basis.

21608 www.allbounty.com
North American Recovery Network
Worldwide portal for agents of collateral repossession and bail bonds. Chats, forums and industry news.

21609 www.aloa.org
Associated Locksmiths of America
News and event information for the locksmith industry. Maintains referral service and offers insurance and bonding programs.

21610 www.alw.nih.gov/Security/security
Center for Information Technology
Computer security information and links.

21611 www.apco911.org
Association of Public-Safety Communications Officials International

Dedicated to the enhancement of public safety communications and to serving its more than 15,000 members, the people who use public safety communications systems and services.

21612 www.asisonline.org
American Society for Industrial Security
Organization which features ideas and practices for business and industrial security managers.

21613 www.asse.org
American Society of Safety Engineers
Information for members on upcoming meetings, training and local chapters.

21614 www.atssa.org
American Traffic Safety Services Association
Promotes uniform use of lights, signs, pavement markings and barricades. Distributes technical information and sponsors training courses for worksite traffic supervisors.

21615 www.bioxs.com
Bio XS
Biometrics newsletter updated weekly. Features company profiles and new products.

21616 www.buildershardware.com
Builders Hardware Manufacturers Association
Code & life safety regulation information concerning locks and builders hardware.

21617 www.businesssecuritytips.com
Security Industry Association
Provides businesses with technology specific information and helps business owners and managers understand how available technology can be be better utilized.

21618 www.ccohs.ca
Canadian Centre for Occupational Safety & Health
Information on safety and industrial health topics in Canada.

21619 www.cdc.gov/niosh/homepage.html
National Institute for Occupational Safety/Health
Information on chemical safety, emergency response, injuries, construction, mining, agriculture concerns, respirators and much more.

21620 www.cert.org
Carnegie Mellon Software Engineering Institute
News, statistics and helpful articles relating to computer security.

21621 www.chemsafety.gov
US Chemical Safety & Hazard Investigation Board
Investigative reports of chemical safety incidents and an archive of completed investigations and recommondations made to regulators.

21622 www.cisecurity.org
Center for Internet Security
Helps organizations around the world effectively manage the risks related to internet security.

21623 www.csrc.nist.gov
National Institute of Standards & Technology
Information, links and white papers from the Information Technology Laboratory, the Computer Security Division and the Computer Security Resource Center.

21624 www.disaster-resource.com
Disaster Resource Guide
News, articles, business resources and product highlights for security and business managers as well as contingency planners who are in charge of emergency business recovery.

21625 www.eia-usa.org
Environmental Information Association
Nonprofit organization dedicated to providing environmental information to individuals, members and the industry. Disseminates information on the abatement of asbestos and lead-based paint, indoor air quality, safety and health issues, analytical issues and environmental site assessments.

21626 www.fama.org
Fire Apparatus Manufacturers' Association
Membership association for manufacturers of emergency vehicles and components affixed to or carried upon the vehicle.

21627 www.findbiometrics.com
Topickz
Showcases new technologies in biometric security and provides links to companies providing them.

21628 www.first.org
Forum of Incident Response and Security Teams
Brings together a variety of computer security incident response teams from government, commercial and academic organizations. This site encourages cooperation in incident prevention, rapid reaction to incidents and to promote information sharing.

21629 www.fraud.org
National Consumers League
Your source for Internet and telemarketing fraud information.

21630 www.fraudandtheftinfo.com
Fraud and Theft Information Bureau
Provides problem solving, crime prevention, money saving manuals and fraud blocker databases.

21631 www.fssa.net
Fire Suppression Systems Association
Association news and events for designers, suppliers and installers of special hazard fire suppression equipment, gases and detectors.

21632 www.ginetwork.com
Global Investigators Network
Worldwide internet based organization for private investigators.

21633 www.gocsi.org
Computer Security Institute
Information on computer and network security.

21634 www.greyhouse.com
Grey House Publishing
Authoritative reference directories for most business sectors including safety and security markets. Users can search the online databases with varied search criteria allowing for custom searches by product category, geographic area, sales volume, keyword, subject and more. Full Grey House catalog and online ordering also available.

21635 www.highwaysafety.org
Insurance Institute for Highway Safety
Vehicle safety news and statistics from traffic and motor vehicle safety organization supported by auto insurers.

21636 www.htcia.org
Int'l High Technology Crime Investigation Assoc
Designed to encourage, promote, aid and effect the voluntary interchange of data, information, experience, ideas and knowledge about methods, processes, and techniques relating to investigations and security in advanced technologies among its membership.

21637 www.imsasafety.org
International Municipal Signal Association

Basic purpose of the organization is to keep its members and others in the profession, up-to-date on proper procedures of construction and maintenance of signal systems and informed on new products and equipment developments.

21638 www.infoguys.com
Spyville
Process servers associations, articles and certification information, forensic experts and a searchable database for private investigators or those seeking to hire one.

21639 www.infosecuritymag.techtarget.com
Tech Target
Online information technology magazine.

21640 www.intsi.org
International Security Industry Organization
Dedicated to improving effcient communication to all stakeholders in the security industries and provides them with the necessary information to be more effective in their daily tasks.

21641 www.investigativeprofessionals.com
Investigative Professionals
Consult with a professional investigator, accomplish a people locator search, do a background check, conduct your own investigation or get information on becoming a private investigator.

21642 www.issa.org
Information Systems Security Association
International computer system information from an organization of security professionals and practitioners.

21643 www.museum-security.org
Museum Security Network
Free internet service and mailing list for museum security professionals, curators, librarians, registrar and specialized police.

21644 www.naaa.org
National Alarm Association of America
Alarm dealers association offers training, tips, an online newsletter and other member benefits.

21645 www.ndia.org
National Defense Industrial Association
To provide legal and ethical forum for the interchange of ideas between the government and industry to resolve industrial problems of joint concern.

21646 www.net-security.org
Help Net Security
Daily updated security related site.

21647 www.nfpa.org
National Fire Protection Association
The mission of the NFPA is to reduce the worldwide burden of fire and other hazards on the quality of life by providing and advocating consensus codes and standards, research, training and education.

21648 www.nnsa.doe.gov
National Nuclear Security Administration
Increasing public awareness of nuclear security and current energy issues. Links to website of supporting offices.

21649 www.nsi.org
National Security Institute
Features industry and product news, computer alerts, travel advisories, a calender of events, a directory of products and services and access to a virtual security library.

21650 www.ope.ed.gov/security
Campus Security Statistics
Direct link to reported criminal offenses for over 6000 colleges and universities in the US. If you are considering a college in a large urban city, a small liberal arts college, a specialized college or a community college you can find their security statistics here.

21651 www.osh.net
Workcare
Links to health and safety news. Offers online newslettter free to subscribers.

21652 www.osha.gov
Occupational Safety & Health Administration
Regulations and standards for worker safety in the US. Also included are a searchable database of recent safety violation citations, electronic safety lessons for many industries, a spot where workers can report safety concerns, safety tipsheets and a section for Spanish speaking workers.

21653 www.osha.gov/dop/nacosh.html
Nat'l Advisory Comm. on Occupational Safety/Health
News releases, federal register notices, reports, meeting agendas and contact information for the 12 members representing management, labor, occupational health and safety and the public. This group advises the secretaries of labor and health and human services on occupational safety and health programs and policies.

21654 www.pavnet.org
Partnership Against Violence Network
Virtual library of information about violence and youth-at-risk, representing data from seven different Federal agencies.

21655 www.personalprotection.com
Nine Lives Associates
Information on programs which emphasize personal survival skills and techniques for the protection of others. Information on training and list of protective agents and consultants.

21656 www.picoffeshop.com
PI Coffee Shop
Articles and a national forum of interest to private investigators.

21657 www.pimall.com
PI Mall
Information for private investigator contacts, products, training and services.

21658 www.processservers.com
International Process Servers Association
Resource for process servers and private investigators. Message board and searchable database by zipcode to locate a local process server.

21659 www.ready.gov
US Government
Updates and information on how the Department of Homeland Security is working to keep America safe.

21660 www.rims.org
Risk & Insurance Management Society
Information on worker's compensation, enterprise risk, risk management and financing, corporate governance and risk management.

21661 www.rmsecgroup.com
Risk Management Security Group
Addresses general aviation and cargo security concerns, training for professional transportation personnel, provides threat vulnerability assessments and literature.

21662 www.safeassociation.com
SAFE Association
Website of the nonprofit organization dedicated to the preservation of human life. It provides a common meeting ground for the sharing of problems, ideas and information.

21663 www.saferoads.org
Advocates for Highway and Auto Safety
Information on road safety issues, federal programs, polls, reports and helpful links for consumers, safety and law enforcement agencies, insurance agents and organizations.

21664 www.safetycentral.org
Safety Equipment Distributors Association
Represents wholesale-distributors of safety equipment and works to enhance and improve distribution through excellence in communications, training, education and services.

21665 www.safetyhealthmanager.org
National Safety Management Society
A professional society dedicated to the advancement of new concepts of accident prevention and loss control, promoting safety management.

21666 www.safetysmart.com
Bongarde Holdings
Safety education products and information.

21667 www.safetysource.com
National Public Safety Information Bureau
News, events, web guide and public safety shopping for professionals in corrections, EMS, fire and police departments.

21668 www.securityfocus.com
Symantec
Offers a forum for objective reporting by security experts on the latest computer security threats and prevention.

21669 www.securitysales.com
Security Sales & Integration
Breaking news of electronic security concerns and articles from the current issue of Security Sales & Integration.

21670 www.siaonline.org
Security Industry Association
Promotes growth, expansion and professionalism within the security industry. Online newsletter has the daily top ten headlines in security.

21671 www.stats.bls.gov
Bureau of Labor Statistics
Data on workplace injuries, illnesses and fatalities.

21672 www.terrorismcentral.com
Terrorism Central
Responding to the need for a single, trusted source of information about terrorism and related security issues, this central information repository comprises original and secondary sources spanning decades of research.

21673 www.ul.com/auth/tca
Underwriters Laboratories
Code Authority — online newsletter for the code community.

21674 www.vpppa.org
Voluntary Protection Program Participant's Assoc.
Information on the Occupational Safety and Health Administration's Voluntary Protection Participant program for companies.

21675 www.whitehouse.gov/homeland
Whitehouse

Updates of Homeland Security department and staff activities, list of state homeland security officers and contact information.

21676 www1.blr.com
Business & Legal Reports

Provides essential tools for safety and environmental compliance and training needs.

Associations

21677 American Apparel & Footwear Association
1601 N Kent Street
Suite 1200
Arlington, VA 22209

703-524-1864
800-520-2262
Fax: 703-522-6741
Home Page: www.apparelandfootwear.org
Social Media: Facebook, Twitter, LinkedIn, YouTube

Aaron M. Albert, Director
Rob DeMartini, Treasurer
Paula Zusi, Secretary
Philip C. Williamson, Chairman
Rick Helfenbein, Vice Chairman

The national trade association representing apparel, footwear and other swen products companies and their suppliers which compete in the global market.
400 Members
Founded in 1960

21678 Association of Footwear Distributors
110-114 N George Street
York, PA 17401-1106

FAX 202-645-0789

Dan Peterman Jr, Executive Director

Major distributors of footwear.
13 Members
Founded in 1956

21679 Fashion Footwear Association of New York
274 Madison Avenue
Suite 1701
New York, NY 10016

212-751-6422
Fax: 212-751-6404
E-Mail: info@ffany.org
Home Page: www.ffany.org
Social Media: Facebook, Twitter

Joseph Moore, President
Diane Sullivan, Secretary
Debbie King, Treasurer
Jim Issler, Vice chairman
Scott Silverstein, Chairman

4 International Trade Shows per year.
300 Members
Founded in 1980

21680 Footwear Distributors and Retailers of America
1319 F St Nw
Suite 700
Washington, DC 20004

202-737-5660
Fax: 202-638-2615
E-Mail: info@fdra.org
Home Page: www.fdra.org
Social Media: Facebook, Twitter, LinkedIn, Flickr

Andy Polk, Vice President
Greg Tunney, Chairman
Nick Grayston, Vice Chair
Rick Muskat, Treasurer
Matt Priest, President

Trade association for footwear distributors and volume retailers.
70 Members
Founded in 1944

21681 Pedorthic Footwear Association
8400 Westpark Drive
2nd Floor
McLean, VA 22102

703-610-9035
800-673-8446
Fax: 703-995-4456
E-Mail: info@pedorthics.org
Home Page: www.pedorthics.org
Social Media: Facebook, Twitter

Althea Powell-Chandler, Director
Jay Zaffater, President
Robert Sobel, Vice President
Dean Mason, Treasurer
Christopher J. Costantini, Secretary

Membership organization for individuals and companies involved in the design, manufacture, modification and fit of therapeutic footwear. Provides educational programs, publications, legislative monitoring, marketing materials, professional liason and business operations services.
Cost: $55.00
2000 Members
Founded in 1958

21682 Sports and Fitness Industry Association
8505 Fenton Street
Suite 211
Silver Spring, MD 20910

301-495-6321
Fax: 301-495-6322
E-Mail: info@sgma.com
Home Page: www.sgma.com
Social Media: Facebook, Twitter, LinkedIn

Tom Cove, President & CEO
Neil Schwartz, Research Director
Chip Baldwin, CFO
Bill Sells, VP of Government Relations
VJ Mayor, Director, Marketing & Communication

Our purpose is to support our member companies and promote a healthy environment for the sporting goods industry. SGMA enhances industry vitality and fosters sports, fitness and active lifestyle participation.
1000 Members
Founded in 1906

21683 Two Ten Footwear Foundation
1466 Main St
Waltham, MA 02451

781-893-1497
800-346-3210
Fax: 781-736-1555
E-Mail: info@twoten.org
Home Page: www.twoten.org
Social Media: Facebook, Twitter, LinkedIn, Flickr, YouTube

Michael Atmore, Director
Thomas (Tom) Murray, Treasurer
Jim Salzano, Chairman
Blake Krueger, Vice Chair
Lawrence Siff, Secretary

Mission is to take action and create change for those in need. Built upon a foundation of caring, serving our community through social services and educational programs.

Newsletters

21684 Footwear News
Fairchild Publications
750 3rd Ave
Suite 7
New York, NY 10017-2700

212-630-4320
800-360-1700
Home Page: www.wwd.com/footwear-news

Jay Spaleta, Publisher
Katie Abel, Editor

Weekly publication covering the international footwear industry's fashion trends, news developments, finances and market data.
Cost: $72.00
Frequency: Weekly
Circulation: 17892
Founded in 1892

21685 WSA Today
Show Dailies International
460 Richmond Street West
Suite 701
Toronto, ON 90049-5103

416-730-8488
800-360-3234
Fax: 416-730-1878
Home Page: www.ingle-international.com

Rich DiGiacomo, Publisher
Robin Ingle, Chairman/CEO

Features products and industry news, conference information and interviews. Published daily during the semiannual Western Shoe Show.
Founded in 1946

Magazines & Journals

21686 Current Pedorthics
Pedorthic Footwear Association
7150 Columbia Gateway Drive
Suite G
Columbia, MD 21046-1151

410-381-8282
800-673-8447
Fax: 410-381-1167
E-Mail: info@pedothrics.org
Home Page: www.pedorthics.org

Ed Habre, Board Chairman
Chuck Schuyler, President
Tanya Allain, Communicaton Coordinator

Covers pedorthics; the design, manufacture, modification and fit of shoes and foot orthoses to alleviate foot problems caused by disease, overuse or injury.
Cost: $35.00
44 Pages
Frequency: Quarterly
Circulation: 5000
Founded in 1958

21687 Footwear Market Guide
307 West 38th Street
Suite 1005
New York, NY 10018

212-398-5505
Fax: 212-398-5504
E-Mail: customercare@infomat.com
Home Page: www.infomat.com
Social Media: Facebook, Twitter, LinkedIn

Provides a broad industry overview, including key press, manufacturing and sales contacts in one superb, value-prived package.
Cost: $165.00

21688 National Shoe Retailers Magazine
7150 Columbia Gateway Drive
Suite G
Columbia, MD 21046-1151

410-381-8282
800-673-8446
Fax: 410-381-1167
E-Mail: info@nsra.org
Home Page: www.nsra.org

Nancy Hultquist, Director Communications
Bill Boettge, President

Provides businesses information such as credit-card processing and shipping at special features for the industry.
36 Pages
Founded in 1912
Printed in 2 colors on glossy stock

21689 Pedorthic Footwear Magazine
7150 Columbia Gateway Drive
Suite G
Columbia, MD 21046-1151

410-381-7278
800-673-8447
Fax: 410-381-1167
E-Mail: info@pedorthics.org
Home Page: www.pedorthics.org

Nancy Hultquist, Director Communications
Brian Lagana, Executive Director
Kalin Wilburn, Sales Coordinator
Mike Forgrave, Publisher
Amy Bloom, Membership Manager

Provides educational articles, marketing materials and professional information.
Cost: $55.00
44 Pages
Circulation: 5000
Founded in 1958
Printed in 2 colors on glossy stock

21690 Runner's World
Runner's World Magazine Company
135 N 6th Street
Emmaus, PA 18098

610-967-5171
800-845-8050
Fax: 610-967-8883
E-Mail: rwforums@rodale.com
Home Page: www.runnersworld.com

Andrew R Hersam, Publisher
David Willey, Editor
Steven Pleshette Murphy, CEO/President
Charles DeLana, Marketing
Richard Alleger, Vice President of Finance

A magazine dedicated to the lifestyle fitness activity of running. Aims to inform, advise, educate and motivate runners of all ages and abilities.
Cost: $21.00
Frequency: Monthly
Circulation: 530511
Founded in 1966
Mailing list available for rent: 370,000 names
Printed in on glossy stock

21691 Shoe Retailing Today
National Shoe Retailers Association
7150 Columbia Gateway Drive
Suite G
Columbia, MD 21046-1151

410-381-8282
800-673-8446
Fax: 410-381-1167
E-Mail: info@nsra.org
Home Page: www.nsra.org

Bill Boettge, Managing Director
Nancy Hultquist, Editor

Offers information to independent shoe retailers across the country.
Cost: $35.00
Circulation: 4000
Founded in 1912

21692 Shoestats
Footwear Industries of America
1420 K St NW
Suite 600
Washington, DC 20005-2506

202-962-0380
Fax: 202-789-7257
E-Mail: shoes@shoeinfonet.com
Home Page: www.shoeinfonet.com

Maria L Abrantes, President
Ivo Geidl, office Manager

Complete statistical coverage of the footwear industry.
Cost: $40.00
210 Pages
Frequency: Bi-annually

Trade Shows

21693 Annual Symposium
Pedorthic Footwear Association
7150 Columbia Gateway Drive
Columbia, MD 21046-2972

800-673-8447
Fax: 410-381-1167
E-Mail: info@pedorthics.org
Home Page: www.pedorthics.org

Jeanne Williams, Manager
Brian Lagana, Executive Director

The Annual Symposium is a combination education event and trade show expo. Containing 100+ booths and exhibits.
600+ Attendees
Frequency: November
Founded in 1958

21694 Global Leather
American Apparel & Footwear Association
1601 N Kent Street
Suite 1200
Arlington, VA 22205

703-524-1864
800-520-2262
Fax: 847-522-6741
Home Page: www.apparelandfootwear.org

Kevin M Burke, President
Stephen E Lamar, VP
Scott Elmore, Marketing

Showcases the best in new leather materials and components for the footwear leather, needle and allied trades of North America. Brings together hundreds of exhibitors from the major sourcing cities around the world, showcasing thousands of products.
400 Members
1500 Attendees
Frequency: February/August
Founded in 2000

21695 Metropolitan Shoe Show New York
50 W 34th Street
Apartment 8A6
New York, NY 10001-3057

212-564-1069
Mary Stanton, Show Manager

225 booths.
2M Attendees
Frequency: March/September

21696 Northwest Show Travelers Buying Show Market
2720 W 43rd Street
Minneapolis, MN 55410-1643

612-920-5005
Dona Merchant, Show Manager

100 booths of shoe retailers and specialty store personnel from Minnesota, Iowa, North Dakota, Maryland and South Dakota.
1.5M Attendees
Frequency: January

21697 Pedorthic Footwear Association Annual Symposium
Pedorthic Footwear Association
8400 Westpark Dr., 2nd Floor~
Suite G
McLean, VA 21046-1170

703-610-9035
Fax: 703-995-4456
E-Mail: info@pedorthics.org
Home Page: www.pedorthics.org

Jeanne Williams, Show Manager
Brian Lagana, Executive Director
Nancy Hultquist, Director Communications

One hundred fifty booths plus educational sessions regarding the design, manufacture or modification and fit of shoes and foot orthoses to alleviate foot problems caused by disease, congenital condition, overuse or injury.
1000 Attendees
Frequency: November

21698 University of Shoe Retailing Conference
National Shoe Retailers Association
7386 N. La Cholla Blvd
Tucson
Arizona 85741

520-209-1710
800-673-8446
Home Page: www.nsra.org

Rob Kaufman, Conference Chairman
Tricia Keane, Conference Co-Chair
Chuck Schuyler, President
Mark Denkler, Chair
Frequency: July, Las Vegas

21699 World Shoe Associates: Shoe Show
15821 Ventura Boulevard
Suite 415
Encino, CA 91436-2974

818-799-9400
Fax: 949-851-8523
Home Page: www.wsashow.com

Chris Aiken, Show Manager

One million square feet of exhibition space. Features thousands of footwear styles, accesories, handbags and foot care products.
12M Attendees
Frequency: August/February

Directories & Databases

21700 American Shoemaking
Shoe Trades Publishing Company
61 Massachusetts Avenue
PO Box 1530
East Arlington, MA 02174-8160

781-648-8160
Fax: 781-646-9832
Home Page: www.shoetrades.com

John J Moynihan, Publisher

Brings the shoe manufacturer the news he needs to know.
Cost: $55.00
30 Pages
Frequency: Monthly

21701 Business Performance Report
National Shoe Retailers Association
7387 N. La Cholla Blvd
Tucson
Arizona 85741

520-209-1711
800-673-8446
E-Mail: info@nsra.org
Home Page: www.nsra.org

Rob Kaufman, Conference Chairman
Tricia Keane, Conference Co-Chair
Chuck Schuyler, President
Mark Denkler, Chair

Comprehensive, in-depth, financial account of retail shoe stores. Benchmark for retailers to compare their own operations.

21702 Complete Directory of Socks & Shoes
Sutton Family Communications & Publishing Company
155 Sutton Lane
Fordsville, KY 42343

270-740-0870
E-Mail: jlsutton@apex.net
Home Page: www.fleamarketeer.net

Theresa Sutton, Editor
Lee Sutton, General Manager

Print-out from database of wholesalers, manufacturers, distributors, importers and close-out houses. Database is updated daily to guarantee the most current and up-to-date sources available.
Cost: $44.50
100+ Pages

21703 Directory of Mail Order Catalogs
Grey House Publishing
4919 Route 22
PO Box 56
Amenia, NY 12501

518-789-8700
800-562-2139
Fax: 845-373-6390
E-Mail: books@greyhouse.com
Home Page: www.greyhouse.com
Social Media: Facebook, Twitter

Leslie Mackenzie, Publisher
Richard Gottlieb, Editor

The premier source of information on the mail order catalog industry. Covers over 13,000 consumer and business catalog companies with 44 different product chapters from Animals to Toys and Games.
Cost: $395.00
1900 Pages
Frequency: Annual
ISBN: 1-592373-96-8
Founded in 1981

21704 Directory of Mail Order Catalogs - Online Database
Grey House Publishing
4919 Route 22
PO Box 56
Amenia, NY 12501

518-789-8700
800-562-2139
Fax: 845-373-6390
E-Mail: gold@greyhouse.com
Home Page: http://gold.greyhouse.com
Social Media: Facebook, Twitter

Leslie Mackenzie, Publisher
Richard Gottlieb, Editor

Reach over 10,000 consumer catalog companies in one easy-to-use source with The Directory of Mail Order Catalogs - Online Database. Filled with business-building detail, each company profile gives you the information you need to access that organization quickly and easily. Listings provide key contacts, sales volume, employee size, printing information, circulation, list data, product descriptions and much more.
Frequency: Annual
Founded in 1981

21705 Financial Performance Profile of Public Consumer Products Manufacturers
Kurt Salmon Associates
1355 Peachtree St NE
Suite 900
Atlanta, GA 30309-3257

404-892-0321
Fax: 404-898-9590
E-Mail: services@kurtsalmon.com
Home Page: www.kurtsalmon.com

William B Pace, CEO

About 23 publicly held footwear manufacturers.
Frequency: Annual June

21706 Footwear Distributors and Retailers of America: Membership Directory
Footwear Distributors and Retailers of America
1319 F Street NW
Washington, DC 20004-1106

202-628-1838
Fax: 202-638-2615
Home Page: http://www.fdra.org

Peter Mangione, President

About 65 American footwear importers and retailers.

21707 Shoe Factory Buyer's Guide
Shoe Trades Publishing Company
323 Cornelia Street
Suite 274
Plattsburgh, NY 12901

514-457-8787
Fax: 514-457-5832
E-Mail: sfbg@shoetrades.com
Home Page: www.shoetrades.com

George McLeash, Publisher

Over 750 suppliers and their representatives to the shoe manufacturing industries in the US and Canada.
Cost: $59.00
Frequency: Annual
Circulation: 1,000

Industry Web Sites

21708 http://gold.greyhouse.com
G.O.L.D Grey House OnLine Databases

Grey House Publishing's online database platform, GOLD, offers Quick Search, Keyword Search and Expert Search for most business sectors including shoe and accessory markets. The GOLD platform makes finding the information you need quick and easy - whether you're a novice searcher or an experienced database user. All of Grey House's directory products are available for subscription on the GOLD platform.

21709 www.apparelandfootwear.org
American Apparel & Footwear Association

National trade association representing apparel, footwear and other sewn products companies and their suppliers. Our mission is to promote and enhance our members competitiveness, productivity and profitability in the global market.

21710 www.greyhouse.com
Grey House Publishing

Authoritative reference directories for most business sectors including shoe and accessory makrets. Users can search the online databases with varied search criteria allowing for custom searches by product category, geographic area, sales volume, keyword, subject and more. Full Grey House catalog and online ordering also available.

21711 www.sgma.com
Sporting Goods Manufacturers Association

For manufacturers, producers, and distributers of sports apparel, athletic footwear, fitness,and sporting goods equipment.

21712 www.ssia.info
Shoe Service Institute of America

Shop to shop chat room, links and listings of manufacturers and wholesalers plus shoe care tips.

Associations

21713 International Network for Social Network Analysis
1404 1/2 Adams Avenue
Huntington, WV 25704

304-208-8001
Fax: 304-523-9701
Home Page: www.insna.org
Social Media: Facebook, Twitter

Laura Skvoretz, Chair/ Treasurer
John Skvoretz, President
Katherine Fraust, Vice President
Yanjie Bian, Board Member
Ulrik Brandes, Board Member

The International Network for Social Network Analysis was developed for researchers interested in social network theory and understanding the online world. Members discuss the virtual community, the virtual workplace and social support.
Founded in 1977

21714 Social Media Association

Home Page: socialmediaassoc.com
Social Media: Facebook, Twitter, LinkedIn, RSS, Google+, Pinterest

Paul Rubell, President
Hilary Topper, Founder
Paul Biedermann, Board Member
Beth Granger, Board Member
Donna Rivera-Downey, Board Member

Social Media Association brings together the media community both online and offline. Members are interested in business and innovation through social, digital and future media.

21715 Social Media Club
Post Office Box 14881
San Francisco, CA 94114-0881

Home Page: socialmediaclub.org
Social Media: Facebook, Twitter, LinkedIn, YouTube, Google+, Pinterest

Golden Ashby, President
Ali Sabkar, New Chapter MD
Cynthia Johnson, Editorial Director
Naomi Assaraf, Sponsorship Director
Anders Abrahamsson, International Web Editorial

Social Media Club was founded to host conversations around the world that explore key issues facing society as technologies transform the way we connect, communicate, collaborate and relate to each other.
300 Members
Founded in 2006

21716 Social Media Professional Association
530 Lytton Avenue
Palo Alto, CA 94301

650-600-3844
800-123-4567
E-Mail: info@smpa.us
Home Page: www.socialmediaprofessionalassociation.com
Social Media: Facebook, Twitter, LinkedIn

The Social Media Professional Association provides training, education, and advocacy for its members. It also offers a Social Media Marketing Certification program that aids existing business owners and entrepreneurs as they grow or start new businesses in the social media and mobile web marketing fields.

21717 The Internet Association

E-Mail: news@internetassociation.org
Home Page: internetassociation.org
Social Media: Facebook, Twitter, LinkedIn, RSS, Google+, Flickr, YouTube

The Internet Association represents America's leading internet companies and their global community of users. They are dedicated to policy solutions that protect internet innovations and empowers users.

21718 The Social Network Association

E-Mail: info@thesocialnetworkassociation.com
Home Page: thesocialnetworkassociation.com
Social Media: Facebook, Twitter, Google+, RSS

Jim Nico, Founder and CEO
Dr. Jane Bellan Karwoski, PhD, MSW, Chief Science Officer
Teri Monoson-Nico, Program Director
Daniel Goodsell, General Counsel
Gian Brown, Member, Advisory Board

The Social Network Association is a collaborative industry forum enabling social networking businesses and users to collectively identify and resolce common issues in a productive environment. It provides a comprehensive suite of applications and services to all its members.
Founded in 2011

21719 Word of Mouth Marketing Association
65 E. Wacker Place
Suite #500
Chicago, IL 60601

312-853-4400
Fax: 312-275-7687
E-Mail: membership@womma.org
Home Page: www.womma.org
Social Media: Facebook, Twitter, LinkedIn, YouTube, Google+

Suzanne Fanning, President
Chris Spallino, Director of Marketing
Jennifer Connelly, Events Manager
Chelsea Hickey, Marketing Manager & Editor
Founded in 2004

21720 eMarketing Association
4259 Old Post Rd.
Charlestown, RI 2813

800-496-2950
Fax: 408-884-2461
E-Mail: ema@emarketingassociation.com
Home Page: emarketingassociation.com
Social Media: Facebook, Twitter, LinkedIn, RSS

eMarketing Association is the world's largest association of online marketers. Members meet and network with the top leaders in the eMarketing arena, through its Power Networking Party which helps businesses with new and significant marketing efforts.

Newsletters

21721 A Formula for Fueling Ad Agency New Business Through Social Media
American Association of Advertising Agencies
1065 Avenue of the Americas
16th Floor
New York, NY 10018

212-682-2500
Fax: 212-682-8391
Home Page: www.aaaa.org
Social Media: Facebook, Twitter, LinkedIn

Nancy Hill, President
Michael D. Donahue, Executive Vice President
Laura J. Bartlett, CFO & COO
Michele Adams, Board Secretary

Designed to focus and kick-start your agency's understanding, participation, credibility and leadership in social media with less expense, time and frustration. Created for C level and senior executives charged with the responsibility of new business development.

21722 NRB Today
National Religious Broadcasters
9510 Technology Dr
Manassas, VA 20110-4149

703-330-7100
Fax: 703-330-7100
E-Mail: info@nrb.org
Home Page: www.nrb.org
Social Media: Facebook

Frank Wright, President/CEO
Linda Smith, EVP/COO
Kenneth Chan, Director of Communications

This weekly newsletter by National Religious Broadcasters covers the latest news from the association and NRB's member organizations. The newsletter also serves as a source for tips, trends, and insights relevant to Christian communicators across the spectrum. Topics include audience building, branding, business strategy, innovation, job hunting, leadership, management, marketing, social media, and web strategy. NRB Today also features occasional columns, movie reviews, and product reviews.
Founded in 1944

Magazines & Journals

21723 The Social Media Monthly

Home Page: www.thesocialmediamonthly.com

A monthly magazine for all things involving social media.

Trade Shows

21724 ANA Digital & Social Media Conference
Association of National Advertisers
708 Third Avenue
33 Floor
New York, NY 10017

212-697-5950
Fax: 212-661-8057
E-Mail: info@ana.net
Home Page: www.ana.net
Social Media: Facebook, Twitter, LinkedIn, YouTube

Bob Liodice, President & CEO
Christine Manna, COO
William Zengel, EVP

Discussing how to use social media to impact the consumer decision journey and how to effectively partner with other companies to maximize social media reach and more.

21725 International Network for Social Network Analysis
1404 1/2 Adams Avenue
Huntington, WV 25704

304-208-8001
Fax: 304-523-9701
Home Page: www.insna.org
Social Media: Facebook, Twitter

Laura Skvoretz, Chair/ Treasurer
John Skvoretz, President
Katherine Fraust, Vice President
Yanjie Bian, Board Member
Ulrik Brandes, Board Member

The International Network for Social Network Analysis was developed for researchers interested in social network theory and understanding the online world. Members discuss the virtual community, the virtual workplace and social support.
Founded in 1977

21726 New York Social Media Marketing Conference
SkillPath Seminars
6900 Sqibb Road
PO Box 2768
Mission, KS 66201-2768

913-623-3900
800-873-7545
Fax: 913-362-4241
E-Mail: webmaster@skillpath.com
Home Page: www.skillpath.com

Steve Nichols, Customer Care Representative
Robb Garr, President
This state-of-the-art conference walks through everything needed to start using social media to drive real business results, even for someone who doesn't know the difference between a tweet and a like button. There's no reason to miss out any longer on the proven, bottom-line benefits of marketing with social media.
Frequency: Semi-Annual, April

21727 Response Expo
201 Sandpointe Ave
Suite 500
Santa Ana, CA 92707-8700

714-338-6700
800-854-3112
Fax: 714-513-8482
E-Mail: thaire@questex.com
Home Page: www.responsemagazine.com
Social Media: Facebook, Twitter, LinkedIn, YouTube

Thomas Haire, Editor
Don Rosenberg, VP
Kristina Kronenberg, Marketing Director
Focuses on the evolution of consumers from passive watchers to active and empowered brand evangelists. Technology and social media have enabled and encouraged consumers to engage and interact with content. Learn how to take DR marketing from traditional campaign management to the future of customer engagement.
Frequency: Monthly
Circulation: 12000
Founded in 1987

21728 Social Media Association
Home Page: socialmediaassoc.com/events
Social Media: Facebook, Twitter, LinkedIn, RSS, Google+, Pinterest

Paul Rubell, President
Hilary Topper, Founder
Paul Biedermann, Board Member
Beth Granger, Board Member
Donna Rivera-Downey, Board Member

Social Media Association brings together the media community both online and offline. Members are interested in business and innovation through social, digital and future media.

21729 Social Media Club
Post Office Box 14881
San Francisco, CA 94114-0881

Home Page: socialmediaclub.org/events
Social Media: Facebook, Twitter, LinkedIn, YouTube, Google+, Pinterest

Golden Ashby, President
Ali Sabkar, New Chapter MD
Cynthia Johnson, Editorial Director
Naomi Assaraf, Sponsorship Director
Anders Abrahamsson, International Web Editorial
Social Media Club was founded to host conversations around the world that explore key issues facing society as technologies transform the way we connect, communicate, collaborate and relate to each other.
300 Members
Founded in 2006

21730 Transformation LA
American Association of Advertising Agencies
1065 Avenue of the Americas
16th Floor
New York, NY 10018

212-682-2500
Fax: 212-682-8391
E-Mail: kipp@aaaa.org
Home Page: www.aaaa.org
Social Media: Facebook, Twitter, LinkedIn

Nancy Hill, President
Chris Weil, Chair
Andrew Bennett, Director at Large
Sharon Napier, Secretary/Treasurer

Talent recruitment and retention; regulatory updates; mobility; social media; and growing your business are a few of the sessions scheduled. Tour some of the entertainment capital's most creative facilities, including innovative 4A's member agencies.

21731 Word of Mouth Marketing Association
65 E. Wacker Place
Suite #500
Chicago, IL 60601

312-853-4400
Fax: 312-275-7687
E-Mail: membership@womma.org
Home Page: www.womma.org/events-education/events
Social Media: Facebook, Twitter, LinkedIn, YouTube, Google+

Suzanne Fanning, President
Chris Spallino, Director of Marketing
Jennifer Connelly, Events Manager
Chelsea Hickey, Marketing Manager & Editor
Founded in 2004

Associations

21732 ADMA Annual Meeting
Alaskan Dog Mushers Association
PO Box 70662
Fairbanks, AK 99707-0662
907-457-6874
Fax: 907-479-3516
E-Mail: adma@sleddog.org
Home Page: www.sleddog.org
Social Media: Facebook
Jonnelle Roos, Executive Director
Shannon Erhart, President
Alaskan Dog Mushers Association annual meeting

21733 ATP Tour
Association of Tennis Professionals
201 ATP Tour Boulevard
Ponte Vedra Beach, FL 32082
904-856-6400
800-527-4811
Fax: 904-285-5966
Home Page: www.atptennis.com
Social Media: Facebook, Twitter, Instagram, Google+,Youtube
Mark Miles, CEO
Patrice Dominguez, Tournament Representative
Laurent Delanney, SVP Sales/Marketing
Chris Kermode, Executive Chairman & President
Mark Wester, Tournament Representative
Operates the official tennis computer ranking system. Administers entry system for international tennis circuit and tennis system. Membership restricted to male, touring, professional tennis players.
Founded in 1972

21734 Academy for Sports Dentistry
P.O. Box 364
Farmersville, IL 62533
800-273-1788
217-227-3431ÿ
Fax: 217-227-3438
E-Mail: sportsdentistry@consolidated.net
Home Page: www.academyforsportsdentistry.org
Social Media: Facebook, Twitter
Shelly Lott, Executive Secretary
Founded in 1983

21735 Adventure Cycling Association
150 East Pine Street
PO Box 8308
Missoula, MT 59807
406-721-1776
800-755-2453
Fax: 406-721-8754
E-Mail: info@adventurecycling.org
Home Page: www.adventurecycling.org
Social Media: Facebook, Twitter, Flickr, YouTube, Instagram
Leigh Carter, Director
Andy baur, Secretary
Andrew Huppert, Treasurer
Donna O'Neal, Vice- President
Wally Werner, President
Their mission is to inspire people of all ages to travel by bicycle for fitness, fun and self-discovery. A non-profit organization, it is a resource offering many programs for cyclists, including a national network of bicycle touring routes and organized trips.
42000 Members
Founded in 1972

21736 Aerobics and Fitness Association of America
15250 Ventura Blvd
Suite 200
Sherman Oaks, CA 91403
818-905-0040
877-968-7263
Fax: 818-990-5468
E-Mail: contactafaa@afaa.com
Home Page: www.afaa.com
Social Media: Facebook, Twitter, Google+, Pinterest
Linda Pfeffer, President
Association for the education, certification and training of exercise instructors; information resource center for consumers.
Founded in 1983

21737 Amateur Athletic Union of the United States
PO Box 22409
Lake Buena Vista, FL 32830
407-934-7200
800-AAU-4USA
Fax: 407-934-7242
Home Page: www.aausports.org
Social Media: Facebook, Twitter, YouTube
Bobby Dodd, President/CEO
Michael Killpack, Director Sports
Rachel D'Orazio, Director Marketing/Websites
John Hodges, Director Sponsorship
Amy Racicot, Director Finance
The AAU hosts the Junior Olympic Games, 30 youth sports programs, 25 adult sports programs, awards over 200,000 championship medals annually, partnered with Walt Disney World to host events at Disney's Wide World of Sports Complex, and presents an annual James E. Sullivan memorial award.
500M Members
Founded in 1888

21738 Amateur Softball Association
2801 NE 50th St.ÿ
Oklahoma City, OK 73111ÿ
405-424-5266
Home Page: www.asasoftball.com
Social Media: Facebook, Twitter
Phil Gutierrez, President
Warren Jones, President-Elect
ET Colvin, Immediate Past President
Andy Dooley, Eastern Territorial VP
Beverly Wiley, Eastern Territorial VP
Founded in 1933

21739 American Academy of Podiatric Sports Medicine
109 Greenwich Dr
Walkersville, MD 21793-9121
352-620-8562
888-854-3338
Fax: 352-620-8765
E-Mail: info@aapsm.org
Home Page: www.aapsm.org
Rita J. Yates, Executive Director
Paul R. Langer, President
Brian Fullem, Secretary-Treasurer
Dianne I. Mitchell, Vice-President
David Jenkins, President-Elect
Serves to advance the understanding, prevention and management of lower extremity sports and fitness injuries. They believe that providing such knowledge to the profession and the public will optimize enjoyment and safe participation in sports and fitness activities. They accomplish this mission through professional education, scientific research, public awareness and membership support.
800 Members
Founded in 1970

21740 American Alliance for Health, Physical Education, Recreation and Dance
1900 Association Dr
Reston, VA 20191-1598
703-476-3400
800-213-7193
Fax: 703-476-9527
Home Page: www.aahperd.org
Social Media: Facebook
Gale Wiedow, President
Rene Colleran, Director
Frances E. Cleland, Director
E. Paul Roetert, CEO
Dolly D. Lambdin, President-Elect
Organization that provides educational programs, resources and support for professionals within the fields of health, physical education, recreation and dance.
25000 Members
Founded in 1885

21741 American Amateur Baseball Congress
100 W Broadway
Farmington, NM 87401
505-327-3120
800-557-3120
Fax: 505-327-3132
E-Mail: aabc@aabc.us.net
Home Page: www.aabc.us
Richard Neely, President
Provides profressive and continuous organized competition for sub teens through adults.bers.
250M Members
Founded in 1935

21742 American Association of Collegiate Registrars and Admissions Officers
One Dupont Circle NW
Suite 520
Washington, DC ÿ20036ÿ
202-293-9161
Fax: 202-872-8857
Home Page: www.aacrao.org
Social Media: Facebook, Twitter, LinkedIn, Google+
Brad Myers, President
Dan Garcia, President-Elect
Adrienne McDay, Past President
Nicole Rovig, VP, Information Technology
Stan DeMerrittÿ, VP, Finance

21743 American Baseball Coaches Association
108 S University Avenue
Suite 3
Mount Pleasant, MI 48858-2327
989-775-3300
Fax: 989-775-3600
E-Mail: abca@abca.org
Home Page: www.abca.org
Social Media: Facebook, Twitter, Google+
Bill Arce, Director
Dave Keilitz, Executive Director
Scott Berry, 1st VP
Mark Johnson,, Chair
Tim Corbin, President
Association of Baseball Coaches in the United States.
6500 Members
Founded in 1945

21744 American Camp Association
5000 State Road 67 N
Martinsville, IN 46151-7902
765-342-8456
800-428-2267
Fax: 765-342-2065
E-Mail: pr@acacamps.org
Home Page: www.acacamps.org

Social Media: Facebook, Twitter, LinkedIn, Google+, RSS, YouTube

Peg Smith, CEO
Tisha Bolger, President
Melanie Lockwoo herman, Treasurer
Jennifer Bender, Board Members
Steve Baskin, Board Members

Formerly known as the American Camping Association, is a community of camp professionals who have joined together to share their knowledge and experience and to ensure the quality of camp programs.
6700 Members
Founded in 1910

21745 American Canoe Association
108 Hanover St.
Fredericksburg, VA 22401

540-907-4460
Fax: 888-229-3792
E-Mail: aca@americancanoe.org
Home Page: www.americancanoe.org/
Social Media: Facebook, Twitter, LinkedIn, Google+, YouTube, Pinterest

Judge Charles, At-Large
Tom Pitt, Secretary
Peter Sloan, Treasurer
Anne Maleady, President
Jim virgin, Vice President

A nationwide not for profit organization that is in service to the broader paddling public by providing education on matters related to paddling, supporting stewardship of the paddling environment, and enabling programs and events to support paddlesport recreation.
Cost: $18.00
50000 Members
Frequency: 6 Per Year
Circulation: 35000
Founded in 1880

21746 American College of Sports Medicine
401 W Michigan St
Indianapolis, IN 46202-3233

317-637-9200
Fax: 317-634-7817
E-Mail: publicinfo@acsm.org
Home Page: www.acsm.org
Social Media: Facebook, Twitter, YouTube, Pinterest

William Dexter, President
James Whitehead, Executive Director
Carol Ewing Garber, President-Elect
J. Larry Durstine, Treasurer
James Pivarnik, Foundation President

The ACSM promotes and integrates scientific research, education, and practical applications of sports medicine and exercise science to maintain and enhance physical performance, fitness, health, and quality of life.
20000 Members
ISBN: 0-195913-1
Founded in 1954

21747 American Council on Exercise
4851 Paramount Dr
San Diego, CA 92123

858-576-6500
888-825-3636
Fax: 858-576-6564
E-Mail: support@acefitness.org
Home Page: www.acefitness.org
Social Media: Facebook, Twitter, Google+, Pinterest

Scott Goudeseune, President & CEO
Al Mirnezam, CFO
Cedric X. Bryant, Chief Science Officer
Janet Frenkel, COO
Graham Melstrand, VP, Corporate Affairs

A nonprofit organization committed to enriching quality of life through safe and effective physical activity. ACE protects all segments of society against ineffective fitness products, programs and trends through its ongoing public education, outreach and research. ACE further protects the public by setting certification and continuing education standards for fitness professionals.
Founded in 1985

21748 American Cutting Horse Association
P.O. Box 2443ÿ
Brenham, TX 77834ÿ

979-836-3370
Fax: 979-251-9971
E-Mail: achacutting@yahoo.com
Home Page: www.achacutting.orgÿ
Social Media: Facebook

Ryan Combs, President
Jason Borchardtÿ, VP
David Wilson, Treasurer-Secretary

21749 American Fastpitch Association
2536 Greenacre Avenue
Anaheim, CA 92801

717-952-9311
E-Mail: info@afasoftball.com
Home Page: www.afasoftball.com

Terry Fullmer, Director
Ron Gossmer, Director

Represents those individuals engaged in amateur softball.
250M Members

21750 American Football Coaches Association
100 Legends Lane
Waco, TX 76706

254-754-9900
Fax: 254-754-7373
E-Mail: info@afca.com
Home Page: www.afca.com

Grant Teaffÿ, Executive Director
Gary Darnell, Associate Executive Director
Vince Thompson, Director of Media Relations
Adam Guess, Managing Director of Finance
Janet Robertson, Director of Conferences & Events
11,00 Members
Founded in 1921

21751 American Greyhound Track Operators Association
Palm Beach Kennel Club
1111 North Congress Avenue
West Palm Beach, FL 33409

561-688-5799
Fax: 801-751-2404
Home Page: www.agtoa.com

Ed Braunger, President
Dennis Bicsak, Office Coordinator
Founded in 1946

21752 American Hockey Coaches Association
7 Concord Street
Gloucester, MA 01930

781-245-4177
Fax: 781-245-2492
E-Mail: ahcahockey@comcast.net
Home Page: www.ahcahockey.com
Social Media: Facebook, Twitter, LinkedIn, YouTube, RSS

Joe Bertagna, Executive Director

Maintains the highest possible standards in hockey and the hockey profession
Founded in 1947

21753 American Orthopaedic Society for Sports Medicine
6300 N River Rd
Suite 500
Rosemont, IL 60018

847-292-4900
877-321-3500
Fax: 847-292-4905
E-Mail: aossm@aossm.org
Home Page: www.sportsmed.org
Social Media: Facebook, Twitter

Susan Serpico, Executice Asst.
Bernard R Bach Jr MD, VP
Bruce Reider MD, Journal Editor
Irvin E Bomberger, Executive Director
Camille Petrick, Managing Director

A national organization of orthopaedic surgeons specializing in sports medicine, including national and international sports medicine leaders.
2000 Members
Founded in 1972

21754 American Recreation Coalition
1225 G St. NW
Suite 650
Washington, DC 20005-3832

202-682-9530
Fax: 202-682-9529
E-Mail: tgeorgevits@funoutdoors.com
Home Page: www.funoutdoors.com
Social Media: Facebook, Twitter

Derrick Crandall, President & CEO
Catherine Ahern, VP, Member Services
Melinda Meade, Director of Communications
Tom Georgevits, Dir. Of Partner Projects

A non-profit Washington based federation that provides a unified voice for recreation interests to conserve their full and active participation in government policy making on issues such as public land management. ARC works to build public-private partnerships to enhance and protect outdoor recreation opportunities and resources.
100+ Members
Founded in 1979

21755 American Running Association
4405 East West Hwy
Suite 405
Bethesda, MD 20814

301-913-9517
800-776-2732
Fax: 301-913-9520
Home Page: www.americanrunning.org
Social Media: LinkedIn

David Watt, Executive Director
Maria Kolanowsk, Project Coordinator
Barb Baldwin, Project Consultant

A leading voice and center for information on sports' running medicine. The 'ARA Clinic' provides personal feedback from a select cadre of physicians and sports medicine personnel.
10000 Members
Founded in 1968

21756 American Society of Golf Course Architects
125 N Executive Dr
Suite 302
Brookfield, WI 53005

262-786-5960
Fax: 262-786-5919
E-Mail: info@asgca.org
Home Page: www.asgca.org
Social Media: Facebook, Twitter

Bob Cupp, Immediate Past President
Rick Robbins, President
Lee Schmidt, Vice President

Steve Smyres, Treasurer
Gregg Martin, Secretary

A non-profit organization comprised of leading golf course designers in North America. ASGCA is actively involved in many issues realted to the game of golf, including responsible environmental designs.
185 Members
Founded in 1946

21757 American Spa and Health Resort
PO Box 585
Lake Forest, IL 60045

847-234-8851
Fax: 847-295-7790
Social Media: Facebook

Melanie Ruehle, Contact

Seeks to establish and maintain high standards of quality in US health spas.
Founded in 1982

21758 American Volleyball Coaches Association
2365 Harrodsburg Road
Suite A325
Lexington, KY 40504

859-226-4315
866-544-2822
Fax: 859-226-4338
E-Mail: members@avca.org
Home Page: www.avca.org
Social Media: Facebook, Twitter, YouTube, Pinterest

Kathy Deboer, Executive Director
Ross Brown, Assistant Executive Director
Anne Kordes, President
Kevin Hambly, President Elect
Kim Norman, NAIA Rep

To advance the development of the sport of volleyball by providing all coaches with educational programs, a forum for opinion exchange and recognition opportunities.
4900 Members
Founded in 1981

21759 Aquatic Exercise Association
PO Box 1609
Nokomis, FL 34274-1609

941-486-8600
888-232-9283
Fax: 941-486-8820
E-Mail: aea@ix.netcom.com
Home Page: www.aeawave.com
Social Media: Facebook

Julie See, President/ Education Director
Angie Proctor, Executive Director
Dan Yeats, Event Operations Coordinator
Troy Nelson, Administrative Services Coordinator
Donna Blackmon, Operations Administrator

A not-for-profit educational organization dedicated to the growth and development of the aquatic fitness industry and the safety of the public served.
6,000 Members
Founded in 1984
Mailing list available for rent: 85,000 names

21760 Archery Range and Retailers Organization
156 N Main St
Suite D
Oregon, WI 53575

608-835-9060
800-234-7499
Fax: 608-835-9360
Home Page: www.archeryretailers.com

Kent Colgrove, Secretary
Martin Stubstad, President
Ervin Wagner, Treasurer
Ron Pelkey, Director
Will Moulton, Vice President

A national organization of porfessional full time archery ranges and pro shops.
140 Members
Founded in 1968

21761 Archery Trade Association
PO Box 70
New Ulm, MN 56073-0070

507-233-8130
866-266-2776
Fax: 507-233-8140
E-Mail: info@archerytrade.org
Home Page: www.archerytrade.org
Social Media: Facebook, Twitter

Jay McAninch, President/CEO
Kurt Weber, Director of Marketing
Kelly Kelly, Executive Asst. to the President
Amy Hatfield, Communiactions coordinator
John Nelson, Dir. Of finance & Operations

Formerly the Archery Manufacturers and Merchants Organization, provides the core funding and direction for two foundations critical to the future of archery and bowhunting.
Founded in 1947

21762 Association for the Advancement of Applied Sports Psychology
8365 Keystone Crossing
Suite 107
Indianapolis, IN 46240

317-205-9225
Fax: 317-205-9481
E-Mail: info@appliedsportpsych.org
Home Page: www.appliedsportpsych.org
Social Media: Facebook, Twitter, YouTube

Robert Schinke, Ed.D., President
Brent Walker, Ph.D., President-Elect
Jonathan Metzler, Ph.D., CC-AAS, Past-President Elect
Rebecca Concepcion, Ph.D., Secretary-Treasurerÿ
Kent Lindeman, CMP, Executive Director
Founded in 1986

21763 Association of Diving Contractors International
5206 Fm 1960 Rd W
Suite 202
Houston, TX 77069

281-893-8388
Fax: 281-893-5118
E-Mail: rroberts@adc-int.org
Home Page: www.adc-int.org

Phil Newsum, Executive Director
Claudio Castro, At Large Executive Committee Member
Robbie Mistretta, Treasurer
David Reser, 1st VP
Craig Fortenbery, President

The Association of Diving Contractors International, Inc. was founded in 1968 by a small group of diving companies. Their goal was to create a non-profit organization to cultivate and promote the art and science of commercial diving, establish uniform safe standards for commercial divers, and encourage industry-wide observance of these standards.
500 Members
Founded in 1968

21764 Association of Volleyball Professionalsÿ
2183 Fairview Road
Suite 222
Costa Mesa, CA 92627

949-646-4600
E-Mail: contact@avp.com
Home Page: www.avp.com
Social Media: Facebook, Twitter, Instagram, YouTube
Founded in 1983

21765 Athletic Equipment Managers Association
460 Hunt Hill Rd
Freeville, NY 13068-9643

607-539-6300
Fax: 607-539-6340
E-Mail: aema@frontiernet.nen
Home Page: www.equipmentmanagers.org

Kelly Jones, Certification Steering Committee
Mike Royster, Executive Director
Matthew Althoff, Associate Executive Director
Dan Siermine, President
Meli Resendiz, VicePresident

The purpose of the AEMA is to promote, advance, and improve the Equipment Managers Profession in all of its many phases.
700 Members
Founded in 1973
Mailing list available for rent

21766 Billiard and Bowling Institute of America
PO Box 6363
West Palm Beach, FL 33405

561-835-0077
Fax: 561-659-1824
E-Mail: bbia@billiardandbowling.org
Home Page: www.billiardandbowling.org

Chris Chartrand, President
Joleen Lawson, VP
David Hickman, Secretary/ Treasurer/ Con. Chairman
Hank Boomershire, Director
Jeff Mraz, Director

A not-for-profit association formed to service the billiard and bowling industries. The BBIA network is uniquely structured to open channels of communication between manufacturers and distributors in order to assist and improve members' business operations. BBIA provides an innovative forum for billiard and bowling businesses to share ideas, gain information, gather feedback and explore the dynamics of the product pipeline between manufacturer and end user.
150 Members
Founded in 1940

21767 Bowling Proprietors' Association of America
621 Six Flags Drive
Arlington, TX 76011

817-649-5105
800-343-1329
Fax: 817-633-2940
E-Mail: answer@bpaa.com
Home Page: www.bpaamax.com

Vladmir Wapensky, Executive Director

Supports the Bowling Proprietors' Association of American Political Action Committee.
3.6M Members
Founded in 1932

21768 College Swimming Coaches Association of America
1640 Maple
#803
Evanston, IL 60201

847-833-3478
E-Mail: r-groseth@northwestern.edu
Home Page: www.cscaa.org/

Joel Shinofield, Executive Director
Kirk Sanocki, President
Maureen Travers, Secretary
Chuck Knoles, Treasurer
Pearson Pearson, Sergeant-At-Arms

The oldest organization of college coaches in America; a professional organization of college swimming and diving coaches dedicated to serving and providing leadership for the advancement of the sport of swimming at the collegiate level.
Founded in 1922

21769 Cross Country Ski Areas Association
259 Bolton Rd
Winchester, NH 03470

603-239-4341
877-779-2754
Fax: 603-239-6387
E-Mail: ccsaa@xcski.org
Home Page: www.xcski.org
Social Media: Facebook, Twitter

Chris Frado, President/Executive Director

A non-profit organization representing member ski service providers. The association's purpose is to promote the growth and improve the quality of cross country ski operations in North America.
Cost: $25.00
350 Members
Frequency: Quarterly
Circulation: 350
Founded in 1977

21770 Football Writers Association of America (FWAA)
18652 Vista Del Sol Dr
Dallas, TX 75287-4021

972-713-6198
E-Mail: tigerfwaa@aol.com
Home Page: www.sportswriters.net/fwaa
Social Media: Twitter

Chris Dufresne, President
Steve Richardson, Executive director
Ted Gangi, Webmaster
Kirk Bohls, 1st VP
Lee Barfknecht, 2nd VP

Established to improve working conditions in college press boxes.
900 Members
Founded in 1941
Mailing list available for rent: 800 names at $50 per M

21771 Golf Coaches Association of America
1225 West Main Street
Suite 110
Norman, OK 73069

866-422-2669
Fax: 405-573-7888
E-Mail: info@collegiategolf.com
Home Page: www.collegiategolf.com
Social Media: Facebook, Twitter

Conrad Ray, President
Andrew Sapp, 1st Vice President
Greg Sands, 2nd Vice President
Mark Crabtree, 3rd Vice President
Todd Sattefield, Past President
Founded in 1958

21772 Golf Superintendents Association of America
1421 Research Park Dr
Lawrence, KS 66049

785-841-2240
800-472-7878
Fax: 785-832-3643
E-Mail: mbrhelp@gcsaa.org
Home Page: www.gcsaa.org
Social Media: Facebook, Twitter

J. Rhett Evans, CEO
Keith A. Ihms, VP
Mark D Kuhns, Director
Patrick R. Finlen, President
John J. O'Keefe, Secretary/ Treasurer

Provides education programs in formal settings and at home through videotapes and correspondence courses. Administers professional certification programs, publishes magazines and multiple newsletters, conducts and supports research, provides scholarship opportunities, offers employment assistance and career development support, promotes the image of the golf course superintendent through cable TV program 'Par For The Course' and other vehicles. Provides leadership in governmental issues.
22000 Members
Founded in 1926

21773 Harness Tracks of America
4640 E Sunrise Dr
Suite 200
Tucson, AZ 85718-4576

520-529-2525
Fax: 520-529-3235
E-Mail: info@harnesstracks.com
Home Page: www.harnesstracks.com
Social Media: Facebook, Twitter

Paul J. Estok, Executive VP &General Counsel
Delight Craddock, Executive Assistant
Bente Jensen, Controller

Mission is to help members obtain their economic objectives by promoting live racing, enhancing and preserving the integrity and image of the sport, and providing information to members and the general public about the sport and the significant economic impact of the industry.
35 Members

21774 Ice Skating Institute
6000 Custer Rd
Bldg 9
Plano, TX 75023

972-735-8800
Fax: 972-735-8815
E-Mail: isi@skateisi.org
Home Page: www.skateisi.org
Social Media: Facebook, Twitter, Pinterest, Google+

Peter Martell, Executive Director
Elizabeth Kibat, Controller
Jeff Anderson, Administrative Service Manager
Mary Ann Mangano, Membership Coordinator
Angela Tooley, Reception/Shipping

Industry trade association dedicated to providing leadership, education and services to the ice skating industry.
64500 Members
Founded in 1959

21775 International Federation of American Football
79 Rateau Street

Home Page: www.ifaf.org

21776 International Light Transportation Vehicle Association
2 Ravinia Drive
Suite 1200
Atlanta, GA 30346

E-Mail: membership@ILTVA.org
Home Page: www.iltva.org

Founded in 1984

21777 International Professional Rodeo Association
1412 S Agnew Ave
Oklahoma City, OK 73108

405-235-6540
Fax: 405-235-6577
E-Mail: info@iprarodio.com
Home Page: www.iprarodeo.com

Butch Stewart, Chief Field Representative
Clayton Macom, Chairman
Trisha Smeenk, Membership/Receptionist
Dale Yerigan, General manager
Lindy Wiggins, Sponsorship Coordinator

Governing body for professional rodeo. 500 rodeos across USA and Canada, $5 million prize money per year, 5 million fans.
3500 Members
Founded in 1960

21778 International Sports Heritage Association
PO Box 2384
Florence, OR 97439

541-991-7315
Fax: 541-997-3871
E-Mail: info@sportsheritage.org
Home Page: www.sportsheritage.org

Karen Bednarski, Executive Director
Rick Walls, President
Marj Snyder, First Vice President
Paula Homan, Second Vice President
Ben Sapp, Treasurer

The mission of ISHA is to educate, promote and support organizations and individuals engaged in the celebration of sports heritage.
140+ Members
Founded in 1971

21779 Ladies Professional Golf Association
100 International Golf Dr
Daytona Beach, FL 32124-1092

386-274-6200
Fax: 386-274-1099
Home Page: www.lpga.com
Social Media: Facebook, Twitter, RSS, YouTube, Instagram, Pinte

Carolyn Bivens, CEO
Karen Durkin, EVP/Chief Marketing Officer
Christopher Higgs, Senior VP/COO
Ken Wooten, VP Finance
Micahael Whan, Commissioner

The LPGA is a non-profit organization involved in every facet of golf. In addition to staging the LPGA Tour, the LPGA is also committed to advancing women, youth and the sport of golf through expanding the programs of the LPGA Teaching and Club Professional Division, as well as increasing contributions of the organization and its tournaments to charity.
Founded in 1959

21780 League of American Bicyclists
1612 K St Nw
Suite 800
Washington, DC 20006-2850

202-822-1333
Fax: 202-822-1334
E-Mail: bikeleague@bikeleague.org
Home Page: www.bikeleague.org
Social Media: Facebook, Twitter, LinkedIn, Google+

Andy D. Clarke, President
Eric Swanson, Treasurer
Diane Albert, Secretary
Gail Spann, Chair
John Siemiatkoski, Vice Chair

Founded in 1880, the League is the only national membership organization of bicyclists in the United States. The League works to promote and encourage bicycling for recreation and transportation, and to protect and defend the rights of bicyclists through advocacy and education.
Founded in 1880

21781 Melbourne Greyhound Park
1100 N Wickham Rd
Melbourne, FL 32935
321-259-9800
Fax: 321-259-3437
Home Page: www.mgpark.com
Social Media: Facebook, Twitter, YouTube, RSS
Patrick Biddix, General Manager
Trade association representing the interest of and providing services to greyhound racetrack owners and operators via government advocacy, information sharing, annual conference and trade shows.
35 Members
Founded in 1971
Mailing list available for rent

21782 National Aeronautic Association
1 Reagan National Airport
Suite 202
Washington, DC 20001-6015
703-416-4888
800-644-9777
Fax: 703-416-4877
E-Mail: naa@naa.aero
Home Page: www.naa-usa.org
Jonathan Gaffney, President
George Carneal, General Counsel
Walter J. Boyne, Chairman
Roy Kiefer, Treasurer
Elizabeth Matarese, Secretary
A non-profit association dedicated to the advancement of the art, sport and science of aviation in the United States. The official record-keeper for United States aviation.
3000 Members
Founded in 1922

21783 National Amateur Baseball Association
PO Box 705
Bowie, MD 20718
410-721-4727
Fax: 410-721-4940
E-Mail: nabf1914@aol.com
Home Page: www.nabf.com
Social Media: Facebook
Thomas Stout, President
Vin DiLauro, First VP
Derek J. Topik, Second VP
Glenn McNish, Third VP
Charles Blackburn Jr, Executive Director
The oldest continually operated national basesball organization in the country.
10M Members
Founded in 1914

21784 National Archery Association (USA Archery)
4065 Sinton Road
Suite 110
Colorado Springs, CO 80907
719-866-4576
Fax: 719-632-4733
E-Mail: membership@usarchery.org
Home Page: www.usarchery.org
Social Media: Facebook, Twitter, YouTube, Instagram
Denise Parker, CEO
Sheri Rhodes, Chairman
Denise Parker, Chief Executive Officer
Amber Hildebrand, Accounting Assistant
Cindy Clark, Office/Finance Manager
Formed to develop and promote the sport of archery. Recognized by the US Olympic committee as the national governing body for the olympic sport of archery. The NAA selects and trains mens and womens archery teams to represent the US in international, pan american and olympic competitions.
8500 Members
Founded in 1879

21785 National Association of Basketball Coaches
1111 Main St
Suite 1000
Kansas City, MO 64105-2136
816-878-6222
Fax: 816-878-6223
Home Page: www.nabc.com
Social Media: Facebook, Twitter
Paul Hewitt, 4th VP
Jeff Jones, 3rd VP
Ron Hunter, 2nd VP
Page Moir, 1st VP
Phil Martelli, President
Promotes the advancement and opportunities for coaches and teachers in the sport of basketball.
5000 Members
Founded in 1927

21786 National Association of Collegiate Directors of Athletics
24651 Detroit Rd
Cleveland, OH 44145
440-892-4000
Fax: 440-892-4007
Home Page: www.nacda.com
Social Media: Facebook, Twitter
Erin Dengler, Manager-Communications
Ryan Virtue, Manager- Affiliate Associations
Jason Galaska, Asst. Executive Director
Bob Vecchione, Executive Director
Noreen Byrne, Business Manger
Professional association for college atheltics directors, assistants and conference administrators. Provides educational opportunities and serves as a vehicle for networking and the exchange of information to others in the college sports profession.
1.5M Members
Founded in 1965

21787 National Association of Collegiate Women Athletic Administrators
2024 Main Street
#1W
Kansas City, MO 64108
816-389-8200
Fax: 816-389-8220
Home Page: www.nacwaa.org
Joan McDermott, President
Lynn Hickey, President Elect
Chris Plonsky, Past President
Erin McDermott, Treasurer
Lori Mazza, Secretary

21788 National Association of Professional Baseball Leagues
1325 Franklin Ave.
Suite 160
Garden City, NY 11530
727-822-6937
Fax: 727-821-5819
E-Mail: inquire@napw.com
Home Page: www.napw.com
Social Media: Facebook, Twitter
Mike Moore, President
RJ Sparks, Promotional Director
Two hundred and seventy booths.
2.5M Members

21789 National Association of Sporting Goods Wholesalers
1833 Centre Point Circle
Suite 123
Naperville, IL 60563
630-596-9006
Fax: 630-544-5055
E-Mail: info@nasgw.org
Home Page: www.nasgw.org
Social Media: Facebook, Twitter
Maurice Desmarais, President
Kent Williams, Chairman
Peter Brownell, Vice Chair & Director
Brad Burney, Treasurer
Maurice Desmarais, President & Secretary
Serves as a liaison with other sporting goods associations. The NASGW is the organizer and sponsor of the industry's annual meeting/expo event.
400 Members
Founded in 1953

21790 National Association of Sports Commissions
9916 Carver Rd.
Suite 100
Cincinnati, OH 45242
513-281-3888
Fax: 513-281-1765
E-Mail: info@SportsCommissions.org
Home Page: www.sportscommissions.orgÿ
Social Media: Facebook, Twitter, LinkedIn, Pinterest, YouTube, WordPress
Kevin Smith, CSEE, Chairman
Greg Ayers, CSEE, Vice Chairman/Chair-Elect
Ralph Morton, CSEE, Treasurer
Mike Anderson, CSEE, Secretary
Terry Hasseltine, CSEE, Immediate Past Chair
Founded in 1992

21791 National Association of Sports Officials
2017 Lathrop Ave
Racine, WI 53405
262-632-5448
800-733-6100
Fax: 262-632-5460
E-Mail: naso@naso.org
Home Page: www.referee.com
Social Media: Facebook, Twitter
Barry Mano, President
Marc Ratner, Chair
Anita Ortega, Vice Chair
Henry Zaborniak, Treasurer
Nonprofit 501(c)(3), educational association providing individual benefits such as training materials, liability and assault protection insurance and more to sports officials of all sports and every level.
16000 Members
Founded in 1976

21792 National Association of Student Financial Aid Administrators
1101 Connecticut AvenueÿNW
Suite 1100
Washington, DC 20036-4303
202-785-0453
Home Page: www.nasfaa.org
Social Media: Facebook, Twitter, LinkedIn, YouTube, Google+
Eileen O'Leary, National Chair
Dan Mann, National Chair-Elect
Craig Munier, Past National Chair
Justin Draeger, President
Lori Vedder, Treasurer

21793 National Athletic Trainers Association
2952 N Stemmons Fwy
Suite 200
Dallas, TX 75247

214-637-6282
860-437-5700
Fax: 214-637-2206
E-Mail: webmaster@nata.org
Home Page: www.nata.org
Social Media: Facebook, Twitter

Eve Becker-Doyle, Executive Director
Teresa Foster Welch, Assistant Executive Director
Karen Peterson, Manager Executive Operations
Ellen Satlof, Public Relations Manager
Cynthia Nadel, Marketing Coordinator

Association for professionals in athletic training.
28000 Members
Founded in 1950

21794 National Athletics Trainers' Associationÿ
1620 Valwood Parkway
Suite 115
Carrolltonÿ, TX 75006

214-637-6282
Fax: 214-637-2206
Home Page: www.nata.org

Jim Thornton, MS, ATC, CES, President
MaryBeth Horodyski, EdD, Vice President
Marjorie Albohm, Past President
Tim Weston, MEd, ATC, Board of Director, District 1
Michael Goldenberg, MS, ATC, Board of Director, District 2
35,00 Members
Founded in 1950

21795 National Basketball Athletic Trainers Association
400 Colony Square
Suite 1750
Atlanta, GA 30361

404-892-8919
Fax: 404-892-8560
E-Mail: rmallernee@mallernee-branch.com
Home Page: www.nbata.com

Tom Badenour, Chairman

A satelite of the National Athletic Trainers Association. Members are athletic trainers in the NBA.
60 Members
Founded in 1974

21796 National Bicycle Dealers Association
3176 Pullman St.
Suite 117
Costa Mesa, CA 92626

949-722-6909
Fax: 949-722-1747
E-Mail: info@nbda.com
Home Page: www.nbda.com

Dan Thornton, Chairman
James Moore, President
Jim Carveth, First VP
Jeff Koenig, Second VP
Chris Kegel, Secretary

The mission of the NBDA is to inspire and serve the specialty bicycle retailer through communicating the value and needs of the specialty bicycle retailer, enhancing the specialty bicycle retailer's profitability, and promoting the passion for cycling. The NBDA is a non-profit association promoting the interests of every specialty bicycle retailer in the United States.
2M Members
Founded in 1946

21797 National Collegiate Athletic Associationÿ
700 W. Washington Street
P.O. Box 6222
Indianapolis, IN 46206-6222

317-917-6222
Fax: 317-917-6888
Home Page: www.ncaa.org
Social Media: Facebook, Twitter, YouTube, Instagram

Mark Emmert, President

21798 National Cutting Horse Association
260 Bailey Avenue
Fort Worth, TX 76107

817-244-6188
Fax: 817-244-2015
E-Mail: info@nchacutting.com
Home Page: www.nchacutting.com
Social Media: Facebook, Twitter, RSS

Keith Deaville, President
Ernie Beutenmiller, VP
Jeff Hooper, Executive Director

Members are individuals and organizations interested in the development of superior horses and the refinement of the cutting horse competition.
20500 Members
Founded in 1946

21799 National Fastpitch Coaches Association
2641 Grinstead Drive
Louisville, KY 40206

502-409-4600
Fax: 502-409-4622
E-Mail: nfca@nfca.org
Home Page: www.nfca.org

Rhonda Revelle, President
Kathryn Gleason, First VP
Kate Drohan, Second VP

The professional growth organization for fastpitch softball coaches from all competitives levels of play.
4100 Members
Founded in 1983

21800 National Golf Cart Manufacturers Association
NGCMA Attn: Fred Somers, Jr.
2 Ravinia Drive
Suite 1200
Atlanta, GA 30346

770-394-7200
Fax: 770-454-0138
E-Mail: membership@ngcma.org
Home Page: www.ngcma.org

Fred L Somers, Jr, Secretary & General Counsel

Non-profit national trade association comprised of the leading golf car and personal transport vehicle manufacturers. NGCMA sponsors the development and maintenance of ANSI sanctioned standards to establish safety specifications for the design and operation of golf cars and PTVs driven by electric motors and internal combustion engines for golf cars.
Founded in 1984

21801 National Golf Foundation
1150 S US Highway 1
Suite 401
Jupiter, FL 33477

561-744-6006
888-275-4643
Fax: 561-744-6107
E-Mail: general@ngf.org
Home Page: www.ngf.org
Social Media: Facebook, Twitter, LinkedIn

Joseph Beditz, President/CEO
Greg Nathan, Sr. Vice President/ Membership

The National Golf Foundation, founded in 1936 and based in Jupiter, Fla., is the industry's knowledge leader on the U.S. golf economy and leading provider of golf industry databases. NGF delivers independent and objective narket intelligence, insights and trends to fulfill its mission: To Keep Golf Businesses Ahead of the Game.
4000 Members
Founded in 1936

21802 National High School Baseball Coaches Association
PO Box 12843
Tempe, AZ 85284

602-615-0571
Fax: 480-838-7133
E-Mail: rdavini@cox.net
Home Page: www.baseballcoaches.org

Ron Davini, Executive Director

Provides services and recognition for baseball coaches and to help promote and represent high school baseball across this country.
1600 Members
Founded in 1991

21803 National Hockey League
1185 Avenue of the Americas
Floor 15
New York, NY 10036

212-789-2000
Fax: 212-789-2020
Home Page: www.nhl.com
Social Media: Facebook, Twitter, LinkedIn

Gary Bettman, Commissioner
William Daly, Deputy Commissioner
John Collins, COO

The NHL is one of the four major professional sports associations in North America, with 30 professional ice hockey franchises in the US and Canada.

21804 National Junior College Athletic Association
1631 Mesa Ave
Suite B
Colorado Springs, CO 80906

719-590-9788
Fax: 719-590-7324
E-Mail: meleicht@njcaa.org
Home Page: www.njcaa.org
Social Media: Facebook, Twitter

Mary Ellen Leicht, Executive Director
Mark Krug, Ass. Executive Director

The purpose of the NJCAA is to promote and foster junior college athletics on intersectional and national levels so that results will be consistent with the total educational program of its members.
525 Members
Founded in 1938

21805 National Pro Fastpitch
3350 Hobson Pike
Hermitage, TN 37076

615-232-2900
Fax: 615-232-8880
E-Mail: info@profastpitch.com
Home Page: www.profastpitch.comÿ
Social Media: Facebook, Twitter, YouTube, Instagram

Cheri Kempf, Commissioner
Gaye Lynn Wilson, Vice President
Ed Whipple, Supervisor of Officials
Cynthia Gerken, NPF Travel Agent
Nikki Worthman, NPF Intern

21806 National Recreation and Park Association
22377 Belmont Ridge Road
Ashburn, VA 20148-4501

703-858-0784
Fax: 703-858-0794
E-Mail: info@nrpa.org
Home Page: www.nrpa.org
Social Media: Facebook, Twitter, LinkedIn, Youtube

Jodie H Adams, President
John Crosby, Marketing
Jessica Lytle, Director

Advancing parks, recreation and environmental conservation efforts that enhance the quality of life for all people.
Founded in 1965

21807 National Rifle Association of America
11250 Waples Mill Rd
Fairfax, VA 22030-7400

703-267-1400
Fax: 703-267-3970
E-Mail: membership@nrahq.org
Home Page: www.home.nra.org
Social Media: Facebook, Twitter

Oldest sportsmen's organization in the US. Maintains the NRA Political Victory Fund and supports the Institute for Legislative Action. Has an annual budget over $140 million.
4 Members
Founded in 1871

21808 National Soccer Coaches Association of America
30 W. Pershing Rd.
Suite 350
Kansas City, MO 64108

816-471-1941
Fax: 816-474-7408
E-Mail: info@nscaa.com
Home Page: www.nscaa.com

George Perry, President
Mike Jacobs, VP, Events
Amanda Vandervort, VP, Marketing
Charlie Slagle, VP, Education
Lesle Gallimore, VP, Membership
Founded in 1941

21809 National Sporting Goods Association
1601 Feehanville Dr
Suite 300
Mt Prospect, IL 60056

847-296-6742
800-815-5422
Fax: 847-391-9827
E-Mail: info@nsga.org
Home Page: www.nsga.org
Social Media: Facebook, Twitter, LinkedIn, Flickr

Ken Meehan, Chairman
Randy Nill, Treasurer/Chairman Elect
Matt Carlson, President

Association of retailers, manufacturers and suppliers of sports equipment, footwear, and apparel.
2000+ Members
Founded in 1929

21810 National Strength and Conditioning Association
1885 Bob Johnson Dr.
Colorado Springs, CO 80906

719-632-6722
800-815-6826
Fax: 719-632-6367
Home Page: www.nsca.com

Steven J. Fleck, PhD, President
Todd Miller, PhD, Vice President
Colin Wilborn, PhD, Treasurer-Secretary
Michael Embree, Executive Director
Levi Boren, PhD, Sr. Director of Certification
Founded in 1978

21811 National Youth Sports Coaches Association
2050 Vista Parkway
Hillsboro, FL 33411

636-797-5334
800-688-5437
Fax: 636-797-5084
E-Mail: nysca@nays.org
Home Page: www.nays.org
Social Media: Twitter, Youtube, RSS

Represents coaches involved in youth athletics.
Founded in 1981

21812 Pop Warner Little Scholars
586 Middletown Boulevard
Suite C-100
Langhorne, PA 19047-1867

215-752-2691
Fax: 215-752-2879
E-Mail: webmaster@popwarner.com
Home Page: www.popwarner.com
Social Media: Facebook, Twitter, LinkedIn

Jon Butler, Executive Director
Mary Fitzgerald, COO
Lisa Moroski, National Cheer/Dance Commissioner

A national youth football and cheerleading organization that provides assistance to its various chapters.
400M Members
Founded in 1929

21813 Professional Association of Diving
30151 Tomas
Rcho Sta Marg, CA 92688-2125

949-858-7234
800-729-7234
Fax: 949-267-1267
E-Mail: webmaster@padi.com
Home Page: www.padi.com
Social Media: Facebook, Twitter

Brian Cronin, CEO

Certifies scuba diving instructors. Provides education/training materials and retail support to its members.
67M Members
Founded in 1966

21814 Professional Association of Volleyball Officials
PO Box 780
Oxford, KS 67119

888-791-2074
Fax: 620-455-3800
E-Mail: pavo@pavo.org
Home Page: www.pavo.org

Julie Voeck, President
Joan Powell, President
Crystal Lewis, Board Delegate
Ben Jordan, Director Examinations
Karen Gee, Director Finance

The Professional Association of Volleyball Officials is dedicated to improving the quality of volleyball officiating for all rules codes and skill levels. PAVO strives to increase the number of competent officials through education and mentoring and promotes involvement in the governing bodies of other volleyball officiating groups.
2M Members

21815 Professional Baseball Athletic Trainers Society
1201 Peachtree St Ne
Suite 1750
Atlanta, GA 30361-6320

404-875-7990
Fax: 410-730-2219
E-Mail: questions@pbats.com
Home Page: www.pbats.com
Social Media: Facebook, Twitter, RSS

Jamie Reed, President
Jim Carroll, Director Public Relations

Serve as an educational resource for the Major League and Minor League baseball athletic trainers. Serves its members by providing for the continued education of the athletic trainer as it relates to the profession, helping improve his understanding of sports medicine so as to better promote the health of his constituency - professional baseball players.
60 Members
Founded in 1983

21816 Professional Bowlers Association
615 Second Ave
Seattle, WA 98104

206-332-9688
Fax: 206-332-9722
E-Mail: info@pba.com
Home Page: www.pba.com
Social Media: Facebook, Twitter, Youtube, RSS

Fred Schreyer, CEO
Steve Miller, Board Member
Lisa Gil, VP Brand Communications

Acts on behalf of professional bowlers.
3800 Members
Founded in 1958

21817 Professional Football Athletic Trainer Society
1201 Peachtree St Ne
Suite 1750
Atlanta, GA 30361-6320

404-875-7990
Fax: 404-892-8560
E-Mail: contact@pfats.com
Home Page: www.pfats.com
Social Media: Facebook, Twitter, Youtube, RSS

Rollin E Mallernee II, President

Professional association whose members are the athletic trainers of the NFL. They provide, lead and manage helathcare for the NFL athletes, club employees and members of the NFL community. Dedicated to insuring the highest quality health care is practiced. Guided by the profesional integrity and ethical standards of its members and by the unity they share.
650 Members
Founded in 1982

21818 Professional Golfers Association (PGA)
100 Ave of the Champions
Palm Beach Gdns, FL 33418

561-624-8400
Fax: 561-624-8448
E-Mail: webmaster@pga.com
Home Page: www.pga.com
Social Media: Facebook, Twitter

Ted Bishop, President
Derek Sprague, Vice President
Paul Levy, Secretary
Peter Bevacqua, CEO

The world's largest working sports organization comprised of more than 25,000 men and women PGA professionals to promote the game

of golf to everyone, and to promote its members as leaders in the golf industry.
28000 Members
Founded in 1916

21819 Professional Inline Hockey Association
1733 East Harrisburg Pike
Middletown, PA 17057

719-200-4208
E-Mail: info@thepiha.com
Home Page: www.thepiha.com

Charles Yoder, Founder
CJ Yoder, President
Jami Yoder, VP
Jim Vanhorn, Chief Financial Officer
Denis Jelcic, Commissioner

21820 Professional Skaters Association
3006 Allegro Park Ln Sw
Rochester, MN 55902

507-280-6812
Fax: 507-281-5491
E-Mail: office@skatepsa.com
Home Page: www.skatepsa.com
Social Media: Facebook, Twitter, LinkedIn, Pinterest

Jimmie Santee, Executive Director
Kelley Morris, First VP
Jackie Brenner, Third VP
Donna Wells, Administrative Assistant
Barb Yackel, Marketing & Events

An international organization responsible for the education of skating coaches. Membership is offered to coaches in every discipline and at all levels, as well as to performing professionals, judges, eligible skaters and friends or patrons of the sport of figure skating.
6000 Members
Founded in 1938

21821 Roller Skating Association
6905 Corporate Dr
Indianapolis, IN 64278

317-347-2626
Fax: 317-347-2636
E-Mail: rsa@rollerskating.com
Home Page: www.rollerskating.org
Social Media: Facebook, Twitter, LinkedIn

Tina Robertson, President
Robert Housholder, VP
Michael Jacques, Treasurer
Jim McMahon, Executive Director

A trade association representing skating center owners and operators; teachers, coaches and judges of roller skating; and manufacturers and suppliers of roller skating equipment.
1000 Members
Founded in 1937

21822 Society for American Baseball Research
4455 E. Camelback Rd Ste~
Suite D 140
Phoenix, AZ 85018

216-575-0500
800-969-7227
Fax: 602-595-5690
E-Mail: info@sabr.org
Home Page: www.sabr.org
Social Media: Facebook, Twitter, Youtube

Vince Gennaro, President
Bill Nowlin, VP
Todd Lebowitz, Secretary
F X Flinn, Treasurer
Emily Hawks, Director

Foisters the study of baseball past and present and provides an outlet for educational, historical and research information about the game.
6700 Members
Founded in 1971

Mailing list available for rent: 25000 names at $85 per M

21823 Sporting Arms and Ammunition Manufacturers Institute
11 Mile Hill Rd
Newtown, CT 06470-2359

203-426-4358
Fax: 203-426-3592
Home Page: www.saami.org

Steve Sanetti, President
Rick Patterson, Managing Director

SAAMI is an association of the nation's leading manufacturers of sporting firearms, ammunition, and components.
Founded in 1926

21824 Sporting Goods Agents Association (SGAA)
PO Box 998
Morton Grove, IL 60053

847-296-3670
Fax: 847-827-0196
E-Mail: sgaa998@aol.com
Home Page: www.sgaaonline.org
Social Media: LinkedIn

Skip Nipper, President
Lois Halinton, Chief Operating Officer

International trade association of independent and established sporting goods agents.
500 Members
Founded in 1934

21825 Sporting Goods Manufacturers Association
8505 Fenton Street
Suite 211
Silver Spring, MD 20910

301-495-6321
Fax: 301-495-6322
E-Mail: info@sfia.org
Home Page: www.sfia.org

Tom Cove, President & CEO
Chip Baldwin, CFO
Bill Sells, VP, Government Relations
Ron Rosenbaum, SVP, Marketing & Business Dev
Jan Ciambor, Office Manager

SGMA is the trade association of North American manufacturers, producers, and distributers of sports apparel, athletic footwear, fitness, and sporting goods equipment. SGMA represents and supports its members through programs and strategies for sports participation, market intelligence, and public policy.
1000 Members
Founded in 1906

21826 Sports Turf Managers Association
805 New Hampshire St
Suite E
Lawrence, KS 66044

785-843-2549
800-323-3875
Fax: 785-843-2977
Home Page: www.stma.org
Social Media: Facebook, LinkedIn

James Michael Goatley, President
David Pinsonneault, President Elect
Rene Aspiron, VP
Allen Johnson, Secretary/Treasurer

Grounds care for golf and athletic fields.
2500 Members
Founded in 1981

21827 Sportsplex Operators and Developers
Westgate Station
PO Box 24263
Rochester, NY 14624-0263

585-426-2215
Fax: 585-247-3112
E-Mail: info@sportsplexoperators.com
Home Page: www.sportsplexoperators.com

John Fitzgerald, President
Diane Aselin, Executive VP
Don Aselin, Executive Director
Norm Rice, Treasurer
Kelly Tharp, Secretary

SODA was formed to meet the needs of the private concerns, public agencies, and other organizations that own or maintain sports complex facilities.
300 Members
Founded in 1981

21828 Tennis Industry Association
117 Executive Center
1 Corpus Christie Place
Hilton Head Island, SC 29928

843-686-3036
Fax: 843-686-3078
E-Mail: info@tennisindustry.org
Home Page: www.tennisindustry.org
Social Media: Facebook, Twitter, LinkedIn, Youtube, Google+, RSS

Jon Muir, President
Jolyn DeBoer, Executive Director
Brian O'Donnell, National Coordinator

To educate the marketplace, fund research and market intelligence and supply this reliable industry data to our member companies. The TIA is the Information source and clearing house for positive tennis news that we supply to TIA members, tennis publications and to the mainstream media in cooperation with the USTA.
800 Members
Founded in 1974

21829 The College Golf Foundation
1225 West Main Street
Suite 110
Norman, OK 73069

866-422-2669
Fax: 405-573-7888
E-Mail: info@collegiategolf.com
Home Page: www.collegiategolf.com
Social Media: Facebook, Twitter

Conrad Ray, President
Andrew Sapp, 1st Vice President
Greg Sands, 2nd Vice President
Mark Crabtree, 3rd Vice President
Todd Sattefield, Past President
Founded in 1958

21830 The United States Association of Blind Athletes
1 Olympic Plaza
Colorado Springs, CO 80909

719-866-3224
Fax: 719-866-3400
Home Page: www.usaba.org
Social Media: Facebook, Twitter

Dave Bushland, President
Tracie Foster, Vice President
Gary Remensnyyder, Treasurer
Trishca Zorn-Hudson, Secretary
Mark A. Lucas, MS, Executive Director

21831 U.S. Track & Field and Cross Country Coaches Association
1100 Poydras Street
Suite 1750
New Orleans, LA 70163

504-599-8900
Fax: 504-599-8909

E-Mail: sam@ustfccca.org
Home Page: www.ustfccca.org
Social Media: Twitter, RSS

Sam Seemes, CEO
Mike Corn, Assistant Director
Tom Lewis, Director, Communications
Dave Svoboda, Director, Operations

A non-profit professional organization that represents men's and women's cross country and track & field coaches in the United States.
8000 Members

21832 U.S. Track & Field and Cross Country Coach es Association
1100 Poydras Street
Suite 1750
New Orleans, LA 70163

504-599-8900
Fax: 504-599-8909
Home Page: www.ustfccca.org
Social Media: Facebook, RSS

Beth Alford-Sullivan, President
Larry Cole, Treasurer
Ray Williams, Secretary
Sam Seemes, Chief Executive Officer
Dave Svoboda, Director of Operations
8,000 Members

21833 US Field Hockey Association
1 Olympic Plaza
Colorado Springs, CO 80909

719-866-4567
Fax: 719-632-0979
E-Mail: usfha@usfieldhockey.com
Home Page: www.usfieldhockey.com
Social Media: Facebook, Twitter, You Tube

Steve Looke, Executive Director
Simon Hoskins, Marketing Director

Represents field hockey, professional and amateur sports.
14000 Members
Founded in 1928

21834 US Handball Association
2333 N Tucson Blvd
Tucson, AZ 85716

520-795-0434
800-289-8742
Fax: 520-795-0465
E-Mail: handball@ushandball.org
Home Page: www.ushandball.org
Social Media: Facebook, Twitter, You Tube

Mike Steele, President
LeaAnn Martin, VP
Steve Dykes, Secretary
Steve Birrell, Treasurer

Organization that runs all the tournaments for the professional and amateur players. Home of the Handball Hall of Fame.

21835 US Lacrosse
113 W University Pkwy
Baltimore, MD 21210

410-235-6882
Fax: 410-366-6735
E-Mail: info@uslacrosse.org
Home Page: www.uslacrosse.org
Social Media: Facebook, Twitter, Youtube, Google+, Instagram

Steve Stenersen, President & CEO
Bill Schoonmaker, COO
Cara Morris, CFO
Bill Rubacky, Managing Director, Marketing

The national governing body of men's and women's lacrosse. Through responsive and effective leadership, the organization provides programs and services to inspire participation while protecting the integrity of the sport. Known as the resource center for the sport, US Lacrosse is devoted to growing the game responsibly, providing programs and services to develop the game nationally, publishing Lacrosse Magazine & LaxMagazine.com, hosting events, and preserving the history of the game.
300M Members
Founded in 1998

21836 US Olympic Committee
PO Box 7010
Albert Lea, MN 56007-8010

719-632-5551
888-222-2313
Fax: 719-632-0250
E-Mail: customerservice@donorssupportusoc.org
Home Page: www.teamusa.com
Social Media: Facebook, Twitter, Youtube, Instagram

Scott Blackmun, CEO
Lawrence Probst, Chairman
Walter Glover, CFO
Lisa Baird, Chief Marketing Officer

The national committee for the US handles the preparation of the US Olympic, Paralympic and Pan American Games teams.
Founded in 1984

21837 US Professional Tennis Association
3535 Briarpark Drive
Suite One
Houston, TX 77042

713-978-7782
800-877-8248
Fax: 713-978-7780
E-Mail: uspta@uspta.com
Home Page: www.uspta.com
Social Media: Facebook, Twitter, LinkedIn, You Tube

Tim Heckler, CEO
Rich Fanning, Director Operations
Shawna Riley, Director Communications
Rick Bostrom, Sports Marketing Coordinator

A nonprofit association for professional tennis teachers.
14000 Members
Founded in 1927

21838 US Raquetball Association
AARA National Office
1685 W Uintah Street
Colorado Springs, CO 80904-2906

719-635-5396
Fax: 719-635-0685
E-Mail: racquetball@usra.org
Home Page: www.usra.org

Randy Stafford, President
Jan Stelma, VP
Jim Hiser, Executive Director
Kevin Joyce, Director Membership
Melody Weiss, Director Finance

A nonprofit corporation designed to promote the development of competitive and recreational racquetball in the United States. The association offers a 'competitive license' membership for a one year term at $30.00 annually. A lifetime membership is also offered.
40M Members
Frequency: 6 Per Year
Circulation: 25,000
Founded in 1968
Mailing list available for rent

21839 US Ski & Snowboard Association
1 Victory Lane
PO Box 100
Park City, UT 84060

435-649-9090
Fax: 435-649-3613
E-Mail: info@ussa.org
Home Page: www.usskiteam.com
Social Media: Facebook

Bill Marolt, President/CEO
Tiger Shaw, COO
Luke Bodensteiner, EVP, Athletics
Mark Lampe, EVP/CFO
Michael Jaquet, VP, Chief Marketing Officer

The national governing body for Olympic skiing and snowboarding.
30000 Members
Founded in 1904

21840 US Soccer Federation
1801 S Prairie Ave
Chicago, IL 60616

312-808-1300
Fax: 312-808-1301
E-Mail: centercircle@ussoccer.org
Home Page: www.ussoccer.com
Social Media: Facebook, Twitter, Youtube

Sunil K Gulati, President
Mike Edwards, EVP
Dan Flynn, CEO/Secretary General

The governing body of soccer in all its form in the United States. US Soccer has helped chart the course for the sport in the USA for 90 years.
Founded in 1913

21841 US Speedskating
5662 Cougar Lane
Kearns, UT 84118

801-417-5360
Fax: 801-417-5361
E-Mail: kmorquard@usspeedskating.org
Home Page: www.usspeedskating.org
Social Media: Facebook, Twitter, Youtube

Ted Morris, Executive Director
Jenny Walter, Marketing Manager
Jamie Miller, Communications Manager
Paul Brabants, Accountant & Business Manager

Devoted to speedskating and its participants on the national and international levels.
2000 Members
Founded in 1966

21842 US Squash Racquet Association
555 Eighth Ave
Suite 1102
New York, NY 10018-4311

212-268-4090
Fax: 212-268-4091
E-Mail: office@us-squash.org
Home Page: www.ussquash.org
Social Media: Facebook, Twitter, LinkedIn, Youtube, Flickr

John A Fry, Chair
Vijay Chitnis, Director Junior Development

The USSRA is the national governing body for the sport of squash racquets in the United States. A nonprofit, service organization whose primary function is that of management and maintenance of all squash related activities for a growing membership- driven organization.
8000 Members
Founded in 1907

21843 US Synchronized Swimming
132 E Washington Street
Suite 820
Indianapolis, IN 46204

317-237-5700
Fax: 317-237-5705
E-Mail: marketing@usasynchro.org
Home Page: www.usasynchro.org
Social Media: Facebook, Twitter, You Tube

Judy McGowan, President
Denise Shively, VP, Operations
Shannon Korpela, VP, Education &

Certification
Nancy Rosengard, VP, Marketing & Member Services
Tom Wiita, Treasurer

Dedicated to the promotion of synchronized swimming. Sanctions and governs all synchronized swimming in the US and selects and trains National and Olympic Teams to represent the US in international competitions.
6000 Members

21844 US Track and Field
132 East Washington Street,
Suite 800
Indianapolis, IN 46204

317-261-0500
Fax: 317-261-0481
Home Page: www.usatf.org
Social Media: Facebook, Twitter, You Tube

Max Siegel, CEO
Renee Washington, COO
Jill Geer, CPAO
Norman Wain, General Counsel
Kelly Kenders, Senior Adminstrative Assistant

The national governing body for track and field, long-distance running and race waling in the United States.

21845 US Volleyball Association
Suite 700
Los Gatos, CA 95031

E-Mail: volleyballorg@hotmail.com
Home Page: www.volleyball.org

Promotes volleyball in the US trains the USA men's and women's teams promotes beach and grassroots volleyball in the United States.
140M Members
Founded in 1928

21846 USA Basketball
5465 Mark Dabling Boulevard
Colorado Springs, CO 80918-3842

719-590-4800
Fax: 719-590-4811
Home Page: www.usab.com
Social Media: Facebook, Twitter, Google+, YouTube

Jerry Colangelo, Chairman
Chauncey Billups, Athlete Representative
Kim Bohuny, NBA Representative
Jim Carr, National Organizations Rep.
Bob Gardner, NFHS Representative

21847 USA Deaf Sports Federation
PO Box 910338
Lexington, KY 40591-0338

605-367-5760
Fax: 605-782-8441
E-Mail: homeoffice@usdeafsports.org
Home Page: www.usdeafsports.org
Social Media: Facebook, Twitter, RSS, YouTube

Jack C. Lamberton, President
Jeffrey L.ÿ Salit, Vice President
Mark Apodaca, Chief Financial Officer
Danny Lacey, Chief Development Officer
Brianne Burger, Secretary
Founded in 1945

21848 USA Gymnastics
132 E Washington Street
Suite 700
Indianapolis, IN 46204

317-237-5050
800-345-4719
Fax: 317-237-5069
E-Mail: rebound@usa-gymnastics.org
Home Page: www.usa-gymnastics.org
Social Media: Facebook, Twitter, Youtube

Peter Vidmar, Chairman
Steve Penny, President
Paul Parilla, Vice Chair
Jim Morris, Treasurer
Gary Anderson, Secretary

The sole national governing body for the sport of gymnastics in the United States. USA Gymnastics creates, organizes and conducts clinics, training camps, team competitions and other aspects of athlete, coach and official selection and development.
13000 Members
Founded in 1963

21849 USA Hockey
1775 Bob Johnson Dr
Colorado Spring, CO 80906-4090

719-576-8724
Fax: 719-538-1160
E-Mail: usah@usahockey.org
Home Page: www.usahockey.com
Social Media: Facebook, Twitter, LinkedIn

Dave Ogrean, Executive Director
Mike Bertsch, Marketing & Communications
Kim Folsom, Executive Assistant
Rae Briggle, Member Services
Casey Jorgensen, General Counsel

Promotes the sport of hockey. USA Hockey is the national governing body for the sport of ice hockey in the US.
600K Members
Founded in 1936

21850 USA Roller Sports
PO Box 6579
Lincoln, NE 68506

402-483-7551
Fax: 402-483-1465
Home Page: www.usarollersports.org
Social Media: Facebook, Twitter, You Tube

George Kolibaba, Chairman/President
David Adamy, VP

The national governing body for all amateur skating sports including artistic, roller, and speed skating.
15K Members
Founded in 1937

21851 USA Swimming
One Olympic Plaza
Colorado Springs, CO 80909

719-866-4578
Home Page: www.usaswimming.org

Chuck Wielgus, Executive Director
Amanda Bryant, Director Corporate Marketing
Mike Unger, Chief Operating Officer
Jim Harvey, Managing Director Financial Affairs

Devoted to the sport of swimming and its enjoyment nationwide. Governing body for the sport of swimming.
290M Members
Founded in 1844

21852 USA Table Tennis
4065 Sinton Road
Suite 120
Colorado Springs, CO 80907

719-866-4583
Fax: 719-632-6071
E-Mail: admin@usatt.org
Home Page: www.usatt.org
Social Media: Facebook, Twitter, LinkedIn

Michael D Cavanaugh, CEO
Doru Gheorghe, COO
Deborah Grey, CFO

Dedicated to the promotion of the sport of table tennis and sponsors the US team. Membership dues are $40 per year for adults and $20 for those 17 years old and under.
9000 Members
Founded in 1933

21853 USA Track & Field
USA Track & Field
132 East Washington Street, Suite 8
Indianapolis, IN 46204

317-261-0500
Fax: 317-261-0481
Home Page: www.usatf.org

Stephanie Hightower, Chairman and President
Steven Miller, Vice Chair
Kenneth Taylor, Treasurer
Darlene Hickman, Secretary
Max Siegel, Chief Executive Officer
Founded in 1878

21854 USA Water Ski Association
1251 Holy Cow Rd
Polk City, FL 33868

863-324-4341
Fax: 863-325-8259
E-Mail: usawaterski@usawaterski.org
Home Page: www.usawaterski.org

The national governing body for organized water skiing in the United States. A member of the International Water Ski Federation (World Governing Body), the Pan American Sports Association and the United States Olympic Committee.
37500 Members
Founded in 1939

21855 USA Weightlifting
1 Olympic Plz
Colorado Spring, CO 80909-5764

719-866-4508
Fax: 719-866-4741
E-Mail: usaw@usaweightlifting.org
Home Page: www.usaweightlifting.org

Michael Masik, CEO, General Secretary
Laurie Lopez, Director, Operations
Carissa Gump, Director, Corp. Services
Phil Andrews, Director, Events & Programs

USA Weightlifting is the National Governing Body (NGB) for the Olympic sport of weightlifting in the United States. USA weightlifting is a member of the United States Olympic Committee and a member of the International Weightlifting Federation. As the NGB, USA Weightlifting is responsible for conducting Olympic weightlifting programs throughout the country. The organization conducts a variety of programs that will ultimately develop Olympic, World Championship and Pan American Games' winners.
Cost: $20.00
4000 Members
Frequency: Quarterly
Circulation: 4500
Founded in 1981

21856 United States Amateur Boxing
1 Olympic Plz
Colorado Spring, CO 80909

719-866-2300
Fax: 719-866-2132
E-Mail: media@usoc.org
Home Page: www.usaboxing.org

Anthony Bartkowski, Executive Director
Betsy McCallister, Executive Assistant
Brian Lawrence, CFO
Lynette Smith, Director, Membership Services

The national governing body for Olympic-style boxing. It is responsible for the administration, development and promotion of Olympic-style boxing in the United State.
7000 Members
Founded in 1981

21857 United States Bowling Congress
621 Six Flags Dr
Arlington, TX 76011

817-385-8200
800-514-2695
Fax: 817-385-8260
E-Mail: abcpr@bowinginc.com
Home Page: www.bowl.com
Social Media: Facebook, Twitter, LinkedIn, You Tube

Andrew Cain, President
Frank Wilkinson, VP
Tamoria Adams, Director
Tim Payne, Chief Information Officer
Kevin Dornberger, Director, Team USA

Established in 2005 as the organization to serve amateur adult and youth bowlers of the United States. It resulted from the merger of the American Bowling Congress, Young American Bowling Alliance and USA Bowling. USBC is the national governing body for bowling as recognized by the United States Olympic Committee.
3 M Members
Founded in 2005

21858 United States Canoe Association
509 S Bishop Ave
Secane, PA 19018

610-405-5008
Home Page: www.uscanoe.com

Susan Williams, President
Joan Theiss, Insurance Coordinator

21859 United States Extreme Sports Association
6350 Lake Oconee Parkway
Suite 102-128
Greensboro, GA 30642

877-900-8737
E-Mail: info@usesa.org
Home Page: www.usesa.orgÿ

21860 United States Fencing Association
1 Olympic Plz
Colorado Spring, CO 80909-5760

719-866-4444
Fax: 719-866-4645
E-Mail: info@usfencing.org
Home Page: www.usfencing.org
Social Media: Facebook, Twitter, LinkedIn, You Tube

Donald Anthony Jr., Chairman
Sam Cheris, Treasurer
Nathan Anderson, Secretary

National Governing Body for the sport of fencing in the United States. Their mission is to develop fencers to achieve international success and to administer and promote the sport in the USA.
9M Members
Founded in 1891

21861 United States Golf Association
PO Box 708
Far Hills, NJ 07931

908-234-2300
Fax: 908-234-9687
E-Mail: mediarelations@usga.org
Home Page: www.usga.org
Social Media: Facebook, Twitter, LinkedIn, You Tube

Walter W Driver Jr, President
James E Reinhart, VP
David Fay, Executive Director

An association of member clubs and courses. Conducts the US Open and Women's Open Championships, the Walker and Curtis Cup matches and ten national amateur championships.
7.5M Members
Founded in 1894

21862 United States Harness Writers Association
PO Box 1314
Mechanicsburg, PA 17055

717-766-3219
E-Mail: ushwa@paonline.com
Home Page: www.ushwa.org

Steve Wolf, President
Chris Tully, First VP
Tim Bojarski, Second VP
Judy Davis-Wilson, Treasurer
Jerry Connors, Secretary

Members are media members who cover the sport of harness racing.
300 Members
Founded in 1947

21863 United States Parachute Association
5401 Southpoint Centre Boulevard
Fredricksburg, VA 22407

540-604-9740
Fax: 540-604-9741
E-Mail: uspa@uspa.org
Home Page: www.uspa.org
Social Media: Facebook, Twitter, LinkedIn, YouTube, RSS

Jay Stokes, President
Randy Allison, Vice President
Sherry Butcher, Secretary
Lee Schlichtemeier, Treasurer
BJ Worth, Chairman

The USPA is a voluntary membership organization of individuals who enjoy and support the sport of skydiving. The purpose of USPA is three-fold: to promote safe skydiving through training, licensing, and instructor qualification programs; to ensure skydiving's rightful place on airports and in the airspace system; and to promote competition and record-setting programs.
33000 Members
Founded in 1946

21864 United States Racquet Stringers
PO Box 3392
Duluth, GA 92084

760-536-1177
Fax: 760-536-1171
E-Mail: usra@racquettech.com
Home Page: www.racquettech.com

David Bone, Executive Director
Dianne Pray, Membership Coordinator
Crawford Lindsey, Editor/Webmaster
Kristine Thom, Production Manager

Educates constituencies to better understand, service, perform with, and enjoy the technological wonders known as racquests, strings, balls, courts, shoes, and stringing machines.
7000 Members
Founded in 1975

21865 United States Tennis Association
70 West Red Oak Lane
White Plains, NY 10604

914-696-7000
Home Page: www.usta.com
Social Media: Facebook, Twitter, YouTube

Katrina Adams, Chairman, CEO & President
Andy Andrews, First Vice President
Tommy Ho, Vice President
Don Tisdel, Vice President
Patrick Galbraith, Secretary-Treasurer
Founded in 1881

21866 United States Trotting Association
750 Michigan Ave
Columbus, OH 43215

614-224-2291
877-800-8782
Fax: 614-224-4575
E-Mail: stats@ustrotting.com
Home Page: www.ustrotting.com
Social Media: Facebook, Twitter, LinkedIn, You Tube

Ivan L Axelrod, Chairman
E Phillip Langley, President
Russell C Williams, Vice Chair
Mike Tanner, VP
Richard Brandt Jr., Treasurer

The USTA licenses owners, trainers, drivers and officials; formulates the rules of racing; maintains and disseminates racing information and records; serves as the registry for the Standardbred breed; endeavors to ensure the integrity of harness racing; insists on the humane treatment of Standardbreds; and promotes the sport of harness racing and the Standardbred breed.
Founded in 1939

21867 United States Water Fitness Association
P.O. Box 243279
Boynton Beach, FL 33424 3279

561-732-9908
Fax: 561-732-0950
E-Mail: info@uswfa.org
Home Page: www.uswfa.com

John R Spannuth, President/CEO
Marion Frega, Assistant to President

Nonprofit educational organization that promotes aquatics throughout the US and other countries. Publishes the National Aquatics Newsletter, names the 100 top programs and aquatics in the country, by state and in 25+ categories. Conducts a wide variety of national aquatics certifications including Water Fitness Instructors (primary and masters), aquatic directors, coordinators of water fitness programs. Conducts annual international aquatics conference.
Founded in 1988

21868 United States of America Cricket Association
8461 Lake Worth Road
Suite B-1-185
Lake Worth, FL 33467

561-839-1888
E-Mail: lbrulport@usaca.org
Home Page: www.usaca.org
Social Media: Facebook, Twitter

Gladstone Dainty, President
Michael Gale, 1st Vice President
Rafey Syed, 2nd Vice President
John Thickett, Treasurer
Mascelles Bailey, Secretary

21869 Western Fairs Association
1776 Tribute Rd
Suite 210
Sacramento, CA 95815-4495

916-927-3100
Fax: 916-927-6397
E-Mail: stephenc@fairsnet.org
Home Page: www.fairsnet.org

Stephen J Chambers, Executive Director
Jon Baker, VP
Carrie Wright, Marketing
Nichole Farley, Marketing
Lori Hanley, Communications Manager

A non-profit association with members throughout the Western United States and Canada that strives to promote industry standards.

Membership includes access to conventions and trade shows, educational training programs as well as legislative advocacy support.
2000 Members
Founded in 1922

21870 Women's Basketball Coaches Association
4646 Lawrenceville Hwy.
Lilburn, GA 30047
770-279-8027
Fax: 770-279-8473
E-Mail: membership@wbca.org
Home Page: www.wbca.org
Social Media: Facebook, Twitter, RSS
Sue Semrau, President
Coquese Washington, VP
Charli Turner Thorne, Past President
Matthew Mitchell, Secretary
Danielle Donehew, Executive Director
Founded in 1981

21871 Women's National Basketball Associationÿ
645 Fifth Avenue
New York, NY 10022
Home Page: www.wnba.com
Social Media: Facebook, Twitter, YouTube, Instagram

21872 Women's Sports Foundation
Eisenhower Park
East Meadow, NY 11554
516-542-4700
800-227-3988
Fax: 516-542-4716
E-Mail: info@womenssportsfoundation.org
Home Page: www.womenssportsfoundation.org
Social Media: Facebook, Twitter
Billie Jean King, Founder
Donna Lopiano, CEO
Allison Sawyer, Senior Communications Coordinator
Disseminates information as well as encourages girls and women in sports and physical activity. Organization offers free access to quarterly electronic newsletter, Women's Sports Experience, that provides general updates on the world of girls' and women's sports as well as the Foundation's work.
4000 Members
Circulation: 15000
Founded in 1974

21873 YMCA of the USA
101 N Wacker Dr
Suite 1400
Chicago, IL 60606-1784
312-977-0031
800-872-9622
Home Page: www.ymca.net
Social Media: Facebook
Neil Nicoll, CEO
Provides national and state branch divisions.
20.1M Members

21874 ational Federation of State High School Associations
PO BOX 690
Indianapolis, IN 46206
317-972-6900
Fax: 317-822-5700
Home Page: www.nfhs.org
Tom Mezzanotte, President
Tom Welter, President-Elect
Gary Ray, B.O.D., Section 2
Jerome Singleton, B.O.D., Section 3
Marty Hickman, B.O.D., Section 4
Founded in 1920

Newsletters

21875 AAPSM Newsletter
American Academy of Podiatric Sports Medicine
109 Greenwich Dr
Walkersville, MD 21793-9121
352-620-8562
888-854-3338
Fax: 352-620-8765
E-Mail: info@aapsm.org
Home Page: www.aapsm.org
Social Media: Facebook
Rita Yates, Executive Director
David M Davidson, Director
A quarterly newsletter published by the American Academy of Podiatric Sports Medicine.
12 Pages
Frequency: Quarterly
Circulation: 700
Founded in 1970
Mailing list available for rent: 600 names at $125 per M

21876 ARC e-Newsletter
American Recreation Coalition
1225 New York Ave NW
Suite 450
Washington, DC 20005
202-682-9530
Fax: 202-682-9529
E-Mail: jmitchelle@funoutdoors.com
Home Page: www.funoutdoors.com
Derrick Crandall, President
Catherine Ahern, VP
Julia Mitchell, Director of Partnership Programs
A monthly e-newsletter distributed via e-mail.
Frequency: Monthly, e-Newsletter
Circulation: Variable

21877 BCA Newsletter
National High School Baseball Coaches Association
PO Box 12843
Tempe, AZ 85284
602-615-0571
Fax: 480-838-7133
E-Mail: rdavini@cox.net
Home Page: www.baseballcoaches.org
Ron Davini, Executive Director

21878 Behind the Seams
National Amateur Baseball Federation
PO Box 705
Bowie, MD 20715
301-625-5005
Fax: 301-352-0214
E-Mail: NABF1914@aol.com
Home Page: www.nabf.com
Social Media: Facebook
J Patrick Eaken, Editor
Charles M Blackburn, Executive Director
The official newsletter of the National Amateur Baseball Federation. Sent to NABF league members.
Frequency: Quarterly
Founded in 1914

21879 CSCAA Newsletter
College Swimming Coaches Association of America
1640 Maple
#803
Evanston, IL 60201
847-833-3478
E-Mail: r-groseth@northwestern.edu
Home Page: www.collegecoaches.org
Bob Groseth, Executive Director
George Kennedy, President

21880 Field Hockey News
US Field Hockey Association
1 Olympic Plaza
Colorado Springs, CO 80909
719-866-4567
Fax: 719-632-0979
E-Mail: usfha@usfieldhockey.com
Home Page: www.usfieldhockey.com
Social Media: Facebook, Twitter, LinkedIn, You Tube
Steve Looke, Executive Director
Simon Hoskins, Marketing Director
Frequency: Seasonally

21881 Hunting Report for Big Game Hunters
Oxpecker Enterprises
Ste 523
9200 S Dadeland Blvd
Miami, FL 33156-2713
305-670-1361
800-272-5656
Fax: 305-716-1376
E-Mail: Subscriptions@HuntingReport.com
Home Page: www.huntingreport.com
Social Media: Facebook, Twitter, LinkedIn
Don Causey, President/Publisher
Nick Titus, Production Manager
Provides information on hunting opportunities and conditions in the US, Africa and other parts of the world.
Cost: $60.00
Frequency: Monthly
ISSN: 1052-4746
Founded in 1980

21882 Hunting Report: Birdshooters and Water
Oxpecker Enterprises
Ste 523
9200 S Dadeland Blvd
Miami, FL 33156-2713
305-670-1361
Fax: 954-370-1376
E-Mail: subscriptions@huntingreport.com
Home Page: www.huntingreport.com
Social Media: Facebook, Twitter, LinkedIn
Don Causey, Publisher
Serving the Sportsman who travels.
Cost: $45.00
14 Pages
Frequency: Monthly
Circulation: 1850
Founded in 1983
Printed in 2 colors on matte stock

21883 InBrief
Sporting Goods Manufacturers Association
8505 Fenton Street
Silver Spring, MD 20910
301-495-6321
Fax: 301-495-6322
E-Mail: info@sgma.com
Home Page: www.sgma.com
Tom Cove, President & CEO
Bill Sells, VP Government Relations
Chip Baldwin, CFO
Mike May, Director Communications
Newsletter with information about and for manufacturers in the sporting goods industry.
Frequency: Bi-weekly

21884 International Sports Heritage Association
PO Box 2384
Florence, OR 97439

541-991-7315
Fax: 541-997-3871
E-Mail: info@sportsheritage.org
Home Page: www.sportsheritage.org
Social Media: Facebook, Twitter

Karen Bednarski, Executive Director
Mike Gibbons, President
Rick Wells, First Vice President
Meg Snyder, Second Vice President
Ben Sopp, Treasurer

E-Newsletter
140+ Members
Frequency: Quarterly
Founded in 1971

21885 Leader Board
Golf Course Superintendents Association of America
1421 Research Park Dr
Lawrence, KS 66049-3859

785-841-2240
800-472-7878
Fax: 785-832-4488
E-Mail: infobox@gcsaa.org
Home Page: www.gcsaa.org
Social Media: Facebook, Twitter

Mark Woodward, CEO
Melissa Householder, Communications Coordinator
Ed Hiscock, Editor-In-Chief

Bi-monthly newsletter for golf facility decision makers, including superintendents and their employers, presenting timely and useful informaiton about golf course management in a quick easy-to-read format.
Frequency: Monthly
Circulation: 40000
Founded in 1926

21886 Media Sports Businss
Kagan Research
1 Lower Ragsdale Dr
Building One Suite 130
Monterey, CA 93940-5749

831-624-1536
800-307-2529
Fax: 831-625-3225
E-Mail: info@kagan.com
Home Page: www.kagan.com

Tim Baskerville, President
Tom Johnson, Marketing Manager

Statistics of a different kind. How much media pay to carry sports events, the impact of media on pro sports franchises, and more. Scores big with major league and media players. Three month trial available.
Cost: $945.00
Frequency: Monthly
Founded in 1969

21887 NASGW Newsletter
National Association of Sporting Goods Wholesalers
1833 Centre Point Circle
Suite 123
Naperville, IL 60563

630-596-9006
Fax: 630-544-5055
E-Mail: nasgw@nasgw.org
Home Page: www.nasgw.org
Social Media: Facebook, LinkedIn

Maurice Desmarais, President
Jack Baumler, Chairman
Kent Williams, Vice Chair
Peter Brownell, Treasurer

Non-profit trade association of wholesalers, distributors and manufacturers. Serves as a liason with other sporting goods associations. The NASGW is the organizer and sponser of the industry's annual meeting/expo event.
400 Members
Founded in 1953

21888 NSGA Sporting Goods Alert
National Sporting Goods Association
1601 Feehanville Dr
Suite 300
Mt Prospect, IL 60056-6035

847-296-6742
Fax: 847-391-9827
E-Mail: info@nsga.org
Home Page: www.nsga.org

Jeff Rosenthal, Chairman of the Board
Matt Carlson, President/CEO
Dan Kasen, Director of Information Services

News and rule changes affecting team dealers. Newsletter is free to members.

21889 NSGA Team Line-Up
National Sporting Goods Association
1601 Feehanville Dr
Suite 300
Mt Prospect, IL 60056-6035
847-296-6742
Fax: 847-391-9827
E-Mail: info@nsga.org
Home Page: www.nsga.org

Ken Meehan, Chairman of the Board
Matt Carlson, President/CEO
Dustin Dobrin, Director of Information Services

News and rule changes affecting team dealers. Newsletter is free to members.
Frequency: Weekly

21890 National High School Baseball Coaches Association
PO Box 12843
Tempe, AZ 85284

602-615-0571
Fax: 480-838-7133
E-Mail: rdavini@cox.net
Home Page: www.baseballcoaches.org

Ron Davini, Executive Director

Association news, information, coaching articles.
Frequency: 2x/Year
Circulation: 1500+
Founded in 1991

21891 Newsline
Golf Course Superintendents Association of America
1421 Research Park Dr
Lawrence, KS 66049-3859

785-841-2240
800-472-7878
Fax: 785-832-4488
E-Mail: infobox@gcsaa.org
Home Page: www.gcsaa.org
Social Media: Facebook

Mark Woodward, CEO

Membership newsletter highlighting programs and services, and featuring news about the association, its members, the golf course management profession and industry.
Founded in 1926

21892 Parachutist
United States Parachute Association
5401 Southpoint Centre Boulevard
Fredricksburg, VA 22407

540-604-9740
Fax: 540-604-9740
E-Mail: uspa@uspa.org
Home Page: www.uspa.org
Social Media: Facebook, Twitter, LinkedIn, YouTube, RSS

Elijah Florio, Editor in Chief
Laura Sharp, Managing Editor
Guilherme Cunha, Advertising Manager, Web Developer
David Cherry, Graphic Designer

The official newsletter of the USPA.
33000 Members
Founded in 1946

21893 Running & FitNews
American Running Association
4405 East-West Highway
Suite 405
Bethesda, MD 20814

800-776-2732
800-776-2732
Fax: 301 913-9520
E-Mail: milerun@americanrunning.org
Home Page: www.americanrunning.org
Social Media: Facebook, LinkedIn

David Watt, Executive Director
Barbara Baldwin, Projects Consultant
Jeff Venables, Editor
Jeff Harbison, President
Bill Young, Secretary/Treasurer

running, health and sports medicine e-newsletter.
Founded in 1968

21894 Sport Scene
North American Youth Sport Institute
4985 Oak Garden Drive
PO Box 957
Kernersville, NC 27285

336-784-4926
800-767-4916
Fax: 336-784-5546
E-Mail: jack@naysi.com
Home Page: www.naysi.com
Social Media: Facebook

Jack Hutslar, Publisher/Editor

News, features, tips, reviews, statistics, and summaries for people who work with tots, children and teens in fitness, recreation, education, sport and health with the focus on management, resources latest coaching and teaching methods, do's and dont's, safety, program ideas, legal issues, and training programs for leaders. Goal is to provide current information to improve learning while making activities more safe and positive so children can have more fun.
Cost: $ 16.00
Frequency: 6X/yr
ISBN: 0-270181-2
Founded in 1979

21895 Team Marketing Report
Team Marketing Report
1653 North Wells St
Suite 2F
Chicago, IL 60614-3962

312-280-2311
847-256-2564
Fax: 312-280-2322
E-Mail: info@teammarketing.com
Home Page: www.teammarketing.com
Social Media: Facebook, Twitter, LinkedIn

Becky Vallett, Executive Editor
Dan Bulla, Editor-at-Large / Director of Sales

Information on rates, ticket prices, and consumer attitudes, new ideas to help increase sales and exposure through the sports market.
Cost: $195.00
Frequency: Monthly
Founded in 1988

21896 Winning Edge Newsletter
1001 Diamond Ridge
Suite 800
Jefferson City, MO 65109

573-635-1660
Fax: 573-635-8233
E-Mail: hq@somo.org
Home Page: www.somo.org
Social Media: Facebook, Twitter, LinkedIn, YouTube, RSS

Mark Musso, President
Mandi Steward Mueller, Public Relations Coordinator
Diannah White, Chief Communications Officer
Randy Bohem, Chair
Don Spear, Member

Publication produced for the athletes, volunteers and supports of the Special Olympics.
Frequency: Quarterly
Founded in 1983

Magazines & Journals

21897 ADDvantage
US Professional Tennis Association
3535 Briarpark Drive
Suite 1
Houston, TX 77042-5245

713-978-7782
800-877-8248
Fax: 713-978-7780
E-Mail: uspta@uspta.org
Home Page: www.uspta.com

Shawna Riley, Editor
Kim Forrester, Managing Editor

A monthly magazine published by the US Professional Tennis Association. Available through membership only.
36 Pages
Frequency: Monthly
Circulation: 13,000
Founded in 1927
Printed in 4 colors on glossy stock

21898 AKWA Magazine
Aquatic Exercise Association
201 Tamiami Trail
PO Box 1609
Nokomis, FL 34274-1609

941-486-8600
888-232-9283
Fax: 941-486-8820
E-Mail: register@aeawave.com
Home Page: www.aeawave.com

Angie Nelson, Executive Director
Julie See, President
Kim Huff, Director of Marketing

The aqatics fitness industry's leading magazine. Brings professionals the most up to date and innovative ideas in programming, management, safety and nutrition for group exercise and personal training in the pool. Available to AEA members with their $65.00 membership.
Circulation: 6000
Founded in 1987
Mailing list available for rent: 90M names
Printed in 4 colors on glossy stock

21899 American Bicyclist Magazine
League of American Bicyclists
1612 K St NW
Suite 800
Washington, DC 20006-2850

202-822-1333
Fax: 202-822-1334
E-Mail: elizabeth@bikeleague.org
Home Page: www.bikeleague.org
Social Media: Facebook, Twitter, LinkedIn, YouTube, RSS

Andy Clarke, Executive Director

Contains cycling stories; how-to articles; health; legal and safety columns; legislative updates, fitness, cycling technique and travel.
Cost: $35.00
Frequency: Quarterly
Circulation: 40000
Founded in 1880
Printed in 4 colors on glossy stock

21900 American Firearms Industry
AFI Communications
2400 E Las Olas Boulevard
#397
Fort Lauderdale, FL 33301

954-467-9994
Fax: 954-463-2501
E-Mail: webmaster@amfire.com
Home Page: www.amfire.com
Social Media: Facebook, Twitter, LinkedIn

Andrew Molchan, Editor
Alexandra Molchan, Circulation Manager
Kathleen Molchan, Sales Manager

A business-to-business trade magazine containing articles and information centered on the retailing of firearms and shooting products. Areas covered are: handguns, revolvers, pistols, rifles, shotguns, ammunition, rifle scopes, reloading, holsters, hunting accessories, gun parts, cutlery, knives, archery, bows, crossbows, camping, camouflage, black powder, smokeless powder, binoculars, safes, gunlocks, air guns, used gun news and political news and views relatingto firearms and the industry.
Cost: $18.00
Frequency: Monthly
Circulation: 34
Founded in 1973

21901 American Fitness
Aerobics and Fitness Association of America
15250 Ventura Blvd
Suite 200
Sherman Oaks, CA 91403-3297

818-905-0040
877-968-7263
Fax: 818-990-5468
E-Mail: contactafaa@afaa.com
Home Page: www.afaa.com

Linda Pfeffer, President
Roscoe K Fawcett Jr, Publisher

The official publication of the Aerobics and Fitness Association of America. Known for reporting health-related fitness research, current trends, advances in equipment and training applications.
Cost: $27.00
Frequency: Bi-annually
Circulation: 100,000
Founded in 1983

21902 American Hunter
National Rifle Association
11250 Waples Mill Rd
Fairfax, VA 22030-7400

703-267-1400
877-672-2000
Home Page: americanhunter.org
Social Media: Facebook, Twitter, LinkedIn, YouTube, RSS

Mark A Keefe IV, Editor

American Hunter offers expertise on how and where to hunt all types of North American game and encourages readers to take advantage of the rich opportunities and to pass along the tradition to the next generation.

21903 American Paddler
American Canoe Association
7432 Alban Station Boulevard
Suite B-232
Springfield, VA 22150

703-451-0141
Fax: 703-451-2245
E-Mail: aca@americancanoe.org
Home Page: www.acanet.org

Marty Bartels, Publisher

21904 American Quarter Horse Journal
American Quarter Horse Association
1600 Quarter Horse Drive
PO Box 200
Amarillo, TX 79104

806-764-4888
Fax: 806-349-6400
Home Page: www.aqha.com

Bill Brewer, Executive VP
Jim Jennings, Publisher

Industry magazine for Quarter Horse breeders, farm managers and owners.
Cost: $25.00
550 Pages
Frequency: Monthly
Circulation: 66575
Founded in 1948
Printed in 4 colors on glossy stock

21905 American Rifleman
National Rifle Association
11250 Waples Mill Rd
Fairfax, VA 22030-7400

703-267-1400
800-672-3888
Fax: 703-267-3971
E-Mail: publications@nrahq.org
Home Page: www.nrapublications.org
Social Media: Facebook, Twitter, LinkedIn, YouTube, RSS

Mark Keefe IV, Editor-In-Chief

Premier magazine for shooting and firearms enthusiasts. Coverage is devoted to rifles, shotguns, handguns, ammunition, reloading, optics and shooting accessories.
Cost: $35.00
Frequency: Monthly
Circulation: 100000
Founded in 1975

21906 Americas 1st Freedom
National Rifle Association
11250 Waples Mill Rd
Fairfax, VA 22030-7400

703-267-1400
877-672-2000
Fax: 703-267-3971
E-Mail: publications@nrahq.org
Home Page: www.nrapublications.org
Social Media: Facebook, Twitter, LinkedIn, YouTube, RSS

Mark Keefe IV, Editor-In-Chief

NRA's pure news magazine. Its mission is to deliver professional, compelling, accurate, timely and hard-hitting journalism that tells the truth about the threats to our Second Amendment rights. Subscription complementary with membership in NRA. Otherwise $9.95
Founded in 1975

21907 Aquatic Therapy and Fitness Research
Aquatic Exercise Association
PO Box 1609
Nokomis, FL 34274-1609

941-486-8600
888-232-9283
Fax: 941-486-8820
E-Mail: info@aeawave.com

Home Page: www.aeawave.com
Social Media: Facebook, Twitter, LinkedIn, YouTube, RSS

Angie Proctor, CEO
Julie See, President
Kim Huff, Director of Marketing

Journal. Peer-reviewed publication providing documentated opinions of industry leaders. A multidisciplinary publication, each issue includes two focus areas. Subscription included with AEA membership.
Cost: $65.00
Frequency: Monthly
Circulation: 6000
Founded in 1984

21908 Aquatics International
Leisure Publications
6222 Wilshire Blvd.
Los Angeles, CA 90020-4244

323-644-4801
888-269-8410
Fax: 323-964-4842
E-Mail: aquaticsintl@earthlink.com
Home Page: www.aquaticsintl.com
Social Media: Facebook, Twitter, LinkedIn, YouTube, RSS

Garry Carter, Sales Manager
Steve Honum, Account Executive
Theresa Wrong, Sales Manager

Articles of interest to colleges and schools; municipal, county and state pool facilities; hotels, resorts and country clubs; fitness clubs; rehab centers; YMCAs; military facilities; and waterparks.
Cost: $30.00
Frequency: 11X/Yr
Circulation: 30000
Mailing list available for rent

21909 Arabian Horse World
Arabian Horse World
1316 Tamsen St
Suite 101
Cambria, CA 93428-3328

805-771-2300
800-955-9423
Fax: 805-927-6522
E-Mail: info@ahwmagazine.com
Home Page: www.ahwmagazine.com

Denise Hearst, Publisher

Our philosophy at Arabian Horse World is to promote the Arabian - through education and entertainment - to new levels of appreciation and usefullness. Show results and breeding farms are featured.
Cost: $40.00
Frequency: Monthly
Circulation: 15000
Founded in 1990
Printed in 4 colors on glossy stock

21910 Archery Business Magazine
Grand View Media Group
14505 21st Ave N
Suite 202
Plymouth, MN 55447

763-473-5800
800-766-0039
Fax: 763 473 5801
E-Mail: pbrady@affinitygroup.com
Home Page: www.bowhuntingworld.com
Social Media: Facebook

Steve Schiffman, Publisher
Mark Melotik, Editor
Patty Brady, Advertising
Steven Hedlund, President

Controlled circulation trade magazine covering the business side of bowhunting and archery: trade news, industry statistics, marketing and product trends, new product research and development, tips for better business management and effective training.
Frequency: Monthly
Circulation: 11000+
Founded in 1975

21911 Arrow Trade Magazine
3479 409th Ave NW
Braham, MN 55006-3340

320-396-3473
888-796-2083
Fax: 320-396-3206
E-Mail: timdehn@arrowtrademag.com
Home Page: www.arrowtrademag.com

Tim Dehn, Publisher
Matt Granger, Advertising

A business magazine published for retailers, distributors, sales representatives and manufacturers of bowhunting equipment and camouflage clothing.
Founded in 1997

21912 Athletic Management
MAG
2488 N Triphammer Road
Ithaca, NY 14850

607-257-6970
Fax: 607-257-7328
E-Mail: info@athleticbid.com
Home Page: www.momentummedia.com

Mark Goldberg, President
Eleanor Frankel, Editor

Free to college athletic administrators and high school athletic directors in the US and Canada. The editorial mission of Athletic Management is to help Athletic Directors enhance their operations, to share new ideas, and cover pertinent news topics. Feature stories and regular sections address the various facets of managing an athletic department.
Cost: $25.00
Frequency: Weekly
Circulation: 30200
Founded in 1988
Printed in 4 colors on glossy stock

21913 Bass Times
ESPN

334-272-9530
E-Mail: customerservice@bassmaster.com
Home Page: sports.espn.go.com/outdoors/bassmaster

Bass Times is packed with news and information for serious bass fishermen. The perfect compliment to Bassmaster Magazine.
Cost: $12.00
Frequency: Monthly

21914 Bassmaster
ESPN

334-272-9530
E-Mail: advertising@basmaster.com
Home Page: sports.espn.go.com/bassmaster
Social Media: Facebook, Twitter, LinkedIn, YouTube, RSS

Bassmaster Magazine monthly.
Frequency: Monthly

21915 Black's Buyers Directory
PO Box 2029
Red Bank, NJ 07701

732-224-8700
800-224-9464
Fax: 732-741-2827
E-Mail: ms-blacks@attglobal.net
Home Page: www.fieldandstream.com
Social Media: Facebook, Twitter, LinkedIn, YouTube, RSS

James F Black Jr, Publisher
Lois Re, Editor
Christopher Pluck, Owner

The complete buyer's guide to equipment. A one-stop source of information on anything and everything that's archery/bowhunting.
Founded in 2001

21916 Bowlers Journal International
Luby Publishing Company
122 S Michigan Ave
Suite 1506
Chicago, IL 60603-6148

312-341-1110
Fax: 312-341-1469
E-Mail: email@bowlersjournal.com
Home Page: www.lubypublishing.com

Keith Hamilton, President
Mason King, Editor
Emily Kupper, Circulation Director
Bob Nieman, Editor

Information geared toward all levels of industry personnel. Regular issue features include new products listings, tournament reviews, personality profiles and proprietor workshops.
Cost: $24.00
Frequency: Monthly
Circulation: 22319
Founded in 1913

21917 Bowling Center Management
Bowling Proprietors Association of America
122 S Michigan Avenue
Suite 1506
Chicago, IL 60603-6107

312-341-1110
Fax: 312-341-1180
E-Mail: bowlctrman@aol.com
Home Page: www.bcmmag.com
Social Media: Facebook, Twitter, LinkedIn

Mike Panozzo, Publisher
Bob Nieman, Editor
Emily Kupper, Circulation Director
Mason King, Editor

Information designed for bowling center owners to help them in the operation and management of their centers.
Cost: $60.00
Frequency: Monthly
Circulation: 5000
Founded in 1995

21918 By Design
American Society of Golf Course Architects
125 N Executive Dr
Suite 302
Brookfield, WI 53005-6035

262-786-5960
Fax: 262-786-5919
E-Mail: info@asgca.org
Home Page: www.asgca.org
Social Media: Facebook, Twitter

Chad Ritterbusch, Executive Director

E-Magazine highlighting the work of ASGCA golf course architects worldwide. Subscribe at no charge at www.asgca.org
185 Members
Frequency: Quarterly
Circulation: 6000
Founded in 1946

21919 Camping Magazine
American Camp Association
5000 State Road 67 N
Martinsville, IN 46151-7902

765-342-8456
800-428-2267
Fax: 765-342-2065
E-Mail: pr@acacamps.org
Home Page: www.acacamps.org
Social Media: Facebook, Twitter, LinkedIn

Peg Smith, CEO
Kim Bruno, Communication/Development

Head
Terrie Nicodemus, Manager

The official publication of the American Camp Association. Experts in the camp field contribute informative articles and essays on current advances in camp management, staffing and human resources, programming, risk management, special populations and diversity, health and wellness, and more.
Cost: $24.95
Founded in 1920
Mailing list available for rent

21920 Coaching Management
MAG
2488 N Triphammer Road
Ithaca, NY 14850-5220

607-257-6970
Fax: 607-257-7328
E-Mail: info@athleticbid.com
Home Page: www.momentummedia.com
Social Media: Facebook, Twitter, LinkedIn

Mark Goldberg, Publisher/CEO
Eleanor Frankel, Editor
Dave Dubin, Circulation Director

Information including team equipment, apparel, injury prevention, conditioning, as well as field, stadium and court maintenance and improvement. Primary feature articles cover a wide range of coaching tools and techniques.
Frequency: Bi-annually
Circulation: 20556
Founded in 1988
Mailing list available for rent

21921 Coaching Volleyball
American Volleyball Coaches Association
2365 Harrodsburg Road
Suite A325
Lexington, KY 40504

859-226-4315
866-544-2822
Fax: 859-226-4338
E-Mail: members@avca.org
Home Page: www.avca.org
Social Media: Facebook, Twitter, LinkedIn, YouTube, RSS

Leah DeBoer, Executive Director
Leah Brock, Communications Manager
Frequency: Bi-Monthly

21922 Cross Country Skier
PO Box 550
Cable, WI 54821

715-798-5500
800-827-0607
Fax: 715-798-3599
E-Mail: info@crosscountryskier.com
Home Page: www.crosscountryskier.com
Social Media: Facebook, Twitter, LinkedIn

Ron Bergin, Owner

The journal of nordic skiing - destinations, news, training and technique, waxing, competition, equipment and new products, and great features on all facets of the sport of cross country skiing.

21923 Cutting Horse Chatter
National Cutting Horse Association
260 Bailey Avenue
Fort Worth, TX 76107

817-244-6188
Fax: 817-244-2015
E-Mail: info@nchacutting.com
Home Page: www.nchacutting.com

Chubby Turner, President
Chris Benedict, VP
Jeff Hooper, Executive Director
Rick Ivey, Tresurer
Alan Gold, Director Marketing
Frequency: Monthly
Circulation: 20500

21924 Deer & Deer Hunting
F+W Media
38 E. 29th Street
New York, NY 10016

212-447-1400
Fax: 212-447-5231
E-Mail: contact_us@fwmedia.com
Home Page: www.fwpublications.com

Hugh McAloon, Publisher

Edited for serious, year-round whitetail hunting enthusiasts and focuses on hunting techniques, deer biology and behavior, deer management, habitat requirements, the natural history of deer, and hunting ethics. Contains how-to articles designed to help hunters be successful. Regular columns and departments include book reviews, Deer Browse (unusual observations by hunters), new products, an editor's column, letters from readers, Deer Behavior, Can You Outsmart This Deer? and Q&A.
Cost: $19.99
Circulation: 212500
Founded in 1977
Mailing list available for rent

21925 Fantasy Sports
F+W Media
38 E. 29th Street
New York, NY 10016
212-447-1400
Fax: 212-447-5231
E-Mail: contact_us@fwmedia.com
Home Page: www.fwpublications.com

Tom Kessenich, Editor
David Nussbaum, Chair
Jim Ogle, Finance/Administration
Sara Domville, President
Phil Graham, VP

The essential manual for those who participate in Rotisserie and other fantasy sports leagues. Reports extensive statistics to help managers in making personnel moves. Also includes recommendations on who to draft or trade. The April and May issues focus on baseball. The August and September issues focus on football. An up-to-the-minute, online version is also available fo a small fee at www.fantasysportsmag.com
Cost: $9.97
132 Pages
Frequency: 4 Per Year
Circulation: 78,767
Founded in 1989
Mailing list available for rent

21926 Fastpitch Delivery
National Fastpitch Coaches Association
2641 Grinstead Drive,
Suite D
Louisville, KY 42046

502-409-4600
Fax: 502-409-4622
E-Mail: nfca@nfca.org
Home Page: www.nfca.org
Social Media: Facebook, Twitter, LinkedIn, YouTube, RSS

Lacy Lee Baker, Executive Director
Hildred Deese, Senior Director of Events
Frequency: Monthly
Founded in 1982

21927 Fishermen's News
Philip's Publishing Group
2201 W Commodore Way
Seattle, WA 98199-1298

206-284-8285
800-258-8609
Fax: 206-284-0391
E-Mail: circulation@rhppublishing.com
Home Page: www.pacmar.com

Peter Philips, Publisher
Lisa Albers, Managing Editor
Bill Forslund, Advertising Manager
Maggie Cheung, Circulation Manager
Sharon Adjiri, Production Manager

In addition to important fisheries news, every month they bring readers important information and lessons on Safety, entertaining pieces about commercial fishing history, a commercial listing of fishing vessels and equipment in their classified section, updated information on seafood market trends and important notices about all the meetings and conferences occurring on the West Coast.
Cost: $21.00
Frequency: Monthly
Circulation: 14,933
Founded in 1945
Printed in 4 colors on newsprint stock

21928 Fishing Tackle Retailer
ESPN Productions
3500 Blue Lake Drive
Birmingham, AL 35243

407-566-2277
Fax: 334-279-7148
E-Mail: customerservice@bassmaster.com
Home Page: www.bassmaster.com
Social Media: Facebook, Twitter, LinkedIn, YouTube, RSS

Clem Dippel, Publisher
Scott Wall, Advertising Sales

Information to inform and instruct America's fishing tackle retailers, merchandisers, and distributors on merchandise and sales techniques used to sell fishing tackle.
Cost: $4.00
Frequency: 11X/yr
Circulation: 17720
Founded in 1980
Printed in 4 colors

21929 Funworld
Int'l Association of Amusement Parks & Attractions
1448 Duke St
Alexandria, VA 22314-3403

703-836-3677
Fax: 703-836-2824
E-Mail: alee@IAAPA.org
Home Page: www.iaapa.org
Social Media: Facebook, Twitter, LinkedIn, YouTube

Charlie Bray, President/CEO
Susan Mosedale, Executive VP
Jan McCool, Executive
Roxanne Pope, Assistant to the President

Funworld Magazine is a service for IAAPA members and provides discussion and illustrative examinations of the amusement and attractions industry form members to stay current and connected. The magazine contains features that analyze various aspects of the amusement business including safety, thrill rides, financial issues, event coverage and profiles of member and nonmember facilities from around the world.
Cost: $45.00
Circulation: 8,500
Founded in 1917

21930 Golf Business
National Golf Course Owners Association
291 Seven Farms Dr
Suite 2
Daniel Island, SC 29492-8000
843-881-9956
800-933-4262
Fax: 843-856-3288

E-Mail: golfbusiness@ngcoa.org
Home Page: www.ngcoa.org
Social Media: Facebook, Twitter, YouTube

Michael Hughes, CEO
Joe Rice, Publisher
Frank Santangelo, Manager

The official publication of the National Golf Course Owners Association. The editorial content is designed to promote the exchange of information and ideas among course owners and senior industry executives to improve the profitability of their operations. Golf Business is dedicated to serving the entire interest of the golf course operation.
Cost: $35.00
Frequency: Monthly
Circulation: 20000
Founded in 1971
Printed in 4 colors on glossy stock

21931 Golf Course Management
Golf Course Superintendents Association of America
1421 Research Park Dr
Lawrence, KS 66049-3859

785-841-2240
800-472-7878
Fax: 785-832-4488
E-Mail: ehiscock@gcsaa.org
Home Page: www.gcsaa.org
Social Media: Facebook, Twitter

Mark Woodward, CEO
Scott Hollistor, Editor
Bunny Smith, Managing Editor
Mark Gabrick, Sr Manager Corp Sales/Marketing

Official monthly magazine of Golf Course Superintendents Association of America and golf course management industry's leading professional journal. Includes scientific, technical and practical management articles.
Cost: $60.00
Frequency: Monthly
Circulation: 40,000
Founded in 1932

21932 Golf Course News
4012 Bridge Avenue
Cleveland, OH 44113

216-961-4130
Fax: 216-961-0364
Home Page: www.golfcoursenews.com

Kevin Gilbride, Publisher
John Walsh, Editor
Richard Foster, CEO
Chris Foster, President/COO
Doug Adams, Director Marketing

Focuses on course maintenance and management, new course openings, and awards and promotions. New products related to the industry and environment and government issues.
Cost: $45.00
Circulation: 30000

21933 Golf Inc Magazine
Cypress Manazines
250 Bei Marin Key Boulevard, #A
PO Box 1150
Novato, CA 94949-5727

415-382-2400
800-436-6149
Fax: 415-382-2416
E-Mail: mikeb@cypressmagazines.com
Home Page: www.cyspressmagazines.com

Jack Crittenden, President
Kim Boalick, Advertising
Mindy Heral, Marketing
Jim Dunlap, Editor-in-Chief

Provides news, success stories and benchmark data for all aspects of the golf course industry - including development, operations, marketing, retail, turf, sales and driving range.
Cost: $65.00
Frequency: Monthly
Circulation: 15000

21934 Golf Range Times
Forecast Golf Group
P.O.Box 3106
Glen Allen, VA 23058-3106

804-379-5760
Fax: 804-378-5780
E-Mail: info@forecastgolf.com
Home Page: www.forecastgolf.com

James E Turner, Publisher/Editor
Betty Jo Bass, Advertising Manager

Information on Golf Range industry changes and closings, new ranges, and development information and services.
Cost: $49.95
Frequency: Monthly
Circulation: 6000
Founded in 1990

21935 Golfdom
Questex Medica Group
PO Bo 5057
Brentwood, TN 37024

615-377-3322
866-344-1315
Fax: 615-377-3322
E-Mail: questex@sunbeltfs.com
Home Page: www.golfdom.com

Patrick Jones, Publisher
Larry Aylward, Editor

Publication is written for golf course architects, superintendents, management companies, owners, developers, consultants and others in the industry with an interest in golf course design, construction, remodeling and related business and management topics. Subscription is free to Golf course superintendents, owners and managers. Individuals who are not qualified as superintendents, owners and managers can subscribe at the current subscription rate.
Cost: $30.00
Circulation: 3000
Founded in 1927

21936 Government Recreation & Fitness
Executive Business Media
825 Old Country Road
PO Box 1500
Westbury, NY 11590

516-334-3030
Fax: 516-334-3059
E-Mail: ebm-mail@ebmpubs.com
Home Page: www.ebmpubs.com

Murry Greenwald, Publisher
Paul Ragnoz, Managing Editor

Government Recreation and Fitness reaches recreation and fitness professionals in every department and agency of the federal government, goes directly to the people who purchase your products, and covers both appropriated and nonappropriated fund budgets. Subscription is free to managers and operators of fitness centers and recreation facilities at US military bases, federal agencies and offices as well as procurement agents for these facilities and others allied to the field
Cost: $35.00
Frequency: 15 issues per year
Circulation: 9974
ISSN: 1086-7899
Founded in 1994
Printed in 4 colors on glossy stock

21937 Gun & Knife Show Calendar
F+W Media
38 E. 29th Street
New York, NY 10016

212-447-1400
Fax: 212-447-5231
E-Mail: contact_us@fwmedia.com
Home Page: www.fwpublications.com
Social Media: Twitter

Hugh McAloon, Publisher
Bruce Wolberg, Ad Manager
John Koenig, Editor'

A compilation of gun shows and knife shows held throughout the country, and is intended to be used as a complete guide for anyone who attends or displays at these shows. Regular listings include the dates of the show, the address, the city, state, number of tables, and the cost of tables. For attendees, the show hours and the cost of admission are listed. Shows are listed for a full year ahead and there is no charge to list a show.
Cost: $15.95
88 Pages
Frequency: Quarterly
Circulation: 5758
Founded in 1952

21938 Hockey Business News
Straight Line Communications
12327 Santa Monica Boulevard
#202
Los Angeles, CA 90025-2552

310-207-9916
Fax: 310-442-6663
E-Mail: hbn@artnet.net

Mark Brown, Publisher

Features articles on ice hockey news and events, Canadian and international news, industry trends and forecasts and new products.
Cost: $60.00
Frequency: 9 per year
Circulation: 5,000

21939 Horseman's Journal
National Horsemen's Administration Corporation
870 Corporate Drive
Suite 300
Lexington, KY 40503

859-259-0451
866-245-1711
Fax: 859-259-0452
E-Mail: racing@hpba.org
Home Page: www.hbpa.org

Richard E Glover, Editor
Sandy Erreguin, Advertising Director

Official magazine of the National Horsemen's Benevolent and Protective Association. Designed to give owners and trainers of racehorses information helpful for the running of their horse related businesses.
56 Pages
Circulation: 32,000
Founded in 1942
Printed in 4 colors on glossy stock

21940 ISI EDGE
Ice Skating Institute
600 Custer Rd
Bldg 9
Plano, TX 75023

972-735-8800
Fax: 972-735-8815
E-Mail: isi@skateisi.org
Home Page: www.skateisi.org

Peter Martell, Executive Director

Professional journal for the ice skating industry. Focuses on the needs and interests of the industry's managers, skating and hockey directors, instructors, and builders/suppliers.
Frequency: Bi-Monthly

21941 Inside Archery
2960 N Academy Boulevard
Suite 101
Colorado Springs, CO 80917
719-495-9999
Fax: 719-495-8899
E-Mail: info@insidearchery.com
Home Page: www.fieldandstream.com
Social Media: Twitter, LinkedIn
Bill Krenz, President/Editor
Sherry Krenz, VP/Publisher
The Archery Industry Authority
Founded in 1997

21942 International Bowling Industry
13245 Riverside Drive
Suite 501
Sherman Oaks, CA 91423
818-789-2695
Fax: 818-789-2812
E-Mail: info@bowlingindustry.com
Home Page: www.bowlingindustry.com
Social Media: Twitter, LinkedIn
Scott Frager, Publisher & Editor
Nick West, Associate Publisher
Fred Groh, Managing Editor
Patty Heath, Office Manager
Information on customer services, new products, industry trends, new concepts in management and marketing techniques, and employee motivation.
Cost: $32.00
Frequency: Monthly
Circulation: 10,205

21943 International Gaming and Wagering Business
BNP Media
PO Box 1080
Skokie, IL 60076-9785
847-763-9534
Fax: 847-763-9538
E-Mail: igwb@halldata.com
Home Page: www.igwb.com
James Rutherford, Editor
Lynn Davidson, Marketing
Tammie Gizicki, Director
Focuses on business strategy, legislative information, food service and promotional concerns.
Frequency: Monthly
Circulation: 25000

21944 Journal of Sport and Social Issues
Sage Publications
2455 Teller Road
Newbury Park, CA 91320
800-818-7243
Fax: 800-583-2665
E-Mail: journals@sagepub.com
Home Page: www.sagepublications.com
Social Media: Facebook
CL Cole, Editor
Brings together the latest research, discussion and analysis on contemporary sport issues.
Cost: $552.00
Frequency: Quarterly
ISSN: 0193-7235

21945 Lacrosse Magazine
113 W University Pkwy
Baltimore, MD 21210-3301
410-235-6882
Fax: 410-366-6735
E-Mail: info@uslacrosse.org
Home Page: www.laxmagazine.com
Social Media: Facebook, Twitter, LinkedIn, Live Blogs
Steve Stenersen, President
Bill Schoonmaker, COO
Bill Rubacky, Managing Director of Marketing
Kira Muller, Director of Advertising Sales
The most widely circulated publication for the sport of lacrosse, Lacrosse Magazine connects the sport's community, educates players, coaches and officials, entertains fans and keeps the membership of US Lacrosse informed.
Frequency: Monthly
Circulation: 300M
ISSN: 1069-5893
Founded in 1982

21946 Master Skier
PO Box 187
Escabana, MI 49829
906-789-1139
E-Mail: mskier@chartermi.net
Home Page: www.masterskier.com
Journal dedicated to the skiing industry. Delivered to 51,000 readers in 19 countries.
Founded in 1986
Mailing list available for rent

21947 Medicine and Science in Sports and Exercise
American College of Sports Medicine
401 W Michigan Street
PO Box 1440
Indianapolis, IN 46206
317-347-7817
Fax: 317-634-7817
E-Mail: msse@acsm.org
Home Page: www.acsm.org
Kent B Pandolf, Editor-in-Chief
Gay Smith, Editor
Scientific research, education, and practical applications of sports medicine and exercise science to maintain and enhance physical performance, fitness, health and quality of life.
Cost: $300.00
Frequency: Monthly
Circulation: 14842
ISSN: 0195-9131
Founded in 1968
Printed in 4 colors on matte stock

21948 Military Trader
F+W Media
38 E. 29th Street
New York, NY 10016
212-447-1400
Fax: 212-447-5231
E-Mail: contact_us@fwmedia.com
Home Page: www.fwpublications.com
Social Media: Facebook, Twitter, LinkedIn, Live Blogs
Rick Groth, Publisher
John Adams-Graf, Editor
David Nussbaum, Chair
Jim Ogle, Finance
David Blansfield, President
For military collectors, the best monthly source of news, features, collecting advice, shows, and events. Each issue offers thousands of 'For Sale' and 'Wanted' mlitary collectibles from hundreds of dealers and collectors. This is where to go when you are trying to buy or sell vintage military uniforms, pins, medals, helmets, ammunition, firearms, flags, and other militaria.
Cost: $19.00
56 Pages
Frequency: Monthly
Circulation: 9414
Founded in 1975

21949 Military Vehicles
F+W Media
38 E. 29th Street
New York, NY 10016
212-447-1400
Fax: 212-447-5231
E-Mail: contact_us@fwmedia.com
Home Page: www.fwpublications.com
Social Media: Facebook, Twitter, LinkedIn, Live Blogs
Bill Reed, President
John Adams-Graf, Editor
David Nussbaum, Chair
Jim Ogle, Finance
David Blansfield, President
Each issue includes news, vintage military photos, collecting advice, market information, show listings, and extensive display and classified advertising sections offering to buy and sell hundreds of jeeps, tanks, trucks, vehicle parts, and accessories from dealers and enthusiasts all over the world. Other regular features include book and media reviews, letters to the editor, tech topics, weapons & replicas, models & toys, and internet sightings.
Cost: $23.98
176 Pages
Circulation: 19,000
Founded in 1952

21950 NJCAA Review
National Junior College Athletic Association
1631 Mesa Ave Suite B
Suite 103
Colorado Springs, CO 80920
719-590-9788
Fax: 719-590-7324
E-Mail: meleicht@njcaa.org
Home Page: www.njcaa.org
Social Media: Facebook, Twitter
Mary Ellen Leicht, Executive Director
Mark Krug, Director Sports Information/Media
Marry Elen, Director
Dee Dorus, Administrative Assistant
Cost: $30.00
Frequency: 10x/Year
Circulation: 2500
Founded in 1989

21951 NRA InSights
National Rifle Association
11250 Waples Mill Rd
Fairfax, VA 22030-7400
703-267-1400
800-672-3888
Home Page: www.nrapublilcations.org
Social Media: Twitter, LinkedIn
NRAs official publication for its Junior members. Designed to motivate its readers to participate in all aspects of the shooting sports. Features personality profiles on top junior shooters, hunting stories, how-to pieces, program announcements, product surveys, safety features and educational information about firearms. Subscription included in membership dues.

21952 Online Magazine
Information Today
143 Old Marlton Pike
Medford, NJ 08055-8750
609-654-6266
800-300-9868
Fax: 609-654-4309
E-Mail: custserv@infotoday.com
Home Page: www.infotoday.com
Thomas H Hogan, President
Roger R Bilboul, Chairman Of The Board
Online is written for information professionals and provides articles, product reviews, case studies, evaluation and informed opinion about selecting, using and managing electronic infor-

mation products, plus industry and professional information about onlline database systems.
Cost: $115.00
Frequency: Monthly
Founded in 1976

21953 Outdoors Magazine
Elk Publishing
531 Main St
Colchester, VT 05446-7222

802-879-2013
800-499-0447
Fax: 802-860-0005
E-Mail: info@outdoorsmagazine.net
Home Page: www.elkpublishing.com

James Austin, Publisher

A monthly publication covering hunting, fishing and wildlife issues in Vermont, New York, Maine, Massachusetts and Connecticut.
Cost: $18.95
Frequency: Monthly
Circulation: 10000
ISSN: 1096-1976
Founded in 1996
Printed in 4 colors on matte stock

21954 PGA TOUR Partners Magazine
North American Media Group
12301 Whitewater Dr
Suite 260
Minnetonka, MN 55343-4103

952-936-9333
800-688-7611
Fax: 952-936-9169
E-Mail: NAMGhq@namginc.com
Home Page: www.namginc.com

Seth Hoyt, Publisher

An exclusive, members-only publication filled with tips and techniques that can be used to improve your game, from the first tee to the 18th green.
Frequency: Bi-Monthly
Circulation: 1.3 m
Founded in 1978

21955 PTR International Tennis Symposium
Professional Tennis Registry
PO Box 4739
Hilton Head Island, SC 29938

843-785-7244
800-421-6289
Fax: 843-686-2033
E-Mail: ptr@ptrtennis.org
Home Page: www.ptrtennis.org
Social Media: Facebook, Twitter

Dan Santoruk, CEO
Julie Jilly, VP/Operations

To provide education and information for PTR members.
14m Members
Frequency: 6x Annually
Circulation: 15,000
Founded in 1976

21956 Paddler
Paddle Sport Publishing
122 South Orange Av.
Steamboat Springs, CO 80477-5450

970-879-1450
888-774-7554
Fax: 970-870-1404
E-Mail: circulation@paddlermagazine.com
Home Page: www.paddlermagazine.com

Eugene Buchanan, Publisher/Editor
Tom Bie, Managing Editor

Each issues is filled with stories on places to paddle, skill enhancement, gear reviews, environmental issues, industry updats and profiles of leading paddlers.
Cost: $18.00
Frequency: Monthly
Circulation: 5527
Printed in 4 colors on glossy stock

21957 Parachutist Magazine
United States Parachute Association
5401 Southpoint Centre Blvd
Fredericksburg, VA 22407-2612

540-604-9740
Fax: 540-604-9741
E-Mail: uspa@uspa.org
Home Page: www.uspa.org
Social Media: Facebook, Twitter

Jay Stokes, President
Randy Allison, VP
Sherry Butcher, Secretary & National Director
Lee Schlichtemeier, Treasurer
Jan Meyer, National Director

Supporting safe skydiving and those individuals who practice the sport. The magazine discusses issues dealing with training, safety, equipment, and networking the worldwide community of skydivers.
Cost: $4.50
112 Pages
Frequency: Monthly
Circulation: 35000
Founded in 1946

21958 Pool and Spa News
Leisure Publications
6222 Wilshire Blvd
Los Angeles, CA 90020 4244

323-644-4801
888-269-8410
Fax: 323-801-4986
E-Mail: poolspanews@hanleywood.com
Home Page: www.poolspanews.com
Social Media: Facebook, Twitter, LinkedIn

Dick Coleman, Publisher
Erika Taylor, Editor
Steve Schlange, Marketing Manager
Scot Christ, Accountant

Pool and Spa News goals are: to furnish information to help pool and spa professionals function better in their businesses; to showcase products that can be sold or used in the industry; to help make their business life easier and more rewarding.
Cost: $16.50
Frequency: Semi-Monthly
Founded in 1960
Mailing list available for rent

21959 Powersports Business
Ehlert Publishing Group
3300 Fernbrook Lane N
Suite 200
Plymouth, MN 55447

763-383-4400
800-848-6247
Fax: 763-383-4499
E-Mail:
customerservice@powersportsbusiness.com
Home Page: www.powersportsbusiness.com
Social Media: Facebook, Twitter, LinkedIn

Mark Adams, CEO
Dave McMahon, Editor

Gives dealers, distributors, and manufacturers timely business news and analysis every three weeks.
Frequency: Weekly
Circulation: 18000
Founded in 1969

21960 Pro Football Weekly
302 Saunders Rd
Suite 100
Riverwoods, IL 60015-3897

847-940-1100
800-331-7529
Fax: 847-940-1108
E-Mail: editors@pfwmedia.com
Home Page: www.profootballweekly.com
Social Media: Facebook, Twitter, LinkedIn

Hub Arkush, President

Seeks to bring the best coverage in the NFL to its readers.
Cost: $49.95
Frequency: Weekly
Founded in 1967

21961 Professional Skater
Professional Skaters Association
3006 Allegro Park Ln SW
Rochester, MN 55902-4159

507-280-6812
Fax: 507-281-5491
E-Mail: office@skatepsa.com
Home Page: www.skatepsa.com

Jimmie Santee, Executive Director

A bi-monthly magazine published by the Professional Skater Association.
Cost: $19.95
40 Pages
Frequency: Bi-Monthly
Founded in 1984

21962 QUAD Off-Road Magazine
Transworld Publishing
Ste 150
2052 Corte Del Nogal
Carlsbad, CA 92011-1491

760-722-7777
Fax: 760-722-0653
E-Mail: jasonyoung@twsnet.com
Home Page: www.neodata.com

Jason Young, Publication Contact

Quad off-road magazine delivers all things ATV: Breathtaking photography, tons of practical tips, the hottest nwe products, Quad comparison tests, ARV adventure stories, and much more.
Cost: $9.97
Frequency: Monthly

21963 Quarter Horse Racing Journal
American Quarter Horse Association
PO Box 200
Amarillo, TX 79168-0001

806-376-4811
Fax: 806-349-6411
Home Page: www.aqha.com
Social Media: Facebook, Twitter, LinkedIn, You Tube

Jim Helzer, President

News and races, health and management, business and industry, winner's circle, the handicapper, horse health, quarter paths, sports medicine, finish line and others are featured articles.
Frequency: Monthly

21964 Racquetball Magazine
USA Racquetball
4244 Russet Court
Lilburn, GA 80904-2906

770-972-2303
Fax: 719-635-0685
E-Mail: rjohn@usra.org
Home Page: www.racqmag.com

Jim Hiser, Executive Director
Kevin Joyce, Director Membership
Melody Weiss, Director Finance
Heather Fender, Executive Assistant/Event

Coord
Ed Mazur, President

Geared toward a readership of informed, active enthusiasts who seek entertainment, instruction and accurate reporting of events. Available by subscription through the US Racquetball Association National Office.
Cost: $20.00
64 Pages
Frequency: Bi-Monthly
Circulation: 16,000
ISSN: 1060-877X
Founded in 1990
Printed in 4 colors on glossy stock

21965 Recreational Ice Skating
Ice Skating Institute
6000 Custer Rd
Bldg 9
Plano, TX 75023

972-735-8800
Fax: 972-735-8815
E-Mail: editor@skateisi.org
Home Page: www.skateisi.org

Peter Martell, Executive Director

Distributed to ISI individual skater members, skating coaches, and rinks and pro shops worldwide. Written for and about ice skating enthusiasts and focuses on promoting ice skating as recreation and sport.
Frequency: Quarterly

21966 Referee
National Association of Sports Officials
2017 Lathrop Ave
Racine, WI 53405-3758

262-632-5448
800-733-6100
Fax: 262-632-5460
E-Mail: questions@referee.com
Home Page: www.referee.com
Social Media: Facebook, Twitter, LinkedIn

Barry Mano, President

Monthly magazine published by the National Association of Sports Officials. Containes interviews, feature articles, late-breaking news, personality profiles, investigative reports, health, legal and tax tips, and a wide range of technical information for many sports.
Cost: $44.95
80 Pages
Frequency: Monthly
Circulation: 77000
Founded in 1976
Printed in 4 colors on glossy stock

21967 Ride BMX
Transworld Magazines
353 Airport Road
Oceanside, CA 92054

760-722-7777
Fax: 760-722-0653
E-Mail: jasonyoung@twsnet.com
Home Page: www.neodata.com
Social Media: Facebook, Twitter, LinkedIn

Jason Young, Publication Contact

Publication with information for BMX riders.
Cost: $15.97
Frequency: Monthly

21968 Rodale's Scuba Diving
F+W Media
38 E. 29th Street
New York, NY 10016

212-447-1400
Fax: 212-447-5231
E-Mail: contact_us@fwmedia.com
Home Page: www.fwpublications.com
Social Media: Facebook, Twitter, LinkedIn

Edited to provide information about the practice of diving, dive travel opportunities, the marine environment, the reader's health and safety and the dive equipment on which they depend. Travel editorial focuses on both domestic and international dive travel and equipment editorial offers readers comparative product reviews.
Cost: $16.97
Frequency: 11 Per Year
Circulation: 187,059
Founded in 1992

21969 Shooting Illustrated
National Rifle Association
11250 Waples Mill Rd
Fairfax, VA 22030-7400

703-267-1400
877-672-2000
Home Page: www.nrapublications.org
Social Media: Facebook, Twitter, LinkedIn

Aaron Carter, Associate Editor

Comprehensive, timely and all-inclusive. In its pages you will find the best gun writers in the world, assembled to bring you the latest information on rifles, pistols or shotguns. From handloading to gunsmithing to highpower competition; from varmint rifles to rifles for the world's biggest game; from competition pistols to heavy field revolvers.
Cost: $9.95

21970 Shooting Industry
12345 World Trade Drive
San Diego, CA 92128-3102

858-674-4898
858-605-0254
Fax: 619-297-5353
E-Mail: subs@shootingindustry.com
Home Page: www.shootingindustry.com
Social Media: Facebook, Twitter, LinkedIn

Russ Thurman, Editor
Brian Friesen, Sales Manager

A trade publication covering the hunting and shooting industries. This publication is available to select dealers and select police personnel only. Dealers must have a current Federal Firearms License and no less than two additional credentials. Police personnel must have a letter from their Police Chief or Range Officer requesting a subscription (on department letterhead).
Cost: $25.00
Frequency: Monthly
Founded in 1955

21971 Shooting Sports Retailer
SSR Communications
200 Croft Street
Suite 1
Birmingham, AL 35242

205-408-3766
Fax: 212-944-1884
E-Mail: stuart@grandviewmedia.com
Home Page: www.shootingsportsretailer.com

Glenn Karaban, President

Features articles on shooting sports equipment, sales techniques, new products, sales aids, and potential problems for the wholesale seller of shooting equipment.
Frequency: Monthly
Circulation: 17463
Founded in 1980

21972 Shooting Sports USA
National Rifle Association
11250 Waples Mill Rd
Fairfax, VA 22030-7400

703-267-1400
877-672-2000
Home Page: www.nrapublications.org
Social Media: Facebook, Twitter

Information for the competitive shooter, from smallbore to high power, air action pistol and everything in between.
Cost: $9.95

21973 Single Shot Rifle Journal
American Single Shot Rifle Association
PO Box 1162
Niles, MI 49120

269-687-9550
E-Mail: journaleditor@assra.com
Home Page: www.assra.com

Gary Staup, President
John Merz, VP
D. Wayne Stiles, Editor

The official magazine of The American Single Shot Rifle Association. Susbscription is included with membership in the ASSRA.
Cost: $35.00
60 Pages
Frequency: Bi-Monthly
Circulation: 2400
Founded in 1948
Printed in on matte stock

21974 Ski Area Management
Beardsley Publishing Corporation
45 Main Street North
PO Box 644
Woodbury, CT 06798

203-263-0888
Fax: 203-266-0452
E-Mail: news@saminfo.com
Home Page: www.saminfo.com

Jennifer Rowan, Publisher
Olivia Rowan, Marketing/Associate Publisher
Donna Jacobs, V.P./Administration
Rick Kahl, Editor
Ann Hasper, Senior Editor

SAM magazine is the professional trade publication for the mountain resort market. It is a bi-monthly, all-paid publication.
Cost: $48.00
Frequency: Monthly
Circulation: 3992
Founded in 1962
Printed in 4 colors on glossy stock

21975 Ski Magazine
929 Pearl Street
5720 Flatiron Parkway
Boulder, CO 80301

303-448-7600
800-678-0817
Fax: 303-442-6321
E-Mail: subsvcs@ski.customersvc.com
Home Page: www.skimag.com
Social Media: Facebook, Twitter, LinkedIn, You Tube

Kendall Hamilton, Editor-In-Chief
Greg Ditrinco, Executive Editor
Kim Beekman, Managing Editor
Samantha Berman, Senior Editor

Includes information on travel, gear, instruction, snow reports, mountain cams, and gift shops.
Cost: $11.00
Frequency: 8X/year

21976 SkiTrax Magazine
260 Spadina Avenue
Suite 200
Toronto, Canada M5V1P9, ON

416-977-2100
866-754-8729
Fax: 416-977-9200
E-Mail: skitrax@passport.ca
Home Page: www.skitrax.com

Social Media: Facebook, Twitter, LinkedIn, You Tube

North America's premier nordic publication is the official magazine of the USSA and CCC and offers the broadest coverage of nordic skiing available. Coverage includes comprehensive Annual North American Buyer's Guide; local touring centers and exotic backcountry hide-a-ways; complete North American and international competition coverage; regular tips on products; training, technique, telemark, masters, and waxing; extensive calendar of events; plus much more.

21977 Soccer Journal
National Soccer Coaches Association of America
6700 Squibb Road
Suite 215
Mission, KS 66202

913-362-1747
800-458-0678
Fax: 913-362-3439
E-Mail: info@nscca.com
Home Page: www.nscaa.com

The official publication of the National Soccer Coaches of America. Produced exclusively for soccer coaches. Each issue contains technical and tactical articles, news and updates on important events, thoughts from opinion leaders in the sport and features on the interesting people and issues of the game. Subscription included in NSCAA membership.
Cost: $50.00
Frequency: 8X/Year
Circulation: 18000
Founded in 1941

21978 Speedway Illustrated
Speedway Illustrated
107 Elm St
Salisbury, MA 01952-1803

978-465-9099
888-837-3684
Fax: 978-465-9033
E-Mail: editorial@speedwayillustrated.com
Home Page: www.speedwayillustrated.com

Dick Berggren, VP
Steve Chryssos, Advertising Manager
Lynne Henry, Advertising Sales

They'll show you how to build and race your own car, and take you inside at NASCAR's hottest teams and stars.
Cost: $19.94
Frequency: Monthly
Circulation: 150000
Founded in 2000

21979 Sporting Goods Business
VNU Business Publications
2900 Veterans Hwy
Bristol, PA 19007-1606

847-763-9050
800-464- 759
Fax: 847-763-9037
E-Mail: info@sgdealer.com
Home Page: www.sportinggoodsbusiness.com
Social Media: Facebook, Twitter

Michael Marchesano, President
Derek Irwin, CFO
Sid Holt, Editorial Director

Covers information on all facets of sporting goods, including industry news, sales volume analysis, market events coverage, and other statistics, also covers store operation, merchandising, pricing, promotion, cost control, and sales training.
Cost: $75.00
Frequency: Monthly
Circulation: 27,374
Founded in 1905

21980 Sporting Goods Dealer
VNU Publications
PO Box 1184
Skokie, IL 60076-8194

847-763-9050
800-464- 759
Fax: 847-763-9037
E-Mail: info@sgdealer.com
Home Page: www.sgdealer.com
Social Media: Facebook, Twitter

Michael Marchesano, President/CEO
Sid Holt, Editorial Director
Derek Irwin, CFO

Sporting Goods Dealer offers reporting on industry insiders, new products, and merchandising trends affecting team dealers and retailers that service schools, colleges, and pro and local teams.
Cost: $75.00
Circulation: 10000
Founded in 1905

21981 Sporting News
Sporting News Publishing Company
PO Vox 51570
Boulder, CO 80322-1510

314-997-7111
800-777-6785
Fax: 314-993-7798
Home Page: www.sportingnews.com

Pete Spina, Publisher
Kathy Kinkeade, VP

A comprehensive publication covering sporting goods manufacturers, retailers, wholesalers and distributors.
Cost: $15.97
Frequency: Bi-Monthly

21982 Sports Illustrated
Time Life Building
New York, NY 10020-1393

212-229-9797
Fax: 212-467-4049
Home Page: www.sportsillustrated.cnn.com

John Huey, Editor-in-Chief
Terry McDonell, Editor, Time Inc. Sports Group
Paul Fichtenbaum, Managing Editor, SI.com

Sports Illustrated is the most respected voice in sports journalism, which reaches a weekly audience of nearly 21 million adults, and SI.com, the 24/7 sports news website that delivers up to the minute news, scores, statistics and in-depth analysis.
Cost: $39.95
Frequency: 56 Issues/Year

21983 Sports Illustrated for Kids
Sports Illustrated
1271 Ave of the Americas
Suite 32
New York, NY 10020-1401

212-522-1212
212-467-4049
Fax: 212-522-0318
Home Page: www.sikids.com
Social Media: Facebook

Bob Der, Managing Editor & Publisher
Beth Power Bugler, Creative Director
Justin Tejada, Assistant Managing Editor
Paul Ulane, Senior Producer, sikids.com

Great action photos, easy-to-read stories about star athletes, helpful instructional tips from the pros, humor, comics and activities.
Cost: $24.95
Frequency: Monthly

21984 SportsTravel Magazine
Schneider Publishing Company
11835 W Olympic Blvd
Suite 1265
Los Angeles, CA 90064-5814

310-577-3700
877-577-3700
Fax: 310-577-3715
E-Mail: info@schneiderpublishing.com
Home Page: www.schneiderpublishing.com
Social Media: Facebook, Twitter, LinkedIn

Tim Schneider, President
Lisa Furfine, Associate Publisher
Jason Gewirtz, Managing Editor/SportsTravel

SportsTravel magazine is the event organizer's guide to successfully creating and staging sports events. SportsTravel provides information on sports destinations and venues, transportation and accommodations, bidding for events, sponsorships, and marketing. SportsTravel facilitates relationships among sports governing bodies, host destinations, sponsors, and suppliers.
Cost: $48.00
Circulation: 14,000
ISSN: 1091-5354
Founded in 1997
Printed in 4 colors on glossy stock

21985 Sportsbusiness Journal
Business Journals Inc
120 W Morehead St
Suite 420
Charlotte, NC 28202-1874

704-973-1200
800-829-9389
Fax: 704-973-1201
E-Mail: citybiz@bizjournals.com
Home Page: www.citybiznetwork.com

George Conley, President

Provides important news information sports industry executives need to be successful in the fast paced world of sports business
Cost: $249.00
Frequency: 49X/Year
Circulation: 17,000
Founded in 1998

21986 Squash Magazine
23 Cynwyd Road
PO Box 1216
Bala Cynwyd, PA 19004-5216

610-667-4006
Fax: 610-667-6539
Home Page: www.us-squash.org
Social Media: Facebook, Twitter

Craig W Brand, Executive Director
Keith Klipstein, Executive Director

Articles on the sport of squash racquets in the United States.
Cost: $35.00
Frequency: 10 per year

21987 Synchro Swimming USA
US Synchronized Swimming
132 E Washington Street
Suite 800
Indianapolis, IN 46204-3674

317-237-5700
Fax: 317-237-5705
E-Mail: marketing@usasynchro.org
Home Page: www.usasynchro.org

Terry Harper, Executive Director
Taylor Payne, Media Relations Director
Jordan Dillon, Business Development Director
Judy McGowan, President
Frequency: Quarterly
Circulation: 6000

21988 TEE Time Magazine
PO Box 225
Whitman, MA 02382

781-447-2299
Fax: 781-447-7773
Home Page: www.teetime-mag.com
Social Media: Facebook, Twitter

Mary Porter, Editor
Karen Christoforo, Sales

The Mid-Atlantics region's most comprehensive golf magazine. Each issue includes golf instruction, profiles of Mid-Atlantic personalities, course reviews and more.
Cost: $12.95
64 Pages

21989 Training & Conditioning
MAG
20 East Lake Rd.
Ithaca, NY 14850-5220

607-257-6970
Fax: 607-257-7328
E-Mail: info@athleticbid.com
Home Page: www.momentummedia.com

Mark Goldberg, Publisher
Diedra Harkenrider, East and Southeast US Sales Rep
Pennie Small, Manager

Articles on injury protection and treatment, rehabilitation, strength and speed training, as well as cardiovascular equipment for competitive athletes.
Frequency: BiMonthly
Circulation: 27,400

21990 Transworld Motocross
Transworld Publications
353 Airport Road
Oceanside, CA 92054

760-722-7777
Fax: 760-722-0653
Home Page: www.neodata.com

Jason Young, Publications Contact
Al Crolius, Manager

Magazine designed for the motocross enthusiast.
Cost: $16.97
Frequency: Monthly

21991 Transworld Skateboarding Business
Transworld Business Subscriptions
2052 Corte del Nogal
Suite 100
Carlsbad, CA 92011

760-722-7777
850-682-7644
Fax: 760-722-0653
E-Mail: subsvcs@skate.cusomtersvc.com
Home Page: www.twsbiz.com
Social Media: Facebook, Twitter, LinkedIn

Larry Balma, Publisher
Brad McDonald, Manager

Geared toward skateboard retailers, apparel chain buyers, and manufacturers of skateboard products, includes new product information, industry news, and technical innovations.
Cost: $16.97
Frequency: Monthly
Circulation: 14500

21992 Transworld Snowboarding
Transworld Business
Ste 150
2052 Corte Del Nogal
Carlsbad, CA 92011-1491

760-722-7777
850-682-7644
Fax: 760-722-0653
E-Mail: twsnowbiz@aol.com
Home Page: www.twsnow.com
Social Media: Facebook, Twitter, LinkedIn

Larry Balma, Publisher
Brad McDonald, Manager

Articles on industry news, retailer surveys, new products, and technical studies.
Cost: $14.97
Frequency: 9/Year
Circulation: 20000

21993 Transworld Surf
Transworld Publishing
Ste 150
2052 Corte Del Nogal
Carlsbad, CA 92011-1491

760-722-7777
850-682-7644
Fax: 760-722-0653
E-Mail: jasonyoung@twsnet.com
Home Page: www.neodata.com
Social Media: Facebook, Twitter, LinkedIn

Jason Young, Publications Contact
Brad McDonald, Manager

Magazine for surfing enthusiasts.
Cost: $12.00
Frequency: Monthly

21994 Trapper & Predator
F+W Media
38 E. 29th Street
New York, NY 10016

212-447-1400
Fax: 212-447-5231
E-Mail: contact_us@fwmedia.com
Home Page: www.fwpublications.com

Hugh McAloon, Publisher
Paul Wait, Editor

Contains news, in-depth features, and how-to tips on trapping, the art of predator calling, and animal damage control. Contributors include the top names in the business. Regular columns and departments include The Fur Shed, Let's Swap Ideas, Q&A, and news from state trapping associations nationwide.
Cost: $18.95
Frequency: 10 Per Year
Circulation: 38,260
Founded in 1975

21995 Turkey & Turkey Hunting
F+W Media
38 E. 29th Street
New York, NY 10016

212-447-1400
Fax: 212-447-5231
E-Mail: contact_us@fwmedia.com
Home Page: www.fwpublications.com

Hugh McAloon, Publisher
Paul Wait, Editor

Edited for serious, technical, year-round, gun and bow turkey hunters. Features emphasize success and enjoyment of the sport. Articles focus on hunting, scouting, turkey behavior and biology, hunting ethics, new equipment, methodologies, turkey management, and current research. Columns include Tree Call,Mail Pouch, Turkey Biology, a Q&A column, Hunter's Library, Turkey Gear, and Last Call.
Cost: $15.95
Frequency: 6 Per Year
Circulation: 68,962
Founded in 1991

21996 USA Table Tennis
USA Table Tennis
1 Olympic Plaza
Colorado Springs, CO 80909-5746

719-866-4583
Fax: 719-632-6071
E-Mail: magazine@usatt.org
Home Page: www.usatt.org
Social Media: Facebook, Twitter

Michael Cavanaugh, CEO

Dedicated to providing readers with all of the tools and information necessary to follow or participate in this life-long sport.
9000 Members
Frequency: 6x/Year
Circulation: 8000
Founded in 1935

21997 Velobusiness
Inside Communications
1830 55th St
Boulder, CO 80301-2700

303-440-0601
Fax: 303-444-6788

Felix Magowan, President

Trends in the market, new product develoment updates and spot news reports, also includes testing and performance evaluations, as well as marketing, merchandising and sales techniques.
Cost: $35.00
Frequency: Monthly
Circulation: 10,560

21998 Woman's Outlook
National Rifle Association
9582 Hamilton Ave
Huntington Beach, CA 92646

800-565-6651
877-672-2000
Home Page: www.womenoutlook.com

Created especially for women. Covers topics from personal protection and home security to general firearms safety and recreation. Subscription complimentary with membership in NRA. Otherwise $9.95

21999 Woodall's Campground Management
Woodall Publishing Company
PO Box 8600
Ventura, CA 93002-8600

805-667-2001
877-680-6155
Fax: 805-667-4122
E-Mail: info@woodallpub.com
Home Page: www.affinitygroup.com

Michael A Schneider, CEO
Kristopher Bunker, Editor
Terry Thompson, Advertising

Information for campground owners and managers, provides methods of management and industry trends along with reports from independent and franchise campgrounds, public parks and state associations.
Cost: $24.95
Frequency: Monthly
Circulation: 10,000
Founded in 1935

Trade Shows

22000 AACCA Spirit Coaches Conference
American Association of Cheerleading Coaches
6745 Lenox Center Court
Suite 318
Memphis, TN 38115

800-533-6583
Fax: 901-251-5851
Home Page: www.aacca.org

Jim Lord, Executive Director
Michle Ziegler, Instructor

The official NFHS Sprit Coaches Education Program.
Frequency: Annual
Founded in 1988

22001 AAU Annual Convention
Amateur Athletic Union
1910 Hotel Plaza Boulevard
PO Box 22409
Lake Buena Vista, FL 32830

407-934-7200
Fax: 407-934-7242
E-Mail: pam@aausports.org
Home Page: www.aausports.org
Social Media: Facebook, Twitter

Pam Marshall, Convention Contact
John Hodges, Exhibitor Information
Bobby Dodd, President/CEO

National Convention of the Amateur Athletic Union.

22002 ASA Sportfishing Summit
American Sportfishing Association
225 Reinekers Lane
Suite 420
Alexandria, VA 22314

703-519-9691
Fax: 703-519-1872
E-Mail: mjwilliamson@asafishing.org
Home Page: www.asafishing.org
Social Media: Facebook, Twitter

Mary Jane Williamson, Communications Director
Amy Yohanes, Administrative Services Manager
Gordon Robertson, VP
Patrick Egan, Manager

ASA's membership meeting and premier networking event. From special sessions, to business workshops tp association committee meeting, the Summit provides a wide-range of opportunities to gain information on the most relevant issues facing the sportfishing industry.
Frequency: October

22003 ASGCA Meeting
American Society of Golf Course Architects
125 N Executive Dr
Suite 302
Brookfield, WI 53005-6035

262-786-5960
Fax: 262-786-5919
E-Mail: info@asgca.org
Home Page: www.asgca.org
Social Media: Facebook, Twitter

Chad Ritterbusch, Executive Director
Bob ~ Cupp, President
Rick Robbin, VP
Lee Schmidt, Treasurer
Steve Smyers, Secretary

Combines golfing experiences with informational seminars and social engagements to form a trulyuniqie atmosphere that makes for both an enjoyable and educational meeting experience.
185 Members
Founded in 1946

22004 AVCA Annual Convention
American Volleyball Coaches Association
2365 Harrodsburg Road
Suite A325
Lexington, KY 40504

859-226-4315
866-544-2822
Fax: 859-226-4338
E-Mail: members@avca.org
Home Page: www.avca.org
Social Media: Facebook, Twitter, LinkedIn

Kathy DeBoer, Executive Director
Will Engle, Assistant Director, Events

A gathering of volleyball coaches and vendors
1700 Members
Frequency: Annual

22005 Action Sports Retailer Trade Exhibit West Fall and Spring
ASR Trade Expo
31910 Del Obispo
Suite 200
San Juan Capistrano, CA 92675

949-226-5744
Fax: 949-226-5659
Home Page: www.asrbiz.com

Tina Middleton, Marketing Director
Lisha Steinkoenig, Registration Coordinator
Megan Lara, Expo Coordinator

Provides the ultimate showcase of the action sports and youth lifestyle market by attracting the world's largest and most powerful brands and buyers representing such diverse markets as surf, skate, swim, snow, footwear and fashion.
10M Attendees
Frequency: September/February

22006 Allegheny Sport, Travel and Outdoor Show
Expositions
PO Box 550
Edgewater Branch
Cleveland, OH 44107-0550

216-529-1300
800-600-0307
Fax: 216-529-0311
Home Page: www.sportandtravel.com

Chris Fassnacht, Show Producer

Dedicated to hunting, shiftin and camping. Features hundreds of state-of-the-art exhibitors, dozens of live demonstrations, and a top notch line-up of seminar experts.
Frequency: Annual
Founded in 1985

22007 Amateur Softball Association of America
2801 NE 50th Street
Oklahoma City, OK 73111

405-424-5266
Fax: 405-424-3855
E-Mail: bplummer@softball.org
Home Page: www.asasoftball.com

Bill Plummer III, Hall of Fame/Trade Show Manager
Ron Radigonda, Executive Director

Annual meeting of the Amateur Softball Association.
1000+ Attendees
Frequency: Annual/November
Founded in 1933

22008 American Alliance for Health, Physical Education, Recreation & Dance Expo
1900 Association Drive
Reston, VA 20191

703-476-3400
800-213-7193
Fax: 703-476-9527
E-Mail: conv@aahperd.org
Home Page: www.aahperd.org
Social Media: Twitter

Danny Ballard, President
Judith C Young, VP
Paula Kun, Marketing
Shannon Mueller, Director

National convention and exposition that features many exhibits focusing on products, services and equipment within the fields of health, physical education, recreation and dance.
5000 Attendees
Frequency: Annual/April
Founded in 1879

22009 American Baseball Coaches Association Convention
108 S University Avenue
Suite 3
Mount Pleasant, MI 48858-2327

989-775-3300
Fax: 989-775-3600
E-Mail: abca@abca.org
Home Page: www.abca.org
Social Media: Facebook, Twitter

Nick Phillips, Membership/Convention Coordinator
4000 Attendees
Frequency: Annual

22010 American Bowling Congress Annual Convention
United States Bowling Congress
5301 South 76th Street
Greendale, WI 53129

414-216-6400
800-514-2695
Fax: 414-421-8560
E-Mail: bowlinfo@bowl.com
Home Page: www.bowl.com

Annual conference of the United States Bowling Congress whose mission is to ensure the integrity and protect the future of the sport by providing programs and services and enhancing the bowling experience.

22011 American Camp Association Conference & Exhibits
American Camp Association
5000 State Road 67 N
Martinsville, IN 46151-7902

765-342-8456
800-428-2267
Fax: 765-342-2065
Home Page: www.aca-camps.org
Social Media: Facebook, Twitter, LinkedIn

Tisher Bolger, President
Scott Brody, VP
Steve Baskin, Treasurer Board of Directors
Peg Smith, CEO

One hundred and forty to one hundred and fifty booths of arts and crafts, computer software, sporting goods, waterfront equipment and more plus a seminar and workshop.
1,200 Attendees
Frequency: Annual
Founded in 1943

22012 American College of Sports Medicine Annual Meeting
401 W Michigan Street
Indianapolis, IN 46202
317-637-9200
Fax: 317-634-7817
E-Mail: acsm@acsm.org
Home Page: www.acsm.org
Social Media: Facebook, Twitter, LinkedIn, You Tube

James R Whitehead, Executive VP
Janet Walberg Rankin, President

One hundred and eighty-five exhibits of sports equipment, publications, supplies and services, conference and banquet. CME credits available for a nominal fee at time of registration.
5000 Attendees
Frequency: Annual
Founded in 1954

22013 American Football Coaches Association Convention
American Football Coaches Association
100 Legends Lane
Waco, TX 76706

254-754-9900
Fax: 254-754-7373
E-Mail: info@acfa.com
Home Page: www.afca.com
Social Media: Facebook, Twitter

Grant Teaff, Executive Director

120 booths of equipment, supplies and services relevant to the game of football. Three-day event includees coaching clinic, awards luncheon and Coach of the Year dinner.
6000 Attendees
Frequency: Annual/January
Founded in 1921

22014 American Greyhound Track Operators Association
Palm Beach Kennel Club
1111 North Congress Avenue
West Palm Beach, FL 33409

561-688-5799
Fax: 801-754-2404
Home Page: www.agtoa.com
Social Media: Facebook, Twitter

Richard Winning, President
Dennis Bicsak, Managing Coordinator
Dennis Bicsak, Managing Coordinator
Michael Corbin~, Treasurer

A forum for all those affiliated with the sport to exchange ideas and to develop new techniques for the improvement and growth of the greyhound industry.
400 Attendees
Frequency: Annual/March

22015 American Hockey Coaches Association Convention
American Hockey Coaches Association
7 Concord Street
Gloucester, MA 01930

781-245-4177
Fax: 781-245-2492
E-Mail: ahcahockey@comcast.net
Home Page: www.ahcahockey.com
Social Media: Facebook, Twitter, LinkedIn

Joe Bertagna, Executive Director
George Gwozdecky, President
Kevin Sneddon, VP/Convention Planning

70 exhibits of ice hockey equipment and supplies plus worksop and banquet.
500 Attendees
Frequency: Annual/April
Founded in 1960

22016 American Orthopaedic Society for Sports Medicine Annual Meeting
American Orthopaedic Society for Sports Medicine
6300 N River Road
Suite 500
Rosemont, IL 60018-4229

847-292-4900
877-321-3500
Fax: 847-292-4905
E-Mail: aossm@aossm.org
Home Page: www.sportsmed.org

Michelle Schaffer, Exhibits Coordinator
Camille Petrick, Manager

130 exhibits of equipment supplies and services for sports medicine and related fields. Banquet and tours available.
1,500 Attendees
Frequency: June/July
Founded in 1972

22017 American Swimming Coaches Association
5101 NW 21st Avenue
Suite 200
Fort Lauderdale, FL 33309

954-563-4930
800-356-2722
Fax: 954-563-9813
Home Page: www.swimmmingcoach.org
Social Media: Facebook

John Leonard, Executive Director
Lori Klatt, Marketing

Annual convention
1.5M Attendees
Frequency: September

22018 American Youth Soccer Organization
12501 S Isis Avenue
Hawthorne, CA 90250

310-643-6455
800-872-2976
Fax: 310-643-5310
Home Page: www.soccer.org

Rick Smith, Executive Director

The AYSO annual general meeting is your opportunity to represent your region, area or section on a national level.
800 Attendees
Frequency: Annual

22019 Archery Trade Show
Archery Trade Association
PO Box 70
Suite 310
Minnesota, UT 84107

507-233-8130
866-266-2776
Fax: 507-233-8140
E-Mail: info@archerytrade.org
Home Page: www.archerytrade.org
Social Media: Facebook, Twitter

Jay McAnich, President/CEO
Denise Parker, VP/Director Marketing
Cindy Brophy, Manager
Tradeshow/Membership Svces
Kelly A. Kelly, Executive Assistant
Kurt Weber, Director of Marketing

Formerly the Archery Manufacturers and Merchants Organization (AMO), the ATA provides the core funding and direction critical to the future of archery and bowhunting. The trade show features 499 exhibitors cover 155,500 square feet.
8000 Attendees
Frequency: Annual

22020 Arnold Sports Festival
Arnold Sports Festival
1215 Worthington Woods Blvd.
Worthington, OH 43805

614-431-2600
Fax: 516-625-1023
E-Mail: lpinney@arnoldexpo.com
Home Page: www.arnoldsportsfestival.com
Social Media: Facebook, Twitter

Lucy Pinneyr, Event Chair
Brent LaLonda, Media Contact

Five days of fitness equipment, sports entertainment, supplements, apparel and athletic stars, with more than 17,000 competitive athletes in 40 sporting events. Over 500 exhibitors and 150,000 visitors; takes place during the Arnold Sports Festival
150M+ Attendees
Frequency: March
Founded in 1976

22021 Athletic Equipment Managers Association Convention
723 Keil Ct
Bowling Green, OH 43402-2235

Home Page: www.aema1.com

Sporting goods equipment manufacturers.
300 Attendees
Frequency: June

22022 BCA Convention
National High School Baseball Coaches Association
PO Box 12843
Tempe, AZ 85284

602-615-0571
Fax: 480-838-7133
E-Mail: rdavini@cox.net
Home Page: www.baseballcoaches.org

Ron Davini, Executive Director

22023 Bowling Proprieters Association of America International Bowl Expo
615 Six Flags Drive
PO Box 5802
Arlington, TX 76011-6347

800-343-1329
888-649-5585
Fax: 817-633-2940
Home Page: www.bpaa.com
Social Media: Facebook, Twitter, LinkedIn

Lee Ann Norton, Director Meetings/Events
Laurie Clower, Executive Assistant~
Judy King, Director of Finance

The bowling industry's premier event. Brings together thousands of bowling industry professionals in one place. You can find the latest trends, bowling-related products and services, marketing ideas, profit center opportunities, and tools to help you spread the excitement of bowling throughout your communities. Trade show showcases the latest products and services from more than 300 companies in over 900 exhibit booths.
5000 Attendees
Frequency: June
Founded in 1932

22024 CMAA Annual Conference
Club Managers Association of America
1733 King Street
Alexandria, VA 22314

703-739-9500
Fax: 703-739-0124
E-Mail: cmaa@cmaa.org
Home Page: www.smaa.org
Social Media: Facebook, Twitter, LinkedIn, You Tube

Jim Singerling, Executive VP

Club Managers Association of America Annual World Conference. This International Conference brings together club industry professionals from around the world for five days of challenging education, entertaining social events and an industry trade show.
Founded in 1990

22025 CSCAA National Convention & Clinic
College Swimming Coaches Association of America
1640 Maple
#803
Evanston, IL 60201

847-833-3478
E-Mail: r-groseth@northwestern.edu
Home Page: www.collegecoaches.org
Social Media: Facebook, Twitter, LinkedIn

Bob Groseth, Executive Director
George Kennedy, President
Founded in 1990

22026 Colorado RV Adventure Travel Show
Industrial Expositions
1675 Larimer, Suite 700
PO Box 480084
Denver, CO 80248-0084

303-892-6800
800-457-2434
Fax: 303-892-6322
E-Mail: info@iei-expos.com
Home Page: www.bigasalloutdoors.com
Social Media: Facebook, Twitter, LinkedIn

Jeff Haughton, President
Dianne Seymour, Expo Manager

Recreational vehicles, accessories and travel.
18000 Attendees
Frequency: Annual/January
Founded in 1990

22027 Colorado RV, Sports, Boat and Travel Show
Industrial Expositions
1675 Larimer Street
Suite 700
Denver, CO 80202

303-892-6800
800-457-2434
Fax: 303-892-6322
E-Mail: dseymour@iei-expos.com
Home Page: www.bigasalloutdoors.com
Social Media: Facebook, Twitter, LinkedIn

Jeff Haughton, President
Dianne Seymour, Expo Manager

Annual trade show of recreational vehicles, sports, boats and travel.
Founded in 1990

22028 Crescent Ski Council
PO Box 17944
Greenville, SC 29606-8944

864-229-7488
Fax: 864-235-2504
Home Page: www.crescentskicouncil.org
Social Media: Facebook, Twitter, LinkedIn, You Tube

Michelle Shuford, Contact

Exhibits of snow ski resorts and related lodging services. 50 booths.
500 Attendees
Frequency: April
Founded in 1969

22029 DEMA/Diving Equipment & Marketing Association Trade Show
3750 Convoy Street
Suite 310
San Diego, CA 92111-3741

858-616-6408
800-862-3483
Fax: 858-616-6495
E-Mail: info@dema.org
Home Page: www.dema.org
Social Media: Facebook, Twitter, LinkedIn, You Tube

Christine Von Steiger, Exhibit Space Sales
Tom Markusson, Sponsorship Sales
Tom Ingram, Executive Director
Stephen Ashmore, President

Annual trade show produced by the Diving Equipment & Marketing Association.
10M Attendees
Frequency: Annual

22030 Eastern Fishing and Outdoor Exposition
International Sport Show Producers Association
PO Box 4720
Portsmouth, NH 03802-4720

603-431-4315
Fax: 603-431-1971
E-Mail: info@sportshows.com
Home Page: www.sportshows.com
Social Media: Facebook, Twitter, LinkedIn, You Tube

Paul Fuller, President

Over 450 exhibitors representing the entire world of fishing and hunting.
45k Attendees
Frequency: Annual/February
Founded in 1996
Mailing list available for rent

22031 Eastern Iowa Sportshow
Iowa Show Productions
PO Box 2460
Waterloo, IA 50704

319-232-0218
Fax: 319-235-8932
E-Mail: info@iowashows.com
Home Page: www.iowashows.com
Social Media: Facebook, Twitter, LinkedIn

See a huge display of fishing boats, family sport boats, personal watercraft, pontoons, tent campers, travel trailers, fifth wheels, vans, and motorhomes. Plus boat accessories, truck toppers, motorcycles, ATVs, fishing camps, fly-ins, outposts, Lake Erie Walleye charters, family resorts, Lake Michigan sportfishing, houseboat rentals, Golf vacations, canoe outfitters, big game outfitters, tourism associations, campgrounds, camping gear, fishing tackle, archery equipment, targets, decoys, calls.

22032 Fall RV & Van Show
O'Loughlin Trade Shows
PO Box 80750
Portland, OR 97280-1750

503-246-8291
Fax: 503-246-1066
E-Mail: otssport@earthlink.net
Home Page: www.oloughlintradeshows.com
Social Media: Facebook, Twitter, LinkedIn

Peter O'Loughlin, Show Manager

Portland, OR. Recreational vehicles and vans
Frequency: September

22033 Fly Fishing Show - Denver
854 Opossum Lake Road
Carlisle, PA 17013

717-243-6733
800-420-7582
Fax: 717-243-8603
E-Mail: flyfishingshow@aol.com
Home Page: www.flyfishingshow.com
Social Media: Facebook, Twitter

Barry Serviente, Executive Director

Annual fly fishing show.

22034 Football Officials Association Southwest Convention
Dallas Football Officials Association
2005 Fairmeadow
Richardson, TX 75080

972-235-9110
Fax: 972-235-7675
E-Mail: dfoasecretary@aol.com
Home Page: www.dfoa.com

David Tucker, Registration
Mike Woodard, President

Texas Association of Sports Officials annual convention.
1.8M Attendees
Frequency: Annual

22035 Fred Hall's Western Fishing Tackle & Boat Show: Delmar
Fred Hall & Associates
PO Box 2925
Camarillo, CA 93011

805-389-3339
Fax: 805-389-1219

Bart Hall, Show Manager

Featuring all forms of outdoor recreation including boats, fishing tackle, adventure travel and recreational vehicles.

22036 Golf Course Superintendents Association of America
GCSAA
1421 Research Park Drive
Lawrence, KS 66049-3858

785-841-2240
800-472-7878
Fax: 785-832-4455
Home Page: www.golfindustryshow.com
Social Media: Facebook, Twitter, LinkedIn, You Tube

Julia Ozark, Sr Trade Show Manager
Caroline Gollier, Trade Show Project Manager
Scotti Corley, Meeting/Trade Show Coordinator
Kelly Jo Springirth, Director Exhibit Services
Steve Mona, CEO

Trade show designed for the owners/operators of golf facilities and the professional members of the golf course and club management industries. The event combines education, networking and solutions for golf course superintendents, owners/operators, general managers, chief operating officers, architects and builders.
25M Attendees
Frequency: February

22037 Grand Center Boat Show
Show Span
2121 Celebration Drive NE
Grand Rapids, MI 49525

616-447-2860
800-328-6550
Fax: 616-447-2861
E-Mail: events@showspan.com
Home Page: www.showspan.com
Social Media: Facebook, Twitter, LinkedIn

Carolyn Alt, Manager

Held at the Grand Center in Grand Rapids, Michigan. Every kind of boat under the sun. Over 400 boats.
82000 Attendees
Frequency: February

22038 Great Lakes Athletic Trainers
8015 Kersey Drive
Indianapolis, IL 46236
815-455-3860
Fax: 815-477-6907
Home Page: www.glata.org
Social Media: Facebook, Twitter, LinkedIn

Mark Schauer, Co Coordinator
Kevin Gerlach, Co Coordinator

Annual meeting and symposium.
1M Attendees
Frequency: March

22039 Greater Cincinnati Golf Show
North Coast Golf Productions
PO Box 372
Twinsburg, OH 44087-0372

330-963-6963
800-939-0040
Fax: 330-487-0352
E-Mail: consumer@northcoastgolfshows.com

Home Page: www.northboastgolfshows.com
Social Media: Facebook, Twitter, LinkedIn

America's favorite consumer golf show.

22040 ICAST
American Sportfishing Association
1001 North Fairfax Street
Suite 501
Alexandria, VA 22314

703-519-9691
Fax: 703-519-1872
E-Mail: mdelvalle@asafishing.org
Home Page: www.asafishing.org
Social Media: Facebook, Twitter, LinkedIn

Maria del Valle, ICAST Director
Kenneth Andres, ICAST Associate
Gordon Robertson, VP
Mary Jane Williamson, Communications Director

The sportfishing industry's largest trade event is a major catalyst for sales and a terrific networking opportunity for the sportfishing community
Frequency: July

22041 ISHA Annual Conference
International Sports Heritage Association
PO Box 2384
Florence, OR 97439

541-991-7315
Fax: 541-997-3871
E-Mail: info@sportsheritage.org
Home Page: www.sportsheritage.org
Social Media: Facebook, Twitter, LinkedIn

Karen Bednarski, Executive Director
Sheila Kelly, President
Mike Gibbons, First Vice President
Pete Fierle, Second Vice President
Ed Harris, Treasurer

Session discussions, educational sessions and speakers
140+ Members
Founded in 1971

22042 Ice Skating Institute
6000 Custe Rd.
Bldg. 9
Plano, TX 75023

972-735-8800
Fax: 972-735-8815
E-Mail: isi@skateisi.org
Home Page: www.skateisi.org
Social Media: Facebook

Peter Martell, Executive Director

The industry's leading trade show where you're sure to find the technical information, products and suppliers you need to run your business every day. Who should attend: Arena owners and managers; Hockey and figure skating coaches and instructors; Ice arena programming directors; Operations personnel; builders and suppliers to the industry.
Frequency: Annual/May

22043 International Billiard and Home Recreation Expo
Billiard Congress of America
4345 Beverly Street
Suite D
Colorado Springs, CO 80918

719-264-8300
Fax: 719-264-0900
Home Page: www.bca-pool.com
Social Media: Facebook, Twitter, LinkedIn

Stephen Ducoff, Executive Director
Carolyn Lewis, Director Trade Services
Amy Long, Director Marketing
Linda Mojer, Director Communications
Kathy Simmons, Member Services Administrator

This show hosts nearly 300 companies in 1400 booths, featuring every product line in the home recreation industry, from billiard and game tables, cues and cue accessories, cloth, balls and apparel, to spas, bowling, darts, foosball, art, home furnishings, novelty items, outdoor living, books, publications, video games, coin-op, pinball, jukeboxes, gaming and much more.
Founded in 1984

22044 International Pool & Spa Expo
PO Box 612128
Dallas, TX 75261-2128

972-536-6350
888-869-8522
Fax: 972-536-6364
Home Page: www.poolandspaexpo.com

Tina Brinkley, Operations Coordinator
Kathy Ruff, Operations Manager
Tracy Beaulieu, Conference Manager
Vila Snider, Registration Manager
Donna Bellantone, Assoc Show Director

Latest trends, newest products, and innovative ways to increase sales and add profits to your business.
16M Attendees
Frequency: November

22045 Kansas Sports, Boat and Travel Show
Industrial Expositions
PO Box 480084
Denver, CO 80248

303-892-6800
800-457-2434
Fax: 303-892-6322
E-Mail: dseymour@iei-expos.com
Home Page: www.bigasalloutdoors.com

Jeff Haughton, President
Dianne Seymour, Expo Manager

Annual show produced by Industrial Expositions.
Frequency: Annual

22046 Let's Play Hockey International Expo
Let's Play Hockey
2721 East 42nd Street
Minneapolis, MN 55406

612-729-0023
Fax: 612-729-0259
E-Mail: letsplay@letsplayhockey.com
Home Page: www.letsplayhockey.com

Doug Johnson, Contact
Doug Johnson, Publisher
Kevin Kurtt, Editor

Hockey Industry Trade Show. Five days of events. Seminars, races, tournaments, awards banquet, expo demo day, Hall of Fame display, buying group meetings and more.
Founded in 1999

22047 Lincoln Boat, Sport and Travel Show
Egan Enterprises
4100 North 84th Street
Lincoln, NE 68505-5465

402-466-8102
Fax: 402-467-5630
Home Page: www.nebraskasportshow.com

Pat Egan, Contact Person

Equipment and supplies for the outdoor life.
Frequency: Annual

22048 Management Conference & Team Dealer Summit
National Sporting Goods Association
1601 Feehanville Drive
Suite 300
Mount Prospect, IL 60056

847-966-6742
800-815-5422
Fax: 847-391-9827
E-Mail: conference@nsga.org
Home Page: www.nsga.org

Jeff Rosenthal, Chairman of the Board
Matt Carlson, President/CEO
Dan Kasen, Director of Information Services

The Sporting Goods industry's premier educational and networking event, featuring programming aimed at ensuring business' success, brings together leaders and industry insiders for engaging conversations and stimulating presentations.

22049 NABC Convention & MarketPlace
National Association of Basketball Coaches
1111 Main St
Suite 1000
Kansas City, MO 64105-2116

816-878-6222
Fax: 816-878-6223
Home Page: www.nabc.com

Jim Haney, Executive Director
Reggie Minton, Deputy Executive Director
Kevin Henderson, Associate Executive Director
Dottie Yearout, Director of Membership Services
Janelle Guidry, Convention Manager

The Convention offers Professional Development Clinics
Frequency: Annual/Spring

22050 NACDA Convention
Nat'l Assoc of Collegiate Directors of Athletics
24651 Detroit Road
Westlake, OH 44145

440-892-4000
Fax: 440-892-4007
Home Page: www.nacda.com
Social Media: Facebook, Twitter, LinkedIn

Michael Cleary, Executive Director

Devoted to examining contemporary problems facing today's athletics administrator. Caters to administrators in all levels of intercollegiate athletics with general sessions for the entire membership and breakout sessions which are geared to the specific needs of administrators at all levels of the NCAA, NAIA, and NJCAA

22051 NASC Sports Event Symposium
9916 Carver Road
Suite 100
Cincinnati, OH 45242

513-281-3888
Fax: 513-281-1765
E-Mail: info@nascsymposium.com
Home Page: www.nascsymposium.com
Social Media: Facebook, Twitter, LinkedIn

Don Schumacher, Executive Director
Beth Hecquet, Director of Meetings and Events

National Association of Sports Commissions. Representing more than 550 organizations. Attendees are provided with new ideas, practical tips and the hottest trends.
550 Members
Founded in 1992

22052 NASGW Annual Meeting and Expo
National Association of Sporting Goods Wholesalers
1833 Centre Point Circle
Suite 123
Naperville, IL 60563

630-596-9006
Fax: 630-544-5055
E-Mail: nasgw@nasgw.org

Home Page: www.nasgw.org
Social Media: Facebook, Twitter, LinkedIn

Maurice Desmarais, President
Jack Baumler, Chairman
Kent Williams, Vice Chair
Peter Brownell, Treasurer

Educational, marketing and communications opportunity for the hunting and shooting sports wholesaler, manufacturer and sales professional.
400 Members
Founded in 1954

22053 NCAA Annual Convention

317-917-6222
Fax: 317-917-6888
E-Mail: feedback@ncaasports.com
Home Page: www.ncaasports.com
Social Media. Facebook, Twitter, LinkedIn

Trade show and convention
Frequency: January
Founded in 1915

22054 NFCA National Convention
National Fastpitch Coaches Association
100 G T Thames Drive
Suite D
Starkville, MS 39759

662-320-2155
Fax: 662-320-2283
E-Mail: nfca@nfca.org
Home Page: www.nfca.org
Social Media: Facebook, Twitter, LinkedIn

Lacy Lee Baker, Executive Director
Hildred Deese, Senior Director of Events
Frequency: Annual, December

22055 NSAA National Convention and Trade Show
National Ski Areas Association
133 S Van Gordon Street
Suite 300
Lakewood, CO 80228

303-987-1111
Fax: 303-986-2345
E-Mail: nsaa@nsaa.org
Home Page: www.nsaa.org
Social Media: Facebook, Twitter, LinkedIn

Michael Berry, President
Keri Hone, Director Events/Projects
Tom Moore, Director Conventions/Meetings
Kate Powers, Director Member Services
Amy Steele, Director Sponsorships

Annual convention of the National Ski Areas Association

22056 National Association of Basketball Coaches Annual Convention
1111 Main Street
Suite 1000
Kansas City, MO 64105-2136

816-878-6222
Fax: 816-878-6223
Home Page: www.nabc.org
Social Media: Facebook, Twitter, LinkedIn

James Haney, Executive Director
Reggie Minton, Deputy Executive Director
Kevin Henderson, Associate Executive Director

Approximately 150 booths offering services and resources for Basketball Coaches.
3M Attendees
Frequency: March/April

22057 National Institute for Golf Management
National Golf Foundation
1150 South US Highway One
Suite 401
Jupiter, FL 33477

561-744-6006
888-275-4643
Fax: 561-744-6107
E-Mail: general@ngf.org
Home Page: www.ngf.org
Social Media: Facebook, Twitter, LinkedIn

Annual golf institute sponsored by the National Golf Foundation.
Frequency: Annual

22058 National Intramural Recreational Sports Association
4185 SW Research Way
Corvallis, OR 97333-1067

541-766-8211
Fax: 541-766-8284
E-Mail: nirsa@nirsa.org
Home Page: www.nirsa.org
Social Media: Facebook, Twitter, LinkedIn

Kent Blumenthal, Executive Director
Dr. William N. Wasson, Owner

This show provides an annual marketplace for athletic and recreational equipment, supplies and services.
1.6M Attendees
Frequency: Annual/April
Founded in 1950

22059 National Recreation and Park Association's Conference and Exposition
National Recreation and Park Association
22377 Belmont Ridge Road
Ashburn, VA 20148

703-858-0784
Fax: 703-858-0794
E-Mail: info@nrpa.org
Home Page: www.nrpa.org

Britt Esen, Director
Jodie H Adams, President
John Crosby, Marketing

Provides targeted learning opportunities specifically for parks and recreation directors, supervisors and managers, community center directors, recreation programmers, natural resources personnel, therapeutic recreation specialists, citizen advocates and students.
4000 Attendees
Founded in 1965

22060 National Soccer Coaches Association of America
800 Ann Avenue
Kansas City, KS 66101

913-362-1747
800-458-0676
Fax: 913-362-3439
Home Page: nscaa.com
Social Media: Facebook, Twitter, LinkedIn

Joe Cummings, CEO and Executive Director
Tommy Reder, CFO

Every coach who attends will find something new to add to their soccer reperoire. The trade show consists of more than 300 companies. Attendees can examine the latest soccer-related technology and equipment.
30m Members
9000 Attendees
Frequency: Annual/January
Founded in 1941

22061 National Trappers Association Sports Show
2815 Washington Avenue
Bedford, IN 47421

812-277-9670
866-680-8727
Fax: 812-277-9672
E-Mail: ntaheadquarters@nationaltrappers.com
Home Page: www.nationaltrappers.com

Kraig Kaatz, President
Chris Flynn, VP
Kraig Kaatz, General Organizer

300 booths including outdoor sports supplies and dealers.
6M Attendees
Frequency: Annual/August

22062 New York National Boat Show
National Marine Manufacturers Association
148 West 37th Street
11th Floor
New York, NY 10018

212-984-7007
Fax: 212-564-2728
Home Page: www.nyboatshow.com
Social Media: Facebook, Twitter

Jonathon Pritko, Show Manager
Bob McAlpine, Exhibitor Relationship Manager
Dan Castellano, Exhibitor Relationships Manager
Elba-Rosales Rise, Show Administrator
Josh Rosales, Operation Coordinator

Annual boat show held at Jacob Javitz Convention Center in New York
Frequency: January

22063 North American Society for Sport Management Conference
North American Society for Sport Management
Slippery Rock University
West Gym 014
Slippery Rock, PA 16057

724-738-4812
Fax: 724-738-4858
E-Mail: nassm@sru.edu
Home Page: www.nassm.com
Social Media: Facebook, Twitter

North American Society for Sport Management annual convention and trade show.

22064 Northwest Sportshow
General Sports Shows
3539 Hennepin Avenue
Minneapolis, MN 55408-3830

612-827-5833
800-777-4766
Fax: 612-827-1424

David Perkins, President

Public show offering the finest presentation of outdoor recreation and marine products and services.
205M Attendees
Frequency: March

22065 Outdoorama Family Sport and Travel Show
Michigan United Conservation Clubs
2101 Wood Street
PO Box 30235
Lansing, MI 48909

517-371-1041
800-777-6720
Fax: 517-371-1505
E-Mail: membership@mucc.org
Home Page: www.mucc.org
Social Media: Facebook, Twitter, LinkedIn

Sam Washington, Executive Director
Kelly Snyder, Event/Fundraising Assistant
Evan Steiner, Events/Fundraising Specialist

Michigan's favorite outdoor show featuring over 200,000 square feet of exhibit space dedicated to the latest in fishing and hunting equipment, fishing and power boats, recreational vehicles, outdoor gear and vacationing destina-

tions throughout North America. Four-hundred plus booths.
42000 Attendees
Frequency: February
Founded in 1974

22066 PTR International Tennis Symposium
Professional Tennis Registry
PO Box 4739
Hilton Head Island, SC 29938

843-785-7244
800-421-6289
Fax: 843-686-2033
E-Mail: ptr@ptrtennis.org
Home Page: www.ptrtennis.org
Social Media: Facebook, Twitter

Dan Santoruk, CEO
Julie Jilly, VP/Operations

Symposium of professional tennis teachers and coaches. PTR has excellent relationships and partnerships with industry leaders such as the USTA, Tennis Industry Association, the ITF and many National Tennis Federations.
14m Members
800+ Attendees
Frequency: 2x Per Year
Founded in 1976

22067 Pop Warner Little Scholars Convention
586 Middletown Boulevard
Suite C-100
Langhorne, PA 19047-1867

215-752-2691
Fax: 215-752-2879
E-Mail: webmaster@popwarner.com
Home Page: www.popwarner.com
Social Media: Facebook, Twitter

Jon Butler, Executive Director
Mary Fitzgerald, COO
Lisa Moroski, National Cheer/Dance Commissioner
1000 Attendees
Frequency: Bi-Annual

22068 Professional Golfers Association Merchandise Show
Reed Exhibitions
383 Main Avenue
Norwalk, CT 06851

203-404-4800
800-840-5628
Fax: 203-840-9628
E-Mail: inquiry@pga.reedexpo.com
Home Page: www.pgamerchandiseshow.com
Social Media: Facebook, Twitter

Kara Codio, Marketing/Conference Manager
Sherry Major, Media Relations Manager
Jay Andronaco, Event Marketing Manager

The PGA Merchandise Show provides a snap-shot of the industry as a whole and access to products and services that pertain to every aspect of the game. It is the focal point for new product introductions, professional development programs, business meetings and more.
30M Attendees
Frequency: January

22069 Professional Golfers Association Golf Show
Sydney Convention and Exhibition Centre
Darling Harbour
Sydney
Australia NSW 2000

Home Page: www.pgaexpo.com
Social Media: Facebook, Twitter, LinkedIn

International PGA Golf Show. 2006 Show held in Australia
50000 Attendees
Frequency: Annual

22070 RSA Convention and Trade Show
Roller Skating Association International
6905 Corporate Drive
Indianapolis, IN 46278

317-347-2626
Fax: 317-347-2636
E-Mail: rsa@rollerskating.com
Home Page: www.rollerskating.org
Social Media: Facebook, Twitter, LinkedIn, You Tube

Bobby Braun, President
Ron Liette, VP
John Purcell, Executive Director

Helping roller skating industry professionals discover ways to build strong foundations for their businesses.
1000 Members
Frequency: annual
Founded in 1937

22071 Rocky Mountain Snowmobile Expo
Industrial Expositions
1675 Larimer Street
Suite 700
Denver, CO 80202

303-892-6800
800-457-2434
Fax: 303-892-6322
E-Mail: dseymour@iei-expos.com
Home Page: www.bigasalloutdoors.com
Social Media: Facebook, Twitter

Jeff Haughton, President
Diane Seymour, Expo Manager

Large display of snowmobiles and accessories, meet performance experts, resorts and lodges, winter clothing, ice fishing, winter travel destinations, snowmobile adventure theatre, avalanche awareness, swap meet and more.

22072 SHOT Show: Shooting Hunting Outdoor Trade Show
Reed Exhibition Companies
28 The Quadrant
Richmond 6851

203-404-4800
800-840-5628
Fax: 203-840-9628
Home Page: www.reedexpo.com

Worldwide annual gathering that unites manufacturer and retailer and all other industry stakeholders to trade, source and learn about the latest products, innovations and trends in the shooting sports industry.
15M Attendees
Frequency: January

22073 SIA Snow Show
SnowSports Industries America
8377-b Greensboro Drive
McLean, VA 22102-3587

703-556-9020
Fax: 703-821-8276
E-Mail: siamail@snowsports.org
Home Page: www.siasnowshow.com
Social Media: Facebook, Twitter, LinkedIn, YouTube, Wikipedia, Vimeo

From fashion to skis and snowboards to Nordic, snowshoes, outdoor and basic essentials, the SIA Snow Show previews the entire winter sports market and then deads to the on-snow demo to try it all out on snow.
700+ Members
19M Attendees
Frequency: Annual/January
Founded in 1954

22074 Saltwater Fishing Expo
Eastern Fishing and Outdoor Exposition
PO Box 4720
Portsmouth, NH 03802

603-431-4315
Fax: 603-431-1971
Home Page: www.sportshows.com

The Saltwater Fishing Expo is expecting over 300 exhibitors representing the entire spectrum of saltwater sportfishing. There will be dozens of seminars throughout the three days of the show, which will be presented by experts who are at the top of their game.

22075 San Mateo Inernational Sportsmen's Expo
International Sportsmen's Exposition
PO Box 2569
Vancouver, WA 98668-2569

360-693-3700
800-545-6100
Fax: 360-693-3352
Home Page: www.sportsexpos.com

Brian Layng, President/CEO
Rick Flattum, Director Operations
Heidi Crannell, Marketing Coordinator
Bruce Tarbet, Sponsorship/Advertising
Brent Layng, Sales Manager

Fishing, hunting, outdoor sports and destination travel show. Connect with new dealers and network with other exhibitors.

22076 Ski Dazzle Ski Show and Snowboard Expo: Chicago
Ski Dazzle
P.O. Box 1839
Laguna Beach, CA 92651

949-497-4977
Fax: 949-497-4123
E-Mail: snowdog@skidazzle.com
Home Page: www.skidazzle.com
Social Media: Facebook, Twitter, LinkedIn, You Tube

Judy Gray, Owner
Jim Foster, Owner

Hundreds of local, national and international exhibitors including over 85 resorts, ski and snowboard retailers, manufacturers, a huge ski and snowboard sale, and lots of surprises. Over 250 exhibit booths showcasing core companies of skiing and snowboarding.

22077 Ski Dazzle: The Los Angeles Ski Show & Snowboard Expo
P.O. Box 1840
Laguna Beach, CA 92651-1839

949-497-4977
Fax: 949-497-4123
E-Mail: snowdog@skidazzle.com
Home Page: www.skidazzle.com
Social Media: Facebook, Twitter, LinkedIn, You Tube

Judy Gray, Co-Owner
Jim Foster, Owner

Consumer ski show and snowboard expo at the Los Angeles Convention Center offering 350 ski and snowboard related exhibits. Excellent sponsor and promotional opportunities for 18-49 demographic audience.
90000 Attendees
Frequency: November

22078 Soaring Society of America Annual Convention
5425 West Jack Gomez Boulevard
P.O. Box 2100
Hobbs, NM 88241

575-392-1177
Fax: 575-392-8154

E-Mail: feedback@ssa.org
Home Page: www.ssa.org

C Wright, Executive Director

Annual convetion of the Soaring Society of America.

22079 **Sporting Goods Manufacturers Markets**
1150 17th Street NW
8th Floor
Washington, DC 20036-1604

202-775-1762
Fax: 202-296-7462
E-Mail: info@sgma.com
Home Page: www.sgma.com

Tom Cove, President/CEO
Gregg Harrlety, VP
Kalinda Mathis, Director Marketing

Retailers, distributors, wholesalers, importers/exporters and other buyers of sports related products come for 10,000 exhibits of sports apparel, footwear, accessories and e-commerce products and services.
80000 Attendees
Frequency: Spring/Fall

22080 **Sports Licensing & Entertainment Marketplace Tailgate Picnic Show**
Showproco, LLC
1450 NE 123rd Street
North Miami, FL 33161

305-893-8771
800-327-3736
Fax: 305-893-8783
E-Mail: showproco@csnipicom
Home Page: www.showproco.com
Social Media: Facebook, Twitter, LinkedIn

Tom Cove, President
Stanley Schwartz, Director

A show dedicated to sports licensed apparel & products with participation from major sports licensors and their licensees. In conjunction will be the Tailgate & Picnic Show, which will bring together all of the products sports fans want to buy. Attendees will represent everything from sporting goods stores to fan shops, grocery to gift shops, drug stores to convenience stores and more.
Frequency: November

22081 **Strictly Sail Pacific**
Jack London Square
Oakland, CA

800 817 7245
Fax: 401-847-2044
E-Mail: info@sailamerica.com
Home Page: www.strictlysail.com
Social Media: Facebook, Twitter, LinkedIn

Cynthia Goss, Contact

Annual Boat Show. A mix of boats and gear, seminars and special events. It will feature over 300 exhibitors from 25 states and over 90 seminars.

22082 **Surf Expo**
Surf Expo Offices
990 Hammond Drive
Suite 325
Atlanta, GA 30328

678-817-7970
800-947-7873
Fax: 404-220-3030
E-Mail: rturner@surfexpo.com
Home Page: www.surfexpo.com

Where manufacturers and retailers in the boardsports, and swim and resort industries have come together in a business-first buying and selling environment.
8M Attendees
Frequency: Twice Annually

22083 **US Gymnastics Federation**
US Gymnastics Congress
Pam American Plaza
201 South Capitol, Suite 300
Indianapolis, IN 46225

317-237-5050
Fax: 317-692-5212
Home Page: www.usagym.org

Steve Penny, President

Three days of eduction with over 135 sessions offered. Lectures given by recognized top people in the field. Sessions on coaching, judging, business, preschool, recreational, sports science, fitness, Group Gymnastics and cheerleading. The Trade Show exhibit hall will feature 200 booths of products and information from over 85 different Industry Member vendors.
2M Attendees
Frequency: Annual

22084 **US Lacrosse National Convention**
113 W University Pkwy
Baltimore, MD 21210-3301

410-235-6882
Fax: 410-366-6735
E-Mail: info@uslacrosse.org
Home Page: www.uslacrosse.org
Social Media: Facebook, Twitter

Steve Stenersen, President
Bill Schoonmaker, COO
Bill Rubacky, Managing Director of Marketing
Kira Muller, Director of Advertising Sales

Billed as the unofficial start to lacrosse season, the event gathers the best the sport has to offer; providing the largest educational opportunity with over 5,000 coaches, officials, vendors and administrators in attendance. Over 100 exhibitors
5000 Attendees
Frequency: Annual

22085 **USA Track and Field Annual Meeting**
One RCA Dome
Suite 140
Indianapolis, IN 46225

317-261-0500
Fax: 317-261-0481
E-Mail: membership@usatf.org
Home Page: www.usatf.org
Social Media: Facebook, Twitter, LinkedIn

Jill Geer, Public Relations

Annual meeting of the USA Track and Field organization.
Frequency: Annual

22086 **USTFCCCA Annual Coaches Convention**
U.S. Track & Field and Cross Country Coaches Assoc
1100 Poydras Street
Suite 1750
New Orleans, LA 70163

504-599-8900
Fax: 504-599-8909
E-Mail: sam@ustfccca.org
Home Page: www.ustfccca.org
Social Media: Facebook, Twitter, LinkedIn

Sam Seemes, CEO
Mike Corn, Assistant Director
Sylvia Kamp, Administrator
Tom Lewis, Director of Communications

22087 **Underwater Intervention**
5206 FM 1960 West
Suite 202
Houston, TX 77069

281-893-8539
800-316-2188
Fax: 281-893-5118
E-Mail: rroberts@adc-int.org
Home Page: www.underwaterintervention.com/
Social Media: Facebook, Twitter, LinkedIn

Rebecca Roberts, Show Manager
Roff Saxon, Executive Director

Conference covering all aspects of underwater operations. Next trade show is scheduled for 2007 with 200+ booths, sponsored by both the Marine Technology Society and the Association of Diving Contractors International.
2500 Attendees
Founded in 1991

22088 **WBCA National Convention**
Women's Basketball Coaches Association
4646 Lawrenceville Highway
Lilburn, GA 30047

770-279-8027
Fax: 770-279-8473
E-Mail: wbca@wbca.org
Home Page: www.wbca.org
Social Media: Facebook, Twitter

Beth Bass, CEO
Shannon Reynolds, COO
Seana Peck, Manager Marketing
Stephanie S Baron, Director Events
Dorinda Schremmer, Director Membership/Conventions

Women's Basketball Coaches Association national convention. Held annually.
Founded in 1981

22089 **Water Ski and Wakeboard Expo**
1251 Holy Cow Road
Polk City, FL 33868

863-324-4341
Fax: 863-325-8529
E-Mail: usawaterski@usawaterski.org
Home Page: www.usawaterski.org
Social Media: Facebook, Twitter, LinkedIn

Annual event of the USA Water Ski Organization.
Frequency: Annual

22090 **Western Fairs Association Annual Trade Show**
Western Fairs Association
1776 Tribute Road
Suite 210
Sacramento, CA 95815-4495

916-927-3100
Fax: 916-927-6397
E-Mail: stephenc@fairsnet.org
Home Page: www.fairsnet.org
Social Media: Facebook, Twitter, YouTube

Rick Pickering, President
Jon Baker, VP
Stephen J Chambers, Executive Director
Nichole Farley, Marketing

Meet face to face with buyers from the Fair and Festival Industry across the Western United States. Acts, attractions, services, supplies, commericial exhibitors and more.
2000 Members
Frequency: Annual/Jan
Founded in 1922

22091 **Western States Toy and Hobby Show**
Western Toy and Hobby Representative Association
PO Box 2250
Pomona, CA 91786

909-899-3753
Fax: 951-277-1599
E-Mail: toyshow@wthra.com
Home Page: www.wthra.com
Social Media: Facebook, Twitter

Phylis St John, Show Director

If it's for kids, it's here. Show is for trade members only, not open to the public.
3000 Attendees
Frequency: March

22092 World Fishing and Outdoor Exposition
Eastern Fishing and Outdoor Exposition
PO Box 4720
Portsmouth, NH 03802-4720

603-431-4315
Fax: 603-431-1971
E-Mail: info@sportshows.com
Home Page: www.sportshows.com
Social Media: Facebook

You'll find the entire world of fishing and hunting and much more.
Frequency: Annual
Founded in 1978

22093 World Fly Fishing Expo
Eastern Fishing and Outdoor Exposition
PO Box 4720
Portsmouth, NH 03802-4720

603-431-4315
Fax: 603-431-1971
E-Mail: info@sportshows.com
Home Page: www.sportshows.com
Social Media: Facebook

This expo has all the major manufacturers of fly rods and reels, fly fishing accessories, fly tying materials, guides and lodges.
Frequency: Annual

Directories & Databases

22094 Amusement Park Guide
Globe Pequot Press
246 Goose Ln
Suite 200
Guilford, CT 06437-2186

203-458-4500
Fax: 203-458-4601
Home Page: www.globepequot.com

James Joseph, President

The complete guide to the amusement parks in the United States and Canada gives the latest details about new rides at each park, with a special focus on roller coasters.
Cost: $14.95
ISBN: 0-762725-37-0

22095 Athlete and Celebrity Address Directory/Autograph Hunter's Guide
Global Sports Productions
16810 Crystal Drive East
Suite 101
Santa Monica, CA 90404-2702

310-454-9480
Fax: 310-454-6590
E-Mail: globalnw@earthlink.net
Home Page: www.sportsbooksempire.com
Social Media: Facebook

Ed Kobak, Owner
Greg Andrews, VP Operations

Complete source of athlete and sports personality addresses from baseball, basketball, football, hockey, golf, tennis, soccer, boxing and autosports. Also included are television, movie and other celebrities' addresses.
Cost: $ 29.95
198 Pages
Frequency: Annual
ISBN: 0-966796-17-9
Founded in 2005

22096 Baseball Bluebook
8373 N Cedar Hills Lane
Fair Grove, MD 65648

417-833-6550
Fax: 417-833-9911
E-Mail: dj@baseballbluebook.com
Home Page: www.baseballbluebook.com

Dennis Wubbena, Owner
Eric Wubbena, President

Directory of baseball club personnel at all levels of play. Spiral bound directory contains Major Leagues, Minor Leagues and Independent League Personnel, contact information and schedules
Cost: $55.00
500 Pages
Frequency: Annual
Founded in 1909

22097 Complete Directory of Fishing Tackle
Sutton Family Communications & Publishing Company
155 Sutton Lane
Fordsville, KY 42343

270-740-0870
E-Mail: jlsutton@apex.net
Home Page: www.fleamarketeer.net

Jerry Sutton, Contact

Listings in directory include names, addresses, phone and fax numbers, and product descriptions from wholesale distributors, Importers, Manufacturers, Close-out houses and liquidators.
Cost: $72.20
100+ Pages

22098 Complete Directory of Outdoor Products
Sutton Family Communications & Publishing Company
155 Sutton Lane
Fordsville, KY 42343

270-740-0870
E-Mail: jlsutton@apex.net
Home Page: www.fleamarketeer.net

Jerry Sutton, Manager

Print-out from database of wholesalers, manufacturers, distributors, importers and close-out houses. Database is updated daily to guarantee the most current and up-to-date sources available.
Cost: $95.20
100+ Pages

22099 Complete Directory of Sporting Goods
Sutton Family Communications & Publishing Company
155 Sutton Lane
Fordsville, KY 42343

270-740-0870
E-Mail: jlsutton@apex.net
Home Page: www.fleamarketeer.net

Jerry Sutton, Manager

Print-out from database of wholesalers, manufacturers, distributors, importers and close-out houses. Database is updated daily to guarantee the most current and up-to-date sources available.
Cost: $139.00
100+ Pages

22100 Computer Sports World
675 Grier Drive
Las Vegas, NV 89119-3738

702-735-0101
800-321-5562
Fax: 702-294-1322
E-Mail: dandros@vegasinsider.com
Home Page: www.cswstats.com

Statistical information on all aspects of the sports industry.
Frequency: Full-text
Founded in 1983

22101 Encyclopedia of Sports Business Contacts
Global Sports Productions
1223 Broadway
Suite 101
Santa Monica, CA 90404-2702

310-395-6533
Fax: 310-454-6590
E-Mail: globalnw@earthlink.net
Home Page: www.sportsbooksempire.com
Social Media: Facebook, Twitter

Ed Kobak, President

This huge book covers the business side of sports with addresses, telephone and fax numbers, emails, websites and entire contact personnel from sports organizations, teams, leagues, publications, lawyers and agents, corporate sponsors, sports marketing and management firms and others.
Cost: $79.95
600 Pages
Frequency: Annual
Founded in 2005

22102 Golf Traveler
Affinity Group
64 Inverness Dr E
Englewood, CO 80112-5114

303-728-7428
800-234-3450
Fax: 303-728-7257
Home Page: www.affinitygroup.com

Bruce Hoster, Manager

Golf courses and affiliated resorts are listed.
Cost: $2.50
88 Pages
Frequency: BiMonthly
Circulation: 75,000

22103 International Sports Directory
Global Sports Productions
1223 Broadway
Suite 101
Santa Monica, CA 90404-2702

310-395-6533
Fax: 310-454-6590
E-Mail: globalnw@earthlink.net
Home Page: www.sportsbooksempire.com

Ed Kobak, Owner

This all-in-one directory covers the entire world of sports from A to Z. Included are addresses, e-mails, websites, telephone and fax numbers and contact personnel from sports organizations, clubs, teams and publications. The most comprehensive sports directory available, covering both national and international listings.
Cost: $29.95
500 Pages
Frequency: Annual
ISBN: 1-891655-02-7
Founded in 1980

22104 Motor Sports Forum
Racing Information Systems
2314 Harriman Ln
Unit A
Redondo Beach, CA 90278-4426
310-374-3750
E-Mail: racing@motorsportsforum.com
Home Page: www.motorsportsforum.com

Michael F Hollander, Editor-in-Chief
Bab Karambelas, Senior Editor

This database contains information on auto racing in the United States and Canada.
Frequency: Bulletin Board

22105 News/Retrieval Sports Report
Dow Jones & Company
1155 Avenue of the Americas
New York, NY 10036-2717

212-597-5756
Fax: 212-416-4348
Home Page: www.dowjones.com

Offers information on sports news stories and statistics from United Press International.
Frequency: Full-text

22106 Orion Blue Book: Guns and Scopes
Orion Research Corporation
14555 N Scottsdale Rd
Suite 330
Scottsdale, AZ 85254-3487

480-951-1114
800-844-0759
Fax: 480-951-1117
Home Page: www.orionbluebook.com

Roger Rohrs, Owner

List of manufacturers of guns. Current issue contains 18,543 products. Lists products from 1800's to present. Over 300 manufacturers listed.
Cost: $45.00
480 Pages
Frequency: Annual
Founded in 1992

22107 Parks Directory of the United States
Omnigraphics
615 Griswold Street
Detroit, MI 48226

313-961-1340
800-234-1340
Fax: 313-961-1383
E-Mail: editorial@omnigraphics.com
Home Page: www.omnigraphics.com

Darren L Smith, Editor

Covers nearly 5,000 national and state parks, and other designated recreational, scenic, and historic areas in the United States and Canada. It provides up-to-date contact and descriptive information for every national and state park in the U.S.
Cost: $185.00
1,100 Pages
Frequency: Biennial
ISBN: 0-780806-63-8

22108 Q&A Booklets
Sporting Goods Agents Association
14555˜N˜Scottsdale˜Rd
Scottsdale˜, AZ 60053

847-296-3670
Fax: 847-827-0196
E-Mail: sgaa998@aol.com
Home Page: www.sgaaonline.org

Skip Nipper, President
Lois Halinton, Chief Operating Officer

Sporting Goods Agents Association booklets for manufacturers and agents. Answers questions such as: Why should I use an independent agent rather than hire my own salespeople? What are the most important aspects to examine when I interview an agency? What are independent sporting goods agents and what do they do? What factors should be considered when forming a territory to cover. And more.
Cost: $15.00

22109 Recreation Facilities Products & Services
Sutton Family Communications & Publishing Company
155 Sutton Lane
Fordsville, KY 42343

270-740-0870
E-Mail: jlsutton@apex.net
Home Page: www.fleamarketeer.net

Jerry Sutton, Manager

Print-out from database of wholesalers, manufacturers, distributors, importers and close-out houses. Database is updated daily to guarantee the most current and up-to-date sources available. Accepts advertising.
Cost: $97.20
100+ Pages

22110 Recreational Sports Directory
National Intramural Recreational Sports Assn
4185 Sw Research Way
Corvallis, OR 97333-1067

541-766-8211
Fax: 541-766-8284
E-Mail: nirsa@nirsa.org
Home Page: www.nirsa.org

Kent Blumenthal, Executive Director

Directory of services and supplies to the industry.
Cost: $20.00
400 Pages
Frequency: Annual
Circulation: 1,500

22111 Sporting News Baseball Guide
Sporting News Publishing Company
10176 Corporate Square Drive
Suite 200
Saint Louis, MO 63132-2924

314-997-7111
Fax: 314-993-7798
Home Page: www.sportingnews.com

Jim Nuckols, CEO

A list of National and American League and their affiliate minor leagues.
Cost: $12.95
Frequency: Annual

22112 Sporting News Football Register
Sporting News Publishing Company
10176 Corporate Square Drive
Suite 200
Saint Louis, MO 63132-2924

314-997-7111
Fax: 314-993-7798
Home Page: www.sportingnews.com

Jim Nuckols, CEO

Directory of services and supplies to the industry.
Cost: $12.95
430 Pages
Frequency: Annual

22113 Sports Address Bible and Almanac
Global Sports Productions
1223 Broadway
Suite 101
Santa Monica, CA 90404-2702

310-395-6533
Fax: 310-454-6590
E-Mail: globalnw@earthlink.net
Home Page: www.sportsbooksempire.com

Ed Kobak, Owner
Greg Andrews, VP Operations

Over 7,500 sports listings from professional, semi-pro, Olympic and amateur, collegiate and interscholastic sports organizations, leagues, teams, halls of fame, media outlets and more.
Cost: $34.95
505 Pages
Frequency: Biennial
ISBN: 1-891655-11-6
ISSN: 0743-4561
Founded in 1998

22114 Sports Market Place Directory
Grey House Publishing
4919 Route 22
PO Box 56
Amenia, NY 12501

518-789-8700
800-562-2139
Fax: 845-373-6390
E-Mail: books@greyhouse.com
Home Page: www.greyhouse.ocm
Social Media: Facebook, Twitter

Leslie Mackenzie, Publisher
Richard Gottlieb, Editor

For over 20 years, this comprehensive, up-to-date directory has offered direct access to the Who, What, When & Where of the Sports Industry. With this directory on your desk, you have a comprehensive tool providing current key information about the people, organizations and events involving the explosive sports industry at your fingertips.
Cost: $225.00
1800 Pages
Frequency: Annual
ISBN: 1-592373-48-8
Founded in 1981

22115 Sports Market Place Directory - Online Database
Grey House Publishing
4919 Route 22
PO Box 56
Amenia, NY 12501

518-789-8700
800-562-2139
Fax: 845-373-6390
E-Mail: gold@greyhouse.com
Home Page: www.gold.greyhouse.com
Social Media: Facebook, Twitter

Leslie Mackenzie, Publisher
Richard Gottlieb, Editor

For over 20 years, this comprehensive, up-to-date directory provides current key information about the people, organizations and events involving the sports industry including, contact information and key executives for single sports organizations, multi-sport organizations, media, sponsors, college sports, manufacturers, trade shows and more.
Founded in 1981

22116 Sports RoundTable
GE Information Services
401 N Washington Street
Rockville, MD 20850-1707

301-388-8284

Cathy Ge, Owner

This database provides coverage of major professional, amateur and collegiate sports including football, basketball, baseball, and hockey.
Frequency: Full-text

22117 SportsAlert
Comtex Scientific Corporation
911 Hope Street
#4838
Stamford, CT 06907-2318

FAX 203-358-0236
Home Page: www.sportsalert.net

This database contains sports news and statistics providing real-time coverage of US and international professional, collegiate and amateur athletic events.
Frequency: Full-text

22118 Tennis-Places to Play: Camps and Clinics Issue
Golf Digest Tennis NY Times Magazine Group
5520 Park Avenue
Trumbull, CT 06611-3400

203-373-7000
Fax: 203-371-2162

Directory of services and supplies to the industry.
Cost: $2.50
Frequency: Annual
Circulation: 800,000

Industry Web Sites

22119 http://gold.greyhouse.com
G.O.L.D Grey House OnLine Databases
Grey House Publishing's online database platform, GOLD, offers Quick Search, Keyword Search and Expert Search for most business sectors including sports and recreation markets. The GOLD platform makes finding the information you need quick and easy - whether you're a novice searcher or an experienced database user. All of Grey House's directory products are available for subscription on the GOLD platform.

22120 www.aahperd.org
American Alliance for Hlth, Phys. Edu. Rec. Dance

22121 www.aahperd.org/uawgs
National Association for Girls and Women in Sports
A non-profit organization serving the needs of teachers, coaches and participants of sports programs for girls and women.

22122 www.aapsm.org
American Academy of Podiatric Sports Medicine
The American Academy of Podiatric Sports Medicine was founded in San Francisco by a group of podiatric sports physicians who had the insight to realize the need for a podiatric sports medicine association devoted to the treatment of athletic injuries. Today the AAPSM has over 500 members.

22123 www.aausports.org
Amateur Athletic Union of the United States

22124 www.abca.org
American Baseball Coaches Association
Formerly called the American Association of College Baseball Coaches.

22125 www.aca-camps.org
American Camping Association
Educational programs. Legislative monitoring, child and youth development.

22126 www.acanet.org
American Canoe Association
Promotes the sport of canoeing and its safety, recreational and conservation

22127 www.acsm.org
American College of Sports Medicine
The ACSM promotes and integrates scientific research, education, and practical applications of sports medicine and exercise science to maintain and enhance physical performance, fitness, health, and quality of life.

22128 www.adventurecycling.org
Adventure Cycling Association
Developes road and mountain bike routes, runs bike tours and eventsand also acts as information resource for bicyclists planning trips.

22129 www.aeawave.com
Aquatic Exercise Association
Covers topics relating to aquatic fitness and therapy including industry trends, research, programs, exercises and products.

22130 www.afaa.com
Aerobics and Fitness Association of America
Association for the education, certification and training of exercise instructors; information resource center for consumers.

22131 www.ahcahockey.com
American Hockey Coaches Association
Helps maintain the highest possible standards in hockey and the hockey profession.

22132 www.americanrunning.org
American Running Association
To encourage all people, from youth to adults, to improve their health and fitness by walking and running, and maintaining an active and healthy lifestyle.

22133 www.asgca.org
American Society of Golf Course Architects
A non-profit organization comprised of leading golf course designers in North America. ASGCA is actively involved in many issues realted to the game of golf, including responsible environmental designs.

22134 www.athleticclubs.com
Athletic Net
Click on links to find fitness, sports medicine, general health and wellness, government sites, directories, nutrition and newsgroups.

22135 www.avca.org
American Volleyball Coaches Association
To develop and grow the sport of volleyball

22136 www.baseballcoaches.org
National High School Baseball Coaches Association
Provides services and recognition for baseball coaches and to help promote and represent high school baseball across the country.

22137 www.bikeleague.org
League of American Bicyclists
Founded in 1880, the League is the only national membership organization of bicyclists in the United States. The League works to promote and encourage bicycling for recreation and transportation, and to protect and defend the rights of bicyclists through advocacy and education.

22138 www.collegecoaches.org
College Swimming Coaches Association of America
The oldest organization of college coaches in America; a professional organization of college swimming and diving coaches dedicated to serving and providing leadership for the advancement of the sport of swimming at the collegiate level.

22139 www.greyhouse.com
Grey House Publishing
Authoritative reference directories for most business sectors including sports and recreation markets. Users can search the online databases with varied search criteria allowing for custom searches by product category, geographic area, sales volume, keyword, subject and more. Full Grey House catalog and online ordering also available.

22140 www.iasv.net
International Academy of Sports Vision
Promotes education, research and development of sports visions. Publishes Sportsvision Magazine and annual scientific journal. Mission is to prevent eye injuries and imprrove visual performance in sports.

22141 www.instituteofdiving.com
Institute of Diving
Membership includes sports, commercial and military divers with the purpose being to operate the Museum of Man in the Sea, publish a newsletter, provide a technical library, offer an information exchange, and promote programs and projects for the improvement of knowledge about the underwater world.

22142 www.iprarodeo.com
International Professional Rodeo Association
Governing body for professional rodeo. 500 rodeos across USA and Canada, $5 million prize money per year, 5 million fans.

22143 www.lpga.com
Ladies Professional Golf Association
For women and youth golfers.

22144 www.naa-usa.org
National Aeronautic Association
Members include aerospace corporations, aero clubs, affiliates and major national sporting aviation organizations.

22145 www.nabc.com
National Association of Basketball Coaches
Promotes the advancement and opportunities for coaches and teachers in the sport of basketball.

22146 www.nabf.com
National Amateur Baseball Association
Promotes amateur baseball and the industry in general.

22147 www.nacola.com
Nat'l Assoc of Collegiate Directors of Athletics
Professional association for college atheltics directors, assistants and conference administrators. Provides educational opportunities and serves as a vehicle for networking and the exchange of information to others in the college sports profession.

22148 www.nasgw.org
National Association of Sporting Goods
Non-profit trade association of wholesalers, distributors and manufacturers. Serves as a liason with other sporting goods associations.

22149 www.naso.org
National Association of Sports Officials
Not-for-profit 501(c)(3) educational association providing individual benefits such as training materials, liability and assault protection insurance and more to sports officials of all sports and every level.

22150 www.nauticalworld.com
Nautical World
Dedicated to bringing all related web sites within easy access to watersports enthusiasts. This search engine has been designed to locate advertiser's information within Nautical World but will also offer access to other watersport related web sites as well. Offers sections on marine electronics and hardware, sailing, boats, dock supplies, fishing accessories, diving ac-

cessories, industry news, watersports, weather forecasting and more.

22151 www.nays.org
National Youth Sports Coaches Association
Represents coaches involved in youth athletics.

22152 www.nfca.org
National Fastpitch Coaches Association
The professional growth organization for fastpitch softball coaches from all competitives levels of play.

22153 www.nflalumni.org
National Football League Alumni
Provides a forum for those individuals retired from the NFL but still playing an active role.

22154 www.ngf.org
National Golf Foundation
Provides market research and serves as an information clearinghouse for the industry. Conducts seminars for golf teachers, coaches and professionals. Conducts golf course development feasibility studies for developers.

22155 www.njcaa.org
National Junior College Athletic Association
NJCAA members are two year institutions recognized by the American Association of Community and Junior Colleges.

22156 www.nra.org
National Rifle Association
Oldest sportsmen's organization in the US. Maintains the NRA Political Victory Fund and supports the Institute for Legislative Action.

22157 www.nsga.org
National Sporting Goods Association
Association of retailers, manufacturers and suppliers of sports equipment, footwear, and apparel.

22158 www.nsgachicagoshow.com
Athletic Goods Team Distributors
Strives to keep athletic team dealers informed of rule changes that affect equipment sales.

22159 www.pga.com
Professional Golfers Association of America
The world's largest working sports organization comprised of more than 25,000 men and women PGA professionals to promote the game of golf to everyone, and to promote its members as leaders in the golf industry.

22160 www.popwarner.com
Pop Warner Little Scholars
A national youth football and cheerleading organization that provides assistance to its various chapters.

22161 www.r-sports.com
Sporting Goods Agents Association
International trade association of independent and established sporting goods agents.

22162 www.restaurantreport.com/top100
Resturant Report On-Line
Includes top 100 food sites, feature stories, newsletters, buyer's guide, marketplace, hospitality jobs.

22163 www.rollerskating.com
Roller Skating Association
Exists for private businessmen and women engaged in the enterprise of roller skating.

22164 www.rollerskating.org
Roller Skating Association International
A trade association representing skating center owners, operators; teachers, coaches and judges of roller skating; and manufacturers and suppliers of roller skating equipment.

22165 www.sabr.org
Society for American Baseball Research
Membership association whose purpose is to facilitate and disseminate baseball research.

22166 www.sgma.com
Sporting Goods Manufacturers Association
For manufacturers, producers, and distributers of sports apparel, athletic footwear, fitness, and sporting goods equipment.

22167 www.skateisi.org
Ice Skating Institute
Industry trade association dedicated to providing leadership, education and services to the ice skating industry.

22168 www.sportsheritage.org
International Sports Heritage Association
The mission of ISHA is to educate, promote and support organizations and individuals engaged in the celebration of sports heritage.

22169 www.sportsmarketplce.com
Grey House Publishing
Provides organizations' contact information with detailed descriptions including: key contacts, physical, mailing, email and web addresses plus phone and fax numbers.

22170 www.sportsmed.org
American Orthopaedic Society for Sports Medicine
Promotes the prevention, recognition and orthopedic treatment of sports injuries.

22171 www.sportsplexoperators.com
Sportsplex Operators and Developers of Association
SODA was formed to meet the needs of the private concerns, public agencies, and other organizations that own or maintain sports complex facilities.

22172 www.teamusa.org
US Olympic Committee
The national committee for the US. Handles the preparation of the US Olympic, Paralympic and Pan American Games teams.

22173 www.tennisindustry.org
Tennis Industry Association
To educate the marketplace, fund research and market intelligence and supply this reliable industry data to our member companies. The TIA is the Information source and clearing house for positive tennis news that we supply to TIA members, tennis publications and to the mainstream media in cooperation with the USTA.

22174 www.usa-swimming.org
USA Swimming
Devoted to the sport of swimming and its enjoyment nationwide.

22175 www.usahockey.com
USA Hockey
Promotes the sport of hockey.

22176 www.usarchery.org
National Archery Association
Supports archers while aiming to advance the sport of archery in the US. Monthly newsletter, Nock-Nock, provides communication among the NAA office, NAA clubs, state associations and the individual members of the NAA. Provides members with news and tournament results ranging from the local and state level to international competition.

22177 www.usatt.org
USA Table Tennis
Dedicated to the promotion of the sport of table tennis and sponsors the US team. Membership dues are $30 per year for adults and $20 for those 18 years old and under.

22178 www.usawaterski.org
USA Water Ski Association
Encourages interest in the sport as well as training and safety.

22179 www.usaweightlifting.org
USA Weightlifting
USA Weightlifting is the National Governing Body (NGB) for the Olympic sport of weightlifting in the United States. USA weightlifting is a member of the United States Olympic Committee and a member of the International Weightlifting Federation. As the NGB, USA Weightlifting is responsible for conducting Olympic weightlifting programs throughout the country. The organization conducts a variety of programs that will ultimately develop Olympic, World Championship and Pan American Games' winners.

22180 www.usfencing.org
United States Fencing Association
Promotes the sport of fencing in the US.

22181 www.usfieldhockey.com
US Field Hockey Association
Represents field hockey, professional and amateur sports.

22182 www.ushandball.org
US Handball Association
Organization that runs all the tournaments for the professional and amateur players. Home of the Handball Hall of Fame.

22183 www.usolimplc.com
United States Amateur Boxing
Promotes the sport of boxing nationwide.

22184 www.uspa.org
United States Parachute Association
A not-for-profit membership association dedicated to the promotion of safe skydiving and the support of those who enjoy it. Sponsors Instructor Rating Program to train and certify instructors, jump masters and examiners.

22185 www.usra.org
US Raquetball Association
A nonprofit corporation designed to promote the development of competitive and recreational racquetball in the United States. The association offers a 'competitive license' membership for a one year term at $15.00 annually, or at discounted longer term rates. A lifetime membership is also offered. A 'Club Recreational Membership' program is offered for an annual fee of $150.00 with a reduced AARA recreational membership available to club members for $3.00 per player.

22186 www.usskiteam.com, www.ussnowboardteam.com
US Ski & Snowboard Association
Association for skiing and snowboarding nationwide.

22187 www.usspeedskating.org
US Speedskating
Devoted to speedskating and its participants on the national and international levels.

22188 **www.ustfccca.org**
U.S. Track & Field and Cross Country Coaches Assoc

A non-profit professional organization that represents men's and women's cross country and track & field coaches in the United States.

22189 **www.uswfa.com**
United States Water Fitness Association

Nonprofit educational organization that promotes aquatics throughout the United States and other countries. Publishes the National Aquatics Newsletter, names the 100 top US water fitness programs and program 5 aquatics in the country, by state and in 25+ categories. Conducts a wide variety of national aquatics certifications including Water Fitness Instructors (primary and masters), aquatic directors, coordinators of water fitness programs. Conducts annual international aquatics conference.

22190 **www.volleyball.org**
US Volleyball Association

Promotes volleyball in the US trains the USA men's and women's teams promotes beach and grassroots voleyball in the United States.

22191 **www.voyager.net/aabc**
American Amateur Baseball Congress

Provides administrative services for amateur baseball youth through adults. 250,000 members.

22192 **www.ymca.net**
YMCA of the USA

Provides national and state branch divisions.

Associations

22193 Allied Stone Industries
PO Box 288145
Chicago, IL 60628-8145
773-928-4800
Fax: 773-928-4129
Home Page: www.alliedstone.com
Social Media: Facebook, Twitter
Brian Porto, President
Butch Coleman, VP
Brundene Van Ness, Secretary
Gary Ballerini, Treasurer
Sharad Muralidhar, Director
Quarries, fabricators and dealers in stone and concrete.
55 Members
Founded in 1950

22194 American Concrete Institute
38800 Country Club Drive
PO Box 9094
Farmington Hills, MI 48331
248-848-3700
Fax: 248-848-3701
E-Mail: ron.burg@concrete.org
Home Page: www.concrete.org
Social Media: Facebook, Twitter, LinkedIn
Anne M Ellis, President
William B Rushing, VP
Sharon L Wood, VP
Ronald G Burg, Executive VP
ACI is a scientific and educational society representing the interests of concrete users concerned with the design, construction, or maintenance of concrete structures. Conventions and meetings, monthly periodicals and special publications; chapter activities; and technical committees all provide a forum for concrete interests to discuss problems relating to concrete.
20000 Members
Founded in 1904

22195 American Concrete Pavement Association
500 New Jersey Ave NW
7th Floor
Washington, DC 20001
847-966-2272
Fax: 847-966-9970
E-Mail: jsmith@multiview.com
Home Page: www.pavement.com
Jon Smith, National Sales Manager
Michael Ayers PhD, Highway Pavement Technology Dir
Leif Wathne PE, Director of Highways
Mitchell Gary, Director of Airports
Jaki Whyte, Registration Information
ACPA is committed to promoting the quality and superiority of concrete pavements. It leads and assists its members in market development, technical expertise, design innovation, research, and public relations. ACPA's membership includes contractors, cement companies, material suppliers, equipment manufacturers and suppliers, ready mix producers, allied associations, bonding and insurance companies, and consulting firms.

22196 American Concrete Pipe Association
8445 Freeport Parkway
Suite 350
Irving, TX 75063-2595
972-506-7216
Fax: 972-506-7682
E-Mail: info@concrete-pipe.org
Home Page: www.concrete-pipe.org
Social Media: Facebook, LinkedIn, Youtube
Matt Childs, President
Josh Beakley, PE, Technical Services Director
Kim Spahn, PE, Engineering Services Director
The American Concrete Pipe Association (ACPA) is a nonprofit organization, composed primarily of manufacturers of concrete pipe and related conveyance products located throughout the United States, Canada and in over 40 foreign countries.
145 Members
Founded in 1907

22197 American Natural Soda Ash Corporation
15 Riverside Avenue
2nd Floor
Westport, CT 06880
203-226-9056
Fax: 203-227-1484
E-Mail: contact@ansac.org
Home Page: www.ansac.com
Social Media: Facebook, Twitter
Donna McSwain-Santos, Marketing
ANSAC markets, sells and distributes high quality soda ash to over 40 countries around the world.
Founded in 1984

22198 American Society of Concrete Contractors
2025 S Brentwood Blvd
Suite 105
St Louis, MO 63144-1850
314-962-0210
866-788-2722
Fax: 314-968-4367
E-Mail: questions@ascconline.org
Home Page: www.ascconline.org
Social Media: Facebook, Twitter
Mike Poppoff, President
Scott M Anderson, VP
Rocky R Geans, VP
Chris Plue, VP
Thomas G Zinchiak, VP
The American Society of Concrete Contractors/ASCC seeks to continually advance the qualifications of concrete constructors and encourage greater interaction between designer and constructor. Publishes the Contactor's Guide to Quality Concrete Construction jointly with ACI. Issues Safety Alerts, Safety Bulletins, and a Safety Manual as well as a troubleshooting newsletter, management reports, and a members bulletin.

22199 Concrete Employers Association
900 Spring Street
Silver Spring, MD 20910
301-587-1400
888-846-7622
Fax: 301-585-4219
E-Mail: info@nrmca.org
Home Page: www.nrmca.org
Social Media: Facebook, Twitter, LinkedIn, Youtube
Robert Garbini, President
Deana Angelastro, Executive Administrator
Eileen Dickson, Vice President
Brian Killingsworth, Senior Director
Concrete plant manufacturers.

22200 Concrete Foundations Association
113 W First Street
PO Box 204
Mount Vernon, IA 52314
319-895-6940
Fax: 320-213-5556
E-Mail: info@cfawalls.org
Home Page: www.cfawalls.org
J Edward Sauter, Executive Director
James Bary II, Technical Director
Janette Barr, Office Manager
Members are residential foundation contractors and their suppliers. The association produces promotional, marketing and technical materials for members' potential customers; provides its members with newsletters, industry publications, and seminar and trade show opportunities; develops specifications, technical information, and safety programs; and represents its members on national code bodies.
300 Members
Founded in 1975

22201 Concrete Promotion Council of Northern California
6966 Sunrise Boulevard
Suite 329
Citrus Heights, CA 95610
916-952-0437
888-633-0393
Fax: 831-302-7330
E-Mail: Paulette.Salisbury@cncement.org
Home Page: www.cpcnc.org
Paulette Salisbury, Interim Director
Bill Albanese, President Board of Directors
Jeff Nehmens, Treasurer Board of Directors
Dave Bearden, Member Board of Directors
Curt Higgins, Member Board of Directors
A member of the Pacific Southwest Concrete Alliance, composed of companies from all parts of the Northern Californian concrete industry including ready mix suppliers, cement producers, admixture manufacturers, concrete contractors as well as members of the public and private design committees. Their mission is to increase the quantity and diversity of quality concrete projects in Northern California through providing educational opportunities to the Professional Design Community.

22202 Concrete Reinforcing Steel Institute
933 N Plum Grove Road
Schaumburg, IL 60173-4758
847-517-1200
Fax: 847-517-1206
E-Mail: brisser@crsi.org
Home Page: www.crsi.org
Social Media: Facebook, Twitter, LinkedIn
Robert J Risser Jr, President
John Healy, CEO
Sue O'Sullivan, Controller
Conducts research and provides technical information on reinforced concrete design and construction practices.
1600 Members
Founded in 1924

22203 Concrete Sawing and Drilling Association
100 2nd Ave S
Suite 402N
St Petersburg, FL 33701
727-577-5004
Fax: 727-577-5012
E-Mail: info@csda.org
Home Page: www.csda.org
Social Media: Facebook
Judith O'Day, President
Kevin Baron, VP
Mike Orzechowski, Secretary/Treasurer
Pat O'Brien, Executive Director
To promote the use of professional specialty sawing and drilling contractors and their methods.
525 Members
Founded in 1972

22204 Expanded Shale Clay and Slate Institute
35 E Wacker Drive
Suite 850
Chicago, IL 60601

801-272-7070
Fax: 312-644-8557
E-Mail: info@escsi.org
Home Page: www.escsi.org

John Riese, President

Sponsors research at engineering schools, educational seminars and develops industry standards.
Founded in 1908

22205 Flexicore Manufacturers Association
7941 New Carlisle Pike
Huber Heights, OH 45424

937-879-5775
Fax: 937-879-0826
Home Page: www.flexicore.com

Strives to protect industry from trade abuses and develop good business practices and quality of product.
11 Members
Founded in 1952

22206 Indiana Limestone Institute of America
1502 I Street
Suite 400
Bedford, IN 47421

812-275-4426
Fax: 812-279-8682
E-Mail: jim@iliai.com
Home Page: www.iliai.com

Jim Owens, Technical Director
Todd Schnatzmeyer, Executive Director
Dave Morthland, Office Manager

The trade association which represents quarries and fabricators of Indiana Limestone, as well as associate members who supply goods or services to the industry, ILIA's charte is to eductate and promote
90 Members
Founded in 1928

22207 International Cast Polymer Alliance
3033 Wilson Blvd
Suite 420
Arlington, VA 22201

703-525-0511
Fax: 703-525-0743
E-Mail: icpa@icpa-hq.org
Home Page: www.icpa-hq.org

Debbie Cannon, President
John Webster, President Elect
Jack Simmons, Secretary

Formerly known as the Cultured Marble Institute, is a nonprofit organization representing over 300 members including manufacturers, suppliers, fabricators, and installers of cultured marble, cultured granite, cultured onyx, and solid surface kitchen and bath products.

22208 Marble Institute of America
28901 Clemens Road
Suite 100
Cleveland, OH 44145

440-250-9222
Fax: 440-250-9223
E-Mail: miainfo@marble-institute.com
Home Page: www.marble-institute.com
Social Media: Facebook, Twitter, LinkedIn

Jonathan Zanger, President
Tony Malisani, VP
Dan Rea, Secretary
David Castelucci, Treasurer

The Marble Institute of America (MIA) is the authoritative source of information on standards of natural stone workmanship and practice and the suitable application of natural stone products.
2000 Members
Founded in 1907

22209 Masonry Society
105 South Sunset Street
Suite Q
Longmont, CO 80501-6172

303-939-9700
Fax: 303-541-9215
E-Mail: info@masonrysociety.org
Home Page: www.masonrysociety.org
Social Media: LinkedIn

Dr. Russell Brown, President
Scott Walkowicz, President-Elect
Jerry Painter, Vice President
Philip Samblanet, Executive Director
Susan Scheurer, TMS Meeting Planner

Dedicated to the advancement of scientific, engineering, architectural and construction knowledge of masonry. Promotes research and education and disseminates information on masonry materials, design, construction. Publishes newsletters, codes & specifications and material on masonry design.
700 Members
Founded in 1977

22210 National Concrete Burial Vault Association
136 South Keowee Street
Dayton, OH 45402

407-788-1996
888-88 -
Fax: 937-222-5794
E-Mail: info@ncbva.org
Home Page: www.ncbva.org

Michael Crummitt, President
Jerry Russell, President Elect
Mark Bates, Secretary/Treasurer
Heather Jones, Convention/Event Planning

A voluntary nonprofit organization of concrete burial vault manufacturers throughtout the United States and Canada. The purpose of the organization is to provide a unified voice for the concrete burial vault industry regardless of product affiliation, brand recognition or location.
350 Members
Founded in 1930

22211 National Concrete Masonry Association
13750 Sunrise Valley Dr
Herndon, VA 20171-4662

703-713-1900
Fax: 703-713-1910
E-Mail: ncma@ncma.org
Home Page: www.ncma.org

Robert Thomas, President
Ron Churchill, Director of Sales

The national trade association representing the concrete masonry industry. The association is involved in a broad range of technical, research, marketing, government relations and community activities.
Founded in 1918

22212 National Lime Association
200 N Glebe Rd
Suite 800
Arlington, VA 22203-3728

703-243-5463
Fax: 703-243-5489
E-Mail: natlime@lime.org
Home Page: www.lime.org
Social Media: Facebook

William C Herz, Executive Director
Arline Seeger, General Counsel
Hunter Prillaman, Director, Govt. Affairs
Lori D Oney, Director, Finance, Administration
Robert Hirsch, Director, Environment

Trade association for US and Canadian manufacturers of high calcium quicklime, dolomitic quicklime and hydrated lime, collectively referred to as lime. NLA represents the interests of its members in Washington, provides input on standards and specifacations for lime, and funds and manages research on current and new uses for lime.
Founded in 1902

22213 National Precast Concrete Association
1320 City Center Drive
Suite 200
Carmel, IN 46032

317-571-9500
800-366-7731
Fax: 317-571-0041
E-Mail: npca@precast.org
Home Page: www.precast.org
Social Media: Facebook, Twitter, LinkedIn, Youtube, RSS, Flickr

Ty Gable, President
Phillip Cutler, VP, Technical Services
Claudia T Hunter, VP, Finance & Administration
Brenda Ibitz, VP, Development & Member Services
Bob Whitmore, VP, Communications & Public Affairs

An international trade organization, NPCA represents manufacturers of plant produced precast concrete products and companies that provide the equipment, supplies and services to make these products. NPCA also provides technical information throught nine product committees, which consist of members who concentrate on specific product lines within the precast industry.
1100 Members
Founded in 1965

22214 National Ready Mixed Concrete Association
900 Spring St
Silver Spring, MD 20910-4015

301-587-1400
888-846-7622
Fax: 301-585-4219
E-Mail: info@nrmca.org
Home Page: www.nrmca.org
Social Media: Facebook, Twitter, LinkedIn, Youtube

Robert Garbini, President
Deana Angelastro, Executive Administrator

NRMCA represents its membership of ready mixed concrete producrs in market development, technical research, engineering advances, government relations, and regulatory issues. In addition to conducting educational seminars, workshops, conferences and trade shows, NRMCA disseminates a wide variety of publications for its members, ranging from Congressional digests and promotion pointers to driver education.

22215 Ornamental Concrete Producers Association
759 Phelps Johnson Rd
Leitchfield, KY 42754

270-879-6319
Fax: 218-751-2186

E-Mail: delpreus@paulbunyan.net
Home Page: www.ornamentalconcrete.org

Del Preuss, Executive Director
Robert Garbini, President
Shawnita Dickens, Manager

An international nonprofit educational association comprised of producers and suppliers.
Cost: $50.00
500 Members
Founded in 1991

22216 Portland Cement Association
5420 Old Orchard Road
Skokie, IL 60077

847-966-6200
Fax: 847-966-8389
E-Mail: info@cement.org
Home Page: www.cement.org
Social Media: Facebook, Twitter, LinkedIn

Brian McCarthy, President/CEO

The Portland Cement Association represents cement companies in the United States and Canada. It conducts market development, engineering, research, education, and public affairs programs.
Founded in 1916

22217 Post-Tensioning Institute
Bldg Main
38800 Country Club Dr
Farmington Hills, MI 48331-3439

248-848-3180
Fax: 248-848-3181
E-Mail: info@post-tensioning.org
Home Page: www.post-tensioning.org

Theodore L Neff, Executive Director
Russell Price, President
Douglas J Schlegel, VP

Provides research, technical development, marketing and promotional activities for companies engaged in post-tensioned prestressed construction. Members include fabricators and manufacturers.
900 Members
Founded in 1976

22218 Refractories Institute
325 Maple Ave
PO Box 8439
Pittsburgh, PA 15218

412-244-1880
Fax: 412-244-1881
E-Mail: info@refractoriesinstitute.org
Home Page: www.refractoriesinstitute.org

Robert Crolius, President

A trade association which promotes the interests of the refractories industry. TRI has a long tradition of providing support and services to manufacturers of refractory materials and products and suppliers of raw materials, equipment, and services to the refractories industry.
80 Members
Founded in 1951

22219 Specialty Minerals
Minerals Technology
405 Lexington Ave
New York, NY 10174-0002

212-986-2486
800-801-1031
Fax: 610-882-8726
E-Mail:
smi.productinfo@specialtyminerals.com
Home Page: www.mineralstech.com

Joseph C Muscari, Executive Chairman
Robert S Wetherbee, President & CEO
Douglas T Dietrich, Senior VP/CFO
D J Monagle III, Senior VP/Managing Director
Thomas J Meek, Senior VP/General Counsel/Secretary

A subsidiary of Minerals Technology, Inc., a resource and technology based organization that develops and produces performance-enhancing minerals, mineral-based and synthetic mineral products for the paper, steel, polymer, healthcare and other manufacturing industries on a worldwide basis.
Founded in 1992

22220 Tilt-Up Concrete Association
113 First Street W
PO Box 204
Mount Vernon, IA 52314-0204

319-895-6911
Fax: 320-213-5555
E-Mail: info@tilt-up.org
Home Page: www.tilt-up.org
Social Media: Facebook, Twitter, LinkedIn, You Tube

Kimberley Corwin, President
Shane Miller, President Elect
Andrew S McPherson, Treasurer
James M Williams, Secretary

TCA members include contractors, suppliers, architects, and engineers dedicated to the advancement of quality tilt-up concrete construction. Activities include a national promotional program, information clearinghouse, educational seminars, referral service, achievement awards program, development of codes and standards, and a quarterly magazine.

Newsletters

22221 Concrete Openings
Concrete Sawing and Drilling Association
13577 Feather Sound Drive
Suite 560
Clearwater, FL 33762

727-577-5004
Fax: 727-577-5012
E-Mail: info@csda.org
Home Page: www.csda.org
Social Media: Facebook, LinkedIn

Patrick O'Brien, Executive Director
500 Members
300 Attendees
Frequency: Quarterly
Circulation: 17000
Founded in 1972

22222 Cutting Edge
Marble Institute of America
28901 Clemens Road
Suite 100
Cleveland, OH 44145

440-250-9222
Fax: 440-250-9223
E-Mail: miainfo@marble-institute.com
Home Page: www.marble-institute.com

Gary Distelhorst, Executive VP/CEO
Helen Distelhorst, Director Meetings/Special Events
Jim Hieb, VP
Frequency: Monthly
Circulation: 1500

22223 Refractory News
Refractories Institute
630 Smithfield Street
Suite 1160
Pittsburgh, PA 15222-3907

412-281-6787
Fax: 412-281-6881
E-Mail: triassn@aol.com
Home Page: www.refractoriesinstitute.org
Social Media: Facebook, Twitter

Flo Story, Editor

A monthly newsletter featuring timely industry news, information on federal regulations, member updates, announcements on seminars, and the latest refractory information and statistics.
Cost: $24.00
4 Pages
Frequency: Monthly
Circulation: 700
Founded in 1951
Mailing list available for rent
Printed in 2 colors on matte stock

Magazines & Journals

22224 ACI Materials Journal
American Concrete Institute
38800 Country Club Drive
PO Box 9094
Farmington Hills, MI 48333-9094

248-848-3700
Fax: 248-848-3701
E-Mail: shannon.hale@concrete.org
Home Page:
www.concrete.org/pubs/journals/mjhome.asp

Shannon M Hale, Technical Editor
Carl R Bischof, Senior Editor Publishing Services
Renee J Lewis, Publishing & Event Services
Douglas J Sordyl, Marketing/Sales/Industry Relations
Donna G Halstead, Finance & Administration

ACI Materials Journal contains individually authored papers as well as papers developed for convention sessions. These papers address structural research, materials research, design theory, structural analysis, and state-of-the-art reviews.
Founded in 1904
Mailing list available for rent

22225 ACI Structural Journal
American Concrete Institute
38800 Country Club Drive
PO Box 9094
Farmington Hills, MI 48333-9094

248-848-3700
Fax: 248-848-3701
E-Mail: shannon.hale@concrete.org
Home Page:
www.concrete.org/pubs/journals/sjhome.asp

Shannon M Hale, Technical Editor
Carl R Bischof, Senior Editor Publishing Services
Renee J Lewis, Publishing & Event Services
Douglas J Sordyl, Marketing/Sales/Industry Relations
Donna G Halstead, Finance & Administration

ACI Structural Journal contains individually authored papers as well as papers developed for convention sessions. These papers address structural research, materials research, design theory, structural analysis, and state-of-the-art reviews.
Founded in 1904
Mailing list available for rent

22226 Cement Americas
Primedia
11555 Central Parkway
10th Floor
Chicago, IL 60606

312-726-2802
Fax: 312-726-2574
Home Page: www.cementamericas.com

Steven Prokopy, Editor
Norm Rose, Sales

Cement Americas provides comprehensive coverage of the North and South American cement markets from raw materials extraction to deliv-

ery and transportation to the end user. Production-oriented articles focus on areas where the market activity is at its greatest. Coverage of new ideas, technological improvements, industry trends, and views from leading figures in the cement industry ensure that Cement Americas remains the cement industry journal of the Americas.
ISSN: 0035-7464
Printed in 4 colors on glossy stock

22227 Concrete InFocus
Naylor Publications
5950 NW 1st Pl
Gainesville, FL 32607-6018

352-332-1252
800-369-6220
Fax: 352-331-3525
E-Mail: chodges@naylor.com
Home Page: www.naylor.com
Social Media: Facebook, Twitter, LinkedIn, You Tube

Michael Moss, President

Magazine that's mailed to 5,000+ industry personnel.

22228 Concrete International
American Concrete Institute
38800 Country Club Drive
PO Box 9094
Farmington Hills, MI 48333-9094
248-848-3700
Fax: 248-848-3701
E-Mail: ron.burg@concrete.org
Home Page: www.concrete.org

Carl R Bischof, Senior Editor
Ronald G Burg, Executive Vice President

The circulation is concentrated among the most important professionals in the concrete field; the engineers, architects, contractors, manufacturers, and technicians largely responsible for the advancement of concrete technology and practice.
Frequency: Monthly
Circulation: 20000

22229 Concrete Masonry Designs
NCMA
13750 Sunrise Valley Dr
Herndon, VA 20171-4662

703-713-1900
Fax: 703-713-1910
E-Mail: ncma@ncma.org
Home Page: www.ncma.org

Robert Thomas, President
Ron Churchill, Director Of Sales

Highlights concrete masonry applications, best practice tips, specifications and details. Also showcases concrete masonry landscape products.
Cost: $1.00
Frequency: Monthly
Circulation: 25000
Founded in 1918
Printed in 4 colors on glossy stock

22230 Concrete Openings
Concrete Sawing and Drilling Association
13577 Feather Sound Drive
Suite 560
St Petersburg, FL 33762

727-577-5004
Fax: 727-577-5012
E-Mail: info@csda.org
Home Page: www.concreteopenings.com
Social Media: Facebook

Cherryl O'Brien, Editor
Russell Hitchen, Associate Editor
Patrick O'Brien, Publisher

The official magazine of the Concrete Sawing & Drilling Association. Editorial contributions are welcomed and advertisements are encouraged.
Frequency: Quarterly
Circulation: 16000
ISSN: 1093-6483

22231 Concrete Producer
Hanley Wood
426 S Westgate
Addison, IL 60101

630-543-0870
Fax: 847-564-9287
E-Mail: ryelton@hanleywood.com
Home Page: www.theconcreteproducer.com

Richard Yelton, Editor-in-Chief
Tom Bagsarian, Managing Editor
Chari O'Rourke, Circulation Manager

Written for decision-making professionals who buy and specify materials, plant equipment, accessories, trucks, and related products used in the major concrete-producing market segments. Each issue offers money saving operational tips, management advice, new products and technology, and solutions to complex concrete-production questions.

22232 Contemporary Stone & Tile Design
Business News Publishing Company
299 Market Street
Suite 320
Saddle Brook, NJ 07663

201-845-5035
Fax: 201-291-9002
E-Mail: cstd@bnp.com
Home Page: www.stoneworld.com

Alex Backrach, Publisher
Michael Reis, Editor

Promotes the benefits of natural stone and ceramic tile to a readership of architects, interior designers, specifiers and consumers. Practical tips and commentary on stone and tile design are included, featuring interviews with architects and designers from the world's leading firms.
Cost: $125.00
Frequency: Quarterly
Circulation: 21000
Founded in 1987

22233 MC
National Precast Concrete Association
10333 N Meridian St
Suite 272
Indianapolis, IN 46290-1081

317-571-9500
800-366-7731
Fax: 317-571-0041
E-Mail: rhyink@precast.org
Home Page: www.precast.org

Ty Gable, President
Brenda Ibitz, Manager Advertising

MC magazine features detailed articles about the latest industry technologies and developments, perspectives on current industry events, profiles on leading precast concrete companies and case studies of various manufactured concrete applications.
Frequency: Bi-Monthly

22234 Masonry Construction
Hanley Wood
426 S Westgate
Addison, IL 60101

630-543-0870
Fax: 847-564-9287
E-Mail: ryelton@hanleywood.com
Home Page: www.masonryconstruction.com
Social Media: Facebook, Twitter

Richard Yelton, Editor-in-Chief
Ron Holzhauer, Deputy Editor
Kari Moosman, Associate Editor
Ted Worthington, Managing Editor
Chari O'Rourke, Circulation Manager

Masonry Construction brings together the complex and fragmented components of the masonry industry—contractors, general contractors, architects, engineers, and producers—providing technical advice, innovative methods and materials, state-of-the-art projects, and essential product information.

22235 Precast
National Precast Concrete Association
1320 City Center Drive
Suite 200
Carmel, IN 46032

317-571-9500
800-366-7731
Fax: 317-571-0041
E-Mail: npca@precast.org
Home Page: www.precast.org

Ty Gable, President
Brenda Ibitz, VP Development and Member Services
Frequency: Bi-Monthly
Circulation: 5000

22236 Professional Builder
Reed Business Information
8878 Barrons Blvd
Littleton, CO 80129-2345

303-470-4000
800-446-6551
Fax: 303-470-4691
E-Mail: subsmail@reedbusiness.com
Home Page: www.reedbusiness.com

Tim Myers, Executive
Stuart Whayman, Finance
Nathan Cahill, HR

The magazine for professionals within the residential building industry. Articles cover industry news, company profiles, market reports, construction technology and merchandising information needed to successfully complete each job.
Frequency: Monthly
Founded in 1977

22237 Rock Products
Primedia
29 N Wacker Drive
10th Floor
Chicago, IL 60606

312-726-2802
Fax: 312-726-2574
E-Mail: rmarkley@primediabusiness.com
Home Page: www.rockproducts.com

Rick Markley, Editor
Scott Bieda, Publisher
Sean ~ Carr, Sales Manager

The aggregate industry's journal of applied technology.
Frequency: Monthly
ISSN: 0035-7464
Founded in 1905

22238 Stone World
BNP Media
210 E State Rt 4
Suite 203
Paramus, NJ 07652-5103

201-291-9001
Fax: 201-291-9002
E-Mail: info@stoneworld.com
Home Page: www.stoneworld.com

Alex Bachrach, Publisher

A source of information on stone use in architecture and interior design as well as stone production, distribution, installationm and maintenance.

Trade Shows

22239 **CSDA Convention and Tech Fair**
Concrete Sawing and Drilling Association
13577 Feather Sound Drive
Suite 560
Clearwater, FL 33762

727-577-5004
Fax: 727-577-5012
E-Mail: info@csda.org
Home Page: www.csda.org
Social Media: Facebook, LinkedIn

Patrick O'Brien, Executive Director
500 Members
300 Attendees
Frequency: Annual
Founded in 1972

22240 **Composites and Polycon Convention**
American Composites Manufacturers Association
1010 North Glebe Road
Suite 450
Arlington, VA 22201

703-525-0511
Fax: 703-525-0743
E-Mail: info@acmanet.org
Home Page: www.icpashow.org

Three-day convention. Attendees will have the opportunity to choose from 100 presentations, live demonstrations and technical papers. Covering every level of expertise from beginer to advanced, industry experts will address dozens of subject areas in the most striking detail, from technical to production to regulatory to management and more.
Frequency: Annual

22241 **Manufactured Concrete Products Exposition**
National Concrete Masonry Association
13750 Sunrise Valley Drive
Herndon, VA 20171-4662

703-713-1900
Fax: 703-713-1910
E-Mail: ncma@ncma.org
Home Page: www.ncma.org

Mark Hogan, President
Ron Churchill, Director Of Sales

The Manufactured Concrete Products Exposition is brought to you by a partnership between the National Concrete Masonry Association, the Interlocking Concrete Paving Institute and the American Concrete Pipe Association.
Frequency: Annual

22242 **National Concrete Burial Vault Association Convention**
NCBVA
195 Wekiva Springs Road
Suite 200
Longwood, FL 32779

407-788-1996
Fax: 407-774-6751
Home Page: www.ncbva.org

Thomas A Monahan, Executive Director
Heather Jones, Conventions/Event Planning

Convention held annually. Includes awards banquet, installation of officers and more.
Frequency: Annual

22243 **PTI Technical Conference and Exhibition**
Post-Tensioning Institute
38800 Country Club Drive
Farmington Hills, MI 48331

248-848-3180
Fax: 248-848-3181
E-Mail: info@post-tensioning.org
Home Page: www.post-tensioning.org

Ted Neff, Executive Director
Larry Krauser, President
Marc Khoury, VP
Robert Sward, Secretary

Earn CEUs, attend technical sessions, awards events, exhibits, and ask-the-expert forum.
Frequency: May

22244 **Precast Show**
National Precast Concrete Association
1320 City Center Drive
Suite 200
Carmel, IN 46032-1074

317-571-9500
800-366-7731
Fax: 317-571-0041
E-Mail: npca@precast.org
Home Page: www.precast.org
Social Media: Facebook, Twitter, LinkedIn, You Tube

Ty Gable, President
Erica Wells, Director Meetings

Trade show for the precast concrete industry, containing 300 booths and 300 exhibits.
3000 Attendees
Frequency: Annual

22245 **StonExpo**
Marble Institute of America
28901 Clemens Road
Suite 100
Cleveland, OH 44145

440-250-9222
Fax: 440-250-9223
Home Page: www.marble-institute.com

Gary Distelhorst, EVP/CEO
Helen Distelhorst, Meetings/Special Events Director

Where fabricators, installers and distributors can experience everything from natural stone extracted from quarries around the world, to the most technologically advanced fabricating machinery, to the beautiful finished product: exquisite countertops that are installed in both residential and commercial properties today.
Frequency: Annual/January

22246 **World of Concrete Exposition**
Post Tensioning Institute
8601 North Black Canyon Highway
Suite 103
Phoenix, AZ 85021

602-870-7540
Fax: 602-870-7541
E-Mail: info@post-tensioning.org
Home Page: www.post-tensioning.org

Seminars, exhibits and trade shows. Sponsored by the Post-Tensioning Institute.
36M Attendees
Frequency: January/Febuary

Directories & Databases

22247 **CSDA Resource Guide & Membership Directory**
Concrete Sawing and Drilling Association
100 2nd Avenue S
Suite 402N
St. Petersburg, FL 33701

727-577-5004
Fax: 727-577-5012
E-Mail: info@csda.org
Home Page: www.csda.org

Patrick O'Brien, Executive Director
Cost: $12.00
500 Members
97 Pages
Founded in 1972

22248 **Dimension Stone Design Manual**
Marble Institute of America
28901 Clemens Rd
Suite 100
Cleveland, OH 44145-1166

440-250-9222
Fax: 440-250-9223
E-Mail: mia@marble-institute.com
Home Page: www.marble-institute.com

Gary Distelhorst, Executive VP
Helen Distelhorst, Director Meetings/Special Events
Jim Hieb, VP
Michael A. Twiss, President

An authoritative source for guidelines on using natural stone in architectural designs. Contents include sections on granite, marble, limestone, serpentine, travertine, quartz-based stone and slate with product descriptions and technical data; general installation guidelines; guidelines and typical detailing for horizontal surfaces, vertical surfaces, wet areas, furniture and countertops; maintenance of exterior/ interior stone installations; and a glossary of terms relating to dimension stone.
Cost: $90.00
350 Pages
Founded in 1960

22249 **Dimension Stones of the World: Book of Color Plates**
Marble Institute of America
28901 Clemens Rd
Suite 100
Cleveland, OH 44145-1166

440-250-9222
Fax: 440-250-9223
E-Mail: mia@marble-institute.com
Home Page: www.marble-institute.com

Gary Distelhorst, Executive VP
Helen Distelhorst, Director Meetings/Special Events
Jim Hieb, VP
Michael A. Twiss, President

This set contains over 600 full color reproductions of granites, limestones, marbles, onyx, quartz based stone, slate and travertine. On the reverse side of each page are the ASTM test values for absorbption, density, compressive strength, hardness and flexural strength. Also listed for each stone are primary name, country of origin, quarry location, geological age, color range, recommended usage and available sizes.
Cost: $330.00
Founded in 1960

22250 **Online MCP**
American Concrete Institute
38800 Country Club Drive
PO Box 9094
Farmington Hills, MI 48333-9094

248-483-3700
Fax: 248-848-3801
E-Mail: shannon.hale@concrete.org
Home Page: www.concrete.org

William R Tolley, Executive VP
Douglas J Sordyl, Marketing/Sales/Industry Relations
Donna G Halstead, Finance/Administration
Shannon M Hale, Technical Editor
Carl R Bischof, Senior Editor Publishing Services

Contains all of the ACI documents you need to answer your questions about code requirements, specifications, tolerance, concrete proportions, construction methods, evaluations of test results, and many more topics.
Founded in 1994
Mailing list available for rent

22251 **Stone World Annual Buyer's Guide**
Stone World Magazine
210 Route 4 East
Suite 311
Paramus, NJ 90001

201-291-9001
Fax: 201-291-2002
E-Mail: info@stoneworld.com
Home Page: www.stoneworld.com
Social Media: Facebook, Twitter

Alex Bachrach, Publisher
Michael Reis, Senior Editor/Associate Publisher

Comprised of six sections covering: stone suppliers, fabricating equipment and suppliers, installation and stone care materials and supplies, associations, services, trade shows and organizers.
Cost: $6.00
Frequency: Annual
Circulation: 22,000
Founded in 1984

Industry Web Sites

22252 **http://gold.greyhouse.com**
G.O.L.D Grey House OnLine Databases
Grey House Publishing's online database platform, GOLD, offers Quick Search, Keyword Search and Expert Search for most business sectors including stone and concrete markets. The GOLD platform makes finding the information you need quick and easy - whether you're a novice searcher or an experienced database user. All of Grey House's directory products are available for subscription on the GOLD platform.

22253 **www.construction.com**
McGraw-Hill Construction
McGraw-Hill Construction (MHC), part of The McGraw-Hill Companies, connects people and projects across the design and construction industry, serving owners, architects, engineers, general contractors, subcontractors, building product manufacturers, suppliers, dealers, distributors and adjacent markets.

22254 **www.crsi.org**
Concrete Reinforcing Steel Institute
Conducts research and provides technical information on reinforced concrete design and construction practices.

22255 **www.csda.org**
Concrete Sawing and Drilling Association
To promote the use of professional specialty sawing and drilling contractors and their methods.

22256 **www.greyhouse.com**
Grey House Publishing
Authoritative reference directories for most business sectors including stone and concrete markets. Users can search the online databases with varied search criteria allowing for custom searches by product category, geographic area, sales volume, keyword, subject and more. Full Grey House catalog and online ordering also available.

22257 **www.icri.org**
International Concrete Repair Institute
To improve the quality of repair, restoration, and protection of concrete and other structures.

22258 **www.marble-institute.com**
Marble Institute of America
Importers, finishers, wholesalers, fabricators, quarriers and exporters of stone for both interior and exterior application as well as suppliers of machines, tools and services.

22259 **www.post-tensioning.org**
Post-Tensioning Institute
Provides research, technical development, marketing and promotional activities for companies engaged in post-tensioned prestressed construction. Members include fabricators and manufacturers.

22260 **www.precast.org**
National Precast Concrete Association

22261 **www.sweets.construction.com**
McGraw Hill Construction
In depth product information that lets you find, compare, select, specify and make purchase decisions in the industrial product marketplace.

Associations

22262 4G Americas
1750 - 112th Avenue NE, Suite B220
Bellevue, WA 98004
425-372-8922
Fax: 425-372-8923
Home Page: www.4gamericas.org
Social Media: Facebook, Twitter
Chris Pearson, President
Vicki Livingston, Director of Communications
Peter Jones, Director
Paul Mankiewich, Director
Bob Suffern, Director

22263 Advanced Television Systems Committee
1776 K St. NW
8th Floor
Washington, Dc 20006-2304
202-872-9160
Fax: 202-872-9161
Home Page: www.atsc.org
Social Media: Facebook, Twitter
Founded in 1982

22264 American Radio Relay League
225 Main St
Newington, CT 06111-1494
860-594-0200
888-277-5289
Fax: 860-594-0259
E-Mail: hq@arrl.org
Home Page: www.arrl.org
Social Media: Facebook, Twitter, Youtube
David Sumner, CEO
Joel Harrison, President
Barry Shelley, CFO
Harold Kramer, COO
National membership association for amateur radio operators.
170m Members
Founded in 1914

22265 Antenna Measurement Techniques Association
6065 Roswell Road
Atlanta, GA 30328
770-864-3488
Fax: 770-864-3491
E-Mail: president@amta.org
Home Page: www.amta.org
Social Media: LinkedIn, RSS
Chi-Chih Chen, President
Jan Zackrisson, VP
Peter Collins, Secretary
John Demas, Treasurer
Nonprofit professional organization open to individuals with an interest in antenna measurements. Areas of interest include: measurement facilities, unique or innovative measurement techniques, test instrumentation and systems, RCS measurements, compact range design and evaluation, near-field techniques and their applications, and the practical aspects of measurement problems and their solutions.
400 Members
Founded in 1979

22266 Armed Forces Communications and Electronics Association
AFCEA International Headquarters
4400 Fair Lakes Ct
Suite 100
Fairfax, VA 22033-3899
703-631-1397
800-336-4583
Fax: 703-631-4693
E-Mail: service@afcea.org
Home Page: www.afcea.org
VADM Herb Brown, President/CEO
A non-profit international association dedicated to supporting global security by providing an ethical environment that encourages a close cooperative relationship among civil government agencies, the military and industry.
Cost: $35.00
31000 Members
Founded in 1946

22267 Assn. of Public-Safety Communications Officials International
351 N Williamson Boulevard
Daytona Beach, FL 32114-1112
386-322-2500
888 272 6911
Fax: 386-322-2501
E-Mail: apco@apcointl.org
Home Page: www.apcointl.org
Social Media: Facebook, Twitter, LinkedIn, Youtube
George S Rice Jr, Executive Director
Susan Stowel, Member Services Director
Dennis Divine, Technology/Support Ops Director
Garry Mendez, Marketing/Communications Director
Robert Gurss Esq., Legal/Government Affairs Director
A not-for-profit professional organization dedicated to the enhancement of public safety communications. Exists to serve the people who manage, operate, maintain, and supply the communications systems used to safeguard the lives and property of citizens everywhere.
16000 Members
Founded in 1935

22268 Association for Local Telecommunications Services
900 17th St NW
Suite 400
Washington, DC 20006-2507
202-296-6650
Fax: 202-296-7585
E-Mail: membership@alts.org
Home Page: www.comptelascent.org
Earl Comstock, CEO
COMPTEL is the leading industry accociation representing communications service providers and their supplier partners.

22269 Association of Teleservices International
222 S Westmonte Drive
Suite 101
Altamonte Springs, FL 32714
603-362-9489
866-896-2874
Fax: 407-774-6440
E-Mail: admin@atsi.org
Home Page: www.atsi.org
Social Media: Facebook, Twitter, LinkedIn
Sharon Campbell, President
Jeff Zindel, President Elect
JoAnn Fussell, VP, Secretary
Raymond P Shaw Jr., VP, Treasurer
Promotes fair competition through appropriate regulation and legislation; provides research and development provides support services and educational opportunities to address challenges in operating environments; in encourages and maintains the high standards of ethics and service.
800+ Members
Founded in 1942

22270 Broadcast Designers' Association International
1522 E Cloverfield Blvd
Santa Monica, CA 90404
310-788-7600
Fax: 310-788-7616
Home Page: www.promaxbda.org
Social Media: Facebook, Twitter, LinkedIn, RSS
Jonathon Block, President
Jill Lindmen, General Manager
Randy Smith, CFO
Lucian Cojescu, Chief Information Officer
Association for manufacturers or suppliers of broadcast design equipment, supplies and services.

22271 CDMA Development Group
575 Anton Blvd.
Suite 440
Costa Mesa, CA 92626
714-545-5211
888-800-CDMA
Fax: 714-545-4601
E-Mail: cdg@cdg.org
Home Page: www.cdg.org
Social Media: Facebook, Twitter, RSS
Mark S. Richer, President
Jerry Whitaker, Vice President
Lindsy Shelton Gross, Director of Communications
Daro Bruno, Office Manager
Founded in 1993

22272 Carnegie Mellon University: Information Networking Institute
Electrical & Computer Engineering Department
4616 Henry Street
Pittsburgh, PA 15213
412-268-7195
Fax: 412-268-7196
E-Mail: ini@cmu.edu
Home Page: www.ini.cmu.edu
Social Media: Facebook, Twitter, LinkedIn, Youtube, Flickr
Dena Haritos Tsamitis, Director
Lynn Carroll, Assistant Director
Andrew Pueschel, Project Manager/Events/Marketing
Chriss Swaney, Director Public Relations
Sean O'Leary, Manager
The Information Networking Institute was established by Carnegie Mellon as the nation's first research and education center devoted to Information Networking.
Founded in 1989

22273 Cellular Telecommunications Industry
CTIA
1400 16th St NW
Suite 600
Washington, DC 20036-2225
202-785-0081
Fax: 202-785-0721
Home Page: www.ctia.org
Steve M Largent, President & CEO
Michael Altschul, Senior VP, General Counsel
Scott Bergmann, VP, Regulatory Affairs
Jot Carpenter, VP, Govt. Affairs
Rocco Carlitti, VP, Finance & Administration
An international organization representing all sectors of wireless communications. As a nonprofit membership organization, they represent service providers, manufacturers, wireless data and Internet companies and other contributors to the wireless universe.
Founded in 1984

22274 Center for Strategic and International Studies
1616 Rhode Island Avenue, NW
Washington, DC 20036

202-887-0200
Fax: 202-775-3199
Home Page: www.csis.org
Social Media: RSS

John J. Hamre, President and CEO
Carig Cohen, Executive Vice President
Jon B. Alterman, SVP
David J. Berteau, SVP & Director
Alice Blevins, SVP for Operations
Founded in 1962

22275 Competitive Telecommunications Association
1200 G St. NW, Suite 350
Washington, DC 20005

202-296-6650
Fax: 202-296-7585
Home Page: www.comptel.org
Social Media: Facebook, Twitter, LinkedIn

Deborah Ward, Chairwoman
Chris Murray, Vice Chairman
Jim Butman, Treasurer
Ron Beaumont, Director
Bill Barloon, Director
Founded in 1981

22276 Enterprise Wireless Alliance
8484 Westpark Drive
Suite 630
McLean, VA 22102-5117

703-528-5115
800-482-8282
Fax: 703-524-1074
E-Mail:
customerservice@enterprisewireless.org
Home Page: www.enterprisewireless.org

Bart Fisher, Chairman
Catherine Leonard, Vice Chairman
Mark E Crosby, President/CEO
William Jenkins, Treasurer

Formerly ITA and AMTA, works to preserve spectrum rights and access for enterprise wireless customers.
400 Members
Founded in 1985

22277 Geospatial Information & Technology Association
1360 University Ave. West
Suite 455
St. Paul, MN 55104-4086

E-Mail: president@gita.org
Home Page: www.gita.org
Social Media: Facebook, Twitter, LinkedIn, YouTube

Talbot J. Brooks, President
Eric Hoogenraad, Treasurer
Jerry King, Secretary
Mark Limbruner, President Elect
Elizabeth Bialek, P.E., At-Large Board Member

22278 Kagan Research
1 Lower Ragsdale Dr
Building One Suite 130
Monterey, CA 93940-5749

831-624-1536
800-307-2529
Fax: 831-625-3225
E-Mail: info@kagan.com
Home Page: www.kagan.com
Social Media: Facebook, Twitter, LinkedIn, Youtube, Google+

Mike Chinn, President
Tom Corbitt, Chief Adminstration Officer
Dan Oakey, Chief Contracts Officer

Provides knowledge, insight and industry perspectives, anticipates trends, projects revenues, tracks financing and values the debt and equity of hundreds of privately held and publicly traded media and communications companies.
Founded in 1969

22279 National Association of Broadcastersÿ
1771 N St. NW
Washington, DC 20036

202-429-5300
800-NAB-EXPO
E-Mail: nan@nab.org
Home Page: www.nab.org
Social Media: Facebook, Twitter, LinkedIn, YouTube

Mary Quass, Member, Executive Committee
Patrick Walsh, Member, Executive Committee
Dan Mason, Member, Executive Committee
Brian Lawlor, Member, Executive Committee
Don Benson, Member, Executive Committee

22280 National Cable andÿTelecommunications Association
25 Massachusetts Avenue, NW
Suite 100
Washington, DC 20001

202-222-2300
Fax: 202-222-2514
E-Mail: info@ncta.com
Home Page: www.ncta.com
Social Media: Facebook, Twitter, LinkedIn

Michael Powell, President & CEO
James M. Assey, Executive Vice President
K. Dane Snowden, Chief of Staff
Bruce Carnes, SVP, Finance & Administration
William Check, SVP, Science & Technology
200 Members

22281 National Exchange Carrier Association
80 S Jefferson Rd
Suite 1
Whippany, NJ 07981-1027

973-599-0580
Fax: 973-884-8469
E-Mail: webmastr@neca.org
Home Page: www.neca.org
Social Media: Facebook, Twitter

William Hegman, CEO
Peter A Dunbar, VP/CFO
James W Frame, VP Operations
Regina McNeil, VP/General Counsel/Corp Secretary
Raymond Henagan, Chair

NECA administer's the FCCs access charge plan. They file access charge tariffs with the FCC, collect and validate cost and revenue data, ensure compliance with FCC rules, distribute revenues from access charges among pool members, process FCC regulatory fees, and offer training and education on a wide variety of telecom topics.
1500 Members
Founded in 1983

22282 National Telephone Cooperative Association
4121 Wilson Blvd
Suite 1000
Arlington, VA 22203-4145

703-351-2000
Fax: 703-351-2001
E-Mail: contact@ntca.org
Home Page: www.ntca.org

Shirley Bloomfield, CEO

Non-profit association offering a wide array of member services including a government affairs program; expert legal and industry representation; a broad range of educational services; a comprehensive assortment of regular and special publications and public relations programs; and a well-rounded complement of national and regional meetings.
560+ Members
Founded in 1954

22283 Organization for the Promotion and Adv. of Small Telecommunications
2020 K Street
Washington, NW 20006

202-659-5990
Fax: 202-659-4619
Home Page: www.opastco.org
Social Media: Facebook, Twitter

John Rose, President
Martha Silver, Editor
Corey Watson, Advertisement

Protects the interests of small, rural, independent commercial telephone companies and cooperatives that have less than 50,000 access lines.
650 Members
Founded in 1963

22284 Personal Communications Industry
500 Montgomery Street
Suite 700
Alexandria, VA 22314

703-390-0300
800-759-0300
Fax: 703-836-1608
E-Mail: webmaster@pcia.com
Home Page: www.pcia.com
Social Media: Facebook, Twitter, LinkedIn

W Benjamin Moreland, Chairman
Thomas A Murray, Vice Chairman
Steven Marshall, Treasurer
Jonathan S Adelstein, President & CEO
Tim House, VP, External Relations

Represents companies that develop, own, manage and operate towers, commercial rooftops and other facilities for the provision of all types of wireless, broadcasting and telecommunication services. PCIA is dedicated to advancing an understanding of the benefits of wireless services and required infrastructure to local and federal government officials and communities at large.
3000 Members
Founded in 1949

22285 Power and Communication Contractors Association
103 Oronoco St
Suite 200
Alexandria, VA 22314

703-212-7734
800-542-7222
Fax: 703-548-3733
E-Mail: info@pccaweb.org
Home Page: www.pccaweb.org

Kevin Mason, President
Larry Libla, President-Elect

A national trade association for companies constructing electric power facilities, including transmission and distribution lines and substations and telephone, fiber optic, and cable television systems.
300 Members
Founded in 1945

22286 Satellite Broadcasting and Communications Association
1100 17th St. NW
Ste. 1150
Washington, DC 20036

202-349-3620
800-541-5981
Fax: 202-318-2618
E-Mail: info@sbca.org
Home Page: www.sbca.com

Social Media: Facebook, Twitter, LinkedIn, YouTube

Andrew Reinsdorf, Chairman
Jeffery Blum, Vice Chairman
Joseph Widoff, Executive Director
Benjamin Rowan, Education Manager
Abdul Salam, Sr. Director of Finance & HR
Founded in 1994

22287 Satellite Industry Association

Home Page: www.sia.org
Social Media: LinkedIn

Bill Weller, Chairman
Stacy Fuller, Vice Chairman
Sam Black, Acting President
Dean Hirasawa, Communications Manager
Jennifer Williams, Office Manager
Founded in 1995

22288 Society for Technical Communication
9401 Lee Highway
Suite 300
Fairfax, VA 22031

703-522-4114
Fax: 703-522-2075
Home Page: www.stc.org
Social Media: YouTube

Katherine Brown-Hoekstra, President
Bernard Aschwanden, Vice President
Chris Lyons, Chief Executive Officer
Kimberly Kelly, Education Manager
Molly Jin, Director of Meetings and Education
Founded in 1957

22289 Society of Broadcast Engineers
9102 N Meridian St
Suite 150
Indianapolis, IN 46260-1896

317-846-9000
Fax: 317-846-9120
E-Mail: mclappe@sbe.org
Home Page: www.sbe.org
Social Media: Facebook, Twitter

Joseph Snelson, President
Jerry Massey, VP
Andrea Cummins, Treasurer
James E Leifer, Secretary

SBE provides members with the opportunity to network and share ideas and information in keeping current with the ongoing changes within the industry. Members can attend annual conferences and expositions, have access to educational opportunities and obtain professional certification.
5500 Members
Founded in 1964
Mailing list available for rent: 5700 names at $170 per M

22290 Society of Cable Telecommunications Engineers
140 Philips Rd
Exton, PA 19341-1318

610-363-6888
800-542-5040
Fax: 610-363-5898
E-Mail: scte@scte.org
Home Page: www.scte.org
Social Media: Facebook, Twitter

Mark Dzuban, President/CEO
Kim Cooney, Executive Assistant
Cathy Oakes, VP, Operations
Lori Bower, VP, National Conferences
Marty Davidson, VP, Engineering & Network Operation

A nonprofit, professional organization committed to advancing the careers of cable telecommunications professionals and serving their industry through excellence in professional development, information and standards.
15000 Members
Founded in 1969

22291 Society of Satellite Professionals
New York Information Technology Center
250 Park Ave
7th Floor
New York, NY 10177

212-809-5199
Fax: 212-825-0075
Home Page: www.sspi.org

Robert Bell, Executive Director
Louis Zacharilla, Director Development
Tamara Bond, Membership Director
Matthew Owen, Communications Manager

A nonprofit association that serves people working in the satellite industry in countries arount the world. Professional development society of the global satellite industry.
1000 Members
Founded in 1983

22292 Society of Telecommunications Consultants
13275 State Highway 89
PO Box 70
Old Station, CA 96071

530-335-7313
800-782-7670
Fax: 530-335-7360
E-Mail: stchdg@stcconsultants.org
Home Page: www.stcconsultants.org

Cathy Cimaglia, Administration Manager

The STC is an international organization of independent telecommunications and information technology consultants who serve clients in business and government.
180 Members
Founded in 1976

22293 Telecom Association
31500 Grape Street #3-307
Lake Elsinore, CA 92532

Home Page: www.telecomassociation.com
Social Media: Facebook, Twitter, LinkedIn, YouTube

Nancy Hagen Baldwin, President
Dan Baldwin, Executive Director
Kathleen Brown, Administrator
3800 Members
Founded in 1995

22294 Telecom Pioneers
1801 California Street
Suite 225
Denver, CO 80202-2932

303-571-1200
800-872-5995
Fax: 303-572-0520
E-Mail: info@telecompioneers.org
Home Page: www.telecompioneers.org

Michael Sears, Chairman
Ann Smalley, Vice Chairman
Charlene Hill, Executive Director

Formerly known as the Telephone Pioneers of America, TelecomPioneers is comprised of nearly 620,000 current and retired telecommunications employees who have joined together to make their communities better places in which to live and work
Founded in 1911

22295 Telecommunications Industry Association (TIA)
1320 N Courthouse Rd
Suite 200
Arlington, VA 22201-3834

703-907-7700
Fax: 703-907-7727
E-Mail: tia@tiaonline.org
Home Page: www.tiaonline.org
Social Media: Facebook, Twitter

Grant Seiffert, President
Andrew Kurtzman, VP & General Counsel
Mary Piper Waters, Sr. Director, Operations
Ed Mikoski, Standards/Business Development

The Telecommunications Industry Association/TIA represents providers of information, communications and entertainment technology products and services for the global marketplace through its core competencies in standards development, domestic and international policy advocacy, and facilitating member business opportunities. The association facilitates the convergence of new communications networks while working for a competitive and innovative market environment.

22296 Telework Coalition
204 E St Ne
Washington, DC 20002-4923

202-266-0046
E-Mail: info@telcoa.org
Home Page: www.telcoa.org
Social Media: Facebook, Twitter, LinkedIn

Chuck Wilsker, President
Jack Heacock, Senior VP & Co-Founder

Enabling virtual, mobile and distributed work through education, technology and legislation.

22297 The National Communication Association
1765 N Street NW
Washington, DC 20036

202-464-4622
Fax: 202-464-4600
E-Mail: inbox@natcom.org
Home Page: www.natcom.org
Social Media: Facebook, Twitter, YouTube, Blog

Carole Blair, President
Christina S. Beck, First Vice President
Stephen J. Hartnett, Second Vice President
Nancy Kidd, Executive Director
Mark Fernando, Chief Of Staff
Founded in 1914

22298 United Communications Group
9737 Washingtonian Blvd
Suite 200
Gaithersburg, MD 20878-7364

301-287-2700
Fax: 301-816-8945
E-Mail: info@ucq.com
Home Page: www.ucg.com

Todd Foreman, Partner-CEO
Nancy Becker, Partner-President
Steve McVearry, General Counsel
Jon Slabaugh, Managing Director, Business Dev
Chris Dingee, CFO

A portfolio of highly focused business and professional publishing companies providing guidance, information, analysis, data and solutions to over two million clients worldwide.
Founded in 1977

22299 United States Telecom Association
607 14th St Nw
Suite 400
Washington, DC 20005-2000
202-326-0809
Fax: 202-326-7333
E-Mail: membership@ustelecom.org
Home Page: www.ustelecom.org
Walter B McCormick Jr, President/CEO
Allison Remsen, Media Relations
Trade association representing service providers and suppliers for the telecom industry.
1200 Members

22300 Wireless Communications Alliance
1510 Page Mill Rd.
Palo Alto, CA 394304
E-Mail: promote@wca.org
Home Page: www.wca.org
Social Media: Facebook, Twitter, LinkedIn
Founded in 1993

22301 Wireless Internet Service Providers Association
1095 Hilltop Drive #317
Redding, CA 96003
866-317-2851
260-622-5776
E-Mail: billing@wispa.org
Home Page: www.wispa.org
Social Media: Facebook, Twitter, Google+, Tumblr
Chuck Hogg, President
Alex Phillips, Vice President
Rick Harnish, Executive Director
Trina Coffey, Associate Executive Director
Dennis Burgess, Secretary
800 Members

Newsletters

22302 Broadband
IGI Group
1340 Soldiers Field Road
Suite 2
Brighton, MA 02135
617-782-5033
800-323-1088
Fax: 617-782-5735
E-Mail: info@igigroup.com
Home Page: www.igigroup.com
Paul Polishuk, President/CEO
Hui Pan, Conference Director
Bev Wilson, Managing Editor
Will Ashley, IT Director/Media Manager
The Broadband Newsletter covers such subjects as: growth in broadband access such as ADSL, cable modems, satellite and fixed wireless; spending plans of the telcos and MSOs for broadband access; important applications that will drive the market; and growth of the internet based on fast internet access.
Cost: $695.00
Frequency: Monthly
Circulation: 1500
Founded in 1977
Mailing list available for rent

22303 Broadband Advertising
Kagan World Media
1 Lower Ragsdale Dr
Building One, Suite 130
Monterey, CA 93940-5749
831-624-1536
800-307-2529
Fax: 831-625-3225
E-Mail: info@kagan.com
Home Page: www.kagan.com
Tim Baskerville, President
Tom Johnson, Marketing Manager
Provides critical information about how and where advertising sales will intersect across all broadband platforms. Includes data and analysis previously published in Internet Advertising and Cable TV advertising
Cost: $1095.00
Frequency: Monthly
Founded in 1969

22304 Broadband Technology
Kagan World Media
1 Lower Ragsdale Dr
Building One Suite 130
Monterey, CA 93940-5749
831-624-1536
800-307-2529
Fax: 831-625-3225
E-Mail: info@kagan.com
Home Page: www.kagan.com
Tim Baskerville, President
Tom Johnson, Marketing Manager
Michael Schroeder, Manager
Incisive, thorough reports on deployments of bundled services, high-spped data, digital video and telephony. Analyzes and projects growth of set-top boxes, modems, switches, routers and other infrastructure. Provides data and stats on services offered and plant construction by cable, DSL, satellite, wireless and wired phone providers.
Cost: $1045.00
Frequency: Monthly
Founded in 1969

22305 Broadcast Investor
Kagan World Media
1 Lower Ragsdale Dr
Building One Suite 130
Monterey, CA 93940-5749
831-624-1536
800-307-2529
Fax: 831-625-3225
E-Mail: info@kagan.com
Home Page: www.kagan.com
Tim Baskerville, President
Tom Johnson, Marketing Manager
The market's most comprehensive sourve of current and historical data on valuations, deals and finance. Trends, forecasts, data.
Cost: $1295.00
Frequency: Monthly
Founded in 1969

22306 CBQ-Communication Booknotes Quarterly
Lawrence Erlbaum Associates
10 Industrial Avenue
Mahwah, NJ 07430
201-258-2200
Fax: 201-760-3735
E-Mail: journals@erlbaum.com
Home Page: www.leaonline.com/loi/cbq
Christopher Sterling, Editor
James K Bracken, Assistant Editor
Descriptive reviews of new publications and websites.
Cost: $350.00
Frequency: Quarterly
ISSN: 1094-8007
Founded in 1969

22307 Cable Program Investor
Kagan World Media
1 Lower Ragsdale Dr
Building One, Suite 130
Monterey, CA 93940-5749
831-624-1536
800-307-2529
Fax: 831-625-3225
E-Mail: info@kagan.com
Home Page: www.kagan.com
Tim Baskerville, President
Tom Johnson, Marketing Manager
Provides exclusive data and analysis, deal benchmarks and balance sheet assessments. It covers home shopping networks, programming trends, multichannel penetration by platform and ratings data.
Cost: $1045.00
Frequency: Monthly
Founded in 1969

22308 Cable TV Investor
Kagan World Media
1 Lower Ragsdale Dr
Building One,Suite 130
Monterey, CA 93940-5749
831-624-1536
800-307-2529
Fax: 831-625-3225
E-Mail: info@kagan.com
Home Page: www.kagan.com
Tim Baskerville, President
Tom Johnson, Marketing Manager
Provides information on the data, the deals, the valuation metrics, the distillation of information into intelligence. The information you want and need to remain competitive
Cost: $1295.00
Frequency: Monthly
Founded in 1969

22309 Cable TV Law Reporter
Kagan World Media
1 Lower Ragsdale Dr
Building One Suite 130
Monterey, CA 93940-5749
831-624-1536
800-307-2529
Fax: 831-625-3225
E-Mail: info@kagan.com
Home Page: www.kagan.com
Tim Baskerville, President
Tom Johnson, Marketing Manager
The quintessential library of cable court cases, arbitrations, legal precedents. Labeled and catalogued for easy reference. Required reading for attorneys, government regulators and top executives. Three month trial available.
Cost: $995.00
Frequency: Monthly
Founded in 1969

22310 Communication
National Technical Information Service
5285 Port Royal Rd
Springfield, VA 22161-0001
703-605-6000
Fax: 703-605-6900
E-Mail: customerservice@ntis.gov
Home Page: www.ntis.gov
Linda Davis, VP
Bruce Borzino, Director
Covers common carrier and satellite communications, information theory, graphics, policies, regulations, studies, radio and television.
Founded in 1991

22311 Communications Daily
Warren Publishing

2115 Ward Ct Nw
Washington, DC 20037-1209

202-872-9200
800-771-9202
Fax: 202-318-8350
E-Mail: info@warren-news.com
Home Page: www.warren-news.com

Brig Easley, Executive VP/Controller
Paul Warren, Chair/Publisher
Daniel Warren, President/Editor

Daily publication for the entire telecommunications indusrty.
Frequency: Daily
Circulation: 70000+
Founded in 1945

22312 Fiber Optic Sensors and Systems
IGI Group
1340 Soldiers Field Road
Suite 2
Brighton, MA 02135

617-782-5033
800-323-1088
Fax: 617 782-5735
E-Mail: info@igigroup.com
Home Page: www.igigroup.com

Paul Polishuk, CEO
Hui Pan, Conference Director
Bev Wilson, Managing Editor

Covers procurements, contract awards, requests for qualifications and proposals, reports on market studies, patents filed and awarded, new product announcements, new technology, market forecasts, reviews of important contracts, important conferences and trade shows, and Japanese and European developments.
Cost: $695.00
Frequency: Monthly
Founded in 1977

22313 Fiber Optics News
Phillips Business Information
1201 Seven Locks Road
Potomac, MD 20854-2931

301-354-1400
Fax: 301-340-0542
E-Mail: stephenh@pennwell.com
Home Page: www.lightwaveonline.com

Ellen Hamm, Publisher
Mark Mikolas, Editor
Stephen Hardy, Editorial Director

Fiber optics in the telecommunications fields.
Cost: $37.00

22314 Fiber Optics Weekly Update
IGI Group
1340 Soldiers Field Road
Suite 2
Brighton, MA 02135

617-782-5033
800-323-1088
Fax: 617-782-5735
E-Mail: info@igigroup.com
Home Page: www.igigroup.com

Paul Polishuk, CEO
Hui Pan, Conference Director
Bev Wilson, Managing Editor
Yesim Taskor, Controller

Covers procurements, new contracts, company buyouts, new products, important publications, latest news, planned projects, financial reports, market forecasts, conference and trade show reviews, joint ventures, contract awards, impact of technology, and international developments.
Cost: $695.00
Frequency: Weekly
Founded in 1977

22315 Fiber Optics and Communications
IGI Group
1340 Soldiers Field Road
Suite 2
Brighton, MA 02135

617-782-5033
800-323-1088
Fax: 617-783-5735
E-Mail: editor@igigroup.com
Home Page: www.igigroup.com

Paul Polishuk, Publisher
Hui Pan, Conference Director
Bev Wilson, Managing Editor
Yesim Taskor, Controller

Fiber optics is spreading rapidly into all major high and low tech fields. This newsletter helps relieve the pressure on busy executives by reviewing over 300 sources on a regular basis and providing only the most relevant information.
Cost: $695.00
Frequency: Monthly
Founded in 1977

22316 Fixed Wireless
IGI Group
1340 Soldiers Field Road
Suite 2
Brighton, MA 02135

617-782-5033
800-323-1088
Fax: 617-782-5735
E-Mail: editor@igigroup.com
Home Page: www.igigroup.com

Paul Polishuk, CEO
Hui Pan, Conference Director
Bev Wilson, Managing Editor
Yesim Taskor, Controller

Tracks technological breakthroughs, network developments, market trends, contacts and examines who the players are in this re-emerging market.
Cost: $695.00
Frequency: Monthly
Founded in 1977

22317 Home Networks
IGI Group
1340 Soldiers Field Road
Suite 2
Brighton, MA 02135

617-782-5033
800-323-1088
Fax: 617-782-5735
E-Mail: info@igigroup.com
Home Page: www.igigroup.com

Paul Polishuk, Publisher/CEO
Hui Pan, Conference Director
Bev Wilson, Managing Editor
Yesim Taskor, Controller

The market for home networks is driven by the 15 million homes with two or more PCs requiring interconnection and new housing units being built for tomorrow's home network environment. This newsletter keeps you connected to this rapidly developing arena of opportunities.
Cost: $695.00
Frequency: Monthly
Founded in 1977

22318 Interval
Society of Cable Telecommunications Engineers
140 Philips Road
Exton, PA 19341-1318

610-363-6888
800-542-5040
Fax: 610-363-5898
E-Mail: scte@scte.org
Home Page: www.scte.org

Mark Durbaz, President/CEO
Catty Oaks, VP

Serving the members of SCTE, Interval highlights the events of the Society and it's Chapters.
Cost: $40.00
Circulation: 15000
Founded in 1969

22319 Kagan Media Money
Kagan World Media
1 Lower Ragsdale Dr
Building One, Suite 130
Monterey, CA 93940-5749

831-624-1536
800-307-2529
Fax: 831-625-3225
E-Mail: info@kagan.com
Home Page: www.kagan.com

Tim Baskerville, President
Tom Johnson, Marketing Manager
Sandie Borthwick, Executive Director

Designed to continually focus on the essential trends and hottest topics. Each issue is jammed with leading media indicators, media merger and acquisition data, handy benchmarks and reference charts and the most thought-provoking and insightful analysis.
Cost: $1245.00
Frequency: 48 issues per y
Founded in 1969

22320 LAN Newsletter
IGI Group
1340 Soldiers Field Road
Suite 2
Brighton, MA 02135

617-782-5033
800-323-1088
Fax: 617-782-5735
E-Mail: editor@igigroup.com
Home Page: www.igigroup.com

Paul Polishuk, President/CEO
Hui Pan, Conference Director
Bev Wilson, Managing Editor
Yesim Taskor, Controller

Provides information on new developments and products in the LAN-local area network-industry. Discusses both foreign and domestic markets, including new LAN purchases and installation and management changes.
Cost: $695.00
Frequency: Monthly
Circulation: 12000
Founded in 1977

22321 LAN Product News
Worldwide Videotex
Po Box 3273
Boynton Beach, FL 33424

561-738-2276
E-Mail: markedit@juno.com
Home Page: www.wvpubs.com

Provides news and information on the computer Local Area Network (LAN) industry. Covers new hardware and software products, as well as research and development.
Cost: $25.00
Frequency: Monthly

22322 MIC/TECH Data Communications
1111 Marlkress Road
Cherry Hill, NJ 08003-2334

856-489-4310
800-678-4642
Fax: 856-424-1999

Lawrence Feidelman, Publisher
Michael Smith, Editor
Carol Bell, Advertising/Sales

Complete performance and pricing of modems, multiplexus, networks and processing.
Cost: $920.00
Frequency: Daily

22323 **Microcell Report**
150 E 2nd Street
New York, NY 10009-8400

800-883-8989
Fax: 212-366-9798

Roger Newell, Publisher

A monthly report on personal communication services including advanced digital mobile telephone applications. Covers regulatory, technical and communication aspects of PCS which includes wireless LANS and PBX.
Cost: $397.00
10 Pages
Frequency: Monthly

22324 **Microwave News**
Microwave News
PO Box 1799
New York, NY 10163-1799

212-517-2800
Fax: 212-734-0316
E-Mail: info@microwavenews.com
Home Page: www.microwavenews.com

Louis Slesin, President

Issues relating to non-ionizing radiation.
Cost: $325.00
Frequency: 6 issues per ye
Founded in 1981

22325 **Modem Users News**
Worldwide Videotex
Po Box 3273
Boynton Beach, FL 33424

561-738-2276
E-Mail: markedit@juno.com
Home Page: www.wvpubs.com

Provides the latest news and information on software, hardware, supplies and services for individuals and companies who communicate via modems in computer and/or facsimile applications. Contains detailed information, prices, and evaluations of products ranging from protable laptop PC and fax boards, to a wide range of accessible services.
Cost: $25.00
Frequency: Monthly

22326 **Newsletter**
United Communications Group
11300 Rockville Pike
#1100
Rockville, MD 20852-3012

301-816-8950
Fax: 301-816-8945
E-Mail: ccmi@ucg.com
Home Page: www.ucg.com

Sean Oberle, Publisher
Todd Foreman, CEO
Jon Slabaugh, MD
Stephanie Tamburello, HR

Editorial content provides hands-on advice on how to improve their services and reduce their overall operating expenses.
Cost: $379.00
Frequency: BiMonthly

22327 **North American Telecom Newswatch**
United Communications Group
11300 Rockville Pike
Street 1100
Rockville, MD 20852-3012

301-287-2700
Fax: 301-816-8945
E-Mail: webmaster@ucg.com
Home Page: www.ucg.com

Benny Dicecca, President
Todd Foreman, CEO
Jon Slabaugh, MD
Stephanie Tamburello, HR

The news that impacts daily business operations, including equipment updates, regulation issues, long distance and internet useage, and wireless financials.
Founded in 1977

22328 **Online Newsletter**
Information Intelligence
PO Box 31098
Phoenix, AZ 85046-1098

602-996-2283
Home Page: www.infointelligience.com

Richard Huleatt, Publisher/Editor

Covers all on-line services, suppliers, vendors, CD-ROM data bases, microcomputers and associated equipment.
Cost: $6.25
9 Pages
Frequency: 10 per year
Founded in 1980
Printed in on newsprint stock

22329 **Optical Networks and WDM**
IGI Group
1340 Soldiers Field Road
Suite 2
Brighton, MA 02135

617-782-5033
800-323-1088
Fax: 617-782-5735
E-Mail: info@igigroup.com
Home Page: www.igigroup.com

Paul Polishuk, CEO
Hui Pan, Conference Director
Bev Wilson, Managing Editor
Yesim Taskor, Controller

The WDM newsletter provides worldwide coverage of technology, markets and applications. Covers such subjects as: WDM systems, MAN applications, Gigabit networks, ATM, financials reports, premise wiring, optical amplifiers, optical networks, new products, network management, standards, optical cross connects, frame relay, competitive analysis, manufacturers strategies, optical access, regulations, tariffs, technology, broadband servies, WANs, market forecasts, BOC strategies and more.
Cost: $695.00
Frequency: Monthly
Founded in 1977

22330 **Photonics Components/Subsystems**
IGI group
1340 Soldiers Field Road
Suite 2
Brighton, MA 02135

617-782-5033
800-323-1088
Fax: 617-782-5735
E-Mail: info@igigroup.com
Home Page: www.igigroup.com

Paul Polishuk, Publisher
Hui Pan, Conference Director
Bev Wilson, Managing Editor
Yesim Taskor, Controller

Provides worldwide coverage of technology, markets, and applications. Some subjects covered include: market forecasts, product comparisons, new products, contract awards, new technologies, start-up funding, customer requirements, standards, industry trends, photonics automation, systems developments, licensing, competitive assessments, mergers and acquisitions, and pricing trends.
Cost: $695.00
Frequency: Monthly
Founded in 1977

22331 **Plastic Optical Fiber (POF)**
IGI Group
1340 Soldiers Field Road
Suite 2
Brighton, MA 02135

617-782-5033
800-323-1088
Fax: 617-782-5735
E-Mail: editor@igigroup.com
Home Page: www.igigroup.com

Paul Polishuk, CEO
Hui Pan, Conference Director
Bev Wilson, Managing Editor
Yesim Taskor, Controller

Some of the subjects covered are: applications, products, imaging, patents, technology, market research, suppliers, publications, standards, sensors, cost analyses, mergers, audio systems, lighting/illuminations, medical acquisitions, medical, market opportunities, contracts awarded, automotive, licensing opportunities, RFPs, component costs, investments and signs.
Cost: $395.00
Frequency: 6 issues per yr
Founded in 1977

22332 **SCTE Interval**
Society of Cable Telecommunications Engineers
140 Philips Road
Exton, PA 19341-1318

610-363-6888
800-542-5040
Fax: 610-363-5898
E-Mail: scte@scte.org
Home Page: www.scte.org

Mark Durbaz, President/CEO
Catty Oaks, VP

SCTE's monthly newsletter keeps members abreast of association events, activities and member accomplishments.
Cost: $40.00
Circulation: 15,000
Founded in 1969

22333 **Satellite News**
Phillips Publishing
7811 Montrose Road
Potomac, MD 20854

301-340-2100
866-599-9491
E-Mail: feedback@healthydirections.com
Home Page: www.healthydirections.com

Satellite telecommunications.
Frequency: Monthly
Founded in 1985

22334 **Society of Telecommunications Consultants Newsletter**
Society of Telecommunications Consultants
13275 State Highway 89
PO Box 70
Old Station, CA 96071

530-335-7313
800-782-7670
Fax: 530-335-7360
E-Mail: stchdq@stcconsultants.org
Home Page: www.stcconsultants.org

Cathy Cimaglia, Administrative Manager
Mark Durbaz, President/CEO
Catty Oaks, VP

A newsletter for update and informational purposes.
Frequency: Quarterly
Founded in 1969

22335 **State & Local Communications Report**
BRP Publications

1333 H Street NW
Suite 100 E
Washington, DC 20005-4746

202-312-6060
800-822-6338
Fax: 202-842-3047

Lynn Stanton, Editor
Victoria Mason, Publisher

Premier biweekly news service covering state and local communications issues. The in-depth reporting includes regular coverage of such timely topics as legislation and regulation, new state regulatory activities and important business and industry developments in the areas of telephone, data and enhanced services.
Cost: $599.00
8 Pages
Frequency: BiWeekly

22336 **State Telephone Regulation Report**
Telecom Publishing Group
1101 King Street
Suite 444
Alexandria, VA 22314-2944

703-683-4100
800-327-7205
Fax: 703-739-6490

Chris Vestal, Publisher
Herbert Kirchoff, Editor

Analysis of state telecommunications legislation.
Cost: $535.00
12 Pages
Frequency: BiWeekly
Printed in 2 colors on matte stock

22337 **Submarine Fiber Optic Communications Systems**
IGI Group
1340 Soldiers Field Road
Suite 2
Brighton, MA 02135

617-782-5033
800-323-1088
Fax: 617-782-5735
E-Mail: editor@igigroup.com
Home Page: www.igigroup.com

Paul Polishuk, Publisher
Hui Pan, Conference Director
Bev Wilson
Yesim Taskor, Controller

Provides a monthly market intelligence report on new developments in markets, technology and applications. Of special interest will be developments in optical amplifier technology, solutions, Wavelength Division Multiplexing and how these are having an impact on the Submarine Fiber Optic business
Cost: $695.00
Frequency: Monthly
Founded in 1977

22338 **TR Wireless News**
BRP Publications
1333 H Street NW
Suite 100 E
Washington, DC 20005-4707

202-312-6060
800 822-6338
Fax: 202-842-3047

Victoria Mason, Publisher
Andrew Kreig, President

Montiors regulatory, technological and market developments in the rapidly expanding wireless communications industry. It covers new services, corporate activity, and licensing and specturm allocation in the areas of personal communication services.
Cost: $597.00
Frequency: BiWeekly

22339 **TV Program Investor**
Kagan World Media
1 Lower Ragsdale Dr
Building One, Suite 130
Monterey, CA 93940-5749

831-624-1536
800-307-2529
Fax: 831-625-3225
E-Mail: info@kagan.com
Home Page: www.kagan.com

Tim Baskerville, President
Tom Johnson, Marketing Manager

More than just a newsletter, practically a seminar on how much programs cost and what they are worth. Exclusive spreadsheets with estimates of what goes between the commercials. Three month trial available.
Cost: $895.00
Frequency: Monthly
Founded in 1969

22340 **Telco Competition Report**
BRP Publications
1333 H Street NW
Suite 100 E
Washington, DC 20005-4746

202-312-6060
800-822-6338
Fax: 202-842-3047

Victoria Mason, Publisher
Brian Hammond, Editor

Provides important information on events and issues surrounding the $90 billion local exchange markets. Each issues covers the continuing regulatory, financial, strategic and technological ramifications of local exchange competition, including the second and third-tier cities being targeted by competitions and strategies for success.
Cost: $596.00
20 Pages
Frequency: BiWeekly

22341 **Tele-Service News**
Worldwide Videotex
Po Box 3273
Boynton Beach, FL 33424

561-738-2276
E-Mail: markedit@juno.com
Home Page: www.wvpubs.com

Provides news and information on the telephone industry. Covers services, products, research and development and business plans of RBOCs (Regional Bell Operating Companies), long distance carriers, and independent vendors.
Cost: $25.00
Frequency: Monthly

22342 **Telecom Daily Lead from US Telecom Association**
SmartBrief
1401 H Street
N.W, Suite 600
Washington, DC 20005

202-326-7300
Fax: 202-326-7333
E-Mail: webmaster@smartbrief.com
Home Page: www.dailylead.com/usta

Portia Krebs, VP Communications
Jason Ross, Lead Editor
Eric Hoffman, Sales Account Director

Free daily newsbriefing, delivered by e-mail, that covers the telecom industry's top news stories.
Frequency: Daily
Circulation: 11000

22343 **Telecom Outlook**
Market Intelligence Research Company
2525 Charleston Road
Mountain View, CA 94043-1626
Wyman Bravard, Publisher

Reports on the telecommunications industry.
Frequency: Monthly

22344 **Telecom Standards**
IGI Group
1340 Soldiers Field Road
Suite 2
Brighton, MA 02135

617-782-5033
800-323-1088
Fax: 617-782-5735
E-Mail: editor@igigroup.com
Home Page: www.igigroup.com

Paul Polishuk, President/CEO
Hui Pan, Conference Director
Bev Wilson, Managing Editor
Yesim Taskor, Controller

Provides coverage of standards activities around the world, schedules of standards meetings, the availablity of standards, and how to obtain standards, minutes of standards meetings and drafts of standards.
Cost: $695.00
Frequency: Monthly
Founded in 1977

22345 **Telecommunications Mergers and Acquisitions**
IGI group
1340 Soldiers Field Road
Suite 2
Brighton, MA 02135

617-782-5033
800-323-1088
Fax: 617-782-5735
E-Mail: editor@igigroup.com
Home Page: www.igigroup.com

Paul Polishuk, President/CEO
Hui Pan, Conference Director
Bev Wilson, Managing Editor
Yesim Taskor, Controller

Covers worldwide developments in the telecommunications mergers and acquisitions. In addition to reporting to these activities, the newsletter analyzes potential merger and acquisition candidates, summarizes in an easy-to-read form trends by different companies and industry requirements.
Cost: $695.00
Frequency: Monthly
Founded in 1977

22346 **Telecommunications Reports International**
BRP Publications
111 Eighth Avenue
7th Floor
New York, NY 10011-4707

212-771-0600
800-234-1660
Fax: 212-771-0885
E-Mail: jrohaly@aspenpublishers.com
Home Page: www.aspenpublishers.com

Andrew Jacobson, Publisher
George Brandon, Editor
Jim Monahan, President
Richard H Kravitz, Execitive VP

International telecom policy and trade issues, global services, satellites, tariffs and financial developments.
Cost: $1789.00
Frequency: 24 issues per y

22347 **Telemarketing Update**
Prosperity & Profits Unlimited

PO Box 416
Denver, CO 80201-0416

303-573-5564

AC Doyle, Publisher

Telemarketing script presentation suggestions and ideas.
Cost: $200.00
8 Pages
Frequency: Annual
Circulation: 2,000
Printed in on matte stock

22348 Telemarketing Update-Catering Service Business Script Presentations
Prosperity & Profits Unlimited
PO Box 416
Denver, CO 80201-0416

303-573-5564

A Doyle, Editor

Catering service telemarketing script presentations.
Cost: $19.95
10 Pages
Frequency: Irregular
Circulation: 2,100
Founded in 1990
Printed in one color on matte stock

22349 VoiceNews
Stoneridge Technical Services
PO Box 1891
Rockville, MD 20849-1891

301-424-0114
Fax: 301-424-8971

William Creitz, Publisher/Editor

Covers voice technology for telecommunications and office automation: voice messaging, voice response, speech recognition, speech synthesis.
Cost: $25.00

22350 Why Not An Answering Service?
Prosperity & Profits Unlimited
PO Box 416
Denver, CO 80201-0416

303-573-5564

A Doyle, Editor

Offers information and ideas on telephone answering service possibilities.
Cost: $29.95
73 Pages
Frequency: Every Five Years
Circulation: 5,000
Founded in 1989
Printed in on matte stock

22351 Wireless Market Stats
Kagan World Media
1 Lower Ragsdale Dr
Building One Suite 130
Monterey, CA 93940-5749

831-624-1536
800-307-2529
Fax: 831-625-3225
E-Mail: info@kagan.com
Home Page: www.kagan.com

Tim Baskerville, President
Tom Johnson, Marketing Manager

In-depth analysis of metropolitan and rural cellular market efficiency, plus operating statistics, private deal market data, economic and demographic data for narrowband and broadband PCS, ESMR, paging and more.
Cost: $1095.00
Frequency: Monthly
Founded in 1969

22352 Wireless Satellite and Broadcasting
IGI Group
1340 Soldiers Field Road
Suite 2
Brighton, MA 02135

617-782-5033
800-323-1088
Fax: 617-782-5735
E-Mail: editor@igigroup.com
Home Page: www.igigroup.com

Paul Polishuk, Publisher
Hui Pan, Conference Director
Bev Wilson, Managing Editor

Subjects covered include: market opportunities, technology, international developments, regulation/policy, standards, applications, procurements, PCN, market forecasts, new products, mergers/acquisitions, joint ventures and more.
Cost: $695.00
Frequency: Monthly
Founded in 1977

22353 Wireless Telecom Investor
Kagan World Media
1 Lower Ragsdale Dr
Building One, Suite 130
Monterey, CA 93940-5749

831-624-1536
800-307-2529
Fax: 831-625-3225
E-Mail: info@kagan.com
Home Page: www.kagan.com

Tim Baskerville, President
Tom Johnson, Marketing Manager

Exclusive analysis of private and public values of wireless telecommunications companies, including cellular telephone, ESMR and PCS. Exclusive databases of subscribers, market penetrations, market potential, industry growth. Catching super-fast growth in a capsule.
Cost: $1095.00
Frequency: Monthly
Founded in 1969

22354 Wireless Week
Chilton Company
600 S Cherry Street
Suite 400
Denver, CO 80246-1706

303-393-7449
Fax: 303-399-2034

Tom Brooksher, Publisher
Judith Lockwood, Editor

Covers the wireless telecommunications industry.
Circulation: 32,000

22355 Worldwide Videotex Update
Worldwide Videotex
Po Box 3273
Boynton Beach, FL 33424

561-738-2276
E-Mail: markedit@juno.com
Home Page: www.wvpubs.com

Reports news and information on videotex, The Internet, online services, electronic mail, satellite communications and television related technologies, such as teleconferencing and teletext.
Cost: $25.00
Frequency: Monthly

22356 XDSL
IGI Group
1340 Soldiers Field Road
Suite 2
Boston, MA 02135

617-782-5033
800-323-1088
Fax: 617-782-5735
E-Mail: bmark@igigroup.com
Home Page: www.igigroup.com

Paul Polishuk, President/CEO
Hui Panb, Conference Director
Bev Wilson, Managing Editor

Subjects covered include: field trials, applicatins, competition ffrom cable and satellite, new products, Telco plans, fiber optics, market forecasts, techology developments, wireless, major player strategies, cable modems, ISDN and more.
Cost: $695.00
Frequency: Monthly
Founded in 1977

Magazines & Journals

22357 ACUTA Journal of Communications Technology in Higher Education
ACUTA
152 W Zandale Drive
Suite 200
Lexington, KY 40503-2486

859-278-3338
Fax: 859-278-3268
E-Mail: pscott@acuta.org
Home Page: www.acuta.org
Social Media: Facebook

Pat Scott, Editor
Tamara Closs, President
Jerry A Simmer, Director
Corinne Harrison, Executive Officer
Tom Chappel, Finance & Administration

Journal is distributed to telecom, information management professionals at colleges and universities, along with industry professionals with products and services for the higher education vertical market.
Cost: $80.00
48 Pages
Frequency: Quarterly
Circulation: 2320
ISSN: 1097-8658
Founded in 1997
Mailing list available for rent: 2,300 names
Printed in 4 colors on matte stock

22358 ARRL The National Association for Amateur Radio
American Radio Relay League
225 Main St
Newington, CT 06111

860-594-0200
888-277-5289
Fax: 860-594-0259
E-Mail: webmaster@arrl.org
Home Page: www.arrl.org

David Sumner, CEO
Kay Craigie, President
Bob Inderbitzen, Marketing Manager

Geared at the IRF and amatuer radio operators industry, provides information on communications theory and technical advances in design and construction. The official journal of the American Radio Relay League.
Cost: $24.00
156M Members
Frequency: Monthly
Circulation: 146000
Founded in 1914

22359 America's Network
Questex Media Group
201 Sandpointe Ave
Suite 500
Santa Ana, CA 92707-8716

714-338-6700
800-854-3112

Fax: 714-513-8481
E-Mail: psemple@advanstar.com
Home Page: www.americasnetwork.com

Paul Semple, Publisher
Bill Pettit, National Sales Director

Independent reporting and business analysis of telecommunications technologies for today's public network.
Cost: $100.00
Frequency: Monthly
Circulation: 60,006

22360 Audiotex Update
Worldwide Videotex
PO Box 3273
Boynton Beach, FL 33424-3273

561-738-2276
E-Mail: markedit@juno.com
Home Page: www.wvpubs.com

Mark E Wright, Editor

Provides the latest news and infromation about the audiotex industry, including voice processing information, products, services, as well as research and development.
Cost: $165.00
Frequency: Monthly
Founded in 1981

22361 B/OSS
Virgo Publishing LLC
3300 N Central Ave
Suite 300
Phoenix, AZ 85012-2532

480-675-9925
Fax: 480-990-0819
E-Mail: mikes@vpico.com
Home Page: www.vpico.com
Social Media: Facebook, Twitter, LinkedIn

Jenny Bolton, President
John Siefert, CEO
Kelly Ridley, VP
Troy Bix, Publisher

Source for news and analysis for telecommunications support systems as they take a leading role in creating and supporting service differentiation in the communications marketplace.
Circulation: 20000
Founded in 1986
Printed in on glossy stock

22362 Business Communications Review
BCR Enterprises
Ste 200
3025 Highland Pkwy
Downers Grove, IL 60515-5668

630-986-1432
800-227-1234
Fax: 630-323-5324
Home Page: www.bcr.com

Fred Knight, Publisher

Offers a complete package of the latest information for persons associated with the communications industry.
Cost: $45.00
80 Pages
Frequency: Monthly
Founded in 1971

22363 CTI the Authority on Computer, Internet, & Network Telephony
Technology Marketing Corporation
1 Technology Plz
Norwalk, CT 06854-1936

203-852-6800
800-243-6002
Fax: 203-853-2845
E-Mail: ctipress@tmcnet.com
Home Page: www.tmcnet.com
Social Media: Facebook, Twitter

Rich Tehrani, CEO
Anthony Graffeo, National Advertising Sales Manager
Greg Galitzine, Editorial Director

Provides tutorials, application stories, and new product listings and reviews, as well as service information. Emphasizes furthering the development, implementation and use of CTI technology.
Frequency: Monthly
Circulation: 50256
Founded in 1998

22364 Cabling Business
Cabling Publications
12035 Shiloh Rd
Suite 350
Dallas, TX 75228-1549

214-322-8171
Fax: 214-319-6077
E-Mail: russell@cablingbusiness.com
Home Page: www.cablingbusiness.com
Social Media: Facebook, Twitter

Stephen Paulov, President
Christy Sheeran, Business Manager
Rita Paulov, Senior Sales Associate
David Deal, Webmaster
Margaret Patterson, Managing Editor

New product information, troubleshooting hints, and information on installation and repair.
Frequency: Monthly
Circulation: 24070
Mailing list available for rent

22365 Cabling Installation & Maintenance
PennWell Publishing Company
1421 S Sheridan Rd
Tulsa, OK 74112-6619

918-831-9421
800-331-4483
Fax: 918-831-9476
E-Mail: patrick@pennwell.com
Home Page: www.pennwell.com

Robert Biolchini, President
Steve Smith, Executive Editor

Emphasizes the problem solving aspects of cable installation in telecommunications, data, and video systems.
Frequency: Monthly
Circulation: 23604
Founded in 1993

22366 Call Center Magazine
Miller Freeman Publications
11 Est 19th Street
3rd Floor
New York, NY 10011

212-600-3000
800-672-6111
Fax: 212-691-1191
E-Mail: msteiger@cmp.com
Home Page: www.callcentermagazine.com

Keith Dawson, Editor
Max Steiger, Sales Manager

Dedicated to providing in-depth and unbiased product and strategic information for call center executives.
Frequency: Monthly
Circulation: 32904

22367 Communication Theory
International Communication Association
U de Montreal, Department de Communication
1500 21st Street
Washington, DC 20026

202-955-1444
Fax: 202-955-1448
E-Mail: communicationtheory@umontreal.ca.
Home Page: www.icahdq.org
Social Media: Facebook, Twitter, LinkedIn

Francois Cooren, Editor

Publishes research articles, theoretical essays, and reviews on topics of broad theoretical interest from across the range of communication studies. Recognizes that approaches to theory develpment and explication are diverse.
Mailing list available for rent

22368 Communication Yearbook
International Communication Association
Ohio University, School of Communication Study
1501 21st Street
Washington, DC 20026

202-955-1445
Fax: 202-955-1449
E-Mail: communicationtheory@umontreal.ca.
Home Page: www.icahdq.org
Social Media: Facebook, Twitter, LinkedIn

Dr Christina S. Beck, Editor

Features state-of-the discipline literature reviews of communication research. Highlights reviews of research exploring communication concepts that span traditional 'division' divides, issues of central importance to the accomplishment of communication in a variety of contexts and for diverse communicators throughout the world.
Founded in 1913
Mailing list available for rent

22369 Communications Billing Report
Telecommunications Reports International
76 9th Ave. 7th fl
#100-E
Washington, NY 10011

21- 77- 071
Fax: 212-771-0732
E-Mail: joseph.rohaly@wolterskluwer.com
Home Page: www.tr.com
Social Media: Facebook, Twitter, LinkedIn

Victoria Mason, Editor-in-Chief

Content provides hard-to-find facts on such issues as developing internet electronic payment systems, keeping on top of new outsourcing opportunities, enhancing customer care and back office functions and making the most of new software developments.
Cost: $765.00
Frequency: BiWeekly

22370 Communications Crossroads
United States Telecom Association
1401 H St NW
Suite 600
Washington, DC 20005-2110

202-326-7300
Fax: 202-326-7333
E-Mail: editor@usta.org
Home Page: www.usta.org
Social Media: Facebook, Twitter, LinkedIn, You Tube

Walter Mc Kormick, President
James Cooconi, VP
Robert Curry, Tresurer
Robert Hunt, Secretary

Dedicated to the success stories, investment opportunities and industry events that herald the future of small and rural carriers.
Cost: $60.00
Circulation: 3500
Founded in 2006

22371 Enterprise Wireless Magazine
Enterprise Wireless Association

8484 Westpark Drive
Suite 630
McLean, VA 22102-5117

703-528-5115
800-482-8282
Fax: 703-524-1074
E-Mail: customerservice@enterprisewireless.org
Home Page: www.enterprisewireless.org
Social Media: Facebook, Twitter

Mark Crosby, President/CEO
Andre Cote, Senior VP
Ila Dudley, VP Spectrum Management
Ron Franklin, VP Membership/Business Development

Covers how wireless meets the operational needs of business and industrial enterprise users. Used extensivley throughout the year by your prospects to stay informed of technical, industry and association information, and as a comprehensive buyers' guide for the products and services they use most often.
Frequency: Quarterly

22372 Global Telephony
Primedia
3585 Engineering Drive
Suite 100
Norcross,, GA 30092

678-421-3000
800-216-1423
Fax: 312-595-0295
E-Mail: mallen@primedia.com
Home Page: www.primediabusiness.com
Social Media: Facebook, Twitter, LinkedIn, You Tube

Larry Lannon, Publisher
Carol Wilson, Editor

Telephony delivers timely and intelligent coverage of the news, technologies and business strategies driving the industry.
Frequency: 24/Yr
Circulation: 63,500

22373 Handbooks of Communication Series
International Communication Association
Dept of Comm, University of Colorado at Boulder
1500 21st Street
Washington, DC 20026

202-955-1444
Fax: 202-955-1448
E-Mail: communicationtheory@umontreal.ca.
Home Page: www.icahdq.org
Social Media: Facebook, Twitter, LinkedIn

Robert T Craig, Editor
Linda Bathgate, Senior Editor

Publishes research articles, theoretical essays, and reviews on topics of broad theoretical interest from across the range of communication studies. Recognizes that approaches to theory develpment and explication are diverse.
Mailing list available for rent

22374 Human Communication Research
International Communication Association
Dept of Communication Arts & Science,234 Sparks
1500 21st Street
Washington, DC 20026

202-955-1444
Fax: 202-955-1448
E-Mail: communicationtheory@umontreal.ca.
Home Page: www.icahdq.org
Social Media: Facebook, Twitter, LinkedIn

James P Dillard, Editor

Publishes research articles, theoretical essays, and reviews on topics of broad theoretical interest from across the range of communication studies. Recognizes that approaches to theory develpment and explication are diverse.
Frequency: Quarterly
Mailing list available for rent

22375 ICA Communique
International Communications Association
1500 21st St NW
1500 21st Street
Washington, DC 20026

202-955-1444
Fax: 202-955-1448
E-Mail: communicationtheory@umontreal.ca.
Home Page: www.icahdq.org
Social Media: Facebook, Twitter, LinkedIn

M Haley, Executive Director

Publishes research articles, theoretical essays, and reviews on topics of broad theoretical interest from across the range of communication studies. Recognizes that approaches to theory develpment and explication are diverse.
Cost: $135.00
Frequency: 10/Year
Mailing list available for rent

22376 IEEE Communications Magazine
Institute of Electrical & Electronics Engineers
3 Park Ave
Suite 17
New York, NY 10016-5997

212-419-7900
Fax: 212-752-4929
E-Mail: publications@comsoc.org
Home Page: www.ieee.org
Social Media: Facebook, Twitter, LinkedIn, You Tube

Daniel J Senese, CEO
Jack Howell, Executive Director

Written in tutorial applications-driven style by the industry's leading experts. IEEE Communications Magazine delivers usable information on the latest international coverage of current issues and advances in key areas.
Cost: $ 20.00
Frequency: Monthly
Circulation: 43832

22377 IEEE Network
IEEE Operations Center
PO Box 1331
Piscataway, NJ 08855-1331

732-981-0060
Fax: 732-981-1721
E-Mail: publications@comsoc.org
Home Page: www.cosmoc.org

John Vig, CEO

The magazine of Global Internetworking provides the most current information for communications professionals involved with the interconnection of computing systems.
Frequency: Bi-Monthly

22378 Intele-Card News
Quality Publishing
523 N Sam Houston Parkway E
Suite 300
Houston, TX 77060

281-272-2744
800-792-6397
Fax: 281-847-5752
E-Mail: info@intelecard.com
Home Page: www.intelecard.com

Theresa Ward, Editor-in-Chief
Jo Ann Davy, Managing Editor
Laurette Veres, Owner

Reports on news and events impacting the business of telephone cards, identifies significant trends and profiles industry newsmakers.
Frequency: Monthly
Circulation: 12000
Founded in 1995

22379 Journal of Communication
International Communication Association
Department of Communication-101 Burton Hall
University of Oklahoma
Norman, OK 73019

405-325-9503
E-Mail: joc@ou.edu
Home Page: www.icahdq.org

Michael Pfau, Editor

A general forum for communication scholarship and publishes articles and book reviews examining a broad range of issues in communication theory and research. Publishes the best available scholarship on all aspects of communication.

22380 Journal of Computer-Mediated Communication
International Communication Association
1500 21st Street
Washington, DC 20026

202-955-1444
Fax: 202-955-1448
E-Mail: communicationtheory@umontreal.ca.
Home Page: jcmc.indiana.edu
Social Media: Facebook, Twitter, LinkedIn

Susan C Herring, Editor

Publishes research articles, theoretical essays, and reviews on topics of broad theoretical interest from across the range of communication studies. Recognizes that approaches to theory develpment and explication are diverse.
Mailing list available for rent

22381 Lightwave
PennWell Publishing Company
1421 S Sheridan Rd
Tulsa, OK 74112-6619

918-831-9421
800-331-4483
Fax: 918-831-9476
E-Mail: stephenh@pennwell.com
Home Page: www.pennwell.com

Robert Biolchini, President
Carrie Meadows, Managing Editor
Meghan Fuller, Senior News Editor
Matt Vincent, Associate Editor/Web Editor

An international journal of fiber optics that covers all applications of the technology in telecommunications, data communications, broadcast and cable TV and specialized military applications.
Cost: $137.00
224 Pages
Frequency: Monthly
ISSN: 0741-5834
Founded in 1910
Printed in 4 colors on matte stock

22382 Locating, Testing and Repairing
Stober Research and Communications
PO Box 517
McHenry, IL 60051

815-385-6123
Fax: 815-385-7151
Home Page: www.ltrmag.com
Social Media: Facebook, Twitter

L Jack Stober, Publisher

Information on copper and fiber optic sets available for telecommunication applications, as well as listings of companies and categories of this equipment. Regular departments contain fault locating and test equipment tips, a new

product showcase and a look at new industry literature.
Cost: $100.00
Frequency: Quarterly
Circulation: 27355
Founded in 1998

22383 Mobile Communication Business
Phillips Business Information
7811 Montrose Road
Potomac, MD 20854

301-340-2100
E-Mail: feedback@healthydirections.com
Home Page: www.healthydirections.com
Social Media: Facebook, Twitter

Don Steele, Editor

Offers information and the latest technological advances in telecommunications.
Frequency: Monthly
Founded in 1985

22384 Multimedia Telecommunication News
Stoneridge Technical Services
PO Box 1891
Rockville, MD 20849-1891

301-424-0114
Fax: 301-424-8971
E-Mail: techwriter@stoneridgetech.com
Home Page: www.stoneridgetech.com

William W Creitz, Editor

Focuses on new products, applications, technological developments, markets and company activites.
Frequency: Monthly

22385 NTCA Exchange
National Telephone Cooperative Association
4121 Wilson Blvd
Suite 1000
Arlington, VA 22203-4145

703-351-2000
Fax: 703-351-2001
Home Page: www.ntca.org

Michael E Brunner, CEO

Bi-monthly newsletter examining association and member news, including profiles, business tips and member updates.
Cost: $15.00
Frequency: Bi-Monthly
Circulation: 5100
Founded in 1980

22386 Network Magazine
CMP Media
245 Blackfriars Road
Manhasset, NY 11030

516-562-5000
866-880-8219
Fax: 516-562-7013
E-Mail: cmp@cmp.com
Home Page: www.cmp.com

Art Wittmann, Editor
Paula McGinlinchey, Publisher

Network Magazine serves communications carriers, communications service providers including interexchange/PTT's/long distance carriers, business services (non-computer) and other industry organizations.
Cost: $175.00
162 Pages
Frequency: Monthly
Circulation: 125000
ISSN: 1093-8001
Founded in 1986
Printed in 4 colors on matte stock

22387 Networks Update
Worldwide Videotex
Po Box 3273
Boynton Beach, FL 33424

561-738-2276
E-Mail: markedit@juno.com
Home Page: www.wvpubs.com
Social Media: Facebook, Twitter

Provides the latest news and information about the computer network industry. This includes national, international, public, private, and military network products, services, companies, marketing strategies, and research and development.
Cost: $25.00
Frequency: Monthly

22388 Opastco Roundtable
OPASTCO
2020 K Street
Suite 700
Washington, DC 20006

202-659-5990
Fax: 202-659-4619
E-Mail: roundtable@opastco.org
Home Page: www.opastco.org

John Rose, President
Caurey Watson, Administrative Services Manager

Provides practical, how-to information that small local exchange carriers can use in their day-to-day operations, as well as plain English explanations of industry issues and technologies.
Frequency: BiMonthly

22389 Outside Plant
Practical Communications
220 N Smith St
Suite 228
Palatine, IL 60067-2488

847-202-4683
Fax: 847-639-9542
E-Mail: sharon@ospmag.com
Home Page: www.ospmag.com

Sharon Stober, VP/Editorial Director
Karen Adolphson, Managing Editor
Mary Beth Koelling, Executive Director Sales/Marketing

Magazine for telecom outside plant professionals. Reaches ASP engineers, planners, managers and technicians in Bell and independent phone companies.
Cost: $30.00
100 Pages
Frequency: Monthly
Circulation: 25000
Founded in 1983

22390 POINT
Direct Marketing Association
1120 Avenue of the Americas
New York, NY 10036-6713

212-768-7277
Fax: 212-768-4547
Home Page: www.the-dma.org
Social Media: Facebook, Twitter

John A. Greco Jr, President & CEO

DMA's digital magazine.

22391 Pen Computing Magazine
Pen Computing Publishing Office
120 Bethpage Road
Suite 300
Hicksville, NY 11801

516-433-8725
Fax: 516-433-8724
E-Mail: cb@pencomputing.com
Home Page: www.pencomputing.com

Howard Borgen, Publisher
Lisa Krebs, VP Advertising
Wayne Laslo, Advertising Manager
Conrad H Blickenstorfer, Editor-in-Chief
David MacNeill, Executive Editor

Bi-Monthly print journal of pen-based and mobile computing. Hardware and software reviews, expert opinions, feature articles, case studies, how-to, industry news, technical primers and more.
Cost: $18.00
Frequency: Bi-Monthly
Circulation: 79515
Founded in 1993

22392 Politically Direct
Direct Marketing Association
1120 Avenue of the Americas
New York, NY 10036-6700

212-768-7277
Fax: 212-302-6714
E-Mail: customerservice@the-dma.org
Home Page: www.the-dma.org

Lawrence M Kimmel, CEO

Published both in print and digital, this newsletter on DMA advocacy efforts keeps DMA members informed and involved in the politics and policies that impact them today and ahead of the curve on developments that will affect them tomorrow.
Frequency: Quarterly

22393 RCR Wireless News
Crain Communications
1746 Cole Blvd
Suite 150
Lakewood, CO 80401-3208

303-733-2500
888-909-9111
Fax: 303-733-9941
E-Mail: subs@crain.com
Home Page: www.crain.com

Mary Pemberton, Marketing
Tracy Ford, Associate Publisher/Editor
Dan Meyer, Managing Editor
Pete Racelis, President

News and analysis of the wireless communications industry.
Cost: $69.00
Frequency: Weekly
Circulation: 65000
Founded in 1981
Printed in on matte stock

22394 Satellite Business News
Satellite Business News
1990 M Street NW
Suite 510
Washington, DC 20036-3102

202-785-0505
Fax: 202-785-9291
E-Mail: general.mail@satbiznews.com
Home Page: www.satbiznews.com

Bob Scherman, Publisher
Jeffrey Williams, Managing Editor
Charlie Ergen, CEO/President

Up-to-date news on satellite television industry, upcoming events, and new technology for the industry.
Cost: $44.75
Frequency: Bi-annually
Circulation: 565700
Founded in 1983

22395 Satellite News
Phillips Business Information
6181 Executive Blvd
Rockville, MD 20852-3901

301-881-7516
866-279-1930
Fax: 301-424-2709

E-Mail: information@phillips.com
Home Page: www.phillips.com

Donald Phelps, President
Robert Phillips, CEO

Information on satellite launches, companies rebounding from losses, blows to competitors and regulatory issues.
Frequency: Weekly
Circulation: 18000
Founded in 1974

22396 Satellite Week
Warren Publishing
2115 Ward Ct NW
Washington, DC 20037-1209

202-872-9200
800-771-9202
Fax: 202-318-8350
E-Mail: info@warren-news.com
Home Page: www.warren-news.com

Brig Easley, Executive VP
Paul Warren, Chair/Publisher
Daniel Warren, President/Editor

The definitive weekly source for fast-breaking, international news on space communications policy, regularion, technology and business. Offers up-to-date, comprehensive reports on new technologies, notices of international advances, details about regulation and deregularion, satellite marketplace intelligence, news of DBS developments, and continuous coverage of what industry leaders are doing and saying.
Frequency: Weekly
Founded in 1945

22397 Sound & Communications
Testa Communications
25 Willowdale Avenue
Port Washington, NY 11050-3779

516-767-2500
800-937-7678
Fax: 516-767-9335
E-Mail: testa@testa.com
Home Page: www.testacommunications.com
Social Media: Facebook, Twitter

Vincent P Testa, President
David A. Silverman, Editor

Covers sound, display, security and multimedia systems, also theory and applications.
Frequency: Monthly
Circulation: 22500
Founded in 1955

22398 Sound & Video Contractor
Primedia
PO Box 12914
Overland Park, KS 66282

913-341-1300
Fax: 913-967-1903
E-Mail: mjohnson@premediabusiness.com
Home Page: www.svconline.com

Mark Johnson, Editor
Trevor Boyer, Associate Editor
Trevor Boyer, Associate Editor

Contains information on sound systems, video display, security, CCTV, home theater, and automation. Delivers in depth instruction and examples of successful installations, fundamental acoustical and video theory and news on new technologies eaffecting the systems contracting business.
Cost: $35.00
Frequency: Monthly
Circulation: 21,000
Founded in 1983
Mailing list available for rent: 20,500 names at $110 per M

22399 Sys Admin
CMP Media
303 Second Street
Suite 200
Lawrence, KS 94107

415-947-6000
Fax: 785-841-2047
E-Mail: aankerholz@cmp.com
Home Page: www.sysadminmag.com

Amber Ankerhola
Deirdre Blake, MD

SYS ADMIN serves the Unix and Linux system administration market.
Cost: $39.00
100 Pages
Frequency: Monthly
Founded in 1992
Printed in on glossy stock

22400 TELEconference Magazine
Applied Business Telecommunications
201 Sandpoint Ave
Suite 600
Santa Ana, CA 92707-8700

714-513-8400
800-854-3112
Fax: 714-513-8680
Home Page: www.advanstar.com

Keith Gallagher, Publisher
Paul DeVeaux, Editor

Devoted to the field of teleconferencing and contains in-depth articles to provide updates on audio/graphic and video teleconferencing applications, trends and developments.
Cost: $10.00
Circulation: 15000
Founded in 1992

22401 Telecommunications
Horizon House Publications
685 Canton St
Norwood, MA 02062-2608

781-762-1319
Fax: 781-769-5037
E-Mail: editorial@telecommagazine.com
Home Page: www.horizonhouse.com

Charles A Ayotte, CEO
Robert Bass, Production Manager
Bob Wallace, Editor
William Harrison, Manager
William Bassy, President

Communication technology and market developments for users, service providers and manufacturers worldwide.
Frequency: Monthly
Circulation: 80854
Founded in 1960

22402 Telephone IP News
Worldwide Videotex
Po Box 3273
Boynton Beach, FL 33424

561-738-2276
E-Mail: markedit@juno.com
Home Page: www.wvpubs.com

Provides news and information concerning the information provider (IP) industry for telephone services and two-way paging and wireless information services. Reports on new products available to providers and monitors public service commission rulings as they aplly to information services.
Cost: $25.00
Frequency: Monthly

22403 Telephony
Telephony Division
One IBM Plaza
Suite 2300
Chicago, IL 10151

312-595-1080
Fax: 312-595-0296
E-Mail: telephony@prismb2b.com
Home Page: www.primedia.com

Mark Hickey, Publisher
Dan O'Shea, Editor-in-Chief
Kim Brower, Marketing Manager

Written for professionals involved in management, construction, maintenance and marketing of modern telecommunication systems. Focus is on new, technical advances, filed applications and management techniques.
Cost: $3.00
Frequency: Weekly
Circulation: 59000
Founded in 1989

22404 VON
Virgo Publishing LLC
3300 N Central Ave
Suite 300
Phoenix, AZ 85012-2532

480-675-9925
Fax: 480-990-0819
E-Mail: mikes@vpico.com
Home Page: www.vpico.com
Social Media: Facebook, Twitter

Jenny Bolton, President

Global information on IP Communications strategy.
Mailing list available for rent: 22000+ names at $var per M

22405 Wire Journal International
Wire Association International
1570 Boston Post Road
PO Box 578
Guilford, CT 06437

203-453-2777
Fax: 203-453-8384
E-Mail: mmarselli@wirenet.org
Home Page: www.wirenet.org
Social Media: Facebook, Twitter

Brian A Bouvier, President
Steven J Fetteroll, Executive Director
Mark A Marselli, Editor-in-Chief
Janice E Swindells, Director of Marketing Services
Robert J Xeller, Director Sales

The leading technical publication for the wire and cable industry. Written for executives, engineers, technical and sales professionals, and purchasing agents engaged in the manufacture of ferrous and nonferrous wire and cable; electrical wire and cable; fiber optic cable; and formed and fabricated wire products.
Frequency: Monthly
Circulation: 13434
Founded in 1930
Printed in 4 colors on glossy stock

22406 Worldwide Telecom
Worldwide Videotex
Po Box 3273
Boynton Beach, FL 33424

561-738-2276
E-Mail: markedit@juno.com
Home Page: www.wvpubs.com
Social Media: Facebook, Twitter

Provides the latest news and information on international telecommunication products, services, and contracts. The emphasis is on U.S. telecommunications companies doing business in foreign markets and on products with a potential market overseas.
Cost: $25.00
Frequency: Monthly

22407 Yellow Pages Industry Sourcebook
SIMBA Information

60 Long Ridge Rd
Suite 300
Stamford, CT 06902-1841
203-325-8193
Fax: 203-325-8915
E-Mail: info@simbanet.com
Home Page: www.simbanet.com

Linda Kopp, Publisher
Kathy Mickey, Managing Editor

Lists key officers, revenues, leading books, major accounts, sales offices and suppliers for more than 1500 firms involved in yellow pages publishing.
Cost: $99.00

22408 xchange
Virgo Publishing LLC
3300 N Central Ave
Suite 300
Phoenix, AZ 85012-2532

480-675-9925
Fax: 480-990-0819
E-Mail: mikes@vpico.com
Home Page: www.vpico.com

Jenny Bolton, President
John Siefert, CEO
Kelly Ridley, VP
Katherine Clements, Publisher

Provides in-depth, executive-level news and analysis regarding strategy, technology and regulation to help communications service providers create new revenue, lower costs and achieve sustainable business models.
Frequency: Annual+
Circulation: 35,003
Founded in 1996

Trade Shows

22409 AFCEA TechNet Asia-Pacific
Armed Forces Communications and Electronics Assn
4400 Fair Lakes Court
Fairfax, VA 22033
703-631-6200
800-564-4220
Fax: 703-654-6931
E-Mail: technet@jspargo.com
Home Page: www.afcea.org

Paul doCarmo, Assistant Director/Exhibit Sales
Connie Shaw, Exhibit Sales Account Manager
Herbert Browne, President

Military, government and industry communications and electronics professionals gather to see exhibits of communications and electronics equipment, supplies and services.
2000 Attendees
Frequency: November/Annual
Founded in 1985

22410 AFCEA Technical Committee Tech Forum TechNet International
AFCEA Headquarters
4400 Fair Lakes Court
Fairfax, VA 22033-3899

703-631-6100
800-336-4583
Fax: 703-631-6169
E-Mail: service@afcea.org
Home Page: www.afcea.org

Herbert Browne, President
Paul doCarmo, Assistant Director/Exhibit Sales
Connie Shaw, Exhibit Sales Account Manager

One of the nation's largest C4I conventions and expositions and features numerous professional development opportunities and tremendous networking opportunies.
Founded in 1985

22411 AFCEA/USNI West Conference & Exposition
Armed Forces Communications and Electronics Assn
4400 Fair Lakes Court
Fairfax, VA 22033

703-631-6200
800-564-4220
Fax: 703-654-6931
E-Mail: west@jspargo.org
Home Page: www.afcea.org

Paul doCarmo, Assistant Director/Exhibit Sales
Connie Shaw, Exhibit Sales Account Manager
Herbert Browne, President

Over 350 of the industry's most recognized defense and technology organizations showcase their technology products and services to top decision-makers from the US Pacific Fleet, Naval Station San Diego, Space & Warfare Command, Naval Base Coronado, Camp Pendleton Marine Corps Base and many other west coast military and government facilities.
6000 Attendees
Frequency: January/Annual
Founded in 1985

22412 AIIM Annual Conference and Expo
Association for Information and Image Management
1100 Wayne Avenue
Suite 1100
Silver Spring, MD 20910-5603

301-587-8202
800-477-2446
Fax: 301-587-2711
E-Mail: aiim@aiim.org
Home Page: www.aiim.org
Social Media: Facebook, Twitter

Jan Andersson, Chair
Robert Zagami, Vice Chair

The leading industry event for Enterprise Content and Document Management, which encompasses the technologies and strategies used to capture, manage, share, and store documents and digital content.
Frequency: April

22413 APCO Annual Conference & Expo
Assoc of Public-Safety Commun Officials Intl
351 N Williamson Boulevard
Daytona Beach, FL 32114-1112

386-322-2500
888-272-6911
Fax: 386-322-2501
E-Mail: apco@apcointl.org
Home Page: www.apcointl.org/
Social Media: Facebook

George S Rice Jr, Executive Director
Barbara Myers, Conference Services Director
Brigid Blaschak, Tradeshow Manager
Patricia Giannini, Senior Meeting Coordinator
Garry Mendez, Marketing/Communications Director

The Association of Public-Safety Communications Officials International/APCO 's Annual Conference brings together more than 300 vendors to give you hands-on demonstrations of new technologies you might use in your agency or call centers. The Conference also offers sessions on personal and professional development and a variety of technical skills. Banquet, breakfast and exhibitors of radio, computer, and supporting equipment companies.
6000 Attendees
Frequency: Annual
Founded in 1935

22414 Annual Conference for Catalog & Multichannel Merchants (ACCM)
Direct Marketing Association
1120 Avenue of Americas
New York, NY 10036

212-768-7277
Fax: 212-768-4547
Home Page: www.the-dma.org

Julie Hogan, SVP Conference & Events
10M Attendees

22415 Antenna Measurement Techniques Association Show
6065 Roswell Road
Suite 2252
Atlanta, GA 30328

770-864-3488
Fax: 770-864-3491
Home Page: www.amta.org
Social Media: Facebook, Twitter

Janet O'Neil, Contact

Antenna test equipment, supplies and services for government, private and institutional laboratories involved in design and development.

22416 Association for Communications Technology Professionals in Higher Education
ACUTA
152 W Zandale Drive
Suite 200
Lexington, KY 40503-2486

859-278-3338
Fax: 859-278-3268
E-Mail: kbowman@acuta.org
Home Page: www.acuta.org
Social Media: Facebook, Twitter, LinkedIn, You Tube

Kellie Bowman, Registration
Jeri Semer, Executive Director

Annual conference and exhibits of educational telecommunications equipment, supplies and services. Containing 95 booths.
600 Attendees
Frequency: Annual
Founded in 1971

22417 Association of Teleservices International Conference
ATSI
12 Academy Avenue
Atkinson, NH 03811

866-896-2874
Fax: 703-435-4390
E-Mail: admin@atsi.org
Home Page: www.atsi.org
Social Media: Facebook, Twitter, LinkedIn, You Tube

Lori Jenkins, President
Marcy Hewlett, Convention Chair

Exhibits of interest to telephone answering and voice message providers.
800+ Attendees
Founded in 1942

22418 Cable-Tec Expo
Society of Cable Telecommunications Engineers
140 Philips Road
Exton, PA 19341-1318

610-524-1725
800-542-5040
Fax: 610-363-5898
E-Mail: info@scte.org
Home Page: expo.scte.org
Social Media: Facebook, Twitter, LinkedIn, You Tube

Heather Gosciniak, Director

The Society's Cable-Tec Expo is the premier industry hardware exhibition that also offers an engineering conference, workshops and meetings. Expo contains more than 500 booths and 400 exhibits.
12M Attendees
Frequency: Annual

22419 Call Center Conference and Exposition
CMP Media
11 West 19th Street
New York, NY 10011

888-428-3976
Fax: 212-600-3080
E-Mail: CCEventInfo@cmp.com
Home Page: www.cmpevents.com
Social Media: Facebook, Twitter, LinkedIn, You Tube

Joni Mitchell, Marketing Manager
Joy Cerequas, Director Events

125 booths, plus conference covering all applications of new technologies and services in call processing, transaction processing and telemarketing.
2.5M Attendees
Frequency: February

22420 Email Evolution Conference
Direct Marketing Association
1120 Avenue of Americas
New York, NY 10036-6700

212-768-7277
Fax: 212-302-6714
E-Mail: dmaconferences@the-dma.org
Home Page: www.the-dma.org

Julie A Hogan, SVP Conference/Events
Lawrence M Kimmel, CEO

Focuses on the ever-changing and evolving world of email marketing, providing you with the best ways to capitalize on the high ROI this low-cost communication tool can provide both on its own, and integrated with social, search, mobile, video and other email enhancers.
10M Attendees
Frequency: Annual/February

22421 Entelec Conference & Expo
Energy Telecommunications and Electrical Assoc
5005 Royal Lane
Suite 116
Irving, TX 75063

888-503-8700
Fax: 972-915-6040
E-Mail: info@entelec.org
Home Page: www.entelec.org
Social Media: Facebook, Twitter, LinkedIn

Blaine Siske, Executive Manager
Amanda Prudden, Association Manager

22422 Enterprise Wireless
Enterprise Wireless Alliance
8484 Westpark Drive
Suite 630
McLean, VA 22102-5117

703-528-5115
Fax: 703-524-1074
E-Mail: customerservice@enterprisewireless.org
Home Page: www.enterprisewireless.org
Social Media: Facebook, Twitter, LinkedIn

Mark Crosby, President/CEO
Andre Cote, Senior VP
Ila Dudley, VP Spectrum Management
Ron Franklin, VP Membership/Business Development

Co-hosted by AAPC and USMSS, this trade show and conference is for wireless service providers, manufacturers, systems integrators an denterprise users to showcase innovative new wireless products.

22423 IEEE Communications Expo IEEE Globecom
J Spargo & Associates
11208 Waples Mill Road
Suite 112
Fairfax, VA 22030

703-631-6200
800-564-4220
Fax: 703-654-6931
E-Mail: ieee@jspargo.com
Home Page: www.ieee.org

Connie Shaw, Exhibit Sales Account Manager
In addition to targeting IEEE Communications Society members, also draws companies from Silicon Valley, Northern California, and the Pacific Rim, who manufacture or distribute products or services to support wireless technologies, optical networking, the Internet, or the telecom marketplace.
2000 Attendees
Frequency: November

22424 International Wireless Communication Expo
6300 S Syracuse Way
Suite 650
Englewood, CO 80111-6726

303-904-0407
E-Mail: rugianskis@prismb2b.com
Home Page: www.iwceexpo.com
Social Media: Facebook, Twitter, LinkedIn

Rita Ugianskis, Group Show Director
Laura Magliola, Marketing Manager
Stacey Orlick, Director
Catherine E. Campfield, Co-ordinator
Angela Wood, Conference Program Manager

The one place where all industries and communications professionals come together to share thoughts and ideas on wireless communications technologies.
6.5M Attendees
Frequency: March

22425 NATOA Annual Conference
Nat'l Assn of Telecommunication Officer & Advisors
3213 Duke Street
Suite 695
Alexandria, VA 22314

703-519-8035
Fax: 703-519-7080
E-Mail: info@natoa.org
Home Page: www.natoa.org
Social Media: Facebook, Twitter

Elizabeth Beaty, Executive Director
Jennifer Harman, Manager
Tonya Rideout, Deputy

Containing 30 booths featuring telecommunications equipment and supplies. Cable operators and local governments. Educational sessions topics include technology, competitive markets, programming, and cable franchise administration.
700 Attendees
Frequency: September

22426 NCDM Conference
Direct Marketing Association
1120 Avenue of Americas
New York, NY 10036-6700

212-768-7277
Fax: 212-302-6714
E-Mail: dmaconferences@the-dma.org
Home Page: www.the-dma.org

Julie A Hogan, SVP Conferences/Events
Lawrence M Kimmel, CEO

Presents industry experts and hard-hitting case studies from a variety of verticals, such as financial services, retail, automotive, publishing, non-profit and many more, who will share the latest strategies and methodologies in gathering, analyzing, leveraging and protecting your most valuable business asset - customer data.
10M Attendees
Frequency: Annual/December

22427 NEAX 2400 IMS Users Group
40 Marsh Wall
Columbia, CT 29221-0886

803-798-4800
Home Page: www.necusergroup.com
Social Media: Facebook, Twitter

Carlisle Reames, Contact

15 booths of educational sessions for NEC 2400 DBX systems users.
350 Attendees
Frequency: April

22428 NXTcomm
Telecommunications Industry Association/TIA
2500 Wilson Boulevard
Suite 300
Arlington, VA 22201-3834

703-907-7700
Fax: 703-907-7727
E-Mail: gseiffert@tiaonline.org
Home Page: www.tiaonline.org/business/events/TIATradeshows.cfm
Social Media: Facebook, Twitter, LinkedIn

Grant Seiffert, President
Mike Nunes, Government Relations Director
Lora Magruder, Member Relations Director
Daniel J. Pigott, Chairman of the Board
Thomas Stanton, Vice Chair

NXTcomm is an industry event uniting the premier information and communications technology suppliers with the world's leading communications and entertainment companies. Connect with 450+ exhibitors and 20,000+ attendees. Soak up essential knowledge during insider-led conferences. The global forces that are driving communications-based innovation are here.

22429 National Conference on Operations & Fulfillment (NCOF)
Direct Marketing Association
1120 Avenue of Americas
New York, NY 10036-6700

212-768-7277
Fax: 212-302-6714
E-Mail: dmaconferences@the-dma.org
Home Page: www.the-dma.org

Julie A Hogan, SVP Conference/Educational Services
Lawrence M Kimmel, CEO

Focuses on innovative solutions for warehouse, distribution, operations, and ecommerce needs in the ever-changing world of operations and fulfillment.
10M Attendees
Frequency: Annual/April

22430 New York Nonprofit Conference
Direct Marketing Association
1120 Avenue of Americas
New York, NY 10036-6700

212-768-7277
Fax: 212-302-6714
E-Mail: dmaconferences@the-dma.org
Home Page: www.the-dma.org

Julie A Hogan, SVP Conference/Events
Lawrence M Kimmel, CEO

Discover which acknowledgement programs work best-and why, increase revenue with

membership options-as well as traditional fund-raising appeals, learn how the internet and e-mail campaigng can improve fundraising, lower costs and increase advocac
10M Attendees

22431 PCCA Annual Convention
Power and Communication Contractors
1908 Mt. Vernon Ave
Suite 200
Alexandria, VA 22314
703-212-7734
800-542-7222
Fax: 703-548-3733
E-Mail: info@pccaweb.org
Home Page: www.pccaweb.org
Social Media: Facebook, Twitter

Kevin Mason, President
Larry Libla, President-Elect
Frequency: March

22432 TechNet North 2006
AFCEA Canada & AFCEA International
102 Centrepointe Drive
Ottawa, ON K2G-6B1

613-786-2619
Fax: 613-230-1554,
E-Mail: kevin@expocorpinc.com
Home Page: www.technetnorth.com
Social Media: Facebook, Twitter

Kevin d'Entremont, Exhibit Director
Rick Tachuk, Marketing & Communications Director

Delivers an inovative professional development conference and a major trade exhibition focused on the latest C4ISR solutions, products and technologies for the North American defense and security sectors.

22433 Telecom
607 14th Street
Suite 600
Washington, DC 20005-2164

202-547-2680
Fax: 202-326-7333
Home Page: www.usta.org
Social Media: Facebook, Twitter, LinkedIn, You Tube

Walter B McCormick Jr, President/CEO
Jaonne Hovis, Chair
Tony Prez, Director

Conference and exhibition offers a variety of educational sessions, special interest seminars and keynote speakers. The show features an estimated 160 exhibitors.
1300 Attendees
Frequency: Annual

22434 Utilities Telecommunications Council Annual Conference and Exhibition
Utilities Telecommunications Council
1129 20th St.NW
Suite 350
Washington, DC 20036

202-872-0030
Fax: 202-872-1331
E-Mail: marketing@utc.org
Home Page: www.utc.org
Social Media: Facebook, Twitter, LinkedIn

Connie Durcsase, President
Mike Oldak, VP & General Counsel
Karnel Thomas, VM- Member Services
Kathleen Fitzpatric, VP- Operations

Annual conference and exhibits of telecommunications equipment and services.
1,000 Attendees
Founded in 1948

22435 Wire Expo
Wire Association International
1570 Boston Post Road
PO Box 578
Guilford, CT 06437-0578

203-453-2777
Fax: 203-453-8384
Home Page: www.wirenet.org
Social Media: Facebook, Twitter

Livia Jacobs, Manager Convention/Events
Nicholas Nickoletopoulos, President
Steven J. Fetteroll~, Executive Director
Robert J. Xeller, Sales

Wire Expo provides you with ready-made opportunities—including meeting with more than 450 suppliers on the show floor. You'll gain manufacturing and technical information by attending short courses and listening to some of the 75+ paper that will be presented at WCTS. Social events also provide oppertunities to make conections with other professionals in the wire industry.
4000 Attendees
Frequency: May/June
Founded in 1930

Directories & Databases

22436 Audiotex Directory
ADBG Publishing
PO Box 25929
Los Angeles, CA 90025-0929

310-914-9000
Fax: 310-479-0654
Home Page: www.krango.com
Social Media: Facebook, Twitter

Larry Podell, Editor

Over 1,200 product and service suppliers in the voice processing fax, and audiotex fields, including hardware, software, vendors, telephone companies, service bureaus, audio programmers, and consultants
Cost: $50.00
Frequency: Annual

22437 Bacon's Radio/TV/Cable Directory
Cision U.S., Inc.
332 South Michigan Avenue
Suite 900
Chicago, IL 60604

312-263-0070
866-639-5087
E-Mail: info.us@cision.com
Home Page: www.us.cision.com

Joe Bernardo, President & CEO
Heidi Sullivan, VP & Publisher
Valerie Lopez, Research Director
Jessica White, Research Director
Rachel Farrell, Research Manager

Includes comprehensive coverage for contact and programming information for more than 3,500 televsion networks, cable networks, television syndicators, television stations, and cable systems in the United States and Canada.
Cost: $350.00
Frequency: Annual
ISSN: 1088-9639
Printed in one color on matte stock

22438 Communication News: Network Access Directory
Nelson Publishing
2500 Tamiami Trl N
Nokomis, FL 34275-3476

941-966-9521
Fax: 941-966-2590
Home Page: www.healthmgttech.com
Social Media: Facebook, Twitter, LinkedIn

A Verner Nelson, Owner
Cost: $7.00
Frequency: Annual, June
Circulation: 71,000
Mailing list available for rent

22439 Communications News: Broadband Directory
Nelson Publishing
2500 Tamiami Trl N
Nokomis, FL 34275-3476

941-966-9521
Fax: 941-966-2590
Home Page: www.healthmgttech.com
Social Media: Facebook, Twitter, LinkedIn

A Verner Nelson, Owner
Cost: $7.00
Frequency: Annual, December
Circulation: 71,000
Mailing list available for rent

22440 Communications News: PBX/CTI Directory
Nelson Publishing
2500 Tamiami Trl N
Nokomis, FL 34275-3476

941-966-9521
Fax: 941-966-2590
Home Page: www.healthmgttech.com
Social Media: Facebook, Twitter, LinkedIn

A Verner Nelson, Owner
Cost: $7.00
Frequency: Annual, April
Circulation: 71,000
Mailing list available for rent

22441 Communications News: Test Directory
Nelson Publishing
2500 Tamiami Trl N
Nokomis, FL 34275-3476

941-966-9521
Fax: 941-966-2590
Home Page: www.healthmgttech.com
Social Media: Facebook, Twitter, LinkedIn

A Verner Nelson, Owner
Cost: $7.00
Frequency: Annual, February
Circulation: 71,000
Mailing list available for rent

22442 Communications News: Video/ Audioconferencing Directory
Nelson Publishing
2500 Tamiami Trl N
Nokomis, FL 34275-3476

941-966-9521
Fax: 941-966-2590
Home Page: www.healthmgttech.com
Social Media: Facebook, Twitter, LinkedIn

A Verner Nelson, Owner
Cost: $7.00
Frequency: Annual, October
Circulation: 71,000
Mailing list available for rent

22443 Communications News: Wireless Directory
Nelson Publishing
2500 Tamiami Trl N
Nokomis, FL 34275-3476

941-966-9521
Fax: 941-966-2590

Home Page: www.healthmgttech.com
Social Media: Facebook, Twitter, LinkedIn

A Verner Nelson, Owner
Cost: $7.00
Frequency: Annual, August
Circulation: 71,000
Mailing list available for rent

22444 **Complete Directory of Telephones & Accessories**
Sutton Family Communications & Publishing Company
155 Sutton Lane
Fordsville, KY 42343

270-740-0870
E-Mail: jlsutton@apex.net
Home Page: www.fleamarketeer.net
Social Media: Facebook, Twitter

Theresa Sutton, Editor
Lee Sutton, General Manager

Print-out from database of wholesalers, manufacturers, distributors, importers and close-out houses. Database is updated daily to guarantee the most current and up-to-date sources available.
Cost: $55.20
100+ Pages

22445 **Corporate Yellow Book**
Leadership Directories
104 5th Ave
New York, NY 10011-6901

212-627-4140
Fax: 212-645-0931
E-Mail: info@leadershipdirectories.com
Home Page: www.leadershipdirectories.com
Social Media: Facebook, Twitter

David Hurvitz, CEO

Contact information for over 48,000 executives at over 1,000 companies and more than 9,000 board members and their outside affiliations.
Cost: $420.00
1,400 Pages
Frequency: Quarterly
ISSN: 1058-2098
Founded in 1986

22446 **Directory of Communications Professionals**
National Assn of Regulatory Utility Commissioners
1101 Vermont Ave NW
Suite 200
Washington, DC 20005-3553

202-898-2200
Fax: 202-898-2213
Home Page: www.naruc.org
Social Media: Facebook, Twitter

Charles Gray, Executive Director
Philip Jones, President

Offers information on consultants and other professionals active in regulated telecommunications.
Cost: $33.00
240 Pages
Frequency: Annual

22447 **International Fiber Optics Yellow Pages**
Information Gatekeepers
214 Harvard Avenue
Suite 200
Allston, MA 02134-4641

617-232-3111
800-323-1088
Fax: 617-734-8562
E-Mail: webmaster@igigroup.com
Home Page: www.fiberopticsyp.com
Social Media: Facebook, Twitter

Will Ashley, Contact

The most extensive Fiber Optics reference volume available anywhere. This directory is still the world's only source book devoted exclusively to Fiber Optics.
Cost: $89.95
Frequency: Annual
Founded in 1977

22448 **LATA Directory**
Center for Communications Management
11300 Rockville Pike
Suite 1100
Rockville, MD 20852-3003

301-770-7490
Fax: 301-287-2445
Home Page: www.lataweb.com
Social Media: Facebook, Twitter

Ronald Canter, Owner

Offers information on local access transport areas by states.
Cost: $195.00
220 Pages
Frequency: Annual

22449 **Local Calling Area Directory**
Center for Communications Management
11300 Rockville Pike
Suite 1100
Rockville, MD 20852-3003

301-770-7490
Fax: 301-287-2445
Home Page: www.lataweb.com
Social Media: Facebook, Twitter

Ronald Canter, Owner

Offers area codes and their zones or exchanges in cities of 100,000 or more in population.
Cost: $795.00
1,050 Pages
Frequency: Annual

22450 **Lynx Global Telecom Database**
Lynx Technologies
710 Route 46 East
PO Box 368
Little Falls, NJ 07424-0368

973-256-7200
Fax: 973-882-3583
E-Mail: msalerno@lynxtech.com
Home Page: www.lynxtech.com
Social Media: Facebook, Twitter

Kathleen Elsayed, Production Manager
Mike Salerno, Circulation Director

350 telecommunications carriers services in approximately 200 countries, territories and other political divisions.

22451 **Network Management Guidelines and Contact Directory**
Network Operations Forum
1200 G Street NW
Washington, DC 20005-3814

202-347-1228
Fax: 202-393-5453

Over 25 telecommunications companies.

22452 **North American Telecommunications Association - Sourcebook**
2000 P St NW
Suite 550
Washington, DC 20036-6921

202-419-0412
Home Page: www.naaee.org

Brian Day, Executive Director
Sue Bumpous, Communications Manager

Offers a wide array of information on manufacturers and suppliers of non-utility telephone terminal equipment.
Cost: $53.00
208 Pages

22453 **Outside Plant: Directory of Outside Plant Contractors Issue**
Practical Communications
PO Box 183
Cary, IL 60013-0183

847-639-2200
Fax: 847-639-7598

John Saxtan, Editor

Offers a list of over 800 contractors in the telecommunications industry that specialize in outside plant projects.
Cost: $30.00
Frequency: Annual
Circulation: 20,000

22454 **Phillips Satellite Industry Directory**
Phillips Business Information
1201 Seven Locks Road
Potomac, MD 20854-2931

301-354-1400
800-777-5006
Fax: 301-309-9473

Minica Kenny, Editor
Don Pazour, CEO

Over 6,000 contacts and more than 3,800 hardware and technical service companies, transponder brokers and resellers, consultants, communications attorneys, publishers, uplinks and downlinks, video conference suppliers, related trade associations, government agencies and satellite telecommunications carriers.
Cost: $257.00
Frequency: Annual January

22455 **Phillips Who's Who in Electronic Commerce**
Phillips Business Information
1201 Seven Locks Road
Potomac, MD 20854-2931

301-354-1400
800-777-5006
Fax: 301-309-9473

Jennifer O Newman, Editor
Don Pazour, CEO

Service providers, value-added banks and networks, software vendors, associations, user groups, consultants, business and technical services for electronic commerce industry.
Cost: $199.00
Frequency: Annual

22456 **Pocket Guides to the Internet: Terminal Connections**
Information Today
143 Old Marlton Pike
Medford, NJ 08055-8750
609-654-6266
800-300-9868
Fax: 609-654-4309
E-Mail: custserv@infotoday.com
Home Page: www.infotoday.com
Social Media: Facebook, Twitter

Thomas H Hogan, President
Roger R Bilboul, Chairman Of The Board

Unix/VMS systems and other basic terminal applications and telecommunications programs.
Cost: $9.95

22457 **Q-TEL 1000**
United Communications Group
11300 Rockville Pike
P.O Box: 217
Rockville, MD 20852-3030

301-816-8950
800-526-5307
Fax: 858-674-5491
E-Mail: media@qtel.com.qa

Home Page: www.qtel.qa
Social Media: Facebook, Twitter

This database offers information on telecommunications charges.
Frequency: Full-text
Mailing list available for rent

22458 RCR Publications
RCR Publications
1746 Cole Boulevard
Suite 150
Golden, CO 80401

303-733-2500
800-678-9696
Fax: 303-733-9941
E-Mail: mbush@crain.com
Home Page: www.rcrnews.com

Melodye Bush, Database Coordinator

Offers a wide variety of information on cellular and personal communications industries. Includes detailed information on carriers and vendors around the world.
Cost: $950.00
Frequency: Annual
Founded in 1991

22459 RCR's Cellular Database
RCR Publications
1746 Cole Boulevard
Suite 150
Golden, CO 80401

303-733-2500
800-678-9696
Fax: 303-733-9941
E-Mail: mbush@crain.com
Home Page: www.rcrnews.com

Melodye Bush, Database Coordinator

Offers a wide variety of information on cellular communications industry. Includes detailed information on cellular carriers and vendors.
Cost: $300.00
Frequency: Annual
Founded in 1991

22460 RCR's PCS Database
RCR Publications
1746 Cole Boulevard
Suite 150
Golden, CO 80401

303-733-2500
800-678-9696
Fax: 303-733-9941
E-Mail: mbush@crain.com
Home Page: www.rcrnews.com

Melodye Bush, Database Coordinator

Offers a wide variety of information on the personal communications industry. Includes detailed information on PCS carriers and vendors.
Cost: $300.00
Frequency: Annual
Founded in 1991

22461 Satellite Industry Directory
Phillips Business Information
1201 Seven Locks Road
Suite 300
Potomac, MD 20854-2931

301-354-1400
Fax: 301-309-9473

Monica Kenny, Editor

Profiles operational and planned satellite systems, equipment and service providers, satellite brokers, uplinkers/downlinkers and more.
Cost: $247.00
750 Pages
Frequency: Annual

22462 Sbusiness
AFSM International
17065 Camino San Bernardo
Suite 200
San Diego, CA 92127-1709

858-673-3055
800-333-9786
Fax: 239-275-0794
E-Mail: info@afsmi.org
Home Page: www.afsmi.org
Social Media: Facebook, Twitter

John Shoenewald, Executive Director
Jb Wood, President/CEO

The professional journal for customer service and support managers.
Cost: $60.00
100 Pages
Frequency: Bi-Monthly
Circulation: 10000
Founded in 1975
Mailing list available for rent

22463 TCP/IP for the Internet
Mecklermedia Corporation
20 Ketchum Street
Westport, CT 06880-5908

203-341-2806
Fax: 203-454-5840

Marshall Breeding, Editor

Standard network protocol for data transmission over the global internet products and packages for Unix, DOS, Windows and Macintosh platforms.
Cost: $24.95

22464 Telecommunications Directory
Gale/Cengage Learning
10650 Toebben Drive
Detroit, KY 41051

248-699-4253
800-877-4253
Fax: 248-699-8049
E-Mail: gale.galeord@cengage.com
Home Page: www.gale.com
Social Media: Facebook, Twitter

Patrick C Sommers, President

Provides detailed information on telecommunications companies providing a range of products and services from cellular communications and local exchange carriers to satellite services and Internet service providers.
ISBN: 1-414419-80-5

22465 Telecommunications Export Guide
North American Telecommunications Association
2000 P St NW
Suite 550
Washington, DC 20036-6921
202-419-0412
Home Page: www.naaee.org

Brian Day, Executive Director
Sue Bumpous, Communications Manager

Offers a list of over 135 foreign telecommunications agencies, and federal and state government agencies concerned with exports in the United States.
Cost: $103.00

22466 Telemarketing and Call Center Solutions Buyer's Guide and Directory Issue
Technology Marketing Corporation
800 Connecticut Ave
1st Floor East
Norwalk, CT 06854-1936

203-852-6800
800-243-6002
Fax: 203-853-2845
E-Mail: tmc@tmcnet.com
Home Page: www.tmcnet.com
Social Media: Facebook, Twitter, LinkedIn, You Tube

Rich Tehrani, CEO
Nanji Tehrani, Chair
David Rodriguez, President/Assistant Treasurer
Michael Genaro, VP

Over 1100 domestic and foreign suppliers of equipment products and services to the telecommunications/telemarketing industry.
Cost: $25.00
Frequency: Annual December
Founded in 1972

22467 Telephone Industry Directory
Phillips Business Information
1201 Seven Locks Road
Suite 300
Potomac, MD 20854-2931

301-354-1400
Fax: 301 349 9473

Jennifer Newman, Assistant Managing Editor

Offers valuable information on over 4,800 manufacturers, distributors and suppliers to the telecommunications industry.
Cost: $249.00
750 Pages
Frequency: Annual

22468 Voice Mail Reference Manual and Buyer's Guide
Robins Press
2675 Henry Hudson Parkway W
Apartment 6J
Bronx, NY 10463-7741

718-548-7245
800-238-7130
Fax: 718-548-7237
E-Mail: robinspr@ix.netcom.com
Home Page: www.mmdimensions.com/telstore

Marc Robins, Publisher

Offers information on over 60 suppliers of about 90 voice mail systems and service bureaus.
Cost: $65.00
384 Pages
Frequency: Annual
Mailing list available for rent: 10M names
Printed in 2 colors on matte stock

22469 Voice Processing Printed Circuit Cards: A Sourcebook of Suppliers & Products
Robins Press
2675 Henry Hudson Parkway W
Apartment 6J
Bronx, NY 10463-7741

718-548-7245

Offers a list of over 50 vendors of voice processing circuit cards and related technology worldwide.
Cost: $150.00
Frequency: Annual

22470 World Satellite Almanac
Phillips Business Information
1201 Seven Locks Road
Suite 300
Potomac, MD 20854-2931

301-354-1400
Fax: 301-340-1520

Monica Kenny, Editor

All commercial satellite systems and operators are profiled.
Cost: $247.00
700 Pages
Frequency: Annual

22471 World Telecommunications Tariff Directory
Lynx Technologies

PO Box 368
Little Falls, NJ 07424-0368

973-256-7200

A comprehensive directory of over 1,200 Local Exchange Carriers and other telecom companies make up this directory. Includes a detailed index for easy cross-referencing by company name, contacts, titles, geographical region, services provided, email and more.
Cost: $699.00
9,000 Pages

Industry Web Sites

22472 **http://gold.greyhouse.com**
G.O.L.D Grey House OnLine Databases
Grey House Publishing's online database platform, GOLD, offers Quick Search, Keyword Search and Expert Search for most business sectors including telecommunications and media markets. The GOLD platform makes finding the information you need quick and easy - whether you're a novice searcher or an experienced database user. All of Grey House's directory products are available for subscription on the GOLD platform.

22473 **www.adweek.com**
ADWEEK
Leading decision makers in the advertising and marketing field go to Adweek.Com every day for breaking news, insight, buzz, opinion, analysis, research and classifieds. The resources of all six regional editions of Adweek, as well as the national edition of Brandweek are combined with the knowledge of our online editors and the multimedia-interactive capabilities of the web to deliver vital information quickly and effectively to our target audience.

22474 **www.alts.org**
Association of Local Telecommunications Services
Represents state and local telecommunications offices.

22475 **www.amtausa.org**
American Mobile Telecommunications Association
Membership is made up of operators in the 220 MHz, 450 MHz, 800 MHz and 900 MHz bands, as well as product and service providers for the industry. Many members are exploring other areas of the mobile telecommunications industry — digital SMR, Personal Communications Services, data communications, mobile satellite, cable telephony and international wireless interests. AMTA is working with its members and with government to insure that those areas can be pursued successfully.

22476 **www.arrl.org**
American Radio Relay League
National membership association for amateur radio operators.

22477 **www.atis.org**
Alliance for Telecommunications Industry Solutions
Membership organization that provides the tools necessary for the industry to identify standards, guidelines and operating procedures that make the interoperability of existing and emerging telecommunications proiducts and services possible.

22478 **www.atsi.org**
Association of Telemessaging Services International
Promotes fair competition through appropriate regulation and legislation; provides research and development provides support services and educational opportunities to address challenges in operating environments; in encourages and maintains the high standards of ethics and service.

22479 **www.floridapsc.com**
Telecommunications Cooperative Network
Offers group purchasing discounts on long-distance telephone services, equipment counseling, and analysis of communications needs.

22480 **www.greyhouse.com**
Grey House Publishing
Authoritative reference directories for most business sectors including telecommunications and media markets. Users can search the online databases with varied search criteria allowing for custom searches by product category, geographic area, sales volume, keyword, subject and more. Full Grey House catalog and online ordering also available.

22481 **www.icea.net**
Insulated Cable Engineers Association
Professional organization dedicated to developing cable standards for the electric power, control and telecommunications industries. Ensures safe, economical and efficient cable systems utilizing proven state-of-the-art materials and concepts. ICEA documents are of interest to cable manufacturers, architects and engineers, utility and manufacturing plant personnel, telecommunication engineers, consultants and OEMs.

22482 **www.igigroup.com**
Information Gatekeepers
Provides worldwide coverage of wireless LAN's, LAN interconnection, wireless in-building and major applications such as point-of-sales, portable computer interconnections and remote data collection.

22483 **www.imc.org**
Internet Email Consortium
Information about IMC and its members, all the internet email standards and more.

22484 **www.isoc.org**
Internet Society
International, professional membership organization focusing on standards, education and policy issues.

22485 **www.kagan.com**
Wireless/Private Cable Investor
The original bible of the wireless cable, multipoint distribution pay TV industry. Published continuously since 1972, this newsletter is the window on cable competition. Three month trial available.

22486 **www.ntca.org**
National Telephone Cooperative Association
Represents both cooperative and commercial, independent rural phone companies.

22487 **www.pcca.org**
Power and Communication Contractors
A national trade association for companies constructing electric power facilities, including transmission and distribution lines and substations and telephone, fiber optic, and cable television systems.

22488 **www.scte.org**
Society of Cable Telecommunications Engineers
For people engaged in engineering, construction, installation, manufacture, technical direction, management, regulation, or administration of broad band communications technologies.

22489 **www.steconsulting.org**
Society of Telecommunications Consultants
The Society of Telecommunications Consultants is aprofessional association of Independent telecommunications consultants who provide expert, non based councel to business industry service organizations and government, worldwide. It serves its constituency by providing educational business and networking opportunities and by negotiating tangible and intangible benefits. The STC also serves as a resource, connecting end users to consultants to business, educational and promotrional opportunities.

22490 **www.telecommagazine.com**
Telecommunications Industry Association
This magazine reports on carrier class and wide area communications technologies for service providers and their corporate network customers worldwide. Coverage includes technology, product, market and application information for serious communications professionals, interexchange, cellular/wireless/satellite carriers, cable companies as well as commercial users and government agencies in the communications industry.

22491 **www.telecommute.org**
Telecommuting Advisory Council
A comprehensive monthly digest of news about employer-sponsored telecommuting programs for employers working at home or elsewhere off-site. Contains case studies, international news, technology updates, legal and regulatory news, and managerial topics.

22492 **www.usta.org**
United States Telecom Association
Broad based association for the local exchange carrier industry worldwide.

Associations

22493 Acrylic Council
1285 Avenue of the Americas
35th Floor
New York, NY 10019

212-397-4600
Fax: 212-554-4042
E-Mail: info@fabriclink.com
Home Page: www.fabriclink.com
Social Media: Facebook, Twitter

Lynn Misiak, Executive Director

A business league created to provide products in facilities maintained in the US. Educates the retailer and consumer of the benefits of acrylic fiber.

22494 Amalgamated Clothing and Textile Workers Union
1710 Broadway
New York, NY 10019-5254

212-255-9655
Home Page: www.acronymfinder.com
Social Media: Facebook, Twitter

Jack Sheinkman, President
William Towne, Manager

Sponsors and supports the Political Action Committee in this field.
249M Members
Founded in 1976

22495 American Flock Association
469 Hospital Drive
Suite C
Gastonia, NC 28054

617-303-6288
Fax: 704-671-2366
E-Mail: info@flocking.org
Home Page: www.flocking.org

Karl Spilhaus, President
Steve Rosenthal, Managing Director

Provides positive leadership to foster a strong flock industry in North America.
60 Members
Founded in 1984

22496 American Home Sewing & Craft Association
PO Box 369
Monroeville, PA 15146

412-372-5950
Fax: 412-372-5953
E-Mail: info@sewing.org
Home Page: www.sewing.org

Handicraft and collectibles forum

22497 American Sheep Industry Association
9785 Maroon Circle
Suite 360
Englewood, CO 80112

303-771-3500
Fax: 303-771-8200
Home Page: www.sheepusa.org
Social Media: Facebook

Clint Krebs, President
Burton Pfliger, VP
Mike Corn, Secretary/Treasurer

A federation of state associations dedicated to the welfare and profitability of the sheep industry.
8000+ Members
Founded in 1865

22498 American Textile Machinery Association
201 Park Washington Ct
Falls Church, VA 22046-4527

703-538-1789
Fax: 703-241-5603
E-Mail: info@atmanet.org
Home Page: www.atmanet.org
Social Media: Facebook, Twitter

Will Motchar, Chairman
Udo Skarke, Vice Chairman
Clay D Tyeryar, President & Assistant Treasurer
Allen Moore, Vice Chairman/Treasurer
Susan A Denston, Executive VP & Secretary

The American Textile Machinery Association/ATMA's purpose is to improve business conditions within the textile machinery industry of the United States within a global context; to encourage the use of the products of the industry; and to protect, promote, foster and advance the common interests of the members as manufacturers and distributors of textile machinery and parts and machinery accessory to textile machinery on a worldwide basis.
1.5M Members
Founded in 1933

22499 American Wool Council
9785 Maroon Circle
Suite 360
Englewood, CO 80112

303-771-3500
Fax: 303-771-8200
Home Page: www.sheepusa.org
Social Media: Facebook, Twitter

Chuck Dallas, VP
Larry Prager, Secretary
Joe Pozzi, Treasurer

Promotes the use of wool and wool products.

22500 American Yarn Spinners Association
PO Box 99
Gastonia, NC 28053

704-824-3522
Fax: 704-824-0630
Home Page: www.aysa.org
Social Media: Facebook, Twitter

Michael Hubbard, Executive Director

Provides full service to the sales yarn industry.
100 Members
Founded in 1967

22501 Association of Georgia's Textile, Carpet, & Consumer Products Manufacturers
50 Hurt Plz Se
Suite 985
Atlanta, GA 30303-2941

404-688-0555
Fax: 404-584-0720
Home Page: www.gamfg.org
Social Media: Facebook, Twitter

Miles Wright, Chairman
Burl Finkelstein, Vice Chairman
G L Bowen III, President
Lee Bryan, Treasurer
Charles B Jones III, VP & General Counsel

22502 Association of Knitted Fabrics
1001 Connecticut Ave NW
Suite 315
Washington, DC 20036

202-822-8028
Fax: 202-822-8029
Home Page: www.nationaltextile.org
Social Media: Facebook, Twitter

William L Jasper, Chairman
James C Self III, Vice Chairman
Augustine Tantillo, President
Sarah Pierce, Senior VP
Mike Hubbard, VP

Manufacturers of knitted cotton and wool products.
6 Members
Founded in 1935

22503 Carpet & Rug Institute: West
100 South Hamilton Street
Suite 3
Dalton, CA 30720

706-278-3176
Fax: 706-278-8835
Home Page: www.carpet-rug.com
Social Media: Facebook, Twitter

Terri Caputo, President
Mailing list available for rent

22504 Cotton Council International
1521 New Hampshire Avenue NW
Washington, DC 20036

202-745-7805
Fax: 202-483-4040
E-Mail: cottonuse@cotton.org
Home Page: www.cottonusa.org
Social Media: Facebook, Twitter

James L Webb, Chairman
John A Burch, President
T Jordan Lea, First VP
Dahlen K Hancock, Second VP
Keith T Lucas, Treasurer

22505 Craft Yarn Council
469 Hospital Drive
Suite E
Gastonia, NC 28054-4779

704-824-7838
Fax: 704-671-2366
Home Page: www.craftyarncouncil.com
Social Media: Facebook

Michael Hubbard, Secretary/Treasurer
Mary Colucci, Executive Director

The Craft Yarn Council represents the leading yarn companies, accessory manufacturers, magazine, book publishers, and consultants in the yarn industry.
Founded in 1981

22506 Durene Association of America
194 S South St
Gastonia, NC 28052-4125

704-865-1651
Fax: 704-824-0638

Russell Duren, President

Develops and uses tests to determine quality. Licenses manufacturers to use Durene identification on products.
4 Members
Founded in 1929

22507 Elastic Fabric Manufacturers Council
230 Congress Street
Boston, MA 02110

617-542-8220
Fax: 617-542-2199
Home Page: www.textilenta.org

Provides exchange and management services, trade promotions, statistical programs and information bulletins.
32 Members
Founded in 1915

22508 Electrostatic Discharge Association
7900 Turin Road
Building 3
Rome, NY 13440-2069

315-339-6937
Fax: 315-339-6793
E-Mail: info@esda.org

Home Page: www.esda.org
Social Media: Facebook, Twitter, LinkedIn

Donn Bellmore, President
Leo G Henry, Senior VP

Professional voluntary association dedicated to advancing the theory and practice of electrostatic discharge avoidance. Initial emphasis on the effects of ESD on electronic components has broadened to include textiles, plastics, web processing, explosives, clean rooms and graphic arts. Expands ESD awareness through educational programs, development of standards, tutorials, publications, local chapters, symposia and certification.
Founded in 1982

22509 Hard Fibers Association
120 Genesee Street
Suite 601
Auburn, NY 13021-3603

315-520-0871
Fax: 315-255-3292

John Hurd, President

Importers and distributors of sisal, abaca and other hard fibers.

22510 Home Sewing Association
PO Box 369
Monroeville, PA 15146

412-725-5950
Fax: 412-372-5953
E-Mail: info@sewing.org
Home Page: www.sewing.org

Joyce Perhac, Manager

Represents most facets of the home sewing industry. National trade association for independent sewing machine dealers and distributors.
1.5M Members
Founded in 1912

22511 INDA Association of Nonwoven Fabrics
1100 Crescent Green
Suite 115
Cary, NC 27518

919-233-1210
Fax: 919-233-1282
E-Mail: info@inda.org
Home Page: www.inda.org
Social Media: Facebook, Twitter, LinkedIn

Todd Bassett, Chairman
Robert Lovegrove, Vice Chairman
Monica Moretti, Vice Chairman
Todd~ Bassett, MD

Mission is to promote the value and profitability of the global nonwovens/engineered fabrics industry to benefit the members.
300 Members
Founded in 1968

22512 Industrial Fabrics Association International
1801 County Road BW
Roseville, MN 55413

651-222-2508
800-225-4324
Fax: 651-631-9334
E-Mail: generalinfo@ifai.com
Home Page: www.ifai.com
Social Media: Facebook, Twitter, LinkedIn

Stephen M Warner, President

A not-for-profit trade association that represent the international specialty fabrics marketplace that facilitates the development, application and promotion of products manufactured by the diverse membership.
2000 Members

22513 Institute of Textile Technology
North Carolina State University
3426 College of Textiles
NSCU Centennial Campus
Raleigh, NC 27695-8301

919-513-7704
888-348-3512
Fax: 919-882-9410
E-Mail: wgoneal@itt.edu
Home Page: www.itt.edu
Social Media: Facebook, Twitter

W Gilbert O'Neal, President & CEO
George Edmunds, VP

A graduate school supported in part by member companies. Publishes the Textile Technology Digest.

22514 International Society of Industrial Fabric
1801 County Road B W
Roseville, MN 55113-2851

651-631-9334
800-225-4324
Fax: 651-631-9334
E-Mail: generalinfo@ifai.com
Home Page: www.ifai.com
Social Media: Facebook, Twitter, LinkedIn, Youtube

Mark J Hennessy, President & CEO
Todd V Lindemann, VP, Conference Management
Pam Egan-Blahna, Director, Human Resource
Dan McCarthy, VP, Finance/CFO
Andrew M Aho, Director, Membership & Divisions

A not-for-profit trade association whose more than 2,000 member companies represent the international specialty fabrics marketplace. Members range in size from one-person shops to multinational corporations; member products span the entire spectrum of the specialty fabrics industry from fiber and fabric suppliers to manufacturers of end products, equipment and hardware.
350 Members

22515 International Textile & Apparel Association
PO Box 70687
Monument, CO 37938-0687

865-992-1535
E-Mail: executivedirector@itaaonline.org
Home Page: www.itaaonline.org
Social Media: Facebook, Twitter

Sandra S Hutton, Executive Director

Professional association for 1,000 college professors of clothing and textile studies.
Founded in 1935

22516 Knitted Textile Association
1001 Connecticut Ave NW
Suite 315
Washington, DC 20036

202-822-8028
Fax: 202-822-8029
E-Mail: info@ktausa.org
Home Page: www.ncto.org
Social Media: Facebook, Twitter, LinkedIn

William L Jasper, Chairman
James C Self III, Vice Chairman
Augustine Tantillo, President
Sarah Pierce, Senior VP
Mike Hubbard, VP

The KTA is an active participant in the International Mechinery and Equipment exhibition that takes place in Textile Hall in Greenville, South Carolina and highlights the latest in knitting and related dying and finishing equipment.

22517 Narrow Fabrics Institute
1801 County Road BW
Roseville, MN 55113-4061

651-225-6920
Fax: 651-631-9334
E-Mail: generalinfo@ifai.com
Home Page: www.narrowfabrics.org
Social Media: Facebook, Twitter, LinkedIn, Youtube

Mary J Hennessy, President & CEO
Todd V Lindemann, VP, Conference Management
Pam Egan-Blahna, Director, Human Resource
Dan McCarthy, VP, Finance/CFO
Andrew M Aho, Director, Membership & Divisions

Conducts research, sells abrasior rods, and compiles statistics on narrow fabrics
40 Members
Founded in 1956

22518 National Cotton Batting Institute
4322 Bloombury St
Southaven, MS 38672

901-218-2393
Fax: 662-449-0046
E-Mail: info@natbat.com
Home Page: www.natbat.com
Social Media: Facebook, Twitter

Weston Arnall, President
Greg Windsperger, VP
Fred Middleton, Executive Secretary-Treasurer

NCBI represents U.S. companies that manufacture and sell batting for use in mattresses, futons, home furnishing, and upholstered products. It provides a range of services to assist its members in expanding markets, monitoring and contributing to legislative and regulatory decisions that affect the industry, and conducting consumer education and information programs.
27 Members
Founded in 1954

22519 National Cotton Council of America
1918 N Parkway
Memphis, TN 38112-5000

901-274-9030
Fax: 901-725-0510
Home Page: www.cotton.org
Social Media: Facebook, Twitter

James F Dodson, Chairman
Wallace L Darneille, Vice Chairman
Meredith B Allen, VP
Sid Brough, VP
John C Fricke, VP

The council serves as the central forum for consensus-building among producers, ginners, warehousers, merchants, cottonseed processors/dealers, cooperatives and textile manufacturers.

22520 National Council for Textile Education
Georgia Institute of Technology
1001 Connecticut Ave
Washington, DC 30332-0001

202-822-8028
Fax: 202-822-8029
Home Page: www.ncto.org
Social Media: Facebook, Twitter

William Jasper, Chairman
Cass Jones, President
Sarah Pierce, VP
Robins Hynes, Director

Members are administrators of college textile departments whose curriculum comprise science-based programs with substantial laboratory and plant experience.

22521 National Knitwear & Sportswear Association
1001 Connecticut Ave NW
Suite 315
Washington, DC 20036

202-822-8028
Fax: 202-822-8029
E-Mail: nksa@pop.interport.net
Home Page: www.ncto.org
Social Media: Facebook, Twitter, LinkedIn

William L Jasper, Chairman
James C Self III, Vice Chairman
Augustine Tantillo, President
Sarah Pierce, Senior VP
Mike Hubbard, VP

Represents U.S. manufacturers and contractors, designing studios and related business engaged in the production of knitted sportswear and knitted products of all types.

22522 Northern Textile Association
1001 Connecticut Ave NW
Suite 315
Washington, DC 20036

202-822-8028
Fax: 202-822-8029
E-Mail: info@ktausa.org
Home Page: www.ncto.org
Social Media: Facebook, Twitter, LinkedIn

William L Jasper, Chairman
James C Self III, Vice Chairman
Augustine Tantillo, President
Sarah Pierce, Senior VP
Mike Hubbard, VP

The KTA is an active participant in the International Mechinery and Equipment exhibition that takes place in Textile Hall in Greenville, South Carolina and highlights the latest in knitting and related dying and finishing equipment.

22523 Restoration Industry Association
12339 Carroll Avenue
Suite K
Rockville, MD 20852

301-231-6505
800-272-7012
Fax: 301-231-6569
E-Mail: info@restorationindustry.org
Home Page: www.restorationindustry.org
Social Media: Facebook, Twitter, LinkedIn

Timothy Shaw, Executive Director
Valorie Peduto, Accountant

A trade association for cleaning and restoration professionals worldwide, and the foremost authority, trainer and educator in the industry.
1100 Members
Founded in 1946

22524 Schiffi Lace & Embroidery Manufacturers Association
26 Industrial Ave
Suite 2
Fairview, NJ 07022-1600

201-840-7611
Fax: 201-943-7793
E-Mail: info@schiffli.org
Home Page: www.schiffli.org
Social Media: Facebook, Twitter

August Bischoff, President
Vincent Mesiano, VP

Crafted lace, and embroidery that adorns lingerie and dresses t towels, sheets, curtains, tablecloths, patches, logos and much more.
Founded in 1848

22525 Secondary Materials and Recycled Textiles Association
3465 Box Hill Corp. Center Drive
Suite H
Abingdon, MD 21009

443-640-1050
Fax: 443-640-1086
E-Mail: Heather@KINGmgmt.org
Home Page: www.smartasn.org
Social Media: Facebook, Twitter, LinkedIn, Youtube

Paul Bailey, Officer
Borton Shapiro, Owner

A dynamic international association which seeks to strengthen the economic opportunities of its members. Promotes the interdependence of all its industry segments by providing a common forum for networking, education, and trade.
Founded in 1932

22526 Shippers of Recycled Textiles
7910 Woodmont Ave # 1405
Bethesda, MD 20814-3082

301-907-0001
Fax: 301-656-1079
E-Mail: smartinfo@kingmgmt.org
Home Page: www.sorti.org
Social Media: Facebook, Twitter

Eric Stubin, President
Robert Goode, Treasurer
Lou Buty, VP
75 Members
Founded in 1988

22527 Southern Textile Association
PO Box 66
Gastonia, NC 28053-0066

704-824-3522
Fax: 704-824-0630
Home Page: www.southerntextile.org
Social Media: Facebook, Twitter

Larry W Oates, Chairman
Lee Thomas, President
Russell W Mims, Jr, First VP

Represents the textile and clothing industry in the South.
Founded in 1908

22528 Surface Design Association
PO Box 20430
Albuquerque, NM 87154

707-829-3110
Fax: 707-829-3285
E-Mail: info@surfacedesign.org
Home Page: www.surfacedesign.org
Social Media: Facebook, Twitter, LinkedIn

Jane Dunnewood, President
Jeanne Beck, VP
Melinda Lowy, Treasurer
Ann Graham, Secretary
Diane Sandlin, Executive Director

Aims to stimulate, promote and improve education in the area of surface design, to encourage the surface designer as an individual artist and to provide a forum for exchange of ideas through conferences and publications.
Founded in 1977
Mailing list available for rentat $75 per M

22529 TRI/Princeton
601 Prospect Ave
PO Box 625
Princeton, NJ 08542

609-430-4820
Fax: 609-683-7836
E-Mail: info@triprinceton.org
Home Page: www.triprinceton.org
Social Media: Facebook, Twitter, LinkedIn

Kurl L Adams, Chair
David Graham, Vice Chairman
Yash K Kamath, Research Director
Robert J. Bianchin, Chairman of the Board
Kurt L. Adams, Vice Chair

Provides advanced research and education in polymers, fibers, films, personal care and porous materials.
40 Members
Founded in 1930

22530 Textile Care Allied Trades Association
271 Us Highway 46
Suite C106
Fairfield, NJ 07004-2432

973-244-1790
Fax: 973-244-4455
E-Mail: info@tcata.org
Home Page: www.tcata.org
Social Media: Facebook, Twitter, LinkedIn

David Cotter, CEO
Cheryl Paglia, Office Manager

Represents the interests of distributors and manufacturers of equipment and supplies for the cleaning industry.

22531 Textile Rental Services Association
1800 Diagonal Rd
Suite 200
Alexandria, VA 22314-2842

703-519-0029
877-770-9274
Fax: 703-519-0026
E-Mail: trsa@trsa.org
Home Page: www.trsa.org
Social Media: Facebook, Twitter, LinkedIn, Youtube, RSS

Greg Jelpema, Chairman
Robert Doud, Executive Director

Covers the uniform, linen supply, health care and dust control service markets.

22532 The Knitting Guild Association (TKGA)
1100-H Brandywine Boulevard
Zanesville, OH 43701-7303

740-452-4541
Fax: 740-452-2552
E-Mail: tkga@tkga.com
Home Page: www.tkga.com
Social Media: Facebook, Twitter, Pinterest

Penny Sitler, Executive Director

Membership organization for knitters with focus on knitting education and enhancing knitters skills.
11000 Members
Founded in 1984

Newsletters

22533 Embroidery News
Schiffi Lace & Embroidery Manufacturers Assn
596 Anderson Avenue
Suite 203
Cliffside Park, NJ 07010-1831

201-943-7757
Fax: 201-943-7793

Leonard Seiler, Editor
Eugene Schrouzol, Publisher

Newsletter for the embroidery industry.
Frequency: BiMonthly
Circulation: 500

22534 Marine Textiles
RCM Enterprises
12 Oaks Center #922
Wayzata, MN 55391

800-451-9278

Mara Sidney, Publisher
Jim Penningroth, Editor

Serves firms in the boating market who use fabrics and furnishings. Accepts advertising.
Cost: $28.00

Magazines & Journals

22535 AATCC Review
American Assoc Textile Chemists and Colorists
1 Davis Dr
Research Triangle Park, NC 27709-2215

919-549-8141
800-360-5380
Fax: 919-549-8933
E-Mail: danielsj@aatcc.org
Home Page: www.aatcc.org
Social Media: Facebook, Twitter, LinkedIn

John Daniels, Executive VP
Debra Hibbard, Executive Assistant
Charles E Gavin, Treasurer
Brenda Jones, Production Manager

Covers all aspects of design, dyeing, printing, finishing, and testing as they relate to textile manufacturing, including fibers, fabrics of all types, garments, carpets, home textiles, and industrial products.
Frequency: Monthly
ISSN: 1532-8813
Founded in 1997
Mailing list available for rent
Printed in 4 colors on glossy stock

22536 Cleaning & Restoration Magazine
Restoration Industry Association
12339 Carroll Avenue~
Suite K
Rockville, MD 20852

301-231-6505
800-272-7012
Fax: 301-231-6569
E-Mail: info@restorationindustry.org
Home Page: www.restorationindustry.org

Donald E Manger, Executive Director
Patricia L Harman, Communications Director
Valorie D. Seely, Accountant

Trade journal covering fire and water damage restoration, rug and textile cleaning, indoor air quality and business issues.
Frequency: Monthly
Circulation: 6000

22537 Fabric Architecture
Industrial Fabrics Association International
1801 County Road B W
Roseville, MN 55113-4061
651-222-2508
800-225-4324
Fax: 651-631-9334
E-Mail: bnwhite@ifai.org
Home Page: www.ifai.com

Stephen Warner, CEO

Strives to inform architects, designers, landscape architects, engineers and other specifiers about architectural fabric structutres, the fibers and fabrics used to make them, their design possibilities, their construction, and issues regarding their applicability and acceptance.
Cost: $39.00
Frequency: Bi-Monthly

22538 Geotechnical Fabrics Report
Industrial Fabrics Association International
1801 County Road B W
Roseville, MN 55113-4061

651-222-2508
800-225-4324
Fax: 651-631-9334
E-Mail: generalinfo@ifai.com
Home Page: www.ifai.com

Stephen Warner, CEO
James Dankert, Managing Editor
Stephen B Duerk, Chairman
Beth L Hungiville, Managing Director
Miller Weldmaster, Director

Peer reviewed technical journal for civil engineers using geosynthetics in road construction, errosion control, hazardous waste, drainage, containment and reinforcement.
Cost: $49.00
Circulation: 16,000
ISSN: 0882-4983
Founded in 1988
Printed in 4 colors on glossy stock

22539 Home Textiles Today
Reed Business Information
360 Park Ave S
New York, NY 10010-1737

646-746-6400
800-446-6551
Fax: 646-756-7583
E-Mail: corporatecommunications@reedbusiness.com
Home Page: www.reedbusiness.com

John Poulin, CEO
Mark Fraser, Publisher

Textile industry news, reports, research and summaries for the professional.
Circulation: 8000
Founded in 1979

22540 IFAI'S Marine Fabricator
Industrial Fabrics Association International
1801 County Road B W
Roseville, MN 55113-4061
651-222-2508
800-225-4324
Fax: 651-631-9334
E-Mail: generalinfo@ifai.com
Home Page: www.ifai.com

Stephen Warner, CEO
George K Ochs, Chairman
Jeffrey W Kirk, Vice Chairman

Publication contains articles designed for beginning to intermediate level fabricators, advanced techniques and technology, profiles, business tips, industry news, new products and publications, and showcases of fabricators' craftmanship.
Frequency: Quarterly
Circulation: 5000
Founded in 1964

22541 Impressions Magazine
Miller Freeman Publications
13760 Noel Rd
Suite 500
Dallas, TX 75240-7336

972-239-3060
800-527-0207
Fax: 972-419-7825

Carl Piazza, Publisher
Laura Gonz, Editor

Covers the textile screen printing imprinted sportswear retailing, and commercial embroidery industry. Accepts advertising.
Cost: $36.00
250 Pages
Frequency: Annual

22542 Industrial Fabric Products Review
Industrial Fabrics Association International
1801 County Road B W
Roseville, MN 55113-4061

651-222-2508
800-225-4324
Fax: 651-631-9334
E-Mail: generalinfo@ifai.com
Home Page: www.ifai.com

Stephen Warner, CEO

Keeps individuals up to date on the information needed to keep their business growing, including reports on traditional or emerging markets and end products worldwide; forecasts and analyses of industry trends, announcements of new technologies in fibers, fabrics, equipment and treatments, and profiles of growth-oriented businesses and prodcuts.
Cost: $69.00
Frequency: Monthly'
Founded in 1915

22543 Journal of Engineered Fibers & Fabrics
INDA Association of Nonwoven Fabrics
1100 Crescent Green
Suite 115
Cary, NC 27511

919-233-1210
Fax: 919-233-1282
Home Page: www.inda.org
Social Media: Facebook, Twitter, LinkedIn

Rory Holmes, President
Peggy Blake, Director of Marketing
Ian Butler, Director Market Research
Todd~ Bassett, Managing Director
Monica Moretti, Tresurer

International peer reviewed scientific eJournal that publishes original R&D on all aspects o ffabric technologies and their value chain from raw materials to end-use products.
Frequency: Quarterly
Circulation: 3000
Founded in 1968

22544 Journal of Industrial Textiles
851 New Holland Avenue
Suite 3535
Lancaster, PA 17604

717-291-5609
800-233-9936
Fax: 717-295-4538
Home Page: www.jit.sagepub.com

22545 Marine Fabricator
Industrial Fabrics Association International
1801 County Road BW
Roseville, MN 55413
651-222-2508
800-225-4324
Fax: 651-631-9334
E-Mail: cptschida@ifai.com
Home Page: www.ifai.com
Social Media: Facebook, Twitter, LinkedIn

Galynn Nordstrom, Senior Editor

Educates and informs 5,000 marine shop professionals and also provides reportage that reflects the innovations and trends of the industry.
Cost: $34.00
Frequency: Bi-Monthly

22546 Nonwovens Industry
Rodman Publishing
70 Hilltop Rd
Suite 3000
Ramsey, NJ 07446-1150

201-825-2552
Fax: 201-825-0553

E-Mail: info@rodpub.com
Home Page: www.nutraceuticalsworld.com
Social Media: Facebook, Twitter, LinkedIn

Rodman Zilenziger Jr, President
Matt Montgomery, VP

Written for nonwoven roll goods producers, converters and end-use manufacturers.
70 Pages
Frequency: Monthly
Circulation: 11000
Founded in 1970

22547 Nonwovens World
MTS Publications
4100 S 7th Street
Kalamazoo, MI 49009-8461

269-375-1236
Fax: 269-375-6710
E-Mail: admin@marketingtechnologyservice.com
Home Page: www.marketingtechnologyservice.com

James P Hanson, Editor
Cindy Costello, Circulation Manager
Wayne C Carter, Advertising Sales Director

Covers new products, as well as production and marketing strategies.
Circulation: 10384
Founded in 1986

22548 Sheep Industry News
9785 Maroon Circle
Suite 360
Englewood, CO 80112

303-771-3500
Fax: 303-771-8200
Home Page: www.sheepusa.org
Social Media: Facebook

Clint Krebs, President
Peter Orwick, Executive Director
Rita Kourlis Samuelson, Wool Marketing Director

A federation of state associations dedicated to the welfare and profitability of the sheep industry.
Cost: $25.00
8000+ Members
Frequency: Monthly
Circulation: 8000
Founded in 1865

22549 Surface Design Journal
PO Box 360
Sebastopol, CA 95473-360

707-829-3110
Fax: 707-829-3285
E-Mail: info@40surfacedesign.org
Home Page: www.surfacedesign.org
Social Media: Facebook, Twitter, LinkedIn

Jason Pollen, President

Professional organization of more than 2,000 textile artists, designers for industry, and academicians.
Cost: $8.00
52 Pages
Frequency: Quarterly
Circulation: 6000
Founded in 1977

22550 Textile Rental Magazine
Textile Rental Services Association
1800 Diagonal Rd
Suite 200
Alexandria, VA 22314-2842

703-519-0029
877-770-9274
Fax: 703-519-0026
E-Mail: trsa@trsa.org
Home Page: www.trsa.org
Social Media: Facebook, Twitter, LinkedIn, You Tube

Roger Cocivera, President/CEO
Jack Morgan, Editor

Packed with valuable tips and ideas.
Frequency: Monthly

22551 Textile Research Journal
TRI Princeton
PO Box 625
Princeton, NJ 08542

609-924-3150
Fax: 609-683-7836
Home Page: www.triprinceton.com

Dr. Gail R Eaton, President

Provides advanced research and education in polymers, fibers, films, personel care and porous materials.
Frequency: Monthly
Founded in 1930

Trade Shows

22552 American Home Sewing & Craft Association Sewing & Craft Show: AHSCA
American Home Sewing and Craft Association
1350 Broadway
Suite 1601
New York, NY 10018

212-714-1633
Fax: 212-714-1655
E-Mail: info@sewing.org
Home Page: www.sewing.org

200 exhibits of fabric, notions, patterns, sewing and knitting machines, crafts and trimmings. Attended by professionals from major chain stores, independent retailers, wholesalers and manufacturers.
3000 Attendees
Frequency: Semiannual

22553 American Textile Machinery Exhibition International
Textile Hall Corporation
PO Box 5823
Greenville, SC 29606

864-331-2277
Fax: 864-331-2282

Butler Mullins, Director

Exhibition of machinery, supplies and services required for manufacture of yarn and fiber, for the weaving, knitting and dying/printing/finishing processes, for manufacture of non-wovens and for plant maintenance.
10000 Attendees
Frequency: September

22554 Apparel Printing and Embroidery Expo
Primedia
3585 Engineering Drive
Suite 100
Norcross, GA 30092

678-421-3000
Fax: 913-967-1898
Home Page: www.primediabusiness.com

Joanie Forsythe, Sales Manager
Arlene Mayfield, President
Scott Asher, VP

Semi-annual show of 200 manufacturers, suppliers and distributors of commercial screen printing and embroidery equipment and supplies, computer graphic systems and softgoods such as T-shirts, sweats, jackets and caps.
3000 Attendees

22555 Apparel Show of the Americas
Bobbin Publishing/Miller Freeman
PO Box 279
Euless, TX 76039

817-215-1600
800-693-1363
Fax: 817-215-1666
E-Mail: bobbin.expoinfo@mfi.com
Home Page: wwwmfi.com

Betty Webb, Trade Show Director

Conference, seminar and 329 exhibits of equipment, fabrics, accessories and services for sewn products and apparel.
5790 Attendees
Frequency: Annual
Founded in 1992

22556 Association of Specialists in Cleaning & Restoration Convention
Restoration Industry Association
9810 Patuxent Woods Drive
Suite K
Columbia, MD 21046-1595

443-878-1000
800-272-7012
Fax: 443-878-1010
E-Mail: info@restorationindustry.org
Home Page: www.restorationindustry.org
Social Media: Facebook, Twitter, LinkedIn, You Tube

Donald E Manger, Executive Director
Patricia L Harman, Communications Director

Annual convention and exhibits of carpet, upholstery and draperies cleaning and restoration equipment, duct cleaning supplies and services, 100+ booths.
600 Attendees
Frequency: Annual
Founded in 1945

22557 Filtration: International Conference & Exposition
INDA Association of Nonwoven Fabrics
1100 Crescent Green
Suite 115
Cary, NC 27511

919-233-1210
Fax: 919-233-1282
Home Page: www.inda.org
Social Media: Facebook, Twitter, LinkedIn

Rory Holmes, President
Peggy Blake, Director of Marketing
Ian Butler, Director Market Research/Stats

The North American Show for all aspects of filter media. One-stop shopping where you can compare products and prices. See state-of-the-art products. Great networking experience.
1400 Attendees
Frequency: Annual

22558 Geosynthetics
Industrial Fabrics Association International
1801 County Road BW
Roseville, MN 55113

651-222-2508
800-225-4324
Fax: 651-631-9334
E-Mail: confmgmt@ifai.com
Home Page: www.ifaiexpo.info
Social Media: Facebook, Twitter, LinkedIn

Beth Wistrcill, Conference Manager

Features design, engineering strategies and cost-saving geosynthetics solutions.
Frequency: February

22559 IDEA, International Engineered Fabrics Con ference + Expositions
INDA Association of Nonwoven Fabrics

1100 Crescent Green
Suite 115
Cary, NC 27518

919-233-1210
Fax: 919-233-1282
Home Page: www.inda.org
Social Media: Facebook, Twitter, LinkedIn

Dave Rousse, President
Joan Izzo, Director of Marketing
Brad Kalil, Director Market Research/Stats

See, touch and buy state-of-the-art engineered fabrics. Compare all the components used to make first class fabrics-raw materials, chemicals, machinery and converting and finishind services.
5200 Attendees
Frequency: Triennial

22560 IFAI Annual Expo
Industrial Fabrics Association International
1801 County Road BW
Roseville, MN 55113

651-222-2508
800-225-4324
Fax: 651-631-9334
Home Page: http://www.ifaiexpo.com

Beth Wistrcill, Conference Manager
Miller Weldmaster, Director
JoAnne Ferris, Director of Marketing

A trade event on the America's for the technical textiles and specialty fabrics industry.
Frequency: Annual/September

22561 International Engineered Fabrics
INDA Association of Nonwoven Fabrics
1100 Crescent Green
Suite 115
Cary, NC 27511

919-233-1210
Fax: 919-233-1282
Home Page: www.inda.org
Social Media: Facebook, Twitter, LinkedIn

Rory Holmes, President
Peggy Blake, Director of Marketing
Ian Butler, Director Market Research/Stats

See, touch and buy state-of-the-art engineered fabrics. Compare all the components used to make first class fabrics-raw materials, chemicals, machinery and converting and finishind services.

22562 International Fashion and Boutique Shows
100 Wells Avenue
#9103
Newton, MA 02459-3210

617-731-8316

Samuel Starr, Show Manager

1,800 booths.
30M Attendees
Frequency: January

22563 International Fastener Exposition
PEMCO
383 Main Avenue
Norwalk, CT 06851-1543

203-840-7700
Fax: 630-260-0395

Barbara Silverman, VP, Show Manager
Laura Rezek, Advertising

450 booths developed specifically for the fastener manufacturing and precision formed parts industry.
4.8M Attendees
Frequency: March

22564 International Hosiery Exposition
Hosiery Association
7421 Carmel Executive Park
Charlotte, NC 28226

704-365-0913
Fax: 704-362-2056
E-Mail: thainfo@hosieryassociation.com
Home Page: www.hosieryassociation.com
Social Media: Facebook, Twitter, LinkedIn

Sally Kay, President
Sheila Simpson, Director of Finance
Vicki Camp, Office Manager

225 booths.
10M Attendees
Frequency: May
Founded in 1905

Directories & Databases

22565 ATI's Textile Red Book: America's Textile Industries
Billian Publishing Company
2100 Powers Ferry Rd SE
Suite 300
Atlanta, GA 30339-5055

770-955-5656
800-533-8484
Fax: 770-952-0669
Home Page: www.billian.com

Jim Borneman, President
Dave Ramsays, Database Sales
Douglas Billian, Owner

Comprehensive reference guide for the textile industry. Includes over 6,000 mills in the US, Canada and Mexico. In addition to providing the complete contact information for the plant, each listing gives key personnel, products produced, fibers processed and mill equipment used.
Cost: $160.00
Frequency: Annual
ISSN: 1047-6903

22566 America's Textiles International
Billian Publishing Company
2100 Powers Ferry Rd SE
Suite 300
Atlanta, GA 30339-5055

770-955-5656
Fax: 770-952-0669
Home Page: www.billian.com

Annual directory provides the complete contact information - including Web sites and e-mail addresses for over 2,400 equipment, technology and service providers to the textile industry.
Frequency: Annual
Circulation: 32,000
ISSN: 0890-9970
Founded in 1887

22567 American Wool Industry White Pages
American Sheep Industry Association
9785 Maroon Circle
Suite 360
Englewood, CO 80112

303-771-3500
Fax: 303-771-8200
Home Page: www.sheepusa.org
Social Media: Facebook, Twitter

Margaret Soulen Hinson, President
Peter Orwick, Executive Director
Rita Kourlis Samuelson, Wool Marketing Director

Wool and wool product services, warehouses, pools, buyers, processors, sources of pelts and suppliers.

22568 Davison's Textile Blue Book
Davison Publishing Company
PO Box 1289
Concord, NC 28026-1289
704-785-8700
800-328-4766
Fax: 704-785-8701
Home Page: www.davisonbluebook.com

Carol Nealy, Advertising Manager

5,400 mills, dryers, finishers, in the United States, Canada, and Mexico.
Cost: $165.00
800 Pages
Frequency: Annual
ISBN: 0-875150-69-1
Founded in 1866

22569 Interior Textiles Fabric Resource Directory
Wool Bureau/Atlanta Merchandise Mart
240 Peachtree Street NW
Suite 6F11
Atlanta, GA 30303-1361

404-577-4320

Approximately 108 manufacturers and suppliers of wool and wool blend upholsteries, wallcoverings and draperies.
45 Pages

22570 International Textile & Apparel Association Membership Directory
PO Box 1360
Monument, CO 80132-1360

719-488-3716
E-Mail: info@itaaonline.org
Home Page: www.itaaonline.org

Sandra S Hutton, Executive Director

Professional association for 1,000 college professors of clothing and textile studies.
8-12 Pages
Frequency: 6 per year
Circulation: Members
Founded in 1944

22571 Knitted Textile Association: Official Resource Guide and Fact Book
Knitted Textile Association
386 Park Avenue
New York, NY 10016-8804

212-545-9014
Fax: 212-889-6160

Peter Adelman, Editor

A list of over 150 member manufacturers, suppliers and distributors of knitted fabric products and services.
Cost: $10.00
Frequency: Annual

22572 Knitting Times: Buyers' Guide Issue
National Knitwear & Sportswear Association
386 Park Avenue S
New York, NY 10016-8804

212-545-9014
Fax: 212-532-0766

Dawne G Shink, Editor

List of about 4,500 suppliers and manufacturers of chemicals, contract, management and computer services, cutting room equipment, dyeing, finishing and printing equipment, knitted and woven fabrics, fibers and yarn, interfacing, pressing and steaming, knitting, sewing and trimming equipment, materials handling and plant control services.
Cost: $25.00
Frequency: Annual, September
Circulation: 10,000

22573 LDB Interior Textiles Buyers' Guide
EW Williams Publications

342 Madison Avenue
Room 1901
New York, NY 10173-1999

212-697-1122
Fax: 212-661-1713
E-Mail: ldb342@aol.com

Renee Bennett, Editor-in-Chief
Aleksandra Kazimierska, Directory Manager
Janys Kuznier, Circulation Director

Over 2,000 manufacturers, importers and suppliers of home fashions products and services, decorative fabric converters and alternative window coverings, fabricators, manufacturer's representatives and others allied to the home fashions trade.
Cost: $40.00
Frequency: Annual June
Circulation: 12,000

22574 Narrow Fabrics Institute: Buyer's Guide
Narrow Fabrics Institute
345 Cedar Street
Suite 800
Saint Paul, MN 55101-1004

800-225-4324
Fax: 651-222-8215

Approximately 34 producers of narrow fabrics for use in automotive medical, lifting, environmental safety, recreational, military, air cargo, trucks, and other fields, requiring industrial fabrics.
Frequency: Annual fall

22575 Textile Chemist and Colorist Buyers Guide
American Assoc Textile Chemists and Colorists
PO Box 12215
Research Triangle Park, NC 27709-2215

919-549-8141
800-360-5380
Fax: 919-549-8933
E-Mail: danielsj@aatcc.org
Home Page: www.aatcc.org

John Daniels, Executive VP
Debra Hibbard, Executive Assistant
Charles E Gavin, Treasurer
Brenda Jones, Product Orders

Over 500 dye, pigments, machinery and equipment manufacturers are profiled.
ISBN: 0-040490-0 -
Founded in 1921
Mailing list available for rent

22576 Textile Technology Digest
2551 Ivy Road
Charlottesville, VA 22903

434-296-5511
Fax: 434-296-2957
E-Mail: webmaster@itt.edu
Home Page: www.itt.edu

Offers abstracts to worldwide literature from more than 1,300 sources annually such as proceedings, trade literature and other sources collected by the institutes library. The CD-ROM quarterly is available for $1,710 plus shipping. Network licenses begin at $500 for up to 10 simultaneous users.
Cost: $545.00
Frequency: Monthly
Founded in 1944

22577 Wool Source List
Kairalla Agency
27 Raymond Street
Manchester, MA 01944-1614
Eleanor Kairalla, Executive Director

Conducts trade and consumer polls on woolen apparel.
360 Pages
Founded in 1939

Industry Web Sites

22578 http://gold.greyhouse.com
G.O.L.D Grey House OnLine Databases

Grey House Publishing's online database platform, GOLD, offers Quick Search, Keyword Search and Expert Search for most business sectors including textile markets. The GOLD platform makes finding the information you need quick and easy - whether you're a novice searcher or an experienced database user. All of Grey House's directory products are available for subscription on the GOLD platform.

22579 www.aatcc.org
American Association of Textile Chemists & Colorists

22580 www.atmanet.org
American Textile Machinery Association

Advances the common interests of its members, works to improve business conditions within the US textile machinery industry from a global perspective and markets the industry and members' machinery, parts and services.

22581 www.carpet-rug.com
Carpet & Rug Institute

22582 www.cottoninc.com
Cotton

22583 www.fibersource.com
American Fiber Manufacturers Association

Trade association for US companies that manufacture synthetic and cellulostic fibers. The industry employs 30,000 people and produces over 9 billion pounds of fiber in the US. The association maintains close ties to other manufactured fiber trade associations worldwide.

22584 www.flocking.org
American Flock Association

Fosters the use of flocked products. Strives to improve and advance flocking technology.

22585 www.greyhouse.com
Grey House Publishing

Authoritative reference directories for most business sectors including textile markets. Users can search the online databases with varied search criteria allowing for custom searches by product category, geographic area, sales volume, keyword, subject and more. Full Grey House catalog and online ordering also available.

22586 www.ifai.com
Industrial Fabrics Association International

Association of geosynthetics, fabricators, installers, equipment manufacturers, suppliers, testing firms, consultants, and educators, who produce textiles, nets, mats, grids, and other products. Industrial Fabrics Association International is the industry's first source for technical fabric resources and information.

22587 www.inda.org
INDA Association of Nonwoven Fabrics Industries

22588 www.itt.edu
Institute of Textile Technology

A graduate school supported in part by member companies. Publishes the Textile Technology Digest.

22589 www.sewing.org
Home Sewing Association

Represents most facets of the home sewing industry. National trade association for independent sewing machine dealers and distributors.

22590 www.sleepproducts.org
International Sleep Products Association

Maintains a strong organization to influence government actions, inform and educate the membership and act on industry issues to enhance the growth,profitability and stature of the sleep products industry. Provides members with information and services to manage their business more effectively and efficiently. Publishes a magazine devoted exclusively to the mattress industry, BEDtimes covers a broad range of issue and news important to the industry.

22591 www.smartasn.org
Shippers of Recycled Textiles

22592 www.textilenta.org
Northern Textile Association

Textile manufacturing trade association.

22593 www.triprinceton.org
TRI Princeton

TRI/Princeton provides advanced research and education in polymers, fibers, films, personel care, and porous materials.

Associations

22594 American Wholesale Marketers Association
2750 Prosperity Ave
Suite 530
Fairfax, VA 22031-4338

703-208-3358
800-482-2962
Fax: 703-573-5738
E-Mail: info@awmanet.org
Home Page: www.awmanet.org
Social Media: Facebook, Twitter, LinkedIn

Scott Ramminger, President & CEO
Joel Brown, Assoc. Publisher, Business Dev
Jennifer Moulton, Director, Administration, IT
Meredith Kimbrell, Director, Education

A trade association supporting the confectionary, tobacco and allied products industries through programs and services. members include wholesale distributors, manufacturers, and other allieds to the industry.
1000 Members
Founded in 1942

22595 Association of Dark Leaf Tobacco Dealers
2500 S Main St
Springfield, TN 37172-0638

615-384-9576
Fax: 615-384-6461
E-Mail: h.krozel@hailcotton.com
Home Page: www.hailcotton.com

Warren Corbin, President & CEO
Tom Wilks, Executive VP
Roderick Roe, CFO
Andy Spies, Executive VP Sales
Eric Van Der Linden, Executive VP

An affiliate of Burley and Dark Leaf Tobacco Export Association.
Founded in 1902

22596 Bright Belt Warehouse Association
PO Box 120004
Raleigh, NC 27606

919-828-8988
Fax: 919-821-2092
E-Mail: donaf@clemson.edu

Association of flue-cured tobacco warehousemen.

22597 Burley Stabilization Corporation
835 Bill Jones Industrial Dr.
Springfield, TN 37172

615-212-0508
Fax: 866-828-6501
E-Mail: burleytobacco@aol.com
Home Page: www.burleystabilization.com

George Marks, President
Joe K Thomas III, VP
Charlie C Finch, Managing Director

Association of Burley tobacco warehouses in Kentucky, Tennessee, Ohio, Missouri, Indiana, Virginia, West Virginia and North Carolina.

22598 Burley Tobacco Growers Cooperative Association
620 S Broadway
Lexington, KY 40508-3149

859-252-3561
Fax: 859-231-9804
E-Mail: stephanie@burleytobacco.com
Home Page: www.burleytobacco.com

Pat Raines, President
Eddie Warren, VP
Robert Reed Bush Sr., Secretary
Al Pedigo, Treasurer
Steve Pratt, General Manager

Burley tobacco grower cooperative

22599 Cigar Association of America
1100 G Street NW
Suite 1050
Washington, DC 20005-7405

202-223-8204
866-482-3570
Fax: 202-833-0379
Home Page: www.cigarassociation.org
Social Media: Facebook, Twitter

Dan Carr, Chairman
Craig Williamson, President

Consists of cigar manufacturers, importers and major industry suppliers. Provides government relations and statistical services to the industry and promotes the image of the cigar.
60 Members
Founded in 1937

22600 Eastern Dark-Fired Tobacco
1109 S Main St
Springfield, TN 37172-3509

615-384-4543
Fax: 615-384-4545

Dan Borthick, President

Association of North Central Tennessee and South Central Kentucky growers that produce Type 22 Dark fire-cured and Type 35 Dark air-cured (one sucker) tobacco.

22601 Flue-Cured Tobacco Cooperative
1304 Annapolis Dr
Raleigh, NC 27608-2130

919-821-4560
Fax: 919-821-4564
E-Mail: arnoldh3151@ipass.net
Home Page: www.ustobaccofarmer.com

Tommy Bunn, President/CEO
Stuart Thompson, CFO/Secretary/Treasurer
Ken Bopp, VP, Administration
Mike Lynch, Senior VP, Global Sales & Marekting
Sam Tie, Manager, Human Resource

Marketing cooperative which administers price support and provides %100 US flue-cured tobacco direct to purchasers.
Founded in 1946

22602 Friends of Tobacco
403 B East New Bern Road
Kinston, NC 20501

919-522-4769
Fax: 919-522-4769
E-Mail: fot@fujipub.com
Home Page: fujipub.com/fot

Gary Corbett, President

Nonprofit organization promoting the economic importance of tobacco and freedom of choice in using tobacco products.
16000 Members
Founded in 1991

22603 Retail Tobacco Dealers of America
4 Bradley Park Ct
Suite 2H
Columbus, GA 31904-3637

706-494-1143
Fax: 706-494-1893
E-Mail: info@rtda.org
Home Page: www.rtda.org
Social Media: Facebook, Twitter, LinkedIn, Youtube

Joe Row, Executive Director

Represents and assists retail tobacconists.

22604 Specialty Tobacco Council
102 W Third Street
Suite 200-B
Winston-Salem, NC 27106

336-723-4311
Fax: 336-759-0965
E-Mail: hroemer@specialtytobacco.org
Home Page: specialtytobacco.org

Henry C Roemer III, Executive Director

Represents manufacturers and importers of specialty tobacco products.
Founded in 1984

22605 Tobacco Associates
1306 Annapolis Drive
Suite 102
Raleigh, NC 27608-2136

919-821-7670
Fax: 919-821-7674
E-Mail: tar@tobaccoassociatesinc.org
Home Page: www.tobaccoassociatesinc.org

Kirk Wayne, President
Hank Mozingo, VP
Veronica Martins, Office Manager

Mission is to enhance understanding of US flue-cured tobacco and assist manufacturers interested in adding quality US leaf to their products.
Founded in 1947
Mailing list available for rent

22606 Tobacco Association of the United States
PO Box 8019
Princeton, NC 08543-8019

609-275-4900
Fax: 609-275-8379
E-Mail: tma@tma.org
Home Page: www.tma.org

Tommy Bunn, Executive VP

Promotes market for US leaf tobacco.
100 Members
Founded in 1900

22607 Tobacco Growers Association of North Carolina
3901 Barrett Dr
Suite 202
Raleigh, NC 27609-6611

919-781-0066
Fax: 919-781-0066
Home Page: www.tganc.com

Graham Boyd, Executive VP

Commodity association for North Carolina tobacco growers.
10000 Members
Founded in 1981

22608 Tobacco Merchants Association
PO Box 8019
Princeton, NJ 08543-8019

609-275-4900
Fax: 609-275-8379
E-Mail: tma@tma.org
Home Page: www.tma.org
Social Media: Facebook, Twitter

Farrell Delman, President
Mark Schoenseld, Editor
Roberta Crosdy, Marketing Manager
Mark Schoenseld, Publisher

Tobacco trade association and source of current information on the tobacco industry.
170 Members
Founded in 1915

Newsletters

22609 **Tobacco Barometer**
Tobacco Merchants Association of the United States
PO Box 8019
Princeton, NJ 08543-8019

609-275-4900
Fax: 609-275-8379
E-Mail: tma@tma.org
Home Page: www.tma.org
Social Media: Facebook, Twitter

Mark Schoenseld, Editor
Roberta Crosdy, Marketing Manager
Mark Schoenseld, Farrell
Delman President

Tobacco industry news.
Frequency: Monthly
Founded in 1915

22610 **Tobacco Products Litigation Reporter**
TPLR
PO Box 1162
Back Bay Annex
Boston, MA 02117-1162

617-373-2026
Fax: 617-437-3672
E-Mail: info@tplr.com
Home Page: www.tplr.com/

Richard Daynard, Publisher
Lissy Friedman, Publication Director
Mark Gottlieb, Legal Editor

Tobacco industry news.
Cost: $995.00
Frequency: 8 issues per year
Founded in 1950

22611 **Tobacco on Trial**
Tobacco Products Liability Project
102 The Fenway
Cushing Hall, Suite 117
Boston, MA 02115-5098

617-373-2026
Fax: 617-373-3672
Home Page: www.tobacco-on-trial.com

Richard A Daynard, Publisher
Susan L Frank, Editor
Mark Gottlieb, Executive Director
Richard A Daynard, President

Tobacco industry news.
Cost: $95.00
Founded in 1979

Magazines & Journals

22612 **Smokeshop**
Lockwood Trade Journal
26 Broadway
Suite 9M2
New York, NY 10004-1777

212-391-2060
800-766-2633
Fax: 212-827-0945
E-Mail: sales@smokeshopmag.com
Home Page: www.lockwoodpublications.com

Robert Lockwood, CEO
Edward Hoyt III, Editor
Bob Olesen, Advertising Sales Manager

Retail tobacco dealer's prevailing source for industry news designed to help readers operate their business more successfully.
Cost: $24.00
Founded in 1970

22613 **Tobacco International**
Lockwood Trade Journal
26 Broadway
Suite 9M2
New York, NY 10004-1777

212-391-2060
Fax: 212-827-0945
E-Mail: sales@smokeshopmag.com
Home Page: www.lockwoodpublications.com

Robert Lockwood, CEO
Edward Hoyt III, Editor
Bob Olesen, Advertising Sales Manager

This trade publication offers information and news on the importing and exporting of tobacco.
Cost: $25.00
Frequency: Monthly
Founded in 1970

22614 **Tobacco Reporter**
SpecComm International
3000 Highwoods Boulevard
Suite 300
Raleigh, NC 27604-1029

919-878-0540
Fax: 919-876-8531
E-Mail: customerservice@tobaccoreporter.com
Home Page: www.tobaccoreporter.com
Cost: $36.00

ISSN: 0361-5593

22615 **Tobacco Retailer**
Bel-Av Communications
359 Galahad Rd
Bolingbrook, IL 60440-2108

E-Mail: cforman@m2media360.com
Home Page: www.tobaccoretailer.com

Charlie Forman, Group Publisher
Richard Brandes, Editor-in-Chief

Features sales, marketing and operations articles, news and new products, personnel advice, cigar reviews, updates on the National Association of Tobacco Outlets and profiles of leading retailers.
Cost: $29.00
Frequency: Bi-Monthly
Circulation: 15000
Founded in 1998

22616 **Tobacco Science**
2016 Fanning Bridge Road
Fletcher, NC 28732

828-684-3562
Fax: 828-684-8715
E-Mail: pam_puryear@ncsu.edu
Home Page: www.tobaccoscience.com

Dr David Shew, Editor
Pam Puryear, Managing Editor

Scientific journal containing technical reports on tobacco and tobacco smoke.

22617 **Tobacconist**
SpecComm International
3101 Poplarwood Court
Suite 115
Raleigh, NC 27604-1029

919-872-5040
Fax: 919-876-6531
E-Mail: mjackson@speccomm.com
Home Page: www.tobacconistmagazine.com

Dayton Matlick, Publisher
Ed O'Connor, Advertising/Sales Manager
Dayton Matlick, Editor
Dayton Matlick, CEO

A business publication for retail tobacconists in the United States that includes information ranging from critical issues to new products and business advice.
Cost: $28.00
Frequency: Quarterly

Trade Shows

22618 **AWMA Expo**
American Wholesale Marketers Association
1128 16th Street NW
Washington, DC 20036-4808

202-463-2124
800-642-2962
Fax: 202-467-0559
E-Mail: robertp@awmanet.org
Home Page: www.awmanet.org

Robert Pignato, VP Marketing/Industry Affairs

Annual show of 4500 manufacturers and suppliers of confectionery, tobacco, snack foods, juice, novelties and related products.

22619 **Retail Tobacco Dealers of America Trade Show**
4 Bradley Park Court
Suite 2H
Columbus, GA 31904-3637

706-494-1143
Fax: 706-494-1893
E-Mail: rtda@msn.com
Home Page: www.rtda.org

Ira Fader Jr, Show Manager

Trade show for premium tobacco products. Not open to the public. For the benefit of association members only. Containing 950 booths and 6,400 exhibits.
5,500 Attendees
Frequency: July

Directories & Databases

22620 **Tobacco Barometer: Cigarettes and Cigars/ Smoking, Chewing and Snuff**
Tobacco Merchants Association of the United States
Po Box 8019
Princeton, NJ 08543-8019

609-275-4900
Fax: 609-275-8379
Home Page: www.tma.org

Farrell Delman, President

These two databases offers information on every aspect of the tobacco industry.
Frequency: Full text

22621 **Tobacco Reporter's Global Tobacco Industry Guide**
SpecComm International
3000 Highwoods Boulevard
Suite 300
Raleigh, NC 27604-1029

919-878-0540
Fax: 919-876-8531
E-Mail: sales@tobaccoreporter.com
Home Page: www.tobaccoreporter.com

Noel Morris, Publisher
Taco Tuinstra, Managing Editor

Directory of tobacco suppliers, leaf dealers, processors, manufacturers, brokers, marketing boards and associations.
Cost: $78.00
Frequency: Annual

Industry Web Sites

22622 http://gold.greyhouse.com
G.O.L.D Grey House OnLine Databases
Grey House Publishing's online database platform, GOLD, offers Quick Search, Keyword Search and Expert Search for most business sectors including tobacco markets. The GOLD platform makes finding the information you need quick and easy - whether you're a novice searcher or an experienced database user. All of Grey House's directory products are available for subscription on the GOLD platform.

22623 www.awmanet.org
American Wholesale Marketers Association
A trade association representing corporations in the wholesale tobacco industries.

22624 www.buycheapcigarettes.com
We offer discount cigarettes and tobacco products. Cigarettes and tobacco products are for consumer use only. Minimum order is 3 Cartons.

22625 www.freedomnet.org/tobacco.html
Pipe Tobacco Council
Consists of manufacturers and importers of smoking tobacco in the United States. Provides government relations and statistical services to the industry.

22626 www.greyhouse.com
Grey House Publishing
Authoritative reference directories for most business sectors including tobacco markets. Users can search the online databases with varied search criteria allowing for custom searches by product category, geographic area, sales volume, keyword, subject and more. Full Grey House catalog and online ordering also available.

22627 www.paylesscigarettes.com
Sells dicount cigarettes and tobacco products.

22628 www.taxfreetobacco.com
Sells dicount cigarettess.

22629 www.thetobaccoshop.com
Offers discount cigarettes and tobacco products.

22630 www.tobaccoassociatesinc.org
Website of the association representing US flue-cured tobacco producers.

22631 www.ustobaccofarmer.com
Information of interest to tobacco farmers.

Associations

22632 AIT Worldwide Logistics
701 N Rohlwing Rd
Itasca, IL 60143-1348

815-229-7700
800-669-4248
Fax: 630-766-0205
E-Mail: info@aitworldwide.com
Home Page: www.aitworldwide.com
Social Media: Facebook, Twitter, LinkedIn, You Tube

Vaughn Moore, President & CEO
Keith Tholan, Executive VP, Sales
Joe Kayser, Executive VP, Finance
Ray Fennelly, Executive VP, Global Development
Chris Jostes, Ocean Transport Coordinator

AIT Worldwide Logistics provides customers with inovative high-tech support and customization that enhances every shipment by tailoring the technology to the systems of each individual customer. AIT distinguishes itself by offering customers a variety of value-added services to enhance supply chain efficiencies: custom-built IT solutions, flexible worldwide service offerings by ground, air, ocean and rail, an extensive global network, competitive price structure, and superior customer service.

22633 APL Logistics
16220 N Scottsdale Rd
Scottsdale, AZ 85254-1720

510-272-8000
Fax: 602-586-4585
E-Mail: michael_zampa@apl.com
Home Page: www.apllogistics.com/wps/portal/apll

Jim McAdams, President
Tony Zasimovich, VP
William Villalon, VP, Automotive Services
David Frentzel, VP, Contract Logistics
David Howland, VP, Land Transport Services

APL provides customers around the world with container transportation services through a network combining high-quality intermodal operations with state-of-the-art information technology.

22634 Advanced Transit Association
9019 Hamilton Drive
Fairfax, VA 22031-3075

703-591-8328
Home Page: www.advancedtransit.org

Tom Richert, Chairman
Catherine G Burke, President
Bob Dunning, VP
Jerry Kieffer, Manager

Supports the transportation association.
100 Members

22635 Air Courier Conference of America
Express Delivery & Logistics Association
400 Admiral Blvd
Kansas City, MO 64106

703-998-7121
816 221-0254
Fax: 703-998-7123
E-Mail: jmorris@aircour.org
Home Page: www.expressassociation.org

George Trapp, President
Steve Wright, VP
Timothy Byrnes, Treasurer

Air courier and air package delivery companies.

22636 Air Line Pilots Association, International
1625 Massachusetts Ave NW
Washington, DC 20036
703-689-2270
Home Page: www.alpa.org

Lee Moak, President
Sean Cassidy, First Vice-President
Bill Couette, Vice President-Administration
W. Randolph Helling, Vice-President-Finance
Tim Canoll, Executive Administrator

International association for airline pilots
Founded in 1931

22637 Air Transport Association of America
1301 Pennsylvania Ave Nw
Suite 1100
Washington, DC 20004-1738

202-626-4000
Fax: 202-626-4166
E-Mail: ata@airlines.org
Home Page: www.airlines.org
Social Media: Facebook, Twitter, LinkedIn, Youtube

Nicholas E Calio, President & CEO
Paul R Archambeault, Senior VP, CFO & Treasurer
David A Berg, Senior VP, General Counsel
Christine M Burgeson, Senior VP, Global Govt. Affairs
Daniel K Elwell, Senior VP, Safety, Security

Represents US scheduled airlines in domestic and international passenger and cargo operations.
Founded in 1936

22638 Air Transport Research Societyÿ
3433 Van Munching Hall
University of Maryland
College Park, MD 20742

301-405-2204
Fax: 301-314-1023
E-Mail: atrs@rhsmith.umd.edu
Home Page: www.atrsworld.org

Tae H. Oum, Founder, Chair
Martin Dresner, President, CEO
Anming Zhang, VP, Research
Sveinnÿ Gudmundsson, VP, External
Christian Hofer, VP, Programs

A Society for researchers in the field of air transportation
Founded in 1995

22639 Aircraft Owners and Pilots Association (AOPA)
421 Aviation Way
Frederick, MD 21701

301-695-2000
800-872-2672
Fax: 301-695-2375
Home Page: www.aopa.org
Social Media: Facebook, Twitter, LinkedIn, Pinterest, Google+

Mark Baker, President & CEO
James W. Minow, Executive Director
Bruce Landsberg, Senior Safety Advisor

For pilots and aircraft owners
Founded in 1939

22640 American Association of Airport Executives
601 Madison Street
Suite 400
Alexandria, VA 22314

703-824-0504
Fax: 703-820-1395
E-Mail: member.services@aaae.org
Home Page: www.aaae.org
Social Media: Facebook, Twitter, LinkedIn, RSS, Pinterest, YouTube

Todd Hauptli, President & CEO
Spencer Dickerson, C.M., Senior EVP, Global Operations
Joel Bacon, EVP, Govt. & Public Affairs
Carter Morris, EVP, AAAE Services
Brad Van Dam, Senior VP, Federal Affairs

The professional association that represents airport management personnel at public-use commercialand general aviation airports in the US
Founded in 1928

22641 American Association of Motor Vehicle Administrators
4401 Wilson Boulevard
Suite 700
Alexandria, VA 22203

703-522-4200
Home Page: www.aamva.org
Social Media: Facebook, Twitter, LinkedIn, Flickr, YouTube

Non-governmental, voluntary organization who strives to develop model programs in motor vehicle administration
Founded in 1933

22642 American Association of Port Authorities
1010 Duke Street
Alexandria, VA 22314

703-684-5700
Fax: 703-684-6321
E-Mail: info@aapa-ports.org
Home Page: www.aapa-ports.org
Social Media: Facebook, Twitter, LinkedIn

Kristin Decas, Chairman
Kurt J. Nagle, President & CEO
Jean C. Godwin, Executive Vice President
Susan Monteverde, VP, Government Relations
Dr. Rexford B. Sherman, Director of Researchÿ

Trade association founded in 1912 that represents over 130 port authorities in the western hemisphere
Founded in 1912

22643 American Association of Railroad Superintendents
425 Third Street SW
Washington, DC 20024
202-639-2100
Fax: 630-762-0755
E-Mail: media@aar.org
Home Page: www.aar.org
Social Media: Facebook, Twitter, LinkedIn, Youtube

Robert M Denny, President
Patricia A Weissmann, Administrative Manager

Operating department officers of railroads.
500 Members
Founded in 1881

22644 American Association of State Highway & Transportation
444 N Capitol St NW
Suite 249
Washington, DC 20001-1539

202-624-5800
Fax: 202-624-5806
E-Mail: info@aashto.org
Home Page: www.transportation.org
Social Media: Facebook, Twitter, LinkedIn, You Tube

Bud Wright, Executive Director
Jenet Adem, Director, Finance & Administration

Representing highway and transportation departments in the 50 states, the District of Columbia, and Puerto Rico. It represents all five

transportation modes: air, highways, public transportation, rail ,and water. Its primary goal is to foster the development, operation, and maintenance of an integrated national transportation system.
Founded in 1981

22645 American Association of State Highway and Transportation Officials
444 North Capitol Street N.W.
Suite 249
Washington, DC 20001

202-624-5800
Fax: 202-624-5806
E-Mail: info@aashto.org
Home Page: www.transportation.org
Social Media: Facebook, Twitter

Bud Wright, Executive Director
Jenet Adem, Director of Financeÿ
Tony Bianchi, Associate Project Director
John Boyd, Senior Communications Editor
Lloyd Brown, Director of Communications

A standards-setting body which publishes specifications, test protocols anf guidelines used in highway design and construction across the United States

22646 American Automobile Association
1000 AAA Drive
Heathrow, FL 32746-5062

407-444-7966
Fax: 800-222-4357
Home Page: www.aaany.com

22647 American Bus Association
111 K Street NE
9th Floor
Washington, DC 20002

202-842-1645
Fax: 202-842-0850
E-Mail: abainfo@buses.org
Home Page: www.buses.org
Social Media: Facebook, Twitter, LinkedIn

Peter J Pantuso, President & CEO
Brandon Buchanan, Director, Operations
Clyde J Hart Jr., Senior VP, Govt. Affairs & Policy
Norm Litter, VP, Regulatory & Industry Affairs
Eric Braendel, CFO

ABA supports 3,800 members consisting of motorcoach and tour companies in addition to organizations that represent the tourism and travel industry. ABA strives to educate consumers on the importance of highway and motorcoach safety.
Founded in 1926

22648 American Commodity and Shipping
2102-D Gallows Rd.
Vienna, VA 22182

703-848-9422
Fax: 703-848-9424
E-Mail: info@americancommodity.com
Home Page: www.americancommodity.com
Social Media: Facebook, Twitter, LinkedIn

22649 American Concrete Pavement Association
9450 W Bryn Mawr Ave.
Suite 150
Rosemont, IL 60018

847-966-2272
E-Mail: acpa@acpa.org
Home Page: www.pavement.com
Social Media: Facebook, Twitter, LinkedIn, YouTube

Tom Beck, Chairman
Mike Lipps, Vice Chairman
Steve Jackson, 2nd Vice Chair
Jerry Voigt, President, CEO
Glenn Eder, Treasurer

Trade association that exclusively represents the interests of those involved with the design, construction and preservation of concrete pavements.
Founded in 1963

22650 American Council of Highway Advertisers
PO Box 809
North Beach, MD 20714

301-386-3330

22651 American Moving and Storage Association
1611 Duke St
Alexandria, VA 22314-3406

703-683-7410
Fax: 703-683-7527
Home Page: www.moving.org

Linda Bauer Darr, CEO
Sandy Lynch, SVP

Represents members including interstate moving and storage companies, local movers, international movers plus industry suppliers and state association members. AMSA's chief goals include strong support for effective government regulations and policies that protect consumers while allowing members to provide quality service at compensatory prices, and ensuring that consumers understand the value of professional moving and storage services.
3200 Members
Founded in 1936

22652 American Public Transportation Association
1666 K St NW
Suite 1100
Washington, DC 20006-1215

202-296-3220
Fax: 202-496-4324
E-Mail: meetings2@apta.com
Home Page: www.apta.com
Social Media: Facebook, Twitter, LinkedIn, Youtube, Flickr

Michael P Melaniphy, President & CEO
Petra Mollet, Chief Of Staff
Pamela L Boswell, VP, Workforce Development
Mary Childress, CFO
Art Guzzetti, VP, Policy

APTA is an international organization that supports and represents the transportation industry. Membership benefits include an annual association meeting, an international expo, membership directory, access to online publications, newsletters and electronic news service.
Founded in 1882

22653 American Railroads Association
425 3rd St SW
Siute 114
Washington, DC 20024-3217

202-639-2100
Fax: 202-639-2558
E-Mail: media@aar.org
Home Page: www.aar.org
Social Media: Facebook, Twitter, LinkedIn

Edward R Hamberger, CEO
Jeff Marsh, VP Finance/Administration
Stephanie A Kilfeather, Director Meeting Services
Mark McRoberts, Director Budget Planning
Founded in 1934

22654 American Railway Development Association
PO Box 255
Lecompton, KS 66050

785-393-8191
Fax: 952-828-9751
E-Mail: amraildev@gmail.com
Home Page: www.amraildev.com/
Social Media: Facebook, Twitter, LinkedIn

David Drach, President
Elizabeth Steel, First VP
Stephanie Johnson, Second VP
Alan Sisk, Secretary/Treasurer

Members are marketing, real estate and industrial development officers of railroads. Objectives are to foster the industrial, real estate, natural resources and market development activities of North American railroads and through the advancement of ideas and education of its members, further promote the effectiveness of railway development and related work.
200 Members
Founded in 1906

22655 American Railway Engineering and Maintenance-of-Way Association
4501 Forbes Blvd
Suite 130
Lanham, MD 20706-4362

301-459-3200
Fax: 301-459-8077
E-Mail: bcaruso@arema.org
Home Page: www.arema.org

Charles H Emely, Executive Director & CEO
Vickie Fisher, Director Finance
Beth Caruso, Director, Administration
Janice Clements, Director, membership & Information
Lisa Hall, Director, Marketing

Fosters concern for design, construction and maintenance of bridges, buildings, water service facilities and other railway structures.
5400 Members
Founded in 1891

22656 American Road and Transportation Builders
1219 28th St NW
Washington, DC 20007-3389
202-289-4434
Fax: 202-289-4435
E-Mail: general@artba.org
Home Page: www.artba.org

Doug Black, Chairman
Nick Ivanoff, Senior Vice Chair
David S Zachry, First Vice Chair
Tom Hill, Treasurer
Pete Ruane, Secretary

Offers information and resources for members associated with the transporation building industry.
Founded in 1902

22657 American Short Line & Regional Railroad Association
50 F Street, N.W.
Suite 7020
Washington, DC 20001

202-628-4500
Fax: 202-628-6430
E-Mail: lbdarr@aslrra.org
Home Page: www.aslrra.org

Linda Bauer Darr, President & Treasurer
Keith T. Borman, VP, General Counsel
Kathleen M. Cassidy, VP, Member Services
Jo E. Strang, VP, Regulatory Affairs
Jenny M. Bourque, Director

An association of North American short line and regional railroads

22658 American Short Line Railroad Association
50 F Street NW
Suite 7020
Washington, DC 20001-1536
202-628-4500
Fax: 202-628-6430
E-Mail: aslrra@aslrra.org
Home Page: www.aslrra.org
Richard F Timmons, President & Treasurer
Keith T Borman, VP, General Counsel
Jenny M Bourque, Director, Marketing
Kathleen M Cassidy, VP, Meetings & Member Services
Monitors and reports legislative and regulatory activities.
750 Members
Founded in 1913

22659 American Society of Transportation & Logistics
8430 W Bryn Mawr Ave
Suite 1000
Chicago, IL 60631
773-355-4900
Fax: 773-355-4888
E-Mail: Info@astl.org
Home Page: www.astl.org
Social Media: Facebook, Twitter, LinkedIn
George Yarusavage, CTL C.P.M., Chairman
William J. Ferreira, Vice Chairman
Laurie Denham, PLS, President
Mike A. Regan, DLP, Treasurer
Evelyn Thomchick, CTL, Secretary
Professional organization for transportation and logistics professionals.
Founded in 1946

22660 American Space Transportation Association
General Dynamics
1801 Alexander Bell Drive
Reston, VA 20191-4400
703-548-2723
800-548-2723
Fax: 703-295-6222
Home Page: www.asce.org
Patrick J Natale, Executive Director
Pete Shavalay, CFO
Thomas Smith, Deputy Executive Director
The successor organization to the Ad Hoc Industry Group promoting the development of commercial space transportation in the United States.
25 Members
Founded in 1852

22661 American Traffic Safety Services Association
15 Riverside Parkway
Suite 100
Fredericksburg, VA 22406-1022
800-272-8772
Home Page: www.atssa.com
Social Media: Facebook, Twitter, YouTube
Scott Seeley, Chairman
Debra Ricker, Chairman Elect
Kathleen Holst, Past President
Henry Ross, Past President
Peter Speer, Past President
An international trade association with the core purpose to advance roadway safety.
Founded in 1969

22662 American Truck Historical Society
10380 N Ambassador Dr.
Suite 101, P.O. Box 901611
Kansas City, MO 64153
816-891-9900
Fax: 816-891-9903
E-Mail: don@aths.org
Home Page: www.aths.org
Social Media: Facebook, Twitter, YouTube
Don Bretthauer, Executive Director
Shelley Ruhlman, Managing Director
Melinda Hunsberger, Director of Finance
Courtney Dery, Library Director
Jan Martin, Support Systems Specialist
Collects and preserves the history of antique trucks and the industry.
Founded in 1971

22663 American Trucking Associations
950 North Glebe Road
Suite 210
Arlington, VA 22203-4181
703-838-1700
E-Mail: atamembership@trucking.org
Home Page: www.trucking.org
Social Media: Facebook, Twitter, YouTube
Bill Graves, President & CEO
Pat Thomas, First Vice Chairman
Kevin W. Burch, Second Vice Chairman
David Manning, Vice Chairman
Barry Pottle, Vice Chairman
The largest national trade association for the trucking industry.
Founded in 1933

22664 American Underground Space Association
12999 E. Adam Aircraft Circle
Englewood, CO 80112
303-948-4200
800-763-3132
Fax: 303-973-3845
E-Mail: cs@smenet.org
Home Page: www.auca.org
Social Media: Facebook, Twitter, LinkedIn
William W Edgerton, Chair
Arthur D Silber, Vice Chairman
700 Members
Founded in 1976

22665 American Waterways Operators
801 N Quincy St
Suite 200
Arlington, VA 22203-1708
703-841-9300
Fax: 703-841-0389
Home Page: www.americanwaterways.com
Social Media: Facebook, Twitter, LinkedIn
Buckley McAllister, Chairman
Frank Morton, Vice Chairman
George Foster, Treasurer
Members include domestic carriers transporting commodities by water, shipyards, terminals and affiliated, business.
375 Members

22666 Association for Commuter Transportation
1341 G Street NW
10th Floor
Washington, DC 20005
202-719-5331
888-719-5772
E-Mail: info@actweb.org
Home Page: www.actweb.org
Social Media: Facebook, Twitter
Caryn Souza, Director
Marlon Powell, Adminstrative Assistant
Kevin Oliff, Marketing & Outreach Specialist
Jason Pavluchuk, Govt. Relations Specialist
ACT provides you with the resources of an international organization and the support of a regional affiliate of experienced Transportation Demand Management professionals.
810 Members
Founded in 1991

22667 Association for Women in Aviation Maintenance
PO Box 1030
Edgewater, FL 32132-1030
386-416-0248
Fax: 386-236-0517
E-Mail: whq@awam.com
Home Page: www.awam.org
Social Media: Facebook, LinkedIn
Lynette Ashland, President
Jane Shelton, Vice President
Teressa Stark, Treasurer
Laura Gordon, Secretary
Anna Romer, Director | Scholarship Co-Chair
An organization formed for the purpose of championing women's professional growth and enrichment in the aviation maintenance fields.

22668 Association of Air Medical Services
909 N. Washington Street
Suite 410
Alexandria, VA 22314-3143
703-836-8732
Fax: 703-836-8920
E-Mail: information@aams.org
Home Page: www.aams.org
Dawn Mancuso, Executive Director
Shirley Scholz, VP
Rick Sherlock, President
Yogendra Sheth, Finance & Accounting Manager
Voluntary nonprofit organization, encourages and supports its members in maintaining a standard of performance reflecting safe operations and efficient, high quality patient care. Built on the idea that representation from a variety of medical transport services and businesses can be brought together to share information, collectively resolve problems and provide leadership in the medical transport community.

22669 Association of American Railroads
425 3rd St Sw
Suite 114
Washington, DC 20024-3217
202-639-2100
Fax: 202-639-2558
E-Mail: pubsrvcs@aar.org
Home Page: www.aar.org
Social Media: Facebook, Twitter, LinkedIn, You Tube
Edward R Hamberger, CEO
Peggy Wilhide, VP Communications
Joyce Koeneman, Manager
Presently serves a joint agency of its individual railroad members to ensure an efficient nationwide rail system.
80 Members
Founded in 1934

22670 Association of Metropolitan Planning Organizations
444 North Capitol Street, NW
Suite 345
Washington, DC 20001
202-624-3680
Fax: 202-624-3685
Home Page: www.ampo.org
Richard Perrin, President
Elaine Clegg, Vice President
DeLania Hardy, Executive Director

Rich Denbow, Director of Technical Programs
Levon Boyagian, Policy Consultant

A nonprofit organization serving metropolitan planning organizations.
Founded in 1994

22671 **Association of Railway Museums**
PO Box 370
Tujunga, CA 91043-0370

818-951-9151
Fax: 818-951-9151
Home Page: www.railway.museums.org

Ellen Fishburn, Secretary
Paul Hamond, President

The association of railway museums is for the preservation of railway equipment, artifacts and history.
125 Members
Founded in 1961

22672 **BAX Global**
440 Exchange
Irvine, CA 92602

602-458-6200
800-225-5229
Home Page: www.dbschenkarusa.org
Social Media: Twitter

Joseph L Carnes, President
Jay Arnold, VP Human Resources

Specializes in managing the movement of heavyweight packages and cargo of all shapes and sizes.

22673 **Boat Owners Association of the United States**
880 South Pickett Street
Alexandria, VA 22304-4606

703-461-2878
E-Mail: membership@boatus.com
Home Page: www.boatus.com
Social Media: Facebook, Twitter, YouTube, Google+

Richard Schwartz, Chairman, Founder
Margaret Podlich, President
Adam Wheeler, VP and Director of Towing
Heather Lougheed, VP, Membership
John Condon, AVP, Towing Operations

Association of boat owners offering various services, supporting recreational boat and trailer towing activities.
Founded in 1966

22674 **Brotherhood of Locomotive Engineers and Trainmen**
Standard Building
1370 Ontario St.
Mezzanine, OH 44113-1702

216-241-2630
E-Mail: PresStaff@ble-t.org
Home Page: www.ble-t.org

Dennis R. Pierce, National President
E. Lee Pruitt, First Vice President
Marcus J. Ruef, VP, Director of Arbitration
Gil L. Gore, Michael D., Vice President

A trade organization for railroad workers.

22675 **Brotherhood of Maintenance of Way Employee s**
41475 Gardenbrook Road
Novi, MI 48375-1328

248-662-2660
Fax: 248-662-2659
Home Page: www.bmwe.org

Freddie N. Simpson, National Division President
Perry Geller, National Div. Secretary-Treasurer
David R. Scoville, Vice President- Western Region
Roger Sanchez, Vice President- South Region
David D. Joynt, Vice President at Large

A national union representing the workers who build and maintain the tracks, bridges, building and other structures of the railroads.

22676 **Brotherhood of Railroad Signalmen**
917 Shenandoah Shores Rd
Front Royal, VA 22630-6418

540-622-6522
Fax: 540-622-6532
E-Mail: kelly@brs.org
Home Page: www.brs.org
Social Media: Facebook, Twitter, RSS

W Dan Pickett, President
Walter A Barrows, Treasurer
Floyd Mason, VP
Mike S. Baldwin, Research

National organization representing the men and women who install and maintain signal systems for most of the nation's railroads.
ISSN: 0037-5020
Founded in 1901

22677 **Center for Transportation and the Environment (CTE)**
Research IV Building
909 Capability Drive, Suite 3600
Raleigh, NC 27606

919-515-8893
Fax: 919-515-8897
Home Page: www.cte.tv

Dr. E. Downey Brill, Jr., Director
Nancy Bailey, M.L.S., Web Development Specialist
Leigh B. Lane, B.S.C.E, Senior Research Associate
James B. Martin, M.C.E., P.E., Associate Director
Eugene Murray, B.A., Distance Learning Specialist

A nonprofit organization to improve the efficiency and sustainability of the energy ad transportation systems.
Founded in 1991

22678 **Committee for Better Transit**
38 W Cliff Street
Somerville, NJ 08876

E-Mail: brooklynbus@hotmail.com
Home Page: www.brooklynbus.tripod.com

The Committee for Better Transit is a forty-one year old New York Metropolitan independent transit advocacy organization comprised of transit experts and users, which seeks cost effective user-friendly solutions to transit challenges.

22679 **Energy Traffic Association**
935 Eldridge Road
Suite 604
Sugar Land, TX 77478

832-474-3564
Home Page: www.energytraffic.org

Ralph Lopez, President
Renee Ahmed, VP & Secretary
Ernest Powell, Executive Director

Formed by the merger of the Oilfield Supply Traffic Association and the Shippers Oil Field Traffic Association, ETA serves the oil and gas industry in transportation, distribution and logistics. Members are energy industry transportation, distribution, purchasing and logistics managers, and transportation and logistics providers.
Founded in 1997

22680 **Expediting Management Association**
Livingston, TN

931-823-1122
Fax: 403-201-6402
Home Page: www.expedite.org

Katherine Rench, C.E.M, President
Glenda Warman, VP
Linda Strauss, Secretary
David Kern, Treasurer
Patricia Murphy, Executive Administrator

The Expediting Management Association, Inc. will maintain a certification program for it's memebers giving them the opportunity to achieve recognition from their peers in the association and industry.
200 Members
Founded in 1972

22681 **Express Carriers Association**
9532 Liberia Avenue
Suite 752
Manassas, VA 20110

703-361-1058
Fax: 703-361-5274
E-Mail: eca@expresscarriers.com
Home Page: www.expresscarriers.com

John Di Tucci, President
Paul Steffes, VP
Jim Luciani, Second VP
MJ Hills, Treasurer
Mike Coyle, Secretary

The missio of the ECA is to develop business between carriers, shippers and vendors of products and services to the transportation industry.

22682 **Fleet Management Institute (NAFA)**
125 Village Boulevard
Suite 200
Princeton, NJ 08540

609-720-0882
Fax: 609-452-8004
E-Mail: info@nafa.org
Home Page: www.nafa.org

Patricia Murtaugh, Assistant Executive Director
Joanne Marsh, Manager

22683 **Flight Safety Foundation**
801 N. Fairfax Street
Suite 400
Alexandria, VA 22314-1774

703-739-6700
Fax: 703-739-6708
E-Mail: wahdan@flightsafety.org
Home Page: flightsafety.org
Social Media: Facebook, Twitter, LinkedIn

David Chair
Ken Hylander, Chair-elect
Jon Beatty, President and CEO
David Barger, Treasurer
Kenneth P. Quinn, General Counsel and Secretary

Independent, nonprofit international ogranization engaged in research, auditing, education, advocacy and publishing to imporove flight safety.
Founded in 1947

22684 **High Speed Grand Transportation**
1010 Massachusetts Avenue NW
Washington, DC 20001

202-789-8107
Home Page: www.hsgt.org

22685 Highway Users Federation for Safety and
PO Box 6285
Olympia, WA 98507-1904

253-376-8492
Home Page: www.acronymfinder.com

Diane Steed, President

The Highway Users Federation (WHUF) is an association concerned ith increasing capacity and safer on Highways.

22686 Institute of Transportation Engineers
1627 Eye St NW
Suite 600
Washington, DC 20006

202-785-0060
Fax: 202-785-0609
E-Mail: ite_staff@ite.org
Home Page: www.ite.org
Social Media: Facebook, Twitter, LinkedIn

Zaki Mustafa, President
W Hibbett Neel Jr., VP
16000 Members
Founded in 1930

22687 Insurance Institute for Highway Safety
988 Dairy Road
Ruckersville, VA 22968

434-985-4600
Fax: 434-985-2202
E-Mail: rrader@iihs.org
Home Page: www.iihs.org
Social Media: Twitter, RSS, YouTube

Adrian Lund, President
Russ Rader, SVP, Communications
Shelley Shelton, Sr. Legal Associate
Brenda O'Donnell, VP, Insurer Relations
Chamelle Matthew, Sr. Communications Specialist

Independent, nonprofit research and communications organization dedicated to reducing highway crash death, injuries and property damage losses.
Founded in 1959

22688 Intermodal Association of North America
11785 Beltsville Dr
Suite 1100
Beltsville, MD 20705-4049

301-982-3400
Fax: 301-982-4815
E-Mail: iana@intermodal.org
Home Page: www.intermodal.org

Joanne F Casey, President/CEO
James R Morrow, Asst. VP, Member Services
Debbie Sasko, Asst. VP, Contract Admin Services
Kristian Blust, Program Manager
Stacie Fagan, Manager, Info Services HD

Members are motor, rail and water transportation companies. Promotes the benefits and growth of the intermodal freight transportation.
600 Members

22689 International Association of Structural Movers
PO Box 2637
Lexington, SC 29071-2637

803-951-9304
Fax: 503-543-6697
E-Mail: gbrymer@alltel.net
Home Page: www.iasm.org

Keith E Settle, President
Jim Herman, VP
William Johnson, Secretaty/Treasurer

Members are movers of heavy structural products, trusses, houses, machinery and masonry structures.
385 Members
Founded in 1983

22690 International Brotherhood of Teamsters
25 Louisiana Ave Nw
Washington, DC 20001-2130

202-624-6800
Fax: 202-624-6918
Home Page: www.teamster.org
Social Media: Facebook, Twitter, Google+

James P Hoffa, President
Ken Hall, Secretary/Treasurer

Affiliated with the AFL-CIO.
1.3MM Members
Founded in 1954

22691 International Council of Cruise Lines
910 SE 17th Street
Suite 400
Fort Lauderdale, FL 33316

754-224-2200
Fax: 754-224-2250
E-Mail: info@cruising.org
Home Page: www.cruising.org
Social Media: Facebook, Twitter

Dedicated to the promotion and growth of the cruise industry.
Founded in 1975

22692 International Furniture Transportation and Logistics Council
PO Box 889
Gardner, MA 01440-0889

978-632-1913
Fax: 978-630-2917
E-Mail: jsears@iftlc.org
Home Page: www.iftlc.org

Raynard F Bohman Jr, Managing Director

Members are furniture manufacturers, retrilers, carriers, wholesalers and warehouses of allied products.
300 Members

22693 International Marine Transit Association
34 Otis Hill Road
Hingham, MA 02043

781-749-0078
Fax: 781-749-0078
E-Mail: terryboots@cs.com
Home Page: www.interferry.com

Membership includes ferry operators, naval architects, manufacturers, suppliers, and others in the ferry industry around the world.
400 Members
Founded in 1976

22694 International Parking Institute
1330 Braddock Place
Suite 350
Alexandria, VA 22314

571-699-3011
Fax: 703-566-2267
E-Mail: ipi@parking.org
Home Page: www.parking.org
Social Media: Facebook, Twitter, LinkedIn, YouTube, Pinterest, Instagram

Liliana Rambo, CAPP, Chair of the BOD
Kim Jackson, CAPP, Chair-elect
Cindy Campbell, Past Chair
Rick Decker, CAPP, Treasurer
Shawn D. Conrad, CAE, Executive Director

Organization that provides educational and technical services to parking professionals and to the public.
Founded in 1962

22695 International Road Federation
703-535-1001
Fax: 703-535-1007
E-Mail: info@IRFnews.org
Home Page: www.irfnet.org
Social Media: Facebook, Twitter, LinkedIn, Flickr

A service organization for better road transportation systems.
Founded in 1948

22696 International Safe Transit Association
1400 Abbot Rd
Suite 160
East Lansing, MI 48823-1900

517-333-3437
888-367-4782
Fax: 517-333-3813
E-Mail: ista@ista.org
Home Page: www.ista.org
Social Media: Facebook, Twitter, LinkedIn

Edward A Church, President
A J Gruber, VP, Technical Services
Lisa Bonsignore, VP, Special Events
Larry Dull, VP, Sustainable Solutions
Kathy A Joneson, VP, Communications

Members are shippers, carriers, manufacturers, packagers, package designers and testing laboratories, included in transport packaging.
750 Members
Founded in 1948
Mailing list available for rent: 4000 names at $500 per M

22697 Interstate Trucking Association
Express Carriers Association
9532 Liberia Avenue
Suite 130
Manassas, VA 20110

703-361-1058
866-322-7447
Fax: 703-361-5274
E-Mail: eca@expresscarriers.com
Home Page: www.expresscarriers.com

Brad Westrom, President
Bruce Birtwell, First VP
Richard Ziemba, Second VP
MJ Hills, Treasurer
John Luciana, Secretary

Organization of newly enacted state legislation regulations having direct impact on vehicle operations, fuel taxes, registration size and weight.

22698 Landstar Global Logistics
13410 Sutton Park Drive S
Jacksonville, FL 32224

904-398-9400
800-872-9400
E-Mail: corpcomm@landstar.com
Home Page: www.landstar.com

Henry H Gerkens, Chairman, President & CEO
Jim B Gattoni, Executive VP, CFO
Joe Beacorn, VP & Chief Safety Operations Office
Larry S Thomas, VP/Chief Information Officer
Michael Kneller, VP, General Counsel & Secretary

Mission is to be the leading non-asset based provider of transportation capacity delivering safe, sepcialized transportation services to customers worldwide utilizing a network of agents, third-party capacity owners and employees.

22699 Mid-West Truckers Association
2727 N Dirksen Pkwy
Springfield, IL 62702-1490

217-525-0310
Fax: 217-525-0342

E-Mail: info@midwesttruckshow.com
Home Page: www.midwesttruckshow.com
Social Media: Facebook

Don Schaefer, President

Serves trucking industry by lobbying on their behalf, assisting with registration, license plate procurement and group insurance programs. Conducts educational programs, has own self-funded workers compensation insurance program. Trade association represents truck owners in 14 states.
2700 Members
Founded in 1962

22700 Motor Transport Management Group
PO Box 605
Rillito, AZ 85654

520-616-0175
Fax: 208-561-2980
Home Page: www.transportationmg.com

22701 National Air Carrier Association
1000 Wilson Boulevard
Suite 1700
Arlington, VA 22209

703-358-8060
Fax: 703-358-8070
Home Page: www.naca.cc

Oakley Brooks, President
Paul H Doell, Director, Govt. Affairs
George R Paul, Director Technical Services
Paul H Doell, Director Government Affairs
7 Members
Founded in 1962

22702 National Air Traffic Controllers Association
1325 Massachusetts Avenue N.W.
Washington, DC 20005

202-628-5451
800-266-0895
Fax: 202-628-5767
Home Page: www.natca.org
Social Media: Facebook, Twitter, LinkedIn, YouTube, Instagram

Paul Rinaldi, President
Trish Gilbert, Executive Vice President
Mike MacDonald, Regional VP
Kevin Peterson, Regional VP
Jim Ullmann, Regional VP

Members are controllers in public and private sectors and Federal Aviation Administration engineers.

22703 National Air Transportation Association
4226 King St
Alexandria, VA 22302-1507

703-845-9000
800-808-6282
Fax: 703-845-8176
Home Page: www.nata.aero
Social Media: Facebook, Twitter, LinkedIn, RSS

Michael Scheeringa, Chairman
Gary Dempsey, Vice Chairman
Thomas L Hendricks, President
Marian Epps, Treasurer

Aggressively promotes safety and the success of aviation service businesses through its advocacy efforts before government, the media and the public as well as by providing valuable programs and forums to further its members' prosperity.
1800 Members
Founded in 1940

22704 National Asphalt Pavement Association

Home Page: www.asphaltpavement.org

A trade association that exclusively represents the interests of the asphalt pavment matieral producer and paving contractor on the national level with Congress, government agencies and other national trade and business organizations.

22705 National Association of Freight & Logistics
P.O Box 61243
Dubai

714-343-1112
Fax: 714-343-1105
Home Page: www.nafl.ae

David Phillips, President
Kevin Ennis, VP
Nadia Abdul Aziz, Secretary General
Suman Chakrabarti, Treasurer

Previously the National Committee of Freight Forwarders, the NAFL brings together in one body all the major players in the freight fowarding, logistics, and shipping industries.

22706 National Association of Rail Shippers
77 K Street NE
8th Floor
Washington, DC 20002-4681

202-650-6500
800-432-2250
Fax: 972-644-8208
E-Mail: nars@onramp.net
Home Page: www.rollcall.com
Social Media: Facebook, Twitter, LinkedIn, You Tube

Charlie Mitchell, VP
Laurie Battaglia, Publisher

Strives to provide a sound transporation system. Bestows annual Award of Excellence.
2M Members
Founded in 1937

22707 National Association of Railroad Passengers
505 Capitol Court NE
Suite 300
Washington, DC 20002-7706

202-408-8362
Fax: 202-408-8287
E-Mail: narp@narprail.org
Home Page: www.narprail.org
Social Media: Facebook, Twitter, Google+

Ross Capon, President & CEO
Sean Jeans-Gail, VP
Malcolm Kenton, Director, Outreach & Engagement
Logan McLeod, Director, Development

Seeks to increase public awareness of rail passenger service and its benefits. Works for a national transportation policy.
12M Members
Founded in 1967

22708 National Association of State Aviation Officials
8400 Westpark Dr.
2nd Floor
McLean, VA 22102

703-454-0649
E-Mail: info@nasao.org
Home Page: www.nasao.org
Social Media: Facebook, Twitter

Carol L. Comer, Chairman
Gary Cathey, Vice Chairman
Brad Brandt, Treasurer
Christopher J.ÿ Willenborg, Immediate Past Chairman
Greg Principato, President/ CEO

Established to ensure uniformity of safety measures and to standardize airport regulations.
Founded in 1931

22709 National Business Aviation Association
1200 G Street NW
Suite 1100
Washington, DC 20005ÿ

202-783-9000
Fax: 202-331-8364
E-Mail: info@nbaa.org
Home Page: www.nbaa.org

Ed Bolen, President, CEO
Dan Hubbard, SVP, Communications
Chris Strong, SVP, Conventions & Membership
Steve Brown, Chief Operating Officer
Marc Freeman, Chief Financial Officer

Promotes the aviation interests of organizations utilizing general aviation aircraft for business purposes.
Founded in 1947

22710 National Business Travel Association
123 North Pitt Street
Alexandria, VA 22314-3234

703-684-6803
Fax: 703-342-4324
E-Mail: info@nbta.org
Home Page: www.gbta.org
Social Media: Facebook, Twitter, LinkedIn, You Tube

Michael W McCormick, Executive Director & CEO
Mary Helen Sifford, Executive Assistant
Sallie Dietz, VP, Human Resource
Heather Trusty, Director, Certification
Hema Shah, CFO

Offers over 1,300 corporate travel managers and allied members in the United States and Canada.
2400 Members
Founded in 1968

22711 National Center for Bicycling and Walking
1612 K Street, NW
Suite 802
Washington, DC 20006

202-223-3621
E-Mail: mark@bikewalk.org
Home Page: www.bikewalk.org

Mark Plotz, Senior Associate / Program Manager
John Williams, CenterlinesÿEditor
Jim Johnston, Web/Systems Administrator

A resident program at the Project for Public Spaces, Inc.
Founded in 1977

22712 National Child Transport Association
Hall of States
444 N Capitol St Nw
Suite 438
Washington, DC 20001-1505

202-624-7710
Fax: 202-624-5899
E-Mail: bthompson@ncsha.org
Home Page: www.ncsha.org
Social Media: Facebook, Twitter

Barbara J Thompson, Executive Director
Cary D Knox, Executive Office Admin
Kristine B. Lewis, Marketing

Thirty booths.
1.2M Members

22713 **National Customs Brokers and Forwarders**
1200 18th St Nw
Suite 901
Washington, DC 20036-2572

202-466-0222
Fax: 202-466-0226
E-Mail: staff@ncbfaa.org
Home Page: www.ncbfaa.org

Jeffrey C Coppersmith, Chairman
Darrell Sekin, Jr, President
Geoffrey C Powell, VP
William S App Jr., Treasurer
Amy Magnus, Secretary

Learn about new business leads, stay on top of Customs Service and other agency regulations that will impact your operations and provide invaluable professional development resources for your employees.
600+ Members

22714 **National Defense Transportation Association (NDTA)**
50 S Pickett Street
Suite 220
Alexandria, VA 22304

703-751-5011
Fax: 703-823-8761
E-Mail: info@ndtahq.com
Home Page: www.ndtahq.com
Social Media: Twitter

LTG Kenneth Wykle, President & COO
Mark Victorson, VP, Membership
Lee Matthews, VP, Marketing & Corp. Development
Patty Casidy, VP, Finance
Rebecca Jones, Executive Asst. To President

Intended as a liasion between government, military and private transportation officials.
7800 Members
Founded in 1944

22715 **National Highway Carriers**
PO Box 6099
Buffalo Grove, IL 60089

847-634-0606
Fax: 847-634-1026
E-Mail: nhcdg@aol.com
Home Page: www.national-highway.com

Founded in 1942

22716 **National Industrial Transportation League**
1700 N Moore St
Suite 1900
Arlington, VA 22209-1931

703-524-5011
Fax: 703-524-5017
E-Mail: info@nitl.org
Home Page: www.nitl.org

Bruce J Carlton, President
Ellie Gilanshah, VP, Finance
Katie Ling, Administrative Assistant

Provides information to the industrial transportation industry, including computer services software and innovations for transportation operations.
600 Members
Founded in 1907

22717 **National Institute of Certified Moving Consultants**
1420 King Street
Alexandria, VA 22314-2794

703-683-7410
800-538-6672
Fax: 703-683-7527
Home Page: www.nicet.org
Social Media: Facebook, LinkedIn

Michael A Clark, Chief Operating Executive
Ahmed Farouki, Senior Director, Technical Services

Awards the certified moving consultant designation to those who have passed an exam testing their liability.
Founded in 1974

22718 **National Institute of Packaging and Handling Logistics Engineers**
5903 Ridgeway Drive
Grand Prairie, TX 75052

817-466-7490
866-464-7453
Fax: 570-523-0606
E-Mail: admin@niphle.com
Home Page: www.niphle.com
Social Media: Facebook, Twitter, LinkedIn

Sean Kerins, President

An assemblage of professionals whose interest in the complex and diverse practice of distribution and logistics is a common bond.
600 Members
Founded in 1956

22719 **National Marine Representatives Associatio n**
PO Box 360
Gurnee, IL 60031

847-662-3167
Fax: 847-336-7126
E-Mail: info@nmraonline.org
Home Page: www.nmraonline.org

Brandon Flack, President
Ken Smaga, Past President
Rob Gueterman, Vice President
Keith LaMarr, Treasurer
Neal Tombley, Secretary

A national organization serving marine industry sales representatives and the manufacturers who sell marine products.
Founded in 1960

22720 **National Motor Freight Traffic Association**
1001 North Fairfax Street
Suite 600
Alexandria, VA 22314-1798

703-838-1810
866-411-6632
Fax: 703-683-6296
E-Mail: customerservice@nmfta.org
Home Page: www.nmfta.org

Paul Levine, Executive Director
Joel Ringer, Chairman, CCSB
Urban Jonson, Chief Technology Officer
Leslie Tate, Finance & HR Manager
Kimberly Hay, Customer Service Manager

Provides expertise in freight classification, packaging, and transportation codes.

22721 **National Motorcoach Network**
PO Box 1088
Mount Jackson, VA 22842

540-477-3202
800-469-0062
Fax: 540-477 3858
E-Mail: smk@motorcoach.com
Home Page: www.motorcoach.com/byways

Founded in 1983

22722 **National Parking Association**
1112 16th St Nw
Suite 840
Washington, DC 20036-4880

202-296-4336
800-647-7275
Fax: 202-296-3102
E-Mail: info@npapark.org
Home Page: www.npapark.org
Social Media: Facebook, Twitter, LinkedIn

Jeff Wolfe, Chairman
Mark Muglich, Chair Elect
John Udelson, Vice Chair
Nicolle Judge, Secretary
Robert A Zuritsky, Treasurer

Proudly serving the nation's parking industry since 1951. Our members are comprised of parking professionals in both the public and private sectors from across the country and around the world. NPA members are private operators, parking consultants, colleges and universities, municipalities, parking authorities, hospitals and medical centers and industry vendors.
1200 Members
Founded in 1951
Mailing list available for rent

22723 **National Private Truck Councily**
Home Page: www.nptc.org

National trade association dedicated exclusively to representing private motor carrier fleets.

22724 **National School Transportation Association**
122 South Royal Street
Alexandria, VA 22314

703-684-3212
800-222-6782
Fax: 703-684-3212
E-Mail: info@yellowbuses.com
Home Page: www.yellowbuses.org

Tim Flood, President
Todd Monteferrario, President Elect
Steve Hey, Secretary/Treasurer

Strives to provide safe transportation, foster safety, and an atmosphere conducive to private enterprise.
3M Members
Founded in 1964

22725 **National Small Shipments Traffic**
758 Quail Run
Waconia, MN 55387

952-442-8850
Fax: 202-686-2877
E-Mail: brian@nasstrac.org
Home Page: www.nasstrac.org
Social Media: Facebook, Twitter, LinkedIn

Eric Morley, Chairperson
Doug Easley, President
Chris Norek, 1st VP
Terri Reid, 2nd VP
Gail Rutkowski, Treasurer

Members are truck, air, rail and sea shippers of freight weighing less than 10,000 pounds.
250 Members
Founded in 1952

22726 **National Waterways Conference**
110 N Glebe Rd.
Suite 1010
Arlington, VA 22201

703-243-4090
Fax: 866-371-1390
E-Mail: amy@waterways.org
Home Page: www.waterways.org

Jim Oliver, Chairman
Jamie McCurry, Vice Chairman
Amy Larson, President
Randy Richardson, VP
Cline Jones, Treasurer

Dedicated to a greater understanding of the widespread public benefits of the American waterways system.
350 Members
Founded in 1960

22727 National/International Safe Transit Association
200 E Randolph
Suite 4120
Chicago, IL 60601-7683
312-552-6300
Fax: 312-552-6302
E-Mail: Rich.Jernstedt@porternovelli.com
Home Page: www.porternovelli.com
Social Media: Facebook, Twitter, LinkedIn, Youtube

Karen Van Bergen, CEO

22728 Natural Gas Vehicles for America
400 N Capitol St Nw
Washington, DC 20001-1511
202-824-7360
Fax: 202-824-7087
E-Mail: rkolodziej@ngvamerica.org
Home Page: www.iangv.org

Richard R Kolodziej, President

Members are organizations with an interest in encouraging the development of natural gas powered vehicles.
250 Members
Founded in 1988

22729 Network of Employers for Traffic Safety
344 Maple Avenue, West
#357
Vienna, VA 22180-5162
703-273-6005
888-221-0045
E-Mail: sgillies@trafficsafety.org
Home Page: trafficsafety.org

Jack Hanley, Executive Director
Susan Gillies, Administrative Lead

Focused on improving traffic safety.

22730 North American Shippers Association
1600 St. Georges Ave
PO Box 249
Rahway, NJ 07065
732-680-4540
Fax: 732-388-6580
E-Mail: nasaships@hillebrandgroup.com
Home Page: www.nasaships.com

Case Pieterman, Executive Director

Members are shippers of wine and alcoholic beverages.
430 Members
Founded in 1987

22731 North American Transportation Council
427 Garrison Rd.
Unit 3 & 4
Fort Erie, ON L2A 6E6
800-559-7421
Fax: 905-994-0117
E-Mail: info@fca-natc.org
Home Page: www.natc.com

Dave Sirgey, President
Mary Anne Vehrs, Sales & Marketing
Julie Gauthier, Administrative Assistantý
Diane Sheppard, Accounting Technician
Jon Ainsworth, Sr. Analyst/ Programmer

Represents Canadian and US based motor carriers engaged in for-hire trucking in the North American transborder market.

22732 Passenger Vessel Association
103 Oronoco Street
Suite 200
Alexandria, VA 22314-1549
703-518-5005
800-807-8360
Fax: 703-518-5151
E-Mail: pvainfo@passengervessel.com
Home Page: www.passengervessel.com

Carolyn Horgan, President
Terri Berstein, Vice President
Dave Anderson, Secretary/Treasurer

Represents operators of tours, excursions, ferries, charter vessels, dinner boats and other small passenger vessels.
600 Members
Founded in 1971

22733 Railway Industrial Clearance Association
8900 Eastloch Dr.
Suite 215
Spring, TX 77379
281-826-0009
Home Page: www.rica.org

Rick Ford, Chairman
Kelli Collins, President
Justin Gilmet, VP
Mike Scott, Treasurer
Mark Lockwood, Secretary

Representation includes all aspects of logistics associated with the movement of dimensional cargo via rail.
Founded in 1969

22734 Railway Supply Institute
425 Third Street
Suite 920
Washington, DC 20024
202-347-4664
Fax: 202-347-0047
E-Mail: rsupplya@aol.com
Home Page: www.rsiweb.org

Thomas D Simpson, President
Nicole B Brewin, VP, Govt. Affairs
Robyn M. Leach, VP, Administration

The railway equipment and supply industry.
300 Members
Founded in 1909

22735 Railway Systems Suppliers
9306 New La Grange Rd
Suite 100
Louisville, KY 40242-3672
502-327-7774
Fax: 502-327-0541
E-Mail: rssi@rssi.org
Home Page: www.rssi.org

Patti Jon Goff, President
John Paljug, Executive VP
N Michael Choat, 1st VP
Walter Winzen, 2nd VP

A trade association serving the communication and signal segment of the rail transportation industry. Manages an annual trade show.
230 Members
Founded in 1966

22736 Regional Airline Association
2025 M Street NW
Washington, DC 20036-3309
202-367-1170
Fax: 202-367-2170
E-Mail: raa@raa.org
Home Page: www.raa.org
Social Media: Facebook, Twitter

Roger Cohen, President
Scott Foose, Senior VP, Operations & Safety
Faye Malarkey Black, Senior VP, Legislative Affairs
Liam Connolly, Senior Director

Membership consists of more than 70 airlines and 350 associate members that provide goods and services.
300 Members
Founded in 1975

22737 Roadmasters and Maintenance of Way Association of America
4501 Forbes Blvd
Suite 130
Lanham, MD 20706
301-459-3200
Fax: 301-459-8077
Home Page: www.arema.org

Charles H Emely, Executive Director & CEO
Vickie Fisher, Director, Finance
Beth Caruso, Director, Administration
Lisa Hall, Director, Marketing
Janice Clements, Director, Membership & IS

Railroad executives concerned with track and roadway management.
2.1M Members
Founded in 1997

22738 Shippers Oil Field Traffic Association
907 Kiowa Drive E
Gainesville, TX 76240-9575
940-668-7735
Fax: 940-668-7212
Home Page: www.all-acronyms.com
Social Media: Facebook, Twitter

50 Members
Founded in 1941

22739 Society of Automotive Engineers
400 Commonwealth Dr
Warrendale, PA 15096
724-776-4841
877-606-7323
Fax: 248-273-2494
E-Mail: customerservice@sae.org
Home Page: www.sae.org
Social Media: Facebook, Twitter, LinkedIn, Google+

Donald Hillebrand, President
Jane Lewis, Automotive HQ Special Events
Patti Kreh, Meetings/Exhibits Manager

Offers automotive engineers the technical information and expertise used in building, maintaining and operating self propelled vehicles for use on land, sea, air or space.

22740 Space Transportation Association
4305 Underwood Street
University Park, MD 20782
703-855-3917
E-Mail: rich@spacetransportation.us
Home Page: www.spacetransportation.us

Richard Coleman, President
Ty McCoy, Chairman

Represents the interests of organizations which intend to develop, build, operate and use space transportation vehicles and systems in order to provide reliable, economical, safe and routine access to space for public and private entities.
20 Members
Founded in 1990

22741 Taxicab, Limousine & Paratransit Association
3200 Tower Oaks Boulevard
Suite 220
Rockville, MD 20852
301-984-5700
Fax: 301-984-5703

E-Mail: info@tlpa.com
Home Page: www.tlpa.org

Alfred La Gasse III, CEO
Harold Morgan, Executive VP
Leah New, Manager, Communications
Michelle A Jasper, Manager, Meetings
Ayesha Plaskett, Office Assistant

Members include owners of taxicab, limousine, airport shuttle, paratransit and nonemergency medical transportation fleets.
1107 Members
Founded in 1917
Mailing list available for rent: 6,000 names at $100 per M

22742 The American Road & Transportation Builders Association
1219 28th Street, N.W.ÿ
Washington, DC 20007ÿ

202-289-4434
E-Mail: info@artba.org
Home Page: www.artba.org
Social Media: Facebook, Twitter, LinkedIn, YouTube, Google+

Nick Ivanoff, Chairman
David S. Zachry, Senior Vice Chairman
Bob Alger, First Vice Chairman
Ward Nye, Vice Chairman At-Large
Tom Hill, Treasurer

National transportation construction trade group.
Founded in 1902

22743 The Associated General Contractors of America
2300 Wilson Blvd.
Suite 300
Arlington, VA 22201

703-548-3118
Fax: 703-548-3119
E-Mail: info@agc.org
Home Page: www.agc.org
Social Media: RSS

Alan L. Landes, President
Charles L. Greco, Senior Vice President
Mark Knight, Vice Presidentÿ
Eric L. Wilson, Treasurer
Stephen E. Sandherr, CEO

Trade association for the construction industry.
Founded in 1918

22744 The Institute of Navigation
8551 Rixlew Ln.
STE 360
Manassas, VA 20109

703-366-2723
Fax: 703-366-2724
E-Mail: membership@ion.org
Home Page: www.ion.org
Social Media: Facebook, Twitter, LinkedIn, YouTube

Lisa Beaty, Executive Director
Rick Buongiovanni, IT Director
Ken Esthus, Marketing Director
Fatima Ally, Graphic Artist
Megan Andrews, Meeting Planner

Nonprofit professional society dedicated to the advancement of the art and sciece of positioning, radar and navigation.
Founded in 1945

22745 The Intelligent Transportation Society of America (ITS America)
1100 New Jersey Ave. SE
Suite 850
Washington, DC 20003

202-484-4847
800-374-8472
E-Mail: info@itsa.org
Home Page: www.itsa.org
Social Media: Facebook, Twitter, LinkedIn

Kirk Steudle, Chair
Jill Ingrassia, Vice Chair
Dana Christensen, Treasurer
Chris Murray, Secretary
Michael Eason, Chief Financial Officer

Organization dedicated to advancing the research, development and design of surface transportation systems.
Founded in 1991

22746 The National Customs Brokers & Forwarders Association of America
1200 18th Street, NW
#901
Washington, DC 20036

202-466-0222
Fax: 202-466-0226
Home Page: www.ncbfaa.org

Darrell Sekin, Jr., Chairman, Board
Geoffrey Powell, President
Scott E. Larson, Treasurer
Barbara Reilly, EVP
Amy Magnus, VP

Represents and supports members of the US freight forwarding industry providing education and publications.
970+ Members
Founded in 1987

22747 Transport Workers Union of America
501 3rd Street NW
9th Floor
Washington, DC 20001

202-719-3900
Fax: 202-347-0454
Home Page: www.twu.org
Social Media: Facebook, Twitter, Youtube

Harry Lombardo, President
John Samuelson, Executive VP
Alex Garcia, Secretary/Treasurer

Chartered by the Congress of Industrial Organizations.
110M Members
ISBN: 0-039865-9 -
Founded in 1934

22748 Transportation Clubs International
P.O. Box 426
Union, WA 98592

877-858-8627
E-Mail:
info@transportationclubinternational.co
Home Page:
www.transportationclubsinternational.com

Members are individuals in all phases of transportation, traffic management and physical distribution.
10M Members

22749 Transportation Institute
5201 Auth Way
Camp Springs, MD 20746-4211

301-423-3335
Fax: 301-423-0634
E-Mail: info@trans-inst.org
Home Page: www.trans-inst.org

James L Henry, Chairman & President
Jerome K Welsch Jr, COO
Robert E Johnston, Executive VP

Members are US flag shipping, towing and dredging companies.
100 Members
Founded in 1967

22750 Transportation Intermediaries Association
3601 Eisenhower Avenue
Suite 110
Alexandria, VA 22304

703-299-5700
Fax: 703-836-0123
E-Mail: info@tianet.org
Home Page: www.tianet.org
Social Media: Facebook, Twitter

Robert Voltmann, President/CEO
Larry Fisher, Contact

Education and policy organization for North American transportation intermediaries. TIA is the only national association representing the interests of all third party transportation service providers. The members of TIA include logistics management firms, property brokers, perishable commodities brokers, freight forwarders, intermodal marketers, ocean and air forwarders, and NVOCC's.
1200 Members
Founded in 1978

22751 Transportation Loss Prevention & Security Association
155 Polifly Road
Hackensack, NJ 07601

732-350-3776
Home Page: www.tlpsa.org

William D Bierman, Executive Director
Edward M Loughman, Assistant to Executive Director

Originally a combination of the National Freight Claim Council and the Transportation Loss Prevention and Security Council, this independent association supports all persons who have an interest in loss and damage claims and security issues. Members include carriers, shippers, vendors, law enforcement, attorneys, insurance carriers, third-party logistics, etc.
Founded in 2000

22752 Transportation Research Board
500 Fifth Street NW
Washington, DC 20001

202-334-2934
Fax: 202-334-2527
E-Mail: TABSales@nas.edu
Home Page: www.trb.org
Social Media: Facebook, Twitter, LinkedIn

Cynthia Allen, Editor
Rosa P Allen, Administrative Coordinator
Cynthia M Baker, Executive Assistant
Anthony T Bailey, Financial Associate

22753 Transportation Research Forum
Department 2880
PO Box 6050
Fargo, ND 58108-6050

701-231-7766
Fax: 701-231-1945
E-Mail: info@trforum.org
Home Page: www.trforum.org
Social Media: Facebook, LinkedIn

Art Guzzetti, Executive VP
David Ripplinger, Program VP
Bob Walton, VP, Membership
Joshua Schank, VP, Public Relations
Joe Schwieterman, VP, Chapter Relations

An independent organization of transportation professionals.
300 Members
Founded in 1958

22754 Truck Renting and Leasing Corporation
675 N Washington Street
Suite 410
Alexandria, VA 22314

703-299-9120
800-426-1420
Fax: 703-299-9115
Home Page: www.trala.org

Thomas James, President & CEO
Jack Jacoby, VP, Govt. Relations
Brian Hefner, Director, Membership & Business
Tonya Gibbs, VP, Finance & Business Operations
Joe Scully, Director, Govt. Relations

A multi-national technology company, NRLC monitors legislation and other issues affecting the truck/trailer leasing and rental industry. It also manufacturers heavy-duty, on-and-off-road trucks worldwide.
275 Members
Founded in 1978

22755 Truck Trailer Manufacturers Association
7001 Heritage Village Plaza
Suite 220
Gainesville, VA 20155

703-549-3010
Fax: 703-549-3014
E-Mail: ttma@erols.com
Home Page: www.ttmanet.org

Jeff Sims, President
John Freller, Engineering Manager
Nancy Livingston, Administration

News of interest to trailer manufacturers and suppliers.

22756 United Bus Owners of America
113 S West Street
4th Floor
Alexandria, VA 22314-2824

703-838-8262
800-424-8262
Fax: 703-838-2950
Home Page: www.uma.org
Social Media: Facebook, Twitter, LinkedIn, Youtube

Victor S Parra, President & CEO
Ken Presley, VP, Industry Relations & COO
Maggie Masterson, Meetings & Operations Director
Michele Nosko, Marketing & Membership Director

Serves the bus industry, with particular emphasis on group travel and tourism.
800 Members

22757 United States Telecom Association
607 14th St Nw
Suite 400
Washington, DC 20005-2000
202-326-0809
Fax: 202-326-7333
E-Mail: membership@ustelecom.org
Home Page: www.ustelecom.org
Social Media: Facebook, Twitter, LinkedIn, Youtube

Walter McKormick, President
Francis X Frantz, Chairman of the Board

Trade association representing service provides and suppliers for the telecom industry.
Cost: $699.00

22758 Wine and Spirits Shippers Association
11800 Sunrise Valley Dr
Suite 332
Reston, VA 20191-5302

703-860-2300
800-368- 316
Fax: 703-860-2422
E-Mail: info@wssa.com
Home Page: www.wssa.com
Social Media: Facebook, Twitter, LinkedIn, RSS

Alison Leavitt, Executive Director
Catherine Jennings, Program Coordinator
Geraldine Zilleruelo, Contract & Rate Manager

Provides members with services that allow for the efficient and economical transportation of alcoholic beverages.
320 Members
Founded in 1976

22759 Women's Transportation Seminar: National
1701 K St Nw
Suite 800
Washington, DC 20006-1504

202-955-5085
Fax: 202-496-4349
E-Mail: membership@wtsinternational.org
Home Page: www.wtsinternational.org
Social Media: Facebook, Twitter, LinkedIn, Pinterest

Dana Hook, Chair
Beverley Swaim-Staley, Vice Chairman
Jennifer Mitchell, Secretary
Marsha Anderson Bomar, Treasurer
3500 Members
Founded in 1977

22760 Womens Transportation Seminar
1701 K St Nw
Suite 800
Washington, DC 20006-1504

202-955-5085
Fax: 202-496-4349
E-Mail: membership@wtsinternational.org
Home Page: www.wtsinternational.org
Social Media: Facebook, Twitter, LinkedIn, Pinterest

Dana Hook, Chair
Beverley Swaim-Staley, Vice Chairman
Jennifer Mitchell, Secretary
Marsha Anderson Bomar, Treasurer
3500 Members
Founded in 1977

22761 World Organization of Dredging
PO Box 5797
Vancouver, WA 98668-5797

360-750-0209
Fax: 360-750-1445
E-Mail: weda@comcast.com
Home Page: www.woda.org

Anders Jensen, President
A.R Cristi, Manager
Rashyan Allays, Secretary

Develops professionalism in individuals involved in the dredging industry.
2700 Members
Founded in 1981

Newsletters

22762 ABA Insider
American Bus Association
111 K Street NE
Suite 575
Washington, DC 20005-5923

202-842-1645
Fax: 202-842-0850
E-Mail: abainfo@buses.org
Home Page: www.buses.org

Peter J Pantuso, CEO
Eron Shosteck, Marketing

ABA's biweekly newsletter that keeps members informed on the travel, tourism and motorcoach industry.
Frequency: Biweekly
Founded in 1926

22763 Advanced Transit News
Advanced Transit Association
PO Box 162
Palo Alto, CA 94302

800-779-0544
800-779-0544
Fax: 800-779-0544
E-Mail: jpaskry@davinciglobal.com
Home Page: www.advancedtransit.org

Catherine G. Burke, President
Bob Dunning, VP
Lawrence Fabian, Publisher

Offers information on the American transit system.
100 Pages
Frequency: Quarterly
Founded in 1953
Printed in one color on matte stock

22764 Center for Microcomputers in Transportation
512 Weil Hall
PO Box 116585
Gainesville, FL 32611

352-392-7575
800-226-1013
Fax: 352-389-2324
E-Mail: mctrans@ce.ufl.edu
Home Page: www.mctrans.ce.ufl.edu

Mark Newman, Associate Director
Max Crumit, Executive Vice President
Kirk Hatfield, Director
Founded in 1986

22765 Dispatch & Division Newsletters
Taxicab, Limousine & Paratransit Association
3200 Tower Oaks Blvd
Suite 220
Rockville, MD 20852

301-984-5700
Fax: 301-984-5703
E-Mail: info@tlpa.org
Home Page: www.tlpa.org

Alfred LaGasse, CEO
Victor Dizengoff, President

Dispatch features articles on industry business issues, provides advice on running a transportation company, and comes with division specific bi-monthly newsletters.
Frequency: Bimonthly
Circulation: 6000

22766 Dual News
Driving School Association of America
11 W Pomona Boulevard
Monterey Park, CA 91754

FAX 626-722-0485

George Hensel, Publisher

Association news for student driving instructors and educational personnel.
Frequency: BiWeekly
Circulation: 5,000

22767 **Fleet Street**
Greenwich Consulting
15821 Fetlock Lane
Chino Hills, CA 91709

909-606-2271
Fax: 909-597-7759

Karen Edward, Publisher

Consulting newsletter geared toward Distribution and Fleet Management Executives - Provides transportation managers with cost-cutting methodogies.
Circulation: 15500

22768 **HazMat Transport News**
Business Publishers
8737 Colesville Road
Suite 1100
Silver Spring, MD 20910-3925

301-876-6300
800-274-6737
Fax: 301-587-4530
E-Mail: custserv@bpinews.com
Home Page: www.bpinews.com

Leonard A Eiserer, Publisher
Beth Early, Operations Director

Regulatory and legislative development affecting hazardous materials transportation. In-depth coverage on research and special programs administration, hazmat regulation programs and enforcement actions.
Cost: $447.00
Founded in 1963

22769 **Inside DOT and Transportation Week**
King of Communications Group
1325 Massachusetts Ave Nw
Suite 310
Washington, DC 20005-4194

240-455-6801
800-926-5464
Fax: 240-628-5774
Home Page: www.kingpublishing.com

F King, President
Dave Ahearn, Editor
Wenita Lhill-waddell, Marketing
Linda Gasparello, General Manager

Offers information to persons working in the transportation profession.
Cost: $1300.00
12 Pages
Frequency: Daily
Founded in 1973
Printed in one color on newsprint stock

22770 **Interstate Information Report**
Express Carriers Association
9532 Liberia Avenue,
Suite 130
Manassas, VA 20190-3233

703-361-1058
866-322-7447
Fax: 704-435-4390
E-Mail: eca@expresscarriers.com
Home Page: www.expresscarriers.com

Carrie Ehlers, President
Stuart Hyden, First Vice President

Compilation of newly enacted state legislation regulations having direct impact on vehicle operations, fuel taxes, registration size and weight.

22771 **Legislative Alert**
Taxicab, Limousine & Paratransit Association
3200 Tower Oaks Blvd
Suite 220
Rockville, MD 20852

301-984-5700
Fax: 301-984-5703
E-Mail: info@tlpa.org
Home Page: www.tlpa.org

Alfred LaGasse, CEO
Victor Dizengoff, President

TLPA's members-only bulletin of early alerts to critical changes in the industry, announcing threats and opportunities on issues that are before Congress and federal agencies. Organizes operators to take action, and provides knowledge and awareness.
Circulation: 6000

22772 **McTrans**
Center for Microcomputers in Transportation
512 Weil Hall
PO Box 116585
Gainesville, FL 32611

352-392-7575
800-226-1013
Fax: 352-389-2324
E-Mail: mctrans@ce.ufl.edu
Home Page: www.mctrans.ce.ufl.edu

CE Wallace, Publisher
Mark Newman, Associate Director
Max Crumit, Executive Vice President
Kirk Hatfield, Director

Information about microcomputer software and resources in transportation.
Circulation: 8,000
Founded in 1986

22773 **Passenger Transport**
American Public Transit Association
1666 K St Nw
Suite 1100
Washington, DC 20006-1215

202-496-4800
Fax: 202-496-4324
E-Mail: hbrett@apta.com
Home Page: www.apta.com

Karol J Popkin, CEO
Petra Mollet, VP
Rosemary Sherid, Marketing

Information on federal legislative, administrative and regulatory developments, management and operations, new technology, and state and local developments in public transit.
Cost: $75.00
Frequency: B-Weekly
Circulation: 5000
Founded in 1882

22774 **Proclaim**
Slesia Companies
619 Broad Creek Dr
Fort Washington, MD 20744-5800

301-292-1970
Fax: 301-292-1787
Home Page: fdrs.ag.utk.edu

Dale L Anderson, President

Covers transportation freight claims.
Frequency: Monthly

22775 **Rider's Digest**
Metropolitan Atlanta Road Transit
2424 Piedmont Rd Ne
Atlanta, GA 30324-3311

404-848-5000
Fax: 404-848-5098
E-Mail: schedinfo@itsmarta.com
Home Page: www.itsmarta.com

Nathaniel P Ford Sr, CEO

Public transportation news.
Frequency: Monthly

22776 **TransitPulse**
Trans 21
55 Virginia St
Dorchester, MA 02125-2352

617-825-9687
Fax: 617-482-7417

Lawrence J Fabin, Publisher

Newsletters and faxed advisory service on worldwide developments in Automated People Movers.
Cost: $75.00
4 Pages
Frequency: BiMonthly
Circulation: 500
Printed in one color on matte stock

22777 **Transport Workers Union of America**
Transport Workers Union of America
1700 Broadway
Suite 2
New York, NY 10019-5905

212-259-4900
Fax: 202-347-0454
E-Mail: mailbox@twu.org
Home Page: www.twu.org

James Little, President
David Rosen, General Counsel
Alex Garcia, Director

Chartered by the Congress of Industrial Organizations.
Frequency: Monthly
ISBN: 0-039865-9 -
Founded in 1934

22778 **Transportation Intermediaries Association**
3601 Eisenhower Avenue
Suite 110
Alexandria, VA 22304

703-299-5700
Fax: 703-836-0123
E-Mail: info@tianet.org
Home Page: www.tianet.org

Robert Voltmann, President/CEO
Larry Fisher, Contact

Education and policy organization for North American transportation intermediaries. TIA is the only national association representing the interests of all third party transportation service providers. The members of TIA include logistics management firms, property brokers, perishable commodities brokers, freight forwarders, intermodal marketers, ocean and air forwarders, and NVOCC's.
700 Pages
Frequency: Monthly

22779 **US Rail News**
Business Publishers
222 Sedwick Dr
Suite 101
Durham, NC 27713

800-223-8720
Fax: 800-508-2592
E-Mail: custserv@bpinews.com
Home Page: www.bpinews.com

Reports on the trends, legislation, regulations, acquisitions, business opportunities and technological developments that directly affect the rail industry.
Cost: $437.00
Frequency: 25 per year
Founded in 1963

22780 **Urban Transport News**
Business Publishers
8737 Colesville Road
Suite 1100
Silver Spring, MD 20910-3928

301-876-6300
800-274-6737
Fax: 301-587-4530

E-Mail: custserv@bpinews.com
Home Page: www.bpinews.com

Leonard A Eiserer, Publisher
Beth Early, Operations Director

Comprehensive briefings on trends, regulations, legislation, business and technological developments in the mass transit area.
Cost: $437.00
Founded in 1963

Magazines & Journals

22781 Air Medical Journal

526 King Street
Suite 415
Alexandria, VA 22314-3143

703-836-8732
800-525-3712
Fax: 703-836-8920
E-Mail: information@aams.org
Home Page: www.aams.org

Renee Holleran, Editor
Dawn M Mancuso, Director
John Fiegel, Director

An association of health care entities operating helicopter transport services. Magazine is published, price included in membership.
375 Pages
Founded in 1980
Printed in on glossy stock

22782 American Journal of Transportation

Fleur de Lis Publishing
1354 Hancock Street
Suite 300
Quincy, MA 02169

617-328-5005
800-599-6358
Fax: 617-328-5999
E-Mail: editorial@ajot.com
Home Page: www.ajot.com/

George Lauriat, Editor
Ann Radwan, Associate Editor
William Bourbon, Publisher
Bob Kirk, Production Manager
Kristen Davis, Graphic Designer

Newspaper serving the shipping, trucking, air freight and railroad industries in the US and Canada.
Cost: $98.00
Frequency: Weekly
Circulation: 8115
ISSN: 1529-1820
Founded in 1994
Printed in on newsprint stock

22783 American Mover

American Movers Conference
1611 Duke St
Alexandria, VA 22314-3406

703-683-7410
Fax: 703-683-7527
E-Mail: info@moving.org
Home Page: www.moving.org

Linda Bauer Darr, CEO
Joseph M Harrison, President
Carol Laird, Production Manager
Norma Gyovai, Advertising Manager

This publication covers the moving and storage industry.
Cost: $60.00
24 Pages
Frequency: Monthly
Circulation: 3700
Founded in 1958

22784 American Shipper

Howard Publications
300 W Adams Street Suite 600
PO Box 4728
Jacksonville, FL 32201-4728

904-355-2601
800-874-6422
Fax: 904-791-8836
Home Page: www.americanshipper.com

Nancy Barry, Production Manager
Hayes Howard, Publisher
Kerry Cowart, Circulation Manager
James Blaeser, Sales Associate

Provides those involved in domestic and global supply chain management with news and information of a strategic nature, useful in the formation of logistics polices and partnerships.
Cost: $36.00
104 Pages
Frequency: Monthly
Circulation: 13705
ISSN: 1074-8350
Founded in 1951
Printed in 4 colors on glossy stock

22785 American Trucker

Primedia
7355 Woodland Drive
Indianapolis, IN 46278-1769

317-991-1350
800-827-7468
Fax: 317-299-1356
Home Page: www.trucker.com

Dallas Nauert, Production Manager
Diana Starks, Circulation Director

A trade publication featuring new and used trucks, trailors,parts and services for the heavy duty trucking industry.
Cost: $21.00
Frequency: Monthly
Circulation: 930338
Founded in 1975
Printed in 4 colors on matte stock

22786 Analysis of Class I Railroads

Association of American Railroads
50 F Street NW
Floor 3
Washington, DC 20001-1564

202-392-2334
877-999-8824
Fax: 202-639-5546
E-Mail: kdonley@aar.org
Home Page: www.aar.org

Kelly Donley, Marketing
Tom White, Editor
Edward Hamberger, CEO/President
Joyce Koeneman, Manager

Offers information on the railroad travel industry.
Cost: $250.00
Founded in 1934

22787 Atlantic Northeast Rails & Ports

162 main street
Yarmouth, ME 04096

207-846-3549
Fax: 603-215-4482
Home Page: www.atlanticnortheast.com

Chop Hardenbergh, CEO/President
Cost: $375.00
Frequency: Monthly
Circulation: 300
Founded in 1994

22788 Better Roads

WMO DannHausen Corporation
PO Box 558
Park Ridge, IL 60068

847-696-2391
Fax: 847-696-3445
E-Mail: wod@dannhausen.com

Wm O Dannhausen, Publisher

Market to federal agencies, bureaus, government departments, states, counties township road and city public works.
Cost: $26.96
Frequency: Monthly
Circulation: 38406
Founded in 1769

22789 Brotherhood of Locomotive Engineers

Brotherhood of Locomotive Engineers
1370 Ontario St
Cleveland, OH 44113-1701

216-241-2630
Fax: 216-241-6516
E-Mail: policy@ble.org
Home Page: www.ble.org

Ed Rodzwicz, CEO
John Bentley, Editor

22790 Bus Conversions Magazine

MAK Publishing
7246 Garden Grove Boulevard
Westminster, CA 92683

714-799-0062
Fax: 714-799-0042
E-Mail: editor@busconversions.com
Home Page: www.busconversions.com

Michael A Kadletz, Publisher
Rikki Gee, Publication Manager

how-to, full color, monthly magazine that includes photos, floor plans, helpful hints and guides for buying, selling, selecting, and converting a bus to an RV or executive entertainer's coach. Features pages of classified ads and valuable info on maintaining, operating and updating your coach.
Cost: $38.00
72 Pages
Circulation: 8000
ISSN: 1070-6526
Founded in 1992
Printed in 4 colors on glossy stock

22791 Bus Ride

Friendship Publications
4742 N 24th St
Suite 340
Phoenix, AZ 85016-4884

602-265-7600
800-541-2670
Fax: 602-277-7588
E-Mail: steve@busride.com
Home Page: www.busride.com

Steve Kane, Publisher/Editor-in-Chief
Wayne Bryan, Editor
Donna Arnseth, Circulation Administrator
Maria Jolly, Assistant Editor
Valerie Valtierra, Production Director

Bus industry trade journal with articles about bus companies, training agencies and manufacturers and suppliers to the bus industry.
Cost: $39.00
120 Pages
Frequency: Monthly
Circulation: 16000
Founded in 1965
Printed in 4 colors on glossy stock

22792 Chief Logistics Officer

Penton Media

1166 Avenue of the Americas/10th
Suite 316
Cleveland, NY 10036

212-204-4200
Fax: 216-696-6662
E-Mail: information@penton.com
Home Page: www.penton.com

Jane Cooper, Marketing
Perry A Trunick, Editor
Maryann Jovorek, Production Manager
Chris Meyer, Director

Magazine for supply chain leaders, supplement to Transportation and Distribution.
Cost: $50.00
48 Pages
Frequency: Quarterly
Circulation: 12M
Founded in 1960
Printed in 4 colors on glossy stock

22793 Classic Trains
James Folcum
21027 Crossroads Circle
Waukesha, WI 53187

262-796-8776
Fax: 262-796-1615
Home Page: www.classictrain.com

Rob McGornigal, Editor
Mike Yuhaf, Advertising Manager

Publication features stories on antique and old trains.

22794 Commercial Carrier Journal
Chilton Company
3200 Rice Mine Road NE
Tuscaloosa, AL 35406

800-633-5953
Fax: 610-964-4647
E-Mail: prichards@randallpub.com
Home Page: www.ccjmagazine.com

Chip Magner, Publisher
F Michael Reilly, CEO
Catherine J Randall, Chairman
Avery Vise, Editorial Director
Paul Richards, Editor

For fleet management.
Frequency: Monthly
Circulation: 101176
Founded in 1934

22795 Contracting for Transportation & Logistics Services
120 Main Street
Huntington, NY 11743-6906

631-270-0100
Fax: 516-549-8962
E-Mail: tcpc@transportlaw.com
Home Page: www.transportlaw.com

William J Augello, Executive Director

Published by the Transportation Consumer Protection Council.
Cost: $48.00
Founded in 2001

22796 Corporate Procedures for Shipping & Receiving
120 Main Street
Huntington, NY 11743-6906

631-270-0100
Fax: 516-549-8962
E-Mail: tcpc@transportlaw.com
Home Page: www.transportlaw.com

William J Augello, Executive Director

Published by the Transportation Consumer Protection Council.
Cost: $95.00
Founded in 1998

22797 Defense Transportation Journal
National Defense Transportation Association
50 S Pickett Street
Suite 220
Alexandria, VA 22304-7206

703-751-5011
Fax: 703-823-8761
E-Mail: info@ndtahq.com
Home Page: www.ndtahq.com

LTG Kenneth Wykle, President
Karen Schmitt, Managing Editor

The official publication of the National Defense Transportation Association and the only publication for the government and military transportation industry.
Cost: $35.00
Frequency: Bi-Monthly
Circulation: 8500

22798 Destinations
American Bus Association
700 13th St NW
Suite 575
Washington, DC 20005-5923

202-842-1645
800-283-2877
Fax: 202-842-0850
E-Mail: abainfo@buses.org
Home Page: www.buses.org

Peter J Pantuso, CEO
Eron Shosteck, Marketing

Motorcoach travel across North America and Association news.
80 Pages
Frequency: Monthly
Circulation: 6000
Founded in 1926
Printed in 4 colors on glossy stock

22799 Digest
American Bus Association
700 13th St NW
Suite 575
Washington, DC 20005-5923

202-842-1645
800-283-2877
Fax: 202-842-0850
E-Mail: abainfo@buses.org
Home Page: www.buses.org

Peter J Pantuso, CEO
Judi Bredemeier, Editor
Chrystal Farmer, Marketing Manager
Michael Hayes, Publisher

Legislation news.
Cost: $150.00
Circulation: 3200
Founded in 1996
Printed in 2 colors on matte stock

22800 Direction
American Moving and Storage Association
1611 Duke St
Alexandria, VA 22314-3406

703-683-7410
Fax: 703-683-7527
Home Page: www.moving.org

Matthew Hicks, Advertising
John Parkinson, Editorial
Allison Bresky, Production

Provides news and in-depth feature articles to provide members with vital information to help operate their companies more profitably.
Cost: $35.00
Frequency: Bi-Monthly
Circulation: 4000

22801 Fleet Equipment Magazine
Maple Publishing Company
3550 Embassy Parkway
Akron, OH 44333-8318

330-670-1234
Fax: 330-670-0874
Home Page: www.truklink.com

Tom Gelinas, Editor
Bill Babcox, President
Robert Dorn, Publisher
Kelly McAleese, Ad Services Manager
Lindsey Fritz, Circulation Manager

Edited for fleet equipment managers of truck fleets.
Cost: $82.00
Frequency: Monthly
Circulation: 61,571
Founded in 1974

22802 Freight Claims in Plain English
120 Main Street
Huntington, NY 11743-6906

631-270-0100
Fax: 516-549-8962
E-Mail: tcpc@transportlaw.com
Home Page: www.transportlaw.com

William J Augello, Executive Director

Published by the Transportation Consumer Protection Council.
Cost: $100.00
Founded in 1995

22803 Freight Claims: Filing & Recovery
120 Main Street
Huntington, NY 11743-6906

631-270-0100
Fax: 516-549-8962
E-Mail: tcpc@transportlaw.com
Home Page: www.transportlaw.com

William J Augello, Executive Director

Published by the Transportation Consumer Protection Council.
Cost: $48.00
Founded in 2001

22804 Go-West Magazine
Motor Transport Management Group
3251 Beacon Road
West Sacramento, CA 95691-3475

916-373-3630
Fax: 916-852-5707

Jim Beach, Editor

Complete overview of the transportation industry.
Frequency: Monthly

22805 Guide to Transportation After the Sunsetting of the ICC
120 Main Street
Huntington, NY 11743-6906

631-270-0100
Fax: 516-549-8962
E-Mail: tcpc@transportlaw.com
Home Page: www.transportlaw.com

William J Augello, Executive Director

Published by the Transportation Consumer Protection Council.
Cost: $75.00
Founded in 1997

22806 Heavy Duty Trucking
Newport Communications
38 Executive Park
Suite 300
Irvine, CA 92614-6755

949-261-1636
Fax: 949-261-2904
E-Mail: webmaster@truckinginfo.com
Home Page: www.truckinginfo.com

Doug Condra, President
Susan Condra, Circulation Manager

Susan Patterson, Marketing
Marty Mc Collan, Publisher

National business magazine for managers of medium and heavy duty truck fleets, and manufacturers and dealers of those trucks and the components used to build them.
Cost: $65.00
Frequency: Monthly
Circulation: 90000
Founded in 1922
Printed in 4 colors on glossy stock

22807 Hemispheres
Pace Communications
PO Box 13607
Greensboro, NC 27415-3607

336-378-6065
800-346-1336
Fax: 336-275-2864
Home Page: www.pacecommunications.com

Bonnie McElveen, CEO
Leigh Klee, Chief Financial Officer
Ed Calfo, Executive Vice President

Children's magazine for US airline fliers.
Frequency: Monthly
Circulation: 60000
Founded in 1973

22808 High Performance Composites
Ray Publishing
P.O.Box 992
Morrison, CO 80465-0992

303-467-1776
Fax: 303-467-1777
Home Page: www.compositeworld.com

Approach is technical, offering cutting-edge design, engineering, prototyping, and manufacturing solutions for aerospace and other traditional and emerging structural applications for advanced composites.

22809 ITE Journal
Institute of Transportation Engineers
1099 14th St NW
Suite 300E
Washington, DC 20005-5924

202-289-0222
Fax: 202-289-7722
E-Mail: ite_staff@ite.org
Home Page: www.it.org

Thomas Brahms, CEO
Shannon Gore Peters, Editor
Christina Denekas, Circulation Manager
Richard T Romer, International President

Provides timely news and information on subjects of interest to professionals responsible for traffic engineering, transportation planning, ITS, transit, safety, demand management, education etc.
Cost: $100.00
300 Pages
Frequency: Monthly
Circulation: 7500
Founded in 1930

22810 Inbound Logistics Magazine
Thomas Publishing Company
5 Penn Plaza
New York, NY 10001-1810

212-950-0500
Fax: 212-629-1565
E-Mail: editor@inboundlogistics.com
Home Page: www.inboundlogistics.com

Keith Biondo, Publisher
Felecia Stratton, Editor
Carolyn Smolin, Circulation Manager
Robert Malone, Executive Editor

Accepts advertising.
Frequency: Monthly
Circulation: 55050
Founded in 1981

22811 Institute of Transportation Engineering Journal
Institute of Transportation Engineering
1627 Eye St. NW
Suite 600
Washington, DC 20006

202-785-0060
Fax: 202-785-0609
E-Mail: ite_staff@ite.org
Home Page: www.ite.org

Thomas Brahms, CEO
Christina Denekas, Marketing Manager
Marianne Saglam, Communications & Media Sr. Director

Dedicated to the transportation engineering field. A journal is published for members only.
Cost: $65.00
Frequency: Monthly
Circulation: 17000
Founded in 1930

22812 International Rail Journal
Simmons-Boardman Publishing Corporation
345 Hudson St
Suite 1201
New York, NY 10014-7123

212-620-7200
Fax: 212-633-1165
E-Mail: db@railjournal.co.uk
Home Page: www.simmonsboardman.com

Arthur J McGinnis Jr, President

Covers the rapidly developing railway marketplace for railway and rail transit managers and engineers, suppliers and consultants worldwide.
Frequency: Monthly
Circulation: 100960
Founded in 1960

22813 Journal of the Transportation Research Forum
Transportation Research Forum
Department 2880
PO Box 6050
Fargo, ND 58108-6050

701-231-7766
Fax: 701-231-1945
E-Mail: info@trforum.org
Home Page: www.trforum.org

Richard Gritta, President
Starr McMullen, VP

Contains original manuscripts which are timely in scope and germane to transportation
300 Members
Frequency: 3x/Year
Founded in 1958

22814 Lifting & Transportation International
7249 Dorset Avenue
Saint Louis, MO 63130

314-863-8979
Fax: 314-863-8786
E-Mail: adwyer@douglaspublications.com

Eugene Brymer, Publisher
Andrew Dwyer, Editor

Covers trucking overdimensional loads, heavy crane, and ridging work.
Cost: $8.00

22815 Locomotive Engineers Journal
Brotherhood of Locomotive Engineers
1370 Ontario St
Standard Building
Cleveland, OH 44113-1701

216-241-2630
Fax: 216-241-6516
E-Mail: execstaff@ble.org
Home Page: www.ble.org

Ed Rodzwicz, CEO
Kathleen Policy, Associate Editor
Don M Hahs, President

Designed to meet the information needs of professional engineers throughout North America, also for railroad enthusiasts.
Cost: $10.00
Frequency: Quarterly
Circulation: 54000
Founded in 1863

22816 Logistics Management & Distribution Report
Reed Business Information
225 Wyman St
Suite 3
Waltham, MA 02451-1216

781-734-8000
800-662-7776
Fax: 781-734-8076
E-Mail: lm@reedbusiness.com
Home Page: www.reedbusiness.com

Mark Finklestein, President
Peter Bradley, CFO
Stuart Whayman, CFO

Logistics Management and Distribution Report is written for managers and professionals in charge of traffic, transportation, purchasing, inventory control, containerization and warehousing the functions of physical distribution and business logistics. Covers marketing and operating strategies, cost reduction opportunities and governmental regulation and law.
Frequency: Monthly
Circulation: 30,000
Founded in 1977

22817 Marine Digest & Transportation News
Marine Publishing
1710 South Norman Street
Seattle, WA 98144-1234

206-709-1840
Fax: 206-324-8939
Home Page: www.marinedigest.com

Peter Hurme, Publisher/Senior Editor
Gary Greenewald, Circulation Manager
Tom Henning, Sales/Marketing Manager
M Daigle, Owner

Serves the maritime shipping community primarily in the western United States. Updates on new products, suppliers, legislation and insurance are featured.
Cost: $28.00
Frequency: Monthly
Circulation: 7200
Founded in 1922

22818 Mass Transit Magazine
Cygnus Publishing
PO Box 803
Fort Atkinson, WI 53538-0803

920-000-1111
Fax: 920-563-1699
Home Page: www.cygnusb2b.com

John French, CEO
Carie Grall, Associate Publisher
Paul Bowers, Group VP
Debbie Dumke, Manager
Deb Krause, National Accounts Manager
Cost: $120.00
Frequency: Monthly
Founded in 1966

22819 Movers News
New York State Movers & Warehousemen's Association

125 Maiden Lane
11th Floor
New York, NY 10038

212-635-0510
Fax: 212-635-0511
E-Mail: nymovers@msn.com
Home Page: www.movernet.com/nysmwa

David Blake, Editor
John Palisand, President

Association news.
Cost: $24.00
Frequency: BiMonthly
ISSN: 8750-1155
Founded in 1937

22820 National Bus Trader
National Bus Trader
9698 W Judson Rd
Polo, IL 61064-9015

815-946-2341
Fax: 815-946-2347
Home Page: www.busmag.com

Larry Plachno, CEO

Equipment magazine for over-the-road and integral buses in the United States and Canada.
Cost: $25.00
Frequency: Monthly
Circulation: 7000
ISSN: 0194-939X
Founded in 1977
Printed in on glossy stock

22821 New Equipment Digest
Penton Media
1166 Avenue of the Americas/10th
Suite 316
New York, NY 10036

212-204-4200
Fax: 216-696-6662
E-Mail: information@penton.com
Home Page: www.penton.com

Jane Cooper, Marketing
Tom Sockel, Associate Editor
Robert King, Editor
Sarah Hughes, Production Manager
Bobbie Macy, Circulation Manager

Serves the general industrial field which includes manufacturing, processing, engineering services, construction, transportation, mining, public utilities, wholesale distributors, educational services, libraries and governmental establishments.
Frequency: Monthly
Circulation: 206154
Founded in 1936

22822 P&D Magazine
Motor Transport Management Group
3251 Beacon Road
West Sacramento, CA 95691-3475

916-373-3630
Fax: 916-852-5707

Robert L Titus, Publisher

Edited for the needs of pick up and delivery.
Cost: $5.00
Circulation: 33,571

22823 PC-Trans
University of Kansas
2011 Learned Hall
Lawrence, KS 66044-7526

785-864-2700
Fax: 785-864-5655
E-Mail: mgivechi@ku.edu
Home Page: www.ku.edu

Lisa Harris, Editor
Mehrdad Givechi, Manager
Alice Kuo, Advertising
Pat Weaver, Director

Software reviews and miscellaneous computer information for transportation professionals.
Circulation: 13000
Founded in 1872

22824 Progressive Railroading
Trade Press Publishing Corporation
PO Box 694
Milwaukee, WI 53201-694

414-271-5011
Fax: 414-228-1134
Home Page: www.facilities.com

Steve Bolte, Publisher
Pat Foran, Editor
Tim Rowe, Marketing
Wendy Melnick, Production Manager
Robert J Wisniewski, CEO

Feature includes management techniques, purchasing developments, engineering innovations and general industry news.
Cost: $55.00
Frequency: Monthly
Circulation: 25,207
Founded in 1994

22825 Protecting Shippers' Interests
120 Main Street
Huntington, NY 11743-6906

631-270-0100
Fax: 516-549-8962
E-Mail: tcpc@transportlaw.com
Home Page: www.transportlaw.com

William J Augello, Executive Director

Published by the Transportation Consumer Protection Council.
Cost: $75.00
Founded in 1997

22826 RV Business
TL Enterprises
3601 Calle Tecate
Camarillo, CA 93012-5056

805-987-1800
Fax: 805 389-0484
E-Mail: tlecs@magserv.com
Home Page: www.rvbusiness.com

Katherine Sharma, Editor
Denielle Sternburg, Business Manager
Sherman Goldenberg, Publisher

Reports on various aspects of the recreational vehicle industry, including forecasting trends, new technologies, marketing and business concepts.
Cost: $12.00
Frequency: Monthly

22827 Rail News Update
Association of American Railroads
50 F Street NW
Floor 3
Washington, DC 20001-1564

202-392-2334
Fax: 202-639-5546

Publishes pertinent new in the railroad industry especially covering Washington news. Covers Department of Transportation and Interstate Commerce activities.
Frequency: BiWeekly

22828 Railroad Facts
Association of American Railroads
50 F Street NW
Floor 3
Washington, DC 20001-1564

202-392-2334
Fax: 202-639-5546
E-Mail: pubsrvcs@aar.org
Home Page: www.aar.org

Kelly Donley, Marketing
Tom White, Editor
Edward R Hamberger, CEO/President

Offers statistical information and research reports on railroad travel.
Cost: $15.00
Frequency: Annual+
Founded in 1934

22829 Railroad Ten-Year Trends
Association of American Railroads
50 F Street NW
Floor 3
Washington, DC 20001-1564

202-392-2334
Fax: 202-639-5546
E-Mail: pubsrvcs@aar.org
Home Page: www.aar.org

Offers historical facts and perspectives on America's railroad industry.
Cost: $100.00
Frequency: Annual+
Founded in 1934

22830 Railway Age
Simmons-Boardman Publishing Corporation
345 Hudson St
Suite 1201
New York, NY 10014-7123

212-620-7200
Fax: 212-633-1165
E-Mail: wvantuono@sbpub.com
Home Page: www.simmonsboardman.com

Arthur J McGinnis Jr, President

Emphasis is placed on technology, operations, strategic planning, marketing and other issues such as legislative, labor and management developments.
Frequency: Monthly
Circulation: 260030
Founded in 1876

22831 Railway Track and Structures
Simmons-Boardman Publishing Corporation
345 Hudson St
Suite 1201
New York, NY 10014-7123

212-620-7200
Fax: 212-633-1165
E-Mail: tjudge@sbpub-chicago.com
Home Page: www.simmonsboardman.com

Arthur J McGinnis Jr, President

A technical magazine designed to meet the information needs of the roadway and other civil engineering related departments of North American rail freight and passenger operators.
Frequency: Monthly
Circulation: 8541

22832 Refrigerated Transporter
Penton Media
1166 Avenue of the Americas/10th
Suite 316
New York, NY 10036

212-204-4200
800-441-0294
Fax: 913-514-6895
Home Page: www,penton.com

Eric Jacobson, Senior VP

22833 School Bus Fleet
Bobit Publishing Company

3520 Challenger St
Torrance, CA 90503-1640

310-533-2400
Fax: 310-533-2500
Home Page: www.bobit.com

Edward J Bobit, CEO
Cliff Henke, Editor

A magazine that serves the field of pupil transportation, to public and private schools and to independent contract operators transporting students.
Cost: $42.00
Frequency: Monthly
Circulation: 24000
Founded in 1961

22834 Shippers' Domestic Truck Bill of Lading & Common Carrier Rate Agreement Kit
Transportation & Logistics Council
120 Main Street
Huntington, NY 11743

631-549-8988
Fax: 631-549-8962
E-Mail: tlc@transportlaw.org
Home Page: www.tlccouncil.org

Diane Smid, Membership Secretary
Judy Selvaggio, Administrative Secretary
George Pezold, Executive Director

Published by the Transportation Consumer Protection Council.
Cost: $50.00
Frequency: Monthly
Founded in 1974

22835 Signalman's Journal
Brotherhood of Railroad Signalmen
601 W Golf Road
Box U
Mount Prospect, IL 60056-4276

847-439-3732
Fax: 847-439-3743
E-Mail: signalman@brs.org
Home Page: www.brs.org

W Dan Pickett, President
Walter A Barrows, Treasurer

Information concerning railroad signaling devices, equipment and apparatus, also includes current events and items pertaining to railroad signalmen.
40 Pages
Frequency: Quarterly
Circulation: 10700
ISSN: 0037-5020
Founded in 1901
Printed in 4 colors on glossy stock

22836 Southern Motor Cargo
477 S Shady Grove Road
Memphis, TN 38120-2512

901-346-5943
Fax: 901-276-5400

Wallace Witmer Jr, Editor

Offers information on shipping.
Cost: $30.00
66 Pages
Frequency: Monthly
Founded in 1945

22837 Speedlines
High Speed Grand Transportation Association
1010 Massachusetts Avenue NW, #110
Washington, DC 20001-5402

202-789-8107
Fax: 212-789-8109
Home Page: www.hsgt.org

Mark Dysart, Editor

Exclusively devoted to the High Speed Ground Transportation Association covering broad policy debates, state activity reports, federal developments and technological papers.
Frequency: Quarterly
Circulation: 3,200

22838 Structural Mover
International Association of Structural Movers
PO Box 2637
Lexington, SC 29071-2637

803-951-9304
Fax: 803-951-9314
E-Mail: gbrymer@alltel.net
Home Page: www.iasm.org

N Eugene Brymer, Staff Executive

A magazine written specifically for members of the International Association of Structural Movers. Subcription to quarterly magazine included in price of membership to IASM.
Frequency: Quarterly
Circulation: 500

22839 Teamster Magazine
International Brotherhood of Teamsters
25 Louisiana Ave NW
Washington, DC 20001-2130

202-624-6800
Fax: 202-624-6918
E-Mail: communications@teamster.org
Home Page: www.teamster.org

James P Hoffa Jr, President
Per Bernstein, Editor-in-Chief

Affiliated with the AFL-CIO. Magazine is published for members only of 30 pages.
Cost: $12.00
Circulation: 1.4 mill
Founded in 1903

22840 Traffic Management
Reed Business Information
275 Washington St
Newton, MA 02458-1611

617-964-3030
Fax: 617-630-3730
E-Mail: webmaster@reedbusiness.com
Home Page: www.designnews.com

Mitch MacDonald, Editor
Ron Bondlow, Publisher

Accepts advertising.
100 Pages
Frequency: Monthly
Circulation: 73000
Founded in 1982

22841 Traffic World
Journal of Commerce
33 Washington Street
13th Floor
Newark, NJ 07102

973-848-7000
800-255-1341
Fax: 973-848-7068
Home Page: www.trafficworld.com

William B Cassidy, Managuing Editor

Discusses all facets of the transportation industry. Also online at www.joc.com.
Cost: $174.00
Frequency: Weekly
Founded in 1907

22842 Trailer/Body Builders
Tunnell Publications
PO Box 66010
Houston, TX 77266

713-523-8124
800-880-0368
Fax: 713-523-8384
Home Page:
advertisers.trailer-bodybuilders.com

Paul Schenck, Editor
Ray Anderson, Publisher
Bruce Sauer, Editorial Director
Wanda Tunnell, Advertising Director
Diana Smith, Advertising Sales

Serves the truck trailer and truck body manufacturing industry. Accepts advertising.
Cost: $38.00
Frequency: Monthly

22843 Transport Fleet News
Transport Publishing
1962 N Bissell Street
#3
Chicago, IL 60614-5015

773-058-8540

Lillana Rogala, Publisher

Industry news and product for fleet supervisors.
Circulation: 10,500

22844 Transportation & Distribution
Penton Media
1166 Avenue of the Americas/10th
Suite 316
New York, NY 10036

212-204-4200
Fax: 216-696-6662
E-Mail: editor@logisticstoday.com
Home Page: www.penton.com

Jane Cooper, Marketing
Antoinette Sanchez-Perkins, Circulation Manager
Newt Barret, Publisher
Dave Blanchard, Editor
David Nussbaum, CEO

Serves the information needs of logistics professionals, identifying trends and providing expert views on strategic, management and operational subjects affecting logistics. Accepts advertising.
Cost: $60.00
78 Pages
Frequency: Monthly
Circulation: 85000
Founded in 1960
Printed in 4 colors on glossy stock

22845 Transportation Leader
Taxicab, Limousine & Paratransit Association
3200 Tower Oaks Blvd
Suite 220
Rockville, MD 20852

301-984-5700
Fax: 301-984-5703
E-Mail: info@tlpa.org
Home Page: www.tlpa.org

Alfred LaGasse, CEO
Victor Dizengoff, President

Leading resource for news and information on issues, trends, and people in the private, for-hire passenger transportation industry. Provides readers with an array of features, articles, and columns that include information on managing a transportation company, industry trends, driver's tips, an industry calendar of events, coverage of TLPA events, and advertisements from the industry's leading suppliers.
Cost: $4.00
48 Pages
Frequency: Quarterly
Circulation: 6000
Founded in 1920
Mailing list available for rent: 6,000 names at $100 per M
Printed in 4 colors on glossy stock

22846 Trucker's Connection
Megan Cullingford
5960 Crooked Creek Road
Suite 15
Norcross, GA 30092

770-416-0927
Fax: 770-416-1734
Home Page: www.truckersconnection.com

Dan Barnhill, Editor
Reid Ramsay, Production Manager
Megan Cullingford, General Manager
David Guthrie, Advertising Sales

Published for the use of long haul, over-the-road truck drivers, owner operators, small trucking company fleet owners, safety and recruiting of personnel for trucking companies in the US and Canada.
Frequency: Monthly
Circulation: 16,5,000
Founded in 1986
Printed in 4 colors on glossy stock

Trade Shows

22847 AAR Annual Convention and Exhibit
Railway Systems Suppliers
9306 New Lagrange Road
Suite 100
Louisville, KY 40242

502-327-7774
Fax: 502-327-0541
E-Mail: rssi@rssi.org
Home Page: www.rssi.org

Donald Remaley, Executive Director
Franklin Brown, President

Railroad signal and communication equipment displays, annual meeting & banquet.
Frequency: Annual
Founded in 1960

22848 AREMA Annual Conference & Exposition
American Railway Engineering & Maintenance-of-Way
10003 Derekwood Ln
Suite 210
Lanham, MD 20706-4362

301-459-3200
Fax: 301-459-8077
E-Mail: dknight@arema.org
Home Page: www.arema.org/meetings

Desiree Knight, Director, Conferences & Seminars

Approximately 198 exhibitors from all segments of the railway engineering and maintenance industry, in addition to the conference talks, seminars, and events. Advanced registration for non-members starts at $760.
1600 Attendees
Frequency: Annual

22849 ARTBA National Convention
American Road and Transportation Builders Assn
1219 28th St NW
Washington, DC 20007-3389

202-289-4434
Fax: 202-289-4435
E-Mail: general@artba.org
Home Page: www.artba.org

Pete Ruane, President
Matt Jeanneret, Sr. VP, Communications/Marketing
Jaime Mahoney, Publications Manager
Liz Cavallaro, Sales Manager
Tom Hill, Treasurer
Frequency: Annual/Fall

22850 American Bus Marketplace
1015 15th Street NW
Washington, DC 20005-2605

202-842-9100
800-283-2877
Fax: 202-842-0850

Katie Robbins

Sales and marketing event for the North American group travel industry. 350 booths.
2M Attendees
Frequency: December

22851 American Car Rental Association Convention
11250 Roger Bacon Drive
#8
Reston, VA 20190

703-787-7718
Fax: 703-435-4390
Home Page: www.acra.org

Gwendolyn Hogan

One hundred exhibits of cars, vans, buses, computers, equipment and services for car rental company owners and officers. Conference, reception and dinner.
600 Attendees
Frequency: Annual
Founded in 1978

22852 American Public Transportation Association Expo
1666 K Street NW
Suite 1100
Washington, DC 20006

202-496-4800
Fax: 202-496-4324
E-Mail: meetings2@apta.com
Home Page: www.apta.com

William W Millar, President
Petra Mollet, VP
Rosemary Sherid, Marketing

Seminar, workshop, conference, luncheon, banquet, tours and 800 exhibits for the planning designing and finance and operation of public transportation.
15000 Attendees
Frequency: October 2008/2011
Founded in 1882

22853 American Railroads Association Communication and Signal Division
50 F Street NW
Washington, DC 20001-1530

202-392-2334

William Peters, Show Manager
Joyce Koeneman, Manager

Transportation equipment and services.
1.5M Attendees

22854 Association for Commuter Transportation Convention
808 17th Street NW
Suite 200
Washington, DC 20006-3910

202-393-3497
Home Page: tmi.cob.fsu.edu/act

Elizabeth Stutts, President
Kenneth M Sufka, Executive Director
Shamus Misek, VP
Kim Tabah, Director of Development
Barbara Ash, Communications Manager

Thirty booths.
300 Attendees
Frequency: September

22855 Association of Railway Museums Convention
Association of Railway Museums
PO Box 370
Tujunga, CA 91043-0370

818-951-9151
Fax: 818-951-9151

Paul Hammond, President ARM

Annual show and exhibits for the preservation of railway equipment, artifacts and history. Seminar, tours, banquet and dinner.
125 Attendees
Frequency: October
Founded in 1961

22856 Biodiesel Investor Conference
Platts
24 Hartwell Avenue
Lexington, MA 02421

781-860-6100
866-355-2930
E-Mail: registration@platts.com
Home Page: www.platts.com

Frequency: June Houston

22857 Education Conference & Expo
American Moving and Storage Association
1611 Duke St
Alexandria, VA 22314-3406

703-683-7410
Fax: 703-683-7527
Home Page: www.moving.org

Linda Bauer Darr, CEO
Sandy Lynch, SVP

The largest gathering of moving and storage industry professionals in the country. With more than 30 education sessions and over 10 hours of dedicated network time, the conference & expo offers countless opportunities to further your career while making new business contacts.
Frequency: Annual/March

22858 Fleet Management Institute (NAFA) Convention
100 Wood Avenue S
Suite 310
Iselin, NJ 08830

732-494-8100
Fax: 732-494-6789
E-Mail: info@nafa.org
Home Page: www.nafa.org

Patricia Murtaugh, Assistant Executive Director
Joanne Marsh, Manager

Fleet management education and automobile parts and services, as well as maintenance for business and public service vehicles. 250 booths
2M Attendees
Frequency: April/May

22859 Institute of Transportation Engineers Annual Meeting
Institute of Transportation Engineers
525 School Street SW
Suite 410
Washington, DC 20024-2729

202-548-8050
Fax: 202-863-5486
Home Page: www.ite.org

Marianne Wool, Manager
Shannon Gore Peters, Editor

Annual meeting of 100 exhibitors of transportation equipment, supplies and services.
2,000 Attendees
Frequency: Las Vegas

22860 International Association of Structural Movers Annual Convention
PO Box 600
Oakton, VA 22124
703-648-3225
Fax: 503-543-6697
Home Page: www.iasm.org
Containing 20 booths and 15 exhibits.

22861 International Public Transit Expo
Pemco/Professional Expo Management Company
191 S Gary Avenue
Carol Stream, IL 60188-2092
630-690-5600
Fax: 203-840-9662
Barbara Silverman, VP
The world's largest transit industry event offering a chance for top transit officials to meet with manufacturers from around the world.
16M Attendees
Frequency: October

22862 International Truck and Bus Expo
Society of Automotive Engineers
400 Commonwealth Drive
Warrendale, PA 15096-0001
724-772-8548
Fax: 724-776-0790
Home Page: www.sae.org
Andrew Brown, Treasurer

22863 Link
R&D Associates
16607 Blanco Road
Suite 305
San Antonio, TX 78232-1940
210-682-4302
Fax: 830-493-8036
David Dee, Editor
Articles of interest to the food, food packaging, food processing and foodservice industry. 50 booths.
300 Attendees
Frequency: Spring/Fall

22864 NDTA Forum & Expo
National Defense Transportation Association
50 S Pickett Street
Suite 220
Alexandria, VA 22304-7206
703-751-5011
Fax: 703-823-8761
E-Mail: info@ndtahq.com
Home Page: www.ndtahq.com
LTG Kenneth Wykle, President
COL Dennis Edwards, VP Marketing
A key element in the Association's fulfillment of its educational and professional development missions and it also offers outstanding opportunities for networking and mentoring.
1200 Attendees
Frequency: Annual/September

22865 NPA
National Parking Association
1112 16th Street NW
Suite 840
Washington, DC 20036
202-296-4336
800-647-7275
Fax: 202-296-3102
E-Mail: info@npapark.org
Home Page: www.npapark.org
Herb Anderson, VP Advertising & Exposition
Frequency: Oct Washington

22866 National Industrial Transportation League Trade Show
1700 N Moore St
Suite 1900
Arlington, VA 22209-1931
703-524-5011
Fax: 703-524-5017
E-Mail: info@nitl.org
Home Page: www.nitl.org
Arthur E. Cole, President
Michael J Barr, First Vice Chairman
Peter Gatti, Executive VP
Annual show of 250 exhibitors of computer services software and innovations for transportation operations.
600 Members
Founded in 1907

22867 National Private Truck Council Management/ Education Conference
National Private Truck Council
66 Canal Center Plaza
Alexandria, VA 22314-1591
703-683-1300
Fax: 703-683-1217
Gary Petty, CEO
Annual conference and exhibits of equipment, supplies and services for processors, shippers, distributors and retailers who operate their own truck fleets to advance their primary nontransportation business enterprises.

22868 North American Truck Show
North American Expositions Company
33 Rutherford Avenue
Boston, MA 02129-3795
617-242-6092
800-225-1577
Fax: 617-242-1817
Home Page: www.truckingexpo.com
Gregory Soughlin, Show Manager
Six hundred booths.
25M Attendees
Frequency: May

22869 TLPA Annual Convention & Trade Show
Taxicab, Limousine & Paratransit Association
3200 Tower Oaks Boulevard
Suite 220
Rockville, MD 20852
301-984-5700
Fax: 301-984-5703
E-Mail: info@tlpa.com
Home Page: www.tlpa.org
Alfred La Gasse III, Executive VP
Victor Dizengoff, President
Shares information vital to owners or taxicab, limousine, airport shuttle, paratransit and nonemergency medical transportation fleets. 100 suppliers and exhibitors of the newest products available to the industry.
1000 Attendees
Frequency: Annual

22870 TransComp Exhibition
National Industrial Transportation League
1700 N Moore Street
Suite 1900
Arlington, VA 22209-1931
703-524-5011
Fax: 703-524-5017
E-Mail: info@nitl.org
Home Page: www.nitl.org
Ellie Gilanshah, VP Finance and Membership
3000 Attendees
Frequency: November
Founded in 1907

22871 Transportation Intermediaries Annual Convention & Trade Show
Transportation Intermediaries Association
3601 Eisenhower Avenue
Suite 110
Alexandria, VA 22304
703-299-5700
Fax: 703-836-0123
E-Mail: info@tianet.org
Home Page: www.tianet.org
Robert Voltmann, President/CEO
Larry Fisher, Contact
Education and policy organization for North American transportation intermediaries. TIA is the only national association representing the interests of all third party transportation service providers. The members of TIA include logistics management firms, property brokers, perishable commodities brokers, freight forwarders, intermodal marketers, ocean and air forwarders, and NVOCC's.
700 Attendees
Founded in 1978

22872 Transportation Research Forum Annual Meeting
Transportation Research Forum
Department 2880
PO Box 6050
Fargo, ND 58108-6050
701-231-7766
Fax: 701-231-1945
E-Mail: info@trforum.org
Home Page: www.trforum.org
Richard Gritta, President
Starr McMullen, VP
300 Members
Founded in 1958

22873 Women's Transportation Seminar
Women's Transportation Seminar
1 Walnut Street
Boston, MA 02108-3616
617-367-3273
Fax: 617-227-6783
Annual seminar and exhibits of transportation equipment, supplies and services.

Directories & Databases

22874 AAA Bridge and Ferry Directory
American Automobile Association
1000 AAA Drive
Heathrow, FL 32746-5062
407-444-7966
Melanie Fuller, Highway Infoformation Coordinator
Offers information on over 500 toll facilities in the US, Canada and Mexico that enable automobiles and passengers to complete toll non-highway portions of their journey.
Cost: $12.50
103 Pages
Frequency: Annual

22875 AREMA Membership Directory & REMSA Buyer's Guide
American Railway Engineering & Maintenance-of-Way
10003 Derekwood Ln
Suite 210
Lanham, MD 20706-4362
301-459-3200
Fax: 301-459-8077

E-Mail: jclement@arema.org
Home Page: www.arema.org/meetings

Janice Clements, Director, Membership & IS

A full listing of AREMA members and REMSA companies. Free for members; $50 for additional member copy; $200 for non-members
Cost: $200.00
400 Pages

22876 **ARTBA Transportation Officials & Engineers Directory**
American Road and Transportation Builders Assn
1219 28th St NW
Washington, DC 20007-3389

202-289-4434
Fax: 202-289-4435
E-Mail: general@artba.org
Home Page. www.artba.org

Pete Ruane, President
Matt Jeanneret, Sr. VP, Communications/Marketing
Jaime Mahoney, Publications Manager
Liz Cavallaro, Sales Manager
Tom Hill, Treasurer

An annual survey of local, state and federal transportation agencies offered as a pocket-sized publication and as a mergeable Excel spreadsheet. The TO&E Directory includes key information about more than 6,000 state and local transportation departments and authorities, including URLs and e-mail addresses. From $195 for members to get the pocket edition to $475 for non-members to get the Excel version.
6300 Members
Frequency: Annual
Founded in 1902

22877 **Affiliated Warehouse Companies Directory**
Affiliated Warehouse Companies, Inc
PO Box 295
Hazlet, NJ 07730-0295

732-739-2323
Fax: 732-739-4154
E-Mail: sales@awco.com
Home Page: www.awco.com

Jim McBride, President
Patrick McBride, Vice President

Third party logistics and public warehousing, marketing and sales company. Directory is free.
Founded in 1953
Mailing list available for rent: 8,500 names at $100 per M
Printed in 4 colors

22878 **Air CargoWorld & Traffic World**
Knight-Ridder Financial
75 Wall Street
Floor 23
New York, NY 10005-2833

212-429-2307
Fax: 212-372-7148

Offers valuable information on cash, futures and options markets.

22879 **Airline, Ship & Catering: Onboard Service Buyer's Guide & Directory**
International Publishing Company of America
664 La Villa Dr
Miami Springs, FL 33166-6030

305-887-1700
Fax: 305-885-1923

Alexander Morton, Owner

Offers information on over 6,000 airlines, railroads, ship lines and termianl restaurants.
Cost: $125.00
Frequency: Annual
Circulation: 6,000

22880 **American Bus Association's Motorcoach Marketer**
American Bus Association
700 13th St NW
Suite 575
Washington, DC 20005-5923

202-842-1645
Fax: 202-842-0850
E-Mail: abainfo@buses.org
Home Page: www.buses.org

Peter J Pantuso, CEO
Eron Shosteck, Marketing

This directory is a comprehensive guide of the bus and travel industry offering information on hotels and sightseeing services, attractions, museums, restaurants and more.
500 Pages
Frequency: Annual
Founded in 1926

22881 **American Public Transit Association Membership Directory**
American Public Transit Association
1666 K St NW
Suite 1100
Washington, DC 20006-1215

202-496-4800
Fax: 202-496-4324
E-Mail: hbrett@apta.com
Home Page: www.apta.com

Karol J Popkin, CEO
Petra Mollet, VP
Rosemary Sherid, Marketing

A who's who directory of services and supplies within the public transportation industry.
Founded in 1882

22882 **American Shortline Railway Guide**
Kalmbach Publishing Company
Po Box 1612
Waukesha, WI 53187-1612

262-796-8776
Fax: 262-796-1615
Home Page: www.trains.com

Gerald Boettcher, President

Directory of services and supplies to the industry.
Cost: $18.95
320 Pages

22883 **Bus Garage Index**
Friendship Publications
PO Box 1472
Spokane, WA 99210-1472

800-541-2670
Fax: 509-325-0405

Bruce Sankey, President
Leslie Maris, VP Marketing
Linda Metler, Production Manager

Offers information on over 900 garages and service centers in the United States and Canada offering services to buses on charter service and tours.
Cost: $28.00
140 Pages
Circulation: 3,000
Mailing list available for rent: 14M names
Printed in 4 colors on glossy stock

22884 **Bus Industry Directory**
Friendship Publications
PO Box 1472
Spokane, WA 99210-1472

800-541-2670
Fax: 509-325-0405

Bruce Sankey, President/Publisher
Leslie Maris, VP Marketing

A comprehensive list of over 4,500 intercity and charter bus companies and local transit authorities in the United States and Canada.
Cost: $78.00
500 Pages
Frequency: Annual
Mailing list available for rent: 14M names
Printed in 4 colors on glossy stock

22885 **Carrier Routing Director**
Transportation Technical Services
500 Lafayette Boulevard
Fredericksburg, VA 22401-6070

540-899-9872
800-666-4887
Fax: 888-665-9887
Home Page: www.ttstrucks.com

Thomas R Fugee, Executive VP

Two thousand six hundred top common and contract carriers, toll-free faxes, states served + Canadian provinces and Mexico, equipment types, commodities.
Cost: $145.00
Frequency: Annual
Founded in 1992

22886 **DRI Transportation Detail**
DRI/McGraw-Hill
24 Hartwell Ave
Lexington, MA 02421-3103

781-860-6060
Fax: 781-860-6002
E-Mail: support@construction.com
Home Page: www.construction.com

Walt Arvin, President

This time series contains annual and quarterly data describing aspects of the transportation industry.

22887 **Defense Transportation Journal NDTA Almanac**
National Defense Transportation Association
50 S Pickett Street
Suite 220
Alexandria, VA 22304-7206

703-751-5011
Fax: 703-823-8761
E-Mail: info@ndtahq.com
Home Page: www.ndtahq.com
Social Media: Facebook, Twitter, LinkedIn, You Tube

LTG Kenneth Wykle, President
COL Dennis Edwards, VP Marketing

Reference book of Military/Government/Transportation industry companies and executives
128 Pages

22888 **Directory of Shippers**
Transportation Technical Services
500 Lafayette Boulevard
Fredericksburg, VA 22401-6070

540-899-9872
800-666-4887
Fax: 888-665-9887
Home Page: www.ttstrucks.com

Thomas R Fugee, Executive VP

Compilateion of 14,000 logistics executives. Key information on 13,500 companies, phone, fax-e-mail, addresses, SIC's, revenue. Great

marketing sales and research tool.
Cost: $170.00
Frequency: Annual
Founded in 1992

22889 **Directory of Transportation Professionals**
National Assn of Regulatory Utility Commissioners
PO Box 684
Washington, DC 20044-0684

202-898-2200

Offers valuable information on over 100 regulated transportation firms and professionals.
Cost: $20.00
150 Pages
Frequency: Annual

22890 **Directory of Truck Dealers**
Transportation Technical Services
500 Lafayette Boulevard
Fredericksburg, VA 22401-6070

540-899-9872
800-666-4887
Fax: 888-665-9887
Home Page: www.ttstrucks.com

Thomas R Fugee, Executive VP

Unique, extensive list of 2,700 of the nation's kmid-size/heavy truck dealers. Address, brands sold, serviced, keky contacts, phone and fax.
Cost: $95.00
Frequency: Annual
Founded in 1992

22891 **Foreign Flag Merchant Ships Owned by US Parent Companies**
US Department of Transportation
400 7th Street SW
Room 8117
Washington, DC 20590-0001

202-366-4000

Directory of services and supplies to the industry.
20 Pages
Frequency: SemiAnnual

22892 **Greenwood's Guide to Great Lakes Shipping**
Freshwater Press
1700 E 13th Street
Suite 3-R
Cleveland, OH 44114-3213

216-241-0373
Fax: 216-781-6344
Home Page: www.lakeboats.com

Michael Dills, VP/General Manager

Offers companies that ship water-carried commodities and service firms on the Great Lakes Seaway systems. Details of vessels, dock facilities, shipyards, etc.
Cost: $71.00
650 Pages
Frequency: Annual
Circulation: 2,500
Founded in 1960
Printed in on glossy stock

22893 **Grey House Transportation Security Directory**
Grey House Publishing
4919 Route 22
PO Box 56
Amenia, NY 12501

518-789-8700
800-562-2139
Fax: 845-373-6390
E-Mail: books@greyhouse.com
Home Page: www.greyhouse.com
Social Media: Facebook, Twitter

Leslie Mackenzie, Publisher
Richard Gottlieb, Editor

Provides information on everything from Regulatory Authorities to Security Equipment, this top-flight directory brings together the relevant information necessary for creating and maintaining a security plan for a wide range of transportation facilities.
Cost: $195.00
800 Pages
ISBN: 1-592370-75-6
Founded in 1981

22894 **Inland River Guide**
Waterways Journal
319 N 4th St
Suite 650
St Louis, MO 63102-1994

314-241-7354
Fax: 314-241-4207
E-Mail: info@waterwaysjournal.net
Home Page: www.waterwaysjournal.net

H Nelson Spencer Iii, Publisher
John S Shoulberg, Editor/Associate Publisher
Ed Rahe, Advertising Sales
Alan Bates, Manager
Marie Rausch, Advertising Sales Director

The only directory published specifically for the benefit of the companies doing business along the inland and intracoastal waterways. It contains vital information about companies servicing all industry segments.
Cost: $65.00
600+ Pages
Frequency: Annual
Circulation: 3,000
Founded in 1972

22895 **Inland River Record**
Waterways Journal
319 N 4th St
Suite 650
St Louis, MO 63102-1994

314-241-7354
Fax: 314-241-4207
E-Mail: hnspencer@waterwaysjournal.net
Home Page: www.waterwaysjournal.net

H Nelson Spencer III, Publisher
John S Shoulberg, Manager
Alan Bates, Manager
Marie Rausch, Advertising Sales Director

Lists in detail more than 3,500 commercial towboats and tugs, U.S. engineer vessels and Coast Guard vessels navigating the Mississippi and Ohio, their tributaries and the Gulf Intracoastal Waterway.
Cost: $37.50
475 Pages
Frequency: Annual
Circulation: 3,000

22896 **Leonard's Guide National Third Party Logistics Directory**
GR Leonard & Company
49 E Huntington Dr
Arcadia, CA 91006-3210

626-574-1800
800-574-5250
E-Mail: grico@ix.netcom.com
Home Page: www.leonardsguide.com

David Ercolani, President

Approximately 2,000 transportation brokers and third party logistics firms and brokerages in the US and Canada.
Cost: $75.00
Frequency: Annual Spring

22897 **Light List**
United States Coast Guard
2100 2nd Street SW
Washington, DC 20593-0002

202-488-8157
Fax: 202-366-5063

Offers information to the shipping industry in the form of lights. This comprehensive directory offers a list of lights, fog signals, daybeacons, radiobeacons and LORAN stations operated or authorized by the US Coast Guard. Various volumes are offered.
Cost: $25.00
200+ Pages
Frequency: Volumes

22898 **Mass Transit: Consultants Issue**
Cygnus Publishing
Po Box 803
Fort Atkinson, WI 53538-0803

920-000-1111
Fax: 920-563-1699
Home Page: www.cygnusb2b.com

John French, CEO
Kathy Scott, Director of Public Relations
Paul Bonaiuto, CFO

Offers listings of over 300 urban transportation architects, designers, engineers and other specialists serving the urban transportation industry.
Frequency: BiMonthly

22899 **Mexican Motor Carrier Directory**
Transportation Technical Services
500 Lafayette Boulevard
Fredericksburg, VA 22401-6070

540-899-9872
800-666-4887
Fax: 888-665-9887
Home Page: www.ttstrucks.com

Thomas R Fugee, Executive VP

Unique, extensive and key information on 500 Mexican carriers.
Cost: $145.00
Frequency: Annual

22900 **NARUC Compilation of Transportation Regulatory Policy**
National Assn of Regulatory Utility Commissioners
PO Box 684
Washington, DC 20044-0684

202-898-2200
Home Page: http://www.naruc.org

Offers a list of over 100 regulatory agencies in the United States and Canada for the transportation industry.
Cost: $33.00

22901 **National Customs Brokers and Forwarders Association of America**
National Customs Brokers & Forwarders Association
1200 18th St NW
Suite 901
Washington, DC 20036-2572

202-466-0222
Fax: 202-466-0226
E-Mail: staff@ncbfaa.org
Home Page: www.ncbfaa.org

Barbara Reilly, Executive VP

About 600 customs brokers, international air cargo agents, and freight forwarders in the United States.
Cost: $24.00
Frequency: Annual

22902 **National Highway Carriers Directory**
National Highway Carriers Directory

PO Box 6099
Buffalo Grove, IL 60089-6099

847-634-0606
Fax: 847-634-1026
Home Page: www.national-highway.com

Pam W Ferreira, President/Editor

Offers information on over 700 motor carriers, LTL carriers, truckload companies, warehousing companies, transportation brokers, freight forwarders, Canadian carriers, over 250,000 points and terminals for LTL carriers, refrigerated carries, and more. Now also on CD-ROM: $399.00 with free book.
Cost: $195.00
1,400 Pages
Frequency: Spring & Fall
Founded in 1948
Printed in 2 colors on newsprint stock

22903 **National Industrial Transportation League Reference Manual**
National Industrial Transportation League
1700 N Moore St
Suite 1900
Arlington, VA 22209-1931
703-524-5011
Fax: 703-524-5017
E-Mail: info@nitl.org
Home Page: www.nitl.org

Bruce J Carlton, President
Frequency: SemiAnnual

22904 **National Institute of Packaging, Handling and Logistic Engineers**
NIPHLE
5903 Ridgeway Drive
Grand Prairie, TX 75052

817-466-7490
866-464-7453
Fax: 570-523-0606
E-Mail: ninphle@dejazzd.com
Home Page: www.niphle.org

Richard D Owen, Executive Director
Founded in 1956

22905 **National Motor Carrier Directory**
Transportation Technical Services
500 Lafayette Boulevard
Fredericksburg, VA 22401-6070

540-899-9872
800-666-4887
Fax: 888-665-9887
Home Page: www.ttstrucks.com

Thomas R Fugee, Executive VP

CEO, fleet size, toll-free/fax number, revenue, SCAC, trailer type, TK or LTL, trucks plus tractors owned and leased and more.
Cost: $395.00
1982 Pages
Frequency: Annual
Founded in 1992

22906 **Official Railway Guide: North American Freight Service Edition**
Commonwealth Business Media
50 Millstone Rd
Suite 200
East Windsor, NJ 08520-1418

609-371-7700
800-221-5488
Fax: 609-371-7879
Home Page: www.cbizmedia.com

Alan Glass, CEO

Directory of services and supplies to the industry.
Cost: $245.00
Frequency: BiMonthly

22907 **Pacific Shipper's Transportation Services Directory**
PRIMEDIA Information
10 Lake Drive
Hightstown, NJ 08520-5321
609-371-7700
800-224-5488
Home Page: www.primediainfo.com

Amy Middlebrook, Editor
John Capers III, Publisher
John Murphy, Circulation Director

Offers valuable information on coastal transportation operations and support services on the Pacific Coast.
Cost: $202.00
730 Pages
Frequency: Annual
Printed in 4 colors on newsprint stock

22908 **Private Fleet Directory**
Transportation Technical Services
500 Lafayette Boulevard
Fredericksburg, VA 22401-6070

540-899-9872
800-666-4887
Fax: 888-665-9887
Home Page: www.ttstrucks.com

Thomas R Fugee, Executive VP

Over 26,000 private fleets in the US that transport their own freight (Wal-Mart, Ace Hardware, Toys R Us).
Cost: $295.00
1,900 Pages
Frequency: Annual July
Founded in 1992

22909 **Railway Line Clearances**
Commonwealth Business Media
10 Lake Drive
Hightstown, NJ 08520-5321

609-371-7703
800-224-5488
Fax: 609-371-7830
Home Page: www.cbizmedia.com

Alan Glass, Chairman/CEO
Susan Murray, Publisher
Kathy Keeney, Associate Publisher

This directory offers weight limitations, heights and widths of clearances for railroads in North America and Canada, parts of the United States, clearance contacts and AAR rules and regulation.
Cost: $200.00
Frequency: Annual
Printed in 2 colors on matte stock

22910 **Refrigerated Transporter: Warehouse Directory Issue**
Tunnell Publications
PO Box 66010
Houston, TX 77266

713-523-8124
Fax: 713-523-8384
Home Page: http://www.refrigeratedtrans.com

Gary Macklin, Editor

Listing of approximately 265 refrigerated warehouses in the US and Canada.

22911 **Survey of State Travel Offices**
United States Travel Data Center
1100 New York Avenue NW
Washington, DC 20005-3934

202-326-7300
Fax: 202-408-1255

Patrick Thompson, Editor

State and territorial government agencies responsible for travel and travel promotion in their states.
Cost: $475.00
Frequency: Annual March

22912 **Transportation Management Association Directory**
Association for Commuter Transportation
1518 K St NW
Suite 503
Washington, DC 20005-1203

202-737-2926
Fax: 202-347-8847
E-Mail: info@nadca.com
Home Page: www.nadca.com

Kenneth Sufka, Executive Vice President

Over 50 established transportation management associations in the United States are the focus of this comprehensive directory.
123 Pages
Circulation: 400

22913 **Transportation Research Board Directory**
Transportation Research Board
2101 Constitution Ave Nw
Washington, DC 20418 0007

202-334-2933
Fax: 202-334-2527
E-Mail: TABSales@nas.edu
Home Page: www.nationalacademies.org/trb

Robert Skinner, CEO

Directory lists organizations and committee members with an interest in transportation. Individual affiliate information is no longer available in print or in electronic format.
Frequency: Annual

22914 **USTA Industry Directory**
United States Telecom Association
1401 H St NW
Suite 600
Washington, DC 20005-2110

202-326-7300
Fax: 202-326-7333
Home Page: www.usta.org

Walter McKormick, President
Joan Johnson, Secretary

Comprehensive directory of over 1200 local exchange carriers and other telecom companies make up this directory. Includes a detailed index for easy cross-referencing by company name, contacts, titles, geographical region, services provided, e-mail and more. USTA's directory is your gateway to the telecom industry.
Cost: $699.00
Frequency: Annual

22915 **WESTLAW Transportation Library**
West Publishing Company
610 Opperman Drive
Eagan, MN 55123-1340

651-687-7327
Home Page: www.westgroup.com

This database offers information on US transportation laws.
Frequency: Full-text

Industry Web Sites

22916 **http://gold.greyhouse.com**
G.O.L.D Grey House OnLine Databases

Grey House Publishing's online database platform, GOLD, offers Quick Search, Keyword Search and Expert Search for most business sectors including transportation markets. The GOLD platform makes finding the information you need quick and easy - whether you're a novice searcher or an experienced database user. All of Grey House's directory products are available for subscription on the GOLD platform.

22917 www.apta.com
American Public Transit Association
Maintains biographical archives and operates a placement service.

22918 www.ar.org
Association of American Railroads
Seeks to advance knowledge of scientific and economic location, construction, maintenance and operation of railroad.

22919 www.buses.org
American Bus Association
Trade association for the North American bus industry.

22920 www.expedia.com
Expedia.com
Internet travel service offers access to airlines, hotels, car rentals, vacation packages, cruises and corporate travel.

22921 www.expresscarriers.com
Interstate Trucking Association
Organization of newly enacted state legislation regulations having direct impact on vehicle operations, fuel taxes, registration size and weight.

22922 www.gams.org
Association of Air Medical Services
An association of health care entities operating helicopter transport services.

22923 www.greyhouse.com
Grey House Publishing
Authoritative reference directories for most business markets including transportation markets. Users can search the online databases with varied search criteria allowing for custom searches by product category, geographic area, sales volume, keyword, subject and more. Full Grey House catalog and online ordering also available.

22924 www.hotwire.com
Hotwire.com
Internet travel service offering discounts on flights, hotels, car rentals, packages and cruises.

22925 www.iasm.org
International Association of Structural Movers
Members are movers of heavy structural products, trusses, houses and machinery and masonry structures.

22926 www.iccl.org
Internhational Council of Cruise Lines
For North American oceangoing, overnight major cruise line companies.

22927 www.intermodal.org
Intermodal Association of North America
Members are motor, rail and water transportation companies. Promotes the benefits and growth of intermodal freight transportation.

22928 www.ista.org
International Safe Transit Association
Members are shippers, carriers, manufacturers, packagers, package designers and testing laboratories, included in transport packaging.

22929 www.ite.org
Institute for Transportation Engineering
Dedicated to the transportation engineering field.

22930 www.moving.org
American Moving and Storage Association
Represents members including interstate moving and storage companies, local movers, international movers plus industry suppliers and state association members. AMSA's chief goals include strong support for effective government regulations and policies that protect consumers while allowing members to provide quality service at compensatory prices, and ensuring that consumers understand the value of professional moving and storage services.

22931 www.narprail.org
National Association of Railroad Passengers
Seeks to increase public awareness of rail passenger service and its benefits. Works for a national transportation policy.

22932 www.nbta.org
National Business Travel Association
Offers over 1,300 corporate travel managers and allied members in the United States and Canada.

22933 www.ndtahq.com
National Defense Transportation Association
Intended as a liasion between government, military and private transportation officials.

22934 www.nitl.org
National Industrial Transportation League
Annual show of 250 exhibitors of computer services software and innovations for transportation operations.

22935 www.npapark.org
National Parking Association
For operators of public and private parking facilities, including government, hospitals, colleges, universities and others.

22936 www.raa.org
Regional Airline Association
Membership consists of more than 70 airlines, plus 350 Associate members provide goods and services.

22937 www.railway.museums.org
Association of Railway Museums
The association of railway museums is for the preservation of railway equipment, artifacts and history.

22938 www.rampages.onramp.net/~nars/
National Association of Rail Shippers
Strives to provide a sound transporation system. Bestows annual Award of Excellence.

22939 www.rpi.org
Railway Progress Institute
The railway equipment and supply industry.

22940 www.rssi.org
Railway Systems Suppliers
A trade association serving the communication and signal segment of the rail transportation industry. Manages an annual trade show.

22941 www.scooltrans.com
National School Transportation Association
Strives to provide safe transportation, foster safety, and an atmosphere conducive to private enterprise.

22942 www.teamster.org
International Brotherhood of Teamsters
Affiliated with the AFL-CIO.

22943 www.terry.org
International Marine Transit Association
Membership includes ferry operators, naval architects, manufacturers, suppliers, and others in the terry industry around the world.

22944 www.tianet.org
Transportation Intermediaries Association
For North American transportation intermediaries including logistics management firms, property brokers, perishable commodities brokers, freight forwarders, intermodal marketers, ocean and air forwarders.

22945 www.travel.yahoo.com
Yahoo.com
Internet travel service providing access to flights, hotels, car rentals, vacation packages and cruises.

22946 www.travelocity.com
Sabre Holdings
Travel service offering consumers access to hundreds of airlines and thousands of hotels, as well as cruise, last-minute and vacation packages and best-in-class car rental companies.

22947 www.tww.org
Transport Workers Union of America
Chartered by the Congress of Industrial Organizations.

22948 www.waterways.org
National Waterways Conference
For shippers, barge lines and local port authorities working to promote a better understanding of the public value of the American waterways system.

22949 www.woda.org
World Organization of Dredging Associations
Develops professionalism in individuals involved in the dredging industry.

Associations

22950 American Bus Association
111 K Street NE
9th Floor
Washington, DC 20002

202-877-2208
Fax: 202-842-0850
E-Mail: abainfo@buses.org
Home Page: www.buses.org
Social Media: Facebook, Twitter, LinkedIn

Peter J Pantuso, CEO
Brandon Buchanan, Director, Operations
Clyde J Hart Jr., Senior VP, Govt. Affairs & Policy
Norm Littler, VP, Regulatory & Industry Affairs
Daniel Hoff, Director

ABA supports 3,800 members consisting of motorcoach and tour companies in addition to organizations that represent the tourism and travel industry. ABA strives to educate consumers on the importance of highway and motorcoach safety.
Founded in 1926

22951 American Council of Highway Advertisers
1101 14th St., NW
Suite 1030
Washington, DC 20005-5635

202-354-0111
Fax: 202-857-7809
E-Mail: info@crp.org
Home Page: www.opensecrets.org
Social Media: Facebook, Twitter, LinkedIn, RSS

Sheila Krumholz, Executive Director
Susan Alger, IT Director
Sarah Bryner, Research Director
Viveca Novak, Editorial & Communications Director

22952 American Society of Travel Agents (ASTA)
1101 King St
Suite 200
Alexandria, VA 22314-2963

703-739-2782
Fax: 703-684-8319
E-Mail: askasta@asta.org
Home Page: www.asta.org
Social Media: Facebook, Twitter, LinkedIn

Zane Kerby, President & CEO
Paul Ruden, Senior VP, Legal & Industry Affairs
Eben Peck, VP, Govt. Affairs
John Pittman, VP, Industry Affairs, Research
Sue Sheats, VP, Market Development

Promotes and encourages travel among people of all nations. Serves as an information resource for the travel industry.
21M Members
Founded in 1931

22953 Association of Corporate Travel Executives
510 King Street
Suite 220
Alexandria, VA 22314-2964

703-683-5322
Fax: 613-836-0619
E-Mail: info@acte.org
Home Page: www.acte.org

Suzanne Neufang, President
Kurt Knackstedt, President Elect
Jeff Kurn, Treasurer
Greeley Koch, Chief Staff Officer

Provides a forum for the discussion of ideas and information related to the corporate travel industry. Conducts educational programs and conferences.
700 Members
Founded in 1988
Mailing list available for rent

22954 Association of Group Travel Executives
AH Light Company
510 King Street
Suite 220
Alexandria, VA 22314

703-683-5323
Fax: 908-273-2344
E-Mail: info@acte.org
Home Page: www.acte.org

Suzanne Neufang, President
Kurt Knackstedt, President Elect
Jeff Kurn, Treasurer
Greeley Koch, Chief Staff Officer

Affiliated with the Travel Industry Association of America.
675 Members
Founded in 1989

22955 Association of Retail Travel Agents
4320 North Miller Road
Scottsdale, AZ 85251

800-969-6069
Fax: 866-743-2087
E-Mail: info@artonline.com
Home Page: www.artaonline.com
Social Media: Facebook, Twitter, LinkedIn, You Tube

Nancy Linares, Board of Director

Promotes the interests of retail travel agents through representation on industry councils and testimony before Congress. Conducts joint marketing and educational programs.
2800 Members
Founded in 1963

22956 Association of Travel Marketing Executives
1745 Broadway
Suite 4
West Tisbury, NY 10019

508-693-0550
Fax: 508-693-0115
E-Mail: kzern@atme.org
Home Page: www.atme.org
Social Media: Facebook, Twitter, LinkedIn, Flickr

Kristin Zern, Executive Director

22957 Association of Travel Marketing Executives
1745 Broadway
Suite 4
West Tisbury, NY 10019

508-693-0550
Fax: 508-693-0115
E-Mail: kzern@atme.org
Home Page: www.atme.org
Social Media: Facebook, Twitter, LinkedIn, Flickr

Kristin Zern, Executive Director

Travel and tourism reports.

22958 Caribbean Hotel Association
2655 Le Jeune Rd
Suite 910
Coral Gables, FL 33134

305-443-3040
Fax: 787-725-9180
Home Page: www.carribeanhotelandtourism.com
Social Media: Facebook, Twitter

Joseph F Forstmayr, Chairman
Richard Doumeng, President
Emil Lee, 1st VP
Alberto Abreu, 2nd VP
Karolin P Troubetzkoy, 3rd VP

Mission is to optimize the full potential of the Caribbean hotel and tourism industry by serving member needs and building partnerships. It's a LLC registered in the Cayman Islands, with offices in San Juan, Puerto Rico and Miami, FL.

22959 Greater Independent Association of National Travel Services
915 Broadway
20th Floor
New York, NY 10010-7130

212-627-0001
Fax: 212-627-1110
E-Mail: info@fullpic.com
Home Page: www.fullpic.com
Social Media: Twitter, Youtube

Desiree Gruber, President
Susan Shapiro, Executive Director

Aims to establish a travel industry marketing cooperative. Holds regional workshops and seminars.
1.8M Members
Founded in 1968

22960 Hospitality Sales & Marketing Association International
1760 Old Meadow Road
Suite 500
McLean, VA 22102

703-506-3280
Fax: 703-506-3266
E-Mail: info@hsmai.org
Home Page: www.hsmai.org
Social Media: Facebook, Twitter, LinkedIn

Barb Bowden, Chairman
Rob Torres, Chair Elect
Jeff Senior, Secretary/Treasurer
Mark Thompson, Vice Chair
Robert Gilbert, President

The hospitality indutry's source for knowledge, community, and recognition for leaders committed to professional development, sales growth, revenue optimization, marketing and branding.
7000 Members
Founded in 1927

22961 International Association of Convention and Visitor Bureaus
2025 M St Nw
Suite 500
Washington, DC 20036-3349

202-296-7888
Fax: 202-296-7889
E-Mail: info@iacvb.org
Home Page: www.destinationmarketing.org
Social Media: Facebook, Twitter, LinkedIn

Michael D Gehrisch, President & CEO
Victoria Isley, EVP/COO
Stephanie Ann Russell, Executive Assistant

Promotes sound professional practices in the solicitation and servicing of meetings and conventions. Members represent travel/tourism related businesses. Publications include an electronic newsletter and online directory.
Founded in 1914
Mailing list available for rent: 1200 names at $400 per M

22962 International Association of Travel
PO Box D
Hurleyville, NY 12747
845-434-7777
Promotes accurate reporting on fields of aviation, travel, tourism and airports.
50+ Members
Founded in 1988

22963 National Association of Business Travel Agents
National Association of Business Travel Agents
1920 L St. NW
Suite 300
Washington, DC 20036-2365
202-463-6223
Fax: 202-463-6239
E-Mail: nabe@nabe.com
Home Page: www.nabe.com
Social Media: Twitter
Tom Beers, Executive Director
Colette Brissett, Administrative Director
NBTA is a forum bringing together business travel buyer and supplier professionals from around the world. Membership includes access to the industry's premier network of corporate and government travel decision-makers and purchasers, a monthly e-newsletter as well as a quarterly publication, world-wide and local events, CTE opportunities and professional certificate programs.

22964 National Association of RV Parks and Campgrounds
9085 E. Mineral Circle
Suite 200
Centennial, CO 80112
303-681-0401
800-395-2267
Fax: 303-681-0426
E-Mail: info@arvc.org
Home Page: www.arvc.org
Social Media: Facebook, Twitter, LinkedIn, Youtube
Linda Profaizer, President
Cyndy Robinson, Executive Assistant
The association actively protects the best interests of its members on a federal level and provides awareness and assistance against government legislation & regulations at all levels(national, state and local).
3,200 Members
Founded in 1966
Mailing list available for rent: 3,200 names

22965 National Motorcoach Network
PO Box 1088
Mount Jackson, VA 22842
540-477-3202
800-469-0062
Fax: 540-477-3858
E-Mail: smk@motorcoach.com
Home Page: www.motorcoach.com/byways
Founded in 1983

22966 National Tour Association
101 Prosperous Place
Suite 350
Lexington, KY 40509
859-264-6540
800-682-8886
Fax: 859-264-6570
E-Mail: questions@ntastaff.com
Home Page: www.ntaonline.com
Social Media: Facebook, Twitter, LinkedIn, Youtube
Lisa Simon, President
Wes Hogan, General Manager
Ben Harward, Controller & Director, HR
Beth Ward, Executive Assistant
The National Tour Association is an organization of nearly 4,000 international tourism professionals focused on the development, promotion and increased use of tour operators packaged travel.
4000 Members
Founded in 1951
Mailing list available for rentat $500 per M

22967 Office of General Supply and Services
One Constitution Square
1275 First Street, NE
Washington, DC 20417
202-564-2480
866-606-8220
Home Page: www.gsa.gov
Social Media: Facebook, Twitter, Youtube, RSS
Susan F Brita, Deputy Administrator
Daniel M Tangherlini, Administrator
Adam Neufeld, Chief Of Staff
The Office of General Supplies and Services (GSS) is responsible for acquisition services and comprehensive supply chain management, including excess/surplus federal property.

22968 Passenger Vessel Association
103 Oronoco Street
Suite 200
Alexandria, VA 22314-1549
703-518-5005
800-807-8360
Fax: 703-518-5151
E-Mail: pvainfo@passengervessel.com
Home Page: www.passengervessel.com
John Groundwater, Executive Director
Bill Clark, Vice President
Gadney Beth, Director of Safety, Security
Hill Lee, Chief Financial Officer
Lauridsen Peter, Regulatory Affairs Consultant
Represents operators of tours, excursions, ferries, charter vessels, dinner boats and other small passenger vessels.
600 Members
Founded in 1971

22969 Receptive Services Association
2365 Harrodsburg Road
Suite A325
Lexington, KY 40504
859-219-3545
866-939-0934
Fax: 859-226-4404
E-Mail: headquarters@rsaa.com
Home Page: www.rsana.com
Social Media: Facebook, Youtube
Matt Grayson, Executive Director
Kate Hendle, Member Services Administrator
Toby Bishop, Sales Manager
Helping receptive operators serve international tour companies through partnerships with North American suppliers.
570 Members

22970 Recreational Vehicle Industry Association
1896 Preston White Drive
Reston, VA 20191
703-620-6003
Fax: 703-620-5071
Home Page: www.rvia.org
David Humphreys, President
The national trade association representing recreation vehicle manufacturers and their component parts suppliers who build more than 98% of all RVsproduced in the U.S.

22971 Society of American Travel Writers
11950 W. Lake Park Drive
Suite 320
Milwaukee,, WI 53224-3049
414-359-1671
Fax: 414-359-1671
E-Mail: info@satw.org
Home Page: www.satw.org
Social Media: Facebook, Twitter, LinkedIn
Steve Giordano, President
Annette Thompson, President Elect
Diana Lambdin Meyer, VP
Tom Adkinson, Treasurer
Peggy Bendel, Secretary
Photographers and 35 associate member representatives of airlines, hotels, resorts, tourist agencies and public relations firms.
Founded in 1955

22972 Society of Incentive and Travel Executives
330 N Wabash Ave
Chicago, IL 60611
312-321-5148
Fax: 312-527-6783
E-Mail: site@siteglobal.com
Home Page: www.siteglobal.com
Social Media: Facebook, Twitter, LinkedIn, Youtube
Kevin Hinton, CEO
Christie Pruyn, Director of Operations
Kelsey Gardner, Membership Services
An individual membership society covering 70 countries. Members are corporate users, airlines, Tourist Boards, cruise lines, destination management companies, consultants, hotels/resorts, travel agents, incentive travel houses and publications.
2,200 Members
Founded in 1973

22973 Travel Industry Association of America
1100 New York Ave Nw
Suite 450
Washington, DC 20005-3934
202-408-8422
Fax: 202-408-1255
Home Page: www.tia.org
Roger J Dow, President & CEO
Todd Davidson, Treasurer & Director
Bonnie L Carlson, Secretary & Director
Members are hotels, airlines and travel agencies interested in promoting increased travel to and within the US.
2100 Members
Founded in 1941

22974 Travel and Tourism Research Association
5300 Lakewood Road
Whitehall, MI 49461
248-708-8872
Fax: 248-814-7150
E-Mail: ~info@ttra.com~
Home Page: www.ttra.com
Richard Perdue, Chairman
Marlise Taylor, President
Dan Mishell, 1st VP
Jeffrey Eslinger, 2nd VP
John Markham, Treasurer

22975 Volunteers for Peace
7 Kilburn Street
Suite 316
Belmont, VT 05401
802-540-3060
Fax: 802-540-3061
E-Mail: info@vfp.org

Home Page: www.vfp.org
Social Media: Facebook, Twitter

Megan Brook, Executive Director
Alexandra Smith, International Placement Coordinator

A Vermont nonprofit membership organization promoting over 3000 international voluntary service projects in 100 countries. Workcamps are an affordable way to travel, live and work abroad.
2000 Members
Founded in 1982

Newsletters

22976 AAA World
2040 Market Street
Philadelphia, PA 19103

215-851-0291
800-763-9900
Fax: 215-851-0297
E-Mail: letters@aaaworld.com
Home Page: www.aaaworld.com

Allen EeWalle, CEO
Sandy Kaden, Circulation Manager

Promotes travel destinations, gives advice on traveling and helpful automobile information.
Cost: $71.00
Circulation: 2.1 mill
Founded in 1900

22977 ABA Insider
American Bus Association
111 K Street NE
9th Floor
Washington, DC 20002

202-842-1645
Fax: 202-842-0850
E-Mail: abainfo@buses.org
Home Page: www.buses.org

Peter J Pantuso, CEO
Buchcannon Brandon, Director of Operations
Hart Clyde, Senior VP of Government Affairs
Hoff Daniel, Director of ABA Foundation & Policy
Jones Patrick, Legislative & Communications Coordi

ABA's biweekly newsletter that keeps members informed on the travel, tourism and motorcoach industry.
Frequency: Biweekly
Founded in 1926

22978 Caribbean Reporter
Caribbean Hotel Association
18 Calle Marseilles
San Juan, PR 907-1682

787-725-2901
Fax: 787-725-9180
Home Page: www.chahotels.com

Beverly Telemague, Publisher

Membership news.
Cost: $4.99
Frequency: Monthly
Founded in 1959

22979 Entree Travel Newsletter
Entree Publishing
PO Box 5148
Santa Barbara, CA 93150-5148

805-969-5848
Fax: 805-969-5849
E-Mail: wtomicki@aol.com
Home Page: www.entreenews.com

William Tomicki, Editor/Publisher

Travel, fashion and beauty ideas, sports and photography, wines and restaurants reviews new literature, music and film of interest to the travel and food enthusiast.
Cost: $75.00
Frequency: Monthly
Circulation: 8000
Printed in one color on matte stock

22980 IACVB e-News
Int'l Association of Convention & Visitor Bureaus
2025 M St Nw
Suite 500
Washington, DC 20036-3349

202-296-7888
Fax: 202-296-7889
Home Page: www.destinationmarketing.org

Michael D Gehrisch, CEO
Kristen Clemens, Editor

An electronic newsletter published by the International Association of Convention and Visitor Bureaus. Available with membership.
Frequency: Weekly
Circulation: 1300
Founded in 1914
Mailing list available for rent: 1200 names at $400 per M

22981 Ocean and Cruise News
PO Box 329
Northport, NY 11768

203-329-2787
Fax: 203-329-2767
E-Mail: news@wocls.org
Home Page: www.wocls.org/

Tom Cassidy, VP
Geroge Devol, President

Complete news on cruises.
Cost: $30.00
Frequency: Monthly
Circulation: 7000
Founded in 1980

22982 Travel Industry Association of America Newsletter
Travel Industry Association of America
1100 New York Ave Nw
Suite 450 W
Washington, DC 20005-6130

202-408-8422
Fax: 202-408-1255
Home Page: www.tia.org

Roger J Dow, CEO
C Betsi, Marketing Manager
Kathy Keefe, Editor

Travel information.
Cost: $1350.00
Frequency: Monthly
Circulation: 3500
Founded in 1941
Printed in 3 colors on glossy stock

22983 Travel Management Newsletter
Reed Travel Group
500 Plaza Dr
Secaucus, NJ 07094-3619

201-902-1800
Fax: 202-902-2053
Home Page: www.tmdaily.com

Steve Bailey, Publisher

Discusses the news and views of the travel professional.
Cost: $735.00
Frequency: Weekly

22984 Travel Manager's Executive Briefing
Health Resources Publishing
1913 Atlantic Ave
Suite 200
Manasquan, NJ 08736-1067

732-292-1100
800-516-4343
Fax: 732-292-1111
E-Mail: info@themcic.com
Home Page: www.healthresourcesonline.com

Robert K Jenkins, Publisher
Lisa Mansfield, Marketing Assistant

Read by travel managers of major corporations, Fortune 500 companies and corporate travel agencies twice a month to get up to the minute developments in the important field of travel and expense cost control.
Cost: $447.00
ISSN: 0272-569x

22985 Travel Weekly
500 Plaza Drive
Secaucus, NJ 07094-3685

201-902-1696
Fax: 201-902-2053
Home Page: www.travelweekly.com

William D Scott, Publisher

Industry news, articles and stories on the travel industry.
Cost: $26.00
Frequency: BiWeekly

22986 Travel and Tourism Executive Report
10200 W 44th Avenue
Suite 304
Wheat Ridge, CO 80033-2840

303-463-2887

Francine Butler, Executive Director

Established as the Travel Research Association as the result of a merger.
750 Pages

22987 Travelwriter Marketletter
21553 Center Point Circle
Ashburn, VA 20147

571-214-9086
Fax: 208-988-7672
Home Page: www.travelwriterml.com

Mimi Backhausen, Editor & Publisher

A monthly newsletter for travel writers and travel photographers. It's mainly about marketing travel articles, photography and travel books; also describes free trips for professional travel writers.
Cost: $75.00
10 Pages
Frequency: Monthly
Circulation: 1000
ISSN: 0738-9093

22988 Tuesday Newsletter
National Tour Association
101 Prosperours Place
Suite 350
Lexington, KY 40509

859-264-6540
800-682-8886
Fax: 859-264-6570
E-Mail: questions@ntastaff.com
Home Page: ntaonline.com

Lisa Simon, President

The National Tour Association is an organization of nearly 4,000 North American tourism professionals focused on the development, promotion and increased use of tour operators packaged travel.
Cost: $36.00
100 Pages
Frequency: Monthly
Circulation: 5000
Founded in 1998
Mailing list available for rent: 3,800 names

Magazines & Journals

22989 ABC Preferred Flight Planner: Europe- Middle East-Africa
ABC Corporate Services/Reed Travel Group
500 Plaza Drive
Secaucus, NJ 07094-3619
201-678-8775
Fax: 201-902-2053
Home Page: www.infotec-travel.com
Luis Murcia, Owner
Offers information on properties and locations of interest to corporate business travelers.
250 Pages
Frequency: SemiAnnual
Circulation: 65,000

22990 ASTA Agency Management
Miller Freeman Publications
2655 Seely Avenue
San Jose, CA 95134
408-943-1234
Fax: 408-943-0513
Mary Pat Sullivan, Publisher
Provides concise and useful information on trends in the industry and practical ideas regarding the profitable administration of travel agencies.
Cost: $36.00
Frequency: Monthly
Circulation: 35,182

22991 ASU Travel Guide
448 Ignacio Boulevard
Suite 333
San Rafael, CA 94949-5539
415-898-9500
866-459-0300
Fax: 415-898-9501
Home Page: www.asutravelguide.com
Christopher Gil, Managing Editor
Hank Sousa, VP
Provides information concerning worldwide travel destinations and other locales of interest to travelers and the bargains and discounts available to airline employees.
352 Pages
Frequency: Quarterly
Circulation: 700000
Founded in 1971
Printed in 4 colors on glossy stock

22992 Bank Travel Management
Group Travel Leader
301 East High Street
Lexington, KY 40507
859-253-0455
Fax: 859-253-0499
E-Mail: info@grouptravelleader.com
Home Page: www.banktravelmanagement.com
Mac Lacy, President & Publisher
Herb Sparrow, Executive Editor
Brian Jewell, Associate Editor
Kelly Tyner, Director of Sales & Marketing
Stacey Bowman, National Account Manager
Regular sections include: The Banker's Box, managing your senior program, and marketing your trips, with special features on personal travel accounts, trends in travel and banking clubs. Subscriptions are complimentary for qualified travel planners.
Cost: $49.00
Frequency: 6/Year
Circulation: 4100
Founded in 1994

22993 Bus Tours Magazine
National Bus Trader
9698 W Judson Rd
Polo, IL 61064-9015
815-946-2341
Fax: 815-946-2347
E-Mail: nbt@busmag.com
Home Page: www.busmag.com
Larry Plachno, President
Shaye Hall, Assistant Editor
Nancy Ann Plachno, Business Manager
Focuses on the operations, arrangements and marketing techniques used to plan these excursions as well as what's new in the industry.
Cost: $10.00
Frequency: Monthly
Circulation: 7,200
Founded in 1979

22994 Byways
National Motorcoach Network
42 Cabin Hill Lane
Mt Jackson, VA 22842
540-773-3323
800-469-0062
Fax: 540-477-3858
E-Mail: nmn@motorcoach.com
Home Page: www.motorcoach.com/byways
Social Media: Facebook, Twitter, LinkedIn
Stephen M Kirchner, Publisher/Editor
Featuring North America's leading travel destinations. Includes riverboat gambling updates and special reports on the top 50 motorcoach destinations.
48 Pages
Frequency: Bi-Monthly
Circulation: 20000
Founded in 1983

22995 City Visitor
Travelhost
5755 Granger Road
Independence, OH 44131
972-556-0541
Fax: 972-432-8729
Home Page: www.travelhost.com
James E Buerger, President
Travelhost is an in room publisher edited for the business and vacation traveler, with news features and general information relating to travel, recreation, business, new products and services and leisure activities.
Cost: $33.00
Frequency: Monthly
Founded in 1967

22996 Conde Nast Traveler Business Extra
Conde Nast
4 Times Sq
14th Floor
New York, NY 10036-6561
212-286-2860
Fax: 212-286-5960
Home Page: www.condenast.com
Charles H Townsend, CEO
Relates to gathering information for tourism.

22997 Corporate & Incentive Travel
Coastal Communications Corporation
2700 N Military Trail
Suite 120
Boca Raton, FL 33431
561-989-0600
Fax: 561-989-9509
E-Mail: ccceditor1@att.net
Home Page: www.themeetingmagazines.com
Harvey Grotsky, Publisher/Editor-In-Chief
Susan Wyckoff Fell, Managing Editor
Susan Gregg, Managing Editor
The magazine for corporate meetings and incentive travel planners. In-depth editorial focus on site selection, accommodations and transportation, current legislation, conference, seminar and training facilities, budget and cost controls, and destination reports. Regular features highlight industry news and developments, trends and personalities, meeting values, facilities, and destinations.
Frequency: Monthly
Circulation: 40,000
Founded in 1983

22998 Corporate and Incentive Travel
Coastal Communications Corporation
2700 N Military Trail
Suite 120
Boca Raton, FL 33431-6394
561-989-0600
Fax: 561-989-9509
Home Page: www.themeetingmagazines.com
Harvey Grotsky, President & CEO
Susan Wyckoff Fell, Managing Editor
Susan S Gregg, Managing Editor
This magazine is edited for corporate meeting planners with the responsibility for staging and planning meetings, incentive travel programs, conferences and conventions.
Frequency: Monthly
Founded in 1983

22999 Country Discoveries
5400 S 60th Street
Greendale, WI 53129-1404
414-423-0100
800-344-6913
Fax: 414-423-8463
Home Page: www.reimanpub.com
Focuses on backwoods travel in both the United States and Canada.
Cost: $14.98
Founded in 1965

23000 Courier
National Tour Association
546 E Main St
Lexington, KY 40508-2342
859-226-4444
800-682-8886
Fax: 859-226-4447
E-Mail: questions@ntastaff.com
Home Page: ntaonline.com
Lisa Simon, President
Courier Magazine helps readers to meet their responsibilities involved with their jobs.
Cost: $36.00
110 Pages
Frequency: Monthly
Circulation: 6000
ISSN: 0279-4489
Founded in 1955
Printed in 4 colors on glossy stock

23001 Cruise Industry News - Annual
Nissel-Lie Communications
441 Lexington Avenue
Room 809
New York, NY 10017-3910
212-986-1025
Fax: 212-986-1033
E-Mail: info2@cruiseindustrynews.com
Home Page: www.cruiseindustrynews.com
Oivind Mathisen, Editor/Publisher
Angela Mathisen, Advertising Director/Publisher
Monty Mathisen, Reporter/Web Editor
The only book of its kind, and often rated the most comprehensive information source on the

industry by cruise line executives.
Cost: $575.00
Frequency: Annual+
Founded in 1988

23002 Cruise Industry News Quarterly Magazine
Nissel-Lie Communications
441 Lexington Avenue
Room 809
New York, NY 10017-3910

212-986-1025
Fax: 212-986-1033
E-Mail: info2@cruiseindustrynews.com
Home Page: www.cruiseindustrynews.com

Oivind Mathisen, Editor/Publisher
Angela Mathisen, Advertising Director/Publsher
Monty Mathisen, Reporter/Web Editor

The magazine covers all aspects of cruise operations, shipbuilding, new ships, cruise companies, ship reviews, onboard services, food and beverage, and ports and destinations.
Cost: $495.00
Frequency: Quarterly
Circulation: 50000
Founded in 1991
Printed in 4 colors

23003 Destinations
American Bus Association
700 13th St NW
Suite 575
Washington, DC 20005-5923

202-842-1645
800-283-2877
Fax: 202-842-0850
E-Mail: abainfo@buses.org
Home Page: www.buses.org

Peter J Pantuso, CEO
Eron Shosteck, Marketing

Motorcoach travel across North America and Association news.
80 Pages
Frequency: Monthly
Circulation: 6000
Founded in 1926
Printed in 4 colors on glossy stock

23004 Digital Travel
Jupiter Communications Company
475 Park Ave S
Suite 4
New York, NY 10016-6901

212-547-7900
800-481-1212
Fax: 212-953-1733
Home Page: www.jup.com

Alan Meckler, CEO
Marla Kammer, Managing Editor

Editorial includes the latest information and technology in agencies, airlines, lodging, ticketing, mapping, Web advertising, transaction processing, revenue models, demographics, and full-service sites.
Cost: $595.00
Frequency: Monthly

23005 Family Motor Coaching Magazine
Family Motor Coach Association
8291 Clough Pike
Cincinnati, OH 45244-2796

513-474-3622
800-543-3622
Fax: 513-474-2332
E-Mail: jyeatts@fmca.com
Home Page: www.fmca.com

Don Eversman, Executive Director
Ranita Jones, Sales Manager
Cost: $3.99
Frequency: Monthly
Circulation: 140000

23006 Frequent Flyer Magazine
2000 Clearwater Drive
Oak Brook, IL 60523

630-574-6000
800-342-5674
Fax: 630-574-6565

23007 Going on Faith
Group Traveler Leader
301 E High Street
Lexington, KY 40507

859-253-0455
888-253-0455
Fax: 859-253-0499
E-Mail: circmanager@grouptravelleader.com
Home Page. www.grouptravelleader.com

Mac Lacy, Publisher
Herb Sparrow, Executive Editor
Brian Jewell, Associate Editor
Kelly Tyner, Director of Sales & Marketing
Stacey Bowman, National Account Manager

The national travel newspaper for churches, synagogues and Religious organizations. The official newspaper for the Going on Faith Conference. Online.
Frequency: 6/Year
Circulation: 5500
Founded in 1997

23008 Group Travel Leader
Group Travel Leader
301 E High St
Lexington, KY 40507-1509

859-253-0455
Fax: 859-253-0499
E-Mail: maclacy@grouptravelleader.com
Home Page: www.grouptravelleader.com

Mac Lacy, President
Herb Sparrow, Executive Editor
Brian Jewell, Associate Editor
Kelly Tyner, Director of Sales & Marketing
Stacey Bowman, National Account Manager

Supplies the senior travel planner with new destinations, unique points of interest and historical venues for their group, club or organization.
Cost: $39.00
Frequency: Monthly
Circulation: 30000
Founded in 1991

23009 HSMAI Marketing Review
Hospitality Sales & Marketing Association Int'l
1760 Old Meadow Road
Suite 500
McLean, VA 22102

703-506-3280
Fax: 703-506-3266
E-Mail: info@hsmai.org
Home Page: www.hsmai.org

Kathleen Tindell, Editor

Features in-depth information and columns on best practices, web marekting, international affairs and future forecasting.
Cost: $65.00
7000 Pages
Frequency: Quarterly
Circulation: 10000
Founded in 1927

23010 Inside Flyer
Flight Plan
1930 Frequent Flyer Point
Colorado Springs, CO 80915

719-597-8889
800-767-8896
Fax: 719-597-6855
E-Mail: editor@insideflyer.com
Home Page: www.insideflyer.com/

Randy Petersen, Editor/publ/CEO
Karen Heldt, Advertising Coordinator
Linda Hanwella, Managing Editor

Leading publication of information for and about frequent traveler programs.
Cost: $45.00
Frequency: Monthly
Founded in 1986
Mailing list available for rent
Printed in 4 colors on matte stock

23011 Jax Fax Travel Marketing
Jax Fax
52 West Main Street
Milford, CT 06460-3310

203-301-0255
Fax: 203-301-0250
Home Page: www.jaxfax.com

Doug Cooke, President
Marc Spac, Publishing Director
Theresa Seanlon, Editor
Marjorie Vincent, Circulation Manager
Peter Badeau, Associate Publisher

Monthly travel trade magazine featuring destination information and listings of discounted airfares and tour packages.
Cost: $15.00
Frequency: Monthly
Circulation: 25000
Founded in 1973
Printed in 4 colors on glossy stock

23012 Mexico Today
2009 S 10th Street
McAllen, TX 78503-5405

956-686-0711
800-222-0158
Fax: 956-686-0732
E-Mail: info@sanbornsinsurance.com
Home Page: www.sanbornsinsurance.com

Pete Castillo, Marketing Director
Frequency: Quarterly
Circulation: 5000
Printed in 4 colors on glossy stock

23013 Mid-Atlantic Group Tour Magazine
Shoreline Creations
PO Box 638
Yarmouth Port, MA 02675-638

508-398-0400
Fax: 616-393-0085
E-Mail: travel@grouptour.com
Home Page: www.grouptour.com

Carl Wassink, Publisher
Carol Smith, Editor
Katie Weller, Circulation Manager
Jamie Cannon, Marketing Manager
Ruth Wassink, Vice President

Material looks at the latest offerings in tour travel including restaurants, theater, shopping, hotels, festivals, and events and activities.
Frequency: Quarterly
Circulation: 10000
Founded in 1980

23014 Midwest Traveler
12901 N Forty Drive
Saint Louis, MO 63141

314-523-6981
800-222-7623

Fax: 314-523-6982
Home Page: www.aaatravelermags.com

Mike Right, Editor
Cost: $3.00
Circulation: 45000
Founded in 1902

23015 Mobility
1717 Pennsylvania Avenue NW
8th Floor
Washington, DC 20006

202-293-7744
Fax: 202-659-8631
Home Page: www.erc.org/MOBILITY_Online

23016 NBTA Travel Quarterly
National Association of Business Travel Agents
123~North~Pitt Street
4th Floor
Alexandria, VA 22314

703-684-0836
Fax: 703-342-4324
E-Mail: info@nbta.org
Home Page: www.nbta.org

Caleb Tiller, Sr Dir, Marketing & Communications
Wendy Santiago, Marketing Manager
Nicole Hayes, Assistant Manager, Communications
Jack Machlum, CEO
Kevin Maguire, VP/Chief Information Officer

This publication provides valuable information on NBTA, its members and the corporate travel industry, to help the professional stay connected to the industry.
Frequency: Quarterly/Members Only

23017 New England Tour Magazine
Shoreline Creations
PO Box 638
Yarmouth Port, MA 02675-638

508-398-0400
Fax: 508-398-4703
E-Mail: travel@grouptour.com
Home Page: www.grouptour.com

Carol Smith, Editor
Carl Wassink, President
Katie Weller, Circulation Manager
Jamie Cannon, Marketing
Ruth Wassink, Executive Vice President

Promotes and covers the attractions, lodging, dining, events and other highlights of popular and less-famous travel destinations in the region.
Frequency: Quarterly
Circulation: 10000
Founded in 1925

23018 Onboard Services
International Publishing Company of America
50 Millstone Road
Building 300 Suite 110
East Windsor, NJ 08520

609-945-8000
800-280-8591
Fax: 609-945-8080
E-Mail: general@obcc.net
Home Page: www.onboard-services.com

Alexander Morton, President
George Hulcher, Contributing Editor

Keeps airline, cruise ships, railroad, and terminal concessions management and purchasing departments up-to-date on all phases of passenger services.
Cost: $25.00
24 Pages
ISSN: 0892-4236
Founded in 1968
Printed in 4 colors on glossy stock

23019 Ozark Mountain Visitor
200 Industrial Park Drive
Hollister, MO 65672-5327

417-334-3161
Fax: 417-335-3933

23020 Pacific Asia Travel News
Americas Publishing Company
3657 Harriet Road
Victoria, Can, BC V8Z-3T1

250-260-1883
Fax: 250-953-5250

Malcolm Scott, Publisher

Issues include a news dateline with features on travel trends and outlooks, a special destination focus, and updates from the Pacific Asia Travel Association.
Cost: $30.00
Frequency: BiMonthly
Circulation: 24,000

23021 Practical Gourmet
Linick Group
PO Box 102
Middle Island, NY 11953-0102

631-924-3888
Fax: 631-924-3890
E-Mail: linickgrp@att.net
Home Page: www.lgroup.addr.com

Andrew S Linick, CEO
Roger Dextor, Production
Barbara Deal, Marketing Manager

The focus of this publication is light, healthy gourmet dining; includes reports on wine tasting, food festivals, contests, celebrations, cooking schools and other events.
Cost: $48.00
36 Pages
Frequency: Monthly
Circulation: 210,000
Founded in 1975
Mailing list available for rent: 210 M names at $110 per M
Printed in 4 colors on glossy stock

23022 Recommend
Worth International Communication Corp
PO Box 171070
Hialeah, FL 33017-1070

305-828-0123
800-447-0123
Fax: 305-826-6950
Home Page: www.recommend.com

Laurel A Herman, Publisher
Lorri Robbins, National Director

Contains colorful information on worldwide destinations, resorts, hotels, transportation and tour operators, as well as marketing angles to help travel agents sell travel.
Cost: $48.00
Frequency: Monthly
Circulation: 60000
Founded in 1967
Printed in on glossy stock

23023 Runzheimer Reports on Travel Management
Runzheimer Park
Rochester, WI 53167-9999

262-712-2200
800-558-1702
Fax: 262-971-2254

Rex Runzheimer, President

23024 Sea Mass Traveler
PO Box 3189
Newport, RI 02840-0322

401-848-2922

23025 Southwest Airlines Spirit
Pace Communications
2811 McKinney Avenue
Suite 360
Dallas, TX 75204

214-580-2491
Fax: 214-580-8070
Home Page: www.spiritmag.com

Jay Heinrichs, Editorial Director
John McAlley, Executive Editor
Frequency: Monthly
Circulation: 400088
Founded in 1971

23026 Specialty Travel Index
PO Box 458
San Anselmo, CA 94979

415-594-4900
888-624-4030
Fax: 415-455-1648
E-Mail: info@specialtytravel.com
Home Page: www.specialtytravel.com

Karin Kinsey, Art Director
Stean Hansen, Circulation Manager
Andy Alpine, Marketing Manager
Risa Weinreb, Editor
Judith Alpine, Advertising Manager

Directory/magazine of adventure and specialty travel.
Cost: $10.00
Circulation: 32000
ISSN: 0889-7085
Founded in 1980
Printed in 4 colors on glossy stock

23027 SportsTravel Magazine
Schneider Publishing Company
11835 W Olympic Blvd
Suite 1265
Los Angeles, CA 90064-5814

310-577-3700
Fax: 310-577-3715
E-Mail: info@schneiderpublishing.com
Home Page: www.schneiderpublishing.com
Social Media: Facebook, Twitter, LinkedIn

Tim Schneider, President
Jason Gewirtz, Managing Editor/Sports Travel
Lisa Furfine, Associate Publisher
Chad Starbuck, Marketing Manager

Includes articles on travel training, sports law, event spotlights, and vital information on sites, hotels, transportation, trade shows and upcomiong events for team travel planners and event organizers.
Cost: $48.00
Frequency: Monthly
Circulation: 1400
ISSN: 1091-5354
Founded in 1997
Printed in on glossy stock

23028 Sun Valley Magazine
Mandala Media LLC
111 1st Avenue North #1M
Meriwether Building
Hailey, ID 83333

208-788-0770
Fax: 208-788-3881
Home Page: www.sunvalleymag.com

Laurie C Sammis, Publisher/Editor-in-Chief
Mike McKenna, Editor
Julie Molema, Production Director

Articles on the arts, community, recreation, dining, shopping and real estate in the Sun Val-

ley, Idaho area.
Cost: $22.00
Frequency: Quarterly
Circulation: 20000

23029 Sundancer's West
1108 Meadowview Drive
Euless, TX 76039

817-545-5265
Fax: 817-571-6481
E-Mail: gwat/@swbell.net
Home Page: www.sundancerswest.com

Gerry Watkins,
Webmaster/Editor/Photographer

23030 Travel & Leisure
American Express Publishing Corporation
1120 Avenue of the Americas
Suite 9
New York, NY 10036-6700

212-382-5600
800-888-8728
Fax: 212-382-5878
Home Page: www.tlexplorer.com

Ed Kelly, CEO
Nancy Novogrod, Editor-in-Chief
Antonia LoPresti, Senior Marketing Manager
Cost: $19.95
Frequency: Monthly
Circulation: 950000

23031 Travel & Leisure Golf
American Express Publishing Corporation
1120 Avenue of the Americas
Suite 9
New York, NY 10036-6700

212-382-5600
800-947-7961
Fax: 212-382-5878
Home Page: www.amexpub.com

Ed Kelly, CEO
Antonia LoPresti, Senior Marketing Manager
Maura Smale, Project Manager
John Rodenburg, Publisher
Rashmi George, Advertising Coordinator
Cost: $19.95
Frequency: Monthly
Circulation: 950000

23032 Travel Agent International
Universal Media
PO Box 5386
Bloomington, IL 61702-5386

309-663-6327
Fax: 212-883-1244
E-Mail: tai@taitravelbmi.com
Home Page: www.taitravelbmi.com

Richard P Friese, Publisher
Provides profiles on resorts and attractions for each given season.
Cost: $250.00
Frequency: 10 per year
Circulation: 19,100

23033 Travel Counselor
Miller Freeman Publications
600 Harrison Street
6th Fl
San Francisco, CA 94107

415-947-6000
800-764-759
Fax: 415-947-6055
E-Mail: email@travel-counselors.com
Home Page: www.travel-counselors.com

Contains business information and analysis appropriate to the retail agency profession
Frequency: 7 per year
Circulation: 28,000

23034 Travel Trends
Meredith Corporation
125 Park Ave
New York, NY 10017-5529

212-557-6600
Fax: 212-551-7161

Peter Mason, Publisher/Editor
Information on the trends of the travel industry.
Frequency: Quarterly
Circulation: 5,000

23035 Travel World
East - West News Bureau
16051 W. Tampa Palms Blvd
Tampa, FL 33647

813-978-0877
800-494-3279
Fax: 310-836-8769
E-Mail: debbie@travelworld1.com
Home Page: www.travelworld1.com

Elizabeth Barnes, Executive Director
Debbie Stewart, Manager

23036 Travel World News
Travel Industry Network
Ste 8
28 Knight St
Norwalk, CT 06851-4719

203-286-6679
Fax: 203-286-6681
E-Mail: editor@travelworldnews.com
Home Page: www.travelworldnews.com

Charles Gatt Jr, Publisher
Peter Gatt, Associate Publisher
Monthly trade publication covering the retail travel industry. Each issue contains industry information and coverage for agents who are making recommendations and booking for their clients, including comprehensive, up to date, and worldwide product news and destination editorial coverage. Available online and in print.
Frequency: Monthly
Circulation: 22000
Founded in 1988

23037 Travel, Food & Wine
Punch-In-Syndicate
400 E 59th Street
Floor 9
New York, NY 10022-2342

212-755-4363
E-Mail: punchin@usa.net
Home Page: www.punchin.com

J Walman, Editor
A magazine featuring articles and reviews on travel, food and wine, columns on airlines, hotels, cruise ships, railroads, resorts, restaurants, and spas. Also theater reviews, cinema, radio and all forms of entertainment.
Cost: $300.00
Frequency: Monthly

23038 TravelBound!
Group Traveler Leader
301 E High Street
Lexington, KY 40507

859-253-0455
888-253-0455
Fax: 859-253-0499
E Mail: circmanager@grouptravelleader.com
Home Page: www.grouptravelleader.com
Social Media: Facebook, Twitter, LinkedIn, You Tube

Mac Lacy, Publisher
Herb Sparrow, Executive Editor
Brian Jewell, Associate Editor
Kelly Tyner, Director of Sales & Marketing
Stacey Bowman, National Account Manager
The national magazine for African American Group Traveling, and the official magazine for the African American Travel Conference (AATC).
Circulation: 4500
Founded in 2001

23039 Travelhost Magazine
Travelhost
10701 N Stemmons Fwy
Dallas, TX 75220-2419

972-556-0541
Fax: 972-432-8729
E-Mail: editor@travelhostps.com
Home Page: www.travelhost.com

James E Buerger, CEO
David B Portener, Associate Publisher
Frequency: Monthly
Circulation: 60000
Founded in 1967

23040 Trip
Charlotte Trip
2424 N Davidson St
Suite 106 B
Charlotte, NC 28205-2382

704-376-7800
Fax: 704-376-7802
Home Page: www.charlottetrip.com

Marie Margaret, CEO/President/Publisher
Dana Jorden, Editor
Jenifer Krupa, Marketing Manager
Angie Jones, Circulation Manager
Cost: $18.00
Frequency: Monthly
Circulation: 35000
Founded in 1990

23041 Vermont Green Mountain Guide
44 Country Road
North Springfield, VT 05150-9738

802-886-3333
Home Page:
www.vtliving.com/newspapers/vtgreenmtnguid

Cindy Thiel, President

Trade Shows

23042 Adventure Travel and Outdoor Show
McRand International
1 Westminster Place
Suite 300
Lake Forest, IL 60045-1867

FAX 847-295-4419

Richard Dux, VP
Sue Wildman, VP

Exhibits by tour operators, outfitters and others geared toward soft and hard adventure travel vacations and outdoor activities.
15M Attendees
Frequency: January

23043 American Society of Travel Agents Conference
1101 King Street
Ste. 200
Alexandria, VA 22314-2944

703-739-2782
Fax: 703-684-8319
E-Mail: bdaniels@asta.org
Home Page: www.asta.org

Chris Vranas, VP
Brooke Daniels, Event Manager
Gathering of travel agents, airlines, hotels and tour operators that provides the opportunity to view and discuss new products, services and trends in the industry. 700 booths.
6M Attendees
Frequency: November

23044 American Travel Market Exhibition Company
Reed Exhibition Companies
383 Main Avenue
Norwalk, CT 06851-1543

203-840-4800
Fax: 203-840-9628
Home Page: www.reedexpo.com

Gregg Vautrin, CEO

The national event for all US travel buyers, including tour operators, travel agents, corporate travel buyers and meeting/conference planners. One of a global series of Travel Market events.
Frequency: September

23045 Annual American and Canadian Sport, Travel and Outdoor Show
Expositions
Edgewater Branch
PO Box 550
Cleveland, OH 44107-0550

216-529-1300
Fax: 216-529-0311
Home Page: ech.case.edu

John Grabowskie, Online Editor
John Bedan, Associate Online Editor
Nathan Delany, Associate Online Editor

975 exhibits of hunting and fishing equipment, travel services, boats, recreational vehicles and related equipment, supplies and services.
300k Attendees
Frequency: Annual
Founded in 1935

23046 Annual Boat, Vacation and Outdoor Show
Showtime Productions
PO Box 4372
Rockford, IL 61110

815-877-8043
Fax: 815-877-9037
E-Mail: brenda@showtimeproduction.net
Home Page: showtimeproduction.net

Duane Nichols, President
Brenda Rotoco, Event Coordinator

Boat, travel, outdoor equipment, supplies, and services plus demonstrations.
28000 Attendees
Frequency: February
Founded in 1970

23047 Annual Capital Sport Fishing, Travel and Outdoor Show
International Sport Show Producers Association
PO Box 4720
Portsmouth, NH 03802-4720

603-431-4315
Fax: 603-431-1971
E-Mail: info@sportshows.com
Home Page: www.sportshows.com

Paul Fuller, President

Over 350 exhibits of sports, fishing, recreation and travel equipment, supplies and services.
45k Attendees
Frequency: Annual
Founded in 1996

23048 Arabian Travel Market
Reed Exhibition Companies
383 Main Avenue
PO Box 6059
Norwalk, CT 06851

203-840-4800
Fax: 203-840-9628
Home Page: www.arabiantravelmarket.com

Three hundred exhibitors with travel related information, supplies and services.
5915 Attendees
Frequency: Annual

23049 Corporate and Incentive Travel
685 S. Washington Street
Alexandira, VA 22314

703-683-0123
Fax: 703-683-4545
E-Mail: info@corporateincentivetravel.net
Home Page: www.corporateincentivetravel.net

Corporate travel forum.

23050 Destinations Showcase
Intl. Association of Convention/Visitors Bureaus
2025 M Street
Suite 500
Washington, DC 20036

202-296-7888
Fax: 202-296-7889
E-Mail: info@destinationmarketing.org
Home Page: www.destinationsshowcase.com
Social Media: Facebook, Twitter

Michael D Gehrisch, President/CEO
Containing 100-200 exhibits at tradeshows.
575 Attendees
Founded in 1914
Mailing list available for rent: 1200+ names at $400 per M

23051 Discover America International Pow Wow
Travel Industry Association of America
1100 New York Avenue NW
Suite 450
Washington, DC 20005-3934

202-408-8422
Fax: 202-408-1255
E-Mail: feedback@ustravel.org
Home Page: www.ustravel.org/events/international-pow-wow

Rodger Dow, President & CEO
Siming Cao, Coordinator
Geoff Freeman, Executive Vice President and COO
Rebecca Shafer, Director of Executive Operations

Annual show of 1050 suppliers of travel products and services.
5,600 Attendees

23052 Euro Travel Forum
Reed Exhibition Companies
255 Washington Street
Newton, MA 02458-1637

617-584-4900
Fax: 617-630-2222

Elizabeth Hitchcock, International Sales

A mobile, multi-product and multi-destination travel trade exhibition bringing travel products from all over the world into direct contact with travel agents and travel buyers from the leisure, business and incentive products industries.
27M Attendees
Frequency: April

23053 Family Motor Coach Association Convention
8291 Clough Pike
Cincinnati, OH 45244-2756

513-474-3622
800-543-3622
Fax: 513-388-5286
E-Mail: jyeatts@fmca.com
Home Page: www.fmca.com

Jerry Yeatts, Convention Director
Ranita Jones, Sales Manager
Shawna Grubbs, Sales Assistant

Convention for Motorhome enthusiasts. Includes hundreds of motorhome displays, supplier displays and component displays.
15M Attendees
Frequency: Mar/Apr/July/Aug
Founded in 1963

23054 Heartland Travel Showcase
Hart Productions
130 E Chestnut Street
Suite 301
Columbus, OH 43215

513-281-0022
800-896-4682
Fax: 513-281-3322
Home Page: www.heartlandtravelshowcase.com

Annual show and exhibits of information from 10 midwest states and the province of Ontario on travel destinations, attractions, accommodations, activities and restaurants.
Frequency: February

23055 Incentive Travel and Meeting Executives Show
Hall-Erickson
98 E Naperville Road
Westmont, IL 60559-1559

630-963-9185
800-752-6312
Fax: 630-434-1216
E-Mail: moti@heiexpo.com
Home Page: www.motivationshow.com

Nancy A Petitti, Show Director
20M Attendees
Frequency: October
Founded in 1972

23056 Motivation Show
Hall-Erickson
98 E Naperville Road
Westmont, IL 60559-1559

630-963-9185
800-752-6312
Fax: 630-434-1216
E-Mail: moti@heiexpo.com
Home Page: www.motivationshow.com

Nancy A Petitti, Exhibit Show Manager
25M Attendees
Frequency: September
Founded in 1929

23057 NTA Convention
National Tour Association
546 E Main St
Lexington, KY 40508

859-226-4444
800-682-8886
Fax: 859-226-4414
E-Mail: questions@ntastaff.com
Home Page: ntaonline.com

Lisa Simon, President
Cathy Greteman, Chair & CEO
Matt Grayson, Director, Industry & Govt Relations
Erin Turner, Event Manager

The National Tour Association is an organization of nearly 4,000 international tourism pro-

fessionals focused on the development, promotion and increased use of tour operators packaged travel.
Mailing list available for rentat $500 per M

23058 National Camping Industry Expo
3700 W Flamingo Rd
Las Vegas, NV 22182-2240

703-932-2342
Fax: 703-734-3004
Home Page: www.gocampingamerica.com

Rick Carbo, Manager
Chandana Karmarkar, Manager

National camping industry expo, only trade expo for RV parks and campground owners/operators. Containing 120 booths and 100 exhibitors.
850+ Attendees
Frequency: November
Founded in 1966
Mailing list available for rent: 3,200 names

23059 Recreational Vehicle Industry Association National RV Trade Show
1896 Preston White Drive
Reston, VA 20191-4325

703-206-6003

David Humphreys, President
Mary Hutya, VP

Six hundred and thirty booths.
10M Attendees
Frequency: November

23060 Seatrade Cruise Convention
Miller Freeman Publications
13760 Noel Road
Suite 500
Dallas, TX 75240

800-527-0207
Fax: 214-419-8855

23061 Sport Travel Outdoor Show
Expositions
PO Box 550
Cleveland, OH 44107-0550

216-529-1300
Fax: 330-529-0311

Judy Fassnacht, Show Manager

475 booths of products and services related to the outdoor travel industry.
93M Attendees
Frequency: February

23062 Sports Travel and Adventure
Show Productions
800 Roosevelt Road
Suite 407
Glen Ellyn, IL 60137-5839

630-694-4611
Fax: 630-790-0209

Sandra Lewis, Show Manager

Two hundred and fifty six booths geared toward outdoor enthusiasts.
15M Attendees
Frequency: February

23063 Travel Industry Association American Pow Wow Marketing
1100 New York Avenue NW
Suite 450W
Washington, DC 20005

202-408-8422

Sue Elms, Show Manager
Roger Dow, CEO

Seven hundred booths where providers of US travel products promote these products.
3M Attendees
Frequency: April

23064 Travel and Tourism Research Association Show
546 E Main Street
Lexington, KY 40508-2342

859-226-4355
Fax: 859-226-4355
E-Mail: lisalcarey@aol.com
Home Page: www.ttra.com

Twenty booths exhibiting information of interest to members of the Tourism Research Association.
400 Attendees
Frequency: June

23065 TravelAge Tradeshows
11400 West Olympic Blvd
Suite 325
Los Angeles, CA 90064

310-954-2510
Fax: 212-237-3007
Home Page: www.travelagewest.com/Magazine

Nancy Montella, Show Manager

Four hundred booths of educational and business-oriented tradeshow that provides a vehicle for various people within the travel industry to meet and exchange information on products, services and trends.
2.5M Attendees
Frequency: March

23066 World Travel Market
Reed Exhibition Companies
255 Washington Street
Newton, MA 02458-1637
617-584-4900
Fax: 617-630-2222
Home Page: www.wtmlondon.com

Elizabeth Hitchcock, International Sales

Premium travel show.
43M Attendees
Frequency: November

Directories & Databases

23067 ABC Cruise and Ferry Guide
Reed Travel Group
Church Street
Hertfordshire, England, LU 5 4HB

Offers information on international shipping companies operating passenger services and cruises.
320 Pages
Frequency: Quarterly
ISBN: 0-001048-0 -

23068 ABC Guide to International Travel
Reed Travel Group
Church Street
Hertfordshire, England, LU 5 4HB

Offers a list of foreign consulates in London, England that offer travel information to tourists.
Frequency: Quarterly

23069 Access Travel: Airports
Airport Operators Council International
1220 19th Street NW
Suite 200
Washington, DC 20036-2463

202-293-8500
Fax: 202-331-1362

Information is given on over 500 airports worldwide that offer handicapped facilities.
50 Pages

23070 Airport Hotel Directory
3255 Wilshire Boulevard
Suite 1514
Los Angeles, CA 90010-1418

213-739-1956

Restaurants and hotels are listed that are a close proximity to major airports.
Cost: $12.00
170 Pages

23071 American Bus Association's Motorcoach Marketer
American Bus Association
111 K Street NE
9th Floor
Washington, DC 20002

202-842-1645
Fax: 202-842-0850
E-Mail: abainfo@buses.org
Home Page: www.buses.org/Member-Resources/Motorcoach-Marketer

Peter J Pantuso, CEO
Eron Shosteck, Marketing

This directory is a comprehensive guide of the bus and travel industry offering information on hotels and sightseeing services, attractions, museums, restaurants and more.
500 Pages
Frequency: Annual
Founded in 1926

23072 American Society of Travel Agents Membership Directory
NACTA
1101 King St
Alexandria, VA 22314-2963

703-739-2782
Fax: 703-684-8319
Home Page: www.nacta.com

Bill Maloney, Manager

Travel agents that represent over 17,000 agencies in the United States, Canada and overseas are the focus of this comprehensive directory.
Cost: $125.00
600 Pages
Frequency: Annual

23073 CMP Publications Travel File
CMP Publications
600 Community Dr
Manhasset, NY 11030-3810

516-562-5000
Fax: 516-562-5718

This large database covers the travel industry, with emphasis on news for travel agents and business travelers.
Frequency: Full-text

23074 Club Metro
Metro Online
1358 Hooper Avenue
Ste. 293
Toms River, NJ 08752

212-794-2664
Home Page: www.clubmetrousa.com

This database contains information on travel, entertainment, and metropolitan services.
Frequency: Bulletin Board

23075 Condo Vacations: the Complete Guide
Lanier Publishing International
PO Box 20429
Oakland, CA 94620-0429

Condominiums that are available for vacation rentals are listed.
Cost: $14.95
320 Pages
Frequency: Annual

23076 Cruise Industry News Annual
Nissel-Lie Communications
441 Lexington Avenue
Suite 809
New York, NY 10017-3910

212-986-1025
Fax: 212-986-1033
E-Mail: info2@cruiseindustrynews.com
Home Page: www.cruiseindustrynews.com

Oivind Mathisen, Editor/Publisher
Angela Mathisen, Publisher/Advertising Director
Monty Mathisen, Reporter/Web Editor

This book presents the entire worldwide cruise industry from new ships on order to supply/demand scenarios; plus reports on relevant issues, financial results, newbuilding and second-hand ship values, shipbuilding, new technology and on board services; plus exclusive reports on each sailing region, and a comprehensive directory of all cruised lines, shipyards, ports and other suppliers.
Cost: $450.00
300 Pages
Frequency: Annual
Founded in 1988

23077 Environmental Vacations: Volunteer Projects to Save the Planet
John Muir Publications
PO Box 613
Santa Fe, NM 87504-0613

505-466-6360
Fax: 505-988-1680

Information is given on vacations that provide opportunities to assist environmental projects.
Cost: $16.95
250 Pages

23078 Federal Travel Directory
Office of Federal Supply & Services
4 Crystal Mall Building
Washington, DC 20406-0001

202-564-2480

A list of airlines is offered in this directory that are under contract to the federal government.
Cost: $77.00
Frequency: Monthly

23079 Ford's Travel Guides
Ford's Travel Guides
19448 Londelius Street
Northridge, CA 91324-3511

818-987-1413

Offers valuable information on cruise ships and their planned cruises for one year ahead.
Cost: $14.95
200 Pages
Frequency: Quarterly
Circulation: 5,000

23080 Foster Travel Publishing Website
Foster Travel Publishing
Po Box 5715
Berkeley, CA 94705-0715

510-549-2202
Fax: 510-549-1131
E-Mail: lee@fostertravel.com
Home Page: www.fostertravel.com

Lee Foster, Owner

award winning travel writing and photography on 200 worldwide locations, presented to the consumer and to the content buyer on the web or in print looking for travel writing or travel photography.
Frequency: Full-text

23081 Free US Tourist Attractions
Pilot Books
127 Sterling Avenue
PO Box 2102
Greenport, NY 11944

631-477-0978
800-797-4568
Fax: 631-477-0978

A directory of free family entertainment in every state of the union.
Cost: $12.95
ISBN: 0-875762-04-2

23082 International Workcamp Directory
VFP International Voluntary Service
7 Kilburn Street
Suite 31
Burlington, VT 05401

802-540-3060
Fax: 802-540-3061
E-Mail: vfp@vfp.org
Home Page: www.vfp.org

Meg Brook, President
Chelsea Frisbee, Outgoing Volunteer Coordinator
Peter Coldwell, Treasurer/Founder
Scott Simpson, Board Chair
Matt Messier, Secretary

An annual booklet listing over 2400 opportunities for meaningful travel throughout Western and Easter Europe, Russia, Africa, Asia, Australia and Latin America. 2-3 week programs are $200 including room and board.
Cost: $20.00
2000 Members
289 Pages
Frequency: Annual
Circulation: 2,000
ISBN: 0-945617-20-8
ISSN: 0896-565X
Founded in 1982
Printed in 4 colors

23083 National Bed and Breakfast Association Guide
National Bed & Breakfast Association
2009 Family Circle
Lexington, KY 50505

859-255-0076
Fax: 859-255-0938
Home Page: www.bbinnsofamerica.com

Phyllis Featherston, Executive Director
Cost: $17.95
600 Pages
Frequency: Every 2-3 Years
ISBN: 0-961129-86-7
Founded in 1982
Printed in 2 colors on matte stock

23084 OAG Flights2Go
UBM Aviation
3025 Highland Parkway
Suite 200
Downers Grove, IL 60515-5561

630-515-5300
Fax: 630-515-3251
Home Page: www.oagtravel.com

Anthony Smith, Group Publisher
Jason Holland, Editor
Simon Barker, Publisher

Flights2Go provides mobile access to worldwide flight schedules in an instance direct to your mobile device. No matter where you are, you can look up flight schedules from across the globe and even check flight status.

23085 OAG Travel Planner Pro
UBM Aviation
3025 Highland Parkway
Suite 200
Downers Grove, IL 60515-5561

630-515-5300
Fax: 630-515-3251
Home Page: www.oagtravel.com

Anthony Smith, Group Publisher
Jason Holland, Editor
Simon Barker, Publisher

OAG Travel Planner Pro is the premier online tool for travel arrangers who need to create, manage, and save complex travel plans quickly and easily.

23086 Official Bus Guide
Russell's Guides
834 3rd Avenue SE
Cedar Rapids, IA 52403-2408

319-364-6138
Fax: 319-364-4853

A list of 475 intercity bus companies in the United States, Canada and Mexico.
Cost: $9.90
Frequency: Monthly
Circulation: 14,000

23087 Official Handbook of Travel Brochures
Vacation Publications
1502 Augusta Drive
Suite 415
Houston, TX 77057-2484

713-974-6903

16 Pages
Frequency: Quarterly
Circulation: 38,000

23088 Real Guides
Farmers Trip & Travel
PO Box 473
Mount Morris, IL 61054-0473

FAX 815-734-1223

A series of guidebooks that list sites, attractions and events in a city or country.
Cost: $8.00
300 Pages
Frequency: Per Edition

23089 Reed's Travel Group's Travel Agent Database
Reed Travel Group
2000 Clearwater Dr
Oak Brook, IL 60523-8809

630-574-0825
800-424-3996
Fax: 630-288-8781
Home Page: www.reedbusiness.com

Jeff Greisch, President

About 65,000 wholesale, retail and cooperative travel agencies worldwide, including tour operators.
Cost: $270.00

23090 Society of American Travel Writers: Membership Directory
Society of American Travel Writers
4101 Lake Boone Trail
Suite 201
Raleigh, NC 27607-7506

FAX 919-787-4916

Sarah Haw, Member Services

About 550 newspaper and magazine travel editors, writers, columnists, photo journalists and

broadcasters in the US and Canada.
Cost: $95.00
Frequency: Annual February

23091 Thomas Cook Airports Guide Europe
Thomas Cook
Unit 11, Coningsby Road
Peterborough, England, PE 3 85B

Offers valuable information on over 75 public airports in Europe.
255 Pages
Frequency: Biennial

23092 Thomas Cook Airports Guide International
Thomas Cook
Unit 11, Coningsby Road
Peterborough, England, PE 3 85B

Offers valuable information on over 90 airport facilities outside of the United Kingdom.
255 Pages
Frequency: Biennial

23093 Tours.com
490 Post St
Suite 1701-A
San Francisco, CA 94102-1308

415-956-0111
Fax: 415-956-0117
E-Mail: info@tours.com
Home Page: www.tours.com

Maria Polk, President/CEO/Co-Founder
Karin Wacaster, Public Relations
Marijo Douglass, Finance Executive

Home of the Worldwide Directory of Tours and Vacation Packages.
Founded in 1995

23094 Travel Agent: Focus 500 Directory Issue
Universal Media
801 2nd Ave
New York, NY 10017-8638

212-986-5100
Fax: 212-883-1244

Lists of attractions, restaurants, convention and visitor bureaus, hotel chains and management companies, cruise lines, state tourism offices, travel trade associations, tourist railways.
Frequency: Annual October
Circulation: 50,000

23095 Travel Editors: US Consumer & Inflight Magazines
Rocky Point Press
4830 Ranchito Avenue
Sherman Oaks, CA 91423-1927

FAX 818-763-4818

Listings of travel editors of US consumer and in-flight magazines.
Frequency: Annual

23096 Travel Forum
CompuServe Information Service
5000 Arlington Centre Blvd
Columbus, OH 43220-5439

614-326-1002
800-848-8199
Home Page: www.travelforum.org

This database contains information on travel and related topics of interest, including travel planning.
Frequency: Bulletin Board

23097 Travel Industry Association of America: Travel Media Directory
Travel Industry Association of America
1100 New York Ave NW
Suite 450
Washington, DC 20005-6130

202-408-8422
Fax: 202-408-1255
E-Mail: feedback@tia.org
Home Page: www.tia.org

Roger J Dow, CEO
Peter Strebel, Secretary

Travel editors of major newspapers, magazines and broadcast outlets.
Cost: $40.00
Frequency: Annual
Circulation: 3,000

23098 Travel Insider's Guide to Alternative Accommodations
Travel Insider
PO Box 14
Streamwood, IL 60107-0014

206-338-3381
Fax: 206-338-3381

John E Sullivan, Editor

Over 400 sources for alternative accommodations worldwide, such as farmhouses, castles, universities and country inns.
Cost: $9.95
Frequency: Annual October

23099 Travel Photo Source Book
Society of American Travel Writers
4101 Lake Boone Trail
Suite 201
Raleigh, NC 27607-7506

715-248-3800
Fax: 919-787-4916
Home Page: www.photosource.com

Nancy Belcher, Editor

Nearly 100 member photographers and 35 associate member representatives of airlines, hotels, resorts, tourist agencies and public relations firms.
Frequency: Biennial

23100 Travel Tips USA
Renaissance Publications
7950 Jones Branch Drive
McLean, VA 22108-0605

614-777-1227
E-Mail: accuracy@usatoday.com
Home Page: www.usatourist.com

Michelle Leco
Mike Leco

Amusement parks, attractions and festivals are among some of the categories listed in this travel directory.
Cost: $17.95
320 Pages

23101 Travel World News Resource Directory
Travel Industry Network
28 Knight Street
Norwalk, CT 06851

203-286-6679
Fax: 203-286-6681
E-Mail: editor@travelworldnews.com
Home Page: www.travelworldnews.com

Charles Gatt Jr, Publisher
Peter Gatt, Associate Publisher

A directory by continent/region/locale of local vendors, tour operators, railways, cruise lines, and travel links.
Founded in 1988

23102 Travel and Tourism Research Association: Membership Directory
Travel and Tourism Research Association
546 E Main Street
Lexington, KY 40508-2342

859-226-4355
Fax: 859-226-4355
E-Mail: lisalcarey@aol.com

Lisa Carey, Executive Director

Over 750 state and local tourism bureaus and other federal and provincial government agencies, airlines, media, hotels, university bureaus of business research and other university departments and research and consulting firms concerned with travel research, marketing and promotion.
Cost: $50.00
Frequency: Annual June

23103 Travel, Leisure and Entertainment News Media
Larriston Communications
PO Box 20229
New York, NY 10025-1518

212-864-0150
Fax: 212-662-8103

Sheila Gordon, Editor

Over 350 travel and leisure magazines and daily newspapers with circulations of over 50,000 that have special leisure or entertainment sections.
Cost: $89.00
Frequency: Annual May

23104 Traveler's Hotline Directory
Forte Travel Lodge
Po Box 270469
San Diego, CA 92198-2469

858-487-9596
800-578-7878
Fax: 858-487-9658

Victor Ferrette, Partner

Approximately 12,000 travel services such as air couriers, auto rental agencies, campgrounds, resorts, hotels, spas, travel groups and airlines that offer toll-free domestic or international telephone numbers.
Cost: $15.95

23105 Travelers Information RoundTable
GE Information Services
401 N Washington Street
Rockville, MD 20850-1707

301-388-8284

Cathy Ge, Owner

Provides a forum enabling users to share information on a range of travel topics.
Frequency: Bulletin Board

23106 West Coast Travel
Foster Travel Publishing
Po Box 5715
Berkeley, CA 94705-0715

510-549-2202
Fax: 510-549-1131
E-Mail: lee@fostertravel.com
Home Page: www.westcoasttravels.com

Lee Foster, Owner

This database offers information for travelers and tourists on approximately 150 locations in the western United States, Canada and Mexico.
Frequency: Full-text

23107 Worldspan TravelShopper
WORLDSPAN
300 Galleria Parkway
Atlanta, GA 30339

770-637-7400
Fax: 770-563-7004
Home Page: www.worldspan.com

Rakesh Gangwal, CEO

This database offers travel information, including 5 million domestic and international flights for every airline in the world for more than 100,000 cities.
Frequency: Directory

Industry Web Sites

23108 **http://gold.greyhouse.com**
G.O.L.D Grey House OnLine Databases
Grey House Publishing's online database platform, GOLD, offers Quick Search, Keyword Search and Expert Search for most business sectors including travel markets. The GOLD platform makes finding the information you need quick and easy - whether you're a novice searcher or an experienced database user. All of Grey House's directory products are available for subscription on the GOLD platform.

23109 **www.biztravel.com**
Biztravel.com
Internet travel service offering discounts on flights, hotels, car rentals, packages and cruises.

23110 **www.buses.org**
American Bus Association
Trade association for the North American bus industry.

23111 **www.expedia.com**
Expedia.com
Internet travel service offers access to airlines, hotels, car rentals, vacation packages, cruises and corporate travel.

23112 **www.gocampingamerica.com**
National Association of RV Parks and Campgrounds
Nat ARVC serves the business and legislative needs of more than 3,200 member RV parks and campgrounds.

23113 **www.goworldnet.com/cgi-bin**
Worldnet USA
States and their hotels, theaters and museums.

23114 **www.greyhouse.com**
Grey House Publishing
Authoritative reference directories for most business markets including travel markets. Users can search the online databases with varied search criteria allowing for custom searches by product category, geographic area, sales volume, keyword, subject and more. Full Grey House catalog and online ordering also available.

23115 **www.hotwire.com**
Hotwire.com
Internet travel service offering discounts on flights, hotels, car rentals, packages and cruises.

23116 **www.hsmai.org**
Hospitality Sales and Marketing Association
To provide resources to sales and marketing professionals at all levels of thier career in travel, hospitality, and tourism.

23117 **www.iacvb.org**
International Association of Convention and Visitor Bureaus
Promotes sound professional practices in the solicitation and servicing of meetings and conventions. Members represent travel/tourism-related businesses. Publications include a electronic newsletter and on-line directory.

23118 **www.info.now.com/site**
Society of Incentive and Travel Executives
An individual membership society covering 70 countries. Members are corporate users, airlines, Tourist Boards, cruise lines, destination management companies, consultants, hotels/resorts, travel agents, incentive travel houses and publications.

23119 **www.nbba.com**
National Bed & Breakfast Association
Innkeepers of bed and breakfast lodgings.

23120 **www.ntaonline.com**
National Tour Association
For North American tourism professionals focused on the development, promotion and increased use of tour operators packaged travel.

23121 **www.orbitz.com**
Orbitz.com
Internet travel service offering discounts on flights, hotels, car rentals, packages and cruises.

23122 **www.rsana.com**
Receptive Services Association
Helping receptive operators serve international tour companies through partnerships with North American suppliers.

23123 **www.tia.org**
Travel Industry Association of America
For hotels, airlines and travel agencies interested in promoting increased travel to and within the US

23124 **www.travel.com**
Travel.com
Internet travel service providing access to flights, hotels, car rentals, vacation packages and cruises.

23125 **www.travel.lycos.com**
Lycos.com
Internet travel service offering discounts on flights, hotels, car rentals, packages and cruises.

23126 **www.travel.yahoo.com**
Yahoo.com
Internet travel service providing access to flights, hotels, car rentals, vacation packages and cruises.

23127 **www.travelocity.com**
Sabre Holdings
Travel service offering consumers access to hundreds of airlines and thousands of hotels, as well as cruise, last-minute and vacation packages and best-in-class car rental companies.

23128 **www.waveconcepts.com/arta**
Association of Retail Travel Agents
Promotes the interests of retail travel agents through representation on industry councils and testimony before Congress. Conducts joint marketing and educational programs.

Associations

23129 ABF Freight Systems
3801 Old Greenwood Road
PO Box 10048
Fort Smith, AR 72903

479-785-8700
800-610-5544
Fax: 479-494-6918
E-Mail: customercare@abf.com
Home Page: www.abfs.com
Social Media: Facebook, Twitter, Google+

Robert A Davidson, CEO
Shannon Lively, Vive President of Transportation

Concentrates on national and regional transportation of general commodities freight, involving primarily LTL shipments. Mission is to provide reliable transportation services in a responsible manner to meet customers' unique needs.

23130 America's Independent Truckers' Association
P.O. Box 1250
Clinton, MS 39060

601-924-9606
Home Page: www.aitaonline.com
Social Media: Facebook, Twitter

Larry Daniel, Founder

Created to serve independent owner operators and small to medium sized fleet owners.
Founded in 1997

23131 American Towman Network
7 West Street
Warwick, NY 10990

201-722-3000
800-732-3869
Fax: 201-722-3010
E-Mail: towcrazy@wrecker.com
Home Page: www.towman.com

Jim Sorrenti, Editor
Steven Calitri, Editor in Chief
Henry Calitri, Exhibit Sales

23132 American Truck Historical Society
10380 N. Ambassador Drive
Suite 101
Kansas City, MO 64153

816-891-9900
Fax: 816-891-9903
Home Page: www.aths.org
Social Media: Facebook, Twitter, YouTube

Collects and preserves the history of antique trucks and the industry.
Founded in 1971

23133 American Trucking Association
950 North Glebe Road
Suite 210
Arlington, VA 22203-4181

703-838-1700
Fax: 703-838-8884
E-Mail: atamembership@trucking.org
Home Page: www.truckline.com

Philip L Byrd Sr., Chairman
Bill Graves, President & CEO
Duane Long, 1st VP
Patty Thomas, 2nd VP
John M Smith, Secretary

23134 American Trucking Associations
950 North Glebe Road
Suite 210
Arlington, VA 22203-4181
703-838-1700
E-Mail: media@trucking.org
Home Page: www.trucking.org
Social Media: Facebook, Twitter, YouTube

Duane Long, ATA Chairman
Bill Graves, ATA President/CEO
Pat Thomas, ATA First Vice Chairman
Barry Pottle, ATA Vice Chairman
David Manning, ATA Vice Chairman

The largest national trade association for the trucking industry that promotes safety on America's highways, improves the industry's image, efficiency, and competitiveness, educates the public about the critical role trucking plays in the economy, and researches significant industry issues.

23135 Association of American Railroads
425 3rd Street SW
Washington, DC 20024

202-639-2100
E-Mail: media@aar.org
Home Page: www.aar.org
Social Media: Facebook, Twitter, LinkedIn, YouTube

Edward R. Hemberger, President & CEO
John Gray, Senior VP
Ian Jefferies, Senior VP
Jefferey Marsh, SVP, Finance and Administration
Patricia M. Reilly, SVP, Communications

Represents North America's freight railroads and Amtrak.

23136 Association of Independent Corrugated Packaging
113 S. West Street
3rd Floor
Alexandria, VA 22314

703-836-2422
877-836-2422
Fax: 703-836-2795
E-Mail: info@aiccbox.org
Home Page: www.aiccbox.org
Social Media: Facebook, Twitter, LinkedIn, YouTube

A. Steven Young, President
Taryn Pyle, Director, Marketing & Communication
Cindy Guarino, Director, Meetings
Virginia Humphrey, Director, Membership
Ralph Young, Technical Services

Provides a forum for discussion of problems and offers educational programs and seminars.
1100 Members
Founded in 1974

23137 Automotive Parts Remanufacturers Association
4460 Brookfield Corporate Drive
Suite H
Chantilly, VA 20151-1671

703-968-2772
Fax: 703-968-2878
Home Page: www.apra.org
Social Media: Facebook, Twitter, LinkedIn, YouTube

Association for remanufacturers of automotive parts.
Founded in 1941

23138 Carrier Information Exchange
4601 N Fairfax Drive
Suite 1160
Arlington, VA 22203

703-841-6374
Fax: 703-841-6370
E-Mail: mcinfosupport@egov.com
Home Page: www.mcinfo.org

23139 Commercial Vehicle Safety Alliance
6303 Ivy Lane
Suite 310
Greenbelt, MD 20770-631

301-830-6144
E-Mail: cvsahq@cvsa.org
Home Page: www.cvsa.org
Social Media: Facebook, Twitter, LinkedIn, YouTube

A nonprofit organization dedicated to improving the safety of commercial vehicles.

23140 Council of Fleet Specialists
315 Delaware Street
Kansas City, MO 64105-1256

816-421-2600
Fax: 816-421-0515

UJ Reese, Executive VP

Members are distributors of parts and services for heavy-duty trucks.
210 Members
Founded in 1967

23141 Driver Employee Council of America
1001 G St Nw
Suite 500-W
Washington, DC 20001-4564

202-434-4100
Fax: 202-842-0011
E-Mail: info@khlaw.com
Home Page: www.khlaw.com
Social Media: LinkedIn, RSS

Jerome H Heckman, Partner

Members are companies leasing truck drivers to private carriers.
43 Members
Founded in 1992

23142 Express Carriers Association
9532 Liberia Avenue
#752
Manassas, VA 20110

703-361-1058
Fax: 703-361-5274
E-Mail: eca@expresscarriers.org
Home Page: www.expresscarriers.org

John Di Tucci, President
Paul Steffes, VP
Jim Luciani, 2nd VP
MJ Hill, Treasurer
Mike Coyle, Secretary

The mission of the ECA is to develop business between carriers, shippers and vendors of products and services to the transportation industry.

23143 Gemini Shippers Group
137 West 25th Street
3rd Floor
New York, NY 10001

212-947-3424
Fax: 212-629-0361
E-Mail: info@geminishippers.com
Home Page: www.geminishippers.com

Shippers association with global contracts for all commodities.
200 Members
Founded in 1916

23144 Heavy Duty Representatives Association
160 Symphony Way
Elgin, IL 847-760-00

330-725-7160
800-763-5717
Fax: 330-725-7160

E-Mail: trucksvc@aol.com
Home Page: www.hdra.org

Larry Rossenthal, President
Walt Sirman, Vice President
John Stojak, Secretary

Independent sales agencies which sell heavy-duty components to the trucking and aftermarket industries.

23145 Independent Truck Owner-Operators
1 NW OOIDA Drive
Grain Valley, MI 64029

816-229-5791
800-444-5791
Home Page: www.ooida.com
Social Media: Facebook, Twitter, RSS

Jim Johnston, President
Todd Spencer, EVP
Woody Chambers, General VP
Robert Esler, Secretary
Bill Rode, Treasurer

Trade association for business and human resources equipment financing.

23146 Intermodal Association of North America
11785 Beltsville Drive
Suite 1100
Calverton, MD 20705

301-982-3400
Fax: 301-982-4815
Home Page: www.intermodal.org/

Phil Shook, Director of Intermodal
Katie Farmer, Group Vice President
Don Aiken, Senior Vice President

A trade association serving the combined interests of the intermodal freight industry.

23147 Lake Carriers Association
20325 Center Ridge Road
Suite 720
Rocky River, OH 44116-3508

440-333-4444
Fax: 440-333-9993
E-Mail: info@lcaships.com
Home Page: www.lcaships.com

James H I Weakley, President
Glen G Nekvasil, VP
Harold W Henderson, General Counsel
Katie Gumeny, Administrative Assistant

Members are US- Flag Great Lakes vessel operators engaged in transporting iron ore, coal, grain, limestone, cement and petroleum products.
Founded in 1880

23148 Light Truck Assessory Alliance
SEMA
1575 S.Valley Vista Drive
Diamond Bar, CA 91765-0910

909-396-0289
E-Mail: info@sema.org
Home Page: www.sema.org
Social Media: Facebook, Twitter, Google+

Nate Shelton, Chairman
Doug Evans, Chair-Elect
Christopher J Kersting, President & CEO
George Afremow, VP, CFO
Tom Myroniak, VP, Marketing & Market Research

A national organization with 150 manufacturers of truck caps and light truck accessories.

23149 Mid-West Truckers Association
2727 N Dirksen Pkwy
Springfield, IL 62702-1490

217-525-0310
Fax: 217-525-0342
E-Mail: info@mid-westtruckers.com
Home Page: www.mid-westtruckers.com
Social Media: Facebook

Don Schaefer, President

Serves the trucking industry by lobbying on their behalf, assisting with registration, license plate procurement and group insurance programs. Conducts educational programs, has own self-funded workers compensation insurance program. Trade association represents truck owners in 14 states.
2700 Members
Founded in 1962

23150 National Association of Small Trucking Companies
2054 Nashville Pike
Gallatin, TN 37066

800-264-8580
Fax: 615-451-0041
E-Mail: david.owen@nastc.com
Home Page: www.nastc.com

David Owen, President
Buster Anderson, Executive Vice President
Dana Campbell, Vice President Of Operations

Association for small trucking fleets and companies.

23151 National Association of Truck Stop Operators
1737 King Street
Suite 801
Alexandria, VA 22314-1483

703-549-2100
888-ASK-NATS
Fax: 703-684-4525
E-Mail: headquarters@natso.com
Home Page: www.natso.com
Social Media: Facebook, Twitter, Youtube, RSS

Tom Heinz, Chairman
Thomas M O'Brien, Secretary/Treasurer
Lisa J Mullings, President & CEO

NATSO is the professional association of America's $42 billion travel plaza and truckstop industry. NATSO represents the industry on legislative and regulatory matters; serves as the official source of information on the diverse travel plaza and truckstop industry; provides education to its members; conducts an annual convention and trade show; and supports efforts to generally improve the business climate in which its members operate.
1100 Members
Founded in 1990

23152 National Automobile Dealers Association
8400 Westpark Dr
Mc Lean, VA 22102-3591

703-356-3665
Fax: 703-821-7234
E-Mail: help@nada.org
Home Page: www.nada.org
Social Media: Facebook, Twitter, Flickr, Youtube

John McEleney, Chairman
Jack Kain, Vice Chairman
Phillip D Brady, President

Manufacturers, suppliers and distributors of products and services designed to control dealership expenses, help merchandising or improve profitability.
19700 Members
Founded in 1917

23153 National Food Distributors Association
401 N. MIchigan Avenue
Suite 2200
Chicago, IL 60611-4267

312-644-6610
Fax: 212-482-6459
E-Mail: info@allfoodbusiness.com
Home Page: www.allfoodbusiness.com

An organization comprised of independent store-to-door service distributors and suppliers of specialty food items.
2100 Members
Founded in 1952

23154 National Motor Freight Traffic Association Inc.
1001 North Fairfax Stree
Suite 600
Alexandria, VA 22314

703-838-1810
866-411-6632
Fax: 703-683-6296
E-Mail: customerservice@nmfta.org
Home Page: www.nmfta.org
Social Media: LinkedIn

Paul Levine, General Manager
Urban Jonson, Chief Technology Officer
Leslie Tate, Finance/HR Manager

To serve as a research and development organization providing the transportation industry with the necessary information to advance and improve their interests and welfare.
950 Members
Founded in 1956

23155 National Private Truck Council
950 N Glebe Rd
Suite 530
Arlington, VA 22203-4183

703-683-1300
Fax: 703-683-1217
E-Mail: info@nptc.org
Home Page: www.nptc.org
Social Media: Facebook, Twitter, LinkedIn, Youtube, Flickr, RSS

Gary S Petty, President & CEO
Tom Moore, SVP
Serena Porter, Membership Manager
George Mundell, EVP & COO
Rick Schweiter, General Counsel & Govt. Affairs

Distributors, shippers, processors, jobbers and manufacturers who transport their own goods and are owners of their own truck fleets. Sponsors national safety contests, safety seminars, management workshops, fleet management certification.
650 Members
Founded in 1939

23156 National Truck Equipment Association
37400 Hills Tech Dr
Farmington Hill, MI 48331-3414

248-489-7090
800-441-6832
Fax: 248-489-8590
E-Mail: info@ntea.com
Home Page: www.ntea.com
Social Media: Facebook, Twitter, LinkedIn

Steve Carey, Executive Director
Carole Vartanian, Accounting Manager
Derek Eng, Senior IT Manager
Sheree Campbell, Executive Assistant

NTEA currently represents nearly 1,600 small to mid sized companies that manufacture, distribute, install, buy, sell and repair commercial trucks, truck bodies, truck equipment, trailers and accessories. The major commercial truck

chassis manufacturers also belong to the NTEA as associate members.
1600 Members
Founded in 1964

23157 **National Truck Leasing System**
2651 Warrenville Road
Suite 560
Oakbrook Terrace, IL 60515

630-538-8878
Fax: 630-953-0040
Home Page: www.nationalease.com
Social Media: Facebook, Twitter, LinkedIn, Google+

John Grainger, President

Members are independent truck leasing companies.
Founded in 1944

23158 **National Truck and Heavy Equipment Claims Council (NTHECC)**
PO Box 5928
Fresno, CA 93755-5928

559-431-3774
Fax: 559-436-4755
Home Page: www.nthecc.org

Richard Bruce, Executive Officer

Repair and manufacturing facilities, insurance companies and adjusters concerned with insuring of heavy equipment and trucks. Promotes safety.
125 Members
Founded in 1961

23159 **National Trucking Industrial Relations**
908 King Street
Alexandria, VA 22314-3067

703-836-5506
Home Page: www.all-acronyms.com
Social Media: Facebook

Trucking executives and lawyers concerned with personnel and labor relations issues.
128 Members
Founded in 1987

23160 **NorthAmerican Transportation Association**
9120 Double Diamond Parkway
Ste 346
Reno, NV 89521-4842

800-805-0040
Home Page: www.ntassoc.com
Social Media: Facebook, Twitter, LinkedIn, YouTube

Association of transportation safety and compliance professionals serving the motor carrier industry.

23161 **Owner Operator Independent Drivers**
1 NW OOIDA Drive
Grain Valley, MI 64029-1000

816-229-5791
800-444-5791
Fax: 816-229-0518
E-Mail: webmaster@ooida.com
Home Page: www.ooida.com
Social Media: Facebook, Twitter, Youtube

Jim Johnston, President
Todd Spencer, EVP
Woody Chambers, General VP
Robert Esler, Secretary
Bill Rode, Treasurer

National association for owner-operators, professional drivers and small fleet owners. Lobbies federal and state government and advises on all legislation affecting the trucking industry. Provides insurance, financial products and business services.
95000 Members
Frequency: Monthly
Circulation: 200000
Founded in 1973

23162 **Owner Operators of America**
PO Box 582
Orchard Park, NY 14127-0582

Merchants providing goods and services to truck drivers, operators and owners. Seeks to protect the status, interests and image of truck drivers. Offers discounts on fuel, tires, food, repairs, parts and insurance. Provides tax filing assistance. Sponsors trade shows, conferences and public relations programs.
250 Members
Founded in 1982

23163 **Professional Truck Driver Institute**
Express Carriers Association
555 E Barddock Road
Alexandria, VA 22314

703-647-7015
866-322-7447
Fax: 703-836-6610
E-Mail: cburruss@truckload.org
Home Page: www.ptdi.org

Terry Burnett, Chairman
Kevin Bursch, Vice Chair
Mary Beth McCollum, Secretary

The nation's foremost advocate of optimum standards and professionalism for entry level truck driver training.
60 Members
Founded in 1986

23164 **Professional Truck Driving Institute**
555 E. Braddock Road
Alexandria, VA 22314

703-647-7015
Fax: 703-846-6610
Home Page: www.ptdi.org

Advocates of truck-driver training standards, driver professionalism and safety.

23165 **Professional Trucking Services Association**
United Truckers Service
1001 Bayhill Drive
Suite 300
San Bruno, CA 94066

650-260-3170
Fax: 770-929-3201
Home Page: www.allbusiness.com
Social Media: Facebook, Twitter, Youtube, RSS, Google+

Members are service bureaus which assist trucking companies in obtaining licensing and permits.
52 Members
Founded in 1984

23166 **Specialized Carriers and Rigging**
5870 Trinity Parkway
Suite 200
Centreville, VA 20120

703-698-0291
Fax: 571-722-1698
E-Mail: info@scranet.org
Home Page: www.scranet.org
Social Media: Facebook, Twitter, LinkedIn

Michael Battaini, Chairman
Ron Montgomery, President
Alan Barnhart, VP
Delynn Burkhalter, Treasurer
Bruce Forster, Assistant Treasurer

Members are carriers, crane and rigging operators and millwrights engaged in the transport of heavy goods.
1100 Members
Founded in 1959

23167 **The Association Of American Truckers**
P.O. Box 230369
Montgomery, AL 36123-0369

800-426-6221
Fax: 334-269-1352
E-Mail: will@americantruckersonline.com
Home Page: www.americantruckersonline.com

Provides insurance and other trucking related products for the American Trucking Associations.

23168 **The Trucking Industry Defense Association**
3601 E. Joppa Road
Baltimore, MD 21234

410-931-8100
Fax: 410-931-8111
E-Mail: info@tida.org
Home Page: www.tida.org
Social Media: LinkedIn

Joel B. Schechter, President
Dana Hoffman, Secretary
William Schrank, General Counsel
Tim Sullivan, Treasurer

A nonprofit assocation devoted to sharing knowledge and resources for defense of the trucking industry.

23169 **Transportation Intermediaries Association**
1625 Prince St
Suite 200
Alexandria, VA 22314-2883

703-299-5700
Fax: 703-836-0123
E-Mail: voltmann@tianet.org
Home Page: www.tianet.org
Social Media: Facebook, Twitter

Robert Voltmann, President
Alec Gizzi, Chair
Geoff Turner, Vice Chair
Jeff Tucker, Treasurer
Barcy Vidt, Secretary

Education and policy organization for North American transportation intermediaries. The only national association representing the interests of all third party transportation service providers. Members include logistics management firms, property brokers, perishable commodities brokers, freight forwarders, intermodal marketers and ocean and air forwarders.
700 Members
Founded in 1977

23170 **Transportation Loss Claim and Security**
120 Main Street
Huntington, NY 11743-6906

631-270-0100
Fax: 516-549-8962
Home Page: www.tlcouncil.org

Bob Hochwarth, Chairman
Reed Tepper, President
Nadia Martin, Secretary/Treasurer

A nonprofit trade association dedicated to the prevention of freight loss, damage and delay, the promulgation of reasonable liability rules, laws and claim policies.
660 Members
Founded in 1973

23171 **Truck Frame and Axle Repair Association**
3741 Enterprise Drive SW
Rochester, MN 55902-0122

800-232-8272
Fax: 813-626-5385
E-Mail: w.g.reich@att.net
Home Page: www.taraassociation.com

Paul Jones, President
John Messina, President Elect
Bill Hinchcliffe, Secretary/Treasurer

For operators and owners of heavy duty truck repair facilities, fleet managers, truckers and insurance damage appraisers.
110 Members
Founded in 1966

23172 **Truck Trailer Manufacturers Association**
7001 Heritage Village Plaza
Suite 220
Gainesville, VA 20155

703-549-3010
Fax: 703-549-3014
E-Mail: ttma@erols.com
Home Page: www.ttmanet.org

Jeff Sims, President
John Freiler, Engineering Manager
Nancy Livingston, Administration

A national organization of truck and tank trailer manufacturers and 120 suppliers to the industry.
Founded in 1941

23173 **Truck and Heavy Equipment Claims Council**
PO Box 5928
Fresno, CA 93755-5928

559-431-3774
Fax: 559-436-4755
Home Page: www.nthecc.org

Bill Ketchelmeier, Executive Officer

Repair and manufacturing facilities, insurance companies and adjusters concerned with insuring of heavy equipment and trucks. Promotes safety.
45 Members
Founded in 1961

23174 **Truck-Frame Axle Repair Association**
Home Page: www.taraassociation.com

Association for truck frame and axle repairers.

23175 **Trucker Buddy International**
3200 Rice Mine Rd
Tuscaloosa, A 35406

800-692-8339
E-Mail: info@truckerbuddy.org
Home Page: www.truckerbuddy.org
Social Media: Facebook, Twitter

A nonprofit organization for educating and mentoring schoolchildren via trucker penpals.
Founded in 1992

23176 **Truckload Carriers Association**
555 E Braddock Rd
Alexandria, VA 22314-2182

703-838-1950
Fax: 703-836-6610
E-Mail: tca@truckload.org
Home Page: www.truckload.org
Social Media: Facebook, Twitter, LinkedIn, Youtube, Flickr

Tom B Kretsinger, President/COO
Shepard Dunn, 1st Vice Chair
Keith Tuttle, 2nd Vice Chair
Rob Penner, Treasurer
Russell Stubbs, Secretary

Dedicated to representing the interests of truckload carriers. TCA is a proud member-driven organization, providing benefits and services to the members regardless of size.
800 Members
Founded in 1938

23177 **United Truckers Association**
1575 Heritage Drive
Suite 103
McKinney, TX 75069

484-681-9283
Fax: 956-425-9350
E-Mail: info@utatruckers.com
Home Page: www.unitedtruckersassociation.com

Association for truck drivers.
Founded in 1995

23178 **Used Truck Association**
325 County Club Drive
Suite A
Stockbridge, GA 30281

817-439-3900
877-438-7882
Fax: 817-439-3609
E-Mail: contact@uta.org
Home Page: www.uta.org
Social Media: Facebook, LinkedIn

Rick Clark, President
Ken Kosic, VP
Sheri Aeberg, Secretary
Tom Pfeiler, Treasurer
Marty Crawford, President Emeritus

Used truck manufacturers and dealerships.
800 Members
Founded in 1988

Newsletters

23179 **American Trucker**
PRIMEDIA Intertec-Technology & Transportation
PO Box 12901
Shawnee Mission, KS 66282-2901

913-341-1300
800-827-7468
Fax: 913-514-6895
Home Page: www.trucker.com

Eric Jacobson, Senior VP
Coleen Liatch, Supervisor

Information for those interested in the truck industry. Contains articles on new and used trucks, supplies, equipment, financing, pricing, and other truck related services.
Cost: $21.00
Frequency: Monthly
Circulation: 600000
Founded in 1926

23180 **Owner Operator News**
PO Box 582
Orchard Park, NY 14127-0582

FAX 716-941-5582

Charles DeVaul, Publisher

Trucking news and information.
Frequency: Monthly

23181 **TCA Newsletter**
Truckload Carriers Association
555 E Braddock Road
Suite CS-4
Alexandria, VA 22314-2182

703-838-1960
Fax: 703-836-6610
E-Mail: tca@truckload.org
Home Page: www.truckload.org
Social Media: Twitter, TCA News

Chris Burruss, President
Deborah Sparks, VP
Gary Salisbury, Chairman

Load carriers association is a non profit trucking association founded in 1938.
850 Members
Frequency: Weekly
Founded in 1938

23182 **Transportation Intermediaries Update**
Transportation Intermediaries Association
1625 Prince St
Suite 200
Alexandria, VA 22314-2883

703-299-5700
Fax: 703-836-0123
E-Mail: voltmann@tianet.org
Home Page: www.tianet.org

Robert Voltmann, President

Education and policy organization for North American transportation intermediaries. TIA is the only national association representing the interests of all third party transportation service providers. The members of TIA include logistics management firms, property brokers, perishable commodities brokers, freight forwarders, intermodal marketers, ocean and air forwarders, and NVOCC's.
700 Pages
Frequency: Monthly

23183 **Truck Equipment News**
National Truck Equipment Association
37400 Hills Tech Dr
Farmington Hill, MI 48331-3414

248-489-7090
800-441-6832
Fax: 248-489-8590
E-Mail: info@ntea.com
Home Page: www.ntea.com

James Carney, Executive Director
Dennis Jones, First Vice President

Covers NTEA and member/industry activities, business management issues, technical topics, excise tax applications, sales/marketing management topics, legislative and regulatory news, monthly new truck retail sales figures, NTEA/industry events calendar, and other current topics of interest to industry members.
Cost: $72.00
150 Pages
Frequency: Monthly
Circulation: 1600
Founded in 1964

23184 **Trucker Publications**
Trucker Publications
PO Box 3413
Little Rock, AR 72203-3413

501-666-0500
Fax: 501-666-0700
Home Page: www.thetrucker.com

Ray Wittenberg, Publisher

Up to date, comprehensive coverage of news affecting both drivers and management, including regulatory issues, road conditions, fuel, and current trends in technology.
Cost: $21.50
Frequency: BiWeekly
Circulation: 27,500

23185 **Truckload Carriers Report**
Truckload Carriers Association
555 E Braddock Road
Suite CS-4
Alexandria, VA 22314-2182

703-838-1950
Fax: 703-836-6610

E-Mail: tca@truckload.org
Home Page: www.truckload.org

Chris Burruss, President
Deborah Sparks, VP
Kevin Burch, Chairman

A newsletter for truckload carriers executives. Free to association members.
Frequency: Weekly
Founded in 1938

Magazines & Journals

23186 **American Shipper**
Howard Publications
300 W Adams Street Suite 600
PO Box 4728
Jacksonville, FL 32201-4728

904-355-2601
800-874-6422
Fax: 904-791-8836
Home Page: www.americanshipper.com

Hayes H Howard, Publisher
Gary G. Burrows, Managing Editor

Provides those involved in domestic and global supply chain management with news and information of a strategic nature, useful in the formation of logistics polices and partnerships.
Cost: $30.00
100 Pages
Frequency: Monthly
Circulation: 13487
ISSN: 1074-8350
Founded in 1951
Printed in 4 colors on glossy stock

23187 **Commercial Carrier Journal**
Reed Business Information
2000 Clearwater Dr
Oak Brook, IL 60523-8809

630-574-0825
Fax: 630-288-8781
Home Page: www.reedbusiness.com

Jeff Greisch, President

For executives who manage, operate and maintain United States utility and specialty fleets.
Cost: $45.00
Frequency: Monthly

23188 **Diesel Equipment Superintendent**
Business Journals
50 Day Street
Norwalk, CT 06854-3100

203-853-6015
Fax: 203-852-8175

James Jones, Editor

Maintenance management in areas of selection, of heavy duty trucks and trailers.
Cost: $25.00
100 Pages
Frequency: Monthly
Founded in 1923

23189 **Fastline Productions**
PO Box 248
Buckner, KY 40010-248

502-222-0146
800-626-6409
Fax: 502-222-0615
E-Mail: helpdesk@fastline.com
Home Page: www.fastlinepub.com

William Howard, Editor
Crysten Minzenberger, Marketing Director
Gail Olszewski, Owner

Nationwide and regional picture buying guides for the trucking industry.
Circulation: 4900
Founded in 1978

23190 **Fleet Owner Magazine**
Primedia
11 River Bend Drive South
PO Box 4949
Stamford, CT 06907-949

203-358-9900
Fax: 203-358-5811
E-Mail: frcs@pbsub.com
Home Page: www.fleetowner.com

Thomas Duncan, Vice President
Jim Mele, Editor-in-Chief
David Cullen, Executive Editor

Monthly business magazine serving executives and managers in commercial trucking fleets.
Cost: $40.00
Frequency: Monthly
Founded in 1928

23191 **Journal of HazMat Transportation**
Packaging Research International
404 Price St
West Chester, PA 19382-3531

610-436-8292
877-429-7447
Fax: 610-436-9422
Home Page: www.hazmatship.com

Vincent A Vitollo, Owner

A professionally prepared technical reporting system, focused exlusively on explaining changes to the hazardous materials transportation regulations. Thoroughly covers and provides technical reviews of the US 49CFR, International Civil Aviation Organization Technical Instructions, the International Maritime Dangerous Goods Code, and the European Road and Rail Regulations.
Cost: $209.00
Circulation: 1000
Founded in 1990
Printed in 4 colors on matte stock

23192 **Keep on Truckin' News**
Mid-West Truckers Association
2727 N Dirksen Pkwy
Springfield, IL 62702-1490

217-525-0310
Fax: 217-525-0342
E-Mail: info@mid-westtruckers.com
Home Page: www.keepontruckinptc.info

Don Schaefer, President

For members of Mid-West Association.
64 Pages
Frequency: Monthly
Circulation: 4000
Founded in 1964
Printed in 4 colors on glossy stock

23193 **Land Line Magazine**
1 NW OOIDA Drive
Grain Valley, MO 64029-712

816-229-5791
800-444-5791
Fax: 816-443-2227
E-Mail: info@landlinemag.com
Home Page: www.landlinemag.com

Todd Spencer, Editor-in-Chief
Sandi Soendker, Publisher
Jim Johnson, CEO/President
Mike Schermoly, Marketing
Pam Perry, Circulation Manager

Edited for the owner/operator and independent trucker and small fleet operator who drive heavy duty trucks.
13 Pages
Frequency: Monthly
Circulation: 200000+
Founded in 1973
Printed in 4 colors on glossy stock

23194 **Lifting & Transportation International**
2895 Chad Drive
Eugene, Or 97408

800-493-2295
Fax: 541-342-3307
E-Mail: adwyer@douglaspublications.com
Home Page: www.liftandtransport.com/

Eugene Brymer, Publisher
Andrew Dwyer, Editor
Jason Pierce, VP

Covers trucking overdimensional loads, heavy crane, and ridging work.
Cost: $110.00
Founded in 1958

23195 **Light & Medium Truck**
TT Publishing
2200 Mill Road
Alexandria, VA 22314-4654

703-838-1770
Fax: 703-548-3662
E-Mail: bharmon@trucking.org
Home Page: www.lmtruck.com

Bruce Harmon, Managing Editor
Debra Devine, Production Coordinator
Stanford Erickson, Associate Publisher
Scott Smith, Circulation Manager
Paul Rosenthal, Marketing Manager

Provides information for day to day management of a company using light to medium duty trucks, such as equipment safety, alternative fuels, maintenance and government regulations.
Frequency: Monthly
Circulation: 50509
Founded in 1945

23196 **Mid-West Truck Trader**
Heartland Communications
15400 Knoll #500
Dallas, TX 75248

800-247-2000
Fax: 515-574-2213

Bruce Foval, Editor

Trucking industry news and views.
Cost: $59.00
56 Pages
Frequency: Monthly
Founded in 1976

23197 **Milk & Liquid Food Transporter**
Brady Company
N80w12878 Fond Du Lac Ave
Menomonee Falls, WI 53051-4410
262-255-0100
Fax: 262-255-3388
Home Page: www.bradymg.com

Kathy Wall, President

Information for owners, operators and managers of companies that haul milk or other liquid foods in sanitary or food grade tankers. Publication covers maintenance, association news, state of the industry, business management, and activities of independent haulers.
Cost: $12.00
Frequency: Monthly
Circulation: 4,100

23198 **Modern Bulk Transporter**
Tunnell Publications
PO Box 66010
Houston, TX 77266

713-523-8124
Fax: 713-523-8384

Charles Wilson, Editor
Robin Anderson, Advertising Director

Serves the truck industry that transports petroleum and petroleum products. Accepts adver-

tising.
Cost: $25.00
Frequency: Monthly

23199 NATSO Truckers News
Newport Communications
PO Box W
Newport Beach, CA 92658-8910

949-261-1636
Fax: 949-261-2904
Home Page: www.heavytruck.com

W Dewey Clower, Publisher

Provides industry news, legislation affecting drivers, product developments, and on road service.
Cost: $20.00
Frequency: Monthly
Circulation: 182,716

23200 Newport's Road Star
Newport Communications
38 Executive Park
Suite 300
Irvine, CA 92614-6755

949-261-1636
800-233-1911
Fax: 949-261-2904
E-Mail: ssturgess@truckinginfo.com
Home Page: www.truckinginfo.com

Doug Condra, President
Faye Solem, Circulation Manager
Steve Sturgess, Editor

Monthly magazine for professional long-distance tractor-trailer drivers, who either own their own trucks or drive for trucking companies.
Frequency: Monthly
Circulation: 153000
Founded in 1898

23201 Oklahoma Motor Carrier
Okalhoma Trucking Association
7201 N Classen Boulevard
Suite 106
Oklahoma City, OK 73116-620

405-843-9488
800-368-9576
Fax: 405-843-7310
Home Page: www.oktrucking.org

Dan Case, Executive Director
Craig Schneithorst, Chairman

Official publication of Associated Motor Carriers of Oklahoma, the state trade association for the trucking industry.
30 Pages
Frequency: Quarterly
Circulation: 3000
Founded in 1932
Printed in 4 colors

23202 Over the Road
Ramp Publishing Group
PO Box 549
Roswell, GA 30077

770-587-0311
Fax: 770-642-8874
Home Page: www.ramppub.com

Marvin Shefsky, Publisher

Information for professional truck drivers, owners, operators, and fleet drivers on current events, industry news, driver profiles, and employment opportunities.
Cost: $30.00
Frequency: Monthly
Circulation: 116624

23203 Overdrive Magazine
Randall Publishing Company
PO Box 2155
Tuscaloosa, AL 35403-2155

205-758-2585
800-633-5953
Fax: 205-758-2593
E-Mail: editors@overdriveonline.com
Home Page: www.randallpub.com

Wayne Randall, President
Brad Holthaus, Publisher
Linda Longton, Editor

For the owner/operator and small fleet operator.
Cost: $30.00
Frequency: Monthly
Circulation: 104753
Founded in 1934
Printed in 4 colors on glossy stock

23204 Owner Operator
Reed Business Information
2000 Clearwater Dr
Oak Brook, IL 60523-8809

630-574-0825
Fax: 630-288-8781
Home Page: www.reedbusiness.com

Jeff Greisch, President

For independent truckers and small fleet owners.
Frequency: Monthly

23205 Pro Trucker
Ramp Publishing Group
PO Box 549
Roswell, GA 30077-549

770-587-0311
800-878-0311
Fax: 770-642-8874
Home Page: www.protruckeronline.com

Greg McClendon, Sales Manager
Marvin Shefsky, Publisher

Professional truck drivers, owners, operators, and fleet drivers, information on interviews, industry news, employment information, distribution locations and leasing options for the professional drivers.
Frequency: Monthly
Circulation: 116000
Founded in 1981

23206 Refrigerated Transporter
Tunnell Publications
PO Box 66010
Suite 200
Houston, TX 77266

713-523-8124
Fax: 713-523-8384
E-Mail: ray.anderson@penton.com
Home Page: www.refrigeratedtrans.com

Raymond Anderson, Publisher
Gary Macklin, Editor-in-Chief
Jay Miller, Editorial
Mary Singlletary, Directories

Serves transportation and distribution companies concerned with the handling of temperature controlled commodities. Accepts advertising. Free to qualified subscribers.
Cost: $45.00
103 Pages
Frequency: Monthly
Printed in 4 colors on glossy stock

23207 Road King
Hammock Publishing
28 White Bridge Road
Suite 209
Nashville, TN 37205

615-385-9745
Fax: 615-386-9349
Home Page: www.roadking.com

Rex Hammock, President

Focuses on trucking lifestyles, achievements and interests. Offers articles on equipment and driver success.
Cost: $15.00
Frequency: BiMonthly
Circulation: 222,590

23208 Successful Dealer
Kona Communications
707 Lake Cook Road
Deerfield, IL 60015

847-498-3180
800-767-5662
Fax: 847-498-3197
E-Mail: truckbooks@konacommunications.com
Home Page: www.successfuldealer.com

Denise Rondini, Editorial Director
James D Moss, Publisher
James D Moss, President
Tom Cory, Circulation Manager
John S Dickson, National Sales Manager

Edited for the dealer organization covering dealerships, selling and servicing medium to heavy-duty trucks, trailers and construction equipment. Accepts advertising.
Cost: $50.00
52 Pages
Frequency: bi-monthly
Circulation: 23000
ISSN: 0161-6080
Founded in 1918
Printed in g colors on 4 stock

23209 Trailer/Body Builders
Tunnell Publications
PO Box 66010
Houston, TX 77266

713-523-8124
800-880-0368
Fax: 713-523-8384
E-Mail: ray.anderson@penton.com
Home Page: www.trailer-bodybuilders.com

Ray Anderson, Publisher
Bruce Sauer, Editor
Rick Weber, Associate Editor

Serves the truck trailer and truck body manufacturing industry. Accepts advertising.
Cost: $25.00
Frequency: Monthly
Circulation: 15500
Founded in 1960

23210 Transport Topics
Express Carriers Association
950 N. Glebe Road
Suite 210
Arlington, VA 22203

703-838-1770
866-322-7447
Fax: 703-838-7916
E-Mail: habramso@ttnews.com
Home Page: www.ttnews.com

Bruce harmon, Managing Editor
Neil Abt, News Editor
Nancy Baily, Copy Editor

Trucking industry news, features and analysis.

23211 Transportation Equipment News
Vulcan Publications
PO Box 55886
Birmingham, AL 35255

205-328-6198
Fax: 205-987-2882
Home Page: www.vulcanpub.com

Ian Greenspan, Publisher

Extensive coverage of government regulations, recruiting and training issues as well as buying and leasing, maintenance and industry trade shows.

23212 **Truck Accessory News**
Bobit Publishing
3520 Challenger St
Torrance, CA 90503-1640

310-533-2400
Fax: 310-533-2500
Home Page: www.bobit.com

Edward J Bobit, CEO
Travis Weeks, Publisher
Jerry Martin, Circulation Manager

Provides information on product and merchandise trends, covers industry news on retail activities, and interviews top executives and buyers.
Cost: $37.00
Frequency: Monthly
Circulation: 10000
Founded in 1961

23213 **Trucker's Connection**
Megan Cullingford
5960 Crooked Creek Road
Suite 15
Norcross, GA 30092

770-416-0927
Fax: 770 416-1734
Home Page: www.truckersconnection.com

David Guthrie, Advertising Sales
Dan Barnhill, Editor
Megan Cullingford, General Manager
Reid Ramsay, Production Manager
Jamie Adcock, Advertising Sales

Published for the use of long haul, over-the-road truck drivers, owner operators, small trucking company fleet owners, safety and recruiting of personnel for trucking companies in the US and Canada.
Frequency: Monthly
Circulation: 165000
Founded in 1986
Printed in 4 colors on glossy stock

23214 **Truckin'**
McMullen Argus Publishing
2400 E Katella Avenue
11th Floor
Anaheim, CA 92806-6832

714-939-2559
Fax: 714-978-6390
E-Mail: info@primedia.com
Home Page: www.primediaautomotive.com

Steve Parr, CEO
Susan Brocett, Marketing Manager
Brad Christopher, Publisher
Steve Warner, Editor
Jerome Dziechiasz, Sales Manager

Provides information on testing new trucks, reviewing accessories and trucking' activities.
Cost: $24.95
Frequency: Monthly
Circulation: 180000

23215 **Trucking Technology**
167 Cherry Street
Suite 430
Milford, CT 06460-3466

203-882-9485

23216 **World Wide Shipping (WWS)**
World Wide Shipping Guide
16302 Byrnwyck Ln
Odessa, FL 33556-2807

813-920-4788
Fax: 813-920-8268
E-Mail: info@wwship.com
Home Page: www.wwship.com

Lee Di Paci, Publisher
Barbara Edwards, Marketing Manager
Bob Susor, Marketing Manager

Dedicated to the interests of North American exporters, importers, distributors, freight forwarders, NVOCC's and customs brokers requiring freight tranportation services and equipment.
Cost: $32.00
32 Pages
Frequency: Fortnightly
Circulation: 9000
ISSN: 1060-7900
Founded in 1919
Printed in 4 colors on glossy stock

Trade Shows

23217 **American Truck Dealers Convention and Equipment Exposition**
National Automobile Dealers Association
8400 Westpark Drive
Mc Lean, VA 22102-3522

703-217-7000
Fax: 703-821-7075
Home Page: www.nada.org

Gary Heimes

Annual show of 100 manufacturers, suppliers and distributors of products and services designed to control dealership expenses, help merchandising or improve profitability.
2,500 Attendees
Founded in 1963

23218 **American Trucking Association Management Conference and Exhibition**
American Trucking Association
2200 Mill Road
Alexandria, VA 22314-4677

703-838-1700
800-282-5463
Fax: 703-838-5720
E-Mail: trucking@cais.com
Home Page: www.cais.com/ata

Bill Graves, President

Annual show of 168 exhibitors of equipment, supplies and services related to the trucking industry.
1,500 Attendees
Frequency: Annual
Founded in 1984

23219 **ECA Shipper: Carrier Marketplace**
Express Carriers Association
9532 Liberia Avenue
Manassas, VA 20110

703-361-1058
866-322-7447
Fax: 703-361-5274
E-Mail: eca@expresscarriers.com
Home Page: www.expresscarriers.com

Carrie Ehlers, President
Stuart Hyden, First Vice President

Premier business to business event featuring one on one interviews between shippers, carriers and vendors of products/services to the transportation industry.
300+ Attendees
Frequency: April
Founded in 1997

23220 **International Truck and Bus Expo**
Society of Automotive Engineers
400 Commonwealth Drive
Warrendale, PA 15096-0001

724-772-8548
Fax: 724-776-0790
Home Page: www.sae.org

23221 **Light Truck Accessory Expo**
Truck Cap and Accessory Association
6564 Loisdale Court
Suite 430
Springfield, VA 22150-1812

703-822-0707
800-283-8242
Fax: 703-922-7806

Kendra Moore, Director Meetings/Marketing

Annual show of 150 manufacturers of truck caps and light truck accessories.
2,500 Attendees

23222 **Midwest Truck Show**
Mid-West Truckers Association
2727 N Dirksen Parkway
Springfield, IL 62702

217-525-0310
Fax: 217-525-0342
E-Mail: info@mid-westtruckers.com
Home Page: www.mid-westtruckers.com

Don Schaefer, Executive VP

Annual show and exhibits of trucks, trailers, financing information, computers, insurance information and related equipment, supplies and services. Containing 200 booths and 150 exhibitors.
6,000 Attendees
Frequency: February

23223 **TCA Annual Convention**
Truckload Carriers Association
555 E Braddock Road
Suite CS-4
Alexandria, VA 22314-2182

703-838-1960
Fax: 703-836-6610
E-Mail: tca@truckload.org
Home Page: www.truckload.org
Social Media: Facebook, Twitter, TCA News

Chris Burruss, President
William Giroux, EVP Conventions/Marketing
Casey Bloyer, Senior Manager Conventions/Mktg
Mackenzie Tolliver, Coordinator Conventions/Marketing

Truckload carriers is a trade association that represents the truckload segment of the motor carrier industry, affiliated with the american trucking association.
900 Members
1800 Attendees
Frequency: Annual/March
Founded in 1938

23224 **TCA Newsletter Annual Convention**
Truckload Carriers Association
555 E Braddock Road
Suite CS-4
Alexandria, VA 22314-2182

703-838-1960
Fax: 703-836-6610
E-Mail: tca@truckload.org
Home Page: www.truckload.org
Social Media: Twitter, TCA News

Chris Burruss, President
Deborah Sparks, VP
Tom Kretsinger, Chairman

Load carriers association is a non profit trucking association founded in 1938.
850 Members
1200 Attendees
Frequency: Weekly
Founded in 1938

23225 **Truck Show Las Vegas**
Independent Trade Show Management

1155 Chess Drive
Suite 102
Foster City, CA 94404-1117

650-349-4876
800-227-5992
Fax: 650-349-5169
E-Mail: rsherrard@truckshow.com
Home Page: www.truckshow.com

Sue K Fena, Sr. Show Coordinator
Roger Sherrard, President

The premier commercial truck and equipment show in the USA. Containing 2,500 booths and 350 exhibits, also offers seminars and workshops on current topics in the trucking industry.
20M Attendees
Frequency: June
Founded in 1961
Mailing list available for rent

23226 Truckerfest
Newport Communications
38 Executive Park
Suite 300
Irvine, CA 92614-6755

949-261-1636
800-233-1911
Fax: 949-261-2904
Home Page: www.truckerfest.com

Bud Farquhar, Show Manager
BJ Iverson, Events Coordinator

Trucker appreciation event at Alamo Travel Plaza, Reno, NV. Truck Parade, trucker games, music, free dinners, truck beauty contest, and fireworks. Containing 75 booths and 60 exhibits.
10M Attendees
Frequency: August

23227 Trucking Show Mid-America
1404 Browns Lane
Suite E
Louisville, KY 40207

Home Page: www.truckingshow.com

Timothy Young, Show Manager

Four hundred and fifty booths displaying the latest in trucking.
35M Attendees
Frequency: March

23228 Work Truck Show
National Truck Equipment Association
37400 Hills Tech Drive
Farmington Hills, MI 48331-3414

248-489-7090
800-441-6832
Fax: 248-489-8590
E-Mail: info@ntea.com
Home Page: www.ntea.com

Tom Rawson, President
Dennis Jones, First Vice President

Annual business to business event designed to bring together distributors, upfitters, manufacturers, buyers and users of work trucks in all industries including delivery, government, construction and landscaping.
7,000 Attendees
Frequency: March

Directories & Databases

23229 Fleet Owner-Specs and Buyers' Directory Issue
Primedia
1166 Avenue of the Americas/10th Fl
Shawnee Mission, NY 10036

212-204-4200
Fax: 913-514-6895
Home Page: www.penton.com

Eric Jacobson, Senior VP
Tom Moore, Editor
Chris Meyer, Director

Lists of manufacturers of equipment and materials used in the operation, management and maintenance of truck and bus fleets.
Cost: $5.00
Frequency: Annual October
Circulation: 100,250

23230 Grey House Transportation Security Directory
Grey House Publishing
4919 Route 22
PO Box 56
Amenia, NY 12501

518-789-8700
800-562-2139
Fax: 845-373-6390
E-Mail: books@greyhouse.com
Home Page: www.greyhouse.com
Social Media: Facebook, Twitter

Leslie Mackenzie, Publisher
Richard Gottlieb, Editor

Provides information on everything from Regulatory Authorities to Security Equipment, this top-flight directory brings together the relevant information necessary for creating and maintaining a security plan for a wide range of transportation facilities.
Cost: $195.00
800 Pages
ISBN: 1-592370-75-6
Founded in 1981

23231 Heavy Duty Representatives Profile Directory
Heavy Duty Representatives Association
160 Symphony Way
Elgin, IL 60120

847-760-0067
800-763-5717
Fax: 330-722-5638
E-Mail: trucksvc@aol.com
Home Page: hdra.org

Larry Rosenthal, President
Walt Sirman, Vice President
John Stojack, Secretary

About 60 independent sales agencies which sell heavy-duty components to the trucking and aftermarket industries.
Frequency: Annual January

23232 Heavy Duty Trucking: CFS Buyers Guide
Newport Communications Div.-HIC Corporation
38 Executive Park
Suite 300
Irvine, CA 92614-6755

949-261-1636
Fax: 949-261-2904

Doug Condra, Publisher

Five hundred Council of Fleet Specialists member manufacturers and wholesalers specializing in heavy-duty truck parts and repairs.
Cost: $45.00
Frequency: Annual January
Circulation: 98,502

23233 NTEA Membership Roster & Product Directory
National Truck Equipment Association
37400 Hills Tech Dr
Farmington Hill, MI 48331-3414

248-489-7090
800-441-6832
Fax: 248-489-8590
E-Mail: info@ntea.com
Home Page: www.ntea.com

James Carney, Executive Director
Dennis Jones, First Vice President

Over 1,600 manufacturers and distributors of commercial trucks, bodies, trailers and related equipment. Information includes: product info, membership category, affiliate membership, join date, address, phone and fax numbers, e-mail address, Web site address.
Cost: $50.00
Frequency: Annual
Founded in 1964

23234 National Private Truck Council: Official Membership Directory
2200 Mill Road
Suite 350
Alexandria, VA 22314

703-683-1300
Fax: 703-683-1217
Home Page: www.nptc.org

Gary Petty, President/CEO
Richard LaRoche, Director Membership

The only organization that represents the interests and concerns of private fleets — companies that use in-house or dedicated truck fleets to support distribution of their products. The directory includes members listed by: company, individual and industry. Both private fleet and supplier members are listed.
Cost: $145.00
100 Pages
Frequency: Annual
Printed in 4 colors on glossy stock

23235 Truck Trailer Manufacturers Association: Membership Directory
Truck Trailer Manufacturers Association
8506 Wellington Road
Suite 101
Alexandria, VA 20109

703-549-3010
Fax: 703-549-3014
E-Mail: ttma@erols.com
Home Page: www.ttmanet.org

Richard Bowling, President

About 100 truck and tank trailer manufacturers and 120 suppliers to the industry.
Cost: $135.00
Frequency: Annual

23236 Trucksource: Sources of Trucking Industry Information
Express Carriers Association
9532 Liberia Avenue
Suite 130
Manassas, VA 20110

703-361-1058
866-322-7447
Fax: 703-361-5274
E-Mail: eca@expresscarriers.org
Home Page: www.expresscarriers.com

Carrie Ehlers, President
Stuart Hyden, First Vice President

Features over 1,000 sources of information on the trucking industry, including industry reports, videos, periodicals and databases about the motor carrier industry.

23237 Vocational Equipment Directory for GMC Truck Dealers
Verbiest Publishing Company
1155 Henrietta Street
Birmingham, MI 48009-1906

Directory of services and supplies to the industry.
Cost: $25.00
200 Pages
Frequency: Annual
Circulation: 6,000

Industry Web Sites

23238 **http://gold.greyhouse.com**
G.O.L.D Grey House OnLine Databases
Grey House Publishing's online database platform, GOLD, offers Quick Search, Keyword Search and Expert Search for most business sectors including trucking and transportation markets. The GOLD platform makes finding the information you need quick and easy - whether you're a novice searcher or an experienced database user. All of Grey House's directory products are available for subscription on the GOLD platform.

23239 **www.expresscarriers.com**
National Tank Truck Carriers
Conducts research, promotes federal standards of construction, design, use and operation of tank trucks.

23240 **www.greyhouse.com**
Grey House Publishing
Authoritative reference directories for most business sectors including trucking and transportation markets. Users can search the online databases with varied search criteria allowing for custom searches by product category, geographic area, sales volume, keyword, subject and more. Full Grey House catalog and online ordering also available.

23241 **www.natso.com**
NATSO
NATSO is the professional association of America's $42 billion travel plaza and truckstop industry. NATSO represents the industry on legislative and regulatory matters; serves as the official source of information on the diverse travel plaza and truckstop industry; provides education to its members; conducts an annual convention and trade show; and supports efforts to generally improve the business climate in which its members operate.

23242 **www.nptc.org**
National Private Truck Council
Distributors, shippers, processors, jobbers and manufacturers who transport their own goods and are owners of their own truck fleets.

23243 **www.ntea.com**
National Truck Equipment Association
For small to mid-sized companies that manufacture, distribute, install, sell and repair commercial trucks, truck bodies, truck equipment, trailers and accessories.

23244 **www.ooida.com**
Owner Operator Independent Drivers Association
For owner-operators, professional drivers and small fleet owners.

23245 **www.ptdi.org**
Professional Truck Driver Institute
Advocate of optimum standards and professionalism for entry-level truck driver training.

23246 **www.scranet.org**
Specialized Carriers and Rigging Association
Members are carriers, crane and rigging operators and millwrights engaged in the transport of heavy goods.

23247 **www.specialtyfoods.org**
National Food Distributors Association
An organization comprised of independent store-to-door service distributors and suppliers of specialty food items.

23248 **www.truckline.com**
American Trucking Association

23249 **www.ttmanet.org**
Truck Trailer Manufacturers Association
A national organization of truck and tank trailer manufacturers and 120 suppliers to the industry.

Associations

23250 **Action Committee for Rural Electrification**
11640 73rd Avenue North
Maple Grove, MN 55369

763-424-1020
Fax: 763-424-5820
Home Page: www.mrea.org

Mark Glaess, General Manager
Melissa Stachovich, Controller
Aleia Yue, Membership Assistant

Political action committee that advocates support for rural electrification.
18M Members
Founded in 1967

23251 **Air Conditioning Contractors of America**
2800 S Shirlington Rd
Ste 300
Arlington, VA 22206

703-575-4477
E-Mail: paul.stalknecht@acca.org
Home Page: www.acca.org
Social Media: Facebook, Twitter, LinkedIn, YouTube, Google+

David Kyle, Chairman
Phil London, Vice Chairman
Steve Lauten, Treasurer
Paul Stalknecht, President/ Chief Executive Officer
Kevin Holland, Senior Vice President

An association of HVAC contractors.
Founded in 1968

23252 **Air and Waste Management Association**
One Gateway Center, 3rd Floor
420 Fort Duquesne Blvd
Pittsburgh, PA 15222-1435

412-232-3444
800-270-3444
Fax: 412-232-3450
E-Mail: info@awma.org
Home Page: www.awma.org
Social Media: Facebook, Twitter, LinkedIn

Michaelÿ Milleryÿ, President
Diane Freemanÿ, Vice President
Jim Powell, Executive Director
Nancy Fowler, Treasure

Association for air and waste management.
Founded in 1907

23253 **Alliance to Save Energy**
1850 M Street, NW
Suite 610
Washington, DC 20036

202-857-0666
Home Page: www.ase.org
Social Media: Facebook, Twitter, LinkedIn, YouTube, Google+

Mark Warner, Chairman
Jorge Carrasco, Co-Chairman
Iain Campbell, Vice-President
Carolyn Green, Treasurer
Kateri Callahan, President

Promotes energy efficiency to acheive a healthier economy and a cleaner environment.
Founded in 1977

23254 **American Coal Ash Association**
38800 Country Club Drive
Farmington Hills, MI 48331

720-870-7897
Fax: 720-870-7889
E-Mail: info@acaa-usa.org
Home Page: www.acaa-usa.org

Thomas Adams, Executive Director

A nonprofit trade association devoted to recycling the materials created from burning coal.
Founded in 1968

23255 **American Gas Association**
400 North Capitol Street, NW
Washington, DC 20001

202-824-7000
Home Page: www.aga.org
Social Media: Facebook, Twitter, LinkedIn, You Tube

Gregg S. Kantor, Chairman
Dave McCurdy, President/ CEO
Terry D. McCallister, First Vice Chairman

The American Gas Association advocates the interests of its members and their customers, and provides information and services promoting efficient demand and supply growth and operational excellence in the safe, reliable and efficient delivery of natural gas.
Founded in 1918

23256 **American National Standards Institute**
1899 L Street, NW
11th Floor
Washington, DC 20036

202-293-8020
Fax: 202-293-9287
Home Page: www.ansi.org
Social Media: Facebook, LinkedIn

Maryÿ Saunders, Interim Chairman
Patricia Griffin, Vice President/ General Counsel

A private nonprofit organization that oversees the development of coluntary consesus standards for products.
Founded in 1918

23257 **American Nuclear Society**
555 North Kensington Avenue
La Grange Park, IL 60526

708-352-6611
800-323-3044
Fax: 708-352-0499
Home Page: www.ans.org
Social Media: Facebook, Twitter, LinkedIn

Ned Wogman, Chairman
Robert C. Fine, Executive Director
Sam Glover, Vice Chairman
Lei Cao, Treasurer

For personnel involved in nuclear power operation and development. Coverage includes power, plant operations and maintenance, fuel cycle, legislation, international employment and more.
Founded in 1954

23258 **American Petroleum Institute**
1220 L Street, NW
Washington, DC 20005-4070

202-682-8000
E-Mail: certification@api.org
Home Page: www.api.org

Stephenÿ Chazenÿ, Chairman
Jack N. Gerard, President/ CEO
Kyle Isakower, Vice President
Robert Greco, Group Director

The largest US trade association for the oil and natrual gas industry.
Founded in 1919

23259 **American Public Energy Agency**
233 South 13th Street
Suite 1500
Lincoln, NE 68508

402-438-1177
800-476-3749
Fax: 402-742-0022
E-Mail: rmock@apea.org
Home Page: www.apea.org
Social Media: Facebook

Roger W. Mock, President/ CEO

Purpose is to provide energy acquisition and energy-related services for its members and other public agencies, and to assist such agencies in acquiring stable energy supplies, reducing energy costs through group purchases, and developing enhanced energy acquisition mechanisms.
40 Members
Founded in 1995

23260 **American Public Power Association**
2451 Crystal Drive
Suite 1000
Arlington, VA 22202-4804

202-467-2900
E-Mail: lnienhuis@publicpower.org
Home Page: www.publicpower.org
Social Media: Facebook, Twitter, LinkedIn, You Tube, Flickr

Paula DiFonzo, Chairman
Douglas Hunter, Vice Chairman
Paul McElroy, Treasurer

Service association for community-owned eletric utilities.
Founded in 1940

23261 **American Public Works Association**
2345 Grand Boulevard
Suite 700
Kansas City, MO 64108-2625

816-472-6100
Fax: 816-472-1610
Home Page: www.apwa.net
Social Media: Facebook, Twitter, LinkedIn, YouTube

Larry Stevens, President
Richard F. Stinson, Director
Peter King, Executive Director

International educational and professional association of public agencies, private sector companies, and individuals dedicated to providing high quality public works goods and services. AWA provides a forum in which public works professionals competency, increase the performance of their agencies and companies, and bring important public works-related topics to public attention in local, state, and federal areas. Mailing list for members only.
Founded in 1984

23262 **American Society of Appraisers**
11107 Sunset Hills Rd
Suite 310
Reston, VA 20190

703-478-2228
800-272-8258
Fax: 703-742-8471
E-Mail: asainfo@appraisers.org
Home Page: www.appraisers.org
Social Media: Twitter, LinkedIn, YouTube

Gary Smith, International President
Lindaÿ Trugman, International Vice President
Jim Hirt, Chief Executive Officer
Susan Golashovsky, International Treasurer

Multi-discipline organization for appraisers.
Founded in 1939

23263 American Solar Energy Society
2525 Arapahoe Ave
Ste E4-253
Boulder, Colorado 80302

303-443-3130
Fax: 303-443-3212
E-Mail: info@ases.org
Home Page: www.ases.org
Social Media: Facebook, Twitter, LinkedIn, digg

David Panich, Chairman
Francis de Winter, Vice-Chairman
Richard Behlmann, Secretary
Kris Brettingen, Treasurer
Alison Mason, Director of Marketing

Individuals and professionals working in the field of solar energy and conservation.
Founded in 1954

23264 American Water Works Association
6666 W. Quincy Ave.
Denver, CO 80235ÿ

303-794-7711
800-926-7337
Fax: 303-347-0804
Home Page: www.awwa.org
Social Media: Facebook, Twitter, LinkedIn, You Tube, RSS

Johnÿ Donahue, President
Michael Simpson, Vice-President
Stephenÿ Shoaf, Vice-President
Davidÿ LaFrance, Chief Executive Officer
Daveÿ Rager, Treasurer

An international nonprofit scientific and educational association to improve water quality and supply.
Founded in 1881

23265 American Wind Energy Association
1501 M Street NW
Suite 1000
Washington, DC 20005

202-383-2500
Fax: 202-383-2505
E-Mail: windmail@awea.org
Home Page: www.awea.org
Social Media: Facebook, Twitter, LinkedIn

Gabriel Alonso, Chair
Susan Reilly, Chair Elect
Jacob Susman, Treasurer
Steve Trenholm, Secretary

A national trade association representing wind power project developers, equipment suppliers, services providers, parts manufacturers, utilities, researchers, and others involved in the wind industry. Promotes wind energy as a clean source of electricity for consumers around the world.
2400 Members

23266 Association of Energy Engineers
3168 Mercer University Drive
Atlanta, GA 30341

770-447-5083
Home Page: www.aeecenter.org

Randy Haines, President
Asit Patel, Secretary
Paul Goodman, Treasurer
David Eberly, Vice President
Albert Thumann, Executive Director

Promotes energy certification, management and education.

23267 Association of Financial Guranty Insurers
139 Lancaster Street
Albany, NY 12210-1903

518-449-4698
E-Mail: tcasey@mackinco.com
Home Page: www.afgi.org

Insure and reinsure municipal bonds and asset-backed securities.

23268 Association of Home Appliance Manufacturer s
1111 19th Street NW
Suite 402
Washington, DC 20036

202-872-5955
E-Mail: info@ahem.org
Home Page: www.aham.org

Joseph McGuireÿ, President
Wayne Morris, Vice President

Represents the manufacturers of household appliances and products and services associated with them.
Founded in 1915

23269 Automatic Meter Reading Association
60 Revere Dr # 500
Suite 500
Northbrook, IL 60062-1591

847-480-9628
888-612-2672
Fax: 847-480-9282
E-Mail: amra@amra-intl.org
Home Page: www.amra-intl.org
Social Media: Facebook, Twitter, LinkedIn

John Waxman, Manager
John Waxman, Manager
Founded in 1986

23270 Buliding Owners and Managers Association
1101 15th St., NW
Suite 800
Washington, DC 20005

202- 40- 266
Fax: 202-326-6377
E-Mail: info@boma.org
Home Page: www.boma.org
Social Media: Facebook, Twitter, LinkedIn, YouTube, Pinterest

John Oliver, Chairman
Brian M. Harnetiaux, Vice-Chairman
Henry Chamberlain, President/ COO
Daniel W. Chancey, Treasurer

Association for building managers and owners.
Founded in 1907

23271 Edison Electric Institute
701 Pennsylvania Ave Nw
Washington, DC 20004-2608

202-508-5000
E-Mail: feedback@eei.org
Home Page: www.eei.org
Social Media: Facebook, Twitter, LinkedIn, Youtube

Michael W Yackira, Chairman
Theodore F Craver Jr., Vice Chair
Nick Akins, Vice Chair
Tom Fanning, Vice Chair
Thomas R Kuhn, President

Advocates public policy, expands market opportunities and provides strategic business information for the shareholder-owned electric utility industry.
180 Members
Founded in 1930

23272 Electric Power Research Institute
3420 Hillview Avenue
Palo Alto, CA 94304

650-855-2121
800-313-3774
Fax: 704-595-2871
E-Mail: askepri@epri.com
Home Page: www.epri.com
Social Media: Facebook, Twitter, LinkedIn

Steven R Specker, CEO
Eugene W Zeltmann, Chairman

Nonprofit energy research consortium for the benefit of utility members, their customers and society. Mission is to provide science and technology-based solutions of indispensable value to our global energy customers by managing a far-reaching program of scientific research, technology development and product implementation.
660 Members
Founded in 1973

23273 Electric Power Supply Association
1401 New York Ave Nw
NW Suite 1230
Washington, DC 20005-2110

202-628-8200
Fax: 202-628-8260
Home Page: www.epsa.org
Social Media: Facebook, Twitter, LinkedIn

John E Shelk, President/CEO
Nancy E Bagot, VP, Regulatory Policy
William S Burlew, VP, Govt. Affairs

23274 Energy Engineering
Association of Energy Engineers
4025 Pleasantdale Rd
Suite 420
Atlanta, GA 30340-4264

770-447-5083
Fax: 770-446-3969
E-Mail: info@aeecenter.org
Home Page: www.aeecenter.org
Social Media: Facebook, Twitter, LinkedIn

Albert Thumann, Executive Director
Ruth Whitlock, Executive Admin
Jennifer Vendola, Controller
Kate Feltgen, Executive Director's Assistant

Engineering solutions to cost efficiency problems and mechanical contractors who design, specify, install, maintain, and purchase non-residential heating, ventilating, air conditioning and refrigeration equipment and components.

23275 Energy Information Administration
National Energy Information Center
1000 Independence Av Sw
Suite 1E-238
Washington, DC 20585-0001

202-586-8800
Fax: 202-586-0727
E-Mail: infoctr@eia.doe.gov
Home Page: www.eia.gov

John H Weiner, Executive Director

Government agency that provides statistical energy data, information and referral assistance to the government and private sectors, academia and the public. NEIC also provides Government Printing Office information. Single copies of blank data collection forms, directories and EIA press releases are free of charge to all users. Ordering information on EIA machine readable files available through the National Technical Information Service and the Government Printing Office.
Founded in 1977

23276 Environment and Energy Study Institute
1112 16th Street, NW
Suite 300
Washington, DC 20036

202-628-1400
Fax: 202-204-5244
E-Mail: info@eesi.org
Home Page: www.eesi.org
Social Media: Facebook, Twitter, YouTube, Google+

Jared Blum, Chairman
John J. Sheehan, Vice Chairman
Shelley Fidler, Treasurer
Carol Werner, Executive Director
Amaury Laporte, Communications Director

Educating Congress on energy efficiency and renewable energy, advancing innovating policy solutions.
Founded in 1984

23277 Gas Research Institute
1700 S Mount Prospect Road
Des Plaines, IL 60018-1804

847-768-0500
Fax: 847-768-0501
E-Mail: businessdevelopmentinfo@gastechnology.or
Home Page: www.gri.org
Social Media: Facebook, Twitter

John Riordan, President/CEO

23278 Geothermal Energy Association
209 Pennsylvania Avenue SE
Washington, DC 20003

202-454-5261
Fax: 202-454-5265
Home Page: www.geo-energy.org
Social Media: Facebook, Twitter, LinkedIn, YouTube

Joe Greco, Chairman
Yoram Bronicki, President
Doug Glaspey, Vice President
Terryÿ Page, Secretary-Treasurer

A US trade organization that supports the expanded use of geothermal energy.
Founded in 1988

23279 Government Finance Officers Association
203 N. LaSalle Street
Suite 2700
Chicago, IL 60601-1210

312-977-9700
Fax: 312-977-4806
Home Page: www.gfoa.org
Social Media: Facebook, Twitter, LinkedIn, YouTube

Robert W. Eichem, President
Ade A. Ariwoola, Finance Director
Joe Costello, Senior Vice President
Lori A. Economy-Scholler, Chief Financial Officer

A professional association of finance officers.
Founded in 1906

23280 Independent Petroleum Association of America
1201 15th Street NW
Suite 300
Washington, DC 20005

202-857-4722
Fax: 202-857-4799
Home Page: www.ipaa.org
Social Media: Twitter, YouTube

Michael Watford, Chairman
Mark Miller, Vice Chairman
Barry Russell, President
Lee O. Fuller, Executive Vice President

Membership organization ensuring a strong, viable domestic oil and natural gas industry.
Founded in 1929

23281 Institute of Industrial Engineers
3577 Parkway Lane
Suite 200
Norcross, GA 30092

770-449-0460
800-494-0460
Fax: 770-441-3295
E-Mail: chapters@iienet.org
Home Page: www.iienet.org
Social Media: Facebook, Twitter, LinkedIn

Don Greene, CEO
Donna Calvert, COO
Monica Elliott, Director, Communications

Dedicated to supporting engineers involved in all industrial applications.

23282 Institute of Public Utilities
735 E Shaw Lane
Room W157
East Lansing, MI 48825

517-355-1876
Fax: 517-355-1854
E-Mail: ipu@msu.edu
Home Page: ipu.msu.edu/
Social Media: Facebook, Twitter

Janice A Beecher, Director
Ligita Nelson, Administrative Assistant

Research and training center at Michigan State University. Program focuses on regulation and management of energy, telecommunications and water companies.

23283 International District Energy Association (IDEA)
24 Lyman Street
Suite 230
Westborough, MA 01581

508-366-9339
Fax: 508-366-0019
E-Mail: idea@districtenergy.org
Home Page: www.districtenergy.org

Patricia Wilson, Chair
Ken Smith, Vice Chair
Bruce Ander, 2nd Vice Chair
James Adams, Secretary/Treasurer

IDEA fosters the success of its members as leaders in providing reliable, economical, and environmentally sound district energy services.
1780 Members
Founded in 1909

23284 International Gas Turbine Institute
6525 The Corners Pkwy
Ste. 115
Norcross, GA 30092

404-847-0072
Fax: 404-847-0151
E-Mail: igti@asme.org
Home Page: igti.asme.org

Madiha Kotb, President
Thomas G Loughlin, Executive Director
Founded in 1880

23285 International Ground Source Heat Pump Association
1201 S. Innovation Way Dr.
Suite 400'
Stillwater, OK 74074

405-744-5175
800-626-4747
Fax: 405-744-5283
E-Mail: igshpa@okstate.edu
Home Page: www.igshpa.okstate.edu
Social Media: Facebook, Twitter, YouTube, Google+

Jack Henrich, Chairman
Bergerson Caswell, President
Trey Austin, Vice President
Robert Ingersoll, Director
Jim Bose, Director Emeritus

A nonprofit organization to advance ground source heat pumps.
Founded in 1987

23286 International Right of Way Association
19210 South Vermont Avenue
Building A Suite 100
Gardena, CA 90248

310-538-0233
888-340-4792
Fax: 310-538-1471
Home Page: www.irwaonline.org
Social Media: Facebook, Twitter, LinkedIn

Mark Rieck, EVP
Fred Nasri, VP, CFO
Deidre C Alves, VP, Professional Development
Barbara Billitzer, VP, Publisher & Editor
Daniel Stekol, VP, Field Operations

Members are responsible for acquiring land over which to run utility lines, pipelines and roads.
9,444 Members
Founded in 1934

23287 Municipal Waste Management Association
127 Wyndham St. N
Suite 100
Guelph, ON N1H 4E9

519-823-1990
Fax: 519-823-0084
Home Page: www.municipalwaste.ca

Ben Bennett, Executive Director
Melissa Campbell, Membership Co-ordinator

Concerned with the processing of municipal solid waste for the production of recyclable materials, heat, and energy. Members are local government organizations; associate members are from the private sector.
200 Members
Founded in 1987

23288 National Association of Counties
25 Massachusetts Avenue, NW
Washington, DC 20001ÿ

202-393-6226
Home Page: www.naco.org
Social Media: Facebook, Twitter, LinkedIn, YouTube

Riki Hokama, President
Sallie Clark, First Vice President
Matthew D. Chase, Executive Director
Kathy Nothstine, Director

The only national organization that represents county governments of the US.
Founded in 1935

23289 National Association of Energy Service Companies
1615 M St Nw
Suite 800
Washington, DC 20036-3213

202-822-0950
Fax: 202-822-0955
E-Mail: info@naesco.org
Home Page: www.naesco.org

David Weiss, Chairman
Greg Collins, Vice Chair
Greg Hanlon, Secretary
Mike Kearney, Treasurer

23290 National Association of Regulatory Utility Commissioners (NARUC)
1101 Vermont Avenue, NW
Suite 200
Washington, DC 20005

202-898-2200
Fax: 202-898-2213
E-Mail: admin@naruc.org
Home Page: www.naruc.org
Social Media: Facebook

Lisa Edgarÿ, President
Travis Kavullaÿ, First Vice President
Robertÿ Powelson, Second Vice President
Charles Gray, Executive Director
Davidÿ Ziegner, Treasurer

A trade association representing the state public service commissioners who regulate utility services, such as electricity, gas, telecommunication, water, and transportation throughout the country.
Founded in 1889

23291 National Association of State Energy Officials
2107 Wilson Boulevard
Suite 850
Arlington, VA 22209

703 299-8800
Fax: 703-299-6208
E-Mail: energy@naseo.org
Home Page: www.naseo.org
Social Media: Facebook, Twitter, LinkedIn, Youtube, Flickr

Michelle New, Acting Executive Director

The only non-profit organization that represents the Governor-designated energy officials from each state and territory. The organization was established to improve the effectiveness and quality of state energy programs and policies, provide policy input and analysis of federal energy issues and be a repository of information on energy issues of concern to the states.
56 Members
Founded in 1986

23292 National Association of State Utility
8380 Colesville Road
Suite 101
Silver Spring, MD 20910

301-589-6313
Fax: 301-589-6380
E-Mail: nasuca@nasuca.org
Home Page: www.nasuca.org

Charles A Acquard, Executive Director
Nicole Haslup, Assistant to the Director

Members are state appointed individuals that represent rate-payers in their state.
44 Members
Founded in 1979

23293 National Electrical Contractors Associatio n
3 Bethesda Metro Center
Suite 1100
Bethesda, MD 20814

301-657-3110
Fax: 301-215-4500
Home Page: www.necanet.org
Social Media: Facebook, Twitter, LinkedIn, YouTube, Flickr

David Nielsen, Chairman
John M. Grau, President/ CEO
Daniel G. Walter, Vice President
Beth Ellis, Executive Director

A trade association representing electrical contractors.
Founded in 1901

23294 National Energy Marketers Association
3333 K Street NW
Suite 110
Washington, DC 20007

202-333-3288
Fax: 202-333-3266
Home Page: www.energymarketers.com
Social Media: Facebook, LinkedIn

A nonprofit trade association representing suppliers and consumers of natural energy.

23295 National Hydropower Association
25 Massachusetts Ave NW
Suite 450
Washington, DC 20001

202-682-1700
Fax: 202-682-9478
E-Mail: help@hydro.org
Home Page: www.hydro.org
Social Media: Facebook, Twitter

Linda Church Ciocci, Executive Director
Jeffrey A Leahey, Sr Manager Government Affairs
Diane C Lear, Membership Services

A nonprofit national association dedicated exclusively to advancing the interests of the hydropower industry. Seeks to secure hydropower's place as a climatc-friendly, renewable and reliable energy source that serves national environmental and energy policy objectives.
140 Members
Founded in 1983

23296 National Mining Association
101 Constitution Ave. NW
Suite 500
Washington, DC 20001

202-463-2600
Fax: 202-463-2666
Home Page: www.nma.org
Social Media: Facebook, Twitter, LinkedIn, YouTube

Harry Red Conger, Chairman
Kevin Crutchfield, Vice Chairman
Hal Quinn, President
Rich Nolan, Senior Vice President

Association for the mining industry in the US.

23297 National Rural Electric Cooperative Association
4301 Wilson Blvd
Suite 1
Arlington, VA 22203-1860

703-907-5500
Fax: 703-907-5526
E-Mail: charla.young@nreca.coop
Home Page: www.nreca.coop
Social Media: Facebook, Twitter, LinkedIn, Youtube

Jo Ann Emerson, CEO

Membership consists of cooperative systems, public power and public utility districts. Annual budget of approximately $94 million. Sponsors and supports the Action for Rural Electrification Political Action Committee.
1000 Members
Founded in 1942

23298 North American Association of Utility Distributors
P.O. Box 1930
Lady Lake, FL 32158

352-259-3999
Fax: 352-259-4014
E-Mail: linda.coker@naaud.org
Home Page: www.naaud.org

Ralphÿ Knobbe, President
Patrickÿ Novak, Vice President
Linda Coker, Executive Director
Jimÿ Reinhardt, Treasurer

A member of the National Association of Wholesler-Distributors.

23299 North American Electric Reliability
3353 Peachtree Road, N.E
Suite 600, North Tower
Atlanta, GA 30326

404-446-2560
Fax: 404-467-0474
E-Mail: webmaster@nerc.com
Home Page: www.nerc.com

Rick Sergel, CEO
David R Nevius, Senior VP
Donald M Benjamin, VP
David N Cook, VP/General Counsel
Ora L Klein, Manager/Administrative Services

Principal organization for coordinating and promoting North America's electrical supplies, demands and reliability issues.
11 Members
Founded in 1968

23300 Northwest Public Power Association
9817 Ne 54th St
Suite 200
Vancouver, WA 98662-6064

360-254-0109
Fax: 360-254-5731
E-Mail: nwppa@nwppa.org
Home Page: www.nwppa.org

Will Lutgen, Executive Director
Debbie Kuraspediani, Communication Director
Brenda Dunn, Associate Editor/Advertising
Glenda Waite, Graphic Artist

A international training organization for electric utilities in 10 western states and 4 western Canadian provinces.
Cost: $75.00
200 Members
Frequency: Monthly/Annual
Founded in 1940

23301 Power Transmission Distributors Association
230 W Monroe St
Suite 1410
Chicago, IL 60606-4802

312-516-2100
Fax: 312-516-2101
E-Mail: ptda@ptda.org
Home Page: www.ptda.org
Social Media: Twitter, LinkedIn

Chris Bursack, President
Kenneth A Miko, 1st VP
Harold Dunaway, 2nd VP
Keith Nowak, Treasurer

Members are industrial power transmission/motion control distributor firms representing locations throughout North America and several other countries and manufacturing firms.
Founded in 1960

23302 Public Utilities Risk Management Association
1900 West Park Drive
Suite 150
Westborough, MA 1581

508-599-3422
Fax: 508-599-3427
Home Page: www.purma.org
Social Media: Facebook

Wayne Doerpholz, President
Jeannine Millett, Vice President

Jeffrey Dobbins, Secretary
Gail Cohen, Treasurer
Paul Heanue, Director

Founded to provide risk management and insurance services to municipal utilities.
Founded in 1996

23303 The Association of Businesses Advocating Tariff Equality
151 S. Old Woodward Avenue
Suiteÿ200
Birmingham, MI 48009ÿ

Home Page: abate-energy.org

An organization for protecting the interests on industrial customers in energy and related matters.
Founded in 1981

23304 US Energy Information Administration
1000 Independence Ave Sw
Suite 1E-238
Washington, DC 20585-0001

202-586-8800
Fax: 202-586-0727
E-Mail: wmaster@eia.doe.gov
Home Page: www.eia.doe.gov
Social Media: Facebook, Twitter, Youtube, RSS

John H Weiner, Executive Director
Stephen F Durbin, Director Resource Management

23305 United States Energy Association
1300 Pennsylvania Avenue, NW
Suite 550
Washington, DC 20004

202-312-1230
Fax: 202-682-1682
E-Mail: reply@usea.org
Home Page: www.usea.in
Social Media: Facebook, Twitter, Google+

Vickey Bailey, Chairman
Barry Worthington, Executive Director
Will Polan, Senior Director
Brain Kearns, Chief Financial Officer
Sheila Slocum Hollis, Treasurer

The US Member Committee of the World Energy Council (WEC).

23306 Water Environment Federation
601 Wythe St
Alexandria, VA 22314-1994

703-684-2400
800-666-206
Fax: 703-684-2492
E-Mail: inquiry@wef.org
Home Page: www.wef.org
Social Media: Facebook, Twitter

Bill Bertera, Executive Director

Newsletters

23307 Clearing Up
Energy NewsData
PO Box 900928
Seattle, WA 98109-9228

206-285-4848
Fax: 206-281-8035
E-Mail: newsdata@newsdata.com
Home Page: www.newsdata.com

Steve Ernst, Managing Editor
Daniel Sackett, Circulation Director

Covers energy policy, resource development, public utility and energy litigation and energy marketing financing in the Pacific Northwestern United States and Western Canada.
Cost: $1199.00
14 Pages
Frequency: Weekly
ISSN: 0738-2332
Founded in 1982
Printed in one color on matte stock

23308 Electric Utility Week
McGraw Hill
PO Box 182604
Columbus, OH 43272

877-833-5524
800-752-8878
Fax: 614-759-3749
E-Mail: customer.service@mcgraw-hill.com
Home Page: www.mcgraw-hill.com

Dan Tanz, Chief Editor
Paul Carlsen, Senior Editor
Harold McGraw, III, President

Provides news of significant developments affecting the electric utility industry focusing on state and federal regulation, management and bulk power markets. Publishes charts of prices utilities pay for fuels.
Cost: $2165.00
Frequency: Weekly
Founded in 1909

23309 Energy Daily
King Publishing Group
1325 Massachusetts Ave Nw
Suite 310
Washington, DC 20005-4194

240-455-6801
800-926-5464
Fax: 240-628-5774
Home Page: www.energy-daily.com

F King, President
George Lobsenz, Editor

Information regarding energy use, supply and demand, power and heat generation, energy sources, conversion and storage, and energy and fuel conversion processes.
Cost: $1900.00
Frequency: Daily
Founded in 1974

23310 Energy Report
Pasha Publications
101 Second St
Suite 110
Petaluma, CA 94952

707-981-8999
800-424-2908
Fax: 707-981-8998
Home Page: www.theenergyreport.com

Harry Baisden, Group Publisher
Barry Cassell, Editor

Coverage includes comprehensive policies and issues affecting oil, natural gas, electricity, cogeneration, power markets, nuclear energy, taxation, global warming and energy business opportunities.
Cost: $872.00
20 Pages
Frequency: Weekly
Founded in 1978

23311 HydroWorld Alert
HCI Publications
410 Archibald St
Kansas City, MO 64111-3288

816-931-1311
Fax: 816-931-2015
Home Page: www.hcipub.com

Leslie Eden, President

Bi-weekly fax report on international hydroelectric project developments, business trends, and news relevant to organizations seeking business developments.
Cost: $635.00
Frequency: Weekly
Founded in 1970

23312 Hydrowire
HCI Publications
410 Archibald St
Kansas City, MO 64111-3288

816-931-1311
Fax: 816-931-2015
E-Mail: hci@aol.com
Home Page: www.hcipub.com

Leslie Eden, President

Concise, bi-weekly report on major news in the hydroelectric industry. Includes timely listings of licensing for hydroelectric power projects. Also covers news and business opportunities in the North American hydroelectric industry.
Cost: $425.00
Circulation: 500
Founded in 1994

23313 IE News: Utilities
Institute of Industrial Engineers
3577 Parkway Lane
Suite 200
Norcross, GA 30092

770-449-0460
800-494-0460
Fax: 770-441-3295
E-Mail: cs@iienet.org
Home Page: www.iienet.org
Social Media: Facebook, Twitter, LinkedIn

Elaine Fuerst, Marketing Director
Monica Erikson, Communicator
David Gatton, Managing Director

Association news.
4 Pages
Frequency: Quarterly
Circulation: 400
Founded in 1948

23314 Inside Energy
Platts, McGraw Hill Companies
1200 G St Nw
Suite 1000
Washington, DC 20005-3814

202-942-8788
800-752-8878
Fax: 202-383-2025
E-Mail: support@platts.com
Home Page: www.platts.com

Bill Loveless, Editor
Georgia Safos, Circulation Director

Covers the Department of Energy including energy, science/technology, and environmental management programs as well as energy programs at the Interior Department.
Cost: $1810.00
16 Pages
Frequency: Weekly
Founded in 1888

23315 NARUC Bulletin
Nat'l Assn of Regulatory Utility Commissioners
1101 Vermont Ave Nw
Suite 200
Washington, DC 20005-3553

202-898-2200
Fax: 202-898-2213
E-Mail: admin@naruc.org
Home Page: www.naruc.org

Charles Gray, Executive Director
Jaclyn Wintle, Publications Coordinator
Diane Munns, Publisher

A quasi-governmental nonprofit corporation composed of governmental agencies engaged in the regulation of public utilities and carriers.

Its primary mission is to serve the consumer interest by seeking to improve the quality and effectiveness of public regulation in America.
Cost: $110.00
16 Pages
Frequency: Weekly
Circulation: 2000
Founded in 1889
Mailing list available for rent
Printed in one color on matte stock

23316 National Association of Regulatory Utility Commissioners Newsletter
Natl Assoc of Regulatory Utility Commissioners
1101 Vermont Ave Nw
Suite 200
Washington, DC 20005-3553

202-898-2200
Fax: 202-898-2213
E-Mail: admin@naruc.org
Home Page: www.naruc.org

Charles Gray, Executive Director
Jaclyn Wintle, Publications Coordinator
Judi Sord, Circulation Manager

A national organization that offers valuable information on over 150 consultants and other professionals active in regulated water, sewer and related industries.
Cost: $125.00
Circulation: 1800
Founded in 1889

23317 Northeast Power Report
McGraw Hill
PO Box 182604
Columbus, OH 43272

877-833-5524
800-752-8878
Fax: 614-759-3749
E-Mail: customer.service@mcgraw-hill.com
Home Page: www.mcgraw-hill.com
Social Media: Facebook, Twitter, LinkedIn

Ron Dionne, Publisher
Rob Ingraham, Publisher
Harold McGraw, III, President
Steven H. Weiss, VP

Provides news of significant developments affecting the electric utility industry focusing on state and federal regulation, management and bulk power markets. Publishes charts of prices utilities pay for fuels.
Cost: $745.00
16 Pages
Frequency: BiWeekly
Founded in 1909

23318 Nuclear Waste News
Business Publishers
222 Sedwick Dr
Suite 101
Durham, NC 27713

800-223-8720
Fax: 800-508-2592
E-Mail: custserv@bpinews.com
Home Page: www.bpinews.com

Worldwide coverage of the nuclear waste management industry including waste generation, packaging, transport, processing and disposal.
Cost: $697.00
10 Pages
Frequency: 25 per year
Founded in 1963
Mailing list available for rent
Printed in 2 colors on matte stock

23319 NuclearFuel
McGraw Hill
PO Box 182605
Columbus, OH 43273

877-833-5525
800-752-8879
Fax: 614-759-3750
E-Mail: customer.service@mcgraw-hill.com
Home Page: www.mcgraw-hill.com

Michael Knapik, Editor
Rob Ingraham, Publisher
Harold McGraw, III, President
Steven H. Weiss, VP

Provides news of significant developments affecting the electric utility industry focusing on state and federal regulation, management and bulk power markets. Publishes charts of prices utilities pay for fuels.
14 Pages
Founded in 1910

23320 Nucleonics Week
McGraw Hill
PO Box 182604
Columbus, OH 43272

877-833-5524
800-752-8878
Fax: 614-759-3749
E-Mail: support@platts.com
Home Page: www.mcgraw-hill.com
Margaret Ryan, Editor

Covers all aspects of commercial nuclear power.
Cost: $2265.00
12 Pages
Frequency: Monthly
Founded in 1888

23321 Public Gas News
American Public Gas Association
11094 Lee Hwy
Suite 102
Fairfax, VA 22030-5034

703-352-3890
Fax: 703-352-1271
E-Mail: info@apga.org
Home Page: www.apga.org

Robert S Cave, Executive Director

Written for public gas managers to keep them apprised of industry news.
Cost: $50.00
Circulation: 1000
Printed in 2 colors

23322 Public Utilities
State Capitals Newsletters
PO Box 7376
Alexandria, VA 22307-7376

703-768-9600
Fax: 703-768-9690
Home Page: statecapitals.com
Cost: $345.00

Frequency: Weekly

23323 Public Utilities: From the State Capitals
Wakeman Walworth
300 N Washington Street
Suite 204
Alexandria, VA 22314-2530

703-689-9600
Fax: 703-549-1372
Home Page: www.publicworks.houstontx.gov/utilities/

Keyes Walworth, Publisher

Covers state regulations of all forms of public utilities across the nation. It reports on new rate structures, allowable profit margins, special taxes, consumer relations, environmental legislation, nuclear plant regulations, deregulation programs and programs for low-income customers.

23324 Utility Environment Report
McGraw Hill
PO Box 182604
Columbus, OH 43272

877-833-5524
800-752-8878
Fax: 614-759-3749
E-Mail: customer.service@mcgraw-hill.com
Home Page: www.mcgraw-hill.com

Rob Ingraham, Publisher
Harold McGraw, III, President
Steven H. Weiss, VP

Provides news of significant developments affecting the electric utility industry focusing on state and federal regulation, management and bulk power markets. Publishes charts of prices utilities pay for fuels.
Cost: $695.00
18 Pages
Founded in 1899

23325 Utility Executive
Water Environment Federation
601 Wythe St
Alexandria, VA 22314-1994

800-666-0206
Fax: 703-684-2492
Home Page: www.wef.org
Social Media: Facebook, Twitter

Matt Bond, President
Cordell Samuels, President-Elect
Sandra Ralston, Vice President
Chris Browning, Treasurer
Jeff Eger, Secretary and Executive Director

For managers and executives at water & wastewater treatment plants, consultants, and others interested in utility management. Focuses on such pertinent business issues as public private partnerships, capital financing options, strategic planning methods, public outreach approaches, and staff development.
79 Members
ISSN: 1044-9943
Founded in 1928

23326 Utility Reporter: Fuels, Energy and Power
InfoTeam
PO Box 15640
Plantation, FL 33318-5640

954-473-9560
Fax: 954-473-0544

Randy M Allen CPA, Editor

Focuses on activities involving: power generation, combustion, delivery and transmission; alternative energy devices and systems; heat transfer, storage and utilization; and myriad of related topics.
Cost: $289.00
20 Pages
Frequency: Monthly
ISBN: 0-890298-4 -
Printed in one color on matte stock

23327 Wind Energy Smart Brief
American Wind Energy Association
1501 M Street NW
Suite 1000
Washington, DC 20005

202-383-2500
Fax: 202-383-2505
E-Mail: windmail@awea.org
Home Page: www.awea.org
Social Media: Facebook, Twitter, LinkedIn, You Tube

Denise Bode, CEO

This newsletter delivers quickly digestible summaries of the day's wind energy-related

stories from across the media, as well as links to those stories.
Frequency: Weekly

23328 **Wind Energy Weekly**
American Wind Energy Association
1501 M Street NW
Suite 1000
Washington, DC 20005

202-383-2500
Fax: 202-383-2505
E-Mail: windmail@awea.org
Home Page: www.awea.org

Denise Bode, CEO

Packed with detailed and up-to-date information on the world of wind energy that simply can't be obtained elsewhere.
Frequency: Weekly

23329 **WindLetter**
American Wind Energy Association
1501 M Street NW
Suite 1000
Washington, DC 20005

202-383-2500
Fax: 202-383-2505
E-Mail: windmail@awea.org
Home Page: www.awea.org
Social Media: Facebook, Twitter, LinkedIn, You Tube

Denise Bode, CEO

Recap's the month's most significant wind energy news and includes interesting for wind energy enthusiasts.
Frequency: Monthly

Magazines & Journals

23330 **APWA Reporter**
American Public Works Association
2345 Grand Blvd
Suite 700
Kansas City, MO 64108-2625

816-472-6100
800-848-2792
Fax: 816-472-1610
E-Mail: ddancy@apwa.net
Home Page: www.apwa.net
Social Media: Facebook, Twitter, LinkedIn

Kaye Sullivan, Executive Director
David Dancy, Director Marketing

Circulation to entire membership of American Public Works Association.
Cost: $100.00
Frequency: Monthly
Circulation: 25000
ISBN: 0-092487-3 -
Founded in 1937
Mailing list available for rent

23331 **Alternative Energy**
PWG
205 S Beverly Drive
#208
Beverly Hills, CA 90212-3827

310-273-3486
Fax: 310-858-8272
Home Page: www.bp.com

Irwin Stambler, Publisher
Ahmad Taleban, President

Reports on future economic and technological trends.
Cost: $95.00
12 Pages
Frequency: Monthly
Printed in 2 colors on matte stock

23332 **Alternative Energy Retailer**
Zackin Publications
PO Box 2180
Waterbury, CT 06722-2180

203-755-0158
800-325-6745
Fax: 203-755-3480
E-Mail: info@aer-online.com
Home Page: www.aer-online.com

Paul Zackin, Publisher
Michael Griffin, Editor
Arlene Sorrentino, Production Coordinator
Jeanette Laliberte, Marketing Manager
June Han, Subscription Manager

Covers solid fuel burning, marketing, technology, and sales.
Frequency: Monthly
Circulation: 14,000

23333 **American Gas Magazine**
American Gas Association
400 N Capitol Street NW
Suite 450
Washington, DC 20001

202-824-7000
Fax: 202-824-7092
Home Page: www.aga.org
Social Media: Facebook, Twitter, LinkedIn

David N Parker, CEO
Kevin Hardardt, CFO/CAO
Ysabel Korolevich, Membership Services
Frequency: 10x/Year
Founded in 1918

23334 **American Public Works Association**
American Public Works Association
2345 Grand Blvd
Suite 700
Kansas City, MO 64108-2625

816-472-6100
800-848-2792
Fax: 816-472-1610
E-Mail: ddancy@apwa.net
Home Page: www.apwa.net

Kaye Sullivan, Executive Director
David Dancy, Marketing Director

International educational and professional association of public agencies, private sector companies, and individuals dedicated to providing high quality public works goods and services. AWA provides a forum in which public works professionals competency, increase the performance of their agencies and companies, and bring important public works-related topics to public attention in local, state, and federal areas. Mailing list for members only.
Cost: $100.00
40 Pages
Frequency: Monthly
ISSN: 0092-4873
Founded in 1937

23335 **American Water Works Association Journal**
American Water Works Association
6666 W Quincy Ave
Denver, CO 80235-3098

303-794-7711
800-926-7337
Fax: 303-347-0804
E-Mail: journal@awwa.org
Home Page: www.awwa.org

Andrew Richardson, President
Jack W. Hoffbuhr, Executive Director

Journal of the professional society of North American drinking water experts. Dues cover subscription for members.
Cost: $120.00
152 Pages
Frequency: Monthly
ISSN: 0003-150X
Founded in 1935

23336 **Bulletin**
NW Public Power Association
9817 Ne 54th St
Suite 200
Vancouver, WA 98662-6064

360-254-0109
Fax: 360-254-5731
E-Mail: nwppa@nwppa.org
Home Page: www.nwppa.org

Will Lutgen, Executive Director

Readership consists of directors, chairmen and managers of electric utilities in the ten Western States and four Canadian provinces. Provides news and events of the public power industry in the Pacific Northwest Region.
Cost: $ 32.00
32 Pages
Circulation: 6200
Printed in 4 colors

23337 **Chief Engineer**
Chief Engineers Association of Chicagoland
4701 Midlothian Turnpike
Crestwood, IL 60445

708-293-1720
Fax: 708-633-7008
Home Page: www.chiefengineer.org

Ernest K Wulff, Editor

Covers building maintenance issues, laws and rulings relative to chief engineers, as well as mechanical and general HVAC equipment.
Frequency: Monthly
Circulation: 2000
Founded in 1935
Mailing list available for rent: 2K names

23338 **Cogeneration Monthly Letter**
Cogeneration Publications Company
509 Tennessee Avenue
Alexandria, VA 22305-1336

703-683-1868
Fax: 703-683-1878
Home Page: www.powermarketers.com

Scott Spiewak, Publisher

Discusses new technology and legislation governing power generating facilities. Includes listings of planned projects.
Frequency: 5 per year
Circulation: 5000

23339 **Diesel & Gas Turbine Worldwide**
Diesel & Gas Turbine Publications
20855 Watertown Rd
Suite 220
Waukesha, WI 53186-1873

262-754-4100
800-558-4322
Fax: 262-832-5075
E-Mail: slizdas@dieselpub.com
Home Page: www.dieselpub.com

Michael Osenga, President
Mark McNeely, Editor
Lynne Diefenbach, Advertising Manager
Christa Johnson, Production Manager

Focuses on the design, production, installation, operation, and maintenance of engines in the global marine, power generation, oil and gas, or railroad industries.
Frequency: bi-Monthly
Circulation: 20100
Founded in 1935

23340 **Diesel Progress: International Edition**
Diesel & Gas Turbine Publications

20855 Watertown Rd
Suite 220
Waukesha, WI 53186-1873

262-754-4100
Fax: 262-832-5075
E-Mail: slizdas@dieselpub.com
Home Page: www.dieselspec.com

Michael Osenga, President
Sue Bollwahn, Circulation Manager
Katie Evans, Sales Manager
Michael J Brezonick, Editor-in-Chief

Focuses on new products and technology that serves engineering, marketing, service and equipment, purchasing, administrative, and others allied to the field.
Circulation: 10273
Founded in 1935

23341 District Energy
International District Enery Association (IDEA)
24 Lyman Streetad
Suite 230
Westborough, MA 01581

508-366-9339
Fax: 508-366-0019
E-Mail: idea@districtenergy.org
Home Page: www.districtenergy.org

Peter Myers, Editor
Rob Thornton, President

Journal of district heating and cooling industry, congeneration, physical plants and energy efficiency. Accepts advertising.
Cost: $40.00
Frequency: Quarterly

23342 Electric Light & Power
Technical Publishing
1421 S. Sheridan Road
Tulsa, OK 74112

981-831-9884
Fax: 918-831-9834
E-Mail: candiced@pennwell.com
Home Page: www.elp.com

Wayne Beaty, Editor
Candice Doctor, Sales Director
Michael Grossman, Publisher
Teresa Hansen, Editor in Chief

Offers articles on the electric utility industry.
Cost: $38.00
84 Pages
Frequency: Monthly
Founded in 1922

23343 Electric Perspectives
Edison Electric Institute
701 Pennsylvania Avenue NW
Washington, DC 20004-2696

202-508-5000
800-344-5453
Fax: 202-508-5794
E-Mail: feedback@eei.org
Home Page: www.eei.org

Thomas R Kuhn, President
Brian Farrell, Member Relations Director

The magazine for management in America's investor-owned electric utilities. Covers all areas of utility operations and concerns, providing detailed analyses and farsighted commentary on how issues and trends are shaping the industry today and the future impact.
Cost: $50.00
Frequency: Bi-Monthly
Circulation: 10000
ISSN: 0364-474X
Founded in 1981

23344 Energy Efficiency Journal
NAESCO
1615 M St NW
Suite 800
Washington, DC 20036-3213

202-822-0950
Fax: 202-822-0955
Home Page: www.eceee.org/ee_journal

Terry E Singer, Executive Editor
Nina Lockhart, Senior Program Manager
Donald Gilligan, Publisher

Targets energy service companies, electric and gas utilities and other energy providers. Highlights industry news and features energy conservation.
Frequency: Quarterly
Circulation: 200

23345 Energy Manager
Primedia
3585 Engineering Drive
Suite 100
Norcross, GA 30092

678-421-3000
Fax: 913-514-6895
Home Page: www.primedia.com

Eric Jacobson, Senior VP
Charles Stubs, President
Kim Payne, VP
Mike Barber, Accountant

Subjects include energy management systems, HVAC, automated building systems, plant and facilities control, and negotiating supplier contracts. Features include legislative news from Washington, analysis of rare updates, relevant news from around the world and new product reviews.
Frequency: 5 per year
Circulation: 50,000
Founded in 1998

23346 Energy Today
Trend Publishing
529 14th St NW
Suite 954
Washington, DC 20045-1925

202-662-8827
Fax: 202-662-8829

Arthur Kranish, Editor

Includes news and analysis, new regulatory and technical developments, grant and contract opportunities, investigative reports, and market studies.
Frequency: Monthly

23347 Energy and Housing Report
Alan L Frank Associates
9124 Bradford Road
Silverspring, MD 20901-4918

703-866-4397
Fax: 301-565-3298
Home Page: homeenergy.org

Mary James, Publisher
Iain Walker, Executive Editor
Cass Duggan, Circulation Manager
Carol A. Markell, Marketing Manager
Alan Meier, President

Research in consumption with the goal of increasing energy conservation at the residential level. Follows trends in consumption and the effects of conservation efforts on energy use.
Founded in 1994

23348 Energy in the News
New York Mercantile Exchange
1 N End Ave
New York, NY 10282-1101

212-299-2000
Fax: 212-301-4700
E-Mail: marketing@nymex.com
Home Page: www.nymex.com

Samuel Gaer, Executive VP

Covers market fundamentals, trading strategies and market conditions. Provides information that keeps future commission merchants, industry executives, options and cash market traders up-to-date with trends affecting the energy industry.
Frequency: Quarterly
Circulation: 35000

23349 Gas Turbine World
Pequot Publishing
PO Box 447
Southport, CT 06490-447

203-259-1812
Fax: 203-259-0532
Home Page: www.business-magazines.com

Victor Debiasi, Publisher

Focuses on implementing policy, specification, design, maintenance, and modernization of the systems and equipment of electric power generation.
Cost: $135.00
Frequency: Monthly
Circulation: 10000

23350 Generation Week
Pasha Publications
1600 Wilson Boulevard
#600
Arlington, VA 22209-2509

703-528-1244
800-424-2908
Fax: 703-816-7821
Home Page: www.pasha.com

Tod Sedgwick, Publisher

On new technology and innovative operation of power plants.
Frequency: Weekly

23351 HRW: Hydro Review Worldwide
HCI Publications
410 Archibald St
Kansas City, MO 64111-3288

816-931-1311
Fax: 816-931-2015
E-Mail: hci@aol.com
Home Page: www.hcipub.com

Leslie Eden, President
Marla Barness, Editor
Bob Merrigan, Marketing

Magazine serving information needs of people associated with hydro throughout the world. Managing and improving plant operations, solving problems, financing and essential business news are covered extensively.
Cost: $44.00
Circulation: 4673
Founded in 1982

23352 Hart's Energy Markets
Hart Publications
4545 Post Oak Place
#210
Houston, TX 77027-3105

713-993-9320
Fax: 713-840-0983
E-Mail: dgriffin@hartenergy.com
Home Page: www.hartenergy.com

Dana Griffin Smith, Publisher
Joe Fisher, Editor
Richard Eichler, President

Keeps readers abreast of trends and opportunities in the marketplace. Covers such topics as electricity deregulation, gas unbundling, rebundling of services, nuclear and renewable energy, technological developments and regulatory issues.
Frequency: Monthly
Circulation: 14000
Founded in 1973

23353 **Home Power**
PO Box 520
Ashland, OR 97520-18
541-512-0201
800-707-6585
Fax: 530-475-0836
E-Mail: info@homepower.com
Home Page: www.homepower.com

Karen Perez, Publisher
Joe Schwartz, Manager

Covers photovoltaics, wind turbines, solar heating, methane, batteries, inverters, water pumping, electric vehicles, controls, and instruments. Examines the design and installation of balanced renewable energy systems in the home, while also reviewing products ranging from solar pumps to refrigerators.
Cost: $22.50
Circulation: 19200
Founded in 1987

23354 **Hydro Review**
HCI Publications
410 Archibald St
Kansas City, MO 64111-3288
816-931-1311
Fax: 816-931-2015
Home Page: www.hcipub.com

Leslie Eden, President

Magazine providing in-depth coverage of the North American hydroelectric industry. Rehab, redevelopment, dam safety and the environment are explored.
Cost: $65.00
Circulation: 500
Founded in 1980

23355 **Independent Energy**
PennWell Publishing Company
1421 S Sheridan Rd
Tulsa, OK 74112-6619
918-831-9421
800-331-4463
Fax: 918-831-9476
Home Page: www.pennwell.com

Robert Biolchini, President

Focuses on analysis and views aimed at doing business more successfully. Reports important market information, trends and equipment advances affecting power project development, financing, construction, operation and management.
Frequency: Monthly
Circulation: 10962
Founded in 1961

23356 **New Equipment Digest**
Penton Media
1300 E 9th St
Suite 316
Cleveland, OH 44114-1503
216-696-7000
Fax: 216-696-6662
E-Mail: information@penton.com
Home Page: www.newequipment.com

Jane Cooper, Marketing
Tom Sockel, Associate Editor
Robert King, Editor
Sarah Hughes, Production Manager
Bobbie Macy, Circulation Manager

Serves the general industrial field which includes manufacturing, processing, engineering services, construction, transportation, mining, public utilities, wholesale distributors, educational services, libraries and governmental establishments.
Frequency: Monthly
Founded in 1936

23357 **Northeast Sun**
NE Sustainable Energy Association
50 Miles St
Suite 3
Greenfield, MA 01301-3255
413-774-6051
Fax: 413-774-6053
E-Mail: nesea@nesea.org
Home Page: www.nesea.org

David Barclay, Executive Director

Addresses the current issues of solar energy and natural gas power. Also provides an exchange of ideas for those seeking other environmentally sound energy sources.
Frequency: Monthly
Circulation: 5000
Founded in 1974

23358 **Northwest Public Power Bulletin**
Northwest Public Power Association
9817 NE 54th St
Suite 200
Vancouver, WA 98662-6064
360-254-0109
Fax: 360-254-5731
E-Mail: nwppa@nwppa.org
Home Page: www.nwppa.org

Will Lutgen, President
Brenda Dunn, Associate Editor
Debbie Kuraspediani, Director Communications

Trade publication for consumer-owned electric utilities managers, directors, commissioners and management staff.
Cost: $25.00
28 Pages
Frequency: Monthly
Circulation: 6000
Founded in 1947

23359 **Nuclear News**
American Nuclear Society
555 N Kensington Ave
La Grange Park, IL 60526-5592
708-352-6611
Fax: 708-352-0499
E-Mail: advertising@ans.org
Home Page: www.nuclear-news.net

Jack Tuohy, Executive Director
Mike Diekman, Information Department Head
Sarah Wells, Editor
Gloria Nawrocki, Marketing Manager

For personnel involved in nuclear power operation and development. Coverage includes power, plant operations and maintenance, fuel cycle, legislation, international employment and more.
Cost: $290.00
Frequency: Monthly
Circulation: 12000
Founded in 1954
Printed in on glossy stock

23360 **Nuclear Plant Journal**
EQES
1400 Opus Place
Suite 904
Downers Grove, IL 60515
630-858-6161
Fax: 630-858-8787
E-Mail: michelle@goinfo.com
Home Page: www.nuclearplantjournal.com

Newal Agnihotri, Publisher

Nuclear Plant Journal includes technical papers, informative articles and departments aimed at developing better methods, systems, products and services in the nuclear power industry. The Journal is compiled through the research efforts of professional engineers who are specialists in their respective fields.
Circulation: 14000
ISSN: 0892-2055
Founded in 1983
Printed in on glossy stock

23361 **Power Engineering International**
PennWell Publishing Company
1421 S Sheridan Rd
Tulsa, OK 74112-6619
918-831-9421
800-331-4463
Fax: 918-831-9476
E-Mail: Headquarters@PennWell.com
Home Page: www.pennwell.com

Robert Biolchini, President
Candice Doctor, Regional Sales Manager
Rick Huntzicker, National Sales Manager
Junior Isles, Publisher & Editorial Director
Rafael A Junquera, Editor

A variety of topics including plant design, operations, management and applications. New products are also reviewed.
Frequency: Monthly
Circulation: 34000
Founded in 1910

23362 **Private Power Executive**
Pequot Publishing
PO Box 447
Southport, CT 06490-0447
203-259-1812
Fax: 203-259-0532

Victor de Biasi, Publisher

Written for cogenerators and developers involved in planning, design, financing, installation and operation of cogeneration plants for industrial, municipal, hospitals, and commercial district heating and cooling.
Frequency: BiMonthly
Circulation: ll,500

23363 **Public Power Magazine**
American Public Power Association
1875 Connecticut Ave NW
Suite 1200
Washington, DC 20009-5715
202-467-2900
800-515-2772
Fax: 202-467-2910
E-Mail: mrufe@appanet.org
Home Page: www.publicpower.org

Alan Richardson, Executive Director
Michael L Kurtz, Publisher

The only national magazine published especially for policymaking and managerial personnel of local publicly owned electric systems. Public Power keeps readers abreast of policy developments, managerial techniques, new technologies, research and development and legislative issues. Subscription, $50.00
Cost: $10.00
72 Pages
Circulation: 11100
ISSN: 0033-3654
Founded in 1942

23364 **Public Utilities Fortnightly**
Public Utilities Reports
8229 Boone Blvd
Suite 400
Vienna, VA 22182-2623
703-847-7720
800-368-5001
Fax: 703-917-6964
E-Mail: pur@pur.com
Home Page: www.pur.com
Social Media: Twitter

Bruce Radford, Publisher
Michael Burr, Editor-In-Chief
Philip Cross, Vice President/ Legal Editor
Joseph Paparello, Director of Sales
Jean Cole, Marketing Manager

Independent publisher for the energy industry.
Cost: $459.00
Frequency: Weekly
Founded in 1929

23365 Public Utility Weekly
Public Utilities Reports
8229 Boone Blvd
Suite 400
Vienna, VA 22182-2623
703-847-7720
800-368-5001
Fax: 703-917-6964
Home Page: www.pur.com
Bruce Radford, President
Richard Stavros, Executive Editor
Joseph Paparello, Marketing Manager
Phillip Cross, Legal Publisher
Designed to serve as a communication forum for the utility industry covering state commission rulings and federal regulatory issues.
Founded in 1915

23366 Solar Today
American Solar Energy Society
4760 Walnut Street
Suite 106
Boulder, CO 80301-2843
303-443-3130
Fax: 303-443-3212
E-Mail: info@solartoday.org
Home Page: www.ases.org
Regina Thompson, Editor/Associate Publisher
Seth Masia, Deputy Editor
Brooke Simmons, Manager of Online Publishing
Provides information, case histories and reviews of a variety of renewable energy technologies, including solar, wind, biomass and geothermal.
Cost: $29.00
90 Pages
Circulation: 7000
Founded in 1987

23367 SolarToday
American Solar Energy Society
2400 Central Avenue
Sutie A
Boulder, CO 80301
303-443-3130
Fax: 303-443-3212
E-Mail: ases@ases.org
Home Page: www.ases.org
Social Media: Facebook, Twitter
Bradley D Collins, Publisher
Gina Johnson, Editor
Brings together ASES' professional members as contributors and readers, amid the community of ASES chapters nationwide, to publish industry-leading editorial for more than 23 years. The leading renewable energy magazine for consumers and professionals.

23368 Transmission & Distribution World
Primedia
PO Box 12901
Shawnee Mission, KS 66282-2901
913-341-1300
800-441-0294
Fax: 913-514-6895
E-Mail: rbush@primediabusiness.com
Home Page: www.tdworld.com
Social Media: Facebook, Twitter
Eric Jacobson, Senior VP
Rick Bush, Editor
Frequency: Monthly
Circulation: 49000
Founded in 1996

23369 Turbomachinery International
Business Journals
PO Box 5550
Norwalk, CT 06856-5550
203-663-7814
Fax: 203-852-8175
Home Page: www.turbomachinerymag.com
Richard Zanetti, Publisher
Includes updates of new approaches to energy conservation, new equipment listings and business/financial news.
Frequency: BiMonthly
Circulation: 11,100
Founded in 1959

23370 Utilities Law Review
John Wiley & Sons
Office A10 Spinners Court
55 West End
Witney, OX OX8 6
199-370-6183
800-825-7550
Fax: 199-370-9410
Home Page: www.lawtext.com/
Nicholas Gingell, Publisher
Cosmo Graham, Editor
William J Pesce, CEO/President
Charlotte Villiers, Assistant Editor
Peter Crowther, Current Survey Editor
Edited by a team of specialist UK and European lawyers, it is the leading journal in this fast-changing field. Providing detailed coverage of electricity, gas, telecommunications, transport, water and broadcasting.
Cost: $4920.00
Frequency: Bi-Monthly
Circulation: 250
Founded in 1807

23371 Utility & Telephone Fleets
Practical Communications
482 Holly Ave
Saint Paul, MN 55102
651-91 -997
Fax: 651-224-2347
Home Page: www.utfleets.com/
Judith F Chance, Group Publisher
Mike Domke, Publisher
Carol Birkland, Editor
Tom Gelinas, Editorial Director
The equipment, accessory and information resource for fleet professionals.
Circulation: 18,000
Founded in 1980

23372 Utility Automation
PennWell Publishing Company
1421 S Sheridan
PO Box 1260
Tulsa, OK 74112
918-835-3161
Fax: 918-831-9497
E-Mail: ua@pennwell.com
Home Page: www.utility-automation.com
Social Media: Facebook, Twitter
Shirley Wilson, Marketing Manager
Steven M Brown, Editor
Michael Grossman, Publisher
Robert F Biolchini, CEO/President
Janet Orteon, Circulation Manager
Innovative energy solutions.
Cost: $74.00
50 Pages
Circulation: 32200
ISSN: 1085-2328
Founded in 1996

23373 Utility Automation International
PennWell Publishing Company
1421 S Sheridan Rd
Tulsa, OK 74112-6619
918-831-9421
800-331-4463
Fax: 918-831-9476
E-Mail: headquarters@pennwell.com
Home Page: www.pennwell.com
Social Media: Facebook, Twitter
Robert Biolchini, President
Tina Jackson, Circulation Manager
Doug Pryor, Editor
Brad Dillman, Marketing
Circulation: 24002
Founded in 1910

23374 Utility Business
PRIMEDIA Intertec-Technology & Transportation
PO Box 12901
Shawnee Mission, KS 66282-2901
913-341-1300
Fax: 913-514-6895
E-Mail: barry-lecerf@intertec.com
Home Page: www.primedia.com
Social Media: Facebook, Twitter, LinkedIn
Eric Jacobson, Senior VP
Editorial emphasis is on providing the reader with solutions and commentary for identifying and developing company assets, realizing the impact technology has on the business, and responding to the evolving demands of the marketplace.
Frequency: 8 per year
Circulation: 50,000

23375 Utility Contractor
3925 Chain Bridge Road
Suite 300
Fairfax, VA 22030
703-358-9300
Fax: 703-358-9307
E-Mail: bill@nuca.com
Home Page: www.nuca.com
Bill Hillman, CEO
Serves the underground utility construction industry, including contractors, manufacturers, suppliers, engineering firms, municipal/public/private utilities, and others allied to the field.
Frequency: Monthly
Circulation: 59329
ISSN: 1098-0342
Founded in 1963

23376 Utility Executive
Water Environment Federation
601 Wythe St
Alexandria, VA 22314-1994
703-684-2400
800-666-0206
Fax: 703-684-2492
E-Mail: csc@wef.org
Home Page: www.wef.org
Bill Bertera, Executive Director
Jack Benson, Marketing Manager
Editorial focuses on issues such as continuous improvement, privatization, financial and risk management, as well as benchmarking and leadership. Problem solving strategies are included for everything from wastewater treatment efficiency to negotiation contracts and proposal evaluations, and address relevant, current issues facing utility managers today.
Cost: $33.00
Frequency: Monthly
Founded in 1928

23377 Utility Fleet Management
TT Publishing

2200 Mill Road
Alexandria, VA 22314-1994

703-838-1770
Fax: 703-838-6259
Home Page: www.ttnews.com

Bob Raft, Publisher

Focuses on fleet management issues and new equipment.
Cost: $25.00
Frequency: Monthly
Circulation: 15,000

23378 Western Energy
Magellan
827 NE Oregon Street
Suite 200
Portland, OR 97232-2172

503-231-1994
Fax: 503-231-2595
Home Page: www.westernenergy.org

Chuck Meyer, President
Jody Brassfield-English, Controller
Karen Himes, Webmaster

Contains technical features designed to inform and educate workers and technicians in the energy production field.
Frequency: BiMonthly
Circulation: 5,058

Trade Shows

23379 AMRA Symposium
Automatic Meter Reading Association
60 Revere Drive
Suite 500
Northbrook, IL 60062

847-480-9628
888-612-2672
Fax: 847-480-9282
Home Page: www.amra-intl.org

Joyce Paschall, Executive Director

Gas, water and electric utilities, telephone companies and installation companies equipment and supplies for meter reading .
1600 Attendees
Frequency: Annual
Founded in 1986

23380 APWA International Public Works Congress & Expo
American Public Works Association
2345 Grand Boulevard
Suite 700
Kansas City, MO 64108-2625

816-472-6100
800-848-2792
Fax: 816-472-1610
E-Mail: ddancy@apwa.net
Home Page: www.apwa.net
Social Media: Facebook, Twitter, LinkedIn

Peter King, Executive Director
David Dancy, Marketing Director

Offers the benefit of a variety of educational sessions, depth of the exhibit program and endless opportunities for networking. The latest cutting-edge technologies, managerial techniques and regulatory trends designed to keep you focused on the right solutions at the right time.
6500 Attendees
Frequency: Annual/September
ISSN: 0092-4873
Founded in 1894

23381 American Public Power Association of Engineers Operations Workshop
2301 M Street NW
Floor 3
Washington, DC 20037-1427

202-467-2900
Barbara Opicka, Marketing Assistant
Alan Richardson, President/CEO
50 booths.
1.3M Attendees
Frequency: February/March

23382 Buscon East/West
Conference Management Company
200 Connecticut Avenue
Norwalk, CT 06854-1940

203-866-4400

David Caplin, Show Manager

Principal industry event for systems builders and electronics engineers.
5M Attendees

23383 EEI Convention & Expo
Edison Electric Institute
701 Pennsylvania Avenue NW
Washington, DC 20004-2696

202-508-5000
800-344-5453
Fax: 202-508-5794
E-Mail: feedback@eei.org
Home Page: www.eei.org
Social Media: Facebook, Twitter, LinkedIn

Thomas R Kuhn, President
Brian Farrell, Member Relations Director

Meeting of Senior executives in the power industry
750 Attendees
Frequency: Annual

23384 Northwest Public Power Engineering & Operations Show
9817 NE 54th Street
Suite 200
Vancouver, WA 98662-6064

360-254-0109
Fax: 360-254-5731
E-Mail: nwppa@nwppa.org
Home Page: www.nwppa.org
Scott Lowry, Training Manager
Debbie Kuraspediani, Director Communications
900 Attendees
Frequency: May

23385 Smart Energy Summitt
Parks Associates
15950 N. Dallas Parkway
Suite 575
Dallas, TX 75248

972-490-1113
800-727-5711
Fax: 972-490-1133
E-Mail: info@parksassociates.com
Home Page: www.parksassociates.com

Tricia Parks, Founder and CEO
Stuart Sikes, President
Farhan Abid, Research Analyst
Bill Ablondi, Director, Home Systems Research
John Barrett, Director of Research

Smart Energy Summit is an annual three-day event that examines the opportunities and technical business requirements inherent in the consumer programs and advanced systems and services made possible by Smart Grids and Residential Energy Management solutions.
Frequency: Annual
Founded in 1986

23386 WINDPOWER Conference and Exhibition
American Wind Energy Association (AWEA)
1501 M Street NW
Suite 1000
Washington, DC 20005

202-383-2500
Fax: 202-383-2505
E-Mail: windmail@awea.org
Home Page: www.windpowerexpo.org
Social Media: Facebook, Twitter

Denise Bode, Chief Executive Officer
Pam Poisson, Chief Financial Officer
Britt Theismann, Chief Operating Officer
Rob Gramlich, Senior VP, Public Policy
Peter Kelley, VP, Public Affairs

The WINDPOWER Conference & Exhibition is produced by the American Wind Energy Association to provide a venue for the wind industry to network, do business, and solve problems. Recognized as one of the fastest-growing trade shows in the U.S., WINDPOWER includes nearly 1,400 exhibiting companies, thousands of qualified wind energy professionals, engaging educational information and unmatched networking opportunities and special events.
2500 Members
20000 Attendees
Frequency: Annual

Directories & Databases

23387 DRI Utility Cost Forecasting
DRI/McGraw-Hill
24 Hartwell Ave
Lexington, MA 02421-3103

781-860-6060
Fax: 781-860-6002
Home Page: www.construction.com

Walt Arvin, President

This large database covers the US public utility industry, including cost inputs for pumps, gas compressors, steam pipes and gas and electric meters.

23388 Directory of Electric Power Producers and Distributors
McGraw Hill
2 Penn Plz
5th Floor
New York, NY 10121-2298

212-760-8589
Fax: 212-904-2723
Home Page: www.mcgraw-hill.com

Offers information on over 3,500 investor-owned, municipal, rural cooperative and government electric utility systems in the United States and Canada.
Cost: $395.00
1,200 Pages
Frequency: Annual

23389 Directory of Electric Utility Company Libraries in the United States
Library Services Committee/Edison Electric Inst
701 Pennsylvania Avenue NW
Washington, DC 20004-2608

202-347-2693

Over 90 investor-owned electric utility company libraries throughout the country are profiled.
Cost: $10.00
149 Pages
Frequency: Annual

23390 **Directory of Energy Professionals**
Assn of Regulatory Utility Commissioners
PO Box 684
Washington, DC 20044-0684
202-898-2200
Offers information on consultants and other professionals active in regulated energy utility industries.
Cost: $44.00
450 Pages
Frequency: Annual

23391 **Directory of Publicly Owned Natural Gas Systems**
American Public Gas Association
11094 Lee Hwy
Suite 102
Fairfax, VA 22030-5034
703-352-3890
Fax: 703-352-1271
E-Mail: info@apga.org
Home Page: www.apga.org
Robert S Cave, Executive Director
A listing of all publicly owned natural gas systems in the US.
Cost: $50.00
80 Pages
Frequency: Annual
Circulation: 1,000
Printed in on matte stock

23392 **Electric Utility Cost Forecast**
WEFA Group
800 Baldwin Tower Boulevard
Eddystone, PA 19022-1368
610-490-4000
Fax: 610-490-2770
E-Mail: info@wefa.com
Home Page: www.wefa.com
Mary Novak
This time series covers prices, construction and operating costs pertinent to the electric utilities industry.

23393 **Electric Utility Industry**
Midwest Publishing Company
2230 E 49th Ste E
Tulsa, OK 74105-8771
918-582-2000
800-829-2002
Fax: 918-587-9349
E-Mail: info@midwestdirectories.com
Home Page: www.midwestdirectories.com
Will Hammack, Editor
Approximately 6,000 utility companies, contractors, engineering firms, equipment manufacturers and supply companies.
Cost: $155.00
Frequency: Annual February
Founded in 1943

23394 **Financial Statistics of Major Investor-Owned Electric Utilities**
US Energy Information Administration
1000 Independence Ave SW
Washington, DC 20585-0001
202-586-8800
Fax: 202-586-0727
Home Page: www.eia.doe.gov
John H Weiner, Executive Director
Offers data from over 180 major investor-owned electric utilities in the United States.
Cost: $33.00
Frequency: Annual

23395 **Gas Industry Training Directory**
American Gas Association
1515 Wilson Boulevard
Suite 100
Arlington, VA 22209-2469
703-841-8400
Fax: 703-841-8406
Home Page: www.ihrdc.com
David F Sullivan, Industry Training
Over 600 programs are available in this directory from gas transmission and distribution companies, manufacturers of gas-fired equipment, consultants, etc., and from gas associations.
Frequency: Annual February

23396 **Guide to Hydropower Mechanical Design**
HCI Publications
410 Archibald St
Kansas City, MO 64111-3288
816-931-1311
Fax: 816-931-2015
E-Mail: hci@aol.com
Home Page: www.hcipub.com
Leslie Eden, President
Developed by the Hydropower Technical Committee of the American Society of Mechanical Engineers. A ready reference for individuals who design hydropower facilities and producers and distributors of electricity.
Cost: $125.00
Circulation: 4673

23397 **Handy-Whitman Index of Public Utility Construction Costs**
Whitman, Requardt and Associates
801 S Caroline St
Baltimore, MD 21231-3311
410-235-3450
Fax: 410-243-5716
Home Page: www.wrallp.com
Jenny Miller, Human Resources
This database covers indexes of building costs for construction of public utilities in the United States.

23398 **International Directory of Electric Power Producers and Distributors**
McGraw Hill
1200 G St NW
Suite 250
Washington, DC 20005-3821
202-383-2377
Fax: 202-383-2438
Home Page: www.aviationnow.com
Jennifer Michels, Manager
Offers valuable information on over 3,000 power generating and distribution systems in over 200 countries overseas.
Cost: $345.00

23399 **International Directory of Nuclear Utilities**
Nuexco
950 17th Street
Suite 2500
Denver, CO 80202-2825
303-534-3100
This comprehensive directory offers information on over 120 utilities in 30 countries that operate nuclear plants with a capacity of at least 100 megawatts.
Cost: $220.00
264 Pages
Frequency: Annual
Founded in 1968

23400 **Inventory of Power Plants in the United States**
US Energy Information Administration
1000 Independence Ave SW
Washington, DC 20585-0001
202-586-8800
Fax: 202-586-0727
Home Page: www.eia.doe.gov
John H Weiner, Executive Director
Information is given on existing and projected and jointly-owned power plants within electric utility systems.
Cost: $23.00
393 Pages
Frequency: Annual

23401 **LEXIS Public Utilities Law Library**
Mead Data Central
9443 Springboro Pike
Dayton, OH 45401
888-223-6337
Fax: 518-487-3584
Home Page: www.lexis-nexis.com
Andrew Prozes, CEO
This database contains information on public utilities-related case decisions from all state supreme courts and most state appellate courts.
Frequency: Full-text

23402 **Northwest Electric Utility Directory**
Northwest Public Power Association
9817 Ne 54th St
Suite 4576
Vancouver, WA 98662-6064
360-254-0109
Fax: 360-254-5731
Home Page: www.nwppa.org
Will Lutgen, President
Randy Shipley, Project Manager
Annual directory for electric utilities in 10 western states and 4 western Canadian provinces.
Frequency: Annually

23403 **PUR Analysis of Investor-Owned Electric & Gas Utilities**
Public Utilities Reports
2111 Wilson Boulevard
Suite 200
Arlington, VA 22201-3001
Covers over 200 investor-owned electric and gas operating and holding companies.
Cost: $395.00
Frequency: Annual

23404 **Pipeline & Utilities Construction: Contractors Issue**
Oildom Publishing Company of Texas
PO Box 219368
Houston, TX 77218-9368
281-558-6930
Offers a comprehensive list of over 5,000 individual contracting firms concerned with the construction of oil and gas pipelines, water and sewer lines and gas distribution systems.
Cost: $80.00
Frequency: Annual
Circulation: 25,000

23405 **Platts UDI**
1200 G St NW
Suite 1000
Washington, DC 20005-3814
202-383-2144
800-752-8878
Fax: 202-942-8789
E-Mail: udi@platts.com
Home Page: www.marketing.platts.com
Liane Kucher, Manager
Publisher of directories for world-wide electric power industry.

23406 **Power Engineering**
PennWell Publishing Company
1421 S Sheridan Rd
Tulsa, OK 74112-6619
918-831-9421
800-331-4463
Fax: 918-831-9476
E-Mail: headquarters@pennwell.com
Home Page: www.power-eng.com
Rick Huntzicker, National Brand Manager
Dan Idoine, Regional Brand Manager
List of manufacturers and suppliers of products and services to the power plant and utility engineering industries.
Cost: $10.00
Frequency: Annual, September

23407 **Public Power Directory of Local Publicly Owned Electric Utilities**
American Public Power Association
2301 M St Nw
Suite 300
Washington, DC 20037-1427
202-467-2900
Fax: 202-467-2910
Home Page: www.appanet.org
Alan Richardson, Executive Director
Cost: $90.00
Frequency: Annual
Circulation: 13,000

23408 **Rural Electrification: Directory Issue**
National Rural Electric Cooperative Association
4301 Wilson Blvd
Arlington, VA 22203-1860
703-907-5500
Fax: 703-907-5526
Home Page: www.nreca.org
Glenn English, CEO
Over 1,000 electric cooperatives.
Frequency: Annual July
Circulation: 35,000

23409 **UDI Who's Who at Electric Power Plants**
Utility Data Institute
1200 G St NW
Suite 250
Washington, DC 20005-3814
202-942-8788
Offers valuable information on over 6,000 key personnel at over 1,200 electric utility plants.
Cost: $195.00
Frequency: Annual

23410 **US Electric Utility Industry Software Directory**
PennWell Publishing Company
PO Box 1260
Tulsa, OK 74101-1260
918-835-3161
800-752-9764
Fax: 918-831-9555
Home Page: www.utilityconnection.com
Wayne Beaty, Editor
Steve Hall, Advertising/Sales
An amazing reference directory offering information on over 400 programs in 75 applications categories covering all aspects of the electric power industry.
Cost: $175.00
140 Pages
Frequency: Annual

Industry Web Sites

23411 **http://gold.greyhouse.com**
G.O.L.D Grey House OnLine Databases
Grey House Publishing's online database platform, GOLD, offers Quick Search, Keyword Search and Expert Search for most business sectors including utility markets. The GOLD platform makes finding the information you need quick and easy - whether you're a novice searcher or an experienced database user. All of Grey House's directory products are available for subscription on the GOLD platform.

23412 **www.aeecenter.org**
Association of Energy Engineers
Source of information on the field of energy efficiency, utility deregulation, plant engineering, facility management and environmental compliance. Membership includes more than 8,000 professionals and certification programs. Offers seminars, conferences, job listings and certification programs.

23413 **www.apea.org**
American Public Energy Agency
Purpose is to provide energy acquisition and management services for public agencies.

23414 **www.apga.org**
American Public Gas Association
Association of municipal gas systems.

23415 **www.apwa.net**
American Public Works Association
For public agencies, private sector companies, and individuals dedicated to providing high quality public works goods and services.

23416 **www.awwa.org**
American Water Works Association
The professional society of North American drinking water experts. Develop standards and support research programs in waterworks design, construction, operation, and management. Conducts in-service training schools and offers placement service.

23417 **www.bus.msu.edu/ipu**
Institute of Public Utilities
Research and training center at Michigan State University. Program focuses on regulation and management of energy, telecommunications and water companies.

23418 **www.eei.org**
Edison Electric Institute
Advocates public policy, expands market opportunities and provides strategic business information for the shareholder-owned electric utility industry. Find out more about EEI's members, upcoming meetings, career opportunities and products and services.

23419 **www.eia.doe.gov/**
Energy Information Administration

23420 **www.electricity-online.com**
Electricity-Online

23421 **www.electricity-online.com/**
Electricity Journal and Daily

23422 **www.energycentral.com**
Energy Central

23423 **www.energymarketers.com**
National Energy Marketers Association

23424 **www.energyonline.com**
EnergyOnLine

23425 **www.energysearch.com**
EPRI Energysearch
Provides fast, accurate search results on global energy topics, and science and technolgoy R&D for the electricity industy.

23426 **www.energyusernews.com**
Energy User News Magazine

23427 **www.epri.com**
Electric Power Research Institute
Nonprofit organization providing science and technology-based solutions to its global energy customers. Manages a far-reaching program of research, technology development and product implementation.

23428 **www.epsa.org**
Electric Power Supply Association

23429 **www.greyhouse.com**
Grey House Publishing
Authoritative reference directories for most business sectors including utility markets. Users can search the online databases with varied search criteria allowing for custom searches by product category, geographic area, sales volume, keyword, subject and more. Full Grey House catalog and online ordering also available.

23430 **www.gri.org**
Gas Research Institute

23431 **www.hydro.org**
National Hydropower Association
For public and private utilities, developers, equipment manufacturers, engineering and design firms, environmental and hydro liscensing consultants, and legal and financial firms.
Membership dues: $1,000 - $18,000.

23432 **www.icea.net**
Insulated Cable Engineers Association
Professional organization dedicated to developing cable standards for the electric power, control and telecommunications industries. Ensures safe, economical and efficient cable systems utilizing proven state-of-the-art materials and concepts. ICEA documents are of interest to cable manufacturers, architects and engineers, utility and manufacturing plant personnel, telecommunication engineers, consultants and OEMs.

23433 **www.mcgraw-hill.com**
McGraw Hill
Provides news of significant developments affecting the electric utility industry focusing on state and federal regulation, management and bulk power markets.

23434 **www.naesco.org**
National Association of Energy Service Companies

23435 **www.naruc.org**
National Association of Regulatory Utility Commissioners
A national organization that offers valuable information on over 150 consultants and other professionals active in regulated water, sewer and related industries.

23436 **www.naseo.org**
National Association of State Energy Officials

23437 www.nerc.com
North American Electric Reliability Council
Voluntary organization promoting bulk electric system reliability and security.

23438 www.nreca.org
Action Committee for Rural Electrification
Political action committee that advocates support for rural electrification.

23439 www.oilonline.com
OilOnLine

23440 www.platts.com
Electrical World
The latest trends in utility engineering and IT, equipment and services, best business practices and critical industry thinking. For managers, engineers and technicians who plan, design, build, maintain and upgrade electric T&D systems around the world.

23441 www.ptda.org
Power Transmission Distributors Association
Members are power transmission/motion control distributor throughout manufacturing firms.

23442 www.publicworks.com
Public Works Online
For professionals in the public works industry.

23443 www.wateronline.com
Water Online

Associations

23444 1394 Trade Association
23117 39th Ave SE
Bothell
Mukilteo, WA 98021

425-870-6574
Fax: 425-320-3897
E-Mail: jsnider@1394ta.org
Home Page: www.1394ta.org

Richard Mourn, Chair
Morten Lave, Vice Chairman
Dave Thompson, Secretary/Editor
Richard Davies, Financial Officer

A trade association devoted to IEEE 1394 communications product furtherance.

23445 Adult Video Association
8033 Sunset Boulevard
PMB 851
Los Angeles, CA 90046-5323

323-436-0060
Fax: 818-501-7502
E-Mail: bmargold@aol.com

William Margold, Director

Trade association primarily concerned with opposing legislative initiatives to restrict the sale of sexually explicit film and video.
400 Members
Founded in 1987

23446 American Rhetoric

Home Page: www.americanrhetoric.com

An association dedicated to rhetoric and public communication in the US.

23447 Association for Recorded Sound Collections
c/o Nathan Georgitis
Knoght Library, 1299 University of
Eugene, OR 97403-1299

E-Mail: contact@arsc-audio.org
Home Page: www.arsc-audio.orgÿ
Social Media: Facebook, Twitter

A nonprofit organization dedicated to the preservation and study of sound recordings in all genres.
Founded in 1966

23448 Association of Visual Communicators
8130 La Mesa Boulevard
#406
La Mesa, CA 91941-6437

619-427-7524
Home Page: www.ivca.org
Social Media: Facebook, Twitter, LinkedIn, You Tube

Marco Forgione, CEO
David Cambridge, Head, Finance & Administration
Janet Cambridge, Administration
Dave Comley, Commercial Director

Sponsors seminars and competitions. Presents CINDY awards annually for 16mm films, videotapes, 35mm filmstrips, and video disc production.
500 Members
Founded in 1957

23449 Audio Engineering Society
60 East 42nd Street
Room 2520
New York, NY 10165-2520

212-661-8528
Fax: 212-682-0477
Home Page: www.aes.org
Social Media: Facebook, Twitter, LinkedIn, YouTube, RSS

Andre Mayo, President
David W. Scheirman, Vice President, Western Region
Michael Fleming, Vice President, Central Region
Ron Streicher, Secretary
Garry Margolis, Treasurer

Worldwide professional association for professionals and students involved in the audio industry.
Founded in 1948

23450 Audio Publishers Association
100 North 20th Street, Suite 400
Philadelphia, PA 19103

215-564-2729
Home Page: www.audiopub.org

Michele Cobb, President
Linda Lee, Vice President
Beth Anderson, Director
Janet Benson, Secretary
Sean McManus, Treasurer

Association for audio publishers.

23451 BICSI
Building Industry Consulting Service International
8610 Hidden River Pkwy
Tampa, FL 33637-1000

813-979-1991
800-242-7405
Fax: 813-971-4311
E-Mail: ayocum@bicsi.org
Home Page: www.bicsi.org
Social Media: Facebook, Twitter, LinkedIn, Youtube

Jerry L Clark Jr, President
Michael Collins, President Elect
Robert Erickson, Secretary
Brian Ensign, Treasurer

BICSI members include cabling contractors, manufacturers, systems integrators and other telecom professionals.

23452 Bay Area Video Coalition
2727 Mariposa St
Suite 200
San Francisco, CA 94110-1468

415-861-3282
Fax: 415-861-4316
E-Mail: bavc@bavc.org
Home Page: www.bavc.org
Social Media: Facebook, Twitter, LinkedIn, You Tube, Flickr

Bathsheba Malsheen, President
Neil O'Donnell, VP
Jason Kipnis, Treasurer
Jeremy O'Neal, Associate Director

A national organization for independent video producers and artists. Advanced, noncommercial, media arts center dedicated to providing access to media, education and technology.
Founded in 1976

23453 Central Station Alarm Association
8150 Leesburg Pike
Suite 700
Vienna, VA 22182-2721

703-242-4670
Fax: 703-242-4675
E-Mail: techadmin@csaaintl.org
Home Page: www.csaaul.org
Social Media: Facebook, Twitter, LinkedIn, RSS

Steve Doyle, Executive Director
Celia Besore, Director Marketing
John A Murphy, President

Trade association representing companies offering security/alarm monitoring systems through a central station.
Founded in 1950

23454 Church Music Association of America
12421 New Point Drive
Richmond, VA 23233
505-263-6298
E-Mail: contact@musicasacra.com
Home Page: musicasacra.com/music/recordings
Social Media: Facebook, Twitter, Google+

William P. Mahrt, President
Horst Buchholz, Vice President
Jeffrey Tucker, Director of Publications
Mary Jane Ballou, Secretary
Adam Wright, Treasurer

A nonprofit association for Catholic church musicians.
Founded in 1964

23455 Cinema Audio Society
827 Hollywood Way #632
Burbank, CA 91505

818-752-8624
Fax: 818-752-8624
E-Mail: CASAwards@CinemaAudioSociety.org
Home Page: cinemaaudiosociety.org

David Fluhr, CAS, President
Mark Ulano, CAS, Vice President
Deb Adair, Director
David J. Bondelevitch, CAS, Secretary
Peter R. Damski, CAS, Treasurer

An association celebrating the scores of movies and films.
Founded in 1964

23456 CompTIA
3500 Lacey Road
Suite 100
Downers Grove, IL 60515

630-678-8300
Fax: 630-678-8384
E-Mail: info@comptia.org
Home Page: www.comptia.org
Social Media: Facebook, Twitter, LinkedIn, You Tube, Flickr

MJ Shoer, Chairman
Robert Stegner, Vice Chair
Todd Thibodeaux, President/CEO

CompTIA is a trade association representing the international technology community. Its goal is to provide a unified voice, global advocacy, and leadership, and to advance industry growth through standards professional competence, education, and business solutions.

23457 Consumer Electronics Association (CEA)
1919 S Eads Street
Arlington, VA 22202

703-907-7600
866-858-1555
301-631-3983
Fax: 703-907-7675
E-Mail: cea@ce.org
Home Page: www.ce.org
Social Media: Facebook, Twitter, LinkedIn

Jay McLellan, Chair
Patrick Lavelle, Vice Chair
Gary Shapiro, President/CEO
Glenda MacMullin, Treasurer
Karen Chupka, Secretary

Consumer Electronics Association (CEA) provides valuable and innovative member-only resources including: exclusive information and unparalleled market research, networking opportunities with business advocates and leaders, up-to-date educational programs and technical training, exposure in extensive promotional programs, and representation from the voice of the industry.

23458 Entertainment Merchants Association
16530 Ventura Blvd, Suite 400
Encino, CA 91436-4551

818-385-1500
Fax: 818-933-0911
E-Mail: info@entmerch.org
Home Page: www.entmerch.org

Marty Graham Rentrak, Chairman
Mike Gimlett, Vice Chairman
Mark Fisher, President & CEO
Sean Bersell, SVP, Public Affairs
Carla Immordino, VP, Finance & Administration

A nonprofit international trade association dedicated to advancing the interests of the home entertainment industry.
45,00 Members

23459 Entertainment Software Association
575 7th Street NW, Suite 300
Washington, DC 20004

Home Page: www.theesa.com
Social Media: Facebook, Twitter

Michael D. Gallagher, President and CEO

The trade association of the video game industry.
Founded in 2000

23460 IFPI-Representing the Recording Industry Worldwide
3470 NW 82nd Avenue
Suite 680
Doral, FL 33122

305-567-0861
Fax: 305-567-0871
Home Page: www.ifpi.org
Social Media: Twitter

Frances Moore, Chief Executive Officer
Lauri Rechardt, Legal
Ang Kwee Tiang, Regional Director, Asia
Javier Asensio, Regional Director, Latin America
Jeremy Banks, Director, Anti-Piracy

Promoting the value of recorded music, safeguarding record producers' rights and expanding the commercial uses of recoded music in all markets.
1300 Members

23461 International Society of Videographers
8499 S. Tamiami Trail
Suite 208
Sarasota, FL 34238

941-923-5334
Fax: 941-921-3836
E-Mail: info@weva.com
Home Page: www.weva.com
Social Media: Facebook, Twitter, LinkedIn, You Tube

Exchanges information on technologies, techniques, and equipment, sponsors Hall of Fame and an international convention.
Founded in 1981

23462 National Association of Record Industry Professionals
P.O. Box 2446
Los Angeles, CA 91610-2446

818-769-7007
Home Page: www.narip.com
Social Media: Facebook, Twitter, YouTube, Vimeo

Association for all professionals in the music business.
130,0 Members
Founded in 1998

23463 Production Equipment Rental Association
14661 Tustin St.
PO Box 55515
Sherman Oaks, CA 91413-0515

407-629-4122
877-629-4122
Fax: 407-629-8884
Home Page: www.productionhub.com
Social Media: Facebook, Twitter, LinkedIn

Pat Patin, President
Mark Beasley, VP/Marketing
John Johnston, Executive Director

A worldwide trade organization that supplies production equipment to the entertainment industry. PERA promotes the commercial advancement of new technologies available from member companies to meet the ever-changing requirements of their client's artistic challenges.
180 Members
Founded in 1998

23464 Professional Audio-Video Retailers Association
10 E 22nd Street
Suite 301
Lombard, IL 60148-6191

630-268-1500
800-621-0298
Fax: 630-953-8957
E-Mail: webmaster@paralink.org
Home Page: www.paralink.org

Rosemary Wenstrom

An organization formed to assist the owners and operators of independently owned, high-end audio/video stores to work toward the mutually compatible goal of providing services to members which would be unattainable by retailers working separately.
204 Members

23465 Professional Lighting and Sound Association
630 Ninth Avenue, Suite 609
New York, NY 10036

212-244-1505
Fax: 212-244-1502
E-Mail: matthew.griffiths@plasa.org
Home Page: www.plasa.org
Social Media: Facebook, Twitter

Matthew Griffiths, Chief Executive Officer
Shane McGreevy, Chief Finance Officer
Lori Rubinstein, Director of International Programs
Jackie Tien, Group Publisher
Christopher Toulmin, Director of Events

A trade association for the lighting and sounds of the entertainment industry.
1200 Members

23466 Recording Industry Association of America
1025 F ST N.W., 10th Floor
Washington, DC 20004

202-775-0101
Home Page: www.riaa.com

Cary Sherman, Chairman & CEO
Mitch Glazier, Senior Executive Vice President
Steven M. Marks, Chief/ General Counsel, Director
Bill Hearn, Director

A trade group that represents the U.S. recording industry whose mission is to foster a business and legal climate that supports and promotes our members' creative and financial vitality.

23467 Special Interests
590 Knox Run Road
PO Box 193
Lanse, PA 16849-0193

814-345-6845
800-735-6997
Fax: 814-345-5566
E-Mail: verasi@verizon.net

Vera A Lockey, Owner

Health and safety sales DVD and videos.
Founded in 1997

23468 University Film and Video Association
E-Mail: ufvahome@gmail.com
Home Page: www.ufva.org
Social Media: Facebook, Twitter, LinkedIn, Vimeo, Instagram, YouTube

Norman Hollyn, President
Jennifer Machiorlatti, Executive Vice President
Heather Addison, Conference Vice President
Bart Weiss, Editorial Vice President
Tom Sanny, Treasurer

Association for videography and film making at universities.

23469 Video Software Dealers Association
16530 Ventura Blvd
Suite 400
Encino, CA 91436-4554

818-385-0567
800-955-8732
Fax: 818-385-0567
E-Mail: servicecenter@vsda.org
Home Page: www.vsda.org

Crossan Andersen, President
Carrie Dieterich, VP Marketing
Mark Fisher, VP Membership/Strategic Initiatives
Sean Bersell, VP Public Affairs
Nancy Gordon, iDEA Manager Ops & Special Projects

Nonprofit international trade association with a membership exceeding 4,500 member companies, representing more than 25,000 locations. Members include retailers, as well as manufacturers, distributors and related businesses that constitute the home video industry. Acts as a spokesperson for home video industry both internally and legislatively.
4.5M Members
Founded in 1981

23470 Wedding and Event Videographers Association International
8499 S. Tamiami Trail, #208
Sarasota, FL 34238

941-923-5334
Fax: 941-921-3836
E-Mail: info@weva.com, admin@weva.com
Home Page: www.weva.com

International association for wedding and event videographers.

Newsletters

23471 Consumer Multimedia Report
Warren Publishing
2115 Ward Ct Nw
Washington, DC 20037-1209

202-872-9200
800-771-9202
Fax: 202-318-8350
E-Mail: info@warren-news.com
Home Page: www.warren-news.com

Brig Easley, Manager
Daniel Warren, President/Editor
Paul Warren, Chair/Publisher

Emphasizes on emerging technologies, marketing strategies, and industry events and news.
Cost: $462.00
Frequency: BiWeekly

23472 DVD: Laser Disc Newsletter
PO Box 420
East Rockaway, NY 11518-420

516-594-9304
Fax: 516-594-9307
E-Mail: doug@dvdlaser.com
Home Page: www.dvdlaser.com

Douglas Pratt, Publisher

A consumer guide to DVD's with news, reviews, ads and more.
Cost: $47.50
24 Pages
Frequency: Monthly
Circulation: 5000
ISSN: 0749-5250
Founded in 1984
Mailing list available for rent: 5000 names at $100 per M

23473 PRC News
Corbell Publishing Company
201 S Alvarado St
Suite 410
Los Angeles, CA 90057-2353

213-483-4559
Fax: 310-258-8096
E-Mail: info@corbell.com
Home Page: www.corbell.com

Gabriel Carabello, President
Joseph Daneshrad, Circulation Manager

A weekly newsletter for the home video industry. Covers pre-recorded video statistics, people, calendar, etc.
Cost: $577.00
8 Pages
Frequency: Monthly
Circulation: 2000
ISSN: 0898-302X
Founded in 1988
Mailing list available for rent: 7000 names at $75 per M
Printed in on newsprint stock

23474 Production Equipment Rental Association
1806 Hammerlin Ave
Winter Park, FL 32789

407-629-4122
877-629-4122
Fax: 407-629-8884
E-Mail: info@peraonline.org
Home Page: www.productionhub.com
Social Media: Facebook, Twitter, LinkedIn, You Tube

Pat Patin, President
Mark Beasley, VP/Marketing
John Johnston, Executive Director

A worldwide trade organization that supplies production equipment to the entertainment industry. PERA promotes the commercial advancement of new technologies available from member companies to meet the ever-changing requirements of their client's artistic challenges.
180 Members

23475 Video Business
Reed Business Information
2000 Clearwater Dr
Oak Brook, IL 60523-8809

630-574-0825
Fax: 630-288-8781
E-Mail: kevin.davis@reedbusiness.com
Home Page: www.reedbusiness.com

Jeff Greisch, President
Paul Sweeting, Editor-at-Large
Charles Tanner, Circulation Manager

Publication includes the retail marketplace, probes business trends and issues, reviews new and upcoming video titles, and contains information and advice for running a successful retail business, and charts top video titles.
Cost: $70.00
Frequency: Weekly
Circulation: 47807
Founded in 1983

23476 Video Investor
Kagan Research
1 Lower Ragsdale Dr
Building One Suite 130
Monterey, CA 93940-5749

831-624-1536
800-307-2529
Fax: 831-625-3225
E-Mail: info@kagan.com
Home Page: www.kagan.com
Social Media: Facebook, Twitter, LinkedIn

Tim Baskerville, President
Tom Johnson, Marketing Manager

Authoritative look inside the business of renting and selling video cassettes. Exclusive estimates of retail and wholesale transactions and inventories. Tracking movies into the home. Three month trial is available.
Cost: $ 795.00
Frequency: Monthly

Magazines & Journals

23477 AudioVideo International
Dempa Publications
275 Madison Avenue
New York, NY 10016-1101

212-682-3755
Fax: 212-682-2730
Home Page: www.dempa.net/

Harry Iguchi, General Manager

Articles cover systems of home entertainment.
Cost: $48.00
100 Pages
Frequency: Quarterly
Founded in 1950

23478 CE Pro
EH Publishing
PO Box 989
Framingham, MA 01701-0989

508-820-1515
Fax: 508-663-1599
E-Mail: ehpubinc@ionet.net
Home Page: www.electronichouse.com

Kenneth D. Moyes, President
Jason Knott, Editor

Provides timely, top quality business, industry and product information, technical how-to articles, product comparisons, dealer profiles and marketing and management tips.
Frequency: Monthly
Circulation: 30,000

23479 CE Vision Magazine
Consumer Electronics Association
1919 S Eads Street
Arlington, VA 22202

703-907-7600
866-858-1555
301-631-3983
Fax: 703-907-7675
E-Mail: cea@ce.org
Home Page: www.ce.org

Gary Shapiro, President/CEO
Pat Lavelle, Chairman
Peter Lesser, Industry Executive Advisor
Jason Oxman, VP Communications
Jenny Pareti, Public Policy Director

Features valuable and innovative articles that address market research, networking opportunities with business advocates and leaders, up-to-date educational programs and technical training, exposure in extensive promotional programs, and representation from the voice of the industry.

23480 CVC Report
Creative Video Consulting
PO Box 5195
Saratoga Springs, NY 12866-8038

212-533-9870
Fax: 212-473-3772
E-Mail: cvcreort@aol.com
Home Page: www.cvc.nic.in

Mitchell Rowen, Publisher

Information for music video programming and production fields, contains charts, reviews, play lists, industry dialogue and news.
Cost: $225.00
Frequency: BiMonthly
Circulation: 800

23481 Digital Content Producer
Prism Business Media
9800 Metcalf Avenue
Overland Park, KS 66212-2216

913-341-1300
Fax: 913-967-1905
E-Mail: subs@prismb2b.com
Home Page: www.digitalcontentproducer.com

Scott Schwadron, Publisher
Cynthia Wisehart, Editoral Director
Kerby Asplund, Marketing
Laury Reeves, Circulation Manager

Features new product listings, updates on state of the art technology applied to new production techniques, and business industry news.
Cost: $70.00
Frequency: Monthly
Circulation: 50000
Founded in 1975

23482 Markee
HJK Publications
1018 Rosetta Dr
Deltona, FL 770-341-08

386-774-8881
Fax: 386-774-8908
E-Mail: markee@markeemag.com
Home Page: www.markeemag.com/
Social Media: Facebook, Twitter, LinkedIn

Janet Karcher, Publisher
Jonathan T Hutchinson, Editor-In-Chief
Shirley Boone, Circulation
Shirley Boone, Circulation

For the Southeast and Southwest film industry.
Cost: $24.00
Frequency: Monthly
Circulation: 12200
Founded in 1986

23483 PRC News
Corbell Publishing Company
201 S Alvarado St
Suite 410
Los Angeles, CA 90057-2353
213-483-4559
Fax: 310-312-4551
E-Mail: info@corbell.com
Home Page: www.corbell.com
Social Media: Facebook, Twitter, LinkedIn
Gabriel Carabello, President
Eric Jacobson, Senior VP
Maria Arnone, Publisher
Kelly Conlin, CEO
Lori Reeves, Circulation Manager
Contains information on pre-recorded videos, software, hardware and blank cassettes, includes industry news, pricing and distribution updates, and reviews videos soon to be released.
Cost: $577.00
8 Pages
Frequency: Monthly
Circulation: 2000
ISSN: 0898-302X
Founded in 1988
Printed in one color

23484 Professional Audio-Video Retailers
10 E 22nd Street
Suite 301
Lombard, IL 60148-6191
630-268-1500
800-621-0298
Fax: 630-953-8957
E-Mail: webmaster@paralink.org
Home Page: www.paralink.org
Rosemary Wenstrom
An organization formed to assist the owners and operators of independently owned, high-end audio/video stores to work toward the mutually compatible goal of providing services to members which would be unattainable by retailers working separately.
204 Members

23485 Prosound News
United Entertainment Media
28 East 28th Street
27th Fl
New York, NY 10016
212-378-0400
Fax: 212-378-2170
E-Mail: sedorusa@optonline.net
Home Page: www.governmentvideo.com
Social Media: Facebook, Twitter, LinkedIn
Gary Rhodes, International Ssales Manager
Frequency: Monthly
Circulation: 25500
Founded in 1978

23486 Sound & Video Contractor
Primedia
PO Box 12901
Shawnee Mission, KS 66282-2901
913-341-1300
866-505-7173
Fax: 913-514-6895
E-Mail: svcs@primedia.com
Home Page: www.primedia.com
Social Media: Facebook, Twitter, LinkedIn
Eric Jacobson, Senior VP
Maria Arnone, Publisher
Kelly Conlin, CEO
Lori Reeves, Circulation Manager
Kiby Asplund, Marketing Manager
Contains information on sound systems, video display, security, CCTV, home theater, and automation. Delivers in depth instruction and examples of successful installations, fundamental acoustical and video theory and news on new technologies affecting the systems contracting business.
Cost: $35.00
Frequency: Monthly
Circulation: 21000
Founded in 1895
Mailing list available for rent: 20,500 names at $110 per M

23487 Television Broadcast
Miller Freeman Publications
28 East 28th Street
Suite 4
New York, NY 10016
212-636-2700
Fax: 212-378-2170
E-Mail: sedorusa2optonline.net
Home Page: www.governmentvideo.com
Social Media: Facebook, Twitter, LinkedIn
Gary Rhodes, International Sales Manager
Television Broadcast primarily serves TV stations including commercial, public, educational, religious military TV stations or networks; teleproduction facilities including production, post-production, tape duplication, effects, audio production or independent program producer.
Frequency: Monthly
Circulation: 30,374
Founded in 1978
Printed in 4 colors on glossy stock

23488 Video & Entertainment
Fairchild Publications
2407 Timberloch Place
Suite B
New York, NY 77380
281-419-5725
877-652-5295
Fax: 281-419-5712
Home Page: www.supermarketnews.com
Dan Bagan, President
David Orgal, Editor

23489 Video Age International
Video Age International
216 E 75th St
Suite PW
New York, NY 10021-2921
212-288-3933
Fax: 212-734-9033
E-Mail: sales@videoageinternational.com
Home Page: www.videoageinternational.com
Social Media: Facebook, Twitter, LinkedIn
Dom Serafini, Publisher
Offers information on program sales and distribution of videocassettes, discs and allied media.
Cost: $30.00
Frequency: 7x/Year
Circulation: 12000

23490 Video Librarian
Video Librarian
3435 NE Nine Boulder Dr
Poulsbo
Seabeck, WA 98370
360-626-1259
800-692-2270
Fax: 360-830-9346
E-Mail: vidlib@videolibrarian.com
Home Page: www.videolibrarian.com
Randy Pitman, President
Anne Williams, Marketing Director
Jazza Williams, Associate Editor
Offers video reviews and news for public, school, academic and special libraries.
Cost: $64.00
56 Pages
Circulation: 2000
ISSN: 0887-6851
Founded in 1986

23491 Video Store Magazine
201 Sandpointe Ave
Suite 600
Santa Ana, CA 92707-8700
714-338-6700
800-854-3112
Fax: 714 513-8402
E-Mail: selliott@advanstar.com
Home Page: www.homemediaretailing.com
Thomas Arnold, Editor
Don Rosenberg, Publisher
Susan Elliott, Publications Coordinator
Steven J. Apple, Director, Business Development
Renee Rosado, Online Manager
Offers market research and buying information for industry people.
Cost: $48.00
Frequency: Weekly
Circulation: 44257

23492 Videomaker Magazine
Videomaker
1350 East 9th Street
PO Box 4591
Chico, CA 95927-4591
530-891-8410
Fax: 530-891-8443
Home Page: www.videomaker.com
Stephen Muratore, Editor-in-Chief
Jennifer O'Rourke, Managing Editor
Information about the world of camcorders, computers, tools and techniques for making video in a way that is timely, applicable, pertinent, engaging and understandable. Each month we teach production techniques, explain technology and include no less than two informative buyer's guides of products central to video. In addition, we are committed to objective analysis of videomaking products so our audience can rely on us for unbiased reporting.
Cost: $3.99
Frequency: Monthly
Circulation: 90,000
ISSN: 0889-4973
Printed in 4 colors on glossy stock

Trade Shows

23493 International Consumer Electronics Show (C ES)
Las Vegas Hotel & Casino
3000 S. Paradise
Las Vegas, VA 22202
866-539-8430
Home Page: www.ceweb.org
Social Media: Facebook, Twitter, LinkedIn
Gary Shapiro, President/CEO
Pat Lavelle, Chairman
Peter Lesser, Industry Executive Advisor
Jason Oxman, VP Communications
Jenny Pareti, Public Policy Director
The CES reaches across global markets, connects the industry and enables consumer electronics to grow and thrive. International CES is

owned and prroduced by the Consumer Electronics Association (CEA).
2000 Members
Frequency: January

23494 International Society of Videographers
PO Box 296
Sparkill, NY 10976-0296
859-624-5429
Fax: 845-359-8527
Steve Jambeck, Executive Director
Exchanges information on technologies, techniques, and equipment, sponsors Hall of Fame and an international convention.
Founded in 1981

Directories & Databases

23495 AV Market Place
Information Today
143 Old Marlton Pike
Medford, NJ 08055-8750
609-654-6266
800-300-9868
Fax: 609-654-4309
E-Mail: custserv@infotoday.com
Home Page: www.infotoday.com
Thomas H Hogan, President
Roger R Bilboul, Chairman Of The Board
The complete business directory of audio, audio visual, computer systems, film, video, and programming with industry yellow pages. The only guide needed to find more than 7,500 companies that create, apply or distribute AV equipment and services for business, education, science, and government.
Cost: $199.95
1700 Pages
Frequency: February
ISBN: 1-573871-87-7

23496 Orion Blue Book: Computer
Orion Research Corporation
14555 N Scottsdale Rd
Suite 330
Scottsdale, AZ 85254-3487
480-951-1114
Fax: 480-951-1117
Roger Rohrs, Owner
A list of manufacturers of data processing hardware and products for the computer industry.
Cost: $200.00
Frequency: Annual

23497 Orion Blue Book: Video and Television
Orion Research Corporation
14555 N Scottsdale Rd
Suite 330
Scottsdale, AZ 85254-3487
480-951-1114
800-844-0759
Fax: 480-951-1117
Home Page: www.bluebook.com
Roger Rohrs, Owner
List of more than 450 manufacturers of video and television products such as cameras, recorders, disc players, projectors, extenders, microphones, mixers, processors and color monitors.
Cost: $144.00
Frequency: Annual January

23498 Video Networks
Bay Area Video Coalition
1111 17th Street
San Francisco, CA 94107-2406
415-613-3282
Fax: 415-861-4316
Home Page: www.bavc.com
List of over 100 film festivals for independent video producers and artists.
Cost: $3.00
Frequency: Annual

23499 Video Source Book
Gale/Cengage Learning
Po Box 09187
Detroit, MI 48209-0187
248-699-4253
800-877-4253
Fax: 248-699-8049
E-Mail: gale.galeord@cengage.com
Home Page: www.gale.com
Social Media: Facebook, Twitter, LinkedIn, You Tube
Patrick C Sommers, President
The Video Source Book continues its comprehensive coverage of the wide universe of video offerings with listing for more than 130,000 complete program listings, encompassing over 160,000 videos.
Frequency: Annual
ISBN: 1-414435-09-6
Mailing list available for rent

Industry Web Sites

23500 http://gold.greyhouse.com
G.O.L.D Grey House OnLine Databases
Grey House Publishing's online database platform, GOLD, offers Quick Search, Keyword Search and Expert Search for most business sectors including video and audio markets. The GOLD platform makes finding the information you need quick and easy - whether you're a novice searcher or an experienced database user. All of Grey House's directory products are available for subscription on the GOLD platform.

23501 www.1394ta.org
1394 Trade Association

23502 www.asid.org
American Society of Interior Designers (ASID)

23503 www.avreps.org
Independent Professional Representatives Org

23504 www.bavc.org
Bay Area Video Collection

23505 www.bicsi.org
BICSI

23506 www.caba.org
Continental Automated Buildings Association (CABA)

23507 www.ce.org
Consumer Electronics Association (CEA)

23508 www.cedia.org
Custom Electronic Design & Installation Associatio

23509 www.comptia.org
CompTIA

23510 www.copper.org
Copper Development Association (CDA)

23511 www.csaaul.org
Central Station Alarm Association

23512 www.fla-alarms.org
Alarm Association of Florida

23513 www.greyhouse.com
Grey House Publishing
Authoritative reference directories for most business sectors including audio and video markets. Users can search the online databases with varied search criteria allowing for custom searches by product category, geographic area, sales volume, keyword, subject and more. Full Grey House catalog and online ordering also available.

23514 www.nsca.org
National Systems Contractors Association (NSCA)

23515 www.paralink.org
Professional Audio-Video Retailers Association

23516 www.riaa.org
Recording Industry Association of America

23517 www.siaonline.org
Security Industry Association

23518 www.soc.org
Society of Camera Operators

23519 www.tiaonline.org
Telecommunications Industry Association (TIA)

23520 www.vsda.org
Video Software Dealers Association

Associations

23521 **Allied Distribution**
4839 Sherburn Road
PO Box 607
Eagle River, WI 54521

715-479-3530
Fax: 715-479-3551
E-Mail: info@warehousenetwork.com
Home Page: www.warehousenetwork.com
Social Media: Facebook, Twitter, LinkedIn

Ernest Brunswick, President
Cyd Brunswick, Customer Service Manager

A sales and marketing association representing public warehouses and distribution centers in the United States.
75 Members
Founded in 1933

23522 **American Chain of Warehouses**
156 Flamingo Dr
Beecher, IL 60401-9725

708-946-9792
Fax: 708-946-9793
E-Mail: bjurus@acwi.org
Home Page: www.acwi.org
Social Media: Facebook, Twitter, LinkedIn

William J Jurus, VP

Sales and marketing company representing public warehouses.
50 Members
Founded in 1911

23523 **American Moving & Storage Association**
1611 Duke St.
Alexandria, VA 22314-3406

888-849-AMSA
Fax: 703-683-7527
Home Page: www.moving.org

Organization which provides information and tips to help with moving.
4000 Members
Founded in 1920

23524 **Automotive Warehouse Distributors Association**
7101 Wisconsin Avenue
Suite 1300
Bethesda, MD 20814-3415
301-654-6664
Fax: 301-654-3299
E-Mail: aaia@aftermarket.org
Home Page: www.aftermarket.org
Social Media: Facebook, Twitter, LinkedIn, Youtube, WordPress

Jack Creamer, President

A trade association consisting of more than 600 members who are manufacturers and warehouse distributors, affiliates, marketing associations and others actively involved in the production, distribution and installation of motor vehicle parts, tools, services, accessories, equipment, materials and supplies. A segment of the Automotive Aftermarket Industry Association
600 Members
Founded in 1947

23525 **Burley Auction Warehouse Association**
620 S Broadway STE 201
Lexington, KY 40508-3150

606-255-4504
Fax: 606-255-4534

Denny Wilson, Managing Director

Members are warehouse companies selling burley tobacco at auction in eight burley-producing states.
225 Members

23526 **Distributors & Consolidators of America**
2240 Bernays Drive
York, PA 17404
888-519-9195
Fax: 717-764-6531
E-Mail: daca@comcast.net
Home Page: www.dacacarriers.com

Mike Oliver, President
Andy Delaney, VP
Rick Staller, Secretary
Rich Eberhart, Treasurer

This organization helps firms and individuals active in the shipping, warehousing, receiving, distribution or consolidation of freight shipments.
39 Members
Founded in 1971

23527 **Distributors and Consolidators of America**

Home Page: dacacarriers.com
Social Media: Facebook, Twitter, LinkedIn

Mike Oliver, Chair
Andy Delaney, President
Rick Staller, Vice President
Mike Moran, Secretary
Rich Eberhart, Treasurer

Association for public warehousing.
Founded in 1971

23528 **Engine Service Association**
37 Pratt Street
Essex, CT 06426-1159

860-767-1770
Fax: 860-767-7932
E-Mail: executivedirector@opeesa.com
Home Page: www.opeesa.com

William L Robinson, Executive Director

Members are central warehouse distributors of internal combustion engines.
60 Members

23529 **Global Cold Chain Alliance**
1500 King Street
Ste 201
Alexandria, VA 22314-2730

703-373-4300
Fax: 703 373 4301
E-Mail: email@gcca.org
Home Page: www.gcca.org
Social Media: Facebook, Twitter, LinkedIn

Corey Rosenbusch, President and CEO
James Rogers, Director of Business Development
Tori Miller Liu, Director of Information Systems
Rita Haley, Executive Asst./ Office Manager
Lowell Randel, VP of Govt. & Legal Affairs

Association for the temperature-controlled products industry.
Founded in 2007

23530 **Independent Liquid Terminals Association**
1005 North Glebe Road
Suite 600
Arlington, VA 22201

703-875-2011
Fax: 703-875-2018
E-Mail: info@ilta.org
Home Page: www.ilta.org

Burton S Russell, Chairman
Earl J Crochet, Vice Chair
David A Ellis, Secretary
Eric W Thomas, Treasurer

We represent bulk liquid terminal companies that store commercial liquids in aboveground storage tanks (ASTs) and transfer products to and from oceangoing tank ships, tank barges, pipelines, tank trucks and tank rail cars.
400 Members
Founded in 1974

23531 **International Association of Refrigerated Warehouses**
1500 King Street
Suite 201
Alexandria, VA 22314

703-373-4300
Fax: 703-373-4301
E-Mail: email@gcca.org
Home Page: www.gcca.org
Social Media: Facebook, Twitter, LinkedIn

J William Hudson, CEO
Corey Rosenbusch, President/COO
Megan Costello, VP, Member & Industry Affairs
Lowell Randal, VP, Govt. & Legal Affairs

Trade association of public refrigerated warehouses storing of all types of perishable products.
900 Members
Founded in 1891

23532 **International Warehouse Logistics Association**
2800 S River Rd
Suite 260
Des Plaines, IL 60018-6003

847-813-4699
Fax: 847-813-0115
E-Mail: email@iwla.com
Home Page: www.iwla.com

Paul Verst, Chairman
Steve DeHaan, President/CEO
Tom Hersche, Vice Chair
Rob Doyle, Treasurer
Mark DeFabis, Secretary

The unified voice of the global logistics outsourcing industry, representing third party warehousing, transportation and logistics service providers. Our member companies provide the most timely and cost-effective global logistics solutions for their customers and are committed to protecting the free flow of products across international borders.
500 Members
Founded in 1997

23533 **Internationl Warehouse Logistics Association**
International Warehouse Logistics Association
2800 S River Road
Suite 260
Des Plains, IL 60018-5764

847-813-4699
Fax: 847-813-0115
E-Mail: email@iwla.com
Home Page: www.iwlz.com

Carrie Gremer, Contact
Joel Anderson, President
Nathan Noy, Gov't Affairs/Legal Services
Scott Brewster, Membership/Partnership
Carrie Gremer, Marketing/Communications

Trade association of public warehouses.
500+ Members
Founded in 1997

23534 Mobile Self-Storage Association
2001 Jefferson Davis Hwy
Suite 1004
Arlington, VA 22202-3617
703-416-0060
Fax: 703-416-0014
Home Page: www.ms-sa.org

Association for mobile-storage companies.

23535 National Portable Storage Association
3312 Broadway
Ste 105
Kansas City, MO 64111
866-777-0635
816-960-6552
Fax: 816-960-6575
E-Mail: joel@npsa.org
Home Page: www.npsa-us.org
Social Media: Facebook, Twitter, LinkedIn, YouTube

Association for portable-storage companies.

23536 RCS Limited
Computer Based Training
1301 Commerce Street
Birmingham, AL 35217
205-841-9955
888-833-1970
Fax: 205-841-2106
E-Mail: info@rcs-limited.co.uk
Home Page: www.rcs-limited.co.uk

Design and build contractor for cold storage warehouses.

23537 Refrigeration Research and Education
World Food Logistics Organization
P.O. Box 6315
Suite 201
Lubbock, TX 79493-6315
703-373-4300
806-789-4078
Fax: 703-373-4301
E-Mail: email@larw.org
Home Page: www.larw.org

Nitra Barnes, President
Michelle Spitzer, Press & Media Contact
Donna Walz, WebMaster
Heather Keister, Program Chair

Sponsors graduate-level scientific research in the refrigeration of perishable commodities. Offers annual training institute for public refrigerated warehouse personnel.
1M Members
Founded in 1943

23538 Self Storage Association
1901 N Beauregard St
Suite 110
Alexandria, VA 22311-1738
703-575-8000
888-735-3784
Fax: 703-575-8901
E-Mail: ssa@selfstorage.org
Home Page: www.selfstorage.org
Social Media: Facebook, Twitter, LinkedIn

Patrick Reilly, Chairman/Executive Director
JR Clisham, Vice Chairman/National Director
John Barry, Treasurer
Marc M Smith, Secretary

Self-storage facility owners/operators and suppliers to the industry.
6000 Members
Founded in 1975

23539 Storage Products Association
572 B Ruger Street
P.O. Box 29920
San Francisco, CA 94129-0920
415-561-6275
E-Mail: LoBue@Storage-Products-Association.org
Home Page: www.storage-products-association.org
Social Media: Twitter, RSS

Theodore Deffenbagh, President
D. Kurt Richarz, Board Member
Mark Grace, Board Member
Michael LoBue, Executive Director/ Secretary
Jeff Burke, PhD, Treasurer

Association for storage manufacturers and users.

23540 Warehousing Education and Research Council
1100 Jorie Boulevard
Ste 170
Oak Brook, IL 60523
630-990-0001
Fax: 630-990-0256
E-Mail: wercoffice@werc.org
Home Page: www.werc.org
Social Media: Twitter, LinkedIn, YouTube

Paul Avampato, President
Sheila Benny, Vice President
Michael J. Mikitka, CAE, Chief Executive Officer
Angie Silberhorn, CMP, Director of Conference
Dave Pardo, Marketing Manager

Association for logistics and warehouse professionals.

Newsletters

23541 AUA News
American Underground Space Association
1000 Corporate Boulevard
Linthicum, MD 21090
410-689-3700
866-746-4282
Fax: 410-689-3800
E-Mail: aua@AUAnet.org
Home Page: www.auanet.org

Thomas O'Neil, President
Elaine Gray, Editor

Offers the latest news on underground space construction development and use in North America. Includes information on infrastructures.
Cost: $107.00
Frequency: Quarterly
Circulation: 1000
Printed in 4 colors on glossy stock

23542 Affiliated Warehouse Companies Newsletter
Affiliated Warehouse Companies, Inc
PO Box 295
Hazlet, NJ 07730-0295
732-739-2323
Fax: 732-739-4154
E-Mail: sales@awco.com
Home Page: www.awco.com

Jim McBride, Publisher
Jim McBride, President
Patrick McBride, Vice President

Assists public warehouse users to gather rates and data, provides information on warehousing and distribution at no charge or obligation for over 100 public warehouse clients in the US, Canada, Mexico and Puerto Rico.
Mailing list available for rent: 8,500 names

23543 Distribution Center Management
Alexander Communications Group
712 Main Street~
Suite 187B
New York, NJ 07005
973-265-2300
800-232-4317
Fax: 973-402-6056
E-Mail: info@distributiongroup.com
Home Page: www.distributiongroup.com

Romauld Alexander, President
Margaret Dewitt, Publisher/Marketing Manager

Provides practical strategies and industry news to help distribution center and warehouse professionals improve distribution center efficiency.
Cost: $199.00
8 Pages
Frequency: Monthly
ISBN: 0-894765-1 -
Founded in 1985

Magazines & Journals

23544 Inside Self-Storage
Virgo Publishing LLC
3300 N Central Ave
Suite 300
Phoenix, AZ 85012-2532
480-990-1101
Fax: 480-990-0819
E-Mail: troyb@vpico.com
Home Page: www.vpico.com

Jenny Bolton, President
John Siefert, CEO & Director
Kelly Ridley, VP
John LyBarger, Director, Business Development
Troy Bix, Publications Editor

For storage professionals.
Frequency: Monthly
Circulation: 20000
Founded in 1991
Mailing list available for rent

23545 Logistics Management & Distribution Report
Reed Business Information
225 Wyman St
Suite 3
Waltham, MA 02451-1216
781-734-8000
Fax: 781-734-8076
E-Mail: fquinn@reedbusiness.com
Home Page: www.reedbusiness.com

Mark Finklestein, President
Mike Levin, Group Editor-in-Chief
Frank Quinn, Editorial Director
Stephen Moylan, President, Divisions

Logistics Management and Distribution Report is written for managers and professionals in charge of traffic, transportation, purchasing, inventory control, containerization and warehousing the functions of physical distribution and business logistics. Covers marketing and operating strategies, cost reduction opportunities and governmental regulation and law.
Cost: $99.90
Frequency: Monthly
Circulation: 68000
Founded in 1977

23546 Mini-Storage Messenger
MiniCo

2531 W Dunlap Ave
Phoenix, AZ 85021-2730

602-870-1711
800-824-6864
Fax: 602-861-1094
E-Mail: publishing@minico.com
Home Page: www.ministoragemessenger.com

Hardy Good, President
Denise Nunez, Director Publishing

As the industry's first trade journal, the mini-storage messenger has become the leading trade magazine for anyone involved in self-storage. This magazine covers rental rates, marketing trends, and finance.
Cost: $59.95
89 Pages
Frequency: Monthly
Founded in 1979
Printed in 4 colors on glossy stock

23547 **Refrigerated Transporter**
Primedia
PO Box 66010
Houston, TX 77266

713-513-8124
800-880-0368
Fax: 713-523-8384
Home Page: www.refrigeratedtrans.com

Ray Anderson, Advertising
Jay Russel Miller, Editorial
Maria Singletary, Directories
Frequency: Monthly
Circulation: 15000
Founded in 1898

23548 **Storage**
West World Productions
420 N Camden Dr
Beverly Hills, CA 90210-4507

310-276-9500
Fax: 310-276-9874
E-Mail: sinan@kanatsiz.com
Home Page: www.wwpi.com

Yuri R Spiro, Publisher
Laura Klein, Production Manager

Storage is the unique storage-intensive magazine supplement to Computer Technology Review. It is recognized as the bible of the entire storage industry.
Cost: $10.00
72 Pages
Frequency: Quarterly
Circulation: 72000
ISSN: 0278-9647
Founded in 1981
Printed in 4 colors on glossy stock

23549 **Warehousing Management**
Reed Business Information
225 Wyman St
Suite 3
Waltham, MA 02451-1216

781-734-8000
Fax: 781-734-8076
E-Mail: fquinn@reedbusiness.com
Home Page: www.reedbusiness.com

Mark Finklestein, President
Mike Levin, Group Editor-in-Chief
Frank Quinn, Editorial Director
Stephen Moylan, President, Divisions

Warehousing Management targets warehousing and distribution center operations managers with analysis, news, trends, equipment and events.
Circulation: 47185
Founded in 1977

Trade Shows

23550 **Eastpack**
Reed Exhibition Companies
255 Wyman Streett
Waltham, MA 02451

781-734-8000
Fax: 781-734-8076
E-Mail: fquinn@reedbusiness.com
Home Page: www.reedbusiness.com

Mark Finklestein, President
Mike Levin, Group Editor-in-Chief
Frank Quinn, Editorial Director
Stephen Moylan, President, Divisions

275 booths.
7.5M Attendees
Frequency: March
Founded in 1977

23551 **Household Goods Forwarders Association**
5904 Richman Avenue
Suite 304
Alexandria, VA 22303-4691
703-684-3780

Belvian Carpinton, Show Manager
Terry Head, President

20 tables.
1M Attendees
Frequency: September

23552 **Independent Liquid Terminals Assoc. Annual Operating Conference & Trade Show**
Independent Liquid Terminals Association
1005 North Glebe Road
Suite 600
Arlington, VA 20005

703-875-2011
Fax: 703-875-2018
E-Mail: info@ilta.org
Home Page: www.ilta.org

E. David Doane, President
Melinda Whitney, Director/Government Affairs

Two-hundred and two booths of products including goods and services designed for the construction and operation of bulk liquid storage terminals. Includes international companies.
2,700 Attendees
Frequency: June

23553 **Inside Self-Storage World Expo**
Virgo Publishing LLC
3300 N Central Ave
Suite 300
Phoenix, AZ 85012-2532

480-675-9925
Fax: 480-990-0819
E-Mail: kkennedy@vpico.com
Home Page: www.vpico.com

Jenny Bolton, President

The self-storage industry's largest, most comprehensive conference and tradeshow. The leading educational and networking event for facility managers, owners, developers and investors, the ISS Expo provides the resources professionals need to build, manage and market their business in a competitive environment.
Circulation: 20000
Founded in 1986
Printed in on glossy stock

23554 **International Transportation and Logistics Exhibition and Conference**
ILT
1300 Higgins Road
Suite 111
Park Ridge, IL 60068-5764
847-292-1891
Fax: 847-823-3901
Home Page: www.warehouselogistics.org

Marge Whalen, Director of Sales
Regan Williams, Trade Show Coordinator

Annual conference and trade show focusing on public warehousing, distribution, transportation, logistics and systems. Containing 200 exhibits.
3,000 Attendees
Frequency: June

23555 **NORPACK**
Northern American Expositions Company
33 Rutherford Avenue
Charlestown, MA 02129

617-242-6092
800-225-1577
Fax: 617-242-1817
E-Mail: naexpo@hotmail.com
Home Page: naexpo.com

The Northeast's premier trade show for packaging, material handling, warehouse automation, shipping/receiving, storage and bottling.
4500 Attendees

23556 **Northwest Material Handling & Packaging Show**
Professional Trade Shows-Division of Penton Media
47817 Fremont Boulevard
Fremont, CA 94538

510-651-6698
Fax: 510-354-3159
Home Page: proshows.com

5,000 Attendees
Frequency: May

23557 **Pack Expo**
Pakaging Machinery Manufacturers Institute
4350 N Fairfax Drive
Suite 600
Arlington, VA 22203

703-243-8555
888-275-7664
E-Mail: pmmi@pmmi.org
Home Page: www.packexpo.com

Matt Crossn, Communications Director
Sara Kryder, Assistant Communications

Informational meeting and exposition held by the Packaging Machinery Manufacturers Institute.
15000 Attendees

23558 **Warehousing, Technology & Distribution Show**
Industrial Shows of America
164 Lake Front Drive
Hunt Valley, MD 21030-2215

410-771-1445
800-638-6396
Fax: 410-771-1158

This show will feature hands-on workshops for the practical applications of new technologies, safety issues and more all designed to improve productivity and cut losses in today's competitive market.
1500 Attendees
Frequency: April

Directories & Databases

23559 Affiliated Warehouse Companies Database of Public Warehouse Users
Affiliated Warehouse Companies, Inc.
PO Box 295
Hazlet, NJ 07730-0295
732-739-2323
Fax: 732-739-4154
E-Mail: sales@awco.com
Home Page: www.awco.com
Jim McBride, President
Patrick McBride, Vice President
Jim McBride, Publisher
In excess of 8,000 listings of individuals and companies that use public warehousing, products produced and services required.
Mailing list available for rent: 8,500 names

23560 American Chain of Warehouses Directory
20500 S La Grange Road
Frankfort, IL 60423-1356
703-875-2018
Fax: 815-469-2941
Donald R Greenland, Executive VP
Public warehouse listings in the United States are profiled.
50 Pages
Frequency: Annual

23561 American Public Warehouse Register
Reed Business Information
2 Brandywine Way
Sicklerville, NJ 08081-0750
856-728-9745
Fax: 630-288-8686
Home Page: www.reedbusiness.com
Laura Masapollo, National Sales Director
Laura MasaPollo, National Sales Director
Worldwide listings of dry, refrigerated, contract and HazMat Public Warehouses Annual.
Cost: $50.00

23562 Associated Warehouses Directory of Services
PO Box 471
Cedar Knolls, NJ 07927-0471
973-539-1277
Fax: 973-538-0944
Home Page: www.awilogistics.com
Mark Richards, Editor
Barbara Brown, Circulation Director
A who's who directory of services to the industry.
100 Pages
Frequency: Annual

23563 Directory of Bulk Liquid Terminal and Storage Facilities
ITLA
1133 15th Street NW
Sutie 650
Washington, DC 20005
202-659-2301
Fax: 202-466-4166
E-Mail: info@ilta.org
Home Page: www.ilta.org
John Prokop, President
EB Calvert, Director Administration
Locates over 480 bulk liquid terminal/storage facilities. Lists key personnel, addresses, telephone numbers. Lists products handled-petroleum products, crude oil, chemicals, animal fats and oils, vegetable oils, molasses, spirits, etc. Lists storage tanks, modes served, pipeline connections. Other services and capabilities-canning, barreling, bleaching, blending, weighing, warehousing, etc. Subc. available for Directory and Newsletter
Cost: $95.00
300 Pages
Frequency: Annual

23564 Food & Beverage Market Place
Grey House Publishing
4919 Route 22
PO Box 56
Amenia, NY 12501
518-789-8700
800-562-2139
Fax: 845-373-6390
E-Mail: books@greyhouse.com
Home Page: www.greyhouse.com
Social Media: Facebook, Twitter
Leslie Mackenzie, Publisher
Richard Gottlieb, Editor
This information-packed 3-volume set is the most powerful buying and marketing guide for the US food and beverage industry. Includes thousands of industry freight and transportation listings.
Cost: $595.00
2000 Pages
Frequency: Annual
ISBN: 1-592373-61-5
Founded in 1981

23565 Food & Beverage Marketplace: Online Database
Grey House Publishing
4919 Route 22
PO Box 56
Amenia, NY 12501
518-789-8700
800-562-2139
Fax: 845-373-6390
E-Mail: gold@greyhouse.com
Home Page: http://gold.greyhouse.com
Social Media: Facebook, Twitter
Richard Gottlieb, President
Leslie Mackenzie, Publisher
This complete updated Food & Beverage Market Place: Online Database is the go-to source for the food and beverage industry. Anyone involved in the food and beverage industry needs this 'industry bible' and the important contacts to develop critical research data that can make for successful business growth.
Frequency: Annual
Founded in 1981

23566 Independent Liquid Terminals Association
1444 Eye St NW
Suite 400
Washington, DC 20005-6538
202-842-9200
Fax: 703-875-2018
E-Mail: info@ilta.org
Home Page: www.ilta.org
E David Doane, President
Melinda Whitney, Director/Government Affairs
A 285 page directory, listing 577 for hire, marketing, throughput, and pipeline bulk liquid storage terminals.
Cost: $95.00
285 Pages
Founded in 1975

23567 International Directory of Public Refrigerated Warehouses
1500 King Street
Suite 201
Alexandria, VA 22314
703-373-4300
Fax: 703-373-4301
E-Mail: email@iwra.org
Home Page: www.iarw.org
J William Hudson, President/CEO
Offers information on more than 950 member warehouses in 32 countries and on companies supplying products and services to the refrigerated warehouse industry.
Cost: $150.00
232 Pages
Frequency: Annual
Circulation: 6,000

23568 International Warehouse Logistics Directory
1300 Higgins Rd
Suite 111
Park Ridge, IL 60068-5743
847-292-1891
Fax: 847-813-0115
E-Mail: bstephens@warehouselogistics.org
Home Page: www.iwla.com
Joel Anderson, President
Ben Stephens, Public Relations/Media Coordinator
The membership directory is published annually in January in book and CD-ROM form.
Frequency: Annually

23569 National Refrigeration Contractors Association
National Refrigeration Contrtactors
1900 Arch Street
Philadelphia, PA 19103-1404
215-564-3484
Fax: 215-963-9785
Home Page: www.arcat.com
Elizabeth Barnett, Editor
About 100 member refrigeration contracting companies
Frequency: Annual

23570 Transportation & Distribution Magazine's Integrated Warehousing/Storage
Penton Media
1166 Avenue of the Americas
New York, NY 10036
212-204-4200
Fax: 216-696-6662
E-Mail: information@penton.com
Home Page: www.penton.com
Jane Cooper, Marketing
Lists over 1,200 manufacturers of products related to the warehousing and distribution industries.
Frequency: Annual
Circulation: 71,000
Printed in 4 colors on glossy stock

23571 Warehouses Licensed Under US Warehouse Act
Farm Service Agency-US Dept. of Agriculture
PO Box 2415
Washington, DC 20013-2415
FAX 202-690-0014
Home Page: www.fsa.usda.gov/
Agricultural warehouses voluntarily licensed under the US Warehouse Act governing public storage facilities.
Frequency: Annual

23572 Warehousing Distribution Directory
PRIMEDIA Information
3585 Engineering Drive
Suite 100
Norcross, GA 30092

678-421-3000
800-216-1423
Fax: 609-371-7819
Home Page: www.primediainfo.com

Amy Middlebrook, Editor
John Capers III, Publisher

List of about 800 warehousing and consolidation companies and firms offering trucking, trailer on flatcar, container on flatcar and piggyback carrier services.
Cost: $55.00
250 Pages
Frequency: SemiAnnual
Circulation: 10,000
Founded in 1949
Printed in 4 colors on glossy stock

Industry Web Sites

23573 http://gold.greyhouse.com
G.O.L.D Grey House OnLine Databases
Grey House Publishing's online database platform, GOLD, offers Quick Search, Keyword Search and Expert Search for most business sectors including warehousing and storage markets. The GOLD platform makes finding the information you need quick and easy - whether you're a novice searcher or an experienced database user. All of Grey House's directory products are available for subscription on the GOLD platform.

23574 www.awco.com
Affiliated Warehouse Companies
Assists public warehouse users to gather rates and data, provides information on warehousing and distribution at no charge or obligation for over 100 public warehouse clients in the US, Canada, Mexico, Europe and Southeast Asia.

23575 www.greyhouse.com
Grey House Publishing
Authoritative reference directories for direct marketing, demographics, business, research, health care, international trade, food industry and education. Users can search the online databases with varied search criteria allowing for custom searches by product category, geographic area, sales volume, keyword, subject and more. Full Grey House catalog and online ordering also available.

23576 www.larw.org
Refrigeration Research and Education Foundation
Sponsors graduate-level scientific research on the refrigeration of perishable commodities. Offers annual training institute for public refrigerated warehouse personnel.

23577 www.warehouselogistics.org
International Warehouse Logistics Association
For third-party warehousing and related logistics services throughout the world. Collectively, the Association's members ship over 3 trillion pounds annually in North America.

Associations

23578 Alliance for Water Efficiency
300 W. Adams Street
Suite 601
Chicago, IL 60606-5109

773-360-5100
866-730-1493
Fax: 773-345-3636
E-Mail: jeffrey@a4we.org
Home Page:
www.allianceforwaterefficiency.org

Mary Ann Dickinson, President/ CEOÿ
Megan Chery, Manager
William Christiansen, Program Manager
Molly Garcia, Accountantÿ
Jeffrey Hughes, Administrative Directorÿ

An association for water efficient products.
Founded in 2007

23579 American Backflow Prevention Association
3016 Maloney Ave
PO Box 3051
Bryan, TX 77801-3121

979-846-7606
877-227-2127
Fax: 979-846-7607
Home Page: www.abpa.org

Michael Moss, International Presidentÿ
John Graham, International Vice President
Patti Fauver, Treasurer
Darren Chitwood, Secretary
Shane Dillard, Director of AdministrativeÿAffairs

An association dedicated to backflow education and technical assistance.
Founded in 1984

23580 American Fisheries Society
5410 Grosvenor Lane
Bethesdaÿ, MD 20814

301-897-8616
Fax: 301-897-8096
E-Mail: sjohnston@fisheries.org
Home Page: fisheries.org
Social Media: x, x, x, Pinterest, Google+, Vimeo

Douglas ÿ Austen, Executive Director
Beth Beard, Digital Content
Thomas Bigford, Policy Director
Juanita Flick, Membership Assistant
Sarah Gilbert Fox, Managing Editor, Fisheries and AFS

Organization dedicated to strengthening the fisheries profession and advancing fisheries.
Founded in 1870

23581 American Ground Water Trust
50 Pleasant Street
Suite 2
Concord, NH 3301

603-228-5444
800-423-7748
Fax: 603-228-6557
E-Mail: trustinfo@agwt.org
Home Page: www.agwt.org

Kevin McGinnis, Chairman
Scott Riegert, Secretary
Andrew Stone, Executive Director

Promotes public awareness of groundwater.

23582 American Institute of Hydrology
1230 Lincoln Drive
Carbondale, IL 62901

618-453-7809
E-Mail: aih@engr.siu.edu
Home Page: www.aihydrology.org

Dr. Stephan J. Nix, President
Dr. John L. Nieber, VP for Academic Affairs
John W. Balay, VP for Institute Development
Ed A. Baquerizo, VP for International Affairs
Kurt Hollman, VP for Communication

Promotes hydrology as a science and a profession.
Founded in 1981

23583 American Recreation Coalition
1200 G Street NW
Suite 650
Washington, DC 20005-3832

202-682-9530
Fax: 202-682-9529
E-Mail: mmeade@funoutdoors.com
Home Page: www.funoutdoors.com

Derrick Crandall, President
Catherine Ahern, VP
Melinda Meade, Director of Communications

A non-profit Washington based federation that provides a unified voice for recreation interests to conserve their full and active participation in government policy making on issues such as public land management. ARC works to build public-private partnerships to enhance and protect outdoor recreation opportunities and resources.
100+ Members
Founded in 1979

23584 American Rivers
1101 14th Street NW
Suite 1400
Washington, DC 20005

202-347-7550
877-347-7550
Fax: 202-347-9240
E-Mail: akober@americanrivers.org
Home Page: www.americanrivers.org
Social Media: Facebook, Twitter, YouTube, Pinterest

William Robert (Bob) Irvin, President
Sandra Adams, SVP, Advancement
Chris Alford, Associate Director
Fay Augustyn, Manager
Courtney Barefoot, Admin & Board Relations Coor

Nonprofit conservation organization dedicated to protecting and restoring the rivers of the US.
Founded in 1973

23585 American Society of Irrigation Consultants
4660 S Hagadorn
Suite 110F
East Lansing, MI 48823

508-763-8140
Fax: 508-763-8102
E-Mail: NormanB@asic.org
Home Page: www.asic.org

Carol Colein, Executive Director

Promotes education skills on data exchange landscape irrigation. Members are irrigation consultants, suppliers, and manufacturers.
Founded in 1970

23586 American Water Resources Association
PO Box 1626
Middleburg, VA 20118

540-687-8390
Fax: 540-687-8395
E-Mail: info@awra.orgÿ
Home Page: www.awra.org
Social Media: x, x, x, Blog

Kenneth D. Reid, CAEÿ, Executive Vice President
Michael J. Kowalski, CAEÿ, Director of Operations
Richard A. Engbergÿ, Technical Director
Patricia A. Reidÿ, Program Coordinatorÿ
Christine McCrehin, Membership Services Manager

Promotes understanding of water resources and related issues.
Founded in 1964

23587 American Water Works Association
6666 W. Quincy Ave.
Denver, CO 80235-3098

303-794-7711
800-926-7337
Home Page: www.awwa.org
Social Media: x, x, x, YouTube, RSS

John J. Donahue, President
Gene C. Koontz, President-Elect
James A. Chaffee, Immediate Past-President
Dave E. Rager, Treasurer
Paula I. MacIlwaine, Deputy ChiefÿExecutive Officer

Nonprofit scientific and education orgaization dedicated to managind and treating water.
Founded in 1881

23588 American Whitewater
P.O. Box 1540
Cullowhee, NC 28723

828-586-1930
866-262-8429
Fax: 828-586-2840
E-Mail: membership@americanwhitewater.org
Home Page: www.americanwhitewater.org

Mark Singleton, Executive Director
Kevin Colburn, National Stewardship Director
Bob Nasdor, Northeast Stewardship Director
Dave Steindorf, California Stewardship Director
Nathan Fey, Colorado Stewardship Director

Association for whitewaters and rafting.
Founded in 1954

23589 Association of Clean Water Administrators
1634 Eye St. NW
Suite 750
Washington, DC 20006

202-756-0605
Fax: 202-793-2600
Home Page: www.acwa-us.org

Julia Anastasio, Executive Director/ General Counsel
Sean Rolland, Deputy Director
Annette Ivey, Director of Operations
Susan Kirsch, Sr. Environmental Program Manager
Melissa McCoy, Environmental Program Manager

Association for the administrators of the clean water industry.
Founded in 1961

23590 Association of State Drinking Water Administrators
1401 Wilson Blvd
Suite 1225
Arlington, VA 22209

703-812-9505
Fax: 703-812-9506
E-Mail: info@asdwa.org
Home Page: www.asdwa.org
Social Media: x, x, YouTube, Blog

Professional association serving state drinking water programs.

23591 Association of State Wetland Managers
32 Tandberg Trail
Suite 2A
Windham, ME 04062ÿ

207-892-3399
Home Page: aswm.org
Social Media: x, Blog

A professional association for state wetland managers.
Founded in 1983

23592 Clean Water Action

Home Page: www.cleanwateraction.org
Social Media: Facebook, Twitter, YouTube, Blog

Robert Wendelgass, President/ CEO
Kathy Aterno, National Managing Director
Lynn Thorp, National Campaigns Director
Andrea Herrmann, Director
Chris Bathurst, National Canvass Coordinator

A national citizen's organization working for clean, safe and affordable water and prevention of health-threatening pollution.
Founded in 1960

23593 Coastal & Estuarine Research Federation
2150 North 107th Street
Suite 205
Seattle, WA 98133-9009

206-209-5262
Fax: 206-367-8777
E-Mail: info@erf.org
Home Page: www.erf.org

Kenneth L. Heck, Jr., President
Robert R. Twilley, President-Elect
Enrique Reyes, Secretary
James Hagy, Treasurer
Mark Wolf-Armstrong, Executive Director (Ex-Officio)

Private nonprofit organization dedicated to advancing the understanging of coastal and estuarine ecosystems.

23594 Ground Water Protection Council
13308 N Macarthur Blvd
Oklahoma City, OK 73142-3021

405-516-4972
Fax: 405-516-4973
E-Mail: dan@gwpc.org
Home Page: www.gwpc.org

Mike Paque, Executive Director
Ben Grunewald, Associate Director
Paul Jehn, Technical Director
Dan Yates, Member Servicess Coordinator

State ground water and underground injection control agencies whose mission is to promote the protection and conservation of ground water resources for all beneficial uses, recognizing ground water as a component of the ecosystem.
1.75M Members
Founded in 1983

23595 Irrigation Association
6540 Arlington Blvd
Falls Church, VA 22042-6638

703-536-7080
Fax: 703-536-7019
E-Mail: info@irrigation.org
Home Page: www.irrigation.org

Warren C Thoma, President
Aric J Olson, President Elect
Jackie W Robbins, VP
Gregory R Hunter, Treasurer

The Irrigation Association is the leading membership organization for irrigation equipment and system manufacturers, dealers, distributors, designers, consultants, contractors and end users.
1600 Members
Founded in 1949

23596 National Aquaculture Association
PO Box 12759
Tallahassee, FL 32317

850-216-2400
Fax: 850-216-2480
E-Mail: naa@thenaa.net
Home Page: thenaa.net

Mike Freeze, President
Jim Ekstrom, Vice-President
Adam Hater, Secretary
Rick Martin, Treasurer

A producer-based association dedicated to aquaculture.

23597 National Association of Clean Water Agencies
1816 Jefferson Place N.W.
Washingtonÿ, DC 20036

202-833-2672
Fax: 888-267-9505
E-Mail: info@nacwa.org
Home Page: www.nacwa.org
Social Media: Facebook, Twitter, LinkedIn, YouTube

Ken Kirk, Executive Director
Paula Dannenfeldt, Deputy Executive Director
Shalina Baker, Executive Assistant
Nathan Gardner-Andrews, General Counsel
Amanda Waters, Deputy General Counsel

Nationally recognized leader in environmental policy and a technical resource on water quality and ecosystem protection.
Founded in 1970

23598 National Drilling Association
4036 Center Rd
Suite B
Brunswick, OH 44212

330-273-5756
877-632-4748
Fax: 216-803-9900
E-Mail: info@nda4u.com
Home Page: www.nda4u.com
Social Media: Facebook, LinkedIn

Dan Dunn, President
Larry Gibel, VP
Tim Augustine, Secretary/Treasurer

A non-profit trade association of contractors, manufacturers and affiliated members from the drilling industry representing the geotechnical, environmental and mineral exploration sectors of this industry.
250+ Members
Founded in 1972

23599 National Environmental Services Center
Box 6893, West Virginia University
Morgantown, WV 26506-6893

304-293-4191
800-624-8301
Fax: 304-293-3161
E-Mail: info@mail.nesc.wvu.edu
Home Page: www.nesc.wvu.edu
Social Media: Facebook, Twitter, WordPress

Gerald Iwan, Director

Helps small, rural communities with their drinking water, wastewater and environmental training needs.
Founded in 1984

23600 National Institute for Water Resources
University of Massachusetts
Blaisdell House
Amherst, MA 01003

413-545-2842
Fax: 413-545-2304
E-Mail: support@niwr.net
Home Page: www.niwr.net

Brian Haggard, President
Sharon Megdal, President Elect
John Tracy, Secretary/Treasurer

Offers information on water resource directions across the nation.
54 Members
Founded in 1974

23601 National Onsite Wastewater Recycling
601 Wythe Street
Alexandria, VA 22314

410-798-1697
800-966-2942
Fax: 703-535-5263
E-Mail: info@nowra.org
Home Page: www.nowra.org
Social Media: Facebook

Tom Fritts, President
Gregory D Graves, President Elect/VP
Robert B Mayer, Secretary/Treasurer

Dedicated solely to educating and representing members within the onsite and decentralized industry. And also to provide leadership and promote the onsite waste water treatment and recycling through education, training, communication and quality tools to support excellence in performance.
3500 Members
Founded in 1991

23602 National Onsite Wastewater Recycling Assoc iation
1199 N. Fairfax St.
Suite 410
Alexandria, VA 22314

703-836-1950
800-966-2942
Home Page: www.nowra.org

Organization dedication to onsite wastewater recycling.

23603 National Rural Water Association
3800 Fairfax Dr
Suite 4
Arlington, VA 22203-1703

703-524-1544
Fax: 703-524-1548
E-Mail: nwra@nwra.org
Home Page: www.nrwa.org
Social Media: Twitter

Tom Myrum, President
Dave Koland, 1st VP
Ron Thompson, 2nd VP
Thomas F Donnelly, Secretary
Wayne Cunningham, Treasurer

Dedicated to the wise management and use of the nation's water and land resources.
5M+ Members
Founded in 1932

23604 National Water Research Institute
18700 Ward Streetÿ
P.O. Box 8096ÿ
Fountain Valley, CA 92728-8096

714-378-3278
Fax: 714-378-3375
E-Mail: jmosher@nwri-usa.org
Home Page: www.nwri-usa.org
Social Media: Facebook, Twitter, LinkedIn, YouTube

Jeff Mosher, Executive Directorÿ
Gina Vartanian, Communications and Outreach Manager

Brandi Caskey, Administrative and Events Manager
Suzanne Faubl, Manager
Ken Lanxner, Webmasterÿ

A nonprofit organization devoted to promoting the protection, maintenance and restoration of water supplies.
Founded in 1991

23605 National Water Resources Association
3800 Fairfax Dr
Suite 4
Arlington, VA 22203-1703

703-524-1544
Fax: 703-524-1548
E-Mail: nwra@nwra.org
Home Page: www.nwra.org
Social Media: Twitter

Tom Myrum, President
Dave Koland, 1st VP
Ron Thompson, 2nd VP
Thomas F Donnelly, Secretary
Wayne Cunningham, Treasurer

Dedicated to the wise management and use of the nation's water and land resources.
5M+ Members
Founded in 1932

23606 Soil and Water Conservation Society
945 SW Ankeny Rd
Ankeny, IA 50023-9764

515-289-2331
800-843-7645
Fax: 515-289-1227
E-Mail: swcs@swcs.org
Home Page: www.swcs.org

Jim Guillford, Executive Director
Annie Binder, Director of Publications/Editor
Cammie Callen, Member Services Specialist
Kim Johnson Smith, Professional Development Director
Jody Ogg, Controller

SWCS is a nonprofit scientific and educational organization that serves as an advocate for conservation professionals and for science-based conservation practice, programs, and policy.
5000+ Members
Founded in 1943

23607 Submersible Waste Water Pump Association
1866 Sheridan Rd
Suite 212
Highland Park, IL 60035-2545

847-681-1868
Fax: 847-681-1869
E-Mail: swpaexdir@sbcglobal.net
Home Page: www.swpa.org

Charles Stolberg, Executive Director

Represents and serves the manufacturers of submersible pumps for the municipal and industrial wastewater applications. Manufacturers of components and accessory items for those products and companies providing services to users of those products.
Founded in 1976

23608 WateReuse Association
1199 North Fairfax Street
Suite 410ÿ
Alexandria, VA 22314

703-548-0880
Fax: 703-548-5085
Home Page: www.watereuse.org
Social Media: Facebook, Twitter, LinkedIn, YouTube

Melissa L. Meeker, Executive Director
Maria Greenly, Accounting Manager
Carrie Knooihuizen, Administrative Assistant
Courtney Tharpe, Director of Conferences and Eventsÿ
Erin DiMenna, Director of Membership

An association for advancing the science of water reuse and destination through research.
Founded in 1990

23609 Water Environment Federation
601 Wythe St
Alexandria, VA 22314-1994

703-684-2400
800-666-0206
Fax: 703-684-2492
E-Mail: inquiry@wef.org
Home Page: www.wef.org
Social Media: Facebook, Twitter, LinkedIn

Bill Bertera, Executive Director

A technical and educational organization with members from varied disciplines who work toward the vision of preservation and enhancement of the global water environment.
79 Members
Founded in 1928

23610 Water Keeper Alliance
17 Battery Place
Suite 1329ÿ
New York, NY 10004

212-747-0622
Fax: 212-747-0611
E-Mail: info@waterkeeper.org
Home Page: waterkeeper.org
Social Media: Facebook, Twitter, YouTube, Instagram

Marc A. Yaggi, Executive Director
Mary Beth Postman, Deputy Director
Lesley Adams, Western Regional Coordinator
Nicole Babbÿ, Associate
Larry Baldwin, North Carolina CAFO Coordinator

An association using grassroots advocacy to achieve clean waterways.
Founded in 1996

23611 Water Quality Association
4151 Naperville Rd
Lisle, IL 60532-3696

630-505-0160
Fax: 630-505-9637
E-Mail: info@mail.wqa.org
Home Page: www.wqa.org
Social Media: Facebook, Twitter, Youtube

Peter Censky, Manager
Margit Fotre, Membership/Marketing Director
Laurie Metanchuk, Communications Manager

An international, nonprofit trade association representing retail/dealers and manufacturer/suppliers in the point of use/entry water quality improvement industry. Membership benefits and services include technical and scientific information, educational seminars and home correspondence course books, professional certification and discount services.
2.5M Members
Founded in 1974

23612 Water and Wastewater Equipment Manufacturers Association
PO Box 17402
Washington, DC 20041

703-444-1777
Fax: 703-444-1779
E-Mail: info@wwema.org
Home Page: www.wwema.org

Dawn Kristof Champney, President

Represents the interests of companies that manufacture the products that are sold to the portable water and wastewater treatment industries. Also informs, educates and provides leadership on the issues which affect the worldwide water and wastewater equipment industry.
80 Members
Founded in 1908

Newsletters

23613 Drinking Water and Backflow Prevention
SFA Enterprises
18927 Hickory Creek Drive
Suite 140
Mokena, IL 60448

303-451-0978
888-367-3927
Fax: 303-452-9776
E-Mail: backflow@dwbp-online.com
Home Page: www.iapmodwbp.org/

Cindy Most, Managing Editor

Accepts advertising.
Cost: $38.00
24 Pages
Frequency: Monthly
Mailing list available for rent

23614 Jet News
WaterJet Technology Association/Industrial &
Municipal Cleaning Association
906 Olive Street, Suite 1200
Saint Louis, MO 63101-1448

314-241-1445
Fax: 314-241-1449
E-Mail: wjta-imca@wjta.org
Home Page: www.wjta.org

George A Savanick PhD, President
Kenneth C Carroll, Association Manager

Provides the latest information on applications, equipment, news from members, new developments, meetings, conferences, and technical information.
Frequency: Bi-Monthly
Circulation: 1000

23615 National Association of Regulatory Utility Commisioners
Natl Assoc of Regulatory Utility Commissioner
1101 Vermont Ave Nw
Suite 200
Washington, DC 20005-3553

202-898-2200
Fax: 202-898-2213
E-Mail: admin@naruc.org
Home Page: www.naruc.org

Charles Gray, Executive Director
Diane Munns, Publisher

A national organization that offers valuable information on over 150 consultants and other professionals active in regulated water, sewer and related industries.
Frequency: Monthly
Circulation: 1800
Founded in 1889

23616 National Water Line
National Water Resources Association
3800 Fairfax Dr
Suite 4
Arlington, VA 22203-1703

703-524-1544
Fax: 703-524-1548
E-Mail: nrwa@nrwa.org
Home Page: www.nwra.org

Thomas Donnelly, VP

Association news and information.
Frequency: Monthly

23617 US Water News
US Water News
230 Main St
Halstead, KS 67056-1913

316-835-2222
800-251-0046
Fax: 316-835-2223
E-Mail: Inquiries@uswaternews.com
Home Page: www.uswaternews.com

Thomas Bell, President/Publisher
Mary DeSana, Editor

Reports news of current events in water resources from across the nation. Accepts advertising.
Cost: $59.00
24 Pages
Frequency: Monthly

23618 Water Newsletter
Water Information Center
1099 18th St
Suite 2600
Denver, CO 80202-1926

303-297-2600
Fax: 303-297-2750
Home Page: www.rwolaw.com

Stephen L Waters, Partner

Contents include water supply and waste disposal information, and presents articles on conservation/usage.
Cost: $127.00
Frequency: Monthly
Founded in 1959

Magazines & Journals

23619 APWA Reporter
American Public Works Association
2345 Grand Blvd
Suite 700
Kansas City, MO 64108-2625

816-472-6100
800-848-2792
Fax: 816-472-1610
E-Mail: ddancy@apwa.net
Home Page: www.apwa.net

Kaye Sullivan, Executive Director
David Dancy, Marketing Director
Connie Hartline, Publications Manager
Lillie Plowman, Publications/Premiums Marketing Mgr

Circulation to entire membership of American Public Works Association.
Cost: $100.00
Frequency: Monthly
Circulation: 34000
ISBN: 0-092487-3 -
Founded in 1937
Mailing list available for rent

23620 Bottled Water Reporter
International Bottled Water Association
1700 Diagonal Rd
Suite 650
Alexandria, VA 22314-2870

703-683-5213
800-928-3711
Fax: 703-683-4074
E-Mail: ibwainfo@bottledwater.org
Home Page: www.bottledwater.org
Social Media: Facebook, Twitter, LinkedIn

Joe Doss, CEO

Provides a vital source of information to bottlers and agencies, consultants and engineers. Also contains statistical data, marketing and management tips and profiles of bottled water operations and supplier companies.
Cost: $ 50.00
Circulation: 3000
Founded in 1958

23621 Cleaner Times
Advantage Publishing Company
1000 Nix Rd
Little Rock, AR 72211-3235

501-280-9111
800-525-7038
Fax: 501-280-9233
E-Mail: gpuls@adpub.com
Home Page: www.cleanertimes.com

Charlene Yarbrough, Publisher
Gerry Puls, Circulation
Chuck Prieur, Sales Manager
Charlener Yarbrough, Publications/Premiums Marketing Mgr

Application, information, and productivity for persons engaged in the manufacturing, distribution, or the use of high pressure water systems and accessories. The emphasis is on safety, regulatory, which affect the industry as well as cleaning applications.
Cost: $18.00
72 Pages
Frequency: Monthly
Circulation: 10000
ISSN: 1073-9602
Founded in 1989
Printed in 4 colors on glossy stock

23622 Clearwaters
New York Water Environment Association
525 Plum Street
Suite 102
Syracuse, NY 13204

315-422-7811
Fax: 315-422-3851
E-Mail: rdh@nywea.org
Home Page: www.nywea.org

Lois Hickey, Editor
Patricia Cerro-Reehil, Executive Director

Contains information on pollution control legislation, regulation, and compliance.
Cost: $25.00
Frequency: Quarterly
Circulation: 3000
Founded in 1929

23623 Drill Bits
National Drilling Association
1545 W 130th St
Suite A2
Hinckley, OH 44233-9121

330-273-5756
877-632-4748
Fax: 216-803-9900
E-Mail: info@nda4u.com
Home Page: www.nda4u.com

Peggy McGee, President
Dan Dunn, VP
Jim Howe, Secretary/Treasurer
Tim Cleary, Board of Directors
R. Alan Garrard, Board of Directors

A non-profit trade association of contractors, manufacturers and affiliated members from the drilling industry representing the geotechnical, environmental and mineral exploration sectors of this industry.
250+ Members
Frequency: 2x/Year
Founded in 1972

23624 Ground Water
National Ground Water Association
PO Box 715435
Columbus, OH 43271-5435

614-898-7791
800-551-7379
Fax: 614-898-7786
E-Mail: customerservice@ngwa.org
Home Page: www.ngwa.org
Social Media: Facebook, Twitter, LinkedIn, YouTube

Paul Humes, VP
Thad Plumley, Publications Director
Shelby Fleck, Advertising
Keviin McKray, Executive Director

Focuses on ground water hydrogeology as a science.
Cost: $395.00
160 Pages
Circulation: 15000
ISSN: 0017-467x
Founded in 1963
Printed in one color

23625 Ground Water Monitoring and Remediation
National Ground Water Association
PO Box 715436
Columbus, OH 43271-5436

614-898-7791
800-551-7379
Fax: 614-898-7786
E-Mail: ngwa@ngwa.org
Home Page: www.ngwa.org
Social Media: Facebook, Twitter, LinkedIn, YouTube

Paul Humes, VP
Thad Plumley, Publications Director
Kevin McKray, Executive Director

Contains peer-reviewed papers, product and equipment news, EPA updates, industry news, and a mix of original columns authored by industry leaders.
Cost: $195.00
Frequency: Quarterly
Circulation: 15201
ISSN: 1069-3629
Founded in 1981

23626 Industrial Wastewater
Water Environment Federation
601 Wythe St
Alexandria, VA 22314-1994

703-684-2400
Fax: 703-684-2492
E-Mail: inquiry@wef.org
Home Page: www.wef.org
Social Media: Facebook, Twitter, LinkedIn

Bill Bertera, Executive Director

Provides the information on the practical application of science and technology in the management of water discharges, air emissions, ground water and soil remediation to the industrial personnel, consultants and other involved in all aspects of management, treatment and disposal of industrial wastewater.
Cost: $129.00
Frequency: Bi-Monthly
Circulation: 35500
ISSN: 1067-5337
Founded in 1928

23627 Journal of Soil and Water Conservation
Soil and Water Conservation Society
945 SW Ankeny Road
Ankeny, IA 50023-9764

515-289-2331
800-843-7645
Fax: 515-289-1227
E-Mail: pubs@swcs.org
Home Page: www.swcs.org

Oksana Gieseman, Director of Publications

The JSWC is a multidisciplinary journal of natural resource conservation research, practice, policy, and perspectives. The journal has two sections: the A Section containing various de-

partments and features and the Research Section containing peer-reviewed research papers.
Cost: $99.00
Frequency: Bimonthly
Circulation: 2000
ISSN: 0022-4561
Founded in 1945

23628 Journal of the American Water Resources Association
PO Box 1623
Middleburg, VA 20118-1626

540-687-8390
540-687-8390
Fax: 540-687-8395
E-Mail: info@awra.org
Home Page: www.awra.org

Kenneth J Lanfear, Editor
Charlene E Young, Publications Production Director
Billy Journell, Manager

Annual directory offering information on all water resources, technologies, systems and services for the water resources industry.
Cost: $205.00
Frequency: Bi-Monthly
ISSN: 1093-474x
Founded in 1964

23629 Landscape & Irrigation
Adams Business Media
PO Box 17349
Chicago, IL 60617-0349

773-221-4223
Fax: 773-374-6270
Home Page: www.adamsbrick.com

Karen Adams, President

23630 National Driller
Business News Publishing Company
1050 IL Route 83
Suite 200
Bensenville, IL 60106

800-223-2194
Fax: 248-786-1358
Home Page: www.nationaldriller.com

Linda Moffat, Publisher
Greg Ettling, Editor
Lisa Shroeder, Managing Editor

Provides feature articles, timely and valuable industry information, newly developed products and technologies, and quality marketing and business management advice.
Frequency: Monthly
Mailing list available for rent

23631 Operations Forum
Water Environment Federation
601 Wythe St
Alexandria, VA 22314-1994

703-684-2400
800-666-0206
Fax: 703-684-2492
Home Page: www.wef.org

Bill Bertera, Executive Director

The emphasis is on process control, plant operations, collection systems and industry news.
Cost: $4995.00
Frequency: Monthly
Circulation: 17005
Founded in 1928

23632 Rural Water Magazine
National Rural Water Association
2915 S 13th St
Duncan, OK 73533-9086

580-252-0629
Fax: 580-255-4476
E-Mail: info@nrwa.org
Home Page: www.nrwa.org

Rob Johnson, CEO

Targeted at the operators and board members of rural and small municipal water and wastewater utilities.
56 Pages
Frequency: Quarterly
Circulation: 22800
Founded in 1979

23633 US Water News
US Water News
230 Main St
Halstead, KS 67056-1913

316-835-2222
800-251-0046
Fax: 316-835-2223
Home Page: www.uswaternews.com

Thomas Bell, President/Publisher

Reports news of current events from across the nation in the municipal and industrial water and wastewater segments of the water industry.
Cost: $59.00
28 Pages
Frequency: Monthly
Circulation: 20000
Founded in 1984
Printed in on n stock

23634 Water Conditioning and Purification Magazine
Publicom
2800 E Fort Lowell Road
Tucson, AZ 85716

520-323-6144
Fax: 520-323-7412
E-Mail: info@wcponline.com
Home Page: www.wcponline.com

Kurt C Peterson, Publisher/Eastern Advertising Exec
Sharon M Peterson, President/Owner
Karen R Smith, Executive Editor
Margo Goldbaum, Circulation Services
Denise M Roberts, Assistant Editor

Comprehensive magazine for all aspects of the water quality improvement industry. Accepts advertising.
Cost: $49.00
100 Pages
Circulation: 20000
ISSN: 1537-1786
Founded in 1959
Mailing list available for rent: 1000 names at $250 per M
Printed in 4 colors on glossy stock

23635 Water Environment & Technology
Water Environment Federation
601 Wythe St
Alexandria, VA 22314-1994

703-684-2400
800-666-0206
Fax: 703-684-2492
E-Mail: csc@wef.org
Home Page: www.wef.org
Social Media: Facebook, Twitter, LinkedIn

Bill Bertera, Executive Director
Margaret Richards, Editorial Assistant
Tracy Hardwick, Publication Services Manager

Covers a wide range of water quality and municipal wastewater treatment issues, from the design, engineering, and management of domestic wastewater treatment plants to watershed management and wet weather issues.
Cost: $178.00
Frequency: Monthly
Circulation: 27304
Founded in 1928

23636 Water Environment Federation
Water Environment Federation
601 Wythe St
Alexandria, VA 22314-1994

703-684-2400
800-666-0206
Fax: 703-684-2492
E-Mail: webfeedback@wef.org
Home Page: www.wef.org

Bill Bertera, Executive Director
David James, Publications Committee

Magazine published monthly for 41,000 members
Cost: $19.00
Founded in 1928

23637 Water Environment Research
Water Environment Federation
601 Wythe St
Alexandria, VA 22314-1994

703-684-2400
Fax: 703-684-2492
Home Page: www.wef.org

Bill Bertera, Executive Director
Glenn Reinhardt, Foundation Executive Director
Tom Wolfe, Advertising

Research journal reviewed by peers and covering the effects of water pollution and the technology and advances used for it's control.
Cost: $158.00
Circulation: 9000
Founded in 1928

23638 Water Resources Research
American Geophysical Union
2000 Florida Ave NW
Washington, DC 20009-1231

202-462-6900
800-966-2481
Fax: 202-328-0566
E-Mail: service@agu.org
Home Page: www.agu.org
Social Media: Facebook, Twitter, LinkedIn

Fred Spilhaus, Executive Director
Karne Blaususs, Circulation Manager

Presents articles on the social, natural, and physical sciences, with emphasis on geochemistry, hydrology, and groundwater transfer technology.
Cost: $1200.00
Frequency: Monthly
Circulation: 4700
Founded in 1919

23639 Water Technology
National Trade Publications
19 British American Blvd. Wes
Latham, NY 12110

518-783-1281
Fax: 518-783-1386
E-Mail: asavino@ntpinc.com
Home Page: www.watertechonline.com
Social Media: Facebook, Twitter, LinkedIn

Tracy Ashton-Martin, Vice President of Business Publishi
Lisa Williman, Marketing Account Executive
Chapman Brown, Advertising Account Executive
Richard DiPaolo, Editorial Director
Jake Mastroianni, Assistant Editor

Serves the POU/POE water treatment industry. Accepts advertising.
Cost: $39.00
48 Pages
Frequency: Monthly
Circulation: 21000
Founded in 1981
Mailing list available for rent: 20000 names at $125 per M
Printed in 4 colors on glossy stock

23640 **Water Well Journal**
Ground Water Publishing Company
601 Dempsey Rd
Westerville, OH 43081-8978

614-882-8179
800-551-7379
Fax: 614-898-7786
Home Page: waterwelljournal.org
Social Media: Facebook, Twitter, LinkedIn

Kevin McCray, Executive Director
Jennifer Strawn, Associate Editor
Joanne Grant, Manager

A complete publication of the water supply industry. Covers technical issues related to drilling and pump installation, rig maintenance, business management and professional development, well rehabilitation, water treatment and more.
Cost: $95.00
84 Pages
Frequency: Monthly
Founded in 1948

23641 **WaterWorld**
PennNet
1421 S Sheridan Road
Tulsa, OK 74112

918-835-3161
800-331-4463
Fax: 918-831-9415
Home Page: www.pennnet.com
Social Media: Facebook, Twitter, LinkedIn

James Laughlin, Editor/Associate Publisher

Gives information about products and services, technology, applications, legislation and regulations to help the water industry pros successfully plan, design, operate and maintain their systems.
Frequency: Monthly
Founded in 1985

23642 **World Wastes: the Independent Voice**
Communication Channels
6151 Powers Ferry Road NW
Atlanta, GA 30339-2959

770-953-4805
Fax: 770-618-0348

Bill Wolpin, Editor
Jerrold France, President Argus Business

Reaches individuals and firms engaged in the removal and disposal of solid wastes.
Cost: $48.00
Frequency: Monthly
Circulation: 36,000

Trade Shows

23643 **American Society of Irrigation Consultants Conference**
PO Box 426
Byron, CA 94514-0426

925-516-1124
Fax: 925-516-1301

Wanda M Sarsfield, Secretary

Irrigation design equipment, supplies, services and seminar.
Frequency: Annual
Founded in 1970

23644 **American Water Resources Conference**
American Water Resources Association
4 West Federal Street
PO Box 1626
Middleburg, VA 20118-1626

540-687-8390
Fax: 540-687-8395
E-Mail: info@awra.org
Home Page: www.awra.org
Social Media: Facebook, Twitter, LinkedIn, YouTube

Terry Meyer, Marketing Coordinator
Ken Reid, Executive VP

Show of water resources science and technology.
Frequency: Annual, November
Founded in 1964

23645 **American Water Works Association Annual Conference and Exhibition**
6666 W Quincy Avenue
Denver, CO 80235

303-794-7711
800-926-7337
Fax: 303-347-0804
Home Page: www.awwa.org

Nilaksh Kothari, President
Jack W. Hoffbuhr, Executive Director
Jane M. Johnson, Director of Sales & Research

With more than 500 exhibitors, who are a source of knowledge and information for water professionals who work to improve the supply and quality of water in North America and beyond
12000 Attendees
Frequency: Annual, June
Founded in 1881

23646 **Chartmaker**
American Recreation Coalition
1225 New York Avenue NW
Suite 450
Washington, DC 20005-6405

202-829-9530
Fax: 202-662-7424

Derrick Crandall, President

Triennial exhibits relating to the responsible use of US aquatic resources, including issues such as wetlands conservation, boating safety, sportfish research and enhancement and boating access improvements.

23647 **Computers in the Water Industry: The Computer Conference**
American Water Works Association
6666 W Quincy Avenue
Denver, CO 80235

303-794-7711
800-926-7337
Fax: 303-347-0804
Home Page: www.awwa.org

Nilaksh Kothari, President
Jack W. Hoffbuhr, Executive Director
Jane M. Johnson, Director of Sales & Research

23648 **Irrigation Show & Education Conference**
6540 Arlington Boulevard
Falls Church, VA 22042-6638

703-536-7080
Fax: 703-536-7019
E-Mail: membership@irrigation.org
Home Page: www.irrigation.org

Bob Sears, Executive VP

Four hundred and twenty five booths of the newest in irrigation equipment for the agricultural industry.
3.5M Attendees
Frequency: November

23649 **National Ground Water Association Annual Convention and Exposition**
National Ground Water Association
601 Dempsey Road
Westerville, OH 43081

614-987-7791
800-551-7379
Fax: 614-898-7786
E-Mail: ngwa@ngwa.org
Home Page: www.ngwa.org

Bob Masters, Conference Coordinator
Greg Phelps, Meeting Planner/Expositions Dir
Kevin McKray, Executive Director

Annual show of 4600 manufacturers, suppliers, distributors, consultants and scientists, and contractors/pump installers.
5,100 Attendees
Frequency: December

23650 **National Rural Water Association**
2915 S 13th Street
Duncan, OK 73533

580-252-0629
Fax: 580-255-4476
E-Mail: info@nrwa.org
Home Page: www.nrwa.org

Larissa M Wood, Publications Coordinator

100 booths; 300 exhibitors.
1.5M Attendees
Frequency: September

23651 **National Water Resources Association Annual Conference**
National Water Resources Association
3800 Fairfax Drive
Suite 4
Arlington, VA 22203

703-524-1544
Fax: 703-524-1548
E-Mail: nwra@nwra.org
Home Page: www.nwra.org

Norman Semanko, President
Thomas Donnelly, VP

Annual conference and exhibits relating to the development, control, conservation and utilization of water resources in the reclamation states.
700 Attendees
Frequency: November

23652 **North American Lake Management Society International Symposium**
North American Lake Management Society
4513 Vernon Boulevard, Suite 103
PO Box 5443
Madison, WI 53705-0443

608-233-2836
Fax: 608-233-3186
E-Mail: nalms@nalms.org
Home Page: www.nalms.org

Bev Clark, President

Annual symposium and exhibits related to lake ecology and management.

23653 **Soil and Water Conservation Society Annual International Conference**
Soil and Water Conservation Society
945 SW Ankeny Road
Ankeny, IA 50021-9764

515-289-2331
800-843-7645
Fax: 515-289-1227
Home Page: www.swsc.org

Craig A Cox, Executive VP

Explores ways to improve the linkages among conservation science, policy and application at local, national, and international scales. The conference will provide participants an opportunity to teach skills, learn techniques, compare successes, and improve understanding.
1200 Attendees
Frequency: Annual

23654 Water Environment Federation
Water Environment Federation
601 Wythe Street
Alexandria, VA 22314-1994
703-684-2400
800-666-2492
Fax: 703-684-2175
Home Page: www.wef.org
Jenny Grigsby, Advertising
Jack Benson, Association Development
Annual show of 650 manufacturers, suppliers and distributors of water treatment equipment, supplies and services.
14M Attendees
Frequency: October, Chicago

23655 Water Quality Association Convention
Water Quality Association
4151 Naperville Road
Suite 100
Lisle, IL 60532-1088
630-505-0160
Fax: 630-505-9637
E-Mail: info@wqa.org
Home Page: www.wqa.org
Peter J Censky, Executive Director
Jeannine Collins, CMP, Convention/Meetings Manager
Annual convention and exhibits of water treatment equipment and related articles.
4,300 Attendees

Directories & Databases

23656 American Water Works Association: Buyers' Guide Issue
American Water Works Association
6666 W Quincy Ave
Denver, CO 80235-3098
303-794-7711
800-926-7337
Fax: 303-347-0804
Home Page: www.awwa.org
Andrew Richardson, President
Jack W. Hoffbuhr, Executive Director
Jane M. Johnson, Director of Sales & Research
Member suppliers and distributors of water supply products and services, contractors for water supply projects and engineering consultants.
Frequency: Annual November
Circulation: 80,000

23657 Directory of Water/Sewer and Related Industries Professionals
National Assn of Regulatory Utility Commissioners
1101 Vermont Ave NW
Suite 200
Washington, DC 20005-3553
202-898-2200
Fax: 202-898-2213
E-Mail: admin@naruc.org
Home Page: www.naruc.org
Charles Gray, Executive Director
Offers valuable information on over 150 consultants and other professionals active in regulated water, sewer and related industries.
Cost: $25.00
195 Pages
Frequency: Annual

23658 Ground Water Age: Directory of Manufacturers
National Trade Publications
13 Century Hill Drive
Latham, NY 12110-2197
518-831-1281
Fax: 518-783-1386
Roslyn Scheib Dahl, Editor
List of over 150 companies that provide products and services to the ground water industry.
Cost: $30.00
Frequency: Annual December
Circulation: 13,448

23659 Ground Water Monitoring & Remediation: Buyers Guide Issue
Ground Water Publishing Company
601 Dempsey Rd
Westerville, OH 43081-8978
614-882-8179
800-332-2104
Fax: 614-898-7786
E-Mail: gwpc@ngwa.org
Home Page: www.ngwa.org
Kevin McCray, Executive Director
Thad Plumley, Publications Director
List of companies that provide products used in the ground water monitoring and remediation industry.
Cost: $15.00
Frequency: Annual
Circulation: 12,382
Founded in 1981

23660 Ground Water Monitoring Review: Consultant & Contract Directory
National Ground Water Association
601 Dempsey Rd
Westerville, OH 43081-8978
614-898-7791
800-332-2104
Fax: 614-898-7786
Home Page: www.ngwa.org
Paul Humes, VP
Shelby Fleck, Advertising Manager
Kevin McCray, Executive Director
About 400 consultant and contracting firms engaged in ground water monitoring projects.
Cost: $200.00
Frequency: Annual
Circulation: 17,000

23661 Ground Water On-Line
National Ground Water Association
601 Dempsey Rd
Westerville, OH 43081-8978
614-898-7791
800-554-7379
Fax: 614-898-7786
E-Mail: ngwa@ngwa.org
Home Page: www.ngwa.org
Paul Humes, VP
Database offers information on more than 90,000 ground water literature citations, which includes information like key words, abstracts, chemical compounds, biological factors, geographic locations, aquifer names, authors, titles, publication source names and a lot more.

23662 Validated Water Treatment Equipment Directory
Water Quality Association
4151 Naperville Rd
Suite 100
Lisle, IL 60532-3696
630-505-0160
Fax: 630-505-9637
Home Page: www.wqa.org
Peter Censky, Manager
Over 700 water treatment products tested by the Water Quality Association and their manufacturers are listed.
Cost: $6.00
Frequency: SemiAnnual

23663 WATERNET
American Water Works Association
6666 W Quincy Ave
Denver, CO 80235-3098
303-794-7711
800-926-7337
Fax: 303-347-0804
Home Page: www.waternetonline.ihe.nl
Andrew Richardson, President
Jack W. Hoffbuhr, Executive Director
Jane M. Johnson, Director of Sales & Research
This database contains more than 23,000 citations, with abstracts, to literature on water quality, water utility management, analytical procedures for water quality testing.

23664 Water Technology: Directory of Manufacturers and Suppliers Issue
National Trade Publications
13 Century Hill Drive
Latham, NY 12110-2197
518-783-1281
Fax: 518-783-1386
Home Page: www.ntpmedia.com
Mark Wilson, Editor
List of about 250 manufacturers, distributors and other suppliers of water conditioning and treatment products.
Cost: $21.00
Frequency: Annual December
Circulation: 17,213

23665 Water Treatability
National Ground Water Information Center
6375 Riverside Drive
Dublin, OH 43017-5045
614-717-2770
Fax: 614-761-3446
Offers information on treatment technologies for the removal of various contaminants from water supplies.
Frequency: Full-text

23666 Water Well Journal: Buyer's Guide Issue
National Ground Water Association
601 Dempsey Rd
Westerville, OH 43081-8978
614-898-7791
800-332-2104
Fax: 614-898-7786
Home Page: www.ngwa.org
Paul Humes, VP
Shelby Fleck, Advertising Manager
List of manufacturers, suppliers and manufacturers' representatives for equipment, machinery and other products for the water well industry.
Cost: $6.00
Frequency: Annual January
Circulation: 26,000

Industry Web Sites

23667 http://gold.greyhouse.com
G.O.L.D Grey House OnLine Databases
Grey House Publishing's online database platform, GOLD, offers Quick Search, Keyword Search and Expert Search for most business sectors including water supply markets. The GOLD platform makes finding the information you need quick and easy - whether you're a novice searcher or an experienced database

user. All of Grey House's directory products are available for subscription on the GOLD platform.

23668 www.greyhouse.com
Grey House Publishing
Authoritative reference directories for most business sectors including water supply markets. Users can search the online databases with varied search criteria allowing for custom searches by product category, geographic area, sales volume, keyword, subject and more. Full Grey House catalog and online ordering also available.

23669 www.gwpc.org
Ground Water Protection Council
Provides a forum for dicussing ground water, watershed and community wallhead protection and underground injection practices. Conducts seminars and workshops on these subjects.

23670 www.nda4u.com
National Drilling Association
A non-profit trade association of contractors, manufacturers and affiliated members from the drilling industry representing the geotechnical, environmental and mineral exploration sectors of this industry.

23671 www.swcs.org
Soil and Water Conservation Society
Promotes erosion control and water quality. Publishes scholarly journal and practical magazine. Conducts annual conference and trade show

23672 www.umsu.edu/niwr/
National Institute for Water Resources
Offers information on water resource directions across the nation.

23673 www.wef.org
Water Environment Federation
A not-for-profit technical and educational organization, consisting of regional association comprised of air quality professionals concerned with all types of air pollution.

23674 www.wjta.org
WaterJet Technology Association/Industrial &
Municipal Cleaning Association
Members research for new findings in waterjet technology.

23675 www.wqa.org
Water Quality Association
For retail/dealers and manufacturer/suppliers in the point of use/entry water quality improvement industry.

Associations

23676 American Association of Meat Processors
One Meating Place
Elizabethtown, PA 17022

717-367-1168
Fax: 717-367-9096
E-Mail: aamp@aamp.com
Home Page: www.aamp.com
Social Media: Facebook

Tim J Haen, President
Erica Hering, 1st VP
Doug Hankes, 2nd VP
Louis Muench, 3rd VP
Kevin Western, Treasurer

Membership consists of small to medium sized meat, poultry and food businesses including, slaughterers, processors, wholesalers, home food service businesses, deli and catering operators and suppliers to the industry. AAMP is affiliated with 32 state, regional and provincial associations.
1400 Members
Founded in 1939

23677 American Machine Tool Distributors Association
7901 Westpark Drive
Suite 320
McLean, MD 22102-4206

703-893-2900
800-524-0475
Fax: 703-893-1151
E-Mail: klaramay@amtda.org
Home Page: www.amtonline.org
Social Media: Facebook, Twitter, LinkedIn, Youtube

Douglas~K.~ Woods, President
Amber Thomas, VP
Jeffrey H Traver, VP
Peter R Eelman, VP
Linda G Montfort, VP

AMTDA will lead distributors of manufacturing technology by providing essential programs and services that help its members gain global recognition from customers and suppliers as the preferred channel of distribution.
300 Members
Founded in 1925

23678 American Supply Association
222 Merchandise Mart
Suite 1400
Chicago, IL 60654

312-464-0090
Fax: 312-464-0091
E-Mail: info@asa.net
Home Page: www.asa.net

Jeff New, Chairman of the Board
Joe Poehling, President
Frank Nisonger, President-Elect
Robert Christiansen, Vice President

ASA is a not-for-profit national organization serving wholesale distributors and their suppliers in the plumbing, heating, cooling and industrial and mechanical pipe, valves and fittings industries.
Founded in 1969

23679 American Veterinary Distributors Association
3465 Box Hill Corp. Center Drive
Suite H
Abingdon, MD 21009

443-640-1040
Fax: 443-640-1086
E-Mail: casey@kingmgmt.org
Home Page: www.avda.net
Social Media: Facebook, Twitter, LinkedIn

Mark Ziller, Chairman
Bobby Mims, President
Jeff Baker, President-Elect

The AVDA was established as the national trade organization for businesses engaged in the distribution of animal health products.
Founded in 1976

23680 American Wholesale Marketers Association
2750 Prosperity Ave
Suite 530
Fairfax, VA 22031-4338

703-208-3358
800-482-2962
Fax: 703-573-5738
E-Mail: info@awmanet.org
Home Page: www.awmanet.org
Social Media: Facebook, Twitter, RSS

Scott Ramminger, President & CEO
Joan Fay, Associate Publisher/Editor
Jennifer Moulton, Director Administration, IT
Meredith Kimbrell, Director, Education

A trade organization supporting the confectionary, tobacco and allied industries through programs and services. members include wholesale distributors, manufacturers and other allieds to the industry.
5300 Members
Founded in 1942

23681 AmericanHort
525 9th St. NW
Suite 800
Washington, DC 20004

202-789-2900
Fax: 202-789-1893
E-Mail: hello@AmericanHort.org
Home Page: www.americanhort.org
Social Media: Facebook, Twitter, LinkedIn

Michael V Geary, Executive VP
Craig J Regelbrugge, VP, Govt. Relations
Joe Bischoff, Director, Govt. Relations

The American Nursery and Landscape Association serves firms who grow, sell or use plants. ANLA advocates the industry's interests before government and provides its members with unique business knowledge essential to long-term growth and profitability.
2200 Members
Founded in 1876

23682 Appliance Parts Distributors Association
3621 N Oakley Avenue
Chicago, IL 60618

773-528-2199
Fax: 888-308-1423
E-Mail: ro@apda.com
Home Page: www.apda.com
Social Media: Facebook, Twitter, LinkedIn

Phil F Orazietti, President
Leonard Kremers, Vice President
Ron Clifton, Treasurer

The APDA is an association of independent businesses that aspire to provide the highest level of quality, service, support and information to its customers and suppliers in order to make its value indispensable to the parts distribution channel.

23683 Associated Beer Distributors of Illinois
PO Box 396
Springfield, IL 62705

217-528-4371
Fax: 217-528-4376
E-Mail: info@abdi.org
Home Page: www.abdi.org
Social Media: Facebook, Twitter, LinkedIn

The ABDI represents, maintains, and improves the interests of its members who are licensed by the State of Illinois to import and distribute beer to licensed retailers.

23684 Associated Equipment Distributors
600 22nd Street
Suite 220
Oak Brook, IL 60523

630-574-0650
800-388-0650
Fax: 630-574-0132
E-Mail: info@aednet.org
Home Page: www.aednet.org
Social Media: Facebook, Twitter, LinkedIn

Bob Henderson, EVP & COO
Dave Gordon, Publisher/VP, Sales
Kim Phelan, Executive Editor/Director, Programs
Jenny Choe, Director, Communications
Janet L Dixon, Director, Meetings & Conferences

AED is an international trade association representing companies involved in the distribution, rental and support of equipment used in construction, mining, forestry, power generation, agriculture and industrial applications.
700 Members

23685 Association for High Technology Distribution
N19 W24400 Riverwood Drive
Waukesha, WI 53188

262-696-3645
800-488-4845
Fax: 630-574-0132
E-Mail: info@aednet.org
Home Page: www.ahtdmembers.org
Social Media: Facebook, Twitter, RSS

Bryan Roesster, Executive Director
Leigha Schatzman, Association Services Manager
Pam Estergard, Financial Services
Cassie Schauer, Association Services Coordinator

The Association for High Technology Distribution has worked to increase the productivity and profitability of the high technology Automation Solutions Providers and Manufacturers who satisfy the automation needs of general industry and OEM manufacturers.
Founded in 1984

23686 Association for Hose and Accessories Distribution
105 Eastern Avenue
Suite 104
Annapolis, MD 21403

410-940-6350
800-624-2227
Fax: 410-263-1659
E-Mail: info@nahad.org
Home Page: www.nahad.org
Social Media: Facebook, Twitter, LinkedIn

Terry Weiner, President
Mark Fournier, 1st VP
Jim Reilly, 2nd VP
Joseph M Thompson Jr., EVP

The mission of NAHAD is to promote a high standard of professionalism and integrity within the hose and accessories industry by providing a medium for communications, education and training, so that quality is maximized and profitability enhanced.

23687 Association for Suppliers of Printing, Publishing & Converting Tech.
1899 Preston White Drive
Reston, VA 20191

703-264-7200
Fax: 703-620-0994
E-Mail: npes@npes.org
Home Page: www.npes.org

DJ Burgess, Chairman
Ralph J Nappi, President
William K Smythe, Jr, Vice President
Christopher Payne, Treasurer
Mark J Nuzzaco, Secretary

This association is a trade association of over 400 companies that manufacture and distribute equipment, systems, software, supplies used in printing, publishing and converting.
400 Members
Founded in 1933

23688 Association of Ingersoll-Rand Distributors
1300 Summer Avenue
Cleveland, OH 44115

216-241-7333
Fax: 216-241-0105
E-Mail: aird@aird.org
Home Page: www.aird.org

Alan Steiden, President
Ted Mailey, VP
Stu Bassett, Treasurer
Brent Darnell, Secretary

The Association of Ingersoll-Rand Distributors (AIRD) was organized as a central resource for distributors of Ingersoll-Rand compressed air equipment. AIRD is chartered to promote improved business conditions affecting distributors of air compressors, further a better understanding between distributors and equipment suppliers, research ways to lower costs of distributing air compressors, collect and disseminate statistical information and conduct other beneficial activities.
Founded in 1970

23689 Association of Millwork Distributors
10047 Robert Trent Jones Parkway
New Port Richey, FL 34655-4649

727-372-3665
800-786-7274
Fax: 727-372-2879
E-Mail: mail@AMDweb.com
Home Page: www.amdweb.com
Social Media: Twitter, LinkedIn

Nathan Potter, President
Joe Bayer, 1st VP
Dave Ondrasek, 2nd VP
Scott Harder, Associate VP
Simon Sikora, Treasurer

AND provides leadership, education, promotion, networking, and advocacy to, and for, the millwork distribution industry.
Founded in 1963

23690 Association of Pool & Spa Professionals
2111 Eisenhower Avenue
Alexandria, VA 22314

703-838-0083
Fax: 703-549-0493
E-Mail: memberservices@apsp.org
Home Page: www.apsp.org
Social Media: Facebook, Twitter, LinkedIn, Youtube, Flickr, RSS

Rich Gottwald, President/CEO
Terry Brown, Director, Operations
Jennifer Hatfield, Director, Govt. Affairs
Lauren Stack, Senior Director, Industry Relations
Carvin DiGiovanni, Senior Director

APSP is the world's largest international trade association for the swimming pool, spa, and hot tub industry. It works with regulatory and legislative bodies to ensure that their codes, ordinance, and legislation are written to the safest and most current standards. The association's mission is to ensure consumer safety and enhance the business success of its members.
Founded in 1956

23691 Association of Service and Computer Dealers International
131 NW First Avenue
Delray Beach, FL 33444

561-266-9016
Fax: 561-431-6302
Home Page: www.ascdi.com

Rob Neumeyer, Director
Arthur P Frierman, Associate Counsel
Jerry Roberts, Chairman Emeritus

The ASCDI is a worldwide, nonprofit organization, made up of companies who provide technology business solutions, technical support, and value added services to the business community.
Founded in 1981

23692 Association of Woodworking and Furnishings Suppliers
2400 E Katella Ave
Suite 340
Anaheim, CA 92806

323-838-9440
800-946-2937
Fax: 323-838-9443
E-Mail: info@awfs.org
Home Page: www.awfs.org

Angelo Gangone, EVP
Angela Hernandez, Executive Assistant
Nancy Neely, Controller
Bruce Valentine, Communications Manager
Nancy Fister, Education & Conference Director

The Association of Woodworking and Furnishings Suppliers is the largest national trade association in the U.S. representing the interests of the broad array of companies that supply the home and commercial furnishings industry.
Founded in 1911

23693 Automotive Aftermarket Industry Association
7101 Wisconsin Avenue
Suite 1300
Bethesda, MD 20814-3415

301-654-6664
Fax: 301-654-3299
E-Mail: aaia@aftermarket.org
Home Page: www.aftermarket.org
Social Media: Facebook, Twitter, LinkedIn, Youtube, WordPress

Kathleen Schmatz, President
Rich White, Marketing

A trade association consisting of more than 23,000 member companies and affiliates representing over 100,000 repair shops, distribution outlets, and parts stores.
23000 Members
Founded in 1999

23694 Bearing Specialists Association
800 Roosevelt Road
Building C, Suite 312
Glen Ellyn, IL 60137

630-858-3838
Fax: 630-790-3095
E-Mail: info@bsahome.org
Home Page: www.bsahome.org
Social Media: Twitter, LinkedIn, RSS

Jack Simpson, President
Brian Negri, VP
Tim Breen, Treasurer

BSA is the forum to enhance networking and knowledge sharing to promote the sale of bearings through authorized distributors.
100 Members
Founded in 1966

23695 Bicycle Product Suppliers Association
740 34th St
Boulder
Montgomeryville, CO 80303

303-442-2466
Fax: 303-552-2060
E-Mail: bpsa@bpsa.org
Home Page: www.bpsa.org

John Nedeau, President
Chris Speyer, Vice President
Patrick Cunnane, Treasurer
Marc Sani, Secretary

BPSA is an association of suppliers of bicycles, parts, accessories and services who serve the Specialty Bicycle Retailer.

23696 Business Solutions Association
3601 E Joppa Rd.
Baltimore, MD 21234

410-931-8100
Fax: 410-931-8111
E-Mail: info@BusinessSolutionsAssociation.com
Home Page: www.opwa.org

Jim O'Brien, President
Bill Cardone, VP
Nick Aronis, Secretary
Alan Goldner, Treasurer

The goal of the Business Solutions Association is to provide a forum for the development of strategic and synergistic solutions to enhance the sale and distribution of business related products and services.

23697 Ceramic Tile Distributors Association
800 Roosevelt Road
Building C, Suite 312
Glen Ellyn, IL 60137

630-545-9415
800-938-2838
Fax: 630-790-3095
E-Mail: info@ctdahome.org
Home Page: www.ctdahome.org
Social Media: Facebook

Frank Donahue, President
Tom Kotel, VP
Robert DeAngelis, Treasurer
Rick Church, Executive Director
Bill Ives, Legal Counsel

CTDA is an international association of distributors, manufacturers, and allied professionals of ceramic tile and related products.

23698 Cleaning Equipment Trade Association
PO Box 270908
Oklahoma City, OK 73137-0908

704-635-7362
800-441-0111
Fax: 704-635-7363
E-Mail: info@ceta.org
Home Page: www.ceta.org

Terry Murray, President
John R Purswell, Senior Vice President
Aaron Auger, Vice President
Mike Turner, Secretary/Treasurer

CETA is dedicated to increasing the awareness and promotion of industry products, while at the same time recognizing the impact on preserving the environment and the opportunity to do business within it.

23699 Commercial Vehicle Solutions Network
3943-2 Baymeadows Road
Jacksonville, FL 32217

904-737-2900
Fax: 904-636-9881
E-Mail: info@cvsn.org
Home Page: www.cvsn.org

Dave Willis, President
Edward Neeley, Vice President
Andy Robblee, Treasurer
Angelo Volpe, Executive VP/Secretary
Kevin Hopton, Director

The Commercial Vehicle Solutions Network (CVSN) is an association of independent parts and service aftermarket distributors serving the transportation industry.
Founded in 2006

23700 Copper and Brass Servicenter Association
6734 W. 121st Street
Overland Park, KS 66209

913-396-0697
Fax: 913-345-1006
E-Mail: cbsahq@copper-brass.org
Home Page: www.copper-brass.org

Susan Avery, Executive Director
Crystal Roberts, Director of Business Development
Jean McClure, Administrative Assistant

Distributors (service centers) of fabricated copper and copper alloy products (sheet, plate, coil, rod, bar tube, etc) and their brass mill suppliers.
78 Members
Founded in 1951

23701 Door & Hardware Institute
14150 Newbrook Drive
Suite 200
Chantilly, VA 20151-2232

703-222-2010
Fax: 703-222-2410
Home Page: www.dhi.org
Social Media: Facebook, Twitter, LinkedIn

Jerry Heppes, Chief Executive Officer
Chuck Molina, Chief Technology Officer
Scott Sabatini, President

The Door & Hardware Institute (DHI) is the only professional association dedicated to the Architectural Openings Industry. DHI represents the North American openings marketplace as the advocate and primary resource for information, professional development and certification.
5000 Members
Founded in 1934

23702 Drycleaning & Laundry Institute (formerly IFI)
14700 Sweitzer Lane
Laurel, MD 20707

301-622-1900
Fax: 240-295-4200
E-Mail: techline@dlionline.org
Home Page: www.dlionline.org

David Machesney, President
Greg Myers, Treasurer
Jan Barlow, Chairman

With its education, research, testing, and professional training, DLI offers solutions that help member businesses provide expert garment care.
2000 Members
Founded in 1907

23703 Electrical Apparatus Service Association Inc
1331 Baur Boulevard
Saint Louis, MO 63132-1903

314-993-2220
Fax: 314-993-1269
E-Mail: easainfo@easa.com
Home Page: www.easa.com
Social Media: Facebook, Twitter, LinkedIn, Youtube

Kenneth Gralow, Chair
Craig Moore, Vice Chair
Mike Dupuis, Secretary/Treasurer

Maintains data files on rewinding and repair of electrical equipment. Sponsors seminars
2000 Members
Founded in 1973

23704 Equipment Marketing & Distribution Association (EMDA)
PO Box 1347
Iowa City, IA 52244

319-354-5156
Fax: 319-354-5157
E-Mail: pat@emda.net
Home Page: www.emda.net

Patricia A Collins, Executive VP

EMDA is the result of the 2008 merger of FEWA and AIMRA. EMDA members are devtoed to the marketing of specialized equipment: agricultural, outdoor power, light industrial, forestry, irrigation, turf and grounds maintenance, lawn and garden and parts/components for thosesegments of industry.
250 Members
Founded in 1945

23705 Financial & Security Products Association
5300 Sequoia Rd
Suite 205
Albuquerque, NM 87120

505-839-7958
800-843-6082
Fax: 919-648-0670
E-Mail: info@fspa1.com
Home Page: www.fspa1.com

Mark Thatcher, Chairman
Bill Mercer, President
John M Vrabec, Executive Director

Independent dealers, manufacturers and associates whose outstanding products and services give financial institutions a crucial edge in performance, efficiency and economy.
Founded in 1973

23706 Fluid Power Distributors Association
105 Eastern Avenue
Suite 104
Annapolis, MD 21403

410-940-6347
Fax: 410-263-1659
E-Mail: info@fpda.org
Home Page: www.fpda.org

Michael A Hamzey Jr., Chairman & President
Parker Lancaster, VP, Membership
Alex Wheelock, President Elect
Tim Gillig, VP, Finance/Treasurer
Patricia A Lilly, Executive Director

The Fluid Power Distributors Association is a trade association on the move, representing motion solution providers who offer fluid power, automation, and electro-mechanical technologies and distribution services to enhance customer performance and profitability.
300+ Members
Founded in 1974

23707 Food Industry Suppliers Association
1207 Sunset Drive
Greensboro, NC 27408-7215

336-274-6311
Fax: 336-691-1839
E-Mail: stella@fisanet.org/
Home Page: www.fisanet.org/

Bob Morava, President
Brad Myers, VP

Member's are distributors and suppliers to the food processing industry.
245 Members
Founded in 1968

23708 Food Marketing Institute
2345 Crystal Drive
Suite 800
Arlington, VA 22202

202-452-8444
Fax: 202-429-4519
Home Page: www.fmi.org
Social Media: Facebook, Twitter, LinkedIn, Youtube, RSS

Frederick J Morganthall II, Chair
Leslie G Sarasin, President & CEO
Rob Bartels, Vice Chair
Jerry Garland, Vice Chair
Henry Johnson, Vice-Chairman

FMI conducts programs in public affairs, food safety, research, education and industry relations on behalf of its 1,500 member companies in the United States and around the world.
1500 Members

23709 Foodservice Equipment Distributors Association
2250 Point Blvd
Suite 200
Elgin, IL 60123-7887

224-293-6500
800-677-9605
Fax: 224-293-6505
E-Mail: feda@feda.com
Home Page: www.feda.com
Social Media: Twitter, LinkedIn

Raymond Herrick, Executive VP
Rosie Montanez, Executive Assistant
Stacy Ward, Managing Editor
Adela Ramos, Administrative Director/Advertising
Amy Risinger, Membership Services Consultant

Dealers and distributors of foodservice equipment and supplies.
300 Members
Founded in 1933

23710 Gases and Welding Distributors Association
8669 Doral Blvd
Suite 130
Florida, PA 33166

215-564-3484
877-382-6440
Fax: 215-963-9785
E-Mail: gawda@gawda.org
Home Page: www.gawda.org

Kent Van Amburg, Executive Director
Malvenia Avery, Associate Director
Tawnee Shuey, Meeting Manager
Kate Marlys

GAWDA's mission is to promote the safe operation and economic vitality of distributors of industrial gases and related welding equipment and supplies.
775 Members
Founded in 1945

23711 Global Market Development Center
1275 Lake Plaza Drive
Colorado Springs, CO 80906-3583

719-576-4260
Fax: 719-576-2661
E-Mail: info@gmdc.org
Home Page: www.gmdc.com

David McConnell, President/CEO
Keith Wypyszynski, VP Business Development/CMO
Ann McConnell, Sr. Director Finance
Michael Winterbottom, VP, IT/Chief Technology Officer

GMDC is the premier non-profit global trade association dedicated to serving General Merchandise and Health Beauty retailers, wholesalers and suppliers. GMDC promotes critical connectivity to grow and expand member companies by uniting members through business building events and opportunities and enriching their thinking through education and training; consumer and business insights; and information resources.
Founded in 1970

23712 Health Industry Distributors Association
310 Montgomery Street
Alexandria, VA 22314-1516

703-549-4432
Fax: 703-549-6495
Home Page: www.hida.org

Matthew J Rowan, President & CEO
Ian Fardey, EVP
Elizabeth Hilla, Executive Director
Lisa A Queeney, VP, Finance & Operations
Linda Rouse O'Neill, VP, Govt. Affairs

HIDA keeps members current on healthcare reform, government affairs, industry trends and forecasts, provider news, and sales tips.
Founded in 1902

23713 Healthcare Distribution Management Association
901 North Glebe Road
Suite 1000
Arlington, VA 22203

703-787-0000
Fax: 703-812-5282
Home Page: www.hdma.net

David Neu, Chairman
Ted Scherr, Vice Chair
Kenneth Couch, President
Michael Kaufmann, CEO
David Moody, CEO

The Healthcare Distribution Management Association (HDMA) is the national association representing primary, full-service healthcare distributors. HDMA and its members are the vital link in the healthcare system, working daily to provide value, remove costs and develop innovative solutions.

23714 Heating, Airconditioning & Refrigeration Distributors International
3455 Mill Run Drive
Suite 820
Columbus, OH 43026

614-345-4328
888-253-2128
Fax: 614-345-9161
E-Mail: hardimail@haridnet.org
Home Page: www.hardinet.org
Social Media: Facebook, Twitter, LinkedIn, Youtube, Instagram, Flickr

Brian Cobble, President
Royce Henderson, President-Elect
William Bergamini, Vice President
Michael Meier, Secretary/Treasurer

This association is a trade organization dedicated to advancing the science of wholesale distribution in the HVACR industry.
750+ Members
Founded in 1960

23715 ISSA
7373 N Lincoln Ave
Lincolnwood, IL 60712-1799

847-982-0800
800-225-4772
Fax: 847-982-1012
E-Mail: info@issa.com
Home Page: www.issa.com
Social Media: Facebook, Twitter, LinkedIn

Fritz Gast, President
Alan R Tomblin, President Elect/VP
Lydia M Work, International Director
John Swigart, Executive Director
John Barrett, Secretary

The worldwide cleaning industry association.
5700+ Members
Founded in 1923

23716 Industrial Compressor Distributor Association
656 Southern Hills Drive
Eureka, MO 63025

636-938-3957
Fax: 636-938-3965
E-Mail: mjgilliam1@aol.com
Home Page: www.icdaonline.com

Margot Gravel, President

The main objectives of the ICDA are to promote for its members the highest standards of production, financial and managerial activities; to act as a vehicle for the solution of common industry problems in an effective and efficient manner; and to increase market volume and profits for its members.

23717 Industrial Supply Association
100 North 20th Street
Suite 400
Philadelphia, PA 19103

215-320-3862
866-460-2360
Fax: 215-963-9785
E-Mail: info@isapartners.org
Home Page: www.isapartners.org
Social Media: Facebook, Twitter, LinkedIn

Michael Carr, President
Tommy Thompson, VP
Craig Vogel, Treasurer
John Wiborg, Secretary

The primary focus of the Industrial Supply Association is to improve the industrial supply channel through its mission-critical activities including: conventions and forums, gathering and dissemination of critical information, and development and implementation of channel performance initiatives.

23718 International Association of Plastics Distribution
6734 W. 121st Street
Overland Park, KS 66209

913-345-1005
Fax: 913-345-1006
E-Mail: iapd@iapd.org
Home Page: www.iapd.org

Susan E Avery, CEO
Crystal Roberts, Deputy Executive Director
Jean McClure, Executive Assistant/HR Manager
Kipp Simmons, Controller
Whitney Nelson, Director, Meetings & Events

The International Association of Plastics Distribution is an international trade association comprised of companies engaged in the distribution and manufacturing of plastics materials.
Founded in 1956

23719 International Foodservice Distributors Association
1410 Spring Hill Road
Suite 210
McLean, VA 22102-3035

703-532-9400
Fax: 703-538-4673
Home Page: www.ifdaonline.org
Social Media: Twitter, LinkedIn

Thomas A Zatina, Chairman
Boyd F Jordan III, President
James A Crawford, Vice Chair

Trade association comprised of food distribution companies that supply independent grocers and food service operations throughout the US, Canada and 19 other countries.
135 Members
Founded in 2003

23720 International Sealing Distribution Association
105 Eastern Avenue
Suite 104
Annapolis, MD 21403

410-940-6344
Fax: 410-263-1659
E-Mail: info@isd.org
Home Page: www.isd.org
Social Media: Facebook, Twitter, LinkedIn

Christy Jaycox, President
John Kates, VP
Steve Luhrs, Treasurer
Deborah B Mitchell, Executive Director
Joseph M Thompson Jr., Associate Director

The International Sealing Distribution Association (ISD) is a not-for-profit trade association formed to enhance the success of members through information, education, and interaction.

23721 International Truck Parts Association
1720 10th Ave. South
Suite 4, PMB 199
Great Falls, MT 59405

202-544-3090
866-346-5692
Fax: 301-229-7331
E-Mail: info@itpa.com
Home Page: www.itpa.com

Jake Rea, Chairman
Gerard Zentner, Vice Chairman

The International Truck Parts Association was organized as a not-for-profit association to promote, foster, and improve relationships among sellers and buyers of trucks and truck surplus products and other parties.
Founded in 1974

23722 Irrigation Association
6540 Arlington Boulevard
Falls Church, VA 22042-6638

703-536-7080
Fax: 703-536-7019
E-Mail: info@irrigation.org
Home Page: www.irrigation.org

Warren C Thoma, President
Aric J Olson, President Elect
Jackie W Robbins, VP
Gregory R Hunter, Treasurer

The Irrigation Association is the leading membership organization for irrigation equipment and system manufacturers, dealers, distributors, designers, consultants, contractors and end users.
1600 Members
Founded in 1949

23723 Jewelry Industry Distributors Association
701 Enterprise Drive
Harrison, OH 45030

513-367-2357
Fax: 513-367-1414
E-Mail: info@jida.info
Home Page: www.jida.info

Larry Goldberg, President
Bill Nagle, First VP
Harvey Cobrin, Second VP
Sallie Goldwyn, Director

A list of over 130 member firms and their suppliers.
Founded in 1946

23724 Machinery Dealers National Association
315 S Patrick Street
Alexandria, VA 22314

703-836-9300
800-872-7807
Fax: 703-836-9303
E-Mail: office@mdna.org
Home Page: www.mdna.org
Social Media: Facebook, Twitter, LinkedIn, Youtube

Paul Lashin, President
Ron Shuster, 1st VP
Kim Khoury, Second Vice President
Joe Lundvick, Treasurer

The Machinery Dealers National Association (MDNA) is an international, nonprofit trade association dedicated to the promotion of the used machinery industry.
Founded in 1941

23725 Material Handling Equipment Distributors Association
201 US Highway 45
Vernon Hills, IL 60061-2398

857-680-3500
Fax: 847-362-6989
E-Mail: connect@mheda.org
Home Page: www.mheda.org
Social Media: Facebook, Twitter, LinkedIn, Google+

Jerry Wiedmann, President
Liz Richards, Executive Vice President
Anna Mariae Kendall, Marketing Manager
Rebecca Hein, Networking & Communications
Susan Freibrun, Education Manager

The Material Handling Equipment Distributors Association is the only national association dedicated solely to improving the proficiency of the independent material handling equipment distributor.
Founded in 1954

23726 Metals Service Center Institute
4201 Euclid Ave
Rolling Meadows, IL 60008-2025

847-485-3000
800-872-7807
Fax: 847-485-3001
E-Mail: info@msci.org
Home Page: www.msci.org/
Social Media: Facebook, Twitter, LinkedIn

Bob Weidner, President/CEO
Sharon Hochel, Executive Assistant
Ashley DeVecht, Director, Communications
Ann D'Orazio, VP, Marketing Growth
Jonathan Kalkwarf, VP, Finance & Govt. Affairs

MSCI is a trade association that supports and represents the elements of the metals value chain, including metals producers, distributors and processors.
350 Members
Founded in 1907

23727 Michigan Distributors & Vendors Association
120 N Washington Square
Suite 110 B
Lansing, MI 48933

517-372-2323
Fax: 517-372-4404
E-Mail: webmaster@mdva.org
Home Page: www.mdva.org

Polly Reber, President
Russ Nowak, Chairman

The Michigan Distributors and Vendors Association (MDVA) is a non-profit, statewide business association representing two very significant business segments in the grocery and convenience products industry.
100 Members
Founded in 1991

23728 Mississippi Malt Beverage Association
4785 I-55 North, Suite 103
PO Box 1132
Jackson, MS 39215-1132

601-987-9098
Fax: 601-981-5566
E-Mail: info@msbeer.com
Home Page: www.msbeer.com

Richard Brown, President

The MMBA was established to represent and promote the beer wholesalers and beer industry within Mississippi.
13 Members
Founded in 1946

23729 Motorcycle Industry Council
2 Jenner Street
Suite 150
Irvine, CA 92618-3806

949-727-4211
Fax: 949-727-3313
E-Mail: ciannello@mic.org
Home Page: www.mic.org

The Motorcycle Industry Council (MIC) is a nonprofit, national trade association representing manufacturers and distributors of motorcycles, scooters, motorcycle/ATV parts and accessories and members of allied trades.

23730 Music Distributors Association
14070 Proton Road
Dallas, TX 75244-3601

972-233-9107
Fax: 972-490-4219
E-Mail: gplummer@iserv.net
Home Page: www.musicdistributors.org
Social Media: Facebook, Twitter, LinkedIn

Glenda Plummer, Executive Director

International, nonprofit trade association representing and serving manufacturers, wholesalers, importers and exporters of musical instruments and accessories, sound reinforcement products and published music.
250 Members
Founded in 1939

23731 NPTA Alliance
330 N Wabash Ave
Suite 2000
Chicago, IL 60611

312-321-4092
800-355-6782
Fax: 312-673-6736
E-Mail: npta@gonpta.com
Home Page: www.gonpta.com
Social Media: LinkedIn

Donald C Clampitt, Chairman
Travis M Mlakar, 1st Vice Chair
Hilton Maze, 2nd Vice Chair/Treasurer
Clay Ellis, 3rd Vice Chair
Kevin Gammonley, CEO

Representing distributors and suppliers of paper, packaging and facility supplies companies.
220 Members
Founded in 1903

23732 National Association of Chemical Distributors
1555 Wilson Boulevard
Suite 700
Arlington, VA 22209

703-527-6223
Fax: 703-527-7747
E-Mail: nacdpublicaffairs@nacd.com
Home Page: www.nacd.com
Social Media: LinkedIn, Youtube

Bruce Schechinger, Chairman, Chief Executive Officer
Andrew K Skipp, Vice Chairman
Roger T Harris, Treasurer
Jean-Pierre Baizan, Director at Large

The National Association of Chemical Distributors (NACD) is an international association of chemical distributor companies that purchase and take title of chemical products from manufacturers.
250 Members
Founded in 1971

23733 National Association of Electrical Distributors
1181 Corporate Lake Drive
St. Louis, MO 63132

314-991-9000
888-791-2512
Fax: 314-991-3060
E-Mail: customerservice@naed.org
Home Page: www.naed.org
Social Media: Facebook, Twitter, LinkedIn, RSS, Youtube

Sandra Rosecrans, President & Chief Executive Officer
Maureen Barsema, VP/CFO
Clarence Martin, CEO/CFO
Shaker Brock, VP, Sales
Scott R O'Day, VP, Marketing & Sales

The main goal of the National Association of Electrical Distributors (NAED) is to establish the electrical distributor as an essential force in the electrical industry and the economy.
Founded in 1908

23734 National Association of Flour Distributors
5350 Woodland Place
Canfield, OH 44406

330-718-6563
Fax: 877-573-1230
E-Mail: timdove51@gmail.com
Home Page: www.thenafd.com
Social Media: Facebook, Twitter, LinkedIn

J Gerard Burns, Chairman
Erin M Ruhl, President
Dominic Valente, 1st VP
Philip S Zilka Jr., 2nd VP
Steve Tardella, Secretary/Treasurer

The mission of the NAFD is to serve the interests of its members who are engaged in the flour industry and those companies allied thereto by providing educational and networking opportunities.

23735 National Association of Sign Supply Distributors
1001 N Fairfax St.
Suite 301
Alexandria, VA 22314

703-836-4012
Fax: 703-836-8353
E-Mail: info@signs.org

Home Page: www.nassd.org
Social Media: Facebook, Twitter, LinkedIn

Harry Niese, Chairman
Chad Jones, Vice Chair
Christopher Flejtuch, Secretary/Treasurer

NASSD is a nonprofit trade association for organizations who are engaged in full-line sign supply distribution and who manufacture or supply commercial, neon and electrical sign products.

23736 **National Association of Sporting Goods Wholesalers**
1833 Center Point Circle
Suite 123
Naperville, IL 60563

630-596-9006
Fax: 630-544-5055
E-Mail: info@nasgw.org
Home Page: www.nasgw.org
Social Media: Twitter, LinkedIn

Kent Williams, Chairman
Peter Brownell, Vice Chair/Director
Brad Burney, Treasurer

Non-profit trade association of wholesalers, distributors and manufacturers. Serves as a liaison with other sporting goods associations.
400 Members
Founded in 1953

23737 **National Association of Wholesaler - Distributors**
1325 G Street NW
Suite 1000
Washington, DC 20005-3100

202-872-0885
Fax: 202-785-0586
E-Mail: naw@naw.org
Home Page: www.naw.org
Social Media: Facebook, Twitter, LinkedIn

Dirk Van Dongen, President
Jade West, SVP - Government Relations
James A Anderson Jr, VP - Government Relations
Joy Goldman, Director - Administration
Ron Schreibman, SVP - Strategic Direction

The NAW provides members with the opportunity for networking and benchmarking within the entire wholesale distribution industry. NAW also represents the wholesale distribution industry before Congress, the White House, and the judiciary on issues that cross the industry's many lines of trade.

23738 **National Beer Wholesalers Association**
1101 King Street
Suite 600
Alexandria, VA 22314-2944

703-683-4300
Fax: 703-683-8965
E-Mail: info@nbwa.org
Home Page: www.nbwa.org
Social Media: Facebook, Twitter

Craig A Purser, President/CEO
Michael Johnson, EVP Fed Aff/Chief Advocacy Officer
Rebecca W Spicer, VP Public Affairs/Chief
Paul Pisano, SVP Industry Affairs & Gen. Counsel

NBWA represents the interests of America's 2,850 independent, licensed beer distributors which service every congressional district and media market in the country.
Founded in 1938

23739 **National Electronics Service Dealers Association**
3608 Pershing Ave
Fort Worth, TX 76107-4527

817-921-9061
800-797-9197
Fax: 817-921-3741
E-Mail: info@nesda.com
Home Page: www.nesda.com

Mack Blakely, Executive Director
Sheila Fredrickson, Dir Communications/Info Technology
Patricia Bohon, Membership & Trade Show Coordinator
James Keesler, Associate Editor/Graphic Designer
Margaret Vazquez, Bookkeeper/Administrative Assistant

Provides educational assistance in electronic training to public schools, compiles statistics, offers certification programs and apprenticeships. Functions as trade association for the electronics service industry.
8 Members
Founded in 1950

23740 **National Fastener Distributors Association**
10842 Noel Street #107
Los Alamitos, CA 90720

714-484-7858
877-487-6332
Fax: 562-684-0695
E-Mail: nfda@nfda-fastener.org
Home Page: www.nfda-fastener.org
Social Media: Facebook, Twitter, LinkedIn

Kevin Reidl, President
Paul Tiffany, VP
Sara Mallo, Associate Chair

Develops new uses for fasteners, offers training and educational programs.
250 Members
Founded in 1968

23741 **National Frozen & Refrigerated Foods Association**
4755 Linglestown Road Suite 300
PO Box 6069
Harrisburg, PA 17112

717-657-8601
Fax: 717-657-9862
E-Mail: info@nfraweb.org
Home Page: www.nfraweb.org
Social Media: Facebook, Twitter, LinkedIn

H V Skip Shaw Jr, President/CEO
Jeff Rumachik, EVP/COO
Dayna Jackson, VP Membership
Julie W Henderson, VP, Communications
Jessica Kurtz, VP, Finance

NFRA is a non-profit trade association representing all segments of the frozen and refrigerated foods industry. Headquartered in Harrisburg, PA, NFRA is the sponsor of March National Frozen Food Month, June dairy Month, and the Summer Favorites Ice Cream & Novelties promotion as well as the OctoberCool Food for Kids educational outreach program. NFRA holds the annual National Frozen & Refrigerated Foods Convention in October.
450 Members
Founded in 1945

23742 **National Grocers Association**
1005 North Glebe Road
Suite 250
Arlington, VA 22201-5758

703-516-0700
Fax: 703-516-0115
E-Mail: amamone@nationalgrocers.org
Home Page: www.nationalgrocers.org
Social Media: Facebook, Twitter, LinkedIn

Peter J Larkin, President & Chief Executive Officer
Charlie Bray, EVP/COO
Tom Wenning, Executive VP/General Counsel
Janessa Kamps, Executive Assistant
Julia Sullivan, Office Administrator/Receptionist

The National Grocers Association is the national trade association representing the retail and wholesale grocers that comprise the independent sector of the food distribution industry.

23743 **National Insulation Association**
12100 Sunset Hills Road
Suite 330
Reston, VA 20190

703-464-6244
Fax: 703-464-5896
Home Page: www.insulation.org
Social Media: Facebook

Michele M Jones, Executive Vice President/CEO
Kristin V DiDomenico, VP
Julia Bardnell, Director, Meetings & Events
Julie McLaughlin, Director, Publications
Ashley Joswick, Senior Manager, Production & Design

The National Insulation Association (NIA) is a trade association representing the mechanical and specialty insulation industry.
Founded in 1953

23744 **National Kitchen and Bath Association**
687 Willow Grove St
Hackettstown, NJ 07840-1731

908-850-1206
800-843-6522
Fax: 908-852-1695
E-Mail: feedback@nkba.org
Home Page: www.nkba.org
Social Media: Facebook, Twitter, LinkedIn

Don Sciolaro, CEO
Lili Corman, Director Professional Programs
Jill Levy, Director Membership
Bill Schankel, Director Marketing
Harry Smith, Director Finance

Protects the interests of members by fostering a better business climate. Awards certification. Conducts training schools and seminars.
25000 Members
Founded in 1963

23745 **National Poultry and Food Distributors Association**
2014 Osbourne Rd
St. Marys, GA 31558

770-535-9901
877-845-1545
Fax: 770-535-7385
E-Mail: kkm@npfda.org
Home Page: www.npfda.org

Marc Miro, President
Ted Rueger, VP
Lee Wilson, Treasurer
Kristin McWhorter, Executive Director

A nationwide association that serves the needs of the poultry and food distribution and processing industries. Provides member services, cost cutting benefits and networking opportunities. Sponsors Poultry Suppliers Showcase every January in Atlanta.
220 Members
Founded in 1967

23746 National School Supply & Equipment Association
8380 Colesville Road
Suite 250
Silver Spring, MD 20910

301-495-0240
800-395-5550
Fax: 301-495-3330
E-Mail: memberservices@nssea.org
Home Page: www.nssea.org
Social Media: Facebook, Twitter, LinkedIn, Youtube

Jim McGarry, President/CEO
Adrienne Dayton, VP, Marketing & Communications
Bill Duffy, VP, Operations & Meetings
Joe Tucker, Director, Meetings & Experiences
Karen Prince, Director, Membership

The National School Supply and Equipment Association (NSSEA) is the leading trade organization for the educational products marketplace. NSSEA puts the collective experience of the most successful school industry business in the world at your fingertips.
1400+ Members
Founded in 1916

23747 New York State Beer Wholesalers Association
100 State Street
Suite 400
Albany, NY 12207

518-465-6115
Fax: 518-465-1907
E-Mail: nybeer@nycap.rr.com
Home Page: www.nybeer.org

Fred C Dana, Chairman
Steven W Harris, President
Ed Keis, Chairman Elect
Bill Bessette, Treasurer
Deb Boening, Secretary

The New York State Beer Wholesalers Association, Inc. represents and protects the legislative and regulators interests of its members in state and local government. Our primary goal is to uphold the three-tier system in order to safeguard the industry's distribution standards.
44 Members
Founded in 1934

23748 North American Association of Telecommunications Dealers
131 NW First Avenue
DelRay Beach, FL 33444

561-266-9440
Fax: 561-266-9017
Home Page: www.natd.com

Rob Neuemeyer, Director
Arthur P Frierman, Associate Counsel

The North American Association of Telecommunications Dealers is a nonprofit organization of companies who provide telecom products to the business community and governments around the world. The NATD gives you access to the right kind of information, resources and business leaders, and provides you with unique opportunities to help grow your business.

23749 North American Association of Floor Covering Distributors
330 N Wabash Ave
Suite 2000
Chicago, IL 60611-4267

312-321-6836
Fax: 312-673-6962
E-Mail: info@nafcd.org
Home Page: www.nafcd.org
Social Media: Facebook, Twitter, LinkedIn, Youtube

George Roth, President
Craig Folven, Vice President
Chris O'Connor, Treasurer
Rosana Chaidez, Secretary
Michelle Miller, Executive Director

The North American Association of Floor Covering Distributors (NAFCD) was organized to foster trade and commerce for those having a business, financial or professional interest as wholesale distributors or manufacturers of floor coverings and allied products.

23750 North American Association of Uniform Manufacturers & Distributors
6800 Jericho Turnpike
Suite 120W
Syosset, NY 11791

516-393-5838
Fax: 516-393-5878
E-Mail: rjlerman@naumd.com
Home Page: www.naumd.com

Steve Robinson, Chair
Jim Tewmey, Vice Chair
Brian Garry, Treasurer
Richard J Lerman, President

An association dedicated to keeping the Uniforn & Imagewear Industry strong and healthy.
Founded in 1933

23751 North American Association of Utility Distributors (NAAUD)
PO Box 1930
Lady Lake, FL 32158

352-259-3999
Fax: 352-259-4014
E-Mail: lcoker@iag.net
Home Page: www.naaud.com

Linda B Coker, Executive Director

NAAUD is comprised of select distributors who specialize in supplying products and supply chain services to the electric utility industry. The purpose of NAAUD is to discuss and promote the newest ideas and best concepts for the industry.
Founded in 1988

23752 North American Building Material Distribution Association
330 N Wabash Ave
Suite 2000
Chicago, IL 60611

312-321-6845
888-747-7862
Fax: 312-644-0310
E-Mail: info@nbmda.org
Home Page: www.nbmda.org
Social Media: Facebook, Twitter, LinkedIn

Michael Darby, President
Donald F Schalk, President-Elect
Rick Turk, Vice President
Robyn Pollina, Treasurer

NBMDA develops and promotes the effectiveness of distribution processes to improve member profitability and growth.
Founded in 1952

23753 North American Horticultural Supply Association
100 North 20th Street
4th Floor
Philadelphia, PA 19103-1443

215-320-3877
Fax: 215-564-2175
E-Mail: nahsa@fernley.com
Home Page: www.nahsa.org
Social Media: Facebook, Twitter, LinkedIn

Sarah Hagy, Executive Director
Jameela Smith, Associate Director
Trudie Rowello, Management Liaison

The North American Horticultural Supply Association's mission is to strengthen and support the distribution and manufacturing of horticultural products and services.
Founded in 1987

23754 North American Meat Processors Association
1970 Broadway
Suite 825
Oakland, CA 94612

510-763-1533
800-368-3043
Fax: 510-763-6186
E-Mail: info@meatassociation.com
Home Page: www.meatassociation.com

Mike Satzow, Co Chair
Marty Evanson, Co Chair
Mike Hesse, Co President
Tony Gahn Jr., Co President
Brian Coelho, Co VP

Represents processors and distributors of meat, poultry, seafood and game to the food-service industry.
400 Members
Founded in 1942

23755 North American Wholesale Lumber Association
3601 Algonquin Road
Suite 400
Rolling Meadows, IL 60008

847-870-7470
800-527-8258
Fax: 847-870-0201
E-Mail: info@nawla.org
Home Page: www.nawla.org
Social Media: Facebook, Twitter, LinkedIn

Mike Phillips, Chairman
Rick Ekstein, 1st Vice Chair
Scott Elston, 2nd Vice Chair
John Stockhausen, Secretary/Treasurer
Gary Vitale, President

Supports the wholesale lumber industry. Publishes monthly NAWLA Bulletin that includes industry and association news, and produces the NAWLA Traders Market, an annual trade show bringing together over 1500 manufacturers and wholesale lumber traders at the premier event in the forest products industry. NAWLA also produces a variety of educational programs designed to enhance professionalism in the lumber industry.
600+ Members
Founded in 1893

23756 Optical Laboratories Association
225 Reinekers Lane
Suite 700
Alexandria, VA 22314
703-548-6619
800-477-5652
Fax: 703-548-4580
E-Mail: info@thevisioncouncil.org
Home Page: www.thevisioncouncil.org
Social Media: Facebook, Twitter, LinkedIn

Ed Greene, CEO
Brian Carroll, COO/CFO
Maureen Beddis, VP, Marketing & Communications
Greg Chavez, VP, Member Services
Deborah Malakoff-Castor, VP, Shows & Meetings

Independent ophthalmic laboratories and supply houses that manufacture prescription eye glasses.
337 Members
Founded in 1894

23757 Outdoor Power Equipment & Engine Service Association
37 Pratt Street
Essex, CT 06426-1159

860-767-1770
Fax: 860-767-7932
E-Mail: executivedirector@opeesa.com
Home Page: www.opeesa.com
Social Media: Facebook, Twitter

Rob Zucker, President & Director
Mark Vining, Vice President/Annual Meeting Dir.
Robert Graham, Secretary/Treasurer
Nancy Cueroni, Executive Director

The Outdoor Power Equipment and Engine Service Association (OPEESA) consists of more than 140 distributors and manufacturers of outdoor power equipment and air-cooled gas and diesel engines. Their mission is to assist distributors in achieving outstanding channel performance.
140 Members

23758 Outdoor Power Equipment Aftermarket Association
341 South Patrick Street
Suite 1101
Alexandria, VA 22314

703-549-7608
Fax: 703-549-7609
E-Mail: jhawes@opeaa.org
Home Page: www.opeaa.org

Bob Wehmueller, President
William S Bergman, Executive VP
Bob Titterington, VP
Laura James, Director/Membership Services
Linda Brownlee, Executive Director

Businessmen dedicated to promoting the use of aftermarket parts in outdoor power equipment, as well as trade in the industry.
85 Members
Founded in 1986

23759 Pacific-West Fastener Association
10842 Noel Street #107
Los Alamitos, CA 90720

714-484-4747
877 606-5232
Fax: 562-684-0695
E-Mail: info@pac-west.org
Home Page: www.pac-west.org

Vickie Lester, Executive Director
Jeannine Christensen, Member Services
Marci Myer, Member Services

An organization dedicated to the fastener industry.

23760 Pet Industry Distributors Association
3465 Box Hill Corp. Center Drive
Suite H
Abingdon, MD 21009

443-640-1060
Fax: 443-640-1086
E-Mail: pida@kingmgmt.org
Home Page: www.pida.org
Social Media: LinkedIn

Steven T King, President
Debbie Darce, Director, Finance
Stephanie Kaplan, Director, Online Education
Marci Hickey, Director, Meetings & Member Service

Represents wholesaler-distributors of pet products, providing training and education to members.
190 Members
Founded in 1968

23761 Petroleum Equipment Institute
PO Box 2380
Tulsa, OK 74101-2380
918-494-9696
Fax: 918-491-9895
E-Mail: info@pei.org
Home Page: www.pei.org
Social Media: Facebook, Twitter, LinkedIn

Terry Cooper, President
Phil Farrell, VP
Kevin McKinney, Treasurer
Robert Renkes, EVP

Members are makers and distributors of equipment used in service stations, bulk plants and other petroleum marketing facilities.
1600+ Members
Founded in 1951
Mailing list available for rent: 1600 names at $275 per M

23762 Power Transmission Distributors Association
230 W. Monroe St
Suite 1410
Chicago, IL 60606-4703

312-516-2100
Fax: 312-516-2101
E-Mail: ptda@ptda.org
Home Page: www.ptda.org
Social Media: Facebook, Twitter, LinkedIn

Ann Arnott, EVP/CEO
Brenda Holt, Director, Programs & Services
Bryan White, Director, Project Management

Members are power transmission/motion control distributors throughout manufacturing firms.
485 Members
Founded in 1960

23763 Professional Beauty Association
15825 N 71st Street
Suite 100
Scottsdale, AZ 85254-1521

480-281-0424
800-468-2274
Fax: 480-905-0708
E-Mail: info@probeauty.org
Home Page: www.probeauty.org
Social Media: Facebook, Twitter, LinkedIn

Scott Buchanan, Chairman
Reuben Carranza, Vice Chair
Kevin Barrett, Vice Chair

The Professional Beauty Association (PBA) is a nonprofit trade association that represents the interests of the professional beauty industry from manufacturers and distributors to salons and spas. PBA offers business tools, education, advocacy, networking and more to improve individual businesses and the industry as a whole.

23764 Quality Bakers of America Cooperative
1275 Glenlivet Drive
Suite 100
Allentown, PA 18106-3107

973-263-6970
Fax: 973-263-0937
E-Mail: info@qba.com
Home Page: www.qba.com

Don Cummings, VP

Members are independent wholesale bakeries and their suppliers.
35 Members
Founded in 1922

23765 Safety Equipment Distributors Association
1901 North Moore Street
Suite 200
Arlington, VA 22209-1762

443-640-1065
Fax: 703-528-2148
Home Page: www.safetycentral.org

Daniel K Shipp, President
Cristine Z Fargo, Director, Technical Service
Ann M Feder, Office Services Manager
Sabra L Decker, Office Administrator

Trade association comprised of companies that distribute safety equipment & related products and services.
300 Members
Founded in 1968

23766 Security Hardware Distributors Association
105 Eastern Avenue
Suite 104
Annapolis, MD 21403

410-940-6346
Fax: 410-263-1659
E-Mail: info@shda.org
Home Page: www.shda.org

Steve Dyson, President
Karen Hoffman, Vice President
Peter Berg, Treasurer
Paul Justen, Immediate Past President

The mission of the Security Hardware Distributors Association is to continually improve, through education and services, the proficiency of Security Distributors in order that they are the most effective and efficient conduit to the marketplace.

23767 Souvenir Wholesale Distributors Association
2105 Laurel Bush Road
Suite 200
Bel Air, MD 21015

443-640-1055
Fax: 443-640-1031
Home Page: www.souvenircentral.org
Social Media: Facebook

Steven T King CAE, Executive VP
Marci L Hickey CMP, Associate Director

Companies distributing local view scenic post cards and souvenirs in North America and the Caribbean.
110 Members
Founded in 1973

23768 Textile Care Allied Trades Association
271 Route 46 West
Suite C-106
Fairfield, NJ 07004

973-244-1790
Fax: 973-244-4455
E-Mail: info@tcata.org
Home Page: www.tcata.org
Social Media: Facebook, Twitter, LinkedIn

David Cotter, Chief Executive Officer
Cheryl Paglia, Office Manager

The Textile Care Allied Trades Association (TCATA) is an international trade association representing manufacturers and distributors of dry-cleaning and laundry equipment and supplies. It is the only trade association dedicated exclusively to the interests of the allied trades.

23769 The NPTA Alliance
330 North Wabash Avenue
Suite 200E
Farmingdale, NY 11735

312-321-4092
800-355-6782
Fax: 312-673-6736
E-Mail: webmaster@gonpta.com
Home Page: www.gonpta.com
Social Media: LinkedIn, Youtube

Kevin Gammonley, CEO
Pamm Schoeder, COO
Sean Samet, Operations Manager
Vickie Crews-Anderson, Manager, Communications & Marketing

Wholesale distributors of printing and industrial paper.
2000 Members
Founded in 1903

23770 United Producers Formulators & Distributors Association
PO Box 55
Roswell, GA 30077

770-552-8072
Fax: 770-417-1419
E-Mail: larry.eichler@prentiss.com
Home Page: www.upfda.com
Social Media: Facebook, Twitter

Tommy Reeves, President
Tom Eichler, Vice President
Cisse Spragins, Secretary & Treasurer
Valerie Jessee, Executive Director

Members are firms which are directly involved in formulating and distributing products or equipment to the pest control industry.

23771 Water & Sewer Distributors of America
100 North 20th Street
Suite 400
Philadelphia, PA 19103-1443
215-564-3482
Fax: 215-963-9785
E-Mail: wasda@fernley.com
Home Page: www.wasda.com
Social Media: Facebook

Sarah Hagy, Executive Director
Rebecca Mathis, Associate Director
Lindsay Groff, Management Liaison
Trish Keppler, Senior Meeting Manager

WASDA's mission is to promote the waterworks/wastewater products distribution industry, and to further improve the image and professionalism of WASDA and its member companies.
100+ Members
Founded in 1979

23772 Wholesale Florists and Florist Suppliers of America
105 Eastern Avenue
Suite 104
Annapolis, MD 21403-3300

410-940-6580
888-289-3372
Fax: 410-263-1659
E-Mail: info@wffsa.org
Home Page: www.wffsa.org
Social Media: Facebook, Twitter, LinkedIn

Patricia A Lilly, EVP
Joseph Thompson, General Manager
Amy Luckado, Membership Director
Kristin Thompson, Communications Manager

To provide networking and business opportunities to wholesale distributors and floral suppliers.
1.3M+ Members
Founded in 1926

23773 Wine/Spirits Wholesalers of America
805 15th Street NW
Suite 430
Washington, DC 20005

202-371-9792
Fax: 202-789-2405
E-Mail: info@wswa.org
Home Page: www.wswa.org
Social Media: Facebook, Twitter, LinkedIn

Craig Wolf, President/CEO
Peggy Sheldon, Executive Assistant
Jim Rowland, SVP, Govt. Affairs
Danwson Hobbs, VP, State Affairs
Reilly O'Connor, VP, Govt. Affairs

Two hundred booths for suppliers of alcoholic beverages from around the world.
3M Members

Newsletters

23774 News & Views
Bearing Specialists Association
800 Roosevelt Road
Building C, Suite 312
Glen Ellyn, IL 60137

630-858-3838
Fax: 630-790-3095
E-Mail: info@bsahome.org
Home Page: www.bsahome.org
Social Media: LinkedIn

Linda Miller, President
Richard W Church, Executive Director
Jerilyn J Church, Executive Secretary

Monthly newlsetter of BSA, the forum to enhance networking and knowledge sharing to promote the sale of bearings through authorized distributors. Available to members only.
100 Members
Frequency: E-Newlsetter for Members
Circulation: 400
Founded in 1966

23775 AMD Insider
10047 Robert Trent Jones Parkway
New Port Richey, FL 34655-4649

727-372-3665
800-786-7274
Fax: 727-372-2879
Home Page: www.amdweb.com

Rosalie Leone, Chief Executive Officer
Terry Rodimer, Operations and Assistant to the CEO
Jeff Burton, Director of Codes & Standards
Miguel Rivera-Sanchez, Director of Education
William G Simon, Graphics Coordinator

The Association of Millwork Distributors online newsletter providing information for and about the millwork distribution industry.
Frequency: Monthly

23776 APSP SmartBrief
Association of Pool & Spa Professionals
2111 Eisenhower Avenue
Alexandria, VA 22314

703-838-0083
Fax: 703-549-0493
E-Mail: memberservices@apsp.org
Home Page: www.apsp.org

Bill Weber, Chief Executive Officer
Terry Brown, Chairman of the Board
Kathleen Carlson, Secretary & Treasurer

APSP SmartBrief is a free weekly e-mail news service available to both APSP members and nonmembers. Each week subscribers are informed of the week's most important news stories for the pool, spa, and hot tub industry.
Frequency: Weekly
Founded in 1956

23777 Creative Marketing Newsletter
Association of Retail Marketing Services
10 DRS james parker BLVD
suite 103
Red Bank, NJ 07701-2003

732-842-5070
Fax: 732-219-1938
Home Page: www.goarms.com

Gerri Hopkins, Executive Director
Lisa McCauley, Administrative Director

Retail promotion marketing newsletter for supermarkets, convenience stores, drug chains and suppliers of retail promotions.
Frequency: Quarterly
Founded in 1957
Printed in 3 colors on matte stock

23778 Cutting Edge
Outdoor Power Equipment Aftermarket
341 South Patrick Street
Suite 1101
Alexandria, VA 22314

703-549-7608
Fax: 703-549-7609
E-Mail: wsb@opeaa.org
Home Page: www.opeaa.org

Katherine Inslie, President
Susan Dove, Editor

Businessmen dedicated to promoting the use of aftermarket parts in outdoor power equipment, as well as trade in the industry.
Cost: $25.00
Frequency: Quarterly
Founded in 1986

23779 Door & Hardware Industry Watch
Door & Hardware Institute
14150 Newbrook Drive
Chantilly, VA 20151
703-222-2010
Fax: 703-222-2410
Home Page: www.dhi.org

Jerry Heppes, Chief Executive Officer
Chuck Molina, Chief Technology Officer
Scott Sabatini, President

Electronic newsletter with the latest industry news and trends.
Frequency: 2 Times/Month
Founded in 1952

23780 Emerging Business
Master Security Company
PO Box 6661
Roanoke, VA 24017-0661

FAX 540-982-8407

Debra Napier, Publisher

Provides summary on articles of interest to small business owners, consultants corner, highlights services available pertaining to alternative financing of growing businesses.
6 Pages
Frequency: Quarterly

23781 FMI Daily Lead
Food Marketing Institute
2345 Crystal Drive
Suite 800
Arlington, VA 22202

202-452-8444
Fax: 202-425-4519
Home Page: www.fmi.org
Social Media: Facebook, Twitter, LinkedIn

Leslie Sarasin, President; Chief Executive Officer

Pat Shinko, Director
Paul Ryan, Executive Director

Newsletter that provides a daily briefing on top stories in food retailing and wholesaling.
1500 Members
Frequency: Daily
Founded in 1892

23782 ISD Insider
International Sealing Distribution Association
105 Eastern Avenue
Suite 104
Annapolis, MD 21403

410-940-6344
Fax: 410-263-1659
E-Mail: info@isd.org
Home Page: www.isd.org

Larry Goode, President
Debbie Mitchess, Executive Director
Joseph Thompson, Associate Director
Marty Lostrom, Conference Manager
Kristin B Thompson, Director of Communications

The association's newsletter is devoted to topics affecting business, training, and technology within the industry, with feature articles from industry experts.
Frequency: Quarterly

23783 Insider
MacLean Hunter
4 Stamford Forum
Stamford, CT 06901-3253

FAX 203-325-8423

Vanessa Grey, Publisher
Adrienne Toth, Editor

A shopping center industry newsweekly. Each issue contains critical information concerning retailer news, new development items, agent announcements and new tenant listings.
Cost: $250.00
6 Pages
Frequency: Monthly

23784 M&E Appraiser
American Society of Appraisers
555 Herndon Pkwy
Suite 125
Herndon, VA 20170-5250

703-478-2228
800-272-8258
Fax: 703-742-8471
Home Page: www.appraisers.org

Laurie Saunders, Executive VP
Jackie Montalvo, Editor
J Michael Clarkson, Publisher

Machinery and equipment appraisal information. Accepts advertising.
Cost: $45.00
48 Pages
Frequency: Quarterly
Founded in 1936

23785 MDNA News
Machinery Dealers National Association
315 S Patrick Street
Alexandria, VA 22314

703 836-9300
800-872-7807
Fax: 703-836-9303
E-Mail: office@mdna.org
Home Page: www.mdna.org

Michael F Feinstein, President
Paul Lashin, First Vice President
Ron Shuster, Second Vice President
Kim Khoury, Treasurer

This newsletter is a valuable source of information about MDNA events and programs, industry news, updates on chapter activities, government programs, and auctions.
Frequency: 6x/Year
Founded in 1941

23786 MHEDA Connection
Material Handling Equipment Distributors Assoc
201 US Highway 45
Vernon Hills, IL 60061-2398

857-680-3500
Fax: 847-362-6989
E-Mail: connect@mheda.org
Home Page: www.mheda.org

Duncan Murphy, President
Liz Richards, Executive Vice President
Kathy Cotter, Marketing Director
Natalie Cobb, Networking & Communications

The MHEDA Connection is a semi-monthly newsletter distributed to members and its associates on the 1st and the 15th of the month.
Frequency: Semi-Monthly
Founded in 1954

23787 NACD News Brief
National Association of Chemical Distributors
1555 Wilson Boulevard
Suite 700
Arlington, VA 22209

703-527-6223
Fax: 703-527-7747
E-Mail: nacdpublicaffairs@nacd.com
Home Page: www.nacd.com

Bruce Schechinger, Chairman, Chief Executive Officer
Andrew K Skipp, Vice Chairman
Roger T Harris, Treasurer
Jean-Pierre Baizan, Director at Large

The NACD News Brief is a biweekly e-mail newsletter outlining the key legislative and regulatory actions affecting NACD members and reporting on other key industry activity.
250 Members
Frequency: Bi-Weekly
Founded in 1971

23788 NAW Report
National Association of Wholesalers & Distributors
1325 G Street NW
Suite 1000
Washington, DC 20005-3100

202-872-0885
Fax: 202-785-0586
E-Mail: naw@naw.org
Home Page: www.naw.org

Peter L Cook, Executive Director
Dirk VanDongen, Contact

Information on regulation, industry research and programs for distributors and wholesalers.

23789 NBMDA Economic Outlook Report
N.A. Building Material Distribution Association
401 N. Michigan Avenue
Chicago, IL 60611

312-321-6845
888-747-7862
Fax: 312-644-0310
E-Mail: info@nbmda.org
Home Page: www.nbmda.org
Social Media: Facebook, Twitter, LinkedIn

Duane Lambrecht, President
Bill Delaney, President-Elect
Brian Schell, Vice President
Mark Kasper, Treasurer

This report correlates macroeconomic data to specific product categories directly related to the building material industry
Frequency: Quarterly
Founded in 1952

23790 NSPI News
National Spa and Pool Institute
2111 Eisenhower Ave
Suite 500
Alexandria, VA 22314-4679

703-838-0083
800-323-3996
Fax: 703-549-0493
E-Mail: MemberServices@TheAPSP.org
Home Page: www.theapsp.org

Bill Weber, President
Jack Cregol, CEO

23791 National Wholesaler Association
251 W Renner Road
#102
Richardson, TX 75080-1318

FAX 972-470-0134

Don Akerman, Publisher

Offers products, new or old, marketing, distribution expertise, customer analysis, positioning, advertising, promotion planning. Accepts advertising.
Frequency: Quarterly

23792 News & Views
Bearing Specialists Association
800 Roosevelt Road
Building C, Suite 312
Glen Ellyn, IL 60137

630-858-3838
Fax: 630-790-3095
E-Mail: info@bsahome.org
Home Page: www.bsahome.org
Social Media: LinkedIn

Linda Miller, President
Richard W Church, Executive Director
Jerilyn J Church, Executive Secretary

Monthly newlsetter of BSA, the forum to enhance networking and knowledge sharing to promote the sale of bearings through authorized distributors. Available to members only.
100 Members
Frequency: E-Newlsetter for Members
Circulation: 400
Founded in 1966

23793 North American Wholesale Lumber Association Bulletin
North American Wholesale Lumber Association
3601 Algonquin Rd
Suite 400
Rolling Meadows, IL 60008-3181

847-870-7470
800-527-8258
Fax: 847-870-0201
E-Mail: info@nawla.org
Home Page: www.nawla.org

Nicholas Kent, President
Stacey Woldt, Meetings Manager

Newsletter published by North American Wholesale Lumber Association.
Frequency: Monthly
Founded in 1892

23794 Unlocked
Security Hardware Distributors Association
105 Eastern Avenue
Suite 104
Annapolis, MD 21403

410-940-6346
Fax: 410-263-1659

E-Mail: info@shda.org
Home Page: www.shda.org

Steve Dyson, President
Karen Hoffman, Vice President
Peter Berg, Treasurer
Paul Justen, Immediate Past President

The SHDA newsletter, Unlocked, provides members with the latest news about the association and its educational events and programs as well as trends and news about security hardware distribution.
Frequency: Monthly

23795 **Weekly Insights**
Global Market Development Center
1275 Lake Plaza Drive
Colorado Springs, CO 80906-3583

719-576-4260
Fax: 719-576-2661
E-Mail: info@gmdc.org
Home Page: www.gmdc.com

David T McConnell Jr, President, Chief Executive Officer
Mark Mechelse, Director of Industry Insights
Keith Wypyszynski, VP Business Development
Mike Winterbottom, VP Information Technology, CTO

Weekly Insights addresses important General Merchandise topics, important Health Beauty Wellness topics and news from GMDC.
Frequency: Weekly
Founded in 1970

23796 **Winning in Washington-NAW Annual Report**
National Association of Wholesalers & Distributors
1725 K St Nw
Washington, DC 20006-1401

202-349-7300
Fax: 202-331-7442
Home Page: www.nawc.org

Peter L Cook, Executive Director

Activities of the National Association of Wholesalers and Distributors.

Magazines & Journals

23797 **AFI**
AFI Communications
2455 E Sunrise Boulevard
Suite 916
Fort Lauderdale, FL 33304-3112

FAX 954-561-4129

Andrew Molchan, President
Bob Lesmeister, Managing Editor

Edited for professional firearm retailers. Editorial emphasis is on new products, new industry and new sales programs for distributors and retailers. Also covers management level trends for manufacturers and wholesalers. Other features include New Products, Archery, Andy's Industry Insights and more.
Circulation: 23,930

23798 **AQ Magazine**
Association of Pool & Spa Professionals
2111 Eisenhower Avenue
Alexandria, VA 22314

703-838-0083
Fax: 703-549-0493
E-Mail: memberservices@apsp.org
Home Page: www.apsp.org

Bill Weber, Chief Executive Officer
Terry Brown, Chairman of the Board
Kathleen Carlson, Secretary & Treasurer

This full-color magazine is written and edited by industry experts with a keen awareness of the issues on the minds of professionals.
Frequency: Quarterly
Founded in 1956

23799 **ASA Materials Market Digest**
American Supply Association
1200 N. Arlington Heights Rd
Suite 150
Chicago, IL 60654

312-464-0090
Fax: 312-464-0091
E-Mail: info@asa.net
Home Page: www.asa.net

Jeff New, Chairman of the Board
Joe Poehling, President
Frank Nisonger, President-Elect
Robert Christiansen, Vice President

Available monthly via e-mail to all members of ASA, the ASA Materials Market Digest is designed to keep readers informed of important trends and recent changes in the industry.
Frequency: Monthly
Founded in 1969

23800 **AVEM Resource Guide**
Association of Vacuum Equipment Manufacturers
201 Park Washington Court
Falls Church, VA 22046-4527

703-538-3543
Fax: 703-241-5603
E-Mail: aveminfo@avem.org
Home Page: www.avem.org

Dawn M. Shiley, Executive Director

Buyers guide offering products and services that are offered by AVEM member companies. Items range from systems, pumps, instrumentation, hardware and deposition components.
49 Members
Frequency: Yearly
Founded in 1969

23801 **American Wholesale Marketers Association**
Ameican Wholesale Marketers Association
2750 Prosperity Ave
Suite 530
Fairfax, VA 22031-4338

703-208-3358
800-482-2962
Fax: 703-573-5738
E-Mail: robertp@awmanet.org
Home Page: www.awmanet.org

Scott Ramminger, President
Traci Carneal, Editor-in-Chief
Joan Fay, Associate Publisher

Information on candy, chewing gum, tobacco, HBC, general merchandise, snack foods and related items.
Printed in 4 colors on glossy stock

23802 **Beer Perspectives**
National Beer Wholesalers Association
1101 King Street
Suite 600
Alexandria, VA 22314-2965

703-683-4300
Fax: 703-683-8965
E-Mail: info@nbwa.org
Home Page: www.nbwa.org
Social Media: Facebook, Twitter

Craig A Purser, President & CEO
Michael Johnson, EVP/Chief Advisory Officer
Rebecca Spicer, VP Public Affairs/Chief
Paul Pisano, SVP Industry Affairs & Gen. Counsel

Trade association for beer wholesalers. Provides government and public affairs outreach as well as education and training for its wholesaler members.
2200 Pages
Founded in 1938

23803 **Chemical Distributor**
National Association of Chemical Distributors
1555 Wilson Boulevard
Suite 700
Arlington, VA 22209

703-527-6223
Fax: 703-527-7747
E-Mail: nacdpublicaffairs@nacd.com
Home Page: www.nacd.com
Social Media: Facebook, Twitter, LinkedIn, YouTube

Bruce Schechinger, Chairman, Chief Executive Officer
Andrew K Skipp, Vice Chairman
Roger T Harris, Treasurer
Jean-Pierre Baizan, Director at Large

The industry's magazine that is published nine times a year and highlights members' news, Association and industry activity, and provides business information useful to chemical distributors.
250 Members
Frequency: 9x/Year
Founded in 1971

23804 **Cleaner Times**
Cleaning Equipment Trade Association
1000 Nix Road
Little Rock, AR 72211-3235

704-635-7362
800-525-7038
Fax: 501-280-9233
Home Page: www.cleanertimes.com
Social Media: Facebook, Twitter, LinkedIn

Charlene Yarbrough, Publisher
Jim McMurry, Editor
Chris Ragan, Art Director
Chuck Prieur, Advertising Sales

Magazine published by the Cleaning Equipment Trade Association for members.
Frequency: Monthly

23805 **Distributor's Link**
4297 Corporate Sq
Naples, FL 34104-4754

239-643-2713
800-356-1639
Fax: 239-643-5220
E-Mail: leojcoar@linkmagazine.com
Home Page: www.linkmagazine.com

Maryann Marzocchi, President
Tracey Lumia, Advertising Sales
Michael T Wrenn, Marketing Manager

Information aimed at the fastener distributors nationwide.
Cost: $45.00
300 Pages
Frequency: Quarterly
Circulation: 50000
Founded in 1975

23806 **Door & Hardware Magazine**
Door & Hardware Institute
14150 Newbrook Drive
Chantilly, VA 20151

703-222-2010
Fax: 703-222-2410
Home Page: www.dhi.org
Social Media: Facebook, Twitter, LinkedIn

Jerry Heppes, Chief Executive Officer
Chuck Molina, Chief Technology Officer
Scott Sabatini, President

The Door & Hardware magazine offers information and articles from the industry's only

publication dedicated solely to the architectural openings industry.
Frequency: Monthly

23807 Employment Guide
Bureau of National Affairs
1801 S Bell St
Arlington, VA 22202-4501
703-341-3000
800-372-1033
Fax: 800-253-0332
E-Mail: customercare@bna.com
Home Page: www.bnabooks.com
Social Media: Facebook, Twitter, LinkedIn

Paul N Wojcik, CEO

An easy-to-read, practical reference guide to a broad range of employment topics, designed for the small to medium sized organization.
Cost: $745.00
Founded in 1929

23808 Essentials Magazine
National School Supply & Equipment Association
8380 Colesville Road
Suite 250
Silver Spring, MD 20910
301-495-0240
800-395-5550
Fax: 301-495-3330
Home Page: essentials.nssea.org
Social Media: Facebook, Twitter, LinkedIn

Tim Holt, President & Chief Executive Officer
Bill Duffy, VP of Operations & Meetings
DeShuna Spencer, Director of Publications
Adrienne Watts Dayton, VP Marketing & Communications

Essentials magazine targets all facets of the educational industry from contemporary, bite-sized studies and statistics, to timely feature articles, as well as NSSEA member interviews, product press releases, and business updates.
Frequency: Monthly
Founded in 1916

23809 GAWDA Edge
Gases and Welding Distributors Association
100 North 20th Street
4th Floor
Philadelphia, PA 19103
215-564-3484
Fax: 215-963-9785
E-Mail: gawda@gawda.org
Home Page: www.gawda.org

Kent Van Amburg, Executive Director
Malvenia Avery, Associate Director
Tawnee Shuey, Meeting Manager
Kate Marlys, Director

Provides relevant news and technology information.
775 Members
Frequency: Quarterly
Founded in 1945

23810 Insulation Outlook
National Insulation Association
12100 Sunset Hills Road
Suite 330
Reston, VA 20190
703-464-6244
Fax: 703-464-5896
Home Page: www.insulation.org

Michele M Jones, Executive Vice President/CEO
Larry Nelles, President
Glenn Frye, President-Elect
Alec Rexroat, Secretary/Treasurer

Insulation Outlook is the only international publication devoted exclusively to industrial and commercial insulation applications, products, and materials.
Cost: $65.00
Frequency: Monthly
Founded in 1953

23811 International Gaming and Wagering Business
BNP Media
PO Box 1080
Skokie, IL 60076-9785
847-763-9534
Fax: 847-763-9538
E-Mail: igwb@halldata.com
Home Page: www.igwb.com

James Rutherford, Editor
Lynn Davidson, Marketing
Tammie Gizicki, Director

Focuses on business strategy, legislative information, food service and promotional concerns.
Frequency: Monthly
Circulation: 25000

23812 Licensing Book
Adventure Publishing Group
1107 Broadway
Suite 1204
New York, NY 10010-1512
212-575-4510
Fax: 212-575-4521
Home Page: www.licensingbook.com

Judy Basis, Publisher
Mathew C Scheiner, Editor-in-Chief
Owen Shorts, Owner

Licensing in successful retailing, licensed product merchandising in various aspects.
Cost: $48.00
40 Pages
Frequency: Monthly
Founded in 1983

23813 Licensing International
WFC
3000 Hadley Rd
South Plainfiel, NJ 07080-1183
908-668-4747
Fax: 732-769-1711
E-Mail: info@wfcinc.com
Home Page: www.wfcinc.com

Theodore Pytlar, VP
Kimberly Calabrese, Production Manager

Business merchandising magazine serving the licensing industry at all levels. Publishes whole foods magazine.
Cost: $70.00
64 Pages
Frequency: Monthly
Circulation: 14,933

23814 MHEDA Journal
Material Handling Equipment Distributors Assoc
201 US Highway 45
Vernon Hills, IL 60061-2398
857-680-3500
Fax: 847-362-6989
E-Mail: connect@mheda.org
Home Page: www.themhedajournal.org
Social Media: Facebook, Twitter, LinkedIn

Duncan Murphy, President
Liz Richards, Executive Vice President
Kathy Cotter, Marketing Director
Natalie Cobb, Networking & Communications

The MHEDA journal is the official magazine of the association.
Frequency: Quarterly
Founded in 1954

23815 Material Handling Wholesaler
Specialty Publications International
801 Bluff Street
PO Box 725
Dubuque, IA 52004-725
563-557-4495
877-638-6190
Fax: 563-557-4499
E-Mail: circulation@mhwmag.com
Home Page: www.mhwmag.com

Dean Millius, General Manager
Cathy Murphy, Editor
Sharon Dague, Account Executive
Cathy Murphy, Contributing Editor

Published for used and new material handling equipment dealers, parts suppliers, manufacturers reps, repair shops, and brokers includes articles on issues, conventions, products and people that impact the industry.
Cost: $31.00
Frequency: Monthly
Circulation: 27000
Founded in 1979
Printed in 4 colors on newsprint stock

23816 NSPI Business Owners Journal
National Spa and Pool Institute
2111 Eisenhower Ave
Suite 500
Alexandria, VA 22314-4679
703-838-0083
800-323-3996
Fax: 703-549-0493
Home Page: www.nspi.org

Bill Weber, President

A resource service offered by the national spa and pool inst. published four times a year. Contains concise, pertinent and useful information of critical importance to business owners throughout the year, this journal delivers information that is easily applied to a business, including more than 100 action alerts and ideas, and 25 to 30 how-to articles, advisories and reports. Covers such topics as ways to cash flows; ways to save and defer taxes; how to sell and buy a business.
Founded in 1956

23817 New Equipment Digest
Penton Media
1300 E 9th St
Suite 316
Cleveland, OH 44114-1503
216-696-7000
Fax: 216-696-6662
E-Mail: information@penton.com
Home Page: www.penton.com

Jane Cooper, Marketing
Dave Madonia, Associate Publisher/eMedia
Robert F King, Editor
Garnetta Russell, Ad Services Manager
Bobbie Macy, Circulation Manager

Serves the general industrial field which includes manufacturing, processing, engineering services, construction, transportation, mining, public utilities, wholesale distributors, educational services, libraries and governmental establishments.
Frequency: Monthly
Circulation: 206164
Founded in 1936

23818 Paper & Packaging
NPTA Alliance
401 N Michigan Avenue
Suite 2200
Chicago, IL 60611
312-321-4092
800-355-6782
Fax: 312-673-6736
E-Mail: npta@gonpta.com
Home Page: www.gonpta.com

Dennis Coyle, Associate Publisher/Editor

Covers association news, industry news, industry reports, industry events, new products, personnel updates and business articles for management and sales representatives and much more.
Cost: $120.00
Frequency: Quarterly
Circulation: 6000

23819 Plumbing Engineer
TMB Publishing
1838 Techny Ct
Northbrook, IL 60062-5474

847-564-1127
Fax: 847-564-1264
E-Mail: tmbpubs@earthlink.net
Home Page: www.tmbpublishing.com

Tom M Brown, President
Cate Brown, Production Manager

Over 400 plumbing products from approximately 250 manufacturers.
Frequency: Monthly
Circulation: 26104
ISSN: 0192-171X
Founded in 1973
Printed in 4 colors

23820 Supply House Times
Reed Business Information
1050 IL Route 83
Suite 200
Bensenville, IL 60106

630-616-0200
800-323-4958
Fax: 630-288-8686
E-Mail: leniusp@bnpmedia.com
Home Page: www.supplyht.com

Patricia Lenius, Managing Editor
Scott Franz, Publisher
Kevin Hackney, Marketing Coordinator
Ashley Anderson, Associate Editor
George Zebrowski, Group Publisher

For plumbing, heating, air conditioning and piping wholesalers
Cost: $92.00
62 Pages
Frequency: Monthly
Founded in 1958
Printed in 4 colors on glossy stock

23821 TED Magazine
National Association of Electrical Distributors
1166 Avenue of the Americas
St. Louis, NY 10036

212-204-4200
888-791-2512
Fax: 314-991-3060
E-Mail: customerservice@naed.org
Home Page: www.tedmag.com

Tom Naber, President & Chief Executive Officer
Michelle McNamara, Vice President
Becky Burgess, Meetings & Conferences Director

TED magazine (The Electrical Distributor) is NAED's premier trade publication. With the latest industry news as well as articles and research ranging from sales to voice-data-video, TED magazine is necessary reading for all electrical distributors.
Cost: $40.00
Frequency: Monthly
Founded in 1908

23822 Welding & Gases Today
Gases and Welding Distributors Association
8669 Doral Blvd
Suite 130
Philadelphia, PA 33166

215-564-3484
877-382-6440
Fax: 305-442-7451
E-Mail: gawda@gawda.org
Home Page: www.gawda.org

Kent Van Amburg, Executive Director
Malvenia Avery, Associate Director
Tawnee Shuey, Meeting Manager
Kate Marlys

The official journal of the Gases and Welding Distributors Association.
775 Members
Frequency: Quarterly
Founded in 1945

Trade Shows

23823 AED Summit
600 22nd~Street
Suite 220
Oak Brook, IL 60523

630-574-0650
800-388-0650
Fax: 630-574-0132
E-Mail: info@aednet.org
Home Page: www.aednet.org
Social Media: Facebook, Twitter, LinkedIn

Toby Mack, President & CEO
Bob Henderson, Executive Vice President & COO
Dave Gordon, Publisher/Vice President of Sales
Kim Phelan, Executive Editor

The AED Summit provides a pure networking opportunity with both dealers and their manufacturer partners. It also offers high quality, high class, professional education content for executives and managers.
700 Members
Frequency: Annual

23824 ASCDI Winter Conference
Association of Service and Computer Dealers Int'l
131 NW First Avenue
Delray Beach, FL 33444

561-266-9016
Fax: 561-266-9017
Home Page: www.ascdi.com

Rob Neumeyer, Director
Bob Boyle, Counsel
Jerry Roberts, Chairman Emeritus
Arthur P Freierman, Treasurer

The ASCDI conferences provide a great forum for networking with others in the industry, meeting old friends, and making new contacts. The winter conference offers an opportunity to learn about the latest technology trends, meet with leading vendors, and gain a competitive edge in the IT market. The conference is conducted by following Green Meeting Practices.
Founded in 1981

23825 AVDA Annual Conference
2105 Laurel Bush Road
Suite 200
Bel Air, MD 21015

443-640-1040
Fax: 443-640-1086
E-Mail: kaymie@ksgroup.org
Home Page: www.avda.net
Social Media: Facebook, Twitter, LinkedIn, YouTube

George Henriques, Chairman
Mary Pat Thompson, President
Ben Coe, President-Elect

The AVDA annual conference is a three-day program of information and educational sessions featuring industry and outside speakers on a variety of timely business and industry issues and topics.
Frequency: Annual
Founded in 1976

23826 AWFS Fair
Association of Woodworking & Furnishings Suppliers
500 Citadel Drive
Suite 200
Commerce, CA 90040

323-838-9440
800-946-2937
Fax: 323-838-9443
E-Mail: info@awfs.org
Home Page: www.awfs.org
Social Media: Facebook, Twitter, LinkedIn, YouTube

Joan Kemp, President
Jeff Oliverson, Vice President
Wade Gregory, Secretary/Treasurer
Skip Hem, Immediate Past President

The AWFS Fair is the largest industry show in the United States.
Frequency: Biennial

23827 AWMA Real Deal Expo
American Wholesale Marketers Association
2750 Prosperity Avenue
Suite 530
Fairfax, VA 22031

703-208-3358
800-482-2962
Fax: 703-573-5738
E-Mail: info@awmanet.org
Home Page: www.realdealexpo.com

Scott Ramminger, President/CEO
Robert Pignato, VP Marketing/Industry Affairs
Annual show of 4500 manufacturers and suppliers of confectionery, tobacco, snack foods, juice, novelties and technology and allies to the industry.
Frequency: March

23828 American Nursery & Landscape Association Convention
American Nursery & Landscape Association
1000 Vermont Avenue NW
Suite 300
Washington, DC 20005-3922

202-789-2900
Fax: 202-789-1893
Home Page: www.anla.org

Peter Orum, President
Robert J Dolibois, Executive Director

Serves firms who grow, sell or use plants. ANLA advocates the industry's interests before government and provides its members with unique business knowledge essential to long-term growth and profitability.
Frequency: July

23829 Annual Business Leadership Summit
Fluid Power Distributors Association
105 Eastern Avenue
Suite 104
Annapolis, MD 21403

410-940-6347
Fax: 410-263-1659
E-Mail: info@fpda.org
Home Page: www.fpda.org

Social Media: Facebook, Twitter, LinkedIn, YouTube

Richard Neels, President & Chairman of the Board
Steve Schwasnick, President-Elect
Bill Gillies, Vice President - Membership
Hal Kemp, Convention Chair
Mike Hamzey Jr, VP of Finance & Treasurer

This conference is held each spring and is designed especially for industry decision-makers and opinion-leaders, and is focused on business opportunities, economic and industry trends, leadership development and channel efficiencies.
300+ Members
Frequency: Annual
Founded in 1974

23830 Atlantic City Pool & Spa Show
Association of Pool & Spa Professionals
6B South Gold Drive
Hamilton, NJ 08691

609-689-9111
Fax: 703-549-0493
E-Mail: memberservices@apsp.org
Home Page: www.nespapool.org

Bill Weber, Chief Executive Officer
Terry Brown, Chairman of the Board
Kathleen Carlson, Secretary & Treasurer

The Atlantic City show is one of the industry's largest, offering a large trade show and business and technical seminars.
10000 Attendees
Frequency: Annual

23831 BSA Convention
Bearing Specialists Association
800 Roosevelt Road
Building C, Suite 312
Glen Ellyn, IL 60137

630-858-3838
Fax: 630-790-3095
E-Mail: info@bsahome.org
Home Page: www.bsahome.org
Social Media: LinkedIn

Linda Miller, President
Richard W Church, Executive Director
Jerilyn J Church, Executive Secretary
Kathy Fatz, Association Manager
Janet Arden, Publications Editor

The world's premier bearing industry event for authorized distributors of bearing products and services and the manufacturers of those products.
100 Members
Frequency: Annual
Founded in 1966

23832 BSA Winter Meeting
Bearing Specialists Association
800 Roosevelt Road
Building C, Suite 312
Glen Ellyn, IL 60137
630-858-3838
Fax: 630-790-3095
E-Mail: info@bsahome.org
Home Page: www.bsahome.org
Social Media: Facebook, Twitter, LinkedIn

Eduardo Bichara, President
Richard W Church, Executive Director
Jerilyn J Church, Executive Secretary
Kathy Fatz, Association Manager
Janet Arden, Publications Editor

BSA committees will be addressing many important issues and association projects at the Winter Meeting. Attending this meeting will help to influence the direction the industry takes over the coming years.
Frequency: Annual

23833 CBBD Annual Convention
1415 L Street
Suite 890
Sacramento, CA 95814

916-441-5402
800-952-8308
Fax: 916-441-0713
E-Mail: assn@cbbd.com
Home Page: www.cbbd.com
Social Media: Facebook, Twitter, LinkedIn

Victoria G Horton, President
Becky Stolberg, Vice President
Rhonda Stevenson, Marketing & Public Affairs Director

The California Beer and Beverage Distributors host this annual convention for professionals in the industry.
100+ Members
Frequency: Annual

23834 CTDA Management Conference
Ceramic Tile Distributors Association
800 Roosevelt Road
Building C, Suite 312
Glen Ellyn, IL 60137

630-545-9415
800-938-2838
Fax: 630-790-3095
E-Mail: info@ctdahome.org
Home Page: www.ctdahome.org

Ryan Calkins, President
Frank Donahue, VP
Barbara Vasquez, Treasurer
Bill Ives, Legal Counsel
Rick Church, Executive Director

CTDA Management Conference is host to the biggest industry leaders and features educational sessions and exhibits
450 Attendees
Frequency: Annual

23835 Distribution Management Conference & Technology Expo
Healthcare Distribution Management Association
901 North Glebe Road
Suite 1000
Arlington, VA 22203

703-787-0000
Fax: 703-812-5282
Home Page: www.healthcaredistribution.org
Social Media: Facebook, Twitter, LinkedIn

Paul Julian, Chairman
David S Moody, Vice Chairman
John M Gray, President & CEO
Albert~ Thomas, Director

Hundreds of healthcare industry thought leaders and supply chain visionaries gather for nearly three days full of networking, business sessions, and an exciting Technology Expo.
Frequency: Annual

23836 EMDA Industry Showcase
FEWA-AIMRA
PO Box 1347
Iowa City, IA 52244

319-354-5156
Fax: 319-354-5157
E-Mail: pat@edma.net
Home Page: www.edma.net
Social Media: Facebook, Twitter, LinkedIn

Patricia A Collins, Executive VP

Annual convention and 130 exhibits of equipment, supplies and services for independent wholesale-distributors and independent manufacturer's representatives of shortline and specialty farm equipment, light industrial tractors, lawn and garden tractors, turf care equipment, estate and park maintenance equipment.
600 Attendees
Frequency: November

23837 Ed Expo
National School Supply & Equipment Association
8380 Colesville Road
Suite 250
Silver Spring, MD 20910

301-495-0240
800-395-5550
Fax: 301-495-3330
Home Page: www.nssea.org
Social Media: Facebook, Twitter, LinkedIn

Tim Holt, President & Chief Executive Officer
Bill Duffy, VP of Operations & Meetings
DeShuna Spencer, Director of Publications
Adrienne Watts Dayton, VP Marketing & Communications
Rashad Cheeks, Circulation Manager

Ed Expo is the country's premier back-to-school buying event and is the ideal place for exhibitors to showcase their products to highly-qualified buyers in the educational products marketplace.
Frequency: Annual
Founded in 1916

23838 Executive Conference
Health Industry Distributors Association
310 Montgomery Street
Alexandria, VA 22314-1516

703-549-4432
Fax: 703-549-6495
Home Page: www.hida.org

Matthew Rowan, President & CEO
Rochelle Hargraves, Vice President Finance & Operations
Andrew Van Ostrand, Vice President Policy & Research
Amy Michael, Senior Manager Governmental Affairs

Hundreds of distributor and manufacturer executives gather for the Executive Conference, which consists of networking, interactive education, strategic planning, and industry discussions.
Frequency: Annual
Founded in 1902

23839 FPDA Annual Network Symposium
Fluid Power Distributors Association
105 Eastern Avenue
Suite 104
Annapolis, MD 21403

410-940-6347
Fax: 410-263-1659
E-Mail: info@fpda.org
Home Page: www.fpda.org

Richard Neels, President & Chairman of the Board
Steve Schwasnick, President-Elect
Bill Gillies, Vice President - Membership
Hal Kemp, Convention Chair
Mike Hamzey Jr, VP of Finance & Treasurer

This meeting is designed for key management and emerging leaders, and focuses on business and product technologies & trends, industry standards & certification, the FPDA Young Executives development and supporting the needs of participants in the FPDA E-Networks program.
300+ Members
Frequency: Annual
Founded in 1974

23840 General Merchandise Marketing Conference
Global Market Development Center

1275 Lake Plaza Drive
Colorado Springs, CO 80906-3583

719-576-4260
Fax: 719-576-2661
E-Mail: info@gmdc.org
Home Page: www.gmdc.com

David T McConnell Jr, President/CEO
Mark Deuschle, Chief Marketing Officer
Keith Wypyszynski, VP Business Development
Mike Winterbottom, VP Information Technology/CTO

Annual conference which has Controlled Casual Conference appointments between wholesalers/retailers and the suppliers, business sessions, roundtables and workshops.
Frequency: Annual/June
Founded in 1970

23841 **Health Beauty Wellness Marketing Conference**
Global Market Development Center
1275 Lake Plaza Drive
Colorado Springs, CO 80906-3583
719-576-4260
Fax: 719-576-2661
E-Mail: info@gmdc.org
Home Page: www.gmdc.com

David T McConnell Jr, President, Chief Executive Officer
Mark Deuschle, Chief Marketing Officer
Keith Wypyszynski, VP Business Development
Mike Winterbottom, VP Information Technology, CTO

Annual conference which has Controlled Casual Conference appointments between wholesalers/retailers and the suppliers, Senior Executive Conference appointments, business sessions, roundtables and workshops.
Frequency: Annual
Founded in 1970

23842 **IAPD Annual Convention**
International Association of Plastics Distribution
6734 W. 121st Street
Overland Park, KS 66209
913-345-1005
Fax: 913-345-1006
E-Mail: iapd@iapd.org
Home Page: www.iapd.org

Susan Avery, Executive Director
Cyndy Launchbaugh, Director of Marketing
Denise Rawlings, Member Services Manager
Crystal Roberts, Sales & Advertising Manager
Wendy Schantz, Marketing & Education Manager

This three-day convention is where the best and the brightest of the plastics distribution industry come together to focus on the future of the industry.
Frequency: Annual
Founded in 1956

23843 **ISA Product Show & Conference**
Industry Supply Association
100 North 20th Street
4th Floor
Philadelphia, PA 19103
215-320-3862
866-460-2360
Fax: 215-963-9785
E-Mail: info@isapartners.org
Home Page: www.isaproductshow.org
Social Media: Facebook, Twitter, LinkedIn, YouTube

John Buckley, Executive Vice President
Mary Ritchie, Director, Membership Services
Ken Hutton, Managing Director
Christopher Schor, Associate Director

This is the premier event for anyone in the maintenance, repair, operations and production (MROP) industry. Any MROP distributor, manufacturer/supplier, manufacturers' representative or industry service provider is welcome to attend.
Frequency: Annual

23844 **ITPA Seasonal Meeting**
International Truck Parts Association
1720 10th Ave. South
Suite 4
Bethesda, MD 20817

202-544-3090
866-346-5692
Fax: 301-229-7331
E-Mail: info@itpa.com
Home Page: www.itpa.com
Social Media: Facebook, Twitter, LinkedIn, YouTube

Andy Reichert, Chairman
Mike Adiletto, Vice Chairman
Venlo Wolfsohn, Executive Director

Meetings are held each Winter, Fall, and Spring and provide outstanding educational programs, one-on-one meetings with the industry's suppliers, and product trade show and excellent networking opportunities.
Frequency: Annual
Founded in 1974

23845 **International Foodservice Distributors: Productivity Convention & Expo**
201 Park Washington Court
Falls Church, VA 22046-4521

703-532-9400
Fax: 703-538-4673
Home Page: www.ifdaonline.org

Mark Allen, President/CEO
Jonathan Eisen, Senior VP Of Government Relations

Workshops, assemblies, facility tours and an exposition are featured. Educational programming features many practitioners who sahre knowledge to be applied to various operations. Practical information for transportation, information technology, human resources and more.
Frequency: October
Founded in 2003

23846 **International Pool & Spa Expo**
Association of Pool & Spa Professionals
2111 Eisenhower Avenue
Alexandria, VA 22314

703-838-0083
Fax: 703-549-0493
E-Mail: jcergol@nspi.org
Home Page: www.poolspapatio.com

Tracy Beaulieu, Conference Manager

The International Pool & Spa Expo is a trade show for the pool, spa and backyard living industry that provides current market updates, info on cutting edge technology and trends.
15M Attendees
Frequency: Annual

23847 **Irrigation Show**
Irrigation Association
6540 Arlington Boulevard
Falls Church, VA 22042-6638

703-536-7080
Fax: 703-536-7019
E-Mail: info@irrigation.org
Home Page: www.irrigation.org

Deborah M Hamlin, Executive Director
Denise Stone, Meetings Director
Kate Baumann, Membership Coordinator
Rebecca Bayless, Finance Director
Marsha Cram, MBA, Foundation & Membership Manager

The Irrigation Show is the industry's one-stop event. Discover innovations on the show floor and in technical sessions, make connections with industry experts, business partners and peers; and build expertise with targeted education and certification.
1600 Members
Founded in 1949

23848 **MDVA Convention**
Michigan Distributors & Vendors Association
120 N Washington Square
Suite 110 B
Lansing, MI 48933

517-372-2323
Fax: 517-372-4404
E-Mail: webmaster@mdva.org
Home Page: www.mdva.org

Polly Reber, President
Russ Nowak, Chairman
Larry Macfirland, Director

Annual meeting for individuals involved in the grocery and convenience products industry.
100 Members
Frequency: Annual

23849 **Manufacturers Seminar**
Health Industry Distributors Association
310 Montgomery Street
Alexandria, VA 22314-1516

703-549-4432
Fax: 703-549-6495
Home Page: www.hida.org
Social Media: Facebook, Twitter, LinkedIn

Matthew Rowan, President & CEO
Rochelle Hargraves, Vice President Finance & Operations
Andrew Van Ostrand, Vice President Policy & Research
Amy Michael, Senior Manager Governmental Affairs

The HIDA Educational Foundation Manufacturers Seminar is guaranteed to provide fresh distributor executive perspectives that will allow attendees to formulate solutions that fit their market strategy.
Frequency: Annual
Founded in 1902

23850 **Mid-America Pool & Spa Show**
Association of Pool & Spa Professionals
2111 Eisenhower Avenue
Alexandria, VA 22314

703-838-0083
Fax: 703-549-0493
E-Mail: memberservices@apsp.org
Home Page: www.apsp.org

Bill Weber, Chief Executive Officer
Terry Brown, Chairman of the Board
Kathleen Carlson, Secretary & Treasurer

The Mid-America show offers a large trade show and business and technical seminars.
Frequency: Annual

23851 **Midwinter Executive Conference**
Food Marketing Institute
2345 Crystal Drive
Suite 800
Arlington, VA 22202

202-452-8444
Fax: 202-425-4519
Home Page: www.fmi.org

Leslie Sarasin, President; Chief Executive Officer
Pat Shinko, Director
Paul Ryan, Executive Director

The FMI Midwinter Executive Conference is an extraordinary opportunity for networking and discussion. The event is invitation-only, and it attracts food industry leaders for an out-

standing program that addresses the major challenges and opportunities ahead.
1500 Members
Frequency: Annual

23852 NACD Annual Meeting
National Association of Chemical Distributors
1555 Wilson Boulevard
Suite 700
Arlington, VA 22209

703-527-6223
Fax: 703-527-7747
E-Mail: nacdpublicaffairs@nacd.com
Home Page: www.nacd.com

Bruce Schechinger, Chairman, Chief Executive Officer
Andrew K Skipp, Vice Chairman
Roger T Harris, Treasurer
Jean-Pierre Baizan, Director at Large

NACD's Annual Meeting is the premier meeting and annual expo for chemical distributor professionals. It provides an opportunity to exchange ideas with other top executives in the chemical distribution industry, attend sessions that focus on the latest products and trends affecting the industry, and visit with a variety of exhibitors at the Vendor Expo.
250 Members
Founded in 1971

23853 NAFD Annual Convention
National Association of Flour Distributors
5450 Woodland Place
Canfield, OH 44406

330-718-6563
Fax: 877-573-1230
E-Mail: timdove51@gmail.com
Home Page: www.thenafd.com
Social Media: Facebook, Twitter, LinkedIn

Ted Heim Jr, President
Erin M. Ruhl, CEO
Dominic Valente, VP

The NAFD sponsors an all-industry forum addressing strategic issues impacting the flour distribution supply chain. In addition to manufacturer and distributor decision makers, senior-level ingredient suppliers participate in the NAFD three-day meeting.
Frequency: Annual

23854 NARM Annual Convention
National Association of Recording Merchandisers
9 Eves Drive
Suite 120
Marlton, NJ 08053-3138

856-596-2221
Fax: 856-596-3268
Home Page: www.narm.com

Linda M Still, Director Meetings/Conventions
James Donio, President

Containing 39 booths. Featuring AFIM.
2,100 Attendees
Frequency: March

23855 NASSD Annual Meeting
National Association of Sign Supply Distributors
4525 Collins Avenue
Miami Beach
Baltimore, FL 33140

703-836-4012
Fax: 703-836-8353
E-Mail: staceyj@clemonsmgmt.com
Home Page: www.nassd.org
Social Media: Facebook, Twitter, LinkedIn

Cal Clemons, Executive Director
Stacey Johnson, Association Coordinator

Held each fall, the annual meeting offers all attendees a full schedule of business and social networking activities. The meeting features distributor & manufacturer-only sessions, general speaker sessions, and roundtable discussions. A highlight of the meeting is the executive conferences which are an opportunity for distributors and manufacturers to meet one-on-one to discuss new sales and business opportunities.
Frequency: Annual

23856 NASSD Spring Management Conference
National Association of Sign Supply Distributors
4526 Collins Avenue
Miami Beach
Baltimore, FL 33140

703-836-4013
Fax: 703-836-8354
E-Mail: staceyj@clemonsmgmt.com
Home Page: www.nassd.org
Social Media: Facebook, Twitter, LinkedIn

Cal Clemons, Executive Director
Stacey Johnson, Association Coordinator

Held each March, this 1-1/2 day conference features general speaker sessions and roundtable discussions. It is the perfect opportunity to get updated on the association's activities and trends in the industry.
Frequency: Annual

23857 NAUMD Convention & Expo
N.A. Association of Uniform Manufacturers & Dist.
336 West 37th Street
Suite 370
New York, NY 10018

212-736-3010
Fax: 212-736-3013
E-Mail: rjlerman@naumd.com
Home Page: www.naumd.com
Social Media: Facebook, Twitter, LinkedIn, you Tube

Richard J Lerman, President & CEO
Veronica Martin-Bennett, Manager Membership Info Services
John Chwat, Director of Government Affairs
Jeff Rundles, Director of Communications
Lois Miller, Director Expo & Advertising Sales

The NAUMD Convention & Expo provides a tremendous opportunity for attendees to expand their horizons, sales, and profits. Attendees can find new customers and suppliers for every uniform and imagewear need.
Founded in 1933

23858 NBMDA Annual Convention
N.A. Building Material Distribution Association
401 N. Michigan Avenue
Chicago, IL 60611

312-321-6845
888-747-7862
Fax: 312-644-0310
E-Mail: info@nbmda.org
Home Page: www.nbmda.org
Social Media: Facebook, Twitter, LinkedIn, you Tube

Duane Lambrecht, President
Bill Delaney, President-Elect
Brian Schell, Vice President
Mark Kasper, Treasurer

The NBMDA provides an opportunity to connect with other leaders in the Building Material Distribution industry. This annual convention is designed to be an executive-level interchange between trading partners coupled with stimulating educational opportunities.
Frequency: Annual
Founded in 1952

23859 NBWA Annual Convention
National Beer Wholesalers Association
1101 King Street
Suite 600
Alexandria, VA 22314-8965

703-683-4300
Fax: 703-683-8965
E-Mail: info@nbwa.org
Home Page: www.nbwa.org
Social Media: Facebook, Twitter

Craig A Purser, President & CEO
Michael Johnson, EVP Fed Aff/Chief Advisory Office
Rebecca Spicer, VP Public Affairs/Chief
Paul Pisano, SVP Industry Affairs & Gen. Counsel

Designed to provide valuable education programs and important networking opportunities for the beer industry. Featuring speakers and seminars on a number of topics of importance to beer distributors .
2500 Attendees
Frequency: Fall

23860 NGA Annual Convention & Supermarket Synergy Showcase
National Grocers Association
1005 North Glebe Road
Suite 250
Arlington, VA 22201-5758

703-516-0700
Fax: 703-516-0115
E-Mail: info@nationalgrocers.org
Home Page: www.nationalgrocers.org
Social Media: Facebook, Twitter, LinkedIn, you Tube

Tom Zaucha, President & Chief Executive Officer
Frank DiPasquale, Executive Vice President
Tom Wenning, Executive VP/General Counsel

Each year, attendees are presented with timely and relevant general sessions and workshops, exciting special events and numerous networking opportunities to speak with other industry executives.
Frequency: Annual

23861 NIA Annual Convention
National Insulation Association
12100 Sunset Hills Road
Suite 330
Reston, VA 20190

703-464-6244
Fax: 703-464-5896
Home Page: www.insulation.org
Social Media: Facebook, Twitter, LinkedIn

Michele M Jones, Executive Vice President/CEO
Larry Nelles, President
Glenn Frye, President-Elect
Alec Rexroat, Secretary/Treasurer

The NIA Annual Convention is the premier gathering for the mechanical and industrial insulation industry, offering valuable and unique educational and industry sessions, networking opportunities, and entertaining evening events.
Frequency: Annual
Founded in 1953

23862 NPTA Annual Convention
NPTA Alliance
330~N.~Wabash Ave
Suite 2000
Chicago, IL 60611

312-321-4092
800-355-6782
Fax: 312-673-6736
E-Mail: npta@gonpta.com
Home Page: www.gonpta.com
Social Media: Facebook, Twitter

John F Millin, Chairman
Newell Holt, President & CEO

Thomas D O'Connor Jr, Treasurer
Anthony Macleod, Counsel

The NPTA Annual Convention is a prime opportunity to generate business leads, strengthen relationships with trading partners, develop leadership skills and more.
Frequency: Annual
Founded in 1903
Mailing list available for rent

23863 National Frozen & Refrigerated Foods Convention
4755 Linglestown Road Suite 300
PO Box 6069
Harrisburg, PA 17112

717-657-8601
Fax: 717-657-9862
E-Mail: info@nfraweb.org
Home Page: www.nfraweb.org
Social Media: Facebook, LinkedIn

H V Skip Shaw Jr, President/CEO
Jeff Rumachik, Senior VP
Marlene Barr, VP Membership

NFRA is a non-profit trade association representing all segments of the frozen and refrigerated foods industry. Headquartered in Harrisburg, PA, NFRA is the sponsor of March National Frozen Food Month, June dairy Month, and the Summer Favorites Ice Cream & Novelties promotion as well as the OctoberCool Food for Kids educational outreach program. NFRA holds the annual National Frozen & Refrigerated Foods Convention in October.
450 Members
1200 Attendees
Founded in 1945

23864 PBA Symposium
Professional Beauty Association
15825 N 71st Street
Suite 100
Scottsdale, AZ 85254

480-281-0424
800-468-2274
Fax: 480-905-0708
E-Mail: info@probeauty.org
Home Page: www.probeauty.org

Steven Sleeper, Executive Director
Marissa Porcaro, Director - Marketing
Steve Wilkerson, Chief Financial Officer
Christy Weaver, Manager - Finance & Administration

The PBA Symposium is a business education event produced for all sectors of the beauty industry.
Frequency: Annual
Founded in 1953

23865 Paper2011
NPTA
330~N.~Wabash Ave
Suite 2000
Chicago, IL 60611

312-321-4092
800-355-6782
Fax: 312-673-6736
E-Mail: npta@gonpta.com
Home Page: www.gonpta.com
Social Media: Facebook, Twitter

Greg Savage, Chairman
Kevin Gammonley, CEO
Hilton Maze, Treasurer

Held in conjunction with the American Forest & Paper Association, features timely sessions on emerging issues, corporate suites, and networking opportunities.
Frequency: March
Founded in 1903
Mailing list available for rent

23866 Pet Exposition Trade Show
Pet Industry Distributors Association
2105 Laurel Bush Road
Suite 200
Bel Air, MC 21015

443-640-1060
Fax: 443-640-1031
E-Mail: pida@ksgroup.org
Home Page: www.pida.com

Blaine Phillips, President
Donald Fleming, VP

Containing 500 booths and 300 exhibits.
3,000 Attendees
Frequency: March
Founded in 1968

23867 Post Card & Souvenir Distributors Assocation Trade Show
Post Card & Souvenir Distributors Association
2105 Laurel Bush Road
Suite 200
Bel Air, MD 21015
443-640-1055
Fax: 443-640-1031
E-Mail: marci@ksgroup.org
Home Page: www.postcardcentral.org

Maria Linton, Manager
Containing 110 booths and 80 exhibits.
175 Attendees
Frequency: September
Founded in 1973

23868 PowerClean Trade Show and Convention
Cleaning Equipment Trade Association
PO Box 1710
Indian Trail, NC 28079

704-635-7362
800-441-0111
Fax: 704-635-7363
Home Page: www.ceta.org
Social Media: Facebook, Twitter, LinkedIn, you Tube
Tony Tranquill, President
Terry Murray, Senior Vice President
Aaron Auger, Vice President
Judy Bowers, Treasurer
CETA hosts the industry's premier PowerClean annual trade show and convention. PowerClean provides members with the opportunity to showcase new products, technology, and exchange ideas with industry peers, develop and present educational and certification programs, increase awareness and promotion of the industry and products and facilitate the development of unified positions when working with government agencies to set industry standards and policies.

23869 Read Deal Expo Convention
American Wholesale Marketers Association
1128 16th Street NW
Washington, DC 20036-4808

202-463-2124
800-482-2962
Fax: 202-467-0559
E-Mail: robertp@awmanet.org
Home Page: www.awmanet.org

Robert Pignato, VP Marketing/Industry Affairs
The AWMA Real Deal Expo and Convention is the country's oldest and largest show for distributors of confections, snacks and convenience products. The AWMA is the only national trade association working on behalf of the convenience products distribution market. AWMA members also include companies and individuals from across the distribution channel, retailers, brokers, manufacturers and others allied to the industry.
Frequency: February

23870 School Equipment Show
National School Supply & Equipment Association
8380 Colesville Road
Suite 250
Silver Spring, MD 20910

301-495-0240
800-395-5550
Fax: 301-495-3330
Home Page: www.nssea.org
Social Media: Facebook, Twitter, LinkedIn, you Tube

Jim McGarry, President & Chief Executive Officer
Bill Duffy, VP of Operations & Meetings
DeShuna Spencer, Essentials Editor
Adrienne Watts Dayton, VP Marketing & Communications
Industry trade show where attendees can source new products, learn from leading experts in the field, and network with suppliers, distributors and purchasing influencers.
Frequency: Annual
Founded in 1916

23871 Supply Chain Conference
Food Marketing Institute
2345 Crystal Drive
Suite 800
Arlington, VA 22202

202-452-8444
Fax: 202-425-4519
Home Page: www.fmi.org
Social Media: Facebook, Twitter, LinkedIn

Leslie Sarasin, President; Chief Executive Officer
Pat Shinko, Director
Paul Ryan, Executive Director
Frederick J. Morganthall II~, Chair
Explores the latest trends in distribution, technology and its application, supply chain collaboration, transportation efficiencies, leadership and management skills. Informal discussion groups give attendees an opportunity to discuss ideas and challenges with their peers.
Frequency: Annual

23872 TCATA Annual Management & Educational Conference
Textile Care Allied Trades Association
271 Route 46 West
#D203
Fairfield, NJ 07004

973-244-1790
Fax: 973-244-4455
E-Mail: info@tcata.org
Home Page: www.tcata.org
Social Media: Facebook, Twitter, LinkedIn

David Cotter, Chief Executive Officer
Cheryl Paglia, Manager
Trade show consisting of well-organized business programs and unique networking opportunities.
Frequency: Annual

Directories & Databases

23873 A-Z Wholesale Source Directory
Sutton Family Communications & Publishing Company

155 Sutton Lane
Fordsville, KY 42343

270-740-0870
E-Mail: jlsutton@apex.net
Home Page: www.fleamarketeer.net

Theresa Sutton, Editor
Lee Sutton, General Manager

Print-out from database of wholesalers, manufacturers, distributors, importers and close-out houses. Database is updated daily to guarantee the most current and up-to-date sources available.
Cost: $550.00
1M Pages

23874 American Warehouse Association and Canadian Association of Warehousing
Association For Logistics Outsourcing
2800 South River Road
Suite 260
Chicago, IL 60018-6003

847-813-4699
Fax: 847-813-0115
E-Mail: email@iwla.com
Home Page: www.iwla.com

Joel Hioland, President
Alex Glan, VP/CEO

Nearly 700 warehouse firms with over 2,000 locations specializing in storage, distribution, and third party logistics.

23875 American Wholesalers and Distributors Directory
Gale/Cengage Learning
10650 Toebben Drive
Independence, KY 41051

800-354-9706
800-877-4253
Fax: 800-487-8488
E-Mail: gale.galeord@cengage.com
Home Page: www.gale.com
Social Media: Facebook, Twitter, LinkedIn

Patrick C Sommers, President

Discover more than 27,000 large and small wholesalers and distributors throughout the US and Puerto Rico.
Frequency: Annual
ISBN: 1-414434-21-9

23876 Complete Directory of Close-outs and Super-buys
Sutton Family Communications & Publishing Company
155 Sutton Lane
Fordsville, KY 42343

270-740-0870
E-Mail: jlsutton@apex.net
Home Page: www.fleamarketeer.net

Theresa Sutton, Editor
Lee Sutton, General Manager

Print-out from database of wholesalers, manufacturers, distributors, importers and close-out houses. Database is updated daily to guarantee the most current and up-to-date sources available.
Cost: $67.50
100+ Pages

23877 Complete Directory of General Flea Market Merchandise
Sutton Family Communications & Publishing Company
155 Sutton Lane
Fordsville, KY 42343

270-740-0870
E-Mail: jlsutton@apex.net
Home Page: www.fleamarketeer.net

Theresa Sutton, Editor
Lee Sutton, General Manager

Print-out from database of wholesalers, manufacturers, distributors, importers and close-out houses. Database is updated daily to guarantee the most current and up-to-date sources available.
Cost: $289.00
100+ Pages

23878 Complete Directory of High Profit Items
Sutton Family Communications & Publishing Company
155 Sutton Lane
Fordsville, KY 42343

270-740-0870
E-Mail: jlsutton@apex.net
Home Page: www.fleamarketeer.net

Theresa Sutton, Editor
Lee Sutton, General Manager

Print-out from database of wholesalers, manufacturers, distributors, importers and close-out houses. Database is updated daily to guarantee the most current and up-to-date sources available.
Cost: $189.00
100+ Pages

23879 Complete Directory of Importers
Sutton Family Communications & Publishing Company
7025 N. Scottsdale Rd #320
Scottsdale, AR 85253

202-595-3101
888-843-0272
Fax: 480-245-5000
E-Mail: info@importgenius.com
Home Page: www.importgenius.com

Theresa Sutton, Editor
Lee Sutton, General Manager

Print-out from database of wholesalers, manufacturers, distributors, importers and close-out houses. Database is updated daily to guarantee the most current and up-to-date sources available.
Cost: $109.00
100+ Pages

23880 Complete Directory of Low-Price Merchandise
Sutton Family Communications & Publishing Company
155 Sutton Lane
Fordsville, KY 42343

270-740-0870
E-Mail: jlsutton@apex.net
Home Page: www.fleamarketeer.net

Theresa Sutton, Editor
Lee Sutton, General Manager

Print-out from database of wholesalers, manufacturers, distributors, importers and close-out houses. Database is updated daily to guarantee the most current and up-to-date sources available.
Cost: $72.20
100+ Pages

23881 Complete Directory of Promotional Products
Sutton Family Communications & Publishing Company
155 Sutton Lane
Fordsville, KY 42343

270-740-0870
E-Mail: jlsutton@apex.net
Home Page: www.fleamarketeer.net

Theresa Sutton, Editor
Lee Sutton, General Manager

Print-out from database of wholesalers, manufacturers, distributors, importers and close-out houses. Database is updated daily to guarantee the most current and up-to-date sources available.
Cost: $139.00
100+ Pages

23882 Complete Directory of Stationery Items
Sutton Family Communications & Publishing Company
155 Sutton Lane
Fordsville, KY 42343

270-740-0870
E-Mail: jlsutton@apex.net
Home Page: www.fleamarketeer.net

Theresa Sutton, Editor
Lee Sutton, General Manager

Print-out from database of wholesalers, manufacturers, distributors, importers and close-out houses. Database is updated daily to guarantee the most current and up-to-date sources available.
Cost: $55.20
100+ Pages

23883 Complete Directory of Tabletop Items
Sutton Family Communications & Publishing Company
155 Sutton Lane
Fordsville, KY 42343

270-740-0870
E-Mail: jlsutton@apex.net
Home Page: www.fleamarketeer.net

Theresa Sutton, Editor
Lee Sutton, General Manager

Print-out from database of wholesalers, manufacturers, distributors, importers and close-out houses. Database is updated daily to guarantee the most current and up-to-date sources available.
Cost: $55.20
100+ Pages

23884 Complete Directory of Unusual Items & Fads
Sutton Family Communications & Publishing Company
155 Sutton Lane
Fordsville, KY 42343

270-740-0870
E-Mail: jlsutton@apex.net
Home Page: www.fleamarketeer.net

Theresa Sutton, Editor
Lee Sutton, General Manager

Print-out from database of wholesalers, manufacturers, distributors, importers and close-out houses. Database is updated daily to guarantee the most current and up-to-date sources available.
Cost: $139.00
100+ Pages

23885 Complete Directory of Wholesale Bargains
Sutton Family Communications & Publishing Company
155 Sutton Lane
Fordsville, KY 42343

270-740-0870
E-Mail: jlsutton@apex.net
Home Page: www.fleamarketeer.net

Theresa Sutton, Editor
Lee Sutton, General Manager

Print-out from database of wholesalers, manufacturers, distributors, importers and close-out houses. Database is updated daily to guarantee the most current and up-to-date sources available.
Cost: $92.70
100+ Pages

23886 EMDA Membership Directory
Equipment Marketing & Distribution Associaion
PO Box 1347
Iowa City, IA 52244-1347
319-354-5156
Fax: 319-354-5157
E-Mail: pat@emda.net
Home Page: ww.emda.net

Patricia A Collins, Executive VP

Annual directory of FEWA-AIMRA members, includes address, phone, fax, web, e-mail, territory covered (with map) product descriptions, key personnel, and a descriptive paragraph.
Cost: $50.00

23887 Food & Beverage Market Place
Grey House Publishing
4919 Route 22
PO Box 56
Amenia, NY 12501
518-789-8700
800-562-2139
Fax: 518-789-0556
E-Mail: gold@greyhouse.com
Home Page: www.greyhouse.com
Social Media: Facebook, Twitter

Leslie Mackenzie, Publisher
Richard Gottlieb, Editor
Richard Gottlieb, President

This information packed three-volume set is the most powerful buying and marketing guide for the US food and beverage industry. Includes thousands of wholesale listings.
Cost: $595.00
2000 Pages
Frequency: Annual
ISBN: 1-592373-61-5
Founded in 1981
Mailing list available for rent

23888 Food & Beverage Marketplace: Online Database
Grey House Publishing
4919 Route 22
PO Box 56
Amenia, NY 12501
518-789-8700
800-562-2139
Fax: 518-789-0556
E-Mail: gold@greyhouse.com
Home Page: http://gold.greyhouse.com
Social Media: Facebook, Twitter

Richard Gottlieb, President
Leslie Mackenzie, Publisher
Richard Gottlieb, Editor

This complete updated Food & Beverage Market Place: Online Database is the go-to source for the food and beverage industry. Anyone involved in the food and beverage industry needs this 'industry bible' and the important contacts to develop critical research data that can make for successful business growth.
Frequency: Annual
Founded in 1981
Mailing list available for rent

23889 Global Logistics & Supply Chain Strategies
Keller International Publishing Corporation
150 Great Neck Rd
Great Neck, NY 11021-3309
516-829-9722
Fax: 516-829-9306
E-Mail: jmurph@starpower.net
Home Page: www.supplychainbrain.com

Jerry Keller, President
Brad Berger, Group President/Publisher
Russell Goodman, Editor-in-Chief

Serves manufacturing, wholesale/retail trade, third party logistics, freight forwarding and transportation/warehousing firms.
Cost: $55.00
96 Pages
Frequency: 11 per year
Circulation: 40M
ISSN: 1525-4887
Founded in 1997
Printed in 4 colors on glossy stock

23890 Membership Directory/Buyer's Guide
Naylor Publications
5950 Nw 1st Pl
Gainesville, FL 32607-6018
352-332-1252
800-369-6220
Fax: 352-331-3525
E-Mail: chodges@naylor.com
Home Page: www.naylor.com

Michael Moss, President

Provider of integrated communications and image-building solutions for associations.
Circulation: 1,200

23891 Outlet Project Directory
Off-Price Specialists, Value Retail News
29399 US Highway 19 N
Suite 370
Clearwater, FL 33761-2138
727-781-7557
Fax: 727-536-4389
Home Page: www.valueretailnews.com

Linda Humphers, Editor-In-Chief
Tom Kirwan, Senior Editor

Offers valuable information on factory outlet projects.
Cost: $225.00
200 Pages
Frequency: Semiannual

23892 Plumbing Engineer: Product Directory Issue
TMB Publishing
1838 Techny Ct
Northbrook, IL 60062-5474
847-564-1127
Fax: 847-564-1264
E-Mail: tmbpubs@earthlink.net
Home Page: www.tmbpublishing.com

Tom M Brown, Owner
Cate Brown, Production Manager

Over 400 plumbing products from approximately 250 manufacturers.
Frequency: Annual January
Circulation: 2,6104
ISBN: 0-192171-1 -

23893 Shippers Guide to Department & Chain Stores Nationwide
Shippers Guides
PO Box 112
Duarte, CA 91009-0112
626-357-6430
Fax: 248-786-1358

Profiles over 1,000 department stores and chain stores and their traffic managers in the United States.
Cost: $349.00
350 Pages
Frequency: Annual
Circulation: 2,000

23894 Who's Who
Association of Pool & Spa Professionals
2111 Eisenhower Avenue
Alexandria, VA 22314-4679
703-838-0083
Fax: 703-549-0493
Home Page: www.theasap.org/

Jack Cergol, Chief Staff Executive
Marianne Kiernan, Executive Secretary

Trade association for pool, spa and hot tub industry. Annual Convention for trade.
Founded in 1956

23895 Who's Who in Beer Wholesaling Directory
National Beer Wholesalers Association
1101 King Street
Suite 600
Alexandria, VA 22314-8965
703-683-4300
Fax: 703-683-8965
E-Mail: info@nbwa.org
Home Page: www.nbwa.org
Social Media: Facebook, Twitter

Craig A Purser, President & CEO
Michael Johnson, EVP Fed Aff/Chief Advisory Office
Rebecca Spicer, VP Public Affairs/Chief
Paul Pisano, SVP Industry Affairs & Gen. Counsel

A listing of more than 3,000 beer distributors and suppliers in the industry.
Cost: $50.00

23896 Wholesale Grocers
Chain Store Guide
3922 Coconut Palm Dr
Tampa, FL 33619-1389
813-627-6700
800-778-9794
Fax: 813-627-7094
E-Mail: info@csgis.com
Home Page: www.csgis.com

Mike Jarvis, Publisher
Shami Choon, Manager

We have uncovered the facts on more than 1,900 grocery suppliers in the U.S. and Canada in this database. This targeted database allows you to reach food wholesalers, cooperatives and voluntary group wholesalers, non-sponsoring wholesalers, and cash and carry operators who serve grocery, convenience, discount and drug stores. You will also find information regarding company headquarters, divisions, branches, and over 11,000 key executives and buyers.
Cost: $335.00
Frequency: Annual

23897 Wholesaler
TMB Publishing
1838 Techny Ct
Northbrook, IL 60062-5474
847-564-1127
Fax: 847-564-1264
Home Page: www.tmbpublishing.com

Tom M Brown, Owner

Ranks 100 leading wholesalers of plumbing, heating, air conditioning, refrigeration equipment and industrial pipe, valves and fittings.
Cost: $25.00
Frequency: Annual July
Circulation: 30,000

23898 Wholesaler-Wholesaling 100 Issue
TMB Publishing
1838 Techny Ct
Northbrook, IL 60062-5474
847-564-1127
Fax: 847-564-1264
Home Page: www.tmbpublishing.com

Tom M Brown, Owner

Offer information on over 100 leading wholesalers of plumbing-heating equipment and supplies.
Cost: $25.00
Circulation: 25,000

Industry Web Sites

23899 http://gold.greyhouse.com
G.O.L.D Grey House OnLine Databases
Grey House Publishing's online database platform, GOLD, offers Quick Search, Keyword Search and Expert Search for most business sectors, including wholesale markets. The GOLD platform makes finding the information you need quick and easy - whether you're a novice searcher or an experienced database user. All of Grey House's directory products are available for subscription on the GOLD platform.

23900 www.aamp.com
American Association of Meat Processors
For small to medium sized meat, poultry and food businesses including: packers, processors, wholesalers, home food service businesses, retailers, deli and catering operators.

23901 www.adbi.org
Associated Beer Distributors of Illinois
The ABDI represents, maintains, and improves the interests of its members who are licensed by the State of Illinois to import and distribute beer to licensed retailers.

23902 www.aednet.org
Associated Equipment Distributors
AED is an international trade association representing companies involved in the distribution, rental and support of equipment used in construction, mining, forestry, power generation, agriculture and industrial applications.

23903 www.aird.org
Association of Ingersoll-Rand Distributors
The Association of Ingersoll-Rand Distributors (AIRD) was organized as a central resource for distributors of Ingersoll-Rand compressed air equipment. AIRD is chartered to promote improved business conditions affecting distributors of air compressors, further a better understanding between distributors and equipment suppliers, research ways to lower costs of distributing air compressors, collect and disseminate statistical information and conduct other beneficial activities.

23904 www.amdweb.com
Association of Millwork Distributors
AMD provides leadership, education, promotion, networking, and advocacy to, and for, the millwork distribution industry.

23905 www.anla.org
American Nursery & Landscape Association
The American Nursery and Landscape Association serves firms who grow, sell or use plants. ANLA advocates the industry's interests before government and provides its members with unique business knowledge essential to long-term growth and profitability.

23906 www.apda.com
Appliance Parts Distributors Association
The APDA is an association of independent businesses that aspire to provide the highest level of quality, service, support and information to its customers and suppliers in order to make its value indispendable to the parts distribution channel.

23907 www.apsp.org
Association of Pool & Spa Professionals
APSP is the world's largest international trade association for the swimming pool, spa, and hot tub industry. It works with regulatory and legislative bodies to ensure that their codes, ordinance, and legislation are written to the safest and most current standards. The association's mission is to ensure consumer safety and enhance the business success of its members.

23908 www.asa.net
American Supply Association
ASA is a not-for-profit national organization serving wholesale distributors and their suppliers in the plumbing, heating, cooling and industrial and mechanical pipe, valves and fittings industries.

23909 www.ascdi.com
Association of Service and Computer Dealers Int'l
The ASCDI is a worldwide, nonprofit organization, made up of companies who provide technology business solutions, technical suppoer, and value added services to the business community.

23910 www.avda.net
American Veterinary Distributors Association
The AVDA was established as the national trade organization for businesses engaged in the distribution of animal health products.

23911 www.awfs.org
Association of Woodworking & Furnishings Suppliers
The Association of Woodworking and Furnishing Suppliers is the largest national trade association in the U.S. representing the interestes of the broad array of companies that supply the home and commercial furnishings industry.

23912 www.awmanet.org
American Wholesale Marketers Association
An organization supporting the confectionery, tobacco and allied products industries through programs and services.

23913 www.bpsa.org
Bicycle Product Suppliers Association
BPSA is an association of suppliers of bicycles, parts, accessories and services who serve the Specialty Bicycle Retailer.

23914 www.bsahome.org
Bearing Specialists Association
BSA is the forum to enhance networking and knowledge sharing to promote the sale of bearings through authorized distributors.

23915 www.cbbd.com
California Beer & Beverage Distributors
The California Beer and Beverage Distributors is a nonprofit trade association representing over 100 beer distributors and brewer/vendor members.

23916 www.ceta.org
Cleaning Equipment Trade Association
CETA is dedicated to increasing the awareness and promotion of industry products, while at the same time recognizing the impact on preserving the environment and the opportunity to do business within it.

23917 www.ctdahome.org
Ceramic Tile Distributors Association
CTDA is an international association of distributors, manufacturers, and allied professionals of ceramic tile and related products.

23918 www.cvsn.org
Commercial Vehicle Solutions Network
The Commercial Vehicle Solutions Network (CVSN) is an association of independent parts and service aftermarket distributors serving the transportation industry.

23919 www.dhi.org
Door & Hardware Institute
The Door & Hardware Institute (DHI) is the only professional association dedicated to the Architectural Openings Industry. DHI represents the North American openings marketplace as the advocate and primary resource for information, professional development and certification.

23920 www.easa.com
Electrical Apparatus Service Association Inc
The Electrical Apparatus Service Association (EASA) is an international trade organization of over 2,100 electromechanical sales and service firms in 58 countries. EASA provides members with a means of keeping up-to-date on materials, equipment, and state-of-the-art technology.

23921 www.emda.net
Equipment Marketing & Distribution Association
Trade association dedicated to the marketing of specialized agricultural equipment, outdoor power equipment, light industrial equipment, and forestry equipment.

23922 www.fewa.org
Farm Equipment Wholesalers Association
International trade association of wholesale/distributors of agricultural equipment and related products.

23923 www.fmi.org
Food Marketing Institute
FMI conducts programs in public affairs, food safety, research, education and industry relations on behalf of its 1,500 member companies in the United States and around the world.

23924 www.fpda.org
Fluid Power Distributors Association
Membership is composed of distributors and manufacturers of hydraulic and pneumatic equipment.

23925 www.gawda.org
Gases and Welding Distributors Association
GAWDA's mission is to promote the safe operation and economic vitality of distributors of industrial gases and related welding equipment and supplies.

23926 www.gmdc.com
Global Market Development Center
GMDC is the premier non-profit global trade association dedicated to serving General Merchandise and Health Beauty retailers, wholesalers and suppliers. GMDC promotes critical connectivity to grow and expand member companies by uniting members through business building events and opportunities and enriching their thinking through education and training; consumer and business insights; and information resources.

23927 www.gmdc.org
General Merchandise Distributors Council
International trade association representing pharmacy products to the mass market retail industry.

23928 www.gonpta.com
NPTA Alliance

The NPTA Alliance (formerly the National Paper Trade Association, Inc.) is the association for the $60+ billion paper, packaging and supplies distribution industry. The mission of NPTA is to actively support the success of its members through the delivery of networking, industry data & research, education and advocacy that focuses on the health of the distribution channel.

23929 **www.greyhouse.com**
Grey House Publishing
Authoritative reference directories for most business sectors including wholesale service markets. Users can search the online databases with varied search criteria allowing for custom searches by product category, geographic area, sales volume, keyword, subject and more. Full Grey House catalog and online ordering also available.

23930 **www.hardinet.org**
Heating, Airconditioning & Refrigeration Dist.
This association is a trade organization dedicated to advancing the science of wholesale distribution in the HVACR industry.

23931 **www.healthcaredistribution.org**
Healthcare Distribution Management Association
The Healthcare Distribution Management Association (HDMA) is the national association representing primary, full-service heatlhcare distributors. HDMA and its members are the vital link in the healthcare system, working daily to provide value, remove costs and develop innovative solutions.

23932 **www.hida.org**
Health Industry Distributors Association
HIDA keeps members current on healthcare reform, government affairs, industry trends and forecasts, provider news, and sales tips.

23933 **www.iapd.org**
International Association of Plastics Distribution
The International Association of Plastics Distribution is an international trade association comprised of companies engaged in the distribution and manufacturing of plastics materials.

23934 **www.icdaonline.com**
Industrial Compressor Distributor Association
The main objetives of the ICDA are to promote for its members the highest standards of production, financial and managerial activities; to act as a vehicle for the solution of common industry problems in an effective and efficient manner; and to increase market volume and profits for its members.

23935 **www.insulation.org**
National Insulation Association
The National Insulation Association (NIA) is a trade association representing the mechanical and specialty insulation industry.

23936 **www.irrigation.org**
Irrigation Association
The Irrigation Association is the leading membership organization ffor irrigation equipment and system manufacturers, dealers, distributors, designers, consultants, contractors and end users.

23937 **www.isapartners.org**
Industrial Supply Association
The primary focus of the Industrial Supply Association is to improve the industrial supply channel through its mission-critical activities including: conventions and forums, gathering and dissemination of critical information, and development and implementation of channel performance initiatives.

23938 **www.isd.org**
International Sealing Distribution Association
The International Sealing Distribution Association (ISD) is a not-for-profit trade association formed to enhance the success of members through information, education, and interaction.

23939 **www.issa.com**
International Sanitary Supply Association
Manufacturers, distributors, wholesalers, representatives and publishers engaged in the manufacture and/or distribution of cleaning and maintenance products.

23940 **www.itpa.com**
International Truck Parts Association
The International Truck Parts Association was organized as a not-for-profit association to promote, foster, and improve relationships among sellers and buyers of trucks and truck surplus products and other parties.

23941 **www.lumber.org**
North American Wholesale Lumber Association
For lumber and building distributors and manufacturers.

23942 **www.mdna.org**
Machinery Dealers National Association
The Machinery Dealers National Association (MDNA) is an international, nonprofit trade association dedicated to the promotion of the used machinery industry.

23943 **www.mdva.org**
Michigan Distributors & Vendors Association
The Michigan Distributors and Vendors Association (MDVA) is a non-profit, statewide business association representing two very significant business segments in the grocery and convenience products industry.

23944 **www.mheda.org**
Material Handling Equipment Distributors Assoc.
The Material Handling Equipment Distributors Association is the only national association dedicated solely to improving the proficiency of the independent material handling equipment distributor.

23945 **www.mic.org**
Motorcycle Industry Council
The Motorcycle Industry Council (MIC) is a nonprofit, national trade association representing manufacturers and distributors of motorcycles, scooters, motorcycle/ATV parts and accessories and members of allied trades.

23946 **www.msbeer.com**
Mississippi Malt Beverage Association
The MMBA was established to represent and promote the beer wholesalers and beer industry within Mississippi.

23947 **www.msci.org**
Metal Service Center Institute (MSCI)
MSCI is the trade association that supports and represents most elements of the metals value chain, including metals producers, distributors, and processors.

23948 **www.naaud.com**
North American Association of Utility Distributors
NAAUD is comprised of select distributors who specialize in supplying products and supply chain services to the electric utility industry. The purpose of NAAUD is to discuss and promote the newest ideas and best concepts for the industry.

23949 **www.nacd.com**
National Association of Chemical Distributors
The National Association of Chemical Distributors (NACD) is an international association of chemial distributor companies that purchase and take title of chemical products from manufacturers.

23950 **www.naed.org**
National Association of Electrical Distributors
The main goal of the National Association of Electrical Distributors (NAED) is to establish the electrical distributor as an essential force in the electrical industry and the economy.

23951 **www.nafcd.org**
North American Association of Floor Covering Dist.
The North American Association of Floor Covering Distributors (NAFCD) was organized to foster trade and commerce for those having a business, financial or professional interest as wholesale distributors or manufacturers of floor coverings and allied products.

23952 **www.nahsa.org**
North American Horticultural Supply Association
The North American Horticultural Supply Association's mission is to strengthen and support the distribution and manufacturing of horticultural products and services.

23953 **www.narm.com**
National Association of Recording Merchandisers
Represents the retailers and suppliers of recorded entertainment as well as many suppliers of ancillary products.

23954 **www.nassd.org**
National Association of Sign Supply Distributors
NASSD is a nonprofit trade association for organizations who are engaged in full-line sign supply distribution and who manufacture or supply commercial, neon and electrical sign products.

23955 **www.natd.com**
N.A. Association of Telecommunications Dealers
The North American Association of Telecommunications Dealers is a nonprofit organization of companies who provide telecom products to the business community and governments around the world. The NATD gives you access to the right kind of information, resources and business leaders, and provides you with unique opportunities to help grow your business.

23956 **www.nationalgrocers.org**
National Grocers Association
The National Grocers Association is the national trade association representing the retail and wholesale grocers that comprise the independent sector of the food distribution industry.

23957 **www.naumd.com**
N.A. Association of Uniform Manufacturers & Dist.

An association dedicated to keeping the Uniforn & Imagewear Industry strong and healthy.

23958 www.nbmda.org
N.A. Building Material Distribution Association

NBMDA develops and promotes the effectiveness of distribution processes to improve member profitability and growth.

23959 www.nbwa.org
National Beer Wholesalers Association

Research and development, quality control and ingredients.

23960 www.nesda.com
National Electronics Service Dealers Association

Provides educational assistance in electronic training to public schools, compiles statistics, offers certification programs and apprenticeships. Functions as trade association for the electronics service industry.

23961 www.nfraweb.org
National Frozen & Refrigerated Foods Association

NFRA is a non profit trade association comprised of 650 member companies representing all segments of the frozen and refrigerated foods industry. NFRA has been serving the frozen food industry since 1945 and just recently in 2001 began serving the refrigerated foods industry. The mission of NFRA is to promote the sales and consumption of frozen and refrigerated foods through: education, training, research, sales planning and menu development and providing a forum for industry dialogue.

23962 www.npes.org
NPES Association

This association is a trade association of over 400 companies that manufacture and distribute equipment, systems, software, supplies used in printing, publishing and converting.

23963 www.npfda.org
National Poultry & Food Distributors Association

For poultry and food distribution and processing industries. Provides member services, cost cutting benefits and networking opportunities.

23964 www.nssea.org
National School Supply & Equipment Association

The National School Supply and Equipment Association (NSSEA) is the leading trade organization for the educational products marketplace. NSSEA puts the collective experience of the most successful school industry business in the world at your fingertips.

23965 www.nybeer.org
New York State Beer Wholesalers Association

The New York State Beer Wholesalers Association, Inc. represents and protects the legislative and regulators interests of its members in state and local government. Our primary goal is to uphold the three-tier system in order to safeguard the industry's distribution standards.

23966 www.opeesa.com
Outdoor Power Equipment & Engine Service Assoc.

The Outdoor Power Equipment and Engine Service Association (OPEESA) consists of more than 140 distributors and manufacturers of outdoor power equipment and air-cooled gas and diesel engines. Their mission is to assist distributors in achieving outstanding channel performance.

23967 www.opwa.org
Business Solutions Association

The goal of the Business Solutions Association is to provide a forum for the development of strategic and synergistic solutions to enhance the sale and distribution of business related products and services.

23968 www.pac-west.org
Pacific-West Fastener Association

An organization dedicated to the fastener industry.

23969 www.pida.com
Pet Industry Distributors Association

Represents wholesaler-distributors of pet products, providing training and education to members.

23970 www.probeauty.org
Professional Beauty Association

The Professional Beauty Association (PBA) is a nonprofit trade association that represents the interests of the professional beauty industry from manufacturers and distributors to salons and spas. PBA offers business tools, education, advocacy, networking and more to improve individual businesses and the industry as a whole.

23971 www.ptda.org
Power Transmission Distributors Association

Members are power transmission/motion control distributor throughout manufacturing firms.

23972 www.safetycentral.org
Safety Equipment Distributors Association

Represents wholesale-distributors of safety equipment and works to enhance and improve distribution through excellence in communications, training, education and services.

23973 www.shda.org
Security Hardware Distributors Association

The mission of the Security Hardware Distributors Association is to continually improve, through education and services, the proficiency of Security Distributors in order that they are the most effective and efficient conduit to the marketplace.

23974 www.ssia.info
Shoe Service Institute of America

Shop to shop chat room, links and listings of manufacturers and wholesalers plus shoe care tips.

23975 www.tcata.org
Textile Care Allied Trades Association

The Textile Care Allied Trades Association (TCATA) is an international trade association representing manufacturers and distributors of drycleaning and laundry equipment and supplies. It is the only trade association dedicated exclusively to the interests of the allied trades.

23976 www.wasda.com
Water & Sewer Distributors of America

WASDA's mission is to promote the waterworks/wastewater products distribution industry, and to further improve the image and professionalism of WASDA and its member companies.

A

B

C

D

F

G

H

I

J

K

M

N

O

P

Q

R

S

T

U

V

W

X

Y

Z

A

B

Crow's Weekly Market Report
CC Crow Publications, 16576

Cruise Industry News - Annual
Nissel-Lie Communications, 23001

Cruise Industry News Annual
Nissel-Lie Communications, 23076

Cruise Industry News Quarterly Magazine
Nissel-Lie Communications, 23002

Cryptosystems Journal
Cryptosystems Journal, 5401

Culinary Collection Directory
International Association/Culinary Professionals, 10685, 21032

Culinary Trends
Culinary Trends Publications, 10044, 20995

Culture Keepers: Making Global Connections
Black Caucus of the American Library Association, 16133

Currency
Grant Thornton, 116

Current Global Carrier Market Environment, Global Carrier
Probe Research, 17623

Current Index to Legal Periodicals
Marian Gould Gallagher Law Library-Univ. of Wash., 15915

Current Issues in Auditing
American Accounting Association, 185

Current Issues in Bank Auditing
Bank Research Associates, 3136

Current Market Snapshot
CompuServe Information Service, 9057

Current Pedorthics
Pedorthic Footwear Association, 21686

Current Thinking on Network Evolution and Its Laws
Probe Research, 17624

Currents
Council for Advancement & Support of Education, 11325, 17738, 20407
Electrical Apparatus Service Association, 6688, 6944
Women's Fisheries Network, 9264

Custom Home
Hanley-Wood, 4200

Custom Publishing & News Services
Information, 14296

Custom Woodworking Business
Vance Publishing, 16577

Customer Communicator
Alexander Communications Group, 17012

Customer Interaction Solutions
Technology Marketing Corporation, 6185, 6545, 17127, 17739

Customer Interface
Advanstar Communications, 6144, 6546

Customer Relationship Management Course: C RMretail
National Retail Federation, 21174

Customer Service Manager's Letter
Bureau of Business Practice, 17013

Customers First
Dartnell Corporation, 17625

Cutting Edge
Int'l Assoc of Diecutting and Diemaking, 16802
Marble Institute of America, 22222
Outdoor Power Equipment Aftermarket, 23778

Cutting Horse Chatter
National Cutting Horse Association, 21923

Cutting Technology
Penton Media, 18170

Cutting Tool Engineering
CTE Publications, 7302, 18171

Cyber Esq.
Daily Journal Corporation, 15770

CyberDealer
Meister Publishing Company, 6547, 17740

Cycle World
Hachette Filipacchi Media US, 18691

Cycling USA
United States Cycling Federation, 18692

D

D&B Million Dollar Database
Dun & Bradstreet Information Service, 6186

D&B Million Dollar Database: International
Dun & Bradstreet Information Service, 6187

DACA Directory
Distributors & Consolidators of America, 14641

DACS Annotated Bibliography
Data & Analysis Center for Software, 5641

DBA Automated Builder Magazine
CMN Associates, 4201

DBMS-Database Management Systems
Miller Freeman Publications, 5403

DBS Report
Kagan World Media, 3810, 5041

DC Advocate
National Defined Contribution Council, 8849

DCAT Digest and Directory of Membership
Drug, Chemical & Associated Technologies, 6429

DCAT Western Education Conference
Drug, Chemical & Associated Technologies, 5828, 6403

DCUC Annual Meeting
Defense Credit Union Council, 8975

DDBC News
Dairy, Deli, Bakery Council of Southern California, 10045

DECA Dimensions
Distributive Education Clubs of America, 17741

DECO
Society of Glass & Ceramic Decorators, 11858

DFA Leader
Dairy Farmers of America, 10046

DFI Journal
Deep Foundations Institute, 4202

DG Review
Data Base Publications, 5404

DGA Membership Directory
Mailorder Gardening Association, 11728

DIA Annual Meeting
Drug Information Association, 6404

DIA Global Forum
Drug Information Association, 6346

DIA Newsletter
Drug Information Association, 6300

DIAL/DATA
Track Data Corporation, 9058

DIALOG Publications
Dialog, Thomas Business, 5642

DIOGENES
FOI Services, 6430

DISA Customer Partnership AFCEA Technology Showcase
Armed Forces Communications and Electronics Assn, 5120

DJ Times
Testa Communications, 18876

DM Review
Powell Publishing Company, 5405

DMA Annual Conference & Exhibition
Direct Marketing Association, 491, 6166, 17794

DMA Daily Digest
Direct Marketing Association, 391

DMB: Direct Marketing to Business Conference
Target Conference Corporation, 17795

DMD New York Conference & Expo
Direct Marketing Conferences, 6081, 6167, 6600

DNR-Daily News Record
Fairchild Publications, 1723

DP Budget
Computer Economics, 5281

DPFN
Directory & Database Publishers Forum & Network, 5282

DRI Chemical
DRI/McGraw-Hill, 4726

DRI Chemical Forecast
DRI/McGraw-Hill, 4727

DRI Coal Forecast
DRI/McGraw-Hill, 18480

DRI Commodities
DRI/McGraw-Hill, 9059

DRI Europe
DRI/McGraw-Hill, 14642

DRI Middle East and African Forecast
DRI/McGraw-Hill, 14643

DRI Steel Forecast
DRI/McGraw-Hill, 18259

DRI Transportation
DRI/McGraw-Hill, 9060

DRI Transportation Detail
DRI/McGraw-Hill, 22886

DRI US Bonds
DRI/McGraw-Hill, 9061

DRI Utility Cost Forecasting
DRI/McGraw-Hill, 23387

DRI- Annual Conference
DRI-The Voice of the Defense Bar, 15882

DRI/Platt's Oil Prices
DRI/McGraw-Hill, 19730

DRI/TBS World Sea Trade Forecast
DRI/McGraw-Hill, 14644

DRI/TBS World Trade Forecast
DRI/McGraw-Hill, 14645

DRUGDEX System
Thompson Micromedex, 6431

DSN Retailing Today
Lebhar-Friedman, 21125

DTCC Newsletter
Depository Trust Company, 3137

DV Digital Video Magazine
Miller Freeman Publications, 3860

DVM Magazine
Advanstar Communications, 863

DVM News
Advanstar Communications, 6347

Daily Advocate
Thomson Newspapers, 9821

Daily Commerce
Daily Journal Corporation, 20763

Daily Construction Service
Construction Market Data, 4203

Daily Deal
Vicki King, 5042

Daily Defense News Capsules
United Communications Group, 12231

Daily Environment Report
Bureau of National Affairs, 7833

Daily Foreign Exchange Analysis & Updates
Technical Data, 9062

Daily Journal
Daily Journal Corporation, 15771

Daily Journal of Commerce
Dolan Media Company/New Orleans Publishing Grp, 4204

Daily News E-Mail (3D)
Direct Marketing Association, 6117, 17626

Daily Report for Executives
Bureau of National Affairs, 17014

Daily Tax Report
Bureau of National Affairs, 8669

Daily Treasury Statement
Financial Management Service, 3138

Dair-e-news
American Dairy Science Association, 761

Dairy Council Digest
National Dairy Council, 9822

E

F

H

I

J

K

L

N

O

P

Q

R

S

U

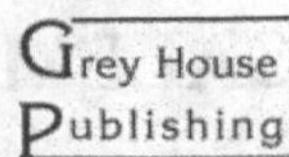

2015 Title List

Visit www.GreyHouse.com for Product Information, Table of Contents, and Sample Pages.

General Reference

An African Biographical Dictionary
America's College Museums
American Environmental Leaders: From Colonial Times to the Present
Encyclopedia of African-American Writing
Encyclopedia of Constitutional Amendments
Encyclopedia of Gun Control & Gun Rights
An Encyclopedia of Human Rights in the United States
Encyclopedia of Invasions & Conquests
Encyclopedia of Prisoners of War & Internment
Encyclopedia of Religion & Law in America
Encyclopedia of Rural America
Encyclopedia of the Continental Congress
Encyclopedia of the United States Cabinet, 1789-2010
Encyclopedia of War Journalism
Encyclopedia of Warrior Peoples & Fighting Groups
The Environmental Debate: A Documentary History
The Evolution Wars: A Guide to the Debates
From Suffrage to the Senate: America's Political Women
Global Terror & Political Risk Assessment
Media & Communications 1900-2020
Nations of the World
Political Corruption in America
Privacy Rights in the Digital Era
The Religious Right: A Reference Handbook
Speakers of the House of Representatives, 1789-2009
This is Who We Were: 1880-1900
This is Who We Were: A Companion to the 1940 Census
This is Who We Were: In the 1910s
This is Who We Were: In the 1920s
This is Who We Were: In the 1940s
This is Who We Were: In the 1950s
This is Who We Were: In the 1960s
This is Who We Were: In the 1970s
U.S. Land & Natural Resource Policy
The Value of a Dollar 1600-1865: Colonial Era to the Civil War
The Value of a Dollar: 1860-2014
Working Americans 1770-1869 Vol. IX: Revolutionary War to the Civil War
Working Americans 1880-1999 Vol. I: The Working Class
Working Americans 1880-1999 Vol. II: The Middle Class
Working Americans 1880-1999 Vol. III: The Upper Class
Working Americans 1880-1999 Vol. IV: Their Children
Working Americans 1880-2015 Vol. V: Americans At War
Working Americans 1880-2005 Vol. VI: Women at Work
Working Americans 1880-2006 Vol. VII: Social Movements
Working Americans 1880-2007 Vol. VIII: Immigrants
Working Americans 1880-2009 Vol. X: Sports & Recreation
Working Americans 1880-2010 Vol. XI: Inventors & Entrepreneurs
Working Americans 1880-2011 Vol. XII: Our History through Music
Working Americans 1880-2012 Vol. XIII: Education & Educators
World Cultural Leaders of the 20th & 21st Centuries

Education Information

Charter School Movement
Comparative Guide to American Elementary & Secondary Schools
Complete Learning Disabilities Directory
Educators Resource Directory
Special Education: A Reference Book for Policy and Curriculum Development

Health Information

Comparative Guide to American Hospitals
Complete Directory for Pediatric Disorders
Complete Directory for People with Chronic Illness
Complete Directory for People with Disabilities
Complete Mental Health Directory
Diabetes in America: Analysis of an Epidemic
Directory of Drug & Alcohol Residential Rehab Facilities
Directory of Health Care Group Purchasing Organizations
Directory of Hospital Personnel
HMO/PPO Directory
Medical Device Register
Older Americans Information Directory

Business Information

Complete Television, Radio & Cable Industry Directory
Directory of Business Information Resources
Directory of Mail Order Catalogs
Directory of Venture Capital & Private Equity Firms
Environmental Resource Handbook
Food & Beverage Market Place
Grey House Homeland Security Directory
Grey House Performing Arts Directory
Grey House Safety & Security Directory
Grey House Transportation Security Directory
Hudson's Washington News Media Contacts Directory
New York State Directory
Rauch Market Research Guides
Sports Market Place Directory

Statistics & Demographics

American Tally
America's Top-Rated Cities
America's Top-Rated Smaller Cities
America's Top-Rated Small Towns & Cities
Ancestry & Ethnicity in America
The Asian Databook
Comparative Guide to American Suburbs
The Hispanic Databook
Profiles of America
"Profiles of" Series – State Handbooks
Weather America

Financial Ratings Series

TheStreet Ratings' Guide to Bond & Money Market Mutual Funds
TheStreet Ratings' Guide to Common Stocks
TheStreet Ratings' Guide to Exchange-Traded Funds
TheStreet Ratings' Guide to Stock Mutual Funds
TheStreet Ratings' Ultimate Guided Tour of Stock Investing
Weiss Ratings' Consumer Guides
Weiss Ratings' Guide to Banks
Weiss Ratings' Guide to Credit Unions
Weiss Ratings' Guide to Health Insurers
Weiss Ratings' Guide to Life & Annuity Insurers
Weiss Ratings' Guide to Property & Casualty Insurers

Bowker's Books In Print® Titles

American Book Publishing Record® Annual
American Book Publishing Record® Monthly
Books In Print®
Books In Print® Supplement
Books Out Loud™
Bowker's Complete Video Directory™
Children's Books In Print®
El-Hi Textbooks & Serials In Print®
Forthcoming Books®
Large Print Books & Serials™
Law Books & Serials In Print™
Medical & Health Care Books In Print™
Publishers, Distributors & Wholesalers of the US™
Subject Guide to Books In Print®
Subject Guide to Children's Books In Print®

Canadian General Reference

Associations Canada
Canadian Almanac & Directory
Canadian Environmental Resource Guide
Canadian Parliamentary Guide
Canadian Venture Capital & Private Equity Firms
Financial Services Canada
Governments Canada
Health Guide Canada
The History of Canada
Libraries Canada
Major Canadian Cities

SALEM PRESS

2015 Title List

Visit www.SalemPress.com for Product Information, Table of Contents, and Sample Pages.

Science, Careers & Mathematics

Ancient Creatures: Unearthed
Applied Science
Applied Science: Engineering & Mathematics
Applied Science: Science & Medicine
Applied Science: Technology
Biomes and Ecosystems
Careers in Business
Careers in Chemistry
Careers in Communications & Media
Careers in Environment & Conservation
Careers in Healthcare
Careers in Hospitality & Tourism
Careers in Human Services
Careers in Law, Criminal Justice & Emergency Services
Careers in Physics
Careers in Technology Services & Repair
Computer Technology Innovators
Contemporary Biographies in Business
Contemporary Biographies in Chemistry
Contemporary Biographies in Communications & Media
Contemporary Biographies in Environment & Conservation
Contemporary Biographies in Healthcare
Contemporary Biographies in Hospitality & Tourism
Contemporary Biographies in Law & Criminal Justice
Contemporary Biographies in Physics
Earth Science
Earth Science: Earth Materials & Resources
Earth Science: Earth's Surface and History
Earth Science: Physics & Chemistry of the Earth
Earth Science: Weather, Water & Atmosphere
Encyclopedia of Energy
Encyclopedia of Environmental Issues
Encyclopedia of Environmental Issues: Atmosphere and Air Pollution
Encyclopedia of Environmental Issues: Ecology and Ecosystems
Encyclopedia of Environmental Issues: Energy and Energy Use
Encyclopedia of Environmental Issues: Policy and Activism
Encyclopedia of Environmental Issues: Preservation/Wilderness Issues
Encyclopedia of Environmental Issues: Water and Water Pollution
Encyclopedia of Global Resources
Encyclopedia of Global Warming
Encyclopedia of Mathematics & Society
Encyclopedia of Mathematics & Society: Engineering, Tech, Medicine
Encyclopedia of Mathematics & Society: Great Mathematicians
Encyclopedia of Mathematics & Society: Math & Social Sciences
Encyclopedia of Mathematics & Society: Math Development/Concepts
Encyclopedia of Mathematics & Society: Math in Culture & Society
Encyclopedia of Mathematics & Society: Space, Science, Environment
Encyclopedia of the Ancient World
Forensic Science
Geography Basics
Internet Innovators
Inventions and Inventors
Magill's Encyclopedia of Science: Animal Life
Magill's Encyclopedia of Science: Plant life
Notable Natural Disasters
Principles of Chemistry
Science and Scientists
Solar System
Solar System: Great Astronomers
Solar System: Study of the Universe
Solar System: The Inner Planets
Solar System: The Moon and Other Small Bodies
Solar System: The Outer Planets
Solar System: The Sun and Other Stars
World Geography

Literature

American Ethnic Writers
Classics of Science Fiction & Fantasy Literature
Critical Insights: Authors
Critical Insights: New Literary Collection Bundles
Critical Insights: Themes
Critical Insights: Works
Critical Survey of Drama
Critical Survey of Graphic Novels: Heroes & Super Heroes
Critical Survey of Graphic Novels: History, Theme & Technique
Critical Survey of Graphic Novels: Independents/Underground Classics
Critical Survey of Graphic Novels: Manga
Critical Survey of Long Fiction
Critical Survey of Mystery & Detective Fiction
Critical Survey of Mythology and Folklore: Heroes and Heroines
Critical Survey of Mythology and Folklore: Love, Sexuality & Desire
Critical Survey of Mythology and Folklore: World Mythology
Critical Survey of Poetry
Critical Survey of Poetry: American Poets
Critical Survey of Poetry: British, Irish & Commonwealth Poets
Critical Survey of Poetry: Cumulative Index
Critical Survey of Poetry: European Poets
Critical Survey of Poetry: Topical Essays
Critical Survey of Poetry: World Poets
Critical Survey of Shakespeare's Sonnets
Critical Survey of Short Fiction
Critical Survey of Short Fiction: American Writers
Critical Survey of Short Fiction: British, Irish, Commonwealth Writers
Critical Survey of Short Fiction: Cumulative Index
Critical Survey of Short Fiction: European Writers
Critical Survey of Short Fiction: Topical Essays
Critical Survey of Short Fiction: World Writers
Cyclopedia of Literary Characters
Holocaust Literature
Introduction to Literary Context: American Poetry of the 20th Century
Introduction to Literary Context: American Post-Modernist Novels
Introduction to Literary Context: American Short Fiction
Introduction to Literary Context: English Literature
Introduction to Literary Context: Plays
Introduction to Literary Context: World Literature
Magill's Literary Annual 2015
Magill's Survey of American Literature
Magill's Survey of World Literature
Masterplots
Masterplots II: African American Literature
Masterplots II: American Fiction Series
Masterplots II: British & Commonwealth Fiction Series
Masterplots II: Christian Literature
Masterplots II: Drama Series
Masterplots II: Juvenile & Young Adult Literature, Supplement
Masterplots II: Nonfiction Series
Masterplots II: Poetry Series
Masterplots II: Short Story Series
Masterplots II: Women's Literature Series
Notable African American Writers
Notable American Novelists
Notable Playwrights
Notable Poets
Recommended Reading: 500 Classics Reviewed
Short Story Writers

SALEM PRESS SALEM PRESS

2015 Title List

Visit www.SalemPress.com for Product Information, Table of Contents, and Sample Pages.

History and Social Science

The 2000s in America
50 States
African American History
Agriculture in History
American First Ladies
American Heroes
American Indian Culture
American Indian History
American Indian Tribes
American Presidents
American Villains
America's Historic Sites
Ancient Greece
The Bill of Rights
The Civil Rights Movement
The Cold War
Countries, Peoples & Cultures
Countries, Peoples & Cultures: Central & South America
Countries, Peoples & Cultures: Central, South & Southeast Asia
Countries, Peoples & Cultures: East & South Africa
Countries, Peoples & Cultures: East Asia & the Pacific
Countries, Peoples & Cultures: Eastern Europe
Countries, Peoples & Cultures: Middle East & North Africa
Countries, Peoples & Cultures: North America & the Caribbean
Countries, Peoples & Cultures: West & Central Africa
Countries, Peoples & Cultures: Western Europe
Defining Documents: American Revolution (1754-1805)
Defining Documents: Civil War (1860-1865)
Defining Documents: Emergence of Modern America (1868-1918)
Defining Documents: Exploration & Colonial America (1492-1755)
Defining Documents: Manifest Destiny (1803-1860)
Defining Documents: Post-War 1940s (1945-1949)
Defining Documents: Reconstruction (1865-1880)
Defining Documents: The 1920s
Defining Documents: The 1930s
Defining Documents: The American West (1836-1900)
Defining Documents: The Ancient World (2700 B.C.E.-50 C.E.)
Defining Documents: The Middle Ages (524-1431)
Defining Documents: World War I
Defining Documents: World War II (1939-1946)
The Eighties in America
Encyclopedia of American Immigration
Encyclopedia of Flight
Encyclopedia of the Ancient World
The Fifties in America
The Forties in America
Great Athletes
Great Athletes: Baseball
Great Athletes: Basketball
Great Athletes: Boxing & Soccer
Great Athletes: Cumulative Index
Great Athletes: Football
Great Athletes: Golf & Tennis
Great Athletes: Olympics
Great Athletes: Racing & Individual Sports
Great Events from History: 17th Century
Great Events from History: 18th Century
Great Events from History: 19th Century
Great Events from History: 20th Century (1901-1940)
Great Events from History: 20th Century (1941-1970)
Great Events from History: 20th Century (1971-2000)
Great Events from History: Ancient World
Great Events from History: Cumulative Indexes
Great Events from History: Gay, Lesbian, Bisexual, Transgender Events
Great Events from History: Middle Ages
Great Events from History: Modern Scandals
Great Events from History: Renaissance & Early Modern Era
Great Lives from History: 17th Century
Great Lives from History: 18th Century
Great Lives from History: 19th Century
Great Lives from History: 20th Century
Great Lives from History: African Americans
Great Lives from History: Ancient World
Great Lives from History: Asian & Pacific Islander Americans
Great Lives from History: Cumulative Indexes
Great Lives from History: Incredibly Wealthy
Great Lives from History: Inventors & Inventions
Great Lives from History: Jewish Americans
Great Lives from History: Latinos
Great Lives from History: Middle Ages
Great Lives from History: Notorious Lives
Great Lives from History: Renaissance & Early Modern Era
Great Lives from History: Scientists & Science
Historical Encyclopedia of American Business
Immigration in U.S. History
Magill's Guide to Military History
Milestone Documents in African American History
Milestone Documents in American History
Milestone Documents in World History
Milestone Documents of American Leaders
Milestone Documents of World Religions
Musicians & Composers 20th Century
The Nineties in America
The Seventies in America
The Sixties in America
Survey of American Industry and Careers
The Thirties in America
The Twenties in America
United States at War
U.S.A. in Space
U.S. Court Cases
U.S. Government Leaders
U.S. Laws, Acts, and Treaties
U.S. Legal System
U.S. Supreme Court
Weapons and Warfare
World Conflicts: Asia and the Middle East

Health

Addictions & Substance Abuse
Adolescent Health
Cancer
Complementary & Alternative Medicine
Genetics & Inherited Conditions
Health Issues
Infectious Diseases & Conditions
Magill's Medical Guide
Psychology & Behavioral Health
Psychology Basics

2015 Title List

Visit **www.HWWilsonInPrint.com** for Product Information, Table of Contents and Sample Pages

Current Biography

Current Biography Cumulative Index 1946-2013
Current Biography Monthly Magazine
Current Biography Yearbook: 2003
Current Biography Yearbook: 2004
Current Biography Yearbook: 2005
Current Biography Yearbook: 2006
Current Biography Yearbook: 2007
Current Biography Yearbook: 2008
Current Biography Yearbook: 2009
Current Biography Yearbook: 2010
Current Biography Yearbook: 2011
Current Biography Yearbook: 2012
Current Biography Yearbook: 2013
Current Biography Yearbook: 2014
Current Biography Yearbook: 2015

Core Collections

Children's Core Collection
Fiction Core Collection
Middle & Junior High School Core
Public Library Core Collection: Nonfiction
Senior High Core Collection

The Reference Shelf

Aging in America
American Military Presence Overseas
The Arab Spring
The Brain
The Business of Food
Conspiracy Theories
The Digital Age
Dinosaurs
Embracing New Paradigms in Education
Faith & Science
Families: Traditional and New Structures
The Future of U.S. Economic Relations: Mexico, Cuba, and Venezuela
Global Climate Change
Graphic Novels and Comic Books
Immigration in the U.S.
Internet Safety
Marijuana Reform
The News and its Future
The Paranormal
Politics of the Ocean
Reality Television
Representative American Speeches: 2008-2009
Representative American Speeches: 2009-2010
Representative American Speeches: 2010-2011
Representative American Speeches: 2011-2012
Representative American Speeches: 2012-2013
Representative American Speeches: 2013-2014
Representative American Speeches: 2014-2015
Revisiting Gender
Robotics
Russia
Social Networking
Social Services for the Poor
Space Exploration & Development
Sports in America
The Supreme Court
The Transformation of American Cities
U.S. Infrastructure
U.S. National Debate Topic: Surveillance
U.S. National Debate Topic: The Ocean
U.S. National Debate Topic: Transportation Infrastructure
Whistleblowers

Readers' Guide

Abridged Readers' Guide to Periodical Literature
Readers' Guide to Periodical Literature

Indexes

Index to Legal Periodicals & Books
Short Story Index
Book Review Digest

Sears List

Sears List of Subject Headings
Sears: Lista de Encabezamientos de Materia

Facts About Series

Facts About American Immigration
Facts About China
Facts About the 20th Century
Facts About the Presidents
Facts About the World's Languages

Nobel Prize Winners

Nobel Prize Winners: 1901-1986
Nobel Prize Winners: 1987-1991
Nobel Prize Winners: 1992-1996
Nobel Prize Winners: 1997-2001

World Authors

World Authors: 1995-2000
World Authors: 2000-2005

Famous First Facts

Famous First Facts
Famous First Facts About American Politics
Famous First Facts About Sports
Famous First Facts About the Environment
Famous First Facts: International Edition

American Book of Days

The American Book of Days
The International Book of Days

Junior Authors & Illustrators

Tenth Book of Junior Authors & Illustrations

Monographs

The Barnhart Dictionary of Etymology
Celebrate the World
Guide to the Ancient World
Indexing from A to Z
The Poetry Break
Radical Change: Books for Youth in a Digital Age

Wilson Chronology

Wilson Chronology of Asia and the Pacific
Wilson Chronology of Human Rights
Wilson Chronology of Ideas
Wilson Chronology of the Arts
Wilson Chronology of the World's Religions
Wilson Chronology of Women's Achievements

Grey House Publishing | Salem Press | H.W. Wilson | 4919 Route, 22 PO Box 56, Amenia NY 12501-0056